WEBSTER'S NEW WORLD®

DICTIONARY OF QUOTATIONS

WILEY

Wiley Publishing, Inc.

For general information on our other products and services or to obtain technical support, please contact our Customer Care Department within the U.S. at 800-762-2974, outside the U.S. at 317-572-3993, or fax 317-572-4002.

Wiley also publishes its books in a variety of electronic formats. Some content that appears in print may not be available in electronic books. For more information about Wiley products, please visit our web site at www.wiley.com.

ISBN: 0-7645-7308-X

Library of Congress Cataloging-in-Publication Data is available from the publisher upon request.

Designed and typeset by Chambers Harrap Publishers Ltd, Edinburgh

Manufactured in the United States of America

10 9 8 7 6 5 4 3 2 1

Contributors

Editor
Una McGovern

Contributors
Don Currie
David Pickering
Alan Taylor
Wilson J Wall
Tim Winter

Consultants
Paul Edmondson
Susan Shatto

Editorial assistance
Hazel Norris
Elaine O'Donoghue

Proofreaders
Hilary Bates
Sheila Ferguson
Rosalind Fergusson
Graham Frankland
Ingalo Thomson

Publishing manager
Patrick White

Prepress manager
Sharon McTeir

Prepress
David Reid

The editors would also like to thank the following members of the public who have
contributed quotations to this edition of the dictionary: Ross Beresford, S S Chubbs,
Ivy Chung, Sue Flavell, Ambrose Kennedy, Richard Little,
Jayne Loughry, Cairns McDevitte, Irving Rosenwater, Mark Snegg, Hugh Tyler

Contributors to the previous edition

Editors
Alison Jones
Stephanie Pickering
Megan Thomson

Contributors
Katherine Acheson
Julia Carlson
John Robert Colombo
Ingrid Cranfield
Wendy Dossett
José Garcia
Graham Giles
W Eric Gustafson
Bruce Henstell
David Horspool
Dean Juniper
Victoria Keller
Grace Kenny
Michael Kinsella
Paul Maloney
Kenny Mathieson
Kevin McGinley
Jim Orton
Patricia Perilli
Michael Petheram
David Pickering
James Robertson
Adrian Room
Donald Rutherford
D W D Shaw
Sean Sheehan
Jane Stewart
Susan Stiles
Onno van Nijf

Political consultant
Kenneth Baker

North American consultant
Rev James B Simpson

Introduction

A quotation can come from any notable source, spoken or written, and from any language at any time. Quotations interest us especially when they express an idea or thought in an interesting or memorable way, or simply amuse us with their sharp wit. Thus this collection contains not only literary quotations from important authors both past and present, but also quotations from people in many other walks of life. As well as writers, critics, politicians and journalists, we have sought out memorable phrases from scientists, industrialists, entertainers, sportspeople, and many more, to reflect the diversity of modern life. And just as the world has changed since the last edition of this dictionary, so many of the hundreds of new quotations we have selected reflect these changes, and important global and local events.

The coverage is truly international, extending to other varieties of English and to other languages where these provide material that is readily quotable in English. Where appropriate, quotations from languages using the Roman alphabet are given in their original form and are followed by a translation. Where no specific translation has been used, we have aimed to give a good working English version.

Quotations are arranged alphabetically by author, and chronologically (as far as possible) within each author entry, with the year of the quotation put first when this is known. This enables the reader to browse through the quotes of a particular person, and see their thoughts or works as they developed over time. This chronological arrangement is specific to this dictionary, and it makes this dictionary much more than a collection of *bons mots*. Where possible, each entry also includes a brief biography of the author, and many quotations are supplemented by contextual notes. These will help the reader to understand and appreciate the quotations more fully.

A dependable source is given for each quotation where possible. Where quotations are known from many secondary sources with no traceable primary source they are given as 'attributed'.

The comprehensive index is arranged by keyword. This allows the reader to find quotations on a particular subject. Once you have located your keyword, each entry in the index refers the user to the author, the page number on which the quotation occurs, and the number of the quotation on the page. Quotations are numbered from 1 to 99 and then start again at 1. So a reference to BACON 47:58 points to the quotation by Francis Bacon numbered 58 on page 47. Cross-references within the text use the same system.

Our aim has been to present the most memorable comments on all aspects of human experience, but we appreciate that no selection can be definitive, and the editors would appreciate suggestions for inclusion in future editions.

Abbreviations

b.	born
bk.	book
c	century (in dates, eg 18c)
c.	circa
ch.	chapter
d.	died
fl.	floruit
l.	line
pt.	part
sc.	scene

Names of months are shortened to their first three letters.

QUOTATIONS

a

Abbott, Diane Julie 1953–

British Labour politician, who became the first black woman Member of Parliament in 1987.

1 Forests of middle-aged men in dark suits…all slightly redfaced from eating and drinking too much…a nightmare of elderly white males.
1988 Of the House of Commons. In the *New York Times*, 3 Jun.

Abelard, Peter 1079–1142

French ecclesiast and theologian. At the age of 38, he fell in love with his 17-year-old pupil Héloïse; when the affair was discovered, he was castrated by her relatives. He became a monk and went on to found the monastic school of the Paraclete and to serve as Abbot of St Gildas-de-Rhuys, Brittany. Declared a heretic by his adversaries, he died on his way to defend himself.

2 *Non enim facile de his, quos plurimum diligimus,*
turpitudinem suspicamur.
We do not easily suspect evil of those whom we love most.
c.1132 *Historia Calamitatum*, ch.6.

3 *Cum itaque membris his vilissimis, quæ pro summæ*
turpitudinis exercitio pudenda vocantur, nec proprium
sustinent nomen, me divina gratia mundavit potius
quam privavit, quid aliud egit quam ad puritatem
munditiæ conservandam sordida removit et vitia.
When divine grace cleansed rather than deprived me of those most vile members which from their grossly depraved activity are called 'pudenda' ['shameful'], having no proper name of their own, what else did it do but remove filth and foulness so as to preserve unblemished purity?
c.1135 Of his castration. Second letter to Héloïse.

4 *O quanta qualia sunt illa sabbata,*
Quae semper celebrat superna curia.
O what their joy and their glory must be,
Those endless sabbaths the blessèd ones see.
Hymnarius Paraclitensis, bk.1, no.29, 'Sabbato. Ad Vesperas' (translated by J M Neale).

Abercrombie, Lascelles 1881–1938

English poet and critic. He wrote several volumes of poetry in the Georgian manner, and a number of works of academic literary criticism.

5 The poet's business is not to describe things to us, or to tell us about things, but to create in our minds the very things themselves.
1932 *Poetry: Its Music and Meaning*, introduction.

Abse, Dannie 1923–

Welsh writer and physician, specialist at a London chest clinic from 1954 to 1989. Best known as a poet, he has also written novels, plays and autobiographical works, including *A Poet in the Family* (1974) and *Goodbye, Twentieth Century* (2001).

6 I know the colour rose, and it is lovely,
But not when it ripens in a tumour;
And healing greens, leaves and grass, so springlike,
In limbs that fester are not springlike.
1968 'Pathology of Colours'.

7 So in the simple blessing of a rainbow,
In the bevelled edge of a sunlit mirror,
I have seen visible, Death's artifact
Like a soldier's ribbon on a tunic tacked.
1968 'Pathology of Colours'.

8 The theme of Death is to Poetry what Mistaken Identity is to Drama.
1984 Journal entry, Feb, collected in *Journals from the Ant-Heap* (1986).

9 We British are an aggressive nation. We seem to have become more violent this last decade: look how we drive fast and furious, with fists clenched; listen, at the stadiums, how the crowds shout, 'Kick his fuckin' head in,' or to the sirens of police cars and ambulances in the shoddy streets of Brixton or Liverpool.
1986 *Journals from the Ant-Heap*, 'Appendix 1: Authors Take Sides'.

Abu'l-'Alá Al-Ma'arri 973–1058

Syrian poet and scholar. He was blinded by smallpox in childhood and devoted himself to study, memorizing the manuscripts of Syrian libraries. As well as poems, he wrote philosophical and mystical works.

10 We live ignorant and die in errancy as we lived.
c.1000 *Luzùmiyyàt*, stanza 4 (translated by R A Nicholson in *Studies in Islamic Poetry*, 1921).

11 The world's best moment is a calm hour passed
In listening to a friend who can talk well.
c.1000 *Luzùmiyyàt*, stanza 32 (translated by R A Nicholson in *Studies in Islamic Poetry*, 1921).

12 We flee from Death's bitter cup; he follows, loving and fain.
c.1000 *Luzùmiyyàt*, stanza 36 (translated by R A Nicholson in *Studies in Islamic Poetry*, 1921).

13 Life is a malady whose one medicine is Death.
c.1000 *Luzùmiyyàt*, stanza 41 (translated by R A Nicholson in *Studies in Islamic Poetry*, 1921).

14 Consider every moment past
A thread from life's frayed mantle cast.
c.1000 *Luzùmiyyàt*, stanza 57 (translated by R A Nicholson in *Studies in Islamic Poetry*, 1921).

Abzug, Bella *originally* **Bella Savitzky** 1920–98

US feminist, lawyer, writer and Congresswoman. She was one of the key figures of the modern feminist movement.

15 Richard Nixon self-impeached…[and] gave us General Ford as his revenge.
1976 In *Rolling Stone*, 2 Dec.

Accius 170–c.86 BC

Roman poet and playwright.

16 *Oderint, dum metuant.*
Let them hate, so long as they fear.
Quoted in Seneca *Dialogues*, 'De Ira'.

Ace, Goodman 1899–1982

US humorist, best known for his radio shows such as *The Easy*

Aces (1928–45), with his wife Jane Epstein Ace. He also wrote for television comedians from 1952.

17 Derived from the words Terrible Vaudeville… We call it a medium because nothing's well done.
1954 Of T V. Letter to Groucho Marx. Collected in *The Groucho Letters* (1967).

Achebe, Chinua *originally* **Albert Chinualumogo** 1930–

Nigerian novelist, poet and essayist. His novel *Things Fall Apart* (1958) explores tensions in 19c African society. Other works include *Anthills of the Savannah* (1987, shortlisted for the Booker Prize).

18 Among the Ibo the art of conversation is regarded very highly, and proverbs are the palm-oil with which words are eaten.
1958 *Things Fall Apart*, ch.1. The title is taken from Yeats's poem 'The Second Coming'.

19 Even now they have not found the mouth with which to tell of their suffering.
1958 *Things Fall Apart*, ch.20.

20 Whenever people have asked me which among my novels is my favourite I have always evaded a direct answer, being strongly of the mind that in sheer invidiousness that question is fully comparable to asking a man to list his children in the order in which he loves them. A paterfamilias worth his salt will, if he must, speak about the peculiar attractiveness of each child.
1974 *Arrow of God*, preface to 2nd edn.

Acheson, Dean Gooderham 1893–1971

US lawyer and politician. As Under-Secretary (1945–7) and then Secretary of State (1949–53) in the Truman administration, he helped to establish the Marshall Plan (1947) and the North Atlantic Treaty Organization.

21 I will undoubtedly have to seek what is happily known as gainful employment, which I am glad to say does not describe holding public office.
1952 On resigning as Secretary of State to resume his career as a lawyer. In *Time*, 22 Dec.

22 Diplomatic problems used to be discussed by ambassadors… Foreign Ministers were called…somebody thought of the summit meetings… We are nearing the moment when political meetings will be held at a divine level.
1959 Comment to reporters in Florence, Sep. Recalled in *This Vast External Realm* (1973).

23 The institution of the throne is an anachronistic, feudal institution perfectly adapted to the use of anachronistic feudal-minded groups.
Opposing US Ambassador Joseph Grew's recommendation for the Emperor's retention in postwar Japan. Quoted in Lee Giovanitti and Fred Freed *The Decision to Drop the Atomic Bomb* (1960).

24 He still had his glorious sense of words drawn from the special reservoir from which Lincoln also drew, fed by Shakespeare and those Tudor critics who wrote the first Prayer Book of Edward VI and their Jacobean successors who translated the Bible.
1961 Of Winston Churchill. *Sketches from Life of Men I Have Known*.

25 The old house carried an assurance, typically

Portuguese, that nothing was urgent.
1961 On the US Embassy residence in Lisbon. *Sketches from Life of Men I Have Known*.

26 He wanted to be independent of the vagaries of butlers.
1961 Of Winston Churchill, who liked to keep a champagne bottle next to his plate. *Sketches from Life of Men I Have Known*.

27 He smiled with the spontaneity of a mechanical tiger.
1961 Of Soviet Foreign Minister V M Molotov. *Sketches from Life of Men I Have Known*.

28 He struck me as looking like a pear on top of two toothpicks.
1962 Of Charles de Gaulle, 22 Oct, after a visit during the Cuban missile crisis. Quoted in David S McLellan and David C Acheson (eds) *Among Friends: Personal Letters of Dean Gooderham Acheson* (1980).

29 Great Britain has lost an Empire and not yet found a role. The attempt to play a separate power role—that is, a role apart from Europe, based on a special relationship with the United States, on being the head of the Commonwealth—is about to be played out. Her Majesty's Government is now attempting, wisely in my opinion, to re-enter Europe.
1962 Speech at West Point military academy, 5 Dec. According to the *New York Times*, 23 Nov 1969, Prime Minister Harold Wilson later countered, 'Mr Acheson is a distinguished figure who has lost a State Department and not yet found himself a role'.

30 Fumbling silence in the White House seeps out over the country like a cold fog over a river bed where no stream runs.
1963 Letter to Harry S Truman, 28 May, alluding to the Eisenhower administration. Quoted in David S McLellan and David C Acheson (eds) *Among Friends: Personal Letters of Dean Gooderham Acheson* (1980).

31 A real Centaur—part man, part horse's ass. A rough appraisal, but curiously true.
1968 Of President Johnson. 13 Apr.

32 Like finding oneself pregnant and trying to fall in love as quickly as possible.
On the weekend of Richard M Nixon's inauguration. Quoted in Douglas Brinkley *Dean Acheson: The Cold War Years 1953–71* (1992).

33 I had shown my colors. Those who took their red straight, without a chaser of white and blue, were not mollified.
1969 *Present at the Creation*.

34 The enormity of the task…[was] just a bit less formidable than that described in the first chapter of Genesis.
1969 Of postwar restructuring. *Present at the Creation*.

35 The first requirement of a statesman is that he be dull.
1970 In the *Observer*, 21 Jun.

36 Much in life cannot be affected…but must be borne…without complaint, because complaints are a bore…and undermine the serenity essential to endurance.
Quoted in Gaddis Smith *American Secretaries of State* (1972).

37 Neither action nor style could have accomplished the result alone. Both were needed.
1975 Of Winston Churchill's charisma. *Grapes from Thorns*.

38 His speeches were prepared with that infinite capacity for taking pains, which is said to be genius.
1975 Of Winston Churchill. *Grapes from Thorns*.

39 Courageous and loyal to the tips of his stubby fingers.
1975 Of British Foreign Secretary Ernest Bevin. *Grapes from Thorns*.

40 Breathless and bewildered like an old lady at a busy intersection.
On the State Dept under Cordell Hull. Quoted in David S McLellan *Dean Acheson: The State Department Years* (1976).

41 Our name for problems is significant. We call them headaches. You take a powder and they are gone.
Quoted in David S McLellan *Dean Acheson: The State Department Years* (1976).

42 You can't argue with a river, it is going to flow. You can dam it up…put it to useful purposes…deflect it, but you can't argue with it.
On the fruitlessness of keeping Russian fishermen from waters that should be off limits. Quoted in David S McLellan *Dean Acheson: The State Department Years* (1976).

43 A memorandum is written not to inform the reader but to protect the writer.
1977 In the *Wall Street Journal*, 8 Sep.

44 The Canadians seem to be held together with string and safety pins.
Quoted in David S McLellan and David C Acheson (eds) *Among Friends: Personal Letters of Dean Gooderham Acheson* (1980).

45 Trust him as much as you would a rattlesnake with a silencer on its rattle.
1980 Advice to President Truman on J Edgar Hoover. Quoted in David S McLellan and David C Acheson (eds) *Among Friends: Personal Letters of Dean Gooderham Acheson* (1980).

46 How gently, wisely, and justly G M Young deals with him. That is not the way to write biography.
Collected in David S McClellan and David C Acheson (eds) *Among Friends: Personal Letters of Dean Gooderham Acheson* (1980). On Young's biography *Stanley Baldwin* (1952).

47 Homage to plain dumb luck.
Of the effectiveness of the US blockade of Soviet ships bringing missiles to Cuba. Quoted in Walter Isaacson and Evan Thomas *The Wise Men* (1986).

48 The Iraqi is really not whacky
Toady, perhaps, even tacky.
When they gave *him* the word
He gave *us* the bird
And joined with the Arabs, by cracky!
Limerick written during dull meeting of Foreign Ministers. Quoted in Walter Isaacson and Evan Thomas *The Wise Men* (1986).

49 Charm never made a rooster.
Of poorly-organized attempts to maintain peace by good intentions. Quoted in James B Reston *Deadline* (1991).

50 It is just as full of propaganda as a dog is full of fleas. In fact, I say it's all fleas and no dog.
Of Russian Foreign Minister Andre Vishinsky's proposal that the US should withdraw from postwar Europe. Quoted in James B Reston *Deadline* (1991).

51 With a nation, as with a boxer, one of the greatest assurances of safety is to add reach to power.
Alluding to US bases in Europe. Quoted in James B Reston *Deadline* (1991).

52 If the best minds in the world had set out to find us the worst possible location in the world to fight this damnable war, politically and militarily, the unanimous choice would have been Korea.
On the Korean War. Quoted in Joseph Goulden *Korea* (1992).

Ackerman, Diane 1948–

US poet and writer. Her poetry is published in many journals and books, which include *Wife of Light* (1978) and *Lady Faustus* (1983). She has published non-fiction and was a staff writer at the *New Yorker* from 1988 to 1994.

53 An occasion, catalyst, or tripwire…permits the poet to reach into herself and haul up whatever nugget of the human condition distracts her at the moment, something that can't be reached in any other way.
Quoted in the *New York Times*, 10 Mar 1991.

Ackroyd, Peter 1949–

English novelist, biographer and critic. He has written a number of erudite and playful novels and scholarly biographies, including studies of Dickens and T S Eliot.

54 And the smell of the library was always the same—the musty odour of old clothes mixed with the keener scent of unwashed bodies, creating what the chief librarian had once described as 'the steam of the social soup'.
1987 *Chatterton*, ch.5.

55 No poet is ever completely lost. He has the secret of his childhood safe with him, like some secret cave in which he can kneel. And, when we read his poetry, we can join him there.
1987 *Chatterton*, ch.10.

56 He had a fear of the dead, and of all inanimate things, rising up around him to claim him; it is the fear of the pre-eminently solitary child and solitary man.
1990 Of Charles Dickens. *Dickens*, prologue.

57 Is it possible to be nostalgic about old fears?
1992 *English Music*, ch.1.

58 Yes, I have inherited the past because I have acknowledged it at last… And, now that I have come to understand it, I no longer need to look back.
1992 *English Music*, ch.19.

Acton, John Emerich Edward Dalberg, 1st Baron Acton of Aldenham 1834–1902

English historian. He sat as a Liberal MP (1859–64) and was created baron by Gladstone in 1869. In 1895 he was appointed Professor of Modern History at Cambridge.

59 Power tends to corrupt, and absolute power corrupts absolutely. Great men are almost always bad men. There is no worse heresy than that the office sanctifies the holder of it.
1887 Letter to Bishop Mandell Creighton, 3 Apr.

Adamov, Arthur 1908–70

Russian-born French playwright. A leading exponent of the Theatre of the Absurd, he was the author of such plays as *Le Professeur Taranne* (1953), *Le Ping Pong* (1955) and *Le Printemps '71* (1961).

60 The reason why Absurdist plays take place in No Man's Land with only two characters is primarily financial.
1962 Speech at Edinburgh, 13 Sep.

Adams, Abigail 1744–1818

US first lady, wife of President John Adams, and early feminist.

61 In the new code of laws which I suppose it will be necessary for you to make I desire you would remember

the ladies, and be more generous and favourable to them than your ancestors. Do not put such unlimited power into the hands of the husbands. Remember all men would be tyrants if they could.
1776 Letter to John Adams, 31 Mar.

62 It is not in the still calm of life, or the repose of a pacific station, that great characters are formed… Great necessities call out great virtues.
1780 Letter to John Quincy Adams, 19 Jan.

Adams, Arthur Henry 1872–1936

New Zealand-born journalist, poet and playwright, whose first collection was *Maoriland: and Other Verses* (1899). His *London Streets* (1906) is a colonist's portrayal of the city. He returned to Sydney, Australia, as editor of *Bulletin* and *Lone Hand*.

63 The land lies desolate and stripped;
Across its waste has thinly strayed
A tattered host of eucalypt.
From whose gaunt uniform is made
A ragged penury of shade.
1913 'Written in Australia', in *The Collected Verses of Arthur H Adams*.

Adams, Charles Francis 1807–86

US diplomat and writer, congressman from Massachusetts (1858–61) and Minister to Britain during the American Civil War (1861–8).

64 It would be superfluous in me to point out to your lordship that this is war.
1863 Despatch to Earl Russell during the Civil War, 5 Sep. Quoted in C F Adams *Charles Francis Adams* (1900), ch.17.

Adams, Douglas Noël 1952–2001

English novelist and scriptwriter. His radio serial *The Hitch-Hiker's Guide to the Galaxy* (1978–80) was a cult success, and it and its sequels were also successful novels.

65 Don't Panic.
1979 *The Hitch-Hiker's Guide to the Galaxy*, preface. These words are said to be written in large friendly letters on the cover of the Guide.

66 The Answer to the Great Question Of…Life, the Universe and Everything…Is…Forty-two.
1979 *The Hitch-Hiker's Guide to the Galaxy*, ch.27.

67 'The first ten million years were the worst,' said Marvin, 'and the second ten million years, they were the worst too. The third ten million I didn't enjoy at all. After that I went into a bit of a decline.'
1980 Marvin, the paranoid android. *The Restaurant at the End of the Universe*, ch.18.

68 So Long, and Thanks for All the Fish.
1984 Title of novel.

69 It can hardly be a coincidence that no language on earth has ever produced the expression 'as pretty as an airport'.
1988 *The Long Dark Tea-Time of the Soul*, ch.1.

70 Kate's spirits sank to the very bottom of her being and began to prowl around there making a low growling noise.
1988 *The Long Dark Tea-Time of the Soul*, ch.1.

71 I love deadlines. I love the whooshing noise they make as they go by.
2001 In *The Guardian*, 14 May.

Adams, Gerry (Gerard) 1948–

Northern Irish politician. He has been President of Sinn Féin since 1983 (Vice-President 1978–83).

72 We want him to be the last British Prime Minister with jurisdiction in Ireland.
1997 On Tony Blair. In *The Irish Times*, 8 Oct.

73 Peace cannot be built on exclusion. That has been the price of the last 30 years.
1998 In the *Daily Telegraph*, 11 Apr.

Adams, Henry Brooks 1838–1918

US historian, son of Charles Francis Adams and grandson of John Quincy Adams. His historical works include *Mont Saint Michel and Chartres* (1904), and his autobiography *The Education of Henry Adams* (published privately 1907, publicly 1918) won the 1919 Pulitzer Prize.

74 Some day science may have the existence of mankind in its power and the human race commit suicide by blowing up the race.
1862 Letter to Charles Francis Adams, Jr, 11 Apr.

75 Politics, as a practice, whatever its professions, has always been the systematic organization of hatreds.
1907 *The Education of Henry Adams*, ch.1.

76 All experience is an arch to build on.
1907 *The Education of Henry Adams*, ch.6.

77 A friend in power is a friend lost.
1907 *The Education of Henry Adams*, ch.7.

78 These questions of taste, of feeling, of inheritance, need no settlement. Everyone carries his own inch-rule of taste, and amuses himself by applying it, triumphantly, wherever he travels.
1907 *The Education of Henry Adams*, ch.12.

79 Chaos often breeds life, when order breeds habit.
1907 *The Education of Henry Adams*, ch.16.

80 A teacher affects eternity; he can never tell where his influence stops.
1907 *The Education of Henry Adams*, ch.20, 'Failure'.

81 One friend in a lifetime is much; two are many; three are hardly possible. Friendship needs a certain parallelism of life, a community of thought, a rivalry of aim.
1907 *The Education of Henry Adams*, ch.20.

82 What one knows is, in youth, of little moment; they know enough who know how to learn.
1907 *The Education of Henry Adams*, ch.21.

83 He had often noticed that six months' oblivion amounts to newspaper death, and that resurrection is rare. Nothing is easier, if a man wants it, than rest, profound as the grave.
1907 *The Education of Henry Adams*, ch.22.

84 Practical politics consists in ignoring the facts.
1907 *The Education of Henry Adams*, ch.22.

85 American art, like the American language and American education, was as far as possible sexless.
1907 *The Education of Henry Adams*, ch.25, 'The Dynamo and the Virgin'.

86 No one means all he says, and yet very few say all they mean, for words are slippery and thought is viscous.
1907 *The Education of Henry Adams*, ch.31, 'The Grammar of Science'.

Adams, John 1735–1826

US statesman and second President, a leader of resistance to Britain and central figure in the Declaration of Independence (1776). He became the first US Vice-President under Washington (1789), and later President (1796–1800).

87 A government of laws, and not of men.
1774 In the *Boston Gazette*, no.7. The phrase was later incorporated into the Massachusetts Constitution (1780).

88 I agree with you that in politics the middle way is none at all.
1776 Letter to Horatio Gates, 23 Mar.

89 The second day of July 1776 will be the most memorable epoch in the history of America. It ought to be solemnised with pomp and parade, with shows, games, sports, guns, bells, bonfires and illuminations from one end of this continent to the other—from this time forward, for ever more.
1776 Letter to his wife, 3 Jul, on the vote of Congress for independence from Britain.

90 You and I ought not to die before we have explained ourselves to each other.
1813 Letter to Thomas Jefferson, 15 Jul.

91 What a poor, ignorant, malicious, short-sighted, crapulous mass is Tom Paine's common sense.
1819 Letter to Thomas Jefferson, 22 Jun, referring to the Republican's treatise on independence entitled *Common Sense*.

Adams, John Quincy 1767–1848

US politician and sixth President. Ambassador to Europe and Secretary of State under Monroe, he negotiated the acquisition of Florida from Spain, before becoming President (1825). He failed to win re-election but continued to oppose slavery as a congressman.

92 *Fiat justitia, pereat coelum.* My toast would be, may our country be always successful, but whether successful or otherwise, always right.
1816 Letter to John Adams, 1 Aug.
➤ *See Decatur 258:8, Ferdinand I 320:1.*

93 The American continents, by the free and independent condition that they have assumed and maintain, are henceforth not to be considered as subjects for future colonisation by any European powers… In the wars of the European powers in matters relating to ourselves, we have never taken any part; nor does it comport with our policy to do so.
1823 The Monroe Doctrine, 2 Dec.

94 I inhabit a weak, frail, decayed tenement; battered by the winds and broken in on by the storms, and, from all I can learn, the landlord does not intend to repair.
1848 Attributed, as he lay on his deathbed. Quoted in Clifton Fadiman *The Faber Book of Anecdotes* (1985).

Adams, Judge Richard 1846–1908

Irish judge. After a Law degree, he became a journalist in Cork until he was called to the Irish Bar in 1873. From 1894 he was Judge of the County Court, Limerick.

95 Look here, sir, tell me no more unnecessary lies. Such lies as your attorney advised you are necessary for the presentation of your fraudulent case I will listen to though I shall decide against you whatever you swear, but if you tell me another unnecessary lie, I'll put you in the dock.
Presiding over Limerick County Court. Quoted in A M Sullivan *Old Ireland*.

96 You have been acquitted by a Limerick jury, and you may now leave the dock without any other stain upon your character.
Quoted in Maurice Healy *The Old Munster Circuit*.

Adams, Samuel 1722–1803

Political leader in the American Revolution, who signed the Declaration of Independence. Clerk of the lower house of Massachusetts legislature, he was involved in the Boston Tea Party.

97 What a glorious morning is this.
1775 On hearing gunfire at Lexington, 19 Apr. Quoted in J K Hosmer *Samuel Adams* (1886), ch.19.

Adamson, Harold 1906–80

US lyricist.

98 Comin' in on a wing and a prayer.
1943 Title of song. The phrase was taken from the words of a fighter pilot from his battered jet to ground control.

Adcock, (Karen) Fleur 1934–

New Zealand poet who settled in Britain in 1963. Her works include *The Eye of the Hurricane* (1964), *Selected Poems* (1983) and *Poems 1960–2000* (2000).

99 Do not ask me for charity now:
Go away until your bones are clean.
1983 *Selected Poems*, 'Advice to a Discarded Lover'.

Addison, Joseph 1672–1719

English poet, playwright and essayist. After a Grand Tour of Europe (1699–1704), he entered Parliament as a Whig in 1708. He contributed numerous essays to the *Tatler* and was co-founder with Richard Steele of the *The Spectator* (1711).

1 Music, the greatest good that mortals know,
And all of heaven we have below.
1694 'A Song for St Cecilia's Day'.

2 For wheresoe'er I turn my ravished eyes,
Gay gilded scenes and shining prospects rise,
Poetic fields encompass me around,
And still I seem to tread on classic ground.
1704 *A Letter from Italy*.

3 A painted meadow, or a purling stream.
1704 *A Letter from Italy*.

4 'Twas then great Marlbro's mighty soul was proved.
1705 *The Campaign*, 1.279.

5 And, pleased th'Almighty's orders to perform,
Rides in the whirl-wind, and directs the storm.
1705 *The Campaign*, 1.291–2.

6 And those who paint 'em truest praise 'em most.
1705 *The Campaign*, 1.476.

7 This republic has been much more powerful than it is at present, as it is still likelier, to sink than increase in its dominions.
1705 On Venice. *Remarks on Several parts of Italy*.

8 I remember when our whole island was shaken with an earthquake some years ago, there was an impudent

mountebank who sold pills which (as he told the country people) were very good against an earthquake.
1710 In *The Tatler*, no.240, 21 Oct.

9 A reader seldom peruses a book with pleasure until he knows whether the writer of it be a black man or a fair man, of a mild or choleric disposition, married or a bachelor.
1711 In *The Spectator*, no.1, 1 Mar.

10 Thus I live in the world rather as a Spectator of mankind, than as one of the species, by which means I have made myself a speculative statesman, soldier, merchant, and artisan, without ever meddling with any practical part of life.
1711 In *The Spectator*, no.1, 1 Mar.

11 Nothing is capable of being well set to music that is not nonsense.
1711 In *The Spectator*, no.18.

12 A perfect tragedy is the noblest production of human nature.
1711 In *The Spectator*, no.39.

13 In all thy humours, whether grave or mellow,
Thou'rt such a touchy, testy, pleasant fellow;
Hast so much wit, and mirth, and spleen about thee,
There is no living with thee, nor without thee.
1711 In *The Spectator*, no.68, 18 May.

14 As Sir Roger is landlord to the whole congregation, he keeps them in very good order, and will suffer nobody to sleep in it [the church] besides himself; for if by chance he has been surprised into a short nap at sermon, upon recovering out of it, he stands up, and looks about him; and if he sees anybody else nodding, either wakes them himself, or sends his servant to them.
1711 In *The Spectator*, no.112, 9 Jul.

15 Sir Roger told them, with the air of a man who would not give his judgement rashly, that much might be said on both sides.
1711 In *The Spectator*, no.122, 20 Jul.

16 It was a saying of an ancient philosopher, which I find some of our writers have ascribed to Queen Elizabeth, who perhaps might have taken occasion to repeat it, that a good face is a letter of recommendation.
1711 In *The Spectator*, no.221, 13 Nov.

17 I have often thought, says Sir Roger, it happens very well that Christmas should fall out in the Middle of Winter.
1712 In *The Spectator*, no.269, 8 Jan.

18 A true critic ought to dwell rather upon excellencies than imperfections, to discover the concealed beauties of a writer, and communicate to the world such things as are worth their observation.
1712 In *The Spectator*, no.291, 2 Feb.

19 These widows, Sir, are the most perverse creatures in the world.
1712 In *The Spectator*, no.335, 25 Mar.

20 Mirth is short and transient, cheerfulness fixed and permanent… Mirth is like a flash of lightning that breaks through a gloom of clouds, and glitters for a moment: cheerfulness keeps up a kind of day-light in the mind, and fills it with a steady and perpetual serenity.
1712 In *The Spectator*, no.381, 17 May.

21 The Knight in the triumph of his heart made several reflections on the greatness of the British Nation; as, that one Englishman could beat three Frenchmen; that we could never be in danger of Popery so long as we took care of our fleet; that the Thames was the noblest river in Europe; that London Bridge was a greater piece of work than any of the Seven Wonders of the World; with many other honest prejudices which naturally cleave to the heart of a true Englishman.
1712 In *The Spectator*, no.383, 20 May.

22 Wide and undetermined prospects are as pleasing to the fancy, as the speculations of eternity or infinitude are to the understanding.
1712 In *The Spectator*, no.412, 23 Jun.

23 An account of it would have been thought fabulous, were not the Wall itself extant.
1712 Commenting on the Great Wall of China, *The Spectator*, no.415, 26 Jun.

24 Through all Eternity to Thee
A joyful Song I'll raise,
For oh! Eternity's too short
To utter all thy Praise.
1712 In *The Spectator*, no.453, 9 Aug.

25 We have in England a particular bashfulness in every thing that regards religion.
1712 In *The Spectator*, no.458, 15 Aug.

26 The spacious firmament on high,
With all the blue ethereal sky,
And spangled heavens, a shining frame,
Their great Original proclaim.
Th' unwearied sun from day to day
Does his Creator's power display;
And publishes to every land
The work of an Almighty hand.
1712 In *The Spectator*, no.465, 23 Aug.

27 In Reason's ear they all rejoice,
And utter forth a glorious voice,
For ever singing, as they shine:
'The hand that made us is divine.'
1712 In *The Spectator*, no.465, 23 Aug.

28 A woman seldom asks advice before she has bought her wedding clothes.
1712 In *The Spectator*, no.475, 4 Sep.

29 Our disputants put me in mind of the skuttle fish, that when he is unable to extricate himself, blackens all the water about him, till he becomes invisible.
1712 In *The Spectator*, no.476, 5 Sept.

30 If we may believe our logicians, man is distinguished from all other creatures by the faculty of laughter.
1712 In *The Spectator*, no.494, 26 Sep.

31 'Tis not in mortals to command success,
But we'll do more, Sempronius; we'll deserve it.
1713 *Cato*, act 1, sc.2, l.43–4.

32 'Tis pride, rank pride, and haughtiness of soul;
I think the Romans call it stoicism.
1713 *Cato*, act 1, sc.4, l.82–3.

33 Were you with these, my prince, you'd soon forget
The pale, unripened beauties of the north.
1713 *Cato*, act 1, sc.4, l.134–5.

34 The woman that deliberates is lost.
1713 *Cato*, act 4, sc.1, l.31.

35 Curse on his virtues! they've undone his country.
Such popular humanity is treason.
1713 *Cato*, act 4, sc.1, l.205–6.

36 What a pity is it
That we can die but once to serve our country!
1713 *Cato*, act 4, sc.1, l.258–9.

37 Content thyself to be obscurely good.
When vice prevails, and impious men bear sway,
The post of honour is a private station.
1713 *Cato*, act 4, sc.1, l.319–21.

38 It must be so—Plato, thou reason'st well!—
Else whence this pleasing hope, this fond desire,
This longing after immortality?
Or whence this secret dread, and inward horror,
Of falling into naught? Why shrinks the soul
Back on herself, and startles at destruction
'Tis the divinity that stirs within us;
'Tis heaven itself, that points out an hereafter,
And intimates eternity to man.
Eternity! thou pleasing, dreadful thought!
1713 *Cato*, act 5, sc.1, l.1–10.

39 From hence, let fierce contending nations know
What dire effects from civil discord flow.
1713 *Cato*, act 5, sc.1, closing words.

40 'We are always doing,' says he, 'something for Posterity,
but I would fain see Posterity do something for us.'
1714 In *The Spectator* no.583, 20 Aug.

41 There is sometimes a greater judgement shewn in
deviating from the rules of art, than in adhering to them;
and…there is more beauty in the works of a great genius
who is ignorant of all the rules of art, than in the works of
a little genius, who not only knows but scrupulously
observes them.
1714 In *The Spectator*, no.592, 10 Sep.

42 I should think myself a very bad woman, if I had done
what I do for a farthing less.
1716 *The Drummer*, act 1, sc.1.

43 See in what peace a Christian can die.
1719 Last words, to his stepson Lord Warwick. Quoted in
Edward Young *Conjectures on Original Composition* (1759).

44 Hunting is not a proper employment for a thinking man.
Quoted in Colin Jarman *The Guinness Dictionary of Sports
Quotations* (1990).

Ade, George 1866–1944

US humorist and dramatist.

45 R-E-M-O-R-S-E!
Those dry Martinis did the work for me;
Last night at twelve I felt immense,
Today I feel like thirty cents.
My eyes are blurred, my coppers hot,
I'll try to eat, but I cannot.
It is no time for mirth and laughter,
The cold, grey dawn of the morning after.
1903 *The Sultan of Sulu*, act 2.

Adelman, Kenneth Lee 1946–

US political scientist, director of the US Arms Control and
Disarmament Agency (1983–8). His works include *The Great
Universal Embrace: Arms Summitry—a skeptic's account* (1989).

46 The history of arms control is a history of great visions
eventually mugged by reality.
1986 In *Newsweek*, 1 Dec.

Adenauer, Konrad 1876–1967

German statesman. Dismissed by the Nazis (1933), he founded
the Christian Democratic Union (1945) and became first
Chancellor of the Federal Republic of Germany (1949–63).

47 We must free ourselves from thinking in terms of nation
states. The countries of western Europe are no longer in a
position to protect themselves individually. Not one of
them is any longer in a position to salvage Europe's
culture.
1953 Speech, May.

Adler, Jerry 1949–

US journalist, a senior editor at *Newsweek*.

48 She…happens to stick out a foot just as history is rushing
by.
1988 Of Fawn Hall, the secretary who helped Col Oliver North to
dispose of top-secret papers, 'the archetype of the Accidental
Celebrity'. In *Newsweek*, 9 Mar.

49 Norman Rockwell, the Brueghel of the 20th century
bourgeoisie, the Holbein of Jell-O ads and magazine
covers; by common assent, the most American artist of
all.
1993 On the opening of the Norman Rockwell Museum at
Stockbridge, Massachusetts. In *Newsweek*, 12 Apr.

50 The widespread belief that Yuppies as a class would
perish from Brie-cheese poisoning turned out to be
over-optimistic.
1995 'The Rise of the Overclass', in *Newsweek*, 31 Jul.

Adler, Larry (Lawrence Cecil) 1914–2001

US musician and virtuoso on the harmonica. He emigrated to
Britain after being blacklisted in the US.

51 His first choice had been Yehudi Menuhin; he was lucky
he got me. Menuhin on the mouth-organ is a mess.
1984 On Henry Koster's casting for the film *Music for Millions*
(1944).

Adler, Polly 1900–62

US writer.

52 A House is not a Home.
1954 Title of a book.

Adorno, Theodor 1903–69

German social philosopher and musicologist, who emigrated
to the US in 1934. His *Negative Dialectics* (1966) expounds his
complex theories, but he also wrote more accessible mass-
culture works.

53 In psychoanalysis nothing is true except the
exaggerations.
1966 *Negative Dialectics*.

Aelius Aristides AD 117–189

Greek orator. He spent much of his life giving rhetorical
demonstrations throughout Asia Minor. He is best known for
his encomium of Rome and his 'Sacred Teachings', an account
of his dreams while seeking a cure in the temple of Asclepius.

54 As the character is, such is the speech.
Pros Platona Peri Rhetorikes, bk.2, 1.392.

St Aelred of Riveaulx   d.1167

English writer, historian and Cistercian monk. Raised at the court of David I of Scotland, he became Abbot of Revesby (1143) and Riveaulx (1147). He aided the England–France alliance in support of Pope Alexander II against Emperor Frederick III.

55 *Inveni fateor in rege monachum, claustrum in curia, in palatio monasterii disciplinam.*
I confess that I found in the king a monk, in the court a cloister, and in the palace the discipline of a monastery.
?c.1160 Lament for David I, King of Scotland. Quoted in John Fordoun *Chronicle of Scotland* (c.1384), bk.5, ch.43.

Aeschylus   c.525–c.456 BC

Greek dramatist, who served in the Athenian army at Marathon (490 BC) and probably in the navy at Salamis (480 BC). He won 13 first prizes in the dramatic contests of Athens from 484 to 458 BC, but only seven of his many works have survived.

56 Ship-destroyer, man-destroyer, city-destroyer.
Of Helen. *Agamemnon*, 1.689.

57 Unworthy was what he did to her, worthy was what he suffered.
Clytemnestra speaks of Agamemnon's sacrifice of their daughter Iphigeneia. *Agamemnon*, 1.1527–8 (translated by H Lloyd-Jones).

58 For by the will of the gods Fate hath held sway since ancient days.
Persae, 1.102 (translated by H Weir Smyth).

59 Now you battle for your all.
Persae, 1.402–5 (translated by H Weir Smyth).

60 Once to die is better than length of days in sorrow without end.
Prometheus Vinctus, 1.750–1.

61 It's a man's job—no place for women's plans here!—what lies outside. Stay home and cause no trouble.
Septem contra Thebas, 1.200–1 (translated by C M Dawson).

62 Obedience, you know, is Good Luck's mother, wedded to Salvation, they say.
Septem contra Thebas, 1.224–5 (translated by C M Dawson).

63 Remember to be submissive, thou art an alien, a fugitive, and in need.
Supplices, 1.202 (translated by H Weir Smyth).

Agassi, Andre   1970–

US tennis player who won the men's singles at Wimbledon in 1992.

64 You expect to leave the dance with the ones you came with.
2003 On his surprise at being the last star of his generation still playing. Quoted in *The Independent*, 29 Dec.

Agassiz, (Jean) Louis (Rodolphe)   1807–73

Swiss-born US zoologist and geologist. A professor of natural history at Neuchâtel, he came to the US (1846) to teach at Harvard University. His works include a study of fossil fish and a *Natural History of the United States* (1857–62).

65 The student must remember, for his consolation…that his failures are almost as important to the cause of science and to those who follow him in the same road, as his successes. It is much to know what we cannot do in any given direction—the first step, indeed, toward the accomplishment of what we can do.
1896 *Geological Sketches*.

66 The study of nature is interwoven with the highest mind. You should never trifle with nature.
Attributed.

Agate, James   1877–1947

English theatre critic. He wrote for the *Sunday Times* from 1923 until his death and also published a notable nine-part autobiography, *Ego* (1935–47).

67 Happy is the country which has no history, and happier still is that musical comedy about which one can find nothing to say.
1920 In the *Sunday Times*.

68 I don't know very much, but what I do know I know better than anybody, and I don't want to argue about it. I know what I think about an actor or an actress, and am not interested in what anybody else thinks. My mind is not a bed to be made and re-made.
1943 Journal entry, 9 Jun. Collected in *Ego 6* (1944).

69 Long experience has taught me that in England nobody goes to the theatre unless he or she has bronchitis.
Attributed.

70 She had a heart as big as Waterloo Station.
Of Marie Lloyd. Attributed.

Agawa, Hiroyuki   1920–

Japanese novelist. His *Citadel in Spring* (1949) is the semi-autobiographical story of a young man fighting on the losing side of World War II. Much of the story is set in Hiroshima, the city of his birth.

71 It quickly swelled into the shape of a gigantic question mark, the middle of which was a vivid crimson, and as this thunderhead-like column billowed upward through the sky, she could see a red ball of fire at its core.
1949 Of the atomic explosion, Hiroshima. *Haru no shiro* (*Citadel in Spring*, translated by Lawrence Rogers), ch.9.

Agnew, Spiro T(heodore)   1918–96

US Republican politician. As liberal Governor of Maryland he introduced anti-racial-discrimination legislation, but by 1968 had become much more conservative. He was Nixon's running mate in the 1968 election, and Vice-President (1969–73).

72 To some extent, if you've seen one city slum, you've seen them all.
1968 Election campaign speech, Detroit, 18 Oct.

73 A spirit of national masochism prevails, encouraged by an effete corps of impudent snobs who characterize themselves as intellectuals.
1969 Of media pundits. Speech, New Orleans, 19 Oct.

74 In the United States today we have more than our fair share of the nattering nabobs of negativism. They have formed their own Four H Club—the hopeless, hysterical, hypochondriacs of history.
1970 Of media pundits. Speech, San Diego, 11 Sep.

75 I was…one of the worst complications he could have had.
1980 On the effect of his no-contest plea to income-tax evasion and subsequent resignation upon Richard M Nixon. *Go Quietly or Else.*

Agustini, Delmira 1886–1914

Uruguayan poet, who was murdered by her estranged husband, who then committed suicide. Her bold sincerity and impassioned lyrics rank her among the most outstanding early modernist poets.

76 *Por todos los senderos de la noche han venido*
a llorar en mi lecho.
¡Fueron tantos, son tantos!
Yo no sé cuáles viven, yo no sé cuál ha muerto.
Me lloraré a mí misma para llorarlos todos.
They have come from all of night's pathways
to cry in my bed.
They were so many, they are so many!
I don't know who lives, I don't know who has died.
I'll cry for myself so that I can cry for all.
1924 *El rosario de Eros*, 'Mis amores' ('My lovers').

St Aidan c.600–651

Irish monk, known as the Apostle of Northumbria. He was summoned from Iona by King Oswald to evangelize the north and established a community on Lindisfarne. He died in the church he had built in Bamburgh.

77 *Nam tibi carior est ille filius equae quam ille filius Dei?*
Is this son of a mare dearer to you, then, than that son of God?
c.645 To King Oswin of Deira, who had objected when Aidan gave to a beggar a horse which he had received as a gift from the king. Quoted in Bede *Historia Ecclesiastica Gentis Anglorum* (731), bk.3, ch.14.

Aitken, Jonathan William Patrick 1942–

British Conservative politician. In 1995 he sued *The Guardian* for libel following articles relating to his dealings with Saudi arms dealers. In 1999 he served a prison sentence for perjury after it was revealed he had lied repeatedly.

78 If it falls to me to start a fight to cut out the cancer of bent and twisted journalism in our country with the simple sword of truth and the trusting shield of British fair play, so be it.
1995 Press statement, 10 Apr.

Akers, John Fellows 1934–

American businessman. He joined IBM as a sales trainee in 1960 and rose to become Chairman 1986–93.

79 Each school can, once again, become what it was always meant to be—a building that has four walls with tomorrow inside.
1991 In the *Wall Street Journal*, 20 Mar.

Akins, Zoë 1886–1958

US poet and playwright. Her works include the play *The Greeks Had a Word for It* (1930) and the Pulitzer Prize-winning stage adaptation of Edith Wharton's novel *The Old Maid* (1935).

80 The Greeks Had a Word for It.
1930 Title of play.

Alain (Émile-Auguste Chartier) 1868–1951

French philosopher, writer and poet.

81 *Rien n'est plus dangereux qu'une idée, quand on n'a qu'une idée.*
Nothing is more dangerous than an idea, when you have only one idea.
1938 *Propos sur la religion*, no.74.

Alan of Lille *also known as* 'Alanus de Insulis' c.1114–1202

French writer and scholar. His major literary works include *De Planctu Natura* and *Anticlaudianus*.

82 *Omnis mundi creatura*
Quasi liber et pictura
Nobis est, et speculum.
Each creature of the world
Is as a book, a picture,
And a mirror to us.
c.1170 *De Incarnatione Christi* (*Rhythmus Alter*), l.1–3.

83 *Post nubila maxima, Phoebus.*
After the greatest clouds, the sun.
1175 *Liber Parabolarum*, ch.1, l.33.

84 *Qui jacet in terra non habet unde cadat.*
He who is lying on the ground has nowhere to fall.
1175 *Liber Parabolarum*, ch.2, l.18.

85 *Mille viae ducunt homines per sæcula Romam.*
Throughout the ages, a thousand roads lead to Rome.
1175 *Liber Parabolarum*, ch.3, l.56.

Alba, Duke of, Ferdinand Alvarez de Toledo 1508–82

Spanish soldier, made a general at 26 and Commander-in-Chief at 30. He led successful campaigns against the Netherlands and Portugal.

86 I have tamed men of iron in my day, shall I not easily crush these men of butter?
1567 On his appointment as Lieutenant-General to the Netherlands. Quoted in J L Motley *The Rise of the Dutch Republic* (1889), vol.2.

Albee, Edward Franklin, III 1928–

US dramatist, influenced by the Theatre of the Absurd, whose plays address the moral ambiguities of US middle-class life. His best-known work is *Who's Afraid of Virginia Woolf?* (1962), but *A Delicate Balance* (1966), *Seascape* (1975) and *Three Tall Women* (1991) all won Pulitzer Prizes.

87 JERRY: I have learned that neither kindness or cruelty by themselves, or independent of each other, create any effect beyond themselves.
1958 *The Zoo Story.*

88 JERRY: When you're a kid you use the cards as a substitute for a real experience, and when you're older you use real experience as a substitute for the fantasy.
1958 On pornographic playing cards. *The Zoo Story.*

89 BESSIE: I am sick of the disparity between things as they are and as they should be. I'm tired. I'm tired of the truth and I'm tired of lying about the truth.
1960 *The Death of Bessie Smith.*

90 Who's Afraid of Virginia Woolf?
1962 Title of play.

91 MARTHA: I have a fine sense of the ridiculous, but no sense of humour.

1962 *Who's Afraid of Virginia Woolf?*, act 1.

92 GEORGE: By God, you gotta have a swine to show you where the truffles are.
1962 *Who's Afraid of Virginia Woolf?*, act 2.

93 I am a Doctor. A.B....M.A....PH.D....ABMAPHID!...a wasting disease of the frontal lobes.
1962 Spoken by a college professor. *Who's Afraid of Virginia Woolf?*

94 American critics are like American universities...both have dull and half-dead faculties.
1969 Speech to the New York Cultural League. Reported in news summaries, 6 Nov.

95 People would rather sleep their way through life than stay awake for it.
Quoted in Joseph F McCrindle (ed) *Behind the Scenes* (1971).

Prince Albert 1819–61

Prince Consort of Queen Victoria, son of the Duke of Saxe-Coburg-Gotha. A patron of the arts and science, he planned the Great Exhibition of 1851. He died of typhoid.

96 I have had wealth, rank and power, but, if these were all I had, how wretched I should be.
1861 Attributed last words.

Alberti, Leon Battista 1404–72

Italian architect, musician, painter and humanist, dubbed 'Alberti the all-sided' by the historian Burckhardt. His work *De re aedificatoria* (c.1450), is considered the first modern work on architecture.

97 Perhaps the artist who seeks dignity above all in his 'historia', ought to represent very few figures; for as paucity of words imparts majesty to a prince, provided his thoughts and orders are understood, so the presence of only the strictly necessary numbers of bodies confers dignity on a picture.
1436 *On Painting* (translated by Cecil Grayson).

98 I prefer you to take as your model a mediocre sculpture rather than an excellent painting, for from painted objects we train our hand only to make a likeness, whereas from sculptures we learn to represent both likeness and correct incidence of light.
1436 *On Painting* (translated by Cecil Grayson).

99 I am really persuaded that if we were to inquire of all the Cities which...have fallen by Siege into the Power of new Masters, who it was that subjected and overcame them, they would tell you, the Architect; and that they were strong enough to have despised the armed Enemy, but not to withstand the Shocks of the Engines, the Violence of the Machines and the Force of other Instruments of War with which the Architect, distressed, demolished and ruinated them. On the contrary, they would inform you that their greatest Defense lay in the Art and Assistance of the Architect.
1451–2 *Architecttura* (translated by James Leoni, 1755).

Alcaeus c.620–c.580 BC

Greek lyric poet. He lived in Mytilene on Lesbos, and was a contemporary of Sappho. Only fragments remain of his ten books of *Odes*.

1 Brave men are a city's strongest tower of defence.
c.600 BC Attributed.

Alcott, Louisa May 1832–88

US writer. Her children's classic *Little Women* (1868) drew on her own experiences. She completed a sequel, *Good Wives*, in 1869 and wrote other novels, including *Little Men* (1871) and *Jo's Boys* (1886).

2 Christmas won't be Christmas without any presents.
1868 *Little Women*, pt.1, ch.1.

3 Conceit spoils the finest genius...and the great charm of all power is modesty.
1868 *Little Women*, pt.1, ch.7.

4 Housekeeping ain't no joke.
1868 *Little Women*, pt.1, ch.11.

5 She had a womanly instinct that clothes possess an influence more powerful over many than the worth of character or the magic of manners.
1869 *Little Women*, pt.2, ch.34.

6 Girls are so queer you never know what they mean. They say no when they mean yes, and drive a man out of his wits just for the fun of it.
1869 *Little Women*, pt.2, ch.35.

7 What *do* girls do who haven't any mothers to help them through their troubles?
1869 *Little Women*, pt.2, ch.46.

Alcuin 735–804

English cleric and scholar. In 771 Charlemagne summoned him to his court as tutor of the royal family. In 778 he became master of his old school at York. His numerous works include treatises on rhetoric, ethics, and theology.

8 *Nec audiendi qui solent dicere, vox populi, vox Dei, quum tumultuositas vulgi semper insaniae proxima sit.*
We should not listen to those who like to affirm that the voice of the people is the voice of God, for the tumult of the masses is truly close to madness.
800 Letter to Charlemagne.

Aldington, Richard *pseudonym of Edward Godfree* 1892–1962

English poet, novelist and biographer. He married fellow Imagist poet Hilda Doolittle ('H.D.'). His best-known work is the novel *Death of a Hero* (1929).

9 Patriotism is a lively sense of collective responsibility. Nationalism is a silly cock crowing on its own dunghill.
1931 *The Colonel's Daughter*, pt.1, ch.6.

Aldiss, Brian Wilson 1925–

English science-fiction writer and novelist. Early novels include *The Hand-Reared Boy* (1970) and *A Soldier Erect* (1971), but his major work has been in science fiction, as a writer, critic and compiler of anthologies.

10 Science fiction is no more written for scientists than ghost stories are written for ghosts.
1961 *Penguin Science Fiction*, introduction.

11 Keep violence in the mind
Where it belongs.
1969 *Barefoot in the Head*, 'Charteris'.

12 The feat represents immense achievement for the neotenic ape, species Homo sapiens. But behind this lie two old attributes of the ape—tribalism and inquisitiveness.
1969 On space flight, in *The Guardian*.

13 Hubris clobbered by Nemesis.
1975 His definition of science fiction. *Science Fiction Art*, introduction.

Aldrich, Henry 1647–1710

English cleric, Dean of Christ Church, Oxford. He designed the Peckwater Quadrangle and wrote the popular catch 'Hark, the bonny Christ-Church Bells', but is best remembered for his *Artis Logicae Compendium* (1691).

14 If all be true that I do think,
There are five reasons why men drink,
Good wine, a friend, or being dry,
Or lest we should be by-and-by,
Or any other reason why.
1689 'Five Reasons for Drinking'.

Aldrin, Edwin E(ugene) Jr *known as* **'Buzz'** 1930–

US astronaut, a crew member on Apollo 11 and the second man to walk on the moon.

15 Houston, Tranquillity Base here. The Eagle has landed.
1969 Radio transmission from the moon, 20 Jul. These were the first words uttered by a human on the moon's surface.

16 Beautiful! Beautiful! Magnificent desolation.
1969 Spoken as he stepped out of the Eagle to join Neil Armstrong on the first moon walk, 20 Jul.

Alembert, Jean le Rond d' 1717–83

French mathematician and philosopher. He wrote a major work on *Dynamics* (1743) and pioneered studies on the mechanics of rigid bodies, the motions of fluids and vibrating strings.

17 Day by day natural science accumulates new riches…
The true system of the World has been recognized, developed and perfected… Everything has been discussed and analyzed, or at least mentioned.
1759 *Elements of Philosophy*.

Alexander the Great 356–323 BC

King of Macedonia. He succeeded his father Philip at the age of 20, and set out to conquer the Persian Empire, campaigning as far as Afghanistan and the Indus valley. He died of a fever in Babylon, and his empire was divided between his generals.

18 Truly, if I were not Alexander, I would be Diogenes.
Quoted in Plutarch *Alexander*, 14.3.
➤ See Diogenes of Sinope 275:21.

19 The end and object of conquest is to avoid doing the same thing as the conquered.
Quoted in Plutarch *Alexander*, 40.2.

Alexander I 1777–1825

Tsar of Russia (1801–25), grandson of Catherine the Great. He spent much of his reign fighting Napoleon and founded the Holy Alliance (1815) to exclude the House of Bonaparte from power in France.

20 Napoleon thinks that I am a fool, but he who laughs last laughs longest.
1808 Letter to his sister, 8 Oct.

Alexander II *known as* **'the Liberator'** 1818–81

Tsar of Russia (1855–81). His reign was marked by the emancipation of the serfs (1861), political and military reform, the expansion of the Russian Empire into Asia and the defeat of Turkey (1877–8). He was assassinated.

21 It is better to abolish serfdom from above than to wait for it to abolish itself from below.
1856 Speech, 30 Mar.

Alexander, Cecil Frances 1818–95

Irish hymnwriter and poet.

22 All things bright and beautiful,
All creatures great and small,
All things wise and wonderful,
The Lord God made them all.
1848 'All Things Bright and Beautiful'.

23 The rich man in his castle,
The poor man at his gate,
God made them, high or lowly,
And ordered their estate.
1848 'All Things Bright and Beautiful'.

24 Once in royal David's city
Stood a lowly cattle-shed,
Where a mother laid her baby
In a manger for his bed.
Mary was that mother mild,
Jesus Christ her little child.
1848 'Once in Royal David's City'.

25 There is a green hill far away,
Without a city wall,
Where the dear Lord was crucified,
Who died to save us all.
1848 'There is a Green Hill Far Away'

26 I bind into myself today
The strong name of the Trinity,
By invocation of the same
The Three in One and One in Three.
1889 'St Patrick's Breastplate', his translation from the Irish.

Alexander, Sir William c.1567–1640

Scottish courtier and poet.

27 The weaker sex, to piety more prone.
1637 Of women. 'Doomsday', Fifth Hour.

Algren, Nelson 1909–81

US novelist, a journalist in Chicago and a migrant worker during the Depression. His hard-bitten, realist novels include *The Man with the Golden Arm* (1949).

28 A Walk on the Wild Side.
1956 Title of novel.

29 Never play cards with a man called Doc. Never eat at a place called Mom's. And never, ever, no matter what else you do in your whole life, never sleep with anyone whose troubles are worse than your own.
1956 In *Newsweek*, 2 Jul. Algren claimed that these were his only principles, taught him by 'a nice old Negro lady'.

30 I went out there for a thousand a week, and I worked Monday, and I got fired Wednesday. The guy that hired me was out of town Tuesday.
In Malcolm Crowley (ed) *Writers at Work* (1958).

31 The hard necessity of bringing the judge on the bench down into the dock has been the peculiar responsibility

of the writer in all ages of man.
1961 Preface to reprint of *Chicago: City On The Make* (first published 1951).

Ali, Muhammad *formerly* **Cassius Clay** 1942–

US boxer. World heavyweight champion in 1964, he was stripped of his title after refusing military service on religious grounds (he was a Black Muslim). His title was restored in 1970, lost to Joe Frazier the next year and regained in 1974 and 1978. He retired in 1981.

32 I am the greatest!
1962 In the *Louisville Times*, 16 Nov. This became his catchphrase.

33 Float like a butterfly, sting like a bee.
c.1964 Of his boxing style. Quoted in G Sullivan *Cassius Clay* (1964), ch.8.

Allainval, Abbé d' 1700–53

French dramatist.

34 *L'embarras des richesses.*
The Embarrassment of Riches.
1726 Title of play.

Allen, Henry Southworth 1941–

US journalist. He is a feature writer and editor for the *Washington Post* (1970–).

35 They are a great tradition…gliding in and out of the corridors of power with the opulent calm of angelfish swimming through an aquarian castle.
1989 Of presidential advisers. In the *Washington Post*, 3 Jan.

36 He long ago learned to eschew the little turf-dances of human encounter.
1989 Of Brent Scowcroft, National Security Council adviser to George Bush. In the *Washington Post*, 3 Jan.

37 It is unlikely that anyone will write his biography, but he will be enshrined in 10,000 indexes.
1989 Of Brent Scowcroft, National Security Council adviser to George Bush. In the *Washington Post*, 3 Jan.

38 Doesn't she know that numberless women have walked past mirrors hoping for a hint of Bacall's slinkiness?
1994 Of Lauren Bacall at age 70. In the *Washington Post*, 27 Oct.

39 Edward Hopper is the great painter of American hell in the 20th century, the limner-laureate of the beauty, poignance, eternity and bone-ache disquietude of life.
1995 In the *Washington Post*, 25 Jun.

Allen, Tim 1953–

US actor and comedian.

40 To infinity and beyond!
1995 As the voice of Buzz Lightyear in *Toy Story* (1995, screenplay by Joss Whedon, Andrew Stanton, Joel Cohen, Joe Ranft, John Lasseter and Pete Docter).

Allen, Woody *pseudonym of* **Allen Stewart Konigsberg** 1935–

US film-maker and writer. He is best known for his comic films, which focus on the neuroses of urban life and relationships, and he has also published collections of essays and stories.

41 I think crime pays. The hours are good, you travel a lot.
1969 *Take the Money and Run.*

42 Not only is there no God, but try getting a plumber on weekends.
1969 'My Philosophy', in the *New Yorker*, 27 Dec.

43 TB or not TB, that is the congestion.
1972 *Everything You Always Wanted to Know about Sex.*

44 The lion and the calf shall lie down together but the calf won't get much sleep.
1974 'The Scrolls', in *The New Republic*, 31 Aug.

45 It's not that I'm afraid to die. I just don't want to be there when it happens.
1975 *Death: A Comedy in One Act.*

46 It immediately doubles your chances for a date on Saturday night.
1975 On bisexuality. In the *New York Times*, 1 Dec.

47 My one regret in life is that I am not someone else.
Quoted as epigraph in Eric Lax *Woody Allen and His Comedy* (1975).

48 Death is an acquired trait.
Quoted in Eric Lax *Woody Allen and His Comedy* (1975), ch.11.

49 I don't want to achieve immortality through my work… I want to achieve it through not dying.
Quoted in Eric Lax *Woody Allen and His Comedy* (1975), ch.12.

50 And my parents finally realize that I'm kidnapped and they snap into action immediately: they rent out my room.
Quoted in Eric Lax *Woody Allen and His Comedy* (1975).

51 On the plus side, death is one of the few things that can be done as easily lying down.
1976 *Without Feathers*, 'Early Essays'.

52 Money is better than poverty, if only for financial reasons.
1976 *Without Feathers*, 'Early Essays'.

53 That was the most fun I ever had without laughing.
1977 Of sex. *Annie Hall* (with Marshall Brickman).

54 Don't knock masturbation. It's sex with someone I love.
1977 *Annie Hall* (with Marshall Brickman).

55 I'm old fashioned. I don't believe in extra-marital relationships. I think people should mate for life, like pigeons or Catholics.
1979 *Manhattan* (with Marshall Brickman).

56 More than at any other time in history, mankind faces a crossroads. One path leads to despair and utter hopelessness. The other, to total extinction. Let us pray we have the wisdom to choose correctly.
1980 *Side Effects*, 'My Speech to the Graduates'.

57 Eighty percent of success is showing-up.
Quoted in Thomas J Peters and Robert H Waterman *Among Friends* (1982).

58 I recently turned sixty. Practically a third of my life is over.
Quoted in the *Observer*, 'Sayings of the Week', 10 Mar 1996.

59 Life does not imitate art. It imitates bad television.
2000 In *The Guardian*, 31 Dec.

Allingham, Margery Louise 1904–66

English writer, creator of the fictional detective Albert Campion. She wrote a series of elegant and witty detective novels, such as *Flowers for the Judge* (1936) and *The China Governess* (1963).

60 Once sex rears its ugly 'ead it's time to steer clear.
1936 *Flowers for the Judge*, ch.4.

Allingham, William   1824–89

Irish poet and editor of *Fraser's Magazine* (from 1874). His *Diary* (published 1907) is a rich recollection of Victorian literary life. Other works include *Day and Night Songs* (1855), illustrated by Dante Gabriel Rossetti and Millais.

61 Up the airy mountain,
Down the rushy glen,
We daren't go a-hunting,
For fear of little men;
Wee folk, good folk,
Trooping all together;
Green jacket, red cap,
And white owl's feather!
1850 'The Fairies'.

62 Four ducks on a pond,
A grass-bank beyond,
A blue sky of spring,
White clouds on the wing;
What a little thing
To remember for years—
To remember with tears!
1888 'A Memory'.

Allsop, (Harold) Bruce   1912–2000

English architect, author, publisher and artist. His many books include *A Modern Theory of Architecture* (1977) and *Should Man Survive?* (1982).

63 For the normal business of living man is most at ease on the ground.
1977 *A Modern Theory of Architecture*.

64 The phenomenon of architecture is a development of the phenomenon of man.
1977 *A Modern Theory of Architecture*.

Almeida, Manuel Antônio de   1831–61

Brazilian writer, translator and journalist, killed in a shipwreck off the Brazilian coast while on a newspaper assignment. His *Memórias de um sargento de milícias* (1953) is considered the first great novel in Brazilian literature.

65 *Espiar a vida alheia, inquirir dos escravos o que se passava no interior das casas, era naquele tempo coisa tão comum e enraizada nos costumes, que ainda hoje, depois de passados tantos anos, restam grandes vestígios dêsse belo hábito.*
Spying on other people's lives, asking slaves what was going on inside their houses was then so common and such a part of our customs that today, after so many years have passed, we have many remnants of such a beautiful habit.
1853 *Memórias de um sargento de milícias* (*Memoirs of a Militia Sergeant*, 1959), ch.3.

Almodóvar, Pedro   1951–

Spanish film director. His first film to attain worldwide success was *Mujeres al Borde de un Ataque de Nervios* (1988, *Women on the Verge of a Nervous Breakdown*).

66 When I was 10, I expressly gave God one year to manifest himself. He didn't.
2004 In *The Guardian*, 7 May.

Alsop, Stewart   1914–74

US political columnist.

67 A fashionable gentleman who much concerns himself with the fashions of gentlemen is neither fashionable nor a gentleman.
1975 In *Newsweek*, 30 Jun.

Alther, Lisa *née Reed*   1944–

US novelist. She achieved success with her comic novel *Kinflicks* (1976), and explored the themes of personal and sexual identity in several subsequent books.

68 If this was adulthood, the only improvement she could detect in her situation was that now she could eat dessert without eating her vegetables.
1976 *Kinflicks*, ch.2.

69 There was nothing wrong with her that a vasectomy of the vocal chords wouldn't fix.
1976 *Kinflicks*, ch.4.

70 I happen to feel that the degree of a person's intelligence is directly reflected by the number of conflicting attitudes she can bring to bear on the same topic.
1976 *Kinflicks*, ch.7.

71 He picked her up out of the dirt and turned her into the clod she was today.
1981 *Original Sins*, pt.4, ch.1.

Altman, Robert   1925–

US film director. His first critical and commercial success was *M*A*S*H* (1970).

72 What's a cult? It just means not enough people to make a minority.
1981 Interview in the *Observer*, 11 Apr.

73 You will never see 'Altman's Great Film of the Seventies: The Director's Cut' because you have never seen a film of mine that wasn't the director's cut. I have never permitted it.
2004 In *The Independent*, 14 May.

Amado, Jorge   1912–2001

Brazilian novelist, born on a cacao plantation in Ferradas. He was imprisoned several times and exiled for leftist activities. Most of his novels are picaresque, ribald tales of lower-class Bahian city life.

74 *Ninguém no cais tem um nome só. Todos têm também um apelido ou abreviam o nome, ou o aumentam, ou lhe acrescentam qualquer coisa que recorde uma história, uma luta, um amor.*
No one on the docks has just one name. Everybody has a nickname too, or the name is shortened, or lengthened, or something is added that recalls a tale, a fight, a woman.
1936 *Mar morto* (*Sea of Death*, 1984), 'Iemanjá'.

St Ambrose   c.339–397 AD

Bishop of Milan. He was much admired by St Augustine.

75 *Ubi Petrus, ibi ergo ecclesia.*
Where Peter is, there, accordingly, is the Church.
Explanatio psalmi 40.

American Library Association

76 The computer is a fast idiot, it has no imagination; it cannot originate action. It is, and will remain, only a tool to man.

1964 Statement of the American Library Association regarding the Univac computer exhibited at the New York World's Fair, 1964.

Amerine, Maynard Andrew 1911–98

US oenologist, Professor at the University of California. His works on viniculture include *Wine: An Introduction for Americans* (1965) and *Introduction to Food Science and Technology* (1973).

77 The fine wine leaves you with something pleasant; the ordinary wine just leaves.
Quoted in Clifton Fadiman *The New Joy of Wine* (1990).

Amery, Leo(pold) Charles Maurice Stennett
1873–1955

English Conservative politician. After working on *The Times* for 10 years he became an MP and served as Colonial Secretary (1919–29) and Secretary of State for India and Burma.

78 For twenty years he has held a season ticket on the line of least resistance and has gone wherever the train of events has carried him, lucidly justifying his position at whatever point he happened to find himself.
1914 Of Herbert Asquith, in *Quarterly Review,* Jul.

79 Speak for England, Arthur!
1939 Shouted to Arthur Greenwood, Labour Opposition spokesman, 2 Sep, as Greenwood began a House of Commons speech calling for the resignation of Prime Minister Neville Chamberlain, immediately preceding the declaration of World War II.

80 Cromwell said to the Long Parliament when he thought it was no longer fit to conduct the affairs of the nation, 'You have sat too long here for any good you have been doing. Depart, I say, and let us have done with you. In the name of God, go!'
1940 Remark addressed to Prime Minister Neville Chamberlain, House of Commons, 7 May.

Amin (Dada), Idi 1925–2003

Ugandan soldier and politician, an army commander who seized power in 1971 and was proclaimed President. He was deposed by exiled Ugandans with the help of the Tanzanian army in 1979 and fled to Libya.

81 Your experience will be a lesson to all of us men to be careful not to marry ladies in very high positions.
1978 Unsolicited advice to Lord Snowdon on the ending of his marriage to Princess Margaret, quoted in A Barrow *International Gossip* (1983).

Amis, Sir Kingsley 1922–95

English novelist and poet. He achieved success with his irreverent novel *Lucky Jim* (1954), and went on to write a substantial body of novels, poetry and non-fiction.

82 The light did him harm, but not as much as looking at things did; he resolved, having done it once, never to move his eyeballs again. A dusty thudding in his head made the scene before him beat like a pulse. His mouth had been used as a latrine by some small creature of the night, and then as its mausoleum.
1953 *Lucky Jim,* ch.6.

83 He thought what a pity it was that all his faces were designed to express rage or loathing. Now that something had happened that really deserved a face, he'd none to celebrate it with. As a kind of token, he made his Sex Life in Ancient Rome face.
1953 *Lucky Jim,* ch.25.

84 Man's love is of man's life a thing apart;
Girls aren't like that.
1956 'A Bookshop Idyll'.
➤ See Byron 181:73.

85 Politics is a thing that only the unsophisticated can really go for.
1957 'Socialism and the Intellectuals'.

86 Work was like cats were supposed to be: if you disliked and feared it and tried to keep out if its way, it knew at once and sought you out and jumped on your lap and climbed all over you to show how much it loved you. Please God, he thought, don't let me die in harness.
1960 *Take A Girl Like You,* ch.5.

87 More will mean worse.
1960 On expanding university intake, in *Encounter,* Jul.

88 Outside every fat man there was an even fatter man trying to close in.
1963 *One Fat Englishman,* ch.3.
➤ See also Connolly 233:82.

89 He was of the faith chiefly in the sense that the church he currently did not attend was Catholic.
1963 *One Fat Englishman,* ch.8.

90 It was no wonder that people were so horrible when they started life as children.
1963 *One Fat Englishman,* ch.14.

91 I was never an Angry Young Man. I am angry only when I hit my thumb with a hammer.
1979 Dissociating himself from that literary grouping, in *The Eton College Chronicle,* Jun.

92 The rewards for being sane may not be very many but knowing what's funny is one of them.
1984 *Stanley and the Women,* ch.2.

93 Alun's life was coming to consist more and more exclusively of being told at dictation speed what he knew.
1986 *The Old Devils,* ch.7.

94 Booze, of course, and then curtains.
1986 His response to being asked how he would spend his Booker Prize cheque, 22 Oct.

95 I wish he'd *shut up* about Flaubert.
Said about Julian Barnes. Quoted in Julian Barnes *Something to Declare* (2002).

Amis, Martin Louis 1949–

English novelist, son of Kingsley Amis. His novels include *The Rachel Papers* (1974), *London Fields* (1989), *Time's Arrow* (1991) and *The Information* (1995).

96 The middle-management of Manhattan stared on, their faces as thin as credit cards.
1984 *Money.*

97 His name was Shadow, short for Shadow That Comes in Sight, an old Indian name, Apache or Cheyenne. I very much approved of this. You don't want dogs called Spot or Pooch. You don't want dogs called Nigel or Keith. The names of dogs should salute the mystical drama of the animal life. *Shadow*—that's a *good* name.
1984 *Money.*

98 My theory is—we don't really go that far into other people, even when we think we do. We hardly ever go in and bring them out. We just stand at the jaws of the cave, and strike a match, and ask quickly if anybody's there.
1984 *Money*.

99 New York is a jungle, they tell you. You could go further, and say that New York is a jungle. New York *is a jungle*. Beneath the columns of the old rain forest, made of melting macadam, the mean Limpopo of swamped Ninth Avenue bears an angry argosy of crocs and dragons, tiger fish, noise machines, sweating rainmakers.
1984 *Money*.

1 My belief is that everything that's written about you is actually secondary showbiz nonsense, and you shouldn't take any notice of it.
1985 Quoted in John Haffenden *Novelists in Interview* (1985).

2 When success happens to an English writer, he acquires a new typewriter. When success happens to an American writer, he acquires a new life.
1986 *The Moronic Inferno*, 'Kurt Vonnegut'.

3 Most writers need a wound, either physical or spiritual.
1987 In the *Observer*, 30 Aug.

4 How do we prevent the use of nuclear weapons? By threatening to use nuclear weapons. And we can't get rid of nuclear weapons, because of nuclear weapons.
1987 *Einstein's Monsters*, introduction.

5 Someone watches over us when we write. Mother. Teacher. Shakespeare. God.
1989 *London Fields*, ch.1.

6 And meanwhile time goes about its immemorial work of making everyone look and feel like shit.
1989 *London Fields*, ch.2.

7 But we mustn't go too far back…in anybody's life… Because if we do…then nobody is to blame for anything, and nothing matters, and everything is allowed.
1989 *London Fields*, ch.10.

8 Insects are what neurosis would sound like, if neurosis could make a noise with its nose.
1995 *The Information*, pt.3.

9 You see tragedy requires persons of heroic stature. It works on the principle of people being more than human—super-human—and also being only too human. But there just aren't many great figures around now, so the tragic mechanisms can't work.
1995 Explaining why only comedy can reflect contemporary reality. Quoted in an interview in *The Scotsman*, 7 Apr.

10 We live in the age of mass loquacity. We are all writing it or at any rate talking it: the memoir, the apologia, the c.v., the *cri de coeur*.
2000 *Experience*.

Ammianus Marcellinus c.330–390 AD

Roman historian, born of Greek parents in Antioch. After a military career he moved to Rome, and devoted himself to literature. He wrote in Latin a history of the Roman Empire.

11 *Etiam parietes arcanorum soli conscii timebantur.*
Even the walls, the only sharers of secrets, were feared.

History, 14.1.7 (translated by J C Rolfe). This became a proverbial expression in the medieval tradition: 'parietes habent aures' (the walls have ears).

Amundsen, Roald Engelbregt Gravning 1872–1928

Norwegian explorer. In 1903–6 he sailed the Northwest Passage in the smack *Gjöa*. Hearing of a British expedition to the South Pole, he made as if sailing for the Arctic but instead turned south. His party beat that of Captain Scott to the South Pole by one month.

12 Beg leave to inform you proceeding Antarctica. Amundsen.
1910 Cable sent from Madeira to Captain Robert F Scott in Melbourne, 12 Oct.

Anaxagoras c.500–428 BC

Greek philosopher. He taught in Athens, and Pericles and Euripides were among his pupils. He denied the divine nature of the celestial bodies, was banned from Athens for impiety, and died in Lampsacus.

13 The sun provides the moon with its brightness.
Fragment in Plutarch *De facie in orbe lunae*, 929b.

Ancona, Ronni 1968–

Scottish comedienne and impressionist.

14 You're sitting in a room with male writers and you say something and it's ignored. You say it again and it's ignored. Then a man will say it and everyone goes 'That's brilliant'.
2004 In the *Observer*, 25 Apr.

Anderson, Admiral George, Jr c.1907–1992

US Chief of Naval Operations in the Cuban missile crisis, 1962. On retirement from the Navy he served as US Ambassador to Portugal.

15 Now, Mr Secretary, if you and your deputy will go back to your offices, the Navy will run the blockade.
1962 On brandishing a manual of procedures to Pentagon officials at the time of the Cuban missile crisis. Recalled on his death, 4 Mar 1992.

Anderson, John Edward 1917–

US businessman.

16 You need enough cash cows to feed your pigs.
1994 On financing. In *Forbes*, 17 Oct.

Anderson, Dame Judith originally *Frances Margaret Anderson* 1898–1992

Australian actress. She achieved fame in the theatre, but is best remembered for her screen role as Mrs Danvers in Alfred Hitchcock's *Rebecca* (1940). In 1984 a Broadway theatre was named after her.

17 I find myself wearing gloves more often.
On how being made a Dame of the British Empire had changed her. Attributed.

Anderson, Lindsay 1932–94

Indian-born British stage and film director. During the 1950s he made documentary films and won an Oscar for his short film *Thursday's Children* (1953). His feature film credits include *This Sporting Life* (1963), *If* (1968) and *The Whales of August* (1987).

18 Perhaps the tendency is to treat the films of one's own country like the prophets—with less than justice.
1947 Comment, quoted in Ian Christie *Arrows of Desire.*

Anderson, Maxwell 1888–1959

US dramatist. He wrote a large number of plays in both prose and verse, many on historical subjects.

19 What Price Glory?
1924 Title of play (with Lawrence Stallings).

20 But it's a long, long while
From May to December;
And the days grow short
When you reach September.
1938 'September Song' (music by Kurt Weill).

Anderson, Poul William 1926–2001

US science fiction and fantasy writer, author of numerous novels and short stories.

21 I have yet to see any problem, however complicated, which, when you looked at it in the right way, did not become still more complicated.
1969 In the *New Scientist*, 25 Sep.

Anderson, Robert Woodruff 1917–

US dramatist and novelist. His plays, confronting the difficulties of human relationships, include *Tea and Sympathy* (1953) and *I Never Sang for My Father* (1968), and he also wrote several screenplays.

22 All you're supposed to do is every once in a while give the boys a little tea and sympathy.
1953 On the duties of a headmaster's wife. *Tea and Sympathy,* act 1.

Anderson, Sherwood 1876–1941

US author, who left a lucrative job as manager of a paint factory to write full-time. His *Winesburg, Ohio* (1919) is a naturalistic study of small-town America in 23 stories.

23 The moment one of the people took one of the truths to himself, called it his truth, and tried to live his life by it, he became a grotesque and the truth he embraced a falsehood.
1919 *Winesburg, Ohio,* 'The Book of the Grotesque'.

Andrade, Carlos Drummond de 1902–87

Brazilian modernist poet. Although trained in pharmacy, he turned to writing and journalism. A friend of Neruda, he shared his devotion to socialism. His writing is characteristically low-key and ironic, focusing on everyday subjects.

24 *O marciano encontrou-me na rua*
e teve medo de minha impossibilidade humana.
Como pode existir, pensou consigo, um ser
que no existir põe sem tamanha anulação de
existência?
The Martian met me in the streets
and was frightened by my human impossibility.
He wondered how such a being could exist
who could not exist without unmaking so much
existence.
1961 *Lição de coisas,* 'Science Fiction'.

Andrade, Mário de 1893–1945

Brazilian modernist writer. His works reflect a deep interest in Brazilian folk culture, and his highly individual prose style imitates colloquial Brazilian speech.

25 *Os guerreiros de cá não buscam mavórticas damas para*
o enlace epitalâmico; mas antes as preferem dóceis e
facilmente trocáveis por pequeninas e voláteis folhas de
papel a que o vulgo chamará dinheiro—o 'curriculum
vitae' da Civilização.
The warriors here do not seek out mettlesome women for epithalamic conjunction, but prefer them docile and willing to exchange with ease their favours for those small and deliquescent leaves of paper which the masses call money—the *curriculum vitae* of Civilization.
1928 *Macunaíma (O Herói sem nenhum caráter) (Macunaima,* 1984), ch.9.

Andreas Capellanus fl. late 12c

French priest and writer, possibly chaplain to the court of Champagne. *De Amore* is his only known work.

26 *Liquide constet inter virum et uxorem amorem sibi*
locum vindicare non posse.
It is clearly certain that between man and wife love can claim no place.
c.1185 *De Amore,* bk.1, ch.6, section 7.

Andrewes, Lancelot 1555–1626

English ecclesiastic, renowned for his memorable sermons. He became Bishop of Chichester, then Ely and finally Winchester.

27 It was no summer progress. A cold coming they had of it, at this time of the year; just, the worst time of the year, to take a journey, and specially a long journey, in. The ways deep, the weather sharp, the days short, the sun farthest off *in solstitio brumali,* the very dead of winter.
1622 *Of the Nativity,* sermon 15.
➤ *See Eliot 306:73.*

28 The nearer the Church, the further from God.
1622 *Of the Nativity,* sermon 15.

Andrews, Julie originally *Julia Elizabeth Wells* 1935–

British singer and actress. She starred in several long-running Broadway musicals, notably *My Fair Lady* (1956) and *Camelot* (1960). Her most popular films have been *Mary Poppins* (1964) and *The Sound of Music* (1965).

29 I'd like to thank all those who made this possible—especially Jack Warner
1965 Speech at the Oscar ceremony when she won an Academy Award for her role in *Mary Poppins,* 5 Apr. Warner had rejected her for the screen role of Eliza in *My Fair Lady,* although she had played it to great acclaim on the stage, preferring Audrey Hepburn whose singing had to be dubbed. Andrews had instead taken the part in *Mary Poppins.*

Angell, Roger 1920–

US journalist. Fiction editor at the *New Yorker,* he is also known for his baseball writing.

30 Such days and moments pass, in ways that this one has not, but there's a weary strength in experience, even in the midst of horror.
2001 Reflecting on the terrorist attacks on 11 Sep. In the *New Yorker.*

Angelou, Maya *originally* **Maya Johnson** 1928–

US writer. A sexual assault on her in childhood left her mute for several years. She became a successful writer with her multi-volume autobiography. She has also published several volumes of verse.

31 If growing up is painful for the Southern Black girl, being aware of her displacement is the rust on the razor that threatens the throat.
1969 *I Know Why The Caged Bird Sings*, opening section.

32 Children's talent to endure stems from their ignorance of alternatives.
1969 *I Know Why The Caged Bird Sings*, ch.17.

33 The quality of strength lined with tenderness is an unbeatable combination, as are intelligence and necessity when unblunted by formal education.
1970 *I Know Why The Caged Bird Sings*, ch.29.

34 At fifteen life had taught me undeniably that surrender, in its place, was as honorable as resistance, especially if one had no choice.
1970 *I Know Why The Caged Bird Sings*, ch.31.

35 The fact that the adult American Negro female emerges a formidable character is often met with amazement, distaste and even belligerence. It is seldom accepted as an inevitable outcome of the struggle won by survivors, and deserves respect if not enthusiastic acceptance.
1970 *I Know Why The Caged Bird Sings*, ch.34

36 Most plain girls are virtuous because of the scarcity of opportunity to be otherwise.
1970 *I Know Why The Caged Bird Sings*, ch.35

37 It is a historical truth. No man can know where he is going unless he knows exactly where he has been and exactly how he arrived at his present place.
1972 On Africa. In the *New York Times*, 16 Apr.

38 There is a kind of strength that is almost frightening in black women. It's as if a steel rod runs right through the head down to the feet.
1973 Television interview, 21 Nov. Collected in *Conversations with Maya Angelou* (1989).

39 We had won… I thought if war did not include killing, I'd like to see one every year. Something like a festival.
1974 On the end of World War II. *Gather Together In My Name*, prologue.

40 Self-pity in its early stage is as snug as a feather mattress. Only when it hardens does it become uncomfortable.
1974 *Gather Together In My Name*, ch.6.

41 The sadness of the women's movement is that they don't allow the necessity of love. See, I don't personally trust any revolution where love is not allowed.
1975 Interview in *California Living*, 14 May. Collected in *Conversations with Maya Angelou* (1989).

42 Oh, the holiness of always being the injured party. The historically oppressed can find not only sanctity but safety in the state of victimization. When access to a better life has been denied often enough, and successfully enough, one can use the rejection as an excuse to cease all efforts.
1976 *Singin' and Swingin' and Getting Merry Like Christmas*, ch.9.

43 Life loves the liver of it.
1977 Interview in *Black Scholar*, Jan–Feb. Collected in *Conversations with Maya Angelou* (1989).

44 Something made greater by ourselves and in turn that makes us greater.
1977 Defining work. Interview in *Black Scholar*, Jan–Feb. Collected in *Conversations with Maya Angelou* (1989).

45 There is an awesome reality to Rent Day. It comes trumpeting, forcing the days before it into a wild scramble.
1981 *The Heart of a Woman*, ch.3.

46 The cliché of whites being ignorant of blacks was not only true, but understandable. Oh, but we knew them with the intimacy of a surgeon's scalpel.
1981 *The Heart of a Woman*, ch.12.

47 Genet had been right at least about one thing. Blacks should be used to play whites. For centuries we had probed their faces, the angles of their bodies, the sounds of their voices and even their odors. Often our survival had depended on the accurate reading of a white man's chuckle or the disdainful wave of a white woman's hand.
1981 *The Heart of a Woman*, ch.12.

48 Poetry is music written for the human voice.
1989 In 'The Power of the Word', Public Broadcasting Service, 15 Sep.

49 Wouldn't Take Nothing for my Journey Now.
1994 Title of book.

Angle, Colin

US businessman. Co-founder and Chief Executive Officer of iRobot.

50 We're not using these robots to hand out flowers.
2004 On the possibility of arming military robots.

Annan, Noël Gilroy, Baron 1916–2000

English scholar, Chair of the Board of Trustees of the National Gallery (1980–5). His works include *Our Age: portrait of a generation* (1990).

51 He cultivated to perfection the sneer which he used like an oyster-knife, inserting it into the shell of his victim, exposing him with a quick-turn of the wrist, and finally flipping him over and inviting his audience to discard him as tainted and inedible.
1991 On the critic F R Leavis. *English Intellectuals Between the World Wars*.

Anne, Queen 1665–1714

Queen of Great Britain and Ireland (1702–14), the last Stuart monarch. Her reign was marked by the union of England and Scotland (1707) and the War of the Spanish Succession. After quarrelling with the Marlboroughs (Whigs), she appointed a Tory government in 1710.

52 Cricket is not illegal, for it is a manly game.
1710 Quoted in Colin Jarman *The Guinness Dictionary of Sports Quotations* (1990).

53 I have changed my Ministers but I have not changed my measures. I am still for moderation, and I will govern by it.
1711 Addressing her new Tory administration, Jan.

Anne Elizabeth Alice Louise 1950–

HRH The Princess Royal, daughter of Queen Elizabeth II and Prince Philip. She has worked on behalf of various charities, notably as President of the Save the Children Fund.

54 It could be said that the AIDS pandemic is a classic own-goal scored by the human race against itself.
1988 In the *Daily Telegraph*, 27 Jan.

Annenberg, Walter H 1908–2002

US publishing tycoon, philanthropist and former US Ambassador to Great Britain and Northern Ireland, a noted art enthusiast and collector.

55 Only when you are moved by a painting should you buy it. Being moved is what collecting is all about.
1991 In *Connoisseur*, Feb.

56 You are asking me to sell members of my family.
1991 In the *New York Times*, 12 Mar. Rejecting a billion-dollar Japanese offer for his art collection.

Anonymous

57 Either with it or upon it.
Traditionally said by a Spartan mother while handing her son his shield when he went to war; he should either return with it (ie as a victor) or on it (ie dead). Plutarch *Lacaenarum Apophthegmata*, 241f.

58 *Cave canem!*
Beware of the dog!
Famous expression, found in mosaics and inscriptions in Pompeii and other Roman towns. See also Petronius *Satyricon*, 29.1: *Ad sinistram enim intrantibus non longe ab ostiarii cella canis ingens, catena vinctus, in pariete erat pictus superque quadrata littera scriptum cave canem* (For on the left hand as you went in, not far from the porter's office, a great dog on a chain was painted on the wall, and over him was written in large letters: 'Beware of the dog'. Translation by W H D Rouse).

59 Not everyone can sail to Corinth.
ie, not everybody has the same opportunities. Greek proverb, which is also mentioned by Horace *Epistulae*, 1. 17.36: 'Non cuivis homini contingit adire Corinthum'.

60 Nothing in excess.
Famous motto in Antiquity. According to Plato, the text was a temple inscription in Delphi (*Hipparchus*, 228e).

61 *Patria est ubicumque est bene.*
One's country is wherever one does well.
Quoted as proverbial by Cicero in *Tusculanes Disputationes*, 5. 108. The saying was attributed to the mythical figure Teucer, ancestor of the Trojans, by the Roman tragedian Pacuvius (220–c.130 BC).

62 *Ave Caesar, morituri te salutant!*
Hail Caesar, we who are about to die salute you!
Traditional formula for gladiators saluting the emperor. One source for the expression is Suetonius *Claudius* 21: 'Ave Imperator, morituri te salutant', ('Hail Emperor, we salute you, we who are about to die!').

63 *Candida me docuit nigras odisse puellas. Odero si potero. Si non, invitus amabo.*
A white girl instructed me to hate black girls. I shall hate them if I can. If not, I shall love them—against my will.
c.1c AD Graffito found in Pompeii. In *Corpus Inscriptionum Latinarum* I V, 1520.

64 *Fures fores, frugi intro!*
Thieves out, profit in!
c.1c AD Graffito found in Pompeii. In *Corpus Inscriptionum Latinarum* I V, 4278.

65 *Fullones ululamque cano, non arma virumque.*
Of fullers and their wailing, I sing, not of arms and the man.

c.1c AD Graffito found in Pompeii. In *Corpus Inscriptionum Latinarum* I V, 9131. This is a parody of the famous opening line of Virgil's *Aeneid* 1.1: 'Arma virumque cano'.

66 Enjoy another glass, for you see what the end is.
c.2c AD Epitaph from Cos for a certain Chrysogonos. Quoted in W Peek *Griechische Versinschriften*, vol.1, no.378.

67 The glory of God is man, and the glory of man is his dress.
c.450 *Babylonian Talmud*. Quoted in Barton Stevenson (ed) *The Macmillan Book of Proverbs, Maxims, and Famous Phrases* (1948).

68 *Gæth a wyrd swa hio scel.*
Fate always goes as it must.
c.800 *Beowulf*, l.455.

69 *Wyrd oft nereth*
unfægne eorl thonne his ellen deah.
Fate often preserves
the undoomed warrior when his courage holds firm.
c.800 *Beowulf*, l.572–3.

70 *Oft seldan hwær*
æfter leodhyre lytle hwile
bongar bugeth.
It is very rare that,
after the fall of a prince,
the deadly spear rests for long.
c.800 *Beowulf*, l.2029–31.

71 He is joyful with swift movement when a mouse sticks in his sharp paw.
I too am joyful when I understand a dearly loved difficult problem.
c.820 'Me and Pangur Bán', by an unidentified cat-owning scholar, translated in Gerard Murphy *Early Irish Lyrics* (1956), no.1.

72 *Lytle hwile leof beoth grene*
thonne hie eft fealewiath, feallath on eorthan
and forweorniath weorthiath to duste.
For a little while the leaves are green.
Then they turn yellow, fall to the ground,
and perish, turning to dust.
c.900 *Second Dialogue of Solomon and Saturn*, l.136–8.

73 *Widgongel wif word gespringeth.*
A roving woman gives rise to gossip.
c.900 *Maxims I*, l.64.

74 *Feoh byth frofur fira gehwylcum*
Sceal theah manna gehwylc miclun hyt dælan.
Money is a comfort to each man,
But everyone should nevertheless give it away freely.
?c.900 *The Rune Poem*, l.1–2.

75 *Ear byth egle eorla gehwylcun.*
The grave is ghastly to every man.
?c.900 *The Rune Poem*, l.90.

76 Thought shall be the harder, heart the keener, courage the greater, as our might lessens.
c.1000 *The Battle of Maldon* (translated by R K Gordon).

77 *La flur de France as perdut.*
The flower of France is lost.
c.1110 *Chanson de Roland*, l.2445.

78 *Mult ad apris ki bien conuist ahan.*
He who has suffered much learns much.
c.1110 *Chanson de Roland*, l.2524.

79 *Man sol sô vrouwen ziehen…*
das si üppeclîche sprüche lasen under wegen.

Women should be trained in such a way
that they avoid idle chatter.
c.1200 *Das Nibelungenlied*, ch.14, l.193–4.

80 And nowe in the winter, when men kill the fat swine
They get the bladder and blow it great and thin,
With many beans and peason put within:
It ratleth, soundeth, and shineth clere and fayre
While it is throwen and caste up in the ayre,
Each one contendeth and hath a great delite
With foote and with hands the bladder for to smite;
If it fall to grounde, they lifte it up agayne,
But this waye to labour they count in no payne.
Medieval verse, one of the earliest descriptions of football in England.

81 *Graeca non leguntur.*
Things in Greek are not read.
Term used by medieval 'glossatores' (commentators) of the *Corpus Iuris*, indicating that the parts in Greek should be skipped. It became a traditional comment to indicate ignorance.

82 Al night by the rose, rose,
Al night by the rose I lay,
Dorst ich nought the rose stele,
And yet I bar the flour away.
c.1210–1240 Untitled lyric.

83 Sumer is icumen in,
Lhude sing cuccu!
Groweth sed, and bleweth med,
And springth the wude nu.
c.1250 'Sumer is icumen in', l.1–4.
➤ See also Pound 664:27.

84 Quhen Alysaunder oure kyng wes dede,
That Scotland led in lauche and le,
Away wes sons of alle and brede,
Off wyne and wax, of gamyn and gle;
Oure gold wes changyd in to lede.
Cryst, borne in to virgynyte,
Succour Scotland, and remede,
That stad is in perplexyte.
c.1286 Lines said to have been written after the death of Alexander II of Scotland, the earliest extant piece of Scottish verse. Quoted in the *Original Chronicle of Andrew Wyntoun* (c.1420), bk.7.

85 Lenten is come with love to toune.
c.1300 'Lenten is come', l.1.

86 *Quamdiu centum viui remanserint, nuncquam Anglorum dominio aliquatenus volumus subjugari.*
As long as one hundred of us shall remain alive, we shall never consent to subject ourselves in any degree to English dominion.
1320 *Declaration of Arbroath*, a letter sent by the barons of Scotland to Pope John XXII, asserting Scotland's independence from England and their right to defend that independence with or without the support of their sovereign.

87 Not what thou arte, ne what thou hast ben, beholdeth
God with his mercyful iye; bot that thou woldest be.
c.1370 *The Cloud of Unknowing*, ch.75.

88 *Patience is a poynt, thagh it displese ofte.*
Patience is a virtue, though it often displeases.
c.1370 *Patience*, l.1.

89 *Ay wolde man of happe more hente
Then moghte by ryght upon hem cleven.*

Man always desires to seize more of happiness,
Than rightfully belongs to him.
c.1370 *Pearl*, l.1195–6.

90 *Of alle chevalry to chose, the chef thyng alosed
Is the lel layk of luf, the lettrure of armes.*
Choosing from all chivalrous actions, the chief things to praise
Are the loyal sport of love and the lore of arms.
c.1370 *Sir Gawain and the Green Knight*, l.1512–3.

91 Yif thou wolte lyve frely, lerne to dye gladly.
c.1375 *The Art of Dieing.*

92 Young men a wooing, for God that you bought,
Be well ware of wedding and think in your thought:
'Had I wist' is a thing, it serves of nought.
c.1425 *The Second Shepherd's Play*, part of the York cycle of Mystery Plays, l.91–3.

93 *Now why that erthe luves erthe, wondere me thinke,
Or why that erthe for erthe sholde other swete or
   swinke:
For when that erthe upon erthe es broghte within brinke,
Thane shall erthe of erthe have a foulle stinke.*
Now, why earth loves earth, I wonder to think,
Or why earth for earth should either sweat or labour:
For when earth upon earth comes within the grave's
   brink,
Then earth upon earth shall have a foul stink.
c.1450 'Erthe oute of erthe', l.19–22.

94 I wyll that my son manhede take
For reson wyll that there be thre—
A man, a madyn, and a tre.
Man for man, tre for tre,
Madyn for madyn; thus shall it be.
?c.1450 God the Father explains how Christ will atone for Adam's sin. *Towneley Annunciation Play*, l.30–5.

95 *Pees maketh plente;
Plente maketh pride;
Pride make plee;
Plee maketh povert;
Povert maketh pees.*
Peace makes plenty;
Plenty makes pride;
Pride makes lawsuits;
Lawsuits make poverty;
Poverty makes peace.
c.1470 Untitled lyric.

96 O God in Heaven, on you we call,
Kyrie eleison,
Help us seize our priests and kill them all,
Kyrie eleison.
1476 Satirical chant. Quoted in Gerald Strauss *Manifestations of Discontent in Germany on the Eve of the Reformation* (1971).

97 Everyman, I will go with thee, and be thy guide.
In thy most need to go by thy side.
c.1485 Knowledge speaks to Everyman. *Everyman*, l.522–3.

98 In youth open your mind, And let all learning in;
Words the head does not shape Are worthless, out
   and in.
Words wit has not salted, No nearer the heart than
   the lip,
Are nothing more than wind, A puppy's insolent yelp.
c.1500 'To a Boy'. Translated from the Irish by Michael O'Donovan ('Frank O'Connor').

99 Westron winde, when wilt thou blow,
The smalle raine downe can raine?
Christ if my love were in my armes,
And I in my bed againe.
c.1500 Untitled lyric.

1 Back and side go bare, go bare,
Both foot and hand go cold;
But, belly, God send thee good ale enough,
Whether it be new or old.
c.1575 Song, included in the play *Gammer Gurton's Needle*, act 2.
William Stevenson (c.1530–75) and John Still (1543–1608) have
both been credited with authorship of the play, but the song
probably predates it.

2 I cannot eat but little meat,
My stomach is not good;
But sure I think that I can drink
With him that wears a hood.
c.1575 Song, included in the play *Gammer Gurton's Needle*, act 2.
'Him that wears a hood' is either a monk or a scholar.

3 And Tib my wife, that as her life
Loveth well good ale to seek,
Full oft drinks she, till ye may see
The tears run down her cheeks.
c.1575 Song, included in the play *Gammer Gurton's Needle*, act 2.

4 Though raging stormes movis us to shake,
And wind makis waters overflow;
We yield thereto bot dois not break
And in the calm bent up we grow.

So baneist men, though princes rage,
And prisoners, be not despairit.
Abide the calm, whill that it 'suage,
For time sic causis has repairit.
1582 *The Maitland Manuscript*, 'The Reeds in the Loch Sayis'.

5 Brissit brawnis and broken banis
Stryfe discorde and waistis wanis
Crukit in eild, syne halt withal,
This are the bewteis of the fute-ball.
1582 *The Maitland Manuscript*, 'The Bewteis of the Fute-ball'.

6 *Flavit deus et dissipati sunt*
God blew and they were scattered.
1588 Inscription on medallion to commemorate the English
defeat of the Spanish Armada.

7 The rose is red, the leaves are green,
God save Elizabeth, our noble queen.
1589 Lines written by a Westminster schoolboy in the margin of
his copy of *Julius Caesar*. Quoted in P W Hasler (ed) *The House
of Commons, 1558–1603* (vol.1), p.474.

8 My Love in her attire doth show her wit,
It doth so well become her;
For every season she hath dressings fit,
For winter, spring, and summer.
No beauty she doth miss
When all her robes are on;
But beauty's self she is
When all her robes are gone.
'Madrigal'. Collected in F Davison (ed) *Poetical Rhapsody* (1602).

9 Nose, nose, jolly red nose,
Who gave thee this jolly red nose?…
Nutmegs and ginger, cinnamon and cloves,
And they gave me this jolly red nose.
Quoted in Francis Beaumont and John Fletcher *The Knight of the*

Burning Pestle (1609) but thought to be a rhyme of earlier
origin.

10 Even when the courtesan farts
She does it as a favour
c.1616–1853 Collected in R H Blyth *Senryō: Japanese Satirical
Verses Translated and Explained* (1949).

11 Possession is nine points of the law.
Proverb, quoted in T Draxe *Adages* (1616) no.163.

12 Too many cooks spoil the broth.
Quoted in Sir Balthazar Gerbier *Three Chief Principles of
Magnificent Building* (1665).

13 O he's a ranting roving blade!
O he's a brisk and a bonnie lad!
Betide what may, my heart is glad
To see my lad wi' his white cockade.
18c 'The White Cockade'.

14 O this is no my ain house,
I ken by the biggin o't.
18c 'This is no my ain house'.

15 A good rider may often be thrown from his horse,
And climb on once again to face forward his course,
Which is how I went forward myself on my way,
And come, Christ, and give me my true judgment day.
18c Traditional Irish poem. Translated by Owen Dudley Edwards.

16 And wasna he a roguey,
A roguey, a roguey,
And wasna he a roguey,
The piper o' Dundee?
18c 'The Piper o' Dundee'.

17 The Campbells are comin', O-ho, O-ho!
c.1715 'The Campbells are comin'. Although its origins are
uncertain, this song may date from John Campbell, Duke of
Argyll's attack on the Jacobite army at Sheriffmuir (1715).

18 Cam ye ower frae France?
Cam ye doun by Lunnon?
Saw ye Geordie Whelps
And his bonnie woman?
Were ye at the place
Ca'd the Kittle Housie?
Saw ye Geordie's grace
Ridin' on a goosie?
c.1715 'Cam Ye Ower Frae France?', stanza 1. This Jacobite song
alludes to George I and his reputed fondness for visiting
brothels.

19 It made Gay Rich and Rich Gay.
c.1728 Alluding to the phenomenal success of *The Beggar's
Opera*, written by John Gay and produced by John Rich.

20 O ye'll tak the high road, and I'll tak the low road,
And I'll be in Scotland afore ye,
But me and my true love will never meet again
On the bonnie, bonnie banks o' Loch Lomond
By yon bonnie banks and by yon bonnie braes,
Where the sun shines bright on Loch Lomond.
1746 'The Bonnie Banks o' Loch Lomond', chorus and stanza 1.
The author was a Jacobite imprisoned in Carlisle.

21 Whaur's yer Wullie Shakespeare noo?
1756 Shout from an enthusiastic member of the audience at the
first production of John Home's *Douglas* at the Canongate
Theatre, Edinburgh.

22 Boston, Boston, Boston!
Thou hast naught to boast on,
But a Grand Sluice, and a high steeple;

A proud conceited ignorant people,
And a coast where souls are lost on.
1766 Comment by visitor at the opening of the Grand Sluice, Boston, Lincolnshire, 15 Oct. Quoted in Jennifer Westwood *Albion* (1985), ch. 6, 'English Shires'.

23 Some hae meat and canna eat
And some wad eat that want it;
But we hae meat and we can eat,
And sae the Lord be thankit.
c.1790 'The Selkirk Grace', sometimes attributed to Robert Burns.

24 I challenge all the men alive
To say they e'er were gladder,
Than boys all striving,
Who should kick most wind out of the bladder.
1794 Charterhouse public school song, celebrating football.

25 Here's tae us; wha's like us?
Gey few, and they're a' deid.
19c Scottish toast of uncertain origin. 'Damn' and other variations are sometimes substituted for 'gey'.

26 This stone commemorates the exploit of William Webb Ellis, who, with a fine disregard for the rules of football as played in his time, first took the ball in his arms and ran with it, thus originating the distinctive feature of the Rugby game. AD 1823.
Plaque at Rugby School.

27 What can be more palpably absurd than the prospect held out of locomotives travelling twice as fast as stagecoaches?
1825 *Quarterly Review*, Mar.

28 There was a girl in our town,
Silk an' satin was her gown,
Silk an' satin, gold an' velvet,
Guess her name, three times I've telled it.
Quoted in James Orchard Halliwell *The Nursery Rhymes of England* (1842). The answer, of course, is 'Ann'.

29 The deceased Gentleman was, we are informed, a native of Ashbourn, Derbyshire, at which place he was born in the Year of Grace, 217, and was consequently in the 1643rd year of his age. For some months the patriotic Old Man had been suffering from injuries sustained in his native town, so far back as Shrovetide in last year; he was at once removed (by appeal) to London, where he lingered in suspense till the law of death put its icy hand upon him, and claimed as another trophy to magisterial interference one who had long lived in the hearts of the people.
1860 'Death of the Right Honourable Game Football', as published in a court circular. There had been recent attempts in the courts to ban the riotous custom of 'Shrovetide football' pursued at Ashbourne, Derbyshire, and other villages.

30 What happens when a game of football is proposed at Christmas among a party of young men assembled from different schools? Alas!… The Eton man is enamoured of his own rules, and turns up his nose at Rugby as not sufficiently aristocratic; while the Rugbeian retorts that 'bullying' and 'sneaking' are not to his taste, and he is not afraid of his shins, or of a 'maul' or 'scrimmage'. On hearing this the Harrovian pricks up his ears, and though he might previously have sided with Rugby, the insinuation against the courage of those who do not allow 'shinning' arouses his ire, and causes him to refuse to lay with one who has offered it. Thus it is found impossible to get up a game.
1861 Editorial in *The Field* newspaper, illustrating the confusion before the codification of the rules of football and rugby.

31 Well-informed people know it is impossible to transmit the voice over wires and that were it possible to do so, the thing would be of no practical value.
1865 Editorial in the *Boston Post*.

32 It is a good plan, if it can previously be so arranged, to have one side with striped jerseys of one colour, say red; and the other with another, say blue. This prevents confusion and wild attempts to run after and wrest the ball from your neighbour. I have often seen this done, and the invariable apology—'I beg your pardon, I thought you were on the opposite side'.
1867 In *Routledge's Handbook of Football*.

33 In affectionate remembrance of English cricket, which died at the Oval on 29th August, 1882. Deeply lamented by a large circle of sorrowing friends and acquaintances. RIP. NB The body will be cremated and the ashes taken to Australia.
1882 Notice in *The Sporting Times*, 2 Sep, after the England cricket team's defeat by the Australians.

34 The climate of Manitoba consists of seven months of Arctic weather and five months of cold weather.
1882 *Settler's Guide to the North-West*, issued by the Northern Pacific Railway Company, New York.

35 The British 'Sphere of Influence'—the cricket ball.
Mr Punch's Book of Sport.

36 £1 per week should be ample remuneration for the best professional footballer that ever existed.
1886 In *The Field* newspaper.

37 To the Glorious, Pious, and Immortal Memory of King William the Third, Prince of Orange, who delivered us from Popes and Popery, Knaves and Knavery, Slaves and Slavery, Brass Money, and Wooden Shoes, and He that Will Not Take this Toast May He Be Damn'd, Cramm'd, and Jamm'd Down the Great Gun of Athlone, and the Gun Fired in the Pope's Belly, and the Pope Fired in the Devil's Belly, and the Devil Fired into Hell, and the Door Lock'd, and the Key Forever in the Pocket of a Stout Orangeman. And Here's a Fart for the Bishop of Cork!
c.1890 'The Orange Toast', traditional Protestant Irish.

38 These Ibsen creatures are 'neither men nor women, they are ghouls', vile, unlovable, morbid monsters, and it were well indeed for society if all such went and drowned themselves at once.
1891 In *The Gentlewoman*. Review of Henrik Ibsen's *Rosmersholm*.

39 How different, how very different, from the home life of our own dear Queen!
c.1892 Overheard from a member of the audience when Sarah Bernhardt appeared in the role of Cleopatra.

40 I don't know, darlin', but I think it was somethin' he did against the English.
1895 Unidentified Irish nurse in the US answering an infant's question on the cause of Oscar Wilde's imprisonment, reported by Kenneth Wiggins Porter.

41 The ordinary 'horseless-carriage' is at present a luxury for the wealthy; and although the price will probably fall in the future, it will never, of course, come into as

common use as the bicycle.
1899 *Literary Digest*, 14 Oct.

42 Far away from where I am now there is a little gap in the hills, and beyond it the sea; and 'tis there I do be looking the whole day long, for it's the nearest thing to yourself that I can see.
c.1900 Letter from an unidentified Irish postboy to his beloved, quoted in Maurice Healy *The Old Munster Circuit*.

43 *Citius, altius, fortius.*
Swifter, higher, stronger.
Motto of the Olympic Games, c.1908. It was apparently adopted by Baron de Coubertin after he spotted it over the doorway of a French lycée, though it has also been attributed to Reverend Father Didon.

44 Skegness is so bracing.
from 1909 Slogan in railway advertisements promoting Skegness, Lincolnshire, as a holiday resort. Quoted in Nigel Rees *Dictionary of Popular Phrases* (1990).

45 That the automobile has practically reached the limit of its development is suggested by the fact that during the past year no improvements of a radical nature have been introduced.
1909 *Scientific American*, 2 Jan.

46 Your country needs you!
1914 First use of British World War I recruiting slogan.

47 Berlin by Christmas.
1914 British press.

48 Say it ain't so, Joe.
1919 Attributed words of a young fan, to US baseball star 'Shoeless Joe' Jackson (1887–1951) who was accused of accepting bribes to throw the 1919 World Series (the 'Black Sox' scandal). Jackson always maintained his innocence, but he and seven other players were barred from baseball for life.

49 Four and twenty Yankees, feeling very dry,
Went across the border to get a drink of rye.
When the rye was opened, the Yanks began to sing,
'God bless America, but God save the King!'
c.1919 Ditty current in Canada, referring to Americans crossing the border to drink during Prohibition. The Duke of Windsor, later Edward VIII, heard it during his tour of Canada (1919) and repeated it to his father, George V, on his return, as he recalled in *A King's Story* (1951).

50 The cure of the id by the odd.
c.1920 Popular definition of psychoanalysis.

51 Dear Sir, your astonishment's odd:
I am always about in the Quad.
And that's why the tree
Will continue to be
Since observed by Yours faithfully, God.
c.1924 Reply to Ronald Knox's limerick. The limericks summarize Bishop George Berkeley's philosophy that everything is dependent at all times on the will of God.
► *See Knox 476:22.*

52 There is no woman who does not dream of being dressed in Paris.
1925 Catalogue of the 1925 Paris Exhibition. Quoted in Colin McDowell *McDowell's Directory of Twentieth Century Fashion* (1984), ch.1.

53 There was a faith-healer of Deal
Who said, 'Although pain isn't real,
If I sit on a pin

And it punctures my skin,
I dislike what I fancy I feel.'
Collected in *The Week-End Book* (1925).

54 Let's get out of these wet clothes and into a dry martini.
c.1925 The origin of this line is disputed; it has been attributed to Billy Wilder, Charles Butterworth, Alexander Woollcott and Robert Benchley's press agent. It was used by Mae West in *Every Day's a Holiday* (1937 film) and by Benchley in *The Major and the Minor* (1942 film).

55 Can't act. Can't sing. Slightly bald. Can dance a little.
c.1930 Studio executive's assessment of Fred Astaire on his first screen test.

56 *Ein Reich, ein Volk, ein Führer.*
One realm, one people, one leader.
1934 German Nazi slogan.

57 Sticks nix hick pix
1935 Headline from *Variety*, 17 Jul. A famous example of the US trade paper's idiosyncratic form of English, referring to the unpopularity of films with rural themes in rural areas.

58 A bayonet is a weapon with a worker at each end.
1940 British pacifist slogan during World War II.

59 A neurotic builds castles in the air, but a psychotic lives in them.
c.1940 Popular saying.

60 *Arbeit macht frei.*
Work liberates.
c.1940 Legend over the gates of the concentration camp at Auschwitz, Poland.

61 Who dares, wins.
1940s Motto of the British Special Air Service regiment.

62 Export or die.
1940s British Board of Trade.

63 Walls have ears.
1940s British war slogan.

64 Coughs and sneezes spread diseases. Trap the germs in your handkerchief.
1942 British Government health slogan, quoted in J Darracott and B Loftus *Second World War Posters* (1972).

65 Went the day well?
Title of an anthology of tributes to men and women killed in the war, used for the title of Cavalcanti's 1942 film about German soldiers invading an English village.

66 No girls, no legs, no jokes, no chance.
1943 Review of the Rodgers and Hammerstein musical *Oklahoma!* wired to theatre critic Walter Winchell by one of his informants after its pre-Broadway tryout in New Haven. Quoted in Peter Hay *Broadway Anecdotes* (1989).

67 If only we might fall
Like cherry blossoms in the spring
So pure and radiant.
c.1945 Quoted in Ivan Morris *The Nobility of Failure* (1975).

68 I like Ike.
1947 Campaign slogan for Dwight D Eisenhower's presidential bid. Irving Berlin presented a song with this title, based on *They Like Ike* from his Broadway musical *Call Me Madam*, to an Eisenhower rally at Madison Square Garden, 8 Feb 1952.

69 Whose finger do you want on the trigger?
1952 Headline in the *Daily Mirror*, 21 Sep, reflecting popular mistrust of both Labour and Conservative leadership in the light of the new destructive potential of the atomic bomb.

70 Massermann, the cat man,
Makes cats neurotic.

Are cats and humans
Similarly symptotic?
1952 Popular jingle. Dr Jules Massermann conducted some
bizarre, behavioural experiments into animal neurosis.

71 No pain—no gain.
Bodybuilding motto. The catchphrase may have had its origins
in Adlai Stevenson's slogan 'There are no gains without pain',
first voiced when accepting the Democratic nomination in 1952.

72 Piping Pebworth, Dancing Marston,
Haunted Hillborough, Hungry Grafton,
Dodging Exhall, Papist Wixford,
Beggarly Broom, and Drunken Bidford.
'Traditional Rhyme on the Vale of Avon Place-Names', quoted in
Arnold Silcock, *Verse and Worse* (1952), 'Whimsies'.

73 Madly for Adlai.
1952 Campaign slogan for Adlai Stevenson's presidential bid.

74 Ban the Bomb.
1953 Used by US nuclear disarmament movement from 1953.

75 Psychology? When my daughter needs psychology I
fetch her a skelp across her backside, which lifts her nigh
six inches in t'air.
1955 Young Yorkshire mother's response on being asked by a
local education psychologist how she felt psychology might
assist her in the upbringing of her difficult daughter.

76 Cambridge has always tried to be more typical and less
exotic than the other place.
1958 In *The Listener*, 14 Aug. 'The other place' has traditionally
come to be used of Cambridge from an Oxford viewpoint and
vice versa.

77 Life's better with the Conservatives…don't let Labour
ruin it.
1959 Conservative Party general election slogan.

78 A chair should be judged by one's pants, a jewel by the
light in a lady's eyes, a typewriter by the hovering
fingers.
1959 On good design. In *Time*, 12 Jan.

79 Nature's way of telling you to slow down.
Of death. Quoted in *Newsweek*, 25 Apr 1960.

80 Let's get America moving again.
1960 John F Kennedy's presidential election slogan.

81 Would you buy a used car from this man?
1960 Democratic slogan to disparage Richard M Nixon in the
1960 presidential campaign. Nixon had come across badly in
television debates, in contrast to the charismatic John F
Kennedy.

82 Never again.
1960 Jewish Defence League.

83 GIGO: Garbage in, garbage out.
c.1960 The great and seemingly most basic principle of the
computer, coined anonymously sometime early in its
development.

84 I have to say Miss Brown, that your methods are
outdated and incorrect. But the children love you and are
learning well. Do not on any account make any changes.
c.1960 Unknown school inspector, quoted in Antony Garrard
Newton Flew *Shephard's Warning. Setting schools back on course*
(1994).

85 Stop The World, I Want to Get Off.
1961 From the musical by Leslie Bricusse and Anthony Newley.

86 Stretch pants—the garment that made skiing a spectator
sport.
1961 In *Time*, 23 Feb.

87 All the egg heads are in one basket.
1961 Of President Kennedy's advisers. Quoted by Harold
Macmillan in a letter to the Queen, 12 Apr.

88 That Was The Week That Was.
1962–3 Title of satirical BBC T V series.

89 Our little bit of grandeur is gone.
1963 Heard on a Dublin bus shortly after the assassination of
John Fitzgerald Kennedy, 22 Nov, reported by Sheila O'Sullivan.

90 Make love, not war.
Flower Power movement, mid-1960s.

91 Thirteen wasted years.
1964 Labour Party general election slogan.

92 Don't report what he says, report what he means.
1964 Unwritten reporters' rule for covering Senator Barry
Goldwater's campaign for presidential nomination. Quoted in
Robert MacNeil *The Right Place at the Right Time* (1982).

93 Hearts and minds.
c.1965 Used by US Defense Department official with regard to
winning public support for its Vietnam policy.

94 An important senior faun.
Description of Prime Minister Harold Macmillan's appearance.
Quoted in John Gunther *Procession* (1965).

95 Hey, hey, LBJ! How many kids did you kill today?
1966 US anti-Vietnam war demonstrators.

96 Black is beautiful.
1966 US black civil rights movement.

97 Black power.
1966 US black civil rights slogan coined by Stokely Carmichael.

98 Magnificent magpiety.
1966 Of the art collection of cosmetic manufacturer Helena
Rubinstein. *Time*, 29 Apr.

99 Bombs away with Curtis LeMay.
1967 Used by US anti-Vietnam demonstrators.

1 Burn, baby, burn!
1967 Radical cry in racial riots and fire-raising in Watts,
California and Newark, New Jersey. Quoted in *Time*, 11 Aug.

2 It became necessary to destroy the town to save it.
1968 Statement issued by the US army, referring to Ben Tre in
Vietnam. In the *New York Times*, 8 Feb.

3 I'm Backing Britain.
1968 Coined by publisher Robert Maxwell to encourage the
public to buy British-made goods.

4 Culture is dead, now let us start creating.
1968 Graffito by Parisian students on the School of Architecture
walls, May.

5 Who Else but Nelse?
1968 Campaign slogan for Nelson Rockefeller's presidential bid.

6 My mother thinks Vietnam is somewhere near Panama.
c.1968 The last words of a US soldier fatally wounded during the
Vietnam War, quoted by Australian film-maker John Pilger in his
1978 film *Do you remember Vietnam?*

7 When you've got it, flaunt it.
1969 Braiff Airlines slogan.

8 Power to the people.
1969 US Black Panther movement slogan.

9 Out of the closets and into the streets.
1969 US Gay rights movement slogan.

10 Here men from the planet Earth first set foot upon the
moon, July 1969 AD. We came in peace for all mankind.
1969 Text of the plaque left on the moon by the first astronauts
to walk there, Buzz Aldrin and Neil Armstrong, 20 Jul.

11 Burn your bra!
1970 US feminists' slogan.

12 Yesterday's men.
1970 Labour Party general election slogan, referring to the Conservative leadership.

13 Send them a message.
1972 Governor George Wallace's presidential election slogan.

14 Nice one, Cyril.
1972 Buy-line in T V advertisement for Wonderloaf. It was adopted in 1973 as the title of a pop song by the Cockerel Chorus, addressed to Tottenham Hotspur left-back Cyril Knowles.

15 The abominable no-man.
Of Sherman Adams, Eisenhower's Chief of Staff. Quoted in William Safire *Before the Fall* (1975).

16 The Grin Will Win.
1976 Campaign slogan for Jimmy Carter's presidential bid.

17 He who has not travelled does not know the value of a man.
Arab proverb. Quoted in Ingrid Cranfield *The Challengers* (1976), preface.

18 Hypochondria is the only disease I haven't got.
1978 Graffito seen in NewYork.

19 Just when you thought it was safe to get back into the water.
c.1978 Publicity slogan for *Jaws 2*.

20 Sick as a parrot.
c.1978 Football cliché. The phrase may have started life as 'sick as a pierrot', an allusion to the sadfaced French Pierrot character of the 18th century, but similar phrases appear in literature as early as the 17th century.

21 To err is human; to blame it on the other party is politics.
1979 In the *Washingtonian*, Nov.

22 Labour isn't working.
1979 Used by the Conservative Party in its general election campaign, referring to high unemployment under the then Labour Government.

23 On yer bike!
1981 Catchphrase derived from Norman Tebbit's Conservative Party conference speech.

24 The Great Communicator.
1981 Tag coined for President Reagan, who was renowned for his ability to put a good spin on speeches prepared for him.

25 Britain is a Morris Minor country, but with Rolls Royce diplomacy.
1982 Remark made during the Falklands crisis by a UN delegate, Apr. Quoted in The Sunday Times Insight Team *The Falklands War* (1982).

26 See Freddy before he sees you!
1984 Publicity for the film *A Nightmare on Elm Street*.

27 It's morning again in America.
1984 Campaign slogan for Ronald Reagan's presidential campaign. Quoted in Hedrick Smith *The Power Game* (1988).

28 A desk is a dangerous place from which to view the world.
1985 Sign on desk of American Express president Louis Gerstner. Quoted in the *New York Times*, 26 Jun.

29 Cannes…is 10,000 people looking for 10 people who really count.
1986 Unknown French publicist speaking on the Cannes Film Festival. Quoted in the *New York Times*, 17 May.

30 Art comes to you proposing to give nothing but the highest quality to your moments as they pass.
Inscription on wall of entrance gallery at Dallas' Lloyd Paxton Art and Antiques. Quoted in *Architectural Digest*, May 1986.

31 Save something for the Third Act.
Show business adage applied by President Reagan to his final months in the White House. Quoted in *Time*, 16 Mar 1987.

32 The future ain't what it used to be.
1987 Anonymous Iowa farmer quoted by President Bush on NBC T V, 10 May.

33 There are checks and balances in government—the checks go to candidates and the balance to the people.
Quoted in *Sunday Morning*, CBS T V broadcast, 17 May 1987.

34 Bill was a tropical fish. His native habitat was hot water.
1987 Of William J Casey of the CI A and his role in the Iran arms sales. Quoted in the *New York Times*, 19 Jul.

35 I know one thing we did right
Was the day we started to fight,
Keep your eye on the prize,
Hold on, hold on!
Civil rights song, quoted in Juan Williams *Eye on the Prize* (1987).

36 Skinny cooks can't be trusted.
1987 Quoted by David Cobb Craig in 'Home Cooking Away From Home', *Life*, Jul.

37 Global double zero.
1987 In *Time*, 3 Aug. This arms control term was applied to Mikhail Gorbachev's agreement for mutual elimination of intermediate and shorter-range missiles in Asia and Europe.

38 Don't die of ignorance.
1987 AIDS awareness campaign slogan.

39 To go to school and finish my schooling without getting pregnant.
1987 15-year-old Detroit girl's definition of the American dream. Reported in *Newsweek*, 29 Jan.

40 Mr Elbows and Knees.
1988 Of Democratic presidential nominee Michael S Dukakis. Quoted in *Time*, 21 Nov.

41 We loved your play. We only have problems with your main character, the second act and the ending.
1988 Fan's comment to playwright Wendy Wasserstein on *The Heidi Chronicles*. Quoted in the *New York Times*, 24 Jan 1991.

42 No duties, only opportunities.
Motto of Princeton, N J, Institute for Advanced Study. Quoted in Ed Regis *Who Got Einstein's Office?* (1988).

43 Before you save the world, you've got to save your seat.
1989 On the need for legislators to keep in close touch with their constituents. Quoted in the *New York Times*, 2 Jan.

44 Life is a sexually transmitted disease.
Graffito, quoted in D J Enright *Faber Book of Fevers and Frets* (1989).

45 We're kuwaiting.
1990 NBC T V broadcast, 16 Aug. The speaker was a US serviceman posted to the Gulf after Iraq's invasion of Kuwait.

46 All the 'isms are wasms.
Attributed comment of a Foreign Office spokesman on the signing of the Molotov–Ribbentrop Pact in Aug 1939. In Peter Hennessy *Whitehall* (1990).

47 Don't iron while the strike is hot.
1991 Women's liberation slogan, quoted in PBS broadcast, 26 Jan.

48 We're here,
We're queer.

Get used to it.
1991 Motto of the homosexual liberation movement, Queer Nation, which rejected use of the term 'gay'. Quoted in the *New York Times*, 6 Apr.

49 Twelve drawers full of political cancer.
1991 FBI agent referring to the files of J Edgar Hoover. Quoted in *Newsweek*, 23 Sep.

50 A fatheaded, boneheaded, dunderheaded, blunderheaded, muttonheaded, knuckleheaded, chuckleheaded, puddingheaded, jobernowled wash-out of a cock-up.
1991 Journalist speaking of the poll tax introduced by Margaret Thatcher. Quoted in *The Economist*, 3 Dec 1994.

51 He who hath the gold maketh the rule.
1991 Inscription on plaque in Armand Hammer's bedroom. Quoted in *Regardie's*, Feb.

52 Polyester…the most valuable word to come out of the 70s, the one that defines tacky for all time.
1991 'Prettier Poly', *New York Times* editorial, 21 Mar.

53 The heraldic equivalent of a pair of furry dice bouncing around in the back of a state coach.
1992 On the title of Countess of Finchley bestowed on former Prime Minister Margaret Thatcher. In the *New Yorker*, 6 Jan.

54 The economy, stupid!
1992 Sign in the Clinton campaign headquarters which became a by-word for the central issue of the 1992 presidential campaign. Quoted in *Fortune*, 19 Oct.

55 It's easier to get a photograph of the Pope in the shower than a picture of her.
1993 On Hillary Rodham Clinton's low profile in the period between her husband's election and inauguration. In *Newsweek*, 25 Jan.

56 Behold the turtle, it only makes progress when it sticks its neck out.
Favourite saying of Harvard's president James B Conant. Quoted in James G Hershberg *James B Conant* (1993).

57 From the cradle to the grave,
Even if I misbehave,
There's a place for me
On government subsidy.
Quoted by a caller from Baltimore on Station W AMU, Washington, 15 Jun 1993.

58 Artists and poets are the raw nerve ends of humanity. By themselves they can do little to save humanity. Without them there would be little worth saving.
Inscription on headstone in Green River Cemetery, Springs NY where Jackson Pollock, Elaine de Kooning, and other artists are buried. Quoted in the *New York Times*, 17 Aug 1993.

59 To have one's credit cards cancelled is now akin to being excommunicated by the medieval church.
1993 In *Reader's Digest*, Sep.

60 Complete the mission, though I be the lone survivor. Never leave a fallen comrade to fall into the hands of the enemy.
1993 *The Ranger's Creed*, quoted in the *New York Times*, 25 Oct. The Rangers, a US Army unit, had stayed to guard the body of a pilot fatally caught in a downed helicopter in Somalia.

61 A potato candidate. The best part of him is underground.
1994 Of Adlai Stevenson and his respectable ancestors. In the *Washington Post*, 9 Jan.

62 I don't know if Mr Kissinger is a great writer, but anyone finishing this book is a great reader.

1994 Unidentified book reviewer quoted by Henry Kissinger on the publication of his 900-page *Diplomacy*. In the *Washington Post*, 11 Apr.

63 The castor oil of the Palestinian peace movement.
1994 Of PLO Chair Yassir Arafat. In NPR broadcast, 4 Jul.

64 He looks like a homeless man in a thousand dollar suit.
1994 On Senator Edward M Kennedy's campaign for re-election at age 62. In the *Washington Post*, 1 Oct.

65 If you are not the lead dog, the view never changes.
Paperweight on the desk of Richard Scott, chief executive officer, Hospital Corp of America. Quoted in *Forbes*, 10 Oct 1994.

66 The President is a walking dead man. He just doesn't know it yet.
1994 Senior legislator on President Clinton's political future as he entered the second half of his term of office. In *Nightline*, ABC T V broadcast, 6 Dec.

67 Running a cemetery is just like being President: you got a lot of people under you and nobody's listening.
Quoted by Bill Clinton, 10 Jan 1995.

68 Has he reconnected with the angry middle?
1995 Listener's question on Clinton's rapport with the middle class after the State of the Union speech. In NPR broadcast, 26 Jan.

69 I'm spending my children's inheritance.
Bumper sticker alluding to the economics of Social Security. Quoted in the *New York Times*, 24 Feb 1995.

70 Louisianans don't tolerate corruption; they demand it.
1995 In the *New York Times*, 5 Mar.

71 Welfare should be a safety-net, not a hammock.
1995 In NPR broadcast, 12 Mar.

72 To avoid criticism, say nothing, do nothing, be nothing.
Inscription on a pillow given Claudia ('Lady Bird') Johnson by her staff. Quoted in *Life*, Apr 1995.

73 Hussein isn't just sitting on the fence; he *is* the fence.
1995 Unknown US diplomat on Jordan's King Hussein prior to making peace with Palestine. Quoted in *The Times*, 22 Jul.

74 The French want to attack, the Americans want to bomb, and the British want to have another meeting.
1995 US diplomat commenting on the war in Bosnia. Quoted by William Safire in the *New York Times*, 27 Jul.

75 You can't expect the Rapid Reaction Force to be ready immediately.
1995 On the British force being sent to Bosnia. Military spokesperson interviewed on BBC Radio 4's *Today* programme.

76 Craft is the handprint of all culture.
1995 On exhibit of metal and ceramic work displayed at the White House. In *Sunday Morning*, CBS T V, 30 Apr.

77 The future's bright, the future's Orange.
1996 Advertising slogan for Orange telecommunications.

78 He may be a minister of the British Government but we are the Walt Disney Corporation and we don't roll over for anyone.
1998 An unidentified Disneyland executive commenting on reports that Peter Mandelson might use the theme park's ideas in the Millennium Dome without permission. In the *Sunday Telegraph*, 18 Jan.

79 Prudence is the other woman in Gordon's life.
1998 On Gordon Brown. Comment from unidentified aide, quoted on BBC News online, 20 Mar.

80 Hear ye! Hear ye! All persons are commanded to keep silent, on pain of imprisonment, while the House of Representatives is exhibiting to the Senate of the United

States articles of impeachment against William Jefferson Clinton, President of the United States.

1999 Formal announcement. Quoted in *The Guardian*, 8 Jan.

81 He who dies with the most shoes wins.

c.2000 Advertising slogan for Nike running shoes, inspired by the earlier T-shirt slogan 'he who has the most stuff when he dies, wins'.

82 The plan is called 'shock and awe', and its goal is 'the psychological destruction of the enemy's will to frighten'.

2003 In the *New Yorker*, 10 Feb.

83 An apple a day keeps the doctor away.

Proverb.

84 It's 105 degrees in Saigon and rising.

Prearranged coded signal for US citizens and their dependents to assemble at evacuation points during Vietnam War. Quoted in Walter Isaacson *Kissinger* (1992).

85 It's what's in the grooves that counts.

Slogan of Tamla Motown Records.

86 Let no-one enter who does not know his geometry.

Inscription at the entrance of Plato's Academy. Reported by commentators on Aristotle (Elias *In Aristotelis categorias commentarium*, 18, 118, 18).

87 Twelve Highlanders and a bagpipe make a rebellion.

Scottish proverb.

88 Wha daur meddle wi' me?

Scots paraphrase of the Scottish royal motto, 'Nemo me impune lacessit' ('No one provokes me with impunity').

89 When the world was made, the rubbish was sent to Stockport.

Quoted in Wolfgang Mieder *Investigations of Proverbs, Proverbial Expressions, Quotations and Clichés* (1984), in turn taken from *Notes and Queries* (1871).

90 *Resta viator et lege!*

Stand still, traveller, and read!

Corpus Inscriptionum Latinarum III, 371 (From Cyzicus in Mysia).

91 *Salud, Dinero, Amor…y Tiempo.*

Health, Wealth, Love…and Time to enjoy them.

Traditional Spanish wedding toast.

Anouilh, Jean 1910–87

French playwright. The author of light comedies, historical pieces and tragedies, his plays include *Antigone* (1944), *Ring Round the Moon* (1947) and *Becket, or the Honour of God* (1959).

92 *Faire l'amour avec une femme qui ne vous plaît pas, c'est aussi triste que de travailler.*

To make love with a woman whom you do not like is as sad as going to work.

1931 *L'Hermine*, act 1.

93 *Je sais de quelles petitesses meurent les plus grandes amours.*

I know how pettiness ruins the greatest loves.

1931 *L'Hermine*, act 2.

94 *Nous voulons tous louer à l'année et nous ne pouvons jamais louer que pour une semaine ou pour un jour. C'est l'image de la vie.*

We would all like to lease for a year and we can only lease for a week or from day to day. That is the image of life.

1937 *Le Rendez-vous de Senlis*, act 1.

95 *Il y aura toujours un chien perdu quelque part qui m'empêchera d'être heureux.*

There will always be a lost dog somewhere that will prevent me being happy.

1938 *La Sauvage*, act 3.

96 *La mort ne fait jamais mal. La mort est douce… Ce qui fait souffrir avec certains poisons, certaines blessures maladroites, c'est la vie. C'est le reste de vie. Il faut se confier franchement à la mort comme à une amie.*

Death never hurts. Death is sweet… Life is what makes us suffer with its poisons and awkward injuries. That's what remains of life. We must confide freely in death as we would in a friend.

1941 *Eurydice*, act 1.

97 *C'est bon pour les hommes de croire aux idées et de mourir pour elles.*

It is good for people to believe in ideas and die for them.

1944 *Antigone*.

98 *C'est plein de disputes, un bonheur.*

Happiness is full of strife.

1944 *Antigone*.

99 *Rien n'est vrai que ce qu'on ne dit pas.*

Nothing is true except that which is unsaid.

1944 *Antigone*.

1 *Chacun de nous a un jour, plus ou moins triste, plus ou moins lointain, où il doit enfin accepter d'être un homme.*

There will come a day for each of us, more or less sad, more or less distant, when we must accept the condition of being human.

1944 *Antigone*.

2 *Mourir, ce n'est rien. Commence donc par vivre. C'est moins drôle et c'est plus long.*

To die is nothing. Begin by living. It's less funny and lasts longer.

1946 *Roméo et Jeannette*, act 3.

3 *Vous savez bien que l'amour, c'est avant tout le don de soi!*

Above all, you must understand that love is the gift of oneself!

1949 *Ardèle*.

4 *Dieu est avec tout le monde… Et, en fin de compte, il est toujours avec ceux qui ont beaucoup d'argent et de grosses armées.*

God is on everyone's side… And, in the last analysis, he is on the side with plenty of money and large armies.

1953 *L'Alouette* (*The Lark*).

St Anselm 1033–1109

Italian cleric, scholar and scholastic philosopher, author of numerous philosophical and devotional treatises. In 1078 he became Abbot of Bec, in Normandy, and in 1093 was appointed Archbishop of Canterbury.

5 *Neque enim quaero ut credem, sed credo ut intelligam.*

For I do not seek to understand so that I may believe; but I believe so that I may understand.

1078 *Proslogion*, ch.1 (translated by M J Charlesworth).

6 *Id quo maius non cogitari potest.*

That than which a greater cannot be thought.

1078 Of God. *Proslogion*, ch.3. His famous ontological argument for the existence of God. Since a being that exists is necessarily greater than a being that does not, God must by this definition exist.

Antheil, George 1900–59

US composer, of Polish descent. His controversial modernistic works included the *Jazz Symphony* (1925) and the *Ballet Mécanique* (1927), written for ten pianos and a variety of eccentric percussion instruments.

7 Art cannot hold its breath too long without dying.
  1945 *Bad Boy of Music.*

Anthony, Susan B(rownell) 1820–1906

US social reformer and women's suffrage leader. A campaigner in temperance and anti-slavery movements, she co-founded the National Women's Suffrage Association with Elizabeth Cady (1869).

8 The true Republic: men, their rights and nothing more; women, their rights and nothing less.
  1868–70 On the front of her newspaper, *The Revolution.*

9 There will never be complete equality until women themselves help to make laws and to elect lawmakers.
  In *The Arena.*

Antiphon 5c BC

Greek philosopher and sophist. Only fragments survive of his works.

10 The greatest cost, namely time.
  Quoted in Plutarch *Antonius*, 28.

Apelles 4c BC

Greek painter, probably born in Colophon on the Ionian coast of Asia Minor.

11 *Ne supra crepidam sutor iudicaret.*
  Let the cobbler stick to his last.
  Quoted in Pliny *Naturalis Historia*, 35.36.85. A cobbler who had criticized Apelles' way of rendering a sandal in one of his paintings, proceeded to criticize the rest of the painting as well. The expression became proverbial.

Apollinaire, Guillaume *originally* **Wilhelm Apollinaris de Kostrowitzki** 1880–1918

French poet and author of Polish–Italian parentage. Associated with avant-garde literary groups, he is said to have invented the word 'surrealism'.

12 *Et toi mon coeur pourquoi bats-tu*
  Comme un guetteur mélancolique
  J'observe la nuit et la mort.
  And you my heart why do you pound
  Like some melancholy watchman
  I watch the night and death.
  1899 *Le Guetteur mélancolique*, préface.

13 *Avant tout, les artistes sont des hommes qui veulent devenir inhumains.*
  Above all, artists are men who want to become inhuman.
  1913 *Les Peintres cubistes; Méditations esthétiques*, 'Sur la peinture, 1'.

14 *Un Picasso étudie un objet comme un chirurgien dissèque un cadavre.*
  A Picasso studies an object like a surgeon dissects a corpse.
  1913 *Les Peintres cubistes; Méditations esthétiques*, 'Sur la peinture, 2'.

15 *La géométrie est aux arts plastiques ce que la grammaire est à l'art de l'écrivain.*
  Geometry is to sculpture what grammar is to the art of the writer.
  1913 *Les Peintres cubistes; Méditations esthétiques*, 'Sur la peinture, 3'.

16 *Sous le pont Mirabeau coule la Seine.*
  Et nos amours, faut-il qu'il m'en souvienne?
  La joie venait toujours après la peine.
  Under Mirabeau Bridge flows the Seine.
  And our loves, must I remember them?
  Joy always came after pain.
  1913 *Les Alcools*, 'Le Pont Mirabeau'.

17 *Vienne la nuit sonne l'heure*
  Les jours s'en vont je demeure.
  Let night come, ring out the hour,
  The days go by, I remain.
  1913 *Les Alcools*, 'Le Pont Mirabeau'.

18 *Je connais gens de toutes sortes*
  Ils n'égalent pas leur destin.
  I know people of all sorts
  They do not measure up to their destiny.
  1913 *Les Alcools*, 'Marizibill'.

19 *L'art, de plus en plus, aura une patrie.*
  Art, more and more, will have a country.
  1913 'L'Esprit nouveau et les poètes', *Mercure de France*.

20 *Il est grand temps de rallumer les étoiles.*
  It's high time we relit the stars.
  1917 *Les Mamelles de Tirésias*, prologue.

21 *Perdre*
  Mais perdre vraiment
  Pour laisser place à la trouvaille
  Perdre
  La vie pour trouver la Victoire.
  To lose
  But really to lose
  And make room for discovery
  To lose
  Life so as to discover Victory.
  1918 *Calligrammes*, 'Toujours'.

Appleton, Sir Edward Victor 1892–1965

English physicist, Professor at London University (1924) and Cambridge (1936). He discovered the Appleton layer of electrically charged particles in the Earth's upper atmosphere, and was awarded the 1947 Nobel prize for physics.

22 You must not miss Whitehall. At one end you will find a statue of one of our kings who was beheaded; at the other, a monument to the man who did it. That is just one example of our attempts to be fair to everybody.
  1948 Speech, Stockholm, 1 Jan.

23 I do not mind what language an opera is sung in so long as it is a language I don't understand.
  1955 In the *Observer*, 28 Aug.

Appleton, Thomas Gold 1812–84

US man of letters and wit, the brother-in-law of Henry Wadsworth Longfellow. His own literary output consisted of formal poetry and pleasant essays and is collected in *Faded Leaves* (1872) and *A Sheaf of Papers* (1875).

24 Good Americans, when they die, go to Paris.
  Quoted in Oliver Wendell Holmes *The Autocrat at the Breakfast*

Table (1858), ch.6. Although the speaker in Holmes's book is not identified by name, he is generally identified as Appleton.

25 Boston is a state of mind.
Attributed. This quotation has also been attributed to Ralph Waldo Emerson and Mark Twain.

26 A Boston man is the east wind made flesh.
Attributed.

Aquinas, St Thomas 1225–74

Italian Dominican monk and leading scholastic theologian, known as The Angelic Doctor. He was the first to attempt a complete theological system, and as Doctor of the Church his work is particularly respected in the Roman Catholic tradition.

27 *Pulchritudo enim creaturae nihil est aliud quam similitudo divinae pulchritudinis in rebus participata.*
The beauty of creatures is nothing other than an image of the divine beauty in which things participate.
c.1260 *Commentarium in Dionysii De Divinibus Nominibus*, bk.4, ch.5.

28 *Pange, lingua, gloriosi*
Corporis mysterium,
Sanguinisque pretiosi,
Quem in mundi pretium
Fructus ventris generosi
Rex effudit gentium.
Now, my tongue, the mystery telling
Of the glorious Body sing,
And the Blood, all price excelling,
Which the Gentiles' Lord and King,
In a Virgin's womb once dwelling,
Shed for this world's ransoming.
1263 *Pange Lingua Gloriosi*, known as the Corpus Christi hymn (translated by J M Neale et al).

29 *Tantum ergo sacramentum*
Veneremur cernui;
Et antiquum documentum
Novo cedat ritui.
Therefore we, before him bending,
This great Sacrament revere;
Types and shadows have their ending,
For the newer rite is here.
1263 *Pange Lingua Gloriosi*, known as the Corpus Christi hymn (translated by J M Neale et al).

30 *Solus homo delectatur in ipsa pulchritudine sensibilium secundum seipsam.*
Only man delights in the beauty of sense objects for their own sake.
c.1268 *Summa Theologia*, bk.1, question 91, article 3.

31 *Ars autem deficit ab operatione naturae.*
Art pales when compared to the workings of nature.
c.1272 *Summa Theologia*, bk. 3, question 66, article 4.

Arbuthnot, John 1667–1735

Scottish physician and writer, who published five satirical pamphlets against the Duke of Marlborough in 1712, under the title *The History of John Bull*.

32 Law is a bottomless pit.
1712 *The History of John Bull*, title of pamphlet.

33 Hame's hame, be it never so hamely.
1712 *The History of John Bull*, 'John Bull Still in His Senses', ch.3.

34 Curle (who is one of the new terrors of Death) has been

writing letters to every body for memoirs of his life.
1733 Letter to Jonathan Swift, 13 Jan.

Archer, Jeffrey Howard, Lord 1940–

English politician and writer. A Conservative MP (1969–74), he resigned from the Commons after a financial disaster and turned to fiction, becoming a best-selling author of political potboilers. In 2001 he received a four-year jail sentence on charges of perjury and perverting the course of justice.

35 Not a Penny More, Not a Penny Less.
1975 Title of novel.

36 First Among Equals.
1984 Title of novel.

37 I am innocent of the charge, and nothing you will say however clever you are in the wording of out-of-context pieces, however clever you are in letting people know what 'on and off the record' means, there is only one thing that matters in this court of law, sir: I have never had sexual intercourse with her. And that is the truth!
Giving evidence at a libel trial in 1987. Quoted in Michael Crick *Jeffrey Archer: Stranger than Fiction* (1996).

Archer, Mary 1944–

English scientist. She is married to Jeffrey Archer.

38 I am cross with Jeffrey, but I have formed the judgement that he is a decent and generous spirited man over 35 years and that will not change over one weekend.
Following the revelation that her husband planned to establish a false alibi in his 1987 libel case. In the *Observer*, 'They said what…?', 28 Nov 1999.

Archimedes c.287–212 BC

Greek mathematician, whose innovations included siege-engines and the Archimedean screw for water raising. He was killed at the Roman siege of Syracuse.

39 Give me a firm spot on which to stand, and I shall move the earth.
Traditionally attributed to Archimedes; a variation can be found in Plutarch *Marcellus*, 14.

40 Eureka, Eureka! (I found it, I found it!).
Vitruvius 9.9.10. Attributed, on discovering the principle of upthrust on a floating body while having a bath. Archimedes had been given the task of establishing whether there was the proper weight of gold in the crown of Hieron of Syracuse. One day when entering his bath he noticed the water which flowed over the sides as he entered and he correctly perceived that the weight of the water displaced was that of the weight of his body.

Arenas, Reinaldo 1943–90

Cuban novelist. He held several minor positions in Cuba before leaving the country in 1980 for the US. He committed suicide in New York while suffering from AIDS.

41 *Nuestro portero descubrió, o creyó descubrir, que su labor no se podía limitar a abrir la puerta del edificio, sino que él, el portero, era el señalado, el elegido, el indicado…para mostrarles a todas aquellas personas una puerta más amplia y hasta entonces invisible o inaccesible; puerta que era la de sus propias vidas.*
Our doorman discovered (or thought he had discovered) that his tasks could not be limited to just opening the door of the building—but that he, the doorman, was the one *chosen, elected, singled out*…to

show everyone who lived there a wider door, until then either invisible or inaccessible: the door to their own lives.
1989 *El portero* (*The Doorman*, 1961), pt.1, ch.1.

Aretino, Pietro 1492–1557

Italian poet, illegitimate son of a nobleman. Banished from his native town, he wandered through Italy. His wit secured the favour of Pope Leo X, subsequently lost with the salacious *Sonetti Lussuriosi*. Later patrons included Giovanni de Medici, Francis I and Charles V. He reputedly died by falling from a stool while laughing.

42 I am a free man, I do not need to copy Petrarch or Boccaccio. My own genius is enough. Let others worry themselves about style and so cease to be themselves. Without a master, without a model, without a guide, without artifice, I go to work and earn my living, my well-being, and my fame. What do I need more? With a goose quill and a few sheets of paper I mock the universe.
Quoted in J H Plumb (ed) *The Horizon Book of the Renaissance* (1961, new edn by Penguin, 1982).

Arguedas, José María 1911–69

Peruvian fiction writer and ethnologist. His works reflect the tensions that underlie Peruvian society, in the marginalization of native peoples. He committed suicide.

43 *Dónde está la patria, amigo? Ni en el corazón ni en la saliva.*
Where is the country, my friend? It is not in the heart or in the saliva.
1971 *El zorro de arriba y el zorro de abajo* ('The Upper and the Lower Fox'), ch.3.

Ariosto, Ludovico 1474–1533

Italian poet. He joined the court of Cardinal Ippolito d'Este at Ferrara in 1503, where he produced his most famous work, the Roland epic, *Orlando Furioso* (completed 1516, enlarged 1532). He also wrote comedies, satires and sonnets.

44 *Natura il fece, e poi roppe la stampa.*
Nature made him, and then broke the mould.
1516 *Orlando Furioso*, canto 10, stanza 84.

Aristophanes c.448–c.388 BC

Greek comic poet. Only 11 comedies survive of his 54 plays; they are characterized by exaggeration, parody and satire of contemporary political and cultural life.

45 Who brings owls to Athens?
Avae (The Birds), l.301. This ancient proverb, quoted by various authors, is the equivalent of 'to carry coals to Newcastle'.

46 Old age is second childhood.
Nubes (The Clouds), l.1417.

47 Till the wolf and the lamb be united.
On the impossibility of peace between sworn enemies. *Pax*, l.1076.

Aristotle 384–322 BC

Greek philosopher, scientist and physician, a student of Plato and tutor to Alexander the Great. His philosophical works include *Metaphysics*, *Politics*, *Rhetoric* and *Poetics*. His influence has been incalculable; in medieval Europe he was known simply as 'The Philosopher'.

48 All men naturally desire knowledge.
Metaphysics, bk.1, ch.1, 980a (translated by H Tredennick).

49 It is through wonder that men now begin and originally began to philosophize; wondering in the first place at obvious perplexities, and then by gradual progression raising questions about the greater matters too.
Metaphysics, bk.1, ch.2, 982 (translated by H Tredennick).

50 Every art and every inquiry, and similarly every action and pursuit, is thought to aim at some good; and for this reason the good has rightly been declared to be that at which all things aim.
Nicomachean Ethics, bk.1, ch.1, 1093 (translated by Sir David Ross).

51 Human good turns out to be activity of soul exhibiting excellence, and if there is more than one sort of excellence, in accordance with the best and most complete. For one swallow does not make a summer, nor does one day; and so too one day, or a short time, does not make a man blessed and happy.
Nicomachean Ethics, bk.1, ch.7, 1098 (translated by Sir David Ross).

52 Virtue, then, is a state of character concerned with choice, lying in a mean…it is a mean between two vices, that which depends on excess and that which depends on defect.
Nicomachean Ethics, bk.2, ch.6, 1006 (translated by Sir David Ross).

53 For man, therefore, the life according to reason is best and pleasantest, since reason more than anything else *is* man.
Nicomachean Ethics, bk.10, ch.7, 1178 (translated by Sir David Ross).

54 Tragedy is thus a representation of an action that is worth serious attention, complete in itself and of some amplitude…by means of pity and fear bringing about the purgation of such emotions.
c.330 BC *Poetics*, ch.6.

55 Now a whole is that which has a beginning, a middle, and an end.
c.330 BC *Poetics*, ch.7, referring to tragedy.

56 Man is by nature a political animal; it is his nature to live in a state.
c.330 BC *Politics*, bk.1, ch.2, 1253a (translated by T A Sinclair).

57 Nature, as we say, does nothing without some purpose; and for the purpose of making man a political animal she has endowed him alone among the animals with the power of reasoned speech.
c.330 BC *Politics*, bk.1, ch.2, 1253b (translated by T A Sinclair).

58 It is a bad thing that many from being rich should become poor; for men of ruined fortunes are sure to stir up revolutions.
c.330 BC *Politics*, bk.4.

59 The flute is not an instrument that has a good moral effect—it is too exciting.
c.330 BC *Politics*.

60 For that which has become habitual, becomes as it were natural.
Rhetorica, 1370a (translated by J H Freese).

61 *Amicus Plato, sed magis amica veritas.*
Plato is dear to me, but dearer still is truth.
Proverbial expression, traditionally attributed to Aristotle, going back to a passage in the *Ethica Nicomachea*, 1069a.

Arlott, (Leslie Thomas) John 1914–91

English cricket commentator and writer, a police detective before joining the BBC in 1945. His voice became the epitome of radio cricket commentary.

62 The Master: records prove the title good:
Yet figures fail you, for they cannot say
How many men whose names you never knew
Are proud to tell their sons they saw you play.

They share the sunlight of your summer day
Of thirty years; and they, with you, recall
How, through those well-wrought centuries, your hand
Reshaped the history of bat and ball.
1952 'To John Berry Hobbs on his Seventieth Birthday'.

63 Cricket, like the novel, is great when it presents men in the round, when it shows the salty quality of human nature.
1953 Quoted in Colin Jarman *The Guinness Dictionary of Sports Quotations* (1990).

64 Most games are skin-deep, but cricket goes to the bone.
1977 *Arlott and Trueman on Cricket*.

65 Cricket is a game of the most terrifying stresses with more luck about it than any other game I know. They call it a team game, but in fact it is the loneliest game of all.
Another Word from Arlott.

Arlt, Roberto 1900–42

Argentinian fiction writer, dramatist and journalist. The son of German immigrants, his works emphasize the anger and disillusionment of the urban middle class.

66 ¡Y yo, yo, Señor, no tendré nunca una querida tan linda como esa querida que lucen los cromos de los libros viciosos!
And I, Sir, I'll never have a mistress as beautiful as those in the pictures of obscene books!
1926 *El juguete rabioso* ('The Rabid Toy'), ch.2.

Armani, Giorgio 1935–

Italian fashion designer.

67 I believe that style is the only real luxury that is really desirable.
Attributed.

Armey, Dick (Richard Keith) 1940–

US Congressman and former economics lecturer.

68 It is like relying on the Flintstones for an understanding of the Stone Age.
1994 On economic data from the Congressional Budget Office. In *Time*, 25 Nov.

69 Entitlement spending—the politics of greed wrapped in the language of love.
1994 On President Johnson's legacy to his party. In the *US News & World Report*, 12 Dec.

Armistead, Lewis Addison 1817–63

Confederate general. Commissioned in the US army from Virginia, he resigned when that state seceded. He took part in Picket's charge at Gettysburg, where he was killed.

70 Give them the cold steel, boys!
1863 Attributed, during the American Civil War.

Armstrong, Lance 1971–

US cyclist. He won the Tour de France a record six times from 1999 to 2004.

71 My illness was also my antidote: it cured me of laziness.
2003 Referring to his recovery from cancer in *Every Second Counts*.

72 You know when I need to die? When I'm done living. When I can't walk, can't eat, can't see, when I'm a crotchety old bastard, mad at the world. Then I can die.
2003 *Every Second Counts*.

73 I'm on my bike.
When, during a furore about drug-taking by professional cyclists, he was asked: 'What are you on?'. Quoted in Graeme Fife *Tour de France—the History, the Legend, the Riders* (2000).

Armstrong, Louis known as **Satchmo** 1900–71

US jazz trumpeter and singer, the first major jazz virtuoso. He led studio groups such as the Hot Five and the Hot Seven as well as working with many big bands, and as a singer introduced the scat style. He toured extensively and appeared in over 50 films as a musician and entertainer.

74 Musicians don't retire; they stop when there's no more music in them.
1968 Quoted in the *Observer*, 21 Apr.

75 If you still have to ask…shame on you.
Habitual response when asked what is jazz? Quoted in M Jones *Salute to Satchmo* (1970).

76 All music is folk music. I ain't never heard no horse sing a song.
Quoted in the *New York Times*, 7 Jul 1971.

77 A lotta cats copy the Mona Lisa, but people still line up to see the original.
Alluding to his many imitators. Quoted in David Pickering *Brewer's Twentieth Century Music* (1994).

Armstrong, Neil A(lden) 1930–

US astronaut. A former fighter pilot, he commanded Gemini 8 (1966) and in 1969 was a crew member of Apollo 11, and the first man to walk on the moon.

78 That's one small step for a man, one giant leap forward for mankind.
1969 His words on becoming the first man to walk on the moon, 20 Jul. Armstrong claimed to have said 'That's one small step for a man…', but tape-recordings seem to confirm that he omitted the 'a', thereby causing some confusion among his listeners.

79 I believe every human has a finite number of heart-beats. I don't intend to waste any of mine running around doing exercises.
Quoted in Colin Jarman *The Guinness Dictionary of Sports Quotations* (1990).

Armstrong, Robert, Baron Armstrong of Ilminster 1927–

English civil servant. In 1970 he became principal private secretary to Prime Minister Edward Heath, and later Secretary to the Cabinet and Head of the Home Civil Service under Margaret Thatcher.

80 It contains a misleading impression, not a lie. It was being economical with the truth.
1986 On a letter, during cross-examination at the 'Spycatcher'

trial, New South Wales, Australia, quoted in the *Daily Telegraph*, 19 Nov.

Arnald Amaury d.1225

French clergyman. Abbot of Citeaux (1202–12), he was the first inquisitor against the Albigensian heresy. In 1212 as Bishop of Narbonne he crusaded against the Moors in Spain.

81 Kill them all. God will recognize his own.
1209 Quoted in Caeserius of Heisterbach *Dialogus Miraculorum* (c.1233), bk.5, ch.21. Cited and translated in Jonathon Sumption *The Albigensian Crusade* (1978), ch.6.

Arnold, Matthew 1822–88

English poet and critic. His poems, mainly elegiac in mood and on pastoral themes, include 'The Forsaken Merman' (1849), 'The Scholar-Gipsy' (1853) and 'Thyrsis' (1867). His critical works include *Essays in Criticism* (1865, 1888) and *Culture and Anarchy* (1869).

82 Come, dear children, let us away;
Down and away below!
1849 *The Strayed Reveller, and Other Poems*, 'The Forsaken Merman', l.1–2.

83 Now the great winds shorewards blow;
Now the salt tides seawards flow;
Now the wild white horses play,
Champ and chafe and toss in the spray.
1849 *The Strayed Reveller, and Other Poems*, 'The Forsaken Merman', l.4–7.

84 Sand-strewn caverns, cool and deep,
Where the winds are all asleep;
Where the spent lights quiver and gleam;
Where the salt weed sways in the stream.
1849 *The Strayed Reveller, and Other Poems*, 'The Forsaken Merman', l.35–8.

85 Where great whales come sailing by,
Sail and sail, with unshut eye,
Round the world for ever and aye.
1849 *The Strayed Reveller, and Other Poems*, 'The Forsaken Merman', l.43–5.

86 Not deep the Poet sees, but wide.
1849 *The Strayed Reveller, and Other Poems*, 'Resignation', l.214.

87 Yet they, believe me, who await
No gifts from chance, have conquered fate.
1849 *The Strayed Reveller, and Other Poems*, 'Resignation', l.247–8.

88 Not milder is the general lot
Because our spirits have forgot,
In action's dizzying eddy whirled,
The something that infects the world.
1849 *The Strayed Reveller, and Other Poems*, 'Resignation', l.275–8.

89 Others abide our question. Thou art free.
We ask and ask: Thou smilest and art still,
Out-topping knowledge.
1849 *The Strayed Reveller, and Other Poems*, 'Shakespeare'.

90 And thou, who didst the stars and sunbeams know,
Self-schooled, self-scanned, self-honoured, self-secure,
Didst tread on Earth unguessed at.—Better so!
All pains the immortal spirit must endure,
All weakness which impairs, all griefs which bow,
Find their sole speech in that victorious brow.
1849 *The Strayed Reveller, and Other Poems*, 'Shakespeare'.

91 Who saw life steadily, and saw it whole:
The mellow glory of the Attic stage;
Singer of sweet Colonus, and its child.
1849 Of Sophocles. *The Strayed Reveller, and Other Poems*, 'To a Friend'.

92 France, famed in all great arts, in none supreme.
1849 *The Strayed Reveller, and Other Poems*, 'To a Republican Friend—Continued'.

93 The sea of faith
Lay like the folds of a bright girdle furled.
But now I only hear
Its melancholy, long, withdrawing roar,
Retreating, to the breath
Of the night-wind, down the vast edges drear
And naked shingles of the world.
1851 'Dover Beach', stanza 3.

94 And we are here as on a darkling plain
Swept with confused alarms of struggle and flight,
Where ignorant armies clash by night.
1851 'Dover Beach', stanza 4.

95 Be neither saint nor sophist-led, but be a man.
1852 'Empedocles on Etna', act 1, sc.2, l.136.

96 Is it so small a thing
To have enjoyed the sun,
To have lived light in the spring,
To have loved, to have thought, to have done.
1852 'Empedocles on Etna', act 1, sc.2, l.397–400.

97 Because thou must not dream, thou needst not then despair!
1852 'Empedocles on Etna', act 1, sc.2, l.426.

98 And we forget because we must
And not because we will.
1852 *Empedocles on Etna and Other Poems*, 'Absence'.

99 Only—but this is rare—
When a beloved hand is laid in ours,
When, jaded with the rush and glare
Of the interminable hours,
Our eyes can in another's eyes read clear,
When our world-deafened ear
Is by the tones of a loved voice caressed—
A bolt is shot back somewhere in our breast,
And a lost pulse of feeling stirs again.
The eye sinks inward, and the heart lies plain,
And what we mean, we say, and what we would, we know.
1852 *Empedocles on Etna and Other Poems*, 'The Buried Life', l.77–87.

1 Come to me in my dreams, and then
By day I shall be well again!
For then the night will more than pay
The hopeless longing of the day.
1852 *Empedocles on Etna and Other Poems*, 'Longing' (later published as 'Faded Leaves' in *Poems: Second Series*, 1855).

2 Calm soul of all things! make it mine
To feel, amid the city's jar,
That there abides a peace of thine,
Man did not make, and cannot mar.
1852 *Empedocles on Etna and Other Poems*, 'Lines written in Kensington Garden'.

3 He spoke, and loosed our heart in tears.
He laid us as we lay at birth

On the cool flowery lap of earth.
1852 Of William Wordsworth. *Empedocles on Etna and Other Poems,* 'Memorial Verses, April 1850', l.47–9.

4   With aching hands and bleeding feet
We dig and heap, lay stone on stone;
We bear the burden and the heat
Of the long day, and wish 'twere done.
Not till the hours of light return,
All we have built do we discern.
1852 *Empedocles on Etna and Other Poems,* 'Morality'.

5   Say, has some wet bird-haunted English lawn
Lent it the music of its trees at dawn?
1852 *Empedocles on Etna and Other Poems,* 'Parting', l.19–20.

6   Resolve to be thyself: and know, that he
Who finds himself, loses his misery.
1852 *Empedocles on Etna and Other Poems,* 'Self-Dependence', l.31–2.

7   Ah! two desires toss about
The poet's feverish blood.
One drives him to the world without,
And one to solitude.
1852 *Empedocles on Etna and Other Poems,* 'Stanzas in Memory of the Author of "Obermann"', l.93–6.

8   Still bent to make some port he knows not where,
Still standing for some false impossible shore.
1852 *Empedocles on Etna and Other Poems,* 'A Summer Night', l.68–9.

9   Yes! in the sea of life enisled,
With echoing straits between us thrown,
Dotting the shoreless watery wild,
We mortal millions live alone.
1852 *Empedocles on Etna and Other Poems,* 'To Marguerite—Continued', l.1–4.

10 A God, a God their severance ruled!
And bade betwixt their shores to be
The unplumbed, salt, estranging sea.
1852 *Empedocles on Etna and Other Poems,* 'To Marguerite—Continued', l.22–4.

11 I am past thirty, and three parts iced over.
1853 Letter to Arthur Hugh Clough, 12 Feb

12 Hark! ah, the Nightingale!
The tawny-throated!
Hark! from that moonlit cedar what a burst!
What triumph! hark—what pain!
1853 *Poems: A New Edition,* 'Philomela', l.1–4.

13 Eternal Passion!
Eternal Pain!
1853 *Poems: A New Edition,* 'Philomela', l.31–2.

14 Her cabined ample Spirit,
It fluttered and failed for breath.
Tonight it doth inherit
The vasty hall of death.
1853 *Poems: A New Edition,* 'Requiescat'.

15 Go, for they call you, Shepherd, from the hill.
1853 *Poems: A New Edition,* 'The Scholar-Gipsy', l.1.

16 All the live murmur of a summer's day.
1853 *Poems: A New Edition,* 'The Scholar-Gipsy', l.20.

17 Tired of knocking at Preferment's door.
1853 *Poems: A New Edition,* 'The Scholar-Gipsy', l.35.

18 Crossing the stripling Thames at Bab-lock-hithe,
Trailing in the cool stream thy fingers wet,

As the slow punt swings round.
1853 *Poems: A New Edition,* 'The Scholar-Gipsy', l.74–6.

19 Rapt, twirling in thy hand a withered spray,
And waiting for the spark from heaven to fall.
1853 *Poems: A New Edition,* 'The Scholar-Gipsy', l.119–20.

20 The line of festal light in Christ-Church hall.
1853 *Poems: A New Edition,* 'The Scholar-Gipsy', l.129.

21 Thou waitest for the spark from heaven! and we,
Light half-believers in our casual creeds…
Who hesitate and falter life away,
And lose tomorrow the ground won today—
Ah, do not we, Wanderer, await it too?
1853 *Poems: A New Edition,* 'The Scholar-Gipsy', l.171–4.

22 O born in days when wits were fresh and clear,
And life ran gaily as the sparkling Thames:
Before this strange disease of modern life,
With its sick hurry, its divided aims,
Its heads o'ertaxed, its palsied hearts, was rife—
Fly hence, our contact fear!
1853 *Poems: A New Edition,* 'The Scholar-Gipsy', l.201–6.

23 Still nursing the unconquerable hope,
Still clutching the inviolable shade.
1853 *Poems: A New Edition,* 'The Scholar-Gipsy', l.211–12.

24 Curled minion, dancer, coiner of sweet words!
1853 *Poems: A New Edition,* 'Sohrab and Rustum', l.458.

25 No horse's cry was that, most like the roar
Of some pained desert lion, who all day
Hath trailed the hunter's javelin in his side,
And comes at night to die upon the sand.
1853 *Poems: A New Edition,* 'Sohrab and Rustum', l.501–4.

26 Truth sits upon the lips of dying men.
1853 *Poems: A New Edition,* 'Sohrab and Rustum', l.656.

27 But the majestic river floated on,
Out of the mist and hum of that low land,
Into the frosty starlight.
1853 *Poems: A New Edition,* 'Sohrab and Rustum', l.875–7.

28 Oxus, forgetting the bright speed he had
In his high mountain cradle in Pamere,
A foiled circuitous wanderer—till at last
The longed-for dash of waves is heard, and wide
His luminous home of waters opens, bright
And tranquil, from whose floor the new-bathed stars
Emerge, and shine upon the Aral Sea.
1853 *Poems: A New Edition,* 'Sohrab and Rustrum', l.886–92.

29 Cruel, but composed and bland,
Dumb, inscrutable and grand,
So Tiberius might have sat,
Had Tiberius been a cat.
1855 *Poems: Second Series,* 'Poor Matthias', l.40–3.

30 For rigorous teachers seized my youth,
And other its faith, and trimmed its fire,
Showed me the high, white star of Truth,
There bade me gaze, and there aspire.
1855 *Poems: Second Series,* 'Stanzas from the Grande Chartreuse', l.67–70.

31 Wandering between two worlds, one dead,
The other powerless to be born,
With nowhere yet to rest my head,
Like these, on earth I wait forlorn.
1855 *Poems: Second Series,* 'Stanzas from the Grande Chartreuse', l.85–8.

32 What helps it now, that Byron bore,
With haughty scorn which mocked the smart,
Through Europe to the Aetolian shore
The pageant of his bleeding heart?
That thousands counted every groan,
And Europe made his woe her own?
1855 *Poems: Second Series*, 'Stanzas from the Grande
Chartreuse', l.133–8.

33 This truth—to prove, and make thine own:
'Thou hast been, shalt be, art, alone.'
1857 'Isolation. To Marguerite', l.29-30.

34 Wordsworth says somewhere that wherever Virgil
seems to have composed 'with his eye on the object',
Dryden fails to render him. Homer invariably composes
'with his eye on the object', whether the object be moral
or a material one: Pope composes with his eye on his
style, into which he translates his object, whatever it is.
1861 *On Translating Homer*, lecture 1.

35 Of these two literatures [French and German], as of the
intellect of Europe in general, the main effort, for now
many years, has been a critical effort; the endeavours, in
all branches of knowledge—theology, philosophy,
history, art, science—to see the object as in itself it really
is.
1861 *On Translating Homer*, lecture 2.

36 [The translator] will find one English book and one only,
where, as in the *Iliad* itself, perfect plainness of speech is
allied with perfect nobleness; and that book is the Bible.
1861 *On Translating Homer*, lecture 3.

37 Nothing has raised more questioning among my critics
than these words—noble, the grand style… I think it will
be found that the grand style arises in poetry, when a
noble nature, poetically gifted, treats with simplicity or
with severity a serious subject.
1862 *On Translating Homer; Last Words*.

38 Nothing could moderate, in the bosom of the great
English middle class, their passionate, absorbing, almost
blood-thirsty clinging to life.
1865 *Essays in Criticism First Series*, preface.

39 Beautiful city! so venerable, so lovely, so unravaged by
the fierce intellectual life of our century, so
serene!…whispering from her towers the last
enchantments of the Middle Age… Home of lost
causes, and forsaken beliefs, and unpopular names, and
impossible loyalties!
1865 Of Oxford. *Essays in Criticism First Series*, preface.

40 I am bound by my own definition of criticism: a
disinterested endeavour to learn and propagate the best
that is known and thought in the world.
1865 *Essays in Criticism First Series*, 'The Function of Criticism at
the Present Time'.

41 Philistinism!—We have not the expression in English.
Perhaps we have not the word because we have so much
of the thing.
1865 *Essays in Criticism First Series*, 'Heinrich Heine'.

42 The great apostle of the Philistine, Lord Macaulay.
1865 *Essays in Criticism First Series*, 'Joubert'.

43 The signal-elm, that looks on Ilsley downs,
The Vale, the three lone weirs, the youthful Thames.
1866 *New Poems*, 'Thyrsis', l.14–15. The poem is an elegy for his
friend Arthur Hugh Clough, who drowned in 1861.

44 And that sweet City with her dreaming spires,
She needs not June for beauty's heightening.
1866 Of Oxford. *New Poems*, 'Thyrsis', l.19–20.

45 So have I heard the cuckoo's parting cry,
From the wet field, through the vext garden trees,
Come with the volleying rain and tossing breeze:
'The bloom is gone, and with the bloom go I.'
1866 *New Poems*, 'Thyrsis', l.57–60.

46 Too quick despairer, wherefore wilt thou go?
Soon will the high Midsummer pomps come on,
Soon will the musk carnations break and swell.
1866 *New Poems*, 'Thyrsis', l.61–3.

47 For Time, not Corydon, hath conquered thee.
1866 *New Poems*, 'Thyrsis', l.80.

48 The foot less prompt to meet the morning dew,
The heart less bounding at emotion new,
And hope, once crushed, less quick to spring again.
1866 *New Poems*, 'Thyrsis', l.138–40.

49 It is not in the outward and visible world of material life
that the Celtic genius of Wales or Ireland can at this day
hope to count for much; it is in the inward world of
thought and science. What it *has* been, what it *is* has done,
what it will be or will do, as a matter of modern politics.
1867 'On the Study of Celtic Literature'.

50 Let us reunite ourselves with our better mind and with
the world through science; and let it be one of our
angelic revenges on the Philistines, who among their
other sins are the guilty authors of Fenianism, to found at
Oxford a chair of Celtic, and to send, through the gentle
ministration of science, a message of peace to Ireland.
1867 'On the Study of Celtic Literature'.

51 Creep into thy narrow bed,
Creep, and let no more be said!
Vain thy onset! all stands fast.
Thou thyself must break at last.
Let the long contention cease!
Geese are swans, and swans are geese.
Let them have it how they will!
Thou art tired; best be still.
1867 *New Poems*, 'The Last Word'.

52 Coldly, sadly descends
The autumn evening. The field
Strewn with its dank yellow drifts
Of withered leaves, and the elms,
Fade into dimness apace,
Silent;—hardly a shout
From a few boys late at their play!
1867 *New Poems*, 'Rugby Chapel, November 1857'.

53 Our society distributes itself into Barbarians, Philistines,
and Populace; and America is just ourselves, with the
Barbarians quite left out, and the Populace nearly.
1869 *Culture and Anarchy*, preface.

54 The pursuit of perfection, then, is the pursuit of
sweetness and light… He who works for sweetness and
light united, works to make reason and the will of God
prevail.
1869 *Culture and Anarchy*, ch.1.

55 The men of culture are the true apostles of equality.
1869 *Culture and Anarchy*, ch.1.

56 That vast portion…of the working-class which, raw and

half-developed has long lain half-hidden amidst its poverty and squalor, and is now issuing from its hiding-place to assert an Englishman's heaven-born privilege of doing as he likes, and is beginning to perplex us by marching where it likes, meeting where it likes, bawling what it likes, breaking what it likes—to this vast residuum we may with great propriety give the name of Populace.
1869 *Culture and Anarchy,* ch.3.

57 Hebraism and Hellenism—between these two points of influence moves our world.
1869 *Culture and Anarchy,* ch.4.

58 'He knows' says Hebraism, 'his Bible!'—whenever we hear this said, we may, without any elaborate defence of culture, content ourselves with answering simply: 'No man, who knows nothing else, knows even his Bible.'
1869 *Culture and Anarchy,* ch.5.

59 Culture, the acquainting ourselves with the best that has been known and said in the world, and thus with the history of the human spirit.
1873 *Literature and Dogma,* preface.

60 Culture is the passion for sweetness and light, and (what is more) the passion for making them prevail.
1873 *Literature and Dogma,* preface.

61 The true meaning of religion is thus not simply morality, but morality touched with emotion.
1873 *Literature and Dogma,* ch.1.

62 Conduct is three-fourths of our life and its largest concern.
1873 *Literature and Dogma,* ch.1.

63 The eternal *not ourselves* that makes for righteousness.
1873 *Literature and Dogma,* ch.8.

64 But there remains the question: what righteousness really is. The method and secret and sweet reasonableness of Jesus.
1873 *Literature and Dogma,* ch.12.

65 So we have the Philistine of genius in religion—Luther; the Philistine of genius in politics—Cromwell; the Philistine of genius in literature—Bunyan.
1879 *Mixed Essays,* 'Lord Falkland'.

66 The theatre is irresistible: organise the theatre.
1882 *Irish Essays,* 'The French Play in London'.

67 In poetry, no less than in life, he is 'a beautiful and ineffectual angel, beating in the void his luminous wings in vain'.
1888 Of Shelley. *Essays in Criticism Second Series,* 'Shelley'. The phrase is a quotation from his own work on Byron.

68 More and more mankind will discover that we have to turn to poetry to interpret life for us, to console us, to sustain us. Without poetry, our science will appear incomplete; and most of what now passes with us for religion and philosophy will be replaced by poetry.
1888 *Essays in Criticism Second Series,* 'The Study of Poetry'.

69 The difference between genuine poetry and the poetry of Dryden, Pope, and all their school, is briefly this: their poetry is conceived and composed in their wits, genuine poetry is conceived and composed in the soul.
1888 *Essays in Criticism Second Series,* 'Thomas Gray'.

70 Poetry is at bottom a criticism of life.
1888 *Essays in Criticism Second Series,* 'Wordsworth'.

71 His expression may often be called bald...but it is bald as

the bare mountain tops are bald, with a baldness full of grandeur.
1888 *Essays in Criticism Second Series,* 'Wordsworth'.

Arnold, Thomas 1795–1842

British educator and historian, educational reformer who introduced mathematics, modern languages, and modern history into the curriculum of his day.

72 My object will be, if possible, to form Christian men, for Christian boys I can scarcely hope to make.
1828 Letter to Rev John Tucker, 2 Mar, on being appointed headmaster of Rugby School.

73 Rather than have it the principal thing in my son's mind, I would gladly have him think that the sun went around the earth, and that the stars were so many spangles set in the bright blue firmament.
1836 Letter to Dr Greenhill, 9 May.

Arnold, Thurman Wesley 1891–1969

US lawyer, Professor at Yale (1930–8), Assistant Attorney General in charge of anti-trust enforcement (1938–43) and Associate Justice at the Court of Appeals (1943–5).

74 We must protect big business from domination by fat-minded men whose principal business policy is to avoid a competitive race for efficiency… They believe in a system of soft enterprise,—soft in the way that an octopus is soft, with tentacles that stifle and suffocate.
1942 'The Abuse of Patents', in *Atlantic Monthly,* Jul.

Aron, Raymond Claude Ferdinand 1905–83

French sociologist and journalist, editor of *La France Libre* in London (1940–4).

75 To customs and beliefs, the very ones we hold sacred, sociology ruthlessly attaches the adjective 'arbitrary'.
1971 *Politics and History.*

76 In a way, all sociologists are akin to Marxists because of their inclination to settle everyone's accounts but their own.
1971 *Politics and History.*

Arras, Jean d' *also known as* **Jean Blondel** fl.c.1375

French writer. He collaborated with Antoine du Val and Fouquart de Cambrai on the *Évangile des Quenouilles,* which provides much information on life at the time.

77 *Bonté vaut mieux que beauté.*
Kindness is worth more than beauty.
c.1393 *Melusine.*

Asahi Shimbun

Leading mass-circulation newspaper in Japan.

78 Are we correct to have changed as much as we have? Or is Yokoi correct not to have changed at all?
1972 Editorial comment, 28 Jan, on the discovery of World War II survivor Sergeant Yokoi in the Pacific jungles.

Ascham, Roger 1515–68

English humanist, Protestant and scholar, reader in Greek at Cambridge, and tutor to Princess Elizabeth. He published a defence of archery, *Toxophilus,* in 1545, and is most famous for his treatise on humanist education, *The Schoolmaster* (1570).

79 He that will write well in any tongue, must follow this counsel of Aristotle, to speak as the common people do, to think as wise men do; and so should every man understand him, and the judgment of wise men allow him.
1545 *Toxophilus*, 'To all Gentlemen and Yeomen of England'.

80 Young children [are] sooner allured by love than driven by beating to attain good learning.
1570 *The Schoolmaster*, 'A Preface to the Reader'.

81 For [the] quick in wit and light in manners be either seldom troubled or very soon weary, in carrying a very heavy purse.
1570 *The Schoolmaster*, bk.2.

Ashbery, John Lawrence 1927–

US poet, critic and novelist. Poetry collections include the award-winning *Self-Portrait in a Convex Mirror* (1976).

82 Darkness falls like a wet sponge.
1956 *Some Trees*, 'The Picture of Little J. A. in a Prospect of Flowers', opening line.

83 And it is the colour of sand,
The darkness, as it sifts through your hand.
1962 *The Tennis Court Oath*, 'How Much Longer Will I Be Able To Inhabit The Divine Sepulcher…'.

84 Self-portrait in a Convex Mirror.
1976 Title of book.

85 Slated for demolition.
1979 Complete text of poem entitled 'The Cathedral Is', in *As We Know*.

86 Still I enjoy
The long sweetness of the simultaneity, yours and mine, ours and mine,
The mosquitoey summer night light.
1981 *Shadow Train*, 'Here Everything Is Still Floating'.

87 My name has gotten to be a household word—at least in certain households. I think there are now people who know my name, but don't know what I do. I'm famous for being famous.
1985 Interview in *PN Review*, no.46.

88 There is the view that poetry should improve your life. I think people confuse it with the Salvation Army.
1989 In the *International Herald Tribune*, 2 Oct.

Ashdown (of Norton-sub-Hamdon), Paddy Ashdown, Baron 1941–

British politician. After working with the Royal Marines (1959–71) and the diplomatic service (1971–6), he was an MP (1983–2001) and leader of the Liberal Democrats (1988–99).

89 Neil Kinnock has travelled the road to Damascus so often, I hear that he has decided to buy himself a season ticket.
1990 At the Liberal Democratic Party conference, Sep.

90 The ringmaster has altered, but the circus remains the same.
1990 On John Major's election as Conservative Party leader, in the *Observer*, 2 Dec.

91 I have learnt from bitter experience that when the armchair theorists and the Whitehall generals start talking of a surgical war, it is time to run for cover.
1991 Referring to plans for the Gulf War. In the *Sunday Times*, 27 Jan.

92 There can be no place in a 21st-century parliament for people with 15th-century titles upholding 19th-century prejudices.
1998 In *The Independent*, 24 Nov.

Ashford, Daisy Mary Margaret 1881–1972

English writer. She wrote her only book, *The Young Visiters*, in 1890, and published the manuscript in 1919. Its childish idiosyncrasies made it a best-seller, and it was adapted for the stage in 1920, and as a musical in 1968.

93 Mr Salteena was an elderly man of 42 and was fond of asking peaple to stay with him.
1890 *The Young Visiters, or Mr Salteena's Plan*, ch.1.

94 You look rather rash my dear your colors don't quite match your face.
1890 *The Young Visiters, or Mr Salteena's Plan*, ch.2.

95 Bernard always had a few prayers in the hall and some whiskey afterwards as he was rather pious but Mr Salteena was not very addicted to prayers so he marched up to bed.
1890 *The Young Visiters, or Mr Salteena's Plan*, ch.3.

96 Oh I see said the Earl but my own idear is that these things are as piffle before the wind.
1890 *The Young Visiters, or Mr Salteena's Plan*, ch.5.

97 I am very fond of fresh air and royalties.
1890 *The Young Visiters, or Mr Salteena's Plan*, ch.5.

98 The bearer of this letter is an old friend of mine not quite the right side of the blanket as they say in fact he is the son of a first rate butcher but his mother was a decent family called Hyssopps of the Glen so you see he is not so bad and is desireus of being the correct article.
1890 *The Young Visiters, or Mr Salteena's Plan*, ch.5.

99 My life will be sour grapes and ashes without you.
1890 *The Young Visiters, or Mr Salteena's Plan*, ch.8.

1 Oh Bernard muttered Ethel this is so sudden. No no cried Bernard and taking the bull by both horns he kissed her violently on her dainty face.
1890 *The Young Visiters, or Mr Salteena's Plan*, ch.9.

2 She had very nice feet and plenty of money.
1890 *The Young Visiters, or Mr Salteena's Plan*, ch.12.

Asimov, Isaac 1920–92

Russian-born US science-fiction novelist and popular scientist. A distinguished biochemist and hugely popular writer, he became a familiar media figure. His works include the 'Foundation' series (1951–3). He coined the term 'robotics'.

3 How many people is the earth able to sustain?
1971 *Der Spiegel*.

4 Science fiction writers foresee the inevitable, and although problems and catastrophes may be inevitable, solutions are not.
1975 'How Easy To See The Future', in *Natural History*, Apr.

5 If there is a category of human being for whom his work ought to speak for itself, it is the writer.
1976 Comment in D L Fitzpatrick (ed) *Contemporary Novelists*.

6 It is change, continuing change, inevitable change, that is the dominant factor in our society today… This, in turn, means that our statesmen, our businessmen, our everyman must take on a science fictional way of thinking.

1978 'My Own View', in R Holdstock (ed) *Encyclopedia of Science Fiction* (1978).

Aslet, Clive William 1955–

English journalist, editor of *Country Life* (1993–).

7 Biography is now more or less a branch of psychiatry.
1994 In *Country Life*, 10 Nov, reviewing Jonathan Dimbleby *The Prince of Wales: A Biography* (1994).

8 We expect the ticking movement of the human timepiece to be revealed.
1994 In *Country Life*, 10 Nov, reviewing Jonathan Dimbleby *The Prince of Wales: A Biography* (1994).

Asquith, Herbert Henry, 1st Earl of Oxford and Asquith 1852–1928

British Liberal politician and Prime Minister. He became an MP (1886), Home Secretary (1892–5), Chancellor (1906) and Prime Minister (1908–16). His period in office was marked by the introduction of old age pensions, the Parliament Act of 1911, the declaration of war (1914) and the Sinn Féin rebellion (1916). A coalition with Conservatives hastened his resignation. He wrote *Memories and Reflections* (1928).

9 We shall never sheath the sword which we have not lightly drawn until Belgium recovers in full measure all and more than all that she has sacrificed, until France is adequately assured against the menace of aggression, until the rights of the smaller nationalities of Europe are placed upon an unassailable foundation and until the military domination of Prussia is wholly and finally destroyed.
1914 Speech at the Guildhall, London, 9 Nov.

10 It is fitting that we should have buried the unknown Prime Minister by the side of the Unknown Soldier.
1923 Remark at the Westminster Abbey funeral of Bonar Law, 5 Nov.

11 One to mislead the public, another to mislead the Cabinet, and the third to mislead itself.
Of the three sets of figures kept by the War Office. Quoted in Alistair Horne *Price of Glory* (1962).

Asquith, Margot 1864–1945

Scottish society figure and wit, wife of Herbert Asquith (married 1894). Her group 'The Souls' advocated greater freedom for women. She continued her extravagant lifestyle through the war, and when Asquith was forced to resign (1916) wrote two sensational autobiographies.

12 If Kitchener is not a great man, he is, at least, a great poster.
Quoted in P Magnus *Kitchener: Portrait of an Imperialist*. Lady Asquith uses the phrase in her *Memories* (1933), but attributes it to her daughter Elizabeth.

13 She tells enough white lies to ice a wedding cake.
Of Lady Desborough. Quoted in *The Listener*, 11 Jun 1953.

14 David Lloyd George could not see a belt without hitting underneath it.
Quoted in *The Listener*, 11 Jun 1953.

15 Stafford Cripps has a brilliant mind, until he makes it up.
Quoted in *The Wit of the Asquiths* (published 1974).

16 F E Smith is very clever, but sometimes he lets his brains go to his head.
Quoted in *The Wit of the Asquiths* (published 1974).

17 The t is silent, as in Harlow.
Attributed riposte to Jean Harlow who was having trouble pronouncing her name. The line may actually have been spoken by Margot Grahame, an English actress in Hollywood in the 1930s.

18 I have no face, only two profiles clapped together.
Attributed.

Asquith of Yarnbury, (Helen) Violet Bonham-Carter, Baroness 1887–1969

English Liberal politician and publicist, daughter of Herbert Asquith. A prominent society figure, she was president of the Liberal Party Organization (1944–5) and governor of the BBC (1941–6).

19 Harold Macmillan held his party together by not allowing his left wing to see what his right wing was doing.
Attributed.

Astell, Mary 1668–1731

English writer, the 'first British feminist'. Orphaned in 1684, she moved alone to London in about 1686. In *A Serious Proposal to the Ladies* (1694) she argues for the education of women. *Some Reflections Upon Marriage* (1700, 2nd edn 1706) highlights the disadvantages of marriage for women.

20 Your glass will not do you half so much service as a serious reflection of your own minds.
1694 *A Serious Proposal to the Ladies For the Advancement of their True and Greatest Interest*, 'By a Lover of Her Sex', pt.1.

21 Women are from their very Infancy debarred those advantages, with the want of which they are afterwards reproached, and nursed up in those vices which will hereafter be upbraided to them. So partial are men as to expect brick where they afford no straw.
1694 *A Serious Proposal to the Ladies For the Advancement of their True and Greatest Interest*, 'By a Lover of Her Sex', pt.1.

22 Fetters of gold are still fetters, and the softest lining can never make them so easy as liberty.
1696 *An Essay in Defence of the Female Sex.*

23 If absolute sovereignty be not necessary in a State, how comes it to be so in a family?
1706 *Some Reflections upon Marriage Occasion'd by the Duke and Duchess of Mazarine's Case which is also consider'd*, preface (1706 edn).

24 If all men are born free, how is it that all women are born slaves? as they must be if the being subjected to the inconstant, uncertain, unknown, arbitrary will of men, be the perfect condition of slavery? and if the essence of freedom consists, as our masters say it does, in having a standing rule to live by? And why is slavery so much condemned and strove against in one case, and so highly applauded, and held so necessary and so sacred in another?
1706 *Some Reflections upon Marriage Occasion'd by the Duke and Duchess of Mazarine's Case which is also consider'd*, preface (1706 edn).

25 But if marriage be such a blessed state, how comes it, may you say, that there are so few happy marriages? Now in answer to this, is it not to be wondered that so few succeed, we should rather be surprized to find so many do, considering how imprudently men engage, the motive they act by, and the very strange conduct they observe throughout.

> **1706** *Some Reflections upon Marriage Occasion'd by the Duke and Duchess of Mazarine's Case which is also consider'd*, preface (1706 edn).

26 A woman indeed can't properly be said to choose, all that is allowed her, is to refuse or accept what is offered.

> **1706** *Some Reflections upon Marriage Occasion'd by the Duke and Duchess of Mazarine's Case which is also consider'd*, preface (1706 edn).

Astley, Sir Jacob 1579–1652

English Royalist commander, leader of Charles I's last remaining army which surrendered in March 1646.

27 O Lord! Thou knowest how busy I must be this day: if I forget thee, do not thou forget me.

> **1642** Prayer before the Battle of Edgehill, 23 Oct. Quoted in Sir Philip Warwick *Memoires* (1702).

28 You have now done your work and may go play, unless you will fall out amongst yourselves.

> **1646** Remark to his Parliamentarian captors, Mar. Quoted in Samuel Rawson Gardiner *History of the Great Civil War, 1642–9* (1911), vol.3.

Astor (of Hever Castle), Nancy Witcher Astor, Viscountess née *Langhorne* 1879–1964

US-born British politician, the first woman MP to sit in the House of Commons. She was especially interested in social problems, including women's rights and temperance.

29 I married beneath me. All women do.

> **1951** Speech, Oldham.

30 You will never get on in politics, my dear, with *that* hair.

> Attributed remark addressed to Shirley Williams.

Asturias, Miguel Ángel 1889–1974

Guatemalan poet, novelist and diplomat, winner of the Nobel prize for literature in 1967 and the Soviet Union's Lenin Peace Prize in 1966.

31 *Como te decía al principio, nadie hace nada y, naturalmente, soy yo, es el Presidente de la República el que lo tiene que hacer todo, aunque salga como el cohetero. Con decir que si no fuera por mí no existiría la fortuna, ya que hasta de diosa ciega tengo que hacer en la lotería.* But, as I told you, nobody ever does a thing, and so naturally it is I, the President of the Republic, who has to do everything, and take all the blame as well. You might almost say that if it weren't for me Fortune wouldn't exist, as I have even to take the part of the blind goddess in the lottery.

> **1946** *El señor presidente* (*The President*, 1963), pt.3, ch.37.

Atatürk, Mustapha Kemal 1880–1938

Turkish soldier and statesman, founder and first President (1923–38) of the Turkish Republic. In the subsequent social and political revolution he encouraged westernization. He took the title Atatürk, 'Father of the Turks', in 1935.

32 It was necessary to abolish the fez, emblem of ignorance, negligence, fanaticism and hatred of progress and civilization, to accept in its place the hat—the headgear worn by the whole civilized world.

> **1927** From his six-day speech to the Turkish Assembly, Oct.

Atkinson, Brooks 1894–1984

US journalist and theatre critic.

33 After each war there is a little less democracy to save.

> **1951** *Once Around the Sun*.

34 Thanks for tomorrow, thanks for last week, thanks for next Friday—in fact thanks for everything except last night.

> Reviewing Le Roy Bailey's *Thanks for Tomorrow*. Quoted in the *New York Times*, 14 Jan 1984.

Atkinson, Ron 1939–

English football manager. He played for Oxford United until 1971 and subsequently managed teams including West Bromwich Albion, Atlético Madrid, Manchester United, Sheffield Wednesday, Aston Villa and Coventry City, before becoming a commentator.

35 It's bloody tough being a legend.

> **1983** Quoted in Peter Ball and Phil Shaw *The Book of Football Quotations* (1989).

Atlas, Charles 1894–1972

US bodybuilder.

36 You too can have a body like mine!

> **c.1922** Advertising slogan.

Atlas, James 1949–

US writer and critic, contributor to the *New Yorker* and former editor at the *New York Times Magazine*.

37 A penumbra of somber dignity has descended over his reputation.

> **1985** Of Edmund Wilson. In the *New York Times*, 28 Jul, reviewing David Castronovo *Edmund Wilson* (1984).

38 To read Wilson…is to be instructed and amused in the highest sense—that is educated.

> **1985** Of Edmund Wilson. In the *New York Times*, 28 Jul, reviewing David Castronovo *Edmund Wilson* (1984).

Attenborough, Sir David Frederick 1923–

English naturalist and broadcaster, a respected and popular wildlife documentary maker. His series include *Life on Earth* (1979), *The Living Planet* (1984) and *Life in the Freezer* (1993).

39 Most of the animals that appeared on British television screens in 1950 did so sitting on door-mats.

> **1982** *The Zoo Quest Expeditions*.

Attlee (of Walthamstow), Clement (Richard) Attlee, 1st Earl 1883–1967

English Labour politician, Deputy Prime Minister in Churchill's war cabinet (1942–5) and Prime Minister (1945–51). During his administration the National Health Service was established and India and Burma were given independence.

40 We believe in a League system in which the whole world should be ranged against an aggressor… We do not think that you can deal with national armaments by piling up national armaments in other countries.

> **1935** House of Commons, 11 Mar.

41 We have seen today a gallant, civilized and democratic people betrayed and handed over to a ruthless despotism.

> **1938** House of Commons speech on Czechoslovakia, 3 Oct.

42 I count our progress by the extent to which what we cried in the wilderness five and thirty years ago has now become part of the assumptions of the ordinary man and woman… It is better to argue from what has been done to what may be done, rather than to suggest that very little has been accomplished.
1944 Of the Labour Party. Letter to Harold J Laski, 1 May.

43 I have been very happy…serving in a state of life to which I had never expected to be called.
1954 *As It Happened.*

44 Few thought he was even a starter
There were many who thought themselves smarter
But he ended PM
CH and OM
An earl and a knight of the garter.
1956 A limerick on himself, in a letter to Tom Attlee, 8 Apr.

45 Russian communism is the illegitimate child of Karl Marx and Catherine the Great.
1956 Speech, Aarhus University, 11 Apr.

46 Democracy means government by discussion, but it is only effective if you can stop people talking.
1957 Speech, Oxford, 14 Jun.

47 The House of Lords is like a glass of champagne that has stood for five days.
Attributed.

Atwood, Margaret Eleanor   1939–

Canadian writer, poet and critic. Her first book of poetry, *The Circle Game* (1966), won the Governor General's Award. Her novels include *The Edible Woman* (1969) and *The Robber Bride* (1993). She won the Booker Prize in 2000 for *The Blind Assassin.*

48 (The photograph was taken
the day after I drowned.
I am in the lake, in the center
of the picture, just under the surface.)
1966 *The Circle Game,* 'This is a Photograph of Me'.

49 we flounder, the air
ungainly in our new lungs
with sunlight streaming merciless on the shores of
  morning
1966 *The Circle Game,* 'Pre-Amphibian'.

50 He stood, a point
on a sheet of green paper
proclaiming himself the center,
with no walls, no borders
anywhere; the sky no height
above him, totally un-
enclosed
and shouted:
Let me out!
1968 *The Animals in that Country,* 'Progressive Insanities of a Pioneer'.

51 Marriage is not
a house or even a tent
it is before that, and colder.
1970 *Procedures from Underground,* 'Habitation'.

52 If the national mental illness of the United States is megalomania, that of Canada is paranoid schizophrenia.
1970 *The Journals of Susanna Moodie: Poems by Margaret Atwood,* afterword.

53 We are all immigrants to this place even if we were born

here: the country is too big for anyone to inhabit completely, and in the parts unknown to us we move in fear, exiles and invaders.
1970 Writing of Canada and Canadians in *The Journals of Susanna Moodie: Poems by Margaret Atwood,* afterword.

54 Possibly the symbol for America is the Frontier… The corresponding symbol for England is the Island… The central symbol for Canada…is undoubtedly Survival, *la Survivance.*
1972 *Survival: a Thematic Guide to Canadian Literature,* ch.1, 'Survival'.

55 This above all, to refuse to be a victim. Unless I can do that I am nothing.
1972 *Surfacing.*

56 Mirrors
are the perfect lovers.
1974 *You are Happy,* 'Tricks with Mirrors'.

57 You are suspended in me
beautiful and frozen, I
preserve you, in me you are safe.
1974 *You Are Happy,* 'Tricks with Mirrors'.

58 To live in prison is to live without mirrors. To live without mirrors is to live without the self.
1978 *Two-headed Poems,* 'Marrying the Hangman'.

59 I would like to be the air
that inhabits you for a moment
only. I would like to be that unnoticed
and that necessary.
1981 *True Stories,* 'Variation on the Word *Sleep*'.

60 At some time during that hour, though not for the whole hour, I forgot what things were called and saw instead what they are.
1983 *Murder in the Dark,* 'Strawberries'.

61 Canada was open for business. And closed for everything else.
1988 Essay on censorship in *The Globe and Mail,* 'The Porn Patrol', 18 Feb. Collected in Douglas Fetherling (ed) *Best Canadian Essays* (1989).

62 Who knows what evil lurks in the hearts of men? An older woman knows. But how much older do you have to get before you acquire that kind of wisdom?
1993 *The Robber Bride,* ch.48.

63 His father was self-made, but his mother was constructed by others, and such edifices are notoriously fragile.
1996 *Alias Grace.*

64 Publishing a book is often very much like being put on trial for some offence which is quite other than the one you know in your heart you've committed.
2002 *Negotiating with the Dead: A Writer on Writing.*

Auber, Daniel-François-Esprit   1782–1871

French composer of operas. His best-known works are *La Muette de Portici,* usually entitled *Masaniello* (1828), and *Fra Diavolo* (1830).

65 Well, there's no help for it. Ageing seems to be the only available way to live a long time.
Attributed, when a friend lamented that they were both getting older. Quoted in Clifton Fadiman *The Faber Book of Anecdotes* (1985).

Aubrey, John 1626–97

English antiquary. Only his credulous *Miscellanies* (1696) of folklore and ghost stories were printed in his lifetime, and his colourful biographical anecdotes were later collected as *Letters by Eminent Persons* (1813), better known as *Brief Lives*.

66 How these curiosities would be quite forgot, did not such idle fellows as I am put them down.
1693 *Brief Lives* (published 1813), 'Venetia Digby'.

67 He had read much, if one considers his long life; but his contemplation was much more than his reading. He was wont to say that if he had read as much as other men, he should have known no more than other men.
1693 Of Thomas Hobbes. *Brief Lives* (published 1813), 'Thomas Hobbes'.

68 His harmonical and ingenious soul did lodge in a beautiful and well proportioned body. He was a spare man.... He was so fair that they called him the *lady* of Christ's College.
1693 Of Milton. *Brief Lives* (published 1813), 'John Milton'.

69 Sir Walter, being strangely surprised and put out of his countenance at so great a table, gives his son a damned blow over the face. His son, as rude as he was, would not strike his father, but strikes over the face the gentleman that sat next to him and said 'Box about: 'twill come to my father anon.'
1693 *Brief Lives* (published 1813), 'Sir Walter Raleigh'.

70 When he killed a calf he would do it in a high style, and make a speech.
1693 *Brief Lives* (published 1813), 'William Shakespeare'. Aubrey had been misinformed that Shakespeare's father was a butcher. He was in fact a glover.

71 The first sense he had of God was when he was eleven years old at Chigwell being retired into a chamber alone: he was so suddenly surprised with a sense of inward comfort and (as he thought) an external glory in the room that he had many times said that from thence he has the Seal of Divinity and Immortality, that there was a God and that the soul of man was capable of enjoying his divine communications.
1693 Of William Penn, early Quaker. *Brief Lives* (published 1813).

Auchincloss, Louis Stanton 1917–

US writer and critic, who studied law. His works chronicle the life of New York City and its inhabitants, particularly the aristocracy. His works include *Venus in Sparta* (1958) and *Pursuit of the Prodigal* (1960).

72 Perfection irritates as well as it attracts, in fiction as in life.
1965 *Pioneers and Caretakers: A Study of Nine American Women Novelists*.

73 A neurotic can perfectly well be a literary genius, but his greatest danger is always that he will not recognize when he is dull.
1965 *Pioneers and Caretakers: A Study of Nine American Women Novelists*.

74 The glittering structure of her cultivation sits on her novels like a rather showy icing that detracts from the cake beneath.
1965 Of Edith Wharton. *Pioneers and Caretakers: A Study of Nine American Women Novelists*.

75 I would rather see the old reservoir on Forty-second

Street or the original Madison Square Garden than I would any of the lost wonders of the ancient world.
Quoted in Carol Gelderman *Louis Auchincloss* (1993).

Auden, W(ystan) H(ugh) 1907–73

English-born US poet. His early work reflects his concern with social problems of the 1930s and his left-wing commitment. His conversion from liberal humanism to Anglo-Catholicism informs his later work. He collaborated with Christopher Isherwood in three plays and *Journey to a War* (1939).

76 Harrow the house of the dead; look shining at New styles of architecture, a change of heart.
1930 'Sir, No Man's Enemy'.

77 Private faces in public places
Are wiser and nicer
Than public faces in private places.
1932 *The Orators*, dedication.

78 What do you think about England, this country of ours where nobody is well?
1932 *The Orators*, 'Address for a Prize Day'.

79 To ask the hard question is simple.
1933 *Poems*, no.27.

80 The sky is darkening like a stain;
Something is going to fall like rain,
And it won't be flowers.
1935 'The Witness'.

81 This is the Night Mail crossing the border
Bringing the cheque and the postal order.
1936 'Night Mail', pt.1, written to accompany a documentary by the Post Office Film Unit.

82 And none will hear the postman's knock
Without a quickening of the heart.
For who can bear to feel himself forgotten?
1936 'Night Mail', written to accompany a documentary by the Post Office Film Unit.

83 Out on the lawn I lie in bed,
Vega conspicuous overhead.
1936 *Look, Stranger*, no.2.

84 August for the people and their favourite islands.
Daily the steamers sidle up to meet
The effusive welcome of the pier.
1936 *Look, Stranger*, no.30.

85 I dread this like the dentist, rather more so:
To me Art's subject is the human clay,
And landscape but a background to a torso;
All Cézanne's apples I would give away
For one small Goya or a Daumier.
1936 'Letter to Byron', pt.3, stanza 20, collected in *Poems, Essays, Dramatic Writings 1927–1939* (1977).

86 The stars are dead. The animals will not look:
We are left alone with our day, and the time is short, and History to the defeated
May say Alas but cannot help nor pardon.
1937 *Spain*.

87 The desires of the heart are as crooked as corkscrews,
Not to be born is the best for man;
The second-best is a formal order,
The dance's pattern; dance while you can.
1937 'Letter to William Coldstream, Esq', in *Letter from Iceland* (with Louis MacNeice).

88 All the others translate: the painter sketches

A visible world to love or reject.
1938 'The Composer' (XXXI V), collected in *The English Auden. Poems 1936–39* (1977).

89 Stop all the clocks, cut off the telephone,
Prevent the dog from barking with a juicy bone,
Silence the pianos and with muffled drum
Bring out the coffin, let the mourners come.
1939 'Stop all the clocks', *Collected Poems*. Featured in the 1994 film *Four Weddings and a Funeral*.

90 About suffering they were never wrong,
The Old Masters: how well they understood
Its human position; how it takes place
While someone else is eating or opening a window or
   just walking dully along.
1940 'Musée des Beaux Arts'.

91 I'll love you dear, I'll love you
Till China and Africa meet
And the river jumps over the mountain
And the salmon sing in the street,
I'll love you till the ocean
Is folded and hung up to dry
And the seven stars go squawking
Like geese about the sky.
1940 'As I Walked Out One Evening'.

92 But all the clocks in the city
Began to whirr and chime:
'O let not Time deceive you,
You cannot conquer Time.'
1940 'As I Walked Out One Evening'.

93 O tell me the truth about love.
When it comes, will it come without warning
Just as I'm picking my nose?
Will it knock on my door in the morning,
Or tread in the bus on my toes?
1940 'Twelve Poems', section 12.

94 Encased in talent like a uniform,
The rank of every poet is well known;
They can amaze us like a thunderstorm,
Or die so young, or live for years alone.
1940 'The Novelist'.

95 When there was peace, he was for peace; when there
was war, he went.
1940 'The Unknown Citizen'.

96 Was he free? Was he happy? The question is absurd:
Had anything been wrong, we should certainly have
heard.
1940 'The Unknown Citizen'.

97 Perfection, of a kind, was what he was after,
And the poetry he invented was easy to understand.
1940 'Epitaph On A Tyrant'.

98 When he laughed, respectable senators burst with
laughter,
And when he cried the little children died in the streets.
1940 'Epitaph On A Tyrant'.

99 To us he is no more a person
Now but a whole climate of opinion.
1940 'In Memory of Sigmund Freud', stanza 17.

1 O all the instruments agree
The day of his death was a dark cold day.
1940 'In Memory of W.B. Yeats', pt.1.

2 You were silly like us: your gift survived it all;

The parish of rich women, physical decay,
Yourself; mad Ireland hurt you into poetry.
Now Ireland has her madness and her weather still,
For poetry makes nothing happen.
1940 'In Memory of W.B. Yeats', pt.2.

3 Earth receive an honoured guest;
William Yeats is laid to rest:
Let the Irish vessel lie
Emptied of its poetry.
1940 'In Memory of W.B. Yeats', pt.3.

4 In the nightmare of the dark
All the dogs of Europe bark,
And the living nations wait,
Each sequestered in its hate.
1940 'In Memory of W.B. Yeats', pt.3.

5 In the deserts of the heart
Let the healing fountain start,
In the prison of his days
Teach the free man how to praise.
1940 'In Memory of W.B. Yeats', pt.3.

6 Lay your sleeping head, my love,
Human on my faithless arm.
1940 'Lullaby'.

7 I and the public know
What all schoolchildren learn,
Those to whom evil is done
Do evil in return.
1940 'September 1, 1939'.

8 There is no such thing as the State
And no one exists alone;
Hunger allows no choice
To the citizen or the police;
We must love one another or die.
1940 'September 1, 1939'.

9 To the man-in-the-street, who, I'm sorry to say,
Is a keen observer of life,
The word 'Intellectual' suggests straight away
A man who's untrue to his wife.
1940 *New Year Letter* (published 1941), note to l.1277.

10 Blessed Cecilia, appear in visions
To all musicians, appear and inspire:
Translated Daughter, come down and startle
Composing mortals with immortal fire.
1941 'Anthem for St Cecilia's Day'.

11 Sob, heavy world,
Sob as you spin
Mantled in mist, remote from the happy.
1944–6 *The Age of Anxiety*, pt.4, 'The Dirge'.

12 In our anguish we struggle
To elude Him, to lie to Him, yet His love observes
His appalling promise; His predilection
As we wander and weep is with us to the end,
Minding our meanings, our least matter dear to Him.
1944–6 *The Age of Anxiety*, pt.6, Epilogue.

13 There is no love;
There are only the various envies, all of them sad.
1951 'In Praise of Limestone', l.58–9.

14 To save your world you asked this man to die:
Would this man, could he see you now, ask why?
1955 'Epitaph for the Unknown Soldier'.

15 No good opera plot can be sensible, for people do not
sing when they are feeling sensible.
Quoted in *Time*, 29 Dec 1961.

16 It is a sad fact about our culture that a poet can earn
much more money writing or talking about his art than
he can by practising it.
1963 *The Dyer's Hand*, foreword.

17 Pleasure is by no means an infallible critical guide, but it
is the least fallible.
1963 *The Dyer's Hand*, 'Reading'.

18 Some books are undeservedly forgotten; none are
undeservedly remembered.
1963 *The Dyer's Hand*, 'Reading'.

19 No poet or novelist wishes he were the only one who
ever lived, but most of them wish they were the only one
alive, and quite a number fondly believe that their wish
has been granted.
1963 *The Dyer's Hand*, 'Writing'.

20 The true men of action in our time, those who transform
the world, are not the politicians and statesmen, but the
scientists… When I find myself in the company of
scientists, I feel like a shabby curate who has strayed by
mistake into a drawing room full of dukes.
1963 *The Dyer's Hand*, 'The Poet and the City'.

21 Man is a history-making creature who can neither repeat
his past nor leave it behind.
1963 *The Dyer's Hand*, 'D.H. Lawrence'.

22 The image of myself which I try to create in my own mind
in order that I may love myself is very different from the
image which I try to create in the minds of others in order
that they may love me.
1963 *The Dyer's Hand*, 'Hic et Ille'.

23 Among those whom I like or admire, I can find no
common denominator, but among those whom I love, I
can: all of them make me laugh.
1963 *The Dyer's Hand*, 'Notes on the Comic'.

24 Geniuses are the luckiest of mortals because what they
must do is the same as what they most want to do.
1964 Foreword to Dag Hammarskjöld, *Markings*.

25 Some thirty inches from my nose
The frontier of my Person goes,
And all the untilled air between
Is private *pagus* or demesne.
Stranger, unless with bedroom eyes
I beckon you to fraternize,
Beware of rudely crossing it:
I have no gun, but I can spit.
1966 'Prologue: The Birth of Architecture', postscript.

26 Youth may be forgiven when it is brash or noisy, but this
does not mean that brashness and noise are virtues.
1966 *Collected Shorter Poems 1927–1957*, introduction.

27 Political history is far too criminal and pathological to be
a fit subject of study for the young. Children should
acquire their heroes and villains from fiction.
1970 *A Certain World*.

28 All sin tends to be addictive, and the terminal point of
addiction is what is called damnation.
1970 *A Certain World*, 'Hell'.

29 Of course, Behaviourism 'works'. So does torture.
1970 *A Certain World*, 'Behaviourism'

30 To my generation no other English poet seemed so
perfectly to express the sensibility of a male adolescent.
If I do not now turn to him very often, I am eternally
grateful to him for the joy he gave me in my youth.
1972 Of A E Housman. 'A Worcestershire Lad', collected in
Forewords and Afterwords (1973).

31 Music is the best means we have of digesting time.
Quoted in Robert Craft *Stravinsky: Chronicle of a Friendship*
(1972).

32 That singular command,
I do not understand,
Bless what there is for being,
What else am I for,
Agreeing or disagreeing?
'Precious Fire', in *Collected Poems* (1976).

33 Thou shall not sin
With statisticians nor commit
A social science.
'Under Which Lyre'.

34 My face looks like a wedding-cake left out in the rain.
Quoted in Humphrey Carpenter *W H Auden* (1981), pt.2, ch.6.

St Augustine *originally* **Aurelius Augustinus**   AD 354–430

Bishop of Hippo from 395. The son of Numidian Roman citizens
(from modern Tunisia), he was converted to Christianity in 386.
His works include his *Confessions* and *The City of God*.

35 *Da mihi castitatem et continentiam, sed noli modo.*
Grant me chastity and continence, but not yet.
AD **397** *Confessions*, bk.8, ch.7 (translated by Henry Chadwick).

36 *Tolle, lege, tolle, lege.*
Pick up and read, pick up and read.
AD **397** *Confessions*, bk.8, ch.12.

37 *Sero te amavi, pulchritudo tam antiqua et tam nova, sero
te amavi!*
Late have I loved you, beauty so old and so new: late
have I loved you.
AD **397** *Confessions*, bk.10, ch.27.

38 *Continentiam iubes; da quod iubes et iube quod vis.*
You command continence; give what you command and
command what you will.
AD **397** *Confessions*, bk.10, ch.29.

39 *Quid est ergo tempus? Si nemo ex me quaerat, scio; si
quaerenti explicare velim, nescio.*
What, then, is time? I know well enough what it is,
provided that nobody asks me; but if I am asked what it is
and try to explain, I am baffled.
AD **397** *Confessions*, bk.11, ch.14 (translated by R S Pine-Coffin).

40 *Multi quidem facilius se abstinent ut non utantur, quam
temperent ut bene utantur.*
For many, total abstinence is easier than perfect
moderation.
AD **401** *On the Good of Marriage*, ch.21.

41 *Dilige et quod vis fac.*
Love, and do what you like
AD **413** *In Epistolam Joannis ad Parthos*, tractatus 7, section 8.

42 What varieties man has found out in buildings, attires,
husbandry, navigation, sculpture and imagery! What
perfection has he shown, in the shows of theatres, in
taming, killing, and catching wild beasts! What millions
of inventions has he against others, and for himself in

poisons, arms, engines, stratagems, and the like! What thousands of medicines for the health, of meats for the throat, of means and figures to persuade, of elegant phrases to delight, of verses for pleasure, of musical inventions and instruments! What excellent inventions are geography, arithmetic, astrology, and the rest! How large is the capacity of man, if we should stand upon particulars!
AD 427 *The City of God*.

43 All the devastation, the butchery, the plundering, the conflagrations, and all the anguish which accompanied the recent disaster at Rome were in accordance with the general practice of warfare.
AD 427 *City of God*, vol.1, ch.1, section 8.

44 If you don't believe it, you won't understand it.
Quoted in Erasmus *De Libero Arbitrio* (1523).

45 Do not plan long journeys, because whatever you believe in you have already seen. When a thing is everywhere, the way to find it is not to travel but to love.
Quoted in Ingrid Cranfield *The Challengers* (1976).

Augustus *originally* Gaius Iulius Caesar Octavianus
63 BC–AD 14

First Roman emperor, a senator's son adopted by Caesar in his will (44 BC). With Marcus Antonius and Lepidus he secured power after the battle of Philippi (42 BC) but the triumvirate collapsed and after Actium (31 BC) Caesar was sole ruler of the Roman Empire. He took the title Augustus in 27 BC and expanded the empire until the loss of three legions in Germany (AD 9).

46 *Quintili Vare, legiones redde.*
Quintilius Varus, give me back my legions.
Quoted in Suetonius, *Augustus*, section 23.

47 *Festina lente.*
Hurry slowly.
Quoted in Suetonius *Augustus*, section 25 (originally quoted in Greek, but better known in the Latin form).

48 *Acta est fabula.*
The play is over.
AD 14 Last words, attributed. In Suetonius *Augustus*, section 99.1, the scene of his death-bed is described: 'He summoned a group of friends and asked: "Have I played my part in the farce of life well enough?" adding the verse: "If it was any good, please applaud for the play, and send us with pleasure on our way".'

Aung San Suu Kyi 1945–

Burmese human rights activist and a leading campaigner for the National League for Democracy before being detained in 1989 by the country's ruling military junta. She has since spent long periods under house arrest. She was awarded the Nobel peace prize in 1991.

49 There is nothing new in Third World governments seeking to justify and perpetuate authoritarian rule by denouncing liberal democratic principles as alien.
1989 *Freedom From Fear*, 'In Quest of Democracy'.

50 Regimented minds cannot grasp the concept of confrontation as an open exchange of major differences with a view to settlement through genuine dialogue.
1989 *Freedom From Fear*, 'In Quest of Democracy'.

51 In societies where men are truly confident of their own worth women are not merely tolerated, they are valued.
1995 Videotaped address at the NGO Forum on Women, Beijing, China, 31 Aug.

Aurelius, Marcus Aurelius Antoninus AD 121–80

Roman emperor. He was consul from 140 to 161, when he succeeded Antoninus Pius to the throne. His *Meditations*, written in Greek, consist of notes made throughout his life.

52 A little flesh, a little breath, and a Reason to rule all—that is myself.
c. AD 170–180 *Meditations*, bk.2, no.2 (translated by M Staniforth).

53 Nowhere can a man find a quieter or more untroubled retreat than in his own soul.
c. AD 170–180 *Meditations*, bk.4, no.3 (translated by M Staniforth).

54 Soon you will have forgotten the world, and the world will have forgotten you.
c. AD 170–180 *Meditations*, bk.7, no.21 (translated by M Staniforth).

55 To live each day as though one's last, never flustered, never apathetic, never attitudinizing—here is perfection of character.
c. AD 170–180 *Meditations*, bk.7, no.69 (translated by M Staniforth).

Austen, Jane 1775–1817

English novelist. Her works satirized fashionable society, exploring the role of women. *Sense and Sensibility* (1811), *Pride and Prejudice* (1813), *Mansfield Park* (1814) and *Emma* (1815) were published anonymously; *Persuasion* and *Northanger Abbey* were both published posthumously (1818).

56 It was too pathetic for the feelings of Sophia and myself—we fainted alternately on the sofa.
1790 *Love and Freindship*, 'Letter the 8th'.

57 She was nothing more than a mere good-tempered, civil and obliging young woman; as such we could scarcely dislike her—she was only an Object of Contempt.
1790 *Love and Freindship*, 'Letter the 13th'.

58 We met…Dr Hall in such very deep mourning that either his mother, his wife, or himself must be dead.
1799 Letter to Cassandra Austen, 17 May.

59 On every formal visit a child ought to be of the party, by way of provisions for discourse.
1811 *Sense and Sensibility*, vol.2, ch.6.

60 It is not time or opportunity that is to determine intimacy; it is disposition alone. Seven years would be insufficient to make some people acquainted with each other, and seven days are more than enough for others.
1811 *Sense and Sensibility*, vol.2, ch.12.

61 It is a truth universally acknowledged, that a single man in possession of a good fortune, must be in want of a wife.
1813 *Pride and Prejudice*, ch.1, opening lines.

62 Her mind was less difficult to develop. She was a woman of mean understanding, little information, and uncertain temper.
1813 Of Mrs Bennet. *Pride and Prejudice*, ch.1.

63 Happiness in marriage is entirely a matter of chance.
1813 *Pride and Prejudice*, ch.6.

64 May I ask whether these pleasing attentions proceed from the impulse of the moment, or are the result of previous study?
1813 *Pride and Prejudice*, ch.14.

65 Mr Wickham is blessed with such happy manners as may ensure his making friends—whether he may be equally capable of retaining them, is less certain.
1813 *Pride and Prejudice*, ch.18.

66 From this day you must be a stranger to one of your parents.—Your mother will never see you again if you do *not* marry Mr Collins, and I will never see you again if you do.
1813 *Pride and Prejudice*, ch.20.

67 Without thinking highly either of men or matrimony, marriage had always been her object; it was the only honourable provision for well-educated young women of small fortune, and however uncertain of giving happiness, must be their pleasantest preservative from want.
1813 *Pride and Prejudice*, ch.22.

68 Next to being married, a girl likes to be crossed in love a little now and then. It is something to think of, and gives her a sort of distinction among her companions.
1813 *Pride and Prejudice*, ch.24.

69 What are men to rocks and mountains? Oh! what hours of transport we shall spend! And when we do return, it shall not be like other travellers, without being able to give one accurate idea of anything. We will know where we have gone—we will recollect what we have seen. Lakes, mountains, and rivers, shall not be jumbled together in our imaginations; nor, when we attempt to describe any particular scene, will we begin quarrelling about its relative situation.
1813 *Pride and Prejudice*, ch.27.

70 You ought certainly to forgive them as a Christian, but never to admit them in your sight, or allow their names to be mentioned in your hearing.
1813 *Pride and Prejudice*, ch.57.

71 For what do we live, but to make sport for our neighbours, and laugh at them in our turn?
1813 *Pride and Prejudice*, ch.57.

72 There is not one in a hundred of either sex who is not taken in when they marry. Look where I will, I see that it is so; and I feel that it must be so, when I consider that it is, of all transactions, the one in which people expect most from others, and are least honest themselves.
1814 *Mansfield Park*, ch.5.

73 Selfishness must always be forgiven you know, because there is no hope for a cure.
1814 *Mansfield Park*, ch.7.

74 We do not look in great cities for our best morality.
1814 *Mansfield Park*, ch.9.

75 Let us have no ranting tragedies. Too many characters—Not a tolerable woman's part in the play.
1814 *Mansfield Park*, ch.14.

76 A large income is the best recipe for happiness I ever heard of. It certainly may secure all the myrtle and turkey part of it.
1814 *Mansfield Park*, ch.22.

77 Shakespeare one gets acquainted with without knowing how. It is part of an Englishman's constitution. His thoughts and beauties are so spread abroad that one touches them everywhere, one is intimate with him by instinct.
1814 *Mansfield Park*, ch.34.

78 I must have a London audience. I could never preach, but to the educated; to those who were capable of estimating my composition.
1814 *Mansfield Park*, ch.34.

79 I think I may boast myself to be, with all possible vanity, the most unlearned and uninformed female who ever dared to be an authoress.
1815 Letter to Rev James Clarke, quoted in Justin Wintle and Richard Kenin (eds) *The Dictionary of Biographical Quotation* (1978).

80 She would not have him really suspect such a circumstance as her not being thought perfect by every body.
1816 *Emma*, ch.1.

81 A real, honest, old-fashioned Boarding-school, where a reasonable quantity of accomplishments were sold at a reasonable price, and where girls might be sent to be out of the way and scramble themselves into a little education, without any danger of coming back prodigies.
1816 *Emma*, ch.3.

82 One half of the world cannot understand the pleasures of the other.
1816 *Emma*, ch.9.

83 The sooner every party breaks up the better.
1816 *Emma*, ch.25.

84 I do not know whether it ought to be so, but certainly silly things do cease to be silly if they are done by sensible people in an impudent way. Wickedness is always wickedness, but folly is not always folly. It depends upon the character of those who handle it.
1816 *Emma*, ch.26.

85 Surprises are foolish things. The pleasure is not enhanced, and the inconvenience is often considerable.
1816 *Emma*, ch.26.

86 One has no great hopes from Birmingham. I always say there is something direful in the sound.
1816 Mrs Elton speaking. *Emma*, ch. 36.

87 Goldsmith tells us, when a lovely woman stoops to folly, she has nothing to do but die; and when she stoops to be disagreeable, it is equally to be recommended as a clearer of ill-fame.
1816 *Emma*, ch.45.
➤ See Goldsmith 361:47.

88 What should I do with your strong, manly, spirited sketches, full of variety and glow?—How could I possibly join them on to the little bit (two inches wide) of ivory on which I work with so fine a brush, as produces little effect after much labour?
1816 Letter to J Edward Austen, 16 Dec.

89 Single women have a dreadful propensity for being poor—which is one very strong argument in favour of matrimony.
1817 Letter to Fanny Knight, 13 Mar.

90 Pictures of perfection as you know make me sick and wicked.
1817 Of heroines in novels. Letter to Fanny Knight, 23 Mar.

91 Oh! it is only a novel!…only some work in which the most thorough knowledge of human nature, the happiest delineation of its varieties, the liveliest effusions of wit and humour are conveyed to the world in the best chosen language.
1818 *Northanger Abbey*, ch.5.

92 But history, real solemn history, I cannot be interested in…it tells me nothing that does not vex or weary me…the men all so good for nothing, and hardly any women at all.
1818 *Northanger Abbey*, vol.1, ch.14.

93 Where people wish to attach, they should always be ignorant. To come with a well informed mind, is to come with an inability of administering to the vanity of others, which a sensible person would always wish to avoid. A woman especially, if she have the misfortune of knowing anything, should conceal it as well she can…imbecility in females is a great enhancement of their personal charms.
1818 *Northanger Abbey*, ch.14.

94 Vanity was the beginning and the end of Sir Walter Elliot's character; vanity of person and of situation.
1818 *Persuasion*, ch.1.

95 'My idea of good company, Mr Elliot, is the company of clever, well-informed people, who have a great deal of conversation; that is what I call good company.' 'You are mistaken,' said he gently, 'that is not good company, that is the best.'
1818 *Persuasion*, ch.16.

96 We cannot help ourselves. We live at home, quiet, confined, and our feelings prey upon us. You are forced on exertion. You have always a profession, pursuits, business of some sort or other, to take you back into the world immediately, and continual occupation and change soon weaken impressions.
1818 Of the difference between women and men. *Persuasion*, ch.23.

97 Men have every advantage of us in telling their story. Education has been theirs in so much higher a degree; the pen has been in their hands.
1818 *Persuasion*, ch.23.

98 All the privilege I claim for my own sex (it is not a very enviable one, you need not covet it) is that of loving longest, when existence or when hope is gone.
1818 *Persuasion*, ch.23.

Auster, Paul *pseudonym of* **Paul Benjamin** 1947–

US novelist, poet and essayist. He is best known for his novels, which include the *New York Trilogy* (1985–7) and *Mr Vertigo* (1994).

99 We construct a narrative for ourselves, and that's the thread we follow from one day to the next. People who disintegrate as personalities are the ones who lose that thread.
1989 In the *Sunday Times*, 16 Apr.

1 More often than not, our lives resemble the stuff of eighteenth-century novels.
2003 *Collected Prose*, 'The National Story Project'.

Austin, Alfred 1835–1913

English poet. Appointed Poet Laureate in 1896, he was the author of *The Season; a Satire* (1861), *The Human Tragedy* (1862), *The Conversion of Winckelmann* (1862), several volumes of poetry and an autobiography (1911).

2 Along the electric wires the message came:
'He is no better, he is much the same.'
1910 'On the Illness of the Prince of Wales'. There is some doubt about the authorship of this satiric poem, but it is usually credited to Austin.

Austin, Mary Hunter 1868–1934

US novelist, short-story writer and suffragist, best known for her fiction about the American West and portraits of Native American life. Her works include *The Land of Little Rain* (1903), *A Woman of Genius* (1912) and her autobiography, *Earth Horizon* (1932).

3 When a woman ceases to alter the fashion of her hair, you guess that she has passed the crisis of her experience.
1903 *The Land of Little Rain*, 'The Basket Maker'.

Austin, Warren R(obinson) 1877–1962

US lawyer and diplomat, a Senator (1931–46) and subsequently US representative at the United Nations (1947–53).

4 It is better that aged diplomats be bored than for young men to die.
On soporifically lengthy debates at the United Nations.

5 Jews and Arabs should settle their differences like good Christians.
Attributed.

Avison, Margaret 1918–

Canadian poet. She has worked as a librarian, lecturer, social worker and embassy secretary. Her first book of poems was *Winter Sun* (1960). Her sixth collection, *Concrete and Wild Carrot*, was published in 2002.

6 Purpose apart, perched like an umpire, dozes,
Dreams golden balls whirring through indigo.
Clay blurs the whitewash but day still encloses
The albinos, bonded in their flick and flow.
Playing in musicked gravity, the pair
Score liquid Euclids in foolscaps of air.
1960 *Winter Sun*, 'Tennis'.

Ayckbourn, Sir Alan 1939–

English playwright. Recognized as a master of farce, his plays often shrewdly observe the English class-structure

7 My mother used to say, Delia, if S-E-X ever rears its ugly head, close your eyes before you see the rest of it.
1977 *Bedroom Farce*, act 2.

Ayer, Sir Alfred Jules 1910–89

English philosopher, professor at Oxford (1947–59). His first book *Language, Truth and Logic* (1936) was an iconoclastic attack on metaphysical speculation. He wrote many more works, and was knighted in 1970.

8 The traditional disputes of philosophers are, for the most part, as unwarranted as they are unfruitful.
1936 *Language, Truth and Logic*, ch.1.

9 We shall maintain that no statement which refers to a 'reality' transcending the limits of all possible sense-experience can possibly have any literal significance.
1936 *Language, Truth and Logic*, ch.1.

10 The criterion which we use to test the genuineness of apparent statements of fact is the criterion of verifiability. We say that a sentence is factually significant to any given person, if, and only if, he knows how to

verify the proposition which it purports to express —
that is, if he knows what observations would lead him,
under certain conditions, to accept the proposition as
being true, or reject it as being false.
1936 *Language, Truth and Logic*, ch.1

11 Sentences which simply express moral judgements do
not say anything. They are pure expressions of feeling
and as such do not come under the category of truth and
falsehood.
1936 *Language, Truth and Logic*, ch.6.

12 It appears, then, that ethics, as a branch of knowledge, is
nothing more than a department of psychology and
sociology.
1936 *Language, Truth and Logic*, ch.6.

13 But if science may be said to be blind without
philosophy, it is true also that philosophy is virtually
empty without science.
1936 *Language, Truth and Logic*, ch.8.

Ayres, Pam 1947–

English poet and broadcaster. She established a reputation as a
popular versifier, reading her own poems on everyday themes
on British television in the 1970s.

14 Medicinal discovery,
It moves in mighty leaps,
It leapt straight past the common cold
And gave it us for keeps.
1976 *Some of Me Poetry*,'Oh no, I got a cold'.

Aytoun, Sir Robert 1570–1638

Scottish poet and courtier at the court of James VI and I in
London. He wrote lyrics in English and Latin, and is credited
with the prototype of 'Auld Lang Syne'.

15 I loved thee once; I'll love no more—
Thine be the grief as is the blame;
Thou art not what thou wast before,
What reason I should be the same?
'To an Inconstant Mistress', stanza 1.

Aytoun, William Edmonstoune 1813–65

Scottish lawyer and humorist, who contributed many parodies
and burlesque reviews to *Blackwood's*. His best-known work
was *Lays of the Scottish Cavaliers and other Poems* (1848).

16 Fhairshon swore a feud
Against the clan M'Tavish;
Marched into their land
To murder and to ravish;
For he did resolve
To extirpate the vipers,
With four-and-twenty men
And five-and-thirty pipers.
1845 'The Massacre of the Macpherson', stanza 1.

17 'He is coming! he is coming!'
Like a bridegroom from his room,
Came the hero from his prison
To the scaffold and the doom.
1848 *Lays of the Scottish Cavaliers and other Poems*, 'The
Execution of Montrose', stanza 14.

18 They bore within their breasts the grief
That fame can never heal—
The deep, unutterable woe

Which none save exiles feel.
1848 *Lays of the Scottish Cavaliers and other Poems*,'The Island
of the Scots', stanza 12.

Babbage, Charles 1792–1871

English mathematician, inventor and scientific theoretician,
who developed the programmable 'analytical engine', which
was able to perform computations.

19 Perhaps the most important principle on which the
economy of a manufacture depends, is the division of
labour amongst the persons who perform the work.
1832 *On the Economy of Machinery and Manufactures*.

Babbitt, Bruce Edward 1938–

US lawyer, Governor of Arizona (1978–87), a Democrat and
noted conservationist.

20 There is room in the west for wolves.
1995 Statement at Yellowstone National Park in Wyoming, 12
Jan, to the House of Representatives Natural Resources
Committee, on the controversial restoration of wildlife.

Babel, Isaac 1894–c.1939

Russian short-story writer.

21 No iron can stab the heart with such force as a full stop
put just at the right place.
1932 *Guy de Maupassant*.

Babeuf, François Noël 1760–97

French communist. As 'Gracchus Babeuf' during the French
Revolution, he plotted to destroy the Directory (1796) and
institute a communist state, but he was discovered and
guillotined.

22 The French Revolution is merely the herald of a far
greater and much more solemn revolution, which will be
the last… The hour has come for founding the Republic
of equals—that great refuge open to every man.
Conjuration des Égaux.

Bacall, Lauren *originally* *Betty Perske* 1924–

US film actress who married Humphrey Bogart in 1945.

23 I think your whole life shows in your face and you should
be proud of that.
1988 In the *Daily Telegraph*, 2 Mar.

Bach, Johann Sebastian 1685–1750

German composer and organist, whose polyphonic works
greatly influenced the course of Western music. He composed
over 200 cantatas, the *Saint John Passion* (1723), the *Saint
Matthew Passion* (1729), the *Mass in B Minor* (1733), and
Christmas and Easter Oratorios, as well as much keyboard
and instrumental music.

24 There is nothing to it. You only have to hit the right notes at the right time and the instrument plays itself.
Of the organ. Quoted in K Geiringer *The Bach Family* (1954).

25 An agreeable harmony for the honour of God and the permissible delights of the soul.
His definition of music. Quoted in Derek Watson *Music Quotations* (1991).

Bach, Richard 1936–

US author, formerly a military pilot. He is best known for *Jonathan Livingston Seagull* (1970).

26 Heaven is not a place, and it is not a time. Heaven is being perfect.
1970 *Jonathan Livingston Seagull.*

27 The gull sees farthest who sees highest.
1970 *Jonathan Livingston Seagull.*

28 'To begin with,' he said heavily, 'you've got to understand that a seagull is an unlimited idea of freedom, an image of the Great Gull, and your whole body, from wingtip to wingtip, is nothing more than your thought itself.'
1970 *Jonathan Livingston Seagull.*

29 There is no such thing as a problem without a gift for you in its hands. You seek problems because you need their gifts.
1977 *Illusions.*

30 Argue for your limitations, and sure enough, they're yours.
1977 *Illusions.*

31 'I don't know they're true,' he said. 'I believe them because it's fun to believe them.'
1977 *Illusions.*

Bacon, Francis, Viscount St Albans 1561–1626

English philosopher and statesman. Educated as a scholar and a lawyer, he entered the service of the crown and eventually became Lord Chancellor. Key works include *Essays* (1597–1625), *The Advancement of Learning* (1605), *Novum Organum* (1620) and *The New Atlantis* (1627).

32 I have taken all knowledge to be my province.
1592 Letter to Lord Burghley.

33 Knowledge is power
1597 *Meditationes sacrae,* 'De Haeresibus' (Of Heresies).

34 Opportunity makes a thief.
1598 Letter to the Earl of Essex.

35 For all knowledge and wonder (which is the seed of knowledge) is an impression of pleasure in itself.
1605 *The Advancement of Learning*, bk.1, ch.1, section 3.

36 So let great authors have their due, as time, which is the author of authors, be not deprived of his due, which is further and further to discover the truth.
1605 *The Advancement of Learning*, bk.1, ch.4, section 12.

37 If a man will begin with certainties, he shall end in doubts; but if he will be content to begin with doubts, he shall end in certainties.
1605 *The Advancement of Learning*, bk.1, ch.5, section 8.

38 Learned men…do many times fail to observe decency and discretion in their behaviour and carriage, so as the vulgar sort of capacities do make a judgment of them in greater matters by that which they find them wanting in smaller.
1605 *The Advancement of Learning*, bk.1.

39 Martin Luther…was enforced to awake all antiquity and to call former times to his succour to make a party against the present time, so that the ancient authors both in divinity and in humanity which had long time slept in libraries began generally to be read and revolved.
1605 *The Advancement of Learning*, bk.1.

40 Vain matter is worse than vain words.
1605 *The Advancement of Learning*, bk.1.

41 Time seemeth to be of the nature of a river or stream, which carrieth down to us that which is light and blown up, and sinketh and drowneth that which is weighty and solid.
1605 *The Advancement of Learning*, bk.1.

42 Antiquities are history defaced, or some remnants of history which have casually escaped the shipwreck of time.
1605 *The Advancement of Learning*, bk.2, ch.2, section 1.

43 [Poesy] was ever thought to have some participation of divineness, because it doth raise and erect the mind, by submitting the shows of things to the desires of the mind; whereas reason doth buckle and bow the mind unto the nature of things.
1605 *The Advancement of Learning*, bk.2, ch.4, section 2.

44 The knowledge of man is as the waters, some descending from above, and some springing from beneath; the one informed by the light of nature, the other inspired by divine revelation.
1605 *The Advancement of Learning*, bk.2, ch.5, section 1.

45 They are ill discoverers that think there is no land, when they can see nothing but sea.
1605 *The Advancement of Learning*, bk.2, ch.7, section 5.

46 A dance is a measured pace, as a verse is a measured speech.
1605 *The Advancement of Learning*, bk.2, ch.16, section 5.

47 But men must know, that in this theatre of man's life it is reserved only for God and angels to be lookers on.
1605 *The Advancement of Learning*, bk.2, ch.20, section 8.

48 We are much beholden to Machiavel and others, that write what men do, and not what they ought to do.
1605 *The Advancement of Learning*, bk.2, ch.21, section 9.

49 Did not one of the fathers in great indignation call poesy *vinum daemonum*?
1605 *The Advancement of Learning*, bk.2, ch.22, section 13. The Latin translates as 'the wine of the devils'.

50 All good moral philosophy is but an handmaid to religion.
1605 *The Advancement of Learning*, bk.2, ch.22, section 14.

51 Of knowledge there is no satiety.
1605 *The Advancement of Learning*, bk.2.

52 It is not granted to man to love and to be wise.
1605 *The Advancement of Learning*, bk.2.

53 Tennis is a game of no use in itself.
1605 *The Advancement of Learning*, bk.2.

54 Man seeketh in society comfort, use, and protection.
1605 *The Advancement of Learning*, bk.2.

55 Fortunes…come tumbling into some men's laps.
1605 *The Advancement of Learning*, bk.2.

56 It is in life as it is in ways, the shortest way is most

commonly the foulest, and surely the fairer way is not much about.
1605 *The Advancement of Learning*, bk.2, ch.23, section 45.

57 Empires and old women are more happy many times in their cures than learned physicians, because they are more exact and religious in holding to the composition and confection of tried medicines.
1605 *The Advancement of Learning*, bk.4, ch.2.

58 The subtlety of nature is greater many times over than the subtlety of the senses and understanding.
1620 *Novum Organum*, bk.1, aphorism 10.

59 *Quod enim mavult homo verum esse, id potius credit.*
For what a man would like to be true, that he more readily believes.
1620 *Novum Organum*, bk.1, aphorism 49.

60 Those who have handled sciences have been either men of experiment or men of dogmas. The men of experiment are like the ant; they only collect and use; the reasoners resemble spiders, who make cobwebs out of their own substance. But the bee takes a middle course; it gathers its material from the flowers of the garden and of the field, but transforms and digests by a power of its own. Not unlike this is the true business of philosophy.
1620 *Novum Organum* bk.1, aphorism 95.

61 *Vim et virtutem et consequentias rerum inventarum notare juvat; quae non in aliis manifestius occurrunt, quam in illis tribus quae antiquis incognitae, et quarum primordia, licet recentia, obscura et ingloria sunt: Artis nimirum Imprimendi, Pulveris Tormentarii, et Acus Nauticae. Haec enim tria rerum faciem et statum in orbe terrarum mutaverunt.*
It is well to observe the force and virtue and consequence of discoveries, and these are to be seen nowhere more conspicuously than in those three which were unknown to the ancients, and of which the origin, though recent, is obscure and inglorious; namely, printing, gunpowder and the magnet [ie the compass]. For these three have changed the whole face and state of things throughout the world.
1620 *Novum Organum*, bk.1, aphorism 129 (translated by James Spedding).

62 *Natura enim non imperatur, nisi parendo.*
For we cannot command Nature except by obeying her.
1620 *Novum Organum*, bk.1, aphorism 129.

63 It would be unsound fancy and self-contradictory to expect that things which have never yet been done can be done except by means which have never yet been tried.
1620 *Novum Organum*.

64 The lame man who keeps the right road outstrips the runner who takes a wrong one. Nay, it is obvious that when a man runs the wrong way, the more active and swift he is the further he will go astray.
1620 *Novum Organum*.

65 *Divitiae bona ancilla, pessima domina.*
Riches are a good handmaid, but the worst mistress.
1623 *De Dignitiate et Augmentis Scientiarum*, Antitheta no.6 (translated by Gilbert Watts, 1640).

66 The voice of the people hath some divineness in it, else how should so many men agree to be of one mind?
1623 *De Dignitiate et Augmentis Scientiarum*, Antitheta no.9 (translated by Gilbert Watts, 1640).

67 *Silentium, stultorum virtus.*
Silence is the virtue of fools.
1623 *De Dignitiate et Augmentis Scientiarum*, Antitheta no.31 (translated by Gilbert Watts, 1640).

68 The end of our foundation is the knowledge of causes, and secret motions of things; and the enlarging of the bounds of human Empire, to the effecting of all things possible.
1624 *New Atlantis* (published posthumously, 1627).

69 Wise nature did never put her precious jewels into a garret four stories high: and therefore…exceeding tall men had ever very empty heads.
1625 *Apophthegms*.

70 Hope is a good breakfast, but it is a bad supper.
1625 *Apophthegms*.

71 What is truth? said jesting Pilate; and would not stay for an answer.
1625 *Essays*, no.1, 'Of Truth'.

72 The inquiry of truth, which is the love-making, or wooing of it, the knowledge of truth, which is the presence of it, and the belief of truth, which is the enjoying of it, is the sovereign good of human nature.
1625 *Essays*, no.1, 'Of Truth'.

73 Men fear death as children fear to go in the dark; and as that natural fear in children is increased with tales, so is the other.
1625 *Essays*, no.2, 'Of Death'.

74 There is no passion in the mind of man so weak, but it mates and masters the fear of death. And therefore death is no such terrible enemy, when a man hath so many attendants about him that can win the combat of him. Revenge triumphs over death; love slights it; honour aspireth to it; grief flieth to it.
1625 *Essays*, no.2, 'Of Death'.

75 It is as natural to die as to be born; and to a little infant, perhaps, the one is as painful as the other.
1625 *Essays*, no.2, 'Of Death'.

76 Death…openeth the gate to good fame, and extinguisheth envy.
1625 *Essays*, no.2, 'Of Death'.

77 All colours will agree in the dark.
1625 *Essays*, no.3, 'Of Unity in Religion'.

78 Revenge is a kind of wild justice, which the more man's nature runs to, the more ought law to weed it out.
1625 *Essays*, no.4, 'Of Revenge'.

79 The virtue of prosperity, is temperance; the virtue of adversity, is fortitude.
1625 *Essays*, no.5, 'Of Adversity'.

80 Prosperity is the blessing of the Old Testament, adversity is the blessing of the New.
1625 *Essays*, no.5, 'Of Adversity'.

81 Prosperity is not without many fears and distastes; and adversity is not without comforts and hopes.
1625 *Essays*, no.5, 'Of Adversity'.

82 Prosperity doth best discover vice, but adversity doth best discover virtue.
1625 *Essays*, no.5, 'Of Adversity'.

83 Let judges also remember that Solomon's throne was

supported by lions on both sides; let them be lions, but yet lions under the throne.
1625 *Essays*, no.6, 'Of Judicature'.

84 The joys of parents are secret, and so are their griefs and fears.
1625 *Essays*, no.7, 'Of Parents and Children'.

85 Children sweeten labours, but they make misfortunes more bitter.
1625 *Essays*, no.7, 'Of Parents and Children'.

86 He that hath wife and children hath given hostages to fortune; for they are impediments to great enterprises, either of virtue or mischief. Certainly the best works, and of greatest merit for the public, have proceeded from the unmarried or childless men, which both in affection and means have married and endowed the public.
1625 *Essays*, no.8, 'Of Marriage and the Single Life'.

87 There are some others that account wife and children but as bills of charge.
1625 *Essays*, no.8, 'Of Marriage and the Single Life'.

88 The most ordinary cause of a single life is liberty, especially in certain self-pleasing and humorous minds, which are so sensible of every restraint, as they will go near to think their girdles and garters to be bonds and shackles.
1625 *Essays*, no.8, 'Of Marriage and the Single Life'.

89 Unmarried men are best friends, best masters, best servants, but not always best subjects, for they are light to run away, and almost all fugitives are of that condition.
1625 *Essays*, no.8, 'Of Marriage and the Single Life'.

90 Certainly wife and children are a kind of discipline of humanity; and single men, though they be many times more charitable, because their means are less exhaust, yet…they are more cruel and hardhearted (good to make severe inquisitors), because their tenderness is not so oft called upon.
1625 *Essays*, no.8, 'Of Marriage and the Single Life'.

91 Wives are young men's mistresses, companions for middle age, and old men's nurses.
1625 *Essays*, no.8, 'Of Marriage and the Single Life'.

92 He was reputed one of the wise men that made answer to the question when a man should marry? 'A young man not yet, an elder man not at all.'
1625 *Essays*, no.8, 'Of Marriage and the Single Life'.

93 It is often seen that bad husbands have very good wives; whether it be that it raiseth the price of their husband's kindness when it comes, or that the wives take a pride in their patience. But this never fails, if the bad husbands were of their own choosing, against their friends' consent; for then they will be sure to make good their own folly.
1625 *Essays*, no.8, 'Of Marriage and the Single Life'.

94 I had rather believe all the fables in the legend, and the Talmud, and the Alcoran, than that this universal frame is without a mind.
1625 *Essays*, no.9, 'Of Atheism'.

95 It is true, that a little philosophy inclineth Man's mind to atheism; but depth in philosophy bringeth men's minds about to religion.
1625 *Essays*, no.9 'Of Atheism'.
➤ *See Berkeley 79:7.*

96 For it is a true Rule that Love is ever rewarded, either with the reciproque, or with an inward and secret contempt.
1625 *Essays*, no.10, 'Of Love'.

97 The speaking in perpetual hyperbole is comely in nothing but love.
1625 *Essays*, no.10, 'Of Love'.

98 All rising to great place is by a winding stair.
1625 *Essays*, no.11, 'Of Great Place'.

99 Men in great place are thrice servants: servants of the sovereign or state, servants of fame, and servants of business.
1625 *Essays*, no.11, 'Of Great Place'.

1 It is a strange desire to seek power and to lose liberty.
1625 *Essays*, no.11, 'Of Great Place'.

2 The rising unto place is laborious, and by pains men come to greater pains; and it is sometimes base, and by indignities men come to dignities. The standing is slippery, and the regress is either a downfall, or at least an eclipse, which is a melancholy thing: *Cum non sis qui fueris, non esse cur velis vivere.*
1625 *Essays*, no.11, 'Of Great Place'. The Latin is taken from Cicero's *Familiar Letters*, and translates as: 'When you are not what you were, there is no reason to live.'

3 Certainly great persons had need to borrow other men's opinions to think themselves happy; for if they judge by their own feeling, they cannot find it; but if they think with themselves what other men think of them, and that other men would fain be as they are, then they are happy.
1625 *Essays*, no.11, 'Of Great Place'.

4 Men in great fortunes are strangers to themselves.
1625 *Essays*, no.11, 'Of Great Place'.

5 Merit and good works is the end of man's motion, and conscience of the same is the accomplishment of man's rest.
1625 *Essays*, no.11, 'Of Great Place'.

6 The vices of authority are chiefly four: delays, corruption, roughness, and facility.
1625 *Essays*, no.11, 'Of Great Place'.

7 In civil business; What first? Boldness; What second, and third? Boldness. And yet boldness is a child of ignorance and baseness.
1625 *Essays*, no.12, 'Of Boldness'.

8 There is in human nature generally more of the fool than of the wise.
1625 *Essays*, no.12, 'Of Boldness'.

9 Mahomet made the people believe that he would call a hill to him, and from the top of it offer up his prayers for the observers of his law. The people assembled: Mahomet called the hill to come to him again and again; and when the hill stood still he was never a whit abashed, but said, 'If the hill will not come to Mahomet, Mahomet will go to the hill.'
1625 *Essays*, no.12, 'Of Boldness'.

10 New nobility is but the act of power, but ancient nobility is the act of time.
1625 *Essays*, no.14, 'Of Nobility'.

11 The surest way to prevent seditions…is to take away the matter of them.
1625 *Essays*, no.15, 'Of Seditions and Troubles'.

12 Money is like muck, not good except it be spread.
  1625 *Essays*, no.15,'Of Seditions and Troubles'.

13 The remedy is worse than the disease.
  1625 *Essays*, no.15,'Of Seditions and Troubles'.

14 It were better to have no opinion of God at all than such an opinion as is unworthy of him.
  1625 *Essays*, no.17,'Of Superstition'.

15 In all superstition wise men follow fools.
  1625 *Essays*, no.17,'Of Superstition'.

16 There is a superstition in avoiding superstition.
  1625 *Essays*, no.17,'Of Superstition'. This is directed against Puritan reformers, who decried both Catholic and Anglican rites as 'superstitious'.

17 It is a miserable state of mind to have few things to desire and many things to fear.
  1625 *Essays*, no.19,'Of Empire'.

18 In things that are tender and unpleasing, it is good to break the ice by some whose words are of less weight, and to reserve the more weighty voice to come in as by chance.
  1625 *Essays*, no.22,'Of Cunning'.

19 Nothing doth more hurt in a state than that cunning men pass for wise.
  1625 *Essays*, no.22,'Of Cunning'.

20 Be so true to thyself as thou be not false to others.
  1625 *Essays*, no.23,'Of Wisdom for a Man's Self'.

21 It is a poor centre of a man's actions, himself.
  1625 *Essays*, no.23,'Of Wisdom for a Man's Self'.

22 It is the nature of extreme self-lovers, as they will set a house on fire, and it were but to roast their eggs.
  1625 *Essays*, no.23,'Of Wisdom for a Man's Self'.

23 It is the wisdom of the crocodiles, that shed tears when they would devour.
  1625 *Essays*, no.23,'Of Wisdom for a Man's Self'.

24 As the births of living creatures at first are ill-shapen, so are all innovations, which are the births of time.
  1625 *Essays*, no.24,'Of Innovations'.

25 He that will not apply new remedies must expect new evils; for time is the greatest innovator.
  1625 *Essays*, no.24,'Of Innovations'.

26 To choose time is to save time.
  1625 *Essays*, no.25,'Of Dispatch'.

27 The French are wiser than they seem, and the Spaniards seem wiser than they are.
  1625 *Essays*, no.26,'Of Seeming Wise'.

28 It had been hard for him that spake it to have put more truth and untruth together, in a few words, than in that speech: 'Whosoever is delighted in solitude is either a wild beast, or a god.'
  1625 *Essays*, no.27,'Of Friendship'.

29 A crowd is not company, and faces are but a gallery of pictures, and talk but a tinkling cymbal, where there is no love.
  1625 *Essays*, no.27,'Of Friendship'.
  ➥ See Bible 121:9.

30 [Friendship] redoubleth joys, and cutteth griefs in half.
  1625 *Essays*, no.27,'Of Friendship'.

31 As if you would call a physician, that is thought good for the cure of the disease you complain of but is unacquainted with your body, and therefore may put you in the way for a present cure but overthroweth your health in some other kind; and so cure the disease and kill the patient.
  1625 *Essays*, no.27,'Of Friendship'.

32 Riches are for spending; and spending for honour and good actions.
  1625 *Essays*, no.28,'Of Expense'.

33 Neither will it be, that a people overlaid with taxes should ever become valiant and martial.
  1625 *Essays*, no.29,'Of the True Greatness of Kingdoms'.

34 Suspicions amongst thoughts are like bats amongst birds, they ever fly by twilight.
  1625 *Essays*, no.31,'Of Suspicion'.

35 There is nothing makes a man suspect much, more than to know little.
  1625 *Essays*, no.31,'Of Suspicion'.

36 If you dissemble sometimes your knowledge of that you are thought to know, you shall be thought, another time, to know that you know not.
  1625 *Essays*, no.32,'Of Discourse'.

37 When the world was young it begat more children; but now it is old it begets fewer: for I may justly account new plantations to be the children of former kingdoms.
  1625 *Essays*, no.33,'Of Plantations'.

38 If you plant where savages are, do not only entertain them with trifles and jingles, but use them justly and graciously.
  1625 *Essays*, no.33,'Of Plantations'.

39 Nature is often hidden, sometimes overcome, seldom extinguished.
  1625 *Essays*, no.38,'Of Nature in Men'.

40 Chiefly the mould of a man's fortune is in his own hands.
  1625 *Essays*, no.40,'Of Fortune'.

41 If a man look sharply, and attentively, he shall see Fortune; for though she be blind, yet she is not invisible.
  1625 *Essays*, no.40,'Of Fortune'.

42 Beauty is as summer-fruits, which are easy to corrupt, and cannot last.
  1625 *Essays*, no.43,'Of Beauty'.

43 Virtue is like a rich stone, best plain set.
  1625 *Essays*, no.43,'Of Beauty'.

44 That is the best part of beauty, which a picture cannot express.
  1625 *Essays*, no.43,'Of Beauty'.

45 There is no excellent beauty that hath not some strangeness in the proportion.
  1625 *Essays*, no.43,'Of Beauty'.

46 God Almighty first planted a garden; and indeed, it is the purest of human pleasures.
  1625 *Essays*, no.46,'Of Gardens'.

47 It is generally better to deal by speech than by letter.
  1625 *Essays*, no.47,'Of Negotiating'.

48 It is better dealing with men in appetite, than with those that are where they would be.
  1625 *Essays*, no.47,'Of Negotiating'.

49 If you would work any man, you must either know his nature and fashions, and so lead him; or his ends, and so persuade him; or his weakness and disadvantages, and

so awe him, or those that have interest in him, and so govern him.
1625 *Essays*, no.47, 'Of Negotiating'.

50 There is little friendship in the world, and least of all between equals.
1625 *Essays*, no.48, 'Of Followers and Friends'.

51 To spend too much time in studies is sloth; to use them too much for ornament is affectation; to make judgment wholly by their rules is the humour of a scholar.
1625 *Essays*, no.50, 'Of Studies'.

52 Read not to contradict and confute, nor to believe and take for granted, nor to find talk and discourse, but to weigh and consider.
1625 *Essays*, no.50, 'Of Studies'.

53 Some books are to be tasted, others to be swallowed, and some few to be chewed and digested; that is, some books are to be read only in parts; others to be read but not curiously; and some few to be read wholly, and with diligence and attention. Some books also may be read by deputy, and extracts made of them by others.
1625 *Essays*, no.50, 'Of Studies'.

54 If a man write little, he had need have a great memory; if he confer little, he had need have a present wit; and if he read little he had need have much cunning, to seem to know that he doth not.
1625 *Essays*, no.50, 'Of Studies'.

55 Histories make men wise; poets, witty; the mathematics, subtle; natural philosophy, deep; moral, grave; logic and rhetoric, able to contend.
1625 *Essays*, no.50, 'Of Studies'.

56 Light gains make heavy purses.
1625 *Essays*, no.52, 'Of Ceremonies and Respects'.

57 A wise man will make more opportunities than he finds.
1625 *Essays*, no.52, 'Of Ceremonies and Respects'.

58 It was prettily devised of Aesop, 'The fly sat upon the axletree of the chariot-wheel and said, what a dust do I raise.'
1625 *Essays*, no.54, 'Of Vain-Glory'.

59 In the youth of a state arms do flourish; in the middle age of a state, learning; and then both of them together for a time; in the declining age of a state, mechanical arts and merchandise.
1625 *Essays*, no.58, 'Of Vicissitude of Things'.

60 I bequeath my soul to God… For my name and memory, I leave it to men's charitable speeches, and to foreign nations, and the next age.
1626 From his will.

61 God's first Creature, which was Light.
New Atlantis (published 1627).

62 The end of our foundation is the knowledge of causes, and secret motions of things; and the enlarging of the bounds of human Empire, to the effecting of all things possible.
1627 Of Solomon's House, the centre of Bacon's scientific utopia. *New Atlantis* (published 1627).

63 No man can tickle himself.
Sylva Sylvarum (published 1627), bk.8.

64 Generally music feedeth that disposition of the spirits which it findeth.
Sylva Sylvarum (published 1627).

65 The world's a bubble; and the life of man
Less than a span.
The World (published 1629).

66 Books must follow sciences, and not sciences books.
A Proposition… Touching Amendment of the Laws of England (published 1657).

67 The government of a woman has been a rare thing at all times; felicity in such government a rarer thing still; felicity and long continuance together the rarest thing of all.
Quoted in J E Neale *The Age of Catherine de Medici and Essays in Elizabethan History* (1963), p.217.

Bacon, Francis 1909–92

Irish-born painter, who settled in England in 1928 and began painting without formal training. His work draws on surrealism and motion photography, often evoking angst. He was a technical perfectionist, and destroyed much of his work.

68 I think of myself as a kind of pulverizing machine into which everything I look at and feel is fed. I believe that I am different from the mixed-media jackdaws who use photographs etc. more or less literally.
On the use of photographs in his art. Quoted in John Russell *Francis Bacon* (1979).

69 Who can I tear to pieces, if not my friends?… If they were not my friends, I could not do such violence to them.
Quoted in John Russell *Francis Bacon* (1979).

Bacon, Martha 1917–81

US educator and author

70 She soothed and solaced and celebrated, destroying her gift by maiming it to suit her hearers.
1965 On Phillis Wheatley. In *Christian Science Monitor*, 24 Jun.

Bacon, Roger *known as* **Doctor Mirabilis** c.1214–c.1292

English philosopher, scientist and alchemist, closely associated with Oxford. His major works include the *Opus Majus*, *Opus Minor* and *Opus Tertium*. He became a Franciscan, but was rejected and persecuted for heresy.

71 All science requires mathematics…the knowledge of mathematical things is almost innate in us…this is the easiest of sciences. A fact which is obvious in that no one's brain rejects it. For laymen and people who are utterly illiterate know how to count and reckon.
1267 *Opus Majus*, pt.4, ch.1 (translated by Robert Belle Burke, 1928).

72 Mathematics is the door and key to the sciences.
1267 *Opus Majus*, pt.4, ch.1 (translated by Robert Belle Burke, 1928).

73 There are two modes of acquiring knowledge, namely, by reasoning and experience. Reasoning draws a conclusion and makes us grant the conclusion, but does not make the conclusion certain, nor does it remove doubt so that the mind may rest on the intuition of truth unless the mind discovers it by the path of experience.
1267 *Opus Majus* (translated by Robert Belle Burke, 1928).

Baden-Powell, Robert Stephenson Smyth, 1st Baron 1857–1941

English soldier. He became a hero for his defence of Mafeking

(1899–1900) during the Boer War but is usually remembered as the founder of the Boy Scout movement in 1908 and for his book *Scouting for Boys* (1908).

74 The scouts' motto is founded on my initials, it is: BE PREPARED, which means, you are always to be in a state of readiness in mind and body to do your DUTY.
1908 *Scouting for Boys*.

75 Football, in itself, is a grand game for developing a lad physically and also morally…but it is a vicious game when it draws crowds of lads away from playing the game themselves to be merely onlookers at a few paid players.
1908 *Scouting for Boys*.

Baedeker, Karl 1801–59

German editor and publisher, famous for his foreign travel guides. The first, for Coblenz, appeared in 1829, and they continued to be published after his death.

76 On arrival at a Syrian port the traveller's passport is sometimes asked for, but an ordinary visiting-card will answer the purpose equally well.
1876 *Palestine and Syria*, 'Passports and Custom House'.

77 Oxford is on the whole more attractive than Cambridge to the ordinary visitor; and the traveller is therefore recommended to visit Cambridge first, or to omit it altogether if he cannot visit both.
1887 *Great Britain*, Route 30: 'From London to Oxford'.

Baer, George Frederick 1842–1914

US lawyer and industrialist, who led the resistance to the strike by the United Mine Workers of America in 1902.

78 The rights and interests of the laboring man will be protected and cared for, not by the labor agitators, but by the Christian men to whom God, in his infinite wisdom, has given control of the property interests of the country.
1902 Letter to the press during the Pennsylvanian miners' strike.

Bagehot, Walter 1826–77

British economist and journalist. His *English Constitution* (1867) is still considered a standard work, and *Physics and Politics* (1872), applying evolution theories to politics, greatly influenced 19c thought.

79 The essence of Toryism is enjoyment…but as far as communicating and establishing your creed is concerned—try a little pleasure. The way to keep up old customs is, to enjoy old customs; the way to be satisfied with the present state of things is, to enjoy that state of things.
1856 Essay on *Macaulay*.

80 No real English gentleman, in his secret soul, was ever sorry for the death of a political economist.
1858 *Estimates of Some Englishmen and Some Scotchmen*, 'The First Edinburgh Reviewers'.

81 Writers, like teeth, are divided into incisors and grinders.
1858 *Estimates of Some Englishmen and Some Scotchmen*, 'The First Edinburgh Reviewers'.

82 It is said that England invented the phrase, 'Her Majesty's Opposition'; that it was the first government which made a criticism of administration as much a part of the polity as administration itself.
1867 *The English Constitution*, ch.2, 'The Cabinet'.

83 *The Times* has made many ministries.
1867 *The English Constitution*, ch.2, 'The Cabinet'.

84 The fancy of the mass of men is incredibly weak; it can see nothing without a visible symbol, and there is much that it can scarcely make out with a symbol.
1867 *The English Constitution*, ch.4, 'The House of Lords'.

85 The order of nobility is of great use, too, not only in what it creates, but in what it prevents. It prevents the rule of wealth—the religion of gold. This is the obvious and natural idol of the Anglo-Saxon… From this our aristocracy preserves us.
1867 *The English Constitution*, ch.4, 'The House of Lords'.

86 A severe though not unfriendly critic of our institutions said that the cure for admiring the House of Lords was to go and look at it.
1867 *The English Constitution*, ch.4, 'The House of Lords'.

87 The great offices, whether permanent or parliamentary, which require mind now give social prestige, and almost only those. An Under-Secretary of State with £2,000 a year is a much greater man than the director of a finance company with £5,000, and the country saves the difference.
1867 *The English Constitution*, ch.4, 'The House of Lords'.

88 Nations touch at their summits.
1867 *The English Constitution*, ch.4, 'The House of Lords'.

89 The best reason why monarchy is a strong government is, that it is an intelligible government. The mass of mankind understand it, and they hardly anywhere in the world understand any other.
1867 *The English Constitution*, ch.6, 'The Monarchy'.

90 Throughout the greater part of his life George III was a kind of 'consecrated obstruction'.
1867 *The English Constitution*, ch.6, 'The Monarchy'.

91 Above all things our royalty is to be revered, and if you begin to poke about it you cannot reverence it… Its mystery is its life. We must not let in daylight upon magic.
1867 *The English Constitution*, ch.6, 'The Monarchy (continued)'.

92 Political economy traces in an abstract way the effects of the desire to be rich; and nations must nowadays abound in that passion if they are to have much power or respect in the world.
1876 'Preliminaries of Political Economy', collected in *Economic Studies* (1880).

93 Men of business have a solid judgment, a wonderful guessing power of what is going to happen, each in his own trade, but they have never practised themselves in reasoning out their judgments and in supporting their guesses by argument; probably if they did so, some of the finer and correcter parts of their anticipations would vanish.
1876 'Postulates of English Political Economy', in *Economic Studies* (1880).

94 Who can tell without instruction what is likely to be the effect of the new loans of England to foreign nations? We press upon half-finished and half-civilized communities incalculable sums; we are to them what the London money-dealers are to students at Oxford and Cambridge.
1876 'Postulates of English Political Economy', in *Economic Studies* (1880).

95 No man has come so near to our definition of a

constitutional statesman—the powers of a first-rate man and the creed of a second-rate man.

1881 *Biographical Studies*, 'The Character of Sir Robert Peel'.

96 A constitutional statesman is in general a man of common opinion and uncommon abilities.

1881 *Biographical Studies*, 'The Character of Sir Robert Peel'.

Bailey, David 1938–

English photographer known particularly for his striking pictures of cultural icons.

97 I never cared for fashion much. Amusing little seams and witty little pleats. It was the girls I liked.

1990 In *The Independent*, 5 Nov.

98 I grew up scared of Hitler. I wanted to kill him because he spent all my childhood trying to kill me.

2001 In *The Mail on Sunday*, 14 Oct.

99 It's funny: you hate authority and then your photography takes on an authority.

2001 In *The Mail on Sunday*, 14 Oct.

Bailey, F(rancis) Lee 1933–

US criminal lawyer, who founded his own detective agency at Harvard. He defended the Boston Strangler and, more recently, he defended O J Simpson at his 1995 murder trial.

1 When you see a lawyer trying to pick a smart jury, you know he's got a strong case.

1972 In the *Los Angeles Times*, 9 Jan.

2 The guilty never escape unscathed. My fees are sufficient punishment for anyone.

1972 In the *Los Angeles Times*, 9 Jan.

3 I think my grandmother actually smelled like a cookie and that's enough to get any child's attention.

Quoted by Phyllis Hanes in *Christian Science Monitor*, 15 Jun 1988.

Bailey, Nathan d.1742

English lexicographer, best known for *An Universal Etymological English Dictionary* (1721), which gives word origins as well as definitions.

4 LONDON…the Metropolis of *Great-Britain*, founded before the City of *Rome*, walled by *Constantine* the Great, no ways inferior to the greatest in *Europe* for Riches and Greatness.

1721 *An Universal Etymological English Dictionary*.

Bailey, Philip James 1816–1902

English poet, father of the Spasmodic school. His great work *Festus* (1839) was expanded in 1889 to incorporate previously published volumes: *The Angel World* (1850), *The Mystic* (1855) and *Universal Hymn* (1867).

5 America, thou half-brother of the world;
With something good and bad of every land.

1839 *Festus*, sc.10.

Baillie, Robert 1599–1662

Scottish Presbyterian leader, an opponent of Archbishop Laud and of episcopacy. He was selected by the Scottish Church to invite Charles II to accept the covenant and crown of Scotland.

6 The Parliament of England cannot have on earth so strong pillars and pregnant supporters of all their

privileges as free protestant assemblies established by law, and kept in their full freedom from the lowest to the highest—from the congregational eldership to the general synod of the nation.

A Dissuasive from the Errors of Time, 1645–6.

Bainbridge, Dame Beryl Margaret 1934–

English novelist and playwright. She worked as an actress and publisher's clerk before publishing *A Weekend with Claude* (1967). Her work is marked by a caustic wit and a finely turned prose style.

7 I am of the firm belief that everybody could write books and I never understand why they don't. After all, everybody speaks. Once the grammar has been learnt it is simply talking on paper and in time learning what not to say.

1976 In D L Kirkpatrick (ed) *Contemporary Novelists*.

8 Being constantly with children was like wearing a pair of shoes that were expensive and too small. She couldn't bear to throw them out, but they gave her blisters.

1977 *Injury Time*, ch.4.

9 We are essentially fragile. We don't have to wait for the sword or some other equally sensational weapon to strike us down… There are so many ways of us dying it's astonishing any of us choose old age.

1978 *Young Adolf*, ch.12.

10 I haven't the humility to find anything beneath me.

1989 *An Awfully Big Adventure*, ch.3.

11 It's all changed now, which is why it mattered to those young men from Liverpool that they should be there to support their team. What other group is going to troop their colours for them, present them with scarves and emblems?

1989 After the Hillsborough football disaster. Quoted in David Pickering *The Cassell Soccer Companion* (1994).

12 The vital accessories to my work are my reference books, such as the complete Shakespeare and a prayer book, and a large refuse bin.

1991 In *The Guardian*, 8 Aug.

13 Women are programmed to love completely, and men are programmed to spread it around.

1996 Interview in the *Daily Telegraph*, 10 Sep.

14 Bugger the writing, I'd have given anything to have had a long-lasting relationship.

2004 In *The Times*, 7 Apr.

Bairnsfather, Bruce 1888–1959

British cartoonist, a soldier in World War I and cartoonist with US troops in World War II. His works include *Fragments from France* (1916), *Bullets and Billets* (1917) and *Jeeps and Jests* (1943).

15 Well, if you knows of a better 'ole, go to it.

1915 Caption to cartoon in *Fragments from France*. The speaker, Ol' Bill, is waist-deep in mud on the Somme. The phrase was used as the title for a 1926 US film based on the character, *The Better 'Ole*.

Baker, Colin 1943–

English actor who played Doctor Who from 1984 to 1986.

16 Love is a human emotion and the doctor isn't human. We

were always told there is one golden rule: no hanky panky in the Tardis.
2004 On playing Doctor Who. Quoted in the *Sunday Times*, 7 Mar.

Baker, Howard Henry, Jr 1925–

US public official, Republican senator from Tennessee and a member of the Watergate Committee (1973). He became Senate Leader and White House Chief of Staff (1987–8) under Reagan.

17 Never speak more clearly than you think.
1987 On becoming President Reagan's third Chief of Staff. In the *New York Times*, 6 Sep.

Baker, James Addison, III 1930–

US lawyer and government official. He managed the campaigns of Ford (1976) and Bush (1980, 1988). As Secretary of State (1989–92) he initiated a round of Middle East peace talks.

18 Sometimes you move publicly, sometimes privately. Sometimes quietly, sometimes at the top of your voice. And sometimes an active policy is best advanced by doing nothing until the right time—or never.
1990 Of statesmanship. In *Time*, 19 Mar.

Baker, John Austin 1928–

English cleric and theologian, Bishop of Salisbury (1982–93).

19 The crucified Jesus is the only accurate picture of God the world has ever seen.
1970 *The Foolishness of God*.

Baker (of Dorking), Kenneth Baker, Baron 1934–

English Conservative politician and writer. He was Secretary of State for the Environment (1985) and introduced a controversial education reform bill as Secretary of State for Education (1986–9) under Margaret Thatcher. He was Home Secretary under John Major (1990–2).

20 If Conservative Backbench MPs want to get on in politics they will have to find a foothold in the narrow strip of land that lies between sycophancy and rebellion.
1979 Queen's Speech in the House of Commons.

21 Why should Scottish and Welsh nationalism be seen as a noble thing, when in England it is seen as something dirty?
2000 In the *Sunday Times*, 'Talking Heads', 6 Jan.

Baker, Russell Wayne 1925–

US newspaper columnist and humorist. In 1979 won a Pulitzer Prize for distinguished commentary.

22 So there he is at last. Man on the moon. The poor magnificent bungler! He can't even get to the office without undergoing the agonies of the damned, but give him a little metal, a few chemicals, some wire and twenty or thirty billion dollars and vroom! there he is, up on a rock a quarter of a million miles up in the sky.
1969 Editoral pages, the *New York Times*, 21 Jul.

23 What is it about sociology that instantly bogs us down in fens of jargon?
1990 In the *New York Times*, 15 Dec.

24 California's power to cloud men's minds must never be

forgot. Under its spell we submitted for eight years to the governance of Ronald Reagan, who had trouble distinguishing history from old movie plots.
1995 'Don't Look Back', in the *New York Times*, 1 Aug.

Bakunin, Mikhail Alekseyevich 1814–76

Russian anarchist. He was sent to Siberia in 1855 but escaped, and became an advocate of anarchism, speaking against Marx at the First Communist International (1868), until he was outvoted and expelled at the Hague Congress (1872).

25 From each according to his faculties, to each according to his needs; that is what we wish, sincerely and energetically.
1870 Anarchists' declaration, signed by the 47 defendants after the failed uprising in Lyons.
➤ *See Marx 558:14*.

Balazs, Bela *originally* Hubert Bauer 1884–1949

Hungarian writer who wrote *Theory of the Film: Character and Growth of a New Art* (1953).

26 Film art has a greater influence on the minds of the general public than any other art.
1953 *Theory of the Film: Character and Growth of a New Art* (translated by Edith Bone).

Balcon, Michael 1896–1977

British film producer.

27 In the absence of money, we'll have to make do with talent.
Quoted in David Puttnam *Michael Balcon: The Pursuit of British Cinema* (1984), preface.

28 Well if you fellows feel so strongly in favour, on my head be it.
Quoted in David Puttnam *Michael Balcon: The Pursuit of British Cinema* (1984), preface.

Baldwin, James Arthur 1924–87

US writer and civil rights activist. His often autobiographical novels include *Go Tell it on the Mountain* (1954) and *Just Above My Head* (1979).

29 At the root of the American Negro problem is the necessity of the American white man to find a way of living with the Negro in order to be able to live with himself.
1953 'Stranger in a Village', in *Harper's*, Oct.

30 It seems to be typical of life in America, where opportunities, real and fancied, are thicker than anywhere else on the globe, that the second generation has no time to talk to the first.
1955 *Notes of a Native Son*, 'Notes of a Native Son'.

31 I learned in New Jersey that to be a Negro meant, precisely, that one was never looked at but was simply at the mercy of the reflexes the color of one's skin caused in other people.
1955 *Notes of a Native Son*, 'Notes of a Native Son'.

32 The writer's greed is appalling. He wants, or seems to want, everything and practically everybody; in another sense, and at the same time, he needs no one at all.
1961 *Nobody Knows My Name*, 'Alas, Poor Richard'.

33 Children have never been very good at listening to their

elders, but they have never failed to imitate them. They must, they have no other models.
1961 *Nobody Knows My Name*, 'Fifth Avenue, Uptown'.

34 Anyone who has ever struggled with poverty knows how extremely expensive it is to be poor.
1961 *Nobody Knows My Name*, 'Fifth Avenue, Uptown'.

35 Freedom is not something that anybody can be given; freedom is something people take and people are as free as they want to be.
1961 *Nobody Knows My Name*, 'Notes for a Hypothetical Novel'.

36 Money, it turned out, was exactly like sex, you thought of nothing else if you didn't have it and thought of other things if you did.
1961 'Black Boy Looks at the White Boy', in *Esquire*, May.

37 If the concept of God has any validity or any use, it can only be to make us larger, freer, and more loving. If God cannot do this, then it is time we got rid of Him.
1962 'Down at the Cross', in the *New Yorker*, 17 Nov.

38 The Fire Next Time.
1963 Title of book of essays. Baldwin took the phrase from the traditional spiritual, 'Home in the Rock'.

39 It comes as a great shock around the age of five, six or seven to discover that the flag to which you have pledged your allegiance, along with everybody else, has not pledged its allegiance to you. It comes as a shock to see Gary Cooper killing off the Indians and, although you are rooting for Gary Cooper, that the Indians are you.
1965 Speech at Cambridge Union, 17 Feb, arguing for the motion that 'The American Dream is at the expense of the American Negro'.

40 If they take you in the morning, they will be coming for us that night.
1971 'Open Letter to my Sister, Angela Davis', in *The New York Review of Books*, 7 Jan.

Baldwin (of Bewdley), Stanley Baldwin, 1st Earl
1867–1947

English Conservative politician, Chancellor (1922–3) and Prime Minister (1923, 1924–9 and 1935–7). His period of office was marked by the abdication of Edward VIII in 1936.

41 A lot of hard-faced men who look as if they had done very well out of the war.
1918 Of the first post-World War I Parliament. Quoted in J M Keynes *Economic Consequences of the Peace* (1919).

42 I met Curzon in Downing Street, and received the sort of greeting a corpse would give an undertaker.
1923 Of his rival for the premiership, Lord Curzon, on the death of Bonar Law. Attributed.

43 A platitude is simply a truth repeated until people get tired of hearing it.
1924 Speech in the House of Commons, 29 May.

44 There are three classes which need sanctuary more than others—birds, wild flowers, and Prime Ministers.
1925 In the *Observer*, 24 May.

45 The work of a Prime Minister is the loneliest job in the world.
1927 Speech, 9 Jan.

46 The papers conducted by Lord Rothermere and Lord Beaverbrook are not newspapers in the ordinary acceptance of the term. They are engines of propaganda

for the constantly-changing policies, desires, personal wishes, and personal likes and dislikes of two men… What the proprietorship of those papers is aiming at is power, and power without responsibility—the prerogative of the harlot throughout the ages.
1931 Speech, 18 Mar. Rudyard Kipling, Baldwin's cousin, is alleged to be the original author of this famous phrase. Harold Macmillan claimed that the Duke of Devonshire (his father-in-law) responded 'Good God, that's done it, he's lost us the tarts.'

47 I think it is well also for the man in the street to realize that there is no power on earth that can protect him from being bombed. Whatever people will tell him, the bomber will always get through. The only defence is in offence, which means that you have to kill more women and children more quickly than the enemy if you want to save yourselves.
1932 Speech in the House of Commons, 10 Nov.

48 When you think about the defence of England, you no longer think of the chalk cliffs of Dover. You think of the Rhine. That is where our frontier lies today.
1934 House of Commons, 30 Jul.

49 There is a wind of nationalism and freedom blowing round the world, and blowing as strongly in Asia as elsewhere.
1934 Speech, Dec.

50 I shall be but a short time tonight. I have seldom spoken with greater regret, for my lips are not yet unsealed. Were these troubles over I would make a case, and I guarantee that not a man would go into the lobby against us.
1935 Speech in the House of Commons, 10 Dec, speaking on the Abyssinian crisis. This is often misquoted as 'My lips are sealed'.

51 You will find in politics that you are much exposed to the attribution of false motives. Never complain and never explain.
1943 Advice to Harold Nicholson.

52 When the call came for me to form a Government, one of my first thoughts was that it should be a Government of which Harrow would not be ashamed.
Attributed.

Balfour, Arthur James Balfour, 1st Earl   1848–1930

Scottish Conservative politician and Prime Minister (1902–5). As Chief Secretary for Ireland (1887–91) his policy of suppression earned him the name 'Bloody Balfour', and as Foreign Secretary (1916–19) he was responsible for the Balfour Declaration, which promised Zionists a national home in Palestine.

53 I look forward to a time when Irish patriotism will as easily combine with British patriotism as Scottish patriotism combines now.
1889 Speech, Glasgow, Dec.

54 His Majesty's Government looks with favour upon the establishment in Palestine of a national home for the Jews.
1917 The Balfour Declaration, made in a letter to Lord Rothschild, 2 Nov.

55 The General Strike has taught the working classes more in four days than years of talking could have done.
1926 Speech in the House of Commons, 7 May.

56 I thought that he was a young man of promise, but it appears that he is a young man of promises.
Of Winston Churchill. Quoted in Churchill *My Early Life* (1930), ch. 17.

57 Herbert Asquith's clarity is a great liability because he
has nothing to say.
Quoted by George Will in *Newsweek*, 9 Sep 1991.

58 Nothing matters very much, and very few things matter
at all.
Attributed.

59 I would rather be an opportunist and float, than go to the
bottom with my principles around my neck.
Attributed.

60 It has always been desirable to tell the truth, but seldom if
ever necessary to tell the whole truth.
Attributed.

Ball, George Wildman 1909–94

US lawyer and diplomat. As Under-Secretary of State (1961–6)
he played a major part in foreign policy, particularly in the Trade
Agreements of 1962. He opposed the war in Vietnam, and left
government for banking in 1966.

61 Once on the tiger's back, we cannot be sure of picking
the place to dismount.
1964 Memo to Secretary of Defense Robert S McNamara, 5 Oct,
on the escalation of the Vietnam War. It became known as 'the
tiger's back memo'. Quoted in Deborah Shapley *Promise and
Power* (1993).

62 Like giving the keys of the world's largest liquor store to a
confirmed alcoholic.
On oil profiteering that permitted an arms-buying spree by
Mohammed Reza Pahlavi, last shah of Iran. Quoted in William
Shawcross *The Shah's Last Ride* (1988).

63 Never to be bored, never to be frustrated, never to be
alone.
Defining what John F Kennedy wanted from the presidency.
President Kennedy (1993).

Ball, John d.1381

English priest, one of the leaders of the Peasants' Revolt of 1381.
He was executed for his part in these events.

64 When Adam delved and Eve span,
Who was then a gentleman?
1381 Sermon on the eve of the Peasants' Revolt. Quoted in
George Holmes *The Later Middle Ages, 1272–1485* (1962), ch.7.

Ballads

65 'Oh, mother, mother, mak my bed,
And mak it saft and narrow;
My love has died for me to-day,
I'll die for him tomorrow.'
'Barbara Allen'.

66 It fell about the Lammas tide,
When the muir-men win their hay,
The doughty Douglas bound him to ride
Into England, to drive a prey.
'The Battle of Otterbourne', opening lines.

67 There was twa sisters in a bower,
Binnorie, O Binnorie;
There came a knight to be their wooer,
By the bonnie mill-dams o' Binnorie.
'Binnorie', stanza 1.

68 Ye Highlands and ye Lawlands,
O where hae ye been?
They hae slain the Earl of Murray

And laid him on the green.
'The Bonnie Earl of Murray', stanza 1.

69 He was a braw gallant,
And he play'd at the ba';
And the bonnie Earl of Murray
Was the flower amang them a'.

He was a braw gallant,
And he play'd at the glove;
And the bonnie Earl of Murray,
O he was the Queen's luve.

O lang will his lady
Look owre the castle Doune,
Ere she sees the Earl of Murray
Come sounding thro' the toun.
'The Bonnie Earl of Murray'.

70 O the broom, the bonnie, bonnie broom,
The broom of Cowdenknowes;
I wish I were with my dear swain,
With his pipe and my yowes.
'The Broom of Cowdenknowes', opening lines.

71 'A bed, a bed,' Clerk Sanders said,
'A bed for you and me!'
'Fye na, fye na,' said may Margaret,
'Till anes we married be!'
'Clerk Sanders'

72 Is there any room at your head, Sanders?
Is there any room at your feet?
Or any room at your twa sides,
Where fain, fain I would sleep?

There is nae room at my head, Margaret,
There is nae room at my feet;
My bed it is the cold, cold grave;
Among the hungry worms I sleep.
'Clerk Sanders'.

73 She hadna sailed a league, a league,
A league but barely three,
When dismal grew his countenance
And drumlie grew his e'e.
They hadna sailed a league, a league,
A league but barely three,
Until she espied his cloven foot,
And she wept right bitterlie.
'The Demon Lover'.

74 Late at e'en, drinkin' the wine,
And ere they paid the lawin',
They set a combat them between,
To fight it at the dawin'.

'O stay at hame, my noble lord,
O stay at hame, my marrow!
My cruel brother will you betray
On the dowie houms o' Yarrow!'
'The Dowie Houms o' Yarrow'.

75 'Yestreen I dreamed a dolefu' dream;
I ken'd here wad be sorrow!
I dreamed I pu'd the heather green,
On the dowie banks o' Yarrow.'

She gaed up yon high, high hill—
I wat she gaed wi' sorrow—
An' in the den spied nine dead men,
On the dowie houms o' Yarrow.
'The Dowie Houms o' Yarrow'.

76 'Why dois your brand sae drap wi' bluid,
Edward, Edward,
Why dois your brand sae drap wi' bluid,
And why sae sad gang ye O?'
'Edward', opening lines.

77 Then up and started our gudewife,
Gied three skips on the floor:
'Gudeman, ye've spoken the foremost word,
Get up and bar the door.'
'Get Up and Bar the Door'.

78 I wish I were where Helen lies,
Night and day on me she cries;
O that I were where Helen lies,
On fair Kirkconnell lea!
'Helen of Kirkconnell', opening lines.

79 'It's I, Jamie Telfer o' the fair Dodhead,
And a harried man I think I be!
There's naething left at the fair Dodhead
But a waefu' wife and bairnies three.'
'Jamie Telfer'.

80 'Will ye gang wi' me, Lizzy Lindsay,
Will ye gang to the Highlands wi' me?
Will ye gang wi' me, Lizzy Lindsay.
My bride and my darling to be?'
'Lizzy Lindsay', opening lines.

81 This ae nighte, this ae nighte,
—*Every nighte and alle*,
Fire and fleet and candle-lighte,
And Christe receive thy saule.
'A Lyke- Wake Dirge', opening lines.

82 Marie Hamilton's to the kirk gane,
Wi' ribbons in her hair;
The king thought mair o' Marie Hamilton
Than ony that were there.
'Marie Hamilton', opening lines.

83 'Yestreen the queen had four Maries,
The night she'll hae but three;
There was Marie Seaton, and Mari Beaton,
And Marie Carmichael, and me.'
'Marie Hamilton'.

84 The king sits in Dunfermline town,
Drinking the blude-red wine;
'O whare will I get a skeely skipper,
To sail this new ship of mine?'
'Sir Patrick Spens', opening lines.

85 'I saw the new moon late yestreen,
Wi' the auld moon in her arm;
And if we gang to sea, master,
I fear we'll come to harm.'
'Sir Patrick Spens'.

86 And lang, lang may the ladyes sit,
Wi' their fans into their hand,
Before they see Sir Patrick Spens
Come sailing to the strand!
'Sir Patrick Spens'.

87 Half-owre, half-owre to Aberdour,
'Tis fifty fathoms deep,
And there lies gude Sir Patrick Spens,
Wi' the Scots lords at his feet.
'Sir Patrick Spens'.

88 'O I forbid you, maidens a',
That wear gowd on your hair,
To come or gae by Carterhaugh,
For young Tam Lin is there.

'There's nane that gaes by Carterhaugh,
But they leave him a wad.
Either their rings or green mantles,
Or else their maidenhead.'

Janet has kilted her green kirtle
A little aboon her knee,
And she has braided her yellow hair
A little aboon her bree,
And she's awa' to Carterhaugh
As fast as she can hie.
'Tam Lin', opening stanzas.

89 True Thomas lay on Huntlie bank,
A ferlie he spied wi' his e'e,
And there he saw a ladye bright,
Come riding down by the Eildon Tree.
'Thomas the Rhymer', opening lines.

90 And see ye not yon braid, braid road,
That lies across the lily leven?
That is the path of Wickedness,
Though some call it the Road to Heaven.
'Thomas the Rhymer'.

91 There were three ravens sat on a tree,
They were as black as they might be.
The one of them said to his make,
'Where shall we our breakfast take?'
'The Three Ravens'.

92 As I was walking all alane,
I heard twa corbies making a mane;
The tane unto the tother say,
'Where sall we gang and dine to-day?'

'In behint yon auld fail dye,
I wot there lies a new-slain knight;
And naebody kens that he lies there,
But his hawk, his hound, and his lady fair.

'His hound is to the hunting gane,
His hawk to fetch the wild-fowl hame,
His lady's ta'en another mate,
So we may mak our dinner sweet.'
'The Twa Corbies', opening stanzas.

93 O'er his white banes, when they are bare,
The wind sall blaw for evermair.
'The Twa Corbies'.

94 O waly, waly up the bank,
And waly, waly doun the brae,
And waly, waly yon burn-side
Where I and my love wont to gae.

I lean'd my back unto an aik,

I thocht it was a trustie tree;
But first it bow'd, and syne it brake—
Sae my true love did lichtlie me.

O waly, waly, gin love be bonnie
A little time while it is new;
But when 'tis auld it waxeth cauld
And fades awa' like morning dew.

O wherefore should I busk my heid,
O wherefore should I kame my hair?
For my true love has me forsook,
And says he'll never lo'e me mair.
pre-1566 'Waly, Waly', opening stanzas.

95 But had I wist, before I kiss'd,
That love had been sae ill to win.
I'd lock'd my heart in a case o' gowd,
And pinn'd it wi' a siller pin.
pre-1566 'Waly, Waly', stanza 4.

96 Tom Pearce, Tom Pearce, lend me your grey mare,
All along, down along, out along lee.
For I want for to go to Widdicombe Fair,
Wi' Bill Brewer, Jan Stewer, Peter Gurney, Peter Davey,
Dan'l Whiddon, Harry Hawk,
Old Uncle Tom Cobleigh and all.
'Widdicombe Fair'.

97 There lived a wife at Usher's Well,
And a wealthy wife was she;
She had three stout and stalwart sons,
And sent them o'er the sea.
'The Wife of Usher's Well', opening lines.

98 The cock doth craw, the day doth daw,
The channerin' worm doth chide.
'The Wife of Usher's Well'.

Ballard, J(ames) G(raham) 1930–

British novelist and science-fiction writer, born in China. His best-known work, the novel *Empire of the Sun* (1984), draws on his childhood experiences in wartime Shanghai, then occupied by Japan.

99 The only truly alien planet is Earth.
1962 'Which Way to Inner Space', in *New Worlds*, May.

1 He believes that science fiction is the apocalyptic literature of the 20th century, the authentic language of Auschwitz, Eniwetok and Aldermaston. He also believes that inner space, not outer, is the real subject of science fiction.
1965 Author's statement contained in a biographical note to *The Drowned World*.

2 Science and technology multiply around us. To an increasing extent they dictate the languages in which we speak and think. Either we use those languages, or we remain mute.
1974 *Crash*.

Balliett, Whitney 1926–

US writer. He became jazz critic of the *New Yorker* in 1957, and has written several books on music.

3 The Sound of Surprise.
1959 Title of book, much cited as a definition of jazz.

4 A bundle of biases held loosely together by a sense of taste.

1962 His definition of a critic. *Dinosaurs in the Morning*, introductory note.

Balzac, Honoré de 1799–1850

French writer, one of the great 19c realist novelists. He created a world of characters whose lives are interwoven in his *Comédie humaine* (1842).

5 *Un homme n'a jamais pu élever sa maîtresse jusqu'à lui; mais une femme place toujours son amant aussi haut qu'elle.*
A man can never elevate his mistress to his rank, but a woman can always place her lover as high as she.
1829 *Physiologie du mariage.*

6 *Le mariage doit incessamment combattre un monstre qui dévore tout: l'habitude.*
Marriage should always combat the monster that devours everything: habit.
1829 *Physiologie du mariage.*

7 *La femme mariée est un esclave qu'il faut savoir mettre sur un trône.*
A married woman is a slave whom one must put on a throne.
1829 *Physiologie du mariage.*

8 *Un mari, comme un gouvernement, ne doit jamais avouer de faute.*
A husband, like a government, never needs to admit a fault.
1829 *Physiologie du mariage.*

9 *En toute chose, nous ne pouvons être jugés que par nos pairs.*
In all things, we should only be judged by our peers.
1830 *La Maison du chat-qui-pelote.*

10 *Dans ces grandes crises, le coeur se brise ou se bronze.*
In times of crisis, the heart either breaks or boldens.
1830 *La Maison du chat-qui-pelote.*

11 *Le bonheur engloutit nos forces, comme le malheur éteint nos vertus.*
Happiness engulfs our strength, just as misfortune extinguishes our virtues.
1831 *La Peau de chagrin.*

12 *La haine est un tonique, elle fait vivre, elle inspire la vengeance; mais la pitié tue, elle affaiblit encore notre faiblesse.*
Hatred is a tonic, it makes one live, it inspires vengeance; but pity kills, it weakens our weaknesses still further.
1831 *La Peau de chagrin.*

13 *Beaucoup d'hommes ont un orgueil qui les pousse à cacher leurs combats et à ne se montrer que victorieux.*
Many men have pride that causes them to hide their combats and to only show themselves victorious.
1831 *La Recherche de l'absolu.*

14 *À lui la foi, à elle le doute, à elle le fardeau le plus lourd: la femme ne souffre-t-elle pas toujours pour deux?*
For him, faith; for her, doubt and for her the heavier load: does not the woman always suffer for both?
1831 *La Recherche de l'absolu.*

15 *L'amour n'est pas seulement un sentiment, il est un art aussi.*
Love is not only a feeling; it is also an art.
1831 *La Recherche de l'absolu.*

16 *L'amour a son instinct, il sait trouver le chemin du coeur comme le plus faible insecte marche à sa fleur avec une irrésistible volonté qui ne s'épouvante de rien.*
Love has its own instinct. It knows how to find the road to the heart just as the weakest insect moves toward its flower by an irresistible will which fears nothing.
1832 *La Femme de trente ans.*

17 *Le coeur d'une mère est un abîme au fond duquel se trouve toujours un pardon.*
A mother's heart is an abyss at the bottom of which there is always forgiveness.
1832 *La Femme de trente ans.*

18 *Les faits ne sont rien, ils n'existent pas, il ne subsiste de nous que des Idées.*
Deeds are nothing. They do not exist. Only our ideas survive.
1832 *Louis Lambert.*

19 *Nos beaux sentiments ne sont-ils pas les poésies de la volonté?*
Aren't our best feelings poetry of the will?
1835 *Le Père Goriot.*

20 *La passion est toute l'humanité. Sans elle, la religion, l'histoire, le roman, l'art seraient inutiles.*
Passion is all of humanity. Without it, religion, history, the novel and art would be useless.
1842 *La Comédie humaine,* foreword.

21 *L'homme n'est ni bon ni méchant, il naît avec des instincts et des aptitudes.*
Man is neither good nor evil; he is born with instincts and abilities.
1842 *La Comédie humaine,* foreword.

22 *L'avarice commence où la pauvreté cesse.*
Greed begins where poverty ends.
1843 *Illusions perdues,*'Les deux poètes'.

23 *Les dettes sont jolies chez les jeunes gens de vingt-cinq ans, plus tard, personne ne les leur pardonne.*
Debts are becoming for 25-year-olds; after this, no one forgives them.
1843 *Illusions perdues,*'Un Grand homme de province'.

Banda, Hastings Kamuzu 1898–1997

Malawian statesman, Prime Minister (1963) and President (1966; Life President from 1971).

24 I wish that I could bring Stonehenge to Nyasaland, to show that there was a time when Britain had a savage culture.
1963 In the *Observer,* 10 Mar.

Bandeira, Manuel 1886–1968

Brazilian poet, literary historian, translator and educator. He achieved enormous popularity and national acclaim.

25 *Estou farto do lirismo comedido*
Do lirismo bem comportado
Do lirismo funcionário público com livro de ponto
expediente protocolo e manifestações de apreço ao Sr
Diretor.
Estou farto do lirismo que pára e vai averiguar no
dicionário o cunho vernáculo de um vocábulo.

Abaixo os puristas

I'm sick of cautious lyricism
of well-behaved lyricism
of a civil servant lyricism complete with time card office hours set procedures and expressions of esteem for Mr Boss, Sir.
I'm sick of the lyricism that has to stop in midstream to look up the precise meaning of a word.

Down with purists!
1930 *Libertinagem,*'Poética' (translated as 'Poetics', 1989).

Bankhead, Tallulah 1903–68

US actress. She made her New York debut in 1918 and subsequently played a range of classical and contemporary roles, attracting notoriety for her scandalous private life. She wrote an autobiography, *Tallulah* (1952).

26 There is less in this than meets the eye.
1922 Attending a revival of Maeterlinck's play *Aglavaine and Selysette.* Quoted in Alexander Woollcott *Shouts and Murmurs* (1923), ch.4.

27 Cocaine habit-forming? Of course not. I ought to know. I've been using it for years.
1939 In conversation at the first night party of Lillian Hellman's *Little Foxes.* Recalled in *Tallulah* (1952), ch.4.

28 I'm as pure as the driven slush.
Quoted by Maurice Zolotow, in *The Saturday Evening Post,* 12 Apr 1947.

29 Darling, they've absolutely ruined your perfectly dreadful play!
1957 Greeting Tennessee Williams at the film première of his play *Orpheus Descending.* Quoted in Peter Hay *Broadway Anecdotes.*

30 Only good girls keep diaries. Bad girls don't have time.
Recalled on her death, 12 Dec 1968.

31 Nobody can be exactly like me. Sometimes even I have trouble doing it.
Attributed.

Banks, Iain Menzies 1954–

Scottish novelist and science-fiction writer. His works include *The Wasp Factory* (1984) and *Complicity* (1993). He writes science-fiction novels using the name Iain M Banks.

32 They are, after all, a language; they do not so much say things about as, they are what is said.
1986 Of clothes. *The Bridge,* ch.2.

33 'You're not upset, are you, Orr?' Brooke says, pouring wine into my glass.
'Merely sober. The symptoms are similar.'
1986 *The Bridge,* ch.3.

34 The choice is not between dream and reality; it is between two different dreams.
1986 *The Bridge,* coda.

35 It was the day my grandmother exploded.
1992 *The Crow Road,* ch.1, opening words.

36 Mr Blawke always reminded me of a heron; I'm not sure why. Something to do with a sense of rapacious stillness, perhaps, and also the aura of one who knows time is on his side.
1992 Of the family lawyer. *The Crow Road,* ch.1.

37 The belief that we somehow moved on to something else—whether still recognisably ourselves, or quite

thoroughly changed—might be a tribute to our evolutionary tenacity and our animal thirst for life, but not to our wisdom.
1992 On the idea of life after death. *The Crow Road*, ch.18.

Banks, Lynne Reid 1929–

English novelist and playwright. Her best-known novel is her first, *The L-Shaped Room* (1960). She has also written plays for radio and television and fiction for children.

38 Jane Austen is the only novelist I know whose peculiar genius lies in taking perfectly ordinary people through ordinary situations, and transmogrifying them into fascinating fiction.
1991 In her entry in *Contemporary Novelists*, 5th edn.

Bannister, Sir Roger Gilbert 1929–

English athlete and neurologist. In 1954 he ran the first 'four-minute mile' (3 mins 59.4 secs). He was knighted in 1975. After a distinguished medical career, he was appointed Master of Pembroke College, Oxford (1985–93).

39 I leapt at the tape like a man taking his last spring to save himself from the chasm that threatens to engulf him.
1955 Of the end of his record-breaking run. *First Four Minutes*.

40 I sometimes think that running has given me a glimpse of the greatest freedom a man can ever know, because it results in the simultaneous liberation of both body and mind.
1955 *First Four Minutes*.

Banting, Frederick Grant 1891–1941

Canadian physician and discoverer of insulin.

41 Diabetus. Ligate pancreatic ducts of dog. Keep dogs alive till acini degenerate leaving Islets. Try to isolate the internal secretion of these to relieve glycosuria.
1920 Note scribbled in his journal, 2.00am, 31 Oct. This led to the discovery of insulin for the treatment of diabetes, as recorded in Michael Bliss *The Discovery of Insulin* (1982).

Barach, Alvan Leroy 1895–1977

US physician. He was Professor of Medicine at Columbia University and a pioneer in respiratory therapy.

42 An alcoholic has been lightly defined as a man who drinks more than his own doctor.
1962 In the *Journal of the American Medical Association*, vol.181, p.393.

Baraka, Amiri *adopted name of* LeRoi (Everett Leroy) Jones 1934–

US poet, playwright and prose writer. He adopted a Muslim identity in 1967 after establishing his reputation as a radical and outspoken black voice.

43 Preface to a Twenty Volume Suicide Note.
1961 Title of poetry collection.

44 A rich man told me recently that a liberal is a man who tells other people what to do with their money.
1962 'Tokenism', in *Kulchur*, spring issue.

45 A man is either free or he is not. There cannot be any apprenticeship for freedom.
1962 'Tokenism', in *Kulchur*, spring issue.

46 But when a man who sees the world one way becomes

the slave of a man who interprets the world in exactly the opposite way, the result is, to my mind, the *worst* possible kind of slavery.
1963 *Blues People*, ch.1.

Barbellion, W(illiam) N(ero) P(ilate) *pseudonym of* Bruce Frederick Cummings 1889–1919

English diarist. He was a self-taught biologist, and worked for the British Museum. His principal work is the self-critical *Journal of A Disappointed Man* (1919).

47 I can remember wondering as a child if I were a young Macaulay or Ruskin and secretly deciding that I was. My infant mind even was bitter with those who insisted on regarding me as a normal child and not as a prodigy.
1919 *Journal of A Disappointed Man*, 23 Oct.

48 Give me the man who will surrender the whole world for a moss or a caterpillar, and impracticable visions for a simple human delight.
1919 *Enjoying Life and Other Literary Remains*, 'Crying for the Moon'.

Barbirolli, Sir John 1899–1970

British conductor and cellist, conductor of the New York Philharmonic in 1937 and of the Hallé Orchestra in Manchester (1943–58). In 1950 he was awarded the Gold Medal of the Royal Philharmonic Society, and he became principal conductor of the Hallé in 1958.

49 Three farts and a raspberry, orchestrated.
Of modern music. Quoted in M Kennedy *Barbirolli, Conductor Laureate* (1971).

50 I want you to sound like 22 women having babies without chloroform.
To a chorus. Quoted in M Kennedy *Barbirolli, Conductor Laureate* (1971).

Barbour, John c.1316–1395

Scottish poet, prelate and scholar, the 'father of Scottish poetry'. His national epic, *The Brus*, is a narrative poem on the life of Robert I, the Bruce. He served as Archdeacon of Aberdeen from c.1357 until his death.

51 Storyss to rede ar delitabill,
Supposs that thai be nocht but fabill.
c.**1375** *The Brus*, bk.1, l.1–2.

52 A! fredome is a noble thing!
Fredome mayss man to haiff liking,
Fredome all solace to man giffis:
He levys at ess that frely levys!
c.**1375** *The Brus*, bk.1, l.225–8.

53 Luff is off sae mekill mycht,
That it all paynis makis lycht.
c.**1375** *The Brus*, bk.2, l.520–1.

Barker, George Granville 1913–91

English poet, novelist and playwright. He was associated with Dylan Thomas and the New Apocalyptic group, but his poetry retained a distinctively individual quality.

54 Sitting as huge as Asia, seismic with laughter,
Gin and chicken helpless in her Irish hand.
1944 'To My Mother'.

55 Honouring itself the clay rears up
To praise its pottering purposes,

But, oh, much sorrow shall it sup
Before fulfilment is.
1954 'Goodman Jacksin and the Angel'.

56 When the guns begin to rattle
And the men to die
Does the Goddess of the Battle
Smile or sigh?
1962 'Battle Hymn of the New Republic'.

Barkley, Alben William 1877–1956

US lawyer and Democratic politician, Vice-President under Truman (1949–53).

57 The best audience is intelligent, well-educated and a little drunk.
Recalled on his death, 30 Apr 1956.

Barlow, Joel 1754–1812

US poet. He is best remembered for his mock-heroic salute to the humble hasty-pudding (a dish of boiled Indian meal), although he considered his turgid epic *The Colombiad* (1807) his major work.

58 I sing the sweets I know, the charms I feel,
My morning incense, and my evening meal,
The sweets of Hasty-Pudding. Come, dear bowl,
Glide o'er my palate, and inspire my soul.
1796 'The Hasty-Pudding', canto 1

Barnard, Frederick R

59 One picture is worth ten thousand words.
1927 In *Printer's Ink*, 10 Mar.

Barnes, Clive Alexander 1927–

English theatre critic. He has written for the *New York Post* since 1977, directing much of his venom against the commercial Broadway stage.

60 This is the kind of show to give pornography a bad name.
1969 Reviewing *Oh, Calcutta!*, *New York Times*, 18 Jun.

Barnes, Djuna 1892–1982

US writer, who spent a large part of her life in Europe. She is best known for her novel *Nightwood* (1936).

61 New York is the meeting place of the peoples, the only city where you can hardly find a typical American.
1916 'Greenwich Village As It Is', in *Pearson's Magazine*, Oct.

62 After all, it is not where one washes one's neck that counts but where one moistens one's throat.
1916 'Greenwich Village As It Is', in *Pearson's Magazine*, Oct.

63 Sleep demands of us a guilty immunity. There is not one of us who, given an eternal incognito, a thumbprint nowhere set against our souls, would not commit rape, murder and all abominations.
1936 Doctor. *Nightwood*, ch.5.

64 Dreams have only the pigmentation of fact.
1936 Doctor. *Nightwood*, ch.5.

65 I'm a fart in a gale of wind, a humble violet under a cow pat.
1936 Doctor. *Nightwood*, ch.5.

Barnes, Julian Patrick 1946–

English novelist, formerly a lexicographer and journalist. His best-known work is *Flaubert's Parrot* (1984), a meditation on fiction and biography.

66 We'd both been to the country and found it disappointingly empty.
1981 *Metroland*, pt.1, ch.4.

67 You can have your cake and eat it: the only trouble is you get fat.
1984 *Flaubert's Parrot*, ch.7.

68 The writer must be universal in sympathy and an outcast by nature: only then can he see clearly.
1984 *Flaubert's Parrot*, ch.10.

69 Do not imagine that Art is something which is designed to give gentle uplift and self-confidence. Art is not a *brassière*. At least, not in the English sense. But do not forget that *brassière* is the French for life-jacket.
1984 *Flaubert's Parrot*, ch.10.

70 Books are where things are explained to you; life is where things aren't… Books make sense of life. The only problem is that the lives they make sense of are other people's lives, never your own.
1984 *Flaubert's Parrot*, ch.13.

71 Women were brought up to believe that men were the answer. They weren't. They weren't even one of the questions.
1986 *Staring At The Sun*, pt.2.

72 Does history repeat itself, the first time as tragedy, the second time as farce? No, that's too grand, too considered a process. History just burps, and we taste again that raw-onion sandwich it swallowed centuries ago.
1989 *A History of the World in 10½ Chapters*, 'Parenthesis'.

73 I've always thought you are what you are and you shouldn't pretend to be anyone else. But Oliver used to correct me and explain that you are whoever it is you're pretending to be.
1991 *Talking It Over*, ch.2.

74 Love is just a system for getting someone to call you darling after sex.
1991 *Talking It Over*, ch.16.

75 Remember that cookery writers are no different from other writers: many have only one book in them (and some shouldn't have let it out in the first place).
2003 *The Pedant in the Kitchen*.

Barnum, P(hineas) T(aylor) 1810–91

US showman. He introduced freak shows, including General Tom Thumb (1842), in his New York museum, and in 1881 co-founded the Barnum and Bailey Circus, 'the greatest show on earth'.

76 There's a sucker born every minute.
Attributed.

Barr, Alfred Hamilton, Jr 1902–81

US art historian, first Director of the Museum of Modern Art, New York. His many works include *Cubism and Abstract Art* (1936).

77 Except the American woman, nothing interests the eye of American man more than the automobile, or seems so important to him as an object of aesthetic appreciation.
1963 In news summaries, 31 Dec.

Barrer, Bruce

78 She endured a five-year marriage to Ernest Hemingway that roughly coincided with and bore more than a passing resemblance to World War II.
1993 Of Martha Gelhorn. In the *Wall Street Journal*, 9 Mar.

Barrie, Sir J(ames) M(atthew) 1860–1937

Scottish novelist and dramatist. After journalism and several autobiographical works, he turned to playwriting in 1890, with such works as *The Admirable Crichton* (1902), *Peter Pan* (1904) and *What Every Woman Knows* (1908, published 1918).

79 The life of every man is a diary in which he means to write one story, and writes another; and his humblest hour is when he compares the volume as it is with what he vowed to make it.
1891 *The Little Minister*, vol.1, ch.1.

80 That is ever the way. 'Tis all jealousy to the bride and good wishes to the corpse.
1901 *Quality Street* (published 1913), act 1.

81 When the first baby laughed for the first time, the laugh broke into a thousand pieces and they all went skipping about, and that was the beginning of fairies.
1904 *Peter Pan* (published 1928), act 1.

82 Every time a child says 'I don't believe in fairies' there is a little fairy somewhere that falls down dead.
1904 *Peter Pan* (published 1928), act 1.

83 To die will be an awfully big adventure.
1904 *Peter Pan* (published 1928), act 3.

84 Charm…it's a sort of a bloom on a woman. If you have it, you don't need to have anything else; and if you don't have it, it doesn't much matter what else you have.
1908 *What Every Woman Knows* (published 1918), act 1.

85 My lady, there are few more impressive sights in the world than a Scotsman on the make.
1908 *What Every Woman Knows* (published 1918), act 2.

86 I have always found that the man whose second thoughts are good is worth watching.
1908 *What Every Woman Knows* (published 1918), act 3.

87 Every man who is high up loves to think that he has done it all himself; and the wife smiles, and lets it go at that. It's our only joke. Every woman knows that.
1908 *What Every Woman Knows* (published 1918), act 4.

88 One's religion is whatever he is most interested in, and yours is Success.
1921 *The Twelve-Pound Look*.

89 I bowl so slow that if after I have delivered the ball and don't like the look of it, I can run after it and bring it back.
Quoted in Colin Jarman *The Guinness Dictionary of Sports Quotations* (1990).

90 What a polite game tennis is. The chief word in it seems to be 'sorry' and admiration of each other's play crosses the net as frequently as the ball.
Quoted in Colin Jarman *The Guinness Dictionary of Sports Quotations* (1990).

91 I am glad you have asked me. I should like you to convey when you are acting it that the man you portray has a brother in Shropshire who drinks port.
Responding to a young actor's urgent request for advice as to how he should play a minor part in one of Barrie's plays. Attributed.

Barrington, Jonah 1941–

English squash player. He was British Open Champion 1967–8 and 1970–3.

92 Squash is boxing with racquets.
Quoted in Colin Jarman *The Guinness Dictionary of Sports Quotations* (1990).

Barry, Marion Shepilov, Jr 1936–

US politician, Mayor of Washington, DC (1979–91). He was arrested and charged with possession of cocaine in 1990.

93 There are two kinds of truth…real truths and made-up truths.
1990 Of the drug charges lodged against him. In the *Washington Post*, 13 May.

Barrymore, Ethel 1879–1959

US actress, one of the most prominent members of the Drew-Barrymore acting dynasty. She made her New York debut in 1901 and went on to excel both in contemporary dramas and in Shakespearean roles. New York's Barrymore Theatre was opened in her honour in 1928.

94 For an actress to be a success she must have the face of Venus, the brains of Minerva, the grace of Terpsichore, the memory of Macaulay, the figure of Juno, and the hide of a rhinoceros.
Quoted in George Jean Nathan *The Theatre in the Fifties* (1953).

95 I never let them cough. They wouldn't dare.
1956 Of her audiences. In the *New York Post*, 7 Jun.

Barrymore, John 1882–1942

US actor of the Drew-Barrymore dynasty. He made his stage debut in 1903 and distinguished himself in Shakespearean and other roles before turning to films. Renowned for his chaotic private life, he suffered increasingly from alcoholism.

96 Die? I should say not, old fellow. No Barrymore would allow such a conventional thing to happen to him.
1942 Quoted in Lionel Barrymore *We Barrymores* (1951), ch.26.

97 My only regret in the theatre is that I could never sit out front and watch me.
Quoted in Eddie Cantor *The Way I See It* (1959), ch.2.

98 Method acting? There are quite a few methods. Mine involves a lot of talent, a glass, and some cracked ice.
Quoted in *Actors about Acting, Loving, Living, Life* (1972).

Barrymore, Lionel 1878–1954

US actor, brother of Ethel and John Barrymore. He gave up a successful stage career for the cinema in 1925, finding fame as Dr Gillespie in a series of *Dr Kildare* films (from 1938).

99 How like father—a curtain call!
1905 Attributed comment, when his father's coffin had to be raised up again after it had snagged on being lowered into the grave.

1 I've played everything but the harp.
Attributed, when asked to suggest his own epitaph.

Barth, John Simmons 1930–

US novelist. His books are much concerned with the processes of story-telling and the making of myths.

2 Everyone is necessarily the hero of his own life story.
1958 *The End of the Road*, ch.1.

3 Every life has a Scheherazadesworth of stories.
1994 *Once Upon A Time*, 'Program Note'.

Barth, Karl 1886–1968

Swiss Reformed theologian, champion of neo-orthodoxy and influential in founding the German Confessing Church, which opposed Nazism. His extensive theological output proved highly influential in 20c Christian theology.

4 Jesus Christ, as he is attested to us in Holy Scripture, is the one Word of God whom we have to hear, and whom we have to trust and obey in life and in death.
1934 *The Barmen Declaration* adopted by the Confessing Church in Germany (translated by D S Bax, 1984).

5 Humanity in its basic form is co-humanity.
1948 *Kirchliche Dogmatik* vol.3, pt.2 (translated by H Knight as *Church Dogmatics*, 1960).

6 Basically and comprehensively, therefore, to be human is to be with God.
1948 *Kirchliche Dogmatik* vol.3, pt.2 (translated by H Knight as *Church Dogmatics*, 1960).

7 It is a bad sign when Christians are frightened by 'political' sermons—as if Christian preaching could be anything but political.
1954 *Gegen den Strom* (translated by E M Delacourt and S Godwin as 'The Christian Community and the Civil Community' in *Against the Stream*, 1954).

8 Whether the angels play only Bach in praising God I am not quite sure; I am sure, however, that *en famille* they play Mozart.
1968 Quoted in the *New York Times*.

Barthelme, Donald 1931–89

US novelist and short story writer.

9 The distinction between children and adults, while probably useful for some purposes, is at bottom a specious one, I feel. There are only individual egos, crazy for love.
1964 *Come Back, Dr Caligari*, 'Me and Miss Mandible'.

10 We like books that have a lot of *dreck* in them, matter which presents itself as not wholly relevant (or indeed, at all relevant), but which, carefully attended to, can supply a kind of 'sense' of what is going on. This 'sense' is not to be obtained by reading between the lines (for there is nothing there, in those white spaces), but by reading the lines themselves.
1967 *Snow White*.

11 'Some people', Miss R. said, 'run to conceits or wisdom but I hold to the hard, brown, nutlike word. I might point out that there is enough aesthetic excitement here to satisfy anyone but a damned fool.'
1968 *Unspeakable Practices, Unnatural Acts*, 'The Indian Uprising'.

12 Endings are elusive, middles are nowhere to be found, but worst of all is to begin, to begin, to begin.
1968 *Unspeakable Practices, Unnatural Acts*, 'The Dolt'.

13 Doubt is a necessary precondition to meaningful action. Fear is the great mover in the end.
1972 *Sadness*, 'The Rise of Capitalism'.

14 The self cannot be escaped, but it can be, with ingenuity and hard work, distracted.
1972 *Sadness*, 'Daumier'.

15 Let me point out, if it has escaped your notice, that what an artist does, is fail.
1972 *Sadness*, 'The Sandman'.

16 The world is sagging, snagging, scaling, spalling, pilling, pinging, pitting, warping, checking, fading, chipping, cracking, yellowing, leaking, stalling, shrinking, and in dynamic unbalance.
1974 *Guilty Pleasures*, 'Down the Line with the Annual'.

17 No tale ever happened in the way we tell it. But the moral is always correct.
1975 *The Dead Father*, ch.6.

Barthes, Roland 1915–80

French literary critic, and major theorist of semiology. He developed a modernist school of criticism which argues for the 'death' of the author, and the need for the reader to recreate the text.

18 *Je crois que l'automobile est aujourd'hui l'équivalent assez exact des grandes cathédrales gothiques: je veux dire une grande création d'époque, conçue passionnément par des artistes inconnus, consommée dans son image, sinon dans son usage, par un peuple entier qui s'approprie en elle un objet parfaitement magique.*
Cars today are almost the exact equivalent of the great Gothic cathedrals...the supreme creation of an era, conceived with passion by unknown artists, and consummated in image if not in usage by a whole population which appropriates them as a purely magical object.
1957 *Mythologies*, 'La nouvelle Citroën'.

19 *Le toucher est le plus démystificateur de tous les sens, à la différence de la vue, qui est le plus magique.*
Touch is the most demystifying of all senses, different from sight which is the most magical.
1957 *Mythologies*, 'La nouvelle Citroën'.

20 *Tout refus du langage est une mort.*
Any refusal of language is a death.
1957 *Mythologies*, 'Le mythe, aujourd'hui'.

21 *L'endroit le plus érotique d'un corps n'est-il pas là où le vêtement bâille?*
Is not the most erotic part of the body wherever the clothing affords a glimpse?
1973 *Le Plaisir du texte*.

22 *L'amoureux qui ne s'oublie pas quelquefois meurt par excès, fatigue et tension de mémoire (tel Werther).*
The lover who does not forget *sometimes* dies from excess, fatigue, and the strain of memory (like Werther).
1977 *Fragments d'un discours amoureux*.

23 *Le langage est une peau: je frotte mon langage contre l'autre.*
Language is a skin; I rub my language against another language.
1977 *Fragments d'un discours amoureux*, 'Déclaration'.

24 *Tout ce qui est anachronique est obscène.*
Everything anachronistic is obscene.
1977 *Fragments d'un discours amoureux*, 'Obscène'.

Bartley, Robert Leroy 1937–2003

US journalist. He joined the *Wall Street Journal* in 1962 as a staff writer, and rose to become Editor and Vice-President. He won a Pulitzer Prize for editorial writing in 1980.

25 You can't beat the market because it's smarter than you are. Intellectually, the only task is trying to determine what the market is telling you.
1992 *The Seven Fat Years*, ch.3.

26 The mystery is why we even collect these figures; if we kept similar statistics for Manhattan Island, Park Avenue could lay awake at night worrying about its trade deficit.
1992 On the balance of payments record. *The Seven Fat Years*.

Bartók, Béla 1881–1945

Hungarian composer and pianist. Much influenced by European folk music, he wrote works for piano and strings as well as music for ballet and opera. He died in poverty in the US, having emigrated in 1940.

27 The trouble is that I have to go with so much still to say.
1945 Spoken on his deathbed. Quoted in David Pickering *Brewer's Twentieth Century Music* (1994).

28 I cannot conceive of music that expresses absolutely nothing.
Quoted in Machlis *Introduction to Contemporary Music* (1963).

Baruch, Bernard Mannes 1870–1965

US financier and statesman. He became a powerful political influence, 'the adviser of presidents', and served on many commissions, including the American Atomic Energy Commission.

29 Let us not be deceived—we are today in the midst of a cold war.
1947 Address to the South Carolina legislature, 16 Apr, using an expression suggested to him by editor Herbert Bayard Swope.

30 The cold war is getting warmer.
1948 Address to a Senate committee.

31 To me old age is always fifteen years older than I am.
1955 In *Newsweek*, 29 Aug.

Barzun, Jacques 1907–

French-born US scholar, Professor of History at Columbia University (1945) and Dean and Provost there (1958–67). His works include *Darwin, Marx, Wagner* (1941) and *The Use and Abuse of Art* (1974).

32 Teaching is not a lost art, but the regard for it is a lost tradition.
1955 In *Newsweek*, 5 Dec.

33 The test and use of man's education is that he finds pleasure in the exercise of the mind.
1958 'Science and the Humanities', in the *Saturday Evening Post*, 3 May.

34 If it were possible to talk to the unborn, one could never explain to them how it feels to be alive, for life is washed in the speechless real.
1959 *The House of Intellect*.

35 Science is an all-pervasive energy, for it is at once a mode of thought, a source of strong emotion, and a faith as fanatical as any in history.
1964 *Science, The Glorious Entertainment*.

36 Whoever wants to know the heart and mind of America had better learn baseball.
Quoted in Michael Novak *The Joy of Sport* (1976), pt 1.

37 Baseball is a kind of collective chess with arms and legs in full play under sunlight.
Quoted in Colin Jarman *The Guinness Dictionary of Sports Quotations* (1990).

38 To watch a football game is to be in prolonged neurotic doubt as to what you're seeing. It's more like an emergency happening at a distance than a game.
Quoted in Colin Jarman *The Guinness Dictionary of Sports Quotations* (1990).

Baselitz, Georg 1938–

German avant-garde artist.

39 I have trouble with beauty.
1995 On the effects of witnessing suffering as a child in Dresden during the war. In the *New York Times*, 21 May.

Basho, Matsuo 1644–94

Japanese poet, regarded as the founder of *haiku* as a significant poetic form, and influenced by Zen Buddhism.

40 An old pond
A frog jumps in
The sound of water
c.1689 Quoted in Hugh Cortazzi *The Japanese Achievement* (1990).

41 Year by year,
the monkey's mask
reveals the monkey
c.1689 *On Love and Barley: Haiku of Basho*, no.3 (translated by Lucien Stryk).

42 Year's end—
still in straw hat
and sandals
c.1689 *On Love and Barley: Haiku of Basho*, no.126 (translated by Lucien Stryk).

43 Orchid—breathing
incense into
butterfly's wings
c.1689 *On Love and Barley: Haiku of Basho*, no.166 (translated by Lucien Stryk).

44 Friends part
forever—wild geese
lost in cloud
c.1689 *On Love and Barley: Haiku of Basho*, no.219 (translated by Lucien Stryk).

45 Learn about a pine tree from a pine tree, and about a bamboo stalk from a bamboo stalk.
Attributed, quoted in *On Love and Barley: Haiku of Basho* (translated by Lucien Stryk), introduction.

Baskin, Leonard 1922–2000

US sculptor and graphic artist, also an influential teacher. His powerful works include *Man with a Dead Bird*.

46 Pop art is the inedible raised to the unspeakable.
1965 In *Publisher's Weekly*, 5 Apr.
➤ *See* Wilde 909:22.

Bastard, Thomas 1566–1618

English poet.

47 Age is deformed, youth unkind,
We scorn their bodies, they our mind.
1598 *Chrestoleros*, bk.7, epigram 9.

Bates, H(erbert) E(rnest) 1905–74

English novelist, playwright and short-story writer. His most popular publications include *Fair Stood the Wind for France* (1944), *The Jacaranda Tree* (1949) and *The Darling Buds of May* (1958).

48 Perfick.
> **1958** Pa Larkin's characteristic summation. *The Darling Buds of May*, ch.1 and passim.

Bates, Katharine Lee 1859–1929

US educator, author and poet. Her works include *College Beautiful and Other Poems* (1887), *Sunshine and Other Verses for Children* (1890), *Hermit Island* (1891) and *Fairy Gold* (1916).

49 O beautiful for spacious skies,
For amber waves of grain,
For purple mountain majesties
Above the fruited plain!
America! America!
God shed His grace on thee.
And crown thy good with brotherhood
From sea to shining sea.
> **1893** 'America the Beautiful', opening lines.

Bateson, Gregory 1904–80

English-born US social scientist, with interests in anthropology and psychology.

50 Information is any difference that makes a difference.
> **1984** Quoted in *Scientific American*, no.41, Sep.

Batman, John 1801–39

Australian explorer, generally accepted as the founder of Melbourne, the site of which he bought from a local Aboriginal group for trinkets.

51 This will be the place for a Village.
> **1835** Journal entry, Jun. The phrase is often quoted as 'a fine place for a Village'.

Battelle, Phyllis 1922–

US columnist.

52 Where great-grandmothers dread to grow old.
> **1958** Of Hollywood. In the New York *Journal-American*, 15 Mar.

Baudelaire, Charles 1821–67

French Symbolist poet and critic. He is best known for his collection *Les Fleurs du mal* (1857), for which author, printer and publisher were prosecuted for impropriety, but was praised by critics and has exerted an influence far into the 20c.

53 *Hypocrite lecteur,—mon semblable,—mon frère!*
Hypocrite reader—my fellow man—my brother!
> **1857** *Les Fleurs du mal*, 'Au lecteur'.
> ➤ See Eliot 306:55.

54 *Je sais la douleur est la noblesse unique*
Où ne mordront jamais la terre et les enfers.
I know that pain is the one nobility
upon which Hell itself cannot encroach.
> **1857** *Les Fleurs du mal*, 'Bénédiction' (translated by Richard Howard, 1982).

55 *Le Poète est semblable au prince des nuées*
Qui hante la tempête et se rit de l'archer;
Exilé sur le sol au milieu des huées,
Ses ailes de géant l'empêchent de marcher.
The Poet is like that prince of the clouds
Who haunts the storms and laughs at the archer;
Exiled to the ground in the midst of jeers,
His giant wings prevent him from walking.
> **1857** *Les Fleurs du mal*, 'L'Albatros'—'Spleen et idéal', no.2.

56 *Les parfums, les couleurs et les sons se répondent.*
Scents, colours, and sounds echo one another.
> **1857** *Les Fleurs du mal*, 'Correspondances'.

57 *Ô douleur! ô douleur! Le Temps mange ma vie.*
Oh pain! Oh pain! time is eating away my life.
> **1857** *Les Fleurs du mal*, 'L'Ennemi'.

58 *Homme libre, toujours tu chériras la mer.*
Free man! You shall always cherish the sea.
> **1857** *Les Fleurs du mal*, 'L'Homme et la mer'.

59 *Quand notre coeur a fait une fois sa vendange,*
Vivre est un mal.
Once our heart has been harvested once,
Life becomes miserable.
> **1857** *Les Fleurs du mal*, 'Semper eadem'.

60 *Ne cherchez plus mon coeur; les bêtes l'ont mangé.*
Don't search any further for my heart; wild beasts ate it.
> **1857** *Les Fleurs du mal*, 'Causerie'.

61 *Là, tout n'est qu'ordre et beauté,*
Luxe, calme et volupté.
There where all is order and beauty.
Lush, calm and voluptuous.
> **1857** *Les Fleurs du mal*, 'L'Invitation au Voyage'.

62 *J'ai plus de souvenirs que si j'avais mille ans.*
I have more memories than if I were one thousand years old.
> **1857** *Les Fleurs du mal*, 'Spleen'.

63 *Souviens-toi que le Temps est un joueur avide*
Qui gagne sans tricher, à tout coup! c'est la loi.
Remember! Time, that tireless gambler, wins
on every turn of the wheel: that is the law.
> **1857** *Les Fleurs du mal*, 'L'Horloge' (translated by Richard Howard, 1982).

64 *Certes, je sortirai quant à moi satisfait*
D'un monde où l'action n'est pas la soeur du rêve.
Indeed, for my part, I shall be happy to leave
A world where action is not sister to the dream.
> **1857** *Les Fleurs du mal*, 'Le Reniement de Saint-Pierre'.

65 *Ah! Seigneur! donnez-moi la force et le courage*
De contempler mon coeur et mon corps sans dégoût.
Lord! give me the strength and the courage
To see my heart and my body without disgust.
> **1857** *Les Fleurs du mal*, 'Un Voyage à Cythère'.

66 *Amer savoir, celui qu'on tire du voyage!*
Bitter is the knowledge gained in travelling.
> **1857** *Les Fleurs du mal*, 'Le Voyage'.

67 If photography is allowed to stand in for art in some of its functions it will soon supplant or corrupt it completely thanks to the natural support it will find in the stupidity of the multitude. It must return to its real task, which is to be the servant of the sciences and the arts, but the very humble servant, like printing and shorthand which have neither created nor supplanted literature.
> **1859** 'Salon of 1859', section 2, in *Curiosités Esthétiques* (1868).

68 Woe betide the man who goes to antiquity for the study of anything other than ideal art, logic and general method!
> **c.1860** Letter, published in *The Painter of Modern Life* (1863).

69 *Il est l'heure de s'enivrer! Pour n'être pas les esclaves martyrisés du Temps, enivrez-vous sans cesse! De vin, de poésie ou de vertu, à votre guise.*
This is the time for drunkenness! Be not the martyred slaves of Time, drink without stopping! Drink wine, poetry, or virtue, as you please.
1869 *Le Spleen de Paris*, 'Enivrez-vous'.

70 *Parce que le Beau est toujours étonnant, il serait absurde de supposer que ce qui est étonnant est toujours beau.*
Just because the beautiful is *always* shocking, it would be absurd to suppose that that which is shocking is *always* beautiful.
1869 *Le Spleen de Paris*, 'Salon de 1859', pt.2.

71 *L'imagination est la reine du vrai, et le possible est une des provinces du vrai.*
Imagination is the queen of the truth and the *possible* is one of the provinces of the truth.
1869 *Le Spleen de Paris*, 'Salon de 1859', pt.3.

72 *Comme l'imagination a créé le monde, elle le gouverne.*
Because imagination created the world, it governs it.
1869 *Le Spleen de Paris*, 'Salon de 1859', pt.4.

73 *Le mal se fait sans effort, naturellement, par fatalité; le bien est toujours le produit d'un art.*
Evil is done without effort, *naturally*, it's destiny; good is always a product of art.
1869 *Le Spleen de Paris*, 'Le Peintre de la vie moderne', pt.11.

74 *L'art moderne a une tendance essentiellement démoniaque.*
Modern art tends towards the demonic.
1869 *L'Art romantique*.

75 *Quand même Dieu n'existerait pas, la religion serait encore sainte et divine—Dieu est le seul être qui, pour régner, n'ait même pas besoin d'exister.*
Even if God did not exist, religion would still be holy and divine. God is the only being who, in order to reign, need not even exist.
1875 *Journaux intimes*. 'Fusées', no.1.

76 *La volupté unique et suprême de l'amour gît dans la certitude de faire le mal.*
The unique, supreme pleasure of love consists in the certainty of doing *evil*.
1875 *Journaux intimes*. 'Fusées', no.2.

77 *La femme est naturelle, c'est-à-dire abominable.*
Woman is *natural*, that is, abominable.
1887 *Mon coeur mis à nu*, pt.5.

78 *Le Dandy doit aspirer à être sublime, sans interruption. Il doit vivre et dormir devant un miroir.*
The dandy must aspire to be sublime at all times. He must live and sleep in front of a mirror.
1887 *Mon coeur mis à nu*, pt.5.

79 *Etre un homme utile m'a paru toujours quelque chose de bien hideux.*
To be useful has always seemed to me quite hideous.
1887 *Mon coeur mis à nu*, pt.9.

80 *Il faut travailler sinon par goût, au moins par désespoir, puisque, tout bien vérifié, travailler est moins ennuyeux que s'amuser.*
We should work: if not by preference, at least out of despair. All things considered, work is less boring than amusement.
1887 *Mon coeur mis à nu*, pt.18.

81 *Il y a dans tout homme, à toute heure, deux postulations simultanées, l'une vers Dieu, l'autre vers Satan.*
Every man at every moment has two simultaneous tendencies: one toward God, the other toward Satan.
1887 *Mon coeur mis à nu*, pt.19.

82 *Il n'existe que trois êtres respectables: le prêtre, le guerrier, le poète. Savoir, tuer et créer.*
There are only three respectable beings: priest, warrior, poet. To know, to kill and to create.
1887 *Mon coeur mis à nu*, pt.22.

83 *L'être le plus prostitué, c'est l'être par excellence, c'est Dieu, puisqu'il est*
l'ami suprême pour chaque individu, puisqu'il est le réservoir commun,
inépuisable de l'amour.
The most prostituted being, the Being par excellence, is God, since he is
supreme friend to every individual, since he is the common, inexhaustible
reservoir of love.
1887 *Mon coeur mis à nu*, pt.46.

84 *Je ne comprends pas qu'une main pure puisse toucher un journal sans une convulsion de dégoût.*
I cannot imagine how a pure hand can touch a newspaper without disgust.
1887 *Mon coeur mis à nu*, pt.81.

85 At its best a poem full of space and reverie.
Of portraits. Quoted in the *New York Times*, 1 Jan 1995.

86 *Il faut épater le bourgeois.*
One must astound the bourgeois.
Attributed.

Baughan, Blanche Edith 1870–1958

New Zealand writer and penal reformer, born in England where she published *Verses* (1898). She emigrated in 1900 and wrote popular verse with an increasingly local flavour.

87 Well, I'm leaving the poor old place, and it cuts as keen as a knife;
The place that's broken my heart—the place where I've lived my life.
1903 *Reuben and Other Poems*, 'The Old Place'.

Baxter, Sir Beverley (Arthur) 1891–1964

British politician and journalist. Canadian-born, he joined the Daily Express in London in 1920 and was editor-in-chief from 1929–33. He became MP for Wood Green 1935–45, and 1945–50 and MP for Southgate from 1950 until his death.

88 Beaverbrook is so pleased to be in the Government that he is like the town tart who has finally married the mayor.
1940 Remark attributed to Baxter in Sir Henry Channon *Chips: the Diaries* (1967), entry for 12 Jun.

89 A great many persons are able to become Members of this House without losing their insignificance.
1946 Speech, House of Commons.

Baxter, Richard 1615–91

English Nonconformist clergyman. Chaplain to Cromwell's army in the English Civil War, he became Royal Chaplain in 1660, but was imprisoned in 1685 for sedition in his *Paraphrase on the New Testament*.

90 Watch against inordinate sensual delight in even the

lawfullest of sports. Excess of pleasure in any such vanity doth very much corrupt and befool the mind.
1678 *A Christian Directory.*

Beachcomber

➤ *See J B Morton*

Beamer, Todd 1968–2001

US businessman, passenger on the hijacked United Airlines Flight 93 on 11 September 2001.

91 Let's roll.
2001 Last known words before he and other passengers tackled the hijackers.

Bearden, Romare 1914–88

US painter, whose bright, bold works deal with the experience of black Americans.

92 The canvas was always saying no to me.
Of early attempts to perfect his medium. Recalled on his death in the *Washington Post*, 14 Mar 1988.

Beasant, Dave 1959–

English goalkeeper, he has played for teams including Wimbledon, Newcastle United and Chelsea. He became the first goalkeeper to captain a team to victory in the FA Cup, 1988.

93 I was a bit disappointed. I should have caught it really.
1988 Of the save that made him the first goalkeeper to stop a penalty in an F A Cup Final. Quoted in Peter Ball and Phil Shaw *The Book of Football Quotations* (1989).

Beattie, Ann 1947–

US short-story writer and novelist.

94 There are things that get whispered about that writers are there to overhear.
1987 *Best American Short Stories*, introduction.

Beattie, James 1735–1803

Scottish philosopher and poet, professor of moral philosophy at Aberdeen. He attacked Hume's scepticism in his *Essay on the Nature and Immutability of Truth* (1770), and wrote an autobiographical poem, *The Minstrel* (1771–4).

95 Some deemed him wondrous wise, and some believed him mad.
1771 *The Minstrel*, bk.1, stanza 16.

96 In the deep windings of the grove no more
The hag obscene, and grisly phantom dwell;
Nor in the fall of mountain-stream, or roar
Of winds, is heard the angry spirit's yell.
1774 *The Minstrel*, bk.2, stanza 47.

Beatty, David, 1st Earl Beatty 1871–1936

British Admiral. After serving in Egypt and Sudan he became Rear Admiral in 1910. Early successes in World War I were followed by a major role in the Battle of Jutland. He commanded the fleet (1916–19) and was First Sea Lord (1919–27).

97 There's something wrong with our bloody ships today, Chatfield.
1916 Comment at the Battle of Jutland, which ended in stalemate, 31 May. Quoted in Winston Churchill *The World Crisis 1916–1918* (1927), pt.1.

Beaumarchais, Pierre Augustin Caron de 1732–99

French writer who led a colourful life as artisan, member of the royal household, music teacher to Louis XV's daughter, speculator, secret agent in England, and munitions runner for the American colonies.

98 *Aujourd'hui, ce qui ne vaut pas la peine d'être dit, on le chante.*
Today, what is not worth being said is sung.
1775 *Le Barbier de Séville*, act 1, sc.2.

99 *Je me presse de rire de tout, de peur d'être obligé d'en pleurer.*
I am quick to laugh at everything so as not to be obliged to cry.
1775 *Le Barbier de Séville*, act 1, sc.2.

1 *On s'intéresse guère aux affaires des autres que lorsqu'on est sans inquiétude sur les siennes.*
We hardly interest ourselves in the affairs of others when things are going well for ourselves.
1775 *Le Barbier de Séville.*

2 *Les vices, les abus, voilà ce qui ne change point, mais se déguise en mille formes sous le masque des moeurs dominantes: leur arracher ce masque et les montrer à découvert, telle est la noble tâche de l'homme qui se voue au théâtre.*
Vices, indulgences, these are the things which never change but which disguise themselves in a thousand forms beneath the mask of prevailing morals: to lift off this mask and expose them, this is the noble task of the person who devotes himself to the theatre.
1784 *Le Mariage de Figaro*, préface.

3 *De toutes les choses sérieuses, le mariage étant la plus bouffonne.*
Of all serious things, marriage is the most farcical.
1784 *Le Mariage de Figaro*, act 1, sc.9.

4 *Boire sans soif et faire l'amour en tout temps, Madame, il n'y a que ça qui nous distingue des autres bêtes.*
We drink when we are not thirsty and make love at any time, Madam. These are the only things which distinguish us from other animals.
1784 *Le Mariage de Figaro*, act 2, sc.21.

5 *Les Anglais, à la vérité, ajoutent par ci, par là, quelques autres mots en conversant; mais il est bien aisé de voir que God-dam est le fond de la langue.*
In truth, the English do add here and there other words when speaking, but it is obvious that *Goddamn* is the basis of their language.
1784 *Le Mariage de Figaro*, act 3, sc.5.

Beaumont, Francis c.1584–1616

English dramatist, a friend of Ben Jonson and his circle, particularly John Fletcher, with whom he wrote at least 10 plays. *The Woman Hater* (1605) and *The Knight of the Burning Pestle* (c.1607) are thought to be mainly Beaumont's work.

6 What things have we seen,
Done at the Mermaid! heard words that have been
So nimble, and so full of subtil flame,
As if that every one from whence they came,
Had meant to put his whole wit in a jest,
And had resolv'd to live a fool, the rest
Of his dull life.
1605 *Letter to Ben Jonson*, verses prefacing Jonson's *Volpone*.

7 She's private to herself, and best of knowledge
Whom she will make so happy as to sigh for.
c.1607 *The Knight of the Burning Pestle*, act 1.

Beaumont, Francis and Fletcher, John c.1584–1616, c.1578–1625

English dramatists.

8 It is always good
When a man has two irons in the fire.
1608 *The Faithful Friends*, act 1.

9 PHILASTER: Oh, but thou dost not know
What 'tis to die.
BELLARIO: Yes, I do know, my Lord:
'Tis less than to be born; a lasting sleep;
A quiet resting from all jealousy,
A thing we all pursue; I know besides,
It is but giving over of a game,
That must be lost.
1609 *Philaster* (published 1620), act 3, sc.1.

10 All your better deeds
Shall be in water writ, but this in marble.
1609 *Philaster* (published 1620), act 5.

11 Kiss till the cow comes home.
c.1610 *The Scornful Lady* (published 1616), act 2, sc.2.

12 There is no other purgatory but a woman.
c.1610 *The Scornful Lady* (published 1616), act 3.

13 Upon my buried body lay
Lightly gentle earth
1610–11 *The Maid's Tragedy*, act 2, sc.1.

14 Those have most power to hurt us that we love.
1610–11 *The Maid's Tragedy*, act 5.

15 The terror of his name has stretched itself
Wherever there is sun.
1611 *A King and No King*, act 2, sc.2.

16 What art thou that dost creep into my breast
And dar'st not see my face? Show forth thyself.
I feel a pair of fiery wings displayed
Hither, from thence. You shall not tarry there;
Up and begone. If thou beest love, begone.
1611 *A King and No King*, act 3, sc.1.

17 I see there's truth in no man, nor obedience
But for his own ends.
1611 *A King and No King*, act 4, sc.2.

18 You are no better than you should be.
1612 *The Coxcomb*, act 4, sc.3.

Beaverbrook, Max (William Maxwell Aitken), 1st Baron 1879–1964

Canadian-born British newspaper magnate and politician. After entering politics in 1910, he bought the *Daily Express* (1916) and made it the world's most widely read newspaper, founding the *Sunday Express* (1921). He was Minister of Supply and Lord Privy Seal during World War II.

19 Churchill on top of the wave has in him the stuff of which tyrants are made.
1928–32 *Politicians and the War*.

20 He has all the qualities that go to the making of a leader of the Conservative Party. He is not stupid, but he is very dull. He is not eloquent, but he talks well. He is not honest, politically, but he is most evangelical. He has a

little money, but not much. He always conforms to the party policy.
1935 Commenting on Sir Samuel Hoare's appointment as Foreign Secretary.

21 Our cock won't fight.
1936 Of Edward VIII. Comment to Winston Churchill during the abdication crisis. Quoted in Francis Donaldson *Edward VIII* (1974).

22 I run the paper purely for the purpose of making propaganda, and with no other motive.
1947 Evidence to the Royal Commission on the Press.

23 With the publication of his private papers in 1952, he committed suicide 25 years after his death.
1956 Of Earl Haig. *Men and Power: 1917–1918*.

24 He did not seem to care which way he travelled providing he was in the driver's seat.
1963 Of Lloyd George. *The Decline and Fall of Lloyd George*, ch.7.

25 I am now in my eighty-fourth year and that is approaching the moment when I must bring out my Late Night Final.
c.1963 Quoted in A J P Taylor *Beaverbrook* (1972), ch.13.

26 Here I must say, in my eighty-sixth year, I do not feel greatly different from when I was eighty-five. This is my final word. It is time for me to become an apprentice once more. I have not settled in which direction. But somewhere, sometime soon.
1964 Address at a farewell banquet in London, hosted for him by Roy Thomson, Lord Thomson of Fleet, 25 May. He died two weeks later.

27 *News, Opinion and Advertisment must all come under the head of Entertainment to a reasonable extent—or they will not be read.* People do not read to be bored. Unless a newspaper can make its material in every department interesting it simply is not read.
Publicity handout for the *Daily Express*, quoted in A J P Taylor *Beaverbrook* (1972), ch.8.

28 Success never depended on pandering to the public taste. It has always been founded on simplicity.
Quoted in A J P Taylor *Beaverbrook* (1972), ch.13.

Beckenbauer, Franz 1945–

German footballer who captained the West German national side to European Nations Cup success in 1972 and to World Cup triumph in 1974.

29 We used to get our old players coming to watch training with football magazines in their hands. Now, more often than not, they're checking their share prices.
2001 In *World Soccer*, Nov.

Becker, Gary Stanley 1930–

US economist, Professor of Economics and Sociology at the University of Chicago. He won the Nobel prize for economics (1992).

30 They talk a good game, but economists hardly know enough about business cycles to figure out where they come from, let alone where they're going.
1989 'How Bad Will the Next Downturn Be?', in *Business Week*, 10 Apr.

Beckett, Margaret (Mary) 1943–

English Labour politician.

31 Being effective is more important to me than being recognized.
2000 In the *Independent on Sunday*, 2 Jan.

Beckett, Samuel 1906–89

Irish author and playwright who lived mostly in France. His best-known play, *En Attendant Godot* (*Waiting for Godot*, 1955), exemplifies his absurdist view of the human condition. He was awarded the Nobel prize for literature (1969).

32 *Je ne supporterai plus d'être un homme, je n'essaierai plus.*
I can no longer bear to be human and I will no longer try.
1951 *Molloy, Malone Meurt.*

33 There is man in his entirety, blaming his shoe when his foot is guilty.
1955 *Waiting for Godot*, act 1.

34 Nothing happens, nobody comes, nobody goes, it's awful!
1955 *Waiting for Godot*, act 1.

35 He can't think without his hat.
1955 Of Lucky. *Waiting for Godot*, act 1.

36 VLADIMIR: That passed the time.
ESTRAGON: It would have passed in any case.
VLADIMIR: Yes, but not so rapidly.
1955 *Waiting for Godot*, act 1.

37 I am like that. I either forget right away or I never forget.
1955 *Waiting for Godot*, act 2.

38 You overdo it with your carrots.
1955 *Waiting for Godot*, act 2.

39 We are not saints, but we have kept our appointment. How many people can boast as much?
1955 *Waiting for Godot*, act 2.

40 We are all born crazy. Some remain that way.
1955 *Waiting for Godot*, act 2.

41 They give birth astride of a grave, the light gleams an instant, then it's night once more.
1955 *Waiting for Godot*, act 2.

42 If I had the use of my body, I would throw it out of the window.
1958 *Malone Dies.*

43 *Tout est faux, il n'y a personne…il n'y a rien.*
Everything is false. There is no one…there is nothing.
1958 *Nouvelles et textes pour rien.*

44 CLOV: Do you believe in the life to come?
HAMM: Mine was always that.
1958 *Endgame.*

45 *Bien choisir son moment et se taire, serait-ce le seul moyen d'avoir être et habitat?*
To carefully choose one's moment and keep quiet, is this the only way one can be and live?
1958 *Nouvelles et textes pour rien.*

46 Joyce was a synthesizer, trying to bring in as much as he could. I am an analyzer, trying to leave out as much as I can.
1981 In the *New York Times*, 19 Apr.

47 Ever tried. Ever failed. No matter. Try again. Fail again. Fail better.
1983 *Worstward Ho.*

48 I was in hospital once. There was a man in another ward, dying of throat cancer. In the silence, I could hear his screams continually. That's the only kind of form my work has.
Attributed, in conversation with Harold Pinter.

Becket, Thomas à, Saint 1118–70

English churchman and martyr. Appointed Chancellor of England by Henry II in 1155, in 1162 he became Archbishop of Canterbury. He proved troublesome to Henry, opposing his remarriage, and was murdered in Canterbury Cathedral by four of the king's soldiers.

49 You will soon hate me as much as you love me now, for you assume an authority in the affairs of the church to which I shall never assent.
c.1160 Remark to Henry II. Quoted in J R Green *A Short History of the English People* (1915), vol.1, ch.2, section 8.

Beckham, David 1975–

English footballer. He was appointed captain of the English national side in 2000, and is a popular icon.

50 It's not easy when someone pulls your ponytail.
2003 In *The Independent*, 29 Dec.

51 I'm very honoured to be given this honour.
2003 On being awarded the OBE. Quoted on bbc.co.uk.

52 I showed that I wasn't just at Real Madrid to sell shirts.
2004 On his first season at the Spanish club, 25 May.

Beckham, Victoria 1975–

English pop singer and former member of The Spice Girls. She is married to the footballer David Beckham.

53 David and I will never split. We're a business.
2004 In *The Scotsman.*

Bede known as 'the Venerable' 673–735

English Benedictine monk, scholar and historian. His numerous works include saints' lives, hymns, grammatical treatises and biblical commentaries. His *Historia Ecclesiastica Gentis Anglorum* (731) is the single most valuable source for early English history.

54 *Talis, inquiens, mihi videtur, rex, vita hominum praesens in terris, ad comparationem eius, quod nobis incertum est, temporis, quale cum te residente, ad caenam cum ducibus ac ministris tuis tempore brumale…adveniens unus passerum domum citissime, pervolaverit; qui cum per unum ostium ingrediens, mox per aliud exierit. Ipso quidem tempore, quo intus est, hiemis tempestate non tangitur, sed tamen parvissimo spatio serenitatis ad momentum excurso, mox de hieme in hiemem regrediens, tuis oculis elabitur. Ita haec vita hominum ad modicum apparet; quid autem sequatur, quidve praecesserit, prorsus ignoramus.*
'Such,' he said, 'O King, seems to me the present life of men on earth, in comparison with that time which to us is uncertain, as if when on a winter's night you sit feasting with your ealdormen and thegns—a single sparrow should fly swiftly into the hall, and coming in at one door, instantly fly out through another. In that time in which it is indoors it is indeed not touched by the fury of the winter, and yet, this smallest space of calmness being passed almost in a flash, from winter going into winter again, it is lost to your eyes. Somewhat like this appears the life of

man; but of what follows or what went before, we are utterly ignorant.'

731 *Historia Ecclesiastica Gentis Anglorum* (*Ecclesiastical History of the English People*, translated by B Colgrave, 1969), bk.2, ch.13.

Bee, Barnard Elliot 1823–61

Confederate General, killed at the First Battle of Bull Run.

55 There is Jackson with his Virginians, standing like a stone wall. Let us determine to die here, and we will conquer.
1861 Of General Thomas J Jackson, whose resistance stopped the Union advance at Bull Run, 21 Jul. Quoted in B Perley Poore *Perley's Reminiscences* (1886), vol.2, ch.7. 'Stonewall Jackson' became a popular nickname for the General.

Beecham, Sir Thomas 1879–1961

British conductor and impresario, famed for his outspokenness and wit, and for a dashing and romantic style of performance. He conducted frequently at Covent Garden from 1910, and founded several orchestras, including the London Philharmonic (1932) and the Royal Philharmonic (1947), with whom he made many recordings.

56 A musicologist is a man who can read music but can't hear it.
1930 Quoted in H Proctor-Gregg *Beecham Remembered* (1976).

57 The English may not like music—but they absolutely love the noise it makes.
Quoted in L Ayre *The Wit of Music* (1930).

58 It is far too large. It ought to be removed.
1940 On his first visit to Sydney, in 1940, being asked by a local journalist his opinion of the Harbour Bridge. Quoted in Gerald Moore *Am I too Loud?* (1962).

59 Good music is that which penetrates the ear with facility and quits the memory with difficulty. Magical music never leaves the memory.
1953 Television broadcast, 17 Nov.

60 Hark! The herald angels sing!
Beecham's Pills are just the thing,
Two for a woman, one for a child,
Peace on earth and mercy mild!
Quoted in Neville Cardus *Sir Thomas Beecham* (1961). Sir Thomas was heir to the Beecham pharmaceutical company.

61 The musical equivalent of the towers of St Pancras Station.
Of Elgar's First Symphony. Quoted in Neville Cardus *Sir Thomas Beecham* (1961).

62 There are two golden rules for an orchestra: start together and finish together. The public doesn't give a damn what goes on in between.
Quoted in Harold Atkins and Archie Newman *Beecham Stories* (1978).

63 Like two skeletons copulating on a corrugated tin roof.
Of the harpsichord's sound. Quoted in Harold Atkins and Archie Newman *Beecham Stories* (1978).

64 British music is in a state of perpetual promise. It might almost be said to be one long promissory note.
Quoted in Harold Atkins and Archie Newman *Beecham Stories* (1978).

65 The function of music is to release us from the tyranny of conscious thought.
Quoted in Harold Atkins and Archie Newman *Beecham Stories* (1978).

66 You have between your legs the most sensitive

instrument known to man, and all you can do is scratch it.
Attributed rebuke to a female cellist. Quoted in Ian Crofton and Donald Fraser *A Dictionary of Musical Quotations* (1985).

Beerbohm, Sir (Henry) Max(imilian) 1872–1956

English writer, caricaturist and theatre critic, of Lithuanian extraction, who succeeded George Bernard Shaw as drama critic of the *Saturday Review*. His criticism was collected in *Around Theatre* (1953) and *More Theatres* (1968). He also wrote a novel, *Zuleika Dobson* (1911), an ironic romance about Oxford student life.

67 Most women are not so young as they are painted.
1894 *The Yellow Book*, vol.1.

68 Fate wrote her a most tremendous tragedy, and she played it in tights.
1894 Of Queen Caroline of Brunswick. *The Yellow Book*, vol.3.

69 There is always something rather absurd about the past.
1895 *The Yellow Book*, vol.4

70 To give an accurate and exhaustive account of the period would need a far less brilliant pen than mine.
1895 *The Yellow Book*, vol.4.

71 I have the satiric temperament: when I am laughing at anyone I am generally rather amusing, but when I am praising anyone, I am always deadly dull.
1898 In *The Saturday Review*, 28 May.

72 [At school] I was a modest, good-humoured boy. It is Oxford that has made me insufferable.
1899 *More*, 'Going Back To School'.

73 When a public man lays his hand on his heart and declares that his conduct needs no apology, the audience hastens to put up its umbrellas against the particularly severe downpour of apologies in store for it. I won't give the customary warning. My conduct shrieks aloud for apology, and you are in for a thorough drenching.
1906 'A Straight Talk' (parody of George Bernard Shaw), in the *Saturday Review*, 22 Dec.

74 She was one of those born to make chaos cosmic.
1911 *Zuleika Dobson*, ch.2.

75 Zuleika, on a desert island, would have spent most of her time in looking for a man's footprint.
1911 *Zuleika Dobson*, ch.2.

76 The dullard's envy of brilliant men is always assuaged by the suspicion that they will come to a bad end.
1911 *Zuleika Dobson*, ch.4.

77 Women who love the same man have a kind of bitter freemasonry.
1911 *Zuleika Dobson*, ch.4.

78 You will find that the woman who is really kind to dogs is always one who has failed to inspire sympathy in men.
1911 *Zuleika Dobson*, ch.6.

79 Beauty and the lust for learning have yet to be allied.
1911 *Zuleika Dobson*, ch.7.

80 You will think me lamentably crude: my experience of life has been drawn from life itself.
1911 *Zuleika Dobson*, ch.7.

81 She was one of the people who say 'I don't know anything about music really, but I know what I like.'
1911 *Zuleika Dobson*, ch.9.

82 You cannot make a man by standing a sheep on its hind-

legs. But by standing a flock of sheep in that position you can make a crowd of men.
1911 *Zuleika Dobson*, ch.9.

83 The Socratic method is not a game at which two can play.
1911 *Zuleika Dobson*, ch.15.

84 I looked out for what the metropolitan reviewers would have to say. They seemed to fall into two classes: those who had little to say and those who had nothing.
1919 *Seven Men*, 'Enoch Soames'.

85 I have known no man of genius who had not to pay, in some affliction or defect either physical or spiritual, for what the gods had given him.
1920 *And Even Now*, 'The Pines'.

86 Not philosophy, after all, not humanity, just sheer joyous power of song, is the primal thing in poetry.
1920 *And Even Now*, 'The Pines'.

87 One might well say that mankind is divisible into two great classes: hosts and guests.
1920 *And Even Now*, 'Hosts and Guests'.

88 I maintain that though you would often in the fifteenth century have heard the snobbish Roman say, in a would-be off-hand tone, 'I am dining with the Borgias tonight,' no Roman ever was able to say, 'I dined last night with the Borgias.'
1920 *And Even Now*, 'Hosts and Guests'.

89 The critic who justly admires all kinds of things simultaneously cannot love any one of them.
1946 'George Moore', in the *Saturday Review*, c.1912.

90 The thought of him has always slightly irritated me. Of course he was a wonderful all-round man, but the act of walking round him has always tired me.
1956 Of William Morris. Letter to Sam Behrman, Feb.

91 Only mediocrity can be trusted to be always at its best.
Quoted in S N Behrman *Conversations with Max* (1960), but also attributed elsewhere to Jean Giraudoux and W Somerset Maugham.

92 The one art-form that has been invented in England.
Of the pantomime. Attributed.

93 Reminds me of a Christmas-tree decorated by a Pre-Raphaelite.
Of the actress Ellen Terry. Attributed.

94 They were a tense and peculiar family, the Oedipuses, weren't they?
Attributed.

Beethoven, Ludwig van　1770–1827

German composer. His prolific output included two masses, the opera *Fidelio*, nine symphonies, five piano concertos, piano sonatas and string quartets. Increasing deafness affected him and his music deeply. His influence, especially on the Romantics, was immense.

95 The immortal god of harmony.
1801 Of Bach. Letter to Christoph Breitkopf.

96 I must confess that I live a miserable life... I live entirely in my music.
1801 Letter to F G Wegeler.

97 *Muss es sein? Es muss sein! Es muss sein!*
Must it be? It must be! It must be!
1826 Written above the opening bars of the String Quartet in F Major, Op 135, his last work.

98 I still hope to create a few great works and then like an old child to finish my earthly course somewhere among kind people.
1826 Letter to F G Wegeler.

99 *Plaudite, amici, comedia finita est.*
Applaud, my friends, the comedy is over.
1827 Quoted in Ian Crofton and Donald Fraser *A Dictionary of Musical Quotations* (1985), quoting the last words of Augustus as he lay dying.
➤ *See Augustus 42:48.*

1 I shall hear in heaven.
1827 Attributed last words. Quoted in Ian Crofton and Donald Fraser *A Dictionary of Musical Quotations* (1985).

Beeton, Isabella Mary *née Mayson*　1836–65

English writer on cookery. Her *Book of Household Management* (1859–60) was published in serial form in a woman's magazine founded by her husband, the publisher Samuel Orchard Beeton.

2 There is no more fruitful source of family discontent than a housewife's badly-cooked dinners and untidy ways.
1861 *The Book of Household Management*, preface.

3 A place for everything and everything in its place.
1861 *The Book of Household Management*, ch.2.

Behan, Brendan Francis　1923–64

Irish playwright, twice imprisoned for IRA activities. He was released by general amnesty (1946), but was rearrested and deported in 1952. His works include *The Quare Fellow* (1956), *The Hostage* (1958) and an autobiography, *Borstal Boy* (1958).

4 When I came back to Dublin, I was courtmartialled in my absence and sentenced to death in my absence, so I said they could shoot me in my absence.
1958 *The Hostage*, act 1.

5 My name is Behan, Brendan Behan, after Saint Brendan, who got into one of our little Irish boats called a curragh one day in the sixth century and sailed across the Atlantic and found America, and when he'd found it, like a sensible man he turned around and sailed back and left it where it fuckin' well was.
1962 Speech in New York.

6 Bless you, Sister. May all your sons be bishops!
1964 Addressing a nursing nun taking his pulse shortly before he died. Attributed.

7 Critics are like eunuchs in a harem. They're in there every night, they see how it should be done every night, but they can't do it themselves.
Quoted in Gyles Brandreth *Great Theatrical Disasters* (1983).

8 I am a daylight atheist.
Quoted in Daniel Farson *Sacred Monsters*, 'Rousting in Dublin' (1988).

9 Other people have a nationality. The Irish and the Jews have a psychosis.
Richard's Cork Leg (1961).

Behn, Aphra *née Amis*　1640–89

English writer. She had an adventurous life, growing up in Surinam and acting as a professional spy in Antwerp. Perhaps the first professional woman author in England, her works include *Oroonoko* (1688), *The Forced Marriage* (1670) and *The Rover* (1678).

10 Variety is the soul of pleasure.
   1678 *The Rover*, pt.2, act 1.

11 Come away; poverty's catching.
   1678 *The Rover*, pt.2, act 1.

12 Money speaks sense in a language all nations understand.
   1678 *The Rover*, pt.2, act 3, sc.1.

13 A brave world, Sir, full of religion, knavery, and change: we shall shortly see better days.
   1682 *The Roundheads*, act 1, sc.1.

14 Be just, my lovely swain, and do not take
   Freedoms you'll not to me allow;
   Or give Amynta so much freedom back
   That she may rove as well as you.

   Let us then love upon the honest square,
   Since interest neither have designed.
   For the sly gamester, who ne'er plays me fair,
   Must trick for trick expect to find.
   1684 *Poems upon Several Occasions*, 'To Lysander, on some Verses he writ, and asking more for his Heart than 'twas worth'.

15 Faith, Sir, we are here to-day, and gone to-morrow.
   1686 *The Lucky Chance*, act 4.

16 Love ceases to be a pleasure, when it ceases to be a secret.
   1686 *The Lover's Watch*, 'Four o'Clock. General Conversation'.

17 Oh, what a dear ravishing thing is the beginning of an Amour!
   1687 *The Emperor of the Moon*, act 1, sc.1.

18 They represented to me an absolute idea of the first state of innocence, before man knew how to sin.
   1688 Of the Indians of Surinam. *Oroonoko, or the Royal Slave*.

19 Simple Nature is the most harmless, inoffensive, and virtuous mistress.
   1688 *Oroonoko, or the Royal Slave*.

20 And though she had some decays in the face, she had none in her sense and wit.
   1688 *Oroonoko, or the Royal Slave*.

21 Since Man with that inconstancy was born,
   To love the absent, and the present scorn.
   Why do we deck, why do we dress
   For such a short-liv'd happiness?
   1688 *Lycidus*, 'To Alexis in Answer to his Poem against Fruition,' stanza 3.

22 The soft, unhappy sex.
   1698 *The Wandering Beauty*.

Behrman, S(amuel) N(athaniel) 1893–1973

US playwright, known for sophisticated comedies such as *No Time for Comedy* (1939) and *Lord Pengo* (1962). Other works include screenplays and biographies.

23 Early in life, Duveen…noticed that Europe had plenty of art and America had plenty of money, and his entire astonishing career was the product of that simple observation.
   1952 *Duveen*, ch.1. Joseph Duveen was a highly successful US art dealer.

Belasco, David *stagename of* **David Valasco** 1859–1931

US actor-manager and dramatist. Nicknamed the 'Bishop of

Broadway', he adapted many successful plays for the theatres he managed in New York.

24 Boxing is show-business with blood.
   Quoted in Colin Jarman *The Guinness Dictionary of Sports Quotations* (1990).

Bell, Alexander Melville 1819–1905

Language instructor, father of Alexander Graham Bell.

25 Yes, Alec, it is I, your father, speaking.
   1876 The first words spoken and heard on the world's first long-distance telephone call, from Alexander Melville Bell in Brantford, Ontario, Canada, to his son Alexander Graham Bell in nearby Paris, 13 km away, 10 Aug.

Bell, Bernard Iddings 1886–1958

US cleric, chaplain at the University of Chicago.

26 A good education is not so much one which prepares a man to succeed in the world, as one which enables him to sustain a failure.
   1950 In *Life*, 16 Oct.

Bell, (Arthur) Clive Howard 1881–1964

English critic of art and literature, an influential member of the Bloomsbury set, husband of Vanessa Bell. His aesthetic theory emphasized form over content in art.

27 It would follow that 'significant form' was form behind which we catch a sense of ultimate reality.
   1914 *Art*, pt.1, ch.3.

28 Art and Religion are, then, two roads by which men escape from circumstance to ecstasy.
   1914 *Art*, pt.2, ch.1.

29 I will try to account for the degree of my aesthetic emotion. That, I conceive, is the function of the critic.
   1914 *Art*, pt.3, ch.3.

30 Materially make the life of the artist sufficiently miserable to be unattractive, and no one will take to art save those in whom the divine daemon is absolute.
   1914 *Art*, pt.5, ch.1.

31 Comfort came in with the middle classes.
   1928 *Civilization*, ch.4.

32 Only reason can convince us of those three fundamental truths without a recognition of which there can be no effective liberty: that what we believe is not necessarily true; that what we like is not necessarily good; and that all questions are open.
   1928 *Civilization*, ch.5.

Bell, Martin 1938–

English journalist and MP. After a career as a television news reporter he stood as an Independent candidate for Tatton in the 1997 general election.

33 I knew when Sir Alec Guinness endorsed my campaign that the force was with us.
   1997 Victory speech on winning the Tatton constituency. In *The Oxford Mail*, 2 May.

34 The great American tradition of telling truth to power was incinerated in New York on 11 September 2001.
   2003 *Through Gates of Fire*.

Bell, Vanessa née *Stephen* 1879–1961

English painter and designer, sister of Virginia Woolf. She married the critic Clive Bell (1907) but left him in 1916 to live with Duncan Grant.

35 Rather lovely descriptions of scenery, don't you think?
> **1928** Remark to Robert Medley and Rupert Doone, when asked what she thought of D H Lawrence's *Lady Chatterley's Lover*. Recalled in Robert Medley *Drawn from the Life: a Memoir* (1983), p.91.

Bellay, Joachim du 1522–60

French poet famous for his sonnets. He was a founding member of the Pléiade and wrote its manifesto, *La défense et illustration de la langue française* (1549).

36 *Rome de Rome est le seul monument,*
Et Rome Rome a vaincu seulement.
Rome is the only monument left of Rome,
And only Rome vanquished Rome.
> **1558** *Antiquitez de Rome*, no.5.

37 *Rome seule pouvait à Rome ressembler,*
Rome seule pouvait Rome fait trembler.
Only Rome can resemble Rome,
And Rome alone can make Rome fall.
> **1558** *Antiquitez de Rome*, no.6.

38 *France, mère des arts, des armes et des lois.*
France, mother of arts, of weapons and of laws.
> **1558** *Les Regrets*, no.9.

39 *Heureux, qui comme Ulysse, a fait un beau voyage,*
Ou comme cestuy là qui conquit la toison,
Et puis est retourné, plein d'usage et raison,
Vivre entre ses parents le reste de son âge!
Happy is he who, like Ulysses, has taken a wondrous journey
Or has won the Golden Fleece,
And then returns home wise and useful
To live in his homeland the rest of his days.
> **1558** *Les Regrets*, no.31.

40 *Celuy vit seulement, lequel vit aujourdhuy.*
Only the person who lives for today lives at all.
> **1558** *Les Regrets*, no.65.

41 *Je n'écris point d'amour, n'estant point amoureux,*
Je n'écris de beauté, n'aiant belle maistresse,
Je n'écris de douceur, n'esprouvant que rudesse,
Je n'écris de plaisir, me trouvant douloureux.
I cannot write of love, as I am not in love,
I cannot write of beauty, as I have no beautiful mistress,
I cannot write of sweetness, as I experience nothing but hardship,
I cannot write of pleasure, as I am always in pain.
> **1558** *Les Regrets*, no.79.

Belli, Carlos Germán 1927–

Peruvian poet, translator and journalist. He travelled widely in South America, Spain, Italy and the United States. His poems are noted for their nihilistic outlook and an orderly precision of language.

42 *De los libros el luminoso plectro*
diríase que pasa
a ser lía del recto,
pues después de tanto leer sin tasa
nada ha quedado en casa.
The luminous plectrum of books
can be said to become
a portion of the rectum,
since after so much eager reading
not a thing remains at home.
> **1961** *¡Oh hada cibernética!*, 'Cuando el seso tiene la altura de un grano de arena' ('When the brain is as high as a grain of sand').

Bellini, Mario 1935–

Italian architect.

43 A design career is a process of learning better and better what you know instinctively.
> **1987** In the *New York Times*, 25 Jun.

44 I designed a bench in a few moments. But, of course, it took me 25 years to do it.
> **1987** In the *New York Times*, 25 Jun.

Belloc, (Joseph) Hilaire Pierre 1870–1953

French-born British writer, poet, Roman Catholic apologist and Liberal MP (1906–10). His works include *The Servile State* (1912), travel books, historical studies and religious books. He is best known for his comic and nonsensical verse for children.

45 Child! do not throw this book about;
Refrain from the unholy pleasure
Of cutting all the pictures out!
Preserve it as your chiefest treasure.
> **1896** *The Bad Child's Book of Beasts*, dedication.

46 A manner rude and wild
Is common at your age.
> **1896** *The Bad Child's Book of Beasts*, introduction.

47 When people call this beast to mind,
They marvel more and more
At such a little tail behind,
So large a trunk before.
> **1896** *The Bad Child's Book of Beasts*, 'The Elephant'.

48 I shoot the Hippopotamus
With bullets made of platinum,
Because if I use the leaden ones
His hide is sure to flatten 'em.
> **1896** *The Bad Child's Book of Beasts*, 'The Hippopotamus'.

49 Mothers of large families (who claim to common sense)
Will find a Tiger will repay the trouble and expense.
> **1896** *The Bad Child's Book of Beasts*, 'The Tiger'.

50 The Microbe is so very small
You cannot make him out at all.
> **1897** *More Beasts for Worse Children*, 'The Microbe'.

51 Whatever happens, we have got
The Maxim Gun, and they have not.
> **1898** *The Modern Traveller*, bk.6.

52 I am a Catholic. As far as possible I go to Mass every day. As far as possible I kneel down and tell these beads every day. If you reject me on account of my religion, I shall thank God that he has spared me the indignity of being your representative.
> **1906** Election campaign speech, Salford.

53 The chief defect of Henry King
Was chewing little bits of string.
> **1907** *Cautionary Tales*, 'Henry King'.

54 Physicians of the utmost fame
Were called at once, but when they came

They answered, as they took their fees,
'There is no cure for this disease.'
1907 *Cautionary Tales*, 'Henry King'.

55 'Oh, my friends, be warned by me,
That breakfast, dinner, lunch, and tea
Are all the human frame requires…'
With that the wretched child expires.
1907 *Cautionary Tales*, 'Henry King'.

56 And always keep a hold of Nurse
For fear of finding something worse.
1907 *Cautionary Tales*, 'Jim'.

57 We had intended you to be
The next Prime Minister but three:
The stocks were sold; the Press was squared;
The Middle Class was quite prepared.
But as it is!… My language fails!
Go out and govern New South Wales!
1907 *Cautionary Tales*, 'Jim'.

58 Matilda told such Dreadful Lies,
It made one Gasp and Stretch one's Eyes;
Her Aunt, who, from her Earliest Youth,
Had kept a Strict Regard for Truth,
Attempted to Believe Matilda:
The effort very nearly killed her.
1907 *Cautionary Tales*, 'Matilda'.

59 She was not really bad at heart,
But only rather rude and wild;
She was an aggravating child.
1907 *Cautionary Tales*, 'Rebecca'.

60 Her funeral sermon (which was long
And followed by a sacred song)
Mentioned her virtues, it is true,
But dwelt upon her vices too.
1907 *Cautionary Tales*, 'Rebecca'.

61 It is the best of trades, to make songs, and the second
best to sing them.
1909 *On Everything*.

62 I said to Heart, 'How goes it?' Heart replied:
'Right as a Ribstone Pippin!' But it lied.
1910 'The False Heart'.

63 When I am living in the Midlands
That are sodden and unkind.
1910 'The South Country'.

64 Everywhere the sea is a teacher of truth. I am not sure
that the best thing I find in sailing is not this salt of reality.
c.1910 *The Cruise of the Nona*.

65 Do you remember an Inn,
Miranda?
Do you remember an Inn,
And the tedding and the spreading
Of the straw for a bedding,
And the fleas that tease in the High Pyrenees
And the wine that tasted of the tar?
1923 'Tarantella'.

66 When I am dead, I hope it may be said,
'His sins were scarlet, but his books were read.'
1923 'On His Books'.

67 And even now, at twenty-five,
He has to WORK to keep alive!
Yes! All day long from 10 till 4!

For half the year or even more;
With but an hour or two to spend
At luncheon with a city friend.
1930 *New Cautionary Tales*, 'Peter Goole'.

68 I am a sundial, and I make a botch
Of what is done much better by a watch.
1938 'On a Sundial'.

69 Statistics are the triumph of the quantitative method, and
the quantitative method is the victory of sterility and
death.
1940 *The Silence of the Sea*.

Bellow, Saul 1915–

Canadian-born US writer. He moved to Chicago in 1924, and was
educated there. His best novels examine Jewish-American
identity and the dilemma of liberal humanist values in a fast-
changing world. He won the Nobel prize for literature in 1976.

70 Everyone knows there is no fineness or accuracy of
suppression. If you hold down one thing you hold down
the adjoining.
1953 *The Adventures of Augie March*.

71 I am an American, Chicago born—Chicago, that somber
city—and go at things as I have taught myself, free-style,
and will make the record in my own way: first to knock,
first admitted; sometimes an innocent knock,
sometimes a not so innocent.
1953 *The Adventures of Augie March*.

72 Of course, in an age of madness, to expect to be
untouched by madness is a form of madness. But the
pursuit of sanity can be a form of madness, too.
1959 *Henderson The Rain King*, ch.3.

73 If I am out of my mind, it's all right with me, thought
Moses Herzog.
1961 *Herzog*, opening words.

74 A man may say, 'From now on I'm going to speak the
truth.' But the truth hears him and runs away and hides
before he's even done speaking.
1961 *Herzog*.

75 I feel that art has something to do with the achievement
of stillness in the midst of chaos.
1965 Interview in *The Paris Review*, no.37, winter issue.

76 No wonder the really powerful men in our society,
whether politicians or scientists, hold writers in
contempt. They do it because they get no evidence from
modern literature that anybody is thinking about any
significant question.
1965 Interview in *The Paris Review*, no.37, winter issue.

77 I am more stupid about some things than about others;
not equally stupid in all directions; I am not a well-
rounded person.
1969 *Mr Sammler's Planet*, ch.2.

78 Conquered people tend to be witty.
1969 *Mr Sammler's Planet*, ch.2.

79 Mr Sammler with his screwy visions! He saw the
increasing triumph of Enlightenment—Liberty, Equality,
Adultery!
1969 *Mr Sammler's Planet*, ch.3.

80 There is much to be said for exotic marriages. If your
husband is a bore, it takes years longer to discover.
1969 *Mr Sammler's Planet*, ch.6.

81 I think that New York is not the cultural centre of America, but the business and administrative centre of American culture.
1969 In radio interview, reported in *The Listener*, 22 May.

82 The idea, anyway, was to ward off trouble. But now the moronic inferno had caught up with me.
1975 *Humboldt's Gift*. Martin Amis used the phrase *The Moronic Inferno* as the title for a book of essays on the US (1986).

83 The only real distinction at this dangerous moment in human history and cosmic development has nothing to do with medals and ribbons. Not to fall asleep is distinguished. Everything else is mere popcorn.
1975 *Humboldt's Gift*.

84 After all these years wallowing in low seriousness—low seriousness, you understand, is high seriousness that's failed.
1975 Interview in the *Sunday Times*, 12 Jan.

85 The feeling individual appeared weak—he felt only his own weakness. But if he accepted his weakness and his separateness and descended into himself, intensifying his loneliness, he discovered his solidarity with other isolated creatures.
1976 Nobel prize lecture, Stockholm, 12 Dec.

86 A novel is balanced between a few true impressions and the multitude of false ones that make up most of what we call life.
1976 Nobel prize lecture, Stockholm, 12 Dec.

87 Tears may be intellectual, but they can never be political. They save no man from being shot, no child from being thrown alive into the furnace.
1982 *The Dean's December*, ch.12.

88 As a rule Corde avoided cemeteries and never went near the graves of his parents. He said it was just as easy for your dead to visit you, only by now he would have to hire a hall.
1982 *The Dean's December*, ch.15.

89 The secret motive of the absent-minded is to be innocent while guilty. Absent-mindedness is spurious innocence.
1987 *More Die of Heartbreak*.

90 Erotic practices have become diversified. Sex used to be a single-crop farming, like cotton or wheat; now people raise all kinds of things.
1987 *More Die of Heartbreak*.

91 The modern reader (or viewer, or listener: let's include everybody) is perilously overloaded. His attention is, to use the latest lingo, 'targeted' by powerful forces… Our consciousness is a staging area, a field of operations for all kinds of enterprises, which make free use of it.
1989 *Something To Remember Me By*, preface.

92 But Fonstein belonged to an even more advanced category…their aim is to convert weaknesses and secrets into burnable energy. A first-class man subsists on the matter he destroys, just as the stars do.
1989 *Something To Remember Me By*, 'The Bellarosa Connection'.

Bemelmans, Ludwig 1898–1962

US writer and restaurateur. He wrote food and travel books, and is best remembered for his 'Madeline' series for children.

93 In an old house in Paris
that was covered with vines

lived twelve little girls in two straight lines.
1939 *Madeline*.

94 And nobody knew so well
How to frighten Miss Clavell.
1939 *Madeline*.

95 Serves you right, you horrid brat
For what you did to that poor cat.
1956 *Madeline and the Bad Hat*.

Benaud, Richie (Richard) 1930–

Australian cricketer and broadcaster. He played in 63 Test matches (28 as captain), scoring 2201 Test runs and taking 248 wickets.

96 Cricket is a batsman's game.
1961 *Way of Cricket*.

Benchley, Robert Charles 1889–1945

US humorist and critic, a member of the famous circle of New York wits and writers known as the Algonquin Round Table. He was drama critic of *Life* and the *New Yorker*, and appeared in cameo roles in many films.

97 In America there are two classes of travel—first class, and with children.
1925 *Pluck and Luck*.

98 The surest way to make a monkey of a man is to quote him.
1936 *My Ten Years in a Quandary*.

99 I haven't been abroad in so long that I almost speak English without an accent now.
1938 *After 1903— What?*

1 One square foot less and it would be adulterous.
On the tiny office he shared with Dorothy Parker, quoted in the *New Yorker*, 5 Jan 1946.

2 My only solution for the problem of habitual accidents…is to stay in bed all day. Even then, there is always the chance that you will fall out.
1949 *Chips Off the Old Benchley*, 'Safety Second'.

3 A great many people have come up to me and asked how I manage to get so much work done and still keep looking so dissipated.
1949 *Chips Off the Old Benchley*, 'How To Get Things Done'.

4 So who's in a hurry?
On being told that the particular drink he was drinking was slow poison. Quoted in Nathaniel Benchley *Robert Benchley* (1955), ch.1.

5 STREETS FLOODED. PLEASE ADVISE.
Telegraph message to the US on arriving in Venice. Quoted in R E Drennan (ed) *Wits End* (1973).

6 Opera is where a guy gets stabbed in the back, and instead of dying, he sings.
Quoted in Ian Crofton and Donald Fraser *A Dictionary of Musical Quotations* (1985).

Bendix, Reinhard 1916–91

German-born US sociologist, Professor at the University of California, Berkeley.

7 In retrospect it always seems as if everything had to develop just the way it did. I call this view the fallacy of retrospective determinism—which looks at the modern world as a victory of the children of light over the

children of darkness if we approve of the development, and of darkness over light if we condemn it.
1984 *Force, Fate, and Freedom: On Historical Sociology.*

Benedetti, Mario 1920–

Uruguayan fiction writer, poet and essayist, who lived in Cuba in the late 1960s. After returning to Uruguay, he helped establish a leftist coalition for future elections. With the military takeover of 1973 he was forced to leave the country.

8   *está demás decirte que a esta altura*
  no creo en predicadores ni en generales
  ni en las nalgas de miss universo
  ni en el arrepentimiento de los verdugos
  ni en el catecismo del confort
  ni en el flaco perdón de dios.
  It's not useless to tell you that, at this stage,
  I don't believe in preachers or generals
  or in Miss Universe's buttocks
  or in the executioner's repentance
  or in the catechism of comfort
  or in God's slim forgiving.
  1974 *Poemas de otros*, 'Credo' ('Creed').

Benét, Stephen Vincent 1898–1943

US poet and novelist. He wrote many evocative poems on the history and national identity of America, of which 'American Names' is the most famous.

9   I have fallen in love with American names,
  The sharp, gaunt names that never get fat,
  The snakeskin-titles of mining-claims,
  The plumed war-bonnet of Medicine Hat,
  Tucson and Deadwood and Lost Mule Flat.
  1927 'American Names'.

10   There are English counties like hunting-tunes
  Played on the keys of a postboy's horn,
  But I will remember where I was born.
  1927 'American Names'.

11   I will get me a bottle of Boston sea
  And a blue-gum nigger to sing me blues.
  I am tired of loving a foreign muse.
  1927 'American Names'.

12   I shall not rest quiet in Montparnasse.
  I shall not lie easy at Winchelsea.
  You may bury my body in Sussex grass,
  You may bury my tongue at Champmédy.
  I shall not be there, I shall rise and pass.
  Bury my heart at Wounded Knee.
  1927 'American Names'. *Bury My Heart At Wounded Knee* was used by Dee Brown as the title of a book on the Indian genocide (1971).

13   One cannot balance tragedy in the scales
  Unless one weighs it with the tragic heart.
  1928 'John Brown's Body'.

14   We thought we were done with these things but we
    were wrong.
  We thought, because we had power, we had wisdom.
  1935 'A Litany for Dictatorships'.

Benn, Tony (Anthony Neil Wedgwood) 1925–

English Labour politician. He became an MP (1950–60), and renounced his hereditary title to be re-elected to the

Commons (1963–83, 1984–2001). He held various government posts, and as a left-wing representative unsuccessfully challenged Neil Kinnock for the leadership of the Labour Party in 1988.

15   The House of Lords is the British Outer Mongolia for retired politicians.
  1962 Speech made during his campaign to disclaim his hereditary peerage, 11 Feb.

16   It is as wholly wrong to blame Marx for what was done in his name, as it is to blame Jesus for what was done in his.
  Quoted in Alan Freeman *The Benn Heresy* (1982).

17   It is beginning to dawn on people that the influence of a nation is not measured by the size of its military budget, but by its industrial strength.
  1991 In *The Independent*, 18 Apr.

18   The dependence of London on Washington for the supply of our so-called independent nuclear weapons is all that remains of the 'special relationship' and…it is really a ball and chain limiting our capacity to play a more positive role in the world.
  1991 In *The Independent*, 18 Apr.
  ➤ *See Churchill 217 : 93.*

19   It is the same each time with progress. First they ignore you, then they say you are mad, then dangerous, then there's a pause, and then you can't find anyone who disagrees.
  1991 Speech at the Labour Party Conference, Oct.

20   It will be Blair, Blair, Blair just as it was Thatcher, Thatcher, Thatcher.
  1997 Replying to a student's question on the supremacy of prime ministerial power.

21   We should put the spin-doctors in spin clinics, where they can meet other spin patients and be treated by spin consultants. The rest of us can get on with the proper democratic process.
  1997 In *The Independent*, 'Quote Unquote', 25 Oct.

22   The Weetabix Years.
  2004 Book title.

Bennard, George 1873–1958

US clergyman and hymn-writer.

23   I will cling to the old rugged cross,
  And exchange it some day for a crown.
  1913 'The Old Rugged Cross'.

Bennett, Alan 1934–

English writer. He came to prominence as an actor and writer in *Beyond the Fringe* (1960), and went on to write wry, mordant plays and monologues for stage and screen. He adapted his play *The Madness of George III* (1991) as an Oscar-winning film (*The Madness of King George*, 1995).

24   Life is rather like a tin of sardines—we're all of us looking for the key.
  1960 *Beyond the Fringe*.

25   I've never understood this liking for war. It panders to instincts already catered for within the scope of any respectable domestic establishment.
  1968 *Forty Years On* (published 1969), act 1.

26   Memories are not shackles, Franklin, they are garlands.
  1968 *Forty Years On* (published 1969), act 2.

27 The Breed never dies. Sapper, Buchan, Dornford Yates, practitioners in that school of Snobbery with Violence that runs like a thread of good-class tweed through twentieth-century literature.
1968 *Forty Years On* (published 1969), act 2. *Snobbery With Violence* was used as a book title by Colin Wilson (1971).

28 It's the one species I wouldn't mind seeing vanish from the face of the earth. I wish they were like the White Rhino—six of them left in the Serengeti National Park, and all males.
1971 Of dogs. *Getting On* (published 1972), act 1.

29 The longer I practise medicine, the more convinced I am there are only two types of cases: those that involve taking the trousers off and those that don't.
1973 *Habeas Corpus*.

30 One of the few things I have learned in life is that there is invariably something odd about women who wear ankle socks.
1977 *The Old Country*, act 1.

31 We were put to Dickens as children but it never took. That unremitting humanity soon had me cheesed off.
1977 *The Old Country*, act 2.

32 There is no such thing as a good script, only a good film, and I'm conscious that my scripts often read better than they play.
1984 *A Private Function*, introduction to published screenplay.

33 I'm going to throw caution to the winds and have a sweet sherry.
1984 Spoken by Maggie Smith as Joyce Chilvers in *A Private Function*.

34 I want a future that will live up to my past.
1984 Spoken by Maggie Smith as Joyce Chilvers in *A Private Function*.

35 They're going to have to be made to sit up and take notice. They're going to have to be made to realise who we are. My father had a chain of dry cleaners.
1984 *A Private Function*.

36 I'm not good at precise, coherent argument. But plays are suited to incoherent argument, put into the mouths of fallible people.
1991 In the *Sunday Times*, 24 Nov.

37 My claim to literary fame is that I used to deliver meat to a woman who became T. S. Eliot's mother-in-law.
1992 In the *Observer*, 26 Apr. The lady in question was the mother of Eliot's wife Valerie Fletcher; Bennett's father was the butcher in the same Yorkshire village.

Bennett, (Enoch) Arnold 1867–1931

English novelist. He was also a journalist, and lived in Paris for ten years. His best-known books are those set in the pottery-making heartland of the Five Towns in the Midlands, notably the *Clayhanger* trilogy (1910–16).

38 Essential characteristic of the really great novelist: a Christ-like, all-embracing compassion.
1896 Journal entry, 15 Oct.

39 'Bah!', she said, 'With people like you, love only means one thing.' 'No,' he replied. 'It means twenty things, but it doesn't mean nineteen.'
1904 Journal entry, 20 Nov.

40 My general impression is that Englishmen act better than Frenchmen, and Frenchwomen better than Englishwomen.
1909 *Cupid and Commonsense*, preface.

41 His opinion of himself, having once risen, remained at 'set fair'.
1911 *The Card*, ch.1.

42 'Ye can call it influenza if ye like,' said Mrs Machin. 'There was no influenza in my young days. We called a cold a cold.'
1911 *The Card*, ch.8.

43 A cause may be inconvenient, but it's magnificent. It's like champagne or high heels, and one must be prepared to suffer for it.
1918 *The Title*, act 1.

44 Being a husband is a whole-time job. That is why so many husbands fail. They cannot give their entire attention to it.
1918 *The Title*, act 1.

45 Journalists say a thing that they know isn't true, in the hope that if they keep on saying it long enough it will be true.
1918 *The Title*, act 2.

46 Mr Lloyd George spoke for 17 minutes, in which period he was detected only once in the use of an argument.
1921 *Things That Have Interested Me*.

47 A test of a first-rate work, and a test of your sincerity in calling it a first-rate work, is that you finish it.
1921 *Things That Have Interested Me*, 'Finishing Books'.

48 In the meantime alcohol produces a delightful social atmosphere that nothing else can produce.
1921 *Things That Have Interested Me*, 'For and Against Prohibition'.

49 Pessimism, when you get used to it, is just as agreeable as optimism.
1921 *Things That Have Interested Me*, 'Slump Into Pessimism'.

50 The price of justice is eternal publicity.
1923 *Things That Have Interested Me* (2nd series), 'Secret Trials'.

51 Between thirty and forty a man may have reached the height of discretion without having tumbled over the top and into the feather-bed of correctitude.
1930 In the *Evening Standard*, 29 May.

52 Good taste is better than bad taste, but bad taste is better than no taste, and men without individuality have no taste—at any rate no taste that they can impose on their publics.
1930 In the *Evening Standard*, 21 Aug.

53 The thing is to produce an impression on the reader—the best you can, the truest you can, but some impression. The newest despisers of form and conventionalization produce no impression at all.
1931 Journal entry, 11 Sep.

54 The saxophone is the embodied spirit of beer.
Quoted in Derek Watson *Music Quotations* (1991).

Bennett, James Gordon, Snr 1795–1872

Scots-born US journalist. In 1835 he started the *New York Herald*, pioneering many journalistic innovations.

55 The Press is the living Jury of the Nation.
1831 In the *Courier and Enquirer*, 6 Aug.

56 An editor must always be with the people—think with

them—feel with them—and he need fear nothing, he will always be right—always be strong—always *free*.
1831 In the *Courier and Enquirer*, 12 Nov.

57 This is the editorial age, and the most intellectual of all ages.
1831 In the *Courier and Enquirer*, 12 Nov.

58 What is to prevent a daily newspaper from being made the greatest organ of social life? Books have had their day—the theatres have had their day—the temple of religion has had its day. A newspaper can be made to take the lead of all these in the great movements of human thought and of human civilisation. A newspaper can send more souls to Heaven, and save more from Hell, than all the churches or chapels in New York—besides making money at the same time.
1836 In the *New York Herald*, 19 Aug.

59 I have infused life, glowing eloquence, philosophy, taste, sentiment, wit, and humor into the daily newspaper… Shakespeare is the great genius of the drama—Scott of the novel—Milton and Byron of the poem—and I mean to be the genius of the daily newspaper press.
c.1836 Quoted in Oliver Carlson *The Man Who Made News: James Gordon Bennett* (1942), ch.10.

Bennis, Warren Gameliel   1925–

US economist and business administrator.

60 Leaders are people who do the right things. Managers are people who do things right…a profound difference.
1994 In *Fortune*, 19 Sep.

Benson, A(rthur) C(hristopher)   1862–1925

English academic writer. He wrote a number of critical studies and biographies of eminent literary Victorians, and is remembered now for his patriotic poem 'Land of Hope and Glory', set to music by Elgar.

61 Land of Hope and Glory, Mother of the Free,
How shall we extol thee who are born of thee?
Wider still and wider shall thy bounds be set;
God who made thee mighty, make thee mightier yet.
1902 'Land of Hope and Glory'.

62 If the dullest person in the world would only put down sincerely what he or she thought about his or her life, about work and love, religion and emotion, it would be a fascinating document.
1906 'From A College Window'.

Benson, Stella   1892–1933

English novelist. Her diary was published long after her death from tuberculosis.

63 Call no man foe, but never love a stranger.
1917 *This is the End*.

Bentham, Jeremy   1748–1832

English philosopher, jurist and writer. His works include *A Fragment of Government* (1776) and *Introduction to the Principles of Morals and Legislation* (1789), which expounds his theory of hedonistic utilitarianism.

64 The community is a fictitious *body*, composed of the individual persons who are considered as constituting as it were its *members*. The interest of the community then, is what? The sum of the interests of the several members who compose it.
1789 *An Introduction to the Principles of Morals and Legislation*, ch.1.

65 The greatest happiness of the greatest number is the foundation of morals and legislation.
1789 *An Introduction to the Principles of Morals and Legislation*, ch.1.
➤ *See Hutcheson 424:52.*

66 All punishment is mischief: all punishment in itself is evil.
1789 *An Introduction to the Principles of Morals and Legislation*, ch.13.

67 Every law is an evil, for every law is an infraction of liberty.
1789 *An Introduction to the Principles of Morals and Legislation*.

68 An absolute and unlimited right over any object of property would be the right to commit nearly every crime. If I had such a right over the stick I am about to cut, I might employ it as a mace to knock down the passengers, or I might convert it into a sceptre as an emblem of royalty, or into an idol to offend the national religion.
Principles of the Civil Code, pt.1, ch.13, final note. Collected in John Bowring (ed) *Works* (1838–43), vol.1.

69 Natural rights is simple nonsense: natural and imprescriptable rights, rhetorical nonsense—nonsense upon stilts.
Anarchical Fallacies. Collected in J Bowring (ed) *Works* (1838–43), vol.2.

70 Publicity is the very soul of justice. It is the keenest spur to exertion, and the surest of all guards against improbity.
Draught of a code for the organization of the judicial establishment in France. Collected in John Bowring (ed) *Works* (1838–43), vol.4.

71 He rather hated the ruling few than loved the suffering many.
Of James Mill. Quoted in *Memories of Old Friends, being Extracts from the Journals and Letters of Caroline Fox* (1882).

72 Prose is when all the lines except the last go on to the end. Poetry is when some of them fall short of it.
Quoted in M St J Packe *The Life of John Stuart Mill* (1954), bk.1, ch.2.

73 To be the most effectively benevolent man who ever lived.
His ambition. Quoted in Mary Peter Mack *International Encyclopedia of the Social Sciences* (1968), vol.2.

Bentley, Edmund Clerihew   1875–1956

English writer and journalist. His books include *Biography for Beginners* (1905), *Baseless Biography* (1939) and the classic detective novel *Trent's Last Case* (1913). He is best known for his humorous verse form, named the clerihew after him.

74 The art of Biography
Is different from Geography.
Geography is about Maps,
But Biography is about Chaps.
1905 *Biography for Beginners*, introduction.

75 What I like about Clive
Is that he is no longer alive.
There is a great deal to be said
For being dead.
1905 *Biography for Beginners*, 'Clive'.

76 Sir Christopher Wren
said, 'I am going to dine with some men.
If anybody calls
Say I am designing St Paul's.'
1905 *Biography for Beginners*, 'Sir Christopher Wren'.

77 Sir Humphrey Davy
Abominated gravy.
He lived in the odium
Of having discovered sodium.
1905 *Biography for Beginners*, 'Sir Humphrey Davy'.

78 John Stuart Mill,
By a mighty effort of will,
Overcame his natural *bonhomie*
And wrote 'Principles of Political Economy'.
1905 *Biography for Beginners*, 'John Stuart Mill'.

79 Henry the Eighth
Took a thuctheththion of mateth.
He inthithted that the monkth
Were a lathy lot of thkunkth.
1929 *More Biography*, 'Henry the Eighth'.

80 George the Third
Ought never to have occurred.
One can only wonder
At so grotesque a blunder.
1929 *More Biography*, 'George the Third'.

81 When their lordships asked Bacon
How many bribes he had taken
He had at least the grace
To get very red in the face.
1939 *Baseless Biography*, 'Bacon'.

Bentley, Nicholas Clerihew 1907–78

English artist and writer, son of Edmund Clerihew Bentley. He was best known for his cartoons, and illustrations to works such as T S Eliot's *Old Possum's Book of Practical Cats* (1939). He edited several editions of *Pick of Punch* (1955–60).

82 Henry Campbell-Bannerman is remembered chiefly as the man about whom all is forgotten.
1974 *An Edwardian Album*.

Bentsen, Lloyd Millard, Jr 1921–

US politician, senator for Texas (1971–93). He was the Democratic nominee for Vice-President in the 1988 elections.

83 America has just passed through…an eight-year coma in which slogans were confused with solutions and rhetoric passed for reality.
1988 Recalling the Reagan administration as he accepted the Democratic nomination for Vice-President, 21 Jul.

84 Senator, I served with Jack Kennedy. I knew Jack Kennedy. Jack Kennedy was a friend of mine. Senator, you're no Jack Kennedy.
1988 On his opponent Dan Quayle's contention that his congressional experience equalled that of President Kennedy when he sought the presidency. Reported in the *New York Times*, 9 Oct.

Benuzzi, Felice 1910–88

Italian diplomat, lawyer and athlete. In Jan 1943 he and two friends escaped from a POW camp at Nanyuki to climb Mt Kenya with minimal equipment and provisions, before breaking back into the camp again and giving themselves up to the British commandant.

85 I emerged at last, stumbled a few steps in the mud and then I saw it: an ethereal mountain emerging from a tossing sea of clouds framed between two dark barracks—a massive, blue-black tooth of sheer rock inlaid with azure glaciers, austere yet floating fairy-like on the near horizon. It was the first 17,000-foot peak I had ever seen.
I stood gazing until the vision disappeared among the shifting cloud banks.
For hours afterwards I remained spell-bound.
I had definitely fallen in love.
1952 *No Picnic on Mount Kenya*.

86 To remember is far worse than to forget.
1952 On being a Prisoner of War. *No Picnic on Mount Kenya*.

Berdyaev, Nicholas 1874–1948

Russian philosopher. He originally supported the communist revolution but subsequently found that Marxism lacked a spiritual element and abandoned it. He founded the Academy of the Philosophy of Religion in Berlin (later transferred to Paris).

87 Man found his form and his identity under the action of religious principles and energies; the confusion in which he is losing them cannot be re-ordered by purely human efforts.
1923 'Konets Rennesansa' in *Sofiya* (translated as 'The End of the Renaissance' in the *Slavonic Review*, Jun/Dec 1925).

Berendt, John 1939–

US writer, journalist and editor. He was a Pulitzer Prize finalist for general non-fiction in 1995 for *Midnight in the Garden of Good and Evil* (1994).

88 In Atlanta, the first question is 'What's your business?' In Macon, it is 'Where do you go to church?' In Augusta they want your grandmother's maiden name. But in Savannah, the first question is 'What would you like to drink?'
1994 *Midnight in the Garden of Good and Evil*.

Berenson, Bernard 1865–1959

Lithuanian-born US art critic. An authority on the Renaissance, he could identify Italian masterworks by style and technique. His works include *Venetian Painters of the Renaissance* (1894) and *Rumor and Reflection* (1952).

89 I earn it by enjoying such authority and prestige that people will not buy expensive Italian pictures without my approval.
Comment on his income, addressed to the Internal Revenue Service. Quoted in *The Making of a Legend* (1987).

Beresford, Lord Charles 1846–1919

British politician.

90 Very sorry can't come. Lie follows by post.
Telegraph to the Prince of Wales, declining a dinner invitation. Quoted in Ralph Nevill *The World of Fashion 1837–1922* (1923), ch.5.

Berg, Alban 1885–1935

Austrian composer, best known for his opera *Wozzeck* (1925), his violin concerto (1935) and the *Lyric Suite* (1926) for string quartet.

91 Why is Schoenberg's Music so Hard to Understand?
1924 Title of essay.

Berger, Bennett Maurice 1926–

US sociologist, Professor at the University of California, San Diego (1973–91, then emeritus).

92 Oversimplification is now a common term of reproach in academic discussions; everyone is against oversimplification. But there is no parallel term nearly as frequently used to describe the opposite phenomenon, which surely occurs as often, if not more so.
1990 *Authors of their Own Lives* (edited by Berger), introduction.

Berger, Gerhard 1959–

Austrian Formula One racing driver.

93 There was something supernatural about him. An aura, as if he came from another planet and therefore had more insight, more brain cells, more power, more energy.
1997 On Ayrton Senna. In his autobiography, *Zielgerade*.

Berger, John Peter 1926–

English writer and art critic. His writing has been strongly influenced by Marxism, and he caused a sensation by denouncing the Booker Corporation in his acceptance speech when awarded the Booker Prize for his novel *G* in 1972.

94 The five senses within whose pentagon each man is alone.
1972 *G*, pt.3, ch.5.

95 If we could all live a thousand years…we would each, at least once during that period, be considered a genius.
1972 *G*, pt.3, ch.6.

96 The camera relieves us of the burden of memory.
1978 *New Statesman*, 17 Aug.

97 It is not usually possible in a poem or a story to make the relationship between particular and universal fully explicit. Those who try to do so end up writing parables.
1979 *Pig Earth*, 'Historical Afterward'.

98 Photography, because it stops the flow of life, is always flirting with death.
1983 In the *New Statesman*, 22/29 Dec.

99 All weddings are similar but every marriage is different. Death comes to everyone but one mourns alone.
1985 *The White Bird*, 'The Storyteller'.

1 Every city has a sex and age which have nothing to do with demography.
1987 In *The Guardian*, 27 Mar.

2 Every painted image of something is also about the absence of the real thing. All painting is about the presence of absence.
1988 In *New Statesman and Society*, 15 Jul.

Bergreen, Laurence 1950–

US journalist and biographer.

3 He was not fit for marriage, only for work. A major writer, he conceded, required major torment.
1984 Of James Agee. *James Agee*.

Berkeley, George 1685–1753

Irish idealist philosopher and Anglican Bishop of Cloyne (1734–52). His philosophical works, such as *A Treatise Concerning the Principles of Human Knowledge* (1710), argue that things in the material world only exist when perceived in the mind.

4 I am inclined to think that the far greater part, if not all, of those difficulties which have hitherto amused philosophers, and blocked up the way to knowledge, are entirely owing to ourselves—that we have first raised a dust and then complain we cannot see.
1710 *A Treatise Concerning the Principles of Human Knowledge*, introduction.

5 Some truths there are so near and obvious to the mind that a man need only open his eyes to see them. Such I take this important one to be, viz. that all the choir of heaven and furniture of the earth, in a word all those bodies which compose the mighty frame of the world, have not any subsistence without a mind—that their *being* is *to be perceived or known*.
1710 *A Treatise Concerning The Principles Of Human Knowledge*, pt.1, section 6.

6 Whatever is immediately perceived is an idea: and can any *idea* exist out of the mind?
1713 *Three Dialogues between Hylas And Philonous*, first dialogue.

7 The same principles which at first lead to scepticism, pursued to a certain point bring men back to common sense.
1734 *Three Dialogues between Hylas and Philonous*, dialogue 3.
➤ See Bacon 48:95.

8 Whose fault is it if poor Ireland still continues poor?
1737 *The Querist*, pt.3.

9 Truth is the cry of all, but the game of the few.
1744 *Siris*.

10 It is impossible that a man who is false to his friends and neighbours should be true to the public.
1750 *Maxims Concerning Patriotism*.

Berlin, Irving originally *Israel Baline* 1888–1989

Russian-born US composer, who began as a singing waiter. He wrote lyrics and music for over 900 songs including 'Alexander's Ragtime Band' and 'White Christmas'. The musical *Annie Get Your Gun* (1946) marked the peak of his career.

11 Come on and hear,
Come on and hear
Alexander's Ragtime Band
1911 'Alexander's Ragtime Band', opening lines, featured in the 1938 film of the same title.

12 A pretty girl is like a melody
That haunts you night and day.
1919 'A Pretty Girl is Like a Melody'.

13 The song is ended
But the melody lingers on.
1927 Song from *Ziegfeld Follies*.

14 I'm puttin' on my top hat
Tyin' up my white tie
Brushin' off my tails
1935 'Top Hat, White Tie and Tails', performed by Fred Astaire in *Top Hat*.

15 There may be trouble ahead

But while there's moonlight and music and love and
  romance
Let's face the music and dance
1936 'Let's Face the Music and Dance', in the film *Follow the Fleet*.

16 I'm dreaming of a white Christmas,
Just like the ones I used to know,
Where the tree-tops glisten
And children listen
To hear sleigh bells in the snow.
1942 'I'm Dreaming of a White Christmas', in the film *Holiday Inn*.

17 There's No Business Like Show Business.
1946 Title of song from the film *Annie Get Your Gun*.

18 Listen kid, take my advice—never hate a song that has
sold half a million copies.
Comment to the young Cole Porter, attributed.

19 No, for prosperity.
Attributed, when asked whether he wrote his songs for posterity.

Berlin, Sir Isaiah 1907–97

Russian-born British philosopher and historian of ideas. He was
Professor of Social and Political Theory at Oxford (1957–67) and
President of Wolfson College (1966–75). He served as a
diplomat to Russia and the US in World War II.

20 Liberty is liberty, not equality or fairness or justice or
human happiness or a quiet conscience.
1958 *Two Concepts of Liberty*, note.

21 The desire not to be impinged upon, to be left to oneself,
has been the mark of high civilisation both on the part of
individuals and communities.
1959 *Four Essays on Liberty*.

22 Man cannot live without seeking to describe and explain
the universe.
1962 In the *Sunday Times*.

23 No perfect solution is, not merely in practice, but in
principle, possible in human affairs, and any determined
attempt to produce it is likely to lead to suffering,
disillusionment and failure.
1978 *The Crooked Timber of Humanity*, 'The Decline of Utopian
Ideals in the West'.

24 Pluralism—that is, the conception that there are many
different ends that men may seek and still be fully
rational, fully men, capable of understanding each other
and sympathising and deriving light from each other.
1978 *The Crooked Timber of Humanity*, 'The Pursuit of the Ideal'.

Berlusconi, Silvio 1936–

Italian businessman and politician who has at times been
criticized for the conflict of interest between his business
empire and the office of Prime Minister and who is a
controversial figure in European politics.

25 I heard that the game was getting dangerous, and that it
was being played in the two penalty areas, with midfield
being left desolately empty… And we decided to fill that
immense space.
On why he founded Forza Italia, a new political party. Quoted in
Paul Ginsberg *Italy and Its Discontents* (2001).

26 Let's talk about football or women.
2003 Comment at a formal lunch at an abortive summit meeting
of EU leaders, Brussels, Dec.

Bernanos, Georges 1888–1948

French novelist who explored the role of the devil and sin in
modern society. A fervent opponent of Fascism, he lost favour
with conservative Catholics after publishing polemical tracts
against Franco.

27 *Le désir de la prière est déjà une prière.*
The wish for prayer is already a prayer.
1936 *Le Journal d'un curé de campagne*, ch.2 (translated by P
Morris as *Diary of a Country Priest*, 1937).

28 *L'enfer, Madame, c'est de ne plus aimer.*
Hell, Madam, is to no longer love.
1936 *Journal d'un curé de campagne*, ch.2.

Bernard of Chartres d. c.1130

French divine and scholar. He taught logic and grammar at
Chartres school from 1114, becoming Chancellor in 1119. In 1124
he began teaching at Paris. Only fragments of his three
philosophical treatises survive.

29 *Nanos gigantium humeris insidentes.*
Dwarfs standing on the shoulders of giants.
c.1128 Of modern scholars in relation to their ancient
predecessors. Quoted in John of Salisbury *Metalogicon* (1159),
bk.3, ch.4.

St Bernard of Clairvaux 1090–1153

Theologian and reformer, first abbot (1115) of the newly-
founded Cistercian monastery of Clairvaux, Champagne.
Renowned for his studious, ascetic life and eloquence (he
spoke in support of the Second Crusade, 1146), he founded
over 70 monasteries.

30 *Omnes nimirum, ex quo monachi sumus, infirmos
stomachos habemus, et tam necessarium Apostoli de
utendo vino consilium merito non negligimus. Modico,
tamen quod ille praemissit, nescio cur praetermisso.*
Being monks, we all naturally have a weak stomach, and
we therefore justly attend to the Apostle's advice to use
wine. He adds, however, the words 'a little'; I can't think
why I have omitted them.
c.1124 *Apologia ad Guillelmum*, ch.9, section 21.

31 You have been called to hold a high position, but not a
safe one; a sublime position, but not a secure one. How
terrible, how very terrible is the place you hold!
c.1145 Letter to Eugenius III shortly after he had become Pope,
on the dangers of the growth of papal power. Collected in B S
James (ed and trans) *The Letters of St Bernard of Clairvaux*
(1953).

32 *Aiunt non vos esse papam, sed me.*
They say it is not you who are pope, but me.
c.1145 Of his own influence within the Cistercian order. Letter to
Pope Eugenius III.

33 You ordered. I obeyed… I opened my mouth; I spoke;
and at once the Crusaders have multiplied to infinity.
Villages and towns are now deserted. You will scarcely
find one man for every seven women. Everywhere you
see widows whose husbands are still alive.
1146 Letter to Pope Eugenius III describing the effects of
preaching the Second Crusade. Collected in J P Migne (ed)
Patrologia Latina, vol.182, letter no.247.

34 *Liberavi animam meam.*
I have freed my soul.
c.1147 Letter to Abbot Suger.

Bernard, Claude 1813–78

French scientist, considered the founder of contemporary experimental medicine on account of his work on the digestive process and on the vasomotor mechanism.

35 Science does not permit exceptions.
1855–6 *Lessons of Experimental Pathology.*

36 In science, the best precept is to alter and exchange our ideas as fast as science moves ahead.
1865 *An Introduction to the Study of Experimental Medicine*, vol.1, ch.1, section 3 (translated by H C Greene).

37 Science rejects the indeterminate.
1865 *An Introduction to the Study of Experimental Medicine*, vol.1, ch.1, section 3 (translated by H C Greene).

38 True science teaches us to doubt and, in ignorance, to refrain.
1865 *An Introduction to the Study of Experimental Medicine*, vol.1, ch.1, section 3 (translated by H C Greene).

39 Particular facts are never scientific; only generalization can establish science.
1865 *An Introduction to the Study of Experimental Medicine*, vol.1, ch.1, section 3 (translated by H C Greene).

Bernardin de Saint-Pierre, Jacques-Henri 1737–1814

French novelist, friend of Rousseau and enemy of many others, naturalist and precursor of the Romantics. He travelled widely in Martinique, Russia and Madagascar.

40 *Les hommes ne veulent connaître que l'histoire des grands et des rois, qui ne sert à personne.*
Men wish to hear no stories but those about the great and powerful, which are no use to anyone.
1788 *Paul et Virginie.*

41 *Après le rare bonheur de trouver une compagne qui nous soit bien assortie, l'état le moins malheureux de la vie est sans doute de vivre seul.*
After the rare happiness of finding a companion with whom we are well matched, the least unpleasant state of life is without doubt to live alone.
1788 *Paul et Virginie.*

42 *La solitude rétablit aussi bien les harmonies du corps que celles de l'âme.*
Solitude restores the harmonies of the body no less than those of the soul.
1788 *Paul et Virginie.*

43 *On se fait une idée précise de l'ordre, mais non pas du désordre. La beauté, la vertu, le bonheur, ont des proportions; la laideur, le vice, et le malheur, n'en ont point.*
We can form a precise idea of order, but not of disorder. Beauty, virtue, happiness, all have their proportions; ugliness, vice and unhappiness have none.
1788 *Paul et Virginie.*

44 *Le parfum de mille roses ne plaît qu'un instant; mais la douleur que cause une seule de leurs épines dure longtemps après la piqûre.*
The perfume of a thousand roses pleases only for an instant; but the pain caused by a single one of their thorns lasts a long time after the prick.
1788 *Paul et Virginie.*

45 *La mort, mon fils, est un bien pour tous les hommes; elle est la nuit de ce jour inquiet qu'on appelle la vie.*
Death, my son, is a good for all; it is the night of this worrisome day that one calls life.
1788 *Paul et Virginie.*

46 *Artistes, poètes, écrivains, si vous copiez toujours, on ne vous copiera jamais.*
Artists, poets, writers, if you copy others all the time, no one will copy you.
1790 *Mémoires sur la ménagerie.*

Bernays, Edward 1891–1995

US pioneer public relations consultant, born in Vienna. His many books include *Crystallizing Public Opinion* (1923) and *The Engineering of Consent* (1955).

47 The engineering of consent.
1955 His definition of public relations, the field he was credited with founding. *The Engineering of Consent.*

Berners, Dame Juliana *or* Juliana Barnes fl.14c

English nun, traditionally Prioress of Sopwell convent, St Albans. She was the author of the *Treatyse perteynynge to Hawkynge, Huntynge, Fyshynge, and Coote Armiris* (1486).

48 A greyhound should be heeded lyke a snake,
And neckyd lyke a drake,
Backed lyke a bream,
Footed lyke a catte,
Taylled lyke a ratte.
1486 *Treatyse perteynynge to Hawkynge, Huntynge, Fyshynge, and Coote Armiris.*

49 The Salmon is the most stately fish that any man may angle to in fresh water.
1486 *Treatyse perteynyne to Hawkynge, Huntynge, Fyshynge, and Coote Armiris.*

Bernhardt, Sarah *stage-name of* Sarah Henriette Rosine Bernard 1844–1923

French actress. Hailed internationally as one of the leading theatrical performers of her generation, she made her stage debut in 1862 and went on to play many of the great tragic roles in Shakespeare, Racine, Hugo, Rostand, Sardou and others.

50 *J'adore ce cricket; c'est tellement Anglais.*
I do so love cricket—it's so very English.
c.1905 On being taken to see a game of football in Manchester. Quoted in R Buckle *Nijinsky* (1971).

51 For the theatre one needs long arms; it is better to have them too long than too short. An *artiste* with short arms can never, never make a fine gesture.
1907 *Memories of My Life.*

Bernini, Gianlorenzo 1598–1680

Italian sculptor, painter and architect, one of the key figures of Italian Baroque art.

52 Sometimes, in order to imitate the original, it is necessary to put something that is not in the original into a portrait in marble.
Attributed remark made to Paul Fréart, in *Diary of Cavalier Bernini's Journey in France* (1665).

Bernstein, Leonard 1918–90

US conductor, pianist and composer. He achieved fame in 1943 as conductor with the New York Philharmonic. His compositions include three symphonies, a television opera and the musical *West Side Story* (1958).

53 It would be nice to hear someone accidentally whistle something of mine, somewhere, just once.
1960 *The Joy of Music*.

Berra, Yogi Lawrence Peter 1925–

US baseball player and coach. A star with the New York Yankees, he took part in a record 14 World Series (1946–63). He went on to manage the New York Yankees, the New York Mets and the Houston Astros.

54 If the people don't want to come out to the park, nobody's gonna stop them.
Quoted in Colin Jarman *The Guinness Dictionary of Sports Quotations* (1990).

55 He made too many wrong mistakes.
Quoted in Colin Jarman *The Guinness Dictionary of Sports Quotations* (1990).

56 You can observe a lot just by watching.
Quoted in Colin Jarman *The Guinness Dictionary of Sports Quotations* (1990).

57 You can't think and hit at the same time.
Quoted in Colin Jarman *The Guinness Dictionary of Sports Quotations* (1990).

58 It ain't over 'til it's over.
Attributed.

Berry, Chuck (Charles Edward Anderson) 1926–

US black rock 'n' roll singer, whose influential hits included 'Maybelline' (1955), 'School Days' (1957), and 'Johnny B Goode' (1958). In 1959 he was charged with transporting a minor over state lines for immoral purposes and jailed for two years (1962).

59 You know my temperature's risin',
The juke box's blowin' a fuse,
My heart's beatin' rhythm,
My soul keeps a singin' the blues—
Roll over Beethoven,
Tell Tchaikovsky the news.
1956 'Roll over Beethoven'.

Berryman, John originally John Allyn Smith 1914–72

US poet and novelist. His reputation rests on his complex, often obscure poetry, collected in *The Dispossessed* (1948), *Homage to Mistress Bradstreet* (1953) and the extended sequence of *Dream Songs* (1964).

60 We must travel in the direction of our fears.
1942 'A Point of Age'.

61 Headstones stagger under great draughts of time
after heads pass out, and their world must reel
speechless, blind in the end
about its chilling star
1953 'Homage to Mistress Bradstreet', stanza 55.

62 Life, friends, is boring. We must not say so.
1964 'Dream Song No.14'.

63 And moreover my mother taught me as a boy
(repeatedly) 'Ever to confess you're bored
means you have no
Inner Resources.' I conclude now I have no
inner resources, because I am heavy bored.
1964 'Dream Song No.14'.

64 I seldom go to films. They are too exciting
said the Honourable Possum.
1964 'Dream Song No.53'.

65 Bats have no bankers and they do not drink
and cannot be arrested and pay no tax
and, in general, bats have it made.
1964 'Dream Song No.63'.

66 A lone letter from a young man: that is fame.
1968 'Dream Song No.342'.

67 My girls suffered during this month or so,
so did my seminars & lectures &
my poetry even. To be a *critic*, ah,
how deeper and more scientific.
1971 'Olympus'.

68 The artist is extremely lucky who is presented with the worst possible ordeal which will not actually kill him.
1972 Interview in *The Paris Review*, winter issue.

Berton, Pierre 1920–

Canadian writer, journalist and broadcaster. His many works include *The Mysterious North* (1956) and *Why We Act Like Canadians* (1982).

69 A Canadian is somebody who knows how to make love in a canoe.
1973 Interviewed by Dick Brown in *The Canadian*, 22 Dec.

Best, George 1946–

Northern Irish footballer who was the leading scorer for Manchester United in the Football League First Division in 1967–8, and in 1968 won a European Cup medal and the title of European Footballer of the Year.

70 Alcoholics Anonymous might have worked for me if I had been anonymous, but I was not. People kept asking me for my autograph.
2001 In the *Observer*, 30 Dec.

71 I *will* respect this liver. After all, it's not mine.
Referring to his liver transplant. In *Scoring at Half Time* (2003).

72 I told the assembled media that I was not the White Pele and that Pele was in fact the Black George Best.
On his arrival in the United States in 1975. In *Blessed* (2003).

Bethell, (Mary) Ursula 1874–1945

New Zealand poet, born in England. Her works, celebrating detail in nature, include *From a Garden in the Antipodes* (1929) and *Day and Night: Poems 1924–1935* (1939).

73 But beside it I have planted a green Bay-tree,
—A sweet Bay, an Olive, and a Turkey Fig,
—A Fig, an Olive, and a Bay.
1929 *From a Garden in the Antipodes*, 'Detail'.

Bethmann Hollweg, Theobald von 1856–1921

German statesman, Imperial Chancellor (1909–17), who played an important part in events leading to war in 1914. Anxious for a negotiated peace, he was forced from office in 1917.

74 Just for a word 'neutrality'—a word which in wartime has so often been disregarded—just for a scrap of paper Great Britain is going to make war on a kindred nation who desires nothing better than to be friends with her.
1914 On Britain's reaction to the German invasion of neutral

Belgium, 4 Aug. Quoted in *British Documents on the Origins of the War 1898–1914* (1926), vol.11.

75 If the iron dice roll, may God help us.
   1914 Speech in the Reichstag.

Bethune, Norman 1890–1939

Canadian physician and revolutionary.

76 The function of the artist is to disturb. His duty is to arouse the sleeper, to shake the complacent pillars of the world. He reminds the world of its dark ancestry, and shows the world its present, and points the way to its new birth. He is at once the product and the preceptor of his time.
   1937 Letter from Madrid, 5 May. Quoted in Ted Allen and Sydney Gordon *The Scalpel, The Sword* (1952).

Betjeman, Sir John 1906–84

English poet, writer and broadcaster, whose nostalgic light verse, often masking an underlying melancholy, achieved great popularity. Appointed Poet Laureate in 1972, he was also a defender of traditional architecture and a perceptive social critic.

77 Oh! Chintzy, chintzy cheeriness,
   Half dead and half alive.
   1930 'Death in Leamington', first published in the *London Mercury*.

78 Sing on, with hymns uproarious,
   Ye humble and aloof,
   Look up! and oh, how glorious
   He has restored the roof!
   1931 *Mount Zion*, 'Hymn'.

79 Broad of Church and broad of Mind,
   Broad before and broad behind,
   A keen ecclesiologist,
   A rather dirty Wykehamist.
   1931 *Mount Zion*, 'The Wykehamist'.

80 Ghastly Good Taste, or a depressing story of the rise and fall of English architecture.
   1933 Title and sub-title of book.

81 He sipped at the weak hock and seltzer
   As he gazed at the London skies
   Through the Nottingham lace of the curtains
   Or was it his bees-winged eyes?
   1937 *Continual Dew*, 'The Arrest of Oscar Wilde at The Cadogan Hotel'.

82 Spirits of well-shot woodcock, partridge, snipe,
   Flutter and bear him up the Norfolk sky:
   In that red house in a red mahogany book-case
   The stamp collection waits with mounts long dry.
   1937 *Continual Dew*, 'Death of King George V'.

83 Come, friendly bombs, and fall on Slough
   It isn't fit for humans now
   There isn't grass to graze a cow
   Swarm over, Death!
   1937 *Continual Dew*, 'Slough'.

84 Pam, I adore you, Pam, you great mountainous
      sports girl,
   Whizzing them over the net, full of the strength of five:
   That old Malvernian brother, you zephyr and khaki
      shorts girl,
   Although he's playing for Woking,

Can't stand up to your wonderful backhand drive.
   1940 *Old Lights for New Chancels*, 'Pot Pourri from a Surrey Garden'.

85 Think of what our Nation stands for,
   Books from Boots' and country lanes,
   Free speech, free passes, class distinction,
   Democracy and proper drains.
   Lord, put beneath Thy special care
   One-eighty-nine Cadogan Square.
   1940 *Old Lights for New Chancels*, 'In Westminster Abbey'.

86 The test of an abstract picture, for me, is not my first reaction to it, but how long I can stand it hanging on the wall of a room where I am living.
   1944 *John Piper*.

87 Miss J. Hunter Dunn, Miss J. Hunter Dunn,
   Furnish'd and burnish'd by Aldershot sun,
   What strenuous singles we played after tea,
   We in the tournament—you against me!
   1945 *New Bats in Old Belfries*, 'A Subaltern's Love-Song'.

88 Miss Joan Hunter Dunn, Miss Joan Hunter Dunn,
   I can hear from the car-park the dance has begun.
   Oh! full Surrey twilight! importunate band!
   Oh! strongly adorable tennis-girl's hand!
   1945 *New Bats in Old Belfries*, 'A Subaltern's Love-Song'.

89 For a full spring-tide of blossom seethed and departed
      hence,
   Leaving land-locked pools of jonquils by sunny garden
      fence.
   1945 *New Bats in Old Belfries*, 'May-Day Song for North Oxford'.

90 And low the mists of evening lie
   And lightly skims the midge.
   1945 *New Bats in Old Belfries*, 'Henley-on-Thames'.

91 Rumbling under blackened girders, Midland, bound for
      Cricklewood,
   Puffed its sulphur to the sunset where that Land of
      laundries stood.
   1945 *New Bats in Old Belfries*, 'Parliament Hill Fields'.

92 Up the hill where stucco houses in Virginia creeper
      drown—
   And my childish wave of pity, seeing children carrying
      down
   Sheaves of drooping dandelions to the courts of Kentish
      Town.
   1945 *New Bats in Old Belfries*, 'Parliament Hill Fields'.

93 Bournemouth is one of the few English towns one can safely call 'her'.
   1949 Radio talk, later collected in *First and Last Loves* (1952), 'Bournemouth'.

94 St Endellion! St Endellion! The name is like a ring of bells.
   1950 Radio talk, later collected in *First and Last Loves* (1952), 'St Endellion'.

95 Imagine the position of the modern architect. Picture the young fellow to be put into a 'profession' because trade is considered beneath him (another antiquarian prejudice). The young fellow hasn't exactly got a legal mind, like father; he's not much good at essays, so he can't write; he faints at the sight of blood so can't be a doctor. What is there for him to do? Architecture of course.
   1952 *First and Last Loves*.

96 Oh prams on concrete balconies, what will your children see?
   1952 *First and Last Loves*.

97 History must not be written with bias, and both sides
must be given, even if there is only one side.
1952 *First and Last Loves.*

98 And girls in slacks remember Dad,
And oafish louts remember Mum.
1954 *A Few Late Chrysanthemums*, 'Christmas'.

99 And is it true? And is it true,
This most tremendous tale of all,
Seen in a stained-glass window's hue,
A Baby in an ox's stall?
The Maker of the stars and sea
Become a Child on earth for me?
1954 *A Few Late Chrysanthemums*, 'Christmas'.

1 Gaily into Ruislip Gardens
Runs the red electric train
With a thousand Ta's and Pardon's
Daintily alights Elaine.
1954 *A Few Late Chrysanthemums*, 'Middlesex'.

2 Then Harrow-on-the-Hill's a rocky island
And Harrow churchyard full of sailor's graves,
And the constant click and kissing of the trolley busses
hissing
Is the level to the Wealdstone turned to waves.
1954 *A Few Late Chrysanthemums*, 'Harrow-on-the-Hill'.

3 But I'm dying now and done for,
What on earth was all the fun for?
I am ill and old and terrified and tight.
1954 *A Few Late Chrysanthemums*, 'Sun and Fun—Song of a
Night-club Proprietress'.

4 Does Mum, the Persil-user, still believe
That there's no Devil and that youth is bliss?
As certain as the sun behind the Downs
And quite as plain to see, the Devil walks.
1954 *A Few Late Chrysanthemums*, 'Original Sin on the Sussex
Coast'.

5 Phone for the fish knives, Norman
As Cook is a little unnerved;
You kiddies have crumpled the serviettes
And I must have things daintily served.
1954 *A Few Late Chrysanthemums*, 'How To Get On In Society'.

6 In the licorice fields at Pontefract
My love and I did meet
And many a burdened licorice bush
Was blooming round our feet;
Red hair she had and golden skin,
Her sulky lips were shaped for sin,
Her sturdy legs were flannel-slack'd,
The strongest legs in Pontefract.
1954 *A Few Late Chrysanthemums*, 'The Licorice Fields at
Pontefract'.

7 In the Garden City Café with its murals on the wall
Before a talk on 'Sex and Civics' I meditated on the Fall.
1954 *A Few Late Chrysanthemums*, 'Huxley Hall'.

8 It's awf'lly bad luck on Diana
Her ponies have swallowed their bits;
She fished down their throats with a spanner
And frightened them all into fits.
1954 *A Few Late Chrysanthemums*, 'Hunter Trails'.

9 Oh wasn't it naughty of Smudges?
Oh, Mummy, I'm sick with disgust.
She threw me in front of the Judges

And my silly old collarbone's bust.
1954 *A Few Late Chrysanthemums*, 'Hunter Trails'.

10 I heard the church bells hollowing out the sky
Deep beyond deep, like never-ending stars.
1960 *Summoned By Bells*, ch.1.

11 Childhood is measured out by sounds and smells
And sights, before the dark of reason grows.
1960 *Summoned By Bells*, ch.4.

12 The dread of beatings! Dread of being late!
And, greatest dread of all, the dread of games!
1960 *Summoned by Bells*, ch.7.

Beuys, Joseph 1921–86

German avant-garde artist. Professor of Sculpture at Düsseldorf
Academy (1961–71), his works were typically 'assemblages' of
rubbish, deliberately anti-formal. He co-founded the German
Green Party.

13 A total work of art is only possible in the context of the
whole of society. Everyone will be a necessary co-
creator of a social architecture, and, so long as anyone
cannot participate, the ideal form of democracy has not
been reached. Whether people are artists, assemblers of
machines or nurses, it is a matter of participating in the
whole.
1972 From an interview with G Jappe (translated by J
Wheelwright), in *Studio International*, vol.184, no.950, Dec.
Quoted in C Harrison and P Wood (eds) *Art in Theory 1900–1990*
(1992).

Bevan, Aneurin 1897–1960

Welsh Labour politician, a miner who took a leading part in the
1926 General Strike, and a brilliant, irreverent orator. He
entered politics in 1929 and joined the Labour Party (1931). As
Minister of Health (1945–51), he introduced the National
Health Service (1948).

14 The worst thing I can say about democracy is that it has
tolerated the right honourable gentleman [Neville
Chamberlain] for four and a half years.
1929 House of Commons, 23 Jul.

15 We have been the dreamers. We have been the sufferers.
Now we are the builders. We want the complete political
extinction of the Tory Party—and 25 years of Labour
Government, for we cannot do in five years what
requires to be done.
1945 Labour Party conference, Blackpool, 18 May.

16 This island is made mainly of coal and surrounded by fish.
Only an organizing genius could produce a shortage of
coal and a shortage of fish at the same time.
1945 Speech at Blackpool. Reported in the *Daily Herald*, 25 May.

17 No amount of cajolery, and no attempts at ethical or
social seduction, can eradicate from my heart a deep
and burning hatred for the Tory Party that inflicted those
experiences on me. So far as I am concerned, they are
lower than vermin.
1948 Speech on the inter-war depression, made at the
inauguration of the National Health Service, 5 Jul.

18 In Place of Fear.
1952 Title of his book about disarmament.

19 We know what happens to people who stay in the
middle of the road. They get run over.
1953 In the *Observer*, Dec.

20 A man suffering from petrified adolescence.
Of Winston Churchill. Quoted in Vincent Brome *Aneurin Bevan* (1953).

21 I am not going to spend any time whatsoever attacking the Foreign Secretary. Quite honestly, I am beginning to feel extremely sorry for him. If we complain about the tune, there is no reason to attack the monkey when the organ grinder is present.
1957 Expressing his wish to address Prime Minister Harold Macmillan rather than Selwyn Lloyd on the Suez crisis in the House of Commons, May.

22 If you carry this resolution, you will send a Foreign Secretary—whoever he may be—naked into the conference chamber. You call that statesmanship. I call it an emotional spasm.
1957 Labour Party conference speech against unilateral disarmament, Oct.

23 I read the newspapers avidly. It is my one form of continuous fiction.
1960 In *The Times*, 29 Mar.

24 Politics is a blood sport.
Quoted in Jennie Lee *My Life with Nye* (1980).

Beveridge, William Henry Beveridge, 1st Baron
1879–1963

British economist, administrator and social reformer, Director of the London School of Economics (1919–37). His *Report on Social Insurance and Allied Services* (The Beveridge Report, 1942) helped to create the Welfare State.

25 The trouble in modern democracy is that men do not approach to leadership until they have lost the desire to lead anyone.
1934 In the *Observer*, 15 Apr.

26 The object of government in peace and in war is not the glory of rulers or of races, but the happiness of the common man.
1942 *Social Insurance and Allied Services*, pt.7.

27 The most urgent tasks in Britain, once war is over, are, on the one hand, the making of a common attack on the giant evils of Want, Disease, Ignorance and Squalor, and on the other hand, the re-equipping of British industry.
1944 *Full Employment in a Free Society.*

28 The state is or can be master of money, but in a free society it is master of very little else.
1948 *Voluntary Action*, ch.12.

Bevin, Ernest 1881–1951

English Labour politician. He formed the National Transport and General Workers' Union, becoming its General Secretary (1921–40), then entered politics. He was appointed Minister of Labour and National Service in the coalition, and later Foreign Secretary (1945–51).

29 The most conservative man in the world is the British trade unionist, when you want to change him.
1927 Speech to Trade Union Congress, 8 Sep.

30 If you open that Pandora's box, you never know what Trojan 'orses will appear.
1948 Expressing doubts about the value of the newly formed Council of Europe. Recalled by his secretary Sir Roderick Barclay in Michael Charlton *The Price of Victory* (1983).

31 Well you know, Chris, we've got to give them something and I think we'll give them this talking shop in Strasbourg—the Council of Europe.
1948 Comment to Christopher Mayhew. Quoted in Michael Charlton *The Price of Victory* (1983).

32 A turn-up in a million.
On himself. Quoted in his entry by Baron Francis-Williams in the *Dictionary of National Biography* (1951–60).

33 Anything you make a mistake about, I will get you out of, and anything you do well I will take the credit for.
Attributed, to a subordinate. Quoted in A J P Taylor *From the Boer War to the Cold War: Essays on Twentieth-Century Europe* (1995).

Bhagavad Gita

A sacred Hindu text, part of the Mahabharata. All translations are from J Mascaro (1978).

34 As the Spirit of our mortal body wanders on in childhood and youth and old age, the Spirit wanders on to a new body: of this the sage has no doubts.
Ch.2, v.13.

35 As a man leaves an old garment and puts on one that is new, the spirit leaves his mortal body and puts on one that is new.
Ch.2, v.22.

36 Leave all things behind, and come unto me for thy salvation. I will make thee free from the bondage of sins. Fear no more.
Ch.18, v.66.

Bible (Old Testament)

All quotations are taken from the King James, or Authorized, translation of the Bible (1611).

37 In the beginning God created the heaven and the earth. And the earth was without form, and void; and darkness was upon the face of the deep. And the spirit of God moved upon the face of the waters.
Genesis 1:1–2.

38 And God said, Let there be light: and there was light.
Genesis 1:3.

39 And God called the light Day, and the darkness he called Night. And the evening and the morning were the first day.
Genesis 1:5.

40 And God saw that it was good.
Genesis 1:10.

41 And God said, Let us create man in our image, after our likeness: and let them have dominion over the fish of the sea, and over the fowl of the air, and over the cattle, and over all the earth, and over every creeping thing that creepeth upon the earth. So God created man in his own image, in the image of God created he him; male and female created he them. And God blessed them, and God said unto them, Be fruitful and multiply, and replenish the earth, and subdue it: and have dominion over the fish of the sea, and over the fowl of the air, and over every living thing that moveth upon the earth.
Genesis 1:26–8.

42 And on the seventh day God ended his work which he had made, and he rested on the seventh day from all his work which he had made. And God blessed the seventh day and sanctified it: because that in it he had rested

from all his work which God created and made.
Genesis 2:2–3.

43 And the LORD God formed man out of the dust of the ground, and breathed into his nostrils the breath of life; and man became a living soul.
Genesis 2:7.

44 And the LORD God planted a garden eastwards in Eden; and there he put the man whom he had formed. And out of the ground made the LORD God to grow every tree that is pleasant for the sight, and good for food; the tree of life also in the midst of the garden, and the tree of knowledge of good and evil.
Genesis 2:8–9.

45 And the LORD God took the man and put him into the garden of Eden to dress it and to keep it. And the LORD God commanded the man, saying, Of every tree of the garden thou mayest freely eat: But of the tree of the knowledge of good and evil, thou shalt not eat of it: for in the day that thou eatest thereof thou shalt surely die.
Genesis 2:15–17.

46 And the LORD God said, It is not good that the man should be alone; I will make him an help meet for him.
Genesis 2:18.

47 And the LORD God caused a deep sleep to fall on Adam, and he slept: and he took one of his ribs, and closed up the flesh instead thereof; And the rib, which the LORD God had taken from man, made he a woman, and brought her unto the man. And Adam said, This is now bone of my bones, and flesh of my flesh: she shall be called Woman, because she was taken out of Man. Therefore shall a man leave his father and his mother, and shall cleave unto his wife: and they shall be one flesh.
Genesis 2:21–4.

48 Now the serpent was more subtil than any beast of the field which the LORD God had made.
Genesis 3:1.

49 And the serpent said unto the woman, Ye shall not surely die: For God doth know that in the day ye eat thereof, then your eyes shall be opened, and ye shall be as gods, knowing good and evil.
Genesis 3:4–5.

50 And when the woman saw that the tree was good for food, and that it was pleasant to the eyes, and a tree to be desired to make one wise she took of the fruit thereof, and did eat, and gave also to her husband with her; and he did eat. And the eyes of them both were opened, and they knew that they were naked; and they sewed fig leaves together, and made themselves aprons. And they heard the voice of the LORD God walking in the garden in the cool of the day: and Adam and his wife hid themselves from the presence of the LORD God amongst the trees of the garden.
Genesis 3:6–8. In the Geneva Bible of 1560, the word 'aprons' was rendered 'breeches', and the version was therefore known as the Breeches Bible.

51 And he said, I heard thy voice in the garden, and I was afraid, because I was naked; and I hid myself. And he said, Who told thee that thou wast naked? Hast thou eaten of the tree, whereof I commanded thee that thou shouldst not eat?
Genesis 3:10–11.

52 And the man said, The woman whom thou gavest to be with me, she gave me of the tree, and I did eat. And the LORD God said unto the woman, What is this that thou hast done? And the woman said, The serpent beguiled me, and I did eat.
Genesis 3:12–13.

53 And the LORD God said unto the serpent, Because thou hast done this, thou art cursed above all cattle, and above every beast of the field; upon thy belly thou shalt go, and dust shalt thou eat all the days of thy life: And I will put enmity between thy seed and her seed; it shall bruise thy head, and thou shalt bruise his heel.
Genesis 3:14–15.

54 Unto the woman he said, I will greatly multiply thy sorrow and conception; in sorrow thou shalt bring forth children; and thy desire shall be for thy husband, and he shall rule over thee.
Genesis 3:16.

55 And unto Adam he said, Because thou hast hearkened unto the voice of thy wife, and hast eaten of the tree, of which I commanded thee, saying, Thou shalt not eat of it: cursed is the ground for thy sake; in sorrow shalt thou eat of it all the days of thy life.
Genesis 3:17.

56 In the sweat of thy face shalt thou eat bread, till thou return to the ground; for out of it wast thou taken: for dust thou art, and unto dust shall return.
Genesis 3:19.

57 And the LORD God said, Behold, the man is become as one of us, to know good and evil: and now, lest he put forth his hand, and take also of the tree of life, and eat, and live for ever: Therefore the LORD God sent him forth from the garden of Eden, to till the ground from whence he was taken. So he drove out the man; and he placed at the east of the garden of Eden Cherubims, and a flaming sword which turned every way, to keep the tree of life.
Genesis 3:21–4.

58 And Adam knew Eve his wife; and she conceived and bare Cain, and said, I have gotten a man from the LORD.
Genesis 4:1.

59 And the LORD said unto Cain, Where is Abel thy brother? And he said, I know not: Am I my brother's keeper? And he said, What hast thou done? the voice of thy brother's blood crieth unto me from the ground.
Genesis 4:9.

60 My punishment is greater than I can bear.
Cain. Genesis 4:10.

61 And the LORD said unto him, Therefore whoever slayeth Cain, vengeance shall be taken on him sevenfold. And the LORD set a mark upon Cain lest any finding him should kill him.
Genesis 4:15.

62 And Cain went out from the presence of the LORD, and dwelt in the land of Nod, on the east of Eden.
Genesis 4:16.

63 And all the days of Methuselah were nine hundred sixty and nine years; and he died.
Genesis 5:27.

64 They went in two and two unto Noah into the ark, the male and the female, as God had commanded Noah.
Genesis 7:9.

65 But the dove found no rest for the sole of her foot.
Genesis 8:9.

66 And the dove came to him in the evening; and, lo, in her mouth was an olive leaf pluckt off: so Noah knew that the waters were abated from off the earth.
Genesis 8:11.

67 I will not again curse the ground any more for man's sake; for the imagination of man is evil from his youth; neither will I again smite any more every thing living, as I have done.While the earth remaineth, seedtime and harvest, and cold and heat, and summer and winter, and day and night shall not cease.
Genesis 8:21–2.

68 At the hand of every man's brother will I require the life of man.Whoso sheddeth man's blood, by man shall his blood be shed: for in the image of God made he man.
Genesis 9:5–6.

69 I do set my bow in the cloud, and it shall be for a token of a covenant between me and the earth.
Genesis 9:13.

70 He was a mighty hunter before the LORD: wherefore it is said, Even as Nimrod the mighty hunter before the LORD.
Genesis 10:9.

71 Therefore is the name of it called Babel; because the LORD did there confound the language of all the earth: and from thence did the LORD scatter them abroad upon the face of all the earth.
Genesis 11:9.

72 Now the LORD had said unto Abram, Get thee out of thy country, and from thy kindred, and from thy father's house, unto a land that I will shew thee: And I will make of thee a great nation, and I will bless thee, and make thy name great; and thou shalt be a blessing: And I will bless them that bless thee, and curse him that curseth thee: and in thee shall all families of the earth be blessed.
Genesis 12:1–3.

73 But the men of Sodom were wicked and sinners before the LORD exceedingly.
Genesis 13:13.

74 Thou shalt be buried in a good old age.
Genesis 15:15.

75 Behold, thou art with child, and shalt bear a son, and shalt call his name Ishmael; because the LORD hath heard thy affliction. And he will be a wild man; his hand will be against every man, and every man's hand against him; and he shall dwell in the presence of all his brethren.
Genesis 16:11–12.

76 And when Abram was ninety years old and nine, the LORD appeared to Abram, and said unto him, I am the Almighty God: walk before me, and be thou perfect.
Genesis 17:1.

77 And I will establish my covenant between me and thee and thy seed after thee in their generations for an everlasting covenant, to be a God unto thee, and to thy seed after thee. And I will give unto thee, and to thy seed after thee, the land wherein thou art a stranger, all the land of Canaan, for an everlasting possession; and I will be their God... Every man child among you shall be circumcised.
Genesis 17:7–10.

78 Shall not the Judge of all the earth do right.
Genesis 18:25.

79 Then the LORD rained upon Sodom and upon Gomorrah brimstone and fire from the LORD out of heaven.
Genesis 19:24.

80 But his wife looked back from behind him, and she became a pillar of salt.
Genesis 19:26.

81 Take now thy son, thine only son Isaac, whom thou lovest.
Genesis 22:2.

82 My son, God will provide himself a lamb for a burnt offering.
Genesis 22:8.

83 Esau sells his birthright for a mess of pottage.
1560 Chapter heading for Genesis 25 (in the Geneva Bible).

84 And the boys grew: and Esau was a cunning hunter, a man of the field; and Jacob was a plain man, dwelling in tents.
Genesis 25:27.

85 Esau said, Behold, I am at the point to die: and what profit shall this birthright do to me? And Jacob said, Swear to me this day: and he sware unto him: and he sold his birthright unto Jacob. Then Jacob gave Esau bread and pottage of lentiles; and he did eat and drink, and rose up, and went his way: thus Esau despised his birthright.
Genesis 25:32–4.

86 And Jacob said to Rebekah his mother, Behold, Esau my brother is a hairy man, and I am a smooth man.
Genesis 27:11.

87 Thy brother came with subtilty, and hath taken away thy blessing.
Genesis 27:35.

88 And he dreamed and behold a ladder set up on the earth, and the top of it reached to heaven: and behold the angels of God ascending and descending on it.
Genesis 28:12.

89 And Jacob awaked out of his sleep, and he said, Surely the LORD is in this place; and I knew it not.
Genesis 28:16.

90 And Jacob served seven years for Rachel; and they seemed unto him but a few days, for the love he had to her.
Genesis 29:20.

91 The LORD watch between me and thee, when we are absent one from another.
Genesis 31:49.

92 I will not let thee go, except thou bless me.
Genesis 32:26.

93 Now Israel loved Joseph more than all his children, because he was the son of his old age: and he made him a coat of many colours.
Genesis 37:3.

94 And they said to one another, Behold, this dreamer cometh.
Genesis 37:19.

95 And all his sons and all his daughters rose up to comfort him; but he refused to be comforted; and he said, For I will go down into the grave unto my son mourning. Thus his father wept for him.
Genesis 37:35.

96 And Onan knew that the seed should not be his; and it came to pass, when he went in unto his brother's wife, that he spilled it on the ground, lest that he should give seed to his brother.
Genesis 38:9.

97 And she caught him by his garment, saying, Lie with me: and he left his garment in her hand, and fled, and got him out.
Genesis 39:12.

98 And the seven thin ears devoured the seven rank and full ears. And Pharaoh awoke, and, behold, it was a dream.
Genesis 41:7.

99 Ye are spies; to see the nakedness of the land ye are come.
Genesis 42:9.

1 And he said, My son shall not go down with you; for his brother is dead, and he is left alone: if mischief befall him by the way in the which ye go, then shall ye bring down my gray hairs with sorrow to the grave.
Genesis 42:38.

2 And the famine was sore in the land.
Genesis 43:1.

3 I will give you the good of the land of Egypt, and ye shall eat the fat of the land.
Genesis 45:18.

4 So he sent his brethren away, and they departed: and he said unto them, See that ye fall not out by the way.
Genesis 45:24.

5 And Jacob said unto Pharaoh, The days of the years of my pilgrimage are an hundred and thirty years: few and evil have the days of the years of my life been, and have not attained unto the days of the years of the life of my fathers in the days of their pilgrimage.
Genesis 47:9.

6 Unstable as water, thou shalt not excel.
Genesis 49:4.

7 And he said, Who made thee a prince and a judge over us? intendest thou to kill me, as thou killedst the Egyptian?
Exodus 2:14.

8 And the angel of the LORD appeared unto him in a flame of fire out of the midst of a bush: and he looked, and, behold, the bush burned with fire, and the bush was not consumed.
Exodus 3:2.

9 And he said, Draw not nigh hither: put off thy shoes from off thy feet, for the place whereon thou standest is holy ground.
Exodus 3:5.

10 And Moses hid his face; for he was afraid to look upon God.
Exodus 3:6.

11 And I am come down to deliver them out of the hand of the Egyptians, and to bring them up out of that land unto a good land and a large, unto a land flowing with milk and honey.
Exodus 3:8.

12 And God said unto Moses, I AM THAT I AM.
Exodus 3:14.

13 But I am slow of speech, and of a slow tongue.
Exodus 4:10.

14 Let my people go.
Exodus 7:16.

15 Your lamb shall be without blemish, a male of the first year.
Exodus 12:5.

16 And thus shall ye eat it; with your loins girded, your shoes on your feet, and your staff in your hand; and ye shall eat it in haste: it is the LORD's passover. For I will pass through the land of Egypt this night, and will smite all the firstborn in the land of Egypt, both man and beast; and against all the gods of Egypt I will execute judgment: I am the LORD.
Exodus 12:11–12.

17 And Pharaoh rose up in the night, he and all his servants, and all the Egyptians; and there was a great cry in Egypt; for there was not a house where there was not one dead.
Exodus 12:30.

18 And the Egyptians were urgent upon the people, that they might send them out of the land in haste; for they said, We be all dead men.
Exodus 12:33.

19 And the LORD went before them by day in a pillar of a cloud, to lead them the way; and by night in a pillar of fire, to give them light; to go by day and night.
Exodus 13:21.

20 The LORD is a man of war: the LORD is his name.
Exodus 15:3.

21 And the children of Israel said unto them, Would to God we had died by the hand of the LORD in the land of Egypt, when we sat by the flesh pots, and when we did eat bread to the full; for ye have brought us forth to this wilderness, to kill this whole assembly with hunger.
Exodus 16:3.

22 And it came to pass, when Moses held up his hand, that Israel prevailed: and when he let down his hand, Amalek prevailed.
Exodus 17:11.

23 And God spake all these words, saying, I am the LORD thy God, which have brought thee out of the land of Egypt, out of the house of bondage.
Thou shalt have no other gods before me.
Thou shalt not make unto thee any graven image, or any likeness of any thing that is in heaven above, or that is in the earth beneath, or that is in the water under the earth:
Thou shalt not bow down thyself to them, nor serve them: for I the LORD thy God am a jealous God, visiting the iniquity of the fathers upon the children unto the third and fourth generation of them that hate me;
And shewing mercy unto thousands of them that love me, and keep my commandments.
Thou shalt not take the name of the LORD thy God in vain; for the LORD will not hold him guiltless that taketh his name in vain.
Remember the sabbath day, to keep it holy. Six days thou shalt labour and do all thy work: But the seventh day is the sabbath of the LORD thy God: in it thou shalt not do any work, thou, nor thy son, nor thy daughter, thy manservant, nor thy maidservant, nor thy cattle, nor thy stranger that is within thy gates:
For in six days the LORD made heaven and earth, the sea,

and all that in them is, and rested the seventh day: wherefore the LORD blessed the sabbath day, and hallowed it.

Honour thy father and thy mother: that thy days may be long upon the land which the LORD thy God giveth thee.

Thou shalt not kill.

Thou shalt not commit adultery.

Thou shalt not steal.

Thou shalt not bear false witness against thy neighbour.

Thou shalt not covet thy neighbour's house, thou shalt not covet thy neighbour's wife, nor his manservant, nor his maidservant, nor his ox, nor his ass, nor any thing that is thy neighbour's.
Exodus 20:1–17.

24 And if any mischief follow, then thou shalt give life for life, Eye for eye, tooth for tooth, hand for hand, foot for foot. Burning for burning, wound for wound, stripe for stripe.
Exodus 21:23–4.

25 And thou shalt put in the breastplate of judgment the Urim and the Thummim; and thy shall be upon Aaron's heart, when he goeth in before the LORD: and Aaron shall bear the judgment of the children of Israel upon his heart before the LORD continually.
Exodus 28:30.

26 And he received them at their hand, and fashioned it with a graving tool, after he had made it a molten calf: and they said, These be thy gods, O Israel, which brought thee up out of the land of Egypt.
Exodus 32:4.

27 And the LORD said unto Moses, I have seen this people, and, behold, it is a stiffnecked people.
Exodus 32:9.

28 Who is on the LORD's side? let him come unto me.
Exodus 32:26.

29 And the LORD spake unto Moses face to face, as a man speaketh unto his friend.
Exodus 33:11.

30 And he said, My presence shall go with thee, and I will give thee rest. And he said unto him, If thy presence go not with me carry us not up hence.
Exodus 33:14–15.

31 And he said, I beseech thee, shew me thy glory.
Exodus 33:18.

32 And he said, I will make all my goodness pass before thee… And he said, Thou canst not see my face: for there shall no man see me, and live.
Exodus 33:19–20.

33 For I am the LORD your God: ye shall therefore sanctify yourselves, and ye shall be holy; for I am holy: neither shall ye defile yourselves with any manner of creeping thing that creepeth upon the earth.
Leviticus 11:44.

34 But the goat, on which the lot fell to be the scapegoat, shall be presented alive before the LORD, to make an atonement with him, and to let him go for a scapegoat into the wilderness.
Leviticus 16:10.

35 Thou shalt not avenge, nor bear any grudge against the children of thy people, but thou shalt love thy neighbour as thyself: I am the LORD.
Leviticus 19:18.

36 The LORD bless thee, and keep thee:
The LORD make his face shine upon thee, and be gracious unto thee:
The LORD lift up his countenance upon thee, and give thee peace.
Numbers 6:24–6.

37 And there we saw the giants, the sons of Anak, which come of the giants: and we were in our own sight as grasshoppers, and so we were in their sight.
Numbers 13:33.

38 The rod of Aaron for the house of Levi was budded, and brought forth buds, and bloomed blossoms, and yielded almonds.
Numbers 17:8.

39 And Moses made a serpent of brass, and put it upon a pole, and it came to pass, that if a serpent had bitten any man, when he beheld the serpent of brass, he lived.
Numbers 21:9.

40 And the LORD opened the mouth of the ass, and she said unto Balaam, What have I done unto thee, that thou hast smitten me these three times?
Numbers 22:28.

41 God is not a man, that he should lie; neither the son of man, that he should repent: hath he said, and shall he not do it? or hath he spoken, and shall he not make it good?
Numbers 23:19.

42 What hath God wrought!
Numbers 23:23. These words were transmitted by Samuel Morse on 24 May 1844, the first electronic telegraph message.

43 Be sure your sin will find you out.
Numbers 32:23.

44 I call heaven and earth to witness against you this day.
Deuteronomy 4:26.

45 Hear, O Israel: the LORD our God is one LORD: And thou shalt love the LORD thy God with all thy soul, and with all thy might.
Deuteronomy 6:4–5.

46 Ye shall not go after other gods, of the gods of the people which are round about you; (For the LORD thy God is a jealous God among you).
Deuteronomy 6:14–15.

47 And he humbled thee, and suffered thee to hunger, and fed thee with manna, which thou knewest not, neither did thy fathers know; that he might make thee know that man doth not live by bread only, but by every word that proceedeth out of the mouth of the LORD doth man live.
Deuteronomy 8:3.

48 Speak not thou in thine heart, after that the LORD thy God hath cast them out from before thee, saying, For my righteousness the LORD hath brought me in to possess this land: but for the wickedness of these nations the LORD doth drive them out from before thee.
Deuteronomy 9:4.

49 If there arise among you a prophet, or a dreamer of dreams, and giveth thee a sign or a wonder… Thou shalt not hearken.
Deuteronomy 13:1–3.

50 When thou cuttest down thine harvest in thy field, and

hast forgot a sheaf in the field, thou shalt not go again to fetch it: it shall be for the stranger, for the fatherless, and for the widow: that the LORD thy God may bless thee in all the work of thine hands.
Deuteronomy 24:19.

51 Thou shalt not muzzle the ox when he treadeth out the corn.
Deuteronomy 25:4.

52 Cursed be he that removeth his neighbour's landmark. And all the people shall say, Amen.
Deuteronomy 27:17.

53 The secret things belong unto the LORD our God; but those things which are revealed belong unto us and our children for ever, that we may do all the words of this law.
Deuteronomy 29:29.

54 I call heaven and earth to record this day against you, that I have set before you life and death, blessing and cursing: therefore choose life, that both thou and thy seed may live.
Deuteronomy 30:19.

55 Give ear, O ye heavens, and I will speak: and hear, O earth, the words of my mouth. My doctrine shall drop as the rain, my speech shall distil as the dew, as the small rain upon the tender herb, and as the showers upon the grass.
Deuteronomy 32:1–2.

56 He found him in a desert land, and in the waste howling wilderness; he led him about, he instructed him, he kept him as the apple of his eye.
Deuteronomy 32:10.

57 Thou art waxen fat, thou art grown thick, thou art covered with fatness.
Deuteronomy 32:15.

58 As thy days, so shall thy strength be.
Deuteronomy 33:25.

59 The eternal God is thy refuge, and underneath are the everlasting arms.
Deuteronomy 33:27.

60 So Moses the servant of the LORD died there in the land of Moab… but no man knoweth of his sepulchre unto this day.
Deuteronomy 34:5–6.

61 There shall not any man be able to stand before thee all the days of thy life: as I was with Moses, so I will be with thee: I will not fail thee, nor forsake thee.
Joshua 1:5.

62 Have I not commanded thee? Be strong and of a good courage: be not afraid, neither be thou dismayed: for the LORD thy God is with thee whithersoever thou goest.
Joshua 1:9.

63 Behold, when we come into the land, thou shalt bind this line of scarlet thread in the window which thou didst let us down by.
Joshua 2:18.

64 So the people shouted when the priests blew with the trumpets: and it came to pass, when the people heard the sound of the trumpet, and the people shouted with a great shout, that the wall fell down flat, so that the people went up into the city, every man straight before him, and they took the city.
Joshua 6:20.

65 I am going the way of all the earth.
Joshua 23:14.

66 Choose you this day whom ye will serve… but as for me and my house, we will serve the LORD.
Joshua 24:15.

67 Then Jael Heber's wife took a nail of the tent, and took an hammer in her hand, and went softly unto him and smote the nail into his temples, and fastened it into the ground: for he was fast asleep and weary. So he died.
Judges 4:21.

68 He asked for water, and she brought him milk; she brought forth butter in a lordly dish. She put her hand to the nail, and her right hand to the workmen's hammer; and with the hammer she smote Sisera, she smote off his head, when she had pierced and stricken through his temples. At her feet he bowed, he fell, he lay down: at her feet he bowed he fell: where he bowed, there he fell down dead. The mother of Sisera looked out at a window, and cried through the lattice, Why is his chariot so long in coming? why tarry the wheels of his chariots?
Judges 5:25–8.

69 The sword of the LORD, and of Gideon.
Judges 7:18.

70 Then said they unto him, Say now Shibboleth: and he said Sibboleth: for he could not frame to pronounce it right. Then they took him, and slew him.
Judges 12:6.

71 And he said unto them, Out of the eater came forth meat, and out of the strong came forth sweetness. And they could not in three days expound the riddle.
Judges 14:14.

72 If ye had not plowed with my heifer, ye had not found out my riddle.
Judges 14:18.

73 He smote them hip and thigh.
Judges 15:8.

74 With the jawbone of an ass, heaps upon heaps, with the jaw of an ass have I slain a thousand men.
Judges 15:16.

75 And she said, The Philistines be upon thee, Samson. And he awoke out of his sleep, and said, I will go out as at other times before, and shake myself. And he wist not that the LORD was departed from him. But the Philistines took him, and put out his eyes, and brought him down to Gaza, and bound him with fetters of brass; and he did grind in the prison house.
Judges 16:20–21.

76 And Samson said, Let me die with the Philistines. And he bowed himself with all his might; and the house fell upon the lords, and upon all the people that were therein. So the dead which he slew at his death were more than they which he slew in his life.
Judges 16:30.

77 In those days there was no king in Israel, but every man did that which was right in his own eyes.
Judges 17:6.

78 The people arose as one man.
Judges 20:8.

79 Intreat me not to leave thee, or to return from following after thee: for whither thou goest, I will go; and where thou lodgest, I will lodge: thy people shall be my people, and thy God my God:

Where thou diest, will I die, and there will I be buried: the LORD do so to me, and more also, if ought but death part thee and me.
Ruth 1:16–17

80 Now the Lord saith, Be it far from me; for them that honour me I will honour, and they that despise me shall be lightly esteemed.
1 Samuel 2:30.

81 The LORD called Samuel: and he answered, Here am I. And he ran unto Eli, and said, Here am I; for thou calledst me. And he said, I called not; lie down again.
1 Samuel 3:4–5.

82 Speak, LORD; for thy servant heareth.
1 Samuel 3:9.

83 Behold, I will do a thing in Israel, at which both the ears of every one that heareth it shall tingle.
1 Samuel 3:11.

84 Be strong, and quit yourselves like men.
1 Samuel 4:9.

85 And it came to pass, when he made mention of the ark of God, that he fell from off the seat backward by the side of the gate, and his neck brake, and he died: for he was an old man, and heavy.
1 Samuel 4:18.

86 Behold, thou art old, and thy sons walk not in thy ways: now make us a king to judge us like all the nations.
1 Samuel 8:5.

87 God save the king.
1 Samuel 10:24.

88 But now thy kingdom shall not continue: the LORD hath sought him a man after his own heart, and the LORD hath commanded him to be captain over his people.
1 Samuel 13:14.

89 Hath the LORD as great delight in burnt offerings and sacrifices, as in obeying the voice of the LORD? Behold, to obey is better than sacrifice, and to hearken than the fat of rams. For rebellion is as the sin of witchcraft, and stubbornness is as iniquity and idolatry.
1 Samuel 15:22–3.

90 Look not on his countenance, or on the height of his stature; because I have refused him: for the LORD seeth not as man seeth; for man looketh on the outward appearance, but the LORD looketh on the heart.
1 Samuel 16:7.

91 Now he was ruddy, and withal of a beautiful countenance, and goodly to look to. And the LORD said, Arise, anoint him: for this is he.
1 Samuel 16:12.

92 I know thy pride, and the naughtiness of thine heart.
1 Samuel 17:28.

93 David said moreover, The LORD that delivered me out of the paw of the lion, and out of the paw of the bear, he will deliver me out of the hand of this Philistine. And Saul said unto David, Go, and the LORD be with thee.
1 Samuel 17:37.

94 And he took his staff in his hand, and chose him five smooth stones out of the brook.
1 Samuel 17:40.

95 And the Philistine said unto David, Am I a dog, that thou comest to me with staves?
1 Samuel 17:43.

96 Saul hath slain his thousands, and David his ten thousands.
1 Samuel 18:7.

97 Behold, I have played the fool, and have erred exceedingly.
1 Samuel 26:21.

98 Saul and Jonathan were lovely and pleasant in their lives, and in their death they were not divided: they were swifter than eagles, they were stronger than lions… I am distressed for thee, my brother Jonathan: very pleasant hast thou been unto me: thy love to me was wonderful, passing the love of women. How are the mighty fallen, and the weapons of war perished!
2 Samuel 1:23–7.

99 And David danced before the LORD with all his might.
2 Samuel 6:14.

1 Set ye Uriah in the forefront of the hottest battle, and retire ye from him, that he may be smitten, and die.
2 Samuel 11:15.

2 But the poor man had nothing, save one little ewe lamb
2 Samuel 12:3.

3 Thou art the man.
2 Samuel 12:7.

4 For we must needs die, and are as water spilt on the ground, which cannot be gathered up again: neither doth God respect any person.
2 Samuel 14:14.

5 And when Ahithophel saw that his counsel was not followed, he saddled his ass, and arose, and gat him home to his house, to his city, and put his household in order, and hanged himself.
2 Samuel 17:23.

6 And the king was much moved, and went up to the chamber over the gate, and wept: and as he went, thus he said, O my son Absalom, my son, my son Absalom! would God I had died for thee, O Absalom, my son, my son!
2 Samuel 18:33.

7 Nay: but I will surely buy it of thee at a price: neither will I offer burnt offerings unto the Lord my God of that which dost cost me nothing.
2 Samuel 24:24.

8 Now king David was old and stricken in years; and they covered him with clothes, but he gat no heat.
1 Kings 1:1.

9 I go the way of all the earth: be thou strong therefore, and shew thyself a man.
1 Kings 2:2.

10 I am but a little child: I know not how to go out or come in.
1 Kings 3:7.

11 But if ye shall at all turn from following me… Then will I cut off Israel out of the land which I have given them; and this house, which I have hallowed for my name, will I cast out of my sight; and Israel shall be a proverb and a byword among all people.
1 Kings 9:6–7.

12 And when the queen of Sheba heard of the fame of Solomon concerning the name of the LORD, she came to prove him with hard questions.
1 Kings 10:1.

13 I believed not the words, until I came, and mine eyes had seen it: and, behold, the half was not told me.
1 Kings 10:7.

14 But king Solomon loved many strange women.
1 Kings 11:1.

15 My little finger shall be thicker than my father's loins. And now whereas my father did lade you with a heavy yoke, I will add to your yoke: my father hath chastised you with whips, but I will chastise you with scorpions.
1 Kings 12:10–11.

16 He slept with his fathers.
1 Kings 14:20.

17 And the ravens brought him bread and flesh in the morning, and bread and flesh in the evening; and he drank of the brook.
Of Elijah. 1 Kings 17:6.

18 Elijah came unto all the people, and said, How long halt ye between two opinions? if the LORD be God, follow him: but if Baal, then follow him. And the people answered him not a word.
1 Kings 18:21.

19 Cry aloud: for he is a god; either he is talking, or he is pursuing, or he is in a journey, or peradventure he sleepeth, and must be wakened.
1 Kings 18:27.

20 There is a sound of abundance of rain.
1 Kings 18:41.

21 Behold, there ariseth a little cloud out of the sea, like a man's hand.
1 Kings 18:44.

22 Elijah…girded up his loins, and ran before Ahab.
1 Kings 18:46.

23 But he himself went a day's journey into the wilderness, and came and sat down under a juniper tree: and he requested for himself that he might die; and said, It is enough, now, O LORD, take away my life; for I am not better than my fathers.
1 Kings 19:4.

24 And, behold, the LORD passed by, and a great and strong wind rent the mountains, and brake in pieces the rocks before the LORD; but the LORD was not in the wind: and after the wind an earthquake; but the LORD was not in the earthquake: And after the earthquake a fire; but the LORD was not in the fire: and after the fire a still small voice.
1 Kings 19:11–12.

25 Elijah passed by him and cast his mantle upon him.
1 Kings 19:19.

26 In the place where dogs licked the blood of Naboth shall dogs lick thy blood, even thine. And Ahab said to Elijah, Hast thou found me, O mine enemy?
1 Kings 21:19–20.

27 A certain man drew a bow at a venture, and smote the king of Israel between the joints of the harness.
1 Kings 22:34.

28 Behold there appeared a chariot of fire, and horses of fire, and parted them both asunder; and Elijah went up by a whirlwind into heaven. And Elisha saw it, and he cried, My father, my father, the chariot of Israel, and the horsemen thereof.
2 Kings 2:11–12.

29 The spirit of Elijah doth rest on Elisha.
2 Kings 2:15.

30 Go up, thou bald head.
2 Kings 2:23.

31 Say unto her, Is it well with thee? is it well with thy husband? is it well with the child? And she answered, It is well.
2 Kings 4:26.

32 Let him come now to me, and he shall know that there is a prophet in Israel.
2 Kings 5:8.

33 Is it peace? and Jehu said, What hast thou to do with peace? turn thee behind me.
2 Kings 9:18.

34 The driving is like the driving of Jehu the son of Nimshi; for he driveth furiously.
2 Kings 9:20.

35 And when Jehu was come to Jezreel, Jezebel heard of it; and she painted her face, and tired her head, and looked out at a window.
2 Kings 9:30.

36 And he lifted up his face to the window, and said, Who is on my side? who? And there looked out to him two or three eunuchs.
2 Kings 9:32.

37 So they threw her down: and some of her blood was sprinkled on the wall, and on the horses: and he trode her under foot.
2 Kings 9:33.

38 And they went to bury her: but they found no more of her than the skull, and the feet, and the palms of her hands.
2 Kings 9:35.

39 Now, behold, thou trustest upon the staff of this bruised reed, even upon Egypt, on which if a man lean, it will go into his hand, and pierce it: so is Pharaoh king of Egypt unto all that trust on him.
2 Kings 18:21.

40 For we are strangers before thee, and soujourners, as were all our fathers: our days on the earth are as a shadow, and there is none abiding.
1 Chronicles 29:15.

41 And he died in a good old age, full of days, riches, and honour: and Solomon his son reigned in his stead.
1 Chronicles 29:28.

42 And king Solomon gave to the queen of Sheba all her desire, whatsoever she asked, beside that which she had brought unto the king.
2 Chronicles 9:12.

43 For the eyes of the LORD run to and fro throughout the whole earth, to shew himself strong in the behalf of them whose heart is perfect toward him. Herein thou hast done foolishly: therefore from henceforth thou shalt have wars.
2 Chronicles 16:9.

44 Be not afraid nor dismayed by reason of this great multitude; for the battle is not yours, but God's.
2 Chronicles 20:15.

45 Every one with one of his hands wrought in the work, and with the other hand held a weapon.
Nehemiah 4:17.

46 So will I go in unto the king, which is not according to the law: and if I perish, I perish.
Esther 4:16.

47 And the LORD said unto Satan, Whence comest thou? Then Satan answered the LORD, and said, From going to and fro in the earth, and from walking up and down in it.
Job 1:7.

48 Naked came I out of my mother's womb, and naked shall I return thither: the LORD gave, and the LORD hath taken away; blessed be the name of the LORD.
Job 1:21.

49 Skin for skin, yea, all that a man hath will he give for his life. But put forth thine hand now, and touch his bone and his flesh, and he will curse thee to thy face.
Job 2:4–5.

50 And he took him a potsherd to scrape himself withal; and he sat down among the ashes. Then said his wife unto him, Dost thou still retain thine integrity? curse God, and die.
Job 2:8–9.

51 Let the day perish wherein I was born, and the night in which it was said, There is a man child conceived.
Job 3:3.

52 There the wicked cease from troubling, and there the weary be at rest.
Job 3:17.

53 Shall mortal man be more just than God? shall a man be more pure than his maker?
Job 4:17.

54 Yet man is born unto trouble, as the sparks fly upward.
Job 5:7.

55 My days are swifter than a weaver's shuttle
Job 7:6.

56 Wherefore then hast thou brought me forth out of the womb? Oh that I had given up the ghost, and no eye had seen me!
Job 10:18.

57 Canst thou by searching find out God? canst thou find out the Almighty unto perfection? It is as high as heaven; what canst thou do? deeper than hell; what canst thou know? The measure thereof is longer than the earth, and broader than the sea.
Job 11:7–9.

58 No doubt but ye are the people, and wisdom shall die with you.
Job 12:2.

59 With the ancient is wisdom; and in length of days understanding.
Job 12:12.

60 Though he slay me, yet will I trust in him: but I will maintain mine own ways before him.
Job 13:15.

61 Man that is born of a woman is of few days, and full of trouble. He cometh forth like a flower, and is cut down:

62 I have heard many such things: miserable comforters are ye all.
Job 16:2.

63 I am escaped with the skin of my teeth.
Job 19:20.

64 For I know that my redeemer liveth, and that he shall stand at the latter day upon the earth: And though after my skin worms destroy this body, yet in my flesh shall I see God.
Job 19:25–6.

65 But ye should say, Why persecute we him, seeing the root of the matter is found in me?
Job 19:28.

66 Behold, my desire is, that the Almighty would answer me, and that mine adversary had written a book.
Job 31:35.

67 Great men are not always wise: neither do the aged understand judgment.
Job 32:9.

68 Therefore doth Job open his mouth in vain; he multiplieth words without knowledge.
Job 35:16.

69 Who is this that darkeneth counsel by words without knowledge? Gird up now thy loins like a man; for I will demand of thee, and answer thou me. Where wast thou when I laid the foundations of the earth? declare, if thou hast understanding.
Job 38:2–4.

70 When the morning stars sang together, and all the sons of God shouted for joy.
Job 38:7.

71 Hitherto shalt thou come, but no further: and here shall thy proud waves be stayed.
Job 38:11.

72 Hath the rain a father? or who hath begotten the drops of dew?
Job 38:28.

73 Canst thou bind the sweet influences of Pleiades, or loose the bands of Orion?
Job 38:31.

74 Hast thou given the horse strength? hast thou clothed his neck with thunder? Canst thou make him afraid as a grasshopper? the glory of his nostrils is terrible. He paweth in the valley and rejoiceth in his strength: he goeth on to meet the armed men.
Job 39:19–21.

75 He swalloweth the ground with fierceness and rage: neither believeth he that it is the sound of the trumpet. He saith among the trumpets, Ha, ha, and he smelleth the battle afar off, the thunder of the captains, and the shouting.
Job 39:24–5.

76 Behold now behemoth, which I made with thee; he eateth grass as an ox.
Job 40:15.

77 The shady trees cover him with their shadow; the willows of the brook compass him about. Behold, he drinketh up a river, and hasteth not: he trusteth that he

can draw up Jordan into his mouth.
Job 40:22–3.

78 Canst thou draw out leviathan with an hook?
Job 41:1.

79 I have heard of thee by the hearing of the ear: but now mine eye seeth thee. Wherefore I abhor myself, and repent in dust and ashes.
Job 42:5–6.

80 So the LORD blessed the latter end of Job more than his beginning.
Job 42:12.

81 Blessed is the man that walketh not in the counsel of the ungodly, nor standeth in the way of sinners, nor sitteth in the seat of the scornful. But his delight is in the law of the LORD; and in his law doth he meditate day and night. And he shall be like a tree planted by the rivers of water, that bringeth forth his fruit in his season; his leaf also shall not wither; and whatsoever he doeth shall prosper. The ungodly are not so: but are like the chaff which the wind driveth away.
Psalms 1:1–4.

82 Why do the heathen rage, and the people imagine a vain thing?
Psalms 2:1.

83 He that sitteth in the heavens shall laugh: the LORD shall have them in derision.
Psalms 2:4.

84 Thou art my Son: this day have I begotten thee. Ask of me, and I shall give thee the heathen for thine inheritance, and the uttermost parts of the earth for thy possession. Thou shalt break them with a rod of iron; thou shalt dash them in pieces like a potter's vessel.
Psalms 2:7–9.

85 Stand in awe, and sin not: commune with your own heart upon your bed, and be still.
Psalms 4:4.

86 O LORD our Lord, how excellent is thy name in all the earth! who hast set thy glory above the heavens. Out of the mouth of babes and sucklings hast thou ordained strength because of thine enemies, that thou mightest still the enemy and the avenger.
Psalms 8:1–2.

87 When I consider thy heavens, the work of thy fingers, the moon and the stars, which thou hast ordained; What is man, that thou art mindful of him? and the son of man, that thou visitest him? For thou hast made him a little lower than the angels, and hast crowned him with glory and honour. Thou madest him to have dominion over the works of thy hands; thou hast put all things under his feet.
Psalms 8:3–6.

88 The fool hath said in his heart, There is no God.
Psalms 14:1.

89 They are all gone aside, they are all together become filthy: there is none that doeth good, no, not one.
Psalms 14:3.

90 LORD, who shall abide in thy tabernacle? who shall dwell in thy holy hill? He that walketh uprightly, and worketh righteousness, and speaketh the truth in his heart.
Psalms 15:1–2.

91 The lines are fallen unto me in pleasant places; yea, I have a goodly heritage.
Psalms 16:6.

92 For thou wilt not leave my soul in hell; neither wilt thou suffer thine Holy One to see corruption.
Psalms 16:10.

93 Keep me as the apple of the eye, hide me under the shadow of thy wings.
Psalms 17:8.

94 For by thee I have run through a troop; and by my God have I leaped over a wall.
Psalms 18:29.

95 He maketh my feet like hinds' feet, and setteth me upon my high places.
Psalms 18:33.

96 Some trust in chariots, and some in horses: but we will remember the name of the LORD our God.
Psalms 20:7.

97 My God, my God, why hast thou forsaken me? why art thou so far from helping me, and from the words of my roaring?
Psalms 22:1.

98 But I am a worm, and no man; a reproach of men, and despised of the people. All they that see me laugh me to scorn: they shoot out the lip, they shake the head, saying, He trusted on the LORD that he would deliver him: let him deliver him, seeing he delighted in him.
Psalms 22:6–8.

99 I am poured out like water, and all my bones are out of joint: my heart is like wax; it is melted in the midst of my bowels.
Psalms 22:14.

1 They pierced my hands and my feet. I may tell all my bones: they look *and* stare upon me. They part my garments among them, and cast lots upon my vesture.
Psalms 22:16–18.

2 The LORD is my shepherd; I shall not want. He maketh me to lie down in green pastures: he leadeth me beside the still waters. He restoreth my soul: he leadeth me in the paths of righteousness for his name's sake. Yea, though I walk through the valley of the shadow of death, I will fear no evil: for thou art with me; thy rod and thy staff they comfort me. Thou preparest a table before me in the presence of mine enemies: thou anointest my head with oil; my cup runneth over. Surely goodness and mercy shall follow me all the days of my life: and I will dwell in the house of the LORD for ever.
Psalms 23:1–6.

3 The earth is the LORD's, and the fulness thereof; the world, and they that dwell therein.
Psalms 24:1.

4 Lift up your heads, O ye gates; and be ye lift up, ye everlasting doors; and the King of glory shall come in. Who is this King of glory? The LORD strong and mighty, the LORD mighty in battle.
Psalms 24:7–8.

5 Remember not the sins of my youth, nor my transgressions.
Psalms 25:7.

6 The LORD is my light and my salvation; whom shall I fear?

the LORD is the strength of my life; of whom shall I be afraid?
Psalms 27:1.

7 Though an host should encamp against me, my heart shall not fear: though war should rise against me, in this will I be confident. One thing have I desired of the LORD, that will I seek after; that I may dwell in the house of the LORD all the days of my life, to behold the beauty of the LORD, and to inquire in his temple.
Psalms 27:3–4.

8 Thou hast turned for me my mourning into dancing: thou hast put off my sackcloth, and girded me with gladness.
Psalms 30:11.

9 Into thine hand I commit my spirit: thou hast redeemed me, O LORD God of truth.
Psalms 31:5.

10 For this shall every one that is godly pray unto thee in a time when thou mayest be found: surely in the floods of great waters they shall not come nigh unto him. Thou *art* my hiding place; thou shalt preserve me from trouble; thou shalt compass me about with songs of deliverance. Selah.
Psalms 32:6–7.

11 I will instruct thee and teach thee in the way which thou shalt go: I will guide thee with mine eye. Be ye not as the horse, or as the mule, which have no understanding: whose mouth must be held in with bit and bridle, lest they come near unto thee.
Psalms 32:8–9.

12 I sought the LORD, and he heard me, and delivered me from all my fears.
Psalms 34:4.

13 O taste and see that the LORD is good: blessed is the man that trusteth in him. O fear the LORD, ye his saints: for there is no want to them that fear him. The young lions do lack, and suffer hunger: but they that seek the LORD shall not want any good thing.
Psalms 34:8–10.

14 The children of men put their trust under the shadow of thy wings.
Psalms 36:7.

15 Delight thyself also in the LORD, and he shall give thee the desires of thine heart. Commit thy way unto the LORD; trust also in him; and he shall bring *it* to pass.
Psalms 37:4–5.

16 But the meek shall inherit the earth; and shall delight themselves in the abundance of peace.
Psalms 37:11.

17 I have been young and now am old; yet have I not seen the righteous forsaken, nor his seed begging bread.
Psalms 37:25.

18 I waited patiently for the LORD, and he inclined unto me, and heard my cry. He brought me up also out of an horrible pit, out of the miry clay, and set my feet upon a rock, and established my goings.
Psalms 40:1–2.

19 Yea, mine own familiar friend, in whom I trusted, which did eat of my bread, hath lifted up his heel against me.
Psalms 41:9.

20 As the hart panteth after the water brooks, so panteth my soul after thee, O God. My soul thirsteth for God, for the living God: when shall I come and appear before God?
Psalms 42:1–2.

21 Why art thou cast down, O my soul? and why art thou disquieted in me? hope thou in God: for I shall yet praise him for the help of his countenance.
Psalms 42:5.

22 Deep calleth unto deep at the noise of thy waterspouts: all thy waves and thy billows are gone over me.
Psalms 42:7.

23 Yea, for thy sake are we killed all the day long; we are counted as sheep for the slaughter.
Psalms 44:22.

24 God is our refuge and strength, a very present help in trouble. Therefore will not we fear, though the earth be removed, and though the mountains be carried into the midst of the sea.
Psalms 46:1–2.

25 There is a river, the streams whereof shall make glad the city of God, the holy place of the tabernacles of the most High. God is in the midst of her; she shall not be moved: God shall help her, and that right early.
Psalms 46:4–5.

26 He maketh wars to cease unto the end of the earth; he breaketh the bow, and cutteth the spear in sunder; he burneth the chariot in the fire.
Be still, and know that I am God: I will be exalted among the heathen, I will be exalted in the earth.
Psalms 46:9–10.

27 Great is the LORD, and greatly to be praised in the city of our God, in the mountain of his holiness. Beautiful for situation, the joy of the whole earth, is mount Zion, on the sides of the north, the city of the great King.
Psalms 48:1–2.

28 For I acknowledge my transgressions: and my sin is ever before me. Against thee, thee only, have I sinned, and done this evil in thy sight: that thou mightest be justified when thou speakest, and be clear when thou judgest. Behold, I was shapen in iniquity; and in sin did my mother conceive me.
Psalms 51:3–5.

29 Behold, thou desirest truth in the inward parts: and in the hidden part thou shalt make me to know wisdom. Purge me with hyssop, and I shall be clean: wash me, and I shall be whiter than snow.
Psalms 51:6–7.

30 Create in me a clean heart, O God; and renew a right spirit within me. Cast me not away from thy presence; and take not thy holy spirit from me. Restore unto me the joy of thy salvation; and uphold me with thy free spirit. Then will I teach transgressors thy ways; and sinners shall be converted unto thee.
Psalms 51:10–13.

31 Deliver me from bloodguiltiness, O God, thou God of my salvation: and my tongue shall sing aloud of thy righteousness. O Lord, open thou my lips; and my mouth shall shew forth thy praise. For thou desirest not sacrifice; else would I give it: thou delightest not in burnt offering. The sacrifices of God are a broken spirit: a

broken and a contrite heart, O God, thou wilt not despise.
Psalms 51:14–17.

32 Oh that I had wings like a dove! for then would I fly away, and be at rest.
Psalms 55:6.

33 Lead me to the rock that is higher than I.
Psalms 61:2.

34 Truly my soul waiteth upon God: from him cometh my salvation. He only is my rock and my salvation; he is my defence; I shall not be greatly moved.
Psalms 62:1–2.

35 O God, thou art my God; early will I seek thee: my soul thirsteth for thee, my flesh longeth for thee in a dry and thirsty land, where no water is.
Psalms 63:1.

36 Thou crownest the year with thy goodness; and thy paths drop fatness.
Psalms 65:11.

37 God be merciful unto us, and bless us; and cause his face to shine upon us; Selah. That thy way may be known upon earth, thy saving health among all nations. Let the people praise thee, O God; let all the people praise thee.
Psalms 67:1–3.

38 Sing unto God, sing praises to his name: extol him that rideth upon the heavens by his name JAH, and rejoice before him. A father of the fatherless, and a judge of the widows, is God in his holy habitation. God setteth the solitary in families: he bringeth out those which are bound with chains: but the rebellious dwell in a dry land.
Psalms 68:4–6.

39 Thou hast ascended on high, thou hast led captivity captive: thou hast received gifts for men; yea, for the rebellious also, that the LORD God might dwell among them.
Psalms 68:18.

40 In thee, O LORD, do I put my trust: let me never be put to confusion.
Psalms 71:1.

41 Truly God is good to Israel, even to such as are of a clean heart. But as for me, my feet were almost gone; my steps had well nigh slipped. For I was envious at the foolish, when I saw the prosperity of the wicked.
Psalms 73:1–3.

42 When I thought to know this, it was too painful for me; Until I went into the sanctuary of God; then understood I their end.
Psalms 73:16–17.

43 Nevertheless I am continually with thee: thou hast holden me by my right hand. Thou shalt guide me with thy counsel, and afterward receive me to glory. Whom have I in heaven but thee? and there is none upon earth that I desire beside thee. My flesh and my heart faileth: but God is the strength of my heart, and my portion for ever.
Psalms 73:23–6.

44 I am the LORD thy God, which brought thee out of the land of Egypt: open thy mouth wide, and I will fill it.
Psalms 81:10.

45 How amiable are thy tabernacles, O LORD of hosts!

My soul longeth, yea, even fainteth for the courts of the LORD: my heart and my flesh crieth out for the living God.
Yea, the sparrow hath found an house, and the swallow a nest for herself, where she may lay her young, even thine altars, O LORD of hosts, my King, and my God.
Psalms 84:1–3.

46 Who passing through the valley of Baca make it a well; the rain also filleth the pools.
They go from strength to strength, every one of them in Zion appeareth before God.
Psalms 84:6–7.

47 For a day in thy courts is better than a thousand. I had rather be a doorkeeper in the house of my God, than to dwell in the tents of wickedness.
Psalms 84:10.

48 Glorious things are spoken of thee, O city of God.
Psalms 87:3.

49 Lord, thou hast been our dwelling place in all generations. Before the mountains were brought forth, or ever thou hadst formed the earth and the world, even from everlasting to everlasting, thou art God.
Psalms 90:1–2.

50 For a thousand years in thy sight are but as yesterday when it is past, and as a watch in the night.
Psalms 90:4.

51 The days of our years are threescore years and ten; and if by reason of strength they be fourscore years, yet is their strength labour and sorrow; for it is soon cut off, and we fly away.
Psalms 90:10.

52 So teach us to number our days that we may apply our hearts unto wisdom.
Psalms 90:12.

53 Surely he shall deliver thee from the snare of the fowler, and from the noisome pestilence.
He shall cover thee with his feathers, and under his wings shalt thou trust: his truth shall be thy shield and buckler.
Thou shalt not be afraid for the terror by night; nor for the arrow that flieth by day;
Nor for the pestilence that walketh in darkness; nor for the destruction that wasteth at noonday.
A thousand shall fall at thy side, and ten thousand at thy right hand, but it shall not come nigh thee.
Psalms 91:3–7.

54 Because thou hast made the LORD, which is my refuge, even the most high, thy habitation.
Psalms 91:9.

55 They shall still bring forth fruit in old age; they shall be fat and flourishing.
Psalms 92:14.

56 He that planted the ear, shall he not hear? he that formed the eye, shall he not see?
Psalms 94:9.

57 O come let us sing unto the LORD: let us make a joyful noise to the rock of our salvation. Let us come before his presence with thanksgiving, and make a joyful noise unto him with psalms.
Psalms 95:1–2.

58 Harden not your heart, as in the provocation, and as in the day of temptation in the wilderness: When your fathers tempted me, proved me, and saw my work. Forty years long was I grieved with this generation, and said, It is a people that do err in their heart, and they have not known my ways: Unto whom I sware in my wrath that they should not enter into my rest.
Psalms 95:8–11.

59 O worship the LORD in the beauty of holiness: fear before him, all the earth.
Psalms 96:9.

60 Make a joyful noise unto the LORD, all ye lands. Serve the LORD with gladness: come before his presence with singing. Know ye that the LORD he is God: it is he that hath made us, and not we ourselves; we are his people, and the sheep of his pasture.
Psalms 100:1–3.

61 Of old hast thou laid the foundation of the earth: and the heavens are the work of thy hands.
Psalms 102:25.

62 Bless the LORD, O my soul: and all that is within me, bless his holy name. Bless the LORD, O my soul, and forget not all his benefits: Who forgiveth all thine iniquities; who healeth all thy diseases; Who redeemeth thy life from destruction; who crowneth thee with loving kindness and tender mercies; Who satisfieth thy mouth with good things; so that thy youth is renewed like the eagle's.
Psalms 103:1–5.

63 The LORD is merciful and gracious, slow to anger, and plenteous in mercy. He will not always chide: neither will he keep his anger for ever. He hath not dealt with us after our sins; nor rewarded us according to our iniquities.
Psalms 103:8–10.

64 For as the heaven is high above the earth, so great is his mercy toward them that fear him. As far as the east is from the west, so far hath he removed our transgressions from us.
Psalms 103:11–12.

65 Like as a father pitieth his children, so the LORD pitieth them that fear him. For he knoweth our frame; he remembereth that we are dust.
Psalms 103:13–14.

66 As for man, his days are as grass: as a flower of the field, so he flourisheth. For the wind passeth over it, and it is gone; and the place thereof shall know it no more.
Psalms 103:15–16.

67 He causeth the grass to grow for the cattle, and herb for the service of man: that he may bring forth food out of the earth; And wine that maketh glad the heart of man, and oil to make his face to shine, and bread which strengtheneth man's heart.
Psalms 104:14–15.

68 Man goeth forth unto his work and to his labour until the evening.
Psalms 104:23.

69 So is this great and wide sea, wherein are things creeping innumerable, both small and great beasts.
There go the ships: there is that leviathan, whom thou hast made to play therein.
These wait all upon thee; that thou mayest give them their meat in due season.
Psalms 104:25–7.

70 Their soul abhorreth all manner of meat; and they draw near unto the gates of death.
Psalms 107:18.

71 They that go down to the sea in ships, that do business in great waters;
These see the works of the LORD, and his wonders in the deep.
Psalms 107:23–4.

72 They reel to and fro, and stagger like a drunken man, and are at their wits' end.
Psalms 107:27.

73 The LORD said unto my Lord, Sit thou at my right hand, until I make thine enemies thy footstool.
Psalms 110:1.

74 The LORD hath sworn, and will not repent, Thou art a priest for ever after the order of Melchizedek.
Psalms 110:4.

75 The fear of the LORD is the beginning of wisdom.
Psalms 111:10.

76 For thou hast delivered my soul from death, mine eyes from tears, and my feet from falling. I will walk before the LORD in the land of the living. I believed, therefore have I spoken: I was greatly afflicted: I said in my haste, All men are liars.
Psalms 116:8–11.

77 Precious in the sight of the LORD is the death of his saints.
Psalms 116:15.

78 The stone which the builders refused is become the head stone of the corner. This is the LORD's doing; it is marvellous in our eyes. This is the day which the LORD hath made; we will rejoice and be glad in it.
Psalms 118:22–4.

79 Blessed be he that cometh in the name of the LORD: we have blessed you out of the house of the LORD.
Psalms 118:26.

80 Wherewithal shall a young man cleanse his way? by taking heed thereto according to thy word.
Psalms 119:9.

81 Thy word have I hid in mine heart, that I might not sin against thee.
Psalms 119:11.

82 I have more understanding than all my teachers: for thy testimonies are my meditation.
Psalms 119:99.

83 How sweet are thy words unto my taste! yea, sweeter than honey to my mouth!
Psalms 119:103.

84 Thy word is a lamp unto my feet, and a light unto my path.
Psalms 119:105.

85 The entrance of thy words giveth light; it giveth understanding unto the simple.
Psalms 119:130.

86 Great peace have they which love thy law: and nothing shall offend them.
Psalms 119:165.

87 I will lift up mine eyes unto the hills, from whence

cometh my help. My help cometh from the LORD, which made heaven and earth. He will not suffer thy foot to be moved: he that keepeth thee will not slumber. Behold, he that keepeth Israel shall neither slumber nor sleep. The LORD is thy keeper: the LORD is thy shade upon thy right hand. The sun shall not smite thee by day, nor the moon by night. The LORD shall preserve thee from all evil: he shall preserve thy soul. The LORD shall preserve thy going out and thy coming in from this time forth, and even for evermore.
Psalms 121:1–8.

88 I was glad when they said unto me, Let us go into the house of the LORD.
Psalms 122:1.

89 Pray for the peace of Jerusalem: they shall prosper that love thee. Peace be within thy walls, and prosperity within thy palaces.
Psalms 122:6–7.

90 They that trust in the LORD shall be as mount Zion, which cannot be removed, but abideth for ever.
Psalms 125:1.

91 They that sow in tears shall reap in joy. He that goeth forth and weepeth, bearing precious seed, shall doubtless come again with rejoicing, bringing his sheaves with him.
Psalms 126:5–6.

92 Except the LORD build the house, they labour in vain that build it: except the LORD keep the city, the watchman waketh but in vain. It is vain for you to rise up early, to sit up late, to eat the bread of sorrows: for so he giveth his beloved sleep.
Psalms 127:1–2.

93 Lo, children are an heritage of the LORD: and the fruit of the womb is his reward. As arrows are in the hand of a mighty man; so are children of the youth. Happy is the man that hath his quiver full of them: they shall not be ashamed, but they shall speak with the enemies in the gate.
Psalms 127:3–5.

94 Thy wife shall be as a fruitful vine by the sides of thine house: thy children like olive plants round about thy table.
Psalms 128:3.

95 Out of the depths have I cried unto thee, O LORD. Lord, hear my voice: let thine ears be attentive to the voice of my supplications. If thou, LORD, shouldest mark iniquities, O LORD, who shall stand? But, there is forgiveness with thee, that thou mayest be feared.
Psalms 130:1–4.

96 Behold, how good and how pleasant it is for brethren to dwell together in unity! It is like the precious ointment upon the head, that ran down upon the beard, even Aaron's beard: that went down to the skirts of his garments; As the dew of Hermon, and as the dew that descended upon the mountains of Zion: for there the LORD commanded the blessing, even life for evermore.
Psalms 133:1–3.

97 O give thanks unto the LORD; for he is good: for his mercy endureth for ever.
Psalms 136:1.

98 By the rivers of Babylon, there we sat down, yea, we wept, when we remembered Zion. We hanged our harps upon the willows in the midst thereof. For there they that carried us away captive required of us a song; and they that wasted us required of us mirth, saying, Sing us one of the songs of Zion. How shall we sing the LORD's song in a strange land?
Psalms 137:1–4.

99 O LORD, thou hast searched me, and known me. Thou knowest my downsitting and mine uprising, thou understandest my thought afar off. Thou compassest my path and my lying down, and art acquainted with all my ways. For there is not a word in my tongue, but, lo, O LORD, thou knowest it altogether. Thou hast beset me behind and before, and laid thine hand upon me. Such knowledge is too wonderful for me; it is high, I cannot attain unto it.
Psalms 139:1–6.

1 Whither shall I go from thy spirit? or whither shall I flee from thy presence?
If I ascend up into heaven, thou art there: if I make my bed in hell, behold, thou art there.
If I take the wings of the morning, and dwell in the uttermost parts of the sea;
Even there shall thy hand lead me, and thy right hand shall hold me.
If I say, Surely the darkness shall cover me; even the night shall be light about me.
Yea, the darkness hideth not from thee; but the night shineth as the day: the darkness and the light are both alike to thee.
Psalms 139:7–12.

2 I will praise thee; for I am fearfully and wonderfully made: marvellous are thy works; and that my soul knoweth right well. My substance was not hid from thee, when I was made in secret, and curiously wrought in the lowest parts of the earth. Thine eyes did see my substance, yet being unperfect; and in thy book all my members were written, which in continuance were fashioned, when as yet there was none of them.
Psalms 139:14–16.

3 Search me, O God, and know my heart: try me, and know my thoughts: And see if there be any wicked way in me, and lead me in the way everlasting.
Psalms 139:23–4.

4 Set a watch, O LORD, before my mouth; keep the door of my lips.
Psalms 141:3.

5 The eyes of all wait upon thee; and thou givest them their meat in due season. Thou openest thine hand, and satisfiest the desire of every living thing.
Psalms 145:15–16.

6 He telleth the number of the stars; he calleth them all by their names.
Psalms 147:4.

7 Let the high praises of God be in their mouth, and a two-edged sword in their hand.
Psalms 149:6.

8 Wisdom crieth without; she uttereth her voice in the streets.
Proverbs 1:20.

9 Trust in the LORD with all thine heart; and lean not unto

thine own understanding. In all thy ways acknowledge him, and he shall direct thy paths.
Proverbs 3:5–6.

10 For whom the Lord loveth he correcteth; even as a father the son in whom he delighteth.
Proverbs 3:12.

11 Wisdom is the principal thing; therefore get wisdom: and with all thy getting get understanding.
Proverbs 4:7.

12 Happy is the man that findeth wisdom, and the man that getteth understanding. For the merchandise of it is better than the merchandise of silver, and the gain thereof than fine gold. She is more precious than rubies: and all the things thou canst desire are not to be compared unto her. Length of days is in her right hand; and in her left hand riches and honour. Her ways are ways of pleasantness, and all her paths are peace. She is a tree of life to them that lay hold upon her: and happy is every one that retaineth her.
Proverbs 3:13–18.

13 For the lips of a strange woman drop as an honeycomb, and her mouth is smoother than oil: But her end is bitter as wormwood, sharp as a two-edged sword. Her feet go down to death; her steps take hold on hell.
Proverbs 5:3–5.

14 Let thy fountain be blessed: and rejoice with the wife of thy youth. Let her be as the loving hind and pleasant roe; let her breasts satisfy thee at all times; and be thou ravished always with her love.
Proverbs 5:18–19.

15 Go to the ant, thou sluggard; consider her ways, and be wise.
Proverbs 6:6.

16 Yet a little sleep, a little slumber, a little folding of the hands to sleep: So shall thy poverty come as one that travelleth, and thy want as an armed man.
Proverbs 6:10–11.

17 Can a man take fire in his bosom and his clothes not be burned? Can one go upon hot coals, and his feet not be burned?
Proverbs 6:27–8.

18 Wisdom hath builded her house, she hath hewn out her seven pillars.
Proverbs 9:1.

19 Stolen waters are sweet, and bread eaten in secret is pleasant.
Proverbs 9:17.

20 The rich man's wealth is his strong city: the destruction of the poor is their poverty.
Proverbs 10:15.

21 A false balance is abomination to the Lord: but a just weight is his delight.
Proverbs 11:1.

22 He that is surety for a stranger shall smart for it: and he that hateth suretiship is sure.
Proverbs 11:15.

23 A virtuous woman is a crown to her husband: but she that maketh ashamed is as rottenness in his bones.
Proverbs 12:4.

24 A wise son heareth his father's instruction: but a scorner

heareth not rebuke.
Proverbs 13:1.

25 Hope deferred maketh the heart sick: but when the desire cometh, it is a tree of life.
Proverbs 13:12.

26 He that spareth his rod hateth his son: but he that loveth him chasteneth him betimes.
Proverbs 13:24.

27 There is a way which seemeth right unto a man, but the end thereof are the ways of death.
Proverbs 14:12.

28 The poor is hated even of his own neighbour: but the rich hath many friends.
Proverbs 14:20.

29 In all labour there is profit: but the talk of the lips tendeth only to penury.
Proverbs 14:23.

30 A soft answer turneth away wrath: but grievous words stir up anger.
Proverbs 15:1.

31 A merry heart maketh a cheerful countenance.
Proverbs 15:13.

32 Better is little with the fear of the Lord than great treasure and trouble therewith. Better is a dinner of herbs where love is, than a stalled ox and hatred therewith.
Proverbs 15:16–17.

33 A word spoken in due season, how good is it!
Proverbs 15:23.

34 A good report maketh the bones fat.
Proverbs 15:30.

35 Commit thy works unto the Lord, and thy thoughts shall be established.
Proverbs 16:3.

36 Pride goeth before destruction, and an haughty spirit before a fall.
Proverbs 16:18.

37 Children's children are the crown of old men; and the glory of children are their fathers.
Proverbs 17:6.

38 A friend loveth at all times, and a brother is born for adversity.
Proverbs 17:17.

39 A merry heart doeth good like a medicine: but a broken spirit drieth the bones.
Proverbs 17:22.

40 The name of the Lord is a strong tower: the righteous runneth into it, and is safe.
Proverbs 18:10.

41 A man that hath friends must shew himself friendly: and there is a friend that sticketh closer than a brother.
Proverbs 18:24.

42 He that hath pity upon the poor lendeth unto the Lord; and that which he hath given will he pay him again.
Proverbs 19:17.

43 The king's heart is in the hand of the Lord, as the rivers of water: he turneth it whithersoever he will.
Proverbs 21:1.

44 Every way of a man is right in his own eyes: but the Lord

 pondereth the hearts.
Proverbs 21:2.

45 It is better to dwell in a corner of the housetop, than with a brawling woman in a wide house.
Proverbs 21:9.

46 Train up a child in the way he should go: and when he is old, he will not depart from it.
Proverbs 22:6.

47 Wilt thou set thine eyes upon that which is not? for riches certainly make themselves wings; they fly away as an eagle toward heaven.
Proverbs 23:5.

48 Remove not the old landmark; and enter not into the fields of the fatherless.
Proverbs 23:10.

49 If thou faint in the day of adversity, thy strength is small.
Proverbs 24:10.

50 A word fitly spoken is like apples of gold in pictures of silver.
Proverbs 25:11.

51 Confidence in an unfaithful man in time of trouble is like a broken tooth, and a foot out of joint.
Proverbs 25:19.

52 If thine enemy be hungry, give him bread to eat; and if he be thirsty, give him water to drink: For thou shalt heap coals of fire upon his head, and the LORD shall reward thee.
Proverbs 25:21–2.

53 As a dog returneth to his vomit, so a fool returneth to his folly.
Proverbs 26:11.

54 The slothful man saith, There is a lion in the way; a lion is in the streets.
Proverbs 26:13.

55 Where no wood is, there the fire goeth out: so where there is no talebearer, the strife ceaseth.
Proverbs 26:20.

56 Boast not thyself of tomorrow; for thou knowest not what a day may bring forth.
Proverbs 27:1.

57 Wrath is cruel, and anger is outrageous; but who is able to stand before envy?
Proverbs 27:4.

58 Open rebuke is better than secret love. Faithful are the wounds of a friend; but the kisses of an enemy are deceitful.
Proverbs 27:5–6.

59 A continual dropping in a very rainy day and a contentious woman are alike.
Proverbs 27:15.

60 Hell and destruction are never full; so the eyes of man are never satisfied.
Proverbs 27:20.

61 A fool uttereth all his mind: but a wise man keepeth it in till afterwards.
Proverbs 29:11.

62 Where there is no vision, the people perish: but he that keepeth the law, happy is he.
Proverbs 29:18.

63 Who can find a virtuous woman? for her price is far above rubies.
Proverbs 31:10.

64 Favour is deceitful, and beauty is vain: but a woman that feareth the LORD, she shall be praised.
Proverbs 31:30.

65 Vanity of vanities, saith the Preacher, vanity of vanities; all is vanity. What profit hath a man of all his labour which he taketh under the sun? One generation passeth away, and another generation cometh: but the earth abideth for ever.
Ecclesiastes 1:2–4.

66 All the rivers run into the sea; yet the sea is not full; unto the place from whence the rivers come, thither they return again.
Ecclesiastes 1:7.

67 The thing that hath been, it is that which shall be; and that which is done is that which shall be done: and there is no new thing under the sun.
Ecclesiastes 1:9.

68 For in much wisdom is much grief: and he that increaseth knowledge increaseth sorrow.
Ecclesiastes 1:18.

69 I said of laughter, It is mad: and of mirth, What doeth it?
Ecclesiastes 2:2.

70 To every thing there is a season, and a time to every purpose under the heaven:
A time to be born, and a time to die; a time to plant, and a time to pluck up that which is planted;
A time to kill, and a time to heal; a time to break down, and a time to build up;
A time to weep, and a time to laugh; a time to mourn, and a time to dance:
A time to cast away stones, and a time to gather stones together; a time to embrace, and a time to refrain from embracing;
A time to get, and a time to lose; a time to keep, and a time to cast away;
A time to rend, and a time to sew; a time to keep silence, and a time to speak;
A time to love, and a time to hate; a time of war, and a time of peace.
Ecclesiastes 3:1–8.

71 Wherefore I perceive that there is nothing better, than that a man should rejoice in his own works; for that is his portion: for who shall bring him to see what shall be after him?
Ecclesiastes 3:22.

72 Wherefore I praise the dead which are already dead more than the living which are yet alive.
Ecclesiastes 4:2.

73 Two are better than one; because they have a good reward for their labour. For if they fall, the one will lift up his fellow: but woe to him that is alone when he falleth; for he hath not another to help him up.
Ecclesiastes 4:9–10.

74 And if one prevail against him, two shall withstand him; and a threefold cord is not quickly broken.
Ecclesiastes 4:12.

75 Better is a poor and a wise child than an old and foolish

king, who will no more be admonished.
Ecclesiastes 4:13.

76 Be not rash with thy mouth, and let not thine heart be hasty to utter any thing before God: for God is in heaven, and thou upon earth: therefore let thy words be few.
Ecclesiastes 5:2.

77 For as the crackling of thorns under a pot, so is the laughter of a fool: this also is vanity.
Ecclesiastes 7:6.

78 Better is the end of a thing than the beginning thereof: and the patient in spirit is better than the proud in spirit.
Ecclesiastes 7:8.

79 Say not thou, What is the cause that the former days were better than these? for thou dost not inquire wisely concerning this.
Ecclesiastes 7:10.

80 There is no man that hath power over the spirit to retain the spirit; neither hath he power in the day of death: and there is no discharge in that war; neither shall wickedness deliver those that are given to it.
Ecclesiastes 8:8.

81 Then I commended mirth, because a man hath no better thing under the sun, than to eat, and to drink, and to be merry: for that shall abide with him of his labour the days of his life, which God giveth him under the sun.
Ecclesiastes 8:15.

82 For to him that is joined to all the living there is hope: for a living dog is better than a dead lion. For the living know that they shall die: but the dead know not any thing, neither have they any more a reward; for the memory of them is forgotten.
Ecclesiastes 9:4–5.

83 Go thy way, eat thy bread with joy, and drink thy wine with a merry heart; for God now accepteth thy works.
Ecclesiastes 9:7.

84 Whatsoever thy hand findeth to do; do it with thy might; for there is no work, nor device, nor knowledge, nor wisdom, in the grave, whither thou goest.
Ecclesiastes 9:10.

85 I returned, and saw under the sun, that the race is not to the swift, nor the battle to the strong, neither yet bread to the wise, nor yet riches to men of understanding, nor yet favour to men of skill; but time and chance happeneth to them all.
Ecclesiastes 9:11.

86 Dead flies cause the ointment of the apothecary to send forth a stinking savour: so doth a little folly him that is in reputation for wisdom and honour.
Ecclesiastes 10:1.

87 He that diggeth a pit shall fall into it; and whoso breaketh an hedge, a serpent shall bite him.
Ecclesiastes 10:8.

88 A feast is made for laughter, and wine maketh merry: but money answereth all things.
Ecclesiastes 10:19.

89 Curse not the king, no not in thy thought; and curse not the rich in thy bedchamber: for a bird of the air shall carry the voice, and that which hath wings shall tell the matter.
Ecclesiastes 10:20.

90 Cast thy bread upon the waters: for thou shalt find it after many days.
Ecclesiastes 11:1.

91 Rejoice, O young man, in thy youth; and let thy heart cheer thee in the days of thy youth, and walk in the ways of thine heart, and in the sight of thine eyes: but know thou, that for all these things God will bring thee into judgment.
Ecclesiastes 11:9.

92 Remember now thy Creator in the days of thy youth, while the evil days come not, nor the years draw nigh, when thou shalt say, I have no pleasure in them;
While the sun, or the light, or the moon, or the stars, be not darkened, nor the clouds return after the rain:
In the day when the keepers of the house shall tremble, and the strong men shall bow themselves, and the grinders cease because they are few, and those that look out of the windows be darkened,
And the doors shall be shut in the streets, when the sound of the grinding is low, and he shall rise up at the voice of the bird, and all the daughters of musick shall be brought low:
Also when they shall be afraid of that which is high, and fears shall be in the way, and the almond tree shall flourish, and the grasshopper shall be a burden, and desire shall fail: because man goeth to his long home, and mourners go about the streets:
Or ever the silver cord be loosed, or the golden bowl be broken, or the pitcher be broken at the fountain, or the wheel broken at the cistern.
Then shall the dust return to the earth as it was: and the spirit shall return unto God who gave it.
Ecclesiastes 12:1–7.

93 And further, by these, my son, be admonished: of making many books there is no end; and much study is a weariness of the flesh.
Ecclesiastes 12:12.

94 Fear God, and keep his commandments: for this is the whole duty of man.
Ecclesiastes 12:13.

95 The song of songs, which is Solomon's.
Song of Solomon 1:1.

96 I am the rose of Sharon, and the lily of the valleys. As the lily among thorns, so is my love among the daughters.
Song of Solomon 2:1–2.

97 He brought me to the banqueting house, and his banner over me was love.
Song of Solomon 2:4.

98 I charge you, O ye daughters of Jerusalem, by the roes, and by the hinds of the field, that ye stir not up, nor awake my love, till he please.
Song of Solomon 2:7.

99 My beloved spake, and said unto me, Rise up, my love, my fair one, and come away. For lo, the winter is past, the rain is over and gone.
Song of Solomon 2:10–11.

1 My beloved is mine, and I am his: he feedeth among the lilies.
Song of Solomon 2:16.

2 Behold, thou art fair, my love; behold, thou art fair; thou hast doves' eyes within thy locks: thy hair is as a flock of

goats, that appear from mount Gilead. Thy teeth are like a flock of sheep that are even shorn, which came up from the washing; whereof every one bear twins, and none is barren among them. Thy lips are like a thread of scarlet, and thy speech is comely: thy temples are like a piece of a pomegranate within thy locks. Thy neck is like the tower of David builded for an armoury, whereon there hang a thousand bucklers, all shields of mighty men. Thy two breasts are like two young roes that are twins, which feed among the lilies. Until the day break, and the shadows flee away, I will get me to the mountain of myrrh, and to the hill of frankincense. Thou art all fair, my love; there is no spot in thee.
Song of Solomon 4:1–7.

3 A garden inclosed is my sister, my spouse; a spring shut up, a fountain sealed.
Song of Solomon 4:12.

4 My beloved put in his hand by the hole of the door, and my bowels were moved for him.
Song of Solomon 5:4.

5 How fair and how pleasant art thou, O love, for delights!
Song of Solomon 7:6.

6 Love is strong as death; jealousy is cruel as the grave: the coals thereof are coals of fire, which hath a most vehement flame. Many waters cannot quench love, neither can the floods drown it: if a man would give all the substance of his house for love, it would utterly be contemned.
Song of Solomon 8:6–7.

7 Come now, and let us reason together, saith the Lord: though your sins be as scarlet, they shall be as white as snow; though they be red like crimson, they shall be as wool.
Isaiah 1:18.

8 They shall beat their swords into plowshares, and their spears into pruninghooks: nation shall not lift up sword against nation, neither shall they learn war any more.
Isaiah 2:4.

9 What mean ye that ye beat my people to pieces, and grind the faces of the poor? saith the Lord God of hosts.
Isaiah 3:15.

10 Woe unto them that rise up early in the morning, that they may follow strong drink; that continue until night, till wine inflame them!
Isaiah 5:11.

11 In the year that king Uzziah died I saw also the Lord sitting upon a throne, high and lifted up, and his train filled the temple. Above it stood the seraphims: each one had six wings; with twain he covered his face, and with twain he covered his feet, and with twain he did fly. And one cried unto another, and said, Holy, holy, holy, is the Lord of hosts: the whole earth is full of his glory. And the posts of the door moved at the voice of him that cried, and the house was filled with smoke.
Isaiah 6:1–4.

12 Then said I, Woe is me! for I am undone; because I am a man of unclean lips, and I dwell in the midst of a people of unclean lips; for mine eyes have seen the King, the Lord of hosts. Then flew one of the seraphims unto me, having a live coal in his hand, which he had taken with the tongs from off the altar: And he laid it upon my mouth, and said, Lo, this hath touched thy lips; and thine iniquity is taken away, and thy sin purged. Also I heard the voice of the Lord, saying, Whom shall I send, and who will go for us? Then said I, Here am I; send me.
Isaiah 6:5–8.

13 Then said I, Lord, how long?
Isaiah 6:11.

14 Therefore the Lord himself shall give you a sign; Behold, a virgin shall conceive, and bear a son, and shall call his name Immanuel.
Isaiah 7:14.

15 And he shall be for a sanctuary; but for a stone of stumbling and for a rock of offence to both the houses of Israel, for a gin and for a snare to the inhabitants of Jerusalem.
Isaiah 8:14.

16 The people that walked in darkness have seen a great light: they that dwell in the land of the shadow of death, upon them hath the light shined.
Isaiah 9:2.

17 For unto us a child is born, unto us a son is given: and the government shall be upon his shoulder: and his name shall be called Wonderful, Counseller, The mighty God, The everlasting Father, The Prince of Peace. Of the increase of his government and peace there shall be no end, upon the throne of David, and upon his kingdom, to order it, and to establish it with judgment and with justice from henceforth even for ever. The zeal of the Lord of hosts will perform this.
Isaiah 9:6–7.

18 And there shall come forth a rod out of the stem of Jesse, and a Branch shall grow out of his roots: And the spirit of the Lord shall rest upon him, the spirit of wisdom and understanding, the spirit of counsel and might, the spirit of knowledge and of the fear of the Lord.
Isaiah 11:1–2.

19 The wolf also shall dwell with the lamb, and the leopard shall lie down with the kid; and the calf and the young lion and the fatling together; and a little child shall lead them. And the cow and the bear shall feed; their young ones shall lie down together: and the lion shall eat straw like the ox. And the sucking child shall play on the hole of the asp, and the weaned child shall put his hand on the cockatrice' den. They shall not hurt nor destroy in all my holy mountain for the earth shall be full of the knowledge of the Lord, as the waters cover the sea.
Isaiah 11:6–9.

20 Therefore with joy shall ye draw water out of the wells of salvation.
Isaiah 12:3.

21 How art thou fallen from heaven, O Lucifer, son of the morning!
Isaiah 14:12.

22 And behold joy and gladness, slaying oxen, and killing sheep, eating flesh, and drinking wine: let us eat and drink; for to morrow we shall die.
Isaiah 22:13.

23 The earth shall reel to and fro like a drunkard, and shall be removed like a cottage; and the transgression thereof shall be heavy upon it; and it shall fall, and not rise again.
Isaiah 24:20.

24 He will swallow up death in victory; and the Lord GOD will wipe away tears from off all faces; and the rebuke of his people shall he take away from off all the earth: for the LORD hath spoken it.
Isaiah 25:8.

25 Thou wilt keep him in perfect peace, whose mind is stayed on thee.
Isaiah 26:3.

26 For precept must be upon precept, precept upon precept; line upon line, line upon line; here a little, and there a little:
For with stammering lips and another tongue will he speak to this people.
Isaiah 28:10–11.

27 We have made a covenant with death, and with hell are we at agreement.
Isaiah 28:15.

28 Behold, I lay in Zion for a foundation a stone, a tried stone, a precious corner stone, a sure foundation: he that believeth shall not make haste. Judgment also will I lay to the line, and righteousness to the plummet: and the hail shall sweep away the refuge of lies, and the waters shall overflow the hiding place.
Isaiah 28:16–17.

29 Forasmuch as this people draw near me with their mouth, and with their lips do honour me, but have removed their heart far from me, and their fear toward me is taught by the precept of men.
Isaiah 29:13.

30 In returning and rest shall ye be saved; in quietness and in confidence shall be your strength: and ye would not.
Isaiah 30:15.

31 And thine ears shall hear a word behind thee, saying, This is the way, walk ye in it, when ye turn to the right hand, and when ye turn to the left.
Isaiah 30:21.

32 And a man shall be as an hiding place from the wind, and a covert from the tempest; as rivers of water in a dry place, as the shadow of a great rock in a weary land.
Isaiah 32:2.

33 Then the eyes of the blind shall be opened, and the ears of the deaf shall be unstopped. Then shall the lame man leap as an hart, and the tongue of the dumb sing: for in the wilderness shall waters break out, and streams in the desert. And the parched ground shall become a pool, and the thirsty land springs of water: in the habitation of dragons, where each lay, shall be grass with reeds and rushes.
Isaiah 35:5–7.

34 And an highway shall be there, and a way, and it shall be called The way of holiness; the unclean shall not pass over it; but it shall be for those: the wayfaring men, though fools shall not err therein.
Isaiah 35:8.

35 Lo, thou trusted in the staff of this broken reed, on Egypt; whereon if a man lean, it will go into his hand, and pierce it: so is Pharaoh king of Egypt to all that trust in him.
Isaiah 36:6.

36 Comfort ye, comfort ye my people, saith your God. Speak ye comfortably to Jerusalem, and cry unto her, that her warfare is accomplished, that her iniquity is pardoned: for she hath received of the LORD's hand double for all her sins.
The voice of him that crieth in the wilderness, Prepare ye the way of the LORD, make straight in the desert a highway for our God.
Every valley shall be exalted, and every mountain and hill shall be made low: and the crooked shall be made straight, and the rough places plain:
And the glory of the LORD shall be revealed, and all flesh shall see it together: for the mouth of the LORD hath spoken it.
The voice said, Cry. And he said, What shall I cry? All flesh is grass, and all the goodliness thereof is as the flower of the field:
The grass withereth, the flower fadeth: because the spirit of the LORD bloweth upon it: surely the people is grass. The grass withereth, the flower fadeth: but the word of our God shall stand for ever.
Isaiah 40:1–8.

37 He shall feed his flock like a shepherd: he shall gather the lambs with his arm, and carry them in his bosom, and shall gently lead those that are with young.
Isaiah 40:11.

38 Who hath measured the waters in the hollow of his hand, and meted out heaven with the span, and comprehended the dust of the earth in a measure, and weighed the mountains in scales, and the hills in a balance?
Isaiah 40:12.

39 Behold, the nations are as a drop of a bucket, and are counted as the small dust of the balance: behold, he taketh up the isles as a very little thing.
Isaiah 40:15.

40 To whom then will ye liken God? or what likeness will ye compare unto him?
Isaiah 40:18.

41 Have ye not known? have ye not heard? hath it not been told you from the beginning? have ye not understood from the foundations of the earth?
Isaiah 40:21.

42 Even the youths shall faint and be weary, and the young men shall utterly fall: But they that wait upon the LORD shall renew their strength; they shall mount up with wings as eagles; they shall run, and not be weary; and they shall walk, and not faint.
Isaiah 40:30–31.

43 A bruised reed shall he not break, and the smoking flax shall he not quench: he shall bring forth judgment unto truth.
Isaiah 42:3.

44 Fear not: for I have redeemed thee, I have called thee by thy name; thou art mine. When thou passest through the waters, I will be with thee; and through the rivers, they shall not overflow thee: when thou walkest through the fire, thou shalt not be burned; neither shall the flame kindle upon thee.
Isaiah 43:1–2.

45 Woe unto him that striveth with his Maker! Let the potsherd strive with the potsherds of the earth. Shall the clay say to him that fashioneth it, What makest thou? or

thy work, He hath no hands?
Isaiah 45:9.

46 Can a woman forget her suckling child, that she should not have compassion on the son of her womb? yea, they may forget, yet will I not forget thee.
Isaiah 49:15.

47 How beautiful upon the mountains are the feet of him that bringeth good tidings, that publisheth peace; that bringeth good tidings of good, that publisheth salvation; that saith unto Zion, Thy God reigneth! Thy watchmen shall lift up the voice; with the voice together shall they sing: for they shall see eye to eye, when the LORD shall bring again Zion.
Isaiah 52:7–8.

48 Break forth into joy, sing together, ye waste places of Jerusalem: for the LORD hath comforted his people, he hath redeemed Jerusalem. The LORD hath made bare his holy arm in the eyes of all the nations; and all the ends of the earth shall see the salvation of our God.
Isaiah 52:9–10.

49 As many were astonished at thee; his visage was so marred more than any man, and his form more than the sons of men: So shall he sprinkle many nations; the kings shall shut their mouths at him: for that which had not been told them shall they see; and that which they had not heard shall they consider.
Isaiah 52:14–15.

50 Who hath believed our report? and to whom is the arm of the LORD revealed? For he shall grow up before him as a tender plant, and as a root out of a dry ground: he hath no form nor comeliness; and when we shall see him, there is no beauty that we should desire him. He is despised and rejected of men; a man of sorrows, and acquainted with grief: and we hid as it were our faces from him; he was despised, and we esteemed him not. Surely he hath borne our griefs, and carried our sorrows.
Isaiah 53:1–4.

51 But he was wounded for our transgressions, he was bruised for our iniquities: the chastisement of our peace was upon him; and with his stripes we are healed. All we like sheep have gone astray; we have turned every one to his own way; and the LORD hath laid on him the iniquity of us all. He was oppressed, and he was afflicted, yet he opened not his mouth: he is brought as a lamb to the slaughter, and as a sheep before her shearers is dumb, so he openeth not his mouth.
Isaiah 53:5–7.

52 He was cut off out of the land of the living: for the transgression of my people was he stricken. And he made his grave with the wicked, and with the rich in his death; because he had done no violence, neither was any deceit in his mouth.
Isaiah 53:8–9.

53 Ho, every one that thirsteth, come ye to the waters, and he that hath no money; come ye, buy, and eat; yea, come, buy wine and milk without money and without price. Wherefore do ye spend money for that which is not bread? and your labour for that which satisfieth not? hearken diligently unto me, and eat ye that which is good, and let your soul delight itself in fatness.
Isaiah 55:1–2.

54 Seek ye the LORD while he may be found, call ye upon him while he is near.
Isaiah 55:6.

55 For my thoughts are not your thoughts, neither are your ways my ways, saith the LORD. For as the heavens are higher than the earth, so are my ways higher than your ways, and my thoughts than your thoughts.
Isaiah 55:8–9.

56 For as the rain cometh down, and the snow from heaven, and returneth not thither, but watereth the earth, and maketh it bring forth and bud, that it may give seed to the sower, and bread to the eater: So shall my word be that goeth forth out of my mouth: it shall not return unto me void, but it shall accomplish that which I please, and it shall prosper in the thing whereto I sent it.
Isaiah 55:10–11.

57 For ye shall go out with joy, and be led forth with peace: the mountains and the hills shall break forth before you into singing, and all the trees of the field shall clap their hands.
Isaiah 55:12.

58 Instead of the thorn shall come up the fir tree, and instead of the brier shall come up the myrtle tree: and it shall be to the LORD for a name, for an everlasting sign that shall not be cut off.
Isaiah 55:13.

59 Peace, peace to him that is far off, and to him that is near, saith the LORD; and I will heal him.
Isaiah 57:19.

60 There is no peace, saith my God, to the wicked.
Isaiah 57:21.

61 Arise, shine; for thy light is come, and the glory of the LORD is risen upon thee.
Isaiah 60:1.

62 The Spirit of the Lord GOD is upon me; because the LORD hath anointed me to preach good tidings unto the meek; he hath sent me, to bind up the brokenhearted, to proclaim liberty to the captives, and the opening of the prison to them that are bound; To proclaim the acceptable year of the LORD, and the day of vengeance of our God; to comfort all that mourn; To appoint unto them that mourn in Zion, to give unto them beauty for ashes, the oil of joy for mourning, the garment of praise for the spirit of heaviness; that they might be called trees of righteousness, the planting of the LORD, that he might be glorified.
Isaiah 61:1–3.

63 But we are all as an unclean thing, and all our righteousnesses are as filthy rags; and we all do fade as a leaf; and our iniquities, like the wind, have taken us away.
Isaiah 64:6.

64 Stand by thyself, come not near to me; for I am holier than thou.
Isaiah 65:5.

65 For, behold, I create new heavens and a new earth: and the former shall not be remembered, nor come into mind.
Isaiah 65:17.

66 The wolf and the lamb shall feed together, and the lion shall eat straw like the bullock: and dust shall be the

serpent's meat. They shall not hurt nor destroy in all my holy mountain, saith the Lord.
Isaiah 65:25.

67 Behold, I have put my words in thy mouth. See, I have this day set thee over the nations and over the kingdoms, to root out, and to pull down, and to destroy, and to throw down, to build, and to plant.
Jeremiah 1:9–10.

68 They have forsaken me the fountain of living waters, and hewed them out cisterns, broken cisterns, that can hold no water.
Jeremiah 2:13.

69 They were as fed horses in the morning: every one neighed after his neighbour's wife.
Jeremiah 5:8.

70 But this people hath a revolting and a rebellious heart; they are revolted and gone.
Jeremiah 5:23.

71 Saying, Peace, peace; when there is no peace.
Jeremiah 6:14.

72 Is this house, which is called by my name, become a den of robbers in your eyes?
Jeremiah 7:11.

73 The harvest is past, the summer is ended, and we are not saved.
Jeremiah 8:20.

74 Is there no balm in Gilead; is there no physician there?
Jeremiah 8:22.

75 Can the Ethiopian change his skin, or the leopard his spots? then may ye also do good, that are accustomed to do evil.
Jeremiah 13:23.

76 The heart is deceitful above all things, and desperately wicked: who can know it? I the Lord search the heart, I try the reins.
Jeremiah 17:9–10

77 The Lord hath appeared of old unto me, saying, Yea, I have loved thee with an everlasting love: therefore with lovingkindness have I drawn thee.
Jeremiah 31:3.

78 A voice was heard in Ramah, lamentation, and bitter weeping; Rachel weeping for her children refused to be comforted for her children, because they were not.
Jeremiah 31:15.

79 How doth the city sit solitary, that was full of people! how is she become as a widow! she that was great among the nations, and princess among the provinces, how is she become tributary!
Lamentations 1:1.

80 Is it nothing to you, all ye that pass by? behold, and see if there be any sorrow like unto my sorrow.
Lamentations 1:12.

81 And I said, My strength and my hope is perished from the Lord: Remembering mine affliction and my misery, the wormwood and the gall.
Lamentations 3:18–19.

82 It is of the Lord's mercies that we are not consumed, because his compassions fail not. They are new every morning: great is thy faithfulness.
Lamentations 3:22–3.

83 It is good for a man that he bear the yoke in his youth.
Lamentations 3:27.

84 The appearance of the wheels and their work was like unto the colour of a beryl: and they four had one likeness: and their appearance and their work was as it were a wheel in the middle of a wheel.
Of his vision in exile. Ezekiel 1:16.

85 For thou art not sent to a people of a strange speech and of an hard language, but to the house of Israel; Not many people of a strange speech and of an hard language, whose words thou canst not understand. Surely, had I sent thee to them, they would have hearkened unto thee.
Ezekiel 3:5–6.

86 And I will give them one heart, and I will put a new spirit within you; and I will take the stony heart out of their flesh, and will give them an heart of flesh.
Ezekiel 11:19.

87 Son of man, eat thy bread with quaking, and drink thy water with trembling and with carefulness.
Ezekiel 12:18.

88 The fathers have eaten sour grapes, and the children's teeth are set on edge.
Ezekiel 18:2.

89 I will accept you with your sweet savour, when I bring you out from the people, and gather you out of the countries wherein you have been scattered; and I will be sanctified in you before the heathen. And ye shall know that I am the Lord, when I shall bring you into the land of Israel, into the country for the which I lifted up mine hand to give it to your fathers. And there shall ye remember your ways, and all your doings, wherein ye have been defiled; and ye shall loath yourselves in your own sight for all your evils that ye have committed.
Ezekiel 20:41–3.

90 As I live, saith the Lord God, I have no pleasure in the death of the wicked; but that the wicked turn from his way and live: turn ye, turn ye from your evil ways; for why will ye die, O house of Israel?
Ezekiel 33:11.

91 The hand of the Lord was upon me, and carried me out in the spirit of the Lord, and set me down in the midst of the valley which was full of bones.
Ezekiel 37:1.

92 Son of man, can these bones live?
Ezekiel 37:3.

93 Prophesy upon these bones, and say unto them, O ye dry bones, hear the word of the Lord. Thus saith the Lord God unto these bones; Behold, I will cause breath to enter into you, and ye shall live: And I will lay sinews upon you, and will bring up flesh upon you, and cover you with skin, and put breath in you, and ye shall live; and ye shall know that I am the Lord.
Ezekiel 37:4–6.

94 Thou, O king, sawest, and behold a great image. This great image, whose brightness was excellent, stood before thee; and the form thereof was terrible. This image's head was of fine gold, his breast and his arms of silver, his belly and his thighs of brass. His legs of iron, his feet part of iron and part of clay. Thou sawest till that a stone was cut out without hands, which smote the image

upon his feet that were of iron and clay, and brake them to pieces.
Daniel 2:31–34.

95 Then Nebuchadnezzar came near to the mouth of the burning fiery furnace, and spake, and said, Shadrach, Meshach, and Abednego, ye servants of the most high God, come forth, and come hither. Then Shadrach, Meshach, and Abednego, came forth of the midst of the fire.
Daniel 3:26.

96 The same hour was the thing fulfilled upon Nebuchadnezzar: and he was driven from men, and did eat grass as oxen, and his body was wet with the dew of heaven, till his hairs were grown like eagles' feathers, and his nails like birds' claws.
Daniel 4:33.

97 In the same hour came forth fingers of a man's hand, and wrote over against the candlestick upon the plaister of the wall of the king's palace: and the king saw the part of the hand that wrote.
Daniel 5:5.

98 And this is the writing that was written, MENE, MENE, TEKEL, UPHARSIN. This is the interpretation of the thing: MENE; God hath numbered thy kingdom, and finished it, TEKEL; Thou art weighed in the balances, and art found wanting. PERES; Thy kingdom is divided, and given to the Medes and Persians.
Daniel 5:25–8.

99 I saw in the night visions and, behold, one like the Son of man came with the clouds of heaven, and came to the Ancient of days, and they brought him near before him.
Daniel 7:13.

1 And they that be wise shall shine as the brightness of the firmament; and they that turn many to righteousness as the stars for ever and ever. But thou, O Daniel, shut up the words, and seal the book, even to the time of the end: many shall run to and fro, and knowledge shall be increased.
Daniel 12:3–4.

2 For they have sown the wind, and they shall reap the whirlwind.
Hosea 8:7.

3 When Israel was a child, then I loved him, and called my son out of Egypt.
Hosea 11:1.

4 And I will restore to you the years that the locust hath eaten, the cankerworm, and the caterpiller, and the palmerworm, my great army which I sent among you.
Joel 2:25.

5 And it shall come to pass afterward, that I will pour out my spirit upon all flesh, and your sons and your daughters shall prophesy, your old men shall dream dreams, your young men shall see visions.
Joel 2:28.

6 Beat your plowshares into swords, and your pruninghooks into spears: let the weak say, I am strong.
Joel 3:10.

7 Can two walk together, except they be agreed?
Amos 3:3.

8 The lion hath roared, who will not fear? the Lord GOD

hath spoken, who can but prophesy?
Amos 3:8.

9 Therefore thus will I do unto thee, O Israel: and because I will do this unto thee, prepare to meet thy God, O Israel.
Amos 4:12.

10 Shall not the day of the LORD be darkness, and not light? even very dark, and no brightness in it?
Amos 5:20.

11 Behold, the days come, saith the Lord GOD, that I will send a famine in the land, not a famine of bread, nor a thirst for water, but of hearing the words of the LORD: And they shall wander from sea to sea, and from the north even to the east, they shall run to and fro to seek the word of the LORD, and shall not find it.
Amos 8:11–12.

12 But thou, Bethlehem, Ephratah, though thou be little among the thousands of Judah, yet out of thee shall he come forth unto me that is to be ruler in Israel.
Micah 5:2.

13 O LORD, revive thy work in the midst of the years, in the midst of the years make known; in wrath remember mercy.
Habakkuk 3:2.

14 He that earneth wages earneth wages to put it into a bag with holes.
Haggai 1:6.

15 I lifted up mine eyes again, and looked, and behold a man with a measuring line in his hand. Then said I, Whither goest thou? And he said unto me, To measure Jerusalem, to see what is the breadth thereof, and what is the length thereof.
Zechariah 2:1–2.

16 For thus saith the LORD of hosts; After the glory hath he sent me unto the nations which spoiled you: for he that toucheth you toucheth the apple of his eye.
Zechariah 2:8.

17 Then he answered and spake unto me, saying, This is the word of the LORD unto Zerubbabel, saying, Not by might, nor by power, but by my spirit, saith the LORD of hosts.
Zechariah 4:6.

18 And I said unto them, If ye think good, give me my price; and if not, forbear. So they weighed for my price thirty pieces of silver.
Zechariah 11:12.

19 Have we not all one father, hath not one God created us? why do we deal treacherously every man against his brother, by profaning the covenant of our fathers?
Malachi 2:10.

20 Bring ye all the tithes into the storehouse, that there may be meat in mine house, and prove me now herewith, saith the LORD of hosts, if I will not open you the windows of heaven, and pour you out a blessing, that there shall not be room enough to receive it.
Malachi 3:10.

21 Then they that feared the LORD spake often one to another: and the LORD hearkened, and heard it, and a book of remembrance was written before him for them that feared the LORD, and that thought upon his name.
Malachi 3:16.

22 For, behold, the day cometh, that shall burn as an oven;

and all the proud, yea, and all that do wickedly, shall be stubble: and the day that cometh shall burn them up, saith the LORD of hosts, that it shall leave them neither root nor branch. But unto you that fear my name shall the Sun of righteousness arise with healing in his wings; and ye shall go forth, and grow up as calves of the stall.
Malachi 4:1–2.

23 Behold, I will send you Elijah the prophet before the coming of the great and dreadful day of the LORD: And he shall turn the heart of the fathers to the children, and the heart of the children to their fathers, lest I come and smite the earth a curse.
Malachi 4:5–6.

Bible (Apocrypha)

24 The first wrote, Wine is the strongest. The second wrote, The king is strongest. The third wrote, Women are strongest: but above all things Truth beareth away the victory.
1 Esdras 3:10–12.

25 By this also ye must know that women have dominion over you: do ye not labour and toil, and give and bring all to the woman? Yea, a man taketh his sword, and goeth his way to rob and to steal, to sail upon the sea and upon rivers; And looketh upon a lion, and goeth in the darkness; and when he hath stolen, spoiled, and robbed, he bringeth it to his love.
1 Esdras 4:22–4.

26 Then were the entrances of this world made narrow, full of sorrow and travail: they are but few and evil, full of perils, and very painful. For the entrances of the elder world were wide and sure, and brought immortal fruit. If then they that live labour not to enter these strait and vain things, they can never receive those that are laid up for them.
2 Esdras 7:12–14.

27 For the world hath lost his youth, and the times begin to wax old.
2 Esdras 14:10.

28 Be not greedy to add money to money: but let it be as refuse in respect of our child.
Tobit 5:18.

29 For the ear of jealousy heareth all things: and the noise of murmurings is not hid.
Wisdom of Solomon 1:10.

30 Nevertheless through envy of the devil came death into the world: and they that do hold of his side do find it.
Wisdom of Solomon 2:24.

31 But the souls of the righteous are in the hand of God, and there shall no torment touch them. In the sight of the unwise they seemed to die: and their departure is taken for misery, And their going from us to be utter destruction: but they are in peace. For though they be punished in the sight of men, yet is their hope full of immortality. And having been a little chastised, they shall be greatly rewarded: for God proved them, and found them worthy for himself.
Wisdom of Solomon 3:1–5.

32 And in the time of their visitation they shall shine, and run to and fro like sparks among the stubble.
Wisdom of Solomon 3:7.

33 For the bewitching of naughtiness doth obscure things that are honest; and the wanderings of concupiscence doth undermine the simple mind. He being made perfect in a short time, fulfilled a long time.
Wisdom of Solomon 4:12–13.

34 Even so we in like manner, as soon as we were born, began to draw to our end, and had no sign of virtue to shew; but were consumed in our own wickedness. For the hope of the ungodly is like dust that is blown away with the wind; like a thin froth that is driven away with the storm; like as the smoke which is dispersed here and there with a tempest, and passeth away as the remembrance of a guest that tarrieth but a day.
Wisdom of Solomon 5:13–14.

35 For all men have one entrance into life, and the like going out.
Wisdom of Solomon 7:6.

36 For thou hast power of life and death: thou leadest to the gates of hell, and bringest up again.
Wisdom of Solomon 16:13.

37 My son, if thou come to serve the Lord, prepare thy soul for temptation.
Ecclesiasticus 2:1.

38 Saying, We will fall into the hands of the Lord, and not into the hands of men: for as his majesty is, so is his mercy.
Ecclesiasticus 2:18.

39 Be not curious in unnecessary matters: for more things are shewed unto thee than men understand.
Ecclesiasticus 3:23.

40 Be not ignorant of any thing in a great matter or a small.
Ecclesiasticus 5:15.

41 A faithful friend is the medicine of life; and they that fear the Lord shall find him.
Ecclesiasticus 6:16.

42 Laugh no man to scorn in the bitterness of his soul: for there is one which humbleth and exalteth.
Ecclesiasticus 7:11.

43 Miss not the discourse of the elders: for they also learned of their fathers, and of them thou shalt learn understanding, and to give answer as need requireth.
Ecclesiasticus 8:9.

44 Open not thine heart to every man, lest he requite thee with a shrewd turn.
Ecclesiasticus 8:19.

45 Give not thy soul unto a woman to set her foot upon thy substance.
Ecclesiasticus 9:2.

46 Forsake not an old friend; for the new is not comparable to him: a new friend is as new wine; when it is old, thou shalt drink it with pleasure.
Ecclesiasticus 9:10.

47 Many kings have sat down upon the ground; and one that was never thought of hath worn the crown.
Ecclesiasticus 11:5.

48 Judge none blessed before his death: for a man shall be known in his children.
Ecclesiasticus 11:28.

49 He that toucheth pitch shall be difiled therewith; and he

that hath fellowship with a proud man shall be like unto him.
Ecclesiasticus 13:1.

50 Burden not thyself above thy power while thou livest; and have no fellowship with one that is mightier and richer than thyself: for how agree the kettle and the earthen pot together? for if the one be smitten against the other, it shall be broken.
Ecclesiasticus 13:2.

51 All flesh waxeth old as a garment: for the covenant from the beginning is, Thou shalt die the death.
Ecclesiasticus 14:17.

52 Desire not a multitude of unprofitable children, neither delight in ungodly sons.
Ecclesiasticus 16:1.

53 Be not made a beggar by banqueting upon borrowing, when thou hast nothing in thy purse: for thou shalt lie in wait for thine own life, and be talked on.
Ecclesiasticus 18:33.

54 A labouring man that is given to drunkenness shall not be rich: and he that contemneth small things shall fall by little and little.
Ecclesiasticus 19:1.

55 Wine and women will make men of understanding to fall away: and he that cleaveth to harlots will become impudent.
Ecclesiasticus 19:2.

56 If thou hast heard a word, let it die with thee; and be bold, it will not burst thee.
Ecclesiasticus 19:10.

57 As the climbing up a sandy way is to the feet of the aged, so is a wife full of words to a quiet man.
Ecclesiasticus 25:20.

58 The stroke of the whip maketh marks in the flesh: but the stroke of the tongue breaketh the bones. Many have fallen by the edge of the sword: but not so many as have fallen by the tongue.
Ecclesiasticus 28:17–18.

59 Envy and wrath shorten the life, and carefulness bringeth age before the time.
Ecclesiasticus 30:24.

60 Leave off first for manners' sake; and be not unsatiable, lest thou offend.
Ecclesiasticus 31:17.

61 Wine is as good as life to a man, if it be drunk moderately: what life is then to a man that is without wine? for it was made to make men glad.
Ecclesiasticus 31:27.

62 Let thy speech be short, comprehending much in few words; be as one that knoweth and yet holdeth his tongue.
Ecclesiasticus 32:8.

63 In all thy works keep to thyself the preeminence; leave not a stain in thine honour.
Ecclesiasticus 33:22.

64 Honour a physician with the honour due unto him for the uses which ye may have of him: for the Lord hath created him. For of the most High cometh healing, and he shall receive honour of the king.
Ecclesiasticus 38:1–2.

65 The wisdom of a learned man cometh by opportunity of leisure: and he that hath little business shall become wise. How can he get wisdom that holdeth the plough, and that glorieth in the goad, that driveth oxen, and is occupied in their labours, and whose talk is of bullocks?
Ecclesiasticus 38:24–5.

66 Let us now praise famous men, and our fathers that begat us.
Ecclesiasticus 44:1.

67 Their bodies are buried in peace; but their name liveth for evermore.
Ecclesiasticus 44:14.

68 Here then will we begin the story: only adding thus much to that which hath been said, that it is a foolish thing to make a long prologue, and to be short in the story itself.
Maccabees 2:32.

69 And when he was at the last gasp, he said, Thou like a fury takest us out of this present life, but the King of the world shall raise us up, who have died for his laws, unto everlasting life.
Maccabees 7:9.

Bible (New Testament)

70 And she shall bring forth a son, and thou shalt call his name JESUS: for he shall save his people from their sins.
St Matthew 1:21.

71 Now all this was done, that it might be fulfilled which was spoken of the Lord by the prophet, saying, Behold, a virgin shall be with child, and shall bring forth a son, and they shall call his name Emmanuel, which being interpreted is, God with us.
St Matthew 1:22–3.

72 Now when Jesus was born in Bethlehem of Judaea in the days of Herod the king, behold, there came wise men from the east to Jerusalem, Saying, Where is he that is born King of the Jews? for we have seen his star in the east, and are come to worship him.
St Matthew 2:1–2.

73 And when they were come into the house, they saw the young child with Mary his mother, and fell down, and worshipped him: and when they had opened their treasures, they presented unto him gifts; gold, and frankincense, and myrrh.
St Matthew 2:11.

74 And saying, Repent ye: for the kingdom of heaven is at hand. For this is he that was spoken of by the prophet Esaias, saying, The voice of one crying in the wilderness, Prepare ye the way of the Lord, make his paths straight.
St Matthew 3:2–3.

75 And the same John had his raiment of camel's hair, and a leathern girdle about his loins; and his meat was locusts and wild honey.
St Matthew 3:4.

76 But when he saw many of the Pharisees and Sadducees come to his baptism, he said unto them, O generation of vipers, who hath warned you to flee from the wrath to come?
St Matthew 3:7.

77 And Jesus, when he was baptized, went up straightway

out of the water: and, lo, the heavens were opened unto him, and he saw the Spirit of God descending like a dove, and lighting upon him: And lo a voice from heaven, saying, This is my beloved Son, in whom I am well pleased.
St Matthew 3:16–17.

78 Then was Jesus led up of the spirit into the wilderness to be tempted of the devil. And when he had fasted forty days and forty nights, he was afterward an hungred. And when the tempter came to him, he said, If thou be the Son of God, command that these stones be made bread. But he answered and said, It is written, Man shall not live by bread alone, but by every word that proceedeth out of the mouth of God.
St Matthew 4:1–4.

79 Jesus said unto him, It is written again, Thou shalt not tempt the Lord thy God.
St Matthew 4:7.

80 Again, the devil taketh him up into an exceeding high mountain, and sheweth him all the kingdoms of the world, and the glory of them; And saith unto him, All these things will I give thee, if thou wilt fall down and worship me. Then saith Jesus unto him, Get thee hence, Satan: for it is written, Thou shalt worship the Lord thy God, and him only shalt thou serve.
St Matthew 4:8–10.

81 The people which sat in darkness saw great light; and to them which sat in the region and shadow of death light is sprung up.
St Matthew 4:16.

82 And he saith unto them, Follow me, and I will make you fishers of men.
St Matthew 4:19.

83 And seeing the multitudes, he went up into a mountain: and when he was set, his disciples came unto him:
And he opened his mouth, and taught them, saying,
Blessed are the poor in spirit: for theirs is the kingdom of heaven.
Blessed are they that mourn: for they shall be comforted.
Blessed are the meek: for they shall inherit the earth.
Blessed are they which do hunger and thirst after righteousness: for they shall be filled.
Blessed are the merciful: for they shall obtain mercy.
Blessed are the pure in heart: for they shall see God.
Blessed are the peacemakers: for they shall be called the children of God.
Blessed are they which are persecuted for righteousness' sake: for theirs is the kingdom of heaven.
Blessed are ye, when men shall revile you, and persecute you, and shall say all manner of evil against you falsely, for my sake.
Rejoice, and be exceeding glad: for great is your reward in heaven: for so persecuted they the prophets which were before you.
St Matthew 5:1–12.

84 Ye are the salt of the earth: but if the salt have lost his savour, wherewith shall it be salted? it is thenceforth good for nothing, but to be cast out, and to be trodden under foot of men.
St Matthew 5:13.

85 Ye are the light of the world. A city that is set on an hill cannot be hid. Neither do men light a candle, and put it under a bushel, but on a candlestick; and it giveth light unto all that are in the house. Let your light so shine before men, that they may see your good works and glorify your Father which is in heaven.
St Matthew 5:14–16.

86 Think not that I am come to destroy the law, or the prophets: I am not come to destroy, but to fulfil. For verily I say unto you, Till heaven and earth pass, one jot or one tittle shall in no wise pass from the law, till all be fulfilled.
St Matthew 5:17–18.

87 For I say unto you, That except your righteousness shall exceed the righteousness of the scribes and Pharisees, ye shall in no case enter into the kingdom of heaven.
St Matthew 5:20.

88 But I say unto you, That whosoever is angry with his brother without a cause shall be in danger of the judgment: and whosoever shall say to his brother, Raca, shall be in danger of the council: but whosoever shall say, Thou fool, shall be in danger of hell fire.
St Matthew 5:22.

89 Ye have heard that it was said by them of old time, Thou shalt not commit adultery: But I say unto you. That whosoever looketh on a woman to lust after her hath committed adultery with her already in his heart.
St Matthew 5:27–8.

90 And if thy right eye offend thee, pluck it out, and cast it from thee: for it is profitable for thee that one of thy members should perish, and not that thy whole body should be cast into hell. And if thy right hand offend thee, cut it off, and cast it from thee: for it is profitable for thee that one of thy members should perish, and not that thy whole body should be cast into hell.
St Matthew 5:29–30.

91 Ye have heard that it hath been said, An eye for an eye, and a tooth for a tooth: But I say unto you, That ye resist not evil: but whosoever shall smite thee on thy right cheek, turn to him the other also.
St Matthew 5:38–9.

92 And whosoever shall compel thee to go a mile, go with him twain.
St Matthew 5:41.

93 Ye have heard that it hath been said, Thou shalt love thy neighbour, and hate thine enemy. But I say unto you, Love your enemies, bless them that curse you, do good to them that hate you, and pray for them which despitefully use you, and persecute you.
St Matthew 5:43–4.

94 That ye may be the children of your Father which is in heaven: for he maketh his sun to rise on the evil and on the good, and sendeth rain on the just and on the unjust.
St Matthew 5:45.

95 Be ye therefore perfect, even as your Father which is in heaven is perfect.
St Matthew 5:48.

96 Therefore when thou doest thine alms, do not sound a trumpet before thee, as the hypocrites do in the synagogues and in the streets, that they may have glory of men, Verily I say unto you, They have their reward. But when thou doest alms, let not thy left hand know what

thy right hand doeth: That thine alms may be in secret: and thy Father which seeth in secret himself shall reward thee openly.
St Matthew 6:2–4.

97 But thou, when thou prayest, enter into thy closet, and when thou hast shut thy door, pray to thy Father which is in secret; and thy Father which seeth in secret shall reward thee openly. But when ye pray, use not vain repetitions, as the heathen do: for they think that they shall be heard for their much speaking.
St Matthew 6:6–7.

98 After this manner therefore pray ye: Our Father which art in heaven, Hallowed be thy name. Thy kingdom come. Thy will be done in earth, as it is in heaven. Give us this day our daily bread. And forgive us our debts, as we forgive our debtors. And lead us not into temptation, but deliver us from evil: For thine is the kingdom, and the power, and the glory, for ever. Amen.
St Matthew 6:9–13

99 Lay not up for yourselves treasures upon earth, where moth and rust doth corrupt, and where thieves break through and steal: But lay up for yourselves treasures in heaven, where neither moth nor rust doth corrupt, and where thieves do not break through nor steal: For where your treasure is, there will your heart be also.
St Matthew 6:19–21.

1 No man can serve two masters: for either he will hate the one, and love the other; or else he will hold to the one, and despise the other. Ye cannot serve God and mammon.
St Matthew 6:24.

2 Behold the fowls of the air: for they sow not, neither do they reap, nor gather into barns; yet your heavenly Father feedeth them. Are ye not much better than they? Which of you by taking thought can add one cubit unto his stature? And why take ye thought for raiment? Consider the lilies of the field, how they grow; they toil not, neither do they spin: And yet I say unto you, That even Solomon in all his glory was not arrayed like one of these.
St Matthew 6:26–9.

3 But seek ye first the kingdom of God, and his righteousness; and all these things shall be added unto you. Take therefore no thought for the morrow: for the morrow shall take thought for the things of itself. Sufficient unto the day is the evil thereof.
St Matthew 6:33–4.

4 Judge not, that ye be not judged. For with what judgment ye judge, ye shall be judged: and with what measure ye mete, it shall be measured to you again.
St Matthew 7:1–2.

5 And why beholdest thou the mote that is in thy brother's eye, but considerest not the beam that is in thine own eye?
St Matthew 7:3.

6 Give not that which is holy unto the dogs, neither cast ye your pearls before swine, lest they trample them under their feet, and turn again and rend you.
St Matthew 7:6.

7 Ask, and it shall be given you; seek, and ye shall find; knock, and it shall be opened unto you: For every one that asketh receiveth; and he that seeketh findeth; and to him that knocketh it shall be opened.
St Matthew 7:7–8.

8 Or what man is there of you, whom if his son ask bread, will he give him a stone? Or if he ask a fish, will he give him a serpent? If ye then, being evil, know how to give good gifts unto your children, how much more shall your Father which is in heaven give good things to them that ask him?
St Matthew 7:9–11.

9 Enter ye in at the strait gate: for wide is the gate, and broad is the way, that leadeth to destruction, and many there be which go in thereat: Because strait is the gate, and narrow is the way, which leadeth unto life, and few there be that find it.
St Matthew 7:13–14.

10 Beware of false prophets, which come to you in sheep's clothing, but inwardly they are ravening wolves.
St Matthew 7:15.

11 Wherefore by their fruits ye shall know them.
St Matthew 7:20.

12 Not every one that saith unto me, Lord, Lord, shall enter into the kingdom of heaven; but he that doeth the will of my Father which is in heaven.
St Matthew 7:21.

13 Therefore whosoever heareth these sayings of mine, and doeth them, I will liken him unto a wise man, which built his house upon a rock: And the rain descended, and the floods came, and the winds blew, and beat upon that house; and it fell not: for it was founded upon a rock. And every one that heareth these sayings of mine, and doeth them not, shall be likened unto a foolish man, which built his house upon the sand: And the rain descended, and the floods came, and the winds blew, and beat upon that house; and it fell: and great was the fall of it.
St Matthew 7:24–7.

14 The centurion answered and said, Lord, I am not worthy that thou shouldest come under my roof: but speak the word only, and my servant shall be healed. For I am a man under authority, having soldiers under me: and I say to this man, Go, and he goeth; and to another, Come, and he cometh; and to my servant, Do this, and he doeth it. When Jesus heard it, he marvelled, and said to them that followed, Verily I say unto you, I have not found so great faith, no, not in Israel.
St Matthew 8:8–10.

15 But the children of the kingdom shall be cast out into outer darkness: there shall be weeping and gnashing of teeth.
St Matthew 8:12.

16 And Jesus saith unto him, The foxes have holes, and the birds of the air have nests; but the Son of man hath not where to lay his head.
St Matthew 8:20.

17 But Jesus said unto him, Follow me; and let the dead bury their dead.
St Matthew 8:22.

18 And his disciples came to him, and awoke him, saying, Lord, save us: we perish. And he saith unto them, Why are ye fearful, O ye of little faith? Then he arose, and rebuked

the winds and the sea; and there was a great calm. But the men marvelled, saying, What manner of man is this, that even the winds and the sea obey him!
St Matthew 8:25–7.

19 And as Jesus passed forth from thence, he saw a man, named Matthew, sitting at the receipt of custom: and he saith unto him, Follow me. And he arose, and followed him.
St Matthew 9:9.

20 But when Jesus heard that, he said unto them, They that be whole need not a physician, but they that are sick. But go ye and learn what that meaneth, I will have mercy, and not sacrifice: for I am not come to call the righteous, but sinners to repentance.
St Matthew 9:12–13.

21 No man putteth a piece of new cloth unto an old garment, for that which is put in to fill it up taketh from the garment, and the rent is made worse. Neither do men put new wine into old bottles: else the bottles break, and the wine runneth out, and the bottles perish: but they put new wine into new bottles, and both are preserved.
St Matthew 9:16–17.

22 But the Pharisees said, He casteth out devils through the prince of the devils.
St Matthew 9:34.

23 But go rather to the lost sheep of the house of Israel.
St Matthew 10:6.

24 Heal the sick, cleanse the lepers, raise the dead, cast out devils: freely ye have received, freely give.
St Matthew 10:8.

25 And whosoever shall not receive you, nor hear your words, when ye depart out of that house or city, shake off the dust of your feet.
St Matthew 10:14.

26 Behold, I send you forth as sheep in the midst of wolves: be ye therefore wise as serpents, and harmless as doves.
St Matthew 10:16.

27 The disciple is not above his master, nor the servant above his lord.
St Matthew 10:24.

28 Are not two sparrows sold for a farthing? and one of them shall not fall on the ground without your Father. But the very hairs of your head are all numbered. Fear ye not therefore, ye are of more value than many sparrows.
St Matthew 10:29–31.

29 Think not that I am come to send peace on earth: I came not to send peace, but a sword.
St Matthew 10:34.

30 He that loveth father or mother more than me is not worthy of me: and he that loveth son or daughter more than me is not worthy of me. And he that taketh not his cross, and followeth after me, is not worthy of me. He that findeth his life shall lose it: and he that loseth his life for my sake shall find it.
St Matthew 10:37–9.

31 And whosoever shall give to drink unto one of these little ones a cup of cold water only in the name of a disciple, verily I say unto you, he shall in no wise lose his reward.
St Matthew 10:42.

32 And said unto him, Art thou he that should come, or do we look for another?
St Matthew 11:3.

33 Jesus answered and said unto them, Go and shew John again those things which ye do hear and see: The blind receive their sight, and the lame walk, the lepers are cleansed, and the deaf hear, the dead are raised up, and the poor have the gospel preached to them.
St Matthew 11:4–5.

34 And as they departed, Jesus began to say unto the multitudes concerning John, What went ye out into the wilderness to see? A reed shaken with the wind? But what went ye out for to see? A man clothed in soft raiment? behold, they that wear soft clothing are in kings' houses. But what went ye out for to see? A prophet? yea, I say unto you, and more than a prophet.
St Matthew 11:7–9.

35 He that hath ears to hear, let him hear.
St Matthew 11:15.

36 And saying, We have piped unto you, and ye have not danced; we have mourned unto you, and ye have not lamented.
St Matthew 11:17.

37 But wisdom is justified of her children.
St Matthew 11:19.

38 Come unto me, all ye that labour and are heavy laden, and I will give you rest. Take my yoke upon you, and learn of me; for I am meek and lowly in heart: and ye shall find rest unto your souls. For my yoke is easy, and my burden is light.
St Matthew 11:28–30.

39 A bruised reed shall he not break, and smoking flax shall he not quench, till he send forth judgment unto victory.
St Matthew 12:20.

40 He that is not with me is against me: and he that gathereth not with me scattereth abroad.
St Matthew 12:30.

41 Wherefore I say unto you, All manner of sin and blasphemy shall be forgiven unto men: but the blasphemy against the Holy Ghost shall not be forgiven unto men.
St Matthew 12:31.

42 O generation of vipers, how can ye, being evil, speak good things? for out of the abundance of the heart the mouth speaketh.
St Matthew 12:34.

43 But he answered and said unto them, An evil and adulterous generation seeketh after a sign; and there shall no sign be given to it, but the sign of the prophet Jonas: For Jonas was three days and three nights in the whale's belly; so shall the Son of man be three days and three nights in the heart of the earth.
St Matthew 12:39–40.

44 The queen of the south shall rise up in the judgment with this generation, and shall condemn it: for she came from the uttermost parts of the earth to hear the wisdom of Solomon; and, behold, a greater than Solomon is here.
St Matthew 12:42.

45 When the unclean spirit is gone out of a man, he walketh through dry places, seeking rest, and findeth none. Then

he saith, I will return into my house from whence I came out; and when he is come, he findeth it empty, swept, and garnished. Then goeth he, and taketh with himself seven other spirits more wicked than himself, and they enter in and dwell there: and the last state of that man is worse than the first. Even so shall it be also unto this wicked generation.
St Matthew 12:43–5.

46 And he stretched forth his hand toward his disciples, and said, Behold my mother and my brethren! For whosoever shall do the will of my Father which is in heaven, the same is my brother, and sister, and mother.
St Matthew 12:49–50.

47 And he spake many things unto them in parables, saying, Behold, a sower went forth to sow; And when he sowed, some seeds fell by the wayside, and the fowls came and devoured them up: Some fell upon stony places, where they had not much earth: and forthwith they sprung up, because they had no deepness of earth: And when the sun was up, they were scorched; and because they had no root, they withered away. And some fell among thorns; and the thorns sprung up, and choked them: But others fell into good ground, and brought forth fruit, some an hundredfold, some sixtyfold, some thirtyfold.
St Matthew 13:3–8.

48 He also that received seed among the thorns is he that heareth the word; and the care of this world, and the deceitfulness of riches, choke the word, and he becometh unfruitful.
St Matthew 13:22.

49 But he that received seed into the good ground is he that heareth the word, and understandeth it; which also beareth fruit, and bringeth forth, some an hundredfold, some sixty, some thirty.
St Matthew 13:23.

50 But while men slept, his enemy came and sowed tares among the wheat, and went his way.
St Matthew 13:25.

51 He said unto them, An enemy hath done this. The servants said unto him, Wilt thou then that we go and gather them up?
St Matthew 13:28.

52 Another parable put he forth unto them, saying, The kingdom of heaven is like to a grain of mustard seed which a man took, and sowed in his field: Which indeed is the least of all seeds: but when it is grown, it is the greatest among herbs, and becometh a tree, so that the birds of the air come and lodge in the branches thereof.
St Matthew 13:31–2.

53 Again the kingdom of heaven is like unto a merchant man, seeking goodly pearls: Who, when he had found one pearl of great price, went and sold all that he had, and bought it.
St Matthew 13:45–6.

54 And they were offended in him. But Jesus said unto them, A prophet is not without honour, save in his own country, and in his own house.
St Matthew 13:57.

55 And they say unto him, We have here but five loaves, and two fishes.
St Matthew 14:17.

56 And in the fourth watch of the night Jesus went unto them, walking on the sea. And when the disciples saw him walking on the sea, they were troubled, saying, It is a spirit; and they cried out for fear. But straightway Jesus spake unto them, saying, Be of good cheer; it is I; be not afraid.
St Matthew 14:25–7.

57 And immediately Jesus stretched forth his hand, and caught him, and said unto him, O thou of little faith, wherefore didst thou doubt?
St Matthew 14:31.

58 Not that which goeth into the mouth defileth a man; but that which cometh out of the mouth, this defileth a man.
St Matthew 15:11.

59 Let them alone: they be blind leaders of the blind. And if the blind lead the blind, both shall fall into the ditch.
St Matthew 15:14.

60 And she said, Truth, Lord: yet the dogs eat of the crumbs which fall from their masters' table.
St Matthew 15:27.

61 He answered and said unto them, When it is evening, ye say, It will be fair weather: for the sky is red. And in the morning, It will be foul weather to day: for the sky is red and lowring. O ye hypocrites, ye can discern the face of the sky; but can ye not discern the signs of the times?
St Matthew 16:2–3.

62 Thou art Peter, and upon this rock I will build my church; and the gates of hell shall not prevail against it. And I will give unto thee the keys of the kingdom of heaven: and whatsoever thou shalt loose on earth shall be loosed in heaven.
St Matthew 16:18–19.

63 But he turned, and said unto Peter, Get thee behind me, Satan: thou art an offence unto me: for thou savourest not the things that be of God, but those that be of men.
St Matthew 16:23.

64 For whosoever will save his life shall lose it: and whosoever will lose his life for my sake shall find it. For what is a man profited, if he shall gain the whole world, and lose his own soul? or what shall a man give in exchange for his soul?
St Matthew 16:25–6.

65 And Jesus said unto them, Because of your unbelief: for verily I say unto you, If ye have faith as a grain of mustard seed, ye shall say unto this mountain, Remove hence to yonder place; and it shall remove; and nothing shall be impossible unto you.
St Matthew 17:20.

66 And said, Verily I say unto you, Except ye be converted, and become as little children, ye shall not enter into the kingdom of heaven.
St Matthew 18:3.

67 And whoso shall receive one such little child in my name receiveth me. But whoso shall offend one of these little ones which believe in me, it were better for him that a millstone were hanged about his neck, and that he were drowned in the depth of the sea.
St Matthew 18:5–6.

68 And if thine eye offend thee, pluck it out, and cast it from thee: it is better for thee to enter into life with one eye,

rather than having two eyes to be cast into hell fire.
St Matthew 18:9.

69 For where two or three are gathered together in my name, there am I in the midst of them.
St Matthew 18:20.

70 Then came Peter to him, and said, Lord, how oft shall my brother sin against me, and I forgive him? till seven times? Jesus saith unto him, I say not unto thee, Until seven times: but, Until seventy times seven.
St Mattthew 18:21–2.

71 What therefore God hath joined together, let not man put asunder.
St Matthew 19:6.

72 Then were there brought unto him little children, that he should put his hands on them, and pray: and the disciples rebuked them. But Jesus said, Suffer little children, and forbid them not, to come unto me: for of such is the kingdom of heaven.
St Matthew 19:13–14.

73 Jesus said unto him, If thou wilt be perfect, go and sell that thou hast, and give to the poor, and thou shalt have treasure in heaven: and come and follow me. But when the young man heard that saying, he went away sorrowful: for he had great possessions.
St Matthew 19:21–2.

74 And again I say unto you, It is easier for a camel to go through the eye of a needle, than for a rich man to enter into the kingdom of God.
St Matthew 19:24.

75 When his disciples heard it, they were exceedingly amazed, saying, Who then can be saved? But Jesus beheld them, and said unto them, With men this is impossible; but with God all things are possible.
St Matthew 19:25–6.

76 But many that are first shall be last; and the last shall be first.
St Matthew 19:30.

77 And about the eleventh hour he went out, and found others standing idle, and saith unto them, Why stand ye here all the day idle?
St Matthew 20:6.

78 Is it not lawful for me to do what I will with mine own? Is thine eye evil, because I am good? So the last shall be first, and the first last: for many be called, but few chosen.
St Matthew 20:15–16.

79 And Jesus went into the temple of God, and cast out all them that sold and bought in the temple, and overthrew the tables of the moneychangers, and the seats of them that sold doves, And said unto them, It is written, My house shall be called the house of prayer; but ye have made it a den of thieves.
St Matthew 21:12–13.

80 Render therefore unto Caesar the things which are Caesar's; and unto God the things that are God's.
St Matthew 22:21.

81 For in the resurrection they neither marry, nor are given in marriage, but are as the angels of God in heaven.
St Matthew 22:30.

82 Jesus said unto him, Thou shalt love the Lord Thy God with all thy heart, and with all thy soul, and with all thy mind. This is the first and great commandment. And the second is like unto it, Thou shalt love thy neighbour as thyself. On these two commandments hang all the law and the prophets.
St Matthew 22:37–40.

83 Ye blind guides, which strain at a gnat, and swallow a camel.
St Matthew 23:24.

84 Woe unto you, scribes and Pharisees, hypocrites! for ye are like unto whited sepulchres, which indeed appear beautiful outward, but are within full of dead men's bones, and of all uncleanness.
St Matthew 23:27.

85 And ye shall hear of wars and rumours or wars: see that ye be not troubled: for all these things must come to pass, but the end is not yet. For nation shall rise against nation, and kingdom against kingdom: and there shall be famines, and pestilences, and earthquakes, in divers places.
St Matthew 24:6–7.

86 Verily I say unto you, This generation shall not pass, till all these things be fulfilled. Heaven and earth shall pass away, but my words shall not pass away.
St Matthew 24:34–5.

87 For as in the days that were before the flood they were eating and drinking, marrying and giving in marriage, until the day that Noe entered into the ark.
St Matthew 24:38.

88 Watch therefore: for ye know not what hour your Lord doth come. But know this, that if the goodman of the house had known in what watch the thief would come, he would have watched, and would not have suffered his house to be broken up.
St Matthew 24:42–3.

89 His lord said unto him, Well done, thou good and faithful servant: thou hast been faithful over a few things, I will make thee ruler over many things: enter thou into the joy of thy lord.
St Matthew 25:21.

90 For unto every one that hath shall be given, and he shall have abundance: but from him that hath not shall be taken away even that which he hath. And cast ye the unprofitable servant into outer darkness: there shall be weeping and gnashing of teeth.
St Matthew 25:29–30.

91 When the Son of man shall come in his glory, and all the holy angels with him, then shall he sit upon the throne of his glory: And before him shall be gathered all nations: and he shall separate them one from another, as a shepherd divideth his sheep from the goats: And he shall set the sheep on his right hand, but the goats on the left.
St Matthew 25:31–3.

92 For I was an hungred, and ye gave me meat: I was thirsty, and ye gave me drink: I was a stranger, and ye took me in: Naked, and ye clothed me: I was sick, and ye visited me: I was in prison, and ye came unto me.
St Matthew 25:35–6.

93 And the King shall answer and say unto them, Verily I say unto you, Inasmuch as ye have done it unto one of the

least of these my brethren, ye have done it unto me.
St Matthew 25:40.

94 For ye have the poor always with you; but me ye have not always.
St Matthew 26:11.

95 Then one of the twelve, called Judas Iscariot, went unto the chief priests, And said unto them, What will ye give me, and I will deliver him unto you? And they covenanted with him for thirty pieces of silver.
St Matthew 26:14–15.

96 And as they were eating, Jesus took bread, and blessed it, and brake it, and gave it to the disciples, and said, Take, eat; this is my body. And he took the cup, and gave thanks, and gave it to them, saying, Drink ye all of it; For this is my blood of the new testament, which is shed for many for the remission of sins.
St Matthew 26:26–8.

97 Jesus said unto him, Verily I say unto thee, That this night, before the cock crow, thou shalt deny me thrice. Peter said unto him, Though I should die with thee yet will I not deny thee. Likewise also said all the disciples.
St Matthew 26:34–5.

98 And he went a little further, and fell on his face, and prayed, saying, O my Father, if it be possible, let this cup pass from me: nevertheless not as I will, but as thou wilt.
St Matthew 26:39.

99 Watch and pray, that ye enter not into temptation: the spirit indeed is willing, but the flesh is weak.
St Matthew 26:41.

1 Then said Jesus unto him, Put up again thy sword into his place: for all they that take the sword shall perish with the sword.
St Matthew 26:52.

2 When Pilate saw that he could prevail nothing, but that rather a tumult was made, he took water, and washed his hands before the multitude, saying I am innocent of the blood of this just person: see ye to it.
St Matthew 27:24.

3 He saved others; himself he cannot save. If he be the King of Israel, let him now come down from the cross, and we will believe him.
St Matthew 27:42.

4 And about the ninth hour Jesus cried with a loud voice, saying Eli, Eli, lama sabachthani? that is to say, My God, my God, why hast thou forsaken me?
St Matthew 27:46.

5 Jesus, when he had cried again with a loud voice, yielded up the ghost. And behold, the veil of the temple was rent in twain from the top to the bottom; and the earth did quake, and the rocks rent; And the graves were opened; and many bodies of the saints which slept arose.
St Matthew 27:50–2.

6 And, lo, I am with you alway, even unto the end of the world. Amen.
St Matthew 28:20.

7 When Jesus heard it, he saith unto them, They that are whole have no need of the physician, but they that are sick: I came not to call the righteous, but sinners to repentance.
St Mark 2:17.

8 And he said unto them, The sabbath was made for man, and not man for the sabbath: Therefore the Son of man is Lord also of the sabbath.
St Mark 2:27–8.

9 And if a kingdom be divided against itself, that kingdom cannot stand. And if a house be divided against itself, that house cannot stand.
St Mark 3:24–5.

10 And he said unto them, He that hath ears to hear, let him hear.
St Mark 4:9.

11 And he said unto them, Take heed what ye hear: with what measure ye mete, it shall be measured to you: and unto you that hear shall more be given.
St Mark 4:24.

12 And he asked him, What is thy name? And he answered, saying, My name is Legion: for we are many.
St Mark 5:9.

13 And Jesus, immediately knowing in himself that virtue had gone out of him, turned him about in the press, and said, Who touched my clothes?
St Mark 5:30.

14 And were beyond measure astonished, saying, He hath done all things well: he maketh both the deaf to hear, and the dumb to speak.
St Mark 7:37.

15 And he looked up, and said, I see men as trees, walking.
St Mark 8:24.

16 And straightway the father of the child cried out, and said with tears, Lord, I believe; help thou mine unbelief.
St Mark 9:24.

17 But when Jesus saw it, he was much displeased, and said unto them, Suffer the little children to come unto me, and forbid them not: for of such is the kingdom of God.
St Mark 10:14.

18 And there came a certain poor widow, and she threw in two mites, which make a farthing. And he called unto him his disciples, and saith unto them, Verily I say unto you, That this poor widow hath cast more in, than all they which have cast into the treasury: For all they did cast in of their abundance; but she of her want did cast in all that she had, even all her living.
St Mark 12:42–4.

19 And when the centurion, which stood over against him, saw that he so cried out, and gave up the ghost, he said, Truly this man was the Son of God.
St Mark 15:39.

20 And he said unto them, Go ye into all the world, and preach the gospel to every creature.
St Mark 16:15.

21 And the angel came in unto her, and said, Hail, thou that art highly favoured, the Lord is with thee: blessed art thou among women. And when she saw him, she was troubled at his saying, and cast in her mind what manner of salutation this should be.
St Luke 1:28–9.

22 And Mary said, Behold the handmaid of the Lord; be it unto me according to thy word. And the angel departed from her.
St Luke 1:38.

23 And Mary said,
  My soul doth magnify the Lord,
  And my spirit hath rejoiced in God my Saviour.
  For he hath regarded the low estate of his handmaiden:
   for, behold, from henceforth all generations shall call
   me blessed.
  For he that is mighty hath done to me great things; and
   holy is his name.
  And his mercy is on them that fear him from generation
   to generation.
  He hath shewed strength with his arm; he hath scattered
   the proud in the imagination of their hearts.
  He hath put down the mighty from their seats, and
   exalted them of low degree.
  He hath filled the hungry with good things; and the rich
   he hath sent empty away.
St Luke 1:46–53.

24 And it came to pass in those days, that there went out a
decree from Caesar Augustus, that all the world should
be taxed.
St Luke 2:1.

25 And so it was, that, while they were there, the days were
accomplished that she should be delivered. And she
brought forth her firstborn son, and wrapped him in
swaddling clothes, and laid him in a manger; because
there was no room for them in the inn.
St Luke 2:6–7.

26 And there were in the same country shepherds abiding
in the field, keeping watch over their flock by night. And,
lo, the angel of the Lord came upon them, and the glory
of the Lord shone round about them: and they were sore
afraid. And the angel said unto them, Fear not: for,
behold, I bring you good tidings of great joy, which shall
be to all people. For unto you is born this day in the city
of David a Saviour, which is Christ the Lord. And this shall
be a sign unto you; Ye shall find the babe wrapped in
swaddling clothes, lying in a manger. And suddenly there
was with the angel a multitude of the heavenly host
praising God, and saying, Glory to God in the highest,
and on earth peace, good will toward men. And it came
to pass, as the angels were gone away from them into
heaven, the shepherds said one to another, Let us now go
even unto Bethlehem, and see this thing which is come
to pass, which the Lord hath made known unto us.
St Luke 2:8–15.

27 Lord, now lettest thou thy servant depart in peace,
according to thy word: For mine eyes have seen thy
salvation, Which thou hast prepared before the face of
all people; A light to lighten the Gentiles, and the glory
of thy people Israel.
St Luke 2:29–32.

28 And Jesus increased in wisdom and stature, and in favour
with God and man.
St Luke 2:52.

29 And he said unto them, Ye will surely say unto me this
proverb, Physician, heal thyself: whatsoever we have
heard done in Capernaum, do also here in thy country.
St Luke 4:23.

30 Woe unto you, when all men shall speak well of you! for
so did their fathers to the false prophets.
St Luke 6:26.

31 Give, and it shall be given unto you; good measure,
pressed down, and shaken together, and running over,
shall men give into your bosom. For with the same
measure that ye mete withal it shall be measured to you
again.
St Luke 6:38.

32 Wherefore I say unto thee, Her sins, which are many, are
forgiven; for she loved much: but to whom little is
forgiven, the same loveth little.
St Luke 7:47.

33 And he said to them all, If any man will come after me, let
him deny himself, and take up his cross daily, and follow
me.
St Luke 9:23.

34 And Jesus said unto him, No man, having put his hand to
the plough, and looking back, is fit for the kingdom of
God.
St Luke 9:62.

35 And into whatsoever house ye enter, first say, Peace be to
this house. And if the son of peace be there, your peace
shall rest upon it: if not, it shall turn to you again. And in
the same house remain, eating and drinking such things
as they give: for the labourer is worthy of his hire.
St Luke 10:5–7.

36 And he said unto them, I beheld Satan as lightning fall
from heaven.
St Luke 10:18.

37 And Jesus answering said, A certain man went down
from Jerusalem to Jericho, and fell among thieves, which
stripped him of his raiment, and wounded him, and
departed, leaving him half dead. And by chance there
came down a certain priest that way: and when he saw
him, he passed by on the other side.
St Luke 10:30–31.

38 But a certain Samaritan, as he journeyed, came where he
was: and when he saw him, he had compassion on him,
And went to him, and bound up his wounds, pouring in
oil and wine, and set him on his own beast, and brought
him to an inn, and took care of him. And on the morrow
when he departed, he took out two pence, and gave
them to the host, and said unto him, Take care of him; and
whatsoever thou spendest more, when I come again, I
will repay thee.
St Luke 10:33–5.

39 And he said, He that shewed mercy on him. Then said
Jesus unto him, Go, and do thou likewise.
St Luke 10:37

40 But Martha was cumbered about much serving, and
came to him, and said, Lord, dost thou not care that my
sister hath left me to serve alone? bid her therefore that
she help me.
  And Jesus answered and said unto her, Martha, Martha,
   thou art careful and troubled about many things:
  But one thing is needful: and Mary hath chosen that
   good part, which shall not be taken away from her.
St Luke 10:40–2.

41 Woe unto you, lawyers! for ye have taken away the key of
knowledge.
St Luke 11:52.

42 And I will say to my soul, Soul, thou hast much goods laid
up for many years; take thine ease, eat, drink, and be

merry. But God said unto him, Thou fool, this night thy soul shall be required of thee.
St Luke 12:19–20.

43 For which of you, intending to build a tower, sitteth not down first, and counteth the cost, whether he have sufficient to finish it?
St Luke 14:28.

44 What man of you, having an hundred sheep, if he lose one of them, doth not leave the ninety and nine in the wilderness, and go after that which is lost, until he find it? And when he hath found it, he layeth it on his shoulders, rejoicing.
St Luke 15:4–5.

45 Either what woman having ten pieces of silver, if she lose one piece, doth not light a candle, and sweep the house, and seek diligently till she find it? And when she hath found it, she calleth her friends and her neighbours together, saying, Rejoice with me; for I have found the piece which I had lost. Likewise, I say unto you, there is joy in the presence of the angels of God over one sinner that repenteth.
St Luke 15:8–10.

46 And not many days after the younger son gathered all together, and took his journey into a far country, and there wasted his substance with riotous living.
St Luke 15:13.

47 And he would fain have filled his belly with the husks that the swine did eat: and no man gave unto him. And when he came to himself, he said, How many hired servants of my father's have bread enough and to spare, and I perish with hunger! I will arise and go to my father, and will say unto him, Father, I have sinned against heaven, and before thee, And am no more worthy to be called thy son: make me as one of thy hired servants.
St Luke 15:16–19.

48 And he arose, and came to his father. But when he was yet a great way off, his father saw him, and had compassion, and ran, and fell on his neck, and kissed him. And the son said unto him, Father, I have sinned against heaven, and in thy sight, and am no more worthy to be called thy son. But the father said to his servants, Bring forth the best robe, and put it on him; and put a ring on his hand, and shoes on his feet: And bring hither the fatted calf, and kill it: and let us eat, and be merry: For this my son was dead, and is alive again; he was lost, and is found. And they began to be merry.
St Luke 15:20–4.

49 It was meet that we should make merry, and be glad: for this thy brother was dead, and is alive again; and was lost, and is found.
St Luke 15:32.

50 And the lord commended the unjust steward, because he had done wisely: for the children of this world are in their generation wiser than the children of light.
St Luke 16:8.

51 And I say unto you, Make to yourselves friends of the mammon of unrighteousness; that, when ye fail, they may receive you into everlasting habitations.
St Luke 16:9.

52 He that is faithful in that which is least is faithful also in

much: and he that is unjust in the least is unjust also in much.
St Luke 16:10.

53 There was a certain rich man, which was clothed in purple and fine linen, and fared sumptuously every day: And there was a certain beggar named Lazarus, which was laid at his gate, full of sores, And desiring to be fed with the crumbs which fell from the rich man's table: moreover the dogs came and licked his sores.
St Luke 16:19–21.

54 And it came to pass, that the beggar died, and was carried by the angels into Abraham's bosom: the rich man also died, and was buried; And in hell he lift up his eyes, being in torments, and seeth Abraham afar off, and Lazarus in his bosom.
St Luke 16:22–3.

55 And beside all this, between us and you there is a great gulf fixed: so that they which would pass from hence to you cannot; neither can they pass to us, that would come from thence.
St Luke 16:26.

56 Neither shall they say, Lo here! or, lo there! for, behold, the kingdom of God is within you.
St Luke 17:21.

57 Remember Lot's wife.
St Luke 17:32.

58 For every one that exalteth himself shall be abased; and he that humbleth himself shall be exalted.
St Luke 18:14.

59 And he answered and said unto them, I tell you that, if these should hold their peace, the stones would immediately cry out.
St Luke 19:40.

60 In your patience possess ye your souls.
St Luke 21:19.

61 Saying, Father, if thou be willing, remove this cup from me: nevertheless not my will, but thine, be done.
St Luke 22:42.

62 And the Lord turned, and looked upon Peter. And Peter remembered the word of the Lord, how he had said unto him, Before the cock crow, thou shalt deny me thrice.
St Luke 22:61.

63 Then said Jesus, Father, forgive them; for they know not what they do. And they parted his raiment, and cast lots.
St Luke 23:34.

64 And he said unto Jesus, Lord, remember me when thou comest into thy kingdom. And Jesus said unto him, Verily I say unto thee, To day shalt thou be with me in paradise.
St Luke 23:42–3.

65 And the sun was darkened, and the veil of the temple was rent in the midst.
St Luke 23:45.

66 And when Jesus had cried with a loud voice, he said, Father, into thy hands I commend my spirit: and having said thus, he gave up the ghost.
St Luke 23:46.

67 And as they were afraid, and bowed down their faces to the earth, they said unto them, Why seek ye the living among the dead? He is not here, but is risen: remember

how he spake unto you when he was yet in Galilee.
St Luke 24:5–6.

68 And their words seemed to them as idle tales, and they believed them not.
St Luke 24:11.

69 And they said one to another, Did not our heart burn within us, while he talked with us by the way, and while he opened to us the scriptures?
St Luke 24:32.

70 And they gave him a piece of a broiled fish, and of an honeycomb.
St Luke 24:42.

71 In the beginning was the Word, and the Word was with God, and the Word was God. The same was in the beginning with God. All things were made by him; and without him was not any thing made that was made.
St John 1:1–3.

72 In him was life; and the life was the light of men. And the light shineth in darkness; and the darkness comprehended it not.
St John 1:4–5.

73 That was the true Light, which lighteth every man that cometh into the world. He was in the world, and the world was made by him, and the world knew him not.
St John 1:9–10.

74 And the Word was made flesh, and dwelt among us, (and we beheld his glory, the glory as of the only begotten of the Father,) full of grace and truth.
St John 1:14.

75 The next day John seeth Jesus coming unto him, and saith, Behold the Lamb of God, which taketh away the sin of the world.
St John 1:29.

76 And Nathanael said unto him, Can there any good thing come out of Nazareth? Philip saith unto him, Come and see.
St John 1:46.

77 Jesus saith unto her, Woman, what have I to do with thee? mine hour is not yet come.
St John 2:4.

78 When the ruler of the feast had tasted the water that was made wine, and knew not whence it was: (but the servants which drew the water knew;) the governor of the feast called the bridegroom, And saith unto him, Every man at the beginning doth set forth good wine; and when men have well drunk, then that which is worse: but thou hast kept the good wine until now.
St John 2:9–10.

79 Jesus answered and said unto him, Verily, verily, I say unto thee, Except a man be born again, he cannot see the kingdom of God.
St John 3:3.

80 The wind bloweth where it listeth, and thou hearest the sound thereof, but canst not tell whence it cometh, and whither it goeth: so is every one that is born of the Spirit.
St John 3:8.

81 For God so loved the world, that he gave his only begotten Son, that whosoever believeth in him should not perish, but have everlasting life.
St John 3:16.

82 And this is the condemnation, that light is come into the world, and men loved darkness rather than light, because their deeds were evil.
St John 3:19.

83 He must increase, but I must decrease.
St John 3:30.

84 God is a Spirit: and they that worship him must worship him in spirit and in truth.
St John 4:24.

85 Say not ye, There are yet four months, and then cometh harvest? behold, I say unto you, Lift up your eyes, and look on the fields; for they are white already to harvest.
St John 4:35.

86 Jesus saith unto him, Rise, take up thy bed, and walk.
St John 5:8.

87 He was a burning and a shining light; and ye were willing for a season to rejoice in his light.
Of John the Baptist. St John 5:35.

88 Search the scriptures; for in them ye think ye have eternal life: and they are they which testify of me.
St John 5:39.

89 There is a lad here, which hath five barley loaves, and two small fishes: but what are they among so many?
St John 6:9.

90 And Jesus said unto them, I am the bread of life: he that cometh to me shall never hunger; and he that believeth on me shall never thirst.
St John 6:35.

91 All that the Father giveth me shall come to me; and him that cometh to me I will in no wise cast out.
St John 6:37.

92 Verily, verily, I say unto you, He that believeth on me hath everlasting life. I am that bread of life.
St John 6:47–8.

93 It is the spirit that quickeneth; the flesh profiteth nothing: the words that I speak unto you, they are spirit, and they are life.
St John 6:63.

94 So when they continued asking him, he lifted up himself, and said unto them, He that is without sin among you, let him first cast a stone at her.
St John 8:7.

95 Then spake Jesus again unto them, saying, I am the light of the world: he that followeth me shall not walk in darkness, but shall have the light of life.
St John 8:12.

96 And ye shall know the truth, and the truth shall make you free.
St John 8:32.

97 If the Son therefore shall make you free, ye shall be free indeed.
St John 8:36.

98 Ye are of your father the devil, and the lusts of the father ye will do. He was a murderer from the beginning, and abode not in the truth, because there is no truth in him. When he speaketh a lie, he speaketh of his own: for he is a liar, and the father of it.
St John 8:44.

99 Whether he be a sinner or no, I know not: one thing I know, that, whereas I was blind, now I see.
St John 9:25.

1 The thief cometh not, but for to steal, and to kill, and to destroy: I am come that they might have life, and that they might have it more abundantly.
St John 10:10.

2 I am the good shepherd: the good shepherd giveth his life for the sheep. But he that is an hireling, and not the shepherd, whose own the sheep are not, seeth the wolf coming, and leaveth the sheep, and fleeth: and the wolf catcheth them, and scattereth the sheep. The hireling fleeth, because he is an hireling, and careth not for the sheep. I am the good shepherd, and know my sheep, and am known of mine. As the Father knoweth me, even so know I the Father: and I lay down my life for the sheep. And other sheep I have which are not of this fold: them also must I bring, and they shall hear my voice; and there shall be one fold, and one shepherd.
St John 10:11–16.

3 I am the resurrection, and the life: he that believeth in me, though he were dead, yet shall he live.
St John 11:25.

4 Jesus wept.
This is the shortest verse in the Bible. St John 11:35.

5 For the poor always ye have with you; but me ye have not always.
St John 12:8.

6 That thou doest, do quickly.
Jesus to Judas. St John 13:27.

7 A new commandment I give unto you, That ye love one another; as I have loved you, that ye also love one another. By this shall all men know that ye are my disciples, if ye have love one to another.
St John 13:34–5.

8 Let not your heart be troubled: ye believe in God, believe also in me.
St John 14:1.

9 In my Father's house are many mansions: if it were not so, I would have told you. I go to prepare a place for you. And if I go and prepare a place for you, I will come again, and receive you unto myself; that where I am, there ye may be also.
St John 14:2–3.

10 Jesus saith unto him, I am the way, the truth, and the life: no man cometh unto the Father, but by me.
St John 14:6.

11 Peace I leave with you, my peace I give unto you: not as the world giveth, give I unto you, Let not your heart be troubled, neither let it be afraid.
St John 14:27.

12 This is my commandment, That ye love one another, as I have loved you. Greater love hath no man than this, that a man lay down his life for his friends.
St John 15:12–13.

13 I have yet many things to say unto you, but ye cannot bear them now.
St John 16:12.

14 These things I have spoken unto you, that in me ye might have peace. In the world ye shall have tribulation: but be of good cheer; I have overcome the world.
St John 16:33.

15 While I was with them in the world, I kept them in thy name: those that thou gavest me I have kept, and none of them is lost, but the son of perdition; that the scripture might be fulfilled.
St John 17:12.

16 Pilate saith unto him, What is truth?
St John 18:38.

17 Then said the chief priests of the Jews to Pilate, Write not, The King of the Jews; but that he said, I am King of the Jews. Pilate answered, What I have written I have written.
St John 19:21–2.

18 When Jesus therefore saw his mother, and the disciple standing by, whom he loved, he saith unto his mother, Woman, behold thy son! Then saith he to the disciple, Behold thy mother! And from that hour that disciple took her unto his own home.
St John 19:26–7.

19 He said It is finished: and he bowed his head, and gave up the ghost.
St John 19:30.

20 But one of the soldiers with a spear pierced his side, and forthwith came there out blood and water.
St John 19:34.

21 The first day of the week cometh Mary Magdalene early, when it was yet dark, unto the sepulchre, and seeth the stone taken away from the sepulchre.
St John 20:1.

22 So they ran both together: and the other disciple did outrun Peter, and came first to the sepulchre.
St John 20:4.

23 Jesus saith unto her, Woman, why weepest thou? whom seekest thou? She, supposing him to be the gardener, saith unto him, Sir, if thou have borne him hence, tell me where thou hast laid him, and I will take him away. Jesus saith unto her, Mary. She turned herself, and saith unto him, Rabboni; which is to say, Master. Jesus saith unto her, Touch me not; for I am not yet ascended to my Father: but go to my brethren, and say unto them, I ascend unto my Father, and your Father; and to my God, and your God.
St John 20:15–17. The Latin Vulgate translation of the Bible, ascribed to St Jerome, famously renders the phrase 'Do not touch me' as 'Noli me tangere'.

24 Except I shall see in his hands the print of the nails, and put my finger into the print of the nails, and thrust my hand into his side, I will not believe.
Thomas. St John 20:25.

25 Be not faithless, but believing. And Thomas answered and said unto him, My Lord and my God. Jesus saith unto him, Thomas, because thou hast seen me, thou hast believed: blessed are they that have not seen, and yet have believed.
St John 20:27–9.

26 When thou wast young, thou girdest thyself, and walkedst whither thou wouldest: but when thou shalt be old, thou shalt stretch forth thy hands, and another shall gird thee, and carry thee whither thou wouldest not.
St John 21:18.

27 It is not for you to know the times or the seasons, which

the Father hath put in his own power. But ye shall receive power, after that the Holy Ghost is come upon you: and ye shall be witnesses unto me both in Jerusalem, and in all Judea, and in Samaria, and unto the uttermost part of the earth.
Acts of the Apostles 1:7–8.

28 Ye men of Galilee, why stand ye gazing up into heaven? this same Jesus, which is taken up from you into heaven, shall so come in like manner as ye have seen him go into heaven.
Acts of the Apostles 1:11.

29 And when the day of Pentecost was fully come, they were all with one accord in one place. And suddenly there came a sound from heaven as of a rushing mighty wind, and it filled all the house where they were sitting. And there appeared unto them cloven tongues like as of fire, and it sat upon each of them. And they were all filled with the Holy Ghost, and began to speak with other tongues, as the Spirit gave them utterance.
Acts of the Apostles 2:1–4.

30 Silver and gold have I none; but such as I have give I thee: In the name of Jesus Christ of Nazareth rise up and walk.
Acts of the Apostles 3:6.

31 And he leaping up stood, and walked, and entered with them into the temple, walking, and leaping, and praising God.
Acts of the Apostles 3:8.

32 Neither is there salvation in any other: for there is none other name under heaven given among men, whereby we must be saved.
Acts of the Apostles 4:12.

33 We ought to obey God rather than men.
Acts of the Apostles 5:29.

34 Then the twelve called the multitude of the disciples unto them, and said, It is not reason that we should leave the word of God, and serve tables.
Acts of the Apostles 6:2–4.

35 And the witnesses laid down their clothes at a young man's feet, whose name was Saul.
Acts of the Apostles 7:57–8.

36 Understandest thou what thou readest? And he said, How can I, except some man should guide me?
Acts of the Apostles 8:30–1.

37 Saul, Saul, why persecutest thou me? And he said, Who art thou, Lord? And the Lord said, I am Jesus whom thou persecutest: it is hard for thee to kick against the pricks.
Acts of the Apostles 9:3–5.

38 Tabitha, which by interpretation is called Dorcas: this woman was full of good works.
Acts of the Apostles 9:36.

39 And saw heaven opened, and a certain vessel descending unto him, as it had been a great sheet knit at the four corners, and let down to the earth:
Wherein were all manner of fourfooted beasts of the earth, and wild beasts, and creeping things, and fowls of the air. And there came a voice to him, Rise, Peter; kill, and eat.
Acts of the Apostles 10:11–13.

40 What God hath cleansed, that call not thou common.
Acts of the Apostles 10:15.

41 Of a truth I perceive that God is no respecter of persons: But in every nation he that feareth Him, and worketh righteousness, is accepted with Him.
Acts of the Apostles 10:34–5.

42 The gods are come down to us in the likeness of men.
Acts of the Apostles 14:11.

43 Sirs, why do ye these things? We also are men of like passions with you, and preach unto you that ye should turn from these vanities unto the living God, which made heaven, and earth, and the sea, and all things that are therein.
Acts of the Apostles 14:15.

44 Sirs, what must I do to be saved? And they said, Believe on the Lord Jesus Christ, and thou shalt be saved, and thy house.
Acts of the Apostles 16:30–1.

45 But the Jews which believeth not, moved with envy, took unto them certain lewd fellows of the baser sort, and gathered a company, and set all the city on an uproar.
Acts of the Apostles 17:5.

46 These that have turned the world upside down are come hither also.
Acts of the Apostles 17:6.

47 What will this babbler say?
Acts of the Apostles 17:18.

48 Ye men of Athens, I perceive that in all things ye are too superstitious. For as I passed by, and beheld your devotions, I found an altar with this inscription, TO THE UNKNOWN GOD. Whom therefore ye ignorantly worship, him declare I unto you.
Acts of the Apostles 17:22–3.

49 God that made the world and all things therein, seeing that he is Lord of heaven and earth, dwelleth not in temples made with hands.
Acts of the Apostles 17:24.

50 For in him we live, and move and have our being.
Acts of the Apostles 17:28.

51 And the times of this ignorance God winked at; but now commandeth all men every where to repent.
Acts of the Apostles 17:30.

52 Have ye received the Holy Ghost since ye believed? And they said unto him, We have not so much as heard whether there be any Holy Ghost.
Acts of the Apostles 19:2.

53 It is more blessed to give than to receive.
Acts of the Apostles 20:35.

54 I am a man which am a Jew of Tarsus, a city in Cilicia, a citizen of no mean city.
Acts of the Apostles 21:39.

55 The chief captain answered, With a great sum obtained I this freedom. And Paul said, But I was free born.
Acts of the Apostles 22:27–8.

56 Paul, thou art beside thyself; much learning doth make thee mad.
Acts of the Apostles 26:24.

57 Almost thou persuadest me to be a Christian.
Acts of the Apostles 26:28.

58 The just shall live by faith.
Romans 1:17.

59 Who changed the truth of God into a lie, and worshipped and served the creature more than the Creator.
Romans 1:25.

60 For when the Gentiles, which have not the law, do by nature the things contained in the law, these, having not the law, are a law unto themselves.
Romans 2:14.

61 God forbid: yea, let God be true, but every man a liar.
Romans 3:4.

62 For all have sinned, and come short of the glory of God.
Romans 3:23.

63 Because the law worketh wrath: for where no law is, there is no transgression.
Romans 4:15.

64 Who against hope believed in hope, that he might become the father of many nations.
Romans 4:18.

65 While we were yet sinners, Christ died for us.
Romans 5:8.

66 Where sin abounded, grace did much more abound.
Romans 5:20.

67 What shall we say then? Shall we continue in sin, that grace may abound? God forbid. How shall we, that are dead to sin, live any longer therein?
Romans 6:1–2.

68 Knowing that Christ being raised from the dead dieth no more; death hath no more dominion over him.
Romans 6:9.

69 For the wages of sin is death; but the gift of God is eternal life through Jesus Christ our Lord.
Romans 6:23.

70 To will is present with me; but how to perform that which is good I find not. For the good that I would I do not: but the evil which I would not, that I do.
Romans 7:19.

71 O wretched man that I am! who shall deliver me from the body of this death?
Romans 7:24.

72 There is therefore now no condemnation to them which are in Christ Jesus, who walk not after the flesh, but after the Spirit.
Romans 8:1.

73 For they that are after the flesh do mind the things of the flesh; but they that are after the Spirit the things of the Spirit. For to be carnally minded is death; but to be spiritually minded is life and peace.
Romans 8:5–6.

74 For ye have not received the spirit of bondage again to fear; but ye have received the Spirit of adoption, whereby we cry, Abba, Father. The Spirit itself beareth witness with our spirit, that we are the children of God: And if children, then heirs; heirs of God, and joint-heirs with Christ; if so be that we suffer with him, that we may be also glorified together.
Romans 8:15–17.

75 For we know that the whole creation groaneth and travaileth in pain together until now.
Romans 8:22.

76 And we know that all things work together for good to them that love God, to them who are the called according to his purpose.
Romans 8:28.

77 If God be for us, who can be against us?
Romans 8:31.

78 I am persuaded, that neither death, nor life, nor angels, nor principalities, nor powers, nor things present, nor things to come, Nor height, nor depth, nor any other creature, shall be able to separate us from the love of God, which is in Christ Jesus our Lord.
Romans 8:38–9.

79 Nay but, O man, who art thou that repliest against God? Shall the thing formed say to him that formed it, Why hast thou made me thus? Hath not the potter power over the clay, of the same lump to make one vessel unto honour, and another unto dishonour?
Romans 9:20–1.

80 I beseech you therefore, brethren, by the mercies of God, that ye present your bodies a living sacrifice, holy, acceptable unto God, which is your reasonable service.
Romans 12:1.

81 Not slothful in business; fervent in spirit; serving the Lord.
Romans 12:11.

82 Rejoice with them that do rejoice, and weep with them that weep.
Romans 12:15.

83 Mind not high things, but condescend to men of low estate. Be not wise in your own conceits. Recompense to no man evil for evil. Provide things honest in the sight of all men. If it be possible, as much as lieth in you, live peaceably with all men. Dearly beloved, avenge not yourselves, but rather give place unto wrath: for it is written, Vengeance is mine; I will repay, saith the Lord.
Romans 12:16–19.

84 Be not overcome of evil, but overcome evil with good.
Romans 12:21.

85 Let every soul be subject unto the higher powers. For there is no power but of God: the powers that be are ordained of God.
Romans 13:1.

86 Render therefore to all their dues: tribute to whom tribute is due; custom to whom custom; fear to whom fear; honour to whom honour. Owe no man any thing, but to love one another: for he that loveth another hath fulfilled the law.
Romans 13:7–8.

87 Love worketh no ill to his neighbour: therefore love is the fulfilling of the law.
Romans 13:10.

88 Doubtful disputations.
Romans 14:1.

89 Whether we live therefore, or die, we are the Lord's.
Romans 14:8.

90 Salute one another with an holy kiss.
Romans 16:16.

91 For after that in the wisdom of God the world by wisdom knew not God, it pleased God by the foolishness of preaching to save them that believe.
1 Corinthians 1:21.

92 But God hath chosen the foolish things of the world to confound the wise; and God hath chosen the weak things of the world to confound the things which are mighty.
1 Corinthians 1:27.

93 I have planted, Apollos watered; but God gave the increase.
1 Corinthians 3:6.

94 We are made a spectacle unto the world, and to angels, and to men.
1 Corinthians 4:9.

95 What? know ye not that your body is the temple of the Holy Ghost which is in you, which ye have of God, and ye are not your own?
1 Corinthians 6:19.

96 It is better to marry than to burn.
1 Corinthians 7:9.

97 For the unbelieving husband is sanctified by the wife.
1 Corinthians 7:14.

98 But he that is married careth for the things that are of the world, how he may please his wife.
1 Corinthians 7:33.

99 I am made all things to all men, that I might by all means save some.
1 Corinthians 9:22.

1 Know ye not that they which run in a race run all, but one receiveth the prize? So run, that ye may obtain.
1 Corinthians 9:24.

2 Wherefore let him that thinketh he standeth take heed lest he fall.
1 Corinthians 10:12.

3 All things are lawful for me, but all things are not expedient: all things are lawful for me, but all things edify not.
1 Corinthians 10:23.

4 For the earth is the Lord's, and the fulness thereof.
1 Corinthians 10:26.

5 If a man have long hair, it is a shame unto him.
But if a woman have long hair, it is a glory to her: for her hair is given her for a covering.
1 Corinthians 11:15.

6 The Lord Jesus the same night in which he was betrayed took bread: And when he had given thanks, he brake it, and said, Take, eat: this is my body, which is broken for you: this do in remembrance of me. After the same manner also he took the cup, when he had supped, saying, This cup is the new testament in my blood: this do ye, as oft as ye drink it, in remembrance of me. For as often as ye eat this bread, and drink this cup, ye do shew the Lord's death till he come.
1 Corinthians 11:23–6.

7 No man can say that Jesus is the Lord, but by the Holy Ghost.
1 Corinthians 12:3.

8 Now there are diversities of gifts, but the same Spirit. And there are differences of administrations, but the same Lord. And there are diversities of operations, but it is the same God which worketh all in all.
1 Corinthians 12:4–6.

9 Though I speak with the tongues of men and of angels, and have not charity, I am become as sounding brass, or a tinkling cymbal. And though I have the gift of prophecy, and understand all mysteries, and all knowledge; and though I have all faith, so that I could remove mountains, and have not charity, I am nothing. And though I bestow all my goods to feed the poor, and though I give my body to be burned, and have not charity, it profiteth me nothing. Charity suffereth long, and is kind; charity envieth not; charity vaunteth not itself, is not puffed up, Doth not behave itself unseemly, seeketh not her own, is not easily provoked, thinketh no evil; Rejoiceth not in iniquity, but rejoiceth in the truth; Beareth all things, believeth all things, hopeth all things, endureth all things. Charity never faileth: but whether there be prophecies, they shall fail; whether there be tongues, they shall cease; whether there be knowledge, it shall vanish away. For we know in part, and we prophesy in part. But when that which is perfect is come, then that which is in part shall be done away. When I was a child, I spake as a child, I understood as a child, I thought as a child: but when I became a man, I put away childish things. For now we see through a glass, darkly; but then face to face: now I know in part; but then shall I know even as also I am known. And now abideth faith, hope, charity, these three; but the greatest of these is charity.
1 Corinthians 13:1–13.

10 For if the trumpet give an uncertain sound, who shall prepare himself to the battle?
1 Corinthians 14:8.

11 Let all things be done decently and in order.
1 Corinthians 14:40.

12 And last of all he was seen of me also, as of one born out of due time. For I am the least of the apostles, that am not meet to be called an apostle, because I persecuted the church of God.
But by the grace of God I am what I am.
1 Corinthians 15:8–9.

13 If in this life only we have hope in Christ, we are of all men most miserable.
1 Corinthians 15:19.

14 But now is Christ risen from the dead, and become the first-fruits of them that slept.
For since by man came death, by man came also the resurrection of the dead.
For as in Adam all die, even so in Christ shall all be made alive.
1 Corinthians 15:20–2.

15 He must reign, till he hath put all enemies under his feet. The last enemy that shall be destroyed is death.
1 Corinthians 15:26.

16 What advantageth it me, if the dead rise not? let us eat and drink; for tomorrow we die.
1 Corinthians 15:32.
➤ *See Parker 638:61.*

17 Evil communications corrupt good manners.
1 Corinthians 15:33.

18 The first man is of the earth, earthy.
1 Corinthians 15:47.

19 Behold, I shew you a mystery; We shall not all sleep, but we shall all be changed, In a moment, in the twinkling of an eye, at the last trump: for the trumpet shall sound, and

the dead shall be raised incorruptible, and we shall be changed.
1 Corinthians 15:51–2.

20 O death, where is thy sting? O grave, where is thy victory?
1 Corinthians 15:55.

21 Watch ye, stand fast in the faith, quit you like men, be strong.
1 Corinthians 16:13.

22 Not that we are sufficient of ourselves to think any thing as of ourselves; but our sufficiency is of God; Who also hath made us able ministers of the new testament; not of the letter, but of the spirit: for the letter killeth, but the spirit giveth life.
2 Corinthians 3:5–6.

23 But we have this treasure in earthen vessels.
2 Corinthians 4:7.

24 We are troubled on every side, yet not distressed; we are perplexed, but not in despair.
2 Corinthians 4:8.

25 For we know that if our earthly house of this tabernacle were dissolved, we have a building of God, an house not made with hands, eternal in the heavens.
2 Corinthians 5:1.

26 For we walk by faith, not by sight.
2 Corinthians 5:7.

27 Therefore if any man be in Christ, he is a new creature: old things are passed away; behold, all things are become new.
2 Corinthians 5:17.

28 Now then we are ambassadors for Christ.
2 Corinthians 5:20.

29 For he saith, I have heard thee in a time accepted, and in the day of salvation have I succoured thee: behold, now is the accepted time; behold, now is the day of salvation.
2 Corinthians 6:2.

30 As unknown, and yet well known; as dying, and, behold, we live; as chastened, and not killed; As sorrowful, yet alway rejoicing; as poor, yet making many rich; as having nothing, and yet possessing all things.
2 Corinthians 6:9–10.

31 So let him give; not grudgingly, or of necessity: for God loveth a cheerful giver.
2 Corinthians 9:7.

32 For ye suffer fools gladly, seeing ye yourselves are wise.
2 Corinthians 11:19.

33 And lest I should be exalted above measure through the abundance of the revelations, there was given to me a thorn in the flesh, the messenger of Satan to buffet me.
2 Corinthians 12:7.

34 My grace is sufficient for thee: for my strength is made perfect in weakness.
2 Corinthians 12:9.

35 They gave to me and Barnabas the right hands of fellowship.
Galatians 2:9.

36 There is neither Jew nor Greek, there is neither bond nor free, there is neither male nor female: for ye are all one in Christ Jesus.
Galatians 3:28.

37 Ye are fallen from grace.
Galatians 5:4.

38 But the fruit of the Spirit is love, joy, peace, longsuffering, gentleness, goodness, faith,
Meekness, temperance: against such there is no law.
Galatians 5:22–3.

39 Be not deceived; God is not mocked: for whatsoever a man soweth, that shall he also reap.
Galatians 6:7.

40 Let us not be weary in well doing: for in due season we shall reap, if we faint not.
Galatians 6:9.

41 See what a large letter I have written unto you with mine own hand.
Galatians 6:11.

42 And came and preached peace to you which were afar off, and to them that were nigh.
Ephesians 2:17.

43 Now therefore ye are no more strangers and foreigners, but fellow citizens with the saints, and of the household of God.
Ephesians 2:19.

44 Unto me, who am less than the least of all saints, is this grace given, that I should preach among the Gentiles the unsearchable riches of Christ.
Ephesians 3:8.

45 That he would grant you, according to the riches of his glory, to be strengthened with might by his Spirit in the inner man; That Christ may dwell in your hearts by faith; that ye, being rooted and grounded in love, May be able to comprehend with all saints what is the breadth, and length, and depth, and height; And to know the love of Christ, which passeth knowledge, that ye might be filled with all the fulness of God.
Ephesians 3:16–19.

46 Now unto him that is able to do exceeding abundantly above all that we ask or think, according to the power that worketh in us, Unto him be glory in the church by Christ Jesus throughout all ages, world without end. Amen.
Ephesians 3:20–1.

47 Wherefore putting away lying, speak every man truth with his neighbour: for we are members one of another. Be ye angry, and sin not: let not the sun go down upon your wrath.
Ephesians 4:25–6.

48 Redeeming the time, because the days are evil.
Ephesians 5:16.

49 Be not drunk with wine, wherein is excess; but be filled with the Spirit.
Ephesians 5:18.

50 Ye fathers, provoke not your children to wrath.
Ephesians 6:4.

51 Not with eyeservice, as menpleasers; but as the servants of Christ, doing the will of God from the heart;
With good will doing service, as to the Lord, and not to men.
Ephesians 6:6–7.

52 Put on the whole armour of God, that ye may be able to stand against the wiles of the devil. For we wrestle not

against flesh and blood, but against principalities, against powers, against the rulers of the darkness of this world, against spiritual wickedness in high places. Wherefore take unto you the whole armour of God, that ye may be able to withstand in the evil day, and having done all, to stand. Stand therefore, having your loins girt about with truth, and having on the breastplate of righteousness; And your feet shod with the preparation of the gospel of peace; Above all, taking the shield of faith, wherewith ye shall be able to quench all the fiery darts of the wicked. And take the helmet of salvation, and the sword of the Spirit, which is the word of God.
Ephesians 6:11–17.

53 For to me to live is Christ, and to die is gain.
Philippians 1:21.

54 Let this mind be in you, which was also in Christ Jesus: Who, being in the form of God, thought it not robbery to be equal with God: But made himself of no reputation, and took upon him the form of a servant, and was made in the likeness of men: And being found in fashion as a man, he humbled himself, and became obedient unto death, even the death of the cross. Wherefore God also hath highly exalted him, and given him a name which is above every name: That at the name of Jesus every knee should bow, of things in heaven, and things in earth, and things under the earth; And that every tongue should confess that Jesus Christ is Lord, to the glory of God the Father.
Philippians 2:5–11.

55 Work out your own salvation with fear and trembling.
Philippians 2:12.

56 Circumcised the eighth day, of the stock of Israel, of the tribe of Benjamin, an Hebrew of the Hebrews; as touching the law, a Pharisee.
Paul lists his religious credentials. Philippians 3:5

57 But what things were gain to me, those I counted loss for Christ.
Philippians 3:7.

58 Forgetting those things which are behind, and reaching forth unto those things which are before, I press toward the mark for the prize of the high calling of God in Christ Jesus.
Philippians 3:13–14.

59 Whose end is destruction, whose God is their belly, and whose glory is in their shame, who mind earthly things.
Philippians 3:19.

60 Rejoice in the Lord alway: and again I say, Rejoice. Let your moderation be known unto all men. The Lord is at hand. Be careful for nothing; but in every thing by prayer and supplication with thanksgiving let your requests be made known unto God. And the peace of God, which passeth all understanding, shall keep your hearts and minds through Christ Jesus.
Philippians 4:4–7.

61 Finally, brethren, whatsoever things are true, whatsoever things are honest, whatsoever things are just, whatsoever things are pure, whatsoever things are lovely, whatsoever things are of good report; if there be any virtue, and if there be any praise, think on these things.
Philippians 4:8.

62 I have learned, in whatsoever state I am, therewith to be content.
Philippians 4:11.

63 I can do all things through Christ which strengtheneth me.
Philippians 4:13.

64 My God shall supply all your need according to his riches in glory by Christ Jesus.
Philippians 4:19.

65 Beware lest any man spoil you through philosophy and vain deceit, after the tradition of men, after the rudiments of the world, and not after Christ.
Colossians 2:8.

66 Set your affection on things above, not on things on the earth.
Colossians 3:2.

67 Lie not one to another, seeing that ye have put off the old man with his deeds; And have put on the new man, which is renewed in knowledge after the image of him that created him: Where there is neither Greek nor Jew, circumcision nor uncircumcision, Barbarian, Scythian, bond nor free: but Christ is all, and in all.
Colossians 3:9–11.

68 Husbands, love your wives, and be not bitter against them.
Colossians 3:19.

69 Let your speech be alway with grace, seasoned with salt, that ye may know how ye ought to answer every man.
Colossians 4:6.

70 Study to be quiet, and to do your own business, and to work with your own hands, as we commanded you.
1 Thessalonians 4:11.

71 Prove all things; hold fast that which is good.
1 Thessalonians 5:21.

72 If any would not work, neither should he eat.
2 Thessalonians 3:10.

73 This is a faithful saying, and worthy of all acceptation, that Christ Jesus came into the world to save sinners; of whom I am chief.
1 Timothy 1:15.

74 If a man desire the office of a bishop, he desireth a good work. A bishop then must be blameless, the husband of one wife, vigilant, sober, of good behaviour, given to hospitality, apt to teach; Not given to wine, no striker, not greedy of filthy lucre; but patient, not a brawler, not covetous.
1 Timothy 3:1–3.

75 But refuse profane and old wives' fables, and exercise thyself rather unto godliness.
1 Timothy 4:7–8.

76 Let no man despise thy youth.
1 Timothy 4:12.

77 Drink no longer water, but use a little wine for thy stomach's sake and thine often infirmities.
1 Timothy 5:23.

78 For we brought nothing into this world, and it is certain we can carry nothing out. And having food and raiment let us be therewith content.
1 Timothy 6:7–8.

79 For the love of money is the root of all evil.
1 Timothy 6:10.

80 Fight the good fight of faith.
1 Timothy 6:12.

81 For God hath not given us the spirit of fear; but of power, and of love, and of a sound mind.
2 Timothy 1:7.

82 I know whom I have believed, and am persuaded that he is able to keep that which I have committed unto him against that day.
2 Timothy 1:12.

83 Hold fast the form of sound words, which thou hast heard of me.
2 Timothy 1:13.

84 All scripture is given by inspiration of God, and is profitable of doctrine, for reproof, for correction, for instruction in righteousness.
2 Timothy 3:16.

85 Preach the word; be instant in season, out of season.
2 Timothy 4:2.

86 I have fought a good fight, I have finished my course, I have kept the faith.
2 Timothy 4:7.

87 The Cretans are always liars, evil beasts, slow bellies.
Titus 1:12.

88 Unto the pure all things are pure: but unto them that are defiled and unbelieving is nothing pure; but even their mind and conscience is defiled.
Titus 1:15.

89 God, who at sundry times and in divers manners spake in time past unto the fathers by the prophets, Hath in these last days spoken unto us by his Son, whom he hath appointed heir of all things, by whom he also made the worlds: Who being the brightness of his glory, and the express image of his person, and upholding all things by the word of his power, when he had by himself purged our sins, sat down on the right hand of the Majesty on high.
Hebrews 1:1–3.

90 For the word of God is quick, and powerful, and sharper than any two-edged sword, piercing even to the dividing asunder of soul and spirit.
Hebrews 4:12.

91 Ye have need that one teach you again which be the first principles of the oracles of God; and are become such as have need of milk, and not of strong meat.
Hebrews 5:12.

92 Without shedding of blood is no remission.
Hebrews 9:22.

93 It is appointed unto men once to die, but after this the judgment.
Hebrews 9:27.

94 It is a fearful thing to fall into the hands of the living God.
Hebrews 10:31.

95 Now faith is the substance of things hoped for, the evidence of things not seen.
Hebrews 11:1.

96 These all died in faith, not having received the promises, but having seen them afar off, and were persuaded of them, and embraced them, and confessed that they were strangers and pilgrims on the earth.
Hebrews 11:13.

97 But now they desire a better country, that is, an heavenly: wherefore God is not ashamed to be called their God: for he hath prepared for them a city.
Hebrews 11:16.

98 Of whom the world was not worthy.
Hebrews 11:38.

99 Wherefore seeing we also are compassed about with so great a cloud of witnesses, let us lay aside every weight, and the sin which doth so easily beset us, and let us run with patience the race that is set before us, Looking unto Jesus the author and finisher of our faith; who for the joy that was set before him endured the cross, despising the shame, and is set down at the right hand of the throne of God.
Hebrews 12:1–2.

1 For whom the Lord loveth he chasteneth.
Hebrews 12:6.

2 For our God is a consuming fire.
Hebrews 12:29.

3 Be not forgetful to entertain strangers: for thereby some have entertained angels unawares.
Hebrews 13:1–2.

4 Jesus Christ the same yesterday, and to day, and for ever.
Hebrews 13:8.

5 He that wavereth is like a wave of the sea driven with the wind and tossed. For let not that man think that he shall receive any thing of the Lord. A double minded man is unstable in all his ways.
James 1:7–8.

6 Every good gift and every perfect gift is from above, and cometh down from the Father of lights, with whom is no variableness, neither shadow of turning.
James 1:17.

7 Be ye doers of the word, and not hearers only, deceiving your own selves. For if any be a hearer of the word, and not a doer, he is like unto a man beholding his natural face in a glass: For he beholdeth himself, and goeth his way, and straightway forgetteth what manner of man he was.
James 1:22–4.

8 If any man among you seem to be religious, and bridleth not his tongue, but deceiveth his own heart, this man's religion is vain.
James 1:26.

9 Pure religion and undefiled before God and the Father is this, To visit the fatherless and widows in their affliction, and to keep himself unspotted from the world.
James 1:27.

10 Thou believest that there is one God; thou doest well: the devils also believe, and tremble.
James 2:19.

11 Faith without works is dead.
James 2:20.

12 Even so the tongue is a little member, and boasteth great things. Behold, how great a matter a little fire kindleth!
James 3:5.

13 And the tongue is a fire, a world of iniquity: so is the tongue among our members, that it defileth the whole

body, and setteth on fire the course of nature; and it is set on fire of hell.
James 3:6.

14 Out of the same mouth proceedeth blessing and cursing. My brethren, these things ought not so to be. Doth a fountain send forth at the same place sweet water and bitter?
James 3:10–11.

15 Submit yourselves therefore to God, Resist the devil, and he will flee from you. Draw nigh to God, and he will draw nigh to you.
James 4:7–8.

16 What is your life? It is even a vapour, that appeareth for a little time, and then vanisheth away. For that ye ought to say, If the Lord will, we shall live, and do this, or that.
James 4:14–15.

17 Grudge not one against another, brethren, lest ye be condemned: behold, the judge standeth before the door.
James 5:9.

18 Swear not, neither by heaven, neither by the earth, neither by any other oath: but let your yea be yea; and your nay, nay.
James 5:12.

19 The effectual fervent prayer of a righteous man availeth much.
James 5:16.

20 He which converteth the sinner from the error of his way shall save a soul from death, and shall hide a multitude of sins.
James 5:20.

21 Wherefore gird up the loins of your mind, be sober, and hope to the end for the grace that is to be brought unto you at the revelation of Jesus Christ.
1 Peter 1:13.

22 For all flesh is as grass, and all the glory of man as the flower of grass. The grass withereth, and the flower thereof falleth away.
1 Peter 1:24.

23 As newborn babes, desire the sincere milk of the word, that ye may grow thereby: If so be you have tasted that the Lord is gracious.
1 Peter 2:2.

24 But ye are a chosen generation, a royal priesthood, an holy nation, a peculiar people; that ye should shew forth the praises of him who hath called you out of darkness into his marvellous light.
1 Peter 2:9.

25 Honour all men. Love the brotherhood. Fear God. Honour the king.
1 Peter 2:17.

26 For ye were as sheep going astray; but are now returned unto the Shepherd and Bishop of your souls.
1 Peter 2:25.

27 Giving honour unto the wife, as unto the weaker vessel.
1 Peter 3:7.

28 And above all things have fervent charity among yourselves: for charity shall cover the multitude of sins.
1 Peter 4:8.

29 Casting all your care upon him; for he careth for you.
1 Peter 5:6–7.

30 Be sober, be vigilant; because your adversary the devil, as a roaring lion, walketh about, seeking whom he may devour.
1 Peter 5:8.

31 The dog is turned to his own vomit again; and the sow that was washed to her wallowing in the mire.
2 Peter 2:22.

32 One day is with the Lord as a thousand years, and a thousand years as one day.
2 Peter 3:8–9.

33 But the day of the Lord will come as a thief in the night.
2 Peter 3:10–11.

34 If we say that we have no sin, we deceive ourselves, and the truth is not in us. If we confess our sins, he is faithful and just to forgive us our sins, and to cleanse us from all unrighteousness.
1 John 1:8–9.

35 If any man sin, we have an advocate with the Father, Jesus Christ the righteous.
1 John 2:1.

36 Behold, what manner of love the Father hath bestowed upon us, that we should be called the sons of God.
1 John 3:1.

37 But whoso hath this world's good, and seeth his brother have need, and shutteth up his bowels of compassion from him, how dwelleth the love of God in him?
1 John 3:17.

38 Beloved, let us love one another: for love is of God; and every one that loveth is born of God, and knoweth God. He that loveth not knoweth not God; for God is love.
1 John 4:7–8.

39 Herein is love, not that we loved God, but that he loved us, and sent his Son to be the propitiation for our sins.
1 John 4:10.

40 There is no fear in love; but perfect love casteth out fear.
1 John 4:18.

41 If a man say, I love God, and hateth his brother, he is a liar: for he that loveth not his brother whom he hath seen, how can he love God whom he hath not seen?
1 John 4:20.

42 John to the seven churches which are in Asia: Grace be unto you, and peace, from him which is, and which was, and which is to come.
Revelation 1:4.

43 Behold, he cometh with clouds; and every eye shall see him, and they also which pierced him: and all kindreds of the earth shall wail because of him. Even so, Amen.
Revelation 1:7.

44 I was in the Spirit on the Lord's day, and heard behind me a great voice, as of a trumpet, Saying, I am Alpha and Omega, the first and the last: and, What thou seest, write in a book, and send it unto the seven churches which are in Asia.
Revelation 1:10–11.

45 And in the midst of the seven candlesticks one like unto the Son of man, clothed with a garment down to the foot, and girt about the paps with golden girdle. His head and his hairs were white like wool, as white as

snow; and his eyes were as a flame of fire;
And his feet like unto fine brass, as if they burned in a furnace; and his voice as the sound of many waters. And he had in his right hand seven stars: and out of his mouth went a sharp two-edged sword: and his countenance was as the sun shineth in his strength. And when I saw him, I fell as his feet as dead.
Revelation 1:13–17.

46 I am he that liveth, and was dead; and, behold, I am alive for evermore, Amen; and have the keys of hell and of death.
Revelation 1:18.

47 I have somewhat against thee, because thou hast left thy first love.
Revelation 2:4.

48 Be thou faithful unto death, and I will give thee a crown of life.
Revelation 2:10.

49 And he shall rule them with a rod of iron; as the vessels of a potter shall they be broken to shivers.
Revelation 2:27.

50 Behold, I have set before thee an open door, and no man can shut it: for thou hast a little strength, and hast kept my word, and hast not denied my name.
Revelation 3:8.

51 I know thy works, that thou art neither cold nor hot: I would thou wert cold or hot. So then because thou art lukewarm, and neither cold nor hot, I will spew thee out of my mouth.
Revelation 3:15–16.

52 Behold, I stand at the door, and knock: if any man hear my voice, and open the door, I will come in to him, and will sup with him, and he with me.
Revelation 3:20.

53 And before the throne there was a sea of glass like unto crystal: and in the midst of the throne, and round about the throne, were four beasts full of eyes before and behind.
Revelation 4:6–7.

54 And the four beasts had each of them six wings about him; and they were full of eyes within: and they rest not day and night, saying, Holy, holy, holy, Lord God Almighty, which was, and is, and is to come.
Revelation 4:8.

55 Cast their crowns before the throne, saying, Thou art worthy, O Lord, to receive glory and honour and power: for thou hast created all things, and for thy pleasure they are and were created.
Revelation 4:10–11.

56 Who is worthy to open the book, and to loose the seals thereof? And no man in heaven, nor in earth, neither under the earth, was able to open the book, neither to look thereon.
Revelation 5:2–3.

57 And I looked, and behold a pale horse: and his name that sat on him was Death, and Hell followed with him.
Revelation 6:8.

58 And said to the mountains and rocks, Fall on us, and hide us from the face of him that sitteth on the throne, and from the wrath of the Lamb: For the great day of his

wrath is come; and who shall be able to stand?
Revelation 6:16–17.

59 A great multitude, which no man could number, of all nations, and kindreds, and people, and tongues, stood before the throne, and before the Lamb, clothed with white robes, and palms in their hands.
Revelation 7:9.

60 These are they which came out of great tribulation, and have washed their robes, and made them white in the blood of the Lamb. Therefore are they before the throne of God, and serve him day and night in his temple: and he that sitteth on the throne shall dwell among them. They shall hunger no more, neither thirst any more; neither shall the sun light on them nor any heat. For the Lamb which is in the midst of the throne shall feed them, and shall lead them unto living fountains of waters: and God shall wipe away all tears from their eyes.
Revelation 7:14–17.

61 And when he had opened the seventh seal, there was silence in heaven about the space of half an hour.
Revelation 8:1.

62 I saw a star fall from heaven unto the earth: and to him was given the key of the bottomless pit.
Revelation 9:1.

63 And there were stings in their tails.
Revelation 9:10.

64 I took the little book out of the angel's hand, and ate it up; and it was in my mouth sweet as honey: and as soon as I had eaten it, my belly was bitter.
Revelation 10:9–10.

65 And there appeared a great wonder in heaven; a woman clothed with the sun, and the moon under her feet, and upon her head a crown of twelve stars.
Revelation 12:1.

66 And there was war in heaven: Michael and his angels fought against the dragon; and the dragon fought and his angels, And prevailed not; neither was their place found any more in heaven. And the great dragon was cast out, that old serpent, called the Devil, and Satan, which deceiveth the whole world: he was cast out into the earth, and his angels were cast out with him.
Revelation 12:7–9.

67 And that no man might buy or sell, save he that had the mark, or the name of the beast, or the number of his name. Here is wisdom. Let him that hath understanding count the number of the beast: for it is the number of a man; and his number is Six hundred threescore and six.
Revelation 13:17–18.

68 And the smoke of their torment ascendeth up for ever and ever: and they have no rest day nor night, who worship the beast and his image, and whosoever receiveth the mark of his name.
Revelation 14:11.

69 Blessed are the dead which die in the Lord from henceforth: Yea, saith the Spirit, that they may rest from their labours; and their works do follow them.
Revelation 14:13.

70 And I saw as it were a sea of glass mingled with fire.
Revelation 15:2.

71 Behold, I come as a thief. Blessed is he that watcheth, and keepeth his garments, lest he walk naked, and they see his shame. And he gathereth them together into a place called in the Hebrew tongue Armageddon.
Revelation 16:15–16.

72 Come hither; I will shew unto thee the judgment of the great whore that sitteth upon many waters.
Revelation 17:1.

73 And upon her forehead was a name written, MYSTERY, BABYLON THE GREAT, THE MOTHER OF HARLOTS AND ABOMINATIONS OF THE EARTH.
Revelation 17:5.

74 And a mighty angel took up a stone like a great millstone, and cast it into the sea, saying, Thus with violence shall that great city Babylon be thrown down, and shall be found no more at all.
Revelation 18:21.

75 And I saw heaven opened, and behold a white horse; and he that sat upon him was called Faithful and True, and in righteousness he doth judge and make war.
Revelation 19:11.

76 And he hath on his vesture and on his thigh a name written, KING OF KINGS, AND LORD OF LORDS.
Revelation 19:16.

77 And he laid hold on the dragon, that old serpent, which is the Devil, and Satan, and bound him a thousand years, And cast him into the bottomless pit, and shut him up, and set a seal upon him, that he should deceive the nations no more, till the thousand years should be fulfilled: and after that he must be loosed a little season.
Revelation 20:2–3.

78 And I saw a great white throne, and him that sat on it, from whose face the earth and the heaven fled away; and there was found no place for them. And I saw the dead, small and great, stand before God; and the books were opened: and another book was opened, which is the book of life: and the dead were judged out of those things which were written in the books, according to their works. And the sea gave up the dead which were in it; and death and hell delivered up the dead which were in them: and they were judged every man according to their works. And death and hell were cast into the lake of fire.
Revelation 20:11–14.

79 And I saw a new heaven and a new earth: for the first heaven and the first earth were passed away; and there was no more sea. And I John saw the holy city, new Jerusalem, coming down from God out of heaven, prepared as a bride adorned for her husband.
Revelation 21:1–2.

80 And God shall wipe away all tears from their eyes; and there shall be no more death, neither sorrow, nor crying, neither shall there be any more pain: for the former things are passed away. And he that sat upon the throne said, Behold, I make all things new. And he said unto me, Write: for these words are true and faithful.
Revelation 21:4–5.

81 I will give unto him that is athirst of the fountain of the water of life freely.
Revelation 21:6.

82 And the street of the city was pure gold, as it were

transparent glass.
Revelation 21:21.

83 And the gates of it shall not be shut at all by day: for there shall be no night there.
Revelation 21:25.

84 And he shewed me a pure river of water of life, clear as crystal, proceeding out of the throne of God and of the Lamb. In the midst of the street of it, and on either side of the river, was there the tree of life, which bare twelve manner of fruits, and yielded her fruit every month: and the leaves of the tree were for the healing of the nations.
Revelation 22:1–2.

85 He which testifieth these things saith, Surely I come quickly. Amen. Even so, come, Lord Jesus. The grace of our Lord Jesus Christ be with you all. Amen.
Revelation 22:20–1.

Bible (Vulgate)

A 4c translation of the Bible into Latin, commissioned by Pope Damasus and undertaken by Jerome (382–405). It became known as the *versio vulgata*, the 'common translation', and is still an official text of the Roman Catholic Church. The quotations given here are those that are well known in their Latin form.

86 *Dominus illuminatio mea, et salus mea, quem timebo?*
The Lord is the source of my light and my safety, so whom shall I fear?
Psalm 26:1.

87 *Asperges me hyssopo, et mundabor; lavabis me, et super nivem dealbabor.*
You will sprinkle me with hyssop, and I shall be made clean; you will wash me and I shall be made whiter than snow.
Psalm 50:9 (Psalm 51:7 Authorized Version).

88 *Cantate Domino canticum novum, quia mirabilia fecit.*
Sing to the Lord a new song, because he has done marvellous things.
Psalm 97:1 (Psalm 98:1 Authorized Version).
➤ *See Book of Common Prayer 143:46.*

89 *Jubilate Deo, omnis terra; servite Domino in laetitia.*
Sing joyfully to God, all the earth; serve the Lord with gladness.
Psalm 99:2 (Psalm 100:2 Authorized Version).
➤ *See Book of Common Prayer 143:66.*

90 *Beatus vir qui timet Dominum, in mandatis ejus volet nimis!*
Happy is the man who fears the Lord, who is only too willing to follow his orders.
Psalm 111:1 (Psalm 112:1 Authorized Version).

91 *Non nobis, Domine, non nobis; sed nomini tuo da gloriam.*
Not unto us, Lord, not unto us; but to thy name give glory.
Psalm 113 (2nd part):1 (Psalm 115:1 Authorized Version).

92 *Laudate Dominum, omnes gentes; laudate eum, omnes populi.*
Praise the Lord, all nations; praise him, all people.
Psalm 116:1 (Psalm 117:1 Authorized Version).

93 *Nisi Dominus aedificaverit domum, in vanum laboraverunt qui aedificant eam.*
Nisi Dominus custodierit civitatem, frustra vigilat qui custodit eam.

Unless the Lord has built the house, its builders have laboured in vain. Unless the Lord guards the city, the watchman watches in vain.
Psalm 126:1 (Psalm 127:1 Authorized Version).

94 *De profundis clamavi ad te, Domine; Domine exaudi vocem meam.*
Up from the depths I have cried to thee, Lord; Lord, hear my voice.
Psalm 129:1 (Psalm 130:1 Authorized Version).

95 *Vanitas vanitatum, dixit Ecclesiastes; vanitas vanitatum, et omnia vanitas.*
Vanity of vanities, said the preacher; vanity of vanities, and everything is vanity.
Ecclesiastes 1:2.
➤ *See Bible (Old Testament) 100:65.*

96 *Rorate, coeli, desuper, et nubes pluant Justum; aperiatur terra, et germinet Salvatorem.*
Drop down dew, heavens, from above, and let the clouds rain down righteousness; let the earth be opened, and a saviour spring to life.
Isaiah 45:8.

97 *Benedicite, omnia opera Domini, Domino; laudate et superexaltate eum in secula.*
Bless the Lord, all the works of the Lord; praise him and exalt him above all things for ever.
Daniel 3:57.

98 *Magnificat anima mea Dominum; et exsultavit spiritus meus in Deo salvatore meo.*
My soul doth magnify the Lord: and my spirit hath rejoiced in God my Saviour.
St Luke 1:46.
➤ *See Bible (New Testament) 115:23.*

99 *Esurientes implevit bonis, et divites dimisit inanes.*
He hath filled the hungry with good things: and the rich he hath sent empty away.
St Luke 1.53.
➤ *See Bible (New Testament) 115:23.*

1 *Nunc dimittis servum tuum, Domine, secundum verbum tuum in pace.*
Lord, now lettest thou thy servant depart in peace: according to thy word.
St Luke 2:29.
➤ *See Bible (New Testament) 115:27.*

2 *Pax Vobis.*
Peace be unto you.
St Luke 24:36.

3 *Quo vadis?*
Where are you going?
St John 16:5.

4 *Ecce homo.*
Behold the man.
St John 19:5.

5 *Noli me tangere.*
Do not touch me.
St John 20:17.
➤ *See Bible (New Testament) 118:23.*

Bickerstaffe, Isaac c.1735–c.1812

Irish playwright. An officer of marines, he was dismissed from the service and later forced to flee the country. He is credited with establishing the comic opera in English theatre.

6 And this the burthen of his song,
For ever used to be,
I care for nobody, not I,
If no one cares for me.
1762 *Love in a Village*, act 1, sc.2.

7 'Tis a sure sign that work goes on merrily, when folks sing at it.
1765 *The Maid of the Mill*, act 1, sc.1.

8 Perhaps it was right to dissemble your love,
But—why did you kick me downstairs?
1789 'An Expostulation'.

Biddle, Francis Beverley 1886–1968

US lawyer, Solicitor General (1940) and Attorney General (1941–5). He served as US judge on the Nuremberg trials of war criminals.

9 The Constitution has never greatly bothered any wartime President.
1962 *In Brief Authority.*

Bierce, Ambrose Gwinett 1842–c.1914

US writer and journalist, best known for his *Cynic's Word Book* (1906, retitled *The Devil's Dictionary*, 1911). His collection of stories *Tales of Soldiers and Civilians* (1892) coincided with his divorce and the death of his son in a gunfight. He is thought to have died in Mexico.

10 That sovereign of insufferables.
1882 *Wasp*, alluding to Oscar Wilde.

11 Accordion, n. An instrument in harmony with the sentiments of an assassin.
1906 *The Cynic's Word Book*. Retitled *The Devil's Dictionary* (1911).

12 Acquaintance, n. A person whom we know well enough to borrow from, but not well enough to lend to.
1906 *The Cynic's Word Book*. Retitled *The Devil's Dictionary* (1911).

13 Advice, n. The smallest current coin.
1906 *The Cynic's Word Book*. Retitled *The Devil's Dictionary* (1911).

14 Alliance, n. In international politics, the union of two thieves who have their hands so deeply inserted in each other's pocket that they cannot separately plunder a third.
1906 *The Cynic's Word Book*. Retitled *The Devil's Dictionary* (1911).

15 Ambition, n. An overmastering desire to be vilified by enemies while living and made ridiculous by friends when dead.
1906 *The Cynic's Word Book*. Retitled *The Devil's Dictionary* (1911).

16 Applause, n. The echo of a platitude.
1906 *The Cynic's Word Book*. Retitled *The Devil's Dictionary* (1911).

17 Battle, n. A method of untying with the teeth a political knot that would not yield to the tongue.
1906 *The Cynic's Word Book*. Retitled *The Devil's Dictionary* (1911).

18 Bore, n. A person who talks when you wish him to listen.
1906 *The Cynic's Word Book*. Retitled *The Devil's Dictionary* (1911).

19 Brain, n. An apparatus with which we think that we think.

1906 *The Cynic's Word Book*. Retitled *The Devil's Dictionary* (1911).

20 Calamity, n. A more than commonly plain and unmistakable reminder that the affairs of this life are not of our own ordering. Calamities are of two kinds: misfortune to ourselves, and good fortune to others.
1906 *The Cynic's Word Book*. Retitled *The Devil's Dictionary* (1911).

21 Circumlocution, n. A literary trick whereby the writer who has nothing to say breaks it gently to the reader.
1906 *The Cynic's Word Book*. Retitled *The Devil's Dictionary* (1911).

22 Conservative, n. A statesman who is enamoured of existing evils, as distinguished from the Liberal, who wishes to replace them with others.
1906 *The Cynic's Word Book*. Retitled *The Devil's Dictionary* (1911).

23 Consult, v.t. To seek another's approval of a course already decided upon.
1906 *The Cynic's Word Book*. Retitled *The Devil's Dictionary* (1911).

24 Corporation, n. An ingenious device for obtaining individual profit without individual responsibility.
1906 *The Cynic's Word Book*. Retitled *The Devil's Dictionary* (1911).

25 Cynic, n. A blackguard whose faulty vision sees things as they are, not as they ought to be.
1906 *The Cynic's Word Book*. Retitled *The Devil's Dictionary* (1911).

26 Diplomacy, n. The patriotic art of lying for one's country.
1906 *The Cynic's Word Book*. Retitled *The Devil's Dictionary* (1911).

27 Education, n. That which discloses to the wise and disguises from the foolish their lack of understanding.
1906 *The Cynic's Word Book*. Retitled *The Devil's Dictionary* (1911).

28 Egotist, n. A person of low taste, more interested in himself than in me.
1906 *The Cynic's Word Book*. Retitled *The Devil's Dictionary* (1911).

29 Faith, n. Belief without evidence in what is told by one who speaks, without knowledge, of things without parallel.
1906 *The Cynic's Word Book*. Retitled *The Devil's Dictionary* (1911).

30 Fashion, n. A despot whom the wise ridicule and obey.
1906 *The Cynic's Word Book*. Retitled *The Devil's Dictionary* (1911).

31 Future, n. That period of time in which our affairs prosper, our friends are true and our happiness is assured.
1906 *The Cynic's Word Book*. Retitled *The Devil's Dictionary* (1911).

32 History, n. An account, mostly false, of events, mostly unimportant, which are brought about by rulers, mostly knaves, and soldiers, mostly fools.
1906 *The Cynic's Word Book*. Retitled *The Devil's Dictionary* (1911).

33 Ink, n. A villainous compound…chiefly used to facilitate the infection of idiocy and promote intellectual crime.
1906 *The Cynic's Word Book*. Retitled *The Devil's Dictionary* (1911).

34 Marriage, n. The state or condition of a community consisting of a master, a mistress and two slaves, making in all, two.
1906 *The Cynic's Word Book*. Retitled *The Devil's Dictionary* (1911).

35 Mayonnaise, n. One of the sauces which serve the French in place of a state religion.
1906 *The Cynic's Word Book*. Retitled *The Devil's Dictionary* (1911).

36 Painting, n. The art of protecting flat surfaces from the weather and exposing them to the critic.
1906 *The Cynic's Word Book*. Retitled *The Devil's Dictionary* (1911).

37 Patience, n. A minor form of despair, disguised as a virtue.
1906 *The Cynic's Word Book*. Retitled *The Devil's Dictionary* (1911).

38 Peace, n. In international affairs, a period of cheating between two periods of fighting.
1906 *The Cynic's Word Book*. Retitled *The Devil's Dictionary* (1911).

39 Philosophy, n. A route of many roads leading from nowhere to nothing.
1906 *The Cynic's Word Book*. Retitled *The Devil's Dictionary* (1911).

40 Piano, n. A parlour utensil for subduing the impenitent visitor. It is operated by depressing the keys of the machine and the spirits of the audience.
1906 *The Cynic's Word Book*. Retitled *The Devil's Dictionary* (1911).

41 Positive, adj. Mistaken at the top of one's voice.
1906 *The Cynic's Word Book*. Retitled *The Devil's Dictionary* (1911).

42 Prejudice, n. A vagrant opinion without visible means of support.
1906 *The Cynic's Word Book*. Retitled *The Devil's Dictionary* (1911).

43 Saint, n. A dead sinner revised and edited.
1906 *The Cynic's Word Book*. Retitled *The Devil's Dictionary* (1911).

44 Talk, v.t. To commit an indiscretion without temptation, from an impulse without purpose.
1906 *The Cynic's Word Book*. Retitled *The Devil's Dictionary* (1911).

45 Vote, n. The instrument and symbol of a freeman's power to make a fool of himself and a wreck of his country.
1906 *The Cynic's Word Book*. Retitled *The Devil's Dictionary* (1911).

Biko, Stephen 1946–77

South African black civil rights activist, founder of the Black Consciousness Movement. In 1973 he was placed under a banning order, and detained four times. He died in police custody, allegedly as a result of beatings.

46 Whites must be made to realise that they are only human, not superior. It's the same with Blacks. They must be made to realise that they are also human, not inferior.
1977 In the *Boston Globe*, 26 Oct.

Billings, Josh *pseudonym of* **Henry Wheeler Shaw** 1818–85

US humorist. He became a popular success with *Josh Billings, His Sayings* (1865).

47 Man was kreated a little lower than the angells and has bin gittin a little lower ever since.
1865 *Josh Billings, His Sayings*, ch.28.

48 It ain't often that a man's reputashun outlasts his munny.
1865 *Josh Billings, His Sayings*, ch.39.

49 Mi advise to them who are about tu begin, in arnest, the jurney ov life, is tu take their harte in one hand and a club in the other.
1865 *Josh Billings, His Sayings*, ch.71.

50 Love iz like the meazles; we kant have it bad but onst, and the latter in life we hav it the tuffer it goes with us.
1874 *Josh Billings' Wit and Humour*.

Binyon, (Robert) Laurence 1869–1943

English poet and art critic. He worked at the British Museum (1913–33) and was Norton Professor of Poetry at Harvard (1933–4). He is best remembered for his patriotic elegy 'For the Fallen', which Elgar set to music.

51 With proud thanksgiving, a mother for her children, England mourns for her dead across the sea.
Flesh of her flesh they were, spirit of her spirit, Fallen in the cause of the free.
1914 'For the Fallen', in *The Times*, 21 Sep.

52 They shall grow not old, as we that are left grow old:
Age shall not weary them, nor the years condemn.
At the going down of the sun and in the morning
We will remember them.
1914 'For the Fallen', in *The Times*, 21 Sep.

53 Now is the time for the burning of the leaves.
1942 'The Burning of the Leaves'.

54 Rootless hope and fruitless desire are there;
Let them go to the fire, with never a look behind.
The world that was ours is a world that is ours no more.
1942 'The Burning of the Leaves'.

55 Earth cares for her own ruins, naught for ours.
Nothing is certain, only the certain spring.
1942 'The Burning of the Leaves'.

Bioy Casares, Adolfo 1914–99

Argentinian fiction writer, known for his lifelong association with Jorge Luis Borges, with whom he published several anthologies and works of fiction. His own writings are examples of fantastic literature.

56 *La eternidad rotativa puede parecer atroz al espectador; es satisfactoria para sus individuos. Libres de malas noticias y de enfermedades, viven siempre como si fuera la primera vez, sin recordar las anteriores.*
A circular eternity may seem atrocious to the spectator, but it is satisfactory to individuals inside. Free from bad news and disease, they always live as if it were the first time, and do not remember previous times.
1940 *La invención de Morel* (*The Invention of Morel*, 1964).

Bird, Isabella *married name Isabella Bishop* 1831–1904

English traveller. She travelled and climbed in Australasia, America and the East; then returned to England to marry. When her husband died in 1886, she set off for Tibet and in 1890 travelled between Persia and the Black Sea. In 1894–7 she again visited the Far East, founding hospitals and orphanages, and her last journey was to Africa.

57 A man who any woman might love, but who no sane woman would marry.
1879 Of Rocky Mountain Jim, her guide on her travels on horseback through the Rockies. *A Lady's Life in the Rocky Mountains*.

58 One eye was entirely gone, and the loss made one side of the face repulsive, while the other might have been modelled in marble. 'Desperado' was written in large letters all over him. I almost repented of having sought his acquaintance.
1879 Of Rocky Mountain Jim, her guide on her travels on horseback through the Rockies. *A Lady's Life in the Rocky Mountains*.

59 I am well as long as I live on horseback…sleep out-of-doors, or in a log cabin, and lead in all respects a completely unconventional life. But each time for a few days…I have become civilised, I have found myself rapidly going down again.
1879 *A Lady's Life in the Rocky Mountains*.

60 Japan offers as much novelty perhaps as an excursion to another planet.
1880 *Unbeaten Tracks in Japan: An Account of Travels on Horseback in the Interior 1880* (published 1885).

61 Appropriating the fruits of Christian civilisation, but rejecting the tree from which they spring.
1880 *Unbeaten Tracks in Japan: An Account of Travels on Horseback in the Interior 1880* (published 1885).

62 It is singular that the Japanese, who rarely commit a solecism in taste in their national costume, architecture, or decorative art, seem to be perfectly destitute of perception when they borrow ours.
1880 *Unbeaten Tracks in Japan: An Account of Travels on Horseback in the Interior 1880* (published 1885).

Birkenhead, F(rederick) E(dwin) Smith, 1st Earl of 1872–1930

English Conservative politician and lawyer, a brilliant orator. In the Irish crisis (1914) he opposed Home Rule, but helped to negotiate the Settlement of 1921. He resigned after criticism over his conduct as Secretary of State for India (1924–8) to pursue commerce.

63 The world continues to offer glittering prizes to those who have stout hearts and stout swords.
1923 Rectorial address, Glasgow University, 7 Nov.

64 We have the highest authority for believing that the meek shall inherit the Earth; though I have never found any particular corroboration of this aphorism in the records of Somerset House.
1924 *Contemporary Personalities*, 'Marquess Curzon'.

65 As a matter of fact, we both are, and the only difference between us is that I am trying to be, and you can't help it.
In response to a judge's observation that Smith was being 'extremely offensive'. Quoted in 2nd Earl of Birkenhead *Frederick Edwin Earl of Birkenhead* (1933), vol.1, ch.9.

66 It is not for me, Your Honour, to attempt to fathom the inscrutable workings of Providence.
In reply to a judge's testy inquiry 'What do you suppose I am on the Bench for, Mr Smith?'. Quoted in 2nd Earl of Birkenhead *F. E.: The Life of F. E. Smith, First Earl of Birkenhead* (1959), ch.9.

67 Possibly not, My Lord, but far better informed.

In reply to a judge who had complained 'I have read your case, Mr Smith, and I am no wiser now than I was when I started'.
Quoted in 2nd Earl of Birkenhead *F. E.: The Life of F. E. Smith, First Earl of Birkenhead* (1959), ch.9.

68 I do not deal with subtleties; I am only a lawyer.
Quoted in Richard Fountain *The Wit of the Wig* (1968).

69 He has devoted the best years of his life to preparing his impromptu speeches.
Of Winston Churchill. Attributed.

Birney, Earle 1904–95

Canadian poet, professor at the universities of Toronto and, after World War II, British Columbia. His first work was *David and Other Poems* (1942).

70 And now he could only
bar himself in and wait
for the great flint to come singing into his heart.
1952 'Bushed'.

71 Through the cold time
she holds me
with evergreen
devotion
she bears up my whiteness.
1977 'She Is'.

Birns, Harold

New York City Buildings Commissioner (1962–5).

72 OG = PLR × AEB: the opportunity for graft equals the plethora of legal requirements multiplied by the number of architects, engineers and builders.
1963 Formula for bribery in building and housing codes. In the *New York Times*, 2 Oct.

Biro, Lajos 1880–1948

Hungarian screenwriter. He worked for Alexander Korda during the 1930s on various films, including *The Private Life of Henry VIII* (1933) and *The Four Feathers* (1939).

73 The things I've done for England.
1933 Line delivered by Charles Laughton as Henry VIII to Else Lanchester as Anne of Cleves in *The Private Life of Henry VIII* (with Arthur Wimperis).

Bishop, Elizabeth 1911–79

US poet. Her work is highly regarded for its precision, elegance and imagination.

74 The ship's ignored. The iceberg rises
and sinks again; its glassy pinnacles
correct elliptics in the sky.
This is a scene where he who treads the boards
is artlessly rhetorical.
1946 'The Imaginary Iceberg'.

75 The armoured cars of dreams, contrived to let us do
so many a dangerous thing.
1946 'Sleeping Standing Up'.

76 All the untidy activity continues,
awful but cheerful.
1955 'The Bight'.

77 Come like a light in the white mackerel sky,
come like a daytime comet
with a long unnebulous train of words,

from Brooklyn, over the Brooklyn Bridge, on this fine morning,
please come flying.
1955 'Invitation to Miss Marianne Moore'.

78 What childishness is it that while there's breath of life
in our bodies, we are determined to rush
to see the sun the other way round?
1965 'Questions of Travel'.

79 Oh, must we dream our dreams
and have them, too?
1965 'Questions of Travel'.

80 The art of losing isn't hard to master;
so many things seem filled with the intent
to be lost that their loss is no disaster.
1969 'One Art'.

Bishop, Jim 1907–87

US syndicated columnist.

81 A good writer is not, per se, a good book critic. No more so than a good drunk is automatically a good bartender.
1957 In the New York *Journal-American*, 26 Nov.

82 The peeping Tom of the sciences…men who care not where they are going: they merely want to know where everyone else has been.
1961 Of archaeology. In the New York *Journal-American*, 14 Mar.

Bismarck, Otto Edward Leopold, Fürst von (Prince of) 1815–98

Prussian statesman, Prime Minister of Prussia. He expanded territory at the expense of Denmark and Austria, forming a new German Empire of which he was Chancellor (1871–90) until he resigned, disapproving of the policies of the new Kaiser, Wilhelm II.

83 The great questions of our day cannot be solved by speeches and majority votes but by iron and blood.
1862 Speech to the Prussian Chamber, 30 Sep. He later altered the concluding words to the more commonly quoted 'blood and iron'.

84 Politics is not an exact science.
1863 Speech to the Prussian Chamber, 18 Dec.

85 Anyone who has ever looked into the glazed eyes of a soldier dying on the battlefield will think hard before starting a war.
1867 Speech, Berlin, Aug.

86 If we are to negotiate, I envisage that we shall play an essentially modest role; that of an honest broker who really intends to do business.
1878 Speech to the Reichstag, 19 Feb, on preventing war in Europe.

87 If there is ever another war in Europe, it will come out of some damned silly thing in the Balkans.
1898 Attributed deathbed remark. Quoted in the House of Commons, 16 Aug 1945.

88 My map of Africa lies in Europe. Here lies Russia and here lies France, and we are in the middle. That is my map of Africa.
Remarking on his preoccupation with European, as opposed to colonial, territorial concerns. Quoted in A J P Taylor *The Struggle for Mastery in Europe 1848–1918* (1954), p.294.

Bissell, Claude T(homas)   1916–2000

Canadian scholar and university administrator, President of the University of Toronto (1958–71).

89 It's ironical that the first people to demand free speech are the first people to deny it to others.
    1969 Of student protesters who disrupted the appearance of Clark Kerr, former President of Berkeley, at the University of Toronto, 5 Feb. Recalled in *Halfway up Parnassus* (1974).

Black, Arthur   1943–

Canadian broadcaster and humorist.

90 I predict that ashtrays will become as obsolete as spitoons in our lifetime.
    1989 *That Old Black Magic*, 'Smoking Can be Dangerous to Your Health'.

Black (of Crossharbour), Conrad Black, Baron   1944–

Canadian newspaper proprietor, Chairman and Chief Executive Officer of Hollinger Inc (1985–2003).

91 Journalists as a group, unlike all other powerful groups, require some protection from themselves, and from their own excesses.
    1988 Speech, Annual Dinner of the Canadian Press, 20 Apr, reported in the *Globe and Mail* the following day.

Black, Hugo LaFayette   1886–1971

US lawyer, senator (1927–37) and Associate Justice of the US Supreme Court (1937–71). He strongly supported civil liberties.

92 Without deviation, without exception, without any ifs, buts, or whereases, freedom of speech means you shall not do something to people for views they have, express, speak, or write.
    Quoted in Irving Dillard (ed) *One Man's Stand for Freedom* (1963).

Blacker, Valentine   1728–1823

Anglo-Irish soldier.

93 Put your trust in God, my boys, and keep your powder dry.
    'Oliver's Advice', collected in E Hayes *Ballads of Ireland* (1856), vol.1, p.192. The words are sometimes attributed to Oliver Cromwell.
    ➥ *See Forgy 330:25.*

Blackstone, Sir William   1723–80

English jurist. Called to the bar in 1746, he became King's Counsel and MP (both 1761), Solicitor-General (1763) and a judge of the court of common pleas (1770). He published *Commentaries on the Laws of England* (1765–9).

94 It is better that ten guilty persons escape than one innocent suffer.
    1769 *Commentaries on the Laws of England*, vol.4, ch.27. A puzzled visitor is apocryphally said to have remarked, 'Better for whom?'

Blainey, Geoffrey Norman   1930–

Australian economic historian and social commentator. He showed in *The Tyranny of Distance* (1966) how geographical isolation had shaped Australian history and people.

95 The Tyranny of Distance.
    1966 Title of book.

Blair, Cherie   1954–

English barrister. She is married to Prime Minister Tony Blair.

96 I am not superwoman. The reality of my daily life is that I am juggling a lot of balls in the air… And sometimes some of the balls get dropped.
    2002 Statement following revelations of her links to the convicted conman Peter Foster, 10 Dec.

Blair, Hamish   *pseudonym of*   Andrew James Fraser Blair   1872–1935

Scottish author and journalist. He moved from England to India where he founded *Empire* (1906) and the *Eastern Bureau* (1912). He wrote a number of short stories as well as articles, sketches and light verse.

97 This bloody town's a bloody cuss—
No bloody trains, no bloody bus,
And no one cares for bloody us—
In bloody Orkney.
    1952 'The Bloody Orkneys', stanza 1. First published in Arnold Silcock *Verse and Worse*, 'Queer People'.

98 Best bloody place is bloody bed,
With bloody ice on bloody head,
You might as well be bloody dead,
In bloody Orkney.
    1952 'The Bloody Orkneys', last stanza. First published in Arnold Silcock *Verse and Worse*, 'Queer People'.

Blair, Tony (Anthony Charles Lynton)   1953–

Scottish-born Labour politician and barrister, elected Prime Minister in 1997.

99 Labour is the Party of law and order in Britain today—tough on crime and tough on the causes of crime.
    1993 Speech as Shadow Home Secretary, Labour Party Conference, Sep.

1 The art of leadership is saying no, not yes. It is very easy to say yes.
    1994 In *The Mail on Sunday*, 2 Oct.

2 I didn't come into politics to change the Labour Party. I came into politics to change the country.
    1995 Speech at the Labour Party Conference, 30 Sep.

3 Ask me my three main priorities for Government, and I tell you: education, education and education.
    1996 Speech at the Labour Party Conference, 1 Oct.

4 People have to know that we will run from the centre and govern from the centre.
    1997 Speech given to The Newspaper Society, London, 16 Mar.

5 We are not the masters. The people are the masters. We are the servants of the people… What the electorate gives, the electorate can take away.
    1997 Addressing Labour MPs on the first day of the new Parliament, 7 May.

6 Sometimes I forget I'm Prime Minister. To me, I'm just Tony Blair.
    1997 In *The Sun*, 29 Jul.

7 She was the people's princess and this is how she will stay.
    1997 On the death of Diana, Princess of Wales. In a press statement, 1 Sep.

8 This is not the time for soundbites. I can feel the hand of

history on our shoulders.
1998 On peace talks in Northern Ireland. In the *Daily Telegraph*, 8 Apr.

9 In future, welfare will be a hand-up, not a hand-out.
1999 Lecture, London, 18 Mar.

10 Britain must, and I am sure will, stand shoulder-to-shoulder with the United States of America and peaceful nations across the world in deploying every possible resource to bring to justice the people responsible, and make sure terrorism never prevails.
2001 Statement, 11 Sep.

11 Jesus was a moderniser.
Quoted in John Rentoul *Tony Blair: Prime Minister* (2001).

12 Every time I have asked us to go to war, I have hated it. I spent months trying to get Milosevic to stop ethnic cleansing in Kosovo, delaying action while we negotiated endlessly.
2003 Speech at the Labour Party Conference, 15 Feb.

13 At every stage, we should seek to avoid war. But if the threat cannot be removed peacefully, please let us not fall for the delusion that it can be safely ignored.
2003 Speech at the Labour Party Conference, 15 Feb.

14 To retreat now, I believe, would put at hazard all that we hold dearest, turn the United Nations back into a talking shop, stifle the first steps of progress in the Middle East; leave the Iraqi people to the mercy of events on which we would have relinquished all power to influence for the better.
2003 Speech to the House of Commons, 18 Mar.

15 I somehow feel I am not being entirely persuasive in certain quarters.
2004 Following protests from the public gallery during a debate on the Iraq war in the House of Commons, 4 Feb.

16 The good news is that it is easy to describe the problem in Iraq today, the bad news is it's tough to tackle it.
2004 Press conference, 22 Apr.

17 There will be no cutting and running in Iraq.
2004 Press conference, 17 May.

18 Now is not the time for a change in direction…but a change in gear.
2004 Press conference, 15 Jun.

Blake, Eubie James Hubert   1883–1983

US jazz musician.

19 If I'd known I was gonna live this long, I'd have taken better care of myself.
1983 Quoted in the *Observer*, 13 Feb. He died 5 days after his 100th birthday.

Blake, Peter   1932–

English painter. A pioneer of the pop art movement in Britain, his most widely-known work is the cover design for the Beatles' album *Sergeant Pepper's Lonely Hearts Club Band* (1967).

20 Most artists go potty as they get older: dafter and madder as they get more celibate. So I am consciously going to do that.
2004 In *The Guardian*, 3 Jun.

Blake, William   1757–1827

English poet, painter, engraver and mystic. His works range from the lyrical *Songs of Innocence* (1789) and *Songs of Experience* (1794) to the mystical poems of *The Marriage of Heaven and Hell* (1791). His best-known engravings are in *The Illustrations to the Book of Job* (1826).

21 Whether on Ida's shady brow,
Or in the chambers of the East,
The chambers of the sun that now
From ancient melody have ceased.
1783 *Poetical Sketches*, 'To The Muses'.

22 How have you left the ancient love
That bards of old enjoyed in you!
The sound is forced, the notes are few!
1783 *Poetical Sketches*, 'To The Muses'.

23 The hills tell each other, and the listening
Valleys hear; all our longing eyes are turned
Up to thy holy feet visit our clime.
Come o'er the eastern hills and let our winds
Kiss thy perfumed garments; let us taste
Thy morn and evening breath. Scatter thy pearls
Upon our love-sick land that mourns for thee.
1783 *Poetical Sketches*, 'To Spring'.

24 O thou who passest through our valleys in
Thy strength, curb thy fierce steeds, ally the heat
That flames from their large nostrils! thou, O Summer,
Beneath our oaks hast slept while we beheld
With joy thy ruddy limbs and flourishing hair.
1783 *Poetical Sketches*, 'To Summer'.

25 O Autumn, laden with fruit, and stained
With the blood of grape, pass not, but sit
Beneath my shady roof; there thou may'st rest,
And tune thy jolly voice to my fresh pipe,
And all the daughters of the year shall dance!
Sing now the lusty song of fruits and flowers.
1783 *Poetical Sketches*, 'To Autumn'.

26 O Winter! bar thine adamantine doors.
The north is thine—there hast thou built thy dark
Deep-founded habitation. Shake not thy roofs,
Nor bend thy pillars with thine iron car.
1783 *Poetical Sketches*, 'To Winter'.

27 Does the eagle know what's in the pit
Or wilt thou go ask the mole?
Can wisdom be put in a silver rod,
Or Love in a golden bowl.
1789 Thel's Motto. *The Book of Thel*.

28 Piping down the valleys wild,
Piping songs of pleasant glee,
On a cloud I saw a child,
And he laughing said to me,
'Pipe a song about a lamb!'
So I piped with merry cheer.
'Piper, pipe that song again!'
So I piped. He wept to hear.
1789 *Songs of Innocence*, 'Introduction'.

29 Little lamb, who made thee?
Dost thou know who made thee?
Gave thee life and bid thee feed
By the stream and o'er the mead;
Gave thee clothing of delight,
Softest clothing, woolly, bright;
Gave thee such a tender voice,
Making all the vales rejoice?

Little lamb, who made thee?
Dost thou know who made thee?
1789 *Songs of Innocence*, 'The Lamb'.

30 My mother bore me in the southern wild,
And I am black, but O! my soul is white;
White as an angel is the English child,
But I am black as if bereaved of light.
1789 *Songs of Innocence*, 'The Little Black Boy'.

31 For Mercy has a human heart
Pity a human face:
And Love, the human form divine,
And Peace, the human dress.
1789 *Songs of Innocence*, 'The Divine Image'.

32 And all must love the human form,
In heathen, Turk or Jew;
Where mercy, Love and Pity dwell
There God is dwelling too.
1789 *Songs of Innocence*, 'The Divine Image'.

33 When my mother died I was very young,
And my father sold me while yet my tongue
Could scarcely cry weep weep weep weep.
So your chimneys I sweep, and in soot I sleep.
1789 *Songs of Innocence*, 'The Chimney Sweep'.

34 'Father! father! where are you going?
O do not walk so fast.
Speak, father, speak to your little boy,
Or else I shall be lost.'
1789 *Songs of Innocence*, 'The Little Boy Lost'.

35 He kissed the hand and by the hand led
And to his mother brought,
Who in sorrow pale, through the lonely dale,
Her little boy weeping sought.
1789 *Songs of Innocence*, 'The Little Boy Found'.

36 Then cherish pity, lest you drive an angel from your door.
1789 *Songs of Innocence*, 'Holy Thursday'.

37 Without contraries is no progression. Attraction and
repulsion, reason and energy, love and hate, are
necessary to human existence.
1790 *The Marriage of Heaven and Hell*, 'The Argument'.

38 Energy is Eternal Delight.
1790 *The Marriage of Heaven and Hell*, 'The Voice of the Devil'.

39 The road of excess leads to the palace of wisdom.
1790 *The Marriage of Heaven and Hell*, 'Proverbs of Hell'.

40 He who desires and acts not, breeds pestilence.
1790 *The Marriage of Heaven and Hell*, 'Proverbs of Hell'.

41 Eternity is in love with the productions of time.
1790 *The Marriage of Heaven and Hell*, 'Proverbs of Hell'.

42 Prisons are built with stones of Law, brothels with bricks
of Religion.
1790 *The Marriage of Heaven and Hell*, 'Proverbs of Hell'.

43 The tygers of wrath are wiser than the horses of
instruction.
1790 *The Marriage of Heaven and Hell*, 'Proverbs of Hell'.

44 The Pride of the peacock is the glory of God.
The lust of the goat is the bounty of God.
The wrath of the lion is the wisdom of God.
The nakedness of woman is the work of God.
1790 *The Marriage of Heaven and Hell*, 'Proverbs of Hell'.

45 Sooner murder an infant in its cradle than nurse unacted
desires.

1790 *The Marriage of Heaven and Hell*, 'Proverbs of Hell'.

46 If the doors of perception were cleansed everything
would appear to man as it is, infinite.
1790 *The Marriage of Heaven and Hell*, 'A Memorable Fancy',
plate 14. Aldous Huxley used this phrase as the title of his work
The Doors of Perception (1954).

47 Mutual forgiveness of each vice,
Such are the Gates of Paradise.
1793 *The Gates of Paradise*, prologue.

48 He who binds to himself a Joy
Doth the winged life destroy;
But he who kisses the Joy as it flies
Lives in Eternity's sunrise.
1793 *MS Notebooks*, p.105.

49 Never pain to tell thy love
Love that never told can be;
For the gentle wind does move
Silently, invisibly.
1793 *MS Notebooks*, p.115.

50 Hear the voice of the Bard!
Who present, past and future sees.
1794 *Songs of Experience*, 'Introduction'.

51 Love seeketh not itself to please,
Nor for itself hath any care,
But for another gives its ease,
And builds a heaven in hell's despair.
1794 *Songs of Experience*, 'The Clod and the Pebble'.

52 Love seeketh only self to please,
To bind another to its delight,
Joys in another's loss of ease
And builds a hell in heaven's despite.
1794 *Songs of Experience*, 'The Clod and the Pebble'.

53 Ah, sunflower, weary of time,
Who countest the steps of the sun,
Seeking after that sweet golden clime
Where the traveller's journey is done;
Where the youth pined away with desire
And the pale virgin shrouded in snow
Arise from their graves, and aspire
Where my sunflower wishes to go.
1794 *Songs of Experience*, 'Ah! Sunflower'.

54 O rose, thou art sick!
The invisible worm
That flies in the night,
In the howling storm,
Has found out thy bed
Of crimson joy,
And his dark secret love
Does thy life destroy.
1794 *Songs of Experience*, 'The Sick Rose'.

55 Is this a holy thing to see
In a rich fruitful land,
Babes reduced to misery,
Fed with cold and usurous hand?
1794 *Songs of Experience*, 'Holy Thursday'.

56 I went to the Garden of Love,
And saw what I never had seen:
A chapel was built in the midst
Where I used to play on the green.
1794 *Songs of Experience*, 'The Garden of Love'.

57 And I saw it was filled with graves,

And tomb-stones where flowers should be;
And priests in black gowns were walking their rounds,
And blinding with briars my joys and desires.
1794 *Songs of Experience*, 'The Garden of Love'.

58 I wander through each charter'd street,
Near where the charter'd Thames does flow,
And mark in every face I meet
Marks of weakness, marks of woe.
1794 *Songs of Experience*, 'London'.

59 I was angry with my friend:
I told my wrath, my wrath did end.
I was angry with my foe:
I told it not, my wrath did grow.
1794 *Songs of Experience*, 'A Poison Tree'.

60 My mother groaned! my father wept.
Into the dangerous world I leapt,
Helpless, naked, piping loud
Like a fiend hid in a cloud.
1794 *Songs of Experience*, 'Infant Sorrow'.

61 Tyger! Tyger! burning bright
In the forests of the night,
What immortal hand or eye
Could frame thy fearful symmetry?
1794 *Songs of Experience*, 'The Tyger'.

62 When the stars threw down their spears,
And watered heaven with their tears,
Did he smile his work to see?
Did he who made the Lamb make thee?
1794 *Songs of Experience*, 'The Tyger'.

63 Dear Mother, dear Mother, the Church is cold,
But the Ale-house is healthy and pleasant and warm.
1794 *Songs of Experience*, 'The Little Vagabond'.

64 Mock on, mock on, Voltaire Rousseau;
Mock on, mock on, 'tis all in vain!
You throw the sand against the wind,
And the wind blows it back again.
1800–3 *MS Notebooks*, p.7.

65 O why was I born with a different face?
Why was I not born like the rest of my race?
1803 Letter to Thomas Butts, 16 Aug.

66 To see a world in a grain of sand,
And heaven in a wild flower,
Hold infinity in the palm of your hand,
And eternity in an hour.
c.1803 *Auguries of Innocence*, l.1–4.

67 A robin red breast in a cage
Puts all Heaven in a rage.
c.1803 *Auguries of Innocence*, l.5–6.

68 Man was made for Joy and Woe,
And when this we rightly know,
Thro' the world we safely go.
Joy and Woe are woven fine,
A clothing for the soul divine.
c.1803 *Auguries of Innocence*, l.56–60.

69 The strongest poison ever known
Came from Ceasar's laurel crown.
c.1803 *Auguries of Innocence*, l.97–8.

70 The whore and gambler, by the state
Licensed build that nation's fate.
The harlot's cry from street to street

Shall weave old England's winding sheet.
c.1803 *Auguries of Innocence*, l.113–6.

71 We are led to believe a Lie
When we see with, not thro' the Eye.
c.1803 *Auguries of Innocence*, l.125–6.

72 The fields from Islington to Marybone,
To Primrose Hill and Saint John's Wood,
Were builded over with pillars of gold;
And there Jerusalem's pillars stood.
c.1804–1807 *Jerusalem*, plate 27.

73 He who would do good to another man must do it in
Minute Particulars.
General Good is the plea of the scoundrel, hypocrite,
and flatterer;
For Art and Science cannot exist but in minutely
organized Particulars.
c.1804–1807 *Jerusalem*, plate 55.

74 I gave you the end of the golden string;
Only wind it into a ball,
It will lead you in at Heaven's gate,
Built in Jerusalem's wall.
c.1804–1807 *Jerusalem*, plate 77.

75 I care not whether a man is good or evil; all that I care
Is whether he is a wise man or a fool. Go! put off
Holiness,
And put on intellect, or my thunderous hammer shall
drive thee,
To wrath which thou condemnest, till thou obey my
voice.
c.1804–1807 *Jerusalem*, plate 91.

76 Painters are noted for being dissipated and wild.
c.1808 *Annotations to Sir Joshua Reynolds' Discourses*.

77 The man who never in his mind and thoughts travelled to
heaven is no artist.
c.1808 *Annotations to Sir Joshua Reynolds' Discourses*.

78 What has Reasoning to do with the Art of Painting?
c.1808 *Annotations to Sir Joshua Reynolds' Discourses*.

79 Knowledge of ideal beauty is not to be acquired. It is
born with us. Innate ideas are in every man, born with
him; they are truly himself.
c.1808 *Annotations to Sir Joshua Reynolds' Discourses*.

80 When Sir Joshua Reynolds died
All Nature was degraded;
The King dropp'd a tear into the Queen's ear,
And all his pictures faded.
c.1808 *Annotations to Sir Joshua Reynolds' Discourses*.

81 Thy friendship oft has made my heart to ache:
Do be my enemy—for friendship's sake.
1808–11 *MS Notebooks*, 'To H[ayley]', p.37.

82 And did those feet in ancient time
Walk upon England's mountains green?
And was the holy Lamb of God
On England's pleasant pastures seen?
1809 *Milton*, preface. Stanza 1.

83 And did the Countenance Divine
Shine forth upon our clouded hills?
And was Jerusalem builded here
Among these dark Satanic mills?
1809 *Milton*, preface. Stanza 2.

84 Bring me my bow of burning gold!

Bring me my arrows of desire!
Bring me my spear! O clouds, unfold!
Bring me my chariot of fire!
1809 *Milton*, preface. Stanza 3.

85 I will not cease from mental fight,
Nor shall my sword sleep in my hand,
Till we have built Jerusalem
In England's green and pleasant land.
1809 *Milton*, preface. Stanza 4.

86 God appears and God is light
To those poor souls who dwell in night,
But does a human form display
To those who dwell in realms of day.
1809 *Milton*, 'And Did Those Feet In Ancient Time'.

Blanch, Lesley 1904–

English biographer, traveller and cookery writer.

87 She was an Amazon. Her whole life was spent riding at
breakneck speed towards the wilder shores of love.
1954 *The Wilder Shores of Love*, pt.2, ch.1.

Blanchflower, Danny (Robert Dennio) 1926–93

Northern Ireland-born footballer. He won numerous titles as
captain of Tottenham Hotspur in the early 1960s and collected
a total of 56 caps playing for Northern Ireland before retiring to
become a noted football commentator and columnist.

88 We try to equalize before the others have scored.
1958 Explaining his tactics as captain of Northern Ireland.
Quoted in Colin Jarman *The Guinness Dictionary of Sports
Quotations* (1990).

89 The great fallacy is that the game is first and last about
winning. It's nothing of the kind. The game is about glory.
It's about doing things in style, with a flourish, about
going out and beating the other lot, not waiting for them
to die of boredom.
Quoted in Hunter Davis *The Glory Game* (1972).

Blass, Bill (William Ralph) 1922–2002

US fashion designer.

90 When in doubt wear red.
1982 In news summaries, 31 Dec.

Blavatsky, Helena Petrovna 1831–91

Russian-born mystic, founder of the Theosophical Society. Her
works include *Isis Unveiled* (1877).

91 'Theosophy' is the essence of all religion and of absolute
truth, a drop of which only underlies every creed.
1889 *The Key to Theosophy.*

92 Theosophy, on earth, is like the white ray of the
spectrum, and each religion only one of the seven
colours.
1889 *The Key to Theosophy.*

Blest Gana, Alberto 1830–1920

Chilean novelist and Ambassador to France and England. He
lived in Paris until the end of his career. He pioneered the
documentary social novel in Spanish American literature.

93 *Entre nosotros el dinero ha hecho desaparecer más
preocupaciones de familia que en las viejas sociedades
europeas. En éstas hay lo que llaman aristocracia de*

*dinero, que jamás alcanza con su poder…a hacer olvidar
enteramente la oscuridad de la cuna, al paso que en
Chile…todo va cediendo su puesto a la riqueza.*
Among us, money has dissolved more worries than
among ancient European societies. The latter have what
they call the moneyed aristocracy, which, despite all its
power, never gets to forget its humble origins; on the
other hand, in Chile everything yields to wealth.
1862 *Martín Rivas*, ch.2 (translated 1918).

Blinder, Alan 1945–

US economist, Professor at Princeton University (1982–) and
Vice Chair of the Federal Reserve System Board (1994–6).

94 Economists have the least influence on policy where
they know the most and are most agreed…the most
influence on policy where they know the least and
disagree most.
1987 *Hard Heads, Soft Hearts.*

95 If you try to give an on-the-one-hand-or-the-other-
hand answer, only one of the hands tends to get quoted.
1995 On economic forecasting. In the *Wall Street Journal*, 23
Jun.

Bliss, Sir Arthur 1891–1975

English composer, Music Director of the BBC (1942–4) and
Master of the Queen's Music (from 1953). His compositions,
sometimes avant-garde, included ballets, an opera, chamber
music and film scores.

96 The jazz band can be used for artificial excitement and
aphrodisiac purposes, but not for spreading eternal
truths.
1941 'Music Policy'.

Blix, Hans 1928–

Swedish diplomat. He was appointed Executive Chairman of
the UN Monitoring, Verification and Inspection Commission for
Iraq in 2000.

97 We have not found any smoking guns.
2003 Of weapons inspections in Iraq. To reporters, 9 Jan.

98 Iraq appears not to have come to a genuine
acceptance—not even today—of the disarmament
which was demanded of it and which it needs to carry
out to win the confidence of the world and to live in
peace.
2003 Security Council update on weapons inspections in Iraq,
27 Jan.

99 These reports do not contend that weapons of mass
destruction remain in Iraq, but nor do they exclude that
possibility. They point to lack of evidence and
inconsistencies, which raise question marks, which must
be straightened out, if weapons dossiers are to be closed
and confidence is to arise.
2003 Security Council update on weapons inspections in Iraq,
27 Jan.

Blixen, Karen, Baroness *pseudonym* **Isak Dinesen**
1885–1962

Danish novelist and story teller. Her book *Out of Africa* (1938) is
set on the Kenyan coffee plantation she managed with her
husband (also cousin) Baron Bror Blixen. She was divorced in
1921, and returned to Denmark in 1931.

1 What is man, when you come to think upon him, but a minutely set, ingenious machine for turning, with infinite artfulness, the red wine of Shiraz into urine?
   1934 *Seven Gothic Tales*, 'The Dreamers'.

2 The true aristocracy and the true proletariat of the world are both in understanding with tragedy. To them it is the fundamental principle of God, and the key, the minor key, to existence. They differ in this way from the bourgeoisie of all classes, who deny tragedy, who will not tolerate it, and to whom the word tragedy means in itself unpleasantness.
   1937 *Out of Africa*, pt.5, ch.1.

Bloom, Allan 1930–92

US writer and educator, Professor of Political Science at the University of Chicago. His best-known work is *The Closing of the American Mind* (1987).

3 The liberally educated person is one who is able to resist the easy and preferred answers, not because he is obstinate but because he knows others worthy of consideration.
   1987 *The Closing of the American Mind*, preface.

4 Education is the taming or demonstration of the soul's raw passions—not suppressing them or excising them, which would deprive the soul of its energy—but forming and informing them as art.
   1987 *The Closing of the American Mind*.

Bloom, André Borisovich, Anthony, Metropolitan of Sourozh 1914–2003

Russian churchman and writer, Head of the Russian Orthodox Church in Great Britain and Ireland.

5 It is not the constant thought of their sins, but the vision of the holiness of God that makes the saints aware of their own sinfulness.
   1966 *Living Prayer*.

6 A miracle is not the breaking of the laws of the fallen world. It is the re-establishment of the laws of the kingdom.
   1966 *Living Prayer*.

Bloom, Harold 1930–

US literary critic and writer, Professor of English (1965–77) and Humanities (1974–) at Yale. His many works include *The Breaking of the Vessels* (1981).

7 The most beautiful prose paragraph yet written by any American.
   1991 On the opening of ch.19 of Mark Twain's *Huckleberry Finn*. *The Western Canon*.

Blough, Roger M(iles) 1904–85

US industrialist.

8 Steel prices cause inflation like wet sidewalks cause rain.
   1967 In *Forbes*, 1 Aug.

Blunden, Edmund Charles 1896–1974

English poet and critic. He served in World War I, an experience reflected both in his poetry and in his prose work *Undertones of War* (1928), but is essentially a nature poet.

9 All things they have in common, being so poor,

And their one fear, Death's shadow at the door. Each sundown makes them mournful, each sunrise Brings back the brightness in their failing eyes.
   1920 'Almswomen'.

10 And night this toppling reed, still as the dead The great pike lies, the murderous patriarch, Watching the water-pit shelving and dark Where through the plash his lithe bright vassals tread.
   1920 'The Pike'.

11 Unrecorded, unrenowned, Men from whom my ways begin, Here I know you by your ground But I know you not within— There is silence, there survives Not a moment of your lives.
   1922 'Forefathers'.

12 Then is not death at watch Within those secret waters? What wants he but to catch Earth's heedless sons and daughters?
   1925 'The Midnight Skaters'.

13 Dance on this ball-floor thin and wan, Use him as though you love him; Court him, elude him, reel and pass, And let him hate you through the glass.
   1925 'The Midnight Skaters'.

14 Cuinchy…was a slaughter yard… Who that had been there for but a few hours could ever forget the sullen sorcery and mad lineaments of Cuinchy?
   1928 *Undertones of War*, 'I V. The Sudden Depths'. Cuinchy, near Arras, was the scene of heavy fighting in 1914.

15 This was my country and it may be yet, But something flew between me and the sun.
   1928 'The Resignation'.

16 I have been young, and now am not too old; And I have seen the righteous forsaken, His health, his honour and his quality taken. This is not what we were formerly told.
   1929 'Report On Experience'.

17 Mastery in poetry consists largely in the instinct for not ruining or smothering or tinkering with moments of vision.
   1930 'Leigh Hunt'.

18 I am for the woods against the world, But are the woods for me?
   1931 'The Kiss'.

19 Cricket to us was more than play, It was a worship in the summer sun.
   'Pride of the Village'. Quoted in Alan Ross (ed) *The Penguin Cricketer's Companion* (1978).

Blunkett, David 1947–

English Labour politician. Blind from birth, he has been MP for Sheffield (Brightside) since 1987 and Home Secretary since 2001.

20 Let me say this very slowly indeed. Watch my lips: no selection by examination or interview under a Labour Government.
   1995 Speech at the Labour Party Conference, 5 Oct.

21 They should go back home and re-create their countries

which we have freed from tyranny, whether it be Kosovo or now Afghanistan. I have no sympathy whatsoever with young men in their twenties who do not get back home and rebuild their countries.
2002 On asylum seekers, 18 Sep.

22 I haven't given up on the idea that we're going to nail this individual.
2004 On the convicted football hooligan Garry Mann, who escaped his sentence when he was repatriated from Portugal before the paperwork was complete, 20 Jun.

Blythe, Ronald George 1922–

English writer. He is best known for his book *Akenfield* (1963), a portrait of an English village told in interviews with linking commentary.

23 As for the British churchman, he goes to church as he goes to the bathroom, with the minimum of fuss and with no explanation if he can help it.
1963 *The Age of Illusion*, ch.12.

24 An industrial worker would sooner have a £5 note but a countryman must have praise.
1969 *Akenfield*, ch.5.

25 Suffolk used to worship Sunday, not God.
1969 *Akenfield*, ch.6.

26 One of the reasons why old people make so many journeys into the past is to satisfy themselves that it is still there.
1979 *The View in Winter*, introduction.

Boccioni, Umberto 1882–1916

Italian artist, futurist painter and sculptor. A key figure in the drafting of the Futurist Manifesto (1910), he later turned to sculpture, attempting to convey motion and light in three-dimensional form.

27 It is necessary to destroy the pretended nobility, entirely literary and traditional, of marble and bronze… The sculptor can use twenty different materials, or even more, in a single work, provided that the plastic emotion requires it.
1912 In the *Technical Manifesto of Futurist Sculpture* (11 Apr, Milan).

Bodenheim, Maxwell 1892–1954

US writer and critic.

28 Poetry is the impish attempt to paint the color of the wind.
Quoted in Ben Hecht's play *Winkelberg* (1958).

Boethius, Anicius Manlius Severinus c.480–524 AD

Roman philosopher and statesman. Under Theodoric he became consul and later chief minister, but was accused of treason and executed. While in prison he wrote *De con-solatione philosophiae* (*The Consolation of Philosophy*, 523).

29 *Nam in omni adversitate fortunae infelicissimum est genus infortunii, fuisse felicem.*
In all adversity of fortune, the most wretched kind is once to have been happy.
523 *De consolatione philosophiae*, bk.2, pt.4 (translated by V E Watts).

Bogan, Louise 1897–1970

US poet and critic, poetry editor of the *New Yorker* for many years. Her work is intense and deeply personal.

30 Women have no wideness in them
They are provident instead,
Content in the tight hot cell of their hearts
To eat dusty bread.
1923 'Women'.

31 But childhood prolonged cannot remain a fairy-land. It becomes a hell.
1940 On Katherine Mansfield. 'Childhood's False Eden'.

32 The intellectual…is the fine nervous flower of the bourgeoisie.
1943 'Some Notes on Popular and Unpopular Poetry'.

Bogarde, Sir Dirk *originally* Derek Jules Ulric Niven van den Bogaerde 1921–99

English actor and novelist.

33 It's always full of all the people I'd hoped were dead.
On the Cannes Film Festival. Quoted in Barry Norman *And Why Not?* (2002).

Bogart, John B 1848–1921

US journalist, an early editor of the *New York Sun*.

34 When a dog bites a man, that is not news, because it happens so often. But if a man bites a dog, that is news.
Quoted in F M O'Brien *The Story of the Sun* (1918), ch.10. The phrase is often attributed to Charles A Dana.

Bohlen, Charles Eustis 1904–74

US diplomat and Soviet specialist, Ambassador to Russia (1953–7, 1959–61).

35 A non-Communist premier with Communist ministers would be like a woman trying to stay half pregnant.
Of Winston Churchill's suggestion that the West share spheres of influence with Joseph Stalin in the post-war development of the Balkans. Quoted in Walter Isaacson and Evan Thomas *The Wise Men* (1986).

36 There are two ways you can tell when a man is lying…when he says he can drink champagne all night and not get drunk…[and] when he says he understands Russians.
Quoted in the *New York Times*, 26 Dec 1993.

Boileau (Despréaux), Nicolas 1636–1711

French critic. His works include satires (1660–6), epistles, critical dissertations (particularly the influential *L'Art poétique*, 'The Art of Poetry', 1674), epigrams and translations.

37 *Si j'écris quatre mots, j'en effacerai trois.*
If I write four words, I strike out three of them.
1665 *Satire no.2 A M Molière*.

38 Often, the fear of one evil leads us into inflicting one that is worse.
1674 *L'Art poétique*.

Bok, Derek 1930–

US educator, President of Harvard University (1971–91) and Professor Emeritus there from 1991. His works include *Beyond the Ivory Tower: Social Responsibilities of the Modern University* (1982).

39 If you think education is expensive—try ignorance.
1979 In *Town and Country*, May.

Bold, Alan 1943–98

Scottish poet, biographer and critic, a prolific full-time writer and anthologizer since 1967. He wrote an award-winning biography of Hugh MacDiarmid (1989).

40 In Scotland, land of the omnipotent No.
1969 'A Memory of Death'.

41 That which once united man
Now drives him apart. We are not helpless
Creatures crashing onwards irresistibly to doom.
There is time for everything and time to choose
For everything. We are that time, that choice.
Everybody gets what he deserves.
1969 'June 1967 at Buchenwald'.

42 The poet lives as long as his lines are imprinted on the minds of his readers.
1989 *MacDiarmid*, epilogue.

Bolingbroke, Henry St John, 1st Viscount 1678–1751

English Jacobite statesman, joint leader of the Tory Party. On the death of Queen Anne he fled to France, where he wrote *Reflections on Exile* (1714). He also wrote the influential *Idea of a Patriot King* (1749).

43 What a world is this, and how does fortune banter us!
1714 Letter to Jonathan Swift, 3 Aug.

44 Faction is to party what the superlative is to the positive. Party is a political evil, and faction is the worst of all parties.
1738 *Idea of a Patriot King*. Published in 1749.

Bolívar, Simón 1783–1830

Venezuelan soldier and statesman. He led revolutions against Spanish rule in New Granada (Colombia), Peru and Upper Peru (Bolivia). He became President of Colombia (1821–30) and of Peru (1823–9), and was a gifted prose writer.

45 *Más grande es el odio que nos ha inspirado la Península, que el mar que nos separa de ella; menos difícil es unir los dos continentes, que reconciliar los espíritus de ambos países.*
The hate that the Iberian peninsula has inspired in us is broader than the sea which separates us from it; it is less difficult to join both continents than to join both countries' souls.
1815 'Carta de Jamaica' (translated as *The Jamaica Letter*, 1977).

Bolles, Richard Nelson 1927–

US writer, famous for his manual for job hunters.

46 What Color is Your Parachute?
1972 Title of a vocational guidance book published annually.

Bolt, Robert Oxton 1924–95

English playwright and screenwriter. His best-known work is the play *A Man for All Seasons* (1960). His screenplays include *Dr Zhivago* (1965) and *The Mission* (1986).

47 A Man for All Seasons.
1960 Play title, originally said by Robert Whittington about his contemporary Sir Thomas More, the central character in Bolt's play.

48 It profits a man nothing to give his soul for the whole world…
But for Wales—!
1960 Thomas More. *A Man for All Seasons*.

49 To be human at all… we must stand fast a little—even at the risk of being heroes.
1960 Thomas More. *A Man for All Seasons*.

50 The courts of Europe are a jungle, compared to which your jungles here are a well-kept garden.
1986 Line delivered by Ray Mc Anally as Cardinal Altamirano in *The Mission*.

Bonavia, David 1940–88

British journalist and Editor of the *Far East Economic Review*. His main field of interest was China.

51 Their civilization is based on the most forthrightly materialistic value system in the history of mankind. If they see pie in the sky, they immediately start figuring out how to get it down onto the dinner table.
1961 *The Chinese*.

Bond, Carrie Jacobs 1862–1946

US songwriter and lyricist.

52 When you come to the end of a perfect day,
And you sit alone with your thought,
While the chimes ring out with a carol gay
For the joy that the day has brought,
Do you think what the end of a perfect day
Can mean to a tired heart,
When the sun goes down with a flaming ray,
And the dear friends have to part?
1910 'A Perfect Day'.

Bonds, Barry Lamar 1964–

US baseball player.

53 Don't talk about him no more.
2003 On the legendary Babe Ruth, whose slugging record he broke. Quoted by Associated Press, 16 Jul.

Bone, Sir David 1874–1959

Scottish novelist. He was a high-ranking sailor, and wrote novels about the sea.

54 It's 'Damn you, Jack—I'm all right!' with you chaps.
1910 *The Brassbounder*, ch.3.

Bonham Carter, Helena 1966–

English actress.

55 It is acting in its purest form. You have to act with your eyes.
2001 On playing a chimp in *Planet of the Apes*. In the *Observer*, 30 Dec.

Bonhoeffer, Dietrich 1906–45

German Lutheran pastor and theologian, executed for implication in a plot against Hitler. His theology, especially his plea for 'religionless Christianity', was influential in mid- and late-20c theology.

56 The Church knows nothing of a sacredness of war. The Church which prays 'Our Father' asks God only for peace.
1932 Draft of a new Catechism with F Hildebrandt, in

Gesammelte Schriften, vol.3 (1947, translated by E Robinson and J Bowden in *No Rusty Sword*, 1965).

57 The cross is God's truth about us, and therefore it is the only power that can make us truthful. When we know the cross we are no longer afraid of the truth.
1937 *Nachfolge* (translated as *The Cost of Discipleship*).

58 *Billige Gnade ist Gnade ohne Nachfolge, Gnade ohne Kreuz, Gnade ohne den lebendigen, menschgewordenen Jesus Christus.*
Cheap grace is grace without discipleship, grace without the cross, grace without Jesus Christ, living and incarnate.
1937 *Nachfolge* (translated as *The Cost of Discipleship*).

59 If religion is only a garment of Christianity—and even this garment has looked very different at different times—then what is religionless Christianity?
1944 Letter to Eberhardt Bethge, 30 Apr. Collected in *Widerstand und Ergebung* (1951, translated 1953).

60 Death is the supreme Festival on the road to freedom.
1945 Letter, collected in *Widerstand und Ergebung* (1951, translated 1953).

61 *Es ist der Vorzug und das Wesen der Starken, dass sie die großen Entscheidungsfragen stellen und zu ihnen klar Stellung nehmen können. Die Schwachen müssen sich immer zwischen Alternativen entscheiden, die nicht die ihren sind.*
It is the nature, and the advantage, of strong people that they can bring out the crucial questions and form a clear opinion about them. The weak always have to decide between alternatives that are not their own.
1951 *Widerstand und Ergebung*, 'Ein paar Gedanken über Verschiedenes' (translated 1953).

62 *Ein Gott, der sich von uns beweisen ließe, wäre ein Götze.*
A God who let us prove his existence would be an idol.
'Glaubst du, so hast du'. Versuch eines Lutherischen Katchismus ('If you believe it, you have it'. Attempt at a Lutheran Catechism). Quoted in E Robinson and J Bowden *No Rusty Sword* (1965).

Bono *real name* **Paul Hewson** 1960–

Irish rock singer with the band U2. He is also known for his charity campaigning and political views.

63 They didn't have Kalashnikovs but U2 tickets in their hands.
1997 Of the audience at the U2 concert in Sarajevo, 24 Sep.

64 Elvis ate America before America ate him.
2004 On Elvis Presley. In *Rolling Stone*, 15 Apr.

Book of Common Prayer

The idea of a new prayer book was developed initially by Thomas Cranmer during the reigns of Edward VI and Elizabeth I. The final text was published in 1662.

65 Dearly beloved brethren, the Scripture moveth us in sundry places to acknowledge and confess our manifold sins and wickedness.
Morning Prayer, Sentences of the Scriptures.

66 We have erred and strayed from thy ways like lost sheep. We have followed too much the devices and desires of our own hearts. We have offended against thy holy laws.

We have left undone those things which we ought to have done. And we have done those things which we ought not to have done. And there is no health in us.
Morning Prayer, General Confession.

67 A godly, righteous, and sober life.
Morning Prayer, General Confession.

68 And forgive us our trespasses, As we forgive them that trespass against us.
Morning Prayer, the Lord's Prayer.

69 Glory be to the Father, and to the Son: and to the Holy Ghost;
As it was in the beginning, is now and ever shall be: world without end. Amen.
Morning Prayer, Gloria.

70 Lord God of Sabaoth.
Morning Prayer, Te Deum.

71 I believe in God the Father Almighty, Maker of heaven and earth: And in Jesus Christ his only Son our Lord, Who was conceived by the Holy Ghost, Born of the Virgin Mary, Suffered under Pontius Pilate, Was crucified, dead, and buried: He descended into hell; The third day he rose again from the dead; He ascended into heaven, And sitteth on the right hand of God the Father Almighty; From thence he shall come to judge the quick and the dead. I believe in the Holy Ghost; The holy Catholick Church; The Communion of Saints; The Forgiveness of sins; The Resurrection of the body, And the life everlasting. Amen.
Morning Prayer, Apostle's Creed.

72 Give peace in our time, O Lord.
Morning Prayer, versicle.

73 The author of peace and lover of concord, in knowledge of whom standeth our eternal life, whose service is perfect freedom.
Morning Prayer, Second Collect, for Peace.

74 Neither run into any kind of danger.
Morning Prayer, Third Collect, for Grace.

75 Pour upon them the continual dew of thy blessing.
Morning Prayer, Prayer for the Clergy and People.

76 O God, from whom all holy desires, all good counsels, and all just works do proceed: Give unto thy servants that peace which the world cannot give.
Evening Prayer, Second Collect.

77 Lighten our darkness, we beseech thee, O Lord; and by thy great mercy defend us from all perils and dangers of this night.
Evening Prayer, Third Collect, for Aid against Perils.

78 Whosoever will be saved: before all things it is necessary that he hold the Catholic Faith.
Athanasian Creed.

79 And yet they are not three Gods: but one God.
Athanasian Creed.

80 O God the Father of heaven: have mercy upon us miserable sinners.
Litany.

81 From envy, hatred, and malice, and all uncharitableness, Good Lord, deliver us.
Litany.

82 All sorts and conditions of men.
Prayer for all Conditions of Men.

83 All who profess and call themselves Christians.
Prayer for all Conditions of Men.

84 We bless thee for our creation, preservation, and all the blessings of this life; but above all for thine inestimable love in the redemption of the world by our Lord Jesus Christ; for the means of grace, and for the hope of glory.
General Thanksgiving.

85 Almighty God, give us grace that we may cast away the works of darkness, and put upon us the armour of light, now in the time of this mortal life.
Collects, 1st Sunday in Advent.

86 Hear them, read, mark, learn, and inwardly digest them.
Of all the holy Scriptures. Collects, 2nd Sunday in Advent.

87 Have mercy upon all Jews, Turks, Infidels, and Hereticks, and take from them all ignorance, hardness of heart, and contempt of thy word.
Collects, Good Friday.

88 Lord of all power and might, who art the author and giver of all good things.
Collects, 7th Sunday after Trinity.

89 Serve thee with a quiet mind.
Collects, 21st Sunday after Trinity.

90 Lord, we beseech thee to keep thy household the Church in continual godliness.
Collects, 22nd Sunday after Trinity.

91 The glory that shall be revealed.
Collects, St Stephen's Day.

92 Almighty God, unto whom all hearts be open, all desires known, and from whom no secrets are hid: Cleanse the thoughts of our hearts by the inspiration of thy Holy Spirit, that we may perfectly love thee, and worthily magnify thy holy Name; through Christ our Lord. Amen.
Holy Communion, Collect.

93 For I the Lord thy God am a jealous God, and visit the sins of the fathers upon the children unto the third and fourth generation of them that hate me, and shew mercy unto thousands in them that love me and keep my commandments.
Holy Communion, Second Commandment.

94 All things visible and invisible.
Holy Communion, Nicene Creed.

95 Very God of very God, Begotten, not made, Being of one substance with the Father, By whom all things were made: Who for us men and for our salvation came down from heaven.
Holy Communion, Nicene Creed.

96 And I believe in the Holy Ghost, The Lord and giver of life, Who proceedeth from the Father and Son, Who with the Father and the Son together is worshipped and glorified, Who spake by the Prophets.
Holy Communion, Nicene Creed.

97 And I believe in one Catholick and Apostolick Church.
Holy Communion, Nicene Creed.

98 Let us pray for the whole state of Christ's Church militant here in earth.
Holy Communion, Introduction to Prayer for the Church militant.

99 Draw near with faith.
Holy Communion, Invitation.

1 Ye that do truly and earnestly repent you of your sins, and are in love and charity with your neighbours, and intend to lead a new life.
Holy Communion, Invitation.

2 We acknowledge and bewail our manifold sins and wickedness, Which we from time to time most grievously have committed, By thought, word, and deed, Against thy Divine Majesty, Provoking most justly thy wrath and indignation against us.
Holy Communion, General Confession.

3 Hear what comfortable words our Saviour Christ saith unto all that truly turn to him.
Holy Communion, Words of Encouragement.

4 It is meet and right so to do.
Holy Communion, versicles and responses.

5 Therefore with Angels, and Archangels, and with all the company of heaven, we laud and magnify thy glorious Name; evermore praising thee, and saying: Holy, holy, holy, Lord God of hosts, heaven and earth are full of thy glory: Glory be to thee, O Lord most High. Amen.
Holy Communion, Praise.

6 A full, perfect, and sufficient sacrifice, oblation, and satisfaction, for the sins of the whole world.
Holy Communion, Prayer of Consecration.

7 We do not presume to come to this thy Table, O merciful Lord, trusting in our own righteousness, but in thy manifold and great mercies. We are not worthy so much as to gather up the crumbs under thy Table. But thou art the same Lord, whose property is always to have mercy: Grant us therefore, gracious Lord, so to eat the flesh of thy dear Son Jesus Christ, and to drink his blood, that our sinful bodies may be made clean by his body, and our souls washed through his most precious blood, and that we may evermore dwell in him, and he in us. Amen.
Holy Communion, Prayer of Humble Access.

8 The Body of our Lord Jesus Christ, which was given for thee, preserve thy body and soul unto everlasting life: Take and eat this in remembrance that Christ died for thee, and feed on him in thy heart by faith with thanksgiving.
Holy Communion.

9 The Blood of our Lord Jesus Christ, which was shed for thee, preserve thy body and soul unto everlasting life: Drink this in remembrance that Christ's Blood was shed for thee, and be thankful.
Holy Communion.

10 The peace of God, which passeth all understanding, keep your hearts and minds in the knowledge and love of God, and of his Son Jesus Christ our Lord: And the blessing of God Almighty, the Father, the Son, and the Holy Ghost, be amongst you and remain with you always. Amen.
Holy Communion, Blessing.

11 O merciful God, grant that the old Adam in this Child may be so buried, that the new man may be raised up in him. Amen.
Publick Baptism of Infants, Blessing.

12 We receive this Child into the Congregation of Christ's flock, and do sign him with the sign of the Cross, in token that hereafter he shall not be ashamed to confess the faith of Christ crucified, and manfully to fight under his banner against sin, the world, and the devil, and to

continue Christ's faithful soldier and servant unto his life's end. Amen.
Publick Baptism of Infants, Reception of the Child.

13 I should renounce the devil and all his works, the pomps and vanity of this wicked world, and all the sinful lusts of the flesh.
Catechism.

14 To keep my hands from picking and stealing, and my tongue from evil-speaking, lying, and slandering.
Catechism.

15 To learn and labour truly to get mine own living, and to do my duty in that state of life, unto which it shall please God to call me.
Catechism.

16 An outward and visible sign of an inward and spiritual grace given unto us.
Catechism.

17 Children being now come to the years of discretion.
Confirmation, Preface.

18 If any of you know cause or just impediment, why these two persons should not be joined together in holy Matrimony, ye are to declare it. This is the first time of asking.
Solemnization of Matrimony, the Banns.

19 Dearly beloved, we are gathered together here in the sight of God, and in the face of this Congregation, to join together this man and this woman in holy Matrimony; which is an honourable estate, instituted of God.
Solemnization of Matrimony, Exhortation.

20 Therefore is not by any to be enterprized, nor taken in hand, unadvisedly, lightly, or wantonly, to satisfy men's carnal lusts and appetites, like brute beasts that have no understanding; but reverently, discreetly, advisedly, soberly, and in the fear of God.
Solemnization of Marriage, Exhortation.

21 First, It was ordained for the procreation of children, to be brought up in the fear and nurture of the Lord, and to the praise of his holy Name.
Solemnization of Marriage, Exhortation.

22 Thirdly, It was ordained for the mutual society, help, and comfort, that the one ought to have of the other, both in prosperity and adversity. Into which holy estate these two persons present come now to be joined.
Solemnization of Marriage, Exhortation.

23 Therefore if any man can shew any just cause, why they may not lawfully be joined together, let him now speak, or else hereafter for ever hold his peace.
Solemnization of Marriage, Exhortation.

24 Wilt thou have this woman to thy wedded wife, to live together after God's ordinance in the holy estate of Matrimony? Wilt thou love her, comfort her, honour, and keep her, in sickness and in health; and, forsaking all other, keep thee only unto her, so long as ye both shall live?
Solemnization of Marriage, Betrothal.

25 Wilt thou have this man to thy wedded husband, to live together after God's ordinance in the holy estate of Matrimony? Wilt thou obey him, and serve him, love, honour and keep him, in sickness and in health; and, forsaking all other, keep thee only unto him, so long as

ye both shall live?
Solemnization of Marriage, Betrothal.

26 To have and to hold from this day forward, for better for worse, for richer for poorer, in sickness and in health, to love and to cherish, till death us do part, according to God's holy ordinance; and thereto I plight thee my troth.
Solemnization of Marriage, Betrothal.

27 To love, cherish, and to obey.
Solemnization of Marriage, Betrothal. This is the bride's form of the oath.

28 With this ring I thee wed, with my body I thee worship, and with all my worldly goods I thee endow.
Solemnization of Marriage, Wedding.

29 Those whom God hath joined together let no man put asunder.
Solemnization of Marriage, Priest's Declaration.

30 Consented together in holy wedlock.
Solemnization of Marriage, Minister's Declaration.

31 Peace be to this house.
Visitation of the Sick.

32 Almighty God, the fountain of all goodness.
Morning Prayer, Prayer for the Royal Family.

33 Man that is born of a woman hath but a short time to live, and is full of misery.
Burial of the Dead, Anthem.

34 In the midst of life we are in death.
Burial of the Dead, Anthem.

35 We therefore commit his body to the ground; earth to earth, ashes to ashes, dust to dust; in sure and certain hope of the Resurrection to eternal life, through our Lord Jesus Christ.
Burial of the Dead, Committal.

36 Why do the heathen so furiously rage together, and why do the people imagine a vain thing? The kings of the earth stand up, and the rulers take counsel together, against the Lord, and against his Anointed.
Psalm 2:1–2.

37 The Lord will abhor both the blood-thirsty and deceitful man.
Psalm 5:6.

38 Make thy way plain before my face.
Psalm 5:8.

39 Let them perish through their own imaginations.
Psalm 5:11.

40 Up, Lord, and let not man have the upper hand.
Psalm 9:19.

41 But they are all gone out of the way, they are altogether become abominable: there is none that doeth good, no not one.
Psalm 14:4.

42 The lot is fallen unto me in a fair ground: yea, I have a goodly heritage.
Psalm 16:7.
➤ *See Kipling 473:53.*

43 The heavens declare the glory of God: and the firmament sheweth his handywork. One day telleth another: and one night certifieth another. There is neither speech nor language: but their voices are heard among them. Their sound is gone out into all lands: and

their words into the ends of the world.
Psalm 19:1–4.

44 Thou shalt prepare a table before me against them that trouble me: thou hast anointed my head with oil, and my cup shall be full.
Psalm 23:5.

45 Into thy hands I commend my spirit.
Psalm 31:6.

46 Sing unto the Lord a new song: sing praises lustily unto him with a good courage.
Psalm 33:3.

47 I myself have seen the ungodly in great power, and flourishing like a green bay-tree. I went by, and lo, he was gone: I sought him, but his place could no where be found. Keep innocency, and take heed unto the thing that is right: for that shall bring a man peace at the last.
Psalm 37:36–8.

48 Lord, let me know mine end, and the number of my days: that I may be certified how long I have to live.
Psalm 39:5.

49 My bones are smitten asunder as with a sword: while mine enemies that trouble me cast me in the teeth; Namely, while they say daily unto me: Where is now thy God?
Psalm 42:12–13.

50 Instead of thy fathers thou shalt have children, whom thou mayest make princes in all lands.
Psalm 45:17.

51 He maketh wars to cease in all the world: he breaketh the bow, and knappeth the spear in sunder, and burneth the chariots in the fire. Be still then, and know that I am God.
Psalm 46:9–10.

52 God is gone up with a merry noise: and the Lord with the sound of the trump.
Psalm 47:5.

53 And I said, O that I had wings like a dove: for then would I flee away, and be at rest.
Psalm 55:6.

54 Be merciful unto me, O God, be merciful unto me, for my soul trusteth in thee: and under the shadow of thy wings shall be my refuge, until this tyranny be over-past.
Psalm 57:1.

55 They are as venomous as the poison of a serpent: even like the deaf adder that stoppeth her ears; Which refuseth to hear the voice of the charmer: charm he never so wisely.
Psalm 58:4–5.

56 They go to and fro in the evening: they grin like a dog, and run about through the city.
Psalm 59:6.

57 He is the God that maketh men to be of one mind in an house, and bringeth the prisoners out of captivity: but letteth the runagates continue in scarceness.
Psalm 68:6.

58 Why hop ye so, ye high hills? this is God's hill, in the which it pleaseth him to dwell: yea, the Lord will abide in it for ever.
Psalm 68:16.

59 Thou art gone up on high, thou hast led captivity captive, and received gifts for men.
Psalm 68:18.

60 Thy rebuke hath broken my heart; I am full of heaviness: I looked for some to have pity on me, but there was no man, neither found I any to comfort me. They gave me gall to eat: and when I was thirsty they gave me vinegar to drink.
Psalm 69:21–2.

61 So the Lord awaked as one out of sleep: and like a giant refreshed with wine.
Psalm 78:66.

62 O how amiable are thy dwellings, thou Lord of hosts!
Psalm 84:1.

63 Lord, thou hast been our refuge from one generation to another. Before the mountains were brought forth, or ever the earth and the world were made: thou art God from everlasting, and world without end.
Psalm 90:1–2.

64 O come, let us sing unto the Lord; let us heartily rejoice in the strength of our salvation. Let us come before his presence with thanksgiving; and shew ourselves glad in him with psalms. For the Lord is a great God; and a great King above all gods. In his hand are all the corners of the earth; and the strength of the hills is his also. The sea is his, and he made it; and his hands prepared the dry land. O come, let us worship and fall down, and kneel before the Lord our Maker. For he is the Lord our God; and we are the people of his pasture, and the sheep of his hand.
Psalm 95:1–7.

65 Today if ye will hear his voice, harden not your hearts: as in the provocation, and as in the day of temptation in the wilderness; When your fathers tempted me: proved me, and saw my works.
Psalm 95:8–9.

66 O be joyful in the Lord, all ye lands: serve the Lord with gladness, and come before his presence with a song.
Psalm 100:1.

67 Whose feet they hurt in the stocks: the iron entered into his soul.
Psalm 105:18.

68 Their soul abhorred all manner of meat: and they were even hard at death's door.
Psalm 107:18.

69 Lord, I am not high-minded: I have no proud looks.
Psalm 131:1.

70 Such knowledge is too wonderful and excellent for me: I cannot attain unto it.
Psalm 139:5.

71 I will give thanks unto thee, for I am fearfully and wonderfully made: marvellous are thy works, and that my soul knoweth right well.
Psalm 139:13.

72 O put not your trust in princes, nor in any child of man: for there is no help in them.
Psalm 146:2.

73 We therefore commit his body to the deep, to be turned into corruption, looking for the resurrection of the body, (when the Sea shall give up her dead).
Forms of Prayer to be Used at Sea, At the Burial of their Dead at Sea.

74 Holy Scripture containeth all things necessary to salvation.
Articles of Religion, VI Of the Sufficiency of the holy Scriptures for Salvation.

75 A fond thing vainly invented.
Articles of Religion, XXII Of Purgatory.

76 The Bishop of *Rome* hath no jurisdiction in this Realm of England.
Articles of Religion, XXXVII Of the Civil Magistrates.

77 It is lawful for Christian men, at the commandment of the Magistrate, to wear weapons, and serve in the wars.
Articles of Religion, XXXVII Of the Civil Magistrates.

78 A Man may not marry his Grandmother.
Table of Kindred and Affinity.

Bookchin, Murray *pseudonym of* *Lewis Herber* 1921–

US writer on social, ecological and environmental issues.

79 Once regarded as the herald of enlightenment in all spheres of knowledge, science is now increasingly seen as a strictly instrumental system of control. Its use as a system of manipulation and its role in restricting human freedom now parallel in every detail its use as a means of natural manipulation.
1982 *The Ecology of Freedom.*

Booth, John Wilkes 1839–65

US actor, usually remembered as the assassin of President Abraham Lincoln. He was hunted down and shot several days after the killing.

80 *Sic semper tyrannis!* The South is avenged!
1865 Attributed, as he shot Lincoln at Ford's Theatre, Washington DC, 14 Apr. 'Sic semper tyrannis', *Thus always to tyrants*, is the motto of the Commonwealth of Virginia.

Booth, Junius Brutus 1796–1852

English-born US actor, a leading rival of Edmund Kean in London, particularly admired as Shylock and Richard III. He continued his success after emigrating in 1821, but succumbed to alcohol-induced melancholia.

81 Where's the stage and what's the play?
Attributed, on being found drunk backstage shortly before making his first entrance.

Booth, Martin 1944–2004

English writer educated in Hong Kong. *The Dragon and the Pearl* (1994) is an account of life there.

82 At any one time, 15 per cent of the buildings of Hong Kong are being either demolished or rebuilt, renovated or restructured.
1994 *The Dragon and the Pearl*, foreword.

Boothby, Sir Robert John Graham, 1st Baron Boothby of Buchan and Rattray Head 1900–86

Scottish Conservative politician, Parliamentary Secretary to Winston Churchill (1926–9) and an original member of the Council of United Europe. His works include *The New Economy* (1943) and *I Fight to Live* (1947).

83 Of all the pygmies, Samuel Hoare was the pygmiest.
Attributed.

Boothroyd, Betty Boothroyd, Baroness 1929–

English Labour politician and first woman Speaker of the House of Commons (1992–2000).

84 My desire to get here [Parliament] was like miners' coal dust, it was under my fingers and I couldn't scrub it out.
Quoted in Glenys Kinnock and Fiona Millar (eds) *By Faith and Daring* (1993).

85 Good temper and moderation are the characteristics of parliamentary language.
1995 In *The Independent*, 9 Feb.

86 Time's up!
2000 On retiring as Speaker of the House of Commons, 26 Jul.

Borah, William Edgar 1865–1940

US Republican politician. Elected Senator for Idaho in 1906, he advocated disarmament and, as a convinced isolationist, was instrumental in blocking US entry into the League of Nations.

87 A democracy must remain at home in all matters that affect the nature of her institutions. They are of a nature to call for the undivided attention and devotion of the entire nation. We do not want the racial antipathies or national antagonisms of the Old World transformed to this continent—as they will, should we become a part of European politics. The people of this country are overwhelmingly for a policy of neutrality.
1936 Radio broadcast, 22 Feb.

Borelli, Giovanni Alfonso 1608–79

Italian mathematician and astronomer, who reasoned that celestial objects follow parabolic paths.

88 No sensible person will deny that the works of Nature are in the highest degree simple, necessary and as economical as possible. Therefore machines devised by mankind will doubtlessly likewise attain most success if they are as far as possible modelled on works of Nature.
1680 *De moto animalium.*

Borges, Jorge Luis 1899–1986

Argentinian writer. He returned to Argentina from Europe in 1921, introducing avant-garde Ultraist theories in essays and poems before publishing his intricate and fantasy-woven short stories in the 1940s. He lost his sight in the 1950s.

89 *Los metafísicos de Tlön no buscan la verdad ni siquiera la verosimilitud: buscan el asombro. Juzgan que la metafísica es una rama de la literatura fantástica.*
The metaphysicians of Tlön do not seek for the truth or even for verisimilitude, but rather for the astounding. They judge that metaphysics is a branch of fantastic literature.
1941 *Ficciones*, 'Tlön, Uqbar, Orbis Tertius' (1963).

90 *Quizá la historia universal es la historia de la diversa entonación de algunas metáforas.*
It may be that universal history is the history of the different intonations given a handful of metaphors.
1952 *Otras inquisiciones*, 'La esfera de Pascal' (translated as *The Fearful Sphere of Pascal*, 1964).

91 *En vano te hemos prodigado el océano,*
En vano el sol, que vieron los maravillados ojos de Whitman;
Has gastado los años y te has gastado,

Y todavía no has escrito el poema.
We have lavished the ocean on you in vain,
In vain the sun that was seen by Whitman's astounded
eyes;
You have spent your years and you have spent yourself,
But you haven't written the poem yet.
1964 *El otro, el mismo*, 'Mateo XX V, 30' ('Matthew 25:30').

92 While we are asleep in this world, we are awake in another one; in this way, every man is two men.
Quoted in John Russell *The Meaning of Modern Art* (1974).

93 Canada is so far away it hardly exists.
1974 Response to the question, 'What do you think of when you think of Canada?', when interviewed in Buenos Aires by Canadian poet and broadcaster Robert Zend, 4 Oct.

94 The Falklands thing was a fight between two bald men over a comb.
1983 In *Time*, 14 Feb.

Borgia, Cesare 1476–1507

Italian soldier, illegitimate son of Pope Alexander VI. He served in the papal army and was created Duke of Romagna, but was defeated in 1506 under Pope Julius II. Macchiavelli praised him as a model prince, but he was commonly perceived as a cruel dictator.

95 *Aut Caesar, aut nihil.*
Either Caesar or nothing.
Motto. It goes back to a couplet composed in 1507, after Borgia's death, by Fausto Maddalena Romano: 'Borgia Caesar erat, factis et nomine Caesar, /aut nihil, aut Caesar dixit: utrumque fuit.' (Borgia was Caesar: he was Caesar in name and in fact. He said / Either Caesar, or nothing: he was both.)

Borman, Frank 1928–

US astronaut, later President of Eastern Airlines.

96 Capitalism without bankruptcy is like Christianity without hell.
1986 In *US*, 21 Apr.

Born, Max 1882–1970

German-born British physicist, Professor of Physics at Göttingen until forced to leave by the Nazis. He won the Nobel prize (1954) for his insights into quantum mechanics.

97 There are two objectionable types of believers: those who believe the incredible and those who believe that 'belief' must be discarded and replaced by 'the scientific method'.
1951 *Natural Philosophy of Cause and Chance*.

98 Science…is so greatly opposed to history and tradition that it cannot be absorbed by our civilization.
1968 *My Life and Views*.

Borotra, Jean 1898–1994

French tennis player. His wins included the men's singles title at Wimbledon in 1924.

99 The only possible regret I have is the feeling that I will die without having played enough tennis.
Quoted in Colin Jarman *The Guinness Dictionary of Sports Quotations* (1990).

Borovoy, A Alan 1932–

General Counsel of the Canadian Civil Liberties Association.

1 I would renounce, therefore, the attempt to create heaven on earth, and focus instead on reducing the hell.
1988 *When Freedoms Collide: A Case for Our Civil Liberties*. His personal maxim.

2 I don't ask employers, for example, to *like* blacks or Jews or native people; I ask employers to *hire* the qualified members of these groups whether they like them or not.
1988 *When Freedoms Collide: A Case for Our Civil Liberties*.

Borrow, George Henry 1803–81

English writer and traveller. His part fictional, part factual books reflect his interest in languages and his love of Romany lore. They include *The Bible in Spain* (1843), *Lavengro* (1851), *The Romany Rye* (1857) and *Wild Wales* (1862).

3 There's night and day, brother, both sweet things; sun, moon, and stars, brother, all sweet things: there's likewise a wind on the heath. Life is very sweet, brother; who would wish to die?
1851 *Lavengro*, ch.25.

4 Fear God, and take your own part.
1857 *The Romany Rye*, ch.16.

5 I never saw such a place for merched anllad [wanton women] as Northampton.
1862 *Wild Wales*, ch.34.

6 'Scotland! a queer country that, your honour!' 'So it is,' said I; 'a queerer country I never saw in all my life.' 'And a queer set of people, your honour.' 'So they are,' said I; 'a queerer set of people than the Scotch you would scarcely see in a summer's day.'
1862 *Wild Wales*, ch.83.

Bosquet, Pierre 1810–61

French soldier, General during the Crimean War.

7 *C'est magnifique, mais ce n'est pas la guerre.*
It is magnificent, but it isn't war.
1854 On seeing the Charge of the Light Brigade at the Battle of Balaclava, 25 Oct. Quoted in Cecil Woodham Smith *The Reason Why* (1953), ch.12.

Bossidy, John Collins 1860–1928

US doctor and versifier.

8 And this is good old Boston,
The home of the bean and the cod,
Where the Lowells talk to the Cabots
And the Cabots talk only to God.
1910 Toast delivered at Holy Cross alumni dinner, Boston.

Boswell, James 1740–95

Scottish man of letters and biographer of Dr Johnson, whom he first met in 1763. Their great friendship led, after Johnson's death, to Boswell's literary masterpiece, the *Life of Samuel Johnson* (1791).

9 I think there is a blossom about me of something more distinguished than the generality of mankind.
1763 Journal entry, 20 Jan. Collected in F A Pottle (ed) *Boswell's London Journal* (1950).

10 JOHNSON: Well, we had a good talk.
BOSWELL: Yes, Sir; you tossed and gored several persons.
1768 Conversation, summer, recorded in *The Life of Samuel Johnson* (1791), vol.2.

11 I am, I flatter myself, completely a citizen of the world. In my travels through Holland, Germany, Switzerland, Italy, Corsica, France, I never felt myself from home.
1773 *Journal of a Tour to the Hebrides* (ed F A Pottle, 1936), entry for 14 Aug.

12 A man, indeed, is not genteel when he gets drunk; but most vices may be committed very genteelly: a man may debauch his friend's wife genteelly: he may cheat at cards genteelly.
1775 *The Life of Samuel Johnson* (1791), vol.2, entry for 6 Apr.

Botha, P(ieter) W(illem) 1932–

South African statesman, Prime Minister (1978–84) and President (1984–9). His attempts at limited constitutional reform were met with a right-wing defection from his ruling National Party (1982).

13 We simply could not go on with policies that were a failure economically and internationally, and which we could not morally justify. To allocate rights and privileges on the basis of a physical characteristic was tantamount to sinning against God.
1991 Interviewed by Donald Woods, BBC T V, Feb.

Botham, Ian Terence 1955–

English cricketer. He established a record number of Test wickets (373) and scored 5,057 runs in Tests for England, including 14 Test centuries.

14 Cricket is full of theorists who can ruin your game in no time.
1980 *Ian Botham on Cricket.*

15 I want to stress again one aspect of the game which is most important. *Never argue with an umpire.*
1980 *Ian Botham on Cricket.*

Bottomley, Gordon 1874–1948

English poet and playwright. His interest in Celtic folklore is reflected in much of his work, and he is best remembered for his *Poetry of Thirty Years* (1925) and some of his plays.

16 When you destroy a blade of grass
You poison England at her roots;
Remember no man's foot can pass
Where evermore no green life shoots.
1912 'To Ironfounders and Others'.

17 Your worship is your furnaces
Which, like old idols, lost obscenes,
Have molten bowels; your vision is
Machines for making more machines.
1912 'To Ironfounders and Others'.

Boucicault, Dion(ysus Lardner) *originally* Dionysius Lardner Bursiquot c.1820–1890

Irish playwright, actor and director. His many works include popular melodramas such as *The Corsican Brothers* (1852), *The Colleen Bawn* (1860) and *The Shaughraun* (1875). He also promoted theatrical reforms, including the box set.

18 Men talk of killing time, while time quietly kills them.
1841 *London Assurance*, act 2, sc.1.

19 It's a mighty pleasant thing to die like this, once in a way, and hear all the good things said about ye afther you're dead and gone, when they can do you no good.
1874 Aside by Conn. *The Shaughraun*, act 3, sc.2.

20 His first holiday.
His own suggested epitaph. Attributed.

Boulanger, Nadia 1887–1979

French musician and teacher. She studied at the Paris Conservatoire (1879–1904) and wrote many vocal and instrumental works.

21 Do not take up music unless you would rather die than not do so.
Advice to her pupils. Quoted in Alan Kendall *The Tender Tyrant: Nadia Boulanger* (1976).

Boulding, Kenneth Ewart 1910–93

British-born US economist and social philosopher (or 'social ecologist'), president of the American Economic Association and professor at the Universities of Michigan and Colorado.

22 We know very little about what it is that moves great masses of men to action, and until we know more about this it is fitting for the social scientist to maintain a becoming modesty in the presence of a great deal to be modest about.
1966 *The Impact of the Social Sciences.*

23 Science might almost be redefined as the process of substituting unimportant questions which can be answered for important questions which cannot.
1969 *The Image.*

24 Almost the whole pollution–environmental problem is summed up in the proposition that all goods are generally produced jointly with bads.
1972 In Sam H Schurr (ed) *Energy, Economic Growth, and the Environment* (1972).

Boulton, Sir Harold Edwin 1859–1935

English songwriter. He compiled and wrote many collections of national songs, including the well-known 'Glorious Devon' (1902) and 'Skye Boat Song' (1908).

25 When Adam and Eve were dispossessed
Of the garden hard by Heaven,
They planted another one down in the west,
'Twas Devon, glorious Devon!
1902 'Glorious Devon'.

26 Speed, bonnie boat, like a bird on the wing,
'Onward!' the sailors cry;
Carry the lad that's born to be king
Over the sea to Skye.
1908 'Skye Boat Song'. The date and authorship of the original song are uncertain, but this is now the most famous version.

Bourassa, Henri 1868–1952

Canadian politician. He entered the Commons as an Independent Liberal (1896) and founded the Quebec Nationalist party, opposing involvement with Britain and the US. He was founding editor of *Le Devoir*, a Montreal newspaper.

27 Our special task, as French Canadians, is to insert into America the spirit of Christian France.
1918 *La Langue, Gardienne de la Foi.*

Bourdillon, F(rancis) W(illiam) 1852–1951

English poet.

28 The night has a thousand eyes,
And the day but one;
Yet the light of the bright world dies,
With the dying sun.

The mind has a thousand eyes,
And the heart but one;
Yet the light of a whole life dies,
When love is done.
1878 *Among the Flowers*, 'Light'.
➤ *See Lyly 523:12.*

Bowen, Catherine Shober *née Drinker* 1897–1973

US writer, biographer and essayist, whose many books include *The Lion and the Throne* (biography of Sir Edward Coke, 1957) and *Miracle at Philadelphia* (1966).

29 In writing biography, fact and fiction shouldn't be mixed. And if they are, the fiction parts should be printed in red ink, the fact parts in black ink.
1958 In *Publisher's Weekly*, 24 Mar. Bowen's biographies were frequently partly fictionalized.

Bowen, Frank Charles 1894–

30 *Irish hurricane*, a flat calm with drizzling rain.
1929 *Sea Slang, a Dictionary of the Old-Timers' Expressions and Epithets*.

Bowie, David *real name David Robert Jones* 1947–

English rock singer and actor. His career blossomed throughout the 1970s as he adopted a range of extreme stage images to suit a variety of musical styles and concepts.

31 You must understand that this is not a woman's dress I'm wearing. It's a man's dress.
Quoted in Maxim Jakubowski *The Wit and Wisdom of Rock and Roll* (1983).

Bowles, Paul Frederick 1910–99

US novelist, poet, travel writer, translator and composer. He studied music in Paris, and began writing fiction after World War II. He lived in Tangier from 1952, and much of his work is set there.

32 The Sheltering Sky.
1947 Title of novel.

33 Too much importance is given the writer and not enough to his work. What difference does it make who he is and what he feels, since he's merely a machine for transmission of ideas. In reality he doesn't exist—he's a cipher, a blank. A spy sent into life by the forces of death. His main objective is to get the information across the border, back into death.
1966 Letter to James Leo Herlihy, 30 Apr.

34 The wind howls and the countryside is the colour of a lion. For a week the cicadas have been screaming; I think by now most of them have burst, for there are far fewer.
1969 Letter to Ned Rorem, 20 Aug.

35 It was an experiment, and I think a successful one, in communal living. It worked largely because Auden ran it; he was exceptionally adept at getting the necessary money out of us when it was due.
1972 On an artist's house in New York. *Without Stopping: An Autobiography*, ch.12.

36 My curiosity about alien cultures was avid and obsessive. I had a placid belief that it was good for me to live in the midst of people whose motives I did not understand; this unreasoned conviction was clearly an attempt to legitimize my curiosity.
1972 *Without Stopping: An Autobiography*, ch.14.

37 The act of living had been enjoyable; at some point when I was not paying attention, it had turned into a different sort of experience, to whose grimness I had grown so accustomed that I now took it for granted.
1972 *Without Stopping: An Autobiography*, ch.17.

38 I envy you if you're able to sustain a uniform degree of interest throughout *Ulysses*. People are always saying they do. People also claim to be clairvoyant and to levitate.
1981 Letter to Millicent Dillon, 1 Jul.

39 The only effort worth making is the one it takes to learn the geography of one's own nature.
1989 In the *Sunday Times*, 23 Jul.

Boycott, Geoffrey 1940–

English cricketer, who made 108 appearances for England. He scored a total of 8,114 Test runs.

40 To have some idea what it's like, stand in the outside lane of a motorway, get your mate to drive his car at you at 95 mph and wait until he's 12 yards away, before you decide which way to jump.
1989 Of the experience of facing fast bowlers. Quoted in Helen Exley *Cricket Quotations* (1992).

Boyd, L(ouis) M(alcolm) 1927–

US journalist.

41 Most business meetings are staged to supply people who'd rather talk than work with people who'd rather listen than work.
1990 'Grab Bag', in the *San Francisco Chronicle*, 7 Apr.

Boyd, William Andrew Murray 1952–

Scottish writer, born in Ghana. A lecturer in English at Oxford (1980–3) and TV critic with the *New Statesman*, he then concentrated on fiction and screenplays. His novels include *A Good Man in Africa* (1981), *Brazzaville Beach* (1990) and *Any Human Heart* (2002).

42 Like Rome, Nkongsamba was built on seven hills, but there all similarity ended. Set in undulating tropical rain forest, from the air it resembled nothing so much as a giant pool of crapulous vomit on somebody's expansive unmown lawn.
1981 *A Good Man in Africa*, ch.1.

43 Morgan liked to imagine the town as some immense yeast culture, left in a deep cupboard by an absent-minded lab technician, festering uncontrolled, running rampant in the ideal growing conditions.
1981 *A Good Man in Africa*, ch.1.

44 My first act on entering this world was to kill my mother.
1988 *The New Confessions*, opening words.

45 The natural world is full of irregularity and random alteration, but in the antiseptic, dust-free, shadowless, brightly lit, abstract realm of the mathematicians they

like their cabbages spherical, please.
1990 *Brazzaville Beach*, 'Cabbages Are Not Spheres'.

46 It seems to me that there are statements about the world and our lives that have no need of formal proof procedures.
1990 *Brazzaville Beach*, 'Fermat's Last Theorem II'.

Boyer, Charles 1899–1978

French actor who moved to Hollywood in 1929 and was particularly successful in romantic roles. His appearances include *The Garden of Allah* (1936), *Mayerling* (1937), *Love Affair* (1939) and *All This and Heaven Too* (1940).

47 Come with me to the Casbah.
1938 Although he never actually spoke this line, it was popularly associated with him as Pepe in the film *Algiers*.

Boyer, Dr Ernest L 1928–95

US educationalist, president of the Carnegie Foundation for the Advancement of Teaching (1979–95).

48 A poor surgeon hurts one person at a time. A poor teacher hurts 30.
1986 In *People*, 17 Mar.

Boyle, Peter G(erard) 1941–

Scottish academic historian.

49 They are the last drops of vintage wine from a musty old bottle.
Of Winston Churchill's letters to President Eisenhower. Quoted in Peter G Boyle (ed) *The Churchill–Eisenhower Correspondence 1953–1955* (1990).

Bracken, Peg 1918–

US writer and humorist. Her books include *The I Hate to Cook Book* (1960) and *I Didn't Come Here to Argue* (1969).

50 Cheese for dessert is rather like *Paradise Lost* in that everyone thinks he *ought* to like it, but still you don't notice too many people actually curling up with it.
1960 *The I Hate to Cook Book*, ch.9.

Bracken, Thomas 1843–98

New Zealand poet, journalist and politician, born in Ireland. He emigrated in 1869. His work, characterized by Victorian sentimentality, includes *Lays and Lyrics: God's Own Country and Other Poems* (1893).

51 Oh, God! that men would see a little clearer,
Or judge less harshly where they cannot see;
Oh, God! that men would draw a little nearer
To one another, they'd be nearer Thee,
And understood.
1905 *Not Understood, and Other Poems*, 'Not Understood'.

Bradbury, Malcolm Stanley 1932–2000

English novelist, critic and teacher. His novels include *The History Man* (1975) and *Rates of Exchange* (1982).

52 It had always seemed to Louis that a fundamental desire to take postal courses was being sublimated by other people into sexual activity.
1959 *Eating People Is Wrong*, ch.5.

53 I like the English. They have the most rigid code of immorality in the world.
1959 *Eating People Is Wrong*, ch.5.

54 Reading someone else's newspaper is like sleeping with someone else's wife. Nothing seems to be precisely in the right place, and when you find what you are looking for, it is not clear then how to respond to it.
1965 *Stepping Westward*, bk.1, ch.1.

55 My experience of ships is that on them one makes an interesting discovery about the world. One finds one can do without it completely.
1965 *Stepping Westward*, bk.1, ch.2.

56 They don't spend themselves in relationships until they know what the odds are; long hours spent as babies lying in the rain outside greengrocers' shops have made them tough.
1965 *Stepping Westward*, bk.2, ch.4.

57 English history is all about men liking their fathers, and American history is all about men hating their fathers and trying to burn down everything they ever did.
1965 *Stepping Westward*, bk.2, ch.5.

58 The English are polite by telling lies. The Americans are polite by telling the truth.
1965 *Stepping Westward*, bk.2, ch.5.

59 'We stay together, but we distrust each other.'
'Ah, yes,…but isn't that a definition of marriage?'
1975 *The History Man*, ch.3.

60 If God had meant us to have group sex, I guess he'd have given us all more organs.
1976 *Who Do You Think You Are?*, 'A Very Hospitable Person'.

61 The British have long had a taste for bad books, but they like them well written.
1981 In the *Observer*, 25 Oct.

62 In Slaka, sex is just politics with the clothes off.
1983 *Rates of Exchange*, pt.4, ch.3.

63 Here we have a saying: a good friend is someone who visits you when you are in prison. But a *really* good friend is someone who comes to hear your lectures.
1983 *Rates of Exchange*, pt.4, ch.3.

64 Conversation is never easy for the British, who are never keen to express themselves to strangers or, for that matter, anyone, even themselves.
1983 *Rates of Exchange*, pt.5, ch.3.

65 You probably know, the better class of Briton likes to send his children away to school until they're old and intelligent enough to come home again. Then they're too old and intelligent to want to.
1983 *Rates of Exchange*, pt.5, ch.3.

66 There were moments when Henry was glad he was a writer, for writers could live in their own minds and didn't have to go out at all.
1987 *Cuts*.

67 The modern novel has been many things, and functioned at many levels. It would keep D.H. Lawrence poor, and make Jilly Cooper and Jeffrey Archer rich.
1993 *The Modern British Novel*, preface.

68 The post-war period has not been marked by a great aesthetic debate about the novel comparable to that of the earlier half of the century, in part because the role of the writer and critic divided, the writer going off to the marketplace and the critic to the university (which eventually turned out to be much the same thing).
1993 *The Modern British Novel*, preface.

Bradbury, Ray(mond Douglas) 1920–

US science-fiction writer, one of the earliest writers in the genre to be recognized for his literary merits. His short-story collections include *The Martian Chronicles* (1950) and *The Illustrated Man* (1951); novels include *Fahrenheit 451* (1953) and *Something Wicked This Way Comes* (1962).

69 The Day it Rained Forever.
1959 Title of story.

70 Where robot mice and robot men, I said, run round in robot towns.
1977 *Where Robot Mice and Robot Men Run Round In Robot Towns*, prologue.

Bradley, Francis Herbert 1846–1924

Welsh philosopher, who spent most of his life at Oxford, a central figure of the 19c British Idealist movement. His important works are *Ethical Studies* (1876) and *Appearance and Reality* (1893).

71 Metaphysics is the finding of bad reasons for what we believe upon instinct, but to find these reasons is no less an instinct.
1893 *Appearance and Reality*, preface.

72 Where everything is bad it must be good to know the worst.
1893 *Appearance and Reality*, preface.

Bradley, Omar Nelson 1893–1981

US soldier. He played a prominent part in World War II, especially in Tunisia and Sicily. Chairman of the joint Chiefs-of-Staff in 1949, he was promoted to General in 1950.

73 We have grasped the mystery of the atom and rejected the Sermon on the Mount.
1948 Speech, 10 Nov, commemorating Armistice Day.

74 The wrong war, at the wrong place, at the wrong time—and with the wrong enemy.
1951 At the Senate inquiry into proposals to escalate the Korean war into China, May.

Bradman, Sir Don(ald George) 1908–2001

Australian cricketer and stockbroker. He played for Australia (1928–48, Captain 1936–48), scoring the highest aggregate and largest number of centuries in Tests against England. In 1949 he became the first Australian cricketer to be knighted.

75 It's hard to bat with tears in your eyes.
1948 When bowled for a duck in his final Test innings. Quoted in Colin Jarman *The Guinness Dictionary of Sports Quotations* (1990).

76 There is probably a greater premium on temperament for a batsman than for any player in any branch of sport.
1958 *The Art of Cricket*.

77 May cricket continue to flourish and spread its wings. The world can only be richer for it.
1958 *The Art of Cricket*.

78 Every ball is for me the first ball, whether my score is 0 or 200, and I never visualize the possibility of anybody getting me out.
Quoted in Colin Jarman *The Guinness Dictionary of Sports Quotations* (1990).

Bradstreet, Anne *née* Dudley 1612–72

English-born American Puritan poet. She emigrated to New England with her husband, a nonconformist minister, later Governor of Massachusetts. Her first collection was published in London by her brother-in-law without her knowledge.

79 In Criticks hands, beware thou dost not come;
And take thy way where yet thou art not known,
If for thy Father askt, say, thou hadst none:
And for thy Mother, she alas is poor,
Which caus'd her thus to send thee out of door.
1650 *The Tenth Muse Lately Sprung Up In America*, 'The Author to Her Book'.

80 I am obnoxious to each carping tongue
Who says my hand a needle better fits,
A poet's pen all scorn I should thus wrong
For such despite they cast on female wits;
If what I do prove well, it won't advance,
They'll say it's stolen, or else, it was by chance.
1678 *Several Poems Compiled with Great Variety of Wit and Learning*, 'The Prologue'.

81 If ever two were one, then surely we.
1678 *Several Poems Compiled with Great Variety of Wit and Learning*, 'To My Dear and Loving Husband'.

Brady, Nicholas F(rederick) 1930–

US financier and politician, Secretary of the Treasury (1988–93) under Presidents Reagan and Bush.

82 If you want to be vice-president, stand out here in the rain in your underwear and let everybody see what you're made of.
1988 On the need to strip the secrecy from selection of vice-presidential candidates instead of having surprise choices such as Dan Quayle. In the *Washington Post*, 28 Aug.

83 We have a habit in this country of correcting things just as they are about to correct themselves.
1989 In the *New York Times*, 1 Feb.

Bragg, Melvyn Bragg, Baron 1939–

English novelist and television arts presenter. He has written a number of novels in the realist tradition, and is well known as a television presenter, notably of the long-running arts series *The South Bank Show*.

84 Patriotism is seen not only as the last refuge of the scoundrel but as the first bolt-hole of the hypocrite.
1976 *Speak For England*, introduction.
➤ *See Johnson 444:8*.

85 There is nothing left to envy about America.
Quoted in Jonathan Freedland *Bringing Home the Revolution: How Britain Can Live in the American Dream* (1998).

Brahms, Johannes 1833–97

German Romantic composer. His compositions include four symphonies and several concertos, a large body of songs, chamber music and music for piano, and *A German Requiem* (1869).

86 When I feel the urge to compose, I begin by appealing directly to my Maker and I first ask Him the three most important questions pertaining to our life here in this world—whence, wherefore, whither.
Quoted in A Hopkins *Music All Around Me* (1967).

Bramante, Donato 1444–1514

Italian High Renaissance architect.

87 The dome of the Pantheon over the vault of the Temple of Peace.

c.1505 Description of his design for St Peter's, Rome. Quoted in Vincent Cronin *The Flowering of the Renaissance* (1969).

Bramston, James c.1694–1744

English cleric and poet.

88 What's not destroyed by Time's devouring hand?
Where's Troy, and where's the Maypole in the Strand?
1729 *The Art of Politics*.

Brando, Marlon 1924–2004

US film and stage actor. He found fame in stage (1947) and screen (1951) productions of *A Streetcar Named Desire*. Subsequent films include *The Wild One* (1953), *On the Waterfront* (1954), for which he won an Academy Award, *Last Tango in Paris* (1972) and *The Godfather* (1972), for which he refused to accept an Academy Award.

89 Sometimes you just get the feeling that here it is 11 o'clock in the morning and you're not in school.
1959 On playing in Western films. In the *New York Post*, 11 May.

90 An actor is a kind of guy who if you ain't talking about him ain't listening.
Quoted in Bob Thomas *Brando* (1973), ch.8.

91 He's the kind of guy that when he dies, he gives God a bad time for making him bald.
1977 On Frank Sinatra. In the *Daily Mail*, 30 Mar.

Braque, Georges 1882–1963

French painter, a developer of Fauvism, and later under the influence of Picasso, of Cubism. He was badly injured in World War I.

92 *L'Art est fait pour troubler, la Science rassure.*
Art was made to disturb, science reassures.
Notebook entry. Collected in *Le Jour et la nuit: Cahiers 1917–52*.

93 *La vérité existe; on n'invente que le mensonge.*
Truth exists; only lies are invented.
Notebook entry. Collected in *Le Jour et la nuit: Cahiers 1917–52*.

Brasch, Charles 1909–73

New Zealand poet. His works include *The Land and Other People* (1939), *Ambulando* (1964) and *Home Ground* (1974). A posthumous book of *Collected Poems* was published in 1984.

94 The ruby and amethyst eyes of anemones
Glow through me, fiercer than stars.
Home Ground (1974), 'Night Cries, Wakari Hospital: Winter Anemones'.

Brathwaite, Edward Kamau originally *Lawson Edward Brathwaite* 1930–

West Indian poet and historian, born in Barbados. His best-known work *The Arrivants: A New World Trilogy* (1973) consists of three earlier long poems, exploring different aspects of Caribbean culture and identity.

95 It is not enough
to be pause, to be hole
to be void, to be silent
to be semicolon, to be semicolony;
1969 *Islands*, no.3 'Rebellion', pt.6 'Negus', collected as *The Arrivants: A New World Trilogy* (1973).

Bratton, John W

British songwriter.

96 If you go down in the woods today
You're sure of a big surprise
If you down in the woods today
You'd better go in disguise.
For every Bear that ever there was
Will gather there for certain because,
Today's the day the Teddy Bears have their Picnic.
1932 'The Teddy Bears' Picnic' (with James B Kennedy).

Braudy, Leo Beal 1941–

US academic. He became Bing Professor of Literature at the University of Southern California in 1985, and University Professor in 1997.

97 People are looking to other lives for answers to questions about their own.
1987 On the increasing popularity of biography. Quoted by Alvin P Sarnoff in *US News and World Report*, 3 Aug.

Braun, Wernher von 1912–77

German-born US rocket scientist and engineer who helped develop the liquid-fuel rocket for the Nazis, and later switched his allegiance to the US. He became technical adviser to the US rocket program and later director of development operations at NASA where he was responsible for development of the Saturn V launch vehicle.

98 Our sun is one of 100 billion stars in our galaxy. Our galaxy is one of billions of galaxies populating the universe. It would be the height of presumption to think that we are the only living things in that enormous immensity.
1960 In the *New York Times*, 29 Apr.

Brautigan, Richard 1935–84

US fabulist and poet, an icon of the 1960s counter-culture movement. His seemingly whimsical fables were also literary experiments. He committed suicide.

99 Language does not leave fossils, at least not until it has become written.
1967 *Trout Fishing In America*, 'Prelude to the Mayonnaise Chapter'.

1 The time is right to mix sentences with dirt and the sun with punctuation and rain with verbs.
1968 *Please Plant This Book*, 'Squash'.

2 If you get hung up on everybody else's hangups, then the whole world's going to be nothing more than one huge gallows.
1970 *The Abortion: An Historical Romance*.

3 Loading Mercury with a Pitchfork.
1976 Title of poetry collection.

4 They used language concentrating emotion, detail and image until they arrived at a form of dew-like steel.
1978 On Japanese poets. *June 30th – June 30th*.

Brecher, Irving 1914–

US screenwriter and director. He wrote the scripts for two of the Marx Brothers' later films—*At the Circus* (1939) and *Go West* (1940).

5 I'll bet your father spent the first year of your life

throwing rocks at the stork.
1939 *At the Circus.*

Brecht, Bertolt Eugen Friedrich   1898–1956

German poet, playwright and theatre director, an innovator of epic theatre and the alienation effect. He fled Nazi Germany when Hitler came to power and returned to settle in East Berlin in 1947, where he directed the *Berliner Ensemble* theatre. His works include *The Threepenny Opera* (1928, with Kurt Weill), *The Life of Galileo* (1938), *Mother Courage and her Children* (1939) and *The Caucasian Chalk Circle* (1945).

6 *Und der Haifisch, der hat Zähne*
Und die trägt er im Gesicht
Und Macheath, der hat ein Messer
Doch das Messer sieht man nicht.
Oh, the shark has pretty teeth, dear,
And he shows them pearly white.
Just a jack-knife has Macheath, dear,
And he keeps it out of sight.
1928 *Die Dreigroschenoper* ('The Threepenny Opera'), prologue (translated by Ralph Manheim and John Willett, 1970).

7 *Erst kommt das Fressen, dann kommt die Moral.*
Food comes first, then morals.
1928 *Die Dreigroschenoper* ('The Threepenny Opera'), act 2, sc.3 (translated by Ralph Manheim and John Willett, 1970).

8 *Von der Wiege bis zur Bahre, zuerst die Wäsche.*
From the cradle to the grave, underwear first, last and all the time.
1928 *Die Dreigroschenoper* ('The Threepenny Opera'), act 2, sc.5 (translated by Ralph Manheim and John Willet, 1970).

9 ANDREA: *Unglücklich das Land das keine Helden hat.*
GALILEI: *Unglücklich das Land das Helden nötig hat.*
ANDREA: Unlucky the land that has no heroes.
GALILEI: Unlucky the land that has need of heroes.
1938 *Leben des Galilei* ('The Life of Galileo'), sc.13.

10 *Angesichts von Hindernissen mag die kürzeste Linie zwischen zwei Punkten die krumme sein.*
When it comes to obstacles, the shortest line between two points may be the crooked one.
1938 *Leben des Galilei* ('The Life of Galileo'), sc.14 (translated by Howard Benton, 1980).
➤ See Lessing 505:47.

11 *Die Wissenschaft kennt nur ein Gebot: den wissenschaftlichen Beitrag.*
Science knows only one commandment: contribute to science.
1938 *Leben des Galilei* ('The Life of Galileo'), sc.14 (translated by Howard Brenton, 1980).

12 *Weil ich ihm nicht traue, sind wir befreundet.*
Because I don't trust him, we are friends.
1939 *Mutter Courage und ihre Kinder* ('Mother Courage and her Children'), sc.3.

13 *Die schönsten Pläne sind schon zuschanden geworden durch die Kleinlichkeit von denen, wo sie ausführen sollten, denn die Kaiser selber können ja nix machen.*
The finest plans have always been spoiled by the pettiness of those who should carry them out. Even emperors cannot do it all by themselves.
1939 *Mutter Courage und ihre Kinder* ('Mother Courage and her Children'), sc.6.

14 *Der Krieg findet immer einen Ausweg.*
War always finds a way.

1939 *Mutter Courage und ihre Kinder* ('Mother Courage and her Children'), sc.6.

Brenan, Gerald   1894–1987

English travel writer, born in Malta. After an itinerant early life he settled in Spain, producing *South from Granada* (1957) and *The Spanish Labyrinth* (1943) among other works.

15 Religions are kept alive by heresies, which are really sudden explosions of faith. Dead religions do not produce them.
1978 *Thoughts in a Dry Season.*

Brennan, William J(oseph), Jr   1906–97

US jurist, Associate Justice of the US Supreme Court (1956–90). He took an active role in liberal decisions handed down under Chief Justice Earl Warren.

16 Sex and obscenity are not synonymous.
1967 Ruling that established a new legal standard for obscenity, 24 Jun.

17 Death is an unusually severe and degrading punishment.
1972 Ruling to outlaw states' right to impose capital punishment, 29 Jun.

Brennus

Gallic king who captured Rome, 390 BC.

18 *Vae victis.*
Down with the defeated!
390 BC His cry on capturing Rome. Quoted in Livy *Ab urbe condita*, bk.5, ch.48, section 9.

Breslin, Jimmy   1930–

US sports journalist, writer and broadcaster. His works include *Can't Anybody Here Play This Game?* (1963). He won a Pulitzer Prize for outstanding commentary (1986).

19 They're killing the game with this phoney mystique—telling people that a guy needs the abilities of a brain surgeon to play left-guard for the Colts. Football is simply a game to keep the coalminers off the streets.
Quoted in Colin Jarman *The Guinness Dictionary of Sports Quotations* (1990).

20 Rage is the only quality which has kept me, or anybody I have ever studied, writing columns for newspapers.
1990 In *The Times*, 9 May.

Brewster, Kingman, Jr   1919–88

US educator, Professor of Law at Harvard (1950–60) and President of Yale (1963–77). He was US Ambassador to Britain (1977–81), and stayed on there as the representative of a US law firm.

21 The most fundamental value of a liberal education is that it makes life more interesting.
Recalled on his death in the *New York Times*, 9 Nov 1988.

Brezhnev, Leonid Ilyich   1906–82

Russian politician. As General Secretary of the Soviet Communist Party Central Committee after Khrushchev (1964), he became the most powerful Soviet leader, the first to hold simultaneously the position of General Secretary and President of the Supreme Soviet (1977–82).

22 She is trying to wear the trousers of Winston Churchill.
   1979 Of Margaret Thatcher. Speech.

23 Whatever may divide us, Europe is our common home. A common fate has linked us through the centuries, and it continues to link us today.
   1981 Speech while visiting the Federal Republic of Germany, 23 Nov.

Bricker, John W(illiam) 1893–1986

US Senator. He was Governor of Ohio (1939–45) and then Senator (1945–49). He ran as Republican vice-presidential candidate in 1944.

24 Joe, you're a dirty son of a bitch but there are times when you've got to have a son of a bitch around, and this is one of them.
   c.1953 Comment to Senator Joseph R McCarthy on rescuing Republic prominence by pressing charges of Communism in government. Recalled in *This Fabulous Century* (1970).

Bridges, Robert Seymour 1844–1930

English Poet Laureate and hymn writer who qualified and practised as a doctor, and a friend of Gerard Manley Hopkins. As wartime Poet Laureate he compiled an anthology *The Spirit of Man* (1916) to lift the nation's spirits.

25 So sweet love seemed that April morn,
   When first we kissed beside the thorn,
   So strangely sweet, it was not strange
   We thought that love could never change.

   But I can tell—let truth be told—
   That love will change in growing old;
   Though day by day is nought to see,
   So delicate his motions be.
   1894 'So Sweet Loved Seemed'.

26 All my hope on God is founded
   He does still my trust renew,
   Me through change and chance he guideth,
   Only good and only true.
   God unknown,
   He alone
   Calls my heart to be his own.
   1899 Hymn.

27 And I replied unto all these things which encompass the door of my flesh, 'Ye have told me of my god, that ye are not he: tell me something of him'. And they cried all with a great voice, 'He made us'. My questioning them was my mind's desire, and their Beauty was their answer.
   1916 *The Spirit of Man: The Confessions of St Augustine*.

Bridges, (Henry) Styles 1898–1961

US Senator. He was Republican Governor of New Hampshire (1935–37) and then Senator (1937–61). He opposed the New Deal and was a supporter of Joseph McCarthy.

28 China asked for a sword, and we gave her a dull paring knife.
   Of China's collapse to Communism. Quoted in David Halberstam *The Fifties* (1993).

Bridie, James *pseudonym of* *Osborne Henry Mavor*
1888–1951

Scottish playwright and doctor. Founder of the Glasgow

Citizens' Theatre, he enjoyed considerable success with such plays as *The Anatomist* (1930) and *Daphne Laureola* (1949).

29 I sat through the first act and heard my lovely lines falling like cold porridge on a damp mattress.
   1939 *One Way of Living*, alluding to a performance of his play *Marriage is no Joke*.

Bright, John 1811–89

British radical statesman and orator, a leading member of the Anti-Corn League (1839), MP from 1843 and an enormous influence on the Unionist party. A member of the Peace Society, he denounced the Crimean War (1854).

30 The Angel of Death has been abroad throughout the land. You may almost hear the beating of his wings.
   1855 Of the Crimean War. Speech, House of Commons, 23 Feb.

31 This regard for the liberties of Europe, this care at one time for the protestant interest, this excessive love for the balance of power, is neither more nor less than a gigantic system of outdoor relief for the aristocracy of Great Britain.
   1858 Speech, Birmingham, 29 Oct.

32 England is the mother of Parliaments.
   1865 Speech, Birmingham, 18 Jan.

33 There is no nation on the continent of Europe that is less able to do harm to England, and there is no nation on the continent of Europe to whom we are less able to do harm, than Russia. We are so separate that it seems impossible that the two nations, by the use of reason or common sense at all, could possibly be brought into conflict with each other.
   1878 Speech, Birmingham, 13 Jan.

Brillat-Savarin, Jean Anthelme 1755–1826

French politician, gastronome and writer, Mayor of Belley in 1793. During the French Revolution he took refuge in Switzerland and America. His *Physiologie du goût* (1825) is an elegant and witty compendium of the art of dining.

34 *Dis-moi ce que tu manges, je te dirai ce que tu es.*
   Tell me what you eat and I will tell you what you are.
   1825 *Physiologie du goût*, aphorism 4 (translated by Anne Drayton, 1970).

35 *La découverte d'un mets nouveau fait plus pour le bonheur du genre humain que la découverte d'une étoile.*
   The discovery of a new dish does more for the happiness of mankind than the discovery of a star.
   1825 *Physiologie du goût*, aphorism 9 (translated by Anne Drayton, 1970).

36 *La volaille est pour la cuisine ce qu'est la toile pour les peintres.*
   Fowls are to the kitchen what his canvas is to the painter.
   1825 *Physiologie du goût*, pt.1, ch.6, section 34 (translated by Anne Drayton, 1970).

37 *La truffe n'est point un aphrodisiaque positif; mais elle peut, en certaines occasions, rendre les femmes plus tendres et les hommes plus aimables.*
   The truffle is not a true aphrodisiac; but in certain circumstances it can make women more affectionate and men more attentive.
   1825 *Physiologie du goût*, pt.1, ch.6, section 44 (translated by Anne Drayton, 1970).

38 *L'alcool est le monarque des liquides, et porte au dernier degré l'exaltation palatale.*
Alcohol is the prince of liquids, and carries the palate to its highest pitch of exaltation.
1825 *Physiologie du goût*, pt.1, ch.9, section 53 (translated by Anne Drayton, 1970).

39 *C'est aussi de tous les arts celui qui nous a rendu le service le plus important pour la vie civile.*
It is also of all arts the one which has done the most to advance the cause of civilization.
1825 Of cooking. *Physiologie du goût*, pt.1, ch.27, section 123 (translated by Anne Drayton, 1970).

Brinkley, David McClure 1920–2003

US news commentator who is best known for the nightly *Huntley–Brinkley Report* (1956–70), co-hosted with Chet Huntley.

40 If you turn on your set and see nothing is happening…do not call a serviceman. You have tuned in the US Senate.
1986 On ABC T V broadcast, 1 Jun.

41 A cavalry commander…said he had just been given a thousand new men who had never seen a horse and a thousand horses who had never seen a man.
1988 On World War II. *Washington Goes to War*.

42 [They] will fearlessly commit both parties to favor mother love and the protection of the whooping crane, and to oppose the man-eating shark and the more unpopular forms of sin.
Of party platforms. Quoted in Marc Gunther *The House That Roone Built* (1994).

Brisbane, Arthur 1864–1936

US newspaper editor and writer. Editor of the *New York Herald*, which was owned by William Randolph Hearst, he was a proponent of 'sensationalist' journalism.

43 Never forget that if you don't hit a newspaper reader between the eyes with your first sentence, there is no need of writing a second one.
c.1900 Quoted in Oliver Carlson *Brisbane: a Candid Biography* (1937), ch.5.

44 Hang your idea on a peg that all can read.
c.1907 Quoted in Oliver Carlson *Brisbane: a Candid Biography* (1937), ch.7.

Britten, Baron (Edward) Benjamin, of Aldeburgh 1913–76

English composer, pianist and conductor, a student of John Ireland and Frank Bridge. His extensive output includes the opera *Peter Grimes* (1945) and other operas, songs, chamber music and orchestral works, and the *War Requiem* (1961), written for the reopening of Coventry Cathedral. With Peter Pears, he founded the Aldeburgh Festival (1948), at which much of his work was first performed.

45 I remember the first time I tried the result looked rather like the Forth Bridge.
1964 Of his first attempts at composition. Quoted in the *Sunday Telegraph*.

Brock, Sir Isaac 1768–1812

British soldier, commander of the British and militia forces in the War of 1812.

46 Push on, brave York Volunteers!
1812 Last command before succumbing to a sniper's bullet in the Battle of Queenston Heights, Upper Canada (modern Ontario), 13 Oct. Quoted in C P Stacey 'Brock's Muniments', in *Books in Canada* (Aug–Sep 1980).

Brodber, Erna 1940–

Jamaican writer, critic and academic. Her works include sociological studies on women and children in Jamaica, books on Caribbean literature, and novels including *Jane and Louisa Will Soon Come Home* (1980) and *Myal* (1988).

47 Different rhymes for different times
Different styles for different climes
Someday them rogues in Whitehall
Be forced to change their tune.
1988 *Myal*, ch.15.

Brodkey, Harold 1930–96

US writer and journalist. He died of AIDS.

48 I have AIDS. I am surprised that I do. I have not been exposed since 1977, which is to say that my experience, my adventures in homosexuality took place largely in the 1960s and '70s, and back then I relied on time and abstinence to indicate my degree of freedom from infection—and to protect others and myself.
1996 *This Wild Darkness: The Story of My Death*.

49 I'm sixty-two, and it's ecological sense to die while you're still productive, die and clear a space for others, old and young.
1996 *This Wild Darkness: The Story of My Death*.

50 Death is not soft-mouthed, vague-footed, nearby. It is in the hall.
1996 *This Wild Darkness: The Story of My Death*.

51 Nothing I have ever written has been admired as much as the announcement of my death.
Remark about his articles tracing the course of his illness in the *New Yorker*. Quoted in his obituary in *The Scotsman*, 29 Jan 1996.

Brodsky, Ioseph 1940–96

Russian-born US poet. Exiled from Russia as a 'social parasite', he took US citizenship in 1977 and was awarded the Nobel prize in 1987. He latterly wrote in English, and translated his earlier Russian poems.

52 Illness and death…the only things that a tyrant has in common with his subjects… In this sense alone, a nation profits from being run by an old man.
1986 *Less Than One*, 'On Tyranny'.

53 The dusty catastrophe of Asia. Green only on the banner of the Prophet. Nothing grows here except mustaches.
1986 *Less Than One*, 'Flight From Byzantium'.

54 Racism? But isn't it only a form of misanthropy?
1986 *Less Than One*, 'Flight From Byzantium'.

55 Snobbery? But it's only a form of despair.
1986 *Less Than One*, 'Flight From Byzantium'.

56 A big step for me, and a small step for mankind.
1987 Response on hearing of his Nobel prize award. Quoted in his obituary in *The Scotsman*, 29 Jan 1996.
➤ *See Armstrong 30:78.*

57 Were we to choose our leaders on the basis of their reading experience and not their political programs, there would be much less grief on earth. I believe—not

empirically, alas, but only theoretically—that for someone who has read a lot of Dickens to shoot his like in the name of an idea is harder than for someone who has read no Dickens.
1987 Nobel prize acceptance speech.

58 There are worse crimes than burning books. One of them is not reading them.
1991 Comment at a press conference in Washington, DC, 15 May, on accepting the US poet laureateship.

59 Russia is my home…and for everything that I have in my soul I am obligated to Russia and its people. And—this is the main thing—obligated to its language.
1992 In the *New York Times*, 1 Oct.

60 They should be in every room in every motel in the land.
1992 Of poetry books. In the *New York Times*, 1 Oct.

Brody, Hugh 1943–

Canadian explorer, anthropologist and writer.

61 Resources left in the ground are saved, not lost.
1981 *Maps and Dreams: Indians and the British Columbia Frontier.*

Bronowski, Jacob 1908–74

Polish-born British mathematician, poet and humanist. He was a popular broadcaster, particularly on the BBC's *Brains Trust* and *The Ascent of Man* (1973).

62 Dissent is the native activity of the scientist, and it has got him into a good deal of trouble in the last years. But if that is cut off, what is left will not be a scientist. And I doubt whether it will be a man.
1953 'The Sense of Human Dignity', lecture at Massachusetts Institute of Technology, 19 Mar.

63 Science has nothing to be ashamed of, even in the ruins of Nagasaki. The shame is theirs who appeal to other values than the human imaginative values which science has evolved.
1953 'The Sense of Human Dignity', lecture at Massachusetts Institute of Technology, 19 Mar.

64 At bottom, the society of scientists is more important than their discoveries. What science has to teach us here is not its techniques but its spirit: the irresistible need to explore.
1956 *Science and Human Values.*

65 Man masters nature not by force but by understanding. This is why science has succeeded where magic failed: because it has looked for no spell to cast on nature.
1956 *Universities Quarterly*, vol.10, issue 3.

66 Sooner or later every one of us breathes an atom that has been breathed before by anyone you can think of who has lived before us—Michelangelo or George Washington or Moses.
1966 Quoted in the *New York Times*, 13 Oct 1969.

67 No science is immune to the infection of politics and the corruption of power.
1971 In *The Listener*.

68 The world can only be grasped by action, not by contemplation… The hand is the cutting edge of the mind.
1973 *The Ascent of Man*, ch.3.

69 That is the essence of science: ask an impertinent question and you are on the way to a pertinent answer.
1973 *The Ascent of Man*, ch.4.

70 Man is a singular creature. He has a set of gifts which make him unique among the animals, so that unlike them he is not a figure in the landscape—he is the shaper of the landscape.
1979 In *The Listener*.

Brontë, Anne 1820–49

English novelist and poet, younger sister of Charlotte and Emily. Her first novel *Agnes Grey* (1847) was published under the pseudonym Acton Bell. She also wrote *The Tenant of Wildfell Hall* (1848).

71 To think a soul so near divine,
Within a form, so angel fair,
United to a heart like thine,
Has gladdened once our humble sphere.
1846 'A Reminiscence', in *Poems by Currer, Ellis and Acton Bell*.

72 My soul is awakened, my spirit is soaring
And carried aloft on the wings of the breeze;
For above and around me the wild wind is roaring,
Arousing to rapture the earth and the seas.
1846 'Line Composed in a Wood on a Windy Day', in *Poems by Currer, Ellis and Acton Bell*.

73 All true histories contain instruction; though in some, the treasure may be hard to find, and when found, so trivial in quantity that the dry, shrivelled kernel scarcely compensates for the trouble of cracking the nut.
1847 *Agnes Grey*, ch.1.

74 He'll be all right when he's married, as Mama says; and reformed rakes make the best husbands, everybody knows. I only wish he were not so ugly—that's all I think about—but then there's no choice here in the country.
1847 *Agnes Grey*, ch.13.

75 What is it that constitutes virtue, Mrs Graham? Is it the circumstance of being able and willing to resist temptation; or that of having no temptation to resist?
1848 *The Tenant of Wildfell Hall*, ch.3.

Brontë, Charlotte 1816–55

English novelist and poet, elder sister of Emily and Anne. Her four novels are *Jane Eyre* (1847), *Shirley* (1849), *Villette* (1853) and *The Professor* (1857).

76 We wove a web in childhood,
A web of sunny air;
We dug a spring in infancy
Of water pure and fair;
We sowed in youth a mustard seed,
We cut an almond rod;
We are now grown up to riper age—
Are they withered in the sod?
1835 'We Wove a Web in Childhood'.

77 But two miles more and then we rest!
Well, there is still an hour of day,
And long the brightness of the west
Sit then, awhile, here in this wood
So total is the solitude,
We safely may delay.
1846 'Regret', in *Poems by Currer, Ellis and Acton Bell*.

78 Women are supposed to be very calm generally: but women feel just as men feel: they need exercise for their faculties, and a field for their efforts as much as their brothers do; they suffer from too rigid a restraint, too

absolute a stagnation, precisely as men would suffer…it is thoughtless to condem them, or laugh at them, if they seek to do more than custom has pronounced necessary for their sex.
1847 *Jane Eyre*, ch.12.

79 I grant an ugly woman is a blot on the fair face of creation; but as to the gentleman, let them be solicitous to possess only strength and valour: let their motto be:—Hunt, shoot, and fight: the rest is not worth a flip.
1847 *Jane Eyre* ch.17.

80 The soul fortunately, has an interpreter—often an unconscious, but still a truthful interpreter—in the eye.
1847 *Jane Eyre*, ch.28.

81 Reader, I married him.
1847 *Jane Eyre*, ch.38.

82 Conventionality is not morality. Self-righteousness is not religion. To attack the first is not to assail the last. To pluck the mask from the face of the Pharisee, is not to lift an impious hand to the Crown of Thorns.
1848 *Jane Eyre* (2nd edn), preface.

83 Of late years an abundant shower of curates has fallen upon the north of England.
1849 *Shirley*, ch.1.

84 I describe imperfect characters. Every character in this book will be found to be more or less imperfect, my pen refusing to draw anything in the model line.
1849 *Shirley*, ch.5.

85 Old maids like the houseless and unemployed poor, should not ask for a place and an occupation in the world: the demand disturbs the happy and the rich.
1849 *Shirley*, ch.22.

86 Liberty lends us her wings and Hope guides us by her star.
1853 *Villette*, ch.6.

87 Out of association grows adhesion, and out of adhesion amalgamation.
1853 *Villette*, ch.25.

88 What animal magnetism drew thee and me together—I know not.
1857 *The Professor*, ch.1.

89 Unlawful pleasure, trenching on another's rights, is delusive and envenomed pleasure—its hollowness disappoints at the time, its poison cruelly tortures afterwards, its effects deprave forever.
1857 *The Professor*, ch.20.

Brontë, Emily Jane 1818–48

English novelist and poet, sister of Anne and Charlotte. Her poems were first published under the pseudonym Ellis Bell. Her only novel is the intense and powerful *Wuthering Heights* (1847).

90 The night is darkening round me,
The wild winds coldly blow;
But a tyrant spell has bound me
And I cannot, cannot go.
1837 'The Night is Darkening Round Me'.

91 The winter wind is loud and wild,
Come close to me, my darling child;
Forsake thy books, and mateless play;
And, while the night is gathering grey,
We'll talk its pensive hours away.

1846 'Faith and Despondency', in *Poems by Currer, Ellis and Acton Bell*.

92 No coward soul is mine,
No trembler in the world's storm-troubled sphere:
I see Heaven's glories shine,
And faith shines equal, arming me from fear.
1846 'No Coward Soul is Mine', in *Poems by Currer, Ellis and Acton Bell*.

93 Cold in the earth—and the deep snow piled above thee,
Far, far, removed, cold in the dreary grave!
Have I forgot, my only Love, to love thee,
Severed at last by Time's all-serving wave?
1846 'Remembrance', in *Poems by Currer, Ellis and Acton Bell*.

94 I've dreamt in my life dreams that have stayed with me ever after, and changed my ideas; they've gone through and through me, like wine through water, and altered the colour of my mind.
1847 *Wuthering Heights*, ch.9.

95 As different as a moonbeam from lightning, or frost from fire.
1847 *Wuthering Heights*, ch.9.

96 My love for Linton is like the foliage in the woods. Time will change it, I'm well aware, as winter changes the trees. My Love for Heathcliff resembles the eternal rocks beneath—a source of little visible delight but necessary. Nelly, I *am* Heathcliff.
1847 *Wuthering Heights*, ch.9.

97 He might as well plant an oak in a flower-pot, and expect it to thrive, as imagine he can restore her to vigour in the soil of his shallow cares!
1847 *Wuthering Heights*, ch.14.

98 The more the worms writhe, the more I yearn to crush out their entrails!
1847 Heathcliff. *Wuthering Heights*, ch.14.

99 I lingered around them, under the benign sky; watched the moths fluttering among the heath and hare-bells; listened to the soft wind breathing through the grass; and wondered how anyone could ever imagine unquiet slumbers, for the sleepers in that quiet earth.
1847 *Wuthering Heights*, ch.34, closing words.

Brooke, Frances née *Moore* 1724–89

English writer. In Canada (1763–8) with her minister husband, she produced 'Canada's first novel', *The History of Emily Montague* (1769). She wrote other novels and plays, and edited a periodical, *The Old Maid*.

1 I no longer wonder the elegant arts are unknown here; the rigor of the climate suspends the very powers of the understanding; and then what must become of those of the imagination?… Genius will never mount high, where the faculties of the mind are benumbed half the year.
1769 *The History of Emily Montague*, 'Letter 49'.

Brooke, Rupert Chawner 1887–1915

English poet, icon of the World War I 'lost generation'. His early verse was published in 1911, and his reputation was established by the posthumous publication of *1914 and Other Poems* (1915). He died of blood poisoning on Skyros.

2 Breathless, we flung us on the windy hill.
Laughed in the sun, and kissed the lovely grass.
1910 'Sonnet'.

3 But there's wisdom in women, of more than they have
   known,
   And thoughts go blowing through them, are wiser than
   their own.
   1913 'There's Wisdom in Women'.

4 Then, the cool kindliness of sheets, that soon
   Smooth away trouble; and the rough male kiss
   Of blankets.
   1914 'The Great Lover'.

5 The benison of hot water; furs to touch;
   The good smell of old clothes.
   1914 'The Great Lover'.

6 If I should die, think only this of me:
   That there's some corner of a foreign field
   That is for ever England.
   There shall be
   In that rich dust a richer dust concealed;
   A dust whom England bore, shaped, made aware,
   Gave, once, her flowers to love, her ways to roam,
   A body of England's, breathing English air,
   Washed by the rivers, blest by suns of home.
   1914 'The Soldier'.

7 In hearts at peace, under an English heaven.
   1914 'The Soldier'.

8 Blow out, you bugles, over the rich Dead!
   There's none of these so lonely and poor of old,
   But, dying, has made us rarer gifts than gold.
   1914 'The Dead'.

9 Naught broken save this body, lost but breath;
   Nothing to shake the laughing heart's long peace there
   But only agony, and that has ending;
   And the worst friend and enemy is but Death.
   1914 'Peace'.

10 Here tulips bloom as they are told;
   Unkempt about those hedges blows
   An English unofficial rose.
   1915 'The Old Vicarage, Grantchester'.

11 And spectral dance, before the dawn,
   A hundred Vicars down the lawn;
   Curates, long dust, will come and go
   On lissom, clerical, printless toe;
   And oft between the boughs is seen
   The sly shade of a Rural Dean.
   1915 'The Old Vicarage, Grantchester'.

12 God! I will pack, and take a train,
   And get me to England once again!
   For England's the one land, I know,
   Where men with Splendid Hearts may go.
   1915 'The Old Vicarage, Grantchester'.

13 For Cambridge people rarely smile,
   Being urban, squat, and packed with guile.
   1915 'The Old Vicarage, Grantchester'.

14 They love the Good; they worship Truth;
   They laugh uproariously in youth;
   (And when they get to feeling old,
   They up and shoot themselves, I'm told).
   1915 'The Old Vicarage, Grantchester'.

15 Stands the Church clock at ten to three?
   And is there honey still for tea?
   1915 'The Old Vicarage, Grantchester'.

16 Fish (fly-replete, in depth of June,
   Dawdling away their wat'ry noon).
   1915 'Heaven'.

17 Fish say, they have their stream and pond;
   But is there anything beyond?
   1915 'Heaven'.

18 But somewhere, beyond Space and Time
   Is wetter water, slimier slime!
   1915 'Heaven'.

19 Unfading moths, immortal flies,
   And the worm that never dies.
   And in that heaven of all their wish,
   There shall be no more land, say fish.
   1915 'Heaven'.

Brookner, Anita 1928–

English novelist and art historian. A spare, elegant stylist, she
won the Booker Prize in 1984 for her novel *Hôtel du Lac*.

20 It is best to marry for purely selfish reasons.
   1981 *A Start in Life*.

21 It is my contention that Aesop was writing for the
   tortoise market…hares have no time to read.
   1984 *Hôtel du Lac*, ch.2.

22 Good women always think it is their fault when
   someone else is being offensive. Bad women never take
   the blame for anything.
   1984 *Hôtel du Lac*, ch.7.

23 Blanche Vernon occupied her time most usefully in
   keeping feelings at bay.
   1986 *Misalliance*, ch.1.

24 I think you always feel braver in another language.
   1988 In the *Observer*, 7 Aug.

25 They were privileged children…they would always
   expect to be greeted with smiles.
   1989 *Lewis Percy*, ch.9.

26 Satire is dependent on strong beliefs, and on strong
   beliefs wounded.
   1989 In *The Spectator*, 23 Mar.

27 I reflected how easy it is for a man to reduce women of a
   certain age to imbecility. All he has to do is give an
   impersonation of desire, or better still, of secret
   knowledge, for a woman to feel herself a source of
   power.
   1993 *A Family Romance*, ch.7.

28 In youth Beatrice had been attractive, but what was
   attractive about her was not her appearance but her
   disposability.
   1998 *Falling Slowly*.

Brooks, Louise 1906–85

US film actress, embodiment of the flapper age, renowned for
her innocent sexuality and natural screen presence.

29 Every actor has a natural animosity toward every other
   actor, present or absent, living or dead.
   1982 *Lulu in Hollywood*.

Brooks, Mel *pseudonym of* **Melvin Kaminsky** 1926–

US director, writer and actor. His successful comedies have
included *The Producers* (1968), *Blazing Saddles* (1974) and
Young Frankenstein (1974).

30 That's it baby. If you've got it, flaunt it.
   1968 *The Producers*.

31 Tragedy is if I cut my finger. Comedy is if I walk into an open sewer and die.
   Attributed.

Brooks, Van Wyck 1886–1963

US author and critic. He wrote biographical studies of Mark Twain (1920), Henry James (1925) and Emerson (1932). His works, which attacked materialism, also include *The Flowering of New England* (1936, Pulitzer Prize).

32 It is not that the French are not profound, but they all express themselves so well that we are led to take their geese for swans.
   1958 *From A Writer's Notebook*.

Brougham, Henry Peter, 1st Baron Brougham and Vaux 1778–1868

Scottish jurist and politician. He was called to the English bar in 1808 and entered parliament in 1810. Noted for his eloquence, he became Lord Chancellor in 1830 and promoted the passage of the Reform Bill.

33 A legal gentleman who rescues your estate from your enemies, and keeps it himself.
   His definition of a lawyer. Quoted in Richard Fountain *The Wit of the Wig* (1968).

Broun, (Matthew) Heywood Campbell 1888–1939

US journalist, humorist and novelist.

34 Except that right side is up is best, there is not much to learn about holding a baby. There are one hundred and fifty-two distinctly different ways—and all are right! At least, all will do.
   1921 *Seeing Things at Night*, 'Holding a Baby'.

35 The tragedy of life is not that man loses, but that he almost wins.
   1922 *Pieces of Hate, and Other Enthusiasms*, 'Sport for Art's Sake'.

36 Just as every conviction begins as a whim so does every emancipator serve his apprenticeship as a crank. A fanatic is a great leader who is just entering the room.
   1928 In *New York World*, 6 Feb.

37 The tradition of baseball always has been agreeably free of chivalry. The rule is 'Do anything you can get away with'.
   Quoted in Colin Jarman *The Guinness Dictionary of Sports Quotations* (1990).

38 Sports do not build character. They reveal it.
   Quoted in Colin Jarman *The Guinness Dictionary of Sports Quotations* (1990).

Brown, (James) Gordon 1951–

Scottish Labour politician, Chancellor of the Exchequer since 1997.

39 We have been prudent for a purpose: a stronger, fairer Britain.
   2000 Budget speech, 21 Mar.

40 It is about time we had an end to the old Britain, where all that matters is the privileges you were born with, rather than the potential you actually have.
   2000 Speech, 25 May.

41 I'm a father, that's what matters most. Nothing matters more.
   2003 Following the birth of his son. Quoted in the *Observer*, 19 Oct.

Brown, John 1800–59

US militant abolitionist. In 1859 he led an unsuccessful raid on the US Armory at Harper's Ferry, Virginia, and was convicted of treason and hanged. He was twice married and had 20 children.

42 I am as content to die for God's eternal truth on the scaffold as in any other way.
   1859 Letter to his children on the eve of his execution, 2 Dec.

Brown, John Mason 1900–69

US theatre critic. He wrote long-running theatre columns in the *New York Post* and *Saturday Review* as well as publishing several books on the theatre.

43 Tallulah Bankhead barged down the Nile last night as Cleopatra—and sank.
   1937 In the *New York Post*, 11 Nov.

44 To many, dramatic criticism must seem like an attempt to tattoo soap bubbles.
   1963 *Stagebill*.

45 He has ears he likes to bathe in sound.
   1963 Of playwright Maxwell Anderson. *Dramatis Personae*.

Brown, Olympia 1835–1900

US religious leader, the first woman ordained in the US.

46 The more we learn of science, the more we see that its wonderful mysteries are all explained by a few simple laws so connected together and so dependent upon each other, that we see the same mind animating them all.
   1895 Sermon in Wisconsin, c.13 Jan.

Brown, Pat (Edmund Gerald, Sr) 1905–96

US lawyer and politician, Governor of California (1959–66).

47 Why, this is the worst disaster since my election.
   1965 Of the Watts riots. Recalled in the *New York Times*, 21 Aug 1994.

Brown, Rita Mae 1944–

US writer and feminist, a campaigner for gay rights. She is the author of a number of popular novels.

48 No government has the right to tell its citizens when or whom to love. The only queer people are those who don't love anybody.
   1982 Speech, 28 Aug, at the opening ceremony of the Gay Olympics, San Francisco.

49 If Michaelangelo were a heterosexual, the Sistine Chapel would have been painted basic white and with a roller.
   1988 In the *New York Times*, 15 May.

50 I think the reward for conformity is that everyone likes you except yourself.
   1988 *Bingo*, ch.35.

Brown, Thomas 1663–1704

English satirical writer.

51 I do not love thee, Dr Fell.

The reason why I cannot tell;
But this I know, and know full well,
I do not love thee, Dr Fell.
Composed while an undergraduate at Christ Church, Oxford,
under the Deanship of Dr Fell.

Brown, Walter   fl.15c

Scottish poet. *Letters of Gold* is his only known surviving poem.

52 Grit riches and prosperitie
Upfosteris vyce.
15c *Letters of Gold*, l.131–2.

Browne, Sir Thomas   1605–82

English writer and physician. His meditative *Religio Medici*
appeared in an authorized version in 1643. Other works
include *Pseudodoxia Epidemica, or Enquiries into…Vulgar and
Common Errors* (1646) and *Hydriotaphia* (Urn Burial) (1658).

53 For my religion, though there be several circumstances
that might persuade the world I have none at all—as the
general scandal of my profession, the natural course of
my studies, the indifferency of my behaviour and
discourse in matters of religion, neither violently
defending one, nor with that common ardour and
contention opposing another—yet in despite hereof I
dare without usurpation assume the honourable style of
a Christian.
1634–5 *Religio Medici* (published 1643), pt.1, section 1.

54 My common conversation I do acknowledge austere, my
behaviour full of rigor, sometimes not without morosity;
yet at my devotion I love to use the civility of my knee, my
hat, and hand, with all those outward and sensible motions
which may express or promote my invisible devotion.
1634–5 *Religio Medici* (published 1643), pt.1, section 3.

55 Those vulgar heads that look asquint on the face of truth.
1634–5 *Religio Medici* (published 1643), pt.1, section 3.

56 In brief, where the Scripture is silent, the church is my
text; where that speaks, 'tis but my comment; where
there is a joint silence of both, I borrow not the rules of
my religion from Rome or Geneva, but the dictates of my
own reason.
1634–5 *Religio Medici* (published 1643), pt.1, section 5.

57 Where we desire to be informed, 'tis good to contest
with men above ourselves; but to confirm and establish
our opinions, 'tis best to argue with judgements below
our own, that the frequent spoils and victories over their
reasons may settle in ourselves an esteem and confirmed
opinion of our own.
1634–5 *Religio Medici* (published 1643), pt.1, section 6.

58 Every man is not a proper champion for truth, nor fit to
take up the gauntlet in the cause of verity.
1634–5 *Religio Medici* (published 1643), pt.1, section 6.

59 Every man's own reason is his best Oedipus.
1634–5 Oedipus here means riddle-solver. *Religio Medici*
(published 1643), pt.1, section 6.

60 For indeed heresies perish not with their authors, but
like the river Arethusa, though they lose their currents in
one place, they rise up again in another.
1634–5 *Religio Medici* (published 1643), pt.1, section 6.

61 Men are lived over again; the world is now as it was in
ages past.
1634–5 *Religio Medici* (published 1643), pt.1, section 6.

62 Methinks there be not impossibilities enough in religion
for an active faith.
1634–5 *Religio Medici* (published 1643), pt.1, section 6.

63 I desire to exercise my faith in the difficultest points, for
to credit ordinary and visible objects is not faith but
persuasion.
1634–5 *Religio Medici* (published 1643), pt.1, section 6.

64 I love to lose myself in a mystery, to pursue my reason to
an *O altitudo!*
1634–5 *Religio Medici* (published 1643), pt.1, section 9.

65 Who can speak of eternity without a solecism, or think
thereof without an ecstasy? Time we may comprehend,
'tis but five days elder than ourselves.
1634–5 *Religio Medici* (published 1643), pt.1, section 11.

66 We carry with us the wonders we seek without us: there
is all Africa and her prodigies in us.
1634–5 *Religio Medici* (published 1643), pt.1, section 15.

67 We are that bold and adventurous piece of nature which
he that studies wisely learns in a compendium what
others labour at in a divided piece and endless
volume.
1634–5 *Religio Medici* (published 1643), pt.1, section 15.

68 Nature is not at variance with art nor art with nature, they
both being the servants of his providence: art is the
perfection of nature.
1634–5 *Religio Medici* (published 1643), pt.1, section 16.

69 All things are artificial, for nature is the art of God.
1634–5 *Religio Medici* (published 1643), pt.1, section 16.

70 Obstinacy in a bad cause, is but constancy in a good.
1634–5 *Religio Medici* (published 1643), pt.1, section 25.

71 Persecution is a bad and indirect way to plant religion.
1634–5 *Religio Medici* (published 1643), pt.1, section 25.

72 There are many…canonized on earth, that shall never
be Saints in Heaven.
1634–5 *Religio Medici* (published 1643), pt.1, section 26.

73 I am not so much afraid of death, as ashamed thereof.
1634–5 *Religio Medici* (published 1643), pt.1, section 40.

74 Certainly there is no happiness within this circle of flesh,
nor is it in the optics of these eyes to behold felicity; the
first day of our Jubilee is death.
1634–5 *Religio Medici* (published 1643), pt.1, section 44.

75 I have tried if I could reach that great resolution…to be
honest without a thought of Heaven or Hell.
1634–5 *Religio Medici* (published 1643), pt.1, section 47.

76 To believe only in possibilities, is not faith, but mere
Philosophy.
1634–5 *Religio Medici* (published 1643), pt.1, section 48.

77 There is no road or ready way to virtue.
1634–5 *Religio Medici* (published 1643), pt.1, section 55.

78 The world was before the creation and at an end before it
had a beginning; and thus was I dead before I was alive.
Though my grave be England, my dying place was
Paradise, and Eve miscarried of me before she
conceived of Cain.
1634–5 *Religio Medici* (published 1643), pt.1, section 59.

79 All places, all airs make unto me one country; I am in
England, everywhere, and under any meridian.
1634–5 *Religio Medici* (published 1643), pt.2, section 1.

80 It is the common wonder of all men, how among so many

millions of faces, there should be none alike.
1634–5 *Religio Medici* (published 1643), pt.2, section 1.

81 I could be content that we might procreate like trees, without conjunction, or that there were any way to perpetuate the World without this trivial and vulgar way of coition: it is the foolishest act a wise man commits in all his life.
1634–5 *Religio Medici* (published 1643), pt.2, section 9.

82 We all labour against our own cure, for death is the cure of all diseases.
1634–5 *Religio Medici* (published 1643), pt.2, section 9.

83 Whilst I study to find how I am a microcosm of little world, I find myself something more than the great. There is surely a piece of divinity in us; something that was before the elements, and owes no homage unto the sun.
1634–5 *Religio Medici* (published 1643), pt.2, section 11.

84 Old mortality, the ruins of forgotten times.
1658 *Hydriotaphia* (Urn Burial), Epistle Dedicatory.

85 Were the happiness of the next world as closely apprehended as the felicities of this, it were a martyrdom to live.
1658 *Hydriotaphia* (Urn Burial), ch.4.

86 The long habit of living indisposeth us for dying.
1658 *Hydriotaphia* (Urn Burial), ch.5.

87 Adversity stretcheth our days.
1658 *Hydriotaphia* (Urn Burial), ch.5.

88 We cannot hope to live so long in our names as some have done in their persons.
1658 *Hydriotaphia* (Urn Burial), ch.5.

89 'Tis too late to be ambitious.
1658 *Hydriotaphia* (Urn Burial), ch.5.

90 There is no antidote against the opium of time.
1658 *Hydriotaphia* (Urn Burial), ch.5.

91 To be nameless in worthy deeds exceeds an infamous history… Who would not rather have been the good thief than Pilate?
1658 *Hydriotaphia* (Urn Burial), ch.5.

92 Man is a noble animal, splendid in ashes, and pompous in the grave.
1658 *Hydriotaphia* (Urn Burial), ch.5.

93 Life is a pure flame, and we live by an invisible sun within us.
1658 *Hydriotaphia* (Urn Burial), ch.5.

94 Life itself is but the shadow of death, and souls departed but the shadows of the living. All things fall under this name. The sun itself is but the dark *simulacrum*, and light but the shadow of God.
1658 *The Garden of Cyrus*, ch.2.

95 The quincunx of heaven runs low, and 'tis time to close the five parts of knowledge.
1658 *The Garden of Cyrus*, ch.5.

96 All things began in order, so shall they end, and so shall they begin again; according to the ordainer of order and mystical mathematics of the city of heaven.
1658 *The Garden of Cyrus*, ch.5.

97 Nor will the sweetest delight of gardens afford much comfort in sleep; wherein the dullness of that sense shakes hands with delectable odours; and though in the bed of Cleopatra, can hardly with any delight raise up

the ghost of a rose.
1658 *The Garden of Cyrus*, ch.5.

Browne, William 1692–1774

English physician and poet.

98 The King to Oxford sent a troop of horse,
For Tories own no argument but force;
With equal skill to Cambridge books he sent,
For Whigs admit no force but argument.
Literary Anecdotes.

Browning, Elizabeth *née Barrett* 1806–61

English poet, who married Robert Browning (1846). Her early work includes her *Essay on Mind, and other Poems* which was published anonymously when she was 19. Her other writings include *Poems* (1884), translations of Aeschylus's *Prometheus Bound* (1833 and a new translation in her *Poems* of 1850), the long narrative poem *Aurora Leigh* (1856), *Sonnets from the Portuguese* (also published in *Poems*, 1850) which were not translations but express her own love, and *Casa Guidi Windows* (1851) on the theme of Italian Liberation. *Last Poems* was published posthumously in 1862.

99 Thou large-brained woman and large-hearted man.
1844 *Poems*, 'To George Sand. A Desire', l.1.

1 And because I was a poet, and because the public praised me,
With their critical deductions for the modern writer's fault;
I could sit at rich men's tables,—though the courtesies that raise me,
Still suggested clear between us, the pale spectrum of the salt.
1844 *Poems*, 'Lady Geraldine's Courtship', stanza 9.

2 And the rolling anapaestic
Curled, like vapour over shrines.
1844 *Poems*, 'Wine of Cyprus', stanza 10.

3 I am floated along, as if I should die
Of Liberty's exquisite pain.
1849 'The Runaway Slave at Pilgrim's Point', stanza 36.

4 Straightway I was 'ware
So weeping, how a mystic shape did move
Behind me, and drew me backward by the hair
And a voice said in mastery while I strove…
'Guess now who holds thee!'—'Death', I said, but there
The silver answer rang… 'Not Death, but Love.'
1850 *Poems*, 'Sonnets from the Portuguese', sonnet 1.

5 If thou must love me, let it be for naught
Except for love's sake only.
1850 *Poems*, 'Sonnets from the Portuguese', sonnet 14.

6 When our two souls stand up erect and strong,
Face to face, silent, drawing nigh and nigher,
Until their lengthening wings break into fire
At either curvèd point,…what bitter wrong,
Can the earth do to us, that we should not long
Be here contented?
1850 *Poems*, 'Sonnets from the Portuguese', sonnet 22.

7 Let the world's sharpness like a clasping knife
Shut in upon itself, and do no harm
In this close hand of love.
1850 *Poems*, 'Sonnets from the Portuguese', sonnet 24.

8 First time he kissed me, but only kissed

The fingers of this hand wherewith I write,
And ever since it grew more clean and white…
1850 *Poems*, 'Sonnets from the Portuguese', sonnet 38.

9 How do I love thee? Let me count the ways!—
I love thee to the depth and breadth and height
My soul can reach, when feeling out of sight
For the ends of Being and Ideal Grace.
1850 *Poems*, 'Sonnets from the Portuguese', sonnet 43.

10 I love thee with the love I seemed to lose
With my lost Saints,—I love thee with the breath
Smiles, tears, of all my life!—and, if God choose,
I shall but love thee better after death.
1850 *Poems*, 'Sonnets from the Portuguese', sonnet 43.

11 God answers sharp and sudden on some prayers,
And thrusts the thing we have prayed for in our face,
A gauntlet with a gift in't.
1856 *Aurora Leigh*, bk.2.

12 The music soars within the little lark,
And the lark soars.
1856 *Aurora Leigh*, bk.3.

13 Since when was genius found respectable?
1856 *Aurora Leigh*, bk.6.

14 Earth's crammed with heaven,
And every common bush afire with God.
1856 *Aurora Leigh*, bk.7.

Browning, Guy 1964–

English writer and broadcaster.

15 A shoal of a million fish might not be able to write *Romeo and Juliet* but they can change direction as one in the blink of an eye. Using language a human team leader can giver an order to a team of six and have it interpreted in six completely different ways.
1999 In *The Guardian*, 24 Jul.

16 Major cities are divided into two parts; the bits that are in the guidebook and the bits that aren't. If you don't take a guidebook, you'll see a different city.
2002 In *The Guardian*, 21 May.

17 Maths is the purest science in that you don't need any test tubes or animal testing to do it. All the other sciences eventually boil down to maths, apart from biology, which boils down to soup.
2004 In *The Guardian*, 19 Jun.

Browning, Robert 1812–89

English poet, who married Elizabeth Browning (1846). His poetry offers a wide range of characters, dramatic situations, and a rich variety of forms and rhythms. His work includes *Men and Women* (1855), *Dramatis Personae* (1864) and *The Ring and the Book* (1868–9).

18 God is the perfect poet,
Who in his person acts his own creations.
1835 *Paracelsus*, pt.2, l.648–9.

19 The year's at the spring,
And days at the morn;
Morning's at seven;
The hill-side's dew-pearled;
The lark's on the wing;
The snail's on the thorn;

God's in His heaven—
All's right with the world.
1841 *Pippa Passes*, pt.1.

20 Like a god going thro' his world there stands
One mountain, for a moment in the dusk,
Whole brotherhoods of cedars on its brow
1841 *Pippa Passes*, pt.2.

21 There's a great text in Galatians,
Once you trip on it, entails
Twenty-nine distinct damnations,
One sure, if another fails.
1842 *Dramatic Lyrics*, 'Soliloquy of the Spanish Cloister'.

22 My scrofulous French novel
On grey paper with blunt type!
1842 *Dramatic Lyrics*, 'Soliloquy of the Spanish Cloister'.

23 The moth's kiss, first!
Kiss me as if you made believe
You were not sure, this eve,
How my face, your flower, had pursed
Its petals up.
1842 *Dramatic Lyrics*, 'In a Gondola'.

24 What's become of Waring
Since he gave us all the slip?
1842 *Dramatic Lyrics*, 'Waring'. The first line was used as the title of a novel by Anthony Powell.

25 Hamelin Town's in Brunswick,
By famous Hanover city;
The river Weser, deep and wide,
Washes its wall on the southern side;
A pleasanter spot you never spied.
1842 *Dramatic Lyrics*, 'The Pied Piper of Hamlin'.

26 Rats!
They fought the dogs and killed the cats,
And bit the babies in the cradles.
And ate the cheeses out of the vats.
1842 *Dramatic Lyrics*, 'The Pied Piper of Hamlin'.

27 I sprang to the stirrup, and Joris, and he;
I galloped, Dirck galloped, we galloped all three.
1845 *Dramatic Romances and Lyrics*, 'How they brought the Good News from Ghent to Aix'.

28 Just for a handful of silver he left us,
Just for a riband to stick in his coat.
1845 Of Wordsworth. *Dramatic Romances and Lyrics*, 'The Lost Leader'.

29 Never glad confident morning again!
1845 *Dramatic Romances and Lyrics*, 'The Lost Leader'.

30 Oh, to be in England
Now that April's there,
And whoever wakes in England
Sees, some morning, unaware,
That the lowest boughs and the brushwood sheaf
Round the elm-tree bole are in tiny leaf,
While the chaffinch sings on the orchard bough
In England—now!
1845 *Dramatic Romances and Lyrics*, 'Home-Thoughts, from Abroad'.

31 That's the wise thrush; he sings each song twice over,
Lest you think he never could recapture
The first fine careless rapture!
1845 *Dramatic Romances and Lyrics*, 'Home-Thoughts, from Abroad'.

32 'Here and here did England help me: how can I help
England?'—say.
1845 *Dramatic Romances and Lyrics*, 'Home- Thoughts, from the
Sea'.

33 And then how I shall lie through centuries,
And hear the blessed mutter of the mass,
And see God made and eaten all day long,
And feel the steady candle-flame, and taste
Good strong thick stupefying incense-smoke!
1845 *Dramatic Romances and Lyrics*, 'The Bishop Orders his
Tomb'.

34 A tap at the pane, the quick sharp scratch
And blue spurt of a lighted match,
And a voice less loud, through its joys and fears,
Than the two hearts beating each to each!
1845 *Dramatic Romances and Lyrics*, 'Meeting at Night'.

35 There may be heaven; there must be hell.
1845 *Dramatic Romances and Lyrics*, 'Time's Revenges'.

36 In the natural fog of the good man's mind.
1850 'Christmas Eve'.

37 Where the quiet-coloured end of evening smiles,
Miles and miles.
1855 *Men and Women*, 'Love among the Ruins'.

38 If you get simple beauty and naught else,
You get about the best thing God invents.
1855 *Men and Women*, 'Fra Lippo Lippi'.

39 This world's no blot for us
Nor blank; it means intensely, and means good:
To find its meaning is my meat and drink.
1855 *Men and Women*, 'Fra Lippo Lippi'.

40 Hark—the dominant's persistence till it must be
answered to!
1855 *Men and Women*, 'A Toccata of Galuppi's'.

41 What of soul was left, I wonder, when the kissing had to
stop?
1855 *Men and Women*, 'A Toccata of Galuppi's'.

42 Dear, dead woman, with such hair, too—what's become
of all the gold
Used to hang and brush their bosoms? I feel chilly and
grown old.
1855 *Men and Women*, 'A Toccata of Galuppi's'.

43 'Tis the Last Judgement's fire must cure this place,
Calcine its clods and set my prisoners free.
1855 *Men and Women*, 'Childe Roland to the Dark Tower Came'.

44 As for the grass, it grew as scant as hair in leprosy—thin
dried blades pricked the mud which underneath looked
kneaded up with blood.
One stiff blind horse, his every bone a-stare, stood
stupefied.
1855 *Men and Women*, 'Childe Roland to the Dark Tower Came'.

45 I never saw a brute I hated so;
He must be wicked to deserve such pain.
1855 *Men and Women*, 'Childe Roland to the Dark Tower Came'.

46 It was roses, roses, all the way.
1855 *Men and Women*, 'The Patriot'.

47 And find a poor devil has ended his cares
At the foot of your rotten-runged rat-riddled stairs?
Do I carry the moon in my pocket?
1855 *Men and Women*, 'Master Huges of Saxe-Gotha'.

48 Just when we are safest, there's a sunset-touch,

A fancy from a flower-bell, some one's death,
A chorus-ending from Euripides,—
And that's enough for fifty hopes and fears
As old and new at once as Nature's self,
To rap and knock and enter in our soul.
Take hands and dance there, a fantastic ring,
Round the ancient idol, on his base again,—
The grand Perhaps.
1855 *Men and Women*, 'Bishop Blougram's Apology'.

49 All we have gained then by our unbelief
Is a life of doubt diversified by faith,
For one of faith diversified by doubt:
We called the chess-board white,—we call it black.
1855 *Men and Women*, 'Bishop Blougram's Apology'.

50 You, for example, clever to a fault,
The rough and ready man who write apace,
Read somewhat seldomer, think perhaps even less.
1855 *Men and Women*, 'Bishop Blougram's Apology'.

51 No, when the fight begins within himself,
A man's worth something.
1855 *Men and Women*, 'Bishop Blougram's Apology'.

52 He said true things but called them by wrong names.
1855 *Men and Women*, 'Bishop Blougram's Apology'.

53 Ah, did you once see Shelley plain,
And did he stop to speak to you
And did you speak to him again?
How strange it seems, and new!
1855 *Men and Women*, 'Memorabilia'.

54 So free we seem, so fretted fast we are!
1855 *Men and Women*, 'Andrea del Sarto'.

55 Ah, but a man's reach should exceed his grasp,
Or what's a heaven for?
1855 *Men and Women*, 'Andrea del Sarto', l.97–8.

56 Your ghost will walk, you lover of trees,
(If love remains)
In an English lane.
1855 *Men and Women*, 'De Gustibus'.

57 Open your heart and you will see
graved inside of it, 'Italy.'
Such lovers old are I and she;
So it always was, so it still shall be!
1855 *Men and Women*, 'De Gustibus'.

58 Stand still, true poet that you are!
I know you; let me try and draw you.
Some night you'll fail us: when afar
You rise, remember one man saw you,
Knew you, and named a star!
1855 *Men and Women*, 'Popularity'.

59 I would that you were all to me,
You that are just so much, no more.
1855 *Men and Women*, 'Two in the Campagna'.

60 Only I discern—
Infinite passion, and the pain
Of finite hearts that yearn.
1855 *Men and Women*, 'Two in the Campagna'.

61 There they are, my fifty men and women
Naming me the fifty poems finished!
Take them, Love, the book and me together.
Where the heart lies, let the brain lie also.
1855 *Men and Women*, 'One Word More. To E.B.B.', stanza 1.

62 Suddenly, as rare things will, it vanished.
   1855 *Men and Women*, 'One Word More. To E.B.B.', stanza 4.

63 Dante, who loved well because he hated,
   Hated wickedness that hinders loving.
   1855 *Men and Women*, 'One Word More. To E.B.B.', stanza 5.

64 Proves she like some portent of an iceberg
   Swimming full upon the ship it founders
   Hungry with huge teeth of splintered crystals?
   1855 *Men and Women*, 'One Word More. To E.B.B.', stanza 17.

65 What's come to perfection perishes.
   Things learned on earth, we shall practise in heaven.
   Work done least rapidly, Art most cherishes.
   1855 *Men and Women*, 'One Word More. To E.B.B.', stanza 17.

66 God be thanked, the meanest of his creatures
   Boasts two soul-sides, one to face the world with,
   One to show a woman when he loves her!
   1855 *Men and Women*, 'One Word More. To E.B.B.', stanza 18.

67 Wrote one song—and in my brain I sing it,
   Drew one angel—borne, see, on my bosom!
   1855 *Men and Women*, 'One Word More. To E.B.B.', closing lines.

68 But God has a few of us to whom he whispers in the ear;
   The rest may reason and welcome; 'tis we musicians know.
   1864 *Dramatis Personae*, 'Abt Vogler'.

69 Grow old along with me!
   The best is yet to be,
   The last of life, for which the first was made:
   Our times are in His hand
   Who saith, 'A whole I planned,
   Youth shows but half; trust God:
   See all nor be afraid!'
   1864 *Dramatis Personae*, 'Rabbi ben Ezra', stanza 1.

70 Time's wheels runs back or stops: Potter and clay endure.
   1864 *Dramatis Personae*, 'Rabbi ben Ezra', stanza 27.

71 My times be in Thy hand!
   Perfect the cup as planned!
   Let age approve of youth, and
   Death complete the same!
   1864 *Dramatis Personae*, 'Rabbi ben Ezra', stanza 32.

72 Stung by the splendour of a sudden thought.
   1864 *Dramatis Personae*, 'A Death in the Desert'.

73 For I say, this is death and the sole death,
   When a man's loss comes to him from his gain,
   Darkness from light, from knowledge ignorance,
   And lack of love from love made manifest.
   1864 *Dramatis Personae*, 'A Death in the Desert'.

74 Progress, man's distinctive mark alone,
   Not God's, and not the beasts'; God is, they are,
   Man partly is and wholly hopes to be.
   1864 *Dramatis Personae*, 'A Death in the Desert'.

75 And it is good to cheat the pair, and gibe,
   Letting the rank tongue blossom into speech.
   Setebos, Setebos, and Setebos!
   Thinketh, He dwelleth i' the cold o' the moon.
   Thinketh He made it, with the sun to match,
   But not the stars; the stars came otherwise.
   1864 *Dramatis Personae*, 'Caliban upon Setebos', stanza 1.

76 Let twenty pass, and stone the twenty-first,
   Loving not, hating not, just choosing so.
   1864 *Dramatis Personae*, 'Caliban upon Setebos', stanza 1.

77 We loved, sir—used to meet:
   How sad and bad and mad it was—
   But then, how it was sweet!
   1864 *Dramatis Personae*, 'Confessions', stanza 9.

78 There's more hateful form of foolery—
   The social sage's, Solomon of saloons
   And philosophic diner-out.
   1864 *Dramatis Personae*, 'Mr Sludge, The Medium', stanza 1.

79 Well, British Public, ye who like me not,
   (God love you!)
   1868–9 *The Ring and the Book*, bk.1, l.410

80 'Go get you manned by Manning and new-manned
   By Newman and, mayhap, wise-manned to boot
   By Wiseman.'
   1868–9 *The Ring and the Book*, bk.1, l.444–6.

81 Youth means love,
   Vows can't change nature, priests are only men.
   1868–9 *The Ring and the Book*, bk.1, l.1056–7.

82 O lyric love half angel and half bird
   And all a wonder and a wild desire.
   1868–9 *The Ring and the Book*, bk.1, l.1391–2.

83 In the great right of an excessive wrong.
   1868–9 *The Ring and the Book*, bk.3, l.1055.

84 Faultless to a fault.
   1868–9 *The Ring and the Book*, bk.9, l.1175.

85 Why comes temptation but for a man to meet
   And master and make crouch beneath his foot,
   And so be pedestalled in triumph?
   1868–9 *The Ring and the Book*, bk.10, l.1184–6.

86 White shall not neutralize the black, nor good
   Compensate bad in man, absolve him so:
   Life's business being just the terrible choice.
   1868–9 *The Ring and the Book*, bk.10, l.1235–7.

87 There's a new tribunal now
   Higher than God's,—the educated man's!
   1868–9 *The Ring and the Book*, bk.10, l.1975–6.

88 Into that sad obscure sequestered state
   Where God unmakes but to remake the soul
   He else made first in vain; which must not be.
   1868–9 *The Ring and the Book*, bk.10, l.2129–31.

89 It is the glory and good of Art,
   That Art remains the one way possible
   Of speaking truth, to mouths like mine, at least.
   1868–9 *The Ring and the Book*, bk.12, l.838–40.

90 But, thanks to wine-less and democracy,
   We've still our stage where truth calls spade a spade!
   1875 'Aristophanes' Apology', stanza 1.

91 Ignorance is not innocence but sin.
   1875 *The Inn Album*, canto 5.

92 I want to know a butcher paints,
   A baker rhymes for his pursuit,
   Candlestick-maker much acquaints
   His soul with song, or, haply mute,
   Blows out his brains upon the flute.
   1876 'Shop', stanza 21.

93 Good, to forgive;
   Best, to forget!
   Living, we fret;
   Dying, we live.
   1878 *La Saisiaz*, prologue.

94 At midnight in the silence of the sleep-time,
When you set your fancies free.
1889 *Asolando*, epilogue.

95 One who never turned his back but marched breast
forward,
Never doubted clouds would break,
Never dreamed, though right were worsted, wrong
would triumph,
Held we fall to rise, are baffled to fight better,
Sleep to wake.
1889 *Asolando*, epilogue.

96 Greet the unseen with a cheer!
1889 *Asolando*, epilogue.

Broyard, Anatole 1920–90

Literary critic, writer and editor at the *New York Times*.

97 She has always ridden the passions as if they were a
magnificent horse.
1978 On Edna O'Brien. In the *New York Times*, 1 Jan.

98 Such a fatigue of adjectives, a drone of alliterations, a
huffing of hyphenated words hurdling the meter like
tired horses. Such a faded upholstery of tears, stars,
bells, bones, flood and blood…a thud of consonants in
tongue, night, dark, dust, seed, wound and wind.
1974 On Dylan Thomas's poetry. *Aroused by Books*.

99 I remember a table in *Barchester Towers* that had more
character than the combined heroes of three recent
novels I've read.
1974 *Aroused by Books*.

1 When Harriet goes to bed with a man, she always takes
her wet blanket with her.
1974 On a character in Iris Owen's *After Claude* (1973). *Aroused
by Books*.

2 Chic is a convent for unloved women.
1988 In the *New York Times*, 10 Jan.

Brummel, George Bryan *called* *Beau Brummell* 1778–1840

English dandy, a leader of 19c fashionable society. A close friend
of the Prince Regent (later George IV), he quarrelled with him in
1813, and was later forced to flee to Calais with gambling debts.
He died a pauper in a lunatic asylum.

3 Who's your fat friend?
c.1813 Of the Prince Regent. Remark addressed to his
companion, whom the Prince had acknowledged while
studiously ignoring Brummell. Quoted in Jesse *Life of George
Brummell* (1844), vol.1.

Brunet, Michel 1917–85

Canadian historian.

4 The thing which amazes me is that I know perfectly well,
as a historian, that there is corruption in any
government—there's always corruption. It's bad when
it's more than fifteen percent.
Interviewed by Ramsay Cook in Eleanor Cook (ed) *The Craft of
History* (1973).

Brunner, John Kilian Houston 1934–95

English science-fiction writer, an important contributor to the
more literary aspirations of the genre. *Stand On Zanzibar* (1969)
is his best-known work.

5 POPULATION EXPLOSION Unique in human experience, an
event which happened yesterday but which everyone
swears won't happen until tomorrow.
1969 *Stand On Zanzibar*, 'The Hipcrime Vocab'.

Bruno, Frank(lin Roy) 1961–

English boxer. He won the European heavyweight title in 1985,
and the World Championship in 1995.

6 Know what I mean, Harry?
Catchphrase, addressed to sports commentator Harry Carpenter.

Bryan, Richard H(udson) 1937–

US politician, Governor of Nevada (1983–9) and Senator
(1989–2001).

7 Being chairman of the Senate Ethics Committee is like
jumping off a cliff. The thrill is very short.
1993 NPR broadcast, 2 Nov.

Bryan, William Jennings 1860–1925

US lawyer, Democratic politician and pacifist. Elected to
Congress in 1890, he ran unsuccessfully in two presidential
elections (1896, 1900). Appointed Secretary of State by
Woodrow Wilson (1913), he resigned in 1915 over the USA's
second *Lusitania* note to Germany.

8 There are two ideas of government. There are those who
believe that, if you will only legislate to make the well-to-
do prosperous, their prosperity will leak through on
those below. The Democratic idea, however, has been
that if you legislate to make the masses prosperous, their
prosperity will find its way up through every class which
rests upon them.
1896 Speech at the Democratic National Convention, 10 Jul.

9 What shall we say of the intelligence, not to say religion,
of those who are so particular to distinguish between
fishes and reptiles and birds, but put a man with an
immortal soul in the same circle with the wolf, the hyena,
and the skunk? What must be the impression made upon
children by such a degradation of man?
Statement issued in Dayton, Tennessee, 28 Jul 1925, by Mrs W J
Bryan, shortly after the end of the Scopes trial and her husband's
death.

Bryant, David 1931–

English bowls player. He was the World Singles Champion in
1966, 1980 and 1988.

10 I'm not an athlete, more a gymnast and golfer, soldered
together.
Quoted in Colin Jarman *The Guinness Dictionary of Sports
Quotations* (1990).

11 Bowls is a young man's game which old men can play.
Quoted in Colin Jarman *The Guinness Dictionary of Sports
Quotations* (1990).

Bryant, William Cullen 1794–1878

US writer and journalist. Originally a lawyer, after the success of
Thanatopsis (1817) he turned increasingly to prose and verse
writing, becoming editor of the New York *Evening Post* (1829).

12 All that tread
The globe are but a handful to the tribes
That slumber in its bosom.
1817 'Thanatopsis', in the *North American Review*, Sep.

13 These are the gardens of the Desert, these
The unshorn fields, boundless and beautiful,
For which the speech of England has no name—
The Prairies.
1832 *Poems*, 'The Prairies'.

Bryson, Bill 1951–

US author, particularly known for his humorous travel memoirs.

14 My mother only ever said two things. She said, 'I don't know, dear.' And she said, 'Can I get you a sandwich, honey?'
1989 *The Lost Continent*, ch.1.

15 There are three things you just can't do in life. You can't beat the phone company, you can't make a waiter see you until he's ready to see you, and you can't go home again.
1989 *The Lost Continent*, ch.2.

16 It sometimes occurs to me that the British have more heritage than is good for them.
1995 *Notes from a Small Island*.

17 I have a small tattered clipping that I sometimes carry with me and pull out for purposes of private amusement. It's a weather forecast from the *Western Daily Mail* and it says, in toto: 'Outlook: Dry and warm, but cooler with some rain.'
1995 *Notes from a Small Island*.

18 Hunters will tell you that a moose is a wily and ferocious forest creature. In fact, a moose is a cow drawn by a three-year-old.
1998 *Notes from a Big Country*.

19 He was the only person in American history for whom attaining the White House was a bad career move.
1998 On Herbert Hoover. *Notes from a Big Country*.

20 In the first three months of this year the US edition of *Time* did not have a single report from France, Italy, Spain or Japan, to name just a few of the countries that seem to have escaped its notice.
1998 *Notes from a Big Country*.

21 According to an opinion poll, 13 per cent of women in the United States cannot say whether they wear their tights under their knickers or over them. That's something like a million women walking around in a state of chronic foundation garment uncertainty.
1998 *Notes from a Big Country*.

Buber, Martin 1878–1965

Austrian Jewish theologian and philosopher, founding editor of *Der Jude* (1916–24, 'The Jew'), known for his important studies in Hasidism and Existentialism. Professor at Frankfurt (1923–33), he fled Germany for Palestine in 1938, becoming Professor of the Sociology of Religion in Jerusalem.

22 Egos appear by setting themselves apart from other egos. Persons appear by entering into relation with other persons.
1923 *Ich und Du* (translated by R G Smith as *I and Thou*, 1936).

23 *Jedes geeinzelte Du ist ein Durchblick zu ihm. Durch jedes geeinzelte Du spricht das Grundwort das Ewige an.* Every particular *Thou* is a glimpse through to the eternal *Thou*; by means of every particular *Thou* the primary word addresses the eternal *Thou*.
1923 *Ich und Du* (translated by R G Smith as *I and Thou*, 1936).

Buchan, John, 1st Baron Tweedsmuir 1875–1940

Scottish author and statesman, best known for his fast-moving adventure stories, particularly *The Thirty-Nine Steps* (1915). He was Governor-General of Canada from 1935 until his death.

24 You think that a wall as solid as the earth separates civilisation from barbarism. I tell you the division is a thread, a sheet of glass.
1916 *The Power-House*, ch.3, 'Tells of a Midsummer Night'.

25 Civilisation is a conspiracy.
1916 *The Power-House*, ch.3, 'Tells of a Midsummer Night'.

26 It's a great life if you don't weaken.
1919 *Mr Standfast*, ch.5.

27 Look at the Irish! They are the cleverest propagandists extant, and managed to persuade most people that they were a brave, generous, humorous, talented, warm-hearted race, cruelly yoked to a dull mercantile England, when, God knows, they were exactly the opposite.
1924 *The Three Hostages*.

28 To live for a time close to great minds is the best kind of education.
1940 *Memory Hold-the-Door*, ch.2.

29 An atheist is a man who has no invisible means of support.
1943 Quoted in H E Fosdick *On Being a Real Person*, ch.10.

Buchanan, James 1791–1868

US statesman and 15th President (1857–61). A Democrat, he tried to maintain a balance between pro-slavery and anti-slavery factions, but was unable to avert the Civil War (1861–5).

30 All the friends that I loved and wanted to reward are dead, and all the enemies that I hated and I had marked out for punishment are turned to my friends.
1857 On finally achieving his country's highest political office at the age of 65.

31 If you are as happy, my dear Sir, on entering this house as I am on leaving it and returning home, you are the happiest man in the country.
1861 Said on welcoming his successor, Abraham Lincoln, to the White House.

Buchman, Sidney 1902–75

US film writer and producer. His films include *Mr Smith Goes to Washington* (1939), *Here Comes Mr Jordan* (1941) and *The Group* (1966).

32 I wouldn't give you two cents for all your fancy rules if, behind them, they didn't have a little bit of plain, ordinary kindness—and a little looking out for the other fella, too.
1939 Line delivered by James Stewart in *Mr Smith Goes to Washington*.

Buchwald, Art 1925–

US writer and humorist. He won a Pulitzer Prize for outstanding commentary (1982).

33 This is not an easy time for humorists because the government is far funnier than we are.
1987 Speech to international meeting of satirists and cartoonists. Reported in the *New York Times*, 28 Jun.

Buck, Gene (Edward Eugene) 1885–1957

US songwriter.

34 That Shakespearian rag,—
Most intelligent, very elegant.
1912 'That Shakespearian Rag' (with Herman Ruby).
➤ *See Eliot 306:57.*

Buck, Pearl née *Sydenstricker* 1892–1973

US novelist, brought up in China and later a teacher and missionary there. Her works include *The Good Earth* (1931), set in China. She won the Nobel prize for literature in 1938.

35 Race prejudice is not only a shadow over the colored—it is a shadow over all of us, and the shadow is darkest over those who feel it least and allow its evil effects to go on.
1943 *What America Means To Me*, ch.1.

36 None who have always been free can understand the terrible fascinating power of the hope of freedom to those who are not free.
1943 *What America Means To Me*, ch.4.

37 Every great mistake has a halfway moment, a split second when it can be recalled and perhaps remedied.
1943 *What America Means To Me*, ch.10.

38 Praise out of season, or tactlessly bestowed, can freeze the heart as much as blame.
1967 *To My Daughters, With Love*, 'First Meeting'.

39 Nothing and no one can destroy the Chinese people. They are relentless survivors... They yield, they bend to the wind, but they never break.
1972 *China, Past and Present*, ch.1.

Bucke, Richard Maurice 1837–1902

Canadian psychiatrist and author. His works include *Cosmic Consciousness: A Study in the Evolution of the Human Mind* (1901).

40 Cosmic consciousness.
1894 Phrase first used in a paper read by Bucke to the American Medico-Psychological Association, Philadelphia, 18 May. He defined it as 'a higher form of consciousness than that possessed by the ordinary man'.

Buckingham, George Villiers, 2nd Duke of 1628–87

English statesman, exiled after the Royalist defeat in the Civil War. He became a member of Charles II's cabal after the Restoration, and was instrumental in Clarendon's downfall (1667), but lost power and was dismissed in 1674.

41 Ay, now the plot thickens very much upon us.
1672 *The Rehearsal*, act 3, sc.1.

42 The world is made up for the most part of fools and knaves.
'To Mr Clifford, on his *Humane Reason*', collected in *The Dramatic Works* (1715), vol.2.

Buechner, (Carl) Frederick 1926–

US clergyman, novelist, poet and essayist. His works include *Lion Country* (1971) and *Godric* (1980).

43 Glory is to God what style is to an artist... To behold God's glory, to sense his style, is the closest you can get this side of Paradise, just as to read King Lear is the closest you can get to Shakespeare.
1973 *Wishful Thinking*.

44 There is no event so commonplace but that God is present in it, always hiddenly, always leaving you room to recognize him or not to recognize him... Listen to your life. See it for the fathomless mystery it is. In the boredom and pain of it no less than in the excitement and gladness: touch, taste, smell your way to the heavenly and hidden heart of it because in the last analysis all moments are key moments, and life itself is grace.
1983 *Now and Then*.

Buffett, Warren Edward 1930–

US investment broker and corporate executive.

45 It is better to be approximately right than precisely wrong.
1994 In *Fortune*, 4 Apr.

Buford, Bill (William Holmes) 1954–

US-born editor and writer who has spent much of his career in Britain. He edited *Granta* (1979–95), then moved to the *New Yorker* as Fiction and Literary Editor (1995–2002) and became its European Correspondent in 2002.

46 I found myself growing increasingly irritated with the notion of a British novel, which was really an irritation with the word British, a grey, unsatisfactory, bad-weather kind of word, a piece of linguistic compromise.
1994 Editorial, *Granta*, no.43.

Bukowski, Charles 1920–94

German-born US poet and writer. His spare, sardonic writing evoked a seamy, low-life urban netherworld in poems, short stories and novels.

47 Show me a man who lives alone and has a perpetually clean kitchen, and 8 times out of 9 I'll show you a man with detestable spiritual qualities.
1967 *Tales of Ordinary Madness*, 'Too Sensitive'.

48 You begin saving the world by saving one man at a time; all else is grandiose romanticism or politics.
1967 *Tales of Ordinary Madness*, 'Too Sensitive'.

49 Erections, Ejaculations, Exhibitions and General Tales of Ordinary Madness.
1972 Title of book.

50 Love is a Dog from Hell.
1977 Title of book.

51 Play the Piano Drunk Like a Percussion Instrument Until the Fingers Begin to Bleed a Bit.
1979 Title of book.

Buller, A(rthur) H(enry) Reginald 1874–1944

Canadian botanist, Professor of Botany at the University of Manitoba.

52 There was a young lady named Bright
Whose speed was far faster than light;
She set out one day
In a relative way
And returned on the previous night.
1923 'Relativity', published anonymously in *Punch*, 19 Dec. Buller's claim to authorship is recorded in W S Baring-Gould *The Lure of the Limerick* (1968).

Bullock, Alan Louis Charles, Baron Bullock
1914–2004

British historian, notably of 20c Europe. He was Master of St Catherine's College, Oxford (1960–80).

53 Hitler showed surprising loyalty to Mussolini, but it never extended to trusting him.
1952 *Hitler: A Study in Tyranny.*

54 The people Hitler never understood, and whose actions continued to exasperate him to the end of his life, were the British.
1952 *Hitler: A Study in Tyranny.*

Bulmer-Thomas, Ivor 1905–93

British politician and writer. He joined *The Times* (1930–7) and was later deputy editor of the *Daily Telegraph* (1953–4). He entered parliament as a Labour MP in 1942, turning Conservative in 1949.

55 If he ever went to school without any boots, it was because he was too big for them.
1949 At the Conservative Party conference, responding to remarks by Harold Wilson about his humble upbringing.
➤ *See Wilson 915:89.*

Bülow, Prince Bernhard Heinrich von 1849–1929

German statesman, Chancellor (1900–9), Foreign Secretary (1897), Count (1899) and Prince (1905). He wrote *Imperial Germany* (translated 1916) and *Memoirs* (translated 1931–2).

56 *Mit einem Worte: wir wollen niemand in den Schatten stellen aber wir verlangen auch unseren Platz an der Sonne.*
In a word, we desire to throw no one into the shade, but we also demand our own place in the sun.
1897 Speech to the Reichstag, 6 Dec.

Bulwer-Lytton, Edward George Lytton, 1st Baron Lytton 1803–73

English writer and politician, known for historical novels such as *The Last Days of Pompeii* (1834), poetry and several plays. A Reform MP (1831–41), he returned as a Conservative in 1852.

57 It was a dark and stormy night.
1830 Opening words of *Paul Clifford.*

58 Beneath the rule of men entirely great, the pen is mightier than the sword.
1839 *Richelieu*, act 2, sc.2.

Bunting, Basil 1900–85

English poet. He was encouraged by Pound and worked with Ford Madox Ford on *The Transatlantic Review*, but never found a wide audience. The long poem *Briggflatts* (1966) is his best-known work.

59 Our doom
is, to be sifted by the wind,

heaped up, smoothed down like silly sands.
We are less permanent than thought.
1925 *Villon*, pt.1.

60 Name and date
split in soft slate
a few months obliterate.
1966 *Briggflatts.*

61 It looks well enough on the page, but never well enough.
1966 *Briggflatts.*

62 Clear Cymric voices carry well this Autumn night,
Aneurin and Taliesin, cruel owls
for whom it is never altogether dark
before the rules made poetry a pedant's game.
1966 *Briggflatts.*

63 Who
swinging his axe
to fell kings,
guesses
where we go?
1966 *Briggflatts*, coda.

Buñuel, Luis 1900–83

Spanish film director, who was successful with early surrealist experiments in collaboration with Dalí. His work is characterized by a poetic, often erotic, use of imagery, black humour and a hatred of Catholicism.

64 *Grâce à Dieu, je suis toujours athée.*
Thanks be to God, I am still an atheist.
1959 In *Le Monde*, 16 Dec.

65 *Le Charme discret de la bourgeoisie.*
The Discreet Charm of the Bourgeoisie.
1972 Title of film.

Bunyan, John 1628–88

English writer and preacher. His father was a tinker and he received little formal education. His works, including an autobiography *Grace Abounding to the Chief of Sinners* (1666) and probably most of *The Pilgrim's Progress* (1st part 1678, 2nd part 1684), were written while imprisoned for nonconformity.

66 Oh, the diligence of Satan! Oh, the desperateness of man's heart!
1666 *Grace Abounding to the Chief of Sinners.*

67 This miry slough, is such a place as cannot be mended: It is the descent whither the scum and filth that attends conviction for sin doth continually run, and therefore is it called the Slough of Despond.
1678 *The Pilgrim's Progress*, pt.1.

68 The valley of Humiliation.
1678 *The Pilgrim's Progress*, pt.1.

69 It beareth the name of Vanity-Fair, because the town where 'tis kept, is lighter than vanity.
1678 *The Pilgrim's Progress*, pt.1.

70 Hanging is too good for him, said Mr Cruelty.
1678 *The Pilgrim's Progress*, pt 1.

71 Now Giant Despair had a wife, and her name was Diffidence.
1678 *The Pilgrim's Progress*, pt.1.

72 Sleep is sweet to the labouring man.
1678 *The Pilgrim's Progress*, pt.1.

73 So I awoke, and behold it was a dream.
1678 *The Pilgrim's Progress*, pt.1.

74 A man that could look no way but downwards, with a muckrake in his hand.
1684 *The Pilgrim's Progress*, pt.2.

75 For though when he was here, he was Fool in every man's mouth, yet now he is gone he is highly

commended of all.
1684 *The Pilgrim's Progress*, pt.2.

76 He that is down needs fear no fall,
He that is low no pride.
He that is humble ever shall
Have God to be his guide.
1684 *The Pilgrim's Progress*, pt.2.

77 My Sword, I give to him that shall succeed me in my Pilgrimage, and my Courage and Skill, to him that can get it. My Marks and Scars I carry with me, to be a witness for me, that I have fought his Battles, who now will be my Rewarder… As he went, he said, Death, where is thy Sting? And as he went down deeper, he said, Grave where is thy Victory? So he passed over, and the Trumpets sounded for him on the other side.
1684 *Mr Valiant-for-Glory. The Pilgrim's Progress*, pt.2.

78 He that lives in sin and looks for happiness hereafter is like him that soweth cockle and thinks to fill his barn with wheat or barley.
1684 *The Pilgrim's Progress*, pt.2.

Burbank, Luther 1849–1926

US plant breeder and natural scientist.

79 Science is knowledge arranged and classified according to truth, facts, and the general laws of nature.
1926 Interview in the *San Francisco Bulletin*, 22 Jan.

Burchard, Samuel Dickinson 1812–91

US Presbyterian minister and staunch Republican supporter.

80 The party whose antecedents are rum, Romanism, and rebellion.
1884 Of the Democratic party. Speech at the Fifth Avenue Hotel, New York City, 29 Oct.

Burgess, Anthony *real name* John Anthony Burgess Wilson 1917–94

English writer. He is widely regarded as among the most important novelists of his generation, notably for his controversial dystopian novel *A Clockwork Orange* (1962).

81 Who ever heard of a clockwork orange? Then I read a malenky bit out loud in a sort of very high type preaching goloss: 'The attempt to impose upon man, a creature of growth and capable of sweetness, to ooze juicily at the last round the bearded lips of God, to attempt to impose, I say, laws and conditions appropriate to a mechanical creation, against this I raise my sword-pen.'
1962 *A Clockwork Orange*.

82 He said it was artificial respiration, but now I find I am to have his child.
1963 *Inside Mr Enderby*, pt.1, ch.4.

83 Bath twice a day to be really clean, once a day to be passably clean, once a week to avoid being a public menace.
1963 *Inside Mr Enderby*, pt.2, ch.1.

84 Rome's just a city like anywhere else. A vastly overrated city, I'd say. It trades on belief just as Stratford trades on Shakespeare.
1963 *Inside Mr Enderby*, pt.2, ch.1.

85 *Pax Romana*. Where they made a desolation they called

it a peace. What absolute nonsense! It was a nasty, vulgar sort of civilization, only dignified by being hidden under a lot of declensions.
1963 *Inside Mr Enderby*, pt.2, ch.2.

86 Keep away from physicians. It is all probing and guessing and pretending to them. They leave it to Nature to cure in her own time, but they take the credit. As well as very fat fees.
1964 *Nothing Like the Sun*.

87 The possession of a book becomes a substitute for reading it.
1966 In the *New York Times Book Review*, 4 Dec.

88 A sure sign of an amateur is too much detail to compensate for too little life.
1971 In the *Times Literary Supplement*, 18 Jun.

89 Death comes along like a gas bill one can't pay—and that's all one can say about it.
1974 Interview in *Playboy*.

90 There is usually something wrong with writers the young like.
1974 Interview in *Playboy*.

91 It was the afternoon of my eighty-first birthday, and I was in bed with my catamite when Ali announced that the archbishop had come to see me.
1980 *Earthly Powers*, opening lines.

92 Reality is what I see, not what you see.
1983 In the *Sunday Times Magazine*, 18 Dec.

93 God was good on the physical and emotional sides and a great one for hate. He generously spilled his own hate into his dearest creation.
1984 *Enderby's Dark Lady*.

94 If Freud had worn a kilt in the prescribed Highland manner he might have had a very different attitude to genitals.
1986 In the *Observer*, 24 Aug.

95 Death, like the quintessence of otherness, is for others.
1987 *Little Wilson and Big God*, ch.6.

96 Music says nothing to the reason: it is a kind of closely structured nonsense.
1989 In the *Observer*, 23 Jul.

97 I could see now that a literary education did not fit one for the popular novelist's trade. Once you had started using words like flavicomous or acroamatic, because you liked the sound of them, you were lost.
1990 *You've Had Your Time*, ch.1.

Burgon, John William 1813–88

English cleric, Dean of Chichester from 1876.

98 Match me such marvel, save in Eastern clime,—
A rose-red city—'half as old as Time'!
1845 *Petra*.

Burke, Edmund 1729–97

Anglo-Irish statesman and political philosopher. He became Secretary for Ireland (1759) and an MP (1765). His works include *Reflections on the French Revolution* (1790).

99 No passion so effectually robs the mind of all its powers of acting than fear.
1757 *On the Sublime and Beautiful*, pt.2, section 2.

1 Custom reconciles us to everything.
    1757 *On the Sublime and Beautiful*, pt.4, section 18.

2 It is a general popular error to imagine the loudest complainers for the public to be the most anxious for its welfare.
    1769 *Observations on a Late Publication on the Present State of the Nation*, 2nd edn.

3 To complain of the age we live in, to murmur at the present possessors of power, to lament the past, to conceive extravagant hopes of the future, are the common dispositions of the greatest part of mankind.
    1770 *Thoughts on the Cause of the Present Discontents.*

4 When bad men combine, the good must associate; else they will fall, one by one, an unpitied sacrifice in a contemptible struggle.
    1770 *Thoughts on the Cause of the Present Discontents.*

5 It is therefore our business carefully to cultivate in our minds, to rear to the most perfect vigour and maturity, every sort of generous and honest feeling that belongs to our nature. To bring the dispositions that are loved in private life into the service and conduct of the commonwealth; so to be patriots, as not to forget we are gentlemen.
    1770 *Thoughts on the Cause of the Present Discontents.*

6 The greater the power, the more dangerous is the abuse.
    1771 Speech on the Middlesex Election, House of Commons, 7 Feb.

7 Parliament is a deliberative assembly of one nation. You choose a Member indeed; but when you have chosen him, he is not the Member for Bristol, but he is a Member of Parliament.
    1774 Speech to Bristol voters.

8 The concessions of the weak are the concessions of fear.
    1775 *On Conciliation with America.*

9 The use of force alone is but temporary. It may subdue for a moment; but it does not remove the necessity of subduing again; and a nation is not governed, which is perpetually to be conquered.
    1775 *On Conciliation with America.*

10 Nothing less will content me, than *whole America*.
    1775 *On Conciliation with America.*

11 All Protestantism, even the most cold and passive, is a sort of dissent. But the religion most prevalent in our northern colonies is a refinement on the principle of resistance; it is the dissidence of dissent, and the Protestantism of the Protestant religion.
    1775 *On Conciliation with America.*

12 It is not, what a lawyer tells me I may do; but what humanity, reason, and justice, tells me I ought to do.
    1775 *On Conciliation with America.*

13 Freedom and not servitude is the cure of anarchy; as religion, and not atheism, is the true remedy for superstition.
    1775 *On Conciliation with America.*

14 Slavery they can have anywhere. It is a weed that grows in every soil.
    1775 *On Conciliation with America.*

15 It is the love of the people; it is their attachment to their government, from the sense of the deep stake they have in such a glorious institution, which gives you your army and your navy, and infuses into both that liberal obedience, without which your army would be a base rabble, and your navy nothing but rotten timber.
    1775 *On Conciliation with America.*

16 A great empire and little minds go ill together.
    1775 *On Conciliation with America.*

17 All government, indeed every human benefit and enjoyment, every virtue and every prudent act, is founded on compromise and barter.
    1775 *On Conciliation with America.*

18 Between craft and credulity, the voice of reason is stifled.
    1777 *Letter to the Sheriffs of Bristol.*

19 Liberty too must be limited in order to be possessed.
    1777 *Letter to the Sheriffs of Bristol.*

20 Among a people generally corrupt, liberty cannot long exist.
    1777 *Letter to the Sheriffs of Bristol.*

21 If any man ask me what a free government is, I answer that for any practical purpose, it is what the people think it so.
    1777 *Letter to the Sheriffs of Bristol.*

22 People crushed by law have no hope but from power. If laws are their enemies, they will be enemies to laws; and those, who have much to hope and nothing to lose, will always be dangerous, more or less.
    1777 Letter to Charles James Fox, 8 Oct.

23 Individuals pass like shadows, but the Commonwealth is fixed and stable.
    1780 Speech, House of Commons, 11 Feb.

24 The people are the masters.
    1780 Speech, House of Commons, 11 Feb.

25 Bad laws are the worst sort of tyranny.
    1780 Speech, Bristol.

26 He was not merely a chip off the old block, but the old block itself.
    1781 Commenting on William Pitt the Younger's maiden speech in the House of Commons, 26 Feb.

27 The people never give up their liberties but under some delusion.
    1784 Speech, Buckinghamshire.

28 Whenever our neighbour's house is on fire, it cannot be amiss for the engines to play a little on our own.
    1790 *Reflections on the Revolution in France.*

29 A state without the means of some change is without the means of its conservation.
    1790 *Reflections on the Revolution in France.*

30 People will not look forward to posterity, who never look backward to their ancestors.
    1790 *Reflections on the Revolution in France.*

31 Those who attempt to level never equalize.
    1790 *Reflections on the Revolution in France.*

32 Whatever each man can separately do, without trespassing upon others, he has a right to do for himself; and he has a right to a fair portion of all which society, with all its combination of skill and force, can do in his favour.
    1790 *Reflections on the Revolution in France.*

33 Government is a contrivance of human wisdom to provide for human wants.
    1790 *Reflections on the Revolution in France.*

34 The age of chivalry is gone.—That of sophisters, economists, and calculators, has succeeded; and the glory of Europe is extinguished for ever.
1790 *Reflections on the Revolution in France.*

35 The unbought grace of life, the cheap defence of nations, the nurse of manly sentiment and heroic enterprise is gone! it is gone, that sensibility of principle, that chastity of honour, which felt a stain like a wound, which ennobled whatever it touched, and under which vice itself lost half its evil, by losing all its grossness.
1790 *Reflections on the Revolution in France.*

36 In the groves of their academy, at the end of every vista, you see nothing but the gallows.
1790 *Reflections on the Revolution in France.*

37 Kings will be tyrants from policy when subjects are rebels from principle.
1790 *Reflections on the Revolution in France.*

38 Man is by his constitution a religious animal; atheism is against not only our reason, but our instincts.
1790 *Reflections on the Revolution in France.*

39 Society is indeed a contract…it becomes a partnership not only between those who are living, but between those who are living, those who are dead, and those who are to be born.
1790 *Reflections on the Revolution in France.*

40 Superstition is the religion of feeble minds.
1790 *Reflections on the Revolution in France.*

41 Our patience will achieve more than our force.
1790 *Reflections on the Revolution in France.*

42 By hating vices too much, they come to love men too little.
1790 *Reflections on the Revolution in France.*

43 We begin our public affection in our families. No cold relation is a zealous citizen.
1790 *Reflections on the Revolution in France.*

44 Good order is the foundation of all good things.
1790 *Reflections on the Revolution in France.*

45 The only infallible criterion of wisdom to vulgar judgements—success.
1791 *Letter to a Member of the National Assembly.*

46 Tyrants seldom want pretexts.
1791 *Letter to a Member of the National Assembly.*

47 Somebody has said, that a king may make a nobleman but he cannot make a gentleman.
1795 Letter to William Smith, 29 Jan.

48 And having looked to government for bread, on the very first scarcity they will turn and bite the hand that fed them. To avoid that evil, government will redouble the causes of it; and then it will become inveterate and incurable.
1795 *Thoughts and Details on Scarcity,* Nov (published 1800).

49 To innovate is not to reform.
1796 *A Letter to a Noble Lord.*

50 All men that are ruined are ruined on the side of their natural propensities.
1796 *Two Letters on the Proposals for Peace with the Regicide Directory,* 9th edn.

51 Example is the school of mankind, and they will learn at no other.

1796 *Two Letters on the Proposals for Peace with the Regicide Directory,* 9th edn.

52 It is necessary only for the good man to do nothing for evil to triumph.
Attributed.

Burke, Johnny   1908–64

US lyricist.

53 Every time it rains, it rains
Pennies from heaven.
1936 'Pennies from Heaven'.
➤ *See also Thatcher 850:18.*

54 Like Webster's dictionary, we're Morocco bound.
1942 Title song in *Road to Morocco,* sung by Bing Crosby and Bob Hope. Music by Jimmy Van Heusen.

55 Or would you like to swing on a star
Carry moonbeams home in a jar
And be better off than you are
Or would you rather be a fish?
1944 *Swinging on a Star,* sung by Bing Crosby in the film *Going My Way.* Music by Jimmy Van Heusen.

Burke, Kathy   1964–

English actress.

56 If they want rough, then I get the phone call.
1997 In the *Observer,* 5 Jan.

Burke, Kenneth   1897–1986

US music and literary critic. His theory of literature as 'symbolic action' was very influential.

57 Any performance is discussable from the standpoint of what it *attains* or what it *misses.* Comprehensiveness can be discussed as superficiality, intensiveness as stricture, tolerance as uncertainty—and the poor *pedestrian* abilities of a fish are clearly explainable in terms of his excellence as a *swimmer.* A way of seeing is also a way of not seeing.
1936 *Permanence and Change.*

Burke, Tim(othy)   c.1942–

Canadian newspaper columnist.

58 There are no lapsed Catholics after a Christmas concert by Pavarotti.
1987 In *The Montreal Gazette,* 8 Dec.

Burns, Ken Lauren   1953–

US film-maker and historian. He has won numerous awards for documentary and historical films on aspects of American life.

59 We are a people starved for self-definition.
1991 On the success of his 11-hour television documentary *The Civil War.* In *People,* 7 Jan.

Burns, Robert   1759–96

Scottish poet and songwriter, the son of a farmer. The Kilmarnock edition (1786) of his poems made his name, and his skill at providing lyrics for old Scottish airs assured his place as one of the world's most popular poets and as his country's national bard. His influence in promoting Scots in literature was enormous.

60 Green grow the rashes, O;
Green grow the rashes, O;
The sweetest hours that e'er I spend,
Are spent amang the lasses, O.
1784 'Green grow the Rashes. A Fragment', chorus.

61 What signifies the life o' man,
An 'twere na for the lasses, O.
1784 'Green grow the Rashes. A Fragment', stanza 1.

62 If honest Nature made you *fools*,
What sairs your grammars.
1785 'Epistle to J. Lapraik, An Old Scotch Bard, 1 April 1785',
stanza 11.

63 They *gang* in Stirks, and *come out* Asses,
Plain truth to speak;
An' syne they think to climb Parnassus
By dint o' Greek!
1785 'Epistle to J. Lapraik, An Old Scotch Bard, 1 April 1785',
stanza 12.

64 Gie me ae spark o' Nature's fire,
That's a' the learning I desire.
1785 'Epistle to J. Lapraik, An Old Scotch Bard, 1 April 1785',
stanza 13.

65 O Thou that in the heavens does dwell!
Wha, as it pleases best Thysel,
Sends ane to heaven, an' ten to hell,
A' for Thy glory,
And no for ony gude or ill
They've done before Thee!
1785 'Holy Willie's Prayer', stanza 1.

66 My curse upon your whunstane hearts,
Ye Enbrugh Gentry!
The tythe o' what ye waste at *cartes*
Wad stow'd his pantry!
1785 'To W. Simpson, Ochiltree', stanza 4, referring to the poet
Robert Fergusson, who died a pauper in the Edinburgh bedlam
in 1774 at the age of 24, and whom Burns considered 'my elder
brother in misfortune, by far my elder brother in the muse'.

67 Some books are lies frae end to end,
And some great lies were never penn'd.
1785 'Death and Doctor Hornbook. A True Story', stanza 1.

68 I was na fou, but just had plenty.
1785 'Death and Doctor Hornbook. A True Story', stanza 3.

69 There's some are fou o' *love divine*;
There's some are fou o' *brandy*.
1785 'The Holy Fair', stanza 27.

70 From scenes like these, old SCOTIA's grandeur springs,
That makes her lov'd at home, rever'd abroad:
Princes and lords are but the breath of kings,
'An honest man's the noble work of GOD'.
1785 'The Cotter's Saturday Night', stanza 19. The last line is in
fact a misquotation of Pope; 'noble' was corrected to 'noblest' in
the 1794 edition of Burns's poems.
➤ *See Pope 660:25.*

71 Wee, sleeket, cowrin, tim'rous *beastie*,
O, what a panic's in thy breastie!
Thou need na start awa sae hasty
Wi' bickering brattle!
I wad be laith to rin an' chase thee,
Wi' murd'ring *pattle*!
1785 'To A Mouse, On turning her up in her Nest with the Plough,
November, 1785', stanza 1.

72 The best-laid schemes o' *Mice* an' *Men*

Gang aft a-gley.
1785 'To A Mouse, On turning her up in her Nest with the Plough,
November, 1785', stanza 7.

73 A fig for those by law protected!
Liberty's a glorious feast!
Courts for Cowards were erected,
Churches built to please the Priest.
c.1786 'The Jolly Beggars', or 'Love and Liberty, a Cantata',
chorus to a song to the tune 'Jolly Mortals, fill your glasses'.

74 His lockèd, letter'd, braw brass-collar,
Show'd him the *gentleman* an' *scholar*.
1786 'The Twa Dogs'.

75 The tither was a *ploughman's collie*,
A rhyming, ranting, raving billie.
1786 'The Twa Dogs'.

76 FREEDOM and WHISKY gang thegither,
Tak aff your *dram!*
1786 'The Author's Earnest Cry and Prayer, to the Right
Honorable and Honorable, the Scotch Representatives in the
House of Commons', stanza 30.

77 O Thou, whatever title suit thee!
Auld Hornie, Satan, Nick, or Clootie.
1786 'Address to the Deil', stanza 1.

78 An' now, auld *Cloots*, I ken ye're thinkan,
A certain *Bardie's* rantin, drinkin,
Some luckless hour will send him linkan,
To your black pit;
But faith! he'll turn a corner jinkan,
An' cheat you yet.
1786 'Address to the Deil', stanza 20.

79 But *Facts* are cheels that winna ding,
And downa be disputed.
1786 'A Dream', stanza 4.

80 Man's inhumanity to Man
Makes countless thousands mourn!
1786 'Man was made to Mourn, A Dirge', stanza 7.

81 O wad some Pow'r the giftie gie us
To see oursels as ithers see us!
It wad frae monie a blunder free us
An' foolish notion.
1786 'To a Louse, On Seeing one on a Lady's Bonnet at Church',
stanza 8.

82 It was upon a Lammas night,
When corn rigs are bonie,
Beneath the moon's unclouded light,
I held awa to Annie.
1786 'Song, The Rigs o' Barley', or 'Corn Rigs Are Bonie', stanza 1.

83 I hae been blythe wi' Comrades dear;
I hae been merry drinking.
1786 'Song, The Rigs o' Barley', or 'Corn Rigs Are Bonie', stanza 4.

84 Corn rigs, an' barley rigs,
An' corn rigs are bonie:
I'll ne'er forget that happy night,
Amang the rigs wi' Annie.
1786 'Song, The Rigs o' Barley', or 'Corn Rigs Are Bonie', chorus.

85 Now westlin winds, and slaught'rin guns
Bring Autumn's pleasant weather.
1786 'Song, composed in August', stanza 1.

86 O ye wha are sae guid yoursel,
Sae pious and sae holy,
Ye've nought to do but mark and tell

Your Neebours' fauts an folly!
1786 'Address to the Unco Guid, or the Rigidly Righteous',
stanza 1.

87 Then gently scan your brother Man,
Still gentler sister Woman;
Tho' they may gang a kennin wrang,
To step aside is human.
1786 'Address to the Unco Guid, or the Rigidly Righteous',
stanza 7.

88 Fair fa' your honest, sonsie face,
Great Chieftain o' the Puddin-race!
Aboon them a' ye tak your place,
Painch, tripe, or thairm:
Weel are ye wordy of a *grace*
As lang's my arm.
1786 'To a Haggis', stanza 1.

89 Auld Scotland wants nae skinking ware That jaups in
luggies;
But, if ye wish her gratefu' prayer,
Gie her a *Haggis!*
1786 'To a Haggis', stanza 8.

90 Edina! *Scotia's* darling seat,
All hail thy palaces and tow'rs,
Where once beneath a monarch's feet
Sat Legislation's sov'reign pow'rs.
1786 'Address to Edinburgh', stanza 1.

91 There was a lad was born in Kyle,
But what na day o' what na style.
I doubt it's hardly worth the while
To be sae nice wi' Robin.
1787 'There was a lad', or 'Rantin' Rovin' Robin', stanza 1.

92 Robin was a rovin' Boy,
Rantin' rovin', rantin', rovin',
Robin was a rovin' Boy,
Rantin' rovin' Robin.
1787 'There was a lad', or 'Rantin' Rovin' Robin', chorus.

93 There was three kings into the east,
Three kings both great and high,
And they hae sworn a solemn oath
John Barleycorn should die.
1787 'John Barleycorn. A Ballad', stanza 1.

94 Bony lassie will ye go
To the birks of Aberfeldey.
1787 'The Birks of Aberfeldey', chorus.

95 Sae rantingly, sae wantonly,
Sae dauntingly gae'd he:
He play'd a spring, and danc'd it round
Below the gallows-tree.
1788 'McPherson's Farewell', chorus.

96 O rattlin, roarin Willie,
O he held to the fair;
An' for to sell his fiddle
And buy some other ware.
1788 'Rattlin, roarin Willie', stanza 1.

97 Rattlin, roarin Willie,
Ye're welcome hame to me!
1788 'Rattlin, roarin Willie', stanza 3.

98 Should auld acquaintance be forgot
And never brought to mind?
Should auld acquaintance be forgot,
And auld lang syne!

1788 'Auld Lang Syne', stanza 1. This is the most familiar version
of an older, traditional song, reworked by Burns.

99 For auld lang syne, my jo,
For auld lang syne,
We'll tak a cup o' kindness yet
For auld lang syne.
1788 'Auld Lang Syne', chorus. This is the most familiar version
of an older, traditional song, reworked by Burns.

1 And there's a hand, my trusty fiere!
And gie's a hand o' thine!
1788 'Auld Lang Syne', stanza 5. This is the most familiar
version of an older, traditional song, reworked
by Burns.

2 Go fetch to me a pint o' wine,
And fill it in a silver tassie,
That I may drink, before I go,
A service to my bonie lassie.
1788 'My Bonie Mary', stanza 1.

3 Of a' the airts the wind can blaw,
I dearly like the West;
For there the bonie Lassie lives,
The Lassie I lo'e best.
1788 'Of a' the airts the wind can blaw', or 'I Love my Jean',
stanza 1.

4 Flow gently, sweet Afton, among thy green braes,
Flow gently, I'll sing thee a song in thy praise.
1789 'Afton Water', stanza 1.

5 The golden Hours, on angel wings,
Flew o'er me and my Dearie;
For dear to me as light and life
Was my sweet Highland Mary.
1789 'Highland Mary', stanza 2.

6 We are na fou, we're nae that fou,
But just a drappie in our e'e;
The cock may craw, the day may daw,
And ay we'll taste the barley bree.
1789 'Willie brew'd a peck o' maut', chorus.

7 Ay waukin, O,
Waukin still and weary:
Sleep I can get nane,
For thinkin on my Dearie.
1790 'Ay waukin O', chorus.

8 My love she's but a lassie yet,
My love she's but a lassie yet;
We'll let her stand a year or twa,
She'll no be half sae saucy yet.
1790 'My love she's but a lassie yet', chorus.

9 My heart's in the Highlands, my heart is not here,
My heart's in the Highlands a chasing the deer;
Chasing the wild deer, and following the roe;
My heart's in the Highlands, wherever I go.
1790 'My heart's in the Highlands', chorus.

10 John Anderson my jo, John,
When we were first acquent;
Your locks were like the raven,
Your bonie brow was brent;
But now your brow is beld, John,
Your locks are like the snaw;
But blessings on your frosty pow,
John Anderson my jo.
1790 'John Anderson my Jo', stanza 1.

11 An ye had been whare I hae been,
Ye wad na been sae canty, O;
An ye had seen what I hae seen,
I' th' braes o' Killiecrankie, O.
1790 'Killiecrankie', chorus.

12 When chapman billies leave the street,
And drouthy neebors, neebors meet,
As market-days are wearing late,
An' folk begin to tak the gate.
1790 'Tam o' Shanter. A Tale'.

13 Whare sits our sulky sullen dame,
Gathering her brows like gathering storm,
Nursing her wrath to keep it warm.
1790 'Tam o' Shanter. A Tale'.

14 Auld Ayr, wham ne'er a town surpasses,
For honest men and bonny lasses.
1790 'Tam o' Shanter. A Tale'.

15 Ah! gentle dames! it gars me greet,
To think how mony counsels sweet,
How mony lengthen'd sage advices,
The husband frae the wife despises!
1790 'Tam o' Shanter. A Tale'.

16 Tam lo'ed him like a vera brither;
They had been fou for weeks thegither.
1790 'Tam o' Shanter. A Tale'.

17 The storm without might rair and rustle,
Tam did na mind the storm a whistle.
1790 'Tam o' Shanter. A Tale'.

18 Kings may be blest but Tam was glorious,
O'er a' the ills o' life victorious!
1790 'Tam o' Shanter. A Tale'.

19 But pleasures are like poppies spread,
You seize the flower, its bloom is shed;
Or like the snow falls in the river,
A moment white—then melts for ever.
1790 'Tam o' Shanter. A Tale'.

20 Nae man can tether time or tide;
The hour approaches Tam maun ride;
That hour, o' night's black arch the key-stane,
That dreary hour Tam mounts his beast in.
1790 'Tam o' Shanter. A Tale'.

21 Inspiring, bold John Barleycorn!
What dangers thou canst make us scorn!
Wi' tippenny, we fear nae evil;
Wi' usquabae, we'll face the devil!
1790 'Tam o' Shanter. A Tale'. 'Usquabae' = whisky.

22 Five tomahawks, wi' blude red-rusted;
Five scymitars, wi' murder crusted.
1790 'Tam o' Shanter. A Tale'.

23 As Tammie glowr'd, amaz'd, and curious,
The mirth and fun grew fast and furious:
The piper loud and louder blew;
The dancers quick and quicker flew.
1790 'Tam o' Shanter. A Tale'.

24 Ah, Tam! Ah, Tam! thou'll get thy fairin!
In hell they'll roast thee like a herrin!
1790 'Tam o' Shanter. A Tale'.

25 Whene'er to drink you are inclin'd,
Or cutty sarks run in your mind,
Think, ye may buy the joys o'er dear—

Remember Tam o' Shanter's mare.
1790 'Tam o' Shanter. A Tale'.

26 Ye banks and braes o' bonie Doon,
How can ye bloom sae fresh and fair;
How can ye chant, ye little birds,
And I sae weary fu' o' care!
1791 'The Banks o' Doon' (2nd version), stanza 1.

27 And my fause Luver staw my rose,
But, ah! he left the thorn wi' me.
1791 'The Banks o' Doon' (2nd version), stanza 2.

28 Ae fond kiss, and then we sever!
Ae fareweel, and then for ever!
Deep in heart-wrung tears I'll pledge thee,
Warring sighs and groans I'll wage thee.
1791 'Ae Fond Kiss', stanza 1.

29 Had we never lov'd sae kindly,
Had we never lov'd sae blindly!
Never met—or never parted,
We had ne'er been broken-hearted.
1791 'Ae Fond Kiss', stanza 4.

30 Fare-thee-weel, thou first and fairest!
Fare-thee-weel, thou best and dearest!
Thine be ilka joy and treasure,
Peace, Enjoyment, Love and Pleasure!
1791 'Ae Fond Kiss', stanza 5.

31 Ye Jacobites by name, give an ear, give an ear!
Ye Jacobites by name, give an ear.
1792 'Ye Jacobites by name', stanza 1.

32 Sic a wife as Willie's wife,
I wad na gie a button for her.
1792 'Willie Wastle', or 'Sic a wife as Willie's wife', stanza 1.

33 Willie Wastle dwalt on Tweed,
The spot they ca'd it Linkumdoddie.
1792 'Willie Wastle', or 'Sic a wife as Willie's wife', stanza 1.

34 Fareweel to a' our Scottish fame,
Fareweel our ancient glory.
1792 'Such a parcel of rogues in a nation', stanza 1.

35 Now Sark rins o'er the Solway sands,
An' Tweed rins to the ocean,
To mark where England's province stands,
Such a parcel of rogues in a nation!
1792 'Such a parcel of rogues in a nation', stanza 1.

36 We're bought and sold for English gold,
Such a parcel of rogues in a nation!
1792 'Such a parcel of rogues in a nation', stanza 3.

37 The deil cam fiddlin thro' the town,
And danc'd awa wi' th' Exciseman;
And ilka wife cries, auld Mahoun,
I wish you luck o' the prize, man!
1792 'The Deil's awa wi' th' Exciseman', stanza 1.

38 There's threesome reels, there's foursome reels,
There's hornpipes and strathspeys, man,
But the ae best dance e'er cam to the Land
Was, the deil's awa wi' th' Exciseman.
1792 'The Deil's awa wi' th' Exciseman', stanza 3.

39 When o'er the hill the eastern star
Tells bughtin-time is near, my jo,
And owsen frae the furrowed field
Return sae dowf and weary O.
1792 'My ain kind dearie', or 'The Lea-rig', stanza 1.

40 I'll meet thee on the lea-rig,
My ain kind Dearie, O.
1792 'My ain kind dearie', or 'The Lea-rig', stanza 1.

41 Scots, wha hae wi' Wallace bled,
Scots, wham Bruce has aften led,
Welcome to your gory bed,—
Or to victorie!—
Now's the day, and now's the hour;
See the front o' battle lour;
See approach proud Edward's power,
Chains and Slaverie!
1793 'Bruce's Address at Bannockburn', stanza 1.

42 Liberty's in every blow!
Let us do or die!
1793 'Bruce's Address at Bannockburn', stanza 3.

43 Though this was fair, and that was braw,
And yon the toast of a' the town,
I sigh'd, and said amang them a',
'Ye are na Mary Morison.'
1793 'Mary Morison', stanza 2.

44 O my Luve's like a red, red rose
That's newly sprung in June;
O my luve's like the melodie
That's sweetly play'd in tune.
As fair art thou, my bonie lass,
So deep in luve am I;
And I will luve thee still, my Dear,
Till a' the seas gang dry.
Till a' the seas gang dry, my Dear,
And the rocks melt wi' the sun:
O I will love thee still, my Dear,
While the sands o' life shall run.
1794 'A red, red rose'.

45 Ca' the yowes to the knowes,
Ca' them whare the heather grows,
Ca' them whare the burnie rowes,
My bonie Dearie!
1794 'Ca' the yowes to the knowes' (2nd version), chorus.

46 Is there for honest Poverty
That hings his head, and a' that;
The coward-slave, we pass him by,
We dare be poor for a' that!
For a' that, and a' that,
Our toils obscure, and a' that,
The rank is but the guinea's stamp,
The man's the gowd for a' that.
1795 'For a' that and a' that', stanza 1.

47 A man's a man for a' that.
1795 'For a' that and a' that', stanza 2.

48 For a' that, and a' that,
It's comin' yet for a' that,
That Man to Man the warld o'er
Shall brothers be, for a' that.
1795 'For a' that and a' that', stanza 5.

49 Gin a body meet a body
Comin thro' the rye,
Gin a body kiss a body
Need a body cry?
1796 'Comin thro' the rye', stanza 2.

50 An' Charlie he's my darling, my darling, my darling,

Charlie he's my darling, the young Chevalier.
1796 'Charlie he's my darling', chorus.

51 It was a' for our rightfu' king,
We left fair Scotland's strand.
1796 'It was a' for our rightfu' king', stanza 1.

52 Now a' is done that men can do,
And a' is done in vain.
1796 'It was a' for our rightfu' king', stanza 2.

53 He turn'd him right and round about,
Upon the Irish shore,
And gae his bridle reins a shake,
With, Adieu for evermore, my dear,
And Adieu for evermore!
1796 'It was a' for our rightfu' king', stanza 3.

54 Oh wert thou in the cauld blast,
On yonder lea, on yonder lea;
My plaidie to the angry airt,
I'd shelter thee, I'd shelter thee.
1796 'Oh wert thou in the cauld blast', stanza 1.

55 There's death in the cup—sae beware!
Nay, more—there is danger in touching;
But wha can avoid the fell snare?
The man and his wine's sae bewitching!
1796 'Inscription on a Goblet'.

Burroughs, Edgar Rice 1875–1950

US novelist. He was a hugely successful writer of popular fiction, much of it in the science-fiction and fantasy genres, and is best known as the creator of Tarzan. The much-quoted line 'Me Tarzan, you Jane', does not appear in any story, and is a misattribution by actor Johnny Weissmuller.

56 Tarzan of the Apes.
1912 Title of story.

Burroughs, William S(eward) 1914–97

US writer. He wandered through the USA and Europe after graduating from Harvard, becoming a heroin addict in New York (1944). His novels draw on his experiences, establishing him as a spokesman of the 'beat' generation.

57 The face of 'evil' is always the face of total need.
1959 The Naked Lunch, introduction.

58 I think there are innumerable gods. What we on earth call God is a little tribal God who has made an awful mess.
1965 In Paris Review, Fall.

59 After one look at this planet any visitor from outer space would say 'I WANT TO SEE THE MANAGER.'
1985 The Adding Machine, 'Women: A Biological Mistake'.

60 You can't fake quality any more than you can fake a good meal.
1987 The Western Lands, ch.2.

61 No problems can be solved, and all solutions lead to more problems.
Comment to Allen Ginsberg. Quoted in Barry Miles Ginsberg (1989), ch.17.

62 Nothing exists until or unless it is observed. An artist is making something exist by observing it.
1992 Painting and Guns, 'The Creative Observer'.

63 Virtue is simply happiness, and happiness is a by-product of function. You are happy when you are functioning.
1992 Painting and Guns, 'The Creative Observer'.

Burt, Benjamin Hapgood 1880–1950

US songwriter.

64 All Dressed Up and No Place to Go.
1913 Song title, *The Beauty Shop* (music by Silvio Hein).

65 One evening in October, when I was one-third sober,
An' taking home a 'load' with manly pride;
My poor feet began to stutter, so I lay down in the gutter,
And a pig came up an' lay down by my side.
Then we sang 'It's all fair weather when good fellows get
together,'
Till a lady passing by was heard to say:
'You can tell a man who boozes by the company he
chooses',
And the pig got up and slowly walked away.
1933 'The Pig Got Up and Slowly Walked Away'.

Burton, C(harles) L(uther) 1876–1961

Canadian businessman.

66 I hold no brief for private enterprise. But I have
unshakeable faith in individual enterprise.
1952 *A Sense of Urgency: Memoirs of a Canadian Merchant.*

67 Life, if you have a bent for it, is a beautiful thing. It
consists, I do believe, of having a sense of urgency.
1952 *A Sense of Urgency: Memoirs of a Canadian Merchant.*

Burton, Robert *pseudonym* *Democritus Junior* 1577–1640

English writer and clergyman. Educated at Oxford, he
remained at Christ Church for life. His *Anatomy of Melancholy*
(1621) is a vast, witty compendium of Jacobean knowledge
and superstition about the 'disease' of melancholy; it went
through several editions in his lifetime.

68 All my joys to this are folly,
Naught so sweet as melancholy.
1621 *Anatomy of Melancholy,* 'The Author's Abstract of
Melancholy'.

69 A loose, plain, rude writer…I call a spade a spade.
1621 *Anatomy of Melancholy,* 'Democritus to the Reader'.

70 All poets are mad.
1621 *Anatomy of Melancholy,* 'Democritus to the Reader'.

71 I may not here omit those two main plagues, and
common dotages of human kind, wine and women,
which have infatuated and besotted myriads of people.
They go commonly together.
1621 *Anatomy of Melancholy,* pt.1, section 2, member 3,
subsection 13.

72 *Hinc quam sit calamus saevior ense patet.*
From this it is clear how much the pen is worse than the
sword.
1621 *Anatomy of Melancholy,* pt.1, section 2, member 4,
subsection 4.

73 See one promontory (said Socrates of old), one
mountain, one sea, one river, and see all.
1621 *Anatomy of Melancholy,* pt.1, section 2, member 4,
subsection 7.

74 One was never married, and that's his hell; another is,
and that's his plague.
1621 *Anatomy of Melancholy,* pt.1, section 2, member 4,
subsection 7.

75 Who cannot give good counsel? 'tis cheap, it costs them
nothing.

1621 *Anatomy of Melancholy,* pt.2, section 3, member 1,
subsection 1.

76 What is a ship but a prison?
1621 *Anatomy of Melancholy,* pt.2, section 3, member 4,
subsection 1.

77 Tobacco, divine, rare, superexcellent tobacco, which
goes far beyond all their panaceas, potable gold, and
philosopher's stones, a sovereign remedy to all
diseases… But, as it is commonly abused by most men,
which take it as tinkers do ale, 'tis a plague, a mischief, a
violent purger of goods, lands, health, hellish, devilish,
and damned tobacco, the ruin and overthrow of body
and soul.
1621 *Anatomy of Melancholy,* pt.2, section 4, member 2,
subsection 1.

78 But this love of ours is immoderate, inordinate, and not to
be comprehended in any bounds. It will not contain itself
within the union of marriage or apply to one object, but
is a wandering, extravagant, a domineering, a
boundless, an irrefragable, a destructive passion.
1621 *Anatomy of Melancholy,* pt.3, section 2, member 1,
subsection 2.

79 No cord nor cable can so forcibly draw, or hold so fast, as
love can do with a twined thread. The scorching beams
under the equinoctial or extremity of cold within the
circle Arctic, where the very seas are frozen, cold or
torrid zone cannot avoid or expel this heat, fury, and rage
of mortal men.
1621 *Anatomy of Melancholy,* pt.3, section 2, member 1,
subsection 2.

80 Of women's unnatural, unsatiable lust, what country,
what village doth not complain?
1621 *Anatomy of Melancholy,* pt.3, section 2, member 1,
subsection 2.

81 A passion of the brain, as all other melancholy, by reason
of corrupt imagination.
1621 Of love. *Anatomy of Melancholy,* pt.3, section 2, member 1,
subsection 2.

82 One religion is as true as another.
1621 *Anatomy of Melancholy,* pt.3, section 4, member 2,
subsection 1.

83 Be not solitary, be not idle.
1621 *Anatomy of Melancholy,* closing words.

Buruma, Ian 1951–

British writer. His works include *The Wages of Guilt* (1994).

84 Isherwood did not so much find himself in Berlin as
reinvent himself; Isherwood became a fiction, a work of
art.
1986 Of Christopher Isherwood. In the *New Republic,* 4 Nov.

85 A nation of people longing to be 12-year-olds or even
younger.
1994 Of Japan. *The Wages of Guilt.*

86 German memory was like a massive tongue seeking out,
over and over, a sore tooth.
1994 *The Wages of Guilt.*

Busby, Sir Matt(hew) 1909–94

Scottish football player and manager. He led Manchester
United to glory in the 1950s, and successfully rebuilt the team
after the Munich air crash in 1958 to win the European Cup in
1968.

87 The theory that the League and Cup double will never be done in modern times is nonsense. I realize no one has done it for sixty years, but there is a simple explanation for that. No club has been good enough.
1957 Attributed, four years before Tottenham Hotspur won both the League Championship and the F A Cup.

Bush, Barbara Pierce 1925–

Former US First Lady. The daughter of a wealthy New York publisher, she married George Bush (1945), who became President in 1989.

88 No other single building is so much a part of the American consciousness.
1992 At the 200th anniversary of the laying of the White House cornerstone. Reported in the *Washington Times*, 24 Jan.

89 I wrote in my diaries about…good meals that I have eaten and am wearing today.
1994 *Barbara Bush: A Memoir*.

90 I am advising the former President, the governor of Florida and the President of the United States—I guess you could say I rule the world.
2003 On her political power. Quoted in *Newsweek*, 31 Mar.

Bush, George Herbert Walker 1924–

US Republican politician and 41st President. After losing to Reagan for the Republican candidacy in the 1980 elections, he became his Vice-President and later President (1989–92). He presided over the US-led UN coalition to defeat Iraq in the Gulf War.

91 The United States is the best and fairest and most decent nation on the face of the earth.
1988 Speech, May.

92 Read my lips: no new taxes.
1988 Accepting the Republican presidential nomination, 19 Aug.

93 It's amazing how many people beat you at golf now that you're no longer president.
1996 In the *Sunday Times*, 22 Dec.

Bush, George W(alker) 1948–

US Republican politician and 43rd President. The son of George Herbert Walker Bush, he was Governor of Texas (1995–2000) before becoming President in 2001.

94 I've inherited 100 per cent of his enemies and only 50 per cent of his friends.
1994 Of the influence of his father, former President George Bush, on his campaign for governor. In the *Washington Times*, 12 Oct.

95 I'm not going to talk about what I did as a child.
1999 On being asked if he ever used marijuana or cocaine. Quoted in *Time*, 22 Feb.

96 Keep good relations with the Grecians.
1999 Quoted in *The Economist*, 12 Jun.

97 New Hampshire has long been known as the bump in the road for front runners—and this year is no exception.
2000 After being defeated in the New Hampshire primary. In the *Sunday Times*, 6 Feb.

98 Reading is the basics for all learning.
2000 Announcing his 'Reading First' initiative in Reston, Virginia, 28 Mar.

99 It's no sign of weakness to talk to your dad.
2000 Denying that he is too much under his father's influence. In the *Sunday Telegraph*, 30 Jul.

1 Well, I think if you say you're going to do something and don't do it, that's trustworthiness.
2000 CNN online chat, 30 Aug.

2 I know the human being and fish can coexist peacefully.
2000 Speaking in Saginaw, Michigan, 29 Sep.

3 I am mindful not only of preserving executive powers for myself, but for my predecessors as well.
2001 Speaking in Washington, 29 Jan.

4 You teach a child to read, and he or her will be able to pass a literacy test.
2001 Speaking in Townsend, Tennessee, 21 Feb.

5 According to the *Oxford English Dictionary*, Mr Jefferson contributed more new words to the language than any other US President. I especially like his term for barbaric pirates: barbaresques. I'm also impressed by his words, debarrass and graffage. The other day I tried a new word for our press corps: misunderestimate. It's not quite in Jefferson's league, but I am giving it my best shot.
2001 Speaking in Washington, 12 Apr.

6 We spent a lot of time talking about Africa, as we should. Africa is a nation that suffers from incredible disease.
2001 Speaking in Gothenburg, Sweden, 14 Jun.

7 We cannot let terrorist and rogue nations hold this nation hostile or hold our allies hostile.
2001 Speaking in Des Moines, Iowa, 21 Aug.

8 Whether we bring our enemies to justice, or bring justice to our enemies, justice will be done.
2001 Address to a joint session of Congress, 20 Sep.

9 Every nation, in every region, now has a decision to make. Either you are with us, or you are with the terrorists. From this day forward, any nation that continues to harbor or support terrorism will be regarded by the United States as a hostile regime.
2001 Address to a joint session of Congress, 20 Sep.

10 States like these, and their terrorist allies, constitute an axis of evil, arming to threaten the peace of the world. By seeking weapons of mass destruction, these regimes pose a grave and growing danger.
2002 State of the Union Address, 29 Jan.

11 Our war on terror is well begun, but it is only begun. This campaign may not be finished on our watch—yet it must be and it will be waged on our watch.
2002 State of the Union Address, 29 Jan.

12 For a century and a half now, America and Japan have formed one of the great and enduring alliances of modern times.
2002 Speaking in Tokyo, Japan, 18 Feb.

13 If this is not evil, then evil has no meaning.
2003 On torture in Iraq. State of the Union Address, 28 Jan.

14 The Columbia is gone. There are no survivors.
2003 On the loss of the space shuttle. Quoted in *Newsweek*, 10 Feb.

15 You're free. And freedom is beautiful. And, you know, it'll take time to restore chaos and order—order out of chaos. But we will.
2003 Speaking in Washington, 13 Apr.

16 Our country puts $1 billion a year up to help feed the hungry. And we're by far the most generous nation in the

world when it comes to that, and I'm proud to report that. This isn't a contest of who's the most generous. I'm just telling you as an aside. We're generous. We shouldn't be bragging about it. But we are. We're very generous.
2003 Speaking in Washington, 16 Jul.

17 The best way to get news is from objective sources. And the most objective sources I have are people on my staff who tell me what's happening in the world.
2003 On Fox News, 22 Sep.

18 See, free nations are peaceful nations. Free nations don't attack each other. Free nations don't develop weapons of mass destruction.
2003 Speaking in Milwaukee, Wisconsin, 3 Oct.

19 The illiteracy level of our children are appalling.
2004 Speaking in Washington, 23 Jan.

20 Iraqis are sick of foreign people coming in their country and trying to destabilize their country. And we will help them rid Iraq of these killers.
2004 Interview on Al Arabiya Television, 4 May.

21 When I speak about the blessings of liberty, coarse videos and crass commercialism are not what I have in mind.
2004 Speaking in Istanbul, 29 Jun.

22 See if Saddam did this. See if he's linked in any way.
In the wake of the 11 September 2001 attacks. Quoted in Richard A Clarke *Against All Enemies: Inside America's War on Terror* (2004).

Bush, Vannevar 1890–1974

US electrical engineer and physicist, Dean of Engineering at the Massachusetts Institute of Technology. He later led the US Office of Scientific Research.

23 To pursue science is not to disparage things of the spirit.
1953 Speech at the Massachusetts Institute of Technology, 5 Oct.

24 It was through the Second World War that most of us suddenly appreciated for the first time the power of man's concentrated efforts to understand and control the forces of nature. We were appalled by what we saw.
1967 *Science is Not Enough.*

25 Knowledge for the sake of understanding, not merely to prevail, that is the essence of our being. None can define its limits, or set its ultimate boundaries.
1967 *Science is Not Enough.*

Bushnell, Candace 1958–

US journalist and author.

26 Let's face it, the unmarried guys in New York suck.
1996 *Sex in the City.*

27 Modelizers are a particular breed. They're a step beyond womanizers, who will sleep with just about anything in a skirt. Modelizers are obsessed not with women but with models. They love them for their beauty and hate them for everything else.
1996 *Sex in the City.*

Busoni, Ferruccio Benvenuto 1866–1924

Italian pianist and composer. An infant prodigy, he taught and played throughout Europe and wrote four operas among other works, mainly for piano. His pupils included Kurt Weill.

28 Music is the art of sounds in the movement of time.
1923 *The Essence of Music.*

Bussy-Rabutin, Comte de 1618–93

French soldier and poet.

29 *L'absence est à l'amour ce qu'est au feu le vent;*
Il éteint le petit, il allume le grand.
Absence is to love what wind is to fire;
It extinguishes the small, it kindles the great.
1665 *Histoire Amoureuse des Gaules. Maximes d'Amour*, pt.2.

30 *Comme vous savez, Dieu est d'ordinaire pour les gros escadrons contre les petits.*
As you know, God is usually on the side of the big squadrons against the small.
1677 Letter to the Comte de Limoges, 18 Oct.

Butler, Joseph 1692–1752

English moral philosopher, cleric and Christian apologist. Originally a dissenter, he joined the Church of England and became Bishop of Bristol, and later of Durham.

31 But to us, probability is the very guide of life.
1736 *The Analogy of Religion*, introduction.

32 Sir, the pretending to extraordinary revelations and gifts of the Holy Ghost is a horrid thing, a very horrid thing.
Comment to John Wesley. Quoted in John Wesley *Works*, pt.13.

Butler (of Saffron Walden), R(ichard) A(usten) Butler, Baron 1902–82

British Conservative politician. He became Chancellor of the Exchequer, Home Secretary and Deputy Prime Minister, and narrowly lost the premiership to Alec Douglas-Home, becoming Foreign Secretary (1963–4).

33 After all, it is not every man who nearly becomes Prime Minister of England.
1957 On being passed over as Harold Macmillan's successor in favour of Alec Douglas-Home, Jan.

34 Politics is the art of the possible.
1971 *The Art of the Possible.*
➤ See Galbraith 343:94.

35 The best Prime Minister we've got.
Attributed comment on Harold Macmillan, made on a train going to the Party Conference in Brighton.

Butler, Samuel 1612–80

English satirist, who served in noble households and in government. His *Hudibras* (1663–78), a burlesque satire on Puritanism, was a special favourite of Charles II. Despite royal favour, he died in penury.

36 A client is fain to hire a lawyer to keep from the injury of other lawyers—as Christians that travel in Turkey are forced to hire Janissaries, to protect them from the insolencies of other Turks.
1660 *Prose Observations.*

37 But here our authors make a doubt
Whether he were more wise or stout.
Some hold the one and some the other;
But howsoe'er they make a pother,
The difference was so small his brain
Outweighed his rage but half a grain;
Which made some take him for a tool

That knaves do work with, called a fool.
1663 *Hudibras*, pt.1, canto 1, l.29–36.

38 We grant, although he had much wit,
He was very shy of using it;
As being loath to wear it out,
And therefore bore it not about,
Unless on holidays, or so,
As men their best apparel do.
1663 *Hudibras*, pt.1, canto 1, l.45–50.

39 'Tis known he could speak Greek
As naturally as pigs squeak.
1663 *Hudibras*, pt.1, canto 1, l.51–2.

40 He was in logic a great critic,
Profoundly skilled in analytic.
He could distinguish and divide
A hair 'twixt south and southwest side.
1663 *Hudibras*, pt.1, canto 1, l.65–8.

41 For every *why* he had a *wherefore*.
1663 *Hudibras*, pt.1, canto 1, l.132.

42 He knew what's what, and that's as high
As metaphysic wit can fly.
1663 *Hudibras*, pt.1, canto 1, l.149–50.

43 And with as delicate a hand
Could twist as tough a rope of sand;
And weave fine cobwebs, fit for skull
That's empty when the moon is full;
Such as take lodgings in a head
That's to be let unfurnishèd.
1663 *Hudibras*, pt.1, canto 1, l.155–60.

44 And still be doing, never done:
As if Religion were intended
For nothing else but to be mended.
1663 *Hudibras*, pt.1, canto 1, l.202–4.

45 For rhyme the rudder is of verses,
With which like ships they steer their courses.
1663 *Hudibras*, pt.1, canto 1, l.457–8.

46 Great actions are not always true sons
Of great and mighty resolutions.
1663 *Hudibras*, pt.1, canto 1, l.877–8.

47 Ay me! what perils do environ
The man that meddles with cold iron!
1663 *Hudibras*, pt.1, canto 3, l.1–2.

48 I'll make the fur
Fly 'bout the ears of the old cur.
1663 *Hudibras*, pt.1, canto 3, l.277–8.

49 I am not now in fortune's power
He that is down can fall no lower.
1663 *Hudibras*, pt.1, canto 3, l.871–2.

50 Learning, that cobweb of the brain,
Profane, erroneous, and vain.
1663 *Hudibras*, pt.1, canto 3, l.1339–40.

51 She that with poetry is won
Is but a desk to write upon.
1664 *Hudibras*, pt.2, canto 1, l.591–2.

52 Love is a boy, by poets styled,
Then spare the rod, and spoil the child.
1664 *Hudibras*, pt.2, canto 1, l.843–4.

53 Oaths are but words, and words but wind.
1664 *Hudibras*, pt.2, canto 2, l.107.

54 For saints may do the same things by

The spirit, in sincerity,
Which other men are tempted to.
1664 *Hudibras*, pt.2, canto 2, l.235–7.

55 Doubtless the pleasure is as great
Of being cheated, as to cheat.
As lookers-on feel most delight,
That least perceive a juggler's sleight,
And still the less they understand,
The more th' admire his sleight of hand.
1664 *Hudibras*, pt.2, canto 3, l.1–6.

56 For in what stupid age or nation
Was marriage ever out of fashion?
1678 *Hudibras*, pt.3, canto 1, l.817–18.

57 What makes all doctrines plain and clear?
About two hundred pounds a year.
And that which was prov'd true before,
Prove false again? Two hundred more.
1678 *Hudibras*, pt.3, canto 1, l.1277–80.

58 For if it be but half denied,
'Tis half as good as justified.
1678 *Hudibras*, pt.3, canto 2, l.803–4.

59 For, those that fly, may fight again,
Which he can never do that's slain.
1678 *Hudibras*, pt.3, canto 3, l.243–4.

60 He that complies against his will
Is of his own opinion still.
1678 *Hudibras*, pt.3, canto 3, l.547.

61 Neither have the heart to stay,
Nor wit enough to run away.
1678 *Hudibras*, pt.3, canto 3, l.569–60.

62 For money has a power above
The stars and fate, to manage love.
1678 *Hudibras*, pt.3, canto 3, l.1279–80.

Butler, Samuel 1835–1902

English writer and parliamentary secretary. His Utopian satire *Erewhon* (1872) and its supplement *Erewhon Revisited* (1901) deal with the origins of religious belief. His autobiographical novel *The Way of All Flesh* was published posthumously (1903).

63 I am forgetting myself into admiring a mountain which is of no use for sheep. This is wrong. A mountain here is only beautiful if it has good grass on it.
1863 Of Mt Cook. *A First Year in Canterbury Settlement.*

64 The wish to spread those opinions that we hold conducive to our own welfare is so deeply rooted in the English character that few of us can escape its influence.
1872 *Erewhon.*

65 Exploring is delightful to look forward to and back upon, but it is not comfortable at the time, unless it be of such an easy nature as not to deserve the name.
1872 *Erewhon.*

66 A hen is only an egg's way of making another egg.
1877 *Life and Habit*, ch.8.

67 It was very good of God to let Carlyle and Mrs Carlyle marry one another and so make only two people miserable instead of four.
1884 Letter to Miss E M A Savage, 21 Nov.

68 Life is like playing a violin solo in public and learning the

instrument as one goes on.
1895 Speech at the Somerville Club, 27 Feb.

69 It has been said that although God cannot alter the past, historians can; it is perhaps because they can be useful to Him in this respect that He tolerates their existence.
1901 *Erewhon Revisited*, ch.14.

70 All animals, except man, know that the principal business of life is to enjoy it.
1903 *The Way of All Flesh*, ch.19.

71 The advantage of doing one's praising for oneself is that one can lay it on so thick and exactly in the right places.
1903 *The Way of All Flesh*, ch.34.

72 Young as he was, his instinct told him that the best liar is he who makes the smallest amount of lying go the longest way.
1903 *The Way of All Flesh*, ch.39.

73 A man's friendships are, like his will, invalidated by marriage.
1903 *The Way of All Flesh*, ch.75.

74 'Getting into the key of C sharp,' he said, 'is like an unprotected female travelling on the Metropolitan Railway, and finding herself at Shepherd's Bush, without quite knowing where she wants to go to. How is she ever to get safe back to Clapham Junction?'
1903 *The Way of All Flesh*.

75 There's many a good tune played on an old fiddle.
1903 *The Way of All Flesh*.

76 As soon as any art is pursued with a view to money, then farewell, in ninety-nine cases out of a hundred, all hope of genuine good work.
Collected in H F Jones (ed) *The Notebooks of Samuel Butler* (1912).

77 Justice is being allowed to do whatever I like. Injustice is whatever prevents my doing it.
Collected in H F Jones (ed) *The Notebooks of Samuel Butler* (1912).

78 An apology for the Devil: It must be remembered that we have only heard one side of the case. God has written all the books.
Collected in H F Jones (ed) *The Notebooks of Samuel Butler* (1912), ch.14.

79 Handel is so great and so simple that no one but a professional musician is unable to understand him.
Collected in H F Jones (ed) *The Notebooks of Samuel Butler* (1912).

80 The healthy stomach is nothing if not conservative. Few radicals have good digestions.
Collected in H F Jones (ed) *The Notebooks of Samuel Butler* (1912).

81 Science, after all, is only an expression for our ignorance of our own ignorance.
Collected in H F Jones (ed) *The Notebooks of Samuel Butler* (1912).

82 To live is like to love—all reason is against it, and all healthy instinct for it.
Collected in H F Jones (ed) *The Notebooks of Samuel Butler* (1912).

83 The three most important things a man has are, briefly, his private parts, his money, and his religious opinions.
Collected in *Further Extracts from the Notebooks* (1934).

84 Jesus! with all thy faults I love thee still.
Collected in *Further Extracts from the Notebooks* (1934).

85 A lawyer's dream of heaven: every man reclaimed his own property at the resurrection, and each tried to recover it from all his forefathers.
Collected in *Further Extracts from the Notebooks* (1934).

Butler, William 1535–1618

English royal physician.

86 Doubtless God could have made a better berry, but doubtless God never did.
Of the strawberry. Quoted in Izaak Walton *The Compleat Angler* (3rd edn, 1661), pt.1, ch.5.

Butterfield, Sir Herbert 1900–79

English historian, Professor of Modern History at Cambridge.

87 We can do worse than remember the principle which both gives us a firm Rock and leaves us the maximum elasticity for our minds—Hold to Christ, and for the rest be totally uncommitted.
1949 *Christianity and History*.

88 In a profound sense we may say that the crucifixion, however else we may interpret it, accuses human nature, accuses all of us in the very things that we think are our righteousness.
1951 *History and Human Relations*.

Byatt, Dame A(ntonia) S(usan) *née Drabble* 1936–

English writer and critic, sister of Margaret Drabble. Her works include critical studies, short stories and novels, such as *Possession* (Booker Prize, 1990), which explores the experience of women in 20c society, and *The Biographer's Tale* (2000).

89 There is something both gratifying and humiliating in watching a man who has taken you for a routinely silly woman begin to take you seriously.
1985 *Still Life*, ch.18, 'Hic Ille Raphael'.

90 Autobiographies tell more lies than all but the most self-indulgent fiction.
1987 'The Day That E.M. Forster Died'.

91 He's one of those men who argues by increments of noise—so that as you open your mouth he says another, cleverer, louder thing.
1990 *Possession*, ch.15.

92 [J K] Rowling speaks to an adult generation that hasn't known and doesn't care about mystery. They are inhabitants of urban jungles, not of the real wild. They don't have the skills to tell ersatz magic from the real thing, for as children they daily invested the ersatz with what imagination they had.
2003 In the *New York Times*, 8 Jul.

Byrd, William 1543–1623

English composer and organist. A firm Catholic, prosecuted as a recusant, he wrote music for both Catholic and Anglican services, as well as madrigals, songs and music for strings.

93 The exercise of singing is delightful to nature and good to preserve the health of Man.
1588 *Psalmes, Sonets and Songs*.

Byrne, David 1952–

Scottish rock singer and guitarist, member of Talking Heads.

94 Book learning, or intelligence of one sort, doesn't
guarantee you intelligence of another sort. You can
behave just as stupidly with a good college education.
2004 In *Scotland on Sunday*, 29 Feb.

Byron, George Gordon, 6th Baron Byron of Rochdale 1788–1824

English Romantic poet. Lame from birth, he later dramatized
himself as a gloomy, romantic man of mystery, the 'Byronic
hero'. Suspected of an incestuous affair with his half-sister, he
left for Venice, where he wrote *Beppo* (1818) and *Don Juan*
(1819–24). He died fervently supporting the Greek war of
independence against the Turks.

95 Yet, when confinement's lingering hour was done,
Our sport, our studies, and our souls were one:
Together we impell'd the flying ball;
Together waited in our tutor's hall;
Together join'd in cricket's manly toil.
1807 *Hours of Idleness*, 'Childish Recollections'. Of his childhood
days at Harrow public school.

96 I'll publish, right or wrong:
Fools are my theme, let satire be my song.
1809 *English Bards and Scotch Reviewers*, l.5–6.

97 A man must serve his time to every trade
Save censure—critics all are ready made.
Take hackneyed jokes from Miller, got by rote,
With just enough of learning to misquote.
1809 *English Bards and Scotch Reviewers*, l.63–6.

98 Be warm, but pure; be amorous, but be chaste.
1809 *English Bards and Scotch Reviewers*, l.306.

99 The petrifactions of a plodding brain.
1809 *English Bards and Scotch Reviewers*, l.416.

1 Then let Ausonia, skilled in every art
To soften manners, but corrupt the heart,
Pour her exotic follies o'er the town,
To sanction Vice, and hunt Decorum down.
1809 *Engish Bards and Scotch Reviewers*, l.618–21.

2 Let simple Wordsworth chime his childish verse,
And brother Coleridge lull the babe at nurse.
1809 *English Bards and Scotch Reviewers*, l.917–18.

3 And glory, like the phoenix midst her fires,
Exhales her odours, blazes, and expires.
1809 *English Bards and Scotch Reviewers*, l.959–60.

4 Never under the most despotic of infidel Governments
did I behold such squalid wretchedness as I have seen
since my return, in the very heart of a Christian country.
And what are your remedies? After months of inaction,
and months of action worse than inactivity, at length
comes forth the grand specific—the never-failing
nostrum of all state physicians from the days of Draco to
the present time; death. Is there not blood enough upon
your penal code that more must be poured forth to
ascend to Heaven and testify against you?
1812 Maiden speech, House of Lords, 27 Feb, against a
proposal to introduce the death penalty for machine-
wrecking.

5 A land of meanness, sophistry and mist.
1812 Of Scotland. 'The Curse of Minerva', l.138.

6 Each breeze from foggy mount and marshy plain
Dilutes with drivel every drizzly brain,
Till, burst at length, each wat'ry head o'er flows,

Foul as their soil, and frigid as their snows.
1812 Of Scotland and the Scots. 'The Curse of Minerva', l.139–42.

7 The laughing dames in who he did delight,
Whose large blue eyes, fair locks, and snowy hands,
Might shake the saintship of an anchorite.
1812–18 *Childe Harold's Pilgrimage*, canto 1, stanza 11.

8 Adieu, adieu! my native shore
Fades o'er the waters blue.
1812–18 *Childe Harold's Pilgrimage*, canto 1, stanza 13.

9 Here all were noble, save Nobility.
1812–18 *Childe Harold's Pilgrimage*, canto 1, stanza 85.

10 None are so desolate but something dear,
Dearer than self, possesses or possessed
A thought, and claims the homage of a tear.
1812–18 *Childe Harold's Pilgrimage*, canto 2, stanza 24.

11 Oh, lovely Spain! renown'd, romantic land!
1812–18 *Childe Harold's Pilgrimage*, canto 2, stanza 35.

12 Dark Sappho! could not verse immortal save
That beast imbued with such immortal fire?
Could she not live who life eternal gave?
1812–18 *Childe Harold's Pilgrimage*, canto 2, stanza 39.

13 Fair Greece! sad relic of departed worth!
Immortal, though no more! though fallen, great!
1812–18 *Childe Harold's Pilgrimage*, canto 2, stanza 73.

14 Hereditary bondsmen! know ye not
Who would be free themselves must strike the blow?
1812–18 *Childe Harold's Pilgrimage*, canto 2, stanza 76.

15 And yet how lovely in thine age of woe,
Land of lost gods and godlike men! art thou!
1812–18 Of Greece. *Childe Harold's Pilgrimage*, canto 2,
stanza 85.

16 Art, Glory, Freedom fail, but Nature still is fair.
1812–18 *Childe Harold's Pilgrimage*, canto 2, stanza 87.

17 What is the worst of woes that wait on age?
What stamps the wrinkle deeper on the brow?
To view each loved one blotted from life's page,
And be alone on earth, as I am now.
1812–18 *Childe Harold's Pilgrimage*, canto 2, stanza 98.

18 Once more upon the waters! yet once more!
And the waves bound beneath me as a steed
That knows his rider.
1812–18 *Childe Harold's Pilgrimage*, canto 3, stanza 2.

19 The wandering outlaw of his own dark mind.
1812–18 *Childe Harold's Pilgrimage*, canto 3, stanza 3.

20 Years steal
Fire from the mind as vigour from the limb;
And life's enchanted cup but sparkles near the brim.
1812–18 *Childe Harold's Pilgrimage*, canto 3, stanza 8.

21 Where rose the mountains, there to him were friends;
Where rolled the ocean, thereon was his home;
Where a blue sky, and glowing clime, extends,
He had the passion and the power to roam.
1812–18 *Childe Harold's Pilgrimage*, canto 3, stanza 13.

22 The very knowledge that he lived in vain,
That all was over on this side the tomb,
Had made Despair a smilingness assume.
1812–18 *Childe Harold's Pilgrimage*, canto 3, stanza 16.

23 There was a sound of revelry by night,
And Belgium's capital had gathered then
Her beauty and her chivalry, and bright

The lamps that shone o'er fair women and brave men;
A thousand hearts beat happily; and when
Music arose with its voluptuous swell,
Soft eyes looked love to eyes which spake again,
And all went merry as a marriage bell;
But hush! hark! a deep sound strikes like a rising knell!
1812–18 *Childe Harold's Pilgrimage*, canto 3, stanza 21.

24 He rushed into the field, and, foremost fighting, fell.
1812–18 *Childe Harold's Pilgrimage*, canto 3, stanza 23.

25 Quiet to quick bosoms is a hell.
1812–18 *Childe Harold's Pilgrimage*, canto 3, stanza 42.

26 I live not in myself, but I become
Portion of that around me; and to me,
High mountains are a feeling, but the hum
Of human cities torture.
1812–18 *Childe Harold's Pilgrimage*, canto 3, stanza 72.

27 His love was passion's essence:—as a tree
On fire by lightning, with ethereal flame
Kindled he was, and blasted.
1812–18 *Childe Harold's Pilgrimage*, canto 3, stanza 78.

28 Sapping a solemn creed with solemn sneer.
1812–18 Of Edward Gibbon. *Childe Harold's Pilgrimage*, canto 3, stanza 107.

29 I have not loved the world, nor the world me.
1812–18 *Childe Harold's Pilgrimage*, canto 3, stanza 113.

30 I stood
Among them, but not of them; in a shroud
Of thoughts which were not their thoughts.
1812–18 *Childe Harold's Pilgrimage*, canto 3, stanza 113.

31 I stood in Venice, on the Bridge of Sighs;
A palace and a prison on each hand:
I saw from out the wave her structures rise
As from the stroke of the enchanter's wand:
A thousand years their cloudy wings expand
Around me, and a dying Glory smiles
O'er the far times, when many a subject land
Look'd to the winged Lion's marble piles,
Where Venice sate in state, thron'd on her hundred isles!
1812–18 *Childe Harold's Pilgrimage*, canto 4, stanza 1.

32 Fair Italy!
Thou art the garden of the world, the home
Of all Art yields, and Nature can decree;
Even in thy desert, what is like to thee?
1812–18 *Childe Harold's Pilgrimage*, canto 4, stanza 26.

33 The moon is up, and yet it is not night;
Sunset divides the sky with her—a sea
Of glory streams along the Alpine height
Of blue Friuli's mountains; Heaven is free
From clouds, but of all colours seems to be
Melted to one vast Iris of the West,
Where the day joins the past eternity.
1812–18 *Childe Harold's Pilgrimage*, canto 4, stanza 27.

34 Italia! oh Italia! thou who hast
The fatal gift of beauty.
1812–18 *Childe Harold's Pilgrimage*, canto 4, stanza 42.

35 Oh Rome! my country! city of the soul!
1812–18 *Childe Harold's Pilgrimage*, canto 4, stanza 78.

36 From mighty wrongs to petty perfidy
Have I not seen what human things could do?
From the loud roar of foaming calumny

To the small whisper of the asp paltry few,
And subtler venom of the reptile crew,
The Janus glance of whose significant eye,
Learning to lie with silence, would seem true,
And without utterance, save the shrug or sigh,
Deal round to happy fools its speechless obloquy.
1812–18 *Childe Harold's Pilgrimage*, canto 4, stanza 136.

37 But I have lived, and have not lived in vain:
My mind may loose its force, my blood its fire,
And my frame perish even in conquering pain;
But there is that within me which shall tire
Torture and Time, and breathe when I expire.
Something unearthly, which they deem not of,
Like the remembered tone of a mute lyre,
Shall on their softened spirits sink, and move
In hearts all rocky now the late remorse of love.
1812–18 *Childe Harold's Pilgrimage*, canto 4, stanza 137.

38 The seal is set.—Now welcome, thou dread power!
Nameless, yet thus omnipotent, which here
Walk'st in the shadow of the midnight hour
With a deep awe, yet all distinct from fear;
Thy haunts are ever where the dead walls rear
Their ivy mantles, and the solemn scene
Derives from thee a sense so deep and clear
That we become a part of what has been,
And grow unto the spot, all-seeing but unseen.
1812–18 *Childe Harold's Pilgrimage*, canto 4, stanza 138.

39 There were his young barbarians all at play,
There was their Dacian mother—he, their sire,
Butchered to make a Roman holiday.
1812–18 *Childe Harold's Pilgrimage*, canto 4, stanza 141.

40 A ruin—yet what ruin! from its mass
Walls, palaces, half-cities, have been reared.
1812–18 *Childe Harold's Pilgrimage*, canto 4, stanza 143.

41 While stands the Coliseum, Rome shall stand;
When falls the Coliseum, Rome shall fall;
And when Rome falls—the World.
1812–18 *Childe Harold's Pilgrimage*, canto 4, stanza 145.

42 Oh! that desert were my dwelling-place,
With one fair spirit for my minister,
That I might all forget the human race,
And, hating no one, love but only her!
1812–18 *Childe Harold's Pilgrimage*, canto 4, stanza 177.

43 There is a pleasure in the pathless woods,
There is a rapture on the lonely shore,
There is society, where none intrudes,
By the deep sea, and music in its roar:
I love not man less, but nature more.
1812–18 *Childe Harold's Pilgrimage*, canto 4, stanza 178.

44 Roll on, thou deep and dark blue Ocean—roll!
Ten thousand fleets sweep over thee in vain;
Man marks the earth with ruin—his control
Stops with the shore.
1812–18 *Childe Harold's Pilgrimage*, canto 4, stanza 179.

45 When for a moment, like a drop of rain,
He sinks into thy depths with bubbling groan,
Without a grave, unkindled, uncoffined, and unknown.
1812–18 *Childe Harold's Pilgrimage*, canto 4, stanza 179.

46 Dark-heaving;—boundless, endless, and sublime—
The image of eternity.
1812–18 Of the sea. *Childe Harold's Pilgrimage*, canto 4, stanza 183.

47 Such hath it been—shall be—beneath the sun
The many still must labour for the one.
1814 *The Corsair*, canto 1, stanza 8.

48 There was a laughing devil in sneer,
That raised emotions both of rage and fear;
And where his frown of hatred darkly fell,
Hope withering fled, and Mercy sighed farewell!
1814 *The Corsair*, canto 1, stanza 9.

49 Deep in my soul that tender secret dwells,
Lonely and lost to light for evermore,
Save when to thine my heart responsive swells,
Then trembles into silence as before.
1814 *The Corsair*, 'Medora's Song', canto 1, stanza 14.

50 The spirit burning but unbent
May writhe, rebel—the weak alone repent!
1814 *The Corsair*, canto 2, stanza 10.

51 Oh! too convincing—dangerously dear—
In woman's eye the unanswerable tear!
1814 *The Corsair*, canto 2, stanza 15.

52 Shakespeare's name, you may depend upon it, stands
absurdly too high and will go down. He had no invention
as to stories, none whatever. He took all his plots from
old novels, and threw their stories into dramatic shape…
That he threw over whatever he did write some flashes
of genius, nobody can deny; but this was all.
1814 Letter to James Hogg, 24 Mar.

53 She walks in beauty like the night
Of cloudless climes and starry skies;
And all that's best of dark and bright
Meet in her aspect and her eyes:
Thus mellowed to that tender light
Which heaven to gaudy day denies.
1815 'She Walks in Beauty'.

54 There's not a joy the world can give like that it takes away.
1816 'Stanzas for Music'.

55 The mind can make
Substance, and people planets of its own
With beings brighter than have been, and give
A breath to forms which can outlive all flesh.
1816 *The Dream*, stanza 1.

56 Sorrow is knowledge: they who know the most
Must mourn the deepest o'er the fatal truth,
The tree of knowledge is not that of Life.
1817 *Manfred*, act 1, sc.1.

57 How beautiful is all this visible world!
How glorious in its action and itself!
But we, who name ourselves its sovereigns, we,
Half dust, half deity, alike unfit
To sink or soar, with our mixed essence make
A conflict of its elements, and breathe
The breath of degradation and of pride.
1817 *Manfred*, act 1, sc.2.

58 In short he was a perfect cavaliero,
And to his very valet seemed a hero.
1818 *Beppo*, stanza 33.

59 His heart was one of those which most enamour us,
Wax to receive, and marble to retain.
1818 *Beppo*, stanza 34.

60 Our cloudy climate, and our chilly women.
1818 *Beppo*, stanza 49.

61 Old man! 'tis not so difficult to die.
1819 *Manfred* (2nd edn), act 3, sc.4.

62 And Coleridge, too, has lately taken wing,
But, like a hawk encumbered with his hood,
Explaining metaphysics to the nation—
I wished he would explain his explanation.
1819–24 *Don Juan*, canto 1, dedication, stanza 2.

63 But—Oh! ye lords of ladies intellectual,
Inform us truly, have they not hen-pecked you all?.
1819–24 *Don Juan*, canto 1, stanza 22.

64 Married, charming, chaste, and twenty-three.
1819–24 *Don Juan*, canto 1, stanza 59.

65 What men call gallantry, and gods adultery,
Is much more common where the climate's sultry.
1819–24 *Don Juan*, canto 1, stanza 63.

66 Christians have burnt each other, quite persuaded
That all the Apostles would have done as they did.
1819–24 *Don Juan*, canto 1, stanza 83.

67 He thought about himself, and the whole earth,
Of man the wonderful, and of the stars,
And how the deuce they ever could have birth;
And then he thought of earthquakes, and of wars,
How many miles the moon might have in girth,
Of air-balloons, and of the many bars
To perfect knowledge of the boundless skies;
And then he thought of Donna Julia's eyes.
1819–24 *Don Juan*, canto 1, stanza 92.

68 A little still she strove, and much repented,
And whispering 'I will ne'er consent'—consented.
1819–24 *Don Juan*, canto 1, stanza 117.

69 Sweet is revenge—especially to women.
1819–24 *Don Juan*, canto 1, stanza 124.

70 'Tis sweet to win, no matter how, one's laurels
By blood or ink; 'tis sweet to put an end
To strife; 'tis sometimes sweet to have our quarrels,
Particularly with a tiresome friend;
Sweet is old wine in bottles, ale in barrels;
Dear is the helpless creature we defend
Against the world; and dear the schoolboy spot
We ne'er forget, though there we are forgot.
1819–24 *Don Juan*, canto 1, stanza 126.

71 But sweeter still than this, than these, than all,
Is first and passionate love—it stands alone,
Like Adam's recollection of his fall;
The tree of knowledge hath been pluck'd—all's known
And life yields nothing further to recall
Worthy of this ambrosial sin, so shown,
No doubt in fable, as the unforgiven
Fire which Prometheus filch'd for us from heaven.
1819–24 *Don Juan*, canto 1, stanza 127.

72 Pleasure's a sin, and sometimes sin is a pleasure.
1819–24 *Don Juan*, canto 1, stanza 133.

73 Man's love is of man's life a thing apart,
'Tis woman's whole existence.
1819–24 *Don Juan*, canto 1, stanza 194.
➤ *See Amis 14:84*.

74 If ever I should condescend to prose,
I'll write poetical commandments, which
Shall supersede beyond all doubt all those
That went before; in these I shall enrich

My text with many things that no one knows,
And carry precept to the highest pitch:
I'll call the work 'Longinus o'er a Bottle,
Or, Every Poet his own Aristotle'.
1819–24 Don Juan, canto 1, stanza 204.

75 Thou shalt believe in Milton, Dryden, Pope;
Thou shalt not set up Wordsworth, Coleridge, Southey;
Because the first is crazed beyond all hope,
The second drunk, the third so quaint and mouthey:
With Crabbe it may be difficult to cope,
And Campbell's Hippocrene is somewhat drouthy:
Thou shalt not steal from Samuel Rogers, nor
Commit flirtation with the muse of Moore.
1819–24 Don Juan, canto 1, stanza 205.

76 So for a good old-gentlemanly vice,
I think I must take up with avarice.
1819–24 Don Juan, canto 1, stanza 216.

77 There's nought, no doubt, so much the spirit calms
As rum and true religion.
1819–24 Don Juan, canto 2, stanza 34.

78 It was a wild and breaker-beaten coast,
With cliffs above, and a broad sandy shore,
Guarded by shoals and rocks as by an host,
With here and there a creek, whose aspect wore
A better welcome to the tempest-tost;
And rarely ceased the haughty billow's roar,
Save on the dead long summer days, which make
The outstretch'd ocean glitter like a lake.
1819–24 Don Juan, canto 2, stanza 177.

79 Few things surpass old wine; and they may preach
Who please,—the more because they preach in vain,
Let us have wine and woman, mirth and laughter,
Sermons and soda water the day after.
1819–24 Don Juan, canto 2, stanza 178.

80 Man, being reasonable, must get drunk;
The best of Life is but intoxication.
Glory, the grape, love, gold, in these are sunk
The hopes of all men, and of every nation.
1819–24 Don Juan, canto 2, stanza 179.

81 They looked up to the sky, whose floating glow
Spread like a rosy ocean, vast and bright;
They gazed upon the glittering sea below,
Whence the broad moon rose circling into sight;
They heard the wave's splash, and the wind so low,
And saw each other's dark eyes darting light
Into each other—and, beholding this,
Their lips drew near, and clung to a kiss.
1819–24 Don Juan, canto 2, stanza 185.

82 In her first passion woman loves her lover,
In all the others all she loves is love.
1819–24 Don Juan, canto 3, stanza 3.

83 'Tis melancholy, and a fearful sign
Of human frailty, folly, also crime,
That love and marriage rarely can combine,
Although they both are born in the same clime;
Marriage from love, like vinegar from wine
A sad, sour, sober beverage—by time
Is sharpened from its high celestial flavour,
Down to a very homely household savour.
1819–24 Don Juan, canto 3, stanza 5.

84 Think you, if Laura had been Petrach's wife,

He would have written sonnets all his life?
1819–24 Don Juan, canto 3, stanza 8.

85 All tragedies are finished by a death,
All comedies are ended by a marriage;
The future states of both are left to faith.
1819–24 Don Juan, canto 3, stanza 9.

86 He was the mildest mannered man
That ever scuttled ship or cut a throat,
With such true breeding of a gentleman,
You never could divine his real thought.
1819–24 Don Juan, canto 3, stanza 41.

87 The mountains look on Marathon—
And Marathon looks on the sea;
And musing there an hour alone,
I dreamed that Greece might still be free.
1819–24 Don Juan, canto 3, stanza 86.

88 And if I laugh at any mortal thing
'Tis that I may not weep.
1819–24 Don Juan, canto 4, stanza 4.

89 But after being fired at once or twice,
The ear becomes more Irish, and less nice.
1819–24 Don Juan, canto 4, stanza 41.

90 I have a passion for the name of 'Mary,'
For once it was a magic sound to me;
And still it half calls up the realms of fairy,
Where I beheld what never was to be.
1819–24 Don Juan, canto 5, stanza 4.

91 There is a tide in the affairs of women,
Which taken at the flood, leads—God knows where.
1819–24 Don Juan, canto 6, stanza 2.

92 Gaunt Famine never shall approach the throne.
Though Ireland starve, great George weighs twenty stone.
1819–24 Don Juan, canto 8, stanza 126.

93 And, after all what is a lie? 'Tis but
The truth in masquerade.
1819–24 Don Juan, canto 11, stanza 37.

94 Now hatred is by far the longest pleasure;
Men love in haste, but they detest at leisure.
1819–24 Don Juan, canto 13, stanza 4.

95 The English winter—ending in July,
To recommence in August.
1819–24 Don Juan, canto 13, stanza 42.

96 Society is now one polished horde,
Formed of two mighty tribes, the Bores and Bored.
1819–24 Don Juan, canto 13, stanza 95.

97 'Tis strange but true; for truth is always stranger;
Stranger than fiction.
1819–24 Don Juan, canto 14, stanza 101.

98 All present life is but an interjection,
An 'Oh!' or 'Ah!' of joy or misery,
Or a 'Ha! ha!' or 'Bah!'—a yawn or 'Pooh!'
Of which perhaps the latter is most true.
1819–24 Don Juan, canto 15, stanza 1.

99 There's music in the sighing of a reed;
There's music in the gushing of a rill;
There's music in all things, if men had ears:
Their earth is but an echo of the spheres.
1819–24 Don Juan, canto 15, stanza 5.

1 Between two worlds life hovers like a star,
'Twixt night and morn, upon the horizon's verge.

How little do we know that which we are!
How less what we may be!
1819–24 *Don Juan*, canto 15, stanza 99.

2 Eat, drink, and love; the rest's not worth a fillip.
1821 *Sardanapalus*, act 1, sc.2.

3 Oh, talk not to me of a name great in story;
The days of our youth are the days of our glory;
And the myrtle and ivy of sweet two-and-twenty
Are worth all your laurels, though ever so plenty.
1821 'Stanzas Written on the Road between Florence and Pisa,
November 1821'.

4 The angels all were singing out of tune,
And hoarse with having little else to do,
Excepting to wind up the sun and moon,
Or curb a runaway young star or two.
1822 *The Vision of Judgement*, stanza 2.

5 As he drew near, he gazed upon the gate
Ne'er to be entered more by him or Sin,
With such a glance of supernatural hate,
As made Saint Peter wish himself within;
He pattered with his keys at a great rate,
And sweated through his apostolic skin:
Of course his perspiration was but ichor,
Or some such other spiritual liquor.
1822 *The Vision of Judgement*, stanza 25.

6 And when the tumult dwindled to a calm,
I left him practising the hundredth psalm.
1822 *The Vision of Judgement*, stanza 106.

7 For what were all these country patriots born?
To hunt, and vote, and raise the price of corn?
1823 *The Age of Bronze*, stanza 14.

8 I awoke one morning and found myself famous.
Of the instant popularity of *Childe Harolde*. Quoted in Thomas
Moore *Letters and Journals of Lord Byron* (1830), vol.1.

Byron, Henry James 1834–84

English playwright and actor. His most successful plays
included *Our Boys* (1874) and the comedies *War to the Knife*
(1865) and *A Hundred Thousand Pounds* (1866), as well as
numerous burlesques and extravaganzas.

9 Life's too short for chess.
1874 *Our Boys*.

Byron, Robert 1905–41

English traveller, critic of art and architecture and historian,
who travelled extensively in Europe and Asia. His best-known
book is *The Road to Oxiana* (1937). He drowned in 1941 when his
ship to the Mediterranean was torpedoed.

10 The existence of St Sophia is atmospheric; that of St
Peter's, overpowering, imminently substantial. One is a
church to God; the other a salon for his agents. One is
consecrated to reality, the other to illusion. St Sophia, in
fact, is large, and St Peter's is vilely, tragically small.
1929 *The Byzantine Achievement*.

11 *Herat, 8 December*. What a day it was! God save me
from any more adventures on a drained stomach.
1937 *The Road to Oxiana*.

12 I shall have warmonger put on my passport.
c.1938 Comment in response to the rise of Nazism, opposing the
policy of appeasement. Quoted in Bruce Chatwin's introduction
to *The Road to Oxiana* (1980 edn).

C

Cabell, James Branch 1879–1958

US novelist and critic. *Jurgen* (1919) is the best known of a
sequence of 18 novels, collectively known as *Biography of
Michael*. His *Preface to the Past* (1936) is a book of criticism.

13 I am willing to taste any drink once.
1919 *Jurgen*, ch.1.

14 A man possesses nothing certainly save a brief loan of his
own body.
1919 *Jurgen*, ch.20.

15 I shall marry in haste and repeat at leisure.
1919 *Jurgen*, ch.26.
➤ *See Congreve 231:1.*

16 Drunkenness is a joy reserved for the Gods: so do men
partake of it impiously, and so are they very properly
punished for their audacity.
1919 *Jurgen*, ch.28.

17 Poetry is man's rebellion against being what he is.
1919 *Jurgen*.

18 The optimist proclaims that we live in the best of all
possible worlds; and the pessimist fears this is true.
1926 *The Silver Stallion*, bk.4, ch.26.

Cabrera Infante, Guillermo 1929–

Cuban novelist, scriptwriter, film critic and diplomat. He
supported Castro's revolutionary forces initially, but later left the
country and settled in London (1965), becoming a British
subject. *Tres tristes tigres* (1967, translated as *Three Trapped Tigers*,
1971) is full of puns, neologisms and humorous word play.

19 *Hablando siempre y siempre contando chismes y
haciendo chistes y siempre y también filosofando o
estetizando o moralizando, siempre: la cuestión era
hacer ver como que no trabajábamos porque en La
Habana, Cuba, esa es la única manera de ser gente bien.*
Talking all the time and telling jokes or gossiping all the
time and always and also philosophizing or
aestheticizing or moralizing, but always: the thing was to
make it look like we didn't have to work because in
Havana, Cuba, this is the only way to be high society . . .
1967 *Tres tristes tigres* (*Three Trapped Tigers*, 1971), 'Bachata'.

Cadoria, Brigadier General Sherian G(race) 1940–

US soldier. In 1985 she became the highest-ranking black
woman in the US military. She retired in 1990.

20 By act of Congress, male officers are gentlemen, but by
act of God, we are ladies.
1989 In *US News and World Report*, 13 Feb.

Caesar, Irving 1895–1996

US librettist and lyricist.

21 Tea for two, and two for tea.
1924 *No! No! Nanette*, 'Tea for Two' (with Otto Harbach. Music by
Vincent Youmans).

Caesar, Gaius Julius 100/102–44 BC

Roman general and statesman. As consul (59 BC) and pro-consul (58–50 BC) he extended Roman power in Gaul and Britain. Refusing to disband his army, he came into conflict with the Senate, supported by Pompey, whom Caesar defeated in the civil war that followed. He became dictator for life, but was assassinated in 44 BC. His works include the *Commentarii* ('War Commentaries'), *De Bello Gallico* ('On the Gallic War', 7 vols) and *De Bello Civili* ('On the Civil War', 3 vols).

22 *Gallia est omnis divisa in partes tres.*
Gaul as a whole is divided into three parts.
51 BC *De Bello Gallico*, bk.1, section 1, opening words.

23 *Fere libenter homines id quod volunt credunt.*
Men are nearly always willing to believe what they wish.
51 BC *De Bello Gallico*, bk.3, section 18.

24 *Iacta est alea.*
The die is cast.
49 BC Comment on crossing the river Rubicon (the border between his province and Italy) with his troops, thereby committing himself to civil war. Quoted in Suetonius *Lives of the Twelve Caesars*, 'Divus Iulius', section 32.

25 *Veni, vidi, vici.*
I came, I saw, I conquered.
46 BC Said to have been written on a *titulus* (placard) carried along in Caesar's triumph after a campaign in Pontus (Asia Minor) during the civil war (46 BC). Quoted in Suetonius *Lives of the Twelve Caesars*, 'Divus Iulius', section 37. Another source reports that Caesar used this expression in a letter to the Senate after the same campaign (cf Plutarch, *Caesar* 50, 3–4).

26 Caesar's wife must be above suspicion.
Attributed. Based on an episode in Plutarch *Caesar* 10.6, which tells that Caesar divorced his wife after accusations of impiety, although he defended her in court.

27 *Et tu, Brute?*
You too, Brutus?
Attributed last words, when struck by his murderers, Cassius and Brutus. The tradition is based on Suetonius *Lives of the Twelve Caesars*, 'Divus Iulius', section 82: 'Some say that when he saw Marcus Brutus about to deliver the second blow, he reproached him in Greek with: 'You too, my son?' (the Greek is *kai su, teknon*).

Cage, John 1912–92

US ultra-modernist composer. His experiments included 'aleatory' music, in which the role of chance determines how a piece will develop. *Silence* (1961), *M* (1973), and *Empty Works* (1979) are among his books.

28 Which is more musical, a truck passing by a factory or a truck passing by a music school?
1961 *Silence*.

29 I have nothing to say
and I am saying it and that is poetry.
1961 'Lecture on Nothing'.

Cagney, James 1899–1986

US film actor. A leading role in *Public Enemy* (1931) established him as the quintessential screen gangster. He won an Academy Award for his performance in *Yankee Doodle Dandy* (1942).

30 Look Ma—top of the world.
1949 Line delivered in *White Heat* (screenplay by Ivan Goff and Ben Roberts).

Cain, James M(allahan) 1892–1977

US crime writer.

31 The Postman Always Rings Twice.
1934 Title of novel.

32 Double Indemnity.
1943 Title of novel.

Calas, Nicolas 1907–88

Greek-born art critic and poet, who associated with the Surrealists in Paris in the 1930s. He moved to the United States in 1939.

33 Art is a form of communication that insinuates. We *expect* the artist to have more to say than what he communicated and *suspect* that what he said was a subterfuge for hiding something.
1968 *Art in the Age of Risk*.

Caldwell, Philip 1920–

US company executive, Chairman of the Ford Motor Co (1980–5).

34 We redesigned everything but the air in the tires.
1995 Of the development of the Taurus, which was to become America's best-selling car. In *Fortune*, 3 Apr.

Calhoun, John Caldwell 1782–1850

US statesman and orator, Vice-President under John Q Adams and then Andrew Jackson. His *Address to the People of South Carolina* (1831) set forth his theory of state rights.

35 The Government of the absolute majority, instead of the Government of the people, is but the Government of the strongest interests; and when not efficiently checked, it is the most tyrannical and oppressive that can be devised.
1833 Speech, US Senate, 15 Feb.

Caligiuri, Paul 1964–

US footballer.

36 The world knows the American athlete is superior. It's only a matter of time before we develop the world's best soccer teams.
2002 In *The Times*, 28 Dec.

Caligula properly *Gaius Julius Caesar Germanicus* AD 12–41

Roman Emperor (AD 37–41), nicknamed Caligula as a child from his little soldier's boots (*caligae*). His extravagant, autocratic, vicious and mentally unstable behaviour resulted in his assassination.

37 *Utinam populus Romanus unam cervicem haberet!*
Would that the Roman people had but one neck!
c.40 AD Quoted in Suetonius *Lives of the Twelve Caesars*, 'Gaius Caligula', section 30.

Callaghan (of Cardiff), (Leonard) James Callaghan, Baron 1912–

English Labour politician. As Chancellor of the Exchequer he introduced controversial corporation and selective employment taxes. He was Home Secretary (1967–70), Foreign Secretary (1974–6) and Prime Minister (1976–9).

38 Britain has lived for too long on borrowed time,

borrowed money, and even borrowed ideas.
1976 Quoted in the *Observer*, 3 Oct.

39 There is no virtue in producing socially well adjusted members of society who are unemployed because they do not have the skills. Nor at the other extreme must they be technically efficient robots.
1976 Speech at Ruskin College, Oxford, reprinted in the *Times Higher Education Supplement*, 15 Oct. This speech began the so-called 'Great Debate' on education.

40 A lie can travel halfway round the world before the truth has got its boots on.
1976 Speech in the House of Commons, Nov.
➤ See *Spurgeon 811:41*.

41 Either back us or sack us.
1977 Speech, Labour Party Conference, 5 Oct.

42 Crisis? What crisis?
1979 Headline in *The Sun*, 11 Jan, alluding to his remark on returning from the Guadaloupe summit to be confronted by widespread strikes. His actual words were, 'I don't think that other people in the world would share the view that there is mounting chaos.'

Callanan, Jeremiah John 1795–1829

Irish poet. Born in Cork and sent by his parents to study for the priesthood, he developed instead his interest in lyrical poetry. He supported himself by teaching and writing. He gained general celebrity with 'Gougane Barra' (1826).

43 There grows the wild ash; and a time-stricken willow
Looks chidingly down on the mirth of the billow,
As, like some gay child that sad monitor scorning,
It lightly laughs back to the laugh of the morning.
1826 'Gougane Barra'.

Callow, Simon Phillip Hugh 1949–

English actor and director.

44 When he speaks, I hear Shakespeare think.
On Sir John Gielgud. Quoted in *The Guardian*, 14 Apr 2004.

Calonne, Charles Alexandre de 1734–1802

French politician. Appointed Controller-General in 1783, he was exiled in 1787 when he failed to provide a statement of accounts to explain the treasury deficit. Napoleon I permitted his return in 1802.

45 *Madame, si c'est possible, c'est fait; impossible? cela se fera.*
Madam, if a thing is possible, consider it done; the impossible? that will be done.
Quoted in J Michelet *Histoire de la Révolution Française* (1847), vol.1, pt.2. This has been adapted as the slogan of the US army: 'The difficult we do immediately; the impossible takes a little longer.'

Calvino, Italo 1923–85

Italian modernist writer and journalist, born in Cuba. A fascist under compulsion, he later joined the Resistance (1943) and wrote for the Communist *L'unità* in the 1940s. His novels combine fantasy with a hard satirical wit.

46 *Lo sguardo dei cani che non capiscono e non sanno che possono aver ragione a non capire.*
The gaze of dogs who don't understand and who don't know that they may be right not to understand.
1957 *Il Barone Rampante*, ch.10.

Cambronne, Pierre, Baron de 1770–1842

French general in the Napoleonic wars.

47 *La Garde meurt, mais ne se rend pas.*
The Guards die but do not surrender.
1815 Attributed, when called upon to surrender at the Battle of Waterloo, 18 Jun.

Cameron, James 1954–

Canadian film director. His film *Titanic* (1997) won eleven Academy Awards, equalling the record set by *Ben Hur* in 1959.

48 I'm king of the world.
1998 Accepting his Best Director Oscar for *Titanic* (1997), 23 Mar, an allusion to a line in *Titanic*.

Campbell, Donald Malcolm 1921–67

English speedboat racer. Son of Sir Malcolm Campbell, he broke all his father's land and water speed records, but was killed when his hydroplane *Bluebird* crashed on Lake Coniston at about 300mph.

49 There is no hope of bailing out of a speedboat. You hit the water and become so much pulp.
Quoted in Douglas Young-James *Donald Campbell: An Informal Biography* (1968).

Campbell, Kim *originally* Avril Phaedra Campbell 1947–

Canadian politician. She entered the Commons in 1988 as a Progressive Conservative, becoming Canada's first woman Prime Minister (Jun–Dec, 1993); she lost her parliamentary seat in the 1993 election.

50 Charisma without substance is a dangerous thing.
1986 Speech, while unsuccessfully contesting the leadership of the Social Credit Party of British Columbia, 22 Oct.

Campbell, Mrs Patrick *née* Beatrice Rose Stella Tanner 1865–1940

English actress. Famed for her stage presence and incisive wit, she made her debut in 1888. She corresponded with George Bernard Shaw, who wrote *Pygmalion* especially for her.

51 When you were quite a little boy somebody ought to have said 'hush' just once.
1912 Letter to George Bernard Shaw, 1 Nov.

52 The deep, deep peace of the double-bed after the hurly-burly of the chaise-longue.
Her definition of marriage, quoted in Alexander Woollcott *While Rome Burns* (1934), 'The First Mrs Tanqueray'.

53 It doesn't matter what you do in the bedroom as long as you don't do it in the street and frighten the horses.
Quoted in Daphne Fielding *The Duchess of Jermyn Street* (1964), ch.2. Sometimes attributed to Edward VII.

54 Watching Tallulah Bankhead on the stage is like watching somebody skating on very thin ice—and the English want to be there when she falls through.
Quoted in *The Times*, 13 Dec 1968.

Campbell, (Ignatius) Roy Dunnachie 1901–57

South African poet, who spent much of his life in Britain. He moved from an early liberalism to outspoken right-wing Catholicism, and is best remembered for his early lyric poems.

55 South Africa, renowned both far and wide

For politics and little else besides.
1928 'The Wayzgoose'.

56 You praise the firm restraint with which they write—
I'm with you there, of course:
They use the snaffle and the curb all right,
But where's the bloody horse?
1930 'On Some South African Novelists'.

57 Of all the clever people round me here
I most delight in Me—
Mine is the only voice I care to hear,
And mine the only face I like to see.
1930 'Home Thoughts in Bloomsbury'.

58 Write with your spade, and garden with your pen,
Shove your couplets to their long repose.
And type your turnips down the field in rows.
1931 'The Georgiad', pt.2.

59 Burn, with Athens and with Rome,
A sacred city of the mind.
1936 'Toledo, July 1936'.

60 I will go stark: and let my meanings show
Clear as a milk-white feather in a crow
Or a black stallion on a field of snow.
1936 'A Good Resolution'.

61 He shouldered high his voluntary Cross,
Wrestled his hardships into forms of beauty,
And taught his gorgon destinies to sing.
1943 'Luis de Camões'.

62 Giraffes!—a People
Who live between the earth and skies,
Each in his own religious steeple,
Keeping a light-house with his eyes.
1946 'Dreaming Spires'.

63 Translations, like wives, are seldom faithful if they are in the least attractive.
1949 *The Poetry Review*, Jun/ Jul.

64 I hate 'Humanity' and all such abstracts: but I love *people*. Lovers of 'Humanity' generally hate *people and children*, and keep parrots or puppy dogs.
1951 *Light On A Dark Horse*, ch.13.

Campbell, Thomas 1777–1844

Scottish poet and journalist, Editor from 1820 to 1830 of *The New Monthly Magazine*, to which he contributed many poems. He is buried in Westminster Abbey.

65 On the green banks of Shannon, when Sheelah was nigh,
No blithe Irish lad was so happy as I;
No harp like my own could so cheerily play,
And wherever I went was my poor dog Tray.
1799 'The Harper', stanza 1.

66 'Tis distance lends enchantment to the view,
And robes the mountain in its azure hue.
1799 *The Pleasures of Hope*, pt.1, l.7–8.

67 Hope, for a season, bade the world farewell,
And Freedom shrieked—as Kosciusko fell!
1799 *The Pleasures of Hope*, pt.1, l.381–2.

68 What millions died—that Caesar might be great!
1799 *The Pleasures of Hope*, pt.2, l.174.

69 What though my wingèd hours of bliss have been,
Like angel-visits, few and far between?
1799 *The Pleasures of Hope*, pt.2, l.375–6.

70 A chieftain to the Highlands bound
Cries 'Boatman, do not tarry!
And I'll give thee a silver pound
To row us o'er the ferry.'
1809 'Lord Ullin's Daughter', stanza 1.

71 And yet, amidst that joy and uproar,
Let us think of them that sleep,
Full many a fathom deep,
By thy wild and stormy steep,
Elsinore!
1809 'The Battle of the Baltic', stanza 8.

72 To-morrow let us do or die!
1809 'Gertrude of Wyoming', pt.3, stanza 37.

73 An original something, fair maid you would win me
To write—but how shall I begin?
For I fear I have nothing original in me—
Excepting Original Sin.
1843 'To a Young Lady, Who Asked Me to Write Something Original for Her Album'.

74 Now Barabbas was a publisher.
Attributed. Quoted in Samuel Smiles *A Publisher and his Friends: Memoir and Correspondence of the late John Murray* (1891), vol.1, ch.14. The quote is sometimes attributed to Byron.

Campion, Jane 1954–

New Zealand film director and writer. She dramatized Janet Frame's autobiography *An Angel at My Table* for television (1990) and won an Academy Award for her screenplay for *The Piano* (1993), which she also directed.

75 Remember your own childhood. That complete certainty you had, looking at the grown-ups, that you would never be like that. It was a lonely feeling, but euphoric, too.
1994 Interview with Sarah Gristwood in *The Times Magazine*, 'Jane Campion: A Childhood', 1 Jan.

Campion, Thomas 1567–1620

English physician, poet and composer. As well as poetry in Latin and English he wrote four *Books of Airs* for voice and lute (1601–17) and *Observations in the Art of English Poesie* (1602), defending classical structures.

76 My sweetest Lesbia, let us live and love,
And though the sager sort our deeds reprove,
Let us not weigh them. Heaven's great lamps do dive
Into their west, and straight again revive,
But soon as once set is our little light,
Then must we sleep one ever-during night.
1601 *A Book of Airs*, no.1, 'My Sweetest Lesbia', translation of a song by Catullus.
➤ *See Catullus 200:5.*

77 As her lute doth live or die,
Led by her passion, so must I:
For when of pleasure she doth sing,
My thoughts enjoy a sudden spring,
But if she doth of sorrow speak,
Ev'n from my heart the strings do break.
1601 *A Book of Airs*, no.6, 'When to Her Lute Corinna Sings'.

78 I care not for these ladies that must be wooed and prayed.
Give me kind Amaryllis, the wanton country maid.
1601 *A Book of Airs*, 'I Care Not for These Ladies'.

79 Rose-cheeked Laura, come,
Sing thou smoothly with thy beauty's
Silent music, either other
Sweetly gracing.
1602 *Second Book of Airs*, 'Rose-Cheeked Laura'.

80 There is a garden in her face,
Where roses and white lilies grow,
A heavenly paradise is that place,
Wherein all pleasant fruits do flow.
There cherries grow, which none may buy
Till 'Cherry ripe!' themselves do cry.
1617 *Fourth Book of Airs*, 'There is a Garden in her Face'.

81 Fain would I wed a fair young man that night and day
could please me,
When my mind or body grieved that had the power to
ease me.
Maids are full of longing thoughts that breed a bloodless
sickness,
And that, oft I hear men say, is only cured by quickness.
1617 *Fourth Book of Airs*, 'Fain Would I Wed'.

82 Yet I would not die a maid, because I had a mother,
As I was by one brought forth, I would bring forth
another.
1617 *Fourth Book of Airs*, 'Fain Would I Wed'.

Campo, Estanislao de 1834–80

Argentinian soldier, political journalist and *gaucho* (pampas
cowboy) poet. *Fausto*, a long poetic dialogue in six episodes,
relates a *gaucho's* impressions of a performance of Gounod's
Faust in Buenos Aires.

83 *Por hembras yo no me pierdo.*
La que me empaca su amor
pasa por el cernidor
y…si te vi, no me acuerdo.
I make no fuss about females.
The one who gives me her love
Gets sifted in my private sieve
and…I don't think we ever met.
1866 *Fausto* (translated as *Faust*, 1943), pt.3.

Camus, Albert 1913–60

French writer. Active in the French Resistance, he found fame
with his Existentialist novel *L'Étranger* (1942). Other works
include *La Peste* (1947), *La Chute* (1956), plays and political
writings. He was awarded a Nobel prize in 1957 and he died in
a car accident.

84 *Intellectuel = celui qui se dédouble.*
Intellectual: someone whose mind watches itself.
Carnets, 1935–42 (published 1962).

85 *La politique et le sort des hommes sont formés par des*
hommes sans idéal et sans grandeur. Ceux qui ont une
grandeur en eux ne font pas de politique.
Politics and the fate of mankind are shaped by men
without ideals and without greatness. Those who have
greatness within them do not go in for politics.
Carnets, 1935–42 (published 1962).

86 *L'absurde est la notion essentielle et la première vérité.*
The absurd is the fundamental idea and the first truth.
1942 *Le Mythe de Sisyphe* (*The Myth of Sisyphus*, 1955).

87 *Il n'y a qu'un problème philosophique vraiment sérieux:*
c'est le suicide. Juger que la vie vaut ou ne vaut pas la
peine d'être vécue, c'est répondre à la question
fondamentale de la philosophie.
There is but one truly serious philosophical problem, and
that is suicide. Judging whether life is or is not worth
living amounts to answering the fundamental question
of philosophy.
1942 *Le Mythe de Sisyphe* (*The Myth of Sisyphus*, 1955), 'Absurdity
and Suicide'.

88 *L'homme se trouve devant l'irrationnel. Il sent en lui son*
désir de bonheur et de raison. L'absurde naît de cette
confrontation entre l'appel humain et le silence
déraisonnable du monde.
Man stands face to face with the irrational. He feels
within him his longing for happiness and for reason. The
absurd is born of this confrontation between the human
need and the unreasonable silence of the world.
1942 *Le Mythe de Sisyphe* (*The Myth of Sisyphus*, 1955), 'The
Absurd Walls'.

89 *Il n'est pas de destin que ne se surmonte par le mépris.*
There is no fate that cannot be surmounted by scorn.
1942 *Le Mythe de Sisyphe* (*The Myth of Sisyphus*, 1955).

90 *La lutte elle-même vers les sommets suffit à remplir un*
coeur d'homme. Il faut imaginer Sisyphe heureux.
The struggle itself towards the heights is enough to
fill a human heart. One must imagine that Sisyphus
is happy.
1942 *Le Mythe de Sisyphe* (*The Myth of Sisyphus*, 1955).

91 *Aujourd'hui, maman est morte. Ou peut-être hier, je ne*
sais pas.
Mother died today. Or perhaps it was yesterday, I don't
know.
1942 *L'Etranger*.

92 *Peut-on être un saint sans Dieu: C'est le seul problème*
concret que je connaisse aujourd'hui.
Can one become a saint without God? That is the only
concrete problem I know of today.
1947 *La Peste*.

93 *Il y a dans les hommes plus de choses à admirer que de*
choses à mépriser.
There are more things to admire in people than to
despise.
1947 *La Peste*.

94 *Qu'est-ce qu'un homme révolté? Un homme qui dit non.*
What is a rebel? A man who says no.
1951 *L'Homme révolté*.

95 *Toutes les révolutions modernes ont abouti à un*
renforcement de l'Etat.
All modern revolutions have ended in a reinforcement of
the State.
1951 *L'Homme révolté*.

96 *Tout révolutionnaire finit en oppresseur ou en hérétique.*
Every revolutionary ends as an oppressor or a heretic.
1951 *L'Homme révolté*.

97 *Le style, comme la popeline, dissimule trop souvent de*
l'eczéma.
Style, like sheer silk, too often hides eczema.
1956 *La Chute*, ch.1 (translated by Stuart Gilbert).

98 *Vous savez ce qu'est le charme: une manière de*
s'entendre répondre oui sans avoir posé aucune
question claire.
You know what charm is: a way of getting the answer yes

without having asked any clear question.
1956 *La Chute* (translated by Stuart Gilbert).

99 *Chacun exige d'être innocent, à tout prix, même si, pour cela, il faut accuser le genre humain et le ciel.*
Everyone insists on his or her innocence, at all costs, even if it means accusing the rest of the human race and heaven.
1956 *La Chute* (translated by Stuart Gilbert).

1 *C'est si vrai que nous nous confions rarement à ceux qui sont meilleurs que nous.*
It is true that we seldom confide in those who are better than ourselves.
1956 *La Chute* (translated by Stuart Gilbert).

2 *N'attendez pas le jugement dernier. Il a lieu tous les jours.*
Do not wait for the last judgment. It happens every day.
1956 *La Chute* (translated by Stuart Gilbert).

3 *Combien de crimes commis simplement parce que leur auteur ne pouvait supporter d'être en faute!*
How many crimes are committed merely because their authors could not endure being wrong!
1956 *La Chute* (translated by Stuart Gilbert).

4 *La vérité, comme la lumière, aveugle. Le mensonge, au contraire, est un beau crépuscule qui met chaque objet en valeur.*
Truth, like light, blinds. A lie, on the contrary, is a beautiful twilight which shows the value of each object.
1956 *La Chute* (translated by Stuart Gilbert).

5 All that I know surely about morality and the obligations of man, I owe to football.
1957 'What I owe to Football', in *France Football*. In his youth, Camus kept goal for the Oran football club in Algiers.

6 A novel is never anything but a philosophy put into images.
Recalled on his death, 4 Jan 1960.

Canmore, Malcolm   d.1093

King of Scotland. The son of Duncan (who was killed by Macbeth), he spent his youth in Northumbria and returned in 1057 to take the throne after Macbeth's death.

7 *Excellentioris personæ semper casus in vitium, minoris lapsum, comparatione scandali multe longius antecedit.*
The scandal of an exalted person's fall into vice, when compared to the lapse of one lesser, always far exceeds it.
c.1057 Quoted in John Fordun's *Chronicle of Scotland* (c.1384), bk.5, ch.4.

Cannadine, David   1950–

English historian and academic.

8 Prince Albert…discovered the impotence of being earnest.
1991 Of Queen Victoria's consort. *The Pleasure of the Past*.

9 Neville Chamberlain had greatness thrust upon him—and in trying to prove he could bear it, collapsed under the weight.
1991 *The Pleasure of the Past*.

Cannan, Edwin   1861–1935

English economist, Professor at the London School of Economics. He was editor of the standard edition of Adam Smith's *Wealth of Nations* in 1904.

10 It often happens that a man of considerable eminence in his own profession, but without the smallest acquaintance with the fundamentals of economics, will make a suggestion which is precisely on a level with the proposition that the locomotive would be much more efficient if its weight were taken off the driving wheels so that they could revolve more easily. The editor of an important magazine accepts with joy the contribution in which he develops his ideas, and the public feebly thinks that there may be something in it, and is confirmed in this view by the fact that professional economists are as disinclined to publish a refutation of it as the Astronomer Royal is to answer the theorists who declare that the world is flat.
1914 *Wealth*, ch.6.

Canning, George   1770–1827

English statesman. He became Foreign Secretary in 1822 on the death of his political opponent Castlereagh, and began a programme of liberalization. On Liverpool's resignation in 1827, he formed his own administration but died the same year.

11 Pitt is to Addington
As London is to Paddington.
c.1803 'The Oracle'. Henry Addington, 1st Viscount Sidmouth (1757–1844) was Prime Minister (1801–4) and a political rival of Pitt, who served in his administration.

12 And finds, with keen discriminating sight,
Black's not so black;—nor white so very white.
1821 'New Morality', l.199–200.

13 Give me the avowed, erect and manly foe;
Firm I can meet, perhaps return the blow;
But of all plagues, good Heaven, thy wrath can send,
Save me, oh, save me, from the candid friend.
1821 'New Morality', l.207–8.

14 In matters of commerce
The fault of the Dutch
Is offering too little
And asking too much.
1826 Dispatch enciphered to Sir Charles Bagehot, English ambassador at The Hague, 31 Jan.

15 I called the New World into existence, to redress the balance of the Old.
1826 Speech to the Commons, on Portugal, 12 Dec.

Cantillon, Richard   c.1680–1734

Irish-born banker and economist who made a fortune in Paris after the collapse of the Mississippi Company. His single surviving work is *Essai sur la nature du Commerce en Général* ('Essay on the Nature of Trade', published 1755).

16 If all the Labourers in a Village breed up several Sons to the same work there will be too many Labourers to cultivate the Lands belonging to the Village, and the surplus Adults must go to seek a livelihood elsewhere, which they generally do in Cities.
1730–4 *Essay on the Nature of Trade*.

17 The Crafts which require the most Time in training or most Ingenuity and Industry must necessarily be the best paid.
1730–4 *Essay on the Nature of Trade*.

18 Men multiply like Mice in a barn if they have unlimited Means of Subsistence.
1730–4 *Essay on the Nature of Trade*.

Cantona, Eric 1966–

French footballer. He retired from football in 1997 to develop an acting career.

19 When the seagulls follow a trawler, it is because they think sardines will be thrown into the sea.
1995 At a press conference, 31 Mar.

20 I was always being creative. I could never have played a defensive role because I would have been forced to destroy the other player's creativity.
2003 In *The Guardian*, 26 Sep.

Capote, Truman 1924–84

US novelist. His best-known works include the semi-documentary novel *In Cold Blood* (1966), *Breakfast at Tiffany's* (1958) and *Music for Chameleons* (1980).

21 Other Voices, Other Rooms.
1948 Title of novel.

22 None of these people have anything interesting to say, and none of them can write, not even Mr Kerouac. What they do isn't writing at all—it's typing.
1959 On the Beat novelists. Television discussion, reported in the *New Republic*, 9 Feb.

23 Venice is like eating an entire box of chocolate liqueurs in one go.
1961 In the *Observer*, 26 Nov.

24 Even an attorney of modest talent can postpone doomsday year after year, for the system of appeals that pervades American jurisprudence amounts to a legalistic wheel of fortune, a game of chance, somewhat fixed in the favor of the criminal, that the participants play interminably.
1965 *In Cold Blood*, ch.4.

25 Buddy, it's fruitcake weather!
1966 Of December in Alabama. *A Christmas Memory*.

26 I don't care what anybody says about me as long as it isn't true.
Quoted in David Frost *The Americans* (1970), 'When Does A Writer Become A Star'.

27 Writing has laws of perspective, of light and shade, just as painting does, or music. If you are born knowing them, fine. If not, learn them. Then rearrange the rules to suit yourself.
1974 Interview in *Paris Review*, Summer.

28 When God hands you a gift, he also hands you a whip; and the whip is intended for self-flagellation solely.
1979 In *Vogue*, Dec. Collected in *Music for Chameleons* (1980), 'Music for Chameleons'.

29 Writing stopped being fun when I discovered the difference between good writing and bad, and then made an even more terrifying discovery—the difference between very good writing and true art: it is subtle, but savage.
1979 In *Vogue*, Dec.

30 Great fury, like great whisky, requires long fermentation.
1980 *Music for Chameleons*, 'Handcarved Coffins'.

31 Finishing a book is just like you took a child out in the yard and shot it.
Quoted in Linda Botts (ed) *Loose Talk* (1980).

32 The chic old blue-haired ladies…chew in mute chandeliered isolation.
Of elderly residents of the Ritz. *Answered Prayers* (1986).

33 The morals of a baboon and the guts of a butterfly.
Of Kenneth Tynan. Quoted in Gerald Clarke *Capote* (1988).

34 The better the actor the more stupid he is.
Attributed.

Capp, Al originally Alfred Gerald Caplin 1909–79

US cartoonist, best known for his strip 'L'il Abner' (1934–77), which satirized current affairs with a hillbilly cast of characters in Dogpatch.

35 A product of the untalented, sold by the unprincipled to the utterly bewildered.
1963 Of abstract art. In the *National Observer*, 1 Jul.

Capra, Frank 1897–1991

Italian-born US film director. He became renowned for his films celebrating the common man, such as *You Can't Take It With You* (1938).

36 There are no rules in filmmaking. Only sins. And the cardinal sin is dullness.
Recalled on his death in *People*, 16 Sep 1991.

Caraway, Hattie Wyatt 1878–1950

US politician. In 1932, she was the first woman to be elected to the US Senate.

37 The windows need washing.
1932 On arriving in the Senate. Recalled on her death, 21 Dec 1950.

38 I haven't the heart to take a minute from the men. The poor dears love it so.
Explaining why she never made a speech during 13 years as the first woman in the US Senate. Quoted in David Brinkley *Washington Goes to War* (1988).

Carballido, Emilio 1925–

Mexican short-story writer and dramatist. He is one of the most popular Latin American playwrights.

39 *Es usted un homo sapiens, mamífero vertebrado… Se encuentra en el periodo de domesticación, y sería colocado en una jaula al menor síntoma de ferocidad. En la escuela, en los laboratorios o en las oficinas de gobierno sabemos todo cuanto puede saberse de usted, de sus semejantes o de los otros seres en la escala zoológica.*
You are a homo sapiens, a vertebrate mammal… You are currently being tamed, and you would be put in a cage if you showed any sign of fierceness. At school, in the laboratories and in government offices we know as much as can be known about you, about your fellow beings and about the other beings in the zoological scale.
1960 *El día que se soltaron los leones* ('The Day When They Let the Lions Loose'), act 1.

Cardus, Sir Neville 1889–1975

English critic and journalist. He joined the *Manchester Guardian* as a music critic (1916), later becoming a cricket writer, and wrote several books on his two passions.

40 Pussycats.
1938 Of Bruch's violin concertos. In the *Manchester Guardian*.

41 Sawdust and spangles.
1938 Of Liszt's Second Piano Concerto. In the *Manchester Guardian*.

42 Like the British constitution, cricket was not made: it has 'grown'.
1945 *English Cricket*.

43 The opera…is the only one in existence that might conceivably have been composed by God.
1961 Of Mozart's *The Magic Flute*. In the *Manchester Guardian*.

44 The laws of cricket tell of the English love of compromise between a particular freedom and a general orderliness, or legality.
Quoted in Sir Rupert Hart-Davis *Cardus on Cricket* (1977).

45 Cricket more than any other game is inclined towards sentimentalism and cant.
Quoted in Sir Rupert Hart-Davis *Cardus on Cricket* (1977).

46 There ought to be some other means of reckoning quality in this the best and loveliest of games; the scoreboard is an ass.
1981 *A Fourth Innings with Cardus*.

47 It is far more than a game, this cricket.
1981 *A Fourth Innings with Cardus*.

48 The elements are cricket's presiding geniuses.
1981 *A Fourth Innings with Cardus*.

Carew, Thomas   1595–1639

English Cavalier poet, courtier and statesman. His most notable works include 'Rapture', 'To Ben Jonson' and an elegy for John Donne.

49 Why should the follies of this dull age
Draw from thy pen such an immodest rage
As seems to blast thy else-immortal bays,
When thine own tongue proclaims thy itch of praise?
Such thirst will argue drought.
1631 'To Ben Jonson, Upon occasion of his Ode of Defiance annexed to his play of *The New Inn*'.

50 The wiser world doth greater thee confess
Than all men else, than thy self only less.
1631 'To Ben Jonson, Upon occasion of his Ode of Defiance annexed to his play of *The New Inn*'.

51 Can we not force from widowed poetry,
Now thou art dead, great Donne, one elegy
To crown thy hearse?
1633 'An Elegy upon the Death of the Dean of Paul's, Dr. John Donne'.

52 Unkneaded dough-baked prose.
1633 'An Elegy upon the Death of the Dean of Paul's, Dr. John Donne'.

53 You committed holy rapes upon our will.
1633 'An Elegy upon the Death of the Dean of Paul's, Dr. John Donne'.

54 The Muses' garden, with pedantic weeds
O'erspread, was purged by thee; the lazy seeds
Of servile imitation thrown away,
And fresh invention planted.
1633 'An Elegy upon the Death of the Dean of Paul's, Dr. John Donne'.

55 Here lies a king, that ruled as he thought fit
The universal monarchy of wit.
1633 'An Elegy upon the Death of the Dean of Paul's, Dr. John Donne'.

56 And so our souls that cannot be embraced
Shall the embraces of our bodies taste.
1640 'A Rapture'.

57 I'll seize the rosebuds in their perfumed bed,
The violet knots, like curious mazes spread
O'er all the garden, taste the ripened cherry,
The warm, firm apple, tipped with coral berry.
Then will I visit with a wandering kiss
The vale of lilies and the bower of bliss,
And where the beauteous region doth divide
Into two milky ways, my lips shall slide
Down those smooth alleys, wearing as I go
A track for lovers on the printed snow.
1640 'A Rapture'.

58 All things are lawful there that may delight
Nature or unrestrainèd appetite.
1640 'A Rapture'.

59 Then tell me why
This goblin Honour which the world adores
Should make men atheists and not women whores.
1640 'A Rapture'.

60 Ask me no more whither dost haste
The nightingale when May is past;
For in your sweet dividing throat
She winters, and keeps warm her note.
1640 'A Song'.

61 Ask me no more if east or west
The Phoenix builds her spicy nest;
For unto you at last she flies,
And in your fragrant bosom dies.
1640 'A Song'.

62 Give me more love or more disdain;
The torrid or the frozen zone:
Bring equal ease unto my pain;
The temperate affords me none.
1640 'Mediocrity in Love Rejected'.

63 So though a virgin, yet a bride
To every Grace, she justified
A chaste polygamy, and died.
1640 'Inscription on the Tomb of Lady Mary Wentworth'.

Carey, John   1934–

English literary critic, Professor of English Literature at Oxford (1976–2001).

64 Given the state of the planet, humans, or some humans, must now be categorized as vermin.
1992 *The Intellectuals and the Masses*, postscript.

Carey, Peter   1943–

Australian novelist and short-story writer, twice winner of the Booker Prize for *Oscar and Lucinda* (1988) and *True History of the Kelly Gang* (2001).

65 Glass is a thing in disguise, an actor, is not solid at all, but a liquid…an old sheet of glass will not only take on a royal and purplish tinge but will reveal its true liquid nature by having grown fatter at the bottom and thinner at the top, and… It is invisible, solid, in short a joyous and paradoxical thing, as good a material as any to build a life from.
1988 *Oscar and Lucinda*, ch.32, 'Prince Rupert's Drops'.

66 The declared meaning of a spoken sentence is only its overcoat, and the real meaning lies underneath its scarves and buttons.
1988 *Oscar and Lucinda*, ch.43, 'Leviathan'.

67 Writers are always envious, mean-minded, filled with rage and envy at other's good fortune. There is nothing like the failure of a close friend to cheer us up.
2002 In the *Observer*, 18 Aug.

Carleton, William 1794–1869

Irish writer, the youngest of 14 children born to peasant parents. His sketches were collected as *Traits and Stories of the Irish Peasantry* (1830, 2nd series 1833). Other works include *The Squanders of Castle Squander* (1852).

68 I remember on one occasion, when she was asked to sing the English version of the touching melody 'The Red-Haired Man's Wife', she replied, 'I will sing it for you; but the English words and the air are like a quarrelling man and wife; *the Irish melts into the tune*, but the English doesn't.'
1830 *Traits and Stories of the Irish Peasantry*, introduction.

Carlyle, Jane Baillie née *Jane Baillie Welsh* 1801–66

Wife of Thomas Carlyle. She married Carlyle in 1826, supporting him loyally through his depressions and ill-health, though resisting his suggestions that she write herself. After her death, Carlyle wrote a memoir of her in *Reminiscences* (1881) and edited her letters and diaries.

69 I am not at all the sort of person you and I took me for.
1822 Letter to Thomas Carlyle, 2 May.

70 Medical men all over the world having merely entered into a tacit agreement to call all sorts of maladies people are liable to, in cold weather, by one name; so that one sort of treatment may serve for all, and their practice thereby be greatly simplified.
1837 Letter to John Welsh, 4 Mar.

71 When I think of what I is
And what I used to was,
I gin to think I've sold myself
For very little cas.
1855 Journal entry, 5 Nov. Collected in James Anthony Froude (ed) *Letters and Memorials of Jane Welsh Carlyle* (1883), vol.2.

72 I scorched my intellect into a cinder of stolidity.
Quoted in Alexander Carlyle (ed) *New Letters and Memorials of Jane Welsh Carlyle* (1903), 'Mrs Carlyle's Notebook'.

73 If you hate a man, though only in secret, never trust him, because hate is hardly to be hidden.
Quoted in Alexander Carlyle (ed) *New Letters and Memorials of Jane Welsh Carlyle* (1903), 'Mrs Carlyle's Notebook'.

Carlyle, Thomas 1795–1881

Scottish historian and essayist. His best-known work, *Sartor Resartus*, on social philosophy, appeared in 1833–4. In 1834 he moved to London, where his major works included *The French Revolution* (3 vols, 1837) and *Frederick the Great* (6 vols, 1858–65).

74 His fellow creatures are still objects of reverence and love, though their basenesses are plainer to no eye than to his. To reconcile these contradictions is the task of all good men.
1824 *Goethe*, vol.4, 'Introduction to German Romance'.

75 A mind that has seen, and suffered, and done, speaks to us of what it has tried and conquered.
1824 *Goethe*, vol.4, 'Introduction to German Romance'.

76 The true Church of England, at this moment, lies in the

Editors of the newspapers.
1829 *Signs of the Times*.

77 It is no very good symptom either of nations or individuals, that they deal much in vaticination.
1829 *Signs of the Times*.

78 Seldom can the unhappy be persuaded that the evil of the day is sufficient for it; and the ambitious will not be content with the present splendour, but paints yet more glorious triumphs, on the cloud curtain of the future.
1829 *Signs of the Times*.

79 Meanwhile, we too admit that the present is an important time… We were wise indeed, could we discern truly the signs of our own time; and by knowledge of its wants and advantages, wisely adjust our own position in it.
1829 *Signs of the Times*.

80 Were we required to characterise this age of ours by any single epithet, we should be tempted to call it, not an Heroical, Devotional, Philosophical, or Moral Age, but above all others, the Mechanical Age. It is the Age of Machinery, in every outward and inward sense of the word.
1829 *Signs of the Times*.

81 We remove mountains, and make seas our smooth highway; nothing can resist us. We war with rude Nature; and, by our resistless engines, come off always victorious, and loaded with spoils.
1829 *Signs of the Times*.

82 Wealth has more and more increased, and at the same time gathered itself more and more into masses, strangely altering the old relations, and increasing the distance between the rich and the poor.
1829 *Signs of the Times*.

83 Men are grown mechanical in head and in the heart, as well as in the hand. They have lost faith in individual endeavour, and in natural force of any kind.
1829 *Signs of the Times*.

84 By our skill in Mechanism, it has come to pass, that in the management of external things we excel all other ages; while in whatever respects the pure mortal nature, in true dignity of soul and character, we are perhaps inferior to most civilised ages.
1829 *Signs of the Times*.

85 We are Giants in physical power: in a deeper than metaphorical sense, we are Titans, that strive, by heaping mountain on mountain, to conquer Heaven also.
1829 *Signs of the Times*.

86 Philosophers…stand among us not to do, nor to create anything, but as a sort of Logic-mill to grind out the true causes and effects of all that is done and created.
1829 *Signs of the Times*.

87 We have a faith in the imperishable dignity of man; in the high vocation to which, throughout this his earthly history, he has been appointed.
1829 *Signs of the Times*.

88 To reform a world, to reform a nation no wise man will undertake; and all but foolish men know, that the only solid, though a far slower reformation, is what each begins and perfects on himself.
1829 *Signs of the Times*.

89 No man who has once heartily and wholly laughed can be altogether irreclaimably bad.
1833–4 *Sartor Resartus*, bk.1, ch.4.

90 He who first shortened the labour of copyists by device of *Movable Types* was disbanding hired armies, and cashiering most Kings and Senates, and creating a whole new democratic world: he had invented the art of printing.
1833–4 *Sartor Resartus*, bk.1, ch.5.

91 Man is a tool-using animal… Without tools he is nothing, with tools he is all.
1833–4 *Sartor Resartus*, bk.1, ch.5.

92 Whoso has sixpence is sovereign (to the length of sixpence) over all men; commands cooks to feed him, philosophers to teach him, kings to mount guard over him,—to the length of sixpence.
1833–4 *Sartor Resartus*, bk.1, ch.5.

93 Man's earthly interests, 'are all hooked and buttoned together, and held up, by Clothes.'
1833–4 *Sartor Resartus*, bk.1, ch.8.

94 Be not the slave of words.
1833–4 *Sartor Resartus*, bk.1, ch.8.

95 Language is called the garment of thought: however, it should rather be, language is the flesh-garment, the body, of thought.
1833–4 *Sartor Resartus*, bk.1, ch.11.

96 The end of man is an action and not a thought, though it were the noblest.
1833–4 *Sartor Resartus*, bk.2, ch.6.

97 The everlasting No.
1833–4 *Sartor Resartus*, bk.2, ch.7, title.

98 Most true it is, as a wise man teaches us, that 'doubt of any sort cannot be removed except by Action.' On which ground, too, let him who gropes painfully in darkness or in uncertain light, and prays vehemently that the dawn may ripen into day, lay this other precept well to heart, which to me was of invaluable service: '*Do the Duty which lies nearest thee*', which thou knowest to be a Duty! Thy second duty will already have become clearer.
1833–4 *Sartor Resartus*, bk.2, ch.9.

99 Man's unhappiness, as I construe, comes of his greatness; it is because there is an Infinite in him, which with all his cunning he cannot quite bury under the Finite.
1833–4 *Sartor Resartus*, bk.2, ch.9.

1 Be no longer a chaos, but a world, or even worldkin. Produce! Produce! Were it but the pitifullest infinitesimal fraction of a product, produce it in God's name! 'Tis the utmost thou hast in thee: out with it, then.
1833–4 *Sartor Resartus*, bk.2, ch.9.

2 Friends! trust not the heart of that man for whom Old Clothes are not venerable.
1833–4 *Sartor Resartus*, bk.3, ch.6.

3 How great a Possibility, how small a realized Result.
1834 Of Samuel Taylor Coleridge. Letter to Emerson, 12 Aug.

4 The public is an old woman. Let her maunder and mumble.
1835 Journal entry.

5 Hope ushers in a Revolution—as earthquakes are preceded by bright weather.
1837 *History of the French Revolution*, vol.1, bk.2, ch.1.

6 A whiff of grapeshot.
1837 *History of the French Revolution*, vol.1, bk.5, ch.3.

7 Under all the roofs of this distracted City is the nodus of a drama, not untragical, crowding towards solution.
1837 *History of the French Revolution*, vol.1, bk.5, ch.6.

8 How true it is, that there is nothing dead in this Universe; that what we call dead is only changed, its forces working in inverse order! 'The leaf that lies rotting in moist winds,' says one, 'has still force; else how could it rot?'
1837 *History of the French Revolution*, vol.2, bk.3, ch.1.

9 The difference between Orthodoxy or My-doxy and Heterodoxy or Thy-doxy.
1837 *History of the French Revolution*, vol.2, bk.4, ch.2.

10 The seagreen Incorruptible.
1837 Of Robespierre. *History of the French Revolution*, vol.2, bk.4, ch.4.

11 Pity is lost in rage and fear.
1837 *History of the French Revolution*, vol.3, bk.2, ch.7.

12 France was long a despotism tempered by epigrams.
1837 *History of the French Revolution*, vol.3, bk.7, ch.7.

13 Aristocracy of the Moneybag.
1837 *History of the French Revolution*, vol.3, bk.7, ch.7.

14 The 'golden-calf of self-love'.
1838 *Critical and Miscellaneous Essays*, 'Burns'.

15 For, strictly considered, what is all knowledge too but recorded experience, and a product of history; of which, therefore, reasoning and belief, no less than action and passion are essential materials?
1838 *Critical and Miscellaneous Essays*, 'History'.

16 History is the essence of innumerable biographies.
1838 *Critical and Miscellaneous Essays*, 'History'.

17 When the oak-tree is fallen, the whole forest echoes with it; but a hundred acorns are planted silently by some unnoticed breeze.
1838 *Critical and Miscellaneous Essays*, 'History'.

18 Laws themselves, political Constitutions, are not our Life; but only the house wherein our Life is led.
1838 *Critical and Miscellaneous Essays*, 'History'.

19 History is philosophy teaching by experience.
1838 *Critical and Miscellaneous Essays*, 'History'.

20 A well-written life is almost as rare as a well-spent one.
1838 *Critical and Miscellaneous Essays*, 'Jean Paul Fredrich Richter'.

21 There is no life of a man, faithfully recorded, but is a heroic poem of its sort, rhymed or unrhymed.
1838 *Critical and Miscellaneous Essays*, 'Sir Walter Scott'.

22 Under all speech there lies a silence that is better. Silence is deep as Eternity; speech is shallow as Time.
1838 *Critical and Miscellaneous Essays*, 'Sir Walter Scott'.

23 A feeling generally exists that the condition and disposition of the Working Class is a rather ominous matter at present; that something ought to be said, something ought to be done, in regard to it.
1839 *Chartism*, ch.1.

24 A witty statesman said, you might prove anything by figures.
1839 *Chartism*, ch.2.

25 To believe practically that the poor and luckless are here

only as a nusiance to be abraded and abated, and in some permissable manner made away with, and swept out of sight, is not an amiable faith.
1839 *Chartism*, ch.3.

26 A man willing to work, and unable to find work, is perhaps the saddest sight that fortune's inequality exhibits under the sun.
1839 *Chartism*, ch.4.

27 Surely of all 'rights of man', this right of the ignorant man to be guided by the wiser, to be, gently or forcibly, held in the true course by him, is the indisputablest.
1839 *Chartism*, ch.6.

28 In epochs when cash payment has become the sole nexus of man to man.
1839 *Chartism*, ch.6.

29 The English are used to suffrage; it is their panacea for all that goes wrong with them.
1839 *Chartism*, ch.9.

30 Books are written by martyr-men, not for rich men alone but for all men. If we consider it, every human being has, by the nature of the case, a *right* to hear what other wise human beings have spoken to him. It is one of the Rights of Men; a very cruel injustice if you deny it to a man!
1840 Letter to John Sterling, collected in *New Letters of Carlyle* (1904), vol.1.

31 It is well said, in every sense, that a man's religion is the chief fact with regard to him.
1841 *On Heroes, Hero- Worship, and the Heroic*, 'The Hero as Divinity' (published 1897).

32 Worship is transcendent wonder.
1841 *On Heroes, Hero- Worship, and the Heroic*, 'The Hero as King'.

33 I hope we English will long maintain our *grand talent pour le silence*.
1841 *On Heroes, Hero- Worship, and the Heroic*, 'The Hero as King'.

34 In books lies the soul of the whole Past Time; the articulate audible voice of the Past, when the body and material substance of it has altogether vanished like a dream.
1841 *On Heroes, Hero- Worship, and the Heroic*, 'The Hero as Man of Letters'.

35 The true University these days is a collection of books.
1841 *On Heroes, Hero- Worship, and the Heroic*, 'The Hero as Man of Letters'.

36 Adversity is sometimes hard upon a man; but for one man who can stand prosperity, there are a hundred that will stand adversity.
1841 *On Heroes, Hero- Worship, and the Heroic*, 'The Hero as Man of Letters'.

37 Heaven's splendour over his head, Hell's darkness under his feet.
1843 *Past and Present*, bk.2, ch.15.

38 Work earnestly at anything, you will by degrees learn to work at all things.
1843 *Past and Present*, bk.3, ch.2.

39 Captains of Industry.
1843 *Past and Present*, bk.4, ch.4, title.

40 Respectable Professors of the Dismal Science.
1850 *Latter-Day Pamphlets*, no.1, 'The Present Time'.

41 Nature admits no lie.
1850 *Latter-Day Pamphlets*, no.5.

42 A Parliament speaking through reporters to Buncombe and the twenty-seven millions mostly fools.
1850 *Latter-Day Pamphlets*, no.6, 'Parliaments'.

43 Transcendental moonshine.
1851 Of the romantic impulses that had led Sterling to the priesthood. *The Life of John Sterling*, pt.1, ch.15.

44 Maid-servants, I hear people complaining, are getting instructed in the 'ologies'.
1866 Inaugural address as Rector of Edinburgh University, 2 Apr.

45 All reform except a moral one will prove unavailing.
1872 *Critical and Miscellaneous Essays*, 'Corn Law Rhymes'.

46 If Jesus Christ were to come today, people would not even crucify him. They would ask him to dinner, and hear what he had to say, and make fun of it.
Quoted in D A Wilson *Carlyle at his Zenith* (1927).

Carman, (William) Bliss 1861–1929

Canadian poet. His vivid and optimistic poetry includes *Songs from Vagabondia* (with Richard Hovey, 1894, 1896 and 1901) and *Pipes of Pan* (1902–5).

47 Have little care that Life is brief,
And less that art is long.
Success is in the silences,
Though fame is in the song.
1923 *Ballads and Lyrics*, 'Envoi'. These lines are reproduced on the plaque erected in his honour at the University of New Brunswick, Fredericton, Canada.

Carnegie, Andrew 1835–1919

Scottish-born US steel magnate and philanthropist. He emigrated with his family in 1848, investing his savings in oil lands as a youth and amassing a vast fortune, with which he endowed numerous institutions and good causes.

48 The man who dies rich…dies disgraced.
1889 'The Gospel of Wealth', in the *North American Review*, Jun.

49 While the law [of competition] may be sometimes hard for the individual, it is best for the race, because it insures the survival of the fittest in every department. We accept and welcome, therefore, as conditions to which we must accommodate ourselves, great inequality of environment, the concentration of business, industrial and commercial, in the hands of a few, and the law of competition between these, as being not only beneficial, but essential to the future progress of the race.
1889 'The Gospel of Wealth', in the *North American Review*, Jun.

Carnegie, Dale *originally* **Dale Carnagey** 1888–1955

US lecturer and writer, a pioneer of self-help psychology.

50 How to Win Friends and Influence People.
1930 Title of book.

Carpentier, Alejo 1904–80

Cuban novelist, musicologist and journalist, Ambassador to Europe for a considerable period of Castro's regime. His style has been called neo-Baroque.

51 *A tal punto me hunden mis palabras, como dichas por* *otro, por un juez que yo llevara dentro sin saberlo y se valiera de mis propios medios físicos para expresarse, que me aterro, al oírme, de lo difícil que es volver a ser hombre cuando se ha dejado de ser hombre.*

As though they were coming from the lips of another, from a judge I carried within me without knowing it, and who made use of my own faculties to express himself, my words took such hold upon me that it frightened me to realize, as I listened to myself, how hard it is to become a man when one has ceased to be a man.
1953 *Los pasos perdidos* (translated as *The Lost Steps*, 1956), ch.1, pt.2.

Carr, E(dward) H(allet) 1892–1982

English political scientist and historian. In the diplomatic service until 1936, he was Assistant Editor of *The Times* (1941–6) and wrote several important historical texts, including biographies of Marx (1934) and Bakunin (1937).

52 The unending dialogue between the present and the past.
Of biography. Quoted in James G Hershberg *James B Conant* (1993).

Carr, Emily 1871–1945

Canadian painter and writer, who recorded the lives of west-coast native Canadians in words and paintings. Her first book *Klee Wyck* (1941) won the Governor-General's Award.

53 The outstanding event was the *doing* which I am still at. Don't pickle me away as done.
c.1940 Quoted in Ira Dilworth's foreword to *Klee Wyck* (1951 edn).

54 There was neither horizon, cloud, nor sound; of that pink, spread silence even I had become part, belonging as much to sky as to earth.
1941 *Klee Wyck*, ch.17, 'Salt Water'.

Carr, J(ames) L(loyd) 1912–94

English novelist. His best-known work is *A Month in the Country* (1980), which was also filmed.

55 'I've never been spoken to like this before in all my thirty years' experience,' she wails. ' *You* have not had thirty years' experience, Mrs Grindle-Jones,' he says witheringly. ' *You* have had one year's experience 30 times.'
1972 *The Harpole Report*, ch.21.

56 In rural England, people live wrapped tight in a cocoon; only their eyes move to make sure that nobody gets more than themselves.
1975 *How Steeple Sinderby Wanderers Won the FA Cup*, pt.2.

57 You must understand, James, that their English God is not so dominant a business institution as ours.
1985 On the US version of God. *The Battle of Pollocks Crossing*.

Carrà, Carlo 1881–1966

Italian painter, involved first in *Pittura metafisica* and then in Futurism.

58 *The painting of sounds, noises and smells calls for:*
1. Reds, rrrrreds, the rrrrrreddest rrrrrrreds that shouuuuuuut.
2. Greens, that can never be greener, greeeeeeeeeeeeens that screeeeeeeam, yellows, as violent as can be: polenta yellows, saffron yellows, brass yellows.

1913 In the *Manifesto of Futurist Painting*, quoted in *Futurismo e Futurismi* (1986).

59 This is the truth! In order to achieve this *total painting*, which requires the active cooperation of all the senses, *a painting which is a plastic state of mind of the universal*, you must paint, as drunkards sing and vomit, sounds, noises and smells!
1913 In the *Manifesto of Futurist Painting*, quoted in *Futurismo e Futurismi* (1986).

Carracci, Annibale 1560–1609

Italian painter, one of a family of artists from Bologna.

60 Poets paint with words, painters speak with works.
Attributed rebuke to his brother Agostino. Quoted in G P Bellori *Vite* (1672).

Carrigan, Jim R(ichard) 1929–

US lawyer, judge at the US Court of Appeals.

61 It is all too rare today to hear the clear, clean ring of a really original insult.
1987 In *Time*, 28 Aug.

Carroll, Lewis *pseudonym of Rev Charles Lutwidge Dodgson* 1832–98

English poet, mathematician and logician. A shy man with a stammer, he was most comfortable in the company of children. He is best known for his children's books *Alice's Adventures in Wonderland* (1865) and *Through the Looking-Glass* (1871).

62 'And what is the use of a book,' thought Alice, 'without pictures or conversations?'
1865 *Alice's Adventures in Wonderland*, ch.1, 'Down the Rabbit-Hole'.

63 'Even if my head *would* go through,' thought poor Alice, 'it would be of very little use without my shoulders.'
1865 *Alice's Adventures in Wonderland*, ch.1, 'Down the Rabbit-Hole'.

64 'Curiouser and curiouser!' cried Alice (she was so much surprised, that for the moment she quite forgot how to speak good English).
1865 *Alice's Adventures in Wonderland*, ch.2, 'The Pool of Tears'.

65 How doth the little crocodile
Improve his shining tail,
And pour the waters of the Nile
On every golden scale!

How cheerfully he seems to grin,
How neatly spreads his claws,
And welcomes little fishes in,
With gently smiling jaws!
1865 *Alice's Adventures in Wonderland*, ch.2, 'The Pool of Tears'.

66 'I'll be judge, I'll be jury,' said cunning old Fury;
'I'll try the whole cause, and condemn you to death.'
1865 *Alice's Adventures in Wonderland*, ch.3, 'A Caucus-Race and a Long Tale', told by the Dormouse.

67 'You are old, Father William,' the young man said,
'And your hair has become very white;
And yet you incessantly stand on your head—
Do you think, at your age, it is right?'

'In my youth,' Father William replied to his son,

'I feared it might injure the brain;
But now that I'm perfectly sure I have none,
Why, I do it again and again.'
1865 *Alice's Adventures in Wonderland*, ch.5, 'Advice from a Caterpillar'.
➤ *See Southey 805:96.*

68 'If everybody minded their own business,' the Duchess said, in a hoarse growl, 'the world would go round a deal faster than it does.'
1865 *Alice's Adventures in Wonderland*, ch.6, 'Pig and Pepper'.

69 Speak roughly to your little boy,
And beat him when he sneezes:
He only does it to annoy,
Because he knows it teases.
1865 The Duchess's lullaby. *Alice's Adventures in Wonderland*, ch.6, 'Pig and Pepper'.

70 'All right,' said the Cat; and this time it vanished quite slowly, beginning with the end of the tail, and ending with the grin, which remained some time after the rest of it had gone.
1865 The disappearance of the Cheshire Cat. *Alice's Adventures in Wonderland*, ch.6, 'Pig and Pepper'.

71 'Then you should say what you mean,' the March Hare went on.
'I do,' Alice hastily replied; 'at least—at least I mean what I say—that's the same thing, you know.'
'Not the same thing a bit!' said the Hatter. 'Why, you might just as well say that "I see what I eat" is the same thing as "I eat what I see!"'
1865 *Alice's Adventures in Wonderland*, ch.7, 'A Mad Tea-Party'.

72 Twinkle, twinkle, little bat!
How I wonder what you're at!
Up above the world you fly!
Like a teatray in the sky.
1865 *Alice's Adventures in Wonderland*, Ch. 7, 'A Mad Tea-Party'.

73 'Take some more tea,' the March Hare said to Alice, very earnestly.
'I've had nothing yet,' Alice replied in an offended tone, 'so I can't take more.'
'You mean you can't take *less*,' said the Hatter: 'It's very easy to take *more* than nothing.'
1865 *Alice's Adventures in Wonderland*, ch.7, 'A Mad Tea-Party'.

74 Off with her head!
1865 The Queen of Hearts. *Alice's Adventures in Wonderland*, ch.8, 'The Queen's Croquet Ground'.

75 Everything's got a moral, if only you can find it.
1865 The Duchess. *Alice's Adventures in Wonderland*, ch.9, 'The Mock Turtle's Story'.

76 Take care of the sense, and the sounds will take care of themselves.
1865 The Duchess. *Alice's Adventures in Wonderland*, ch.9, 'The Mock Turtle's Story'.

77 'Just about as much right,' said the Duchess, 'as pigs have to fly.'
1865 *Alice's Adventures in Wonderland*, ch.9, 'The Mock Turtle's Story'.

78 'That's the reason they're called lessons,' the Gryphon remarked: 'because they lessen from day to day.'
1865 *Alice's Adventures in Wonderland*, ch.9, 'The Mock Turtle's Story'.

79 'I only took the regular course.'
'What was that?' inquired Alice.

'Reeling and Writhing, of course, to begin with,' the Mock Turtle replied; 'and then the different branches of Arithmetic—Ambition, Distraction, Uglification, and Derision.'
1865 *Alice's Adventures in Wonderland*, ch.9, 'The Mock Turtle's Story'.

80 The Drawling-master was an old conger-eel, that used to come once a week: *he* taught us Drawling, Stretching, and Fainting in Coils.
1865 *Alice's Adventures in Wonderland*, ch.9, 'The Mock Turtle's Story'.

81 'Will you walk a little faster?' said a whiting to a snail,
'There's a porpoise close behind us and he's treading on my tail.'
1865 *Alice's Adventures in Wonderland*, ch.10, 'The Lobster-Quadrille'.

82 Will you, won't you, will you, won't you, will you join the dance?
1865 *Alice's Adventures in Wonderland*, ch.10, 'The Lobster-Quadrille'.

83 Beautiful Soup, so rich and green,
Waiting in a hot tureen!
Who for such dainties would not stoop?
Soup of the evening, beautiful Soup!
1865 Song of the Mock Turtle. *Alice's Adventures in Wonderland*, ch.10.

84 'Tis the voice of the lobster; I heard him declare,
'You have baked me too brown, I must sugar my hair.'
1865 *Alice's Adventures in Wonderland*, ch.10, 'The Lobster-Quadrille'.

85 The Queen of Hearts, she made some tarts,
All of a summer day:
The Knave of Hearts, he stole those tarts
And took them quite away!
1865 *Alice's Adventures in Wonderland*, ch.11, 'Who Stole the Tarts?'.

86 'Where shall I begin, please your Majesty?' he asked.
'Begin at the beginning,' the King said, gravely, 'and go on till you come to the end; then stop.'
1865 *Alice's Adventures in Wonderland*, ch.12, 'Alice's Evidence'.

87 'That's not a regular rule: you invented it just now.'
'It's the oldest rule in the book,' said the King.
'Then it ought to be Number One,' said Alice.
1865 *Alice's Adventures in Wonderland*, ch.12, 'Alice's Evidence'.

88 'No, no!' said the Queen. 'Sentence first—verdict afterwards.'
1865 *Alice's Adventures in Wonderland*, ch.12, 'Alice's Evidence'.

89 'Why,' said the Dodo, 'the best way to explain it is to do it.'
1865 *Alice's Adventures in Wonderland*, ch.3, 'A Caucus-Race and a Long Tale'.

90 'Twas brillig, and the slithy toves
Did gyre and gimble in the wabe;
All mimsy were the borogoves,
And the mome raths outgrabe.

'Beware the Jabberwock, my son!
The jaws that bite, the claws that catch!
Beware the Jubjub bird, and shun
The frumious Bandersnatch!'
1871 *Through the Looking-Glass*, ch.1, 'Looking-Glass House'.

91 And, as in uffish thought he stood,

The Jabberwock, with eyes of flame,
Came whiffling through the tulgey wood,
And burbled as it came!

One, two! One, two! And through and through
The vorpal blade went snicker-snack!
He left it dead and with its head
He went galumphing back.

'And hast thou slain the Jabberwock?
Come to my arms, my beamish boy!
Oh frabjous day! Callooh! Callay!'
He chortled in his joy.
1871 *Through the Looking-Glass*, ch.1, 'Looking-Glass House'.

92 Curtsey while you're thinking what to say. It saves time.
1871 *Through the Looking-Glass*, ch.2, 'The Garden of Live Flowers'.

93 'When you say "hill",' the Queen interrupted, 'I could show you hills, in comparison with which you'd call that a valley.'
'No, I shouldn't,' said Alice, surprised into contradicting her at last: 'a hill *can't* be a valley, you know. That would be nonsense—'
The Red Queen shook her head. 'You may call it "nonsense" if you like,' she said, 'but *I've* heard nonsense, compared with which that would be as sensible as a dictionary!'
1871 *Through the Looking-Glass*, ch.2, 'The Garden of Live Flowers'.

94 Now, *here*, you see, it takes all the running *you* can do, to keep in the same place. If you want to get somewhere else, you must run at least twice as fast as that!
1871 *Through the Looking-Glass*, ch.2, 'The Garden of Live Flowers'.

95 Speak in French when you can't think of the English for a thing—turn out your toes as you walk—and remember who you are!
1871 The Red Queen's advice to Alice as she begins the chess game. *Through the Looking-Glass*, ch.2, 'The Garden of Live Flowers'.

96 'You shouldn't make jokes,' Alice said, 'if it makes you so unhappy.'
1871 Alice to the gnat. *Through the Looking-Glass*, ch.3, 'Looking-Glass Insects'.

97 Tweedledum and Tweedledee
Agreed to have a battle;
For Tweedledum said Tweedledee
Had spoilt his nice new rattle.
1871 *Through the Looking-Glass*, ch.4, 'Tweedledum and Tweedledee'.

98 'Contrariwise,' continued Tweedledee, 'if it was so, it might be; and if it were so, it would be: but as it isn't it ain't. That's logic.'
1871 *Through the Looking-Glass*, ch.4, 'Tweedledum and Tweedledee'.

99 The sun was shining on the sea,
Shining with all his might:
He did his very best to make
The billows smooth and bright—
And this was odd, because it was
The middle of the night.
1871 Tweedledee. *Through the Looking-Glass*, ch.4, 'Tweedledum and Tweedledee'.

1 The Walrus and the Carpenter
Were walking close at hand;
They wept like anything to see
Such quantities of sand:
'If this were only cleared away,'
They said, 'it would be grand!'
1871 Tweedledee. *Through the Looking-Glass*, ch.4, 'Tweedledum and Tweedledee'.

2 'The time has come,' the Walrus said,
'To talk of many things:
Of shoes—and ships—and sealing-wax—
Of cabbages—and kings—
And why the sea is boiling hot—
And whether pigs have wings.'
1871 Tweedledee. *Through the Looking-Glass*, ch.4, 'Tweedledum and Tweedledee'.

3 'You know,' he said very gravely, 'it's one of the most serious things that can possibly happen to one in a battle—to get one's head cut off.'
1871 *Through the Looking-Glass*, ch.4, 'Tweedledum and Tweedledee'.

4 The rule is, jam to-morrow and jam yesterday—but never jam to-day.
1871 The White Queen. *Through the Looking-Glass*, ch.5, 'Wool and Water'.

5 'It's a poor sort of memory that only works backwards,' the Queen remarked.
1871 *Through the Looking-Glass*, ch.5, 'Wool and Water'.

6 Consider anything, only don't cry!
1871 *Through the Looking-Glass*, ch.5, 'Wool and Water'.

7 Alice laughed. 'There's no use trying,' she said: 'one can't believe impossible things.'
'I daresay you haven't had much practice,' said the Queen. 'When I was your age, I always did it for half-an-hour a day. Why, sometimes I've believed as many as six impossible things before breakfast.'
1871 *Through the Looking-Glass*, ch.5, 'Wool and Water'.

8 'It's *very* provoking,' Humpty Dumpty said after a long silence, looking away from Alice as he spoke, 'to be called an egg—*very!*'
1871 *Through the Looking-Glass*, ch.6, 'Humpty Dumpty'.

9 With a name like yours you might be any shape, almost.
1871 *Through the Looking-Glass*, ch.6, 'Humpty Dumpty'.

10 'They gave it me,' Humpty Dumpty continued thoughtfully… 'for an un-birthday present.'
1871 *Through the Looking-Glass*, ch.6, 'Humpty Dumpty'.

11 'The question is,' said Humpty Dumpty, 'which is to be master—that's all.'
1871 *Through the Looking-Glass*, ch.6, 'Humpty Dumpty'.

12 'That's a great deal to make one word mean,' Alice said in a thoughtful tone.
'When I make a word do a lot of work like that,' said Humpty Dumpty, 'I always pay it extra.'
1871 *Through the Looking-Glass*, ch.6, 'Humpty Dumpty'.

13 'Slithy' means 'lithe and slimy'… You see it's like a portmanteau—there are two meanings packed up into one word.
1871 Humpty Dumpty explaining the *Jabberwock* poem. *Through the Looking-Glass*, ch.6, 'Humpty Dumpty'.

14 'I can repeat poetry as well as other folk if it comes to that—'

'Oh, it needn't come to that!' Alice hastily said.
> 1871 *Through the Looking-Glass*, ch.6, 'Humpty Dumpty'.

15 'There's glory for you!'
'I don't know what you mean by "glory",' Alice said.
'I meant, "there's a nice knock-down argument for you!"'
'But "glory" doesn't mean "a nice knock-down argument",' Alice objected.
'When I use a word,' Humpty Dumpty said in a rather scornful tone, 'it means just what I choose it to mean—neither more nor less.'
> 1871 *Through the Looking-Glass*, ch.6, 'Humpty Dumpty'.

16 The Lion and the Unicorn were fighting for the crown:
The Lion beat the Unicorn all round the town.
Some gave them white bread, some gave them brown;
Some gave them plum-cake and drummed them out of town.
> 1871 *Through the Looking-Glass*, ch.7, 'The Lion and the Unicorn'.

17 He's an Anglo-Saxon Messenger—and those are Anglo-Saxon attitudes.
> 1871 *Through the Looking-Glass*, ch.7, 'The Lion and the Unicorn'.

18 The Lion looked at Alice wearily. 'Are you animal—or vegetable—or mineral?' he said, yawning at every other word.
> 1871 *Through the Looking-Glass*, ch.7, 'The Lion and the Unicorn'.

19 I must have *two* you know—to come and go. One to come, and one to go.
> 1871 The King speaking of his messengers. *Through the Looking-Glass*, ch.7, 'The Lion and the Unicorn'.

20 It's as large as life and twice as natural!
> 1871 *Through the Looking-Glass*, ch.7, 'The Lion and the Unicorn'.

21 'It's long,' said the Knight, 'but it's very, *very* beautiful. Everybody that hears me sing it—either it brings the *tears* into their eyes, or else—'
'Or else what?' said Alice, for the Knight had made a sudden pause.
'Or else it doesn't, you know.'
> 1871 *Through the Looking-Glass*, ch.8, 'It's My Own Invention'.

22 I'll tell thee everything I can:
There's little to relate.
I saw an aged, aged man,
A-sitting on a gate.
> 1871 *Through the Looking-Glass*, ch.8, 'It's My Own Invention'.

23 Or madly squeeze a right-hand foot
Into a left-hand shoe.
> 1871 *Through the Looking-Glass*, ch.8, 'It's My Own Invention'.

24 Un-dish-cover the fish, or dishcover the riddle.
> 1871 *Through the Looking-Glass*, ch.9, 'Queen Alice'.

25 'Fan her head!' the Red Queen anxiously interrupted. 'She'll be feverish after so much thinking.'
> 1871 *Through the Looking-Glass*, ch.9, 'Queen Alice'.

26 'Do you know Languages? What's the French for fiddle-de-dee?'
'Fiddle-de-dee's not English,' Alice replied gravely.
'Who ever said it was?' said the Red Queen.
Alice thought she saw a way out of the difficulty this time. 'If you'll tell me what language "fiddle-de-dee" is, I'll tell you the French for it!' she exclaimed triumphantly.
But the Red Queen drew herself up rather stiffly, and said 'Queens never make bargains.'
> 1871 *Through the Looking-Glass*, ch.9, 'Queen Alice'.

27 What I tell you three times is true.
> 1876 *The Hunting of the Snark*, 'Fit the First: The Landing'.

28 He would answer to 'Hi!' or to any loud cry,
Such as 'Fry me!' or 'Fritter-my-wig!'
> 1876 *The Hunting of the Snark*, 'Fit the First: The Landing'.

29 His intimate friends called him 'Candle-ends',
And his enemies, 'Toasted-cheese'.
> 1876 *The Hunting of the Snark*, 'Fit the First: The Landing'.

30 'What's the good of Mercator's North Poles and Equators,
Tropics, Zones and Meridian lines?'
So the Bellman would cry: and the crew would reply,
'They are merely conventional signs!'
> 1876 *The Hunting of the Snark*, 'Fit the Second: The Bellman's Speech'.

31 But the principal failing occurred in the sailing,
And the Bellman, perplexed and distressed,
Said he *had* hoped, at least, when the wind blew due East,
That the ship would *not* travel due West!
> 1876 *The Hunting of the Snark*, 'Fit the Second: The Bellman's Speech'.

32 They sought it with thimbles, they sought it with care;
They pursued it with forks and hope;
They threatened its life with a railway-share;
They charmed it with smiles and soap.
> 1876 *The Hunting of the Snark*, 'Fit the Fifth: The Beaver's Lesson'.

33 He thought he saw an Elephant,
That practised on a fife:
He looked again, and found it was
A letter from his wife.
'At length I realize,' he said
'The bitterness of life!'
> 1889 *Sylvie and Bruno*, ch.5.

34 He thought he saw a Rattlesnake
That questioned him in Greek,
He looked again and found it was
The Middle of Next Week.
'The one thing I regret,' he said,
'Is that it cannot speak!'
> 1889 *Sylvie and Bruno*, ch.6.

Carson, Edward Henry, Baron 1854–1935

Irish Unionist politician, Solicitor General in the Conservative Government (1900–5). He successfully defended the Marquis of Queensberry against Oscar Wilde's libel suit in 1895. In 1912, he forced the Government to exclude Ulster from the Home Rule settlement. During World War I, he served as Attorney General (1915), First Lord of the Admiralty (1916–17) and a member of the war cabinet (1917–18).

35 A sentence of death with a stay of execution for six years.
> 1914 On the British Government's compromise terms by which Ireland was to be allowed to defer Home Rule for six years. Speech, Mar.

36 My only great qualification for being put at the head of the navy is that I am wholly at sea.
> c.1916 Quoted in I Colvin *Life of Lord Carson* (1936), vol.3, ch.23.

Carter, Angela Olive 1940–92

English novelist and essayist, whose works combine fantasy and genre pastiche. They include *The Magic Toyshop* (1967) and *The Sadeian Woman* (1979).

37 Clothes are our weapons, our challenges, our visible insults.
1967 'Notes for a Theory of Sixties Style', in *New Society* (1967). Collected in *Nothing Sacred* (1982).

38 Solitude and melancholy, that is a woman's life.
1977 *The Passion of New Eve*, ch.9.

39 Myth deals in false universals, to dull the pain of particular circumstances.
1979 *The Sadeian Woman*, 'Polemical Preface'.

40 What is marriage but prostitution to one man instead of many?
1985 *Nights at the Circus*, 'London 2'.

41 I notice that I'm getting more sentimental as I get older; I feel I owe it to myself somehow.
Quoted in John Haffenden *Novelists in Interview* (1985).

42 He was a man with a great future behind him, already.
1991 *Wise Children*, ch.3.

43 She looked like a million dollars, I must admit, even if in well-used notes.
1991 *Wise Children*, ch.5.

Carter, Jimmy (James Earl) 1924–

US Democratic politician and 39th President (1977–81). He helped to effect the Egypt–Israel peace treaties (1979), but after the Iran hostage crisis and the Soviet invasion of Afghanistan he was defeated by Reagan in 1980. Latterly he has been a prolific human rights campaigner and negotiator. He won the Nobel peace prize in 2002.

44 Why not the best?
1976 Presidential campaign slogan.

45 I am convinced that UFOs exist, because I have seen one.
1976 T V interview, 16 Jun.

46 We become not a melting pot but a beautiful mosaic. Different people, different beliefs, different yearnings, different hopes, different dreams.
1976 Speech at Pittsburgh, 27 Oct.

47 I have looked on a lot of women with lust. I have committed adultery in my heart many times. God recognizes I will do that, and forgives me.
1976 *Playboy* interview, Nov.

48 The experience of democracy is like the experience of life itself—always changing, infinite in its variety, sometimes turbulent and all the more valuable for having been tested by adversity.
1978 Address to the Parliament of India, 2 Jun.

49 If you fear making anyone mad, then you ultimately probe for the lowest common denominator of human achievement.
1978 Address to the Future Farmers of America, Kansas City, 9 Nov.

50 All of you have met another Democratic President. I've never had that opportunity yet.
1991 On greeting former Presidents Bush, Reagan, Ford and Nixon at the dedication of the Reagan Library. Reported in the *New York Times*, 5 Nov.

51 My role is one of filling vacuums.
1994 On his work with 105 countries since leaving the White House. Broadcast on ABC TV, 13 Dec.

52 I feel truer to myself…more of a missionary than a politician.

1995 On the Carter Library as a centre for the study of international issues. In *Life*, Nov.

Carter, Lillian 1898–1983

Mother of US President Jimmy Carter.

53 Sometimes when I look at my children, I say to myself, 'Lillian, you should have stayed a virgin.'
1977 In *Woman* magazine, 9 Apr.

Cartier, Jacques 1491–1557

French navigator and explorer in North America, discoverer of the St Lawrence river.

54 In fine I am rather inclined to believe that this is the land God gave to Cain.
1534 Of Canada, as he sailed past the bleak northern shore of the Gulf of St Lawrence. Journal entry, summer. Quoted in H P Biggar (ed) *The Voyages of Jacques Cartier* (1924).

Cartland, Dame (Mary) Barbara Hamilton 1901–2000

English romantic novelist. A prolific writer of popular romances, she became a media celebrity for her garish dress and well-honed sense of social status.

55 At fifty you have the choice of keeping your face or your figure and it's *much* better to keep your face.
1981 In the *Daily Mail*, 10 Jul.

56 I answer 20,000 letters a year and so many couples are having problems because they are not getting the right proteins and vitamins.
1986 Quoted in the *Observer*, 31 Aug.

Cartwright, John 1740–1824

English reformer, 'The Father of Reform', and political writer.

57 One man shall have one vote.
1780 *The People's Barrier Against Undue Influence*, ch.1, 'Principles, maxims, and primary rules of politics'.

Caruso, Enrico 1873–1921

Italian operatic tenor renowned for the power and musical purity of his voice.

58 You know whatta you do when you shit? Singing, it's the same thing, only up!
Quoted in H Brown *Whose Little Boy Are You?* (1983).

Cary, (Arthur) Joyce Lunel 1888–1957

English novelist. His best-known books are *Mister Johnston* (1939), set in Africa, and *The Horse's Mouth* (1944), the final work in a trilogy exploring the pretensions of the art world.

59 This is not to pretend that reading is a passive act. On the contrary, it is highly creative, or re-creative; itself an art.
1939 *Mister Johnston*, preface.

60 I ain't complaining—it's a duty laid down upon us by God—but the Pax Britannia takes a bit of keeping up—with 'arf the world full of savages and 'arf the other 'arf just getting in the way.
1939 *Mister Johnston*.

61 She had a mannish manner of mind and face, able to feel hot and think cold.
1940 *Herself Surprised*, ch.7.

62 It is the misfortune of an old man that though he can put things out of his head he can't put them out of his feelings.
1942 *To Be A Pilgrim*, ch.8.

63 Sara could commit adultery at one end and weep for her sins at the other, and enjoy both at once.
1944 *The Horse's Mouth*, ch.8.

64 Remember I'm an artist. And you know what that means in a court of law. Next worse to an actress.
1944 *The Horse's Mouth*, ch.14.

65 To a real anarchist a poke in the eye is better than a bunch of flowers. It makes him see stars.
1944 *The Horse's Mouth*, ch.16.

66 The only good government…is a bad one in a hell of a fright.
1944 *The Horse's Mouth*, ch.32.

67 It is the tragedy of the world that no one knows what he doesn't know; and the less a man knows, the more sure he is that he knows everything.
1958 *Art and Reality*, introduction.

Casal, Julián del 1863–93

Cuban poet, forerunner of the *modernista* movement, influenced by Baudelaire and the Parnassian poets. He was a chronic invalid and frequently took a morbid view of life.

68 *Tengo el impuro amor de las ciudades,*
y a este sol que ilumina las edades
prefiero yo del gas las claridades.
I have an impure love for cities,
and I prefer the light coming from gaslamps
rather than this sun that lights the ages.
1893 *Bustos y rimas*, 'En el campo' ('In the Countryside').

Casals, Pablo 1876–1973

Spanish cellist, conductor and composer. In 1936 he emigrated because of the Civil War.

69 The most perfect technique is that which is not noticed at all.
Quoted in Julian Lloyd Webber *The Song of the Birds* (1985).

Cassini, Oleg Lolewski 1913–

French-born US fashion designer, raised in Italy.

70 I imagined her as an ancient Egyptian princess.
1987 On designing for Jacqueline Kennedy as First Lady. *In My Own Fashion*.

71 Fashion anticipates, and elegance is a state of mind.
1987 *In My Own Fashion*.

Casson, Sir Hugh Maxwell 1910–99

English architect and artist, Director of Architecture for the Festival of Britain (1948–51). Among his works are *Homes by the Million* (1947) and a series, *Hugh Casson's London* (1983), *Oxford* (1988) and *Cambridge* (1992).

72 Architecture cannot be understood without some knowledge of the society it serves.
1948 *An Introduction to Victorian Architecture*.

73 The Victorians expected every building, like every painting, to tell a story, and preferably to point to a moral as well.
1948 *An Introduction to Victorian Architecture*.

Castle (of Blackburn), Barbara Anne Castle, Baroness 1910–2002

English Labour politician.

74 Dogs make you walk. Politics make you think. Only boredom makes you old.
1997 In the *Daily Mail*, 11 Jan.

Castle (of Islington), Ted (Edward Cyril) Castle, Baron 1907–79

English journalist, Assistant Editor (1944–50) and Editor (1951–2) of *Picture Post*.

75 In Place of Strife.
1969 Title of a White Paper on industrial relations, 17 Jan. Suggested by Castle to his wife Barbara Castle, Secretary of State for Employment and Productivity.

Castro (Ruz), Fidel 1927–

Cuban revolutionary. He landed in Cuba in 1956 with a small band of insurgents. In 1958 Batista was forced to flee and Castro became Prime Minister (1959–76) and President (1976–), instituting a Marxist–Leninist programme.

76 *La historia me absolverá.*
History will absolve me.
1953 Title of propaganda pamphlet.

77 We are not politicians. We made our revolution to get the politicians out.
1961 Speech on assuming the presidency, two years after overthrowing the Batista regime.

78 A man who does not believe in human beings is not a revolutionary.
1967 Speech, 29 Jan.

79 I was a man lucky enough to have discovered a political theory, a man who was caught up in the whirlpool of Cuba's political crisis long before becoming a fully-fledged communist. Discovering Marxism was like finding a map in a forest.
1971 Speech, Chile, 18 Nov.

Caswall, Edward 1814–78

English hymnwriter and translator.

80 Jesu, the very thought of Thee
With sweetness fills the breast.
1849 *Hymns and Poems*, 'Jesu, the Very Thought of Thee' (a translation from 12c Latin, often attributed to St Bernard).

81 When morning gilds the skies.
1854 Title and first line of hymn.

82 See amid the winter's snow,
Born for us on earth below,
See, the Lamb of God appears,
Promised from eternal years!

Hail thou ever-blessèd morn!
Hail, redemption's happy dawn!
Sing through all Jerusalem:
Christ is born in Bethlehem!
1858 'See Amid the Winter's Snow'.

Cather, Willa Sibert 1873–1947

US novelist, poet and journalist. Her best-known books are the trilogy on pioneering life, *O Pioneers!* (1913), *The Song of the*

Lark (1915) and *My Antonia* (1918).

83 The history of every country begins in the heart of a man or a woman.
1913 *O Pioneers!*, pt.1, ch.5.

84 Isn't it queer: there are only two or three human stories, and they go on repeating themselves as fiercely as if they had never happened before; like the larks in this country, that have been singing the same five notes over for thousands of years.
1913 *O Pioneers!*, p.2, ch.4.

85 I like trees because they seem more resigned to the way they have to live than other things do.
1913 *O Pioneers!*, pt.2, ch.8.

86 Artistic growth is, more than it is anything else, a refining of the sense of truthfulness.
1915 *The Song of the Lark*, pt.6, ch.11.

87 Winter lies too long in country towns; hangs on until it is stale and shabby, old and sullen.
1918 *My Antonia*, bk.2, ch.7.

88 The dead might as well speak to the living as the old to the young.
1922 *One of Ours*, bk.2, ch.6.

89 When it has left a place where we have always found it, it is like shipwreck; we drop from security into something malevolent and bottomless.
1926 Of kindness. *My Mortal Enemy.*

90 Oh, the Germans classify, but the French arrange.
1927 *Death Comes to the Archbishop*, prologue.

91 The irregular and intimate quality of things made entirely by the human hand.
1927 *Death Comes to the Archbishop*, bk.1, ch.3.

92 Most of the basic material a writer works with is acquired before the age of fifteen.
Quoted in René Rapin *Willa Cather* (1930).

93 Only solitary men know the full joys of friendship. Others have their family—but to a solitary and an exile his friends are everything.
1931 *Shadows On The Rock*, bk.3, ch.5.

94 Religion and art spring from the same root and are close kin. Economics and art are strangers.
1936 In *Commonweal*, 17 Apr.

95 Every fine story must leave in the mind of the sensitive reader an intangible residuum of pleasure, a cadence, a quality of voice that is exclusively the writer's own, individual, unique.
1936 *Not Under Forty*, 'Miss Jewett'.

Catiline *full name* **Lucius Sergius Catilina** c.108–62 BC

Roman conspirator, from an obscure senatorial family. In 63 BC, he plotted to murder Cicero and other hostile senators, and to seize power, but was arrested and executed.

96 *Idem velle atque idem nolle, ea demum firma amicitia est.*
Agreements in likes and dislikes—this, and only this is what constitutes true friendship.
Quoted in Sallust *De Catilinae coniuratione*, bk.20, pt.4 (translated by J C Rolfe).

Cato *full name* **Marcus Porcius Cato** *known as* **'the Elder'** *or* **'the Censor'** 234–149 BC

Roman statesman and orator, renowned for his strict morality and conservatism. Appointed censor in 184 BC, he discharged his duties rigorously. He was sent on a mission to Carthage in 175 BC.

97 All mankind rules its women, and we rule all mankind, but our women rule us.
Criticizing the prevalent domination of women. Quoted (in Greek) in Plutarch *Regum et imperatorum apophthegmata*, pt.198d (translated by F C Babbitt).

98 *Orator vir bonus dicendi peritus.*
An orator is a good man, skilled in speaking.
Quoted in Quintilian *Institutio Oratoria*, bk.12, pt.1, section 1 (translated by H E Butler).

99 *Rem tene, verba sequentur.*
Stick to your subject, and words will follow.
Attributed advice to orators. Quoted in Gaius Julius Victor *Ars Rhetorica*, 'De inventione'.

1 *Delenda est Carthago.*
Carthage must be destroyed.
Attributed. Quoted in Florus *Epitome*, bk.1, pt.31 (*Cato inexpiabili odio delendam esse Carthaginem, et cum de alio consuletur, pronuntiabat*, Cato bore an unquenchable hatred to Carthage and used to announce that Carthage had to be destroyed, even when he was consulted on a different subject) and Pliny *Naturalis Historia*, bk.15, ch.74.

Cattell, Raymond B(ernard) 1905–98

British psychologist, designer of intelligence and personality tests. Associated with the eugenics movement in the 1930s, he believed that the large size and low IQs of lower-class families would undermine the nation's intellect.

2 The Fight for our National Intelligence.
1937 Title of book.

Catto, Henry E(dward) 1930–

US government official, chief of protocol at the White House (1974–6), Ambassador to the UK (1989–91) and Director of the US Information Agency (1991–3).

3 Like being the captain of a mine-sweeper, if you do your job well, nobody notices. If you don't, there's a hell of an explosion.
1988 On his role as chief of protocol. In the *Washington Post*, 22 Mar.

Catullus *full name* **Gaius Valerius Catullus** c.84–c.54 BC

Latin poet, mainly known for his passionate love poems for Lesbia. Her true name was Clodia, and she was probably the sister of Cicero's enemy P Clodius Pulcher.

4 *Cui dono lepidum novum libellum*
arida modo pumice expolitum?
Corneli, tibi.
Who shall I give my nice new little book to, my little book polished with dry pumice? To you, Cornelius.
Dedication to Cornelius Nepos, the biographer.
Carmina, no.1.

5 *Vivamus, mea Lesbia, atque amemus,*
rumoresque senum severiorum
omnes unius aestimemus assis.
Let us live, my Lesbia, and let us love! Let us not give one penny if old men protest and disapprove.

Carmina, no.5.
➤ See Campion 186:76.

6 *Quaeris, quot mihi basiationes*
tuae, Lesbia, sint satis superque?
You ask me, Lesbia, how many kisses
it will take to make me fully satisfied?
Carmina, no.7.

7 *Nam risu inepto res ineptior nulla est.*
For there is nothing more ridiculous than a ridiculous
laugh.
Carmina, no.39.

8 *Ille mi par esse Deo videtur,*
ille, si fas est, superare Divos,
qui sedens adversus identidem te
spectat et audit
dulce ridentem.
He seems to me to be like a god,
even superior to the Gods, if it is
permitted to say so, the man who sits
gazing on you all day and listens to
your sweet laughter.
Carmina, no.51.

9 *Otium et reges prius et beatas*
perdidit urbes.
Often has leisure ruined great kings and fine cities.
Carmina, no.51.

10 *Odi et amo. quare id faciam, fortasse requiris.*
nescio sed fieri sentio et excrucior.
I hate and I love. You ask me to explain, perhaps.
I don't know. But I feel it happen and the pain is dreadful.
Carmina, no.85.

Caulfield, Sir Bernard 1914–94

English high court judge.

11 Remembering Mary Archer in the witness box. Your
vision of her probably will never disappear. Has she
elegance? Has she fragrance? Would she have, without
the strain of this trial, radiance?
Summing up in 1987 libel trial in which Jeffrey Archer contested
a newspaper's claim that he had sex with a prostitute. Quoted in
Michael Crick *Jeffrey Archer: Stranger than Fiction* (1996).

Causley, Charles 1917–2003

English poet of verse for adults and children, much of it set in
his native Cornwall.

12 You must take off your clothes for the doctor
And stand as straight as a pin,
His hand of stone on your white breastbone
Where the bullets all go in.
1953 'Recruiting Drive'.

13 Timothy Winters comes to school
With eyes as wide as a football pool,
Ears like bombs and teeth like splinters:
A blitz of a boy is Timothy Winters.
1957 'Timothy Winters'.

14 Who is the smiling stranger
With hair as white as gin,
What is he doing with the children
And who could have let him in?
1961 'Innocent's Song'.

Cavafy, Constantine *pseudonym of* **Konstantínos Pétron Kaváfis** 1863–1933

Egyptian-born Greek poet who spent much of his life working
as a civil servant in Alexandria. Most of his work was published
posthumously, including in English translation *Poems* (1951)
and *Complete Poems* (1961).

15 And now, what will become of us without any barbarians?
Those people were a kind of solution.
1904 'Waiting for the Barbarians' (translated by E Keeley and P
Sherrard).

16 Have Ithaka always in your mind
Your arrival there is what you are destined for.
1911 'Ithaka' (translated by E Keeley and P Sherrard).

17 New places you will not find, you will not find another
sea
The city will follow you.
1911 'The Town' (translated by E Keeley and P Sherrard).

Cavell, Edith Louisa 1865–1915

English nurse, matron of a Red Cross hospital in Brussels during
World War I. She was arrested by the Germans in 1915, charged
with helping Allied soldiers escape to Holland, and executed
when she did not deny the charges.

18 Standing, as I do, in view of God and eternity, I realize
that patriotism is not enough. I must have no hatred or
bitterness towards anyone.
1915 On the eve of her execution. Reported in *The Times*, 23 Oct.

Cavendish, Margaret, Duchess of Newcastle 1624–74

English writer and playwright. She was a maid of honour at the
court of Charles I, and married the Duke of Newcastle in 1645.
They lived in exile in Europe during the Civil War.

19 Marriage is the grave or tomb of wit.
1662 *Plays*, 'Nature's Three Daughters', pt.2, act 5, sc.20.

20 If Nature had not befriended us with beauty, and other
good graces, to help us to insinuate our selves into men's
affections, we should have been more enslaved than any
other of Nature's creatures she hath made.
1664 *Sociable Letters*.

Caxton, William c.1422–c.1491

English printer responsible for printing the first book in English.

21 I, according to my copy, have done set it in imprint, to the
intent that noble men may see and learn the noble acts of
chivalry, the gentle and virtuous deeds that some
knights used in those days.
1485 Thomas Malory *Le Morte D'Arthur*, prologue.

Cecil, Lord (Edward Christian) David Gascoyne 1902–86

English literary critic and essayist, Professor of English
Literature at Oxford (1948-70) and a respected literary
biographer. His traditional approach to literary criticism
earned him the scorn of F R Leavis.

22 It does not matter that Dickens's world is not life-like; it is
alive.
1934 *Early Victorian Novelists*.

23 The primary object of a student of literature is to be
delighted.
1949 *Reading as One of the Fine Arts*.

24 Funny you should ask. As a matter of fact I did have a light
temperature when I set out.

Response to a Berlin nightclubber's ambiguous question, 'Sind
Sie normal?'. Quoted in Jonathan Keates 'The Delightful Lord
David', in the *Times Literary Supplement*, 1 Mar 1991. Keates also
describes how Cecil had confessed that, had he visited Sodom
and Gomorrah, he would probably only have noticed the
cathedral.

Cecil, Robert Arthur James Gascoyne, 5th Marquis of Salisbury 1893–1972

English Conservative statesman. Opposition Leader in the
Lords (1945–51), he became Secretary of State for
Commonwealth Relations in Churchill's Government and
Leader of the Lords (1951–7).

25 The Colonial Secretary [Iain Macleod] has been too
clever by half. I believe that he is a very fine bridge player.
It is not considered immoral, or even bad form, to outwit
one's opponent at bridge. It almost seems to me as if the
Colonial Secretary, when he abandoned the sphere of
bridge for the sphere of politics, brought his bridge
technique with him.

1961 Speech, House of Lords.

Cecil, Robert Arthur Talbot Gascoyne, 3rd Marquis of Salisbury 1830–1903

English Conservative statesman and three times Prime Minister
(1885–6, 1886–92, 1895–1902), often serving as his own Foreign
Secretary. He remained as head of government during the Boer
War (1899–1902), and then retired.

26 Peace without honour is not only a disgrace, but, except
as a temporary respite, it is a chimera.

1864 In the *Quarterly Review*, Apr.

27 Under a more heroic Minister, and in a less self-seeking
age, it is probable that England would have preferred the
risk, whatever its extent, to the infamy of betraying an
ally whom she had enticed into peril. But our Ministry is
not heroic; and our generation, though not indifferent to
glory, prefers it when it is safe and cheap.

1864 On Palmerston's failure to defend Denmark against
Prussia, in the *Quarterly Review*, Jul.

28 Horny-handed sons of toil.

1873 In the *Quarterly Review*, Oct.

29 English policy is to float lazily downstream, occasionally
putting out a diplomatic boathook to avoid collisions.

1877 Letter to Lord Lytton, 9 Mar.

30 The commonest error in politics is sticking to the
carcasses of old policies.

1877 Speech, Hatfield, 25 May.

31 Randolph and the Mahdi have occupied my thoughts
about equally. The Mahdi pretends to be half mad, but is
very sane in reality. Randolph occupies exactly the
converse position.

1884 Of Lord Randolph Churchill. Letter to Lady John Manners,
May.

32 We are part of the community of Europe, and we must do
our duty as such.

1888 Speech, Caernarvon, 10 Apr.

33 It is a superstition of an antiquated diplomacy that there
is any necessary antagonism between Russia and Great
Britain.

1896 Speech, London Guildhall, 9 Nov.

Céline, Louis-Ferdinand *pseudonym of* Louis Ferdinand Destouches 1894–1961

French novelist, author of *Journey to the End of Night* (1932),
and other misanthropic works. He wrote anti-Semitic tracts
before World War II and collaborated with the Germans. He
escaped to Denmark after the war, but returned to France in
1951.

34 *Entre le pénis et les mathématiques…il n'existe rien.
Rien!*

Between the penis and mathematics…there's nothing.
Nothing!

1932 *Voyage au bout de la nuit* (*Journey to the End of Night*,
translated by John H P Marks, 1960).

35 *Voyager, c'est bien utile, ça fait travailler l'imagination.
Tout le reste n'est que déceptions et fatigues. Notre
voyage à nous est entièrement imaginaire. Voilà sa force.*

To travel is useful. It engages the imagination. Everything
else is deceitful and boring. Our own voyage is entirely
imaginary. And therein lies its force.

1932 *Voyage au bout de la nuit* (*Journey to the End of Night*,
translated by John H P Marks, 1960).

36 *Quand on a pas d'imagination, mourir c'est peu de
chose, quand on en a, mourir c'est trop.*

For those who have no imagination, death means little.
For those who have one, death is often too much.

1932 *Voyage au bout de la nuit* (*Journey to the End of Night*,
translated by John H P Marks, 1960).

37 *C'est l'actuel qui compte. Invoquer sa postérité, c'est faire
un discours aux asticots.*

It is the present that counts. To invoke one's posterity is to
make a speech to maggots.

1932 *Voyage au bout de la nuit* (*Journey to the End of Night*,
translated by John H P Marks, 1960).

38 *La plupart des gens ne meurent qu'au dernier moment;
d'autres commencent et s'y prennent vingt ans d'avance
et parfois davantage. Ce sont les malheureux de la terre.*

Most people only die at the last moment; others begin
early and take twenty years and sometimes more. These
are the most miserable people on earth.

1932 *Voyage au bout de la nuit* (*Journey to the End of Night*,
translated by John H P Marks, 1960).

39 *Des pauvres, c'est-à-dire des gens dont la mort
n'intéresse personne.*

The poor—that is, the people whose death interests no
one.

1932 *Voyage au bout de la nuit* (*Journey to the End of Night*,
translated by John H P Marks, 1960).

40 *Les Anglais, c'est drôle quand même comme dégaine,
c'est mi-curé, mi-garçonnet.*

The English are funny and peculiar, half-clergymen and
half-little boys.

1936 *Mort à crédit.*

Cellini, Benvenuto 1500–71

Italian goldsmith and sculptor, known for his autobiography as
much as for his art.

41 A painting is merely the image of a tree, a man, or any
other object reflected in a fountain. The difference
between a painting and sculpture is the difference
between a shadow and the thing which casts it.

1547 Letter to Benedetto Varchi.

Cennini, Cennino c.1370–c.1440

Florentine painter and writer, best remembered for his *Il Libro dell'Arte*, a practical guide for the art student.

42 Do not fail, as you go on, to draw something every day, for no matter how little it is it will be well worth while, and it will do you a world of good.
c.1400 *Il Libro dell'Arte* ('The Craftsman's Handbook').

43 There is another cause which, if you indulge it, can make your hand so unsteady that it will waver more, and flutter far more, than leaves do in the wind, and this is indulging too much in the company of women.
c.1400 *Il Libro dell'Arte* ('The Craftsman's Handbook').

Cervantes, Miguel de 1547–1616

Spanish writer, best known for his novel *Don Quixote* (in two parts 1605, 1615), the first part of which is thought to have been written in prison in La Mancha. Other works include *La Galatea* (1585), a pastoral romance, and many plays, only two of which survive.

44 *La mejor salsa del mundo es el hambre.*
Hunger is the best sauce in the world.
1615 *Don Quixote*, pt.2, ch.5.

45 *El pan comido y la compañía deshecha.*
With the bread eaten, the company breaks up.
1615 *Don Quixote*, pt.2, ch.7.

46 *Para todo hay remedio, si no es para la muerte.*
There's a remedy for everything except death.
1615 *Don Quixote*, pt.2, ch.10.

47 *Dos linajes sólo hay en el mundo, como decía una abuela mía, que son el tener y el no tener.*
There are but two families in the world, as my grandmother used to say—the Haves and the Havenots.
1615 *Don Quixote*, pt.2, ch.20.

48 *Digo, paciencia y barajar.*
What I say is, patience, and shuffle the cards.
1615 *Don Quixote*, pt.2, ch.23.

Césaire, Aimé Fernand 1913–

Caribbean poet known for his visionary, surrealist style and as a Marxist and anti-colonialist.

49 *Ma bouche sera la bouche des malheurs qui n'ont point de bouche, ma voix, la liberté de celles qui s'affaissent au cachot du désespoir.*
My voice will be the voice of those who suffer and have no voice. My voice, the freedom of those weakened in the dungeon of despair.
1939 *Cahier d'un retour au pays natal.*

50 *Je vois l'Afrique multiple et une verticale dans la tumultueuse péripétie avec ses bourrelets, ses nodules, un peu à part, mais à portée du siècle, comme un coeur de réserve.*
I see several Africas and one vertical in the tumultuous event with its screens and nodules, a little separated, but within the century, like a heart in reserve.
1960 *Ferrements*, 'Pour saluer le Tiers-Monde'.

Cézanne, Paul 1839–1906

French Post-Impressionist painter, a friend of Zola who persuaded him to go to Paris to paint in 1862. His paintings foreshadow Cubism, emphasizing underlying forms with glowing colours.

51 May I repeat what I told you here: treat nature by the cylinder, the sphere, the cone, everything in perspective.
1904 Letter to Émile Bernard, 15 Apr.

52 The Louvre is the book in which we learn to read.
1905 Letter to Émile Bernard.

53 Monet is only an eye, but my God what an eye!
Attributed, in conversation with Ambroise Vollard. Quoted in Cooper *Claude Monet* (1957).

54 I wished to copy nature but I could not. But I was satisfied when I discovered that the sun could not be reproduced but that it must be represented by something else—colour.
Quoted in D Hooker (ed) *Art of the Western World* (1989).

Chalmers, Patrick Reginald 1872–1942

English writer and banker, an authority on field sports.

55 What's lost upon the roundabouts we pulls up on the swings!
1912 *Green Days and Blue Days*, 'Roundabouts and Swings'.

Chamberlain, Sir (Joseph) Austen 1863–1937

English Conservative politician, successively Chancellor of the Exchequer, Secretary for India, Unionist leader, Foreign Secretary and First Lord of the Admiralty. He received the 1925 Nobel peace prize for negotiating the Locarno Pact.

56 I yield to no one in my devotion to this great League of Nations, but not even for this will I destroy that smaller but older league of which my own country was the birthplace, and of which it remains the centre… Beware how you so draw tight the bonds, how you so pile obligation on obligation and sanction on sanction, lest at last you find that you are not living nations but dead states.
1927 Speech, League of Nations Assembly, Geneva, 9 Sep.

Chamberlain, Joseph 1836–1914

English Liberal politician. He was President of the Board of Trade, but resigned over Gladstone's Home Rule bill (1880). Leader of the Liberal Unionists from 1889, he was also Secretary of State for the Colonies (1895), and retired in 1903.

57 Lord Salisbury constitutes himself the spokesman of a class, of the class to which he himself belongs, who 'toil not neither do they spin'.
1883 Speech, 30 Mar.

58 Provided that the City of London remains, as it is at present, the clearing-house of the world, any other nation may be its workshop.
1904 Speech at the Guildhall, 19 Jan.

59 The day of small nations has passed away. The day of Empires has come.
1904 Speech at Birmingham, 12 May, advocating preferential trade within the British Empire as a means of ensuring Britain's security.

Chamberlain, (Arthur) Neville 1869–1940

English politician, who played a leading part in the formation of the National Government (1931). As Prime Minister (1937–40) he advocated appeasement of Italy and Germany. He resigned as a result of criticism of his war leadership.

60 In war, whichever side may call itself the victor, there are no winners, but all are losers.
1938 Speech at Kettering, 3 Jul.

61 How horrible, fantastic, incredible it is that we should be digging trenches and trying on gas-masks here because of a quarrel in a far away country between people of whom we know nothing.
1938 Radio broadcast, 27 Sep, referring to Germany's annexation of the Sudetenland.

62 This morning I had another talk with the German Chancellor, Herr Hitler, and here is the paper that bears his name upon it as well as mine: 'We regard the agreement signed last night and the Anglo-German naval agreement, as symbolic of the desire of our two people never to go to war with one another again.'
1938 Speech on the signing of the Munich Agreement, Heston airport, 30 Sep.

63 My good friends, this is the second time in our history that there has come back from Germany to Downing Street peace with honour. I believe it is peace for our time. Go home and have a nice, quiet sleep.
1938 Speech from the window of No. 10 Downing Street to the crowds outside, 30 Sep, having returned that day from signing the Munich Agreement. The earlier peace referred to was the Treaty of Berlin which Beaconsfield brought back in 1878.
➤ *See also Disraeli 277:85.*

64 We should seek by all means in our power to avoid war, by analysing possible causes, by trying to remove them, by discussion in a spirit of collaboration and good will. I cannot believe that such a programme would be rejected by the people of this country, even if it does mean the establishment of personal contact with the dictators.
1938 Speech in the House of Commons, 6 Oct.

65 This morning, the British ambassador in Berlin handed the German Government a final note stating that, unless we heard from them by 11 o'clock, that they were prepared at once to withdraw their troops from Poland, a state of war would exist between us. I have to tell you that no such undertaking has been received, and that consequently this country is at war with Germany.
1939 Radio broadcast, 3 Sep.

66 Whatever may be the reason—whether it was that Hitler thought he might get away with what he had got without fighting for it, or whether it was that after all the preparations were not sufficiently complete—however, one thing is certain—he missed the bus.
1940 Speech at Central Hall, Westminster, 4 Apr.

Chamberlain, Wilt(on Norman) 1936–99

US basketball player. Over seven feet tall, he set many individual scoring records.

67 Nobody roots for Goliath.
1967 Quoted in Colin Jarman *The Guinness Dictionary of Sports Quotations* (1990).

Chamfort, Sébastien-Roch Nicolas 1741–94

French writer. He joined the Jacobins at the outbreak of the French Revolution, but his remarks on the terror brought him into disfavour. Threatened with arrest, he attempted suicide, dying several days later.

68 *Guerre aux châteaux, paix aux chaumières.*
War to the castles, peace to the cottages.
1790 Motto for the Revolution.

69 Society is composed of two large classes; those who have more dinners than appetites, and those with more appetites than dinners.
Maximes et Pensées (1795), ch.1.

70 *Vivre est une maladie dont le sommeil nous soulage toutes les 16 heures. C'est un palliatif. La mort est le remède.*
Living is an illness to which sleep provides relief every 16 hours. It's a palliative. Death is the remedy.
Maximes et Pensées (1795), ch.2.

71 *Sois mon frère, ou je te tue.*
Be my brother, or I kill you.
His interpretation of the motto 'Fraternité ou la mort'. Quoted in P R Angus (ed) *Oeuvres Complètes* (1824), vol.1.

Chandler, Raymond 1888–1959

US crime writer, brought up in England. He returned to America and lived in California. He is best known for his creation of Philip Marlowe, a cynically philosophical, wise-cracking private detective whose career is closely involved with a series of beautiful and seductive *femmes fatales*.

72 I was neat, clean, shaved and sober, and I didn't care who knew it.
1939 Philip Marlowe. *The Big Sleep*, ch.1.

73 The General spoke again, slowly, using his strength as carefully as an out-of-work showgirl uses her last good pair of stockings.
1939 *The Big Sleep*, ch.2.

74 He looked about as inconspicuous as a tarantula on a slice of angel food.
1940 Of Moose Malloy. *Farewell, My Lovely*, ch.1.

75 It was a blonde. A blonde to make a bishop kick a hole in a stained glass window.
1940 *Farewell, My Lovely*, ch.13.

76 She gave me a smile I could feel in my hip pocket.
1940 *Farewell, My Lovely*, ch.18

77 Down these mean streets a man must go who is not himself mean, who is neither tarnished nor afraid.
1944 'The Simple Art of Murder'. In *Atlantic Monthly*, Dec.

78 The English may not always be the best writers in the world, but they are incomparably the best dull writers.
1944 'The Simple Art of Murder'. In *Atlantic Monthly*, Dec.

79 If my books had been any worse, I should not have been invited to Hollywood, and if they had been any better, I should not have come.
1945 Letter to Charles W Morton, 12 Dec.

80 Just don't get too complicated Eddie. When a guy gets too complicated he's unhappy. And when he's unhappy—his luck runs out.
1945 *The Blue Dahlia*.

81 Would you convey my compliments to the purist who reads your proofs and tell him or her that I write in a sort of broken-down patois which is something like the way a Swiss waiter talks, and that when I split an infinitive, God damn it, I split it so it will stay split.
1947 Letter to Edward Weeks at *Atlantic Monthly*, 18 Jan.

82 By the way, do you ever read the Bible? I suppose not

very often, but I had occasion to the other night and believe me it is a lesson in how not to write for the movies. The worst kind of overwriting. Whole chapters that could have been said in one paragraph. And the dialogue!
1947 Letter to Edgar Carter, 28 Mar.

83 It wasn't exactly carelessness; her knowledge of literate English contained such vast areas of desert that she took it for granted that half of what she wrote would be meaningless to her.
1947 On the shortcomings of his ex-secretary. Letter to Erle Stanley Gardner, 1 Jul.

84 California, the department-store state. The most of everything and the best of nothing.
1949 *The Little Sister*, ch.13.

85 A big hard-boiled city with no more personality than a paper cup.
1949 Of Los Angeles. *The Little Sister*, ch.26.

86 It is pretty obvious that the debasement of the human mind caused by a constant flow of fraudulent advertising is no trivial thing. There is more than one way to conquer a country.
1951 Letter to Carl Barndt, 15 Nov.

87 Some people are better off dead—like your wife and my father for instance.
1951 Line delivered by Robert Walker as Bruno in the film *Strangers on a Train* (with Czenzi Ormonde), based on the novel by Patricia Highsmith.

88 A preoccupation with words for their own sake is fatal to good film-making. It's not what films are for.
1951 To Dale Warren, 7 Nov.

89 If people could deal with each other honestly, they would not need agents.
1952 'Ten Per Cent of Your Life', in *Atlantic Monthly*, Feb.

90 Alcohol is like love… The first kiss is magic, the second is intimate, the third is routine. After that you take the girl's clothes off.
1953 *The Long Good-Bye*, ch.4.

91 A dead man is the best fall guy in the world. He never talks back.
1953 *The Long Good-Bye*, ch.10.

92 By his standards anyone who noticed how many walls the room had would be observant.
1953 On an interviewer. Letter to Roger Machell, 15 Mar.

93 I suppose all writers are crazy, but if they are any good, I believe they have a terrible honesty.
1957 Letter to Edgar Carter, 3 Jun.

94 Dashiell Hammett took murder out of the Venetian vase and dropped it into the alley.
On the moving of murder mysteries from the English country house to more realistic areas. Quoted in *Contemporary Authors* (1979).

95 As elaborate a waste of human intelligence as you can find outside an advertising agency.
Of chess. Quoted in Colin Jarman *The Guinness Dictionary of Sports Quotations* (1990).

96 The streets were dark with something more than night.
Quoted in the *Smithsonian*, May 1994.

Chanel, Gabrielle *known as* Coco 1883–1971

French couturier. In the 1920s she came to prominence with designs notable for simple elegance and comfort, such as her 'chemise' dress and collarless cardigan jacket. She also developed a perfume, Chanel No.5.

97 Fashion is made to become unfashionable.
1957 In *Life*, 19 Aug.

98 Youth is something very new: twenty years ago no one mentioned it.
Quoted in Marcel Haedrich *Coco Chanel: Her Life, Her Secrets* (1972), ch.1 (translated by Charles Lam Markmann).

99 A fashion for the young? That is a pleonasm: there is no fashion for the old.
Quoted in Marcel Haedrich *Coco Chanel: Her Life, Her Secrets* (1972), ch.1 (translated by Charles Lam Markmann).

1 Nature gives you the face you have when you are twenty. Life shapes the face you have at thirty. But it is up to you to earn the face you have at fifty.
Quoted in Marcel Haedrich *Coco Chanel: Her Life, Her Secrets* (1972), ch.1 (translated by Charles Lam Markmann).
➤ *See Orwell 630:7, Cartland 198:55.*

2 Fashion is architecture: it is a matter of proportions.
Quoted in Marcel Haedrich *Coco Chanel: Her Life, Her Secrets* (1972), ch.1 (translated by Charles Lam Markmann).

3 You ask if they were happy. This is not a characteristic of a European. To be contented—that's for the cows.
Quoted in A Madsen *Coco Chanel* (1990), ch.35.

Channing, Carol Elaine 1921–

US comedienne. A star of US cabaret, she has made occasional appearances in films, notably in *Thoroughly Modern Millie* (1967).

4 Laughter is much more important than applause. Applause is almost a duty. Laughter is a reward. Laughter means they trust and like you.
Attributed.

5 I am terribly shy, but of course no one believes me. Come to think of it, neither would I.
Attributed.

Channon, Sir Henry 1897–1958

English Conservative politician. He became an MP in 1935, becoming a parliamentary private secretary in 1938. He kept a witty diary recording the political and society figures of the time.

6 This afternoon I slept for two hours in the Library of the House of Commons. A deep House of Commons sleep. There is no sleep to compare with it—rich, deep, and guilty.
Attributed.

7 I love the House of Commons so passionately that were I to be offered a peerage, I should be tempted to refuse it. Only tempted, of course.
Attributed.

Chao AD 168–89

Chinese poet. Little is known of him and only fragments of his poetry have survived.

8 Obsequiousness is glorified:
While honest worth must wait outside.
c.180 AD 'Poems of Disgust, no.1', collected in *A Golden Treasury of Chinese Poetry* (translated by John Turner, 1976).

Chaplin, Charlie (Sir Charles Spencer) 1889–1977

English film actor and director. He developed his skill in comedy under Fred Karno and moved to Hollywood in 1914. His early short comedies were extremely popular. His feature films included *Modern Times* (1936), *The Great Dictator* (1940) and *Limelight* (1952).

9 They are spoiling the oldest art in the world—the art of pantomime. They are ruining the great beauty of silence.
1929 Of the advent of talking pictures. Interview in *Motion Picture Magazine*, May.

10 All I need to make a comedy is a park, a policeman and a pretty girl.
1964 *My Autobiography*, ch.10.

Chapman, Arthur 1873–1935

US poet and author, best known for his long poem *Out Where The West Begins* (1916).

11 Out where the handclasp's a little stronger,
Out where the smile dwells a little longer,
That's where the West begins.
1916 *Out Where the West Begins*, stanza 1.

Chapman, (Anthony) Colin Bruce 1928–82

English motor racing manager, founder of the Lotus racing team.

12 Money is how we keep the score in motor racing nowadays.
1974 Quoted in Colin Jarman *The Guinness Dictionary of Sports Quotations* (1990).

Chapman, Dinos 1962–

English installation artist, who works with his brother Jake under the name the Chapman Brothers.

13 We will just make it again—it's only art.
2004 After the installation *Hell* was destroyed in a fire in east London. Quoted in *The Scotsman*, 5 Jun.

Chapman, George c.1559–1634

English dramatist, poet and translator. His plays include *The Blind Beggar of Alexandria* (1595) and *Bussy d'Ambois* (1607). In 1598 he wrote a continuation of Marlowe's unfinished *Hero and Leander*, and he made important translations of Homer (1598–1624).

14 Man is a torch borne in the wind; a dream
But of a shadow, summed with all his substance.
1607 *Bussy d'Ambois*, act 1, sc.1.

15 Who to himself is law, no law doth need,
Offends no law, and is a king indeed.
1607 *Bussy d'Ambois*, act 1, sc.1.

16 Perfect happiness, by princes sought,
Is not with birth born, nor exchequers bought.
1611 *The Iliads of Homer Prince of Poets*, 'Epistle Dedicatory'.

17 Fate's such a shrewish thing.
1611 *The Iliads of Homer Prince of Poets*, bk.4, l.21.

18 We have watered our houses in Helicon.
1611 *May-Day*, act 3, sc.3. This is sometimes misquoted as 'We have watered our horses in Helicon'.

19 A poem, whose subject is not truth, but things like truth.
1613 *The Revenge of Bussy d'Ambois*, dedication.

20 Danger, the spur of all great minds.
1613 *The Revenge of Bussy d'Ambois*, act 5, sc.1.

21 I know an Englishman
Being flattered, is a lamb; threatened, a lion.
Alphonsus, Emperor of Germany (published posthumously, 1654), act 1. Although this is credited to Chapman, his authorship is doubtful.

22 I am ashamed the law is such an ass.
Revenge for Honour (published posthumously, 1654), act 3, sc.2. Although this is credited to Chapman, his authorship is doubtful.
➤ See Dickens 267:96.

Chapman, Jake 1966–

English installation artist, who works with his brother Dinos under the name the Chapman Brothers.

23 I hold God personally responsible.
2004 After the installation *Hell* was destroyed in a fire in east London. In the *London Evening Standard*, 26 May.

Chapman, John 1900–72

US theatre critic.

24 It is three and a half hours long, four characters wide, and a cesspool deep.
1962 In the *New York Daily News*, 15 Oct, reviewing Edward Albee's *Who's Afraid of Virginia Woolf?*

Chardin, Jean-Baptiste-Siméon 1699–1779

French painter of genre scenes and still-life.

25 The man who has not realized the difficulty of art never does anything worthwhile; the man who realizes it too soon does nothing at all.
1765 Quoted in Frank Elgar *Mondrian* (1968).

Chargaff, Erwin 1905–2002

Czech-born US biochemist. He settled at Columbia University in 1935, where his pioneering research on nucleic acids laid the foundations for modern molecular biology.

26 What counts…in science is to be not so much the first as the last.
1971 In *Science*, vol.172.

Charles, Elizabeth 1828–96

British writer.

27 To know how to say what others only know how to think is what makes men poets or sages; and to dare to say what others only dare to think makes men martyrs or reformers—or both.
Chronicle of the Schönberg-Cotta Family.

Charles I 1600–49

King of Scotland and England. His marriage to the Catholic French princess, Henrietta Maria, his expensive foreign wars and his high-handed treatment of Parliament (he dismissed three parliaments and ruled for 11 years without one) culminated in the Civil War and his execution.

28 A rule that may serve for a statesman, a courtier, or a lover—never make a defence or an apology before you be accused.
1636 Letter to Lord Wentworth, 3 Sep.

29 I see all the birds are flown.
1642 After his unsuccessful attempt to arrest the Five Members in the House of Commons, 4 Jan.

30 I tell you (and I pray God it be not laid to your charge) that I am the martyr of the people.
1649 Speech upon the scaffold.

Charles II 1630–85

King of Scotland and England. Exiled during the Civil War, on the execution of his father Charles I (1649) he was proclaimed king in Edinburgh but was not recalled as king to England until 1660. His childless marriage produced a succession crisis and contributed to much political and religious tension.

31 Whereas, women's parts in plays have hitherto been acted by men in the habits of women…we do permit and give leave for the time to come that all women's parts be acted by women.
1662 Royal licence, sanctioning the appearance of actresses on the English stage.

32 Better than a play.
1670 Commenting on the debates in the House of Lords over the Divorce Bill. Quoted in A Bryant *King Charles II* (1931).

33 This is very true—for my words are my own, and my actions are my Ministers'.
Riposte to 'The King's Epitaph'.
➤ *See Rochester 692:72.*

34 Let not poor Nelly starve.
c.1685 Worrying on his deathbed about his mistress, Nell Gwynn. Quoted in Bishop Gilbert Burney *History of My Own Time* (1724), vol.1, bk.2.

Charles V 1500–58

Holy Roman Emperor (1519–58) and King of Spain (1516–56), founder of the Habsburg dynasty. His wars against France led to the formation of the Holy League against him. After numerous wars, he divided his Empire between his son and brother and retired to a monastery in Spain.

35 I came, I saw, God conquered.
1547 Attributed remark after the Battle of Muhlberg, 23 Apr.
➤ *See also Caesar 184:25, John III Sobieski 438:59.*

36 Remember, the prince is like a mirror exposed to the eyes of all his subjects who continually look to him as a pattern on which to model themselves, and who in consequence without much trouble discover his vices and virtues.
1555 *Instructions à Philippe II son Fils* (*Advice To His Son*, translated 1788). Quoted in G R Elton *Renaissance and Reformation, 1300–1648* (2nd edn, 1968), p.137.

37 To God I speak Spanish, to women Italian, to men French, and to my horse—German.
Attributed.

Charles, Prince of Wales 1948–

HRH The Prince of Wales, son of Elizabeth II.

38 Yes…whatever that may mean.
1981 On being asked whether he was in love, after the announcement of his engagement, 24 Feb.

39 What is proposed is like a monstrous carbuncle on the face of a much-loved and elegant friend.
1984 On the proposed extension to the National Gallery, London. Speech at the 150th anniversary of the Royal Institute of British Architects, 30 May.

40 I just come and talk to the plants, really—very important to talk to them, they respond I find.
1986 In a television interview, 21 Sep.

41 Both myself and the Respondent recognized there were irreconcilable differences and that accordingly we could no longer live together.
1996 On why he and Diana, Princess of Wales, were getting a divorce. Quoted in *The Times*, 16 Jul.

42 It's really the result of talking to trees too often.
2001 Explaining his appearance in public wearing an eyepatch.

Charlton, Sir Bobby (Robert) 1937–

English footballer. He won 106 caps for England and played in the victorious World Cup team of 1966.

43 Some people tell me that we professional players are soccer slaves. Well, if this is slavery, give me a life sentence.
1960 Quoted in Peter Ball and Phil Shaw *The Book of Football Quotations* (1989).

44 They know on the Continent that European football without the English is like a hot dog without the mustard.
1988 Quoted in Peter Ball and Phil Shaw *The Book of Football Quotations* (1989). There was at the time a European ban in force against English clubs.

Charlton, Jack (John) 1935–

English footballer, brother of Sir Bobby Charlton. He played in the victorious World Cup team of 1966, and later managed the Republic of Ireland team (1986–95).

45 Soccer is a man's game; not an outing for mamby-pambies.
1967 *For Leeds and England.*

46 I have a little black book with two players in it, and if I get a chance to do them I will. I will make them suffer before I pack this game in. If I can kick them four years over the touch-line, I will.
1970 Remark to reporters, which led to severe trouble with the soccer authorities. Quoted in Colin Jarman *The Guinness Dictionary of Sports Quotations* (1990).

Charpak, Georges 1924–

French physicist, born in Poland. He was awarded the Nobel prize for physics in 1992.

47 I can buy a new pair of shoes this afternoon.
1992 On being awarded $1.2 million for his work on atom smashers. In the *Washington Post*, 15 Oct.

Chase, Edna Woolman 1877–1954

US fashion journalist, editor of *Vogue* (1914–52).

48 Fashion can be bought. Style one must possess.
1954 *Always in Vogue*, ch.12.

Chatwin, Bruce 1940–89

English travel writer and novelist. His travels in the Sudan, Patagonia and Australia converted him to nomadic asceticism. His prize-winning books are a mixture of documentary, fiction, anthropology and philosophy.

49 That will not bring back the things we love: the high, clear days and the blue icecaps on the mountains; the lines of white poplars fluttering in the wind, and the long

white prayer flags… Nor shall we get back the smell of
the beanfields; the sweet, resinous smell of deodar
wood burning, or the whiff of a snow leopard at 14,000
feet. Never. Never. Never.
1980 Introduction to Robert Byron's *The Road to Oxiana*.

50 Being lost in Australia gives you a lovely feeling of
security.
1987 *The Songlines*, ch.10.

51 Tyranny sets up its own echo-chamber.
1988 *Utz*.

52 Like all self-possessed people, he was prey to doubt.
1989 *What Am I Doing Here*, 'Heavenly Horses'.

Chaucer, Geoffrey   c.1345–1400

English poet. He served in the King's household, travelling
extensively on state business. Much influenced by Boccaccio,
his spirited and often humorous poetry established the literary
language of English. He lost his offices in 1386 and fell on hard
times, but in 1399 was awarded a pension.

53 Ful craftier to pley she was
Than Athalus, that made the game
First of the ches, so was his name.
c.1370 *The Book of the Duchess*, l.662–4.

54 That lyf so short, the craft so long to lerne,
Th'assay so hard, so sharp the conquerynge.
c.1380 *The Parliament of Fowls*, l.1–2.

55 But love a womman that she woot it nought,
And she wol quyte it that thow shalt nat fele;
Unknowe, unkist, and lost, that is unsought.
c.1385 *Troilus and Criseyde*, bk.1, l.807–9.

56 So longe mote ye lyve, and alle proude,
Til crowes feet be growen under youre y'.
c.1385 *Troilus and Criseyde*, bk 2, l.402–3.

57 It is nought good a slepyng hound to wake.
c.1385 *Troilus and Criseyde*, bk.3, l.764.

58 For I have seyn of a ful misty morwe
Folowen ful ofte a myrie someris day.
c.1385 *Troilus and Criseyde*, bk.3, l.1060–1.

59 Right as an aspes leef she gan to quake.
c.1385 *Troilus and Criseyde*, bk.3, l.1200.

60 For of fortunes sharpe adversitee
The worst kynde of infortune is this,
A man to han ben in prosperitee,
And it remembren, whan it passed is.
c.1385 *Troilus and Criseyde*, bk.3, l.1625–8.

61 Oon ere it herde, at tother out it went.
c.1385 *Troilus and Criseyde*, bk.4, l.434.

62 For tyme ylost may nought recovered be.
c.1385 *Troilus and Criseyde*, bk.4, l.1283.

63 Ek gret effect men write in place lite;
Th'entente is al, and nat the lettres space.
c.1385 *Troilus and Criseyde*, bk.5, l.1629–30.

64 Go, litel bok, go, litel myn tragedye,
Ther God thi makere yet, er that he dye,
So sende myght to make in som comedye!
c.1385 *Troilus and Criseyde*, bk.5, l.1786–8.

65 And for ther is so gret diversite
In Englissh and in writing of oure tonge,
So prey I God that non myswrite the,
Ne the mysmetre for defaute of tonge.

And red wherso thow be, or elles songe,
That thow be understonde, God I biseche!
c.1385 *Troilus and Criseyde*, bk.5, l.1793–8.

66 Whan that Aprill with his shoures soote
The droghte of March hath perced to the roote.
1387 *Canterbury Tales*, 'General Prologue', l.1–2.

67 And smale foweles maken melodye,
That slepen al the nyght with open ye
(So priketh hem nature in hir corages);
Thanne longen folk to goon on pilgrimages.
1387 *Canterbury Tales*, 'General Prologue', l.9–12.

68 He loved chivalrie,
Trouthe and honour, fredom and curteisie.
1387 *Canterbury Tales*, 'General Prologue', l.45–6.

69 He was a verray, parfit gentil knyght.
1387 *Canterbury Tales*, 'General Prologue', l.72.

70 Ful weel she soong the service dyvyne,
Entuned in hir nose ful semely,
And Frenssh she spak ful faire and fetisly,
After the scole of Stratford atte Bowe,
For Frenssh of Parys was to hire unknowe.
1387 *Canterbury Tales*, 'General Prologue', l.122–6.

71 A Clerk ther was of Oxenford also,
That unto logyk hadde longe ygo.
As leene was his hors as is a rake.
1387 *Canterbury Tales*, 'General Prologue', l.285–7.

72 But al be that he was a philosophre,
Yet hadde he but litel gold in cofre.
1387 *Canterbury Tales*, 'General Prologue', l.298–9.

73 Nowher so bisy a man as he ther nas,
And yet he semed bisier than he was.
1387 *Canterbury Tales*, 'General Prologue', l.321–2.

74 And thries hadde she been at Jerusalem;
She hadde passed many a straunge strem;
At Rome she hadde been, and at Boloigne,
In Galice at Seint-Jame, and at Coloigne.
1387 *Canterbury Tales*, 'General Prologue', l.463–6.

75 If gold ruste, what shall iren do?
1387 *Canterbury Tales*, 'General Prologue', l.500.

76 But Cristes lore, and his apostles twelve,
He taughte, but first he folwed it him-selve.
1387 *Canterbury Tales*, 'General Prologue', l.527–8.

77 And therefore, at the kynges court, my brother,
Ech man for hymself, ther is noon oother.
1387 *Canterbury Tales*, 'The Knight's Tale', l.1181–2.

78 Ther is no newe gyse that it nas old.
1387 *Canterbury Tales*, 'The Knight's Tale', l.1267.

79 The bisy larke, messager of day.
1387 *Canterbury Tales*, 'The Knight's Tale', l.1491.

80 Pitee renneth soone in gentil herte.
1387 *Canterbury Tales*, 'The Knight's Tale', l.1761.

81 The smylere with the knyf under the cloke.
1387 *Canterbury Tales*, 'The Knight's Tale', l.1999.

82 What is this world? what asketh men to have?
Now with his love, now in his colde grave.
1387 *Canterbury Tales*, 'The Knight's Tale', l.2777–8.

83 This world nys but a thurghfare ful of wo,
And we been pilgrymes, passynge to and fro.
1387 *Canterbury Tales*, 'The Knight's Tale', l. 2847–8.

84 'The gretteste clerkes been noght wisest men.'
1387 *Canterbury Tales*, 'The Reeve's Tale', l.4054.

85 Yblessed be god that I have wedded fyve!
Welcome the sixte, whan that evere he shal.
1387 *Canterbury Tales*, 'The Wife of Bath's Prologue', l.44–5.

86 Crist wole we claym of him oure gentilleesse,
Nat of oure eldres for hire old richesse.
1387 *Canterbury Tales*, 'The Wife of Bath's Tale', l.1117–8.

87 Love wol nat been constreyned by maistrye.
Whan maistrie comth, the God of Love anon
Beteth his wynges, and farewel he is gon!
1387 *Canterbury Tales*, 'The Franklin's Tale', l.764–6.

88 Wommen, of kynde, desiren libertee,
And nat to been constreyned as a thral;
And so doon men, if I sooth seyen shal.
1387 *Canterbury Tales*, 'The Franklin's Tale', l.768–70.

89 Til that the brighte sonne loste his hewe;
For th'orisonte hath reft the sonne his lyght;
This is as muche to seye as it was nyght!
1387 *Canterbury Tales*, 'The Franklin's Tale', l.1016–8.

90 Trouthe is the hyest thyng that man may kepe.
1387 *Canterbury Tales*, 'The Franklin's Tale', l.1479.

91 O wombe! O bely! O stynkyng cod
Fulfilled of dong and of corrupcioun!
1387 *Canterbury Tales*, 'The Pardoner's Tale', l.534–5.

92 'By God,' quod he, 'for pleynly, at a word,
Thy drasty rymyng is nat worth a toord!'
1387 *Canterbury Tales*, 'Sir Thopas', l.929–30.

93 What is bettre than gold? Jaspre. What is bettre than
jaspre? Wisedoom.
1387 *Canterbury Tales*, 'The Tale of Melibee', l.1106–7.

94 And what is bettre than wisedoom? Womman. And what
is bettre than a good womman? Nothyng.
1387 *Canterbury Tales*, 'The Tale of Melibee', l.1107–8.

95 His coomb was redder than the fyn coral,
And batailled as it were a castle wal;
His byle was blak, and as the jeet it shoon;
Lyk asure were his legges and his toon;
His nayles whitter than the lylye flour,
And lyk the burned gold was his colour.
1387 Of Chauntecleer. *Canterbury Tales*, 'The Nun's Priest's Tale',
l.2859–64.

96 Mordre wol out, that see we day by day.
1387 *Canterbury Tales*, 'The Nun's Priest's Tale', l.3052.

97 Thou shalt make castels thanne in Spayne
And dreme of joye, all but in vayne.
The Romaunt of the Rose, l.2573–4. This translation of the *Roman
de la Rose* has been attributed to Chaucer but it is thought now to
be the work of several authors, including Chaucer.

Cheever, John William 1912–82

US short-story writer and novelist. He sold his first short story,
'Expelled', after being thrown out of school at the age of 17, and
became a regular contributor to the *New Yorker*, writing lyrical
tales of alcoholism, adultery and loss. His novels include *The
Wapshot Chronicle* (1957) and *Falconer* (1977).

98 The city is old, out of step with the century, but age only
seems to have quickened its elements… Relics from the
past continually pierce the present. Some dream of love
survives the sandstone apartment houses.
1934 Of Boston. Letter to Elizabeth Ames.

99 When the beginnings of self-destruction enter the heart
it seems no bigger than a grain of sand.
1952 Collected in *The Journals*, 'The Late Forties and Fifties'.

1 Wisdom we know is the knowledge of good and
evil—not the strength to choose between the two.
1956 Collected in *The Journals*, 'The Late Forties and Fifties'.

2 Neither you nor I nor anyone else can describe the
volcanic landscapes a poor girl strays into when she
marries a literary man.
1965 Letter to Frederick Exley, 16 Jun.

3 A lonely man is a lonesome thing, a stone, a bone, a
stick, a receptacle for Gilbey's gin, a stooped figure
sitting at the edge of a hotel bed, heaving copious sighs
like the autumn wind.
1966 Collected in *The Journals*, 'The Sixties'.

4 We travel by plane, oftener than not, and yet the spirit of
our country seems to have remained a country of
railroads.
1969 On the US. *Bullet Park*, pt.1, ch.1.

5 My veins are filled once a week with a Neapolitan carpet
cleaner distilled from the Adriatic and I am as bald as an
egg. However I still get around and am mean to cats.
1982 On his cancer treatment. Letter to Philip Roth, 10 May.

6 Yevtushenko has…an ego that can crack crystal at a
distance of 20 feet.
Recalled on Cheever's death, 18 Jun 1982.

7 Trust your editor, and you'll sleep on straw.
Favourite axiom, quoted in Susan Cheever *Home Before Dark*
(1984).

Chekhov, Anton 1860–1904

Russian playwright and short-story writer. His first play, *The
Seagull* (1896), failed initially but was revived in Moscow in
1898. Others include *Uncle Vanya* (1897), *The Three Sisters* (1901)
and *The Cherry Orchard* (1904).

8 Brevity is the sister of talent.
1889 Letter to Alexander Chekhov, 11 Apr.

9 MEDVEDENKO: Why do you wear black all the time?
MASHA: I'm in mourning for my life.
1896 *The Seagull*, act 1.

10 Women can't forgive failure.
1896 *The Seagull*, act 2.

11 The chief thing, my dear fellows, is to play it simply,
without any theatricality: just very simply. Remember
that they are all ordinary people.
1896 Attributed advice to actors, during a rehearsal of *The Seagull*.

12 A woman can become a man's friend only in the
following stages—first an acquaintance, next a mistress,
and only then a friend.
1897 *Uncle Vanya*, act 2.

13 When a woman isn't beautiful, people always say, 'You
have lovely eyes, you have lovely hair.'
1897 *Uncle Vanya*, act 3.

14 If a lot of cures are suggested for a disease, it means that
the disease is incurable.
1904 *The Cherry Orchard*, act 1 (translated by Elisaveta Fen).

15 To begin to live in the present, we must first atone for our
past and be finished with it, and we can only atone for it
by suffering, by extraordinary, unceasing exertion.
1904 *The Cherry Orchard*, act 2 (translated by Elisaveta Fen).

Chelmsford, Frederick John Napier Thesiger, 1st Viscount 1868–1933

English colonial administrator, Governor of Queensland (1905–9) and of New South Wales (1909–13), Viceroy of India (1916–21) and First Lord of the Admiralty (1924).

16 We have here an educated class 95 per cent of whom hate us.
1918 Of the situation in India. Letter to George V.

Cheney, Dick (Richard Bruce) 1946–

US politician. He was Secretary of Defense under George Bush from 1989 to 1993 and in 2001 was sworn in as Vice-President under George W Bush.

17 Except for the occasional heart attack, I never felt better.
2003 In *Newsweek*, 16 Jun.

18 The days of looking the other way while despotic regimes trample human rights, rob their nations' wealth, and then excuse their failings by feeding their people a steady diet of anti-Western hatred are over.
2004 Speaking at the World Economic Forum in Davos, Switzerland, 24 Jan.

19 When diplomacy fails, we must be prepared to face our responsibilities and be willing to use force if necessary. Direct threats require decisive action.
2004 Speaking at the World Economic Forum in Davos, Switzerland, 24 Jan.

Cher originally Cheryl Sarkisian La Pier 1946–

US pop singer and film actress.

20 Do I enjoy getting older? No. I'm thrilled and delighted for those people who enjoy the experience. I just don't happen to be one of them.
2004 In *The Scotsman*, 11 May.

Chereskin, Alvin 1928–

US advertising executive, founder and president of AC & R Advertising (later affiliated with Saatchi & Saatchi).

21 Sex! What is that but *life*, after all? We're all of us selling sex, because we're all selling life.
1986 In the *New Yorker*, 15 Sep.

Chernow, Ron 1949–

US journalist, a columnist with *The Wall Street Journal* (1990–).

22 Capitalism requires people to be pious souls in the workplace, wild pagans at the cash register.
1993 In *The Wall Street Journal*, 31 Aug.

Cherry-Garrard, Apsley 1886–1959

Polar explorer and a member of Scott's last expedition. His group found the bodies of Scott and his companions in 1912.

23 At once the cleanest and most isolated way of having a bad time which has ever been devised.
1952 Of polar exploration. Recalled in *The Worst Journey in the World*.

Chesnut, Mary Boykin Miller 1823–86

US diarist, daughter of a South Carolina senator and wife of the heir to a large plantation. Her diary of the Civil War, *A Diary from Dixie*, was published in 1905.

24 Mrs. Stowe did not hit the sorest spot. She makes Legree a bachelor.
1861 Diary entry, 26 Aug, recording the conversation of a group of southern white women on the subject of men and slavery. The reference is to the principal slaveholder in Harriet Beecher Stowe's *Uncle Tom's Cabin*.

Chesnutt, Charles Waddell 1858–1932

US writer, the first black fiction writer to gain national acclaim when his stories were published in the *Atlantic Monthly* in the 1880s. He also wrote a biography of Frederick Douglass (1899).

25 Those who set in motion the forces of evil cannot always control them afterwards.
1901 *The Marrow of Tradition*, ch.35.

Chesterfield, Philip Dormer Stanhope, 4th Earl of 1694–1773

English statesman and orator, a member of the Pelham ministry (1744), Irish Lord-Lieutenant (1745) and Secretary of State (1746–8). His *Letters to his Son* (published 1774) are a worldly guide to manners and success.

26 The difference in this case between a man of sense and a fop, is, that the fop values himself upon his dress; the man of sense laughs at it, at the same time that he knows he must not neglect it.
1745 Letter to his son, 19 Nov.

27 Whatever is worth doing at all is worth doing well.
1746 Letter to his son, 10 Mar.

28 An injury is much sooner forgotten than an insult.
1746 Letter to his son, 9 Oct.

29 I recommend you to take care of the minutes, for hours will take care of themselves.
1747 Letter to his son, 6 Nov.

30 Advice is seldom welcome; and those who want it the most always like it the least.
1748 Letter to his son, 29 Jan.

31 Wear your learning, like your watch in a private pocket: and do not merely pull it out and strike it, merely to show that you have one.
1748 Letter to his son, 22 Feb.

32 There is nothing so illiberal and so ill-bred, as audible laughter.
1748 Letter to his son, 9 Mar.

33 It must be owned, that the Graces do not seem to be natives of Great Britain; and I doubt, the best of us here have more of rough than polished diamond.
1748 Letter to his son, 11 Nov.

34 Style is the dress of thoughts.
1749 Letter to his son, 24 Nov.

35 Fashion is more tyrannical at Paris than in any other place in the world; it governs even more absolutely than their king, which is saying a great deal. The least revolt against it is punished by proscription. You must observe and conform to all the minutiae of it, if you will be in fashion there yourself; and if you are not in fashion, you are nobody.
1750 Letter to his son, 30 Apr.

36 The chapter of knowledge is very short, but the chapter of accidents is a very long one.
1753 Letter to Solomon Dayrolles, 16 Feb.

37 In matters of religion and matrimony I never give any advice; because I will not have anybody's torments in this world or the next laid to my charge.
1765 Letter to Arthur Charles Stanhope, 12 Oct.

38 In case my godson Philip Stanhope shall at any time keep or be concerned in keeping any racehorse or pack of hounds, or reside one night at Newmarket, that infamous seminary of iniquity and ill-manners, during the course of the races there, or shall resort to the said races or shall lose in one day at any game or bet whatsoever the sum of £500 then in any of the cases aforesaid it is my express will that he, my said godson, shall forfeit and pay out of my estate the sum of £50,000 to and for the use of the Dean and Chapter of Westminster.
1773 Clause in his will.

39 David, you are an actor everywhere but upon the stage.
Attributed, in conversation with the actor David Garrick.

40 The pleasure is momentary, the position ridiculous, and the expense damnable.
Of sex. Attributed.

Chesterton, G(ilbert) K(eith) 1874–1936

English critic, novelist and poet, one of the most colourful and provocative writers of his day. His amiable detective-priest Father Brown first appeared in *The Innocence of Father Brown* (1911). Many of his essays and articles were published in his own *G.K.'s Weekly*.

41 I share all your antipathy to the noisy Plebeian excursionist. A visit to Ramsgate during the season and the vision of the crowded, howling sands has left in me feelings which all my Radicalism cannot allay. At the same time I think that the lower orders are seen unfavourably when enjoying themselves. In labour and trouble they are more dignified and less noisy.
1891 Letter to E C Bentley. Collected in Maisie Ward *Gilbert Keith Chesterton* (1943).

42 With monstrous head and sickening cry
And ears like errant wings,
The devil's walking parody
Of all four-footed things.
1900 'The Donkey'.

43 Fools! For I also had my hour;
One far fierce hour and sweet:
There was a shout about my ears,
And palms before my feet.
1900 'The Donkey'.

44 Literature is a luxury; fiction is a necessity.
1901 *The Defendant*, 'Defence of Penny Dreadfuls'.

45 All slang is metaphor, and all metaphor is poetry.
1901 *The Defendant*, 'Defence of Slang'.

46 'My country right or wrong', is a thing that no patriot would think of saying except in a desperate case. It is like saying, 'My mother, drunk or sober'.
1901 *The Defendant*, 'Defence of Patriotism'.
➤ *See Decatur 258:8.*

47 The human race, to which so many of my readers belong, has been playing at children's games from the beginning, and will probably do it till the end, which is a nuisance for the few people who grow up.
1904 *The Napoleon of Notting Hill*, ch.1.

48 The word 'orthodoxy' not only no longer means being right; it practically means being wrong.
1905 *Heretics*, ch.1.

49 There is no such thing on earth as an uninteresting subject; the only thing that can exist is an uninterested person.
1905 *Heretics*, ch.3.

50 In the case of Smith, the name is so poetical that it must be an arduous and heroic matter for the man to live up to it... The name shouts poetry at you.
1905 *Heretics*, ch.3.

51 Charity is the power of defending that which we know to be indefensible. Hope is the power of being cheerful in circumstances which we know to be desperate.
1905 *Heretics*, ch.12.

52 Science in the modern world has many uses; its chief use, however, is to provide long words to cover the errors of the rich.
1905 *Heretics*, ch.13.

53 A good novel tells us the truth about its hero; but a bad novel tells us the truth about its author.
1905 *Heretics*, ch.15.

54 The artistic temperament is a disease that afflicts amateurs. It is a disease which arises from men not having sufficient power of expression to utter and get rid of the element of art in their being.
1905 *Heretics*, ch.17.

55 Bigotry may be roughly defined as the anger of men who have no opinions.
1905 *Heretics*, ch.20.

56 There is a great man who makes every man feel small. But the real great man is the man who makes every man feel great.
1906 *Charles Dickens*, ch.1.

57 The madman is not the man who has lost his reason. The madman is the one who has lost everything except his reason.
1908 *Orthodoxy*, ch.2.

58 Poets do not go mad; but chess players do.
1908 *Orthodoxy*, ch.2.

59 The men who really believe in themselves are all in lunatic asylums.
1908 *Orthodoxy*, ch.2.

60 It is an act of faith to assert that our thoughts have any relation to reality at all.
1908 *Orthodoxy*, ch.3.

61 Tradition means giving votes to the most obscure of all classes, our ancestors. It is the democracy of the dead.
1908 *Orthodoxy*, ch.4.

62 All conservatism is based upon the idea that if you leave things alone you leave them as they are. But you do not. If you leave a thing alone you leave it to a torrent of change.
1908 *Orthodoxy*, ch.7.

63 Angels can fly because they take themselves lightly.
1908 *Orthodoxy*, ch.7.

64 Thieves respect property. They merely wish the property to become their property that they may more perfectly respect it.
1908 *The Man who was Thursday*, ch.4.

65 An adventure is only an inconvenience rightly

considered. An inconvenience is only an adventure wrongly considered.
1908 *All Things Considered*, 'On Running After One's Hat'.

66 No animal ever invented anything so bad as drunkenness—or so good as drink.
1908 *All Things Considered*, 'Wine When It Is Red'.

67 Lying in bed would be an altogether perfect and supreme experience if only one had a coloured pencil long enough to draw on the ceiling.
1909 'On Lying In Bed'.

68 He desired all beautiful things—even God.
1909 Of Oscar Wilde. In the *Daily News*, 19 Oct.

69 The Christian ideal has not been tried and found wanting. It has been found difficult; and left untried.
1910 *What's Wrong with the World*, ch.1, 'The Unfinished Temple'.

70 Compromise used to mean that half a loaf was better than no bread. Among modern statesmen, it really seems to mean that half a loaf is better than a whole loaf.
1910 *What's Wrong with the World*, ch.3.

71 She was maintaining the prime truth of woman, the universal mother…that if a thing is worth doing, it is worth doing badly.
1910 *What's Wrong with the World*, pt.4, 'Folly and Female Education'.

72 I tell you naught for your comfort,
Yea, naught for your desire,
Save that the sky grows darker yet
And the sea rises higher.
1911 *Ballad of the White Horse*, bk.1.

73 For the great Gaels of Ireland
Are the men that God made mad,
For all their wars are merry,
And all their songs are sad.
1911 *Ballad of the White Horse*, bk.2.

74 There is always a forgotten thing,
And love is not secure.
1911 *Ballad of the White Horse*, bk.3.

75 When all philosophies shall fail,
This word alone shall fit;
That a sage feels too small for life,
And a fool too large for it.
1911 *Ballad of the White Horse*, bk.8.

76 He could not think up to the height of his own towering style.
1912 Of Tennyson. *The Victorian Age in Literature*, ch.3.

77 And Noah he often said to his wife when he sat down to dine.
'I don't care where the water goes if it doesn't get into the wine.'
1914 *The Flying Inn*, ch.5, stanza 1. Collected as 'Wine and Water' in *Wine, Water and Song* (1915).

78 The rich are the scum of the earth in every country.
1914 *The Flying Inn*, ch.15.

79 Tea is like the East he grows in,
A great yellow Mandarin
With urbanity of manner
And unconsciousness of sin.
1914 *The Flying Inn*, ch.18, stanza 2. Collected as 'The Song of Right and Wrong' in *Wine, Water and Song* (1915).

80 Tea, although an Oriental,

Is a gentleman at least;
Cocoa is a cad and coward,
Cocoa is a vulgar beast.
1914 *The Flying Inn*, ch.18, stanza 3. Collected as 'The Song of Right and Wrong' in *Wine, Water and Song* (1915).

81 When red wine had brought red ruin
And the death-dance of our times,
Heaven sent us Soda Water
As a torment for our crimes.
1914 *The Flying Inn*, ch.18, stanza 4. Collected as 'The Song of Right and Wrong' in *Wine, Water and Song* (1915).

82 The folk that live in Liverpool, their heart is in their boots;
They go to hell like lambs, they do, because the hooter hoots.
1914 'Me Heart'.

83 They haven't got no noses,
The fallen sons of Eve.
1914 'Song of Quoodle'.

84 And goodness only knowses
The Noselessness of Man.
1914 'Song of Quoodle'.

85 Before the Roman came to Rye or out to Severn strode,
The rolling English drunkard made the rolling English road.
1914 'The Rolling English Road'.

86 A merry road, a mazy road, and such as we did tread
The night we went to Birmingham by way of Beachy Head.
1914 'The Rolling English Road'.

87 For there is good news yet to hear and fine things to be seen,
Before we go to Paradise by way of Kensal Green.
1914 'The Rolling English Road'.

88 To be clever enough to get all that money, one must be stupid enough to want it.
1914 *The Wisdom of Father Brown*, 'Paradise of Thieves'.

89 Journalism largely consists in saying 'Lord Jones Dead' to people who never knew Lord Jones was alive.
1914 *The Wisdom of Father Brown*, 'The Purple Wig'.

90 We only know the last sad squires ride slowly towards the sea,
And a new people takes the land: and still it is not we.
1915 'The Secret People'.

91 The souls most fed with Shakespeare's flame
Still sat unconquered in a ring,
Remembering him like anything.
1915 'Shakespeare Memorial'.

92 John Grubby, who was short and stout
And troubled with religious doubt,
Refused about the age of three
To sit upon the curate's knee.
1915 'The New Freethinker'.

93 And I dream of the days when work was scrappy,
And rare in our pockets the mark of the mint,
When we were angry and poor and happy,
And proud of seeing our names in print.
1915 'Song of Defeat'.

94 The gallows in my garden, people say,
Is new and neat and adequately tall.
1915 'Ballade of Suicide'.

95 The strangest whim has seized me… After all
I think I will not hang myself today.
1915 'Ballade of Suicide'.

96 They died to save their country and they only saved the
world.
1922 'English Graves'.

97 Democracy means government by the uneducated,
while aristocracy means government by the badly
educated.
1931 In the *New York Times*, 1 Feb.

98 A great deal of contemporary criticism reads to me like a
man saying: 'Of course I do not like green cheese: I am
very fond of brown sherry'.
1933 *All I Survey*, 'On Jonathan Swift'.

99 Why do you rush through the fields in trains,
Guessing so much and so much.
Why do you flash through the flowery meads,
Fat-head poet that nobody reads;
And why do you know such a frightful lot
About people in gloves and such?
1933 'The Fat White Woman Speaks', a response to Frances
Cornford's poem.
➤ *See Cornford 237:69.*

1 It isn't that they can't see the solution. It is that they can't
see the problem.
1935 *The Scandal of Father Brown*, 'Point of a Pin'.

2 Am in Market Harborough. Where ought I to be?
Attributed. Chesterton remarks in his *Autobiography* (1936),
ch.16, 'I cannot remember whether this story is true; but it is not
unlikely, or, I think, unreasonable.'

3 Music with dinner is an insult both to the cook and the
violinist.
Quoted in *The New York Times*, 16 Nov 1967.

4 I regard golf as an expensive way of playing marbles.
Quoted in Colin Jarman *The Guinness Dictionary of Sports
Quotations* (1990).

Chiang Kai-Shek 1887–1975

Chinese general and nationalist, defeated by Mao Zedong's
forces. In 1948 he was forced to withdraw to Taiwan where he
retained the office of President.

5 The sky cannot have two suns.
c.1945 Quoted in Ross Merrill *Mao* (1993) ch.10.

Chilcott, Gareth 1956–

English rugby union player.

6 I thought I would have a quiet pint…and about 17 noisy
ones.
1993 On playing his last game of rugby for Bath.

Child, Julia McWilliams 1912–2004

US cookery expert.

7 Life itself is the proper binge.
1980 In *Time*, 7 Jan.

8 The view of history that we get through the kitchen
window is a more gentle view, not of war and politics,
but of family and community and sharing.
1993 On studying cookbooks dating back to the 1400s in the
Library of Congress. In *Memory and Imagination*, PBS TV,
15 Aug.

Ch'in Chia c.150 BC

Chinese poet and civil servant about whom very little is known.
He wrote a series of three poems on his separation from his
wife, the result of a posting to Beijing.

9 I sent a carriage to bring you back
But it went empty, and empty it returned.
c.150 BC 'To My Wife 1', collected in *A Book of Chinese Verse*
(translated by N L Smith and R H Kotewall).

10 Sorrow comes as in a circle
And cannot be rolled up like a map.
c.150 BC 'To My Wife 2', collected in *A Book of Chinese Verse*
(translated by N L Smith and R H Kotewall).

11 One separation breeds ten thousand regrets.
c.150 BC 'To My Wife 2', collected in *A Book of Chinese Verse*
(translated by N L Smith and R H Kotewall).

Chirac, Jacques René 1932–

French Conservative politician, Prime Minister (1974–6,
1986–8) and President (1995–) of France.

12 What's it for?
On being shown a scale model of the Millennium Dome. Quoted
in *Servants of the People: The Inside Story of New Labour* (2000).

13 Tony Blair is very convincing, he will sway public
opinion.
2004 On the proposed British referendum on the EU
Constitution, 9 May.

14 This cuisine here in America was certainly on a par with
French cuisine.
2004 At the G8 meeting on Sea Island, Georgia, 10 Jun.

Chirico, Giorgio de 1888–1978

Italian painter, born in Greece, the developer of 'metaphysical
painting', based on semi-abstract geometric figures. In the
1930s he renounced his earlier work and returned to an
academic style.

15 If a work of art is to be truly immortal, it must pass quite
beyond the limits of the human world, without any sign
of common sense and logic. In this way the work will
draw nearer to dream and to the mind of a child.
Quoted in Saranne Alexandrian *Surrealist Art* (1970).

Chisholm, Caroline née Jones 1808–77

English-born Australian social worker and philanthropist.
She married an army officer and settled in New South Wales in
1838, where she worked with impoverished immigrant women
and children. Her petition to Earl Grey helped persuade the
British Government to grant free passage to the families of
convicts.

16 If Her Majesty's Government be really desirous of
seeing a well-conducted community spring up in
these Colonies, the social wants of the people
must be considered… For all the clergy you can
despatch, all the schoolmasters you can appoint,
all the churches you can build, and all the books you
can export, will never do much good without what a
gentleman in that Colony very appropriately called
'God's police'—wives and little children—good and
virtuous women.
1847 *Emigration and Transportation Relatively Considered; in a
Letter, Dedicated, by Permission, to Earl Grey*, 17 Jun. The phrase
'God's police' was adopted by Australian feminist Anne

Summers in her feminist critique of Australian culture, *Damned Whores and God's Police* (1975).
➤ See Clark 219:54.

Chocano, José Santos 1875–1934

Peruvian poet, teacher, editor and diplomat. He visited almost every Central and South American country, often being expelled for political intrigue. He was assassinated in Chile.

17 *Soy el cantor de América autóctono y salvaje;*
mi lira tiene un alma, mi canto un ideal.
Mi verso no se mece colgado de un ramaje
con un vaivén pausado de hamaca tropical.
I am the aboriginal and savage singer of America;
my lyre has a soul, my song has an ideal.
My poetry does not swing from the branches
with the slow movement of a tropical hammock.
1906 *Alma América*, 'Blasón' (translated as 'Blazon', 1935).

Chomsky, (Avram) Noam 1928–

US linguist and social critic. His theories revolutionized the study of language and remain controversial. In the political arena, he has criticized many aspects of US foreign policy.

18 An obscenity, a depraved act by weak and miserable men, including all of us, who have allowed it to go on and on with endless fury.
1969 Of US involvement in the war in Vietnam. *American Power and the New Mandarins.*

19 As soon as questions of will or decision arise, human science is at a loss.
1978 Television interview, 30 Mar, reported in *The Listener*, 6 Apr.

20 The military system is, to a substantial extent, a method whereby the population provides a subsidy to the high technology industry.
1988 Interview, Public Broadcasting System, 4 Nov.

Chopin, Kate (Katherine) née *O'Flaherty* 1851–1904

US novelist and short-story writer. After the death of her husband she began to write sketches of Creole life, including *Bayou Folk* (1894). Her novel *The Awakening* (1899) was harshly condemned for its frank treatment of female sexuality.

21 The voice of the sea speaks to the soul. The touch of the sea is sensuous, enfolding the body in its soft, close embrace.
1899 *The Awakening*, ch.6.

22 The past was nothing to her... The future was a mystery which she never attempted to penetrate. The present alone was significant.
1899 *The Awakening*, ch.15.

23 She was becoming herself and daily casting aside that fictitious self which we assume like a garment with which to appear before the world.
1899 *The Awakening*, ch.19.

24 The artist must possess the courageous soul that dares and defies.
1899 *The Awakening*, ch.39.

25 I trust I will not be giving away professional secrets to say that many readers would be surprised, perhaps shocked, at the questions which some newspaper editors will put to a defenseless woman under the guise of flattery.
1899 'On Certain Brisk Days', in the *St Louis Post–Dispatch*, 26 Nov.

Christiansen, Arthur 1904–63

British journalist, Editor of the *Daily Express* (1933–58).

26 Whenever possible print a woman's age.
1957 Quoted in Francis Williams *Dangerous Estate.*

27 The people who lived behind those clean lace curtains in row after row of identical boxes were newspaper readers, and every word in at any rate *my* newspaper must be clear and comprehensible to them, must be interesting to them, must encourage them to break away from littleness, stimulate their ambition, help them to want to build a better land.
1961 *Headlines all my Life*, ch.1.

28 Remember the people in the back streets of Derby.
1961 *Headlines all my Life*, ch.1.

29 Show me a contented newspaper editor and I will show you a bad newspaper.
1961 *Headlines all my Life*, ch.15.

30 No matter how many media for the dissemination of news are created, there is one rule that should never be broken: TELL THE PEOPLE!
1961 *Headlines all my Life*, ch.18.

31 My approach to newspapers was based on the idea that when you looked at the front page you said: 'Good heavens', when you looked at the middle page you said: 'Holy smoke', and by the time you got to the back page—well, I'd have to utter a profanity to show how exciting it was.
1961 *Headlines all my Life*, ch.19.

Christie, Dame Agatha Mary Clarissa née *Miller* 1890–1976

English author, who wrote more than 70 classic detective novels including *The Mysterious Affair at Styles* (1920), *Murder on the Orient Express* (1934) and *Death on the Nile* (1937).

32 He tapped his forehead. 'These little grey cells. It is up to them—as you say over here.'
1920 *The Mysterious Affair at Styles*, ch.10.

33 Life nowadays is dominated and complicated by the remorseless Zip. Blouses zip up, skirts zip down, ski-ing suits zip everywhere... Why? Is there anything more deadly than a Zip that turns nasty on you?
1946 *Come, Tell Me How You Live*, ch.1.

34 Here, in the west of Ireland, the Romans had never marched, tramp, tramp, tramp: had never fortified a camp: had never built a well-ordered, sensible, useful road. It was a land where common sense and an orderly way of life were unknown.
Hercule Poirot looked down at the tips of his patent-leather shoes and sighed. He felt forlorn and very much alone. The standards by which he lived were here not appreciated.
1947 *The Labours of Hercules.*

35 War settles *nothing*... to *win* a war is as disastrous as to lose one.
1977 *An Autobiography*, ch.10.

Christie, Linford 1960–

English athlete who won an Olympic gold medal for the 100m at the 1992 games in Barcelona.

36 I could have been a god, but people only allow you to get so far in this country.
2002 In *The Independent*, 20 Dec.

Christine de Pisan 1364–1430

Italian-born French writer. Taken to the court of Charles V as a child, married at 15 and widowed at 25, she became the first professional woman poet and official biographer of Charles V. Other works include lyrics and essays on politics and the status of women in society.

37 *En la hauteur ou abaissement des gens ne gist mie es corps selonc le sexe, mais en la perfeccion des meurs et vertus.*
The dignity or baseness of a person lies not in their body according to the sex, but in the perfection of behaviour and virtues.
1405 *Le livre de la Cité des Dames*, bk.1, ch.9.

38 *De tant comme femmes ont le corps plus delie que les hommes, plus foible et moins habille a plusieurs choses faire, de tant ont elles l'entendement plus a delivre et plus agu ou elles s'appliquent.*
Just as women's bodies are more delicate than men's, weaker and less able for many things, so, where they apply themselves, their understanding is freer and sharper.
1405 *Le livre de la Cité des Dames*, bk.1, ch.27.

Christopher, Warren Minor 1925–

US lawyer and government official, Secretary of State (1993–6). In 1980 he negotiated for the release of US hostages in Iran.

39 I wish the meeting had been as good as the lunch.
1994 On beginning talks in Beijing with China's Prime Minister. In the *New York Times*, 13 Mar.

40 Sometimes you have to learn how to give the right answer to the wrong question.
1994 On Syrian President Hafez Assad's complaint that he had been put off by a hostile question in a news conference shared with President Clinton. In *US News and World Report*, 19 Dec.

Church, Richard 1893–1972

English author, known for his poems, novels, literary criticism, travel books and children's stories.

41 We have to accept the verbal portraits, as indeed we have to accept paintings and sculptures, as well as photographs, of the immortals whose influence on our lives is often greater than that of our own family members.
In praise of biography. Quoted in *Christian Science Monitor*, 30 Apr 1963.

42 He delights to expose the raw nerves of evil, showing it as a force in the world, a skeletonlike figure working visible mischief in the ordinary everyday affairs of men and women and children.
Of Graham Greene. Recalled on Greene's death in the *New York Times*, 4 Apr 1991.

Churchill, Charles 1731–64

English satirical poet. His works savagely attacked many well-known figures of his time, including Samuel Johnson, Tobias Smollett and William Hogarth. He is best known for *The Rosciad* (1761).

43 A pert, prim Prater of the northern race, Guilt in his heart, and famine in his face.
1761 Of the Scottish-born judge Alexander Wedderburn, later Lord Loughborough. *The Rosciad*, l.75–6.

44 Fashion—a word which knaves and fools may use, Their knavery and folly to excuse.
1761 *The Rosciad*, l.455–6.

45 So much they talked, so very little said.
1761 *The Rosciad*, l.550.

46 But, spite of all the criticizing elves, Those who would make us feel, must feel themselves.
1761 *The Rosciad*, l.961–2.

47 Keep up appearances; there lies the test; The world will give thee credit for the rest. Outward be fair, however foul within; Sin if thou wilt, but then in secret sin.
1762 *Night*, l.311–12.

48 Just to the windward of the law.
1763 *The Ghost*, bk.3, l.56.

49 A joke's a very serious thing.
1763 *The Ghost*, bk.3, l.1386.

50 Apt Alliteration's artful aid.
1763 *The Prophecy of Famine*, l.86.

51 The danger chiefly lies in acting well; No crime's so great as daring to excel.
1763 *An Epistle to William Hogarth*, l.51–2.

52 Be England what she will, With all her faults, she is my country still.
1764 *The Farewell*, l.27–8.

53 It can't be Nature, for it is not sense.
1764 *The Farewell*, l.200.

Churchill, Jeanette née *Jeanette Jerome* 1852–1921

US-born wife of Lord Randolph Henry Spencer Churchill, daughter of a prominent New York businessman.

54 There is no such thing as a moral dress… It's people who are moral or immoral.
1921 'That Moral Dress', in the *Daily Chronicle*, 16 Feb.

Churchill, Lord Randolph Henry Spencer 1849–95

English politician, the leader of a guerrilla band of Conservatives known as the 'Fourth Party' (from 1880) and father of Sir Winston Churchill. He was Chancellor of the Exchequer and leader of the House of Commons (1886).

55 Ulster will not be a consenting party. Ulster, at the proper time, will resort to the supreme arbitrament of force; Ulster will fight and Ulster will be right.
1886 Public letter, 7 May.

56 This monstrous mixture of imbecility, extravagance and political hysteria, better known as the Bill for the future government of Ireland—this farrago of superlative nonsense, is to be put in motion for this reason and no other: to gratify the ambition of an old man in a hurry.
1886 Pamphlet attacking Gladstone's Home Rule Bill, Jun.

57 I could never make out what those damned dots meant.
Of decimal points. Quoted in Winston Churchill *Lord Randolph Churchill* (1906).

58 The duty of an Opposition is to oppose.
Remark attributed by his son, Winston Churchill. The phrase

was used earlier by Edward Stanley, 14th Earl of Derby, who attributed it to Mr Tierney (4 Jun 1841).

Churchill, Sir Winston Leonard Spencer 1874–1965

English statesman, Prime Minister (1940–5, 1951–2) and writer. He became a Conservative MP in 1900 but turned Liberal in 1904 and was made First Lord of the Admiralty (1911) and Chancellor of the Exchequer (1924–9). He returned to the Conservative Party in 1929 and on Chamberlain's defeat formed a coalition government to pursue the war with Germany.

59 Business carried on as usual during alterations on the map of Europe.
1914 Of the British people's view of World War I. Speech at the Guildhall, London, 9 Nov.

60 In war: resolution. In defeat: defiance. In victory: magnanimity. In peace: goodwill.
c.1918 *The Second World War* (1948), vol.1, epigraph. According to Sir Edward Marsh, in *A Number of People* (1939), the phrase occurred to Churchill shortly after the end of World War I. Some sources attribute it to Marsh himself.

61 Of all tyrannies in history, the Bolshevik tyranny is the worst, the most destructive, the most degrading. Every British and French soldier killed last year was really done to death by Lenin and Trotsky—not in fair war, but by the treacherous desertion of an ally without parallel in the history of the world.
1919 Speech, London, 11 Apr.

62 The community lacks goods and a million and a quarter people lack work. It is certainly one of the highest functions of national finance and credit to bridge the gap between the two.
1925 Letter to Otto Niemeyer, 22 Feb. Collected in D E Moggridge *Maynard Keynes* (1992).

63 The day must come when the nation's whole scale of living must be reduced. If that day comes, Parliament must lay the burden equally on all classes.
1925 Speech as Chancellor of the Exchequer, House of Commons, 7 Aug.

64 Jellicoe was the only man on either side who could lose the war in an afternoon.
1927 On Admiral Jellicoe, commander of the Grand Fleet in World War I. *The World Crisis*, pt.1, ch.5.

65 The loss of India would mark and consummate the downfall of the British Empire. That great organism would pass at a stroke out of life into history. From such a catastrophe there could be no recovery.
1930 Speech to the Indian Empire Society, London, 12 Dec.

66 Mr Gladstone read Homer for fun, which I thought served him right.
1930 *My Early Life*.

67 Those who can win a war well can rarely make a good peace, and those who could make a good peace would never have won the war.
1930 *My Early Life*.

68 The War was decided in the first twenty days of fighting, and all that happened afterwards consisted in battles which, however formidable and devastating, were but desparate and vain appeals against the decision of Fate.
1930 His preface to E L Spears *Liaison 1914*.

69 I remember, when I was a child, being taken to the celebrated Barnum's circus, which contained an exhibition of freaks and monstrosities, but the exhibit on the programme which I most desired to see was the one described as 'The Boneless Wonder'. My parents judged that the spectacle would be too revolting and demoralizing for my youthful eyes, and I have waited 50 years to see the boneless wonder sitting on the Treasury Bench.
1931 Alluding to Ramsay MacDonald. Speech in the House of Commons, 28 Jan.

70 It is alarming and odious to see Mr Gandhi, a seditious Middle Temple lawyer, now posing as a fakir of a type well-known in the East, striding half-naked up the steps of the vice-regal palace, while he is still conducting a defiant campaign of civil disobedience, to parley on equal terms with the representative of the King-Emperor.
1931 Speech, 23 Feb.

71 That long frontier from the Atlantic to the Pacific oceans, guarded only by neighbourly respect and honourable obligations, is an example to every country and a pattern for the future of the world.
1939 Address at the Canada Club, London, 20 Apr.

72 This is no war for domination or imperial aggrandisement or material gain… It is a war…to establish, on impregnable rocks, the rights of the individual and it is a war to establish and revive the stature of man.
1939 Speech in the House of Commons, 3 Sep, on the declaration of war against Germany by Britain and France.

73 I cannot forecast to you the action of Russia. It is a riddle wrapped inside a mystery inside an enigma. But perhaps there is a key; that key is Russian national interest.
1939 Radio broadcast, 1 Oct.

74 You ask what is our aim. I can answer in one word—victory. Victory at all costs, victory in spite of all terror, victory, however long and hard the road may be.
1939 Radio broadcast, 1 Oct.

75 I have nothing to offer but blood, toil, tears and sweat.
1940 Speech in the House of Commons on assuming the premiership, 13 May.

76 We shall not flag or fail. We shall go on to the end. We shall fight in France, we shall fight on the seas and oceans, we shall fight with growing confidence and growing strength in the air, we shall defend our island whatever the cost may be. We shall fight on the beaches, we shall fight on the landing grounds, we shall fight in the fields and in the streets, we shall fight in the hills. We shall never surrender.
1940 Speech in the House of Commons, 4 Jun, after the Dunkirk evacuation.

77 Let us therefore brace ourselves to our duties, and so bear ourselves that, if the British Empire and its Commonwealth last for a thousand years, men will still say: 'This was their finest hour.'
1940 Speech, 18 Jun. Quoted in A J P Taylor *English History 1914–45*, p.491.

78 Never in the field of human conflict has so much been owed by so many, to so few.
1940 On the Battle of Britain pilots. Speech, House of Commons, 20 Aug.

79 No one can guarantee success in war, but only deserve it.
1940 Letter to Lord Wavell, 26 Nov. Quoted in Winston Churchill *The Second World War*, vol.2 (1949), ch.27.

80 Here is the answer that I will give to President Roosevelt… Give us the tools, and we will finish the job.
1941 Radio broadcast, 9 Feb.

81 No one has been a more consistent opponent of Communism than I have for the last 25 years. I will unsay no word that I have spoken about it, but all that fades away before the spectacle that is now unfolding. The past, with its crimes, its follies, and its tragedies, flashes away. I see the Russian soldiers standing on the threshold of their native land, guarding the fields that their fathers have tilled from time immemorial. Any man or state who fights on against Nazidom will have our aid. Any man or state who marches with Hitler is our foe.
1941 Radio broadcast on the German invasion of Russia, 22 Jun.

82 When I warned the French that Britain would fight on alone, General Weygand told their Prime Minister and his divided Cabinet that in three weeks England will have her neck wrung like a chicken. Some chicken, some neck!
1941 Speech to the Canadian Parliament, 30 Dec.

83 What kind of people do they think we are?
1941 Of the Japanese. Speech to Congress, Dec.

84 Commanders and senior officers should die with troops. The honour of the British Empire and the British Army is at stake.
1942 Telegram to Wavell, the commander in chief of armed forces in Singapore, 10 Feb, after being told that a Japanese victory was inevitable. Recalled in *The Second World War*, vol.4 (1951).

85 The latest refinements of science are linked with the cruelties of the Stone Age.
1942 Speech, 26 Mar, in devastated war-time London.

86 Now this is not the end. It is not even the beginning of the end. But it is, perhaps, the end of the beginning.
1942 Speech at the Mansion House, London, 10 Nov, referring to the Battle of Egypt.

87 I have not become the King's First Minister in order to preside over the liquidation of the British Empire.
1942 Speech at the Mansion House, London, 10 Nov.

88 We make this wide encircling movement in the Mediterranean, having for its primary object the recovery of the command of that vital sea, but also having for its object the exposure of the under-belly of the Axis, especially Italy, to heavy attack.
1942 Speech in the House of Commons, 11 Nov.

89 There is no finer investment for any community than putting milk into babies. Healthy citizens are the greatest asset any country can have.
1943 Speech on BBC radio, 21 Mar.

90 The Bomb brought peace, but man alone can keep that peace.
1945 Speech in the House of Commons, 16 Aug.

91 If this is a blessing, it is certainly very well disguised.
1945 On his defeat in the first post-war general election, quoted in Richard Nixon *Memoirs* (1978).

92 From Stettin in the Baltic to Trieste in the Adriatic, an iron curtain has descended across the Continent.
1946 Speech at Fulton, Missouri, 5 Mar. He had used the phrase in a telegraph to President Truman, 12 May 1945, when he said of the Russian-held territories that 'An iron curtain is drawn down upon their front'.

93 Would a special relationship between the United States and the British Commonwealth be inconsistent with our overriding loyalty to the world organization?
1946 Speech at Fulton, Missouri, Mar.

94 No one pretends that democracy is perfect or all-wise. Indeed, it has been said that democracy is the worst form of Government except all those other forms that have been tried from time to time.
1947 Speech in the House of Commons, 11 Nov.

95 Science bestowed immense new powers on man, and, at the same time, created conditions which were largely beyond his comprehension and still more beyond his control.
1949 Speech, Massachusetts Institute of Technology, 31 Mar.

96 I am ready to meet my maker. Whether my maker is ready for the ordeal of meeting me is another matter.
1949 Speech, Nov.

97 I have only one purpose—the destruction of Hitler, and my life is much simplified thereby. If Hitler invaded Hell, I would at least make a favourable reference to the Devil in the House of Commons.
Recalled in *The Second World War*, vol.3 (1950), ch.20.

98 Perhaps it is better to be irresponsible and right than to be responsible and wrong.
1950 Radio broadcast, 26 Aug.

99 If you recognize anyone, it does not mean that you like him. We all, for instance, recognize the honourable Member for Ebbw Vale.
1952 Of Ernest Bevin, in a House of Commons debate on 1 Jul on British recognition of communist China.

1 I have lived 78 years without hearing of bloody places like Cambodia.
1953 Comment, 28 Apr. Quoted in Lord Moran *Winston Churchill, The Struggle for Survival* (1966).

2 Talking jaw is better than going to war.
1954 White House speech, 26 Jun. His comment is often rendered 'To jaw-jaw is always better than to war-war.'

3 I have never accepted what many people have kindly said—that I inspired the nation. It was the nation and the race living around the globe that had the lion heart. I had the luck to be called upon to give the roar.
1954 Speech to both Houses of Parliament in Westminster Hall, Nov, on the occasion of his 80th birthday.

4 An appeaser is someone who feeds a crocodile, hoping it will eat him last.
Attributed. Quoted in *Reader's Digest*, Dec 1954.

5 In defeat unbeatable: in victory unbearable.
Of Montgomery. Quoted in Sir Edward Howard Marsh *Ambrosia and Small Beer* (1964), ch.5.

6 Scientists should be on tap, but not on top.
Quoted in Randolph S Churchill *Twenty-One Years* (1965).

7 An empty taxi arrived at 10 Downing Street, and when the door was opened Attlee got out.
Attributed. Quoted in Kenneth Harris *Attlee* (1982), ch.16.

8 An ineffectual attempt to direct an uncontrollable sphere into an inaccessible hole with instruments ill-adapted for the purpose.
Quoted in Michael Hobbs *The Golf Quotations Book* (1992).

9 All I wanted was compliance with my wishes after reasonable discussion.

Attributed. Quoted in A J P Taylor *From the Boer War to the Cold War: Essays on Twentieth-Century Europe* (1995).

10 Do not criticize your Government when out of the country. Never cease to do so when at home.
Attributed.

11 There, but for the grace of God, goes God.
Of Sir Stafford Cripps. Attributed.

12 I am so bored with it all.
Attributed last words.

Ciardi, John 1916–85

US poet, critic and translator. His translation of Dante's *Inferno* is much admired.

13 This island rock in space turns flowering endlessly
To peaks of cloud still mounting where you took
Your last high passage and your faltering luck.
1947 'Elegy for Kurt Porjescz, Missing in Action, 1 April, 1945'.

14 At the next vacancy for God, if I am elected,
I shall forgive last the delicately wounded
who, having been slugged no harder than anyone else,
never got up again, neither to fight back,
nor to finger their jaws in painful admiration.
1959 'In Place of a Curse'.

15 You don't have to suffer to be a poet. Adolescence is enough.
1962 In the *Saturday Review*, Fall issue.

Cibber, Colley 1671–1757

English actor and dramatist. He worked for most of his career at the Theatre Royal in Drury Lane, and in 1696 established himself as both playwright and actor with his first comedy, *Love's Last Shift*. From 1730 he was Poet Laureate.

16 One had as good be out of the World, as out of the Fashion.
1696 *Love's Last Shift: or, The Fool in Fashion*, act 2, sc.1.

17 Perish the thought!
1700 *Richard III*, act 5 (his adaptation of Shakespeare's play).

18 Stolen sweets are best.
1709 *The Rival Fools*, act 1.

Cicero *full name* **Marcus Tullius Cicero** 106–43 BC

Roman orator and statesman, exiled after his unconstitutional execution of the Catiline conspirators. Although recalled by the people (57 BC) he lost the respect of both Caesar and Pompey by his vacillations. He wrote most of his major works on rhetoric and philosophy in retirement in Rome. His speeches against Mark Antony after Caesar's death (*The Philippics*) cost him his life.

19 *Quo usque tandem abutere, Catilina, patientia nostra?*
In heaven's name, Catiline, how long will you abuse our patience?
63 BC Opening line of the first of four speeches against the conspirator L Sergius Catilina, 8 Nov. *In Catilinam* 1.1.

20 *Salus populi suprema est lex.*
The good of the people is the chief law.
52 BC *De Legibus*, bk.3, ch.3.

21 *Silent enim leges inter arma.*
For laws are silent in time of war.
51 BC *Pro Milone*, ch.11.

22 *Cui bono?*
Who benefits?
51 BC *Pro Milone*, ch.12 (and elsewhere).

23 *Nervos belli, pecuniam infinitam.*
The sinews of war, unlimited money.
44 BC *Fifth Philippic*, ch.5.

24 *Nihil tam absurde dici potest quo non dicatur ab aliquo philosophorum.*
There is nothing so absurd that it has not been said by some philosopher.
c.44 BC *De Divinatione*, bk.2, section 58.

25 *Civis Romanus sum.*
I am a Roman citizen.
In Verrem 5.147. This is a reference to the tradition that Roman citizens in foreign courts could often expect preferential treatment. The Roman governor Verres, whom Cicero was prosecuting, had ignored this fact altogether, even executing Roman citizens.

26 *Cedant arma togae, concedant laurea laudi.*
Let war yield to peace, laurels to paeans.
De Officiis, bk.1, ch.77.

27 *Mens cuiusque is est quisque: non ea figura quae digito demonstrari potest.*
The mind is the true self, not the person that can be pointed to with the finger.
De Republica bk.6, ch.24.

28 *O fortunatam natam me consule Romam!*
O lucky Rome, born when I was consul!
Cicero was consul in 63 BC. His only extant line of poetry, quoted in Juvenal, *Satires* 10, 1.122.

29 *O tempora, o mores!*
What times! what morals!
Favourite phrase, used on various occasions. See *In Catilinam* 1.1, *In Verrem* 4.25 and *Pro rege Deiotaro* 11.31.

Cisneros, Henry 1947–

US politician, Secretary of Housing and Urban Development (1993–7).

30 Like piles of dry wood with red-hot coals underneath.
1993 Of US cities, rife with racial tension. In *US News and World Report*, 19 Apr.

31 We have to be honest, we have to be truthful and speak to the one dirty secret in American life, and that is racism.
1993 In *US News and World Report*, 19 Apr.

Cixous, Hélène 1937–

French feminist author and critic who has argued that women write differently from men by virtue of their bodies.

32 *On dit que la vie et la mort sont au pouvoir de la langue.*
It is said that life and death are under the power of language.
1969 *Dedans*.

33 *La seule différence incontestable n'est pas celle des sexes ou des âges ou des forces, mais celle des vifs et des morts.*
The only incontestable difference is not that of sex or age or strength, but that of the living and the dead.
1969 *Dedans*.

34 *J'ai peu de mots. Mon père qui les avait tous, est parti si précipitamment, qu'il n'a pas eu le temps de me les donner.*

I have few words. My father, who had all of them, left so suddenly that he did not have the time to give them all to me.
1969 *Dedans.*

35 *Le temps et le monde et la personne ne se rencontrent qu'une seule fois.*
Time, the world and the person only encounter one another once.
1969 *Dedans.*

36 *Je me cherche à travers les siècles et je ne me vois nulle part.*
I have searched for myself across time and have not found myself anywhere.
1974 *Prénoms du soleil* (translated by Morag Shiach in *Hélène Cixous: A Politics of Writing*).

37 *Des mots sont arrachés vivants à la langue défunte.*
Words are taken alive from a defunct language.
1976 *La.*

38 *On ne s'éveille qu'au contact de l'amour. Et avant ce temps, on n'est que jardins sans douleurs, espaces fourmillant de corps érotiques, champs de mers poissonneuses, chairs sans soucis.*
One wakes only to the touch of love. Before then, we are only gardens without sorrows, spaces swarming with erotic bodies, landscapes of seas full of fish, flesh without cares.
1976 *La.*

39 *Quand je n'écris pas, c'est comme si j'étais morte.*
When I do not write, it's as though I'm dead.
Quoted in Jean-Louis Rambures *Comment travaillent les écrivains* (1978).

40 *Je ne suis pas innocente. L'innocence est une science du sublime. Et je ne suis qu'au tout début de l'apprentissage.*
I am not innocent. Innocence is a science of the sublime. And I am only at the very beginning of the apprenticeship.
1979 *Vivre l'orange/ To Live the Orange* (bilingual text, translated by Ann Liddle and Sarah Cornell).

41 *Je voudrais tant être une femme sans y penser.*
I would like so much to be a woman without thinking about it.
1983 *Le Livre de Promethea.*

Clare, John 1793–1864

English poet, whose work reflects the harsh rural world of the 19c. He became mentally unstable in 1823 and spent the last 23 years of his life in a lunatic asylum.

42 When badgers fight and everyone's a foe.
1836 'Badger'.

43 A quiet, pilfering, unprotected race.
1841 'The Gipsy Camp'.

44 The present is the funeral of the past,
And man the living sepulchre of life.
1845 'The Present is the Funeral of the Past'.

45 I am—yet what I am, none cares or knows;
My friends forsake me like a memory lost:
I am the self-consumer of my woes.
1848 'I Am'.

46 I long for scenes where man hath never trod
A place where woman never smiled or wept
There to abide with my Creator God

And sleep as I in childhood sweetly slept,
Untroubling and untroubled where I lie
The grass below, above, the vaulted sky.
1848 'I Am'.

47 He could not die when the trees were green,
For he loved the time too well.
'The Dying Child' (published 1873).

Clark, Alan Kenneth McKenzie 1928–99

English Conservative politician, noted for his diaries, which were published from 1993. He was the son of the art historian Kenneth Clark.

48 There are no true friends in politics. We are all sharks circling, and waiting, for traces of blood to appear in the water.
1990 Diary entry, 30 Nov.

49 Safe is spelled D-U-L-L. Politics has got to be a fun activity.
1997 On being selected as parliamentary candidate for Kensington and Chelsea, 24 Jan. In the *Daily Telegraph*, 25 Jan.

50 If I can comport myself with the dignity and competence of Ms Mo Mowlam, I shall be very satisfied.
1999 After surgery for a brain tumour. In the *Sunday Times*, 'Talking Heads', 6 Jun.

Clark, Eleanor 1913–

US writer, wife of Robert Penn Warren. Her works include *Eyes, Etc.* (1977), on her experience of blindness. She won the National Book Award, 1965, for *The Oysters of Locmariaquer.*

51 If you don't love life you can't enjoy an oyster.
1964 *The Oysters of Locmariaquer*, ch.1.

Clark, Kenneth Mackenzie Clark, Baron 1903–83

English art historian, particularly remembered for his pioneering television series, *Civilisation* (1969).

52 All great civilisations, in their early stages, are based on success in war.
1969 *Civilisation*, ch.1.

53 Medieval marriages were entirely a matter of property, and, as everyone knows, marriage without love means love without marriage.
1969 *Civilisation*, ch.3.

Clark, Ralph c.1755–1794

British lieutenant of the First Fleet to Australia.

54 The damned whores the moment that they got below fell a fighting amongst one and another and Capt Meridith order the Sergt. not to part them but to let them fight it out.
c.1789 *The Journal and Letters of Lt Ralph Clark 1787–1792*. The phrase 'damned whores' was adopted by Australian feminist Anne Summers in her feminist critique of Australian culture, *Damned Whores and God's Police* (1975).
► *See Chisholme 213:16.*

Clark, Ramsey 1927–

US lawyer, appointed Attorney General (1967–9), known for his staunch defence of civil liberties and his opposition to the Vietnam War.

55 A right is not what someone gives you; it's what no one

can take from you.
1977 In the *New York Times*, 2 Oct.

Clark, William R and Michael Grunstein

US scientists.

56 Why are human beings so different from one another?
2000 *Are We Hardwired? The Role of Genes in Human Behaviour.*

Clarke, Sir Arthur C(harles) 1917–

English author, a prolific and entertaining writer of works of science fiction, popular science, mysticism and speculative thought. His story 'The Sentinel' was the basis of Stanley Kubrick's film *2001: A Space Odyssey* (1968).

57 Overhead without any fuss the stars were going out.
1958 'The Nine Billion Names of God'.

58 Any sufficiently advanced technology is indistinguishable from magic.
1962 *Profiles of the Future*, introduction.

59 When a distinguished but elderly scientist states that something is possible he is almost certainly right. When he states that something is impossible, he is very probably wrong.
1962 *Profiles of the Future*.

60 For the radiance of eternity is not white: it is infra-red.
1993 *By Space Possessed.*

Clarke, Kenneth Harry 1940–

English Conservative politician.

61 I do not wear a bleeper. I can't speak in soundbites. I refuse to repeat slogans… I hate focus groups. I absolutely hate image consultants.
1999 In the *New Statesman*, 12 Feb.

Claudel, Paul 1868–1955

French dramatist, poet and diplomat, whose writing reflects his mystical Catholicism. He was ambassador to Japan (1921–7), the US (1927–33) and Belgium (1933–35). His works include the play *Tidings Brought to Mary* (1912) and *Five Great Odes* (1910).

62 You explain nothing, O poet, but thanks to you all things become explicable.
Recalled on his death, 23 Feb 1955.

63 A cocktail is to a glass of wine as rape is to love.
Quoted by William Grimes in 'The American Cocktail', *Americana*, Dec 1992.

Claudius Caecus, Appius 4c–3c BC

Roman statesman and lawgiver. He oversaw the construction of Rome's first aqueduct, the Aqua Appia. He later became blind, hence his surname, Caecus.

64 *Faber est suae quisque fortunae.*
Each man is the architect of his own fate.
Quoted in Sallust *Ad Caesarem Senem de Re Publica Oratio*, ch.1, section 2.

Clausewitz, Karl von 1780–1831

Prussian general, Director of the Prussian army school in Berlin (1818–30) and Gneisenau's Chief-of-Staff. His treatise *Vom Kriege* ('On War', 1833) had a major impact on strategic studies.

65 Battles decide everything.
1812 *Principles of War* (translated by J J Graham).

66 Only the study of military history is capable of giving those who have no experience of their own a clear picture of what I have just called the friction of the whole machine.
1812 *Principles of War* (translated by J J Graham).

67 *Der Krieg ist nichts als eine Fortsetzung des politischen Verkehrs mit Einmischung anderer Mittel.*
War is merely the continuation of policy with the admixture of other means.
1833 *Vom Kriege*, bk.8, ch.6, section b. The phrase is commonly rendered 'War is the continuation of politics by other means.'

Clavell, James du Maresq 1924–94

Australian-born US novelist. His first novel, *King Rat* (1962), is set in Singapore's Changi prison, where the Japanese kept prisoners of war (1942–5). Clavell was himself a prisoner of war in Java.

68 These men too were criminals. Their crime was vast. They had lost a war. And they had lived.
1962 *King Rat.*

Cleaver, Eldridge 1935–98

US political activist.

69 You're either part of the solution, or you're part of the problem.
1968 Speech, San Francisco.

Cleese, John 1939–

British actor, comedian and writer, best known for his contribution to the satirical television series, *Monty Python's Flying Circus* (1969–74).

70 I wish to complain about this parrot what I have purchased not half an hour ago from this very boutique.
1968 As Mr Praline in the 'Dead Parrot' sketch, *Monty Python's Flying Circus.*

71 Don't mention the war. I mentioned it once but I think I got away with it.
1975 As Basil Fawlty in *Fawlty Towers*, 'The Germans'.

72 Loving your neighbour as much as yourself is practically bloody impossible… You might as well have a commandment that states, 'Thou shalt fly'.
1993 In *The Times*.

Clemenceau, Georges 1841–1929

French statesman, leader of the extreme left, known as 'The Tiger'. He was Premier (1906–9, 1917–20) and presided at the 1919 Peace Conference.

73 *La guerre, c'est une chose trop grave pour la confier à des militaires.*
War is too serious a business to be left to generals.
Quoted in Hampden Jackson *Clemenceau and the Third Republic* (1946), but also attributed elsewhere to others.

74 He died as he had lived—like a second lieutenant.
1891 On the death of General Boulanger, who had shot himself on the grave of his mistress, who had died two months earlier. In *La Justice*. Quoted in Edgar Holt *The Tiger: The Life of Georges Clemenceau 1841–1929* (1976).

75 Your verdict, gentlemen, will be less upon us than upon yourselves. We appear before you. You appear before history.

1898 Addressing the jury as a member of the defence at Zola's trial, 22 Feb, following the publication of *J'Accuse*.

76 *Politique intérieure, je fais la guerre; politique extérieure, je fais toujours la guerre. Je fais toujours la guerre.*
My home policy? I wage war. My foreign policy? I wage war. Always, everywhere, I wage war.
1918 Speech to the Chamber of Deputies, 8 Mar.

77 *Il est plus facile de faire la guerre que la paix.*
It is far easier to make war than to make peace.
1919 Speech at Verdun, 20 Jul.

78 America is the only country in history that miraculously has gone directly from barbarism to decadence without the usual interval of civilization.
Attributed. This has also been attributed to George Bernard Shaw.

79 We have won the war. Now we have to win the peace—and that may be more difficult.
Quoted in David R Watson *George Clemenceau; A Political Biography* (1974).

Cleveland, (Stephen) Grover 1837–1908

22nd and 24th US President (1885–9, 1893–7). He supported civil service reform and lower tariffs, and in his second term he took a strong stance against Britain in its boundary dispute with Venezuela.

80 I have considered the pension list of the republic a roll of honour.
1888 Veto of the Dependent Pension Bill, 5 Jul.

Cleveland, John 1613–1658

English poet, a satirical propagandist for the Royalists in the Civil War, and for a time a political prisoner. Two collections of his poems were published during his lifetime, one in 1651 and the other in 1653.

81 Had Cain been Scot, God would have changed his doom
Nor forced him wander, but confined him home.
1647 'The Rebel Scot'.

82 Mystical grammar of amorous glances,
Feeling of pulses the physic of love,
Rhetorical courtings, and musical dances;
Numbering of kisses arithmetic prove.
1651 'Mark Antony'.

83 Virtue's no more in womankind
But the green sickness of the mind.
Philosophy, their new delight,
A kind of charcoal appetite.
1653 'The Antiplatonic'.

84 Give me a lover bold and free,
Not eunuched with formality.
1653 'The Antiplatonic'.

85 Like an ambassador that beds a queen
With the nice caution of a sword between.
1653 'The Antiplatonic'.

Clifford, Clark M(cAdams) 1906–98

US lawyer, adviser to Truman and Kennedy and later Secretary of Defense (1968–9) under Johnson.

86 The amiable dunce.
Of Ronald Reagan. Quoted in Haynes Johnson *Sleep-Walking Through History* (1991).

Clinton, Bill (William) 1946–

US Democratic politician and 42nd President. He became Governor of Arkansas in 1978 and served for five terms (1979–81, 1983–92). In 1992 he became the first Democrat President for twelve years and in 1996 the first Democrat to gain re-election since Roosevelt in 1936. In 1998 his initial denial of an affair with White House intern Monica Lewinsky was followed by charges of perjury and obstruction of justice, although he was subsequently acquitted by the Senate. He is married to Hillary Rodham Clinton.

87 Cash for trash.
1992 On tabloid payments to his alleged mistress Gennifer Flowers. On ABC T V, 23 Jan.

88 I experimented with marijuana a time or two. And I didn't like it, and I didn't inhale.
1992 In the *Washington Post*, 30 Mar.

89 On this day with high hopes and brave hearts, in massive numbers, the American people have voted to make a new beginning.
1992 Accepting victory in the election, 3 Nov.

90 When somebody tells you it is not a money problem, they're talking about somebody else's money.
1992 In *USA Today*, 20 Dec.

91 That hallowed piece of earth, that land of light and revelation, is the home to the memories and dreams of Jews, Muslims and Christians throughout the world.
1993 On the signing of Palestinian–Israeli peace accord at the White House, 13 Sep.

92 I have had a drill to the tooth of America for the last two years.
1994 Of painful political decisions. In the *US News & World Report*, 13 Feb.

93 I can't stop being President.
1994 Comment after a suicide plane attack and two incidents of gunfire on the White House. Reported in the *New York Times*, 18 Dec.

94 If something makes you cry, you have to do something about it. That's the difference between politics and guilt.
On what makes a liberal. Quoted in Meredith Oakley *On the Make* (1994).

95 Half the time when I see the evening news, I wouldn't be for me, either.
1995 Comment, 2 Jun.

96 Hillary was born 40, and she'll always be 40… I was born 16, and I'll always be 16.
Quoted in Gore Vidal *Virgin Islands: Essays 1992–1997* (1997).

97 I did not have sexual relations with that woman.
1998 On Monica Lewinsky, in a television interview. Quoted in the *Daily Telegraph*, 27 Jan.

98 I did have a relationship with Ms Lewinsky that was not appropriate. In fact, it was wrong.
1998 Television broadcast to America, 18 Aug. In *The Times*, 19 Aug.

99 It depends on what the meaning of 'is' is.
1998 Evidence to the grand jury. Quoted in *The Guardian*, 2 Sep.

1 I believe any person who asks for forgiveness has to be prepared to give it.
1999 Statement after being acquitted by the Senate, 12 Feb.

2 Golf is like life in a lot of ways. The most important competition is the one against yourself.
2000 Quoted in *The Independent*, 23 Dec.

3 A terrible moral error.
2004 On his affair with Monica Lewinsky. In an interview on CBS television programme *60 Minutes*, 20 Jun.

4 I did something for the worst possible reason. Just because I could.
2004 On his affair with Monica Lewinsky. In an interview on CBS television programme *60 Minutes*, 20 Jun.

5 Don't ask, don't tell.
2004 The Clinton family motto. In *My Life*.

6 Do I have regrets? Sure, both private and public ones.
2004 *My Life*.

7 During the government shutdowns I was engaged in two titanic struggles: a public one with Congress over the future of our country, and a private one to hold the old demons at bay. I had won the public fight and lost the private one.
2004 *My Life*.

Clinton, Hillary Rodham 1947–

US politician and lawyer, wife of President Bill Clinton. As a lawyer she specialized in family issues and children's rights, and after her husband's election she served as chief presidential adviser. In 2001 she became Senator for New York, the first First Lady to be elected to public office.

8 I suppose I could have stayed home, baked cookies, and had teas.
1992 Rejecting charges of a conflict of interest between politics and her legal career. In the *New York Times*, 18 May.

9 I'd be a terrific governor…a terrific president.
1992 Statement during her husband's presidential campaign. Reported in the *Washington Post*, 22 Feb 1995.

10 It is time for us to say here in Beijing, and the world to hear, that it is no longer acceptable to discuss women's rights as separate from human rights.
1995 Addressing the 4th World Conference on Women. Reported in the *New York Times*, 6 Sep.

11 I was talking to one of the Secret Service men about security the other day, and he said that as far as they were concerned, they'd be happier if we lived in a bunker and travelled the streets in a tank.
Quoted in Gore Vidal *Virgin Islands: Essays 1992–1997* (1997).

12 The great story here…is this vast right-wing conspiracy that has been conspiring against my husband since the day he announced for president.
1998 Interview on NBC television's *Today*, 27 Jan.

13 A hard dog to keep on the porch.
1999 On her husband. In *The Guardian*, 2 Aug.

Clive, Kitty 1711–85

English comic actress. Though she longed to be a tragic actress, she excelled in light comedy under the management of David Garrick at Drury Lane. She retired in 1769.

14 Damn him, he could act a gridiron.
On watching a performance by David Garrick. Quoted in William Archer's introduction to *Dramatic Essays of Leigh Hunt* (1894).

Clive, Robert, 1st Baron of Plassey 1725–74

English soldier and administrator in India, who defeated a large Indian–French force at Plassey (1757). After a spell in Parliament in Britain he returned to Calcutta (1765) to reform the civil service and the military, but was criticized for his drastic measures.

15 It is scarcely hyperbole to say that tomorrow the whole Moghul Empire is in our power.
1757 Letter, 24 Jun, following victory at Plassey the previous day.

16 By God, Mr Chairman—at this moment I stand astonished at my own moderation!
1773 At a parliamentary inquiry into his rapacious policies on India.

Clough, Arthur Hugh 1819–61

English poet. A friend of Ruskin, Arnold and Carlyle, he experienced a religious crisis in Oxford which pervades much of his writing.

17 Sesquipedalian blackguard.
1848 *The Bothie of Tober-na-Vuolich*, pt.2, l.223.

18 Grace is given of God, but knowledge is bought in the market.
1848 *The Bothie of Tober-na-Vuolich*, pt.4, l.159.

19 What shall we do without you? Think where we are. Carlyle has led us all out into the desert, and he has left us there.
1848 Parting words to Ralph Waldo Emerson, 15 Jul. Quoted in E E Hale *James Russell Lowell and His Friends* (1898), ch.9.

20 Say not the struggle naught availeth
The labour and the wounds are vain,
The enemy faints not, nor faileth,
And as things have been, things remain.
1849 'Say Not the Struggle Naught Availeth'.

21 If hopes were dupes, fears may be liars.
1849 'Say Not the Struggle Naught Availeth'.

22 And not by eastern windows only,
When daylight comes, comes in the light,
In front the sun climbs slow, how slowly,
But westward, look, the land is bright.
1849 'Say Not the Struggle Naught Availeth'.

23 Afloat. We move: Delicious! Ah,
What else is like the gondola?
1850 *Dipsychus* (published 1865), sc.5.

24 This world is bad enough maybe;
We do not comprehend it;
But in one fact can all agree
God won't, and we can't mend it.
1850 *Dipsychus* (published 1865), sc.5.

25 'There is no God', the wicked saith,
'And truly it's a blessing,
For what he might have done with us
It's better only guessing.'
1850 *Dipsychus* (published 1865), sc.6.

26 And almost every one when age,
Disease, or sorrow strike him,
Inclines to think there is a God,
Or something very like him.
1850 *Dipsychus* (published 1865), sc.6.

27 'Tis better to have fought and lost,
Than never to have fought at all.
1854 'Peschiera'.
➤ See Tennyson 843:34.

28 Rome, believe me, my friend, is like its own Monte Testaceo,

Merely a marvellous mass of broken and castaway wine-pots.
1858 *Amours de Voyage*, canto 1, pt.2.

29 The horrible pleasure of pleasing inferior people.
1858 *Amours de Voyage*, canto 1, pt.11.

30 Am I prepared to lay down my life for the British female? Really, who knows?…
Ah, for a child in the street I could strike; for the full-blown lady—
Somehow, Eustace, alas! I have not felt the vocation.
1858 *Amours de Voyage*, canto 2, pt.4.

31 I do not like being moved: for the will is excited; and action
Is a most dangerous thing: I tremble for something factitious,
Some malpractice of heart and illegitimate process;
We are so prone to these things with our terrible notions of duty.
1858 *Amours de Voyage*, canto 2, pt.11.

32 But for his funeral train which the bridegroom sees in the distance,
Would he so joyfully, think you, fall in with the marriage-procession?
1858 *Amours de Voyage*, canto 3, pt.6.

33 Allah is great, no doubt, and Juxtaposition his prophet.
1858 *Amours de Voyage*, canto 3, pt.6.

34 Mild monastic faces in quiet collegiate cloisters.
1858 *Amours de Voyage*, canto 3, pt.9.

35 Whither depart the souls of the brave that die in the battle,
Die in the lost, lost fight, for the cause that perishes with them?
1858 *Amours de Voyage*, canto 5, pt.6.

36 Thou shalt have one God only: who
Would be at the expense of two?
1862 *The Latest Decalogue*.

37 Thou shalt not kill; but need'st not strive
Officiously to keep alive.
1862 *The Latest Decalogue*.

38 Do not adultery commit;
Advantage rarely comes of it.
1862 *The Latest Decalogue*.

39 Thou shalt not steal; an empty feat,
When it's so lucrative to cheat.
1862 *The Latest Decalogue*.

40 Thou shalt not covet; but tradition
Approves all forms of competition.
1862 *The Latest Decalogue*.

Clough, Brian 1935–2004

English football player and manager. As a player, he set a postwar goal-scoring record of 254 goals, and also won two England caps. He went on to become a controversial and outspoken but successful manager.

41 Football hooligans? Well, there are 92 club chairmen for a start.
Quoted in Colin Jarman *The Guinness Dictionary of Sports Quotations* (1990).

42 Say nowt, win it, then—talk your head off.
Quoted in Colin Jarman *The Guinness Dictionary of Sports Quotations* (1990).

43 My wife says OBE stands for Old Big 'Ead.
Quoted in Phil Shaw *The Book of Football Quotations* (2003).

44 Resignations are for Prime Ministers and those caught with their trousers down, not for me.
Quoted in Phil Shaw *The Book of Football Quotations* (2003).

Cobain, Kurt (Donald) 1967–94

US singer and guitarist, founder member of the band Nirvana.

45 Here we are now, entertain us.
1991 'Smells Like Teen Spirit'.

46 Here's the one who likes all our pretty songs
And he likes to sing along
And he likes to shoot his gun
But he don't know what it means.
1991 'In Bloom'.

Cobbett, William 1762–1835

English radical politician and journalist. His pioneering essays on the the conditions of the rural poor were collected in his best-known work, *Rural Rides* (1830).

47 Protestations of impartiality I shall make none. They are always useless and are besides perfect nonsense, when used by a news-monger.
1797 In the first issue of *Porcupine's Gazette*, 4 Mar, 'Address to the public'.

48 All Middlesex is *ugly*, notwithstanding the millions upon millions which it is continually sucking up from the rest of the kingdom.
1822 *Rural Rides* (published 1830), entry for 25 Sep.

49 DEAL is a most villainous place. It is full of filthy-looking people. Great desolation of abomination has been going on here.
1823 On Deal, Kent. *Rural Rides* (published 1830), entry for 3 Sep.

50 The town of GUILDFORD, which (taken with its environs) I, who have seen so many, many towns, think the prettiest, and, taken all together, the most agreeable and most happy-looking, that I ever saw in my life.
1825 On Guildford, Surrey. *Rural Rides* (published 1830), entry for 23 Oct.

51 WESTBURY, a nasty odious *rotten-borough*, a really *rotten* place.
1826 On Westbury, Wiltshire. *Rural Rides* (published 1830), entry for 3 Sep.

52 From a very early age, I had imbibed the opinion, that it was every man's duty to do all that lay in his power to leave his country as good as he had found it.
1832 *Political Register*, 22 Dec.

Cobden, Richard 1804–65

English economist and politician, known as 'The Apostle of Free Trade'. In 1838 he co-founded the Anti-Corn League, and as MP from 1841 he spoke in support of the cause, bringing about the repeal of the Corn Laws in 1846.

53 Are we to be the Don Quixotes of Europe—to go about fighting for every cause where we find that someone has been wronged?
1854 Referring to the Crimean War, House of Commons, 22 Dec.

Cockburn, Alison née *Rutherford* 1713–94

Scottish poet, whose best-known lyric 'The Flowers of the Forest' commemorates a calamity in Ettrick Forest. Walter Scott was her protégé.

54 I've seen the smiling of Fortune beguiling,
  I've felt all its favours and found its decay;
  Sweet was its blessing, kind its caressing,
  But now it is fled, fled far, far away.
  1765 'The Flowers of the Forest'.

55 O fickle Fortune, why this cruel sporting?
  Why thus torment us poor sons of day?
  Nae mair your smiles can cheer me, nae mair your
  frowns can fear me,
  For the flowers of the forest are a' wade away.
  1765 'The Flowers of the Forest'. wade = weeded. The last line is often rendered 'For the flowers of the forest are withered away'.

Cocker, Jarvis 1963–

English singer, member of the band Pulp.

56 Let's all meet up in the year 2000
  Won't it be strange when we're all fully grown?
  1995 'Disco 2000'.

Cocteau, Jean 1889–1963

French poet, playwright and film director, a key figure in Surrealism and Dadaism, elected to the French Academy in 1955. His works explore the problems of adolescence and family relationships.

57 *Le tact dans l'audace c'est de savoir jusqu'où on peut aller trop loin.*
  Being tactful in audacity is knowing how far one can go too far.
  1918 *Le Coq et l'Arlequin.*

58 *Le pire drame pour un poète, c'est d'être admiré par malentendu.*
  The worst tragedy for a poet is to be admired through being misunderstood.
  1918 *Le Coq et l'Arlequin.*

59 *S'il faut choisir un crucifié, la foule sauve toujours Barabbas.*
  If it has to choose who is to be crucified, the crowd will always save Barabbas.
  1918 *Le Coq et l'Arlequin.*

60 *Vivre est une chute horizontale.*
  Life is a horizontal fall.
  1930 *Opium.*

61 Art produces ugly things which frequently become beautiful with time. Fashion, on the other hand, produces beautiful things which always become ugly with time.
  1960 In the *New York World-Telegram and Sun*, 21 Aug.

Coen, Joel 1954–

US film director and screenwriter who often works in collaboration with his brother Ethan Coen.

62 We'll gladly enter the mainstream any time the mainstream will have us.
  2004 In *The Guardian*, 15 Jun.

Coffee, Lenore 1900–84

US screenwriter, Oscar-nominated for *Four Daughters* (1938).

63 What a dump!
  1949 Spoken by Bette Davis in *Beyond the Forest*.

Coffinhal, Jean Baptiste 1754–94

Presiding judge at the trial of chemist Antoine Lavoisier.

64 The Republic has no need for scientists.
  1794 Quoted in the *Encyclopedia Britannica* (1911), vol.16.

Cohan, George M(ichael) 1878–1942

US actor-manager and playwright. Having started out in vaudeville, he became one of the great Broadway personalities, appearing in plays by himself and others at his own George M Cohan Theatre from 1911.

65 I'm a Yankee Doodle Dandy
  A Yankee Doodle, do or die;
  A real live nephew of my Uncle Sam's,
  Born on the fourth of July.
  1904 'Yankee Doodle Boy'.

66 I don't care what you say about me, as long as you say *something* about me, and as long as you spell my name right.
  Quoted in John McCabe *George M Cohan, The Man Who Owned Broadway* (1973), ch.13.

Cohen, Sacha Baron 1972–

English comedian, best known for the character Ali G.

67 Is it because I is black?
  1998 Frequently, as comic character Ali G.

Coke, Sir Edward 1552–1634

English jurist, prosecutor of Essex, Raleigh and the Gunpowder conspirators. After 1606 he vindicated national liberties against the royal prerogative. Dismissed in 1617, he led the popular party in Parliament from 1620 and instigated the Petition of Right (1628).

68 How long soever it hath continued, if it be against reason, it is of no force in law.
  1628 *The First Part of the Institutes of the Laws of England*, bk.1, ch.10, section 80.

69 We have a saying in the House of Commons; that old ways are the safest and surest ways.
  1628 Speech, London, 8 May.

70 A man's house is his castle.
  1628 *The Third Part of the Institutes of the Laws of England*, ch.73.

Coke, F T Desmond 1879–1931

English novelist. A schoolmaster, he wrote several popular novels set in English public schools and universities, notably *The Bending of a Twig* (1906) and *Sandford of Merton* (1908).

71 His blade struck the water a full second before any other…until, as the boats began to near the winning post his own was dipping in the water twice as fast as any other.
  1908 *Sandford of Merton*, ch.12. Often misquoted as 'All rowed fast but none so fast as stroke'.

Cole, Mac

Founder, Cole Carnival Shows.

72 The first carnival person was Christopher Columbus. When he sailed, he didn't know where he was going. When he got there, he didn't know where he was. And when he got back, he didn't know where he'd been.
1989 In the *Washington Times*, 18 Aug.

Cole, W Sterling 1904–88

Chair, Joint Committee on Atomic Energy.

73 It is more sinful to conceal the power of the atom than it is to reveal it.
1954 Statement, 9 Mar, endorsed by Winston Churchill in a letter to President Eisenhower. Quoted in Peter G Boyle (ed) *The Churchill – Eisenhower Correspondence 1953–55*.

Cole, William 1919–2000

US children's writer. His output consisted chiefly of humorous verse, such as *A Boy Named Mary Jane* (1975). He also edited many poetry and verse collections.

74 Said Jerome K. Jerome to Ford Madox Ford,
'There's something, old boy, that I've always abhorred:
When people address me and call me 'Jerome',
Are they being standoffish, or too much at home?'
Said Ford, 'I agree;
It's the same thing with me.'
'Mutual Problem', collected in *The Oxford Book of American Light Verse* (1979).

Coleman, Ornette 1930–

US jazz saxophonist and composer. A controversial figure when he first appeared in New York in the late 1950s, he went on to become a key figure in the development of Free Jazz, and beyond.

75 The creation of music is just as natural as the air we breathe. I believe music is really a free thing, and any way you can enjoy it, you should.
1958 Sleeve-note, *Something Else!*

76 Many people apparently don't trust their reactions to art or to music unless there is a verbal *explanation* for it. In music the only thing that matters is whether you *feel* it or not.
1959 Sleeve-note, *Change of the Century*.

77 When I have them working together, it's like a beautiful kaleidoscope.
1981 On the music of his band Prime Time. Quoted in John Litweiler *The Freedom Principle* (1984).

Coleridge, Samuel Taylor 1772–1834

English poet, with Wordsworth one of the founders of the Romantic movement. Among his best-known poems are 'The Rime of the Ancient Mariner' (1798), 'Christabel' (1816) and 'Kubla Khan' (1816).

78 So for the mother's sake the child was dear,
And dearer was the mother for the child.
1797 'Sonnet to a Friend Who Asked Me How I Felt When the Nurse First Presented My Infant to Me'.

79 No sound is dissonant which tells of life.
1797 'This Lime-Tree Bower my Prison'.

80 It is an ancient Mariner,
And he stoppeth one of three.
'By thy long grey beard and glittering eye,
Now wherefore stopp'st thou me?'
1798 'The Rime of the Ancient Mariner', pt.1.

81 He holds him with his glittering eye—
The Wedding-Guest stood still,
And listens like a three years' child:
The Mariner hath his will.
The Wedding-Guest sat on a stone:
He cannot choose but hear;
And thus spake on that ancient man,
The bright-eyed Mariner.
1798 'The Rime of the Ancient Mariner', pt.1.

82 'God save thee, ancient Mariner!
From the fiends that plague thee thus!
Why look'st thou so?'—With my cross-bow
I shot the Albatross.
1798 'The Rime of the Ancient Mariner', pt.1.

83 We were the first that ever burst
Into that silent sea.
1798 'The Rime of the Ancient Mariner', pt.2.

84 As idle as a painted ship
Upon a painted ocean.
1798 'The Rime of the Ancient Mariner', pt.2.

85 Water, water, everywhere,
Nor any drop to drink.
The very deep did rot: O Christ!
That ever this should be!
Yes, slimy things did crawl with legs
Upon the slimy sea.
1798 'The Rime of the Ancient Mariner', pt.2.

86 I fear thee ancient Mariner!
I fear thy skinny hand!
And thou art long, and lank, and brown,
As is the ribbed sea-sand.
1798 'The Rime of the Ancient Mariner', pt.4.

87 And a thousand thousand slimy things
Lived on; and so did I.
1798 'The Rime of the Ancient Mariner', pt.4.

88 A spring of love gushed from my heart,
And I blessed them unaware.
1798 'The Rime of the Ancient Mariner', pt.4.

89 We were a ghastly crew.
1798 'The Rime of the Ancient Mariner', pt.5.

90 Like one, that on a lonesome road
Doth walk in fear and dread,
And having once turned round walks on,
And turns no more his head;
Because he knows, a frightful fiend
Doth close behind him tread.
1798 'The Rime of the Ancient Mariner', pt.6.

91 No voice, but oh! the silence sank
Like music on my heart.
1798 'The Rime of the Ancient Mariner', pt.6.

92 He prayeth well, who loveth well
Both man and bird and beast.
He prayeth best, who loveth best
All things both great and small.
1798 'The Rime of the Ancient Mariner', pt.7.

93 He went like one that hath been stunned,
And is of sense forlorn:
A sadder and wiser man,
He rose the morrow morn.
1798 'The Rime of the Ancient Mariner', pt.7.

94 O let me be awake, my God!
Or let me sleep alway.
1798 'The Rime of the Ancient Mariner', pt.7.

95 The frost performs its secret ministry,
Unhelped by any wind.
1798 'Frost at Midnight'.

96 Bells, the poor man's only music.
1798 'Frost at Midnight'.

97 And hark! the Nightingale begins its song,
'Most musical, most melancholy' bird!
A melancholy bird?…his song
Should make all Nature lovelier, and itself
Be loved like Nature!
1798 'The Nightingale'.

98 Belovèd, what are names but air?
Choose thou whatever suits the line;
Call me Sappho, call me Chloris,
Call me Lalage or Doris,
Only, only call me Thine.
1799 'Names', a translation from G E Lessing's German original
(first published in the *Morning Post*, 1803).

99 All thoughts, all passions, all delights
Whatever stirs this mortal frame,
All are but ministers of Love,
And feed his sacred flame.
1799 'Love'.

1 Those sounds which oft have raised me, whilst they awed,
And sent my soul abroad,
Might now perhaps their wonted impulse give,
Might startle this dull pain, and make it move and live!
1802 'Dejection: An Ode', stanza 1.

2 I may not hope from outward forms to win
The passion and the life, whose fountains are within.
1802 'Dejection: An Ode', stanza 3.

3 Ah! from the soul itself must issue forth
A light, a glory, a fair luminous cloud
Enveloping the Earth—
And from the soul itself must there be sent
A sweet and potent voice, of its own birth
Of all sweet sounds the life and element!
1802 'Dejection: An Ode', stanza 4.

4 O pure of heart! thou need'st not ask of me
What this strong music in the soul may be!
What, and wherein it doth exist,
This light, this glory, this fair luminous mist,
This beautiful and beauty-making power.
1802 'Dejection: An Ode', stanza 5.

5 'Alas!' said she, 'we ne'er can be
Made happy by compulsion!'
1809 'The Three Graves', pt.4, stanza 12.

6 What is an Epigram? a dwarfish whole,
Its body brevity, and wit its soul.
1809 'Epigram'.

7 Alas! they had been friends in youth;
But whispering tongues can poison truth;
And constancy lives in realms above;
And life is thorny; and youth is vain;
And to be wroth with one we love
Doth work like madness on the brain.
1816 'Christabel', pt.2.

8 On awaking he…instantly and eagerly wrote down the
lines that are here preserved. At this moment he was
unfortunately called out by a person on business from
Porlock.
1816 Preliminary note to 'Kubla Khan', explaining the reasons for
the fragmented end of the poem.

9 In Xanadu did Kubla Khan
A stately pleasure-dome decree:
Where Alph, the sacred river, ran
Through caverns measureless to man
Down to a sunless sea.
1816 'Kubla Khan', opening lines.

10 A savage place! as holy and enchanted
As e'er beneath a waning moon was haunted
By woman wailing for her demon-lover!
1816 'Kubla Khan'.

11 And from this chasm, with ceaseless turmoil seething,
As if this earth in fast thick pants were breathing,
A mighty fountain momently was forced.
1816 'Kubla Khan'.

12 It was a miracle of rare device,
A sunny pleasure-dome with caves of ice!
1816 'Kubla Khan'.

13 Through wood and dale the sacred river ran,
Then reached the caverns measureless to man,
And sank in tumult to a lifeless ocean:
And 'mid this tumult Kubla heard from far
Ancestral voices prophesying war!
1816 'Kubla Khan'.

14 A damsel with a dulcimer
In a vision once I saw:
It was an Abyssinian maid,
And on her dulcimer she played,
Singing of Mount Abora.
1816 'Kubla Khan'.

15 And all who heard should see them there,
And all should cry, Beware! Beware!
His flashing eyes, his floating hair!
Weave a circle round him thrice,
And close your eyes with holy dread,
For he on honey-dew hath fed,
And drunk the milk of Paradise.
1816 'Kubla Khan'.

16 Until you understand a writer's ignorance, presume
yourself ignorant of his understanding.
1817 *Biographia Literaria*, ch.12.

17 That willing suspension of disbelief for the moment,
which constitutes poetic faith.
1817 *Biographia Literaria*, ch.14.

18 Kean is original; but he copies from himself. His rapid
descents from the hyper-tragic to the infra-colloquial,
though sometimes productive of great effect, are often
unreasonable. To see him act, is like reading
Shakespeare by flashes of lightning.
1823 Of Edmund Kean. *Table Talk* (published 1835), entry for
27 Apr.

19 He who begins by loving Christianity better than
Truth will proceed by loving his own sect or church
better than Christianity, and end by loving himself
better than all.
1825 *Aids to Reflection: Moral and Religious Aphorisms*.

20 Summer has set in with its usual severity.
  1826 Letter to Vincent Novello, 9 May.

21 Prose = words in their best order;—poetry = the *best*
  words in the best order.
  1827 *Table Talk* (published 1835), entry for 12 Jul.

22 The man's desire is for the woman; but the woman's
  desire is rarely other than for the desire of the man.
  1827 *Table Talk* (published 1835), entry for 23 Jul.

23 In Köhln, a town of monks and bones,
  And pavements fang'd with murderous stones
  And rags, and hags, and hideous wenches;
  I counted two and seventy stenches,
  All well defined, and several stinks!
  Ye Nymphs that reign o'er sewers and sinks,
  The river Rhine, it is well known,
  Doth wash your city of Cologne;
  But tell me, Nymphs, what power divine
  Shall henceforth wash the river Rhine?
  1828 'Cologne', first published in *Friendship's Offering* (1834), as
  'Lightheartedness in Rhyme', no.4.

24 If men could learn from history, what lessons it might
  teach us! But passion and party blind our eyes, and the
  light which experience gives is a lantern on the stern,
  which shines only on the waves behind us!
  1831 *Table Talk* (published 1835), entry for 18 Dec.

25 Farce is nearer tragedy in its essence than comedy is.
  1833 *Table Talk* (published 1835), entry for 25 Aug.

26 Of no age—nor of any religion, or party or profession.
  The body and substance of his works came out of the
  unfathomable depths of his own oceanic mind.
  1834 Of Shakespeare. *Table Talk* (published 1835), entry for
  15 Mar.

27 Iago's soliloquy—the motive-hunting of motiveless
  malignity.
  The Literary Remains of Samuel Taylor Coleridge (published
  1836), bk.2, 'Notes on the Tragedies of Shakespeare: Othello'.

Colette *full name* **Sidonie Gabrielle Colette** 1873–1954

French writer. Her first husband, Henri Gauthier-Villars,
published her early *Claudine* series under his pen-name
'Willy'. Her writing is marked by its exploration of the sensual.
Later works include *Chéri* (1920) and *Gigi* (1944).

28 *Quand elle lève ses paupières, on dirait qu'elle se déshabille.*
  When she raises her eyelids it's as if she were taking off all
  her clothes.
  1903 *Claudine et Annie*, ch.3 (translated by Antonia White).

29 *Il découvrait…le monde des émotions qu'on nomme, à
  la légère, physiques.*
  He was discovering…the world of the emotions that are
  so lightly called physical.
  1923 *Le Blé en herbe*.

30 *Ne porte jamais de bijoux artistiques, ça déconsidère
  complètement une femme.*
  Don't ever wear artistic jewellery; it wrecks a woman's
  reputation.
  1944 *Gigi*.

Collingwood, Cuthbert, Baron 1748–1810

English admiral. He rose from midshipman to become second-
in-command to Nelson at Trafalgar, on board the *Royal
Sovereign*.

31 Now, gentlemen, let us do something today which the
  world may talk of hereafter.
  1805 Remark to troops before the Battle of Trafalgar, 21 Oct.
  Quoted in G L Newnham Collingwood (ed) *A Selection from the
  Correspondence of Lord Collingwood* (1828), vol.1.

Collingwood, R(obin) G(eorge) 1889–1943

English philosopher and historian, with a strong archaeological interest. He wrote widely on the philosophy of history
although his work was not well known until well after his death.

32 Perfect freedom is reserved for the man who lives by his
  own work and in that work does what he wants to do.
  1924 *Speculum Mentis*.

33 A man ceases to be a beginner in any given science and
  becomes a master in that science when he has learned
  that…he is going to be a beginner all his life.
  1942 *New Leviathan*, pt.1 ch.1.

Collins, Billy 1941–

US poet.

34 The name of the author is the first to go
  followed obediently by the title, the plot,
  the heartbreaking conclusion, the entire novel
  which suddenly becomes one you have never read,
  never even heard of.
  2000 *Taking off Emily Dickinson's Clothes: Selected Poems*,
  'Forgetfulness'.

Collins, Charles 1874–1926

English songwriter. He wrote rapid patter songs for use by
music-hall stars of the day such as Harry Champion.

35 Any old iron, any old iron,
  Any any old old iron?
  You look neat
  Talk about a treat,
  You look dapper from your napper to your feet.
  Dressed in style, brand new tile,
  And your father's old green tie on,
  But I wouldn't give you tuppence for your old watch
  chain;
  Old iron, old iron?
  1911 'Any Old Iron' (with E A Sheppard and Fred Terry). The
  second line is commonly rendered 'Any any any old iron?'.

36 My old man said, 'Follow the van,
  Don't dilly-dally on the way!'
  Off went the cart with the home packed in it,
  I walked behind with my old cock linnet.
  But I dillied and dallied, dallied and dillied,
  Lost the van and don't know where to roam.
  You can't trust the 'specials' like the old time 'coppers'
  When you can't find your way home.
  1919 'Don't Dilly-Dally on the Way' (with Fred Leigh).

Collins, Michael 1890–1922

Irish patriot and leader of the IRA. He signed the treaty of 1921
giving Ireland dominion status, believing it the best possible at
the time, and after attempting to form a government under the
terms of the treaty was killed in an ambush by hardline
republicans.

37 Think—what I have got for Ireland? Something which
  she has wanted these past seven hundred years. Will

anyone be satisfied with the bargain? Will anyone? I tell you this—early this morning I signed my death warrant. I thought at the time how odd, how ridiculous—a bullet may just as well have done the job five years ago.
1921 Letter, written after signing the peace treaty with Great Britain, 6 Dec.

Collins, Michael 1930–

Italian-born US astronaut who as a crew member of Apollo 11 piloted the spacecraft during its historic mission to the moon (1969). He orbited the moon alone in the command unit while Neil Armstrong and Buzz Aldrin made the first manned lunar landing.

38 I knew I was alone in a way that no earthling has ever been before.
1972 In *Time*, Dec 11.

Collins, Phil 1951–

English singer, drummer and songwriter. He joined Genesis as drummer in 1970, and took over as lead vocalist when Peter Gabriel left the group (1985). He has also had a successful solo career.

39 I suppose Phil Collins offers something for everybody, and in hipdom that's not cool. But in the real world, there's no shame in that at all.
Quoted in *Guinness Rockopedia* (1998).

Collins, William 1721–59

English poet, first published at the age of 17. His poetry, which is original and even experimental for the day, includes the 'Ode to Simplicity', 'Dirge in Cymbeline', 'Ode to Evening' and 'How Sleep the Brave'.

40 Too nicely Jonson knew the critic's part,
Nature in him was almost lost in Art.
1743 'Verses addressed to Sir Thomas Hanmer'.

41 To fair Fidele's grassy tomb
Soft maids and village hinds shall bring
Each opening sweet of earliest bloom,
And rifle all the breathing spring.
1744 'Dirge in Cymbeline'.

42 How sleep the brave, who sink to rest,
By all their country's wishes blest!
1746 'How Sleep the Brave' (published 1748), no.1.

43 By fairy hands their knell is rung,
By forms unseen their dirge is sung.
1746 'How Sleep the Brave' (published 1748), no.2.

44 O thou, the friend of man assigned,
With balmy hands his wounds to bind,
And charm his frantic woe:
When first Distress with dagger keen
Broke forth to waste his destined scene,
His wild unsated foe!
1747 *Odes on Several Descriptive and Allegoric Subjects*, 'Ode to Pity', no.1.

45 Ah Fear! Ah frantic Fear!
I see, I see thee near.
1747 *Odes on Several Descriptive and Allegoric Subjects*, 'Ode to Fear', l.5–6.

46 Though taste, though genius bless
To some divine excess,
Faints the cold work till thou inspire the whole;

What each, what all supply
May court, may charm our eye,
Thou, only thou can'st raise the meeting soul!
1747 *Odes on Several Descriptive and Allegoric Subjects*, 'Ode to Simplicity', no.8.

47 Now air is hushed, save where the weak-eyed bat
With short shrill shriek flits by on leathern wing,
Or where the beetle winds
His small but sullen horn,
As oft he rises midst the twilight path,
Against the pilgrim borne in heedless hum.
1747 *Odes on Several Descriptive and Allegoric Subjects*, 'Ode to Evening', l.9–14.

48 While Spring shall pour his showers, as oft he wont,
And bathe thy breathing tresses, meekest Eve!
While Summer loves to sport
Beneath thy lingering light;
While sallow Autumn fills thy lap with leaves,
Or Winter, yelling through the troublous air,
Affrights thy shrinking train,
And rudely rends thy robes.
1747 *Odes on Several Descriptive and Allegoric Subjects*, 'Ode to Evening', l.41–8.

49 With eyes up-raised, as one inspired,
Pale Melancholy sate retired,
And from her wild sequestered seat,
In notes by distance made more sweet,
Poured thro' the mellow horn her pensive soul.
1747 'The Passions, An Ode for Music', l.57–61.

50 Love of peace, and lonely musing,
In hollow murmurs died away.
1747 'The Passions, An Ode for Music', l.67–8.

Colombo, John Robert 1936–

Canadian editor and poet.

51 Canada could have enjoyed:
English government,
French culture,
And American know-how.
Instead it ended up with:
English know-how,
French government,
And American culture.
1965 'O Canada', collected in Al Purdy (ed) *The New Romans* (1968).

Colton, Charles Caleb 1780–1832

British clergyman and writer. He was also a successful sportsman and was known for his gambling, which eventually led to his financial ruin and suicide.

52 Men will wrangle for religion; write for it; fight for it—anything but live for it.
1820 *Lacon*, vol.1, no.25.

53 When you have nothing to say, say nothing.
1820 *Lacon*, vol.1, no.183.

54 Imitation is the sincerest form of flattery.
1820 *Lacon*, vol.1, no.217.

55 Examinations are formidable even to the best prepared, for the greatest fool may ask more than the wisest man can answer.
1820 *Lacon*, vol.1, no.322.

56 If you would be known, and not know, vegetate in a village; if you would know, and not be known, live in a city.
1820 *Lacon*, vol.1, no.334.

Coltrane, John 1926–67

US jazz saxophonist. He was the most influential tenor and soprano saxophonist of the postwar era.

57 The main thing a musician would like to do is to give a picture to the listener of the many wonderful things he knows and senses in the universe.
1966 Quoted in sleeve-note to the re-issue of *Coltrane's Sound* (originally published 1961).

Colum, Padraic 1881–1972

Irish poet, playwright, novelist, biographer, critic and children's writer, a central figure in the Irish Literary Renaissance. Reflecting a peasant background, his work was realistic rather than romantic. His collections include *Wild Earth* (1907).

58 Sunset and silence! A man: around him earth savage, earth broken;
Beside him two horses—a plough!

Earth savage, earth broken, the brutes, the dawn-man there in the sunset,
And the Plough that is twin to the Sword, that is founder of cities!
1907 *Wild Earth*, 'The Plougher'.

59 My young love said to me, 'My brothers won't mind,
And my parents won't slight you for your lack of kind.'
Then she stepped away from me, and this she did say,
'It will not be long, love, till our wedding day.'
1907 *Wild Earth*, 'She Moved through the Fair'.

60 Then the wet, winding roads,
Brown bogs with black water;
And my thoughts on white ships
And the King o' Spain's daughter.
1907 'A Drover'.

61 Oh, to have a little house!
To own the hearth and stool and all!
The heaped-up sods upon the fire,
The pile of turf against the wall!
To have a clock with weights and chains
And pendulum swinging up and down,
A dresser filled with shining delph,
Speckled and white and blue and brown!
c.1907 'An Old Woman of the Roads'.

Columbus, Christopher *Spanish name* **Cristóbal Colón**
1451–1506

Genoese explorer, and discoverer of the New World (1492). His *Carta del descubrimiento* (1493) is the first European historical document about America.

62 *Toda la cristiandad debe tomar alegría y hacer grandes fiestas, y dar gracias solemnes a la Santa Trinidad, con muchas oraciones solemnes por el tanto ensalzamiento que habrán, en tornándose tantos pueblos a nuestra Santa Fe, y después por los bienes temporales que no solamente a la España, mas a todos los cristianos tendrán aquí refigerio y ganancia.*
All Christendom ought to feel joyful and make great celebrations and give solemn thanks to the Holy Trinity with many solemn prayers for the great exaltation which it will have, in the turning of so many people to our holy faith, and afterwards for material benefits, since not only Spain but all Christians will hence have refreshment and profit.
1493 *Carta del descubrimiento* (translated as *The Letter in Spanish of Christopher Columbus*, 1889).

Comden, Betty *pseudonym of* **Elizabeth Cohen** 1919–

US screenwriter and lyricist, who worked with Adolph Green on a number of musicals. Her scripts include *On the Town* (1949), *Singin' in the Rain* (1952) and *Bells are Ringing* (1960).

63 I can stand anything but failure.
1953 Line delivered by Oscar Levant in *The Band Wagon*.

64 The party's over, it's time to call it a day.
1956 'The Party's Over' (with Adolphe Green, music by Jule Styne).

Commoner, Barry 1917–

US biologist closely associated with issues of ecology, public health and environmental policy.

65 Science is triumphant with far-ranging success, but its triumph is somehow clouded by growing difficulties in providing for the simple necessities of human life on earth.
1966 *Science and Survival*.

66 The gap between brute power and human need continues to grow, as the power fattens on the same faulty technology that intensifies the need.
1972 'The Closing Circle', in *Technology*.

Comnena, Anna 1083–1153

Byzantine princess and historian, daughter of Emperor Alexius I. She retired to a convent to write an account of her father's reign after failing to secure the imperial throne for her husband, Nicephorus Bryennius.

67 A mounted Kelt is irresistible; he would bore his way through the walls of Babylon.
c.1148 Her description of the Frankish knights who passed through Constantinople on the First Crusade, 1097. *The Alexiad of Anna Comnena*, bk.13, ch.8 (translated by E R A Sewter).

Compton-Burnett, Dame Ivy 1892–1969

English novelist. Her novels, which explore the nuances of human relationships, include *Pastors and Masters* (1925), *Brothers and Sisters* (1929), *More Women than Men* (1933) and *Mother and Son* (1955).

68 'Well, of course, people are only human,' said Dudley to his brother, as they walked to the house behind the women. 'But it really does not seem much for them to be.'
1939 *A Family and a Fortune*, ch.2.

69 People don't resent having nothing nearly as much as too little.
1939 *A Family and a Fortune*, ch.4.

70 It will be a beautiful family talk, mean and worried and full of sorrow and spite and excitement. I cannot be asked to miss it in my weak state. I should only fret.
1939 *A Family and a Fortune*, ch.10.

71 As regards plots I find real life no help at all. Real life

seems to have no plots.
1945 *Orion*, no.1, 'A Conversation'.

72 And people in life hardly seem definite enough to appear in print. They are not good or bad enough, or clever or stupid enough, or comic or pitiful enough.
1945 *Orion*, no.1, 'A Conversation'.

73 We must use words as they are used, or stand aside from life.
1955 *Mother and Son*, ch.9.

74 There is more difference within the sexes than between them.
1955 *Mother and Son*, ch.10.

75 When I die people will say it is the best thing for me. It is because they know it is the worst. They want to avoid the feeling of pity.
1961 *The Mighty and Their Fall*, ch.4.

76 There are different kinds of wrong. The people sinned against are not always the best.
1961 *The Mighty and Their Fall*, ch.7.

77 There's not much to say. I haven't been at all deedy.
1969 When asked about her life. In *The Times*, 30 Aug.

Comte, Auguste Isidore Marie Françoise 1798–1857

French social scientist, mathematician and philosopher of social science, whose work in logical positivism laid the foundations for contemporary social science.

78 To understand a science it is necessary to know its history.
1851–4 *Système de politique positive* (*Positive Philosophy*).

Conant, James Bryant 1893–1978

US educator, President of Harvard University (1933–53).

79 There is only one proved method of assisting the advancement of pure science—that of picking men of genius, backing them heavily, and leaving them to direct themselves.
1945 Letter to the *New York Times*, 13 Aug.

80 It seems as though I were in a lunatic asylum, but I am never sure who is the attendant and who the inmate.
1950 Of Washington. Letter to Bernard Baruch, Feb. Quoted in James G Hershberg *James B Conant* (1993).

81 A Harvard education consists of what you learn at Harvard while you are not studying.
Quoted in *Time*, 29 Sep 1986.

Condon, Richard 1915–96

US writer. He made his reputation with his successful novel of political intrigue, *The Manchurian Candidate* (1959).

82 In Mexico the gods ruled, the priests interpreted and interposed, and the people obeyed. In Spain, the priests ruled, the king interpreted and interposed, and the gods obeyed. A nuance in an ideological difference is a wide chasm.
1961 *A Talent for Loving*, bk.1, ch.6.

83 He was an unzipped fly caught in forever amber.
1967 *The Ecstasy Business*, ch.1.

84 What is art is not likely to be decided for decades or longer after the work has been produced—and then is often redecided—so we must not think badly if we

regard literature as entertainment rather than as transcendent enlightenment.
1976 Comment in D L Fitzpatrick (ed) *Contemporary Novelists*.

85 She felt sexual urgings towards Yvonne in the manner that politicians feel an enormous sexual pull towards mirrors.
1978 *Bandicoot*, ch.21.

Confucius or K'ung Fu–tse, 'The Master K'ung' 551–479 BC

Chinese philosopher. He was Governor of Chung-tu, Minister of Works and later Minister of Justice. Although his social reform measures were popular, his enemies forced him into exile. His sayings are collected in the *Confucian Analects*, compiled by his pupils after his death.

86 Man has three ways of acting wisely. First, on meditation; that is the noblest. Secondly, on imitation; that is the easiest. Thirdly, on experience; that is the bitterest.
c.479 BC *The Analects*.

87 The people may be made to follow a course of action, but they may not be made to understand it.
c.479 BC *The Analects*.

88 When you meet someone better than yourself, turn your thoughts to becoming his equal. When you meet someone not as good as you are, look within and examine your own self.
c.479 BC *The Analects*.

89 When I have pointed out one corner of a square to anyone and he does not come back with the other three, I will not point it out to him a second time.
c.479 BC *The Analects*.

90 You can rob an army of its commander-in-chief, but you cannot deprive the humblest man of his free will.
c.479 BC *The Analects*.

91 But without the trust of the people, no government can stand.
c.479 BC *The Analects*.

92 He that in his studies wholly applies himself to labour and exercise, and neglects meditation, loses his time, and he that only applies himself to meditation, and neglects labour and exercise, only wanders and loses himself.
Quoted in Colin Jarman *The Guinness Dictionary of Sports Quotations* (1990).

Congreve, William 1670–1729

English dramatist and poet. His first publication was the novel *Incognita* (1692), and he translated Juvenal and wrote original verse. He is best remembered for his witty plays, including *Love for Love* (1695) and *The Way of the World* (1700).

93 I am always of the opinion with the learned, if they speak first.
1692 *Incognita*.

94 In my conscience I believe the baggage loves me, for she never speaks well of me herself, nor suffers any body else to rail at me.
1693 Bellemore to Sharper. *The Old Bachelor*, act 1, sc.3.

95 Man was by Nature Woman's cully made:
We never are, but by ourselves, betrayed.
1693 Lucy to Silvia. *The Old Bachelor*, act 3, sc.1.

96 Bilbo's the word, and slaughter will ensue.
1693 Bluffe to Sir Joseph. *The Old Bachelor*, act 3, sc.7.

97 If this be not love, it is madness, and then it is pardonable.
  1693 Heartwell to Sylvia. *The Old Bachelor*, act 3, sc.10.

98 Eternity was in that moment.
  1693 Bellmore to Laetitia. *The Old Bachelor*, act 4, sc.7.

99 Now am I slap-dash down in the mouth.
  1693 Sir Joseph to Bluffe. *The Old Bachelor*, act 4, sc.9.

1 Thus grief still treads upon the heels of pleasure:
  Married in haste, we may repent at leisure.
  1693 Sharper to Setter. *The Old Bachelor*, act 5, sc.1.

2 Some by experience find those words mis-placed:
  At leisure married, they repent in haste.
  1693 Setter to Sharper. *The Old Bachelor*, act 5, sc.1.

3 I could find it in my heart to marry thee, purely to be rid
  of thee.
  1693 Belinda to Bellmore. *The Old Bachelor*, act 5, sc.10.

4 Courtship to marriage, as a very witty prologue to a very
  dull play.
  1693 Bellmore to Belinda. *The Old Bachelor*, act 5, sc.10.

5 It is the business of a comic poet to paint the vices and
  follies of human kind.
  1693 *The Double Dealer*, epistle dedicatory.

6 Retired to their tea and scandal, according to their
  ancient custom.
  1693 Mellefont to Charles. *The Double Dealer*, act 1, sc.1.

7 There is nothing more unbecoming a man of quality than
  to laugh; Jesu, 'tis such a vulgar expression of the passion!
  1693 Lord Froth to Brisk. *The Double Dealer*, act 1, sc.4.

8 Tho' marriage makes man and wife one flesh, it leaves
  'em still two fools.
  1693 Cynthia to Mellefont. *The Double Dealer*, act 2, sc.3.

9 She lays it on with a trowel.
  1693 Brisk to Lord Froth. *The Double Dealer*, act 3, sc.10.

10 See how love and murder will out.
  1693 *The Double Dealer*, act 4, sc.6.

11 No mask like open truth to cover lies,
  As to go naked is the best disguise.
  1693 *The Double Dealer*, act 5, sc.6.

12 Has he not a rogue's face?…a haunting-look to me…has
  a damned Tyburn-face, without the benefit o' the
  Clergy.
  1695 Of Sir Sampson. *Love for Love*, act 2, sc.7.

13 I came upstairs into the world; for I was born in a cellar.
  1695 Jeremy. *Love for Love*, act 2, sc.7.

14 I know that's a secret, for it's whispered every where.
  1695 Tattle to Scandal. *Love for Love*, act 3, sc.3.

15 He that first cries out stop thief, is often he that has stolen
  the treasure.
  1695 Scandal to Mrs Foresight. *Love for Love*, act 3, sc.14.

16 Women are like tricks by sleight of hand, which, to
  admire, we should not understand.
  1695 Valentine. *Love for Love*, act 4, sc.21.

17 A branch of one of your antediluvian families, fellows
  that the flood could not wash away.
  1695 Sir Sampson to Angelica. *Love for Love*, act 5, sc.2.

18 To find a young fellow that is neither a wit in his own
  eye, nor a fool in the eye of the world, is a very hard
  task.
  1695 Sir Sampson to Angelica. *Love for Love*, act 5, sc.2.

19 Aye, 'tis well enough for a servant to be bred at an
  University. But the education is a little too pedantic for a
  gentleman.
  1695 Tattle to Jeremy. *Love for Love*, act 5, sc.3.

20 Nay, for my part I always despised Mr Tattle of all things;
  nothing but his being my husband could have made me
  like him less.
  1695 Mrs Frail to Mrs Foresight. *Love for Love*, act 5, sc.11.

21 I confess freely to you, I could never look long upon a
  Monkey, without very Mortifying Reflections.
  1695 Letter to John Dennis, 10 Jul.

22 Music hath charms to soothe a savage breast,
  To soften rocks, or bend a knotted oak.
  1697 Almeria to Leonora. *The Mourning Bride*, act 1, sc.1.

23 Heaven has no rage, like love to hatred turned,
  Nor Hell a fury, like a woman scorned.
  1697 Zara. *The Mourning Bride*, act 3, sc.8.

24 Is he then dead?
  What, dead at last, quite, quite for ever dead!
  1697 Almeria to Leonora. *The Mourning Bride*, act 5, sc.11.

25 They come together like the Coroner's Inquest, to sit
  upon the murdered reputations of the week.
  1700 Fainall to Mirabell. *The Way of the World*, act 1, sc.1.

26 She once used me with that insolence that in revenge I
  took her to pieces; sifted her, and separated her failings; I
  studied 'em, and got 'em by rote. The catalogue was so
  large that I was not without hopes, one day or other, to
  hate her heartily.
  1700 *The Way of the World*, act 1, sc.3.

27 Ay, ay, I have experience: I have a wife, and so forth.
  1700 Fainall to Mirabell. *The Way of the World*, act 1, sc.3.

28 FAINALL: 'Tis for the honour of England that all Europe
  should know that we have blockheads of all ages.
  MIRABELL: I wonder there is not an Act of Parliament to
  save the credit of the nation, and prohibit the
  exportation of fools.
  1700 *The Way of the World*, act 1, sc.5.

29 A wit should no more be sincere than a woman constant;
  one argues a decay of parts, as t'other of beauty.
  1700 *The Way of the World*, act 1, sc.6.

30 What, he speaks unseasonable truths sometimes,
  because he has not wit enough to invent an evasion.
  1700 *The Way of the World*, act 1, sc.6.

31 I always take blushing either for a sign of guilt, or of ill
  breeding.
  1700 Petulant to Mirabell. *The Way of the World*, act 1, sc.9.

32 To pass over youth in dull indifference, to refuse the
  sweets of life because they once must leave us, is as
  preposterous as to wish to have been born old, because
  we one day may be old. For my part, my youth may wear
  and waste, but it shall never rust in my possession.
  1700 *The Way of the World*, act 2, sc.1.

33 Say what you will, 'tis better to be left than never to have
  been loved.
  1700 Mrs Warwood to Mrs Fainall. *The Way of the World*, act 2,
  sc.1.

34 Beauty is the lover's gift.
  1700 Mirabell. *The Way of the World*, act 2, sc.4.

35 Here she comes i' faith full sail, with her fan spread and
  streamers out, and a shoal of fools for tenders.
  1700 Of Mirabell. *The Way of the World*, act 2, sc.5.

36 Nobody knows how to write letters; and yet one has 'em, one does not know why.—They serve one to pin up one's hair.
1700 *The Way of the World*, act 2, sc.5.

37 WITWOUD: Madam, do you pin up your hair with all your letters?
MILLAMANT: Only with those in verse, Mr Witwoud. I never pin up my hair with prose.
1700 *The Way of the World*, act 2, sc.5.

38 To please a fool is some degree of folly.
1700 *The Way of the World*, act 2, sc.6.

39 A fellow that lives in a windmill has not a more whimsical dwelling than the heart of a man that is lodged in a woman.
1700 *The Way of the World*, act 2, sc.7.

40 A little disdain is not amiss; a little scorn is alluring.
1700 Lady Wishfort to Foible. *The Way of the World*, act 3, sc.5.

41 Love's but the frailty of the mind,
When 'tis not with ambition joined;
A sickly flame, which if not fed expires;
And feeding, wastes in self-consuming fires.
1700 *The Way of the World*, act 3, sc.12.

42 Marriage is honourable, as you say; and if so, wherefore should cuckoldom be a discredit, being derived from so honourable a root?
1700 *The Way of the World*, act 3, sc.12.

43 I confess I have deserted the high place I once held of sighing at your feet.
1700 *The Way of the World*, act 3, sc.12.

44 O, nothing is more alluring than a levee from a couch in some confusion.
1700 Lady Wishfort to Foible. *The Way of the World*, act 4, sc.1.

45 Don't let us be familiar or fond, nor kiss before folks, like my Lady Fadler and Sir Francis: nor go to Hyde-Park together the first Sunday in a new chariot, to provoke eyes and whispers, and then never be seen there together again; as if we were proud of one another the first week, and ashamed of one another ever after… Let us be very strange and well-bred: Let us be as strange as if we had been married a great while, and as well-bred as if we were not married at all.
1700 Millamant to Mirabell. *The Way of the World*, act 4, sc.5.

46 These articles subscribed, if I continue to endure you a little longer, I may by degrees dwindle into wife.
1700 Millamant to Mirabell. *The Way of the World*, act 4, sc.5.

47 I hope you do not think me prone to any iteration of nuptials.
1700 Lady Wishfort to Whitwell disguised as Sir Roland. *The Way of the World*, act 4, sc.12.

48 Music alone with sudden charms can bind
The wand'ring sense, and calm the troubled mind.
c.1701 'Hymn to Harmony'.

49 Would I were free from this restraint,
Or else had hopes to win her;
Would she could make of me a saint,
Or I of her a sinner.
'Pious Selinda Goes to Prayers'.

Conklin, Edwin G(rant) 1863–1952

Professor of Embryology at Princeton. He was a specialist in the embryology of marine organisms.

50 Wooden legs are not inherited but wooden heads may be.
Recalled on his death, 21 Nov 1952.

Connally, John Bowden 1917–93

US politician and lawyer. He was Governor of Texas (1963–9).

51 A chess tournament disguised as a circus.
1964 Of US political conventions. In the *National Observer*. Quoted in Edwin A Roberts Jr *Elections 1964* (1964).

52 It's not a sin to be rich anymore—it's a miracle.
1988 In *Time*, 18 Jan.

53 All hat and no cattle.
1989 Responding to George Bush's claim to be a Texan. In the *New York Times*, 14 Feb.

Connally, Tom (Thomas Terry) 1877–1963

US Congressman and lawyer. He was Representative for Texas (1917–29) and a Senator (1929–53). A Democrat, he supported southern business interests and opposed anti-lynching legislation. He was a strong supporter of the UN and NATO.

54 Don't you ever shake that lanky Yankee finger at me.
1963 To Senator Charles Tobey. Reported in *Time*, 8 Nov.

Connell, James 1852–1929

Irish socialist and songwriter.

55 The people's flag is deepest red;
It shrouded oft our martyred dead.
And ere their limbs grew stiff and cold,
Their heart's blood dyed its every fold.
Then raise the scarlet standard high!
Within its shade we'll live or die.
Tho' cowards flinch and traitors sneer,
We'll keep the red flag flying here.
1889 'The Red Flag', official anthem of the Labour Party.

Connery, Sir Sean 1930–

Scottish actor who became an international film star in the role of secret agent James Bond.

56 It is Scotland's rightful heritage that its people should create a modern Parliament… This entire issue is above and beyond any political party.
1997 Speech in Edinburgh. In the *Daily Record*, 8 Sep.

57 We have waited nearly 300 years. My hope is that it will evolve with dignity and integrity and it will truly reflect the new voice of Scotland. My position on Scotland has never changed in 30-odd years. Scotland should be nothing less than an equal of other nations in the world.
1999 On the Scottish Parliament. In the *Daily Telegraph*, 27 Apr.

Connolly, Billy 1942–

Scottish comedian and actor.

58 Marriage is a wonderful invention; but then again so is a bicycle repair kit.
Duncan Campbell *Billy Connolly* (1976).

59 I spent the whole time battering people I liked and singing with my arm round people I loathed.
Talking about his drinking days. Quoted in Pamela Stephenson *Billy* (2001).

60 I decided to stop drinking while it was still my idea.
Quoted in Pamela Stephenson *Billy* (2001).

61 For me, it's about the desire to win. My audience becomes a crowd of wild animals and I have to be the lion-tamer or be eaten.

Quoted in Pamela Stephenson *Billy* (2001).

Connolly, Cyril Vernon 1903–74

English author and journalist. He founded and edited the influential cultural journal *Horizon* (1939–50). His best-known books are *Enemies of Promise* (1938) and *The Unquiet Grave* (1944).

62 Better to write for yourself and have no public, than to write for the public and have no self.

1933 In the *New Statesman*, 25 Feb.

63 Destroy him as you will, the bourgeois always bounces up—execute him, expropriate him, starve him out *en masse*, and he reappears in your children.

1937 In the *Observer*, 7 Mar.

64 A great writer creates a world of his own and his readers are proud to live in it. A lesser writer may entice them in for a moment, but soon he will watch them filing out.

1938 *Enemies of Promise*, ch.1.

65 Literature is the art of writing something that will be read twice; journalism what will be read once.

1938 *Enemies of Promise*, ch.3.

66 As repressed sadists are supposed to become policemen or butchers, so those with an irrational fear of life become publishers.

1938 *Enemies of Promise*, ch.10.

67 I should like to see the custom introduced of readers who are pleased with a book sending the author some small cash token… Not more than a hundred pounds—that would be bad for my character—not less than half a crown—that would do no good to yours.

1938 *Enemies of Promise*, ch.13.

68 Whom the gods wish to destroy they first call promising.

1938 *Enemies of Promise*, ch.13.

69 There is no more sombre enemy of good art than the pram in the hall.

1938 *Enemies of Promise*, ch.14.

70 All charming people have something to conceal, usually their total dependence on the appreciation of others.

1938 *Enemies of Promise*, ch.16.

71 Humorists are not happy men. Like Beachcomber or Saki or Thurber they burn while Rome fiddles.

1938 *Enemies of Promise*, ch.16.

72 A private school has all the faults of a public school without any of its compensations.

1938 *Enemies of Promise*, ch.19.

73 I have called this style the Mandarin style… It is the style of those writers whose tendency is to make their language convey more than they mean or more than they feel, it is the style of most artists and all humbugs.

1938 *Enemies of Promise*, ch.20.

74 Were I to deduce any system from my feelings on leaving Eton, it might be called *The Theory of Permanent Adolescence*.

1938 *Enemies of Promise*, ch.24.

75 The more books we read, the sooner we perceive that the only function of a writer is to produce a masterpiece.

No other task is of any consequence.

1944 *The Unquiet Grave*, pt.1.

76 There is no fury like an ex-wife looking for a new lover.

1944 *The Unquiet Grave*, pt.1.

77 In the sex war thoughtlessness is the weapon of the male, vindictiveness of the female.

1944 *The Unquiet Grave*, pt.1.

78 Life is a maze in which we take the wrong turning before we have learnt to walk.

1944 *The Unquiet Grave*, pt.1.

79 Everything is a dangerous drug to me except reality, which is unendurable.

1944 *The Unquiet Grave*, pt.1.

80 The civilization of one epoch becomes the manure of the next.

1944 *The Unquiet Grave*, pt.2.

81 The disasters of the world are due to its inhabitants not being able to grow old simultaneously.

1944 *The Unquiet Grave*, pt.2.

82 Imprisoned in every fat man a thin one is wildly signalling to be let out.

1944 *The Unquiet Grave*, pt.2.

83 The true index of a man's character is the health of his wife.

1944 *The Unquiet Grave*, pt.2.

84 We are all serving a life-sentence in the dungeon of self.

1944 *The Unquiet Grave*, pt.2.

85 Our memories are card-indexes consulted, and then put back in disorder by authorities whom we do not control.

1944 *The Unquiet Grave*, pt.2.

86 It is closing time in the gardens of the West and from now on an artist will be judged only by the resonance of his solitude or the quality of his despair.

1949 *Horizon*, no.120–1, Dec 1949– Jan 1950 (double issue, the final issue of the journal).

87 A romantic interest in our own sex, not necessarily carried as far as physical experiments, was the intellectual fashion.

Of Oxford during his student days. Quoted in Peter Quennell *The Marble Foot* (1977).

Connolly, James 1868–1916

Irish Labour leader and insurgent. He organized the Irish Socialist Republican party and founded *The Workers' Republic*, the first Irish socialist paper. He lectured in the US and organized strikes in Ireland, and was executed for his part in the 1916 Easter rebellion.

88 It is an axiom enforced by all the experience of the ages, that they who rule industrially will rule politically.

1909 *Socialism Made Easy*.

89 Don't be 'practical' in politics. To be practical in that sense means that you have schooled yourself to think along the lines, and in the grooves that those who rob you would desire you to think.

1909 *Socialism Made Easy*.

90 The day has passed for patching up the capitalist system; it must go. And in the work of abolishing it the Catholic and the Protestant, the Catholic and the Jew, the Catholic and the Freethinker, the Catholic and the Buddhist, the Catholic and the Mahometan will co-

operate together… For, as we have said elsewhere, Socialism is neither Protestant nor Catholic, Christian nor Freethinker, Buddhist, Mahometan, nor Jew; it is only HUMAN.
1910 *Labour, Nationality, and Religion.*

91 The worker is the slave of capitalist society, the female worker is the slave of that slave.
1915 *The Re-conquest of Ireland.*

Connor, Sir William Neil *pseudonym* *Cassandra*
1909–67

English journalist, a columnist with the *Daily Mirror* from 1935 until his death.

92 As I was saying when I was interrupted, it is a powerful hard thing to please all of the people all of the time.
1946 On resuming his Cassandra column in the *Daily Mirror,* Sep, after the end of World War II.

Conrad, Joseph *originally* *Jozef Teodor Konrad Nalecz Korzeniowski* 1857–1924

Polish-born British novelist who joined an English merchant ship in 1878, and was naturalized in 1884 as a master mariner. The sea provided the background for much of his work, notably *Heart of Darkness* (1899) and *Lord Jim* (1900).

93 It is only those who do nothing that make no mistakes, I suppose.
1896 *An Outcast of the Islands,* pt.3, ch.2.

94 Any work that aspires, however humbly, to the condition of art should carry its justification in every line.
1897 *The Nigger of the Narcissus,* preface.

95 My task which I am trying to achieve is, by the power of the written word to make you hear, to make you feel—it is, before all, to make you *see.* That—and no more, and it is everything.
1897 *The Nigger of the Narcissus,* preface.

96 The conquest of the earth, which mostly means the taking it away from those who have a different complexion or slightly flatter noses than ourselves, is not a pretty thing when you look into it too much. What redeems it is an idea only.
1899 *Heart of Darkness,* pt.1 (first published in *Blackwood's Magazine,* collected in *Youth: A Narrative, and Two Other Stories,* 1902).

97 We live, as we dream—alone.
1899 *Heart of Darkness,* pt.1 (first published in *Blackwood's Magazine,* collected in *Youth: A Narrative, and Two Other Stories,* 1902).

98 Exterminate all the brutes!
1899 *Heart of Darkness,* pt.2 (first published in *Blackwood's Magazine,* collected in *Youth: A Narrative, and Two Other Stories,* 1902).

99 He cried in a whisper at some image, at some vision—he cried out twice, a cry that was no more than a breath: 'The horror! The horror!'
1899 Kurtz's final words. *Heart of Darkness,* pt.3 (first published in *Blackwood's Magazine,* collected in *Youth: A Narrative, and Two Other Stories,* 1902).

1 Mistah Kurtz—he dead.
1899 *Heart of Darkness,* pt.3 (first published in *Blackwood's Magazine,* collected in *Youth: A Narrative, and Two Other Stories,* 1902).

2 A man that is born falls into a dream like a man who falls into the sea… The way is to the destructive element submit yourself, and with the exertions of your hands and feet in the water make the deep, deep sea keep you up.
1900 *Lord Jim,* ch.20.

3 You shall judge a man by his foes as well as by his friends.
1900 *Lord Jim,* ch.34.

4 Suddenly a puff of wind, a puff faint and tepid and laden with strange odours of blossoms, of aromatic wood, comes out of the still night—the first sigh of the east on my face.
1902 'Youth'.

5 The mysterious East, perfumed like a flower, silent like death, dark like a grave.
1902 'Youth'.

6 I remember my youth and the feeling that it will never come back any more—the feeling that I could last for ever, outlast the sea, the earth, and all men; the deceitful feeling that lures us on to joys, to perils, to love, to vain effort—to death; the triumphant conviction of strength, the heat of life in the handful of dust, the glow in the heart that with every year grows dim, grows cold, grows small, and expires—and expires, too soon, too soon—before life itself.
1902 'Youth'.

7 Action is consolatory. It is the enemy of thought and the friend of flattering illusions.
1904 *Nostromo,* pt.1, ch.6.

8 Liberty of the imagination should be the most precious possession of a novelist.
1905 'Books'.

9 To be hopeful in an artistic sense it is not necessary to think that the world is good. It is enough to believe that there is no impossibility of it being made so.
1905 'Books'.

10 Of all the inanimate objects, of all men's creations, books are the nearest to us, for they contain our very thoughts, our ambitions, our indignations, our illusions, our fidelity to truth, and our persistent leaning towards error. But most of all they resemble us in their precarious hold on life.
1905 'Books'.

11 The terrorist and the policeman both come from the same basket.
1907 *The Secret Agent,* ch.4.

12 Some kind of moral discovery should be the object of every tale.
1911 *Under Western Eyes,* prologue.

13 Words, as is well known, are the great foes of reality.
1911 *Under Western Eyes,* prologue.

14 The scrupulous and the just, the noble, humane, and devoted natures; the unselfish and the intelligent may begin a movement—but it passes away from them. They are not the leaders of a revolution. They are its victims.
1911 *Under Western Eyes,* pt.2, ch.3.

15 A belief in a supernatural source of evil is not necessary; men alone are quite capable of every wickedness.
1911 *Under Western Eyes,* pt.2, ch.4.

16 All ambitions are lawful except those which climb upwards on the miseries or credulities of mankind.
1912 *Some Reminiscences,* preface.

17 On the contrary, the mere fact of dealing with matters outside the general run of everyday experience laid me under the obligation of a more scrupulous fidelity to the truth of my own sensations. The problem was to make unfamiliar things credible.
1915 *Within the Tides*, preface.

18 Thinking is the great enemy of perfection. The habit of profound reflection, I am compelled to say, is the most pernicious of all the habits formed by civilized man.
1915 *Victory*, author's note.

19 It is not the clear-sighted who rule the world. Great achievements are accomplished in a blessed, warm fog.
1915 *Victory*, author's note.

20 It was amazing to think that in those miles of human habitations there was not probably half a dozen pounds of nails.
1917 Of Bangkok. *The Shadow-Line*.

21 In plucking the fruit of memory one runs the risk of spoiling its bloom.
1920 *The Arrow of Gold*, author's note.

Conran, Shirley Ida née *Pearce* 1932–

English designer, fashion editor and author, first wife of the designer and businessman Sir Terence Conran. Her books include *Superwoman* (1975) and *Lace* (1982).

22 Our motto: Life is too short to stuff a mushroom.
1975 *Superwoman*, epigraph.

Conroy, (Donald) Pat(rick) 1945–

US writer. His works include *The Prince of Tides* (1986) and *Beach Music* (1997).

23 It was like walking down the street with the Statue of Liberty.
1995 On walking in Manhattan with the instantly recognizable Barbra Streisand. In *WAMU*, 4 Sep.

Constable, John 1776–1837

English landscape painter. With Turner, one of Britain's most important and best-loved landscape painters.

24 A gentleman's park is my aversion. It is not beauty because it is not nature.
1822 In R B Beckett (ed) *Constable's Correspondence*, Suffolk Records Society (1962–70).

25 In Claude's landscape all is lovely—all amiable—all is amenity and repose;—the calm sunshine of the heart.
1836 Lecture, 2 Jun. Quoted in C R Leslie *Memoirs of the Life of John Constable* (1843).

26 When I set down to make a sketch from nature, the first thing I try to do is to forget that I have ever seen a picture.
Quoted in C R Leslie *Memoirs of the Life of John Constable* (1843).

27 There is nothing ugly; *I never saw an ugly thing in my life*: for let the form of an object be what it may—light, shade and perspective will always make it beautiful.
Quoted in C R Leslie *Memoirs of the Life of John Constable* (1843).

28 He seems to paint with tinted steam.
Of Turner. Quoted in *Treasures of the Fitzwilliam Museum* (1982).

Constant (de Rebecque), (Henri) Benjamin 1767–1830

French novelist and politician. He supported the Revolution in Paris (1795) and was banished (1802) for opposing Napoleon. On his return in 1814 he became leader of the liberal opposition. His best-known novel *Adolphe* (1816) is based on his relationship with Mme de Staël.

29 *L'art pour l'art, sans but, car tout but dénature l'art. Mais l'art atteint au but qu'il n'a pas.*
Art for art's sake, with no purpose, for any purpose perverts art. But art achieves a purpose which is not its own.
1804 *Journal intime*, 11 Feb, quoted in the *Revue Internationale*, 10 Jan 1887.

Constantine *full name* **Flavius Valerius Aurelius Constantinus** c.274–337 AD

Roman Emperor, who adopted Christianity c.312 AD. He founded a royal residence at Byzantium (Constantinople), an act of great historical importance.

30 *In hoc signo vinces.*
In this sign thou shalt conquer.
AD 312 'Constantine's Vision', quoted in Eusebius *Life of Constantine*.

Cook, Arthur James 1883–1931

Welsh miners' leader, General Secretary of the national union and a key figure in the General Strike of 1926.

31 Not a penny off the pay; not a second on the day.
1926 Miners' strike slogan, coined in a speech, 3 Apr. It is often rendered 'not a minute on the day'.

Cook, Captain James 1728–79

English navigator. He undertook expeditions to the Pacific, the Antarctic and the west coast of North America, charting all these regions. He was killed in Hawaii by local people as he landed to recover a stolen boat.

32 As to a Southern Continent, I do not believe any such thing exists, unless in a high altitude.
1768–71 *Captain Cook's Journal during his First Voyage Round the World made in H. M. Bark 'Endeavour'*.

33 Curse the scientists, and all science into the bargain.
Quoted in J C Beaglehole (ed) *The Voyage of the Resolution* (1961).

Cook, Peter 1937–94

English comedian. He appeared in revue at Cambridge University and went on to write and star in the revue *Beyond the Fringe* (1960).

34 We exchanged many frank words in our respective languages.
1961 Impersonation of Harold Macmillan. *Beyond the Fringe*.

35 I go to the theatre to be entertained. I don't want to see plays about rape, sodomy and drug addiction—I can get all that at home.
Comedy routine. Also used as a cartoon caption in the *Observer*, 8 Jul 1962.

Cook, Robin *originally* **Robert Finlayson Cook** 1946–

Scottish Labour politician. In 2001 he became Leader of the House of Commons, a position he resigned in 2003 over the war with Iraq.

36 Chicken masala is now Britain's true national dish, not only because it is the most popular, but because it is a

perfect illustration of the way Britain absorbs and adapts external influences.
2001 Speech to the Social Market Foundation, London, 19 Apr.

37 Iraq probably has no weapons of mass destruction in the commonly understood sense of the term—namely a credible device capable of being delivered against a strategic city target.
2003 Speech to the House of Commons, following his resignation as Leader of the House, 17 Mar.

38 What has come to trouble me most over past weeks is the suspicion that if the hanging chads in Florida had gone the other way and Al Gore had been elected, we would not now be about to commit British troops.
2003 Speech to the House of Commons, following his resignation as Leader of the House, 17 Mar.

Cooke, (Alfred) Alistair 1908–2004

English-born US journalist and broadcaster, best known for his 'Letter from America', first broadcast by the BBC in 1946, which became the world's longest-running radio series with the same presenter. He retired shortly before his death.

39 All Presidents start out pretending to run a crusade, but after a couple of years they find they are running something much less heroic, much more intractable: namely, the Presidency.
1963 In *The Listener*.

40 An episode out of George Orwell rewritten by Charles Dickens.
1979 Of Gerald R Ford's succession to the US presidency on Richard M Nixon's resignation. *The Americans*.

41 Like a christening, a wedding, a graduation ceremony, a holy war, a revolution even…a fireworks display, a gaudy promise of what life ought to be, not life itself.
1979 Of elections. *The Americans*.

42 But after all it's not the winning that matters, is it? Or is it? It's—to coin a word—the amenities that count: the smell of the dandelions, the puff of the pipe, the click of the bat, the rain on the neck, the chill down the spine, the slow, exquisite coming on of sunset and dinner and rheumatism.
Quoted in Helen Exley *Cricket Quotations* (1992).

43 Canned music is like audible wallpaper.
Quoted in David Pickering *Brewer's Twentieth Century Music* (1994).

Coolidge, (John) Calvin 1872–1933

US Republican politician and 30th President (1923–9). A strong supporter of US business interests, he was re-elected in 1924 but refused renomination in 1928.

44 Civilization and profits go hand in hand.
1920 Speech, New York, 27 Nov.

45 There is no right to strike against the public safety by anybody, anywhere, at any time.
1919 Telegram to the President of the American Federation of Labor, while Coolidge was Governor of Massachusetts during the Boston police strike.

46 The chief business of the American people is business.
1925 Speech to the Society of Newspaper Editors, Washington, 17 Jan.

47 Prosperity is only an instrument to be used, not a deity to be worshipped.
1928 Speech, Boston, 11 Jun.

48 Perhaps one of the most important accomplishments of my Administration has been minding my own business.
1929 Press conference, Mar.

49 Patriotism is easy to understand in America. It means looking out for yourself while looking out for your country.
Attributed.

Cooper, Dame Gladys 1888–1971

English actress. She made her stage debut in 1905 and subsequently achieved stardom with her performance in Pinero's *The Second Mrs Tanqueray* (1922).

50 If this is what virus pneumonia does to one, I really don't think I shall bother to have it again.
1971 Last words.

Cooper, James Fenimore 1789–1851

US writer, a prolific novelist and essayist. He is now chiefly remembered for his 5-volume *Leatherstocking Tales*, which includes *The Last of the Mohicans* (1826).

51 The tendency of democracies is, in all things, to mediocrity.
1838 *The American Democrat*, 'On the Disadvantages of Democracy'.

52 Equality of condition is incompatible with civilization, and is found only to exist in those communities that are but slightly removed from the savage state. In practice, it can only mean a common misery.
1838 *The American Democrat*, 'On the Disadvantages of a Monarchy'.

53 Individuality is the aim of political liberty.
1838 *The American Democrat*, 'Individuality'.

54 It is a misfortune that necessity has induced men to accord greater license to this formidable engine, in order to obtain liberty, than can be borne with less important objects in view; for the press, like fire, is an excellent servant, but a terrible master.
1838 *The American Democrat*, 'On the Press'.

Cooper, William *pseudonym of* Harry Summerfield Hoff 1910–2002

English novelist. A barbed and witty satirist, he was a forerunner of the 'angry young man' school of the 1950s.

55 I would gladly have thrashed her for it. Unfortunately, thrashing your young woman doesn't make her admire you more as a novelist.
1950 *Scenes from Provincial Life*, pt.3, ch.1.

56 If girls aren't ignorant, they're cultured… You can't avoid suffering.
1950 *Scenes from Provincial Life*, pt.3, ch.2.

57 The trouble about finding a husband for one's mistress, is that no other man seems quite good enough.
1950 *Scenes from Provincial Life*, pt.3, ch.5.

Coover, Robert Lowell 1932–

US novelist, short-story writer and playwright, best known for his experimental stories.

58 The narrative impulse is always with us; we couldn't imagine ourselves through a day without it.
1986 In *Time Out*, 7 May.

Cope, Wendy 1945–

English poet. Her collections include *Making Cocoa for Kingsley Amis* (1986) and *If I Don't Know* (2001).

59 I used to think all poets were Byronic—
  Mad, bad and dangerous to know.
  And then I met a few.
  1986 'Triolet'.
  ► *See Lamb 486:25.*

60 There are so many kinds of awful men—
  One can't avoid them all. She often said
  She'd never make the same mistake again:
  She always made a new mistake instead.
  1986 'Rondeau Redoublé'.

61 Bloody men are like bloody buses—
  You wait for about a year
  And as soon as one approaches your stop
  Two or three others appear.
  1992 *Serious Concerns*, 'Bloody Men', stanza 1.

62 My heart has made its mind up
  And I'm afraid it's you.
  1992 *Serious Concerns*, 'Valentine'.

63 Some socks are loners
  They can't live in pairs.
  2001 *If I Don't Know*, 'The Sorrow of Socks'.

64 Never trust a journalist.
  2001 *If I Don't Know*, 'How to Deal with the Press'.

Copland, Aaron 1900–90

US composer. His early works employed jazz idioms, and he later drew on US folk tradition, as in the ballets *Billy the Kid* (1938) and *Appalachian Spring* (1944). He also composed film scores, operas and symphonies.

65 The whole problem can be stated quite simply by asking, 'Is there a meaning to music?' My answer would be, 'Yes'. And 'Can you state in so many words what the meaning is?' My answer to that would be 'No'.
  1939 *What to Listen for in Music.*

66 The difference between Beethoven and Mahler is the difference between watching a great man walk down the street and watching a great actor act the part of a great man walking down the street.
  Quoted in the *Wall Street Journal*, 9 Jun 1995.

Coppola, Francis Ford 1939–

US film director, screenwriter and producer. Among his films are *The Godfather* (1972; Part II 1974; Part III, 1990) and his controversial study of the Vietnam War, *Apocalypse Now* (1979).

67 When you start you want to make the greatest film in the world, but when you get into it, you just want to get it done, let it be passable and not embarrassing.
  Quoted in Michael Schumacher *Francis Ford Coppola: A Film-Maker's Life* (1999).

Cornford, Frances née *Darwin* 1886–1960

English poet, the granddaughter of Charles Darwin. She lived most of her life in Cambridge, and her poetry deals with the minute details of emotion.

68 A young Apollo, golden-haired,
  Stands dreaming on the verge of strife,
  Magnificently unprepared

For the long littleness of life.
  1910 Of Rupert Brooke. 'Youth'.

69 O fat white woman whom nobody loves,
  Why do you walk through the fields in gloves,
  When the grass is soft as the breast of doves
  And shivering-sweet to the touch?
  Oh why do you walk through the fields in gloves,
  Missing so much and so much?
  1910 'To a Fat Lady Seen from a Train'.
  ► *See Chesterton 213:99.*

70 Now we know nothing, nothing is richer now
  Because of all he was. O friend we have loved
  Must it be thus with you?—and if it must be
  How can men bear laboriously to live?
  1915 'Rupert Brooke'.

71 I hope to meet my Maker brow to brow
  And find my own the higher.
  1954 'Epitaph for a Reviewer'.

Cornforth, Sir John Warcup 1917–

Australian organic chemist. Despite being totally deaf from childhood, he pioneered the study of enzyme stereochemistry and was awarded the Nobel prize for chemistry in 1975.

72 In a world where it is so easy to neglect, deny, pervert and suppress the truth, the scientist may find his discipline severe. For him, truth is so seldom the sudden light that shows new order and beauty; more often, truth is the uncharted rock that sinks his ship in the dark.
  1975 Nobel prize speech.

Corwin, Thomas 1794–1865

US politician, Governor of Ohio (1840–2), Senator (1845–50) and Secretary of the Treasury (1850–3) under President Fillmore.

73 If I were a Mexican, I would tell you, 'Have you not enough room in your own country to bury your dead men? If you come into mine, we will greet you with bloody hands and hospitable graves.'
  1846 Speech to the Senate against the American–Mexican War, 11 Feb.

Cory, William originally *William Johnson* 1823–92

English academic, translator and poet. He was assistant master at Eton (1845–72), when he wrote the 'Eton Boat Song', but he resigned over controversy about his friendships with pupils. He also tutored Mary Coleridge (1861–1907).

74 They told me, Heraclitus, they told me you were dead,
  They brought bitter news to hear, and bitter tears to shed.
  I wept as I remembered how often you and I
  Had tired the sun with talking and sent him down the sky.
  1858 *Ionica, Poems*, 'Heraclitus', his translation of an epigram by Callimachus.

75 A handful of grey ashes, long long ago at rest.
  1858 *Ionica, Poems*, 'Heraclitus', his translation of an epigram by Callimachus.

76 You promise heavens free from strife,
  Pure truth, and perfect change of will;
  But sweet, sweet is this human life,
  So sweet, I fain would breathe it still;
  Your chilly stars I can forgo,

This warm kind world is all I know.
1858 *Ionica, Poems*, 'Mimnermus in Church'.

77 All beauteous things for which we live
By laws of space and time decay.
But Oh, the very reason why
I clasp them, is because they die.
1858 *Ionica, Poems*, 'Mimnermus in Church'.

78 Jolly boating weather
And a hay-harvest breeze,
Blade on the feather,
Shade off the trees;
Swing, swing together,
With your body between your knees.
1865 'Eton Boat Song'.

Coryate, Thomas c.1577–1617

English traveller and wit. In 1608 he set out on a journey on foot through central Europe, later travelling east as far as India. In 1611 he published *Coryat's Crudities Hastily Gobled Up in Five Moneths' Travells*.

79 Of all the pleasures in the world, travel is (in my opinion) the sweetest and most delightful.
1611 *Coryat's Crudities Hastily Gobled Up in Five Moneths' Travells*.

Costello, Elvis *real name* **Declan Patrick McManus** 1954–

English singer-songwriter and composer.

80 It would be like comparing blancmange and mustard gas.
2002 Asked how he would compare Tony Blair and Margaret Thatcher. Quoted on www.independent.co.uk.

81 There is something kind of absurd about people who live in such a comfortable, cushioned, spoiled society tattooing themselves and piercing themselves to make them appear tribal.
2002 In *Interview Magazine*, May.

82 Some music that I don't take to in modern orchestral stuff just seems to be trying to do something with an orchestra that Jimi Hendrix could do so much better with an electric guitar and a fuzzbox. Why create a hideous sound with violas when they were made to sound melodious and agreeable?
2002 In *The Irish Times*, 23 Mar.

83 The songs weren't theirs any more. They were everybody's.
2004 On why the Beatles stopped performing. *Rolling Stone*, 15 Apr.

Cotman, John Sell 1782–1842

English landscape painter and etcher, best known for his work in watercolour.

84 Three quarters of mankind, you know, mind more what is represented than how it is done.
Quoted in William Vaughn *Romantic Art* (1978).

Coubertin, Pierre de, Baron 1863–1937

French educationalist. He revived the Olympic Games at Athens in 1896, in the hope that they would foster national and international understanding through sport.

85 Women have but one task, that of crowning the winner with garlands.
1902 Quoted in Colin Jarman *The Guinness Dictionary of Sports Quotations* (1990).

86 The most important thing in the Olympic games is not winning but taking part—just as the most important thing in life is not the triumph but the struggle. The essential thing in life is not conquering but fighting well.
1908 Speech to Olympic Games officials, London, 24 Jul.

Coué, Émile 1857–1926

French pharmacist, pioneer of 'auto-suggestion'. He opened a free clinic in Nancy in 1910 and 'Couéism' subsequently attracted followers all round the world.

87 *Tous les jours, à tous points de vue, je vais de mieux en mieux.*
Every day, in every way, I am getting better and better.
1915 *De la suggestion et de ses applications*. Maxim recommended by Coué to his patients, to be repeated several times over on rising and on going to bed.

Coupland, Douglas 1961–

Canadian novelist. His *Generation X: Tales for an Accelerated Culture* (1991) was a cult novel defining the angst of the children of the baby boomers.

88 Generation X.
1991 From the title of his satiric novel *Generation X: Tales for an Accelerated Culture*. The phrase refers to young people born in the mid-1960s who are in no hurry to 'find themselves'.

89 MCJOB: A low-pay, low-prestige, low-dignity, no-future job in the service sector. Frequently considered a satisfying career choice for people who have never held one.
1991 *Generation X*, 'The Sun Is Your Enemy'.

90 HISTORICAL OVERDOSING: To live in a period of time when too much seems to happen.
1991 *Generation X*, 'The Sun Is Your Enemy'.

91 HISTORICAL SLUMMING: the act of visiting locations such as diners, smokestack industrial sites, rural villages—locations where time appears to have been frozen many years back—so as to experience relief when one returns back to 'the present'.
1991 *Generation X*, 'Our Parents Had More'.

92 BRAZILIFICATION: The widening gulf between the rich and the poor and the accompanying disappearance of the middle classes.
1991 *Generation X*, 'Our Parents Had More'.

93 CONSENSUS TERRORISM: The process that decides in-office attitudes and behavior.
1991 *Generation X*, 'Quit Recycling the Past'.

94 Marketing is essentially about feeding the poop back to diners fast enough to make them think they're still getting real food.
1991 *Generation X*, 'Quit Your Job'.

95 Shopping is Not Creating.
1991 *Generation X*, chapter heading.

96 Their talk was endless, compulsive, and indulgent, sometimes sounding like the remains of the English language after having been hashed over by nuclear war survivors for a few hundred years.
1991 *Generation X*, 'It Can't Last'.

97 I want to tell them that I envy their upbringings that were so clean, so free of *futurelessness*. And I want to throttle

them for blithely handing over the world to us like so much skid-marked underwear.
1991 Claire speaking of her parents. *Generation X*, 'Eat Your Parents'.

98 BRADYISM: A multisibling sensibility derived from having grown up in large families…symptoms of *Bradyism* include a facility for mind games, emotional withdrawal in situations of overcrowding, and a deeply felt need for a well-defined personal space.
1991 *Generation X*, 'Define Normal'.

99 STRANGELOVE REPRODUCTION: Having children to make up for the fact that one no longer believes in the future.
1991 *Generation X*, 'Define Normal'.

1 PERSONALITY TITHE: A price paid for becoming a couple; previously amusing human beings become boring: '*Thanks for inviting us, but Noreen and I are going to look at flatware catalogs tonight. Afterward we're going to watch the shopping channel.*'
1991 *Generation X*, 'M T V Not Bullets'.

2 NOSTALGIA IS A WEAPON
1991 *Generation X*, 'Welcome Home from Vietnam, Son'.

Cousins, Norman 1915–90

US editor and activist. As director of the *Saturday Review* (1942–71, 1973–7), he broadened its scope and circulation, campaigning on issues such as nuclear disarmament. His works include *Who Speaks for Man?* (1953).

3 The poet reminds men of their uniqueness and it is not necessary to possess the ultimate definition of this uniqueness. Even to speculate is a gain.
1978 In the *Saturday Review*, 15 Apr.

4 President Nixon's motto was, if two wrongs don't make a right, try three.
1979 In the *Daily Telegraph*, 17 Jul.

Cousteau, Jacques Yves 1910–97

French underwater explorer, who helped develop the Aqua-Lung (1943) and later became famous for a series of documentaries about the world's oceans.

5 The sea is the universal sewer.
1971 Testimony before the House Committee on Science and Astronautics, 28 Jan.

Coventry, Thomas, 1st Baron 1578–1640

English judge.

6 The dominion of the sea, as it is an ancient and undoubted right of the crown of England, so it is the best security of the land… The wooden walls are the best walls of this kingdom.
1635 Speech to the Star Chamber, 17 Jun. 'Wooden walls' refers to ships.

Coward, Sir Noël Peirce 1899–1973

English playwright, actor, director, composer and singer. His witty, stylish and sometimes biting plays include *Hay Fever* (1925), *Private Lives* (1930), *Blithe Spirit* (1941) and *Present Laughter* (1943). His films include the Academy Award-winning *In Which We Serve* (1941).

7 Poor Little Rich Girl.
1925 Title of song.

8 There's sand in the porridge and sand in the bed,
And if this is pleasure we'd rather be dead.
1928 'The English Lido' (song).

9 I believe that since my life began
The most I've had is just
A talent to amuse.
Heigho, if love were all!
1929 'If Love Were All'.

10 Very flat, Norfolk.
1930 *Private Lives*, act 1.

11 Extraordinary how potent cheap music is.
1930 *Private Lives*, act 1.

12 Certain women should be struck regularly, like gongs.
1930 *Private Lives*, act 3.

13 Mad dogs and Englishmen
Go out in the midday sun.
1931 'Mad Dogs and Englishmen' (song).

14 In the Philippines, there are lovely screens
To protect you from the glare.
1931 'Mad Dogs and Englishmen' (song).

15 Mad about the boy,
It's pretty funny but I'm mad about the boy.
He has a gay appeal
That makes me feel
There may be something sad about the boy.
1932 'Mad About the Boy' (song).

16 People are wrong when they say the opera isn't what it used to be. It is what it used to be. That's what's wrong with it.
1933 *Design for Living*.

17 Don't put your daughter on the stage, Mrs Worthington,
Don't put your daughter on the stage.
1935 'Mrs Worthington' (song).

18 The stately homes of England,
How beautiful they stand,
To prove the upper classes
Have still the upper hand.
1938 'The Stately Homes of England' (song).

19 Dear Mrs A,
Hooray, hooray,
At last you are deflowered.
On this as every other day
I love you—Noël Coward.
1940 Telegram sent to Gertrude Lawrence the day after her marriage, quoted in Gertrude Lawrence *A Star Danced* (1945).

20 It's discouraging to think how many people are shocked by honesty and how few by deceit.
1941 *Blithe Spirit*.

21 Don't Let's Be Beastly to the Germans.
1943 Song title.

22 Speak clearly, don't bump into people, and if you must have motivation think of your pay packet on Friday.
1962 Speech, Gallery First-Nighters' Club, sharing his advice to young actors. On other occasions he repeated it in the form 'Just say your lines and don't trip over the furniture'.

23 I never realised before that Albert married beneath him.
c.1964 Quoted in Kenneth Tynan *Tynan on Theatre* (1964), alluding to the performance of a particular actress in the role of Queen Victoria.

24 Squash—that's not exercise, it's flagellation.

Quoted in Colin Jarman *The Guinness Dictionary of Sports Quotations* (1990).

25 I love criticism just so long as it's unqualified praise.
Attributed.

26 Two things should have been cut. The second act and that youngster's throat.
After watching a play featuring a 14-year-old child star (sometimes identified as Bonnie Langford). Attributed.

27 He must have been a marvellously good shot.
On hearing that an impresario he disliked had blown his brains out. Attributed.

28 I'm not very keen on Hollywood. I'd rather have a nice cup of cocoa really.
Attributed.

Cowley, Abraham 1618–67

English poet, essayist and Royalist. He served Queen Henrietta Maria in exile during the Civil War, and only returned to England permanently at the Restoration. His works include a lyric collection, *Poetical Blossoms* (1633), and the epic *Davideis* (1656).

29 The world's a scene of changes, and to be
Constant, in Nature were inconstancy.
1647 *The Mistress*, 'Inconstancy'.

30 Such were the numbers which could call
The stones into the Theban wall.
Such miracles are ceased, and now we see
No towns or houses raised by poetry.
1656 *Poems*, 'Ode: Of Wit'.

31 Ye fields of Cambridge, our dear Cambridge, say,
Have ye not seen us walking every day?
Was there a tree about which did not know
The love betwixt us two?
1656 'On the Death of Mr William Harvey'.

32 Life is an incurable disease.
1656 'To Dr Scarborough', stanza 6.

33 Fill all the glasses there, for why
Should every creature drink but I,
Why, man of morals, tell me why?
1656 'Drinking'.

34 God the first garden made, and the first city Cain.
1668 *Essays, in Verse and Prose*, 'The Garden'.

35 This only grant me, that my means may lie
Too low for envy, for contempt too high.
1668 *Essays, in Verse and Prose*, 'Of Myself'.

Cowley, Hannah 1743–1809

English playwright and poet, an early exponent of the comedy of manners. She also wrote long narrative verses (1780–94).

36 But what is woman?—only one of Nature's agreeable blunders.
1779 *Who's the Dupe?*, act 2.

37 Five minutes! Zounds! I have been five minutes too late all my life-time!
1780 *The Belle's Stratagem*, act 1, sc.1.

Cowley, Malcolm 1898–1989

US writer and critic, known for his studies of US expatriate writers in the 1920s and for his works on William Faulkner.

38 A new generation does not appear every 30 years. It

appears when writers of the same age join in a common revolt against the fathers and when, in the process of adopting a new life style, they find their own models and spokesmen.
Quoted in the *New York Times*, 29 Mar 1989.

39 I...chopped the manuscript down to size, or sawed it into fireplace lengths.
Quoted in the *New York Times*, 29 Mar 1989.

40 Going back to Hemingway's work after several years is like going back to a brook where you had often fished and finding the woods as deep and cool as they used to be.
Quoted in Pete Hamill *A Drinking Life* (1994).

Cowper, William 1731–1800

English poet, whose work reflects the evangelical revival. Regarded as a precursor of Wordsworth, he wrote *The Task* (1785), a long rural poem, and a collection of moral satires, *Poems* (1782).

41 Damned below Judas; more abhorred than he was.
c.1774 Of himself. 'Hatred and Vengeance, my eternal portion'.

42 O make this heart rejoice or ache;
Decide this doubt for me;
And if it be not broken, break—
And heal it if it be.
1779 *Olney Hymns*, 'The Contrite Heart'.

43 God moves in a mysterious way
His wonders to perform;
He plants his footsteps in the sea,
And rides upon the storm.
1779 *Olney Hymns*, 'Light Shining out of Darkness'.

44 Blind unbelief is sure to err,
And scan his work in vain;
God is his own interpreter,
And he will make it plain.
1779 *Olney Hymns*, 'Light Shining out of Darkness'.

45 Behind a frowning providence
He hides a smiling face.
1779 *Olney Hymns*, 'Light Shining out of Darkness'.

46 Oh! for a closer walk with God,
A calm and heav'nly frame;
A light to shine upon the road
That leads me to the Lamb!
1779 *Olney Hymns*, 'Walking with God'.

47 A tale should be judicious, clear, succinct;
The language plain, and incidents well linked;
Tell not as new what ev'ry body knows,
And new or old, still hasten to a close.
1782 *Poems*, 'Conversation', l.235–8.

48 The pipe with solemn interposing puff,
Makes half a sentence at a time enough;
The dozing sages drop the drowsy strain,
Then pause, and puff—and speak, and pause again.
1782 *Poems*, 'Conversation', l.245–8.

49 His wit invites you by his looks to come,
But when you knock it never is at home.
1782 *Poems* 'Conversation', l.303–4.

50 The discumbered Atlas of the state.
1782 *Poems*, 'Retirement'.

51 He likes the country, but in truth must own,

Most likes it, when he studies it in town.
1782 *Poems*, 'Retirement'.

52 Religion Caesar never knew
Thy posterity shall sway,
Where his eagles never flew,
None as invincible as they.
1782 *Poems*, 'Boadicea: an Ode'.

53 Rome shall perish—write that word
In the blood that she has spilt.
1782 *Poems*, 'Boadicea: an Ode'.

54 I am monarch of all I survey,
My right there is none to dispute;
From the centre all round to the sea,
I am lord of the fowl and the brute.
O Solitude! where are the charms
That sages have seen in thy face?
Better dwell in the midst of alarms,
Than reign in this horrible place.
1782 *Poems*, 'Verses Supposed to be Written by Alexander Selkirk, During His Solitary Abode in the Island of Juan Fernandez'.

55 I am out of humanity's reach.
1782 *Poems*, 'Verses Supposed to be Written by Alexander Selkirk, During His Solitary Abode in the Island of Juan Fernandez'.

56 When I think of my own native land,
In a moment I seem to be there;
But alas! recollection at hand
Soon hurries me back to despair.
1782 *Poems*, 'Verses Supposed to be Written by Alexander Selkirk, During His Solitary Abode in the Island of Juan Fernandez'.

57 Grief is itself a med'cine.
1782 *Poems*, 'Charity', l.159.

58 He found it inconvenient to be poor.
1782 *Poems*, 'Charity', l.189.

59 Spare the poet for his subject's sake.
1782 *Poems*, 'Charity', l.636.

60 The man that hails you Tom or Jack,
And proves by thumps upon your back
How he esteems your merit,
Is such a friend, that one had need
Be very much his friend indeed
To pardon or to bear it.
1782 *Poems*, 'Friendship', l.169–74.

61 Remorse, the fatal egg by pleasure laid.
1782 *Poems*, 'The Progress of Error', l.239.

62 As creeping ivy clings to wood or stone,
And hides the ruin that it feeds upon,
So sophistry, cleaves close to, and protects
Sin's rotten trunk, concealing its defects.
1782 *Poems*, 'The Progress of Error', l.285–8.

63 How much a dunce that has been sent to roam
Excels a dunce that has been kept at home.
1782 *Poems*, 'The Progress of Error', l.415–6.

64 Laugh at all you trembled at before.
1782 *Poems*, 'The Progress of Error', l.592.

65 Our severest winter, commonly called the spring.
1783 Letter to Rev William Unwin, 8 Jun.

66 There is a mixture of evil in everything we do;
indulgence encourages us to encroach, while we

exercise the rights of children, we become childish.
1783 Letter to Rev William Unwin, 7 Sep.

67 Thus first necessity invented stools,
Convenience next suggested elbow-chairs,
And luxury the accomplished sofa last.
1785 *The Task*, bk.1, 'The Sofa', l.86–8.

68 God made the country, and man made the town.
1785 *The Task*, bk.1, 'The Sofa', l.749.

69 At eve
The moonbeam, sliding softly in between
The sleeping leaves, is all the light they wish,
Birds warbling all the music.
1785 *The Task*, bk.1, 'The Sofa'.

70 England, with all thy faults I love thee still—
My country!
1785 *The Task*, bk.2, 'The Timepiece', l.206–7.

71 There is a pleasure in poetic pains
Which only poets know.
1785 *The Task*, bk.2, 'The Timepiece', l.285–6.

72 Variety's the spice of life,
That gives it all its flavour.
1785 *The Task*, bk.2, 'The Timepiece', l.606–7.

73 Defend me, therefore, common sense, say I,
From reveries so airy, from the toil
Of dropping buckets into empty wells,
And growing old in drawing nothing up!
1785 *The Task*, bk.3, 'The Garden', l.187–90.

74 Detested sport,
That owes its pleasure to another's pain.
1785 Of hunting. *The Task*, bk.3, 'The Garden', l.326–7.

75 Studious of laborious ease.
1785 *The Task*, bk.3, 'The Garden', l.361.

76 Now stir the fire, and close the shutters fast,
Let fall the curtains, wheel the sofa round,
And, while the bubbling and loud-hissing urn
Throws up a steamy column, and the cups,
That cheer but not inebriate, wait on each,
So let us welcome peaceful evening in.
1785 *The Task*, bk.4, 'The Winter Evening', l.34–9.

77 But war's a game, which, were their subjects wise,
Kings should not play at. Nations would do well
To extort their truncheons from the puny hands
Of heroes, whose infirm and baby minds
Are gratified with mischief, and who spoil,
Because men suffer it, their toy the world.
1785 *The Task*, bk.5, 'The Winter Morning Walk', l.187–92.

78 Knowledge dwells
In heads replete with thoughts of other men;
Wisdom in minds attentive to their own.
1785 *The Task*, bk.6, 'The Winter Walk at Noon', l.89–91.

79 Knowledge is proud that he has learned so much;
Wisdom is humble that he knows no more.
1785 *The Task*, bk.6, 'The Winter Walk at Noon', l.96–7.

80 Nature is but a name for an effect,
Whose cause is God.
1785 *The Task*, bk.6, 'The Winter Walk at Noon', l.223.

Crabbe, George 1754–1832

English poet and clergyman, whose early career was spent in

poverty until Edmund Burke befriended him. His best-known poem, *The Village* (1783), is a bleak account of rural life.

81 Lo! the poor toper whose untutored sense,
Sees bliss in ale, and can with wine dispense;
Whose head proud fancy never taught to steer,
Beyond the muddy ecstasies of beer.
1775 *Inebriety, a Poem*, pt.1, l.132–5.

82 With awe, around these silent walks I tread;
These are the lasting mansions of the dead.
1781 *The Library* (published 1808), l.105–6.

83 Lo! all in silence, all in order stand,
And mighty folios first, a lordly band:
Then quartos their well-ordered ranks maintain,
And light octavos fill a spacious plain;
See yonder, ranged in more frequented rows,
A humbler band of duodecimos.
1781 *The Library* (published 1808), l.128–33.

84 Fashion, though Folly's child, and guide of fools,
Rules e'en the wisest, and in learning rules.
1781 *The Library* (published 1808), l.167–8.

85 Coldly profane and impiously gay.
1781 *The Library* (published 1808), l.265.

86 Yes, thus the Muses sing of happy swains,
Because the Muses never knew their pains:
They boast their peasants' pipes, but peasants now
Resign their pipes and plod behind the plough.
1783 *The Village*, bk.1, l.21–4.

87 I grant indeed that fields and flocks have charms,
For him that gazes or for him that farms.
1783 *The Village*, bk.1, l.39–40.

88 I paint the cot,
As truth will paint it, and as bards will not.
1783 *The Village*, bk.1, l.53–4.

89 Where Plenty smiles—alas! she smiles for few,
And those who taste not, yet behold her store,
Are as the slaves that dig the golden ore,
The wealth around them makes them doubly poor.
1783 *The Village*, bk.1, l.136–9.

90 The cold charities of man to man.
1783 *The Village*, bk.1, l.245.

91 A potent quack, long versed in human ills,
Who first insults the victim whom he kills;
Whose murd'rous hand a drowsy bench protect,
And whose most tender mercy is neglect.
1783 *The Village*, bk.1, l.282.

92 The murmuring poor, who will not fast in peace.
1785 *The Newspaper*, l.158.

93 A master passion is the love of news.
1785 *The Newspaper*, l.279.

94 Our farmers round, well pleased with constant gain,
Like other farmers, flourish and complain.
1807 *Poems*, 'The Parish Register', pt.1, l.273–4.

95 'What is a church?'—Our honest sexton tells,
''Tis a tall building, with a tower and bells.'
1810 *The Borough*, letter 2, 'The Church', l.11–12.

96 Virtues neglected then, adored become,
And graces slighted, blossom on the tomb.
1810 *The Borough*, letter 2, 'The Church', l.133–4.

97 Ye Lilies male! think (as your tea you sip,
While the Town small-talk flows from lip to lip;
Intrigues half-gathered, conversation-scraps,
Kitchen-cabals, and nursery-mishaps),
If the vast world may not some scene produce,
Some state where your small talents might have use.
1810 *The Borough*, letter 3, 'The Vicar', l.69–74.

98 Habit with him was all the test of truth,
'It must be right: I've done it from my youth.'
1810 *The Borough*, letter 3, 'The Vicar', l.138–9.

99 There anchoring, Peter chose from man to hide,
There hang his head, and view the lazy tide
In its hot slimy channel slowly glide;
Where the small eels that left the deeper way
For the warm shore, within the shallows play;
Where gaping mussels, left upon the mud,
Slope their slow passage to the fallen flood.
1810 *The Borough*, letter 22, 'Peter Grimes', l.185–91.

1 He nursed the feelings these dull scenes produce,
And loved to stop beside the opening sluice;
Where the small stream, confined in narrow bound,
Ran with a dull, unvaried, sad'ning sound;
Where all presented to the eye or ear,
Oppressed the soul! with misery, grief, and fear.
1810 *The Borough*, letter 22, 'Peter Grimes', l.194–9.

2 That all was wrong because not all was right.
1812 *Tales*, 'The Convert', l.313.

3 He tried the luxury of doing good.
1819 *Tales of the Hall*, 'Boys at School', l.139.

4 'The game,' said he, 'is never lost till won.'
1819 *Tales of the Hall*, 'Gretna Green', l.334.

5 The face the index of a feeling mind.
1819 *Tales of the Hall*, 'Lady Barbara', l.124.

6 Secrets with girls, like loaded guns with boys,
Are never valued till they make a noise.
1819 *Tales of the Hall*, 'The Maid's Story', l.84–5.

Craik, Dinah Maria *née Mulock* 1826–87

English novelist, essayist and poet. She published over 20 novels, the best known being *John Halifax, Gentleman* (1858). Although sentimental, her work emphasizes the self-reliance of women.

7 Leonora, Leonora,
How the word rolls—*Leonora*—
Lion-like, in full-mouthed sound,
Marching o'er the metric ground
With a tawny tread sublime;
So your name moves, Leonora,
Down my desert rhyme.
1881 *Collected Poems*, 'Leonora'.

Crane, (Harold) Hart 1899–1932

US poet. He was an alcoholic who led a troubled life which ended in suicide. He has come to be regarded as one of the most important US poets of the 20c.

8 The Cross alone has flown the wave.
But since the Cross sank, much that's warped and cracked
Has followed in its name, has heaped its grave.
1920 'The Mermen', in *The Dial*, no.85, Jul.

9 The bottom of the sea is cruel.
1926 *White Buildings*, 'Voyages', pt.1.

10 And onwards, as bells off San Salvador
Salute the crocus lustres of the stars,
In these poinsettia meadows of her tides.
1926 *White Buildings*, 'Voyages', pt.2.

11 Bequeath us no earthly shore until
Is answered in the vortex of our grave
The seal's wide spindrift gaze toward paradise.
1926 *White Buildings*, 'Voyages', pt.2.

12 Light wrestling there incessantly with light,
Star kissing star through wave on wave unto
Your body rocking!
1926 *White Buildings*, 'Voyages', pt.3.

13 Slow tyranny of moonlight, moonlight loved
And changed.
1926 *White Buildings*, 'Voyages', pt.5.

14 O Sleepless as the river under thee,
Vaulting the sea, the prairies' dreaming sod,
Unto us lowliest sometime sweep, descend
And of the curveship lend a myth to God.
1927 'To Brooklyn Bridge', in *The Dial*, Jun.

15 You who desired so much—in vain to ask—
Yet fed your hunger like an endless task,
Dared dignify the labor, bless the quest—
Achieved that stillness ultimately best,
Being, of all, least sought for: Emily, hear!
1929 'To Emily Dickinson', in *The Nation*, 29 Jun.

16 The last bear, shot drinking in the Dakotas
Loped under wires that span the mountain stream.
Keen instruments, strung to a vast precision
Bind town to town and dream to ticking dream.
1930 *The Bridge*, 'The River'.

17 Hobo-trekkers that forever search
An empire wilderness of freight and rails.
1930 *The Bridge*, 'The River'.

18 Dead echoes! But I knew her body there,
Time like a serpent down her shoulder, dark,
And space, an eaglet's wing, laid on her hair.
1930 *The Bridge*, 'The River'.

19 Few evade full measure of their fate.
1930 *The Bridge*, 'The River'.

20 Thin squeaks of radio static,
The captured fume of space foams in our ears.
1930 *The Bridge*, 'Cape Hatteras'.

21 Stars scribble on our eyes the frosty sagas,
The gleaming cantos of unvanquished space.
1930 *The Bridge*, 'Cape Hatteras'.

22 Cowslip and shad-blow, flaked like tethered foam
Around bared teeth of stallions, bloomed that spring
When first I read thy lines, rife as the loam
Of prairies, yet like breakers cliffward leaping!
1930 Of Walt Whitman. *The Bridge*, 'Cape Hatteras'.

23 Our Meistersinger, thou set breath in steel;
And it was thou who on the boldest heel
Stood up and flung the span on even wing
Of that great Bridge, our Myth, whereof I sing.
1930 On Whitman and Brooklyn Bridge. *The Bridge*, 'Cape Hatteras'.

24 Our tongues recant like beaten weather vanes.

1930 *The Bridge*, 'The Tunnel'.

25 The phonographs of hades in the brain
Are tunnels that re-wind themselves, and love
A burnt match skating in a urinal.
1930 *The Bridge*, 'The Tunnel'.

26 The bell-rope that gathers God at dawn
Dispatches me as though I dropped down the knell
Of a spent day.
1932 'The Broken Tower', in the *New Republic*, 8 Jun.

Crane, Stephen 1871–1900

US writer. His reputation rests on *The Red Badge of Courage* (1895), which relates the experience of a soldier in the Civil War. His well-known short stories include *The Open Boat* (1898). He died of tuberculosis in Baden Baden.

27 The Red Badge of Courage.
1895 Title of novel.

28 'It is bitter—bitter,' he answered;
'But I like it
Because it is bitter,
And because it is my heart.'
1895 *The Black Riders*, 'The Heart'. The speaker is a 'naked, bestial' creature which the narrator sees eating its heart in the desert.

29 None of them knew the color of the sky.
1898 *The Open Boat*.

30 A man said to the universe:
'Sir, I exist!'
'However,' replied the universe,
'The fact has not created in me
A sense of obligation.'
1899 *A Man Said to the Universe*.

Cranfield, Ingrid 1945–

Australian-born writer and journalist. Her books on adventurers and travellers include *The Challengers* (1976) and *Skiing down Everest and Other Crazy Adventures* (1983).

31 To Hunt an 'assault' on the mountain merely meant a concerted, military-style operation; whereas to Shipton 'assault' sounded more like a criminal offence.
1978 Of the contrast in approach to the climbing of Mt Everest between Eric Shipton, originally appointed as leader of the 1953 expedition, and John Hunt, who replaced him. In *Expedition*, vol.8, no.4, Jul.

Cranmer, Thomas 1489–1556

English Protestant prelate, Archbishop of Canterbury (1533–53), largely responsible for the Book of Common Prayer (1549, 1552). He was convicted of treason for his part in the plan to divert the succession of the English Crown to Lady Jane Grey, and was burned at the stake.

32 This hath offended! Oh this unworthy hand!
1556 Last words at the stake, referring to the hand which had signed several recantations, later withdrawn.

Crashaw, Richard c.1613–1649

English metaphysical poet. He abandoned Puritanism for Catholicism, but lost his fellowship at Cambridge in 1643 and went to the Continent. His works include *Steps to the Temple* (1646) and *The Delights of the Muses* (1646).

33 *Nympha pudica Deum vidit, et erubuit.*
The conscious water saw its God, and blushed.

1634 Of the water which Jesus turned into wine at Cana.
Epigrammata Sacra, 'Aquae in Vinum Versae' (translated by
Dryden).

34 Wellcome, all Wonders in one sight!
Eternity shut in a span.
Summer in Winter, Day in Night.
Heaven in Earth and God in Man.
1646 'Hymn of the Nativity' (published 1652), l.79.

35 I would be married, but I'd have no wife,
I would be married to a single life.
1646 'On Marriage'.

36 Th' have left thee naked, Lord, O that they had!
This garment too I would they had denied.
Thee with thyself they have too richly clad,
Opening the purple wardrobe of thy side.
O never could be found garments too good
For thee to wear, but these, of thine own blood.
1646 'On Our Crucified Lord, Naked and Bloody'.

37 And now where'er he strays
Among the Galilean mountains
Or more unwelcome ways,
He's followed by two faithful fountains;
Two walking baths; two weeping motions;
Portable and compendious oceans.
1646 'Saint Mary Magdalene, or The Weeper'.

38 What heaven-entreated heart is this,
Stands trembling at the gate of bliss,
Holds fast the door, yet dares not venture
Fairly to open it, and enter?
1646 'To the Noblest and Best of Ladies, the Countess of
Denbigh'.

39 Say, lingering fair! why comes the birth
Of your brave soul so slowly forth?
1646 'To the Noblest and Best of Ladies, the Countess of
Denbigh'.

40 What yet fantastic bands
Keep the free heart from its own hands!
1646 'To the Noblest and Best of Ladies, the Countess of
Denbigh'.

41 Yield, then, O yield, that love may win
The fort at last, and let life in.
1646 'To the Noblest and Best of Ladies, the Countess of Denbigh'.

42 In love's field was never found
A nobler weapon than a wound.
'The Flaming Heart Upon the Book and Picture of Saint Teresa',
collected in *Carmen Deo Nostro* (published posthumously, 1652).

43 All thy brim-filled bowls of fierce desire
'The Flaming Heart Upon the Book and Picture of Saint Teresa',
collected in *Carmen Deo Nostro* (published posthumously, 1652).

Craster, Mrs Edmund d.1874

44 The centipede was happy quite,
Until the toad in fun
Asked him which leg went after which,
Which drove him into such a pitch
He lay distracted in a ditch,
Considering how to run.
Attributed.

Crawford, Joan *originally Lucille Fay le Sueur* 1904–77

US film actress. Originally a nightclub dancer, she began in
silent films in 1925 and found fame in the 1930s and 1940s.

45 I found that incredible thing, a public.
Quoted in Alexander Walker *Joan Crawford* (1983).

Crichton, Michael 1942–

US writer and film-maker. His many scientific and medical
thrillers include *The Andromeda Strain* (1969), *Jurassic Park*
(1990) and *Timeline* (1999).

46 Physics was the first of the natural sciences to become
fully modern and highly mathematical. Chemistry
followed in the wake of physics, but biology, the
retarded child, lagged far behind.
1969 *The Andromeda Strain*.

Crick, Francis Harry Compton 1916–2004

English molecular biologist, winner (with James Watson and
Maurice Wilkins) of the Nobel prize for physiology or medicine
in 1962 for work on the structure of DNA.

47 We have discovered the secret of life!
1953 Announcement, with James Watson, to the patrons of The
Eagle public house in Cambridge on solving the structure of DNA.
➤ *See* Watson 890:96.

48 Almost all aspects of life are engineered at the molecular
level, and without understanding molecules we can only
have a very sketchy understanding of life itself.
1988 *What Mad Pursuit*, ch.5.

Cripps, Arthur S(hearly) 1869–1952

English clergyman. He was the writer of occasional verse,
mainly on rural or religious themes.

49 England has greater counties—
Their peace to hers is small;
Low hills, rich fields, calm rivers,
In Essex seek them all.
Quoted in S P B Mais and Tom Stephenson (eds) *Lovely Britain*
(c.1930).

Cripps, Sir (Richard) Stafford 1889–1952

English Labour politician and economist, expelled from the
Party for his opposition to appeasement (1939). In 1945 he was
readmitted and subsequently became Chancellor of the
Exchequer, with a successful austerity policy.

50 There is only a certain sized cake to be divided up, and if
a lot of people want a larger slice they can only take it
from others who would, in terms of real income, have a
smaller one.
1948 Speech, Trades Union Congress, 7 Sep.

Crisp, Quentin 1908–99

English writer. He achieved notoriety with the publication of
The Naked Civil Servant (1968), an account of his experiences
growing up as a flamboyant gay young man in England.

51 Keeping up with the Joneses was a full-time job with my
mother and father. It was not until many years later when
I lived alone that I realized how much cheaper it was to
drag the Joneses down to my level.
1968 *The Naked Civil Servant*, ch.1.

52 As soon as I stepped out of my mother's womb on to dry
land, I realized that I had made a mistake…but the
trouble with children is that they are not returnable.
1968 *The Naked Civil Servant*, ch.2.

53 This woman did not fly to extremes, she lived there.
1968 *The Naked Civil Servant*, ch.3.

54 I don't hold with abroad and think that foreigners speak English when our backs are turned.
1968 *The Naked Civil Servant*, ch.4.

55 If one is not going to take the necessary precautions to avoid having parents, one must undertake to bring them up.
1968 *The Naked Civil Servant*, ch.5.

56 There was no need to do any housework after all. After the first four years the dirt doesn't get any worse.
1968 *The Naked Civil Servant*, ch.15.

57 Life was a funny thing that happened to me on the way to the grave.
1968 *The Naked Civil Servant*, ch.18.

58 I became one of the stately homos of England.
1968 *The Naked Civil Servant*, ch.24.

59 An autobiography is an obituary in serial form with the last instalment missing.
1968 *The Naked Civil Servant*, ch.29.

60 In England, the system is benign and the people are hostile. In America, the people are friendly—and the system is brutal!
1985 In *The Guardian*, 23 Oct.

Critchfield, Richard Patrick 1931–94

US journalist. His books include *The Long Charade: Political Subversion in the Vietnam War* (1968) and *An American Looks at Britain* (1990).

61 What people read most of the time should be as worth mentioning as what they read almost none of the time.
1990 *An American Looks at Britain*.

Critchley, Sir Julian Michael Gordon 1930–2000

English Conservative MP, writer and broadcaster, known for his acerbic and witty comments on Westminster life.

62 I was told when a young man that the two occupational hazards of the Palace of Varieties were alcohol and adultery. The hurroosh that follows the intermittent revelation of the sexual goings-on of an unlucky MP has convinced me that the only safe pleasure for a parliamentarian is a bag of boiled sweets.
1982 In *The Listener*, 10 Jun.

63 She has been beastly to the Bank of England, has demanded that the BBC 'set its house in order' and tends to believe the worst of the Foreign and Commonwealth Office. She cannot see an institution without hitting it with her handbag.
1982 Profile of Margaret Thatcher in *The Times*, 21 Jun.

Critias c.460–403 BC

Athenian aristocrat and politician, one of the 30 tyrants who ruled Athens after the Peloponnesian war (404 BC). He was killed in the democratic revolution of 404/3. Only fragments of his poetry and tragedies survive.

64 Is not living at all not better than living badly?
Fragment, quoted in H Diels and W Kranz (eds) *Die Fragmente der Vorsokratiker* (1952), vol.2, 385, no.23.

Croker, John Wilson 1780–1857

Irish politician and essayist, known for his satires on the Irish stage and Dublin society. He became an MP (1807) and helped found the *Quarterly Review* (1809).

65 We are now, as we have always been, decidedly and conscientiously attached to what is called the Tory, and which might with more propriety be called the Conservative party.
1830 *Quarterly Review*, Jan.

Cromer, Evelyn Baring, Earl 1841–1917

English colonial administrator.

66 It is well that Gordon should be under my orders, but a man who habitually consults the prophet Isaiah when he is in difficulty is not apt to obey the orders of anyone.
Of General Charles George Gordon. Quoted in Charles Chevenix Trench *Charley Gordon* (1978).

Crompton, Richmal *originally* Richmal Samuel Lamburn 1890–1969

English writer, a classics teacher until she contracted polio in 1923. Her best-known children's books are those in the 'William' series, beginning with *Just William* (1922).

67 I'll thcream and thcream and thcream until I'm thick.
1925 Violet Elizabeth. *Still—William*, ch.8.

Cromwell, Oliver 1599–1658

English soldier and Puritan statesman. In the Civil War he led his New Model Army to victory at Naseby (1645). After the execution of Charles I, he established a Commonwealth, and later, on dissolving the Rump Parliament (1653) and refusing the crown, a Protectorate.

68 A few honest men are better than numbers.
1643 Letter to Sir William Spring, Sep. Quoted in Thomas Carlyle *Letters and Speeches of Oliver Cromwell* (1845).

69 I had rather have a plain, russet-coated Captain, that knows what he fights for, and loves what he knows, than that which you call a Gentle-man and is nothing else.
1643 Letter to Sir William Spring, Sep. Quoted in Thomas Carlyle *Letters and Speeches of Oliver Cromwell* (1845).

70 The state, in choosing men to serve it, takes no notice of their opinions. If they be willing faithfully to serve it, that satisfies.
1644 Said before the Battle of Marston Moor, 2 Jul.

71 EARL OF MANCHESTER: If we beat the King ninety-nine times, yet he is King still so will his posterity be after him; but if the King beat us once we shall be hanged, and our posterity made slaves.
OLIVER CROMWELL: My Lord, if this be so, why did we take up arms at first? This is against fighting hereafter. If so, let us make peace, be it never so base.
1644 Recorded in *The Calendar of State Papers*, 10 Nov.

72 I beseech you, in the bowels of Christ, think it possible you may be mistaken.
1650 Letter to the General Assembly of the Church of Scotland, 3 Aug.

73 Mr Lely, I desire you would use all your skill to paint my picture truly like me, and not flatter me at all; but remark all these roughnesses, pimples, warts, and everything as you see me, otherwise I will never pay a farthing for it.

1650 Remark to Sir Peter Lely, who was about to paint his portrait. Quoted in H Walpole *Anecdotes of Painting in England*, vol.3 (1763).

74 You have sat too long here for any good you have been doing. Depart, I say, and let us have done with you. In the name of God, go!
1653 On dismissing the Rump Parliament, 20 Apr.

75 Take away that fool's bauble—the Mace.
1653 On dismissing the Rump Parliament, 20 Apr.

76 My desire is to make what haste I can to be gone.
1658 Last words. Quoted in John Morley *Oliver Cromwell* (1900), bk.5, ch.10.

Cronenberg, David 1943–

Canadian sci-fi and horror film director. His films include *The Fly* (1986), *Crash* (1996) and *eXistenZ* (1999).

77 More blood! More blood!
Characteristic on-set declaration. Quoted in Neil Gaiman and Kim Newman *Ghastly Beyond Belief* (1985).

78 I don't have a moral plan. I'm a Canadian.
Quoted in Leslie Halliwell *Halliwell's Filmgoer's and Video Viewer's Companion* (9th edn, 1988).

Cronkite, Walter 1916–

US journalist.

79 And that's the way it is.
Catchphrase, used at the end of the CBS *Evening News* (1962–81).

Cronyn, Hume 1911–2003

Canadian-born actor, writer and director. He was married to Jessica Tandy, with whom he acted many times.

80 The most magical moment in the theater is a silence so complete that you can't even hear people breathe. It means that you've got them.
1990 In *Time*, 2 Apr.

Crosby, Bing *originally* **Harry Lillis Crosby** 1904–77

US film actor and singer. His many successful films include the *Road to* series with Bob Hope and Dorothy Lamour.

81 That was a great game of golf.
1977 Last words, as he finished play at the 18th hole before suffering a heart attack.

82 He was an average guy who could carry a tune.
Suggesting his own epitaph. Quoted in David Pickering *Brewer's Twentieth Century Music* (1994).

Cross, Douglas

US songwriter.

83 I Left My Heart in San Francisco.
1954 Title of song.

Crossman, Richard Howard Stafford 1907–74

British Labour politician. He chronicled his ministerial career and the workings of government in a series of diaries, begun in 1952, which were published in four volumes (1975–81), despite attempts to suppress them.

84 My Minister's room is like a padded cell, and in certain ways I am like a person who is suddenly certified a lunatic and put safely into this great, vast room, cut off

from real life. Of course they don't behave *quite* like nurses, because the Civil Service is profoundly deferential—'Yes, Minister! No, Minister! If you wish it, Minister!'
1964 *The Diaries of a Cabinet Minister*, vol.1 (1975), 22 Oct.

Crowley, (Edward) Aleister 1875–1947

English writer and occultist. He founded his own order and became notorious for rumours of orgies, drugs and the sacrifice of babies in the course of black magic ceremonies.

85 Do what thou wilt shall be the whole of the Law.
1909 *Book of the Law*.

Cruyff, Johan 1947–

Dutch footballer, European Footballer of the Year (1971, 1973, 1974).

86 I am no longer a footballer. I am an industry.
1973 On being transferred from Ajax to Barcelona for a record £922,000. Quoted in Peter Ball and Phil Shaw *The Book of Football Quotations* (1989).

Cruz, Sor Juana Inés de la 1651–95

Mexican intellectual, nun and poet. After she took her vows at the age of 16, attempts were made to stop her writing. Two years after writing her defence, *Respuesta a sor Filotea* (1691), she sold her books and devoted herself to religion.

87 *En perseguirme, Mundo, Qué interesas?*
En qué te ofendo, cuando sólo intento
poner bellezas en mi entendimiento
y no mi entendimiento en las bellezas?
World, in hounding me, what do you gain?
How can it harm you if I choose, astutely,
rather to stock my mind with things of beauty,
than waste its stock on every beauty's claim?
1688 *Poesía, teatro y prosa*, 'Quéjase de la suerte' (translated as 'She Complains about Her Fate', 1985).

88 *Aprendamos a ignorar,*
pensamiento, pues hallamos
que cuanto añado al discurso,
tanto le usurpo a los años.
Thought, let's learn not to know,
since so plainly it appears
that whatever we add to our minds
we take away from our years.
1688 *A Sor Juana Anthology*, 'Acusa la hidropesía de mucha ciencia' (translated as 'She Condemns the Bloatedness of Much Learning', 1985).

89 *Este natural impulso que Dios puso en mí…su Majestad sabe por qué y para qué; y sabe que le he pedido que apague la luz de mi entendimiento dejando sólo lo que baste para guardar su Ley, pues lo demás sobra, (según algunos) en una mujer; y aun hay quien dice que daña.*
This natural impulse which God has implanted in me…only His Majesty knows why and wherefore and His Majesty also knows that I have prayed to Him to extinguish the light of my mind, only leaving sufficient to keep His Law, since any more is overmuch, so some say, in a woman, and there are even those who say it is harmful.
1691 *Poesía, teatro y prosa*, 'Respuesta a sor Filotea' ('An Answer to Sister Filotea', 1982).

Cuarón, Alfonso 1961–

Mexican film director.

90 You speed up and up then you realise that your scarf has got caught in the machinery and if you don't keep up you're going to be strangled.
2004 On the pace of work involved in directing *Harry Potter and the Prisoner of Azkaban*. Quoted in the *Sunday Herald*, 23 May.

Cullen, Countee 1903–46

Black US poet and novelist, an important figure in the Harlem Renaissance of the 1920s.

91 She even thinks that up in heaven
Her class lies late and snores,
While poor black cherubs rise at seven
To do celestial chores.
1925 *On These I Stand*, 'For a Lady I Know'.

92 What is Africa to me:
Copper sun or scarlet sea,
Jungle star or jungle track,
Strong bronzed men, or regal black
Women from whose loins I sprang
When the birds of Eden sang?
1925 *On These I Stand*, 'Heritage'.

93 One three centuries removed
From the scenes his fathers loved,
Spicy grove, cinnamon tree,
What is Africa to me?
1925 *On These I Stand*, 'Heritage'.

94 So I lie, whose fount of pride,
Dear distress, and joy allied,
Is my somber flesh and skin,
With the dark blood dammed within.
1925 *On These I Stand*, 'Heritage'.

95 Ever at Thy glowing altar
Must my heart grow sick and falter,
Wishing He I served were black.
1925 *On These I Stand*, 'Heritage'.

96 Lord, forgive me if my need
Sometimes shapes a human creed.
1925 *On These I Stand*, 'Heritage'.

cummings, e e *pen name of* *Edward Estlin Cummings*
1894–1962

US writer and painter, best known as an eccentric innovator in lyrical poetry, using idiosyncratic typography. He also wrote a novel, plays and essays.

97 He had no nose, properly speaking, but a large beak of preposterous widthlessness, which gave his whole face the expression of falling gravely downstairs, and quite obliterated the unimportant chin.
1922 *The Enormous Room*, ch.3.

98 Subconsciously every one was, of course, fearful that he himself would go nuts—everyone with the exception of those who had already gone nuts, who were in the wholly pleasant situation of having no fear.
1922 *The Enormous Room*, ch.5.

99 To create is first of all to destroy…there is and can be no such thing as authentic art until the *bons trucs* (whereby we are taught to see and imitate on canvas and in stone and by words this so-called world) are entirely and

thoroughly and perfectly annihilated by that vast and painful process of Unthinking which may result in a minute bit of purely personal Feeling. Which minute bit is Art.
1922 *The Enormous Room*, ch.12.

1 The tall, impossibly tall, incomparably tall, city shoulderingly upwards into hard sunlight leaned a little through the octaves of its parallel edges, leaningly strode upwards into firm, hard, snowy sunlight; the noises of America nearingly throbbed with smokes and hurrying dots which are men and which are women and which are things new and curious and hard and strange and vibrant and immense, lifting with a great ondulous stride firmly into immortal sunlight…
1922 *The Enormous Room*, ch.13, closing words.

2 spring
when the world is puddle wonderful
1923 *Tulips and Chimneys*, 'Chanson Innocente'.

3 the Cambridge ladies who live in furnished souls
are unbeautiful and have comfortable minds
1923 *Tulips and Chimneys*, 'Sonnets-Realities', no.1.

4 Buffalo Bill's
defunct
—who used to
—ride a watersmooth-silver
——stallion
and break onetwothreefourfive pigeonsjustlikethat
1923 *Tulips and Chimneys*, 'Portraits', no.8.

5 Humanity i love you because you
are perpetually putting the secret of
life in your pants and forgetting
it's there and sitting down
on it.
1925 *XLI Poems*, no.2, 'La Guerre'.

6 who knows if the moon's
a balloon, coming out of a keen city
in the sky—filled with pretty people?
1925 'Seven Poems, VII'. David Niven used the phrase for his autobiography, *The Moon's a Balloon* (1975).

7 If a poet is anybody, he is somebody to whom things made matter very little—somebody who is obsessed by Making.
1926 *is 5*, foreword.

8 'next to of course god america i
love you land of the pilgrims' and so forth oh
say can you see by the dawn's early my
country 'tis of centuries come and go
and are no more what of it we should worry
in every language even deafanddumb
they sons acclaim you glorious name by gorry
by jingo by gee by gosh by gum
1926 *is 5*, 'Two, III'.

9 why talk of beauty what could be more beautiful than these heroic happy dead
who rushed like lions to the roaring slaughter
they did not stop to think they died instead
then shall the voices of liberty be mute?

He spoke. And drank rapidly a glass of water.
1926 *is 5*, 'Two, III'.

10 America makes prodigious mistakes, America has

colossal faults, but one thing cannot be denied: America is always on the move. She may be going to Hell, of course, but at least she isn't standing still.
1927 'Why I Like America', in *Vanity Fair*, May.

11 nobody, not even the rain, has such small hands
1931 *w*, 'somewhere I have never travelled'.

12 unless statistics lie he was
more brave than me: more blond than you
1931 *w*, 'i sing of Olaf glad and big'.

13 What about the world, Mr Cummings?
I live in so many: which one do you mean?
1934 Introduction to revised edition of *The Enormous Room*.

14 my father moved through dooms of love
through sames of am through haves of give,
singing each morning out of each night
my father moved through depths of height
1940 *50 poems*, 'my father moved through dooms of love'.

15 because my father lived his soul
love is the whole and more than all
1940 *50 poems*, 'my father moved through dooms of love'.

16 a politician is an arse upon
which everyone has sat except a man
1944 *1x1*, no.10.

17 pity this busy monster, manunkind,
not. Progress is a comfortable disease.
1944 *1x1*, no.14.

18 We doctors know
a hopeless case if—listen: there's a hell
of a good universe next door; let's go
1944 *1x1*, no.14.

19 anyone lived in a pretty how town
(with up so floating many bells down)
spring summer autumn winter
he sang his didn't he danced his did
1949 *50 poems*, no.29.

20 Knowledge is a polite word for dead but not buried imagination.
1951 'Jottings', in *Wake*, no.10.

21 for whatever we lose (like a you or a me)
it's always ourselves we find in the sea
'maggie and milly and molly and may'.

22 Humane, but not human.
On Ezra Pound. Recalled on Cummings's death, 3 Sep 1962.

23 A draftsman of words.
Self-description. Quoted in the *New York Times*, 30 Oct 1963.

Cunningham, Allan 1784–1842

Scottish poet, friend and acquaintance of James Hogg and Walter Scott.

24 A wet sheet and a flowing sea,
A wind that follows fast,
And fills the white and rustling sail,
And bends the gallant mast
1825 'A Wet Sheet and a Flowing Sea', stanza 1.

25 Wha the deil hae we got for a King,
But a wee, wee German lairdie!
1847 *Poems and Songs*, 'The Wee, Wee German Lairdie', stanza 1.

Cunningham, Roseanna 1951–

Scottish advocate and politician. She was an MP (1995–2001)

before becoming an MSP in 1999 and Deputy Leader of the Scottish National Party in 2000.

26 Until a woman is free to be as incompetent as the average male then she will never be completely equal.
1995 By-election campaign speech, May.

Cuomo, Mario Matthew 1932–

US lawyer and Democratic politician, Governor of New York (1983–95).

27 We propose it, we massage it, and we often have to ram it.
1988 Of legislation. In the *US News and World Report*, 25 Jan.

28 If there's a plastic surgeon who claims to be responsible for this face, then New York State will decertify him immediately.
1991 On reports that he had undergone plastic surgery. In *Newsweek*, 11 Nov.

29 President Bush…seems to think that the ship [of state] will be saved by imperceptible undercurrents, directed by the invisible hand of some cyclical economic god, that will gradually move the ship so that at the last moment it will miraculously glide past the rocks to safer shores.
1992 Address nominating Bill Clinton as Democratic presidential candidate, 15 Jul.

30 It is as if Homer not only chronicled the siege of Troy, but conducted the siege as well. As if Shakespeare set his play writing aside to lead the English against the Armada.
1992 Tribute to Lincoln's literary and political genius. In the *New York Times*, 18 Nov.

31 Commitment seems to live more in the poetry of our aspirations than in the prose of the realities we have created.
1992 In the *New York Times*, 18 Nov.

32 Ever since the Republican landslide on Nov 8, it's been getting dark outside a little earlier every day. You notice that?
1994 In the *New York Times*, 17 Dec.

33 Dog eat dog produces, inevitably, just one dog.
1994 In the *New York Times*, 31 Dec.

Cupitt, Rev Don 1934–

English radical theologian, Dean of Emmanuel College, Cambridge (1966–91).

34 A belief is made religious, not so much by its content, as rather by the way it is held.
1984 *The Sea of Faith*.

35 It is hardest of all to give up the last slivers and shreds of objectivity, but only by doing so can faith finally free itself from all that is outworn and become as fully voluntary, creative and courageous as it is required to be today.
1984 *The Sea of Faith*.

Curie, Marie originally *Marya Sklodowska* 1867–1934

Polish-born French chemist, who shared a 1903 Nobel prize with her husband Pierre and with Henri Becquerel for research on radioactivity. In 1911 she again won the Nobel prize for the discovery of radium and polonium.

36 In science, we must be interested in things, not in persons.
Quoted in Eve Curie *Madame Curie* (1937), ch.16 (translated by Vincent Sheean, 1943).

Curnow, (Thomas) Allen Munro 1911–2001

New Zealand poet and critic, whose works focus on his country's past and its quest for national identity.

37 Fluent in all the languages dead or living,
the sun comes up with a word of worlds all spinning
in a world of words.
1979 *An Incorrigible Music*, 'A Balanced Bait in Handy Pellet Form'.

Curran, Charles

US journalist.

38 One of nature's Balkans.
Of his friend and fellow journalist, Rebecca West. Quoted by V S Pritchett in the *New Yorker*, 21 Dec 1987.

39 [She] has several skins fewer than any other human being…a kind of psychological haemophilia, which is one reason why she writes so well, and why she is so vulnerable.
Of his friend and fellow journalist, Rebecca West. Quoted by V S Pritchett in the *New Yorker*, 21 Dec 1987.

Curran, John Philpot 1750–1817

Irish judge and orator, called to the Irish bar in 1775. He entered Parliament in 1783, and although a staunch Protestant strongly opposed the Union.

40 But as in wailing there's nought availing,
And Death unfailing will strike the blow,
Then for that reason, and for a season,
Let us be merry before we go.
?1773 'Let Us Be Merry Before We Go'.

41 The condition upon which God hath given liberty to man is eternal vigilance; which condition if he break, servitude is at once the consequence of his crime, and the punishment of his guilt.
1790 Speech, Dublin, 10 Jul.

42 Like the silver plate on a coffin.
Of Sir Robert Peel's smile. Quoted by Daniel O'Connell in the House of Commons, 26 Feb 1835.

Currie, Edwina 1946–

English Conservative politician and novelist. She was appointed Health Minister (1986–8), and attracted notoriety for her outspoken comments on various health issues.

43 My message to the businessmen of this country when they go abroad on business is that there is one good thing above all they can take with them to stop them catching AIDS—and that is the wife.
1987 Speech as Health Minister, 12 Feb.

44 The strongest possible piece of advice that I could give to any young woman is: Don't screw around and don't smoke.
1988 In the *Observer*, 3 Apr.

45 Most of the egg production in this country, sadly, is now infected with salmonella.
1988 Radio interview as junior Health Minister, 3 Dec, which outraged both the domestic poultry industry and those of her own back-benchers who represented agricultural constituencies, forcing her resignation two weeks later.

Curtis, Charles P

46 Literature is a power line and the motor, mark you, is the reader.
1957 *A Commonplace Book*.

Curtis, Lionel 1872–1955

British writer on international affairs.

47 In private conversation he tries on speeches like a man trying on ties in his bedroom, to see how he would look in them.
1912 Of Winston Churchill. Letter to Nancy Astor.

Curtis, Richard Whalley Anthony 1956–

British writer for film and television, best known for the TV series *Not the Nine O'Clock News* (1979–83) and *Blackadder* (1984–9), and for films including *Four Weddings and a Funeral* (1994), *Notting Hill* (1999) and *Love Actually* (2003).

48 Whatever your script is like, no matter how much stewing and rewriting—if the punters don't want to sleep with the star, you may never be asked to write another one.
1994 Introduction to the published script of *Four Weddings and a Funeral*.

Curtis, Tony *pseudonym of* Bernie Schwartz 1925–

US film actor.

49 Like kissing Hitler.
Of working with Marilyn Monroe on *Some Like It Hot*. Attributed.

Curtiz, Michael *originally* Mihaly Kertesz 1888–1962

Hungarian-born film director.

50 Bring on the empty horses!
1936 Instructions during the filming of *The Charge of the Light Brigade*, subsequently used by David Niven for the title of one of his books. Curtiz's less-than-perfect English was renowned for producing such felicitous phrases.

Curzon (of Kedleston), Lord George Nathaniel 1859–1925

English statesman. As Viceroy of India from 1898 he introduced many social and political reforms and partitioned Bengal. He resigned after a disagreement with Kitchener (1905), but returned to politics as Lord Privy Seal (1915) and Foreign Secretary (1919–24).

51 It is only when you get to see and realize what India is—that she is the strength and the greatness of England—that you feel that every nerve a man may strain, every energy he may put forward, cannot be devoted to a nobler purpose than keeping tight the cords that hold India to ourselves.
1893 Speech at Southport, 15 May.

52 I hesitate to say what the functions of the modern journalist may be, but I imagine that they do not exclude the intelligent anticipation of the facts even before they occur.
1898 House of Commons, 29 Mar.

53 To fight for the right, to abhor the imperfect, the unjust, or the mean, to swerve neither to the right hand nor the left, to care nothing for flattery or applause or odium or abuse—it is so easy to have any of them in India—never to let your enthusiasm be soured or your courage grow dim but to remember that the Almighty has placed your hand on the greatest of his ploughs, in whose furrow the nations of the future are germinating and taking shape, to drive the blade a little forward in your time and to feel that somewhere among those millions you have left, a little justice, or happiness or prosperity, a sense of manliness or moral dignity, a spring of patriotism, a dawn of intellectual enlightenment or a stirring of duty where it did not exist before—that is enough, that is the Englishman's justification in India.

1906 Farewell speech on departing from Bombay as Viceroy of India.

54 I never knew that the lower classes had such white skins.

c.1915 Remark made during a visit of front-line British troops in World War I, after observing some of them bathing in old beer barrels.

55 Gentlemen do not take soup at luncheon.

Attributed. Quoted in E L Woodward *Short Journey* (1942), ch.7.

St Cyprian *full name* Thascius Caecilius Cyprianus
c.200–258 AD

Christian martyr and Father of the Church. Probably born in Carthage, he became a bishop and theologian. He was excommmunicated for his views on baptism and beheaded in Valerian's reign.

56 *Habere non potest Deum patrem qui ecclesiam non habet matrem.*
He cannot have God for his father who has not the church for his mother.
AD **251** *De Ecclesiae Catholicae Unitate*, ch 6.

57 *Salus extra ecclesiam non est.*
There is no salvation outside the church.
AD **256** *Letters*, no.73.

Cyrano de Bergerac, Savinien de 1619–55

French poet and soldier, famous as a duellist. He was a student of Gassendi, who influenced him in the philosophy of free-thinking.

58 *Peut-on être innocent, lorsqu'on aime un coupable?*
Can one be innocent when one loves a guilty person?
1653 *La Mort d'Agrippine*, act 5, sc.5.

59 *Un Philosophe doit juger le vulgaire, et non pas juger comme le vulgaire.*
A philosopher should judge the masses and should not judge like the masses.
1654 *Lettres diverses*, *Contre les sorciers* (later published as *Voyage dans la lune*).

60 *Non, non, si ce Dieu visible éclaire l'homme, c'est par accident, comme le flambeau du roi éclaire par accident au crocheteur qui passe par la rue.*
No, no, if this manifest God enlightens men, it is purely by accident, just as the king's torch throws its light upon a labourer who passes him in the street.
1656 *L'Autre Monde; ou, Les Estats et empires de la lune* (later published as *Voyage dans la lune*).

d

Daché, Lilly 1904–89

French-born US milliner. Her autobiography, *Talking Through My Hats*, was published in 1946.

61 Glamour is what makes a man ask for your telephone number. But it also is what makes a woman ask for the name of your dressmaker.
1955 'Lilly Daché's Secrets of Lifelong Glamour Book', in *Woman's Home Companion*, vol.82, Jul.

Dafoe, John W 1866–1944

Canadian publisher and editor.

62 A journalist is hardly an authority upon anything—unless perhaps upon the appraisal of the drift of public opinion.
1923 Convocation address at the University of Manitoba, Winnipeg, May. Quoted in Murray Donnelly *Dafoe of the Free Press* (1968).

63 There are only two kinds of government, the scarcely tolerable and the absolutely unbearable.
Characteristic remark, quoted in Murray Donnelly *Dafoe of the Free Press* (1968).

Daily Express

British tabloid newspaper.

64 Britain will not be involved in a European war this year, or next year either.
1938 Headline, 30 Sep. The newspaper used similar phrases frequently, up to 11 Aug 1939, three weeks before the outbreak of World War II.

Daily Mail

British tabloid newspaper.

65 Nobel Prize for British Wife.
1964 Headline announcing that the Nobel prize for chemistry had been awarded to Professor Dorothy Hodgkin.

Daily Mirror

British tabloid newspaper.

66 Whose finger do you want on the trigger?
1951 Headline, 21 Sep, referring to the atom bomb.

Dalai Lama *originally* Tenzin Gyatso 1935–

Spiritual and temporal leader of Tibet since 1940. He negotiated an autonomy agreement for Tibet with the Chinese in 1951 but went into exile after the suppressed nationalist uprising in 1959. Now living in India, he continues to move for Tibetan independence. He was awarded the Nobel peace prize in 1989.

67 Frankly speaking, it is difficult to trust the Chinese. Once bitten by a snake, you feel suspicious even when you see a piece of rope.
1981 Quoted in the *Observer Colour Magazine*, 5 Apr.

Dalglish, Kenny 1951–

Scottish footballer and manager. As manager of Liverpool, he won the League and Cup double in 1986.

68 The saddest and most beautiful sight I have ever seen.
> **1989** Of the display of flowers and club scarfs that were piled on Liverpool's Anfield pitch in memory of those who died in the Hillsborough football disaster. Quoted in Peter Ball and Phil Shaw *The Book of Football Quotations* (1989).

Dalí, Salvador 1904–89

Spanish painter, graphic artist and sculptor, the most flamboyant of the Surrealist artists. His work draws on the symbolism of dreams and, later, religion.

69 At the age of six I wanted to be a cook. At seven I wanted to be Napoleon. And my ambition has been growing steadily ever since.
> **1942** *The Secret Life of Salvador Dalí*, prologue.

70 I do not paint a portrait to look like the subject, rather does the person grow to look like his portrait.
> Quoted in Esar *A Treasury of Humorous Quotations* (1951).

71 The first man to compare the cheeks of a young woman to a rose was obviously a poet; the first to repeat it was possibly an idiot.
> **1968** *Dialogues with Marcel Duchamp*, preface.

72 The famous soft watches are nothing else than the tender, extravagant, solitary, paranoic-critical camembert of time and space.
> **1969** *Conquest of the Irrational*.

73 Every good painter who aspires to the creation of genuine masterpieces should first of all marry my wife.
> Quoted in Saranne Alexandrian *Surrealist Art* (1970).

74 *Le surréalisme, c'est moi.*
> I am surrealism.
> Quoted in Saranne Alexandrian *Surrealist Art* (1970), ch.5.
> ➤ *See Louis XIV 518:93.*

Dallek, Robert 1934–

US historian, Professor at the University of California, Los Angeles.

75 What makes war interesting for Americans is that we don't fight war on our soil, we don't have direct experience of it, so there's an openness about the meanings we give it.
> **1991** In the *New York Times*, 24 Feb.

Daly, Daniel 1874–1937

US gunnery sergeant in World War I.

76 Come on you sons of bitches! Do you want to live forever?
> **1918** Attributed, to his troops at Belleau Wood, 4 Jun.
> ➤ *See Frederick the Great 335:33.*

Daly, John 1966–

US golfer.

77 I spent $3m on drink and $3m on gambling, but I wasted the rest.
> **2000** On spending his winnings. Quoted in *The Independent*, 23 Dec.

Daly, Mary 1928–

US feminist theorist and theologian. She advocates a feminist

spirituality in *Beyond God the Father* (1973) and *Gyn/Ecology: the Metaethics of Radical Feminism* (1978).

78 Mister-ectomy n.: guaranteed solution to The Contraceptive Problem, tried and true and therefore taboo birth control method, recommended by Gyn/Ecologists, insisted upon by spinsters.
> **1987** *Webster's First New Intergalactic Wickedary of the English Language* (with Jane Caputi), Word Web 2.

St Peter Damian *or* **Pietro Damiani** 1007–72

Italian cleric and saint. A swineherd in his youth, he rose to become Bishop of Ostia and a Cardinal. He was active in attempts to reform the clergy in order to correct immorality.

79 *Sanctum Satanum meum.*
> My holy Satan.
> **c.1070** Of Hildebrand, later Pope Gregory VII. Letter to Pope Alexander II and Cardinal Archdeacon Hildebrand.

Damrosch, Walter Johannes 1862–1950

German-born US conductor and composer. Having established a reputation as a conductor of Wagner, he became a champion of works by contemporary composers.

80 If a young man at the age of twenty-three can write a symphony like that, in five years he will be ready to commit murder.
> **1925** After conducting Aaron Copland's *Symphony for Organ and Orchestra*. Quoted in Machlis *Introduction to Contemporary Music* (1963).

Dana, Charles Anderson 1819–97

US newspaper editor. From 1848 to 1862 he edited the New York *Tribune*. From 1863 to the end of the Civil War he was Assistant-Secretary of War. In 1867 he purchased the New York *Sun*.

81 I have always felt that whatever Divine Providence permitted to occur I was not too proud to report.
> **1888** *The Art of Newspaper Making*, 'The Modern American Newspaper'.

82 Get the news, get all the news, and nothing but the news.
> **1888** *The Art of Newspaper Making*, 'The Modern American Newspaper'.

83 The invariable law of the newspaper is to be interesting.
> **1888** *The Art of Newspaper Making*, 'The Making of a Newspaper Man'.

Danforth, John Claggett 1936–

US lawyer and politician, Senator of Missouri (1976–95).

84 It has locked candidates into ridiculous positions because only ridiculous positions can be compacted into 30-second commercials.
> **1990** Of television in politics. In the *New York Times*, 18 Mar.

Dangarembga, Tsitsi 1959–

Zimbabwean writer. Her novel *Nervous Conditions* (1988) portrays the effect of white values on black African society, especially women.

85 This business of womanhood is a heavy burden… And these days it is worse, with the poverty of blackness on one side and the weight of womanhood on the other.
> **1988** *Nervous Conditions*, ch.1.

Dangerfield, George

86 Ireland is one of the few countries—perhaps the last—where the boundaries between politics and art have never been fixed.
1935 *The Strange Death of Liberal England.*

Daniel, Samuel 1562–1619

English poet and dramatist. A private tutor and courtier, he wrote masques, plays and epistles. His poetic works include the sonnet sequence *Delia* (1592) and the epic *Civil Wars Between the Two Houses of Lancaster and York* (1594–1609).

87 I that have loved thee thus before thou fadest,
My faith shall wax, when thou art in thy waning.
The world shall find this miracle in me,
That fire can burn when all the matter's spent.
1592 *Delia*, sonnet 33.

88 Care-charmer Sleep, son of the sable Night,
Brother to Death, in silent darkness born,
Relieve my languish and restore the light;
With dark forgetting of my care return.
And let the day be time enough to mourn
The shipwreck of my ill adventured youth:
Let waking eyes suffice to wail their scorn
Without the torment of the night's untruth.
1592 *Delia*, sonnet 54.

89 O thou whom envy ev'n is force t'admire!
1594 'To the Right Honourable, the Lady Mary, Countess of Pembroke'. Daniel was part of the group of writers who met at Wilton, which also included Jonson and Drayton, and he tutored Pembroke's son.

90 Unless above himself he can
Erect himself, how poor a thing is man!
1594 'To the Lady Margaret, Countess of Cumberland'.

91 Custom that is before all law, Nature that is above all art.
1603 *A Defence of Rhyme.*

92 But years hath done this wrong,
To make me write too much, and live too long.
1605 *Philotas*, 'To the Prince', dedication.

Dante Alighieri *originally* **Durante** 1265–1321

Italian poet and scholar, author of *The Divine Comedy* (a poet's journey through hell, purgatory and paradise, begun c.1307). A White Guelf, he was exiled from his native Florence when the Black Guelfs triumphed in 1309. He died in Ravenna.

93 *Nel mezzo del cammin di nostra vita*
mi ritrovai per una selva oscura
ché la diritta via era smarrita.
In the middle of the journey of our life
I found myself in a dark wood
where the straight path was lost.
c.1320 *Divina Commedia*, 'Inferno', canto 1, l.1–3.

94 *Lasciate ogni speranza voi ch'entrate.*
Abandon all hope ye who enter here.
c.1320 Inscription above the gates of Hell. *Divina Commedia*, 'Inferno', canto 3, l.9.

95 *Nessun maggior dolore,*
Che ricordarsi del tempo felice
Nella miseria.
There is no greater pain than to remember a happy time when one is in misery.
c.1320 *Divina Commedia*, 'Inferno', canto 5, l.121–3.

96 *E quindi uscimmo a riveder le stelle.*
Thence we came forth to see the stars again.
c.1320 *Divina Commedia*, 'Inferno', canto 34, l.139.

97 *Lì si vedrà la superbia ch'asseta,*
che fa lo Scotto e l'Inghilese folle,
sì che non può soffrir dentro a sua meta.
There shall you see the pride which causes thirst,
which makes the Scots and the English mad,
so that they cannot remain within their boundaries.
c.1320 *Divina Commedia*, 'Paradiso', canto 1, l.121–3.

98 *E'n la sua voluntade è nostra pace.*
In His will is our peace.
c.1320 *Divina Commedia*, 'Paradiso', canto 3, l.85.

99 *L'amor che move il sole e l'altre stelle.*
The love that moves the sun and the other stars.
c.1320 *Divina Commedia*, 'Paradiso', canto 33, l.145.

Danton, Georges Jacques 1759–94

French revolutionary leader. As Minister of Justice (1792) he voted for the king's death. He tried to moderate the severity of the Revolutionary Tribunal, but lost the leadership to Robespierre and was executed for conspiracy.

1 *De l'audace, et encore de l'audace, et toujours de l'audace!*
Boldness, and again boldness, and always boldness!
1792 Speech to the Legislative Committee of General Defence, 2 Sep.

Darío, Rubén *pseudonym of* **Félix Rubén García Sarmiento** 1867–1916

Nicaraguan poet, journalist and diplomat. From 1886 he travelled extensively throughout Latin America and Europe. A key figure of Spanish-American Modernism, he experimented with rhythm, metre and imagery.

2 *Si hay poesía en nuestra América, ella está en las cosas viejas: en Palenke y Uatlán, en el indio legendario y el inca sensual y fino y en el gran Moctezuma de la silla de oro. Lo demás es tuyo, demócrata Walt Whitman.*
If there is poetry in our America, it is in ancient items: in Palenke and Uatlán, in the legendary Indian and in the sensuous and elegant Inca and the great Moctezuma. The rest is yours, democratic Walt Whitman.
1896 *Prosas profanas*, 'Palabras liminares'.

3 *Yo persigo una forma que no encuentra mi estilo,*
botón de pensamiento que busca ser la rosa;
se anuncia con un beso que en mis labios se posa
al abrazo imposible de la Venus de Milo.
I seek a form that my style cannot discover,
a bud of thought that wants to be a rose;
it is heralded by a kiss that is placed on my lips
in the impossible embrace of the Venus de Milo.
1896 *Prosas profanas*, 'Yo persigo una forma…' (translated as 'I seek a form…', 1922).

4 *Dichoso el árbol que es apenas sensitivo,*
y más la piedra dura porque ésa ya no siente,
pues no hay dolor más grande que el dolor de ser vivo,
ni mayor pesadumbre que la vida consciente.
Blessed is the almost insensitive tree,
more blessed is the hard stone that doesn't feel,
for no pain is greater than the pain of being alive,
and no sorrow more intense than conscious life.
1901 *Cantos de vida y esperanza*, 'Lo fatal' ('Fatalism').

Dark, Eleanor *née O'Reilly pseudonym Patricia O'Rane*
1901–85

Australian novelist and poet. Her works include the historical trilogy *The Timeless Land* (1941), *Storm of Time* (1948) and *No Barrier* (1953).

5 Silence ruled this land. Out of silence mystery comes, and magic, and the delicate awareness of unreasoning things.
1941 *The Timeless Land*, pt.1, '1788'.

Darman, Richard G(ordon) 1943–

US government official and businessman, Director of the Office of Management and the Budget in President Bush's Cabinet (1988–93).

6 I am now celebrating the 20th anniversary of the first request for my resignation. I look forward to many more.
Address to the White House press room. Quoted in Brian Kelly *Adventures in Porkland* (1992).

Darnell, Bill c.1940–

Canadian ecologist and activist, one of the original founders of the Greenpeace Foundation in Vancouver, British Columbia.

7 Make it a *green* peace.
1970 Quoted in Robert Hunter *Warriors of the Rainbow* (1979).

Darrow, Clarence Seward 1857–1938

US lawyer. He undertook the defence of John T Scopes (1925) for the teaching of Darwinism in school.

8 I do not consider it an insult but rather a compliment to be called an agnostic. I do not pretend to know where many ignorant men are sure—that is all that agnosticism means.
1925 Speech in defence of John T Scopes, 15 Jul.

Darwin, Charles Robert 1809–82

English naturalist. He joined the HMS *Beagle* scientific survey (1831–6) to South America and Australasia, which led eventually to his theory of evolution and the publication of many scientific works, including *The Origin of Species by Means of Natural Selection* (1859).

9 The naturalist in England, in his walks, enjoys a great advantage over others in frequently meeting with something worthy of attention; here he suffers a pleasant nuisance in not being able to walk a hundred yards without being fairly tied to the spot by some new and wondrous creature.
1832 In Brazil. *Journey of Researches into the Geology and Natural History of the Various Countries Visited during the Voyage of HMS 'Beagle' Round the World* (published 1839).

10 I have called this principle, by which each slight variation, if useful, is preserved, by the term of Natural Selection, in order to mark its relation to man's power of selection.
1859 *The Origin of Species by Means of Natural Selection*, ch.3.

11 From the war of nature, from famine and death, the most exalted object which we are capable of conceiving, namely, the production of the higher animals, directly follows. There is grandeur in this view of life.
1859 *The Origin of Species by Means of Natural Selection*, ch.14.

12 Great is the power of steady misrepresentation—but the history of science shows how, fortunately, this power does not long endure.
1859 *The Origin of Species by Means of Natural Selection*.

13 I have tried lately to read Shakespeare, and found it so intolerably dull that it nauseated me.
1860 *The Life and Letters of Charles Darwin*, vol.1.

14 False facts are highly injurious to the progress of science, for they often long endure; but false views, if supported by some evidence, do little harm, as every one takes a salutary pleasure in proving their falseness.
1871 *The Descent of Man and Selection in Relation to Sex*, ch.13.

15 The chief distinction in the intellectual powers of the two sexes is shewn by man's attaining to a higher eminence in whatever he takes up, than can woman—whether requiring deep thought, reason, or imagination, or merely the use of the senses and hands.
1871 *The Descent of Man and Selection in Relation to Sex*, ch.19.

16 We must however acknowledge, as it seems to me, that man with all his noble qualities…still bears in his bodily frame the indelible stamp of his lowly origin.
1871 *The Descent of Man and Selection in Relation to Sex*, ch.21.

17 I must begin with a good body of facts and not from a principle (in which I always suspect some fallacy) and then as much deduction as you please.
1874 Letter to J Fiske, 8 Dec.

18 A mathematician is a blind man in a dark room looking for a black cat which isn't there.
Quoted in John D Barrow *Pie in the Sky, Counting, Thinking and Being* (1992).

Darwin, Sir Francis 1848–1925

English botanist, son of Charles Darwin. He became a Reader in Botany at Oxford (1888) and produced his father's *Life and Letters* (1887–1903).

19 In science the credit goes to the man who convinces the world, not to the man to whom the idea first occurs.
1914 'Francis Galton', in *Eugenics Review*, vol.6, issue 1, Apr.

Daugherty, Harry Micajah 1860–1941

US politician, manager of Warren G Harding's political career from 1902. He was tried and acquitted (1927) on fraud charges.

20 A group of senators, bleary eyed for lack of sleep, will have to sit down at about two o'clock in the morning around a table in a smoke-filled room in some hotel, and decide the nomination.
1920 On the Republicans' failure to choose a presidential candidate at their convention.

David, Hal 1921–

US lyricist. He frequently worked with Burt Bacharach. His lyrics include *What the World Needs Now Is Love* and *Do You Know the Way to San Jose*.

21 Raindrops Keep Fallin' on My Head.
1969 Title of song. (Music by Burt Bacharach.)

Davidson, John 1857–1909

Scottish poet and writer. He moved to London in 1885, publishing *Fleet Street Eclogues* (1893) and *Ballads and Songs* (1894). He committed suicide by drowning himself at Penzance.

22 The difficultest job a man can do,

is to come it brave and meek with thirty bob a week,
and feel that that's the proper thing for you.
1894 *Ballads and Songs*, 'Thirty Bob a Week', stanza 15.

23 It's naked child against hungry wolf;
it's playing bowls upon a splitting wreck;
it's walking on a string across a gulf
with millstones fore-and-aft about your neck;
but the thing is daily done by many and many a one;
and we fall, face forward, fighting, on the deck.
1894 *Ballads and Songs*, 'Thirty Bob a Week', stanza 16.

24 In anguish we uplift
A new unhallowed song:
The race is to the swift,
The battle to the strong.
1899 'War Song', stanza 1.
➤ See *Bible 101:85*.

25 And blood in torrents pour
In vain—always in vain,
For war breeds war again.
1899 'War Song', stanza 7.

26 When the pods went pop on the broom, green broom,
And apples began to be golden-skinned,
We harboured a stag in the Priory coomb.
1906 *Holiday and Other Poems*, 'A Runnable Stag', stanza 1.

27 A stag of warrant, a stag, a stag,
A runnable stag, a kingly crop,
Brow, bay and tray and three on top,
A stag, a runnable stag.
1906 *Holiday and Other Poems*, 'A Runnable Stag', stanza 1.

Davie, George Elder   1912–

Scottish philosopher, a pioneer in studies of the Scottish Enlightenment.

28 The Democratic Intellect.
1961 Title of book.

Davies, (Sarah) Emily   1830–1921

English feminist and educational reformer who campaigned vigorously for equal opportunities for women in education.

29 If neither governesses or mothers *know*, how can they teach? So long as education is not provided *for* them, how can it be provided *by* them?
1868 Paper read at the Annual Meeting of the National Association for the Promotion of Social Sciences, published in *Thoughts on Some Questions Relating to Women 1860–1908*.

30 We have persuaded ourselves that Englishmen of the present day are such a nervously excitable race, that the only chance for their descendants is to keep the mothers in a state of coma. The fathers, we think are incurable.
1868 Paper read at the Annual Meeting of the National Association for the Promotion of Social Sciences, published in *Thoughts on Some Questions Relating to Women 1860–1908*.

Davies, Sir John   1569–1626

English poet and civil servant. He held high office in Ireland where he supported severe repressive measures and was nominated Chief Justice (1626). His poems include *Orchestra, or a Poem of Dancing* (1596) and *Hymns to Astrea* (1599).

31 Dancing is a frenzy and a rage.
1596 *Orchestra, or a Poem of Dancing*, stanza 16.

32 This wondrous miracle did Love devise,

For dancing is love's proper exercise.
1596 *Orchestra, or a Poem of Dancing*, stanza 18.

33 Learn then to dance, you that are princes born,
And lawful lords of earthly creatures all;
Imitate them, and thereof take no scorn,
(For this new art to them is natural)
And imitate the stars celestial.
For when pale death your vital twist shall sever,
Your better parts must dance with them forever.
1596 *Orchestra, or a Poem of Dancing*, stanza 60.

34 Skill comes so slow, and life so fast doth fly,
We learn so little and forget so much.
1599 *Nosce Teipsum*, stanza 19.

35 I know my life's a pain and but a span,
I know my sense is mocked in every thing;
And to conclude, I know myself a man,
Which is a proud and yet a wretched thing.
1599 *Nosce Teipsum*, stanza 45.

36 Wedlock, indeed, hath oft compared been
To public feasts where meet a public rout,
Where they that are without would fain go in
And they that are within would fain go out.
1608 'A Contention Betwixt a Wife, a Widow, and a Maid for Precedence', l.193–6.

Davies, Nigel   1960–

English chess player.

37 One very important aspect of actually achieving something is, I believe, the ability to avoid making excuses, in all their guises.
Quoted on www.chessville.com.

Davies, Ray(mond Douglas)   1944–

British songwriter and rock musician, founder of The Kinks (1963). His lyrics are noted for their lightly satirical commentary.

38 One week he's in polka-dots, the next week he's in stripes
'Cos he's a dedicated follower of fashion.
1966 'Dedicated Follower of Fashion'.

Davies, Robertson   1913–95

Canadian novelist, playwright, critic and essayist. After the Deptford trilogy (1970–5) he wrote another trilogy, including *What's Bred in the Bone* (1985), shortlisted for the Booker Prize.

39 There is more to marriage than four bare legs under a blanket.
1957 *Love and Libel*.

40 'Mary, what made you do it?'
She looked him honestly in the face and gave the answer that became famous in Deptford: 'He was very civil, 'Masa. And he wanted it so badly.'
1970 Mrs. Dempster explains to her parson husband why she had sex with a tramp. *Fifth Business*, pt.1, ch.10.

41 I saw corpses, and grew used to their unimportant look, for a dead man without any of the panoply of death is a desperately insignificant object.
1970 Of World War I. *Fifth Business*, pt.2, ch.1.

42 When a man is down on his luck he seems to consume all

he can get of coffee and doughnuts.
1970 *Fifth Business*, pt.4, ch.1.

43 He was killed by the usual cabal: by himself, first of all; by the woman he knew; by the woman he did not know; by the man who granted his inmost wish; and by the inevitable fifth, who was keeper of his conscience and keeper of the stone.
1970 *Fifth Business*, pt.6, ch.8.

44 Canada is not really a place where you are encouraged to have large spiritual adventures.
1972 Interviewed by Peter C Newman, 'The Master's Voice', in *Maclean's*, Sep.

45 The ideal companion in bed is a good book.
Interviewed by Terence M Green, recorded in J Madison Davis (ed) *Conversations with Robertson Davies* (1989).

Davies, Ron(ald) 1946–

Welsh Labour politician, Secretary of State for Wales (1997–8).

46 It was a moment of madness for which I have subsequently paid a very, very heavy price.
1998 Talking about the episode on Clapham common which led to his resignation as Welsh Secretary. Television interview, 30 Oct.

Davies, W(illiam) H(enry) 1871–1940

Welsh poet, who emigrated to the US at the age of 22. He lost a leg there while jumping a train and returned to England, where he lived as a tramp until his poetry found a public. He also wrote novels and autobiographical works.

47 It was the Rainbow gave thee birth,
And left thee all her lovely hues.
1910 'The Kingfisher'.

48 What is this life if, full of care,
We have no time to stand and stare?
1911 'Leisure'.

49 A rainbow and a cuckoo's song
May never come together again;
May never come
This side the tomb.
1914 'A Great Time'.

50 And hear the pleasant cuckoo, loud and long—
The simple bird that thinks two notes a song.
1916 'April's Charms'.

da Vinci, Leonardo

▸ *See* Leonardo da Vinci

Davis, Adelle 1904–74

US nutritionist.

51 People in nutrition do get the idea that they are going to live to be 150. And they never do.
1973 Quoted in Daniel Yergin's 'Supernutritionist', *New York Times* magazine, 20 May.

Davis, Bette *originally* *Ruth Elizabeth Davis* 1908–89

US film actress. She made her screen debut in 1931 and in the late 1930s and 1940s starred in a string of romantic melodramas such as *The Old Maid* (1939) and *Now Voyager* (1942).

52 Mother of three; divorcee; American. Twenty years experience as an actress in motion pictures. Mobile still

and more affable than rumour would have it. Wants steady employment in Hollywood. (Has had Broadway). References upon request.
1962 Advertisement placed in the Hollywood trade papers.

53 Evil people…you never forget them. And that's the aim of any actress—never to be forgotten.
1966 On her favourite character roles. In the New York State Theater programme, Jun.

54 The best time I ever had with Joan Crawford was when I pushed her down the stairs in *Whatever Happened to Baby Jane?*
Quoted in Doug McClelland *Star Speak* (1987).

55 I have eyes like a bullfrog, a neck like an ostrich and long, limp hair. You just have to be good to survive with that equipment.
Attributed.

56 She's the original good time who was had by all.
On an anonymous starlet. Attributed.

Davis, Jefferson 1808–89

US statesman. He led the Senate's extreme State Rights Party, supported slavery, and was President of the rebel Confederate States during the Civil War (1861–5). Later imprisoned, he was never brought to trial.

57 All we ask is to be let alone.
1861 Inaugural address, 18 Feb.

Davis, Miles Dewey, III 1926–91

US jazz trumpeter and composer. A leading figure in postwar jazz, he also won wide acceptance with rock audiences in the 1970s and 1980s.

58 An artist's first responsibility is to himself.
1961 *Ebony*, Jan.

59 You could be a great musician, an innovative and important artist, but nobody cared if you didn't make the white people who were in control some money.
1989 *Autobiography*, ch.10.

Davis, Sammy, Jnr 1925–90

US jazz musician, actor, dancer and comedian.

60 Being a star has made it possible for me to get insulted in places where the average Negro could never hope to go and get insulted.
1965 *Yes I Can*, pt.3, ch.23.

Davis, Steve 1957–

English snooker player. He won the world championships six times.

61 Billiards is very similar to snooker, except there are only three balls and no one watches it.
1988 Quoted in Colin Jarman *The Guinness Dictionary of Sports Quotations* (1990).

Davis, Stuart 1894–1964

US Cubist painter.

62 An artist who has travelled on a steam train, driven an automobile, or flown in an airplane doesn't feel the same way about form and space as one who has not.
1940 'Is There a Revolution in the Arts?', in *Bulletin of America's Town Meeting of the Air*, vol.5, no.19 (19 Feb).

63 It has been often said, even by proponents of those pictures known in aesthetic slang as Cubist and Abstract, that they have no subject matter. Such a statement is equivalent to saying that life has no subject matter.
1943 'The Cube Root', in *Art News*, vol.41, 1 Feb.

Davis, Thomas Osborne 1814–45

Irish poet and politician, head of the Young Ireland Movement. He cofounded the weekly *Nation* in 1842, and wrote patriotic verses which became anthems of the Sinn Féin movement.

64 'Did they dare, did they dare, to slay Owen Roe O'Neil?'
'Yes, they slew with poison him they feared to meet with steel.'
'May God wither up their hearts! May their blood cease to flow!
May they walk in living death, who poisoned Owen Roe!'
1842 'Lament for the Death of Owen Roe O'Neil'.

65 Sagest in the council was he, kindest in the hall:
Sure we never won a battle—'twas Owen won them all.
Had he lived, had he lived, our dear country had been free;
But he's dead, but he's dead, and 'tis slaves we'll ever be.
1842 'Lament for the Death of Owen Roe O'Neil'.

66 They fought as they revelled, fast, fiery, and true,
And, though victors, they left on the field not a few;
And they who survived fought and drank as of yore,
But the land of their heart's hope they never saw more,
For in far, foreign fields, from Dunkirk to Belgrade
Lie the soldiers and chiefs of the Irish Brigade.
1845 *The Spirit of the Nation*, 'The Battle-Eve of the Brigade'.

67 Our colonel comes from Brian's race,
His wounds are in his breast and face.
1845 *The Spirit of the Nation*, 'Clare's Dragoons'.

68 Viva la the New Brigade!
Viva la the Old One, too!
Viva la, the Rose shall fade,
And the Shamrock shine for ever new!
1845 *The Spirit of the Nation*, 'Clare's Dragoons'.

69 Come in the evening, or come in the morning,
Come when you're looked for, or come without warning.
1846 'The Welcome'.

Davison, Emily Wilding 1872–1913

English militant suffragette, who campaigned fiercely for women's emancipation. She was frequently imprisoned, and died after running in front of the King's horse at the 1913 Derby.

70 As I am a woman and women do not count in the State, I refuse to be counted. Rebellion against tyrants is obedience to God.
1911 Comment on uncompleted Census paper, quoted in Gertrude Colmore *The Life of Emily Wilding Davison* (1913).

Dawkins, Richard 1941–

British ethologist, Professor at Oxford. He has done much to popularize the theories of Charles Darwin, most notably in his work *The Selfish Gene* (1976).

71 There is a better reason for studying zoology than its possible 'usefulness', and the general likeableness of animals. This reason is that we animals are the most complicated and perfectly designed pieces of machinery in the known universe. Put it like that, and it is hard to see why anybody studies anything else!
1976 *The Selfish Gene*, preface.

72 We are survival machines—robot vehicles blindly programmed to preserve the selfish molecules known as genes. This is a truth which still fills me with astonishment.
1976 *The Selfish Gene*, ch.2.

73 It has no vision, no foresight, no sight at all. If it can be said to play the role of watchmaker in nature, it is the *blind* watchmaker.
1986 Of natural selection. *The Blind Watchmaker*, ch.1.
➤ See Paley 635:16.

74 However many ways there may be of being alive, it is certain that there are vastly more ways of being dead.
1986 *The Blind Watchmaker*, ch.1.

Day, Clarence Shepard 1874–1935

US humorist, best known for his writings in the *New Yorker* and for his autobiographical sketches in *Life With Father* (1935).

75 The poets of each generation seldom sing a new song. They turn themes men always have loved, and sing them in the mode of their times.
1921 *The Crow's Nest*, 'Humpty-Dumpty and Adam'.

76 The real world is not easy to live in. It is rough; it is slippery. Without the most clear-eyed adjustments we fall and get crushed. A man must stay sober: not always, but most of the time.
1921 *The Crow's Nest*, 'In His Baby Blue Ship'.

77 I meant to be prompt, but it never occurred to me that I had better try to be early.
1935 *Life With Father*, 'Father teaches me to be prompt'.

78 Imagine the Lord talking French! Aside from a few odd words in Hebrew, I took it for granted that God had never spoken anything but the most dignified English.
1935 *Life With Father*, 'Father interferes'.

79 'If you don't go to other men's funerals,' he told Father stiffly, 'they won't go to yours.'
1935 *Life With Father*, 'Father interferes'.

80 Father declared he was going to buy a new plot in the cemetery, a plot all for himself. 'And I'll buy one on a corner,' he added triumphantly, 'where I can get out.'
1935 *Life With Father*, penultimate paragraph.

Day, Doris originally **Doris Kappelhoff** 1924–

US singer and film actress, whose sunny personality and girl-next-door image made her a star of 1950s musicals.

81 The really frightening thing about middle age is the knowledge that you'll grow out of it.
Quoted in A E Hotchner *Doris Day* (1978).

Dayan, Moshe 1915–81

Israeli soldier and politician. He left the Labour Party in 1966 to set up the Rafi Party with Ben Gurion. His heavily outnumbered forces were successful in the Six-Day War (1967), and as Foreign Minister he helped secure peace with Egypt (1977).

82 Whenever you accept our views, we shall be in full agreement with you.

Remark to US envoy Cyrus Vance during the Arab–Israeli negotiations, quoted in the *Observer*, 14 Aug 1977.

Day-Lewis, Cecil 1904–72

Irish poet and critic. Professor at Oxford (1951–6) and Harvard (1964–5), he became Poet Laureate in 1968. As well as poetry he wrote criticism, translation and, under the pseudonym Nicholas Blake, detective novels.

83 Tempt me no more; for I
Have known the lightning's hour,
The poet's inward pride,
The certainty of power.
1933 *The Magnetic Mountain*, pt.3, no.24.

84 You that love England, who have an ear for her music,
The slow movement of clouds in benediction,
Clear arias of light thrilling over her uplands,
Over the chords of summer sustained peacefully.
1933 *The Magnetic Mountain*, pt.4, no.32.

85 Do not expect again a phoenix hour,
The triple-towered sky, the dove complaining,
Sudden the rain of gold and heart's first ease
Traced under trees by the eldritch light of sundown.
1935 'From Feathers to Iron'.

86 Now we lament one
Who danced on a plume of words,
Sang with a fountain's panache,
Dazzled like slate roofs in sun
After rain, was flighty as birds
And alone as a mountain ash.
The ribald, inspired urchin
Leaning over the lip
Of his world, as over a rock pool
Or a lucky dip,
Found everything brilliant and virgin.
1953 'In Memory of Dylan Thomas'.

Dean, John 1938–

US lawyer and author. As White House adviser to President Nixon, he was implicated in the Watergate scandal.

87 I am convinced that we are going to make the whole road and put this thing in the funny pages of the history books.
1973 Taped conversation with the President, Feb.

88 We have a cancer within, close to the presidency, that is growing. It is growing daily.
1973 Taped conversation with the President, Mar.

89 Doing time is like climbing a mountain wearing roller skates.
1977 On conviction after the Watergate scandal. In *Newsweek*, 4 Jul.

90 History never exactly repeats itself, but it does some rather good impressions.
Comparing the presidential styles of Richard Nixon and George W Bush. Quoted in *Worse than Watergate* (2004).

de Beauvoir, Simone 1906–86

French philosopher, feminist and writer, who maintained a lifelong association with fellow-existentialist Jean-Paul Sartre. Her *Le Deuxième Sexe* (*The Second Sex*, 1949–50) is a pioneering feminist text.

91 There is a good case for showing that airplanes,

machines, the telephone and the radio do not make men of today happier than those of former times.
1948 *Ethics of Ambiguity*.

92 *On ne naît pas femme: on le devient.*
One is not born a woman: one becomes a woman.
1949 *Le Deuxième Sexe* (*The Second Sex*), bk.2, pt.1, ch.1.

93 *Ce n'est guère que dans les asiles que les coquettes gardent avec entêtement une foi entière en des regards absents; normalement, elles réclament des témoins.*
Women fond of dress are hardly ever entirely satisfied not to be seen, except among the insane; usually they want witnesses.
1949 *Le Deuxième Sexe* (*The Second Sex*), bk.2, pt.5, ch.18 (translated by H M Parshley, 1952).

94 *La femme…sait que quand on la regarde on ne la distingue pas de son apparence: elle est jugée, respectée, désirée à travers sa toilette.*
Woman…knows that when she is looked at she is not considered apart from her appearance: she is judged, respected, desired, by and through her toilette.
1949 *Le Deuxième Sexe* (*The Second Sex*), bk.2, pt.7, ch.25 (translated by H M Parshley, 1952).

95 *Si l'on vit assez longtemps, on voit que toute victoire se change un jour en défaite.*
If you live long enough, you'll find that every victory turns into a defeat.
1955 *Tous les hommes sont mortels* (*All Men Are Mortal*).

de Bernières, Louis 1954–

English author who achieved international fame with *Captain Corelli's Mandolin* (1994), a love story set on a small island in Greece during World War II.

96 Writing today is like being stood stark naked in Trafalgar Square and being told to get an erection.
2001 On being asked how he was making progress on a successor to *Captain Corelli's Mandolin* (1994), Apr.

de Botton, Alain 1969–

British author, born in Switzerland.

97 How generous was it to offer gifts to people one knew would never accept them?
1994 *The Romantic Movement*, 'Martyrdom'.

98 How Proust Can Change Your Life.
1997 Book title.

Debray, Regis 1941–

French Marxist theorist. He gained international fame through his association with Che Guevara in Latin America.

99 Since the Cuban Revolution and since the invasion of Santo Domingo *a state of emergency* has existed in Latin America. The Marines shoot at anything that moves, regardless of party affiliation.
1967 *Révolution dans la Révolution?*

1 *Vedi Napoli, e poi muori? Oui, mais pour voir Venise, mourez d'abord.*
See Naples and die? Yes, but to see Venice, die first.
1995 *Contre Venise*.

2 *À Naples, personne ne vous demande dans quel hôtel ou chez qui vous êtes descendu: c'est indifférent. À Venise, impossible d'échapper la question: Gritti? Danieli?*

Palazzo du duc de C.? Appartement de M.?
(Consternation si vous répondez: auberge de jeunesse,
ou dortoir de l'institut universitaire.)
In Naples, no one asks you which hotel you're in or who
you're staying with: it doesn't matter. In Venice, you can't
avoid the question: the Gritti? the Danieli? the Duke of
C.'s palazzo? M.'s apartment? (Dismay if you reply: the
youth hostel, or the university halls of residence.)
1995 *Contre Venise.*

Debussy, Claude Achille 1862–1918

French composer. His writing for piano was described as 'musical
Impressionism'. He translated it to the orchestra in *La Mer* (1905),
to his opera, *Pelléas et Mélisande*, and to other works.

3 The colour of my soul is iron-grey and sad bats wheel
about the steeple of my dreams.
1894 Letter.

4 That old poisoner.
1896 Letter, alluding to Wagner.

5 People don't very much like things that are
beautiful—they are so far from their nasty little minds.
1900 Letter.

6 A pink bonbon stuffed with snow.
1903 Of the music of Edvard Grieg. *Gil Blas.*

7 A century of aeroplanes deserves its own music. As
there are no precedents, I must create anew.
1913 Quoted in *La Revue S.I.M.*

Decatur, Stephen 1779–1820

US naval officer, who distinguished himself in the war with
Tripoli (1801–5) and fought against Britain, capturing the
frigate *Macedonian* (1812), but surrendering in 1814.

8 Our country! In her intercourse with foreign nations,
may she always be in the right; but our country, right or
wrong.
1816 Speech made in Norfolk, Virginia, Apr.
➤ *See Adams 5:92, Chesterton 211:46.*

Deedes, William Francis Deedes, Baron 1913–

English Conservative politician and journalist. He was an MP
(1950–1974), and later pursued a career in journalism,
becoming Editor of the *Daily Telegraph* (1974–86).

9 One golden rule for people who want to get on in
politics is to keep their traps shut in August.
1999 In *The Mail on Sunday,* 22 Aug.

Deffand, Marquise du 1697–1780

French noblewoman, famous for her wit and beauty. Her salon
was frequented by leading figures in Paris literary society,
including Voltaire, Montesquieu and D'Alembert.

10 The distance does not matter; it is only the first step that
counts.
1763 Commenting on the legend of St Denis, said to have carried
his severed head for six miles following his execution. Letter,
7 Jul.

Defoe, Daniel 1660–1731

English writer, best known for his novels *Robinson Crusoe* (1719)
and *Moll Flanders* (1722), and for his partly factual *Journal of the
Plague Year* (1724). He also wrote a travel book, *A Tour Through
the Whole Island of Great Britain* (1724–7).

11 The soul is placed in the body like a rough diamond, and
must be polished, or the lustre of it will never appear.
1697 *An Essay upon Projects,* 'Of Academies: An Academy for
Women'.

12 The best of men cannot suspend their fate:
The good die early, and the bad die late.
1697 'Character of the Late Dr Annesley'.

13 Wherever God erects a house of prayer,
The Devil always builds a chapel there;
And 'twill be found, upon examination,
The latter hast the largest congregation.
1701 *The True-Born Englishman,* pt.1, l.1–4.

14 From this amphibious ill-born mob began
That vain, ill-natured thing, an Englishman.
1701 *The True-Born Englishman,* pt.1, l.132–3.

15 Your Roman-Saxon-Danish-Norman English.
1701 *The True-Born Englishman,* pt.1, l.139.

16 His lazy, long, lascivious reign.
1701 Of Charles II. *The True-Born Englishman,* pt.1, l.236.

17 Actions receive their tincture from the times,
And as they change are virtues made or crimes.
1703 *A Hymn to the Pillory,* l.29–30.

18 It happened one day, about noon, going towards my
boat, I was exceedingly surprised with the print of a
man's naked foot on the shore, which was very plain to
be seen in the sand. I stood like one thunderstruck, or as
if I had seen an apparition.
1719 *Robinson Crusoe.*

19 My man Friday.
1719 *Robinson Crusoe.*

20 Vice came in always at the door of necessity, not at the
door of inclination.
1722 *Moll Flanders.*

21 Manchester, one of the greatest, if not really the greatest
mere village in England.
1724–7 *A Tour Through the Whole Island of Great Britain,* letter 10.

22 Here is a pleasant situation, and yet nothing pleasant to
be seen. Here is a harbour without ships, a port without
trade, a fishery without nets, a people without business;
and, that which is worse than all, they do not seem to
desire business, much less do they understand it.
1724–7 Of Kirkcudbright, Scotland. *A Tour Through the Whole
Island of Great Britain,* letter 12.

23 A very fine city; the four principal streets are the fairest
for breadth, and the finest built that I have ever seen in
one city together… In a word, 'tis the cleanest and
beautifullest, and best built city in Britain, London
excepted.
1724–7 Of Glasgow. *A Tour Through the Whole Island of Great
Britain,* letter 12.

24 Pleasure is a *thief* to business.
1725 *The Complete English Tradesman,* vol.1, ch.9.

25 Things as certain as death and taxes, can be more firmly
believed.
1726 *History of the Devil,* bk.2, ch.6.
➤ *See also Franklin 335:18.*

De Forest, Lee 1873–1961

US inventor, pioneer in the development of wireless telegraphy
and radio.

26 While theoretically and technically television may be feasible, commercially and financially I consider it an impossibility, a development of which we need waste little time dreaming.
1926 In the *New York Times*.

Degas, (Hilaire Germain) Edgar 1834–1917

French artist. After a trip to Italy, where he was influenced by Renaissance painters, he returned to Paris and exhibited with the Impressionists (1874–86).

27 Art does not expand, it repeats itself.
1872 Letter to Paul Frölich, 27 Nov.

28 It is essential to do the same subject over again, ten times, a hundred times.
1886 Letter to Bartholomé, 17 Jan.

29 Aren't all beautiful things made by renunciation?
Quoted in P Lafond *Degas* (1918–9).

30 Drawing is not the form; it is the way of seeing the form.
Quoted in P Valéry *Degas, danse, dessin* (1938).

31 Art cannot be made with an intent to please.
Quoted in R H Ives Gammell *The Shop-Talk of Edgar Degas* (1961).

32 It is all very well to copy what you see; it is much better to draw what you see only in memory.
Quoted in R H Ives Gammell *The Shop-Talk of Edgar Degas* (1961).

33 Everybody has talent at twenty-five. The difficult thing is to have it at fifty.
Quoted in R H Ives Gammell *The Shop-Talk of Edgar Degas* (1961).

de Gaulle, Charles 1890–1970

French general. Leader of the Free French during World War II, he became head of the provisional government, and later Prime Minister (1958). As President of the Fifth Republic, he implemented an assertive foreign policy, but in 1969 resigned after the defeat of his referendum proposals for senate and regional reforms.

34 Nothing great will ever be achieved without great men—and men only become great if they are determined to be so.
1934 *Le Fil de l'épée*.

35 *La France a perdu une bataille! Mais la France n'a pas perdu la guerre!*
France has lost a battle! But France has not lost the war!
1940 Proclamation, 18 Jun. Collected in *Discours, messages et déclarations du Général de Gaulle* (1941).

36 *Puisque ceux qui avaient le devoir de manier l'épée de la France l'ont laissée tomber brisée, moi, j'ai ramassé le tronçon du glaive.*
Since those whose duty it was to wield the sword of France have let it fall shattered to the ground, I have taken up the broken blade.
1940 Speech, 13 Jul.

37 The French will only be united under the threat of danger. How else can one govern a country that produces 246 different types of cheese?
1951 Speech. Quoted in *Les Mots du Général* (1962).

38 *Les traités, voyez-vous, sont comme les jeunes filles et comme les roses: ça dure ce que ça dure.*
Treaties are like girls and roses—they last while they last.

1963 Speech at the Elysée Palace, 2 Jul. Quoted in Brian Crozier *De Gaulle the Statesman* (1973).

39 I myself have become a Gaullist only little by little.
1963 In the *Observer*, 29 Dec.

40 I respect only those who resist me, but I cannot tolerate them.
1966 In the *New York Times*, 12 May.

41 Vive le Québec! Vive le Québec libre! Vive le Canada français! Vive la France!
1967 Address to the crowd before Montreal's City Hall, 24 Jul. The slogan 'Québec libre' was identified with the separatist cause.

42 When I want to know what France thinks, I ask myself.
Sons of France.

43 In order to become the master, the politician poses as the servant.
Attributed.

44 Politics is too important to be left to the politicians.
Atrributed.

Dekanahwideh fl.c.1450

Native American leader, traditional founder of the Six Nations Confederacy.

45 I, Dekanahwideh, and the Confederated Chiefs, now uproot the tallest pine tree, and into the cavity thereby made we cast all weapons of war… Thus shall the Great Peace be established.
Traditional words from the Six Nations Confederacy (present-day Ontario and the Northeastern United States), one of the world's oldest constitutions, quoted in Paul A W Wallace *The White Roots of Peace* (1946).

Dekker, Thomas c.1570–c.1641

English dramatist. He wrote dramas for both public and private stages, masques, pageants and topical pamphlets, and was imprisoned for debt for three years. He frequently collaborated with other dramatists.

46 Ill is the weather that bringeth no gain.
1600 *The Shoemaker's Holiday*, 'The First Three-men's Song'.

47 Dost thou not know that love respects no blood, Cares not for difference of birth or state?
1600 *The Shoemaker's Holiday*, act 5, sc.5.

48 Golden slumbers kiss your eyes,
Smiles awake you when you rise;
Sleep, pretty wantons, do not cry,
And I will sing a lullaby,
Rock them, rock them, lullaby.
1603 *The Pleasant Comedy of Patient Grisill*, act 4, sc.2.

49 That great fishpond.
1604 Of the seas. *The Honest Whore*, pt.1, act 1, sc.2.

50 This wench we speak of strays so from her kind,
Nature repents she made her; 'tis a mermaid
Has tolled my son to shipwreck
1611 *The Roaring Girl* (with Thomas Middleton), act 1, sc.2.

51 'Tis the maddest fantasticalest girl. I never knew so much flesh and so much nimbleness put together.
1611 *The Roaring Girl* (with Thomas Middleton), act 2, sc.2.

52 I have no humour to marry; I love to lie o' both sides of the bed myself; and again, o' th' other side.
1611 *The Roaring Girl* (with Thomas Middleton), act 2, sc.2.

53 I have the head now of myself, and am man enough for a woman.
  1611 *The Roaring Girl* (with Thomas Middleton), act 2, sc.2.

54 Thou'rt one of those
  That thinks each woman thy fond flexible whore.
  1611 *The Roaring Girl* (with Thomas Middleton), act 3, sc.1.

de Klerk, F(rederik) W(illem) 1936–

South African politician. He was President of South Africa (1989–94) and in 1993 was jointly awarded the Nobel peace prize with Nelson Mandela.

55 Today we have closed the book on apartheid.
  1992 On the endorsement of his government's reform programme following a referendum of white South Africans. In *The Independent*, 19 Mar.

de Kooning, Willem 1904–97

Dutch-born US painter, who emigrated to the US in 1926 and became a leader of Abstract Expressionism, especially in action painting. His works, which focus on the human form, include the controversial series *Woman I–V* (1952–3).

56 Style is a fraud. I always felt the Greeks were hiding behind their columns.
  1949 'A Desperate View', lecture given in New York.

57 Flesh was the reason why oil painting was invented.
  1980 In *Bulletin*, Pittsburgh International Museum.

Delacroix, (Ferdinand Victor) Eugène 1798–1863

French Romantic painter, whose loose drawing and vivid colour aroused controversy. He continued to experiment with non-classical techniques and the use of colour.

58 What makes men of genius, or rather, what they make, is not new ideas, it is that idea—possessing them—that what has been said has still not been said enough.
  1824 *The Journal of Eugène Delacroix* (translated by W Pach, 1948), entry for 15 May.

59 I live in company with a body, a silent companion, exacting and eternal. He it is who notes that individuality which is the seal of the weakness of our race. My soul has wings, but the brutal jailer is strict.
  1824 *The Journal of Eugène Delacroix* (translated by W Pach, 1948), entry for 4 Jun.

60 A taste for simplicity cannot endure for long.
  1847 *The Journal of Eugène Delacroix* (translated by W Pach, 1948).

61 Painters who are not colourists produce illumination and not painting.
  1852 *The Journal of Eugène Delacroix* (translated by W Pach, 1948).

de la Mare, Walter 1873–1956

English poet and novelist. He worked for an oil company until 1908, when he became a full-time writer. His work included volumes of verse, novels, prose fantasy and short stories for both children and adults.

62 Oh, no man knows
  Through what wild centuries
  Roves back the rose.
  1912 'All That's Past'.

63 'Is there anybody there?' said the Traveller,
  Knocking on the moonlit door;

And his horse in the silence champed the grasses
  Of the forest's ferny floor.
  1912 'The Listeners'.

64 'Tell them I came, and no one answered,
  That I kept my word,' he said.
  1912 'The Listeners'.

65 Aye, they heard his foot upon the stirrup,
  And the sound of iron on stone,
  And how the silence surged softly backward,
  When the plunging hoofs were gone.
  1912 'The Listeners'.

66 He is crazed with the spell of far Arabia,
  They have stolen his wits away.
  1912 'Arabia'.

67 But beauty vanishes; beauty passes;
  However rare—rare it be;
  And when I crumble, who will remember
  This lady of the West Country?
  1912 'Epitaph'.

68 Ann, Ann!
  Come! quick as you can!
  There's a fish that *talks*
  In the frying pan.
  1913 'Alas, Alack'.

69 Slowly, silently, now the moon
  Walks the night in her silver shoon.
  1913 'Silver'.

70 A face peered. All the grey night
  In chaos of vacancy shone;
  Nought but vast Sorrow was there—
  The sweet cheat gone.
  1918 'The Ghost'.

71 When I lie where shades of darkness
  Shall no more assail mine eyes.
  1918 'Fare Well'.

72 Look thy last on all things lovely,
  Every hour. Let no night
  Seal thy sense in deathly slumber
  Till to delight
  Thou have paid thy utmost blessing.
  1918 'Fare Well'.

73 Too late for fruit, too soon for flowers.
  Attributed, when asked, while ill, if he would prefer fruit or flowers. Quoted in Clifton Fadiman *The Faber Book of Anecdotes* (1985).

Delaney, Shelagh 1939–

English playwright and screenwriter, whose best-known play, *A Taste of Honey* (produced 1958), was written when she was 17.

74 Women never have young minds. They are born three thousand years old.
  1958 *A Taste of Honey*, act 1, sc.2.

DeLillo, Don 1936–

US novelist. His ambitious dissection of modern cultural codes in such novels as *White Noise* (1985), *Libra* (1988) and *Underworld* (1998) have made him an important voice in contemporary fiction.

75 I've come to think of Europe as a hardcover book,

America as the paperback version.
1982 Owen Brademas. *The Names*, ch.1.

76 Tourism is the march of stupidity.
1982 James Axton. *The Names*, ch.3.

77 If I were a writer, how I would enjoy being told the novel is dead. How liberating to work in the margins, outside a central perception. You are the ghoul of literature. Lovely.
1982 Owen Brademas. *The Names*, ch.4.

78 To a writer, madness is a final distillation of self, a final editing down. It's the drowning out of false voices.
1982 Owen Brademas. *The Names*, ch.5.

79 Men with secrets tend to be drawn to each other, not because they want to share what they know but because they need the company of the like-minded, the fellow-afflicted.
1988 Walter Everett, Jr. *Libra*, pt.1, '17 April'.

80 A conspiracy is everything that ordinary life is not. It's the inside game, cold, sure, undistracted, forever closed off to us. We are the flawed ones, the innocents, trying to make some rough sense of the daily jostle. Conspirators have a logic and a daring beyond our reach.
1988 *Libra*, pt.2, 'In Dallas'.

81 The dead have come to take the living. The dead in winding-sheets, the regimented dead on horseback, the skeleton that plays a hurdy-gurdy.
1998 *Underworld*.

Delius, Frederick 1862–1934

English composer of German-Scandinavian descent. He settled in France in 1890, establishing himself as a prolific and highly original composer. In 1924 he became paralysed and blind, but continued to work with the help of his amanuensis Eric Fenby.

82 It is only that which cannot be expressed otherwise that is worth expressing in music.
1920 'At the Crossroads'.

Deming, W(illiam) Edwards 1900–93

US statistician, inventor of modern quality control.

83 What's the aim of the school of business, for example? They teach students how business is conducted today and how to perpetuate it. Any wonder we're in trouble? They ought to be preparing students for the future, not for the past.
1990 Interview in the *Wall Street Journal*, 4 Jun.

Democritus c.460–c.370 BC

Greek philosopher. Only fragments of his extensive work on ethics have survived.

84 Nothing exists except atoms and empty space; everything else is opinion.
Diogenes Laertius, vol.9.

85 Strength and beauty are the blessings of youth; temperance, however, is the flower of old age.
Fragment quoted in H Diels and W Kranz (eds) *Die Fragmente der Vorsokratiker*, vol.2 (1952), no.294.

Dempsey, (William Harrison) Jack 1895–1983

US boxer. He won the world heavyweight title in 1919 and lost it to Gene Tunney in 1926. He retired in 1940 and became a successful restaurateur.

86 Honey, I forgot to duck.
1926 Attributed, to his wife after he was knocked out by Gene Tunney. US President Ronald Reagan repeated the phrase to his wife when wounded in an attempted assassination, 1981.

87 When you're fighting, you're fighting for one thing—money.
Quoted in Colin Jarman *The Guinness Dictionary of Sports Quotations* (1990).

Deng Xiaoping 1904–97

Chinese political leader who rose to power (1978) after disgrace during the Cultural Revolution. His international esteem suffered after he sanctioned the Tiananmen Square massacre of pro-democracy supporters, Jun 1989.

88 It doesn't matter whether the cat is black or white, as long as it catches mice.
1962 Speech at Communist Youth League conference, Jul.

89 A fundamental contradiction does not exist between socialism and a market economy.
1985 Address to US businessmen organized by *Time* magazine, 18 Dec.

90 Even if they're functioning out of ignorance, they are still participating and must be suppressed. In China, even one million people can be considered a small sum.
1989 Of pro-democracy demonstrators. In *The Times*, 5 Jun.

Denham, Sir John 1615–69

Irish poet and Royalist, who undertook secret missions for Charles I and Charles II during the Civil War and Protectorate, and was knighted in 1661. He is credited with introducing to English verse the couplet form which later dominated 18c poetry.

91 Can knowledge have no bound, but must advance
So far, to make us wish for ignorance?
1642 *Cooper's Hill*, l.145–6.

92 O could I flow like thee, and make thy stream
My great example, as it is my theme!
Though deep, yet clear, though gentle, yet not dull,
Strong without rage, without o'erflowing full.
1642 Of the Thames. *Cooper's Hill*, l.189–92.

93 Such is our pride, our folly, or our fate,
That few, but such as cannot write, translate.
1648 'To Richard Fanshaw'.

94 Old Mother Wit, and Nature gave
Shakespeare and Fletcher all they have;
In Spenser, and in Jonson, Art
Of slower Nature got the start.
1667 'On Mr Abraham Cowley'.

95 Youth, what man's age is like to be doth show;
We may our ends by our beginnings know.
1668 'Of Prudence', l.225–6.

Deniehy, Daniel Henry 1828–65

Australian lawyer, politician, orator and writer, who formed his own famous library.

96 A Bunyip Aristocracy.
1853 Quoted in *The Australian Dictionary of Biography*, vol 4. The bunyip is a mythical, chimerical animal of Australian folklore.

Denis, Maurice 1870–1943

French painter and art theorist, associated with the Nabis group ('prophets' influenced by Gauguin), and Symbolism.

97 Remember that a painting—before it is a battlehorse, a nude woman, or some anecdote—is essentially a flat surface covered with colours assembled in a certain order.
1912 *Théories: 1890–1910*.

Denman, Thomas, 1st Baron 1779–1854

English jurist. A Whig MP (1818–26), he was Attorney-General in Earl Grey's administration (1830–2) and Lord Chief Justice (1832–50).

98 Trial by jury itself, instead of being a security to persons who are accused, will be a delusion, a mockery, and a snare.
1844 Judgement in *O'Connell* v *The Queen*, 4 Sep.

Denning, Alfred Thompson, Lord 1899–1999

English judge. As Master of the Rolls (1962–82) he earned a reputation for his outspoken opinions.

99 A wrong decision can make me very miserable. But I have trust in God. If you have this trust you don't have to worry, as you don't have the sole responsibility.
1982 Speech on his retirement.

Dennis, C(larence Michael) J(ames) 1876–1938

Australian poet and journalist. His poems have been popular for their vernacular humour.

1 Me pal 'e trots 'er up an' does the toff—
'E allus wus a bloke fer showin' off.
'This 'ere's Doreen,' 'e sez. 'This 'ere's the Kid.'
I dips me lid.
1915 *Songs of a Sentimental Bloke*, 'The Intro'. Bill persuades his friend to introduce him to a girl.

Dennis, John 1657–1734

English playwright and critic. He was among the most famous critics of his day, but his own plays met with little success and he was one of the targets of Alexander Pope's satire in *The Dunciad*.

2 Damn them, see how the rascals use me! They will not let my play run, and yet they steal my thunder!
1709 Attributed, when watching a production of *Macbeth* that featured a thunder machine he had designed for use in his own play *Appius and Virginia*, which had been denied a long run. Said to be the origin of the phrase 'to steal one's thunder'.

3 A man who could make so vile a pun would not scruple to pick a pocket.
Of Dennis. In the *Gentleman's Magazine* 1781, editorial note.

Depp, Johnny (John Christopher) 1963–

US actor.

4 If you were waiting for the opportune moment, that was it.
2003 As Captain Jack Sparrow in *Pirates of the Caribbean* (screenplay by Ted Elliott and Terry Rossio).

5 I'm not swimming in the soup bowl. I'm not getting overcooked in that big stew pot.
2004 On why he lives in France rather than in Los Angeles. Quoted in *Scotland on Sunday*, 2 May.

De Quincey, Thomas 1785–1859

English writer. He ran away from school in 1802, lived with a prostitute in London, became an opium addict at Oxford, lived for a time in the Lake District and moved to Edinburgh in 1828.

6 A duller spectacle this earth of ours has not to show than a rainy Sunday in London.
1821 *Confessions of an English Opium Eater* (originally serialized in the *London Magazine*, published 1822).

7 Thou hast the keys of Paradise, oh just, subtle, and mighty opium!
1821 *Confessions of an English Opium Eater* (originally serialized in the *London Magazine*, published 1822).

8 Books, we are told, propose to *instruct* or to *amuse*. Indeed!… The true antithesis to knowledge, in this case, is not *pleasure*, but *power*. All that is literature seeks to communicate power; all that is not literature, to communicate knowledge.
1823 *Letters to a Young Man whose Education has been Neglected*, no.3, in the London Magazine, Jan–Jul.

9 Murder Considered as One of the Fine Arts.
1827 Title of essay, in *Blackwood's Magazine*, Feb.

10 If once a man indulges himself in murder, very soon he comes to think little of robbing; and from robbing he comes next to drinking and sabbath-breaking, and from that to incivility and procrastination.
1839 'On Murder Considered as One of the Fine Arts' (supplementary paper), in *Blackwood's Magazine*, Nov.

Derby, Edward Geoffrey Smith Stanley, 14th Earl of 1799–1869

English statesman and Conservative Prime Minister (1852, 1858–9, 1866–8), formerly a Whig. He entered the Lords in 1844 and headed the Protectionists from 1846, the year he became Party leader.

11 The foreign policy of the noble Earl, Lord Russell, may be summed up in two truly expressive words: meddle and muddle.
1864 Speech in the House of Lords, Feb, referring to the Prime Minister's policy on the American Civil War.

Desai, Anita née Mazumbar 1937–

Indian novelist, who writes for children and adults. Her novels *The Clear Light of Day* (1980), *In Custody* (1984) and *Fasting, Feasting* (1999) were all shortlisted for the Booker Prize.

12 Do you know anyone who would—secretly, sincerely, in his innermost self—*really* prefer to return to childhood?
1980 *The Clear Light of Day*, ch.1.

Desbiens, Jean-Paul 1927–

Canadian writer and educator.

13 Education is impossible without love, without loving a few of the great men of the past.
1965 *For Pity's Sake* (translated by Frédéric Côte).

Desbordes-Valmore, Marceline 1786–1859

French poet. She worked in the theatre and published children's stories before turning to poetry. Her poems are written in an open, informal style, often as dialogues.

14 *Par toi tout le bonheur que m'offre l'avenir*
Est dans mon souvenir.

Through you, all the happiness that the future offers
Is in my memory.
1819 *Élegies, Marie et romances*, 'Le Souvenir'.

15 *Ce qu'on donne à l'amour est à jamais perdu.*
What one gives in love is forever lost.
1830 *Poésies*, 'L'Isolement'.

16 *J'ai vécu d'aimer, j'ai donc vécu de larmes.*
I lived to love. I lived, therefore, in tears.
1860 *Poésies posthumes*, 'Rêve intermittent d'une nuit triste'.

Descartes, René 1596–1650

French philosopher and mathematician. He travelled widely
before settling in Holland and writing his major works (both
popular, in French, and scholarly, in Latin): the *Discours de la
méthode* (1637), *Meditationes de prima philosophia* (1641), and
Principia philosophiae (1644).

17 *La lecture de tous les bons livres est comme une
conversation avec les plus honnêtes gens des siècles
passés, qui en ont été les auteurs, et même une
conversation étudiée en laquelle ils ne nous découvrent
que les meilleures de leurs pensées.*
The reading of good books is like a conversation with the
best men of past centuries—in fact like a prepared
conversation, in which they reveal their best thoughts.
1637 *Discours de la méthode* (*Discourse on Method*), 1st
discourse (translated by G E M Anscombe and Peter Geach).

18 *Le bon sens est la chose du monde la mieux partagée: car
chacun pense en être si bien pourvu, que ceux même qui
sont les plus difficiles à contenter en toute autre chose
n'ont point coutume d'en désirer plus qu'ils ont. En quoi
il n'est pas vraisemblable que tous se trompent; mais
plutôt cela témoigne que la puissance de bien juger et
distinguer le vrai d'avec le faux, qui est proprement ce
qu'on nomme le bon sens ou la raison, est naturellement
égale en tous les hommes.*
Good sense is the most fairly distributed thing in the
world; for everyone thinks himself so well supplied with
it, that even those who are hardest to satisfy in every
other way do not usually desire more of it than they
already have. In this matter it is not likely that everybody
is mistaken; it rather goes to show that the power of
judging well and distinguishing truth from falsehood,
which is what we properly mean by good sense or
reason, is naturally equal in all men.
1637 *Discours de la méthode* (*Discourse on Method*), 1st
discourse (translated by G E M Anscombe and Peter Geach).

19 *Pour ce qu'alors je désirais vaquer seulement à la
recherche de la vérité, je pensai qu'il fallait que
je…rejetasse comme absolument faux tout ce en quoi je
pourrais imaginer le moindre doute, afin de voir s'il ne
resterait point, après cela, quelque chose en ma créance
qui fût entièrement indubitable.*
Since my present aim was to give myself up to the pursuit
of truth alone, I thought I must…reject as if absolutely
false anything as to which I could imagine the least
doubt, in order to see if I should not be left at the end
believing something that was absolutely indubitable.
1637 *Discours de la méthode* (*Discourse on Method*), 4th
discourse (translated by G E M Anscombe and Peter Geach).

20 *Je pris garde que, pendant que je voulais ainsi penser que
tout était faux, il fallait nécessairement que moi, qui le
pensais, fusse quelque chose.*

I noticed that while I was trying to think everything false,
it must needs be that I, who was thinking this, was
something.
1637 *Discours de la méthode* (*Discourse on Method*), 4th
discourse (translated by G E M Anscombe and Peter Geach).

21 *Je pense, donc je suis.*
I think, therefore I am.
1637 *Discours de la méthode* (*Discourse on Method*), 4th
discourse (translated by G E M Anscombe and Peter Geach).
Often quoted as 'Cogito, ergo sum', but Descartes wrote the
French version before the Latin.

22 *Je pouvais prendre pour règle générale, que les choses
que nous concevons fort clairement et fort distinctement
sont toutes vraies.*
I could take it as a general rule that whatever we
conceive very clearly and very distinctly is true.
1637 *Discours de la méthode* (*Discourse on Method*), 4th
discourse (translated by G E M Anscombe and Peter Geach).

23 *Animadverti jam ante aliquot annos quam multa, ineunte
aetate, falsa pro veris admiserim, et quam dubia sint
quaecunque istis postea superextruxi, ac proinde funditus
omnia semel in vita esse evertenda, atque a primis
fundamentis denno inchoandum, si quid aliquando
firmum et mansurum cupiam in scientiis stabilire.*
Some years ago now I observed the multitude of
errors that I had accepted as true in my earliest years,
and the dubiousness of the whole superstructure I
had since then reared on them; and the consequent need
of making a clean sweep for once in my life,
and beginning again from the very foundations, if
I would establish some secure and lasting result in science.
1641 *Meditationes*, 1st meditation (translated by G E M
Anscombe and Peter Geach).

24 *Supponam igitur non optimum Deum, fontem veritatis,
sed genium aliquum malignum, eundemque summe
potentem et callidum, omnem suam industriam in eo
posuisse, ut me falleret.*
I will suppose then, not that there is a supremely good
God, the source of truth; but that there is an evil spirit,
who is supremely powerful and intelligent, and does his
utmost to deceive me.
1641 *Meditationes*, 1st meditation (translated by G E M
Anscombe and Peter Geach).

25 *Agnoscam fieri non posse ut existam talis naturae qualis
sum, nempe ideam Dei in me habens, nisi revera Deus
etiam existeret, Deus, inquam, ille idem cujus idea in me
est.*
I could not possibly exist with the nature I actually have,
that is, one endowed with the idea of God, unless there
really is a God; the very God, I mean, of whom I have an
idea.
1641 *Meditationes*, 3rd meditation (translated by G E M
Anscombe and Peter Geach)

Deschamps, Eustache c.1345–1406

French poet, soldier and courtier.

26 *Rien ne se peut comparer à Paris.*
Nothing can compare to Paris.
c.1370 'Ballade de Paris', refrain.

Deschamps, Yvon 1935–

Canadian entertainer, known for his separatist allegiances.

27 All we want is an independent Quebec within a strong and united Canada.
Quoted by Peter C Newman in *Maclean's*, 13 Nov 1978. This has become the classic formulation of Quebec's national and political aspirations.

Destouches, Philippe *originally* **Néricault** 1680–1754

French playwright, a diplomat in England (1717–23). His early comedies are undistinguished, but his masterpiece is *Le Glorieux* (1732, 'The Boaster').

28 *Les absents ont toujours tort.*
The absent are always in the wrong.
1717 *L'Obstacle imprévu*, act 1, sc.6.

Dettori, Frankie (Lanfranco) 1970–

Italian jockey. He was Champion Jockey (1994, 1995) and in 1996 achieved the unparalleled feat of winning all seven races on the card at Ascot.

29 When I'm good, I can be really good—I can do things even I didn't think I could do. I would say my worst is still not so bad, either.
2003 Quoted in *The Times*, 27 Sep.

De Valera, Éamon 1882–1975

Irish statesman, born in the US. He narrowly escaped execution for his part in the 1916 Easter Rebellion, and became leader of Sinn Féin (1917–26). He was Prime Minister (1932–48, 1951–4, 1957–9) and President (1959–73).

30 Why doesn't he use a spoon?
1921 On being told that David Lloyd George had said talking to him was like trying to pick up mercury with a fork.

31 Whenever I wanted to know what the Irish people wanted, I had only to examine my own heart and it told me straight off what the Irish people wanted.
1922 Speech to the Irish Parliament, 6 Jan.

Devlin, Denis 1908–59

Irish poet and diplomat, born in Scotland. His poetry, which assimilates Christian iconography into cosmopolitan settings, was not appreciated until after his death.

32 And sad, Oh sad, that glen with one thin stream
He met his death in; and a farmer told me
There was but one small bird to shoot: it sang
'Better Beast and know your end, and die
Than Man with murderous angels in his head.'
c.1956 'The Tomb of Michael Collins'.

De Voto, Bernard 1897–1955

US historian and writer, known for 'The Easy Chair' in *Harper's Magazine* from 1935. His works include the historical trilogy beginning with *The Year of Decision: 1846* (1943) and he edited Twain's work.

33 The proper union of gin and vermouth is a great and sudden glory; it is one of the happiest marriages on earth, and one of the shortest lived.
1949 In *Harper's Magazine*, Dec.

34 Novelists, whatever else they may be besides, are also children talking to children—in the dark.
1950 *The World of Fiction*.

35 When evening quickens in the street, comes a pause in

the day's occupation that is known as the cocktail hour.
1951 *The Hour*.

36 You can no more keep a martini in the refrigerator than you can keep a kiss there.
1951 *The Hour*.

De Vries, Peter 1910–93

US novelist and humorist, best known for *The Tunnel of Love* (1954).

37 It is the final proof of God's omnipotence that he need not exist in order to save us.
1958 *The Mackerel Plaza*, ch.1.

38 Look at it this way: Psychoanalysis is a permanent fad.
1973 *Forever Panting*.

Dewar, Donald Campbell 1937–2000

Scottish Labour politician. He was Secretary of State for Scotland (1997–9) and the first First Minister of the new Scottish Parliament (1999–2000).

39 He could start a party in an empty room—and often did—filling it with good cheer, Gaelic songs, and argument.
1994 Of John Smith, leader of the Labour Party, at his funeral, 19 May.

40 'There shall be a Scottish Parliament.' Through long years, those words were first a hope, then a belief, then a promise. Now they are a reality.
1999 Speech at the official opening of the Scottish Parliament, 1 Jul.

41 We look forward to the time when this moment will be seen as a turning point: the day when democracy was renewed in Scotland, when we revitalized our place in this our United Kingdom.
1999 Speech at the official opening of the Scottish Parliament, 1 Jul.

42 This is about more than our politics and our laws. This is about who we are, how we carry ourselves.
1999 Speech at the official opening of the Scottish Parliament, 1 Jul.

Dewey, John 1859–1952

US philosopher and educator. A leading pragmatist, he developed an influential philosophy of education which stressed learning through experience. His writings include *The Quest for Certainty* (1929) and *The Child and the Curriculum* (1902).

43 When physics, chemistry, biology, medicine, contribute to the detection of concrete human woes and to the development of plans for remedying them and relieving the human estate, they become moral; they become part of the apparatus of moral inquiry or science... When the consciousness of science is fully impregnated with the consciousness of human value, the greatest dualism which now weighs humanity down, the split between the material, the mechanical and the scientific and the moral and ideal will be destroyed.
1920 *Reconstruction in Philosophy*.

44 The function of criticism is the reeducation of perception of works of art... The conception that its business is to appraise, to judge in the legal and moral sense, arrests the perception of those who are

influenced by the criticism that assumes this task.
1934 *Art as Experience*.

De Wolfe, Elsie 1865–1950

English actress, interior decorator and hostess, the wife of the British diplomat Sir Charles Mendl.

45 Beige! Just my color.
On seeing the Acropolis for the first time. Quoted in Nina Campbell and Caroline Seebohm *Elsie de Wolfe: A Decorative Life* (1992), ch.1.

Diaghilev, Sergei 1872–1929

Russian impresario. His Ballets Russes company, formed in 1911, created a sensation throughout Europe and launched the careers of such dancers as Balanchine, Fokine, Nijinsky and Pavlova.

46 *Étonne-moi!*
Astonish me!
1912 Attributed, when Jean Cocteau complained that he was getting insufficient direction when designing the scenario for a new ballet. Quoted in Wallace Fowlie (ed) *Journals of Jean Cocteau* (1956), ch.1.

Diana, Princess of Wales 1961–97

British princess. She married Charles, Prince of Wales, in 1981 and they were divorced in 1996.

47 I'm as thick as a plank.
Remark quoted in *Sunday Today*, 25 Jan 1987.

48 There were three of us in this marriage, so it was a bit crowded.
1995 Of her marriage to Charles, Prince of Wales, and his relationship with Camilla Parker-Bowles. Television interview on BBC1's *Panorama*, 20 Nov.

49 I'd like to be a queen in people's hearts but I don't see myself being Queen of this country.
1995 Television interview on BBC1's *Panorama*, 20 Nov.

Díaz, Jorge 1930–

Chilean dramatist, born in Argentina. He has lived in Spain since 1965. His plays are influenced by the theatre of the absurd and other avant-garde experimental movements.

50 ¡Pero la verdad es que estoy cansada, horriblemente cansada de ser la esposa femenina de ese animal masculino que se rasca, pierde el pelo sistemáticamente y canta tangos pasados de moda!… Quisiera…quisiera engordar, fumar un puro y enviudar de una manera indolora y elegante.
The truth is, I'm tired, frightfully tired of being the feminine spouse to the masculine animal who scratches himself, systematically loses his hair and sings outdated tangos!… I'd like… I'd like to get fat, to smoke cigars and to become a widow in a painless and elegant fashion.
1961 *El cepillo de dientes* (*The Toothbrush*), act 1.

Diaz, Porfirio 1830–1915

President of Mexico. He supported Juarez in the War of Reform and gained the presidency through rebellion in 1877.

51 Poor Mexico, so far from God and so close to the United States.
1846 Attributed, at the beginning of the American–Mexican War (1846–8).

Dibdin, Charles 1745–1814

English songwriter, who wrote his first operetta (*The Shepherd's Artifice*, performed at Covent Garden 1762) as a boy. He wrote nearly 100 sea songs and 70 dramatic pieces.

52 For a soldier I listed, to grow great in fame,
And be shot at for sixpence a day.
1791 'Charity'.

53 Did you ever hear of Captain Wattle?
He was all for love, and a little for the bottle.
1797 'Captain Wattle and Miss Roe'.

54 Then trust me, there's nothing like drinking
So pleasant this side of the grave;
It keeps the unhappy from thinking,
And makes e'en the valiant more brave.
'Nothing Like Grog'. First published 1803.

55 What argufies pride and ambition?
Soon or late death will take us in tow:
Each bullet has got its commission,
And when our time's come we must go.
'Each Bullet Has Got Its Commission'. First published 1803.

Dick, Philip K(indred) 1928–82

US science-fiction writer. His output was prolific, marked by a strong literary sensibility as well as a powerful, often chilling imagination and humour.

56 Dr Bloodmoney, Or How We Got Along After The Bomb.
1965 Title of novel.

57 I mean, after all; you have to consider that we're only made out of dust. That's admittedly not much to go on and we shouldn't forget that. But even considering, I mean, it's sort of a bad beginning, we're not doing too bad. So I personally have faith that even in this lousy situation we're faced with we can make it. You get me?
1966 *The Three Stigmata of Palmer Eldritch*, closing words.

58 Do Androids Dream Of Electric Sheep?
1968 Title of novel, later the basis for the film *Blade Runner*.

59 Reality is that which, when you stop believing in it, doesn't go away.
1972 Quoted in introduction to *I Hope I Shall Arrive Soon* (1986).

60 Drug misuse is not a disease, it is a decision, like the decision to step out in front of a moving car. You would call that not a disease but an error of judgement.
1977 *A Scanner Darkly*, author's note.

61 The basic tool for the manipulation of reality is the manipulation of words. If you can control the meaning of words, you can control the people who must use the words.
1986 *I Hope I Shall Arrive Soon*, 'How To Build A Universe That Doesn't Fall Apart Two Days Later'.

Dickens, Charles John Huffam 1812–70

English novelist. After a childhood of poverty and hardship, during which his father was sent to a debtors' prison, he became one of England's most popular and prolific novelists, exposing the inhumanities of the 19c with an idiosyncratic blend of wit, satire, sentiment and seriousness and a gallery of memorable characters.

62 Grief never mended no broken bones, and as good people's wery scarce, what I says is, make the most on 'em.
1836–7 *Sketches by Boz*, 'Gin Shops'.

63 We shall never forget the mingled feelings of awe and respect with which we used to gaze on the exterior of Newgate in our schoolboy days…[the doors] looking as if they were made for the express purpose of letting people in, and never letting them out again.
1836–7 *Sketches by Boz*, 'Criminal Courts'.

64 A smattering of everything, and a knowledge of nothing.
1836–7 *Sketches by Boz*, 'Sentiment'.

65 He had used the word in its Pickwickian sense.
1836–7 Of Mr Blotton, a member of the Pickwick Club. *Pickwick Papers*, ch.1.

66 'Heads, heads—take care of your heads!' cried the loquacious stranger, as they came out under the low archway, which in those days formed the entrance to the coachyard. 'Terrible place—dangerous work—five children—mother—tall lady, eating sandwiches—forgot the arch—crash—knock—children look round—mother's head off—sandwich in her hand—no mouth to put it in—head of a family off—shocking, shocking!
1836–7 Jingle. *Pickwick Papers*, ch.2.

67 'I was ruminating,' said Mr Pickwick, 'on the strange mutability of human affairs.' 'Ah! I see—in at the palace door one day, out at the window the next. Philosopher, Sir?' 'An observer of human nature, sir,' said Mr Pickwick.
1836–7 *Pickwick Papers*, ch.2.

68 'Ah! You should keep dogs—fine animals—sagacious creatures—dog of my own once—Pointer—surprising instinct—out shooting one day—entering enclosure—whistled—dog stopped—whistled again—Ponto—no go; stock still—called him—Ponto, Ponto—wouldn't move— dog transfixed—staring at a board—looked up, saw an inscription—"Gamekeeper has orders to shoot all dogs found in this enclosure"— wouldn't pass it—wonderful dog—valuable dog that—very.'
1836–7 Jingle. *Pickwick Papers*, ch.2.

69 Kent, sir—everyone knows Kent—apples, cherries, hops and women.
1836–7 Jingle. *Pickwick Papers*, ch.2.

70 There are very few moments in a man's existence when he experiences so much ludicrous distress, or meets with so little charitable commiseration, as when he is in pursuit of his own hat.
1836–7 *Pickwick Papers*, ch.4.

71 There was a fine gentle wind, and Mr Pickwick's hat rolled sportively before it. The wind puffed, and Mr Pickwick puffed, and the hat rolled over and over as merrily as a lively porpoise in a strong tide.
1836–7 *Pickwick Papers*, ch.4.

72 I wants to make your flesh creep.
1836–7 The Fat Boy. *Pickwick Papers*, ch.8.

73 'It's always best on these occasions to do what the mob do.' 'But suppose there are two mobs?' suggested Mr Snodgrass. 'Shout with the largest,' replied Mr Pickwick.
1836–7 *Pickwick Papers*, ch.13.

74 And a wery good name it is—only one I know, that ain't got a nickname to it.
1836–7 Sam Weller comments on Job Trotter's Christian name. *Pickwick Papers*, ch.16.

75 Tongue; well, that's a wery good thing when it an't a woman's.
1836–7 Sam Weller's father. *Pickwick Papers*, ch.19.

76 Poverty and oysters always seem to go together.
1836–7 Sam Weller. *Pickwick Papers*, ch.22.

77 Dumb as a drum vith a hole in it, sir.
1836–7 Sam Weller. *Pickwick Papers*, ch.25.

78 Our noble society for providing the infant negroes in the West Indies with flannel waistcoats and moral pocket handkerchiefs.
1836–7 Rev Mr Stiggins. *Pickwick Papers*, ch.27.

79 Poetry's unnat'ral; no man ever talked poetry 'cept a beadle on boxin' day, or Warren's blackin', or Rowland's oil, or some o' them low fellows; never you let yourself down to talk poetry, my boy.
1836–7 Sam Weller's father. *Pickwick Papers*, ch.33.

80 It's my opinion, sir, that this meeting is drunk, sir!
1836–7 Rev Mr Stiggins. *Pickwick Papers*, ch.33.

81 'Yes, I have a pair of eyes,' replied Sam, 'and that's just it. If they wos a pair o' patent double million magnifyin' gas microscopes of hextra power, p'raps I might be able to see through a flight o' stairs and a deal door; but bein' only eyes, you see, my wision's limited.'
1836–7 *Pickwick Papers*, ch.34.

82 Miss Bolo rose from the table considerably agitated, and went straight home, in a flood of tears, and a sedan chair.
1836–7 *Pickwick Papers*, ch.35.

83 *We* know, Mr. Weller—*we*, who are men of the world—that a good uniform must work its way with the women, sooner or later.
1836–7 The Gentleman in Blue. *Pickwick Papers*, ch.37.

84 You're a amiably-disposed young man, sir, I don't think.
1836–7 Sam Weller's father. *Pickwick Papers*, ch.38.

85 It's a regular holiday to them—all porter and skittles.
1836–7 *Pickwick Papers*, ch.41.

86 Anythin' for a quiet life, as the man said wen he took the sitivation at the lighthouse.
1836–7 Sam Weller. *Pickwick Papers*, ch.43.

87 The fact is, that there was considerable difficulty in inducing Oliver to take upon himself the office of respiration—a troublesome practice, but one which custom has rendered necessary to our easy existence; and for some time he lay gasping on a little flock mattress, rather unequally poised between this world and the next: the balance being decidedly in favour of the latter. Now, if during this brief period, Oliver had been surrounded by careful grandmothers, anxious aunts, experienced nurses, and doctors of profound wisdom, he would most inevitably and indubitably have been killed in no time.
1837–9 *Oliver Twist*, ch.1.

88 Please, sir, I want some more.
1837–9 Oliver. *Oliver Twist*, ch.2.

89 It was a nice sickly season just at this time. In commercial phrase, coffins were looking up.
1837–9 *Oliver Twist*, ch.6.

90 What a fine thing capital punishment is! Dead men never repent; dead men never bring awkward stories to light. Ah, it's a fine thing for the trade! Five of 'em strung up in a

row; and none left to play booty, or turn white-livered!
1837–9 Fagin. *Oliver Twist*, ch.9.

91 'Hard,' replied the Dodger. 'As nails,' added Charley Bates.
1837–9 *Oliver Twist*, ch.9.

92 There is a passion for hunting something deeply implanted in the human breast.
1837–9 *Oliver Twist*, ch.10.

93 I'll eat my head.
1837–9 Mr Grimwig. *Oliver Twist*, ch.14.

94 I only know two sorts of boys. Mealy boys, and beef-faced boys.
1837–9 Mr Grimwig. *Oliver Twist*, ch.14.

95 This ain't the shop for justice.
1837–9 The Artful Dodger. *Oliver Twist*, ch.43.

96 'If the law supposes that,' said Mr Bumble…'the law is a ass—a idiot.'
1837–9 *Oliver Twist*, ch.51.

97 The delights—the ten thousand million delights of a pantomime.
1838 *Memoirs of Joseph Grimaldi*, ed Dickens.

98 United Metropolitan Improved Hot Muffin and Crumpet Baking and Punctual Delivery Company.
1838–9 *Nicholas Nickleby*, ch.2.

99 EDUCATION.—At Mr Wackford Squeers's Academy, Dotheboys Hall, at the delightful village of Dotheboys, near Greta Bridge in Yorkshire. Youth are boarded, clothed, booked, furnished with pocket-money, provided with all necessaries, instructed in all languages, living and dead, mathematics, orthography, geometry, astronomy, trigonometry, the use of the globes, algebra, single stick (if required), writing, arithmetic, fortification, and every other branch of classical literature. Terms, twenty guineas per annum. No extras, no vacations, and diet unparalleled.
1838–9 *Nicholas Nickleby*, ch.3.

1 Mr Squeers's appearance was not prepossessing. He had but one eye, and the popular prejudice runs in favour of two.
1838–9 *Nicholas Nickleby*, ch.4.

2 Subdue your appetites, my dears, and you've conquered human nature.
1838–9 *Nicholas Nickleby*, ch.5.

3 There are only two styles of portrait painting, the serious and the smirk.
1838–9 Miss LaCreevy. *Nicholas Nickleby*, ch.10.

4 Oh! They're too beautiful to live, much too beautiful!
1938–9 Mrs Kenwigs, of her four daughters. *Nicholas Nickleby*, ch. 14.

5 Sir, My pa requests me to write to you. The doctors considering it doubtful whether he will ever recuvver the use of his legs which prevents his holding a pen.
1838–9 Fanny Squeers. *Nicholas Nickleby*, ch.15.

6 'What's the water in French, sir?' 'L'eau,' replied Nicholas. 'Ah!' said Mr Lillyvick, shaking his head mournfully, 'I thought as much. Lo, eh? I don't think anything of that language—nothing at all.'
1838–9 *Nicholas Nickleby*, ch.16.

7 'It's very easy to talk,' said Mrs Mantalini. 'Not so easy when one is eating a demnition egg,' replied Mr Mantalini; 'for the yolk runs down the waistcoat, and yolk of egg does not match any waistcoat but a yellow waistcoat, demmit.'
1838–9 *Nicholas Nickleby*, ch.17.

8 Language was not powerful enough to describe the infant phenomenon.
1838–9 *Nicholas Nickleby*, ch.23.

9 'I'm always ill after Shakespeare,' said Mrs Wititterly. 'I scarcely exist the next day; I find the re-action so very great after a tragedy…and Shakespeare is such a delicious creature.'
1838–9 *Nicholas Nickleby*, ch.27.

10 Every baby born into the world is a finer one than the last.
1838–9 *Nicholas Nickleby*, ch.36.

11 Bring in the bottled lightning, a clean tumbler, and a corkscrew.
1838–9 The Gentleman in the Small-Clothes. *Nicholas Nickleby*, ch.49.

12 All is gas and gaiters.
1838–9 The Gentleman in the Small-Clothes. *Nicholas Nickleby*, ch.49.

13 My life is one demd horrid grind!
1838–9 Mr Mantalini. *Nicholas Nickleby*, ch.64.

14 What is the odds so long as the fire of soul is kindled at the taper of conwiviality, and the wing of friendship never moults a feather!
1840–1 Dick Swiveller. *The Old Curiosity Shop*, ch.2.

15 Fan the sinking flame of hilarity with the wing of friendship; and pass the rosy wine.
1840–1 Dick Swiveller. *The Old Curiosity Shop*, ch.7.

16 She's all my fancy painted her, Sir, that's what she is.
1840–1 Dick Swiveller. *The Old Curiosity Shop*, ch.7.

17 Codlin's the friend, not Short.
1840–1 Codlin. *The Old Curiosity Shop*, ch.19.

18 And don't you think you must be a very wicked little child…to be a wax-work child at all?
1840–1 Miss Monflathers to Nell. *The Old Curiosity Shop*, ch.31.

19 'Did you ever taste beer?'
'I had a sip of it once,' said the small servant.
'Here's a state of things!' cried Mr. Swiveller, raising his eyes to the ceiling. 'She *never* tasted it—it can't be tasted in a sip!'
1840–1 *The Old Curiosity Shop*, ch.57.

20 They moved so gently, that their footsteps made no noise; but there were sobs from among the group, and sounds of grief and mourning.
1840–1 The death of little Nell. *The Old Curiosity Shop*, ch.71.

21 Something will come of this. I hope it mayn't be human gore!
1841 Simon Tappertit. *Barnaby Rudge*, ch.4.

22 Polly put the kettle on, we'll all have tea.
1841 Grip, the raven. *Barnaby Rudge*, ch.17.

23 'There are strings,' said Mr Tappertit…'in the human heart that had better not be wibrated.'
1841 Mr Tappertit. *Barnaby Rudge*, ch.22.

24 Oh gracious, why wasn't I born old and ugly?
1841 Miss Miggs. *Barnaby Rudge*, ch.70.

25 Was there ever such a sunny street as this Broadway! The pavement stones are polished with the tread of feet until

they shine again… Heaven save the ladies, how they dress! We have seen more colours in these ten minutes, than we should have seen elsewhere, in as many days. What various parasols! what rainbow silks and satins! what pinking of thin stockings and pinching of thin shoes, and fluttering of ribbons and silk tassels, and display of rich cloaks with gaudy hoods and linings!
1842 *American Notes.*

26 Politics are much discussed, so are banks, so is cotton. Quiet people avoid the question of the Presidency…the great constitutional feature of this institution being, that directly the acrimony of the last election is over, the next one begins.
1842 *American Notes.*

27 'Bah!' said Scrooge, 'Humbug!'
1843 *A Christmas Carol*, stave 1.

28 'You are fettered,' said Scrooge, trembling. 'Tell me why?' 'I wear the chain I forged in life,' replied the Ghost. 'I made it link by link, and yard by yard; I girded it on of my own free will, and of my own free will I wore it.'
1843 *A Christmas Carol*, stave 1.

29 'God bless us every one!' said Tiny Tim, the last of all.
1843 *A Christmas Carol*, stave 3.

30 But however and whenever we part from one another, I am sure we shall none of us forget poor Tiny Tim.
1843 *A Christmas Carol*, stave 4.

31 It *was* a turkey! He could never have stood upon his legs, that bird. He would have snapped 'em off short in a minute, like sticks of sealing-wax.
1843 *A Christmas Carol*, stave 5.

32 The Lord No Zoo.
1843–4 Toby Chuzzlewit. *Martin Chuzzlewit*, ch.1.

33 'The name of those fabulous animals (pagan, I regret to say) who used to sing in the water, has quite escaped me.' Mr George Chuzzlewit suggested 'Swans'. 'No,' said Mr Pecksniff. 'Not swans. Very like swans, too. Thank you.' The nephew…propounded 'Oysters'. 'No,' said Mr Picksniff…'nor oysters. But by no means unlike oysters… Wait! Sirens. Dear me! sirens, of course.'
1843–4 *Martin Chuzzlewit*, ch.4.

34 Any man may be in good spirits and good temper when he's well dressed. There an't much credit in that. If I was very ragged and very jolly, then I should begin to feel I had gained a point, Mr. Pinch.
1843–4 Mark Tapley. *Martin Chuzzlewit*, ch.5.

35 His moral character…was full of promise, but of no performance.
1843–4 Of Mr Pecksniff. *Martin Chuzzlewit*, ch.5.

36 Affection beaming in one eye, and calculation shining out of the other.
1843–4 Of Mrs Todgers. *Martin Chuzzlewit*, ch.8.

37 Let us be moral. Let us contemplate existence.
1843–4 Mr Pecksniff. *Martin Chuzzlewit*, ch.9.

38 Here's the rule for bargains: 'Do other men, for they would do you.' That's the true business precept.
1843–4 Jonas Chuzzlewit. *Martin Chuzzlewit*, ch.11.

39 Buy an annuity cheap, and make your life interesting to yourself and everybody else that watches the speculation.
1843–4 Jonas Chuzzlewit. *Martin Chuzzlewit*, ch.18.

40 'Mrs Harris,' I says, 'leave the bottle on the chimley-piece, and don't ask me to take none, but let me put my lips to it when I am so dispoged.'
1843–4 Mrs Gamp. *Martin Chuzzlewit*, ch.19.

41 Features are an index to the heart.
1843–4 *Martin Chuzzlewit*, ch.24.

42 At the same moment a peculiar fragrance was borne upon the breeze, as if a passing fairy had hiccuped, and had previously been to a wine vaults.
1843–4 On Mrs Gamp's entering a room. *Martin Chuzzlewit*, ch.25.

43 Gamp would certainly have drunk its little shoes right off its feet, as with our precious boy he did, and arterwards send the child a errand to sell his wooden leg for any money it 'ud fetch as matches in the rough, and bring it home in liquor.
1843–4 Mrs Gamp. *Martin Chuzzlewit*, ch.25.

44 She's the sort of woman…one would almost feel disposed to bury for nothing: and do it neatly, too!
1843–4 Mould speaking about Mrs Gamp. *Martin Chuzzlewit*, ch.25.

45 He'd make a lovely corpse.
1843–4 Mrs Gamp speaking of Jonas Chuzzlewit. *Martin Chuzzlewit*, ch.25.

46 We never knows wot's hidden in each other's hearts; and if we had glass winders there, we'd need keep the shutters up, some on us, I do assure you!
1843–4 Mrs Gamp. *Martin Chuzzlewit*, ch.29.

47 A lane was made; and Mrs Hominy…came slowly up it, in a procession of one.
1843–4 *Martin Chuzzlewit*, ch.34.

48 'Mind and matter,' said the lady in the wig, 'glide swift into the vortex of immensity. Howls the sublime, and softly sleeps the calm Ideal, in the whispering chambers of Imagination.'
1843–4 A Transcendental literary lady. *Martin Chuzzlewit*, ch.34.

49 Farewell! Be the proud bride of a ducal coronet, and forget me!… Unalterably, never yours, Augustus.
1843–4 Augustus Moddle. *Martin Chuzzlewit*, ch.54.

50 Oh let us love our occupations,
Bless the squire and his relations,
Live upon our daily rations,
And always know our proper stations.
1844 Lady Bowley. *The Chimes*, second quarter.

51 The earth was made for Dombey and Son to trade in, and the sun and moon were made to give them light. Rivers and seas were formed to float their ships; rainbows gave them promise of fair weather; winds blew for or against their enterprises; stars and planets circled in their orbits, to preserve inviolate a system of which they were the centre.
1846–8 *Dombey and Son*, ch.1.

52 Dombey and Son had often dealt in hides, but never in hearts. They left that fancy ware to boys and girls, and boarding-schools and books.
1846–8 *Dombey and Son*, ch.1.

53 'The sea, Floy, what is it that it keeps on saying?' She told him that it was only the noise of the rolling waves. 'Yes, yes,' he said. 'But I know that they are always saying something. Always the same thing. What place is over there?'…

She told him there was another country opposite, but he said he didn't mean that; he meant farther away—farther away!

Very often afterwards, in the midst of their talk, he would break off, to try to understand what it was that the waves were always saying; and would rise up in his couch to look towards that invisible region, far away.
1846–8 Of little Paul Dombey. *Dombey and Son*, ch.8.

54 She was dry and sandy with working in the graves of deceased languages. None of your live languages for Miss Blimber. They must be dead—stone dead—and then Miss Blimber dug them up like a Ghoul.
1846–8 *Dombey and Son*, ch.11.

55 As to Mr Feeder, B.A., Doctor Blimber's assistant, he was a kind of human barrel-organ, with a little list of tunes at which he was continually working, over and over again, without any variation.
1846–8 *Dombey and Son*, ch.11.

56 When found, make a note of.
1846–8 Captain Cuttle. *Dombey and Son*, ch.15.

57 Train up a fig-tree in the way it should go, and when you are old sit under the shade of it.
1846–8 Captain Cuttle. *Dombey and Son*, ch.19.

58 The bearings of this observation lays in the application on it.
1846–8 Captain Bunsby. *Dombey and Son*, ch.23.

59 Say, like those wicked Turks, there is no What's-his-name but Thingummy, and What-you-may-call-it is his prophet!
1846–8 Mrs Skewton. *Dombey and Son*, ch.27.

60 If you could see my legs when I take my boots off, you'd form some idea of what unrequited affection is.
1846–8 Mr Toots. *Dombey and Son*, ch.48.

61 I am a lone lorn creetur…and everythink goes contrairy with me.
1849–50 Mrs Gummidge. *David Copperfield*, ch.3.

62 'I feel it more than other people,' said Mrs Gummidge.
1849–50 *David Copperfield*, ch.3.

63 I'd better go into the house, and die and be a riddance!
1849–50 Mrs Gummidge. *David Copperfield*, ch.3.

64 Barkis is willin'.
1849–50 Barkis's proposal of marriage to Peggotty. *David Copperfield*, ch.5.

65 Experientia does it—as papa used to say.
1849–50 Mrs Micawber. *David Copperfield*, ch.11.

66 I never will desert Mr Micawber.
1849–50 Mrs Micawber. *David Copperfield*, ch.12.

67 Annual income twenty pounds, annual expenditure nineteen nineteen six, result happiness. Annual income twenty pounds, annual expenditure twenty pounds ought and six, result misery.
1849–50 Mr Micawber. *David Copperfield*, ch.12.

68 I am well aware that I am the umblest person going… My mother is likewise a very umble person. We live in a numble abode.
1849–50 Uriah Heep. *David Copperfield*, ch.16.

69 We are so very umble.
1849–50 Uriah Heep. *David Copperfield*, ch.17.

70 The mistake was made of putting some of the trouble out of King Charles's head into my head.
1849–50 Mr Dick. *David Copperfield*, ch.17.

71 'Orses and dorgs is some men's fancy. They're wittles and drink to me—lodging, wife, and children—reading, writing and 'rithmetic—snuff, tobacker, and sleep.
1849–50 Man on the Canterbury coach. *David Copperfield*, ch.19.

72 I only ask for information.
1849–50 Rosa Dartle. *David Copperfield*, ch.20.

73 'It was as true,' said Mr Barkis, '…as taxes is. And nothing's truer than them.'
1849–50 *David Copperfield*, ch.21.

74 What a world of gammon and spinnage it is, though, ain't it?
1849–50 Miss Mowcher. *David Copperfield*, ch.22.

75 Accidents will occur in the best-regulated families.
1849–50 Mr Micawber. *David Copperfield*, ch.28.

76 'People can't die, along the coast,' said Mr Peggotty, 'except when the tide's pretty nigh out. They can't be born, unless it's pretty nigh in—not properly born, till flood. He's a going out with the tide.'
1849–50 On the death of Barkis. *David Copperfield*, ch.30.

77 Mrs Crupp had indignantly assured him that there wasn't room to swing a cat there; but, as Mr Dick justly observed to me… 'You know, Trotwood, I don't want to swing a cat. I never do swing a cat. Therefore, what does that signify to me!'
1849–50 *David Copperfield*, ch.35.

78 'No better opening anywhere,' said my aunt, 'for a man who conducts himself well, and is industrious.'
1849–50 Of Mr Micawber's prospects in Australia. *David Copperfield*, ch.52.

79 Fog everywhere. Fog up the river, where it flows among green aits and meadows; fog down the river, where it rolls defiled among the tiers of shipping, and the waterside pollutions of a great (and dirty) city. Fog on the Essex marshes, fog on the Kentish heights. Fog creeping into the cabooses of collier-brigs; fog lying out on the yards, and hovering in the rigging of great ships… And hard by Temple Bar, in Lincoln's Inn Hall, at the very heart of the fog, sits the Lord High Chancellor in his High Court of Chancery.
1852–3 *Bleak House*, ch.1.

80 But Jarndyce and Jarndyce still drags its dreary length before the court, perennially hopeless.
1852–3 *Bleak House*, ch.1.

81 The evil of it is, that it is a world wrapped up in too much jeweller's cotton and fine wool, and cannot hear the rushing of the larger worlds, and cannot see them as they circle round the sun. It is a deadened world, and its growth is sometimes unhealthy for want of air.
1852–3 Of the world of fashion. *Bleak House*, ch.2.

82 This is a London particular… A fog, miss.
1852–3 Mr Guppy to Esther. *Bleak House*, ch.3.

83 I expect a judgement. Shortly.
1852–3 Miss Flyte. *Bleak House*, ch.3. The judgement predicted, in the case of *Jarndyce* v *Jarndyce*, fails to materialize for many decades.

84 The wind's in the east… I am always conscious of an uncomfortable sensation now and then when the wind is blowing in the east.
1852–3 Mr Jarndyce. *Bleak House*, ch.6.

85 It is said that the children of the poor are not brought up, but dragged up.
1852–3 Mr Jarndyce. *Bleak House*, ch.6.

86 I don't feel any vulgar gratitude to you. I almost feel as if *you* ought to be grateful to *me*, for giving you the opportunity of enjoying the luxury of generosity… For anything I can tell, I may have come into the world expressly for the purpose of increasing your stock of happiness.
1852–3 Harold Skimpole. *Bleak House*, ch.6.

87 An oyster of the old school whom nobody can open.
1852–3 Of Mr Tulkinghorn. *Bleak House*, ch.10.

88 He wos wery good to me, he wos!
1852–3 Jo speaking of Nemo. *Bleak House*, ch.11.

89 'For I don't,' says Jo, 'I don't know nothink.'
1852–3 *Bleak House*, ch.16.

90 You are a human boy, my young friend. A human boy. O glorious to be a human boy!…
O running stream of sparkling joy
To be a soaring human boy!
1852–3 Rev Mr Chadband. *Bleak House*, ch.19.

91 Jobling, there *are* chords in the human mind.
1852–3 Mr Guppy. *Bleak House*, ch.20.

92 'It is,' says Chadband, 'the ray of rays, the sun of suns, the moon of moons, the star of stars. It is the light of Terewth.'
1852–3 *Bleak House*, ch.25.

93 'Old girl,' said Mr Bagnet, 'give him my opinion. You know it.'
1852–3 *Bleak House*, ch.27.

94 It is a melancholy truth that even great men have their poor relations.
1852–3 *Bleak House*, ch.28.

95 Never have a mission.
1852–3 Mr Jellyby. *Bleak House*, ch.30.

96 The one great principle of the English law is, to make business for itself. There is no other principle distinctly, certainly, and consistently maintained through all its narrow turnings.
1852–3 *Bleak House*, ch.39.

97 He is not a genuine foreign-grown savage; he is the ordinary home-made article. Dirty, ugly, disagreeable to all the senses, in body a common creature of the common streets, only in soul a Heathen. Homely filth begrimes him, homely parasites devour him, homely sores are in him, homely rags are on him: native ignorance, the growth of English soil and climate, sinks his immortal nature lower than the beasts that perish.
1852–3 Of Jo. *Bleak House*, ch.47.

98 Dead, your Majesty. Dead, my lords and gentlemen. Dead, Right Reverends and Wrong Reverends of every order. Dead, men and women, born with Heavenly compassion in your hearts. And dying thus around us every day.
1852–3 On the death of Jo. *Bleak House*, ch.47.

99 Now, what I want is, Facts. Teach these boys and girls nothing but Facts. Facts alone are wanted in life.
1854 Mr Gradgrind. *Hard Times*, bk.1, ch.1.

1 The speaker, and the schoolmaster, and the third grown person present, all backed a little, and swept with their eyes the inclined plane of little vessels then and there

arranged in order, ready to have imperial gallons of facts poured into them until they were full to the brim.
1854 *Hard Times*, bk.1, ch.1.

2 'Girl number twenty unable to define a horse!' said Mr Gradgrind… 'Girl number twenty possessed of no facts, in reference to one of the commonest of animals!'…
'Bitzer' said Thomas Gradgrind. 'Your definition of a horse.'
'Quadruped. Graminivorous. Forty teeth, namely twenty-four grinders, four eye-teeth, and twelve incisive. Sheds coat in the spring; in marshy countries, sheds hoofs, too. Hoofs hard, but requiring to be shod with iron. Age known by marks in mouth.' Thus (and much more) Bitzer.
'Now girl number twenty,' said Mr Gradgrind. 'You know what a horse is.'
1854 *Hard Times*, bk.1, ch.2.

3 It was a town of red brick, or of brick that would have been red if the smoke and ashes had allowed it; but, as matters stood it was a town of unnatural red and black as the painted face of a savage.
1854 Of Coketown. *Hard Times*, bk.1, ch.5.

4 Coketown…ugly citadel, where Nature was as strongly bricked out as killing airs and gases were bricked in.
1854 *Hard Times*, bk.1, ch.10.

5 I see traces of the turtle soup, and venison, and gold spoon in this.
1854 Mr Bounderby. *Hard Times*, bk.1, ch.11.

6 Ah, Rachel, aw a muddle! Fro' first to last, a muddle!
1854 Stephen Blackpool. *Hard Times*, bk.3, ch.6.

7 People mutht be amuthed. They can't be alwayth a learning, nor yet they can't be alwayth a working, they an't made for it.
1854 Mr Sleary. *Hard Times*, bk.3, ch.8.

8 Whatever was required to be done, the Circumlocution Office was beforehand with all the public departments in the art of perceiving—HOW NOT TO DO IT.
1855–7 *Little Dorrit*, bk.1, ch.10.

9 Take a little time—count five-and-twenty, Tattycoram.
1855–7 Mr Meagles. *Little Dorrit*, bk.1, ch.16.

10 In company with several other old ladies of both sexes.
1855–7 *Little Dorrit*, bk.1, ch.17.

11 It was not a bosom to repose upon, but it was a capital bosom to hang jewels upon.
1855–7 Of Mrs Merdle. *Little Dorrit*, bk.1, ch.21.

12 There's milestones on the Dover Road!
1855–7 Mr F's Aunt. *Little Dorrit*, bk.1, ch.23.

13 I revere the memory of Mr F. as an estimable man and most indulgent husband, only necessary to mention Asparagus and it appeared or to hint at any little delicate thing to drink and it came like magic in a pint bottle it was not ecstasy but it was comfort.
1855–7 Flora Finching. *Little Dorrit*, bk.1, ch.24.

14 As to marriage on the part of a man, my dear, Society requires that he should retrieve his fortunes by marriage. Society requires that he should gain by marriage. Society requires that he should found a handsome establishment by marriage. Society does not see, otherwise, what he has to do with marriage.
1855–7 Mrs Merdle. *Little Dorrit*, bk.1, ch.33.

15 Mrs General had no opinions. Her way of forming a mind was to prevent it from forming opinions…Mrs General was not to be told of anything shocking. Accidents, miseries, and offences, were never to be mentioned before her. Passion was to go to sleep in the presence of Mrs General, and blood was to change to milk and water. The little that was left in the world, when all these deductions were made, it was Mrs General's province to varnish.
1855–7 *Little Dorrit*, bk.2, ch.2.

16 Father is rather vulgar, my dear. The word Papa, besides, gives a pretty form to the lips. Papa, potatoes, poultry, prunes, and prism, are all very good words for the lips: especially prunes and prism.
1855–7 Mrs General. *Little Dorrit*, bk.2, ch.5.

17 That it is at least as difficult to stay a moral infection as a physical one; that such a disease will spread with the malignity and rapidity of the Plague; that the contagion, when it has once made head, will spare no pursuit or condition, but will lay hold on people in the soundest health, and become developed in the most unlikely constitutions; is a fact as firmly established by experience as that we human creatures breathe an atmosphere.
1855–7 *Little Dorrit*, bk.2, ch.13.

18 Once a gentleman, and always a gentleman.
1855–7 Rigaud. *Little Dorrit*, bk.2, ch.28.

19 It was the best of times, it was the worst of times, it was the age of wisdom, it was the age of foolishness, it was the epoch of belief, it was the epoch of incredulity, it was the season of Light, it was the season of Darkness, it was the spring of hope, it was the winter of despair, we had everything before us, we had nothing before us, we were all going direct to Heaven, we were all going direct the other way.
1859 *A Tale of Two Cities*, bk.1, ch.1.

20 I pass my whole life, miss, in turning an immense pecuniary Mangle.
1859 Mr Lorry. *A Tale of Two Cities*, bk.1, ch.4.

21 If it was ever intended that I should go across salt water, do you suppose Providence would have cast my lot in an island?
1859 Miss Pross. *A Tale of Two Cities*, bk.1, ch.4.

22 If you must go flopping yourself down, flop in favour of your husband and child, and not in opposition to 'em.
1859 Jerry Cruncher. *A Tale of Two Cities*, bk.2, ch.1.

23 I care for no man on earth, and no man on earth cares for me.
1859 Sydney Carton. *A Tale of Two Cities*, bk.2, ch.4.

24 Although it's a long time on the road, it is on the road and coming. I tell thee it never retreats, and never stops.
1859 Madame Defarge. *A Tale of Two Cities*, bk.2, ch.16.

25 It is a far, far better thing that I do, than I have ever done; it is a far, far better rest that I go to than I have ever known.
1859 Sydney Carton. *A Tale of Two Cities*, bk.3, ch.15.

26 Cleanliness is next to Godliness, and some people do the same by their religion.
1860–1 *Great Expectations*, ch.4.

27 I was always treated as if I had insisted on being born in opposition to the dictates of reason, religion, and morality.
1860–1 Pip. *Great Expectations*, ch.4.

28 Your sister is given to government.
1860–1 Joe Gargery. *Great Expectations*, ch.7.

29 In the little world in which children have their existence, whosoever brings them up, there is nothing so finely perceived and so finely felt, as injustice.
1860–1 *Great Expectations*, ch.8.

30 I had cherished a profound conviction that her bringing me up by hand, gave her no right to bring me up by jerks.
1860–1 *Great Expectations*, ch.8.

31 It is a most miserable thing to feel ashamed of home.
1860–1 *Great Expectations*, ch.14.

32 Probably every new and eagerly expected garment ever put on since clothes came in, fell a trifle short of the wearer's expectation.
1860–1 *Great Expectations*, ch.19.

33 You wouldn't mind being at once introduced to the Aged, would you?
1860–1 Wemmick introduces Pip to his father. *Great Expectations*, ch.25.

34 I loved Estella… I loved her against reason, against promise, against peace, against hope, against happiness, against all discouragement that could be.
1860–1 *Great Expectations*, ch.29.

35 Words cannot state the amount of aggravation and injury wreaked upon me by Trabb's boy, when passing abreast of me, he pulled up his shirt-collar, twined his side-hair, stuck an arm akimbo, and smirked extravagantly by, wriggling his elbows and body, and drawling to his attendants, 'Don't know yah, don't know yah, 'pon my soul don't know yah!'
1860–1 *Great Expectations*, ch.30.

36 'Halloa! Here's a church!… Let's go in!… Here's Miss Skiffins! Let's have a wedding.'
1860–1 *Great Expectations*, ch.55.

37 I listened with hadmiration amounting to haw.
1864–5 Mr Boffin. *Our Mutual Friend*, bk.1, ch.5.

38 A literary man—*with* a wooden leg—and all Print is open to him.
1864–5 Mr Boffin speaking of Silas Wegg. *Our Mutual Friend*, bk.1, ch.5.

39 Mrs Boffin…is a highflyer at Fashion.
1864–5 *Our Mutual Friend*, bk.1, ch.5.

40 'Was you thinking at all of poetry?' Mr Wegg inquired, musing.
'Would it come dearer?' Mr Boffin asked.
'It would come dearer,' Mr Wegg returned. 'For when a person comes to grind off poetry night after night, it is but right he should expect to be paid for its weakening effect on his mind.'
1864–5 *Our Mutual Friend*, bk.1, ch.5.

41 These two ignorant and unpolished people had guided themselves so far on in their journey of life, by a religious sense of duty and desire to do right.
1864–5 Of Mr and Mrs Boffin. *Our Mutual Friend*, bk.1, ch.9.

42 Mr Podsnap was well to do, and stood very high in Mr Podsnap's opinion.
1864–5 *Our Mutual Friend*, bk.1, ch.11.

43 A certain institution in Mr Podsnap's mind which he called 'the young person' may be considered to have been embodied in Miss Podsnap, his daughter…The

question about everything was, would it bring a blush into the cheek of the young person?
1864–5 *Our Mutual Friend*, bk.1, ch.11.

44 'Our Language,' said Mr Podsnap, with a gracious consciousness of being always right, 'is Difficult. Ours is a Copious Language, and Trying to Strangers. I will not Pursue my Question… It merely referred,' Mr Podsnap explained, with a sense of meritorious proprietorship, 'to our Constitution, Sir. We Englishmen are Very Proud of our Constitution, Sir. It Was Bestowed Upon Us By Providence. No Other Country is so Favoured as This Country.'
1864–5 *Our Mutual Friend*, bk.1, ch.11.

45 Mr Podsnap settled that whatever he put behind him he put out of existence… 'I don't want to know about it; I don't choose to discuss it; I don't admit it!'
1864–5 *Our Mutual Friend*, bk.1, ch.11.

46 I think…that it is the best club in London.
1864–5 Mr Twemlow's description of the House of Commons. *Our Mutual Friend*, bk.2, ch.3.

47 Come up and be dead! Come up and be dead!
1864–5 Jenny Wren. *Our Mutual Friend*, bk.2, ch.5.

48 A slap-up gal in a bang-up chariot.
1864–5 The scout's description of Bella. *Our Mutual Friend*, bk.2, ch.8.

49 I want to be something so much worthier than the doll in the doll's house.
1864–5 Bella. *Our Mutual Friend*, bk.4, ch.5.

50 Stranger, pause and ask thyself the question, Canst thou do likewise? If not, with a blush retire.
1870 Mr Sapsea's epitaph for his wife. *Edwin Drood*, ch.4.

Dickinson, Emily Elizabeth 1830–86

US poet who spent her life in seclusion in Massachusetts, writing over 1000 intensely lyrical and personal poems, few of which were published during her lifetime.

51 Success is counted sweetest
By those who ne'er succeed.
c.1859 *Complete Poems*, no.67 (first published 1890).

52 Can I expound the skies?
How still the Riddle lies!
c.1859 *Complete Poems*, no.89 (first published 1890).

53 Surgeons must be very careful
When they take the knife!
Underneath their fine incisions
Stirs the culprit—*Life!*
c.1859 *Complete Poems*, no.108 (first published 1891).

54 To fight aloud, is very brave,
But gallanter, I know,
Who charge within the bosom
The Cavalry of Woe.
c.1859 *Complete Poems*, no.126 (first published 1890).

55 Musicians wrestle everywhere—
All day—among the crowded air
I hear the silver strife—
And—waking—long before the morn—
Such transport breaks upon the town
I think it that 'New Life!'
c.1860 *Complete Poems*, no.157 (first published 1891).

56 'Faith' is a fine invention

When Gentlemen can *see*—
But *Microscopes* are prudent
In an Emergency.
c.1860 *Complete Poems*, no.185 (first published 1891).

57 Inebriate of Air—am I—
And Debauchee of Dew—
Reeling—thro endless summer days—
From inns of Molten Blue—
c.1860 *Complete Poems*, no.214 (first published 1861).

58 'Hope' is the thing with feathers—
That perches in the soul—
And sings the tune without the words—
And never stops—at all—
c.1860 *Complete Poems*, no.254 (first published 1891).

59 Some keep the Sabbath going to Church—
I keep it, staying at Home—
With a Bobolink for a Chorister—
And an Orchard, for a Dome—
c.1860 *Complete Poems*, no.324 (first published 1864).

60 After great pain, a formal feeling comes—
The Nerves sit ceremonious, like Tombs.
c.1862 *Complete Poems*, no.341 (first published 1929).

61 Much Madness is divinest Sense—
To a discerning Eye—
Much Sense—the starkest Madness—
c.1862 *Complete Poems*, no.435 (first published 1890).

62 They shut me up in Prose—
As when a little girl
They put me in the Closet—
Because they liked me 'still'.
c.1862 *Complete Poems*, no.613 (first published 1935).

63 The Brain—is wider than the Sky.
c.1862 *Complete Poems*, no.632 (first published 1896).

64 I cannot live with You—
It would be Life—
And Life is over there—
Behind the Shelf.
c.1862 *Complete Poems*, no.640 (first published 1890).

65 One need not be a Chamber—to be Haunted—
One need not be a House—
The brain has Corridors—surpassing
Material Place—
c.1863 *Complete Poems*, no.670 (first published 1891).

66 Because I could not stop for Death—
He kindly stopped for me—
The carriage held but just Ourselves—
And Immortality.
c.1863 *Complete Poems*, no.712 (first published 1890).

67 Ample make this Bed—
Make this Bed with Awe—
In it wait till Judgement break
Excellent and Fair.
c.1864 *Complete Poems*, no.829 (first published 1891).

68 Of Consciousness, her awful Mate
The soul cannot be rid—
As easy the secreting her
Behind the Eyes of God.
c.1864 *Complete Poems*, no.894 (first published 1945).

69 Faith—is the Pierless Bridge
Supporting what We see

Unto the Scene that We do not.
c.**1864** *Complete Poems*, no.915 (first published 1929).

70 Death is a dialogue between
The Spirit and the Dust.
c.**1864** *Complete Poems*, no.976 (first published 1890).

71 Tell all the Truth but tell it slant—
Success in Circuit lies
Too bright for our infirm Delight
The Truth's superb surprise.
c.**1868** *Complete Poems*, no.1129 (first published 1945).

72 A word is dead
When it is said,
Some say.
I say it just
Begins to live
That day.
?**1872** *Complete Poems*, no.1212 (first published 1894).

73 The abdication of Belief
Makes the Behavior small—
Better an ignis fatuus
Than no illume at all.
c.**1882** *Complete Poems*, no.1551 (first published 1945).

74 He ate and drank the precious Words,
His Spirit grew robust;
He knew no more that he was poor,
Nor that his frame was Dust.
c.**1883** *Complete Poems*, no.1587 (first published 1890).

75 The Pedigree of Honey
Does not concern the Bee—
A Clover, any time, to him,
Is Aristocracy—
c.**1884** *Complete Poems*, no.1627 (first published 1890).

76 'Eternity' is there,
We say, as of a station.
Meanwhile, he is so near,
He joins me in my Ramble—
Divides abode with me—
No Friend have I that so persists
As this Eternity.
Complete Poems, no.1684 (first published 1914).

77 Parting is all we know of heaven,
And all we need of hell.
Complete Poems, no.1732 (first published 1896).

78 Rearrange a 'Wife's' affection!
When they dislocate my Brain!
Amputate my freckled Bosom!
Make me bearded like a man!
Complete Poems, no.1737 (first published 1891).

79 The distance that the dead have gone
Does not at first appear—
Their coming back seems possible
For many an ardent year.
Complete Poems, no.1742 (first published 1896).

80 Let us go in; the fog is rising.
Last words, attributed.

Dickinson, John 1732–1808

US revolutionary statesman, leader of conservative opposition to the British. His draft formed the basis of the Articles of Confederation.

81 Then join hand in hand, brave Americans all—
By uniting we stand, by dividing we fall.
1768 'The Liberty Song'.

82 We have counted the cost of this contest, and find nothing so dreadful as voluntary slavery… Our cause is just, our union is perfect.
1775 Declaration of reasons for taking up arms against Britain, 8 Jul, presented to Congress. Quoted in C J Stille *The Life and Times of John Dickinson* (1891), ch.5.

Diderot, Denis 1713–84

French philosopher, novelist, essayist, playwright and critic. A leading figure in the Enlightenment, he is best remembered for his ambitious *Encyclopédie* (1751–72). Other writings include sentimental dramas and theoretical studies of the theatre.

83 *Il ne faut point donner d'esprit à ses personnages; mais savoir les placer dans des circonstances qui leur en donnent.*
You should not give wit to your characters, but know instead how to put them in situations which will make them witty.
1757 *Entretiens sur le fils naturel*, pt.2.

84 *Les passions détruisent plus de préjugés que la philosophie. Et comment le mensonge leur résisterait-il? Elles ébranlent quelquefois la vérité.*
Passions destroy more prejudices than philosophy. And how would lies resist passions? Passions sometimes weaken the truth.
1757 *Entretiens sur le fils naturel*, pt.2.

85 *Les beautés ont, dans les arts, le même fondement que les vérités dans la philosophie. Qu'est-ce que la vérité? La conformité de nos jugements avec les êtres. Qu'est-ce que la beauté d'imitation? La conformité de l'image avec la chose.*
Beauty has in art the same foundation as does truth in philosophy. What is the truth? The conformity of our judgements with beings. What is the beauty of imitation? The conformity of the image with the thing.
1757 *Entretiens sur le fils naturel*, pt.3.

86 *Une danse est un poème.*
A dance is a poem.
1757 *Entretiens sur le fils naturel*, pt.3.

87 *Soit donc que vous composiez, soit donc que vous jouiez, ne pensez non plus au spectateur que s'il n'existait pas. Imaginez sur le bord du théâtre, un grand mur qui vous sépare du parterre; jouez comme si la toile ne se levait pas.*
Whether you compose or act, think no more of the spectator than if he did not exist. Imagine at the edge of the stage a large wall which separates you from the orchestra; act as if the curtain never rose.
1758 *Discours sur la poésie dramatique*, introducing the theatrical concept of the 'fourth wall'.

88 *Le génie se sent; mais il ne s'imite point.*
Genius is felt, but it is not imitated.
1758 *Discours sur la poésie dramatique*.

89 *En général, plus un peuple est civilisé, poli, moins ses mœurs sont poétiques; tout s'affaiblit en s'adoucissant.*
In general, the more civilized and refined the people, the less poetic are its morals; everything weakens as it mellows.
1758 *Discours sur la poésie dramatique*.

90 *La poésie veut quelque chose d'énorme, de barbare et de sauvage.*
Poetry needs something on the scale of the grand, the barbarous, the savage.
1758 *Discours sur la poésie dramatique.*

91 *Le public ne sait pas toujours désirer le vrai.*
The public does not always know how to desire the truth.
1758 *Discours sur la poésie dramatique.*

92 *Le rôle d'un auteur est un rôle assez vain; c'est celui d'un homme qui se croit en état de donner des leçons au public. Et le rôle du critique? Il est bien plus vain encore; c'est celui d'un homme qui se croit en état de donner des leçons à celui qui se croit en état d'en donner au public.*
The role of the author is vain enough; it is that of a person who considers himself able to give lessons to the public. And the role of the critic? It is vainer still; it is that of a person who considers himself able to give lessons to he who considers himself able to give them to the public.
1758 *Discours sur la poésie dramatique.*

93 *Ce n'est que par la mémoire que nous sommes un même individu pour les autres et pour nous-mêmes. Il ne me reste peut-être pas, à l'âge que j'ai, une seule molécule du corps que j'apportai en naissant.*
It is only in memory that we are the same person for others and for ourselves. At the age I am now, there is probably not a single molecule of my body that I had when born.
1758 *Discours sur la poésie dramatique.*

94 *Mes pensées sont mes catins.*
My thoughts are my prostitutes.
1761–74 *Le Neveu de Rameau.*

95 *Rien ne dissemble plus de lui que lui-même.*
Nothing resembles him less than himself.
1761–74 *Le Neveu de Rameau.*

96 *Voyez-vous cet oeuf. C'est avec cela qu'on renverse toutes les écoles de théologie, et tous les temples de la terre.*
See this egg. It is with this that all the schools of theology and all the temples of the earth are to be overturned.
1769 *Le Rêve de d'Alembert* (published 1830), pt.1.

97 *Tous les jours on couche avec des femmes qu'on n'aime pas, et l'on ne couche pas avec des femmes qu'on aime.*
Every day we sleep with women we do not love and don't sleep with the women we do love.
c.1773 *Jacques le fataliste et son maître* (published 1796).

98 *L'esprit de l'escalier.*
Staircase wit.
1773–8 That is, the witty reply that comes to mind after leaving the company, while descending the stairs. *Paradoxe sur le comédien* (published 1830).

99 Two qualities essential for the artist: morality and perspective.
1776–81 *Pensées détachées sur la peinture.*

1 One composition is meagre, though it has many figures; another is rich, though it has few.
1776–81 *Pensées détachées sur la peinture.*

2 Paint as they spoke in Sparta.
1776–81 *Pensées détachées sur la peinture.*

3 *L'homme est né pour la société; séparez-le, isolez-le, ses idées se désuniront, son caractère se tournera, mille affections ridicules s'élèveront dans son coeur; des*

pensées extravagantes germeront dans son esprit, comme les ronces dans une terre sauvage.
Man is born to live in society: separate him, isolate him, and his ideas disintegrate, his character changes, a thousand ridiculous affectations rise up in his heart; extreme thoughts take hold in his mind, like the brambles in a wild field.
1796 *La Religieuse.*

Didion, Joan 1934–

US writer, a respected essayist on US life and culture. Her works include the novel *A Book of Common Prayer* (1977) and the non-fiction titles *The White Album* (1979) and *Political Fictions* (2001).

4 Innocence ends when one is stripped of the delusion that one likes oneself.
1961 'On Self Respect', collected in *Slouching Towards Bethlehem* (1968).

5 Was there ever in anyone's life span a point free in time, devoid of memory, a night when choice was any more than the sum of all the choices gone before?
1963 *Run River*, ch.4.

6 New York was no mere city. It was instead an infinitely romantic notion, the mysterious nexus of all love and money and power, the shining and perishable dream itself. To think of 'living' there was to reduce the miraculous to the mundane; one does not 'live' at Xanadu.
1967 'Goodbye To All That', collected in *Slouching Towards Bethlehem* (1968).

7 We tell ourselves stories in order to live.
1979 *The White Album*, 'The White Album, 1'.

8 Everything was unmentionable but nothing was unimaginable.
1979 Of Los Angeles in 1968–9. *The White Album*, 'The White Album, 10'.

9 To believe in 'the greater good' is to operate, necessarily, in a certain ethical suspension.
1979 *The White Album*, 'The Woman's Movement'.

Dietz, Howard 1896–1983

US writer and lyricist.

10 That's Entertainment.
1953 Title of song reputedly written by Dietz and Arthur Schwartz for the film *The Band Wagon* in less than an hour.

11 More stars than there are in heaven.
MGM slogan.

Dillard, Annie 1945–

US writer. She is best known for her essay collection *Pilgrim at Tinker Creek* (1974), and has also written poetry and fiction.

12 It was a bitter birthday present from evolution.
1974 Of self-consciousness. *Pilgrim at Tinker Creek*, ch.6.

13 I don't know what it is about fecundity that so appals. I suppose it is the teeming evidence that birth and growth, which we value, are ubiquitous and blind, that life itself is so astonishingly cheap, that nature is as careless as it is bountiful, and that with extravagance goes a crushing waste that will one day include our own cheap lives.
1974 *Pilgrim at Tinker Creek*, ch.10.

14 I think the dying pray at the last not please but thank you as a guest thanks his host at the door.
1974 *Pilgrim at Tinker Creek*, ch.15.

Dillingham, Charles 1868–1934
US theatre producer.

15 I bet you, Ziggie, a hundred bucks that he ain't in here.
1926 Attributed whisper to Florenz Ziegfeld as they acted as pall-bearers at the funeral of escapologist Harry Houdini.

Dillon, Wentworth c.1633–1685
Irish poet and critic.

16 Choose an author as you choose a friend.
1684 *Essay on Translated Verse*, l.96.

17 Immodest words admit of no defence,
For want of decency is want of sense.
1684 *Essay on Translated Verse*, l.113.

DiMaggio, Joe (Joseph Paul) 1914–99
US baseball player. A powerful and elegant centre fielder and hitter, he played for 15 seasons with the New York Yankees, voted Most Valuable Player three times. In 1954 he married (briefly) Marilyn Monroe.

18 There's no skill involved. Just go up there and swing at the ball.
Of baseball. Quoted in Colin Jarman *The Guinness Dictionary of Sports Quotations* (1990).

19 It's no fun being married to an electric light.
Of his marriage to Marilyn Monroe. Quoted in Colin Jarman *The Guinness Dictionary of Sports Quotations* (1990).

Dimbleby, Richard 1913–65
English broadcaster, best known for his commentaries on state occasions. He joined the BBC's news team in 1936, becoming its first war correspondent (1939).

20 The moment of the Queen's crowning is come.
1953 Commentary on the coronation at Westminster Abbey, 2 Jun.

Dinesen, Isak
➤ *See Blixen, Karen, Baroness*

Diogenes of Sinope c.410–c.320 BC
Greek Cynic philosopher and moralist, student of Antisthenes.

21 Yes…stand out of my sun a little.
His reply when asked by Alexander the Great if he lacked anything. Quoted in Plutarch *Parallel Lives*, 'Alexander'.
➤ *See Alexander the Great 11:18.*

22 I am looking for an honest man.
His reply when asked why he was wandering the streets of Athens during the day with a lantern.

Dior, Christian 1905–57
French couturier who founded his own Paris house in 1947 and achieved worldwide fame with his 'New Look' in the same year.

23 Women are most fascinating between the ages of thirty-five and forty, after they have won a few races and know how to pace themselves. Since few women ever pass forty, maximum fascination can continue indefinitely.
1955 In *Collier's Magazine*, 10 Jun.

24 In the world today *haute couture* is one of the last repositories of the marvellous, and the *couturiers* the last possessors of the wand of Cinderella's Fairy Godmother.
Dior by Dior (translated by Antonia Fraser, 1957).

Dirksen, Everett M(cKinley) 1896–1969
US Republican politician.

25 The oil can is mightier than the sword.
1964 In *Life*, 5 Jun.

26 I am a man of fixed and unbending principles, the first of which is to be flexible at all times.
Recalled on his death, 7 Sep 1969.

27 A billion here, a billion there. Pretty soon it runs into real money.
Quoted in 'Half a Trillion in Real Money', editorial in the *New York Times*, 2 Dec 1979.

Disch, Thomas M(ichael) 1940–
US writer and critic, best known for his sophisticated, politically conscious science fiction, such as *Camp Concentration* (1968). He has also written several volumes of poetry.

28 Mankind Under The Leash.
1966 Title of novel.

29 A predilection for genre fiction is symptomatic of a kind of arrested development.
1986 In *The Face*, Mar.

30 Science fiction, like Brazil, is where the nuts come from.
1987 In the *Observer*, 23 Aug.
➤ *See Thomas 852:53.*

Diski, Jenny 1947–
English author and journalist.

31 Statistics are designed to keep you safe.
1997 *Skating to Antarctica*.

32 For the most part, quantum theory has been of little practical value in my life.
1997 *Skating to Antarctica*.

Disney, Walt(er Elias) 1901–66
US artist and film producer. His animated characters such as Mickey Mouse (1928) featured in *Silly Symphonies* (from 1929) and later full-length animated films.

33 Fancy being remembered around the world for the invention of a mouse!
c.1966 Comment to his wife during his last illness. Quoted in Leonard Mosley *Disney's World* (1985).

Disraeli, Benjamin, 1st Earl of Beaconsfield 1804–81
British statesman, first known for his political novels *Coningsby* (1844) and *Sybil* (1845). He became a Tory MP in 1837, Chancellor of the Exchequer (1852, 1858–9 and 1866), and Prime Minister (1868, 1874–80). His second administration (1874–80) was notable both for diplomacy and social reform.

34 Experience is the child of Thought, and Thought is the child of Action. We cannot learn men from books.
1826–7 *Vivian Grey*, bk.5, ch.1.

35 I repeat…that all power is a trust—that we are accountable for its exercise—that, from the people, and for the people, all springs, and all must exist.
1826–7 *Vivian Grey*, bk.6, ch.10.

36 A good eater must be a good man; for a good eater must have a good digestion, and a good digestion depends upon a good conscience.
1831 *The Young Duke*, bk.1, ch.14.

37 'The age of chivalry is past,' said May Dacre. 'Bores have succeeded to dragons.'
1831 *The Young Duke*, bk.2, ch.5.

38 Read no history: nothing but biography, for that is life without theory.
1832 *Contarini Fleming*, pt.1, ch.23.

39 The practice of politics in the East may be defined by one word—dissimulation.
1832 *Contarini Fleming*, pt.5, ch.10.

40 Time is the great physician.
1837 *Henrietta Temple*, bk.6, ch.9.

41 Though I sit down now, the time will come when you will hear me.
1837 On being barracked during his overly ornate maiden speech in the House of Commons, 7 Dec.

42 The Continent will not suffer England to be the workshop of the world.
1838 House of Commons, 15 Mar.

43 No Government can be long secure without a formidable Opposition.
1844 *Coningsby*, bk.2, ch.1.

44 Conservatism discards Prescription, shrinks from Principle, disavows Progress; having rejected all respect for antiquity, it offers no redress for the present, and makes no preparation for the future.
1844 *Coningsby*, bk.2, ch.5.

45 Youth is a blunder; Manhood a struggle; Old Age a regret.
1844 *Coningsby*, bk.3, ch.1.

46 It seems to me a barren thing this Conservatism—an unhappy cross-breed, the mule of politics that engenders nothing.
1844 *Coningsby*, bk.3, ch.5.

47 What Art was to the ancient world, Science is to the modern.
1844 *Coningsby*, bk.4, ch.1.

48 The depository of power is always unpopular.
1844 *Coningsby*, bk.4, ch.13.

49 Man is only truly great when he acts from the passions.
1844 *Coningsby*, bk.4, ch.13.

50 Consider Ireland. Thus you have a starving population, an absentee aristocracy, and an alien Church—and in addition, the weakest executive in the world. That is the Irish Question.
1844 Speech, House of Commons, 16 Feb.

51 I am neither a Whig nor a Tory. My politics are described in one word, and that word is England.
1844 Speech, House of Commons.

52 To do nothing and get something, formed a boy's ideal of a manly career.
1845 *Sybil*, bk.1, ch.5.

53 'Two nations; between whom there is no intercourse and no sympathy; who are as ignorant of each other's habits, thoughts and feelings, as if they were dwellers in different zones, or inhabitants of different planets; who are formed by a different breeding, are fed by a different food, are ordered by different manners, and are not governed by the same laws.' 'You speak of—' said Egremont, hesitatingly. 'THE RICH AND THE POOR.'
1845 *Sybil*, bk.2, ch.5.

54 Little things affect little minds.
1845 *Sybil*, bk.3, ch.2.

55 The Youth of a Nation are the trustees of Posterity.
1845 *Sybil*, bk.6, ch.13

56 The right honourable gentleman caught the Whigs bathing and walked away with their clothes.
1845 House of Commons speech, 28 Feb, attacking Prime Minister Sir Robert Peel for bullying his back-benchers into supporting the Government's action in intercepting the private mail of radical MPs.

57 A Conservative government is an organized hypocrisy.
1845 Speech, House of Commons, 17 Mar.

58 A majority is always the best repartee.
1847 *Tancred*, bk.2, ch.14.

59 London is a modern Babylon.
1847 *Tancred*, bk.5, ch.5.

60 Justice is truth in action.
1851 Speech, House of Commons, 11 Feb.

61 He has to learn that petulance is not sarcasm, and that insolence is not invective.
1852 Of Sir Charles Wood. Speech, House of Commons, 16 Dec.

62 England does not love coalitions.
1852 Speech, House of Commons, 17 Dec.

63 The blue ribbon of the turf.
1852 Of the Derby race. *Life of Lord George Bentinck*, ch.26.

64 If a traveller were informed that such a man was Leader of the House of Commons, he may well begin to comprehend how the Egyptians came to worship an insect.
1852 Of Lord John Russell. Attributed.

65 His temper, naturally morose, has become licentiously peevish. Crossed in his Cabinet, he insults the House of Lords and plagues the most eminent of his colleagues with the crabbed malice of a maundering witch.
1855 Of Lord Aberdeen, whose disagreements with his Whig–Peelite coalition over the Crimean War eventually forced his resignation.

66 Finality is not the language of politics.
1859 Speech, House of Commons, 28 Feb.

67 I hold that the characteristic of the present age is craving credulity.
1864 Speech, Oxford, 25 Nov.

68 Party is organized opinion.
1864 Speech, Oxford, 25 Nov.

69 The question is this: is man an ape or an angel? I am on the side of the angels.
1864 Speech, Oxford, 25 Nov.

70 Assassination has never changed the history of the world.
1865 Speech, House of Commons, 1 May, paying tribute to US President Abraham Lincoln who had been assassinated in Washington, 14 Apr.

71 I have climbed to the top of the greasy pole.
1868 On becoming Prime Minister.

72 The pursuit of science leads only to the insoluble.
1870 *Lothair*, ch.17.

73 A Protestant, if he wants aid or advice on any matter, can only go to his solicitor.
1870 *Lothair*, ch.27.

74 When a man fell into his anecdotage it was a sign for him to retire from the world.
1870 *Lothair*, ch.28.

75 Every woman should marry—and no man.
1870 *Lothair*, ch.30.

76 You know who the critics are? The men who have failed in literature and art.
1870 *Lothair*, ch.35.

77 'My idea of an agreeable person,' said Hugo Bohun, 'is a person who agrees with me.'
1870 *Lothair*, ch.35.

78 Increased means and increased leisure are the two civilizers of man.
1872 Speech at Manchester, 3 Apr.

79 A University should be a place of light, of liberty, and of learning.
1873 Speech, House of Commons, 11 Mar.

80 An author who speaks about his own books is almost as bad as a mother who talks about her own children.
1873 Rectorial address, Glasgow, 19 Nov.

81 Upon the education of the people of this country the fate of this country depends.
1874 Speech, House of Commons, 15 Jun.

82 Posterity will do justice to that unprincipled maniac Gladstone—an extraordinary mixture of envy, vindictiveness, hypocrisy and superstition and with one commanding characteristic. Whether Prime Minister or Leader of the Opposition, whether preaching, praying, speechifying, or scribbling—never a gentleman. He is so vain that he wants to figure in history as the settler of all the great questions; but a parliamentary Constitution is not favourable to such ambitions. Things must be done by parties, not by persons using parties as tools.
c.1874 Letter.

83 I am dead: dead, but in the Elysian fields.
1876 On his elevation to the House of Lords.

84 Gladstone, like Richelieu, cannot write. Nothing can be more unmusical, more involved, or more uncouth than all his scribblement.
1877 Letter, 3 Oct.

85 Lord Salisbury and myself have brought you peace—but a peace, I hope, with honour.
1878 Declaration, 16 Jul, on returning from the Berlin Congress with the guarantees it had produced of continuing peace in Europe.
➤ *See also Chamberlain 204:63.*

86 A sophistical rhetorician inebriated with the exuberance of his own verbosity.
1878 Of Gladstone. Speech reported in *The Times*, 29 Jul.

87 His Christianity was muscular.
1880 *Endymion*, ch.14.

88 You must dress according to your age, your pursuits, your object in life.
1880 *Endymion*, ch.23.

89 What all men should avoid is the 'shabby genteel'. No man ever gets over it… You had better be in rags.
1880 *Endymion*, ch.23.

90 'Sensible men are all the same religion.' 'And pray what is that?' inquired the prince. 'Sensible men never tell.'
1880 Waldershire. *Endymion*, ch.81.

91 I believe they went out, like all good things, with the Stuarts.
1880 *Endymion*, ch.99.

92 I will not go down to posterity talking bad grammar.
1881 On correcting proofs of his last parliamentary speech, 31 Mar. Quoted in Robert Blake *Disraeli*, ch.32.

93 There are three kinds of lies: lies, damned lies and statistics.
Attributed. Quoted in Mark Twain *Autobiography*, vol.1 (published 1924).

94 Millstones around our neck.
Of the colonies. Quoted in Robert Blake *The Conservative Party from Peel to Churchill* (1970).

95 England is unrivalled for two things—sport and politics.
Quoted in Colin Jarman *The Guinness Dictionary of Sports Quotations* (1990).

Dobson, (Henry) Austin 1840–1921

English poet. He published several volumes of carefully crafted, often humorous verse, and prose studies of famous writers.

96 Time goes, you say? Ah no!
Alas, Time stays, we go.
1877 'Paradox of Time'.

97 Fame is a food that dead men eat,
I have no stomach for such meat.
1906 'Fame is a Fool'.

Dobzhansky, Theodosius G 1900–75

Russian-born US geneticist, Professor at Columbia University and the University of California at Davis.

98 Nature's stern discipline enjoins mutual help at least as often as warfare. The fittest may also be the gentlest.
1962 *Mankind Evolving*.

Docherty, Tommy (Thomas Henderson) 1928–

Scottish footballer and manager. In a tempestuous career he played for Scotland and managed ten clubs, including Manchester United and Queen's Park Rangers, and was briefly manager of Scotland (1971–2).

99 The ideal board of directors should be made up of three men—two dead and the other dying.
1977 Quoted in Colin Jarman *The Guinness Dictionary of Sports Quotations* (1990).

1 Our strikers couldn't score in a brothel.
1985 Of the forwards at Wolverhampton Wanderers. Quoted in Peter Ball and Phil Shaw *The Book of Football Quotations* (1989).

Doctorow, E(dgar) L(awrence) 1931–

US novelist, best known for *Ragtime* (1975) and *Billy Bathgate* (1989).

2 A few professional alienists understood his importance, but to most of the public he appeared as some kind of German sexologist, an exponent of free love who used big words to talk about dirty things. At least a decade would have to pass before Freud would have his revenge and see his ideas begin to destroy sex in America forever.
1975 *Ragtime*, ch.5.

3 There is no longer any such thing as fiction or non-fiction; there's only narrative.
> **1988** In the *New York Times Book Review*, 27 Jan.

4 Like art and politics, gangsterism is a very important avenue of assimilation into society.
> **1990** In the *International Herald Tribune*, 1 Oct.

Dodd, Christopher J 1944–
US Democratic politician.

5 Time is the 101st Senator…the ally of the people who want to do nothing.
> **1994** On the difficulty of passing President Clinton's health programme when legislators were longing for the holidays. In the *New York Times*, 26 Aug.

Dodd, Ken(neth) 1927–
English stand-up comedian, singer and actor.

6 The trouble with Freud is that he never had to play the old Glasgow Empire on a Saturday night after Rangers and Celtic had both lost.
> **1965** Television interview, discussing Freud's theory of catharsis through laughter, whereby jokes produce a feeling of elation.

Doddridge, Philip 1702–51
English nonconformist minister and hymn-writer.

7 Hark, the glad sound! The Saviour comes,
The Saviour promised long;
Let every heart exult with joy,
And every voice be song!
> *Hymns*, 'Hark, the Glad Sound' (published 1755).

8 O God of Bethel! by whose hand
Thy people still are fed,
Who through this weary pilgrimage
Hast all our fathers led.
> *Hymns*, 'O God of Bethel' (published 1755).

9 Ye servants of the Lord,
Each in his office wait,
Observant of the heavenly word,
And watchful at his gate.
> *Hymns*, 'Ye Servants of the Lord' (published 1755).

10 Father of Peace, and God of love!
We own Thy power to save,
That power by which our Shepherd rose
Victorious o'er the grave.
> *Hymns*, 'Father of Peace' (published 1755).

Dole, Bob (Robert Joseph) 1923–
US Republican politician. Having run unsuccessfully for presidential nomination in 1980 and 1988, he became a presidential candidate in 1996, but lost the election to Bill Clinton.

11 George Meany could run for President, but then why should he step down?
> **1976** On Meany's status as president of the American Federation of Labor. In the *Wall Street Journal*, 7 Sep.

12 It is inside work with no heavy lifting.
> **1988** On the vice presidency. ABC TV broadcast, 24 Jul.

13 Contrary to reports that I took the loss badly, I slept like a baby—every two hours I woke up and cried.
> **1988** On losing the presidential nomination. ABC TV broadcast, 14 Aug.

14 Putting a majority together is like a one-armed man wrapping cranberries.
> Quoted in Hedrick Smith *The Power Game* (1988).

15 This President will go down in history as the only President who raised taxes before he took office and cut spending after he left office.
> **1993** On Bill Clinton's retroactive tax increases and promises of future spending cuts. In the *Los Angeles Times*, 16 Feb.

16 I thought about it a lot and I think every country ought to have a President.
> **1995** To television host David Letterman on his decision to seek high office. Reported in *Time*, 13 Feb.

17 We really win if we win. But we may even win if we lose.
> **1995** On the prospect of gaining popularity by reintroducing a balanced budget amendment. In the *New York Times*, 2 Mar.

Dole, Elizabeth Hanford 1936–
US lawyer and Republican politician, former President of the American Red Cross. She is married to Bob Dole.

18 Sometimes I think we're the only two lawyers in Washington who trust each other.
> **1987** On her marriage to Senator Bob Dole. In *Newsweek*, 3 Aug.

Domínguez Camargo, Hernando 1606–59
Colombian epic poet. A Jesuit, he probably abandoned this calling at the end of his life. His major work, the unfinished *Poema heroyco*, is a long, ambitious narrative in a highly Baroque style.

19 ¡En tantas de la muerte librerías,
los cuerpos de esos huesos, mal seguro,
estudia, Julio; y en su letra advierte,
que son abecedarios de la muerte!
Julio, in those libraries of death
study the bodies of those bones—an assured evil;
and learn from those characters
that they form the abecedary of death!
> **1666** *San Ignacio de Loyola, Poema heroyco* ('Heroic Poem of Saint Ignatius of Loyola'), bk.4, canto 6.

Donaghy, Siobhan 1985–
English pop singer, former member of the band the Sugababes.

20 Everyone else gets themselves dressed in the morning so why can't I?
> **2003** When asked why, unlike other pop stars, she had no stylist. Quoted in the *Sunday Times*, 21 Sep.

Donahue, Phil 1935–
US broadcaster, host of the daytime talk show *Donahue* (1967–96) and credited with inventing the genre. His political talk show was axed after six months in 2003.

21 The breasts, the hallmark of our culture. You cannot sell anything in America without the breasts.
> **1990** On NBC TV, Aug.

Donald, David Herbert 1920–
US historian and writer, Professor at Harvard (1973–91, emeritus from 1991). His many works include *Charles Sumner and the Coming of the Civil War* (1960, Pulitzer Prize) and *Lincoln* (1995).

22 Their correspondence was something like a duet between a tuba and a piccolo.

1987 On letters of Thomas Wolfe and Aline Bernstein. *Look Homeward: A Life of Thomas Wolfe*.

Donleavy, J(ames) P(atrick) 1926–

US-born Irish writer, best known for his picaresque novel *The Ginger Man* (1955).

23 To marry the Irish is to look for poverty.
1955 *The Ginger Man*, ch.2.

24 But Jesus, when you don't have any money the problem is food. When you have money, it's sex. When you have both it's health, you worry about getting ruptured or something. If everything is simply jake then you're frightened of death.
1955 *The Ginger Man*, ch.5.

25 When I die I want to decompose in a barrel of porter and have it served in all the pubs in Dublin. I wonder would they all know it was me?
1955 *The Ginger Man*, ch.31.

26 I got disappointed in human nature as well and gave it up because I found it too much like my own.
1973 *A Fairy Tale of New York*, ch.18.

27 Writing is turning one's worst moments into money.
1979 In *Playboy*, May.

Donne, John c.1572–1631

English priest and poet. He converted from Catholicism to Anglicanism, becoming Dean of St Paul's.

28 Shall I leave all this constant company,
And follow headlong, wild uncertain thee?
1594–5 *Satires*, no.1.

29 For if one eat my meat, though it be known
The meat was mine, the excrement is his own.
1594–5 *Satires*, no.2.

30 Kind pity chokes my spleen.
1594–5 *Satires*, no.3.

31 On a huge hill,
Cragged, and steep, Truth stands, and he that will
Reach her, about must, and about must go.
1594–5 *Satires*, no.3.

32 Are not your kisses then as filthy, and more,
As a worm sucking an envenomed sore?
Doth not thy fearful hand in felling quake,
As one which gathering flowers, still fears a snake?
Is not your last act harsh, and violent,
As when a plough a stony ground doth rent?
c.1595 *Elegies*, no.8, 'The Comparison'.

33 Filled with her love, may I be rather grown
Mad with much heart than idiot with none.
c.1595 *Elegies*, no.10, 'The Bracelet'.

34 I will not look upon the quickening sun,
But straight her beauty to my sense shall run;
The air shall note her soft, the fire most pure;
Water suggest her clear, and the earth sure;
Time shall not lose our passages.
c.1595 *Elegies*, no.12, 'His Parting from Her'.

35 Come, madam, come, all rest my powers defy,
Until I labour, I in labour lie.
The foe oft-times having the foe in sight,
Is tired with standing though he never fight.
Off with that girdle, like heaven's zone glistering,

But a far fairer world encompassing.
Unpin that spangled breastplate which you wear,
That busy fools may be stopped there.
Unlace yourself, for that harmonious chime
Tells me from you that now 'tis your bed time.
c.1595 *Elegies*, no.19, 'To His Mistress Going to Bed'.

36 License my roving hands, and let them go
Before, behind, between, above, below.
O my America! my new-found-land,
My kingdom, safeliest when with one man manned.
c.1595 *Elegies*, no.19, 'To His Mistress Going to Bed'.

37 I wonder, by my troth, what thou and I
Did, till we loved? were we not weaned till then?
But sucked on country pleasures, childishly?
c.1595–1605 'The Good Morrow', collected in *Songs and Sonnets* (1633).

38 Now thou hast loved me one whole day,
Tomorrow when thou leav'st, what wilt thou say?
c.1595–1605 'Woman's Constancy', collected in *Songs and Sonnets* (1633).

39 Go, and catch a falling star,
Get with child a mandrake root,
Tell me, where all past years are,
Or who cleft the Devil's foot.
c.1595–1605 'Song: Go and catch a falling star', collected in *Songs and Sonnets* (1633).

40 Sweetest love I do not go,
For weariness of thee,
Nor in hope the world can show
A fitter Love for me;
But since that I
Must die at last, 'tis best,
To use myself in jest
Thus by feigned deaths to die.
c.1595–1605 'Song: Sweetest love I do not go', collected in *Songs and Sonnets* (1633).

41 Busy old fool, unruly sun,
Why dost thou thus,
Through windows, and through curtains, call on us?
Must to thy motions lovers' seasons run?
Saucy pedantic wretch, go chide
Late schoolboys, and sour prentices,
Go tell court-huntsmen that the King will ride,
Call country ants to harvest offices;
Love, all alike, no season knows, nor clime,
Nor hours, days, months, which are the rags of time.
c.1595–1605 'The Sun Rising', collected in *Songs and Sonnets* (1633).

42 She's all states, and all princes I,
Nothing else is.
Princes do but play us; compared to this,
All honour's mimic, all wealth alchemy.
c.1595–1605 'The Sun Rising', collected in *Songs and Sonnets* (1633).

43 For God's sake, hold your tongue, and let me love,
Or chide my palsy, or my gout,
My five grey hairs, or ruined fortune flout,
With wealth your state, your mind with arts improve,
Take you a course, get you a place,
Observe his honour, or his grace,
Or the King's real, or his stamped face
Contemplate; what you will, approve,

So you will let me love.
c.1595–1605 'The Canonization', collected in *Songs and Sonnets* (1633).

44 Alas, alas, who's injured by my love?
What merchant's ships have my sighs drowned?
Who says my tears have overflowed his ground?
When did my colds a forward spring remove?
When did the heats which my veins fill
Add one more to the plaguey bill?
Soldiers find wars, and lawyers find out still
Litigious men, which quarrels move,
Though she and I do love.
c.1595–1605 'The Canonization', collected in *Songs and Sonnets* (1633).

45 'Tis the year's midnight, and it is the day's.
c.1595–1605 'Nocturnal upon St Lucy's Day', collected in *Songs and Sonnets* (1633).

46 I sing the progress of a deathless soul.
c.1595–1605 'The Progress of the Soul', stanza 1, collected in *Songs and Sonnets* (1633).

47 Nature's great masterpiece, an Elephant.
c.1595–1605 'The Progress of the Soul', stanza 39, collected in *Songs and Sonnets* (1633).

48 I am two fools, I know,
For loving, and for saying so
In whining poetry.
c.1595–1605 'The Triple Fool', collected in *Songs and Sonnets* (1633).

49 Twice or thrice had I loved thee,
Before I knew thy face or name;
So in a voice, so in a shapeless flame
Angels affect us oft, and worshipped be;
Still when, to where thou wert, I came,
Some lovely glorious nothing did I see.
c.1595–1605 'Air and Angels', collected in *Songs and Sonnets* (1633).

50 He which hath business, and makes love, doth do
Such wrong, as when a married man doth woo.
c.1595–1605 'Break of Day', collected in *Songs and Sonnets* (1633).

51 O more than moon,
Draw not up seas to drown me in thy sphere,
Weep me not dead, in thine arms, but forbear
To teach the sea what it may do too soon.
c.1595–1605 'A Valediction: Of Weeping', collected in *Songs and Sonnets* (1633).

52 Mark but this flea, and mark in this
How little that which thou deny'st me is;
It sucked me first, and now sucks thee,
And in this flea our two bloods mingled be.
c.1595–1605 'The Flea', collected in *Songs and Sonnets* (1633).

53 Come live with me, and be my love,
And we will some new pleasures prove
Of golden sands, and crystal brooks:
With silken lines, and silver hooks.
c.1595–1605 'The Bait', collected in *Songs and Sonnets* (1633).
➤ *See Marlowe 553:17, Raleigh 677:98.*

54 As virtuous men pass mildly away,
And whisper to their souls, to go,
Whilst some of their sad friends do say,
The breath goes now, and some say, no:

So let us melt, and make no noise,
No tear-floods, nor sigh-tempests move;
'Twere profanation of our joys
To tell the laity of our love.
c.1595–1605 'A Valediction: Forbidding Mourning', collected in *Songs and Sonnets* (1633).

55 Our two souls therefore, which are one,
Though I must go, endure not yet
A breach, but an expansion,
Like gold to airy thinness beat.
c.1595–1605 'A Valediction: Forbidding Mourning', collected in *Songs and Sonnets* (1633).

56 Thy firmness makes my circle just,
And makes me end, where I begun.
c.1595–1605 'A Valediction: Forbidding Mourning', collected in *Songs and Sonnets* (1633).

57 Where, like a pillow on a bed,
A pregnant bank swelled up, to rest
The violet's reclining head,
Sat we two, one another's best.
c.1595–1605 'The Ecstasy', collected in *Songs and Sonnets* (1633).

58 Our eye-beams twisted, and did thread
Our eyes, upon one double string.
c.1595–1605 'The Ecstasy', collected in *Songs and Sonnets* (1633).

59 So to engraft our hands, as yet
Was all the means to make us one,
And pictures in our eyes to get
Was all our propagation.

And whilst our souls negotiate there,
We like sepulchral statues lay;
All day, the same our postures were,
And we said nothing all the day.
c.1595–1605 'The Ecstasy', collected in *Songs and Sonnets* (1633).

60 I had rather owner be
Of thee one hour, than all else ever.
c.1595–1605 'A Fever', collected in *Songs and Sonnets* (1633).

61 To what a cumbersome unwieldiness
And burdenous corpulence my love had grown,
But that I did, to make it less,
And keep it in proportion,
Give it a diet, made it feed upon
That which love worst endures, *discretion*.
?1595–1605 'Love's Diet', collected in *Songs and Sonnets* (1633).

62 And seeing the snail, which everywhere doth roam,
Carrying his own house still, still is at home,
Follow (for he is easy paced) this snail,
Be thine own palace, or the world's thy gaol.
1597–8 'To Sir Henry Wotton'.

63 More than kisses, letters mingle souls.
1597–8 'To Sir Henry Wotton'.

64 John Donne, Anne Donne, Un-done.
1602 Letter to his wife from prison. Quoted in Izaak Walton *The Life of Doctor Donne* (1640).

65 Immensity cloistered in thy dear womb.
1609 *La Corona*, 'Nativity'.

66 At the round earth's imagined corners, blow
Your trumpets, angels, and arise, arise

From death, you numberless infinities
Of souls, and to your scattered bodies go.
c.1610–1615 *Holy Sonnets*, no.7.

67 Death be not proud, though some have called thee
Mighty and dreadful, for thou art not so,
For those, whom thou think'st thou dost overthrow,
Die not, poor death, nor yet canst thou kill me.
From rest and sleep, which but thy pictures be,
Much pleasure, then from thee much more must flow,
And soonest our best men with thee do go,
Rest of their bones and soul's delivery.
c.1610–1615 *Holy Sonnets*, no.10.

68 One short sleep past, we wake eternally,
And Death shall be no more: Death, thou shalt die!
c.1610–1615 *Holy Sonnets*, no.10.

69 Oh let me then His strange love still admire.
c.1610–1615 *Holy Sonnets*, no.11.

70 Batter my heart, three-personed God; for You
As yet but knock, breathe, shine, and seek to mend.
c.1610–1615 *Holy Sonnets*, no.14.

71 Take me to You, imprison me, for I,
Except You enthrall me, never shall be free,
Nor ever chaste, except You ravish me.
c.1610–1615 *Holy Sonnets*, no.14.

72 I am a little world made cunningly
Of elements and an angelic sprite.
c.1610–1615 *Holy Sonnets*, no.15.

73 What if this present were the world's last night?
c.1610–1615 *Holy Sonnets*, no.19.

74 And new philosophy calls all in doubt,
The element of fire is quite put out;
The sun is lost, and th'earth, and no man's wit
Can well direct him, where to look for it.
1611 'An Anatomy of the World: The First Anniversary'.

75 If man were anything, he's nothing now.
1611 'An Anatomy of the World: The First Anniversary'.

76 'Tis all in pieces, all coherence gone.
1611 'An Anatomy of the World: The First Anniversary'.

77 She, she is dead; she's dead; when thou know'st this,
Thou know'st how dry a cinder this world is.
1611 'An Anatomy of the World: The First Anniversary'.

78 Verse hath a middle nature: heaven keeps souls,
The grave keeps bodies, verse the fame enrols.
1611 'An Anatomy of the World: The First Anniversary'.

79 It comes equally to us all, and makes us all equal when it
comes. The ashes of an oak in the chimney are no
epitaph of that oak, to tell me how high or how large
that was; it tells me not what flocks it sheltered while it
stood, nor what men it hurt when it fell…and when a
whirlwind hath blown the dust of the churchyard into the
church, and the man sweeps out the dust of the church
into the churchyard, who will undertake to sift those
dusts again, and to pronounce, This is the Patrician, this
the noble flower, and this the yeomanly, this the
Plebeian bran.
c.1621 Of death. Sermon, 8 Mar.

80 Since I am coming to that holy room
Where, with Thy choir of saints forevermore,
I shall be made Thy Music, as I come
I tune the instrument here at the door,

And what I must do then, think now before.
c.1623 'Hymn to God My God, in My Sickness'.

81 Wilt thou forgive that sin, where I begun,
Which is my sin, though it was done before?
Wilt thou forgive those sins through which I run
And do them still, though still I do deplore?
When thou hast done, thou hast not done,
For I have more.
c.1623 'Hymn to God the Father'.

82 It is too little to call man a little world; except God, man is
a diminutive to nothing.
1624 *Devotions upon Emergent Occasions*, Meditation no.4.

83 But I do nothing upon my self, and yet I am mine own
executioner.
1624 *Devotions upon Emergent Occasions*, Meditation no.12.

84 No man is an island, entire of itself; every man is a piece
of the continent, a part of the main.
1624 *Devotions upon Emergent Occasions*, Meditation no.17.

85 Any man's death diminishes me, because I am involved
in mankind; and therefore never send to know for whom
the bell tolls; it tolls for thee.
1624 *Devotions upon Emergent Occasions*, Meditation no.17.

86 My God, my God, thou art a direct God, may I not say a
literal God… But thou art also…a figurative, a
metaphorical God too.
1624 *Devotions upon Emergent Occasions*, Expostulation 19, 'The
Language of God'.

87 The air is not so full of motes, of atoms, as the church is of
mercies.
1624 *Sermons*, 'Christmas Day, 1624'.

88 He brought light out of darkness, not out of a lesser light;
he can bring thy summer out of winter, though thou have
no spring… God comes to thee, not as in the dawning of
the day, not as in the bud of the spring, but as the sun at
noon to illustrate all shadows, as the sheaves in harvest to
fill all penuries. All occasions invite his mercies, and all
times are his seasons.
1624 *Sermons*, 'Christmas Day, 1624'.

89 All the four Monarchies, with all their thousands of
years, and all the powerful Kings and all the beautiful
Queens of this world, were but as a bed of flowers, some
gathered at six, some at seven, some at eight, all in one
morning, in respect to this day.
1626 On eternity. Sermon, 30 Apr.

90 I throw myself down in my Chamber, and I call in, and
invite God, and his Angels thither, and when they are
there, I neglect God and his Angels, for the noise of a fly,
for the rattling of a coach, for the whining of a door.
1626 Sermon preached at the funeral of Sir William Cockayne,
12 Dec.

91 How imperfect is all our knowledge!
1626 Sermon preached at the funeral of Sir William Cockayne,
12 Dec.

92 Young men mend not their sight by using old men's
spectacles.
1626 Sermon preached at the funeral of Sir William Cockayne,
12 Dec.

93 And if there be any addition to knowledge, it is rather a
new knowledge than a greater knowledge; rather a
singularity in a desire of proposing something that was
not known at all before than an improving, an advancing,

a multiplying of former inceptions; and by that means, no knowledge comes to be perfect.

1626 Sermon preached at the funeral of Sir William Cockayne, 12 Dec.

94 He that purchases a manor will think to have an exact survey of the land, but who thinks of taking so exact a survey of his conscience, how that money was got that purchased that manor? We call that a man's means, which he hath; but that is truly his means, what way he came by it.

1626 Sermon preached at the funeral of Sir William Cockayne, 12 Dec.

95 The world is a great volume, and man the index of that book.

1626 'Sermon preached at the Funeral of Sir William Cockayne', 12 Dec.

96 Let man's soul be a sphere, and then, in this, The intelligence that moves, devotion is.

'Good Friday, 1613. Riding Westward', published 1635.

Donoghue, Denis 1928–

Irish literary critic, Professor at New York University.

97 If there is a distinctive Irish experience, it is one of division, exacerbated by the fact that division in a country so small seems perverse. But the scale doesn't matter.

1986 *We Irish.*

Donoso, José 1924–96

Chilean novelist. After teaching at several universities in Chile and the US, he lived in Europe for 15 years before returning to Chile. *El obsceno pájaro de la noche* (1970), his masterpiece, presents a hallucinatory and grotesque vision of Chilean society.

98 *Los servidores acumulan los privilegios de la miseria…conservan los instrumentos de la venganza porque van acumulando en sus manos ásperas y verrugosas esa otra mitad de sus patrones, la mitad inútil, descartada, lo sucio y lo feo que ellos…les han ido entregando con el insulto de cada enagua gastada que les regalan.*
Servants accumulate the privileges of misery… They save up the instruments of vengeance because their coarse warty hands collect, bit by bit, that other side of their employers—the useless, discarded side, the filth and the sordidness that…they've been putting into their servants' hands with the insult of each shabby skirt they gave them.

1970 *El obsceno pájaro de la noche*, ch.4 (translated as *The Obscene Bird of Night*, 1973).

Doolittle, James Harold 1896–1993

US air force officer. He was the Commanding General, US 8th Air Force, in the ETO (European Theatre of Operations) in 1944.

99 Next to a letter from home, Captain Miller, your organization is the greatest morale builder in the ETO.

1944 Of Glenn Miller's wartime band. Comment on stage after a concert for the troops at Wycombe Abbey, 29 Jul. The words were later attributed to General Eisenhower in the publicity for the film *The Glenn Miller Story* (1954).

Doram-Smith, Sir Reginald Hugh 1899–1977

Irish-born British politician, a former army colonel who became an MP in 1935, Minister of Agriculture and Fisheries (1939–40) and Governor of Burma (1941–6).

1 Let 'Dig for Victory' be the motto of everyone with a garden and of every able-bodied man and woman capable of digging an allotment in their spare time.

1939 Radio broadcast, 3 Oct.

Dorgan, Tad (Thomas Aloysius) 1877–1929

US cartoonist and sportswriter. He was known for his satiric cartoons and colourful use of slang.

2 Yes, We Have No Bananas.

1922 Cartoon caption, later used as the title of a song by Irving Conn and Frank Silver (1923) and as an advertising slogan for Elders and Fyffes, British banana importers.

Dos Passos, John Roderigo 1896–1970

US novelist, playwright, travel writer and poet. He is best known for his novels such as *Manhattan Transfer* (1925) and the massive, formally experimental epic trilogy *U.S.A.* (1930–6).

3 U.S.A. is the slice of a continent. U.S.A. is a group of holding companies, some aggregations of trade unions, a set of laws bound in calf, a radio network, a chain of moving picture theatres, a column of stock quotations rubbed out and written in by a Western Union boy on a black-board, a public library full of old newspapers and dogeared history books with protests scrawled in the margins in pencil. U.S.A. is the world's greatest river valley fringed with mountains and hills. U.S.A. is a set of bigmouthed officials with too many bank accounts. U.S.A. is a lot of men buried in their uniforms in Arlington Cemetery. U.S.A. is the letters at the end of an address when you are away from home. But mostly U.S.A. is the speech of the people

1938 *U.S. A.*, 'U.S. A.' (new prologue to collected trilogy).

4 People don't choose their careers. They are engulfed by them.

1959 In the *New York Times*, 25 Oct.

Dostoevsky, Fyodor Mikhailovich 1821–81

Russian novelist. He was condemned to death in 1849 for his revolutionary connections, but was instead sent to hard labour in Siberia until 1859.

5 The formula 'Two and two is five' is not without its attractions.

1864 *Notes from Underground.*

6 All people seem to be divided into 'ordinary' and 'extraordinary'. The ordinary people must lead a life of strict obedience and have no right to transgress the law because…they are ordinary. Whereas the extraordinary people have the right to commit any crime they like and transgress the law in any way just because they happen to be extraordinary.

1866 *Crime and Punishment*, pt.3, ch.5 (translated by David Magarshak).

7 Power is given only to him who dares to stoop and take it…one must have the courage to dare.

1866 *Crime and Punishment*, pt.5, ch.4 (translated by David Magarshak).

8 If you were to destroy in mankind the belief in
immortality, not only love but every living force
maintaining the life of the world would at once be dried
up.
1879–80 *The Brothers Karamazov*, bk.2, ch.6.

9 If the devil doesn't exist, but man has created him, he has
created him in his own image and likeness.
1879–80 *The Brothers Karamazov*, bk.5, ch.4.

10 So long as man remains free he strives for nothing so
incessantly and so painfully as to find someone to
worship.
1879–80 *The Brothers Karamazov*, bk.5, ch.5.

11 Love all God's creation, the whole of it and every grain of
sand in it. Love every leaf, every ray of God's lights. Love
the animals, love the plants, love everything. If you love
everything, you will perceive the divine mystery in
things.
1879–80 *The Brothers Karamazov*, bk.6, ch.3.

Douglas, Lord Alfred Bruce   1870–1945

English poet. He is remembered chiefly for his relationship with
Oscar Wilde, which precipitated Wilde's downfall.

12 I am the love that dare not speak its name.
1894 'Two Loves'.

13 All good poetry is forged slowly and patiently, link by
link, with sweat and blood and tears.
1919 *Collected Poems*, introduction.

Douglas, Charles   1840–74

New Zealand explorer, who travelled over much uncharted
territory in the South Island of New Zealand.

14 I am perfectly aware that the mosquito and sandfly have
a purpose in this world, but why don't they attend to it?
Their destiny is to keep down microscopic insects…but
their sphere of use is when they are in the grub state. Why
don't they stick at that and not trouble innocent
unoffending prospectors who can't carry a curtain?
1891 Quoted in J Pascoe (ed) *Mr Explorer Douglas* (1957).

15 I believe the reason I escaped, both this time and on
other occasions, was the idea of perishing never entered
my head. Nothing is so bad as terror for lowering a man's
stamina.
1891 Quoted in J Pascoe (ed) *Mr Explorer Douglas* (1957).

Douglas, Gavin   c.1474–1522

Scottish poet and, from 1515, Bishop of Dunkeld. His translation
of Virgil's *Aeneid* is considered to be one of the greatest
achievements of Scots vernacular literature.

16 First I protest, beau schiris, by your leif
Beis weill adivisit my werk or ye reprief;
Consider it warely, read ofter than anis,
Weill, at ane blenk, slee poetry nocht ta'en is.
c.1513 *Eneados*, bk.1, prologue.

17 Riveris ran reid on spate with water broun,
And burnis hurlis all their bankis doun.
c.1513 *Eneados*, bk.7, prologue.

18 And all small fowlys singis on the spray:
Welcum the lord of lycht and lamp of day.
c.1513 *Eneados*, bk.12, prologue.

Douglas, Keith Castellain   1920–44

English poet. Only one volume of his poems was published in
his lifetime, and he was killed in action shortly after the D-Day
landings in Normandy.

19 Remember me when I am dead
and simplify me when I'm dead.
1941 'Simplify Me When I'm Dead'.

20 For here the lover and killer are mingled
who had one body and one heart.
And death, who had the soldier singled
has done the lover mortal hurt.
1943 'Vergissmeinnicht'.

21 If at times my eyes are lenses
through which the brain explores
constellations of feeling
my ears yielding like swinging doors
admit princes to the corridors
into the mind, do not envy me.
I have a beast on my back.
1944 'Bête Noire'.

22 And all my endeavours are unlucky explorers
come back, abandoning the expedition;
the specimens, the lilies of ambition
still spring in their climate, still unpicked;
but time, time is all I lacked
to find them, as the great collectors before me.
1944 'On a Return from Egypt, 1943–44' (published 1946).

Douglas, (George) Norman   1868–1952

Scottish novelist, travel writer and essayist. His works include
Siren Land (1911), an account of his travels in Italy, and the novel
South Wind (1917).

23 Bouillabaisse is only good because cooked by the
French, who, if they cared to try, could produce an
excellent and nutritious substitute out of cigar stumps
and empty matchboxes.
1911 *Siren Land*, 'Rain on the Hills'.

24 Don Francesco was a fisher of men, and of women. He
fished *ad maiorem Dei gloriam*, and for the fun of the
thing. It was his way of taking exercise.
1917 *South Wind*, ch.2.

25 You can tell the ideals of a nation by its advertisements.
1917 *South Wind*, ch.6.

26 Many a man who thinks to found a home discovers that
he has merely opened a tavern for his friends.
1917 *South Wind*, ch.20.

27 It is the drawback of all sea-side places that half the
landscape is unavailable for purposes of human
locomotion, being covered by useless water.
1921 *Alone*, 'Mentone'.

28 As to abuse—I thrive on it. Abuse, hearty abuse, is a
tonic to all save men of indifferent health.
1928 *Some Limericks*.

29 Education is a state-controlled manufactory of echoes.
1929 *How About Europe?*

30 To find a friend one must close one eye. To keep
him—two.
1941 *Almanac*.

31 A child of eight is many-sided. By eighteen most of his
auspicious angles have been polished away; he is

standardised; transformed, perhaps into the perfect citizen. Your perfect citizen may be a fine fellow, but he is not the perfect man.

1946 *Late Harvest.*

Douglas, William Orville 1898–1980

US lawyer, Associate Justice of the US Supreme Court (1939–80). His consistently liberal decisions were occasionally controversial, such as the stay of execution granted to the Rosenbergs, convicted spies, in 1953.

32 It is procedure that spells much of the difference between rule by law and rule by whim or caprice.

1951 Ruling to strike the Joint Anti-Fascist Refugee Committee and two other organizations from the Attorney General's list of subversive groups until final adjudication, 30 Apr.

33 We are a religious people whose institutions presuppose a Supreme Being.

1952 Ruling to allow the release of public school students for religious instruction, 28 Apr.

34 If the individual is no longer to be sovereign, if the police can pick him up whenever they do not like the cut of his jib…we enter a new regime.

1968 Dissenting opinion in ruling to uphold the police right 'to stop and frisk', 10 Jun.

Douglass, Frederick *originally* **Frederick Augustus Washington Bailey** 1817–95

US abolitionist. Born a slave, in 1838 he escaped and changed his name. He lectured on slavery in Great Britain (1845–47) and £150 was collected so that he could purchase his freedom.

35 The white man's happiness cannot be purchased by the black man's misery.

1849 'The Destiny of Colored Americans' in *The North Star*, 16 Nov.

36 To imagine that we shall ever be eradicated is absurd and ridiculous. We can be remodified, changed, and assimilated, but never extinguished.

1849 'The Destiny of Colored Americans' in *The North Star*, 16 Nov.

37 Where justice is denied, where poverty is enforced, where ignorance prevails, and where one class is made to feel that society is an organized conspiracy to oppress, rob, and degrade them, neither persons nor property will be safe.

1886 Speech in Washington DC, commemorating the 24th anniversary of emancipation.

38 No man can point to any law in the U.S. by which slavery was originally established. Men first make slaves and then make laws.

1889 Speech, Bethel Literary and Historical Association, Washington DC, Apr.

Dove, Rita Frances 1952–

US poet. Her poetry collections include *Thomas and Beulah* (1986, Pulitzer Prize), *On the Bus with Rosa Parks* (1999) and *American Smooth* (2004). From 1993 to 1995 she was US Poet Laureate.

39 A good poem is like a bouillon cube. It's concentrated and it nourishes you when you need it.

1989 In *Time*, 18 Oct.

Dowd, Maureen 1952–

US newspaper columnist, winner of the 1999 Pulitzer Prize for distinguished commentary.

40 President Clinton returned today…to the university where he didn't inhale, didn't get drafted, and didn't get a degree.

1994 On President Clinton's visit to Oxford where as a Rhodes Scholar he had tried marijuana, avoided conscription, and left to attend Yale Law School. In the *New York Times*, 9 Jun.

41 Don't write anything down, but save everything that anyone else writes down.

1995 Advice for political survival in Washington. In the *US News and World Report*, 9 Jan.

Dowland, John 1563–1626

English lutenist and songwriter. Having failed, as a Catholic, to win a place at the court of Elizabeth I, he made his name in Europe before returning home. His *First Book of Songes* appeared in 1597 and ran to five editions by 1613.

42 Who loves not music and the heavenly muse, That man God hates.

1614 Commendatory poem to William Leighton's *Teares or Lamentations of a Sorrowfull Soule*.

Downey, Dr Richard 1881–1953

English prelate, Bishop of Liverpool.

43 If Stalin had learned to play cricket, the world might now be a better place.

1948 Quoted in Colin Jarman *The Guinness Dictionary of Sports Quotations* (1990).

Dowson, Ernest 1867–1900

English poet. A member of the 'decadent' school, he studied at Oxford and became part of the Rhymers' Club. He developed friendships with W B Yeats and Arthur Symons and lived in France, where he died of alcoholism.

44 I have forgot much, Cynara! Gone with the wind, Flung roses, roses, riotously with the throng, Dancing, to put thy pale, lost lilies out of mind; But I was desolate and sick of an old passion, Yea, all the time, because the dance was long: I have been faithful to thee, Cynara! in my fashion.

1896 *Verses*, 'Non Sum Qualis Eram Bonae Sub Regno Cynarae'.

45 They are not long, the days of wine and roses: Out of a misty dream Our path emerges for a while, then closes Within a dream.

1896 'Vitae Summa Brevis'.

Doyle, Sir Arthur Conan 1859–1930

Scottish physician and writer. His stories of the brilliant and resourceful detective Sherlock Holmes and his assistant, Dr Watson, are among the most enduringly popular works of crime fiction ever written. He also wrote historical romances and other novels.

46 London, that great cesspool into which all the loungers and idlers of the Empire are irresistibly drained.

1887 *A Study in Scarlet*, ch.1.

47 It is a capital mistake to theorize before one has all the evidence. It biases the judgement.

1887 *A Study in Scarlet*, ch.3.

48 Where there is no imagination there is no horror.
1887 *A Study in Scarlet*, ch.5.

49 It is a mistake to confound strangeness with mystery.
1887 *A Study in Scarlet*, ch.7.

50 Our ideas must be as broad as Nature if they are to interpret Nature.
1887 *A Study in Scarlet*, ch.7.

51 Detection is, or ought to be, an exact science, and should be treated in the same cold and unemotional manner. You have attempted to tinge it with romanticism, which produces much the same effect as if you worked a love-story or an elopement into the fifth proposition of Euclid.
1890 *The Sign of Four*, ch.1.

52 The most winning woman I ever knew was hanged for poisoning three little children for their insurance money.
1890 *The Sign of Four*, ch.2.

53 I never make exceptions. An exception disproves the rule.
1890 *The Sign of Four*, ch.2.

54 How often have I said to you that when you have eliminated the impossible, whatever remains, *however improbable*, must be the truth?
1890 *The Sign of Four*, ch.6.

55 You know my methods. Apply them.
1890 *The Sign of Four*, ch.6.

56 'It is the unofficial force—the Baker Street irregulars.' As he spoke, there came a swift pattering of naked feet upon the stairs, a clatter of high voices, and in rushed a dozen dirty and ragged little street Arabs.
1890 *The Sign of Four*, ch.8.

57 The bow was made in England,
Of true wood, of yew wood,
The wood of English bows.
1891 *The White Company*, 'Song of the Bow'.

58 Singularity is almost invariably a clue. The more featureless and commonplace a crime is, the more difficult it is to bring it home.
1892 *The Adventures of Sherlock Holmes*, 'The Boscombe Valley Mystery'.

59 You know my method. It is founded upon the observance of trifles.
1892 *The Adventures of Sherlock Holmes*, 'The Boscombe Valley Mystery'.

60 It has long been an axiom of mine that the little things are infinitely the most important.
1892 *The Adventures of Sherlock Holmes*, 'A Case of Identity'.

61 Depend upon it, there is nothing so unnatural as the commonplace.
1892 *The Adventures of Sherlock Holmes*, 'A Case of Identity'.

62 The case has, in some respects, been not entirely devoid of interest.
1892 *The Adventures of Sherlock Holmes*, 'A Case of Identity'.

63 It is quite a three-pipe problem, and I beg that you won't speak to me for fifty minutes.
1892 *The Adventures of Sherlock Holmes*, 'The Red-Headed League'.

64 To Sherlock Holmes she is always *the* woman. I have seldom heard him mention her under any other name. In his eyes she eclipses and predominates the whole of her sex.

1892 Of Irene Adler. *The Adventures of Sherlock Holmes*, 'Scandal in Bohemia'.

65 You see, but you do not observe.
1892 *The Adventures of Sherlock Holmes*, 'Scandal in Bohemia'.

66 A man should keep his little brain attic stocked with all the furniture that he is likely to use, and the rest he can put away in the lumber room of his library, where he can get it if he wants it.
1892 *The Adventures of Sherlock Holmes*, 'The Five Orange Pips'.

67 It is my belief, Watson, founded upon my experience, that the lowest and vilest alleys in London do not present a more dreadful record of sin than does the smiling and beautiful countryside.
1892 *The Adventures of Sherlock Holmes*, 'The Copper Beeches'.

68 Crime is common. Logic is rare. Therefore it is upon the logic rather than upon the crime that you should dwell.
1892 *The Adventures of Sherlock Holmes*, 'The Copper Beeches'.

69 A long shot, Watson; a very long shot!
1894 *The Memoirs of Sherlock Holmes*, 'Silver Blaze'.

70 Ex-Professor Moriarty of mathematical celebrity…is the Napoleon of crime, Watson.
1894 *The Memoirs of Sherlock Holmes*, 'The Final Problem'.

71 'Excellent!', I cried.
'Elementary', said he.
1894 *The Memoirs of Sherlock Holmes*, 'The Crooked Man'. The famous phrase 'Elementary, my dear Watson' does not in fact appear in any of the Conan Doyle books. It may have originated with a review of the film *The Return of Sherlock Holmes* in the *New York Times*, 19 Oct 1929.

72 They were the footprints of a gigantic hound!
1902 *The Hound of the Baskervilles*, ch.2.

73 A study of family portraits is enough to convert a man to the doctrine of reincarnation.
1902 *The Hound of the Baskervilles*, ch.13.

74 You mentioned your name as if I should recognise it, but I assure you that, beyond the obvious facts that you are a bachelor, a solicitor, a Freemason, and an asthmatic, I know nothing whatever about you.
1905 *The Return of Sherlock Holmes*, 'The Norwood Builder'.

75 Now, Watson, the fair sex is your department.
1905 *The Return of Sherlock Holmes*, 'The Second Stain'.

76 It is horrible, yet fascinating, this struggle between a set purpose and an utterly exhausted frame.
1908 Of the final moments of the 1908 Olympic marathon, in which the Italian runner Dorando Pietri had to be helped over the finishing line and was thus disqualified. Quoted in Colin Jarman *The Guinness Dictionary of Sports Quotations* (1990).

77 'I am inclined to think—' said I.
'I should do so,' Sherlock Holmes remarked, impatiently.
1915 *The Valley of Fear*, ch.1.

78 Mediocrity knows nothing higher than itself, but talent instantly recognises genius.
1915 *The Valley of Fear*, ch.1.

79 All other men are specialists, but his specialism is omniscience.
1917 *His Last Bow*, 'Bruce-Partington Plans'.

80 Good old Watson! You are the one fixed point in a changing age.
1917 *His Last Bow*, title story.

81 There is but one step from the grotesque to the horrible.
1917 *His Last Bow*, 'Wisteria Lodge'.

82 Matilda Briggs…was a ship which is associated with the giant rat of Sumatra, a story for which the world is not yet prepared.
  1927 *The Case-Book of Sherlock Holmes*, 'The Sussex Vampire'.

Doyle, Charles (Mike) 1928–

New Zealand poet, primarily of the city and suburbs. His collections include *A Splinter of Glass* (1956) and *Messages for Herod* (1965). He has lived in Canada since 1968.

83 If only to be born were being invented
  Merely, or, better still, to concoct oneself
  From an antique alembic, a receipt. How splendid
  To take the phial cleanly from its shelf;

  Powders and liquids, all one's favourite hues
  Making the being one would be, the looker at stars
  Or storks on the spires of Denmark, drinker of dews,
  Or an eye simply.
  'Phials', collected in *Quadrant*, 1964.

Doyle, Roddy 1958–

Irish novelist. His works include the 'Barrytown trilogy'—*The Commitments* (1987), *The Snapper* (1990) and *The Van* (1991)—and the Booker Prize-winning *Paddy Clarke Ha Ha Ha* (1993).

84 The Irish are the niggers of Europe…An' Dubliners are the niggers of Ireland…An' the northside Dubliners are the niggers o' Dublin—Say it loud. I'm black and I'm proud.
  1987 *The Commitments*.

85 'A song belongs to no man,' said Joey The Lips. 'The Lord holds copyright on all songs.'
  'Me arse,' said Outspan.
  1987 *The Commitments*.

86 I said one Hail Mary and four Our Fathers, because I preferred the Our Father to the Hail Mary and it was longer and better.
  1993 *Paddy Clarke Ha Ha Ha*.

Drabble, Margaret 1939–

English novelist, critic and editor. Her novels often deal with the experiences and difficulties of educated young women.

87 Sometimes it seems the only accomplishment my education ever bestowed on me was the ability to think in quotations.
  1963 *A Summer Birdcage*, ch.1.

88 Perhaps the rare and simple pleasure of being seen for what one is compensates for the misery of being it.
  1963 *A Summer Birdcage*, ch.7.

89 What fools middle-class girls are to expect other people to respect the same gods as themselves and E M Forster.
  1963 *A Summer Birdcage*, ch.11.

90 Lord knows what incommunicable small terrors infants go through, unknown to all.
  1965 *The Millstone*.

91 England's not a bad country… It's just a mean, cold, ugly, divided, tired, clapped-out, post-imperial, post-industrial slag-heap covered in polystyrene hamburger cartons.
  1989 *A Natural Curiosity*.

Drake, Sir Francis c.1540–1596

Elizabethan seaman, the first Englishman to circumnavigate the world. In 1585 he sailed on a successful expedition to the Spanish Indies. He commanded the fleet that defended England against the Spanish Armada in 1588.

92 The singeing of the King of Spain's beard.
  1587 His description of an expedition to Cadiz, quoted in Francis Bacon *Considerations Touching a War with Spain* (1629).

93 The advantage of time and place in practical actions is half the victory; which being lost is irrecoverable.
  1588 Letter to Elizabeth I, 13 Apr.

94 There is plenty of time to win this game, and to thrash the Spaniards too.
  1588 Attributed, while finishing a game of bowls at Plymouth Hoe, 20 Jul, before sailing to meet the Armada. Quoted in the *Dictionary of National Biography* (1917–), vol.5, p.1342.

Drapeau, Jean 1916–99

Canadian politician, Mayor of Montreal (1954–57, 1960–86).

95 The Montreal Olympics can no more have a deficit than a man can have a baby.
  1973 Comment at press conference, Montreal, 29 Jan. The games went well over budget.

Drayton, Michael 1563–1631

English poet and dramatist. After his first work *The Harmony of the Church* (1591) was condemned by the Church, he turned to pastoral and historical themes. *Polyolbion* (1616–22) is a topographical survey of Britain. Only one play survives, *The First Part of Sir John Oldcastle* (1600).

96 She wore a frock of frolic green.
  1593 *Idea, the Shepherd's Garland*, 'The Eighth Eclogue'.

97 So in all humours sportively I range;
  My muse is rightly of the English strain,
  That cannot long one fashion entertain.
  1594 *Ideas Mirrour*, 'To the Reader of These Sonnets'.

98 Dear, why should you command me to my rest,
  When now the night doth summon all to sleep?
  Methinks this time becometh lovers best;
  Night was ordained together friends to keep.
  1594 *Ideas Mirrour*, sonnet 37.

99 When Time shall turn those amber locks to grey,
  My verse again shall gild and make them gay.
  1597 *England's Heroic Epistles*, 'Henry Howard, Earl of Surrey, to the Lady Geraldine'.

1 Fair stood the wind for France
  When we our sails advance,
  Nor now to prove our chance
  Longer will tarry.
  1606 *Poems Lyrick and Pastorall*, 'To the Cambro-Britons and Their Harp, His Ballad of Agincourt', describing Henry V's expedition to France, 1415.

2 Upon Saint Crispin's day
  Fought was this noble fray,
  Which fame did not delay
  To England to carry;
  Oh, when shall English men
  With such acts fill a pen,
  Or England breed again
  Such a King Harry?

1606 Of the Battle of Agincourt. *Poems Lyrick and Pastorall*, 'To the Cambro-Britons and Their Harp, His Ballad of Agincourt'.

3 But she, good sir,
Did not prefer
You, for that I was ranging;
But for that she
Found faith in me
And she loved to be changing.
1606 *Poems Lyrick and Pastorall*, 'To His Rival'.

4 That shire which we the Heart of England well may call.
1612–22 Of Warwickshire. *Polyolbion*, song 13, l.2.

5 Neat Marlowe, bathed in the Thespian springs,
Had in him those brave translunary things
That the first poets had; his raptures were
All air and fire, which made his verses clear,
For that fine madness still he did retain
Which rightly should possess a poet's brain.
1619 'To My Most Dearly Loved Henry Reynolds, Esquire, of Poets and Poesie'.

6 Since there's no help, come let us kiss and part;
Nay, I have done, you get no more of me,
And I am glad, yea glad with all my heart
That thus so cleanly I myself can free;
Shake hands forever, cancel all our vows,
And when we meet at any time again,
Be it not seen in either of our brows
That we one jot of former love retain.
1619 *Idea*, sonnet 61.

7 The walls of spiders' legs are made,
Well mortised and finely laid;
He was the master of his trade
It curiously builded;
The windows of the eyes of cats,
And for the roof, instead of slats,
Is covered with the skins of bats,
With moonshine that are gilded.
1627 *Nymphidia, the Court of Fairy.*

Drennan, William   1754–1820

Irish patriot and poet.

8 Nor one feeling of vengeance presumed to defile
The cause, or the men, or the Emerald Isle.
1795 *Erin*, stanza 3.

Drexler, Arthur

US art administrator, Director of Architecture and Design at the Metropolitan Museum of Art, New York (1956–87).

9 History is written for the victors and what they leave out is the losers.
1975 In the *New York Review*, 27 Nov.

Driberg, Tom (Thomas Edward Neil), Baron of Bradwell   1905–76

English journalist, broadcaster and politician. On the editorial staff of the *Daily Express* (1928–43), he became an independent (1942) then Labour (1945) MP and was created a life peer in 1975.

10 Sincerity is all that counts is a widespread modern heresy. Think again. Bolsheviks are sincere. Fascists are sincere. Lunatics are sincere. People who believe that the earth is flat are sincere. They can't all be right. Better make certain first that you have something to be sincere about, and with.
1937 In the *Daily Express.*

Drucker, Peter Ferdinand   1909–

Austrian-born US management consultant, Professor of Social Science and Management at Claremont Graduate University, California.

11 Entrepreneurship can be learned, but it can't be taught, so schools are not much good.
1988 Interviewed in 'Adam Smith' *The Roaring '80s* (1988), ch.2.

12 If you ever run into an industry that says it needs better people, sell its shares. There *are* no better people. You have to use ordinary, every-day people and make them capable of doing the work.
1991 In the *Los Angeles Times*, 17 Sep.

Drummond, Thomas   1797–1840

Scottish engineer and statesman, developer of the Drummond Light (limelight). He was appointed Under-Secretary for Ireland in 1835.

13 Property has its duties as well as its rights.
1838 Letter to the Earl of Donoughmore, 22 May.

Dryden, John   1631–1700

English poet, critic and playwright. He was made Poet Laureate in 1668 and his satirical verses such as *Absalom and Achitophel* (1681) were highly regarded. Among his best plays are *Marriage-à-la-Mode* (1672) and *All for Love* (1678); his works were prefaced with critical essays, including the seminal *Essay of Dramatic Poesy* (1668). He became a Catholic in 1685 and on refusing to swear allegiance to William and Mary was deprived of his laureateship.

14 An horrid stillness first invades the ear,
And in that silence we the tempest fear.
1660 *Astraea Redux*, l.7–8.

15 His colours laid so thick on every place,
As only showed the paint, but hid the face.
1660 Epistle 'To my honoured friend Sir Robert Howard', l.75–6.

16 I strongly wish for what I faintly hope:
Like the day-dreams of melancholy men,
I think and think on things impossible,
Yet love to wander in that golden maze.
1664 *The Rival Ladies*, act 3, sc.1.

17 And love's the noblest frailty of the mind.
1665 *The Indian Emperor*, act 2, sc.2.

18 Repentance is the virtue of weak minds.
1665 *The Indian Emperor*, act 3, sc.1.

19 For all the happiness mankind can gain
Is not in pleasure, but in rest from pain.
1665 *The Indian Emperor*, act 4, sc.1.

20 By viewing nature, nature's handmaid art,
Makes mighty things from small beginnings grow:
Thus fishes first to shipping did impart,
Their tail the rudder, and their head the prow.
1667 *Annus Mirabilis*, stanza 155.

21 For secrets are edged tools,
And must be kept from children, and from fools.
1667 *Sir Martin Mar-All*, act 2, sc.2.

22 I am resolved to grow fat and look young till forty, and then slip out of the world with the first wrinkle and the reputation of five-and-twenty.
1668 *The Maiden Queen*, act 3, sc.1.

23 Every age has a kind of universal genius, which inclines those that live in it to some particular studies.
1668 *An Essay of Dramatic Poesy*, 'Shakespeare and Ben Jonson Compared'.

24 A thing well said will be wit in all languages…though it may lose something in the translation.
1668 *An Essay of Dramatic Poesy*, 'The Wit of the Ancients: The Universal'.

25 Shakespeare…was the man who of all modern, and perhaps ancient poets, had the largest and most comprehensive soul. All images of Nature were still present to him, and he drew them, not laboriously, but luckily; when he describes anything, you more than see it, you feel it too. Those who accuse him to have wanted learning, give him the greater commendation: he was naturally learned; he needed not the spectacles of books to read Nature; he looked inwards, and found her there… He is many times flat, insipid; his comic wit degenerating into clenches, his serious swelling into bombast. But he is always great.
1668 *An Essay of Dramatic Poesy*, 'Shakespeare and Ben Jonson Compared'.

26 He invades authors like a monarch; and what would be theft in other poets, is only victory in him.
1668 Of Ben Jonson. *An Essay of Dramatic Poesy*, 'Shakespeare and Ben Jonson Compared'.

27 If by the people you understand the multitude, the *hoi polloi*, 'tis no matter what they think; they are sometimes in the right, sometimes in the wrong: their judgement is a mere lottery.
1668 *An Essay of Dramatic Poesy*, 'Shakespeare and Ben Jonson Compared'.

28 One cannot say he wanted wit, but rather that he was frugal of it.
1668 Of Ben Jonson. *An Essay of Dramatic Poesy*, 'Shakespeare and Ben Jonson Compared'.

29 You seldom find him making love in any of his scenes or endeavouring to move the passions; his genius was too sullen and saturnine to do it gracefully, especially when he knew he came after those who had performed both to such an height.
1668 Of Ben Jonson. *An Essay of Dramatic Poesy*, 'Shakespeare and Ben Jonson Compared'.

30 If I would compare [Jonson] with Shakespeare, I must acknowledge him the more correct poet, but Shakespeare the greater wit.
1668 *An Essay of Dramatic Poesy*, 'Shakespeare and Ben Jonson Compared'.

31 Shakespeare was the Homer, or father of our dramatic poets; Jonson was the Virgil, the pattern of elaborate writing; I admire him, but I love Shakespeare.
1668 *An Essay of Dramatic Poesy*, 'Shakespeare and Ben Jonson Compared'.

32 And he, who servilely creeps after sense,
Is safe, but ne'er will reach an excellence.
1669 *Tyrannic Love*, prologue.

33 All delays are dangerous in war.
1669 *Tyrannic Love*, act 1, sc.1.

34 Pains of love be sweeter far
Than all other pleasures are.
1669 *Tyrannic Love*, act 4, sc.1.

35 I am as free as nature first made man,
Ere the base laws of servitude began,
When wild in woods the noble savage ran.
1670 *The Conquest of Granada*, pt.1, act 1, sc.1.

36 Forgiveness to the injured does belong;
But they ne'er pardon, who have done the wrong.
1670 *The Conquest of Granada*, pt.2, act 1, sc.2.

37 Thou strong seducer, opportunity!
1670 *The Conquest of Granada*, pt.2, act 4, sc.3.

38 I am to be married within these three days; married past redemption.
1672 *Marriage-à-la-Mode*, act 1, sc.1.

39 The very Janus of poets; he wears almost everywhere two faces; and you have scarce begun to admire the one, ere you despise the other.
1672 Of Shakespeare. *Essay on the Dramatic Poetry of the Last Age*.

40 So poetry, which is in Oxford made
An art, in London only is a trade.
1673 'Prologue to the University of Oxon…at the Acting of *The Silent Woman*'.

41 Sure the poet…spewed up a good lump of clotted nonsense at once.
1674 *Notes and Observations on the Empress of Morocco*, 'The First Act'.

42 Death, in itself, is nothing; but we fear,
To be we know not what, we know not where.
1675 *Aureng-Zebe*, act 4, sc.1.

43 None would live past years again,
Yet all hope pleasure in what yet remain;
And, from the dregs of life, think to receive,
What the first sprightly running could not give.
1675 *Aureng-Zebe*, act 4, sc.1.

44 They, who would combat general authority with particular opinion, must first establish themselves a reputation of understanding better than other men.
1677 'The Author's Apology for Heroic Poetry and Heroic Licence', an essay prefacing *State of Innocence*, a libretto based on *Paradise Lost*.

45 Virgil and Horace [were] the severest writers of the severest age.
1677 'The Author's Apology for Heroic Poetry and Heroic Licence', an essay prefacing *State of Innocence*, a libretto based on *Paradise Lost*.

46 A propriety of thoughts and words; or, in other terms, thought and words elegantly adapted to the subject.
1677 Definition of wit. 'The Author's Apology for Heroic Poetry and Heroic Licence', an essay prefacing *State of Innocence*, a libretto based on *Paradise Lost*.

47 All human things are subject to decay,
And, when fate summons, monarchs must obey.
1678 *MacFlecknoe* (published 1682), l.1–2.

48 Shadwell alone, of all my sons, is he
Who stands confirmed in full stupidity.
1678 Richard Flecknoe selects Shadwell as heir to the kingdom of dullness. *MacFlecknoe* (published 1682), l.17–18.

49 The rest to some faint meaning make pretence,
But Shadwell never deviates into sense.
Some beams of wit on other souls may fall,

Strike through and make a lucid interval;
But Shadwell's genuine night admits no ray,
His rising fogs prevail upon the day.
1678 *MacFlecknoe* (published 1682), l.19–24.

50 Thy genius calls thee not to purchase fame
In keen iambics, but mild anagram:
Leave writing plays, and choose for thy command
Some peaceful province in Acrostic Land.
There thou mayest wings display and altars raise,
And torture one poor word ten thousand ways.
1678 *MacFlecknoe* (published 1682), l.203–8.

51 Errors, like straws, upon the surface flow;
He who would search for pearls must dive below.
1678 *All for Love, or The World Well Lost*, prologue.

52 Then he defies the world and bids it pass.
1678 Of Antony. *All for Love, or The World Well Lost*, act 1.

53 Virtue's his path; but sometimes 'tis too narrow
For his vast soul; and then he starts out wide,
And bounds into a vice.
1678 Of Antony. *All for Love, or The World Well Lost*, act 1.

54 Sure there's contagion in the tears of friends.
1678 *All for Love, or The World Well Lost*, act 1.

55 My love's a noble madness.
1678 Cleopatra to Iris. *All for Love, or The World Well Lost*, act 2, sc.1.

56 Give, you gods,
Give to your boy, your Caesar,
The rattle of a globe to play withal,
This gewgaw world, and put him cheaply off:
I'll not be pleased with less than Cleopatra.
1678 Anthony. *All for Love, or The World Well Lost*, act 2, sc.1.

57 Moderate sorrow
Fits vulgar love, and for a vulgar man:
But I have lov'd with such transcendent passion,
I soar'd, at first, quite out of reason's view,
And now am lost above it.
1678 *All for Love, or The World Well Lost*, act 2.

58 O that faint word, *respect*! how I disdain it!
1678 *All for Love, or The World Well Lost*, act 2.

59 My heart's so full of joy,
That I shall do some wild extravagance
Of love in public; and the foolish world,
Which knows not tenderness, will think me mad.
1678 *All for Love, or The World Well Lost*, act 2.

60 We were so clos'd within each other's breasts
The rivets were not found that join'd us first.
That does not reach us yet: we were so mix'd,
As meeting streams, both to ourselves were lost;
We were one mass; we could not give or take,
But from the same; for he was I, I he!
1678 Antony speaking of his friendship with Dollabella. *All for Love, or The World Well Lost*, act 3.

61 What I have left is from my native spring;
I've still a heart that swells, in scorn of fate,
And lifts me to my banks.
1678 *All for Love, or The World Well Lost*, act 3.

62 The worst your malice can,
Is but to say the greatest of mankind
Has been my slave. The next, but far above him
In my esteem, is he whom law calls yours,
But whom his love made mine.

1678 Cleopatra boasts to Octavia of her conquest of Caesar and Antony. *All for Love, or The World Well Lost*, act 3.

63 Men are but children of a larger growth;
Our appetites as apt to change as theirs,
And full as craving too, and full as vain.
1678 Dollabella. *All for Love, or The World Well Lost*, act 4, sc.1.

64 Nature meant me
A wife, a silly, harmless, household dove,
Fond without art, and kind without deceit;
But Fortune, that has made a mistress of me,
Has thrust me out to the wide world, unfurnish'd
Of falsehood to be happy.
1678 Cleopatra. *All for Love, or The World Well Lost*, act 4.

65 Welcome, thou kind deceiver!
Thou best of thieves; who with an easy key,
Dost open life, and, unperceived by us,
Even steal us from ourselves.
1678 Cleopatra speaking of love. *All for Love, or The World Well Lost*, act 5, sc.1.

66 My whole life
Has been a golden dream of love and friendship.
1678 *All for Love, or The World Well Lost*, act 5.

67 All the learn'd are cowards by profession.
1678 *All for Love, or The World Well Lost*, act 5.

68 In pious times, ere priestcraft did begin,
Before polygamy was made a sin.
1681 *Absalom and Achitophel*, pt.1, l.1–2.

69 Then Israel's monarch, after Heaven's own heart,
His vigorous warmth did, variously, impart
To wives and slaves: and, wide as his command,
Scattered his Maker's image through the land.
1681 *Absalom and Achitophel*, pt.1, l.7–10. An oblique reference to Charles II, who had no legitimate, but many illegitimate, children.

70 Whate'er he did was done with so much ease,
In him alone, 'twas natural to please.
1681 *Absalom and Achitophel*, pt.1, l.27–8.

71 His motions all accompanied with grace;
And paradise was opened in his face.
1681 *Absalom and Achitophel*, pt.1, l.29–30.

72 The Jews, a headstrong, moody, murmuring race.
1681 *Absalom and Achitophel*, pt.1, l.45.

73 But when to sin our biased nature leans,
The careful Devil is still at hand with means;
And providently pimps for ill desires.
1681 *Absalom and Achitophel*, pt.1, l.79–81.

74 Plots, true or false, are necessary things,
To raise up commonwealths and ruin kings.
1681 Alluding to the alleged Popish plot to murder the King, which brought about the Exclusion crisis. *Absalom and Achitophel*, pt.1, l.83–4.

75 Some truth there was, but dashed and brewed with lies,
To please the fools, and puzzle all the wise.
1681 *Absalom and Achitophel*, pt.1, l.114–15.

76 Pleased with the danger, when the waves went high
He sought the storms; but for a calm unfit,
Would steer too nigh the sands to boast his wit.
1681 Alluding to Anthony Ashley Cooper, first Earl of Shaftesbury, leader of the Exclusion forces. *Absalom and Achitophel*, pt.1, l.160–2.

77 Great wits are sure to madness near allied,
And thin partitions do their bands divide.
1681 *Absalom and Achitophel*, pt.1, l.163–4.

78 Why should he, with wealth and honour blest,
Refuse his age the needful hours of rest?
Punish a body which he could not please;
Bankrupt of life, yet prodigal of ease?
And all to leave what with his toil he won
To that unfeathered two-legged thing, a son.
1681 *Absalom and Achitophel*, pt.1, l.165–70.

79 In friendship false, implacable in hate:
Resolved to ruin or to rule the state.
1681 *Absalom and Achitophel*, pt.1, l.173–4.

80 He stood at bold defiance with his prince;
Held up the buckler of the people's cause
Against the crown, and skulked behind the laws.
1681 *Absalom and Achitophel*, pt.1, l.205–7.

81 Politicians neither love nor hate.
1681 *Absalom and Achitophel*, pt.1, l.223.

82 The people's prayer, the glad diviner's theme,
The young men's vision and the old men's dream!
1681 *Absalom and Achitophel*, pt.1, l.238–9.
➤ See Bible 106:5.

83 What cannot praise effect in mighty minds,
When flattery soothes, and when ambition blinds!
1681 *Absalom and Achitophel*, pt.1, l.303–4.

84 Desire of power, on earth a vicious weed,
Yet, sprung from high, is of celestial seed:
In God 'tis glory; and when men aspire,
'Tis but a spark too much of heavenly fire.
1681 *Absalom and Achitophel*, pt.1, l.305–9.

85 All empire is no more than power in trust.
1681 *Absalom and Achitophel*, pt.1, l.411.

86 Better one suffer, than a nation grieve.
1681 *Absalom and Achitophel*, pt.1, l.416.

87 But far more numerous was the herd of such
Who think too little and who talk too much.
1681 *Absalom and Achitophel*, pt.1, l.533–4.

88 A man so various that he seemed to be
Not one, but all mankind's epitome.
Stiff in opinions, always in the wrong;
Was everything by starts, and nothing long:
But, in the course of one revolving moon,
Was chemist, fiddler, statesman, and buffoon.
1681 *Absalom and Achitophel*, pt. 1, l.545–60.

89 In squandering wealth was his peculiar art:
Nothing went unrewarded, but desert.
Beggared by fools, whom still he found too late:
He had his jest, and they had his estate.
1681 *Absalom and Achitophel*, pt.1, l.559–62.

90 Youth, beauty, graceful action seldom fail:
But common interest always will prevail:
And pity never ceases to be shown
To him, who makes the people's wrongs his own.
1681 *Absalom and Achitophel*, pt.1, l.723–6.

91 For who can be secure of private right,
If sovereign sway may be dissolved by might?
Nor is the people's judgement always true:
The most may err as grossly as the few.
1681 *Absalom and Achitophel*, pt.1, l.779–82.

92 Government itself at length must fall
To nature's state, where all have right to all.
1681 *Absalom and Achitophel*, pt.1, l.793–4.

93 The court he practised, not the courtier's art:
Large was his wealth, but larger was his heart.
1681 Of the loyalist James Butler, Duke of Ormond. *Absalom and Achitophel*, pt.1, l.825–6.

94 Swift was the race, but short the time to run.
1681 *Absalom and Achitophel*, pt.1, l.837.

95 Never was patriot yet, but was a fool.
1681 *Absalom and Achitophel*, pt.1, l.968.

96 From plots and treasons Heaven preserve my years,
But save me most from my petitioners.
Unsatiate as the barren womb or grave;
God cannot grant so much as they can crave.
1681 *Absalom and Achitophel*, pt.1, l.985–8.

97 Beware the fury of a patient man.
1681 *Absalom and Achitophel*, pt.1, l.1005.

98 For lawful power is still superior found,
When long driven back, at length it stands the ground.
1681 *Absalom and Achitophel*, pt.1, l.1024–5.

99 Doeg, though without knowing how or why,
Made still a blund'ring kind of melody;
Spurred boldly on, and dashed through thick and thin,
Through sense and nonsense, never out nor in;
Free from all meaning, whether good or bad,
And in one word, heroically mad.
1681 *Absalom and Achitophel*, pt.2, l.412–17.

1 Rhyme is the rock on which thou art to wreck.
1681 *Absalom and Achitophel*, pt.2, l.486.

2 But 'tis the talent of our English nation,
Still to be plotting some new reformation.
1681 *Sophonisba* (2nd edn).

3 There is a pleasure sure,
In being mad, that none but madmen know!
1681 *The Spanish Friar*, act 1, sc.1.

4 And, dying, bless the hand that gave the blow.
1681 *The Spanish Friar*, act 2, sc.2.

5 We loathe our manna, and we long for quails.
1682 *The Medal*, l.131.

6 But treason is not owned when 'tis descried;
Successful crimes alone are justified.
1682 *The Medal*, l.207–8.

7 And this unpolished rugged verse I chose
As fittest for discourse and nearest prose.
1682 *Religio Laici*, l.453–4.

8 Farewell, too little, and too lately known,
Whom I began to think and call my own.
1684 'To the Memory of Mr Oldham'. John Oldham was the author of *Satires upon the Jesuits* (1681).

9 Bold knaves thrive without one grain of sense,
But good men starve for want of impudence.
1684 *Constantine the Great*, epilogue.

10 Mute and magnificent, without a tear.
1685 *Threnodia Augustalis*, stanza 2.

11 Freedom which in no other land will thrive,
Freedom an English subject's sole prerogative.
1685 *Threnodia Augustalis*, stanza 10.

12 Her pencil drew whate'er her soul designed,

And oft the happy draft surpassed the image in her mind.
1686 'To the Pious Memory of the Accomplished Young Lady
Mrs Anne Killigrew'.

13 O double sacrilege on things divine,
To rob the relic, and deface the shrine!
1686 'To the Pious Memory of the Accomplished Young Lady
Mrs Anne Killigrew'. Killigrew had died of smallpox.

14 And doomed to death, though fated not to die.
1687 *The Hind and the Panther*, pt.1, l.8.

15 For truth has such a face and such a mien
As to be loved needs only to be seen.
1687 *The Hind and the Panther*, pt.1, l.33–4.

16 My thoughtless youth was winged with vain desires,
My manhood, long misled by wandering fires,
Followed false lights; and when their glimpse was gone
My pride struck out new sparkles of her own…
Good life be now my task: my doubts are done;
(What more could fright my faith than Three in One?)
1687 *The Hind and the Panther*, pt.1, l.71–6.

17 Reason to rule, but mercy to forgive:
The first is law, the last prerogative.
1687 *The Hind and the Panther*, pt.1, l.261–2.

18 Either be wholly slaves or wholly free.
1687 *The Hind and the Panther*, pt.2, l.285.

19 Much malice mingled with a little wit
Perhaps may censure this mysterious writ.
1687 *The Hind and the Panther*, pt.3, l.1–2.

20 For present joys are more to flesh and blood
Than a dull prospect of a distant good.
1687 *The Hind and the Panther*, pt.3, l.364–5.

21 By education most have been misled;
So they believe, because they so were bred.
The priest continues what the nurse began,
And thus the child imposes on the man.
1687 *The Hind and the Panther*, pt.3, l.389–92.

22 T'abhor the makers, and their laws approve,
Is to hate traitors and the treason love.
1687 *The Hind and the Panther*, pt.3, l.706–7.

23 For those whom God to ruin has designed,
He fits for fate, and first destroys their mind.
1687 *The Hind and the Panther*, pt.3, l.1093–4.

24 Three poets, in three distant ages born,
Greece, Italy, and England did adorn.
The first in loftiness of thought surpassed,
The next in majesty, in both the last:
The force of Nature could no farther go;
To make a third, she joined the former two.
1688 'Epigram on Milton', engraved on the frontispiece to the
1688 edition of *Paradise Lost*. The three poets are Homer, Virgil
and Milton.

25 That fairy kind of writing which depends only upon the
force of imagination.
1691 *King Arthur*, dedication.

26 War is the trade of kings.
1691 *King Arthur*, act 2, sc.2.

27 Fairest Isle, all isles excelling,
Seat of pleasures, and of loves;
Venus here will choose her dwelling,
And forsake her Cyprian groves.
1691 *King Arthur*, act 5, 'Song of Venus'.

28 Music, Music for a while
Shall all your cares beguile.
1692 *Oedipus* (with Nathaniel Lee).

29 How easy it is to call rogue and villain, and that wittily!
But how hard to make a man appear a fool, a blockhead,
or a knave, without using any of those opprobrious
terms! To spare the grossness of the names, and to do the
thing yet more severely, is to draw a full face, and to make
the nose and cheeks stand out, and yet not to employ
any depth of shadowing.
1693 *A Discourse Concerning the Original and Progress of Satire*,
'The Art of Satire'.

30 A man may be capable, as Jack Ketch's wife said of his
servant, of a plain piece of work, a bare hanging; but to
make a malefactor die sweetly was only belonging to her
husband.
1693 *A Discourse Concerning the Original and Progress of Satire*,
'The Art of Satire'.

31 Ovid, the soft philosopher of love.
1694 *Love Triumphant*, act 2, sc.1.

32 Thou tyrant, tyrant Jealousy,
Thou tyrant of the mind!
1694 *Love Triumphant*, act 3, sc.1, 'Song of Jealousy'.

33 Happy, happy, happy, pair!
None but the brave,
None but the brave,
None but the brave deserves the fair.
1697 *Alexander's Feast*, l.4–7.

34 With ravished ears
The monarch hears,
Assumes the god,
Affects to nod,
And seems to shake the spheres.
1697 *Alexander's Feast*, l.42–6.

35 Drinking is the soldier's pleasure;
Rich the treasure;
Sweet the pleasure;
Sweet is pleasure after pain.
1697 *Alexander's Feast*, l.57–60.

36 Fallen from his high estate,
And welt'ring in his blood:
Deserted at his utmost need
By those his former bounty fed;
On the bare earth expos'd he lies,
With not a friend to close his eyes.
1697 *Alexander's Feast*, l.78–83.

37 Revolving in his altered soul
The various turns of chance below.
1697 *Alexander's Feast*, l.85–6.

38 War, he sung, is toil and trouble;
Honour but an empty bubble.
Never ending, still beginning,
Fighting still, and still destroying,
If the world be worth thy winning,
Think, oh think, it worth enjoying.
1697 *Alexander's Feast*, l.97–102.

39 Sighed and looked, and sighed again.
1697 *Alexander's Feast*, l.120.

40 Let old Timotheus yield the prize,
Or both divide the crown:
He raised a mortal to the skies;

She drew an angel down.
1697 Of 'Divine Cecilia'. *Alexander's Feast*, l.177–80.

41 We must beat the iron while it is hot, but we may polish it at leisure.
1697 *Aeneis* (his translation of Virgil's *Aeneid*), dedication.

42 Arms, and the man I sing, who, forced by fate,
And haughty Juno's unrelenting hate,
Expelled and exiled, left the Trojan shore.
1697 *Aeneis* (his translation of Virgil's *Aeneid*), bk.1, l.1–3.

43 What judgement I had increases rather than diminishes; and thoughts, such as they are, come crowding in so fast upon me, that my only difficulty is to choose or reject; to run them into verse or give them the other harmony of prose.
1700 *Fables Ancient and Modern*, preface.

44 We can only say that he lived in the infancy of our poetry, and that nothing is brought to perfection at the first.
1700 *Fables Ancient and Modern*, preface, 'In Praise of Chaucer'.

45 [Chaucer] must have been a man of a most wonderful comprehensive nature, because, as it has been truly observed of him, he has taken into the compass of his *Canterbury Tales* the various manners and humours of the whole English nation in his age.
1700 *Fables Ancient and Modern*, preface, 'In Praise of Chaucer'.

46 A perpetual fountain of good sense.
1700 Of Chaucer. *Fables Ancient and Modern*, preface.

47 'Tis sufficient to say, according to the proverb, that here is God's plenty.
1700 Of the *Canterbury Tales*. *Fables Ancient and Modern*, preface, 'In Praise of Chaucer'.

48 One of our great poets is sunk in his reputation, because he could never forgive any conceit which came in his way; but swept like a drag-net, great and small. There was plenty enough, but the dishes were ill-sorted; whole pyramids of sweetmeats, for boys and women; but little of solid meat for men.
1700 Of Abraham Cowley. *Fables Ancient and Modern*, preface.

49 Refined himself to soul, to curb the sense
And made almost a sin of abstinence.
1700 'The Character of a Good Parson', l.10–11.

50 He trudged along unknowing what he sought,
And whistled as he went, for want of thought.
1700 *Cymon and Iphigenia*, l.84–5.

51 She hugged the offender, and forgave the offence.
1700 *Cymon and Iphigenia*, l.367.

52 Of seeming arms to make a short essay,
Then hasten to be drunk, the business of the day.
1700 *Cymon and Iphigenia*, l.407–8.

53 Better to hunt in fields, for health unbought,
Than fee the doctor for a nauseous draught.
The wise, for cure, on exercise depend;
God never made his work, for man to mend.
1700 Epistle, 'To my honoured kinsman John Driden', l.92–5.

54 Even victors are by victories undone.
1700 Epistle, 'To my honoured kinsman John Driden', l.164.

55 But love's a malady without a cure.
1700 *Palamon and Arcite*, bk.2, l.110.

56 Fool, not to know that love endures no tie,
And Jove but laughs at lovers' perjury.
1700 *Palamon and Arcite*, bk.2, l.148–9.

57 And Antony, who lost the world for love.
1700 *Palamon and Arcite*, bk.2, l.607.

58 Repentance is but want of power to sin.
1700 *Palamon and Arcite*, bk.3, l.813.

59 Since every man who lives is born to die,
And none can boast sincere felicity,
With equal mind, what happens, let us bear,
Nor joy nor grieve too much for things beyond our care.
Like pilgrims to th'appointed place we tend;
The world's an inn, and death the journey's end.
1700 *Palamon and Arcite*, bk.3, l.883–8.

60 A virgin-widow, and a mourning bride.
1700 *Palamon and Arcite*, bk.3, l.927.

61 A very merry, dancing, drinking,
Laughing, quaffing, and unthinking time.
1700 *The Secular Masque*, l.39–40.

62 Joy ruled the day, and Love the night.
1700 *The Secular Masque*, l.81.

63 All, all of a piece throughout;
Thy chase had a beast in view;
Thy wars brought nothing about;
Thy lovers were all untrue.
'Tis well an old age is out,
And time to begin a new.
1700 *The Secular Masque*, l.92–7.

Dubin, Al 1891–1945

Swiss-born US lyricist.

64 Come and meet those dancing feet
On the avenue I'm taking you to
Forty-Second Street.
1932 From the title song, *Forty-Second Street*. Music by Harry Warren.

65 You're Getting to be a Habit with Me.
1932 Title of song in *Forty-Second Street*. Music by Harry Warren.

66 We're in the money, we're in the money
We've got a lot of what it takes to get along.
1933 From the song 'We're in the Money' featured in *Gold Diggers of 1933*. Music by Harry Warren.

67 I Only Have Eyes For You.
1934 Title of song from the film *Dames*. Music by Harry Warren.

68 You may not be an angel
Cause angels are so few
But until the day that one comes along
I'll string along with you.
1934 From the song 'I'll String Along With You' in *Twenty Million Sweethearts*. Music by Harry Warren.

69 Come on along and listen to
The Lullaby of Broadway
The hip hooray and bally hoo
The Lullaby of Broadway.
1935 From the song 'Lullaby of Broadway' in *Gold Diggers of 1935*. Music by Harry Warren.

Du Bois, W(illiam) E(dward) B(urghardt) 1868–1963

US writer. He became a leading figure in and spokesman for the black community, and wrote a number of pioneering books on black life and social reform.

70 The problem of the twentieth century is the problem of the colour line.

1900 Address to the Pan-African Conference, London.

71 To be a poor man is hard, but to be a poor race in a land of dollars is the very bottom of hardships.
1903 *The Souls of Black Folk*, ch.1.

72 Herein lies the tragedy of the age: not that men are poor…not that men are wicked…but that men know so little of men.
1903 *The Souls of Black Folk*, ch.12.

73 If there is anybody in this land who thoroughly believes that the meek shall inherit the earth they have not often let their presence be known.
1924 *The Gift of Black Folk*, ch.9.

74 One thing alone I charge you. As you live, believe in life! Always human beings will live and progress to a greater, broader and fuller life. The only possible death is to lose belief in this truth simply because the great end comes slowly, because time is long.
1957 Written 26 Jun, and read as an oration at his funeral.

75 Today I see more clearly than yesterday that back of the problem of race and color, lies a greater problem which both obscures and implements it: and that is the fact that so many civilized persons are willing to live in comfort even if the price of this is poverty, ignorance and disease of the majority of their fellowmen; that to maintain this privilege men have waged war until today war tends to become universal and continuous, and the excuse for this war continues largely to be color and race.
Preface to reprint of *The Souls of Black Folk* (1969).

Du Bos, Jean-Baptiste 1670–1742

French critic, whose work influenced aesthetic theory.

76 *Les larmes d'un inconnu nous émeuvent même avant que nous sachions le sujet qui le fait pleurer.*
The tears of someone we do not know move us even before we know the reason why he weeps.
1719 *Réflexions critiques sur la poésie et la peinture.*

77 *Le sentiment enseigne bien mieux si l'ouvrage touche que toutes les dissertations composées par les critiques.*
Feeling teaches much more than all the writing of critics if the work touches us.
1719 *Réflexions critiques sur la poésie et la peinture.*

Dudek, Louis 1918–2001

Canadian poet, critic, teacher and aphorist, whose works attempt to liberate Candian poetry from its British influences. His early lyric poetry was followed by longer poems such as *En México* (1958).

78 Aphorisms give you more for your time and money than any other literary form. Only the poem comes near to it, but then most good poems either start off from an aphorism or arrive at one… Aphorisms and epigrams are the corner-stones of literary art.
Collected in *Notebooks 1960–1994* (1994).

79 Fame is based on what people say about you, reputation on what they think of you.
Collected in *Notebooks 1960–1994* (1994).

80 If there is a heaven it's no doubt already filled—with horses, chickens, lambs, and other poor creatures. People will simply not get in.
Collected in *Notebooks 1960–1994* (1994).

81 All the ills of mankind spring from belonging to a race, a nation, a city, a group of some kind. The ideal would be to belong to none, and to care for all—but who is capable of that?
Collected in *Notebooks 1960–1994* (1994).

82 Intellectually, most people never wash. They never free their minds of the accumulated rubbish of centuries.
Collected in *Notebooks 1960–1994* (1994).

83 Imagination should be integrated with life, not turned into a separate activity, art, that monopolizes one's whole existence.
Collected in *Notebooks 1960–1994* (1994).

84 Hatred is generalized, but love is for the particular.
Collected in *Notebooks 1960–1994* (1994).

85 The twentieth century had a wonderful capacity for seeing nothing as the sum of everything.
Collected in *Notebooks 1960–1994* (1994).

Duell, Charles H

US government official, Commissioner of the Office of Patents.

86 Everything that can be invented has been invented.
1899 Letter to President William McKinley, suggesting that an Office of Patents was no longer necessary.

Duesenberry, James Stemble 1918–

US economist, Emeritus Professor at Harvard.

87 Economics is all about how people make choices. Sociology is all about why they don't have any choices to make.
1960 In the National Bureau of Economic Research's *Demographic and Economic Change in the Developed World.*

Duffield, George 1818–88

US Presbyterian minister and hymnwriter.

88 Stand Up! Stand Up For Jesus!
1858 *The Psalmist*, title of hymn. Duffield's inspiration for the hymn came from the dying words of the evangelist Dudley Atkins Tyng to him: 'Tell them to stand up for Jesus.'

Dugommier, General Jean François Coquille 1736–94

General of the French Republic.

89 *Récompensez, avancez ce jeune homme; car, si l'on était ingrat envers lui, il s'avancerait de lui-même.*
Reward that young man, promote him; for if his services are not recognised, he will promote himself.
1794 Comment to the Minister for War, speaking of the 24-year-old Napoleon Bonaparte, after the siege of Toulon. Quoted in John Julius Norwich *Venice* (1981).

Dulles, John Foster 1888–1959

US Republican politician, Secretary of State from 1953 until his resignation just a week before his death. His vigorous diplomacy led to many personal conferences with statesmen in other countries.

90 You have to take chances for peace, just as you must take chances in war… The ability to get to the verge without getting into the war is the necessary art. If you try to run away from it, if you are scared to go to the brink, you are lost.
1956 Quoted in 'How Dulles Averted War', in *Life* magazine,

16 Jan. His biographer Peter Grose in *Gentleman Spy* (1994) claims Dulles 'never actually used the word '*brinkmanship*', but the label stuck to him as the legacy of a diplomatic strategy that was reckless for the nuclear age'.

91 The Soviets sought not a place in the sun, but the sun itself. Their objective was the world. They would not tolerate compromise on goals, only on tactics.
Comment to his brother Allen. Quoted in Peter Grose *Gentleman Spy* (1994).

Dumas, Alexandre, *père* 1802–70

French novelist and playwright. He began writing plays, but turned to travelogues and historical novels, including *Le Comte de Monte Cristo* (*The Count of Monte Cristo*, 1844–5).

92 *Tous pour un, un pour tous.*
All for one, one for all.
1844 *Les Trois Mousquetaires*, ch.9.

93 *Cherchons la femme.*
Let us look for the woman.
1854–5 *Les Mohicans de Paris.*

Dumas, Alexandre, *fils* 1824–95

French writer, illegitimate son of Dumas père. In addition to his novel *La Dame aux camélias* (1848), he produced many brilliant dramas, essays, letters and speeches, and may have aided George Sand with her work for the stage.

94 The demi-monde does not represent the crowd of courtesans, but the class of declassed women… It is divided from that of honest women by public scandal, and divided from that of the courtesans by money.
1855 On the first performance of his play *La Dame aux camélias*, 20 Mar, the first recorded use of the phrase. Quoted in Joanna Richardson *The Courtesans* (1967), p.227.

95 All generalizations are dangerous, even this one.
Attributed.

du Maurier, Dame Daphne 1907–89

English novelist and short-story writer.

96 Last night I dreamt I went to Manderley again.
1938 *Rebecca*, opening words.

97 Every book is like a purge; at the end of it one is empty…like a dry shell on the beach, waiting for the tide to come in again.
1956 In the *Ladies Home Journal*, Nov.

Dunbar, Paul Laurence 1872–1906

US poet, the son of escaped slaves. He wrote several volumes of poetry in dialect, including *Lyrics of Lowly Life* (1896).

98 We wear the mask that grins and lies,
It hides our cheeks and shades our eyes.
1895 'We Wear the Mask', stanza 1.

99 I know why the caged bird sings!
1895 'Sympathy', stanza 3. This was used by Maya Angelou as the title of her autobiography in 1970.

Dunbar, William c.1460–c.1520

Scottish poet, thought to have graduated from St Andrew's University in 1479. He was a courtier of James IV, and wrote many short poems, remarkable for their range of style and subject.

1 He that may be but sturt or stryfe,

And leif ane lusty plesand lyfe,
And syne with mariege dois him mell,
And bindis him with ane wicket wyfe,
He wirkis sorrow to him sell.
early 16c 'Ane His Awin Ennemy', l.6–10.

2 Now of wemen this I say for me,
Off erthly thingis nane may bettir be;
Thay suld haif wirschep and great honoring
Off men, aboif all uthir erthly thing.
early 16c 'In Prais of Wemen', l. 1–4.

3 Be riche in patience, gif thow in gudis be pure;
Quho levis mirry, he levis michtely:
Without glaidnes availis no tresour.
early 16c 'No Tressour Availis without Glaidnes', l.22–4.

4 Be courtly ay in clething and costly arrayit,
That hurtis yow nought worth a hen; yowr husband pays for all.
early 16c *The Tua Mariit Wemen and the Wedo*, l.268–9.

5 London, thou art of townes *A per se.*
Soveraign of cities, someliest in sight,
Of high renoun, riches, and royaltie;
Of lordis, barons, and many goodly knyght;
Of most delectable lusty ladies bright;
Of famous prelatis in habitis clericall;
Of merchauntis full of sybstaunce and myght;
London, thou art the flour of Cities all.
c.1501 'To the City of London', attributed to 'A Rhymer of Scotland'. Dunbar was a member of the Scots party negotiating the marriage of James IV to Margaret Tudor, and is popularly credited with the verse.

6 I that in heill wes and gladnes
Am trublit now with gret seiknes
And feblit with infermite:
Timor mortis conturbat me.
c.1505 'Lament for the Makaris', stanza 1. The Latin is from the Office for the Dead: 'The fear of death disturbs me'.

7 Sen for the deid remeid is none,
Best is that we for dede dispone
Eftir our deid that lif may we:
Timor mortis conturbat me.
c.1505 'Lament for the Makaris', stanza 25.

8 In to thir dirk and drublie dayis,
Quhone sabill all the hevin arrayis
With mystie vapouris, cluddis and skyis,
Nature all curage me denyis
Off sangis, ballattis, and of playis.
'Meditatioun in Wyntir', stanza 1.

Duncan, Isadora *originally* **Angela Duncan** 1878–1927

US dancer. She was hailed as one of the most innovative dancers of her day, espousing a free-flowing interpretative style of dance that was quite distinct from conventional ballet.

9 *Adieu, mes amis. Je vais à la gloire!*
Farewell, my friends. I am going to glory!
1927 Last words, shortly before she broke her neck when her long scarf caught in the wheels of her open-topped Bugatti sportscar. Quoted in Mary Desti *Isadora Duncan's End* (1929), ch.25.

Duncan, Robert Edwards *originally* **Edward Howard Duncan** 1919–88

US poet. He was associated with the Black Mountain Poets

including Charles Olsen and Robert Creeley.

10 Among my friends love is a payment.
It is an old debt for a borrowing foolishly spent.
1946 *Early Poems 1939–46*, 'Among My Friends Love Is a Great Sorrow'.

11 Neither our vices nor our virtues
further the poem.
1960 *The Opening of the Field*, 'Poetry, a Natural Thing'.

12 Noble men in the quiet of morning hear
Indians singing the continent's violent requiem.
1960 *The Opening of the Field*, 'A Poem Beginning with a Line by Pindar'.

13 Desire paces Eternity as if it had bounds, craving death.
The Word climbs upward into Its crown.
1964 *Roots and Branches*, 'Structure of Rime X VII'.

14 I would be a falcon and go free.
I tread her wrist and wear the hood,
Talking to myself, and would draw blood.
1968 *Bending the Bow*, 'My Mother Would Be a Falconress'.

15 The great house of our humanity
No longer stands.
1984 *Ground Work: Before the War*, 'Bring It Up from the Dark'.

Dunlop, Ian 1925–

English art historian.

16 The Shock of the New: seven historic exhibitions of modern art.
1972 Title of book.

Dunn, Douglas Eaglesham 1942–

Scottish poet, essayist and anthologizer. A librarian at Hull University, he was encouraged by Philip Larkin. He is one of Scotland's most respected contemporary poets.

17 This masculine invisibility makes gods of them,
A pantheon of boots and overalls.
1969 'Men of Terry Street'.

18 And all their lives, like that, they'll have to rush
Forwards in reverse, always holding their caps.
1979 'Glasgow Schoolboys, Running Backwards'.

19 Snow has begun to fall on the guilty secrets of Europe.
1981 'The Deserter'.

20 Nationalism, and its chum, patriotism, encourage unedifying hyperbole.
1992 'Language and Liberty', introduction to the *Faber Book of Twentieth Century Scottish Poetry*.

21 What I tell my students is there are three places where poems must happen and a poem must happen in these three places simultaneously for it to be a good poem. It happens between the ears, that's intelligence; behind the left nipple, heart and feeling; between the tongue and teeth, the noise it makes.
1999 Interview in *The Dark Horse*, Autumn.

Dunne, Finley Peter 1867–1936

US humorist, editor of the *Chicago Journal* (1897–1900). His philosopher-bartender Mr Dooley became the exponent of Irish-American topical satire.

22 Glory Be, whin Business gets above sellin' tinpinny nails

in a brown paper cornucopy, 'tis hard to tell it fr'm murther.
1901 *Mr Dooley's Opinions*, 'On Wall Street'.

23 Even an Englishman was niver improved by bein' blown up.
'Revolution'. Collected in Louis Filler (ed) *The World of Mr Dooley* (1962).

Dunne, Philip 1908–92

US screenwriter. His films include *Suez* (1938), *How Green Was My Valley* (1941), *Forever Amber* (1947) and *The Robe* (1953).

24 A perfumed parlor snake.
1947 Daniel Gregg's description of Miles Fairley in *The Ghost and Mrs Muir*.

Dunning, John 1731–1820

British lawyer and politician.

25 The influence of the Crown has increased, is increasing, and ought to be diminished.
1780 Motion passed by the House of Commons.

Duplessis, Maurice 1890–1959

Canadian statesman, Premier of Quebec (1936–9, 1944–59).

26 The bishops eat from my hand.
Characteristic remark, recalled in Conrad Black *Duplessis* (1977).

Durant, William James 1885–1981

US historian and essayist. He wrote a series of popular works culminating in the massive *Story of Civilization* (11 vol, 1935–67), written with his wife.

27 There is nothing in Socialism that a little age or a little money will not cure.
Attributed.

Dürer, Albrecht 1471–1528

German painter and engraver. He travelled widely (1490–4) and in 1498 published his first major series of woodcuts, illustrations of the Apocalypse. He was employed by Emperor Maximilian I and later Charles V.

28 The art of painting cannot be truly judged save by such as are themselves good painters; from others verily it is hidden even as a strange tongue.
c.1512 Quoted in William Martin Conway *Literary Remains of Albrecht Dürer* (1889).

29 He that would be a painter must have a natural turn thereto. Love and delight are better teachers of the Art of Painting than compulsion is.
c.1512 *On Painting*. Quoted in William Martin Conway *Literary Remains of Albrecht Dürer* (1889).

Durkheim, Émile 1858–1917

French sociologist, appointed to the first chair of sociology in France in 1913.

30 The economic services that it can render are picayune compared to the moral effect that it produces, and its true function is to create in two or more persons a feeling of solidarity.
1893 Of labour. *The Division of Labor in Society* (translated by George Simpson, 1933).

31 The division of labor does not present individuals to one another, but social functions.
   1893 *The Division of Labor in Society* (translated by George Simpson, 1933).

32 Our excessive tolerance of suicide is due to the fact that, since the state of mind from which it springs is a general one, we cannot condemn it without condemning ourselves; we are too saturated with it not partly to excuse it.
   1897 *Suicide: a Study in Sociology* (translated by John A Spaulding and George Simpson, 1952).

33 All known religious beliefs, whether simple or complex, present one common characteristic: they presuppose a classification of all things, real and ideal, of which men think, into two classes or opposed groups, generally designated…*profane* and *sacred*.
   1912 *The Elementary Forms of the Religious Life* (translated by Joseph Ward Swain, 1965).

34 If the idea of society were extinguished in individual minds and the beliefs, traditions and aspirations of the group were no longer felt and shared by individuals, society would die. We can say of it what we just said of divinity: it is real only in so far as it has a place in the human consciousness, and this place is whatever we may give it.
   1912 *The Elementary Forms of the Religious Life* (translated by Joseph Ward Swain, 1965).

Durocher, Leo 1906–91

US baseball manager, noted for his toughness.

35 Nice guys finish last.
   1946 When asked if he regretted beating the New York Giants, who had been described as a 'nice bunch of guys'. He later used this as a book title, 1975.

36 Show me a good loser and I'll show you an idiot.
   1950 Attributed.

Durranc, Edouard

37 How beautiful the Republic was—under the Empire.
   Quoted in Edgar Holt *The Tiger: The Life of Georges Clemenceau 1841–1929* (1976).

Durrell, Lawrence George 1912–90

English novelist, poet, travel writer and playwright, born in India. His best-known works are the novel sequences *The Alexandria Quartet* (1957–60) and *The Avignon Quincunx* (1974–85).

38 I love to feel events overlapping each other, crawling over one another like wet crabs in a basket.
   1958 *Balthazar*, pt.1.

39 No one can go on being a rebel too long without turning into an autocrat.
   1958 *Balthazar*, pt.2.

40 Poggio's, where people go to watch each other watch each other.
   1968 *Tunc*, ch.1.

41 History is the endless repetition of the wrong way of living, and it'll start again tomorrow, if it's moved from here today.
   1978 In *The Listener*, 20 Apr.

Dürrenmatt, Friedrich 1921–90

Swiss writer. After several novels he established an international reputation as a playwright with works such as *The Physicists* (1962) and *Play Strindberg* (1969).

42 What was once thought can never be unthought.
   1962 *The Physicists*.

Dury, Ian 1942–2000

British rock singer, associated with the punk era of the late 1970s.

43 Sex 'n' drugs 'n' rock 'n' roll.
   1977 Title of song.

Duvall, Robert 1931–

US actor.

44 The English have Shakespeare, the Russians have Chekhov, the French Molière but we have the western.
   2004 In the *Sunday Times*, 21 Mar.

Dvořák, Antonin 1841–1904

Czech composer and organist. His work, basically classical but with colourful Slavonic motifs, became increasingly popular throughout Europe.

45 I have composed too much.
   Letter to Sibelius.

Dworkin, Andrea 1946–

US radical feminist, civil-rights activist and writer, whose work examines the relationship between male power and pornography. In 1983 she made an unsuccessful attempt to define pornography as sexual discrimination under law.

46 A man wants what a woman has—sex. He can steal it (rape), persuade her to give it away (seduction), rent it (prostitution), lease it over the long term (marriage in the United States), or own it outright (marriage in most societies).
   1976 In *Ms*, vol.5, no.6, Dec. Collected as 'Phallic Imperialism: why economic recovery will not work for us' in *Letters from a War Zone* (1988).

47 The power of money is a distinctly male power. Money speaks, but it speaks with a male voice. In the hands of women, money stays literal, count it out, it buys what it is worth or less. In the hands of men, money buys women, sex, status, dignity, esteem, recognition, loyalty, all manner of possibility.
   1981 *Pornography: Men Possessing Women*.

48 One of the differences between marriage and prostitution is that in marriage you only have to make a deal with one man.
   1984 In *The A.B.C.s of Reading*, winter issue. Collected as 'Feminism: An Agenda' in *Letters from a War Zone* (1988).

49 Violation is a synonym for intercourse.
   1987 *Intercourse*, 'Occupation/Collaboration'.

Dyer, Sir Edward c.1545–1607

English poet, diplomat and courtier, a friend of Sir Philip Sidney. Only a few of his poems survive.

50 My mind to me a kingdom is;
   Such perfect joy therein I find

That it excels all other bliss
That world affords or grows by kind.
Though much I want which most men have,
Yet still my mind forbids to crave.
1588 'In Praise of a Contented Mind'.

51 No princely pomp, no wealthy store,
No force to win the victory,
No wily wit to salve a sore,
No shape to feed each gazing eye;
To none of these I yield as thrall.
For why my mind doth serve for all.
1588 'In Praise of a Contented Mind'.

52 Some weigh their pleasure by their lust,
Their wisdom by their rage of will,
Their treasure is their only trust;
And cloakèd craft their store of skill.
But all the pleasure that I find
Is to maintain a quiet mind.
1588 'In Praise of a Contented Mind'.

53 My wealth is health and perfect ease;
My conscience clear my chief defence;
I neither seek by bribes to please,
Nor by deceit to breed offence.
Thus do I live; thus will I die.
Would all did so well as I!
1588 'In Praise of a Contented Mind'.

Dylan, Bob *pseudonym of* **Robert Allen Zimmerman** 1941–

US singer and song-writer. His early acoustic, folk-influenced songs such as 'Blowin' in the Wind' were succeeded in 1965 by rock 'n' roll, with 'Mr Tambourine Man' and 'Like a Rolling Stone'.

54 How many roads must a man walk down
Before you can call him a man?…
The answer, my friend, is blowin' in the wind,
The answer is blowin' in the wind.
1962 'Blowin' in the Wind'.

55 But I can't think for you,
You'll have to decide,
Whether Judas Iscariot
Had God on his side.
1963 'With God on Our Side'.

56 Ah, but I was so much older then,
I'm younger than that now.
1964 'My Back Pages'.

57 The Times They Are A' Changing.
1964 Title of song.

58 The motorcycle black madonna
Two-wheeled gypsy queen.
1965 'Gates of Eden'.

59 Money doesn't talk, it swears.
1965 'It's Alright, Ma (I'm Only Bleeding)'.

60 Hey! Mr Tambourine Man, play a song for me.
I'm not sleepy and there is no place I'm going to.
1965 'Mr Tambourine Man'.

61 Folk music is a bunch of fat people.
Quoted in David Pickering *Brewer's Twentieth Century Music* (1994).

Dyson, Freeman J(ohn) 1923–

English-born US theoretical physicist, a nuclear weapons designer who has subsequently undertaken major work in arms control and disarmament. His works include *Weapons and Hope* (1984) and *The Sun, the Genome, and the Internet* (1999).

62 For insight into human affairs I turn to stories and poems rather than to sociology. This is the result of my upbringing and background. I am not able to make use of the wisdom of the sociologists because I do not speak their language.
1979 *Disturbing the Universe*, ch.1.

63 Science and technology, like all original creations of the human spirit, are unpredictable. If we had a reliable way to label our toys good and bad, it would be easy to regulate technology wisely. But we can rarely see far enough ahead to know which road leads to damnation. Whoever concerns himself with big technology, either to push it forward or to stop it, is gambling in human lives.
1979 *Disturbing the Universe*, ch.1.

Dyson, Will(iam Henry) 1880–1938

Australian-born radical cartoonist of the London *Daily Herald*.

64 Curious! I seem to hear a child weeping.
1919 Cartoon caption in the *Daily Herald*, 17 May. French minister Clemenceau is shown leaving the Palais de Versailles with Woodrow Wilson and Lloyd George after signing the peace treaty with Germany. The 'child' is the generation of 1940.

e

Eagleton, Terry 1943–

English literary critic and Professor of Cultural Theory in the Department of English and American Studies at the University of Manchester.

65 Homosexuality was the badge of the upper class and the sign of a revolt against it; and it is small wonder that someone locked for a lifetime in this impossible contradiction should end up with cirrhosis of the liver.
1993 Review of Sean French's *Patrick Hamilton: a Life* (1993). In the *London Review of Books*, 2 Dec.

66 If there are indeed any iron laws of history, one of them is surely that in any major crisis of the capitalist system, a sector of the liberal middle class will shift to the left, and then shift smartly back again once the crisis has blown over.
1993 In the *London Review of Books*, 2 Dec.

Earhart, Amelia 1897–1937

US aviator. In 1932 she was the first woman to fly solo across the Atlantic and in 1935 she was the first person to fly alone from Hawaii to California.

67 Of course I realized there was a measure of danger. Obviously I faced the possibility of not returning when first I considered going. Once faced and settled there really wasn't any good reason to refer to it.
1928 *20 Hours: 40 Minutes—Our Flight in the Friendship*, ch.5.

Eastwood, Clint 1930–

US actor and director. He achieved fame initially for his roles in westerns, but more recently has directed several well-respected films, including *Unforgiven* (1992) and *Mystic River* (2003).

68 You've got to ask yourself a question. Do I feel lucky. Well do you punk?
1971 As Harry Callahan in *Dirty Harry* (screenplay by Harry Julian Fink, Rita M Fink and Dean Riesner).

69 Nothing wrong with shooting so long as the right people get shot.
1973 As Harry Callahan in *Magnum Force* (screenplay by John Milius and Michael Cimino).

Eban, Abba *originally* **Aubrey Solomon** 1915–2002

Israeli diplomat and politician, born in South Africa. He was Israeli UN representative (1948), Ambassador to Washington (1950–9) and Foreign Minister (1966–74), but was unexpectedly defeated in the 1989 general election.

70 History teaches us that men and nations behave wisely once they have exhausted all other alternatives.
1970 Speech, London, 16 Dec.

Ebbinghaus, Hermann 1850–1909

German experimental psychologist. He carried out pioneering research on memory to investigate higher mental processes, and published his findings in *Über das Gedächtnis* (1885).

71 Psychology has a long past, but only a short history.
1885 *Summary of Psychology.*

Eberhart, Richard Ghormley 1904–

US poet and academic.

72 If I could only live at the pitch that is near madness
When everything is as it was in my childhood
Violent, vivid and of infinite possibility.
1947 'If I Could Only Live at the Pitch That Is Near Madness'.

73 You would think the fury of aerial bombardment
Would rouse God to relent; the infinite spaces
Are still silent. He looks on shock-pried faces.
History, even, does not know what is meant.
1951 'The Fury of Aerial Bombardment'.

74 Was man made stupid to see his own stupidity?
Is God by definition indifferent, beyond us all?
Is the eternal truth man's fighting soul
Wherein the Beast ravens in its own avidity?
1951 'The Fury of Aerial Bombardment'.

Eberts, Jake 1941–

Canadian-born film producer. In 1977 he founded Goldcrest Films which made *Chariots of Fire* (1981) and *Local Hero* (1983).

75 My Indecision Is Final.
1990 Title of his book on Goldcrest Films.

Echeverría, Esteban 1805–51

Argentinian poet and fiction writer. An opponent of the dictator Rosas, he was exiled in 1839 and lived in Uruguay until his death. He was the innovator of the Romantic school in Spanish American literature.

76 *A pesar de que la mía es historia, no la empezaré por el arca de Noé y la genealogía de sus ascendientes como acostumbraban hacerlo los antiguos historiadores españoles de América, que deben ser nuestros prototipos.*
I'm going to tell a true story, but I won't start with Noah's Ark and the genealogy of his forefathers, as is usual among the ancient Spanish historians of America, who we consider our prototypes.
1838 *El matadero* (*The Slaughter-House*, 1959).

Eco, Umberto 1932–

Italian novelist and semiotician. He is, perhaps, best known for *The Name of the Rose* (1980), a suspense story set in a medieval monastery.

77 In the United States there's a Puritan ethic and a mythology of success. He who is successful is good. In Latin countries, in Catholic countries, a successful person is a sinner.
1988 In the *International Herald Tribune*, 14 Dec.

78 I enjoyed your article, but I preferred my own.
Speaking to Jeremy Treglown, editor of the *Times Literary Supplement*. Quoted in Derwent May *Critical Times: The History of the Times Literary Supplement* (2001).

The Economist

British journal, founded in 1843.

79 Michael Harrington…was America's leading socialist; a position, one might have thought, that almost epitomized marginality.
1989 *The Economist*, 12 Aug.

80 Corruption is more than a poison afflicting Chinese business life. It *is* Chinese business life.
1994 *The Economist*, 29 Jan.

81 One of the saddest features of the real world is that goods do not spontaneously present themselves for distribution.
1994 *The Economist*, 5 Nov.

82 Why Silvio Berlusconi is unfit to lead Italy.
2001 Front cover headline. In *The Economist*, 28 Apr.

Eddington, Sir Arthur Stanley 1882–1944

English astronomer and physicist, Professor of Astronomy (from 1913) and Director of the Observatory (from 1914) at Cambridge University.

83 Let us draw an arrow arbitrarily. If as we follow the arrow we find more and more of the random element in the world, then the arrow is pointing towards the future; if the random element decreases the arrow points towards the past… I shall use the phrase 'time's arrow' to express this one-way property of time which has no analogue in space.
1928 *The Nature of the Physical World*, ch.4. Martin Amis used the phrase 'Time's Arrow' for the title of his 1991 novel.

84 I ask you to look both ways. For the road to a knowledge of the stars leads through the atom; and important knowledge of the atom has been reached through the stars.
1928 *Stars and Atoms*, lecture 1.

85 I think it is something of the same sort of security we should seek in our relationship with God. The most flawless proof of the existence of God is no substitute for

it; and if we have that relationship, the most convincing disproof is turned aimlessly aside. If I may say it with reverence, the soul and God laugh together over so odd a conclusion.
1929 *Science and the Unseen World.*

86 I believe that there are 15,747,724,136,275,002,577,605, 653,961,181,555,468,044,717,914,527,116,709,366,231, 425,076,185,631,031,296 protons in the universe, and the same number of electrons.
1938 Tarner Lecture.

Eddy, Mary Baker 1821–1910

US founder of the Christian Science Church.

87 Christian Science explains all cause and effect as mental, not physical.
1875 *Science and Health with Key to the Scriptures.*

88 Jesus of Nazareth was the most scientific man that ever trod the globe. He plunged beneath the material surface of things, and found the spiritual cause.
1875 *Science and Health with Key to the Scriptures.*

Eden, Sir (Robert) Anthony, 1st Earl of Avon
1897–1977

Anglo-Irish politician and Conservative Prime Minister (1955–7). He ordered British forces to occupy the Suez Canal Zone (1956), an action which caused widespread condemnation.

89 Everybody is always in favour of general economy and particular expenditure.
1956 In the *Observer*, 17 Jun.

90 We best avoid wars by taking even physical action to stop small ones. Everybody knows that the United Nations is not in a position to do that… We must face the fact that the United Nations is not yet the internal equivalent of our own legal system and rule of law. Police action must be to separate the belligerents and to prevent a resumption of hostilities.
1956 House of Commons, 1 Nov.

91 We are not at war with Egypt. We are in armed conflict.
1956 On the Suez crisis, House of Commons, 4 Nov.

Eden, Lady Clarissa 1920–

Wife of Sir Anthony Eden.

92 During the past few weeks, I felt sometimes that the Suez canal was flowing through my drawing room.
1956 Speech, Nov.

Edgeworth, Maria 1767–1849

Anglo-Irish novelist, whose novels reflect the rhythms of Irish country speech in their wry observation and humour. She is best remembered for *Castle Rackrent* (1800) and *The Absentee* (1812).

93 Possessed, as are all the fair daughters of Eve, of a hereditary propensity, transmitted to them undiminished through succeeding generations, to be 'soon moved with the slightest touch of blame'; very little precept and practice will confirm them in the habit, and instruct them all the maxims, of self-justification.
1795 *Letters for Literary Ladies*, 'An Essay on the Noble Science of Self-Justification'.

94 Man is to be held only by the *slightest* chains; with the idea that he can break them at pleasure, he submits to them in sport.
1795 *Letters for Literary Ladies*, 'Letters of Julia and Caroline', no.1.

95 Sir Patrick died that night—just as the company rose to drink his health with three cheers, he fell down in a sort of fit, and was carried off—they sat it out, and were surprised, on enquiry, in the morning, to find it was all over with poor Sir Patrick.
1800 *Castle Rackrent*, 'An Hibernian Tale'.

96 Sir Patrick Rackrent lived and died a monument of old Irish hospitality.
1800 *Castle Rackrent*, 'An Hibernian Tale'.

97 I've a great fancy to see my funeral before I die.
1800 Sir Cody to Thady. *Castle Rackrent*, 'History of Sir Conolly Rackrent'.

98 Did the Warwickshire militia, who were chiefly artisans, teach the Irish to drink beer, or did they learn from the Irish how to drink whiskey?
1800 *Castle Rackrent*, 'History of Sir Conolly Rackrent'.

99 Come when you're called;
And do as you're bid;
Shut the door after you;
And you'll never be chid.
1804 *The Contrast*, ch.1.

1 What a misfortune it is to be born a woman!… Why seek for knowledge, which can prove only that our wretchedness is irremediable? If a ray of light break in upon us, it is but to make darkness more visible; to show us the new limits, the Gothic structure, the impenetrable barriers of our prison.
1806 *Leonora*, letter 1.

2 There need, at all events, be none of this, if people would but live upon their own estates, and kill their own mutton.
1812 Sir Terence O'Fay. *The Absentee*, ch.5.

3 Those enemies to Ireland—those cruel absentees!
1812 Count O'Halloran. *The Absentee*, ch.8.

4 Deeds, not words.
1812 Sir James Brooke's motto. *The Absentee*, ch.9.

5 Let me not, even in my own mind, commit the injustice of taking a speck for the whole.
1812 *The Absentee*, ch.11.

6 Her son saw that the *Londonmania* was now stronger than ever upon her.
1812 *The Absentee*, ch.14.

7 In marrying, a man does not, to be sure, marry his wife's mother; and yet a prudent man, when he begins to think of the daughter, would look sharp at the mother; ay, and back to the grandmother too, and along the whole female line of ancestry.
1812 Count O'Halloran's advice to Lord Colambare. *The Absentee*, ch.15.

Edinburgh, Prince Philip, Duke of 1921–

Consort of Elizabeth II, son of Prince Andrew of Greece and Princess Alice of Battenberg. He entered the Royal Navy in 1939, became a naturalized British subject in 1947, and was created Duke of Edinburgh on the eve of his marriage (20 Nov). In 1956 he began the Duke of Edinburgh Award Scheme to foster the leisure activities of young people.

8 I have very little experience of self-government. In fact, I am one of the most governed people in the world.
1959 In the *New York Times*, 30 Dec.

9 We are suffering a national defeat comparable to any lost military campaign, and what is more, it is self-inflicted… It is about time that we pulled our fingers out… The rest of the world most certainly does not owe us a living.
1961 Speech to British industrialists, London, 17 Oct.

10 There is a widely held and quite erroneously held belief that cricket is just another game.
1975 In *Wisden: Cricketers' Almanack*, 'The Pleasures of Cricket'.

11 The grouse are in no danger at all from people who shoot grouse.
1988 Quoted in *Private Eye*, no.693, 8 Jul.

Edison, Thomas Alva 1847–1931

US inventor, one of the most productive of his time. Among his inventions were the gramophone and the motion picture.

12 The phonograph…is not of any commercial value.
c.1860 Comment to his assistant, Samuel Insull. Edison hoped that his invention would find a place in businesses and offices, rather than in the entertainment world. Quoted in Robert A Conot *A Streak of Luck: The Life and Legend of Thomas Edison* (1979).

13 Genius is one per cent inspiration, ninety-nine per cent perspiration.
c.1903 Quoted in *Harper's Monthly Magazine*, Sep 1932.

Edmeston, John 1721–1867

English architect and hymnwriter.

14 Lead us, Heavenly Father, lead us
O'er the world's tempestuous sea.
1821 *Sacred Lyrics*, *Set 2*, 'Lead us, Heavenly Father'.

Edward II 1284–1327

King of England (from 1307). His invasion of Scotland resulted in defeat by Robert the Bruce at Bannockburn (1314). He was eventually murdered.

15 Forasmuch as there is great noise in the city caused by hustling over large balls, from which many evils may arise, which God forbid, we command and forbid on behalf of the King, on pain of imprisonment, such game to be used in the city in future.
1314 Royal proclamation, banning football from the streets of London.

Edward III 1312–77

King of England (from 1327). He started hostilities against France in 1337 and assumed the title of King of France in 1340. Victories at Crecy (1346) and Poitiers (1356) led to a large concession of territory by the French. He also invaded Scotland.

16 Also say to them, that they suffre hym this day to wynne his spurres, for if god be pleased, I well this journey be his, and the honoure thereof.
1346 Of his 16-year-old son, Edward the Black Prince. Quoted in the *Chronicle of Froissart* (translated by Sir John Bourchier, Lord Berners, 1523–5), ch.130.

17 *Honi soit qui mal y pense.*
Evil be to him that evil thinks.
c.1348 Motto of the Order of the Garter. Said to have been uttered by Edward when adjusting the Countess of Salisbury's garter, which had slipped down.

Edward VII 1841–1910

King of the UK (from 1901), son of Queen Victoria. In 1863 he married Alexandra of Denmark. His scandalous behaviour as Prince of Wales led to his exclusion from affairs of state, but as King he made several visits to improve international relations.

18 Because a man has a black face and a different religion from ours, there is no reason why he should be treated as a brute.
1875 Letter from India to Lord Granville, 30 Nov.

Edward VIII 1894–1972

King of the UK (1936). He succeeded his father George V in 1936, but abdicated (11 Dec) because of his proposed marriage to divorcee Mrs Wallis Simpson. As Duke of Windsor, he lived in Paris except during his governorship of the Bahamas (1940–5).

19 These works brought all these people here. Something should be done to get them at work again.
1936 Comment while viewing the derelict Dowlais Iron and Steel Works, 18 Nov. It is often rendered 'Something must be done'.

20 I have found it impossible to carry the heavy burden of responsibility, and to discharge my duties as King as I would wish, without the help and support of the woman I love.
1936 Radio broadcast to the nation, 11 Dec, following his abdication to marry Wallis Simpson.

Edwards, Bob (Robert Chambers) 1864–1922

Canadian publisher and writer.

21 One can always tell when one is getting old and serious by the way that holidays seem to interfere with one's work.
1913 In *Eye Opener*, 20 Dec.

Edwards, Oliver 1711–91

English lawyer, an acquaintance of Samuel Johnson.

22 You are a philosopher, Dr Johnson. I have tried too in my time to be a philosopher; but, I don't know how, cheerfulness was always breaking in.
1778 In conversation with Dr Johnson, 17 Apr. Quoted in James Boswell *Life of Samuel Johnson* (1791).

Edwards, Otis C(arl), Jr 1928–

US theologian and educator, ordained into the Episcopal Church in 1954. After serving in several churches as curate and rector, he taught at Nashotah House (1969–74) before being appointed Dean of Seabury-Western Theological Seminary (1974–83).

23 To be loose with grammar is to be loose with the worst woman in the world.
1966 New Testament lecture, Nashotah House, 10 Jan.

Egan, Pierce 1772–1849

English sporting writer. A London journalist, he wrote *Boxiana: or Sketches of Ancient and Modern Pugilism* (1812–13), and is best remembered for *Life in London* (1821), a description of the life of a 'man about town'.

24 Here lies, bowl'd out by Death's unerring ball,
A cricketer renowned, by name John Small;
But though his name was small, yet great was his fame,
For nobly did he play the 'noble game'.
His life was like his innings—long and good;
Full ninety summers had Death withstood,
At length the ninetieth winter came—when (Fate
Not leaving him one solitary mate)
This last of Hambledonians, old John Small,
Gave up his bat and ball—his leather, wax and all.
1832 Epitaph on cricketer John Small. *Pierce Egan's Book of Sports*.

Eggers, Dave 1970–
US magazine editor and novelist.

25 A Heartbreaking Work of Staggering Genius.
2000 Book title.

Ehrlich, Paul Ralph 1932–
US biologist, Professor at Stanford University.

26 The first rule of intelligent tinkering is to save all the parts.
1971 In the *Saturday Review*, 5 Jun.

Ehrlichman, John 1925–99
US government official, Special Counsel to the Nixon White House, implicated in the Watergate scandal.

27 He's the Big Enchilada.
1973 On the possibility of pinning the blame for Watergate on Attorney General John Mitchell. Taped conversation, 27 Mar.

28 I think we ought to let him hang there. Let him twist slowly, slowly in the wind.
1973 Of Patrick Gray, regarding his nomination as Director of the FBI. Taped conversation with John Dean, reported in the *Washington Post*, 27 Jul.

Eichelbaum, Samuel 1894–1969
Argentinian playwright and fiction writer. He began writing in a naturalistic style, but later adopted an emotional realism to show the effect of social environment on the individual.

29 ¡No hay políticos malos! Y buenos, tampoco, ¡qué caray! *Los políticos no son ni buenos ni malos. Son hombres de oficio. Como los carpinterios y los albañiles.*
There are no bad politicians! There aren't any good ones either, damn it! Politicians are neither bad nor good. They are professionals, like carpenters or masons.
1940 *Un guapo del 900* ('A Handsome Man from the Nineteen Hundreds'), act 1.

Einstein, Albert 1879–1955
German-born theoretical physicist, who took Swiss (1901) and US (1940) citizenship. His early work on the photoelectric effect pioneered quantum theory and won him the 1921 Nobel prize. He is best known for his special (1905) and general (1916) theories of relativity. After Hitler's rise to power he lectured in the US, and later urged international control of atomic weapons.

30 $E = mc^2$
1905 *Zur Elektrodynamik bewegter Körper* ('The Electrodynamics of Moving Bodies').

31 *Raffiniert ist der Herrgott, aber boshaft ist er nicht.*
God is subtle, but he is not malicious.
1921 Said on a visit to Princeton University, May, and later carved above a fireplace there.

32 *Jedenfalls bin ich überzeugt, dass der nicht würfelt.*
Anyway, I am sure that he [God] does not play dice.
1926 Letter to Max Born, 4 Dec.
➤ See Hawking 385:31.

33 One of the strongest motives that lead people to give their lives to art and science is the urge to flee from everyday life, with its drab and deadly dullness and thus to unshackle the chains of one's own transient desires, which supplant one another in an interminable succession so long as the mind is fixed on the horizon of daily environment.
1933 Prologue to Max Planck *Where is Science Going?* (1933).

34 I think and think for months and years. Ninety-nine times, the conclusion is false. The hundredth time I am right.
1934 *The World as I See It*.

35 It may be possible to set up a nuclear reaction in uranium by which vast amounts of power could be released… This new phenomenon would also lead to the construction of…extremely powerful bombs of a new type.
1939 Letter to President Franklin D Roosevelt.

36 Science without religion is lame, religion without science is blind.
1941 *Science, Philosophy and Religion: A Symposium*, ch.13.

37 The most beautiful emotion we can experience is the mystical. It is the power of all true art and science. He to whom this emotion is a stranger, who can no longer wonder and stand rapt in awe, is as good as dead. To know that what is impenetrable to us really exists, manifesting itself as the highest wisdom and the most radiant beauty, which our dull faculties can comprehend only in their most primitive forms—this knowledge, this feeling, is at the center of true religiousness. In this sense, and in this sense only, I belong to the rank of devoutly religious men.
Quoted in Philipp Frank *Einstein: His Life and Times* (1947), ch.12, section 5.

38 Science can only state what is, not what should be.
1950 *Out of My Later Years*.

39 Perfections of means and confusion of goals seem—in my opinion—to characterize our age.
1950 *Out of My Later Years*.

40 The man of science is a poor philosopher.
1950 *Out of My Later Years*.

41 The whole of science is nothing more than a refinement of everyday thinking.
1950 *Out of My Later Years*.

42 Education is what remains, if one has forgotten everything one learned in school.
1950 *Out of My Later Years*.

43 If *A* is success in life, then *A* equals *x* plus *y* plus *z*. Work is *x*; *y* is play; and *z* is keeping your mouth shut.
1950 In the *Observer*, 15 Jan.

44 The most incomprehensible thing about the world is that it is comprehensible.
1950 In *Life Magazine*.

45 If only I had known, I would have become a watchmaker.
1955 On his part in developing the atom bomb. In the *New Statesman*, 16 Apr.

46 The grand aim of all science is to cover the greatest number of empirical facts by logical deduction from the smallest number of hypotheses or axioms.
1970 Quoted in *Life Magazine*, 9 Jan.

47 As far as the laws of mathematics refer to reality, they are not certain, and as far as they are certain, they do not refer to reality.
Quoted in Fritjof Capra *The Tao of Physics* (1975), ch.2.

48 Everything should be made as simple as possible, but not simpler.
Quoted in *Newsweek*, 16 Apr 1979.

Eisenhower, Dwight D(avid)   1890–1969

US soldier and Republican politician, whose success as Supreme Commander of Allied forces during World War II and later of NATO swept him to victory as 34th US President (1953–61). His main concerns were foreign policy and anti-communism.

49 The eyes of the world are upon you. The hopes and prayers of liberty-loving people everywhere march with you.
1944 Despatch to US forces on D-Day, 6 Jun.

50 Neither a wise man nor a brave man lies down on the tracks of history to wait for the train of the future to run over him.
1952 In *Time*, 6 Oct.

51 I shall go to Korea, to try to end the war.
1952 Presidential campaign pledge, Oct.

52 A soldier's pack is not so heavy a burden as a prisoner's chains.
1953 Inaugural address, 20 Jan.

53 History does not long entrust the care of freedom to the weak or the timid.
1953 Inaugural address, 20 Jan.

54 I just won't get into a pissing contest with that skunk.
1953 Comment to his brother Milton, refusing to publicly contend with Senator Joseph R McCarthy. Quoted in Piers Brandon *Ike* (1986).

55 You have a row of dominoes set up. You knock over the first one, and what will happen to the last is that it will go over very quickly.
1954 Explaining the domino theory in relation to SE Asia, 7 Apr.

56 There can be no law if we were to invoke one code of international conduct for those who oppose us and another for our friends.
1956 Speech on the Suez crisis, 31 Oct.

57 If the United Nations once admits that international disputes can be settled by using force, we will have destroyed the foundation of the organization and our best hope of establishing a world order.
1957 Address to the nation on Israel's invasion of Egypt, 20 Feb.

58 In the councils of government, we must guard against the acquisition of unwarranted influence, whether sought or unsought, by the military-industrial complex. The potential for the disastrous rise of misplaced powers exists and will persist.
1961 Farewell address to the nation, 17 Jan.

59 Now, on Friday noon, I am to become a private citizen. I am proud to do so. I look forward to it.
1961 Concluding his farewell address to the nation, 17 Jan.

60 I want…the $60 GI job and no medals on my chest.
1963 To President Truman, 25 Nov. Quoted in Michael R Beschloss *Eisenhower* (1990).

61 There's one thing to be said about being President—nobody can tell you when to sit down.
1964 Speech.

62 A fine man who, in the middle of a stormy lake, knows nothing of swimming.
His initial impression of President Harry S Truman while he was military chief of staff. Quoted in Michael R Beschloss *Eisenhower* (1990).

63 Just what does he think the Presidency *is*?
On being warned by a doctor to avoid 'irritation, frustration, anxiety, fear, and above all else, anger'. Quoted in Michael R Beschloss *Eisenhower* (1990).

64 This embattled shore, portal of freedom, is forever hallowed by the ideals, the valor and the sacrifices of our fellow countrymen.
Inscription at US cemetery near St-Laurent. Quoted in the *New York Times*, 5 Jun 1994.

Eisenstaedt, Alfred   1898–1995

German-born US photographer and photojournalist, renowned for his candid pictures of both everyday life and historic occasions.

65 The most important thing about photographing people is not clicking the shutter…it is clicking with the subject.
1966 *Witness to Our Time*.

66 I want to be a mouse in a mousehole.
1995 On the unobtrusiveness of the photographer. In NPR broadcast, 24 Aug.

Elgar, Sir Edward   1857–1934

English composer. His *Enigma Variations* (1899) and the oratorio *The Dream of Gerontius* (1900) established his reputation as the leading English composer of his generation. He was Master of the King's Musick from 1924.

67 To my friends pictured within.
1899 Dedication to the *Enigma Variations*.

68 My idea is that there is music in the air, music all around us, the world is full of it and you simply take as much as you require.
Quoted in R J Buckley *Sir Edward Elgar* (1905), ch.4.

Elgin, James Bruce   1811–63

English government official. In 1860 he was in China, enforcing the treaty of Tientsin (1858), and his actions included the burning of the Summer Palace in Beijing.

69 You can scarcely imagine the beauty and magnificence of the buildings we burnt.
1860 Letter, 18 Aug. Quoted in Nigel Cameron *Barbarians and Mandarins* (1989), ch.16.

Eliot, George   *pseudonym of* Mary Ann Evans   1819–80

English novelist, renowned for her powers of observation and characterization. Her novels include *Adam Bede* (1859), *The Mill on the Floss* (1860), *Silas Marner* (1861) and her masterpiece, *Middlemarch* (1871–2).

70 Life is too precious to be spent in this weaving and unweaving of false impressions, and it is better to live quietly under some degree of misrepresentation than to attempt to remove it by the uncertain process of letter-writing.
1856 Letter to Mrs Peter Taylor, 8 Jun. Collected in G S Haight (ed) *The George Eliot Letters* (1954), vol.2.

71 In every parting there is an image of death.
1858 *Scenes of Clerical Life*, ch.10.

72 Errors look so very ugly in persons of small means—one feels they are taking quite a liberty in going astray; whereas people of fortune may naturally indulge in a few delinquencies.
1858 *Scenes of Clerical Life*, ch.25.

73 He knew two kinds of Methodists—the ecstatic and the bilious.
1859 *Adam Bede*, ch.2.

74 We are apt to be kinder to the brutes that love us than to the women that love us. Is it because the brutes are dumb?
1859 *Adam Bede*, ch.4.

75 Young souls, in such pleasant delirium as hers, are as unsympathetic as butterflies sipping nectar.
1859 Of Hetty. *Adam Bede*, ch.9.

76 I aspire to give no more than a faithful account of men and things as they have mirrored themselves in my mind.
1859 *Adam Bede*, ch.17.

77 Our deeds determine us, as much as we determine our deeds; and until we know what has been or will be the peculiar combination of outward with inward facts, which constitute a man's critical actions, it will be better not to think ourselves wise about his character.
1859 *Adam Bede*, ch.29.

78 A maggot must be born i' the rotten cheese to like it.
1859 *Adam Bede*, ch.32.

79 There's no pleasure i' living, if you're to be corked up for iver, and only dribble your mind out by the sly, like a leaky barrel.
1859 Mrs Poyser. *Adam Bede*, ch.32.

80 He was like a cock who thought the sun had risen to hear him crow.
1859 *Adam Bede*, ch.33.

81 Deep, unspeakable suffering may well be called a baptism, a regeneration, the initiation into a new state.
1859 *Adam Bede*, ch.42.

82 We hand folks over to God's mercy, and show none ourselves.
1859 *Adam Bede*, ch.42.

83 The mother's yearning, that completest type of the life in another life which is the essence of real human love, feels the presence of the cherished child even in the debased, degraded man.
1859 *Adam Bede*, ch.43.

84 If art does not enlarge men's sympathies, it does nothing morally.
1859 Letter to Charles Bray, 5 Jul.

85 He would punish everyone who deserved it: why, he wouldn't have minded being punished himself if he deserved it; but, then, he never did deserve it.
1860 Of Tom Tulliver. *The Mill on the Floss*, bk.1. ch.5.

86 Anger and jealousy can no more bear to lose sight of their objects than love.
1860 *The Mill on the Floss*, bk.1, ch.10.

87 The Catholics, bad harvests, and the mysterious fluctuations of trade—three evils mankind had to fear.
1860 *The Mill on the Floss*, bk.1, ch.12.

88 In a mind charged with an eager purpose and an unfinished vindictiveness, there is no room for new feelings.
1860 *The Mill on the Floss*, bk.4, ch.3.

89 Our life is determined for us—and it makes the mind very free when we give up wishing and only think of bearing what is laid upon us and doing what is given us to do.
1860 *The Mill on the Floss*, bk.5, ch.1.

90 The dead level of provincial existence.
1860 *The Mill on the Floss*, bk.5, ch.3.

91 The happiest women, like the happiest nations, have no history.
1860 *The Mill on the Floss*, bk.6, ch.3.

92 I should like to know what is the proper function of women, if it is not to make reasons for husbands to stay at home, and still stronger reasons for bachelors to go out.
1860 *The Mill on the Floss*, bk.6, ch.6.

93 'Character' says Novalis, in one of his questionable aphorisms, 'character is destiny.'
1860 *The Mill on the Floss*, bk.6, ch.6.

94 Half the sorrows of women would be averted if they could repress the speech they know to be useless; nay, the speech they have resolved not to make.
1866 *Felix Holt*, ch.2.

95 There is no private life which has not been determined by a wider public life.
1866 *Felix Holt*, ch.3.

96 An election is coming. Universal peace is declared, and the foxes have a sincere interest in prolonging the lives of the poultry.
1866 *Felix Holt*, ch.5.

97 Speech is often barren; but silence also does not necessarily brood over a full nest. Your still fowl, blinking at you without remark, may all the while be sitting on one addled egg; and when it takes to cackling will have nothing to announce but that addled delusion.
1866 *Felix Holt*, ch.15.

98 A woman can hardly ever choose…she is dependent on what happens to her. She must take meaner things, because only meaner things are within her reach.
1866 *Felix Holt*, ch.27.

99 There's many a one who would be idle if hunger didn't pinch him; but the stomach sets us to work.
1866 *Felix Holt*, ch.30.

1 Women were expected to have weak opinions; but the great safeguard of society and of domestic life was, that opinions were not acted on. Sane people did what their neighbours did, so that if any lunatics were at large, one might know and avoid them.
1871–2 *Middlemarch*, bk.1, ch.1.

2 A woman dictates before marriage in order that she may have an appetite for submission afterwards.
1871–2 *Middlemarch*, bk.1, ch.9.

3 He said he should prefer not to know the sources of the Nile, and that there should be some unknown regions preserved as hunting-grounds for the poetic imagination.
1871–2 *Middlemarch*, bk.1, ch.9.

4 Among all forms of mistake, prophecy is the most gratuitous.
1871–2 *Middlemarch*, bk.1, ch.10.

5 Plain women he regarded as he did the other severe facts of life, to be faced with philosophy and investigated by science.
1871–2 *Middlemarch*, bk.1, ch.11.

6 Any one watching keenly the stealthy convergence of human lots, sees a slow preparation of effects from one life on another, which tells like a calculated irony on the indifference or the frozen stare with which we look at our unintroduced neighbour.
1871–2 *Middlemarch*, bk.1, ch.11.

7 To point out other people's errors was a duty that Mr Bulstrode rarely shrank from.
1871–2 *Middlemarch*, bk.2, ch.13.

8 If we had a keen vision and feeling of all ordinary human life, it would be like hearing the grass grow and the squirrel's heart beat, and we should die of that roar which lies on the other side of silence.
1871–2 *Middlemarch*, bk.2, ch.20.

9 We do not expect people to be deeply moved by what is not unusual. That element of tragedy which lies in the very fact of frequency, has not yet wrought itself into the coarse emotion of mankind.
1871–2 *Middlemarch*, bk.2, ch.20.

10 A woman, let her be as good as she may, has got to put up with the life her husband makes for her.
1871–2 *Middlemarch*, bk.3, ch.25.

11 It is an uneasy lot at best, to be what we call highly taught and yet not to enjoy: to be present at this great spectacle of life and never to be liberated from a small hungry shivering self.
1871–2 *Middlemarch*, bk.3, ch.29.

12 A man is seldom ashamed of feeling that he cannot love a woman so well when he sees a certain greatness in her: nature having intended greatness for men.
1871–2 *Middlemarch*, bk.4, ch.39.

13 Gossip is a sort of smoke that comes from the dirty tobacco-pipes of those who diffuse it: it proves nothing but the bad taste of the smoker.
1876 *Daniel Deronda*, bk.2, ch.13.

14 A difference of taste in jokes is a great strain on the affections.
1876 *Daniel Deronda*, bk.2, ch.15.

15 There is a great deal of unmapped country within us which would have to be taken into account in an explanation of our gusts and storms.
1876 *Daniel Deronda*, bk.3, ch.24.

16 Friendships begin with liking or gratitude—roots that can be pulled up.
1876 *Daniel Deronda*, bk.4, ch.32.

Eliot, T(homas) S(tearns) 1888–1965

US-born English poet, dramatist and critic, whose work enshrined the disillusionment of the post-World War I generation and the advance of modernism. His most significant poetic works are *The Waste Land* (1922) and *Four Quartets* (1935–42). In 1948 he was awarded the Nobel prize for literature.

17 Let us go then, you and I,
When the evening is spread out against the sky
Like a patient etherized upon a table.
1915 'The Love Song of J Alfred Prufrock' (first published in *Poetry* magazine, collected in *Prufrock and Other Observations*, 1917), opening lines.

18 In the room the women come and go
Talking of Michelangelo.
1915 'The Love Song of J Alfred Prufrock' (first published in *Poetry* magazine, collected in *Prufrock and Other Observations*, 1917).

19 Should I, after tea and cakes and ices,
Have the strength to force the moment to its crisis?
1915 'The Love Song of J Alfred Prufrock' (first published in *Poetry* magazine, collected in *Prufrock and Other Observations*, 1917).

20 For I have known them all already, known them all—
Have known the evenings, mornings, afternoons,
I have measured out my life with coffee spoons;
I know the voices dying with a dying fall
Beneath the music from a farther room.
1915 'The Love Song of J Alfred Prufrock' (first published in *Poetry* magazine, collected in *Prufrock and Other Observations*, 1917).

21 I should have been a pair of ragged claws
Scuttling across the floors of silent seas.
1915 'The Love Song of J Alfred Prufrock' (first published in *Poetry* magazine, collected in *Prufrock and Other Observations*, 1917).

22 I am no prophet—and here's no great matter;
I have seen the moment of my greatness flicker,
And I have seen the eternal Footman hold my coat, and snicker,
And in short, I was afraid.
1915 'The Love Song of J Alfred Prufrock' (first published in *Poetry* magazine, collected in *Prufrock and Other Observations*, 1917).

23 No! I am not Prince Hamlet, nor was meant to be;
Am an attendant lord, one that will do
To swell a progress, start a scene or two,
Advise the prince.
1915 'The Love Song of J Alfred Prufrock' (first published in *Poetry* magazine, collected in *Prufrock and Other Observations*, 1917).

24 I grow old…I grow old…
I shall wear the bottoms of my trousers rolled.
1915 'The Love Song of J Alfred Prufrock' (first published in *Poetry* magazine, collected in *Prufrock and Other Observations*, 1917).

25 Do I dare to eat a peach?
1915 'The Love Song of J Alfred Prufrock' (first published in *Poetry* magazine, collected in *Prufrock and Other Observations*, 1917).

26 I have heard the mermaids singing, each to each.
I do not think that they will sing to me.
1915 'The Love Song of J Alfred Prufrock' (first published in *Poetry* magazine, collected in *Prufrock and Other Observations*, 1917).

27 The winter evening settles down
With smell of steaks in passageways
Six o'clock.
The burnt-out ends of smoky days.
1917 *Prufrock and Other Observations*, 'Preludes', pt.1.

28 The morning comes to consciousness
Of faint stale smells of beer
From the sawdust-trampled street.
1917 *Prufrock and Other Observations*, 'Preludes', pt.2.

29 Held in a lunar synthesis,
Whispering lunar incantations
Dissolve the floors of memory
And all its clear relations
Its divisions and precisions.
1917 *Prufrock and Other Observations*, 'Rhapsody on a Windy Night'.

30 Midnight shakes the memory
As a madman shakes a dead geranium.
1917 *Prufrock and Other Observations*, 'Rhapsody on a Windy Night'.

31 Stand on the highest pavement of the stair—
Lean on a garden urn—
Weave, weave the sunlight in your hair.
1917 *Prufrock and Other Observations*, 'La Figlia Che Piange'.

32 Sometimes these cogitations still amaze
The troubled midnight and the noon's repose.
1917 *Prufrock and Other Observations*, 'La Figlia Che Piange'.

33 I am aware of the damp souls of housemaids
Sprouting despondently at area gates.
1917 *Prufrock and Other Observations*, 'Morning at The Window'.

34 Webster was much possessed by death
And saw the skull beneath the skin;
And breastless creatures under ground
Leaned backward with a lipless grin.
1919 'Whispers of Immortality'.

35 Uncorseted, her friendly bust
Gives promise of pneumatic bliss.
1919 'Whispers of Immortality'.

36 Polyphiloprogenitive
The sapient sutlers of the Lord
Drift across the window-panes
In the beginning was the Word.
1919 'Mr Eliot's Sunday Morning Service'.

37 Apeneck Sweeney spreads his knees
Letting his arms hang down to laugh,
The zebra stripes along his jaw
Swelling to maculate giraffe.
1919 'Sweeney among the Nightingales'.

38 And let their liquid siftings fall
To stain the stiff dishonoured shroud.
1919 'Sweeney among the Nightingales'.

39 Here I am, an old man in a dry month,
Being read to by a boy, waiting for rain.
1919 'Gerontion'.

40 Signs are taken for wonders. 'We would see a sign!'
The word within the word, unable to speak a word,
Swaddled with darkness. In the juvescence of the year
Came Christ the tiger.
1919 'Gerontion'.

41 After such knowledge, what forgiveness? Think now

History has many cunning passages, contrived corridors
And issues, deceives with whispering ambitions,
Guides us by vanities.
1919 'Gerontion'.

42 Neither fear nor courage saves us. Unnatural vices
Are fathered by our heroism. Virtues
Are forced upon us by our impudent crimes.
1919 'Gerontion'.

43 Tenants of the house,
Thoughts of a dry brain in a dry season.
1919 'Gerontion'.

44 Where are the eagles and the trumpets?
Buried beneath some snow-deep Alps.
Over buttered scones and crumpets
Weeping, weeping multitudes
Droop in a hundred A.B.C.'s.
1920 'Cooking Egg'.

45 The emotion of art is impersonal.
1920 *The Sacred Wood*, 'Tradition and Individual Talent'.

46 Poetry is not a turning loose of emotion, but an escape from emotion; it is not the expression of personality but an escape from personality.
1920 *The Sacred Wood*, 'Tradition and Individual Talent'.

47 The only way of expressing emotion in the form of art is by finding an 'objective correlative'…such that when the external facts, which must terminate in sensory experience, are given, the emotion is immediately evoked.
1920 *The Sacred Wood*, 'Hamlet and His Problems'.

48 The bad poet dwells partly in a world of objects and partly in a world of words, and he never can get them to fit.
1920 *The Sacred Wood*, 'Swinburne as a Poet'.

49 Immature poets imitate; mature poets steal; bad poets deface what they take, and good poets make it into something better, or at least something different.
1920 *The Sacred Wood*, 'Philip Massinger'.

50 In the seventeenth century a dissociation of sensibility set in from which we have never recovered; and this dissociation, as is natural, was due to the influence of the two most powerful poets of the century, Milton and Dryden.
1921 *Selected Essays* (1932), 'The Metaphysical Poets'.

51 When a poet's mind is perfectly equipped for its work, it is constantly amalgamating disparate experience…in the mind of the poet these experiences are always forming new wholes.
1921 *Selected Essays* (1932), 'The Metaphysical Poets'.

52 April is the cruellest month, breeding
Lilacs out of the dead land, mixing
Memory and desire, stirring
Dull roots with spring rain.
1922 *The Waste Land*, pt.1, 'The Burial of the Dead'.

53 And I will show you something different from either
Your shadow at morning striding behind you
Or your shadow at evening rising to meet you;
I will show you fear in a handful of dust.
1922 *The Waste Land*, pt.1, 'The Burial of the Dead'.

54 Unreal City,
Under the brown fog of a winter dawn,

A crowd flowed over London Bridge, so many,
I had not thought death had undone so many.
1922 *The Waste Land*, pt.1, 'The Burial of the Dead'.

55 'You! hypocrite lecteur!—mon semblable,—mon frère!'
1922 *The Waste Land*, pt.1, 'The Burial of the Dead'.
➤ *See Baudelaire 64:53.*

56 The Chair she sat in, like a burnished throne,
Glowed on the marble.
1922 *The Waste Land*, pt.2, 'A Game of Chess'.
➤ *See Shakespeare 764:23.*

57 O O O O that Shakespeherian Rag—
It's so elegant
So intelligent.
1922 *The Waste Land*, pt.2, 'A Game of Chess'.

58 Hurry up please it's time.
1922 *The Waste Land*, pt.2, 'A Game of Chess'.

59 Sweet Thames, run softly till I end my song,
Sweet Thames, run softly, for I speak not loud or long.
But at my back in a cold blast I hear
The rattle of the bones, and chuckle spread from ear
  to ear.
1922 *The Waste Land*, pt.3, 'The Fire Sermon'.
➤ *See Marvell 556:62.*

60 I Tiresias, old man with wrinkled dugs
Perceived the scene, and foretold the rest—
I too awaited the expected guest.
He, the young man carbuncular, arrives,
A small house agent's clerk, with one bold stare,
One of the low on whom assurance sits
As a silk hat on a Bradford millionaire.
1922 *The Waste Land*, pt.3, 'The Fire Sermon'.

61 When lovely woman stoops to folly and
Paces about her room again, alone,
She smoothes her hair with automatic hand,
And puts a record on the gramophone.
1922 *The Waste Land*, pt.3, 'The Fire Sermon'.
➤ *See Goldsmith 361:47.*

62 A current under sea
Picked his bones in whispers.
1922 *The Waste Land*, pt.4, 'Death by Water'.

63 O you who turn the wheel and look to windward,
Consider Phlebas, who was once handsome and tall
  as you.
1922 *The Waste Land*, pt.4, 'Death by Water'.

64 He who was living is now dead
We who were living are now dying
With a little patience.
1922 *The Waste Land*, pt.5, 'What the Thunder Said'.

65 Who is the third who walks always beside you?
When I count, there are only you and I together
But when I look ahead up the white road
There is always another one walking beside you.
1922 *The Waste Land*, pt.5, 'What the Thunder Said'.

66 In this decayed hole among the mountains
In the faint moonlight, the grass is singing
Over the tumbled graves.
1922 *The Waste Land*, pt.5, 'What the Thunder Said'.

67 The awful daring of a moment's surrender
Which an age of prudence can never retract.
1922 *The Waste Land*, pt.5, 'What the Thunder Said'.

68 These fragments I have shored against my ruins.
1922 *The Waste Land*, pt.5, 'What the Thunder Said'.

69 We are the hollow men
We are the stuffed men
Leaning together
Headpiece filled with straw. Alas!
1925 'The Hollow Men'.

70 This is the dead land
This is cactus land
Here the stone images
Are raised, here they receive
The supplication of a dead man's hand
Under the twinkle of a fading star.
1925 'The Hollow Men'.

71 Between the idea
And the reality
Between the motion
And the act
Falls the shadow.
1925 'The Hollow Men'.

72 This is the way the world ends
Not with a bang but a whimper.
1925 'The Hollow Men', closing lines.

73 A cold coming we had of it,
Just the worst time of the year
For a journey, and such a long journey:
The ways deep and the weather sharp,
The very dead of winter.
1927 'The Journey of the Magi'.

74 But set down
This, set down
This: were we led all that way for
Birth or Death? There was a Birth, certainly,
We had evidence and no doubt. I had seen birth and
  death
But had thought they were different; this Birth was
Hard and bitter agony for us, like Death, our death.
We returned to our places, these Kingdoms,
But no longer at ease here, in the old dispensation,
With an alien people clutching their gods.
I should be glad of another death.
1927 'The Journey of the Magi'.

75 All great poetry gives the illusion of a view of life.
1927 'Shakespeare and the Stoicism of Seneca'.

76 We know too much and are convinced of too little. Our
literature is a substitute for religion, and so is our
religion.
1928 'A Dialogue on Dramatic Poetry', collected in *Selected Essays* (1932).

77 Genuine poetry can communicate before it is
understood.
1929 *Dante.*

78 Because I do not hope to turn again
Because I do not hope
Because I do not hope to turn.
1930 'Ash Wednesday'.

79 Because these wings are no longer wings to fly
But merely vans to beat the air
The air which is now thoroughly small and dry
Smaller and dryer than the will.
1930 'Ash Wednesday'.

80 Teach us to care and not to care
Teach us to sit still.
1930 'Ash Wednesday'.

81 Lady, three white leopards sat under a juniper-tree
In the cool of the day.
1930 'Ash Wednesday'.

82 Birth, and copulation, and death.
That's all the facts when you come to brass tacks:
Birth, and copulation, and death.
I've been born, and once is enough.
1932 *Sweeney Agonistes*, 'Fragment of an Agon'.

83 Any man has to, needs to, wants to
Once in a lifetime, do a girl in.
1932 *Sweeney Agonistes*, 'Fragment of an Agon'.

84 The people which ceases to care for its literary
inheritance becomes barbaric; the people which ceases
to produce literature ceases to move in thought and
sensibility.
1933 *The Use of Poetry and the Use of Criticism*.

85 Poetry is not a career, but a mug's game.
1933 *The Use of Poetry and the Use of Criticism*.

86 But the essential advantage for a poet…is to be able to
see beneath both beauty and ugliness; to see the
boredom, and the horror, and the glory.
1933 *The Use of Poetry and the Use of Criticism*.

87 Where is the Life we have lost in living?
Where is the wisdom we have lost in knowledge?
Where is the knowledge we have lost in information?
1934 *The Rock*, pt.1.

88 And the wind shall say: 'Here were decent godless
people:
Their only monument the asphalt road
And a thousand lost golf balls.'
1934 *The Rock*, pt.1.

89 What life have you if you have not life together?
There is not life that is not in community,
And no community not lived in praise of God.
1934 Choruses from *The Rock*.

90 A book is not harmless merely because no one is
consciously offended by it.
1935 *Religion and Literature*.

91 Those who talk of the Bible as a 'monument of English
prose' are merely admiring it as a monument over the
grave of Christianity.
1935 *Religion and Literature*.

92 Time present and time past
Are both perhaps present in time future,
And time future contained in time past.
1935 *Four Quartets*, 'Burnt Norton', pt.1.

93 Footfalls echo in the memory
Down the passage which we did not take
Towards the door we never opened
Into the rose-garden. My words echo
Thus, in your mind.
1935 *Four Quartets*, 'Burnt Norton', pt.1.

94 Go, go, go, said the bird: human kind
Cannot bear very much reality.
1935 *Four Quartets*, 'Burnt Norton', pt.1.

95 At the still point of the turning world. Neither flesh nor
fleshless;

96 Neither from nor towards; at the still point, there the
dance is,
But neither arrest nor movement.
1935 *Four Quartets*, 'Burnt Norton', pt.2.

96 Time past and time future
Allow but a little consciousness.
1935 *Four Quartets*, 'Burnt Norton', pt.2.

97 Only through time time is conquered.
1935 *Four Quartets*, 'Burnt Norton', pt.2.

98 Time and the bell have buried the day,
The black cloud carries the sun away.
1935 *Four Quartets*, 'Burnt Norton', pt.4.

99 After the kingfisher's wing
Has answered light to light, and is silent, the light is still
At the still point of the turning world.
1935 *Four Quartets*, 'Burnt Norton', pt.5.

1 Or say that the end precedes the beginning,
And the end and the beginning were always there
before the beginning and after the end.
And all is always now.
1935 *Four Quartets*, 'Burnt Norton', pt.5.

2 Words strain,
Crack and sometimes break, under the burden,
Under the tension, slip, slide, perish,
Decay with imprecision, will not stay in place,
Will not stay still.
1935 *Four Quartets*, 'Burnt Norton', pt.5.

3 Yet we have gone on living,
Living and partly living.
1935 *Murder in the Cathedral*, pt.1.

4 The last temptation is the greatest treason:
To do the right deed for the wrong reason.
1935 *Murder in the Cathedral*, pt.1.

5 Clear the air! clean the sky! wash the wind! take the
stone from the stone, take the skin from the arm, take the
muscle from bone, and wash them.
1935 *Murder in the Cathedral*, pt.2.

6 How unpleasant to meet Mr Eliot!
With his features of clerical cut,
And his brow so grim
And his mouth so prim.
1936 'Five-Finger Exercises'.

7 Success is relative:
It is what we can make of the mess we have made of
things.
1939 *The Family Reunion*, pt.2, sc.3.

8 Round and round the circle
Completing the charm
So the knot be unknotted
The cross be uncrossed
The crooked be made straight
And the curse be ended.
1939 *The Family Reunion*, pt.2, sc.3.

9 At first you may think I'm as mad as a hatter
When I tell you a cat must have THREE DIFFERENT NAMES.
1939 *Old Possum's Book of Practical Cats*, 'The Naming of Cats'.

10 When you notice a cat in profound meditation
The reason, I tell you, is always the same:
His mind is engaged in a rapt contemplation
Of the thought, of the thought, of the thought of

his name:
His ineffable effable
Effanineffable
Deep and inscrutable singular name.
1939 *Old Possum's Book of Practical Cats*, 'The Naming of Cats'.

11 Macavity, Macavity, there's no one like Macavity,
There never was a Cat of such deceitfulness and suavity.
He always has an alibi, and one or two to spare:
At whatever time the deed took place—MACAVITY WASN'T
THERE!
1939 *Old Possum's Book of Practical Cats*, 'Macavity: The Mystery
Cat'.

12 No *vers* is *libre* for the man who wants to do a good job.
1940 Introduction to Ezra Pound *Poems*.

13 In my beginning is my end.
1940 *Four Quartets*, 'East Coker', pt.1.

14 I said to my soul, be still, and wait without hope
For hope would be hope for the wrong thing; wait
without love
For love would be love of the wrong thing; there is
yet faith
But the faith and the hope and the love are all in the
waiting.
Wait without thought, for you are not ready for thought,
So the darkness shall be the light and the stillness the
dancing.
1940 *Four Quartets*, 'East Coker', pt.1.

15 A periphrastic study in a worn-out poetical fashion,
Leaving one still with the intolerable wrestle
With words and meanings.
1940 *Four Quartets*, 'East Coker', pt.1.

16 There is, it seems to us,
At best, only a limited value
In the knowledge derived from experience.
1940 *Four Quartets*, 'East Coker', pt.2.

17 Do not let me hear
Of the wisdom of old men, but rather of their folly.
1940 *Four Quartets*, 'East Coker', pt.2.

18 The only wisdom we can hope to acquire
Is the wisdom of humility: humility is endless.
1940 *Four Quartets*, 'East Coker', pt.2.

19 O dark dark dark. They all go into the dark,
The vacant interstellar spaces, the vacant into the
vacant.
1940 *Four Quartets*, 'East Coker', pt.3.

20 And what you do not know is the only thing you know
And what you own is what you do not own
And where you are is where you are not.
1940 *Four Quartets*, 'East Coker', pt.3.

21 The wounded surgeon plies the steel
That questions the distempered part;
Beneath the bleeding hands we feel
The sharp compassion of the healer's art
Resolving the enigma of the fever chart.
1940 *Four Quartets*, 'East Coker', pt.4.

22 The dripping blood our only drink,
The bloody flesh our only food:
In spite of which we like to think
That we are sound, substantial flesh and blood—
Again, in spite of that, we call this Friday good.
1940 *Four Quartets*, 'East Coker', pt.4.

23 And so each venture
Is a new beginning, a raid on the inarticulate
With shabby equipment always deteriorating
In the general mess of imprecision of feeling,
Undisciplined squads of emotion.
1940 *Four Quartets*, 'East Coker', pt.5.

24 There is only the fight to recover what has been lost
And found and lost again and again: and now, under
conditions
That seem unpropitious. But perhaps neither gain
nor loss.
For us, there is only the trying. The rest is not our
business.
1940 *Four Quartets*, 'East Coker', pt.5.

25 Home is where one starts from. As we grow older
The world becomes stranger, the pattern more
complicated
Of dead and living.
1940 *Four Quartets*, 'East Coker', pt.5.

26 Love is most nearly itself
When here and now cease to matter.
1940 *Four Quartets*, 'East Coker', pt.5.

27 I do not know much about gods; but I think that the river
Is a strong brown god—sullen, untamed and intractable,
1941 *Four Quartets*, 'The Dry Salvages', pt.1.

28 The river is within us, the sea is all about us.
1941 *Four Quartets*, 'The Dry Salvages', pt.1.

29 The tolling bell
Measures time not our time, rung by the unhurried
Ground swell, a time
Older than the time of chronometers.
1941 *Four Quartets*, 'The Dry Salvages', pt.1.

30 We had the experience but missed the meaning,
And approach to the meaning restores the experience
In a different form, beyond any meaning
We can assign to happiness.
1941 *Four Quartets*, 'The Dry Salvages', pt.2.

31 Time the destroyer is time the preserver.
1941 *Four Quartets*, 'The Dry Salvages', pt.2.

32 You cannot face it steadily, but this thing is sure,
That time is no healer: the patient is no longer here.
1941 *Four Quartets*, 'The Dry Salvages', pt.3.

33 And right action is freedom
From past and future also.
1941 *Four Quartets*, 'The Dry Salvages', pt.5.

34 For most of us, there is only the unattended
Moment, the moment in and out of time.
1941 *Four Quartets*, 'The Dry Salvages', pt.5.

35 These are only hints and guesses,
Hints followed by guesses; and the rest
Is prayer, observance, discipline, thought and action.
The hint half guessed, the gift half understood, is
Incarnation.
1941 *Four Quartets*, 'The Dry Salvages', pt.5.

36 Here the impossible union
Of spheres of existence is actual,
Here the past and future
Are conquered, and reconciled.
1941 *Four Quartets*, 'The Dry Salvages', pt.5.

37 Midwinter Spring is its own season

Sempiternal though sodden towards sundown,
Suspended in time, between pole and tropic.
1942 *Four Quartets*, 'Little Gidding', pt.1.

38 And glow more intense than blaze of branch, or brazier,
Stirs the dumb spirit: no wind, but pentecostal fire
In the dark time of the year. Between melting and
    freezing
The soul's sap quivers.
1942 *Four Quartets*, 'Little Gidding', pt.1.

39 And what you thought you came for
Is only a shell, a husk of meaning
From which the purpose breaks only when it is fulfilled
If at all. Either you had no purpose
Or the purpose is beyond the end you figured
And is altered in fulfilment.
1942 *Four Quartets*, 'Little Gidding', pt.1.

40 And what the dead had no speech for, when living,
They can tell you, being dead: the communication
Of the dead is tongued with fire beyond the language of
    the living.
1942 *Four Quartets*, 'Little Gidding', pt.1.

41 Dust in the air suspended
Marks the place where a story ended.
1942 *Four Quartets*, 'Little Gidding', pt.2.

42 In the uncertain hour before the morning
Near the ending of interminable night
At the recurrent end of the unending.
1942 *Four Quartets*, 'Little Gidding', pt.2.

43 Since our concern was speech, and speech impelled us
To purify the dialect of the tribe
And urge the mind to aftersight and foresight.
1942 *Four Quartets*, 'Little Gidding', pt.2.

44 From wrong to wrong the exasperated spirit
Proceeds, unless restored by that refining fire
Where you must move in measure, like a dancer.
1942 *Four Quartets*, 'Little Gidding', pt.2.

45 History may be servitude,
History may be freedom.
1942 *Four Quartets*, 'Little Gidding', pt.3.

46 This is the use of memory:
For liberation—not less of love but expanding
Of love beyond desire, and so liberation
From the future as well as the past.
1942 *Four Quartets*, 'Little Gidding', pt.3.

47 The dove descending breaks the air
With flame of incandescent terror
Of which the tongues declare
The one discharge from sin and error.
1942 *Four Quartets*, 'Little Gidding', pt.4.

48 We shall not cease from exploration
And the end of all our exploring
Will be to arrive where we started
And know the place for the first time.
1942 *Four Quartets*, 'Little Gidding', pt.4.

49 What we call the beginning is often the end
And to make an end is to make a beginning.
The end is where we start from.
1942 *Four Quartets*, 'Little Gidding', pt.5.

50 A people without history
Is not redeemed from time, for history is a pattern

Of timeless moments.
1942 *Four Quartets*, 'Little Gidding', pt.5.

51 And all shall be well and
All manner of thing shall be well
When the tongues of flame are in-folded
Into a crowned knot of fire
And the fire and the rose are one.
1942 *Four Quartets*, 'Little Gidding', pt.5.

52 Culture may even be described simply as that which
makes life worth living.
1948 *Notes towards a Definition of Culture*, ch.1.

53 You've missed the point completely, Julia:
There *were* no tigers. *That* was the point.
1950 *The Cocktail Party*, act 1, sc.1, opening lines.

54 What is hell?
Hell is oneself,
Hell is alone, the other figures in it
Merely projections. There is nothing to escape from
And nothing to escape to. One is always alone.
1950 *The Cocktail Party*, act 1, sc.3.

Elizabeth I 1533–1603

Queen of England (from 1558), daughter of Henry VIII and Anne Boleyn. Imprisoned by her Catholic half-sister Mary (later Mary I), she ascended the throne as a Protestant ruler on Mary's death. After several conspiracies she had Mary, Queen of Scots executed (1587) and her subsequent persecution of Catholics led Philip of Spain to send an Armada, which was defeated (1588). Elizabeth never married.

55 If I am to disclose to you what I should prefer if I follow
the inclination of my nature, it is this: beggar-woman and
single, far rather than queen and married!
1563 Attributed reply to an imperial envoy. Quoted in J E Neale *Queen Elizabeth I* (1979).

56 Though I be a woman yet I have as good a courage
answerable to my place as ever my father had. I am your
anointed queen. I will never be by violence constrained
to do anything. I thank God I am indeed endued with
such qualities that if I were turned out of the realm in
my petticoat I were able to live in any place of
Christendom.
1566 Speech to a parliamentary delegation, 5 Nov. Quoted in
Christopher Haigh *Elizabeth I* (1988).

57 The doubt of future foes exiles my present joy.
c.1568 'The Doubt of Future Foes'.

58 No foteball player be used or suffered within the City
of London and the liberties thereof upon pain of
imprisonment.
1572 Royal proclamation, banning football from the streets of
London.

59 My care is like my shadow in the sun,
Follows me flying, flies when I pursue it,
Stands and lies by me, doth what I have done.
c.1582 'On Monsieur's Departure'.

60 I know that I have the body of a weak and feeble woman,
but I have the heart and stomach of a king—and a king of
England too; and think foul scorn that Parma or Spain, or
any Prince of Europe, should dare to invade the borders
of my realm.
1588 Address at Tilbury on the approach of the Spanish
Armada.

61 My lord, we make use of you, not for your bad legs, but for your good head.

> **c.1590** To her gout-stricken courtier William Cecil. Quoted in F Chamberlain *Sayings of Queen Elizabeth* (1923).

62 To be a King and to wear a crown is a thing more glorious to them that see it than it is pleasant to them that bear it.

> **1601** Address to parliament. Quoted in G R Elton *Renaissance and Reformation 1300–1648* (2nd edn, 1968), p.134.

63 Little man, little man! The word 'must' is not to be used to princes!

> **1603** To Robert Cecil when, during her last illness, he told her that she must go to bed. Quoted in Christopher Haigh *Elizabeth I* (1988), p.24.

64 Like strawberry wives, that laid two or three great strawberries at the mouth of their pot, and all the rest were little ones.

> Of the Commission of Sales. Quoted in Francis Bacon *Apophthegms New and Old* (1625), no.54.

Elizabeth II 1926–

Queen of the UK and Head of the Commonwealth, daughter of George VI. She was proclaimed Queen on 6 February 1952, and crowned on 2 June 1953. She married Philip, Duke of Edinburgh, in 1947.

65 I think that people will concede that, on this of all days, I should begin my speech with the words, 'My husband and I'.

> **1972** Speech at a banquet to celebrate her silver wedding anniversary, 20 Nov.

66 Experience shows that great enterprises seldom end with a tidy and satisfactory flourish. Together, we are doing our best to re-establish peace and civil order in the Gulf region, and to help those members of civil and ethnic minorities who continue to suffer through no fault of their own. If we succeed, our military success will have achieved its true objective.

> **1991** Commenting on the aftermath of the Gulf War in the first address by a British monarch to Congress, 16 May.

67 1992 is not a year I shall look back on with undiluted pleasure. In the words of one of my more sympathetic correspondents, it has turned out to be an *annus horribilis*.

> **1992** Speech at the Guildhall, 24 Nov.

Elizabeth, Queen, the Queen Mother 1900–2002

Queen Consort of King George VI, mother of Elizabeth II. Until her marriage to the King in 1923, she was Lady Elizabeth Bowes-Lyon.

68 I'm glad we've been bombed. It makes me feel I can look the East End in the face.

> **1940** Comment to a London policeman, 13 Sep. Quoted in John Wheeler-Bennet *King George VI* (1948), pt.3, ch.6.

Elkin, Stanley Lawrence 1930–95

US novelist and short-story writer. His novels include *Boswell* (1964), *The Magic Kingdom* (1985) and *The MacGuffin* (1991).

69 All books *are* the Book of Job, high moral tests and tasks set in fairy tales, landmined and unforgiving as golf greens, as steeplechase and gameboard and obstacle course.

> **1991** 'The Future of the Novel', in the *New York Times*, 17 Feb.

70 Story is just just deserts…man in the crucible like jack in the box.

> **1991** 'The Future of the Novel', in the *New York Times*, 17 Feb.

Ellerton, John 1826–93

English cleric, hymnologist, hymnwriter and translator.

71 God the Omnipotent! King, who ordainest
Great winds Thy clarions, lightnings Thy sword.

> **1866** Hymn (with Henry Fothergill Chorley, 1808–72).

72 The day Thou gavest, Lord, is ended,
The darkness falls at Thy behest.

> **1870** *A Liturgy for Missionary Meetings*, 'The Day Thou Gavest'.

Ellington, Duke (Edward Kennedy) 1899–1974

US composer, bandleader and pianist. He founded his first regular group in New York in 1924 and became a key figure in orchestral jazz. He composed about 2,000 works, including 'Mood Indigo' and 'Sophisticated Lady'.

73 Playing bop is like playing Scrabble with all the vowels missing.

> **1954** In *Look*, 10 Aug.

74 When it sounds good, it *is* good.

> **1957** *Such Sweet Thunder*, programme note.

75 Bubber was the first man I heard use the expression, 'it don't mean a thing if it ain't got that swing.' Everything, and I repeat, everything had to swing.

> **1965** Of trumpeter Bubber Miley. 'The Most Essential Instrument', in *Jazz Journal*, Dec.

76 New music? Hell, there's been no new music since Stravinsky.

> **1970** Quoted in D Jewell *Duke* (1977).

77 Music is my mistress, and she plays second fiddle to none.

> **1973** *Music Is My Mistress*.

Elliot, Jean *also known as* **Jane Elliot** 1727–1805

Scottish poet and songwriter, whose only surviving work, based on traditional versions, was written as a lament for the Battle of Flodden.

78 I've heard the lilting at our yowe-milking,
Lasses a-lilting before the dawn o' day;
But now they are moaning on ilka green loaning:
'The Flowers of the Forest are a' wede away'.

> **1769** 'The Flowers of the Forest', stanza 1.
> ➤ See Cockburn 224:55.

Elliott, Charlotte 1789–1871

English religious poet and hymnwriter.

79 Just as I am, without one plea
But that Thy blood was shed for me,
And that Thou bid'st me come to Thee,
O Lamb of God, I come!

> **1834** *Invalid's Hymn Book*, 'Just As I Am'.

Elliott, Sir Claude Aurelius 1888–1973

English schoolmaster, head and Provost of Eton College.

80 I've often thought I should like to have a set of postcards printed: 'Dear Sir or Madam, Thank you for your communication. Go to hell. Yours sincerely.'

> Quoted in the *Times Literary Supplement*, 22 Jan 1988.

Ellis, George   1753–1815

British poet, born in the West Indies. He co-founded the Tory *Anti-Jacobin* (1797) and made important translations of Middle English verse.

81 Snowy, Flowy, Blowy,
  Showery, Flowery, Bowery,
  Hoppy, Croppy, Droppy,
  Breezy, Sneezy, Freezy.
  'The Twelve Months'.

Ellis, Havelock   1859–1939

English physician and writer. His seven-volume *Studies in the Psychology of Sex* (1897–1928, rev edn 1936), caused tremendous controversy, and was banned in Great Britain.

82 All civilization has from time to time become a thin crust over a volcano of revolution.
  1922 *Little Essays of Love and Virtue.*

83 What we call morals is simply blind obedience to words of command.
  1923 *The Dance of Life.*

Ellison, Harlan Jay   1934–

US novelist, essayist, critic and editor. He has written mainly in the genres of science fiction and fantasy, where he has been a radical and outspoken contributor.

84 I Have No Mouth And I Must Scream.
  1967 Title of story collection.

85 The reason men are greater than animals isn't because we can dream of the stars…it's because we have something they haven't. Greed.
  1970 *The Glass Teat*, introduction.

86 Our childhoods are sowing the wind, our adulthoods are reaping the whirlwind.
  1974 *Approaching Oblivion*, introduction.

87 All The Lies That Are My Life.
  1989 Title of autobiography.

Ellison, Ralph Waldo   1914–94

US novelist, best known for his classic account of black urban existence, *Invisible Man* (1952), his only completed novel. He also wrote essays on music and culture.

88 I am an invisible man. No, I am not a spook like those who haunted Edgar Allen Poe; nor am I one of your Hollywood-movie ectoplasms. I am a man of substance, of flesh and bone, fibre and liquids—and I might even be said to possess a mind. I am invisible, understand, simply because people refuse to see me… When they approach me they see only my surroundings, themselves, or figments of their imagination—indeed, everything and anything except me.
  1952 *Invisible Man*, prologue.

89 I was never more hated than when I tried to be honest… On the other hand, I've never been more loved and appreciated than when I tried to 'justify' and affirm someone's mistaken beliefs; or when I've tried to give my friends the incorrect, absurd answers they wished to hear.
  1952 *Invisible Man*, epilogue.

90 All novels are about certain minorities: the individual is a minority.
  1955 Interview in *Paris Review*, Spring.

91 Part of the problem for the invisible man was that he was invisible to himself, that he didn't grasp his own complexity.
  1992 Quoted by Keith Botsford in Ellison's obituary, 18 Apr 1994, in *The Independent.*

Ellwood, David T   1953–

US economist, Professor at John F Kennedy School of Government, Harvard University.

92 The chief source of economic insecurity in America used to be growing old; now it's being born into or raised in a single-parent family.
  1991 In the *Washington Post*, 22 Feb.

Eltit, Diamela   1949–

Chilean novelist. Her novels are complex and experimental, but she has found a devoted readership among intellectuals and feminist circles.

93 *Para decirlo de otra manera, no es la herida la que causó el grito, sino exactamente a la inversa; para herirse es preciso el grito, todo lo demás es un pretexto.*
  In other words, it was not the wound that caused the scream, but precisely the opposite: to get wounded one needs the scream; the rest is only a pretext.
  1983 *Lumpérica*, 1.

Elton, Ben   1959–

English comedian and writer.

94 I did not vote Labour because they've heard of Oasis and nobody is going to vote Tory because William Hague has got a baseball cap.
  1998 In *The Radio Times*, 18 Apr.

Elton, Sir Geoffrey Rudolph   1921–94

British historian, Professor at Cambridge University.

95 When I meet a historian who cannot think that there have been great men, great men moreover in politics, I feel myself in the presence of a bad historian; and there are times when I incline to judge all historians by their opinion of Winston Churchill—whether they can see that, no matter how much better the details, often damaging, of man and career become known, he still remains, quite simply, a great man.
  1970 *Political History*, ch.2.

Éluard, Paul   *pseudonym of* **Eugène Grindel**   1895–1952

French poet, a founder of the Surrealist movement with which he later parted (1938). He was active in political affairs, in the Resistance and the Communist Party.

96 *Le poète est celui qui inspire bien plus que celui qui est inspiré.*
  The poet is more the inspirer than the one who is inspired.
  1936 *L'Évidence poétique.*

97 *Je suis né pour te connaître*
  Pour te nommer
  Liberté.
  I was born to know you
  To give you your name:
  Freedom.
  1942 *Poésie et vérité*, 'Liberté'.

98 *Adieu tristesse*
Bonjour tristesse.
Farewell sadness
Hello sadness.
1942 *Poésie et vérité*,'La Vie immédiate'.

Emecheta, Buchi   1944–

Nigerian-born British writer.

99 Sometimes it seemed that matrimony, apart from being a way of getting free sex when men felt like it, was also a legalized way of committing assault and getting away with it.
1972 *In the Ditch.*

1 I am a woman and a woman of Africa. I am a daughter of Nigeria and if she is in shame, I shall stay and mourn with her in shame.
1982 *Destination Biafra.*

Emerson, Ralph Waldo   1803–82

US philosopher and poet, a central figure of the transcendentalist movement. He was a minister in the Unitarian church, but resigned after a controversy over his belief in spiritual independence.

2 By the rude bridge that arched the flood,
Their flag to April's breeze unfurled,
Here once the embattled farmers stood
And fired the shot heard around the world.
1837 'Concord Hymn', opening lines. This poem was sung on 4 Jul 1837 at the dedication of the monument commemorating the battle of 19 Apr 1775.

3 This time, like all times, is a very good one, if we but know what to do with it.
1837 'The American Scholar', lecture at Harvard University.

4 All are needed by each one;
Nothing is fair or good alone.
1839 'Each and All', l.11–12.

5 In every work of genius we recognize our own rejected thoughts: they come back to us with a certain alienated majesty.
1841 *Essays: First Series*,'Self-Reliance'.

6 Every Stoic was a Stoic; but in Christendom where is the Christian?
1841 *Essays: First Series*,'Self-Reliance'.

7 Whoso would be a man must be a nonconformist.
1841 *Essays: First Series*,'Self-Reliance'.

8 A foolish consistency is the hobgoblin of little minds, adored by little statesmen and philosophers and divines.With consistency a great soul has simply nothing to do.
1841 *Essays: First Series*,'Self-Reliance'.

9 To be great is to be misunderstood.
1841 *Essays: First Series*,'Self-Reliance'.

10 Nothing can bring you peace but yourself.
1841 *Essays: First Series*,'Self-Reliance'.

11 The dice of God are always loaded.
1841 *Essays: First Series*,'Compensation'.

12 There is properly no history; only biography.
1841 *Essays: First Series*,'History'.

13 All mankind love a lover.
1841 *Essays: First Series*,'Love'.

14 A friend may well be reckoned the masterpiece of nature.
1841 *Essays: First Series*,'Friendship'.

15 The only reward of virtue is virtue; the only way to have a friend is to be one.
1841 *Essays: First Series*,'Friendship'.

16 In skating over thin ice, our safety is in our speed.
1841 *Essays: First Series*,'Prudence'.

17 People wish to be settled: only as far as they are unsettled is there any hope for them.
1841 *Essays: First Series*,'Circles'.

18 Nothing great was ever achieved without enthusiasm.
1841 *Essays: First Series*,'Circles'.

19 Though we travel the world over to find the beautiful, we must carry it with us, or we find it not.
1841 *Essays: First Series*,'Art'.

20 In sculpture, did ever anybody call the Apollo a fancy piece? Or say of the Laocoön how it might be made different? A masterpiece of art has in the mind a fixed place in the chain of being, as much as a plant or a crystal.
1841 'Thoughts on Art', in *The Dial*, vol.1, no.3, Jan.

21 Have I a lover
Who is noble and free?
I would he were nobler
Than to love me.
1841 'The Sphinx', stanza 12.

22 The reward of a thing well done is to have done it.
1844 'New England Reformers', lecture to the Society, 3 Mar.

23 It is not metres, but a metre-making argument, that makes a poem.
1844 *Essays: Second Series*,'The Poet'.

24 Let the Stoics say what they please, we do not eat for the good of living, but because the meat is savory and the appetite is keen.
1844 *Essays: Second Series*,'Nature'.

25 The only gift is a portion of thyself.
1844 *Essays: Second Series*,'Gifts'.

26 Every man is wanted, and no man is wanted much.
1844 *Essays: Second Series*,'Nominalist and Realist'.

27 Things are in the saddle,
And ride mankind.
1847 *Poems*,'Ode', dedicated to W H Channing.

28 Belief consists in affirming the affirmations of the soul; unbelief, in denying them.
1850 *Representative Men*,'Montaigne; or, The Skeptic'.

29 Is not marriage an open question, when it is alleged, from the beginning of the world, that such as are in the institution wish to get out; and such as are out wish to get in.
1850 *Representative Men*,'Montaigne; or, The Skeptic'.

30 Keep cool: it will be all one a hundred years hence.
1850 *Representative Men*,'Montaigne; or, The Skeptic'.

31 I can reason down or deny everything, except this perpetual Belly: feed he must and will, and I cannot make him respectable.
1850 *Representative Men*,'Montaigne; or, The Skeptic'.

32 The world is upheld by the veracity of good men: they make the earth wholesome.

1850 *Representative Men*, 'Uses of Great Men'.

33 Every hero becomes a bore at last.
1850 *Representative Men*, 'Uses of Great Men'.

34 Perpetual modernness is the measure of merit in every work of art.
1850 *Representative Men*, 'Plato'.

35 Men's actions are too strong for them. Show me a man who has acted, and who has not been the victim and slave of his action.
1850 *Representative Men*, 'Goethe'.

36 The aristocrat is the democrat ripe, and gone to seed.
1850 *Representative Men*, 'Napoleon, the Man of the World'.

37 As long as our civilization is essentially one of property, of fences, of exclusiveness, it will be mocked by delusions. Our riches will leave us sick; there will be bitterness in our laughter; and our wine will burn our mouth.
1850 *Representative Men*, 'Napoleon, the Man of the World'.

38 They have in themselves what they value in their horses, mettle and bottom.
1856 Of Englishmen. *English Traits*, 'Manners'.

39 If the red slayer think he slays,
Or if the slain think he is slain,
They know not well the subtle ways
I keep, and pass, and turn again.
1857 'Brahma'. Collected in *May Day* (1867).
➤ *See Lang 488:90.*

40 A person seldom falls sick, but the bystanders are animated with a faint hope that he will die.
1860 *The Conduct of Life*, 'Considerations by the Way'.

41 Art is a jealous mistress, and if a man have a genius for painting, poetry, music, architecture, or philosophy, he makes a bad husband and an ill provider.
1860 *The Conduct of Life*, 'Wealth'.

42 We are born believing. A man bears beliefs as a tree bears apples.
1860 *The Conduct of Life*, 'Worship'.

43 Immortality will come to such as are fit for it, and he who would be a great soul in future must be a great soul now.
1860 *The Conduct of Life*, 'Worship'.

44 The louder he talked of his honour, the faster we counted our spoons.
1860 *The Conduct of Life*, 'Worship'.

45 The revelation of Thought takes men out of servitude into freedom.
1860 *The Conduct of Life*, 'Fate'.

46 He has not learned the lesson of life who does not every day surmount a fear.
1870 *Society and Solitude*, 'Courage'.

47 Raphael paints wisdom; Handel sings it, Phidias carves it, Shakespeare writes it, Wren builds it, Columbus sails it, Luther preaches it, Washington arms it, Watt mechanizes it.
1870 *Society and Solitude*, 'Art'.

48 Hitch your wagon to a star.
1870 *Society and Solitude*, 'Civilization'.

49 We boil at different degrees.
1870 *Society and Solitude*, 'Eloquence'.

50 Can anybody remember when the times were not hard, and money was not scarce?
1870 *Society and Solitude*, 'Works and Days'.

51 We do not count a man's years, until he has nothing else to count.
1870 *Society and Solitude*, 'Old Age'.

52 America is a country of young men.
1870 *Society and Solitude*, 'Old Age'.

53 A rogue alive to the ludicrous is still convertible. If that sense is lost, his fellow-men can do little for him.
1876 *Letters and Social Aims*, 'The Comic'.

54 Music is the poor man's Parnassus.
1876 *Letters and Social Aims*, 'Poetry and Imagination'.

Emery, Jane c.1918–

US biographer and academic.

55 As thin and neat as a furled umbrella.
1992 On Rose Macaulay. *Rose Macaulay*.

Emin, Tracey 1964–

English artist. She gained widespread public attention with various 'confessional' installation works such as *Everyone I Have Ever Slept With, from 1963 to 1995* (1995), which was later destroyed in a fire.

56 The wheel that squeaks gets the oil.
2001 In the *Observer*, 22 Apr.

57 The majority of the British public have no regard or no respect for what me and my peers do to the point where they actually laugh at a disaster like a fire.
2004 After some of her work (and the work of other contemporary artists) was destroyed in a fire in London. Quoted in *The Scotsman*, 31 May.

58 Just love me.
2004 Words spelled out in a neon light installation she created.

Emmet, Robert 1778–1803

Irish patriot, member of the United Irishmen. In 1803 he plotted an insurrection against the English, and was hanged after returning from the Wicklow Mountains for a last meeting with his sweetheart.

59 I have but one request to make at my departure from this world, it is—the charity of its silence. Let no man write my epitaph; for as no man who knows my motives, dare now vindicate them, let no prejudice or ignorance asperse them. Let them rest in obscurity and peace! Let my memory be left in oblivion, and my tomb remain uninscribed, until other times and other men can do justice to my character. When my country takes her place among the nations of the earth, *then*, and *not till then*, let my epitaph be written.
1803 Speech before being sentenced.

Empson, Sir William 1906–84

English critic and poet. He established his reputation with his first book on textual criticism, *Seven Types of Ambiguity* (1930, revised 1947). An edition of *Collected Poems* was published in 1955.

60 Seven Types of Ambiguity.
1930 Title of book.

61 Slowly the poison the whole blood stream fills.
It is not the effort or the failure tires.

The waste remains, the waste remains and kills.
1935 'Missing Dates'.

62 Ripeness is all; her in her cooling planet
Revere; do not presume to think her wasted.
1935 'To an Old Lady'.

63 But as to risings, I can tell you why.
It is on contradiction that they grow.
It seemed the best thing to be up and go.
Up was the heartening and the strong reply.
The heart of standing is we cannot fly.
1935 'Aubade'.

64 Waiting for the end, boys, waiting for the end.
What is there to be or do?
What's become of me or you?
1940 'Just a Smack at Auden'.

Engels, Friedrich 1820–95

German socialist philosopher, founder of 'scientific socialism'.
He first met Karl Marx in Brussels in 1844, collaborated with him
on the *Communist Manifesto* (1848), and later edited and
translated Marx's writings.

65 [The] English proletariat is becoming more and more
bourgeois, so that this most bourgeois of all nations is
apparently aiming ultimately at the possession of a
bourgeois aristocracy and a bourgeois proletariat *as well
as* a bourgeoisie. For a nation which exploits the whole
world this is of course to a certain extent justifiable.
1858 Letter to Karl Marx, 7 Oct.

66 *Der Staat wird nicht 'abgeschafft', er stirbt ab.*
The state is not 'abolished'; it withers away.
1878 *Anti-Dühring*, pt.3, ch.2.

67 The British Labour movement is today, and for many
years has been, working in a narrow circle of strikes that
are looked upon, not as an expedient, and not as a
means of propaganda, but as an ultimate aim.
1878 Letter to Eduard Bernstein, 17 Jul.

68 The society that will organize production on the basis of
a free and equal association of the producers will put the
whole machinery of the state where it will then belong:
into the museum of antiquities, by the side of the
spinning wheel and the bronze axe.
1884 *The Origin of the Family, Private Property, and the State.*

Engle, Paul Hamilton 1908–91

US poet, novelist and critic, whose writing is formal, elegant
and accessible. He ran courses in literature and writing in his
native Iowa.

69 Poetry—tries to tell you about a vision in the unvisionary
language of farm, city and love.
1956 In *Life*, 28 May.

Ennius, Quintus Ennius c.239–169 BC

Roman poet, probably of Greek extraction. He was a friend of
Scipio Africanus the Elder, and he introduced the hexameter
into Latin. Only fragments have survived of his work.

70 *Quod est ante pedes nemo spectat, caeli scrutantur
plagas.*
No one regards the things before his feet, but views with
care the regions of the sky.
Fragment of *Iphigeneia*, quoted in Cicero *De Divinatione*, bk.2
(translated by W A Falconer, 1979).

71 How like us is that ugly brute, the ape!
Quoted in Cicero *De Divinatione*, bk.50 (translated by
H Rackham, 1942).

Enright, D(ennis) J(oseph) 1920–2002

English poet, critic and literary journalist. He held posts in
universities around the world (1947–60), although his
humanistic work rejects academic politics.

72 Metaphysical lederhosen.
On the murky philosophizing and cumbrous symbolism of
German novels. Quoted by John Gross in the *New York Times*,
20 Jan 1987.

Ephorus of Cumæ c.400–330 BC

Greek historian.

73 Music was invented to deceive and delude mankind.
History, preface.

Ephron, Nora 1941–

US screenwriter and director.

74 I always say that a successful parent is one who raises a
child so that they can pay for their own psychoanalysis.
1995 In *The Guardian*, 26 Jun.

Epstein, Jacob 1880–1959

US-born British sculptor.

75 Why don't they stick to murder and leave art to us?
Attributed. On hearing that his statue, Lazarus, in New College
chapel, Oxford, kept Nikita Khrushchev awake at night.

Epstein, Julius J 1909–2000

US screenwriter, twin brother of Philip G Epstein. The two
worked as a screenwriting team for many years on films such
as *Casablanca* (1942) and *My Foolish Heart* (1949).

76 Of all the gin joints in all the towns in all the world, she
walks into mine.
1942 Humphrey Bogart as Rick in *Casablanca* (with Philip G
Epstein and Howard Koch).

77 If she can stand it, I can. Play it!
1942 Humphrey Bogart as Rick in *Casablanca* (with Philip G
Epstein and Howard Koch). The line is commonly rendered 'Play
it again, Sam', a conflation with an earlier line of Ingrid Bergman,
'Play it, Sam. Play *As Time Goes By*.'

78 Here's looking at you, kid.
1942 Humphrey Bogart as Rick in *Casablanca* (with Philip G
Epstein and Howard Koch).

79 I'm no good at being noble, but it doesn't take much to
see that the problems of three little people don't amount
to a hill of beans in this crazy world.
1942 Humphrey Bogart as Rick in *Casablanca* (with Philip G
Epstein and Howard Koch).

80 If that plane leaves the ground and you're not with him,
you'll regret it. Maybe not today, maybe not tomorrow,
but soon and for the rest of your life.
1942 Humphrey Bogart as Rick in *Casablanca* (with Philip G
Epstein and Howard Koch).

81 Major Strasser has been shot. Round up the usual
suspects.
1942 Claude Rains as Captain Louis Renault in *Casablanca* (with
Philip G Epstein and Howard Koch).

82 A woman is beautiful only when she is loved.
1944 *Mr Skeffington* (with Philip Epstein).

83 Honeymoon's over—time to get married.
1972 *Pete 'n Tillie*.

84 When you've reached my age, and your friends are beginning to worry about you, blind dates are a way of life.
1972 *Pete 'n Tillie*.

85 Dear J W, have the bank president finish the script.
Response to a note from Jack Warner which had read 'Railroad presidents get in at nine o'clock, bank presidents get in at nine o'clock, read your contract, you're coming in at nine o'clock.' Quoted in Aljean Harmetz *Round Up the Usual Suspects* (1993).

Erasmus, Desiderius *originally* **Gerrit Gerritszoon**
1466–1536

Dutch humanist and scholar, author of the satire *Encomium Moriae* (*Praise of Folly*, 1509) and *Colloquia familiaria* (1519), an audacious treatment of Church abuses. Other works include the first translation of the Greek New Testament.

86 *In regione caecorum rex est luscus.*
In the country of the blind the one-eyed man is king.
c.1500 *Adages*, bk.3, century 4, no.96.

87 Let a king recall that it is better to improve his realm than to increase his territory.
1517 *Querela Pacis*.

Eriksson, Sven Goran 1948–

Swedish football coach, manager of the England football team from 2001.

88 There is more politics in football than in politics.
2004 In *Varsity*, 23 Jan.

Ernst, Max 1891–1976

German-born artist, a founder of the Dada group and later a key figure of Surrealism. He settled in the US in 1941 but returned to France in 1953.

89 The artist is a spectator, indifferent or impassioned, at the birth of his work, and observes the phases of its development.
Quoted in Saranne Alexandrian *Surrealist Art* (1970).

90 Collage is a supersensitive and scrupulously accurate instrument, similar to a seismograph, which is able to record the exact amount of the possibility of human happiness at any period.
Quoted in Saranne Alexandrian *Surrealist Art* (1970).

Ertz, Susan *pseudonym of* **Mrs Ronald McCrindle**
c.1894–1985

US novelist, born in England. She was the author of a great many popular novels.

91 Someone has somewhere commented on the fact that millions long for immortality who don't know what to do with themselves on a rainy Sunday afternoon.
1943 *Anger in the Sky*, ch.5.

Etherege, Sir George c.1635–1691

English dramatist, who spent most of his life in royal service abroad. Inspired by Molière, he founded the comedy of intrigue in English literature.

92 Like dancers on the ropes poor poets fare,
Most perish young, the rest in danger are.
1676 *The Man of Mode or, Sir Fopling Flutter*, prologue.

93 What a dull, insipid thing is a billet-doux written in cold blood, after the heat of the business is over!
1676 *The Man of Mode or, Sir Fopling Flutter*, act 1, sc.1.

94 Next to the coming to a good understanding with a new mistress, I love a quarrel with an old one.
1676 *The Man of Mode or, Sir Fopling Flutter*, act 1, sc.1.

95 I know he is a devil, but he has something of the angel yet undefaced in him, which makes him so charming and agreeable that I must love him, be he never so wicked.
1676 *The Man of Mode or, Sir Fopling Flutter*, act 2, sc.2.

96 We are not masters of our own affections; our inclinations daily alter: now we love pleasure, and anon we shall dote on business. Human frailty will have it so, and who can help it?
1676 *The Man of Mode or, Sir Fopling Flutter*, act 2, sc.2.

97 When love grows diseased, the best thing we can do is to put it to a violent death. I cannot endure the torture of a lingering and consumptive passion.
1676 *The Man of Mode or, Sir Fopling Flutter*, act 2, sc.2.

98 I must confess I am a fop in my heart; ill customs influence my very senses, and I have been so used to affectation that without the help of the air of the court what is natural cannot touch me.
1688 Letter to Mr Poley, 12 Jan.

Eubank, Chris 1966–

English boxer.

99 All the rudiments of life are to be found ironing trousers.
2003 Quoted in *The Independent*, 29 Dec.

Euclid 4c BC

Greek mathematician, best known for his 13-volume work *The Elements*, dealing with plane and solid geometry and arithmetic.

1 That which was to be proved.
c.300 BC *Elementa*, bk.1, proposition 5. Although originally written in Greek, this phrase is usually quoted in its Latin form, 'Quod erat demonstrandum', sometimes abbreviated to 'QED'.

2 There is no 'royal road' to geometry.
c.300 BC Response to Ptolemy I, when asked if there were an easier way to solve theorems. Quoted in Proclus *Commentary on the First Book of Euclid's Elementa*, prologue.

Eudamidas 4c BC

King of Sparta, the brother of Agis I whom he succeeded in 331/330 BC.

3 The speech is admirable, but the speaker is not to be trusted; for he has never been amid the blare of trumpets.
Of a philosopher who had claimed that philosophers were the only good generals. Quoted in Plutarch *Apophthegmata Laconica*, 220E (translated by F C Babbitt, 1931).

Euripides 480 or 484–406 BC

Greek dramatist. Of more than 80 plays only 18 survive complete. He won the tragic prize only five times, but his plays gained popularity after his death.

4 Regard this day's life as yours, but all else as Fortune's.
Alcestis, l.788–9 (translated by D Kovacs, 1994).

5 I have found nothing stronger than Necessity.
Alcestis, l.965 (translated by D Kovacs, 1994).

6 Nothing else that a wife may suffer, equals this: if she loses her husband, she loses her life.
Andromacha, l.375–6.

7 Women's love is for their men, not for their children.
Electra, l.265.

8 None wise dares hopeless venture.
Helena, l.811 (translated by A S Way, 1959).

9 The life of men is painful.
Hippolytus, l.190.

10 It is necessary for mortals to be worn with toil.
Hippolytus, l.207.

11 Your very silence is your confession.
Clytemnestra to Agamemnon, realizing that he plans to sacrifice their daughter, Iphigenia, to secure favourable winds during the Greek expedition against Troy. *Iphigenia Aulidensis*, l.1142.

12 The meanest life is better than the most glorious death.
Iphigenia Aulidensis, l.1252 (translated by W S Merwin and G E Dimock Jr, 1978).

13 Wrath brings mortal men their gravest hurt.
Medea, l.1080 (translated by D Kovacs, 1994).

14 A change is always nice.
Orestes, l.234 (translated by M L West, 1987).

15 Lucky is the man who has been successful with his children and not got ones who are notorious disasters.
Orestes, l.542–3 (translated by M L West, 1987).

16 And wealth abides not, it is but for a day.
Phoenissae, l.558.

Evans, Bergen 1904–78

US scholar and literary critic, Professor of English at Indiana University.

17 It was said of Metternich that he was so conservative that had *he* been present at the Creation, he would have begged God to have retained Chaos.
1968 Note in his *Dictionary of Quotations*.

Evans, Dame Edith 1888–1976

English actress, best remembered for her starchy Lady Bracknell in Oscar Wilde's *The Importance of Being Earnest* (1939), which she also played on film.

18 People always ask me the most ridiculous questions. They want to know, 'How do you approach a role?' Well, I don't know. I approach it by first saying yes, then getting on with the bloody thing.
Attributed.

Evans, George Essex 1863–1909

Australian poet, born in England. A journalist and literary editor, he is best known for his patriotic ceremonial verse.

19 Not as the songs of other lands
Her song shall be.
'An Australian Symphony', in *Collected Verse* (1920).

Evans, Walker 1903–75

US photographer, chronicler of the harsh life in the rural South during the Great Depression of the 1930s. His photographs appear in James Agee's *Let Us Now Praise Famous Men* (1941).

20 People out of work are not given to talking much about the one thing on their minds. You only sense by indirection, degrees of anger, shades of humiliation and echoes of fear.
Quoted in *Fortune*, 11 Feb 1980.

Evelyn, John 1620–1706

English diarist. His *Diary*, which covers the years 1641–1706, offers an insight into life in post-Restoration England.

21 This knight was indeed a valiant Gent: but not a little given to romance, when he spake of himself.
1651 Diary entry, 6 Sep.

22 I saw *Hamlet Prince of Denmark* played, but now the old plays begin to disgust this refined age.
1661 Diary entry, 26 Nov.

Ewart, Gavin Buchanan 1916–95

Scottish-born poet. His poems are often humorous or scatological in nature, and frequently mimic comic popular forms like the limerick. He published his first book of poems in 1939.

23 Miss Twye was soaping her breasts in the bath
When she heard behind her a meaning laugh
And to her amazement she discovered
A wicked man in the bathroom cupboard.
1939 'Miss Twye'.

24 Sex suppressed will go berserk,
But it keeps us all alive.
It's a wonderful change from wives and work
And it ends at half past five.
1966 'Office Friendships'.

25 Would you rather live in lively London
or where a young penguin lies screaming?
1977 *Where a Young Penguin Lies Screaming*, epigraph.

26 He's very popular among his mates.
I think I'm Auden, he thinks he's Yeats.
1986 'Seamus Heaney'.

27 On the Last Day the wrecks will surface over the sea.
1986 'Resurrection'.

Ewer, William Norman 1885–1976

British writer.

28 How odd
Of God
To choose
The Jews.
1924 In *The Week-End Book*.

Ewing, Winnie 1929–

Scottish Nationalist politician.

29 The Scottish Parliament which adjourned on 25 March in the year 1707 is hereby reconvened.
1999 Speech at the opening of the new Scottish Parliament, 12 May.

30 Time after time, on matters great and small, we are still standing on the sidelines, mutely accepting what is decided elsewhere instead of raising our voices and

making our own choices. Scotland's much vaunted partnership of Jonah and the whale.
Quoted in Michael Russell (ed) *Stop the World: The Autobiography of Winnie Ewing* (2004).

Fackenheim, Emil L 1916–2003

Jewish rabbi and philosopher. He was Professor at the University of Toronto until 1984, when he moved to Jerusalem, where he continued to teach and write.

31 Had every Christian in Hitler's Europe followed the example of the king of Denmark and decided to put on the yellow star, there would be today neither despair in the church nor talk of the death of God.
1968 *Quest for Past and Future.*

Fadiman, Anne 1953–

US writer.

32 Sharing a bed and a future was child's play compared to sharing my copy of *The Complete Poems of W B Yeats.*
1998 On the joys and pain of combining libraries when couples move in together. In *Ex Libris: Confessions of a Common Reader.*

33 If my father were still writing essays, every full-grown 'girl' would probably be transformed into a 'woman'.
1998 On her father, Clifton Fadiman, a renowned man-of-letters. In *Ex Libris: Confessions of a Common Reader.*

Fadiman, Clifton 1904–99

US writer, literary critic and lecturer. He worked as a book reviewer for the *New Yorker.*

34 Liquor is not a necessity. It is a means of momentarily sidestepping necessity.
1955 *Party of One,* 'From My Notebooks'.

35 The mama of dada.
1955 Of Gertrude Stein. *Party of One.*

36 Cheese, milk's leap toward immortality.
1957 *Any Number Can Play,* 'The Cheese Stands Alone'.

37 The police dog of American fiction, except that his hatred is not the result of mere crabbedness but of an eye that sees too deep for comfort.
Of US writer Ring Lardner. Quoted in Scott Meredith *George S Kaufman and His Friends* (1974).

38 Poetry in a bottle.
1985 Of wine. In *Manhattan Inc,* Jul.

Falkland, Lucius Cary, Viscount 1610–43

English statesman and writer, whose house at Tew attracted the brightest intellects of Oxford and London. A Royalist during the Civil War, he was Secretary of State in 1642 and was killed at the first Battle of Newbury.

39 When it is not necessary to change, it is necessary not to change.
1641 Speech, House of Commons, 22 Nov. Collected as 'A Speech concerning Episcopacy' in *Discourses of Infallibility* (1660).

Faludi, Susan 1960–

US journalist and writer. She has written *Backlash: The Undeclared War Against American Women* (1991), a controversial and award-winning study of feminism, and *Stiffed: The Betrayal of Modern Man* (2000).

40 The more women are paid, the less eager they are to marry.
1992 *Backlash* (UK edn), ch.2, 'Man Shortages and Barren Wombs'.

41 Social scientists *could* supply plenty of research to show that one member of the family, at least, is happier and more well adjusted when mum stays home and looks after the children. But that person is dad—a finding of limited use to backlash publicists.
1992 *Backlash* (UK edn), ch.2, 'Man Shortages and Barren Wombs'.

42 A backlash against women's rights is nothing new. Indeed, it's a recurring phenomenon: it returns every time women begin to make some headway towards equality, a seemingly inevitable early frost to the brief flowerings of feminism.
1992 *Backlash* (UK edn), ch.3, 'Backlashes Then and Now'.

Fanon, Frantz Omar 1925–61

French West Indian psychoanalyst and social philosopher, editor of *El Moudjahid* in Tunis and Ambassador to Ghana. He is best remembered for his critiques of colonialism.

43 *Aux colonies, l'infrastructure économique est également une superstructure. La cause est conséquence: on est riche parce que blanc, on est blanc parce que riche.*
In the colonies the economic substructure is also a superstructure. The cause is the consequence; you are rich because you are white, you are white because you are rich.
1961 *Les Damnés de la terre (The Wretched of the Earth,* translated by Constance Farrington, 1965), ch.1, 'Concerning Violence'.

44 *Le colonialisme ne se satisfait pas d'enserrer le peuple dans ses mailles, de vider le cerveau colonisé de toute forme et de tout contenu. Par une sorte de perversion de la logique, il s'oriente vers le passé du peuple opprimé, le distort, le défigure, l'anéantit.*
Colonialism is not satisfied merely with holding a people in its grip and emptying the native's brain of all form and content. By a kind of perverted logic, it turns to the past of the oppressed people, and distorts, disfigures and destroys it.
1961 *Les Damnés de la terre (The Wretched of the Earth,* translated by Constance Farrington, 1965), ch.4, 'On National Culture'.

45 *Le colonialisme accule le peuple dominé à se poser constamment la question: 'Qui suis-je en réalité?'*
Colonialism forces the people it dominates to ask themselves the question constantly: 'In reality, who am I?'
1961 *Les Damnés de la terre (The Wretched of the Earth,* translated by Constance Farrington, 1965), ch.5, 'Colonial War and Mental Disorders'.

Fanthorpe, U(rsula) A(skham)   1929–

English poet.

46 I wasn't good
At growing up. Never learned
The natives' art of life.
1984 'Growing Up'.

Farjeon, Eleanor   1881–1965

English children's writer. Her copious output comprises stories, poems, recountings, fables, saints' lives and prayers, and includes *Nursery Rhymes of London Town* (1916) and 'A Morning Song' (1957).

47 Morning has broken
Like the first morning,
Blackbird has spoken
Like the first bird.
Praise for the singing!
Praise for the morning!
Praise for them springing
Fresh from the Word!
1957 *Children's Bells*, 'A Morning Song'.

48 There's Carol like a rolling car,
And Martin like a flying bird,
And Adam like the Lord's First Word,
And Raymond like the Harvest Moon,
And Peter like a piper's tune,
And Alan like the flowing on
Of water. And there's John, like John.
1958 *Then There Were Three*, 'Boys' Names'.

Farjeon, Herbert   1887–1945

English actor, theatre manager and critic.

49 I've danced with a man, who's danced with a girl, who's danced with the Prince of Wales.
1927 *The Picnic*.

Farquhar, George   c.1677–1707

Irish playwright, who turned to soldiering after an early career as an actor. His comic plays include *Love and a Bottle* (1698), *The Recruiting Officer* (1706) and, most famously, *The Beaux' Stratagem* (1707).

50 Poetry's a mere drug, Sir.
1698 *Love and a Bottle*, act 3, sc.2.

51 I hate all that don't love me, and slight all that do.
1699 *The Constant Couple*, act 1, sc.2.

52 Crimes, like virtues, are their own reward.
1702 *The Inconstant*, act 4, sc.2.

53 Hanging and marriage, you know, go by destiny.
1706 *The Recruiting Officer*, act 3, sc.2.

54 Sir, you shall taste my Anno Domini.
1707 *The Beaux' Stratagem*, act 1, sc.1.

55 I have fed purely upon ale; I have eat my ale, drank my ale, and I always sleep upon ale.
1707 *The Beaux' Stratagem*, act 1, sc.1.

56 There is no scandal like rags, nor any crime so shameful as poverty.
1707 *The Beaux' Stratagem*, act 1, sc.1.

57 Since a woman must wear chains, I would have the pleasure of hearing 'em rattle a little.

1707 *The Beaux' Stratagem*, act 2, sc.2.

58 No woman can be a beauty without a fortune.
1707 *The Beaux' Stratagem*, act 2, sc.2.

Farragut, David Glasgow   1801–70

US admiral. He served in the War of 1812 and had minor commands in the American–Mexican War before leading a Union fleet in the Civil War. He was the US navy's first vice-admiral (1864) and admiral (1866).

59 Damn the torpedoes! Full speed ahead.
1864 At the Battle of Mobile Bay, 5 Aug. Quoted in A T Mahan *Great Commanders: Admiral Farragut* (1892), ch.10.

Fassbinder, Rainer Werner   1946–82

German film director, who made over 40 films.

60 I hope to build a house with my films. Some of them are the cellar, some are the walls, and some are the windows. But I hope in time there will be a house.
Quoted in Leslie Halliwell *Halliwell's Filmgoer's Companion* (1993).

Faulkner, William Harrison   1897–1962

US novelist, known for his experiments in literary form and style and for his treatment of social and racial problems in the US South in a series of novels beginning with *Sartoris* (1929). He was awarded the Nobel prize for literature in 1949.

61 *Yes*, he thought, *between grief and nothing I will take grief*.
1939 Wilborne. *The Wild Palms*, 'Wild Palms', no.5.

62 No man can cause more grief than that one clinging blindly to the vices of his ancestors.
1948 *Intruder in the Dust*, ch.3.

63 He must teach himself that the basest of all things is to be afraid and, teaching himself that, forget it forever, leaving no room in his workshop for anything but the old verities and truths of the heart, the old universal truths lacking which any story is ephemeral and doomed—love and honour and pity and compassion and sacrifice.
1950 Nobel prize acceptance speech.

64 I believe man will not merely endure, he will prevail. He is immortal, not because he, alone among creatures, has an inexhaustible voice but because he has a soul, a spirit capable of compassion and sacrifice and endurance.
1950 Nobel prize acceptance speech.

65 Maybe the only thing worse than having to give gratitude constantly all the time, is having to accept it.
1951 *Requiem for a Nun*, act 2, sc.1.

66 Since his capacity to do is forced into channels of evil through environment and pressures, man is strong before he is moral. The world's anguish is caused by people between twenty and forty.
1956 Interview in *Paris Review*, Spring.

67 An artist is a creature driven by demons.
1956 Interview in *Paris Review*, Spring.

68 The writer's only responsibility is to his art. He will be completely ruthless if he is a good one.
1956 Interview in *Paris Review*, Spring.

69 If a writer has to rob his mother, he will not hesitate; the *Ode on a Grecian Urn* is worth any number of old ladies.
1956 Interview in *Paris Review*, Spring.

70 The aim of every artist is to arrest motion, which is life, by artificial means and hold it fixed so that a hundred years later, when a stranger looks at it, it moves again since it is life.
   1956 Interview in *Paris Review*, Spring.

71 All of us failed to match our dreams of perfection. So I rate us on the basis of our splendid failure to do the impossible.
   1956 On his generation of writers. Interview in *Paris Review*, Spring.

72 If I were reincarnated, I'd want to come back as a buzzard. Nothing hates him or envies him or wants him or needs him. He is never bothered or in danger, and he can eat anything.
   1956 Interview in *Paris Review*, Spring.

73 Success is feminine and like a woman; if you cringe before her she will override you. So the way to treat her is to show her the back of your hand. Then maybe she will do the crawling.
   1956 Interview in *Paris Review*, Spring.

74 No man can write who is not first a humanitarian.
   1957 In *Time*, 25 Feb.

75 The last sound on the worthless earth will be two human beings trying to launch a homemade spaceship and already quarreling about where they are going next.
   1959 Speech to UNESCO Commission, in the *New York Times*, 3 Oct.

76 But a man shouldn't fool with booze until he's fifty; then he's a damn fool if he doesn't.
   Quoted in Webb and Wigfall Green *William Faulkner of Oxford* (1965).

Fauré, Gabriel Urbain 1845–1924

French composer. Director of the Conservatoire (1905–20), he is remembered chiefly for his songs and instrumental music, and for his *Requiem* (1887–90).

77 If that was music, I have never understood what music was.
   1902 After attending the première of Debussy's *Pelléas et Mélisande*. Quoted in R Orledge *Gabriel Fauré* (1979).

Favre, Jules Claude Gabriel 1809–80

French lawyer and politician. He took part in the July Revolution (1830), becoming a Republican leader and, after the fall of Napoleon III, Foreign Minister. He negotiated the Treaty of Frankfurt (1871).

78 Not an inch of our territory or a stone of our fortresses.
   1870 Reply to Bismarck's demands for concessions, 18 Sep, following France's defeat in the Franco-Prussian War. Quoted in A J P Taylor *The Struggle for Mastery in Europe 1848–1918* (1954), p.212.

Fawcett, Percy Harrison 1867–c.1925

English explorer. After military service he made several expeditions to Brazil (1906–25) in search of traces of ancient civilizations, disappearing with his son and a companion in the Mato Grosso region. Their fate is a mystery.

79 There, I believed, lay the greatest secrets of the past yet preserved in our world of today. I had come to the turn of the road; and for better or worse I chose the forest path.
   1911 Of South America. Collected in Brian Fawcett (ed) *Exploration Fawcett* (1953).

80 You need have no fear of any failure.
   1925 Last words written to his wife. Collected in Brian Fawcett (ed) *Exploration Fawcett* (1953).

Fawkes, Guy 1570–1606

English conspirator. He converted to Catholicism at an early age, and served in the Spanish army in the Netherlands (1593–1604). He was involved in the Gunpowder Plot, and was caught red-handed and hanged.

81 A desperate disease requires a dangerous remedy.
   1605 When questioned after his arrest on 5 Nov.

Feibleman, Peter 1930–

US novelist, playwright and literary executor of Lillian Hellmann. His novels include *A Place Without Twilight* (1958) and *The Daughters of Necessity* (1959). With Lillian Hellmann he wrote *Eating Together* (1985).

82 The biggest difference between Lillian as a grown-up and Lillian as a child was that she was taller.
   1988 On Lillian Hellman. *Lily*.

Feiffer, Jules 1929–

US cartoonist and writer. His early cartoons in *Village Voice* (1956) were followed by *Little Murders* (a black comedy, 1965), novels and screenplays, including *Carnal Knowledge* (1971). He currently writes and illustrates children's books.

83 I used to think I was poor. Then they told me I wasn't poor, I was needy. They told me it was self-defeating to think of myself as needy, I was deprived. Then they told me underprivileged was overused. I was disadvantaged. I still don't have a dime. But I have a great vocabulary.
   1956 Cartoon caption.

84 As a matter of racial pride we want to be called *blacks*. Which has replaced the term *Afro-American*. Which replaced *Negroes*. Which replaced *colored people*. Which replaced *darkies*. Which replaced *blacks*.
   Quoted in William Safire *Language Maven Strikes Again* (1990).

Feininger, Lyonel 1871–1956

US Cubist painter, also associated with the German painters of the Blaue Reiter.

85 Each individual work serves as an expression of our most personal state of mind at that particular moment and of the inescapable, imperative need for release by means of an appropriate act of creation: in the rhythm, form, colour and mood of a picture.
   1917 Letter to Paul Westheim, quoted in Wolf-Dieter Dube *The Expressionists* (1972).

Fellini, Federico 1920–93

Italian film director. His most famous and controversial work, *La Dolce Vita* (1960, 'The Sweet Life'), was a cynical evocation of modern Roman high life.

86 I always direct the same film. I can't distinguish one from the other.
   Quoted in Leslie Halliwell *Halliwell's Filmgoer's Companion* (1993).

Fenton, James 1949–

English satirical poet and critic, formerly a foreign correspondent. He was Professor of Poetry at Oxford (1994–9).

87 It is not what they built. It is what they knocked down.
It is not the houses. It is the spaces between the houses.
It is not the streets that exist. It is the streets that no longer exist.
It is not your memories which haunt you.
It is not what you have written down.
It is what you have forgotten, what you must forget.
What you must go on forgetting all your life.
1981 'A German Requiem'.

88 And I'm afraid, reading this passage now,
That everything I knew has been destroyed
By those whom I admired but never knew;
The laughing soldiers fought to their defeat
And I'm afraid most of my friends are dead.
1982 'In a Notebook'.

89 Oh let us not be condemned for what we are.
It is enough to account for what we do.
1983 'Children in Exile'.

90 English poetry begins whenever we decide to say the modern English language begins, and it extends as far as we decide to say that the English language extends.
2002 An Introduction to English Poetry.

Fenwick, Millicent Hammond   1910–93

US politician and diplomat, congresswoman from New Jersey (1975–83). She compiled the Vogue Book of Etiquette (1948).

91 The gentle and respectful ways of saying 'To hell with you' are being abandoned.
Recalled on her death, 16 Sep 1993.

Ferber, Edna   1887–1968

US writer. She wrote a number of novels and short stories, and is remembered as the writer of Show Boat (1926), which inspired the successful musical.

92 Mother Knows Best.
1923 Title of story.

93 I am not belittling the brave pioneer men but the sunbonnet as well as the sombrero has helped to settle this glorious land of ours.
1929 Cimarron, ch.23.

94 America—rather, the United States—seems to me to be the Jew among the nations. It is resourceful, adaptable, maligned, envied, feared, imposed upon. It is warm-hearted, overfriendly; quick-witted, lavish, colorful; given to extravagant speech and gestures; its people are travellers and wanderers by nature, moving, shifting, restless; swarming in Fords, in ocean liners; craving entertainment; volatile.
1939 A Peculiar Treasure, ch.1.

95 It was part of the Texas ritual… We know about champagne and caviar but we talk hog and hominy.
1952 Giant, ch.2.

96 A woman can look both moral and exciting—if she also looks as if it was quite a struggle.
1954 In Reader's Digest, Dec.

97 Science had married the wilderness and was taming the savage shrew.
1958 Of Alaska. Ice Palace.

98 Being an old maid is like death by drowning, a really delightful sensation after you cease to struggle.

Quoted in 'Completing the Circle', in R E Drennan Wit's End (1973).

99 Dinner parties are for eating, not mating.
Reminder to hostesses who only invite people in pairs. In the New York Times, 25 Sep 1984.

Ferdinand I   1503–64

Holy Roman Emperor from 1558, heir to his elder brother, Charles V, whom he joined in battling against Ottoman incursions. He was mainly responsible for the compromise at Augsburg (1555) which ended the religious wars.

1 Fiat justitia et pereat mundus.
Let justice be done, though the world may perish.
Motto.
➤ See Watson 891:1.

Ferguson, Sir Alex   1941–

Scottish football manager. In 1999 he led Manchester United to the treble (the League Championship, FA Cup and European Championship).

2 Never use sarcasm on players. It doesn't work.
2002 In the Observer, 19 May.

Ferguson, Niall   1964–

Scottish historian.

3 It is of course a truth universally acknowledged that large overseas military commitments cannot be sustained without even larger economic resources.
2004 Colossus: The Rise and Fall of the American Empire.

4 The United States today is an empire—but a peculiar kind of empire. It is vastly wealthy. It is militarily peerless. It has astonishing cultural reach. Yet by comparison with other empires it often struggles to impose its will beyond its shores.
2004 Colossus: The Rise and Fall of the American Empire.

Ferguson, Sir Samuel   1810–86

Irish poet and Celtic scholar, president of the Royal Irish Academy and a key figure in the study of early Irish art. His spirited poetry draws on Irish myth.

5 Wider comprehensions, deeper insights to the dead belong:—
Since for Love thou wakest not, sleeper, yet awake for sake of Song!
c.1864 'The Tain-Quest'.

Fergusson, Robert   1750–74

Scottish poet, much admired by Burns. He wrote primarily of Edinburgh life and died in its lunatic asylum aged 24.

6 For thof ye had as wise a snout on
As Shakespeare or Sir Isaac Newton,
Your judgement fouk wou'd hae a doubt on,
I'll tak my aith,
Till they cou'd see ye wi' a suit on
O' gude Braid Claith.
1772 'Braid Claith', stanza 9.

7 Wanwordy, crazy, dinsome thing,
As e'er was fram'd to jow or ring,
What gar'd them sic in steeple hing
They ken themsel',

But weel wat I they coudna bring
Waur sounds frae hell.
1772 'To the Tron-Kirk Bell', stanza 1.

8 Auld Reikie! wale o' ilka town
That Scotland kens beneath the moon;
Whare couthy chiels at e'ening meet
Their bizzing craigs and mous to weet.
1773 'Auld Reikie, A Poem'.

9 Now gae your wa's—Tho'anes as gude
As ever happit flesh and blude,
Yet part we maun—the case sae hard is,
Amang the writers and the bardies
That lang they'll brook the auld I trow,
Or neibours cry, 'Weel brook the new'.
1773 'To My Auld Breeks'.

Ferlinghetti, Lawrence 1919–

US poet and publisher. A member of the Beat Generation of poets, he founded the important radical bookstore and publishing house, City Lights, in San Francisco.

10 A Coney Island of the Mind.
1958 Title of book.

11 the poet like an acrobat
climbs on rime
to a high wire of his own making.
1958 'A Coney Island of the Mind', section 15.

12 I have a feeling I'm falling
on rare occasions
but most of the time I have my feet on the ground
I can't help it if the ground itself is falling.
1973 'Mock Confessional'.

13 For even bad poetry has relevance
for what it does not say
for what it leaves out.
1988 'Uses of Poetry'.

14 As I get older I perceive
Life has its tail in its mouth.
1988 'Poet as Fisherman'.

Fermat, Pierre de 1601–65

French lawyer, mathematician and founder of number theory. A great deal of his fame stems from Fermat's Last Theorem.

15 To divide a cube into two other cubes, a fourth power or in general any power whatever into two powers of the same denomination above the second is impossible, and I have assuredly found an admirable proof of this, but the margin is too narrow to contain it.
Scribbled note in the margins of his copy of Diophantus's *Arithmetica*. He did not live to provide the promised proof, and the conjecture became famous as Fermat's Last Theorem. In 1993 Andrew Wiles, a British mathematician, claimed to have discovered the proof.

Fermi, Enrico 1901–54

Italian-born US physicist, discoverer of the element neptunium and winner of the 1938 Nobel prize. In 1942 he created the first self-sustaining chain reaction in uranium, which led to the atomic bomb.

16 Whatever Nature has in store for mankind, unpleasant as it may be, men must accept, for ignorance is never better than knowledge.
Quoted in Laura Fermi *Atoms in the Family* (1954).

Fern, Fanny née *Willis* 1811–72

US writer, whose witty sketches were collected in *Fern Leaves from Fanny's Portfolio* (1853). When he made his famous attack on women writers, Nathaniel Hawthorne was careful to exempt her.

17 Well, it is a humiliating reflection, that the straightest road to a man's heart is through his palate.
1854 *Fern Leaves from Fanny's Portfolio, Second Series*, 'Hungry Husbands'. Often quoted as 'The way to a man's heart is through his stomach.'

Fernández, Macedonio 1874–1952

Argentinian philosopher, poet and novelist. He lived a secluded life, reluctant to publish his manuscripts. His philosophical postulates anticipate the work of later writers such as Borges and Bioy Casares.

18 *Todo se ha escrito, todo se ha dicho, todo se ha hecho, oyó Dios que le decían y aún no había creado el mundo, todavía no había nada. También eso ya me lo han dicho, repuso quizá desde la vieja, hendida Nada. Y comenzó.*
Everything has been written, everything has been said, everything has been made: that's what God heard before creating the world, when there was nothing yet. I have also heard that one, he may have answered from the old, split Nothingness. And then he began.
1967 *Museo de la novela de la Eterna* ('The Museum of Eternity's Novel'), 'Prólogo a la eternidad'.

Ferré, Rosario 1943–

Puerto Rican novelist and critic, who has lived and taught in both Puerto Rico and the US.

19 *Dios sólo nos tiene aquí prestados, en este valle de lágrimas no estamos más que de paso. Si llegara algún día a pensar que ha perdido a su hija para el mundo de los hombres, la habrá ganado para el de los ángeles.*
God has us here only on loan, we are transitory in this vale of tears. If you ever come to think that you have lost your daughter to the world of men, think also that you have given her to that of the angels.
1976 *La Bella Durmiente* ('Sleeping Beauty').

Ferrier, Kathleen 1912–53

English contralto. The range and richness of her voice, together with her remarkable technical control, rapidly won her a great reputation until her early death from cancer.

20 Now I'll have eine kleine pause.
1953 Last words. Quoted in Gerald Moore *Am I Too Loud?* (1962).

Feuerbach, Ludwig 1804–72

German philosopher, famous for his interpretation of Christian doctrine in secular terms and for its adaptation by Karl Marx.

21 While Socrates empties the cup of poison with unshaken soul, Christ exclaims, 'If it is possible, let this cup pass from me'. Christ in this respect is the self-confession of human sensibility.
1841 *Das Wesen des Christentums* (translated by Mary Ann Evans (George Eliot) as *The Essence of Christianity*, 1854).

22 The power of miracle is the power of imagination.

1841 *Das Wesen des Christentums* (translated by Mary Ann Evans (George Eliot) as *The Essence of Christianity*, 1854).

23 *Der Mensch ist, was er isst.*
Man is what he eats.
Quoted in Jacob Moleschott *Lehre der Nahrungsmittel: Für das Volk* (1850).

Feynman, Richard P(hillips) 1918–88

US physicist who shared (1965) the Nobel prize in physics for his work on quantum electrodynamics.

24 We have a habit in writing articles published in scientific journals to make the work as finished as possible, to cover up all the tracks, to not worry about the blind alleys or describe how you had the wrong idea first, and so on. So there isn't any place to publish, in a dignified manner, what you actually did in order to do the work.
1966 Nobel lecture.

25 You know how it always is, every new idea, it takes a generation or two until it becomes obvious that there's no real problem. I cannot define the real problem, therefore I suspect there's no real problem, but I'm not sure there's no real problem.
1982 Explaining his feelings on quantum mechanics. In the *International Journal of Theoretical Physics*, vol.21.

26 If I could explain it to the average person, I wouldn't have been worth the Nobel prize.
1985 In *People Magazine*, 22 Jul.

27 For a successful technology, reality must take precedence over public relations, for nature cannot be fooled.
1988 *What Do YOU Care What Other People Think?*

Fiedler, Leslie A(aron) 1917–92

US critic and novelist. His reputation rests on his influential and often controversial books on US 'literary anthropology', of which *Love and Death in the American Novel* (1960) is the best known.

28 Come Back To The Raft Again, Huck Honey!
1955 Title of essay on the repressed homoerotic undercurrent in US writing.

29 To be an American (unlike being English or French or whatever) is precisely to *imagine* a destiny rather than to inherit one; since we have always been, insofar as we are Americans at all, inhabitants of myth rather than history.
1969 'Cross the Border—Close the Gap', in *Playboy*, Dec.

Field, Barron 1786–1846

Australian jurist, born in London. He went to Sydney in 1817 as Judge of the New South Wales Supreme Court and published the first collection of Australian verse, *First Fruits of Australian Poetry* (1819).

30 Kangaroo, Kangaroo!
Thou Spirit of Australia,
That redeems from utter failure,
From perfect desolation,
And warrants the creation
Of this fifth part of the Earth.
1819 *First Fruits of Australian Poetry*, 'The Kangaroo'.

Field, Eugene 1850–95

US writer and theatre critic. A columnist for the *Chicago*

Morning News, he achieved a reputation as a humorist and poet with his column 'Sharps and Flats'. He also published several books of children's verse.

31 Mr Creston Clarke played King Lear at the Tabor Grand last night. All through five acts of Shakespeare's tragedy he played the king as though under momentary apprehension that someone else was about to play the ace.
c.1880 Attributed review in the *Denver Post*.

32 Wynken, Blynken, and Nod one night
Sailed off in a wooden shoe—
Sailed on a river of crystal light,
Into a sea of dew.
1889 'Wynken, Blynken, and Nod'.

33 I never lost a little fish. Yes, I am free to say.
It always was the biggest fish I caught that got away.
Attributed.

Field, Frank 1942–

English Labour politician. Director of the Child Poverty Action Group (1969–79) and the Low Pay Unit (1974–80), he became an MP in 1979 and has campaigned strenuously for social justice.

34 The House of Lords is a model of how to care for the elderly.
1981 In the *Observer*, 24 May.

Fielding, Henry 1707–54

English novelist and playwright. After the introduction of the Theatrical Licensing Act in 1737 he turned to fiction, with works such as *The Adventures of Joseph Andrews* (1742), *Tom Jones* (1749) and *Amelia* (1751). He died in Lisbon.

35 Love and scandal are the best sweeteners of tea.
1728 *Love in Several Masques*, act 4, sc.11.

36 Map me no maps, sir, my head is a map, a map of the whole world.
1730 *Rape upon Rape*, act 2, sc.5.

37 Oh! The roast beef of England,
And old England's roast beef!
1731 *Grub Street Opera*, act 3, sc.3.

38 All Nature wears one universal grin.
1731 *Tom Thumb the Great*, act 1, sc.1.

39 I am as sober as a Judge.
1734 *Don Quixote in England*, act 3, sc.14.

40 He in a few minutes ravished this fair creature, or at least would have ravished her, if she had not, by a timely compliance, prevented him.
1743 *Jonathan Wild*, bk.3, ch.7.

41 Thwackum was for doing justice, and leaving mercy to heaven.
1749 *Tom Jones*, bk.3, ch.10.

42 What is commonly called love, namely the desire of satisfying a voracious appetite with a certain quantity of delicate white human flesh.
1749 *Tom Jones*, bk.6, ch.1.

43 His designs were strictly honourable, as the phrase is; that is, to rob a lady of her fortune by way of marriage.
1749 *Tom Jones*, bk.11, ch.4.

44 It hath been often said, that it is not death, but dying, which is terrible.
1751 *Amelia*, bk.3, ch.4.

45 One fool at least in every married couple.
1751 *Amelia*, bk.9, ch.4.

Fields, Dorothy 1905–74

US author and lyricist, daughter of comedian Lew Fields. She wrote the books and lyrics for many Broadway shows and films, often with Jimmy McHugh or Jerome Kern.

46 Grab your coat, and get your hat,
Leave your worry on the doorstep,
Just direct your feet
To the sunny side of the street.
1930 'On the Sunny Side of the Street'.

47 I might as well play bridge with my old maid aunts
I haven't got a chance
This is a fine romance.
1934 'A Fine Romance', song featured in the film *Swing Time* (music by Jerome Kern).

Fields, W C originally *William Claude Dukenfield* 1880–1946

US comedian. He wrote and performed in several classic comedies including *The Bank Dick* (1940), *My Little Chickadee* (1940) and *Never Give a Sucker an Even Break* (1940).

48 It ain't a fit night out for man or beast.
1932 *The Fatal Glass of Beer*.

49 Women are like elephants to me. I like to look at them, but I wouldn't want to own one.
1935 *Mississippi*.

50 Egbert, is it true that married people live longer?
No, it just seems longer.
1940 *The Bank Dick*.

51 Never Give a Sucker an Even Break.
1941 Title of film, but an earlier catchphrase of Fields's that may have originated in the 1923 film *Poppy*.

52 I was in love with a beautiful blonde once, dear. She drove me to drink. That's the one thing I'm indebted to her for.
1941 *Never Give a Sucker an Even Break*.

53 Anybody who hates children and dogs can't be all bad.
Attributed.

54 Fish fuck in it.
Attributed, his reason for not drinking water.

Fiennes, Sir Ranulph 1944–

English explorer.

55 To write about hell it helps if you have been there.
2004 *Captain Scott*.

Fierstein, Harvey Forbes 1954–

US playwright and actor. He began as a female impersonator and acts on stage and screen. He has won awards for the semi-autobiographical *Torch Song Trilogy* (produced 1982) and for the book of the Broadway musical *La Cage Aux Folles* (1983).

56 I assume everyone is gay, unless told otherwise.
1994 In *Life*, Jan.

50 Cent originally *Curtis Jackson* 1976–

US rapper.

57 Where I grew up if you have two parents you're spoilt.
2003 In the *Sunday Times*, 15 Jun.

Findley, Timothy 1931–2002

Canadian writer and actor. His novels include *The Wars* (1977), *The Piano Man's Daughter* (1995) and *Pilgrim* (1999).

58 He did the thing that no one else would even dare to think of doing. And that to me's as good a definition of a 'hero' as you'll get. Even when the thing that's done is something of which you disapprove.
1977 Juliet D'Orsey. *The Wars*, pt.1, section 3.

59 Dead men are serious.
1977 *The Wars*, pt.1, section 20.

60 Any man whose love of horses is stronger than his fear of being an absurdity is all right with me.
1977 Rodwell. *The Wars*, pt.2, section 8.

Firbank, (Arthur Annesley) Ronald 1886–1926

English novelist. Solitary and somewhat eccentric, he wrote slight but witty and innovative novels. His works include *Valmouth* (1919) and *Prancing Nigger* (1924).

61 There was a pause—just long enough for an angel to pass, flying slowly.
1915 *Vainglory*, ch.6.

62 The world is disgracefully managed, one hardly knows to whom to complain.
1915 *Vainglory*, ch.10.

63 All millionaires love a baked apple.
1915 *Vainglory*, ch.13.

64 She stands, I fear, poor thing, now, for something younger than she looks.
1919 *Valmouth*, ch.1.

65 'I know of no joy,' she airily began, 'greater than a cool white dress after the sweetness of confession.'
1919 *Valmouth*, ch.4.

66 There was really no joy in pouring out one's sins while he sat assiduously picking his nose.
1919 *Valmouth*, ch.6.

67 His Weariness the Prince entered the room in all his tinted orders.
1923 *The Flower Beneath the Foot*, ch.1.

68 'O! help me heaven,' she prayed, 'to be decorative and to do right!'
1923 *The Flower Beneath the Foot*, ch.2.

69 Beneath the strain of expectation even the little iced sugar cakes upon the tea-table looked green with worry.
1923 *The Flower Beneath the Foot*, ch.3.

70 Looking back, I remember the average curate at home as something between a eunuch and a snigger.
1923 *The Flower Beneath the Foot*, ch.4.

71 'Basta!' his master replied with all the brilliant glibness of the Berlitz-school.
1923 *The Flower Beneath the Foot*, ch.5.

72 She looks at other women as if she would inhale them.
1923 *The Flower Beneath the Foot*, ch.5.

73 'I've never travelled,' Dona Consolation blandly confessed, 'but I dare say, dear, you can't judge Egypt by Aïda.'
1926 *Concerning the Eccentricities of Cardinal Pirelli*, ch.9.

Fish, Michael 1944–

English weather forecaster.

74 A woman rang to say she heard there was a hurricane on the way. Well don't worry, there isn't.
1987 Television weather forecast prior to severe gales in southern England, 15 Oct.

Fisher (of Lambeth), Geoffrey Francis Fisher, Baron 1887–1972

English prelate and Archbishop of Canterbury (1945–61). He officiated at the coronation of Elizabeth II in Westminster Abbey (1953).

75 The long and distressing controversy over capital punishment is very unfair to anyone meditating murder.
1957 In the *Sunday Times*, 24 Feb.

Fisher, H(erbert) A(lbert) L(aurens) 1865–1940

English historian. As Education Minister (1916–22) he sponsored the Fisher Act (1918). He wrote on Napoleon, and is best known for his *History of Europe* (1936).

76 Men wiser and more learned than I have discerned in history a plot, a rhythm, a predetermined pattern. Those harmonies are concealed from me. I can see only one emergency following upon another, as wave follows upon wave; only one real fact with respect to which, since it is unique, there can be no generalizations. Only one safe rule for the historian: that he should recognize in the development of human destinies the play of the contingent and the unforeseen.
1936 *History of Europe*, introduction.

77 Purity of race does not exist. Europe is a continent of energetic mongrels.
1936 *History of Europe*, ch.1.

Fisher, M(ary) F(rances) K(ennedy) 1908–92

US cookery writer.

78 Sharing food with another human being is an intimate act that should not be indulged in lightly.
1949 *An Alphabet for Gourmets*, 'A Is for Dining Alone'.

79 In America we eat, collectively, with a glum urge for food to fill us. We are ignorant of flavor. We are as a nation taste-blind.
1976 *The Art of Eating*.

Fiske, John 1842–1901

US historian, tutor and librarian at Harvard. He wrote many popular books on US history, Spencerian philosophy and Darwinism.

80 The element of chance…is expelled. Nobody would now waste his time in theorizing about a fortuitous concourse of atoms. We have so far spelled out the history of creation as to see that all has been done in strict accordance with law. The method has been the method of evolution, and the more we study it the more do we discern in it intelligible coherence.
1900 *Through Nature to God*.

Fitt, Gerry (Gerard) Fitt, Baron 1926–

Northern Ireland politician.

81 The people have spoken and the politicians have had to listen.
1998 In the *Sunday Telegraph*, 24 May.

Fitzgerald, Edward 1809–83

English scholar, poet and translator, a friend of Thackeray, Carlisle and Tennyson. His translation of the *Rubáiyát of Omar Khayyám* was first published anonymously in 1859.

82 Awake! for Morning in the bowl of night
Has flung the stone that puts the stars to flight:
And Lo! the Hunter of the East has caught
The Sultan's turret in a noose of light.
1859 *The Rubáiyát of Omar Khayyám of Naishapur*, stanza 1.

83 Here with a loaf of bread beneath the bough,
A flask of wine, a book of verse—and Thou
Beside me singing in the wilderness—
And wilderness is paradise enow.
1859 *The Rubáiyát of Omar Khayyám of Naishapur*, stanza 12. In the 1879 edn this was changed to 'A Book of Verses underneath the Bough, / A Jug of Wine, a loaf of Bread—and Thou / Beside me singing in the Wilderness— / Oh, Wilderness were Paradise enow!'

84 The moving finger writes; and, having writ,
Moves on: nor all thy piety nor wit
Shall lure it back to cancel half a line,
Nor all thy tears wash out a word of it.
1859 *The Rubáiyát of Omar Khayyám of Naishapur*, stanza 51.

85 Drink! for you know not whence you came, nor why:
Drink! for you know not why you go nor where.
1859 *The Rubáiyát of Omar Khayyám of Naishapur*, stanza 74.

86 And when Thyself with shining foot shall pass
Among the guests star-scattered on the grass,
And in thy joyous errand reach the spot
Where I made one—turn down an empty glass!
1859 *The Rubáiyát of Omar Khayyám of Naishapur*, stanza 75. In the 1879 edition this was changed to 'And when like her, O Saki, you shall pass…'.

Fitzgerald, F(rancis) Scott Key 1896–1940

US novelist who epitomized the Jazz Age in his best-known book, *The Great Gatsby* (1925). He wrote about US expatriates in *Tender is the Night* (1934).

87 At eighteen our convictions are hills from which we look; at forty-five they are caves in which we hide.
1920 'Bernice Bobs Her Hair', in the *Saturday Evening Post*, 1 May.

88 The wise writer, I think, writes for the youth of his own generation, the critics of the next, and the schoolmasters of ever afterward.
1920 Interview in the *New York Tribune*, 7 May.

89 She had once been a Catholic, but discovering that priests were infinitely more attentive when she was in process of losing or regaining faith in Mother Church, she maintained an enchantingly wavering attitude.
1921 Of Beatrice Blaine. *This Side of Paradise*, bk.1, ch.1.

90 If I start to hold somebody's hand they laugh at me, and *let* me, just as if it wasn't part of them. As soon as I get hold of a hand they sort of disconnect it from the rest of them.
1921 *This Side of Paradise*, bk.1, ch.1.

91 The Beautiful and the Damned.
1922 Title of novel.

92 Personality is an unbroken series of successful gestures.
1925 *The Great Gatsby*, ch.1.

93 One of those men who reach such an acute limited excellence at twenty-one that everything afterward savors of anti-climax.
1925 Of Tom Buchanan. *The Great Gatsby*, ch.1.

94 In his blue gardens, men and girls came and went like moths among the whisperings and the champagne and the stars.
1925 *The Great Gatsby*, ch.3.

95 Everyone suspects himself of at least one of the cardinal virtues, and this is mine: I am one of the few honest people that I have ever known.
1925 Nick Carraway, the narrator. *The Great Gatsby*, ch.3.

96 There are only the pursued, the pursuing, the busy, and the tired.
1925 *The Great Gatsby*, ch.4.

97 Reach me a rose, honey, and pour me a last drop into that there crystal glass.
1925 *The Great Gatsby*, ch.4.

98 Her voice is full of money.
1925 *The Great Gatsby*, ch.7.

99 They were careless people, Tom and Daisy—they smashed up things and creatures and then retreated back into their money or their vast carelessness, or whatever it was that kept them together, and let other people clean up the mess they had made.
1925 *The Great Gatsby*, ch.9.

1 And as the moon rose higher the unessential houses began to melt away until gradually I became aware of the old island here that flowered once for Dutch sailors' eyes—a fresh, green breast of the new world… For a transitory enchanted moment man must have held his breath in the presence of this continent, compelled into an aesthetic contemplation he neither understood nor desired, face to face for the last time in history with something commensurate to his capacity for wonder.
1925 *The Great Gatsby*, ch.9.

2 Gatsby believed in the green light, the orgiastic future that year by year recedes before us. It eluded us then, but that's no matter—to-morrow we will run faster, stretch out our arms further… And one fine morning… So we beat on, boats against the current, borne back ceaselessly into the past.
1925 *The Great Gatsby*, ch.9.

3 Let me tell you about the very rich. They are different from you and me.
1926 *All the Sad Young Men*, 'The Rich Boy'. Hemingway published an ironic rejoinder in 'The Snows of Kilimanjaro': 'Yes, they have more money'.
☛ *See Hemingway 394:12.*

4 Though the Jazz Age continued, it became less and less of an affair of youth. The sequel was like a children's party taken over by the elders.
1931 'Echoes of the Jazz Age', *Scribner's Magazine*, Nov.

5 Mostly, we authors repeat ourselves—that's the truth.
1933 'One Hundred False Starts', in the *Saturday Evening Post*, 4 Mar.

6 Tender is the Night.
1934 Title of novel.

7 When people are taken out of their depths they lose their heads, no matter how charming a bluff they may put up.
1934 *Tender is the Night*, bk.3, ch.12.

8 The test of a first-rate intelligence is the ability to hold two opposed ideas in the mind at the same time, and still retain the ability to function.
1936 'The Crack-Up', in *Esquire*, Feb.

9 In a real dark night of the soul, it is always three o'clock in the morning, day after day.
1936 'Handle With Care', in *Esquire*, Mar.

10 Often I think writing is a sheer paring away of oneself leaving always something thinner, barer, more meagre.
1940 Letter, 27 Apr.

11 The faces of most American women over thirty are relief maps of petulant and bewildered unhappiness.
1940 Letter, 5 Oct.

12 It's not a slam at *you* when people are rude—it's a slam at the people they've met before.
1941 *The Last Tycoon*, ch.1.

13 No grand idea was ever born in a conference, but a lot of foolish ideas have died there.
Note Books, E, in Edmund Wilson (ed) *The Crack-Up* (1945).

14 Show me a hero and I will write you a tragedy.
Note Books, E, in Edmund Wilson (ed) *The Crack-Up* (1945).

15 Great art is the contempt of a great man for small art.
Note Books, L, in Edmund Wilson (ed) *The Crack-Up* (1945).

16 When the first-rate author wants an exquisite heroine or a lovely morning, he finds that all the superlatives have been worn shoddy by his inferiors. It should be a rule that bad writers must start with plain heroines and ordinary mornings, and, if they are able, work up to something better.
Note Books, L, in Edmund Wilson (ed) *The Crack-Up* (1945).

Fitzgerald, Penelope Mary 1916–2000

English novelist and biographer. She won the Booker Prize in 1979 for *Offshore*.

17 Patience is passive, resignation is active.
1986 *Innocence*.

18 A human being is old when he has survived long enough to name, with absolute confidence, a year, one of the next thirty, which he won't be there to see.
A House of Air—Selected Writings, 'Last Words' (2003).

19 Twice in your life you know that you are approved of by everyone: when you learn to walk, and when you learn to read.
A House of Air—Selected Writings, 'Schooldays' (2003).

Flanagan, Bud *stage name of* Robert Winthrop 1896–1968

English comedian. He was immensely popular both as one of the Crazy Gang of comedians and in a duo with Chesney Allen.

20 Underneath the Arches,
I dream my dreams away,
Underneath the Arches,
On cobble-stones I lay.
1932 'Underneath the Arches' (song).

21 No dog can go as fast as the money you bet on him.
Quoted in Colin Jarman *The Guinness Dictionary of Sports Quotations* (1990).

Flanders, Michael and Swann, Donald 1922–75, 1923–94

English songwriting team, who made their name with *At the Drop of a Hat* (1956).

22 Mud! Mud! Glorious mud!
Nothing quite like it for cooling the blood.
So follow me, follow,
Down to the hollow,
And there let us wallow
In glorious mud.
1952 'The Hippopotamus'.

23 Eating people is wrong!
1956 'The Reluctant Cannibal'. Malcolm Bradbury took the phrase as the title of his 1959 novel.

24 Ma's out, Pa's out—let's talk rude:
Pee, po, belly, bum, drawers.
c.1956 'P, P, B, B, D'.

25 The English, the English, the English are best!
I wouldn't give tuppence for all of the rest!
1963 'Song of Patriotic Prejudice'.

Flaubert, Anne Justine Caroline 1793–1872

Mother of Gustave Flaubert.

26 Your mania for sentences has dried up your heart.
To her son. Quoted in D J Enright *A Mania for Sentences* (1983), p.101.

Flaubert, Gustave 1821–80

French novelist, master of the realistic novel. He studied law at Paris before turning to writing. His works include *Madame Bovary* (1857) and *Trois contes* (1877). He intended to include a *Dictionnaire des idées reçues* in the second volume of *Bouvard et Pécuchet*.

27 *Je suis autant Chinois que Français.*
I am as much Chinese as French.
1846 Letter to Mme Louise Colet, 8 Aug.

28 *L'Idée seule est éternelle et nécessaire.*
The idea alone is eternal and necessary.
1846 Letter to Mme Louise Colet, 9 Aug.

29 *Il ne faut pas toujours croire que le sentiment soit tout. Dans les arts, il n'est rien sans la forme.*
You must not think that feeling is everything. Art is nothing without form.
1846 Letter to Mme Louise Colet, 12 Aug.

30 *On fait de la critique quand on ne peut pas faire de l'art, de même qu'on se met mouchard quand on ne peut pas être soldat.*
Someone is a critic when he cannot be an artist in the same way that a man becomes an informer when he cannot be a soldier.
1846 Letter to Mme Louise Colet, 22 Oct.

31 *Les oeuvres les plus belles sont celles où il y a le moins de matière; plus l'expression se rapproche de la pensée, plus le mot colle dessus et disparaît, plus c'est beau. Je crois que l'avenir de l'art est dans ces voies.*
The most beautiful works are those that have the least content; the closer the expression is to the thought, the more indistinguishable the word from the content, the more beautiful is the work. I believe that the future of art lies in this direction.

1852 Letter to Mme Louise Colet, 16 Jan.

32 *La courtisane est un mythe. Jamais une femme n'a inventé une débauche.*
The courtesan is a myth. No woman has ever invented any new sensual pleasure.
1852 Letter to Mme Louise Colet, Aug.

33 *L'amour, croyait-elle, devait arriver tout à coup, avec de grands éclats et des fulgurations.*
She believed that love should appear instantaneously, with the brilliance of a lightning storm.
1857 *Madame Bovary*, pt.1, ch.8.

34 *La parole humaine est comme un chaudron fêlé où nous battons des mélodies à faire danser les ours, quand on voudrait attendrir les étoiles.*
Human speech is like a cracked kettle on which we beat out tunes for bears to dance to, when all the time we are longing to move the stars to pity.
1857 *Madame Bovary*, pt.1, ch.12.

35 *Le charme de la nouveauté, peu à peu tombant comme un vêtement, laissait voir à nu l'éternelle monotonie de la passion, qui a toujours les mêmes formes et le même langage.*
The charm of novelty, falling little by little like a robe, revealed the eternal monotony of passion, which has always the same forms and the same language.
1857 *Madame Bovary*, pt.2, ch.12.

36 *Il faut écrire pour soi, avant tout. C'est la seule chance de faire beau.*
It is necessary to write for oneself, above all. It is the only hope of creating something beautiful.
1858 Letter to Mlle Leroyer de Chantepie, 11 Jul.

37 *Un romancier, selon moi, n'a pas le droit de dire son avis sur les choses de ce monde. Il doit, dans sa vocation, imiter Dieu dans la sienne, c'est-à-dire faire et se taire.*
A novelist, in my opinion, does not have the right to give advice on the affairs of the world. He must, in his occupation, imitate God in His; that is to say, create and keep quiet.
1866 Letter to Mlle Bosquet.

38 *Axiome: la haine du bourgeois est le commencement de la vertu.*
Axiom: Hatred of the bourgeois is the beginning of wisdom.
1867 Letter to George Sand, 10 May.

39 *Il tournait dans son désir, comme un prisonnier dans son cachot.*
He was circling in his desire, like a prisoner in his dungeon.
1869 *L'Education sentimentale*, pt.1, ch.5.

40 My kingdom is as wide as the universe and my wants have no limits. I go forward always, freeing spirits and weighing words, without fear, without compassion, without love, without God. I am called science.
1874 *The Temptation of St Antony*.

41 *Antiquité. —en tout ce qui s'y rapporte: Est poncif, embêtant! etc.*
Antiquity. And everything to do with it, clichéd and boring.
Bouvard et Pécuchet avec un choix des scénarios, du Sottisier, L'Album de la Marquise et Le Dictionnaire des idées reçues.
(published 1881, translated by Geoffrey Wall, 1994).

42 *Homère. Célèbre par sa façon de rire: rire homérique.*
N'a jamais existé.
Homer. Famous for his laugh. 'Homeric laughter'. Never
existed.
Bouvard et Pécuchet avec un choix des scénarios, du Sottisier,
L'Album de la Marquise et Le Dictionnaire des idées reçues.
(published 1881, translated by Geoffrey Wall, 1994).

43 *Latin. Langage naturel de l'homme. Gâte l'écriture. Est*
seulement utile pour comprendre les inscriptions des
fontaines publiques. Il faut se méfier des citations en
Latin; elles cachent toujours quelque chose de leste.
Latin. Man's natural language. Spoils your style. Useful
only for reading the inscriptions on public fountains.
Beware of quotations in Latin: they always conceal
something improper.
Bouvard et Pécuchet avec un choix des scénarios, du Sottisier,
L'Album de la Marquise et Le Dictionnaire des idées reçues.
(published 1881, translated by Geoffrey Wall, 1994).

Flecker, James Elroy   1884–1915

English poet. He studied Oriental languages and joined the
consular service, symptoms of a fascination with the East
which is reflected in much of his verse.

44 O friend unseen, unborn, unknown,
Student of our sweet English tongue,
Read out my words at night, alone:
I was a poet, I was young.
1910 'To a Poet a Thousand Years Hence'.

45 We who with songs beguile your pilgrimage
And swear that Beauty lives though lilies die,
We Poets of the proud old lineage
Who sing to find your hearts, we know not why—
What shall we tell you? Tales, marvellous tales
Of ships and stars and isles where good men rest.
1913 'The Golden Journey to Samarkand', epilogue.

46 For lust of knowing what should not be known,
We take the Golden Road to Samarkand.
1913 'The Golden Journey to Samarkand', epilogue.

47 How splendid in the morning glows the lily; with what
grace he throws
His supplication to the rose.
1913 'Yasmin'.

48 The dragon-green, the luminous, the dark, the serpent-
haunted sea.
1913 'The Gates of Damascus'.

49 For pines are gossip pines the wide world through
And full of runic tales to sigh or sing.
1913 'Brumana'.

50 Half to forget the wandering and pain,
Half to remember days that have gone by,
And dream and dream that I am home again!
1913 'Brumana'.

51 West of these out to seas colder than the Hebrides
I must go
Where the fleet of stars is anchored and the young
Star captains glow.
1913 'The Dying Patriot'.

52 A ship, an isle, a sickle moon—
With few but with how splendid stars
The mirrors of the sea are strewn
Between their silver bars!

1913 'A Ship, an Isle, a Sickle Moon'.

53 I have seen old ships sail like swans asleep.
1915 'The Old Ships'.

Fleming, Ian Lancaster   1908–64

English novelist. He is best known for his creation of the hugely
popular secret service agent, James Bond.

54 Live and Let Die.
1954 Title of novel.

55 From Russia with Love.
1957 Title of novel.

56 I would like a medium Vodka dry Martini—with a slice of
lemon peel. Shaken and not stirred, please. I would
prefer Russian or Polish vodka.
1958 *Dr No*, ch.14.

Fleming, Marjory   1803–11

Scottish child writer, the subject of an essay by Dr John Brown
which popularized her image as 'Pet Marjorie' and invented an
affectionate relationship with her distant relative Walter Scott.

57 The most Devilish thing is 8 times 8 and 7 times 7 it is
what nature itselfe cant endure.
1810 'Journal 2' in F Sidgwick (ed) *The Complete Marjory*
Fleming (1934).

58 Many girls have not the advantage I have and I [am] very
very glad that satan has not geven me boils and many
other Misfortunes.
1810 'Journal 2' in F Sidgwick (ed) *The Complete Marjory*
Fleming (1934).

59 To Day I pronunced a word which should never come out
of a ladys lips it was that I called John a Impudent Bitch.
1810 'Journal 2' in F Sidgwick (ed) *The Complete Marjory*
Fleming (1934).

60 I would rather have a man dog then a women dog
because they do not bear like women dogs, it is a hard
case it is shoking.
1810 'Journal 2' in F Sidgwick (ed) *The Complete Marjory*
Fleming (1934).

61 I hope I will be religious again but as for reganing my
charecter I despare for it.
1810 'Journal 2' in F Sidgwick (ed) *The Complete Marjory*
Fleming (1934).

62 An annibaptist is a thing I am not a member of:—I am a
Pisplikan just now & a Prisbeteren at Kercaldy my native
town which thugh dirty is clein in the country.
1811 'Journal 3' in F Sidgwick (ed) *The Complete Marjory*
Fleming (1934).

63 Love is a very papithatick thing as well as troublesom &
tiresome but O Isabella forbid me to speak about it.
1811 'Journal 3' in F Sidgwick (ed) *The Complete Marjory*
Fleming (1934).

Fletcher (of Saltoun), Andrew   1655–1716

Scottish patriot, fierce opponent of Stuart policy and of union
with England. After the Union he retired in disgust and
devoted himself to agriculture.

64 This will be the issue of that darling Plea, of being one
and not two; it will be turned upon the Scots with a
Vengeance; and their 45 Scots Members may dance
round to all Eternity, in this Trap of their own making.
1706 *State of the Controversy betwixt United and Separate*

Parliaments, a critique of the proposed Union.

65 It is only fit for the slaves who sold it.
1707 Of Scotland, on leaving it after the signing of the Treaty of Union. Quoted in G W T Ormond *Fletcher of Saltoun* (1897).

Fletcher, John 1579–1625

English dramatist, who collaborated with Beaumont until the latter's marriage in 1613, and also with Shakespeare, Jonson, Middleton, Massinger and Rowley, as well as writing on his own. He died of plague.

66 Care-charming Sleep, thou easer of all woes,
Brother to Death.
c.1610–1614 *Valentinian*, act 5, sc.7.

67 Best while you have it use your breath,
There is no drinking after death.
1616 *The Bloody Brother*, act 2, sc.2, song (with Ben Jonson, George Chapman and Philip Massinger).

68 And he that will go to bed sober,
Falls with the leaf still in October.
1616 *The Bloody Brother*, act 2, sc.2, song (with Ben Jonson, George Chapman and Philip Massinger).

69 We are stark naught all, bad's the best of us.
1616 *The Bloody Brother*, act 4, sc.2 (with Ben Jonson, George Chapman and Philip Massinger).

70 We are beasts now, and the beasts are our masters.
c.1621 *The Wild-Goose Chase*, act 1, sc.1.

71 Blush at your faults.
c.1621 *The Wild-Goose Chase*, act 1, sc.1.

72 Give me the plump Venetian, fat, and lusty,
That meets me soft and supple, smiles upon me
As if a cup of full wine leaped to kiss me.
c.1621 *The Wild-Goose Chase*, act 1, sc.2.

73 Health and an able body are two jewels.
c. 1621 *The Wild-Goose Chase*, act 2, sc.1.

74 Nothing is thought rare
Which is not new and follow'd, yet we know
That what was worne some twenty yeare agoe,
Comes into grace againe.
c.1623 *The Noble Gentleman*, prologue.

75 Are you at ease now? Is your heart at rest?
Now you have got a shadow, an umbrella
To keep the scorching world's opinion
From your fair credit.
1624 *Rule a Wife and Have a Wife*, act 3, sc.1.

Florio, John c.1553–1625

English scholar, writer and translator, born of Italian Protestant family in London. His most famous work is his translation of Montaigne's *Essays* (1603); he also published an Italian–English dictionary, *A World of Words* (1598), and two compendiums of Italian proverbs.

76 England is the paradise of women, the purgatory of men, and the hell of horses.
1591 *Second Frutes*, ch.12.

Flynn, Errol 1909–59

Hollywood actor born in Tasmania. He starred in historical swashbucklers such as *Captain Blood* (1935), *The Adventures of Robin Hood* (1938) and *The Sea Hawk* (1940). His off-screen reputation for drinking, drug-taking and womanizing became legendary and eventually affected his career.

77 The public has always expected me to be a playboy and a decent chap never lets his public down.
Quoted in Gary Herman *The Book of Hollywood Quotes* (1979).

78 Inside this Hollywood playboy is a someway decent actor waiting for a chance to prove it. But, since Hollywood will never give me that chance, I drink to obliviate that decent actor.
Quoted in Michael Wilding and Pamela Wilcox *Apple Sauce* (1982).

Fo, Dario 1926–

Italian playwright and actor-manager, whose often controversial plays and revues deal with political themes. His plays include *Accidental Death of an Anarchist* (1970) and *Trumpets and Raspberries* (1984). He was awarded the Nobel prize for literature in 1997.

79 *Non si paga, non si paga.*
We won't pay, we won't pay.
1974 Play title, translated into English in 1981 as *Can't pay? Won't pay!*

Foch, Ferdinand 1851–1929

French marshal, born in Tarbes. He taught at the École de Guerre, and proved himself a great strategist at the Battles of the Marne and Ypres. He commanded the Allied armies in 1918.

80 *Mon centre cède, ma droite recule, situation excellente, j'attaque.*
My centre is giving way, my right is retreating, situation excellent, I am attacking.
1914 Message sent during the first Battle of the Marne, Sep. Quoted in R Recouly *Foch* (1919), ch.6.

81 *Ce n'est pas un traité de paix, c'est un armistice de vingt ans.*
This is not a peace treaty, it is an armistice for twenty years.
1919 At the signing of the Treaty of Versailles. Quoted in Paul Reynaud *Memoires* (1963), vol.2.

Follett, Ken 1949–

Welsh novelist.

82 They are the rent boys of politics.
2000 Of those who give off-the-record briefings against ministers. In the *Observer*, 2 Jul.

83 The polite fiction that the Prime Minister's advisers are responsible is absurd. Control-freak Tony doesn't let Alastair Campbell and Peter Mandelson go around saying anything they like… Peter isn't the Prince of Darkness, though he may be Lady Macbeth.
2000 In the *Observer*, 2 Jul.

Fontenelle, Bernard le Bovier de 1657–1757

French writer, the nephew of Corneille. He introduced mathematics and the natural sciences into the conversation of the salons, and expressed scientific ideas through literature. He was secretary of the Académie des Sciences (1699–1741).

84 *Ah! si l'on ôtait les chimères aux hommes, quel plaisir leur resterait?*
Oh! If man were robbed of his fantasies, what pleasure would be left him?
1683 *Dialogue des morts*.

85 *L'univers…je l'en estime plus depuis que je sais qu'il* *ressemble à une montre; il est surprenant que l'ordre de la nature, tout admirable qu'il est, ne roule que sur des choses si simples.*

I have come to esteem the universe more now that I know it resembles a watch; it is surprising that the order of nature, as admirable as it is, only runs on such simple things.

1686 *Entretiens sur la pluralité des mondes.*

86 *Les mouvements les plus naturels, et les plus ordinaires, sont ceux qui se font le moins sentir; cela est vrai jusque dans la morale. Le mouvement de l'amour-propre nous est si naturel que, le plus souvent, nous ne le sentons pas.*

The most natural and ordinary movements are those which are the least felt; this is also true in morals. Pride is so natural to us that, most often, we never feel it.

1686 *Entretiens sur la pluralité des mondes, Premier soir.*

87 *Les vrais philosophes sont comme les éléphants, qui en marchant ne posent jamais le second pied à terre que le premier ne soit bien affermi.*

True philosophers are like elephants, who when walking never place their second foot on the ground until the first is steady.

1686 *Entretiens sur la pluralité des mondes, Sixième soir.*

88 *Un grand obstacle au bonheur, c'est de s'attendre à un trop grand bonheur.*

The greatest obstacle to happiness is the expectation of too great a happiness.

1724 *Du bonheur.*

89 *Leibniz n'était point marié; il y avait pensé à l'âge de cinquante ans; mais la personne qu'il avait en vue voulut avoir le temps de faire ses réflexions. Cela donne à Leibniz le loisir de faire aussi les siennes, et il ne se maria point.*

Leibniz never married; he had considered it at the age of fifty, but the person he had in mind desired time to think about it. This gave Leibniz time to reflect, also, and he didn't marry.

Éloge des académiciens, Leibniz.

Foot, Michael Mackintosh 1913–

English Labour politician. He resigned the leadership of the Labour Party in 1983, after a heavy defeat in the general election. A pacifist and CND supporter, his prolific writings include a two-volume biography of Aneurin Bevan.

90 The only man I knew who could make a curse sound like a caress.

1962 Of Aneurin Bevan. *Aneurin Bevan 1897–1945*, vol.1.

91 The members of our secret service have apparently spent so much time looking under the bed for Communists that they haven't had time to look in the bed.

1963 Attributed comment on the Profumo scandal.

92 A Royal Commission is a broody hen sitting on a china egg.

1964 Speech, House of Commons.

93 Men of power have not time to read; yet men who do not read are unfit for power.

1980 *Debts of Honour.*

Foote, Samuel 1720–77

English actor-manager and playwright. Dubbed the 'English

Aristophanes', he excelled in satirical comedy at the Haymarket Theatre, which he managed. He won a limited theatrical patent as compensation when he lost a leg in a practical joke involving the Duke of York. His plays include *The Englishman in Paris* (1753) and *The Minor* (1760).

94 So she went into the garden to cut a cabbage-leaf, to make an apple-pie; and at the same time a great she-bear coming up the street, pops its head into the shop. 'What! no soap?' So he died and she very imprudently married the barber; and there were present the Picninnies, and the Joblillies, and the Garyulies, and the Grand Panjandrum himself, with the little round button at top; and they all fell to playing the game of catch-as-catch-can till the gunpowder ran out of the heels of their boots.

Responding to a challenge from the actor Charles Macklin that there was no speech he could not repeat from memory after just one hearing. Macklin had to acknowledge defeat. Foote's phrases 'no soap' and 'the grand Panjandrum' became widely adopted. Quoted in Maria Edgeworth *Harry and Lucy* (1825), vol.2.

Forbes, (Malcolm Stevenson) 'Steve', Jr 1947–

US publisher. He is President and Chief Executive Officer of Forbes and Editor-in-Chief of *Forbes* magazine and ran for the Republican presidential nomination in 1996 and 2000.

95 People who never get carried away, should be.

1976 In *Town and Country*, Nov.

96 It is unfortunate we can't buy many business executives for what they are worth and sell them for what they think they are worth.

Quoted in David Mahoney *Confessions of a Street-Smart Manager* (1988).

Ford, Anna 1943–

English television news presenter.

97 Let's face it, there are no plain women on television.

1979 In the *Observer*, 23 Sep.

Ford, Ford Madox originally *Ford Hermann Hueffer* 1873–1939

English writer and editor. He was associated with the modernist movement, and launched the *English Review* and later the *Transatlantic Review*. His best-known novels are *The Good Soldier* (1915) and the *Parade's End* (1924–8) tetralogy.

98 God knows that the lesson we learn from life is that our very existence in the nature of things is a perpetual harming of somebody else—if only because every mouthful of food that we eat is a mouthful taken from somebody else.

1911 *Ancient Lights*, dedication.

99 I should say that Rossetti was a man without principles at all, who earnestly desired to find salvation along the lines of least resistance.

1911 Of Dante Gabriel Rossetti. *Memories and Impressions.*

1 You cannot be absolutely dumb when you live with a person unless you are an inhabitant of the North of England or the State of Maine.

1915 *The Good Soldier*, pt.3, ch.4.

2 Alas, it does indeed seem a monstrous thing, but after all, what is chaste in Constantinople may have the aspect of

lewdness in Liverpool, and what in Liverpool may pass for virtue in Constantinople is frequently regarded as vice.
1915 Letter to John Lane, 17 Dec.

3 Only two classes of books are of universal appeal. The very best and the very worst.
1924 *Joseph Conrad, a Personal Remembrance*, pt.1.

4 We used to say that a passage of good style began with a fresh, usual word, and continued with fresh, usual words to the end; there was nothing more to it.
1924 *Joseph Conrad, a Personal Remembrance*, pt.3.

5 We agreed that the novel is absolutely the only vehicle for the thought of our day.
1924 *Joseph Conrad, a Personal Remembrance*, pt.3.

6 I have always had the greatest contempt for novels written with a purpose. Fiction should render, not draw morals. But…I sinned against my gods to the extent of saying that I was going—to the level of the light vouchsafed me—to write a work that should have for its purpose the obviating of all future wars.
1934 On *Parade's End*.

Ford, Henry 1863–1947

US automobile engineer and manufacturer. In 1903 he started the Ford Motor Company, pioneering 'assembly line' mass-production techniques for his famous Model T (1908–9), 15 million of which were produced up to 1928.

7 History is more or less bunk. It's tradition.
1916 Interview, *Chicago Tribune*, May.

8 Any color—so long as it's black.
Of the Model T Ford. Quoted in Allan Nevins *Ford* (1957), vol.2.

9 Exercise is bunk. If you are healthy, you don't need it: if you are sick, you shouldn't take it.
Attributed.

Ford, Henry 1917–87

US businessman, grandson of Henry Ford, president of the Ford Motor Co from 1945 and chairman from 1960. He introduced many modernizing measures.

10 My name is on the building.
His habitual justification for having the last word. Recalled on his death, 29 Sep 1987.

Ford, John c.1586–c.1640

English dramatist, who collaborated with Dekker, Fletcher, Rowley and Webster. His works include *The Broken Heart* (1633), *'Tis Pity She's a Whore* (1633) and *Perkin Warbeck* (1634), a historical play.

11 I am…a mushroom
On whom the dew of heaven drops now and then.
1633 *The Broken Heart*, act 1, sc.3.

12 The joys of marriage are the heaven on earth,
Life's paradise, great princess, the soul's quiet,
Sinews of concord, earthly immortality,
Eternity of pleasures; no restoratives
Like to a constant woman.
1633 *The Broken Heart*, act 2, sc.2.

13 He hath shook hands with time.
1633 *The Broken Heart*, act 5, sc.2.

14 Nice philosophy
May tolerate unlikely arguments,

But heaven admits no jest.
1633 *'Tis Pity She's a Whore*, act 1, sc.1.

15 'Tis my destiny
That you must either love, or I must die.
1633 *'Tis Pity She's a Whore*, act 1, sc.2.

16 Busy opinion is an idle fool.
1633 *'Tis Pity She's a Whore*, act 5, sc.3.

17 Why, I hold fate
Clasped in my fist, and could command the course
Of time's eternal motion, hadst thou been
One thought more steady than an ebbing sea.
1633 *'Tis Pity She's a Whore*, act 5, sc.4.

18 Of one so young, so rich in nature's store,
Who could not say, 'tis pity she's a whore?
1633 *'Tis Pity She's a Whore*, act 5, sc.6.

19 Tell us, pray, what devil
This melancholy is, which can transform
Men into monsters.
1638 *The Lady's Trial*, act 3, sc.1.

Ford, Lena Guilbert 1870–1916

English songwriter.

20 Keep the Home-fires burning,
While your hearts are yearning,
Though your lads are far away
They dream of Home.
There's a silver lining
Through the dark clouds shining;
Turn the dark cloud inside out,
Till the boys come Home.
1914 'Till the Boys Come Home', a wartime anthem (music by Ivor Novello).

Ford, Richard 1944–

US writer. He has edited anthologies and written short stories and novels, including *The Sportswriter* (1986) and *Independence Day* (1996, Pulitzer Prize).

21 If there's another thing that sportswriting teaches you, it is that there are no transcendent themes in life. In all cases things are here and they're over, and that has to be enough.
1986 *The Sportswriter*, ch.1.

22 Married life requires shared mystery even when all the facts are known.
1986 *The Sportswriter*, ch.5.

23 Leaving reminds us what we can part with and what we can't, then offers us something new to look forward to, to dream about.
1992 'An Urge for Going', in *Harper's*, Feb.

Foreman, George 1949–

US boxer, world heavyweight champion (1973–4, 1994–5).

24 A boxer never sees the big one that hits him.
Quoted in Colin Jarman *The Guinness Dictionary of Sports Quotations* (1990).

Forgy, Howell Maurice 1908–83

US naval chaplain.

25 Praise the Lord and pass the ammunition.
1941 At Pearl Harbor, 7 Dec. Reported in the *New York Times*,

1 Nov 1942, and used as a song title by Frank Loesser, 1942.
➤ *See Blacker 132:93.*

Formby, George 1904–61

English entertainer. He developed a music-hall act featuring a ukulele and comic songs which translated well to film, and became one of Britain's most popular pre-war stars.

26 When I'm Cleaning Windows.
1936 Title of song (with Harry Gifford and Fred E Cliffe), first featured in the film *Keep Your Seats Please.*

27 It's me Auntie Maggie's home-made remedy
Guaranteed never to fail
Now that's the stuff that will do the trick
It's sold at ev'ry chemist for 'one and a kick'.
1941 'Auntie Maggie's Remedy' (with Eddie Latta), song featured in the film *Turned Out Nice Again.*

Forster, E(dward) M(organ) 1879–1970

English novelist and critic, a member of the Bloomsbury circle. His novels include *Howards End* (1910) and *A Passage to India* (1924). *Maurice* (written 1913–14), on homosexuality, was published posthumously in 1971. He was a prolific essayist and critic.

28 Here is the heart of our island: the Chilterns, the North Downs, the South Downs radiate hence. The fibres of England unite in Wiltshire, and did we condescend to worship her, here should we erect our national shrine.
1907 *The Longest Journey,* ch.13.

29 A Room with a View.
1908 Title of novel.

30 They are our gates to the glorious and the unknown. Through them we pass out into adventure and sunshine, to them, alas! we return.
1910 On railway termini. *Howards End,* ch.2.

31 It will be generally admitted that Beethoven's Fifth Symphony is the most sublime noise that has ever penetrated into the ear of man.
1910 *Howards End,* ch.5.

32 He believed in sudden conversion, a belief which may be right, but which is peculiarly attractive to the half-baked mind.
1910 *Howards End,* ch.6.

33 She felt that those who prepared for all the emergencies of life beforehand may equip themselves at the expense of joy.
1910 *Howards End,* ch.7.

34 The poor cannot always reach those whom they want to love, and they can hardly ever escape from those whom they no longer love.
1910 *Howards End,* ch.7.

35 Personal relations are the important thing for ever and ever, and not this outer life of telegrams and anger.
1910 *Howards End,* ch.19.

36 Only connect! That was the whole of her sermon. Only connect the prose and the passion, and both will be exalted, and human love will be seen at its height. Live in fragments no longer.
1910 *Howards End,* ch.22.

37 Death destroys a man: the idea of death saves him.
1910 *Howards End,* ch.27.

38 There is much to be said for apathy in education.
1913–14 *Maurice* (published 1971), ch.1.

39 Religion is far more acute than science, and if it only added judgement to insight, would be the greatest thing in the world.
1913–14 *Maurice* (published 1971), ch.44.

40 'I don't think I understand people very well. I only know whether I like or dislike them.' 'Then you are an Oriental.'
1924 *A Passage to India,* ch.2.

41 The so-called white races are really pinko-grey.
1924 *A Passage to India,* ch.7.

42 Nothing in India is identifiable, the mere asking of a question causes it to disappear or to merge in something else.
1924 *A Passage to India,* ch.8.

43 The echo began in some indescribable way to undermine her hold on life. Coming at a moment when she chanced to be fatigued, it had managed to murmur, 'Pathos, piety, courage—they exist, but are identical, and so is filth. Everything exists, nothing has value.'
1924 *A Passage to India,* ch.14.

44 Yes—oh dear yes—the novel tells a story.
1927 *Aspects of the Novel,* ch.2.

45 *Ulysses*…is a dogged attempt to cover the universe with mud, an inverted Victorianism, an attempt to make crossness and dirt succeed where sweetness and light failed, a simplification of the human character in the interests of Hell.
1927 Of James Joyce's 1922 novel. *Aspects of the Novel,* ch.6.

46 They go forth into a world…of men who are as various as the sands of the sea; into a world of whose richness and subtlety they have no conception. They go forth into it with well-developed bodies, fairly developed minds, and undeveloped hearts.
1936 On public schoolboys. *Abinger Harvest,* 'Notes on English Character'.

47 It is not that the Englishman can't feel—it is that he is afraid to feel.
1936 *Abinger Harvest,* 'Notes on English Character'.

48 It is frivolous stuff, and how rare, how precious is frivolity! How few writers can prostitute all their powers! They are always implying 'I am capable of higher things.'
1936 *Abinger Harvest,* 'Ronald Firbank'.

49 The historian must have a third quality as well: some conception of how men who are not historians behave. Otherwise he will move in a world of the dead.
1936 *Abinger Harvest,* 'Captain Edward Gibbon'.

50 Works of art, in my opinion, are the only objects in the material universe to possess internal order, and that is why, though I don't believe that only art matters, I do believe in Art for Art's sake.
1951 *Two Cheers for Democracy,* 'Art for Art's Sake'.

51 I do not believe in Belief… Lord I disbelieve—help thou my unbelief.
1951 *Two Cheers for Democracy,* 'What I Believe'.

52 I hate the idea of causes, and if I had to choose between betraying my country and betraying my friend, I hope I should have the guts to betray my country.
1951 *Two Cheers for Democracy,* 'What I Believe'.

53 So two cheers for democracy: one because it admits variety and two because it permits criticism. Two cheers are quite enough: there is no occasion to give three. Only Love the Beloved Republic deserves that.
1951 *Two Cheers for Democracy*, 'What I Believe'. The phrase 'Love the Beloved Republic' is taken from Swinburne's poem 'Hertha'.

54 Think before you speak is criticism's motto; speak before you think creation's.
1951 *Two Cheers for Democracy*, 'Raison d'être of Criticism'.

55 Creative writers are always greater than the causes that they represent.
1951 *Two Cheers for Democracy*, 'Gide and George'.

56 I would suggest that the only books that influence us are those for which we are ready, and which have gone a little farther down our particular path than we have yet got ourselves.
1951 *Two Cheers for Democracy*, 'Books That Influenced Me'.

57 One was left, too, with a gap in Christianity: the canonical gospels do not record that Christ laughed or played. Can a man be perfect if he never laughs or plays? Krishna's jokes may be vapid, but they bridge a gap.
1953 *The Hill of Devi*, 'Gokul Ashtami'.

Foster, Sir George   1847–1931

Canadian politician.

58 These somewhat troublesome days when the great Mother Empire stands splendidly isolated in Europe.
1896 Speech in the House of Commons, 16 Jan. *The Times* reported the speech under the heading of 'Splendid Isolation', 22 Jan.

Foster, Stephen Collins   1826–64

US songwriter. His 125 compositions include 'The Old Folks at Home', 'Camptown Races' and 'Jeannie with the Light Brown Hair', but despite their success, he died in poverty and obscurity.

59 Gwine to run all night,
Gwine to run all day,
I'll bet my money on de bob-tail nag,
Somebody bet on de bay.
1850 'Camptown Races', chorus.

60 Way down upon the Swanee River,
Far, far away,
There's where my heart is turning ever;
There's where the old folks stay.
1851 'The Old Folks at Home'.

61 I dream of Jeannie with the light brown hair,
Floating, like a vapour, on the soft summer air.
1854 'Jeannie with the Light Brown Hair'.

62 Beautiful dreamer, wake unto me,
Starlight and dewdrop are waiting for thee.
1864 'Beautiful Dreamer'.

Foster, Vince(nt W, Jr)   1945–93

US lawyer. Deputy Counsel in the Clinton White House.

63 I was not meant for the spotlight of public life in Washington. Here running people down is considered sport.
1993 Note found after his suicide. Reported in the *New York Times*, 13 Aug.

Foucault, Michel   1926–84

French philosopher and historian of ideas.

64 For the nineteenth century, the initial model of madness would be to believe oneself to be God, while for the preceding centuries it had been to deny God.
1967 *Madness and Civilization*.

Fowles, John Robert   1926–

English novelist. He scored a cult success with *The Magus* (1965, revised 1977), and consolidated his reputation as an ambitious experimental writer with *The French Lieutenant's Woman* (1969, filmed 1981).

65 All perfect republics are a perfect nonsense. The craving to risk death is our last great perversion. We come from night, we go into night. Why live in night?
1965 *The Magus*, ch.19.

66 And if you are wise you will never pity the past for what it did not know, but pity yourself for what it did.
1965 *The Magus*, ch.24.

67 That is the great distinction between the sexes. Men see objects, women see the relationship between objects… It is an extra dimension of feeling which we men are without and one that makes war abhorrent to all real women—and absurd.
1965 *The Magus*, ch.52.

68 In essence the Renaissance was simply the green end of one of civilization's hardest winters.
1969 *The French Lieutenant's Woman*, ch.10.

69 We all write poems; it is simply that poets are the ones who write in words.
1969 *The French Lieutenant's Woman*, ch.19.

70 The more abhorrent a news item the more comforting it was to be the recipient since the fact that it had happened elsewhere proved that it had not happened here, was not happening here, and would therefore never happen here.
1974 *The Ebony Tower*, 'Poor Koko'.

71 Cricket remains for me the game of games, the sanspareil, the great metaphor, the best marriage ever devised of mind and body… For me it remains the Proust of pastimes, the subtlest and most poetic, the most past-and-present; whose beauty can lie equally in days, in a whole, or in one tiny phrase, a blinding split second.
Quick Singles, 'Vain Memories'. Quoted in Helen Exley *Cricket Quotations* (1992).

72 The diary will really try and tell people who you are and what you were. The alternative is writing nothing, or creating a totally lifeless, as it is leafless, garden.
2003 *The Journals: Volume 1*.

73 One degrades oneself sometimes in the effort not to be lonely.
2003 After a late night socializing. In *The Journals: Volume 1*, 24 Dec 1950.

Fox, Charles James   1749–1806

English Liberal statesman. He formed an administration with Lord North in 1783, and on its failure became Pitt's leading parliamentary adversary. He was a strong opponent of the war with France, and an advocate of non-intervention.

74 How much the greatest event it is that ever happened in

the world—and how much the best.
1779 On the fall of the Bastille. Letter to Richard Fitzpatrick, 30 Jul.

75 The worst of a revolution is a restoration.
1785 House of Commons, 10 Dec.

76 I die happy.
1806 Last words. Quoted in Lord John Russell *Life and Times of C J Fox*, vol.3 (1860), ch.9.

Fox, George 1624–91

English itinerant Puritan preacher and writer, who was imprisoned for dissent. He was the founder of Society of Friends (known as 'Quakers').

77 One morning, as I was sitting by the fire, a great cloud came over me, and a temptation beset me, and I sate still… And as I sate still under it and let it alone, a living hope rose in me, and a true voice arose in me which cried: There is a living God who made all things. And immediately the cloud and temptation vanished away, and the life rose over it all, and my heart was glad, and I praised the living God.
1648 *Journal of George Fox*.

78 Walk cheerfully over the world, answering that of God in everyone.
1656 *Journal of George Fox*.

Frame, Janet Paterson *also known as* Jean Paterson Frame 1924–2004

New Zealand poet and writer. She was misdiagnosed as schizophrenic, and spent eight years in psychiatric hospitals. Her autobiographical trilogy *To the Is-land* (1982), *An Angel at My Table* (1984) and *The Envoy from Mirror City* (1985) was made into an award-winning film by Jane Campion.

79 What use the green river, the gold place, if time and death pinned human in the pocket of my land not rest from taking underground the green all-willowed and white rose and bean flower and morning-mist picnic of song in pepper-pot breast of thrush?
1961 *Owls Do Cry*, pt.1, ch.4.

80 From the first place of liquid darkness, within the second place of air and light, I set down the following record with its mixture of fact and truths and memories of truths and its direction always toward the Third Place, where the starting point is myth.
1982 *To the Is-land*, ch.1, 'In the Second Place'.

81 I was born…with ready-made parents and a sister and brother who had already begun their store of experience, inaccessible to me except through their language and the record, always slightly different, of our mother and father, and as each member of the family was born, each, in a sense with memories on loan, began to supply the individual furnishings of each Was-land, each Is-land, and the hopes and dreams of the Future.
1982 *To the Is-land*, ch.1, 'In the Second Place'.

82 The word *permanent*…had its own kind of revenge on those who misused it, for the Bible said that nothing was permanent and everything came and went.
1982 *To the Is-land*, ch.2, 'Toward the Is-Land'.

France, Anatole *pseudonym of* Jacques Anatole François Thibault 1844–1924

French novelist, poet and essayist, who won the Nobel prize for literature in 1921. Along with Émile Zola, he championed the cause of Dreyfus.

83 *Le bon critique est celui qui raconte les aventures de son âme au milieu des chefs-d'oeuvres.*
The good critic is one who recognizes the adventures of his soul in great works of art.
1892 *La Vie littéraire*, préface.

84 *Le livre est l'opium de l'Occident.*
Books are the opium of the West.
1892 *La Vie littéraire*, préface.
➡ *See Marx 557:94.*

85 *La faim et l'amour sont les deux axes du monde.*
Hunger and love are the two axes of the world.
1892 *La Vie littéraire*, pt.3.

86 *L'histoire est condamnée, par un vice de nature, au mensonge.*
History is condemned, by a defect of nature, to lies.
1892 *La Vie littéraire*, pt.17.

87 *Les vérités découvertes par l'intelligence demeurent stériles.*
Truths discovered by intelligence are sterile.
1892 *La Vie littéraire*, pt.21.

88 *Je tiens à mon imperfection comme à ma raison d'être.*
I hold on to my imperfection as tightly as my reason for being.
1894 *Le Jardin d'Epicure*.

89 *Il y a toujours un moment où la curiosité devient un péché, et le diable s'est toujours mis du côté des savants.*
There is always a moment when curiosity becomes a sin and the devil is always on the side of the learned.
1894 *Le Jardin d'Epicure*.

90 *L'histoire n'est pas une science, c'est un art. On n'y réussit que par l'imagination.*
History is not a science. It is an art. One can succeed in it only through the imagination.
1894 *Le Jardin d'Epicure*.

91 To disarm the strong and arm the weak would be to change the social order which it's my job to preserve. Justice is the means by which established injustices are sanctioned.
1901 *Crainquebille*.

92 *Le poireau, c'est l'asperge du pauvre.*
The leek is the asparagus of the poor.
1906 *Crainquebille*.

93 *La majestueuse égalité des lois, qui interdit au riche comme au pauvre de coucher sous les ponts, de mendier dans les rues et de voler du pain.*
The majestic equality of laws forbids the rich as well as the poor to sleep under bridges, to beg in the streets and to steal bread.
1910 *Le Lys rouge*.

Francis I 1494–1547

King of France (1515–47) after his father-in-law Louis XII. The chief feature of his reign was his military conflict with Emperor Charles V.

94 *De toutes choses ne m'est demeuré que l'honneur et la vie qui est saulve.*
Of all I had, only honour and life have been spared.
1525 Letter to his mother, Louise of Savoy, after his defeat and

capture by Charles V at Pavia, 24 Feb. Collected in *Collection des documents inédits sur l'histoire de France* (1847), vol.1.

95 *Souvent femme varie,*
   Mal habil qui s'y fie
   Woman is often fickle,
   Foolish the man who trusts her.
   Couplet scratched by the King on the glass of a window at Chambord. Quoted in Vincent Cronin *Louis XI V* (1964), p.175.

96 But is he a patriot for me?
   On being assured of the loyalty of a candidate for high office. The phrase was later used as a title by John Osborne for his 1965 play.

St Francis of Assisi c.1181–1226

Italian monk and saint, founder of the Franciscan order. The son of a wealthy merchant, in 1206 he renounced his patrimony and became a hermit, attracting followers who rejected all forms of property. His works include sermons, ascetic treatises and hymns.

97 *Bene veniat soror mea mors.*
   Welcome, my sister Death.
   1226 Last words. Quoted in Thomas of Celano *Life of St Francis* (c.1245), bk.2, ch.163.

98 Lord, make me an instrument of Your peace.
   Where there is hatred, let me sow love;
   Where there is injury, pardon;
   Where there is doubt, faith;
   Where there is despair, hope;
   Where there is darkness, light;
   Where there is sadness, joy.

   O divine Master, grant that I may not so much seek
   To be consoled as to console;
   To be understood as to understand;
   To be loved as to love.
   For it is in giving that we receive;
   It is in pardoning that we are pardoned;
   And it is in dying that we are born to eternal life.
   Attributed prayer, traditionally known as the 'Prayer of St Francis'.

Francis, Dick (Richard Stanley) 1920–

English jockey and writer. In the Grand National of 1956 he was on the point of winning when his horse collapsed. Subsequently he became a writer of popular thrillers with a racing background.

99 I approach chapter one each year with a deeper foreboding than I ever felt facing Becher's.
   Quoted in Colin Jarman *The Guinness Dictionary of Sports Quotations* (1990).

Frank, Anne 1929–45

German Jewish diarist, whose diary covers her time in hiding in Amsterdam. She died in Bergen–Belsen concentration camp.

1 It was a terrible time through which I was living. The war raged about us, and nobody knew whether or not he would be alive the next week.
   1944 Diary entry, 25 Mar.

2 I want to go on living even after death!
   1944 Diary entry, 4 Apr.

3 We all live with the objective of being happy; our lives are all different and yet the same.
   1944 Diary entry, 6 Jul.

Frankenthaler, Helen 1928–

US artist, a key figure in the Abstract Expressionism school. Her innovative, colourful works include *The Human Edge* (1967). The Museum of Modern Art in New York presented her retrospective in 1989.

4 A picture that is beautiful, or that comes off, or that works, looks as if it was all made at one stroke.
   1972 Quoted in Ian Crofton (ed) *A Dictionary of Art Quotations* (1988).

5 I follow the rules until I go against them all.
   1993 On translating her large, lyrical abstracts from paintings to prints. In the *Washington Times*, 16 Apr.

Franklin, Benjamin 1706–90

US statesman, author and scientist, whose popular *Poor Richard's Almanack* first appeared in 1732. He proved that lightning and electricity are identical and suggested that buildings should be protected by lightning conductors. He was involved in the Declaration of Independence (1775), and helped secure British recognition (1783).

6 The body of
   Benjamin Franklin, printer,
   (Like the cover of an old book,
   Its contents worn out,
   And stripped of its lettering and gilding)
   Lies here, food for worms!
   Yet the work itself shall not be lost,
   For it will, as he believed, appear once more
   In a new
   And more beautiful edition,
   Corrected and amended
   By its Author!
   1728 Proposed epitaph for himself.

7 To lengthen thy Life, lessen thy Meals.
   1733 *Poor Richard's Almanack*, Jun.

8 He that drinks fast, pays slow.
   1733 *Poor Richard's Almanack*, Aug.

9 Necessity never made a good bargain.
   1735 *Poor Richard's Almanack*, Apr.

10 Nothing but Money,
   Is sweeter than Honey.
   1735 *Poor Richard's Almanack*, Jun.

11 Time is money.
   1748 *Advice to a Young Tradesman*.

12 Fond Pride of Dress is sure an Empty Curse;
   E'er Fancy you consult, consult your Purse.
   1751 *Poor Richard Improved*, May.

13 A little neglect may breed mischief…for want of a nail, the shoe was lost; for want of a shoe, the horse was lost; and for want of a horse the rider was lost.
   1758 *Poor Richard's Almanack*, preface.

14 Some punishment seems preparing for a people who are so ungratefully abusing the best Constitution and the best king that any nation was ever blessed with.
   1768 Speech in London during the Wilkes riots, May.

15 There never was a good war or a bad peace.
   1773 Letter, 11 Sep.

16 We must indeed all hang together or, most assuredly, we shall all hang separately.
1776 On signing the Declaration of Independence, 4 Jul.

17 Furnished as all Europe is with Academies of Science, with nice instruments and the spirit of experimentation, the progress of human knowledge will be rapid and discoveries made of which we have at present no conception. I begin to be almost sorry I was born since I cannot have the happiness of knowing what will be known a hundred years hence.
1783 Letter to Sir Joseph Banks, President of the Royal Society, 27 Jul.

18 In this world nothing can be said to be certain, except death and taxes.
1789 Letter to Jean Baptiste Le Roy, 13 Nov.
➤ See Defoe 258:25.

19 What is the use of a new-born child?
Reply when questioned as to the use of a new invention. Quoted in J Parton *Life and Times of Benjamin Franklin* (1864), pt.4, ch.17.

Franklin, (Stella Marian Sarah) Miles *pseudonym* Brent of Bin Bin 1879–1954

Australian novelist, journalist and feminist. After writing *My Brilliant Career* (1901), she moved to the US (1906) then England (1915), returning to Australia in 1927. Other work includes the *Brent of Bin* series (1928), the autobiographical *My Career Goes Bung* (1946) and critical essays.

20 This was life—my life—my career, my brilliant career!
1901 *My Brilliant Career*, ch.5.

21 Grannie remarked that I might have the spirit of an Australian but I had by no means the manners of a lady.
1901 *My Brilliant Career*, ch.19.

22 I am proud that I am an Australian, a daughter of the Southern Cross, a child of the mighty bush. I am thankful I am a peasant, a part of the bone and muscle of my nation, and earn my bread by the sweat of my brow, as man was meant to do. I rejoice I was not born a parasite, one of the blood-suckers who loll on velvet and satin, crushed from the proceeds of human sweat and blood and souls.
1901 *My Brilliant Career*, ch.38.

Franz Josef I 1830–1916

Emperor of Austria (1848) and King of Hungary (1867).

23 Farewell youth!
1848 On signing the document that made him Emperor, following the abdication of Ferdinand. Attributed, quoted in A J P Taylor *From Napoleon to the Second International* (1993).

Franzen, Jonathan 1959–

US novelist. *The Corrections* (2001) won the National Book Award.

24 It's the fate of most Ping-Pong tables in home basements eventually to serve the ends of other, more desperate games.
2001 *The Corrections*.

25 Just as the camera draws a stake through the heart of serious portraiture, television has killed the novel of social reportage.
2002 *How to Be Alone*.

Fraser, Lady Antonia 1932–

English writer, best known for her historical biographies.

26 As with all forms of liberation, of which the liberation of women is only one example, it is easy to suppose in a time of freedom that the darker days of repression can never come again.
1984 *The Weaker Vessel*, epilogue.

Fraser, George MacDonald 1925–

English writer of historical fiction.

27 I have observed, in the course of a dishonest life, that when a rogue is outlining a treacherous plan, he works harder to convince himself than to move his hearers.
1969 *Flashman*.

Fraser, Major Sir Keith Alexander 1867–1935

British politician. After his army career he became MP for Leicestershire (1918–23) and a Justice of the Peace for Ross and Cromarty.

28 I never met anyone in Ireland who understood the Irish question, except one Englishman who had been there only a week.
1919 House of Commons, May.

Fraser, (John) Malcolm 1930–

Australian politician. He became an MP in 1955 and leader of the Liberals in 1975. He formed a caretaker government until becoming Prime Minister. Defeated in the 1983 elections, he retired soon afterwards.

29 Life is not meant to be easy.
1971 The Deakin Lecture, Melbourne, 20 Jul.

Frayne, Trent 1918–

Canadian sportswriter.

30 It is an axiom of sports that the legs go first. For sportswriters, it's the enthusiasm.
1990 *The Tales of an Athletic Supporter*.

Frederick II 1194–1250

Holy Roman Emperor, last of the Hohenstaufen line. His plans to consolidate his power in Italy were frustrated by the Lombard cities and the popes. During the Fifth Crusade in 1228 he took possession of Jerusalem, and crowned himself king there (1229).

31 Our work is to present things that are as they are.
De Ate Venandi cum Avibus.

Frederick II, the Great 1712–86

King of Prussia from 1740. He fought against the Austrians in the War of the Austrian Succession (1740–8) and seized Silesia in 1741. In 1772 he shared in the first partition of Poland. By the time of his death, Prussia had become a world power.

32 Troops always ready to act, my well-filled treasury, and the liveliness of my disposition—these were my reasons for making war on Maria Theresa.
1741 Letter to Voltaire.

33 Rascals, would you live for ever?
1757 Attributed, to hesitant guards at the Battle of Kolin, 18 Jun.
➤ See Daly 251:76.

34 *Chassez les préjugés par la porte, ils rentreront par la fenêtre.*

Drive out prejudices through the door, and they will return through the window.

1771 Letter to Voltaire, 19 Mar.

35 *Vanité des Vanités; Vanité de la géométrie.*

Vanity of vanities! Vanity of mathematics!

1778 Letter to Voltaire, 25 Jan, protesting against the increasing use of mathematical calculation in engineering projects, which he saw as theory triumphing over practical experience.

36 My people and I have come to an agreement that satisfies us both. They are to say what they please, and I am to do what I please.

Attributed.

Freed, Arthur *pseudonym of* *Arthur Grossman* 1894–1973

US producer and lyricist. He came to Hollywood in 1929 and worked for MGM, producing many well-known musicals. As a lyricist he frequently worked with composer Nacio Herb Brown.

37 I'll walk down the lane with a happy refrain
And singin' just singin' in the rain.

1929 'Singin' in the Rain' featured in *Hollywood Revue of 1929* and other films, including the famous musical of the same title (music by Nacio Herb Brown).

38 You Are My Lucky Star.

1935 Title of song featured in *Broadway Melody of 1936* (music by Nacio Herb Brown).

Freeman, Bud (Lawrence) 1906–91

US jazz saxophonist. He was a leading figure in the evolution of the Chicago style in the 1920s and 1930s.

39 I think audiences come to hear older musicians like me just to see if we can pick up a horn without falling over.

1989 *Crazeology: The Autobiography of a Chicago Jazzman* (as told to Robert Wolf), ch.9.

Freeman, Edward Augustus 1823–92

English historian, Regius Professor of Modern History at Oxford. Among his prolific output were his *History of Federal Government* (1863) and *History of the Norman Conquest* (1867–76).

40 This would be a grand land if only every Irishman would kill a negro, and be hanged for it.

1881 Of America. Letter to F H Dickinson from New Haven, 4 Dec.

41 Nobody can't do nothing never at all for Ireland—you can't help people against their will; that's what it comes to—let it go, let it go.

1882 Letter to Edith Thompson, 29 Jan.

42 History is past politics, and politics is present history.

1886 *Methods of Historical Study.*

Freeman, John 1880–1929

English poet.

43 In that sharp light the fields did lie
Naked and stone-like; each tree stood
Like a tranced woman, bound and stark,
Far off the wood
With darkness ridged the riven dark.

1916 'Stone Trees'.

44 Than these November skies
Is no sky lovelier. The clouds are deep;
Into their grey the subtle spies
Of colour creep,
Changing their high austerity to delight,
Till ev'n the leaden interfolds are bright.

1916 'November Skies'.

45 It was the lovely moon—she lifted
Slowly her white brow among
Bronze cloud-waves that ebbed and drifted
Faintly, faintlier afar.

1916 'It Was the Lovely Moon'.

Freleng, Friz *born* *Isadore Freleng* 1905–95

US cartoon director.

46 That's all folks!

Porky Pig's stammered trademark, sign-off line for Warner Brothers' *Looney Tunes.*

French, Marilyn 1929–

US writer and feminist scholar. She enjoyed a huge success with her bestselling first novel, *The Women's Room* (1977), and has written further novels and feminist studies.

47 'I hate discussions of feminism that end up with who does the dishes,' she said. So do I. But at the end, there are always those damned dishes.

1977 *The Women's Room*, bk.1, ch.21.

48 Whatever they may be in public life, whatever their relations with men, in their relations with women, all men are rapists, and that's all they are. They rape us with their eyes, their laws, and their codes.

1977 *The Women's Room*, bk.5, ch.19.

Freud, Sir Clement 1924–

English writer and broadcaster.

49 If you resolve to give up smoking, drinking and loving, you don't actually live longer; it just seems longer.

1964 In the *Observer*, 27 Dec.

Freud, Sigmund 1856–1939

Austrian neurologist, founder of psychoanalysis. He published his controversial but influential ideas in such works as *The Interpretation of Dreams* (1900), *The Psychopathology of Everyday Life* (1904) and *Ego and Id* (1923).

50 I am actually not at all a man of science… I am by temperament nothing but a conquistador, an adventurer.

1900 Letter to Wilhelm Fliess, Feb.

51 Congratulations and bouquets keep pouring in, as if the role of sexuality had been suddenly recognised by His Majesty, the interpretation of dreams confirmed by the Council of Ministers, and the necessity of the psychoanalytic therapy of hysteria carried by a two-thirds majority in Parliament.

1902 Letter to Wilhelm Fliess, 11 Mar, describing the public enthusiasm in Vienna that greeted his appointment to an associate professorship at the age of 45.

52 The principal task of civilisation, its actual raison d'être, is to defend us against nature.

1903 *Introductory Lectures.*

53 A woman who is very anxious to get children always reads 'storks' for 'stocks'.

1904 *The Psychopathology of Everyday Life.*

54 *Die Anatomie ist das Schicksal.*
Anatomy is destiny.

1924 *Collected Works*, vol.5.

55 At bottom God is nothing more than an exalted father.

1927 *The Future of an Illusion.*

56 The more the fruits of knowledge become accessible to men, the more widespread is the decline of religious belief.

1927 *The Future of an Illusion.*

Friday, Nancy 1937–

US feminist and writer, whose works include *My Secret Garden* (1973), *My Mother, My Self* (1977) and *Women on Top* (1991).

57 If you believe in the maternal instinct and fail at mother love, you fail as a woman. It is a controlling idea that holds us in an iron grip.

1977 *My Mother, My Self*, ch.1.

58 The older I get, the more of my mother I see in myself.

1977 *My Mother, My Self*, ch.1.

Friedan, Betty (Elizabeth) Naomi *née Goldstein* 1921–

US feminist and writer, founder of the National Organization for Women (1966) and author of the seminal feminist text *The Feminine Mystique* (1963).

59 The problem lay buried, unspoken, for many years in the minds of American women. It was a strange stirring, a sense of dissatisfaction, a yearning that women suffered in the middle of the twentieth century in the United States. Each suburban wife struggled with it alone. As she made the beds, shopped for groceries, matched slipcover material, ate peanut butter sandwiches with her children, chauffeured Cub Scouts and Brownies, lay beside her husband at night—she was afraid to ask even of herself the silent question—'Is this all?'

1963 *The Feminine Mystique*, ch.1, 'The Problem that has No Name'.

60 Women, even though they are almost too visible as sex objects in this country, are invisible people.

1969 Speech at First National Conference for Repeal of Abortion Laws, Chicago.

61 Motherhood will only be a joyous and responsible human act when women are free to make, with full conscious choice and full human responsibility, the decisions to become mothers.

1969 Speech at First National Conference for Repeal of Abortion Laws, Chicago.

Friedman, Milton 1912–

US economist. A leading monetarist, his work includes the permanent income theory of consumption, and the role of money in determining events, particularly the US Great Depression. He was awarded the Nobel prize for economics in 1976.

62 Economics as a positive science is a body of tentatively accepted generalizations about economic phenomena that can be used to predict the consequences of changes in circumstances.

1953 'The Methodology of Positive Economics' in *Essays in Positive Economics.*

63 There is no such thing as a free lunch.

1973 Lecture. The phrase is thought to have been coined anonymously, perhaps referring to the 19c US tradition of supplying food in bars to patrons buying drinks.

64 The price that the market sets on the services of our resources is similarly affected by a bewildering mixture of chance and choice. Frank Sinatra's voice was highly valued in twentieth-century United States. Would it have been highly valued in twentieth-century India, if he had happened to be born and to live there?

1981 *Free to Choose* (with Rose Friedman).

65 No major institution in the US has so poor a record of performance over so long a period as the Federal Reserve, yet so high a public reputation.

1988 'The Fed Has No Clothes', in *The Wall Street Journal*, 15 Apr.

Friedrich, Carl J(oachim) 1901–84

German political theorist. He taught at the universities of Harvard and Heidelberg.

66 To be an American is an ideal, while to be a Frenchman is a fact.

1987 In *Time*, 9 Nov.

Friedrich, Caspar David 1774–1840

German painter, who depicted landscape as vast and desolate expanses in which man is a melancholy spectator.

67 Just as the pious man prays without speaking a word and the Almighty hearkens unto him, so the artist with true feelings *paints* and the sensitive man understands and recognizes it.

Quoted in S Hinz *Caspar David Friedrich in Briefen und Bekenntnissen* (1968).

68 The Divine is everywhere, even in a grain of sand, here I have represented it in bull-rushes.

Remark to the German artist Peter Cornelius, quoted in S Hinz *Caspar David Friedrich in Briefen und Bekenntnissen* (1968).

69 Close your bodily eye, so that you may see your picture first with the spiritual eye. Then bring to the light of day that which you have seen in the darkness so that it may react on others from the outside inwards.

Quoted in *Caspar David Friedrich 1774–1840*, Tate Gallery (1972).

70 Despite what even many artists appear to believe, art is not and should not be merely a skill. It should actually be completely and utterly the language of our feelings, our frame of mind; indeed, even of our devotion and our prayers.

Quoted in *Caspar David Friedrich 1774–1840*, Tate Gallery (1972).

71 The artist should not only paint what he sees before him, but also what he sees within him. If, however, he sees nothing within him, then he should also omit to paint that which he sees before him.

Quoted in *Caspar David Friedrich 1774–1840*, Tate Gallery (1972).

72 Every true work of art must express a distinct feeling.

Quoted in William Vaughn *Romantic Art* (1978).

Friel, Brian 1929–

Northern Irish playwright and short-story writer.

73 Two such wonderful phrases—'I understand perfectly'

and 'That is a lie'—a précis of life, aren't they?
1983 *The Communication Cord.*

74 Do you want the whole countryside to be laughing at us?—women of our years?—mature women, *dancing*?
1990 *Dancing at Lughnasa.*

Frisch, Max Rudolph 1911–91

Swiss writer, novelist and playwright. His novels include *I'm Not Stiller* (1954), *Homo Faber* (1957), and *A Wilderness of Mirrors* (1964). His plays include *The Firebugs* (1953) and *Andorra* (1961, translated 1962).

75 *Ich kann nur berichten, was ich weiß.*
I can only report on what I know.
1957 *Homo Faber*, pt.1.

76 *Technik…Kniff, die Welt so einzurichten, dass wir sie nicht erleben müssen.*
Technology…the knack of so arranging the world that we don't have to experience it.
1957 *Homo Faber*, pt.2.

77 *Kein Mensch, wenn er die Welt sieht, die sie ihm hinterlassen, versteht seine Eltern.*
No one understands their parents when we look at the world that they have bequeathed us.
1961 *Andorra*, sc.9.

78 *Ich habe kein Gemüt, sondern Angst.*
I have no comfort, only anxiety.
1961 *Andorra*, sc.9.

79 *Man kann sich seinen Vater nicht wählen.*
A person cannot choose his father.
1961 *Andorra*, 10.

80 *Ich gehe ins Theater ja auch nicht als Voyeur.*
I do not go into the theatre as a voyeur.
1967 *Biographie.*

Frohman, Charles 1860–1915

US theatre manager. Among his many successful productions were several plays by J M Barrie.

81 Why fear death? It's the most beautiful adventure in life.
1915 Last words, paraphrasing a line in J M Barrie's *Peter Pan*, said to the actress Rita Jolivet as the *Lusitania* went down after being torpedoed by a German submarine, 7 May.

Fromm, Erich 1900–80

German-born US psychoanalyst and author, who emigrated in 1934 to the US, where he practised psychoanalysis and lectured at various institutions.

82 The pace of science forces the pace of technique. Theoretical physics forces atomic energy on us; the successful production of the fission bomb forces upon us the manufacture of the hydrogen bomb. We do not choose our problems, we do not choose our products; we are pushed, we are forced—by what? By a system which has no purpose and goal transcending it, and which makes man its appendix.
1955 *The Sane Society.*

Frost, Robert Lee 1874–1963

US poet, whose work is rooted in New England. He established his reputation with *A Boy's World* (1913) and *North of Boston* (1914) and won Pulitzer Prizes in 1924, 1931, 1937 and 1943.

83 Most of the change we think we see in life
Is due to truths being in and out of favour.
1914 *North of Boston*, 'The Black Cottage'.

84 Something there is that doesn't love a wall,
That sends the frozen-ground-swell under it,
And spills the upper boulders in the sun;
And makes gaps even two can pass abreast.
1914 *North of Boston*, 'Mending Wall'.

85 Before I built a wall I'd ask to know
What I was walling in or walling out,
And to whom I was like to give offence.
1914 *North of Boston*, 'Mending Wall'.

86 Part of a moon was falling down the west,
Dragging the whole sky with it to the hills.
1914 *North of Boston*, 'The Death of the Hired Man'.

87 'Home is the place where, when you have to go there,
They have to take you in.'
'I should have called it
Something you somehow haven't to deserve.'
1914 *North of Boston*, 'The Death of the Hired Man'.

88 A sentence is a sound in itself on which sounds called words may be strung.
1914 Letter to John Bartlett, 22 Feb.

89 I shall be telling this with a sigh
Somewhere ages and ages hence:
Two roads diverged in a wood, and I—
I took the one less traveled by,
And that has made all the difference.
1916 'The Road Not Taken'.

90 We love the things we love for what they are.
1916 'Hyla Brook'.

91 The question that he frames in all but words
Is what to make of a diminished thing.
1916 'The Oven Bird'.

92 I'd like to go by climbing a birch tree
And climb black branches up a snow-white trunk
Toward heaven, till the tree could bear no more,
But dipped its top and set me down again.
That would be good both going and coming back.
One could do worse than be a swinger of birches.
1916 'Birches'.

93 They listened at his heart.
Little—less—nothing!—and that ended it.
No more to build on there. And they, since they
Were not the one dead, turned to their affairs.
1916 'Out, Out—'.

94 No wonder poets sometimes have to *seem*
So much more businesslike than businessmen.
Their wares are so much harder to get rid of.
1923 'New Hampshire'.

95 He knew too well for any earthly use
The line where man leaves off and nature starts,
And never overstepped it save in dreams.
1923 'New Hampshire'.

96 Never tell me that not one star of all
That slip from heaven at night and softly fall
Has been picked up with stones to build a wall.
1923 'A Star in a Stoneboat'.

97 Some say the world will end in fire,
Some say in ice.

From what I've tasted of desire
I hold with those who favour fire.
But if I had to perish twice,
I think I know enough of hate
To say that for destruction ice
Is also great
And would suffice.
1923 'Fire and Ice', complete poem.

98 The woods are lovely, dark and deep.
But I have promises to keep,
And miles to go before I sleep,
And miles to go before I sleep.
1923 'Stopping by Woods on a Snowy Evening'.

99 I have been one acquainted with the night.
1928 'Acquainted with the Night'.

1 It is this backward motion toward the source,
Against the stream, that most we see ourselves in.
The tribute of the current to the source.
1928 'West-Running Brook'.

2 The land may vary more;
But wherever the truth may be—
The water comes ashore,
And the people look at the sea.
1928 'Neither Far Out Nor in Deep'.

3 A poet is a person who thinks there is something special about a poet and about his loving one unattainable woman. You'll usually find he takes the physical out on whores. I am defining a romantic poet—and there is no other kind. An unromantic poet is a self-contradiction.
1930 Letter to Louis Untermeyer, 6 Jun.

4 Writing free verse is like playing tennis with the net down.
1935 Address at Milton Academy, Mass, 17 May.

5 What brought the kindred spider to that height,
Then steered the white moth thither in the night?
What but design of darkness to appall?—
If design govern in a thing so small.
1936 'Design'.

6 I never dared be radical when young
For fear it would make me conservative when old.
1936 'Ten Mills, 1. Precaution'.

7 Like a piece of ice on a hot stove the poem must ride on its own melting. A poem may be worked over once it is in being, but may not be worried into being.
1939 'The Figure a Poem Makes', preface to *Collected Poems*.

8 Happiness Makes Up in Height for What It Lacks in Length.
1942 Title of poem.

9 The land was ours before we were the land's.
She was our land more than a hundred years
Before we were her people.
1942 'The Gift Outright'.

10 And were an epitaph to be my story
I'd have a short one ready for my own.
I would have written of me on my stone:
I had a lover's quarrel with the world.
1942 'The Lesson for Today'.

11 We dance round in a ring and suppose,
But the Secret sits in the middle and knows.
1942 'The Secret Sits', complete poem.

12 I have never started a poem yet whose end I knew.
Writing a poem is discovering.
1955 In the *New York Times*, 7 Nov.

13 Forgive, O Lord, my little jokes on Thee
And I'll forgive Thy great big one on me.
1959 'The Preacher', complete poem.

14 Poetry is a way of taking life by the throat.
Quoted in Elizabeth S Sergeant *Robert Frost: The Trial By Existence* (1960).

15 Summoning artists to participate
In the august occasions of the state
Seems something artists ought to celebrate.
1961 'For John F Kennedy: His Inauguration', 20 Jan. Snow-blindness prevented the aged poet from reading beyond the first three lines on the occasion.

16 Courage is in the air in bracing whiffs.
1961 'For John F Kennedy: His Inauguration', 20 Jan.

17 Education is… hanging around until you've caught on.
Recalled on his death, 29 Jan 1963.

18 The mind skating circles around itself as it moves forward.
His definition of style. Recalled on his death, 29 Jan 1963.

19 The right reader of a good poem can tell the moment it strikes him that he has taken an immortal wound—that he will never get over it.
Recalled on his death, 29 Jan 1963.

20 Poetry is what is lost in translation. It is also what is lost in interpretation.
Quoted in Louis Untermeyer *Robert Frost: A Backward Look* (1964).

Froude, James Anthony 1818–94

English writer and historian, who resigned his Oxford fellowship after controversy over his early novels. He wrote a *History of England from the Fall of Wolsey to the Spanish Armada* (12 vols, 1856–69).

21 Wild animals never kill for sport. Man is the only one to whom the torture and death of his fellow-creatures is amusing in itself.
1886 *Oceana*.

Fry, C(harles) B(urgess) 1872–1956

English all-round sportsman, who represented his country in athletics, cricket and soccer. As a cricketer, he played 26 Tests for England, some as captain. After World War II he served as India's delegate to the League of Nations and declined an offer of the throne of Albania.

22 It is a standing insult to sportsmen to have to play under a rule which assumes that players intend to trip, hack and push their opponents, and to behave like cads of the most unscrupulous kidney. The lines marking a penalty area are a disgrace to the playing fields of a public school.
1907 Quoted in Colin Jarman *The Guinness Dictionary of Sports Quotations* (1990).

23 In football it is widely acknowledged that if both sides agree to cheat, cheating is fair.
1911 Quoted in Colin Jarman *The Guinness Dictionary of Sports Quotations* (1990).

24 The game is so full of plot-interest and drama.
Of rugby union. Quoted in E H D Sewell *Rugger: The Man's Game* (1950).

Fry, Christopher *pseudonym of* *Christopher Harris* 1907–

English playwright. His early poetic drama was succeeded by comedies and tragi-comedies such as *A Phoenix Too Frequent* (1946) and *Venus Observed* (1950).

25 The Lady's Not for Burning.
1949 Play title, subsequently reworked by Margaret Thatcher in the form 'The lady's not for turning' at the Conservative Party Conference, 1980.

26 What after all
Is a halo? It's only one more thing to keep clean.
1949 *The Lady's Not for Burning*, act 1.

27 Where in this small-talking world can I find
A longitude with no platitude?
1949 *The Lady's Not for Burning*, act 3.

28 I hope
I've done nothing so monosyllabic as to cheat.
A spade is never so merely a spade as the word
Spade would imply.
1950 *Venus Observed*, act 1.

29 The Dark Is Light Enough.
1954 Title of play.

Fry, Elizabeth 1780–1845

English Quaker prison reformer who devoted her life to prison and asylum reform at home and abroad.

30 Does capital punishment tend to the security of the people? By no means. It hardens the hearts of men, and makes the loss of life appear light to them; and it renders life insecure, inasmuch as the law holds out that property is of greater value than life.
Quoted in Rachel E Cresswell and Katharine Fry *Memoir of the Life of Elizabeth Fry* (1848).

31 Punishment is not for revenge, but to lessen crime and reform the criminal.
Quoted in Rachel E Cresswell and Katharine Fry *Memoir of the Life of Elizabeth Fry* (1848).

Fry, Roger Eliot 1866–1934

English artist and art critic, who championed modern artists such as Cézanne, organizing the first London exhibition of Post-Impressionists in 1910. He devised an aesthetic theory of 'significant form'.

32 The trouble with Moore is that he knows what a work of art is, and is trying to make one.
c.1930 Of Henry Moore. Quoted in Robert Medley *Drawn from the Life: a Memoir* (1983).

33 Art is significant deformity.
Quoted in Virginia Woolf *Roger Fry* (1940), ch.8.

Fry, Stephen 1957–

English actor, writer and broadcaster.

34 Only my tongue, sir.
2004 When asked by a security guard at Heathrow Airport whether he had any sharp objects on him. Quoted in the *Observer*, 6 Jun.

Frye, Northrop 1912–91

Canadian literary critic and Episcopalian priest. His influential *Anatomy of Criticism* (1957) explores the common motifs and myths underlying literature.

35 Literature is a human apocalypse, man's revelation to man, and criticism is not a body of adjudications, but the awareness of that revelation, the last judgment of mankind.
1963 *The Educated Imagination*, 'The Keys of Dreamland'.

36 Literature is conscious mythology: as society develops, its mythical stories become structural principles of story-telling, its mythical concepts, sun-gods and the like, become habits of metaphoric thought. In a fully mature literary tradition the writer enters into a structure of traditional stories and images.
1971 *The Bush Garden*, 'Conclusion'.

37 Where is here?
'Haunted by Lack of Ghosts', in David Staines (ed) *The Canadian Imagination* (1977).

38 Most of my writing consists of an attempt to translate aphorisms into continuous prose.
Quoted in Richard Kostelanetz, 'The Literature Professors' Literature Professor', in *The Michigan Quarterly Review*, Fall 1978.

39 The knowledge that you can have is inexhaustible, and what is inexhaustible is benevolent. The knowledge that you cannot have is of the riddles of birth and death, of our future destiny and the purposes of God. Here there is no knowledge, but illusions that restrict freedom and limit hope. Accept the mystery behind knowledge: It is not darkness but shadow.
1988 Address, Metropolitan United Church, Toronto, 10 Apr, quoted by Alexandra Johnston in *Vic Report*, spring 1991.

40 Even the human heart is slightly left of centre.
Quoted by Paul Wilson in 'Growing Up with Orwell', in *The Idler*, Jul–Aug 1989.

Fuentes, Carlos 1928–

Mexican novelist and playwright, press secretary with the UN and Ambassador to France (1975–7). His works include short stories, and novels such as *Terra nostra* (1975), *The Old Gringo* (1985) and *The Years with Laura Diaz* (1999).

41 *Yo soy un artista. El placer de la carne le resta fuerzas a mi vocación pictórica, prefiero sentir que los jugos de mi sexo fluyen hacia un cuadro, lo irrigan, lo fertilizan, lo realzan; cástrame el goce de la carne, satisfáceme el goce del arte.*
I am an artist. The pleasure of the flesh robs strength from my artistic vocation, I prefer to feel my sexual juices flow toward a painting, wash over it, fertilize it, realize it; the delights of the flesh castrate me, the delights of art satisfy me.
1975 *Terra nostra*, 'El cronista'.

42 What America does best is to understand itself. What it does worst is to understand others.
1986 In *Time*, 16 Jun.

Fulbright, J(ames) William 1905–95

US Democratic politician, lawyer and author. As Chairman of the Senate Committee on Foreign Relations, he became a major critic of the Vietnam War (1964–75).

43 We have the power to do any damn fool thing we want to do, and we seem to do it every 10 minutes.
1952 In *Time*, 4 Feb.

44 In a democracy dissent is an act of faith. Like medicine, the test of its value is not in its taste, but its effects.

1966 Speech to the US Senate, 21 Apr.

45 Fearful and hostile behavior is not rational but neither is it uncommon, either to individuals or to nations, including our own.
1995 On the 'arrogance of power' of US policy on Vietnam. In the *New Yorker*, 6 Mar.

Fulford, Robert 1932–

Canadian cultural commentator.

46 My generation of Canadians grew up believing that, if we were very good or very smart, or both, we would someday *graduate* from Canada.
1970 'Notebook', in *Saturday Night*, Oct.

Fuller, (Sarah) Margaret, Marchioness Ossoli 1810–50

US feminist and literary critic. She edited *Dial* (a transcendentalist journal, 1840–2) and moved to New York (1844) then Italy (1847), where she married Marquis Ossoli and was involved in the Revolution. She was shipwrecked returning to New York.

47 Beware of over-great pleasure in being popular or even beloved.
1840 Letter to her brother, 20 Dec. Collected in Alice Rossi *The Feminist Papers* (1973).

48 As the friend of the negro assumes that one man cannot, by right, hold another in bondage, should the friend of woman assume that man cannot, by right, lay even well-meant restrictions on woman.
1843 'The Great Lawsuit', in *Dial*, vol.4, Jul.

49 It is well known that of every strong woman they say she has a masculine mind.
1843 'The Great Lawsuit', in *Dial*, vol.4, Jul.

Fuller, Peter 1947–90

English art critic, writer and founder of the magazine *Modern Painters*.

50 It is only a mild exaggeration to say that now no one wants Fine Artists, except Fine Artists, and that neither they nor anyone else have the slightest idea what they should be doing, or for whom they should be doing it.
1981 *Beyond the Crisis in Art*.

Fuller, R(ichard) Buckminster 1895–1983

US architect, inventor, engineer and philosopher, whose revolutionary technological designs reflect his personal vision of a better-designed and more efficient future. In 1962 he became Norton Professor of Poetry at Harvard.

51 God, to me, it seems,
is a verb
not a noun
proper or improper.
1940 Poem, published in *No More Secondhand God* (1963).
➤ *See Hugo 421:83*.

52 I just invent, then wait until man comes around to needing what I've invented.
1964 On his innovative geodesic domes. In *Time*, 10 Jun.

53 Either war is obsolete or men are.
1966 In the *New Yorker*, 8 Jan.

54 I am a passenger on the spaceship, Earth.

1969 *Operating Manual for Spaceship Earth*, ch.1.

55 Now there is one outstandingly important fact regarding Spaceship Earth, and that is that no instruction book came with it.
1969 *Operating Manual for Spaceship Earth*, ch.4.

56 If we do more with less, our response will be adequate to take care of everybody.
1972 In *Playboy*.

Fuller, Roy Broadbent 1912–91

English poet and novelist. His work is marked by careful construction and acute observation.

57 As horrible thoughts,
Loud fluttering aircraft slope above his head
At dusk.
The ridiculous empires break like biscuits.
1942 'The Middle of a War'.

58 The poets get a quizzical ahem.
They reflect time, I am the very ticking.
1944 'A Wry Smile'.

59 Anyone happy in this age and place
Is daft or corrupt. Better to abdicate
From a material and spiritual terrain
Fit only for barbarians.
1954 'Translation'.

Fuller, Thomas 1608–61

English antiquarian and divine. His 11-volume *Church History of Britain* (1655) was attacked as a 'rhapsody'. The unfinished *Great Worthies of England*, a biographical miscellany, was published by his son in 1661.

60 Know most of the rooms of thy native country before thou goest over the threshold thereof.
1642 *The Holy and Profane State*, bk.2, ch.4, 'Of Travelling'.

61 *Mon Mam Cymbry*. That is, Anglesea is the Mother of Wales.
1662 *History of the Worthies of England*, 'Anglesea'. The saying is an old one, meaning that Anglesey's corn is enough to sustain all Wales.

Fuller, Thomas 1654–1734

English physician and writer.

62 Bacchus hath drowned more men than Neptune.
1732 *Gnomologia*, no.830.

63 Borrowed garments never fit well.
1732 *Gnomologia*, no.1008.

64 Eat-well is drink-well's brother.
1732 *Gnomologia*, no.1357.

65 Fine cloth is never out of fashion.
1732 *Gnomologia*, no.1537.

66 God sends meat, and the devil sends cooks.
1732 *Gnomologia*, no.1687.

67 Good clothes open all doors.
1732 *Gnomologia*, no.1705.

68 It is in vain to mislike the current fashion.
1732 *Gnomologia*, no.2968.

69 The present fashion is always handsome.
1732 *Gnomologia*, no.4718.

70 Often drunk, and seldom sober

Falls like the leaves in October.
1732 *Gnomologia*, no.6219.

71 It signifies nothing to play well and lose.
1732 Quoted in Colin Jarman *The Guinness Dictionary of Sports Quotations* (1990).

Furthman, Jules 1888–1966

US screenwriter. His credits include *Shanghai Express* (1932), *Mutiny on the Bounty* (1935), *To Have and Have Not* (1945) and *The Big Sleep* (1946).

72 You know you don't have to act with me, Steve. You don't have to say anything and you don't have to do anything. Not a thing. Oh, maybe just whistle. You know how to whistle, don't you, Steve? You just put your lips together—and blow.
1945 Lauren Bacall as Slim to Humphrey Bogart (Steve) in *To Have and Have Not* (with William Faulkner).

Fuseli, Henry 1741–1825

Swiss-born British painter and art critic. He was a key figure of the Romantic movement.

73 Art, like love, excludes all competition and absorbs the man.
1789 *Aphorisms on Art*, no.3 (published 1831).

74 The superiority of the Greeks seems not so much the result of climate and society, as of the simplicity of their end and the uniformity of their means.
1789 *Aphorisms on Art*, no.148 (published 1831).

75 Art among a religious race produces reliques; among a military one, trophies, among a commercial one, articles of trade.
1789 *Aphorisms on Art*, no.149 (published 1831).

76 The forms of virtue are erect, the forms of pleasure undulate.
1789 *Aphorisms on Art*, no.194 (published 1831).

77 Selection is the invention of the landscape painter.
1789 *Aphorisms on Art*, no.237, (published 1831).

Fyffe, Will 1885–1947

Scottish comedian, singer and actor. He wrote several sketches for Harry Lauder and when they were rejected performed them himself, thereby launching a long and successful career on stage and in film.

78 I belong to Glasgow
Dear old Glasgow town!
But what's the matter with Glasgow?
For it's going round and round.
I'm only a common old working chap,
As anyone can see,
But when I get a couple of drinks on a Saturday,
Glasgow belongs to me.
1921 'I Belong to Glasgow', chorus.

Fyleman, Rose 1877–1957

English children's writer.

79 There are fairies at the bottom of our garden.
1918 *Fairies and Chimneys*, 'The Fairies'.

Gabor, Dennis 1900–79

Hungarian-born British physicist. Gabor studied and worked in Germany but left in 1933 to become professor of electronics at Imperial College, London. He did important work on the electronic microscope and is generally recognized as the main contributor to the discovery of holography.

80 Till now man has been up against Nature: from now on he will be up against his own nature.
1964 *Inventing the Future*.

81 The most important and urgent problems of the technology of today are no longer the satisfactions of the primary needs or of archetypal wishes, but the reparation of the evils and damages wrought by the technology of yesterday.
1970 *Innovations*.

Gabor, Zsa Zsa 1919–

Hungarian-born US actress, sister of Eva Gabor. Her films include *Moulin Rouge* (1953), *Touch of Evil* (1958) and *Arrivederci Baby* (1966).

82 I never hated a man enough to give him diamonds back.
Quoted in the *Observer*, 28 Aug 1957.

83 A girl must marry for love and keep on marrying until she finds it.
Attributed.

Gagarin, Yuri A(lekseyevich) 1934–68

Soviet cosmonaut, the first person to achieve orbital space flight, on 12 Apr 1961.

84 I could have gone on flying through space forever.
1961 In the *New York Times*, 14 Apr.

Gainsborough, Thomas 1727–88

English portrait and landscape painter.

85 I wish you would recollect that Painting and Punctuality mix like Oil and Vinegar, and that Genius and regularity are utter Enemies and must be to the end of time.
1772 Letter to Edward Stratford, 1 May, excusing himself for not yet finishing the portrait of him and his wife.

86 We are all going to heaven, and Vandyke is of the company.
1788 Last words (attributed), quoted in William B Boulton *Thomas Gainsborough* (1905), ch.9.

Gaitskell, Hugh 1906–63

English Labour politician, Leader of the Opposition (1955–63). He opposed Eden's Suez action (1956), and refused to accept a narrow conference vote for unilateral disarmament (1960), surviving the subsequent leadership challenge.

87 Some of us will fight and fight again to save the party we love. We will fight and fight again to bring back sanity and honesty and dignity, so that our party, with its great past,

may retain its glory and its greatness.
1960 Denouncing unilateralists trying to gain control of the party. Labour Party conference speech, Oct.

88 Let us not forget that we can never go farther than we can persuade at least half the people to go.
1961 Labour Party conference speech, Oct.

89 It does mean the end of Britain as an independent European state. It means the end of a thousand years of history.
1962 On Britain joining the European Community. Labour Party conference speech, Oct.

Galbraith, John Kenneth 1908–

Canadian-born US economist and diplomat, Professor at Harvard (1949–75), Ambassador to India (1961–3) and adviser to Presidents Kennedy and Johnson.

90 The charge that an idea is radical, impractical, or long-haired is met by showing that a prominent businessman has favored it…an additional tactic in this strategy of defense…is to assert that Winston Churchill once sponsored the particular idea. If one is challenged, a sufficiently careful investigation will show that he did.
1955 *Economics and the Art of Controversy.*

91 Few things are as immutable as the addiction of political groups to the ideas by which they have once won office.
1958 *The Affluent Society.*

92 In the affluent society, no useful distinction can be made between luxuries and necessities.
1958 *The Affluent Society.*

93 It takes a certain brashness to attack the accepted economic legends but none at all to perpetuate them. So they are perpetuated.
1960 *The Liberal Hour.*

94 Politics is not the art of the possible. It consists in choosing between the disastrous and the unpalatable.
1962 Letter to John F Kennedy, 2 Mar.
➡ *See Butler 176:34.*

95 The line dividing the state from what is called private enterprise, or at least from the highly organized part of it, is a traditional fiction.
1967 *The New Industrial State.*

96 The real accomplishment of modern science and technology consists in taking ordinary men, informing them narrowly and deeply and then, through appropriate organization, arranging to have their knowledge combined with that of other specialized but equally ordinary men. This dispenses with the need for genius. The resulting performance, though less inspiring, is far more predictable.
1967 *The New Industrial State.*

97 There are times in politics when you must be on the right side and lose.
1968 In the *Observer*, 11 Feb.

98 It is the good fortune of the affluent country that the opportunity cost of economic discussion is low and hence it can afford all kinds.
1971 *Economics, Peace, and Laughter.*

99 In a world where for pedagogic and other purposes a very large number of economists is required, an arrangement which discourages many of them from rendering public advice would seem to be well conceived.
1971 *Economics, Peace, and Laughter.*

1 Much discussion of money involves a heavy overlay of priestly incantation.
1975 *Money*, p.4.

2 Much of the world's work, it has been said, is done by men who do not feel quite well. Marx is a case in point.
1977 *The Age of Uncertainty*, ch.3.

3 We have escapist fiction…why not escapist biography?
1980 In the *New York Times*, 27 Jul.

4 Speeches in our culture are the vacuum that fills a vacuum.
1984 Speech at the American University, Washington DC. Quoted in *Time* magazine, 18 Jun.

Galeano, Eduardo 1940–

Uruguayan writer and journalist. His books include *Days and Nights of Love and War* (1978) and the trilogy *Memory of Fire* (1985–8).

5 In the house of words was a table of colors. They offered themselves in great fountains and each poet took the color he needed: lemon yellow or sun yellow, ocean blue or smoke blue, crimson red, blood red, wine red.
1991 *The Book of Embraces.*

Galen *or* Claudius Galenus c.130–c.201AD

Greek physician, imperial physician to Marcus Aurelius, Commodus and Severus. He wrote extensively on medical and philosophical matters, and his theories have been highly influential.

6 Much music marreth men's manners.
Quoted in Roger Ascham *Toxophilus* (1545).

Galilei, Galileo 1564–1642

Italian astronomer, mathematician and physicist, credited with anticipating Newton's laws of motion. He constructed the first astronomical telescope, and controversially argued that the earth revolved around the sun.

7 *Eppur si muove.*
Nevertheless, it moves.
1632 Attributed muttered remark, after being compelled to publicly renounce his arguments against a geocentric universe. This famous quotation is almost certainly an invention.

8 Light held together by moisture.
Attributed, a description of wine.

Gallagher, Noel 1967–

English rock star, founder member of the band Oasis.

9 Some might say they don't believe in heaven
Go and tell it to the man who lives in hell.
1995 'Some Might Say'.

10 I would hope we mean more to people than putting money in a church basket and saying ten Hail Marys on a Sunday. Has God played Knebworth recently?
1997 On the attraction of Oasis. In the *New Musical Express*, 12 Jul.

11 The funny thing is, that mouthing off three years ago about how we were going to be the biggest band in the world, we actually went and done it. And it was a piece of piss.

1998 Quoted in the *Guinness Rockopedia*.

Gallico, Paul William 1897–1976

US journalist, novelist and short-story writer. His works include *The Snow Goose* (1941) and *The Poseidon Adventure* (1969).

12 College football today is one of the last great strongholds of genuine old-fashioned American hypocrisy.

1938 *Farewell to Sport*.

13 When in Doubt—Wash.

1950 *Jennie*, ch.5, chapter title. Peter, having turned into a cat, is taught the proper etiquette.

14 I have covered boxing, promoted boxing, watched it, thought about it, and after long reflection I cannot find a single thing that is good about it either from the point of view of participant or spectator.

Quoted in Edith Summerskill *The Ignoble Art* (1956).

15 No one can be as calculatedly rude as the British, which amazes Americans, who do not understand studied insult and can only offer abuse as a substitute.

1962 In the *New York Times*, 14 Jan.

Galloway, George 1954–

Scottish Labour politician.

16 I saw 'New Labour' conceived, watched it gestate, witnessed its birth and growth. Now I fervently hope I will be present at its death.

2004 *I'm Not the Only One*.

Galloway, Janice 1956–

Scottish writer. She worked as a teacher, but became a full-time writer after the success of her first novel *The Trick Is to Keep Breathing* (1989), chronicling a mental breakdown. Other works include the short-story collection *Blood* (1991) and the novel *Clara* (2002).

17 The Trick Is to Keep Breathing.

1989 Title of first novel.

18 I write because I hate being told HOW IT IS. I didn't realise that for a long while. I thought it was LIFE I hated: that the unfairnesses that were explained as JUST HOW IT IS were JUST HOW IT IS. BUT HOW IT IS wasn't.

1993 'Objective Truth and the Grinding Machine'. In Brown and Munro (eds) *Writers Writing* (1993).

19 Quiet book-learning in monasteries and ethereal music, sonnets and courtly love—that stuff is all fantasy and veneer… You couldn't afford to let the beauty of the thing seduce you too far or you forgot the truth and the truth was always hard as iron bloody bars.

1994 *Foreign Parts*, ch.7.

Gallup, George Horace 1901–84

US statistician and public opinion expert. He developed the Gallup polls for testing public opinion, which proved their worth by correctly predicting Franklin Roosevelt's 1936 election victory.

20 Polling is merely an instrument for gauging public opinion. When a president or any other leader pays attention to poll results, he is, in effect, paying attention to the views of the people. Any other interpretation is nonsense.

1979 NBC news, 1 Dec.

21 I could prove God statistically.

Attributed.

Galsworthy, John 1867–1933

English novelist and playwright, best known for his series of novels *The Forsyte Saga* (1906–28). His plays, including *Strife* (1909), illustrate his interest in social and ethical issues. He was awarded the Nobel prize in 1932.

22 From all *I* can learn, he's got no business, no income, and no connection worth speaking of; but then, I know nothing—nobody tells me anything.

1906 *The Man of Property*, pt.1, ch.1.

23 When a Forsyte was engaged, married, or born, the Forsytes were present; when a Forsyte died—but no Forsyte had as yet died; they did not die; death being contrary to their principles, they took precautions against it, the instinctive precautions of highly vitalised persons who resent encroachments on their property.

1906 *The Man of Property*, pt.1, ch.1.

24 It is not good enough to spend time and ink in describing the penultimate sensations and physical movements of people getting into a state of rut, we all know them so well.

1914 On D H Lawrence's *Sons and Lovers*, in a letter to Edward Garnett, 13 Apr.

25 He was afflicted by the thought that where Beauty was, nothing ever ran quite straight, which, no doubt, was why so many people looked on it as immoral.

1920 *In Chancery*, pt.1, ch.13.

26 When we began this fight, we had clean hands—are they clean now? What's gentility worth if it can't stand fire?

1920 *The Skin Game*, act 3.

27 Slang is vigorous and apt. Probably most of our vital words were once slang.

1927 *Castles in Spain and Other Screeds*.

Galt, John 1779–1839

Scottish novelist and Canadian pioneer. After a failed business venture in London he travelled in the Levant (1809–11) and later turned to writing.

28 In a word, man in London is not quite so good a creature as he is out of it.

1821 *The Ayrshire Legatees*, ch.7, 'Discoveries and Rebellions', letter 22.

29 From the lone shieling of the misty island
Mountains divide us, and the waste of seas—
Yet still the blood is strong, the heart is Highland,
And we in dreams behold the Hebrides!
Fair these broad meads, these hoary woods are grand;
But we are exiles from our fathers' land.

1829 'Canadian Boat Song', a translation from the Gaelic attributed to Galt, published in *Blackwood's Magazine*, Sep. It has also been attributed to Walter Scott.

Galtieri, Leopoldo Fortunato 1926–2003

Argentinian soldier and politician, President of Argentina (1981–3). In 1982, he ordered the invasion of the disputed

Malvinas (Falkland) Islands; their recovery by Britain led to his downfall.

30 Why are you telling me this? The British won't fight.
1982 Responding to a warning from US Secretary of State Alexander Haig about the consequence of the invasion.

Galton, Sir Francis 1822–1911

English scientist. He travelled widely in Africa and wrote *The Art of Travel* (1855), which became the explorer's standard handbook.

31 There are even times when any assumption of dignity becomes ludicrous, and the traveller must, as Mungo Park once had to do, 'lay down as a rule to make himself as useless and as insignificant as possible, as the only means of recovering his liberty'.
1855 *The Art of Travel.*

Gandhi, Indira Priyad Arshini 1917–84

Indian politician and Prime Minister (1966–77, 1980–4). Although a leader of the developing nations, she failed to suppress sectarian violence at home and was assassinated by Sikh extremists, members of her bodyguard.

32 Even if I die in the service of this nation, I would be proud of it. Every drop of my blood, I am sure, will contribute to the growth of this nation and make it strong and dynamic.
1984 Speech at Orissa, 31 Oct, the day before her assassination.

Gandhi, Mohandas Karamchand *known as* **Mahatma** [*great soul*] 1869–1948

Indian nationalist leader, who advocated peaceful non-cooperation to achieve independence, but was jailed for conspiracy (1922–4) following his civil disobedience campaign. After independence (1947), his attempts to stop the Hindu–Muslim conflict in Bengal led to his assassination by a Hindu fanatic.

33 I claim that in losing the spinning wheel we lost our left lung. We are, therefore, suffering from galloping consumption. The restoration of the wheel arrests the progress of the…disease.
1921 Speech, 13 Oct.

34 Non-violence is the first article of my faith. It is also the last article of my creed.
1922 Speech at Shahi Bag, 18 Mar.

35 Non-violence is not a garment to be put on and off at will. Its seat is in the heart, and it must be an inseparable part of our very being.
1926 *War or Peace*, 'Young India'.

36 What do I think of Western civilization? I think that it would be a good idea.
Attributed.

Gandhi, Sonia 1946–

Italian-born Indian politician, widow of Rajiv Gandhi and daughter-in-law of Indira Gandhi.

37 There is no question. It is my inner voice, it is my conscience.
2004 On turning down the office of Indian prime minister, 18 May.

Garbo, Greta *pseudonym of* **Greta Lovisa Gustafsson** 1905–90

Swedish-born actress who went to the US in 1925 with director Mauritz Stiller. Her films at MGM during the 1930s include *Queen Christina* (1933), *Anna Karenina* (1936) and *Ninotchka* (1939). She retired in 1941.

38 I want to be alone.
1932 The media have famously attributed these words to Garbo although she always denied she said them. In the film *Grand Hotel* (1932) Grusinskaya (played by Garbo) says 'I want to be left alone'.

39 One day, there's a hand that goes over the face and changes it. You look like an apple that isn't young anymore.
Quoted in *Vanity Fair*, Feb 1994.

García Márquez, Gabriel 1928–

Colombian novelist and journalist, awarded the Nobel prize for literature (1982). His fiction, typically set in the imaginary village of Macondo, tends to magic realism.

40 *No se le había ocurrido pensar hasta entonces que la literatura fuera el mejor juguete que se había inventado para burlarse de la gente.*
It had never occurred to him until then to think that literature was the best plaything that had ever been invented to make fun of people.
1967 *Cien años de soledad* (translated as *One Hundred Years of Solitude*, 1970).

41 The last optimist left in Colombia.
Attributed.

Garcilaso de la Vega, Inca 1539–1616

Peruvian soldier, translator and historian, son of a Spanish father and an Inca princess. He went to Spain in 1560 and became a soldier. His historical compositions draw on both indigenous sources and imagination.

42 *Porque allá los españoles y las otras naciones…como tienen historias divinas y humanas, saben por ellas cuándo empezaron a reinar sus Reyes y los ajenos…todo esto y mucho más saben por sus libros. Empero vosotros, que carecéis de ellos, Qué memoria tenéis de vuestras antiguallas?, Quién fue el primero de nuestros Incas?*
Over there Spaniards and other nations know from their divine and human history when their Kings and other peoples' Kings began their reigns… Their books teach them all of this, and much more. But you, who have no books, what memories do you have of your ancient past? Who was our first Inca?
1609 *Comentarios reales* (*The Royal Commentaries of Peru*, 1688), bk.1, ch.15.

Gardner, Ava *originally* **Lucy Johnson** 1922–90

US film actress. Signed for MGM as a teenager, she achieved fame in *The Killers* (1946) and later *The Barefoot Contessa* (1954) and *Night of the Iguana* (1964). She was married to Mickey Rooney, Artie Shaw and Frank Sinatra.

43 *On the Beach* is a story about the end of the world, and Melbourne sure is the right place to film it.
1959 Alleged comment to Australian journalist Neil Jillett of the Melbourne *Age* at the shooting of a film based on the book by British–Australian novelist Nevil Shute.

44 What I'd really like to say about stardom is that it gave me everything I never wanted.
1990 *Ava: My Story.*

Gardner, John William 1912–77

US public official, Secretary of Health, Education and Welfare (1965–8). In 1970 he founded the citizens' lobby Common Force, which he chaired until his death.

45 We are all faced with a series of great opportunities—brilliantly disguised as insoluble problems.
Quoted in *Reader's Digest*, Mar 1966.

46 We get richer and richer in filthier and filthier communities until we reach a final stage of affluent misery—a crocus on a garbage heap.
1969 In the *New York Times*, 9 Oct.

Garibaldi, Giuseppe 1807–82

Italian patriot, twice forced to flee the country for his revolutionary activities. He returned in 1859 for Italy's war of liberation, leading his thousand 'Red Shirts', conquering Sicily and Naples for the unified kingdom of Italy.

47 England is a great and powerful nation, foremost in human progress, enemy to despotism, the only safe refuge for the exile, friend of the oppressed. If ever England should be so circumstanced as to require the help of any ally, cursed be the Italian who would not step forward with me in her defence.
1854 Letter, 12 Apr.

48 *Soldati, io esco da Roma. Chi vuole continuare la guerra contro lo straniero venga con me. Non posso offrigli né onori né stipendi; gli offro fame, sete, marce forzate, battaglie e morte. Chi ama la Patria me segua.*
Soldiers, I'm getting out of Rome. Anyone who wants to carry on the war against the outsiders, follow me. I can offer you neither honours nor wages, I offer you hunger, thirst, forced marches, battles and death. Anyone who loves his country, follow me.
Quoted in Giuseppe Guerzoni *Garibaldi* (1882), vol.1.

Garland, (Hannibal) Hamlin 1860–1940

US writer. He is remembered chiefly for his stories of Midwest farm life in books including *Main-Travelled Roads* (1891) and *Prairie Folks* (1892), but also wrote novels, essays and memoirs.

49 Like the main-travelled road of life it is traversed by many classes of people, but the poor and the weary predominate.
1891 *Main-Travelled Roads*, 'The Main-Travelled Road of the West'.

50 There is no gilding of setting sun or glamor of poetry to light up the ferocious and endless toil of the farmers' wives.
1899 *Boy Life on the Prairie*, 'Melons and Early Frost'.

Garner, John Nance 1868–1967

US lawyer and politician, Speaker of the House (1931–3) and Vice-President under President Roosevelt (1933–41). He opposed Roosevelt's third-term candidacy and retired in 1941.

51 Worst damnfool mistake I ever made was letting myself be elected Vice-President of the United States. Should have stuck…as Speaker of the House… Gave up the second most important job in Government for eight long years as Roosevelt's spare tire.
1963 In the *Saturday Evening Post*, 2 Nov.

52 The vice-presidency isn't worth a pitcher of warm piss. It doesn't amount to a hill of beans.
Quoted in O C Fisher *Cactus Jack* (1978), ch.11.

Garrick, David 1717–79

English actor and theatre manager. He revolutionized acting with his naturalistic Shakespearean heroes and in 1747 became manager of the Drury Lane theatre, introducing many theatrical reforms.

53 Here lies Nolly Goldsmith, for shortness called Noll, Who wrote like an angel, but talked like poor Poll.
1773 Of Oliver Goldsmith. 'Impromptu Epitaph'.

54 Are these the choice dishes the Doctor has sent us? Is this the great poet whose works so content us? This Goldsmith's fine feast, who has written fine books? Heaven sends us fine meat, but the Devil sends cooks.
1777 'On Doctor Goldsmith's Characteristical Cookery'.

55 Comedy is a very serious thing.
Attributed, in conversation with the actor Jack Bannister.

Garvey, Marcus 1887–1940

Jamaican activist and advocate of black nationalism. In 1914 he founded the Universal Negro Improvement Association (UNIA). Rejecting integration, he called for a 'back to Africa' movement.

56 We are not engaged in domestic politics, in church building or in social uplift work, but we are engaged in nation building.
1922 Speech to the Principles of the Universal Negro Improvement Association, New York, 25 Nov.

57 There is no humanity before that which starts with yourself.
1923 'African Fundamentalism, a Racial Hierarchy and Empire for Negroes'.

Gaskell, Mrs Elizabeth Cleghorn née *Stevenson* 1810–65

English novelist. She is best known for her novels of social realism, including *North and South* (1855), in which she criticized the conditions in English factories, and *Cranford* (1851–3).

58 Their dress is very independent of fashion; as they observe, 'What does it signify how we dress here at Cranford, where everybody knows us?' And if they go from home, their reason is equally cogent, 'What does it signify how we dress here, where nobody knows us?'
1851–3 Of the Cranford ladies. *Cranford*, ch.1.

59 A man…is *so* in the way in the house!
1851–3 *Cranford*, ch.1.

Gass, William H(oward) 1924–

US novelist, literary theorist and philosopher, best known for his experimental story collection *In the Heart of the Heart of the Country* (1968). His massive autobiographical novel, *The Tunnel* (1995), was in progress for more than 20 years.

60 I love metaphor the way some people love junk food.
1977 Interview in *Paris Review*, Summer.

61 One's complete sentences are attempts, as often as not, to complete an incomplete self with words.

1977 Interview in *Paris Review*, Summer.

Gates, Bill (William Henry III) 1955–

US businessman, who founded the Microsoft Corporation with Paul Allen in 1974. In 1980 the company bought an operating system and adapted it for the IBM personal computer; the company is now the world's chief software producer for personal computers.

62 I think business is very simple. Profit. Loss. Take the sales, subtract the costs, you get this big positive number. The math is quite straightforward.
1993 Quoted in the *US News and World Report*, 15 Feb.

63 Technology is just a tool. In terms of getting the kids working together and motivating them, the teacher is the most important.
1997 In the *Independent on Sunday*, 12 Oct.

64 A fundamental new rule for business is that the Internet changes everything.
1999 *Business@the Speed of Thought* (co-written with Collins Hemingway).

65 The Internet is becoming the town square for the global village of tomorrow.
1999 *Business@the Speed of Thought* (co-written with Collins Hemingway).

Gauguin, Paul 1848–1903

French Post-Impressionist painter, printmaker and sculptor.

66 There are noble tones, ordinary ones, tranquil harmonies, consoling ones, others which excite by their vigour.
1885 Letter to Emile Schuffenecker.

67 Some advice: do not paint too much after nature. Art is an abstraction; derive this abstraction from nature while dreaming before it, and think more of the creation which will result than of nature.
1888 Letter to Emile Schuffenecker.

68 You may dream freely when you listen to music as well as when you look at painting. When you read a book you are the slave of the author's mind.
c.1888 *Notes Synthétiques*, quoted in J Rewald *Gauguin* (1938).

Gautier, Théophile 1811–72

French poet, novelist and critic. He propounded the theory of 'art for art's sake', and was honoured by Baudelaire. His many novels include the celebrated *Mademoiselle de Maupin* (1835).

69 *Virginité, mysticisme, mélancolie! Trois mots inconnus, trois maladies nouvelles apportées par le Christ.*
Virginity, mysticism, melancholy! Three unknown words, three new illnesses brought by Christ.
1835 *Mademoiselle de Maupin.*

70 *Hélas! Les femmes n'ont lu que le roman de l'homme et jamais son histoire.*
Alas, women have read only the novel of mankind, not the history.
1835 *Mademoiselle de Maupin.*

71 *L'orgueil sort du coeur le jour où l'amour y entre.*
Pride leaves the heart the moment love enters it.
1835 *Mademoiselle de Maupin.*

72 The religion of money is today the only one which has no unbelievers.

1860s On the France of the Second Republic. Quoted in Joanna Richardson *The Courtesans* (1967), p.2.

Gavarni *real name* *Guillaume Sulpice Chevalier* 1804–88

French lithographer.

73 *Les Enfants Terribles.*
The Little Terrors.
1842 Title of a series of prints.

Gay, James 1810–91

Canadian poet, the self-styled 'Poet Laureate of Canada'.

74 Hail our Great Queen in her regalia;
One foot in Canada, the other in Australia.
Attributed to Gay by William Arthur Deacon in *The Four Jameses* (1927).

Gay, John 1685–1732

English poet, best known for his extraordinarily popular *The Beggar's Opera* (1728), set to music by Pepusch. In his final years he lived chiefly with his patrons, the Duke and Duchess of Queensberry.

75 Praising all alike, is praising none.
1714 'A Letter to a Lady', l.114.

76 Life is a jest; and all things show it.
I thought so once; but now I know it.
1720 'My Own Epitaph'.

77 A woman's friendship ever ends in love.
1720 *Dione*, act 4, sc.6.

78 And when a lady's in the case,
You know, all other things give place.
1727 *Fables*, 'The Hare and Many Friends', l.41.

79 She who trifles with all
Is less likely to fall
Than she who but trifles with one.
1727 'The Coquet Mother and the Coquet Daughter'.

80 How, like a moth, the simple maid
Still plays around the flame!
1728 *The Beggar's Opera*, act 1, sc.4, air 4.

81 Do you think your mother and I should have lived comfortably so long together, if ever we had been married?
1728 *The Beggar's Opera*, act 1, sc.8.

82 Money, wife, is the true fuller's earth for reputations, there is not a spot or a stain but what it can take out.
1728 *The Beggar's Opera*, act 1, sc.9.

83 The comfortable estate of widowhood, is the only hope that keeps up a wife's spirits.
1728 *The Beggar's Opera*, act 1, sc.10.

84 If with me you'd fondly stray
Over the hills and far away.
1728 *The Beggar's Opera*, act 1, sc.13, air 16.

85 I must have women. There is nothing unbends the mind like them.
1728 *The Beggar's Opera*, act 2, sc.3.

86 To cheat a man is nothing; but the woman must have fine parts indeed who cheats a woman!
1728 *The Beggar's Opera*, act 2, sc.4.

87 How happy I could be with either,
Were t'other dear charmer away!

1728 *The Beggar's Opera*, act 2, sc.13.

88 Music might tame and civilize wild beasts, but 'tis evident it never yet could tame and civilize musicians.
1729 *Polly*.

89 From wine what sudden friendship springs!
1738 *Fables*, 'The Squire and His Cur', l.4.

Gay, Noel *pseudonym of* **Richard Moxon Armitage** 1898–1954

British songwriter who wrote for stage and screen. His song 'Leaning on a Lamp-Post' became one of George Formby's greatest successes.

90 I'm leaning on a lamp-post at the corner of the street
In case a certain little lady comes by.
1937 Song sung by George Formby, featured in the film *Feather Your Nest*.

Geddes, Sir Eric Campbell 1875–1937

British politician, a member of the War Cabinet in 1918. He presided over the 'Geddes Axe' committee on national expenditure in 1922.

91 The Germans, if this Government is returned, are going to pay every penny. They are going to be squeezed as a lemon is squeezed—until the pips squeak. My only doubt is not whether we can squeeze hard enough, but whether there is enough juice.
1918 Speech at Cambridge Guildhall, 10 Dec.

Gee, Maggie 1948–

English novelist. She has written a number of highly regarded literary novels.

92 There are people not spoken about, people not written about, people whose name is a way of saying they are not there. *Hibakusha*, atomic victims—the scarred who carry our scars.
1983 Of the victims of the bombing of Hiroshima and Nagasaki. *The Burning Book*, ch.1.

93 The alcohol made the present enough, it held her in its golden hand, where past and future were comprehended, where nothing mattered, nothing was lost, where everything could be known and forgiven, where she herself could be whole at last.
1994 *Lost Children*, ch.35.

Geldof, Bob 1954–

Irish rock musician and philanthropist, founder of the Boomtown Rats (1975–86). He established the pop charity Bandaid in 1984 for African famine relief, and organized simultaneous Live Aid concerts in Philadelphia and London in 1985. He was awarded an honorary KBE in 1986.

94 Most people get into bands for three very simple rock and roll reasons: to get laid, to get fame, and to get rich.
1977 In *Melody Maker*, 27 Aug.

95 Irish Americans are about as Irish as Black Americans are African.
1986 In the *Observer*, 22 Jun.

96 Rock 'n' roll is instant coffee.
Quoted in David Pickering *Brewer's Twentieth Century Music* (1994).

Gellhorn, Martha Ellis 1908–98

US journalist and novelist. She covered numerous wars throughout the world between 1936 and 1985 and also wrote essays and fiction. Her first husband (1940–5) was Ernest Hemingway.

97 I see mysteries and complications wherever I look, and I have never met a steadily logical person.
1959 *The Face of War*, introduction.

98 It would be a bitter cosmic joke if we destroy ourselves due to atrophy of the imagination.
1959 *The Face of War*, introduction.

99 Gradually I came to realize that people will more readily swallow lies than truth, as if the taste of lies was homey, appetizing: a habit.
1959 *The Face of War*, introduction.

1 You define your own horror journey, according to your taste. My definition of what makes a journey wholly or partially horrible is boredom. Add discomfort, fatigue, strain in large amounts to get the purest-quality horror, but the kernel is boredom. I offer that as a universal test of travel; boredom, called by any other name, is why you yearn for the first available transport out. But what bores whom?… The threshold of boredom must be like the threshold of pain, different in all of us.
1979 *Travels with Myself and Another*.

2 We savaged them, though they had never hurt us, and we cannot find it in our hearts, our honor, to give them help—because the government of Vietnam is Communist. And perhaps because they won.
1986 On the Vietnamese. *The Face of War* (rev edn), 'The War in Vietnam— Vietnam Again, 1986'.

Genet, Jean 1910–86

French playwright, author and poet who spent much of his youth in jail. Once his literary talent was discovered, many, including Sartre, came to champion his cause, even dubbing him 'Saint Genet'.

3 *Jean Cocteau me croit un mauvais voleur. C'est parce qu'auprès de lui je suis d'abord un écrivain. Les voleurs me croient un mauvais écrivain.*
Jean Cocteau thinks that I am a poor thief. That's because next to him I am primarily a writer. Thieves think that I am a poor writer.
1949 *Journal du voleur*.

4 *L'artiste n'a pas—ou le poète—pour fonction de trouver la solution pratique des problèmes du mal.*
It is not up to the artist or to the poet to find practical solutions to the problems of evil.
1956 *Le Balcon*, 'Avertissement'.

5 *Prisons, cachots, lieux bénis où le mal est impossible, puisqu'ils sont le carrefour de toute la malédiction du monde. On ne peut pas commettre le mal dans le mal.*
Prison, dungeons, blessed places where evil is impossible because they are the crossroads of all the evil in the world. One cannot commit evil in hell.
1956 *Le Balcon*, 'Deuxième tableau'.

6 *Ce qu'il nous faut, c'est la haine. D'elle naîtront nos idées.*
Hatred is what we need. Ideas are born from hatred.
1958 *Les Nègres*, épigraphe.

7 *Dans les villes actuelles, le seul lieu,—hélas encore vers la périphérie—où un théâtre pourrait être construit, c'est le cimetière.*

In today's cities, the only place—unfortunately on the outskirts—to construct a theatre is a cemetery.

1959 *L'Étrange Mort d'…*

Genghis Khan *originally* **Temujin** c.1167–1227

Mongol conqueror. Leader of the Mongols from 1206, he conquered widely throughout Asia, penetrating Persia and Eastern Europe as far as the Dnieper River. His empire was divided between his sons and grandsons on his death.

8 Happiness lies in conquering one's enemies, in driving them in front of oneself, in taking their property, in savouring their despair, in outraging their wives and daughters.

c.1210 Quoted in Witold Rodzinski *The Walled Kingdom: A History of China* (1979).

Geoffrey de Breteuil fl.12c

French ecclesiastic.

9 *Claustrum sine armario quasi castrum sine armamentario. Ipsum armarium nostrum est armamenturium.*

A cloister without a library is like a castle without an armoury. For the library is our armoury.

c.1165 Letter to Peter Mangot.

George I 1660–1727

King of Great Britain and Ireland and Elector of Hanover. He succeeded to the British throne in 1714 on the death of Queen Anne in accordance with the Act of Settlement (1701) and was the first Hanoverian King of Great Britain and Ireland. He never mastered English.

10 I hate all Boets and Bainters.

In John Campbell *Lives of the Chief Justices*, 'Lord Mansfield' (1849).

George II 1683–1760

King of Great Britain and Ireland (1727–60) and Elector of Hanover, last British king to command in the field, at Dettingen, 1743. His reign saw the Jacobite defeat at Culloden (1746), British involvement in India after Plassey (1757) and the onset of the Seven Years War.

11 Oh! he is mad is he? Then I hope he will *bite* some of my other generals.

c.1759 Replying to remarks made about General James Wolfe by the Duke of Newcastle. Quoted in Henry Beckles Wilson *Life and Letters of James Wolfe* (1909), ch.17.

George III 1738–1820

King of Great Britain and Ireland (1760–1820). In the 1770s he was blamed with North for the loss of the American colonies. In 1783 he called Pitt (the Younger) to office, ending the supremacy of the old Whig families. As a result of his supposed insanity (now believed to have been porphyria), his son George was made Regent.

12 I can never suppose this country so far lost to all ideas of self-importance as to be willing to grant America independence; if that could ever be adopted, I shall despair of this country being ever preserved from a state of inferiority, and consequently falling into a very low class among the European states.

1780 Letter to Lord North, 7 Mar.

13 I was the last to consent to the separation, but the separation having been made, and having become inevitable, I have always said that I would be the first to meet the friendship of the United States as an independent power.

1785 Letter to John Adams, first US Ambassador to England, 1 Jun.

George V 1865–1936

King of Great Britain and Northern Ireland (1910–36). He served in the navy and travelled widely in the Empire. His reign saw the Union of South Africa (1910), World War I (1914–18), the Irish Free State Settlement (1922) and the General Strike (1926).

14 I have many times asked myself whether there can be more potent advocates of peace on earth through the years to come than this massed multitude of silent witnesses to the desolation of war.

1922 Message read at the Terlincthun Cemetery, Boulogne, 13 May.

15 Today 23 years ago, dear Grandmama died. I wonder what she would have thought of a Labour government.

1924 Of Queen Victoria. Diary entry, 22 Jan, on having invited Ramsay Macdonald to form the first Labour administration.

16 Bugger Bognor.

1929 or 1936 Reply to a courtier who had remarked 'Cheer up, your Majesty, you will soon be at Bognor again', either during his convalescence or on his deathbed. Quoted in Kenneth Rose *King George V* (1983), ch.9.

17 I will not have another war. If there is another and we are threatened with being brought into it, I will go to Trafalgar Square and wave a red flag myself sooner than allow this country to be brought in.

1935 To David Lloyd George, 10 May.

18 Golf always makes me so damned angry.

Quoted in Colin Jarman *The Guinness Dictionary of Sports Quotations* (1990).

George VI 1895–1952

King of Great Britain and Northern Ireland (1936–52). After ascending the throne (on the abdication of his elder brother, Edward VIII), he remained in bomb-damaged Buckingham Palace during World War II and delivered many broadcasts, mastering a speech impediment.

19 The British Empire has advanced to a new conception of autonomy and freedom, to the idea of a system of British nations, each freely ordering its own individual life, but bound together in unity by allegiance to one Crown, and co-operating in all that concerns the common weal.

1927 Opening, as Duke of York, the first Australian Parliament to assemble in Canberra, 9 May.

20 Abroad is bloody.

Quoted in W H Auden *A Certain World* (1970), 'Royalty'.

George, Chief Dan 1899–1981

Canadian native spokesperson.

21 The heart never knows the colour of the skin.

1974 *My Heart Soars.*

George, Daniel *pseudonym of* *Daniel George Bunting*
1890–1967

English author and critic.

22 O Freedom, what liberties are taken in thy name!
1963 *The Perpetual Pessimist.*

George-Brown, George (Alfred) Brown, Baron
1914–85

English Labour politician. He was Vice-Chairman and Deputy Leader of the party (1960–70), and unsuccessfully contested Harold Wilson for party leadership in 1963.

23 Most British statesmen have either drunk too much or womanised too much. I never fell into the second category.
1974 In the *Observer*, Nov.

24 Lovely creature in scarlet, dance with me!
Drunken invitation to a red-robed apostolic delegate.
Attributed.

Geracimos, Ann

US journalist and feature writer.

25 Washington is a town where more people probably contemplate writing a book than finish reading one.
1989 In the *Washington Times*, 29 Mar.

Gerald of Wales *also called* *Giraldus Cambrensis*
c.1146–c.1223

Welsh bishop and historian. He wrote 17 books and planned several others, all in Latin. His best-known works are *The History and Topography of Ireland* (1185) and *Journey through Wales* (1191).

26 Among the smaller islands there is one of fair size that is now called the Isle of Man… There was a great controversy in antiquity concerning the question: to which of the two countries should the island properly belong? Eventually, however, the matter was settled. All agreed that since it allowed poisonous reptiles to live in it, it should belong to Britain.
1185 *The History and Topography of Ireland*, pt.2 (translated by John J O'Meara, 1951).

Gerbert *later* *Pope Sylvester II*   940–1003

French divine and scholar, whose chemical, mathematical and philosophical expertise led to claims that he was in league with the devil. In 982 he became Abbot of Bobbio, and was appointed Archbishop of Ravenna in 988. He was elected Pope in 999. He opposed the separatist tendencies of the French Church.

27 *Cum studio bene vivendi semper conjunxi studium bene dicendi.*
I have always combined the study of how to live well with the study of how to speak well.
985 Letter to Ebrard, Abbot of Tours.

28 *An quicquam melius amicas divinitas mortalibus concesserit nescio.*
I do not know if the divinity has provided mortals with anything better than friends.
985 Letter to Abbot Gerald of Aurillac.

29 *Delegimus certum otium studiorum, quam incertum negotium bellorum.*

We have opted for the certain leisure of study, rather than the uncertain business of war.
985 Letter to Monk Raymond.

Gergen, David Richmond   1942–

US government official, an assistant and later adviser to Presidents Nixon, Ford, Reagan and Clinton. He is editor-at-large at *US News & World Report*.

30 About the time you are writing a line that you have written so often that you want to throw up, that is the first time the American people will hear it.
1993 On working as a speech-writer in the Nixon White House. In the *New York Times*, 31 Oct.

31 A naked moment in politics.
1993 On the vulnerability of the President. In the *New York Times*, 31 Oct.

32 We are making politics a spectator sport in which our only duty is to vote somebody into office and then retire to the grandstands.
1993 In *US News & World Report*, 10 May.

Gerhardie, William Alexander   1895–1977

English novelist, born and educated in St Petersburg. His best-known books are the novels *Futility* (1922) and *Polyglots* (1925).

33 She even sighed offensively…as if she meant to charge me with the necessity of doing so.
1922 *Futility*, pt.3, ch.3.

34 There are as many fools at a university as anywhere… But their folly, I admit, has a certain stamp—the stamp of university training, if you like. It is trained folly.
1925 *Polyglots*, ch.7.

35 We are like icebergs in the ocean: one-eighth part consciousness and the rest submerged beneath the surface of articulate apprehension.
1925 *Polyglots*, ch.14.

Gershwin, George   1898–1937

US composer. His early works are Broadway musicals, such as *Lady Be Good* (1924), written with his brother Ira. Other works include *Rhapsody in Blue* (1924, a concert piece in the jazz idiom), *An American in Paris* (1928) and the opera *Porgy and Bess* (1935).

36 Not many composers have ideas. Far more of them know how to use strange instruments which do not require ideas.
1930 'The Composer in the Machine Age'.

37 Jazz is the result of the energy stored up in America.
Quoted in D Morgenstern *Composers on Music* (1958).

Gershwin, Ira *originally* *Israel Gershowitz*   1896–1983

US lyricist. He worked exclusively with his brother George Gershwin until George died, and then with other composers including Kurt Weill and Jerome Kern.

38 I got rhythm,
I got music,
I got my man—
Who could ask for anything more.
1930 'I Got Music', featured in the film *Girl Crazy* (music by George Gershwin).

39 Away with the music of Broadway!

Be off with your Irving Berlin!
Oh, I'd give no quarter
to Kern or Cole Porter
and Gershwin keeps pounding on tin.
How can I be civil
when hearing this drivel?
It's only for night-clubbing souses.
Oh, give me the free 'n' easy
waltz that is Viennesey
And go tell the band
if they want a hand
the waltz must be Strauss's!
1936 'By Strauss'.

40 The way you wear your hat,
The way you sip your tea,
The mem'ry of all that—
No, no! They can't take that away from me!
1937 'They Can't Take That Away from Me', song from the film
musical *Shall We Dance?* (music by George Gershwin).

41 The way your smile just beams
The way you sing off key
The way you haunt my dreams
No, no! They can't take that away from me!
1937 'They Can't Take That Away from Me', song from the film
musical *Shall We Dance?* (music by George Gershwin).

42 You say potato and I say po-tah-to
You say tomato and I say to-mah-to...
Let's call the whole thing off!
1937 'Let's Call the Whole Thing Off', song from the film musical
Shall We Dance? (music by George Gershwin).

43 A foggy day in London Town
Had me low and had me down.
1937 'A Foggy Day', song from the musical *Damsel in Distress*
(music by George Gershwin).

44 Holding hands at midnight
'Neath a starry sky,
Nice work if you can get it,
And you can get it if you try.
1937 'Nice Work If You Can Get It', song from the musical *Damsel
in Distress* (music by George Gershwin).

45 In time the Rockies may crumble
Gibraltar may tumble
They're only made of clay,
But our love is here to stay.
1938 'Love Is Here to Stay', sung by Kenny Baker in *The Goldwyn
Follies* (music by George Gershwin).

Gervais, Ricky 1961–

English comic writer and performer, whose comedy series *The
Office* won two Golden Globes (2004).

46 If you work for Nasa or the Cosa Nostra, I bet it's all the
same. Why's his chair bigger than my chair? I've been an
assassin longer than him and he gets to sit nearest the
water cooler.
2002 In *The Guardian*, 7 Sep.

47 Fact is stranger than fiction. You see people walking
down the street that would never be allowed on
television. You have to tone it down.
2002 On the Jo Whiley show, BBC Radio 1, 30 Sep.

48 If David Brent is the best thing that I ever come up with,
then so be it. What are you supposed to do—time the

best thing you do for just before you die?
2003 On his character in the television series *The Office*. Quoted
in the *Observer*, 14 Dec.

Getty, Jean Paul 1892–1976

US oil executive, multimillionaire and art collector. He entered
the oil business in his early 20s, and merged his father's fortune
with his own in 1930. Despite his legendary wealth, he acquired
a reputation for miserliness.

49 If you can actually count your money, then you are not
really a rich man.
1957 In the *Observer*, 3 Nov.

50 Some people find oil, some don't.
His entire submission when asked by a magazine editor to
submit an article entitled 'The Secret of My Success'. Quoted by
L M Boyd in the *San Francisco Chronicle*, 2 Mar 1991.

Giacosa, Giuseppe 1847–1906

Italian librettist.

51 *Che gelida manina.*
Your tiny hand is frozen.
1896 Rodolpho to Mimi. *La Bohème* (with Luigi Illica, music by
Puccini).

Gibbon, Edward 1737–94

English historian. After a visit to Rome (1764) he embarked on a
history of the Roman Empire. He became an MP in 1774, and the
first volume of *The Decline and Fall of the Roman Empire*
appeared in 1776. Lord Sheffield published his *Miscellaneous
Works* (1796), including his autobiography.

52 If a man were called to fix the period in the history of the
world during which the condition of the human race was
most happy and prosperous, he would, without
hesitation, name that which elapsed from the death of
Domitian to the accession of Commodus.
1776–88 *The Decline and Fall of the Roman Empire*, ch.3.

53 The principles of a free constitution are irrevocably lost
when the legislative power is nominated by the
executive.
1776–88 *The Decline and Fall of the Roman Empire*, ch.3.

54 In every age and country, the wiser, or at least the
stronger, of the two sexes, has usurped the powers of the
state, and confined the other to the cares and pleasures
of domestic life.
1776–88 *The Decline and Fall of the Roman Empire*, ch.6.

55 Corruption, the most infallible symptom of
constitutional liberty.
1776–88 *The Decline and Fall of the Roman Empire*, ch.21.

56 The Huns...chanted a funeral song to the memory of a
hero, glorious in his life, invincible in his death, the father
of his people, the scourge of his enemies, and the terror
of the world.
1776–88 Description of the funeral of Attila the Hun. *The Decline
and Fall of the Roman Empire*, ch.35.

57 The Rhine is not more impassable than the Nile or
Euphrates, and the Arabian fleet might have sailed
without a naval combat into the mouth of the Thames.
Perhaps the interpretation of the Koran would now be
taught in the schools of Oxford, and her pupils might
demonstrate to a circumcised people the sanctity and
truth of the revelation of Mahomet.

1776–88 *The Decline and Fall of the Roman Empire*, ch.52.

58 Persuasion is the resource of the feeble; and the feeble can seldom persuade.
1776–88 *The Decline and Fall of the Roman Empire*, ch.68.

59 All that is human must retrograde if it does not advance.
1776–88 *The Decline and Fall of the Roman Empire*, ch.71.

60 To the University of Oxford I acknowledge no obligation; and she will as cheerfully renounce me for a son, as I am willing to disclaim her for a mother. I spent fourteen months at Magdalen College: they proved the fourteen months the most idle and unprofitable of my whole life.
Memoirs of My Life (published 1796), ch.3.

61 It was here that I suspended my religious inquiries (aged 17).
Memoirs of My Life (published 1796), ch.4.

62 I sighed as a lover, I obeyed as a son.
On his enforced visit to Lausanne, leaving behind Suzanne Curchod. *Memoirs of My Life* (published 1796), ch.4. This passage was inserted (from a draft) by Lord Sheffield.

63 It was at Rome, on the fifteenth of October 1764, as I sat musing amidst the ruins of the Capitol, while the barefooted friars were singing vespers in the temple of Jupiter, that the idea of writing the decline and fall of the City first started to my mind.
Memoirs of My Life (published 1796), ch.6, note. Variations of the lines can be found in the various drafts of Gibbon's autobiography and in the last lines of the *Decline and Fall*: 'It was among the ruins of the Capitol that I first conceived the idea of a work which has amused and exercised near twenty years of my life, and which, however inadequate to my own wishes, I finally deliver to the curiosity and candour of the public' (vol.6, ch.71).

64 My English text is chaste, and all licentious passages are left in the obscurity of a learned language.
Memoirs of My Life (published 1796), ch.8.

Gibbon, Lewis Grassic 1901–35

Scottish novelist.

65 So that was Chris and her reading and schooling, two Chrisses there were that fought for her heart and tormented her. You hated the land and the coarse speak of the folk and learning was brave and fine one day and the next you'd waken with the peewits crying across the hills, deep and deep, crying in the heart of you, and the smell of the earth in your face, almost you'd cry for that, the beauty of it and the sweetness of the Scottish land and skies.
1932 *Sunset Song*.

66 For the cleansing of that horror, if cleanse it they could, I would welcome the English in suzerainty over Scotland till the end of time. I would welcome the end of Braid Scots and Gaelic, our culture, our history, our nationhood under the heels of a Chinese army of occupation if it could cleanse the Glasgow slums, give a surety of food and play—the elementary right of every human being—to those people of the abyss...
1934 *Scottish Scene*, 'Glasgow' (with Hugh MacDiarmid).

Gibbons, Kaye 1960–

US novelist. Her first novel, *Ellen Foster* (1986), was widely acclaimed. Other works include *A Virtuous Woman* (1989) and *Divining Women* (2004).

67 I read about writers' lives with the fascination of one slowing down to get a good look at an automobile accident.
1990 In the *New York Times*, 7 Jan.

Gibbons, Orlando 1583–1625

English composer and organist of Westminster Abbey (from 1623). He wrote little, but some of his anthems, services and madrigals are regarded as masterpieces.

68 The silver swan, who living had no note,
When death approached, unlocked her silent throat;
Leaning her breast against the reedy shore,
Thus sung her first and last, and sung no more:
'Farewell, all joys; Oh death, come close mine eyes;
More geese than swans now live, more fools than wise.'
1612 *The First Set of Madrigals and Motets of Five Parts*, 'The Silver Swan'.

Gibbons, Stella Dorothea 1902–89

English writer. She worked as a journalist, and wrote novels, poetry and short stories. Her reputation rests on her famous parody of rural fiction, *Cold Comfort Farm* (1932).

69 The life of the journalist is poor, nasty, brutish and short. So is his style.
1932 *Cold Comfort Farm*, foreword.

70 And when the spring comes her hour is upon her again. 'Tes the hand of Nature and we women cannot escape it.
1932 Judith Starkadder, of Meriam. *Cold Comfort Farm*, ch.5.

71 Something nasty in the woodshed.
1932 Aunt Ada Doom. *Cold Comfort Farm*, ch.10.

72 He said that, by god, D. H. Lawrence was right when he had said there must be a dumb, dark, dull, bitter belly-tension between a man and a woman, and how else could this be achieved save in the long monotony of marriage?
1932 Mr Mybug, proposing to Rennet. *Cold Comfort Farm*, ch.20.

Gibbs, Wolcott 1902–58

US journalist and critic.

73 Backward ran sentences until reeled the mind.
1936 Parody of *Time* magazine's literary style. 'Time... Fortune...Life...Luce', in the *New Yorker*, 28 Nov.

Gibran, Kahlil 1883–1931

Syrian mystic, author and artist, whose most famous work is *The Prophet* (1923).

74 Your children are not your children.
They are the sons and daughters of Life's longing for itself.
They came through you but not from you
And though they are with you yet they belong not to you.
You may give them your love but not your thoughts,
For they have their own thoughts.
You may house their bodies, but not their souls.
1923 *The Prophet*, 'On Children'.

Gibson, Wilfred Wilson 1878–1962

English poet. He was a prolific writer of both poetry and plays, rooted in the reality of everyday life.

75 But we, how shall we turn to little things

And listen to the birds and winds and streams
Made holy by their dreams,
Nor feel the heart-break in the heart of things?
1918 'Lament'.

Gibson, William Ford 1948–

US science-fiction writer, best known as the author of *Neuromancer* (1984), which spawned the genre of cyberpunk fiction.

76 Cyberspace. A consensual hallucination experienced daily by billions of legitimate operators, in every nation, by children being taught mathematical concepts… A graphical representation of data abstracted from the banks of every computer in the human system. Unthinkable complexity. Lines of light ranged in the non-space of the mind, clusters and constellations of data. Like city lights, receding.
1984 *Neuromancer*. This is the first recorded use of the term 'cyberspace'.

77 Cyberspace is where you are when you're on the telephone.
1994 In the *US News & World Report*, 21 Jun.

Gide, André Paul Guillaume 1869–1951

French writer of fiction, poetry, plays, criticism, biography and translations. His novels focus on the conflict between the spiritual and the physical. He won the Nobel prize for literature in 1947.

78 *Nous avons bâti sur le sable*
Des cathédrales impérissables.
We have built immovable cathedrals
In the sand.
1895 *Paludes*.

79 *Que mon livre t'enseigne à t'intéresser plus à toi qu'à lui-même—puis à tout le reste plus qu'à toi.*
May my book teach you to be more interested in yourself than in it—then, in everyone else more than yourself.
1897 *Les Nourritures terrestres*, pt.1.

80 *La sagesse n'est pas dans la raison, mais dans l'amour.*
Wisdom comes not from reason but from love.
1897 *Les Nourritures terrestres*, pt.1.

81 *Familles! je vous hais! Foyers clos; portes refermées; possessions jalouses du bonheur.*
Families! I hate you! Enclosed hallways, shut doors, jealous possessions of happiness.
1897 *Les Nourritures terrestres*, pt.4.

82 *Chaque instant de notre Vie est essentiellement irremplaçable: sache parfois t'y concentrer uniquement.*
Every instant of Life is essentially irreplaceable: concentrate on it fully from time to time.
1897 *Les Nourritures terrestres*, pt.4.

83 *C'est avec de beaux sentiments qu'on fait de la mauvaise littérature.*
Bad literature is written with beautiful sentiments.
1928 Letter to François Mauriac.

84 *Le bonheur de l'homme n'est pas dans la liberté, mais dans l'acceptation d'un devoir.*
Man's happiness does not come from freedom but in the acceptance of a task.
1932 Journal entry, 8 Feb.

Gielgud, Sir (Arthur) John 1904–2000

English actor and producer. A leading Shakespearean actor, he appeared in many films, notably as Cassius in *Julius Caesar* (1952) and in *Prospero's Books* (1991).

85 When you're my age, you just never risk being ill—because then everyone says: Oh, he's done for.
1988 In the *Sunday Express*, 17 Jul.

86 Daniel Day Lewis has what every actor in Hollywood wants: talent. And what every actor in England wants: looks.
1995 In *The Independent*, 13 May.

87 Being another character is more interesting than being yourself.
Attributed.

Gilbert, Sir Humphrey 1537–83

English navigator and explorer. He took Newfoundland for the crown in 1583, establishing a colony at St John's. He was drowned on the journey home.

88 We are as near to heaven by sea as by land!
1583 Dying words as his frigate *Squirrel* sank in the Atlantic Ocean near the Azores, 5 Aug. Quoted in Richard Hakluyt *Third and Last Volume of the Voyages…of the English Nation* (1600).

Gilbert, Sir W(illiam) S(chwenck) 1836–1911

English parodist and librettist. His humorous verse was collected in 1869 as the *Bab Ballads*. His partnership with Sir Arthur Sullivan, from 1871, produced a succession of light operas, from *Trial by Jury* (1875) to *The Grand Duke* (1896).

89 So I fell in love with a rich attorney's
Elderly, ugly daughter.
1875 *Trial by Jury*.

90 She may very well pass for forty-three
In the dusk with a light behind her!
1875 *Trial by Jury*.

91 I'm called little Buttercup—dear Little Buttercup,
Though I could never tell why.
1878 *HMS Pinafore*, act 1.

92 CAPT: Bad language or abuse,
I never, never use,
Whatever the emergency;
Though 'Bother it' I may
Occasionally say,
I never use a big, big D—
ALL: What, never?
CAPT: No, never!
ALL: What *never*?
CAPT: Well, hardly ever!
ALL: Hardly ever swears a big, big D—
Then give three cheers, and one cheer more,
For the well-bred Captain of the *Pinafore*!
1878 *HMS Pinafore*, act 1.

93 I am the monarch of the sea,
The Ruler of the Queen's Navee,
Whose praise Great Britain loudly chants
And we are his sisters, and his cousins, and his aunts!
1878 *HMS Pinafore*, act 1.

94 When I was a lad I served a term
As office boy to an attorney's firm.
I cleaned the windows and I swept the floor,

And I polished up the handle of the big front door.
I polished up that handle so carefullee
That now I am the Ruler of the Queen's Navee!
1878 *HMS Pinafore*, act 2.

95 In spite of all temptations
To belong to other nations,
He remains an Englishman!
1878 *HMS Pinafore*, act 2.

96 Climbing over rocky mountain,
Skipping rivulet and fountain.
1879 Girls' chorus, *The Pirates of Penzance*, act 1.

97 It is, it is a glorious thing
To be a Pirate King.
1879 Pirate King's song, *The Pirates of Penzance*, act 1.

98 Oh, is there not one maiden here
Whose homely face and bad complexion
Have caused all hopes to disappear
Of ever winning man's affection?
1879 Frederic's song, *The Pirates of Penzance*, act 1.

99 I am the very model of a modern Major-General,
I've information vegetable, animal and mineral,
I know the kings of England, and I quote the fights historical,
From Marathon to Waterloo, in order categorical.
1879 The Major-General's song, *The Pirates of Penzance*, act 1.

1 I can hum a fugue of which I've heard the music's din afore,
And whistle all the airs from that infernal nonsense *Pinafore*.
1879 The Major-General's song, *The Pirates of Penzance*, act 1.

2 Stay, Frederic, stay!
Nay, Mabel, nay!
1879 Mabel and Frederic's duet, *The Pirates of Penzance*, act 2.

3 When a felon's not engaged in his employment
Or maturing his felonious little plans
His capacity for innocent enjoyment
Is just as great as any honest man's—
Ah! When constabulary duty's to be done
A policeman's lot is not a happy one.
1879 Sergeant's song, *The Pirates of Penzance*, act 2.

4 And everyone will say,
As you walk your mystic way,
'If this young man expresses himself in terms too deep for me,
Why, what a very singularly deep young man this deep young man must be!'
1881 Bunthorne's song, *Patience*, act 1.

5 Sing 'Booh to you—
Pooh, pooh to you'—
And that's what I shall say!
1881 Jane and Bunthorne's duet, *Patience*, act 2.

6 A commonplace young man,
A matter-of-fact young man,
A steady and stolid-y, jolly Bank-Holiday
Every-day young man!
1881 Bunthorne and Grosvenor's duet, *Patience*, act 2.

7 A Japanese young man,
A blue and white young man,
Francesca di Rimini, miminy, piminy,
Je-ne-sais-quoi young man.
1881 Bunthorne and Grosvenor's duet, *Patience*, act 2.

8 A Chancery Lane young man,
A Somerset House young man,
A very delectable, highly respectable,
Threepenny-bus young man!
1881 Bunthorne and Grosvenor's duet, *Patience*, act 2.

9 A pallid and thin young man,
A haggard and lank young man,
A greenery-yallery, Grosvenor Gallery,
Foot-in-the-grave young man!
A Sewell & Cross young man,
A Howell & James young man,
A push-ing young par-ti-cle—
'What's the next ar-ti-cle?'—
Wa-ter-loo House young man!
1881 Bunthorne and Grosvenor's duet, *Patience*, act 2.

10 Bow, bow, ye lower middle classes!
Bow, bow, ye tradesmen, bow ye masses!
1882 Chorus, *Iolanthe*, act 1 (first performed 25 Nov, simultaneously in London and New York).

11 The Law is the true embodiment
Of everything that's excellent.
It has no kind of fault or flaw,
And I, my Lords, embody the Law.
1882 *Iolanthe*, act 1.

12 When I went to the Bar as a very young man,
(Said I to myself—said I),
I'll work on a new and original plan,
(Said I to myself—said I).
1882 *Iolanthe*, act 1.

13 I often think it's comical
How Nature always does contrive
That every boy and every gal
That's born into the world alive
Is either a little Liberal
Or else a little Conservative!
1882 Private Willis's song, *Iolanthe*, act 2.

14 The House of Peers, throughout the war,
Did nothing in particular,
And did it very well:
Yet Britain set the world ablaze
In good King George's glorious days!
1882 Lord Mountarat's song, *Iolanthe*, act 2.

15 When you're lying awake with a dismal headache, and repose is taboo'd by anxiety,
I conceive you may use any language you choose to indulge in, without impropriety.
1882 Lord Chancellor's nightmare song, *Iolanthe*, act 2.

16 Expressive glances
Shall be our lances
And pops of Sillery
Our light artillery.
1884 Trio, *Princess Ida*, act 1.

17 I've an irritating chuckle, I've a celebrated sneer,
I've an entertaining snigger, I've a fascinating leer.
To everybody's prejudice I know a thing or two;
I can tell a woman's age in half a minute—and I do.
But although I try to make myself as pleasant as I can,
Yet everybody says I'm such a disagreeable man!
1884 Gama's song, *Princess Ida*, act 1.

18 Oh, doughty sons of Hungary!
May all success

Attend and bless
Your warlike ironmongery!
1884 Chorus, *Princess Ida*, act 3.

19 A wandering minstrel I—
A thing of shreds and patches
Of ballads, songs and snatches
And dreamy lullaby!
1885 Nanki-Poo's song, *The Mikado*, act 1.

20 As in a month you've got to die
If Ko-Ko tells us true,
'Twere empty compliment to cry
'Long life to Nanki-Poo!'
But as one month you have to live
As fellow-citizen,
This toast with three times three we'll give—
'Long life to you—till then!'
1885 Pooh-Bah's solo, *The Mikado*, act 1.

21 As some day it may happen that a victim must be found,
I've got a little list—I've got a little list
Of society offenders who might well be underground,
And who never would be missed— who never would be
    missed!
There's the pestilential nuisances who write for
    autographs—
All people who have flabby hands and irritating laughs.
1885 Ko-Ko's song, *The Mikado*, act 1.

22 The idiot who praises, with enthusiastic tone,
All centuries but this, and every country but his own;
And the lady from the provinces, who dresses like a guy,
And who 'doesn't think she dances, but would rather like
    to try';
And that singular anomaly, the lady novelist—
I don't think she'd be missed—I'm *sure* she'd not be
    missed!
1885 Ko-Ko's song, *The Mikado*, act 1.

23 Defer, defer,
To the Lord High Executioner!
1885 Chorus, *The Mikado*, act 1.

24 Three little maids from school are we,
Pert as a school-girl well can be
Filled to the brim with girlish glee.
1885 Trio for Yum-yum, Peep-Bo and Pitti Sing, with Chorus of
Girls, *The Mikado*, act 1.

25 To sit in solemn silence in a dull, dark dock,
In a pestilential prison, with a life-long lock,
Awaiting the sensation of a short, sharp shock,
From a cheap and chippy chopper on a big black block!
1885 Trio, *The Mikado*, act 1.

26 Here's a how-de-do!
1885 Trio, *The Mikado*, act 2.

27 My object all sublime
I shall achieve in time—
To let the punishment fit the crime.
1885 The Mikado's song, *The Mikado*, act 2.

28 And there he plays extravagant matches
In fitless finger-stalls
On a cloth untrue
With a twisted cue
And elliptical billiard balls.
1885 The doom of the billiard sharp. *The Mikado*, act 2.

29 On a tree by a river a little tom-tit

Sang 'Willow, titwillow, titwillow!'
1885 Ko-Ko's song, *The Mikado*, act 2.

30 This particularly rapid unintelligible patter
Isn't generally heard, and if it is it doesn't matter!
1887 *Ruddigore*, act 2.

31 For I have a song to sing, O!…
It is sung to the moon
By a love-lorn loon,
Who fled from the mocking throng, O!
It's the song of a merryman moping mum,
Whose soul was sad and whose glance was glum
Who sipped no sup and who craved no crumb,
As he sighed for the love of a ladye!
1888 Jack Point's song, *The Yeomen of the Guard*.

32 In enterprise of martial kind,
When there was any fighting,
He led his regiment from behind—
He found it less exciting.
But when away his regiment ran,
His place was at the fore, O—
That celebrated,
Cultivated
Underrated
Nobleman,
The Duke of Plaza-Toro!
1889 Duke's song, *The Gondoliers*, act 1.

33 I am a courtier grave and serious
Who is about to kiss your hand:
Try to combine a pose imperious
With a demeanour nobly bland.
1889 *The Gondoliers*, act 2.

34 Take a pair of sparkling eyes.
1889 Marco's song, *The Gondoliers*, act 2.

35 Funny without being vulgar.
1893 Of Sir Henry Beerbohm Tree's performance as Hamlet.
Attributed.

36 Do you know how they are going to decide the
Shakespeare–Bacon dispute? They are going to dig up
Shakespeare and dig up Bacon; they are going to get Tree
to recite *Hamlet* to them. And the one who turns in his
coffin will be the author of the play.
Letter.

37 My dear chap! Good isn't the word!
To an actor who had just given a very weak performance.
Attributed.

Gill, Brendan 1914–97

US writer and critic of film, theatre and architecture. His works
include *The Day the Money Stopped* (1957) and *A New York Life: of
friends and others* (1990). He received the national Book Award
for *The Trouble of One House* (1951).

38 In the later nineteenth century, the tops of skyscrapers
often took the shape of domes, surmounted by jaunty
gilded lanterns; later came ziggurats, mausoleums,
Alexandrian lighthouses, miniature Parthenons. These
charming follies contained neither royal corpses nor
effigies of gods and goddesses; rather they contained
large wooden tanks filled with water.
1982 Quoted in Laura Rosen *Top of the City: New York's hidden
rooftop world* (1990), foreword.

39 He stared the assorted meannesses and failed promises

of American life straight in the face, and they stared back.
1990 On Walker Evans's photographs for James Agee's book on the destitute South. *A New York Life*.

40 The big houses sat in self-congratulatory propinquity on their level green lawns…stout matrons seated elbow to elbow, implacably chaperoning a ball.
1990 On a residential boulevard of Rochester, New York. *A New York Life*.

41 A vain attempt to subdue that unsubduable country.
1990 Of Cromwell's settlement of Scots in the north of Ireland. *A New York Life*.

Gill, (Arthur) Eric Rowton 1882–1940

English artist, type designer and writer.

42 That state is a state of Slavery in which a man does what he likes to do in his spare time and in his working time that which is required of him.
1929 *Art-nonsense and Other Essays*, 'Slavery and Freedom'.

43 The artist is not a special kind of man but every man a special kind of artist.
1934 *Art*, introduction.

44 Man cannot live on the human plane, he must be either above or below it.
1940 *Autobiography*, closing words.

45 Science is analytical, descriptive, informative. Man does not live by bread alone, but by science he attempts to do so. Hence the deadliness of all that is purely scientific.
'Art'. Collected in *Essays* (1948).

Gillespie, Dizzy (John Birks) 1917–93

US jazz trumpeter, composer and bandleader. A leading exponent of bebop in the 1940s, he formed several big bands and led an international touring orchestra (1956).

46 It's taken me all my life to learn what not to play.
Quoted in N Hentoff *Jazz Is* (1978).

47 When I first heard Charlie Parker, I said, 'That's how our music should be played.'… After we got it together, yeah, I knew we were making something new. It was magic. Nobody on the planet was playing like that but us.
1991 On bebop. In the *San Francisco Chronicle*, 25 May.

48 Now, our music is universal. It shares the rhythmic content of African music, music of the Western Hemisphere and various lands of the East, and has merged this rhythm with European harmonies, the soul of the slaves, the blues, and the spirituals to create jazz.
1979 *Dizzy– To Be Or Not To Bop* (with Al Fraser), 'Evolutions'.

Gillette, King Camp 1855–1932

US inventor of the safety razor (c.1895), founder of the Gillette Safety Razor Company (1901).

49 To be successful in business, you should produce something cheap, habit-forming, and consumed by use.
Attributed.

Gilligan, Andrew 1968–

English journalist.

50 I have spoken to a British official who was involved in the preparation of the dossier… He said: 'It was transformed in the week before it was published, to make it sexier.'
2003 Referring to the Government's dossier on weapons of mass destruction in Iraq. On BBC Radio 4's *Today* programme, 29 May.

Gilman, Charlotte Anna *pen names* **Charlotte Perkins Gilman** *and* **Charlotte Perkins Stetson** 1860–1935

US feminist and writer. She lectured on women's and other social issues, and her *Women and Economics* (1898) is regarded as a feminist landmark. Her fiction includes the story 'The Yellow Wall-Paper' (1892), a feminist study of madness.

51 The economic status of women generally depends on that of men generally, and…the economic status of women individually depends upon that of men individually, those men to whom they are related.
1898 *Women and Economics: A Study of the Economic Relation between Men and Women as a Factor in Social Evolution*, ch.1.

52 The labor of women in the house, certainly, enables men to produce more wealth than they otherwise could; and in this way [they] are economic factors in society. But so are horses.
1898 *Women and Economics: A Study of the Economic Relation between Men and Women as a Factor in Social Evolution*, ch.1.

53 Whatever the economic value of the domestic industry of women is, they do not get it. The women who do the most work get the least money, and the women who have the most money do the least work.
1898 *Women and Economics: A Study of the Economic Relation between Men and Women as a Factor in Social Evolution*, ch.1.

54 His dominance is not that of one chosen as best fitted to rule…but it is sovereignty based on the accident of sex.
1898 *Women and Economics: A Study of the Economic Relation between Men and Women as a Factor in Social Evolution*, ch.1.

Gilmore, Dame Mary Jean *née* **Mary Jean Cameron** 1865–1962

Australian writer and poet. She sailed to Paraguay in 1893 to help establish the New Australia Movement Utopian community, and when this failed returned to Australia (1902), becoming a journalist. A lifelong supporter of aboriginal rights, in 1936 she was awarded the DBE.

55 I span and Eve span
A thread to bind the heart of man!
1918 *The Passionate Heart and Other Poems*, 'Eve-song'.

56 Lone, lone, and lone I stand,
With none to hear my cry,
As the black feet of the night
Go walking down the sky.
1932 *Under the Wilgas*, 'The Myall in Prison'.

Gilmour of Craiglockhart, Ian Gilmour, Baron 1926–

English Conservative politician, Secretary of State for Defence (1970–4) and Lord Privy Seal (1979–81). He has published several books on politics.

57 It does no harm to throw the occasional man overboard, but it does not do much good if you are steering full speed ahead for the rocks.
1981 In *The Times*, after he was sacked by Margaret Thatcher for publicly criticizing her anti-European stance.

Gingold, Hermione 1897–1987

English actress. A star of intimate revue, she also appeared with success in plays by Noël Coward and in musicals by Stephen Sondheim.

58 I got all the schooling any actress needs. That is, I learned to write enough to sign contracts.
Attributed.

Gingrich, Newt(on Leroy) 1943–

US politician. Originally a history professor, he became representative from Georgia in 1978 and subsequently leader of conservative Republicans in the House. He was Speaker of the House (1995–99).

59 One reason I try to get people to call me Newt is to break down barriers. It's a whole lot easier for someone to say, 'Newt, you've got a spot on your tie,' than it is to say 'Congressman'.
1979 Attributed comment.

Ginsberg, Allen 1926–97

US poet, a key member of the Beat movement with Jack Kerouac and William Burroughs. Despite his anti-establishment views, he was a popular poet and performer. His works include *Kaddish and Other Poems* (1961).

60 A naked lunch is natural to us,
we eat reality sandwiches.
But allegories are so much lettuce.
Don't hide the madness.
1954 'On Burroughs' Work'.

61 The madman bum and angel beat in Time, unknown, yet putting down here what might be left to say in time come after death.
1956 *Howl and Other Poems*, 'Howl, I'.

62 Moloch whose mind is pure machinery! Moloch whose blood is running money! Moloch whose fingers are ten armies! Moloch whose breast is a cannibal dynamo! Moloch whose ear is a smoking tomb!
1956 *Howl and Other Poems*, 'Howl, II'.

63 You were never no locomotive, Sunflower, you were a sunflower!
And you Locomotive, you are a locomotive, forget me not!
1956 *Howl and Other Poems*, 'Sunflower Sutra'.

64 America I've given you all and now I'm nothing.
1956 *Howl and Other Poems*, 'America'.

65 America I'm putting my queer shoulder to the wheel.
1956 *Howl and Other Poems*, 'America'.

66 Democracy! Bah! When I hear that word I reach for my feather Boa!
1960 Journal entry, Oct. Collected in *Journals: Early Fifties Early Sixties*, 'New York City'.

67 and poets should stay out of politics or become monsters
I have become monsterous with politics.
1961 *Kaddish and Other Poems*, 'Death to Van Gogh's Ear!'.

68 A very unique cat…a French Canadian Hinayana Buddhist Beat Catholic savant.
1970 Of Jack Kerouac. *This Fabulous Century 1950–1960*.

69 What if someone gave a war & Nobody came?
Life would ring the bells of Ecstasy and Forever be Itself again.
1973 *The Fall of America*, 'Graffiti 12th Cubicle Men's Room Syracuse Airport'.
➡ *See Sandburg 713 : 6.*

70 All this time [San Francisco, from 1955] I realized we were involved as a community with a historical change of consciousness and some kind of cultural revolution… I thought it was really in some respects a contest between further liberation or 1984 authoritarianism, police state; that it was creeping police state or creeping socialism-libertarianism.
1984 Quoted in Gordon Ball (ed) *Allen Ginsberg: Journals Mid-Fifties* (1995), 'Meditations on Record Keeping by Poet, Transcribed by Editor'.

71 Poetry is not an expression of the party line. It's that time of night, lying in bed, thinking what you really think, making the private world public, that's what the poet does.
Quoted in Barry Miles *Ginsberg* (1989), ch.5.

Giovanni, Nikki *in full Yolande Cornelia Giovanni, Jr* 1943–

US poet, a significant voice in the development of black consciousness. Her early work was more radical in tone than subsequent more introspective volumes.

72 Mistakes are a fact of life
It is the response to error that counts.
1968 *Black Judgement*, 'Of Liberation', stanza 16.

73 and I really hope no white person ever has cause to write about me
because they never understand Black love is Black wealth and they'll
probably talk about my hard childhood and never understand that
all the while I was quite happy
1968 *Black Judgement*, 'Nikki–Rosa'.

74 it's a sex object if you're pretty
and no love
or love and no sex if you're fat
1968 *Black Judgement*, 'Woman Poem'.

75 White people really deal more with God and black people with Jesus.
1971 Conversation with James Baldwin, London, 4 Nov. Collected in *A Dialogue* (1973).

76 A white face goes with a white mind. Occasionally a black face goes with a white mind. Very seldom a white face will have a black mind.
1971 Conversation with James Baldwin, London, 4 Nov. Collected in *A Dialogue* (1973).

Gipp, George 1895–1920

US American football player. His success on the field inspired Notre Dame to two unbeaten seasons (1919 and 1920), though his career was cut short by his death from pneumonia.

77 Some time, Rock, when the team's up against it, when things are wrong and the breaks are beating the boys – tell them to go in there with all they've got and win just one for the Gipper.
1920 Last words, to coach Knute Rockne. Rockne told the team about Gipp's request in 1928, when their fortunes were low, and inspired the squad to new efforts. 'Win one for the Gipper' subsequently became a catchphrase throughout US sport.

Giraudoux, (Hippolyte) Jean 1882–1944

French writer, head of propaganda in World War II. He is best known for his poetic plays, including *La Guerre de Troie n'aura pas lieu* (1935, translated as *The Tiger at the Gates*, 1955) and *Pour Lucrèce* (1953, translated as *Duel of Angels*, 1958).

78 *Le plagiat est la base de toutes les littératures, excepté de la première, qui d'ailleurs est inconnue.*
Plagiarism is the base of all literature except the first text which, however, is unknown.
1922 *Siegfried et le Limousin.*

79 *L'humanité est…une entreprise surhumaine.*
Humanity is…a superhuman undertaking.
1933 *Intermezzo*, act 1, sc.6.

80 A golf course is the epitome of all that is purely transitory in the universe, a space not to dwell in, but to get over as quickly as possible.
1933 Quoted in Colin Jarman *The Guinness Dictionary of Sports Quotations* (1990).

81 *Nous savons tous ici que le droit est la plus puissante des écoles de l'imagination. Jamais poète n'a interprété la nature aussi librement qu'un juriste la réalité.*
We all know here that the law is the most powerful of schools for the imagination. No poet ever interpreted nature as freely as a lawyer interprets the truth.
1935 *La Guerre de Troie n'aura pas lieu*, act 2, sc.5.

82 *Il n'est pas très prudent d'avoir des dieux et des légumes trop dorés.*
It is not wise to have either your gods or your vegetables too gilded.
1935 *La Guerre de Troie n'aura pas lieu*, act 2, sc.13.

83 *C'est de là que vient tout le mal: Dieu est un homme.*
All evil comes from this fact: God is a man.
1937 *Sodome et Gomorrhe*, act 1, sc.2.

Girondo, Oliverio 1891–1967

Argentinian poet, who travelled extensively in Europe and Africa and had close contact with the French avant garde. He edited the Ultraist manifesto in the avant-garde magazine *Martín Fierro* (1924).

84 *Cansado,*
sobre todo,
de estar siempre conmigo,
de hallarme cada día,
cuando termina el sueño,
allí, donde me encuentre,
con las mismas narices
y con las mismas piernas.
Tired,
above all,
of being always with myself,
of finding myself everyday,
when the dream comes to an end,
wherever I am,
with the same old nose
and with the same old legs.
1942 *Persuasión de los días*, 'Cansancio' ('Fatigue').

Giscard d'Estaing, Valéry 1926–

French politician, born in Germany. A Resistance worker during World War II, he was Finance Minister (1962–6) before launching the National Federation of Independent Republicans. He was President of France (1974–81) and in 1989 he resigned from the French National Assembly to play, instead, a leading role in the EU.

85 During my seven years in office, I was in love with seventeen million French women… I know this

declaration will inspire irony and that English language readers will find it very French.
1988 *Le Pouvoir et la vie.*

Gitlin, Todd

US academic and columnist. He is Professor of Journalism and Sociology at Columbia University. He has written on culture, politics and the media and is also a published poet.

86 There is a misunderstanding by marketers in our culture about what freedom of choice is. In the market, it is equated with multiplying choice. This is a misconception. If you have infinite choice, people are reduced to passivity.
1990 In the *New York Times*, 14 Feb.

Giuliani, Rudy (Rudolph William) 1944–

US lawyer and politician. He was mayor of New York City at the time of the 11 September terrorist attacks on the World Trade Center.

87 Show your confidence. Show you're not afraid. Go to restaurants. Go shopping.
2001 Encouraging the people of New York to resume their normal lives after the terrorist attack of 11 Sep. Press conference, 12 Sep.

88 Our hearts are broken, but they continue to beat, and the spirit of our City has never been stronger.
2001 *One Nation: America Remembers September 11, 2001*, introduction.

Gladstone, W(illiam) E(wart) 1809–98

English Liberal statesman. He entered Parliament as a Conservative (1832), and in 1867 became leader of the Liberal Party. As Prime Minister (1868–74, 1880–5, 1886, 1892–4) he established a system of national education (1870), introduced parliamentary reforms aimed at universal male suffrage and argued for Irish Home Rule.

89 It is upon those who say that it is necessary to exclude forty-nine fiftieths of the working classes [from the vote] to show cause, and I venture to say that every man who is not presumably incapacitated by some consideration of personal unfitness or of political danger, is morally entitled to come within the pale of the Constitution.
1864 House of Commons, 11 May.

90 One cannot fight against the future. Time is on our side.
1866 Speech on the Reform Bill, House of Commons, 27 Apr.

91 Remember the rights of the savage, as we call him. Remember that the happiness of his humble home, remember that the sanctity of life in the hill villages of Afghanistan, among the winter snows, is as inviolable in the eye of Almighty God as can be your own.
1879 Speech at Edinburgh Foresters' Hall, during the Midlothian Campaign, 26 Nov.

92 England's foreign policy should always be inspired by the love of freedom. There should be a sympathy with freedom, a desire to give it scope, founded not upon visionary ideas but upon the long experience of many generations within the shores of this happy isle, that in freedom one lays the firmest foundations both of loyalty and order.
1879 Speech, West Calder, 27 Nov.

93 All the world over, I will back the masses against the classes.
1886 Speech, Liverpool, 28 Jun.

94 We are part of the community of Europe, and we must do our duty as such.
1888 Speech, 10 Apr.

95 What that Sicilian mule was to me, I have been to the Queen.
1894 Memorandum on his relationship with Queen Victoria, 20 Mar.

96 It is not a Life at all. It is a Reticence, in three volumes.
Of J W Cross's *Life of George Eliot*. Quoted in E F Benson *As We Were* (1930), ch.6.

Glasgow, Ellen Anderson Gholson 1874–1945

US novelist. Much of her fiction was set in the South. She won a Pulitzer Prize in 1941 for *In This Our Life*.

97 It was not the matter of the work, but the mind that went into, that counted—and the man who was not content to do small things well would leave great things undone.
1900 *The Voice of the People*, bk.2, ch.4.

98 Women like to sit down with trouble as if it were knitting.
1932 *The Sheltered Life*, pt.3, section 3.

99 No matter how vital experience might be while you lived it, no sooner was it ended and dead than it became as lifeless as the piles of dry dust in a school history book.
1941 *In This Our Life*, pt.3, ch.9.

Gleick, James 1954–

US software designer and science writer. His books include *Faster: The Acceleration of Just About Everything* (1999) and *Isaac Newton* (2003).

1 To some physicists chaos is a science of process rather than state, of becoming rather than being.
1987 *Chaos*.

2 The Internet has taken shape with startlingly little planning… The most universal and indispensable network on the planet somehow burgeoned without so much as a board of directors, never mind a mergers-and-acquisitions department. There is a paradoxical lesson here for strategists. In economic terms, the great corporations are acting like socialist planners, while old-fashioned free-market capitalism blossoms at their feet.
1994 In the *New York Times Magazine*, 1 May.

Glen, Iain 1961–

Scottish actor.

3 I used to have this terrible wish. I didn't mind dying as long as the rest of the world ground to a halt when I did.
2001 In *The Herald*, 8 Jul.

Glennie, Evelyn 1965–

Scottish percussion player. Judged to be a percussionist of outstanding abilities, she is additionally remarkable in her achievements as she experienced a gradual but total loss of hearing in her early teens.

4 If we cannot spare some patience towards a piece of music or art, what hope do we have for showing it to another human being?
2004 In *Scotland on Sunday*, 30 May.

Gloucester, William Henry, 1st Duke of 1743–1805

British nobleman and military officer. He was the son of Frederick Louis, Prince of Wales and Augusta of Saxe-Gotha.

5 Another damned, thick, square book! Always scribble, scribble, scribble! Eh! Mr Gibbon?
1781 Attributed, when presented with the second volume of *The Decline and Fall of the Roman Empire*. These words have also been attributed to George III and the Duke of Cumberland.

Godard, Jean-Luc 1930–

French film critic and director. His first feature *À bout de souffle* (1959) established him as one of the leading members of the 'New Wave'. Other notable films include *Pierrot Le Fou* (1965), *Alphaville* (1965) and *Week-end* (1967).

6 *La photographie, c'est la vérité. Le cinéma: la vérité vingt-quatre fois par seconde.*
Photography is truth. And cinema is truth twenty-four times a second.
1960 *Le Petit Soldat*.

Goebbels, (Paul) Joseph 1897–1945

German Nazi official. In 1926 Hitler appointed him district party leader for Berlin and in 1928 he entered the Reichstag. As Minister for Propaganda from 1933 he was a vociferous and virulent anti-Semite. He killed his family and committed suicide as Berlin fell in 1945.

7 *Ohne Butter werden wir fertig, aber nicht beispielsweise ohne Kanonen. Wenn wir einmal überfallen werden, dann können wir uns nicht mit Butter, sondern nur mit Kanonen verteidigen.*
We can manage without butter but not, for example, without guns. If we are attacked, we can only defend ourselves with guns not butter.
1936 Speech in Berlin, 17 Jan.

8 *Wenn das deutsche Volk die Waffen niederlegte, würden die Sowjets…ganz Ost- und Südosteuropa zuzüglich des größten Teiles des Reiches besetzen. Vor diesem einschließlich der Sowjetunion riesigen Territorium würde sich sofort ein eiserner Vorhang heruntersenken.*
Should the German people lay down their arms, the Soviets…would occupy all eastern and south-eastern Europe together with the greater part of the Reich. Over all this territory, which with the Soviet Union would be of enormous extent, an iron curtain would at once descend.
1945 In *Das Reich*, a Nazi propaganda weekly, quoted in *The Times* and the *Manchester Guardian* on 23 Feb.
➤ *See also Churchill* 217:92.

Goering, Hermann Wilhelm 1893–1946

German soldier and Nazi leader, commander of the Hitler storm troopers and head of the Gestapo. He was sentenced to death at the Nuremberg Trials, but committed suicide.

9 Our movement took a grip on cowardly Marxism, and from it, extracted the meaning of socialism. It also took from the cowardly, middle-class parties their nationalism. Throwing both into the cauldron of our way of life there emerged, as clear as crystal, the synthesis —German National Socialism.
1933 Speech, Berlin, 9 Apr.

10 Would you rather have butter or guns? …preparedness

makes us powerful. Butter merely makes us fat.
1936 Speech, Hamburg.
➡ *See Goebbels 359:7.*

11 I hereby commission you to carry out all the preparations with regard to…a total solution of the Jewish question, in those territories of Europe that are under German influence.
1941 Directive to the Nazi High Command, 31 Jul, quoted in William Shirer *The Rise and Fall of the Third Reich* (1962).

Goethe, Johann Wolfgang von 1749–1832

German poet, dramatist and scientist. His early nationalistic, 'Sturm und Drang' dramas were followed by lyric poetry and poetical drama. His masterpiece was *Faust* (1808), on which he worked for most of his life.

12 English plays,
Atrocious in content,
Absurd in form,
Objectionable in action,
Execrable English Theatre!
1749 Attributed.

13 For a woman, she has extraordinary talent. One must look for what she does, not what she fails to do.
1786–8 Of the painter Angelica Kauffman. *Italienische Reise* (published 1816–17, translated by W H Auden and Elizabeth Mayer as *Italian Journey*, 1962).

14 *Wenn es eine Freude ist das Gute zu genießen, so ist es eine größere das Bessere zu empfinden, und in der Kunst ist das Beste gut genug.*
As it is a joy to enjoy what is good, so it is a greater joy to experience what is better, and in art the best is good enough.
1787 *Italienische Reise* 3 Mar (published 1816–17, translated by W H Auden and Elizabeth Mayer as *Italian Journey*, 1962).

15 *Wer nie sein Brot mit Tränen aß,*
Wer nie die kummervollen Nächte,
Auf seinem Bette weinen saß,
Der kennt euch nicht, ihr himmlischen Mächte.
Who never ate his bread in sorrow,
Who never spent the darksome hours
Weeping and watching for the morrow
He knows ye not, ye heavenly powers.
1795–6 *Wilhelm Meisters Lehrjahre* (translated by Carlyle in 1824 as *Wilhelm Meister's Apprenticeship*).

16 *Es irrt der Mensch, so lang er strebt.*
Man will err while yet he strives.
1808 *Faust*, pt.1, 'Prolog im Himmel'.

17 *Grau, teurer Freund, ist alle Theorie.*
Und grün des Lebens goldner Baum.
All theory, dear friend, is grey, but the golden tree of actual life springs ever green.
1808 *Faust*, pt.1, 'Studierzimmer'.

18 *Alles Gescheite ist schon gedacht worden; man muss nur versuchen, es noch einmal zu denken.*
Everything clever has been thought of before. We must try to think it again.
1819 *Sprüche in Prosa, Maximen und Reflexionen*, pt.1.

19 *Der Aberglaube ist die Poesie des Lebens.*
Superstition is the poetry of life.
1819 *Sprüche in Prosa, Maximen und Reflexionen*, pt.3.

20 *Neuere Poeten tun viel Wasser in die Tinte.*

Modern poets mix a lot of water with their ink.
1819 *Sprüche in Prosa, Maximen und Reflexionen*, pt.6.

21 *Das Erste und Letzte, was vom Genie gefordert wird, ist Wahrheitsliebe.*
The first and the last thing demanded of genius is the love of truth.
1819 *Sprüche in Prosa, Maximen und Reflexionen*, pt.6.

22 *Klassisch ist das Gesunde, romantisch das Kranke.*
The classical period was healthy; the romantic diseased.
1819 *Sprüche in Prosa, Maximen und Reflexionen*, pt.7.

23 Lord Byron is only great as a poet; as soon as he reflects he is a child.
1825 Eckermann's *Conversations with Goethe*, 18 Jan.

24 *Ich kenne mich auch nicht und Gott soll mich auch davor behuten.*
I do not know myself, and God forbid that I should.
1829 Eckermann's *Conversations with Goethe*, 10 Apr.

25 *Mehr Licht!*
More light!
1832 Last words.

26 *Ach da ich irrte, hatt' ich viel Gespielen,*
Da ich dich kenne, bin ich fast allein.
Ah! while I erred I had many friends.
Now that I know you, I am alone.
Gedichte, Zuneigung (published 1910).

Goheen, Robert F(rancis) 1919–

US classical scholar and educator, born in India. He joined Princeton University in 1948, and became President there (1957–72). He was Ambassador to India (1977–80).

27 If you feel that you have both feet planted on level ground, then the university has failed you.
1961 Baccalaureate address. Reported in *Time* magazine, 23 Jun.

Golding, Sir William (Gerald) 1911–93

English novelist. He achieved fame with his first novel *Lord of the Flies* (1954), and was awarded the Nobel prize for literature in 1983.

28 Ralph wept for the end of innocence, the darkness of man's heart, and the fall through the air of a true, wise friend called Piggy.
1954 *Lord of the Flies*, ch.12.

29 Sleep is when all the unsorted stuff comes flying out as from a dustbin upset in a high wind.
1956 *Pincher Martin*, ch.6.

30 Philip is a living example of natural selection. He was as fitted to survive in this modern world as a tapeworm in an intestine.
1959 *Free Fall*, ch.2.

31 Eighteen is a good time for suffering. One has all the necessary strength, and no defences.
1967 *The Pyramid*.

32 With lack of sleep and too much understanding I grow a little crazy, I think, like all men at sea who live too close to each other and too close thereby to all that is monstrous under the sun and moon.
1980 *Rites of Passage*, closing words.

33 The theme defeats structuralism, for it is an emotion. The

theme of *Lord of the Flies* is grief, sheer grief, grief, grief, grief.
1982 'Moving Target'.

34 It really means nothing in this country whatsoever—but then being a writer here means nothing either.
1983 On winning the Nobel prize. Quoted in the *Observer*, 31 May.

35 Life should serve up its feast of experience in a series of courses.
1987 *Close Quarters*.

Goldman, William 1931–

US screenwriter, who has written the scripts for films such as *Butch Cassidy and the Sundance Kid* (1969, Academy Award), *All the President's Men* (1976, Academy Award) and *Misery* (1990).

36 Boy, I got vision. The rest of the world wears bifocals.
1969 Anachronistic line delivered by Paul Newman in *Butch Cassidy and the Sundance Kid*.

Goldmark, Peter Carl, Jr 1940–

US government official, President of the Rockefeller Foundation (1988–97) and Director of the Global and Regional Air Program at Environmental Defense (2003–).

37 Welfare is hated by those who administer it; mistrusted by those who pay for it; and held in contempt by those who receive it.
1977 In the *New York Times*, 24 May.

Goldsmith, Oliver 1728–74

Irish novelist, poet, and playwright. After studying medicine and attempting to join the Church, he began a literary career. He is best known for the novel *The Vicar of Wakefield* (1766), the poem *The Deserted Village* (1770) and the play *She Stoops to Conquer* (1773).

38 The doctor found, when she was dead,
Her last disorder mortal.
1759 'Elegy on Mrs Mary Blaize'.

39 Where'er I roam, whatever realms to see,
My heart untravelled fondly turns to thee;
Still to my brother turns with ceaseless pain,
And drags at each remove a lengthening chain.
1764 *The Traveller*, l.7–10.

40 Such is the patriot's boast, where'er we roam,
His first, best country ever is, at home.
1764 *The Traveller*, l.73–4.

41 Laws grind the poor, and rich men rule the law.
1764 *The Traveller*, l.386.

42 How small, of all that human hearts endure,
That part which laws or kings can cause or cure!
1764 *The Traveller*, l.429–30.

43 I was ever of the opinion, that the honest man who married and brought up a large family, did more service than he who continued single and only talked of population.
1766 *The Vicar of Wakefield*, ch.1.

44 Let us draw upon content for the deficiencies of fortune.
1766 *The Vicar of Wakefield*, ch.3.

45 Conscience is a coward, and those faults it has not strength enough to prevent it seldom has justice enough to accuse.

1766 *The Vicar of Wakefield*, ch.13.

46 It seemed to me pretty plain, that they had more of love than of matrimony in them.
1766 *The Vicar of Wakefield*, ch.16.

47 When lovely woman stoops to folly
And finds too late that men betray,
What charm can soothe her melancholy,
What art can wash her guilt away?
1766 *The Vicar of Wakefield*, ch.29.

48 Friendship is a disinterested commerce between equals; love, an abject intercourse between tyrants and slaves.
1768 *The Good-Natured Man*, act 1.

49 Silence is become his mother tongue.
1768 *The Good-Natured Man*, act 2.

50 Sweet Auburn, loveliest village of the plain,
Where health and plenty cheered the labouring swain.
1770 *The Deserted Village*, l.1–2.

51 How often have I paused on every charm,
The sheltered cot, the cultivated farm,
The never-failing brook, the busy mill,
The decent church that topped the neighbouring hill.
1770 *The Deserted Village*, l.9–12.

52 Ill fares the land, to hastening ills a prey
Where wealth accumulates and men decay:
Princes and lords may flourish or may fade;
A breath can make them, as a breath has made;
But a bold peasantry, their country's pride,
When once destroyed, can never be supplied.
1770 *The Deserted Village*, l.51–6.

53 The village preacher's modest mansion rose.
A man he was to all the country dear,
And passing rich with forty pounds a year.
1770 *The Deserted Village*, l.140–2.

54 The village master taught his little school;
A man severe he was and stern to view;
I knew him well, and every truant knew;
Well had the boding tremblers learned to trace
The day's disasters in his morning face;
Full well they laughed, with counterfeited glee,
At all his jokes, for many a joke had he.
1770 *The Deserted Village*, l.196–202.

55 In arguing too, the parson owned his skill,
For e'en though vanquished, he could argue still;
While words of learned length, and thund'ring sound
Amazed the gazing rustics ranged around,
And still they gazed, and still the wonder grew,
That one small head could carry all he knew.
1770 *The Deserted Village*, l.211–16.

56 And, even while fashion's brightest arts decoy,
The heart distrusting asks, if this be joy.
1770 *The Deserted Village*, l.263–4.

57 The rich man's joys increase, the poor's decay,
'Tis yours to judge how wide the limits stand
Between a splendid and a happy land.
1770 *The Deserted Village*, l.266–8.

58 Thus fares the land, by luxury betrayed.
1770 *The Deserted Village*, l.295.

59 In all the silent manliness of grief.
1770 *The Deserted Village*, l.384.

60 I see the rural virtues leave the land.

1770 *The Deserted Village*, l.398.

61 Though very poor, may still be very blest.
1770 *The Deserted Village*, l.426.

62 I love everything that's old: old friends, old times, old manners, old books, old wine.
1773 *She Stoops to Conquer*, act 1, sc.1.

63 Is it one of my well-looking days, child? Am I in face to-day?
1773 *She Stoops to Conquer*, act 1, sc.1.

64 Let school-masters puzzle their brain,
With grammar, and nonsense, and learning;
Good liquor, I stoutly maintain,
Gives genius a better discerning.
1773 *She Stoops to Conquer*, act 1, sc.2.

65 I'll be with you in a squeezing of a lemon.
1773 *She Stoops to Conquer*, act 1, sc.2.

66 It's a damned long, dark, boggy, dirty, dangerous way.
1773 *She Stoops to Conquer*, act 1, sc.2.

67 The first blow is half the battle.
1773 *She Stoops to Conquer*, act 2, sc.1.

68 But there's no love lost between us.
1773 *She Stoops to Conquer*, act 4, sc.1.

69 Our Garrick's a salad; for in him we see
Oil, vinegar, sugar, and saltness agree.
1774 *Retaliation*, l.11–12.

70 Who, too deep for his hearers, still went on refining,
And thought of convincing, while they thought of dining;
Though equal to all things, for all things unfit,
Too nice for a statesman, too proud for a wit.
1774 Of Edmund Burke. *Retaliation*, l.29–32.

71 On the stage he was natural, simple, affecting;
'Twas only that when he was off he was acting.
1774 Of Garrick. *Retaliation*, l.101–2.

72 When they talked of their Raphaels, Correggios, and stuff,
He shifted his trumpet, and only took snuff.
1774 Of Reynolds. *Retaliation*, l.145–6.

Goldwater, Barry M(orris) 1909–98

US politician, Senator from Arizona (1952–64, 1969–87) and leader of the extreme right Republican wing. He was defeated in the 1964 presidential election by Lyndon B Johnson.

73 Extremism in the defence of liberty is no vice, and moderation in the pursuit of justice is no virtue.
1964 Speech to the Republican convention, 16 Jul.

74 In your heart, you know I'm right.
1964 Presidential campaign slogan.

75 He had probably been vaccinated with a phonograph needle.
1979 On the windy presidential candidate Hubert Humphrey. *With No Apologies*.

76 You don't need to be 'straight' to fight and die for your country. You just need to shoot straight.
1993 On homosexuals in the military. In *Life*, Dec.

Goldwyn, Sam(uel) originally Schmuel Gelbfisz
1882–1974

Polish-born US film producer. In 1917 he founded Goldwyn Pictures Corporation and in 1925 the Metro-Goldwyn-Mayer Company. His films include *Wuthering Heights* (1939), *The Little Foxes* (1941) and *Guys and Dolls* (1955). He is credited with many artless Goldwynisms, most probably apocryphal.

77 I'll cable Hitler and ask him to shoot around you.
1939 Remark to David Niven, Sep, when Niven left Hollywood to return to England. Quoted in David Niven *Bring on the Empty Horses* (1975).

78 I don't care if it doesn't make a nickel. I just want every man, woman and child in America to see it!
1946 Of *The Best Years of Our Lives*. Quoted in Leslie Halliwell *Halliwell's Filmgoer's and Video Viewer's Companion* (9th edn, 1989).

79 Any man who goes to a psychiatrist should have his head examined.
Quoted in Norman Zierold *Moguls* (1969), ch.3.

80 Please write music like Wagner, only louder.
Note to a composer of a forthcoming film soundtrack. Recalled on his death, 31 Jan 1974.

81 You ought to take the bull between the teeth.
Recalled on his death, 31 Jan 1974.

82 Now why did you name your baby 'John'? Every Tom, Dick and Harry is named 'John'.
Attributed. Quoted in Fred Metcalf (ed) *The Penguin Dictionary of Humorous Quotations* (1986).

83 I seriously object to seeing on the screen what belongs in the bedroom.
Attributed maxim. Quoted in Leslie Halliwell *Halliwell's Filmgoer's and Video Viewer's Companion* (9th edn, 1989).

84 What we want is a story that starts with an earthquake and works its way up to a climax.
Quoted in Leslie Halliwell *Halliwell's Filmgoer's and Video Viewer's Companion* (9th edn, 1989).

85 A verbal contract isn't worth the paper it's written on.
Attributed. Quoted in A Scott Berg *Goldwyn* (1989).

86 I'll give you a definite maybe.
Attributed. Quoted in A Scott Berg *Goldwyn* (1989).

87 Include me out.
Attributed. Quoted in A Scott Berg *Goldwyn* (1989).

88 We are dealing in facts, not realities.
Attributed. Quoted in A Scott Berg *Goldwyn* (1989).

89 You gotta take the sour with the bitter.
Remark allegedly said to Billy Wilder when one of his films flopped. Quoted in A Scott Berg *Goldwyn* (1989).

90 The most important thing in acting is honesty. Once you've learned to fake that, you're in.
Attributed.

91 The only reason so many people showed up at his funeral was because they wanted to make sure he was dead.
Of Louis B Mayer. Attributed.

Gomez, Vernon Louis known as 'Lefty' 1908–89

US baseball player, pitcher for the New York Yankees in the 1930s.

92 Tell you what, you keep the salary and pay me the cut.
When asked to take a cut in salary from $20,000 to $7,500 following a poor season. Quoted in Colin Jarman *The Guinness Dictionary of Sports Quotations* (1990).

Goncharov, Ivan Alexandrovich 1812–91

Russian novelist. He led an uneventful life in the civil service and produced *Oblomov* (1857, translated 1915), one of the greatest works of Russian realism.

93 The trouble is that no devastating or redeeming fires have ever burnt in my life… My life began by flickering out.
1859 *Oblomov*, pt.2, ch.4 (translated by David Magarshak).

94 You lost your ability for doing things in childhood… It all began with your inability to put on your socks and ended by your inability to live.
1859 *Oblomov*, pt.4, ch.2 (translated by David Magarshak).

Gonne, Maud 1865–1953

Irish nationalist and actress. She met W B Yeats in the early 1890s and, though Yeats wished to marry her, she ultimately rejected him and married Major John MacBride.

95 Poets should never marry. The world should thank me for not marrying you.
Attributed. Said to W B Yeats.

González Prada, Manuel 1848–1918

Peruvian reformer, journalist and poet. Nationalistic, pro-Indian, anti-Spanish and anti-clerical, he was a virtuoso in the vocabulary of invective, combining intensity of emotion with a pervasive sense of form.

96 *Aunque chillen los pedantes*
y arruguen todos el ceño,
lo declaro yo: Cervantes
suele producirme sueño
Pedants may cry out loud
or frown at me,
but I must say it: Cervantes
usually puts me to sleep.
1937 *Grafitos*, 'Hombres y libros' ('Men and Books').

Gooch, George Peabody 1873–1968

English historian and politician. He wrote several works on political and diplomatic history.

97 We can now look forward with something like confidence to the time when war between civilised nations will be considered as antiquated as a duel.
1911 *History of Our Time 1855–1911*.

Goodall, John 1863–1942

English footballer, captain of Preston North End. He also captained England, winning a total of 14 caps. He subsequently played cricket at county level for Derbyshire.

98 The one passion of my life has been football—the most exhilarating game I know, and the strongest protest against selfishness, without sermonizing, that was ever put before a thoughtful people.
Quoted in Andrew Ward and Anton Rippon *The Derby County Story* (1983).

Gorbachev, Mikhail Sergeyevich 1931–

Russian politician, President of the Supreme Soviet of the USSR (1988–90) and first executive President of the USSR. Despite his historic achievements as the father of *glasnost* (openness of information) and *perestroika* (a radical reform programme), which ended the Cold War, he was forced to resign on 25 Dec 1991. He was awarded the Nobel peace prize in 1990.

99 Some comrades apparently find it hard to understand that democracy is just a slogan.
1987 In the *Observer*, 1 Feb.

1 If the Russian word 'perestroika' has easily entered the international lexicon, it is due to more than just interest in what is going on in the Soviet Union. Now the whole world needs restructuring; that is, progressive development, a fundamental change.
1987 *Perestroika: New Thinking for Our Country and the World*.

2 The Soviet people want full-blooded and unconditional democracy.
1988 Speech, Jul.

3 Life is making us abandon established stereotypes and outdated views; it is making us discard illusions.
1988 Speech, United Nations, 7 Dec.

4 Mitterrand has 100 lovers. One has AIDS, but he doesn't know which one. Bush has 100 bodyguards. One is a terrorist, but he doesn't know which one. Gorbachev has 100 economic advisers. One is smart, but he doesn't know which one.
1990 In the *Sunday Times*, 9 Dec.

Gordon, Adam Lindsay 1833–70

Australian poet, born in the Azores. A series of personal tragedies led to a mental breakdown, and he committed suicide.

5 Question not, but live and labour
Till yon goal be won,
Helping every feeble neighbour,
Seeking help from none;
Life is mostly froth and bubble,
Two things stand like stone:
KINDNESS in another's trouble,
COURAGE in your own.
1866 'Ye Wearie Wayfarer: Hys Ballad. In Eight Fyttes', in *Bell's Life in Victoria*, Nov 1866, collected in *Sea Spray and Smoke Drift* (1867).

6 I would that with sleepy, soft embraces
The sea would fold me—would find me rest
In luminous shades of her secret places,
In depths where her marvels are manifest;
So the earth beneath her should not discover
My hidden couch—nor the heaven above her—
As a strong love shielding a weary lover,
I would have her shield me with shining breast.
'The Swimmer', stanza 5, collected in *Bush Ballads and Galloping Rhymes* (1870).

7 A little season of love and laughter,
Of light and life, and pleasure and pain,
And horror of outer darkness after,
And dust returneth to dust again.
Then the lesser life shall be as the greater,
And the lover of life shall join the hater,
And the one thing cometh sooner or later,
And no one knoweth the loss or gain.
'The Swimmer', stanza 10, collected in *Bush Ballads and Galloping Rhymes* (1870).

Gordon, Mack 1904–59

Polish-born US lyricist.

8 Pardon me boy is that the Chattanooga Choo-choo,

Track twenty nine,
Boy you can give me a shine.
1941 Song 'Chattanooga Choo Choo', featured in *Sun Valley Serenade* (music by Harry Warren).

9 Dinner in the diner
nothing could be finer
than to have your ham'n eggs in Carolina.
1941 Song 'Chattanooga Choo Choo', featured in *Sun Valley Serenade* (music by Harry Warren).

Gordon, Ruth 1896–1985

US actress and playwright, best known for the screenplays she wrote with her husband Garson Kanin, *Adam's Rib* (1949) and *Pat and Mike* (1952). She won an Oscar for her performance in *Rosemary's Baby* (1968).

10 MAX: Say, is it too early for a drink?
POLLY: What's early about it? It's tomorrow in Europe and yesterday in China.
1943 *Over Twenty-One*, act 3.

Gore, Al(bert,)r 1948–

US Vice-President under Bill Clinton (1992–2000). In 2000 he ran for President in what turned out to be the closest contest in over 100 years, losing to Republican George W Bush by the narrowest of margins.

11 You get all the French-fries the President can't get to.
1994 On being Vice-President. In the *New York Times*, 8 Apr.

12 It makes no more sense to launch an assault on our civil liberties as the best way to get at terrorists than it did to launch an invasion on Iraq as the best way to get at Osama Bin Laden.
2003 Speech calling for the repeal of the US Patriot Act, 9 Nov.

Gorman, Dave 1971–

English comedian.

13 Fictional comedy tells us that the writer is remarkable. Factual comedy tells us that the world is remarkable. I suppose I prefer to live in a remarkable world.
2004 In *Varsity*, 23 Jan.

Gorostiza, José 1901–73

Mexican poet and diplomat. The most famous member of the avant-garde *Contemporáneos* group, his published poems are few but complex.

14 *¡Oh inteligencia, soledad en llamas,*
que todo lo concibe sin crearlo!
Oh intelligence, flaming solitude,
envisioning all without creating!
1939 *Muerte sin fin*, pt.1 (translated as *Death without End*, 1969).

Gorostiza, Manuel Eduardo de 1789–1851

Mexican dramatist and diplomat. He spent his youth in Spain, returning to Mexico in 1833 where he fought in the US invasion. He was a key figure in Latin American neoclassical theatre.

15 *Yo no digo por eso que el té no sea saludable…cuando*
duelen las tripas…pero al cabo no pasa de ser agua
caliente; sólo podía habernos venido de Inglaterra, que
como allí son herejes, ni tendrán vino, ni bueyes
cebones.
I'm not saying that tea is not healthy…when you have a

stomach ache…but, all in all, it is only hot water; it could only come from the English, who, being heretics as they are, probably have no wine or good beer.
1833 *Contigo pan y cebolla*, act 1.

Gosse, Sir Edmund 1849–1928

English critic and translator. He wrote biographies of many notable literary figures, and translated the plays of Henrik Ibsen.

16 A sheep in sheep's clothing.
Of Sturge Moore, a poet. Quoted in F Greenslet *Under the Bridge* (1943), ch.10.

17 We were as nearly bored as enthusiasm would permit.
Of a play by Algernon Swinburne. Quoted in C Hassall *Biography of Edward Marsh*.

Gottfried von Strassburg fl.c.1200

German poet. His major work is a version of the Tristan and Isolde legend, *Tristan* (c.1210), but his appraisals of the works of other writers are a striking early example of literary criticism.

18 *Wan swelh wîp tugendet wider ir art,*
diu gerne wider ir art bewart
ir lop, ir êre unde ire lîp,
diu ist niwan mit namen ein wîp
und ist ein man mit muote.
When a woman grows in virtue despite her nature
and gladly preserves the integrity
of her honour, her reputation, and her person,
she is only a woman in name:
in spirit she is a man.
c.1210 *Tristan*, l.17971–3.

Gottlieb, Adolph 1903–74

US painter, one of the leaders of Abstract Expressionism.

19 Certain people always say we should go back to nature. I notice they never say we should go forward to nature. It seems to me they are more concerned that we should go back, than about nature.
1947 In *Tiger's Eye*, vol.1, no.2, Dec, quoted in C Harrison and Paul Wood (eds) *Art in Theory 1900–1990* (1992).

Gould, Glenn 1932–82

Canadian pianist and musical theorist. He performed his last live concert in 1964, thereafter confining himself to recording.

20 The concert is dead.
Quoted in Richard Kostelanetz *Master Minds* (1969).

21 The purpose of art is the lifelong construction of a state of wonder.
Quoted by Lorraine Monk at the Commencement Address, York University, Toronto, 6 Nov 1982.

Gould, Philip 1950–

English political strategist and senior adviser to Tony Blair.

22 The New Labour brand has been badly contaminated. It is the object of constant criticism and, even worse, ridicule.
2000 Internal memo, May, later leaked to the press. In *The Guardian*, 20 Jul.

Gould, Stephen Jay 1941–2002

US palaeontologist, evolutionary biologist and science writer,

Professor at Harvard University (1967–2002).

23 A man does not attain the status of Galileo merely
because he is persecuted, he must also be right.
1977 *Ever Since Darwin*.

24 Science must be understood as a social phenomenon,
a gutsy, human enterprise, not the work of robots
programmed to collect pure information.
1981 *The Mismeasure of Man*.

25 Science is an integral part of culture. It's not this foreign
thing, done by an arcane priesthood. It's one of the
glories of the human intellectual tradition.
1990 In *The Independent*, 24 Jan.

Gounod, Charles François 1818–93

French composer. His works include operas, masses, hymns
and oratorios, and he was popular as a songwriter. He fled to
England in the Franco-Prussian War (1870), becoming a
commander of the Legion of Honour in 1877.

26 God grant me a failure like that!
1861 Of Wagner's opera *Tannhäuser*, after the disastrous
première of its revised version at the *Opéra*, 13 Mar, when it was
withdrawn after only three performances. Quoted in Joanna
Richardson *La Vie Parisienne* (1971).
➤ See Mérimée 567:13.

Gourmont, Rémy de 1858–1915

French writer and critic, leader of the Symbolist movement. He
founded the periodical *Le Mercure de France*, and wrote essays,
literary criticism and novels.

27 Science is the only truth and it is the great lie. It knows
nothing, and people think it knows everything. It is
misrepresented. People think that science is electricity,
automobilism, and dirigible balloons. It is something
very different. It is life devouring itself. It is the sensibility
transformed into intelligence. It is the need to know
stifling the need to live. It is the genius of knowledge
vivisecting the vital genius.
1905 *Promenades philosophiques* (translated by Glen S Burne,
1966).

Gowers, Sir Ernest Arthur 1880–1966

English civil servant, called to the bar in 1906. His *Plain Words*
(1948) and *ABC of Plain Words* (1951) are guides for officials in
writing clear English. He revised Fowler's *Dictionary of Modern
English Usage* (1965).

28 It is not easy nowadays to remember anything so
contrary to all appearances as that officials are the
servants of the public; and the official must try not to
foster the illusion that it is the other way round.
1948 *Plain Words*, ch.3.

29 Sociology is a new science concerning itself not
with esoteric matters outside the comprehension of
the layman, as the older sciences do, but with the
ordinary affairs of ordinary people. This seems to
engender in those who write about it a feeling that
the lack of any abstruseness in their subject matter
demands a compensatory abstruseness in their
language.
1965 'Sociologese', in H F Fowler *A Dictionary of Modern English
Usage* (2nd rev edn).

Goya, Francisco de 1746–1828

Spanish painter and graphic artist, perhaps best known for his
series of etchings *The Disasters of War*.

30 But where do they find these lines in nature? Personally I
only see forms that are lit up and forms that are not,
planes which advance and planes which recede, relief
and depth. My eye never sees outlines or particular
features or details. I do not count the hairs in the beard of
the man who passes by any more than the buttonholes
on his jacket attract my notice. My brush should not see
better than I do.
Quoted in Enriqueta Harris *Goya* (1969).

Grace, W(illiam) G(ilbert) 1848–1915

English cricketer and physician. He made his debut in first-
class cricket in 1864; by the time he retired in 1908 he had
scored 126 first-class centuries and 54,896 runs, and taken
2,864 wickets.

31 Let's be getting at them before they get at us.
His reason for always choosing to bat first if his team won the
toss. Quoted in Colin Jarman *The Guinness Dictionary of Sports
Quotations* (1990).

32 They haven't come to see you umpiring, they have come
to see me bat.
On refusing to leave the crease after an umpire gave him out
before he had scored, attributed. Other versions of the story
have the umpire refusing to call out on the first ball, explaining
to the outraged bowler that the crowd had paid not to see him
bowl, but to see Grace bat.

Graham, Harry 1874–1936

English writer of light verse. His blackly comic rhymes in
Ruthless Rhymes for Heartless Homes (1899) and the later *More
Ruthless Rhymes* (1930) won widespread popularity.

33 Aunt Jane observed, the second time
She tumbled off a bus,
'The step is short from the Sublime
To the Ridiculous.'
1899 *Ruthless Rhymes for Heartless Homes*, 'Equanimity'.

34 O'er the rugged mountain's brow
Clara threw the twins she nursed,
And remarked, 'I wonder now
Which will reach the bottom first?'
1899 *Ruthless Rhymes for Heartless Homes*, 'Calculating Clara'.

35 Billy, in one of his nice new sashes,
Fell in the fire and was burnt to ashes;
Now, although the room grows chilly,
I haven't the heart to poke poor Billy.
1899 *Ruthless Rhymes for Heartless Homes*, 'Tender-
Heartedness'.

36 Weep not for little Léonie
Abducted by a French *Marquis*!
Though loss of honour was a wrench
Just think how it's improved her French.
1930 *More Ruthless Rhymes for Heartless Homes*, 'Compensation'.

Grahame, Kenneth 1859–1932

Scottish children's writer and Secretary of the Bank of England
(1898–1908). He wrote essays and country tales but is best
remembered for *The Wind in the Willows* (1908).

37 Believe me, my young friend, there is *nothing*—

absolutely nothing—half so much worth doing as simply messing about in boats.
1908 *The Wind in the Willows*, ch.1.

38 The poetry of motion! The *real* way to travel! The *only* way to travel! Here today—in next week tomorrow! Villages skipped, towns and cities jumped—always somebody else's horizon!
1908 Toad rhapsodizes about the motor car. *The Wind in the Willows*, ch.2.

39 The smell of buttered toast simply talked to Toad, and with no uncertain voice; talked of warm kitchens, of breakfasts on bright frosty mornings, of cosy parlour firesides on winter evenings, when one's ramble was over and slippered feet were propped on the fender; of the purring of contented cats, and the twitter of sleepy canaries.
1908 *The Wind in the Willows*, ch.8.

40 The clever men at Oxford
Know all that there is to be knowed.
But they none of them know one half as much
As intelligent Mr Toad.
1908 *The Wind in the Willows*, ch.10.

Gramm, Phil (William Philip) 1942–

US Senator (1985–2002) and economist.

41 If I had to decide today, I would run. But I may come to my senses.
1994 On seeking presidential nomination. In *Time*, 26 Sep.

42 I didn't come to Washington to be loved and I haven't been disappointed.
1995 In NPR broadcast, 24 Feb.

43 Sophia Loren is not a citizen.
1995 On being asked if he would choose a woman as a running mate. In *Newsweek*, 13 Mar.

44 I have the most reliable friend that you can have in American politics—ready money.
1995 On seeking presidential nomination. In the *New York Times*, 23 Apr.

Grand, Sarah *pseudonym of* Frances Elizabeth McFall *née* Clarke 1854–1943

British novelist and feminist, born in Ireland. She was Mayoress of Bath (1923, 1925–9), and is best known for her novels which explore sexual double standards.

45 Both the cow-woman and the scum-woman are well within range of the comprehension of the Bawling Brotherhood, but the new woman is a little above him, and he never thought of looking up to where she has been sitting apart in silent contemplation all these years.
1894 *North American Review*, 'The New Aspect of the Woman Question', Mar.

Grant, Cary *pseudonym of* Archibald Leach 1904–86

English-born US film star. He made his film debut in 1932 and developed a reputation as a suave, debonair performer in sophisticated light comedy. His films include *Bringing up Baby* (1938), *His Girl Friday* (1940), *An Affair to Remember* (1957) and *North by Northwest* (1959).

46 Not only will I not play it, but if Rex Harrison doesn't do it, I won't even go to see it.

c.1963 Response when offered the role of Professor Henry Higgins in the film of *My Fair Lady*. Attributed.

47 Old Cary Grant fine. How you?
His response to a journalist's terse cable to his press agent, 'How old Cary Grant?' Attributed.

Grant, George P 1918–

Canadian philosopher and teacher.

48 We listen to others to discover what we ourselves believe.
Quoted in *CBC Times*, 18 Feb 1959.

Grant, Hugh 1960–

English actor, who became an international star after starring in *Four Weddings and a Funeral* (1994). Subsequent films include *Notting Hill* (1999) and *Bridget Jones's Diary* (2001).

49 I play the sort of character who would sell his grandmother for career advancement, something I've come across a lot with actors.
1994 On his role in *Restoration*. In *Screen International*, 2 Sep.

50 If *Pulp Fiction* had been set in the Sussex countryside— and I'm sure it could have worked—then things might have turned out very differently.
1995 Contrasting *Four Weddings and a Funeral* with a notoriously violent urban US drama. Speech at the British Academy of Film and Television Arts award ceremony, reported in *Screen International*, 28 Apr.

51 I just don't believe in love at first sight any more, even though I've based my whole career on the concept.
Quoted in the *Daily Telegraph*, 1 Jan 2004.

Grant, Sir Robert 1779–1838

English lawyer and politician, Advocate-General and Governor of Bombay.

52 O worship the King, all glorious above;
O gratefully sing his power and his love:
Our Shield and Defender, the Ancient of Days,
Pavilioned in splendour, and girded with praise.
1833 'O worship the King, all glorious above', collected in *Sacred Poems* (1839).

53 O tell of his might, O sing of his grace,
Whose robe is the light, whose canopy space.
His chariots of wrath the deep thunder-clouds form,
And dark is his path on the wings of the storm.
1833 'O worship the King, all glorious above', collected in *Sacred Poems* (1839).

Grant, Ulysses S(impson) 1822–85

US soldier and 18th President (1869–77), Union general in the Civil War, who accepted the Confederate surrender at Appomattox Court House (1865). He presided over the reconstruction of the South, but his administration was marred by scandal and corruption.

54 No terms except unconditional and immediate surrender can be accepted. I propose to move immediately upon your works.
1862 Message to Simon Bolivar Buckner, besieged at Fort Donelson, 16 Feb. Quoted in P C Headley *The Life and Campaigns of General U. S. Grant* (1869), ch.6.

55 I purpose to fight it out on this line, if it takes all summer.
1864 Despatch to Washington from Spottsylvania, 11 May.

Quoted in P C Headley *The Life and Campaigns of General U. S. Grant* (1869), ch.23.

56 I know no method to secure the repeal of bad or obnoxious laws so effective as their stringent execution.
1869 Inaugural address, 4 Mar.

57 I only know two tunes. One of them is 'Yankee Doodle', and the other isn't.
Attributed. Quoted in Derek Watson *Music Quotations* (1991).

Grass, Günter Wilhelm 1927–

German novelist, poet and playwright. Intellectual and experimental in form, theme and language, his books consistently challenge the status quo and question our reading of the past. He was awarded the Nobel prize for literature in 1999.

58 *Ich bin Schriftsteller von Beruf. Ich versuche, gegen die vergehende Zeit anzuschreiben, damit das Vergangene nicht unbekannt bleibt.*
I am a writer by profession. I seek in my writing to hold back time so that the past is not forgotten.
1978 *Denkzettel: Politische Reden und Aufsätze.*

59 *Ich sei nicht nur als Autor, sondern auch als Mann betroffen. Und zwar irgendwie schuldhaft.*
I am moved, not only as an author, but as a person. And feel somehow guilty.
1977 *Der Butt* (translated as *The Flounder*, 1978).

60 We of the long tails! We of the presentient whiskers! We of the perpetually growing teeth! We, the serried footnotes to man, his proliferating commentary. We, indestructible!
1987 *Die Ratten* (translated as *The Rat*, 1987).

Grattan, Henry 1746–1820

Irish statesman. He abandoned law for politics in 1775, leading the fight for independence. Unable to prevent the Act of Union, he sat at Westminster until his death.

61 She hears the ocean protesting against separation, but she hears the sea protesting against union. She follows therefore her physical destination when she protests against the two situations, both equally unnatural— separation and union.
Of Ireland. Quoted in Conor Cruise O'Brien *Parnell and His Party* (1957).

Graves, Robert von Ranke 1895–1985

English writer. He lived abroad for much of his adult life. His works include novels, poems, essays, studies of mythology, criticism, and his autobiography, *Goodbye to All That* (1929).

62 His eyes are quickened so with grief,
He can watch a grass or a leaf
Every instant grow.
1921 'Lost Love'.

63 Love shall come at your command
Yet will not stay.
1923 'Song of Contrariety'.

64 Children are dumb to say how hot the day is,
How hot the scent is of the summer rose.
1927 'The Cool Web'.

65 Goodbye to All That.
1929 Title of autobiography.

66 Take your delight in momentariness,
Walk between dark and dark—a shining space
With the grave's narrowness, though not its peace.
1938 'Sick Love'.

67 In fear begotten, I begot in fear.
Would you have had me cast fear out
So that you should not be?
1938 'Parents to Child'.

68 What, then, was war?
No mere discord of flags
But an infection of the common sky
That sagged ominously upon the earth
Even when the season was the airiest May?
1938 'Recalling War'.

69 To evoke posterity
Is to weep on your own grave,
Ventriloquizing for the unborn.
1938 'To Evoke Posterity'.

70 To bring the dead to life
Is no great magic.
Few are wholly dead:
Blow on a dead man's embers
And a live flame will start.
1938 'To Bring the Dead to Life'.

71 Truth-loving Persians do not dwell upon
The trivial skirmish fought near Marathon.
1945 'The Persian Version'.

72 Stirring suddenly from long hibernation,
I knew myself once more a poet
Guarded by timeless principalities
Against the worm of death.
1945 'Mid- Winter Waking'.

73 To be a poet is a condition rather than a profession.
1946 Response to a questionnaire from the editor of *Horizon*.

74 The function of poetry is religious invocation of the Muse; its use is the experience of mixed exaltation and horror that her presence excites.
1948 *The White Goddess*, foreword.

75 For a woman to have a *liaison* is almost always pardonable, and occasionally, when the lover chosen is sufficiently distinguished, even admirable.
1950 *Occupation: Writer*, 'Lars Porsena'.

76 In love as in sport, the amateur status must be strictly maintained.
1950 *Occupation: Writer*, 'Lars Porsena'.

77 Counting the slow heart beats,
The bleeding to death of time in slow heart beats,
Wakeful they lie.
1951 'Counting the Beats'.

78 Prose books are the show dogs I breed and sell to support my cat.
1958 On writing novels to support his love of writing poetry. In the *New York Times*, 13 Jul.

79 Why have such scores of lovely, gifted girls
Married impossible men?
1958 'A Slice of Wedding Cake'.

80 Julia: how Irishly you sacrifice
Love to pity, pity to ill-humour,
Yourself to love, still haggling at the price.
'Reproach to Julia', collected in *Collected Poems* (1959).

81 Love is a universal migraine
A bright stain on the vision
Blotting out reason.
1961 'Symptoms of Love'.

82 A well-chosen anthology is a complete dispensary of medicine for the more common mental disorders, and may be used as much for prevention as cure.
1962 On English Poetry, 'Definitions'.

83 Nine-tenths of English poetic literature is the result either of vulgar careerism, or of a poet trying to keep his hand in. Most poets are dead by their late twenties.
1962 In the Observer, 11 Nov.

84 If there's no money in poetry, neither is there poetry in money.
1963 Speech at London School of Economics, 6 Dec.

85 The remarkable thing about Shakespeare is that he is really very good—in spite of all the people who say he is very good.
1964 Attributed.

86 The poet is the unsatisfied child who dares to ask the difficult question which arises from the schoolmaster's answer to his simple question, and then the still more difficult question which arises from that.
Recalled on his death, 7 Dec 1985.

87 Love without hope, as when the young bird-catcher
Swept off his tall hat to the Squire's own daughter,
So let the imprisoned larks escape and fly
Singing about her head, as she rode by.
'Love without Hope'.

Gray, Alasdair James 1934–

Scottish novelist, painter and playwright. His novel *Lanark* (1981) is an inventive semi-fantasy based in Glasgow. He has subsequently written and illustrated several equally unconventional novels.

88 Of course in nature the only ending is death, but death hardly ever happens when people are at their best. That is why we like tragedies. They show men energetically with their wits about them and deserving to do it.
1981 *Lanark*, bk.1, interlude.

89 Art is the only work open to people who can't get along with others and still want to be special.
1981 *Lanark*, bk.3, ch.1.

90 Glasgow, the sort of industrial city where most people live nowadays but nobody imagines living.
1981 *Lanark*, bk.3, ch.11.

Gray, Alexander 1882–1968

Scottish economist, Professor at Aberdeen and Edinburgh Universities.

91 The services of a menial servant, taking him as an example of unproductive labour, 'generally perish in the very instant of their performance'—and forthwith into this galley, along with the menial servant, goes the sovereign, accompanied by all the army, the navy, and the civil service, followed by churchmen, lawyers, buffoons and opera dancers. All these—and it is a hard saying—render services which perish in the very instant of their performance.
1931 *The Development of Economic Doctrine*.

Gray, Thomas 1716–71

English poet. In 1742 he wrote his *Ode on a Distant Prospect of Eton College* (1747) and began the famous *Elegy Written in a Country Churchyard* (1751). He declined the Laureateship (1757), and became Professor of History and Modern Languages at Cambridge (1768).

92 Ye distant spires, ye antique towers,
That crown the wat'ry glade.
1742 *Ode on a Distant Prospect of Eton College* (published 1747), l.1–2.

93 Still as they run they look behind,
They hear a voice in every wind,
And snatch a fearful joy.
1742 *Ode on a Distant Prospect of Eton College* (published 1747), l.38–40.

94 Alas, regardless of their doom,
The little victims play!
No sense have they of ills to come,
Nor care beyond to-day.
1742 *Ode on a Distant Prospect of Eton College* (published 1747), l.51–4.

95 To each his suff'rings, all are men,
Condemned alike to groan;
The tender for another's pain,
Th'unfeeling for his own.

Yet ah! why should they know their fate?
Since sorrow never comes too late,
And happiness too swiftly flies.
Thought would destroy their paradise.
No more; where ignorance is bliss,
'Tis folly to be wise.
1742 *Ode on a Distant Prospect of Eton College* (published 1747), l.91–100.

96 The language of the age is never the language of poetry, except among the French, whose verse, where the thought or image does not support it, differs in nothing from prose.
1742 Letter to Richard West, 8 Apr. Collected in H W Starr (ed) *Correspondence of Thomas Gray* (1971).

97 Demurest of the tabby kind,
The pensive Selima reclined,
Gazed on the lake below.
1747 *Ode on the Death of a Favourite Cat, Drowned in a Tub of Gold Fishes*, l.4–6.

98 The velvet of her paws,
Her coat that with the tortoise vies,
Her ears of jet and emerald eyes,
She saw; and purred applause.
1747 *Ode on the Death of a Favourite Cat, Drowned in a Tub of Gold Fishes*, l.9–12.

99 What female heart can gold despise?
What cat's averse to fish?
1747 *Ode on the Death of a Favourite Cat, Drowned in a Tub of Gold Fishes*, l.23–4.

1 A favourite has no friend!
1747 *Ode on the Death of a Favourite Cat, Drowned in a Tub of Gold Fishes*, l.36.

2 Not all that tempts your wandering eyes
And heedless hearts, is lawful prize;
Nor all that glisters gold.
1747 *Ode on the Death of a Favourite Cat, Drowned in a Tub of*

Gold Fishes, l.40–3. Derived from 'All that glitters is not gold', *The Merchant of Venice*, act 2, scene 7.

3 The Attic warbler pours her throat,
Responsive to the cuckoo's note,
The untaught harmony of spring.
1748 *Ode on the Spring*, l.5–7.

4 Where'er the oak's thick branches stretch
A broader browner shade;
Where'er the rude and moss-grown beech
O'er-canopies the glade,
Beside some water's rushy brink
With me the Muse shall sit, and think.
1748 *Ode on the Spring*, l.11–16.

5 How low, how little are the proud,
How indigent the great!
1748 *Ode on the Spring*, l.19–20.

6 The insect youth are on the wing,
Eager to taste the honeyed spring,
And float amid the liquid noon:
Some lightly o'er the current skim,
Some show their gaily-gilded trim
Quick-glancing to the sun.
1748 *Ode on the Spring*, l.25–30.

7 Methinks I hear in accents low
The sportive kind reply:
Poor moralist! and what art thou?
A solitary fly!
1748 *Ode on the Spring*, l.41–4.

8 Shame of the versifying tribe!
Your history whither are you spinning?
Can you do nothing but describe?
1750 *A Long Story*, l.17–20.

9 To celebrate her eyes, her air—
Coarse panegyrics would but tease her.
Melissa is her nom de guerre.
Alas, who would not wish to please her!
1750 *A Long Story*, l.33–6.

10 The curfew tolls the knell of parting day,
The lowing herd wind slowly o'er the lea,
The ploughman homeward plods his weary way,
And leaves the world to darkness and to me.

Now fades the glimmering landscapes on the sight,
And all the air a solemn stillness holds,
Save where the beetle wheels his droning flight,
And drowsy tinklings lull the distant folds.
1751 *Elegy Written in a Country Churchyard*, l.1–8.

11 Save that from yonder ivy-mantled tower
The moping owl does to the moon complain.
1751 *Elegy Written in a Country Churchyard*, l.9–10.

12 Beneath those rugged elms, that yew-tree's shade,
Where heaves the turf in many a mouldering heap,
Each in his narrow cell for ever laid,
The rude forefathers of the hamlet sleep.

The breezy call of incense-breathing Morn,
The swallow twitt'ring from the straw-built shed,
The cock's shrill clarion, or the echoing horn,
No more shall rouse them from their lowly bed.
1751 *Elegy Written in a Country Churchyard*, l.13–20.

13 For them no more the blazing hearth shall burn,

Or busy housewife ply her evening care:
No children run to lisp their sire's return,
Or climb upon his knees the envied kiss to share.
1751 *Elegy Written in a Country Churchyard*, l.21–4.

14 Let not Ambition mock their useful toil,
Their homely joys and destiny obscure;
Nor Grandeur hear, with a disdainful smile,
The short and simple annals of the poor.

The boast of heraldry, the pomp of power,
And all that beauty, all that wealth e'er gave,
Awaits alike th' inevitable hour,
The paths of glory lead but to the grave.
1751 *Elegy Written in a Country Churchyard*, l.29–36.

15 Can storied urn or animated bust
Back to its mansion call the fleeting breath?
Can Honour's voice provoke the silent dust,
Or Flattery soothe the dull cold ear of Death?
1751 *Elegy Written in a Country Churchyard*, l.41–4.

16 But knowledge to their eyes her ample page
Rich with the spoils of time did ne'er unroll;
Chill Penury repressed their noble rage,
And froze the genial current of the soul.
1751 *Elegy Written in a Country Churchyard*, l.49–52.

17 Full many a gem of purest ray serene
The dark unfathomed caves of ocean bear:
Full many a flower is born to blush unseen
And waste its sweetness on the desert air.
1751 *Elegy Written in a Country Churchyard*, l.52–6.

18 Some mute inglorious Milton here may rest,
Some Cromwell guiltless of his country's blood.
1751 *Elegy Written in a Country Churchyard*, l.59–60.

19 Their lot forbad: nor circumscribed alone
Their growing virtues, but their crimes confined:
Forbad to wade through slaughter to a throne,
And shut the gates of mercy on mankind.
1751 *Elegy Written in a Country Churchyard*, l.65–8.

20 Far from the madding crowd's ignoble strife
Their sober wishes never learned to stray;
Along the cool sequestered vale of life
They kept the noiseless tenor of their way.
1751 *Elegy Written in a Country Churchyard*, l.73–6. Thomas Hardy popularized the phrase as the title of his novel *Far From the Madding Crowd* (1874).

21 Their name, their years, spelt by the unlettered muse,
The place of fame and elegy supply:
And many a holy text around she strews,
That teach the rustic moralist to die.
1751 *Elegy Written in a Country Churchyard*, l.81–4.

22 For who to dumb Forgetfulness a prey,
This pleasing anxious being e'er resigned,
Left the warm precincts of the cheerful day,
Nor cast one longing ling'ring look behind?
1751 *Elegy Written in a Country Churchyard*, l.85–8.

23 Mindful of the unhonoured dead.
1751 *Elegy Written in a Country Churchyard*, l.93.

24 Oft have we seen him at the peep of dawn
Brushing with hasty steps the dews away
To meet the sun upon the upland lawn.
1751 *Elegy Written in a Country Churchyard*, l.98–100.

25 Here rest his head upon the lap of earth

A youth to fortune and to fame unknown.
Fair Science frowned not on his humble birth,
And Melancholy marked him for her own.
1751 *Elegy Written in a Country Churchyard*, l.117–20, 'The Epitaph'.

26 No farther seek his merits to disclose,
Or draw his frailties from their dread abode,
(There they alike in trembling hope repose)
The bosom of his Father and his God.
1751 *Elegy Written in a Country Churchyard*, l.125–8, 'The Epitaph'.

27 Ruin seize thee, ruthless King!
Confusion on thy banners wait,
Tho' fanned by Conquest's crimson wing
They mock the air with idle state.
1757 *The Bard. A Pindaric Ode*, l.1–4.

28 To save thy secret soul from nightly fears.
1757 *The Bard. A Pindaric Ode*, l.6.

29 Loose his beard, and hoary hair
Streamed, like a meteor, to the troubled air.
1757 *The Bard. A Pindaric Ode*, l.19–20.

30 Cold is Cadwallon's tongue,
That hushed the stormy main.
1757 *The Bard. A Pindaric Ode*, l.29–30.

31 Dear as the light that visits these sad eyes,
Dear as the ruddy drops that warm my heart,
Ye died amidst your dying country's cries.
1757 *The Bard. A Pindaric Ode*, l.40–2.

32 Weave the warp, and weave the woof,
The winding-sheet of Edward's race.
Give ample room, and verge enough
The characters of hell to trace.
1757 *The Bard. A Pindaric Ode*, l.49–52.

33 Mighty victor, mighty lord,
Low on his funeral couch he lies!
No pitying heart, no eye, afford
A tear to grace his obsequies.
1757 *The Bard. A Pindaric Ode*, l.63–6.

34 Fair laughs the morn and soft the zephyr blows,
While proudly riding o'er the azure realm
In gallant trim the gilded vessel goes;
Youth on the prow, and Pleasure at the helm;
Regardless of the sweeping whirlwind's sway,
That, hushed in grim repose, expects his evening prey.
1757 *The Bard. A Pindaric Ode*, l.71–6.

35 In buskined measures move
Pale Grief and pleasing Pain,
With Horror, tyrant of the throbbing breast.
1757 *The Bard. A Pindaric Ode*, l.128–30.

36 'Be thine despair and sceptred care;
To triumph, and to die, are mine.'
He spoke, and headlong from the mountain's height
Deep in the roaring tide he plunged to endless night.
1757 *The Bard. A Pindaric Ode*, l.141–4.

37 Far from the sun and summer-gale,
In thy green lap was Nature's darling laid.
1757 Of William Shakespeare. *The Progress of Poesy*, l.83–4.

38 Nor second he, that rode sublime
Upon the seraph-wings of ecstasy,
The secrets of th'abyss to spy.
He passed the flaming bounds of place and time:

The living throne, the sapphire-blaze,
Where angels tremble, while they gaze,
He saw; but blasted with excess of light,
Closed his eyes in endless night.
1757 Of Milton. *The Progress of Poesy*, l.95–102.

39 Thoughts, that breathe, and words, that burn.
1757 *The Progress of Poesy*, l.110.

40 Beyond the limits of a vulgar fate,
Beneath the good how far—but far above the great.
1757 *The Progress of Poesy*, l.122–3.

41 It has been usual to catch a mouse or two (for form's sake) in public once a year.
1757 On refusing the Laureateship. Letter to William Mason, 19 Dec.

42 Too poor for a bribe, and too proud to importune,
He had not the method of making a fortune.
1761 'Sketch of His Own Character'.

43 I shall be but a shrimp of an author.
1768 Letter to Horace Walpole, 25 Feb.

44 Any fool may write a most valuable book by chance, if he will only tell us what he heard and saw with veracity.
1768 Letter to Horace Walpole, 25 Feb.

Greeley, Horace   1811–72

US journalist, founding editor of the *New York Tribune*.

45 Go West, young man, and grow up with the country.
1850 *Hints toward Reforms*.

Greenaway, Peter   1942–

English film-maker and painter. His films include *The Cook, the Thief, His Wife and Her Lover* (1989) and *Prospero's Books* (1991).

46 Most cinema is built along 19th-century models. You would hardly think that the cinema had discovered James Joyce sometimes. Most of the cinema we've got is modelled on Dickens and Balzac and Jane Austen.
2004 In *The Guardian*, 10 May.

Greenberg, Clement   1909–94

US art critic.

47 When you don't like something the words come more readily.
1991 Aged 82, on the relative ease of negative criticism over positive. In the *New York Times*, 3 Oct.

48 For every good art critic there may be ten great artists.
1991 In the *New York Times*, 3 Oct.

Greene, (Henry) Graham   1904–91

English writer. His writings included novels (which he divided into 'entertainments' and more serious works), short stories, essays, plays, biography, criticism, travel books and two volumes of autobiography.

49 At one with the One, it didn't mean a thing beside a glass of Guinness on a sunny day.
1938 *Brighton Rock*, pt.1, ch.1.

50 He trailed the clouds of his own glory after him; hell lay about him in his infancy. He was ready for more deaths.
1938 *Brighton Rock*, pt.2, ch.2.
➤ See Wordsworth 926:24.

51 I couldn't eat, just went on drinking coffee, and sweating it out again. Liquid had no time to be digested; it came through the pores long before it reached the stomach. I lay wet through with sweat for four hours—it was very nearly like happiness.

1939 In Mexico. *The Lawless Roads* (published in the US as *Another Mexico*).

52 There is always one moment in childhood when the door opens and lets the future in.
1940 *The Power and the Glory*, pt.1, ch.1.

53 A virtuous man can almost cease to believe in Hell, but he carried Hell about with him. Sometimes at night he dreamed of it… Evil ran like malaria in his veins.
1940 *The Power and the Glory*, pt.3, ch.1.

54 They had been corrupted by money, and he had been corrupted by sentiment. Sentiment was the more dangerous, because you couldn't name its price.
1948 *The Heart of the Matter*, bk.1, pt.1, ch.2, iii.

55 He felt the loyalty we all feel to unhappiness—the sense that that is where we really belong.
1948 *The Heart of the Matter*, bk.2, pt.2, ch.1, i.

56 His hilarity was like a scream from a crevasse.
1948 *The Heart of the Matter*, bk.3, pt.1, ch.1, i.

57 Of those four winters which I passed in Indo-China opium has left the happiest memory.
1955 *The Quiet American*, introduction.

58 That feeling of exhilaration which a measure of danger brings to the visitor with a return ticket.
1955 *The Quiet American*, introduction.

59 Death was the only absolute value in my world. Lose life and one would lose nothing again for ever… Death was far more certain than God, and with death there would no longer be the daily possibility of love dying.
1955 *The Quiet American*, pt.1, ch.3.

60 Our Man in Havana.
1958 Title of novel.

61 Hail Mary, quite contrary!
1958 *Our Man in Havana*, pt.1, ch.2.

62 Those who marry God…can become domesticated too—it's just as humdrum a marriage as all the others.
1961 *A Burnt-Out Case*, ch.1.

63 Fame is a powerful aphrodisiac.
1964 In the *Radio Times*, 10 Sep.

64 His slang…was always a little out of date, as though he had studied in a dictionary of popular usage, but not in the latest edition.
1966 *The Comedians*, pt.1, ch.1.

65 The man who offers a bribe gives away a little of his own importance; the bribe once accepted, he becomes the inferior, like a man who has just paid for a woman.
1966 *The Comedians*, pt.1, ch.4.

66 We mustn't complain too much of being comedians—it's an honourable profession. If only we could be good ones the world might gain at least a sense of style.
1966 *The Comedians*, pt.2, ch.5.

67 An autobiography is only 'a sort of life'—it may contain less errors of fact than a biography, but it is of necessity even more selective: it begins later and it ends prematurely.
1971 *A Sort of Life*, preface.

68 And the motive for recording these scraps of the past? It

is much the same motive that has made me a novelist: a desire to reduce a chaos of experience to some sort of order, and a hungry curiosity.
1971 *A Sort of Life*, preface.

69 I put the muzzle of the revolver into my right ear and pulled the trigger… I was out by one. I remember an extraordinary sense of jubilation, as if carnival lights had been switched on in a drab street. My heart knocked in its cage, and life contained an infinite number of possibilities.
1971 Recalling a game of Russian roulette with his brother's revolver in 1923. *A Sort of Life*, ch.6, pt.2.

70 He would certainly have despised Christ for being the son of a carpenter, if the New Testament had not proved in time to be such a howling commercial success.
1980 *Dr Fischer of Geneva*, ch.7.

71 Writing a novel does not become easier with practice.
1980 *Ways of Escape*, ch.5.

72 Writing is a form of therapy; sometimes I wonder how all these people who do not write, compose or paint can manage to escape the madness, the melancholia, the panic fear which is inherent in the human situation.
1980 *Ways of Escape*, ch.9.

73 Perhaps we are all fictions, father, in the minds of God.
1982 *Monsignor Quixote*, pt.1, ch.1.

74 The believer will fight another believer over a shade of difference: the doubter fights only with himself.
1982 *Monsignor Quixote*, pt.1, ch.4.

75 A solitary laugh is often a laugh of superiority.
1982 *Monsignor Quixote*, pt.1, ch.9.

76 The world is not black and white. More like black and grey.
1982 Quoted in 'Sayings of the Year', the *Observer*, Dec.

77 What's the good of a lie if it's seen through? When I tell a lie no-one can tell it from the gospel truth. Sometimes I can't even tell it myself.
1988 The Captain. *The Captain and the Enemy*, pt.1, ch.1.

Greene, Robert 1558–92

English dramatist. His many plays and romances include the prose romance *Pandosto* (1588) and the comedy *Friar Bacon and Friar Bungay* (c.1589). He laid the foundations of English drama.

78 Love taught me that your honour did but jest.
c.1589 *Friar Bacon and Friar Bungay* (published 1594), sc.8.

79 Only your hearts be frolic, for the time
Craves that we taste of naught but jouissance.
c.1589 *Friar Bacon and Friar Bungay* (published 1594), sc.16.

80 For there is an upstart crow, beautified with our feathers, that with his tiger's heart wrapped in a player's hide, supposes he is as well able to bombast out a blank verse as the best of you; and being an absolute *Iohannes fac totum*, is in his own conceit the only Shake-scene in a country.
1592 Of Shakespeare. *The Groatsworth of Wit, Bought with a Million of Repentance. Iohannes fac totum* = 'Jack-of-all-trades'.

Greenspan, Alan 1926–

US financier and economist, chairman of the board of governors of the Federal Reserve System.

81 Since I've become a central banker, I've learned to mumble with great coherence… If I seem unduly clear to you, you must have misunderstood what I said.
1987 Address to Congress, Sep. Quoted by Jonathan Marshall in the *San Francisco Chronicle*, 9 Jun 1995.

82 The buck starts here.
Sign on his desk. Quoted in Bob Woodward *The Agenda* (1994).
➤ *See* Truman 869:45.

83 The gut-feel of the 55-year old trader is more important than the mathematical elegance of the 25-year old genius.
1995 In the *New York Times*, 6 Mar, shortly after the collapse of Barings in Singapore brought about by a young derivatives trader.

84 I worry incessantly that I might be too clear.
1995 In the *New York Times*, 25 Jun.

85 The free lunch has still to be invented.
2004 On the US budget deficit, 6 May.

Greer, Germaine 1939–

Australian feminist, author and lecturer. Her first book *The Female Eunuch* (1970) challenges male dominance and the misrepresentation of female sexuality, which she attributes to Freud.

86 A full bosom is actually a millstone around a woman's neck.
1970 *The Female Eunuch*, 'Body: Curves'.

87 Freud is the father of psychoanalysis. It had no mother.
1970 *The Female Eunuch*, 'Soul: The Psychological Sell'.

88 If women understand by emancipation the adoption of the masculine role then we are lost indeed.
1970 *The Female Eunuch*, 'Soul: Womanpower'.

89 English children have lost their innocence, for their first lessons have been in the exploitation of their adult slave.
1970 Of the mother's subjugation to her family's demands. *The Female Eunuch*, 'Love: Family'.

90 Many a housewife staring at the back of her husband's newspaper, or listening to his breathing in bed is lonelier than any spinster in a rented room.
1970 *The Female Eunuch*, 'Love: Security'.

91 Libraries are reservoirs of strength, grace and wit, reminders of order, calm and continuity, lakes of mental energy, neither warm nor cold, light nor dark.
1991 In the *New York Times*, 24 Mar.

92 Football is an art more central to our culture than anything the Arts Council deigns to recognize.
1996 In *The Independent*, 28 Jun.

Pope Gregory I *known as* 'the Great' 540–604

Italian divine. He resigned as Praetor of Rome in 575, distributing his wealth to the poor, and entered a monastery. Reluctantly elected Pope in 590, he carried out many reforms. He wrote numerous biblical commentaries and homilies.

93 *Non Angli, sed angeli.*
Not Angles, but angels.
c.580 Reference to Angle slave children seen by Gregory in Rome, which inspired him with the desire to convert Britain to Christianity. Quoted in Bede *Historia Ecclesiastica gentis Anglorum* (c.731), bk.2, ch.1. His exact words according to Bede were 'Nam et angelicam habent faciem, et tales angelorum in caelis decet esse coheredes' ('Since they have the faces of angels, they should be the co-heirs of the angels in heaven').

94 *Scriptura sacra mentis oculis quasi quoddam speculum opponitur, ut interna nostra facies in ipsa videatur.*
Holy scripture is placed before the eyes of our mind like a mirror, so that we may view our inner face therein.
c.582 *Moralia in Job*, bk.2, ch.1, section 1.

Pope Gregory VII *also known as* **Hildebrand** c.1020–1085

Italian cleric. He was appointed Cardinal by Leo IX and as Pope from 1073 instituted many reforms to the clergy. He asserted the right of the Pope to direct temporal authorities, and conflicted violently with Emperor Henry IV, who appointed an anti-Pope (Clement III) and seized Rome (1084).

95 *Dilexi iustitiam et odi iniquitatem, propterea morior in exilio.*
I have loved righteousness and hated iniquity, and therefore I die in exile.
1085 Last words. Quoted in Christopher Brooke *Europe in the Central Middle Ages 962–1154* (1964), ch.15.

Gregory, Lady Isabella Augusta *née* **Persse** 1852–1932

Irish playwright. After marrying Sir William Gregory, Governor of Ceylon (1880), she founded with W B Yeats Dublin's Abbey Theatre. Her plays include *Spreading the News* (1904), and she also wrote Irish legends and translated Molière.

96 His eyesight has always been weak, a sort of film over the eyes. A doctor advised him not to read, but he said, 'Then I should be ignorant', and he refused an operation because there was a thousandth chance he might go blind and so remain ignorant.
1924 Of Sean O'Casey. Journal entry, 8 Jun.

Gregory, John Walter 1864–1932

English geologist, geographer and explorer, Professor of Geology at Melbourne University (1900–4), and then at Glasgow. In 1932 he joined an expedition to Peru, where he was drowned on a canoeing trip.

97 The Dead Heart of Australia.
1906 Title of book, dealing with the central deserts of Australia.

Grellet, Stephen 1773–1855

French-born missionary to America.

98 I expect to pass through this world but once. Any good thing, therefore, that I can do, or any kindness that I can show to any fellow-creature, let me do it now…for I shall not pass this way again.
Attributed.

Grenfell, Joyce *née* **Phipps** 1910–79

English comedienne. She starred in intimate revue in the 1940s and developed a fine line in the art of comic monologues; occasional film appearances included parts in such comedies as *Laughter in Paradise* (1951) and *The Belles of St Trinian's* (1954).

99 George—don't do that.
Catchphrase from one of her comic monologues, also the title of her autobiography, 1977.

1 Stately as a galleon, I sail across the floor, Doing the Military Two-step, as in the days of yore.
1978 'Stately as a Galleon' (song).

Grenfell, Julian Henry Francis   1888–1915

English poet, killed in action during World War I. He is largely remembered for his patriotic poem 'Into Battle'.

2   And life is colour and warmth and light
  And a striving evermore for these;
  And he is dead, who will not fight;
  And who dies fighting has increase.
  1915 'Into Battle', in *The Times*, 27 May.

Grenfell, Sir Wilfred   1865–1940

English medical missionary and writer.

3   The service we render to others is really the rent we pay for our room on this earth.
  1938 *A Labrador Logbook*.

Grenville, George   1712–70

English statesman. He became Prime Minister in 1763, and his period of office was marked by the prosecution of John Wilkes and the passing of the American Stamp Act before his resignation in 1765.

4   It is clear that both England and America are now to be governed by the mob.
  1765 On the repeal of the Stamp Act, Jul.

Grey of Fallodon, Edward Grey, 1st Viscount
1862–1933

British statesman. He was Liberal MP for Berwick-on-Tweed (1885–1916), and Secretary for Foreign Affairs (1905–16), distinguishing himself in the Balkans peace negotiations (1913) and on the outbreak of World War I in 1914. He was subsequently Ambassador to Washington (1919–20) and Chancellor of Oxford University from 1928.

5   It is the lees left by Bismarck that still foul the cup.
  1906 On the duplicity of international diplomacy as practised in the early 20c. Letter to President Roosevelt, Dec. Quoted in G M Trevelyan *Grey of Fallodon* (1937).

6   If there is war, there will be Labour governments in every country—and quite right too.
  1914 In conversation with the Italian Ambassador, Jul.

7   The lamps are going out all over Europe. We shall not see them lit again in our lifetime.
  1914 Remark made on the eve of World War I, 3 Aug, in his room at the Foreign Office, recounted in *Twenty-Five Years* (1925), vol.2, ch.18.

8   In 1914, Europe had arrived at a point at which every country except Germany was afraid of the present, and Germany was afraid of the future.
  1924 House of Lords, 24 Jul.

Greyser, Stephen A

US marketing expert, Professor of Business Administration (Marketing/ Communications) Emeritus at Harvard Business School.

9   The poets of commerce.
  1987 Of advertising copywriters. In the *New York Times*, 28 Apr.

Grieg, Edvard Hagerup   1843–1907

Norwegian composer, whose works, much influenced by folk heritage, include orchestral suites, incidental music for Ibsen's *Peer Gynt*, choral music and piano pieces.

10   I am sure my music has a taste of codfish in it.
  1903 Speech. Quoted in Ian Crofton and Donald Fraser *A Dictionary of Musical Quotations* (1985).

Griffith, D(avid Lewelyn) W(ark)   1874–1948

US film director. He began as an actor and short-story writer before entering the infant film industry, learning his trade in hundreds of short films. He is best known for *The Birth of a Nation* (1915) and *Intolerance* (1916).

11   Viewed as a drama, the war is somewhat disappointing.
  c.1915 Comment on World War I. Quoted in Leslie Halliwell *Halliwell's Filmgoer's Companion* (1984).

12   Out of the cradle, endlessly rocking.
  1916 *Intolerance*.

Grillparzer, Franz   1791–1872

Austrian politician, poet and playwright. He was prone to hypochondria and depression.

13   *Es binden Sklavenfesseln nur die Hände,*
  Der Sinn, er macht den Freien und den Knecht.
  The chains of slavery can only bind the hands.
  The mind makes us either free or enslaved.
  1818 *Sappho*, act 2, sc.4.

14   *Gold schenkt die Eitelkeit, der rauhe Stolz,*
  Die Freundschaft und die Liebe schenken Blumen.
  Gold is the gift of vanity and pride,
  Friendship and love offer flowers.
  1818 *Sappho*, act 2, sc.4.

15   *Ich suchte dich und habe mich gefunden.*
  I sought you and I found myself.
  1818 *Sappho*, act 5, sc.6.

Grimaldi, Joseph   1779–1837

English comedian, of Italian descent. His Clown figure transformed English pantomime, though his career was virtually over by 1824 as a result of the injuries he suffered in slapstick routines on stage.

16   Here we are again!
  c.1800 His customary greeting to the audience on making his entrance as Clown, later adopted as a catchphrase by clowns everywhere.

Grisham, John   1955–

US author, known for his suspenseful courtroom dramas.

17   I cannot write as well as some people; my talent is in coming up with good stories about lawyers. That is what I am good at.
  1994 In the *Independent on Sunday*, 5 Jun.

Griswold, Alfred Whitney   1906–63

US educator, President of Yale University (1950–63).

18   A Socrates in every classroom.
  1951 On his hopes for the Yale faculty. In *Time*, 11 Jun.

19   Could Hamlet have been written by a committee, or the *Mona Lisa* painted by a club? Could the New Testament have been composed as a conference report?
  1957 Baccalaureate address, 9 Jun.

20   Self-respect…comes to us when we are alone, in quiet moments in quiet places when we suddenly realize that, knowing the good, we have done it; knowing the beautiful, we have served it; knowing the truth, we have spoken it.

1957 Baccalaureate address, 9 Jun.

Gromyko, Andrei Andreyevich 1909–89

Soviet politician, notorious for his austere and humourless demeanour. As Foreign Minister (1957–85) he influenced Soviet relations with the West during the Cold War. President in 1985, he was replaced by Gorbachev.

21 Every night, whisper 'Peace' in your husband's ear.

1984 Said to Nancy Reagan at a White House reception, 28 Sep.

22 This man, Comrades, has a nice smile, but he has iron teeth.

1985 Speech to the Supreme Soviet on proposing Mikhail Gorbachev as the new party leader.

Grossmith, George 1847–1912

English comedian and entertainer. He took leading parts in Gilbert and Sullivan operettas (1877–89) and with his brother, Weedon, wrote *The Diary of a Nobody*, first serialized in *Punch* (published 1892).

23 What's the good of a home if you are never in it?

1892 *The Diary of a Nobody* (with Weedon Grossmith), ch.1.

24 I left the room with silent dignity, but caught my foot in the mat.

1892 *The Diary of a Nobody* (with Weedon Grossmith), ch.7.

Grosvenor, Gilbert M 1875–1966

US geographer and editor, Director then President of the National Geographic Society (1899–1954) and editor of its magazine. He pioneered the use of colour photography, and encouraged conservation and wildlife protection.

25 If you don't know where you are, you're nowhere.

On the NGS's establishment of a $20-million foundation to fight ignorance of geography. Quoted in the *Washington Post*, 14 Jan 1988.

Guare, John 1938–

US dramatist.

26 Everybody on this planet is separated by only six other people. Six degrees of separation. Between us and everybody else on this planet.

1990 *Six Degrees of Separation*.

Guedalla, Philip 1889–1944

English historian and biographer, known for his irreverent wit. His books include *Supers and Supermen* (1920), *Palmerston* (1926), a biography of Wellington, *The Duke* (1931), and *Mr Churchill* (1941).

27 The work of Henry James has always seemed divisible by a simple dynastic arrangement into three reigns: James I, James II, and the Old Pretender.

1920 *Supers and Supermen*, 'Some Critics'.

28 History repeats itself. Historians repeat each other.

1920 *Supers and Supermen*, 'Some Historians'.

29 The Crimean War is one of the bad jokes of history.

1943 *The Two Marshals*.

Guibert of Nogent fl.c.1097

Medieval historian.

30 God has instituted in our time holy wars, so that the order of knights and the crowd running in their wake, who following the example of the ancient pagans have been engaged in slaughtering one another, might find a new way of gaining salvation.

c.1097 *Gesta Dei per Francos*, in *Recueil des historiens de croisades occidentaux*, edited by L'Académie des Inscriptions et Belles-Lettres (1847–95), vol.4, p.124.

Guillén, Nicolás 1902–89

Cuban poet, of mixed African and European descent, a leader of the Afro-Cuban movement. An outspoken member of the Communist Party, he was active in Castro's regime.

31 *Según un yanqui que debe*
    ser todo un derrochador,
    es Cuba donde mejor
    se come siempre y se bebe.
    According to a gringo who must
    be a true spendthrift,
    Cuba is always the best place
    to eat and to drink.

1953 *Sátira política*, 'Depende' ('It Depends').

Guimarães Rosa, João 1908–67

Brazilian novelist. He practised medicine, then joined the foreign service. *Grande Sertão* (1956) is derived from the oral tradition of the hinterland of Brazil.

32 *Um está sempre no escuro, só no último derradeiro é que clareiam a sala.*
    One is always in the dark, and it is only at the last moment that they turn on the lights in the room.

1956 *Grande Sertão: Verédas* (translated as *The Devil to Pay in the Backlands*, 1963).

Guiraldes, Ricardo 1886–1927

Argentinian poet and novelist, renowned for his masterful blending of the gaucho (cowboy) tale with modernist techniques.

33 *Si sos gaucho en de veras, no has de mudar, porque andequiera que vayas irás con tu alma por delante.*
    If you're really a gaucho, you can't change, because wherever you go, you'll go with your soul leading the way.

1926 *Don Segundo Sombra* (translated 1935), ch.26.

Guitry, Sacha 1885–1957

French actor and playwright. Born in Russia, he established himself as a popular light comedian as well as writing a number of screenplays and directing several films.

34 The others were only my wives. But you, my dear, will be my widow.

Attributed reply to his fifth wife, when she expressed jealousy of her predecessors.

Gulbenkian, Nubar Sarkis 1896–1972

British industrialist and philanthropist. He worked with his father in the oil business, advising on Middle East oil negotiations (1926–8, 1948–54), and was honorary counsellor at the Turkish embassy (1966–72).

35 The best number for a dinner party is two—myself and a damn good head waiter.

1965 In the *Daily Telegraph*, 14 Jan.

Gullit, Ruud 1962–

Dutch footballer and manager. He transferred to the Italian club AC Milan for a record £6 million in 1987.

36 If I'd wanted to be an individual, I'd have taken up tennis.
Quoted in Colin Jarman *The Guinness Dictionary of Sports Quotations* (1990).

37 I'm looking forward to seeing some sexy football.
1996 Comment as BBC TV pundit at Euro 96.

Gunn, Jeannie *known as* **Mrs Aeneas Gunn** 1870–1961

Australian writer. In 1901 she married Aeneas James Gunn and went with him to Elsey Station, Northern Territory. When her husband died in 1903 she returned to Melbourne and wrote of her experiences in the outback.

38 There's time enough for everything in the Never-Never.
1908 *We of the Never-Never*, ch.5.

Gunn, Thom(son William) 1929–2004

English poet. He lived in the US from 1954 until his death. He is recognized as one of the major poets of his generation.

39 I saw that lack of love contaminates,
You know I know you know I know you know.
1954 'Carnal Knowledge'.

40 At worst, one is in motion; and at best,
Reaching no absolute, in which to rest,
One is always nearer by not keeping still.
1957 'On the Move'.

Gunther, John 1901–70

US author and journalist. He established his reputation with the best-selling *Inside Europe* (1939), and followed it with a series of *Inside* books.

41 Bright grayness. Both the clothes and hair were neat and gray. The gray-framed spectacles magnified the gray hazel eyes, but there was no grayness in the mind.
Of Harry S Truman. Quoted in David McCullough *Truman* (1992).

Gurney, Dorothy Frances 1858–1932

English poet and hymnwriter.

42 The kiss of the sun for pardon,
The song of the birds for mirth,
One is nearer God's Heart in a garden
Than anywhere else on earth.
1913 'God's Garden'.

Gurney, Ivor 1890–1937

English poet and composer, especially renowned for his war poems.

43 The songs I had are withered
Or vanished clean.
Yet there are bright tracks
Where I have been.
1922 'The Songs I Had'.

44 I paid the prices of life
Standing where Rome immortal heard October's strife,
A war poet whose right of honour cuts falsehood like a knife.
c.1922 'Poem for End'.

Gurney, John Hampden 1802–62

English clergyman and hymnwriter.

45 Ye holy angels bright,
Who wait at God's right hand,
Or through the realms of light
Fly at your Lord's command,
Assist our song,
Or else the theme too high doth seem
For mortal tongue.
1838 'Ye Holy Angels Bright', based on a poem by Richard Baxter (1615–91).

Gustavus II (Adolphus) 1594–1632

King of Sweden (1611), who entered the Thirty Years War by invading Poland in 1621. His armies conquered much of Germany in 1631, and he was killed at the Battle of Lützen, 1632.

46 All the wars that are now afoot in Europe have been fused together, and have become a single war.
1630 Letter to Axel Oxenstierna, referring to the Thirty Years War, 1618–48.

Guston, Philip 1913–80

Canadian-born painter. He moved with his family to California in 1916. His early paintings combine realism with surrealism and his later work is characterized by its cartoon-like style.

47 I go to my studio every day, because one day I may go and the angel will be there. What if I don't go and the angel came?
1991 Quoted by Gail Godwin in the *Washington Post*, 7 Mar.

Guthrie, Woody (Woodrow Wilson) 1912–67

US folk-singer, songwriter and author. His songs draw on traditional country music and blues themes and reflect his social and political concerns.

48 This land is your land, this land is my land,
From California to the New York Island.
From the redwood forest to the Gulf Stream waters
This land was made for you and me.
1956 'This Land is Your Land'.

49 You can't write a good song about a whore-house unless you been in one.
1964 Quoted in *Broadside*.

Guy, Ray 1939–

Canadian columnist.

50 Pity the poor creatures in warmer countries where the seasons never change. Where summer is eternal and they never know the pain of waiting and the joy at last when summer comes.
1976 *That Far Greater Bay*, 'Catching Conners'.

Gwyn, Nell 1650–87

English actress. Originally an orange-seller at Drury Lane, she became a popular performer in comedies; her admirers included Charles II, whose mistress she became in about 1669. She retired from the stage in 1670.

51 Pray, good people, be civil; I am the Protestant whore.
1675 Attributed, when angry crowds pressed round her carriage in the belief that she was Charles II's unpopular Catholic mistress Louise de Kérouaille.

Haas, Ernst Bernard 1921–

Austrian photographer and author. Known for his early black and white photojournalism (particularly his 'Returning Prisoners of War' story in 1949), he was a pioneer of early colour, and his work on colour-blur made his fame. His film assignments include *Moby Dick* (1956), *The Misfits* (1961), *West Side Story* (1961) and *Heaven's Gate* (1980).

52 Beauty pains, and when it pained most, I shot.
1955 In *Life*, 1 Aug. 'The Glow of Paris'.

Habington, William 1605–54

English writer, one of the metaphysical followers of Donne. He published a book of lyrics, *Castara* (1634), a play, *The Queen of Aragon* (1640) and *The History of Edward the Fourth* (1640).

53 O empty boast of flesh.
1634 *Castara*, 'Upon Beauty'.

54 'Cause some make forfeit of their name,
And slave themselves to man's desire;
Shall the sex free
From guilt, damn'd to the bondage be?
1634 *Castara*, 'Against Them Who Lay Unchastity to the Sex of Women'.

Haeckel, Ernst Heinrich 1834–1919

German biologist and philosopher, who popularized Darwinism in the German-speaking world. He became Professor of Comparative Anatomy at the University of Jena.

55 God…a gaseous vertebrate.
1899 *Welträtsel* ('The Riddle of the Universe').

Hagen, Walter 1892–1969

US golfer. The first great professional US golfer, he won the US Open twice and the British Open four times.

56 Give me a man with big hands and big feet and no brains and I'll make a golfer out of him.
Quoted in Michael Hobbs *The Golf Quotation Book* (1992).

Haggai, Thomas 1939–

US businessman.

57 Cast your bread upon the waters, but wait until the tide is coming in to do it.
1988 In *Fortune*, 7 Nov.

Haggard, Sir (Henry) Rider 1856–1925

English novelist. He travelled to Natal and the Transvaal (1875–9) before embarking on a literary life. His first successful novel was *King Solomon's Mines* (1885), followed by *She* (1887) and *Ayesha* (1905), among others.

58 A little while and I will be gone from among you, whither I cannot tell. From nowhere we came, into nowhere we go. What is Life? It is a flash of a firefly in the night. It is a breath of a buffalo in the winter time. It is as the little

shadow that runs across the grass and loses itself in the sunset.
1885 Dying words of the African chief Umbopa in *King Solomon's Mines*. John Peter Turner in *The North-West Mounted Police* (1950) credited them to Crowfoot (c.1830–1890), chief of the Blackfoot Indians, who died in his teepee overlooking the Bow River, Alberta, 25 Apr 1890, and this attribution gained popular acceptance.

59 She who must be obeyed.
1887 *She*, ch.6, and passim.

60 What a terrifying reflection it is, by the way, that nearly all our deep love for women who are not our kindred depends—at any rate, in the first instance—upon their personal appearances. If we lost them, and found them again dreadful to look on, though otherwise they were the very same, should we still love them?
1887 *She*, ch.26 'What We Saw', narrator's note.

Hague, William 1961–

English Conservative politician. He was Leader of the Conservative Party from 1997 to 2001.

61 It was inevitable the Titanic was going to set sail, but that doesn't mean it was a good idea to be on it.
1998 In *The Mail on Sunday*, 'Quotes of the Week', 11 Jan.

62 This is a candidate of probity and integrity—I am going to back him to the full.
1999 On Jeffrey Archer as a London mayoral candidate, at the Conservative Party conference, Oct.

63 People work hard and save hard to own a car. They do not want to be told that they cannot drive it by a Deputy Prime Minister whose idea of a park and ride scheme is to park one Jaguar and drive away in another.
1999 Of John Prescott. In the House of Commons, 17 Nov.

Haig, Alexander Meigs, Jr 1924–

US soldier and Republican politician, White House Chief of Staff at the end of Nixon's presidency and Supreme NATO Commander. He was Secretary of State under Reagan (1981–2), and unsuccessfully sought presidential nomination in 1988.

64 As of now, I am in control here in the White House.
1981 Said immediately after the attempted assassination of President Reagan, 30 Mar, in Vice-President George Bush's absence from Washington DC.

65 I take it as a compliment when an agent of the largest and most heinous bully of the century, the Soviet Union, accuses me of being a bully.
1995 On how he was seen as US Secretary of State by former Soviet Ambassador Anatoly Dobrynin. In the *Washington Post*, 27 Oct.

Haig (of Bemersyde), Douglas Haig, 1st Earl 1861–1928

Scottish field marshal. He became Commander of the British Expeditionary Force in 1915. His war of attrition was costly and widely criticized; he led the final successful offensive of World War I in Aug 1918.

66 Every position must be held to the last man: there must be no retirement. With our backs to the wall, and believing in the justice of our cause, each one of us must fight on until the end.
1918 Order to British troops facing the German offensive across

the Somme battlefields, 12 Apr. Quoted in A Duff Cooper *Haig* (1936), vol.2, ch.23.

Haile Selassie *originally* Prince Ras Tafari Makonnen
1891–1975

Emperor of Ethiopia (1930–6, 1941–74), leader of the revolution against Lij Yasu (1916). He was exiled after the Italian conquest of Abyssinia (1935–6), and restored after British liberation. Although deposed after the famine of 1973, he is still much revered, notably by Rastafarians.

67 Throughout history it has been the inaction of those who could have acted, the indifference of those who should have known better, the silence of the voice of justice when it mattered most, that has made it possible for evil to triumph.
   1963 Address to a special session of the UN General Assembly, 4 Oct, making him the first head of state to address both that organization and the League of Nations.

Hailsham, Quintin (McGarel) Hogg, 2nd Viscount
1907–2001

English Conservative politician. After succeeding to his title (1950), he held a number of senior state posts. In 1963 he renounced his peerage in an unsuccessful bid to become Leader of the Conservative Party. He was later Lord Chancellor.

68 Conservatives do not believe that the political struggle is the most important thing in life… The simplest of them prefer fox-hunting, the wisest religion.
   1947 *The Case for Conservatism*, pt.1.

69 A great party ought not to be brought down because of a squalid affair between a woman of easy virtue and a proved liar.
   1963 On the Profumo affair, BBC TV, 13 Jun.

70 If the British public falls for this, I say that it will be stark, staring bonkers.
   1964 Press conference on the Labour election manifesto, 12 Oct.

71 I've known every prime minister to a greater or lesser extent since Balfour, and most of them have died unhappy.
   Attributed.

Halberstam, David 1934–

US journalist and author, staff writer and correspondent for the *New York Times* (1960–7). His books include *The Powers That Be* (1979) and *Firehouse* (2002).

72 He has seen the future and it is hamburgers.
   1993 On Ray Kroc's decision to buy and expand the original McDonald's. *The Fifties*.
   ➤ See Steffens 814:6.

Haldane, J(ohn) B(urdon) S(anderson) 1892–1964

Anglo-Indian biologist. He wrote many popular books on biology and genetics, and was Chairman of the *Daily Worker* (1940–9), but left the Communist Party in 1956.

73 Bad as our urban conditions often are, there is not a slum in the country which has a third of the infantile death-rate of the royal family in the middle ages.
   1924 *Daedalus, or Science and the Future*.

74 Now, my own suspicion is that the universe is not only queerer than we suppose, but queerer than we *can* suppose.

1927 *Possible Worlds and Other Essays*, 'Possible Worlds'.

75 You can drop a mouse down a thousand-yard mine shaft; and, on arriving at the bottom, it gets a slight shock and walks away. A rat is killed, a man is broken, a horse splashes.
   1927 *Possible Worlds and Other Essays*, 'On Being the Right Size'.

76 I believe that the scientist is trying to expand absolute truth and the artist absolute beauty, so that I find in art and science, and in an attempt to live a good life, all the religion I want.
   1931 *Living Philosophies*.

77 My final word, before I'm done,
Is 'Cancer can be rather fun'.
Thanks to the nurses and Nye Bevan
The NHS is quite like heaven
Provided one confronts the tumour
With a sufficient sense of humour.
I know that cancer often kills,
But so do cars and sleeping pills;
And it can hurt one till one sweats,
So can bad teeth and unpaid debts.
   1964 'Cancer's a Funny Thing'.

Hale, Nathan 1755–76

American revolutionary soldier. In 1776 he volunteered to penetrate British lines on Long Island and procure intelligence for Washington, but was detected and hanged as a spy.

78 I only regret that I have but one life to lose for my country.
   1776 At his execution, 22 Sep.

Hale, Robert Beverly 1901–85

US artist, teacher and curator. He has works in the Whitney, the Metropolitan Museum of Art, New York City, and in many private collections. He was curator at the Metropolitan (1949–85) and lectured at Pennsylvania Academy of Fine Arts (1968–85) and Columbia University. He wrote, edited and translated books on art.

79 New artists must break a hole in the subconscious and go fishing there.
   1960 In *Time*, 11 Apr.

Hale, Sarah Josepha *née* Buell 1788–1879

US writer. In 1828 she became editor of the *Ladies' Magazine* in Boston. She wrote a novel, *Northwood* (1827), and *Poems for Our Children* (1830).

80 Mary had a little lamb,
Its fleece was white as snow,
And everywhere that Mary went
The lamb was sure to go.
   1830 *Poems for Our Children*, 'Mary's Little Lamb'.

Hales, Stephen 1677–1761

English clergyman and physiologist, considered the founder of plant physiology. His investigations are reported in his work *Statickal Essays*, the first of which, *Vegetable Staticks*, was published in 1727.

81 Since we are assured that the all-wise Creator has observed the most exact proportions of number, weight and measure in the make of all things, the most likely way therefore to get any insight into the nature of those parts of the Creation which come within our observation must

in all reason be to number, weigh and measure.
1727 *Vegetable Staticks.*

Haliburton, Thomas Chandler 1796–1865

Canadian lawyer and satirist. In 1835 he began a series of satiric sketches later enlarged as *The Clockmaker; or The Sayings and Doings of Samuel Slick* (1836). *The Old Judge; or Life in a Colony* (1849) combines social history and satire.

82 I was always well mounted. I am fond of a horse, and always piqued myself on having the fastest trotter in the Province. I have made no great progress in the world. I feel doubly, therefore, the pleasure of not being surpassed on the road.
1836 *The Clockmaker* (first series), 'The Trotting Horse'.

83 If a chap seems bent on cheatin' himself, I like to be neighbourly and help him to do it.
1838 *The Clockmaker* (second series), 'A Cure for Smuggling'.

Halifax, Edward Frederick Lindley Wood, 1st Earl of 1881–1959

English Conservative politician, Viceroy of India (1926–31). He was Foreign Secretary (1938–40) under Neville Chamberlain, whose 'appeasement' policy he implemented, and Ambassador to the US (1941–6).

84 I often think how much easier the world would have been to manage if Herr Hitler and Signor Mussolini had been at Oxford.
1937 Speech, York, 4 Nov.

Halifax, George Savile, 1st Marquis of 1633–95

English statesman, created viscount (1668) at the Restoration. Under James II, he was dismissed as President of the Council for opposing the repeal of the Test and Habeas Corpus Acts. He gave allegiance to William of Orange, but joined the Opposition in 1689.

85 Men are not hanged for stealing horses, but that horses may not be stolen.
c.1687 *Political Thoughts and Reflections*, 'Of Punishment'.

86 Anger is never without an argument, but seldom with a good one.
c.1687 *Political Thoughts and Reflections*, 'Of Anger'.

87 Malice is of a low stature, but it hath very long arms.
c.1687 *Political Thoughts and Reflections*, 'Of Malice and Envy'.

88 The best way to suppose what may come, is to remember what is past.
c.1687 *Political Thoughts and Reflections*, 'Miscellaneous Experience'.

89 When the people contend for their liberty, they seldom get anything by their victory but new masters.
c.1687 *Political Thoughts and Reflections*, 'Of Prerogative, Power and Liberty'.

90 Most men's anger about religion is as if two men should quarrel for a lady they neither of them care for.
Collected in *Complete Works* (published 1912).

Hall, Charles 1745–1825

English physician educated in Holland, best known for his socialist work *The Effects of Civilization on the People in European States* (1805). In 1805 he was impoverished by a lawsuit and, refusing aid, later died in prison determined to show that he had been unjustly treated.

91 The effect of trade and commerce with respect to most civilized states is to send out of their countries what the poor, that is, the great mass of mankind, have occasion for, and to bring back, in return, what is consumed almost wholly by a small part of those nations, viz. the rich. Hence it appears that the greater part of manufactures, trade and commerce is highly injurious to the poor as being the chief means of depriving them of the necessaries of life.
1805 *The Effects of Civilization on the People in European States.*

Hall, J(oyce) C(lyde) 1891–1982

US businessman, founder of Hallmark Cards Inc.

92 The art of the masses.
Of illustrated greetings cards. Recalled on his death, quoted in *The Annual Obituary 82* (1983).

Halliwell, Geri 1972–

English pop star, former member of The Spice Girls.

93 The Ginger character was my own invention, of course. It was like putting on a uniform. You don't have to think. You don't have to deal with being a human being.
2002 *Geri— Just For The Record.*

Halsey, W(illiam) F(rederick) *known as* **'Bull' Halsey** 1882–1959

US naval officer, commander at the Battle of Leyte Gulf (1944) and others. He received the formal Japanese surrender on his flagship, the USS *Missouri*, on 2 Sep 1945.

94 The Third Fleet's sunken and damaged ships have been salvaged and are retiring at high speed toward the enemy.
1944 Comment, 14 Oct, on hearing claims that the Japanese had virtually annihilated the US fleet. Quoted in E B Potter *Bull Halsey* (1985), ch.17.

Hamer, Robert 1911–63

British film director and screenwriter. He is best known for *It Always Rains on Sunday* (1947), *Kind Hearts and Coronets* (1949, with John Dighton) and *School for Scoundrels* (1960).

95 I shot an arrow in the air. She fell to earth in Berkeley Square.
1949 *Kind Hearts and Coronets* (with John Dighton).

96 Every lunch time I went to see how my inheritance was proceeding. Sometimes the deaths column brought good news. Sometimes the births column brought bad. The advent of twin sons to the Duke was a terrible blow. Fortunately an epidemic of diphtheria restored the status quo almost immediately.
1949 *Kind Hearts and Coronets* (with John Dighton).

97 I always say that my west window has all the exuberance of Chaucer without, happily, any of the concomitant crudities of his period.
1949 *Kind Hearts and Coronets* (with John Dighton).

Hamilton, Alexander c.1755–1804

US statesman, Washington's aide-de-camp in the American Revolution and later a congressman. As Secretary of the Treasury (1789–95) he restored the country's finances, but he was killed in a duel with a rival.

98 A national debt, if it is not excessive, will be to us a national blessing.
1781 Letter to Robert Morris, 30 Apr.

99 To model our political systems upon speculations of lasting tranquillity is to calculate on the weaker springs of the human character.
1787–8 *The Federalist Papers*.

Hamilton, Edith 1867–1963

German-born US classicist, whose popular works include *The Greek Way* (1930).

1 To be able to be caught up into the world of thought—that is educated.
Quoted in the *Saturday Evening Post*, 27 Sep 1958.

Hamilton, (Robert) Ian 1938–2001

English poet. He was editor of *Review* (1962–72) and poetry and fiction editor of the *Times Literary Supplement* (1965–73).

2 If my life were like hers, I'd rather be dead. Come to think of it, if my life were like mine, I'd rather be dead.
Quoted by Al Alvarez in D Harsent (ed) *Another Road at the Pillars: Essays, Poems and Reflections on Ian Hamilton* (1972).

3 Back in the early Sixties, when I first started out, insolvency spelt glamour.
1998 *The Trouble with Money and Other Essays*.

4 Show me an enemy of literature, and I will show him my accounts.
1998 *The Trouble with Money and Other Essays*.

Hammarskjöld, Dag Hjalmar Agne Carl 1905–61

Swedish statesman. As Secretary-General of the United Nations from 1953 he took part in conciliation moves in the Middle East. He was awarded the Nobel peace prize posthumously, after he was killed in an air crash while involved in the Congo crisis.

5 For what has been—thanks!
For what shall be—yes!
1950 *Vägmarken* (translated by L Sjöberg and W H Auden as *Markings*, 1964).

6 God does not die on the day when we cease to believe in a personal deity, but we die on the day when our lives cease to be illumined by the steady radiance, renewed daily, of a wonder, the source of which is beyond all reason.
1950 *Vägmarken* (translated by L Sjöberg and W H Auden as *Markings*, 1964).

7 Before Thee in humility, with Thee in faith, in Thee in peace.
1955 *Vägmarken* (translated by L Sjöberg and W H Auden as *Markings*, 1964).

8 The 'men of the hour', the self-assured who strut among us in the jingling harness of their success and importance, how can you let yourself be irritated by them. Let them enjoy their triumph—on the level to which it belongs.
1956 *Vägmarken* (translated by L Sjöberg and W H Auden as *Markings*, 1964).

9 I didn't know Who—or what—put the question, I don't know when it was put. I don't even remember answering. But at some moment I did answer Yes to Someone—or Something—and from that hour I was certain that existence is meaningful and that, therefore, my life, in self-surrender, had a goal.
1961 *Vägmarken* (translated by L Sjöberg and W H Auden as *Markings*, 1964).

10 Weep
If you can,
Weep,
But do not complain—
And you must be thankful.
1961 *Vägmarken* (translated by L Sjöberg and W H Auden as *Markings*, 1964).

11 Never let success hide its emptiness from you; achievement its nothingness; toil its desolation. Keep alive the incentive to push on further, that pain in the soul that drives us beyond ourselves. Do not look back, and do not dream about the future either. It will neither give you back the past, nor satisfy your other daydreams. Your duty, your reward, your destiny are here and now.
1961 *Vägmarken* (translated by L Sjöberg and W H Auden as *Markings*, 1964).

Hammer, Armand 1898–1990

US business executive and art collector.

12 The art world is a jungle echoing to the calls of vicious jealousies and ruthless combat between dealers and collectors; but I have been walking in the jungles of business all my life, and fighting tooth and nail for pictures comes as a form of relaxation to me.
1987 *Hammer, Witness to History*, his autobiography.

13 My Van Gogh is better than *Irises*. I have the whole garden.
On ranking his own Van Gogh, *Hospital at Saint-Rémy*, over the *Irises* that brought £53.9 million at auction. In *Connoisseur*, Jan 1991.

Hammerstein, Oscar, II 1895–1960

US lyricist–librettist. In collaboration with composer Richard Rodgers he wrote such hit musicals as *Oklahoma!* (1943), *South Pacific* (1949) and *The Sound of Music* (1959).

14 Fish got to swim and birds got to fly
I got to love one man till I die
Can't help lovin' dat man of mine.
1927 Song from *Show Boat* (music by Jerome Kern).

15 Ol' Man River.
1927 Title of song from *Show Boat* (music by Jerome Kern).

16 When I grow too old to dream
Your love will live in my heart.
1935 Song from *The Night is Young* (music by Sigmund Romberg).

17 As you walk through the storm,
Hold your head up high,
And don't be afraid of the dark,
At the end of the storm,
Is a golden sky,
And the sweet silver song of the lark,
Walk on through the wind,
Walk on through the rain,
Though your dreams be tossed and blown.
Walk on, walk on,
With hope in your hearts,
And you'll never walk alone,
You'll never walk alone.
1945 *Carousel*, 'You'll Never Walk Alone' (music by Richard Rodgers). The song was subsequently released in a pop version

by Gerry and the Pacemakers in 1963 and adopted as a club song by Liverpool football club.

18 I'm Gonna Wash That Man Right Outa My Hair.
1949 Title of song sung by Mitzi Gaynor in *South Pacific* (music by Richard Rodgers).

19 You've got to be taught to be afraid
Of people whose eyes are oddly made,
Of people whose skin is a different shade.
You've got to be carefully taught.

You've got to be taught before it's too late,
Before you are six or seven or eight,
To hate all the people your relatives hate.
You've got to be carefully taught.
1949 'You've Got to Be Carefully Taught', song from *South Pacific* (music by Richard Rodgers).

20 The hills are alive with the sound of music
With the songs they have sung
For a thousand years.
1959 *The Sound of Music*, title song (music by Richard Rodgers).

Hammett, (Samuel) Dashiell 1894–1961

US crime writer. He joined the Pinkerton Detective Agency as an operator, and later translated his experiences into literature. He suffered from alcohol abuse, which broke his health, and like his partner Lillian Hellman, came into conflict with McCarthy in the anti-Communist trials.

21 He looked rather pleasantly like a blond satan.
1930 Of Sam Spade. *The Maltese Falcon*, 'Spade and Archer'.

22 'I mean that you paid us more than if you'd been telling the truth,' he explained blandly, 'and enough more to make it all right.'
1930 *The Maltese Falcon*, 'The Black Bird'.

23 I distrust a man that says when. If he's got to be careful not to drink too much it's because he's not to be trusted when he does.
1930 *The Maltese Falcon*, 'The Fat Man'.

24 Murder doesn't round out anybody's life except the murdered's and sometimes the murderer's.
1932 *The Thin Man*, ch.31.

Hampton, Christopher 1946–

English playwright and screenwriter. He established his reputation with such plays as *The Philanthropist* (1970). He adapted *Les Liaisons Dangereuses* (1986) from the novel by Laclos and Graham Greene's *The Quiet American* (2002) for screen.

25 Masturbation is the thinking man's television.
1970 *The Philanthropist*.

26 I always divide people into two groups. Those who live by what they know to be a lie, and those who live by what they believe, falsely, to be the truth.
1970 *The Philanthropist*.

27 If I had to give a definition of capitalism, I would say: the process whereby American girls turn into American women.
1974 *Savages*, sc.16.

28 Asking a working writer what he thinks about critics is like asking a lamp-post how it feels about dogs.
Attributed.

Hancock, Lang(ley George) 1909–92

Australian mining industrialist, who discovered iron ore in the Pilbara region with his light aircraft. His various claims, including Rhodes Ridge, made him one of Australia's richest men.

29 The best way to help the poor is not to become one of them.
Quoted in R W Kent (ed) *Money Talks* (1985).

Hand, (Billings) Learned 1872–1961

US jurist, senior judge at the US Court of Appeals for the Second Circuit (1924–51). His legal judgements had enormous influence on the Supreme Court.

30 The spirit of liberty is the spirit which is not too sure that it is right.
1944 Address at 'I Am An American Day' in New York's Central Park, recalled on his death, 18 Aug 1961.

Handel, George Frideric 1685–1759

German-born English composer. He settled in England in 1712, becoming first Director of the Royal Academy of Music (1720). He turned from opera to oratorio in 1739, most notably with *Messiah* (1742). Other works include *Water Music* (1717) and *Music for the Royal Fireworks* (1749).

31 Whether I was in my body or out of my body as I wrote it I know not. God knows.
Of the 'Hallelujah Chorus' in his *Messiah*. Quoted in Romain Rolland *Essays on Music* (1948).

Handy, Charles Brian 1932–

Irish writer and management theorist. His works include *The Making of Managers* (1988) and *The New Alchemists* (1999).

32 Words are the bugles of social change.
1991 *The Age of Unreason*.

Hankey, Katherine 1834–1911

English evangelist and hymnwriter.

33 Tell me the old, old story,
Of unseen things above.
1866 *The Story Wanted*, 'Tell Me the Old, Old Story'.

Hansberry, Lorraine Vivian 1930–65

US playwright. Her semi-autobiographical *A Raisin in the Sun* (1959), the first Broadway play written by a black woman, dealt with the problems facing a black family in a white neighbourhood.

34 Though it be a thrilling and marvelous thing to be merely young and gifted in such times, it is doubly so—doubly dynamic—to be young, gifted and black.
Speech to entrants in the United Negro College Fund writers competition. The phrase was later used as the title of her biography *Young, Gifted and Black* (1969).

Harburg, E(dgar) Y(ip) 1898–1981

US lyricist–librettist, born in New York, who contributed to many Broadway shows. He is best known for the songs in *The Wizard of Oz* (1939).

35 Brother can you spare a dime?
1932 Title of song.

36 Say, it's only a paper moon,

Sailing over a cardboard sea.
1933 'It's Only a Paper Moon' (with Billy Rose, music by Harold Arlen).

37 Lydia the Tattooed Lady.
1939 Title of song featured in the Marx Brothers film *At the Circus* (music by Harold Arlen).

38 Somewhere over the rainbow
Way up high,
There's a land that I heard of
Once in a lullaby.
1939 'Over the Rainbow', sung by Judy Garland in *The Wizard of Oz* (music by Harold Arlen).

Hardie, (James) Keir 1856–1915

Scottish Labour politician, a former miner. He founded and edited the *Labour Leader*, and was Chairman of the Independent Labour Party and of the Labour Party (1906–8), which he helped to found. He was a strong pacifist, and lost his seat opposing the Boer War.

39 From his childhood onward this boy will be surrounded by sycophants and flatterers by the score, and will be taught to believe himself as of a superior creation. A line will be drawn between him and the people whom he is to be called upon some day to reign over. In due course, following the precedent which has already been set, he will be sent on a tour round the world, and probably rumours of a morganatic alliance will follow, and the end of it all will be that the Country will be called upon to pay the bill.
1894 Speech in the House of Commons, 28 Jun, opposing an Address of Congratulation to the Queen being passed in the House of Commons, on the birth of a son (the future Edward VIII) to the Duke and Duchess of York.

40 Can a Man be a Christian on a Pound a Week?
1901 Title of pamphlet.

Hardie, Robert 1904–73

Scottish doctor who, when Singapore fell in 1942, became one of the 61,000 Allied prisoners of war forced by the Japanese to work on the Burma–Siam railway. He kept a secret diary while a prisoner.

41 This is the last day of 1943, a year to be said goodbye to without regret, holding as it did nothing beyond captivity and depression, weary waiting, and above all the sight of immeasurable human misery, suffering and death.
1943 Diary entry, 31 Dec.

Harding, Warren G(amaliel) 1865–1923

US politician and 29th President. A successful journalist, he emerged as a power in the Republican Party, won its nomination and became President (1920–3) when he campaigned against US membership of the League of Nations.

42 America's present need is not heroics but healing; not nostrums but normalcy; not revolution but restoration.
1920 Speech, Boston, Jun.

Hardwicke, Sir Cedric 1893–1964

English actor and director. He made his stage debut in 1912 and appeared in plays by George Bernard Shaw, Emlyn Williams and Shakespeare among others, receiving acclaim on both sides of the Atlantic.

43 I can't act. I have never acted. And I shall never act. What I do is suspend my audience's power of judgement till I've finished.
1945 Attributed.

44 When in doubt, shout—that's the motto.
Attributed, repeating advice that was given to him as a young actor.

Hardy, Godfrey Harold 1877–1947

English mathematician, a professor at Oxford and Cambridge. With Srinivasa Ramanujan, he found an exact formula for the partition function, which expresses the number of ways a number can be written as a sum of smaller numbers.

45 Beauty is the first test: there is no permanent place in the world for ugly mathematics.
1941 *A Mathematician's Apology.*

46 A science is said to be useful if its development tends to accentuate the existing inequities in the distribution of wealth, or more directly promotes the destruction of human life.
1941 *A Mathematician's Apology.*

Hardy, Oliver originally *Norvell Hardy Jr* 1892–1957

US comic actor. He is best known for his partnership with Stan Laurel, and together they produced more than 100 films.

47 Here's another fine mess you've gotten me into.
Of Laurel. Line delivered in *Another Fine Mess* (1930) and other films.

Hardy, Thomas 1840–1928

English novelist and poet. His novels include *The Mayor of Casterbridge* (1886), *Tess of the D'Urbervilles* (1891) and *Jude the Obscure* (1896). His poetry was collected in *Wessex Poems* (1898), and he also wrote a drama, *The Dynasts* (1903–8).

48 Good, but not religious-good.
1872 *Under the Greenwood Tree*, ch.2.

49 That man's silence is wonderful to listen to.
1872 *Under the Greenwood Tree*, ch.14.

50 No man likes to see his emotions the sport of a merry-go-round of skittishness.
1874 *Far from the Madding Crowd*, ch.4.

51 Men thin away to insignificance and oblivion quite as often by not making the most of good spirits when they have them as by lacking good spirits when they are indispensable.
1874 *Far from the Madding Crowd*, ch.22.

52 He was moderately truthful towards men, but to women lied like a Cretan.
1874 Of Sergeant Troy. *Far from the Madding Crowd*, ch.25.

53 It is hard for a woman to define her feelings in language which is chiefly made by men to express theirs.
1874 *Far from the Madding Crowd*, ch.81.

54 Human beings, in their generous endeavour to construct a hypothesis that shall not degrade a First Cause, have always hesitated to conceive a dominant power of a lower moral quality than their own.
1878 *The Return of the Native*, bk.6, ch.1.

55 There was a natural instinct to abjure man as the blot on an otherwise kindly universe.
1886 *The Mayor of Casterbridge*, ch.1.

56 Her bygone simplicity was the art that conceals art.
   1886 *The Mayor of Casterbridge*, ch.15.

57 Sex had never before asserted itself in her so
   strongly, for in former days she had perhaps been
   too impersonally human to be distinctively
   feminine.
   1886 Of Miss Newson. *The Mayor of Casterbridge*, ch.15.

58 Her occasional pretty and picturesque use of dialect
   words—those terrible marks of the beast to the truly
   genteel.
   1886 *The Mayor of Casterbridge*, ch.20.

59 It is not by what is, in this life, but by what appears, that
   you are judged.
   1886 *The Mayor of Casterbridge*, ch.25.

60 She whose youth had seemed to teach that happiness
   was but the occasional episode in a general drama of
   pain.
   1886 *The Mayor of Casterbridge*, ch.45.

61 It was one of those sequestered spots outside the gates
   of the world.
   1887 *The Woodlanders*, ch.1.

62 Why it was that upon this beautiful feminine tissue,
   sensitive as gossamer, and practically blank as snow as
   yet, there should have been traced such a coarse pattern
   as it was doomed to receive; why so often the coarse
   appropriates the finer thus, the wrong man the woman,
   the wrong woman the man, many thousand years of
   analytical philosophy have failed to explain to our sense
   of order.
   1891 *Tess of the D'Urbervilles*, ch.11.

63 'Justice' was done, and the President of the Immortals (in
   Aeschylean phrase) had ended his sport with Tess.
   1891 *Tess of the D'Urbervilles*, ch.59.

64 A novel is an impression, not an argument.
   1892 *Tess of the D'Urbervilles*, preface to 5th edn.

65 His face wearing the fixity of a thoughtful child's who has
   felt the pricks of life somewhat before his time.
   1896 *Jude the Obscure*, pt.1, ch.1.

66 What was good for God's birds was bad for God's
   gardener.
   1896 *Jude the Obscure*, pt.1, ch.2.

67 It was better to love a woman than to be a graduate, or a
   parson; ay, or a pope!
   1896 *Jude the Obscure*, pt.1, ch.7.

68 Cruelty is the law pervading all nature and society; and
   we can't get out of it if we would!
   1896 *Jude the Obscure*, pt.5, ch.8.

69 Done because we are too menny.
   1896 The note left by Jude's young son, who had hanged his
   siblings and himself. *Jude the Obscure*, pt.6, ch.2.

70 An aged thrush, frail, gaunt and small,
   In blast-beruffled plume,
   Had chosen thus to fling his sail
   Upon the growing gloom.

   So little cause for carollings
   Of such ecstatic sound
   Was written on terrestrial things
   Afar or nigh around,
   That I could think there trembled through

His happy good-night air
Some blessed Hope, whereof he knew
And I was unaware.
   1902 'The Darkling Thrush'.

71 If way to the Better there be, it exacts a full look at the
   worst.
   1902 'De Profundis'.

72 What we gain by science is, after all, sadness, as the
   Preacher saith. The more we know of the laws and nature
   of the Universe the more ghastly a business we perceive
   it all to be—and the non-necessity of it.
   1902 Letter to Edward Clodd, 27 Feb.

73 A local thing called Christianity.
   1904 *The Dynasts*, pt.1, act 1, sc.6.

74 War makes rattling good history; but Peace is poor
   reading.
   1904 *The Dynasts*, pt.1, act 2, sc.5.

75 Woman much missed, how you call to me, call to me,
   Saying that now you are not as you were
   When you had changed from the one who was all to me,
   But as at first, when our day was fair.
   1914 'The Voice'.

76 This is the weather the cuckoo likes,
   And so do I;
   When showers betumble the chestnut spikes,
   And nestlings fly:
   And the little brown nightingale bills his best,
   And they sit outside at 'The Travellers' Rest',
   And maids come forth sprig-muslin drest,
   And citizens dream of the south and west,
   And so do I.
   1922 *Late Lyrics and Earlier*, 'Weathers'.

77 Well, World, you have kept faith with me,
   Kept faith with me;
   Upon the whole you have proved to be
   Much as you said you were.
   1928 *Winter Words*, 'He Never Expected Much'.

Hargreaves, W F 1846–1919

English songwriter. Married to US singer Ella Shields, he wrote
such music-hall standards as 'I Must Go Home Tonight'.

78 I acted so tragic the house rose like magic,
   The audience yelled, 'You're sublime'.
   They made me a present of Mornington Crescent,
   They threw it a brick at a time.
   'The Night I Appeared as Macbeth' (song).

Harington, Sir John 1561–1612

English courtier and writer, godson of Elizabeth I. He translated
Ariosto's *Orlando Furioso* (1591) and published the satiric *The
Metamorphosis of Ajax* (1596), which contained the first design
of a flushing toilet. His government work in Ireland inspired *A
Short View of the State of Ireland* (1605).

79 When I would make a feast
   I would my guests should praise it, not the cooks.
   1618 *Epigrams*, bk.1, no.5, 'Against Writers That Carp at Other
   Men's Books'.

80 Treason doth never prosper, what's the reason?
   For if it prosper, none dare call it treason.
   1618 *Epigrams*, bk.4, no.5.

Harkin, Tom (Thomas) 1939–

US politician, Democratic Senator from Iowa.

81 The Gulf War was like teenage sex. We got in too soon and we got out too soon.
1991 Quoted in the *Independent on Sunday*, 29 Sep.

Harkness, Richard Long 1907–77

US radio and television news commentator. He was also a journalist and government official. As the Washington correspondent for NBC (1943–72) he covered the Roosevelt–Churchill war conferences, as well as UN sessions, NATO and domestic political campaigns.

82 A group of the unwilling, picked from the unfit, to do the unnecessary.
1960 Definition of a committee. In the *New York Herald Tribune*, 15 Jun.

Harlech, William David Ormsby Gore, 5th Baron 1918–85

English Conservative politician and businessman, British Ambassador in Washington (1961–5). On his return he obtained the franchise for Harlech Television (1967). He was President of the British Board of Film Censors at a time of increasing permissiveness.

83 It would indeed be the ultimate tragedy if the history of the human race proved to be nothing more noble than the story of an ape playing with a box of matches on a petrol dump.
1960 In the *Christian Science Monitor*, 25 Oct.

Harlow, Jean *pseudonym of* **Harlean Carpentier** 1911–37

US actress, best known for her roles as a fast-talking wisecracking blonde in *Hell's Angels* (1930), *Red Dust* (1932) and *Libelled Lady* (1936). She died young from cerebral oedema.

84 Excuse me while I slip into something more comfortable.
1930 Line delivered in *Hell's Angels* (screenplay by Howard Estabrook and Harry Behn).

Harold II c.1019–1066

Earl of Wessex and King of England (1066). Shipwrecked in Normandy, he swore an oath to support Duke William's claim to the English throne. When he was elected king, William invaded, and Harold was killed at Hastings.

85 He will give him seven feet of English ground, or as much more as he may be taller than other men.
1066 His offer to the invading Norse King Harald Hardrada, quoted in Snorri Sturluson *Heimskringla* (c.1260), 'King Harald's Saga', section 91 (translated by Samuel Laing as *History of the Norse Kings*, 1844).

Harpur, Charles 1813–68

Australian poet. He used traditional, ornate 18c English verse patterns, overlaid with pastoral Australian imagery, in an attempt to create an appropriate colonial style.

86 Stale is their gladness who were never sad.
'Sonnet XIII', collected in C W Salier (ed) *Rosa: Love Sonnets to Mary Doyle* (1949).

Harrington, James 1611–77

English political theorist. Although a republican, he was an attendant of Charles I and was with him at the scaffold. His semi-romance *The Commonwealth of Oceana* (1656) proposed a commonwealth based on property. He was arrested and imprisoned in 1661.

87 No man can be a politician except he first be an historian or a traveller; for except he can see what must be, or what may be, he is no politician.
1656 *The Commonwealth of Oceana*.

Harrington, Michael 1928–89

US political activist and writer. In 1973 he set up the Democratic Socialist Organizing Committee. *The Other America: Poverty in the United States* (1962) is an indictment of poverty in the US.

88 If there is technological advance without social advance, there is, almost automatically, an increase in human misery, in impoverishment.
1962 *The Other America: Poverty in the United States*, ch.1.

89 Clothes make the poor invisible too: America has the best-dressed poverty the world has ever known.
1962 *The Other America: Poverty in the United States*, ch.1.

Harris, Joel Chandler 1848–1908

US author, who worked for the Atlanta *Constitution* (1876–1900). His reputation rests on his Uncle Remus stories, told in dialect. They include *Uncle Remus: His Songs and His Sayings* (1880) and *Nights with Uncle Remus* (1883).

90 Tar-Baby, she stay still, en Brer Fox, he lay low.
1880 *Uncle Remus: His Songs and His Sayings*, 'The Wonderful Tar-Baby Story'.

91 Bred en bawn in a brier-patch!
1880 *Uncle Remus: His Songs and His Sayings*, 'How Mr. Rabbit Was Too Sharp for Mr. Fox'.

92 Licker talks mighty loud w'en it git loose fum de jug.
1880 *Uncle Remus: His Songs and His Sayings*, 'Plantation Proverbs'.

93 Hongry rooster don't cackle w'en he fine a wum.
1880 *Uncle Remus: His Songs and His Sayings*, 'Plantation Proverbs'.

94 Watch out w'en you'er gittin all you want. Fattenin' hogs ain't in luck.
1880 *Uncle Remus: His Songs and His Sayings*, 'Plantation Proverbs'.

95 When folks git ole en strucken wid de palsy, dey mus' speck ter be laff'd at.
1883 *Nights with Uncle Remus*, 'Mr. Man Has Some Meat'.

96 All by my own-alone self.
1883 *Nights with Uncle Remus*, 'Brother Wolf Falls a Victim'.

Harris, Robert 1957–

English writer. He has worked as a news reporter and journalist and has also published novels.

97 The only leaders Labour loves are dead ones.
1996 In the *Sunday Times*, 11 Aug.

Harris, Rolf 1930–

Australian entertainer and artist. He went to London in 1952 to study art, and began working with the BBC children's department. More recently he has been the presenter of the television series *Animal Hospital* (1994–).

98 Tie Me Kangaroo Down, Sport.

1950s Title and chorus of song, passim in BBC children's programme.

Harris, (Theodore) Wilson *pseudonym of* **Kona Waruk** 1921–

British novelist, born in Guyana. His best-known work is *The Guyana Quartet* (1960–3).

99 The dark notes rose everywhere, so dark, so sombre, they broke into a fountain—light as the rainbow— sparkling and immaterial as invisible sources and echoes. The savannahs grew lonely as the sea and broke again into a wave and forest. Tall trees with black marching boots and feet were clad in the spurs and sharp wings of a butterfly.
1960 *The Palace of the Peacock*, ch.11.

Harrison, Tony 1937–

English poet. His work has focused on giving voice to working class culture. His best-known work is the inflammatory poem *V* (1985), a denunciation of contemporary British life.

1 Articulation is the tongue-tied's fighting.
1978 'On Not Being Milton'.

2 This pen's all I have of magic wand.
1985 *V*.

3 I have always disliked the idea of an arts ghetto in which poetry is kept on a life-support system.
1989 In the *Observer*, 23 Jul.

Harrison, Wallace K(irkman) 1895–1981

US architect, whose best-known designs include the UN Secretariat building and the Metropolitan Opera House, both in New York. He married into the Rockefeller dynasty.

4 When we started the UN we were not trying to make a monument. We were building a workshop—a workshop for world peace. And we tried to make it the best damn workshop we could.
1952 In *Time*, 22 Sep.

Harrod, Sir Roy 1900–78

English economist, Professor at Oxford (1922–67), noted for his work on international economics and economic growth.

5 The most basic law of economics…that one cannot get something for nothing.
1948 *Towards a Dynamic Economics*.

6 No economy ever stands still.
1963 *The British Economy*.

Hart, Gary *originally* **Gary Hartpence** 1936–

US lawyer and Democrat politician. He entered the Senate in 1974, and was narrowly defeated for the presidential nomination by Walter Mondale in 1984. He made a further unsuccessful bid for the presidency in 1988.

7 You can get awful famous in this country in seven days.
1984 Rueful comment after reports of his marital infidelity ended his presidential campaign. In the *New York Times*, 7 Oct.

8 This is one Hart that you will not leave in San Francisco.
1984 Said after his failed bid for the presidential nomination at the Democratic National Convention in San Francisco.

Hart, Ian 1964–

English actor.

9 There's a statistical theory that if you gave a million monkeys typewriters and set them to work, they'd eventually come up with the entire works of Shakespeare. Thanks to the internet, we now know this isn't true.
2001 In the *Sunday Herald*, 30 Dec.

Hart, Lorenz 1895–1943

US songwriter.

10 When love congeals
It soon reveals
The faint aroma of performing seals,
The double-crossing of a pair of heels.
I wish I were in love again!
1937 'I Wish I Were in Love Again' (music by Richard Rodgers), from *Babes in Arms*.

11 I get too hungry for dinner at eight.
I like the theater, but never come late.
I never bother with people I hate.
That's why the lady is a tramp.
1937 'The Lady Is a Tramp' (music by Richard Rodgers), from *Babes in Arms*.

12 I'm wild again
Beguiled again
A simpering, whimpering child again,
Bewitched, bothered and bewildered am I.
1941 'Bewitched' (music by Richard Rodgers), from *Pal Joey*.

Hart, Moss 1904–61

US playwright and author. He won a Pulitzer Prize for *You Can't Take It With You* (1937) and a Perry award for directing his own play *My Fair Lady* (1957). He also wrote *Once in a Lifetime* (1930).

13 A play for me never really takes on an aspect of reality until it has left the dry air of the study and begins to sniff the musty breezes of a bare stage.
1959 *Act One*.

14 The four most dramatic words in the English language: 'Act One, Scene One.'
1959 *Act One*.

Harte, (Francis) Bret 1836–1902

US writer, who wrote sketches of California miners in works such as 'The Luck of Roaring Camp' (1868). Secretary of the US Mint in San Francisco (1864–70), he became US consul at Krefeld (1878–80) and Glasgow (1880–5).

15 I reside at Table Mountain, and my name is Truthful James;
I am not up to small deceit or any sinful games.
1868 'The Society upon the Stanislaus', stanza 1.

16 Which I wish to remark—
And my language is plain—
That for ways that are dark
And for tricks that are vain,
The heathen Chinee is peculiar,
Which the same I would rise to explain.
1870 'Plain Language from Truthful James', stanza 1. The poem became popularly known as 'That Heathen Chinee'.

17 We are ruined by Chinese cheap labour.

1870 'Plain Language from Truthful James', stanza 7.

18 And on that grave where English oak and holly
And laurel wreaths entwine,
Deem it not all a too presumptuous folly,
This spray of Western pine!
1870 On the death of Charles Dickens.'Dickens in Camp',
stanza 10.

19 If, of all words of tongue and pen,
The saddest are, 'It might have been,'

More sad are these we daily see:
'It is, but hadn't ought to be.'
1871 'Mrs. Judge Jenkins'.

Hartley, L(eslie) P(oles) 1895–1972

English writer. His early published works were short stories of a macabre turn. He went on to write successful novels of considerable psychological acuity.

20 The past is a foreign country: they do things differently there.
1953 *The Go-Between*, prologue.

Harvey, P(olly) J(ean) 1969–

English singer and songwriter.

21 There would be more women in the rock scene if they were any good. But there are so few who are.
2004 In *Scotland on Sunday*, 30 May.

Harvey, William 1578–1657

English physician and scientist, who established the foundations of modern medicine. He was the first to demonstrate the function of the heart and the complete circulation of the blood.

22 Nature is nowhere accustomed more openly to display her secret mysteries than in cases where she shows tracings of her workings apart from the beaten paths; nor is there any better way to advance the proper practice of medicine than to give our minds to the discovery of the usual law of nature, by careful investigation of cases of rarer forms of disease.
1657 Letter to John Vlackveld, 24 Apr.

Harvey-Jones, Sir John 1924–

English industrial executive.

23 All in all, if one sought to design a life style which was destructive of the individual, the way that business has structured itself would seem to be almost ideal.
1987 *Making It Happen: Reflections on Leadership*.

Haskell, Molly 1939–

US author and film critic.

24 The propaganda arm of the American Dream machine.
1973 Of Hollywood. *From Reverence to Rape: the treatment of women in the movies*.

Haskins, Minnie Louise 1875–1951

English author and educationist.

25 And I said to the man who stood at the gate of the year: 'Give me a light that I may tread safely into the unknown.'

And he replied: 'Go out into the darkness and put your hand into the hand of God. That shall be to you better than light and safer than a known way.'
1908 *Desert*,'God Knows'. Quoted by King George VI, Christmas address, 25 Dec 1939.

Hattersley, Roy Sydney George Hattersley, Baron 1932–

English Labour politician and writer. He was an MP from 1964 to 1997 and served in the Callaghan government.

26 As a boy I genuinely believed in the man who never ate bacon because its red and white stripes reminded him of Sheffield United—indeed in my blue and white Wednesday heart I applauded and supported his loyalty.
1976 *Goodbye to Yorkshire*.

27 Politicians are entitled to change their minds. But when they adjust their principles some explanation is necessary.
1999 In the *Observer*, 21 Mar.

Haughey, Charles James 1925–

Irish politician and Prime Minister (1979–81, 1982, 1987–92). He became a Fianna Fáil MP (1957), but was dismissed from the Cabinet in 1970 after a quarrel with the Prime Minister, Jack Lynch. His career has been controversial, but he is also responsible for introducing tax exemption for artists.

28 It seems that the historic inability in Britain to comprehend Irish feelings and sensitivities still remains.
1988 In the *Observer*, Feb.

Havel, Václav 1936–

Czech playwright and politician. He was a co-founder of Charter '77, President of Czechoslovakia (1989–1992) and first President of the Czech Republic (1993–2003).

29 The worst thing is that we live in a contaminated moral environment.We fell morally ill because we became used to saying something different from what we thought.
1990 Speech, 1 Jan.

Hawes, Hampton 1928–77

US jazz pianist. He was an important (but often undervalued) figure in West Coast jazz.

30 The worst thing that can happen to old good music is that it might become dated for a while, but watch out, in twenty years it will come drifting back like bell-bottoms and W.C. Fields movies.
1974 *Raise Up Off Me* (with Don Asher), ch.22.

Hawking, Stephen William 1942–

English theoretical physicist, theorist of the astronomical bodies known as black holes. He has written several bestselling popular science books including *A Brief History of Time* (1988) and *The Universe in a Nutshell* (2001). From the 1960s he has suffered from a progressive motor neurone disease.

31 God not only plays dice. He also sometimes throws the dice where they cannot be seen.
1975 In *Nature*, vol.257.
➤ *See Einstein 301:32*.

32 If we find the answer to that, it would be the ultimate triumph of human reason—for then we would know the mind of God.
1988 Referring to the question of why we and the universe exist. *A Brief History of Time*, ch.11.

33 What is it that breathes fire into the equations and makes a universe for them to describe… Why does the universe go to all the bother of existing?
1988 *A Brief History of Time*, ch.11.

Hawthorn, Mike 1929–59

English racing driver. Driving for Ferrari, he won the Formula One World Championship in 1958 but then retired from the sport, only to be killed in a road accident a few months later.

34 Motor racing is dangerous; but what is danger? It is dangerous to climb a mountain. It is dangerous to cross main roads. It is dangerous to explore a jungle. One cannot frame regulations to make everything safe.
1959 Shortly before his death. Quoted in Colin Jarman *The Guinness Dictionary of Sports Quotations* (1990).

Hawthorne, Nathaniel 1804–64

US novelist, who worked in the Salem custom house and was Consul at Liverpool (1853–7). Between 1850 and 1852 he lived in Lenox near Herman Melville, where he wrote *The Scarlet Letter* (1850) and *The House of the Seven Gables* (1851).

35 We sometimes congratulate ourselves at the moment of waking from a troubled dream: it may be so the moment after death.
c.1836 *The American Notebooks*, ch.1.

36 The love of posterity is a consequence of the necessity of death. If a man were sure of living forever here, he would not care about his offspring.
1840 *The American Notebooks* (published 1868), ch.3.

37 Bees are sometimes drowned in the honey which they collect—so some writers are lost in their collected learning.
1842 *The American Notebooks* (published 1868), ch.5.

38 Human nature will not flourish, any more than a potato, if it be planted and replanted, for too long a series of generations, in the same worn-out soil.
1850 *The Scarlet Letter*, 'The Custom-House'.

39 The founders of a new colony, whatever Utopia of human virtue and happiness they might originally project, have invariably recognized it among their earliest practical necessities to allot a portion of the virgin soil as a cemetery, and another portion as the site of a prison.
1850 *The Scarlet Letter*, ch.1.

40 Let men tremble to win the hand of woman, unless they win along with it the utmost passion of her heart!
1850 *The Scarlet Letter*, ch.15.

41 No man, for any considerable period, can wear one face to himself, and another to the multitude, without finally getting bewildered as to which may be the true.
1850 *The Scarlet Letter*, ch.20.

42 When a writer calls his work a Romance, it need hardly be observed that he wishes to claim a certain latitude, both as to its fashion and material, which he would not have felt himself entitled to assume had he professed to be writing a Novel.

1851 *The House of the Seven Gables*, preface.

43 Life is made up of marble and mud.
1851 *The House of the Seven Gables*, ch.2.

44 Life, within doors, has few pleasanter prospects than a neatly arranged and well-provisioned breakfast-table.
1851 *The House of the Seven Gables*, ch.7.

45 The world, that grey-bearded and wrinkled profligate, decrepit, without being venerable.
1851 *The House of the Seven Gables*, ch.12.

46 The world owes all its onward impulse to men ill at ease. The happy man inevitably confines himself within ancient limits.
1851 *The House of the Seven Gables*, ch.20.

47 In the depths of every heart, there is a tomb and a dungeon, though the lights, the music, and revelry above may cause us to forget their existence, and the buried ones, or prisoners whom they hide.
1851 *Twice-Told Tales*, 'The Haunted Mind'.

48 The greatest obstacle to being heroic is the doubt whether one may not be going to prove one's self a fool; the truest heroism is to resist the doubt; and the profoundest wisdom, to know when it ought to be resisted and when to be obeyed.
1852 *The Blithedale Romance*, ch.2.

49 America is now wholly given over to a d—d mob of scribbling women.
1855 Quoted in Caroline Ticknor *Hawthorne and His Publisher* (1913).

50 The present is burthened too much with the past.
1856 Entry for 27 Mar at the British Museum, collected in *The English Notebooks* (1870).

51 Nobody has any conscience about adding to the improbabilities of a marvelous tale.
1860 *The Marble Faun*, ch.4.

52 How is it possible to say an unkind or irreverential word of Rome? The city of all time, and of all the world!
1860 *The Marble Faun*, ch.12.

53 Dr Johnson's morality was as English an article as a beefsteak.
1863 *Our Old Home*.

Hay, Ian *pseudonym of Major–General John Hay Beith* 1876–1952

Scottish novelist and dramatist. His light popular novels (eg *Pip*, 1907) were followed by war books, including *The First Hundred Thousand* (1915). His best-known comedies are *Tilly of Bloomsbury* (1919) and *The Housemaster* (1936).

54 What do you mean, funny? Funny peculiar, or funny ha-ha?
1936 *The Housemaster*, act 3.

Hayakawa, S(amuel) I(chiye) 1906–92

Canadian-born US philologist and politician. His semantics works include *Language in Action* (1941, later retitled *Language in Thought and Action*). He was president of San Francisco State College (1968–73) and entered the House as Senator for California (1977–83).

55 In a real sense, people who have read good literature have lived more than people who cannot or will not read.
1941 *Language in Action*.

56 It's ours.We stole it fair and square.
Of the Panama Canal Zone. Attributed.

Haydn, Franz Joseph 1732–1809

Austrian composer. Kapellmeister to the Esterházy family from 1761, he twice visited England and several works were first performed in London. His works include piano music, string quartets, concertos, symphonies, masses and choral works such as the oratorio *The Creation* (1798).

57 But all the world understands my language.
1790 Reply to Mozart, who had advised him against visiting England because he could not speak the language. Quoted in Ian Crofton and Donald Fraser *A Dictionary of Musical Quotations* (1985).

Haydon, Benjamin Robert 1786–1846

English historical painter. He was twice imprisoned for debt, and, after a number of bitter disappointments, shot himself.

58 The French had a more martial air than the English. There seemed to be a species of military instinct in all classes. No young man appeared to have finished his education till after a bloody campaign… They were at this singular period, without the least exaggeration, a century behind us in notions of legal and moral responsibility.
Autobiography (published 1847).

Hayek, Friedrich August von 1899–1992

Austrian-born British political economist and libertarian moral philosopher. Professor at the London School of Economics (1932–50), Chicago (1950–72) and Freiburg (1962–5) and a guru of the New Right, in 1974 he was awarded the Nobel prize for economics with Gunnar Myrdal.

59 The more the state 'plans' the more difficult planning becomes for the individual.
1944 *The Road to Serfdom.*

60 We are only beginning to understand on how subtle a communication system the functioning of an advanced industrial society is based—a communications system which we call the market and which turns out to be a more efficient mechanism for digesting dispersed information than any that man has deliberately designed.
1978 *New Studies in Philosophy, Politics, Economics and the History of Ideas*, 'The Pretence of Knowledge'.

61 [There is] a delusion that macro-economics is both viable and useful (a delusion encouraged by its extensive use of mathematics, which must always impress politicians lacking any mathematical education, and which is really the nearest thing to the practice of magic that occurs among professional economists).
1989 *The Fatal Conceit: The Errors of Socialism*, ch.6.

Hayes, J Milton 1884–1940

British author.

62 There's a one-eyed yellow idol to the north of Khatmandu,
There's a little marble cross below the town,
There's a broken-hearted woman tends the grave of Mad Carew,
And the Yellow God forever gazes down.
1911 *The Green Eye of the Yellow God.*

Hayes, Rutherford B(irchard) 1822–93

US Republican statesman and 19th President (1877–81). Under his presidency, the country recovered commercial prosperity, and his policy included the reform of the civil service and the conciliation of the Southern states.

63 He serves his party best who serves his country best.
1877 Inaugural address, 5 Mar.

Hayward, Thomas Bibb 1924–

US admiral, Chief of Operations in the US Navy (1978–83). He served in both Korea and Vietnam.

64 We are…a one-and-a-half ocean navy with a three-ocean commitment.
1982 Congressional testimony, reported in the *New York Times*, 11 Apr.

Hazlitt, William 1778–1830

English essayist, whose controversial and witty work ranges from theatre and literature to politics and even sports. His various collections of essays include *Table Talk* (1821) and *Spirit of the Age, or Contemporary Portraits* (1825).

65 There is in Kean, an infinite variety of talent, with a certain monotony of genius.
1815 Of the actor Edmund Kean. In *The Examiner*, 10 Dec.

66 Mr Kemble sacrifices too much to decorum. He is chiefly afraid of being contaminated by too close an identity with the character he represents. This is the greatest vice in an actor, who ought never to *bilk* his part.
1816 Of John Philip Kemble's performance as Sir Giles Overreach in Massinger's *A New Way to Pay Old Debts*. In *The Examiner*, 5 May.

67 There is nothing good to be had in the country, or if there is, they will not let you have it.
1817 *The Round Table*, 'Observation on Mr Wordsworth's Poem *The Excursion*'.

68 The art of pleasing consists in being pleased.
1817 *The Round Table*, 'On Manner'.

69 He talked on for ever; and you wished him to talk on for ever.
1818 Of Coleridge. *Lectures on the English Poets*, 'On the Living Poets'.

70 Fashion constantly begins and ends in the two things it abhors most, singularity and vulgarity.
1818 'On Fashion', in the *Scots Magazine*.

71 The love of liberty is the love of others; the love of power is the love of ourselves.
1819 *Political Essays*, 'The Times Newspaper'.

72 Those who make their dress a principal part of themselves, will, in general, become of no more value than their dress.
1819 *Political Essays*, 'On the Clerical Character'.

73 You will hear more good things on the outside of a stagecoach from London to Oxford than if you were to pass a twelvemonth with the undergraduates, or heads of colleges, of that famous university.
1821 *Table Talk*, vol.1, 'The Ignorance of the Learned'.

74 We can scarcely hate any one that we know.
1822 *Table Talk*, vol.2, 'On Criticism'.

75 Give me the clear blue sky over my head, and the green turf beneath my feet, a winding road before me, and a

three hours' march to dinner—and then to thinking! It is hard if I cannot start some game on these lone heaths.
1822 *Table Talk*, vol.2, 'On Going a Journey'.

76 *The Times* is, we suppose, entitled to the character it gives of itself, of being the 'leading journal of Europe', and is perhaps the greatest engine of temporary opinion in the world.
1823 In the *Edinburgh Review*, May.

77 It is a commercial paper, a paper of business, and it is conducted on principles of trade and business. It floats with the tide: it sails with the stream. It has no other principle.
1823 Of *The Times*. In the *Edinburgh Review*, May.

78 It takes up no falling cause; fights no uphill battle; advocates no great principle; holds out a helping hand to no oppressed or obscure individual. It is 'ever strong upon the stronger side'.
1823 Of *The Times*. In the *Edinburgh Review*, May.

79 Paris is a beast of a city to be in—to those who cannot get out of it. Rousseau said well, that all the time he was in it, he was only trying how he should leave it… The continual panic in which the passenger is kept, the alarm and the escape from it, the anger and the laughter at it, must have an effect on the Parisian character, and tend to make it the whiffling, skittish, snappish, volatile, inconsequential, unmeaning thing it is.
1824 *Notes on a Journey through France and Italy* (published 1856).

80 He is a kind of *fourth estate* in the politics of the country.
1825 Of the journalist and reformer William Cobbett. *Spirit of the Age*, 'Mr Cobbett'.

81 Death cancels everything but truth; and strips a man of everything but genius and virtue. It is a sort of natural canonization.
1825 *Spirit of the Age*, 'Lord Byron'.

82 The present is an age of talkers, and not of doers; and the reason is, that the world is growing old. We are so far advanced in the Arts and Sciences, that we live in retrospect, and dote on past achievement.
1825 *Spirit of the Age*, 'Mr Coleridge'.

83 He writes as fast as they can read, and he does not write himself down… His worst is better than any other person's best… His works (taken together) are almost like a new edition of human nature. This is indeed to be an author!
1825 *Spirit of the Age*, 'Sir Walter Scott'.

84 Mr Wordsworth's genius is a pure emanation of the Spirit of the Age. Had he lived in any other period of the world, he would never have been heard of.
1825 *Spirit of the Age*, 'Mr Wordsworth'.

85 The dupe of friendship, and the fool of love; have I not reason to hate and to despise myself? Indeed I do; and chiefly for not having hated and despised the world enough.
1826 *The Plain Speaker*, 'On the Pleasure of Hating'.

86 His sayings are generally like women's letters; all the pith is in the postscript.
1826–7 Of Charles Lamb. *Conversations of James Northcote*.

87 The origin of all science is in the desire to know causes; and the origin of all false science and imposture is in the desire to accept false causes rather than none; or, which

is the same thing, in the unwillingness to acknowledge our own ignorance.
1829 In *The Atlas*, 15 Feb.

88 Well, I've had a happy life.
1830 Last words. Quoted in W C Hazlitt *Memoirs of William Hazlitt* (1867).

89 So have I loitered my life away, reading books, looking at pictures, going to plays, hearing, thinking, writing on what pleased me best. I have wanted only one thing to make me happy, but wanting that have wanted everything.
Literary Remains (published 1836), 'My First Acquaintance with Poets'.

90 But of all footmen the lowest class is *literary footmen*.
Sketches and Essays (published 1839), 'Footmen'.

91 A nickname is the heaviest stone that the devil can throw at a man.
Sketches and Essays (published 1839), 'Nicknames'.

92 The greatest offence against virtue is to speak ill of it.
Sketches and Essays (published 1839), 'On Cant and Hypocrisy'.

93 There is an unseemly exposure of mind, as well as of the body.
Sketches and Essays (published 1839), 'On Disagreeable People'.

94 Rules and models destroy genius and art.
Sketches and Essays (published 1839), 'On Taste'.

95 All is without form and void. Someone said of his landscapes that they were pictures of nothing and very like.
Of Turner's painting, quoted in J Lindsay *Turner: The Man and his Art* (1985).

Hazzard, Shirley 1931–

Australian-born US novelist. Her works include short stories, the satirical *People in Glass Houses* (1967) and novels including *The Transit of Venus* (1980) and *The Great Fire* (2003).

96 Nothing…makes a more fanatical official than a Latin. Organization is alien to their natures, but once they get the taste for it they take to it like drink.
1967 *People in Glass Houses*, 'Official Life'.

Head, Bessie 1937–86

South African novelist.

97 Love is mutually feeding each other, not one living on another like a ghoul.
1973 *A Question of Power*.

98 Poverty has a home in Africa—like a quiet second skin. It may be the only place on earth where it is worn with unconscious dignity.
1989 *Tales of Tenderness and Power*.

Healey, Denis Winston Healey, Baron 1917–

English Labour politician, Secretary of State for Defence (1964–70) and Chancellor of the Exchequer (1974–9). Unsuccessful in the Labour leadership contests of 1976 and 1980, he became Deputy Leader (1980–3) and shadow Foreign Secretary (1980–7).

99 That part of his speech was rather like being savaged by a dead sheep.
1978 Responding to a speech by Chancellor of the Exchequer Sir Geoffrey Howe, House of Commons, Jun.

1 For the past few months, [Margaret Thatcher] has been charging around like some bargain-basement Boadicea.
1982 In the *Observer*, 7 Nov.

2 The great She-elephant, the great She-who-must-be-obeyed, the Catherine the Great of Finchley.
1985 Of Margaret Thatcher. Comment when Trade Union recognition was withdrawn for employees working in GCHQ.

Heaney, Seamus Justin 1939–

Irish poet and critic, born in Northern Ireland. He moved to Dublin in 1976, was Professor of Poetry at Oxford (1989–94) and also teaches at Harvard (1981–). His works include *Death of a Naturalist* (1966) and *The Spirit Level* (1997) as well as translations. He won the Nobel prize for literature in 1995.

3 Between my finger and my thumb
The squat pen rests.
I'll dig with it.
1966 *Death of a Naturalist*, 'Digging'.

4 My father worked with a horse-plough,
His shoulders globed like a full sail strung
Between the shafts and the furrow.
1966 *Death of a Naturalist*, 'Follower'.

5 Love, you shall perfect for me this child
Whose small imperfect limits would keep breaking:
Within new limits now, arrange the world
And square the circle: four walls and a ring.
1966 *Death of a Naturalist*, 'Poem: For Marie'.

6 My poor scapegoat,

I almost love you
but would have cast, I know,
the stones of silence.
1975 *North*, 'Punishment'.

7 I hold my lady's head
like a crystal

and ossify myself
by gazing: I am screes
on her escarpments,
a chalk giant

carved upon her downs.
Soon my hands, on the sunken
fosse of her spine
move towards the passes.
1975 *North*, 'Bone Dreams', no.4.

8 He had gone miles away
For he drank like a fish
Nightly, naturally
Swimming towards the lure
Of warm lit-up places.
1979 *Field Work*, 'Casualty'.

9 How culpable was he
That last night when he broke
Our tribe's complicity?
'Now you're supposed to be
An educated man,'
I hear him say. 'Puzzle me
The right answer to that one.'
1979 *Field Work*, 'Casualty'. On a man killed breaking the curfew.

10 Don't be surprised,

If I demur, for, be advised,
My passport's green.
No glass of ours was ever raised
To toast *The Queen*.
1983 'An Open Letter to Blake and Andrew, Editors, Contemporary British Verse, Penguin Books, Middlesex'. Heaney was complaining at his inclusion in the book edited by Blake Morrison and Andrew Motion on the grounds of his Irish nationality.

11 Need I go on? I hate to bite
Hands that led me to the limelight
In the Penguin book, I regret
The awkwardness.
But British, no, the name's not right.
Yours truly, Seamus.
1983 'An Open Letter to Blake and Andrew, Editors, Contemporary British Verse, Penguin Books, Middlesex'. Heaney was complaining at his inclusion in the book edited by Blake Morrison and Andrew Motion on the grounds of his Irish nationality.

12 The riverbed, dried-up, half full of leaves.
Us, listening to a river in the trees.
1987 *The Haw Lantern*, 'For Bernard and Jane McCabe', complete poem.

13 When I landed in the republic of conscience
it was so noiseless when the engines stopped
I could hear a curlew high above the runway.
1987 *The Haw Lantern*, 'From the Republic of Conscience', pt.1, stanza 1.

14 Their embassies, he said, were everywhere
but operated independently
and no ambassador would ever be relieved.
1987 *The Haw Lantern*, 'From the Republic of Conscience', pt.3, stanza 4.

15 She taught me what her uncle once taught her:
How easily the biggest coal block split
If you got the grain and hammer angled right.

The sound of that relaxed alluring blow,
Its co-opted and obliterated echo,
Taught me to hit, taught me to loosen,

Taught me between the hammer and the block
To face the music. Teach me now to listen,
To strike it rich behind the linear black.
1987 *The Haw Lantern*, 'Clearances: In Memoriam M.K.H., 1911–1984'.

16 The Nobel is just another prize; it changes something but it doesn't change your being the way your first writing does.
Quoted in Annalena Mc Afee (ed) *Lives and Works: Profiles of Leading Novelists, Poets and Playwrights* (2002).

Hearst, William Randolph 1863–1951

US newspaper proprietor. He revolutionized journalism with innovations such as the banner headline, in papers such as the *Chicago Examiner*, *Boston American*, *Cosmopolitan* and *Harper's Bazaar*.

17 You furnish the pictures and I'll furnish the war.
1898 Telegram to the artist Frederic Remington at the beginning of the Spanish–American War in Cuba, Mar. This may be apocryphal, but it inspired a famous line of dialogue in Orson Welles's film *Citizen Kane*.

Heath, Sir Edward Richard George *also called* Ted
1916–

English Conservative politician, chief negotiator for Britain's entry into the European Common Market, and Prime Minister (1970–4). He was replaced as leader by Margaret Thatcher, whose policies he openly criticized.

18 We are the trade union for pensioners and children; the trade union for the disabled and the sick; the trade union for the nation as a whole.
1970 Election campaign speech, 20 Feb.

19 This would, at a stroke, reduce the rise in prices, increase productivity, and reduce unemployment.
1970 Statement on proposed tax cuts and a price freeze by nationalized industries, 16 Jun. These words were contained in a press release, and were never actually spoken by Heath.

20 It is the unpleasant and unacceptable face of capitalism, but one should not suggest that the whole of British industry consists of practices of this kind.
1973 House of Commons, 15 May, referring to the Lonrho tax-avoidance scandal involving 'Tiny' Rowland, owner of Harrods and the London and Rhodesia company.

21 If you want to see the acceptable face of capitalism, go out to an oil rig in the North Sea.
1974 Election campaign speech, 18 Feb.

22 Rejoice! Rejoice! Rejoice!
1990 On hearing of Margaret Thatcher's resignation, Nov.

23 British Conservatives base their entire approach to politics on the rule of law, and rightly so.
1998 *The Course of My Life: My Autobiography.*

24 It was not totally inconceivable that she could have joined me as my wife at No.10.
2000 Of the film star Jayne Mansfield. In the *Sunday Times*, 'Talking Heads', 6 Feb.

25 Ocean racing is like standing under a cold shower tearing up £5 notes.
Quoted in Colin Jarman *The Guinness Dictionary of Sports Quotations* (1990).

Heat-Moon, William Least *originally* William Trogdon
1939–

US writer. He made his name with *Blue Highways: A Journey Into America* (1983), a travelogue of America which, like *Prairyerth* (1991), also explored his Native American heritage.

26 Beware thoughts that come in the night. They aren't turned properly; they come in askew, free of sense and restriction, deriving from the most remote of sources.
1983 *Blue Highways: A Journey Into America*, opening words.

27 There are two kinds of adventurers: those who go truly hoping to find adventure and those who go secretly hoping they won't.
1983 *Blue Highways: A Journey Into America.*

28 To say nothing is out here is incorrect; to say the desert is stingy with everything except space and light, stone and earth is closer to the truth.
1983 *Blue Highways: A Journey Into America.*

29 Motels can be big, but never grand.
1983 *Blue Highways: A Journey Into America.*

30 Whoever the last true cowboy in America turns out to be, he's likely to be an Indian.
1983 *Blue Highways: A Journey Into America.*

Hebbel, Friedrich   1813–63

German dramatist, whose plays typically have a legendary or historical setting, exploring the conflict between the individual and humanity as a whole.

31 *Dies Österreich ist eine kleine Welt,*
In der die große ihre Probe hält.
Austria is a little world in which the big one holds its tryouts.
On the social and political disintegration affecting the Austro-Hungarian Empire in the late 1890s. Quoted in Heinrich Benedikt (ed) *Geschichte der Republik Oesterreich* (1954).

Heber, Reginald   1783–1826

English divine and hymnwriter, Bishop of Calcutta from 1823.

32 Brightest and best of the sons of the morning!
Dawn on our darkness and lend us Thine aid!
1811 In the *Christian Observer*, Nov.

33 By cool Siloam's shady rill
How sweet the lily grows!
1812 In the *Christian Observer*, Apr.

34 From Greenland's icy mountains,
From India's coral strand,
Where Afric's sunny fountains
Roll down their coral strand.
1819 Quoted in the *Christian Observer*, Feb 1823.

35 Holy, Holy, Holy! Lord God Almighty!
Early in the morning our song shall rise to Thee:
Holy, Holy, Holy! merciful and mighty!
God in Three Persons, blessèd Trinity.
1826 'Holy, Holy, Holy!'.

Hecht, Ben   1894–1964

US writer. A journalist in Chicago, he began to write novels, plays and filmscripts. From 1946 he was dedicated to the Zionist cause.

36 The movie-makers are able to put more reality into a picture about the terrors of life at the ocean bottom than into a tale of two Milwaukeans in love.
1954 In news reports, 13 Jun.

Hedin, Sven Anders   1865–1952

Swedish explorer and geographer, who travelled in unexplored regions of central Asia, where he made the first detailed map (1908). He was outspoken in his political beliefs, including sympathy for Nazi Germany.

37 But the adventure, the conquest of an unknown country, the struggle against the impossible, all have a fascination which draws me with an irresistible force.
1926 *My Life as an Explorer.*

Heffer, Simon   1960–

English journalist and writer.

38 If there is writing on Hadrian's Wall, it reads that the English should leave Scotland to its own devices.
1999 *Nor Shall My Sword: The Reinventing of England.*

39 The more a climate can be created in which neither the English nor the Scots are given cause to resent each other, the better.
1999 *Nor Shall My Sword: The Reinventing of England.*

Hegel, Georg Wilhelm Friedrich 1770–1831

German idealist philosopher. His first major work *Phänomenologie des Geistes* (1807, 'The Phenomenology of the Mind') attacked romantic intuitionism. Other works include *Enzyklopädie der philosophischen Wissenschaften* (1817, 'Encyclopedia of the Philosophical Sciences'), in which he set out his tripartite system of logic, philosophy of nature and of mind.

40 In England, even the poorest of people believe that they have rights; that is very different from what satisfies the poor in other lands.
1821 *The Philosophy of Right.*

41 Experience and history teach…that nations and governments have never learned anything from history, or acted upon any lessons they might have drawn from it.
1830 *Lectures on the Philosophy of World History*, introduction.

42 Political genius consists in identifying oneself with a principle.
Constitution of Germany.

Heidegger, Martin 1889–1976

German philosopher, student of Husserl and Professor of Philosophy at Freiburg. He was an important theoretician of phenomenology. His major work is *Being and Time* (1927).

43 The essence of technology is by no means anything technological.
1949 'The Question Concerning Technology', collected in *Basic Writings* (1977).

44 The mathematical is that evident aspect of things within which we are always already moving and according to which we experience them as things at all, and as such things. The mathematical is this fundamental position we take toward things by which we take up things as already given to us, and as they must and should be given. Therefore, the mathematical is the fundamental presupposition of the knowledge of things.
'Modern Science, Metaphysics and Mathematics', collected in *Basic Writings* (1977).

Heifetz, Jascha 1901–87

US violinist of Russo-Polish birth. A child prodigy, he settled in the US after the Russian Revolution, becoming a citizen in 1924. He first appeared in Britain in 1920.

45 I occasionally play works by contemporary composers and for two reasons. First, to discourage the composer from writing any more, and secondly to remind myself how much I appreciate Beethoven.
1961 In *Life.*

Heine, Heinrich 1797–1856

German poet and critic, who lived most of his life in Paris. An incurable spinal disease left him bedridden from 1848. He became a prominent radical political journalist, writing essays on French and German culture and composing satirical verse.

46 *Alle kräftige Menschen lieben das Leben*
All great, powerful souls love life.
1835 *Ideén, Das Buch Le Grand*, pt.3.

47 *Das Leben ist der Güter höchstes, und das schlimmste Übel ist der Tod.*
Life is the greatest of blessings, and death the worst of evils.
1835 *Ideén, Das Buch Le Grand*, pt.3.

48 *Ich glaube sogar, durch Leidenskämpfe könnten die Tiere zu Menschen werden.*
I believe that by suffering even animals could be made human.
1836 *Französische Zustände.*

49 Nothing is more futile than theorizing about music. No doubt there are laws, mathematically strict laws, but these laws are not music; they are only its conditions… The essence of music is revelation.
1837 *Letters on the French Stage.*

50 *Ich kenn es wohl, dein Missgeschick:*
Verfehltes Leben, verfehlte Liebe!
I know it well, your mishap:
A missed life, a missed love!
1840–4 *Neue Gedichte, Unterwelt*, pt.5.

51 *Dieu me pardonnera. C'est son métier.*
God will forgive me. It is His trade.
1856 Attributed, on his deathbed.

Heinse, Wilhelm 1746–1803

German novelist and art critic, whose work influenced the writers and artists of the Romantic movement.

52 Drawing is only a necessary evil, proportions are easily determined: colour is the goal, the beginning and end of art.
1787 *Ardinghello.*

53 The best subjects for artists, surely, are animals and plants, grasses and trees; these they can represent, but human beings they ought to leave to poets.
1787 *Ardinghello.*

54 Every form is individual, there exists none which is abstract.
Quoted in J J W Heinse *Sämmtliche Werke* (1903–25).

Heisenberg, Werner 1901–76

German physicist, a founder of quantum theory. His 'uncertainty principle' states that it is impossible to determine both the position and momentum of a subatomic particle. He received the 1932 Nobel prize for physics.

55 Natural science does not simply describe and explain nature; it is part of the interplay between nature and ourselves; it describes nature as exposed to our method of questioning.
1959 *Physics and Philosophy.*

56 Unless you stake your life, life will not be won.
1969 *Der Teil und das Ganze*, translated by A J Pomerans as *Physics and Beyond* (1971).

57 An expert is someone who knows some of the worst mistakes that can be made in his subject and who manages to avoid them.
1969 *Der Teil und das Ganze*, translated by A J Pomerans as *Physics and Beyond* (1971).

Heller, Joseph 1923–99

US novelist. He drew on his wartime experience for his black comedy *Catch-22* (1961), which became an international bestseller. Later books include *Something Happened* (1974), *God Knows* (1984) and *Picture This* (1988).

58 He was a self-made man who owed his lack of success to nobody.
1961 Of Colonel Cargill. *Catch-22*, ch.3.

59 He had decided to live forever or die in the attempt, and his only mission each time he went up was to come down alive.
1961 Of Yossarian. *Catch-22*, ch.3.

60 There was only one catch and that was Catch-22, which specified that a concern for one's safety in the face of dangers that were real and immediate was the process of a rational mind. Orr was crazy and could be grounded. All he had to do was ask; and as soon as he did, he would no longer be crazy and would have to fly more missions. Orr would be crazy to fly more missions and sane if he didn't, but if he was sane he had to fly them. If he flew them he was crazy and didn't have to; but if he didn't want to he was sane and had to. Yossarian was moved very deeply by the absolute simplicity of this clause of Catch-22, and let out a respectful whistle.
'That's some catch, that Catch-22,' he observed.
'It's the best there is,' Doc Daneeka agreed.
1961 *Catch-22*, ch.5.

61 'Yossarian? Is that his name? Yossarian? What the hell kind of a name is Yossarian?' Lieutenant Scheisskopf had the facts at his finger tips. 'It's Yossarian's name, sir,' he explained.
1961 *Catch-22*, ch.8.

62 Hungry Joe collected lists of fatal diseases and arranged them in alphabetical order so that he could put his finger without delay on any one he wanted to worry about.
1961 *Catch-22*, ch.17.

63 Frankly, I'd like to see the government get out of the war altogether and leave the whole field to private industry.
1961 Milo Minderbinder. *Catch-22*, ch.24.

64 Success and failure are both difficult to endure. Along with success come drugs, divorce, fornication, bullying, travel, meditation, medication, depression, neurosis and suicide. With failure comes failure.
1975 Interview in *Playboy*, Jun.

65 If Richard Nixon was second-rate, what in the world *is* third-rate?
1979 *Good as Gold*, ch.6.

66 And a man who lay with a beast, said the Lord, would surely die. And if he doesn't lie with a beast, I would have countered, he won't die?
1984 King David. *God Knows*, ch.2.

67 Mankind is resilient: the atrocities that horrified us a week ago become acceptable tomorrow.
1988 *Picture This*, ch.37.

68 I used to joke—and it wasn't much of an exaggeration—that a story I would mail to the *New Yorker* in the morning would be back with its concise, slighting rejection slip in the afternoon mail that same day.
1998 *Now and Then: A Memoir*.

69 There were reviews that were good, a good many that were mixed, and there were reviews that were bad, very bad, almost venomously spiteful, one might be tempted to say (and I am the one that might say it).
1998 Recalling the critical reception to *Catch-22*. In *Now and Then: A Memoir*.

70 Who has?
On being asked why he hadn't written another novel as good as *Catch-22*. Quoted by Peter Guttridge in the postscript of *Now and Then: A Memoir* (1998).

Heller, Walter Wolfgang 1915–87

Chairman of the US Council of Economic Advisers to the President under Kennedy and Johnson (1961–64).

71 An economist is someone who, when he finds something which works in practice, wonders if it will work in theory.
1992 Attributed.

Hellman, Lillian Florence 1907–84

US playwright, whose plays include *The Children's Hour* (1934) and *The Little Foxes* (1939). In 1952 she came before McCarthy's House Un-American Activities Committee. She lived for many years with Dashiell Hammett.

72 That's cynical. [Smiles.] Cynicism is an unpleasant way of saying the truth.
1939 Ben. *The Little Foxes*, act 1.

73 It's an indulgence to sit in a room and discuss your beliefs as if they were a juicy piece of gossip.
1941 Sara. *Watch on the Rhine*, act 2.

74 I do not like subversion or disloyalty in any form and if I had ever seen any I would have considered it my duty to have reported it to the proper authorities. But to hurt innocent people whom I knew many years ago in order to save myself is to me inhuman and indecent and dishonorable.
1952 Letter to John S Wood, 19 May, on being asked to give information for the McCarthy trials. Collected in *US Congress Committee Hearing on Un-American Activities* (1952), pt.8.

75 I cannot and will not cut my conscience to fit this year's fashions, even though I long ago came to the conclusion that I was not a political person and could have no comfortable place in any political group.
1952 Letter to John S Wood, 19 May, on being asked to give information for the McCarthy trials. Collected in *US Congress Committee Hearing on Un-American Activities* (1952), pt.8.

76 That's what you always said, success isn't everything but it makes a man stand straight, and you were right.
1960 Julian. *Toys in the Attic*, act 1.

77 Well, people change and forget to tell each other. Too bad—causes so many mistakes.
1960 Anna. *Toys in the Attic*, act 3.

78 If I had to give young writers advice, I would say don't listen to writers talking about writing or themselves.
1960 In the *New York Times*, 21 Feb.

79 Intellectuals can tell themselves anything, sell themselves any bill of goods, which is why they were so often patsies for the ruling classes in nineteenth-century France and England, or twentieth-century Russia and America.
1967 Journal entry, 30 Apr. Collected in *An Unfinished Woman* (1969), ch.13.

80 It is a mark of many famous people that they cannot part with their brightest hour.
1973 *Pentimento*, 'Theatre'.

81 The English don't raise their voices, Arthur, although they may have other vulgarities.

1973 *Pentimento*, 'Arthur W. A. Cowan'.

82 I am suspicious of guilt in myself and in other people: it is usually a way of not thinking, or of announcing one's own fine sensibilities the better to be rid of them.
1976 *Scoundrel Time*.

83 He was getting over a four-day drunk, and I was getting over a 4-year marriage.
1985 On meeting Dashiell Hammett. In the *Christian Science Monitor*, 13 Oct.

Helmholtz, Hermann Ludwig Ferdinand von 1821–94

German scientist and investigator of thermodynamics and electrodynamics. He was Professor of Physics at the University of Berlin.

84 Whoever, in the pursuit of science, seeks after immediate practical utility may rest assured that he seeks in vain.
1862 Lecture at Heidelberg, collected in *Popular Lectures on Scientific Subjects* (1873).

Helmsley, Leona (Mindy) née *Rosenthal* 1920–

US businesswoman. Convicted of tax evasion in 1989, she received a four-year jail sentence, but avoided jail until 1992. She was released in 1994.

85 We don't pay taxes. Only the little people pay taxes.
1989 Remark to a former hotel housekeeper which became a byword of her trial and conviction for tax fraud. Reported in the *New York Times*, 13 Jul.

Héloïse 1101–64

French abbess. At 17 she had a child by her tutor, Peter Abelard. After Abelard was castrated by her family, she entered the convent of Argenteuil, becoming prioress there, and later became abbess at the Paraclete, founded by Abelard.

86 *Et si uxoris nomen sanctius ac validius videtur, dulcius mihi semper exstitit amicæ vocabulum; aut si non indigneris, concubinæ vel scorti.*
If the name of wife seems more blessed or more binding, always sweeter to me will be the word lover, or if I may, concubine or whore.
c.1135 First letter to Peter Abelard.

87 *Non enim quo quisque ditior sive potentior, ideo et melior: fortunae illud est, hoc virtutis.*
To be wealthier or more powerful is not necessarily to be worthier: the former are products of fortune, the latter stems from virtue.
c.1135 First letter to Peter Abelard.

88 *Non enim rei effectus, sed efficientis affectus in crimine est. Nec quæ fiunt, sed quo animo fiunt, æquitus pensat.*
Crime lies not in the deed, but in the doer's intention: it is not what was done, but the spirit in which it was done that justice should consider.
c.1135 First letter to Peter Abelard.

Helpmann, Sir Robert Murray 1909–86

Australian dancer, actor and choreographer. He debuted in Adelaide (1923), studied with Pavlova and in 1931 went to Britain. Star of the new Sadler's Wells Ballet (1933–50), he danced in many films and also acted with the Royal Shakespeare Company. His choreographic work includes *Hamlet* (1942) and *Miracle in the Gorbals* (1944).

89 You see there are portions of the human anatomy which would keep swinging after the music had finished.
c.1968 Disagreeing with the suggestion that there might be a future for nudity in dance. Quoted in Elizabeth Salter *Helpmann* (1978), ch.21. It is sometimes quoted as a comment on the opening night of the musical *Oh, Calcutta!*, as 'The trouble with nude dancing is that not everything stops when the music stops.'

Hemans, Felicia née *Browne* 1793–1835

English poet.

90 The stately homes of England,
How beautiful they stand!
Amid their tall ancestral trees,
O'er all the pleasant land.
1849 'The Homes of England'.
➤ *See Coward 239:18.*

91 The boy stood on the burning deck
Whence all but he had fled;
The flame that lit the battle's wreck
Shone round him o'er the dead.
1849 'Casabianca'.

Hemingway, Ernest Millar 1899–1961

US novelist, short-story writer and journalist, whose terse prose style was much imitated. He was a legendary figure known for his drinking, big-game hunting, and deep-sea fishing. He won the Nobel prize for literature in 1954. Depressed by his failing powers, he later committed suicide.

92 Switzerland is a small, steep country, much more up and down than sideways, and is all stuck over with large brown hotels built on the cuckoo clock style of architecture.
1922 In the *Toronto Star Weekly*, 4 Mar.

93 A man's got to take a lot of punishment to write a really funny book.
1924 Letter, 6 Dec.

94 God knows people who are paid to have attitudes toward things, professional critics, make me sick: camp-following eunuchs of literature.
1925 Letter to Sherwood Anderson, 23 May.

95 Don't you like to write letters? I do because it's such a swell way to keep from working and yet feel you've done something.
1925 Letter to F Scott Fitzgerald, 1 Jul.

96 Soon I was alone and began cursing the bloody bible because there were no titles in it—although I found the source of practically every good title you ever heard of. But the boys, principally Kipling, had been there before me and swiped all the good ones so I called the book Men Without Women hoping it would have a large sale among the fairies and old Vassar Girls.
1927 Letter to F Scott Fitzgerald, 15 Sep.

97 I did not say anything. I was always embarrassed by the words sacred, glorious and sacrifice and the expression in vain. We had heard them, sometimes standing in the rain almost out of earshot, so that only the shouted words came through, and had read them, on proclamations that were slapped up by billposters over other proclamations, now for a long time, and I had seen nothing sacred, and the things that were glorious had no

glory and the sacrifices were like the stock-yards at Chicago if nothing was done with the meat except to bury it.
1929 Frederic Henry. *A Farewell to Arms*, ch.27.

98 I had the paper but I did not read it because I did not want to read about the war. I was going to forget the war. I had made a separate peace.
1929 Frederic Henry. *A Farewell to Arms*, ch.34.

99 The world breaks everyone and afterwards many are strong at the broken places. But those that will not break it kills. It kills the very good and the very gentle and the very brave impartially. If you are none of these you can be sure it will kill you too but there will be no special hurry.
1929 Frederic Henry. *A Farewell to Arms*, ch.34.

1 I mean grace under pressure.
1929 His definition of 'guts'. Interview with Dorothy Parker in the *New Yorker*, 30 Nov.

2 Hail nothing full of nothing, nothing is with thee.
1932 End of the older waiter's 'nada' prayer. *Winner Take Nothing*, 'A Clean, Well-Lighted Place'.

3 When you have shot one bird flying you have shot all birds flying. They are all different and they fly in different ways but the sensation is the same and the last one is as good as the first.
1932 *Winner Take Nothing*, 'Fathers and Sons'.

4 About morals, I know only that what is moral is what you feel good after and what is immoral is what you feel bad after.
1932 *Death in the Afternoon*, ch.1.

5 Bullfighting is the only art in which the artist is in danger of death and in which the degree of brilliance in the performance is left to the fighter's honor.
1932 *Death in the Afternoon*, ch.9.

6 There is no lonelier man in death, except the suicide, than the man who has lived many years with a good wife and then outlived her. If two people love each other there can be no happy end to it.
1932 *Death in the Afternoon*, ch.11.

7 Madame, all stories, if continued far enough, end in death, and he is no true story-teller who would keep that from you.
1932 *Death in the Afternoon*, ch.11.

8 The great thing is to last and get your work done, and see and hear and understand and write when there is something that you know and not before and not too damn much after.
1932 *Death in the Afternoon*, ch.16.

9 The hardest thing to do is to write straight honest prose on human beings.
1934 'Old Newsman Writes', in *Esquire*, Dec.

10 All modern American literature comes from one book by Mark Twain called *Huckleberry Finn*. American writing comes from that. There was nothing before. There has been nothing good since.
1935 *The Green Hills of Africa*, ch.1.

11 The only time it isn't good for you is when you write or when you fight. You have to do that cold. But it always helps my shooting. Modern life, too, is often a mechanical oppression and liquor is the only mechanical relief.
1935 Of whisky. Letter to Ivan Kashkin, 19 Aug.

12 He remembered poor Julian and his romantic awe of them and how he had started a story once that began, 'The very rich are different from you and me.' And somebody had said to Julian, 'Yes, they have more money.'
1936 'The Snows of Kilimanjaro', in *Esquire*, Aug. In the original version 'Julian' was named as F Scott Fitzgerald, but the pseudonym was used for book publication in *The Fifth Column and Other Stories* (1938).
➤ *See Fitzgerald 325:3.*

13 'A man…ain't got no hasn't got any can't really isn't any way out… One man alone ain't got…no chance.
1937 Harry Morgan's dying words. *To Have and Have Not*.

14 'Oh,' she said, 'I die each time. Do you not die?'
'No. Almost. But did thee feel the earth move?'
'Yes. As I died. Put thy arm around me, please.'
1940 *For Whom the Bell Tolls*, ch.7.

15 He was just a coward and that was the worst luck any man could have.
1940 *For Whom the Bell Tolls*, ch.30.

16 Cowardice, as distinguished from panic, is almost always simply a lack of ability to suspend the functioning of the imagination.
1942 Introduction to *Men At War*.

17 It wasn't by accident that the Gettysburg address was so short. The laws of prose writing are as immutable as those of flight, of mathematics, of physics.
1945 Letter, 23 Jul.

18 I started out very quiet and I beat Mr Turgenev. Then I trained hard and I beat Mr De Maupassant. I've fought two draws with Stendhal, and I think I had an edge in the last one. But nobody's going to get me in any ring with Mr Tolstoy unless I'm crazy or I keep getting better.
1950 In the *New Yorker*, 13 May.

19 Writing and travel broaden your ass if not your mind and I like to write standing up.
1950 Letter, 9 Jul.

20 All the contact I have had with politics has left me feeling as though I had been drinking out of spittoons.
1950 In the *New York Times*, 17 Sep.

21 A man can be destroyed but not defeated.
1952 *The Old Man and the Sea*.

22 It is because we have had such great writers in the past that a writer is driven out far past where he can go, out to where no one can help him.
1954 Nobel prize acceptance speech, 10 Dec.

23 No classic resembles any previous classic, so do not be discouraged.
1956 Advice to young writers, in *McCall's*, May.

24 Once writing has become your major vice and greatest pleasure only death can stop it.
1958 Interview in the *Paris Review*, Spring.

25 Under the black hat, when I had first seen them, the eyes had been those of an unsuccessful rapist.
1964 Of Percy Wyndham-Lewis. *A Moveable Feast*, ch.12 (published posthumously).

26 I always try to write as good as the best picture that was ever painted.
Quoted in the *Saturday Review*, 9 May 1964.

27 Never confuse movement with action.
Quoted in A E Hotchner *Papa Hemingway* (1966), pt.1, ch.1.

28 Hesitation increases in relation to risk in equal proportion to age.
Quoted in A E Hotchner *Papa Hemingway* (1966), pt.1, ch.3.

29 To be a successful father, there's one absolute rule: when you have a kid, don't look at it for the first two years.
Quoted in A E Hotchner *Papa Hemingway* (1966), pt.2, ch.5.

30 Wearing underwear is as formal as I ever hope I get.
Quoted in A E Hotchner *Papa Hemingway* (1966).

31 My writing is nothing, my boxing is everything.
Quoted in Colin Jarman *The Guinness Dictionary of Sports Quotations* (1990).

Hempstone, Smith 1929–

US journalist, writer and diplomat, Ambassador to Kenya (1989–93). His works include *Africa, Angry Young Giant* (1961) and *Rogue Ambassador: An African Memoir* (1997).

32 If you liked Beirut, you'll love Mogadishu.
1992 To US Marines in Somalia some years after the Corps' losing battle against Kenyan terrorists. Reported in the *Guardian Weekly*, 19 Dec.

33 It will take five years to get Somalia not on its feet but just on its knees.
1992 Reported in the *Guardian Weekly*, 19 Dec.

Henderson, Leon 1895–1986

US economist.

34 Having a little inflation is like being a little pregnant.
Attributed.

Henderson, Sir Nevile Meyrick 1882–1942

English diplomat. He served as Minister to Yugoslavia (1929–35) and as Ambassador to Argentina (1935–7) and to Germany until the outbreak of World War II.

35 When I go to see Herr Hitler I give him the Nazi salute because that is the normal thing. It carries no hint of approval of anything he or his regime may do. And, if I do it, why should you or your team object?
1938 When asked for advice by the England football team in 1938 about giving the Nazi salute before a match in Berlin against Germany. The England team gave the salute, and thereby attracted considerable notoriety at home.

Hendrix, Jimi (James Marshall) 1942–70

US rock guitarist and singer, based in Britain from 1966. Born into poverty, he taught himself guitar and became one of rock music's most innovative and influential instrumentalists before drugs and alcohol caused his death.

36 Purple haze is in my brain
Lately things don't seem the same.
1967 'Purple Haze'.

37 You can't mess with people's heads, that's for sure. But that's what music's all about, messing with people's heads.
Quoted in Nat Shapiro *An Encyclopedia of Quotations about Music* (1978).

Henley, W(illiam) E(rnest) 1849–1903

English poet, playwright, critic and editor. He collaborated with his friend R L Stevenson in four plays. He edited the *Scots Observer* (1889), renaming it *The National Observer*. The best known of his poetry collections is *In Hospital* (1903).

38 In the fell clutch of circumstance,
I have not winced nor cried aloud:
Under the bludgeonings of chance
My head is bloody but unbowed.
1888 'Invictus', collected in *In Hospital* (1903).

39 It matters not how strait the gate,
How charged with punishments the scroll,
I am the master of my fate:
I am the captain of my soul.
1888 'Invictus', collected in *In Hospital* (1903).

40 What have I done for you,
England, my England?
1900 'Pro Rege Nostro'.

Henri, Adrian Maurice 1932–2000

English poet, associated with the Mersey poets of the 1960s.

41 Beautiful boys with bright red guitars
In the spaces between the stars.
1967 'Mrs Albion You've Got a Lovely Daughter'.

42 Love is a fanclub with only two fans.
1967 'Love Is…'.

43 I wanted your soft verges
But you gave me the hard shoulder.
1967 'Song of a Beautiful Girl Petrol-pump Attendant'.

Henry II 1133–89

King of England from 1154. He instituted numerous political reforms aimed at diminishing the power of the barons and of the Church.

44 Will no one rid me of this turbulent priest?
1170 Of Thomas à Becket. Quoted in W L Warren *Henry II*, p508. Four of Henry's soldiers took his words to heart and proceeded to Canterbury, where they murdered Becket in the cathedral.

Henry V 1387–1422

King of England from 1413. He won a famous victory against the French at Agincourt in 1415, despite numerical disadvantage.

45 War has three handmaidens ever waiting on her, Fire, Blood, and Famine, and I have chosen the meekest maid of the three.
1418 Comment during the English army's siege of Rouen. Quoted in J R Green *A Short History of the English People*, vol.1 (1915), ch.5, section 6.

Henry VIII 1491–1547

King of England (1509–47). His desire to divorce his first wife, Catherine of Aragon, against papal decree led to ecclesiastical revolution, with Henry as sole head of the Church of England. In all he married six wives. His reign also saw the judicial murder of Sir Thomas More and others who dared to oppose him.

46 We at no time stand so highly in our estate royal as in the time of Parliament, wherein we as head, and you as members, are conjoined and knit together into one body politic, so as whatsoever offence or injury is offered to the meanest member of the House is to be judged as done against our person and the whole

Court of Parliament.
1543 Address to a deputation from the House of Commons, 31 Mar.

Henry, Philip 1631–96

English clergyman.

47 All this, and heaven too!
Quoted in Matthew Henry *Life of Mr Philip Henry* (1698), ch.5.

Henry, Thierry 1977–

French footballer.

48 When you look at other sports, like golf, the players earn a lot more money without running around.
2003 In *The Times*, 31 Dec.

Henryson, Robert c.1425–c.1508

Scottish poet, usually designated 'schoolmaster of Dunfermline', whose surviving poems include *The Testament of Cresseid* (c.1470) and metrical versions of Aesop's fables.

49 For to be yong I wald not, for my wis,
Off all this warld to mak me lord and king:
The more of age, the nerar hevynnis blis.
c.1460 'The Praise of Age', l.5–9.

50 The man that will nocht quhen he may
Sall haif nocht quhen he wald.
c.1460 'Robene and Makeyne', l.91–2.

51 The nuttis schell, thocht it be hard and teuch,
Haldis the kirnell, sueit and delectabill;
Sa lyis thair ane doctrine wyse aneuch
And full of frute vnder ane fenyeit fabill.
c.1470 *Moral Fables*, prologue, l.15–19.

52 Ane bow that is ay bent
Worthis ay unsmart and dullis on the string;
Sa dois the mynd that is ay diligent
In ernistfull thochtis and in studying.
c.1470 *Moral Fables*, prologue, l.21–5.

53 Best thing in eird, I say for me,
Is merry hart with small possessioun.
c.1470 *Moral Fables*, 'The Two Mice', l.387–8.

54 Louers be war and tak gude heid about
Quhome that ye lufe, for quhome ye suffer paine.
I lat yow wit, thair is richt few thairout
Quhome ye may traist to haue trew lufe agane.
c.1470 *The Testament of Cresseid*, l.561–4.

55 Nocht is your fairnes bot ane faiding flour,
Nocht is your famous laud and hie honour
Bot wind inflat in uther mennis eiris.
c.1470 *The Testament of Cresseid*, stanza 65.

Henze, Hans Werner 1926–

German composer. His stage works, often reflecting his socialist commitment, include the operas *Der Junge Lord* (1965) and *The English Cat* (1983). He has also composed orchestral, chamber, vocal and piano music.

56 There is no such thing as an unmusical person.
1969 'Does Music Have to Be Political?'

57 My profession…consists of bringing truths nearer to the point where they explode.
1982 *Music and Politics*.

Hepburn, Katharine 1907–2003

US film and stage actress. She made her professional stage debut in *The Czarina* (1928). Her films included *Bringing up Baby* (1938) and *The African Queen* (1951). *The Lion in Winter* (1968) and *On Golden Pond* (1981) both won her Academy Awards. She was the professional and personal partner of Spencer Tracy.

58 The average Hollywood film star's ambition is to be admired by an American, courted by an Italian, married to an Englishman and have a French boyfriend.
1954 In the *Journal American*, 22 Feb.

59 When a man says he likes a woman in a skirt, I tell him to try one.
1994 WETA TV broadcast, Washington, 27 Jun.

60 She gave him sex and he gave her class.
Explaining the success of the Fred Astaire and Ginger Rogers partnership. Attributed.

Hepworth, Dame Barbara 1903–75

English sculptor. She was an important figure in the development of British abstract art.

61 Carving is interrelated masses conveying an emotion: a perfect relationship between the mind and the colour, light and weight which is the stone, made by the hand which feels.
1934 *Unit One*.

62 There is an inside and an outside to every form.
1970 *A Pictorial Autobiography*.

63 My left hand is my thinking hand. The right is only a motor hand.
1970 *A Pictorial Autobiography*.

Heraclitus fl.500 BC

Greek philosopher, born in Ephesus. Only fragments survive of his book 'On Nature', which was written in an aphoristic style.

64 All is flux, nothing is stationary.
c.500 BC Quoted in Aristotle *De caelo*, bk.3, pt.1.18.

65 The path up and down is one and the same.
c.500 BC Quoted in Kirk, Raven and Schofield (eds) *The Presocratic Philosophers* (1957), ch.6.

66 Upon those that step into the same rivers different and different waters flow. They scatter and gather, come together and flow away, approach and depart.
c.500 BC Quoted in Kirk, Raven and Schofield (eds) *The Presocratic Philosophers* (1957), ch.6. Often quoted as 'It is not possible to step into the same river twice', from Plato, *Cratylus* 402a.

67 The world is an ever-living fire.
c.500 BC Quoted in Kirk, Raven and Schofield (eds) *The Presocratic Philosophers* (1957), ch.6.

68 You would not find out the boundaries of the soul, even by travelling along every path: so deep a measure does it have.
c.500 BC Quoted in Kirk, Raven and Schofield (eds) *The Presocratic Philosophers* (1957), ch.6.

69 Education is another sun to the educated.
Fragment quoted in H Diels and W Kranz (eds) *Die Fragmente der Vorsokratiker*, vol.1 (1951), 181, no.134.

70 If you do not expect the unexpected, you will not find it; for it is hard to be sought out, and difficult.
Collected in Charles H Kahn *The Art and Thought of Heraclitus* (1979).

71 The fairest order in the world is a heap of random
sweepings.
Collected in Charles H Kahn *The Art and Thought of Heraclitus*
(1979).

Herbert, Sir A(lan) P(atrick) 1890–1971

English writer and politician. He was called to the bar but never
practised, having established himself as a humorist. His
'Misleading Cases' were accounts of unusual trials, in such
collections as *Uncommon Law* (1935). He was an MP (1935–50).

72 Don't tell my mother I'm living in sin,
Don't let the old folks know.
1925 'Don't Tell My Mother I'm Living in Sin'.

73 Don't let's go to the dogs tonight
For mother will be there.
1926 'Don't Let's Go to the Dogs Tonight'.

74 Not huffy, or stuffy, not tiny or tall,
But fluffy, just fluffy, with no brains at all.
1927 Of women. 'I Like Them Fluffy'.

75 Let's find out what everyone is doing
And then stop everyone from doing it.
1930 'Let's Stop Somebody from Doing Something'.

76 As my poor father used to say
In 1863,
Once people start on all this Art
Goodbye, moralitee!
1930 'Lines for a Worthy Person'.

77 Other people's babies—
That's my life!
Mother to dozens,
And nobody's wife.
1930 'Other People's Babies'.

78 Well, fancy giving money to the Government!
Might as well have put it down the drain.
Fancy giving money to the Government!
Nobody will see the stuff again.
1931 'Too Much!'.

79 For Kings and Governments may err
But never Mr Baedeker.
1931 'Mr Baedeker, or Britons Abroad'.

80 Holy Deadlock.
1934 Title of novel.

81 Milord, in that case an Act of God was defined as
'something which no reasonable man could have
expected'.
1935 *Uncommon Law*, 'Act of God'.

82 People must not do things for fun. We are not here for
fun. There is no reference to fun in any Act of Parliament.
1935 *Uncommon Law*, 'Is it a Free Country?'.

83 The Common Law of England has been laboriously built
about a mythical figure—the figure of 'The Reasonable
Man'.
1935 *Uncommon Law*, 'The Reasonable Man'.

84 The critical period in matrimony is breakfast-time.
1935 *Uncommon Law*, 'Is Marriage Lawful?'.

85 The Englishman never enjoys himself except for a noble
purpose.
1935 *Uncommon Law*, 'Fox-Hunting Fun'.

86 It may be life, but ain't it slow?
1941 'It May be Life'.

87 Nothing is wasted, nothing is in vain:
The seas roll over but the rocks remain.
c.1949 From an operetta, *Tough at the Top*, published in *My Life
and Times* (1970), ch.7.

Herbert, George 1593–1633

English metaphysical poet and clergyman. His religious lyrics
are collected in *The Temple, Sacred Poems and Private
Ejaculations*, published posthumously in 1633.

88 Drink not the third glass, which thou canst not tame,
When once it is within thee.
'The Church-porch', collected in *The Temple, Sacred Poems and
Private Ejaculations* (published posthumously, 1633).

89 A broken Altar, Lord, thy servant rears,
Made of a heart, and cemented with tears.
'The Altar', collected in *The Temple, Sacred Poems and Private
Ejaculations* (published posthumously, 1633).

90 Avoid, Profaneness; come not here:
Nothing but holy, pure, and clear,
Or that which groaneth to be so,
May at his peril further go.
'Superliminare', collected in *The Temple, Sacred Poems and
Private Ejaculations* (published posthumously, 1633).

91 Let all the world in ev'ry corner sing
My God and King.
'Antiphon', collected in *The Temple, Sacred Poems and Private
Ejaculations* (published posthumously, 1633).

92 I got me flowers to strew Thy way,
I got me boughs off many a tree;
But Thou wast up by break of day,
And brought'st Thy sweets along with Thee.
'Easter Song', collected in *The Temple, Sacred Poems and Private
Ejaculations* (published posthumously, 1633).

93 A servant with this clause
Makes drudgery divine;
Who sweeps a room as for Thy laws
Makes it and th' action fine.
'The Elixir', collected in *The Temple, Sacred Poems and Private
Ejaculations* (published posthumously, 1633).

94 Teach me, my God and King,
In all things Thee to see,
And what I do in any thing
To do it as for Thee.
'The Elixir', collected in *The Temple, Sacred Poems and Private
Ejaculations* (published posthumously, 1633).

95 Whereas my birth and spirit rather took
The way that takes the town;
Thou didst betray me to a lingering book,
And wrap me in a gown.
'Affliction (1)', collected in *The Temple, Sacred Poems and Private
Ejaculations* (published posthumously, 1633).

96 Sorrow was all my soul; I scarce believed,
Till grief did tell me roundly, that I lived.
'Affliction (1)', collected in *The Temple, Sacred Poems and Private
Ejaculations* (published posthumously, 1633).

97 I read, and sigh, and wish I were a tree;
For sure then I should grow
To fruit or shade: at least some bird would trust
Her household to me, and I should be just.
'Affliction (1)', collected in *The Temple, Sacred Poems and Private
Ejaculations* (published posthumously, 1633).

98 Love bade me welcome: yet my soul drew back;

Guilty of dust and sin.
But quick-ey'd Love, observing me grow slack
From my first entrance in,
Drew nearer to me, sweetly questioning
If I lacked any thing.
'Love', collected in *The Temple, Sacred Poems and Private Ejaculations* (published posthumously, 1633).

99 'You must sit down,' says Love, 'and taste my meat,'
   So I did sit and eat.
'Love', collected in *The Temple, Sacred Poems and Private Ejaculations* (published posthumously, 1633).

1 I know the ways of Pleasure, the sweet strains,
   The lullings and the relishes of it.
'The Pearl', collected in *The Temple, Sacred Poems and Private Ejaculations* (published posthumously, 1633).

2 King of glory, King of peace
   I will love Thee
   And that love may never cease,
   I will move Thee.
'Praise', collected in *The Temple, Sacred Poems and Private Ejaculations* (published posthumously, 1633).

3 My God, I heard this day,
   That none doth build a stately habitation,
   But that he means to dwell therein.
   What house more stately hath there been,
   Or can be, than is Man? to whose creation
   All things are in decay.
'Man', collected in *The Temple, Sacred Poems and Private Ejaculations* (published posthumously, 1633).

4 Man is all symmetry,
   Full of proportions, one limb to another.
'Man', collected in *The Temple, Sacred Poems and Private Ejaculations* (published posthumously, 1633).

5 O mighty love! Man is one world, and hath
   Another to attend him.
'Man', collected in *The Temple, Sacred Poems and Private Ejaculations* (published posthumously, 1633).

6 Who says that fictions only and false hair
   Become a verse? Is there in truth no beauty?
   Is all good structure in a winding stair?
'Jordan (1)', collected in *The Temple, Sacred Poems and Private Ejaculations* (published posthumously, 1633).

7 I sought out quaint words, and trim invention;
   My thoughts began to burnish, sprout, and swell,
   Curling with metaphors a plain intention,
   Decking the sense, as if it were to sell.
'Jordan (2)', collected in *The Temple, Sacred Poems and Private Ejaculations* (published posthumously, 1633).

8 So did I weave my self into the sense.
'Jordan (2)', collected in *The Temple, Sacred Poems and Private Ejaculations* (published posthumously, 1633).

9 I struck the board, and cried, 'No more.
   I will abroad.'
   What? shall I ever sigh and pine?
   My lines and life are free; free as the road,
   Loose as the wind, as large as store.
'The Collar', collected in *The Temple, Sacred Poems and Private Ejaculations* (published posthumously, 1633).

10 Sure there was wine
   Before my sighs did dry it; there was corn
   Before my tears did drown it.
'The Collar', collected in *The Temple, Sacred Poems and Private*

Ejaculations (published posthumously, 1633).

11 My crooked winding ways, wherein I live.
'A Wreath', collected in *The Temple, Sacred Poems and Private Ejaculations* (published posthumously, 1633).

12 The soul in paraphrase.
'Prayer (1)', collected in *The Temple, Sacred Poems and Private Ejaculations* (published posthumously, 1633).

13 O that thou shouldst give dust a tongue
   To cry to thee,
   And then not hear it crying!
'Denial', collected in *The Temple, Sacred Poems and Private Ejaculations* (published posthumously, 1633).

14 Sweet day, so cool, so calm, so bright,
   The bridal of the earth and sky:
   The dew shall weep thy fall tonight,
   For thou must die.
'Virtue', collected in *The Temple, Sacred Poems and Private Ejaculations* (published posthumously, 1633).

15 Joy, I did lock thee up; but some bad man
   Hath let thee out again.
'The Bunch of Grapes', collected in *The Temple, Sacred Poems and Private Ejaculations* (published posthumously, 1633).

16 When God at first made man,
   Having a glass of blessings standing by,
   'Let us,' said he, 'pour on him all we can:
   Let the world's riches, which dispersèd lie,
   Contract into a span'.
'The Pulley', collected in *The Temple, Sacred Poems and Private Ejaculations* (published posthumously, 1633).

17 Let him be rich and weary, that at least,
   If goodness lead him not, yet weariness
   May toss him to My breast.
'The Pulley', collected in *The Temple, Sacred Poems and Private Ejaculations* (published posthumously, 1633).

18 Farewell, sweet phrases, lovely metaphors:
   But will ye leave me thus? when ye before
   Of stews and brothels only knew the doors,
   Then did I wash you with my tears, and more,
   Brought you to church well-dressed and clad:
   My God must have my best, even all I had.
'The Forerunners', collected in *The Temple, Sacred Poems and Private Ejaculations* (published posthumously, 1633).

19 Throw away thy rod,
   Throw away thy wrath:
   O my God,
   Take the gentle path.
'Discipline', collected in *The Temple, Sacred Poems and Private Ejaculations* (published posthumously, 1633).

20 He that makes a good war makes a good peace.
Outlandish Proverbs (published posthumously, 1640), no.420.

21 Music helps not the toothache.
Jacula Prudentum (published posthumously, 1651). This is probably an older proverb.

22 God's mill grinds slow, but sure.
Jacula Prudentum (published posthumously, 1651).

23 He that will learn to pray, let him go to sea.
Jacula Prudentum (published posthumously, 1651).

Herbert, Xavier 1901–84

Australian writer. His novel *Capricornia* won the Sesquicentennial Literary Prize (1938) and the 1939 Australian Literary Society Gold Medal.

24 Since no normal humble man can help but feel magnificent in a brand-new suit of clothes, it is not surprising that those who don a fresh suit of bright white linen every day should feel magnificent always. Nor is it surprising that a normal humble head should swell beneath a solar topee, since a topee is more a badge of authority than a hat, as is the hat of a soldier.
1938 *Capricornia*, 'Psychological Effect of a Solar Topee'.

Herfindahl, Orris C 1918–72

US economist.

25 Conservation of one resource may entail the sacrifice of another resource which others want to conserve.
1974 *Resource Economics: Selected Writings*, p.6.

Hernández, Felisberto 1902–64

Uruguayan novelist and pianist. He led an obscure life and wrote stories describing banal events with fantastic resolutions. His surrealistic sense of humour paved the way for literary experiments in Latin America and beyond.

26 *Se ha hecho para los vivos y no para los muertos el porqué metafísico y las reflexiones sobre la vida y la muerte, pero no les hace falta aclarar todo el misterio, les hace falta distraerse y soñar en aclararlo.*
Metaphysical questions and reflections on life and death were created for people alive and not for the dead. However, they do not have to solve all mystery; it is enough for them to create some distraction and to dream that they clarify.
1929 *Libro sin tapas*, 'La piedra filosofal' ('The Philosopher's Stone').

Hernández, José 1834–86

Argentinian poet. He had little formal education and was a gaucho (pampas cowboy) in his youth, later becoming a soldier in the civil wars, a newspaper editor and a minor government official.

27 *Yo he conocido cantores*
que era un gusto el escuchar;
mas no quieren opinar
y se divierten cantando;
pero yo canto opinando,
que es mi modo de cantar.
I have known singers
it was a pleasure to listen to;
they amuse themselves singing
and don't care to give opinions;
but I sing giving opinions
and that's my kind of song.
1879 *La vuelta de Martín Fierro*, pt.1 (translated as *Martín Fierro*, 1923).

28 *Hay hombres que de su ciencia*
tienen la cabeza llena;
hay sabios de todas menas,
mas digo, sin ser muy ducho:
es mejor que aprender mucho
el aprender cosas buenas.
There are some men who have their heads
full up with the things they know.
Wise men come in all sizes,
but I don't need so much sense to say

that better than learning a lot of things
is learning things that are good.
1879 *La vuelta de Martín Fierro*, pt.32 (translated as *Martín Fierro*, 1923).

Herodotus c.485 BC–c.425 BC

Greek historian. His *Histories* deal with the wars between the Persians and the Greeks. He is often called 'The Father of History'.

29 In peace, children inter their parents; war violates the order of nature and causes parents to inter their children.
c.440 BC *The Histories of Herodotus*, bk.1, ch.87 (translated by Aubrey de Selincourt).

Herr, Michael 1940–

US journalist and war correspondent. He collaborated on the screenplays of *Apocalypse Now* (1979) and *Full Metal Jacket* (1987).

30 Vietnam was what we had instead of happy childhoods.
1977 *Dispatches*, 'Colleagues', section 3.

31 All the wrong people remember Vietnam. I think all the people who remember it should forget it, and all the people who forgot it should remember it.
1989 In the *Observer*, 15 Jan.

Herrick, Robert 1591–1674

English poet and clergyman, a Royalist who lost his living during the Civil War. His writing, both secular and religious, is collected in *Hesperides* and *Noble Numbers* (both 1648).

32 I write of *Hell*; I sing (and ever shall)
Of *Heaven*, and hope to have it after all.
1648 *Hesperides*, 'The Argument of His Book'.

33 I sing of brooks, of blossoms, birds, and bowers:
Of April, May, of June, and July-flowers.
I sing of May-poles, Hock-carts, wassails, wakes,
Of bride-grooms, brides, and of their bridal-cakes.
1648 *Hesperides*, 'The Argument of His Book'.

34 Is there no way to beget
In my limbs their former heat?
Aeson had (as *Poets* fain)
Baths that made him young again:
Find that *Medicine* (if you can)
For your dry-decrepit man:
Who would but fain his strength renew,
Were it but to pleasure you.
1648 'To His Mistress'.

35 But ah! if empty dreams so please,
Love give me more such nights as these.
1648 'The Vision to *Electra*'.

36 But thou liv'st fearless; and thy face ne'er shows
Fortune when she comes, or goes.
1648 'A Country Life: To His Brother, *M. Tho. Herrick*'.

37 Wealth cannot make a life, but Love.
1648 'A Country Life: To His Brother, *M. Tho. Herrick*'.

38 Soul of my life, and fame!
Eternal lamp of love! whose radiant flame
Out-glares the Heav'ns *Osiris*; and thy gleams
Out-shine the splendour of his mid-day beams.
1648 'The Welcome to Sack'.

39 'Tis thou, alone, who with thy mystic fan,

Work'st more than Wisdom, Art, or Nature can,
To rouse the sacred madness; and awake
The frost-bound-blood, and spirits; and to make
Them frantic with thy raptures, flashing through
The soul, like lightning, and as active too.
1648 'His Fare-well to Sack'.

40 Let others drink thee freely; and desire
Thee and their lips espous'd; while I admire,
And love thee; but not taste thee. Let my Muse
Fail of thy former helps; and only use
Her inadult'rate strength: what's done by me
Hereafter, shall smell of the lamp, not thee.
1648 'His Fare-well to Sack'.

41 Her legs were such *Diana* shows,
When tuckt up she a hunting goes;
With buskins shortened to descry
The happy dawning of her thigh.
1648 'The Vision'.

42 Get up, get up for shame, the blooming morn
Upon her wings presents the god unshorn.
1648 'Corinna's Going a Maying'.

43 See how *Aurora* throws her fair
Fresh-quilted colours through the air:
Get up, sweet-slug-a-bed, and see
The dew-bespangling herb and tree.
1648 'Corinna's Going a Maying'.

44 So when or you or I are made
A fable, song, or fleeting shade;
All love, all liking, all delight
Lies drowned with us in endless night.
Then while time serves, and we are but decaying;
Come, my *Corinna*, come, let's go a Maying.
1648 'Corinna's Going a Maying'.

45 Gather ye rose-buds while ye may,
Old Time is still a flying:
And this same flower that smiles to day,
Tomorrow will be dying.
1648 'To the Virgins, to Make Much of Time'.

46 Go happy rose, and interwove
With other flowers, bind my love.
Tell her too, she must not be,
Longer flowing, longer free,
That so oft has fetter'd me.
1648 'To the Rose: Song'.

47 Then come on, come on, and yield
A savour like unto a blessed field,
When the bedabbled morn
Washes the golden ears of corn.
1648 'A Nuptial Song, or Epithalamion, on Sir Clipseby Crew and His Lady'.

48 Her eyes, the glow-worm lend thee,
The shooting stars attend thee;
And the elves also,
Whose little eyes glow,
Like the sparks of fire, befriend thee.
1648 'The Night-piece, to Julia', written for his young daughter.

49 When as in silks my *Julia* goes,
Then, then (me thinks) how sweetly flows
That liquefaction of her clothes.
1648 'Upon Julia's Clothes'.

50 A sweet disorder in the dress

Kindles in clothes a wantonness:
A lawn about the shoulders thrown
Into a fine distraction…
A careless shoe-string, in whose tie
I see a wild civility:
Do more bewitch me, than when Art
Is too precise in every part.
1648 'Delight in Disorder'.

51 Where we such clusters had,
As made us nobly wild, not mad;
And yet each verse of thine
Out-did the meat, out-did the frolic wine.
1648 'An Ode for [Ben Jonson]'.

Herriot, James *pseudonym of* James Alfred Wight 1916–95

Scottish-born veterinary surgeon and writer of a series of highly popular novels on the adventures of a country vet.

52 I have long held the notion that if a vet can't catch his patient there's nothing much to worry about.
1976 *Vet in Harness*.

Hersey, John Richard 1914–93

US author, born in China. As Far East correspondent for *Time* magazine, his most famous piece was his eye-witness report in the *New Yorker* (31 Aug 1946) of the bombing of Hiroshima. His novels include *A Bell for Adano* (1944) and *The Walnut Door* (1977).

53 A gifted glassblower of language.
1988 On the British poet and critic I A Richards. In the *New Yorker*, 18 Jul.

Herzen, Alexander Ivanovich 1812–70

Russian political thinker and writer, a revolutionary socialist active in the Paris revolution of 1848. He settled in London (1851), producing propagandist novels and treatises, and smuggling into Russia his journal *Kolokol* (1857–67, 'The Bell').

54 Science, which cuts its way through the muddy pond of daily life without mingling with it, casts its wealth to right and left, but the puny boatmen do not know how to fish for it.
1855 Notebook entry, collected in *Byloe i dumy* (*My Past and Thoughts*), vol.3 (published 1861–7, translated by Constance Garnett, 1924).

55 There are those who prefer to get away *inwardly*, some with the help of a powerful imagination and an ability to abstract themselves from their surroundings…some with the help of opium or alcohol… I prefer shifting my whole body to shifting my brain, and going round the world to letting my head go round.
1861–7 *Byloe i dumy* (*My Past and Thoughts*), translated by Constance Garnett, 1924).

56 There is a certain basis of truth in the fear that the Russian government is beginning to have of communism, for communism is Tsarist autocracy turned upside down.
1861–7 *Byloe i dumy* (*My Past and Thoughts*), translated by Constance Garnett, 1924).

Herzl, Theodor 1860–1904

Hungarian Zionist leader. He graduated in law but wrote essays and plays until the anti-Semitism aroused by the Dreyfus trial (1894) roused him to political action and he convened the First Zionist Congress (1897).

57 Do you know out of what the German Empire arose?
Out of dreams, songs, fantasies and black-red-gold
ribbons… Bismarck merely shook the tree that fantasies
had planted.
Quoted in Carl E Schorske *Fin-de-Siècle Vienna* (1961), p.165.

Herzog, Maurice 1919–

French engineer and mountaineer. He led the French
Himalayan Expedition of 1950, which made the first ascent of
Annapurna, losing several fingers and toes through frostbite.
Annapurna was dictated during his subsequent three-year
period in hospital.

58 The mountains were there and so was I.
1952 His reason for becoming a mountain climber. Quoted in
Annapurna: Conquest of the First 8000-metre Peak (1952,
translated by Nea Morin and Janet Adam Smith).

59 Annapurna, to which we had gone empty-handed, was a
treasure on which we should live the rest of our lives.
With this realization we turn the page: a new life begins.
There are other Annapurnas in the lives of men.
1952 Quoted in *Annapurna: Conquest of the First 8000-metre
Peak* (translated by Nea Morin and Janet Adam Smith).

Heseltine, Michael Ray Dibdin Heseltine, Baron 1933–

British Conservative politician. He was Defence Secretary
under Margaret Thatcher, and resigned on the issue of the
takeover of Westland Helicopters (1986). Defeated by John
Major in the 1990 leadership contest, he became Secretary of
State for the Environment (1990–2) and for Trade and Industry
(1992–5). He was Deputy Prime Minister from 1995 to 1997 and
MP until 2001.

60 It is the only time that I can ever remember the Prime
Minister reading out the conclusions of a meeting that
did not take place. They were already written before it
started.
1986 Of the Cabinet meeting, Jan, on the Westland affair at
which he resigned as Defence Minister.

61 I can foresee no circumstance in which I would allow my
name to be put forward for the leadership of the
Conservative Party.
1990 Said on numerous occasions in the autumn.

62 I am persuaded now that I have a better prospect than
Mrs Thatcher of leading the Conservatives to a fourth
electoral victory and preventing the ultimate calamity of
a Labour government.
1990 On announcing his decision to stand for the leadership,
Nov.

63 You can't wield a handbag from an empty chair.
1999 At the launch of 'Britain in Europe', London, 14 Oct.

Hesiod c.8c BC

One of the earliest Greek poets, best known for *Opera et dies*
(*Works and Days*), which depicts rural life in archaic Greece,
and *Theogony*.

64 Potter is piqued with potter, joiner with joiner,
beggar begrudges beggar, and singer singer.
Of a quarrel within a village. *Opera et dies*, 25 (translated by M L
West, 1988).

65 The ill design is most ill for the designer.
Opera et dies, 266 (translated by M L West, 1988).

66 Inhibition is no good provider for a needy man,

inhibition, which does men great harm and great good,
inhibition attaches to poverty, boldness to wealth.
Opera et dies, 317–9 (translated by M L West, 1988).

Hess, Moses 1812–75

German political writer, and an early friend of Marx.

67 Imagine Rousseau, Voltaire, Holbach, Lessing, Heine,
and Hegel united in one person—I say united, not
lumped together—and you have Dr Marx.
Quoted in A J P Taylor's introduction to the Penguin edition of
The Communist Manifesto (1967).

Heston, Charlton 1923–

US actor. His major early successes were the Cecil B De Mille
films *The Greatest Show on Earth* (1952) and *The Ten
Commandments* (1956). He is also remembered for larger-than-
life roles in *Ben Hur* (1959, Academy Award) and *El Cid* (1961).

68 I'll give up my gun when you take it from my cold, dead
hands.
2000 In his capacity as President of the National Rifle
Association, in *The Guardian*, 31 Dec.

Hewart, Gordon Hewart, 1st Viscount 1870–1943

British barrister. He was called to the Bar in 1902 and attended
the Paris Peace Conference in 1919 as Attorney-General. He was
Lord Chief Justice of England (1922–40).

69 Justice should not only be done, but should manifestly
and undoubtedly be seen to be done.
1923 Case of *Rex v. Sussex Justices*, 9 Nov.

Hewett, Dorothy Coade *later* Davies *and* Lilley 1923–2002

Australian playwright and poet. Her poetic works include
Windmill Country (1965) and *Halfway up the Mountain* (2001),
and her plays include *The Chapel Perilous* (1971) and *This Old
Man Comes Rolling Home* (1976).

70 I had a tremendous world in my head and more than
three-quarters of it will be buried with me.
1971 Sally Banner. *The Chapel Perilous*, act 2.

Hewlett, Sylvia Ann

US economist and writer.

71 What we've done in this country in the past few decades
is socialize the cost of growing old and privatize the cost
of childhood.
1991 In the *Washington Post*, 22 Feb.

Heyerdahl, Thor 1914–2002

Norwegian anthropologist and adventurer, best known for his
voyages and journeys, particularly the *Kon-Tiki* and *Ra*
expeditions, which reproduced the methods and materials
used by early peoples.

72 Just occasionally you find yourself in an odd situation.
You get into it by degrees and in the most natural way, but
when you are right in the midst of it you are suddenly
astonished and ask yourself how in the world it all came
about. If, for example, you put to sea on a wooden raft
with a parrot and five companions, it is inevitable that
sooner or later you will wake up one morning out at sea,
perhaps a little better rested than ordinarily, and begin to

think about it.

1948 *The Kon-Tiki Expedition: By Raft across the South Seas* (translated by F H Lyon).

Heyward, Du Bose 1885–1940

US lyricist.

73 Summer time an' the livin' is easy,
Fish are jumpin' an' the cotton is high.
Oh, yo' daddy's rich, and yo' ma is good-lookin',
So hush, little baby, don' yo' cry.
1935 'Summertime' from *Porgy and Bess* (with Ira Gershwin, music by George Gershwin).

74 It ain't necessarily so,
De t'ings dat yo' li'ble
To read in the Bible
It ain't necessarily so.
1935 'It Ain't Necessarily So' from *Porgy and Bess* (with Ira Gershwin, music by George Gershwin).

Heywood, Thomas c.1574–1641

English dramatist, poet and actor. He claimed to have contributed to 220 plays, but much of his work has been lost, including his unpublished 'Lives of All the Poets…'.

75 Content's a kingdom, and I wear that crown.
c.1607 *A Woman Killed with Kindness*, sc.7.

76 That Time could turn up his swift sandy glass,
To untell the days.
c.1607 *A Woman Killed with Kindness*, sc.13.

77 With this kiss I wed thee once again.
c.1607 *A Woman Killed with Kindness*, sc.16.

Hicks, Sir Edward Seymour 1871–1949

English actor-manager and author. A popular light comedian, he appeared in many successful plays written by himself.

78 You will recognize, my boy, the first sign of old age: it is when you go out into the streets of London and realize for the first time how young the policemen look.
Quoted in C R D Pulling *They Were Singing* (1952), ch.7.

Hicks, Sir John Richard 1904–89

English economist, Professor of Political Economy at Manchester (1938–46) and Oxford (1952–65). He laid the foundation of modern welfare economics, and was awarded the Nobel prize for economics in 1972 with Kenneth Arrow.

79 The best of all monopoly profits is a quiet life.
1935 *Econometrica*, 'The Theory of Monopoly'.

80 We ought to define a man's income as the maximum value which he can consume during a week, and still expect to be as well off at the end of the week as he was at the beginning.
1946 *Value and Capital* (2nd edn).

81 Weapons grow rusty if unused, and a Union which never strikes may lose the ability to organise a formidable strike, so that its threats become less effective.
1963 *The Theory of Wages* (2nd edn).

82 There is much of economic theory which is pursued for no better reason than its intellectual attraction; it is a good game.
1979 *Causality in Economics*.

Hickson, William Eward 1803–70

British educator and writer on singing.

83 If at first you don't succeed,
Try, try again.
'Try and Try Again'.

Highfield, Roger

English chemist, science editor of the *Daily Telegraph*.

84 Can Reindeer Fly? The Science of Christmas.
1998 Book title.

85 There is now evidence to suggest that Santa's grotto lies not in icy Lapland, but among Mediterranean olive groves on Gemiler, a tiny island off Turkey.
1998 *Can Reindeer Fly? The Science of Christmas*.

Higley, Brewster d.1911

US songwriter.

86 Oh give me a home where the buffalo roam,
Where the deer and the antelope play,
Where seldom is heard a discouraging word
And the skies are not cloudy all day.
c.1873 'Home on the Range'.

Hill, (Norman) Graham 1929–75

English racing driver. He won the Formula One World Championship in 1962 in a BRM. In 1967 he rejoined Lotus and won the world title for a second time (1968). He retired in 1975 and was killed in an air crash a few months later.

87 It is like balancing an egg on a spoon while shooting the rapids.
On motor racing. Quoted in Colin Jarman *The Guinness Dictionary of Sports Quotations* (1990).

Hill, Joe originally *Joel Hägglund* 1879–1915

US labour leader and songwriter.

88 You will eat, by and by,
In that glorious land above the sky;
Work and pray, live on hay,
You'll get pie in the sky when you die.
1911 *Songs of the Workers*, 'The Preacher and the Slave'.

Hill, Rowland 1744–1833

English popular preacher. He helped to found the Religious Tract Society and the London Missionary Society, and in 1801 published the popular *Village Dialogues*.

89 I do not see any reason why the devil should have all the good tunes.
Quoted in E W Broome *The Rev. Rowland Hill* (1881), ch.7.

Hillaby, John 1917–96

English writer, naturalist and prodigious walker. He journeyed on foot, usually alone, through Africa, across Europe and across the length of Britain.

90 Walking is a way of being somewhere, rather than striving to arrive.
1964 *Journey to the Jade Sea*.

91 Fortunately for poets and those who like to walk about in the open air, the beauty of landscape is not something that can be reduced easily to basic geology or a few

ready-wrapped phrases about what places are used for. Preference and prejudice creep in.
1968 *Journey through Britain.*

Hillary, Sir Edmund Percival 1919–

New Zealand mountaineer and explorer. He was a member of John Hunt's Everest expedition, and reached the summit with Sherpa Tenzing Norgay on 29 May 1953. He was New Zealand High Commissioner to India (1984–89) and has raised funds to provide hospitals and schools in the Himalayan region.

92 We knocked the bastard off!
1953 On returning from the summit of Everest, Jun. Quoted in his autobiography *Nothing Venture, Nothing Win* (1975), ch.10.

93 Better if he had said something natural like, 'Jesus, here we are.'
1974 Criticizing Neil Armstrong's premeditated words on first stepping onto the moon. Quoted in the *Sunday Times*.
➤ *See Armstrong 30:78.*

Hillebrand, Fred 1893–1963

US musical comedy actor and songwriter. He wrote *Ghosts of Broadway* for television and *Southlands*, an American opera.

94 Home James, and Don't Spare the Horses.
1934 Title of song.

Hillingdon, Lady 1857–1940

95 I am happy now that Charles calls on my bedchamber less frequently than of old. As it is, I now endure but two calls a week and when I hear his steps outside my door I lie down on my bed, close my eyes, open my legs, and think of England.
1912 Journal entry. Quoted in J Gathorne-Hardy *The Rise and Fall of the British Nanny* (1972), ch.3. The phrase is often rendered 'Lie back and think of England'.

Hilton, James 1900–54

English novelist. Several of his books have been filmed, including *Lost Horizon* (1933), *Goodbye, Mr Chips* (1934) and *Random Harvest* (1941).

96 Nothing really wrong with him—only anno domini, but that's the most fatal complaint of all, in the end.
1934 *Goodbye, Mr Chips*, ch.1.

Hindemith, Paul 1895–1963

German composer. His early neo-classical compositions gave way to chromatic works such as *Konzertmusik* (1930–3). His symphony *Mathis der Maler* (1934) was banned by the Nazis and he emigrated to Turkey then Britain, where he continued composing.

97 Tonality is a natural force, like gravity.
1937 *The Craft of Musical Composition.*

98 There are only two things worth aiming for: good music and a clean conscience.
1938 Letter to Willy Strecker.

99 There are only twelve notes. You must treat them carefully.
Quoted in Derek Watson *Music Quotations* (1991).

Hippocrates c.460 BC – c.370 BC

Greek physician, the 'father of medicine', associated with the profession's 'Hippocratic oath'. He practised on Cos. The

'Hippocratic Corpus' is a collection of 72 medical and surgical treatises, but probably not written by him.

1 *Ars longa vita brevis.*
The craft so long [to learn], the life so short.
Quoted in Seneca *De brevitate vitae*, 1. The original was in Greek.

2 Science is the father of knowledge, but opinion breeds ignorance.
The Canon, vol. 4 (translated by John Chadwick).

Hirohito 1901–89

Emperor of Japan during World War II. In 1945 he announced the Japanese surrender in a broadcast to his people and called for their support.

3 We declared war on America and Britain out of Our sincere desire to ensure Japan's self-preservation and the stabilisation of East Asia.
1945 Declaration, 15 Aug. Quoted in Edward Behr *Hirohito* (1989).

4 Endure what is difficult to endure and to suffer what is difficult to suffer.
1945 Declaration, 15 Aug. Quoted in Hugh Cortazzi *The Japanese Achievement* (1990).

5 It was not clear to me that our course was unjustified. Even now I am not sure how historians will allocate the responsibility for the war.
1945 Remark to General Mac Arthur, quoted in Edward Behr *Hirohito* (1989), introduction.

Hirsch, E(ric) D(onald), Jr 1928–

US educational reformer, Professor Emeritus of Education and Humanities at the University of Virginia. His works include *Cultural Literacy: What Every American Needs to Know* (1987) and *The Schools We Need and Why We Don't Have Them* (1996).

6 Cultural literacy is the oxygen of social intercourse.
1987 *Cultural Literacy: What Every American Needs to Know*, introduction.

Hirschfeld, Al 1903–

US artist, theatrical caricaturist for the *New York Times* for over 70 years.

7 I was a sculptor. But that's really drawing—a drawing you fall over in the dark, a three-dimensional drawing.
1988 In the *New York Times*, 21 Jun. 85th birthday interview.

8 The opening-night audience is mostly friends of the cast and backers of the show, and they come to applaud their money.
1988 In the *New York Times*, 21 Jun.

9 Writers who drew, they all seemed to draw the same way. They managed to keep that childlike creativity in their line.
Of Edward Lear and James Thurber. Quoted in Neil A Grauer *Remember Laughter* (1994).

Hirst, Damien 1965–

English painter and installation artist. In 1993 he caused a sensation at the Venice Biennale with his *Mother and Child, Divided*, where a cow and a calf, both sliced in half, expressed the severing of the closest bonds. He was awarded the 1995 Turner Prize.

10 What I really like is minimum effort for maximum effect.

Like with Picasso's *Bull's Head*—a bike seat and handlebars.
1995 In the *Idler*, 10 Jul.

11 You have to step over the boundaries sometimes just to find out where they are.
2002 Quoted on www.bbc.co.uk, 20 Sep.

12 Sometimes I have nothing to say. I often want to communicate this.
Quoted on www.bbc.co.uk.

Hitchcock, Sir Alfred Joseph 1899–1980

English film director, a master of suspense thrillers. His films include (in Britain) *The Thirty Nine Steps* (1935) and *The Lady Vanishes* (1938), (in Hollywood) *Rebecca* (1940), *Psycho* (1960) and many others.

13 If I made *Cinderella*, the audience would immediately be looking for a body in the coach.
1956 In *Newsweek*, 11 Jun.

14 Television has brought back murder into the home— where it belongs.
1965 In the *Observer*, 19 Dec.

15 The more successful the villain, the more successful the picture.
Quoted in François Truffaut *Hitchcock* (1968).

16 Actors are cattle. Disney probably has the right idea. He draws them and if he doesn't like them he tears them up.
Quoted in Doug McClelland *Star Speak* (1987).

Hitler, Adolf 1889–1945

German dictator, Leader of the Third Reich for 12 years. He was defeated by the Allies in World War II, during which over six million people were killed by the Nazis in concentration camps. He died in a Berlin bunker in 1945.

17 *Die breite Masse eines Volkes…einer großen Lüge leichter zum Opfer fällt als einer kleinen.*
The broad mass of a nation…will more easily fall victim to a big lie than to a small one.
1925 *Mein Kampf (My Struggle*, 1939), ch.10.

18 *Wer in Europa die Brandfackel des Krieges erhebt, kann nur das Chaos wünschen.*
Whoever lights the torch of war in Europe can wish for nothing but chaos.
1935 Speech in the Reichstag, Berlin, 21 May.

19 *Ich gehe mit traumwandlerischer Sicherheit den Weg, den mich die Vorsehung gehen heißt.*
I go the way that Providence dictates with the assurance of a sleepwalker.
1936 Speech in Munich, 14 Mar, in Max Domarus (ed) *Hitler: Reden und Proklamationen 1932–1945* (1962), p.606.

20 *Es ist die letzte territoriale Forderung, die ich Europa zu stellen habe, aber es ist die Forderung, von der ich nicht abgehe, und die ich, so Gott will, erfüllen werde.*
It is the last territorial claim which I have to make in Europe, but it is the claim from which I will not recede and which, God-willing, I will make good.
1938 On the Sudetenland. Speech in Berlin, 26 Sep. In Max Domarus (ed) *Hitler: Reden und Proklamationen 1932–1945* (1962), p.927.

21 *In Bezug auf das sudetendeutsche Problem meine Geduld jetzt zu Ende ist!*
With regard to the problem of the Sudeten Germans, my patience is now at an end!
1938 Speech in Berlin, 26 Sep, in Max Domarus (ed) *Hitler: Reden und Proklamationen 1932–1945* (1962), p.932.

Hobbes, Thomas 1588–1679

English political philosopher. He wrote several works on government, and at the exiled English court in Paris wrote his major work, *Leviathan* (1651), combining metaphysics, psychology and political philosophy. In 1652 he returned to England and submitted to Cromwell.

22 Science [is] knowledge of the truth of Propositions and how things are called.
1650 *Human Nature*, ch.6.

23 In Geometry (which is the only science that it hath pleased God hitherto to bestow on mankind) men begin at settling the significations of their words; which…they call Definitions.
1651 *Leviathan*, pt.1, ch.4.

24 Science is the knowledge of consequences and the dependence of one fact upon another.
1651 *Leviathan*, pt.1, ch.5.

25 The value, or worth of a man, is as of all other things, his price; that is to say, so much as would be given for the use of his power.
1651 *Leviathan*, pt.1, ch.10.

26 I put for a general inclination of all mankind, a perpetual and restless desire of power after power, that ceaseth only in death.
1651 *Leviathan*, pt.1, ch.11.

27 Whatsoever therefore is consequent to a time of war, where every man is enemy to every man; the same is consequent to the time wherein men live without other security than what their own strength, and their own invention shall furnish them withall. In such condition, there is no place for industry; because the fruit thereof is uncertain: and consequently no culture of the earth; no navigation, nor use of the commodities that may be imported by sea; no commodious building; no instruments of moving, and removing such things as require much force; no knowledge of the face of the Earth; no account of Time; no Arts; no Letters; no Society; and which is worst of all, continual fear, and danger of violent death; and the life of man, solitary, poor, nasty, brutish, and short.
1651 *Leviathan*, pt.1, ch.13.

28 They that are discontented under monarchy call it tyranny; and they that are displeased with aristocracy call it oligarchy; so also, they which find themselves grieved under a democracy call it anarchy, which signifies the want of government; and yet I think no man believes that want of government is any new kind of government.
1651 *Leviathan*, pt.2, ch.19.

29 A Free Man is he, that in those things, which by his strength and wit he is able to do, is not hindered to do what he has a will to.
1651 *Leviathan*, pt.2, ch.21.

30 The Enemy has been here in the night of our natural ignorance, and sown the tares of spiritual errors.
1651 *Leviathan*, pt.4, ch.44.

Hobhouse, John Cam, 1st Baron Broughton
1786–1869

English statesman. He wrote *Journey through Albania* with Lord Byron (1813), entered Parliament as a radical in 1820, and after succeeding to his baronetcy held several Cabinet posts.

31 It is said to be hard on His Majesty's Ministers to raise objections to this proposition. For my part, I think it no more hard on His Majesty's Opposition to compel them to take this course.
  1826 House of Commons, 27 Apr. This is the first recorded use of the term 'His Majesty's Opposition'.

Hobsbawm, Eric (John Ernest) 1917–

English historian, Professor Emeritus at Birkbeck College, London University. He is the author of numerous works of history including *Bandits* (1969) and *The Age of Extremes* (1994).

32 There is not much that even the most socially responsible scientists can do as individuals, or even as a group, about the social consequences of their activities.
  1970 In the *New York Review of Books*, 18 Nov.

33 Megalomania is the occupational disease of global victors, unless controlled by fear.
  2002 *Interesting Times: A Twentieth-Century Life*.

34 History may judge my politics…readers may judge my books.
  2002 *Interesting Times: A Twentieth-Century Life*.

Hobson, John Atkinson 1858–1940

English economist. An unorthodox figure, he believed 'under-consumption' to be the cause of unemployment. His works include an autobiography, *Confessions of an Economic Heretic* (1938).

35 Organised outdoor sports for the old ruling classes.
  1902 On militarism and colonialism. *Imperialism*.

Hoby, Sir Edward 1560–1617

English politician.

36 On the 5th November we began our Parliament, to which the King should have come in person but refrained, through a practice but that morning discovered. The plot was to have blown up the King…at one instant to have ruined the whole estate and kingdom of England.
  1605 Letter to the British Ambassador to Brussels, describing the Gunpowder Plot, 19 Nov.

Ho Chi Minh originally *Nguyen That Thanh* 1892–1969

Vietnamese political leader, who became President of North Vietnam in 1954. He led his country, first in the independence movement against the French (1946–54) and later in the war against US-backed South Vietnam in the 1960s.

37 Let him who has a rifle use his rifle, let him who has a sword use his sword! And let those who have no sword take up pick-axes and sticks.
  1946 Rallying call, Dec. Quoted in J Facouture *Ho Chi-Minh*.

38 It is better to sniff France's dung for a while than eat China's all our lives.
  1946 Attributed. Quoted in J Facouture *Ho Chi-Minh*.

Hockney, David 1937–

English painter, photographer, set designer and printmaker.

39 It's a myth that if you're liked by only four people it must be good. It might also be very bad: they might be your mother, your brother, your uncle and your aunt.
  1978 *David Hockney*.

40 Art has to move you and design does not, unless it's a good design for a bus.
  1988 In *The Guardian*, 26 Oct.

Hodges, Andrew

British mathematician.

41 When the history of science reaches Alan Turing, it hardly feels like history at all.
  1987 *Man Masters Nature*.

Hodgson, Ralph 1871–1962

English poet. He published three volumes of Georgian poems, on the themes of nature and England (1907–17). After lecturing in Japan, he settled in the US.

42 Time, you old gipsy man,
  Will you not stay,
  Put up your caravan
  Just for one day?
  1917 'Time, You Old Gipsy Man'.

43 I climbed a hill as light fell short,
  And rooks came home in scramble sort,
  And filled the trees and flapped and fought
  And sang themselves to sleep.
  1917 'Song of Honour'.

44 I stood upon that silent hill
  And stared into the sky until
  My eyes were blind with stars and still
  I stared into the sky.
  1917 'Song of Honour'.

45 When stately ships are twirled and spun
  Like whipping tops and help there's none
  And mighty ships ten thousand ton
  Go down like lumps of lead.
  1917 'Song of Honour'.

46 'Twould ring the bells of heaven
  The widest peal for years,
  If Parson lost his senses
  And people came to theirs,
  And he and they together
  Knelt down with angry prayers
  For tamed and shabby tigers
  And dancing dogs and bears,
  And wretched, blind, pit ponies,
  And little hunted hares.
  1917 'Bells of Heaven'.

Hoffer, Eric 1902–83

Migratory farm labourer, box factory worker and later longshoreman in San Francisco, who turned to writing social philosophy. His most influential work was *The True Believer* (1951), on mass movements in politics.

47 Where there is the necessary technical skill to move mountains, there is no need for the faith that moves mountains.

1955 *The Passionate State of Mind.*

Hoffman, Abbie 1936–89

US radical activist and writer. In 1968 he helped organize violent anti-Vietnam war demonstrations in Chicago, and was prominent in the 'Chicago Seven' trial in 1969. He was active in public demonstrations until 1986.

48 I always held my flower in a clenched fist.
1980 On his social activism as a 1960s flower child. *Soon to Be a Major Motion Picture.*

Hoffman, Dustin 1937–

US actor. He made his Broadway debut in 1961 and after a modest start achieved fame in the cinema with *The Graduate* (1967). He subsequently won Oscars for *Kramer vs Kramer* (1979) and *Rain Man* (1988).

49 If I'd seen me at a party, I'd never have gone up and met me.
1995 In *Dateline*, NBC TV broadcast, 8 Mar.

Hoffman, Hans 1880–1966

German-born US painter, who emigrated to the US in 1930. His work is characterized by bold, clashing colours.

50 The ability to simplify means to eliminate the unnecessary so that the necessary may speak.
1967 *Search for the Real.*

Hoffmann, Heinrich 1809–94

German physician and children's writer. His character Struwwelpeter is a slovenly, naughty boy who features in a book of cautionary tales written for his four-year-old son. He also wrote poetry, satire and medical works.

51 Augustus was a chubby lad;
Fat, ruddy cheeks Augustus had:
And everybody saw with joy
The plump and hearty, healthy boy.
He ate and drank as he was told,
And never let his soup get cold.
But one day, one cold winter's day,
He screamed out, 'Take the soup away!
O take the nasty soup away!
I won't have any soup today.'
1845 *Struwwelpeter*, 'Augustus'.

52 Look at little Johnny there,
Little Johnny Head-in-Air!
1845 *Struwwelpeter*, 'Johnny Head-in- Air'.

53 The door flew open, in he ran,
The great, long, red-legged scissor-man.
1845 *Struwwelpeter*, 'The Little Suck-a- Thumb'.

Hofstadter, Douglas R(ichard) 1945–

US cognitive scientist and writer, Professor of Cognitive Science and Computer Science at the University of Indiana. His *Gödel, Escher, Bach: An Eternal Golden Braid* (1979, Pulitzer Prize) is a series of ruminations on computers and cognition.

54 Hofstadter's Law: It always takes longer than you expect, even when you take into account Hofstadter's Law.
1979 *Gödel, Escher, Bach: An Eternal Golden Braid.*

Hofstadter, Richard 1916–70

US historian, Professor at Columbia University (1946–70). He applied theories of natural selection and ideology to the study of US capitalism and politics in works such as *The Age of Reform* (1955).

55 The nation seems to slouch onward into its uncertain future like some huge inarticulate beast, too much attainted by wounds and ailments to be robust, but too strong and resourceful to succumb.
Quoted in Hedrick Smith *The Power Game* (1988).

56 It has been our fate as a nation not to have ideologies but to be one.
Quoted in the *New York Times*, 2 Jul 1989.

Hogarth, William 1697–1764

English painter and engraver. He is known for his moral paintings and prints of low life (such as the *Industry and Idleness* series, 1747).

57 Simplicity, without variety, is wholly insipid.
1753 *The Analysis of Beauty.*

Hogg, James 1770–1835

Scottish poet and novelist. The self-taught 'Ettrick Shepherd' divided his time between literary Edinburgh and his native Borders countryside. His best-known work is the psychological novel *The Private Memoirs and Confessions of a Justified Sinner* (1824).

58 Lock the door, Lariston, lion of Liddesdale;
Lock the door, Lariston, Lowther comes on;
The Armstrongs are flying,
The widows are crying,
The Castletown's burning, and Oliver's gone!
c.1810 'Lock the Door, Lariston', stanza 1.

59 'What a wonderful boy he is!' said my mother.
'I'm feared he turn out to be a conceited gowk,' said old Barnet, the minister's man.
1824 *The Private Memoirs and Confessions of a Justified Sinner.*

60 Where the pools are bright and deep,
Where the grey trout lies asleep,
Up the river and o'er the lea,
That's the way for Billy and me.
1831 'A Boy's Song', stanza 1. From *A Poetic Mirror* 1829–31.

Hoggart, Simon David 1946–

English political commentator and broadcaster, political columnist with *Punch* (1979–85) and parliamentary reporter with *The Guardian* (1993–).

61 The nanny seemed to be extinct until 1975, when, like the coelacanth, she suddenly and unexpectedly reappeared in the shape of Margaret Thatcher.
1983 In *Vanity Fair*, Aug.

62 Everything we hear from Buckingham Palace suggests that [the Queen] is surrounded by stupid, blind, stuffy, self-promoting, rivalrous, gin-drinking courtiers, who haven't realised that a modern constitutional Monarch exists no longer by right but by consent and free will.
1997 Following the death of Diana, Princess of Wales. In *The Guardian*, 5 Sep.

63 Peter Mandelson is someone who can skulk in broad daylight.
1998 In *The Guardian*, 10 Jul.

Holiday, Billie 1915–59

US jazz singer. She was one of the most influential singers in jazz, and during the 1940s appeared in several films, although by the end of that decade she was falling victim to drug addiction.

64 Mama may have, papa may have,
But God bless the child that's got his own!
That's got his own.
1941 'God Bless the Child', with Arthur Herzog Jr.

65 People don't understand the sort of fight it takes to record what you want, to record the way you want to record it.
1956 *Lady Sings the Blues*, with William Duffy.

66 You can be up to your boobies in white satin, with gardenias in your hair and no sugar cane for miles, but you can still be working on a plantation.
1956 *Lady Sings the Blues*, with William Duffy.

Holland, Henry Scott 1847–1918

English clergyman and theologian, renowned for his eloquent preaching.

67 Death is nothing at all; it does not count. I have only slipped away into the next room.
1910 Sermon, Whit Sunday.

Hollander, Anne 1930–

US art historian. She explores the connections between fashion and art in *Seeing Through Clothes* (1975) and *Fabric of Vision: Dress and Drapery in Painting* (2002).

68 Dress is a form of visual art, a creation of images with the visible self as its medium.
1975 *Seeing Through Clothes*, ch.5.

Hollinghurst, Alan 1954–

English novelist. His novels include *The Swimming Pool Library* (1988), a highly acclaimed account of gay life; *The Folding Star* (1994); and *The Line of Beauty* (2004).

69 My life was a strange one that summer, the last summer of its kind there was ever to be. I was riding high on sex and self-esteem—it was my time, my *belle époque*—but all the while with a faint flicker of calamity, like flames around a photograph, something seen out of the corner of the eye.
1988 *The Swimming Pool Library*, ch.1.

Holman, James 1786–1857

English naval officer. Although blind from the age of 25 he continued travelling, firstly to the Continent (1819–22), then to the Russian Empire and later to Brazil, South Africa, South Asia, Tasmania, New South Wales and New Zealand.

70 On the summit of the precipice and in the deep green woods emotions as palpable and as true have agitated me as if I were surveying them with the blessing of sight. There was an intelligence in the winds of the hills and in the solemn stillness of the buried foliage that could not be misleading. It entered into my heart and I could have wept, not that I did not see, but that I could not portray all I felt.
1834 *A Voyage round the World*.

Holme (of Cheltenham), Richard Holme, Baron 1936–

British electoral reformer and writer. He represents the Liberal Democrat Party in the House of Lords and was appointed to the Privy Council in 2000.

71 She is the Enid Blyton of economics. Nothing must be allowed to spoil her simple plots.
1980 Of Margaret Thatcher. Speech at the Liberal Party conference, 10 Sep.

Holmes, John Clellon 1926–88

US writer. He is credited with first use of the phrase 'The Beat Generation'. His own novels include *Go* (1952) and *The Horn* (1958).

72 To Walden the saxophone was, at once, his key to the world in which he found himself, and the way by which that world was rendered impotent to brand him either a failure or madman or Negro or saint.
1958 *The Horn*, 'Chorus: Walden'.

73 Jazz music has haunted America for seventy years. It has tempted us out of our lily-white reserve with its black promise of untrammeled joy.
1979 Preface to reprint of *The Horn*.

74 Some books accrete things to themselves like a magnet. The writer risks sterility by subjecting the mysterious power of imagination to the devices of mere comprehension.
1979 Preface to reprint of *The Horn*.

Holmes, Oliver Wendell 1809–94

US physician and writer, who in 1842 discovered that puerperal fever was contagious. His essays in the *Atlantic Monthly* were collected in four volumes, including *The Autocrat of the Breakfast Table* (1857–8) and *The Professor at the Breakfast Table* (1858–9). He also published three novels and several volumes of poetry.

75 Man wants but little drink below,
But wants that little strong.
1848 'A Song of Other Days'.

76 And, when you stick on conversation's burrs,
Don't strew your pathway with those dreadful *urs*.
1848 'A Rhymed Lesson'.

77 They are the brute beasts of the intellectual domain.
1857–8 Of facts. *The Autocrat of the Breakfast Table*, ch.1.

78 A thought is often original, though you have uttered it a hundred times.
1857–8 *The Autocrat of the Breakfast Table*, ch.1.

79 When one has had *all* his conceit taken out of him, when he has lost *all* his illusions, his feathers will soon soak through, and he will fly no more.
1857–8 *The Autocrat of the Breakfast Table*, ch.1.

80 Some of the sharpest men in argument are notoriously unsound in judgment.
1857–8 *The Autocrat of the Breakfast Table*, ch.1.

81 Put not your trust in money, but put your money in trust.
1857–8 *The Autocrat of the Breakfast Table*, ch.2.

82 Build thee more stately mansions, O my soul,
As the swift seasons roll!
Leave thy low-vaulted past!
1857–8 *The Autocrat of the Breakfast Table*, ch.4.

83 Truth is tough. It will not break, like a bubble, at a touch; nay, you may kick it about all day like a football, and it will be round and full at evening.
1857–8 *The Autocrat of the Breakfast Table*, ch.5.

84 Sin has many tools, but a lie is the handle which fits them all.
1857–8 *The Autocrat of the Breakfast Table*, ch.6.

85 Boston State-House is the hub of the solar system. You couldn't pry that out of a Boston man, if you had the tire of all creation straightened out for a crowbar.
1857–8 *The Autocrat of the Breakfast Table*, ch.6.

86 The world's great men have not commonly been great scholars, nor its great scholars great men.
1857–8 *The Autocrat of the Breakfast Table*, ch.6.

87 Talk about those subjects you have had long in your mind, and listen to what others say about subjects you have studied but recently. Knowledge and timber shouldn't be much used till they are seasoned.
1857–8 *The Autocrat of the Breakfast Table*, ch.6.

88 Shabby gentility has nothing so characteristic as its hat.
1857–8 *The Autocrat of the Breakfast Table*, ch.8.

89 Have you heard of the wonderful one-hoss shay
That was built in such a logical way,
It ran a hundred years to a day.
1857–8 *The Autocrat of the Breakfast Table*, ch.11.

90 Nothing is so common-place as to wish to be remarkable.
1857–8 *The Autocrat of the Breakfast Table*, ch.12.

91 Fate tried to conceal him by calling him Smith.
1858 Of Samuel Francis Smith.'The Boys'.

92 Depart,—be off,—excede,—evade,—erump!
1858 'Aestivation'.

93 We must have a weak spot or two in a character before we can love it much.
1858–9 *The Professor at the Breakfast Table*, ch.3.

94 Apology is only egotism wrong side out.
1858–9 *The Professor at the Breakfast Table*, ch.6.

95 Fashion is only the attempt to realize Art in living forms and social intercourse.
1858–9 *The Professor at the Breakfast Table*, ch.6.

96 A moment's insight is sometimes worth a life's experience.
1857–8 *The Professor at the Breakfast Table*, ch.10.

97 Lord of all being, throned afar,
Thy glory flames from sun and star;
Centre and soul of every sphere,
Yet to each loving heart how near!
1858–9 *The Professor at the Breakfast Table*,'A Sun-Day Hymn'.

98 It is the province of knowledge to speak, and it is the privilege of wisdom to listen.
1872 *The Poet at the Breakfast Table*, ch.10.

99 To be seventy years young is sometimes far more cheerful and hopeful than to be forty years old.
1879 Letter to Julia Ward Howe, 27 May.

1 The morning cup of coffee has an exhilaration about it which the cheering influence of the afternoon or evening cup of tea cannot be expected to reproduce.
1891 *Over the Teacups*, ch.1.

Holmes, Oliver Wendell, Jr   1841–1935

US lawyer, Professor at Harvard Law School, Justice of the US Supreme Court for 30 years.

2 For the rational study of the law the blackletter man may be the man of the present, but the man of the future is the man of statistics and the master of economics.
1897 'The Path of the Law', in the *Harvard Law Review*, 10:469.

Holroyd, Michael de Courcy Fraser   1935–

English biographer. He is married to the novelist Margaret Drabble.

3 Between history and the novel stands biography, their unwanted offspring, which has brought a great embarrassment to them both.
2002 *Works on Paper: The Craft of Biography & Autobiography*, 'The Case against Biography'.

4 In the historian's view biography is a kind of frogspawn—it takes ten thousand biographies to make one small history.
2002 *Works on Paper: The Craft of Biography & Autobiography*, 'The Case against Biography'.

Holst, Gustav Theodore   1874–1934

British composer, of Swedish origin. Prevented by neuritis in his hand from becoming a concert pianist, he learned the trombone and taught music before establishing himself as a composer.

5 Never compose anything unless the not composing of it becomes a positive nuisance to you.
1921 Letter to W G Whittaker.

Holt, Harold Edward   1908–67

Australian politician. He succeeded Robert Menzies as Prime Minister in 1966 but disappeared while swimming in the sea off Victoria the following year. He was a supporter of US policy in Vietnam.

6 All the way with LBJ.
1966 Speech, Washington DC, Jun.

Holub, Miroslav   1923–98

Czech poet and immunologist.

7 Humankind can generally be divided into hunters and people who cope with consequences.
1990 *The Dimensions of the Present Moment and Other Essays*.

Homans, George C   1910–89

US sociologist, Professor at Harvard University.

8 It is really intolerable that we can say only one thing at a time; for social behavior displays many features at the same time, and so in taking them up one by one we necessarily do outrage to its rich, dark, organic unity.
1961 *Social Behavior: Its Elementary Forms*.

9 The rule of distributive justice is a statement of what ought to be, and what people say ought to be is determined in the long run and with some lag by what they find in fact to be the case.
1974 *Social Behavior: Its Elementary Forms* (rev edn).

Home of the Hirsel, Alec (Alexander Frederick) Douglas-Home, Baron 1903–95

Scottish Conservative statesman. An MP from 1931, he was Chamberlain's secretary during negotiations with Hitler and Mussolini (1937–9). He succeeded as 14th Earl of Home (1951), but after Macmillan's resignation he renounced his peerage and became Prime Minister (1963–4).

10 As far as the fourteenth earl is concerned, I suppose Mr Wilson, when you come to think of it, is the fourteenth Mr Wilson.
1963 Response to Harold Wilson's claim that the democratic process had 'ground to a halt with a fourteenth earl' when Home won the premiership. Reported in the *Daily Telegraph*, 22 Oct.

11 There are two problems in my life. The political ones are insoluble, and the economic ones are incomprehensible.
1964 Speech, Jan.

12 When I read economic documents, I have to have a box of matches and start moving them into position, to illustrate and simplify the points to myself.
1965 *The Making of the Prime Minister.*

13 Fishing is undoubtedly a form of madness but, happily for the once-bitten, there is no cure.
1976 Quoted in Colin Jarman *The Guinness Dictionary of Sports Quotations* (1990).

14 My wife had an uncle who could never walk down the nave of his abbey without wondering whether it would take spin.
In *The Twentieth Century Revisited*, BBC T V programme, 1982.

15 Oh God, if there be cricket in heaven, let there also be rain.
Quoted in Helen Exley *Cricket Quotations* (1992).

Homer 8c BC

Greek epic poet, in antiquity said to have been blind, to whom are attributed the *Iliad* (dealing with episodes in the Trojan War) and the *Odyssey* (dealing with the subsequent wanderings of Odysseus). Scholars now date the poems to the 8c BC, as the culmination of an oral tradition dating back to the Bronze Age.

16 He who battles with the immortals does not live long, nor do his children prattle about his knees when he has returned from battle.
c.700 BC *Iliad*, bk.5, l.407 (translated by Martin Hammond).

17 Like that of leaves is a generation of men.
c.700 BC *Iliad*, bk.6, l.146 (translated by Martin Hammond).

18 Always to be best, and to be distinguished above the rest.
c.700 BC Motto of the hero Glaucus. *Iliad*, bk.6, l.208 (translated by Martin Hammond).

19 Victory switches from man to man.
c.700 BC *Iliad*, bk.6, l.339 (translated by Martin Hammond).

20 One omen is best of all—to fight for your country.
c.700 BC *Iliad*, bk.7, l.243 (translated by Martin Hammond).

21 Tribeless, lawless, homeless is he who loves the horror of civil war.
c.700 BC *Iliad*, bk.9, l.63–4 (translated by Martin Hammond).

22 This is the best portent, to fight in defence of one's country.
c.700 BC *Iliad*, bk.12, l.243 (translated by Martin Hammond).

23 It is no shame for a man to die fighting for his country.
c.700 BC *Iliad*, bk.15, l.496 (translated by Martin Hammond).

24 Tell me, Muse, of the man of many ways, who was driven
far journeys, after he had sacked Troy's sacred citadel.
Many were they whose cities he saw, whose minds he learned of,
many the pains he suffered in his spirit on the wide sea,
struggling for his own life and the homecoming of his companions.
c.700 BC *Odyssey*, bk.1, l.1–5 (translated by Richmond Lattimore).

Homer, Winslow 1836–1910

US painter, known for his watercolours of rural and domestic scenes and especially for his seascapes after 1881.

25 The life that I have chosen gives me my full hours of enjoyment for the balance of my life. The sun will not rise, or set, without my notice, and thanks.
1895 Letter to his brother, Charles, 23 Feb.

26 I regret very much that I have painted a picture that requires any description.
On being asked about the meaning of a painting by a dealer. Quoted by Andrea Bennett in the *New York Times Book Review*, 15 Sep 1991.

Honegger, Arthur 1892–1955

French composer of Swiss descent. One of the group of Parisian composers known as *Les Six*, he established his reputation with the oratorio *King David* (1921). Subsequent works include the dramatic oratorio *Joan of Arc at the Stake* (1936).

27 The modern composer is a madman who persists in manufacturing an article which nobody wants.
1951 *I Am a Composer.*

28 Composing is not a profession. It is a mania—a harmless madness.
1951 *I Am a Composer.*

29 To write music is to raise a ladder without a wall to lean it against. There is no scaffolding: the building under construction is held in balance only by the miracle of a kind of internal logic, an innate sense of proportion.
1951 *I Am a Composer.*

30 The public doesn't want new music: the main thing it demands of a composer is that he be dead.
1951 *I Am a Composer.*

Honorius of Autun fl.1106–35

French ecclesiastic, and the author of numerous philosophical, theological and devotional works.

31 *Universitas in modo citharae sit disposita, in qua diversa genera in modo chordarum sit consonantia.*
The universe is arranged like a cithera, in which different kinds of things sound together harmoniously, just as they do in a chord.
c.1120 *Liber Duodecim Questionum*, ch.2.

32 *Quid confert animae pugna Hectoris, vel disputatio Platonis, aut carmina Maronis, vel neniae Nasonis?*
Of what benefit to the soul are the struggles of Hector, the disputations of Plato, the songs of Virgil, or the dirges of Ovid?
c.1130 *Gemma Animae*, prologue.

Hood, Thomas 1799–1845

English poet and journalist. His collection *Odes and Addresses* (1825) was followed by several volumes of humorous verse and political poems such as 'The Song of the Shirt' (1843).

33 I saw old Autumn in the misty morn
Stand shadowless like Silence, listening
To silence.
1823 'Ode: Autumn'.

34 Ben Battle was a soldier bold,
And used to war's alarms:
But a cannon-ball took off his legs,
So he laid down his arms!
1826 'Faithless Nelly Gray'.

35 For here I leave my second leg,
And the Forty-second Foot!
1826 'Faithless Nelly Gray'.

36 The love that loves a scarlet coat
Should be more uniform.
1826 'Faithless Nelly Gray'.

37 I remember, I remember,
The house where I was born,
The little window where the sun
Came peeping in at morn;
He never came a wink too soon,
Nor brought too long a day,
But now, I often wish the night
Had borne my breath away!
1826 'I Remember'.

38 I remember, I remember,
The fir trees dark and high;
I used to think their slender tops
Were close against the sky:
It was a childish ignorance,
But now 'tis little joy
To know I'm farther off from heav'n
Than when I was a boy.
1826 'I Remember'.

39 She stood breast high amid the corn,
Clasped by the golden light of morn,
Like the sweetheart of the sun,
Who many a glowing kiss had won.
1827 'Ruth'.

40 The sedate, sober, silent, serious, sad-coloured sect.
1839 Of the Quakers. *Comic Annual*, 'The Doves and the Crows'.

41 'Extremes meet', as the whiting said with its tail in its mouth.
1839 *Comic Annual*, 'The Doves and the Crows'.

42 Holland…lies so low they're only saved by being dammed.
1840 *Up the Rhine*, 'Letter from Martha Penny to Rebecca Page'.

43 Home-made dishes that drive one from home.
1841–3 *Miss Kilmansegg and her Precious Leg*, 'Her Misery'.

44 When Eve upon the first of Men
The apple pressed with specious cant,
Oh! what a thousand pities then
That Adam was not Adamant!
1842 'A Reflection'.

45 With fingers weary and worn,
With eyelids heavy and red,
A woman sat, in unwomanly rags

Plying her needle and thread—
Stitch! stitch! stitch!
In poverty, hunger, and dirt.
And still with a voice of dolorous pitch
She sang the 'Song of the Shirt'.
1843 'The Song of the Shirt'.

46 O! men with sisters dear,
O! men with mothers and wives!
It is not linen you're wearing out,
But human creatures' lives!
1843 'The Song of the Shirt'.

47 Oh! God! that bread should be so dear,
And flesh and blood so cheap!
1843 'The Song of the Shirt'.

48 Take her up tenderly,
Lift her with care;
Fashioned so slenderly,
Young, and so fair!
1844 'The Bridge of Sighs'.

49 Mad from life's history,
Glad to death's mystery,
Swift to be hurled—
Anywhere, anywhere,
Out of the world!
1844 'The Bridge of Sighs'.

50 But evil is wrought by want of thought,
As well as want of heart!
1844 'The Lady's Dream'.

51 No sun—no moon!
No morn—no noon
No dawn—no dusk—no proper time of day.
1844 'No'.

52 No warmth, no cheerfulness, no healthful ease,
No comfortable feel in any member—
No shade, no shine, no butterflies, no bees,
No fruits, no flowers, no leaves, no birds,—
November!
1844 'No'.

53 What is a modern poet's fate?
To write his thoughts upon a slate;
The critic spits on what is done,
Gives it a wipe—and all is gone.
'A Joke'. Collected in Hallam Tennyson *Alfred Lord Tennyson* (1897), vol.2, ch.3.

Hooker, Richard 1554–1600

English theologian, writer of an extensive treatise on the basis of Church government, which had a powerful influence on Anglican doctrine.

54 See we not plainly that obedience of creatures unto the law of nature is the stay of the whole world?
1594 *Laws of Ecclesiastical Polity*.

55 Man doth seek a triple perfection: first a sensual, consisting in those things which very life itself requireth either as necessary supplements, or as beauties and ornaments thereof; then an intellectual, consisting in those things which none underneath man is either capable of or acquainted with; lastly a spiritual and divine, consisting in those things whereunto we tend by supernatural means here, but cannot here attain unto them.

1594 *Laws of Ecclesiastical Polity.*

56 They must have hearts very dry and tough, from whom the melody of psalms doth not sometime draw that wherein a mind religiously affected delighteth.
1594 *Laws of Ecclesiastical Polity.*

Hoover, Herbert Clark 1874–1964

US Republican politician. As 31st President (1929–33), his opposition to direct assistance for the unemployed in the recession led to defeat by Roosevelt in 1932. He assisted with various US–European economic relief programmes after World War II.

57 The grass will grow in the streets of a hundred cities, a thousand towns; the weeds will overrun the fields of millions of farms if [tariff protection] is taken away.
1923 Presidential campaign speech, 22 Oct.

58 We are nearer today to the ideal of the abolition of poverty and fear from the lives of men and women than ever before in any land.
1923 Presidential campaign speech, 22 Oct.

59 The American system of rugged individualism.
1928 Speech, New York City, 22 Oct.

60 People moved in hushed and anxious hours while his life lingered on. It was thus I learned that some great man was at the helm of our country.
1951 On President Garfield's assassination, 2 Jul 1881. *The Memoirs of Herbert Hoover*, vol 1.

61 I should have been glad to have humanity forget all about stray alcoholic drinks…but in the present stage of human progress, this vehicle of joy could not be generally suppressed by federal law.
1951 On prohibition. *The Memoirs of Herbert Hoover*, vol.1.

62 All men are equal before a fish.
1951 Quoted in Colin Jarman *The Guinness Dictionary of Sports Quotations* (1990).

63 Democracy is not a polite employer… The only way out of elective office is to get sick or die or get kicked out.
1952 *The Memoirs of Herbert Hoover*, vol.2.

64 The White House…a palace more comfortable than that of most kings.
1952 *The Memoirs of Herbert Hoover*, vol.2.

65 A chameleon on plaid.
On his opponent Franklin D Roosevelt. Quoted in James MacGregor Burns *The Lion and the Fox* (1956).

66 Honour is not the exclusive property of any political party.
1964 In *Christian Science Monitor*, 21 May.

67 Sportsmanship, next to the Church, is the greatest teacher of morals.
Quoted in John Rickards Betts *America's Sporting Heritage: 1850–1950* (1974).

68 Dewey has no inner reserve of knowledge on which to draw for his thinking. A man couldn't wear a moustache like that without having it affect his mind.
Quoted in Richard Norton Smith *An Uncommon Man* (1984).

Hoover, J(ohn) Edgar 1895–1972

US public servant, director of the Federal Bureau of Investigation (1924–72). He remodelled it, making it more efficient, but his vendettas against liberal activists in later years were criticized.

69 We of the FBI are powerless to act in cases of oral–genital intimacy, unless it has in some way obstructed interstate commerce.
Quoted in the *New York Times*, 6 Oct 1980.

70 You are honored by your friends…distinguished by your enemies. I have been very distinguished.
Address to the House Sub-Committee on Appropriations. Quoted in Curt Gentry *J Edgar Hoover* (1991).

Hope, A(lec) D(erwent) 1907–2000

Australian poet and critic. He retired from academic life in 1972 to concentrate on poetry. Works include *The Wandering Isles* (1955), *The Drifting Continent* (1979) and *Orpheus* (1991).

71 Historians spend their lives and lavish ink
Explaining how great commonwealths collapse
From great defects of policy—perhaps
The cause is sometimes simpler than they think.
… Have more states perished, then,
For having shackled the enquiring mind,
Than those who, in their folly not less blind,
Trusted the servile womb to breed free men?
1965 'Advice to Young Ladies', in *Collected Poems 1930–1970* (1972).

72 They call her a young country, but they lie:
She is the last of lands, the emptiest,
A woman beyond her change of life, a breast
Still tender but within the womb is dry.
'Australia', in *Collected Poems 1930–1970* (1972).

Hope, Anthony *pseudonym of Sir Anthony Hope Hawkins* 1863–1933

English novelist. His novel *The Prisoner of Zenda* (1894), a romantic adventure set in fictitious Ruritania, established him as one of the most popular of all Victorian writers.

73 Oh, for an hour of Herod!
1904 On witnessing the first performance of J M Barrie's children's play *Peter Pan*. Quoted in Denis Mackail *Story of JMB* (1941), ch.17. Records exist of something similar having been said by the English actress Dorothea Jordan when watching the child actor William Betty and his imitators in the early 19c.

Hope, Bob *originally Leslie Townes Hope* 1903–2003

English-born US actor and humorist. With Bing Crosby and Dorothy Lamour he appeared in the successful *Road to…* comedies (1940–52). An entertainer of troops in World War II and a noted golfer and humanitarian, he became a show-business institution.

74 If you watch a game, it's fun. If you play it, it's recreation. If you work at it, it's golf.
Quoted in the *Reader's Digest*, Oct 1958.

75 I don't know what people have got against Jimmy Carter. He's done nothing.
1980 Campaign speech for Ronald Reagan, 2 Nov.

76 Fish don't applaud.
1989 When asked why he didn't retire and go fishing, in the *New York Times*, 28 Sep.

Hopkins, Sir Anthony 1937–

Welsh-born US film and stage actor.

77 I always check the last page of the script to see if I'm on it.

I have a bit of an ego, you know.
1997 In the *Toronto Sun*, 24 Sep.

Hopkins, Gerard Manley 1844–89

English poet and Jesuit priest. His work is characterized by religious subjects and the use of natural imagery. His poems include 'The Wreck of the Deutschland' (1876), 'Pied Beauty' (1877) and 'The Windhover' (1877). His poetry was written in secret, only published 30 years after his death.

78 I have desired to go
Where springs not fail,
To fields where flies no sharp and sided hail
And a few lilies blow
And I have asked to be
Where no storms come,
Where the green swell is in the havens dumb,
And out of the swing of the sea.
1864 'Heaven-Haven'.

79 Crystal sincerity hath found no shelter but in a fool's cap.
1864 'Floris in Italy'. Collected in H House and G Storey (eds) *The Journals and Papers of Gerard Manley Hopkins* (1959), p.42.

80 Elected Silence, sing to me
And beat upon my whorled ear,
Pipe me to pastures still and be
The music that I care to hear.
1866 'The Habit of Perfection'.

81 Palate, the hutch of tasty lust,
Desire not to be rinsed with wine:
The can must be so sweet, the crust
So fresh that come in fasts divine!
1866 'The Habit of Perfection'.

82 I did say yes
O at lightning and lashed rod;
Thou heardst me truer than tongue confess
Thy terror, O Christ, O God.
1876 'The Wreck of the Deutschland', pt.1, stanza 2.

83 The world is charged with the grandeur of God.
It will flame out like shining from shook foil…
Generations have trod, have trod, have trod;
And all is seared with trade; bleared, smeared with toil;
And wears man's smudge and shares man's smell: the soil
Is bare now, nor can foot feel, being shod.
1877 'God's Grandeur'.

84 Because the Holy Ghost over the bent
World broods with warm breast and with ah! bright
wings.
1877 'God's Grandeur'.

85 Glory be to God for dappled things.
1877 'Pied Beauty'.

86 All things counter, original, spare, strange;
Whatever is fickle, freckled (who knows how?)
With swift, slow; sweet, sour; adazzle, dim;
He fathers-forth whose beauty is past change:
Praise him.
1877 'Pied Beauty'.

87 The glassy peartree leaves and blooms, they brush
The descending blue; that blue is all in a rush
With richness.
1877 'Spring'.

88 Look at the stars! look, look up at the skies!
O look at all the fire-folk sitting in the air!

The bright boroughs, the circle-citadels there!
1877 'The Starlight Night'.

89 I caught this morning morning's minion, kingdom of
Daylight's dauphin, dapple-dawn-drawn Falcon.
1877 'The Windhover'.

90 My heart in hiding
Stirred for a bird,—the achieve of, the mastery of the
thing!
1877 'The Windhover'.

91 Towery city and branchy between towers;
Cuckoo-echoing, bell-swarmèd, lark-charmèd, rook-
racked, river-rounded.
1879 Of Oxford. 'Duns Scotus's Oxford', published 1918.

92 Ten or twelve, only ten or twelve
Strokes of havoc unselve
The sweet especial scene
Rural scene, a rural scene
Sweet especial rural scene.
1879 'Binsey Poplars'.

93 Margaret, are you grieving
Over Goldengrove unleaving?
1880 'Spring and Fall: to a young child'.

94 Ah! as the heart grows older
It will come to such sights colder
By and by, not spare a sigh
Though worlds of wanwood leafmeal lie;
And yet you *will* weep and know why.
1880 'Spring and Fall: to a young child'.

95 It is the blight man was born for,
It is Margaret you mourn for.
1880 'Spring and Fall: to a young child'.

96 I can scarcely fancy myself to ask a superior to publish a
volume of my verse and I own that humanly there is very
little likelihood of that ever coming to pass. And to be
sure if I chose to look at things on one side and not the
other I could of course regret this bitterly. But there is
more peace and it is the holier lot to be unknown than to
be known.
1881 Letter to Richard Watson Dixon, 29 Oct. Collected in C C
Abbott (ed) *The Correspondence of Gerard Manley Hopkins and
Richard Watson Dixon* (1935).

97 What would the world be, once bereft
Of wet and wildness? Let them be left,
O let them be left, wildness and wet;
Long live the weeds and the wilderness yet.
1881 'Inversnaid'.

98 Time has three dimensions and one positive pitch or
direction. It is therefore not so much like any river or any
sea as like the Sea of Galilee, which has the Jordan
running through it and giving a current to the whole.
1881 'Creation and Redemption: The Great Sacrifice'. Collected
in C Devlin (ed) *The Sermons and Devotional Writings of Gerard
Manley Hopkins* (1959), ch.8.

99 God…is so great that all things give him glory if you
mean they should.
1882 'The Principle or Foundation', closing words. Collected in
G Roberts (ed) *Gerard Manley Hopkins. Selected Prose* (1980).

1 Wild air, world-mothering air,
Nestling me everywhere.
1883 'The Blessed Virgin Compared to the Air We Breathe'.

2 Not, I'll not, carrion comfort, Despair, not feast on thee;

Not untwist—slack they may be—these last strands of man
In me or, most weary, cry *I can no more*. I can;
Can something, hope, wish day come, not choose not to be.
1885 'Carrion Comfort'.

3 That night, that year
Of now done darkness I wretch lay wrestling with (my God!) my God.
1885 'Carrion Comfort'.

4 No worst, there is none. Pitched past pitch of grief,
More pangs will, schooled at forepangs, wilder wring.
Comforter, where, where is your comforting?
1885 'No worst, there is none'.

5 O the mind, mind has mountains; cliffs of fall
Frightful, sheer, no-man-fathomed. Hold them cheap
May who ne'er hung there.
1885 'No worst, there is none'.

6 Here! creep,
Wretch, under a comfort serves in a whirlwind: all
Life death does end and each day dies with sleep.
1885 'No worst, there is none'.

7 The fine pleasure is not to do a thing but to feel that you could... If I could but get on, if I could but produce a work I should not mind its being buried, silenced, and going no further; but it kills me to be time's eunuch and never to beget.
1885 Letter to Robert Bridges, 1 Sep. Collected in C C Abbott (ed) *The Correspondence of Gerard Manley Hopkins and Robert Bridges* (1935).

8 I am all at once what Christ is, since he was what I am, and
This Jack, joke, poor potsherd, patch, matchwood, immortal diamond,
Is immortal diamond.
1888 'That Nature is a Heraclitean Fire'.

9 Thou art indeed just, Lord, if I contend
With thee; but, sir, so what I plead is just.
Why do sinners' ways prosper? and why must
Disappointment all I endeavour end?
1889 'Thou art indeed just, Lord'.

10 Birds build—but not I build; no, but strain,
Time's eunuch, and not breed one work that wakes.
Mine, O thou lord of life, send my roots rain.
1889 'Thou art indeed just, Lord'.

11 The male quality is the creative gift.
Quoted in C C Abbott (ed) *Correspondence of Gerard Manley Hopkins and Richard Watson Dixon* (1935).

12 I always knew in my heart Walt Whitman's mind to be more like my own than any other man's living.
Quoted in Denis Donoghue *England, Their England* (1988).

Hopkins, J Castell 1864–1923

Canadian editor and writer.

13 Canada only needs to be known in order to be great.
1901 *The Story of the Dominion*, preface.

Hopper, Edward 1882–1967

US painter, known for his haunting, atmospheric paintings of empty streets and houses. His works include *Early Sunday Morning* (1930).

14 A nation's art is greatest when it most reflects the character of its people.
Quoted in Anatole Broyard *Aroused by Books* (1974).

15 It's probably a reflection of my own, if I may say, loneliness. I don't know. It could be the whole human condition.
On the mood and content of his paintings. Quoted in the *Washington Post*, 25 Jun 1995.

Hopper, Grace Murray 1906–92

US computer scientist and naval officer, developer of the Cobol computer language.

16 Life was simple before World War II. After that, we had systems.
Quoted in the OCLC Newsletter, no.167, Mar/Apr 1987.

17 We've tended to forget that no computer will ever ask a new question.
Quoted in the OCLC Newsletter, no.167, Mar/Apr 1987.

18 A ship in port is safe but that's not what ships are built for.
1987 Address at Trinity College, Washington. Reported in *Time*, 22 Jun.

Horace *full name* ***Quintus Horatius Flaccus*** 65 BC–8 BC

Roman poet of the Augustan age. His works, which survive in their entirety, include the *Satires* (c.35 BC), *Odes* (c.23–13 BC), *Epistles* (c.19 BC) and the *Ars Poetica* (c.19 BC). His poetry is characterized by an urbane sociability and a love of the country.

19 *Carpe diem.*
Seize the day.
Odes, bk.1, no.11, l.8.

20 *Nunc est bibendum!*
Now is the time to drink!
Odes, bk.1, no.37, l.1.

21 *Eheu fugaces, Postume, Postume,*
labuntur anni.
Oh, my Postumus, Postumus, the fleeting years are slipping by.
Odes, bk.2, no.14, l.1–2.

22 *Odi profanum vulgus et arceo;*
Favete linguis; carmina non prius
Audita Musarum sacerdos
Virginibus puerisque canto.
I despise the uninitiated mob and I warn them off: keep your tongues well-omened; I, priest of the Muses, am singing songs, never heard before, to girls and boys.
Odes, bk.3, no.1, l.1–4 (translated by G Williams).

23 *Dulce et decorum est pro patria mori.*
It is a sweet and seemly thing to die for one's country.
Odes, bk.3, no.2, l.13.
➤ See Owen 632:57.

24 *Exegi monumentum, aere perennius.*
I have completed a memorial more lasting than bronze.
Odes, bk.3, no.30, l.1.

25 *Vixere fortes ante Agamemnona*
Multi; sed omnes illacrimabiles
Urgentur ignotique longa
Nocte, carent quia vate sacro.
Many brave men lived before Agamemnon's time; but

they are all unmourned and unknown, covered by the long night, because they lack their sacred poet.
Odes, bk.4, no.9, l.25–8.

26 *Dulce est desipere in loco.*
Frivolity is sweet, at the right time.
Odes, bk.4, no.12, l.28.

27 *Quo semel est imbuta recens servabit odorem testa diu.*
The first scent you pour in a jar lasts for years.
Epistulae, bk.1, no.2, l.69.

28 *Concordia discors.*
Harmony in discord.
Epistulae, bk.1, no.12, l.7.

29 *Graecia capta ferum victorem cepit et artes Intulit agresti Latio.*
Captive Greece overcame her savage conqueror and brought the arts into rustic Latium.
Epistulae, bk.2, no.1, l.156–7.

30 *Brevis esse laboro, Obscurus fio.*
I try hard to be succinct, and am merely obscure.
Ars Poetica, l.25–6.

31 *Si vis me flere, dolendum est Primum ipse tibi.*
If you wish me to shed tears you must first feel pain yourself.
Ars Poetica, l.102–3.

32 *Parturiunt montes; nascetur ridiculus mus.*
The mountains are in labour, and there will be born an absurd little mouse.
Ars Poetica, l.139.

33 *Omne tulit punctum, qui miscuit utile dulci.*
The man who has mixed profit with pleasure wins everyone's approval.
Ars Poetica, l.343.

34 *Indignor quandoque bonus dormitat Homerus.*
I am vexed when the worthy Homer nods.
Ars Poetica, l.359.

35 *Est modus in rebus.*
There is a measure in things.
Satirae, bk.1, no.1, l.106.

Horner, Jack 1946–

Curator of Palaeontology, Museum of the Rockies.

36 In the lifetime of one person, we went from figuring out where we came from to figuring out how to get rid of ourselves.
1993 On the 80-year period from Darwin's *Origin of Species* to the first nuclear bomb. In *Time*, 26 Apr.

Hornung, E(rnest) W(illiam) 1866–1921

English novelist. Brother-in-law of Arthur Conan Doyle, he created Raffles the gentleman burglar, hero of *The Amateur Cracksman* (1899), *Mr Justice Raffles* (1909) and many other adventure stories.

37 'Cricket,' said Raffles, 'like everything else, is a good enough sport until you discover a better. As a source of excitement it isn't in it with other things you wot of Bunny, and the involuntary comparison becomes a bore. What's the satisfaction of taking a man's wicket when you want his spoons?'
1899 *The Amateur Cracksman.*

Horsley, Samuel 1733–1806

English prelate, most famous for his theological controversy (1783–9) with Joseph Priestley over the uncreated divinity of Christ. He published several scientific works.

38 In *this* country, my Lords…the individual subject…has nothing to do with the laws but to obey them.
1795 Speech in the House of Lords, 13 Nov.

Hoskins, Bob 1942–

English actor.

39 It's good to talk.
1996 Advertising slogan for British Telecom.

Houllier, Gerard 1947–

French football manager. He was appointed joint manager at Liverpool in 1998, later becoming sole manager (1999–2004).

40 It used to be the rat race. Now it's the sack race.
2004 On being a football manager. In *The Guardian*, 1 Mar.

Housman, A(lfred) E(dward) 1859–1936

English scholar and poet. He was a distinguished classical scholar, and is known primarily for his poetry, particularly *A Shropshire Lad* (1896), an anti-pastoral view of country life which was widely popular after an initially cool reception.

41 Loveliest of trees, the cherry now
Is hung with bloom along the bough,
And stands about the woodland ride
Wearing white for Eastertide.
1896 *A Shropshire Lad*, no.2.

42 Now, of my threescore years and ten,
Twenty will not come again,
And take from seventy springs a score,
It only leaves me fifty more.
1896 *A Shropshire Lad*, no.2.

43 And since to look at things in bloom
Fifty springs are little room,
About the woodlands I will go
To see the cherry hung with snow.
1896 *A Shropshire Lad*, no.2.

44 Clay lies still, but blood's a rover;
Breath's a ware that will not keep.
Up, lad: when the journey's over
There'll be time enough to sleep.
1896 *A Shropshire Lad*, no.4.

45 And naked to the hangman's noose
The morning clocks will ring
A neck God made for other use
Than strangling in a string.
1896 *A Shropshire Lad*, no.9.

46 When I was one-and-twenty
I heard a wise man say,
'Give crowns and pounds and guineas
But not your heart away;
Give pearls away and rubies,
But keep your fancy free.'
But I was one-and-twenty
No use to talk to me.
1896 *A Shropshire Lad*, no.13.

47 Oh, when I was in love with you,

Then I was clean and brave,
And miles around the wonder grew
How well I did behave.
1896 *A Shropshire Lad*, no.18.

48 And now the fancy passes by,
And nothing will remain,
And miles around they'll say that I
Am quite myself again.
1896 *A Shropshire Lad*, no.18.

49 And silence sounds no worse than cheers
After dying has stopped the ears.
1896 *A Shropshire Lad*, no.19.

50 Twice a week the winter through
Here I stood to keep the goal:
Football then was fighting sorrow
For the young man's soul.
1896 *A Shropshire Lad*, no.21.

51 In summertime in Bredon
The bells they sound so clear;
Round both the shires they ring them
In steeples far and near,
A happy noise to hear.
1896 *A Shropshire Lad*, no.21.

52 Here of a Sunday morning
My love and I would lie,
And see the coloured counties,
And hear the larks so high
About us in the sky.
1896 *A Shropshire Lad*, no.21.

53 'Come all to church, good people,'—
Oh, noisy bells, be dumb;
I hear you, I will come.
1896 *A Shropshire Lad*, no.21.

54 The lads in their hundreds to Ludlow come in for the fair,
There's men from the barn and the forge and the mill and
     the fold,
The lads for the girls and the lads for the liquor are
     there,
And there with the rest are lads that will never be old.
1896 *A Shropshire Lad*, no.23.

55 On Wenlock Edge the wood's in trouble;
His forest fleece the Wrekin heaves;
The wind it plies the saplings double,
And thick on Severn snow the leaves.
1896 *A Shropshire Lad*, no.31.

56 The gale, it plies the saplings double,
It blows so hard, 'twill soon be gone:
To-day the Roman and his trouble
Are ashes under Uricon.
1896 *A Shropshire Lad*, no.31.

57 From far, from eve and morning
And yon twelve-winded sky,
The stuff of life to knit me
Blew hither: here am I.
1896 *A Shropshire Lad*, no.32.

58 Speak now, and I will answer;
How shall I help you, say;
Ere to the wind's twelve quarters
I take my endless way.
1896 *A Shropshire Lad*, no.32.

59 Into my heart an air that kills
From yon far country blows:
What are those blue remembered hills,
What spires, what farms are those?
1896 *A Shropshire Lad*, no.40.

60 That is the land of lost content,
I see it shining plain,
The happy highways where I went
And cannot come again.
1896 *A Shropshire Lad*, no.40.

61 And bound for the same bourn as I,
On every road I wandered by,
Trod beside me, close and dear,
The beautiful and death-struck year.
1896 *A Shropshire Lad*, no.41.

62 Clunton and Clunbury,
Clungunford and Clun,
Are the quietest places
Under the sun.
1896 *A Shropshire Lad*, no.50, epigraph.

63 With rue my heart is laden
For golden friends I had,
For many a rose-lipt maiden
And many a lightfoot lad.
1896 *A Shropshire Lad*, no.54.

64 By brooks too broad for leaping
The lightfoot boys are laid;
The rose-lipt girls are sleeping
In fields where roses fade.
1896 *A Shropshire Lad*, no.54.

65 Say, for what were hop-yards meant,
Or why was Burton built on Trent?
Oh many a peer of England brews
Livelier liquor than the Muse,
And malt does more than Milton can
To justify God's ways to man.
Ale, man, ale's the stuff to drink
For fellows whom it hurts to think.
1896 *A Shropshire Lad*, no.62.

66 Oh I have been to Ludlow fair
And left my necktie God knows where,
And carried half-way home, or near,
Pints and quarts of Ludlow beer.
1896 *A Shropshire Lad*, no.62.

67 Then the world seemed none so bad,
And I myself a sterling lad;
And down in lovely muck I've lain,
Happy till I woke again.
1896 *A Shropshire Lad*, no.62.

68 I tell the tale that I heard told.
Mithridates, he died old.
1896 *A Shropshire Lad*, no.62.

69 This great College, of this ancient University, has seen
some strange sights. It has seen Wordsworth drunk and
Porson sober. And here am I, a better poet than Porson,
and a better scholar than Wordsworth, betwixt and
between.
1911 Speech on taking up the Chair of Latin at Trinity College,
Cambridge.

70 Pass me the can, lad; there's an end of May.
1922 *Last Poems*, no.9.

71 May will be fine next year as like as not:
Oh, ay, but then we shall be twenty-four.
    1922 *Last Poems*, no.9.

72 We for a certainty are not the first
Have sat in taverns while the tempest hurled
Their hopeful plans to emptiness, and cursed
Whatever brute and blackguard made the world.
    1922 *Last Poems*, no.9.

73 The troubles of our proud and angry dust
Are from eternity, and shall not fail.
Bear them we can, and if we can we must.
Shoulder the sky, my lad, and drink your ale.
    1922 *Last Poems*, no.9.

74 But men at whiles are sober
And think by fits and starts,
And if they think, they fasten
Their hands upon their hearts.
    1922 *Last Poems*, no.10.

75 The laws of God, the laws of man,
He may keep that will and can;
Not I: let God and man decree
Laws for themselves and not for me;
And if my ways are not as theirs
Let them mind their own affairs.
    1922 *Last Poems*, no.12.

76 And how am I to face the odds
Of man's bedevilment and God's?
I, a stranger and afraid
In a world I never made.
    1922 *Last Poems*, no.12.

77 The candles burn their sockets,
The blinds let through the day,
The young man feels his pockets
And wonders what's to pay.
    1922 *Last Poems*, no.21.

78 To think that two and two are four
And neither five nor three
The heart of man has long been sore
And long 'tis like to be.
    1922 *Last Poems*, no.35.

79 These, in the day when heaven was falling,
The hour when earth's foundations fled,
Followed their mercenary calling
And took their wages and are dead.
    1922 *Last Poems*, no.37,'Epitaph on an Army of Mercenaries'.

80 Their shoulders held the sky suspended;
They stood, and earth's foundations stay;
What God abandoned, these defended,
And saved the sum of things for pay.
    1922 *Last Poems*, no.37,'Epitaph on an Army of Mercenaries'.

81 For nature, heartless, witless nature,
Will neither care nor know
What stranger's feet may find the meadow
And trespass there and go,
Nor ask amid the dews of morning
If they are mine or no.
    1922 *Last Poems*, no.40.

82 Experience has taught me, when I am shaving of a
morning, to keep watch over my thoughts, because, if a
line of poetry strays into my memory, my skin bristles so
that the razor ceases to act.

1933 'The Name and Nature of Poetry', Lecture at Cambridge,
9 May.

83 The seat of this sensation is the pit of the stomach.
    1933 'The Name and Nature of Poetry', Lecture at Cambridge,
9 May.

84 The stroke of midnight ceases,
And I lie down alone.
    1936 *More Poems*, no.11.

85 Life, to be sure, is nothing much to lose;
But young men think it is, and we were young.
    1936 *More Poems*, no.36.

86 Good-night. Ensured release
Imperishable peace,
Have these for yours,
While earth's foundations stand
And sky and sea and land
And heaven endures.
    1936 *More Poems*, no.48.

87 That is indeed very good. I shall have to repeat that on the
Golden Floor!
    1936 Remark made to his doctor after the latter had told him a
risqué story on his deathbed.

88 The Grizzly bear is huge and wild;
He has devoured the infant child.
The infant child is not aware
He has been eaten by the bear.
    'Infant Innocence', collected *The Oxford Book of Light Verse*
(1938).

89 Oh who is that young sinner with the handcuffs on his
    wrist?
And what has he been after that they groan and shake
    their fists?
And wherefore is he wearing such a conscience-stricken
    air?
Oh they're taking him to prison for the colour of his hair.
    'Additional Poems', no.18, in *Collected Poems* (1939).

90 'Tis a shame to human nature, such a head of hair as his;
In the good old time 'twas hanging for the colour that
    it is;
Though hanging isn't bad enough and flaying would be
    fair
For the nameless and abominable colour of his hair.
    'Additional Poems', no.18, in *Collected Poems* (1939).

91 Now hollow fires burn out to black
And lamps are guttering low.
Square your shoulders, lift your pack,
And leave your friends and go.

Oh, never fear, man, nought's to dread
Look not left nor right.
In all the endless road you tread,
There's nothing but the night.
    Quoted in Bernard Levin *Hannibal's Footsteps* (1985).

How, William Walsham 1823–97

English churchman and religious writer, the first Bishop of
Wakefield.

92 For all the Saints who from their labours rest,
Who Thee by faith before the world confess'd,
Thy name, O Jesu, be for ever blest,
Alleluia!

1864 'For All the Saints', in Earl Nelson *Hymns for Saints' Days*.

93 From earth's wide bounds, from ocean's farthest coast,
Through gates of pearl streams in the countless host,
Singing to Father, Son, and Holy Ghost,
Alleluia!
1864 'For All the Saints', in Earl Nelson *Hymns for Saints' Days*.

Howard, Thomas, Earl of Surrey and 2nd Duke of Norfolk 1443–1524

English nobleman and soldier. He fought for Richard III at Bosworth (1485) and was imprisoned by Henry VII, but regained his estates and led successful campaigns against the Scots, including Flodden (1513).

94 He was my crowned King, and if the Parliamentary authority of England set the crown upon a stock, I will fight for that stock: And as I fought then for him, I will fight for you, when you are established by the said authority.
1485 Explaining before the future Henry VII his reasons for siding with Richard III at Bosworth, 22 Aug. Quoted in William Camden *Remains Concerning Britain* (1605).

Howe (of Aberavon), (Richard Edward) Geoffrey Howe, Baron 1926–

English Conservative politician. In 1989 he became Deputy Prime Minister, Lord President of the Council and Leader of the House of Commons. His resignation from Margaret Thatcher's government in Nov 1990, and his subsequent resignation speech, were instrumental in her downfall.

95 Megaphone diplomacy leads to a dialogue of the deaf.
1985 Quoted in the *Observer*, 29 Sep.

96 How on earth are the Chancellor of the Exchequer and the Governor of the Bank of England…to be taken seriously against that kind of background noise? It is rather like sending your opening batsmen to the crease, only for them to find, the moment the first balls are bowled, that their bats have been broken before the game by the team captain.
1990 Personal statement on his resignation, House of Commons, 13 Nov.

97 If some of my former colleagues are to be believed, I must be the first minister in history to have resigned because he was in full agreement with government policy.
1990 Personal statement on his resignation, House of Commons, 13 Nov.

Howe, Gordie (Gordon) 1928–

Canadian hockey player.

98 All pro athletes are bilingual. They speak English and profanity.
Dismissing Canadian bilingualism. Quoted by George Gamester in the *Toronto Star*, 27 May 1975.

Howe, Joseph 1804–73

Anglo-Canadian journalist and statesman.

99 A wise nation preserves its records, gathers up its muniments, decorates the tombs of its illustrious dead, repairs its great public structures, and fosters national pride and love of country, by perpetual references to the sacrifices and glories of the past.

1871 Address at Framingham, Massachusetts, 31 Aug. Collected in *Poems and Essays* (1874).

Howe, Julia Ward 1819–1910

US feminist and writer, influential in suffragette and Unitarian causes. Her poetry collections include *Passion Flowers* (1854). She made history as the first woman member of the American Academy.

1 Mine eyes have seen the glory of the coming of the Lord:
He is trampling out the vintage where the grapes of wrath are stored.
He hath loosed the fatal lightning of his terrible swift sword:
His truth is marching on.
1862 'Battle Hymn of the Republic'.

Howe, Louis McHenry 1871–1936

US diplomat.

2 You can't adopt politics as a profession and hope to remain honest.
1933 Speech, Columbia University, 17 Jan.

Hoyle, Edmond 1672–1769

English authority on card games. He published manuals on whist, backgammon, brag, quadrille, piquet and chess.

3 When in doubt, win the trick.
A Short Treatise on the Game of Whist (first published 1742, this edn edited by Charles Jones, 1790). This may be an addition by Jones.

Hoyle, Sir Fred 1915–2001

English astronomer and mathematician, one of the first to apply modern physics to cosmology. He was knighted in 1972.

4 To take an almost religious view, this earth is nothing very special. There have probably been millions of earths just like ours each producing a particular intelligent species. That is not to say that they all developed well, that they all achieved some sort of perfection. And if the planner made lots of them and some of them chose to destroy themselves, then we can only suppose that the planner is a hard and practical man.
1974 In the *Daily Mail*.

5 Space isn't remote at all. It's only an hour's drive away if your car could go straight upwards.
1979 Quoted in the *Observer*, 'Sayings of the Week', 9 Sep.

Hubbard, Elbert Green 1856–1915

US writer, editor and printer.

6 Life is just one damned thing after another.
1909 In *The Philistine*, Dec.

7 Little minds are interested in the extraordinary; great minds in the commonplace.
1911 *Thousand and One Epigrams*.

8 One machine can do the work of fifty ordinary men. No machine can do the work of one extraordinary man.
1911 *Thousand and One Epigrams*.

9 Editor: a person employed by a newspaper, whose business it is to separate the wheat from the chaff, and to see that the chaff is printed.
1914 *The Roycroft Dictionary*.

10 College football is a sport that bears the same relation to education that bullfighting does to agriculture.

Quoted in Colin Jarman *The Guinness Dictionary of Sports Quotations* (1990).

Hubble, Edwin Powell 1889–1953

US astronomer. In 1929 he formulated Hubble's law: galaxies recede with speeds directly proportionate to their distance from us, confirming that the universe is expanding. The space telescope launched in 1990 was named in his honour.

11 We measure shadows, and we search among ghostly errors of measurement for landmarks that are scarcely more substantial.

Quoted in Dennis Overbye *Lonely Hearts of the Cosmos* (1991).

Hügel, Friedrich von, Baron 1852–1925

Austrian-born British theologian and Bible critic, son of the Austrian Ambassador in Italy. He settled in England in 1871. His works include *The Mystical Element in Religion* (1908–9) and *The Reality of God* (published 1931).

12 I take these to be the seven great facts and doctrines concerning God—his richness; his double action, natural and supernatural; his perfect freedom; his delightfulness; his otherness; his adorableness and his prevenience.

The Life of Prayer (published 1927).

13 Christianity has taught us to care. Caring is the greatest thing, caring matters most.

Letter to his niece.

Hugh of St Victor c.1096–1141

German divine and scholar, who entered the Augustinian order despite his parents' objections. In 1115 he was sent to the Abbey of St Victor in Paris, where he completed his vows, later becoming master of the school. He composed many treatises on theological, philosophical and devotional subjects.

14 *Delicatus ille est adhuc cui patria dulcis est. Fortis autem jam cui omne solum patria est, perfectus vero cui mundus totus exsilium est.*

He whose own homeland is sweet to him is a mere beginner. He to whom every soil is as his native land is strong. But he to whom the whole world is a place of exile has achieved perfection.

c.1127 *Didascalicon*, bk.3, ch.20.

Hughes, Howard Robard 1905–76

US millionaire businessman, film producer and aviator. Known as an eccentric, he left Hollywood in 1932 to design, build and fly aircraft before returning to film production. After 1966 he lived in complete seclusion.

15 That man's ears make him look like a taxi-cab with both doors open.

Of Clark Gable. Quoted in Charles Higham and Joel Greenbert *Celluloid Muse* (1969).

Hughes, (James Mercer) Langston 1902–67

US poet, a leading figure of the Harlem Renaissance, whose poetry and sketches reflect folk culture, jazz, blues and colloquial speech. His works include *Weary Blues* (1926) and the autobiographical *The Big Sea* (1940).

16 I, too, sing America.

I am the darker brother.
They send me to eat in the kitchen
When company comes.
But I laugh
And eat well,
And grow strong.

1925 'I, Too', in *Survey Graphic*, Mar.

17 Tomorrow
I'll sit at the table
When company comes
Nobody'll dare
Say to me,
'Eat in the kitchen'
Then.

1925 'I, Too', in *Survey Graphic*, Mar.

18 Swaying to and fro on his rickety stool
He played that sad raggy tune like a musical fool.
Sweet blues!

1926 'The Weary Blues'.

19 I swear to the Lord,
I still can't see,
Why Democracy means,
Everybody but me.

1943 'The Black Man Speaks'.

20 What happens to a dream deferred?

Does it dry up
like a raisin in the sun?

1951 'Dream Deferred'. Lorraine Hansberry used the phrase for the title of her play *A Raisin in the Sun* (1959).

21 Maybe it just sags
like a heavy load.

Or does it explode?

1951 'Dream Deferred'.

22 You are white—
yet a part of me, as I am a part of you.
That's American.

1951 'Theme for English B'.

23 A wonderful time—the War:
when money rolled in
and blood rolled out.

1951 'Green Memory'.

24 'It's powerful,' he said.
'What?'
'That one drop of Negro blood—because just *one* drop of black blood makes a man coloured. *One* drop—you are a Negro!'

1953 *Simple Takes a Wife*.

Hughes, Richard Arthur Warren 1900–76

English novelist. He is best known for his adventure tale *A High Wind in Jamaica* (1929, entitled *The Innocent Voyage* in the US). Other works include *Hazard: A Sea Story* (1938), *The Fox in the Attic* (1961) and *The Wooden Shepherdess* (1972).

25 Nature is as wasteful of promising young men as she is of fish-spawn. It's not just getting them killed in wars: mere middle age snuffs out ten times more talent than ever wars and sudden death do.

1961 *The Fox in the Attic*, bk.1, ch.18.

26 For a politician rises on the backs of his friends (that's probably all they're good for), but it's through his enemies he'll have to govern afterwards.
1961 *The Fox in the Attic*, bk.2, ch.20.

27 Do your bit to save humanity from lapsing back into barbarity by reading all the novels you can.
1975 Speech at Foyle's Literary Luncheon, London, in honour of his 75th birthday.

Hughes, Robert Studley Forrest 1938–

Australian-born US art critic, writer with *Time* magazine (1970–). His books include *The Fatal Shore* (1987) and *Goya* (2003). He has also written and narrated art documentaries for television including the series *American Visions* (1997).

28 Lentil-soup colors.
1981 Of the paints used by French realists. In *Time*, 13 Apr.

29 The protein of our cultural imagination.
1984 Of the US Museum of Modern Art. In *Time*, 14 May.

30 Close by the Hudson, in MANHATTAN'S TOWN,
The iron palaces of Art glare down
On such as, wandering in the streets below,
Perambulate in glamorous SoHo,
A spot acclaimed by savant and by bard
As forcing chamber of the Avant-Garde.
1984 'The SoHoiad', in the *New York Review of Books*.

31 Popular in our time, unpopular in his. So runs the stereotype of rejected genius.
1985 On a Caravaggio exhibition. In *Time*, 11 Mar.

32 Landscape is to American painting what sex and psychoanalysis are to the American novel.
1985 In *Time*, 30 Dec.

33 [A Gustave Courbet] portrait of a trout…has more death in it than Rubens could get in a whole Crucifixion.
1986 In *Time*, 15 Sep.

34 Its clones have hung on so many suburban walls over the decades that it has become the *Mona Lisa* of the vegetable world.
1987 On Vincent Van Gogh's *Sunflowers*. In *Time*, 13 Apr.

35 The self is now the sacred cow of American culture, self-esteem is sacrosanct, and so we labour to turn arts education into a system in which no one can fail. In the same spirit, tennis could be shorn of its elitist overtones: you just get rid of the net.
1994 *Culture of Complaint: The Fraying of America*.

36 America came up with the idea of therapeutic avant-gardism, and built museums in its name. These temples stood on two pillars. The first was aestheticism… The second was the familiar one of social benefit.
1994 *Culture of Complaint: The Fraying of America*.

37 My idea of a contact sport was chess.
1999 *A Jerk on One End: Reflections of a Mediocre Fisherman*.

Hughes, Ted (Edward James) 1930–98

English poet. His elemental, highly symbolic works include *The Hawk in the Rain* (1957) and *Crow* (1970). Other works include *Birthday Letters* (1998) and books for children. He was Poet Laureate (1984–98).

38 The world rolls under the long thrust of his heel.
Over the cage floor the horizons come.

1957 'The Jaguar'.

39 It took the whole of Creation
To produce my foot, my each feather:
Now I hold Creation in my foot.
1960 'Hawk Roosting'.

40 Nothing has changed since I began.
My eye has permitted no change.
I am going to keep things like this.
1960 'Hawk Roosting'.

41 Pike, three inches long, perfect
Pike in all parts, green tigering the gold.
Killers from the egg: the malevolent aged grin.
1960 'Pike'.

42 The gash in its throat was shocking, but not pathetic.
1960 'View of a Pig'.

43 The deeps are cold:
In that darkness camaraderie does not hold:
Nothing touches but, clutching, devours.
1960 'Relic'.

44 The brassy wood-pigeons
Bubble their colourful voices, and the sun
Rises upon a world well-tried and old.
1967 'Stealing Trout on a May Morning'.

45 No, the serpent did not
Seduce Eve to the apple.
All that's simply
Corruption of the facts.

Adam ate the apple.
Eve ate Adam.
The serpent ate Eve.
This is the dark intestine.

The serpent, meanwhile,
Sleeps his meal off in Paradise—
Smiling to hear
God's querulous calling.
1967 'Theology'.

46 Who owns the whole rainy, stony earth? *Death*.
Who owns all of space? *Death*.
1970 'Examination at the Womb-door'.

47 But who is stronger than death?
Me, evidently.
1970 'Examination at the Womb-door'.

48 And he shivered with the horror of Creation.
1970 'Crow Alights'.

49 But Oedipus he had the luck
For when he hit the ground
He bounced up like a jackinabox
And knocked his Daddy down.
1970 'Song for a Phallus'.

50 And the elephant sings deep in the forest-maze
About a star of deathless and painless peace
But no astronomer can find where it is.
1972 'Crow's Elephant Totem Song'.

51 Black village of gravestones.
1979 'Heptonstall'.

52 Only the rain never tires.
1979 'Heptonstall'.

53 You were the jailer of your murderer—

Which imprisoned you.
And since I was your nurse and your protector
Your sentence was mine too.
1998 In *Birthday Letters*, a collection of poems addressed to
Sylvia Plath, his first wife.

Hughes, Thomas 1822–96

English reformer and novelist. Called to the Bar in 1848, a
Liberal MP (1865–74) and a county court judge (1882), he is
best remembered for his semi-autobiographical classic, *Tom
Brown's Schooldays* (1856).

54 Life isn't all beer and skittles—but beer and skittles, or
something better of the same sort, must form a good
part of every Englishman's education.
1856 *Tom Brown's Schooldays*, pt.1, ch.2.

55 He never wants anything but what's right and fair, only
when you come to settle what's right and fair, it's
everything that he wants and nothing that you want. And
that's his idea of a compromise. Give me the Brown
compromise when I'm on his side.
1856 *Tom Brown's Schooldays*, pt.2, ch.2.

56 It's more than a game. It's an institution.
1856 Of cricket. *Tom Brown's Schooldays*, pt.2, ch.7.

Hughes, William Morris 1864–1952

Welsh-born Australian statesman. He emigrated in 1884 and
became Minister for External Affairs (1904) in the first Labour
government and subsequently Prime Minister (1915–23). He
founded the United Australian Party.

57 Mr President, I speak for sixty thousand dead!
1919 Reply to Woodrow Wilson at the Versailles Peace
Conference, Jan, referring to the ANZAC fatalities in World War
I. Wilson had asked 'Mr Hughes, I speak for very many millions
of people. For whom do you speak?'.

58 Without the Empire we should be tossed like a cork in
the cross current of world politics. It is at once our sword
and our shield.
1926 Speech, Melbourne.

Hugo, Victor Marie 1802–85

French poet, dramatist and novelist. His great epics are *Notre-
Dame de Paris* (1831, *The Hunchback of Notre Dame*) and *Les
Misérables* (1862). His writings and theories were enormously
influential.

59 *Le beau n'a qu'un type; le laid en a mille.*
Beauty has only one form; ugliness has a thousand.
1827 *Cromwell*, préface.

60 *Les temps primitifs sont lyriques, les temps antiques sont
épiques, les temps modernes sont dramatiques.*
The primitive era was lyrical, the classical era was epic
and the modern era is dramatic.
1827 *Cromwell*, préface.

61 *Il n'y a ni règles ni modèles; ou plutôt il n'y a d'autres
règles que les lois générales de la nature qui planent sur
l'art tout entier, et les lois spéciales qui, pour chaque
composition, résultent des conditions d'existence
propres à chaque sujet.*
There are no rules or models; that is, there are no rules
except general laws of nature which hover over art and
special laws which apply to specific subjects.
1827 *Cromwell*, préface.

62 *La vérité de l'art ne saurait jamais être…la réalité
absolue. L'art ne peut donner la chose même.*
The truth of art should never be…absolute reality. Art
cannot show the thing itself.
1827 *Cromwell*, préface.

63 *Le but de l'art est presque divin: ressusciter, s'il fait de
l'histoire; créer, s'il fait de la poésie.*
The goal of art is almost divine: to resuscitate, if it
concerns history; to create, if it concerns poetry.
1827 *Cromwell*, préface.

64 *Le vers est la forme optique de la pensée. Voilà pourquoi
il convient surtout à la perspective scénique.*
Verse is the optical form of thought. That is the reason a
scenic perspective suits it.
1827 *Cromwell*, préface.

65 *La langue française n'est point fixée et ne se fixera point.*
French is not a *static* language and will never become
static.
1827 *Cromwell*, préface.

66 *Sois donc ami sincère ou sincère ennemi,
Et ne reste pas traître et fidèle à demi.*
Be either a sincere friend or a sincere enemy,
And never be half-traitor and half-faithful.
1827 *Cromwell*, act 1, sc.1.

67 *L'Angleterre toujours sera sœur de la France.*
England will always be the sister of France.
1827 *Cromwell*, act 2, sc.2.

68 *Vous me manquez, je suis absente de moi-même.*
I miss you, I am estranged from myself.
1830 *Hernani*, act 1, sc.2.

69 *Nos pères avaient un Paris de pierre, nos fils auront un
Paris de plâtre.*
Our fathers had a Paris made of stone; our sons will have
a Paris made of plaster.
1831 *Notre-Dame de Paris*, pt.3, ch.2.

70 *Rêver, c'est le bonheur; attendre, c'est la vie.*
To dream is happiness; to wait is life.
1831 *Les Feuilles d'automne*, no.27, 'À mes amis L.B. et S.-B.'.

71 *Au banquet du bonheur bien peu sont conviés.*
Few are invited to the banquet of happiness.
1831 *Les Feuilles d'automne*, no.32, 'Pour les pauvres'.

72 *Mêlez toute votre âme à la création!*
Involve all of your soul in creation!
1831 *Les Feuilles d'automne*, no.38, 'Pan'.

73 *O Virgile! ô poète! ô mon maître divin!*
Oh Virgil! Oh poet! Oh my divine master!
1837 *Les Voix intérieures*, no.7, 'À Virgile'.

74 *Le drame tient de la tragédie par la peinture des passions
et de la comédie par la peinture des caractères. Le drame
est la troisième grande forme de l'art.*
In drama, tragedy paints the passions and comedy paints
characters. Drama is the third great form of art.
1838 *Ruy Blas*, préface.

75 *Je ne veux pas tomber, non, je veux disparaître.*
I do not want to fall; I want to disappear.
1838 *Ruy Blas*, act 1, sc.1.

76 *Visage de traître!
Quand la bouche dit oui, le regard dit peut-être.*
Face of a traitor!
When the mouth says yes, the look says maybe.

1838 *Ruy Blas*, act 1, sc.2.

77 *Sous l'habit d'un valet, les passions d'un roi.*
Beneath the clothing of a manservant, the passions of a king.
1838 *Ruy Blas*, act 1, sc.3.

78 *Les femmes aiment fort à sauver qui les perd.*
Women love to save those who damn them.
1838 *Ruy Blas*, act 1, sc.4.

79 *Dieu s'est fait homme; Soit! Le diable s'est fait femme.*
God made himself a man. So be it! The devil made himself a woman.
1838 *Ruy Blas*, act 2, sc.5.

80 *Tout se fait par intrigue et rien par loyauté.*
Everything is done by intrigue, not by loyalty.
1838 *Ruy Blas*, act 3, sc.2.

81 *Ah! toute nation bénit qui la délie.*
Ah! every nation blesses what undoes it.
1838 *Ruy Blas*, act 3, sc.5.

82 *La popularité? c'est la gloire en gros sous.*
Popularity? It is glory in large coins.
1838 *Ruy Blas*, act 3, sc.5.

83 *Le mot, c'est le Verbe, et le Verbe, c'est Dieu.*
The word is the Verb, and the Verb is God.
1856 *Contemplations*, bk.1, no.8.

84 *Cette cloison qui nous sépare du mystère des choses et que nous appelons la vie.*
Life is a screen which separates us from the mystery of things.
1862 *Les Misérables*, vol.1, bk.1, ch.2.

85 *Ce génie particulier de la femme qui comprend l'homme mieux que l'homme ne se comprend.*
A woman's particular talent is to understand a man better than he understands himself.
1862 *Les Misérables*, vol.1, bk.1, ch.9.

86 *Les livres sont des amis froids et sûrs.*
Books are cold and certain friends.
1862 *Les Misérables*, vol.1, bk.5, ch.3.

87 *Conscience déchirée entraîne vie décousue.*
A torn conscience brings about a disconnected life.
1862 *Les Misérables*, vol.2, bk.1, ch.16.

88 *La symétrie, c'est l'ennui, et l'ennui est le fond même du deuil. Le désespoir bâille.*
Symmetry is boredom and boredom is the foundation of grief. Despair yawns.
1862 *Les Misérables*, vol.2, bk.4, ch.1.

89 *Personne ne garde un secret comme un enfant.*
No one keeps a secret like a child.
1862 *Les Misérables*, vol.2, bk.7, ch.8.

90 *Respirer Paris, cela conserve l'âme.*
To inhale Paris preserves the soul.
1862 *Les Misérables*, vol.3, bk.1, ch.6.

91 *On jugerait bien plus sûrement un homme d'après ce qu'il rêve que d'après ce qu'il pense.*
We would judge a man more certainly according to his dreams than to his thoughts.
1862 *Les Misérables*, vol.3, bk.5, ch.5.

92 *On a voulu, à tort, faire de la bourgeoisie une classe. La bourgeoisie est tout simplement la portion contentée du peuple. Le bourgeois, c'est l'homme qui a maintenant le temps de s'asseoir. Une chaise n'est pas une caste.*

Wrongly, one wanted to make the bourgeoisie a class. The bourgeoisie is simply a contented section of the public. A bourgeois is a man who now has the time to sit down. A chair is not a caste.
1862 *Les Misérables*, vol.4, bk.1, ch.2.

93 *La première égalité, c'est l'équité.*
The first equality is equity.
1862 *Les Misérables*, vol.4, bk.1, ch.4.

94 *Le premier symptôme de l'amour vrai chez un jeune homme, c'est la timidité, chez une jeune fille, c'est la hardiesse.*
The first symptom of true love in a young man is timidity; in a young woman, it is boldness.
1862 *Les Misérables*, vol.4, bk.3, ch.6.

95 *Le dix-neuvième siècle est grand, mais le vingtième sera heureux.*
The nineteenth century is great, but the twentieth will be happy.
1862 *Les Misérables*, vol.5, bk.1, ch.4.

96 *Le suicide, cette mystérieuse voie de fait sur l'inconnu.*
Suicide: that mysterious route towards the unknown.
1862 *Les Misérables*, vol.5, bk.3, ch.10.

97 *Jésus a pleuré, Voltaire a souri; c'est de cette larme divine et de ce sourire humain qu'est faite la douceur de la civilisation actuelle.*
Jesus wept; Voltaire smiled. Of that divine tear and of that human smile the sweetness of present civilization is composed.
1878 Speech on Voltaire's centenary, 30 May.

98 Science says the first word on everything and the last word on nothing.
Attributed.

Huidobro, Vicente 1893–1948

Chilean poet, who wrote in French as well as Spanish. He created the movement known as *creacionismo*, which abandons traditional descriptive poetry.

99 *Que se rompa el andamio de los huesos*
Que se derrumben las vigas del cerebro
Y arrastre el huracán los trozos a la nada al otro lado
En donde el viento azota a Dios
Smash the scaffold of the bones
Pull down the rafters of the brain
Let the hurricane drag the pieces to the nothing on the other side
Where the wind thrashes God
1931 *Altazor o el viaje en paracaídas*, canto 1 (translated as *Altazor, or, A Voyage in a Parachute*, 1988).

Humboldt, Alexander, Baron von 1769–1859

German naturalist and traveller. He travelled through Central and South America (1799–1804), and his observations laid the foundations for the sciences of physical geography and meteorology.

1 In the sphere of natural investigation, as in poetry and painting, the delineation of that which appeals most strongly to the imagination, derives its collective interest from the vivid truthfulness with which the individual features are portrayed.
1845–62 *Kosmos* (translated as *Cosmos*, 1897).

2 The great and solemn spirit that pervades the intellectual labour (of science) arises from the sublime consciousness of striving toward the infinite, and of grasping all that is revealed to us amid the boundless and inexhaustible fullness of creation, development and being.

1845–62 *Kosmos* (translated as *Cosmos*, 1897).

Hume, David 1711–76

Scottish philosopher and historian. His most important work, the empiricist *A Treatise of Human Nature*, was published anonymously (1739–40). He published a five-volume *History of England* (1754–62) and was secretary to the British Ambassador in Paris (1763–5).

3 Let us fix our attention out of ourselves as much as possible; let us chase our imagination to the heavens, or to the utmost limits of the universe; we never really advance a step beyond ourselves, nor can conceive any kind of existence, but those perceptions, which have appeared in that narrow compass.

1739 *A Treatise of Human Nature*, bk.1, pt.2, section 6.

4 We have no other notion of cause and effect, but that of certain objects, which have been *always conjoined* together, and which in all past instances have been found inseparable.

1739 *A Treatise of Human Nature*, bk.1, pt.3, section 6.

5 For my part, when I enter most intimately into what I call *myself*, I always stumble on some particular perception or other, of heat or cold, light or shade, pain or pleasure. I never can catch *myself* at any time without a perception, and never can observe anything but the perception.

1739 *A Treatise of Human Nature*, bk.1, pt.4, section 6.

6 In all the events of life, we ought still to preserve our scepticism. If we believe that fire warms, or water refreshes, it is only because it costs us too much pains to think otherwise.

1739 *A Treatise of Human Nature*, bk.1, pt.4, section 7.

7 Reason is, and ought only to be the slave of the passions, and can never pretend to any other office than to serve and obey them.

1739 *A Treatise of Human Nature*, bk.2, pt.3, section 3.

8 It is not contrary to reason to prefer the destruction of the whole world to the scratching of my finger.

1739 *A Treatise of Human Nature*, bk.2, pt.3, section 3.

9 It is not, therefore, reason, which is the guide of life, but custom.

1739 *A Treatise of Human Nature*, abstract.

10 Art may make a suit of clothes; But nature must produce a man.

1741–2 *Essays Moral, Political and Literary*, 'The Epicurean'.

11 It cannot reasonably be doubted, but a little miss, dressed in a new gown for a dancing-school ball, receives as complete enjoyment as the greatest orator, who triumphs in the splendour of his eloquence, while he governs the passions and resolutions of a numerous assembly.

1741–2 *Essays Moral, Political and Literary*, 'The Sceptic'.

12 The increase of riches and commerce in any one nation, instead of hurting, commonly promotes the riches and commerce of all its neighbours.

1741–2 *Essays Moral, Political and Literary*, 'Of the Jealousy of Trade'.

13 All the objects of human reason or enquiry may naturally be divided into two kinds, to wit, *Relations of Ideas*, and *Matters of Fact*.

1748 *An Enquiry Concerning Human Understanding*, section 4, pt.1.

14 A wise man proportions his belief to the evidence.

1748 *An Enquiry Concerning Human Understanding*, section 10, pt.1.

15 When we run over libraries, persuaded of these principles, what havoc must we make? If we take in our hand any volume; of divinity or school metaphysics, for instance; let us ask, *Does it contain any abstract reasoning concerning quantity or number?* No. *Does it contain any experimental reasoning concerning matter of fact or existence?* No. Commit it then to the flames: for it can contain nothing but sophistry and illusion.

1748 *An Enquiry Concerning Human Understanding*, section 12, pt.3.

16 Never literary attempt was more unfortunate than my Treatise of Human Nature. It fell *dead-born from the press*, without reaching such distinction, as even to excite a murmur among the zealots.

1777 *My Own Life*, ch.1.

Humphrey, Hubert Horatio 1911–78

US politician. He served as Vice-President under Lyndon B Johnson but failed to win the Democratic candidature in 1968.

17 There are not enough jails, not enough policemen, not enough courts to enforce a law not supported by the people.

1965 Speech, 1 May.

Humphry, Derek 1930–

British journalist and co-founder of the Hemlock Society, which supports euthanasia for the terminally ill.

18 We're not lawbreakers, we're law reformers.

1992 In *Time*, 28 Dec.

Humphrys, John 1943–

Welsh broadcaster, particularly known as a tenacious presenter on BBC Radio 4's *Today* programme (since 1987).

19 It is largely on television and radio that real probing of what politicians are up to has to happen.

2000 *The Devil's Advocate*.

20 It is no good saying we [journalists] must report only what is true because what is true cannot always be proven.

2004 In the *Sunday Times*, 8 Feb.

Hunt, G W 1829–1904

English composer, lyricist and painter.

21 We don't want to fight, but by jingo if we do,
We've got the ships, we've got the men, we've got the money too!

1878 Music-hall song, inspired by Disraeli's speech of 9 Nov 1876 threatening Russia with war if it sent volunteers into Serbia and Montenegro. This is the origin of 'jingoism'.

Hunt, Johnnie B(ryan) 1924–

US businessman of poor origins.

22 I was hungry once and once you're hungry, you're different.
1992 In *Forbes*, 19 Oct.

Hunt, Lamar 1932–

US founder of the Kansas City Chiefs American football club.

23 My definition of utter waste is a coachload of lawyers going over a cliff, with three empty seats.
Quoted in Colin Jarman *The Guinness Dictionary of Sports Quotations* (1990).

Hunt, (James Henry) Leigh 1784–1859

English poet, critic and essayist. With his brother he edited *The Examiner* (1808–21) and popularized Keats and Shelley. His house in Hampstead was a literary meeting-place, and he was caricatured by Dickens as Harold Skimpole in *Bleak House*.

24 Never lay yourself open to what is called conviction: you might as well open your waist-coat to receive a knock-down blow.
1808 'Rules for the Conduct of Newspaper Editors', in *The Examiner*, 6 Mar.

25 A playful moderation in politics is just as absurd as a remonstrative whisper to a mob.
1808 'Rules for the Conduct of Newspaper Editors', in *The Examiner*, 6 Mar.

26 She can overpower, astonish, afflict, but she cannot win; her majestic presence and commanding features seem to disregard love, as a trifle to which they cannot descend.
1808 Of Sarah Siddons. *Critical Essays on the Performers of the London Theatres*.

27 The two divinest things this world has got,
A lovely woman in a rural spot!
1816 'The Story of Rimini', canto 3, l.257–8.

28 The laughing queen that caught the world's great hands.
1818 Of Cleopatra. 'The Nile'.

29 Stolen sweets are always sweeter,
Stolen kisses much completer,
Stolen looks are nice in chapels,
Stolen, stolen, be your apples.
1830 'Song of Fairies Robbing an Orchard'.

30 Poetry, in the most comprehensive application of the term, I take to be the flower of any kind of experience, rooted in truth, and issuing forth into beauty.
1832 *The Story of Rimini*, preface to rev edn.

31 The pretension is nothing; the performance everything. A good apple is better than an insipid peach.
1832 *The Story of Rimini*, preface to rev edn.

32 'No love,' quoth he, 'but vanity, sets love a task like that.'
1836 'The Glove and the Lions'.

33 Abou Ben Adhem (may his tribe increase!)
Awoke one night from a deep dream of peace.
1838 'Abou Ben Adhem'.

34 I pray thee then,
Write me as one that loves his fellow-men.
1838 'Abou Ben Adhem'.

35 Jenny kissed me when we met,
Jumping from the chair she sat in;
Time, you thief, who love to get
Sweets into your list, put that in:

Say I'm weary, say I'm sad,
Say that health and wealth have missed me,
Say I'm growing old, but add,
Jenny kissed me.
1838 'Rondeau'.

36 That man must be very much absorbed in reflection, or stupid, or sulky, or unhappy, or a mere hog at his trough, who is not moved to say something when he dines.
1851 *Table-Talk*, 'Table-Talk'.

37 If you are ever at a loss to support a flagging conversation, introduce the subject of eating.
1851 *Table-Talk*, 'Eating'.

Hunt, Sir Rex 1926–

Governor of the Falkland Islands at the time of the Argentine invasion of 1982.

38 It is very uncivilised to invade British territory. You are here illegally.
1982 Attributed remark to an Argentinian general. Quoted in *Life*, Jan 1983.

Hunter, William 1718–83

Scottish anatomist and obstetrician, appointed physician-extraordinary to Queen Charlotte Sophia (1764) and first Professor of Anatomy to the Royal Academy (1768). His Hunterian Museum was bequeathed to Glasgow University.

39 Some physiologists will have it that the stomach is a mill;—others, that it is a fermenting vat;—others again that it is a stew-pan;—but in my view of the matter, it is neither a mill, a fermenting vat, nor a stew-pan—but a *stomach*, gentlemen, a *stomach*.
Quoted in J A Paris *A Treatise on Diet* (1824), epigraph, from a note made by Hunter on one of his lectures.

Hupfeld, Herman 1894–1951

US composer of popular songs, best known for 'Sing Something Simple' and 'As Time Goes By'.

40 You must remember this, a kiss is still a kiss,
A sigh is just a sigh;
The fundamental things apply,
As time goes by.
1931 'As Time Goes By', sung by Dooley Wilson in the film *Casablanca* (1943).

Hussein, ibn Talal 1935–99

King of Jordan (1952–99), four times married. The longest-serving Arab leader, pro-Western in attitude, he moved towards democracy in Jordan.

41 After all the doors were shut, our region is facing a deep abyss after the turning of the Gulf crisis into an imminent catastrophe. We have not left a door that we did not knock on, or a road that we did not take to find a political settlement of this crisis.
1991 On his attempts to intercede for peace in the Gulf War, Jan.

Hussein, Saddam 1937–

Iraqi politician, a key figure in Iraq's 1968 revolution and later President (1979–2003). He engaged in the Iran–Iraq War (1980–8) and in 1990 invaded Kuwait and was repulsed by a coalition of Western and Arab forces. He made further raids on

Iran in 1993, defying UN ceasefire resolutions. He was captured by US forces in Iraq in December 2003.

42 The devil Bush and his treacherous gang, with criminal Zionism, have begun the great showdown, the mother of all battles between good and evil.
1991 Speech in Baghdad, 6 Jan, describing Operation Desert Storm. Quoted in the *Sunday Times*, 27 Jan.

43 There is no other course but the one we have chosen, except the course of humiliation and darkness, after which there will be no bright sign in the sky or brilliant light on earth… All this will make us more patient and steadfast, and better prepared for the battle which God blesses and which good men support. Then there will only be a glorious conclusion, where a brilliant sun will clear the dust of battle, and where the clouds of battles will be dispelled.
1991 Baghdad radio broadcast, 21 Feb.

44 Baghdad is determined to force the Mongols of our age to commit suicide at its gates.
2003 Speech on the anniversary of the Gulf War, 17 Jan.

45 At dawn prayers today on March 20 2003 (17 Muharram 1424), the criminal, reckless little Bush and his aides committed this crime that he was threatening to commit against Iraq and humanity.
2003 Address to the nation of Iraq, broadcast on state television, after a US strike on Baghdad. Quoted in *The Guardian*, 20 Mar.

46 We do not have weapons of mass destruction.
Quoted in George Galloway *I'm Not the Only One* (2004).

47 If they come we are ready. We will fight them on the streets, from the rooftops, from house to house. We will never surrender our independence no matter what happens in any invasion.
Quoted in George Galloway *I'm Not the Only One* (2004).

Huston, John 1906–87

US actor, screenwriter and director, son of Walter Huston. He made his directorial debut with *The Maltese Falcon* (1941). Other successes include *Key Largo* (1948), *The African Queen* (1951), *Moulin Rouge* (1952) and *The Man Who Would Be King* (1975).

48 You're good, you're real good.
1941 Line delivered by Humphrey Bogart in *The Maltese Falcon*.

49 A work of art doesn't dare you to realize it. It germinates and gestates by itself.
1982 Reply to a tribute from the Directors Guild of America. Reported in *Variety*, 26 Apr.

Hutchens, John Kennedy 1905–95

US journalist and editor. He was theatre critic with the *New York Times* (1929–32, 1934–8), editor of the *New York Times Book Review* (1946–8), and was on the editorial board of the Book-of-the-Month Club (1963–88).

50 A writer and nothing else: a man alone in a room with the English language, trying to get human feelings right.
1961 On Stephen Crane. In the *New York Herald Tribune*, 10 Sep.

Hutcheson, Francis 1694–1746

Scottish philosopher, born in Ulster, a Professor of Moral Philosophy at Glasgow (1729–46) and exponent of the theory of moral sense. His ideas were later expanded by David Hume and taken up by the Utilitarians.

51 Wisdom denotes the pursuing of the best ends by the best means.
1725 *An Inquiry into the Original of Our Ideas of Beauty and Virtue*, treatise 1, sect.5.

52 That action is best, which procures the greatest happiness for the greatest numbers.
1725 *An Inquiry into the Original of Our Ideas of Beauty and Virtue*, treatise 2, sect.3. This is the classic exposition of pragmatism.
➤ *See Bentham 77:65.*

Hutchins, Robert M 1899–1977

US educationalist, Chancellor of the University of Chicago.

53 On the principle laid down by Gilbert and Sullivan that when everybody is somebody, nobody is anybody; if everybody is abnormal, we don't need to worry about anybody.
1951 Farewell address to students at the University of Chicago.

54 Whenever I feel like exercise, I lie down until the feeling passes.
Quoted in Colin Jarman *The Guinness Dictionary of Sports Quotations* (1990).

Huxley, Aldous Leonard 1894–1963

English novelist and essayist. His satirical novels *Crome Yellow* (1921) and *Antic Hay* (1923) established his reputation, and his best-known work is the dystopian novel *Brave New World* (1932). Other works include *Eyeless in Gaza* (1936) and *Time Must Have a Stop* (1944).

55 I can sympathize with people's pains, but not with their pleasures. There is something curiously boring about somebody else's happiness.
1920 *Limbo*, 'Cynthia'.

56 The proper study of mankind is books.
1921 *Crome Yellow*, ch.28.
➤ *See Pope 660:16.*

57 There are few who would not rather be taken in adultery than in provincialism.
1923 *Antic Hay*, ch.10.

58 Mr Mercaptan went on to preach a brilliant sermon on that melancholy sexual perversion known as continence.
1923 *Antic Hay*, ch.18.

59 Lady Capricorn, he understood, was still keeping open bed.
1923 *Antic Hay*, ch.21.

60 I'm afraid of losing my obscurity. Genuineness only thrives in the dark. Like celery.
1925 *Those Barren Leaves*, pt.1, ch.1.

61 Science has 'explained' nothing: the more we know the more fantastic the world becomes and the profounder the surrounding darkness.
1925 *Views of Holland*.

62 Facts do not cease to exist because they are ignored.
1927 *Proper Studies*, 'Note on Dogma'.

63 Those who believe that they are exclusively in the right are generally those who achieve something.
1927 *Proper Studies*, 'Note on Dogma'.

64 That all men are equal is a proposition to which, at

ordinary times, no sane human being has ever given his assent.
1927 *Proper Studies*, 'The Idea of Equality'.

65 Several excuses are always less convincing than one.
1928 *Point Counter Point*, ch.1.

66 A bad book is as much of a labour to write as a good one; it comes as sincerely from the author's soul.
1928 *Point Counter Point*, ch.13.

67 There is no substitute for talent. Industry and all the virtues are of no avail.
1928 *Point Counter Point*, ch.13.

68 Brought up in an age when ladies apparently rolled along on wheels, Mr Quarles was peculiarly susceptible to calves.
1928 *Point Counter Point*, ch.20.

69 Parodies and caricatures are the most penetrating of criticisms.
1928 *Point Counter Point*, ch.28.

70 Happiness is like coke—something you get as a by-product in the process of making something else.
1928 *Point Counter Point*, ch.30.

71 Too much consistency is as bad for the mind as it is for the body. Consistency is contrary to nature, contrary to life.
1929 *Do What You Will*, 'Wordsworth in the Tropics'.

72 After silence, that which comes nearest to expressing the inexpressible is music.
1931 *Music at Night*.

73 Experience is not what happens to a man; it is what a man does with what happens to him.
1932 *Texts and Pretexts*, introduction.

74 Only man behaves with such gratuitous folly. It is the price he has to pay for being intelligent but not, as yet, quite intelligent enough.
1932 *Texts and Pretexts*, 'Amor Fati'.

75 The escalator from the Social Predestination Room… One circuit of the cellar at ground level, one on the first gallery, half on the second, and on the two hundred and sixty-seventh morning, daylight in the Decanting Room. Independent existence—so called.
1932 *Brave New World*, ch.1.

76 Our Ford…had been the first to reveal the appalling dangers of family life.
1932 *Brave New World*, ch.3.

77 Oh, she's a splendid girl. Wonderfully pneumatic.
1932 *Brave New World*, ch.3.

78 The sexophones wailed like melodious cats under the moon.
1932 *Brave New World*, ch.5.

79 The real pitch lake is simply about two hundred asphalt tennis courts, in very bad condition, set in the midst of some gently undulating green meadows. I am inclined to ask for my money back.
1934 On the Trinidad Pitch Lake. *Beyond the Mexique Bay*.

80 Official dignity tends to increase in inverse ratio to the importance of the country in which the office is held.
1934 *Beyond the Mexique Bay*.

81 'Death,' said Mark Staithes. 'It's the only thing we haven't succeeded in completely vulgarizing.'
1936 *Eyeless in Gaza*, ch.31.

82 The end cannot justify the means, for the simple and obvious reason that the means employed determine the nature of the ends produced.
1937 *Ends and Means*, ch.1.

83 We are living now, not in the delicious intoxication induced by the early successes of science, but in a rather grisly morning-after, when it has become apparent that what triumphant science has done hitherto is to improve the means for achieving unimproved or actually deteriorated ends.
1937 *Ends and Means*, ch.1.

84 So long as men worship the Caesars and Napoleons, Caesars and Napoleons will duly arise and make them miserable.
1937 *Ends and Means*, ch.8.

85 The propagandist's purpose is to make one set of people forget that certain other sets of people are human.
1937 *The Olive Tree*.

86 What is science? Science is angling in the mud—angling for immortality and for anything else that may happen to turn up.
1939 *After Many a Summer Dies the Swan*.

87 The quality of moral behaviour varies in inverse ratio to the number of human beings involved.
1941 *Grey Eminence*, ch.10.

88 There's only one corner of the universe you can be certain of improving, and that's your own self.
1944 *Time Must Have a Stop*.

89 You learn to love by loving—by paying attention and doing what one thereby discovers has to be done.
1944 *Time Must Have a Stop*.

90 Facts are ventriloquist's dummies. Sitting on a wise man's knee they may be made to utter words of wisdom; elsewhere they say nothing, or talk nonsense.
1944 *Time Must Have a Stop*.

91 Most human beings have an infinite capacity for taking things for granted.
1950 'Variations on a Philosopher'.

92 We participate in a tragedy; at a comedy we only look.
1952 *The Devils of Loudun*, ch.11.

93 I was seeing what Adam had seen on the morning of his creation—the miracle, moment by moment, of naked existence.
1954 *The Doors of Perception*.

94 I have spoken so far only of the blissful visionary experience… But visionary experience is not always blissful. It's sometimes terrible. There is hell as well as heaven.
1956 *Heaven and Hell*.

95 'Bed,' as the Italian proverb succinctly puts it, 'is the poor man's opera.'
1956 *Heaven and Hell*.

96 The most distressing thing that can happen to a prophet is to be proved wrong. The next most distressing thing is to be proved right.
1956 'Brave New World Revisited', in *Esquire*.

97 But liberty, as we all know, cannot flourish in a country that is permanently on a war footing, or even a near-war footing. Permanent crisis justifies permanent control of everybody and everything by the agencies of central

government.
1956 'Brave New World Revisited', in *Esquire*.

98 But some of us still believe that, without freedom, human beings cannot become fully human and that freedom is therefore supremely valuable.
1956 'Brave New World Revisited', in *Esquire*.

99 That men do not learn very much from the lessons of history is the most important of all the lessons that history has to teach.
1959 'A Case of Voluntary Ignorance'.

1 Science is the reduction of the bewildering diversity of unique events to manageable uniformity within one of a number of symbol systems, and technology is the art of using these symbol systems so as to control and organize unique events. Scientific observation is always a viewing of things through the refracting medium of a symbol system, and technological praxis is always handling of things in ways that some symbol system has dictated. Education in science and technology is essentially education on the symbol level.
1962 In *Daedalus*, spring issue.

2 Idealism is the noble toga that political gentlemen drape over their will to power.
Quoted in his *New York Herald Tribune* obituary, 24 Nov 1963.

Huxley, Sir Julian Sorell 1887–1975

English biologist and humanist, grandson of T H Huxley. He was the first Director-General of UNESCO, and formulated a pragmatic ethical theory of 'evolutionary humanism'.

3 We all know how the size of sums of money appears to vary in a remarkable way according as they are being paid in or paid out.
1923 *Essays of a Biologist*, ch.5.

4 Operationally, God is beginning to resemble not a ruler but the last fading smile of a cosmic Cheshire cat.
1957 *Religion without Revelation* (rev edn), ch.3.

Huxley, T(homas) H(enry) 1825–95

English biologist, who made significant contributions to palaeontology and comparative anatomy. He famously supported Darwin's controversial theory of evolution by natural selection, and the term 'agnostic' has been attributed to him.

5 The generalizations of science sweep in ever-widening circles, and more aspiring flights, through a limitless creation.
1859 Letter to *The Times*, 26 Dec.

6 Sit down before fact as a little child, be prepared to give up every preconceived notion, follow humbly wherever and to whatsoever abysses Nature leads, or you shall learn nothing.
1860 Letter to Charles Kingsley.

7 Most of my colleagues were *-ists* of one sort or another; and however kind and friendly they might be, I, the man without a rag of a label to cover himself with, could not fail to have some of the uneasy feelings which must have beset the historical fox when, after leaving the trap in which his tail remained, he presented himself to his normally elongated companions. So I took thought, and invented what I conceived to be the appropriate title of 'agnostic'.

1869 *Science and Christian Tradition*.

8 The central propositions [of Descartes]...are these: There is a path that leads to the truth so surely that any one who will follow it must needs reach the goal... And there is one guiding rule by which a man may always find this path...give unqualified assent to no propositions but those the truth of which is so clear and distinct that they cannot be doubted.
1870 *Lay Sermons, Addresses, and Reviews*.

9 The great tragedy of Science—the slaying of a beautiful hypothesis by an ugly fact.
1870 'Biogenesis and Abiogenesis', in the *British Association Annual Report*.

10 Our reverence for the nobility of manhood will not be lessened by the knowledge that man is in substance and in structure, one with the brutes; for he alone possesses the marvellous endowment of intelligible and rational speech whereby...he has slowly accumulated and organized the experience which is almost wholly lost with the cessation of individual life in other animals; so that he now stands raised above it as on a mountain-top, far above the level of his humble fellows, and transfigured from his grosser nature by reflecting, here and there, a ray from the infinite source of truth.
1880 *Man's Place in Nature*.

11 It is the customary fate of new truths to begin as heresies and to end as superstitions.
1880 *Science and Culture and Other Essays*, 'The Coming of Age of the Origin of the Species'.

12 Irrationally held truths may be more harmful than reasoned errors.
1880 *Science and Culture and Other Essays*, 'The Coming of Age of the Origin of the Species'.

13 Science is nothing but trained and organized common sense, differing from the latter only as a veteran may differ from a raw recruit: and its methods differ from those of common sense only as far as the guardsman's cut and thrust differ from the manner in which a savage wields his club.
1893–4 *Collected Essays*, no.4, 'The Method of Zadig'.

14 Some experience of popular lecturing had convinced me that the necessity of making things plain to uninstructed people was one of the very best means of clearing up the obscure corners in one's own mind.
1894 *Man's Place in Nature* (rev edn), preface.

15 Next to being right in this world, the best of all things is to be clearly and definitely wrong. If you go buzzing about between right and wrong, vibrating and fluctuating, you come out nowhere; but if you are absolutely and thoroughly and persistently wrong you must, some of these days, have the extreme good fortune of knocking your head against a fact, and that sets you all straight again.
Attributed.

Huxtable, Ada Louise *née Landman* c.1921–

US architectural critic. In her columns for the *New York Times* (1963–82), she denounced new buildings and property speculation which spoiled American cities. Her work helped promote the preservation of historic buildings. She won the first Pulitzer Prize for criticism in 1970.

16 I got a terrible case of the Fountainblues.

1970 On Miami Beach. In the *New York Times*, 15 Oct.

17 America the beautiful,
Let me sing of thee;
Burger King and Dairy Queen
From sea to shining sea.
1971 'Goodbye History, Hello Hamburger', in the *New York Times*,
21 Mar.

18 New York, thy name is irreverence and hyperbole. And grandeur.
1975 In the *New York Times*, 20 Jul.

Hyde, Robin *pseudonym of* **Iris Guiver Wilkinson** 1906–39

New Zealand novelist, poet and journalist, born in South Africa. She was one of the few women career journalists of the 1930s. Brief affairs led to the births of two sons; the first, whose name she adopted, was stillborn. Her works include the autobiographical novel *The Godwits Fly* (1938).

19 Something there had been, something delicate, wild and far away. But it was shut out behind the doors of yesterday, lost beyond the hills.
1938 *The Godwits Fly*, ch.3.

20 You were English and not English. It took time to realize that England was far away.
1938 *The Godwits Fly*, ch.3.

21 We live half our lives in England…there can't have been anything quite like this since the Roman colonists settled in Britain: not the hanging on with one hand, and the other hand full of seas.
1938 *The Godwits Fly*, ch.8.

22 Having a lover isn't much to write home about.
1938 *The Godwits Fly*, ch.17.

23 She stands an instant in the sun
Athwart her harsh land's red and green—
Hands of a serf, and warrior eyes
Of some flame-sceptred Irish queen.
… As if she does not care that life
Has reft the jewels from her hair—
But grieves that menial needs and base
Were those that left her palace bare.
1938 *The Godwits Fly*, ch.23. This poem is an adaptation of 'The Farmer's Wife', first published in *The Desolate Star* (1929).

Hyde-White, Wilfred 1903–91

English film actor.

24 The suaveness isn't born of confidence; it's born of fright.
Quoted in his obituary, in the *San Francisco Chronicle*, 7 May 1991.

Hynde, Chrissie 1951–

US singer, member of The Pretenders.

25 I feel displaced when I'm back in America, like a visitor. I feel like if I don't get a cup of tea I'm going to lose my mind.
2003 In the *Daily Telegraph*, 19 Apr.

26 There's the meat eaters and there's us. And that's the way I look at the world.
2003 In *The Independent*, 13 Sep.

Hytner, Nicholas 1956–

English film and theatre director. He has been artistic director

at the National Theatre since 2003.

27 The theatre on its own can't and doesn't change society, but plays can define a moment. *The Marriage of Figaro* did seem to predict a revolution, but I doubt it sent anybody onto the streets.
2004 In *Varsity*, 6 Feb.

Iacocca, Lee (Lido Anthony) 1924–

US businessman, president of the Ford Motor Company and later head of Chrysler Corporation (1979–1992).

28 People want economy and they will pay any price to get it.
1974 In the *New York Times*, 13 Oct.

29 Everybody in an organization has to believe their livelihood is based on the quality of the product they deliver.
1988 *Talking Straight*.

30 If you want to continue being leaders in the world, start by getting some of that [Federal] debt off your backs. Debtors can't be leaders. It's the guy holding the IOUs who can call the shots; the other guy is called a hostage.
1992 Quoted in the *New York Times*, 26 May.

Ibarruri Gomez, Dolores *known as* **La Pasionaria** 1895–1989

Spanish writer and politician, a founder of the Spanish Communist Party (1920). She urged the fight against the Fascist forces, and left for the USSR when Franco came to power. On returning to Spain in 1977, she was re-elected to the National Assembly.

31 It is better to die on your feet than live on your knees. *No pasarán*!
1936 Speech in Paris, 3 Sep, at the onset of the Spanish Civil War, imploring the people to defend the Republic against the Fascist uprising. 'No pasarán', meaning 'they will not pass' and associated with the World War I Battle of Verdun, was to become the battle-cry of the Republican cause.
➤ See Pétain 649:74.

Ibn Battutah 1304–68

Arab traveller and geographer, who spent 30 years visiting parts of Africa, Asia and southern Europe. He then settled in Fez and wrote the history of his journeys.

32 Never to travel any road a second time.
His guiding principle. *Travels in Asia and Africa 1325–1354* (translated by H A R Gibb, 1929).

Ibsen, Henrik Johan 1828–1906

Norwegian playwright, the founder of modern prose drama. His realistic plays on sensitive social issues revolutionized modern European drama. They include *En dukkehjem* (*A Doll's House*, 1879), *Vildanden* (*The Wild Duck*, 1884) and *Hedda Gabler* (1890).

33 *Flertallet har aldrig retten på sin side. Aldrig, siger jeg!*
Det er en af disse samfundsløgnere, som en fri,
tænkende mand må gøre oprør imod. Hvem er det, som
udgør flertallet af beboerne i et land? Er det de kloge
folk, eller er det dè dumme? Jeg tænker, vi får vaere enige
om, at dumme mennesker er tilstede i en ganske
forskrækkelig overvældende majoritet rundt omkring
på den hele vide jord.
The majority never has right on its side. Never, I say! That
is one of the social lies that a free, thinking man is bound
to rebel against. Who makes up the majority in any given
country? Is it the wise men or the fools? I think we must
agree that the fools are in a terrible overwhelming
majority, all the wide world over.
1882 *En folkefiende (An Enemy of the People)*, act 4.

34 *En skulde aldrig ha' sine bedste buxer på, nå r en er ude*
og strider for frihed og sandhed.
You should never have your best trousers on when you
turn out to fight for freedom and truth.
1882 *En folkefiende (An Enemy of the People)*, act 5.

35 *Luftslotter,—de er så nemme at ty ôûnd i, de. Og nemme*
at bygge også.
Castles in the air—they are so easy to take refuge in. And
so easy to build, too.
1892 *Bygmester Solness (The Master Builder)*, act 3.

36 On the contrary!
1906 Last words, refuting a nurse's suggestion that he was
feeling better.

I Ching c.2000 BC

I Ching (*The Book of Changes*) is reputed to have been
composed by a Chinese king and his son under guidance from
a Taoist sage. It is a compendium of observations and advice
regarding the rise and fall of individuals and their power
groups and was later annotated by Confucius.

37 It is unlucky to sound off about happiness.
c.2000 BC *I Ching*, no.16 (translated by Thomas Cleary).

38 Change proves true on the day it is finished.
c.2000 BC *I Ching*, no.49 (translated by Thomas Cleary).

39 Cultured people practise self-examination with
trepidation and fear.
c.2000 BC *I Ching*, no.51 (translated by Thomas Cleary).

Ignatieff, Michael 1947–

Canadian author, broadcaster and academic.

40 The medium's gaze is brief, intense, and promiscuous.
The shelf life of the moral causes it makes its own is
brutally short.
1988 'Is Nothing Sacred? The Ethics of Television', in *Daedalus:*
Journal of the American Academy of Arts and Sciences, Fall.

Ignatow, David 1914–97

US poet and academic. He published several volumes of poetry,
much of it highly autobiographical in content.

41 Faster and faster it rolled,
with me running after it
bent low, gritting my teeth,
and I found myself doubled over
and rolling down the street
head over heels, one complete somersault
after another like a bagel

and strangely happy with myself.
1968 *Rescue the Dead*, 'The Bagel'.

42 To love is to be a fish.
My boat wallows in the sea.
You who are free,
rescue the dead.
1968 *Rescue the Dead*, 'Rescue the Dead'.

Ihimaera, Witi Tame 1944–

New Zealand writer and diplomat. His novel *Tangi* (1973), about
a son's return home to his father's funeral and to his Maori roots,
was the first written by a Maori to have been published. Other
works include *The Matriarch* (1986), *The Whale Rider* (1987) and
Sky Dancer (2003).

43 The sunlight falls across the country, lighting up the
greenstone years of a boy with his father.
1973 *Tangi*, ch.14.

44 *Titiro ki te rangi tahuri rawa ake, Kahore he whenua*
e…Kua riro: We looked up to heaven and before we
knew where we were there was no land left…gone.
1986 *The Matriarch*, ch.3.

Illich, Ivan 1926–2002

Austrian-born social critic, former priest and polymath. His
works include *Deschooling Society* (1971) and *In the Vineyard of*
the Text (1993).

45 Current nationalism is merely the affirmation of the right
of colonial elites to repeat history and follow the road
travelled by the rich toward the universal consumption
of internationally marketed packages, a road which can
ultimately lead only to universal pollution and universal
frustration.
1970 *Celebration of Awareness*, ch.12.

46 In both rich and poor nations consumption is polarized
while expectation is equalized.
1970 *Celebration of Awareness*, ch.12.

47 In a consumer society there are inevitably two kinds of
slaves: the prisoners of addiction and the prisoners of
envy.
1973 *Tools for Conviviality*, ch.3.

Independent on Sunday

48 Floral fascism and an explosion of almost medieval
irrationality.
1997 Editorial reflecting on the response to the death of Diana,
Princess of Wales, 9 Nov.

Inge, William Ralph 1860–1954

English prelate and theologian, known as 'The Gloomy Dean'
for his pessimistic sermons as Dean of St Paul's (1911–34). His
books include *Outspoken Essays* (1919, 1922), *Lay Thoughts of a*
Dean (1926, 1931) and more serious theological works.

49 It takes in reality only one to make a quarrel. It is useless
for the sheep to pass resolutions in favour of
vegetarianism, while the wolf remains of a different
opinion.
1919 *Outspoken Essays* (first series), 'Patriotism'.

50 A man may build himself a throne of bayonets, but he
cannot sit on it.
1923 *Philosophy of Plotinus*, vol.2, lecture 22.

51 Many people believe that they are attracted by God, or by Nature, when they are only repelled by man.
    1931 *More Thoughts of a Lay Dean*, pt.4, ch.1.

52 The enemies of freedom do not argue; they shout and they shoot.
    1948 *The End of an Age*, ch.4.

53 The effect of boredom on a large scale in history is underestimated. It is a main cause of revolutions, and would soon bring to an end all the static Utopias and the farmyard civilization of the Fabians.
    1948 *The End of an Age*, ch.6.

54 A nation is a society united by a delusion about its ancestry and by a common hatred of its neighbours.
    Sagittarius and George.

Ingersoll, Robert 1833–99

US lawyer, orator and freethinker, called 'The Great Agnostic' for his anti-religious views.

55 The hope of science is the perfection of the human race. The hope of theology is the salvation of a few and the damnation of almost everybody.
    1867 *The Age of Reason*, Mar.

56 An honest God is the noblest work of man.
    1876 *The Gods*, pt.1.
    ➤ See Pope 660:25.

57 In nature there are neither rewards nor punishments—there are consequences.
    1881 *Some Reasons Why*, pt.8, 'The New Testament'.

Ingham, Sir Bernard 1932–

English journalist and businessman, particularly known as Margaret Thatcher's chief press secretary (1979–90).

58 Blood sport is brought to its ultimate refinement in the gossip columns.
    1986 Speech, 5 Feb.

Ingram, John Kells 1823–1907

Irish economist and poet, Professor of Oratory then of Greek at Trinity College, Dublin. In 1847 he co-founded the Dublin Statistical Society, attempting in his works to formulate a social rather than purely mathematical science of economics.

59 Who fears to speak of Ninety-Eight?
Who blushes at the name?
When cowards mock the patriot's fate,
Who hangs his head for shame?
He's all a knave or half a slave
Who slights his country thus:
But a *true* man, like you, man,
Will fill your glass with us.
    1845 *The Spirit of the Nation*, 'The Memory of the Dead'.

Ingrams, Richard Reid 1937–

English writer, former editor of the satirical magazine *Private Eye.*

60 I have come to regard the law courts not as a cathedral but rather as a casino.
    1977 Referring to libel suits against him. Quoted in *The Guardian*, 30 Jul.

Ingres, Jean Auguste Dominique 1780–1867

French painter, leading exponent of the Classical tradition in 19c France. He painted many of his famous nudes while living in Rome (1806–20).

61 Is there anyone among the great men who has not imitated? Nothing is made with nothing.
    1821 Quoted in Henri Delaborde *Ingres, sa vie, ses travaux, sa doctrine* (1870).

62 What do these so-called artists mean when they preach the discovery of the 'new'? Is there anything new? Everything has been done, everything has been discovered.
    1821 Quoted in Henri Delaborde *Ingres, sa vie, ses travaux, sa doctrine* (1870).

63 Anti-classic art, if it may even be called an art, is merely the art of the idle. It is the doctrine of those who desire to produce without working, to know without learning.
    1821 Quoted in Henri Delaborde *Ingres, sa vie, ses travaux, sa doctrine* (1870).

64 Make copies, young man, many copies. You can only become a good artist by copying the masters.
    1855 Attributed comment to Degas. Quoted in A Vollard *Souvenirs d'un marchand de tableaux* (1937).

65 They have let the wolf into the sheepfold!
    1859 Attributed remark on hearing that Delacroix had been elected to the Academy. Quoted in P Amaury-Duval *L'Atelier d'Ingres* (1878).

66 One must go after the modelling like a fly crawling over a piece of paper.
    Attributed aphorism. Quoted in P Valéry *Degas, Danse, Dessin* (1938).

Innis, Harold Adams 1894–1952

Canadian political economist.

67 Canadian nationalism was systematically encouraged and exploited by American capital. Canada moved from colony to nation to colony.
    1948 'Great Britain, the United States and Canada', collected in Mary Quayle Innis (ed) *Essays in Canadian Economic History* (1956).

68 Property like incest holds the family together.
    Quoted in William Christian (ed) *The Idea File of Harold Adams Innis* (1980).

Pope Innocent III *originally* Lotario de' Conti di Segni 1160–1216

Italian prelate and scholar, elected Pope in 1198. He asserted the authority of the papacy over secular princes, and strongly promoted the Fourth Crusade.

69 *Omnis cupidus at avarus contra naturam nititur et molitur. Natura namque pauperem adducit in mundum; natura pauperem reducit a mundo.*
Every covetous and avaricious man struggles and strives against nature. For nature brings him into the world poor, and takes him out of it poor.
    1195 *De Miseraria Condicionis Humanae*, bk.2, ch.12.

70 *Gula carum tributem exigit, sed vilissimum reddit, quia quanto sunt delicaciora cibavia, tanto fetidiora sunt stercora.*
Gluttony demands a heavy tribute but gives the basest returns: the more delicate the food, the more reeking

the dung.
1195 *De Miseraria Condicionis Humanae*, bk.2, ch.20.

71 This [Magna Carta] has been forced from the King. It constitutes an insult to the Holy See, a serious weakening of the royal power, a disgrace to the English nation, a danger to all Christendom, since this civil war obstructs the crusade. Therefore…we condemn the charter and forbid the King to keep it, or the barons and their supporters to make him do so, on pain of excommunication.
1215 Papal Bull, 24 Aug.

Inouye, Daniel Ken 1924–

US politician, Democratic senator from Hawaii since 1962. He served on the committees investigating Watergate (1973–4) and (as chairman) the Iran-Contra affair (1987).

72 No times were more dangerous than when our country was born, when revolution was our midwife.
1987 Response to Adm John M Poindexter and Lt Col Oliver L North's contention that their actions were greatly influenced by 'a dangerous world'. In the *New York Times*, 24 Jul.

73 These hearings will be remembered longest not for the facts they elicited, but for the extraordinary and extraordinarily frightening views of government they exposed.
1987 On the Iran-Contra hearings. In the *New York Times*, 24 Jul.

74 A great nation betrayed the principles which have made it great, and thereby became hostage to hostage-takers.
1987 Of the Iran-Contra scandal. In the *New York Times*, 24 Jul.

Ionesco, Eugène 1912–94

French playwright. He pioneered a new style of drama that came to be called the Theatre of the Absurd.

75 *Un fonctionnaire ne plaisante pas.*
A civil servant doesn't make jokes.
1958 *Tueur sans gages*, act 1.

76 *C'est une chose anormale de vivre.*
Living is abnormal.
1959 *Rhinocéros*, act 1.

Irigaray, Luce c.1932–

Belgian-born French feminist literary critic and philosopher who has applied Lacan's psychoanalytic writings to the question of the difference between women's and men's writing.

77 *Il faut renouveler le langage.*
We must re-invent language.
1981 *Corps-à-corps avec la mère*.

Irving, Washington 1783–1859

US essayist. Under the pseudonym 'Geoffrey Crayon' he wrote *The Sketch Book* (1819–20) which included 'Rip Van Winkle' and 'The Legend of Sleepy Hollow'. Several collections are devoted to his European travels, including *Tales of a Traveller* (1824). He was US Ambassador to Spain (1842–6).

78 What is history, in fact, but a kind of Newgate calendar, a register of the crimes and miseries that man has inflicted on his fellow-man?
1809 *A History of New York*, bk.4, ch.1.

79 My native country was full of youthful promise; Europe was rich in the accumulated treasures of age.
1819–20 *The Sketch Book*, 'The Author's Account of Himself'.

80 A tart temper never mellows with age, and a sharp tongue is the only edged tool that grows keener with constant use.
1819–20 *The Sketch Book*, 'Rip Van Winkle'.

81 A woman's whole life is a history of the affections.
1819–20 *The Sketch Book*, 'The Broken Heart'.

82 Whenever a man's friends begin to compliment him about looking young, he may be sure that they think he is growing old.
1822 *Bracebridge Hall*, 'Bachelors'.

83 I am always at a loss to know how much to believe of my own stories.
1824 *Tales of a Traveller*, 'To the Reader'.

84 There is a certain relief in change, even though it be from bad to worse… I have often found in travelling in a stage-coach, that it is often a comfort to shift one's position, and be bruised in a new place.
1824 *Tales of a Traveller*, 'To the Reader'.

85 The almighty dollar, that great object of universal devotion throughout our land.
1855 *Wolfert's Roost*, 'The Creole Village'.

Isaacs, Jorge 1837–95

Colombian novelist. He worked variously as a journalist, businessman, government official and consul to Chile. His much-imitated romantic novel *María* (1867) is notable for its idyllic descriptions of nature.

86 *Las grandes bellezas de la creación no pueden a un tiempo ser vistas y cantadas: es necesario que vuelvan al alma empalidecidas por la memoria infiel.*
The most beautiful things on earth cannot be seen and sung at the same time: they must return to the soul weakened by unfaithful memory.
1867 *María*, ch.2 (translated as *María: A South American Romance*, 1977).

Isaacson, Walter Seff 1952–

US journalist and writer. He has been the managing editor of *Time* magazine (1996–2001) and chairman and chief executive officer of CNN. His books include *Kissinger: A Biography* (1992) and *Benjamin Franklin: An American Life* (2003).

87 He was something between an epitome and a parody.
1992 On Harvard Professor William Elliott, Kissinger's mentor. *Kissinger: A Biography*.

88 No one could shine his shoes, much less fill them.
1992 On President Nixon's self-image at the time of his resignation. *Kissinger: A Biography*.

Isherwood, Christopher William Bradshaw 1904–86

English novelist. He collaborated with Auden in the 1930s. He moved to California in 1939, and became a US citizen in 1946.

89 I am a camera with its shutter open, quite passive, recording, not thinking… Some day, all this will have to be developed, carefully printed, fixed.
1930 'A Berlin Diary', in *Goodbye to Berlin* (1939).

90 Like Shelley and like Baudelaire it may be said of him that he suffered, in his own person, the neurotic ills of an entire generation.
1937 Of T E Lawrence, 'Lawrence of Arabia'. Collected in *Exhumations* (1966).

91 They share the insult of each other's presence.
1962 On characters in his novels. *Down There on a Visit.*

Ishiguro, Kazuo 1954–

British novelist, born in Japan. His first book, *A Pale View of Hills* (1982), was set in Japan, but later works have been English in tone and subject, notably *The Remains of the Day* (1989, Booker Prize).

92 An Artist of the Floating World.
1988 Title of novel.

93 A 'great' butler can only be, surely, one who can point to his years of service and say that he has applied his talents to serving a great gentleman—and through the latter, to serving humanity.
1989 *The Remains of the Day,* 'Day Two— Afternoon'.

94 Perhaps it is indeed time that I began to look at this whole matter of bantering more enthusiastically. After all, when we think about it, it is not such a foolish thing to indulge in—particularly if it is the case that in bantering lies the key to human warmth.
1989 *The Remains of the Day,* 'Day Six—Evening'.

Issigonis, Sir Alec (Alexander Arnold Constantine) 1906–88

Turkish-born British car designer. He came to the English Midlands where he designed some of Britain's most popular and influential cars, including the Morris Minor and the Mini.

95 All creative people hate mathematics. It's the most uncreative subject you can study.
Recalled on his death. Quoted in *The Australian,* 5 Oct 1988.

96 Styling is designing for obsolescence.
Recalled on his death. Quoted in *The Australian,* 5 Oct 1988.

97 A camel is a horse designed by a committee.
Attributed to him in *The Guardian,* 14 Jan 1991.

Ito, Lance Allan 1950–

US jurist, presiding judge at the Los Angeles Superior Court (1989–). His most famous case is the O J Simpson murder trial (1994–5).

98 Rule 1: Be cautious, careful and when in doubt, keep your mouth shut. Rule 2: When tempted to say something, take a deep breath and refer to Rule 1.
1994 In the *New York Times,* 23 Jul.

Ivan IV *known as* Ivan the Terrible 1530–84

Grand Prince of Moscow (1533–84), the first to assume the title of 'tsar' (Latin *Caesar*). In 1564 he began a reign of terror, directed mainly at the aristocracy.

99 To shave the beard is a sin that the blood of all the martyrs cannot cleanse. It is to deface the image of man created by God.
Quoted in David Maland *Europe in the Seventeenth Century* (1968).

Iverson, Allen 1975–

US basketball player.

1 The basket looked like an ocean, and I was just throwing rocks in.
2003 After scoring 55 points for the Philadelphia 76ers against the New Orleans Hornets. Quoted on SI.com, 20 Apr.

Ives, Charles Edward 1874–1954

US composer. His innovative, experimental works were unappreciated for most of his life, but in 1947 he was awarded a Pulitzer Prize for his 3rd symphony (composed 1911).

2 Please don't try to make things nice! All the wrong notes are *right*… I want it that way.
c.1914 Note to the copyist of *The Fourth of July.*

Izzard, Eddie 1962–

British comedian and actor.

3 It's my manifest destiny to wear a skirt in all countries.
2001 Quoted on www.theonionavclub.com, 31 Jan.

4 Drama is a complete meal, vitamins, proteins, carbohydrates. It's a slow burn thing. It's got an arc. Comedy is more like coke.
2004 In *The Guardian,* 17 May.

Jackson, Jesse Louis 1941–

US clergyman and Democratic politician, founder and President of the Rainbow/PUSH (People United to Save Humanity) coalition. In 1984 and 1988 he sought nomination for the presidency, the first black American to be a serious candidate for the office.

5 I cast my bread on the waters long ago. Now it's time for you to send it back to me—toasted, and buttered on both sides.
1984 Addressing black voters, New York, 30 Jan.

6 My constituency is the desperate, the damned, the disinherited, the disrespected, and the despised.
1984 Speech at the Democratic National Convention, San Francisco, 17 Jul.

7 Our flag is red, white and blue, but our nation is a rainbow—red, yellow, brown, black and white—and we are all precious in God's sight… America is not like a blanket—one piece of unbroken cloth, the same color, the same texture, the same size. America is more like a quilt—many patches, many pieces, many colors, many sizes; all woven and held together by a common thread.
1984 Launching his 'rainbow coalition' at the Democratic National Convention, San Francisco, 17 Jul.

8 If I can conceive it and believe it, I can achieve it. It's not my aptitude but my attitude that will determine my altitude—*with a little intestinal fortitude!*
1988 *Ebony,* Aug.

Jackson, Peter 1961–

New Zealand film director, best known for directing the *Lord of the Rings* trilogy (*The Fellowship of the Ring,* 2001; *The Two Towers,* 2002; *The Return of the King,* 2003).

9 I read the book when I was 18 years old and thought 'I can't wait till the movie comes out'. Twenty years later no one had done it—so I got impatient.

2003 On how he came to direct the *Lord of the Rings*. Quoted in the *Observer*, 30 Nov.

Jackson, Robert Houghwout 1892–1954

US jurist, Associate Justice of the US Supreme Court (1941–54). He took leave to be US Chief Counsel at the Nuremberg war trials (1945–6). His decisions upheld freedom of speech and religion.

10 We are not final because we are infallible, but we are infallible only because we are final.

1953 Ruling to uphold the Supreme Court as the bench of last appeal, 9 Feb.

11 He who must search a haystack for a needle is likely to end up with the attitude that the needle is not worth the search.

1953 Ruling to uphold the Supreme Court as the bench of last appeal, 9 Feb.

Jacobs, Andrew, Jr 1932–

US lawyer and Democratic politician. He retired from Congress in 1997.

12 It's like saying that the patient died but the good news is that he's eating less.

1982 Of the Reagan administration's claim to have reduced inflation. In the *Washington Post*, 6 Jun.

Jacobs, Herman

Pharmaceutical store supplier.

13 It is not the mouse who is the thief, it is the hole that allows the mouse in.

1994 His interpretation of Talmudic principles applied in business. In *Forbes*, 21 Nov.

Jacobs, Joe 1896–1940

US boxing manager. He was manager of boxer Max Schmeling.

14 We wuz robbed!

1932 After Schmeling's unexpected defeat by Jack Sharkey, 21 Jun. Quoted in Peter Heller *In This Corner* (1975). Jack Dempsey in 1927 claimed 'I was robbed of the championship' when he lost to Gene Tunney. The cry was subsequently widely adopted by aggrieved losers.

Jacobs, W(illiam) W(ymark) 1863–1943

English short-story writer. He specialized in colourful yarns about the watermen on the Thames, and macabre stories.

15 'Dealing with a man,' said the night-watchman, 'is as easy as a teetotaller walking along a nice wide pavement; dealing with a woman is like the same teetotaller, after four or five whiskies, trying to get up a step that ain't there.'

1919 *Deep Waters*, 'Husbandry'.

Jagger, Mick and Richards, Keith 1943–, 1943–

English rock musicians, who with Bill Wyman, Charlie Watts and Brian Jones formed The Rolling Stones (1961). Their rebellious image and controversial lifestyles added to the extraordinary success of their music.

16 I can't get no satisfaction
I can't get no girl reaction.

1966 '(I Can't Get No) Satisfaction'.

17 Mother needs something today to calm her down,
And though she's not really ill,
There's a little yellow pill:
She goes running for the shelter
Of a mother's little helper,
And it helps her on her way,
Gets her through her busy day.

1966 'Mother's Little Helper'.

18 Please allow me to introduce myself
I'm a man of wealth and taste.
I've been around for a long, long year
Stole many a man's soul and faith.
And I was around when Jesus Christ
Had his moments of doubt and pain,
Made damn sure that Pilate
Washed his hands and sealed his fate.
Pleased to meet you, hope you guess my name
But what's puzzling you
Is the nature of my game.

1968 'Sympathy for the Devil'.

19 I shouted out, 'Who killed the Kennedys?'
When after all it was you and me.

1968 'Sympathy for the Devil'.

20 It's Only Rock and Roll.

1974 Title of song.

James I 1394–1437

King of Scotland (from 1424). He was imprisoned by the English for 18 years before returning to Scotland to take the throne. His measures to curb the nobles' power led to his murder. *The Kingis Quair* (c.1435), his only surviving work, is thought to have introduced Chaucerian style to Scotland.

21 The bird, the beste, the fisch eke in the see,
They lyve in fredome, euerich in his kynd,
And I, a man, and lakkith libertee!

c.1435 *The Kingis Quair*, stanza 27.

James IV 1473–1513

King of Scotland (from 1488). His marriage to Margaret Tudor, daughter of Henry VII of England, led ultimately to the union of the crowns. He was defeated and killed at Flodden.

22 It is statute and ordained that in na place of the Realme there be used Fute-ball, Golfe, or uther sik unproffitable sportes.

1491 Royal decree.

James V 1512–42

King of Scotland (from 1513). He succeeded to the throne as an infant, amid quarrelling pro-French and pro-English factions. As an adult he ruled with a mixture of good judgement and vindictiveness, strengthening the Crown's power and revenues.

23 Adieu, Farewell, it came with a lass, it will pass with a lass.

1542 Said on his deathbed, 14 Dec, on hearing of the birth of his daughter Mary, referring to the Crown of Scotland passing from the Stewarts. Quoted in Robert Lindsay of Pitscottie (c.1532–1580) *The Historie and Cronicles of Scotland* (published 1728), vol.1.

James, Alice 1848–92

US diarist, sister of Henry and William James. She spent her childhood travelling with her family in Europe. A semi-invalid for much of her life, she lived in England to be near her brother

Henry. Her diary was published posthumously.

24 How heroic to be able to suppress one's vanity to the extent of confessing that the game is too hard.
1889 On suicide. Diary entry, 5 Aug.

25 When will women begin to have the first glimmer that above all other loyalties is the loyalty to Truth, i.e., to yourself, that husband, children, friends and country are as nothing to that.
1889 Diary entry, 19 Nov.

26 How sick one gets of being 'good', how much I should respect myself if I could burst out and make every one wretched for 24 hours.
1889 Diary entry, 11 Dec.

27 I suppose one has a greater sense of intellectual degradation after an interview with a doctor than from any human experience.
1890 Diary entry, 27 Sep.

James, Clive Vivian Leopold 1939–

Australian journalist, writer and broadcaster, famous as a witty and perceptive cultural commentator.

28 A country so precipitously convoluted that the rivers flowing through it look like the silver trails of inebriated slugs.
1978 'Postcard from Japan', in the *Observer* magazine, 4 Jun.

29 She sounded like the book of Revelations read out over a railway station public-address system by a headmistress of a certain age wearing calico knickers.
1979 Of Margaret Thatcher. In the *Observer*.

30 I feared for her as I loved her, and the fear intensified the love.
1997 On the death of Diana, Princess of Wales. In the *New Yorker*, 15 Sep.

31 When you say a man writes badly, you are trying to hurt him. When you say it in words better than his, you have succeeded.
2003 In the *New York Times*, 7 Sep.

James, C(yril) L(ionel) R(obert) 1901–89

Trinidadian writer, lecturer and political activist. Arguing for the freedom of blacks through Marxism and revolution, he was deported from the US and placed under house arrest in Trinidad.

32 Body-line was not an incident, it was not an accident, it was not a temporary aberration. It was the violence and ferocity of our age expressing itself in cricket.
1963 *Beyond the Boundary.*

James, Henry 1843–1916

US-born British novelist, brother of William and Alice James. He took British citizenship in 1915. Many of his novels explore his 'international theme', including *The Ambassadors* (1903) and *The Golden Bowl* (1904). His critical theory is defined in 'The Art of Fiction' (1884).

33 It's a complex fate, being an American, and one of the responsibilities it entails is fighting against a superstitious valuation of Europe.
1872 Letter to Charles Eliot Norton, 4 Feb.

34 It takes a great deal of history to produce a little literature.
1879 *Hawthorne*, ch.1.

35 It is, I think, an indisputable fact that Americans are, as Americans, the most self-conscious people in the world, and the most addicted to the belief that the other nations of the earth are in a conspiracy to under value them.
1879 *Hawthorne*, ch.6.

36 Cats and monkeys—monkeys and cats—all human life is there!
1879 *The Madonna of the Future*, vol.1. The *News of the World* took 'All human life is there' as its slogan from the late 1950s.

37 There are few hours in life more agreeable than the hour dedicated to the ceremony known as afternoon tea.
1881 *The Portrait of a Lady*, ch.1.

38 An Englishman's never so natural as when he's holding his tongue.
1881 Isabel Archer. *The Portrait of a Lady*, ch.10.

39 Money's a horrid thing to follow, but a charming thing to meet.
1881 Gilbert Osmond. *The Portrait of a Lady*, ch.35.

40 Art derives a considerable part of its beneficial exercise from flying in the face of presumptions.
1884 'The Art of Fiction', collected in *Partial Portraits* (1988).

41 The only obligation to which in advance we may hold a novel, without incurring the accusation of being arbitrary, is that it be interesting.
1884 'The Art of Fiction', collected in *Partial Portraits* (1888).

42 Experience is never limited, and it is never complete; it is an immense sensibility, a kind of huge spider-web of the finest silken threads suspended in the chamber of consciousness, and catching every air-borne particle in its tissue.
1884 'The Art of Fiction', collected in *Partial Portraits* (1888).

43 Try to be one of the people on whom nothing is lost!
1884 'The Art of Fiction', collected in *Partial Portraits* (1888).

44 What is character but the determination of incident? What is incident but the illustration of character?
1884 'The Art of Fiction', collected in *Partial Portraits* (1888).

45 The superiority of one man's opinion over another's is never so great as when the opinion is about a woman.
1890 *The Tragic Muse*, ch.9.

46 We work in the dark—we do what we can—we give what we have. Our doubt is in our passion and our passion is our task. The rest is madness.
1893 Dencombe speaking of the artist. 'The Middle Years', in *Scribner's Magazine*, May.

47 The time-honored bread-sauce of the happy ending.
1894–5 *Theatricals, Second Series*, preface.

48 Most English talk is a quadrille in a sentry box.
1899 The Duchess. *The Awkward Age*, bk.5, ch.4.

49 People talk about the conscience, but it seems to me one must just bring it up to a certain point and leave it there. You can let your conscience alone if you're nice to the second housemaid.
1899 Nanda Brookenham. *The Awkward Age*, bk.6, ch.3.

50 Live all you can; it's a mistake not to. It doesn't so much matter what you do in particular, so long as you have your life. If you haven't had that what *have* you had?
1903 Lambert Strether. *The Ambassadors*, bk.5, ch.11.

51 In art economy is always beauty.
1909 Preface for revised New York edn of *The Altar of the Dead* (first published 1895).

52 The terrible *fluidity* of self-revelation.
1909 Preface for revised NewYork edn of *The Ambassadors* (first published 1903).

53 I'm glad you like adverbs—I adore them; they are the only qualifications I really much respect.
1912 Letter to Miss M Bentham Edwards, 5 Jan, quoted in Percy Lubbock (ed) *The Letters of Henry James* (1920).

54 Summer afternoon—summer afternoon; to me those have always been the two most beautiful words in the English language.
Quoted in Edith Wharton *A Backward Glance* (1934), ch.10, section 6.

55 So here it is at last, the distinguished thing!
Quoted in Edith Wharton *A Backward Glance* (1934), ch.14, section 3. According to Wharton, these were James's last words.

56 I hate American simplicity. I glory in the piling up of complications of every sort.
Remark to his niece. Quoted in Leon Edel *The Letters of Henry James* (1953–72), vol.4, introduction.

James (of Holland Park), P(hyllis) D(orothy) James, Baroness 1920–

English writer. She specializes in carefully detailed crime fiction.

57 I thought that writing a detective story would be a wonderful apprenticeship because, whatever people tell you, a crime novel is not easy to write well. As I continued with my craft I became increasingly fascinated by the form and realized that you can use the formula to say something true about men and women and the society in which they live.
1991 'Series Detectives', collected in Brown and Munro (eds) *Writers Writing* (1993).

58 Murder is a unique crime for which we can never make reparation.
1991 'Series Detectives', collected in Brown and Munro (eds) *Writers Writing* (1993).

James, William 1842–1910

US philosopher and psychologist, brother of Henry and Alice James. A 'radical empiricist', he is often considered the founder of pragmatism. *The Principles of Psychology* (1890) places psychology on a physiological basis. Other works include *The Will to Believe* (1897) and *Pragmatism* (1907).

59 Man lives by science as well as bread.
1875 *Vivisection.*

60 Metaphysics means nothing but an unusually obstinate effort to think clearly.
1890 *The Principles of Psychology*, ch.6.

61 But facts are facts, and if we only get enough of them they are sure to combine.
1890 *The Principles of Psychology*, ch.7.

62 The aim of science is always to reduce complexity to simplicity.
1890 *The Principles of Psychology*, ch.9.

63 Consciousness, then, does not appear to itself chopped up in bits. Such words as 'chain' or 'train' do not describe it fitly as it presents itself in the first instance. It is nothing jointed; it flows. A 'river' or a 'stream' are the metaphors by which it is most naturally described. *In talking of it*

hereafter, let us call it the stream of thought, of consciousness, or of subjective life.
1890 *The Principles of Psychology*, ch.9. This is the coining of the phrase 'stream of consciousness', later applied to the narrative technique used by Joyce and others.

64 The baby, assailed by eyes, ears, nose, skin, and entrails at once, feels it all as one great blooming, buzzing confusion.
1890 *The Principles of Psychology*, ch.13.

65 As the art of reading (after a certain stage in one's education) is the art of skipping, so the art of being wise is the art of knowing what to overlook.
1890 *The Principles of Psychology*, ch.22.

66 Man is essentially *the* imitative animal. His whole educability and in fact the whole history of civilization depend on this trait, which his strong tendencies to rivalry, jealousy, and acquisitiveness reinforce.
1890 *The Principles of Psychology*, ch.24.

67 If this life be not a real fight, in which something is eternally gained for the universe by success, it is no better than a game of private theatricals from which one may withdraw at will.
1897 *The Will to Believe.*

68 Sobriety diminishes, discriminates, and says no; drunkenness expands, unites, and says yes.
1902 *The Varieties of Religious Experience*, 'Mysticism'.

69 The philosophy which is so important in each of us is not a technical matter; it is our more or less dumb sense of what life honestly and deeply means… it is our individual way of just seeing and feeling the total push and pressure of the cosmos.
1907 *Pragmatism*, lecture 1.

70 Tender-minded and tough-minded.
1907 His terms for two kinds of philosophical temperament. *Pragmatism*, lecture 1.

71 You must bring out of each word its practical cash-value, set it at work within the stream of your experience.
1907 *Pragmatism*, lecture 2.

72 First, you know, a new theory is attacked as absurd; then it is admitted to be true, but obvious and insignificant; finally it is seen to be so important that its adversaries claim that they themselves discovered it.
1907 *Pragmatism*, lecture 6.

73 'The true' to put it very briefly, is only the expedient in the way of our thinking, just as 'the right' is only the expedient in the way of our behaving.
1907 *Pragmatism*, lecture 6.

74 Many persons nowadays seem to think that any conclusion must be very scientific if the arguments in favor of it are derived from twitching of frogs' legs—especially if the frogs are decapitated—and that—on the other hand—any doctrine chiefly vouched for by the feelings of human beings—with heads on their shoulders—must be benighted and superstitious.
1907 *Pragmatism.*

75 Hogamus, higamous
Man is polygamous
Higamous, hogamous
Woman monogamous.
Quoted in the *Oxford Book of Marriage* (1990).

Janeway, Elizabeth Hall 1913–

US author and critic.

76 As long as mixed grills and combination salads are popular, anthologies will undoubtedly continue in favor.
Quoted in Helen Hull (ed) *The Writer's Book* (1950), ch.32.

Janowitz, Tama 1957–

US writer. She has written novels and short stories, and scored a cult success with the story collection *Slaves of New York* (1986).

77 Long after the bomb falls and you and your good deeds are gone, cockroaches will still be here, prowling the streets like armoured cars.
1986 *Slaves of New York*, 'Modern Saint 271'.

78 With publicity comes humiliation.
1992 In the *International Herald Tribune*, 8 Sep.

Jarrell, Randall 1914–65

US poet and critic. A passionate poet and incisive critic, he also wrote one satirical novel, *Pictures from an Institution* (1954), and children's books. He committed suicide.

79 I felt quite funny when Freud died. It was like having a continent disappear.
1939 Letter to Allen Tate, Sep.

80 Six miles from earth, loosed from its dream of life, I woke to black flak and the nightmare fighters. When I died they washed me out of the turret with a hose.
1945 'The Death of the Ball Turret Gunner'.

81 A good poet is someone who manages, in a lifetime of standing out in thunderstorms, to be struck by lightning five or six times; a dozen or two dozen times and he is great.
1953 *Poetry and the Age*, 'The Obscurity of the Poet'.

82 President Robbins was so well adjusted to his environment that sometimes you could not tell which was the environment and which was President Robbins.
1954 *Pictures from an Institution*, pt.1, ch.4.

83 To Americans, English manners are far more frightening than none at all.
1954 *Pictures from an Institution*, pt.1, ch.4.

84 She looked at me the way you'd look at a chessman if it made its own move.
1954 *Pictures from an Institution*, pt.2, ch.1.

85 It's better to entertain an idea than to take it home to live with you for the rest of your life.
1954 *Pictures from an Institution*, pt.4, ch.9.

86 You Americans do not rear children, you *incite* them; you give them food and shelter and applause.
1954 *Pictures from an Institution*, pt.4, ch.10.

87 Is an institution always a man's shadow shortened in the sun, the lowest common denominator of everybody in it?
1954 *Pictures from an Institution*, pt.5, ch.9.

88 One of the most obvious facts about grown-ups, to a child, is that they have forgotten what it is like to be a child.
Introduction to Christina Stead *The Man Who Loved Children* (1965).

Jarry, Alfred 1873–1907

French playwright and humorist, best known for the creation of the petty tyrant in *Ubu Roi* (1896), a play first written when he was only 15.

89 *Quant à l'action, elle se passe en Pologne, c'est à dire, nulle part.*
The action takes place in Poland; in other words, nowhere.
1896 *Ubu Roi*, introduction.

90 *Mère Ubu, tu es bien laide aujourd'hui. Est-ce parce que nous avons du monde?*
Mother Ubu, you are very ugly today. Is it because we have company?
1896 *Ubu Roi*, act 1, sc.1.

91 *La mort n'est que pour les médiocres.*
Death is only for the mediocre.
1898 *Gestes et opinions du Docteur Faustroll Pataphysicien*, vol.8, pt.37.

92 *Dieu est le point tangent de zéro et de l'infini.*
God is the tangential point of zero and the infinite.
1898 *Gestes et opinions du Docteur Faustroll Pataphysicien*, vol.8, pt.41.

93 *S'apercevoir que sa mère est vierge.—Les 36 situations dramatiques; trente-septième situation.*
The thirty-seventh dramatic situation out of 36: To become aware that one's mother is a virgin.
1899 *L'Amour absolu*, pt.3, épigraphe.

Jason, David 1940–

English actor, known for a variety of television roles.

94 Why do they call me David 'Del Boy' Jason? You never hear anyone talking about Alec 'Bridge Over the River Kwai' Guinness.
On his ongoing association with his character in *Only Fools and Horses*. Quoted in Stafford Hildred and Tim Ewbank *Arise Sir David Jason* (2003).

Jaurès, (Auguste Marie Joseph) Jean 1859–1914

French socialist leader, writer and orator. He co-founded the socialist paper *L'Humanité* (1904), and was central in the founding of the French Socialist Party. He was assassinated in Paris.

95 There is, then, over the affairs of the army a universal conspiracy of silence, of childlike mysteries, of clannishness, routine and intrigue.
1910 *L'Armée nouvelle*.

Jay, Sir Antony Rupert 1930–

English writer and television producer. He joined the BBC in 1955, editing *Tonight* (1962–3) and co-writing the successful *Yes, Minister* and *Yes, Prime Minister* (1980–8). He was knighted in 1988.

96 From now on you can keep the lot.
Take every single thing you've got,
Your land, your wealth, your men, your dames,
Your dream of independent power,
And dear old Konrad Adenauer,
And stick them up your Eiffel Tower.
1963 On France's rejection of British membership of the Common Market, in *Time*, 8 Feb.

97 The great modern corporations are so similar to independent or semi-independent states of the past that they can only be fully understood in terms of political or constitutional history, and management can only be properly studied as a branch of government.
1967 *Management and Machiavelli.*

98 Efficiency…is measured at the extremities. You do not find the efficiency of an army at headquarters, nor of a firm in head office. It is at the remotest point—the private soldier or humble legionary on the distant frontier, the girl at the counter or the branch-office junior salesman —that the really decisive test of an army or a firm is made. It is there that all the instruction and knowledge of relevant facts and procedural disciplines bear fruit—or wither on the tree.
1967 *Management and Machiavelli.*

99 The bigger the organization, the fewer the jobs worth doing.
1967 *Management and Machiavelli.*

Jay (of Paddington), Margaret Jay, Baroness 1939–

English Labour peer, Leader of the House of Lords (1998–2001).

1 I never aim to be unpredictable.
2000 In the *Observer*, 'They Said What…?', 20 Feb.

Jay, Peter 1937–

English economist, broadcaster and diplomat, Ambassador to the US (1977–9), later economics editor at the BBC (1990–2001).

2 [Prince Charles] is entitled to be as underwhelmed by the prospect of reigning over a fourth-class nation as the rest of us are by the prospect of living in it.
1986 Of Prince Charles. In the *London Illustrated News*, Apr.

Jeffers, (John) Robinson 1887–1962

US poet and dramatist. A number of his works drew on themes from biblical stories and Greek drama. His veneration of nature often went hand in hand with a contempt for the works of humanity.

3 While this America settles in the mould of its vulgarity, heavily
thickening to empire.
1924 *Tamar and Other Poems*, 'Shine, Perishing Republic'.

4 And boys, be in nothing so moderate as in love of man, a clever servant,
insufferable master.
1924 *Tamar and Other Poems*, 'Shine, Perishing Republic'.

5 The poet as well
Builds his monument mockingly;
For man will be blotted out, the blithe earth die, the brave sun
Die blind, his heart blackening:
Yet stones have stood for a thousand years, and pained thoughts found
The honey peace in old poems.
1924 *Tamar and Other Poems*, 'To the Stone-Cutters'.

6 The wing trails like a banner in defeat,
No more to use the sky forever but live with famine
And pain a few days.
1928 *Cawdor*, 'Hurt Hawks'.

7 He is strong and pain is worse to the strong, incapacity is worse.
1928 *Cawdor*, 'Hurt Hawks'.

8 The wild God of the world is sometimes merciful to those
That ask mercy, not often to the arrogant.
You do not know him, you communal people, or you have forgotten him;
Intemperate and savage, the hawk remembers him;
Beautiful and wild, the hawks, and men that are dying, remember him.
1928 *Cawdor*, 'Hurt Hawks'.

9 I'd sooner, except the penalties, kill a man than a hawk.
1928 *Cawdor*, 'Hurt Hawks'.

10 This wild swan of a world is no hunter's game.
Better bullets than yours would miss the white breast,
Better mirrors than yours would crack in the flame.
1935 *Solstice*, 'Love the Wild Swan'.

11 Praise life, it deserves praise, but the praise of life
That forgets the pain is a pebble
Ruttled in dry ground.
1948 *The Double Axe and Other Poems*.

Jefferson, Thomas 1743–1826

US statesman, third President (1801–9). Prominent in the first Continental Congress (1774), he drafted the Declaration of Independence. His administration saw war with Tripoli, the Louisiana Purchase (1803) and the prohibition of the slave trade.

12 We hold these truths to be sacred and undeniable; that all men are created equal and independent; that from that equal creation they derive rights inherent and inalienable, among which are the preservation of life, and liberty, and the pursuit of happiness.
c.1776 Draft of the American Declaration of Independence. Collected in J P Boyd et al *Papers of Thomas Jefferson* (1950), vol.1.

13 Were it left to me to decide whether we should have a government without newspapers, or newspapers without a government, I should not hesitate a moment to prefer the latter.
1787 Letter to Col Edward Carrington, 16 Jan.

14 A little rebellion now and then is a good thing.
1787 Letter to James Madison, 30 Jan.

15 The tree of liberty must be refreshed from time to time with the blood of patriots and tyrants. It is its natural manure.
1787 Letter to W S Smith, 13 Nov.

16 A bill of rights is what the people are entitled to against every government on earth, general or particular, and what no just government should refuse or rest on inference.
1787 Letter to James Madison, 20 Dec.

17 I have seen enough of one war never to wish to see another.
1794 Letter to John Adams, 25 Apr.

18 I am for encouraging the progress of science in all its branches; and not for…awing the human mind by stories of raw-head and bloody bones to a distrust of its own vision and to repose implicitly on that of others.
1799 Letter, 26 Jan.

19 Equal and exact justice to all men…freedom of religion, freedom of the press, freedom of the person under the protection of the habeas corpus; and trial by juries impartially selected—these principles form the bright constellation that has gone before us.
1801 Inaugural address, 4 Mar.

20 When a man assumes a public trust, he should consider himself as public property.
1807 Letter to Baron von Humboldt.

21 Some men look at Constitutions with sanctimonious reverence and deem them like the Ark of the Covenant —too sacred to be touched.
1816 Letter to Samuel Kercheval, 12 Jul.

22 Games played with the ball, and others of that nature, are too violent for the body, and stamp no character on the mind.
Quoted in Colin Jarman *The Guinness Dictionary of Sports Quotations* (1990).

Jeffrey, Lord Francis 1773–1850

Scottish critic, lawyer and judge, founder of the *Edinburgh Review*.

23 This will never do.
1814 Of Wordsworth's *The Excursion* (1814). In the *Edinburgh Review*, Nov.

Jenkins, David Edward 1925–

English churchman, Bishop of Durham (1984–94). He became notorious for his radical and often controversial views.

24 A conjuring trick with bones only proves that it is as clever as a conjuring trick with bones… A resuscitated corpse might be a resuscitated corpse and might be the sign of something, but there is still the question of what it is the symbol of.
1984 Of the Christian doctrine of Christ's physical resurrection. 'Poles Apart', BBC radio broadcast, 4 Oct.

25 Christians are not called to win battles, but to find ways of being in battles.
1988 *Spirituality for Conflict*.

Jenkins (of Hillhead), Roy Harris Jenkins, Baron 1920–2003

Welsh Labour politician and author.

26 I have become increasingly convinced that great men have strong elements of comicality in them.
2001 *Churchill*.

Jensen, Albert D

US soldier, colonel in the air force.

27 We're going faster and lower than anything out there. And we can bomb the knot off a tree.
1987 On the capabilities of the B-1 bomber 10 years after its initial development. In the *New York Times*, 4 Jul.

Jerome, Jerome K(lapka) 1859–1927

English humorous novelist and playwright. He became joint editor of *The Idler* (1892) and started his own weekly, *To-Day*. He is best known for his classic *Three Men in a Boat* (1889).

28 It is impossible to enjoy idling thoroughly unless one has plenty of work to do.

1886 *Idle Thoughts of an Idle Fellow*, 'On Being Idle'.

29 Love is like the measles; we all have to go through it.
1886 *Idle Thoughts of an Idle Fellow*, 'On Being in Love'.

30 We drink one another's healths, and spoil our own.
1886 *Idle Thoughts of an Idle Fellow*, 'On Eating and Drinking'.

31 It is a most extraordinary thing, but I never read a patent medicine advertisement without being impelled to the conclusion that I am suffering from the particular disease therein dealt with in its most virulent form.
1889 *Three Men in a Boat*, ch.1.

32 But there, everything has its drawbacks, as the man said when his mother-in-law died, and they came down upon him for the funeral expenses.
1889 *Three Men in a Boat*, ch.3.

33 I like work: it fascinates me. I can sit and look at it for hours. I love to keep it by me: the idea of getting rid of it nearly breaks my heart.
1889 *Three Men in a Boat*, ch.15.

34 It is always the best policy to speak the truth—unless, of course, you are an exceptionally good liar.
1892 In *The Idler* (edited by Robert Barr and Jerome), Feb.

35 I want a house that has got over all its troubles; I don't want to spend the rest of my life bringing up a young and inexperienced house.
1909 *They and I*, ch.11.

36 I did not know I was a humorist. I have never been sure about it. In the middle ages, I should probably have gone about preaching and got myself burned or hanged.
1926 *My Life and Times*, ch.6.

Jerome, William 1865–1932

US songwriter.

37 Any Old Place I Can Hang My Hat Is Home Sweet Home to Me.
1901 Title of song.

Jerrold, Douglas William 1803–57

English author, dramatist and wit. His works include the play *Black-ey'd Susan* (1829), various comedies and a series of novels. He wrote for *Punch* under the pseudonym 'Q' and edited several magazines.

38 Religion's in the heart, not in the knees.
1830 *The Devil's Ducat*, act 1, sc.2.

39 Earth is here so kind, that just tickle her with a hoe and she laughs with a harvest.
Of Australia. *The Wit and Opinions of Douglas Jerrold* (published 1859), 'A Land of Plenty'.

40 Love's like the measles—all the worse when it comes late in life.
The Wit and Opinions of Douglas Jerrold (published 1859), 'Love'.

41 The best thing I know between France and England is—the sea.
The Wit and Opinions of Douglas Jerrold (published 1859), 'The Anglo-French Alliance'.

42 If an earthquake were to engulf England tomorrow, the English would manage to meet and dine somewhere among the rubbish, just to celebrate the event.
Quoted in Blanchard Jerrold *The Life and Remains of Douglas Jerrold* (1859), ch.14.

43 The only athletic sport I mastered was backgammon.
Quoted in W Jerrold *Douglas Jerrold* (1914), vol.1, ch.1.

Jevons, William Stanley 1835–82

English economist, Professor of Political Economy at University College London (1876–81).

44 Economics, if it is to be a science at all, must be a mathematical science.
1871 *The Theory of Political Economy.*

45 The point of equilibrium will be known by the criterion that an infinitely small amount of commodity exchanged in addition, at the same rate, will bring neither gain nor loss of utility.
1871 *The Theory of Political Economy.*

46 Labour once spent has no influence on the future value of any article; it is gone and lost for ever. In commerce bygones are for ever bygones; and we are always starting clear at each moment, judging the values of things with a view to future utility.
1871 *The Theory of Political Economy.*

47 All classes of society are trade unionists at heart, and differ chiefly in the boldness, ability, and secrecy with which they pursue their respective interests.
1882 *The State in Relation to Labour*, introduction.

48 It is requisite from time to time to remind one generation of the experience which led a former generation to important legislative actions.
1882 *The State in Relation to Labour.*

Jiang Qing *or Chiang Ch'ing* 1914–91

Chinese politician, third wife of Mao Zedong. After Mao's death in 1976 she was arrested—as one of the 'gang of four'—and sentenced to death in 1980, later commuted to life imprisonment. She committed suicide.

49 Sex is engaging in the first rounds but what sustains interest in the long run is power.
c.1970 Quoted in Ross Merrill *Mao* (1993), ch.10.

50 Man's contribution to human history is nothing more than a drop of sperm.
1984 In *Newsweek*, 20 Feb.

51 Today the revolution has been stolen by the revisionist clique of Deng.
1991 Remark, May. Quoted in Ross Merrill *Mao* (1993), introduction.

St Joan of Arc 1412–31

French patriot and saint. As a 13-year-old peasant she heard saintly voices bidding her to free Paris from the English, and in 1429 she led troops into Orleans and successfully raised the siege. She was later sold to the English, who burned her as a witch.

52 And as for you, archers, soldiers, gentlemen, and all others who are besieging Orleans, depart in God's name to your own country… I assure you that wherever I find your people in France I shall fight them, and pursue them, and expel them from here, whether they will or not.
1429 Letter to the English at Poitiers, 22 Mar. Quoted in *Les Procès de Jeanne d'Arc* (translated by C Larrington), p.33.

53 Si je n'y suis, Dieu m'y veuille mettre; et si j'y suis, Dieu

m'y veuille tenir.
If I am not in grace, may God set me there; and if I am, may God keep me there.
1431 Quoted in the record of her trial at Rouen, 24 Feb.

Joel, Billy 1949–

US singer, pianist and songwriter.

54 The piano is a percussion instrument, like a drum. You don't strum a piano. You don't bow a piano. You bang and strike a piano. You beat the shit out of a piano.
2004 *Rolling Stone*, 15 Apr.

Pope John XXIII *originally Angelo Giuseppe Roncalli* 1881–1963

Italian prelate, Pope (1958–63). He convened the 21st Ecumenical Council and in 1963 issued the encyclical *Pacem in Terris* ('Peace on Earth'), advocating reconciliation between East and West.

55 In order to imbue civilization with sound principles and enliven it with the spirit of the gospel, it is not enough to be illumined with the gift of faith and enkindled with the desire of forwarding a good cause. For this end it is necessary to take an active part in the various organizations and influence them from within. And since our present age is one of outstanding scientific and technical progress and excellence, one will not be able to enter these organizations and work effectively from within unless he is scientifically competent, technically capable and skilled in the practice of his own profession.
1963 *Pacem in Terris*, 10 Apr.

56 If civil authorities legislate for or allow anything that is contrary to that order and therefore contrary to the will of God, neither the laws made nor the authorizations granted can be binding on the consciences of the citizens, since God has more right to be obeyed than man.
1963 *Pacem in Terris*, 10 Apr.

57 The social progress, order, security and peace of each country are necessarily connected with the social progress, order, security and peace of all other countries.
1963 *Pacem in Terris*, 10 Apr.

St John of the Cross *originally Juan de Yepes y Álvarez* 1542–91

Spanish Christian mystic, founder of the Order of Discalced Carmelites.

58 God passes through the thicket of the world, and wherever his glance falls he turns all things to beauty.
Cántico espiritual (translated by K Kavanaugh and O Rodriguez as *The Spiritual Canticle*).

John III Sobieski of Poland 1624–96

King of Poland (from 1674), elected after a distinguished military career. He formed the Holy League alliance with Pope Innocent XI and the Holy Roman Emperor, Leopold I, in 1688, campaigning against the Turks.

59 I came, I saw, God conquered.
1683 Message sent to the Pope after the defeat of the Turks at the Battle of Vienna, 12 Sep.
➤ See Caesar 184:25, Charles V 207:35.

Pope John Paul II *originally* **Karol Jozef Wojtyła** 1920–

Polish priest and theologian. He became Archbishop and Metropolitan of Cracow in 1964, was elected Cardinal (1967) and then Pope (1978), the first non-Italian pope in 456 years.

60 It is unbecoming for a cardinal to ski badly.
c.1968 Attributed, responding to criticism that it was unbecoming for him, then a cardinal, to be seen skiing.

61 The command 'Thou shalt not kill' must be binding on the conscience of humanity if the terrible tragedy and destiny of Cain is not to be repeated.
1979 Speech at Drogheda, Ireland, 29 Sep.

62 Violence is a lie, for it goes against the truth of our faith, the truth of our humanity… Violence is a crime against humanity, for it destroys the very fabric of society. On my knees I beg you to turn away from the paths of violence.
1979 Speech at Drogheda, Ireland, 29 Sep.

63 Commitment to the poor is based on the Gospel: it does not have to rely on some political manifesto.
1979 Speech at the Third Conference of Latin American Bishops, Puebla.

64 A process of genocide is being carried out before the eyes of the world.
1989 Of the situation in Beirut. In *The Independent*, 16 Aug.

John, Sir Elton Hercules *originally* **Reginald Kenneth Dwight** 1947–

English pop singer, songwriter and pianist. In a prolific career his albums have included *Tumbleweed Connection* (1970), *Don't Shoot Me I'm Only the Piano Player* (1973), *A Single Man* (1978), *Too Low for Zero* (1983), *Sleeping with the Past* (1989) and *Made in England* (1995).

65 Goodbye England's Rose;
May you ever grow in our hearts.
1997 From 'Candle in the Wind', sung at the funeral of Diana, Princess of Wales, co-written with Bernie Taupin. The song was a reworking of an earlier song to Marilyn Monroe.

66 I'm not a nest-egg person.
2000 On how he manages to spend £2m a month. In *The Guardian*, 31 Dec.

John, Gwen 1876–1939

Welsh painter, sister of Augustus John. From 1904 she worked in Paris as an artist's model, becoming Rodin's mistress. She converted to Roman Catholicism in 1913 and became increasingly reclusive.

67 My religion and my art—they are all my life.
Quoted in K Petersen and J J Wilson *Women Artists* (1979).

Johns, Jasper 1930–

US painter and sculptor, a pioneer of Pop Art in the US. He challenged the relationship between art and reality, painting ordinary objects in a deliberately banal style (eg *Flag*, 1954).

68 Things that are seen but not looked at.
1988 Defining the subject of his art. Quoted by Deborah Solomon in 'The Unflagging Artistry of Jasper Johns', in the *New York Times*, 19 Jun.

Johnson, Ben 1961–

Jamaican-born Canadian sprinter.

69 I have never, ever knowingly taken illegal drugs, and I would never embarrass my family, my friends, my country, and the kids who love me.
1988 Statement at press conference, Toronto, 4 Oct. Johnson tested positive to the use of banned substances, was stripped of his Olympic gold medal, and subsequently admitted using anabolic steroids.

Johnson, Boris 1964–

English journalist and Conservative politician. He has been editor of *The Spectator* since 1999 and MP for Henley since 2001.

70 My chances of being PM are about as good as the chances of finding Elvis on Mars, or my being reincarnated as an olive.
2004 In the *Observer*, 20 Jun.

Johnson, Claudia Alta Taylor *known as* **Lady Bird** 1912–

US First Lady (1963–9), the widow of President Lyndon B Johnson. She was active in conservation and improvement programmes. After the presidency she published *A White House Diary* (1970).

71 We had a delicious dinner of too much.
1970 On dining at Manhattan's Plaza Hotel. *A White House Diary*.

72 Somehow that was one of the most poignant sights —that immaculate woman, exquisitely dressed, and caked in blood.
1970 On Jacqueline Kennedy after her husband's assassination. *A White House Diary*.

73 I face the prospect of another campaign like an open-ended stay in a concentration camp.
1970 *A White House Diary*.

74 Mrs Kennedy is going to marry Aristotle Socrates Onassis!… I feel strangely freer! No shadow walks behind me down the halls of the White House.
1970 *A White House Diary*.

75 We were distant. But that suited both of us.
1995 On her relationship with Jacqueline Kennedy Onassis. In the *Washington Post*, 23 Mar.

76 This country needs to be united. And sadly, sadly, he wasn't the man who could do it.
1995 On Lyndon B Johnson's decision not to seek a second term during the Vietnam War. In the *Washington Post*, 23 Mar.

Johnson, Earvin ('Magic') 1959–

US basketball player. He played with the Los Angeles Lakers (1979–91, 1996) and was a member of the gold medal-winning US Olympic basketball team ('Dream Team') in 1992.

77 We've dominated sports and we've dominated entertainment, but our problem has been we've never been able to dominate money. We still don't own our share of business, and it's killing us. It's killing our communities.
2003 On African Americans. Quoted in *Los Angeles Magazine*, Oct.

Johnson, Hiram Warren 1866–1945

US politician. He entered the Senate from California (1917–45) and as a founder of the Progressive Party was Theodore Roosevelt's running mate in his unsuccessful 1912 campaign. He outspokenly opposed the League of Nations.

78 The first casualty when war comes is truth.
1917 Speech, US Senate.

Johnson, Lindley

US scientist, a member of NASA's Near Earth Object Observation Program.

79 It is as likely to happen next week as in a randomly selected week a thousand years from now.
2004 Report to the US Senate on the probability of an object hitting the earth.

Johnson, Lyndon B(aines) *also called LBJ* 1908–73

US politician, 36th President (1963–9). He came to power after Kennedy's assassination, and was returned with a huge majority in 1964. He presided over the Civil Rights Act (1964) and the Voting Rights Act (1965), but the Vietnam War made him unpopular.

80 I am a free man, an American, a United States Senator, and a Democrat, in that order.
1958 *Texas Quarterly*, winter issue.

81 I want to be progressive without getting both feet off the ground at the same time…a progressive who is prudent.
1964 Interview, 16 Mar.

82 You let a bully come into your front yard, and the next day he'll be on your porch.
1964 In *Time*, Apr.

83 We are not about to send American boys 9,000 or 10,000 miles away from home to do what Asian boys ought to be doing for themselves.
1964 On the war in Vietnam. Speech at Akron University, 21 Oct.

84 Better to have him inside the tent pissing out, than outside pissing in.
Of J Edgar Hoover. Quoted in David Halberstam *The Best and the Brightest* (1971), ch.20.

85 I want loyalty. I want him to kiss my ass in Macy's window at high noon and tell me it smells like roses. I want his pecker in my pocket.
Of a potential assistant. Quoted in David Halberstam *The Best and the Brightest* (1971), ch.20.

86 So dumb he can't fart and chew gum at the same time.
Of Gerald Ford. Quoted in Richard Reeves *A Ford, Not a Lincoln.* (1975), ch.2.

87 Let's press the flesh.
Of shaking voters' hands. Quoted in Alistair Cooke *The Americans* (1980).

88 I want every family in America to have a carpet on the floor and a picture on the wall. After bread, you've got to have a picture on the wall.
On visiting Pittsburgh's Polish–Czech area. Quoted in Alistair Cooke *The Americans* (1980).

89 I don't believe I'll ever get credit for anything I do in foreign affairs, no matter how successful it is, because I didn't go to Harvard.
To columnist Hugh Sidey. Quoted in Alistair Cooke *The Americans* (1980).

90 I can teach it round or flat.
When asked by a school board about the shape of the earth. Quoted in Tom Wicker *One of Us* (1991).

Johnson, Michael 1967–

US track athlete. At the 1996 Olympics in Atlanta he won gold medals in both the 200-metre and 400-metre events, the first man ever to do so.

91 Pressure is nothing more than the shadow of great opportunity.
Attributed.

Johnson, Paul 1928–

English author.

92 Hell is being trapped in a night-club with the 'beautiful people' and forced to live in a 'luxury penthouse flat'.
1996 *To Hell With Picasso, and Other Essays*.

93 If we want foxes, to observe and delight in, we must have hunting.
1996 *To Hell With Picasso, and Other Essays*.

Johnson, Pauline 1861–1913

Native Canadian poet and patriot.

94 The Dutch may have their Holland, the Spaniard have his Spain,
The Yankee to the south of us must south of us remain;
For not a man dare lift a hand against the men who brag
That they were born in Canada beneath the British flag.
1903 'Canadian Born', collected in *Flint and Feather* (1912).

Johnson, Philander Chase 1866–1939

US journalist.

95 Cheer up—the worst is yet to come.
1920 In *Everybody's Magazine*, May.

Johnson, Philip Cortelyou 1906–

US architect, best known for his book *The International Style* (1932). His designs include the Lincoln Center (1964) and the American Telephone and Telegraph Headquarters Building (1978) in New York City.

96 American megalomania is largely responsible for the growth of the Skyscraper School.
1931 'The Skyscraper School of Modern Architecture', in *Arts*, X VII (May). Collected in *Writings* (1979).

97 They say a building is good architecture if it works. Of course, this is poppycock. All buildings work… You expect any architect, a graduate of Harvard or not, to be able to put the kitchen in the right place.
1954 'The Seven Crutches of Architecture', informal talk to students, School of Architectural Design, Harvard University, 7 Dec. Published in *Perspecta 3* (1955).

98 It's got to be clear, back in your own mind, that serving the client is one thing and the art of architecture another.
1954 'The Seven Crutches of Architecture', informal talk to students, School of Architectural Design, Harvard University, 7 Dec. Published in *Perspecta 3* (1955).

99 Surely architecture is the organization for pleasure of enclosed space. And what more magnificent enclosure than a town, a *place*, a place where the spirit is cuddled, made serene, made proud, happy, or excited depending on the ceremony, the day, the hour.
1954 'The Seven Crutches of Architecture', informal talk to students, School of Architectural Design, Harvard University, 7 Dec. Published in *Perspecta 3* (1955).

1 You can't learn architecture any more than you can learn a sense of music or of painting. You shouldn't talk about art, you should do it.
1954 'The Seven Crutches of Architecture', informal talk to students, School of Architectural Design, Harvard University,

7 Dec. Published in *Perspecta 3* (1955).

2 The automobile is the greatest catastrophe in the entire history of City architecture.
1955 'The Town and the Automobile or the Pride of Elm Street', published in *Writings* (1979).

3 The delicate operation of separating an American from the four-wheeled part of him has to be performed with tact.
1955 'The Town and the Automobile or the Pride of Elm Street', published in *Writings* (1979).

4 Some of the opera houses in Italy had to be burnt down because people could *neither* see nor hear. They gave up seeing years ago, but they did enjoy the music.
1960 Informal talk, Architectural Association School of Architecture, 28 Nov. Collected in *Writings* (1979).

5 Architecture is the art of how to waste space.
1964 In the *New York Times*, 27 Dec.

6 I'm about four skyscrapers behind.
Excusing himself from a dinner party. Quoted in the *Wall Street Journal*, 20 Jun 1984.

Johnson, Samuel *known as* **Dr Johnson** 1709–84

English lexicographer, critic, poet and conversationalist, best known for his *A Dictionary of the English Language* (1755) and an edition of Shakespeare (1765). In 1773 he toured Scotland with James Boswell, and wrote *A Journey to the Western Isles of Scotland* (1775). Other works include *Rasselas* (1759) and *Lives of the English Poets* (1779–81).

7 Sir, we are a nest of singing birds.
1730 Of Pembroke College, Oxford. Quoted in James Boswell *The Life of Samuel Johnson* (1791), vol.1.

8 It is incident to physicians, I am afraid, beyond all other men, to mistake subsequence for consequence.
1734 Review of Dr Lucas's *Essay on Waters*, 25 Nov.

9 It is not easy to forbear reflecting with how little reason these men profess themselves the followers of Jesus, who left this great characteristic to his disciples, that they should be known by loving one another, by universal and unbounded charity and benevolence.
1735 Of the Jesuit missionaries in Abyssinia. Johnson's preface to Fr J de Lobo's *Voyage to Abyssinia*.

10 Unmoved though witlings sneer and rivals rail; Studious to please, yet not ashamed to fail.
c.1737 *Irene*, prologue (first produced 1749).

11 A thousand horrid Prodigies foretold it. A feeble government, eluded Laws, A factious Populace, luxurious Nobles, And all the maladies of stinking states.
c.1737 *Irene*, act 1, sc.1 (first produced 1749).

12 There Poetry shall tune her sacred voice, And wake from ignorance the Western World.
c.1737 *Irene*, act 4, sc.1 (first produced 1749).

13 For who would leave, unbrib'd, *Hibernia's* Land, Or change the rocks of *Scotland* for the *Strand*?
1738 *London: a Poem*, l.9–10.

14 By numbers here from shame or censure free, All crimes are safe, but hated poverty. This, only this, the rigid law pursues, This, only this, provokes the snarling muse.
1738 *London: a Poem*, l.158–61.

15 The stage but echoes back the public voice.

The drama's laws the drama's patrons give, For we, who live to please, must please to live.
1747 Prologue, written for David Garrick on the occasion of the opening of his management of the Theatre Royal, Drury Lane.

16 Let observation with extensive view, Survey mankind, from China to Peru.
1749 *The Vanity of Human Wishes*, l.1–2.

17 Yet hope not life from grief or danger free, Nor think the doom of man reversed for thee: Deign on the passing world to turn thine eyes, And pause awhile from letters, to be wise; There mark what ills the scholar's life assail, Toil, envy, want, the patron and the jail.
1749 *The Vanity of Human Wishes*, l.155–60.

18 Enlarge my life with multitude of days, In health, in sickness, thus the suppliant prays; Hides from himself his state, and shuns to know, That life protracted is protracted woe. Time hovers o'er, impatient to destroy, And shuts up all the passages of joy.
1749 *The Vanity of Human Wishes*, l.255–60.

19 Must helpless man, in ignorance sedate, Roll darkling down the torrent of his fate?
1749 *The Vanity of Human Wishes*, l.345–6.

20 Still raise for good the supplicating voice, But leave to heaven the measure and the choice.
1749 *The Vanity of Human Wishes*, l.351–2.

21 A man may write at any time, if he will set himself doggedly to it.
1750 Comment, Mar. Quoted in James Boswell *The Life of Samuel Johnson* (1791), vol.1.

22 I'll come no more behind your scenes, David: for the silk stockings and white bosoms of your actresses excite my amorous propensities.
1750 In conversation with the actor-manager David Garrick. Quoted in James Boswell *The Life of Samuel Johnson* (1791), vol.1.

23 There are minds so impatient of inferiority, that their gratitude is a species of revenge, and they return benefits, not because recompense is a pleasure, but because obligation is a pain.
1750–2 In *The Rambler*.

24 No place affords a more striking conviction of the vanity of human hopes, than a public library.
1750–2 In *The Rambler*.

25 Wit, you know, is the unexpected copulation of ideas, the discovery of some occult relation between images in appearance remote from each other.
1750–2 In *The Rambler*.

26 Almost every man wastes part of his life in attempts to display qualities which he does not possess, and to gain applause which he cannot keep.
1750–2 In *The Rambler*.

27 The love of life is necessary to the vigorous prosecution of any undertaking.
1750–2 In *The Rambler*.

28 I have laboured to refine our language to grammatical purity, and to clear it from colloquial barbarisms, licentious idioms, and irregular combinations.
1750–2 In *The Rambler*.

29 A fly, Sir, may sting a stately horse and make him wince;

but one is but an insect, and the other is a horse still.
1754 Of Edwards's criticism of Thomas Warburton. Quoted in
James Boswell *The Life of Samuel Johnson* (1791), vol.1.

30 They teach the morals of a whore, and the manners of a
dancing master.
1754 Of Lord Chesterfield's letters. Quoted in James Boswell *The
Life of Samuel Johnson* (1791), vol.1.

31 This man I thought had been a Lord among wits; but, I
find, he is only a wit among Lords.
1754 Of Lord Chesterfield. Quoted in James Boswell *The Life of
Samuel Johnson* (1791), vol.1.

32 Ignorance, madam, pure ignorance.
1755 Reply to a lady who had asked why he had defined *pastern*
as the 'knee' of a horse. Quoted in James Boswell *The Life of
Samuel Johnson* (1791), vol.1.

33 I had done all I could; and no man is well pleased to have
his all neglected, be it ever so little.
1755 Letter to Lord Chesterfield, 7 Feb. Quoted in James
Boswell *The Life of Samuel Johnson* (1791), vol.1.

34 Is not a Patron, my lord, one who looks with unconcern
on a man struggling for life in the water, and, when he has
reached ground, encumbers him with help? The notice
which you have been pleased to take of my labours, had
it been early, had been kind; but it has been delayed till I
am indifferent, and cannot enjoy it; till I am solitary, and
cannot impart it; till I am known, and do not want it.
1755 Letter to Lord Chesterfield, 7 Feb. Quoted in James
Boswell *The Life of Samuel Johnson* (1791), vol.1.

35 There are two things which I am confident I can do very
well: one is an introduction to a literary work, stating
what it is to contain, and how it should be executed in
the most perfect manner; the other is a conclusion,
shewing from various causes why the execution has not
been equal to what the author promised to himself and
to the public.
1755 Quoted in James Boswell *The Life of Samuel Johnson*
(1791), vol.1.

36 If a man does not make new acquaintance as he
advances through life, he will soon find himself left
alone. A man, Sir, should keep his friendship in constant
repair.
1755 Quoted in James Boswell *The Life of Samuel Johnson*
(1791), vol.1.

37 Change is not made without inconvenience, even from
worse to better.
1755 *A Dictionary of the English Language*, preface.

38 It is the fate of those who toil at the lower employments
of life…to be exposed to censure, without hope of
praise; to be disgraced by miscarriage or punished for
neglect… Among these unhappy mortals is the writer of
dictionaries… Every other author may aspire to praise;
the lexicographer can only hope to escape reproach.
1755 *A Dictionary of the English Language*, preface.

39 I am not yet so lost in lexicography as to forget that words
are the daughters of earth, and that things are the sons of
heaven. Language is only the instrument of science, and
words are but the signs of ideas: I wish, however, that the
instrument might be less apt to decay, and that signs
might be permanent, like the things which they denote.
1755 *A Dictionary of the English Language*, preface.

40 I have protracted my work till most of those whom I
wished to please have sunk into the grave; and success

and miscarriage are empty sounds.
1755 *A Dictionary of the English Language*, preface.

41 Every quotation contributes something to the stability or
enlargement of the language.
1755 *A Dictionary of the English Language*, preface.

42 But these were the dreams of a poet doomed at last to
wake a lexicographer.
1755 *A Dictionary of the English Language*, preface.

43 If the changes we fear be thus irresistible, what remains
but to acquiesce with silence, as in the other
insurmountable distresses of humanity? It remains that
we retard what we cannot repel, that we palliate what
we cannot cure.
1755 *A Dictionary of the English Language*, preface.

44 *Dull*. To make dictionaries is dull work.
1755 *A Dictionary of the English Language*.

45 *Excise*. A hateful tax levied upon commodities.
1755 *A Dictionary of the English Language*.

46 *Lexicographer*. A writer of dictionaries, a harmless drudge.
1755 *A Dictionary of the English Language*.

47 *Net*. Any thing reticulated or decussated at equal
distances, with interstices between the intersections.
1755 *A Dictionary of the English Language*.

48 *Oats*. A grain, which in England is generally given to
horses, but in Scotland supports the people.
1755 *A Dictionary of the English Language*.

49 *Patron*. Commonly a wretch who supports with
insolence, and is paid with flattery.
1755 *A Dictionary of the English Language*.

50 *Pension*. Pay given to state hireling for treason to his
country.
1755 *A Dictionary of the English Language*.

51 The only end of writing is to enable the readers better to
enjoy life, or better to endure it.
1757 Reviewing Soame Jenyns *A Free Inquiry into the Nature and
Origin of Evil*, in the *Literary Magazine*, Apr–Jul.

52 To us, who are regaled every morning and evening with
intelligence, and are supplied from day to day with
materials for conversation, it is difficult to conceive how
man can subsist without a newspaper.
1758 In *The Idler*, no.7, 27 May.

53 When two Englishmen meet, their first talk is of the
weather.
1758 In *The Idler*, no.11, 24 Jun.

54 To these compositions is required neither genius nor
knowledge, neither industry nor spriteliness, but
contempt of shame, and indifference to truth are
absolutely necessary.
1758 Of journalistic reporting. In *The Idler*, no.31, 11 Nov.

55 Among the calamities of War may be justly numbered
the diminution of the love of truth, by the falsehoods
which interest dictates and credulity encourages.
1758 In *The Idler*, no.31, 11 Nov.

56 Nothing is more hopeless than a scheme of merriment.
1759 In *The Idler*, no.58, 26 May.

57 The Europeans have scarcely visited any coast, but to
gratify avarice, and extend corruption; to arrogate
dominion without right, and practice cruelty without
incentive… But there is reason to hope…that the light of
the gospel will at last illuminate the sands of Africa, and

the deserts of America, though its progress cannot but be slow when it is so much obstructed by the lives of Christians.
1759 Introduction to *The World Displayed*.

58 Marriage has many pains, but celibacy has no pleasures.
1759 *Rasselas*, ch.26.

59 No man will be a sailor who has contrivance enough to get himself into jail; for being in a ship is being in a jail, with the chance of being drowned… A man in a jail has more room, better food, and commonly better company.
1759 Remark, 16 Mar. Quoted in James Boswell *The Life of Samuel Johnson* (1791), vol.1.

60 Liberty is, to the lowest rank of every nation, little more than the choice of working or starving.
1760 'The Bravery of the English Common Soldier', in *The British Magazine*, Jan.

61 The notion of liberty amuses the people of England, and helps to keep off the taedium vitae. When a butcher tells you that his heart bleeds for his country he has, in fact, no uneasy feeling.
1763 Remark, 16 May. Quoted in James Boswell *The Life of Samuel Johnson* (1791), vol.1.

62 Yes, Sir, many men, many women, and many children.
1763 Remark, 16 May, on being asked if any man of a modern age could have written *Ossian*. Quoted in James Boswell *The Life of Samuel Johnson* (1791), vol.1.

63 The noblest prospect which a Scotchman ever sees, is the high road that leads him to England!
1763 Remark, 6 Jul. Quoted in James Boswell *The Life of Samuel Johnson* (1791), vol.1.

64 A man ought to read just as inclination leads him; for what he reads as a task will do him little good.
1763 Remark, 14 Jul. Quoted in James Boswell *The Life of Samuel Johnson* (1791), vol.1.

65 But if he does really think that there is no distinction between virtue and vice, why, Sir, when he leaves our houses, let us count our spoons.
1763 Remark, 14 Jul. Quoted in James Boswell *The Life of Samuel Johnson* (1791), vol.1.

66 A man with a good coat upon his back meets with a better reception than he who has a bad one.
1763 Remark, 20 Jul. Quoted in James Boswell *The Life of Samuel Johnson* (1791), vol.1.

67 All the arguments which are brought to represent poverty as no evil, show it to be evidently a great evil. You never find people labouring to convince you that you may live very happily upon a plentiful fortune.
1763 Remark, 20 Jul. Quoted in James Boswell *The Life of Samuel Johnson* (1791), vol.1.

68 Truth, Sir, is a cow, that will yield such people no more milk, and so they are gone to milk the bull.
1763 Of sceptics. Remark, 21 Jul. Quoted in James Boswell *The Life of Samuel Johnson* (1791), vol.1.

69 Young men have more virtue than old men; they have more generous sentiments in every respect.
1763 Remark, 21 Jul. Quoted in James Boswell *The Life of Samuel Johnson* (1791), vol.1.

70 In my early years I read very hard. It is a sad reflection, but a true one, that I knew almost as much at eighteen as I do now.
1763 Remark, 21 Jul. Quoted in James Boswell *The Life of Samuel Johnson* (1791), vol.1.

71 Your levellers wish to level down as far as themselves; but they cannot bear levelling up to themselves.
1763 Remark, 21 Jul. Quoted in James Boswell *The Life of Samuel Johnson* (1791), vol.1.

72 It is burning a farthing candle at Dover, to shew light at Calais.
1763 Summarizing the influence of the plays of Thomas Sheridan upon English literature, 28 Jul. Quoted in James Boswell *The Life of Samuel Johnson* (1791), vol.1.

73 Sir, a woman's preaching is like a dog walking on its hinder legs. It is not done well; but you are surprised to find it done at all.
1763 Remark, 31 Jul. Quoted in James Boswell *The Life of Samuel Johnson* (1791), vol.1.

74 He who does not mind his belly will hardly mind any thing else.
1763 Remark, 5 Aug. Quoted in James Boswell *The Life of Samuel Johnson* (1791), vol.1.

75 'I refute it *thus*.'
1763 Johnson refutes Bishop Berkeley's theory of the non-existence of matter by kicking a large stone, 6 Aug. Quoted in James Boswell *The Life of Samuel Johnson* (1791), vol.1.

76 Nature has given women so much power that the law has very wisely given them little.
1763 Letter to John Taylor, 18 Aug.

77 A very unclubbable man.
1764 Of Sir John Hawkins. Remark quoted in James Boswell *The Life of Samuel Johnson* (1791), vol.1.

78 Nothing can please many, and please long, but just representations of general nature.
1765 *Plays of William Shakespeare*, preface.

79 He that tries to recommend him by select quotations, will succeed like the pedant in Hierocles, who, when he offered his house to sale, carried a brick in his pocket as a specimen.
1765 Of Shakespeare. *Plays of William Shakespeare*, preface.

80 Love is only one of many passions.
1765 *Plays of William Shakespeare*, preface.

81 Notes are often necessary, but they are necessary evils.
1765 *Plays of William Shakespeare*, preface.

82 That all who are happy, are equally happy, is not true. A peasant and a philosopher may be equally satisfied, but not equally happy. Happiness consists in the multiplicity of agreeable consciousness.
1766 Remark, Feb. Quoted in James Boswell *The Life of Samuel Johnson* (1791), vol.2.

83 It is our first duty to serve society, and, after we have done that, we may attend wholly to the salvation of our own souls. A youthful passion for abstracted devotion should not be encouraged.
1766 Remark, Feb. Quoted in James Boswell *The Life of Samuel Johnson* (1791), vol.2.

84 Our tastes greatly alter. The lad does not care for the child's rattle, and the old man does not care for the young man's whore.
1766 Quoted in James Boswell *The Life of Samuel Johnson* (1791), vol.2.

85 It was not for me to bandy civilities with my sovereign.
1767 Remark, Feb. Quoted in James Boswell *The Life of Samuel Johnson* (1791), vol.2.

86 Now, sir, there is the liberty of the press, which you know is a constant topic. Suppose you and I and two hundred

more were restrained from printing our thoughts: what then? What proportion would that restraint upon us bear to the private happiness of the nation?

1768 Remark, May. Quoted in James Boswell *The Life of Samuel Johnson* (1791), vol.2.

87 Sir, if a man has a mind to *prance*, he must study at Christ-Church and All-Souls.

1769 Remark, Autumn. Quoted in James Boswell *The Life of Samuel Johnson* (1791), vol.2.

88 We know our will is free, and there's an end on't.

1769 Remark, 16 Oct. Quoted in James Boswell *The Life of Samuel Johnson* (1791), vol.2.

89 It matters not how a man dies, but how he lives. The act of dying is not of importance, it lasts so short a time.

1769 Remark, 26 Oct. Quoted in James Boswell *The Life of Samuel Johnson* (1791), vol.2.

90 That fellow seems to me to possess but one idea, and that is a wrong one.

1770 Quoted in James Boswell *The Life of Samuel Johnson* (1791), vol.2.

91 The triumph of hope over experience.

1770 On a friend's second marriage shortly after the death of his first, troublesome, wife. Quoted in James Boswell *The Life of Samuel Johnson* (1791), vol.2.

92 I do not care to speak ill of any man behind his back, but I believe the gentleman is an *attorney*.

1770 Quoted in James Boswell *The Life of Samuel Johnson* (1791), vol.2.

93 Every man has a lurking wish to appear considerable in his native place.

1771 Letter to Sir Joshua Reynolds, 17 Jul. Quoted in James Boswell *The Life of Samuel Johnson* (1791), vol.2.

94 I would not give half a guinea to live under one form of government rather than another. It is of no moment to the happiness of an individual.

1772 Remark, 31 Mar. Quoted in James Boswell *The Life of Samuel Johnson* (1791), vol.2.

95 There is more knowledge of the heart in one letter of Richardson's, than in all *Tom Jones*.

1772 Remark, 6 Apr. Quoted in James Boswell *The Life of Samuel Johnson* (1791), vol.2.

96 Grief is a species of idleness.

1773 Letter to Mrs Thrale, whose son had just died, 17 Mar.

97 He has, indeed, done it very well; but it is a foolish thing well done.

1773 Of Oliver Goldsmith, who had responded to Thomas Evans's uncomplimentary open letter with a physical assault, and then published an apology in the *London Chronicle*. Remark, 3 Apr. Collected in James Boswell *The Life of Samuel Johnson* (1791), vol.2.

98 Read over your compositions, and where ever you meet with a passage which you think is particularly fine, strike it out.

1773 Remark, 30 Apr, quoting an old college tutor. Collected in James Boswell *The Life of Samuel Johnson* (1791), vol.2.

99 A lawyer has no business with the justice or injustice of the cause which he undertakes, unless his client asks his opinion, and then he is bound to give it honestly. The justice or unjustice of the cause is to be decided by the judge.

1773 Remark, 15 Aug. Quoted in James Boswell *The Journal of a Tour to the Hebrides* (1785).

1 I inherited a vile melancholy from my father, which has made me mad all my life, at least not sober.

1773 Remark, 16 Sep. Quoted in James Boswell *The Journal of a Tour to the Hebrides* (1785).

2 I am always sorry when any language is lost, because languages are the pedigrees of nations.

1773 Remark, 18 Sep. Quoted in James Boswell *The Journal of a Tour to the Hebrides* (1785).

3 A cucumber should be well sliced, and dressed with pepper and vinegar, and then thrown out, as good for nothing.

1773 Remark, 5 Oct. Quoted in James Boswell *The Journal of a Tour to the Hebrides* (1785).

4 At seventy-seven it is time to be in earnest.

1775 *A Journey to the Western Isles of Scotland*, 'Col'.

5 There are few ways in which a man can be so innocently employed than in getting money.

1775 Remark, 27 Mar. Collected in James Boswell *The Life of Samuel Johnson* (1791), vol.2. This is sometimes rendered 'A man is seldom so innocently occupied as when he is making money.'

6 It is wonderful, when a calculation is made, how little the mind is actually employed in the discharge of any profession.

1775 Remark, 6 Apr. Collected in James Boswell *The Life of Samuel Johnson* (1791), vol.2.

7 The greatest part of a writer's time is spent in reading, in order to write: a man will turn over half a library to make one book.

1775 Remark, 6 Apr. Collected in James Boswell *The Life of Samuel Johnson* (1791), vol.2.

8 Patriotism is the last refuge of a scoundrel.

1775 Remark, 7 Apr. Collected in James Boswell *The Life of Samuel Johnson* (1791), vol.2.

9 Knowledge is of two kinds. We know a subject ourselves, or we know where we can find information upon it.

1775 Remark, 18 Apr. Quoted in James Boswell *The Life of Samuel Johnson* (1791), vol.2.

10 Politics are now nothing more than means of rising in the world.

1775 Remark, 18 Apr. Quoted in James Boswell *The Life of Samuel Johnson* (1791), vol.2.

11 Players, Sir! I look upon them as no better than creatures set upon tables and joint stools to make faces and produce laughter, like dancing dogs.

1775 Letter to James Macpherson.

12 How is it that we hear the loudest yelps for liberty among the drivers of negroes?

1775 *Taxation No Tyranny*.

13 In lapidary inscriptions a man is not upon oath.

1775 Quoted in James Boswell *The Life of Samuel Johnson* (1791), vol.2.

14 There is nothing which has yet been contrived by man, by which so much happiness is produced as by a good tavern or inn.

1776 Remark, 21 Mar. Quoted in James Boswell *The Life of Samuel Johnson* (1791), vol.2.

15 Marriages would in general be as happy, and often more so, if they were all made by the Lord Chancellor, upon a due consideration of characters and circumstances, without the parties having any choice in the matter.

1776 Remark, 22 Mar. Quoted in James Boswell *The Life of Samuel Johnson* (1791), vol.2.

16 I had often wondered why young women should marry, as they have so much more freedom, and so much more attention paid to them while unmarried, than when married.
1776 Remark, 25 Mar. Quoted in James Boswell *The Life of Samuel Johnson* (1791), vol.2.

17 Fine clothes are good only as they supply the want of other means of procuring respect.
1776 Remark, 27 Mar. Quoted in James Boswell *The Life of Samuel Johnson* (1791), vol.2.

18 Consider, Sir, how should you like, though conscious of your innocence, to be tried before a jury for a capital crime, once a week.
1776 Remark, 3 Apr. Quoted in James Boswell *The Life of Samuel Johnson* (1791), vol.3.

19 We would all be idle if we could.
1776 Remark, 3 Apr. Quoted in James Boswell *The Life of Samuel Johnson* (1791), vol.3.

20 No man but a blockhead ever wrote, except for money.
1776 Remark, 5 Apr. Quoted in James Boswell *The Life of Samuel Johnson* (1791), vol.3.

21 It is better that some should be unhappy than that none should be happy, which would be the case in a general state of equality.
1776 Remark, 7 Apr. Quoted in James Boswell *The Life of Samuel Johnson* (1791), vol.3.

22 A man who has not been in Italy, is always conscious of an inferiority, from his not having seen what it is expected a man should see.
1776 Remark, 11 Apr. Quoted in James Boswell *The Life of Samuel Johnson* (1791), vol.3.

23 Every man of any education would rather be called a rascal, than accused of deficiency in the graces.
1776 Remark, May. Quoted in James Boswell *The Life of Samuel Johnson* (1791), vol.3.

24 Sir, you have but two topics, yourself and me. I am sick of both.
1776 Remark, May. Quoted in James Boswell *The Life of Samuel Johnson* (1791), vol.3.

25 If I had no duties, and no reference to futurity, I would spend my life in driving briskly in a post-chaise with a pretty woman.
1777 Remark, 19 Sep. Quoted in James Boswell *The Life of Samuel Johnson* (1791), vol.3.

26 Depend upon it, Sir, when a man knows he is to be hanged in a fortnight, it concentrates his mind wonderfully.
1777 Remark, 19 Sep, alluding to the forthcoming execution of Dr Dodd. Quoted in James Boswell *The Life of Samuel Johnson* (1791), vol.3.

27 When a man is tired of London, he is tired of life; for there is in London all that life can afford.
1777 Remark, 20 Sep. Quoted in James Boswell *The Life of Samuel Johnson* (1791), vol.3.

28 All argument is against it; but all belief is for it.
1778 Remark, 31 Mar, on the existence of ghosts. Quoted in James Boswell *The Life of Samuel Johnson* (1791), vol.3.

29 Seeing Scotland, Madam, is only seeing a worse England.
1778 Remark quoted in a letter to Boswell, 7 Apr. Quoted in James Boswell *The Life of Samuel Johnson* (1791), vol.3.

30 The more contracted that power is, the more easily it is destroyed. A country governed by a despot is an inverted cone.
1778 Remark, 14 Apr. Quoted in James Boswell *The Life of Samuel Johnson* (1791), vol.3.

31 As the Spanish proverb says, 'He, who would bring home the wealth of the Indies, must carry the wealth of the Indies with him.' So it is in travelling; a man must carry knowledge with him, if he would bring home knowledge.
1778 Remark, 17 Apr. Quoted in James Boswell *The Life of Samuel Johnson* (1791), vol.3.

32 Sir, the insolence of wealth will creep out.
1778 Remark, 18 Apr. Quoted in James Boswell *The Life of Samuel Johnson* (1791), vol.3.

33 Wine makes a man better pleased with himself. I do not say that it makes him more pleasing to others.
1778 Remark, 28 Apr. Quoted in James Boswell *The Life of Samuel Johnson* (1791), vol.3.

34 BOSWELL: There is more learning in their [Chinese] language than in any other, from the immense number of their characters.
JOHNSON: It is only more difficult from its rudeness, as there is more labour in hewing down a tree with a stone than with an axe.
1778 Conversation, 8 May. Quoted in James Boswell *The Life of Samuel Johnson* (1791), vol.3.

35 Were it not for imagination, Sir, a man would be as happy in the arms of a chambermaid as of a Duchess.
1778 Remark, 9 May. Quoted in James Boswell *The Life of Samuel Johnson* (1791), vol.3.

36 A man who exposes himself when he is intoxicated, has not the art of getting drunk.
1779 Remark, 24 Apr. Quoted in James Boswell *The Life of Samuel Johnson* (1791), vol.3.

37 Claret is the liquor for boys; port, for men; but he who aspires to be a hero [smiling] must drink brandy.
1779 Remark, 7 Aug. Quoted in James Boswell *The Life of Samuel Johnson* (1791), vol.3.

38 Remember that all tricks are either knavish or childish.
1779 Letter to Boswell, 9 Sep. Quoted in James Boswell *The Life of Samuel Johnson* (1791), vol.3.

39 BOSWELL: Is not the Giant's Causeway worth seeing?
JOHNSON: Worth seeing? Yes, but not worth going to see.
1779 Conversation, 12 Oct. Quoted in James Boswell *The Life of Samuel Johnson* (1791), vol.3.

40 If you are idle, be not solitary; if you are solitary, be not idle.
1779 Letter to Boswell, 27 Oct. Quoted in James Boswell *The Life of Samuel Johnson* (1791), vol.3.

41 Trade could not be managed by those who manage it, if it had much difficulty.
1779 Letter to Hester Thrale, 16 Nov.

42 The true genius is a mind of large general powers, accidentally determined to some particular direction.
1779–81 *Lives of the English Poets*, 'Cowley'.

43 The father of English criticism.
1779–81 Of Dryden. *Lives of the English Poets*, 'Dryden'.

44 To charge all unmerited praise with the guilt of flattery, and to suppose that the encomiast always knows and feels the falsehood of his assertions, is surely to discover great ignorance of human nature and human life. In determinations depending not on rules, but on

experience and comparison, judgement is always to some degree subject to affection. Very near to admiration is the wish to admire.
1779–81 *Lives of the English Poets*, 'Halifax'.

45 It…had the effect, as was ludicrously said, of making Gay *rich*, and Rich *gay*.
1779–81 Of the *Beggar's Opera*, written by Gay and produced by Rich. *Lives of the English Poets*, 'John Gay'.

46 An exotic and irrational entertainment.
1779–81 Of Italian opera. *Lives of the English Poets*, 'Hughes'.

47 I am disappointed by that stroke of death, which has eclipsed the gaiety of nations, and impoverished the public stock of harmless pleasure.
1779–81 His tribute to the recently deceased actor David Garrick. *Lives of the English Poets*, 'Edmund Smith'.

48 Every man has a right to utter what he thinks truth, and every other man has a right to knock him down for it. Martyrdom is the test.
1780 Quoted in James Boswell *The Life of Samuel Johnson* (1791), vol.4.

49 Depend upon it, said he, that if a man talks of his misfortunes there is something in them that is not disagreeable to him; for where there is nothing but pure misery, there never is any recourse to the mention of it.
1780 Quoted in James Boswell *The Life of Samuel Johnson* (1791), vol.4.

50 A wise Tory and a wise Whig, I believe, will agree. Their principles are the same, though their modes of thinking are different.
1781 Written note given to Boswell, May. Quoted in James Boswell *The Life of Samuel Johnson* (1791), vol.4.

51 Classical quotations is the parole of literary men all over the world.
1781 Remark, 8 May. Quoted in James Boswell *The Life of Samuel Johnson* (1791), vol.4.

52 Sir, I have two very cogent reasons for not printing any list of subscribers;—one, that I have lost all the names,—the other, that I have spent all the money.
1781 Remark, May. Quoted in James Boswell *The Life of Samuel Johnson* (1791), vol.4.

53 Why, that is, because, dearest, you're a dunce.
1781 To Lady Corke, who had said that she was affected by Sterne's writings. Quoted in James Boswell *The Life of Samuel Johnson* (1791), vol.4.

54 Always, Sir, set a high value on spontaneous kindness. He whose inclination prompts him to cultivate your friendship of his own accord, will love you more than one whom you have been at pains to attract to you.
1781 Remark, May. Quoted in James Boswell *The Life of Samuel Johnson* (1791), vol.4.

55 I hate a fellow whom pride, or cowardice, or laziness drives into a corner, and who does nothing when he is there but sit and growl; let him come out as I do, and bark.
1782 Remark, 10 Oct, alluding to Jeremiah Markland. Quoted in James Boswell *The Life of Samuel Johnson* (1791), vol.4.

56 Resolve not to be poor; whatever you have, spend less. Poverty is a great enemy to human happiness; it certainly destroys liberty, and it makes some virtues impracticable, and others extremely difficult.
1782 Letter to Boswell, 7 Dec. Quoted in James Boswell *The Life of Samuel Johnson* (1791), vol.4.

57 How few of his friends' houses would a man choose to be at when he is sick.
1783 Quoted in James Boswell *The Life of Samuel Johnson* (1791), vol.4.

58 There is a wicked inclination in most people to suppose an old man decayed in his intellects. If a young or middle-aged man, when leaving a company, does not recollect where he laid his hat, it is nothing; but if the same inattention is discovered in an old man, people will shrug up their shoulders, and say, 'His memory is going.'
1783 Quoted in James Boswell *The Life of Samuel Johnson* (1791), vol.4.

59 Sir, there is no settling the point of precedency between a louse and a flea.
1783 On the relative merits of two minor poets. Quoted in James Boswell *The Life of Samuel Johnson* (1791), vol.4.

60 My dear friend, clear your mind of cant… You may talk in this manner; it is a mode of talking in Society: but don't think foolishly.
1783 Remark, 15 May. Quoted in James Boswell *The Life of Samuel Johnson* (1791), vol.4.

61 It is as bad as bad can be: it is ill-fed, ill-killed, ill-kept, and ill-drest.
1783 Of the roast mutton he was served at an inn, 3 Jun. Quoted in James Boswell *The Life of Samuel Johnson* (1791), vol.4.

62 As I know more of mankind I expect less of them, and am ready now to call a man a good man, upon easier terms than I was formerly.
1783 Remark, Sep. Quoted in James Boswell *The Life of Samuel Johnson* (1791), vol.4.

63 Milton, Madam, was a genius that could cut a Colossus from a rock; but could not carve heads upon cherry-stones.
1784 Remark to Hannah More, 13 Jun, who had commented with surprise that Milton's sonnets failed to compare with his epic *Paradise Lost*. Quoted in James Boswell *The Life of Samuel Johnson* (1791), vol.4.

64 Talking of the Comedy of 'The Rehearsal', he said 'It has not enough wit to keep it sweet.' This was easy;—he therefore caught himself, and pronounced a more rounded sentence; 'It has not vitality enough to preserve it from putrefaction.'
1784 Remark, Jun. Quoted in James Boswell *The Life of Samuel Johnson* (1791), vol.4.

65 Sir, I have found you an argument; but I am not obliged to find you an understanding.
1784 Remark, Jun. Quoted in James Boswell *The Life of Samuel Johnson* (1791), vol.4.

66 No man is a hypocrite in his pleasures.
1784 Remark, Jun. Quoted in James Boswell *The Life of Samuel Johnson* (1791), vol.4.

67 Dictionaries are like watches, the worst is better than none, and the best cannot be expected to go quite true.
1784 Letter to Francesco Sastres, 21 Aug. Quoted in James Boswell *The Life of Samuel Johnson* (1791), vol.4.

68 Sir, I look upon every day to be lost, in which I do not make a new acquaintance.
1784 Remark, Nov. Quoted in James Boswell *The Life of Samuel Johnson* (1791), vol.4.

69 I will be conquered; I will not capitulate.
1784 Of his increasing ill health, Nov. Quoted in James Boswell *The Life of Samuel Johnson* (1791), vol.4.

70 An odd thought strikes me:—we shall receive no letters in the grave.

> **1784** Remark, Dec. Quoted in James Boswell *The Life of Samuel Johnson* (1791), vol.4.

71 Difficult do you call it, Sir? I wish it were impossible.

> Of the playing of a famous violinist. Quoted in G B Hill *Johnsonian Miscellanies*, vol.2 (1784).

72 It is the only sensual pleasure without vice.

> **1784** Of music. Quoted in Sir John Hawkins *Johnsoniana* (1787).

73 I would rather see the portrait of a dog that I know, than all the allegorical paintings they can show me in the world.

> Quoted in Mrs Piozzi *Anecdotes of the Late Samuel Johnson* (1786).

74 Corneille is to Shakespeare…as a clipped hedge is to a forest.

> Quoted in Mrs Piozzi *Anecdotes of the Late Samuel Johnson* (1786).

75 It is very strange, and very melancholy, that the paucity of human pleasures should persuade us ever to call hunting one of them.

> Quoted in Mrs Piozzi *Anecdotes of the Late Samuel Johnson* (1786).

76 Of all noises I think music the least disagreeable.

> Quoted in *The Morning Chronicle*, 1816.

77 Fly fishing may be a very pleasant amusement; but angling or float fishing I can only compare to a stick and a string, with a worm at one end and a fool at the other.

> Quoted in Hawker *Instructions to Young Sportsmen* (1859). The attribution is doubtful, and Swift has also been credited with the remark.

78 The use of travelling is to regulate imagination by reality, and instead of thinking how things may be, to see them as they are.

> Attributed.

Johnston, Brian 1912–94

English cricket commentator.

79 The bowler's Holding, the batsman's Willey.

> **1976** Radio commentary, during a Test match between England and the West Indies.

80 Turner looks a bit shaky and unsteady, but I think he's going to bat on—one ball left!

> Radio commentary, during an England Test match after batsman Glenn Turner was hit on the box by a cricket ball on the fifth ball of the over.

Johst, Hanns 1890–1978

German dramatist.

81 *Wenn ich Kultur höre…entsichere ich meinen Browning!* When I hear anyone talk of culture…I take off the safety catch on my Browning!

> **1933** *Schlageter*, act 1, sc.1. The phrase is often attributed to Hermann Goering, in the form 'Whenever I hear the word culture, I reach for my gun!'.

Jolson, Al *pseudonym of* **Asa Yoelson** 1886–1950

Russian-born US actor and singer. He emigrated to the US in 1893 and made his stage debut in *The Children of the Ghetto* (1899). He was the star of the first talking picture *The Jazz Singer* in 1927.

82 You Ain't Heard Nothin' Yet.

> **1919** Title of a song, allegedly taken from an earlier impromptu remark in a café in which Jolson was performing. It is popularly recognized as a line from *The Jazz Singer* (screenplay by Alfred Cohn), the first major film with sound.

Jonas, George 1935–

Hungarian-born Canadian author and journalist.

83 There are many wrongs in the world, but none that could be righted by the terrorist's program.

> **1987** *Crocodiles in the Bathtub and Other Perils*.

84 Maybe that's what is crazy: to want to be free. A lot of people wouldn't cross the street for it.

> **1989** *A Passion Observed: The Story of a Motorcycle Racer*.

Jones, Bobby (Robert Tyre) 1902–71

US golfer. He won the US Open four times, the British Open three times, the US Amateur Championship five times and the British Amateur Championship once. In 1930 he won the 'Grand Slam', and retired from competitive golf.

85 Golf is a game that is played on a five inch course—the distance between your ears.

> Quoted in Colin Jarman *The Guinness Dictionary of Sports Quotations* (1990).

Jones, Henry Arthur 1851–1929

English playwright. His early melodramas were followed by more realistic plays and social comedies.

86 O God! Put back Thy universe and give me yesterday.

> **1907** *The Silver King* (with Henry Herman), act 2, sc.4.

Jones, James 1921–77

US writer. He is best known for his novel set in the run-up to the bombing of Pearl Harbor, *From Here to Eternity* (1951), and its sequel, *The Thin Red Line* (1962).

87 From Here to Eternity.

> **1951** Title of novel.

88 I therefore solemnly declare to all young men trying to be writers that they do not actually have to become drunkards first.

> **1959** Interview in the *Paris Review*, Winter.

89 To me politics is like one of those annoying and potentially dangerous, but generally just painful, chronic diseases that you just have to put up with all your life if you happen to have contracted it. Politics is like having diabetes.

> **1959** Interview in the *Paris Review*, Winter.

90 Conversation is more often likely to be an attempt at deliberate evasion, deliberate confusion, rather than communication. We're all cheats and liars, really.

> **1959** Interview in the *Paris Review*, Winter.

Jones, John Paul 1747–92

US admiral. He fought the English fleet in the American Revolution, and later became rear-admiral in the Russian navy.

91 Sir, I have not yet begun to fight.

> **1779** His reply to a request for surrender when his ship was sinking, 23 Sep. He lashed his ship to his enemy's and boarded it, accepting the enemy captain's surrender. Quoted in Anna de Koven *Life and Letters of John Paul Jones* (1913).

Jones, Quincy Delight 1933–

US jazz trumpeter, songwriter and record producer. His many albums include *Body Heat* (1974) and *The Dude* (1981). As Vice-President of Mercury Records he promoted Frank Sinatra and Michael Jackson among others.

92 Jazz has always been a man telling the truth about himself.
Quoted in Alan Kendall *The Tender Tyrant: Nadia Boulanger* (1976).

93 To try to talk to the young people who will run the future—in ten minutes—is a little like trying to put a cantaloupe in a coke bottle.
1995 At Claremont College commencement. Reported in the *New York Times*, 29 May.

Jones, Tom 1940–

Welsh pop singer.

94 My pants are not as tight any more, I don't open my shirt so far and I don't pick up the underwear.
2004 On getting older. Quoted in *Mojo*, May.

Jong, Erica née *Mann* 1942–

US novelist and poet. She achieved notoriety with her controversial first novel, *Fear of Flying* (1973).

95 Everyone has talent. What is rare is the courage to follow the talent to the dark place where it leads.
1972 'The Artist as Housewife', in *The First Ms. Reader*.

96 If sex and creativity are often seen by dictators as subversive activities, it's because they lead to the knowledge that you own your own body (and with it your own voice), and that's the most revolutionary insight of all.
1972 'The Artist as Housewife', in *The First Ms. Reader*.

97 The zipless fuck is absolutely pure. It is free of ulterior motives. There is no power game. The man is not 'taking' and the woman is not 'giving'. No one is attempting to cuckold a husband or humiliate a wife. No one is trying to prove anything or get anything out of anyone. The zipless fuck is the purest thing there is. And it is rarer than the unicorn. And I have never had one.
1973 *Fear of Flying*, ch.1.

98 Solitude is un-American.
1973 *Fear of Flying*, ch.1.

99 Gossip is the opiate of the oppressed.
1973 *Fear of Flying*, ch.6.

1 Horrible as successful artists often are, there is nothing crueller or more vain than a failed artist.
1973 *Fear of Flying*, ch.9.

2 Jealousy is all the fun you *think* they had.
1977 *How To Save Your Own Life*.

3 Advice is what we ask for when we already know the answer but wish we didn't.
1977 *How To Save Your Own Life*.

4 Friends *love* misery, in fact. Sometimes, especially if we are too lucky or too successful or too pretty, our misery is the only thing that endears us to our friends.
1977 *How To Save Your Own Life*.

5 Every country gets the circus it deserves. Spain gets bullfights. Italy gets the Catholic Church. America gets Hollywood.
1977 *How To Save Your Own Life*.

6 Women are the only exploited group in the world who have been idealized into powerlessness.
1978 In *Time*.

7 Fear of Fifty.
1994 Title of memoir.

Jonson, Ben 1572–1637

English dramatist. Imprisoned for killing a man in a duel, he became a Catholic but later recanted. His plays reject romantic comedy for a more realistic mode and include *Volpone* (1606), *The Silent Woman* (1609) and *The Alchemist* (1610). He was regarded as superior to Shakespeare in his day.

8 Well, I will scourge those apes,
And to these courteous eyes oppose a mirror,
As large as is the stage whereon we act;
Where they shall see the time's deformity
Anatomised in every nerve, and sinew,
With constant courage, and contempt of fear.
1600 *Every Man out of His Humour*, Induction.

9 GENT: He hath been beyond-sea, once, or twice.
CARL: As far as *Paris*, to fetch over a fashion, and come back again.
1600 *Every Man out of His Humour*, act 2, sc.2.

10 Good morning to the day; and next, my gold!
1609 *Volpone*, act 1, sc.1.

11 Yet I glory
More in the cunning purchase of my wealth
Than in the glad possession.
1609 *Volpone*, act 1, sc.1.

12 What should I do,
But cocker up my genius, and live free
To all delights my fortune calls me to?
1609 *Volpone*, act 1, sc.2.

13 Hood an ass with reverend purple,
So you can hide his two ambitious ears,
And he shall pass for a cathedral doctor.
1609 *Volpone*, act 1, sc.3.

14 Give 'em words;
Pour oil into their ears, and send them hence.
1609 *Volpone*, act 1, sc.4.

15 He has no faith in physic. He does think
Most of your doctors are the greater danger,
And worse disease, t'escape.
1609 *Volpone*, act 1, sc.4.

16 'Fore heaven, I wonder at the desperate valour
Of the bold English, that they dare let loose
Their wives to all encounters!
1609 *Volpone*, act 1, sc.5.

17 Calumnies are answered best with silence.
1609 *Volpone*, act 2, sc. 2.

18 Ay, a plague on't,
My conscience fools my wit!
1609 *Volpone*, act 2, sc.7.

19 Success hath made me wanton.
1609 *Volpone*, act 3, sc.1.

20 All my house,
But now, steamed like a bath with her thick breath.
A lawyer could not have been heard; nor scarce

Another woman, such a hail of words
She has let fall.
1609 Of Lady Politic Would-be. *Volpone*, act 3, sc.5.

21 Come, my Celia, let us prove,
While we can, the sports of love,
Time will not be ours for ever,
He, at length, our good will sever;
Spend not then his gifts in vain:
Suns that set may rise again;
But if once we lose this light,
'Tis with us perpetual night.
Why should we defer our joys?
Fame and rumour are but toys.
1609 *Volpone*, 'Song', act 3, sc.7.

22 His soul moves in his fee.
1609 Of the lawyer. *Volpone*, act 4, sc.5.

23 I'd have your tongue, sir, tipped with gold for this.
1609 *Volpone*, act 4, sc.6.

24 A pox of her autumnal face, her pieced beauty!
1609–10 *Epicoene*, act 1, sc.1.

25 Still to be neat, still to be drest,
As you were going to a feast;
Still to be powdered, still perfumed,
Lady, it is to be presumed,
Though art's hid causes are not found,
All is not sweet, all is not sound.

Give me a look, give me a face,
That makes simplicity a grace;
Robes loosely flowing, hair as free:
Such sweet neglect more taketh me,
Than all the adulteries of art;
They strike mine eyes, but not my heart.
1609–10 *Epicoene*, act 1, sc.1.

26 Let me see: all discourses but mine own afflict me; they
seem harsh, impertinent, and irksome.
1609–10 *Epicoene*, act 2, sc.1.

27 A man of your head and hair should owe more to that
reverend ceremony, and not mount the marriage bed like
a town-bull, or a mountain-goat; but stay the due season
and ascend it then with religion and fear.
1609–10 *Epicoene*, act 3, sc.5.

28 Fortune, that favours fools.
1610 *The Alchemist*, act 1, sc.4.

29 [The play] is like to be a very conceited scurvy one, in
plain English.
1614 *Bartholomew Fair*, Induction.

30 WIN LITTLEWIT: Come, indeed, la, you are such a fool, still!
LITTLEWIT: No, but half a one, Win; you are the t'other half:
man and wife make one fool, Win.
1614 *Bartholomew Fair*, act 1, sc.1.

31 He is a fellow of a most arrogant and invincible dullness, I
assure you.
1614 *Bartholomew Fair*, act 1, sc.1.

32 There is a doing of right out of wrong, if the ways be
found.
1614 *Bartholomew Fair*, act 2, sc.2.

33 I see compassion may become a justice, though it be a
weakness, I confess, and nearer a vice than a virtue.
1614 *Bartholomew Fair*, act 4, sc.2.

34 There's reason good, that you good laws should make:
Men's manners ne'er were viler, for your sake.
1616 *Epigrams*, 'To the Parliament'.

35 Nor shall our cups make any guilty men:
But, at our parting, we will be, as when
We innocently met. No simple word,
That shall be utter'd at our mirthful board,
Shall make us sad next morning: or affright
The liberty, that we'll enjoy tonight.
1616 *Epigrams*, 'On Inviting a Friend to Supper'.

36 Thou art not, Penshurst, built to envious show
Of touch or marble, nor canst boast a row
Of polished pillars, or a roof of gold;
Thou hast no lantern whereof tales are told,
Or stair, or courts; but standst an ancient pile,
And these grudged at, art reverenced the while.
1616 *The Forest*, 'To Penshurst'.

37 Then hath thy orchard fruit, thy garden flowers,
Fresh as the air, and new as are the hours.
The early cherry, with the later plum,
Fig, grape, and quince, each in his time doth come:
The blushing apricot, and woolly peach
Hang on thy walls, that every child may reach.
1616 *The Forest*, 'To Penshurst'.

38 Freedom doth with degree dispense.
1616 *The Forest*, 'To Sir Robert Wroth'.

39 Nor for my peace will I go far,
As wanderers do, that still do roam,
But make my strengths, such as they are,
Here in my bosom, and at home.
1616 *The Forest*, 'To the World'.

40 Drink to me, only, with thine eyes,
And I will pledge with mine;
Or leave a kiss but in the cup,
And I'll not look for wine.
1616 *The Forest*, 'To Celia'.

41 'Tis grown almost a danger to speak true
Of any good mind, now: There are so few.
1616 *The Forest*, 'Epistle to Katherine, Lady Aubigny'.

42 Rest in soft peace, and, asked, say here doth lie
Ben Jonson his best piece of poetry.
1616 'On My First Son'.

43 Soul of the Age!
The applause, delight, the wonder of our stage!
1623 'To the Memory of My Beloved, the Author, Mr. William
Shakespeare, and What He Hath Left Us'.

44 Thou hadst small Latin, and less Greek.
1623 'To the Memory of My Beloved, the Author, Mr. William
Shakespeare, and What He Hath Left Us', prefatory dedication to
the first folio of Shakespeare's plays.

45 He was not of an age, but for all time!
1623 'To the Memory of My Beloved, the Author, Mr. William
Shakespeare, and What He Hath Left Us', prefatory dedication to
the first folio of Shakespeare's plays.

46 Sweet Swan of Avon! What a sight it were
To see thee in our waters yet appear,
And make those flights upon the banks of Thames
That so did take Eliza, and our James!
1623 'To the Memory of My Beloved, the Author, Mr. William
Shakespeare, and What He Hath Left Us', prefatory dedication to
the first folio of Shakespeare's plays.

47 O rare Ben Jonson.
   1637 His epitaph in Westminster Abbey. It is thought that the words were inscribed on his gravestone at the order of a certain Sir John Young, possibly in error for 'Orare Ben Jonson' ('Pray for Ben Jonson').

48 For Love's sake, kiss me once again,
   I long, and should not beg in vain,
   Here's none to spy, or see;
   Why do you doubt, or stay?
   I'll taste as lightly as the Bee,
   That doth but touch his flower, and flies away.
   Once more, and (faith) I will be gone:
   Can he that loves, ask less than one?
   The Underwood, 'A Celebration of Charis', no.7 (published 1640).

49 Minds that are great and free,
   Should not on fortune pause,
   'Tis crown enough to virtue still, her own applause.
   The Underwood, 'An Ode to Himself' (published 1640).

50 Helen, did Homer never see
   Thy beauties, yet could write of thee?
   The Underwood, 'An Ode' (published 1640).

51 Come, let us here enjoy the shade;
   For love in shadow best is made.
   Though envy oft his shadow be,
   None brooks the sunlight worse than he.
   The Underwood, 'A Song' (published 1640).

52 'Tis true, I'm broke! Vows, oaths, and all I had
   Of credit lost. And I am now run mad,
   Or do upon my self some desperate ill;
   This sadness makes no approaches, but to kill.
   The Underwood, 'An Elegy', no.40 (published 1640).

53 Wisdom without honesty is mere craft and cozenage. And therefore the reputation for honesty must first be gotten; which cannot be but by living well. A good life is a main argument.
   Timber: or Discoveries made upon Men and Matter (published 1640).

54 Poetry in this latter age hath proved but a mean mistress to such as have wholly addicted themselves to her, or given their names up to her family. They who have but saluted her on the by, and now and then tendered their visits, she hath done much for, and advanced in the way of their own professions (both the law and the gospel) beyond all they could have hoped, or done for themselves without her favour.
   Timber: or Discoveries made upon Men and Matter (published 1640).

55 I remember that the players have often mentioned it as an honour to Shakespeare that in his writing, whatsoever he penned, he never blotted out a line. My answer hath been, Would he had blotted a thousand: which they thought a malevolent speech…[but] I loved the man and do honour his memory, on this side idolatry, as much as any.
   Timber: or Discoveries made upon Men and Matter (published 1640).

56 There was ever more in him to be praised than to be pardoned.
   Of Shakespeare. *Timber: or Discoveries made upon Men and Matter* (published 1640).

57 The fear of every man that heard him was, lest he should make an end.
   Of Francis Bacon. *Timber: or Discoveries made upon Men and Matter* (published 1640).

58 For a man to write well, there are required three necessaries: to read the best authors, observe the best speakers, and much exercise of his own style.
   Timber: or Discoveries made upon Men and Matter (published 1640).

59 Ready writing makes not good writing, but good writing brings on ready writing.
   Timber: or Discoveries made upon Men and Matter (published 1640).

60 Custom is the most certain mistress of language, as the public stamp makes the current money.
   Timber: or Discoveries made upon Men and Matter (published 1640).

61 Our composition must be more accurate in the beginning and end than in the midst, and in the end more than in the beginning; for through the midst the stream bears us.
   Timber: or Discoveries made upon Men and Matter (published 1640).

62 Our style should be as a skein of silk, to be carried and found by the right thread, not ravelled and perplexed; then all is a knot, a heap.
   Timber: or Discoveries made upon Men and Matter (published 1640).

Joplin, Janis 1943–70

US rhythm and blues singer.

63 Lord, won't you buy me a Mercedes-Benz,
   My friends all drive Porsches,
   I must make amends.
   1970 'Mercedes-Benz', co-written with Michael McClure and Bob Neuwirth.

Jordan, June 1936–2002

US poet, essayist, political activist and writer for children. Her work was marked by a strong commitment to black consciousness.

64 Body and soul, Black America reveals the extreme questions of contemporary life, questions of freedom and identity: *How can I be who I am?*
   1969 'Black Studies: Bringing Back the Person', in the *Evergreen Review*, Oct.

65 We do not deride the fears of prospering white America. A nation of violence and private property has every reason to dread the violated and the deprived.
   1969 'Black Studies: Bringing Back the Person', in the *Evergreen Review*, Oct.

66 To rescue our children we will have to let them save us from the power we embody: we will have to trust the very difference that they forever personify.
   1978 Keynote address for Child Welfare League of America. Collected as 'Old Stories: New Lives' in *Moving Towards Home* (1989).

67 I am a feminist, and what that means to me is much the same as the meaning of the fact that I am Black: it means that I must undertake to love myself as though my very life depends upon self-love and self-respect.
   1978 Address to Black Writers Conference, Howard University. Collected as 'Where Is the Love?' in *Moving Towards Home* (1989).

Jordan, Michael 1963–

US basketball player. He played with the Chicago Bulls (1984–93, 1995–8), set numerous records, and was a member of the US Olympic gold medal-winning basketball teams in 1984 and 1992.

68 Talent wins games, but teamwork wins championships.
Attributed.

Jordan, Neil 1950–

Irish film-maker and writer. His films include *The Crying Game* (1992), *Interview with the Vampire* (1994), *The Butcher Boy* (1997) and *The End of the Affair* (1999).

69 The action movie in the 1980s became like what the silent movie used to be. The same movie could be seen in Los Angeles and Taiwan and Hong Kong and you didn't need subtitles because everybody understands Bruce Willis blowing things up in a torn vest.
2004 In *The Scotsman*, 22 May.

Joseph II 1741–90

Holy Roman Emperor (1756–90), known as 'the revolutionary emperor' for his programme of modernization. He suppressed papal power and in 1781 published an Edict of Toleration for Protestants and Greeks.

70 As I have just come from making my Easter confession on Good Friday and have forgiven all those who trespass against me, I cannot harbour any thoughts of revenge, only contempt for an arrant shit who is bursting with pride, although he is simply being taken for a ride by his women.
1786 Of the senior dignitary of the Holy Roman Empire, the Elector-Archbishop of Mainz. Letter to Trauttmansdorff (his representative at Mainz), 14 Apr. Quoted in T C W Blanning *Joseph II* (1994), p.148.

71 Here lies a prince whose intentions were pure, but who had the misfortune to see all his plans collapse.
Epitaph for himself. Quoted in T C W Blanning *Joseph II* (1994), p.1.

Joseph of Exeter fl.12c

English poet.

72 The youths at cricks did play
Throughout the merry day.
1180 Quoted in Ivor Brown *A Book of England* (1958). This is thought to be the first mention of the game of cricket in English literature.

Josephus, Flavius AD 37–100

Jewish historian and soldier, commander of Galilee. He surrendered to the Romans rather than commit suicide, and later won imperial patronage and lived in Rome. His works include *The Antiquities of the Jews*.

73 Their exercises are unbloody battles, and their battles bloody exercises.
c.75–79 AD Of the Romans. *A History of the Jewish War*, bk.3, ch.5, section 1 (translated by William Whiston).

Jourdan, Louis *originally* **Louis Gendre** 1921–

French-born actor. He appeared in French films (1940–6), then moved to the US. His many American and European film credits since include *Gigi* (1958), *Can Can* (1960) and *Octopussy* (1983).

74 In New York people don't go to the theater—they go to see hits.
1950 In the *New York Herald Tribune*, 1 Jan.

Jouvet, Louis 1887–1951

French actor and director. Appointed director of the Comédie des Champs-Élysées in 1922, he had a profound impact on the development of French theatre between the wars, making many reforms.

75 The one thing constant in a changing world is the avant-garde.
Attributed.

Jovanovich, William 1920–2001

US publisher. He joined Harcourt Brace Jovanovich Inc in 1947, eventually becoming president and director.

76 The most important single thing in publishing is the English sentence, and the editor who cannot contemplate it again and again with a sense of wonder has not yet gained respect for the complexity of learning.
1964 *Now, Barabbas*.

Jowell, Tessa 1947–

English Labour politician, Secretary of State for Culture, Media and Sport since 2001.

77 In the last Parliament, the House of Commons had more MPs called John than all the women MPs put together.
1999 In the *Independent on Sunday*, 'Quotes', 14 Mar.

Jowett, Benjamin 1817–93

English classical scholar, Professor of Greek at Oxford (1855–93), ordained as an Anglican priest in 1845.

78 One man is as good as another until he has written a book.
Quoted in Evelyn Abbott and Lewis Campbell (eds) *Life and Letters of Benjamin Jowett* (1897), vol.1.

79 Nowhere probably is there more true feeling, and nowhere worse taste, than in a churchyard.
Quoted in Evelyn Abbott and Lewis Campbell (eds) *Letters of Benjamin Jowett* (1899), ch.6.

Joyce, James Augustine Aloysius 1882–1941

Irish writer who lived in exile on the Continent and was plagued for most of his life with deteriorating eyesight. His fiction includes *Dubliners* (1914), *Ulysses* (1922), one of the most influential works of 20c fiction, and *Finnegans Wake* (1939).

80 'O, pa!' he cried. 'Don't beat me, pa! And I'll…I'll say a *Hail Mary* for you… I'll say a *Hail Mary* for you, pa, if you don't beat me.'
1914 *Dubliners*, 'Counterparts'.

81 His soul swooned slowly as he heard the snow falling faintly through the universe and faintly falling, like the descent of their last end, upon all the living and the dead.
1914 *Dubliners*, 'The Dead'.

82 The fellows were practising long shies and bowling lobs and slow twisters. In the soft grey silence he could hear the bump of the balls: and from here and from there through the quiet air the sound of the cricket bats: pick, pack, pock, puck: like drops of water in a fountain falling

softly in the brimming bowl.
1916 *A Portrait of the Artist as a Young Man.*

83 At the door Dante turned round violently and shouted down the room, her cheeks flushed and quivering with rage:
—Devil out of hell! We won! We crushed him to death! Fiend!
The door slammed behind her. Mr Casey, freeing his arms from his holders, suddenly bowed his head on his hands with a sob of pain.
—Poor Parnell! he cried loudly. My dead king!
1916 *A Portrait of the Artist as a Young Man.*

84 The snotgreen sea. The scrotumtightening sea.
1922 *Ulysses.*

85 It is a symbol of Irish art. The cracked looking-glass of a servant.
1922 *Ulysses.*

86 When I makes tea I makes tea, as old mother Grogan said. And when I makes water I makes water…*Begob, ma'am,* says Mrs. Cahill, *God send you don't make them in the one pot.*
1922 *Ulysses.*

87 History, Stephen said, is a nightmare from which I am trying to awake.
1922 *Ulysses.*

88 Lawn Tennyson, gentleman poet.
1922 *Ulysses.*

89 Come forth, Lazarus! And he came fifth and lost the job.
1922 *Ulysses.*

90 A man of genius makes no mistakes. His errors are volitional and are the portals of discovery.
1922 *Ulysses.*

91 Greater love than this, he said, no man hath that a man lay down his wife for his friend. Go thou and do likewise. Thus, or words to that effect, saith Zarathustra, sometime regius professor of French letters to the university of Oxtail.
1922 *Ulysses.*

92 Mr. Leopold Bloom ate with relish the inner organs of beasts and fowls. He liked thick giblet soup, nutty gizzards, a stuffed roast heart; liver slices fried with crustcrumbs, fried hencod's roes. Most of all he liked grilled mutton kidneys which gave to his palate a fine tang of faintly scented urine.
1922 *Ulysses.*

93 A woman loses a charm with every pin she takes out.
1922 *Ulysses.*

94 Heavenly weather. If life was always like that. Cricket weather. Sit around under sunshades. Over after over. Out. They can't play it here. Still, Captain Buller broke a window in Kildare Street Club with a slog to square leg.
1922 *Ulysses.* Legend has it that W G Grace performed the feat of breaking the Kildare Street Club window while playing at the distant College Park in the 1870s.

95 Her crocus dress she wore, lowcut, belongings on show.
1922 *Ulysses.*

96 yes and how he kissed me under the Moorish wall and I thought well as well him as another and then I asked him with my eyes to ask again yes and then he asked me

would I yes to say yes my mountain flower and first I put my arms around him yes and drew him down to me so he could feel my breasts all perfume yes and his heart was going like mad and yes I said yes I will Yes.
1922 *Ulysses*, last words.

97 I read the first 2 pages of the usual sloppy English and [Stuart Gilbert] read me a lyrical bit about nudism in the wood and the end which is a piece of propaganda in favour of something which, outside of D. H. L.'s country at any rates, makes all the propaganda for itself.
1931 On D H Lawrence's *Lady Chatterley's Lover.* Letter to Harriet Weaver, 17 Dec.

98 That ideal reader suffering from an ideal insomnia.
1939 *Finnegans Wake.*

99 Gentes and laitymen, fullstoppers and semicolonials, hybreds and lubberds!
1939 *Finnegans Wake.*

1 All moanday, tearsday, wailsday, thumpsday, frightday, shatterday till the fear of the Law.
1939 *Finnegans Wake.*

Joyce, Nora d.1951

Wife of James Joyce.

2 Well, Jim, I haven't read any of your books but I'll have to someday because they must be good considering how well they sell.
To her husband James Joyce. Recalled on her death, 12 Apr 1951.

Joyce, William *known as* **Lord Haw Haw** 1906–46

British traitor. He fled to Germany before World War II, from where he broadcast anti-British propaganda in his upper-class drawl until captured at Flensburg and executed.

3 The Twenty Thousand Thieves.
c.1941 Of the Australian 9th Division troops who were besieged at Tobruk, North Africa. Radio broadcast from Nazi Germany.

Julian of Norwich *known as* **Lady Julian** c.1342–1416

English anchoress, who spent much of her life enclosed in a cell attached to the Church of St Julian, Norwich. In 1373 she experienced a series of religious visions which she set down in her *Revelations of Divine Love.*

4 He showed me something small, no bigger than a hazelnut, lying in the palm of my hand, as it seemed to me, and it was as round as a ball. I looked at it with the eye of my understanding, and thought: What can this be? I was amazed that it could last, for I thought that because of its littleness it would suddenly have fallen into nothing. And I was answered in my understanding: It lasts and always will, because God loves it; and thus every thing has being through the love of God.
1373–c.1393 *Revelations of Divine Love*, ch.5.

5 It is true that sin is the cause of all this pain; but all shall be well, and all shall be well, and all manner of things shall be well.
1373–c.1393 *Revelations of Divine Love*, ch.27.

6 Pray inwardly, even though you do not enjoy it. It does good though you feel nothing, even though you think you are doing nothing.
1373–c.1393 *Revelations of Divine Love*, ch.41.

Jumblatt, Walid 1949–

Lebanese politician and hereditary Druze chieftain, who succeeded his father Jumblatt on the latter's assassination in 1977.

7 Here, even the law of the jungle has broken down.
1985 Of the situation in Beirut, in the *Sunday Times*, 29 Dec.

Jung, Carl Gustav 1875–1961

Swiss psychiatrist. After collaborating with Sigmund Freud he published *The Psychology of the Unconscious* (1911–12), departing from Freud's psychosexual emphasis. Subsequently he developed analytical psychology and the concept of the 'collective unconscious'.

8 The pendulum of the mind oscillates between sense and nonsense, not between right and wrong.
1962 *Memories, Dreams and Reflections*.

9 Show me a sane man and I will cure him for you.
Quoted in the *Observer*, 19 Jul 1975.

'Junius' *possibly the pseudonym of* **Sir Philip Francis** (1740–1818)

The identity of Junius, whose scathing political letters were printed in the *Public Advertiser* between 1769 and 1771 and collected in 1772, has never been established. Sir Philip Francis is a favourite candidate.

10 There is a holy mistaken zeal in politics as well as in religion. By persuading others, we convince ourselves.
1769 *Public Advertiser*, 19 Dec, Letter 35.

11 Let it be impressed upon your minds, let it be instilled into your children, that the liberty of the press is the *Palladium* of all the civil, political, and religious rights of an Englishman.
1772 *Letters*, Dedication to the Authorized Edition.

Just, Ward Swift 1935–

US journalist and writer. He was a correspondent with *Newsweek* (1963–5) and the *Washington Post* (1965–70), before turning full time to fiction with works such as *The American Blues* (1984) and *Echo House* (1997).

12 The place where bulls and foxes dine very well, but lambs end up head down on the hook.
1988 Of Chicago. *Jack Gance*.

Justinian I AD 482–565

Emperor of the East Roman Empire (from 527). His reign saw the restoration of the Roman Empire to its ancient limits and many legal reforms, collected in the *Corpus Juris Civilis*, which had a considerable influence on European law.

13 Justice is the constant and perpetual wish to render to every one his due.
AD 533 *Institutiones*, pt.1.

Juvenal *full name* **Decimus Iunius Iuvenalis** c.55–c.140 AD

Roman lawyer and satirist. He was banished to Egypt for some years by Domitian for his 16 verse satires (c.100–128 AD), which deal with the corruption and immorality of the times.

14 *Difficile est saturam non scribere.*
It is difficult not to write satire.
Satirae, no.1, l.30.

15 *Quis tulerit Gracchos de seditione querentes?*

Who can bear the Gracchi deploring revolution?
Satirae, no.2, l.24. The brothers Gaius and Tiberius Sempronius Gracchus (2c BC) attempted radical agrarian reforms, and were both killed by political opponents.

16 *Nil habet infelix paupertas durius in se Quam quod ridiculos homines facit.*
The hardest thing to bear in poverty is the fact that it makes men ridiculous.
Satirae, no.3, l.152–3 (translated by Peter Green).

17 *Sed quis custodiet ipsos custodes?*
But who is to guard the guards themselves?
Satirae, no.6, l.347.

18 *Cantabit vacuus coram latrone viator.*
Travel light and you can sing in the robber's face.
Satirae, no.10, l.22.

19 *Nam qui dabat olim imperium, fasces, legiones, omnia, nunc se continet atque duas tantum res anxius optat, panem et circenses.*
Time was when their plebiscite elected generals, Heads of State, commanders of legions: but now they've pulled in their horns, there's only two things that concern them: bread and games.
Of the people of Rome. *Satirae*, no.10, l.78–81 (translated by Peter Green). 'Panem et circenses' is sometimes translated as 'bread and circuses'.

20 *Orandum est ut sit mens sana in corpore sano.*
One should pray to have a sound mind in a sound body.
Satirae, no.10, l.356.

21 *Maxima debetur puero reverentia, si quid turpe paras.*
If you are planning any misdeed, never forget that a child has a first claim on your respect.
Satirae, no.14, l.47 (translated by Peter Green).

Kael, Pauline 1919–2001

US film critic. She was film critic of the *New Yorker* from 1968 to 1991.

22 The words 'Kiss Kiss Bang Bang' which I saw on an Italian movie poster, are perhaps the briefest statement imaginable of the basic appeal of movies.
1968 *Kiss Kiss Bang Bang*.

23 Good movies make you care, make you believe in possibilities again.
1970 *Going Steady*.

Kafka, Franz 1883–1924

Czech novelist and short-story writer who wrote in German. After studying law he worked in Prague at a workers' accident insurance company. He is best known for his bleak studies of the absurdity of the human condition.

24 *Ich glaube, mann sollte überhaupt nur solche Bücher*

lesen, die einen beißen und stechen.
I think we ought to read only the kind of books that wound and stab us.
1904 Letter to Oskar Pollack. Collected in Richard and Clara Winston (eds and trans) *Letters to Friends, Family, and Editors* (1977).

25 *Ist es schwer und kann es ein Außenseiter begreifen, dass man eine Geschichte von ihrem Anfang in sich erlebt, vom fernen Punkt bis zu der heranfahrenden Lokomotive aus Stahl, Kohl und Dampf, sie aber auch jetzt noch nicht verlässt, sondern von ihr gejagt wird und aus eigenem Schwung vor ihr läuft, wohin sie nur stößt und wohin man sie lockt.*
It is so difficult and can an outsider understand that you experience a story within yourself from its beginning, from the distant point up to the approaching locomotive of steel, coal and steam, and you don't abandon it even now, but want to be pursued by it and have time for it, therefore are pursued by it and of your own volition run before it wherever it may thrust and wherever you may lure it.
1911 Diary entry, Aug. Collected in Max Brod (ed) *The Diaries of Franz Kafka, 1910–1913* (1948).

26 *Als Gregor Samsa eines Morgens aus unruhigen Träumen erwachte, fand er sich in seinem Bett zu einem ungeheueren Ungeziefer verwandelt.*
When Gregor Samsa awoke one morning from uneasy dreams he found himself transformed in his bed into a gigantic insect.
1915 *Metamorphosis*, ch.1.

27 *Es ist oft besser, in Ketten als frei zu sein.*
It is often safer to be in chains than to be free.
1925 *Der Prozess* (translated as *The Trial*, 1937).

28 *Ich bin so weit, dass ich Gewissheit gar nicht haben will.*
I have reached the stage where I no longer wish to have certainty.
'Der Bau', collected in Nahum N Glatzer (ed) *The Complete Stories* (1971).

29 *Er lächelte und sagte: 'Von mir willst du den Weg erfahren?' 'Ja,' sagte ich, 'da ich ihn selbst nich finden kann.' 'Gibs auf, gibs auf,' sagte er und wandte sich mit einem großen Schwunge ab, so wie Leute, die mit ihrem Lachen allein sein wollen.*
He smiled and said: 'You asking me the way?' 'Yes,' I said, 'since I cannot find it myself.' 'Give it up! Give it up!' said he, and turned with a sudden jerk, like someone who wants to be alone with his laughter.
'Gibs Auf!', collected in Nahum N Glatzer (ed) *The Complete Stories* (1971).

Kahn, Gus 1886–1941

US lyricist and author. He supplied the lyrics for many classic hit songs of the 1920s and 1930s, among them 'Toot, Toot, Tootsie', 'Carolina in the Morning', 'Yes Sir, That's My Baby', and 'Makin' Whoopee'.

30 There's nothing surer,
The rich get rich and the poor get children.
In the meantime, in between time,
Ain't we got fun.
1921 'Ain't We Got Fun' (with Raymond B Egan).

31 All God's Chillum Got Rhythm.
1937 Title of song.

Kaiko, Takeshi 1930–89

Japanese novelist. His first novel to be translated into English was *Darkness in Summer* (1972).

32 I don't trust anybody who's never eaten bread with the salt of tears.
1963 'The Laughing Stock', in *Five Thousand Runaways* (translated by Cecilia Segawa Seigle).

33 Late one morning, I awoke in the capital of a certain country and found myself—not changed overnight into a large brown beetle, nor feeling exactly on top of the world—merely ready to go home.
1978 'The Crushed Pellet', in *Five Thousand Runaways* (translated by Cecilia Segawa Seigle).

Kames, Henry Home, Lord 1696–1782

Scottish judge, philosopher and agricultural improver, a central figure of the Scottish Enlightenment.

34 Fare ye a' weel, ye bitches!
1782 His alleged words on taking leave of his fellow judges in the Court of Session. He died eight days later. Quoted in Robert Chambers *Traditions of Edinburgh* (1824), 'The Parliament House'.

Kandinsky, Wassily 1866–1944

Russian-born painter and writer on art. He was an important pioneer of abstract art. With Franz Marc he edited the *Blaue Reiter Almanac*.

35 The force that propels the human spirit on the clear way forward and upward is the abstract spirit.
1912 'On the Question of Form', in *Blaue Reiter Almanac*.

36 We should never make a god out of form. We should struggle for form only as long as it serves as a means of expression for the inner sound.
1912 'On the Question of Form', in *Blaue Reiter Almanac*.

37 Every work of art is the child of its time, often it is the mother of our emotions.
1912 *Concerning the Spiritual in Art*.

38 In general, therefore, color is a means of exerting a direct influence upon the soul. Color is the keyboard. The eye is the hammer. The soul is the piano, with its many strings.
Quoted in K C Lindsay and P Vergo (eds and trans) *Kandinsky: Complete Writings on Art* (1982).

Kant, Immanuel 1724–1804

German philosopher, Professor of Logic and Metaphysics at Konigsberg (1770), who developed a theory of knowledge depending on perception and propounded the 'moral argument' for the existence of God. His great work is the *Kritik der reinen Vernunft* (*Critique of Pure Reason*, 1781).

39 *Der Verstand vermag nichts anzuschauen, und die Sinne nichts zu denken. Nur daraus, dass sie sich vereinigen, kann Erkenntnis entspringen.*
The understanding can intuit nothing, the senses can think nothing. Only through their union can knowledge arise.
1781 *Kritik der reinen Vernunft* (*Critique of Pure Reason*), B75 (translated by N Kemp Smith).

40 *Ich habe also demnach keine Erkenntnis von mir, wie ich bin, sondern bloß, wie ich mir selbst erscheine. Das Bewusstsein seiner selbst ist also noch lange nicht eine Erkenntnis seiner selbst.*

I have no *knowledge* of myself as I am but merely as I appear to myself. The consciousness of myself is thus very far from being a knowledge of the self.
1781 *Kritik der reinen Vernunft* (*Critique of Pure Reason*), B158 (translated by N Kemp Smith).

41 *Eben darin Philosophie besteht, seine Grenzen zu kennen.*
It is precisely in knowing its limits that philosophy consists.
1781 *Kritik der reinen Vernunft* (*Critique of Pure Reason*), B755 (translated by N Kemp Smith).

42 *Sapere aude,* have the courage to know: that is the motto of enlightenment.
1783 His reply to a newspaper's challenge to define enlightenment. Quoted in *The Economist*, 16 Mar 1996.

43 *Aus so krummen Holze, als woraus der Mensch gemacht ist, kann nichts ganz Gerades gezimmert werden.*
Out of the crooked timber of humanity, no straight thing can ever be made.
1784 *Idee zu einer allgemeinen Geschichte in weltbürgerlicher Absicht* (*Idea for a General History with a Cosmopolitan Purpose*), prop.6.

44 *Ich solle niemals anders verfahren, als so, dass ich auch wollen könne, meine Maxime solle ein allgemeines Gesetz werden.*
I ought never to act except in such a way *that I can also will that my maxim should become a universal law.*
1785 *Grundlagen zur Metaphysik der Sitten* (*Groundwork to a Metaphysic of Morals*), ch.1 (translated by H J Paton).

45 *Handle so, dass du die Menschheit, sowohl in deiner Person, als in der Person eines jeden andern, jederzeit zugleich als Zweck, niemals bloß als Mittel brauchst.*
Act in such a way that you always treat humanity, whether in your own person or in the person of any other, never simply as a means, but always at the same time as an end.
1785 *Grundlagen zur Metaphysik der Sitten* (*Groundwork to a Metaphysic of Morals*), ch.2 (translated by H J Paton).

46 *Ich musste also das Wissen aufheben, um zum Glauben Platz zu bekommen.*
I have therefore found it necessary to deny *knowledge,* in order to make room for *faith.*
1787 *Kritik der reinen Vernunft* (*Critique of Pure Reason*), preface to 2nd edn (translated by N Kemp Smith).

47 *Zwei Dinge erfüllen das Gemüt mit immer neuer und zunehmender Bewunderung und Ehrfurcht, je öfter und anhaltender sich das Nachdenken damit beschäftigt: der bestirnte Himmel über mir, und das moralische Gesetz in mir.*
Two things fill the mind with ever new and increasing admiration and awe, the oftener and more steadily we reflect on them: *the starry heavens above me and the moral law within.*
1788 *Kritik der praktischen Vernunft* (*Critique of Practical Reason*) (translated by T K Abbott).

Kapitsa, Peter Leonidovich 1894–1984

Soviet physicist who studied in Britain under Ernest Rutherford. Director of the Institute of Physical Problems, he was dismissed by Stalin for refusing to work on an atomic bomb, but was later reinstated.

48 Theory is a good thing but a good experiment lasts forever.
1980 *Experiment, Theory, Practice.*

Karloff, Boris originally *William Henry Pratt* 1887–1969

English-born US film star. He went to Canada and the US aiming at a diplomatic career, but turned to acting, finding fame as the monster in *Frankenstein* (1931) and other horror roles.

49 The monster was indeed the best friend I could ever have.
On his success as Frankenstein's monster. Quoted in *Connoisseur,* Jan 1991.

Karpov, Anatoly 1951–

Russian chess player.

50 Chess is everything—art, science and sport.
Attributed.

Karr, Alphonse 1808–90

French writer and journalist.

51 *Plus ça change, plus c'est la même chose.*
The more things change, the more they stay the same.
1849 *Les Guêpes,* Jan.

Karsh, Yousuf 1908–2002

Turkish-born Canadian portrait photographer.

52 I said, 'Forgive me, sir,' and plucked the cigar out of his mouth. By the time I got back to my camera, he looked so belligerent he could have devoured me. It was at that instant that I took the photograph. The silence was deafening.
1983 Recalling how he snapped the celebrated 'bulldog' photograph of Sir Winston Churchill in the Speaker's Chambers, House of Commons, Ottawa, on 30 Dec 1941. *Karsh: A Fifty-Year Retrospective.*

Kaufman, George S(imon) 1889–1961

US playwright, director and journalist, a member of the Algonquin Round Table circle of literary wits. He collaborated on several successful comedies with Moss Hart, notably *The Man Who Came to Dinner* (1939), and also worked with Edna Ferber and George Gershwin.

53 Am sitting in the last row. Wish you were here.
1932 Telegram sent during a performance of *Of Thee I Sing* to the actor William Gaxton, who was taking various liberties with Kaufman's lines while playing the leading role.

54 Massey won't be satisfied until he's assassinated.
1938 Of Raymond Massey in the title role of *Abe Lincoln in Illinois.* Recalled on Kaufman's death, 2 Jun 1961.

55 Satire is what closes Saturday night.
Quoted in Howard Teichmann *George S Kaufman* (1972).

56 I saw his play under bad conditions. The curtain was up.
Of Alexander Woollcott. Quoted in Scott Meredith *George S Kaufman and His Friends* (1974).

57 Like the Arabs, I fold my tens and silently steal away.
On winning at poker. Quoted in Scott Meredith *George S Kaufman and His Friends* (1974).
➤ *See Longfellow 516:50.*

58 It's what God would have done if he'd had the money.
On visiting Pocantico Hills, the Rockefeller family's 3,000-acre Hudson River estate. Quoted in Michael Kramer and Sam Roberts *I Never Wanted to Be Vice-President of Anything!* (1976).

59 God finally caught his eye.
Epitaph for a deceased waiter. Quoted in Jon Winokur *The Portable Curmudgeon* (1987).

60 There was scattered laughter in the rear of the theatre, leading to the belief that somebody was telling jokes back there.
Play review.

61 Close the play and keep the store open nights.
Reply when asked by one of his backers, the owner of Bloomingdale's department store, how the première of Kaufman's latest play had gone. Attributed.

62 Over my dead body.
Suggestion for his own epitaph. Attributed.

Kaufman, Gerald 1930–
English Labour politician.

63 We would prefer to see the House run by a philistine with the requisite financial acumen than by the succession of opera and ballet lovers who have brought a great and valuable institution to its knees.
1997 Report of the Commons' Culture, Media and Sport Select Committee on Covent Garden, 3 Dec.

Kaufmann, Christoph 1753–95
Swiss-born German author and critic.

64 *Sturm und Drang.*
Storm and stress.
c.1775 Suggested title for a romantic historical play of F M Klinger, adopted as the defining term for late-18c German drama.

Kaunitz-Rietberg, Wenzel Anton, Prince von 1711–94
Austrian statesman, Ambassador to the French court (1750–2). Appointed Chancellor in 1753, he directed Austrian politics for almost 40 years. Active in the ecclesiastical reforms of Joseph II, he was a liberal patron of arts and sciences.

65 That was very good of him.
1790 Attributed, on hearing that Joseph II had died. Quoted in T C W Blanning *Joseph II* (1994), p.198.

Kavanagh, P(atrick) J(oseph Gregory) 1931–
English poet and novelist. His works include the autobiographical *The Perfect Stranger* (1966) and *A Kind of Journal* (2003), a collection of his *Spectator* columns.

66 Charlie Parker…always filled me with a kind of despair, because he played the way I would have liked to write, and this wasn't possible for me or anyone else. He made poetry seem word-bound.
1966 *The Perfect Stranger*, ch.5.

67 Try not to despise yourself too much—it's only a conceit.
1968 *A Song and Dance*, ch.6.

68 But years ago he had decided never to be afraid of the deafeningly obvious, it is always news to somebody.
1968 *A Song and Dance*, ch.6.

69 Mary lived by wondering what lay round the corner. I lived by knowing there was no corner.
1973 *A Happy Man*, ch.12.

Kazantzakis, Nikos 1883–1957
Greek writer, best known for his novel *Zorba the Greek* (1946, filmed 1964) and the long autobiographical narrative poem,

The Odyssey, a Modern Sequel (1938).

70 My entire soul is a cry, and all my work is a commentary on that cry.
1965 *Report to Greco.*

Kazin, Alfred 1915–98
US writer, best known for influential books of literary criticism such as *On Native Grounds* (1942) and the autobiographical *A Walker in the City* (1951).

71 In a very real sense, the writer writes in order to teach himself, to understand himself, to satisfy himself; the publishing of his ideas, though it brings gratifications, is a curious anti-climax.
1963 In *Think*, Feb.

72 Only power can get people into a position where they may be noble.
Quoted in M Korda *Power in the Office* (1976).

Keane, Roy 1971–
Irish footballer.

73 They have a few drinks, and maybe the prawn sandwiches, and they don't realise what's going on out on the pitch.
2000 On spectators in the corporate boxes at Manchester United games. In the *Sunday Times*, 31 Dec.

74 I don't give people hell. I tell them the truth and they think it's hell.
2002 On RTE, 28 May.

Keating, Paul John 1944–
Australian Republican politician. He became President of the New South Wales Labor Party (1979–83) and in 1991 was elected Leader of the Australian Labor Party. He was Prime Minister from 1991 to 1996.

75 A banana republic.
1986 On Australia's balance-of-payments crisis and cycle of recession. Radio broadcast, Radio 2GB, Sydney, 14 May.

Keats, John 1795–1821
English Romantic poet. His long mythological poem *Endymion* (1818) was fiercely criticized but *Lamia, Isabella, The Eve of St. Agnes and Other Poems* (1820), containing the romances 'The Eve of St Agnes' and 'Lamia', the epic 'Hyperion' and his major odes, was better received. He died of tuberculosis in Rome.

76 Much have I travell'd in the realms of gold.
1815 'On First Looking into Chapman's Homer', l.1. (Published in *The Examiner* 1816.)

77 Then felt I like some watcher of the skies
When a new planet swims into his ken;
Or like stout Cortez when with eagle eyes
He star'd at the Pacific—and all his men
Look'd at each other with a wild surmise—
Silent, upon a peak in Darien.
1815 'On First Looking into Chapman's Homer', l.9–14. (Published in *The Examiner* 1816.)

78 Sweetly they slept
On the blue fields of heaven, and then there crept
A little noiseless noise among the leaves,
Born of the very sign that silence heaves.
1816 'I Stood Tip-Toe upon a Little Hill', l.9–12.

79 Here are sweet peas, on tiptoe for a flight,
With wings of gentle flush o'er delicate white.
1816 'I Stood Tip-Toe upon a Little Hill', l.57–8.

80 Morality
Weighs heavily on me like unwilling sleep.
1817 'On Seeing the Elgin Marbles'.

81 Yet the sweet converse of an innocent mind,
Whose words are images of thoughts refined,
Is my soul's pleasure; and it sure must be
Almost the highest bliss of human-kind,
When to thy haunts two kindred spirits flee.
1817 'O Solitude! If I Must withThee Dwell'.

82 Stop and consider! life is but a day;
A fragile dew-drop on its perilous way
From a tree's summit; a poor Indian's sleep
While his boat hastens to the monstrous steep
Of Montmorenci.
1817 'Sleep and Poetry', l.85–9.

83 O for ten years, that I may overwhelm
Myself in poesy; so I may do the deed
That my own soul has to itself decreed.
1817 'Sleep and Poetry', l.96–8.

84 They swayed about upon a rocking horse,
And thought it Pegasus.
1817 'Sleep and Poetry', l.186–7.

85 And they shall be accounted poet kings
Who simply tell the most heart-easing things.
1817 'Sleep and Poetry', l.267–8.

86 It keeps eternal whisperings around
Desolate shores—and with its mighty swell
Gluts twice ten thousand Caverns.
1817 'On the Sea'.

87 I had a dove and the sweet dove died;
And I have thought it died of grieving:
O, what could it grieve for? Its feet were tied,
With a silken thread of my own hands' weaving.
1817 'I had a Dove and the Sweet Dove Died'.

88 A long poem is a test of invention which I take to be the
Polar star of poetry, as fancy is the sails, and imagination
the rudder.
1817 Letter to Benjamin Bailey, 8 Oct.

89 I am certain of nothing but the holiness of the heart's
affections and the truth of the imagination—what the
imagination seizes as beauty must be truth—whether it
existed before or not.
1817 Letter to Benjamin Bailey, 22 Nov.

90 O for a life of sensations rather than of thoughts!
1817 Letter to Benjamin Bailey, 22 Nov.

91 Negative Capability; that is, when a man is capable of
being in uncertainties, mysteries, doubts, without any
irritable reaching after fact and reason.
1817 Letter to G and T Keats, 21 Dec.

92 Souls of Poets dead and gone
What Elysium have ye known,
Happy field or mossy cavern,
Choicer than the Mermaid Tavern?
1818 'Lines on the Mermaid Tavern'.

93 When I have fears that I may cease to be
Before my pen has gleaned my teeming brain,
Before high-piled books, in charactery,

Hold like rich garners the full ripened grain.
1818 'When I Have FearsThat I May Cease to Be'.

94 When I behold, upon the night's starred face
Huge cloudy symbols of a high romance,
And think that I may never live to trace
Their shadows, with the magic hand of chance;
And when I feel, fair creature of an hour,
That I shall never look upon thee more,
Never have relish in the faery power
Of unreflecting love;—then on the shore
Of the wide world I stand alone, and think
Till love and fame to nothingness so sink.
1818 'When I Have FearsThat I May Cease to Be'.

95 If poetry comes not as naturally as leaves to a tree it had
better not come at all.
1818 Letter to John Taylor, 27 Feb.

96 Scenery is fine—but human nature is finer.
1818 Letter to Benjamin Bailey, 13 Mar.

97 It is impossible to live in a country which is continually
under hatches… Rain! Rain! Rain!
1818 Letter to J H Reynolds, 10 Apr.

98 I think I shall be among the English Poets after my death.
1818 Letter to George and Georgiana Keats, 14 Oct.

99 The imagination of a boy is healthy, and the mature
imagination of a man is healthy; but there is a space of
life between, in which the soul is in a ferment, the
character undecided, the way of life uncertain, the
ambition thick-sighted: thence proceeds mawkishness.
1818 *Endymion*, preface.

1 A thing of beauty is a joy for ever:
Its loveliness increases; it will never
Pass into nothingness; but still will keep
A bower quiet for us, and a sleep
Full of sweet dreams, and health, and quiet breathing.
1818 *Endymion*, bk.1, l.1–5.

2 The grandeur of the dooms
We have imagined for the mighty dead.
1818 *Endymion*, bk.1, l.20–1.

3 They always must be with us, or we die.
1818 *Endymion*, bk.1, l.33.

4 Who, of men, can tell
That flowers would bloom, or that green fruit would
   swell
To melting pulp, that fish would have bright mail,
The earth its dower of river, wood, and vale,
The meadows runnels, runnels pebble-stones,
The seed its harvest, or the lute its tones,
Tones ravishment, or ravishment its sweet,
If human souls did never kiss and greet?
1818 *Endymion*, bk.1, l.835–42.

5 Here is wine,
Alive with sparkles—never, I aver,
Since Ariadne was a vintager,
So cool a purple.
1818 *Endymion*, bk.2, l.441–4.

6 To Sorrow,
I bade good-morrow,
And thought to leave her far away behind;
But cheerly, cheerly,
She loves me dearly;

She is so constant to me, and so kind.
1818 *Endymion*, bk.4, l.173–8.

7 Their smiles,
Wan as primroses gathered at midnight
By chilly fingered spring.
1818 *Endymion*, bk.4, l.969–71.

8 Turn the key deftly in the oiled wards,
And seal the hushed Casket of my Soul.
1819 'To Sleep'.

9 Call the world if you please 'The vale of soul-making'.
1819 Letter to George and Georgiana Keats, 14 Feb.

10 I have met with women whom I really think would like to be married to a poem, and to be given away by a novel.
1819 Letter to Fanny Brawne, 8 Jul.

11 I have two luxuries to brood over in my walks, your loveliness and the hour of my death. O that I could have possession of them both in the same minute.
1819 Letter to Fanny Brawne, 25 Jul.

12 My friends should drink a dozen of Claret on my Tomb.
1819 Letter to Benjamin Bailey, 14 Aug.

13 Give me books, fruit, french wine and fine weather and a little music out of doors, played by somebody I do not know.
1819 Letter to Fanny Keats, 29 Aug.

14 Fanatics have their dreams, wherewith they weave
A paradise for a sect.
1819 'The Fall of Hyperion', l.1–2.
(Published 1856.)

15 'None can usurp this height,' returned that shade,
'But those to whom the miseries of the world
Are misery, and will not let them rest.'
1819 'The Fall of Hyperion', l.147–9.
(Published 1856.)

16 The poet and the dreamer are distinct,
Diverse, sheer opposite, antipodes.
The one pours out a balm upon the world,
The other vexes it.
1819 'The Fall of Hyperion', l.199–202.
(Published 1856.)

17 Oh what can ail thee, knight at arms,
Alone and palely loitering;
The sedge has wither'd from the lake,
And no birds sing.
1820 'La Belle Dame Sans Merci', stanza 1.

18 She found me roots of relish sweet,
And honey wild, and manna dew;
And sure in language strange she said,
'I love thee true.'
1820 'La Belle Dame Sans Merci', stanza 7.

19 I saw pale kings, and princes too,
Pale warriors, death-pale were they all;
Who cry'd—'La belle Dame sans Merci
Hath thee in thrall!'
1820 'La Belle Dame Sans Merci', stanza 10.

20 She was a gordian shape of dazzling hue,
Vermilion-spotted, golden, green, and blue;
Striped like a zebra, freckled like a pard,
Eyed like a peacock, and all crimson barr'd.
1820 *Lamia, Isabella, The Eve of St. Agnes and Other Poems*,
'Lamia', pt.1, l.47–50.

21 Real are the dreams of Gods, and smoothly pass
Their pleasures in a long immortal dream.
1820 *Lamia, Isabella, The Eve of St. Agnes and Other Poems*,
'Lamia', pt.1, l.127–8.

22 Love in a hut, with water and a crust,
Is—Love, forgive us!—cinders, ashes, dust;
Love in a palace is perhaps at last
More grievous torment than a hermit's fast.
1820 *Lamia, Isabella, The Eve of St. Agnes and Other Poems*,
'Lamia', pt.2, l.1–4.

23 That purple-lined palace of sweet sin.
1820 *Lamia, Isabella, The Eve of St. Agnes and Other Poems*,
'Lamia', pt.2, l.31.

24 In pale contented sort of discontent.
1820 *Lamia, Isabella, The Eve of St. Agnes and Other Poems*,
'Lamia', pt.2, l.135.

25 Do not all charms fly
At the mere touch of cold philosophy?
There was an awful rainbow once in heaven:
We know her woof, her texture; she is given
In the dull catalogue of common things.
Philosophy will clip an Angel's wings.
1820 *Lamia, Isabella, The Eve of St. Agnes and Other Poems*,
'Lamia', pt.2, l.229–34.

26 Why were they proud? again we ask aloud,
Why in the name of Glory were they proud?
1820 *Lamia, Isabella, The Eve of St. Agnes and Other Poems*,
'Isabella; or, The Pot of Basil', stanza 16.

27 So the two brothers and their murdered man
Rode past fair Florence.
1820 *Lamia, Isabella, The Eve of St. Agnes and Other Poems*,
'Isabella; or, The Pot of Basil', stanza 27.

28 And she forgot the stars, the moon, and sun,
And she forgot the blue above the trees,
And she forgot the dells where waters run,
And she forgot the chilly autumn breeze;
She had no knowledge when the day was done,
And the new morn she saw not: but in peace
Hung over her sweet Basil evermore,
And moistened it with tears unto the core.
1820 *Lamia, Isabella, The Eve of St. Agnes and Other Poems*,
'Isabella; or, The Pot of Basil', stanza 53.

29 'To steal my Basil-pot away from me.'
1820 *Lamia, Isabella, The Eve of St. Agnes and Other Poems*,
'Isabella; or, The Pot of Basil', stanza 62.

30 St. Agnes' Eve—Ah, bitter chill it was!
The owl, for all his feathers, was a-cold;
The hare limped trembling through the frozen grass,
And silent was the flock in woolly fold.
1820 *Lamia, Isabella, The Eve of St. Agnes and Other Poems*, 'The
Eve of St. Agnes', stanza 1.

31 The silver, snarling trumpets 'gan to chide.
1820 *Lamia, Isabella, The Eve of St. Agnes and Other Poems*, 'The
Eve of St. Agnes', stanza 4.

32 And soft adorings from their loves receive
Upon the honeyed middle of the night.
1820 *Lamia, Isabella, The Eve of St. Agnes and Other Poems*, 'The
Eve of St. Agnes', stanza 6.

33 The music, yearning like a God in pain.
1820 *Lamia, Isabella, The Eve of St. Agnes and Other Poems*, 'The
Eve of St. Agnes', stanza 7.

34 Sudden a thought came like a full-blown rose,

Flushing his brow, and in his painted heart
Made purple riot.
1820 *Lamia, Isabella, The Eve of St. Agnes and Other Poems*, 'The Eve of St. Agnes', stanza 16.

35 A poor, weak, palsy-stricken, churchyard thing.
1820 *Lamia, Isabella, The Eve of St. Agnes and Other Poems*, 'The Eve of St. Agnes', stanza 18.

36 A casement high and triple-arched there was,
All garlanded with carven imag'ries
Of fruits, and flowers, and bunches of knot-grass,
And diamonded with panes of quaint device,
Innumerable of stains and splendid dyes,
As are the tiger-moth's deep-damasked wings.
1820 *Lamia, Isabella, The Eve of St. Agnes and Other Poems*, 'The Eve of St. Agnes', stanza 24.

37 Full on this casement shone the wintry moon,
And threw warm gules on Madeleine's fair breast,
As down she knelt for heaven's grace and boon;
Rose-bloom fell on her hands, together prest,
And on her silver cross soft amethyst,
And on her hair a glory like a saint:
She seemed a splendid angel, newly drest,
Save wings, for heaven.
1820 *Lamia, Isabella, The Eve of St. Agnes and Other Poems*, 'The Eve of St. Agnes', stanza 25.

38 By degrees
Her rich attire creeps rustling to her knees.
1820 *Lamia, Isabella, The Eve of St. Agnes and Other Poems*, 'The Eve of St. Agnes', stanza 26.

39 As though a rose should shut, and be a bud again.
1820 *Lamia, Isabella, The Eve of St. Agnes and Other Poems*, 'The Eve of St. Agnes', stanza 27.

40 And still she slept an azure-lidded sleep,
In blanched linen, smooth, and lavendered,
While he from forth the closet brought a heap
Of candied apple, quince, and plum, and gourd;
With jellies soother than the creamy curd,
And lucent syrops, tinct with cinnamon;
Manna and dates, in argosy transferred
From Fez; and spiced dainties, every one,
From silken Samarcand to cedared Lebanon.
1820 *Lamia, Isabella, The Eve of St. Agnes and Other Poems*, 'The Eve of St. Agnes', stanza 30.

41 He played an ancient ditty, long since mute,
In Provence called, 'La belle dame sans mercy'.
1820 *Lamia, Isabella, The Eve of St. Agnes and Other Poems*, 'The Eve of St. Agnes', stanza 33.

42 And the long carpets rose along the gusty floor.
1820 *Lamia, Isabella, The Eve of St. Agnes and Other Poems*, 'The Eve of St. Agnes', stanza 40.

43 And they are gone: aye, ages long ago
These lovers fled away into the storm.
1820 *Lamia, Isabella, The Eve of St. Agnes and Other Poems*, 'The Eve of St. Agnes', stanza 42.

44 Deep in the shady sadness of a vale
Far sunken from the healthy breath of morn,
Far from the fiery noon and eve's one star,
Sat gray-haired Saturn, quiet as a stone,
Still as the silence round about his lair.
1820 *Lamia, Isabella, The Eve of St. Agnes and Other Poems*, 'Hyperion', bk.1, l.1–5.

45 Where the dead leaf fell, there did it rest.

1820 *Lamia, Isabella, The Eve of St. Agnes and Other Poems*, 'Hyperion', bk.1, l.10.

46 But oh! How unlike marble was that face.
1820 *Lamia, Isabella, The Eve of St. Agnes and Other Poems*, 'Hyperion', bk.1, l.34.

47 That large utterance of the early Gods.
1820 *Lamia, Isabella, The Eve of St. Agnes and Other Poems*, 'Hyperion', bk.1, l.51.

48 Season of mists and mellow fruitfulness,
Close bosom-friend of the maturing sun;
Conspiring with him how to load and bless
With fruit the vines that round the thatch-eaves run.
1820 *Lamia, Isabella, The Eve of St. Agnes and Other Poems*, 'To Autumn', stanza 1.

49 Where are the songs of Spring? Ay, where are they?
Think not of them, thou hast thy music too.
1820 *Lamia, Isabella, The Eve of St. Agnes and Other Poems*, 'To Autumn', stanza 3.

50 Thou still unravished bride of quietness,
Thou foster-child of silence and slow time.
1820 *Lamia, Isabella, The Eve of St. Agnes and Other Poems*, 'Ode on a Grecian Urn', stanza 1.

51 What men or Gods are these? What maidens loth?
What mad pursuit? What struggle to escape?
What pipes and timbrels? What wild ecstasy?
1820 *Lamia, Isabella, The Eve of St. Agnes and Other Poems*, 'Ode on a Grecian Urn', stanza 1.

52 Heard melodies are sweet, but those unheard
Are sweeter; therefore, ye soft pipes, play on;
Not to the sensual ear, but, more endeared,
Pipe to the spirit ditties of no tone.
1820 *Lamia, Isabella, The Eve of St. Agnes and Other Poems*, 'Ode on a Grecian Urn', stanza 2.

53 She cannot fade, though thou hast not thy bliss,
For ever wilt thou love, and she be fair!
1820 *Lamia, Isabella, The Eve of St. Agnes and Other Poems*, 'Ode on a Grecian Urn', stanza 2.

54 O Attic shape! Fair attitude!
1820 *Lamia, Isabella, The Eve of St. Agnes and Other Poems*, 'Ode on a Grecian Urn', stanza 5.

55 Thou, silent form, dost tease us out of thought
As doth eternity: Cold Pastoral!
1820 *Lamia, Isabella, The Eve of St. Agnes and Other Poems*, 'Ode on a Grecian Urn', stanza 5.

56 'Beauty is truth, truth beauty,'—that is all
Ye know on earth, and all ye need to know.
1820 *Lamia, Isabella, The Eve of St. Agnes and Other Poems*, 'Ode on a Grecian Urn', stanza 5.

57 My heart aches, and a drowsy numbness pains
My sense, as though of hemlock I had drunk,
Or emptied some dull opiate to the drains
One minute past, and Lethe-wards had sunk:
'Tis not through envy of thy happy lot,
But being too happy in thine happiness
That thou, light-winged Dryad of the trees,
In some melodious plot
Of beechen green, and shadows numberless,
Singest of summer in full-throated ease.
1820 *Lamia, Isabella, The Eve of St. Agnes and Other Poems*, 'Ode to a Nightingale', stanza 1.

58 O, for a draught of vintage! that hath been
Cooled a long age in the deep-delved earth,

Tasting of Flora and the country green,
Dance, and Provençal song, and sunburnt mirth!
O for a beaker full of the warm South,
Full of the true, the blushful Hippocrene,
With beaded bubbles winking at the brim,
And purple-stained mouth;
That I might drink, and leave the world unseen,
And with thee fade away into the forest dim.
1820 *Lamia, Isabella, The Eve of St. Agnes and Other Poems*, 'Ode to a Nightingale', stanza 2.

59 Fade far away, dissolve, and quite forget
What thou among the leaves hast never known,
The weariness, the fever, and the fret
Here, where men sit and hear each other groan;
Where palsy shakes a few, sad, last grey hairs,
Where youth grows pale, and spectre-thin, and dies;
Where but to think is to be full of sorrow
And leaden-eyed despairs.
1820 *Lamia, Isabella, The Eve of St. Agnes and Other Poems*, 'Ode to a Nightingale', stanza 3.

60 Already with thee! tender is the night.
1820 *Lamia, Isabella, The Eve of St. Agnes and Other Poems*, 'Ode to a Nightingale', stanza 4.

61 Fast fading violets covered up in leaves;
And mid-May's eldest child,
The coming musk-rose, full of dewy wine,
The murmurous haunt of flies on summer eves.
1820 *Lamia, Isabella, The Eve of St. Agnes and Other Poems*, 'Ode to a Nightingale', stanza 5.

62 Darkling I listen; and, for many a time
I have been half in love with easeful Death,
Called him soft names in many a musèd rhyme,
To take into the air my quiet breath;
Now more than ever seems it rich to die,
To cease upon the midnight with no pain,
While thou art pouring forth thy soul abroad
In such an ecstasy!
1820 *Lamia, Isabella, The Eve of St. Agnes and Other Poems*, 'Ode to a Nightingale', stanza 6.

63 Thou wast not born for death, immortal Bird!
1820 *Lamia, Isabella, The Eve of St. Agnes and Other Poems*, 'Ode to a Nightingale', stanza 7.

64 Forlorn! the very word is like a bell
To toll me back from thee to my sole self!
Adieu! the fancy cannot cheat so well
As she is famed to do, deceiving elf.
1820 *Lamia, Isabella, The Eve of St. Agnes and Other Poems*, 'Ode to a Nightingale', stanza 8.

65 I know the colour of that blood; it is arterial blood;
I cannot be deceived in that colour; that drop of blood
is my death-warrant—I must die.
1821 On examining a drop of blood that fell from his mouth as he lay dying from tuberculosis. Quoted in John Sutherland *The Oxford Book of Literary Anecdotes* (1975).

66 Here lies one whose name was writ in water.
Epitaph for himself. Quoted in Richard Monckton Milnes *Life, Letters and Literary Remains of John Keats* (1848), vol.2.

Keble, John 1792–1866

English churchman, the father of the Tractarian movement. He was also influential in the Oxford Movement after J H Newman's secession to Rome.

67 New every morning is the love
Our wakening and uprising prove.
1827 *The Christian Year*, 'Morning'.

Keenan, Brian 1950–

Northern Irish teacher and writer. He was kidnapped on 11 April 1986 while working at the American University of Beirut by Iranian terrorists and held hostage for four years.

68 I'm going to visit every country in the world, eat all the food of the world, drink all the drink of the world—and, I hope, make love to every woman in the world. Then I might get a good night's sleep.
1990 Said on his release, BBC TV, 25 Aug.

Keillor, (Gary Edward) Garrison 1942–

US humorous writer and broadcaster. In 1974 he began his live radio show, *A Prairie Home Companion*, telling tales of small-town Minnesota set in fictional Lake Wobegon. His works include *Lake Wobegon Days* (1985) and *Love Me* (2004).

69 Where all the women are strong, all the men are good-looking, and all the children are above average.
from 1974 His description of the fictional mid-Western town Lake Wobegon, used regularly in *A Prairie Home Companion*.

70 Peanut butter has survived everything that has been done to improve it.
1990 In NPR broadcast, 29 Dec.

71 Public radio is a ghetto of good taste.
1991 In National Public Radio broadcast, 9 Feb.

72 March is the month that God designed to show those who don't drink what a hangover is like.
1991 In NPR broadcast, 1 Dec.

73 It's a play that after you've been there for a short while, you wonder how long this is going to take.
1995 Of Edward Albee's *Three Tall Women*. In *New York*, 2 Jan.

74 I look like a tree toad who was changed into a boy but not completely.
2001 *Lake Wobegon Summer 1956*.

Keller, Helen Adams 1880–1968

US writer. She became deaf and blind at 19 months, but educated by Anne Sullivan she learned to speak, graduated in 1904 and became a distinguished lecturer and writer.

75 Everything has its wonders, even darkness and silence, and I learn, whatever state I may be in, therein to be content.
1902 *The Story of My Life*.

76 As the eagle was killed by the arrow winged with its own feather, so the hand of the world is wounded by its own skill.
1912 In the *American Magazine*, Dec.

Kelman, James 1946–

Scottish novelist, whose novels and short stories set in working-class Glasgow are characterized by an uncompromising vernacular style and vocabulary. In 1994 his novel *How late it was, how late* won the Booker Prize.

77 Theoretical webs, dirty webs, fusty webs, old and shrivelling away into nothingness, a fine dust. Who needs that kind of stuff. Far far better getting out into the open air and doing it, actually doing it, something solid

and concrete and unconceptualisable.
1989 *A Disaffection.*

78 Yes, they say, go and write whatever story you want, but
don't use whatever language is necessary… By
implication those in authority ask the writer to censor
and suppress her or his own work. They demand it. If you
don't comply then your work isn't produced.
1992 *Some Recent Attacks*, 'The Importance of Glasgow in My
Work'.

79 My culture and my language have the right to exist, and
no one has the authority to dismiss that.
1994 Speech at the Booker Prize award ceremony, 11 Oct.

80 Ye wake in a corner and stay there hoping yer body will
disappear, the thoughts smothering ye; these thoughts;
but ye want to remember and face up to things, just
something keeps ye from doing it, why can ye no do it;
the words filling yer head: then the other words; there's
something far far wrong; ye're no a good man, ye're just
no a good man.
1994 *How late it was, how late*, opening words.

Kelvin, William Thomson, 1st Baron   1824–1907

Irish-born Scottish physician and mathematician, who
developed the temperature scale named after him.

81 At what time does the dissipation of energy begin?
When his wife proposed an afternoon walk. Quoted in A
Fleming *Memories of a Scientific Life* (1934).

Kemble, Charles   1775–1854

English actor-manager. A celebrated comic actor, he became
manager of Covent Garden in 1822 but subsequently ran into
financial difficulties, mitigated in the early 1830s when he
presented his daughter Fanny Kemble's stage debut.

82 Sir, I now pay you this exorbitant charge, but I must ask
you to explain to Her Majesty that she must not in future
look upon me as a source of income.
When reluctantly obliged to pay overdue income tax.
Attributed.

Kemble, John Philip   1757–1823

English actor-manager, brother of Sarah Siddons and Charles
Kemble. A successful tragic actor, he was manager of the
Theatre Royal, Drury Lane and subsequently of Covent
Garden, where riots greeted his decision to raise ticket prices.

83 Ladies and gentlemen, unless the play is stopped, the
child cannot possibly go on.
Addressing the audience during a performance that was being
much disrupted by a child crying. Attributed.

Kempis, St Thomas à   c.1380–1471

German monk and author. In 1400 he entered the Augustinian
convent of Agnetenberg, near Zwolle, where he was Sub-Prior
at the time of his death.

84 *Vere magnus est, qui magnam habet caritatem.*
He is truly great who has great charity.
c.1413 *De Imitatione Christi*, bk.1, ch.4, section 6.

85 *Quam cito transit gloria mundi.*
How quickly the glory of the world passes.
c.1413 *De Imitatione Christi*, bk.1, ch.4, section 6.

86 *Homo proponit, sed Deus disponit.*
Man proposes, but God disposes.

87 *Nemo secure præcipit, nisi qui bene obedire didicit.*
Nobody rules safely, but he who has learned well how to
obey.
c.1413 *De Imitatione Christi*, bk.1, ch.20, section 2.

88 *Transeunt omnia, et tu cum eis pariter.*
All things perish, and you along with them.
c.1413 *De Imitatione Christi*, bk.2, ch.1, section 4.

89 *Gloria boni hominis, testimonium bonæ conscientiæ.*
The testimony of a good conscience is the good man's
glory.
c.1413 *De Imitatione Christi*, bk.2, ch.6, section 1.

90 *In cruce salus, in cruce vita.*
In the cross is salvation, in the cross is life.
c.1413 *De Imitatione Christi*, bk.2, ch.12, section 2.

91 *Si libenter crucem portas, portabit te.*
If you bear your cross willingly, it will bear you.
c.1413 *De Imitatione Christi*, bk.2, ch.12, section 5.

92 *De duobus malis minus est semper eligendum.*
Of two evils the lesser should always be chosen.
c.1413 *De Imitatione Christi*, bk.3, ch.12, section 2.

Ken, Thomas   1637–1711

English churchman and royal chaplain. He became Bishop of
Bath and Wells (1685), and was deposed in 1691 when he
refused to take the oath of allegiance to William III.

93 Awake my soul, and with the sun
Thy daily stage of duty run.
1709 *Manual of Prayers for the use of the Scholars of Winchester
College.*

94 Praise God, from whom all blessings flow,
Praise Him, all creatures here below,
Praise Him above, ye heavenly host,
Praise Father, Son, and Holy Ghost.
1709 *Manual of Prayers for the use of the Scholars of Winchester
College.*

Kendall, Henry Clarence   1839–82

Australian poet who worked variously as a civil servant,
freelance writer, timber merchant and inspector of forests. His
great love of the Australian countryside is evident in his
collections *Poems and Songs* (1862), *Leaves from Australian
Forests* (1869), and *Songs from the Mountains* (1880).

95 Through breaks of the cedar and sycamore bowers
Struggles the light that is love to the flowers;
And, softer than slumber and sweeter than singing,
The notes of the bell-birds are running and ringing.
The silver-voiced bell-birds, the darlings of daytime!
They sing in September their songs of the May-time.
1869 *Leaves from Australian Forests*, 'Bell-Birds'.

Kennan, George Frost   1904–

US diplomat and historian, adviser to Secretary of State Dean
Acheson (1949–52) and US Ambassador in Moscow (1952–53)
and Yugoslavia (1961–63). Initially in favour of 'containment' of
the USSR, he later called for US disengagement from Europe.

96 The best that an American can look forward to is the
lonely pleasure of one who stands at long last on a chilly
and inhospitable mountain top where few have been,
where few can follow, and where few will consent to
believe that he has been.

On negotiating with the Soviets. Quoted in Walter Isaacson and Evan Thomas *The Wise Men* (1986).

97 A guest of one's time and not a member of the household.
Of the feeling of being viewed as a pragmatist. Quoted in Walter Isaacson and Evan Thomas *The Wise Men* (1986).

98 Fig leaves of democratic procedure to hide the nakedness of Stalinist dictatorship.
Of postwar agreements to govern Eastern Europe. Quoted in Walter Isaacson and Evan Thomas *The Wise Men* (1986).

Kennedy, A(lison) L(ouise)   1965–

Scottish novelist. Her short stories and novels have established her as a leading writer of her generation.

99 Night Geometry and the Garscadden Trains.
1990 Title of short story collection.

1 Words just say what you want them to; they don't know any better.
1990 'The Role of Notable Silences in Scottish History'.

2 4. The chosen and male shall go forth unto professions while the chosen and female shall be homely, fecund, docile and slightly artistic.
1993 *Looking for the Possible Dance*, 'The Scottish Method for the Perfection of Children'.

3 7. Joy is fleeting, sinful and the forerunner of despair.
1993 *Looking for the Possible Dance*, 'The Scottish Method for the Perfection of Children'.

4 We all have it in us to be an opium for every conceivable mass.
1995 *So I Am Glad*, ch.1.

5 I am not calm, I am unspontaneous. When something happens to me, I don't know how to feel.
1995 *So I Am Glad*, ch.1.

Kennedy, Edward M(oore)   1932–

US Democratic politician, son of Joseph and brother of John and Robert. His political career was dogged by his involvement in a car accident at Chappaquiddick in 1969, in which a female companion was drowned, and he withdrew as presidential candidate in 1980.

6 I don't mind not being President. I just mind that someone else is.
1986 Speech, Washington, 22 Mar.

7 Sunlight is the best disinfectant.
1990 On sponsoring legislation for the disclosure of graduation rates and crime figures on campuses. In the *New York Times*, 8 Oct.

8 We are the most hated nation in the world as a result of this disastrous policy in the prisons.
2004 Following news coverage of the abuse of Iraqi prisoners by US soldiers, 13 May.

Kennedy, John F(itzgerald)   1917–63

US Democratic politician, 35th President. His *Profiles in Courage* (1956) won the Pulitzer Prize. The first Catholic, and the youngest person, to be elected President (1961–3), he initiated education and civil rights reform and induced the USSR to withdraw its missiles from Cuba (1962). He was assassinated, allegedly by Lee Harvey Oswald, while being driven in an open car through Dallas, Texas.

9 We stand today on the edge of a new frontier. But the new frontier of which I speak is not a set of promises. It is a set of challenges. It sums up not what I intend to offer the American people, but what I intend to ask of them. It appeals to their pride, not their pocketbook—it holds out the promise of more sacrifice instead of more security.
1960 On accepting the Democratic Convention's presidential nomination, 15 Jul.

10 Let us never negotiate out of fear, but let us never fear to negotiate. Together let us explore the stars.
1961 Inaugural address, Washington, 20 Jan.

11 All this will not be finished in the first 100 days, nor will it be finished in the first 1,000 days, nor in the life of this Administration—nor even, perhaps, in our lifetime on this planet. But let us begin.
1961 Inaugural address, Washington, 20 Jan.

12 Let the word go forth from this time and place, to friend and foe alike, that the torch has been passed to a new generation of Americans, born in this century, tempered by war, disciplined by a hard and bitter peace, proud of our ancient heritage, and unwilling to witness or permit the slow undoing of those human rights to which this nation has always been committed, and to which we are committed today at home and around the world. Let every nation know, whether it wishes us well or ill, that we shall pay any price, bear any burden, meet any hardship, support any friend, oppose any foe, to assure the survival and success of liberty.
1961 Inaugural address, Washington, 20 Jan.

13 And so, my fellow Americans, ask not what your country can do for you. Ask what you can do for your country.
1961 Inaugural address, Washington, 20 Jan.

14 I believe that this nation should commit itself to achieving the goal, before this decade is out, of landing a man on the moon and returning him safely to earth.
1961 State of the Union message to Congress, May.

15 Now we have a problem in making our power credible, and Vietnam is the place.
1961 Attributed remark to journalist James Reston, following Kennedy's meeting with Khrushchev, Jun.

16 A form of atomic blackmail.
1961 On the Soviet decision to resume nuclear testing, 31 Aug.

17 The cold reaches of the universe must not become the new area of an even colder war.
1961 Address to the United Nations, 25 Sep.

18 Mankind must put an end to war or war will put an end to mankind.
1961 Address to the United Nations, 25 Sep.

19 Those who make peaceful revolution impossible will make violent revolution inevitable.
1962 Speech to Latin American diplomats, 12 Mar.

20 This is the most extraordinary collection of talent, of human knowledge, that has ever been gathered in the White House—with the possible exception of when Thomas Jefferson dined alone.
1962 Address at a dinner for 49 Nobel laureates, 29 Apr.

21 The cost of freedom is always high, but Americans have always paid it. And one path we shall never choose, and that is the path of surrender, or submission.
1962 Address to the nation, 22 Oct.

22 If you take the wrong course...the President bears the burden of the responsibility quite rightly. The advisers may move on—to new advice.

1962 Comment to White House Special Counsel Theodore C Sorensen, Dec, after the ill-fated Bay of Pigs invasion of Cuba.

23 His stately ship of life, having weathered the severest storms of a troubled century, is anchored in tranquil waters, proof that courage and faith and zest for freedom are truly indestructible. The record of his triumphant passage will inspire free hearts all over the globe.

1963 On conferring honorary US citizenship on Winston Churchill, 9 Apr.

24 [Winston Churchill] mobilized the English language and sent it into battle.

1963 On conferring honorary US citizenship on Winston Churchill, 9 Apr.

25 Equality of opportunity does not mean equality of responsibility.

1963 Address at Vanderbilt University, 19 May.

26 Man is still the most extraordinary computer of all.

1963 Speech, 21 May.

27 History teaches us that enmities between nations…do not last forever. We must conduct our affairs in such a way that it becomes in the communists' interests to agree on a genuine peace…to let each nation choose its own future, so long as that choice does not interfere with the choices of others. If we cannot now end our differences, at least we can help make the world safe for diversity.

1963 Speech, American University, Washington DC, 10 Jun.

28 The rights of every man are diminished when the rights of one man are threatened.

1963 On sending national guardsmen to ensure peaceful integration at the University of Alabama. Address to the nation, 11 Jun.

29 He [John Hoban] believed by incorporating several features of the Dublin style he would make it more home-like for any President of Irish descent. It was a long wait, but I appreciate his efforts.

1963 On the Irish-American architect's design of the White House. Speech to the Irish Parliament reported in the *New York Times*, 19 Jun.

30 Let it not be said of this Atlantic generation that we left ideals and visions to the past, nor purpose and determination to our adversaries. We have come too far, we have sacrificed too much to disdain the future now.

1963 Speech to the West German Parliament, Frankfurt, 25 Jun.

31 There are many people in the world who really don't understand, or say they don't, what is the great issue between the free world and the Communist world. Let them come to Berlin!

1963 Address in Berlin's Rudolf Wilde Platz, 26 Jun, 22 months after the erection of the wall dividing the city.

32 We have never had to put a wall up to keep our people in, to prevent them from leaving us.

1963 Address in Berlin's Rudolf Wilde Platz, 26 Jun, 22 months after the erection of the wall dividing the city.

33 All free men, wherever they may live, are citizens of Berlin, and therefore, as a free man, I take pride in the words, 'Ich bin ein Berliner.' I am a Berliner!

1963 Speech at West Berlin City Hall, Rudolf Wilde Platz, 26 Jun. Unfortunately for Kennedy, his phrase translated into colloquial German as 'I am a doughnut.'

34 For the first time, we have been able to reach an agreement which can limit the dangers of this age.

1963 On the ratification of a treaty to limit nuclear testing, 7 Oct.

35 The highest duty of the writer, the composer, the artist is to remain true to himself… In serving his vision of the truth, the artist best serves his nation.

1963 At the dedication of Amherst College Robert Frost Library, 25 Oct.

36 When power leads man towards arrogance, poetry reminds him of his limitations. When power narrows the area of man's concern, poetry reminds him of the richness and diversity of existence. When power corrupts, poetry cleanses.

1963 At the dedication of Amherst College Robert Frost Library, 25 Oct.

37 I look forward to…a future in which our country will match its military strength with our moral restraint; its wealth with our wisdom; its power with our purpose.

1963 Last major public speech, Amherst College, 26 Oct.

38 The definition of happiness of the Greeks…is full use of your powers along lines of excellence. I find, therefore, the Presidency provides some happiness.

1963 News conference, 31 Oct.

39 We're heading into nut country today.

1963 Spoken to his wife in Fort Worth a few hours before the assassination in Dallas. Quoted in William Manchester *The Death of a President* (1967).

40 We in this country, in this generation, are—by destiny, rather than choice—the watchmen on the walls of the world.

1963 Address prepared for Dallas luncheon on the day he was assassinated, 22 Nov.

41 What your government believes is its own business; what it does in the world is the world's business.

Letter to Nikita Khrushchev. Quoted in Theodore C Sorensen *Kennedy* (1965).

42 The three most overrated things in the world are the state of Texas, the FBI, and hunting trophies.

Quoted in William Manchester *The Death of a President* (1967).

43 You don't fire God.

Expressing reluctance to replace FBI Director J Edgar Hoover. Reported after Kennedy's death in Senate committee findings on US intelligence activities, 1976.

44 You never know what's hit you. A gunshot is the perfect way.

Comment on methods of assassination. Quoted in Peter Collier and David Horowitz *The Kennedys* (1984).

Kennedy, Joseph Patrick 1888–1969

US businessman and diplomat, a supporter of Roosevelt and the 'New Deal'. The grandson of an Irish immigrant, he placed his fortune at the political disposal of his nine children, all of whom except the eldest son, killed in a flying accident, achieved international fame.

45 With the money I spent I could have elected my chauffeur.

Of his contributions to John F Kennedy's presidential campaign. Quoted in Nigel Hamilton *JFK: Reckless Youth* (1992).

46 Don't get mad, get even.

Attributed.

Kennedy, Joseph P(atrick) II 1952–

Former US Democratic congressman (1987–99) and founder of

the Citizens Energy Corporation. He is the son of Joseph Patrick Kennedy.

47 I've had a tough time learning how to act like a Congressman. Today I accidentally spent some of my own money.
1987 In *Newsweek*, 9 Feb.

Kennedy, Nigel 1956–

English violinist.

48 I'd never accept a knighthood because the Queen knows nothing about music, man. How can she say I'm good or bad?
2004 In *The Independent*, 17 Jun.

Kennedy, Robert F(rancis) 1925–68

US politician, son of Joseph. Manager of his brother John's presidential campaign, he became Attorney-General (1961–4) and Senator for New York from 1965. In 1968 he was assassinated after winning the California primary election.

49 Courage is the most important attribute of a lawyer.
1962 Speech at the University of San Francisco Law School, 29 Sep.

50 One fifth of the people are against everything all the time.
1964 In the *Observer*, May.

51 My thanks to you all—and now it's on to Chicago, and let's win there.
1968 Last public remark after winning the Californian primary for the Democratic presidential nomination in Los Angeles, before being assassinated as he left the rally, 4 Jun.

52 It isn't the first step that concerns me, but both sides escalating to the fourth or fifth step—and we don't go to the sixth because there is no one around to do so.
On the possibility of initiating nuclear warfare. *Thirteen Days* (published 1969).

53 Many times…I had heard the military take positions which, if wrong, had the advantage that no one would be around at the end to know.
Recalling discussions on Soviet placement of nuclear missiles in Cuba. *Thirteen Days* (published 1969).

54 Well, we Kennedys, we eat Rockefellers for breakfast.
Quoted in Peter Collier and David Horowitz *The Rockefellers* (1976).

Kennedy, Roger George 1926–

Former director, US National Park Service (1993–97). He has also been a correspondent for NBC and Director, National Museum of American History, Smithsonian Institution. He has written books on architecture, houses and historic America.

55 How do you put a price on the Washington Monument?
1995 On presenting his annual budget to Congress and being asked to produce a price list setting a market value on each of the nation's 368 park units. Reported in the *US News and World Report*, 3 Apr.

Kennedy, William (Joseph) 1928–

US novelist and screenwriter. He won a Pulitzer Prize for *Ironweed* (1983).

56 I don't hold no grudges more'n five years.
1983 Francis Phelan. *Ironweed*.

57 That year an ill wind blew over the city and threatened to destroy flowerpots, family fortunes, reputations, true love, and several types of virtue.
2002 *Roscoe*, opening lines.

Kent, Bruce 1929–

British peace campaigner and former cleric, Chairman (1987–90) and Vice-President (1990–) of the Campaign for Nuclear Disarmament.

58 Preparing for suicide is not a very intelligent means of defence.
1989 Speech.

Kent, Corita *known as* '*Sister Corita*' 1918–86

US artist, best remembered for her prints and her 'Love' postage stamp (1985).

59 Women's liberation is the liberation of the feminine in the man and the masculine in the woman.
1974 In the *Los Angeles Times*, 11 Jul.

Kent, Rockwell 1882–1971

US artist and writer, best known for his stark woodcuts, often accompanying his travel writing. His major works include the paintings *Toilers of the Sea* and *Winter* and writings such as *Wilderness* (1921).

60 Sledgehammer sentimentality.
Of his wholesome depiction of contemporary America. Quoted in the *Washington Post*, 6 Jun 1993

Kerouac, Jack (John) 1922–69

US novelist. His fast-moving, stream of consciousness novel *On The Road* (1957) became the quintessential text of the Beat Generation.

61 All of life is a foreign country.
1949 Letter, 24 Jun.

62 But then they danced down the street like dingle-dodies, and I shambled after as I've been doing all my life after people who interest me, because the only people for me are the mad ones, the ones who are mad to live, mad to talk, mad to be saved, desirous of everything at the same time, the ones who never yawn or say a commonplace thing, but burn, burn, burn, like fabulous yellow roman candles exploding like spiders across the stars and in the middle you see the blue centerlight pop and everybody goes 'Awww!'
1957 *On The Road*, pt.1, ch.1.

63 I have nothing to offer anybody except my own confusion.
1957 *On The Road*, pt.2, ch.3.

64 The road is life.
1957 *On The Road*, pt.3, ch.5.

65 John Clellon Holmes…and I were sitting around trying to think up the meaning of the Lost Generation and the subsequent Existentialism and I said, 'You know, this is really a beat generation' and he leapt up and said, 'That's it, that's right!'
1959 Interview in *Playboy*, Jun.

66 Desolation Angels.
1965 Title of novel.

Kerr, Jean *née Collins* 1923–2003

US playwright. Her works include successful Broadway plays and humorous autobiographies. She collaborated with her husband Walter Kerr on several projects, including an adaptation of Werfel's *Song of Bernadette* (1946).

67 Even though a number of people have tried, no one has yet found a way to drink for a living.
    1964 *Poor Richard*, act 1.

Kerry, John F 1943–

US politician. Senator for Massachusetts, he ran against President George W Bush in the 2004 presidential election.

68 No young American in uniform should ever be held hostage to America's dependence on oil from the Middle East.
    2004 Speech in New Hampshire, 27 Jan.

69 Like father, like son, one term and you're done.
    2004 Referring to his contender's chances in the presidential election.

Kesey, Ken Elton 1935–2001

US novelist. He achieved a major success with his novel *One Flew Over the Cuckoo's Nest* (1962), set in a mental hospital, and became a hero of the US counter-culture in the 1960s.

70 One Flew Over the Cuckoo's Nest.
    1962 Title of novel, derived from a traditional rhyme.

71 But it's the truth even if it didn't happen.
    1962 *One Flew Over The Cuckoo's Nest*, pt.1.

72 I'd rather be a lightning rod than a seismograph.
    Quoted in Tom Wolfe *The Electric Kool-Aid Acid Test* (1968), ch.1.

73 We are always acting on what just finished happening. It happened at least 1/30th of a second ago. We think we're in the present, but we aren't. The present we know is only a movie of the past.
    Quoted in Tom Wolfe *The Electric Kool-Aid Acid Test* (1968), ch.11.

74 You don't lead by pointing and telling people some place to go. You lead by going to that place and making a case.
    1970 Interview in *Esquire*, Jun.

Kethe, William d. c.1608

English divine, army chaplain and hymnwriter. His hymns are characteristically written in metre, like psalms.

75 All people that on earth do dwell,
    Sing to the Lord with cheerful voice;
    Him serve with fear, His praise forth tell,
    Come ye before Him, and rejoice.
    1560 *Daye's Psalter*, 'All People That on Earth Do Dwell'.

Key, Francis Scott 1779–1843

US lawyer and poet, best known for his devotional verse and prose. His poem 'The Star-Spangled Banner' was officially adopted as the national anthem of the US in 1931.

76 O say, can you see, by the dawn's early light,
    What so proudly we hailed at the twilight's last gleaming—
    Whose broad stripes and bright stars, through the clouds of the fight,
    O'er the ramparts we watched were so gallantly streaming!

And the rocket's red glare, the bombs bursting in air,
Gave proof through the night that our flag was still there;
O! say, does that star-spangled banner yet wave
O'er the land of the free, and the home of the brave?
    1814 'The Star-Spangled Banner', originally published as 'The Defence of Fort M'Henry' in the *Baltimore Patriot*, 20 Sep; it commemorates the bombardment of Fort McHenry, Baltimore, by the British, 13–14 Sep.

Keynes (of Tilton), John Maynard, 1st Baron 1883–1946

English economist. His major works, *A Treatise on Money* (1930) and the revolutionary *General Theory of Employment, Interest and Money* (1936), were inspired by the unemployment crisis. His views influenced Roosevelt's 'New Deal' administration and underpin modern macroeconomics.

77 I work for a government I despise for ends I think criminal.
    1917 Letter to Duncan Grant, 15 Dec.

78 Like Odysseus, the President looked wiser when he was seated.
    1919 Of Woodrow Wilson. *The Economic Consequences of the Peace*.

79 Lenin was right. There is no subtler, no surer means of overturning the existing basis of society than to debauch the currency. The process engages all the hidden forces of economic law on the side of destruction, and does it in a manner which not one man in a million is able to diagnose.
    1919 *The Economic Consequences of the Peace*.

80 England still stands outside Europe. Europe's voiceless tremors do not reach her. Europe is apart, and England is not of her flesh and body.
    1919 *The Economic Consequences of the Peace*.

81 The *long run* is a misleading guide to current affairs. *In the long run*, we are all dead. Economists set themselves too easy, too useless a task if in tempestuous seasons they can only tell us that when the storm is long past the ocean is flat again.
    1923 *A Tract on Monetary Reform*.

82 If Enterprise is afoot, Wealth accumulates whatever may be happening to Thrift; and if Enterprise is asleep, Wealth decays, whatever Thrift may be doing.
    1930 *A Treatise on Money*.

83 A 'sound' banker, alas! is not one who foresees danger and avoids it, but one who, when he is ruined, is ruined in a conventional and orthodox way along with his fellows, so that no one can really blame him.
    1931 *Essays in Persuasion*.

84 It is *not* a correct deduction from the Principles of Economics that enlightened self-interest always operates in the public interest… Experience does *not* show that individuals when they make up a social unit are always less clear-sighted than when they act separately.
    1931 *Essays in Persuasion*.

85 I agree that our methods of control are unlikely to be sufficiently delicate or sufficiently powerful to maintain continuous full employment. I should be quite content with a reasonable approximation to it, and in practice I should probably relax my expansionist measures a little

before technical full employment had actually been reached.
1936 Letter to E F M Durbin, 30 Apr.

86 It might have been supposed that competition between expert professionals, possessing judgement and knowledge beyond that of the average private investor, would correct the vagaries of the ignorant individual left to himself. It happens, however, that the energies and skills of the professional investor and speculator are mainly occupied elsewhere. For most of these persons are, in fact, largely concerned, not with making superior long-term forecasts of the probable yield on an investment over its whole life, but with foreseeing changes in the conventional basis of valuation a short time ahead of the general public… This battle of wits to anticipate the basis of conventional valuation a few months hence, rather than the prospective yield of an investment over a long term of years, does not even require gulls amongst the public to feed the maws of the professional; it can be played by professionals amongst themselves.
1936 *The General Theory of Employment, Interest, and Money.*

87 Speculators may do no harm as bubbles on a steady stream of enterprise. But the position is serious when enterprise becomes the bubble on a whirlpool of speculation. When the capital development of a country becomes a by-product of the activities of a casino, the job is likely to be ill-done.
1936 *The General Theory of Employment, Interest, and Money.*

88 If the Treasury were to fill old bottles with banknotes, bury them at suitable depths in disused coalmines which are then filled up to the surface with town rubbish, and leave it to private enterprise on well-tried principles of *laissez-faire* to dig the notes up again…there need be no more unemployment and, with the help of the repercussions, the real income of the community, and its capital wealth also, would probably become a good deal greater than it actually is. It would, indeed, be more sensible to build houses and the like; but as there are political and practical difficulties in the way of this, the above would be better than nothing.
1936 *The General Theory of Employment, Interest and Money.*

89 The ideas of economists and political philosophers, both when they are right and when they are wrong, are more powerful than is commonly understood. Indeed the world is ruled by little else. Practical men, who believe themselves to be quite exempt from any intellectual influences, are usually the slaves of some defunct economist. Madmen in authority, who hear voices in the air, are distilling their frenzy from some academic scribbler of a few years back. I am sure the power of vested interests is vastly exaggerated compared with the gradual encroachment of ideas.
1936 *The General Theory of Employment, Interest and Money.*

90 The outstanding faults of the economic society in which we live are its failure to provide for full employment and its arbitrary and inequitable distribution of wealth and incomes.
1936 *The General Theory of Employment, Interest and Money.*

91 We take it as a fundamental psychological rule of any modern community that, when its real income is increased, it will not increase its consumption by an

equal absolute amount.
1936 *The General Theory of Employment, Interest, and Money.*

92 Worldly wisdom teaches us that it is better for the reputation to fail conventionally than to succeed unconventionally.
1936 *The General Theory of Employment, Interest and Money.*

93 I believe that there is social and psychological justification for significant inequalities of incomes and wealth, but not for such large disparities as exist today.
1936 *The General Theory of Employment, Interest and Money.*

Khayyám, Omar c.1050– c.1123

Persian poet and scholar. Born in Nishapur, he was summoned to Merv by the sultan, where he reformed the Muslim calendar. A renowned astronomer, he also composed mathematical treatises, and is best remembered for his *Rubáiyát* (c.1100).

94 Know yourself as a snowdrift on the sand
Heaped for two days, or three, then thawed and gone.
c.1100 *Rubáiyát*, stanza 16 (translated by Robert Graves and Omar Ali-Shah, 1972).

95 Never anticipate tomorrow's sorrow;
Live always in this paradisal now.
c.1100 *Rubáiyát*, stanza 21 (translated by Robert Graves and Omar Ali-Shah, 1972).

96 The cheerful bird of youth flutters away—
I hardly noticed how it came or went.
c.1100 *Rubáiyát*, stanza 103 (translated by Robert Graves and Omar Ali-Shah, 1972).

Khomeini, Ayatollah Ruhollah 1900–89

Iranian religious and political leader. Exiled in 1964, he returned to Iran in 1979 after the collapse of the Shah's government and became virtual head of state. He instigated a fundamentalist 'Islamic Revolution'.

97 Music is no different from opium. Music affects the human mind in a way that makes people think of nothing but music and sensual matters… Music is a treason to the country, a treason to our youth, and we should cut out all this music and replace it with something instructive.
1979 Ramadan speech, 23 Jul. Quoted in Lebrecht *Discord* (1982).

Khrushchev, Nikita Sergeyevich 1894–1971

Soviet politician. On the death of Stalin he became First Secretary of the Communist Party (1953–64), and subsequently denounced Stalinism. His period of office was marked by the 1956 Poznan riots, the Hungarian uprising, and the Cuban missile crisis (1962).

98 Those who wait for the USSR to reject Communism must wait until a shrimp learns to whistle.
1955 Speech in Moscow, 17 Sep.

99 Whether you like it or not, history is on our side. We will bury you.
1956 Remark to Western diplomats at the Kremlin, 18 Nov. Khrushchev later claimed that he had meant 'We will overtake you [economically]', rather than this more sinister version.

1 Politicians are the same all over. They promise to build a bridge even where there is no river.
1960 Press conference, New York, Oct.

2 When you are skinning your customers, you should leave some skin on to grow so that you can skin them again.
1961 Speech to British industrialists, May.

3 They talk about who won and who lost. Human reason won. Mankind won.
1962 Of the ending of the Cuban missile crisis. In the *Observer*, 11 Nov.

4 We had no use for the teachings of the Gospels: if someone slaps you, just turn the other cheek. We had shown that anyone who slapped us on our cheek would get his head kicked off.
1970 *Khrushchev Remembers*. This biography, published in the West, is of dubious authenticity.

5 What the scientists have in their briefcases is terrifying.
Attributed.

Kidder, Tracy 1945–

US author. He won a Pulitzer Prize for *The Soul of a New Machine* (1981), which was also awarded a National Book Award.

6 The Soul of A New Machine
1981 Book title.

Kierkegaard, Sören Aabye 1813–55

Danish philosopher and religious thinker, who attacked dogmatism and the established Lutheran church and foreshadowed Existentialism.

7 The thing is to find a truth *for me*, to find *the idea for which I can live and die*.
1835 Journal entry (translated by Alexander Dru, 1938).

8 There are many people who reach their conclusions about life like schoolboys; they cheat their master by copying the answer out of a book without having worked out the sum for themselves.
1837 Journal entry (translated by Alexander Dru, 1938).

9 Without risk there is no faith.
1846 *Concluding Unscientific Postscript*, bk.2, pt.2, ch.2 (translated by Swenson and Lowrie).

10 The ethical reality of the individual is the only reality.
1846 *Concluding Unscientific Postscript*, bk.2, pt.2, ch.3 (translated by Swenson and Lowrie).

11 If a man in truth *will* the Good then he must be willing to suffer *for* the Good.
1846 *Purity Of Heart Is To Will One Thing* (translated by D Steere, 1938).

12 It is perfectly true, as philosophers say, that life must be understood backwards. But they forget the other proposition, that it must be lived forwards. And if one thinks over that proposition it becomes more and more evident that life can never really be understood in time simply because at no particular moment can I find the necessary resting-place from which to understand it—backwards.
Journal entry (translated by Alexander Dru, 1938).

13 Father in Heaven, when the thought of Thee wakes in our hearts, let it not awaken like a frightened bird that flies about in dismay, but like a child waking from its sleep with a heavenly smile.
Journal entry (translated by Alexander Dru, 1938).

14 Most people really believe that the Christian commandments (e.g. to love one's neighbour as oneself) are intentionally a little too severe—like putting

the clock on half an hour to make sure of not being late in the morning.
Journal entry (translated by Alexander Dru, 1938).

15 The bird on the branch, the lily in the meadow, the stag in the forest, the fish in the sea, the countless joyful creatures sing, God is Love. But beneath all these sopranos, as it were a sustained bass part, is the *De profundis* of the Sacrificed, God is Love.
Journal entry (translated by Alexander Dru, 1938).

Killy, Jean-Claude 1943–

French ski racer. He won the downhill and combined gold medals at the World Championship in Chile in 1966 and a further three gold medals at the Winter Olympics in 1968, after which he turned professional.

16 Skiing is a battle against yourself, always to the frontiers of the impossible. But most of all, it must give you pleasure. It is not an obligation but a joy.
1968 In *Sports Illustrated*, 18 Nov.

Kilmer, Joyce 1886–1918

US poet.

17 I think that I shall never see
A poem lovely as a tree.
1914 'Trees'.

Kilmer, Val 1959–

US actor.

18 On set, you've got 50 people asking if you want a cup of coffee. You throw your shoes in a corner, someone puts them neatly together. It's corrupting.
2004 In the *Observer*, 9 May.

Kilpatrick, James J 1920–

US writer and broadcaster.

19 A whore may be *naked*, but a mistress is *nude*. We are talking class.
1993 *Fine Print: Reflections on the Writing Art*.

Kim Il Sung 1912–94

North Korean soldier and political leader. After proclaiming his country a Republic in 1948 he remained in political control until his death. Within his country he was regarded with awe by the majority of citizens.

20 Everything is decided by a person's thoughts and if he is ideologically motivated, there is nothing he cannot do.
1969 Speech, 20 Apr. Collected in *Selected Works* (1992), vol.1, 'Work with Artists Should be Carried Out in Line with Political Principles'.

Kimball, Donald M

US business executive.

21 There's no place where success comes before work, except in the dictionary.
1986 In *USA Today*, 21 Apr.

Kincaid, Jamaica *originally* Elaine Potter Richardson 1949–

Antiguan writer; living in the US. Her works include *At the Bottom of the River* (1983), *Annie John* (1985), *Mr Potter* (2002) and a critique of colonialism and tourism, *A Small Place* (1988).

22 There was nothing noble-minded men could not do when they discovered they could slap time on their wrists just like that.
   1988 *A Small Place*.

23 A tourist is an ugly human being.
   1988 *A Small Place*.

King, Anthony 1934–

Canadian academic and political commentator. Professor of Government at the University of Essex since 1969.

24 It is an asteroid hitting the planet and destroying practically all life on earth.
   1997 Attempting to define the scale of Labour's victory in the general election, on BBC1's 'Election Night', 2 May.

King, Billie Jean *née Moffitt* 1943–

US tennis player, who won 20 titles at Wimbledon (1965–80).

25 Ask Nureyev to stop dancing, ask Sinatra to stop singing, then you can ask me to stop playing.
   1982 Quoted in Colin Jarman *The Guinness Dictionary of Sports Quotations* (1990).

26 If you're up against a girl with big boobs, bring her to the net and make her hit backhand volleys.
   1982 *Billie Jean King*.

King, Carlyle 1907–

Canadian political scientist and socialist.

27 The main business of socialist parties is not to form governments but to change minds.
   Attributed, 1940s.

King, Don 1932–

US boxing promoter.

28 Only in America could a Don King happen.
   Quoted in Colin Jarman *The Guinness Dictionary of Sports Quotations* (1990). King adopted 'Only in America' as a catchphrase, billing himself as Don 'Only in America' King.

29 This fight is bigger than life itself.
   2001 On the heavyweight title bout between Lennox Lewis and Hasim Rahman. In the *Observer*, 30 Dec.

King, Martin Luther Jr 1929–68

US civil rights leader. He advocated passive resistance to segregation and led a boycott (1955–6) against segregated bus lines in Montgomery, Alabama. In 1964 he received both the Kennedy and Nobel peace prizes. He was assassinated by James Earl Ray.

30 He who passively accepts evil is as much involved in it as he who helps to perpetuate it.
   1958 *Strides Towards Freedom*.

31 It may be true that the law cannot make a man love me, but it can keep him from lynching me, and I think that's pretty important.
   1962 Speech at Cornell College, Mt Vernon, Iowa. Reported in the *Wall Street Journal*, 13 Nov.

32 Injustice anywhere is a threat to justice everywhere.
   1963 Letter from Birmingham jail, Alabama, 16 Apr.

33 I have a dream. I have a dream that my four little children

will one day live in a nation where they will not be judged by the colour of their skin but by the content of their character.
   1963 Washington civil rights rally, 15 Jun.

34 If a man hasn't discovered something he will die for, he isn't fit to live.
   1963 Speech in Detroit, 23 Jun.

35 When the architects of our republic wrote the magnificent words of the Constitution and the Declaration of Independence, they were signing a promissory note to which every American was to fall heir… America has defaulted on this promissory note insofar as her citizens of color are concerned.
   1963 Speech at the Lincoln Memorial, 28 Aug, during the March on Washington.

36 We have…come to this hallowed spot to remind America of the fierce urgency of now.
   1963 Speech at the Lincoln Memorial, 28 Aug, during the March on Washington.

37 Let us not seek to satisfy our thirst for freedom by drinking from the cup of bitterness and hatred…[nor] allow our creative protests to degenerate into physical violence.
   1963 Speech at the Lincoln Memorial, 28 Aug, during the March on Washington.

38 You have been the victim of creative suffering.
   1963 Speech at the Lincoln Memorial, 28 Aug, during the March on Washington.

39 I have a dream that one day…the sons of former slaves and the sons of former slave owners will be able to sit together at the table of brotherhood.
   1963 Speech at the Lincoln Memorial, 28 Aug, during the March on Washington.

40 We have genuflected before the god of science only to find that it has given us the atomic bomb, producing fears and anxieties that science can never mitigate.
   1963 *Strength to Love*, ch.13.

41 The church must be reminded that it is not the master or servant of the state, but rather the conscience of the state.
   1963 *Strength to Love*.

42 Discrimination is a hellhound that gnaws at negroes in every waking moment of their lives, to remind them that the lie of their inferiority is accepted as truth in the society dominating them.
   1967 Speech at the Christian leadership conference, Atlanta, 16 Aug.

43 I've been to the mountain top. I've looked over, and I've seen the promised land. I may not get there with you, but I want you to know tonight that we as a people will get to the promised land. So, I'm happy tonight. Mine eyes have seen the glory of the coming of the Lord.
   1968 Speech at Memphis, 3 Apr, the day before he was assassinated.

44 Love is the only force capable of transforming an enemy into a friend.
   Attributed, collected in *The Words of Martin Luther King*.

King, Stephen 1947–

US author, known for his highly suspenseful horror novels. His works include *Carrie* (1974), *The Shining* (1976), *Misery* (1988) and *Bag of Bones* (1998).

45 Terror…often arises from a pervasive sense of disestablishment; that things are in the unmaking.
1981 *Danse Macabre*.

46 I believe there is an unseen world all around us.
1993 *Nightmares and Dreamscapes*, introduction.

King, William Lyon Mackenzie 1874–1950

Canadian Liberal politician, Prime Minister 1921–6, 1926–30 and 1935–48. His view that the dominions should be autonomous within the British Empire resulted in the Statute of Westminster (1931).

47 If some countries have too much history, we have too much geography.
1936 Address to the House of Commons, Ottawa, 18 Jun.

Kingsley, Charles 1819–75

English writer. Among his best-known works are the historical novels *Westward Ho!* (1855), and the children's book *The Water Babies* (1863). A Christian Socialist, he also published an immense number of articles on current topics.

48 'Oh Mary, go and call the cattle home,
And call the cattle home,
And call the cattle home,
Across the sands of Dee.'
The western wind was wild and dank with foam,
And all alone went she.
1850 *Alton Locke*, ch.26, 'The Sands of Dee'.

49 Come; and strong within us
Stir the Vikings' blood;
Bracing brain and sinew;
Blow, thou wind of God!
1857 'Ode to the North-East Wind'.

50 Be good, sweet maid, and let who will be clever;
Do noble things, do not dream them, all day long:
And so make life, death, and that vast for-ever
One grand, sweet song.
1858 'A Farewell'.

51 Once upon a time there was a little chimney-sweep, and his name was Tom.
1863 *The Water Babies*, ch.1.

52 The great elm-trees in the gold-green meadows were fast asleep above, and the cows fast asleep beneath them; nay, the few clouds which were about were fast asleep likewise, and so tired that they had lain down on the earth to rest, in long white flakes and bars, among the stems of the elm-trees, and along the tops of the alders by the stream.
1863 *The Water Babies*, ch.1.

53 When all the world is young, lad,
And all the trees are green;
And every goose a swan, lad,
And every lass a queen;
Then hey for boot and horse, lad,
And round the world away:
Young blood must have its course, lad,
And every dog his day.
1863 Song. *The Water Babies*, ch.2.

54 He was as thorough an Englishman as ever coveted his neighbour's goods… [He was] chief professor of Necrobioneopalaeonthydrochthonanthropopithek-ology.

1863 Professor Ptthmllnsprts. *The Water Babies*, ch.4.

55 The healthiest situation in England, on Easthampstead Plain. Free run of Windsor Forest. *The Times* every morning. A double-barrelled gun and pointers, and leave to shoot three Wellington College boys a week (not more) in case black game was scarce.
1863 The reward for criminal lunacy. *The Water Babies*, ch.4.

56 I am the ugliest fairy in the world, and I shall be till people behave themselves as they ought to do. And then I shall grow as handsome as my sister…Mrs Doasyouwouldbedoneby.
1863 Mrs Bedonebyasyoudid. *The Water Babies*, ch.5.

57 How long would it take a school-inspector of average activity to tumble head over heels from London to York?
1863 *The Water Babies*, ch.8.

58 So Tom went home with Ellie…and he is now a great man of science…and knows everything about everything, except why a hen's egg don't turn into a crocodile, and two or three other little things which no one will know till the coming of the Cocqcigrues. And all this from what he learnt when he was a water-baby, underneath the sea. 'And of course, Tom married Ellie?' My dear child, what a silly notion! Don't you know that no one ever marries in a fairy tale, under the rank of a prince or a princess?
1863 *The Water Babies*, ch.8.

59 We have used the Bible as if it was a constable's handbook—an opium-dose for keeping beasts of burden patient while they are being overloaded.
Letters to the Chartists, no.2.

60 To be discontented with the divine discontent, and to be ashamed with the noble shame, is the very germ and first upgrowth of all virtue.
1874 *Health and Education*.

Kingsley, Mary Henrietta 1862–1900

English writer and traveller. After the death of her invalid parents she travelled to West Africa (1893 and 1895), living among the natives, and wrote accounts of both journeys. She died of enteric fever while serving as a nurse in the second Boer War.

61 A certain sort of friendship soon arose between the Fans and me. We each recognized that we belonged to that same section of the human race with whom it is better to drink than to fight. We knew we would each have killed the other, if sufficient inducement were offered, and so we took a certain amount of care that the inducement should not arise.
1893 *Travels in West Africa* (published 1899).

62 It is at these times that you realise the blessings of a good thick skirt… Save for a good many bruises, here I was with the fulness of my skirt tucked under me, sitting on nine ebony spikes some twelve inches long, in comparative comfort.
1893 *Travels in West Africa* (published 1899).

63 The sooner the Crown Colony system is removed from the sphere of practical politics and put under a glass case in the South Kensington Museum, labelled 'Extinct', the better for everyone.
1899 *West African Studies*.

64 West Africa today is just a quarry of paving stones for Hell, and those stones were cemented in place with

men's blood mixed with wasted gold.
1899 *West African Studies*.

Kington, Miles 1941–

British writer and columnist. He is best known as a humorist, and also writes on jazz.

65 Nobody has ever been able to define jazz satisfactorily. This is probably because anyone who was capable of doing so never really wanted to, knowing how much you would have to leave out of the definition.
1992 *The Jazz Anthology*, ch.1

Kinnock, Neil Gordon 1942–

Welsh Labour politician. In 1983 he succeeded Michael Foot as Party leader, but resigned after the 1992 election defeat. He was Vice-President of the European Commission until 2004, subsequently becoming Chair of the British Council.

66 We cannot remove the evils of capitalism without taking its source of power: ownership.
1975 In *Tribune*.

67 I want to retire at 50. I want to play cricket in the summer and geriatric football in the winter, and sing in the choir.
1980 In *The Times*, 28 Jul.

68 Like Brighton Pier—all right as far as it goes, but inadequate for getting to France.
1981 On Conservative European policy, House of Commons, 2 Feb.

69 It's a pity others had to leave theirs on the ground at Goose Green to prove it.
1983 Reply to a heckler who had said Mrs Thatcher had shown 'guts' in the Falklands Crisis. Quoted in *The Times*, 6 Jun.

70 If Margaret Thatcher wins on Thursday, I warn you not to be ordinary, I warn you not to be young, I warn you not to fall ill, I warn you not to get old.
1983 Speech one day before polling, Jun.

71 I have a lot of sympathy with him. I too was once a young, bald Leader of the Opposition.
1999 On William Hague. In *The Independent*, 3 Oct.

Kinsella, W(illiam) P(atrick) 1935–

Canadian novelist.

72 There was silence in the room. Then a voice, stunning as thunder, clear and common as a train whistle—the voice of a ball-park announcer: 'If you build it, he will come.'
1980 'Shoeless Joe Jackson Comes to Iowa', a short story later expanded into the novel *Shoeless Joe* (1982) and filmed as *Field of Dreams* (1989).

Kipling, (Joseph) Rudyard 1865–1935

English writer, born in Bombay, who lived for several years in India. His verse both celebrated and satirized the British Imperial presence, and won him widespread popularity, while the stories in *The Jungle Book* (1894) are considered classics of their kind. He also wrote novels and a biography, and was awarded the Nobel prize in 1907.

73 The toad beneath the harrow knows
Exactly where each tooth-point goes;
The butterfly upon the road
Preaches contentment to that toad.
1886 'Pagett, MP'.

74 Never praise a sister to a sister, in the hope of your compliments reaching the proper ears.
1888 *Plain Tales from the Hills*, 'False Dawn'.

75 Take my word for it, the silliest woman can manage a clever man; but it takes a very clever woman to manage a fool.
1888 *Plain Tales from the Hills*, 'Three and—an Extra'.

76 Every one is more or less mad on one point.
1888 *Plain Tales from the Hills*, 'On the Strength of a Likeness'.

77 The Man who Would be King.
1888 *Wee Willie Winkie*, title of short story.

78 Being kissed by a man who didn't wax his moustache was—like eating an egg without salt.
1888 *The Story of the Gadsbys*, 'Poor Dear Mamma'.

79 Down to Gehenna or up to the Throne,
He travels fastest who travels alone.
1888 *The Story of the Gadsbys*, 'L'Envoi'. The poem was later renamed 'The Winners' (1912).

80 We're poor little lambs who've lost our way,
Baa! Baa! Baa!
We're little black sheep who've gone astray,
Baa-aa-aa!
Gentlemen-rankers out on the spree,
Damned from here to eternity,
God ha' mercy on such as we,
Baa! Yah! Bah!
1889 'The Gentlemen-Rankers'.

81 Oh, East is East, and West is West, and never the twain shall meet,
Till earth and sky stand presently at God's great Judgement seat;
But there is neither East nor West, Border, nor Breed, nor Birth,
When two strong men stand face to face, tho' they come from the ends of the earth.
1889 'The Ballad of East and West'.

82 A man lives well and happily until he begins to feel unwell. Then he feels worse because the climate allows him no chance of pulling himself together—and then he dies.
1889 Of life in Singapore. *From Sea to Sea*.

83 The Japanese should have no concern with business.
1889 *From Sea to Sea*.

84 Moulmein is situated up the mouth of a river which ought to flow through South America.
1889 *From Sea to Sea*.

85 By the old Moulmein Pagoda, lookin' eastward to the sea,
There's a Burma girl a-settin', and I know she thinks o' me;
For the wind is in the palm trees, an' the temple bells they say:
'Come you back, you British soldier'; come you back to Mandalay!'
1890 'Mandalay'.

86 Come you back to Mandalay,
Where the old Flotilla lay:
Can't you 'ear their paddles chunkin' from Rangoon to Mandalay?
On the road to Mandalay,
Where the flyin'-fishes play,

An' the dawn comes up like thunder outer China 'crost the Bay!
1890 'Mandalay'.

87 An' I seed her first a-smokin' of a whackin' white cheroot,
An' a-wastin' Christian kisses on an 'eathen idol's foot.
1890 'Mandalay'.

88 Ship me somewhere east of Suez, where the best is like the worst,
Where there aren't no Ten Commandments an' a man can raise a thirst.
1890 'Mandalay'.

89 For they're hangin' Danny Deever, you can hear the Dead March play,
The regiment's in 'ollow square—they're hangin' him to-day;
They've taken of his buttons off an' cut his stripes away,
An' they're hangin' Danny Deever in the mornin'.
1890 'Danny Deever'.

90 O it's Tommy this, an' Tommy that, an' 'Tommy, go away';
But it's 'Thank you, Mister Atkins,' when the band begins to play.
1890 'Tommy'.

91 Then it's Tommy this, an' Tommy that, and 'Tommy 'ow's yer soul?'
But it's 'Thin red line of 'eroes' when the drums begin to roll.
1890 'Tommy'.
➤ *See Russell 706:69.*

92 For it's Tommy this, an' Tommy that, and 'Chuck him out, the brute!'
But it's 'Saviour of 'is country' when the guns begin to shoot.
1890 'Tommy'.

93 When you're wounded and left on Afghanistan's plains
And the women come out to cut up what remains
Just roll to your rifle and blow out your brains
An' go to your Gawd like a soldier.
1890 'The Young British Soldier'.

94 So 'ere's *to* you, Fuzzy-Wuzzy, at your 'ome in the Soudan;
You're a pore benighted 'eathen but a first-class fightin' man;
An' 'ere's *to* you, Fuzzy-Wuzzy, with your 'ayrick 'ead of 'air—
You big black boundin' beggar—for you broke a British square!
1890 'Fuzzy-Wuzzy'.

95 The uniform 'e wore
Was nothin' much before,
An' rather less than 'arf o' that be'ind.
1890 'Gunga Din'.

96 Though I've belted you and flayed you,
By the livin' Gawd that made you,
You're a better man than I am, Gunga Din!
1890 'Gunga Din'.

97 'Ave you 'eard o' the Widow at Windsor
With a hairy gold crown on 'er 'ead?
She 'as ships on the foam—she 'as millions at 'ome,
An' she pays us poor beggars in red.
1890 'The Widow at Windsor'.

98 And the talk slid north, and the talk slid south,
With the sliding puffs from the hookah-mouth.
Four things greater than all things are,—
Women and Horses and Power and War.
1890 'The Ballad of the King's Jest'.

99 Winds of the World, give answer! They are whimpering to and fro—
And what should they know of England who only England know?—
The poor little street-bred people that vapour and fume and brag.
1891 'The English Flag'.

1 If I were damned of body and soul,
I know whose prayers would make me whole,
Mother o' mine, O mother o' mine.
1891 *The Light That Failed*, dedication.

2 There ain't twelve hundred people in the world who understand pictures. The others pretend and don't care.
1891 *The Light That Failed*.

3 When the flush of a new-born sun fell first on Eden's green and gold,
Our father Adam sat under the Tree and scratched with a stick in the mould;
And the first rude sketch that the world had seen was joy to his mighty heart,
Till the Devil whispered behind the leaves, 'It's pretty, but is it Art?'
1892 'The Conundrum of the Workshops'.

4 We know that the tail must wag the dog, for the horse is drawn by the cart;
But the Devil whoops, as he whooped of old: 'It's clever, but is it Art?'
1892 'The Conundrum of the Workshops'.

5 And the end of the fight is a tombstone white, with the name of the late deceased,
And the epitaph drear: 'A fool lies here who tried to hustle the East.'
1892 *The Naulahka*, ch.5.

6 For the sin ye do by two and two ye must pay for one by one!
1892 'Tomlinson'.

7 There be triple ways to take, of the eagle or the snake,
Or the way of a man with a maid;
But the sweetest way to me is a ship's upon the sea
In the heel of the North-East Trade.
1892 'The Long Trail'.

8 There are nine and sixty ways of constructing tribal lays,
And—every—single—one—of—them—is—right!
1892 'In the Neolithic Age'.

9 A man-cub is a man-cub, and he must learn *all* the Law of the Jungle.
1894 *The Jungle Book*, 'Kaa's Hunting'.

10 'We be one blood, thou and I,' Mowgli answered. 'I take my life from thee to-night. My kill shall be thy kill if ever thou art hungry, O Kaa.'
1894 *The Jungle Book*, 'Kaa's Hunting'.

11 Brother, thy tail hangs down behind!
1894 *The Jungle Book*, 'The Road Song of the Bandar-Log'.

12 Now this is the Law of the Jungle—as old and as true as the sky;

And the Wolf that shall keep it may prosper, but the Wolf that shall break it must die.
1895 *The Second Jungle Book*, 'The Law of the Jungle'.

13 Keep ye the law—be swift in all obedience—
Clear the land of evil, drive the road and bridge the ford.
Make ye sure to each his own
That he reap where he hath sown;
By the peace among our peoples let men know we serve the Lord!
1896 'A Song of the English'.

14 We have fed our sea for a thousand years
And she calls us, still unfed,
Though there's never a wave of all her waves
But marks our English dead.
1896 'A Song of the Dead'.

15 If blood be the price of admiralty
Lord God, we ha' paid in full!
1896 'A Song of the Dead'.

16 I've taken my fun where I've found it,
An' now I must pay for my fun,
For the more you 'ave known o' the others
The less will you settle for one;
1896 'The Ladies'.

17 For the Colonel's Lady an' Judy O'Grady
Are sisters under their skins!
1896 'The Ladies'.

18 The 'eathen in 'is blindness bows down to wood an' stone;
'E don't obey no orders unless they is 'is own.
1896 'The 'Eathen'.

19 The 'eathen in 'is blindness must end where 'e began.
But the backbone of the Army is the non-commissioned man!
1896 'The 'Eathen'.

20 And only the Master shall praise us, and only the Master shall blame;
And no one shall work for money, and no one shall work for fame,
But each for the joy of working, and each, in his separate star,
Shall draw the Thing as he sees It for the God of Things as They are!
1896 'When Earth's Last Picture is Painted'.

21 The tumult and the shouting dies—
The captains and the kings depart—
Still stands Thine ancient Sacrifice,
An humble and a contrite heart.
Lord God of Hosts, be with us yet,
Lest we forget—lest we forget!
1897 'Recessional'.
➤ See Bible 95:31.

22 If, drunk with sight of power, we loose
Wild tongues that have not Thee in awe—
Such boasting as the Gentiles use,
Or lesser breeds without the Law.
1897 'Recessional'.

23 What the horses o' Kansas think to-day, the horses of America will think tomorrow; an' I tell *you* that when the horses of America rise in their might, the day o' the Oppressor is ended.
1898 *The Day's Work*, 'A Walking Delegate'.

24 Take up the White Man's burden—
Send forth the best ye breed—
Go, bind your sons to exile
To serve your captives' need.
1899 'The White Man's Burden'.

25 Your new-caught, sullen peoples,
Half devil and half child.
1899 'The White Man's Burden'.

26 By all ye will or whisper,
By all ye leave or do,
The silent sullen peoples
Shall weigh your God and you.
1899 'The White Man's Burden'.

27 When you've shouted 'Rule Britannia', when you've sung 'God save the Queen'—
When you've finished killing Kruger with your mouth—
Will you kindly drop a shilling in my little tambourine
For a gentleman in *Kharki* ordered South?
1899 *The Absent-Minded Beggar*.

28 Mr Raymond Martin, beyond question, was born in the gutter, and bred in a Board-School, where they played marbles. He was further (I give the barest handful from great store) a Flopshus Cad, an Outrageous Stinker, a Jelly-bellied Flag-flapper (this was Stalky's contribution), and several other things which it is not seemly to put down.
1899 *Stalky & Co.*

29 Being human, she must have been afraid of something, but one never found out what it was.
c.1900 Of Mary Kingsley (1862–1900), the enterprising English traveller in West Africa. Attributed.

30 Little Friend of all the World.
1901 Kim's nickname. *Kim*, ch.1.

31 Men are as chancy as children in their choice of playthings.
1901 *Kim*, ch.10.

32 One does not own to the possession of money in India.
1901 *Kim*, ch.11.

33 'Noble and generous Cetacean, have you ever tasted Man?' 'No,' said the Whale. 'What is it like?' 'Nice,' said the small 'Stute Fish. 'Nice but nubbly.'
1902 *Just So Stories*, 'How the Whale Got His Throat'.

34 You must not forget the suspenders, Best Beloved.
1902 *Just So Stories*, 'How the Whale Got His Throat'.

35 He had his Mummy's leave to paddle, or else he would never have done it, because he was a man of infinite-resource-and-sagacity.
1902 *Just So Stories*, 'How the Whale Got His Throat'.

36 The camel's hump is an ugly lump
Which well you may see at the Zoo;
But uglier yet is the hump we get
From having too little to do.
1902 *Just So Stories*, 'How the Camel Got His Hump'.

37 The cure for this ill is not to sit still,
Or frowst with a book by the fire;
But to take a large hoe and a shovel also,
And dig till you gently perspire.
1902 *Just So Stories*, 'How the Camel Got His Hump'.

38 Most 'scruciating idle.
1902 *Just So Stories*, 'How the Camel Got His Hump'.

39 'Humph yourself!'
And the Camel humphed himself.
1902 *Just So Stories*, 'How the Camel Got His Hump'.

40 There lived a Parsee from whose hat the rays of the sun
were reflected in more-than-oriental splendour.
1902 *Just So Stories*, 'How the Rhinoceros Got His Skin'.

41 But there was one Elephant—a new Elephant—an
Elephant's Child—who was full of 'satiable curtiosity,
and that means he asked ever so many questions.
1902 *Just So Stories*, 'The Elephant's Child'.

42 The great grey-green, greasy Limpopo River, all set
about with fever-trees.
1902 *Just So Stories*, 'The Elephant's Child'.

43 Led go! You are hurtig be!
1902 *Just So Stories*, 'The Elephant's Child'.

44 And I'd like to roll to Rio
Some day before I'm old!
1902 *Just So Stories*, 'The Beginning of the Armadilloes'.

45 'You are making my spots ache,' said Painted Jaguar.
1902 *Just So Stories*, 'The Beginning of the Armadillos'.

46 But the wildest of all the wild animals was the Cat. He
walked by himself, and all places were alike to him.
1902 *Just So Stories*, 'The Cat That Walked By Himself'.

47 And he went back through the Wet Wild Woods, waving
his wild tail and walking by his wild lone. But he never
told anybody.
1902 *Just So Stories*, 'The Cat That Walked By Himself'.

48 He would surprise them out of their jumpsome lives.
1902 *Just So Stories*, 'How the Leopard Got His Spots'.

49 Something lost behind the Ranges.
1903 *The Five Nations*, 'The Explorer'.

50 Who hath desired the Sea?—the sight of salt water
unbounded—
The heave and the halt and the hurl and the crash of the
comber wind-hounded?
The sleek-barrelled swell before storm, grey, foamless,
enormous, and growing—
Stark calm on the lap of the Line or the crazy-eyed
Hurricane blowing.
1903 'The Sea and the Hills'.

51 And here the sea-fogs lap and cling,
And here, each warning each,
The sheep-bells and the ship-bells ring
Along the hidden beach.
1903 'Sussex'.

52 God gives all men all earth to love,
But since man's heart is small,
Ordains for each one spot shall prove
Belovèd over all.
1903 'Sussex'.

53 Each to his choice, and I rejoice
The lot has fallen to me
In a fair ground—in a fair ground—
Yea, Sussex by the sea!
1903 'Sussex'.
▶ See Book of Common Prayer 142:42.

54 Then ye returned to your trinkets; then ye contented
your souls
With the flannelled fools at the wicket or the muddied
oafs at the goals.

1903 'The Islanders'.

55 An' it all goes into the laundry
But it never comes out in the wash.
1903 'Stellenbosh'.

56 'Tisn't beauty, so to speak, nor good talk necessarily. It's
just It. Some women'll stay in a man's memory if they
once walked down a street.
1904 *Traffics and Discoveries*, 'Mrs Bathhurst'.

57 The God who Looks after Small Things had caused
the visitor that day to receive two weeks' delayed mails
in one.
1904 *Traffics and Discoveries*, 'The Captive'

58 Of all the trees that grow so fair,
Old England to adorn,
Greater are none beneath the Sun,
Than Oak, and Ash, and Thorn.
1906 *Puck of Pook's Hill*, 'Tree Song'.

59 England shall bide till Judgement Tide
By Oak, and Ash, and Thorn.
1906 *Puck of Pook's Hill*, 'Tree Song'.

60 What is a woman that you forsake her,
And the hearth-fire and the home-acre,
To go with the old grey Widow-maker?
1906 *Puck of Pook's Hill*, 'Harp Song of the Dane Women'.

61 If you wake at midnight, and hear a horse's feet,
Don't go drawing back the blind, or looking in the street,
Them that asks no questions isn't told a lie.
Watch the wall, my darling, while the Gentlemen go by!
1906 *Puck of Pook's Hill*, 'Smuggler's Song'.

62 Land of our birth, we pledge to thee
Our love and toil in the years to be;
When we are grown and take our place,
As men and women with our race.
1906 *Puck of Pook's Hill*, 'Children's Song'.

63 Teach us delight in simple things
And mirth that has no bitter springs;
Forgiveness free of evil done,
And love to all men 'neath the sun!
1906 *Puck of Pook's Hill*, 'Children's Song'.

64 But I consort with long-haired things
In velvet collar-rolls,
Who talk about the Aims of Art,
And 'theories' and 'goals',
And moo and coo with women-folk
About their blessed souls.
1909 'In Partibus'.

65 There is sorrow enough in the natural way
From men and women to fill our day;
But when we are certain of sorrow in store,
Why do we always arrange for more?
Brothers and Sisters, I bid you beware
Of giving your heart to a dog to tear.
1909 'The Power of the Dog'.

66 They shut the road through the woods
Seventy years ago.
Weather and rain have undone it again,
And now you would never know
There was once a road through the woods.
1910 *Rewards and Fairies*, 'The Way Through the Woods'.

67 If you can keep your head when all about you

Are losing theirs and blaming it on you;
If you can trust yourself when all men doubt you,
But make allowance for their doubting too;
If you can wait and not be tired by waiting,
Or being lied about, don't deal in lies,
Or being hated, don't give way to hating,
And yet don't look too good, nor talk too wise;
If you can dream—and not make dreams your master;
If you can think—and not make thoughts your aim,
If you can meet with Triumph and Disaster
And treat those two imposters just the same.
1910 *Rewards and Fairies*, 'If—'.

68 If you can talk with crowds and keep your virtue,
Or walk with Kings—nor lose the common touch,
If neither foes nor loving friends can hurt you,
If all men count with you, but none too much;
If you can fill the unforgiving minute
With sixty seconds' worth of distance run,
Yours is the Earth and everything that's in it.
And—which is more—you'll be a Man, my son!
1910 *Rewards and Fairies*, 'If—'.

69 One man in a thousand, Solomon says,
Will stick more close than a brother.
1910 *Rewards and Fairies*, 'The Thousandth Man'

70 It is always a temptation to a rich and lazy nation,
To puff and look important and to say:
'Though we know we should defeat you, we have not
   the time to meet you,
We will therefore pay you cash to go away.'

And that is called paying the Dane-geld;
But we've proved it again and again,
That if once you have paid him the Dane-geld
You never get rid of the Dane.
1911 'Dane-Geld'.

71 'Oh, where are you going to, all you Big Steamers,
With England's own coal, up and down the salt seas?'
'We are going to fetch you your bread and your butter,
Your beef, pork, and mutton, eggs, apples and cheese.'
1911 'Big Steamers'.

72 Our England is a garden that is full of stately views,
Of borders, beds and shrubberies and lawns and
   avenues,
With statues on the terraces and peacocks strutting by;
But the Glory of the Garden lies in more than meets the
   eye.
1911 'The Glory of the Garden'.

73 Our England is a garden, and such gardens are not made
By singing:—'Oh, how beautiful!' and sitting in the
   shade,
While better men than we go out and start their working
   lives
At grubbing weeds from gravel paths with broken
   dinner-knives.
1911 'The Glory of the Garden'.

74 Oh, Adam was a gardener, and God who made him sees
That half a proper gardener's work is done upon his
   knees,
So when your work is finished, you can wash your hands
   and pray
For the Glory of the Garden that it may not pass away!
1911 'The Glory of the Garden'.

75 We know the war prepared
On every peaceful home,
We know the hells declared
For such as serve not Rome,
The terror, threats and dread
In market, hearth and field:
We know when all is said
We perish if we yield.
1912 'Ulster'.

76 For all we have and are,
For all our children's fate,
Stand up and take the war.
The Hun is at the gate!
1914 'For All We Have and Are'.

77 There is but one task for all—
For each one life to give.
What stands if freedom fall?
Who dies if England live?
1914 'For All We Have and Are'.

78 It's north you may run to the rime-ringed sun,
Or south to the blind Horn's hate;
Or east all the way into Mississippi Bay,
Or west to the Golden Gate.
1918 *Twenty Poems*, 'The Long Trail'.

79 Pull out, pull out on the Long Trail—the trail that is always
new!
1918 *Twenty Poems*, 'The Long Trail'.

80 Their Name Liveth for Evermore.
1919 His suggestion for the text to be carved over the lists of
the dead in the Commonwealth war cemeteries after World
War I.
➤ *See Bible 108:67.*

81 If any question why we died,
Tell them, because our fathers lied.
1919 *Rudyard Kipling's Verse*, 'Common Form'.

82 The female of the species is more deadly than the
male.
1919 *Rudyard Kipling's Verse*, 'The Female of the Species'.

83 Words are, of course, the most powerful drug used by
mankind.
1923 Speech, 14 Feb, collected in *A Book of Words*.

84 As it will be in the future, it was at the birth of Man—
There are only four things certain since Social Progress
   began:—
That the Dog returns to his Vomit and the Sow returns to
   her Mire,
And the burnt Fool's bandaged finger goes wabbling
   back to the Fire.
1927 *Rudyard Kipling's Verse*, 'The Gods of the Copybook
Headings'.

85 England's on the anvil—hear the hammers ring—
Clanging from the Severn to the Tyne!
1927 *Rudyard Kipling's Verse*, 'The Anvil'.

Kirkland, (Joseph) Lane 1922–99

US labour leader.

86 My pappy told me never to bet my bladder against a
brewery or get into an argument with people who buy
ink by the barrel.
Quoted in David Olive *Business Babble* (1993).

Kirkup, James 1923–

English poet. He held academic posts in Japan from the early 1960s, and his work has been greatly influenced by Japanese culture and literature.

87 But the river remains unchanged, sad, refusing rehabilitation.
   1962 'No More Hiroshimas'.

Kishen fl.c.1840

Chinese diplomatist.

88 It appears to Your Majesty's slave that we are very deficient in means, and have not the shells and rockets used by the barbarians. We must, therefore, adopt other methods to stop them, which will be easy, as they have opened negotiations.
   1841 Report, Mar, to the Chinese Emperor during the 1st Opium War, 1839–42.

Kissinger, Henry Alfred 1923–

US academic and statesman. He was the main US figure in the negotiations to end the Vietnam War (for which he shared the 1973 Nobel peace prize), and Secretary of State (1973–7). His 'shuttle diplomacy', aimed at improving Israeli–Egyptian relations, had much success.

89 It is not often that nations learn from the past—even rarer that they draw the correct conclusions from it. For the lessons of historical experience, as of personal experience, are contingent. They teach the consequences of certain actions, but they cannot force a recognition of comparable situations.
   1957 A World Restored: Castlereagh, Metternich and the Restoration of Peace, 1812–22.

90 We lost sight of one of the cardinal maxims of guerrilla war: the guerrilla wins if he does not lose. The conventional army loses if it does not win.
   1969 On the Vietnam War. In Foreign Affairs, Jan.

91 Power is the ultimate aphrodisiac.
   1969 Comment at the end of his first year as head of the National Security Council. Quoted in Walter Isaacson Kissinger (1992).

92 We are all the President's men, and we must behave accordingly.
   1970 On the US invasion of Cambodia, alluding to the nursery rhyme Humpty Dumpty ('All the king's men…'). The phrase was used in the title of the book by Washington Post reporters Bob Woodward and Carl Bernstein on the Watergate scandal.

93 No foreign policy, no matter how ingenious, has any chance of success if it is born in the minds of a few and carried in the heart of none.
   1973 Speech to International Platform Association, 2 Aug.

94 Every civilization that has ever existed has ultimately collapsed.
   1974 In the New York Times, 13 Oct.

95 History is a tale of efforts that failed…aspirations that weren't realized, or wishes that were fulfilled and then turned out to be different from what one expected.
   1974 In the New York Times, 13 Oct.

96 There can't be any crisis next week. My schedule is already full.
   1977 In Time, Jan.

97 High office teaches decision-making, not substance. It consumes intellectual capital; it does not create it. Most high officials leave office with the perceptions and insights with which they entered: they learn how to make decisions, but not what decisions to make.
   1979 The White House Years.

98 The statesman's duty is to bridge the gap between his nation's experience and his vision.
   1982 Years of Upheaval.

99 The nice thing about being a celebrity is that when you bore people, they think that it's their fault.
   Quoted in Reader's Digest, Apr 1985.

1 Whatever must happen ultimately should happen immediately.
   1986 Of the Iran–Contra scandal. In Time, 8 Oct.

2 Any people who have been persecuted for 2,000 years must be doing something wrong.
   Of Israel, after its attack on Egypt. Quoted in Walter Isaacson Kissinger (1992).

3 I'd do anything for caviar and probably did.
   On his visit to Moscow. Quoted in Walter Isaacson Kissinger (1992).

Kitchener of Khartoum and Broome, (Horatio) Herbert, 1st Earl 1850–1916

British field marshal. He served in Palestine, Cyprus and the Sudan, which he regained for the British Empire at Omdurman (1898), and was chief-of-staff and commander-in-chief in the Boer War. In World War I he was Secretary of State for War, but was drowned when HMS Hampshire struck a mine.

4 You are ordered abroad as a soldier of the King to help our French comrades against the invasion of a common enemy… In this new experience you may find temptations both in wine and women. You must entirely resist both temptations, and while treating all women with perfect courtesy, you should avoid any intimacy. Do your duty bravely. Fear God. Honour the King.
   1914 Message to the soldiers of the British Expeditionary Force, reported in The Times, 19 Aug.

5 I don't mind your being killed, but I object to your being taken prisoner.
   1914 To the Prince of Wales, later Edward VIII, who had asked to be allowed to the Front, 18 Dec.

Klee, Paul 1874–1940

Swiss painter and graphic artist, one of the most influential teachers of the German Bauhaus.

6 I have now reached the point where I can look over the great art of antiquity and its Renaissance. But, for myself, I cannot find any artistic connection with our own times. And to want to create something outside of one's own age strikes me as suspect.
   1901–2 The Diaries of Paul Klee 1898–1918, entry 294.

7 The worst state of affairs is when science begins to concern itself with art.
   1906 Collected in The Notebooks of Paul Klee (published 1957).

8 Color possesses me. I don't have to pursue it. It will possess me always, I know it. That is the meaning of this happy hour: Color and I are one. I am a painter.
   1914 The Diaries of Paul Klee 1898–1918, entry 926.

9 Art is like Creation: it holds good on the last day as on the first.

1916 *The Diaries of Paul Klee 1898–1918*, entry 1008.

10 *Kunst gibt nicht das Sichtbare wieder, sondern macht sichtbar.*
Art does not reproduce the visible; rather it makes visible.
1920 'Creative Credo', in *Inward Vision* (1958).

Klein, Calvin Richard 1942–

US fashion designer.

11 You have to take things to an extreme and then bring them back to reality.
1988 On the fluctuating length of hemlines. In the *New York Times*, 9 Mar.

Kline, Nancy

12 Withholding information from someone is an act of intellectual imperialism. Not bothering to seek accurate information is an act of intellectual recklessness.
1999 *Time to Think*.

Kneller, Godfrey 1646–1723

German-born painter who spent most of his working life in England, particularly renowned as a portrait painter.

13 Painters of history make the dead live, and do not begin to live themselves till they are dead. I paint the living, and they make me live!
When asked why he preferred portraits to more prestigious history scenes. Quoted in A Cunningham *The Lives of the Most Eminent Painters, Sculptors and Architects* (1829).

Knight, Frank Hyneman 1885–1972

US economist, Professor at the University of Chicago (1927–58) and an opponent of social planning. His most famous works were *Risk, Uncertainty and Profit* (1921) and *The Ethics of Competition* (1923).

14 Costs merely register competing attractions.
1921 *Risk, Uncertainty and Profit*.

15 I have been increasingly moved to wonder whether my job is a job or a racket, whether economists, and particularly economic theorists, may not be in the position that Cicero, citing Cato, ascribed to the augurs of Rome—that they should cover their faces or burst into laughter when they met on the street.
1950 Collected in *Essays on the History and Method of Economics* (1956).

16 Sociology is the science of talk, and there is only one law in sociology. Bad talk drives out good.
Quoted in Paul A Samuelson *The Samuelson Sampler* (1973).

Knox, John c.1513–1572

Scottish Protestant reformer and architect of the Church of Scotland, whose single-minded determination to establish Presbyterianism brought him into conflict with the Catholic Queen Mary.

17 The Monstrous Regiment of Women.
1558 From the title of his pamphlet, *The First Blast of the Trumpet Against the Monstrous Regiment of Women*.

18 To promote a woman to bear rule, superiority, dominion, or empire above any realm, nation, or city, is repugnant to nature, contumely to God, a thing most contrarious to his revealed will and approved ordinance; and,

finally, it is the subversion of good order, of all equity and justice.
1558 *First Blast of the Trumpet against the Monstrous Regiment of Women*.

19 If there be not in her, a proud mind, a crafty wit, and an indurate heart against God and his truth, my judgment faileth me.
1561 After his first meeting with Mary, Queen of Scots. *History of the Reformation in Scotland*, vol.2.

20 *Un homme avec Dieu est toujours dans la majorité.*
One man with God is always a majority.
Inscription on the Reformation Monument, Geneva, attributed to Knox.

Knox, Philander Chase 1853–1921

US lawyer and politician. He served as US Attorney General (1901–4) and Secretary of State (1909–13).

21 Oh, Mr President, do not let so great an achievement suffer from any taint of legality.
1903 Quoted in Tom Buckley *Violent Neighbours* (1983), alluding to Theodore Roosevelt's desire to find legal grounds for the seizure of the Panama Canal by the US.

Knox, Ronald Arbuthnot 1888–1957

English writer and Roman Catholic theologian. He wrote many theological works and Bible translations, and also detective novels.

22 There was once a man who said 'God
Must think it exceedingly odd
If he finds that this tree
Continues to be
When there's no-one about in the Quad.'
Attributed. Quoted in Langford Reed *Complete Limerick Book* (1924).
The limericks summarise Bishop George Berkeley's philosophy that everything is dependent at all times on the will of God.
➤ *See Anonymous 22:51*.

23 It is stupid of modern civilization to have given up believing in the devil, when he is the only explanation of it.
1939 *Let Dons Delight*, ch.8.

24 A loud noise at one end and no sense of responsibility at the other.
His definition of a baby. Attributed.

Knudsen, Semon Emil 1912–98

US automotive executive.

25 Before you tell someone how good you are, you must tell him how bad you used to be.
1959 In *Time* magazine, 25 May.

Koch, Edward I(rving) 1924–

US lawyer and Mayor of New York City (1978–89).

26 You're not a nice guy if you have a gun, even if you are a nice guy.
1980 In *Time*, 3 Mar.

27 Each diploma is a lighted match… Each one of you is a fuse.
1983 Addressing students at NY State University. In the *New York Times*, 10 Jun.

Koestler, Arthur 1905–83

Hungarian-born British writer and journalist. He wrote on science and parapsychology, and is best known for his anti-communist novel *Darkness at Noon* (1940). He and his wife committed suicide after he became terminally ill.

28 The definition of an individual was: a multitude of one million divided by one million.
   1940 *Darkness at Noon*, 'The Grammatical Fiction', pt.2.

29 A writer's ambition should be…to trade a hundred contemporary readers for ten readers in ten years' time and for one reader in a hundred years.
   1951 In the *New York Times Book Review*, 1 Apr.

30 Space-ships and time machines are no escape from the human condition. Let Othello subject Desdemona to a lie-detector test; his jealousy will still blind him to the evidence. Let Oedipus triumph over gravity; he won't triumph over his fate.
   1953 'The Boredom of Fantasy', collected in *The Trail of the Dinosaur* (1955), pt.2.

31 Among all forms of mentation, verbal thinking is the most articulate, the most complex, and the most vulnerable to infectious diseases. It is liable to absorb whispered suggestions, and to incorporate them as hidden persuaders into the code.
   1964 *The Act of Creation*.

32 Creativity in science could be described as the act of putting two and two together to make five.
   1964 *The Act of Creation*.

33 The most persistent sound that reverberates through men's history is the beating of war drums.
   1978 *Janus; A Summing Up*, 'Prologue: The New Calendar', sect.1.

Koffler, Murray 1924–

Canadian pharmacist and philanthropist.

34 Dress British, look Irish, think Yiddish.
   His formula for success, quoted in Frank Rasky *Just a Simple Pharmacist: The Story of Murray Koffler, Builder of the Shoppers Drug Mart Empire* (1988).

Koh, Harold Hongju 1954–

US lawyer, Professor of International Law at Yale University.

35 Silence has a sound, and the sound is 'no.'
   1991 Testimony to the US Senate Judiciary Committee on the presidential right to enter the Gulf War without congressional approval. Quoted by Senator Joseph R Biden, Jr in NPR broadcast, 10 Jan.

Kohl, Helmut 1930–

German statesman. He was Chancellor from 1982 to 1998.

36 The policy of European integration is in reality a question of war and peace in the 21st century.
   1996 Speech, 2 Feb.

Kohlberg, Jerome, Jr 1925–

US investment banker.

37 An ethic is not an ethic, and a value not a value without some sacrifice for it. Something given up, something not gained.
   Quoted in Sarah Bartlett *The Money Machine* (1991).

Kollwitz, Käthe 1867–1945

German sculptor and graphic artist. She had two sons, Peter and Hans. Peter was killed at the beginning of World War I, in 1914.

38 As you, the children of my body, have been my tasks, so too are my other works.
   1915 Letter to her son Hans, 21 Feb.

39 I have never done any work cold… I have always worked with my blood, so to speak.
   1917 Letter to her son Hans, 16 Apr.

The Koran

All quotations are taken from the Arthur J Arberry (1955) translation of The Koran. Line numbers refer to the standard numeration.

40 In the name of God, the Merciful, the Compassionate.
   Praise belongs to God, the Lord of all Being,
   the All-merciful, the All-compassionate
   the Master of the Day of Doom.
   Thee only we serve; to Thee alone we pray for succour.
   Guide us in the straight path,
   the path of those whom Thou hast blessed,
   not of those against whom Thou art wrathful,
   nor of those who are astray.
   Sura 1, l.1–7.

41 We have sent among you, of yourselves, a Messenger, to recite Our signs to you and to purify you, and to teach you the Book and the Wisdom, and to teach you that you knew not. So remember Me, and I will remember you; and be thankful to Me; and be you not ungrateful towards Me.
   Sura 2, l.151–2.

42 O all you who believe, seek you help in patience and prayer; surely God is with the patient.
   Sura 2, l.153.

43 Surely in the creation of the heavens and the earth and the alternation of night and day and the ship that runs in the sea with profit to men, and the water God sends down from heaven therewith reviving the earth after it is dead and His scattering abroad in it all manner of crawling thing, and the turning about of the winds and the clouds compelled between heaven and earth— surely there are signs for a people having understanding.
   Sura 2, l.164.

44 It is not piety that you turn your faces to the East and to the West. True piety is this: to believe in God, and the Last Day, the angels, the Book, and the Prophets, to give of one's substance, however cherished, to kinsmen, and orphans, the needy, the traveller, beggars, and to ransom the slave, to perform the prayer, to pay the alms.
   Sura 2, l.177.

45 And fight in the way of God with those who fight with you, but aggress not: God loves not the aggressors.
   Sura 2, l.190.

46 God charges no soul save to its capacity; standing to account is what it has earned, and against its account what it has merited.
   Sura 2, l.286.

47 And when the angels said: 'Mary, God has chosen thee, and purified thee; He has chosen thee above all women.

Mary be obedient to thy Lord, prostrating and bowing before Him.'
Sura 3, l.42–3

48 You will not attain piety until you expend of what you love.
Sura 3, l.92.

49 It was by some mercy of God that thou wast gentle to them; hadst thou been harsh and hard of heart, they would have scattered from about thee. So pardon them, and pray forgiveness for them, and take counsel with them in the affair; and when thou art resolved, put thy trust in God.
Sura 3, l.159.

50 Every soul shall taste of death; you shall surely be paid in full your wages on the Day of Resurrection. Whosoever is removed from the Fire and admitted to Paradise, shall win the triumph. The present life is but the joy of delusion.
Sura 3, l.185.

51 Surely in the creation of the heavens and earth and in the alternation of night and day there are signs for men possessed of minds who remember God, standing and sitting and on their sides, and reflect upon the creation of the heavens and the earth. 'Our Lord, thou has not created this for vanity!'
Sura 3, l.191.

52 Mankind, fear your Lord, who created you of a single soul, and from it created its mate, and from the pair of them scattered abroad many men and women; and fear God by whom you demand one of another, and the wombs; surely God ever watches over you.
Sura 4, l.1.

53 God commands you to deliver trusts back to their owners.
Sura 4, l.58.

54 How is it with you, that you do not fight in the way of God, and for the men, women, and children who, being abased, say, 'Our Lord, bring us forth from this city whose people are evildoers, and appoint to us a protector from Thee?'
Sura 4, l.75.

55 O believers, be you securers of justice, witnesses for God, even though it be against yourselves, or your parents and kinsmen, whether the man be rich or poor.
Sura 4, l.135

56 We have revealed to thee as We revealed to Noah, and the Prophets after him, and We revealed to Abraham, Ishmael, Isaac, Jacob, and the Tribes, Jesus and Job, Jonah and Aaron and Solomon, and We gave to David Psalms, and Messengers We have already told thee of before, and Messengers We have not told thee of; and unto Moses God spoke directly—Messengers bearing good tidings, and warning, so that mankind might have no argument against God, after the Messengers; God is All-mighty, All-wise.
Sura 4, l.163–4.

57 People of the Book, go not beyond the bounds in your religion, and say not as to God but the truth. The Messiah, Jesus son of Mary, was only the Messenger of God, and His Word that He committed to Mary, and a spirit from Him. So believe in God and His Messengers,

and say not, 'Three'. Refrain; better is it for you. God is only One God. Glory be to Him—that He should have a son! To Him belongs all that is in the heavens and the earth; God suffices for a guardian. The Messiah will not disdain to be a servant of God, neither the angels who are near stationed to Him.
Sura 4, l.171–2.

58 O believers, be you securers of justice, witnesses for God. Let not detestation for a people move you not to be equitable.
Sura 5, l.8.

59 No creature is there crawling on the earth, no bird flying with its wings, but they are nations like unto yourselves.
Sura 6, l.38.

60 With Him are the keys of the Unseen; none knows them but He. He knows what is in land and sea; not a leaf falls, but He knows it.
Sura 6, l.59.

61 It is God who splits the grain and the date-stone, brings forth the living from the dead; He brings for the dead too from the living. So that then is God; then how are you perverted? He splits the sky into dawn, and has made the night for a repose, and the sun and moon for a reckoning.
Sura 6, l.96–7.

62 Say: 'As for me, my Lord has guided me to a straight path, a right religion, the creed of Abraham, a man of pure faith; he was no idolater.' Say: 'My prayer, my ritual sacrifice, my living, my dying—all belongs to God, the Lord of all Being.'
Sura 6, l.162.

63 To every nation a term; when their term comes they shall not put it back by a single hour nor put it forward.
Sura 7, l.34.

64 Of the people of Moses there is a nation who guide by the truth, and by it act with justice.
Sura 7, l.159.

65 And when thy Lord took from the Children of Adam, from their loins, their seed, and made them testify touching themselves, 'Am I not your Lord?' They said, 'Yes, we testify'—lest you should say on the Day of Resurrection, 'As for us, we were heedless of this.'
Sura 7, l.172.

66 To God belong the Names Most Beautiful; so call Him by them.
Sura 7, l.180.

67 O believers, fear God, and be with the truthful ones.
Sura 9, l.119.

68 And God summons to the Abode of Peace.
Sura 10, l.26.

69 Surely God wrongs not men anything, but themselves men wrong.
Sura 10, l.45.

70 And the king said: 'I saw in a dream seven fat kine, and seven lean ones devouring them; likewise seven green ears of corn, and seven withered. My counsellors, pronounce to me upon my dream, if you are expounders of dreams.' 'A hotchpotch of nightmares!' they said.
Sura 12, l.43–4.

71 It is He who shows you the lightning, for fear and hope,

and produces the heavy clouds; the thunder proclaims His praise, and the angels, in awe of Him.
Sura 13, l.13.

72 Hast thou not seen how God has struck a similitude? A good word is as a good tree—its roots are firm, and its branches are in heaven; it gives its produce every season by the leave of its Lord. So God strikes similitudes for men; haply they will remember. And the likeness of a corrupt word is as a corrupt tree—uprooted from the earth, having no stablishment. God confirms those who believe with the firm word, in the present life and in the world to come.
Sura 14, l.24–7.

73 And when thy Lord said to the angels, 'See, I am creating a mortal of a clay of mud moulded. When I have shaped him, and breathed My spirit in him, fall you down, bowing before him!'
Sura 15, l.28–9.

74 He created man of a sperm-drop; and behold, he is a manifest adversary.
Sura 16, l.4.

75 Man prays for evil, as he prays for good; man is ever hasty.
Sura 17, l.11.

76 Thy Lord has decreed you shall not serve any but Him, and to be good to parents, whether one or both of them attains old age with thee; say not to them 'Fie' neither chide them, but speak unto them words respectful, and lower to them the wing of humbleness out of mercy and say: 'My Lord, have mercy on them, as they raised me up when I was little.'
Sura 17, l.23–4.

77 They will question thee concerning the Spirit. Say: 'The Spirit is of the bidding of my Lord. You have been given of knowledge nothing except a little.'
Sura 17, l.85.

78 Say: 'If the sea were ink for the Words of my Lord, the sea would be spent before the Words of my Lord are spent.'
Sura 18, l.110.

79 Whosoever turns away from My remembrance, his shall be a life of narrowness.
Sura 20, l.124.

80 God is the Light of the heavens and the earth; the likeness of His Light is as a niche wherein is a lamp (the lamp in a glass, the glass as it were a glittering star) kindled from a Blessed Tree, an olive that is neither of the East nor of the West whose oil wellnigh would shine, even if no fire touched it; Light upon Light; (God guides to His Light whom He will). (And God strikes similitudes for men, and God has knowledge of everything.)
Sura 24, l.35.

81 Hast thou not seen how that whatsoever is in the heavens and in the earth extols God, and the birds spreading their wings? Each—He knows its prayer and its extolling.
Sura 24, l.41.

82 And of His signs is that He created for you, of yourselves, spouses, that you might repose in them, and He has set between you love and mercy.
Sura 30, l.21.

83 And of His signs is the creation of the heavens and the earth and the variety of your tongues and hues.
Sura 30, l.22.

84 Not a nation there is, but there has passed away in it a warner.
Sura 35, l.24.

85 And when We bless man, he turns away and withdraws aside; but when evil visits him, he is full of endless prayers.
Sura 41, l.51.

86 Hast thou seen him who has taken his caprice to be his God?
Sura 45, l.23.

87 They say: 'There is nothing but our present life; we die, and we live, and nothing but Time destroys us.' Of that they have no knowledge; they merely conjecture.
Sura 45, l.24.

88 Find not fault with one another, neither revile one another by nicknames.
Sura 49, l.11.

89 O mankind, We have created you male and female, and appointed you races and tribes, that you may know one another. Surely the noblest among you in the sight of God is the most godfearing of you. God is All-knowing, All-aware.
Sura 49, l.13.

90 Be not as those who forgot God, and so He caused them to forget their souls.
Sura 59, l.18.

91 They fulfil their vows, and fear a day whose evil is upon the wing; they give food, for the love of Him, to the needy, the orphan, the captive: 'We feed you only for the Face of God; we desire no recompense from you, no thankfulness.'
Sura 76, l.7–9.

92 But as for him who feared the Station of his Lord and forbade the soul its caprice, surely Paradise shall be the refuge.
Sura 79, l.40.

93 When the sun shall be darkened, when the stars shall be thrown down, when the mountains shall be set moving, when the pregnant camels shall be neglected, when the savage beasts shall be mustered, when the seas shall be set boiling, when the souls shall be coupled, when the buried infant shall be asked for what sin she was slain, when the scrolls shall be unrolled, when heaven shall be stripped off, when Hell shall be set blazing, when Paradise shall be brought nigh, then shall a soul know what it has produced.
Sura 81, 1–14.

94 No! I swear by the slinkers, the runners, the sinkers, by the night swarming, by the dawn sighing, truly this is the word of a noble Messenger.
Sura 81, 15–19.

95 By heaven of the returning rain, by earth splitting with verdure, surely it is a decisive word; it is no merriment.
Sura 86, l.11–14.

96 By the snorting chargers, by the strikers of fire, by the dawn raiders blazing a trail of dust, cleaving there with a host! Surely Man is ungrateful to his Lord.

Sura 100, 1–6.

97 Woe to those that pray and are heedless of their prayers, to those who make display and refuse charity.
Sura 107, 1.4–7.

Korda, Sir Alexander 1893–1956

Hungarian-born British film producer. He worked in Vienna, Berlin and Hollywood before coming to Britain in the early 1930s where he founded London Film Productions and the Denham Studios.

98 One can be unhappy before eating caviar, even after, but at least not *during*.
1979 In *Newsweek*, 26 Nov.

99 Inside every banker, even the governor of the Bank of England, there lies a gambling streak. In me, they recognise one of their own kind.
Quoted in Michael Wilding and Pamela Wilcox *Apple Sauce* (1982).

1 It's not enough to be Hungarian, you must have talent too.
Attributed. The predominance of Eastern European employees at Denham Studios in the 1930s was a topical joke.

Korn, Arthur 1891–1978

German-born architect, planner and teacher.

2 A new glass age has begun, which is equal in beauty to the old one of Gothic windows.
1926 *Glas im Bau und als Gebrauchsgegenstand* (translated as *Glass in Modern Architecture*, 1967).

Korthals, Robert 1933–

Canadian bank president (1981–95).

3 The easiest way to steal from a bank is to own one.
Quoted by Diane Francis in *Controlling Interest: Who Owns Canada?* (1986).

Kosinski, Jerzy Nikodem 1933–91

Polish-born US novelist. His best-known books are *The Painted Bird* (1965) and *Being There* (1971).

4 I rent everything, other than the gift of life itself, which was given to me without any predictable lease, a gift that can be withdrawn at any time.
1991 Interview given three days before his suicide, in the *Weekend Guardian*, 25–6 May.

Kramer, Larry (Lawrence) 1935–

US novelist, playwright and screenwriter. He is best known for his controversial gay novel *Faggots* (1978), and his plays dealing with AIDS, notably *The Normal Heart* (1985).

5 We're all going to go crazy, living this epidemic every minute, while the rest of the world goes on out there, all around us, as if nothing is happening, going on with their own lives and not knowing what it's like, what we're going through. We're living through war, but where they're living it's peacetime, and we're all in the same country.
1985 Ned speaking of gay men with AIDS. *The Normal Heart*, act 2, sc.11.

Krasna, Norman 1909–84

US playwright and screenwriter. He won an Academy Award for

Princess O'Rourke (1943). Other films include *Bachelor Mother* (1939) and *Indiscreet* (1958).

6 How dare he make love to me and not be a married man?
1958 Line delivered by Ingrid Bergman in *Indiscreet*.

Kraus, Karl 1874–1936

Austrian critic and dramatist, publisher and sole writer of the radical satirical magazine *Die Fackel* ('The Torch', 1899–1936). He wrote the apocalyptic satirical play *The Last Days of Mankind* (1919), and collections of aphorisms.

7 Today's literature: prescriptions written by patients.
Aphorism collected in Heinrich Fischer (ed) *Beim Wort genommen* (1955). Translated by Harry Zohn in *Half-truths and one-and-a-half truths* (1986).

8 Why didn't Eternity have this deformed age aborted? Its birthmark is the stamp of a newspaper, its medium is printer's ink, and in its veins flows ink.
Aphorism collected in Heinrich Fischer (ed) *Beim Wort genommen* (1955). Translated by Harry Zohn in *Half-truths and one-and-a-half truths* (1986).

9 The making of a journalist: no ideas and the ability to express them.
Aphorism collected in Heinrich Fischer (ed) *Beim Wort genommen* (1955). Translated by Harry Zohn in *Half-truths and one-and-a-half truths* (1986).

10 A historian is often only a journalist facing backwards.
Aphorism collected in Heinrich Fischer (ed) *Beim Wort genommen* (1955). Translated by Harry Zohn in *Half-truths and one-and-a-half truths* (1986).

11 How is the world ruled and led to war? Diplomats lie to journalists and believe these lies when they see them in print.
Aphorism collected in Heinrich Fischer (ed) *Beim Wort genommen* (1955). Translated by Harry Zohn in *Half-truths and one-and-a-half truths* (1986).

12 One ought to acknowledge the significance for mankind of the simultaneous invention of gunpowder and printer's ink.
Aphorism collected in Heinrich Fischer (ed) *Beim Wort genommen* (1955). Translated by Harry Zohn in *Half-truths and one-and-a-half truths* (1986).

Krishnamurti, Jiddu 1895–1986

Indian-born mystic and spiritual teacher. The theosophist Annie Besant in 1925 proclaimed him Messiah and from then on he travelled the world, teaching a way of life free from the conditioning of culture, race or religion.

13 I maintain that truth is a pathless land, and you cannot approach it by any path whatsoever, by any religion, by any sect.
1929 Speech in Holland. Quoted in Terry Lynn Taylor *Messengers of Light*, ch.32.

14 The authority of a belief imposed by religion surely destroys the discovery of reality. One relies on authority because one is afraid to stand alone.
1970 BBC interview, 7 Dec.

Kristol, Irving 1920–

US economist and academic, often considered as the founder of neoconservatism.

15 History does not provide us with any instance of a society that repressed the economic liberties of the

individual while being solicitous of his other liberties.
1978 *Two Cheers for Capitalism*, introduction.

16 The fact of affluence is indisputable… Nevertheless, not many of us *feel* that well off. The instinct for contentment seems to have withered even as our economic condition has radically improved.
1978 *Two Cheers for Capitalism*, ch.1.

17 The elitist attitude is basically suspicious of, and hostile to, the market precisely because the market is so vulgarly democratic—one dollar, one vote.
1978 *Two Cheers for Capitalism*, ch.2.

Kroc, Ray(mond) A 1902–84

US entrepreneur, developer of the McDonald's fast-food chain.

18 Luck is a dividend of sweat. The more you sweat, the luckier you get.
1988 Quoted by Penny Moser 'The McDonald's Mystique', in *Fortune*, 4 Jul.

19 If they were drowning to death, I would put a hose in their mouth.
1988 On competitors. In *Fortune*, 4 Jul.

Kronecker, Leopold 1823–91

German mathematician, who worked in algebraic number theory and the foundations of analysis, and lectured widely. He held that mathematics should be based on whole numbers, rejecting the infinite, irrational and imaginary.

20 God made the integers, man made the rest.
Quoted in F Cajori *A History of Mathematics* (1919).

Kronenberger, Louis 1904–80

US writer, lecturer and critic. His books include novels and autobiographical reminiscences as well as critical works on literature and culture, and biographies.

21 Kings and Desperate Men.
1942 Title of book on 18c England.

22 The trouble with our age is that it is all signpost and no destination.
1954 *Company Manners*, 'The Spirit of The Age'.

Kruger, Paulus 1825–1904

South African soldier and statesman, President of the Transvaal (1883–1902) and head of the provisional government in the first Boer War. During the second Boer War he was forced to flee to Europe, and he died in Switzerland.

23 They have asked me for my trousers, and I have given them; for my coat, and I have given that also; now they want my life, and that I cannot give.
1899 Speech in the Raad, 7 Sep, at the beginning of the second Boer War, 1899–1902.

Krugman, Paul R 1953–

US economist and columnist, Professor of Economics and International Affairs at Princeton University.

24 The trouble with poverty, as an issue, is that it has basically exhausted the patience of the general public.
1992 *The Age of Diminished Expectations*.

25 Given that the deepest problem with the US economy is slow productivity growth, it is difficult to argue for tax increases that might reduce incentives… There seems to be a public consensus that Donald Trump is the price of progress.
1992 *The Age of Diminished Expectations*.

26 The exchange rate is only a statistic, not a symbol of national honor and virility.
1994 Quoted in the *New York Times*, 26 Jun.

Krutch, Joseph Wood 1893–1970

US author, teacher and critic. He is the author of *The Modern Temper* (1929) and *The Measure of Man* (1954).

27 A tragic writer does not have to believe in God, but he must believe in man.
1929 *The Modern Temper*, 'The Tragic Fallacy'.

28 Electronic calculators can solve problems which the man who made them cannot solve; but no government subsidized commission of engineers and physicists could create a worm.
1949 *The Twelve Seasons*, 'February'.

29 The most serious charge which can be brought against New England is not Puritanism but February.
1949 *The Twelve Seasons*, 'February'.

30 Cats seem to go on the principle that it never does any harm to ask for what you want.
1949 *The Twelve Seasons*, 'February'.

Kubrick, Stanley 1928–99

US screenwriter, film producer and director. His films include *Spartacus* (1960), *2001: A Space Odyssey* (1969), the controversial *A Clockwork Orange* (1971) and *Full Metal Jacket* (1987).

31 Gentlemen, you can't fight in here. This is the war room.
1963 *Dr Strangelove: or How I stopped worrying and learned to love the bomb* (with Terry Southern and Peter George).

32 The great nations have always acted like gangsters, and the small nations like prostitutes.
1963 In *The Guardian*.

33 The very meaninglessness of life forces man to create his own meaning. If it can be written or thought, it can be filmed.
Quoted in *Halliwell's Filmgoer's and Video Viewer's Companion* (1999).

Kuhn, Maggie 1905–95

US writer and social reformer, founder of the Gray Panthers.

34 The ultimate indignity is to be given a bedpan by a stranger who calls you by your first name.
1978 In the *Observer*, 20 Aug.

Kuhn, Thomas S(amuel) 1922–96

US historian and philosopher of science. His major work is *The Structure of Scientific Revolutions* (1962), a cornerstone of modern approaches to the philosophy and history of science.

35 Effective research scarcely begins before a scientific community thinks it has acquired firm answers to questions like the following: What are the fundamental entities of which the universe is composed? How do these interact with each other and with the senses? What questions may legitimately be asked about such entities and what techniques employed in seeking solutions?
1962 *The Structure of Scientific Revolutions*.

Kundera, Milan 1929–

Czech-born French novelist.

36 The Unbearable Lightness of Being.
  1984 Title of novel.

Küng, Hans 1928–

Swiss Roman Catholic theologian. His questioning of received doctrine aroused controversy, and the Vatican withdrew his authority to teach as a Catholic theologian in 1979. He defended himself in *Why I Am Still A Christian* (1987).

37 A Church which abandons the truth abandons itself.
  Die Kirche (translated by Ray and Rosalee Ockenden as *The Church*, 1967).

Kunitz, Stanley Jasspon 1905–

US poet and editor, whose style is at once intellectual and passionate. His poetry collections include *Selected Poems, 1928–1958* (1958, Pulitzer Prize winner) and *Next-to-Last Things: New Poems and Essays* (1985). In 2000 he became the US Poet Laureate.

38 A poem is at once the most primitive and most sophisticated use of language, but my emphasis is on the former.
  1985 *Next-to-Last Things*, 'The Wisdom of the Body'.

39 The deepest thing I know is that I am living and dying at once, and my conviction is to report that dialogue.
  1987 In the *New York Times*, 11 Mar.

Kuralt, Charles 1934–97

US writer and broadcaster.

40 It takes an earthquake to remind us that we walk on the crust of an unfinished earth.
  1994 In *Sunday Morning*, CBS T V, 23 Jan.

Kurosawa, Akira 1910–98

Japanese film director and winner of numerous international awards for his films. Best known in the West for his full-blooded adaptations of Shakespeare.

41 Like a steak spread with butter and topped with good, rich, broiled eels.
  1965 His concept of a great film. In *Japan Quarterly*, vol.12.

42 The Japanese see self-assertion as immoral and self-sacrifice as the sensible course to take in life.
  1982 *Something like an Autobiography.*

Kushner, Tony 1956–

US playwright, whose highly political plays include the two-part *Angels in America* (1991–2, Pulitzer Prize 1993), on the effects of AIDS in New York.

43 I wanted to attempt something of ambition and size even if that meant I might be accused of straying too close to ambition's ugly twin, pretentiousness.
  1993 Of his *Angels in America*, written in two parts. In the *New York Times*, 21 Nov.

Kurz, Mordecai 1934–

US economist, Professor at Stanford University.

44 There is only one truth, and many opinions. Therefore, most people are wrong most of the time.
  1985 In *Fortune*, 3 Apr.

Kyd, Thomas 1558–94

English dramatist.

45 In time the savage bull sustains the yoke;
  In time all haggard hawks will stoop to lure;
  In time small wedges cleave the hardest oak,
  In time the flint is pierced with softest shower,
  And she in time will fall from her disdain,
  And rue the sufferance of your friendly pain.
  c.1589 *The Spanish Tragedy*, act 2, sc.1.

46 Where words prevail not, violence prevails;
  But gold doth more than either of them both.
  c.1589 *The Spanish Tragedy*, act 2, sc.1.

47 Oh eyes, no eyes, but fountains fraught with tears;
  Oh life, no life, but lively form of death;
  Oh world, no world, but mass of public wrongs.
  c.1589 *The Spanish Tragedy*, act 3, sc.2.

48 I'll trust myself, myself shall be my friend.
  c.1589 *The Spanish Tragedy*, act 3, sc.2.

49 Thus must we toil in other men's extremes,
  That know not how to remedy our own.
  c.1589 *The Spanish Tragedy*, act 3, sc.6.

50 For what's a play without a woman in it?
  c.1589 *The Spanish Tragedy*, act 4, sc.1.

L

Labé, Louise 1526–66

A poet of the École Lyonnaise who wrote sonnets, elegies and a prose work, *Débat de Folie et d'Amour* (1555, 'Debate Between Folly and Love').

51 *Quelque rigueur qui loge en votre coeur,*
  Amour s'en peut un jour rendre vainqueur.
  That little harshness which resides in your heart,
  Love will vanquish someday.
  1555 *Elégies*, no.1.

52 *Où donc es-tu, ô âme bien-aimée?*
  Where are you now, oh soul desired?
  1555 *Sonnets*, no.6.

53 *Je vis, je meurs; je me brûle et me noie.*
  I live, I die; I am on fire and I drown.
  1555 *Sonnets*, no.8.

54 *Ne reprenez, dame, si j'ai aimé,*
  Si j'ai senti mille torches ardentes,
  Mille travaux, mille douleurs mordantes,
  Si, en pleurant, j'ai mon temps consumé.
  Do not blame me, madam, if I loved,
  If I felt one thousand burning torches,
  One thousand labours, or one thousand scathing pains,
  If, in crying, I spent all my time.
  1555 *Sonnets*, no.24.

Labouchère, Henry Du Pré 1831–1912

English radical journalist and politician. A Liberal MP (1865–8, 1880–1906), in 1876 he founded the investigative journal *Truth*.

55 Nothing has conduced more to shake that decent respect for the living symbol of the state that goes by the name of royalty than the ever-recurring rattle of the money box.
1884 In the *Fortnightly Review*, Feb.

La Bruyère, Jean de 1645–96

French moralist author who tutored Louis de Bourbon, grandson of the Great Condé. His *Caractères de Théophraste* (1688) made his reputation but won him many enemies.

56 *Tout est dit, et l'on vient trop tard depuis plus de sept mille ans qu'il y a des hommes et qui pensent.*
Everything has been said. After seven thousand years of human thought, we have come too late.
1688 *Les Caractères ou les mœurs de ce siècle*, 'Des ouvrages de l'esprit', no.1.

57 *C'est un métier que de faire un livre, comme de faire une pendule; il faut plus que de l'esprit pour être auteur.*
It is as much a trade to write a book as it is to make a watch; it takes more than wit to make an author.
1688 *Les Caractères ou les mœurs de ce siècle*, 'Des ouvrages de l'esprit', no.3.

58 *Une belle femme qui a les qualités d'un honnête homme est ce qu'il y a au monde d'un commerce plus délicieux: l'on trouve en elle tout le mérite des deux sexes.*
A beautiful woman who has the qualities of a gentleman is the most pleasing person in all the world: one finds in her all the merit of both sexes.
1688 *Les Caractères ou les mœurs de ce siècle*, 'Des femmes', no.13.

59 *Les femmes sont extrêmes: elles sont meilleures ou pires que les hommes.*
Women are all in extremes: they are either better or worse than men.
1688 *Les Caractères ou les mœurs de ce siècle*, 'Des femmes', no.53.

60 *Un homme est plus fidèle au secret d'autrui qu'au sien propre; une femme au contraire garde mieux son secret que celui d'autrui.*
A man keeps another person's secret better than his own; a woman, on the contrary, keeps her own secrets better than those of others.
1688 *Les Caractères ou les mœurs de ce siècle*, 'Des femmes', no.58.

61 *Une femme insensible est celle qui n'a pas encore vu celui qu'elle doit aimer.*
A dispassionate woman is one who has yet to see the one she should love.
1688 *Les Caractères ou les mœurs de ce siècle*, 'Des femmes', no.81.

62 *Le temps, qui fortifie les amitiés, affaiblit l'amour.*
Time, which strengthens friendships, weakens love.
1688 *Les Caractères ou les mœurs de ce siècle*, 'Du cœur', no.4.

63 *L'amour et l'amitié s'excluent l'un l'autre.*
Love and friendship exclude one another.
1688 *Les Caractères ou les mœurs de ce siècle*, 'Du cœur', no.7.

64 *L'amour qui naît subitement est le plus long à guérir.*
Love which strikes suddenly takes the longest to cure.
1688 *Les Caractères ou les mœurs de ce siècle*, 'Du cœur', no.12.

65 *Les amours meurent par le dégoût, et l'oubli les enterre.*
Loves die from disgust, and forgetting buries them.
1688 *Les Caractères ou les mœurs de ce siècle*, 'Du cœur', no.32.

66 *Qu'il est difficile d'être content de quelqu'un!*
How difficult it is to be happy with someone!
1688 *Les Caractères ou les mœurs de ce siècle*, 'Du cœur', no.65.

67 *L'esclave n'a qu'un maître; l'ambitieux en a autant qu'il y a des gens utiles à sa fortune.*
A slave has but one master; an ambitious person has as many as he needs to make his fortune.
1688 *Les Caractères ou les mœurs de ce siècle*, 'Du cœur', no.70.

68 *Il fera demain ce qu'il fait aujourd'hui et ce qu'il fit hier; et il meurt ainsi après avoir vécu.*
What he does tomorrow will be what he did today and yesterday; and he shall die after having lived this way.
1688 *Les Caractères ou les mœurs de ce siècle*, 'De la ville', no.12.

69 *La vie est courte et ennuyeuse: elle se passe toute à désirer.*
Life is short and bothersome: all we do is desire what we do not have.
1688 *Les Caractères ou les mœurs de ce siècle*, 'De l'homme', no.19.

70 *Si la vie est misérable, elle est pénible à supporter; si elle est heureuse, il est horrible de la perdre. L'un revient à l'autre.*
If life is miserable, it is difficult to endure; if it is happy, it is horrible to lose. They come to the same thing.
1688 *Les Caractères ou les mœurs de ce siècle*, 'De l'homme', no.33.

71 *A parler humainement, la mort a un bel endroit, qui est de mettre fin à la vieillesse.*
To speak humanely, death has a useful function: it puts an end to old age.
1688 *Les Caractères ou les mœurs de ce siècle*, 'De l'homme', no.45.

72 *Il n'y a pour l'homme que trois événements: naître, vivre et mourir. Il ne se sent pas naître, il souffre à mourir, et il oublie de vivre.*
There are only three great events for a person: to be born, to live and to die. He does not feel his own birth, he suffers upon death and he forgets to live.
1688 *Les Caractères ou les mœurs de ce siècle*, 'De l'homme', no.48.

73 *Les enfants sont hautains, dédaigneux, colères, envieux, curieux, intéressés, paresseux, volages, timides, intempérants, menteurs, dissimulés…ils ne veulent point souffrir de mal, et aiment à en faire: ils sont déjà des hommes.*
Children are haughty, disdainful, angry, envious, curious, interested, lazy, fickle, shy, self-indulgent, liars, deceivers…they do not wish to suffer evil, but like to do evil: they are already adults.
1688 *Les Caractères ou les mœurs de ce siècle*, 'De l'homme', no.50.

74 *Les enfants n'ont ni passé ni avenir, et, ce qui ne nous arrive guère, ils jouissent du présent.*
Children have neither past nor future. They live in the present, something which rarely happens to us.
1688 *Les Caractères ou les mœurs de ce siècle*, 'De l'homme', no.51.

75 *Il y a une espèce de honte d'être heureux à la vue de certaines misères.*
There is a type of shame which comes from being happy at another's distress.
1688 *Les Caractères ou les mœurs de ce siècle*, 'De l'homme', no.82.

76 *La plupart des hommes emploient la meilleure partie de leur vie à rendre l'autre misérable.*
Most people spend the greater part of their lives making others miserable.
1688 *Les Caractères ou les mœurs de ce siècle*, 'De l'homme', no.102.

77 *Le flatteur n'a pas assez bonne opinion de soi ni des autres.*
The flatterer does not have a good opinion of himself or of others.
1688 *Les Caractères ou les mœurs de ce siècle*, 'Des jugements', no.90.

78 *Ceux qui emploient mal leur temps sont les premiers à se plaindre de sa brièveté.*
Those who make poor use of their time are the first to complain of its brevity.
1688 *Les Caractères ou les mœurs de ce siècle*, 'Des jugements', no.101.

79 *L'impossibilité où je suis de prouver que Dieu n'est pas me découvre son existence.*
The impossibility I find myself in to prove that God does not exist proves to me his existence.
1688 *Les Caractères ou les mœurs de ce siècle*, 'Des esprits forts', no.13.

Laclos, Pierre-Ambroise Choderlos de 1741–1803

French artillery officer, best known for his study of human vices and virtues in *Les Liaisons dangereuses* (1782), as well as his advocacy of women's education in *De l'Education des femmes* (1785).

80 *J'ai bien besoin d'avoir cette femme, pour me sauver du ridicule d'en être amoureux.*
I need to possess this woman in order to save myself from the absurdity of being in love with her.
1782 *Les Liaisons dangereuses*, letter 4.

81 *Nos deux passions favorites, la gloire de la défense et le plaisir de la défaite.*
The glory of the resistance and the pleasure of the defeat are our two favourite passions.
1782 *Les Liaisons dangereuses*, letter 10.

82 *Il ne faut se permettre d'excès qu'avec les gens qu'on veut quitter bientôt.*
We should never permit ourselves to behave in excess except with those whom we will leave soon.
1782 *Les Liaisons dangereuses*, letter 10.

83 *En vérité, plus je vis, et plus je suis tenté de croire qu'il n'y a que vous et moi dans le monde, qui valions quelque chose.*
In truth, the more I live, the more I am tempted to believe that only you and I are of any value at all in the world.
1782 *Les Liaisons dangereuses*, letter 100.

84 *J'avoue bien que l'argent ne fait pas le bonheur; mais il faut avouer aussi qu'il le facilite beaucoup.*
I will admit that money does not bring happiness, but it must also be admitted that it facilitates much.
1782 *Les Liaisons dangereuses*, letter 104.

85 *Ce n'est pas assez pour moi de la posséder, je veux qu'elle se livre.*
It's not enough to possess her. I want her to abandon herself.
1782 *Les Liaisons dangereuses*, letter 110.

86 *La haine est toujours plus clairvoyante et plus ingénieuse que l'amitié.*
Hate is always more clairvoyant and ingenious than friendship.
1782 *Les Liaisons dangereuses*, letter 113.

87 *Pour les hommes, l'infidélité n'est pas l'inconstance.*
For men, infidelity is not inconstancy.
1782 *Les Liaisons dangereuses*, letter 134.

88 *On s'ennuie de tout, mon Ange, c'est une loi de la Nature; ce n'est pas ma faute.*
One gets bored of everything, my Angel, it's a law of nature; it's not my fault.
1782 *Les Liaisons dangereuses*, letter 141.

89 *Quand une femme frappe dans le coeur d'une autre, elle manque rarement de trouver l'endroit sensible, et la blessure est incurable.*
When one woman touches another's heart, she rarely has trouble finding the sensitive spot and the wound is incurable.
1782 *Les Liaisons dangereuses*, letter 145.

90 *Apprenez qu'on ne sort de l'esclavage que par une grande révolution.*
Learn that one never escapes slavery except by a great revolution.
1785 *De l'Éducation des femmes.*

Ladd, Alan 1913–64

US film star, best known for *The Blue Dahlia* (1946), *The Great Gatsby* (1949) and *Shane* (1953).

91 A man's gotta do what a man's gotta do.
1953 Line delivered in *Shane* (screenplay by A B Guthrie).

La Fayette, Marie-Madeleine Pioche de La Vergne 1634–93

French novelist. Although married to François Motier, she lived with La Rochefoucauld.

92 *L'amour était toujours mêlé aux affaires et les affaires à l'amour.*
Love has always mixed with politics and politics with love.
1678 *La Princesse de Clèves.*

93 *On persuade aisément une vérité agréable.*
It is easy to persuade one with an agreeable truth.
1678 *La Princesse de Clèves.*

94 *Les passions peuvent me conduire; mais elles ne sauraient m'aveugler.*
Passions can lead me on, but never blind me.
1678 *La Princesse de Clèves.*

95 *La honte est la plus violente de toutes les passions.*
Shame is the most violent of all the passions.
1678 *La Princesse de Clèves.*

La Fontaine, Jean de 1621–95

French poet and moralist. His *Contes et nouvelles en vers* ('Tales and Novels in Verse', 1665) was followed by *Fables choisies mises en vers* ('Selected Fables in Verse', 1668–94).

96 *Je me sers d'animaux pour instruire les hommes.*
I use animals to educate people.
1668 *Fables, à Monseigneur le Dauphin.*

97 *Nous n'écoutons d'instincts que ceux qui sont les nôtres,*
Et ne croyons le mal que quand il est venu.
We only trust our own instincts
And only believe the worst when it comes true.
1668 *Fables*, pt.1, no.8, 'L'hirondelle et les petits oiseaux'.

98 *La raison du plus fort est toujours la meilleure.*
The reason of the strongest is always the best.
1668 *Fables*, pt.1, no.10, 'Le loup et l'agneau'.

99 *Il accusait toujours les miroirs d'être faux.*
He was always blaming mirrors for being untrue.
1668 *Fables*, pt.1, no.11, 'L'homme et son image'.

1 *Plutôt souffrir que mourir,*
C'est la devise des hommes.
It is better to suffer than to die.
That is the motto of mankind.
1668 *Fables*, pt.1, no.16, 'La mort et le bûcheron'.

2 *Je plie, et ne romps pas.*
I bend but do not break.
1668 *Fables*, pt.1, no.22, 'Le chêne et le roseau'. The reed speaks
to the oak tree.

3 *Le mensonge et les vers de tout temps sont amis.*
Lies and literature have always been friends.
1668 *Fables*, pt.2, no.1, 'Contre ceux qui ont le goût difficile'.

4 *Patience et longueur de temps*
Font plus que force ni que rage.
Patience and longevity
Are worth more than force and rage.
1668 *Fables*, pt.2, no.11, 'Le lion et le rat'.

5 *C'est double plaisir de tromper le trompeur.*
It's doubly sweet to deceive the deceiver.
1668 *Fables*, pt.2, no.15, 'Le coq et le renard'.

6 *Tout au monde est mêlé d'amertume et de charmes:*
La guerre a ses douceurs, l'hymen a ses alarmes.
Everything in the world is a mixture of the sweet and the
sour:
War has its own sweetness and marriage its alarms.
1668 *Fables*, pt.3, no.1, 'Le meunier, son fils et l'âne'.

7 *En toute chose il faut considérer la fin.*
One must consider the end in everything.
1668 *Fables*, pt.3, no.5, 'Le renard et le bouc'.

8 *Amour est un étrange maître.*
Heureux qui peut ne le connaître
Que par récit, lui ni ses coups!
Love is a cruel conqueror.
Happy is he who knows him through stories
And not by his blows!
1668 *Fables*, pt.4, no.1, 'Le lion amoureux'.

9 *Le geai paré des plumes du paon.*
A bluejay in peacock feathers.
1668 *Fables*, pt.4, no.9, 'Le geai paré des plumes du paon'.

10 *Chacun se dit ami; mais fol qui s'y repose:*
Rien n'est plus commun que ce nom,
Rien n'est plus rare que la chose.
Everyone calls himself a friend; foolish is he who
believes it:
Nothing is more common than the name friend,

And nothing is more rare than the real thing.
1668 *Fables*, pt.4, no.17, 'Parole de Socrate'.

11 *Ne possédait pas l'or; mais l'or le possédait.*
He never owned his gold; his gold owned him.
1668 *Fables*, pt.4, no.20, 'L'avare qui a perdu son trésor'.

12 *Une ample Comédie à cent actes divers,*
Et dont la scène est l'Univers.
A grand comedy in one hundred different acts,
On the stage of the universe.
1668 *Fables*, pt.5, no.1, 'Le bûcheron et Mercure'.

13 *Un auteur gâte tout quand il veut trop bien faire.*
An author spoils everything when he wants too much to
do good.
1668 *Fables*, pt.5, no.1, 'Le bûcheron et Mercure'.

14 *Garde-toi, tant que tu vivras,*
De juger des gens sur la mine.
Beware as long as you live,
Of judging others according to appearance alone.
1668 *Fables*, pt.6, no.5, 'Le cochet, le chat et le souriceau'.

15 *Sur les ailes du Temps la tristesse s'envole.*
Grief is carried off by the wings of time.
1668 *Fables*, pt.6, no.21, 'La jeune veuve'.

16 *Quand l'eau courbe un bâton, ma raison la redresse.*
When water curves a stick, my reason straightens it out.
1668 *Fables*, pt.7, no.18, 'Un animal dans la lune'.

17 *Fortune aveugle suit aveugle hardiesse.*
Blind fortune pursues inconsiderate rashness.
1668 *Fables*, pt.10, no.13, 'Les deux aventuriers et le talisman'.

18 *Tout est mystère dans l'Amour.*
Everything about love is a mystery.
1668 *Fables*, pt.12, no.14, 'L'Amour et la folie'.

19 *Tous chemins vont à Rome.*
All roads lead to Rome.
1668 *Fables*, pt.12, no.29, 'Le juge arbitre, l'hospitalier, et le
solitaire'.

Lagerfeld, Karl 1938–

German-born French fashion designer.

20 She never wanted to be sexy, but in those days ambitions
were different, and she was the most ambitious of them
all.
1993 Of Wallis Simpson, Duchess of Windsor. In the *New York
Times*, 19 Sep.

21 Fashion is the image of an age and can tells its story
better than a speech.
1994 In the *Daily Telegraph*, 20 Oct.

Lamartine, Alphonse Marie Louis de 1790–1869

French poet and revolutionary politician, a minister in the
provisional government after 1848. His best-known work is his
first volume of lyrical poems, *Méditations poétiques* (1820). His
historical works include the *Histoire de la Révolution de 1848*
(1849).

22 *Un seul être vous manque, et tout est dépeuplé.*
One being only is wanting, and your whole world is
bereft of people.
1820 *Méditations poétiques*, 'L'Isolement'.

23 France is revolutionary or she is nothing at all. The
revolution of 1789 is her political religion.
1847 *Histoire des Girondins*.

24 At its birth, the republic gave voice to three words—Liberty, Equality, Fraternity! If Europe is wise and just, each of those words signifies Peace.
    1848 *A Manifesto to the Powers*, 4 Mar.

Lamb, Lady Caroline 1785–1828

English novelist and aristocrat, daughter of the Earl of Bessborough and wife of Prime Minister William Lamb, 2nd Viscount Melbourne, notorious for her nine-month devotion (1812–3) to Lord Byron.

25 Mad, bad, and dangerous to know.
    1812 Of Byron. Journal entry, Mar, after meeting the poet at a ball. Quoted in Elizabeth Jenkins *Lady Caroline Lamb* (1932), ch.6.

Lamb, Charles 1775–1834

English essayist and critic. Together with his sister Mary, he wrote *Tales from Shakespeare* (1807), and his *Specimens of English Dramatic Poets* (1808) contributed to a revival of interest in Elizabethan plays. As 'Elia', he contributed essays to the *London Magazine* from 1820.

26 I have something more to do than feel.
    1796 Letter to Samuel Taylor Coleridge, 27 Sep, on the death of his mother at his sister Mary's hands. Collected in E W Marrs *Letters of Charles and Mary Lamb*, vol.1 (1975).

27 Cultivate simplicity, Coleridge.
    1796 Letter to Samuel Taylor Coleridge, 8 Nov. Collected in E W Marrs *Letters of Charles and Mary Lamb*, vol.1 (1975).

28 The man must have a rare recipe for melancholy, who can be dull in Fleet Street.
    1802 Letter to Thomas Manning, 15 Feb. Collected in E W Marrs *Letters of Charles and Mary Lamb*, vol.2 (1975).

29 Nursed amid her noise, her crowds, her beloved smoke—what have I been doing all my life, if I have not lent out my heart with usury to such scenes?
    1802 Of London. Letter to Thomas Manning, 15 Feb. Collected in E W Marrs *Letters of Charles and Mary Lamb*, vol.2 (1975).

30 Gone before
    To that unknown and silent shore.
    1803 'Hester', stanza 7.

31 Nothing puzzles me more than time and space; and yet nothing troubles me less, as I never think about them.
    1806 Letter to Thomas Manning, 2 Jan. Collected in E W Marrs (ed) *Letters of Charles and Mary Lamb*, vol.3 (1978).

32 A child's a plaything for an hour.
    1809 'Parental Recollections'. This is often attributed to his sister Mary.

33 Anything awful makes me laugh.
    1815 Letter to Robert Southey, 9 Aug. Collected in E W Marrs (ed) *Letters of Charles and Mary Lamb*, vol.3 (1978).

34 This very night I am going to leave off tobacco! Surely there must be some other world in which this unconquerable purpose shall be realized.
    1815 Letter to Thomas Manning, 26 Dec. Collected in E W Marrs (ed) *Letters of Charles and Mary Lamb*, vol.3 (1978).

35 An Archangel a little damaged.
    1816 Of Coleridge. Letter to Wordsworth, 26 Apr. Collected in E W Marrs (ed) *Letters of Charles and Mary Lamb*, vol.3 (1978).

36 The rogue gives you Love Powders, and then a strong horse drench to bring 'em off your stomach that they mayn't hurt you.

1816 Of Coleridge. Letter to Wordsworth, 23 Sep. Collected in E W Marrs (ed) *Letters of Charles and Mary Lamb*, vol.3 (1978).

37 Fanny Kelly's divine plain face.
    1818 Letter to Mary Wordsworth, 18 Feb. Collected in H H Harpter (ed) *Letters of Charles Lamb*, vol.4 (1905).

38 Newspapers always excite curiosity. No one ever lays one down without a feeling of disappointment.
    1822 In the *London Magazine*, May – Jul. Collected in *Essays of Elia*, 'Detached Thoughts of Books and Reading'.

39 Who first invented work—and tied the free
    And holy-day rejoicing spirit down
    To the ever-haunting importunity
    Of business?
    1822 Letter to Bernard Barton, 11 Sep. Collected in H H Harpter (ed) *Letters of Charles Lamb*, vol.4 (1905).

40 I hate a man who swallows it, affecting not to know what he is eating. I suspect his taste in higher matters.
    1823 *Essays of Elia*, 'Grace Before Meat'.

41 In everything that relates to science, I am a whole Encyclopedia behind the rest of the world.
    1823 *Essays of Elia*, 'The Old and the New Schoolmaster'.

42 I know that a sweet child is the sweetest thing in nature…but the prettier the kind of a thing is, the more desirable it is that it should be pretty of its kind.
    1823 *Essays of Elia*, 'A Bachelor's Complaint of the Behaviour of Married People'.

43 If the husband be a man with whom you have lived on a friendly footing before marriage,—if you did not come in on the wife's side,—if you did not sneak into the house in her train, but were an old friend in first habits of intimacy before their courtship was so much as thought on,—look about you… Every long friendship, every old authentic intimacy, must be brought into their office to be new stamped with their currency, as a sovereign Prince calls in the good old money that was coined in some reign before he was born or thought of, to be new marked and minted with the stamp of his authority, before he will let it pass current in the world.
    1823 *Essays of Elia*, 'A Bachelor's Complaint of the Behaviour of Married People'.

44 Ceremony is an invention to take off the uneasy feeling which we derive from knowing ourselves to be less the object of love and esteem with a fellow-creature than some other person is. It endeavours to make up, by superior attentions in little points, for that invidious preference which it is forced to deny in the greater.
    1823 *Essays of Elia*, 'A Bachelor's Complaint of the Behaviour of Married People'.

45 Sentimentally I am disposed to harmony. But organically I am incapable of a tune.
    1823 *Essays of Elia*, 'A Chapter on Ears'.

46 I have no ear.
    1823 *Essays of Elia*, 'A Chapter on Ears'.

47 Presents, I often say, endear Absents.
    1823 *Essays of Elia*, 'A Dissertation upon Roast Pig'.

48 She unbent her mind afterwards—over a book.
    1823 *Essays of Elia*, 'Mrs Battle's Opinions on Whist'.

49 A votary of the desk—a notched and cropt scrivener—one that sucks his substance, as certain sick people are said to do, through a quill.
    1823 *Essays of Elia*, 'Oxford in the Vacation'.

50 The uncommunicating muteness of fishes.
    1823 *Essays of Elia*, 'A Quakers' Meeting'.

51 The human species, according to the best theory I can form of it, is composed of two distinct races, the men who borrow, and the men who lend.
    1823 *Essays of Elia*, 'The Two Races of Men'.

52 Your *borrowers of books*—those mutilators of collections, spoilers of the symmetry of shelves, and creators of odd volumes.
    1823 *Essays of Elia*, 'The Two Races of Men'.

53 Not many sounds in life, and I include all urban and rural sounds, exceed in interest a knock at the door.
    1823 *Essays of Elia*, 'Valentine's Day'.

54 Credulity is the man's weakness, but the child's strength.
    1823 *Essays of Elia*, 'Witches and Other Night-Fears'.

55 How sickness enlarges the dimensions of a man's self to himself.
    1823 *Essays of Elia*, 'The Convalescent'.

56 If dirt were trumps, what hands you would hold!
    1828 Quoted in Leigh Hunt *Lord Byron and his Contemporaries*, p.299.

57 How sickness enlarges the dimensions of a man's self to himself.
    1833 *Last Essays of Elia*, 'The Convalescent'.

58 The drinking man is never less himself than during his sober intervals.
    1833 *Last Essays of Elia*, 'Confessions of a Drunkard'.

59 Books think for me.
    1833 *Last Essays of Elia*, 'Detached Thoughts on Books and Reading'.

60 Things in book's clothing.
    1833 *Last Essays of Elia*, 'Detached Thoughts on Books and Reading'.

61 A poor relation is the most irrelevant thing in nature.
    1833 *Last Essays of Elia*, 'Poor Relations'.

62 A pistol let off at the ear; not a feather to tickle the intellect.
    1833 Of puns. *Last Essays of Elia*, 'Popular Fallacies', no.9.

63 The greatest pleasure I know, is to do good action by stealth, and to have it found out by accident.
    1834 'Table Talk by the late Elia', in *The Athenaeum*, 1834.

64 The last breath I drew in he wished might be through a pipe and exhaled in a pun.
    Quoted in W Toynbee *Diaries of William Charles Macready 1833–1851* (1912).

Lamb, Marjorie 1949–

Canadian ecologist.

65 Suppose our ancestors had discovered nuclear power in the middle ages, and had decided to bury their radioactive fuel.
    1990 *Two Minutes a Day for a Greener Planet*.

Lambert, Constant 1905–51

English composer, conductor and critic. His first success came with the ballet *Romeo and Juliet*, commissioned by Diaghilev in 1926. Subsequently he worked as conductor for the Camargo Society and for Sadler's Wells Ballet.

66 The Appalling Popularity of Music.
    1934 *Music Ho!*, chapter title.

67 There is a definite limit to the length of time a composer can go on writing in one dance rhythm. This limit is obviously reached by Ravel toward the end of *La Valse* and toward the beginning of *Boléro*.
    1934 *Music Ho!*

68 To put it vulgarly, the whole trouble with a folk song is that once you have played it through there is nothing much you can do except play it over again and play it rather louder.
    1934 *Music Ho!*

Lamming, George Eric 1927–

Barbadian novelist. Winner of the Somerset Maugham Prize for literature for his novel *In the Castle of My Skin* (1953), he has also published *The Emigrants* (1954), *Seasons of Adventure* (1960), and *Natives of My Person* (1972).

69 Histr'y ain't got eyes to see everything.
    1953 *In the Castle of My Skin*, ch.6.

70 If you aren't native to a place you have an excellent chance of becoming a gentleman in it.
    1953 *In the Castle of My Skin*, ch.14.

Lamport, Allan 1903–

Canadian politician, Mayor of Toronto (1952–42) and a renowned malapropist.

71 If somebody's gonna stab me in the back, I wanna be there.
    1990 *Quotations from Chairman Lamport*.

Lancaster, Sir James c.1554–1618

English navigator, soldier and merchant. He visited the East Indies in 1591–4 and in 1595 captured Pernambuco. In 1600–3 he commanded the first fleet of the East India Company to visit the East Indies. He promoted the voyages of Hudson, Baffin and others in search of the Northwest Passage.

72 I cannot tell where you should look for me, if you send out any pinnace to seek me; because I live at the devotion of the wind and seas. And thus fare you well; desiring God to send us a merry meeting in this world, if it be his good will and pleasure.
    c.1594 Letter to the East India Company written on the homeward voyage when the two English ships ran into storms off the Cape of Good Hope. Lancaster's ship lost her rudder. Unwilling to risk the other ship, Lancaster ordered her captain to sail straight home, taking the letter with him. *A voyage with three tall ships, the Penelope, admirall, the Marchant Royall, vice-admiral, and the Edward Bonaventure, rear-admiral, to the East Indies… Begun By M. George Raymond, in the yeere 1591, and performed by M. James Lancaster; and written from the mouth of Edmund Barker of Ipswich (his lieutenant in the sayd voyage) by M. Richard Hakluyt*.

Lance, Bert

Former US White House Budget Director.

73 Go out on the front porch of the house, turn the *Washington Post* over with your big toe, and if your name's above the fold, you know you're not going to have a good day.
    1993 Of the Bert Lance Toe Test which he devised for his nine months in the Carter administration. In the *Washington Post*, 6 Oct.

Landers, Ann 1918–2002

US newspaper columnist and 'agony aunt', who offered advice and information on topics such as family life, marriage, social issues and health.

74 Women complain about sex more often than men. Their gripes fall into two major categories: (1) Not enough. (2) Too much.
1968 *Truth Is Stranger…*, ch.2.

Landor, Walter Savage 1775–1864

English writer and poet. His *Imaginary Conversations of Literary Men and Statesmen* (1824–9) was celebrated in its day but has lost popularity. Other works include *Hellenics* (1847) and *Dry Sticks Fagoted* (1858).

75 Ah, what avails the sceptred race!
Ah, what the form divine!
1806 'Rose Aylmer'.

76 Clear writers, like clear fountains, do not seem so deep as they are; the turbid look the most profound.
1824 *Imaginary Conversations of Literary Men and Statesmen*, 'Southey and Porson'.

77 Fleas know not whether they are upon the body of a giant or upon one of ordinary size.
1824 *Imaginary Conversations of Literary Men and Statesmen*, 'Southey and Porson'.

78 Past ruined Ilion Helen lives,
Alcestis rises from the shades;
Verse calls them forth; 'tis verse that gives
Immortal youth to mortal maids.
1831 'To Ianthe'.

79 There is delight in singing, tho' none hear
Beside the singer.
1846 'To Robert Browning'.

80 Thee gentle Spenser fondly led;
But me he mostly sent to bed.
1846 'To Wordsworth: Those Who Have Laid the Harp Aside'.

81 There are no fields of amaranth on this side of the grave.
1846 *Imaginary Conversations of Literary Men and Statesmen*, 'Aesop and Rhodope'.

82 Death stands above me, whispering low
I know not what into my ear;
Of his strange language all I know
Is, there is not a word of fear.
1853 'Death stands above me'.

83 I strove with none; for none was worth my strife;
Nature I loved, and, next to Nature, Art.
1853 'Dying Speech of an Old Philosopher'.

84 Ireland never was contented…
Say you so? You are demented.
Ireland was contented when
All could use the sword and pen,
And when Tara rose so high
That her turrets split the sky,
And about her courts were seen
Liveried Angels robed in green,
Wearing, by St. Patrick's bounty,
Emeralds big as half a county.
1853 'Ireland never was contented'.

85 Prose on certain occasions can bear a great deal of poetry: on the other hand, poetry sinks and swoons under a moderate weight of prose.
1853 *Imaginary Conversations of Greeks and Romans*, 'Archdeacon Hare and Walter Landor'.

Landowska, Wanda 1879–1959

Polish pianist, harpsichordist and musical scholar, who founded the École de Musique Ancienne near Paris in 1927, and stimulated a new interest in the harpsichord. She also composed songs and piano and orchestral pieces and wrote on music.

86 You play Bach your way and I'll play him *his* way.
Refusing to adapt her technique to suit another Bach specialist. Quoted in Clifton Fadiman *The Faber Book of Anecdotes* (1985).

Lane, Anthony 1962–

English journalist, film critic at the *New Yorker* since 1993.

87 There is more suspense, more dramatic torque, in one page of [Nathaniel] Hawthorne's heart-racked ruminations on the Christian conscience than in all Demi Moore's woodland gallops and horizontal barn dancing.
On the film adaptation of *The Scarlet Letter*, directed by Roland Joffé. In *Nobody's Perfect: Writings from The New Yorker* (2002).

88 If you are going to spend two hundred million dollars on a movie, this is the way to do it.
Admiring the film *Titanic*. In *Nobody's Perfect: Writings from The New Yorker* (2002).

Lang, Andrew 1844–1912

Scottish man of letters. He specialized in mythology, famously arguing against Max Müller that folktale was the foundation of literary mythology. He also wrote history texts, popular fairy books, studies of literary figures and poetry.

89 Politicians use statistics in the same way that a drunk uses lamp-posts—for support rather than illumination.
1910 Speech. Quoted in Alan L Mackay *The Harvest of a Quiet Eye* (1977).

90 If the wild bowler thinks he bowls
Or if the batsman thinks he's bowled,
They know not, poor misguided souls,
They too shall perish unconsoled.
I am the batsman and the bat,
I am the bowler and the ball,
The umpire, the pavilion cat,
The roller, pitch, and stumps and all.
'Brahma'. Quoted by Alan Richardson in a letter to *The Times*, 18 May, 1963.
➤ *See Emerson 313:39.*

Lang, Fritz 1890–1976

Austrian-born US film director. His many films include *Metropolis* (1926), *You Only Live Once* (1937) and *Beyond a Reasonable Doubt* (1956).

91 Don't forget the western is not only the history of this country, it is what the Saga of the Nibelungen is for the European.
Quoted in Peter Bogdanovich *Fritz Lang in America* (1967).

Langbridge, Frederick 1849–1923

English religious writer.

92 Two men look out through the same bars:

One sees the mud, and one the stars.
1896 *A Cluster of Quiet Thoughts*.

Langland, William c.1332–c.1400

English poet. Little is known of his life but he seems to have been in London in 1362 when he began his only known work, the long poem *Vision of William concerning Piers the Plowman*, the greatest poem of the Middle English Alliterative Revival. It deals with the themes of truth, integrity and social justice. Three versions survive in over 60 manuscipts. It was first printed in 1550.

93 In a somer seson, whan softe was the sonne,
I shoop me into shroudes as I a sheep were,
In habite an heremite unholy of werkes,
Went wide in this world wondres to here.
c.1377 *Piers Plowman* (B text), prologue, l.1–4.
(shoop = got, shroudes = garments)

94 A gloten of wordes.
c.1377 *Piers Plowman* (B text), prologue, l.139.
(gloten = glutton)

95 'Though we hadde ykilled the cat, yat sholde there come another
To cracchen us ans al oure kynde, though we cropen under benches.'
c.1377 The wise mouse advises against belling the cat. *Piers Plowman* (B text), prologue, l.185–6.
(cracchen = scratch, cropen = crept)

96 He was bitelbrowed and baberlipped, with two blered eighen,
And as a letheren purs lolled his chekes.
c.1377 A description of the sin of Envy. *Piers Plowman* (B text), 'Passus 5,' l.188–9. (eighen = eyes, letheren = leather)

97 Al the povere peple tho pescoddes fetten;
Benes and baken apples thei broghte in hir lappe,
Chibolles and chervelles and ripe chiries manye,
And profrede Piers this present to plese with Hunger.
c.1378 A description of the sin of Envy. *Piers Plowman* (B text), 'Passus 6,' l.291–4.
(pescoddes = pea-pod, fetten = fetched, chibolles = spring-onions, chervelles = chervil, plese with Hunger = please hunger with)

98 Ac thorough his science soothy was nevere no soule ysaved,
Ne broght by hir bokes to blisse ne to joye.
c.1378 *Piers Plowman* (B text), 'Passus 12', l.134–5.
The 'science' and 'books' are those of pagan scholars who developed natural science from empirical observation only.

99 'Counseilleth me, Kynde,' quod I, 'what craft be best to lerne?'
'Lerne to love,' quod kynde, 'and leef alle othere.'
c.1378 *Piers Plowman* (B text), 'Passus 20', l.207–8.

Langner, Lawrence 1890–1962

Co-founder, US Theater Guild.

1 I have no interest in anything but *genius*, so please sit down.
To Tennessee Williams. Recalled in Williams *Memoirs* (1975).

Lanier, Sidney 1842–81

US poet. He fought in the Civil War for the Confederacy. His critical study *The Science of English Verse* (1880) establishes a musical basis for poetry which he tries to exemplify in his verse.

2 Music is Love in search of a word.
1875 *The Symphony*.

Lanyer, Aemilia 1569–1645

English poet. One of the very few professional early female poets, she was unable to secure patronage and published only one work, *Salve Deus Ex Judaeorum* (1611). It has been argued (unconvincingly) that she is the 'dark lady' of Shakespeare's *Sonnets*.

3 Our mother Eve, who tasted of the tree,
Giving to Adam what she held most dear,
Was simply good, and had no power to see.
1611 *Salve Deus Ex Judaeorum*, 'Eve's Apology in Defense of Women'.

4 But surely Adam cannot be excused;
Her fault though great, yet he was most to blame;
What weakness offered, strength might have refused,
Being lord of all, the greater was the shame.
1611 *Salve Deus Ex Judaeorum*, 'Eve's Apology in Defense of Women'.

5 Not Eve, whose fault was only too much love,
Which made her give this present to her dear,
That what she tasted he likewise might prove,
Whereby his knowledge might become more clear;
He never sought her weakness to reprove
With those sharp words which he of God did hear;
Yet men will boast of knowledge, which he took
From Eve's fair hand, as from a learned book.
1611 *Salve Deus Ex Judaeorum*, 'Eve's Apology in Defense of Women'.

6 Then let us have our liberty again,
And challenge to yourselves no sovereignty.
You came not in the world without our pain,
Make that a bar against your cruelty;
Your fault being greater, why should you disdain
Our being your equals, free from tyranny?
1611 *Salve Deus Ex Judaeorum*, 'Eve's Apology in Defense of Women'.

7 Farewell (sweet *Cooke-ham*) where I first obtained
Grace from that grace where perfect grace remained;
And where the muses gave their full consent,
I should have power the virtuous to content;
Where princely palace willed me to indite,
The sacred story of the soul's delight.
1611 *Salve Deus Ex Judaeorum*, 'The Description of Cooke-ham'.
Probably the first 'country-house' poem in English, this work is dedicated to Margaret Russell Clifford, Countess of Cumberland, and her daughter, Anne Clifford, whose family home was Cookham.

8 Never shall my sad eyes again behold
Those pleasures which my thoughts did then unfold.
1611 *Salve Deus Ex Judaeorum*, 'The Description of Cooke-ham'.

Lao-Tzu 6c BC

Chinese philosopher regarded as the inspiration for Taoism. Its major work, the *Tao-te Ching* was compiled some 300 years after his death but is traditionally ascribed to him.

9 Free from desire, you realise the mystery.
Caught in desire, you see only the manifestations.
c.250 BC *Tao-te Ching*, no.1 (translated by Stephen Mitchell, 1988).

10 He who defines himself can't know who he really is.

c.250 BC *Tao-te Ching*, no.24 (translated by Stephen Mitchell, 1988).

11 Even in victory, there is no beauty, and he who calls it beautiful is one who delights in slaughter.
c.250 BC *Tao-te Ching*, no.31. Collected in Lin Yutang (trans and ed) *The Wisdom of China and India* (1942).

12 A victory should be celebrated with the funeral rite.
c.250 BC *Tao-te Ching*, no.31. Collected in Lin Yutang (trans and ed) *The Wisdom of China and India* (1942).

13 When two equally matched armies meet, it is the man of sorrow who wins.
c.250 BC *Tao-te Ching*, no.69. Collected in Lin Yutang (trans and ed) *The Wisdom of China and India* (1942).

Lardner, Dionysus 1793–1859

Irish scientific writer, Professor of Natural Philosophy and Astronomy at University College London (1827). He is best known as the originator and editor of *Lardner's Cabinet Cyclopaedia* (133 vols, 1829–49).

14 Men might as well project a voyage to the Moon as attempt to employ steam navigation against the stormy North Atlantic Ocean.
1838 Speech to the British Association for the Advancement of Science, London.

Lardner, James

US journalist, former staff writer for the *New Yorker*. He is the director and founder of Inequality.org, a non-profit organization.

15 If…Americans do not succeed in engineering an economic revival, we can look forward to being remembered as, of all the nations that have prospered and declined, the one that has done so in the highest state of self-awareness.
1993 'The Declining Middle', in the *New Yorker*, 3 May.

Lardner, Ring(old Wilmer) 1885–1933

US short story writer, novelist and columnist. He is best known for his vernacular, comic, satirical and usually pessimistic short stories.

16 Are you lost daddy I arsked tenderly.
Shut up he explained.
1920 *The Young Immigrunts*, ch.10.

17 I have known what it was like to be hungry, but I always went right to a restaurant.
1927 *The Lardners: My Family Remembered*, ch.1.

18 'Babe' Ruth and Old Jack Dempsey,
Both Sultans of Swat,
One hits where the other people are,
The other where they're not.
Attributed.

Larionov, Mikhail 1881–1964

Russian painter and designer.

19 We declare: the genius of our days to be: trousers, jackets, shoes, tramways, buses, aeroplanes, railways, magnificent ships—what an enchantment—what a great epoch unrivalled in world history.
1913 'Rayonnist Manifesto', quoted in C Gray *The Russian Experiment in Art* (revised edn 1986).

Larkin, Philip Arthur 1922–85

English poet, novelist and essayist. He was librarian at Hull University, and a jazz critic. His meticulously phrased, frequently pessimistic but often tongue-in-cheek poems include 'The Whitsun Weddings' (1964) and 'High Windows' (1974).

20 Always too eager for the future, we
Pick up bad habits of expectancy.
1951 'Next, Please'.

21 What are days for?
Days are where we live.
They come, they wake us
Time and time over.
They are to be happy in:
Where can we live but days?
1953 'Days'.

22 What calls me is that lifted, rough-tongued bell
(Art, if you like) whose individual sound
Insists I too am an individual.
1953 'Reasons for Attendance'.

23 And the case of butterflies so rich it looks
As if all summer settled there and died.
1953 'Autumn'.

24 Nothing, like something, happens anywhere.
1954 'I Remember, I Remember'.

25 On me your voice falls as they say love should,
Like an enormous yes.
1954 'For Sidney Bechet'.

26 Hatless, I take off
My cycle-clips in awkward reverence.
1954 'Church Going'.

27 A serious house on serious earth it is,
In whose blent air all our compulsions meet,
Are recognised, and robed as destinies.
1954 'Church Going'.

28 Why should I let the toad *work*
Squat on my life?
Can't I use my wit as a pitchfork
And drive the brute off?
Six days of the week it soils
With its sickening poison—
Just for paying a few bills!
That's out of proportion.
1954 'Toads'.

29 Marrying left your maiden name disused.
1955 'Maiden Name'.

30 Time has transfigured them into
Untruth. The stone fidelity
They hardly meant has come to be
Their final blazon, and to prove
Our almost-instinct almost true:
What will survive of us is love.
1956 'An Arundel Tomb'.

31 Never such innocence,
Never before or since,
As changed itself to past
Without a word—the men
Leaving the gardens tidy,
The thousands of marriages
Lasting a little while longer:

Never such innocence again.
1960 'MCMXI V'.

32 Get stewed:
Books are a load of crap.
1960 'A Study of Reading Habits'.

33 The widening river's slow presence,
The piled gold clouds, the shining gull-marked mud,
Gathers to the surprise of a large town:
Here domes and statues, spires and cranes cluster
Beside grain-scattered streets, barge-crowded water,
And residents from raw estates.
1961 Of Hull.'Here'.

34 Give me your arm, old toad;
Help me down Cemetery Road.
1962 'Toads Revisited'.

35 Life is first boredom, then fear.
1963 'Dockery and Son'.

36 I thought of London spread out in the sun,
Its postal districts packed like squares of wheat.
1964 'The Whitsun Weddings'.

37 Sexual intercourse began
In nineteen sixty-three
(Which was rather late for me)—
Between the end of the *Chatterly* ban
And the Beatles' first LP.
1967 'Annus Mirabilis'.

38 They fuck you up, your mum and dad.
They may not mean to, but they do.
They fill you with the faults they had
And add some extra, just for you.
1971 'This Be the Verse'.

39 Man hands on misery to man.
It deepens like a coastal shelf.
Get out as early as you can,
And don't have any kids yourself.
1971 'This Be the Verse'.

40 I should never call myself a book lover, any more than a
people lover: it all depends what's inside them.
1972 In the London Antiquarian Book Fair programme.

41 Perhaps being old is having lighted rooms
Inside your head, and people in them, acting.
People you know, yet can't quite name.
1973 'The Old Fools'.

42 You can't put off being young until you retire,
And however you bank your screw, the money you save
Won't in the end buy you more than a shave.
1973 'Money'.

43 And beyond it, the deep blue air, that shows
Nothing, and is nowhere, and is endless.
1974 'High Windows'.

44 That sure extinction that we travel to
And shall be lost in always. Not to be here,
Not to be anywhere,
And soon; nothing more terrible, nothing more true.
1977 'Aubade'.

45 That vast moth-eaten musical brocade
Created to pretend we never die.
1977 Of religion.'Aubade'.

46 Far too many relied on the classic formula of a
beginning, a muddle, and an end.

1978 On judging the Booker Prize entries for 1977, in *New Fiction*,
no.15, Jan.

47 Deprivation is for me what daffodils were for
Wordsworth.
1983 *Required Writing*.

La Rochefoucauld, François, 6th Duc de 1613–80

French writer. A supporter of the queen, Marie de Médicis, and
an opponent of Richelieu, he was entangled in a series of
amorous adventures and political intrigues. His *Mémoires*,
published secretly in 1662, caused wide offence and were
followed by his *Réflexions, ou sentences et maximes morales*
(1664).

48 The love of justice in most men is simply the fear of
suffering injustice.
1664 *Réflexions, ou sentences et maximes morales*, no.78.

49 *Dans l'adversité de nos meilleurs amis, nous trouvons
toujours quelque chose qui ne nous déplaît pas.*
In the misfortune of our best friends, we always find
something which is not displeasing to us.
1664 *Réflexions, ou sentences et maximes morales*, no.99.

50 *On n'est jamais si malheureux qu'on croit, ni si heureux
qu'on espère.*
One is never as unhappy as one thinks, nor as happy as
one hopes.
1664 *Réflexions, ou sentences et maximes morales*, no.128.

51 *Nous avons tous assez de force pour supporter les maux
d'autrui.*
We are all strong enough to bear the misfortunes of
others.
1678 *Maximes*, no.19.

52 *L'hypocrisie est un hommage que le vice rend à la vertu.*
Hypocrisy is a tribute which vice pays to virtue.
1678 *Maximes*, no.218.

53 *L'absence diminue les médiocres passions, et augmente
les grandes, comme le vent éteint les bougies, et allume le
feu.*
Absence diminishes commonplace passions, and
increases great ones, as wind extinguishes candles and
kindles fire.
1678 *Maximes*, no.276.

54 *L'accent du pays où l'on est né demeure dans l'esprit et
dans le cœur comme dans le langage.*
The accent of the place in which one was born lingers in
the mind and in the heart as it does in one's speech.
1678 *Maximes*, no.342.

Larwood, Harold 1904–95

English cricketer. He became notorious in the 1932–3 tour of
Australia, employed by D R Jardine to bowl 'Bodyline', which
led to several batsmen being seriously hurt. He retired from
Test cricket as a result of the ensuing furore and eventually
settled in Australia.

55 A cricket tour in Australia would be a most delightful
period in one's life if one was deaf.
1933 *Body-line*.

56 Bodyline was devised to stifle Bradman's batting genius.
They said I was a 'killer with the ball', without taking into
account that Bradman, with the bat, was the greatest
killer of all.
1965 Of the 'Bodyline' controversy. Quoted in Colin Jarman *The*

Guinness Dictionary of Sports Quotations (1990).

57 I darned near bowled him that time.
> Attributed. Said to an umpire who had disallowed two previous appeals, on clean bowling a batsman, knocking down the entire wicket.

Lasky, Jesse 1880–1958

US film pioneer. He formed his own production company in 1914 and had his first hit with *The Squaw Man*, going on to produce for Paramount, Fox and Warner.

58 I yearned to trespass on Quality Street.
> On his desire to produce better films. Quoted in the *New Yorker*, 21 Mar 1994.

Lassels, Richard c.1603–1668

English classical scholar and priest. As tutor to the young English nobility, he travelled widely in Europe. His *Voyage of Italy* was published posthumously in Paris in 1670, and in London in 1698.

59 Pick out of every country what's best in it.
> **c.1650** *The Voyage of Italy, or a Compleat Journey through Italy* (published 1670).

60 [Travel] preserves my young nobleman from surfeiting of his parents, and weans him from a dangerous fondness of his mother. It teacheth him wholesome hardship…
Whereas the country gentleman that never travelled, can scarce go to London without making his will, at least without wetting his handkerchief.
> **c.1650** *The Voyage of Italy, or a Compleat Journey through Italy* (published 1670).

Latimer, Hugh c.1485–1555

English theologian, Bishop of Worcester and Protestant martyr. After Mary I's accession he was tried for heresy and burned at the stake in Oxford.

61 Be of good comfort Master Ridley, and play the man. We shall this day light such a candle by God's grace in England, as (I trust) shall never be put out.
> **1555** Spoken to Nicholas Ridley, as they waited together to be burned at the stake, 16 Oct. Quoted in Foxe *Acts and Monuments* (1563).

Lauder, Sir Harry (Hugh MacLennan) 1870–1950

Scottish comedian and music-hall entertainer.

62 Will yer stop yer tickling, Jock!
Oh, stop yer tickling, Jock!
Dinna mak' me laugh so hearty, or you'll mak' me choke.
Oh! I wish you'd stop yer nonsense—just look at all the folk.
Will yer stop yer tickling—tickle-ickle-ickle-ing—
Stop yer tickling, Jock!
> **1904** 'Stop Yer Tickling, Jock!', chorus.

63 I love a lassie, a bonnie, bonnie lassie,
She's as pure as the lily in the dell.
She's as sweet as the heather
The bonnie bloomin' heather—
Mary, ma Scotch Bluebell.
> **1905** 'I Love a Lassie', or 'Ma Scotch Bluebell', chorus.

64 Roamin' in the gloamin' on the bonnie banks o' Clyde.
Roamin' in the gloamin' wae my lassie by my side.
When the sun has gone to rest,

That's the time that we love best—
O, it's lovely roamin' in the gloamin'!
> **1911** 'Roamin' in the Gloamin', chorus.

65 Keep right on to the end of the road,
Keep right on to the end.
Tho' the way be long let your heart be strong,
Keep right on round the bend.
Tho' you're tired and weary
Still journey on, till you come to your happy abode,
Where all you love you've been dreaming of
Will be there, at the end of the road.
> **1924** 'The End of the Road', chorus.

Laughlin, J Laurence 1850–1933

US economist, Professor at the University of Chicago.

66 Anything from plumbing to philosophy.
> His definition of the scope of sociology. Quoted in Joseph Dorfman *Thorstein Veblen and his America* (1934), p.93.

Laughton, Charles 1899–1962

British actor. His many roles include Henry VIII in *The Private Life of Henry VIII* (1933), Captain Bligh in *Mutiny on the Bounty* (1935) and Quasimodo in *The Hunchback of Notre Dame* (1939).

67 But they can't censor the gleam in my eye.
> **1934** Of his role of Mr Barrett in *The Barretts of Wimpole Street*.

Lauren, Ralph 1939–

US fashion designer.

68 I don't design clothes, I design dreams.
> **1986** In the *New York Times*, 19 Apr.

Laurence, Margaret 1926–87

Canadian novelist. Her first works were set in Africa, where she lived for seven years. In London she wrote the five Manawaka novels (1964–74). She has received numerous honours, including the Order of Canada.

69 Privacy is a privilege not granted to the aged or the young.
> **1964** *The Stone Angel*, ch.1.

70 Even if heaven were real, and measured as Revelation says, so many cubits this way and that, how gimcrack a place it would be, crammed with its pavements of gold, its gates of pearl and topaz, like a gigantic chunk of costume jewelry.
> **1964** *The Stone Angel*, ch.4.

71 In bygone days, Morag had once believed that nothing could be worse than killing a person. Now she perceived river-slaying as something worse.
> **1974** *The Diviners*, ch.1.

Laurencin, Marie 1885–1956

French artist, best known for her portraits of women in misty pastel colours. She also illustrated many books with watercolours and lithographs. She exhibited at the Salon des Indépendents in 1907.

72 My ambition is that men should have a voluptuous feeling when they look at the portraits I paint of women. Love interests me more than painting. My pictures are the love stories I tell to myself and which I want to tell others.

Quoted in Gabrielle Buffet 'Marie Laurencin', in *The Arts 3* (1903).

Lautréamont, Comte de *properly Isidore Ducasse*
1846–70

French writer, hailed by the Surrealists as one of their forerunners for his psychological poetry. His death at the age of twenty-four remains a mystery.

73 *Il n'était pas menteur, il avouait la vérité et disait qu'il était cruel.*
He was not a liar. He admitted the truth and said that he was cruel.
1868 *Les Chants de Maldoror*, pt.1.

74 *Oui, quel est le plus profond, le plus impénétrable des deux: l'océan ou le cœur humain?*
What is deeper, more impenetrable: the ocean or the human heart?
1868 *Les Chants de Maldoror*, pt.1.

75 *Moi, je n'aime pas les femmes! Ni même les hermaphrodites! Il me faut des êtres qui me ressemblent, sur le front desquels la noblesse humaine soit marquée en caractères plus tranchés et ineffaçables!*
Me, I do not like women! Nor even hermaphrodites! I need beings who resemble me, on whose foreheads nobility is engraved in sharp and unerasable characters.
1868 *Les Chants de Maldoror*, pt.5.

76 *Si vous êtes malheureux, il ne faut pas le dire au lecteur. Gardez cela pour vous.*
If you are miserable, you should not say so to the reader. Keep it for yourself.
1870 *Poésies*, pt.1.

77 *Il faut que la critique attaque la forme, jamais le fond de vos idées, de vos phrases. Arrangez-vous.*
A critic must attack the form, never the foundation of your ideas and phrases. See to it.
1870 *Poésies*, pt.1.

78 *Si la morale de Cléopâtre eût été moins courte, la face du monde aurait changé. Son nez n'en serait pas devenu plus long.*
If Cleopatra's morality had been less short, the face of the world would have been altered. Her nose would not thereby have grown longer.
1870 *Poésies*, pt.2.

79 *La poésie doit être faite par tous. Non par un. Pauvre Hugo!*
Poetry should be composed by everyone. Not by one. Poor Hugo!
1870 *Poésies*, pt.2.

80 *On ne peut juger de la beauté de la vie que par celle de la mort.*
One can only judge the beauty of life through death.
1870 *Poésies*, pt.2.

Laver, James 1899–1975

English poet, writer and art critic, and Keeper at the Victoria and Albert Museum (1922–59). He made a substantial contribution to the history of English costume.

81 The same costume will be
Indecent…10 years before its time
Shameless…5 years before its time
Outré (daring)…1 year before its time

Smart
Dowdy…1 year after its time
Hideous…10 years after its time
Ridiculous…20 years after its time
Amusing…30 years after its time
Quaint…50 years after its time
Charming…70 years after its time
Romantic…100 years after its time
Beautiful…150 years after its time.
1937 *Taste and Fashion*, ch.18.

82 A visitor from Mars contemplating a man in a frock coat and top hat and a woman in a crinoline might well have supposed that they belonged to different species.
1969 *The Concise History of Costume and Fashion*, ch.8.

Lavoisier, Antoine Laurent 1743–94

French chemist and physicist, one of the fathers of modern chemistry. He was one of the first to use effective quantitative methods to study chemical reactions.

83 We must trust to nothing but facts. These are presented to us by Nature, and cannot deceive. We ought, in every instance, to submit our reasoning to the test of experiment, and never to search for truth but by the natural road of experiment and observation.
1789 *Traité élémentaire de la chimie* ('Elements of Chemistry', translated by Robert Kerr).

Law, (Andrew) Bonar 1858–1923

Canadian-born British Unionist politician. He was Chancellor of the Exchequer (1916–18) and from 1916 Leader of the House of Commons. He retired in 1921, but returned to serve as Prime Minister (1922–3).

84 I can imagine no length of resistance to which Ulster can go in which I should not be prepared to support them, and in which, in my belief, they would not be supported by the overwhelming majority of the British people.
1912 During the Irish Home Rule crisis, 27 Jul.

Law, William 1686–1761

English divine, whose writings expounded the mysticism of Jakob Boehme.

85 I take it for granted that every Christian that is in health is up early in the morning; for it is much more reasonable to suppose a person up early because he is a Christian than because he is a labourer or a tradesman or a servant or has business that wants him.
1728 *A Serious Call to a Devout and Holy Life*.

86 If, therefore, a man will so live as to show that he feels and believes the most fundamental doctrines of Christianity, he must live above the world.
1728 *A Serious Call to a Devout and Holy Life*.

Lawrence, D(avid) H(erbert) 1885–1930

English novelist, poet and essayist. He was the son of a miner, and much of his fiction reflected his upbringing. His candid treatment of emotion and physical love led to prosecution for obscenity with *The Rainbow* in 1915, and *Lady Chatterley's Lover* in 1928 (and 1961). He lived in Italy and Mexico from 1919.

87 'Be a good animal, true to your instincts,' was his motto.
1911 *The White Peacock*, pt.2, ch.2.

88 Curse the blasted, jelly-boned swines, the slimy, the

belly-wriggling invertebrates, the miserable sodding rotters, the flaming sods, the snivelling, dribbling, dithering, palsied, pulse-less lot that make up England today.
1913 Letter to Edward Garnett, 3 Jul, after the rejection of *Sons and Lovers* by Heinemann.

89 I like to write when I feel spiteful; it's like having a good sneeze.
1913 Letter to Lady Cynthia Asquith, Nov.

90 You mustn't look in my novel for the old stable *ego* of the character.
1914 Letter to Edward Garnett, 5 Jun.

91 People are not fallen angels, they are merely people.
1916 Letter to J Middleton Murry and Katherine Mansfield, 17 Feb.

92 I am only half there when I am ill, and so there is only half a man to suffer. To suffer in one's whole self is so great a violation, that it is not to be endured.
1916 Letter to Catherine Carswell, 16 Apr.

93 Not I, not I, but the wind that blows through me!
A fine wind is blowing the new direction of Time.
1917 'Song of a Man Who Has Come Through'.

94 The glamour
Of childish days is upon me, my manhood is cast
Down in the flood of remembrance, I weep like a child for the past.
1918 'Piano'.

95 Don't you find it a beautiful clean thought, a world empty of people, just uninterrupted grass, and a hare sitting up?
1920 *Women in Love*, ch.11.

96 In China the bat is a symbol of happiness
Not for me!
1921 'Bat'.

97 I like Australia less and less. The hateful newness, the democratic conceit, every man a little pope of perfection.
1922 Letter, 28 May.

98 Morality which is based on ideas, or on an ideal, is an unmitigated evil.
1922 *Fantasia of the Unconscious*, ch.7.

99 Every race which has become self-conscious and idea-bound in the past has perished.
1922 *Fantasia of the Unconscious*, ch.7.

1 Death is the only pure, beautiful conclusion of a great passion.
1922 *Fantasia of the Unconscious*, ch.15.

2 Better passion and death than any more of these 'isms'. No more of the old purpose done up in aspic. Better passion and death.
1922 *Fantasia of the Unconscious*, ch.15.

3 In the *established* sense it is socially nil. Happy-go-lucky, don't-you-bother, we're-in-Australia. But there also seems to be no inside life of any sort: just a long lapse and drift. A rather fascinating indifference, a *physical* indifference to what we call soul or spirit. It's really a weird show.
1922 Of Australia. Letter, collected in A Huxley (ed) *The Letters of D H Lawrence* (1932).

4 I do not want peace nor beauty nor even freedom from pain. I want to fight and to feel new gods in the flesh.
1922 Letter to E H Brewster, 2 Jan.

5 The wonderful Southern night-sky that makes a man feel so lonely, alien: with Orion standing on his head in the west, and his sword-belt upside down, and his Dog-star prancing in mid-heaven, high above him; and with the Southern Cross insignificantly mixed in with the other stars, democratically inconspicuous.
1923 Of night over Sydney. *Kangaroo*, ch.1.

6 What do the facts we know *about* a man amount to? Only two things we can know of him, and this by pure soul-intuition: we can know if he is true to the flame of life and love which is inside his heart, or if he is false to it.
1923 *Kangaroo*, ch.7.

7 The indifference—the fern-dark indifference of this remote golden Australia. Not to care—from the bottom of one's soul not to care.
1923 *Kangaroo*, ch.10.

8 Life makes no absolute statement. It is all Call and Answer.
1923 *Kangaroo*, ch.10.

9 And so, I missed my chance with one of the lords
Of life.
And I have something to expiate;
A pettiness.
1923 'Snake'.

10 Men! The only animal in the world to fear.
1923 'Mountain Lion'.

11 Hanging upside down like rows of disgusting old rags
And grinning in their sleep.
1923 'Bats'.

12 Evil, what is evil?
There is only one evil, to deny life.
1923 'Cypresses'.

13 The dead don't die. They look on and help.
1923 Letter to J Middleton Murry, 2 Feb, on the death of Katherine Mansfield.

14 Never trust the artist. Trust the tale.
1924 *Studies in Classic American Literature*, ch.1.

15 I want to go south, where there is no autumn, where the cold doesn't crouch over one like a snow-leopard waiting to pounce. The heart of the North is dead, and the fingers of cold are corpse fingers.
1924 Letter to J Middleton Murry, 3 Oct.

16 The identifying ourselves with the visual image of ourselves has become an instinct; the habit is already old. The picture of me, the me that is *seen*, is me.
1925 'Art and Morality'.

17 Damn all absolutes. Oh damn, damn, damn all absolutes!
1925 'The Novel'.

18 After the funeral, my father struggled through half a page, and it might as well have been Hottentott.
'And what dun they gi'e thee for that, lad?'
'Fifty pounds, father.' 'Fifty pounds!' He was dumbfounded, and looked at me with shrewd eyes, as if I were a swindler. 'Fifty pounds! An' tha's niver done a day's hard work in thy life.'
1925 Preface to Edward D McDonald (ed) *A Bibliography of D. H. Lawrence*.

19 I'm not sure if a mental relation with a woman doesn't

make it impossible to love her. To know the *mind* of a woman is to end in hating her.
1927 Letter to Dr Trigant Burrow, 3 Aug.

20 You have to have something vicious in you to be a creative writer… God save me from being 'nice'.
1927 Book review, reprinted in *Phoenix*.

21 Ours is essentially a tragic age, so we refuse to take it tragically.
1928 *Lady Chatterley's Lover*, ch.1.

22 John Thomas says goodnight to Lady Jane, a little droopingly, but with a hopeful heart.
1928 *Lady Chatterley's Lover*, ch.19.

23 My God, what a clumsy *olla putrida* James Joyce is! Nothing but old fags and cabbage-stumps of quotations from the Bible and the rest, stewed in the juice of deliberate, journalistic dirty-mindedness.
1928 Letter to Aldous and Maria Huxley, 15 Aug.

24 Sentimentalism is the working off on yourself of feelings you haven't really got.
1928 'John Galsworthy'.

25 I am tired of being told there is no such animal by animals who are merely different.
1929 Letter to J Middleton Murry, 20 May.

26 How beastly the bourgeois is
Especially the male of the species.
1929 'How Beastly the Bourgeois Is'.

27 I never saw a wild thing
Sorry for itself.
1929 'Self-Pity'.

28 When I read Shakespeare I am struck with wonder
That such trivial people should muse and thunder
In such lovely language.
1929 'When I Read Shakespeare'.

29 Pornography is the attempt to insult sex, to do dirt on it.
1929 'Pornography and Obscenity'.

30 Now man cannot live without some vision of himself. But still less can he live with a vision that is not true to his inner experience and inner feeling.
1929 'The Risen Lord'.

31 Now it is autumn and the falling fruit
And the long journey towards oblivion…
Have you built your ship of death, O have you?
1932 'The Ship of Death'.

32 To the Puritan all things are impure, as somebody says.
1932 *Etruscan Places*, 'Cerveteri'.

33 And being a novelist, I consider myself superior to the saint, the scientist, the philosopher, and the poet, who are all great masters of different bits of man alive, but never get the whole hog.
1936 'Why The Novel Matters'.

34 Nothing is more difficult than to determine what a child takes in, and does not take in, of its environment and its teaching. This fact is brought home to me by the hymns which I learned as a child, and never forgot. They mean more to me almost than the finest poetry, and they have for me a more permanent value, somehow or other.
Collected in *Phoenix II: Uncollected, Unpublished and Other Prose Works* (1968).

35 The sense of wonder
that is the sixth sense.

And it is the natural religious sense.
'Hymns in a Man's Life'. Collected in *Pheonix II: Uncollected, Unpublished and Other Prose Works* (1968).

Lawrence, Gertrude 1898–1952

English actress. A star of revue on both sides of the Atlantic, she was highly popular as the lead in Noël Coward's comedies. She died while appearing in the hit Broadway musical *The King and I*.

36 Pardon my long preamble. It's like a chorus girl's tights—it touches everything and covers nothing.
During an after-dinner speech. Attributed.

Lawrence, T(homas) E(dward) *known as* Lawrence of Arabia 1888–1935

Anglo-Irish soldier and writer. In World War I he worked for army intelligence in North Africa (1914–16). Espousing the Arab cause, he led the Arabs in their revolt against the Turks.

37 I loved you, so I drew these tides of men into my hands
—and wrote my will across the sky in stars
To earn you Freedom, the seven pillared worthy house,
—that your eyes might be shining for me
When we came.
1926 *Seven Pillars of Wisdom*, dedication.

38 All men dream, but not equally. Those who dream by night in the dusty recesses of their minds wake in the day to find that it was vanity; but the dreamers of the day are dangerous men, for they may act their dream with open eyes, to make it possible.
1926 *Seven Pillars of Wisdom*, introductory chapter.

39 We were a self-centred army without parade or gesture, devoted to freedom, the second of man's creeds, a purpose so ravenous that it devoured all our strength, a hope so transcendent that it devoured our earlier ambitions faded in its glare.
1926 *Seven Pillars of Wisdom*, ch.1.

40 Many men would take the death sentence without a whimper to escape the life-sentence which fate carries in her other hand.
1936 *The Mint*, pt.1, ch.4.

41 A man hates to be moved to folly by a noise.
1936 Of the emotion aroused by the military trumpets. *The Mint*, pt.3, ch.9.

42 The test of nomadism, that most deeply biting of social disciplines.
Introduction to an edition of Charles Montagu Doughty *Travels in Arabia Deserta*.

Lawson, Henry Hertzberg 1867–1922

Australian writer, son of the writer and feminist Louisa Lawson. His writings for the *Bulletin*, 'The Bushman's Bible', have been collected in *Short Stories in Prose and Verse* (1894) and *While the Billy Boils* (1896).

43 And the sun sank again on the grand Australian bush—the nurse and tutor of eccentric minds, the home of the weird, and of much that is different from things in other lands.
1892 'The Bush Undertaker', first published in *The Antipodean*.

44 The departed was a 'Roman', and the majority of the town were otherwise—but unionism is stronger than creed. Drink, however, is stronger than unionism; and, when the hearse presently arrived, more than two-thirds

of the funeral were unable to follow.
1893 'The Union Buries its Dead', first published in *Truth*, Apr.

45 Type of a coming nation,
In the land of cattle and sheep,
Worked on Middleton's station,
'Pound a week and his keep.'
'Middleton's Rouseabout', collected in Colin Roderick (ed) *Henry Lawson: Collected Verse* (3 vols, 1967–9).

46 Have you seen the bush by moonlight, from the train, go running by?
Blackened log and stump and sapling, ghostly trees all dead and dry;
Here a patch of glassy water; there a glimpse of mystic sky?
Have you heard the still voice calling—yet so warm, and yet so cold:
'I'm the Mother-Bush that bore you! Come to me when you are old'?
'On the Night Train', collected in Colin Roderick (ed) *Henry Lawson: Collected Verse* (3 vols, 1967–9).

Layamon fl.c.1190

English author and priest who lived at Arley Regis in Worcestershire. He wrote the *Brut*, the first English version of the story of Arthur, largely based on Wace's French *Roman de Brut*.

47 And I will fare to Avalun, to the fairest of all maidens, to Argante the queen, an elf most fair, and she shall make my wounds all sound.
c.1190 *Brut* (translated by Eugene Mason, 1912).

Layton, Irving 1912–

Romanian-born Canadian poet, who came to Montreal as an infant. His 35 books of poetry include *The Black Huntsman* (1951), *The Cold Green Element* (1955) and *A Red Carpet for the Sun* (1959).

48 Death is a name for beauty not in use.
1953 'Composition in Late Spring', collected in *The Collected Poems of Irving Layton* (1971).

49 It amazes me that organs that piss
Can give human beings such perfect bliss.
1969 *The Whole Bloody Bird*, 'Aphs'.

50 Only the tiniest fracton of mankind want freedom. All the rest want someone to tell them they are free.
1969 *The Whole Bloody Bird*.

Lazarus, Emma 1849–87

US poet, a champion of oppressed Jewry. Her poems include *Songs of a Semite* (1882) and *By the Waters of Babylon* (1887). She is best known for her sonnet, 'The New Colossus' which is inscribed on the Statue of Liberty.

51 Give me your tired, your poor,
Your huddled masses yearning to breathe free,
The wretched refuse of your teeming shore,
Send these, the homeless, tempest-tossed, to me:
I lift my lamp beside the golden door.
1883 'The New Colossus', inscribed at the foot of the Statue of Liberty, New York harbour, 1886.

52 Still on Israel's head forlorn
Every nation heaps its scorn.
1886 'The World's Justice'.

Leach, Jim (James Albert Smith) 1942–

US Republican politician.

53 The only thing the Balkans export is history.
1995 WAMU broadcast, Washington, 25 Nov.

Leacock, Stephen Butler 1869–1944

English-born Canadian humorist and economist. Head of Economics at McGill University from 1908, he wrote several books on economics and literary biographies, and is usually remembered for his short stories, essays and parodies, which include *Literary Lapses* (1910), *Nonsense Novels* (1911) and *Winsome Winnie* (1920).

54 There are no handles to a horse, but the 1910 model has a string to each side of its face for turning its head when there is anything you want it to see.
1910 *Literary Lapses*, 'Reflections on Riding'.

55 It takes a good deal of physical courage to ride a horse. This, however, I have. I get it at about forty cents a flask, and take it as required.
1910 *Literary Lapses*, 'Reflections on Riding'.

56 The great man…walks across his century and leaves the marks of his feet all over it, ripping out the dates on his galoshes as he passes.
1910 *Literary Lapses*, 'The Life of John Smith'.

57 I detest life-insurance agents; they always argue that I shall some day die, which is not so.
1910 *Literary Lapses*, 'Insurance Up to Date'.

58 The landlady of a boarding-house is a parallelogram—that is, an oblong angular figure, which cannot be described, but which is equal to anything.
1910 *Literary Lapses*, 'Boarding-House Geometry'.

59 Astronomy teaches the correct use of the sun and the planets.
1910 *Literary Lapses*, 'A Manual of Education'.

60 Electricity is of two kinds, positive and negative. The difference is, I presume, that one comes a little more expensive, but is more durable; the other is a cheaper thing, but the moths get into it.
1910 *Literary Lapses*, 'A Manual of Education'.

61 Get your room full of good air, then shut up the windows and keep it. It will keep for years. Anyway, don't keep using your lungs all the time. Let them rest.
1910 *Literary Lapses*, 'How to Live to Be 200'.

62 Lord Ronald said nothing; he flung himself from the room, flung himself upon his horse and rode madly off in all directions.
1911 *Nonsense Novels*, 'Gertrude the Governess: or, Simple Seventeen'.

63 When you meet Mr. Smith first you think he looks like an over-dressed pirate. Then you begin to think him a character. You wonder at his enormous bulk. Then the utter hopelessness of knowing what Smith is thinking by merely looking at his features gets on your mind and makes the Mona Lisa seem an open book and the ordinary human countenance as superficial as a puddle in the sunlight.
1912 *Sunshine Sketches of a Little Town*, 'The Hostelry of Mr. Smith'.

64 His life was one round of activity which he himself might deplore but was powerless to prevent.

1912 *Sunshine Sketches of a Little Town*, 'The Ministrations of the Rev. Mr. Drone'.

65 The classics are only primitive literature. They belong to the same class as primitive machinery and primitive music and primitive medicine.
1913 *Behind the Beyond*, 'Homer and Humbug'.

66 The parent who could see his boy as he really is, would shake his head and say: 'Willie is no good; I'll sell him.'
1916 *Further Foolishness*, 'The Lot of the Schoolmaster'.

67 A decision of the courts decided that the game of golf may be played on a Sunday, not being a game within the view of the law, but being a form of moral effort.
1923 *Over the Footlights*, 'Why I Refuse to Play Golf'.

68 Advertising may be described as the science of arresting human intelligence long enough to get money from it.
1924 *The Garden of Folly*, 'The Perfect Salesman'.

69 The general idea, of course, in any first-class laundry, is to see that no shirt or collar ever comes back twice.
1926 *Winnowed Wisdom*, ch.6.

70 I am what is called a *professor emeritus*—from the Latin *e*, 'out', and *meritus*, 'so he ought to be'.
1938 *Here are my Lectures*, ch.14.

71 A sportsman is a man who, every now and then, simply has to go out and kill something. Not that he's cruel. He wouldn't hurt a fly. It's not big enough.
1942 *My Remarkable Uncle*.

72 Presently I shall be introduced as 'this venerable old gentleman' and the axe will fall when they raise me to the degree of 'grand old man'. That means on our continent any one with snow-white hair who has kept out of jail till eighty.
1942 *My Remarkable Uncle*, 'Three Score and Ten'.

73 I have a suspicion it's inevitable, but give me my stick. I'll face it.
1942 On being asked what he thought about death, following a serious throat operation, quoted in John Stevens's introduction to *My Remarkable Uncle* (1965 edn).

Leadbelly *pseudonym of* **Huddie William Ledbetter** 1889–1949

US blues and folk singer, songwriter and guitarist. He was 'discovered' while serving one of several prison sentences. His recordings include 'Midnight Special' and 'Rock Island Line'.

74 No white man ever had the blues.
Quoted in Joachim Berendt *The Jazz Book* (1984).

Lear, Edward 1812–88

English artist, humorist and traveller, famous for his nonsense verse such as that collected in *A Book of Nonsense* (1846, enlarged 1861, 1863 and 1870), as well as his illustrations and landscapes.

75 There was an Old Man with a beard,
Who said, 'It is just as I feared!—
Two Owls and a Hen,
Four Larks and a Wren,
Have all built their nest in my beard!'
1846 *A Book of Nonsense*.

76 When awful darkness and silence reign
Over the great Gromboolian plain,
Through the long, long wintry nights,
When the angry breakers roar

As they beat on the rocky shore—
When storm-clouds brood on the towering heights
Of the Hills of the Chankly Bore.
1871 *Nonsense Songs*, *Stories*, *Botany and Alphabets*, 'The Dong with a Luminous Nose'.

77 And those who watch at that midnight hour
From Hall or Terrace or lofty Tower,
Cry as the wild light passes along,
'The Dong!—the Dong!
The wandering Dong through the forest goes!
The Dong!—the Dong!
The Dong with a Luminous Nose!'
1871 *Nonsense Songs*, *Stories*, *Botany and Alphabets*, 'The Dong with a Luminous Nose'.

78 They went to sea in a sieve, they did
In a sieve they went to sea.
1871 *Nonsense Songs*, *Stories*, *Botany and Alphabets*, 'The Jumblies'.

79 Far and few, far and few,
Are the lands where the Jumblies live;
Their heads are green, and their hands are blue,
And they went to sea in a Sieve.
1871 *Nonsense Songs*, *Stories*, *Botany and Alphabets*, 'The Jumblies'.

80 They called aloud 'Our Sieve ain't big,
But we don't care a button! We don't care a fig!'
1871 *Nonsense Songs*, *Stories*, *Botany and Alphabets*, 'The Jumblies'.

81 And they brought an Owl, and a useful Cart,
And a pound of Rice, and a Cranberry Tart,
And a hive of silvery Bees.
And they brought a Pig, and some green Jack-daws,
And a lovely Monkey with lollipop paws, and forty Bottles of Ring-Bo-Ree,
And no end of Stilton Cheese.
1871 *Nonsense Songs*, *Stories*, *Botany and Alphabets*, 'The Jumblies'.

82 Till Mrs Discobbolos said
'Oh! W! X! Y! Z!
It has just come into my head—
Suppose we should happen to fall!!!!
Darling Mr Discobbolos?'
1871 *Nonsense Songs*, *Stories*, *Botany and Alphabets*, 'Mr and Mrs Discobbolos'.

83 The Owl and the Pussy-Cat went to sea
In a beautiful pea-green boat.
They took some honey, and plenty of money,
Wrapped up in a five-pound note.
The Owl looked up to the Stars above
And sang to a small guitar,
'Oh lovely Pussy! O Pussy, my love,
What a beautiful Pussy you are'.
1871 *Nonsense Songs*, *Stories*, *Botany and Alphabets*, 'The Owl and the Pussy-Cat'.

84 Pussy said to the Owl, 'You elegant Fowl!
How charmingly sweet you sing!
O let us be married! too long we have tarried:
But what shall we do for a ring?'
They sailed away for a year and a day,
To the land where the Bong-tree grows,
And there in a wood a Piggy-wig stood
With a ring at the end of his nose.

1871 *Nonsense Songs, Stories, Botany and Alphabets*, 'The Owl and the Pussy-Cat'.

85 'Dear Pig, are you willing to sell for one shilling
Your ring?' Said the Piggy, 'I will.'
1871 *Nonsense Songs, Stories, Botany and Alphabets*, 'The Owl and the Pussy-Cat'.

86 They dined on mince, and slices of quince,
Which they ate with a runcible spoon;
And hand in hand, on the edge of the sand,
They danced by the light of the moon.
1871 *Nonsense Songs, Stories, Botany and Alphabets*, 'The Owl and the Pussy-Cat'.

87 The Pobble who has no toes
Had once as many as we;
When they said, 'Some day you may lose them all';
He replied—'Fish fiddle de-dee!'
His Aunt Jobiska made him drink
Lavender water tinged with pink,
For she said, 'The world in general knows
There's nothing so good for a Pobble's toes!'
1871 *Nonsense Songs, Stories, Botany and Alphabets*, 'The Pobble Who Has No Toes'.

88 When boats or ships came near him
He tinkledy-binkledy-winkled a bell.
1871 *Nonsense Songs, Stories, Botany and Alphabets*, 'The Pobble Who Has No Toes'.

89 He has gone to fish, for his Aunt Jobiska's
Runcible Cat with crimson whiskers!
1871 *Nonsense Songs, Stories, Botany and Alphabets*, 'The Pobble Who Has No Toes'.

90 'But the longer I live on this Crumpetty Tree
The plainer than ever it seems to me
That very few people come this way
And that life on the whole is far from gay!'
Said the Quangle-Wangle Quee.
1871 *Nonsense Songs, Stories, Botany and Alphabets*, 'The Quangle Wangle's Hat'.

91 And what can we expect if we haven't any dinner,
But to lose our teeth and eyelashes and keep on growing thinner?
1871 *Nonsense Songs, Stories, Botany and Alphabets*, 'The Two Old Bachelors'.

92 Nasticreechia Krorluppia.
1872 *More Nonsense, Pictures, Rhymes, Botany Etc*, 'Nonsense Botany'.

93 There was an old person of Ware,
Who rode on the back of a bear:
When they asked, 'Does it trot?'
He said, 'Certainly not!
He's a Moppsikon Floppsikon bear.'
1872 *More Nonsense, Pictures, Rhymes, Botany Etc*, 'One Hundred Nonsense Pictures and Rhymes'.

94 There was an old man of Thermopylae,
Who never did anything properly;
But they said, 'If you choose
To boil eggs in your shoes,
You shall never remain in Thermopylae.'
1872 *More Nonsense, Pictures, Rhymes, Botany Etc*, 'One Hundred Nonsense Pictures and Rhymes'.

Leary, Timothy Francis 1920–96

US psychologist, Professor at the Universities of California and

Harvard, best known for his advocacy of the drug LSD and his association with the counter-cultural movement of the 1960s and 1970s.

95 My advice to people today is as follows: If you take the game of life seriously, if you take your nervous system seriously, if you take your sense organs seriously, if you take the energy process seriously, you must turn on, tune in, and drop out.
1966 Lecture, Jun, collected in *The Politics of Ecstasy* (1968), ch.21.

96 Science is all metaphor.
1980 Interview, 24 Sep, collected in *Contemporary Authors* vol.107.

Lease, Mary Elizabeth Cylens 1853–1933

US reformer, who spoke out for women's suffrage, Irish Home Rule, prohibition and other causes.

97 The farmers of Kansas must raise less corn and more hell.
1890 Speech, Kansas. This phrase became the slogan of the Populist Party.

Leavis, F(rank) R(aymond) 1895–1978

English critic. He taught at Cambridge University, and was a hugely influential figure, although his ideas have now been superseded by new approaches to textual and cultural criticism.

98 Poetry can communicate the actual quality of experience with a subtlety and precision unapproachable by any other means.
1932 *New Bearings in English Poetry*, ch.2.

99 The Sitwells belong to the history of publicity rather than of poetry.
1932 *New Bearings in English Poetry*, ch.2.

1 It is well to start by distinguishing the few really great—the major novelists who count in the same way as the major poets, in the sense that they not only change the possibilities of the art for practitioners and readers, but that they are significant in terms of the human awareness they promote; awareness of the possibilities of life.
1948 *The Great Tradition*, ch.1.

2 The only way to escape misrepresentation is never to commit oneself to any critical judgement that makes an impact—that is, never *say anything*.
1948 *The Great Tradition*, ch.1.

Leavis, Q(ueenie) D(orothy) 1906–81

British literary critic.

3 Really I suppose what I hate myself most on is showing other people where to dig, not having time to do intensive and exclusive digging myself. I am a dowser and not a navvy.
Quoted in the *Times Literary Supplement*, 8 Sep 1989.

Le Bon, Gustave 1841–1931

French psychologist and sociologist, whose works aim to identify national characteristics and thereby racial superiority.

4 Science has promised us truth—an understanding of such relationships as our minds can grasp; it has never promised us either peace or happiness.

1895 *Psychologie des foules*, introduction.

Lebowitz, Fran(ces Ann) 1951–

US writer. Her work is marked by an aphoristic sensibility and a caustic, world-weary and rather cynical wit.

5 There is no such thing as inner peace. There is only nervousness or death. Any attempt to prove otherwise constitutes unacceptable behaviour.
1978 *Metropolitan Life*, 'Manners'.

6 Nothing succeeds like address.
1978 *Metropolitan Life*, 'The Nail Bank'.

7 Sleep is death without the responsibility.
1978 *Metropolitan Life*, 'Why I Love Sleep'.

8 It is by this painstaking method of careful examination and eventual rejection that we reach a conclusion: life is something to do when you can't get to sleep.
1978 *Metropolitan Life*, 'Mars'.

9 Salad is not a meal. It is a style.
1978 *Metropolitan Life*, 'Food For Thought and Vice Versa'.

10 Perhaps the least cheering statement ever made on the subject of art is that life imitates it.
1978 *Metropolitan Life*, 'Arts'.

11 Original thought is like original sin: both happened before you were born to people you could not possibly have met.
1981 *Social Studies*, 'People'.

12 Great people talk about ideas, average people talk about things, and small people talk about wine.
1981 *Social Studies*, 'People'.

13 The opposite of talking isn't listening. The opposite of talking is waiting.
1981 *Social Studies*, 'People'.

14 There are two modes of transport in Los Angeles: car and ambulance.Visitors who wish to remain inconspicuous are advised to choose the latter.
1981 *Social Studies*, 'Lesson One'.

15 If you're going to America, bring your own food.
1981 *Social Studies*, 'Fran Lebowitz's Travel Hints'.

16 Being offended is the natural consequence of leaving one's home.
1981 *Social Studies*, 'When Smoke Gets In Your Eyes…Shut Them'.

17 War is, undoubtedly, hell, but there is no earthly reason why it has to start so early in the morning.
1981 *Social Studies*, 'War Stories'.

Leboyer, Frédérick 1918–

French gynaecologist and obstetrician, who first drew attention to birth trauma, and has always emphasized the intimate associations between sex, depression and anxiety.

18 Making love is the sovereign remedy for anguish.
1991 *Birth without Violence*.

Le Carré, John *pseudonym of* David John Moore Cornwell 1931–

English novelist. He taught at Eton and entered the Foreign Service, resigning in 1964 to become a full-time writer. His works, many of which have been filmed, are set in the dark underworld of international diplomacy and espionage.

19 The Spy who Came in from the Cold.
1963 Title of novel.

20 A committee is an animal with four back legs.
1974 *Tinker, Tailor, Soldier, Spy*, pt.3, ch.34.

21 Sometimes…we have to do a thing in order to find out the reason for it. Sometimes our actions are questions, not answers.
1986 *A Perfect Spy*, ch.1.

22 The only decent diplomat is a deaf Trappist.
1986 *A Perfect Spy*, ch.3.

23 A society that admires its shock troops had better be bloody careful about where it's going.
1986 *A Perfect Spy*, ch.18.

24 Publishers can get their minds halfway round anything.
1989 *The Russia House*, ch.5.

25 One long act of sadism.
1991 On his boyhood at Sherborne School. In *The Times*, 21 Feb.

26 As a maker of fictions, I invent versions of myself, never the real thing, if it exists.
2002 In the *New Yorker*, 18 Feb.

27 How Bush and his junta succeeded in deflecting America's anger from Bin Laden to Saddam Hussein is one of the great public relations conjuring tricks in history.
2003 In *Time*, 27 Jan.

Le Corbusier *pseudonym of* Charles Édouard Jeanneret 1887–1965

Swiss architect, co-author of the Purist manifesto. His buildings, which demonstrate the interrelation of machine forms and architectural techniques, include the Cité Universitaire, Paris, and his city planning designs include Buenos Aires (1938). His books have had a worldwide influence.

28 It is a question of building which is at the root of the social unrest of today: architecture or revolution.
1923 *Vers une architecture* (translated as *Towards a New Architecture*, 1927).

29 The day consists of twenty-four hours only. This regulates the size of the house and the rôle it has to fulfil. For the twenty-four hour day is short, and our acts and thoughts are spurred on *by time*. If we were taught to regard the hand of the clock as a beneficent but implacable god, we should order our lives more rationally.
1930 'Twentieth-century living and twentieth-century building'. Collected in Dennis Sharp (ed) *The Rationalists: Theory and Design in the Modern Movement* (1978).

30 Architecture provides the framework for a civilization (housing, work, leisure, circulation); so architecture is also town planning. It is no longer possible to separate architecture and town planning—they are one and the same thing.
1943 'If I had to teach you architecture'. Collected in Dennis Sharp (ed) *The Rationalists: Theory and Design in the Modern Movement* (1978).

Lee, Gypsy Rose *stage-name of* Rose Louise Hovick 1914–70

US actress. Her career as a striptease artist in burlesque on Broadway in the 1930s provided the basis for the film *Gypsy* (1959).

31 I know men aren't attracted to me by my mind. They're attracted by what I don't mind.
Attributed.

32 God is love, but get it in writing.
Attributed.

Lee, (Nelle) Harper 1926–

US writer. She wrote only one novel, *To Kill a Mockingbird* (1960, Pulitzer Prize 1961), but it has become a classic of its time.

33 Until I feared I would lose it, I never loved to read. One does not love breathing.
1960 Scout. *To Kill A Mockingbird*, pt.1, ch.2.

34 Shoot all the bluejays you want, if you can hit 'em, but remember it's a sin to kill a mockingbird.
1960 Atticus Finch. *To Kill A Mockingbird*, pt.1, ch.10.

35 The one thing that doesn't abide by majority rule is a person's conscience.
1960 Atticus Finch. *To Kill A Mockingbird*, pt.1, ch.11.

36 Folks don't like to have somebody around knowin' more than they do. It aggravates 'em.
1960 Calpurnia. *To Kill A Mockingbird*, pt.2, ch.12.

37 A court is only as sound as its jury, and a jury is only as sound as the men who make it up.
1960 Atticus Finch. *To Kill A Mockingbird*, pt.2, ch.20.

38 As you grow older, you'll see white men cheat black men every day of your life, but let me tell you something and don't you forget it—whenever a white man does that to a black man, no matter who he is, how rich he is, or how fine a family he comes from, that white man is trash.
1960 Atticus Finch. *To Kill A Mockingbird*, pt.2, ch.23.

Lee, Hsien Loong 1952–

Singaporean politician, son of the former Prime Minister Lee Kuan Yew.

39 In Singapore you don't volunteer to go into politics—you are invited to enter.
1984 Remark. Quoted in Alan Chong *Goh Tok Chong* (1991), ch.4.

Lee, Kuan Yew 1923–

Singaporean politician, the country's first Prime Minister (1959–90), renowned for his authoritarianism and intolerance of political opponents.

40 I have decided that we shall make and build and never give way.
1966 Remark, 27 Dec. Quoted in James Minchin *No Man is an Island* (1986), ch.8.

41 Even from my sick bed, even if you are going to lower me into the grave, and I feel something is wrong, I will get up.
1988 Remark, Aug. Quoted in C M Turnbull *A History of Singapore* (1989).

Lee, Laurie 1914–97

English writer. He fought in the Spanish Civil War, but is best known for *Cider With Rosie* (1959), his evocative account of growing up in an English village between the wars.

42 Such a morning it is when love
leans through geranium windows
and calls with a cockerel's tongue.
1947 'Day of these Days'.

43 I was set down from the carrier's cart at the age of three; and there with a sense of bewilderment and terror my life in the village began.
1959 *Cider With Rosie*, 'First Light'.

44 Effie M. was a monster. Six foot high and as strong as a farm horse. No sooner had she decided that she wanted Uncle Tom than she knocked him off his bicycle and told him.
1959 *Cider With Rosie*, 'The Uncles'.

45 As for me—for me, the grass grew longer, and more sorrowful, and the trees were surfaced like flesh, and girls were no longer to be treated lightly but were creatures of commanding sadness, and all journeys through the valley were now made alone, with passion in every bush, and the motions of wind and cloud and stars were suddenly for myself alone, and voices elected me of all men living and called me to deliver the world, and I groaned from solitude, blushed when I stumbled, loved strangers and bread and butter, and made long trips through the rain on my bicycle, stared wretchedly through lighted windows, grinned wryly to think how little I was known, and lived in a state of raging excitement.
1959 *Cider With Rosie*, 'Last Days'.

Lee, Robert E 1807–70

US Confederate General. He fought in the Mexican War and in Texas. During the Civil War, although he defeated McClellan at Richmond, he surrendered to General Grant at Appomatox, Virginia in 1865.

46 It is well that war is so terrible. We should grow too fond of it.
1862 Attributed, after the Battle of Fredericksburg, Dec.

Lee-Potter, Linda

British journalist.

47 Powerful men often succeed through the help of their wives. Powerful women only succeed in spite of their husbands.
1984 In the *Daily Mail*, 16 May.

Lees-Milne, James 1908–97

English diarist and founding Secretary of the National Trust's Country House Scheme.

48 All creatures give out a smell when aroused, it seems; certainly humans do.
Ancient as the Hills: Diaries, 1973–1974 (1997).

49 Watched [Vladimir] Horowitz playing his first concert in England for over thirty years. His fingers turn up at the ends, like a pig's nose.
Holy Dread: Diaries, 1982–1984 (2001).

Lees-Smith, Hastings Bernard 1878–1941

British politician. He was associated with Ruskin College, Oxford from its foundation in 1899. He was Liberal MP for Northampton (1910–18), and joined the Labour Party in 1919. He was Labour MP for Keighley (1922–23, 1924–31 and 1935–41).

50 Security can only be obtained by a scheme by which the nations of Europe and outside agree together that all will guarantee each, and each will guarantee all. The purposes of the war will be attained if there is a League of Nations with an absolute and decisive veto upon any mere aggression, and consideration of any legitimate claims that any of the countries engaged in the war may be able to make good.

1916 House of Commons, 21 Oct.

Leeson, Nick 1967–

British derivatives trader, who lost over £600 million trading on the Tokyo stockmarket and caused the collapse of Barings Bank.

51 My sincere apologies for the predicament I have left you in.

1995 Part of a faxed letter of resignation.

Léger, Fernand 1881–1946

French painter, a major force in the Cubist movement, although his paintings are more 'tubist' than 'cubist'. He executed murals for the UN building in New York (1952).

52 Modern man lives more and more in a preponderantly geometric order. All human creation mechanical or industrial is dependent upon geometric intentions.

1924 'The Aesthetic of the Machine', in *Bulletin de l'Effort Moderne*.

53 The thing depicted is less stationary, even the object in itself is less discernible than it used to be. A landscape broken into and traversed in a car or an express train loses in descriptive value but gains in synthetic value; the window of the railroad carriage or the windshield of the car, combined with the speed at which you are traveling, have changed the familiar look of things. Modern man registers one hundred times more impressions than did an eighteenth century artist.

Quoted in D Cooper *The Cubist Epoch* (1970).

Le Guin, Ursula *née Kroeber* 1929–

US writer. She is best known for her literate, politically aware works of science fiction, and her children's fantasy novels, notably the *Earthsea* trilogy (1968–72) and its overtly feminist sequel, *Tehanu* (1990).

54 It is a terrible thing, this kindness that human beings do not lose. Terrible because when we are finally naked in the dark and cold, it is all we have.

1969 *The Left Hand of Darkness*, ch.13.

55 To be, the will to power must increase with each fulfilment, making the fulfilment only a step to a further one. The vaster the power gained the vaster the appetite for more.

1971 *The Lathe of Heaven*, ch.9.

56 In so far as one denies what is, one is possessed by what is not, the compulsions, the fantasies, the terrors that flock to fill the void.

1971 *The Lathe of Heaven*, ch.10.

57 The years before and after the menstrual years are vestigial: the only meaningful condition left to women is that of fruitfulness.

1976 'The Space Crone', in *The Co-Evolution Quarterly*, Summer.

58 To me the 'female principle' is, or at least historically has been, basically anarchic. It values order without constraint, rule by custom not by force. It has been the male who enforces order, who constructs power structures, who makes, enforces, and breaks laws.

'Is Gender Necessary?', in Anderson and McIntyre (eds) *Aurora* (1976).

59 The preservation of life seems to be rather a slogan than a genuine goal of the anti-abortion forces; what they want is control. Control over behavior: power over women.

1982 Address to the National Abortion Rights Action League, Jan. Collected as 'The Princess' in *Dancing at the Edge of the World* (1989).

60 Success is the American Dream we can keep dreaming because most people in most places, including thirty million of ourselves, live wide awake in the terrible reality of poverty.

1983 Address at Mills College. Collected as 'A Left-Handed Commencement Address' in *Dancing at the Edge of the World* (1989).

61 We are volcanoes. When we women offer our experience as our truth, as human truth, all the maps change. There are new mountains.

1983 Address at Mills College. Collected as 'A Left-Handed Commencement Address' in *Dancing at the Edge of the World* (1989).

62 The children of the revolution are always ungrateful, and the revolution must be grateful that it is so.

1983 Address to Folger Library Poetry Series, Washington. Collected as 'Reciprocity of Prose and Poetry' in *Dancing at the Edge of the World* (1989).

63 When either the political or the scientific discourse announces itself as the voice of reason, it is playing God, and should be spanked and stood in the corner.

1986 Commencement address at Bryn Mawr College. Collected in *Dancing at the Edge of the World* (1989).

64 My imagination makes me human and makes me a fool; it gives me all the world and exiles me from it.

1990 'Winged Creatures On My Mind', in *Harper's*, Aug.

Lehmann-Haupt, Christopher Charles Herbert 1934–

US literary critic, born in Scotland. He was senior book reviewer on the *New York Times*.

65 One misses the hiss of acid.

1984 On Gore Vidal's biography *Lincoln* (1984). In the *New York Times*, 30 May.

66 We breathe, we think, we conceive of our lives as narratives.

1984 On Peter Brooks *Reading for the Plot* (1984). In the *New York Times*, 11 Jul.

67 The beginning of a plot…is the prompting of desire.

1984 On Peter Brooks *Reading for the Plot* (1984). In the *New York Times*, 11 Jul.

68 Happiest when he is trying to sculpture fog.

1989 On Robert C Christopher. In the *New York Times*, 29 May.

69 Stevenson's convictions were sometimes too complex for the binary political arena to which he devoted his life.

1989 In the *New York Times*, 31 Jul.

70 The only trouble with this book is that its covers are too close together.

1992 On Florence King *With Charity Toward None* (1992). In the *New York Times*, 9 Apr.

Lehrer, Tom (Thomas Andrew) 1928–

US teacher, songwriter and social satirist.

71 In one word he told me the secret of success in mathematics: Plagiarize…only be sure always to call it please 'research'.
1953 'Lobachevski', satirical song.

72 We'll all go together when we go,
Every Hottentot and every Eskimo,
When the air becomes uranious,
We'll all go simultaneous,
Yes, we'll all go together when we go.
1953 'We'll All Go Together When We Go', satirical song.

Leisen, Mitchell 1898–1972

US film director. His films include *Hold Back the Dawn* (1941), *Frenchman's Creek* (1944) and *Kitty* (1945).

73 He was God out there. He wanted it a certain way, that was the MGM style, and that's what you got.
On working for Cedric Gibbons on *Young Man with Ideas* (1952), quoted in David Chierichetti *Hollywood Director* (1972).

Lekota, Mosiuoa 1948–

South African Defence Minister (1999–).

74 When will we cease to be Africans, Coloureds, Indians and Whites and merely South Africans? This is the question we must ask ourselves.
2004 Briefing the South African parliament's portfolio committee on defence, 1 Jun.

LeMay, Curtis Emerson 1906–90

US general and air force chief. After commanding in World War II he became air force Chief of Staff (1961–5) and ran unsuccessfully for Vice-President as George Wallace's running mate, 1968.

75 My solution to the problem would be to tell them that they've got to draw in their horns, or we're going to bomb them into the Stone Age.
Of the North Vietnamese. *Mission with LeMay* (1965).

76 A man should have dinner with his friends, and the commanding general has no friends.
On declining to dine with a group of colonels. Recalled on his death, 1 Oct 1990.

Lemmon, Jack (John Uhler) 1925–2001

US actor. He made his film debut in *It Should Happen to You* (1954), beginning a career as a comic, bittersweet underdog which won him eight Academy Award nominations and two Oscars.

77 I won't quit until I get run over by a truck, a producer or a critic.
1986 In *Newsweek*, 5 May.

78 I would rather play Hamlet with no rehearsal than TV golf.
Quoted in Michael Hobbs *The Golf Quotation Book* (1992).

79 If you think it's hard to meet new people, try picking up the wrong golf ball.
Attributed.

Lemmy 1945–

English heavy metal singer and bass player, member of the band Motörhead.

80 People don't know how to be outrageous any more.
2004 In *The Guardian*, 31 May.

L'Engle, Madeleine *married name* **Mrs Hugh Franklin** 1918–

US writer, best known for her children's trilogy *A Wrinkle in Time* (1962), *A Wind in the Door* (1973) and *A Swiftly Tilting Planet* (1978). Her many other works include *Troubling the Star* (1994) and the autobiographical *Summer of Great-Grandmother* (1974).

81 Artistic temperament…sometimes seems a battleground for a dark angel of destruction and a bright angel of creativity wrestling.
1982 *A Severed Wasp*.

Lenin, Vladimir Ilyich *originally* **Vladimir Ilyich Ulyanov** 1870–1924

Russian Marxist revolutionary and politician. After the Feb 1917 revolution he urged the proletariat to seize power, and in Oct 1917 led the Bolshevik Revolution and headed the first Soviet government. After the Civil War (1918–21) he introduced the New Economic Policy, which his critics saw as a retreat from strict socialism.

82 A small, compact core, consisting of reliable, experienced and hardened workers, with responsible agents…connected by all the rules of strict secrecy with the organisations of revolutionists, can, with the wide support of the masses and without an elaborate set of rules, perform all the functions of a trade union.
1902 *What Is to be Done?*

83 One Step Forward, Two Steps Back
1904 Title of book.

84 I greet you as the advance guard of the world proletarian army. The hour is not far off when…the German people will turn their weapons against their capitalist exploiters. The sun of the socialist revolution has already risen.
1917 Speech, Petrograd, 16 Apr.

85 We will now proceed to the building of socialism.
1917 Speech, Oct. Quoted in A J P Taylor *From the Boer War to the Cold War: Essays on Twentieth-Century Europe* (1995), p.192.

86 A good man fallen among Fabians.
Of George Bernard Shaw. Quoted in Arthur Ransome *Six Weeks in Russia in 1919* (1919).

87 Chess is the gymnasium of the mind.
Quoted in Colin Jarman *The Guinness Dictionary of Sports Quotations* (1990).

Lennon, John Winston 1940–80

English rock singer, guitarist and songwriter. A member of The Beatles, he wrote with Paul McCartney many of the hits of the 1960s. He later established himself as a solo artist. He was shot dead by a deranged fan outside his Manhattan apartment.

88 On this next number I want you all to join in. Would those in the cheap seats clap their hands? The rest of you can rattle your jewellery.
1963 Addressing the audience during a Royal Command performance. Quoted in Bill Harry *The Ultimate Beatles Encyclopedia* (1992).

89 We're more popular than Jesus Christ now. I don't know which will go first, rock and roll or Christianity.
1966 In the *Evening Standard*.

90 All we are saying is give peace a chance.
1969 Song (with his wife, Yoko Ono), used widely in protests against the Vietnam War.

91 Imagine there's no heaven,
It's easy if you try,
No hell below us,
Above us only sky,
Imagine all the people
Living for today.
1971 'Imagine'.

92 Women should be obscene and not heard.
Attributed.

Lennon, John Winston and McCartney, Sir (James) Paul   1940–80, 1942–

English songwriters and composers who formed The Beatles in 1960. They gained international fame with their songs and performances. They disbanded in 1970.

93 For I don't care too much for money,
For money can't buy me love.
1964 'Can't Buy Me Love'.

94 It's been a hard day's night,
And I've been working like a dog.
1964 'A Hard Day's Night'.

95 She's got a ticket to ride, but she don't care.
1965 'Ticket to Ride'.

96 Eleanor Rigby picks up the rice in a church where a wedding has been,
Lives in a dream.
Waits at the window, wearing the face that she keeps in a jar by the door,
Who is it for?
All the lonely people, where do they all come from?
1966 'Eleanor Rigby'.

97 Oh I get by with a little help from my friends,
Mm, I get high with a little help from my friends.
1967 'With a Little Help From My Friends'.

98 Will you still need me, will you still feed me,
When I'm sixty four?
1967 'When I'm Sixty Four'.

99 Strawberry fields forever.
1967 Title of song.

1 Back in the USSR.
1968 Title of song.

Lenthall, William   1591–1662

English lawyer and parliamentarian, Speaker of the Long Parliament (1640–53) and Master of the Rolls from 1643. He was again made Speaker in 1654 and 1659, and in 1657 became one of Cromwell's peers.

2 May it please your Majesty, I have neither eye to see nor tongue to speak in this place, but as this House is pleased to direct me, whose servant I am.
1642 To Charles I, on his arrival in the Chamber to arrest five Members, House of Commons, 4 Jan.

Leonard, Elmore John   1925–

US novelist and screenwriter. He has written mainly in the field of crime fiction, where he is widely regarded as the foremost practitioner of his era.

3 The Chekhov of the suburbs.
Of John Cheever. Quoted in *The Annual Obituary 1982* (1983).

4 I try to leave out the parts that people skip.
1985 In *Publisher's Weekly*, 8 Mar.

5 If it sounds like writing, I rewrite it.
1985 In *Newsweek*, 22 Apr.

6 Easy on the Adverbs, Exclamation Points and Especially Hooptedoodle.
2003 Essay title.

Leonard, Sugar Ray   1956–

US boxer.

7 We're all endowed with certain God-given talents. Mine happens to be punching people in the head.
Quoted in Colin Jarman *The Guinness Dictionary of Sports Quotations* (1990).

Leonardo da Vinci   1452–1519

Italian painter, sculptor, architect and engineer, the epitome of the 'Renaissance' man. He entered the service of Cesare Borgia in 1500 as architect and engineer, working alongside Michelangelo, and worked for Louis XII of France in 1506.

8 To devise is the work of the master, to execute the act of the servant.
Treatise on Painting (published 1651, translated by A P McMahon, 1956).

9 I do not find any difference between painting and sculpture except that the sculptor pursues his work with greater physical fatigue than the painter and the painter pursues his with greater mental fatigue.
Treatise on Painting (published 1651, translated by A P McMahon, 1956).

10 Shun those studies in which the work that results dies with the worker.
The Notebooks of Leonardo da Vinci (translated by Edward MacCurdy, 1938), vol.1, pt.1.

11 Painting is poetry which is seen and not heard, and poetry is a painting which is heard but not seen.
Quoted in J P and Irma A Richter *The Literary Works of Leonardo da Vinci* (2 vols, 1939).

12 Force is the same throughout and the whole is in every part of it. Force is a spiritual power, an invisible energy which is imparted by violence from without to all bodies out of their natural balance.
Quoted in Jean-Paul Richter (ed) *The Literary Works of Leonardo da Vinci* (1939).

13 If a man have a tent made in linen of which the apertures have all been stopped up, and it be twelve *braccia* across and twelve in depth, he will be able to throw himself down from any great height without sustaining injury.
Description of a parachute. *Notebooks*. Quoted in Vincent Cronin *The Flowering of the Renaissance* (1969).

14 The air moves like a river and carries the clouds with it; just as running water carries all the things that float upon it.
Notebooks. Quoted in Vincent Cronin *The Flowering of the Renaissance* (1969).

15 He is a poor disciple who does not excel his master.
Quoted in Irma A Richter (ed) *Selections from the Notebooks of Leonardo da Vinci* (1977).

16 A good painter has two chief objects to paint, man and

the intention of his soul; the former is easy, the latter harder, because he has to represent it by the attitudes and movements of the limbs.
Quoted in Irma A Richter (ed) *Selections from the Notebooks of Leonardo da Vinci* (1977).

17 Perspective is the bridle and rudder of painting.
Quoted in Irma A Richter (ed) *Selections from the Notebooks of Leonardo da Vinci* (1977).

18 The span of a man's outspread arms is equal to his height.
Quoted in Irma A Richter (ed) *Selections from the Notebooks of Leonardo da Vinci* (1977).

19 Do not despise my opinion, when I remind you that it should not be hard for you to stop sometimes and look into the stains of walls, or ashes of a fire, or clouds, or mud or like places, in which, if you consider them well, you may find really marvellous ideas.
Quoted in Irma A Richter (ed) *Selections from the Notebooks of Leonardo da Vinci* (1977).

20 Just as a stone flung into the water becomes the centre and cause of many circles, and as sound diffuses itself in circles in the air; so any object, placed in the luminous atmosphere, diffuses itself in circles, and fills the surrounding air with infinite images of itself.
Quoted in Irma A Richter (ed) *Selections from the Notebooks of Leonardo da Vinci* (1977).

21 The painter who draws by practice and judgement of the eye without the use of reason is like a mirror which copies everything placed in front of it without knowledge of the same.
Quoted in Irma A Richter (ed) *Selections from the Notebooks of Leonardo da Vinci* (1977).

Leonidas d.480 BC

King of Sparta, commander of the Greeks when the Persian army of Xerxes invaded mainland Greece. At the narrow pass of Thermopylae he made a heroic stand with 300 Spartans.

22 Come and take them.
Attributed reply when Xerxes summoned him to surrender his weapons at Thermopylae. Quoted in Plutarch, *Apophthegmata Laconica*.

Lerner, Alan Jay 1918–86

US lyricist, screenwriter and producer. He frequently worked in collaboration with Frederick Loewe, and is best known for *Brigadoon* (1955), *Gigi* (1958), *My Fair Lady* (1964) and *Camelot* (1967).

23 Those little eyes so helpless and appealing
One day will flash and send you crashing through the ceiling.
1958 'Thank Heaven for Little Girls', in the musical *Gigi* (music by Frederick Loewe).

24 We met at nine
—We met at eight
I was on time
—No, you were late
Ah yes! I remember it well.
1958 'I Remember it Well', in the musical *Gigi* (music by Frederick Loewe).

25 I've Grown Accustomed To Her Face.
1964 Title of song, in *My Fair Lady* (music by Marcus Loewe).

26 Oozing charm from every pore
He oiled his way around the floor.

1964 'You Did It', from *My Fair Lady* (music by Marcus Loewe).

27 Why can't a woman be more like a man?
Men are so honest, so thoroughly square;
Eternally noble, historically fair;
Who, when you win, will always give your back a pat.
Why can't a woman be like that?
1964 'A Hymn to Him', from *My Fair Lady* (music by Frederick Loewe).

28 Because it saves time.
When Andrew Lloyd Webber asked him 'Why do people take an instant dislike to me?' Quoted by Leah Garchik in the *San Francisco Chronicle*, 27 Nov 1990.

Le Sage, Alain René 1668–1747

French novelist and playwright. He is best remembered for his play *Turcaret* (1709), which satirized the financial world, and the picaresque novel *Gil Blas de Santillane* (1715–35).

29 Justice is such a fine thing that we cannot pay too dearly for it.
1707 *Crispin rival de son maître*, pt.9.

Leslie, David 1601–82

Scottish soldier. He fought at Marston Moor (1644), and defeated Montrose at Philiphaugh (1645). Routed by Cromwell at Dunbar in 1650, he was subsequently imprisoned and held in the Tower until the Restoration. He was made Lord Newark in 1651.

30 How glorious it would be in the eyes of God and men, if we managed to hunt the Catholics from England, follow them to France, and, like the bold King of Sweden, rouse the Protestants in France, plant our religion in Paris by agreement or force, and go from there to Rome to chase the Antichrist and burn the town whence superstition comes.
1643 Said to Lord Hume, Council of Scottish Nobles, Aug.

Lessing, Doris May *née Tayler* 1919–

Rhodesian writer, born in Iran. She has lived much of her adult life in England after being exiled for her opposition to the white Southern Rhodesian government. She was a communist for a time, and later an icon of the women's movement. Her best-known works are the novel sequence *Children of Violence* (1952–69) and *The Golden Notebook* (1962).

31 When old settlers say 'One has to understand the country,' what they mean is, 'You have to get used to our ideas about the native.' They are saying, in effect, 'Learn our ideas, or otherwise get out; we don't want you.'
1950 *The Grass Is Singing*, ch.1.

32 When a white man in Africa by accident looks into the eyes of a native and sees the human being (which it is his chief preoccupation to avoid), his sense of guilt, which he denies, fumes up in resentment and he brings down the whip.
1950 *The Grass Is Singing*, ch.8.

33 I had learned that if one cannot call a country to heel like a dog, neither can one dismiss the past with a smile in an easy gush of feeling, saying: I could not help it, I am also a victim.
1951 *This was the Old Chief's Country*, 'The Old Chief Mshlanga'.

34 For she was suffering that misery peculiar to the young, that they are going to be cheated by circumstances out

of the full life every nerve and instinct is clamouring for.
1952 *Martha Quest*, pt.1, ch.1.

35 She was thinking—for, since she had been formed by literature, she could think in no other way—that all this had been described in Dickens, Tolstoy, Hugo, Dostoevsky, and a dozen others. All that noble and terrific indignation had done nothing, achieved nothing, the shout of anger from the nineteenth century might as well have been silent—for here came the file of prisoners, handcuffed two by two, and on their faces was that same immemorial look of patient, sardonic understanding.
1952 *Martha Quest*, ch.2.

36 In every city there is a group of middle-aged and elderly women who in fact run it. The extent to which they are formally organised is no gauge of their real power. The way in which they respond to danger is that gauge; and from the frankness with which they express their intentions can be measured the extent of the danger.
1954 *A Proper Marriage*, pt.3, ch.1.

37 Martha and Jasmine smiled at each other…the future they dreamed of seemed just around the corner; they could almost touch it. Each saw an ideal town, clean, noble and beautiful, soaring up over the actual town they saw, which consisted in this area of sordid little shops and third-rate cafés.
1958 *A Ripple from the Storm*, pt.1, ch.1.

38 There is only one real sin, and that is to persuade oneself that the second-best is anything but the second-best.
1962 *The Golden Notebook*, 'The Blue Notebook'.

39 It occurred to her that she was going mad… Yet it did not seem to her that she was even slightly mad; but rather that people who were not as obsessed as she was with the inchoate world mirrored in the newspapers were all out of touch with an awful necessity.
1962 *The Golden Notebook*, 'Free Women 5'.

40 But this novel was not a trumpet for Women's Liberation. It described many female emotions of aggression, hostility, resentment. It put them into print. Apparently what many women were thinking, feeling, experiencing came as a great surprise.
1971 *The Golden Notebook*, preface to new edition.

41 Briefing for a Descent into Hell.
1971 Title of novel.

42 It does no harm to repeat, as often as you can, 'Without me the literary industry would not exist'.
1980 In *The Author*, spring.

43 To be in love with a country or a political regime is a tricky business. You get your heart broken even more surely than by being in love with a person.
1992 *African Laughter*, 'Next Time 1988'.

Lessing, Gotthold Ephraim 1729–81

German philosopher and playwright, an important Enlightenment figure, best known for his essay on aesthetics, *Laokoon* (1766).

44 *Wie manches würde in der Theorie unwidersprechlich scheinen, wenn es dem Genie nicht gelungen wäre, das Widerspiel durch die Tat zu erweisen.*
How many things would have appeared incontestable in theory if genius had not proved them wrong in practice.

1766 *Laokoon: an essay upon the limits of painting and poetry*, pt.4.

45 *Ein einziger dankbarer Gedanke gen Himmel ist das vollkommenste Gebet.*
One single grateful thought raised to heaven is the most perfect prayer.
1767 *Minna von Barnhelm*, act 2, sc.7.

46 *Wer richtig räsonniert, erfindet auch; und wer erfinden will, muss räsonnieren können. Nur die glauben, dass sich das eine von dem anderen trennen lasse, die zu keinem von beiden aufgelegt sind.*
The man who can reason properly can invent; and anyone who wants to invent must be able to reason. The only people who think that the one can be separated from the other are those who have no inclination for either.
1769 *Hamburgische Dramaturgie*.

47 *Es ist nicht wahr, dass die kürzeste Linie immer die Gerade ist.*
It is not true that the shortest line is always the straight one.
1780 *Die Erziehung des Menschengeschlechts*.
➤ See also Brecht 151:10.

L'Estrange, Sir Roger 1616–1704

English journalist and pamphleteer. During the Restoration he was Licenser of the Press.

48 Supposing the Press in order, the people in their right wits, and news or no news to be the question, a Public Mercury should not have my Vote, because I think it makes the Multitude too familiar with the actions and counsels of their superiors, too pragmatical and censorious, and gives them not only an itch but a kind of colourable right to be meddling with the government.
1663 *The Intelligencer*, 31 Aug.

Leupold, Jakob 1674–1727

German mechanic, machinery constructor and government mining commissioner, who wrote a large and comprehensive work on the tasks the engineer faced.

49 As in earlier days were our mechanics, such today are our engineers, who may be required not only to tear down a fortress, and then to build it up again, but also to produce all sorts of engines based on mechanical principles, and with equal ease to defend or to annihilate a fortress.
1724 *Theatrum machinarum*.

50 The best machines and to be chosen above all others are those which consist of the fewest parts or which are the simplest, which produce the least friction; which are not too heavily loaded, and where the power can be conveniently applied without any waste.
1724 *Theatrum machinarum*.

Levant, Oscar 1906–72

US composer, pianist, writer, actor and conductor. He played Gershwin's 'Rhapsody in Blue' on its first performance in 1932.

51 It's a right step in the wrong direction.
1935 Attributed remark at the first performance of George

Gershwin's *Porgy and Bess*. He in fact had the deepest respect for Gershwin's music.

52 Chutzpah—that quality which enables a man who has murdered his mother and father to throw himself on the mercy of the court as an orphan.
1968 *The Unimportance of Being Oscar.*

Levenson, Michael

US literary critic, a professor of English at the University of Virginia.

53 Although Brooke never succeeded in becoming the first modern poet, he may deserve to be called the first modern undergraduate, a title of comparable significance.
1987 Of Rupert Brooke. 'Budding Brooke', in the *New Republic*, 31 Aug.

Levenstein, Ros

US copywriter.

54 I'm only here for the beer.
1971 British advertising slogan for Double Diamond beer.

Leverson, Ada 1895–1936

English novelist and journalist, she was friendly with Beerbohm and Wilde, who called her 'the Sphinx'. She wrote six novels.

55 You don't know a woman until you have had a letter from her.
1912 *Tenterhooks*, ch.7.

56 He seemed at ease and to have the look of the last gentleman in Europe.
1930 Of Oscar Wilde. *Letters to the Sphinx.*

Levertov, Denise 1923–97

English-born US poet. She is associated with the Black Mountain group of poets led by Charles Olsen, but has a distinctive voice of her own, reflected in numerous collections.

57 Let's go—much as that dog goes,
intently haphazard.
1958 *Overland to the Islands*, 'Overland to the Islands'.

58 Pergo Park knew me, and Clavering, and Havering-atte-Bower,
Stanford Rivers lost me in osier-beds, Stapleford Abbots sent me safe home on the dark road after Simeon-quiet evensong,
Wanstead drew me over and over into its basic poetry, in its serpentine lake I saw bass-viols among the golden dead
leaves,
through its trees the ghost of a great house.
1961 *The Jacob's Ladder*, 'A Map of the Western Part of the County of Essex in England'.

59 The world is
not with us enough.
1964 *O Taste and See*, 'O Taste and See'.
➤ See Wordsworth 925:4.

60 Death and pain dominate this world, for though many are cured, they leave still weak,

still tremulous, still knowing mortality

has whispered to them; have seen in the folding of white bedspreads according to rule

the starched pleats of a shroud.
1972 *Footprints*, 'The Malice of Innocence'.

Levi, Primo 1919–87

Italian writer and the author of a series of major works of remembrance and analysis of his experiences in Nazi concentration camps in World War II.

61 The future of humanity is uncertain, even in the most prosperous countries, and the quality of life deteriorates; and yet I believe that what is being discovered about the infinitely large and infinitely small is sufficient to absolve this end of the century and millennium. What a very few are acquiring in knowledge of the physical world will perhaps cause this period not to be judged as a pure return of barbarism.
1985 *Other People's Trades*, 'News from the Sky' (translated by Raymond Rosenthal, 1989).

Levin, (Henry) Bernard 1928–2004

English writer, journalist and critic. In 1985 he crossed the Alps on foot, following the path of the Carthaginian general, Hannibal.

62 The musical equivalent of blancmange.
1983 Of the music of Frederick Delius. *Enthusiasms.*

63 I dislike almost all dogs, but Alsatians, I do truly believe, should be prohibited by law in any civilised country…
The more I see of dogs, the more I admire men.
1985 *Hannibal's Footsteps.*

64 Baedeker is astonishingly enduring; travellers can use nineteenth-century editions with confidence, providing they take some elementary precautions. Many hotels will long since have disappeared, and the prices will be somewhat different, but if Baedeker says 'On leaving the tunnel, the best view is on the right', it probably still is, unless somebody has shifted the mountain, and his descriptions of scenery and where to go to see it at its best are still valid, as is practically all of his potted history.
1985 *Hannibal's Footsteps.*

Lévis, Duc de 1764–1830

French soldier and writer.

65 *Noblesse oblige.*
Nobility brings obligations.
1812 *Maximes et réflexions*, 'Morale: Maximes et Préceptes', no.73.

Lévi-Strauss, Claude 1908–

French social anthropologist.

66 *La langue est une raison humaine qui a ses raisons, et que l'homme ne connaît pas.*
Language is a form of human reason, and has its reasons which are unknown to man.
1962 *La Pensée sauvage*, ch.9.
➤ See Pascal 641:23.

67 The scientific mind does not so much provide the right answers as ask the right questions.
1964 *The Raw and the Cooked* (translated by John and Doreen Weightman 1983).

68 I can't help thinking that science would be more appealing if it had no practical use.

1964 *The Raw and the Cooked* (translated by John and Doreen Weightman 1983).

Lewin, Albert 1895–1968

US screenwriter and director. His films include *The Moon and Sixpence* (1943), *The Picture of Dorian Gray* (1945) and *Pandora and the Flying Dutchman* (1950).

69 The measure of love is what one is willing to give up for it.

1950 *Pandora and the Flying Dutchman*.

Lewis, C(live) S(taples) 1898–1963

English novelist, literary scholar and theological writer. His most widely read works include the children's series *The Chronicles of Narnia* (1950–6), several allegorical science-fiction novels, and the Christian apologetics, *The Screwtape Letters* (1942).

70 Humanity does not pass through phases as a train passes through stations: being alive, it has the privilege of always moving yet never leaving anything behind.

1936 *The Allegory of Love*, ch.1.

71 Out of the Silent Planet.

1938 Title of novel.

72 There is wishful thinking in Hell as well as on earth.

1942 *The Screwtape Letters*, preface.

73 Gratitude looks to the past and love to the present: fear, avarice, lust and ambition look ahead.

1942 *The Screwtape Letters*, no.15.

74 He has a vulgar mind.

1942 Of God. *The Screwtape Letters*, no.22.

75 She's the sort of woman who lives for others—you can always tell the others by their hunted expression.

1942 *The Screwtape Letters*, no.26.

76 Fatigue makes women talk more and men less.

1942 *The Screwtape Letters*, no.30.

77 Courage is not simply one of the virtues but the form of every virtue at the testing point.

Quoted in Cyril Connolly *The Unquiet Grave* (1944), ch.3.

78 I remember summing up what I took to be our destiny, in conversation with my best friend at Chartres, by the formula, 'Term, holidays, term, holidays, till we leave school, and then work, work, work till we die.'

1955 *Surprised by Joy*, ch.4.

79 A sick society must think much about politics, as a sick man must think much about his digestion.

1980 *The Weight of Glory*.

80 All except the best men would rather be called wicked than vulgar.

Quoted in *The Guardian*, 21 Aug 1980.

Lewis, Esther *married name* Clark fl.1747–89

English poet.

81 Are simple women only fit
To dress, to darn, to flower or knit,
To mind the distaff, or the spit?
Why are the needle and the pen
Thought incompatible by men?

1754 'A Mirror for Detractors', l.146–50.

Lewis, Joe E 1902–71

US comedian.

82 I distrust camels and anyone else who can go a week without a drink.

Recalled on his death, 4 Jun 1971.

Lewis, John L(lewellyn) 1880–1969

US labour leader.

83 No tin hat brigade of goose-stepping vigilantes or bibblebabbling mob of blackguarding and corporation-paid scoundrels will prevent the onward march of labor, or divert its purpose to play its natural and rational part in the development of the economic, political, and social life of our nation.

1937 Address, 3 Sep. Recalled on his death 11 Jun 1969.

84 All forms of government fall when it comes up to the question of bread—bread for the family, something to eat. Bread to a man with a family comes first—before his union, before his citizenship, before his church affiliation. Bread!

1963 In the *Saturday Evening Post*, 12 Oct.

Lewis, (Harry) Sinclair 1885–1951

US novelist. His novels satirized the materialism and intolerance of US small-town life. He is best known for his novel *Babbitt* (1922), a study of middle-class philistinism. In 1930 he became the first American to receive the Nobel prize for literature.

85 He never put on BVDs without thanking the God of Progress that he didn't wear tight, long, old-fashioned undergarments.

1922 *Babbitt*, ch.1, section 4. BVD is a trademark for a brand of US underwear.

86 His name was George F. Babbitt. He was forty-six years old now, in April, 1920, and he made nothing in particular, neither butter nor shoes nor poetry, but he was nimble in the calling of selling houses for more than people could afford to pay.

1922 *Babbitt*, ch.1.

87 To George F. Babbitt, as to most prosperous citizens of Zenith, his motor car was poetry and tragedy, love and heroism. The office was his pirate ship but the car his perilous excursion ashore.

1922 *Babbitt*, ch.3.

88 In other countries, art and literature are left to a lot of shabby bums living in attics and feeding on booze and spaghetti, but in America the successful writer or picture-painter is indistinguishable from any other decent business man.

1922 *Babbitt*, ch.14.

89 Damn the great executives, the men of measured merriment, damn the men with careful smiles, damn the men that run the shops, oh, damn their measured merriment.

1925 *Arrowsmith*, ch.25.

90 Our American professors like their literature clear and cold and pure and very dead.

1930 Nobel prize address, 12 Dec.

91 Intellectually I know that America is no better than any other country; emotionally I know she is better than

every other country.
1930 Interview in Berlin, 29 Dec.

92 It Can't Happen Here.
1935 Title of novel.

93 A man takes a drink, a drink takes another, and the drink takes the man.
Words to his future wife, Dorothy Thompson. Quoted in Vincent Sheean *Dorothy and Red* (1963).

Lewis, (Percy) Wyndham 1882–1957

English novelist, painter and critic. He co-founded the Vorticist movement with Ezra Pound, and remained an important experimental writer and painter between the wars. He became blind in 1951, but continued to write. His works include *The Apes of God* (1930) and the autobiographical *The Self Condemned* (1954).

94 'Dying for an idea,' again, sounds well enough, but why not let the idea die instead of you?
1926 *The Art of Being Ruled*, pt.1, ch.1.

95 When we say 'science' we can either mean any manipulation of the inventive and organizing power of the human intellect: or we can mean such an extremely different thing as the religion of science, the vulgarized derivative from this pure activity manipulated by a sort of priestcraft into a great religious and political weapon.
1926 *The Art of Being Ruled*.

96 The puritanical potentialities of science have never been forecast. If it evolves a body of organized rites, and is established as a religion, hierarchically organized, things more than anything else will be done in the name of 'decency'. The coarse fumes of tobacco and liquors, the consequent tainting of the breath and staining of white fingers and teeth, which is so offensive to many women, will be the first things attended to.
1926 *The Art of Being Ruled*.

97 The revolutionary simpleton is everywhere.
1927 *Time and Western Man*, pt.1, ch.6.

98 Gertrude Stein's prose song is a cold, black suet-pudding…of fabulously reptilian length.
1927 *Time and Western Man*, pt.1, ch.13.

99 If you must go nowhere, step out.
1928 *The Childermass*, final words.

1 It is to what I have called the Apes of God that I am drawing your attention—those prosperous mountebanks who alternately imitate and mock at and traduce those figures they at once admire and hate.
1930 *The Apes of God*, pt.3.

2 The soul started at the knee-cap and ended at the navel.
1930 *The Apes of God*, pt.12.

3 Give me the *outside* of all things, I am a fanatic for the externality of things.
1937 *Blasting and Bombardiering*, ch.1.

4 Then down came the lid—the day was lost, for art, at Sarajevo. World-politics stepped in, and a war was started which has not ended yet: 'a war to end war'. But it merely ended art. It did not end war.
1937 *Blasting and Bombardiering*, pt.5, 'Toward an Art-Less Society'.

5 'The Art of Being Ruled' might be described from some points of view as an infernal Utopia.
1950 *Rude Assignment*, ch.31.

6 An account…of the decadence occupying the trough between the two world wars introduces us to a moronic inferno of insipidity and decay.
1950 *Rude Assignment*, ch.31.

LeWitt, Sol 1928–

US artist, one of the developers of the branch of Conceptual art referred to as 'Minimalism'.

7 In Conceptual art the idea or concept is the most important aspect of the work…all planning and decisions are made beforehand and the execution is a perfunctory affair. The idea becomes the machine that makes the art.
1967 'Paragraphs on Conceptual Art', in *Artforum*, summer.

8 One usually understands the art of the past by applying the conventions of the present thus misunderstanding the art of the past.
1969 'Sentences on Conceptual Art', in *Art-Language*, vol.1, no.1, May.

Lewontin, Richard Charles 1929–

US evolutionary biologist, geneticist and writer, Professor of Zoology at Harvard.

9 It is characteristic of the design of scientific research that exquisite attention is devoted to methodological problems that can be solved, while the pretense is made that the ones that cannot be solved are really nothing to worry about.
1995 'Sex, Lies, and Social Science', in the *New York Review of Books*, 20 Apr.

10 The social scientist is in a difficult, if not impossible position. On the one hand there is the temptation to see all of society as one's autobiography writ large, surely not the path to general truth. On the other hand, there is the attempt to be general and objective by pretending that one knows nothing about the experience of being human, forcing the investigator to pretend that people usually know and tell the truth about important issues, when we all know from our own lives how impossible that is.
1995 'Sex, Lies, and Social Science', in the *New York Review of Books*, 20 Apr.

Leybourne, George *pseudonym of* **Joseph Saunders** 1842–84

English singer, entertainer and songwriter, a star of the Victorian music-hall.

11 O, he flies through the air with the greatest of ease, This daring young man on the flying trapeze.
1868 'The Daring Young Man on the Flying Trapeze'.

Lezama Lima, José 1910–76

Cuban poet, novelist and essayist. His autobiographical novel *Paradiso* (1966) is considered his masterpiece, and he is the key figure of Cuban neo-Baroque literature.

12 *Más que una costumbre, parece como un conjuro para una divinidad que todos desconocemos, que al reunirse varios cubanos…se permanece en un silencio de suspensión, hasta que se oye una voz cualquiera que dice o canta algo, que no tiene relación con la convocatoria para la reunión.*

Rather than custom, it feels more like an invocation to an unknown deity when Cubans get together...they hold a suspenseful silence until any voice is heard saying or singing something that has nothing to do with the purpose of the meeting.
1966 *Paradiso*, ch.3.

Li Po 701–62

Chinese poet, patronized by Emperor Ming Huang until banished from the court. He is said to have drowned after falling intoxicated from a barge, in an attempt to embrace the moon's reflection in the water.

13 Since Life is but a Dream,
Why toil to no avail?
c.750 'A Homily on Ideals in Life, Uttered in Springtime on Rising from a Drunken Slumber', collected in *A Golden Treasury of Chinese Poetry* (translated by John Turner, 1967).

Liberace *pseudonym of* **Wladziu Valentino Liberace** 1919–87

US pianist and entertainer, renowned for his flamboyant lifestyle.

14 What you said hurt me very much. I cried all the way to the bank.
1973 Responding to a hostile critic. *Autobiography.*

Liberman, Alexander 1912–99

Russian-born US artist and editor, artistic director of Vogue (1943–62). His works include *Olympic Iliad* (1984) and *Faith* (1987). He published *The Artist in his Studio* (1960).

15 All art is solitary and the studio is a torture area.
1979 In the *New York Times*, 13 May.

Lichtenberg, Georg Christoph 1742–99

German scientist and philosopher, a lecturer at the University of Göttingen. His philosophical reputation rests on his aphorisms, collected in notebooks throughout his adult life.

16 Every man also has his moral backside which he refrains from showing unless he has to and keeps covered as long as possible with the trousers of decorum.
c.1770 *Aphorisms*, Notebook B (translated by R J Hollingdale, 1990).

17 If an angel were ever to tell us anything of his philosophy I believe many propositions would sound like 2 times 2 equals 13.
c.1770 *Aphorisms*, Notebook B (translated by R J Hollingdale, 1990).

18 When a book and a head collide and a hollow sound is heard, must it always have come from the book?
c.1773–1775 *Aphorisms*, Notebook D (translated by R J Hollingdale, 1990).

19 What they call 'heart' lies much lower than the fourth waistcoat button.
c.1776–1779 *Aphorisms*, Notebook F (translated by R J Hollingdale, 1990).

20 It is almost impossible to bear the torch of truth through a crowd without singeing someone's beard.
c.1779–1783 *Aphorisms*, Notebook G (translated by R J Hollingdale, 1990).

21 To err is human also in so far as the animals seldom or never err, or at least only the cleverest of them do so.
c.1779–1783 *Aphorisms*, Notebook G (translated by R J Hollingdale, 1990).

22 Once he has stolen his 100,100 thalers a rogue can walk through the world an honest man.
c.1784–1788 *Aphorisms*, Notebook H (translated by R J Hollingdale, 1990).

23 A golden rule: we must judge men, not by their opinions, but by what their opinions make of them.
c.1791 *Aphorisms*, Notebook J (translated by R J Hollingdale, 1990).

24 Doubt everything at least once, even the proposition that two times two equals four.
c.1796 *Aphorisms*, Notebook K (translated by R J Hollingdale, 1990).

Lichtenstein, Roy 1923–97

US painter, a key figure of Pop Art. He moved from Abstract Expressionism in the 1950s to illustrations from popular magazines and cartoon strips, duplicating the dots of newspaper reproduction in colourful, large-scale works.

25 Paintings are Rorschach ink blots. They are what you want them to be.
1993 In *The Times*, 27 Mar.

Liebermann, Max 1847–1935

German painter and graphic artist. His early works are open-air studies and sentimental scenes of humble life, and he later found a more colourful, romantic style, influenced by Impressionism.

26 The art of drawing is the art of omission.
Quoted in Paul Klee *On Modern Art* (1979).

Liebman, David 1946–

US jazz saxophonist, highly regarded as a performer and teacher.

27 A jazz performance centers upon the process of creation. The final objective is not only the finished product, but the path and process taken towards it.
1988 *Self-Portrait of a Jazz-Artist*, ch.3.

Ligne, Charles Joseph, Prince de 1735–1814

Belgian soldier and man of letters, who served in the Seven Year's War (1756–63) and the Russo-Turkish war (1787–93). A skilful diplomat and royal favourite, he also wrote extensively.

28 *Le congrès ne marche pas, il danse.*
The Congress makes no progress; it dances.
1814 On the Congress of Vienna (1814–15). Quoted in Auguste de la Garde-Chambonas *Souvenirs du Congrès de Vienne, 1814–1815* (1820), ch.1.

29 One could forgive the fiend for becoming a torrent, but to become an earthquake was really too much.
1814 Of Napoleon I. Attributed.

Lillie, Beatrice Gladys *stage-name of* **Constance Sylvia Munston, Lady Peel** 1898–1989

Canadian-born actress. A star of light comedy and revue, she married Sir Robert Peel in 1920 and published an autobiography, *Every Other Inch a Lady* (1973).

30 Heard there was a party. Came.
Explaining her presence after staggering to the nearest house, that of film actor John Gilbert, when she was involved

in a car accident in Hollywood. Attributed.

Lillo, George 1693–1739

English dramatist and jeweller, of Dutch extraction. His seven plays were among the first to put middle-class rather than royal characters on the English stage.

31 There's sure no passion in the human soul,
But finds its food in music.
1736 *Fatal Curiosity*, act 1, sc.2.

Lin Yutang 1895–1976

Chinese author and philologist. He lived mainly in the US and was Chancellor of Singapore University (1954–5). He is best known for his novels and essays on Chinese culture and wisdom.

32 All women's dresses, in every age and country, are merely variations on the eternal struggle between the admitted desire to dress and the unadmitted desire to undress.
1945 In the *Ladies Home Journal*.

Lincoln, Abraham 1809–65

US Republican statesman, 16th President (1861–5) and opponent of slavery. In the Civil War he defined the issue in terms of national integrity, not anti-slavery, but proclaimed freedom for all slaves in areas of rebellion. He was shot at Ford's Theatre, Washington, by John Wilkes Booth, an actor, and he died next morning.

33 No man is good enough to govern another man without that other's consent.
1854 Speech, Peoria, 16 Oct.

34 'A house divided against itself cannot stand': I believe that this Government cannot endure permanently half-slave and half-free. I do not expect the Union to be dissolved. I do not expect the house to fall—but I do expect it will cease to be divided. It will become all one thing, or all the other.
1858 Speech, Springfield, 16 Jun.

35 You can fool some of the people some of the time, and some of the people all the time, but you cannot fool all the people all of the time.
1858 Speech, Clinton, 8 Sep.

36 The patent system…added the fuel of *interest* to the *fire* of genius.
1859 Collected in Roy B Basler (ed) *Collected Works* (1953).

37 What is conservatism? Is it not adherence to the old and tried, against the new and untried?
1860 Speech, New York, 27 Feb.

38 Let us have faith that right makes might; and in that faith let us to the end dare to do our duty as we understand it.
1860 Speech, New York, 27 Feb.

39 Four score and seven years ago our fathers brought forth upon this continent a new nation, conceived in liberty and dedicated to the proposition that all men are created equal…we here highly resolve that the dead shall have not died in vain; that this nation, under God, shall have a new birth of freedom; and that government of the people, by the people, and for the people, shall not perish from the earth.
1863 Dedication address, Gettysburg National Cemetery, 19 Nov.

40 The brave men, living and dead, who struggled here, have consecrated [this ground], far above our poor power to add or detract. The world will little note, nor long remember what we say here, but it can never forget what they did here.
1863 Dedication address, Gettysburg National Cemetery, 19 Nov.

41 With malice toward none, with charity for all, with firmness in the right, as God gives us to see the right, let us strive on to finish the work we are in, to bind up the nation's wounds, to care for him who shall have borne the battle, and for his widow and his orphan, to do all which may achieve and cherish a just and and lasting peace among ourselves, and with all nations.
1865 Second inaugural address, 4 Mar, a month before the end of the Civil War.

Lindbergh, Anne Spencer Morrow 1906–2001

US writer, widow of the aviator Charles Augustus Lindbergh. Her works include *North to the Orient*, an account of flights with her husband (1935), and an essay collection, *Earth Shine* (1970).

42 Thoughts die and are buried in the silences between sentences.
1980 Of the conversational style of US Secretary of State John Foster Dulles. *War Within and Without*.

Lindbergh, Charles A(ugustus) 1902–74

US aviator who made the first solo, non-stop transatlantic flight in *The Spirit of St Louis*, landing in Paris on 21 May 1927. He spoke in favour of isolationism at the beginning of World War II, but subsequently flew in combat missions.

43 I have seen the science I worshipped and the aircraft I loved, destroying the civilization I expected them to serve.
1967 In *Time*, 26 May.

Lindsay, John Vliet 1921–2000

US politician, Mayor of New York City (1966–74).

44 You'll make the mummies dance.
To Thomas Hoving, new director of the Metropolitan Museum of Art, who later adopted the phrase as a book title. Quoted in Thomas Hoving *Making the Mummies Dance* (1993).

Lindsay, (Nicholas) Vachel 1879–1931

US poet. He functioned for a time almost as a travelling troubadour across the US, trading his incantatory verses for hospitality. He suffered serious depression in later years, and committed suicide.

45 Booth led boldly with his big brass drum—
(Are you washed in the blood of the Lamb?)
The saints smiled gravely and they said 'He's come.'
1913 *General Booth Enters Into Heaven*, 'General Booth Enters Into Heaven'.

46 Drabs from the alleyways and drug fiends pale—
Minds still passion-ridden, soul-power frail:—
Vermin-eaten saints with moldy breath,
Unwashed legions with the ways of Death—
(Are you washed in the blood of the Lamb?)
1913 *General Booth Enters Into Heaven*, 'General Booth Enters Into Heaven'.

47 Booth died blind and still by faith he trod,

Eyes still dazzled by the ways of God.

1913 *General Booth Enters Into Heaven*, 'General Booth Enters Into Heaven'.

48 Then I saw the Congo, creeping through the black,
Cutting through the forest with a golden track.

1914 *The Congo and Other Poems*, 'The Congo', pt.1.

49 Mumbo-Jumbo is dead in the jungle.

1914 *The Congo and Other Poems*, 'The Congo', pt.3.

50 It is portentous, and a thing of state
That here at midnight, in our little town
A mourning figure walks, and will not rest,
Near the old courthouse pacing up and down.

1914 *The Congo and Other Poems*, 'Abraham Lincoln Walks At Midnight'.

51 And who will bring white peace
That he may sleep upon his hill again?

1914 *The Congo and Other Poems*, 'Abraham Lincoln Walks At Midnight'.

52 The flower-fed buffalos of the spring
In the days of long ago,
Ranged where the locomotives sing
And the prairie flowers lie low.

1926 *Going to the Stars*, 'The Flower-Fed Buffaloes'.

53 They gore no more, they bellow no more,
They trundle around the hills no more:—
With the Blackfeet, lying low,
With the Pawnees, lying low,
Lying low.

1926 *Going to the Stars*, 'The Flower-Fed Buffaloes'.

Linklater, Eric Robert 1889–1974

Scottish journalist and writer, born in Wales. While in the US (1928–30) he wrote *Poet's Pub* (1929), the first of a series of satirical novels which include *Juan in America* (1931) and *Private Angelo* (1946). Other works include books for children, such as *The Wind on the Moon* (1944), plays and memoirs.

54 All I've got against it is that it takes you so far from the club house.

1929 Of golf. *Poet's Pub*, ch.3.

55 Authors and uncaptured criminals…are the only people free from routine.

1929 *Poet's Pub*, ch.23.

56 With a heavy step Sir Matthew left the room and spent the morning designing mausoleums for his enemies.

1931 *Juan in America*, prologue.

57 It is notorious that we speak no more than half-truths in our ordinary conversation, and even a soliloquy is likely to be affected by the apprehension that walls have ears.

1931 *Juan in America*, bk.2, pt.4.

58 She looks like a million dollars, but she only knows a hundred and twenty words and she's only got two ideas in her head. The other one's hats.

1931 *Juan in America*, bk.2, pt.5.

59 There won't be any revolution in America… The people are all too clean. They spend all their time changing their shorts and washing themselves. You can't feel fierce and revolutionary in a bathroom.

1931 Isadore. *Juan in America*, bk.5, pt.3.

60 I dislike burdens…and at my back I often hear Time's winged chariot changing gear.

1937 Juan. *Juan in China*, 'End-Piece'.

➤ *See Marvell 556:62*.

61 Wanting to know an author because you like his books is like wanting to know a goose because you like pâté.

Quoted by Kenneth Murphy in the *Washington Post*, 27 Nov 1994.

Linnaeus, Carolus 1707–78

Swedish botanist and taxonomist, the founder of modern scientific classification of plants and animals.

62 Nature does not make jumps.

1750 *Philosophia Botanica*, no.77.

63 Minerals grow, plants grow and live, animals grow and live and feel.

'Systema Naturae', collected in E A Hackel *Generelle Morphologie* (1866).

Lippard, Lucy 1937–

US art critic and feminist.

64 The New York Pop artists are often asked whether or not they like their subjects. This, as Dorothy Seckler has noted, is as irrelevant as asking whether Cézanne liked apples, Géricault corpses, or Picasso guitars.

1966 *Pop Art*.

Lippmann, Walter 1899–1974

US journalist, a columnist with the New York *Herald Tribune*, awarded a Pulitzer Prize for international reporting (1962). He also wrote *Public Opinion* (1922) and *The Cold War* (1947).

65 The present crisis of Western democracy is a crisis in journalism.

1920 *Liberty and the News*, 'Journalism and the Higher Law'.

66 There can be no higher law in journalism than to tell the truth and shame the devil.

1920 *Liberty and the News*, 'Journalism and the Higher Law'.

➤ *See Shakespeare 742:17*.

67 The news of the day as it reaches the newspaper office is an incredible medley of fact, propaganda, rumor, suspicion, clues, hopes, and fears, and the task of selecting and ordering that news is one of the truly sacred and priestly offices in a democracy. For the newspaper is in all literalness the bible of democracy, the book out of which a people determines its conduct.

1920 *Liberty and the News*, 'What Modern Liberty Means'.

68 Newspapers necessarily and inevitably reflect, and therefore, in greater or lesser measure, intensify, the defective organization of public opinion.

1922 *Public Opinion*, ch.1.

69 Usually it is the stereotyped shape assumed by an event at an obvious place that uncovers the run of the news.

1922 *Public Opinion*, ch.23.

70 The news is not a mirror of social conditions, but the report of an aspect that has obtruded itself.

1922 *Public Opinion*, ch.23.

71 The function of news is to signalize an event, the function of truth is to bring to light the hidden facts, to set them into relation with each other, and make a picture of reality on which men can act. Only at those points, where social conditions take recognizable and measurable shape, do the body of truth and the body of news coincide.

1922 *Public Opinion*, ch.23.

72 Successful politicians…are insecure and intimidated men. They advance politically only as they placate, appease, bribe, seduce, bamboozle, or otherwise manage to manipulate the demanding and threatening elements in their constituencies.
1955 *The Public Philosophy*, ch.2, sect.4.

73 The public interest may be presumed to be what men would choose if they saw clearly, thought rationally, acted disinterestedly and benevolently.
1955 *The Public Philosophy*, ch.4.

Lispector, Clarice 1925–77

Brazilian novelist, born in the Ukraine. Her artistic vision transcends time and place, and her characters (often female) are only incidentally modern or Brazilian.

74 *Dessa civilização só pode sair quem tem como função especial a de sair: a um cientista é dada a licença, a um padre é dada a permissão. Mas não a uma mulher que nem sequer tem as garantias de um título.*
Only he whose special function is departure can depart from that civilization: a scientist is given license, a priest is given permission. But these are not given to a woman who does not even have the guarantee of a title.
1964 *A Paixão Segundo G.H.* (The Passion According to G.H.).

75 *O bom era ter uma inteligência e não entender. Era uma bênção estranha como a de ter loucura sem ser doida. Era um desinteresse manso em relação às coisas ditas do intelecto, uma doçura de estupidez.*
What was good was to have intelligence and yet not understand. It was a strange blessing like experiencing madness without being mad. It was a gentle lack of interest with respect to the so-called things of the intellect, a sweet stupidity.
1969 *Uma Aprendizagem ou O Livro dos Prazeres*, 'Luminescência' (translated as *An Apprenticeship or The Book of Delights*, 1986).

Liszt, Franz 1811–86

Hungarian composer and pianist. An acclaimed technical and lyrical player, his works include symphonic poems, sacred works, masses and vocal and piano works in which he often experimented with new musical forms.

76 *Ich kann warten.*
I can wait.
When it was suggested to him that his music was being neglected. Quoted in F Lamond *Memoirs* (1949).

Littlewood, John Edensor 1885–1977

English mathematician, whose research included the distribution of prime numbers and ballistics (in World War I). Depite a severe nervous affliction, he continued working into old age. He published the popular *Mathematician's Miscellany* (1953).

77 They are not clever school boys or scholarship candidates, but 'Fellows of another college'.
1953 Of the ancient Greeks. *A Mathematician's Miscellany.*

Lively, Penelope (Margaret) 1933–

English writer. She is best known as a novelist, and has also written a memoir of her early childhood in Egypt, children's books, and an introduction to landscape history.

78 One never, of course, knows what people in portraits are thinking.
1982 *Next to Nature, Art*, ch.10.

79 Wars are fought by children—conceived by their mad demonic elders, and fought by boys.
1987 *Moon Tiger*, ch.8.

80 I believe that the experience of childhood is irretrievable. All that remains, for any of us, is a handful of brilliant frozen moments, already dangerously distorted by the wisdoms of maturity.
1994 *Oleander, Jacaranda*, preface.

81 All habits are geared towards the linear, the sequential, but memory refuses such orderliness.
1994 *Oleander, Jacaranda*, ch.3.

82 Literature has a lot to answer for, where concepts of the countryside are concerned.
2001 *A House Unlocked.*

Livingstone, Dr David 1813–73

Scottish missionary, doctor and explorer. He devoted his life to fighting the Portuguese slave trade, and to establishing settlements for missions in central Africa. He also explored widely, discovering Lakes Ngami, Shirwa and Nyasa and exploring the course of the Zaire River.

83 The mere animal pleasure of travelling in a wild unexplored country is also great… The effect of travel on a man whose heart is in the right place is that the mind is made more self-reliant: it becomes more confident of its own resources—there is greater presence of mind… The sweat of one's brow is no longer a curse when one works for God: it proves a tonic to the system, and actually a blessing. No one can truly appreciate the charm of repose unless he has undergone severe exertion.
Collected in H Waller (ed) *The Last Journals of David Livingstone in Central Africa*; *continued by a narrative of his last moments and sufferings, obtained from his faithful servants, Chuma and Susi* (1874).

Livingstone, Ken 1945–

English Labour politician. He was leader of the Greater London Council from 1981 to 1986, and in 2000 was elected to the newly created post of Mayor of London.

84 The problem is that many MPs never see the London that exists beyond the wine bars and brothels of Westminster.
1987 In *The Times*, 19 Feb.

85 I feel like Galileo going before the Inquisition to explain that the Sun doesn't revolve around the Earth. I hope I have more success.
1999 Before his interview for selection as Labour's nominee for Mayor of London

86 I've met serial killers and professional assassins and nobody scared me as much as Mrs T.
2000 On Margaret Thatcher. In *The Times*, 7 Mar.

87 Every year the international finance system kills more people than the Second World War. But at least Hitler was mad, you know.
2000 In the *Sunday Times*, 'Talking Heads', 16 Apr.

Livy *full name* **Titus Livius** 59 BC–AD 17

Roman historian, admitted to the court of Augustus c.29 BC. His

Ab urbe condita libri (History of Rome from its Foundations) consisted of 142 books, of which only parts have survived.

88 *Vae victis!*
Down with the defeated!
Attributed to the Gallic King Brennus, who had captured Rome in 390 BC, bk.5, ch.48.

89 *Dum Romae consulitur, Saguntum expugnatur.*
While they were deliberating in Rome, Saguntum was captured.
Oral tradition deriving from Livy's description of the siege and capture of the Spanish city of Saguntum by the Carthaginians in 219 BC. The Roman senate deliberated endlessly before deciding to take action when it was already too late. Cf. Livy 21.7.1 'Dum ea Romani parant consultantque, iam Saguntum summa vi oppugnabatur'.

Llewellyn, Richard *originally* Richard Doyle Vivian Llewellyn Lloyd   1907–83

Welsh author, who made his name with *How Green was my Valley* (1939), set in a Welsh mining village and later filmed.

90 How Green was my Valley.
1939 Title of book.

Lloyd, Henry Demarest   1847–1903

US journalist, financial writer and editor with the *Chicago Tribune* (1872–85). He crusaded against monopoly, and was a pioneer 'muckraker' journalist.

91 Monopoly is Business at the end of its journey.
1894 *Wealth against Commonwealth*, ch.1.

Lloyd, John   1946–

British journalist and author.

92 There are few hauteurs higher than foreign reporters' disdain for those who have not shared their craft.
2004 *What the Media Are Doing to Our Politics*.

Lloyd, Marie *stage-name of* Matilda Alice Victoria Wood 1870–1922

English singer. Known simply as 'Our Marie', she became a major star of music hall and pantomime, notorious for her suggestive delivery of such songs as 'A Little of What You Fancy Does You Good'.

93 If we didn't laugh at him, we'd cry our eyes out.
c.1891 Of the singer and comedian Dan Leno, who died insane in 1904. Attributed.

Lloyd George (of Dwyfor), David, 1st Earl   1863–1945

British Liberal Prime Minister. Elected MP for Caernarvon in 1890. President of the Board of Trade 1905–8 and Chancellor of the Exchequer 1905–15. Secretary of War in 1916 and coalition Prime Minister in the same year. After the war, his downfall came when he conceded the Irish Free State in 1921.

94 You cannot feed the hungry on statistics.
1904 Speech advocating tariff reform.

95 This is the trusty mastiff that is to watch over our interests, but which runs away at the first snarl of the trade unions. A mastiff? It is the right honourable gentleman's poodle. It fetches and carries for him. It barks for him. It bites anybody that he sets it on.
1908 Speech to the House of Commons, 21 Dec, referring to the obstructive Conservative majority in the House of Lords

exploited by the then Tory leader, A J Balfour.

96 There are no credentials. They do not even need a medical certificate. They need not be sound either in body or mind. They only require a certificate of birth—just to prove that they were the first of the litter. You would not choose a spaniel on those principles.
1909 Referring to the House of Lords, Budget speech, Mar.

97 We are placing the burdens on the broadest shoulders. I made up my mind that, in forming the Budget, no cupboard should be barer, no lot should be harder to bear.
1909 Speech on the People's Budget, London, 30 Jul.

98 Four spectres haunt the poor—old age, accident, sickness, and unemployment. We are going to exorcise them. We are going to drive hunger from the hearth. We mean to banish the workhouse from the horizon of every workman in the land.
1910 Speech, Reading, 1 Jan.

99 We have been too comfortable and too indulgent—many, perhaps, too selfish—and the stern hand of fate has scoured us to an elevation where we can see the great everlasting things that matter for a nation; the great peaks we had forgotten, of honour, duty, patriotism, and, clad in glittering white, the great pinnacle of sacrifice pointing like a rugged finger to Heaven. We shall descend into the valleys again, but as long as men and women of this generation last, they will carry in their hearts the image of those great mountain peaks, whose foundations are not shaken, though Europe rock and sway in the convulsions of a great war.
1914 Speech, London, 19 Sep.

1 By the test of our faith the highest standard of civilization is the readiness to sacrifice for others.
1914 Speech in Queen's Hall, London, 21 Sep.

2 It is a great war for the emancipation of Europe from the thralldom of a military caste which has thrown its shadows upon two generations of men, and is now plunging the world into a welter of bloodshed and death.
1914 Speech in Queen's Hall, London, 21 Sep.

3 At eleven o'clock this morning came to an end the cruellest and most terrible war that has ever scourged mankind. I hope we may say that thus, this fateful morning, came to an end all wars.
1918 Speech in the House of Commons, 11 Nov, announcing the armistice.

4 What is our task? To make Britain a fit country for heroes to live in.
1918 Speech at Wolverhampton, Nov, at the end of World War I.

5 Give it because it is right. Give it because it is just. Give it because it is good for Ireland and good for the United Kingdom. Give it because it brings peace and good will, but do not give it because you are bullied by assassins.
1920 Speech on an Irish settlement, Caernarvon, 9 Oct.

6 Every man has a House of Lords in his own head. Fears, prejudices, misconceptions—those are the peers, and they are hereditary.
1927 Speech, Cambridge.

7 It is the old trouble—too late in dealing with Czechoslovakia, too late with Poland, and certainly too late with Finland. It is always too late, or too little, or both. That is the road to disaster.

1940 House of Commons, 13 Mar.

8 A good lord mayor of Birmingham in a lean year.
Of Neville Chamberlain. Quoted in A J P Taylor *From the Boer War to the Cold War: Essays on Twentieth-Century Europe* (1995), p.363

9 A politician is a person with whose politics you don't agree; if you agree with him, he is a statesman.
Attributed.

Lloyd Webber, Julian 1951–

English cellist.

10 Cello players, like other great athletes, must keep their fingers exercised.
2001 In the *Observer*, 30 Dec.

Loach, Ken 1936–

English film-maker. As well as television work, he has directed such films as *Kes* (1969), *Raining Stones* (1993), *Carla's Song* (1997), *My Name is Joe* (1998) and *Bread and Roses* (2000).

11 If the cinema is any kind of force for social change, then it's a force for the bad, because most films are about one guy with a gun solving a problem.
1998 In *Cineaste*, Winter issue.

Lochhead, Liz 1947–

Scottish poet and dramatist.

12 Sexual Etiquette
Sexual Etiquette
How to get more of it
and get more out of what you get.
2003 *The Colours of Black & White: Poems 1984–2000*, 'Sexual Etiquette'.

Locke, John 1632–1704

English philosopher, a formative influence on British Empiricism and on theories of liberal democracy. His most important work is the *Essay Concerning Human Understanding*, published in 1690. His treatises *On Government* (1690) were also influential, inspiring both American and French revolutionaries.

13 Government has no other end but the preservation of property.
1681 *Second Treatise on Civil Government* (published anonymously 1690).

14 Every man has a property in his person. This no body has any right to but himself. The labour of his body, and the work of his hands, we may say, are properly his.
1681 *Second Treatise on Civil Government* (published anonymously 1690).

15 Freedom of men under government is to have a standing rule to live by, common to every one of that society, and made by the legislative power vested in it; a liberty to follow my own will in all things when the rule prescribes not, and not to be subject to the inconstant, uncertain, unknown, arbitrary rule of another man.
1681 *Second Treatise on Civil Government* (published anonymously 1690).

16 It is ambition enough to be employed as an under-labourer in clearing ground a little, and removing some of the rubbish that lies in the way to knowledge.
1690 *Essay Concerning Human Understanding*, 'Epistle to the Reader'.

17 Let us then suppose the mind to be, as we say, white paper, void of all characters, without any ideas; how comes it to be furnished? Whence comes it by that vast store which the busy and boundless fancy of man has painted on it with an almost endless variety? Whence has it all the materials of reason and knowledge? To this I answer, in one word, from *experience*.
1690 *Essay Concerning Human Understanding*, bk.2, pt.1, section 2.

18 These two, I say, viz. external material things, as the objects of SENSATION, and the operations of our own minds within, as the objects of REFLECTION, are to me the only originals from whence all our ideas take their beginnings.
1690 *Essay Concerning Human Understanding*, bk.2, pt.1, section 4.

19 For should the soul of a prince enter and inform the body of a cobbler, as soon as deserted by his own soul, everyone sees he would be the same *person* with the prince, accountable only for the prince's actions; but who would say it was the same *man*?
1690 *Essay Concerning Human Understanding*, bk.2, pt.27, section 15.

20 A sound mind in a sound body is a short but full description of a happy state in this world. He that has those two, has little more to wish for; and he that wants either of them will be little the better for anything else.
1693 *Some Thoughts Concerning Education*, opening words.
➤ *See Juvenal 453:20.*

Lodge, David John 1935–

English novelist, playwright and critic. His best-known novels are set in academic circles, such as *Changing Places* (1975). Other works include *Thinks* (2001) and *Author, Author: A Novel* (2004).

21 Literature is mostly about having sex and not much about having children. Life is the other way round.
1965 *The British Museum is Falling Down*, ch.4.

22 The British, he thought, must be gluttons for satire: even the weather forecast seemed to be some kind of spoof, predicting every possible combination of weather for the next twenty-four hours without actually committing itself to anything specific.
1975 *Changing Places*, ch.2.

23 He understood…Walt Whitman, who laid end to end words never seen in each other's company before outside of a dictionary, and Herman Melville who split the atom of the traditional novel in the effort to make whaling a universal metaphor.
1975 *Changing Places*, ch.5.

24 Conversation is like playing tennis with a ball made of Krazy Putty that keeps coming back over the net in a different shape.
1984 *Small World*, pt.1, ch.1.

25 The world is a global campus, Hilary, you'd better believe it. The American Express card has replaced the library pass.
1984 *Small World*, pt.1, ch.2.

26 I gave up screwing around a long time ago. I came to the conclusion that sex is a sublimation of the work instinct.
1984 *Small World*, pt.1, ch.2.

27 Another law of academic life: *it is impossible to be excessive in flattery of one's peers.*
1984 *Small World*, pt.3, ch.1.

28 As to our universities, I've come to the conclusion that they are élitist where they should be egalitarian, and egalitarian where they should be élitist.
1988 *Nice Work*, pt.5, ch.4.

Lodge, Henry Cabot 1850–1924

US Republican politician and Senator.

29 The businessman dealing with a large political question is really a painful sight. It does seem to me that businessmen, with a few exceptions, are worse when they come to deal with politics than men of any other class.
1902 Letter to Theodore Roosevelt, 20 Oct.

Loengard, John Borg 1934–

US photographer, picture editor of *Life* (1973–87). His works include *Pictures Under Discussion* (1987) and many essays in *Life*.

30 A bit like God confessing he'd never gotten the hang of the thunderstorms.
1987 On Henri Cartier-Bresson's remark that he was only good at casual photography. In *Life*, Dec.

Lofthouse, Nat 1925–

English footballer. A star centre-forward with Bolton Wanderers in the 1950s, he led the team to victory in the 1958 FA Cup final and also scored 30 goals in 33 internationals for England.

31 There was plenty of fellers who would kick your bollocks off. The difference was that at the end they'd shake your hand and help you look for them.
Comparing football in the 1950s with that of later eras. Quoted in Peter Ball and Phil Shaw *The Book of Football Quotations* (1989).

Logau, Friedrich von 1605–55

German writer, author of epigrams.

32 *Gottes Mühlen mahlen langsam, mahlen aber trefflich klein;*
Ob aus Langmut Er sich säumet, bringt mit Schärf' Er alles ein.
Though the mills of God grind slowly, yet they grind exceeding small;
Though with patience He stands waiting, with exactness grinds He all.
1654 *Sinngedichte*, bk.3, pt.2, no.24 (translated as *Retribution* by Henry Wadsworth Longfellow). Logau used an anonymous classical source for the first line.

Lombardi, Vince(nt Thomas) 1913–70

US American football coach.

33 Winning isn't everything; it's the only thing.
Attributed. His exact words were 'Winning isn't everything, but making the effort is'. Some sources attribute the saying to Red Sanders, coach of the University of California team.

34 If you aren't fired with enthusiasm, you'll be fired with enthusiasm.
Attributed.

35 Once you learn to quit, it becomes a habit.
Attributed.

London, Jack (John Griffith) 1876–1916

US writer. His books, such as *The Call of the Wild* (1903) and *White Fang* (1907), reflect his experiences as a sailor, tramp, gold miner in the Klondike and alcoholic. He also wrote a futuristic political novel *The Iron Heel* (1907).

36 The Call of the Wild.
1903 Title of book.

37 In an English ship, they say, it is poor grub, poor pay, and easy work; in an American ship, good grub, good pay, and hard work. And this is applicable to the working populations of both countries.
1903 *The People of the Abyss*, ch.20.

Longden, Robert Paton 1903–40

English classical scholar and historian, writer of limericks on famous figures of Roman history.

38 The Emperor Caligula
's Habits were somewhat irrigula.
When he sat down to lunch
He got drunk at onch.
Quoted and first published in Arnold Silcock *Verse and Worse* (1952), 'Potted Biography'.

39 The Emperor Claudius
Used to keep a baudius.
When he got more criminal
He ran a den on the Viminal.
1952 Quoted and first published in Arnold Silcock, *Verse and Worse* (1952), 'Potted Biography'.

Longfellow, Henry Wadsworth 1807–82

US poet, Professor of Modern Languages and Literature at Harvard for nearly 18 years. His narrative skill made him one of the most popular poets of his day. His best-known poems include *Evangeline* (1847), *Hiawatha* (1855) and *Tales of a Wayside Inn* (1863).

40 Music is the universal language of mankind.
1835 *Outre Mer*. Also attributed to Christopher North (1865–1954).

41 Life is real, life is earnest!
And the grave is not its goal;
Dust thou art, to dust returnest,
Was not spoken of the soul.
1838 'A Psalm of Life'. In *Knickerbocker or New York Monthly Magazine*, Sep. Collected in *Voices of the Night* (1839).

42 Art is long, and time is fleeting,
And our hearts, though stout and brave,
Still, like muffled drums, are beating
Funeral marches to the grave.
1838 'A Psalm of Life', stanza 4. In *Knickerbocker or New York Monthly Magazine*, Sep. Collected in *Voices of the Night* (1839).

43 Lives of great men all remind us
We can make our lives sublime,
And departing, leave behind us
Footprints on the sands of time.
1838 'A Psalm of Life', stanza 7. In *Knickerbocker or New York Monthly Magazine*, Sep. Collected in *Voices of the Night* (1839).

44 Under a spreading chestnut-tree
The village smithy stands;
The smith a mighty man is he,
With large and sinewy hands;
And the muscles of his brawny arms

Are strong as iron bands.
1840 ' The Village Blacksmith', stanza 1. Collected in *Ballads and other Poems* (1841).

45 His brow is wet with honest sweat,
He earns whate'er he can,
And looks the whole world in the face,
For he owes not any man.
1840 'The Village Blacksmith', stanza 2. Collected in *Ballads and other Poems* (1841).

46 Each morning sees some task begin,
Each evening sees it close;
Something attempted, something done,
Has earned a night's repose.
1840 'The Village Blacksmith', stanza 7. Collected in *Ballads and other Poems* (1841).

47 It was the schooner Hesperus,
That sailed the wintry sea.
1841 *Ballads and other Poems*, 'The wreck of the Hesperus'.

48 The shades of night were falling fast,
As through an Alpine village passed
A youth, who bore, 'mid snow and ice,
A banner with a strange device,
Excelsior!
1841 'Excelsior'.

49 I like that ancient Saxon phrase, which calls,
The burial-ground God's-Acre.
1841 'God's- Acre'.

50 And the night shall be filled with music,
And the cares, that infest the day,
Shall fold up their tents like Arabs,
And as silently steal away.
1844 *The Waif*, 'The Day Is Done', stanza 11.
➤ *See Kaufman 455:57.*

51 I shot an arrow into the air,
It fell to earth, I knew not where.
1845 'The Arrow and the Song'.

52 This is the forest primeval.
1847 *Evangeline*, prologue.

53 Sorrow and silence are strong, and patient endurance is godlike.
1847 *Evangeline*, pt.2, section 1.

54 Thou, too, sail on, O Ship of State!
Sail on, O UNION, strong and great!
Humanity with all its fears,
With all the hopes of future years,
Is hanging breathless on thy fate!
1849 *The Seaside and Fireside*, 'The Building of the Ship', l.377–81.

55 In the moonlight and the starlight,
Fair Nokomis bore a daughter.
And she called her name Wenonah,
As the first-born of her daughters.
1855 The naming of Hiawatha's mother. *The Song of Hiawatha*, pt.3, 'Hiawatha's Childhood'. The name is now usually spelt Winona.

56 By the shore of Gitche Gumee
By the shining Big-Sea-Water,
Stood the wigwam of Nokomis,
Daughter of the Moon, Nokomis.
Dark behind it rose the forest,
Rose the black and gloomy pine-trees,

Rose the firs with cones upon them;
Bright before it beat the water,
Beat the clear and sunny water,
Beat the shining Big-Sea-Water.
1855 *The Song of Hiawatha*, pt.3, 'Hiawatha's Childhood'.

57 From the waterfall he named her,
Minnehaha, Laughing Water.
1855 *The Song of Hiawatha*, pt.4, 'Hiawatha and Mudjekeewis'.

58 A boy's will is the wind's will,
And the thoughts of youth are long, long thoughts.
1855 'My Lost Youth', in *Putnam's Monthly Magazine*, vol.6, Aug. Collected in *The Courtship of Miles Standish and Other Poems*, 1858. In his diary Longfellow notes that these lines are from an 'old Lapland song'.

59 But ah! what once has been shall be no more!
The groaning earth in travail and in pain
Brings forth its races, but does not restore,
And the dead nations never rise again.
1855 'The Jewish Cemetery at Newport'.

60 A Lady with a Lamp shall stand
In the great history of the land,
A noble type of good,
Heroic womanhood.
1857 Of Florence Nightingale. 'Santa Filomena'.

61 Between the dark and the daylight,
When the night is beginning to lower,
Comes a pause in the day's occupations,
That is known as the Children's Hour.
1863 'The Children's Hour', stanza 1.

62 Listen, my children, and you shall hear
Of the midnight ride of Paul Revere,
On the eighteenth of April in Seventy-five.
1863 *Tales of a Wayside Inn*, pt.1, 'The Landlord's Tale: Paul Revere's Ride'.

63 Our ingress into the world
Was naked and bare;
Our progress through the world
Is trouble and care.
1872 *Tales of a Wayside Inn*, pt.2, 'The Student's Tale: The Cobbler of Hagenau'.

64 Ships that pass in the night, and speak each other in passing,
Only a signal shown and a distant voice in the darkness;
So on the ocean of life, we pass and speak one another,
Only a look and a voice, then darkness again and a silence.
1873 *Tales of a Wayside Inn*, pt.3. 'The Theologian's Tale: Elizabeth'.

65 If you would hit the mark, you must aim a little above it;
Every arrow that flies feels the attraction of earth.
1881 *Elegaic Verse*, stanza 9.

66 The men that women marry,
And why they marry them, will always be
A marvel and a mystery to the world.
1883 *Michael Angelo*, pt.1, sc.5.

67 There was a little girl
Who had a little curl
Right in the middle of her forehead;
And when she was good
She was very, very good,

But when she was bad, she was horrid.
Attributed to Longfellow by Blanch Roosevelt Tucker Macchetta in *The Home Life of Henry W. Longfellow* (1882).

Longworth, Alice Roosevelt 1884–1980

US political hostess, daughter of Theodore Roosevelt, renowned for her wit.

68 If you can't say something good about someone, sit right here by me.
Motto embroidered on a sofa pillow. Quoted in *Time*, 9 Dec 1966.

Lonsdale, Hugh Cecil Lowther, 5th Earl of 1857–1944

English sportsman. As president of the National Sporting Club, he founded and presented the 'Lonsdale belts' for boxing.

69 I have always considered that boxing really combines all the finest and highest inclinations of a man—activity, endurance, science, temper, and, last, but not least, presence of mind.
1915 Foreword in Eugene Corri *Thirty Years a Boxing Referee*.

Loos, Adolf 1870–1933

Austrian architect and design theorist, a major figure of the 'Modern Movement', whose designs reflect his rejection of ornament and an emphasis on elegant functionalism.

70 I have emerged victorious from my thirty years of struggle. I have freed mankind from superfluous ornament.
1930 *Trotzdem 1900–1930.*

71 The evolution of culture is synonymous with the removal of ornament from utilitarian objects.
1931 *Trotzdem 1900–1930.*

Loos, Anita c.1893–1981

US writer, best known for her satirical novel *Gentleman Prefer Blondes* (1925). She also wrote plays, screenplays and memoirs.

72 Gentlemen Prefer Blondes.
1925 Title of novel, and subsequently a film starring Marilyn Monroe and Jane Russell (1953).

73 So this gentleman said a girl with brains ought to do something more with them besides think.
1925 *Gentlemen Prefer Blondes*, ch.1.

74 Gentlemen always seem to remember blondes.
1925 *Gentlemen Prefer Blondes*, ch.1.

75 She said she always believed in the old adage, 'Leave them while you're looking good.'
1925 *Gentlemen Prefer Blondes*, ch.1.

76 You have got to be a Queen to get away with a hat like that.
1925 *Gentlemen Prefer Blondes*, ch.4.

77 Any girl who was a lady would not even think of having such a good time that she did not remember to hang on to her jewelry.
1925 *Gentlemen Prefer Blondes*, ch.4.

78 The Eyefull Tower is devine.
1925 *Gentlemen Prefer Blondes*, ch.4.

79 So I really think that American gentlemen are the best after all, because kissing your hand may make you feel very very good but a diamond and safire bracelet lasts forever.
1925 *Gentlemen Prefer Blondes*, ch.4.

80 Fun is fun but no girl wants to laugh all of the time.
1925 *Gentlemen Prefer Blondes*, ch.4.

81 So then Dr Froyd said that all I needed was to cultivate a few inhibitions and get some sleep.
1925 *Gentlemen Prefer Blondes*, ch.5.

82 So then he said that he used to be a member of the choir himself, so who was he to cast the first rock at a girl like I.
1925 *Gentlemen Prefer Blondes*, ch.5.

83 Tallulah never bored anyone, and I consider that humanitarianism of a very high order indeed.
1968 Eulogy at Tallulah Bankhead's funeral. Reported in the *New York Times*, 17 Dec.

84 I'm furious about the Woman's Liberationists. They keep getting up on soap-boxes and proclaiming that women are brighter than men. That's true, but it should be kept very quiet or it ruins the whole racket.
Quoted in the *Observer*, 30 Dec 1973.

Lorca, Federico García 1898–1936

Spanish poet and playwright, assassinated on the order of the Nationalist Civil Governor early in the Civil War. He is best known for his gypsy songs and powerful, elemental tragedies such as *Bodas de Sangre* (1933, translated as *Blood Wedding*, 1947).

85 *Verde que te quiero verde.*
Verde viento. Verdes ramas.
El barco sobre la mar
y el caballo en la montaña.
Green how I love you green.
Green wind. Green boughs.
The ship on the sea
and the horse on the mountain.
1924–7 *Romance sonámbulo.*

86 Spain is the only country where death is the national spectacle.
Quoted in Colin Jarman *The Guinness Dictionary of Sports Quotations* (1990).

Loren, Sophia *pseudonym of* **Sofia Scicolone** 1934–

Italian actress. Her films include *El Cid* (1961) and *Two Women* (1961), for which she won an Academy Award.

87 Everything you see I owe to spaghetti.
Attributed.

Lorenz, Konrad 1903–89

Austrian zoologist and ethnologist. Lorenz studied the organization of individual animal and group behaviour patterns. He shared the 1973 Nobel prize in physiology or medicine with Karl von Frisch.

88 *Überhaupt ist es für den Forscher ein guter Morgensport, täglich vor dem Frühstück eine Lieblingshypothese einzustampfen—das erhält jung.*
It is a good morning exercise for a research scientist to discard a pet hypothesis every day before breakfast. It keeps him young.
1963 *Das sogenannte Böse* ('The So-Called Evil', translated by Marjorie Latzke as *On Aggression*, 1966), ch.2.

89 Man appears to be the missing link between anthropoid apes and human beings.
1965 In the *New York Times*, 11 Apr.

Louis IX *also called* **St Louis** 1214–70

King of France (1226–70). He led the Seventh Crusade (1248), but was defeated, imprisoned and ransomed. On his return to France (1254) he carried out reforms and encouraged the arts and literature. He began a new Crusade in 1270, but died of plague in Tunis.

90 I would rather have a Scot come from Scotland to govern the people of this kingdom well and justly, than that you should govern them ill in the sight of all the world.
1244 To his son, Louis, at Fontainebleau.

Louis XI 1423–83

King of France (1461–83). By a mixture of force and cunning, he broke the power of the nobility and by 1483 had united most of France under the Crown.

91 I have chased the English out of France more easily than my father ever did, for my father drove them out by force of arms, whereas I have driven them out with venison pies and good wine.
1475 Said after the signing of the Treaty of Picquigny, Sep.

Louis XIV *known as* **the Great** *or* **le Roi Soleil [the Sun King]** 1638–1715

King of France (1643–1715). His aggressive foreign and commercial policies and his attempt to create a Franco–Spanish Bourbon bloc led to the War of the Spanish Succession (1701–13). Although his old age saw military disaster and its financial toll, he was a model of royal absolutism and courtly brilliance.

92 Everyone knows how much trouble your meetings have caused in my State, and how many dangerous results they have had. I have learnt that you intend to continue them. I have come here expressly to forbid you to do this, which I do absolutely.
1655 Address to the Parlement of Paris, 13 Apr.

93 *L'État, c'est moi.*
I am the State.
1655 Address to the Parlement of Paris, 13 Apr. This is probably apocryphal.

94 Every time that I fill a high office, I make one hundred men discontented and one ungrateful.
c.1669 After the disgrace of the Duke of Lauzun. Quoted in Voltaire *Le Siècle de Louis XI V* (1751), ch.26.

95 How could God do this to me after all I have done for him?
1704 On hearing the news of the French defeat at Blenheim, Aug. Quoted in L Norton *Saint-Simon at Versailles* (1958).

96 The function of kings consists primarily of using good sense, which always comes naturally and easily. Our work is sometimes less difficult than our amusements.
Mémoires for the Instruction of the Dauphin.

Louis XVI 1754–93

King of France (1774–93), deposed during the Revolution. He was tried before the National Convention for conspiracy with foreign powers, and executed in Paris.

97 Louis XVI: Is this a revolt?
Duke of Rochefoucauld-Liancourt: No, sir, it's a revolution.
1789 Exchange after the fall of the Bastille, 14 Jul. Quoted in F Dreyfus *La Rochefoucauld-Liancourt* (1903), ch.2, section 3.

Louis XVIII *originally* **Stanislas Xavier** 1755–1824

King of France (from 1795). He fled to Belgium in 1791, proclaiming himself Regent for Louis XVII in 1793 and King in 1795. On the fall of Napoleon, he landed at Calais (1814) and began a severe rule, until Napoleon's return for the Hundred Days (1815). His rule was subsequently more moderate.

98 *L'exactitude est la politesse des rois.*
Punctuality is the politeness of kings.
Quoted in *Souvenirs de J Lafitte* (1844), bk.1, ch.3.

Louis Philippe *known as* **the Citizen King** 1773–1850

King of France (1830–48). Eldest son of the Duc d'Orléans, he renounced his titles and fought in the wars of the Republic, becoming 'Citizen King' after the Revolution of 1830. Demands for electoral reform led to the uprising of 1848 and his forced abdication.

99 Died, has he? Now I wonder what he meant by that.
1838 Said on the death of Talleyrand, his calculating and self-serving adviser, 18 Mar.

1 The entente cordiale.
1843 Speech, 27 Dec. Quoted in Collingham *The July Monarchy* (1988), p.320.

2 What perished in France in 1830 was not respect for a dynasty, but respect for anything.
Of the Revolution which brought him to power. Quoted in A J P Taylor *From Napoleon to the Second International* (1993).

Louis, Joe *pseudonym of* **Joseph Louis Barrow** 1914–81

US boxer. Known as the 'Brown Bomber', he won the world heavyweight title in 1937 and held it for a record 12 years, defending it 25 times. He retired in 1949, attempting two unsuccessful comebacks (1950–1). In all he won 68 of his 71 professional fights.

3 He can run, but he can't hide.
1941 Said during a bout against Billy Conn.

4 Everybody wants to go to heaven, but nobody wants to die.
1965 In *Sports Illustrated*, 'Scorecard', 19 Jul.

5 Every man's got to figure to get beat some time.
Quoted in Colin Jarman *The Guinness Dictionary of Sports Quotations* (1990).

6 I don't like money, actually, but it quiets my nerves.
Quoted in Colin Jarman *The Guinness Dictionary of Sports Quotations* (1990).

7 Why should I? When somebody insulted Caruso, did he sing an aria for him?
When a friend asked why he did not punch a motorist who swore at him following a minor traffic accident. Quoted in Colin Jarman *The Guinness Dictionary of Sports Quotations* (1990).

Love, James *pseudonym of* **James Dance** 1722–74

English actor and writer.

8 Hail Cricket! glorious, manly, British game!
First of all Sports! be first alike in fame!
1744 'Cricket: An Heroic Poem'.

Lovelace, Richard 1618–58

English Cavalier poet. Twice imprisoned (1642 and 1648–49) by the Puritans for his Royalist sympathies, he spent much of his time behind bars writing poetry, which he published in 1649 as the collection *Lucasta*.

9 When I lie tangled in her hair,
And fettered to her eye;
The Gods, that wanton in the air
Know no such liberty.
1649 *Lucasta*, 'To Althea, from Prison'.

10 Stone walls do not a prison make,
Nor iron bars a cage;
Minds innocent and quiet take
That for a hermitage;
If I have freedom in my love,
And in my soul am free;
Angels along that soar above,
Enjoy such liberty.
1649 *Lucasta*, 'To Althea, from Prison'.

11 If to be absent were to be
Away from thee;
Or that when I am gone,
You or I were alone;
Then my *Lucasta* might I crave
Pity from blust'ring wind, or swallowing wave.
1649 *Lucasta*, 'To Lucasta, Going beyond the Seas'.

12 *Amarantha* sweet and fair,
Ah braid no more that shining hair!
As my curious hand or eye,
Hovering round thee let it fly.
1649 *Lucasta*, 'To Amarantha, That She Would Dishevel Her Hair'.

13 Tell me not, Sweet, I am unkind,
That from the nunnery
Of thy chaste breast, and quiet mind,
To war and arms I fly.
1649 *Lucasta*, 'To Lucasta, Going to the Wars'.

14 I could not love thee, Dear, so much,
Loved I not honour more.
1649 *Lucasta*, 'To Lucasta, Going to the Wars'.

15 Thus did they live: Thus did they love,
Repeating only joys above;
And Angels were, but with clothes on,
Which they would put off cheerfully,
To bathe them in the galaxy,
Then gird them with the Heavenly zone.
1649 *Lucasta*, 'Love Made in the First Age'.

16 The asp doth on his feeder feed.
1649 *Lucasta*, 'A Fly Caught in a Cobweb'.

Loveless, George 1805–40

English Methodist preacher, who in 1833 organized the agricultural labourers of Tolpuddle, Dorset, into a trade union. When the men were convicted of taking illegal oaths and transported, a public outcry ensued and they were eventually pardoned.

17 If we have violated any law, it was not done intentionally. We have injured no man's reputation, character, person, or property. We were meeting together to preserve ourselves, our wives, and our children from utter degradation and starvation.
1833 Statement to the Dorchester Assizes, Mar, on behalf of the Tolpuddle martyrs.

Lovell, Sir (Alfred Charles) Bernard 1913–

English astronomer. He was the instigator of the funding, construction and use of the radio telescope at Jodrell Bank.

18 The fate of human civilization will depend on whether the rockets of the future carry the astronomer's telescope or a hydrogen bomb.
1959 *The Individual and the Universe*.

19 A study of history shows that civilizations that abandon the quest for knowledge are doomed to disintegration.
1972 In the *Observer*, 'Sayings of the Week', 14 May.

Lowe, Emily fl.1850s

Englishwoman, who travelled in Norway with her mother.

20 The only use of a gentleman in travelling is to look after the luggage.
1857 *Unprotected Females in Norway*.

Lowell, Amy 1874–1925

US poet. A descendant of James Russell Lowell, she was associated with the Imagist movement, and wrote free verse in a style she named 'unrhymed cadence'. She also wrote prose and criticism.

21 For books are more than books, they are the life
The very heart and core of ages past,
The reason why men lived and worked and died,
The essence and quintessence of their lives.
1912 'The Boston Atheneum'.

22 All books are either dreams or swords,
You can cut, or you can drug, with words.
1914 'Sword Blades and Poppy Seeds'.

23 And the softness of my body will be guarded by embrace
By each button, hook, and lace.
For the man who should loose me is dead,
Fighting with the Duke in Flanders,
In a pattern called a war.
Christ! What are patterns for?
1916 'Patterns'.

24 A man must be sacrificed now and again
To provide for the next generation of men.
1922 'A Critical Fable'.

25 I must be mad, or very tired,
When the curve of a blue bay beyond a railroad track
Is shrill and sweet to me like the sudden springing of a tune,
And the sight of a white church above thin trees in a city square
Amazes my eyes as though it were the Parthenon.
1925 'Meeting-House Hill'.

Lowell, James Russell 1819–91

US poet, essayist and diplomat. His popular satiric poems in Yankee dialect were published as *The Biglow Papers* (1848 and 1867). A lecturer at Harvard, he was also editor of the *Atlantic Monthly* and US Minister to Spain (1877–80) and Britain (1880–85).

26 It is mediocrity which makes laws and sets mantraps and spring-guns in the realm of free song, saying thus far shall you go and no further.
1843 'Elizabethan Dramatists, Omitting Shakespeare: John Webster'.

27 Once to every man and nation comes the moment to decide,

In the strife of Truth with Falsehood, for the good or evil
side.
1844 'The Present Crisis', in the *Boston Courier*, 11 Dec. Collected
in *Poems: Second Series*, 1848. The poem was written in the midst
of the controversy over whether Texas should be annexed and
slavery extended.

28 They talk about their Pilgrim blood,
Their birthright high and holy!
A mountain-stream that ends in mud
Methinks is melancholy.
1846 'An Interview with Miles Standish', stanza 11.

29 Ez fer war, I call it murder,—
There you hev it plain an' flat;
I don't want to go no furder
Than my Testyment fer that;
God hez sed so plump an' fairly,
It's ez long ez it is broad,
An' you've gut to git up airly
Ef you want to take in God.
1846 'A Letter'. In the *Boston Courier*, 17 Jun. Collected in *The
Biglow Papers, First Series* (1848), no.1.

30 'Slavery's a thing thet depends on complexion,
It's God's law thet fetters on black skins don't chafe;
Ef brains wuz to settle it (horrid reflection!)
Wich of our onnable body'd be safe?'
1848 'The Debate in the Sennit', in the *Boston Courier*, 3 May,
collected in *The Biglow Papers: First Series* (1848), no. 5.

31 And what is so rare as a day in June?
Then, if ever come perfect days.
1848 'The Vision of Sir Launfal', prelude.

32 There comes Poe, with his raven, like Barnaby Rudge,
Three-fifths of him genius and two-fifths sheer fudge.
1848 'A Fable for Critics'.

33 A reading machine, always wound up and going,
He mastered whatever was not worth knowing.
1848 Of a scholar. 'A Fable for Critics'.

34 Books are the bees which carry the quickening pollen
from one to another mind.
1849 'Nationality in Literature', in the *North American Review*,
Jul.

35 Every man feels instinctively that all the beautiful
sentiments in the world weigh less than a single lovely
action.
1867 'Rousseau and the Sentimentalists', in the *North American
Review*, Jul.

36 The mind can weave itself warmly in the cocoon of its
own thoughts, and dwell a hermit anywhere.
1869 'On a Certain Condescension in Foreigners', in the *Atlantic
Monthly*, Jan.

37 Sorrow, the great idealizer.
1876 *Among My Books*, 'Spenser'.

38 There is no good in arguing with the inevitable. The only
argument available with an east wind is to put on your
overcoat.
1884 'On Democracy', Lowell's inaugural address when he
became president of the Birmingham and Midland Institute,
6 Oct.

39 Compromise makes a good umbrella but a poor roof.
1884 'On Democracy', speech in Birmingham, 6 Oct.

40 As life runs on, the road grows strange
With faces new,—and near the end
The milestones into headstones change,

'Neath every one a friend.
1887 'Sixty-Eighth Birthday'.

Lowell, Robert Traill Spence, Jr   1917–77

US poet. His poems are intensely personal and confessional.
His public involvement and outspoken comments, especially
during the Vietnam War, have made him one of the best known
of all contemporary poets.

41 Let there pass
A minute, ten, ten trillion; but the blaze
Is infinite, eternal: this is death.
To die and know it. This is the Black Widow, death.
1950 'Mr Edwards and the Spider'.

42 They died
When time was open-eyed,
Wooden and childish; only bones abide
There, in the nowhere, where their boats were tossed
Sky-high, where mariners had fabled news
of IS, the whited monster.
1950 'The Quaker Graveyard in Nantucket', pt.3.

43 This is the end of the whaleroad and the whale
Who spewed Nantucket bones on the thrashed swell
And stirred the troubled waters to whirlpools
To send the Pequod packing off to hell
1950 'The Quaker Graveyard in Nantucket', pt.4. The Pequod
was the ship that sailed after Moby Dick in Melville's novel.

44 The Lord survives the rainbow of his will.
1950 'The Quaker Graveyard in Nantucket', last line.

45 I keep no rank nor station.
Cured, I am frizzled, stale and small.
1956 'Home After Three Months Away'.

46 I myself am hell.
1956 'Skunk Hour'.

47 I often sigh still
for the dark downward and vegetating kingdom
of the fish and reptile.
1964 'For the Union Dead'.

48 William James could almost hear the bronze Negroes
breathe.

Their monument sticks like a fishbone
in the city's throat.
1964 'For The Union Dead'.

49 Everywhere,
giant finned cars nose forward like fish;
a savage servility
slides by on grease.
1964 'For the Union Dead'.

50 He is out of bounds now. He rejoices in man's lovely
peculiar power to choose life and die—
when he leads his black soldiers to death,
he cannot bend his back.
1964 'For The Union Dead'. 'He' refers to Colonel Shaw, the white
commander of the black regiment commemorated in the
monument.

51 The man is killing time—there's nothing else.
1964 'The Drinker'.

52 But I suppose even God was born
too late to trust the old religion—
all those settings out
that never left the ground,

beginning in wisdom, dying in doubt.
1964 'Tenth Muse'.

53 The elect, the elected…they come here bright as dimes,
and die dishevelled and soft.
1964 'July in Washington'.

54 Yours the lawlessness
of something simple that has lost its law.
1964 'Caligula'.

55 O that the spirit could remain
tinged but untarnished by its strain!
1967 'Waking Early Sunday Morning'.

56 Pity the planet, all joy gone
from this sweet volcanic cone
1967 'Waking Early Sunday Morning'.

57 Life is too short to silver over this tarnish.
The gods, employed to haunt and punish husbands,
have no hand for trigger-fine distinctions,
their myopia makes all error mortal.
1968 'New Year's Eve'.

58 My Darling, prickly hedgehog of the heart,
chocolates, cherries, hairshirts, pinks and glass—
when we joined in the sublime blindness of courtship
loving lost all its vice with half its virtue.
1968 'New Year's Eve'.

59 Age is our reconciliation with dullness.
1973 'Last Summer at Milgate'.

60 We feel the machine slipping from our hands
As if someone else were steering;
If we see the light at the end of the tunnel,
It's the light of the oncoming train.
1977 *Day by Day*, 'Since 1939'.

61 Those blessed structures, plot and rhyme —
why are they no help to me now
I want to make
something imagined, not recalled?
1977 *Day by Day*, 'Epilogue'.

62 Pray for the grace of accuracy
Vermeer gave to the sun's illumination
stealing like the tide across a map
to his girl solid with yearning.
1977 *Day by Day*, 'Epilogue'.

Lowenthal, Leo 1900–93

German-born US sociologist.

63 We call the heroes of the past heroes of production. We
feel entitled to call the present day magazine heroes
'idols of consumption'. Indeed, almost every one of them
is directly, or indirectly, related to the sphere of leisure
time.
1944 'The Triumph of Mass Idols', collected in *Literature and
Mass Culture* (1984).

Lowndes, William 1652–1724

English politician.

64 Take care of the pence, and the pounds will take care of
themselves.
Quoted by Lord Chesterfield in a letter to his son, 5 Feb 1750. In
an earlier letter, 6 Nov 1747, he refers to the same adage in the
form 'for the pounds'.

Lowry, (Clarence) Malcolm 1909–57

English novelist. He went to sea as a young man and lived in
Mexico and Vancouver. He is best known for his novel, *Under
the Volcano* (1947), one of the great 20c explorations of
alcoholism. He died after choking in his sleep.

65 Nothing in the world was more terrible than an empty
bottle! Unless it was an empty glass.
1947 *Under the Volcano*, ch.3.

66 Where are the children I might have had?… Drowned to
the accompaniment of the rattling of a thousand douche
bags.
1947 *Under the Volcano*, ch.10.

67 How alike are the groans of love to those of the dying.
1947 *Under the Volcano*, ch.12.

68 Dark as the Grave Wherein my Friend is Laid.
Title of novel, published posthumously (1968).

Lucan full name Marcus Annaeus Lucanus AD 39–65

Latin poet, born in Spain, nephew of the philosopher Seneca.
A favourite at the court of Nero, he lost imperial favour and in
AD 65 joined Piso's conspiracy against Nero, but was betrayed
and compelled to commit suicide. His epic poem *Bellum Civile*
(or *Pharsalia*) deals with the civil war between Caesar and
Pompey.

69 *Victrix causa deis placuit, sed victa Catoni.*
A victorious case pleased the gods, but a lost one Cato.
Pharsalia, bk.1, l.126.

70 *Stat magni nominis umbra.*
There stands the shade of a great name.
Of Pompey. *Pharsalia*, bk.1, l.135.

71 *Coniunx est mihi, sunt nati: dedimus tot pignora fatis.*
I have a wife, I have sons: we have given so many
hostages to the fates.
Pharsalia, bk.6, l.661–2.
➤ See Bacon 48:86.

Lucas, E(dward) V(errell) 1868–1938

English essayist and biographer. He was assistant editor of
Punch, and wrote novels and travel books.

72 I have noticed that people who are late are often so
much jollier than the people who have to wait for them.
1926 *365 Days and One More*.

73 Readers of novels are strange folk, upon whose
probable or even possible tastes no wise book-maker
would ever venture.
1932 *Reading, Writing and Remembering*, ch.1.

74 There can be no defence like elaborate courtesy.
1932 *Reading, Writing and Remembering*, ch.8.

Lucas, F(rank) L(awrence) 1894–1967

English teacher, critic and poet.

75 Unintelligible, the borrowings cheap and the notes
useless.
1923 On T S Eliot's *The Waste Land*, in the *New Statesman and
Nation*, Nov.

76 The virtues common to good living and good poetry
seem to me not so much matters of what used to be
called 'virtue' as, above all, of sane vitality.
1936 *The Decline and Fall of the Romantic Ideal*, ch.1.

77 Human temperaments are too diverse; we can never agree how drunk we like our art to be.
1951 *Literature and Psychology*, ch.10.

78 Every author's fairy godmother should provide him not only with a pen but also with a blue pencil.
1955 *Style*, introduction.

Lucas, George 1944–

US film-maker, best known for the series of *Star Wars* and *Indiana Jones* films.

79 May the Force be with you.
1977 Line delivered by Alec Guinness as Obi-Wan Kenobi in *Star Wars*.

80 Art is the retelling of certain themes in a new light, making them accessible to the public of the moment.
1988 In the *New York Times*, 9 Jun.

Luce, Clare Booth 1903–87

US writer, socialite and wit, associate editor of *Vogue* (1930), US Ambassador to Italy (1953–7) and author of several Broadway successes including *Kiss the Boys Goodbye* (1938).

81 Communism is the opiate of the intellectuals, with no cure except as a guillotine might be called a cure for dandruff.
1955 In *Newsweek*, 24 Jan.

Lucretius full name Titus Lucretius Carus 98–c.55 BC

Roman poet and philosopher, author of *De Rerum Natura*, a hexameter poem in six books expounding the physical system of Epicurus, in which release from fear, and the mortality of the soul, are central concerns.

82 *Nil posse creari*
De nilo.
Nothing can be created from nothing.
De Rerum Natura, bk.1, line 155–6.

83 *Suave, mari magno turbantibus aequora ventis,*
E terra magnum alterius spectare laborem;
Non quia vexari quemquamst iucunda voluptas,
Sed quibus ipse malis careas quia cernere suave est.
Suave etiam belli certamina magna tueri
Per campos instructa tua sine parte pericli.
Sed nil dulcius est, bene quam munita tenere
Edita doctrina sapientum templa serena,
Despicere unde queas alios passimque videre
Errare atque viam palantis quaerere vitae,
Certare ingenio, contendere nobilitate,
Noctes atque dies niti praestante labore
Ad summas emergere opes rerumque potiri.
What joy it is, when out at sea the stormwinds are lashing the waters, to gaze from the shore at the heavy stress some other man is enduring. Not that anyone's afflictions are in themselves a source of delight; but to realize from what troubles you yourself are free is joy indeed. What joy, again, to watch opposing hosts marshalled on the field of battle when you have yourself no part in their peril! But this is the greatest joy of all: to possess a quiet sanctuary, stoutly fortified by the teaching of the wise, and to gaze down from that elevation on others wandering aimlessly in search of a way of life, pitting their wits one against another, disputing for precedence, struggling night and day with

unstinted effort to scale the pinnacles of wealth and power.
De Rerum Natura, bk.2, lines 1–13 (translated by R. E. Latham).

84 *Vitaque mancipio, nulli datur, omnibus usu.*
To none is life given in freehold; to all on lease.
De Rerum Natura, bk.3, line 971 (translated by R. E. Latham).

85 *Ut quod ali cibus est aliis fuat acre venenum.*
What is food to one may be literally poison to others.
De Rerum Natura, bk.4, line 637 (translated by R. E. Latham).

Lugones, Leopoldo 1874–1938

Argentinian poet and critic. As a socialist journalist, he joined the *Modernista* group, later becoming a conservative nationalist and, in 1929, a Fascist.

86 *Si tengo la fortuna*
de que con tu alma mi dolor se integre,
te diré entre melancólico y alegre
las singulares cosas de la luna.
If I am fortunate enough
for your soul to mix with my sorrow,
I will tell you, half with melancholy, half with gladness,
Unique things about the moon.
1909 *Lunario sentimental*, 'Divagación lunar' ('Lunar digression').

Lukács, Georg 1885–1971

Hungarian-born Marxist scholar, philosopher and aesthetician.

87 Nature is a social category.
1923 *History and Class Consciousness*.

Lumière, Auguste Marie Louis Nicolas 1862–1954

French film pioneer, brother of Louis Lumière. The brothers owned a factory in Lyons where photographic products were made. They invented the first successful cine camera and projector and presented their film of workers leaving the Lumière factory in 1895.

88 *Mon frère, en une nuit, avait inventé le cinématographe.*
My brother, in one night, had invented the cinema.
Of the night his brother Louis had a flash of inspiration which resulted in the 'Kinetoscope de projection' patented in 1895.
Quoted in C W Ceram *Archaeology of the Cinema* (1965).

Lurie, Alison 1926–

US novelist and academic. She has written a number of acutely observed novels, often with academic settings, as well as non-fiction and children's literature.

89 That is the worst thing about being a middle-class woman…you have more knowledge of yourself and the world: you are equipped to make choices, but there are none left to make.
1974 *The War Between The Tates*, ch.3.

90 Fashion is free speech, and one of the privileges, if not always one of the pleasures, of a free world.
1981 *The Language of Clothes*.

91 The most desirable mental state for a potential consumer…is a kind of free-floating anxiety and depression, combined with a nice collection of unrealistic goals and desires.
1983 Of advertising. In the *New York Review of Books*, 2 Jun.

Luther, Martin 1483–1546

German theologian. Originally an Augustinian monk, he became the leader of Protestant Reformation in Europe. When he publicly burned the Papal Bull against him he was summoned before the Diet at Worms and banned. His followers later founded the Lutheran Church.

92 *Hier stehe ich. Ich kann nicht anders. Gott helfe mir. Amen.*

Here I stand; I can do no other; God help me; Amen.
1521 Speech in defence of his doctrines at the Diet of Worms, 18 Apr. The Diet subsequently denounced his ideas as heretical.

93 I cannot and will not recant anything, for to go against conscience is neither right nor safe.
1521 Speech in defence of his doctrines at the Diet of Worms, 18 Apr.

94 *Esto peccator et pecca fortiter, sed fortius fide et gaude in Christo.*

Be a sinner and sin boldly, but more boldly believe and rejoice in Christ.
1521 Letter to Melanchthon.

95 *Wenn ich gewusst hätte, dass so viel Teufel auf mich gezielet hätten, als Ziegel auf den Dächern waren zu Worms, wäre ich dennoch eingeritten.*

I would have gone into Worms though there were as many devils as tiles on the roof.
1524 Letter to Frederick, Elector of Saxony, 21 Aug.

96 It is better that all of these peasants should be killed rather than that the sovereigns and magistrates should be destroyed, because the peasants take up the sword without God's authority.
1525 Letter to Nicholas von Ansdorf, 30 May.

97 *Ein' feste Burg ist unser Gott,*
Ein' gute Wehr und Waffen.

A safe stronghold our God is still,
A trusty shield and weapon.
1529 *Ein' feste Burg ist unser Gott* (translated by Thomas Carlyle).

98 *Wo rauff du nu…dein Hertz engest und verlessest, das ist eygentlich dein Gott.*

Whatever your heart clings to and confides in, that is really your God.
1529 *Large Catechism*, 'The First Commandment'.

99 Rough, boisterous, stormy and altogether warlike, I am born to fight against innumerable monsters and devils.
Quoted in Vincent Cronin *The Flowering of the Renaissance* (1969).

1 *Wer nicht liebt Wein, Weib und Gesang,*
Der bleibt ein Narr sein Leben lang.

Who loves not woman, wine and song
Remains a fool his whole life long.
Attributed. This was inscribed in the Luther room at Wartburg, but is probably apocryphal.

Lutyens, Sir Edwin Landseer 1869–1944

English architect. His designs include the Cenotaph, Whitehall and Liverpool Roman Catholic Cathedral.

2 There will never be great architects or great architecture without great patrons.
1915 In *Country Life*, 8 May.

Lydgate, John c.1370–c.1451

English poet and Benedictine monk, who travelled widely in Europe. In 1423 he became Prior of the monastery of Hatfield Broadoak. His many works include *The Siege of Thebes* (1420–2) and *The Fall of Princes* (1431–8).

3 Off our language he was the lodesterre.
1431–8 Of Chaucer. *The Fall of Princes*, prologue, l.252.

4 Lat no man booste of conning nor vertu,
Of tresour, richesse, nor of sapience,
Of worldly support, for all cometh of Jesu.
c.1450 'Lat no man booste', l.1–3.

5 Woord is but wynd; leff woord and tak the dede.
Secrets of Old Philosophers, l.224.

Lyly, John c.1554–1606

English writer and dramatist. He published his prose romance *Euphues, or the Anatomy of Wit* in 1578, and wrote eight plays between 1584 and 1590, including *Endymion, or The Man in the Moon* (1588).

6 Be valiant, but not too venturous. Let thy attire be comely, but not costly.
1578 *Euphues, or the Anatomy of Wit*.

7 What bird so sings, yet so does wail?
O 'tis the ravished nightingale.
Jug, jug, jug, jug, tereu, she cries,
And still her woes at midnight rise.
1584 *Campaspe*, act 5, sc.1.

8 How at heaven's gates she claps her wings,
The morn not waking till she sings.
1584 Of the lark. *Campaspe*, act 5, sc.1.

9 A heat full of coldness, a sweet full of bitterness, a pain full of pleasantness, which maketh thoughts have eyes and hearts ears, bred by desire, nursed by delight, weaned by jealousy, killed by dissembling, buried by ingratitude, and this is love. Fair lady, will you any?
1588 *Gallathea*, act 1, sc.2. The passage gently satirizes the conventions of love sonnets, and is characterized by the yoked opposites called Euphuisms, after Lyly's earlier work, a style later used by the metaphysical poets.

10 If love be a god, why should not lovers be virtuous?
1588 *Gallathea*, act 3, sc.1.

11 Yield, ladies, yield to love, ladies, which lurketh under your eyelids whilst you sleep and playeth with your heartstrings whilst you wake, whose sweetness never breedeth satiety, labour weariness, nor grief bitterness.
1588 *Gallathea*, epilogue.

12 Night hath a thousand eyes.
1600 *The Maydes Metamorphosis*, act 3, sc.1.
➤ See Bourdillon 147:28.

Lynd, Robert 1879–1949

Irish essayist and critic, literary editor of the *Daily News* and a contributor to the *New Statesman* (1913–45). His essay collections include *The Art of Letters* (1920), *The Blue Lion* (1923) and *In Defence of Pink* (1939).

13 It may be that all games are silly. But then, so are humans.
Quoted in Colin Jarman *The Guinness Dictionary of Sports Quotations* (1990).

14 It is almost impossible to remember how tragic a place this world is when one is playing golf.
Attributed.

Lyndon, Neil 1946–

British journalist and writer. His critique of feminism, *No More Sex War: The Failures of Feminism*, was published in 1992.

15 The cardinal tenets of feminism divided my generation, effectively disempowering and disenfranchising its members. It does make me bitterly angry that my generation, which prided itself so complacently on its soul, on its powers of intelligence and analysis, should have fallen so cloddishly for totalitarian simplicities which declared a war of eternal opposition between men and women.
1992 *No More Sex War: The Failures of Feminism.*

Lyte, Henry Francis 1793–1847

Scottish hymn writer, curate of Lower Brixham, Devon, from 1823.

16 Praise, my soul, the King of Heaven;
To his feet thy tribute bring.
Ransomed, healed, restored, forgiven,
Who like me his praise should sing?
1834 'Praise, my Soul, the King of Heaven'.

17 Abide with me; fast falls the eventide;
The darkness deepens; Lord, with me abide;
When other helpers fail and comforts flee,
Help of the helpless, O, abide with me.
1847 *Remains*, 'Abide with Me' (published 1850).

Lyttelton, Humphrey Richard Adeane 1921–

English jazz trumpeter, bandleader and broadcaster. An Old Etonian and former guardsman, he is the *doyen* of the English jazz scene, both as a musician and as a writer and broadcaster.

18 It is this tendency to play with manic enthusiasm on every possible occasion that distinguishes the amateur jazz musician from the professional, often to the public detriment of the latter, who are regarded as snooty and unfriendly.
1984 *Why No Beethoven?*, ch.1.

McAleese, Mary 1951–

Irish politician, elected President of Ireland in 1997.

19 Apart from shamrock, the President should not wear emblems or symbols of any kind.
1997 On why she would not be wearing a poppy at her inauguration on 11 Nov. In *The Guardian*, 13 Apr.

20 The day of the dinosaurs is over. The future belongs to the bridge-builders, not the wreckers.
1998 On the Northern Ireland Assembly. In *The Irish Times*, 27 Jun.

MacArthur, Douglas 1880–1964

US soldier. He commanded troops in the Far East (1941) in World War II, directed the recapture of the SW Pacific (1942–5), formally accepted Japan's surrender, and commanded its occupation (1945–51). He led the UN forces in the Korean War, but was relieved of command when he tried to continue the war against China.

21 I came through and I shall return.
1942 On reaching Australia, having broken through Japanese lines en route from Corregidor, 20 Mar. Reported in the *New York Times*, 21 Mar.

22 There lies the Holy Grail.
1943 Remark, 6 May, one year after the fall of Corregidor to the Japanese, recalled in *A Soldier Speaks*.

23 A great tragedy has ended. A great victory has been won. A new era is upon us… We have had our last chance. If we do not devise some greater and more equitable system, Armageddon will be at our door.
1945 National radio broadcast on the surrender of Japan, 2 Sep.

24 An unsinkable air-craft carrier.
1950 Of Taiwan's military significance for the US. Remark, 27 Aug, recalled in *A Soldier Speaks*.

25 In war, indeed, there can be no substitute for victory.
1951 Address to Congress, 19 Apr. In the *Congressional Record*, vol.97, pt.3, p.4125.

26 The world has turned over many times since I took the oath on the plain at West Point…but I still remember the refrain of one of the most popular ballads of that day which proclaimed most proudly that old soldiers never die; they just fade away.
1951 Address to Congress after being relieved of his duty by President Truman, 19 Apr.

27 I now close my military career and just fade away, an old soldier who tried to do his duty as God gave him the light to see that duty.
1951 Address to Congress after being relieved of his duty by President Truman, 19 Apr.

28 It isn't just dust that is settling in Korea, Senator, it is American blood.
1951 During the Senate inquiry on MacArthur's dismissal. Reported in the *New York Times*, 2 May.

29 He'll make a fine president. He was the best clerk who ever served under me.
1952 On Dwight D Eisenhower's election as President. In news summaries, 31 Dec.

30 The chickens are coming home to roost, and you happen to have just moved into the chicken house.
Comment to John F Kennedy on the presidential crisis. Kennedy enjoyed the remark and often quoted it. Quoted in Theodore C Sorensen *Kennedy* (1965).

Macarthur, James 1937–

Actor, only son of Helen Hayes.

31 What a wonderful sight, a full house—my mother would have loved it!
1993 Speaking at the memorial service at New York's Shubert's Theater for his mother, Helen Hayes. Reported in the *New York Times*, 19 Jun.

Macaulay, Dame (Emilie) Rose 1881–1958

English novelist and travel writer whose book, *Pleasure of Ruins* (1953), includes an account of her visit to Cambodia and the ruins of Angkor.

32 You should always believe all you read in newspapers, as

this makes them more interesting.
1925 *A Casual Commentary,* 'Problems of a Reader's Life'.

33 My point of view has sadly changed. For now, should all the books in the world be laid before me, my problem would be how many of them I could avoid. Most books are like that.
1925 *A Casual Commentary,* 'Problems of a Reader's Life'.

34 Here is one of the points about this planet which should be remembered; into every penetrable corner of it, and into most of the impenetrable corners, the English will penetrate.
1926 *Crewe Train,* pt.1, ch.1.

35 Gentlemen know that fresh air should be kept in its proper place—out of doors—and that, God having given us indoors and out-of-doors, we should not attempt to do away with that distinction.
1926 *Crewe Train,* pt.1, ch.5.

36 All is now desolate, fantastic, and ambushed with ghosts; the archaeologists twitter among them like bats.
1953 Of Angkor Thom. *Pleasure of Ruins.*

37 'Take my camel, dear,' said my aunt Dot, as she climbed down from this animal on her return from High Mass.
1956 *The Towers of Trebizond,* ch.1.

Macaulay (of Rothley), Thomas Babington Macaulay, 1st Baron   1800–59

English essayist and historian, an MP from 1830 and a skilful orator in the Reform Bill debates. He wrote the highly popular *Lays of Ancient Rome* (1842) and contributed to the *Edinburgh Review,* but his major work was the *History of England from the Accession of James II* (1848–61, fifth volume unfinished).

38 Then, beneath the nine-tailed cat
Shall they who use it writhe, sir;
And curates lean, and rectors fat,
Shall dig the ground they tithe, sir.
Down with your Bayleys, and your Bests,
Your Giffords, and your Gurneys;
We'll clear the island of the pests,
Which mortals name attorneys.
1820 'A Radical War Song', stanza 8. The names are those of lawyers and judges who figured in the trial of the Cato Street conspirators.

39 Free trade, one of the greatest blessings which a government can confer on a people, is in almost every country unpopular.
1824 'Essay on Mitford's *History of Greece*', collected in *Works* (published 1906), vol.7, p.688–9.

40 The men of our time are not to be converted or perverted by quartos.
1825 'Milton', in the *Edinburgh Review,* Aug.

41 Perhaps no person can be a poet, or can even enjoy poetry, without a certain unsoundness of mind.
1825 'Milton', in the *Edinburgh Review,* Aug.

42 There is only one cure for the evils which newly acquired freedom produces; and that is freedom… The blaze of truth and liberty may at first dazzle and bewilder nations which have become half blind in the house of bondage. But let them gaze on, and they will soon be able to bear it.
1825 'Milton', in the *Edinburgh Review,* Aug.

43 Many politicians of our time are in the habit of laying it down as a self-evident proposition, that no people ought to be free till they are fit to use their freedom. The maxim is worthy of the fool in the old story, who resolved not to go into the water till he had learnt to swim. If men are to wait for liberty till they become wise and good in slavery, they may indeed wait for ever.
1825 'Milton', in the *Edinburgh Review,* Aug.

44 Every man who has seen the world knows that nothing is so useless as a general maxim.
1827 'Machiavelli', in the *Edinburgh Review,* Mar.

45 It has lately been brought to my knowledge
That the Ministers fully design
To suppress each cathedral and college,
And eject every learned divine.
To assist this detestable scheme
Three nuncios from Rome are come over;
They left Calais on Monday by steam,
And landed to dinner at Dover.
1827 'The Country Clergyman's Trip to Cambridge', stanza 2. A satirical poem against the opposition to Catholic emancipation.

46 Knowledge advances by steps, and not by leaps.
1828 'History' in the *Edinburgh Review,* May.

47 History, at least in its ideal state of perfection, is a compound of poetry and philosophy.
1828 'Hallam's *Constitutional History*' in the *Edinburgh Review,* Sep.

48 We know of no spectacle so ridiculous as the British public in one of its periodical fits of morality.
1828 In the *Edinburgh Review.*

49 The gallery in which the reporters sit has become a fourth estate of the realm.
1828 'Hallam's *Constitutional History*' in the *Edinburgh Review,* Sep.
➤ *See Hazlitt 388:80.*

50 His writing bears the same relation to poetry which a Turkey carpet bears to a picture.
1830 'Robert Montgomery', in the *Edinburgh Review,* Apr.

51 Mr Robert Montgomery's genius [is] far too free and aspiring to be shackled by the rules of syntax… [His] readers must take such grammar as they can get and be thankful.
1830 'Robert Montgomery', in the *Edinburgh Review,* Apr.

52 From the poetry of Lord Byron they drew a system of ethics, compounded of misanthropy and voluptuousness, a system in which the two great commandments were, to hate your neighbour, and to love your neighbour's wife.
1831 Of the young Byron enthusiasts who emulated and hero-worshipped him. 'Moore's *Life of Lord Byron*', in the *Edinburgh Review,* Jun.

53 Many of the greatest men that ever lived have written biography. Boswell was one of the smallest men that ever lived and he has beaten them all.
1831 'Croker's new edition of *The Life of Samuel Johnson*', in the *Edinburgh Review,* Sep.

54 In the foreground is that strange figure which is as familiar to us as the figures of those among whom we have been brought up, the gigantic body, the huge massy face, seamed with the scars of disease, the brown coat, the black worsted stockings, the grey wig with the scorched foretop, the dirty hands, the nails bitten and

pared to the quick.
1831 Of Dr Samuel Johnson. 'Croker's new edition of *The Life of Samuel Johnson*', in the *Edinburgh Review*, Sep.

55 Dark and terrible beyond any season within my remembrance of political affairs was the day of their flight. Far darker and more terrible will be the day of their return.
1831 On the defeat of the Tory Government, House of Commons, 20 Sep.

56 He [John Hampden] knew that the essence of war is violence, and that moderation in war is imbecility.
1831 'Lord Nugent's *Memorials of Hampden*', in the *Edinburgh Review*, Dec.

57 It is not easy to make a simile go on all fours.
1831 Of the task of the allegorist. 'Robert Southey's edition of Bunyan's *Pilgrims Progress*', in the *Edinburgh Review*, Dec.

58 A broken head in Cold Bath Fields produces a greater sensation among us than three pitched battles in India.
1833 House of Commons, 20 Sep.

59 There was a time when the most powerful of human intellects were deluded by the gibberish of the astrologer and the alchemist… But time advances; facts accumulate; doubts arise… The highest intellects, like the tops of mountains, are the first to catch and to reflect the dawn.
1835 'Sir James Mackintosh's *History of the Revolution in England, in 1688*' in the *Edinburgh Review*, Jul.

60 The history of England is emphatically the history of progress.
1835 'Sir James Mackintosh's *History of the Revolution in England, in 1688*' in the *Edinburgh Review*, Jul.

61 But even Archimedes was not free from the prevailing notion that geometry was degraded by being employed to produce anything useful. It was with difficulty that he was induced to stoop from speculation to practice. He was half ashamed of those inventions which were the wonder of hostile nations, and always spoke of them slightingly as mere amusements, as trifles in which a mathematician might be suffered to relax his mind after intense application to the higher parts of his science.
1837 'Basil Montagu's edition of *The Works of Francis Bacon, Lord Chancellor of England*', in the *Edinburgh Review*, Jul.

62 Lars Porsena of Clusium
By the nine gods he swore
That the great house of Tarquin
Should suffer wrong no more.
1842 *Lays of Ancient Rome*, 'Horatius', stanza 1.

63 Then out spake brave Horatius,
The Captain of the Gate:
'To every man upon this earth
Death cometh soon or late.
And how can man die better
Than facing fearful odds,
For the ashes of his fathers
And the temples of his God?'
1842 *Lays of Ancient Rome*, 'Horatius', stanza 27.

64 'Now who will stand on either hand,
And keep the bridge with me?'
1842 *Lays of Ancient Rome*, 'Horatius', stanza 29.

65 Was none who would be foremost
To lead such dire attack;
But those behind cried 'Forward!'

And those before cried 'Back!'
1842 *Lays of Ancient Rome*, 'Horatius', stanza 50.

66 Alone stood brave Horatius,
But constant still in mind;
Thrice thirty thousand foes before,
And the broad flood behind.
1842 *Lays of Ancient Rome*, 'Horatius', stanza 57.

67 And even the ranks of Tuscany
Could scarce forbear to cheer.
1842 *Lays of Ancient Rome*, 'Horatius', stanza 60.

68 With weeping and with laughter
Still is the story told,
How well Horatius kept the bridge
In the brave days of old.
1842 *Lays of Ancient Rome*, 'Horatius', stanza 70.

69 The rugged miners poured to war from Medip's sunless caves.
1842 'The Armada', in the *Quarterly Magazine*.

70 And broader still became the blaze, and louder still the din,
And fast from every village round the horse came spurring in.
1842 'The Armada', in the *Quarterly Magazine*.

71 We hardly know any instance of the strength and weakness of human nature so striking, and so grotesque, as the character of this haughty, vigilant, resolute, sagacious blue-stocking—half Mithridates and half Trissotin, bearing up against a world in arms, with an ounce of poison in one pocket, and a quire of bad verses in the other.
1843 Of Frederick the Great. *Historical Essays*. 'Frederic the Great', in the *Edinburgh Magazine*, Apr.

72 Forget all feuds, and shed one English tear
O'er English dust. A broken heart lies here.
1845 'A Jacobite's Epitaph', closing lines.

73 I hardly know which is the greater pest to society: a paternal Government; that is to say, a prying meddlesome Government, which intrudes itself into every part of human life and which thinks that it can do everything for everybody better than anyone can do for himself, or a careless, lounging Government, which suffers grievances, such as it could at once remove, to grow and multiply, and which to all complaint and remonstrance has only one answer, 'We must let things take their course, we must let things find their own level.'
1846 House of Commons, 22 May.

74 Persecution produced its natural effect on them. It found them a sect; it made them a faction.
1846 On the Puritans, House of Commons, 22 May.

75 The history of England is emphatically the history of progress.
1846 House of Commons, 22 May.

76 Thus our democracy was, from an early period, the most aristocratic, and our aristocracy the most democratic in the world.
1848 *History of England*, vol.1, ch.1.

77 The Puritan hated bear-baiting, not because it gave pain to the bear, but because it gave pleasure to the spectators.
1849 *History of England*, vol.1, ch.2.

78 The Mountjoy began to move, and soon passed safe through the broken stakes and floating spars. But her brave master was no more. A shot from one of the batteries had struck him; and he died by the most enviable of all deaths, in sight of the city which was his birthplace, which was his home, and which had just been saved by his courage and self-devotion from the most frightful form of destruction.
  1849 *History of England*, on the relief of Londonderry, vol.2, ch.12.

McAuliffe, Anthony 1898–1975
US soldier, a general in World War II.

79 Nuts!
  1944 Replying to the German demand for surrender at Bastogne, Belgium, 23 Dec. His response was reported in this form in the *New York Times*, 28 Dec; the original may have been more explicit.

MacBeth, George Mann 1932–92
Scottish writer. He is best known as a poet, but also wrote novels and children's books.

80 To leave great themes unfinished is
  Perhaps the most satisfying exercise
  Of power.
  1963 'The Spider's Nest'.

81 No one can read a poem unless he realises that it is a physical object as well as an abstract vehicle for conveying ideas. A poem has a material existence like a piece of music or sculpture or a plate of meat.
  1967 Introduction to *Poetry 1900 to 1965*.

82 Heap high the
  groaning platter with pink fillets, sucking pig and thick gammon, celestial chef. Be generous with the crackling. Let your hand slip with the gravy trough, dispensing plenty.
  1977 'An Ode to English Food'.

MacCaig, Norman Alexander 1910–96
Scottish poet. He was a school-teacher for much of his working life. He was one of Scotland's most distinguished poets.

83 A man's boots with a woman in them
  Clatter across the floor.
  1960 'Crofter's Kitchen, Evening'.

84 The stone remains, and the cross, to let us know
  Their unjust, hard demands, as symbols do.
  1960 'Celtic Cross'.

85 A cubic inch of some stars
  weighs a hundred tons—Blue tit,
  who could measure the power
  of your tiny spark of energy?
  1980 'Blue Tit on a String of Peanuts'.

McCain, John 1936–
US Republican politician, Senator from Arizona.

86 I will not take the low road to the highest office in the land.
  2000 Conceding victory in the South Carolina primary to George W Bush. In *The Guardian*, 24 Feb.

McCann, M(ichael) J(oseph) 1824–1883
Irish teacher, journalist and ballad-writer.

87 Proudly the note of the trumpet is sounding,
  Loudly the war-cries arise on the gale,
  Fleetly the steed by Loc Suilig is bounding
  To join the thick squadrons in Saimear's green vale.
  On, every mountaineer,
  Strangers to flight and fear:
  Rush to the standard of dauntless Red Hugh!
  Bonnought and gallowglass,
  Throng from each mountain-pass!
  On for old Erin—O'Donnell abu!
  1845 *The Spirit of the Nation*, 'O'Donnell Abu'.

88 Wildly o'er Desmond the war-wolf is howling,
  Fearless the eagle sweeps over the plain,
  The fox in the streets of the city is prowling—
  All, all who would scare them are banished or slain!
  1845 *The Spirit of the Nation*, 'O'Donnell Abu'.

McCarthy, Eugene J(oseph) 1916–
US Democratic politician, Senator from Minnesota (1958–70). An opponent of the Vietnam War, in 1968 he challenged President Johnson for nomination but the bid failed and he left politics to devote himself to teaching and writing.

89 The war in Vietnam…[is] of questionable loyalty and constitutionality…diplomatically indefensible… morally wrong.
  1967 Speech to the Conference of Concerned Democrats, 2 Dec, an address noted for crystallizing dissent against the Vietnam War.

90 The message from the administration today is a message of fear—even a message of fear of fear.
  1967 Speech to the Conference of Concerned Democrats, 2 Dec.

91 Let us pick up again these lost strands and weave them again into the fabric of America…sort out the music from the sounds and again respond to the trumpet and the steady drum.
  1967 Speech to Conference of Concerned Democrats, 2 Dec.

92 Being in politics is like being a football coach. You have to be smart enough to know the game and stupid enough to think it is important.
  1991 In the *Los Angeles Times*, 7 Dec.

McCarthy, Joseph R(aymond) 1909–57
US Republican politician and inquisitor. As Chairman of the Permanent Subcommittee on Investigations from 1953, he used hectoring cross-examination and innuendo to arraign many often innocent citizens for communist sympathies.

93 While I cannot take time off to name all the men in the State Department who have been named as members of the Communist Party and members of a spy ring, I have here in my hand a list of 205 that were known to the Secretary of State as being members of the Communist Party, and who nevertheless are still working and shaping the policy of the State Department.
  1950 Speech at Wheeling, West Virginia, 9 Feb, which marked the beginning of the McCarthy 'witch hunts' for communists.

94 McCarthyism is Americanism with its sleeves rolled.
  1952 Re-election campaign slogan.

McCarthy, Mary Thérèse 1912–89

US writer, critic and social commentator. She is best known for her novel *The Group* (1963).

95 When an American heiress wants to buy a man, she at once crosses the Atlantic. The only really materialistic people I have ever met have been Europeans.
1947 'America the Beautiful', in *Commentary*, Sep.

96 The American character looks always as if it just had a rather bad haircut, which gives it, in our eyes at any rate, a greater humanity than the European, which even among its beggars has an all too professional air.
1947 'America the Beautiful', in *Commentary*, Sep.

97 American life, in large cities, is a perpetual assault on the senses and the nerves; it is out of asceticism, out of unworldliness, precisely, that we bear it.
1947 'America the Beautiful', in *Commentary*, Sep.

98 The happy ending is our national belief.
1947 'America the Beautiful', in *Commentary*, Sep.

99 Liberty, as it is conceived by current opinion, has nothing inherent about it; it is a sort of gift or trust bestowed on the individual by the state pending *good behavior*.
1952 Speech. Collected as 'The Contagion of Ideas', in *On the Contrary* (1961).

1 Every age has a keyhole to which its eye is pasted.
1953 'My Confession'. Collected in *On the Contrary* (1961).

2 In the unreal realms of the canals, as in a Swiftian Lilliput, the real world, with its contrivances, appears as a vast folly.
1956 Of Venice. *Venice Observed*, ch.1.

3 To care for the quarrels of the past, to identify oneself passionately with a cause that became, politically speaking, a losing cause with the birth of the modern world, is to experience a kind of straining against reality, a rebellious nonconformity that, again, is rare in America, where children are instructed in the virtues of the system they live under, as though history had achieved a happy ending in American civics.
1957 Of Catholicism. *Memories of a Catholic Girlhood*, 'To the Reader'.

4 Bureaucracy, the rule of no one, has become the modern form of despotism.
1958 'Vita Activa', in the *New Yorker*, 18 Oct.

5 There are no new truths, but only truths that have not been recognized by those who have perceived them without noticing.
1958 'Vita Activa', in the *New Yorker*, 18 Oct.

6 The labor of keeping house is labor in its most naked state, for labor is toil that never finishes, toil that has to be begun again the moment it is completed, toil that is destroyed and consumed by the life process.
1958 'Vita Activa', in the *New Yorker*, 18 Oct.

7 In violence, we forget who we are.
1961 *On the Contrary*, 'Characters in Fiction'.

8 An interviewer asked me what book I thought best represented the modern American woman. All I could think of to answer was: *Madame Bovary*.
1961 *On the Contrary*, 'Characters in Fiction'.

9 Being abroad makes you conscious of the whole imitative side of human behavior. The ape in man.
1965 *Birds of America*, 'Epistle from Mother Carey's Chicken'.

10 In politics, it seems, retreat is honorable if dictated by military considerations and shameful if even *suggested* for ethical reasons.
1967 *Vietnam*, 'Solutions'.

11 I once said in an interview that every word she writes is a lie, including 'and' and 'the'.
1980 In response to Lillian Hellman's memoir, *Scoundrel Time*, in the *New York Times*, 16 Feb.

McCartney, Sir (James) Paul 1942–

British rock singer, musician and songwriter. With fellow-Beatle John Lennon, he formed the most successful songwriting team of the 1960s.

12 Pop music is the classical music of now.
Quoted in Tony Palmer *All You Need Is Love* (1976).
➤ *See also Lennon 502:89.*

13 You can't reheat a souffle.
Explaining why The Beatles would not be reforming. Quoted in the *Chronicle of the 20th Century* (1977).

McCarty, Maclyn 1911–

US biologist.

14 An alternative device for the recovery of bacteria from large volumes of culture had become available by modification of a machine originally designed as a cream separator.
1985 *The Transforming Principle: Discovering that Genes Are Made of DNA*.

McClellan, George Brinton 1826–85

Union general in the American Civil War, given command of troops in and around Washington after the Battle of Bull Run in 1861. He ran unsuccessfully for election against Abraham Lincoln and resigned from the army in 1864.

15 All quiet along the Potomac.
1862 Attributed.

MacColl, Ewan James Miller 1915–89

English folksinger, composer, collector, author, playwright and socialist, whose work was an important influence on the Scottish and worldwide folk music revivals of the 1950s and 1960s.

16 The first time ever I saw your face
I thought the sun rose in your eyes,
And the moon and the stars were the gifts you gave
To the dark and the empty skies.
1962 'The First Time Ever I Saw Your Face', stanza 1.

McCourt, Frank 1931–

US author known for the bestselling memoir *Angela's Ashes* (1996).

17 Worse than the ordinary miserable childhood is the miserable Irish childhood, and worse yet is the miserable Irish Catholic childhood.
1996 *Angela's Ashes*, ch.1.

McCoy, John B(onnet) 1943–

US banker.

18 I was trying to make it as friendly as you can make an unfriendly offer.

1995 On his unsolicited $5 billion bid in an unsuccessful attempt to acquire the Bank of Boston. In *Fortune*, 21 Aug.

McCrae, John 1872–1915

Canadian soldier, physician, and poet, First Brigade surgeon in the Canadian Field Artillery. His most famous poem, 'In Flanders Fields', was written during the Second Battle of Ypres, Belgium, 3 May 1915.

19 In Flanders fields the poppies blow
Between the crosses, row on row,
That mark our place; and in the sky
The larks, still bravely singing, fly
Scarce heard amid the guns below.
1915 'In Flanders Fields', stanza 1.

McCullers, (Lula) Carson *née Smith* 1917–67

US writer. Her novels, tragic and often symbolic, have been labelled Southern Gothic. She also wrote a novella, *The Ballad of the Sad Café* (1951) as well as short stories and plays.

20 The Heart Is A Lonely Hunter.
1940 Title of novel.

21 All men are lonely. But sometimes it seems to me that we Americans are the loneliest of all. Our hunger for foreign places and new ways has been with us almost like a national disease.
1940 'Look Homeward, Americans', in *Vogue*, 1 Dec.

22 There's nothing that makes you so aware of the improvisation of human existence as a song unfinished. Or an old address book.
1951 *The Ballad of the Sad Café*, 'The Sojourner'.

23 Nothing is so musical as the sound of pouring bourbon for the first drink on a Sunday morning. Not Bach or Schubert or any of those masters.
1953 *Clock Without Hands*.

McCurry, Michael D

Clinton White House Press Secretary (1995–98).

24 There are people around here who think Hillary Clinton is responsible for the weather.
1995 In the *New York Times*, 7 Jan. New revelations about the First Lady's role in Whitewater land sales and the firing of the presidential travel office had coincided with a heavy Washington snowfall.

MacDiarmid, Hugh *pseudonym of Christopher Murray Grieve* 1892–1978

Scottish poet, nationalist and communist, the driving-force behind the modern Scottish literary Renaissance. He used complex forms of both Scots and English in his lyrical, philosophical and polemical verse.

25 I myself believe that we have lost this war—in everything but actuality. When I see scores of sheep go to a slaughter-house I do not feel constrained to admire their resignation.
1918 Letter to George Ogilvie, 12 Nov.

26 Earth, thou bonnie broukit bairn!
1925 *Sangschaw*, 'The Bonnie Broukit Bairn'.
Broukit = neglected.

27 But greet, an' in your tears ye'll droun
The haill clanjamfrie.
1925 *Sangschaw*, 'The Bonnie Broukit Bairn'.

28 An' see the deid come loupin' owre
The auld grey wa's.
1925 *Sangschaw*, 'Crowdieknowe', stanza 1.

29 I met ayont the cairney
A lass wi' tousled hair
Singin' till a bairnie
That was nae langer there.
1926 *Penny Wheep*, 'Empty Vessel', stanza 1.

30 No' wan in fifty kens a wurd Burns wrote
But misapplied is a'body's property
1926 *A Drunk Man Looks at the Thistle*, l.41–2.

31 I'll hae nae hauf-way hoose, buy aye be whaur
Extremes meet—it's the only way I ken
To dodge the curst conceit o' bein' richt
That damns the vast majority o' men.
1926 *A Drunk Man Looks at the Thistle*, l.141–4.

32 The thistle yet'll unite
Man and the Infinite!
1926 *A Drunk Man Looks at the Thistle*, l.481–2.

33 To be yersel's—and to mak' that worth bein'.
Nae harder job to mortals has been gi'en.
1926 *A Drunk Man Looks at the Thistle*, l.745–6.

34 A'thing that ony man can be's
A mockery o' his soul at last.
1926 *A Drunk Man Looks at the Thistle*, l.1415–7.

35 Be like the thistle, O my soul,
Heedless o' praise and quick to take affront
1926 *A Drunk Man Looks at the Thistle*, l.1709–10.

36 'Let there be Licht,' said God, and there was
A little: but He lacked poo'er
To licht up mair than pairt o' space at aince,
And there is lots o' darkness that's the same
As gin He'd never spoken
1926 *A Drunk Man Looks at the Thistle*, l.2101–5.

37 And Jesus and a nameless ape
Collide and share the selfsame shape
That nocht terrestial can escape?
1926 *A Drunk Man Looks at the Thistle*, l.2476–8.

38 He canna Scotland see wha yet
Canna see the Infinite,
And Scotland in true scale to it.
1926 *A Drunk Man Looks at the Thistle*, l.2527–9.

39 O wha's the bride that cairries the bunch
O' thistles blinterin' white?
Her cuckold bridegroom little dreids
What he sall ken this nicht.
1926 *A Drunk Man Looks at the Thistle*.

40 The number of people who can copulate properly may be few; the number who can write well are infinitely fewer.
1928 Review of D H Lawrence's *Lady Chatterley's Lover* in *The New Age*, 27 Sep. This may very well have been the first published review of Lawrence's novel.

41 Lourd on my hert as winter lies
The state that Scotland's in the day.
Spring to the North has aye come slow
But noo dour winter's like to stay
For guid,
And no' for guid!
1930 *To Circumjack Cencrastus, or The Curly Snake*.

42 Better a'e gowden lyric
Than a social problem solved.
1930 *To Circumjack Cencrastus, or The Curly Snake.*

43 Are my poems spoken in the factories and fields,
In the streets o' the toon?
Gin they're no', then I'm failin' to dae
What I ocht to ha' dune.
1932 *Second Hymn to Lenin.*

44 Scotland is not wholly surrounded by the
sea—unfortunately.
1934 *Scottish Scene,* 'The Sea'.

45 We must reconcile ourselves to the stones,
Not the stones to us.
1934 'On a Raised Beach'.

46 The rose of all the world is not for me.
I want for my part
Only the little white rose of Scotland
That smells sharp and sweet—and breaks the heart.
1934 *Stony Limits and other poems,* 'The Little White Rose'.

47 My aim all along has been (in Ezra Pound's term) the
most drastic *desuetization* of Scottish life and letters,
and, in particular, the de-Tibetanization of the Highlands
and Islands, and getting rid of the whole gang of high
mucky-mucks, famous fatheads, old wives of both
sexes, stuffed shirts, hollow men with headpieces
stuffed with straw, bird-wits, lookers-under-beds,
trained seals, creeping Jesuses, Scots Wha Ha'evers,
village idiots, policemen, leaders of white-mouse
factions and noted connoisseurs of bread and butter,
glorified gangsters, and what 'Billy' Phelps calls Medlar
Novelists (the medlar being a fruit that becomes rotten
before it is ripe), Commercial Calvinists, makers of
'noises like a turnip', and all the touts and toadies and
lickspittles o the English Ascendancy, and their infernal
women-folk, and all their skunkoil skulduggery.
1943 *Lucky Poet,* ch.3, 'The Kind of Poetry I Want'.

48 We do not like the confiding, the intimate, the
ingratiating, the hail-fellow-well-met, but prefer the
unapproachable, the hard-bitten, the recalcitrant, the
sinister, the malignant, the saturnine, the cross-grained
and the cankered, and the howling wilderness to the
amenities of civilization, the irascible to the affable, the
prickly to the smooth. We have no damned fellow-
feeling at all.
1952 'The Dour Drinkers of Glasgow', in *The American Mercury,*
Mar.

49 So this is what our lives have been given to find,
A language that can serve our purposes,
A marvellous lucidity, a quality of fiery aery light,
Flowing like clear water, flying like a bird
Burning like a sunlit landscape.
1955 'The Task'.

50 My job, as I see it, has never been to lay a tit's egg, but to
erupt like a volcano emitting not only flame but a lot of
rubbish.
1964 Letter to George Bruce, 1 Jul.

51 Scotland small? Our multiform, infinite Scotland small?
1974 'Direadh'.

McDonald, Alonzo L

US government official and businessman, former chief

executive officer of McKinsey & Company and of the Bendix
Corporation and staff director at the White House (1979–81).

52 Very few factors help produce economies of scale.
Technology may be one, but not people. When it comes
to motivating people and using their brainpower, you hit
diseconomies of scale early. At that point, bigger isn't
better.
1986 'Of Floating Factories and Mating Dinosaurs', in the
Harvard Business Review, Nov/Dec.

MacDonald, George 1824–1905

Scottish pastor, poet and novelist who wrote fantastical and
allegorical works for both adults and children.

53 Here lie I, Martin Elginbrodde:
Hae mercy o' my soul, Lord God;
As I wad do, were I Lord God,
And ye were Martin Elginbrodde.
1863 *David Elginbrod,* bk.1, ch.13.

54 The love of our neighbour is the only door out of the
dungeon of self, where we mope and mow, striking
sparks, and rubbing phosphorescence out of the walls,
and blowing our own breath in our own nostrils, instead
of issuing to the fair sunlight of God, the sweet winds of
the universe.
1867 *Unspoken Sermons.*

55 Where did you come from, baby dear?
Out of the everywhere into here.
1871 *At the Back of the North Wind,* ch.33, 'Song'.

56 They all were looking for a king
To slay their foes and lift them high:
Thou cam'st, a little baby thing
That made a woman cry.
1883 'That Holy Thing', stanza 1.

57 There is no strength in unbelief. Even the unbelief of what
is false is no source of might. It is the truth shining from
behind that gives the strength to disbelieve.
The Marquis of Lossie (published 1906).

58 To be trusted is a greater compliment than to be loved.
The Marquis of Lossie (published 1906).

Macdonald, (James) Ramsay 1866–1937

Scottish politician, Prime Minister and Foreign Secretary of the
first British Labour government (1924, 1929–31). He met the
financial crisis of 1931 by forming a 'National' coalition
government, which he led after a general election (1931–5).

59 The League of Nations grows in moral courage. Its frown
will soon be more dreaded than a nation's arms, and
when that happens, you and I shall have security and
peace.
1929 Speech, London, 9 Nov.

60 We hear war called murder. It is not: it is suicide.
1930 Quoted in the *Observer,* 3 May.

MacDonnell, A(rchibald) G(ordon) 1895–1941

Scottish writer who lived most of his life in England, the subject
of his best-known satirical novel.

61 England, their England.
1933 Title of novel.
➤ *See Henley 395:40.*

MacDougall, Ranald 1915–73

US screenwriter whose credits include *The Hasty Heart* (1949), *The Naked Jungle* (1954), *Queen Bee* (1955) and *The Mountain* (1956).

62 Alligators have the right idea, they eat their young.
1945 *Mildred Pierce* (with Catherine Turney).

McElligott, Tom (Thomas James) 1943–

US advertising executive.

63 You're never too bad to win.
1987 In the *Wall Street Journal*, 26 Mar.

McEnroe, John Patrick 1959–

US tennis player. He won four US Open singles titles and three Wimbledon titles. He was known for temperamental behaviour on court.

64 You cannot be serious!
1981 In protest at an umpire's decision at Wimbledon.

65 Being a celebrity is like being raped, and there's absolutely nothing a player can do about it.
Quoted in Colin Jarman *The Guinness Dictionary of Sports Quotations* (1990).

McEwan, Ian Russell 1948–

English writer. He established his reputation with two volumes of short stories before turning to novels. He has also written screenplays.

66 Her eyes, nose, mouth, skin, all might have been designed in committee to meet the barest requirements of feasibility.
1981 *The Comfort of Strangers*, ch.6.

67 Shall there be womanly times? Or shall we die?
1983 Refrain from *Or Shall We Die*, an oratorio.

68 Looking after children is one of the ways of looking after yourself.
1992 *Black Dogs*, preface.

McFadden, Robert D(ennis) 1937–

US journalist and writer. He has worked for the *New York Times* as a senior journalist since 1961, and is the author of two journalism-related books. His numerous press awards have included an Excellence in Journalism award (1994).

69 That rarest of political creatures—a Labor leader who could actually win elections.
1995 Of Harold Wilson. In the *New York Times*, 25 May.

70 He was rotund, provincial, resolutely middle-class, studiously ambiguous and sometimes wavering in his opinions.
1995 Of Harold Wilson. In the *New York Times*, 25 May.

71 In an era of precipitous decline for Britain and its once-global empire, Harold Wilson was a fixture for 30 years, a solid workingman's socialist in a rumpled ready-to-wear suit and his trademark Gannex mackintosh.
1995 Of Harold Wilson. In the *New York Times*, 25 May.

72 The silver-haired, pipe-smoking northerner was a consummate British politician: tenacious, shrewd, manipulative, a blend of homespun tastes, acid wit and pragmatic, often shifting policies…the symbol of an emerging middle-class Briton.

1995 Of Harold Wilson. In the *New York Times*, 25 May.

McFarlane, J A, and Clements, Warren 1944–, 1952–

Canadian journalists.

73 Say *quotes* from the shortstop or the Prime Minister, but *quotations* from the Bible, Browning or Churchill.
1990 *The Globe and Mail Style Book*.

74 The patron saint of journalists, officially named by the church, is St. Francis de Sales. The traditional patron saint of editors is St. John Bosco. (The protector of computer-age journalists may well be St. Anthony of Padua, patron saint of searchers for lost articles.)
1990 *The Globe and Mail Style Book*.

McFarlane, Robert 'Bud' Carl 1937–

US government official. After serving with the Marines, he became National Security adviser to President Reagan (1983–5) and later founder of Global Energy Investors (GEI).

75 He knows so little and accomplishes so much.
Of President Reagan. Quoted in George P Shultz *Turmoil and Triumph* (1993).

MacGill, Patrick 1890–1963

Irish navvy, novelist and poet. Sold into servitude by his farming parents, he escaped to Scotland where he laboured and hawked his verses before coming to literary attention. He emigrated to the US in 1930, where he fell into poverty and developed muscular sclerosis.

76 All the night the frogs go chuckle, all the day the birds are
    singing
In the pond beside the meadow, by the roadway poplar-lined,
In the field between the trenches are a million blossoms
    springing
'Twixt the grass of silver bayonets where the lines of
    battle wind
Where man has manned the trenches for the maiming of
    his kind.
1917 *Soldier Songs*, 'The Trench'.

McGonagall, William c.1825–1902

Scottish self-styled 'poet and tragedian' from Dundee, most of his work was doggerel. The majority of his poems were originally produced as broadsheets and not collected until after his death.

77 Alas! Lord and Lady Dalhousie are dead, and buried at
    last,
Which causes many people to feel a little downcast.
1890 *Poetic Gems*, 'The Death of Lord and Lady Dalhousie', stanza 1.

78 Beautiful Railway Bridge of the Silv'ry Tay!
Alas! I am very sorry to say
That ninety lives have been taken away
On the last Sabbath day of 1879,
Which will be remember'd for a very long time.
1890 *Poetic Gems*, 'The Tay Bridge Disaster', stanza 1.

79 Ye lovers of the picturesque, if ye wish to drown your
    grief,
Take my advice, and visit the ancient town of Crieff;
The climate is bracing, and the walks lovely to see
Besides, ye can ramble over the district, and view the

beautiful scenery.
More Poetic Gems (published 1962), 'Beautiful Crieff', stanza 1.

80 The man that gets drunk is little else than a fool,
And is in the habit, no doubt, of advocating for Home Rule;
But the best Home Rule for him, as far as I can understand,
Is the abolition of strong drink from the land.
Last Poetic Gems (published 1968), 'The Demon Drink', stanza 9.

McGough, Roger 1937–

English poet, playwright and performer, associated with the 1960s Liverpool pop scene. His poetry is characterized by a dry, ironic wit and a feeling for the diction and rhythms of the street. He has also written children's books.

81 Let me die a youngman's death
not a clean and in-between-
the-sheets, holy-water death.
1967 'Let Me Die A Youngman's Death'.

82 Discretion is the better part of Valerie
(though all of her is nice).
1969 'Discretion'.

83 by thus keeping one pace ahead of myself
I need never catch up with the truth.
1973 'unlikely now'.

84 I could never begin a poem: 'When I am dead'
In case it tempted Fate, and Fate gave way.
1982 'When I Am Dead'.

85 Do people who wave at trains
Wave at the driver, or at the train itself?
Or, do people who wave at trains
Wave at the passengers? Those hurtling strangers,
The unidentifiable flying faces?
1982 'Waving At Trains'.

86 This is the mother
who one day chose
to smother the child
with kisses, and blows and blows and blows.
1982 'Kisses and Blows'.

MacGowan, Shane 1957–

English singer, member of The Pogues.

87 They died in their hundreds with no sign to mark where
Save the brass in the pocket of the entrepreneur
By landslide and rockblast they got buried so deep
That in death if not life they'll have peace while they sleep.
1985 'Navigator' (co-written with Jim Finer).

88 You're a bum
You're a punk
You're an old slut on junk
Lying there almost dead on a drip in that bed
You scumbag, you maggot
You cheap lousy faggot
Happy Christmas your arse I pray God it's our last.
1988 'Fairytale of New York' (co-written with Jim Finer).

89 Never mind Dylan and the Dead, this'll be Dylan and the Nearly Dead.
1997 On a gig in which he was to be support act for Bob Dylan. Quoted in *Q Magazine*, Apr.

90 Cram as much pleasure as you can into life, and rail against the pain that you have to suffer as a result.
1997 In *Loaded*, Nov.

91 I don't believe in the Hebrew God, some big hairy bastard with thunderbolts.
1999 In the *Irish Voice*, 9 Jun.

McGovern, George S(tanley) 1922–

US Democratic politician, Senator for South Dakota (1963–81). He made a bid for the presidential nomination in 1968, and unsuccessfully opposed Nixon in the 1972 presidential election. He tried again for the presidential nomination in 1984, but withdrew.

92 To those who charge that liberalism has been tried and found wanting, I answer that the failure is not in the idea but in the course of recent history. The New Deal was ended by World War II. The New Frontier was closed by Berlin and Cuba even before it was opened. And the Great Society lost its greatness in the jungles of Indochina.
1973 Lecture at Oxford University, 21 Jan.

McGregor, Ewan 1971–

Scottish actor.

93 I'm sometimes asked 'Can you lose the accent?' and I say 'No, but I can put on another one'.
2001 In *In Style*, Sep.

McGuigan, Barry 1961–

Irish boxer.

94 There is nothing like wealth for dulling desire.
2003 In *The Independent*, 29 Dec.

Machado de Assis, Joaquim Maria 1839–1908

Brazilian poet and novelist, writer of romantic stories and poems. *Memórias Póstumas de Brás Cubas* (1881) marks the beginning of his mature style, informed by both pessimism and wit.

95 *Cada estação da vida é uma edição, que corrige a anterior, e que será corrigida também, até a edição definitiva, que o editor dá de graça aos vermes.*
Each stage in life is an edition that supersedes the previous one and will also be superseded until the definitive edition: the one that the editor gives to the worms.
1881 *Memórias Póstumas de Brás Cubas*, ch.27 (translated as *Epitaph of a Small Winner*, 1952).

96 *A vida é tão bela que a mesma idéia da morte precisa de vir primeiro a ela, antes de se ver cumprida. Já me vás entendendo; lê agora outro capítulo.*
Life is so beautiful that even the idea of death must be born before it can be realized. You must already understand. Now read another chapter.
1899 *Dom Casmurro*, ch.133.

Machiavelli, Niccolò di Bernardo dei 1469–1527

Italian politician and political theorist. Obliged to withdraw from public life after an accusation of conspiracy (1513), he devoted himself to literature. His masterpiece is the pragmatic manual for statesmen, *Il Principe* ('The Prince', written in 1513, published in 1532).

97 *Gli uomini si debbano o vezzeggiare o spegnere; perché si vendicano delle leggeri offese, delle gravi non possono.*
Men should be either treated generously or destroyed, because they take revenge for slight injuries—for heavy ones they cannot.
1513 *Il Principe,* ch.3 (translated by Alan Gilbert).

98 *Nasce da questo una disputa: s'egli è meglio essere amato che temuto, o è converso. Rispondesi che si vorebbe essere l'uno e l'altro; ma perché egli è difficile accozzarli insieme, è molto più sicuro essere temuto che amato, quando si abbia a mancare dell'uno de'due.*
This leads to a debate: is it better to be loved than feared, or the reverse? The answer is that it is desirable to be both, but because it is difficult to join them together, it is much safer for a prince to be feared than loved, if he is to fail in one of the two.
1513 *Il Principe,* ch.8 (translated by Alan Gilbert).

99 It never or rarely happens that a republic or monarchy is well constituted, or its old institutions entirely reformed, unless it is only done by one individual.
1513–17 *Discourses on First Ten Books of Livy.*

McIlvanney, William Angus 1936–

Scottish writer. He is best known for his Ayrshire novels *Docherty* (1975) and *The Big Man* (1985), and his series of crime novels featuring the Glaswegian detective, Laidlaw. He has also written poetry, essays and short stories.

1 There is a kind of laughter people laugh at public events, as if a joke were a charity auction and they want to be seen to be bidding.
1985 *The Big Man,* ch.1.

2 That would have been a nice place, inside an idea, but it wasn't a place to live. It was necessary to live where the idea and the fact collided.
1985 *The Big Man,* ch.8.

McInerney, Jay 1955–

US author.

3 I'm glad I don't have a book coming out this month.
2001 Comment made by Jay McInerney to Brett Easton Ellis on 11 Sep, when the World Trade Center was destroyed. Ellis replied, 'I was just thinking the same thing'. Quoted in *The Guardian,* 15 Sep.

MacInnes, Colin 1914–79

English writer. He gave a voice to sections of society often ignored. He is best known for his novel *Absolute Beginners* (1959).

4 And I thought, 'My lord, one thing is certain, and that's that they'll make musicals one day about the glamour-studded 1950s.' And I thought, my heaven, one thing is certain too, I'm miserable.
1959 *Absolute Beginners.*

5 Tradition, if not constantly recreated, can be as much a millstone as a mill-wheel.
1961 *England, Half English,* 'England, Half English'.

6 In England, pop art and fine art stand resolutely back to back.
1961 *England, Half English,* 'Pop Songs and Teenagers'.

7 A coloured man can tell, in five seconds dead, whether a white man likes him or not. If the white man *says* he does, he is instantly—and usually quite rightly—mistrusted.
1961 *England, Half English,* 'A Short Guide for Jumbles'.

8 The decorations are like those of the embassy of a nation about to go into voluntary liquidation.
1961 *England, Half English,* 'See You At Mabel's'.

MacInnis, Joseph 1937–

Canadian doctor, environmentalist and undersea explorer.

9 The larger the island of knowledge, the longer the shoreline of wonder.
Quoted by Donald Grant in *The Globe and Mail,* 8 Nov 1986.

Mackay, Alan Lindsay 1926–

British scientist and Fellow of the Royal Society.

10 How can we have any new ideas or fresh outlooks when 90 per cent of all the scientists who have ever lived have still not died?
1969 In *Scientific World,* vol.13.

McKay, Claude *originally* Festus Claudius 1890–1948

Jamaican born US writer. He wrote poetry, novels, autobiography and a study of life in Harlem, and was a key figure in the Harlem Renaissance of the 1920s.

11 If we must die, let it not be like hogs
Hunted and penned in an inglorious spot
While round us bark the mad and hungry dogs,
Making their mock at our accursed lot.
1922 *Harlem Shadows,* 'If We Must Die'.

12 Like men we'll face the murderous cowardly pack,
Pressed to the wall, dying, but fighting back!
1922 *Harlem Shadows,* 'If We Must Die'.

Mackaye, Dorothy Disney 1904–92

US journalist and agony aunt, best known for editing the 'Can This Marriage be Saved?' column for the *Ladies Home Journal* for more than 30 years.

13 'He never listens' is universal in the institution of marriage.
Recalled on her death, 5 Sep 1992.

Macke, August 1887–1914

German painter, one of the founder members of the *Blaue Reiter* group of Expressionist artists.

14 To create forms means: to live. Are not children more creative in drawing directly from the secret of their sensations than the imitator of Greek forms? Are not savages artists who have forms of their own powerful as the form of thunder?
1912 *The Blaue Reiter Almanac.*

Mackellar, (Isobel Marion) Dorothea 1885–1968

Australian popular poet and novelist. Her works include *The Witch Maid* (1914), *Dreamharbour* (1923) and the novel *The Little Blue Devil* (1912). She wrote little after the mid-1920s, but translated widely from various European poets.

15 The love of field and coppice,
Of green and shaded lanes,
Of ordered woods and gardens

Is running in your veins.
Strong love of grey-blue distance
Brown streams and soft, dim skies—I know
but cannot share it,
My love is otherwise.

I love a sunburnt country,
A land of sweeping plains,
Of ragged mountain ranges,
Of droughts and flooding rains.
I love her far horizons,
I love her jewel-sea,
Her beauty and her terror—
The wide brown land for me!

1905 'Core of My Heart', first published in the London *Spectator*. Collected as 'My Country' in *The Closed Door, and Other Verses* (1911).

McKellen, Sir Ian Murray 1939–

English stage and film actor and director.

16 I can't be absolutely certain, 30 years ago when I made the decision to become an actor, but certainly one of the reasons was it was the way to meet other queer men.
Quoted in Blake Green 'A Kingly McKellen as a Fascist in *Richard II*', in the Pink Pages, *San Francisco Chronicle*, 16 Aug 1992.

17 You can always pick out stage actors at the Oscars: they know how to walk.
2002 In the *Observer*, 17 Feb.

MacKenzie, Sir (Edward Montague) Compton
1883–1972

English writer and editor. His best-known books are *Sinister Street* (1913–14) and *Whisky Galore* (1947), which became a famous film.

18 Prostitution. Selling one's body to keep one's soul…one might say of most modern marriages that they were selling one's soul to keep one's body.
1918 *The Adventures of Sylvia Scarlett*, bk.2, ch.5.

19 You are offered a piece of bread and butter that feels like a damp handkerchief and sometimes, when cucumber is added to it, like a wet one.
1927 *Vestal Fire*, bk.1, ch.3.

20 Women do not find it difficult nowadays to behave like men, but they often find it extremely difficult to behave like gentlemen.
1933 *Literature in My Time*, ch.22.

MacKenzie, Lewis W 1940–

Canadian Major-General, retired, United Nations Chief of Staff for peacekeeping in Sarajevo, Bosnia-Herzegovina.

21 Countries that have soldiers in charge seem, more often than not, to be the ones where democracy is but a flickering candle sitting in an open window with a forecast of rain.
1993 Letter about his retirement, in *The Globe and Mail*, 21 Jan.

Mackintosh, Sir James 1765–1832

Scottish writer, philosopher and historian. He studied medicine, but settled in London as a journalist. His *Vindiciae Gallicae* (1791) was a defence of the French Revolution (he later recanted his views, 1815). He spent seven years in Bombay, becoming an MP on his return.

22 Men are never so good or so bad as their opinions.
1830 *Dissertation on the Progress of Ethical Philosophy*, section 6, 'Jeremy Bentham'.

23 Henry VIII perhaps approached as nearly to the ideal standard of perfect wickedness as the infirmities of human nature will allow.
1831 Of Henry's actions in executing Thomas More and Anne Boleyn. *History of England*, vol.2.

MacLaine, Shirley *pseudonym of Shirley MacLean Beatty*
1934–

US actress, sister of Warren Beatty. Her films include *The Apartment* (1959), *Irma La Douce* (1963), *Sweet Charity* (1968), *Terms of Endearment* (1983) and *Steel Magnolias* (1989).

24 I've played so many hookers they don't pay me in the regular way any more. They leave it on the dresser.
1989 In *New Woman*, Jul.

McLean, Don 1945–

US singer and songwriter. He enjoyed a series of hits in the early 1970s, among them the classic singles 'American Pie' (1972) and 'Vincent' (1972). He later concentrated on country music.

25 I can't remember if I cried
When I read about his widowed bride.
Something touched me deep inside
The day the music died.
1972 Of the death of Buddy Holly. 'American Pie'.

26 So bye, bye, Miss American Pie,
Drove my Chevy to the levee
But the levee was dry.
Them good old boys was drinkin' whiskey and rye
Singin' 'This'll be the day that I die.'
1972 'American Pie'.

27 And the three men I admired most,
The Father, Son and Holy Ghost,
They caught the last train for the coast
The day the music died.
1972 'American Pie'.

Maclean, Sir Fitzroy Hew 1911–96

English diplomat, soldier and traveller. Sent at his own request to Moscow, he travelled in Central Asia. During World War II he joined the Special Air Service in North Africa and later he was parachuted into Yugoslavia as Churchill's personal representative to contact Tito, then a guerrilla leader.

28 At first sight, landing by plane had seemed an infinitely more normal and agreeable method of entering the country than what Mr Churchill called 'jumping out of a parachute'.
1949 *Eastern Approaches*.

29 A spirit of contradiction has always, to some extent, guided my behaviour.
1949 *Eastern Approaches*.

30 It was unhealthy and unsafe, and of no interest whatever. 'But what,' I said, 'about the tigers ?' 'Tigers, perhaps,' he replied pityingly, 'but no culture.'
1949 Of Lenkoran, Azerbaijan, in discussion with an Armenian official. *Eastern Approaches*.

Maclean, John 1879–1923

Scottish Marxist and revolutionary of almost legendary status in Glasgow, appointed Soviet Consul on the Clyde after the Russian Revolution. Ill health accentuated by frequent prison sentences led to his early death.

31 No government is going to take from me my right to speak, my right to protest against wrong, my right to do everything that is for the benefit of mankind. I am not here, then, as the accused; I am here as the accuser of capitalism dripping with blood from head to foot.
1918 Speech at his trial at the High Court, Edinburgh, 9 May, quoted in Nan Milton *John Maclean* (1973), ch.3.

MacLean, Sorley *Gaelic name* **Somhairle MacGill–Eain** 1911–96

Scottish poet. He wrote in Gaelic, in which language he was the most important late 20th century poet, and prepared his own English translations.

32 *Ma thubhairt ar cainnt gu bheil a' chiall*
co-ionann ris a' ghaol
chan fhior dhi.
If our language has said that reason
is identical with love,
it is not speaking the truth.
1943 'A Chiall's a Ghràidh' ('Reason and Love').

33 *Mairg an t-sòil a chì air fairge*
ian mór marbh na h-albann.
Pity the eye that sees on the ocean
the great dead bird of Scotland.
1943 'An t-Eilean', 'The Island'.

34 *Tha tìm, am fiadh, an coille Hallaig.*
Time, the deer, is in the wood of Hallaig.
1970 'Hallaig', epitaph.

35 *Mura tig's ann theànas ni a Hallaig*
a dh' ionnsaigh sàbaid nam marbh,
far a bheil an sluagh a' tathaich,
gach aon ghinealach a dh' fhalbh.
If it does not, I will go down to Hallaig,
to the Sabbath of the dead,
where the people are frequenting,
every single generation gone.
1970 'Hallaig'.

MacLeish, Archibald 1892–1982

US poet, Librarian of Congress (1939–44), Assistant Secretary of State (1944–5) and Professor of Rhetoric at Harvard (1949–62). He won Pulitzer Prizes for *Conquistador* (1932), *Collected Poems 1917–52* (1952) and his verse drama *J.B.* (1958).

36 A Poem should be palpable and mute
As a globed fruit.
1926 'Ars Poetica'.

37 A poem should be wordless
As the flight of birds.
1926 'Ars Poetica'.

38 A poem should not mean
But be.
1926 'Ars Poetica'.

39 We have learned the answers, all the answers:
It is the question that we do not know.
1928 'The Hamlet of A. MacLeish'.

40 If the poem can be improved by its author's explanations, it should never have been published.
1933 Author's note in *Poems*.

41 Keepers of books, keepers of print and paper on the shelves, librarians are keepers also of the records of the human spirit—the records of men's watch upon the world and on themselves.
1941 A Time to Speak, 'Of the Librarian's Profession'.

42 The dissenter is every human being at those moments in his life when he resigns momentarily from the herd and thinks for himself.
1956 'In Praise of Dissent', in the *New York Times*, 16 Dec.

43 Anything can make us look, only art can make us see.
1961 *Poetry and Experience*. 'Riverside'.

44 History, like a badly constructed concert hall, has occasional dead spots where the music can't be heard.
1967 In the *Observer*, 12 Feb.

45 Wildness and silence disappeared from the countryside, sweetness fell from the air, not because anyone wished them to vanish or fall but because throughways had to floor the meadows with cement to carry the automobiles which advancing technology produced.
1968 'The Great American Frustration', in the *Saturday Review*, 9 Jul.

46 To see the earth as we now see it, small and beautiful in that eternal silence where it floats, is to see ourselves as riders on the earth together, brothers on that bright loveliness in the unending night—brothers who *see* now they are truly brothers.
1968 On the first pictures from the moon. In the *New York Times*, 25 Dec.

47 The business of the law is to make sense of the confusion of what we call human life—to reduce it to order but at the same time to give it possibility, scope, even dignity.
1972 'Apologia', in the *Harvard Law Review*, Jun.

48 Poets…are literal-minded men who will squeeze a word till it hurts.
1972 'Apologia', in the *Harvard Law Review*, Jun.

49 We are great as our belief in human liberty—no greater. And our belief in human liberty is only ours when it is larger than ourselves.
1976 'Now Let Us Address The Main Question: Bicentennial of What?', in the *New York Times*, 3 Jul.

50 Poetry is the art of understanding what it is to be alive.
1982 Recalled on his death, 20 Apr 1982.

51 If the art of poetry is…the art of making sense of the chaos of human experience, it's not a bad thing to see a lot of chaos.
On his work in government. Quoted in Scott Donaldson *Archibald MacLeish* (1992).

52 Mr Morgan struck me as a healthy and childish Britisher probably inhabiting the early 19th century.
Of financier J P Morgan. Quoted in Scott Donaldson *Archibald MacLeish* (1992).

MacLennan, Hugh 1927–90

Canadian novelist and essayist.

53 Boy Meets Girl in Winnipeg and Who Cares?
1960 Title of a magazine article in *Scotchman's Return and Other Essays*. It refers to the preference of Canadian editors,

publishers, and readers for romance and drama set in foreign locales.

Macleod, Fiona

➤ See Sharp, William

Macleod, Iain Norman 1913–70

English Conservative politician, Chairman of the Conservative Party (1961–3). He refused to serve under Lord Home (having supported R A Butler's leadership claim), and spent two years editing the *Spectator*. He was shadow Chancellor under Heath (1965–70), and briefly Chancellor (1970).

54 The Socialists can scheme their schemes and the Liberals can dream their dreams, but we, at least, have work to do.
1960 Speech at the Conservative Party Conference.

55 We now have the worst of both worlds—not just inflation on the one side or stagnation on the other, but both of them together. We have a sort of stagflation situation.
1965 Speech in the House of Commons, Nov.

McLuhan, (Herbert) Marshall 1911–80

Canadian critic and cultural theorist. He claimed that it is the communication media *per se*, not the information and ideas which they broadcast, that influence society. His books include *The Gutenberg Galaxy* (1962) and *The Medium is the Message* (1969).

56 For tribal man space was the uncontrollable mystery. For technological man it is time that occupies the same role.
1951 *The Mechanical Bride*, 'Magic that Changes Mood'.

57 The medium is the message.
1959 Speech at the University of British Columbia, 30 Jun, following a symposium in Vancouver on the subject of music and the mass media. The phrase was later used as the title of ch.1 in *Understanding Media* (1964), and as a book title (1969).

58 The new electronic independence recreates the world in the image of a global village.
1962 *The Gutenberg Galaxy*.

59 The car has become an article of dress without which we feel uncertain, unclad, and incomplete in the urban compound.
1964 *Understanding Media*, ch.22.

60 Persons grouped around a fire or candle for warmth or light are less able to pursue independent thoughts, or even tasks, than people supplied with electric light. In the same way, the social and educational patterns latent in automation are those of self-employment and artistic autonomy.
1964 *Understanding Media*, ch.33.

61 If the nineteenth century was the age of the editorial chair, ours is the century of the psychiatrist's couch.
1964 *Understanding Media*.

62 Canada is the only country in the world that knows how to live without an identity.
1967 'Canada: A Borderline Case', CBC radio broadcast, 29 May.

63 Life. Consider the alternative.
1968 *War and Peace in the Global Village*.

64 Television brought the brutality of war into the comfort of the living room. Vietnam was lost in the living rooms of America, not on the battlefields of Vietnam.

1975 Quoted in the *Montreal Gazette*, May.

65 Gutenburg made everybody a reader. Xerox makes everybody a publisher.
1977 In the *Guardian Weekly*, 12 Jun.

Macmillan, Sir (Maurice) Harold, 1st Earl of Stockton 1894–1986

English Conservative politician. He succeeded Eden as Prime Minister (1957), and was re-elected in 1959. He resigned through ill health in 1963.

66 We have not overthrown the divine right of kings to fall down for the divine right of experts.
1950 Speech, Strasbourg, 16 Aug.

67 I thought that the best thing to do was to settle up these little local difficulties, and then turn to the wider vision of the Commonwealth.
1956 On departing for a Commonwealth conference, after sacking several members of his Cabinet in his Night of the Long Knives, Jan.

68 Forever poised between a cliché and an indiscretion.
1956 On the role of a Foreign Secretary, in *Newsweek*, Apr.

69 Let us be frank about it. Most of our people have never had it so good. Go around the country, go to the industrial towns, go to the farms, and you will see a state of prosperity such as we have never had in my lifetime—nor indeed ever in the history of this country.
1957 Speech, Bedford, 20 Jul. This is the original form of the oft-misquoted 'You never had it so good'.

70 At home, you always have to be a politician. When you are abroad, you almost feel yourself to be a statesman.
1958 Speech during the first visit of a British Prime Minister to Australia, 17 Feb.

71 The most striking of all the impressions that I have formed since I left London a month ago is of the strength of African national consciousness. In different places it may take different forms, but it is happening everywhere. The wind of change is blowing through this continent. Whether we like it or not, the growth of national consciousness is a political fact.
1960 Speech to the South African Parliament, 3 Feb.

72 Are we so sure that with 15 representatives…in NATO, acting under the unanimity rule, the deterrent would continue to deter? There may be one finger on the trigger, but there will be 15 fingers on the safety catch.
1960 House of Commons, 30 May.

73 I was determined that no British government should be brought down by the action of two tarts.
1963 On the Profumo scandal, referring specifically to Christine Keeler and Mandy Rice-Davies, Jul.

74 I have never found, in a long experience of politics, that criticism is ever inhibited by ignorance.
1963 In the *Wall Street Journal*, 13 Aug.

75 A man who trusts nobody is apt to be the kind of man whom nobody trusts.
1963 In the *New York Herald Tribune*, 17 Dec.

76 Tradition does not mean that the living are dead; it means that the dead are living.
1963 In the *Manchester Guardian*, 18 Dec.

77 There are three bodies no sensible man directly challenges: the Roman Catholic Church, the Brigade of Guards, and the National Union of Mineworkers.

1981 In the *Observer*, 22 Feb.

78 There is a growing division in our comparatively prosperous society between the South and the North and Midlands, which are ailing, that cannot be allowed to continue. There is a general sense of tension. The old English way might be to quarrel and have battles, but they were friendly. I can only describe as wicked the hatred that has been introduced, and which is to be found among different types of people today. Not merely an intellectual but a moral effort is required to get rid of it.
1984 Maiden speech as the Earl of Stockton (60 years after first entering the House of Commons), House of Lords, 13 Nov.

79 First of all the Georgian Silver goes, and then all that nice furniture that used to be in the salon. Then the Canalettos go.
1985 Speech at a private dinner of the Tory Reform Group, 8 Nov, in a reference to privatization and the selling of profitable state-owned enterprises.

80 Margaret Thatcher is a brilliant tyrant surrounded by mediocrities.
1986 In *Newsweek*, 12 Oct.

81 A man who was alleged to have the rigidity of a poker without its occasional warmth.
Of Charles de Gaulle, whose nickname was 'Ramrod'. Quoted by Henry Fairlie in the *New Republic*, 20 Mar 1989.

82 If people want a sense of purpose, they should get it from their archbishop, they should certainly not get it from their politicians.
Quoted in *The Life of Politics*.

83 You've reached the stage where you must decide whether you're going to be a good writer or a good public servant. You can't be both.
Attributed comment to Michael O'Donovan (real name of the writer Frank O'Connor).

McMurtry, Larry Jeff 1936–

US novelist. Several of his novels have been filmed successfully, but his most significant work is the epic fusion of generic western and historical novel in *Lonesome Dove* (1985).

84 The Last Picture Show.
1966 Title of novel, subsequently filmed.

85 Terms of Endearment.
1975 Title of novel, subsequently filmed.

86 'We'll be the Indians, if we last another twenty years,' Augustus said. 'The way this place is settling up it'll be nothing but churches and dry-goods stores before you know it. Next thing you know they'll have to round up us old rowdies and stick us on a reservation to keep us from scaring the ladies.'
1985 *Lonesome Dove*, ch.42

87 The cowboys had lived for months under the great bowl of the sky, and yet the Montana skies seemed deeper than the skies of Texas or Nebraska. Their depth and blueness robbed even the sun of its harsh force—it seemed smaller, in the vastness, and the whole sky no longer turned white at noon as it had in the lower plains. Always, somewhere to the north, there was a swath of blueness, with white cloads floating in it like petals in a pond.
1985 *Lonesome Dove*, ch.93.

88 Self-parody is the first portent of age.
1989 *Some Can Whistle*, pt.1, ch.14.

89 But the sorrowing are nomads, on a plain with few landmarks and no boundaries; sorrow's horizons are vague and its demands are few.
1989 *Some Can Whistle*, pt.4, ch.9.

McNamara, Robert Strange 1916–

US Democratic politician and businessman, Secretary of Defense in the Kennedy administration (1961) during the Vietnam War. He resigned to become President of the World Bank (1968–81), and later emerged as a critic of the nuclear arms race and of the Vietnam conflict, expressing regret for his role in the latter.

90 I don't object to it being called 'McNamara's war' ... It is a very important war and I am pleased to be identified with it and do whatever I can to win it.
1964 On the Vietnam War. In the *New York Times*, 25 Apr.

91 A test case of US capacity to help a nation meet a Communist 'war of liberation'.
1964 Of the Vietnam War. Quoted in N Sheehan *The Pentagon Papers*.

92 Neither conscience nor sanity itself suggests that the United States is, or should or could be the global gendarme.
1966 Speech to US newspaper editors. Reported in the *New York Times*, 19 May.

93 I wondered if I'd ever see another Saturday night.
On the threat of nuclear war from Russian warheads in Cuba, Oct 1962. Quoted in Elie Abel *Missile Crisis* (1966).

94 One cannot fashion a credible deterrent out of an incredible action.
1968 On nuclear weapons. *The Essence of Security*.

95 We had a two-track approach, one political and the other military, and the military was designed to move us along the political track.
On the Vietnam War in late 1967. Quoted in Deborah Shapley *Promise and Power* (1993).

96 We tend to justify our actions and in a sense we color history to achieve that objective.
Quoted in Robert Siegel (ed) *The NPR Interviews* (1994).

97 Although we sought to do the right thing—and believed we were doing the right thing—in my judgement, hindsight proves us wrong.
1995 *In Retrospect: The tragedy and lessons of Vietnam* (with Brian Van de Mark).

MacNeice, (Frederick) Louis 1907–63

Irish poet born in Belfast. He was closely associated with the British left-wing poets of the 1930s, especially W H Auden with whom he wrote *Letters from Iceland* (1937). He also wrote radio drama, including *The Dark Tower* (broadcast 1946, published 1947). His *Collected Poems* was published in 1966.

98 Something of glass about her, of dead water,
Chills and holds us,
Far more fatal than painted flesh or the lodestone of live hair
This despair of crystal brilliance.
1935 *Poems*, 'Circe'.

99 World is crazier and more of it than we think,
Incorrigibly plural.

1935 *Poems*, 'Snow'.

1 The little sardine men crammed in a monster toy
Who tilt their aggregate beast against our crumbling
    Troy.
1935 *Poems*, 'Turf-stacks'.

2 It's no go the merrygoround, it's no go the rickshaw,
All we want is a limousine and a ticket for the peepshow.
Their knickers are made of crêpe-de-chine, their shoes
    are made of python,
Their halls are lined with tiger rugs and their walls with
    the heads of bison.
1937 'Bagpipe Music', stanza 1.

3 It's no go my honey love, it's no go my poppet;
Work your hands from day to day, the winds will blow
    the profit.
The glass is falling hour by hour, the glass will fall for ever,
But if you break the bloody glass, you won't hold up the
    weather.
1937 'Bagpipe Music', stanza 10.

4 And the gods are absent and the men are still—
Noli me tangere, my soul is forfeit.

Some are now happy in the hive of home,
Thigh over thigh and a light in the night nursery,
And some are hungry under the starry dome
And some sit turning handles.
1938 *Autumn Journal*, part 2.

5 Spider, spider, spin
Your register and let me sleep a little,
Not now in order to end but to begin
The task begun so often.
1938 *Autumn Journal*, part 2.

6 All of London littered with remembered kisses.
1938 *Autumn Journal*, part 4.

7 Tonight we sleep
On the banks of Rubicon—the die is cast;
There will be time to audit
The accounts later, there will be sunlight later
And the equation will come out at last.
1938 *Autumn Journal*, part 24.

8 Time was away and somewhere else.
1939 'Meeting Point'. Collected in *Collected Poems 1925–1948*
(1949).

9 In my childhood trees were green
And there was plenty to be seen.

Come back early or never come.
1941 *Plant and Phantom*, 'Autobiography', l.1–3.

10 The dark was talking to the dead;
The lamp was dark beside my bed.
1941 *Plant and Phantom*, 'Autobiography', l.13–14.

11 The best people never land, sir.
1946 Steward to Roland. *The Dark Tower* (published 1947).

12 For the last blossom is the first blossom
And the first blossom is the best blossom
And when from Eden we take our way
The morning after is the first day.
'Apple Blossom', in *Collected Poems*, 1966.

13 His father gave him a box of truisms
Shaped like a coffin, then his father died;

The truisms remained on the mantelpiece.
'The Truisms', in *Collected Poems*, 1966.

McNeil, Robert

14 Mein Banff.
Suggested title for a biography of Alex Salmond, leader of the
Scottish Nationalist Party and MP for Banff and Buchan.

MacQueen, Robert, Lord Braxfield 1722–99

Scottish judge who presided over many famous trials in
Edinburgh. Notorious for his harsh sentencing and cruel
humour, he was known as the 'hanging judge', and was the
original for R L Stevenson's Lord Hermiston in *Weir of Hermiston*.

15 Muckle he made o' that; he was hanget.
1794 Riposte at the trial of a political reformer, when the
defendant remarked that all great men had been reformers,
'even our Saviour himself'. Quoted in Lord Cockburn *Memorials
of his Time* (1856), ch.2.

16 Ye're a verra clever chiel', man, but ye wad be nane the
waur o' a hanging.
Quoted in John G Lockhart *Memoirs of the Life of Sir Walter Scott,
Bart.* (1837–8), ch.48.

17 Let them bring me prisoners, and I'll find them law.
Quoted in Lord Cockburn *Memorials of his Time* (1856), ch.2.

MacRéamoinn, Sean Seamas Criostoir 1921–

Irish broadcaster and journalist.

18 I am becoming like the Irish Census, broken down by
Age, Sex, and Religion.
1991 Chairing a lecture on Parnell, Merriman Summer School.

Madan, Geoffrey 1895–1947

English aphorist.

19 Conservative ideal of freedom and progress: everyone
to have an unfettered opportunity of remaining exactly
where they are.
Collected in *Geoffrey Madan's Notebooks* (published 1981).

Madison, James 1751–1836

US politician and 4th President (1809–17), co-author of the
Federalist Papers (1787–8). Originator of the Virginia Plan, his
compromise measure on the status of slaves ensured
adoption of the Constitution in slave states. He presided over
the 1812 war with Britain.

20 The diversity in the faculties of men, from which the
rights of property originate, is not less an insuperable
obstacle to a uniformity of interests. The protection of
those faculties is the first object of government.
1787 *The Federalist*, Nov.

21 What is government itself but the greatest of all
reflections on human nature? If men were angels, no
government would be necessary. If angels were to
govern men, neither external nor internal controls on
government would be necessary.
1788 *The Federalist*, Jan.

Madonna *full name* Madonna Louise Veronica Ciccone
1958–

US pop singer and actress.

22 We are living in a material world

And I am a material girl.
1985 'Material Girl'.

23 Many people see Eva Perón as either a saint or as the incarnation of Satan. That means I can definitely identify with her.
1996 On playing Eva Perón in the film *Evita*. Quoted in *Newsweek*, 5 Feb.

24 If I had known I would be so universally misunderstood, maybe I wouldn't have been so rebellious and outspoken.
Quoted in the *Guinness Rockopedia* (1998).

Maeterlinck, Maurice 1862–1949

Belgian playwright and poet. The success enjoyed by his play *Pelléas et Mélisande* (1892) established him as the leading playwright of the Symbolist movement. He was awarded a Nobel prize in 1911.

25 *L'Oiseau bleu.*
The Blue Bird.
1908 Title of play.

Magidson, Herb 1906–86

US songwriter.

26 Music, Maestro, Please.
1938 Title of song.

Magna Carta

The Great Charter obtained from King John in 1215, the basis of English political and personal liberty.

27 *Nullius liber homo capiatur, vel imprisonetur, aut dissaisiatur, aut utlagetur, aut exuletur, aut aliquo modo destruator, nec super eum ibimus, nec super eum mittemus, nisi per legale judicium parium suorum vel per legem terrae.*
No free man shall be taken or imprisoned or dispossessed, or outlawed or exiled, or in any way destroyed, nor will we go upon him, nor will we send against him except by the lawful judgement of his peers or by the law of the land.
1215 Clause 39.

28 *Nulli vendemus, nulli negabimus aut differemus, rectum aut justitiam.*
To no man will we sell, or deny, or delay, right or justice.
1215 Clause 40.

Mahathir, Mohamad 1925–

Malaysian politician and the country's longest serving Prime Minister, holding office from 1981 to 2003.

29 I'm brash and abrasive but that's because I've noticed when people are nice and polite they never get anywhere.
c.1990 Quoted in the *Eastern Express*, 24 Apr 1995.

30 If you can't be famous, at least you can be notorious.
c.1994 Quoted in the *Eastern Express*, 24 Apr 1995.

Mahler, Gustav 1860–1911

Austrian composer, conductor and artistic director at the Vienna State Opera (1897). He resigned after 10 years to conduct the New York Philharmonic (1908–11). He is best known for the song-symphony *Das Lied von der Erde* ('The Song of the Earth').

31 A symphony must be like the world, it must embrace everything.
1907 In conversation with Sibelius. Quoted in Ian Crofton and Donald Fraser *A Dictionary of Musical Quotations* (1985).

32 *Endlich fortissimo!*
Fortissimo at last!
1907 On seeing the Niagara Falls. Quoted in Charles Osborne *The Dictionary of Composers* (1977).

33 He is young and perhaps he is right. Maybe my ear is not sensitive enough.
Of Schoenberg's music. Quoted in Lebrecht *Discord* (1982).

Mahony, Francis Sylvester *pseudonym* Father Prout 1804–66

Irish priest and humorous writer. He became a Jesuit priest but was expelled after a late-night frolic. After a spell as a priest in Italy, he turned to journalism in London.

34 And cymbals glorious
Swinging uproarious
In the gorgeous turrets
Of Notre Dame.
'The Bells of Shandon'.

35 O the bells of Shandon
Sound far more grand on
The pleasant waters
Of the River Lee.
'The Bells of Shandon'.

Mailer, Norman Kingsley 1923–

US novelist and journalist. An inveterate polemicist and high-profile public figure, he is arguably the most controversial figure in post-war US letters.

36 The Naked and the Dead.
1948 Title of novel.

37 Hip is the sophistication of the wise primitive in a giant jungle.
1957 In *Dissent*, Summer.

38 Each day a few more lies eat into the seed with which we are born, little institutional lies from the print of newspapers, the shock waves of television, and the sentimental cheats of the movie screen.
1959 *Advertisements for Myself*, 'First Advertisement for Myself'.

39 America is a hurricane, and the only people who do not hear the sound are those fortunate if incredibly stupid and smug White Protestants who live in the center, in the serene eye of the big wind.
1959 *Advertisements for Myself*, 'Advertisement for "Games and Ends"'.

40 There is probably no sensitive heterosexual alive who is not preoccupied with his latent homosexuality.
1959 *Advertisements for Myself*, 'The Homosexual Villain'.

41 The final purpose of art is to intensify, even, if necessary, to exacerbate, the moral consciousness of people.
1959 'Hip, Hell, and The Navigator', in *Western Review*, no.23, Winter.

42 Every moment of one's existence one is growing into more or retreating into less. One is always living a little more or dying a little bit.
1959 'Hip, Hell, and The Navigator', in *Western Review*, no. 23, Winter.

43 Once a newspaper touches a story, the facts are lost

forever, even to the protagonists.
1960 In *Esquire*, Jun.

44 A modern democracy is a tyranny whose borders are undefined; one discovers how far one can go only by traveling in a straight line until one is stopped.
1963 *The Presidential Papers*, preface.

45 In America few people will trust you unless you are irreverent.
1963 *The Presidential Papers*, preface.

46 Ultimately a hero is a man who would argue with the gods, and so awakens devils to contest his vision.
1963 *The Presidential Papers*, preface.

47 In America all too few blows are struck into flesh. We kill the spirit here, we are experts at that. We use psychic bullets and kill each other cell by cell.
1963 *The Presidential Papers*, 'Fourth Presidential Paper'.

48 A high church for the true mediocre.
1963 Of the FBI. *The Presidential Papers*, 'Sixth Presidential Paper'.

49 Writing books is the closest men ever come to childbearing.
1965 'Mr Mailer Interviews Himself', in the *New York Times Book Review*, 17 Sep.

50 The sense of a long last night over civilization is back again.
1966 *Cannibals and Christians*, 'Introducing Our Argument'.

51 Sentimentality is the emotional promiscuity of those who have no sentiment.
1966 *Cannibals and Christians*, 'My Hope For America'.

52 There is one expanding horror in American life. It is that our long odyssey toward liberty, democracy and freedom-for-all may be achieved in such a way that utopia remains forever closed, and we live in freedom and hell, debased of style, not individual from one another, void of courage, our fear rationalized away.
1966 *Cannibals and Christians*, 'My Hope For America'.

53 What characterizes a member of a minority group is that he is forced to see himself as both exceptional and insignificant, marvelous and awful, good and evil.
1966 *Cannibals and Christians*, 'A Speech At Berkeley on Vietnam Day'.

54 The surest way not to be remembered is to talk about the way you want to be.
1968 Interview in *Playboy*, Aug.

55 New York is one of the capitals of the world and Los Angeles is a constellation of plastic. San Francisco is a lady, Boston has become Urban Renewal, Philadelphia and Baltimore and Washington blink like dull diamonds in the smog of Eastern Megalopolis, and New Orleans is unremarkable past the French Quarter. Detroit is a one-trade town, Pittsburgh has lost its golden triangle. St Louis has become the golden arch of the corporation, and nights in Kansas City close early. The oil depletion allowance makes Houston and Dallas naught but checkerboards for this sort of game. But Chicago is a great American city. Perhaps it is the last of the great American cities.
1969 *Miami and the Siege of Chicago*, 'The Siege of Chicago'.

56 The horror of the Twentieth Century was the size of each event, and the paucity of its reverberation.
1970 Of *A Fire On The Moon*, pt.1, ch.2.

57 The difference between writing a book and being on television is the difference between conceiving a child and having a baby made in a test tube.
1971 'The Siege of Mailer: Hero to Historian', in *Village Voice*, 21 Jan.

58 So we think of Marilyn who was every man's love affair with America, Marilyn Monroe who was blonde and beautiful and had a sweet little rinky-dink of a voice and all the cleanliness of all the clean American backyards.
1973 *Marilyn*.

59 No physical activity is so vain as boxing. A man gets into the ring to attract admiration. In no sport, therefore, can you be more humiliated.
1976 *The Fight*.

60 The true religion of America has always been America.
1984 Interview in *Time Out*, 27 Sep–3 Oct.

61 All the security around the American President is just to make sure the man who shoots him gets caught.
1990 In the *Sunday Telegraph*, 4 Mar.

62 When a novel comes, it's a grace. Something in the cosmos has forgiven you long enough so that you can start.
1991 In *The Guardian*, 5 Oct.

63 Writing a best-seller with conscious intent to do so is, after all, a state of mind that is not without comparison to the act of marrying for money only to discover that the absence of love is more onerous that anticipated.
2003 *The Spooky Art: Some Thoughts on Writing*.

64 Movies are more likely than literature to reach deep feelings in people.
2003 *The Spooky Art: Some Thoughts on Writing*.

Maillart, Ella Kini 1903–97

Swiss explorer, writer, actress and athlete. She captained the Swiss women's hockey team and represented Switzerland in skiing and sailing. In 1932 she travelled alone to Russian Turkestan and in 1934 to northeastern China.

65 No. Cost what it may I am determined to go East. The nomad's life enthralls me. Its restlessness pursues me: it is as much part of me as of the sailor. All parts and none are home to me, and all arriving only a new setting forth.
1934 *Des Monts Célestes aux Sables Rouges* (translated by John Rodder as *Turkestan Solo: One Woman's Expedition from the Tien Shan to the Kizil Kum*).

66 Wherever I go, it is always the secret life of such simple, straightforward races that I seek, people whom a fair face is sufficient to content. Only by returning to their way of life, can we ever hope to find a way out of the bogs in which we vainly stumble.
1934 *Des Monts Célestes aux Sables Rouges* (translated by John Rodder as *Turkestan Solo: One Woman's Expedition from the Tien Shan to the Kizil Kum*).

67 So far I like India.
1935 On crossing the Mintaka Pass at the extreme border of China. Quoted in Peter Fleming *News from Tartary* (1936).

Maimonides *properly* **Moses ben Maimon** 1135–1204

Spanish-born Jewish philosopher, rabbi and physician, one of the greatest Hebrew scholars. His philosophical work *Guide to the Perplexed* (1190) attempts to reconcile Greek philosophy and Judaism.

68 There is one [disease] which is widespread, and from which men rarely escape. This disease varies in degree in different men… I refer to this: that every person thinks his mind…more clever and more learned than it is… I have found that this disease has attacked many an intelligent person… They…express themselves [not only] upon the science with which they are familiar, but upon other sciences about which they know nothing… If met with applause…so does the disease itself become aggravated.
Aphorisms. Quoted in *Bulletin of the History of Medicine*, vol.3, p.555 (1935).

Maintenon, Françoise d'Aubigné, Marquise de *known as Madame de Maintenon* 1635–1719

Second wife of Louis XIV of France. Impoverished widow of the crippled poet Paul Scarron, in 1669 she became governess to Louis' sons. After the queen's death (1683) he married her secretly. She retired to her educational foundation at St-Cyr after his death.

69 You must make use of people according to their abilities, and realize that absolutely no one is perfect.
1679 Letter to Count d'Aubigné, 25 Sep.

Major, John 1943–

English Conservative politician and Prime Minister (1990–7). He rose quickly under Margaret Thatcher to become Chancellor of the Exchequer on Lawson's resignation (1989). After Thatcher's downfall he became Prime Minister, and his government was re-elected in 1992.

70 I hope…to build a society of opportunity. By opportunity, I mean an open society—a society in which what people fulfil will depend upon their talent, their application, and their good fortune. What people achieve should depend particularly on those things, and I hope increasingly in the future that that will be the case.
1990 Address on entering No.10 Downing Street for the first time as Prime Minister, 27 Nov.

71 I think that we had better start again, somewhere else.
1991 Attributed remark during a Cabinet meeting when the Cabinet Room was rocked by an IRA mortar attack on No.10 Downing Street, 7 Feb.

72 Only in Britain could it be thought a defect to be 'too clever by half'. The probability is that too many people are too stupid by three-quarters.
1991 Quoted in the *Observer*, 7 Jul.

73 When the final curtain comes down, it's time to get off the stage.
1997 Outside 10 Downing Street on 2 May, leaving office as Prime Minister and announcing that he would resign as Party Leader. In *The Guardian*, 3 May.

74 So right. OK. We lost.
1997 On election night. In *The Guardian*, 3 May.

75 Margaret has been at her happiest confronting political dragons: I chose consensus.
1999 On the difference between his approach to politics and that of Margaret Thatcher. In *The Autobiography*.

Makin, Bathsua b. c.1600

English poet and educator. She was appointed tutor to Princess Elizabeth in the 1640s, a post usually held by a man.

76 A Learned Woman is thought to be a Comet, that bodes Mischief, when ever it appears.
1673 *An Essay to Revive the Antient Education of Gentlewomen In Religion, Manners, Art and Tongues, With An Answer to the Objections against this Way of Education.*

Makwetu, Clarence 1931–

South African politician, president of the radical Pan-Africanist Congress (1990–7). Initially opposed to negotiation, he agreed to talks with other parties in the early 1990s.

77 We are determined to confront the oppressor with one voice.
1991 Addressing the first formal joint meeting for 30 years of the PAC and the rival African National Congress, 15 Apr.

Malamud, Bernard 1914–86

US Jewish writer. Novels including *The Assistant* (1957), *The Fixer* (1966), *Dublin's Lives* (1979) and *God's Grace* (1982) established his reputation as one of the finest novelists of the post-war period.

78 Levin wanted friendship and got friendliness; he wanted steak and they offered spam.
1961 *A New Life*, pt.6.

79 'Mourning is a hard business,' Cesare said. 'If people knew there'd be less death.'
1963 *Idiot's First*, 'Life Is Better Than Death'.

80 There comes a time in a man's life when to get where he has to go—if there are no doors or windows he walks through a wall.
1973 *Rembrandt's Hat*, 'The Man in the Drawer'.

81 I think I said 'All men are Jews except they don't know it.' I doubt I expected anyone to take the statement literally. But I think it's an understandable statement and a metaphoric way of indicating how history, sooner or later, treats all men.
'An Interview', in L and J Fields (eds) *Bernard Malamud* (1975).

82 Comedy, I imagine, is harder to do consistently than tragedy, but I like it spiced in the wine of sadness.
1975 Interview in *Paris Review*, Spring.

83 I love metaphor. It provides two loaves where there seems to be one. Sometimes it throws in a load of fish.
1975 Interview in *Paris Review*, Spring.

84 The past exudes legend: one can't make pure clay of time's mud. There is no life that can be recaptured wholly; as it was. Which is to say that all biography is ultimately fiction.
1979 *Dubin's Lives*.

Malcolm X *originally Malcolm Little* 1925–65

US black nationalist leader. Converted to the Black Muslims while in prison, on his release he assumed a new name and promoted the sect. He later founded his own organization, for Afro-American Unity, and in the resulting factional feuding was assassinated.

85 If you're born in America with a black skin, you're born in prison.
1963 Interview, Jun.

86 It has always been my belief that I, too, will die by violence. I have done all that I can to be prepared.
1965 *The Autobiography of Malcolm X*.

87 We didn't land on Plymouth Rock. It landed on us.
Quoted in *Life*, Fall issue 1990.

Malevich, Kasimir 1878–1935

Russian painter and designer. A pioneer of abstract art.

88 Only when the habit of one's consciousness to see in paintings bits of nature, madonnas and shameless nudes has disappeared, shall we see a pure-painting composition.
1915 Manifesto, quoted in C Gray *The Russian Experiment in Art* (rev edn 1986).

Mallarmé, Stéphane 1842–98

French poet, a leading writer in the Symbolist movement.

89 *Il n'y a que la Beauté—et elle n'a qu'une expression parfaite, la Poésie.*
There is only beauty—and it has only one perfect expression, poetry.
1867 Letter to Cazalis.

90 *Le vierge, le vivace et le bel aujourd'hui.*
The virgin, the vibrant and the beautiful today.
1881 *Plusieurs Sonnets*, no.1.

91 *La Poésie est l'expression, par le langage humain ramenée à son rythme essentiel, du sens mystérieux des aspects de l'existence; elle doue ainsi d'authenticité notre séjour et constitue la seule tâche spirituelle.*
Poetry is an expression, through human language restored to its essential rhythm, of the mysteriousness of existence; it endows our life with authenticity and constitutes our only spiritual task.
1884 Letter to M. Léo d'Orfer, 27 Jun.

92 *La chair est triste, hélas! et j'ai lu tous les livres.*
The flesh is sad, alas! and I've read all the books.
1887 'Brise marine', in *Poésies, Du Parnasse Contemporain* (1893).

93 *Dire au peintre qu'il faut prendre la nature comme elle est, vaut de dire au virtuose qu'il peut s'asseoir sur le piano.*
Telling a painter that he must take nature as it is is like telling a virtuoso that he can sit on the piano.
1888 *Le 'ten o'clock' de M. Whistler*.

94 *Nuit blanche de glaçons et de neige cruelle!*
White night of icicles and bitter snow!
1893 *Poésies, Hérodiade*,'La Nourrice'.

95 *Donner un sens plus pur aux mots de la tribu.*
Bestow a purer sense on the language of the horde.
1893 *Poésies, Hommages et Tombeaux*,'Le Tombeau d'Edgar Poe' (translated by Henry Weinfield, 1994).

96 *Tel qu'en Lui-même enfin l'éternité le change.*
As for Himself at last eternity changes him.
1893 *Poésies, Hommages et Tombeaux*,'Le Tombeau d'Edgar Poe' (translated by Henry Weinfield, 1994).

97 *Un coup de dés n'abolira jamais le hasard.*
A throw of the dice will never abolish chance.
1914 Title of poem, in *Cosmopolis*, May.

Mallet-Stevens, Robert 1886–1945

French architect.

98 Architecture is an art which is basically geometrical. The cube is the basis of architecture because the right angle is necessary—the steps of a staircase consist of vertical and horizontal planes and the corners of rooms are nearly always right angles. We need right angles.

1924 'Architecture and Geometry', in *Bulletin de la Vie Moderne*, Paris.

Mallory, George Leigh 1886–1924

English mountaineer. He disappeared while attempting to climb Everest.

99 Because it's there.
1923 When asked 'Why do you want to climb Mount Everest?'. Quoted in the *New York Times*, 18 Mar.

Malory, Sir Thomas d.1471

English writer. His masterpiece, the *Morte d'Arthur*, a cycle of Arthurian legends, influenced Tennyson and other. It was completed c.1470 and a version was printed by Caxton in 1485.

1 The third sister, Morgan le Fey, was put to scole in a nonnery, and ther she lerned so moche that she was a grete clerke of nygromancye.
c.1470 *Morte d'Arthur*, bk.1, ch.2.

2 So the child was delyverd unto Merlyn, and so he bare it forth unto syre Ector and made an holy man to crysten hym and named hym Arthur.
c.1470 *Morte d'Arthur*, bk.1, ch.2.

3 'WHOSO PULLETH OUTE THIS SWERD OF THIS STONE AND ANVYLD IS RIGHTWYS KYNGE BORNE OF ALL ENGLOND'
c.1470 *Morte d'Arthur*, bk.1, ch.4. Inscription on the sword. Arthur was able to remove the sword with ease, and thus became king.

4 And there had Arthure the firste syght of queene Gwenyvere, the kyngis doghter of the londe of Camylarde, and ever afftir he loved hir.
c.1470 *Morte d'Arthur*, bk.1, ch.18.

5 'That is the Ladye of the Lake,' seyde Merlion. 'There ys a grete roche, and therein ys as fayre a paleyce as ony on erthe, and rychely besayne. And thys dameseL woll come to you anone, and than speke ye fayre to hir, that she may gyff you that swerde.'
c.1470 To Arthur. *Morte d'Arthur*, bk.1, ch.25.

6 And so kyng Lodgreaunce delyverd hys doughtir Gwenyver unto Merlion, and the Table Rounde.
c.1470 *Morte d'Arthur*, bk.3, ch.1.

7 'What tydynges at Camelot?' seyde that on knyght. 'By my hede, there have I been and aspied the courte of kynge Arthure, and there ys such a felyshyp that they may never be brokyn, and well-nyghe all the world holdith with Arthure, for there ys the floure of chevalry.'
c.1470 *Morte d'Arthur*, bk.3, ch.14.

8 And so at that tyme sir Launcelot had the grettyste name of ony knyght of the worlde, and moste he was honoured of hyghe and lowe.
c.1470 *Morte d'Arthur*, bk.6, ch.18.

9 'But one thyng begyled us, that we myght nat se the Holy Grayle hit was so precyously coverde. Wherefore I woll make here a vow that to-morne, withoute longer abydynge, I shall laboure in the queste of the Sankgreall.'
c.1470 Sir Gawain. *Morte d'Arthur*, bk.13, ch.7.

10 And thus hit passes on frome Candylmas untyll Ester, that the moneth of May was com, whan every lusty harte begynnith to blossom and to burgyne. For, lyke as trees and erbys burgenyth and florysshyth in May, lyke wyse every lusty harte that is ony maner of lover spryngith, burgenyth, buddyth, and florysshyth in lusty dedis.

c.1470 *Morte d'Arthur*, bk.18, ch.25.

11 And there he bounde the gyrdyll aboute the hyltis, and threw the swerde as farre into the watir as he myght. And there cam an arme and an honde above the watir, and toke hit and cleyght hit, and shoke hit thryse and braundysshed, and than vanysshed with the swerde into the watir.
c.1470 *Morte d'Arthur*, bk.21, ch.5.

12 Yet som men say in many partys of Inglonde that kynge Arthur ys nat dede…and men say that he shall com agayne, and he shall win the Holy Crosse. Yet I woll nat say that hit shall be so, but rather I wolde sey: here in thys there ys wrytten uppon the tumbe thys: HIC IACET ARTHURUS, REX QUONDAM REXQUE FUTURUS. [Here lies Arthur, the once and future king].
c.1470 *Morte d'Arthur*, bk.21, ch.7.

13 Herein may be seen noble chyvalrye, curtosye, humanyté, frendlynesse, hardynesse, love, frendshyp, cowardyse, murdre, hate, vertue, and synne.
c.1485 *Morte d'Arthur*, Caxton's preface.

Malouf, David 1934–

Australian novelist and librettist, of Lebanese and English extraction. His works include *An Imaginary Life* (1978), *Remembering Babylon* (1993) and *Dream Stuff* (2000).

14 'Do not shoot,' it shouted. 'I am a B-b-british object!'
1993 *Remembering Babylon*, ch.1.

Malthus, Thomas Robert 1766–1834

English economist. His anonymous *Essay on the Principle of Population* (1798) argued that population tends to increase faster than the means of subsistence, and that efforts should be made to cut the birth rate. He also wrote *Principles of Political Economy* (1820).

15 Population, when unchecked, increases in geometrical ratio. Subsistence only increases in arithmetical ratio.
1798 *An Essay on the Principle of Population.*

16 All the immediate checks to population—seem to be resolvable into moral restraint, vice and misery.
1798 *An Essay on the Principle of Population.*

17 The perpetual struggle for room and food.
1798 *An Essay on the Principle of Population.*

18 A man who is born into a world already possessed, if he cannot get subsistence from his parents on whom he has a just demand, and if the society do not want his labour, has no claim of *right* to the smallest portion of food, and, in fact, has no business to be where he is.
1803 *An Essay on the Principle of Population* (revised edn).

19 The employment of the poor in roads and public works, and a tendency among landlords and persons of property to build, to improve and beautify their grounds, and to employ workmen and menial servants, are the means most within our power and most directly calculated to remedy the evils arising from disturbance in the balance of produce and consumption.
1820 *Principles of Political Economy.*

Mamet, David Alan 1947–

US dramatist, screenwriter and director. His demotic language and hard-hitting social observation have made him a significant voice in modern US theatre. He has translated works by Chekhov and written various screenplays. He has also directed films and published essay collections.

20 Sexual Perversity in Chicago.
1976 Title of play.

21 We respond to a drama to that extent to which it corresponds to our dream life.
1986 *Writing in Restaurants*, 'A National Dream-Life'.

22 We live in oppressive times. We have, as a nation, become our own thought police; but instead of calling the process by which we limit our expression of dissent and wonder 'censorship', we call it 'concern for commercial viability'.
1986 *Writing in Restaurants*, 'Radio Drama'.

23 Policemen so cherish their status as keepers of the peace and protectors of the public that they have occasionally been known to beat to death those citizens or groups who question that status.
1986 *Writing in Restaurants*, 'Some Thoughts On Writing In Restaurants'.

24 In a world we find terrifying, we ratify that which doesn't threaten us.
1986 *Writing in Restaurants*, 'Notes For a Catalogue for Raymond Saunders'.

25 We recipients of the boon of liberty have always been ready, when faced with discomfort, to discard any and all first principles of liberty, and, further, to indict those who do not freely join with us in happily arrogating those principles.
1986 *Writing in Restaurants*, 'First Principles'.

26 The product of the artist has become less important than the *fact* of the artist. We wish to absorb this person. We wish to devour someone who has experienced the tragic. In our society this person is much more important than anything he might create.
1986 *Writing in Restaurants*, 'Exuvial Magic: An Essay Concerning Magic'.

27 The absence of the urge to create is decadence.
1986 *Writing in Restaurants*, 'Decadence'.

28 Our semantic chickens have come home to roost… We have come to accept all sorts of semantic inversions, just as George Orwell told us we would.
1986 *Writing in Restaurants*, 'Semantic Chickens'.

29 We live in a world ruined by Reason.
1986 *Writing in Restaurants*, 'Oscars'.

30 We Americans have always considered Hollywood, at best, a sinkhole of depraved venality. And, of course, it is. It is not a Protective Monastery of Aesthetic Truth.
1986 *Writing in Restaurants*, 'A Playwright in Hollywood'.

31 There is such a thing as luck. There is such a thing as a *run of luck*. This is an instructive insight I have gained from poker—that all things have a rhythm, even the most seemingly inanimate of statistics.
1986 *Writing in Restaurants*, 'Things I Have Learned Playing Poker On The Hill'.

32 The poker player learns that sometimes both science and common sense are wrong; that the bumblebee *can* fly; that, perhaps, one should never trust an expert; that there are more things in heaven and earth than are dreamt of by those with an academic bent.
1986 *Writing in Restaurants*, 'Things I Have Learned Playing Poker On The Hill'.

33 All plays are about decay… That is why the theater has always been essential to human psychic equilibrium.
1986 *Writing in Restaurants*, 'Decay: Some Thoughts for Actors'.

34 The problems of the world, AIDS, cancer, nuclear war, pollution, are, finally, no more solvable than the problems of a tree which has borne fruit: the apples are overripe and they are falling—what can be done?… What can be done about the problems which beset our life? *Nothing* can be done, and nothing needs to be done. Something *is* being done—the organism is preparing to rest.
1986 *Writing in Restaurants*, 'Decay: Some Thoughts for Actors'.

35 The Film Industry is the American Monarchy: it is strict entailed succession and Horatio Alger in one. Except for the money manipulators and speculators on the top, it is a society built on work, achievement, and fealty to those in power.
1986 *Writing in Restaurants*, 'Observations of a Backstage Wife'.

36 Life in the movie business is like the beginning of a new love affair: it's full of surprises and you are constantly getting fucked.
1988 Charlie. *Speed The Plough*, sc.1.

37 A good film script should be able to do completely without dialogue.
1988 In *The Independent*, 11 Nov.

38 Film is the least realistic of art forms.
1989 In *The Guardian*, 16 Feb.

39 All of us write plays in our heads all the time…before we're going to visit our girl friend, before we're going to talk to a boss—we rehearse.
Quoted in Susan Stamberg *Talk* (1993).

Manchester, William Raymond 1922–

US novelist, foreign correspondent and contemporary historian, born in Attleboro, Massachusetts. His chief work is *The Death of a President* (1967), a landmark account written at the behest of the Kennedys.

40 A leader cut from whipcord.
1967 Of Governor John B Connally Jr. *The Death of a President*.

41 Johnson approached a strongly fortified position by outflanking it, or burrowing under it, or surprising the defenders from the rear, or raining down obstacles upon them from the sky, or starving them into submission… Rarely, and then only reluctantly, would he proceed directly from A to B, to him the shortest distance between two points was a tunnel.
1967 Of Lyndon B Johnson. *The Death of a President*.

42 His critics called him a wheeler-dealer. They overlooked the subtlety of Johnsonian strategy, his use of wheels within wheels.
1967 Of Lyndon B Johnson. *The Death of a President*.

43 Actors who have tried to play Churchill and MacArthur have failed abysmally because each of those men was a great actor playing himself.
1983 In *Book of the Month Club News*, Jun.

44 He resolved to lead Britain and her fading empire in one last great struggle…to arm the nation, not only with weapons but also with the mace of honor, creating in every English breast a soul beneath the ribs of death.
1988 Of Winston Churchill. *The Last Lion*.

45 It would be inaccurate to say that Churchill and I conversed. Like Gladstone speaking to Victoria, he addressed me as though I were a one-man House of Commons.
1988 *The Last Lion*.

Mandela, Nelson Rolihlahla 1918–

African Nationalist leader, sentenced to life imprisonment in 1964. A potent symbol of black resistance, he was released in Feb 1990, and elected President (1991) of the ANC. In 1993 he was jointly awarded the Nobel peace prize with F W de Klerk, and in 1994 became South Africa's first black President. His term ended in 1999.

46 During my lifetime I have dedicated my life to this struggle of the African people. I have fought against white domination, and I have fought against black domination. I have cherished the ideals of a democratic and free society in which all persons live together in harmony with equal opportunities. It is an ideal which I hope to live for, and to see realized. But My Lord, if needs be, it is an ideal for which I am prepared to die.
1964 Speech in court, 20 Apr, when charged under the Suppression of Communism Act and facing the death penalty.

47 We are not a political party. We have not changed at all. On the contrary, the ANC is a Government in waiting.
1991 Interviewed for BBC T V, Feb.

48 My fellow South Africans, today we are entering a new era for our country and its people. Today we celebrate not the victory of a party, but a victory for all the people of South Africa.
1994 Speech after his election to the presidency, Cape Town, 9 May.

49 No one is born hating another person because of the colour of his skin, or his background, or his religion. People must learn to hate, and if they can learn to hate, they can be taught to love, for love comes more naturally to the human heart than its opposite.
1994 *Long Walk to Freedom*.

50 One of the things I learnt when I was negotiating was that until I changed myself I could not change others.
2000 In the *Sunday Times*, 16 Apr.

Mandela, (Nomzano) Winnie 1934–

South African civil rights activist, who joined her husband Nelson Mandela in his work with the ANC and on release from prison became controversially involved in the militant politics of the townships. She was divorced by her husband in 1996.

51 With that stick of matches, with our necklaces, we shall liberate this country.
1986 Speech in the black townships, reported in *The Guardian*, 15 Apr. The 'necklaces' were home-made bombs, car tyres filled with petrol.

Mandelson, Peter 1953–

English Labour politician, he has twice resigned from government posts and in 2004 was appointed European Commissioner.

52 Few politicians are good at taking the high ground and throwing themselves off it.
1996 Of Tony Blair and the revision of Clause Four. In the *New Yorker*, 5 Feb.

53 You'll say that I'm in charge of a Mickey Mouse project.

1998 Declining to be photographed holding a balloon at Disney World, while in charge of the ill-fated Millennium Dome project. In the *Daily Telegraph*, 5 Jan.

Mandeville, Bernard 1670–1733

Dutch-born English satirist. After obtaining an MD degree from Leiden in 1691 he practised as a physician in London. He was widely denounced for encouraging immorality through his principle 'private vices are public benefits'.

54 The root of Evil, Avarice
That damn'd ill-natur'd, baneful Vice,
Was Slave to Prodigality,
That noble Sin; whilst Luxury
Employed a Million of the Poor,
And odious Pride a Million more;
Envy itself, and Vanity,
Were Ministers of Industry;
Their darling Folly, Fickleness,
In Diet, Furniture and Dress
That strange ridic'lous Vice, was made
That very Wheel that turned the Trade.

1723 *The Fable of the Bees, or, Private Vices, Publick Benefits* (2nd edn.).

Manguel, Alberto 1948–

Argentinian-born Canadian writer.

55 The world that is a book is devoured by a reader who is a letter in the world's text; thus a circular metaphor is created for the endlessness of reading; We are what we read.

1996 *A History of Reading*.

Manilow, Barry 1946–

US singer and songwriter.

56 I think my music is like anchovies—some people love it, some people get nauseous.

2003 In *Readers Digest*, Mar.

Mankiewicz, Herman 1897–1953

US journalist, screenwriter and film producer. He initially worked in newspapers as a foreign correspondent in Berlin and as a drama editor in New York, moving to Hollywood in 1926 where he worked on his screenplays. He is best remembered for his Academy Award-winning film *Citizen Kane* (1941), although Orson Welles originally claimed this script as his own work. He is the elder brother of the film director Joseph Mankiewicz.

57 Old age…it's the only disease you don't look forward to being cured of.

1941 *Citizen Kane* (with Orson Welles).

58 Rosebud.

1941 Kane's last word, the opening word of the film, and constantly referred to throughout. *Citizen Kane* (with Orson Welles).

59 Don't believe everything you hear on the radio.

1941 *Citizen Kane* (with Orson Welles).

60 There are millions to be grabbed out here and your only competition is idiots. Don't let this get around.

Cable to Ben Hecht in the early days of Hollywood. Quoted in the *New York Times*, 8 Jan 1993.

Mankiewicz, Joseph 1909–93

US director, producer and writer, brother of Herman. He won an Oscar for the script of *A Letter for Three Wives* (1949) and an Oscar for the direction and script of *All About Eve* (1950).

61 Fasten your seat belts, it's going to be a bumpy night!

1950 Bette Davis as Margo Channing in *All About Eve*.

62 We are a breed apart from the rest of humanity, we theatre folk. We are the original displaced personalities, concentrated gatherings of neurotics, egomaniacs, emotional misfits and precocious children.

1950 George Sanders as Addison De Witt in *All About Eve*.

Mann, Thomas 1875–1955

German novelist and short story writer who left Germany during World War II and settled in California. He received the Nobel prize for literature in 1929.

63 *Wahrscheinlich sind sie der interessanteste Reiz und Stoff unseres Nachdenkens und unserer Tätigkeit.*
Probably they are the most interesting stimulus and object of our meditation and our activity.

1924 Of illnesses. *Der Zauberberg* (*The Magic Mountain*), vol.1.

64 *Bier, Tabak und Musik. Da haben wir Ihr Vaterland!*
Beer, tobacco, and music. There we have the Fatherland!

1924 *Der Zauberberg* (*The Magic Mountain*), vol.1.

65 *Leben ist, dass im Wechsel der Materie die Form erhalten bleibt.*
Life is that the form is maintained through the change of substance.

1924 *Der Zauberberg* (*The Magic Mountain*), vol.1.

66 *Dass nicht alles auf einmal da ist, bleibt als Bedingung des Lebens und der Erzählung zu achten, und man wird sich doch wohl gegen die gottgegebenen Formen menschlicher Erkenntnis nich auflehnen wollen.*
Let us not forget the condition of life as narration: that we can never see the whole picture at once—unless we propose to throw overboard all the God-conditioned forms of human knowledge.

1924 *Der Zauberberg* (*The Magic Mountain*), vol.2.

67 *Zum Leben gibt es zwei Wege: Der eine ist der gewöhnliche, direkte und brave. Der andere ist schlimm, er führt über den Tod, und das ist der geniale Weg!*
There are two paths in life: one is the regular one, direct, honest. The other is bad, it leads through death—that is the way of genius!

1924 *Der Zauberberg* (*The Magic Mountain*), vol.2.

68 *Und wenn man sich für das Leben interessiert, so interessiert man sich namentlich für den Tod.*
If a person concerns himself with life, he also concerns himself with death.

1924 *Der Zauberberg* (*The Magic Mountain*), vol.2.

69 *Die Zeit hat in Wirklichkeit keine Einschnitte, es gibt kein Gewitter oder Drommetengetön beim Beginn eines neuen Monats oder Jahres, und selbst bei dem eines neuen Säkulums sind es nur wir Menschen, die schießen und läuten.*
Time has no divisions to mark its passage, there is never a thunderstorm or blare of trumpets to announce the beginning of a new month or year. Even when a new century begins it is only we mortals who ring bells and

fire off pistols.
1924 *Der Zauberberg* (*The Magic Mountain*), ch.4, section 4 (translated by H T Lowe-Porter).

70 *Unser Sterben ist mehr eine Angelegenheit der Weiterlebenden als unserer selbst.*
A man's dying is more the survivors' affair than his own.
1924 *Der Zauberberg* (*The Magic Mountain*), ch.6, section 8 (translated by H T Lowe-Porter).

71 *Die Zeit ist das Element der Erzählung, wie sie das Element des Lebens ist,—unlösbar damit verbunden, wie mit den Körpern im Raum. Sie ist auch das Element der Musik, als welche die Zeit misst und gliedert, sie kurzweilig und kostbar auf einmal macht.*
For time is the medium of narration, as it is the medium of life. Both are inextricably bound up with it, as are bodies in space. Similarly, time is the medium of music; music divides, measures, articulates time, and can shorten it, yet enhance its value, both at once.
1924 *Der Zauberberg* (*The Magic Mountain*), ch.7, section 1 (translated by H T Lowe-Porter).

72 *Liebe zu sich selbst ist immer der Anfang eines romanhaften Lebens.*
Self-love is always the beginning of a novelistic affair.
1933 *Joseph und seine Brüder* ('Joseph and his Brothers').

73 *Man kann sehr wohl in einer Geschichte sein, ohne sie zu verstehen.*
A person can be fully involved in a story without understanding it.
1933 *Joseph und seine Brüder* ('Joseph and his Brothers').

74 *Denn dem Menschen ist am Wiedererkennen gelegen; er möchte das Alte im Neuen wiederfinden und das Typische im Individuellen.*
For man always searches for recognition: he would like to find the old in the new and the ordinary in the individual.
1936 *Freud und die Zukunft.*

75 *Ist die Liebe das Beste im Leben, so ist in der Liebe das Beste der Kuss.*
If love is the best thing in life, then the best part of love is the kiss.
1939 *Lotte im Weimar.*

76 *Das Seelische [ist] immer das Primäre und eigentlich Motivierende; die politische Aktion ist zweiter Ordnung, Reflex, Ausdruck, Instrument.*
The mental state is always the primary and ultimately the motivating state. Political action is of second rank, reflex, expression, instrument.
1947 *Doktor Faustus.*

Mann, Thomas Edward 1944–

US political scientist. He is Senior Fellow in Governance Studies at the Brookings Institution and is the author and co-editor of many books on American political science and congressional election studies, such as *Renewing Congress* (1992) and *Vital Statistics on Congress* (2002).

77 He's a great ex-president. It's a shame he couldn't have gone directly to the ex-presidency.
1994 Of Jimmy Carter and his successful visit to Korea. In *Newsweek*, 27 Jun.

Mannheim, Karl 1893–1947

Hungarian-born German sociologist, who taught at the University of Heidelberg until expelled by Hitler and later at the LSE, known for his contributions to the sociology of knowledge.

78 Even the categories in which experiences are subsumed, collected, and ordered vary according to the social position of the observer.
1936 *Ideology and Utopia.*

Manning, Henry Edward 1808–92

English Roman Catholic prelate. He succeeded as Archbishop of Westminster in 1865 and became a cardinal in 1875. Noted for his support for the temperance and benevolent movements, he was also a keen cricketer and captained the Harrow Eleven team.

79 That bat that you were kind enough to send, Seems (for as yet I have not tried it) good: And if there's anything on earth can mend My wretched play, it is that piece of wood.
1826 Verse sent to Charles Wordsworth, nephew of the poet William Wordsworth, after the latter sent him the present of a cricket bat.

80 To put labour and wages first and human or domestic life second is to invert the order of God and of nature.
1889 On the London dock strike.

Mansfield, Katherine *pseudonym of* *Kathleen Mansfield Beauchamp* 1881–1923

New Zealand writer. She moved to London to pursue a literary career and married John Middleton Murry. She died prematurely of tuberculosis. She is best known for her finely crafted short stories, in collections such as *Bliss and Other Stories* (1920). Her *Journal* was published in 1927.

81 Talk of our enlightened days and our emancipated country—pure nonsense! We are firmly held with the self-fashioned chains of slavery. Yes, now I see that they *are* self-fashioned, and must be self-removed.
1908 Journal entry, May.

82 The trouble with women like me is—they can't keep their nerves out of the job in hand… I walk about with a mind full of ghosts of saucepans and primus stoves and 'Will there be enough to go round?' I loathe myself, today. I detest this woman who 'superintends' you and rushes about, slamming doors and slopping water—all untidy with her blouse out and her nails grimed.
1913 Letter to John Middleton Murry, summer.

83 Why haven't I got a real 'home'—a real life—why haven't I got a Chinese nurse with green trousers and two babies who rush at me and clasp my knees? I'm not a girl—I'm a woman. I *want* things…all this love and joy that fights for outlet—and all this life drying up, like milk in an old breast.
1915 Letter to John Middleton Murry, 23 Mar.

84 I want for one moment to make our undiscovered country leap into the eyes of the Old World. It must be mysterious, as though floating. It must take the breath. It must be 'one of those islands…'.
1916 Journal entry, 22 Jan.

85 E M Forster never gets any further than warming the teapot. He's a rare fine hand at that. Feel this teapot. Is it not beautifully warm? Yes, but there ain't going to be no tea. And I can never be perfectly certain whether Helen

was got with child by Leonard Bast or by his fatal forgotten umbrella. All things considered, I think it must have been the umbrella.
1917 Journal entry, May.

86 Her underlip protruded a little; she had a way of sucking it in that somebody else had told her was awfully fascinating.
1920 *Bliss and Other Stories*, 'Prelude'.

87 True to oneself! Which self? Which of my many…hundreds of selves?… There are moments when I feel I am nothing but the small clerk of some hotel without a proprietor, who has all his work cut out to enter the names and hand the keys to the wilful guests.
1920 Journal entry, Apr.

88 I believe that people are like portmanteaux—packed with certain things, started going, thrown about, tossed away, dumped down, lost and found, half emptied suddenly, or squeezed fatter than ever, until finally the Ultimate Porter swings them on to the Ultimate Train and away they rattle.
1920 *Bliss and Other Stories*, 'Je Ne Parle Pas Français'.

89 Is it not possible that the rage for confession, autobiography, especially for memories of earliest childhood, is explained by our persistent yet mysterious belief in a self which is continuous and permanent; which, untouched by all we acquire and all we shed, pushes a green spear through the dead leaves and through the mould, thrusts a scaled bud through years of darkness until, one day, the light discovers it and shakes the flower free and—we are alive—we are flowering for our moment upon the earth? This is the moment which after all, we live for—the moment of direct feeling when we are most ourselves and least personal.
1920 Journal entry, Apr.

90 If there was one thing he hated more than another it was the way she had of waking him in the morning… It was her way of establishing her grievance for the day.
1920 *Bliss and Other Stories*, 'Mr Reginald Peacock's Day'.

91 The aloe seemed to ride…like a ship with the oars lifted. Bright moonlight hung upon the lifted oars like water, and on the green wave glittered the dew.
1920 *Bliss and Other Stories*, 'Prelude'.

92 He stands, smiling encouragement, like a clumsy dentist.
1922 *The Garden Party and Other Stories*, 'Bank Holiday'.

93 She couldn't possibly go back to the gentleman's flat; she had no right to cry in strangers' houses.
1922 *The Garden Party and Other Stories*, 'The Life of Ma Parker'.

94 What would father say when he found out? For he was bound to find out sooner or later. He always did. 'Buried. You two girls had me *buried*!' She heard his stick thumping. Oh, what would they say? What possible excuse could they make? It sounded such an appallingly heartless thing to do. Such a wicked advantage to take of a person because he happened to be helpless at the moment.
1922 *The Garden Party and Other Stories*, 'The Daughters of the Late Colonel'.

95 Whenever I prepare for a journey I prepare as though for death. Should I never return, all is in order. This is what life has taught me.
1922 Journal entry, 29 Jan.

96 The longer I live the more I turn to New Zealand. I thank God I was born in New Zealand. A young country is a real heritage, though it takes one time to recognize it. But New Zealand is in my very bones. What I wouldn't give to have a look at it!
1922 Letter to her father, Sir Harold Beauchamp, 18 Mar.

97 Looking back, I imagine I was always writing. Twaddle it was, too. But better far write twaddle or anything, anything, than nothing at all.
1922 Journal entry.

Mansfield, Michael Joseph 1903–2001

US Democratic senator and ambassador. A professor of history and political science (1933–42), he became a congressional member (1943–53) and Senator for Montana (1953–77). As US Ambassador to Japan (1977–89) in Tokyo, he represented the US on several trips to China.

98 A half-creature of the Senate and a half-creature of the executive.
1969 On the role of the Vice-President as the Senate's presiding officer. In *Time*, 14 Nov.

Mansfield, William Murray, 1st Earl 1705–93

English judge and MP. He was chief-justice of the king's Bench (1756) and a member of the Cabinet. His rulings developed the law of maritime contracts, insurance and bills, and influenced international law.

99 We must not regard political consequences, however formidable they may be. If rebellion was the certain consequence, we are bound to say, 'Justitia fiat, ruat coelum' (Let Justice be done, though the skies may fall).'
1768 Judgement against the sentence imposed on John Wilkes for publishing the anti-ministerial political newspaper *North Briton*, 28 Apr.
➤ See Ferdinand I 320:1.

1 Every man who comes to England is entitled to the protection of the English law, whatever oppression he may heretofore have suffered, and whatever may be the colour of his skin, whether it is black or whether it is white.
1772 Judgement on the Somersett slavery case, May.

Mao Zedong *or Mao Tse-tung* 1893–1976

Chinese military and political leader who became the first Chairman (1949) of the People's Republic. After the failure of the 1958–60 'Great Leap Forward' economic programme, his hold on power was weakened but he regained control by launching the 1966–9 'Cultural Revolution'.

2 But just think how good communism is! The state won't bother us anymore.
1919 Attributed remark. Quoted in Ross Terrill *Mao: A Biography* (1980), ch.4.

3 A revolution is not a dinner party.
1927 *The Little Red Book*, section 2.

4 A single spark can start a forest fire. Our forces, although small at present, will grow rapidly.
1930 Letter, 5 Jan.

5 If you want to know the taste of a pear, you must taste the pear by eating it for yourself. If you want to know the theory and methods of revolution, you must take part in

Map   548

revolution. All genuine knowledge originates in direct experience.

1937 Address to the Anti-Japanese Military and Political College, Jul.

6   Politics is war without bloodshed; war is politics with bloodshed.

1938 'On Protracted War', speech, May.

7   Every Communist must grasp the truth that political power grows out of the barrel of a gun.

1938 'Problems of War and Strategy', speech, 6 Nov.

8   China has stood up.

1949 Proclaiming the establishment of the People's Republic of China, 1 Oct.

9   When a man reaches old age, he will die and the same is true of a party.

1950 Collected in *Selected Works* (1975), vol.4.

10   If the worst came to the worst and half of mankind died, the other half would remain while imperialism would be razed to the ground and the whole world could become socialist.

1954 Quoted in the *Peking Review*, 9 Jun 1963.

11   All the so-called powerful reactionaries are paper tigers, for they are cut off from their people. Was not Hitler a paper tiger, and was he not overthrown? US imperialism has not yet been overthrown, and it has atomic bombs—but I believe that it too will be overthrown. It, too, is a paper tiger.

1957 Speech to Communist International Congress, Moscow, Nov.

12   Letting a hundred flowers blossom and a hundred schools of thought contend is the policy for promoting the progress of the arts and the sciences and a flourishing culture in our land.

1957 Speech, Peking, 27 Feb.

13   The east wind prevails over the west wind.

1957 Spoken at an international conference of Communist leaders in Moscow. Quoted in Ross Terrill *Mao: A Biography* (1980), ch.14.

14   People of the world, unite and defeat the US aggressors and all their running dogs.

1958 Speech, Jul.

15   I have seen Lenin's manuscripts, which are filled with changes. He too made mistakes.

1959 Quoted in Ross Terrill *Mao: A Biography* (1980), ch.15.

16   Water too pure breeds no fish.

Quoted in Han Suyin *Wind in the Tower* (1974).

17   The more books one reads, the more stupid one becomes.

1976 Quoted in Ross Terrill *Mao: A Biography* (1980), ch.22.

Map, Walter   c.1140–c.1209

Welsh poet and ecclesiast, author of *De Nugis Curialium* (c.1181) and possibly new versions of the Arthurian Romances.

18   *Dura est manus cirurgi, sed sanans.*
     The hand of the surgeon is hard, but healing.

c.1181 *De Nugis Curialium*, Distinction 4, ch.4.

19   *Numquam enim audiendi quod aliquis monachus super puerum incubuisset, quin statim post ipsum surrexisset puer.*
     I have heard before of a monk throwing himself on a boy,

but the boy always rose again afterwards.

c.1181 On hearing of an unsuccessful attempt by Saint Bernard of Clairvaux to revive a dead boy by throwing himself on the body and praying. *De Nugis Curialium*, Distinction 4, ch.5.

20   *Hoc solum deliqui, quod uiuo.*
     My only fault is that I am alive.

c.1181 On the refusal of many of his contemporaries to believe that his *Dissuasio Valerii ad Rufinum* could have been composed by a modern writer. *De Nugis Curialium*, Distinction 4, ch.5.

Maradona, Diego   1960–

Argentinian footballer.

21   It was the hand of God.

1986 To reporters after Argentina's World Cup defeat of England in which he scored a goal with his hand, 22 Jun.

Maraniss, David   1949–

US journalist and author. As a journalist for the *Washington Post* (of which he later became an associate editor) he received the Pulitzer Prize for national reporting in 1993, and has written a biography of President Bill Clinton.

22   It is…classic Bill Clinton, sincere and deceptive at the same time, requiring a careful reading between the lines.

1995 On President Clinton's letter as a graduate student, 3 Dec 1969, to arrange RO TC enlistment to avoid being drafted for the Vietnam War, a position that was to haunt his future campaigning. *First in His Class*.

23   Natural politicians are skilled actors, recreating reality, adjusting and ad-libbing, synthesizing the scenes, saying the same thing over and over again and making it seem that they are saying it for the first time.

1995 Of Bill Clinton. *First in His Class*.

24   At 34, he fit the ironic description of the quintessential Rhodes Scholar: someone with a great future behind him.

1995 Of Bill Clinton, the youngest defeated state governor in US history. *First in His Class*.

25   He is a congenital campaigner.

1995 Predicting that Bill Clinton would always be a candidate for office or an advocate. CNBC broadcast, 7 Mar.

Marc, Franz   1880–1916

German painter, founder member of the Munich-based Blaue Reiter (Blue Rider) group. Most of his paintings were of animals (eg *Blue Horses*, 1911) portrayed in forceful colours. He was killed at Verdun during World War I.

26   Today art is moving in a direction of which our fathers would never even have dreamed. We stand before the new pictures as in a dream and we hear the apocalyptic horsemen in the air.

1912 Subscription prospectus of the *Blaue Reiter Almanac*, Jan.

27   Art will liberate itself from the needs and desires of men. No longer will we paint a forest or a horse as we like or as they appear to us, but as they really are.

1914–15 *Aphorisms*.

28   Traditions are lovely things—to create traditions, that is, not to live off them.

1914–15 *Aphorisms*.

29   Who is able to paint the existence of a dog as Picasso paints the existence of a cubic shape?

Quoted in *Briefe, Aufzeichnungen und Aphorismen* (2 vols, 1920), translated by Chipp in his *Theories of Modern Art* (1968).

Marceau, Marcel 1923–

French mime artist. Celebrated for his performances in the role of the white-faced Bip, he is the foremost exponent of the mime theatre of Charles Dullin and Jean-Louis Barrault.

30 Life is a cycle, and mime is particularly suitable for showing fluidity, transformation, metamorphosis. Words can keep people apart; mime can be a bridge between them.
Attributed.

Marcos, Ferdinand Edralin 1917–89

Filipino politician, elected President in 1965 and again in 1969. His years of office became increasingly notorious for widespread corruption but US backing helped keep him in power. He declared martial law in 1972 but was overthrown in 1986 by a popular 'People's Power' campaign.

31 It is easier to run a revolution than a government.
1977 In *Time*, 6 Jun.

32 Some people say the president is incapable of enforcing the law. Let them say that once more and I will set the tanks on them.
1986 Quoted in 'The Snap Revolution', in James Fenton *All the Wrong Places*.

33 History isn't through with me yet.
1986 Remark, quoted in Sterling Seagrave *The Marcos Dynasty*.

Marcos, Imelda Romualdez 1927–

Wife of President Ferdinand Marcos of the Philippines, with whom she fled in 1986. She later faced charges of theft and corruption.

34 Some are smarter than others.
c.1985 Her reply to a question about the great wealth she had accumulated. Quoted in Sterling Seagrave *The Marcos Dynasty*.

35 The real index of this country is the smiles of the people, not the economic index.
c.1985 Quoted in Sterling Seagrave *The Marcos Dynasty*.

Marcus Aurelius *full name* *Marcus Aelius Aurelius Antoninus* AD 121–180

Roman emperor and philosopher. His spiritual reflections, the *Meditations*, are considered a classic work of Stoicism.

36 Nothing is so conducive to greatness of mind as the ability to examine systematically and honestly everything that meets us in life.
Meditations, vol.3, pt.2 (translated by Charles Reginald Haines, 1901).

Marguerite d'Angoulême 1492–1549

Queen of Navarre and sister of François I. She was a patron of the arts, and wrote poetry.

37 Je n'ai plus ni père, ni mère,
Ni sœur, ni frère
Sinon Dieu seul auquel j'espère.
I no longer have a father, nor a mother,
Nor a sister, nor a brother.
I only have God to trust in.
1547 *Cantique spirituel*.

38 Plus j'ai d'amour plus j'ai de fâcherie.
The more I love, the more I quarrel.
1547 *Dizains*.

39 Depuis qu'Ève fit pécher Adam, toutes les femmes ont pris possession de tourmenter, tuer et damner les hommes.
Ever since Eve made Adam sin, women have taken it upon themselves to torment, kill and damn men.
1558 *Heptaméron*, pt.1.

40 Seulement les sots sont punis, et non les vicieux.
Only the foolish are punished, never the truly vicious.
1558 *Heptaméron*, pt.13.

41 Un malheureux cherche l'autre.
One unhappy person seeks out another.
1558 *Heptaméron*, pt.21.

42 Le scandale est souvent pire que le péché.
The scandal is often worse than the sin itself.
1558 *Heptaméron*, pt.25.

43 Votre plaisir gît déshonorer les femmes, et votre honneur tuer les hommes en guerre; qui sont deux points formellement contraires à la loi de Dieu.
Your pleasure lies in dishonouring women and your honour lies in killing men at war; two acts which stand in contradiction to the law of God.
1558 *Heptaméron*, pt.26.

44 Mariage est un état de si longue durée qu'il ne doit être commencé légèrement, ni sans l'opinion de nos meilleurs amis et parents.
Marriage is a state of such long duration that it should not begin lightly, nor without the opinion of our best friends and parents.
1558 *Heptaméron*, pt.40.

45 L'amour n'est pas un feu que l'on tient dans la main.
Love is not a flame that one holds in the hand.
1558 *Heptaméron*, pt.47.

46 À force de jurer, on engendre quelque doute à la vérité.
When forced to swear an oath, one can encounter doubt about the truth.
1558 *Heptaméron*, pt.61.

Marhabal fl.216 BC

Carthaginian soldier, a cavalry commander under Hannibal at the Battle of Cannae (216 BC).

47 You know how to gain a victory, Hannibal: you know not how to use one.
216 BC Comment to Hannibal after victory at Cannae. Quoted in Livy *Ab urbe condita*, bk.22.

Mariátegui, José Carlos 1895–1930

Peruvian political leader and essayist, who applied Marxist principles to Peruvian problems, while acknowledging the value of religion and myth to the indigenous peoples.

48 Mientras en Norteamérica la colonización depositó los gérmenes de un espíritu y una economía que se plasmaban entonces en Europa y a los cuales pertenecía el porvenir, a la América española trajo los efectos y los métodos de un espíritu y una economía que declinaban ya y a los cuales no pertenecía sino el pasado.
Whereas in North America colonization planted the seeds of the spirit and economy then growing in Europe

and representing the future, the Spaniard brought to America the effects and methods of an already declining spirit and economy that belonged to the past.

1928 *Siete ensayos de interpretación de la realidad peruana*, 'El problema de la tierra' (translated as *Seven Interpretive Essays on Peruvian Reality*, 1971).

Marie de France   fl.1160–70

French poet, author of *Lais* and *Fables*. Born in Normandy, she spent most of her life in England. Her *Lais* in particular were of great influence on French literature.

49 *Qui Deus a duné esciënce*
e de parler bone eloquence,
ne s'en deit taisir ne celer,
ainz se deit voluntiers mustrer.
Whoever God has given knowledge
and eloquence in speaking,
should not be silent or secretive,
but should willingly show it.
c.1170 *Lais*, prologue, l.1–4.

50 *Ki qu'en plurt ne ki qu'en chant,*
le dreit estuet aler avant.
Whether it makes one cry or sing,
justice must be carried out.
c.1170 *Lanval*, l.437–8.

51 *Mult est fole, ki hume creit.*
She is a fool, who trusts a man.
c.1170 *Eliduc*, l.1084.

Marinetti, Emilio Filippo Tomasso   1876–1944

Italian dramatist, novelist and poet. He published his influential manifesto for Futurism in *Figaro* in 1909, and became a Fascist in 1919. His writings glorify war, the machine age and dynamism, disparaging all traditional forms of art.

52 We sing the love of danger. Courage, rashness, and rebellion are the elements of our poetry. Hitherto literature has tended to exalt thoughtful immobility, ecstasy, and sleep, whereas we are for aggressive movement, febrile insomnia, mortal leaps, and blows with the fist. We proclaim that the world is richer for a new beauty of speed, and our praise is for the man at the wheel. There is no beauty now save in struggle, no masterpiece can be anything but aggressive, and hence we glorify war, militarism and patriotism.
1909 *Manifesto of Futurism*. Quoted in Denis Mack Smith *Italy: A Modern History* (1959), p.270.

53 We affirm that the world's magnificence has been enriched by a new beauty: the beauty of speed. A racing car whose hood is adorned with great pipes, like serpents of explosive breath—a roaring car that seems to ride on grapeshot is more beautiful than the *Victory of Samothrace*.
1909 *Manifesto of Futurism*.

54 It is from Italy that we launch through the world this violently upsetting incendiary manifesto of ours. With it, today, we establish *Futurism*, because we want to free this land from its smelly gangrene of professors, archaeologists, *ciceroni* and antiquarians. For too long has Italy been a dealer in second-hand clothes. We mean to free her from the numberless museums that cover her like so many graveyards.
1909 *Manifesto of Futurism*.

Marion, Frances   originally *Frances Marion Owens*   1888–1973

US screenwriter and novelist. She wrote prolifically for the silent screen before working as a war correspondent, and subsequently translated her skills to talking pictures. She later turned to novel writing.

55 Gimme visky…ginger ale on the side. And don't be stingy baby.
1931 Opening lines delivered by Greta Garbo in *Anna Christie*.

56 I read somewhere that machinery is going to take the place of every profession.
Oh my dear that's something you'll never have to worry about.
1933 Dialogue between Jean Harlow and Marie Dressler in *Dinner At Eight* (with Herman Mankiewicz).

Maritain, Jacques   1882–1973

French philosopher and critic. He converted from Protestantism to Catholicism (1906) and gained renown for his interpretations of St Thomas Aquinas. He based his own philosophy on Aristotle and Aquinas.

57 Poetry proceeds from the totality of man, sense, imagination, intellect, love, desire, instinct, blood and spirit together.
Quoted in Robert Fitzgerald (ed) *Enlarging the Change* (1985).

58 The poet knows himself only on the condition that things resound in him, and that in him, at a single awakening, they and he come forth together out of sleep.
Quoted in Robert Fitzgerald (ed) *Enlarging the Change* (1985).

Marivaux, Pierre Carlet de Chamblain de   1688–1763

French author best known for his comedies in which language, more than characters, dictates the action.

59 *Un mari porte un masque avec le monde, et une grimace avec sa femme.*
A husband wears a mask in the world and a smirk with his wife.
1730 *Le jeu de l'amour et du hasard*, act 1, sc.2.

60 *Dans ce monde, il faut être un peu trop bon pour l'être assez.*
In this world, one must be a little too good in order to be good enough.
1730 *Le jeu de l'amour et du hasard*, act 1, sc.2.

61 *Les bienfaits des hommes sont accompagnés d'une maladresse si humiliante pour les personnes qui les reçoivent!*
The generosity of men is accompanied by such a humiliating embarrassment for those who benefit from it.
1731 *La vie de Marianne*, ch.1.

62 *C'est presque toujours le péché qui prêche la vertu dans nos chaires.*
It's almost always sin which preaches virtue in our pulpits.
1731 *La vie de Marianne*, ch.4.

63 *Qu'est-ce qu'une charité qui n'a point de pudeur avec le misérable, et qui, avant de le soulager, commence par écraser son amour-propre.*
What is that charity worth which does not spare the wretched person's feelings, which instead, before

providing comfort, begins by wiping out his self-esteem.
1731 *La vie de Marianne*, ch.14.

64 *L'âme se raffine à mesure qu'elle se gâte.*
The soul refines itself in proportion to how it spoils itself.
1735 *Le paysan parvenu*, ch.4.

Markham, Dewey 'Pigmeat' 1906–81

US songwriter and comedy writer.

65 Here comes the judge.
1968 Song title, co-written with Dick Alen, Bob Astor and Sarah Harvey. Often quoted as a vaudeville catchphrase, 'Here come de judge'.

Marks, Leo 1920–2001

British writer. He acted as adviser on the film *Carve Her Name With Pride* (1958), partly based on his own wartime work in cryptography. He also wrote the script of *Peeping Tom* (1960).

66 The life that I have is all that I have
and the life that I have is yours
The love that I have of the life that I have
Is yours and yours and yours.
1958 Poem recited by Virginia McKenna as Violette Szabo in *Carve Her Name With Pride*.

Marlborough, John Churchill, 1st Duke of 1650–1722

English general. He helped quell Monmouth's rebellion at Sedgemoor, but deserted to William of Orange in 1688. Under Queen Anne he was appointed supreme commander of British forces in the War of the Spanish Succession, rewarded for his success with a dukedom.

67 I have not time to say any more, but to beg you will give my duty to the Queen, and let her know her army has had a glorious victory. Monsieur Tallard and two other generals are in my coach, and I am following the rest.
1704 Note written on a tavern bill to his wife, Sarah, 13 Aug, after the Battle of Blenheim.

Marley, Bob (Robert Nesta) 1945–81

Jamaican singer, guitarist, and composer of reggae music. His hits include 'No woman, no cry', 'I Shot the Sheriff', and 'Exodus'. Among his albums were *Catch a Fire* (1972), *Rastaman Vibration* (1976) and *Uprising* (1980).

68 Get up, stand up
Stand up for your rights
Get up, stand up
Don't give up the fight.
1973 'Get Up, Stand Up'.

69 Don't just move to the music, listen to what I'm saying.
Quoted in Johnson and Pines *Reggae* (1982).

Marlowe, Christopher 1564–93

English poet and playwright. It is thought that he was a spy for the English in the Netherlands, and that he was killed in a tavern brawl. His many dramatic works include *Doctor Faustus* (1592), and his poems include the unfinished *Hero and Leander* and lyrics such as 'The Passionate Shepherd to his Love'.

70 From jigging veins of rhyming mother-wits,
And such conceits as clownage keeps in pay,
We'll lead you to the stately tents of war.
1587 *Tamburlaine the Great* (published 1590), pt.1, prologue.

71 Come, lady, let not this appall your thoughts.

1587 *Tamburlaine the Great* (published 1590), pt.1, act 1, sc.2.

72 Tamburlaine!—
A Scythian shepherd so embellishèd
With nature's pride and richest furniture!
His looks do menace heaven and dare the gods.
His fiery eyes are fixed upon the earth.
1587 *Tamburlaine the Great* (published 1590), pt.1, act 1, sc.2.

73 Accurst be he that first invented war.
1587 *Tamburlaine the Great* (published 1590), pt.1, act 2, sc.4.

74 A god is not so glorious as a king.
I think the pleasure they enjoy in Heaven,
Cannot compare with kingly joys in earth.
To wear a crown enchased with pearl and gold,
Whose virtues carry with it life and death;
To ask and have, command and be obeyed;
When looks breed love, with looks to gain the prize,
Such power attractive shines in princes' eyes!
1587 *Tamburlaine the Great* (published 1590), pt.1, act 2, sc.5.

75 Nature that framed us of four elements,
Warring within our breasts for regiment,
Doth teach us all to have aspiring minds:
Our souls, whose faculties can comprehend
The wondrous architecture of the world,
And measure every wandering planet's course,
Still climbing after knowledge infinite,
And always moving as the restless spheres,
Wills us to wear ourselves, and never rest,
Until we reach the ripest fruit of all,
That perfect bliss and sole felicity,
The sweet fruition of an earthly crown.
1587 *Tamburlaine the Great* (published 1590), pt.1, act 2, sc.7.

76 Virtue is the fount whence honour springs.
1587 *Tamburlaine the Great* (published 1590), pt.1, act 4, sc.4.

77 What is beauty, saith my sufferings, then?
If all the pens that ever poets held
Had fed the feeling of their masters' thoughts,
And every sweetness that inspired their hearts,
Their minds, and muses on admirèd themes;
If all the heavenly quintessence they still
From their immortal flowers of poesy,
Wherein, as in a mirror, we perceive
The highest reaches of a human wit;
If these had made one poem's period,
And all combined in beauty's worthiness,
Yet should there hover in their restless heads
One thought, one grace, one wonder, at the least,
Which into words no virtue can digest.
1587 *Tamburlaine the Great* (published 1590), pt.1, act 5, sc.1.

78 And every warrior that is rapt with love
Of fame, of valour, and of victory,
Must needs have beauty beat on his conceits:
I thus conceiving and subduing both,
That which hath stopped the tempest of the gods,
Even from the fiery-spangled veil of heaven,
To feel the lovely warmth of shepherds' flames,
And march in cottages of strowèd weeds,
Shall give the world to note, for all my birth,
That virtue solely is the sum of glory,
And fashions men with true nobility.
1587 *Tamburlaine the Great* (published 1590), pt.1, act 5, sc.1.

79 Helen, whose beauty summoned Greece to arms,

And drew a thousand ships to Tenedos.
1587 *Tamburlaine the Great* (published 1590), pt.2, l.3055–6.

80 More childish valorous than manly wise.
1587 *Tamburlaine the Great* (published 1590), pt.2, l.3690.

81 Holla, ye pampered Jades of Asia;
What, can ye draw but twenty miles a day?
1587 *Tamburlaine the Great* (published 1590), pt.2, l.3980–1.

82 I count religion but a childish toy,
And hold there is no sin but ignorance.
c.1589 *The Jew of Malta* (published 1633), 'Prologue to the Stage,
At the Cock-pit'.

83 Might first made kings, and laws were then most sure
When…they were writ in blood.
c.1589 *The Jew of Malta* (published 1633), 'Prologue'.

84 Thus methinks should men of judgement frame
Their means of traffic from the vulgar trade,
And as their wealth increaseth, so enclose
Infinite riches in a little room.
c.1589 *The Jew of Malta* (published 1633), act 1, sc.1.

85 The sad presaging raven, that tolls
The sick man's passport in her hollow beak,
And in the shadow of the silent night
Doth shake contagion from her sable wings.
c.1589 *The Jew of Malta* (published 1633), act 2, sc.1.

86 As for myself, I walk abroad o'nights
And kill sick people groaning under walls:
Sometimes I go about and poison wells.
c.1589 *The Jew of Malta* (published 1633), act 2, sc.3.

87 Barnardine: Thou hast committed—
Barabas: Fornication—but that was in another country;
and besides, the wench is dead.
c.1589 *The Jew of Malta* (published 1633), act 4, sc.1.

88 'My father is deceased. Come, Gaveston,
And share the kingdom with thy dearest friend.'
Ah, words that make me surfeit with delight!
What greater bliss can hap to Gaveston
Than live and be the favourite of a king?
Sweet prince, I come; these, these thy amorous lines
Might have enforced me to have swum from France,
And, like Leander, gasped upon the sand,
So thou would'st smile, and take me in thy arms.
c.1591 Gaveston is reading a letter from King Edward. *Edward II*
(published 1594), act 1, sc.1.

89 My men, like satyrs grazing on the lawns,
Shall with their goat feet dance an antic hay.
c.1591 *Edward II* (published 1594), act 1, sc.1.

90 The griefs of private men are soon allayed,
But not of kings.
c.1591 *Edward II* (published 1594), act 5, sc.1.

91 But what are kings, when regiment is gone,
But perfect shadows in a sunshine day?
c.1591 *Edward II* (published 1594), act 5, sc.1.

92 He hath a body able to endure
More than we can inflict: and therefore now
Let us assail his mind another while.
c.1591 *Edward II* (published 1594), act 5, sc.4.

93 Sweet Analytics, 'tis thou has ravished me!
c.1592 *Doctor Faustus* (published 1604), act 1, sc.1.

94 I'll have them fly to India for gold,
Ransack the ocean for orient pearl.
c.1592 *Doctor Faustus* (published 1604), act 1, sc.1.

95 Is, to dispute well, logic's chiefest end?
Affords this art no greater miracle?
c.1592 *Doctor Faustus* (published 1604), act 1, sc.1.

96 Oh, what a world of profit and delight,
Of power, of honour, and omnipotence,
Is promised to the studious artisan!
c.1592 *Doctor Faustus* (published 1604), act 1, sc.1.

97 All things that move between the quiet poles
Shall be at my command: emperors and kings
Are but obeyed in their several provinces,
Nor can they raise the wind, or rend the clouds;
But his dominion that exceeds in this
Stretcheth as far as doth the mind of man;
A sound magician is a demi-god.
c.1592 *Doctor Faustus* (published 1604), act 1, sc.1.

98 How am I glutted with conceit of this!
Shall I make spirits fetch me what I please,
Resolve me of all ambiguities,
Perform what desperate enterprise I will?
I'll have them fly to India for gold,
Ransack the ocean for orient pearl,
And search all corners of the new found world
For pleasant fruits and princely delicates.
c.1592 *Doctor Faustus* (published 1604), act 1, sc.1.

99 Why, this is hell, nor am I out of it:
Thinkst thou that I who saw the face of God,
And tasted the eternal joys of heaven,
Am not tormented with ten thousand hells
In being deprived of everlasting bliss!
c.1592 *Doctor Faustus* (published 1604), act 1, sc.3.

1 Hell hath no limits, nor is circumscribed
In one self place; but where we are is hell,
And where hell is, there must we ever be:
And, to be short, when all the world dissolves,
And every creature shall be purified,
All places shall be hell that is not heaven.
c.1592 *Doctor Faustus* (published 1604), act 2, sc.1.

2 But think'st thou heaven is such a glorious thing?
I tell thee, Faustus, it is not half so fair
As thou, or any man that breathes on earth.
c.1592 *Doctor Faustus* (published 1604), act 2, sc.2.

3 Have I not made blind Homer sing to me?
c.1592 *Doctor Faustus* (published 1604), act 2, sc.2.

4 O gentle Faustus, leave this damnèd art,
This magic, that will charm thy soul to hell.
c.1592 *Doctor Faustus* (published 1604), act 5, sc.1.

5 Was this the face that launched a thousand ships,
And burnt the topless towers of Ilium?
Sweet Helen, make me immortal with a kiss!
Her lips suck forth my soul: see, where it flies!
Come Helen, come give me my soul again.
Here will I dwell, for heaven be in these lips,
And all is dross that is not Helena.
c.1592 *Doctor Faustus* (published 1604), act 5, sc.1.

6 Now hast thou but one bare hour to live,
And then thou must be damned perpetually!
Stand still, you ever-moving spheres of heaven,
That time may cease, and midnight never come.
Fair nature's eye, rise, rise, again, and make
Perpetual day; or let this hour be but

A year, a month, a week, a natural day,
That Faustus may repent and save his soul!
O lente, lente currite, noctis equi:
The stars move still, time runs, the clock will strike,
The devil will come, and Faustus must be damned.
Oh, I'll leap up to my God!—Who pulls me down?—
See, see, where Christ's blood streams in the
    firmament!
One drop would save my soul, half a drop, ah, my Christ.
c.1592 *Doctor Faustus* (published 1604), act 5, sc.2.

7 You stars that reigned at my nativity,
Whose influence hath allotted death and hell,
Now draw up Faustus like a foggy mist,
Into the entrails of yon labouring cloud,
That when you vomit forth into the air,
My limbs may issue from your smoky mouths,
So that my soul may but ascend to heaven.
c.1592 *Doctor Faustus* (published 1604), act 5, sc.2.

8 Ah, Pythagoras' metempsychosis, were that time,
This soul should fly from me, and I be changed
Unto some brutish beast.
c.1592 *Doctor Faustus* (published 1604), act 5, sc.2.

9 Cut is the branch that might have grown full straight,
And burnèd is Apollo's laurel bough,
That sometime grew within this learned man.
c.1592 *Doctor Faustus* (published 1604), epilogue.

10 Where Venus in her naked glory strove
To please the careless and disdainful eyes
Of proud Adonis.
1593 *Hero and Leander* (published 1598), pt.1, l.12–14.

11 So lovely fair was Hero, Venus' nun,
As Nature wept, thinking she was undone.
1593 *Hero and Leander* (published 1598), pt.1, l.45–6.

12 His body was as straight as Circe's wand;
Jove might have sipped out nectar from his hand.
1593 *Hero and Leander* (published 1598), pt.1, l.61–2.

13 It lies not in our power to love, or hate,
For will in us is overruled by fate.
When two are stripped, lo ere the course begin
We wish that one should lose, the other win;
And one especially do we affect
Of two gold ingots, like in each respect.
The reason no man knows, let it suffice,
What we behold is censured by our eyes.
Where both deliberate, the love is slight;
Who ever loved, that loved not at first sight?
1593 *Hero and Leander* (published 1598), pt.1, l.167–76.

14 Virginity, albeit some highly prize it,
Compared with marriage, had you tried them both,
Differs as much as wine and water doth.
1593 *Hero and Leander* (published 1598), pt.1, l.268–9.

15 And as she wept, her tears to pearl he turned,
And wound them on his arm, and for her mourned.
1593 The mourner is Cupid. *Hero and Leander* (published 1598),
pt.1, l.375–6.

16 And to this day is every scholar poor;
Gross gold from them runs headlong to the boor.
1593 *Hero and Leander* (published 1598), pt.1, l.477–8.

17 Come live with me and be my love,
And we will all the pleasures prove
That valleys, groves, hills, and fields,

Woods, or steepy mountain yields.

And we will sit upon the rocks,
Seeing shepherds feed their flocks,
By shallow rivers to whose falls
Melodious birds sing madrigals.

And I will make thee beds of roses
And a thousand fragrant posies,
A cap of flowers, and a kirtle
Embroidered all with leaves of myrtle.
'The Passionate Shepherd to His Love' (published 1599).
➤ *See Raleigh 677:98.*

Marples, Morris

English writer and traveller.

18 The soul of a journey is liberty, perfect liberty to think,
feel, do just as one pleases. We go on a journey chiefly to
be free of all impediments and of all inconveniences; to
leave ourselves behind, much more to get rid of others. It
is because I want a little breathing space to muse on
different matters…that I absent myself from the town for
a while.
Quoted in John Hillaby *Journey through Britain* (1968).

Marquand, John P(hillips) 1893–1960

US novelist. He began as a writer of popular stories for
magazines, and later turned to realist novels in the manner of
Sinclair Lewis.

19 His father watched him across the gulf of years and
pathos which always must divide a father from his son.
1937 *The Late George Apley*, ch.10.

Marqués, René 1919–79

Puerto Rican playwright, short-story writer and nationalist.
Most of his plays and essays are concerned with the problem
of national identity in relation to language, literature and the
prevailing social conditions of Puerto Rico.

20 *Hombre, tienes un hijo, un hijo que te hicieron creer
podría inmortalizarte llevando el germen de ti mismo
por siglos de generaciones… Tu carne, Hombre, carne
deleznable, carne podrida que no puede soportar el
peso de tu inmortalidad. No, no hay nada de ti mismo en
esa carne. ¡Tu hijo no te hará inmortal!'*
Man, you have a son, a son who they made you believe
would make you immortal by carrying your seed
through centuries of generations… Your flesh, O man,
your despicable and rotten flesh that cannot bear the
sight of your immortality. No: there's nothing of yourself
in that flesh. Your son won't make you immortal!'
1948 *El hombre y sus sueños* ('Man and His Dreams'), act 2.

Marquis, Don(ald Robert Perry) 1878–1937

US novelist, playwright and poet. He worked as a journalist and
wrote serious work, but is remembered for his comic poems,
notably in the *archy and mehitabel* series, the tales of a
cockroach who can't reach the upper-case keys of the
typewriter, and an alley cat.

21 but wotthehell wotthehell
oh i should worry and fret
death and i will coquette

there s a dance in the old dame yet
toujours gai toujours gai.
1927 *archy and mehitabel*, 'the song of mehitabel'.

22 live so that you
can stick out your tongue
at the insurance.
1927 *archy and mehitabel*, 'certain maxims of archy'.

23 procrastination is the
art of keeping
up with yesterday.
1927 *archy and mehitabel*, 'certain maxims of archy'.

24 millionaires and
bums taste
about alike to me.
1927 *archy and mehitabel*, 'certain maxims of archy'.

25 an optimist is a guy
that has never had
much experience.
1927 *archy and mehitabel*, 'certain maxims of archy'.

26 coarse
jocosity
catches the crowd
shakespeare
and i
are often
low browed
1927 *archy and mehitabel*, 'archy confesses'.

27 persian pussy from over the sea
demure and lazy and smug and fat
none of your ribbons and bells for me
ours is the zest of the alley cat
1927 *archy and mehitabel*, 'mehitabels extensive past'.

28 but wotthehell archy wotthehell
jamais triste archy jamais triste
that is my motto.
1927 *archy and mehitabel*, 'mehitabel sees paris'.

29 honesty is a good
thing but
it is not profitable to
its possessor
unless it is
kept under control.
1933 *archys life of mehitabel*, 'archygrams'.

30 did you ever
notice that when
a politician
does get an idea
he usually
gets it all wrong.
1933 *archys life of mehitabel*, 'archygrams'.

31 now and then
there is a person born
who is so unlucky
that he runs into accidents
which started to happen
to somebody else.
1933 *archys life of mehitabel*, 'archy says'.

32 boss there is always
a comforting thought
in time of trouble when
it is not our trouble

1935 *archy does his part*, 'comforting thoughts'.

33 Writing a book of poetry is like dropping a rose petal
down the Grand Canyon and waiting for the echo.
Quoted in E Anthony *O Rare Don Marquis* (1962), ch.6.

34 The art of newspaper paragraphing is to stroke a
platitude until it purrs like an epigram.
Quoted in E Anthony *O Rare Don Marquis* (1962), ch.11.

35 By the time a bartender knows what drink a man will
have before he orders, there is little else about him
worth knowing.
Quoted in E Anthony *O Rare Don Marquis* (1962), ch.11.

36 Bores bore each other, too; but it never seems to teach
them anything.
Quoted in E Anthony *O Rare Don Marquis* (1962), ch.11.

37 A demagogue is a person with whom we disagree as to
which gang should mismanage the country.
Quoted in E Anthony *O Rare Don Marquis* (1962), ch.11.

38 Fishing is a delusion entirely surrounded by liars in old
clothes.
Attributed.

Marshall, George C(atlett) 1880–1959

US soldier and statesman. He directed the US army throughout
the war as chief of staff (1939–45), and as Secretary of State
(1947–9) he originated the Marshall Aid plan for the post-war
reconstruction of Europe. He was awarded the Nobel peace
prize in 1953.

39 Our policy is directed not against any country or
doctrine, but against hunger, poverty, desperation and
chaos. The purpose shall be the revival of a working
economy in the world so as to permit the emergence of
political and social conditions in which free institutions
can exist.
1947 Speech at Harvard, 5 Jun, announcing the European
Recovery Plan (ER A) that became known as the Marshall Plan.

40 We want you to feel unhampered tactically and
strategically to proceed north of the 38th parallel.
1950 Telegram to General Douglas MacArthur during the
Korean War, Sep, later used by MacArthur as justification for
continuing operations after the Chinese had made their
presence known. Quoted in David S McLellan *Dean Acheson:
The State Department Years* (1976).

Marshall, Thurgood 1908–93

US jurist and civil rights advocate. He worked with the National
Association for the Advancement of Colored People and the
Court of Appeals (1961–5). Solicitor General (1965–7), he
became the first black Justice of the US Supreme Court
(1967–91).

41 If the United States is indeed the great melting pot, the
negro either didn't get in the pot or he didn't get melted
down.
1987 In the *New York Times*, 9 Sep.

Martel, Yann 1963–

Canadian author. His novel *Life of Pi* (2002) was awarded the
Booker Prize.

42 If we, citizens, do not support our artists, then we sacrifice
our imagination on the altar of crude reality and we end up
believing in nothing and having worthless dreams.
2002 *Life of Pi*.

43 In the literature can be found legions of examples of animals that could escape but did not, or did and returned.
2002 *Life of Pi.*

Martí, José 1853–95

Cuban national hero. A journalist, editor and poet, he was a key figure in Cuba's struggle for independence. Exiled for his revolutionary activities, he travelled in Europe and the Americas. He died fighting at Boca de Dos Ríos.

44 *¡Robaron los conquistadores una página al Universo! Aquellos eran los pueblos que llamaban a la Vía Láctea 'el camino de las almas'; para quienes el Universo estaba lleno del Grande Espíritu, en cuyo seno se encerraba toda luz.*
The conquistadores stole a page from the Universe! Those were the good people who called the Milky Way 'the souls' path'; for them the Universe was full of the Great Spirit, within which all light was contained.
1884 *Obra literaria*, 'El hombre antiguo de América y sus artes primitivas' ('Ancient Man in America and his Primitive Arts').

45 *Yo soy un hombre sincero De donde crece la palma, Y antes de morirme quiero Echar mis versos del alma.*
I am a sincere man from where the palm tree grows; and before I die I want to loose my verses from my heart.
1891 *Versos sencillos* ('Simple Verses'), no.1.

Martial *full name* Marcus Valerius Martialis c. 40–104 AD

Latin poet, born in Spain. He went to Rome and became an associate of Lucan and the younger Seneca, who were also Spanish. Martial's most important work is the twelve books of *Epigrams*, each a concise expression of one idea or theme.

46 *Non est, crede mihi, sapientis dicere 'Vivam': Sera nimis vita est crastina: vive hodie.*
Believe me, wise men do not say 'I shall live on.' Tomorrow's life's too late; live today.
Epigrams, bk.1, no.15.

47 *Non amo te, Sabidi, nec possum dicere quare: Hoc tantum possum dicere, non amo te.*
I do not love you, Sabidius, and I can't tell you why; all I can say is this, I don't love you.
Epigrams, bk.1, no.32.

48 *Laudant illa sed ista legunt.*
They praise those works, but read these.
Epigrams, bk.4, no.49, l.9–10.

49 *Bonosque Soles effugere atque abire sentit, Qui nobis pereunt et imputantur.*
Each of us feels the good days speed and depart, and they're lost to us and counted against us.
Epigrams, bk.5, no.20, l.11–13.

50 *Non est vivere, sed valere vita est.*
Life is not just to be alive, but to be well.
Epigrams, bk.6, no.70.

51 *Difficilis facilis, iucundus acerbus es idem: Nec tecum possum vivere nec sine te.*
Difficult or easy, pleasant or bitter, you are the same:

I cannot live with you—or without you.
Epigrams, bk.12, no.46.

52 *Rus in urbe.*
Country in the town.
Epigrams, bk.12, no.57, l.21.

Martin, Sir George 1926–

English record producer, particularly known for his association with The Beatles.

53 If you were poor fifty years ago, it meant you didn't have enough to eat. If you're poor now, it means you only have one car.
2003 In *Esquire*, Jan.

Marvell, Andrew 1621–78

English poet. Educated at Cambridge, he held various government posts. His poems cover a variety of genres and classical forms, but he also published anonymously political and satirical prose works.

54 The inglorious arts of peace.
1650 'An Horatian Ode upon Cromwell's Return from Ireland'.

55 He nothing common did or mean Upon that memorable scene: But with his keener eye The axe's edge did try.
1650 Of Charles I. 'An Horatian Ode upon Cromwell's Return from Ireland'.

56 How fit he is to sway That can so well obey.
1650 'An Horatian Ode upon Cromwell's Return from Ireland'.

57 See how the Orient dew, Shed from the bosom of the morn Into the blowing roses, Yet careless of its mansion new; For the clear region where 'twas born Round in its self encloses: And in its little globes extent, Frames as it can its native element.
c.1650–1652 'On a Drop of Dew' (published 1681).

58 There is not such another in The world, to offer for their sin.
c.1650–1652 'The Nymph Complaining for the Death of her Fawn' (published 1681).

59 Had it lived long, it would have been Lilies without, roses within.
c.1650–1652 'The Nymph Complaining for the Death of her Fawn' (published 1681)

60 I have a garden of my own, But so with roses overgrown, And lilies, that you would it guess To be a little wilderness.
c.1650–1652 'The Nymph Complaining for the Death of her Fawn' (published 1681).

61 Had we but world enough, and time, This coyness Lady were no crime. We would sit down, and think which way To walk, and pass our long love's day. Thou by the Indian Ganges' side Shouldst rubies find: I by the tide Of Humber would complain. I would Love you ten years before the flood.

c.1650–1652 'To His Coy Mistress' (published 1681).

62 My vegetable love should grow
Vaster than empires, and more slow,
An hundred years should go to praise
Thine eyes, and on thy forehead gaze.
Two hundred to adore each breast:
But thirty thousand to the rest.
An age at least to every part,
And the last age should show your heart.
For Lady you deserve this state;
Nor would I love at lower rate.
But at my back I always hear
Time's winged chariot hurrying near:
And yonder all before us lie
Deserts of vast eternity.
c.1650–1652 'To His Coy Mistress' (published 1681).

63 Then worms shall try
That long preserved virginity:
And your quaint honour turn to dust;
And into ashes all my lust.
The grave's a fine and private place,
But none I think do there embrace.
c.1650–1652 'To His Coy Mistress' (published 1681).

64 Now let us sport us while we may;
And now, like amorous birds of prey,
Rather at once our time devour,
Than languish in his slow-chapped power.
c.1650–1652 'To His Coy Mistress' (published 1681).

65 Let us roll all our strength, and all
Our sweetness, up into one ball:
And tear our pleasures with rough strife,
Through the iron gates of life.
Thus, though we cannot make our sun
Stand still, yet we will make him run.
c.1650–1652 'To His Coy Mistress' (published 1681), closing lines.

66 My love is of a birth as rare
As 'tis for object strange and high:
It was begotten by Despair
Upon Impossibility.

Magnanimous Despair alone
Could show me so divine a thing,
Where feeble Hope could ne'er have flown
But vainly flapped its tinsel wing.
c.1650–1652 'The Definition of Love' (published 1681).

67 As lines so loves oblique may well
Themselves in every angle greet
But ours so truly parallel,
Though infinite can never meet.

Therefore the love which doth us bind,
But fate so enviously debars,
Is the conjunction of the mind,
And opposition of the stars.
c.1650–1652 'The Definition of Love' (published 1681).

68 Ye living lamps, by whose dear light
The nightingale does sit so late,
And studying all the summer night,
Her matchless songs does meditate.
c.1650–1652 'The Mower to the Glo- Worms' (published 1681).

69 And now, when I have summed up all my store,
Thinking (so I myself deceive)
So rich a chaplet thence to weave
As never yet the King of Glory wore,
Alas! I find the serpent old,
That, twining in his speckled breast,
About the flowers disguised does fold
With wreaths of fame and interest.
c.1650–1652 'The Coronet' (published 1681).

70 My mind was once the true survey
Of all these meadows fresh and gay;
And in the greenness of the grass
Did see its hopes as in a glass.
c.1650–1652 'The Mower's Song' (published 1681).

71 How vainly men themselves amaze
To win the palm, the oak, or bays;
And their uncessant labours see
Crown'd from some single herb or tree.
Whose short and narrow verged shade
Does prudently their toils upbraid;
While all flow'rs and all trees do close
To weave the garlands of repose.
c.1650–1652 'The Garden' (published 1681).

72 Fair quiet, have I found thee here,
And Innocence thy Sister dear!
Mistaken long, I sought you then
In busy companies of men.
c.1650–1652 'The Garden' (published 1681).

73 Society is all but rude,
To this delicious solitude.
c.1650–1652 'The Garden' (published 1681).

74 What wondrous life is this I lead!
Ripe apples drop about my head;
The luscious clusters of the vine
Upon my mouth do crush their wine;
The nectarine, and curious peach,
Into my hands themselves do reach;
Stumbling on melons, as I pass,
Ensnared with flowers, I fall on grass.
c.1650–1652 'The Garden' (published 1681), stanza 5.

75 Annihilating all that's made
To a green thought in a green shade.
c.1650–1652 'The Garden' (published 1681), stanza 6.

76 Such was that happy garden-state,
While man there walked without a mate.
c.1650–1652 'The Garden' (published 1681), stanza 8.

77 'Twas beyond a mortal's share
To wander solitary there:
Two paradises 'twere in one
To live in paradise alone.
c.1650–1652 'The Garden' (published 1681), stanza 8.

78 No creature loves an empty space;
Their bodies measure out their place.
c.1650–1652 'Upon Appleton House, to My Lord Fairfax' (published 1681), stanza 2.

79 'Tis not, what once it was, the world;
But a rude heap together hurl'd.
c.1650–1652 'Upon Appleton House, to My Lord Fairfax' (published 1681), stanza 96.

80 Oh thou, that dear and happy isle
The garden of the world ere while,

Thou paradise of four seas,
Which heaven planted us to please,
But, to exclude the world, did guard
With watery if not flaming sword;
What luckless apple did we taste,
To make us mortal, and thee waste?
c.1650–1652 'Upon Appleton House, to My Lord Fairfax'
(published 1681), stanza 41.

81 What should we do but sing the praise
That led us through the watery maze,
Unto an isle so long unknown,
And yet far kinder than our own?
c.1653 'Bermudas' (published 1681).

Marvell, Holt originally *Eric Maschwitz* 1901–69

English songwriter.

82 These Foolish Things Remind Me of You.
1935 Title of song.

Marx, Chico originally *Leonard Marx* 1891–1961

US film comedian, one of the Marx Brothers, best known as the piano player.

83 I wasn't kissing her, I was just whispering in her mouth.
Explanation to his wife, on being discovered in a compromising position with a chorus girl. Quoted in Groucho Marx and Richard J Anobile *Marx Brothers Scrapbook* (1973), ch.24.

Marx, Groucho originally *Julius Henry Marx* 1895–1977

US film comedian, one of the Marx Brothers. He appeared in many films including *Animal Crackers* (1930), *Monkey Business* (1931), *Horse Feathers* (1932) and *Duck Soup* (1933).

84 What's a thousand dollars? Mere chicken feed. A poultry matter.
1929 Line delivered in *The Cocoanuts* (screenplay by George Kaufman and Morrie Ryskind).

85 One morning I shot an elephant in my pyjamas. How he got into my pyjamas I don't know.
1930 Line delivered in *Animal Crackers* (screenplay by George Kaufman and Morrie Ryskind).

86 You go Uruguay and I'll go mine.
1930 Line delivered in *Animal Crackers* (screenplay by George Kaufman and Morrie Ryskind).

87 I could dance with you till the cows come home. On second thoughts I'll dance with the cows and you come home.
1933 Line delivered in *Duck Soup* (screenplay by Bert Kalmar, Harry Ruby and Arthur Sheekman).

88 There ain't no Sanity Claus.
1935 Line delivered in *A Night at the Opera* (screenplay by George Kaufman and Morrie Ryskind).

89 Either he's dead or my watch has stopped.
1937 Line delivered in *A Day at the Races* (screenplay by George Seaton, Robert Pirosh and George Oppenheimer).

90 Marry me and I'll never look at another horse.
1937 Line delivered in *A Day at the Races* (screenplay by George Seaton, Robert Pirosh and George Oppenheimer).

91 Please accept my resignation. I don't want to belong to any club that will accept me as a member.
1959 Recalled in his autobiography, *Groucho and Me* (1959), ch.26.

92 When's the game itself going to begin?

While watching a game of cricket at Lord's. Quoted in Colin Jarman *The Guinness Dictionary of Sports Quotations* (1990).

Marx, Harpo originally *Adolf Marx* 1893–1961

US film comedian, one of the Marx Brothers. His role within the team was that of dumb clown and harp maestro. He published an autobiography in 1961.

93 No worse than a bad cold.
His winning suggestion when a critic set up a competition for readers' reviews of the long-running play *Abie's Irish Rose* by Anne Nichols. Attributed.

Marx, Karl Heinrich 1818–83

German-born political and economic theorist who began his career as a journalist in 1843. With his lifelong literary collaborator Friedrich Engels he wrote *The Communist Manifesto* (1848), and settled in London the next year, where he began his unfinished *Das Kapital* (vol.1, 1867, the rest posthumously).

94 Religion is the sigh of the oppressed creature, the feelings of a heartless world, and the spirit of conditions that are unspiritual. It is the opium of the people.
1843–4 *A Contribution to the Critique of Hegel's Philosophy of Right*.

95 The worker becomes poorer the more wealth he produces and the more his production increases in power and extent. The worker becomes an ever cheaper commodity the more good he creates. The *devaluation* of the human world increases in direct relation with the *increase in value* of the world of things. Labour does not only create goods; it also produces itself and the worker *as a commodity*, and indeed in the same proportion as it produces goods.
1844 Collected in T B Bottomore (trans and ed) *Early Writings* (1964), p.121.

96 Political economy thus does not recognize the unoccupied worker, the working man so far as he is outside this work relationship. Swindlers, thieves, beggars, the unemployed, the starving, poverty-stricken and criminal working man, are figures which do not exist for political economy, but only for other eyes; for doctors, judges, grave-diggers, beadles, etc. They are ghostly figures outside the domain of political economy.
1844 Collected in T B Bottomore (trans and ed) *Early Writings* (1964), p.137–9.

97 The *division of labour* is nothing but the *alienated* establishment of human activity.
1844 Collected in T B Bottomore (trans and ed) *Early Writings* (1964), p.181.

98 The philosophers have only interpreted the world in various ways; the point is to change it.
1845 *Theses on Feuerbach*, no.11.

99 In communist society, where nobody has one exclusive sphere of activity but each can become accomplished in any branch he wishes, society regulates the general production and thus makes it possible for me to do one thing today and another tomorrow, to hunt in the morning, fish in the afternoon, rear cattle in the evening or criticize after dinner, just as I desire, without ever becoming hunter, fisherman, shepherd or critic.
1845 *The German Ideology* (with Friedrich Engels).

1 Assume a particular state of development in the

productive facilities of man and you will get a particular form of commerce and consumption. Assume particular stages of development in production, commerce and consumption and you will have a corresponding social constitution, a corresponding organisation of the family, of orders or of classes, in a word, a corresponding civil society. Assume a particular civil society and you will get particular political conditions which are only the official expression of civil society.
1846 Letter to P V Annenkov, 26 Dec.

2 The history of all hitherto existing society is the history of class struggles.
1848 *The Communist Manifesto* (with Friedrich Engels, translated by Samuel Moore, 1888), opening sentence.

3 The theory of the Communists may be summed up in the single sentence: Abolition of private property.
1848 *The Communist Manifesto* (with Friedrich Engels, translated by Samuel Moore, 1888).

4 A spectre is haunting Europe—the spectre of communism. All the powers of old Europe have entered into a holy alliance to exorcise this spectre; Pope and Tsar, Metternich and Guizot, French Radicals and German police spies.
1848 *The Communist Manifesto* (with Friedrich Engels, translated by Samuel Moore, 1888).

5 Let the ruling classes tremble at a communist revolution. The proletarians have nothing to lose but their chains. they have a world to win. Working men of all countries, unite!
1848 *The Communist Manifesto* (with Friedrich Engels, translated by Samuel Moore, 1888), closing words. This translation was approved by Engels, but the phrase is also known as 'Workers of the world, unite'. The literal translation of the German is 'Proletarians of all lands, unite.'

6 If capital is growing rapidly, wages may rise; the profit of capital rises incomparably more rapidly. The material position of the worker has improved, but at the cost of his social position. The social gulf that divides him from the capitalist has widened.
1849 'Wage Labour and Capital', collected in Robert C Tucker (ed) *The Marx–Engels Reader* (2nd edn, 1972), p.211.

7 Hegel says somewhere that all great events and personalities in the world reappear in one fashion or another. He forgot to add: the first time as tragedy, the second as farce.
1852 *The Eighteenth Brumaire of Louis Bonaparte*, section 1.

8 All our inventions have endowed material forces with intellectual life and degraded human life into material force.
1856 Speech, 14 Apr.

9 Society does not consist of individuals; it expresses the sum of connections and relationships in which individuals find themselves.
1857–8 *The Grundrisse* (translated by David McLellan, 1971), p.77.

10 The product of mental labour—science—always stands far below its value, because the labour-time necessary to reproduce it has no relation at all to the labour-time required for its original production.
1862 *Theory of Surplus Value.*

11 The production of surplus-value, or the extraction of surplus labour, is the specific end and aim, the sum and substance, of capitalist production.
1867 *Das Kapital.*

12 The instruments of labour, when they assume the form of machinery, acquire a kind of material existence which involves the replacement of human forces by the forces of Nature, and of rule-of-thumb methods by the purposeful application of natural science.
1867 *Das Kapital.*

13 In manufacture and in handicrafts, the worker uses a tool; in the factory, he serves a machine.
1867 *Das Kapital.*

14 Only in a higher phase of communist society…can the narrow horizon of bourgeois right be crossed in its entirety, and society inscribe on its banners, 'From each according to his ability, to each according to his needs!'
1875 Critique of the Gotha Programme, May.
▬ *See Bakunin 53:25.*

15 All I know is that I am not a Marxist.
Recalled by Friedrich Engels in letter to Conrad Schmidt, 3 Aug 1890.

16 What I did that was new was to prove that the existence of classes is only bound up with particular, historical phases in the development of production; that the class struggle necessarily leads to the dictatorship of the proletariat; and that dictatorship itself only constitutes the transition to the abolition of all classes and to a classless society.
In Karl Marx and Friedrich Engels *Correspondence* (1934).

Mary of Teck *formerly* **Princess Victoria Mary Augusta Louise Olga Pauline Claudine Agnes** *known as* **Princess May** 1867–1953

Queen-Consort of George V of Britain (married 1893). She helped mould her husband into a 'people's king' and throughout her son's reign was involved in women's war work and philanthropy.

17 God grant that we may not have a European war thrust upon us, and for such a stupid reason too, no I don't mean stupid, but to have to go to war on account of tiresome Serbia beggars belief.
1914 Letter to her aunt Princess Augusta, Grand-Duchess of Mecklenburg-Strelitz, 28 Jul.

Mary, Queen of Scots 1542–87

Queen of Scotland, the daughter of James V. A Catholic, she succeeded to the throne at the age of one week but was forced to sign an act of abdication in favour of her son James VI in 1567. She fled to England and was imprisoned by Elizabeth I for 20 years before being executed.

18 *En ma fin git mon commencement.*
In my end is my beginning.
Embroidered motto, quoted in Antonia Fraser *Mary Queen of Scots* (1969), ch.21, 'My Norfolk'.

Mary Tudor *also known as* **Mary I** 1516–58

Queen of England and Ireland (from 1553). On Edward VI's death she ousted Lady Jane Grey with popular support and repealed anti-Catholic legislation. Public anger at her persecutions of Protestants and her unpopular marriage, and the loss of Calais to the French, broke her down.

19 When I am dead and opened, you shall find 'Calais' lying
in my heart.
Quoted in Holinshed *Chronicles* (1808), vol.4.

Masaryk, Tomás Garrigue 1850–1937

Czechoslovak statesman. An ardent Slovak, while in exile
during World War I he organized the Czech independence
movement. As the first President of Czechoslovakia (1918–35),
he was re-elected on three occasions.

20 Our whole history inclines us towards the democratic
powers. Our renaissance is a logical link between us and
the democracies of the west.
1918 Inaugural address, 23 Dec.

Masefield, John Edward 1878–1967

English poet and novelist. He served his apprenticeship in the
merchant navy, before ill-health forced him to concentrate on
writing about the sea rather than sailing it. He became Poet
Laureate in 1930.

21 I must down to the seas again, to the lonely sea and the
sky,
And all I ask is a tall ship and a star to steer her by,
And the wheel's kick and the wind's song and the white
sail's shaking,
And a grey mist on the sea's face and a grey dawn
breaking.
1902 'Sea Fever'.

22 I must down to the seas again, for the call of the running
tide
Is a wild call and a clear call that may not be denied.
1902 'Sea Fever'.

23 I must down to the seas again, to the vagrant gypsy life,
To the gull's way and the whale's way where the wind's
like a whetted knife;
And all I ask is a merry yarn from a laughing fellow-rover,
And quiet sleep and a sweet dream when the long trick's
over.
1902 'Sea Fever'.

24 It's a warm wind, the west wind, full of bird's cries;
I never hear the west wind but tears are in my eyes.
1902 'West Wind'.

25 It is good to be out on the road, and going one knows not
where.
1902 'Tewkesbury Road'.

26 Quinquireme of Nineveh from distant Ophir
Rowing home to haven in sunny Palestine,
With a cargo of ivory,
And apes and peacocks,
Sandalwood, cedarwood, and sweet white wine.
1903 'Cargoes'.

27 Dirty British coaster with a salt-caked smoke-stack,
Butting through the Channel in the mad March days.
1903 'Cargoes'.

28 I have seen dawn and sunset on moors and windy hills
Coming in solemn beauty like slow old tunes of Spain.
1903 'Beauty'.

29 Oh some are fond of Spanish wine, and some are fond of
French,
And some'll swallow tay and stuff fit only for a wench.
1903 'Captain Stratton's Fancy'.

30 Most roads lead men homewards,
My road leads me forth.
1903 'Roadways'.

31 My road leads me seawards
To the white dipping sails.
1903 'Roadways'.

32 Death opens unknown doors. It is most grand to die.
1910 *Pompey the Great*, act 2.

33 In the dark room where I began
My mother's life made me a man.
Through all the months of human birth
Her beauty fed my common earth.
I cannot see, nor breathe, nor stir,
But through the death of some of her.
1910 'C.L.M.'.

34 Out into the street I ran uproarious
The devil dancing in me glorious.
1911 'The Everlasting Mercy'.

35 And he who gives a child a treat
Makes joy-bells ring in Heaven's street,
And he who gives a child a home
Builds palaces in Kingdom come,
And she who gives a baby birth
Brings Saviour Christ again to Earth.
1911 'The Everlasting Mercy'.

36 In this life he laughs longest who laughs last.
1912 *The Widow in Bye Street*, ch.4.

37 The days that make us happy make us wise.
1914 'Biography'.

38 Life's battle is a conquest for the strong;
The meaning shows in the defeated thing.
1914 'The Wanderer'.

39 I have seen flowers come in stony places
And kind things done by men with ugly faces,
And the gold cup won by the worst horse at the races,
So I trust, too.
1914 'An Epilogue'.

40 And all the way that wild high crying,
To cold his blood with the thought of dying.
1919 *Reynard the Fox*, pt.2, stanza 49.

41 People who leave their own time out of their work
cannot be surprised if their time fails to find them
interesting.
1925 'With the Living Voice'.

Massinger, Philip 1583–1640

English dramatist. He attended Oxford, but left to join
Henslowe's company. He collaborated with Thomas Dekker,
Ben Jonson and George Chapman, and particularly John
Fletcher, with whom he is buried. His works include *A New
Way to Pay Old Debts* (1633).

42 He that would govern others, first should be
The master of himself.
1623 *The Bondman*, act 1, sc.3.

43 Soar not too high to fall; but stoop to rise.
1623 *The Duke of Milan*, act 1, sc.2.

44 Oh that thou hadst like others been all words,
And no performance.
1624 *The Parliament of Love*, act 4, sc.2.

45 Pleasures of worse natures

Are gladly entertained, and they that shun us
Practice in private sports the stews would blush at.
1626 Of the theatre. *The Roman Actor*, act 1, sc.1.

46 Nay, droop not, fellows; innocence should be bold.
1626 *The Roman Actor*, act 1, sc.1.

47 They are only safe
That know to soothe the prince's appetite
And serve his lusts.
1626 *The Roman Actor*, act 1, sc.1.

48 O master doctor, he is past recovery;
A lethargy hath seized him.
1626 *The Roman Actor*, act 2, sc.1.

49 How strangely hopes delude men.
1626 *The Roman Actor*, act 5, sc.2.

50 Greatness, with private men
Esteem'd a blessing, is to me a curse;
And we, whom, for our high births, they conclude
The happy freemen, are the only slaves.
Happy the golden mean!
1627 *The Great Duke of Florence*, act 1, sc.1.

51 Virgin me no virgins!
I must have you lose that name, or you lose me.
1633 *A New Way to Pay Old Debts*, act 3, sc.2.

Masters, Edgar Lee 1869–1950

US poet. Although he wrote a number of books of both poetry and prose, he is chiefly remembered for the satirical free verse epitaphs on real and imaginary occupants of a midwestern cemetery in *Spoon River Anthology* (1915).

52 Where are Elmer, Herman, Bert, Tom and Charley,
The weak of will, the strong of arm, the clown, the boozer, the fighter?
All, all, are sleeping on the hill.
1915 *Spoon River Anthology*, 'The Hill'.

53 Why, a moral truth is a hollow tooth
Which must be propped with gold.
1915 *Spoon River Anthology*, 'Sersmith the Dentist'.

54 Your eight-page paper—behind which you huddle,
Bawling through the megaphone of big type:
'This is I, the giant.'
1915 *Spoon River Anthology*, 'Editor Whedon'.

Matak, Sirik c.1930–1975

Cambodian politician and business leader who joined with Lol Nol to overthrow Sihanouk in 1970. Prime Minister of the US-backed Khmer Republic (1970–5), he was executed by the Khmer Rouge after refusing to leave with the US Ambassador.

55 But mark it well, if I shall die here on the spot and in my country that I love, it is too bad because we are all born and must die one day. I have only committed this mistake of believing in you, the Americans.
1975 Letter to John Dean, US Ambassador to Cambodia (1974–5), Apr.

Mathew, Sir James Charles 1830–1908

Irish judge. He was appointed judge (1881–1901) and Lord Justice of Appeal (1901–6).

56 In England, justice is open to all—like the Ritz Hotel.
Quoted in R E Megarry *Miscellany-at-Law* (1955). Sometimes attributed to Lord Darling.

Mathews, Harry Burchell 1930–

US writer and translator. His fiction is marked by a rich vein of lexical experiment and unconventional fantasy. He also translates and has written original literary works in French.

57 Translation is the paradigm, the exemplar of all writing…
It is translation that demonstrates most vividly the yearning for transformation that underlies every act involving speech, that supremely human gift.
1980 *Country Cooking and Other Stories*, 'The Dialect of the Tribe'.

58 Syntax and vocabulary are overwhelming constraints—the rules that run us. Language is using *us* to talk—we think we're using the language, but language is doing the thinking, we're its slavish agents.
1988 Interview in *City Limits*, 26 May.

Mathias, Charles McCurdy, Jr 1922–

US lawyer and Republican politician. He was a Congressman (1961–69), then Senator from Maryland (1969–87).

59 Most of us are honest all the time, and all of us are honest most of the time.
1967 Of congressional ethics. In *Time*, 31 Mar.

Mathison, Melissa 1949–

US screenwriter, best known for *E.T.—the Extraterrestrial* (1982).

60 E.T. phone home.
1982 *E.T.—the Extraterrestrial*.

61 How do you explain school to a higher intelligence?
1982 *E.T.—the Extraterrestrial*.

Matisse, Henri Émile Benoît 1869–1954

French painter, sculptor, designer and graphic artist, from 1904 leader of the Fauves. His paintings typically display bold use of colour organized within a rhythmic two-dimensional design.

62 Expression, for me, does not reside in passions glowing in a human face or manifested by violent movement. The entire arrangement of my picture is expressive: the place occupied by the figures, the empty spaces around them, the proportions, everything has its share.
1908 'Notes d'un peintre', in *La Grande Revue*.

63 What I dream of is an art of balance, of purity and serenity…a soothing, calming influence on the mind, rather like a good armchair which provides relaxation from physical fatigue.
1908 'Notes d'un peintre', in *La Grande Revue*.

64 If drawing belongs to the realm of the Spirit and colour to that of the Senses, you must draw first, to cultivate the Spirit and to be able to lead colour through the paths of the Spirit.
1948 Letter to Henry Clifford, quoted in Jack D Flam *Matisse on Art* (1973).

Matlovich, Leonard 1943–88

US soldier, the first active-duty soldier openly to acknowledge his homosexuality.

65 A Gay Vietnam Veteran—They gave me a medal for killing two men, and a discharge for loving one.
Tombstone inscription. Quoted in the *Washington Post*, 22 Apr 1988.

Matos, Gregório de c.1623–1696

Brazilian poet and epigrammatist, born into the slave-owning gentry. His scandalous private life brought him into conflict with the clergy, government and respectable society, but his frankness and rebellious spirit made him a cultural hero.

66 *De dois ff se compõe*
Esta cidade a meu ver:
Um furtar, outro foder.
Of two f's,
as I see it,
is this city composed:
one fraud, the other fornication.
'Define a sua cidade' ('He defines his city'), collected in *Crônica do viver bahiano* (published 1882).

Matthews, Christopher J

US journalist. Former political aide and speechwriter for President Carter. He has written several books, including *Kennedy Nixon: The Rivalry that Shaped Postwar America* (1996).

67 Hang a lantern on your problem.
1987 Advice to political candidates to expose their personal frailties before they can be discovered by the media. In the *New York Times*, 10 Jul.

68 The key is to be a porcupine—have a reputation for being difficult.
Advice for success in the political world. Quoted in Hedrick Smith *The Power Game* (1988).

Matthews, Sir Stanley 1915–2000

English footballer. He was acclaimed the finest winger of his generation and won a total of 54 caps before his eventual retirement in 1955.

69 I played 33 years and never got cautioned. I like that.
1995 Television interview, on his 80th birthday.

Matthiessen, Peter 1927–

US writer, naturalist and explorer. His novels include *Far Tortuga* (1975) and *Killing Mister Watson* (1990). He also writes non-fiction and he won a National Book Award in 1978 for his account of a mystical journey through Tibet, *The Snow Leopard*.

70 At Play In The Fields Of The Lord.
1965 Title of novel.

71 For some time I watch the coming of the night… Above is the glistening galaxy of childhood, now hidden in the Western world by air pollution and the glare of artificial light; for my children's children, the power, peace and healing of the night will be obliterated.
1978 Of the night sky in Nepal. *The Snow Leopard*, 'Northward, October 18'.

Mature, Victor 1915–99

US actor whose credits include *Samson and Delilah* (1949), *Androcles and the Lion* (1952) and *The Robe* (1953).

72 Actually, I am a golfer. That is my real occupation. I never was an actor; ask anybody, particularly the critics.
Attributed.

Maugham, W(illiam) Somerset 1874–1965

British writer, born in Paris of Irish descent. He served as a secret agent in World War II, and travelled widely in south-east Asia. His works include the autobiographical novel *Of Human*

Bondage (1915) and his satirical masterpiece, *Cakes and Ale* (1930).

73 At a dinner party one should eat wisely but not too well, and talk well but not too wisely.
1896 *A Writer's Notebook* (published 1949).

74 Impropriety is the soul of wit.
1919 *The Moon and Sixpence*.

75 I hate people who play bridge as though they were at a funeral and knew their feet were getting wet.
1921 Quoted in Colin Jarman *The Guinness Dictionary of Sports Quotations* (1990).

76 Hypocrisy is the most difficult and nerve-racking vice that any man can pursue; it needs an unceasing vigilance and a rare detachment of spirit. It cannot, like adultery or gluttony, be practised at spare moments; it is a whole-time job.
1930 *Cakes and Ale*, ch.1.

77 There is no silence in the East.
1930 *The Gentleman in the Parlour*.

78 Mandalay has its name; the falling cadence of the lovely word has gathered about itself the chiaroscuro of romance.
1930 *The Gentleman in the Parlour*.

79 The Chinese are the aristocracy of the East.
1930 *The Gentleman in the Parlour*.

80 They are like a face full of character that intrigues and excites you, but that on closer acquaintance you discover is merely the mask of a vulgar soul. Such is Tourane.
1930 Of Tourane, now Da Nang, Vietnam. *The Gentleman in the Parlour*.

81 Observing these people I am no longer surprised that there is such a scarcity of domestic servants at home.
1960 Said in an uncharacteristically loud voice after being refused entry to the premier British expatriate club in Singapore. Quoted in Robert Calder *Willie* (1989).

Maupassant, Guy de 1850–93

French writer, best known for his captivating short stories which explored a wide range of characters and, often, the supernatural world.

82 *L'histoire, cette vieille dame exaltée et menteuse.*
History, this old, honoured and lying woman.
1876 *Sur l'eau*.

83 *Le talent provient de l'originalité, qui est une manière spéciale de penser, de voir, de comprendre et de juger.*
Talent comes from originality which is a special manner of thinking, of seeing, of understanding and of judging.
1888 *Pierre et Jean*, préface.

84 *Raconter tout serait impossible.*
To tell all would be impossible.
1888 *Pierre et Jean*, préface.

85 *Les grands artistes sont ceux qui imposent à l'humanité leur illusion particulière.*
Great artists impose their particular illusion on humanity.
1888 *Pierre et Jean*, préface.

86 *La moindre chose contient un peu d'inconnu. Trouvons-le.*
The least thing contains something mysterious. Find it.
1888 *Pierre et Jean*, préface.

87 *On finirait par devenir fou, ou par mourir, si on ne pouvait pas pleurer.*
We would end by becoming crazy or by dying, if we could not cry.
1889 *Fort comme la mort*, bk.2, ch.1.

Maxton, James 1885–1946

Socialist politician, born in Glasgow, elected as a Labour MP in 1922. One of the group of 'Red Clydesiders', he was a brilliant and colourful orator rather than a skilful political tactician.

88 In the interests of economy they condemned hundreds of children to death and I call it murder.
1923 Speech against the withdrawal of child benefits, including the supply of milk, in Scotland. In *Hansard*, 27 Jun.

89 All I say is, if you cannot ride two horses you have no right in the circus.
1931 On the Scottish Independent Labour Party's proposed disaffiliation from the Labour Party. In the *Daily Herald*, 12 Jan.

May, Elaine *originally Elaine Berlin* 1932–

US actress, director and screenwriter. She wrote screenplays for *A New Leaf* (1971) and *Primary Colours* (1998).

90 All I am or was is rich, and that's all I ever wanted to be.
1971 Line delivered by Walter Matthau in *A New Leaf*.

Mayakovsky, Vladimir 1894–1930

Russian Futurist poet, a supporter of the Bolsheviks in the 1917 Revolution. His works include plays, poems and satirical plays. He committed suicide in Moscow.

91 I'll be irreproachably tender;
not a man, but—a cloud in trousers!
1915 'The Cloud in Trousers' (translated by Samuel Charteris).

92 We do not need art museums to worship dead works, we need living factories of the soul—in the streets, in the trams, in the factories, in studios, and in the workers' houses.
1918 Quoted in *Futurismo e Futurismi* (1986).

93 To us love says humming that the heart's stalled motor has begun working again.
1928 'Letter from Paris to Comrade Kostorov on the Nature of Love' (translated by Samuel Charteris).

Maybeck, Bernard Ralph 1862–1957

US architect, renowned for his eclectic combinations of styles and materials. His works include the Palace of Fine Arts, San Francisco (1915) and Clyde, a town in California (1917).

94 Let the thing fall down in peace.
On the crumbling remains of his Corinthian classic Palace of Fine Arts, designed for San Francisco's 1915 Panama–Pacific Exposition. Recalled in the *New York Times*, 9 May 1965.

Mayer, Louis B(urt) *originally Eliezer Mayer* 1885–1957

Russian-born US film mogul. A co-founder of Metro Films in 1915, he joined with Sam Goldwyn to form Metro-Goldwyn-Mayer (MGM) in 1924. He received an honorary Academy Award in 1950.

95 We are the only company whose assets all walk out the gates at night.
Quoted in Leslie Halliwell *The Filmgoer's Book of Quotes* (1973).

Mayhew, Alex

Professor of Political Science, Georgetown University.

96 The future of America is based on one generation sacrificing for the next.
Quoted by David Maraniss in CNBC broadcast, 7 Mar 1995. The phrase was popularized by Mayhew's former student, Bill Clinton.

Mayo, Charles Horace 1865–1939

US surgeon. An authority on the treatment of goitre, he co-founded the Mayo Clinic with his brother in 1905 within what is now St Mary's Hospital, Rochester.

97 The definition of a specialist as one who 'knows more and more about less and less' is good and true.
1939 In *Modern Hospital*, Sep.

Mazarin, Jules, Cardinal 1602–61

Neapolitan statesman. He entered Louis XIII's service in 1639, and succeeded Richelieu as Chief Minister (1642), becoming the lover of Anne of Austria. His domestic policy was problematic, but he negotiated the Peace of Westphalia (1648) and the Treaty of the Pyrenees (1659).

98 The French are nice people. I allow them to sing and to write, and they allow me to do whatever I like.
Attributed by the Duchess of Orléans in a letter dated 25 Oct 1715.

Mazzini, Giuseppe 1805–72

Italian patriot, a leader of the Risorgimento and founder of the revolutionary Young Italy Association. His underground journal, *La Giovine Italia*, fomented revolt throughout Europe.

99 Insurrection—by means of guerrilla bands—is the true method of warfare for all nations desirous of emancipating themselves from a foreign yoke.
1833 *General Instructions for the Members of Young Italy*, section 4.

1 I had thought to evoke the soul of Italy but all I find before me is its corpse.
Attributed. Quoted in Denis Mack Smith *Italy: A Modern History* (1959).

2 A nation is the universality of citizens speaking the same tongue.
In *La Giovine Italia* ('Young Italy').

Mead, Margaret 1901–78

US anthropologist. After expeditions to Samoa and New Guinea she wrote books on her experiences, arguing that personality characteristics are shaped by conditioning rather than heredity.

3 The greatest invention since the novel.
1974 Of television. Comment, 31 Dec.

Meat Loaf 1947–

US rock singer.

4 I don't have a rock voice. I have to force it. I am like an opera singer.
2003 In the *Observer*, 7 Dec.

Medawar, Sir Peter Brian 1915–87

British zoologist and immunologist, born in Rio de Janeiro.

Professor of Anatomy at University College London, he pioneered experiments in immunological toleration and skin and organ grafting, winning a Nobel prize with Sir Macfarlane Burnet in 1960.

5 I cannot give any scientist of any age better advice than this: the intensity of a conviction that a hypothesis is true has no bearing over whether it is true or not.
   1979 *Advice to a Young Scientist.*

6 A scientist soon discovers that he has become a member of the cast of 'them' in the context 'what mischief are they up to now?'
   1979 *Advice to a Young Scientist.*

7 Good scientists often possess old-fashioned virtues of the kind school teachers have always professed to despair of ever inculcating in us. These are: a sanguine temperament that expects to solve a problem; power of application and the kind of fortitude that keeps scientists erect in the face of much that might otherwise cast them down; and above all, persistence, a refusal bordering upon obstinacy to give in and admit defeat.
   1984 *The Limits of Science.*

Meijer, Frederik 1919–

US retail executive and Chairman Emeritus of Meijer Inc.

8 I am more poor than you think.
   On trying to secure a low profile. Quoted in *Forbes*, 19 Oct 1992.

Meilhac, Henri 1831–97

French playwright. From 1855 he produced a long series of light comedies, often in conjunction with Ludovic Halévy, with whom he also wrote the librettos for Offenbach's operettas and Bizet's *Carmen*.

9 *L'amour est un oiseau rebelle*
   Que nul ne peut apprivoiser.
   Love's a bird that will live in freedom
   That no man ever learned to tame.
   1875 The *Habañera. Carmen*, act 1.

10 *La fleur que tu m'avais jetée*
   Here is the flower that you threw me
   1875 *Carmen*, act 2, 'Flower Song' (Don José).

11 *Toreador, en garde!*
   1875 *Carmen*, act 2, 'Couplets' (Escamillo).

Meir, Golda 1898–1978

Israeli politician. She was elected Prime Minister in 1969, but her efforts for peace in the Middle East were halted by the fourth Arab–Israeli War (1973) and she resigned in 1974.

12 Those that perished in Hitler's gas chambers were the last Jews to die without standing up to defend themselves.
   1967 Speech in New York, 11 Jun.

13 Women's Liberation is just a lot of foolishness. It's the men who are discriminated against. They can't bear children. And no-one's likely to do anything about that.
   1972 In *Newsweek*, 23 Oct.

Melba, Dame Nellie *real name* **Helen Mitchell** 1861–1931

Australian soprano, who took her stage name from her native Melbourne. Notorious for her many 'farewell' performances, her earthy Australian character contrasted oddly with the graces she adopted in her stage persona.

14 What are you going to sing? All I can say is—sing 'em muck! It's all they can understand!
   c.1907 Advice to Dame Clara Butt on her first tour of Australia. Quoted in Winifred Ponder *Clara Butt: Her Life-Story* (1928).

15 If you wish to understand me at all (and to write an autobiography is only to open a window into one's heart) you must understand first and foremost, that I am an Australian… I shall always come back to rest in the shadow of the blue mountains, in the heart of this vast, deserted continent which gave me birth.
   1925 *Melodies and Memories*, ch.1.

16 The first rule in opera is the first rule in life: see to everything yourself.
   1925 *Melodies and Memories.*

17 If I'd been a housemaid I'd have been the best in Australia—I couldn't help it. It's got to be perfection for me.
   Said to the conductor Fritz Hart. Quoted in John Thompson *On Lips of Living Men* (1962).

Melbourne, William Lamb, 2nd Viscount 1779–1848

English statesman, Chief Secretary for Ireland (1827–8), Home Secretary (1830–4), and Whig Prime Minister (1834, 1835–41), a confidante of the young Queen Victoria. Defeated in the election of 1841, he resigned and thereafter took little part in public affairs.

18 I wish that I was as cocksure of anything as Tom Macaulay is of everything.
   1889 Attributed by Earl Cowper.

Melchett, Peter Robert Henry Mond, Baron 1948–

English Labour peer, executive director of Greenpeace UK (1989–2000).

19 The menu could not guarantee GM-free food but I ate vegetarian shepherd's pie.
   1999 After spending two days in prison for leading a raid to destroy GM crops. In the *Sunday Times*, 'Talking Heads', 1 Aug.

Mellor, D H 1938–

British Emeritus Professor of Philosophy at Cambridge University. He has written several books on philosophy.

20 Appeals to rationality are mostly bluff. There is no good theory of what it is nor of how to recognize it.
   1983 'Objective Decision Making', in *Social Theory and Practice*, Summer–Fall.

Melly, George 1926–

English jazz singer.

21 Jazz is an impure art. There's a great deal of romantic nostalgia involved.
   1965 *Owning Up*, ch.2.

Melville, Andrew 1545–c.1622

Scottish religious and educational reformer, consolidating the Presbyterianism of the reformed Church of Scotland, and a fierce critic of royal authority where it impinged on that of the Kirk. In 1596 he headed a deputation to 'remonstrate' with James VI.

22 God's silly vassal.

> **1596** Said of (and to) King James VI, as reported in his nephew James Melville's *Diary*: 'Mr Andrew bore him down and uttered the commission as from the mighty God, calling him but "God's silly vassal".'

Melville, Herman 1819–91

US novelist. Between 1839 and 1844 he spent time at sea, working as a cabin-boy and on whaling ships. His experiences gave him material for many of his best-known books, including *Typee* (1846) and his masterpiece, *Moby Dick* (1851).

23 We may have civilized bodies and yet barbarous souls.

> **1849** *Redburn*, ch.58.

24 Toil is man's allotment; toil of brain, or toil of hands, or a grief that's more than either, the grief and sin of idleness.

> **1849** *Mardi*, ch.63.

25 Call me Ishmael.

> **1851** *Moby Dick*, ch.1, opening words.

26 Better sleep with a sober cannibal than a drunken Christian.

> **1851** *Moby Dick*, ch.3.

27 Faith, like a jackal, feeds among the tombs, and even from these dead doubts she gathers her most vital hope.

> **1851** *Moby Dick*, ch.7.

28 A whale ship was my Yale College and my Harvard.

> **1851** *Moby Dick*, ch.24.

29 Old age is always wakeful; as if, the longer linked with life, the less man has to do with aught that looks like death.

> **1851** *Moby Dick*, ch.29.

30 All visible objects, man, are but as pasteboard masks. But in each event—in the living act, the undoubted deed—there, some unknown but still reasoning thing puts forth the mouldings of its features from behind the unreasoning mask. If man will strike, strike through the mask!

> **1851** Captain Ahab. *Moby Dick*, ch.36.

31 Though in many of its aspects this visible world seems formed in love, the invisible spheres were formed in fright.

> **1851** *Moby Dick*, ch.42.

32 It was the whiteness of the whale that above all things appalled me…for all these accumulated associations, with whatever is sweet, and honourable, and sublime, there yet lurks an elusive something in the innermost idea of this hue, which strikes more of a panic to the soul than that redness which affrights in blood.

> **1851** Ishmael. *Moby Dick*, ch.42.

33 It may seem strange that of all men sailors should be tinkering at their last wills and testaments, but there are no people in the world more fond of that diversion.

> **1851** *Moby Dick*, ch.49.

34 There is a wisdom that is woe; but there is a woe that is madness.

> **1851** *Moby Dick*, ch.96.

35 To produce a mighty book, you must choose a mighty theme. No great and enduring volume can ever be written on the flea, though many there be who have tried it.

> **1851** *Moby Dick*, ch.104.

36 For whatever is truly wonderous and fearful in man, never yet was put into words or books.

> **1851** *Moby Dick*, ch.110.

37 Come; let us squeeze hands all round; nay, let us all squeeze ourselves into each other; let us squeeze ourselves universally into the very milk and sperm of kindness.

> **1851** Ishmael. *Moby Dick*, ch.114.

38 Warmest climes but nurse the cruellest fangs: the tiger of Bengal crouches in spiced groves of ceaseless verdure.

> **1851** *Moby Dick*, ch.119.

39 Oh God! that man should be a thing for immortal souls to sieve through!

> **1851** Captain Ahab. *Moby Dick*, ch.125.

40 Let me look into a human eye; it is better than to gaze into sea or sky; better than to gaze upon God.

> **1851** Captain Ahab. *Moby Dick*, ch.132.

41 Guinea-coast slavery of solitary command!

> **1851** Captain Ahab. *Moby Dick*, ch.132.

42 He says NO! in thunder; but the Devil himself cannot make him say yes. For all men who say *yes*, lie; and all men who say *no*,—why, they are in the happy condition of judicious, unencumbered travellers in Europe; they cross the frontiers into Eternity with nothing but a carpet bag.

> **1851** Of Nathaniel Hawthorne.

43 The calm, the coolness, the silent grass-growing mood in which a man *ought* always to compose,—that, I fear, can seldom be mine. Dollars damn me; and the malicious Devil is forever grinning in upon me, holding the door ajar… What I feel most moved to write, that is banned,—it will not pay. So the product is a final hash, and all my books are botches.

> **1851** Letter to Nathaniel Hawthorne, Jun.

44 Why, ever since Adam, who has got to the meaning of this great allegory—the world? Then we pygmies must be content to have our paper allegories but ill comprehended.

> **1851** Letter to Nathaniel Hawthorne, Nov.

45 Nothing so aggravates an earnest person as a passive resistance.

> **1853** 'Bartleby the Scrivener', in *Putnam's Monthly Magazine*, Nov–Dec.

46 If some books are deemed most baneful and their sale forbid, how, then, with deadlier facts, not dreams of doting men? Those whom books will hurt will not be proof against events. Events, not books, should be forbid.

> **1854** 'The Encantadas, Sketch Eighth', in *Putnam's Monthly Magazine*, May.

47 Who in the rainbow can draw the line where the violet tint ends and the orange tint begins? Distinctly we see the difference of the colors, but where exactly does the one first blendingly enter into the other? So with sanity and insanity.

> **1891** *Billy Budd, Foretopman* (first published 1924), ch.21.

48 There is nothing nameable but that some men will, or undertake to, do it for pay.

> **1891** *Billy Budd, Foretopman* (first published 1924), ch.21.

Menander c.343–291 BC

Greek comic poet, born in Athens. He wrote more than 100

comedies, most of which are lost. Various fragments and one complete play (*Dyscolus*) have been rediscovered in recent times.

49 He whom the gods love dies young.
Dis Exapaton, fragment 4.

50 The man who runs away will fight again.
Fragment quoted in Aulus Gellius *Noctes Atticae*, 17.21.31 (translated by J C Rolfe, 1967).

Mencius *properly* Meng-tzu c.371–c.289 BC

Chinese philosopher and sage. He helped to develop and popularize Confucian ideas and founded a school to promote their study. His sayings were recorded by his pupils after his death, and included proposals for social and political reform.

51 If the king loves music, there is little wrong in the land.
3c BC *Discourses*.

Mencken, H(enry) L(ouis) 1880–1956

US journalist and critic. He wrote much literary and political criticism as editor of *The Smart Set* (1914–23) and co-founder and editor of the *American Mercury* (1924–33), and various essays were collected in *Prejudices* (6 vols, 1919–27). Other publications included autobiographical writings and *The American Language* (1919).

52 Democracy is the theory that the common people know what they want, and deserve to get it good and hard.
1916 *Little Book in C Major*.

53 Conscience: the inner voice which warns us that someone may be looking.
1916 *Little Book in C Major*.

54 I can't remember a single masculine figure created by a woman who is not, at bottom, a booby.
1918 *In Defence of Women*, ch.1, pt.1.

55 All successful newspapers are ceaselessly querulous and bellicose.
1919 *Prejudices*, 1st series, ch.13.

56 If, after I depart this vale, you ever remember me and have thought to please my ghost, forgive some sinner and wink your eye at some homely girl.
1921 In *The Smart Set*, Dec.

57 Poetry is a comforting piece of fiction set to more or less lascivious music.
1922 *Prejudices*, 3rd series, ch.7.

58 Faith may be defined briefly as an illogical belief in the occurrence of the improbable.
1922 *Prejudices*, 3rd series, ch.14.

59 The man who boasts that he habitually tells the truth is simply a man with no respect for it. It is not a thing to be thrown about loosely, like small change; it is something to be cherished and hoarded, and disbursed only when absolutely necessary.
1922 *Prejudices*, 3rd series, ch.14.

60 [Jeremy] Bentham held no post at the mercy of bankers and tripe sellers; he was a man of independent means, a lawyer and politician and a heretic in general practice. It is impossible to imagine such a man occupying a chair at Harvard or Princeton. He had a hand in too many pies; he was too rebellious and contumacious; he had too little respect for authority, either academic or worldly. Moreover, his mind was too wide for a professor; he

could never remain safely in a groove; the whole field of social organization invited his inquiries and experiments.
1922 'The Dismal Science', in *The Smart Set*, Jun.

61 Hygiene is the corruption of medicine by morality.
1922 *Prejudices*.

62 The opera…is to music what a bawdy house is to a cathedral.
1925 Letter to Isaac Goldberg.

63 No one in this world, so far as I know—and I have searched the record for years, and employed agents to help me—has ever lost money by underestimating the intelligence of the great masses of the plain people.
1926 'Notes on Journalism' in the *Chicago Sunday Tribune*, 19 Sep. The phrase is commonly quoted as 'No one ever went broke underestimating the intelligence of the American people.'

64 The saddest life is that of a political aspirant under democracy. His failure is ignominious and his success is disgraceful.
1929 In the *Baltimore Evening Sun*, 9 Dec.

65 Here, indeed, was his one peculiar Fach, his one really notable talent. He slept more than any other President, whether by day or night. Nero fiddled, but Coolidge only snored.
1933 Of Calvin Coolidge. In the *American Mercury*, Apr.

66 Roosevelt will probably go down into American history as a great hero. It is one of our Heavenly Father's characteristic jokes upon the American people, and in the usual bad taste.
1944 Journal entry. Collected in *The Diary of H. L. Mencken* (published 1990).

67 I've made it a rule never to drink by daylight and never to refuse a drink after dark.
1945 In the *New York Post*, 18 Sep.

68 When women kiss it always reminds one of prize-fighters shaking hands.
1949 *Chrestomathy*, ch.30.

69 Love is the delusion that one woman differs from another.
1949 *Chrestomathy*, ch.30.

70 Men have a much better time of it than women. For one thing, they marry later. For another thing, they die earlier.
1949 *Chrestomathy*, ch.30

71 Puritanism. The haunting fear that someone, somewhere, may be happy.
1949 Chrestomathy, ch.30.

72 He is a man who sits in the outer office of the White House hoping to hear the President sneeze.
Of the Vice-President. Recalled on his death, 29 Jan 1956.

73 Science, at bottom, is really anti-intellectual. It always distrusts pure reason, and demands the production of objective fact.
'Minority Report'. Collected in *Notebooks* (1956).

74 Some people read too much: the bibliobuli…who are constantly drunk on books, as other men are drunk on whiskey or religion. They wander through the most diverting and stimulating of worlds in a haze, seeing nothing and hearing nothing.
'Minority Report'. Collected in *Notebooks* (1956).

75 We must respect the other fellow's religion, but only in the sense and to the extent that we respect his theory that his wife is beautiful and his children smart.
'Minority Report'. Collected in *Notebooks* (1956).

76 Men always try to make virtues of their weaknesses. Fear of death and fear of life become piety.
'Minority Report'. Collected in *Notebooks* (1956).

77 It is now quite lawful for a Catholic woman to avoid pregnancy by a resort to mathematics, though she is still forbidden to resort to physics and chemistry.
'Minority Report'. Collected in *Notebooks* (1956).

78 The capacity of human beings to bore one another seems to be vastly greater than that of any other animals. Some of their most esteemed inventions have no other apparent purpose, for example, the dinner party of more than two, the epic poem, and the science of metaphysics.
'Minority Report'. Collected in *Notebooks* (1956).

79 Men are the only animals who devote themselves assiduously to making one another unhappy. It is, I suppose, one of their godlike qualities.
'Minority Report'. Collected in *Notebooks* (1956).

80 War will never cease until babies begin to come into the world with larger cerebrums and smaller adrenal glands.
'Minority Report'. Collected in *Notebooks* (1956).

81 Whenever one comes to close grips with so-called idealism, as in war time, one is shocked by its rascality.
'Minority Report'. Collected in *Notebooks* (1956).

82 I hate all sports as rabidly as a person who likes sports hates common sense.
Quoted in Fred Metcalfe *The Penguin Dictionary of Modern Humorous Quotations* (1986).

83 The greatest of all the contributions of the American way of life to the salvation of humanity.
Of the cocktail. Quoted by William Grimes in 'The American Cocktail', *Americana*, Dec 1992.

84 The varnishers and veneerers have been busily converting Abe into a plaster saint...to pump all his human weaknesses out of him, and so leave him a mere moral apparition, a sort of amalgam of John Wesley and the Holy Ghost.
Of popular perceptions of Abraham Lincoln. Quoted in Fred Hobson *Mencken: A Life* (1994).

85 His whole carcass seemed to be made of iron. There was no give in him—no bounce, no softness. He sailed through American history like a steel ship loaded with monoliths made of granite.
Of President Grover Cleveland. Quoted in Fred Hobson *Mencken: A Life* (1994).

86 A third-rate political wheel-horse, with the face of a moving-picture actor, the intelligence of a respectable agricultural implement dealer, and the imagination of a lodge joiner...a benign blank—a decent, harmless, laborious, hollow-headed mediocrity.
Of President Warren G Harding. Quoted in Fred Hobson *Mencken: A Life* (1994).

87 His English reminds me of tattered washing on the line...of stale bean-soup, of college yells, of dogs barking idiotically through endless nights. It is so bad that a sort of grandeur creeps into it.
Of President Warren G Harding. Quoted in Fred Hobson *Mencken: A Life* (1994).

88 He was, on his plane, as insufferable as a Methodist on his.
Of Oscar Wilde. Introduction to a new edition of Wilde *A House of Pomegranates*.

Menzies, Sir Robert Gordon 1894–1978

Australian statesman, Prime Minister (1939–41), Leader of the Opposition (1943–9) and thereafter Premier of the coalition government. He headed the Five Nations Committee which sought a settlement with Nasser on the question of Suez (1956).

89 What Great Britain calls the Far East is to us the near north.
1939 Quoted in the *Sydney Morning Herald*, 27 Apr. Menzies was one of the first Australian statesmen to recognize the importance to his country of Asia.

90 If I were the Archangel Gabriel, madam, I'm afraid you would not be in my constituency.
Attributed reply to a woman who had heckled him with the words 'I wouldn't vote for you if you were the Archangel Gabriel.' Quoted in Ray Robinson *The Wit of Robert Menzies* (1966).

Mercer, David 1928–80

English playwright. Such plays as *A Climate of Fear* (1962) and *In Two Minds* (1967) explored his fascination with mental health, psychiatry and his struggle to reconcile a belief in socialism with the repression revealed during his stays in Eastern Europe. Other writings included the films *Morgan* (1965) and *Providence* (1977) and several plays for television.

91 A Suitable Case for Treatment.
1962 Play title.

Mercer, Johnny 1909–76

US songwriter. His songs include 'Accentuate the Positive', 'Black Magic', 'In the Cool Cool of the Evening' and 'Something's Gotta Give'.

92 Hooray for Hollywood.
1937 Title of song which first appeared in the film *Hollywood Hotel*, performed by Johnny Davis and Frances Langford.

Meredith, George 1828–1909

English novelist and poet. He married the daughter of Thomas Love Peacock but she left him for the painter Henry Wallis, for whose *Death of Chatterton* Meredith was the model. His volumes of poetry include *Modern Love* (1862) and *Poems and Lyrics of the Joy of the Earth* (1883). His novels include *The Ordeal of Richard Feverel* (1859), *Evan Harrington* (1860) and *The Egoist* (1879).

93 Lovely are the curves of the white owl sweeping
Wavy in the dusk lit by one large star.
Lone on the fir-branch, his rattle-note unvaried,
Brooding o'er the gloom, spins the brown eve-jar.
1851 *Poems*, 'Love in the Valley', stanza 5. The poem was revised and republished in 1878.

94 Happy happy time, when the white star hovers
Low over dim fields fresh with blooming dew,
Near the face of dawn, that draws athwart the darkness,
Threading it with colour, like yewberries the yew.
1851 *Poems*, 'Love in the Valley', stanza 7. The poem was revised and republished in 1878.

95 I expect that Woman will be the last thing civilized by Man.
1859 *The Ordeal of Richard Feverel*, ch.1.

96 Away with systems! Away with a corrupt world! Let us breathe the air of the Enchanted island. Golden lie the meadows; golden run the streams; red gold is on the pine-stems. The sun's coming down to earth, and walks the fields and the waters. The sun is coming down to earth, and the fields and the waters shout to him golden shouts.
1859 *The Ordeal of Richard Feverel*, ch.19.

97 Kissing don't last: cookery do!
1859 *The Ordeal of Richard Feverel*, ch.28.

98 Speech is the small change of silence.
1859 *The Ordeal of Richard Feverel*, ch.34.

99 It became known that death had taken Mr Melchisedec Harrington, and struck one off the list of living tailors.
1860 *Evan Harrington*, ch.1.

1 He fainted on his vengefulness, and strove
To ape the magnanimity of love.
1862 *Modern Love*, 2.

2 O have a care of natures that are mute!
1862 *Modern Love*, 35.

3 Much benevolence of the passive order may be traced to a disinclination to inflict pain upon oneself.
1866 *Vittoria*, ch.24.

4 A dainty rogue in porcelain.
1879 *The Egoist*, ch.5

5 Cynicism is intellectual dandyism.
1879 *The Egoist*, ch.7.

6 'But do care a bit for flattery, my lady,' said De Craye. ''Tis the finest of the Arts; we might call it moral sculpture. Adepts in it can cut their friends to any shape they like.'
1879 De Craye to Lady Busshe. *The Egoist*, ch.36.

7 Enter these enchanted woods,
You who dare.
1883 *Poems and Lyrics of the Joy of Earth*, 'The Woods of Westermain'.

8 Soaring through wider zones that pricked his scars
With memory of the old revolt from Awe,
He reached the middle height, and at the stars,
Which are the brain of heaven, he looked, and sank.
Around the ancient track marched, rank on rank,
The army of unalterable law.
1883 *Poems and Lyrics of the Joy of Earth*, 'Lucifer in Starlight'.

9 For singing till his heaven fills
'Tis love of earth that he instils,
And ever winging up and up,
Our valley is his golden cup,
And he the wine which overflows.
1883 *Poems and Lyrics of the Joy of Earth*, 'The Lark Ascending'.

10 'Tis Ireland gives England her soldiers, her generals too.
1885 *Diana of the Crossways*, ch.2.

11 Affairs of the world he could treat competently; he had a head for high politics and the management of men; the feminine half of the world was a confusion and a vexation to his intelligence, characterless; and one woman at last appearing decipherable, he fancied it must be owing to her possession of character, a thing prized the more in women because of his latent doubt of its existence.
1885 Percy Dacier's opinion of Diana. *Diana of the Crossways*, ch.28.

12 A wind sways in the pines,

And below
Not a breath of wild air;
Still as the mosses that glow
On the flooring and over the lines
Of the roots here and there.
The pine tree drops its dead;
They are quiet, as under the sea.
Overhead, overhead
Rushes life in a race,
As the clouds the clouds chase;
And we go,
And we drop like the fruits of the tree,
Even we,
Even so.
1888 *A Reading of Earth*, 'Dirge in the Woods'.

Mérimée, Prosper 1803–70

French novelist, Inspector-General of Historical Remains in France (1833) and a Senator (1853). He wrote many short stories and novels, including *Colomba* (1841) and *Carmen* (1847), as well as archaeological and historical dissertations and travel stories.

13 A colossal bore… I feel I could write something like it tomorrow, if my cat inspired me by walking over the piano.
1861 Of Wagner's opera *Tannhäuser*, after the disastrous première of its revised version at the Paris Opéra, 13 Mar. Quoted in Joanna Richardson *La Vie Parisienne* (1971), p.262.
➤ See Gounod 365:26.

Merman, Ethel *stage-name of* *Ethel Agnes Zimmermann* 1909–84

US singer and actress. Nicknamed 'The Golden Foghorn' because of her powerful singing voice, she established her reputation in cabaret and subsequently starred in such musicals as *Annie Get Your Gun* (1946) and *Hello, Dolly!* (1970).

14 She's OK, if you like talent.
1958 Of Mary Martin. In *Theater Arts*, Sep.

15 Can you imagine the name Zimmermann in bright lights? It would burn you to death!
Explaining why she took a stage-name. Attributed.

Merrifield, D(udley) Bruce 1921–

US former government official and Professor Emeritus of the Wharton Business School. He was Assistant Secretary of Commerce in the Reagan administration.

16 Innovate, automate—or evaporate!
1987 Address at London's Guildhall to Britain's senior industrialists and bankers. Reported in *The Times*, 19 Feb.

Merrill, James Ingram 1926–95

US poet, the 'ouija poet', whose interest in the occult led him to use a ouija board to communicate with the spirit world. The experience is recorded in an epic poem, *The Changing Light at Sandover* (1982, rev 1992). His collections include *Nights and Days* (1966) and *Divine Comedies* (1976, Pulitzer Prize), and he also wrote plays and novels.

17 Here one is in Later Life, and it's perfectly pleasant really, not for a moment that garden of cactus and sour grapes I'd always assumed it *must* be.
1972 Letter to a friend at age 46.

18 What one wants in this world isn't so much to 'live' as to…*be* lived, to be used by life for its own purposes.
Quoted in the *New Yorker*, 27 Mar 1995.

Merrin, Edward H

Antiquities dealer.

19 The price was quite reasonable. It just happened to be a lot of money.
1989 In the *New York Times*, 16 Jul. On paying $2.09 million for a nine-inch, 5,000-year-old Greek head.

Merton, Paul 1957–

English comedian.

20 They say the closer you sit to the stage, the better chance you have of winning. Angus Deayton is sitting in Row G—at the Theatre Royal, Drury Lane.
2003 At the BAFTA television awards night at the London Palladium—assessing his fellow TV presenter's chances, 13 Apr.

21 I don't consider myself a fashion victim. I consider fashion a victim of me.
2003 In the *Daily Telegraph*, 21 Apr.

Merton, Robert King 1910–2003

US sociologist, Columbia University (1941–2003). He was awarded the National Medal of Science in 1994.

22 The self-fulfilling prophecy is, in the beginning, a *false* definition of the situation evoking a new behavior which makes the originally false conception come *true*. The specious validity of the self-fulfilling prophecy perpetuates a reign of error.
1948 'The Self-Fulfilling Prophecy', in *Social Theory and Social Structure* (rev. edn, 1968), p.477. This is the first use of the phrase 'self-fulfilling prophecy'.

23 It would be a curious reading of the history of thought to suggest that the absence of disagreement testifies to a developing discipline.
1961 Defending internal disputes among sociologists. 'Now the Case for Sociology', in the *New York Times Magazine*, 16 Jul.

24 The sociologists of knowledge have been among those raising high the banner which reads: 'We don't know if what we say is true, but it is at least significant.' The sociologists and psychologists engaged in the study of public opinion and mass communications are most often found in the opposed camp of the empiricists… 'We don't know that what we say is particularly significant, but it is at least true.'
1968 *Social Theory and Social Structure* (rev. edn), pt.3, introduction.

Merwin, W(illiam) S(tanley) 1927–

US poet. His poetry includes *A Mask for Janus* (1952), *The Carrier of Ladders* (1970, Pulitzer Prize), *Opening the Hand* (1983) and *The River Sound* (1999). He is also a translator, notably of *The Cid* (1959).

25 The thing that makes poetry different from all of the other arts…[is] you're using language, which is what you use for everything else—telling lies and selling socks, advertising, and conducting law. Whereas we don't write little concerts or paint little pictures.

1994 On receiving the $100,000 Tanning Prize for Poetry. In the *Washington Post*, 30 Sep.

Metternich, Prince Clemens Lothar Wenzel
1773–1859

Austrian statesman, Foreign Minister from 1809. He was a powerful influence for conservatism in Europe, contributing to the tension that produced the upheavals of 1848 and popular rebellions in many countries.

26 When Paris sneezes, Europe catches cold.
1830 Letter, 26 Jan.

27 Italy is a geographical expression.
1847 Letter, 6 Aug.

28 I have been a rock of order.
1859 Attributed, shortly before his death. Quoted in Andrew Milne *Metternich* (1975).

29 Error has never approached my spirit.
Said to Guizot on the steps of the British Museum. Quoted in A J P Taylor *From the Boer War to the Cold War: Essays on Twentieth-Century Europe* (1995).

Meyer, Karl Ernest 1928–

US journalist and author, formerly of the *Washington Post* and the *New York Times*.

30 Whatever his private behavior, the man and his work existed in different realms. Mencken's defects were commonplace; his virtues were not. So wonderfully uninhibited was his style that even a single sentence in a routine article proclaimed its begetter.
1994 Of H L Mencken. In the *New York Times Book Review*, 8 May.

Michael, George *originally* *Georgios Kyriacos Panayiotou*
1963–

English pop singer and songwriter.

31 I have never felt any ethnic connection between the Greeks and me other than how hairy I am.
2004 In *Scotland on Sunday*, 14 Mar.

Michelangelo *full name* *Michelangelo Buonarroti*
1475–1564

Italian painter, sculptor, architect, draughtsman and poet. Born near Florence, he is one of the most important figures of the Italian Renaissance.

32 I've finished that chapel I was painting. The Pope is quite satisfied.
1512 Letter written to his father after 18 months of painting the vault of the Sistine Chapel, quoted in Robert J Clements (ed) *Michelangelo: A Self-Portrait* (1968).

33 Nothing the greatest artist can conceive
That every marble block doth not confine
Within itself; and only its design
The hand that follows intellect can achieve.
c.1538 Quoted in Robert J Clements (ed) *Michelangelo: A Self-Portrait* (1968).

34 Your Lordship sends to tell me that I should paint and have no doubts. I answer that painting is done with the brain, not the hands.
1542 Letter written to a Cardinal, Oct, collected in Creighton Gilbert (ed and trans) *Complete Poems and Selected Letters of Michelangelo* (1963).

35 I have only too much of a wife in this art of mine, who has

always kept me in tribulation, and my children shall be
the works I leave, which, even if they are naught, will live
a while.

In response to a priest and friend who had said it was a pity he
had not married and had children to whom he could leave his
works. Attributed in Giorgio Vasari *Lives of the Artists* (1568).

36 They are so beautiful that they would grace the entrance
to Paradise.

Of Ghiberti's doors for the Florence Baptistery. Quoted in
Giorgio Vasari *Lives of the Artists* (1568).

37 In my opinion painting should be considered excellent in
proportion as it approaches the effect of relief, while
relief should be considered bad in proportion as it
approaches the effect of painting.

Quoted in Robert J Clements (ed) *Michelangelo: A Self-Portrait*
(1968).

Middleton, Thomas　c.1570–1627

English dramatist, who collaborated with Dekker, Webster,
Rowley, Massinger, Beaumont and Fletcher and probably
Shakespeare. His works include *A Mad World, My Masters*
(1608), *Women Beware Women* (1620–7) and *A Chaste Maid in
Cheapside* (published 1630). He also wrote pageants and
masques for the city of London.

38 But you are dull, nothing comes nimbly from you; you
dance like a plumber's daughter and deserve two
thousand pound in lead to your marriage, and not in
goldsmith's ware.

1613 *A Chaste Maid in Cheapside* (published 1630), act 1, sc.1.

39 Lie soft, sleep hard, drink wine, and eat good cheer.

1613 *A Chaste Maid in Cheapside* (published 1630), act 1, sc.1.

40 Nay, good sir, be not so violent; with speed
I cannot render satisfaction
Unto the dear companion of my soul,
Virginity, whom I thus long have lived with,
And part with it so rude and suddenly.
Can such friends divide, never to meet again,
Without a solemn farewell?

1622 *The Changeling* (with William Rowley), act 1, sc.1.

41 Our eyes are sentinels unto our judgements
And should give certain judgement what they see;
But they are rash sometimes and tell us wonders
Of common things, which when our judgements find,
They can then check the eyes and call them blind.

1622 *The Changeling* (with William Rowley), act 1, sc.1.

42 Now I know
She had rather wear my pelt tanned in a pair
Of dancing pumps.

1622 *The Changeling* (with William Rowley), act 1, sc.1.

43 There's scarce a thing but is both loved and loathed.

1622 *The Changeling* (with William Rowley), act 1, sc.1.

44 I shall run mad with joy.

1622 *The Changeling* (with William Rowley), act 2, sc.2.

45 I'm up to the chin in heaven.

1622 *The Changeling* (with William Rowley), act 2, sc.2.

46 Paper blushes not.

1622 *The Changeling* (with William Rowley), act 3, sc.4.

47 Y'are the deed's creature.

1622 *The Changeling* (with William Rowley), act 3, sc.4.

48 Beneath the stars, upon yon meteor
Ever hung my fate, 'mongst things corruptible;

I ne'er could pluck it from him. My loathing
Was prophet to the rest, but ne'er believed.

1622 *The Changeling* (with William Rowley), act 5, sc.3.

Midler, Bette　1945–

US comedienne, singer and actress, whose bawdy nightclub act
led to a successful career on Broadway and then in films.

49 There comes a time when you have to let your clothes go
out in the world and try to make it on their own.

1987 On relinquishing the mermaid costume she wore in the
1970s film *Clams on the Half Shell*. In *People*, 31 Aug.

Mies van der Rohe, Ludwig　1886–1969

German-born US architect and furniture designer, a pioneer of
glass skyscrapers. He was director of the Bauhaus in Dessau
(1930–3) and emigrated to the US in 1937.

50 Architecture is the will of the age conceived in spatial
terms.

1922 *De Stijl*, vol.6.

Mikes, George　1912–87

Hungarian-born writer who wrote humorous books about his
experience of being a foreigner in England.

51 On the Continent people have good food; in England
people have good table manners.

1946 *How to Be an Alien*.

52 Many continentals think life is a game, the English think
cricket is a game.

1946 *How to be an Alien*.

Milestone, Lewis　*pseudonym of* **Levis Milstein**　1895–1980

US film director, best known for *All Quiet on the Western Front*
(1930), which won an Academy Award.

53 I've got your happy ending. We'll let the Germans win the
war.

c.1929 Response when asked to provide an upbeat ending for *All
Quiet on the Western Front*.

Milius, John　1944–

US screenwriter and director. His writing credits include *The
Life and Times of Judge Roy Bean* (1973), *Magnum Force* (1973),
Apolcalyse Now (co-writer, 1979) and *The Wind and the Lion*
(1975) which he also directed.

54 I know the law since I have spent my entire life in its
flagrant disregard.

1972 *The Life and Times of Judge Roy Bean*.

Mill, James　1773–1836

Scottish philosopher, historian and economist. He was a friend
of Jeremy Bentham and an enthusiastic proponent of
Utilitarianism.

55 The government and the people are under a moral
necessity of acting together; a free press compels them
to bend to one another.

1811 In the *Edinburgh Review*, May – Aug.

Mill, John Stuart　1806–73

English empiricist philosopher, MP (1863–8) and reformer, a
supporter of women's suffrage (*Subjection of Women*, 1869) and
liberalism. His works include *System of Logic* (1843), *Principles*

of Political Economy (1848), On Liberty (1859) and Utilitarianism (1863).

56 Unlike the Laws of Production, those of Distribution are partly of human institution, since the manner in which wealth is distributed in any given society, depends on the statutes or usages therein obtaining.
1848 *Principles of Political Economy, with Some Applications to Social Philosophy.*

57 A stationary condition of capital and population implies no stationary state of human improvement. There could be as much scope as ever for all kinds of mental culture, and moral and social progress.
1848 *Principles of Political Economy, with Some Applications to Social Philosophy.*

58 Happily, there is nothing in the laws of value which remains for the present or any future writer to clear up; the theory of the subject is complete.
1848 *Principles of Political Economy, with Some Applications to Social Philosophy.*

59 I am not charmed with the ideal of life held out by those who think that the normal state of human beings is that of struggling to get on. I know not why it should be a matter of congratulation that persons who are already richer than any one needs to be, should have doubled their means of consuming things which give little or no pleasure except as representative of wealth.
1848 *Principles of Political Economy, with Some Applications to Social Philosophy.*

60 The average condition of the people improving or deteriorating, depends upon whether population is advancing faster than improvement, or improvement than population.
1848 *Principles of Political Economy, with Some Applications to Social Philosophy.*

61 That the whole or any part of the education of the people should be in State hands, I go so far as anyone in deprecating… A general State education is a mere contrivance for molding people to be exactly like one another.
1856 *Utilitarianism, Liberty and Representative Government.*

62 The only purpose for which power can be rightfully exercised over any member of a civilized community, against his will, is to prevent harm to others.
1859 *On Liberty.*

63 A party of order or stability, and a party of progress or reform, are both necessary elements of a healthy state of political life.
1859 *On Liberty.*

64 Everyone who receives the protection of society owes a return for the benefit, and the fact of living in a society renders it indispensable that each should be bound to observe a certain line of conduct towards the rest. That conduct consists…in each person bearing his share of the labours and sacrifices incurred for defending the society or its members from injury and molestation.
1859 *On Liberty.*

65 If all mankind minus one were of one opinion, and only one person were of the contrary opinion, mankind would no more be justified in silencing that one person than he, if he had the power, would be justified in silencing mankind.
1859 *On Liberty.*

66 If the roads, the railways, the banks, the insurance offices, the great joint-stock companies, the universities, and the public charities, were all of them branches of government; if, in addition, the municipal corporations and local boards, with all that now devolves on them, became departments of the central administration; if the employees of all these different enterprises were appointed and paid by the government, and looked to the government for every rise in life; not all the freedom of the press and popular constitution of the legislature would make this or any other country free otherwise than in name.
1859 *On Liberty.*

67 The Conservatives, as being by the law of their existence the stupidest party.
1861 *Considerations on Representative Government*, ch.7, note.

68 The worth of the State, in the long run, is the worth of the individuals composing it.
1861 *Considerations on Representative Government.*

69 It is better to be a human being dissatisfied than a pig satisfied; better to be Socrates dissatisfied than a fool satisfied.
1863 *Utilitarianism*, ch.2.

70 The creed which accepts as the foundation of morals, Utility, or the Greatest Happiness Principle, holds that actions are right in proportion as they tend to promote happiness, wrong as they tend to produce the reverse of happiness.
1863 *Utilitarianism*, ch.2.

71 The sole evidence it is possible to produce that anything is desirable, is that people do actually desire it.
1863 *Utilitarianism*, ch.4.

72 If the universe had a beginning, its beginning, by the very condition of the cases, was supernatural; the laws of Nature cannot account for their own origin.
1865 *Auguste Comte and Positivism.*

73 It is always easy to find fault with a classification. There are a hundred ways of arranging any set of objects, and something may almost always be said against the best, and in favour of the worst of them. But the merits of a classification depend on the purposes to which it is instrumental.
1865 *Auguste Comte and Positivism.*

74 I never was a boy, never played at cricket; it is better to let Nature take her course.
1867 *Autobiography.*

75 It may be asserted without scruple, that no other class of dependants have had their character so entirely distorted from its natural proportions by their relations with their masters.
1869 *The Subjection of Women*, ch.1.

76 With equality of experience and of general faculties, a woman usually sees much more than a man of what is immediately before her.
1869 *The Subjection of Women*, ch.3.

77 Women cannot be expected to devote themselves to the emancipation of women, until men in considerable number are prepared to join with them in the undertaking.
1869 *The Subjection of Women*, ch.3.

78 Marriage is the only actual bondage known to our law. There remain no legal slaves, except the mistress of every house.
1869 *The Subjection of Women*, ch.4.

79 The self-worship of the monarch, or of the feudal superior, is matched by the self-worship of the male.
1869 *The Subjection of Women*, ch.4.

Millay, Edna St Vincent 1892–1950

US poet. Despite her contemporary subject matter, she was a formalist and her poems show a strong technical skill. Her collections include *The Harp-Weaver* (1923), which won a Pulitzer Prize.

80 World, world, I cannot get thee close enough!
Long have I known a glory in it all,
But never knew like this;
Here such a pattern is
As stretcheth me apart. Lord, I do fear
Thou'st made the world too beautiful this year:
My soul is all but out of me—let fall
No burning leaf; prithee, let no bird call.
1917 *God's World.*

81 My candle burns at both ends;
It will not last the night;
But ah, my foes, and oh, my friends—
It gives a lovely light.
1920 *A Few Figs From Thistles*, 'First Fig'.

82 Safe upon solid rock the ugly houses stand:
Come and see my shining palace built upon the sand.
1920 *A Few Figs From Thistles*, 'Second Fig'.

83 Death devours all lovely things;
Lesbia with her sparrow
Shares the darkness—presently
Every bed is narrow.
1921 *Second April*, 'Passer Mortuus Est'.

84 After all, my erstwhile dear,
My no longer cherished,
Need we say it was not love,
Now that love is perished?
1921 *Second April*, 'Passer Mortuus Est'.

85 What lips my lips have kissed, and where, and why,
I have forgotten, and what arms have lain
Under my head till morning; but the rain
Is full of ghosts tonight, that tap and sigh
Upon the glass and listen for reply
1923 *Harp-Weaver and Other Poems*, 'Sonnet 19: What lips my lips have kissed'.

86 Thus in the winter stands the lonely tree,
Nor knows what birds have vanished one by one,
Yet knows its boughs more silent than before
1923 *Harp-Weaver and Other Poems*, 'Sonnet 19: What lips my lips have kissed'.

87 I only know that summer sang in me
A little while, that in me sings no more.
1923 *Harp-Weaver and Other Poems*, 'Sonnet 19: What lips my lips have kissed'.

88 Euclid alone
Has looked on Beauty bare. Fortunate they
Who, though once only and then but far away,
Have heard her massive sandal set on stone.
1923 *Harp-Weaver and Other Poems*, 'Sonnet 22: Euclid alone

has looked on Beauty bare'.

89 Down, down, down into the darkness of the grave
Gently they go, the beautiful, the tender, the kind;
Quietly they go, the intelligent, the witty, the brave.
I know. But I do not approve. And I am not resigned.
1928 *The Buck in the Snow*, 'Dirge Without Music'.

90 It's not true that life is one damn thing after another—it's one damn thing over and over.
1930 Letter to Arthur Davison Ficke, 24 Oct.

91 Love is not all; it is not meat nor drink.
1931 *Fatal Interview*, title of poem.

92 Childhood is not from birth to a certain age and at a certain age
The child is grown, and puts away childish things.
Childhood is the kingdom where nobody dies.
Nobody that matters, that is.
1934 *Wine From These Grapes*, 'Childhood is the Kingdom where Nobody dies'.

Miller, Arthur 1915–

US playwright. *Death of a Salesman* (1949) won a Pulitzer Prize and established him as a leading contemporary playwright, dealing with the realities of family life. Subsequent plays have included *After the Fall* (1964), thought to have been inspired by his unhappy marriage to Marilyn Monroe.

93 A small man can be just as exhausted as a great man.
1949 Linda. *Death of a Salesman*, act 1.

94 Willie was a salesman. And for a salesman, there is no rock bottom to life… He's a man way out there in the blue, riding on a smile and a shoeshine. And when they start not smiling back—that's an earthquake.
1949 Charley. *Death of a Salesman*, 'Requiem'.

95 A salesman is got to dream, boy. It comes with the territory.
1949 Charley. *Death of a Salesman*, 'Requiem'.

96 They believed, in short, that they held in their steady hands the candle that would light the world. We have inherited this belief, and it has helped and hurt us.
1953 Of the settlers in Salem in 1692. *The Crucible*, act 1.

97 Spare me! You forget nothin' and forgive nothin'. Learn charity, woman. I have gone tiptoe in this house all seven month since she is gone. I have not moved from there to there without I think to please you, and still an everlasting funeral marches around your heart.
1953 Proctor to Elizabeth. *The Crucible*, act 2.

98 Theology, sir, is a fortress; no crack in a fortress may be accounted small.
1953 Hale. *The Crucible*, act 2.

99 Oh, no, the machine, the machine is necessary. A man comes into a great hotel and says, I am a messenger. Who is this man? He disappears walking, there is no noise, nothing. Maybe he will never come back, maybe he will never deliver the message. But a man who rides up on a great machine, this man is responsible, this man exists. He will be given messages.
1955 Rodolpho. *A View From the Bridge*, act 1.

1 A genuine invention in the realm of ideas must first emerge as an abstruse and even partial concept… At first blush a new idea appears to be very close to insanity because to be new it must reverse important basic beliefs and assumptions which, in turn, have been

institutionalized and are administered by one or another kind of priesthood with a vested interest in an old idea.
1958 *The Collected Plays*, 'Introduction, II'.

2 A good newspaper, I suppose, is a nation talking to itself.
1961 In the *Observer*, 26 Nov.

3 How few the days are that hold the mind in place; like a tapestry hanging on four or five hooks. Especially the day you stop becoming; the day you merely are. I suppose it's when the principles dissolve, and instead of the general gray of what ought to be you begin to see what is… The word 'Now' is like a bomb through the window, and it ticks.
1964 Quentin. *After the Fall*, act 1.

4 A suicide kills two people, Maggie. That's what it's for.
1964 Quentin. *After the Fall*, act 2.

5 Part of knowing who we are is knowing we are not someone else. And Jew is only the name we give to that stranger, the agony we cannot feel, the death we look at like a cold abstraction. Each man has his Jew; it is the other.
1964 Leduc. *Incident at Vichy*, act 1.

6 The concentration camp is the final expression of human separateness and its ultimate consequence. It is organized abandonment.
1966 Interview in the *Paris Review*, Summer.

7 Success, instead of giving freedom of choice, becomes a way of life.
1966 Interview in the *Paris Review*, Summer.

8 [Plays that would] cut through time like a knife through a layer cake or a road through a mountain revealing its geologic layers.
1987 Describing the plays he always wished to write. *Timebends: A Life*.

9 Without alienation, there can be no politics.
1988 In *Marxism Today*, Jan.

10 I'm the end of the line; absurd and appalling as it may seem, serious New York theater has died in my lifetime.
1989 In *The Times*, 11 Jan.

11 Maybe all one can do is hope to end up with the right regrets.
1991 Tom. *The Ride Down Mount Morgan*, act 1.

12 Witch-hunts are always spooked by women's horrifying sexuality awakened by the superstud Devil.
1998 On President Clinton's relationship with Monica Lewinsky. In the *New York Times*, 15 Oct.

13 Mr Clinton, according to Toni Morrison, the Nobel prize-winning novelist, is our first black President, the first to come from the broken home, the alcoholic mother, the under-the-bridge shadows of our ranking system.
1998 In the *New York Times*, 15 Oct.

Miller, Henry Valentine 1891–1980

US novelist. An exile in Paris in the 1930s, he later returned to live in California. His novels, notorious for sexual explicitness, include *Tropic of Cancer* (1934) and *Tropic of Capricorn* (1939), both at one time banned in the US.

14 The wallpaper with which the men of science have covered the world of reality is falling to tatters.
1934 *The Tropic of Cancer*.

15 This is not a book in the ordinary sense of the word. No, this is a prolonged insult, a gob of spit in the face of Art, a kick in the pants to God, Man, Destiny, Time, Love, Beauty…what you will. I am going to sing for you, a little off-key perhaps, but I will sing.
1934 *Tropic of Cancer*.

16 Chaos is the score upon which reality is written.
1934 *Tropic of Cancer*.

17 Every man with a bellyful of the classics is an enemy of the human race.
1934 *Tropic of Cancer*.

18 We live in the mind, in ideas, in fragments.
1936 *Black Spring*, 'The Fourteenth Ward'.

19 There are passages of Ulysses which can be read only in the toilet—if one wants to extract the full flavour of their content.
1936 *Black Spring*, 'A Saturday Afternoon'.

20 The world is the mirror of myself dying.
1936 Black Spring, 'Third or Fourth Day of Spring'.

21 I see America as a black curse upon the world. I see a long night settling in and that mushroom which has poisoned the world withering at the roots.
1936 *Black Spring*, 'Third or Fourth Day of Spring'.

22 What does it matter how one comes by the truth so long as one pounces upon it and lives by it.
1939 *Tropic of Capricorn*.

23 The artist does not tinker with the universe; he recreates it out of his own experience and understanding of life.
1939 *The Cosmological Eye*, 'An Open Letter to Surrealists Everywhere'.

24 Example moves the world more than doctrine.
1939 *The Cosmological Eye*, 'An Open Letter to Surrealists Everywhere'.

25 Life has no other discipline to impose, if we would but realize it, than to accept life unquestioningly… Every moment is a golden one for him who has the vision to recognize it as such.
1940 *The World of Sex*.

26 Morally, spiritually, we are fettered. What have we achieved in mowing down mountain ranges, harnessing the energy of mighty rivers, or moving whole populations about like chess pieces, if we ourselves remain the same restless, miserable, frustrated creatures we were before. To call such activity progress is utter delusion.
1940 *The World of Sex*.

27 Until we do lose ourselves there is no hope of finding ourselves.
1940 *The World of Sex*.

28 All that matters is that the miraculous becomes the norm.
1940 *The World of Sex*.

29 Though I've never read a line of Homer I believe the Greek of today is essentially unchanged. If anything he is more Greek than he ever was.
1941 *The Colossus of Maroussi*, pt.1.

30 If men cease to believe that they will one day become gods then they will surely become worms.
1941 *The Colossus of Maroussi*, pt.3.

31 To live without killing is a thought which could electrify the world, if men were only capable of staying awake long enough to let the idea soak in.

1944 *Sunday After The War*, 'Reunion in Brooklyn'.

32 No man would set a word down on paper if he had the courage to live out what he believed in.
1945 *Sexus*, ch.1.

33 The world has *not* to be put in order: the world *is* order incarnate. It is for us to put ourselves in unison with this order.
1945 *Sexus*, ch.9.

34 The great joy of the artist is to become aware of a higher order of things, to recognize by the compulsive and spontaneous manipulation of his own impulses the resemblance between human creation and what is called 'divine' creation.
1945 *Sexus*, ch.9.

35 Imagination is the voice of daring. If there is anything Godlike about God it is that. He dared to imagine everything.
1945 *Sexus*, ch.14.

36 Nowhere have I encountered such a dull, monotonous fabric of life as here in America. Here boredom reaches its peak.
1945 *The Air-Conditioned Nightmare*, preface.

37 Man has demonstrated that he is master of everything—except his own nature.
1945 *The Air-Conditioned Nightmare*, 'With Edgar Varèse in the Gobi Desert'.

38 The world goes on because a few men in every generation believe in it utterly, accept it unquestioningly, underwrite it with their lives.
1945 *The Air-Conditioned Nightmare*, 'With Edgar Varèse in the Gobi Desert'.

39 Back of every creation, supporting it like an arch, is faith. Enthusiasm is nothing: it comes and goes. But if one *believes*, then miracles occur.
1945 *The Air-Conditioned Nightmare*, 'With Edgar Varèse in the Gobi Desert'.

40 The study of crime begins with the knowledge of oneself. All that you despise, all that you loathe, all that you reject, all that you condemn and seek to convert by punishment springs from you.
1945 *The Air-Conditioned Nightmare*, 'The Soul of Anaesthesia'.

41 Art is only a means to life, to the life more abundant. It is not in itself the life more abundant… In becoming an end it defeats itself.
1947 *The Wisdom of the Heart*, 'Reflections on Writing'.

42 I have always looked upon decay as being just as wonderful an expression of life as growth.
1947 *The Wisdom of the Heart*, 'Reflections on Writing'.

43 It is the creative nature of man which has refused to let him lapse back into that unconscious unity with life which characterizes the animal world from which he made his escape.
1947 *The Wisdom of the Heart*, 'Creative Death'.

44 The poem is the dream made flesh, in a two-fold sense: as work of art, and as life, which is a work of art.
1947 *The Wisdom of the Heart*, 'Creative Death'.

45 All growth is a leap in the dark, a spontaneous unpremeditated act without benefit of experience.
1947 *The Wisdom of the Heart*, 'The Absolute Collective'.

46 Life, as it is called, is for most of us one long postponement.
1947 *The Wisdom of the Heart*, 'The Enormous Womb'.

47 It is the American vice, the democratic disease which expresses its tyranny by reducing everything unique to the level of the herd.
1947 On democracy. *The Wisdom of the Heart*, 'Raimu'.

48 History is the myth, the true myth, of man's fall made manifest in time.
1949 *Plexus*, ch.12.

49 In this age, which believes that there is a short cut to everything, the greatest lesson to be learned is that the most difficult way is, in the long run, the easiest.
1951 *The Books in My Life*, preface.

50 Every genuine boy is a rebel and an anarch.
1951 *The Books in My Life*, ch.4.

51 Words divested of their magic are but dead hieroglyphs.
1951 *The Books in My Life*, ch.7.

52 If we are always arriving and departing, it is also true that we are eternally anchored. One's destination is never a place but rather a new way of looking at things.
1957 *Big Sur and the Oranges of Hieronymous Bosch*, 'The Oranges of the Millennium'.

53 We resist only what is inevitable.
1957 *Big Sur and the Oranges of Hieronymous Bosch*, 'Paradise Lost'.

54 Obscenity is a cleansing process, whereas pornography only adds to the murk.
1962 Interview in the *Paris Review*, Summer.

55 The word 'civilization' to my mind is coupled with death. When I use the word, I see civilization as a crippling, thwarting thing, a stultifying thing… Civilization is the arteriosclerosis of culture.
1962 Interview in the *Paris Review*, Summer.

56 The moment you praise a book too highly you waken a resistance in your listener.
1957 *The Books in My Life*.

57 One has to be a lowbrow, a bit of a murderer, to be a politician; ready and willing to see people sacrificed, slaughtered, for the sake of an idea—whether a good one or a bad one.
In Malcolm Crowley (ed) *Writers at Work* (1958).

Miller, Jonathan Wolfe 1934–

British stage and opera director and writer, trained as a doctor.

58 In fact, I'm not really a *Jew*. Just *Jew-ish*. Not the whole hog you know.
1960 *Beyond the Fringe*, 'Real Class'.

59 The human species is, to some extent, the result of mistakes which arrested our development and prevented us from assuming the somewhat unglamorous form of our primitive ancestors.
1977 *The Body in Question*.

60 I wasn't driven into medicine by a social conscience but by rampant curiosity.
1983 In the *Observer*, 5 Feb.

Miller, William 1810–72

Scottish poet, born in Glasgow, known as the 'Laureate of the Nursery' for his children's rhymes, of which only 'Willie Winkie' is now remembered.

61 Wee Willie Winkie rins through the toun,
Up stairs and doun stairs in his nicht-gown,
Tirling at the window, crying at the lock,
'Are the weans in their bed, for it's now ten o'clock?'
1841 'Willie Winkie', stanza 1.

Millett, Kate (Katherine) *née Murray* 1934–

US feminist critic, activist and sculptor. Her PhD thesis was published as *Sexual Politics* (1970). Other works include the autobiographical *Flying* (1974), *The Loony Bin Trip* (1991) and *Mother Millett* (2001).

62 Patriarchy's chief institution is the family. It is both a mirror of and a connection with the larger society; a patriarchal unit within a patriarchal whole.
1970 *Sexual Politics*, ch.2, 'Theory of Sexual Politics'.

63 Aren't women prudes if they don't and prostitutes if they do?
1975 Speech at the Women Writers' Conference, Los Angeles, 22 Mar.

Milligan, Spike 1918–2002

Irish humorist.

64 Money couldn't buy friends but you got a better class of enemy.
1963 *Puckoon*, ch.6.

65 I am not going to thank anybody—because I did it all myself.
1994 Acceptance speech after being awarded the British Comedy Award for Lifetime Achievement.

66 Dúirt mé leat go raibh mé breoite.
2002 Gaelic inscription on his gravestone at Winchelsea, East Sussex. English translation: I told you I was ill.

Millman, Dan 1946–

US writer, who was world trampoline champion before meeting a remarkable gas station attendant called Socrates. He now writes self-help books and runs courses helping athletes and others make the most of their potential.

67 There are no ordinary moments.
1980 *The Way of the Peaceful Warrior*.

Mills, C(harles) Wright 1916–62

US sociologist, a professor at Columbia University.

68 No social study that does not come back to the problems of biography, of history and of their intersections within a society has completed its intellectual journey.
1959 *The Sociological Imagination*, ch.1.

69 In so far as the family as an institution turns women into darling little slaves and men into their chief providers and unweaned dependents, the problem of a satisfactory marriage remains incapable of purely private solution.
1959 *The Sociological Imagination*, ch.1.

70 If everything is caused by innumerable 'factors,' then we had best be very careful in any practical actions we undertake. We must deal with many details, and so it is advisable to proceed to reform this little piece and see what happens, before we reform that little piece too.
1959 *The Sociological Imagination*, ch.4.

Mills, Irving 1884–1985

US jazz manager, music publisher and lyricist.

71 It don't mean a thing
If it ain't got that swing.
1932 Song (music by Duke Ellington).

Mills, Sir John Lewis Ernest Watts 1908–

English actor, known for his stiff-upper-lip heroes in such films as *In Which We Serve* (1942), *Scott of the Antarctic* (1948) and *The Colditz Story* (1954). He won an Academy Award for his role in *Ryan's Daughter* (1970).

72 I played the young Earl of Dudley and was beheaded in the third reel—not, in my opinion, a moment too soon.
1980 Of his role in the 1936 film *Tudor Rose*. *Up in the Clouds, Gentlemen Please*.

Milne, A(lan) A(lexander) 1882–1956

English writer. He was an editor at *Punch* and wrote comedies and light essays. His works for children, which he began writing for his son Christopher Robin, are *When We Were Very Young* (1924), *Winnie-the-Pooh* (1926), *Now We Are Six* (1927) and *The House at Pooh Corner* (1928).

73 It is impossible to win gracefully at chess. No man has yet said 'Mate!' in a voice which failed to sound to his opponent bitter, boastful and malicious.
1919 *Not That It Matters*.

74 They're changing guard at Buckingham Palace—
Christopher Robin went down with Alice.
Alice is marrying one of the guard.
'A soldier's life is terribly hard,'
Says Alice.
1924 *When We Were Very Young*, 'Buckingham Palace'.

75 Little Boy kneels at the foot of the bed,
Droops on the little hands, little gold head;
Hush! Hush! Whisper who dares!
Christopher Robin is saying his prayers.
1924 *When We Were Very Young*, 'Vespers'.

76 The King said
'Butter, eh?'
And bounced out of bed.
1924 *When We Were Very Young*, 'The King's Breakfast'.

77 I have just been thinking, and I have come to a very important decision. *These are the wrong sort of bees.*
1926 *Winnie-the-Pooh*, ch.1.

78 Would you read a Sustaining Book, such as would help and comfort a Wedged Bear in Great Tightness?
1926 Pooh, stuck in the entrance to Rabbit's house after eating too much honey. *Winnie-the-Pooh*, ch.2.

79 I am a Bear of Very Little Brain, and long words Bother me.
1926 *Winnie-the-Pooh*, ch.4.

80 'Help, help!' cried Piglet, 'a Heffalump, a Horrible Heffalump!' and he scampered off as hard as he could, still crying out, 'Help, help, a Herrible Hoffalump! Hoff, Hoff, a Hellible Horralump! Holl, Holl, a Hoffable Hellerump!'
1926 *Winnie-the-Pooh*, ch.5.

81 'I ought to say,' explained Pooh as they walked down to the shore of the island, 'that it isn't just an ordinary sort of boat. Sometimes it's a Boat, and sometimes it's more of

an Accident. It all depends.'
'Depends on what?'
'On whether I'm on the top of it or underneath it.'
1926 *Winnie-the-Pooh*, ch.9.

82 The more it
SNOWS-tiddely-pom,
The more it
GOES-tiddely-pom
The more it
GOES-tiddely-pom
On
Snowing.
1928 *The House at Pooh Corner*, ch.1.

83 'It's snowing still,' said Eeyore gloomily.
'So it is.'
'And freezing.'
'Is it?'
'Yes,' said Eeyore. 'However,' he said, brightening up a
little, 'we haven't had an earthquake lately.'
1928 *The House at Pooh Corner*, ch.1.

84 But whatever his weight in pounds, shillings, and ounces,
He always seems bigger because of the bounces.
1928 Pooh's song about Tigger. *The House at Pooh Corner*, ch.2.

85 I could spend a happy morning
Seeing Roo,
I could spend a happy morning
Being Pooh,
For it doesn't seem to matter,
If I don't get any fatter
(And I don't get any fatter),
What I do.
1928 *The House at Pooh Corner*, ch.4.

86 Then he dropped two in at once, and leant over the
bridge to see which of them would come out first; and
one of them did; but as they were both the same size, he
didn't know if it was the one which he wanted to win, or
the other one. So the next time he dropped one big one
and one little one, and the big one came out first, which
was what he had said it would do, and the little one came
out last, which was what he had said it would do, so he
had won twice… And that was the beginning of the
game called Poohsticks.
1928 *The House at Pooh Corner*, ch.6.

87 But what care I? It's the game that calls me—
Simply to be on the field of play;
How can it matter what fate befalls me,
With ten good fellows and one good day!
Quoted in Helen Exley *Cricket Quotations* (1992).

88 Golf is so popular simply because it is the best game in
the world at which to be bad.
Attributed.

Milner, Alfred, 1st Viscount Milner   1854–1925

English statesman. He held a succession of top administrative
posts, including High Commissioner for South Africa during the
Boer Wars, Secretary for War (1918–19) and Colonial Secretary
(1921). He recommended virtual independence for Egypt.

89 If we believe a thing to be bad, and if we have a right to
prevent it, it is our duty to try to prevent it and damn the
consequences.
1909 On the blocking by the Conservative majority in the House

of Lords of the Liberal Government's budget. Speech at Glasgow,
Nov.

Milosevic, Slobodan   1941–

Serbian politician. He became Presdient of Serbia in 1988. In
1996 he was re-elected amidst furious accusations of electoral
rigging and from 1998 onwards oversaw Serb military
incursions into the province of Kosovo. This led to NATO air
strikes and the establishment of a NATO-led peacekeeping
force in the province, forcing a Serb withdrawal. He was
defeated at the polls in 2000 by opposition candidate Vojislav
Kostunica. He was subsequently indicted for crimes against
humanity by the International Criminal Tribunal in the Hague
and arrested in 2001 to face trial.

90 Kosovo is not a part of Serbia. It is the very heart of
Serbia.
Quoted in Dusko Doder and Louise Branson *Milosevic: Portrait
of a Tyrant* (1999).

91 I'm the Ayatollah Khomeini of Serbia. The Serbs will
follow me no matter what!
Quoted in Dusko Doder and Louise Branson *Milosevic: Portrait
of a Tyrant* (1999).

Milton, John   1608–74

English poet and controversial pamphleteerist, official
apologist for the Commonwealth. Blind from 1652, he devoted
himself to poetry after the Restoration. His best-known work is
the religious epic *Paradise Lost* (1667), followed by *Paradise
Regained* and *Samson Agonistes* (both 1671).

92 This is the month, and this the happy morn
Wherein the son of Heaven's eternal King,
Of wedded maid and virgin mother born,
Our great redemption from above did bring.
1629 'On the Morning of Christ's Nativity', 'The Hymn', stanza 1.

93 It was the winter wild
While the Heaven born child
All meanly wrapped in the rude manger lies;
Nature in awe to him
Had doffed her gaudy trim
With her great Master so to sympathize;
It was no season then for her
To wanton with the sun, her lusty paramour.
1629 'On the Morning of Christ's Nativity', 'The Hymn', stanza 3.

94 But peaceful was the night
Wherein the Prince of Light
His reign of peace upon the earth began:
The winds, with wonder whist,
Smoothly the waters kissed,
Whispering new joys to the mild oceàn,
Who now hath quite forgot to rave,
While birds of calm sit brooding on the charmèd wave.
1629 'On the Morning of Christ's Nativity', 'The Hymn', stanza 3.

95 The stars with deep amaze
Stand fixed in steadfast gaze.
1629 'On the Morning of Christ's Nativity', 'The Hymn', stanza 6.

96 Nature that heard such sound
Beneath the hollow round
Of Cynthia's seat, the airy region thrilling,
Now was almost won
To think her part was done,
And that her reign had here its last fulfilling;
She knew such harmony alone

Could hold all heaven and earth in happier uniòn.
1629 'On the Morning of Christ's Nativity', 'The Hymn', stanza 10.

97 Ring out, ye crystal spheres,
Once bless our human ears
(If ye have power to touch our senses so),
And let your silver chime
Move in melodious time,
And let the bass of Heaven's deep organ blow;
And with your ninefold harmony
Make up full consort to th'angelic symphony.
1629 'On the Morning of Christ's Nativity', 'The Hymn', stanza 13.

98 For if such holy song
Enwrap our fancy long,
Time will run back, and fetch the age of gold,
And speckled vanity
Will sicken soon and die.
1629 'On the Morning of Christ's Nativity', 'The Hymn', stanza 14.

99 The oracles are dumb;
No voice or hideous hum
Runs through the archèd roof in words deceiving.
1629 'On the Morning of Christ's Nativity', 'The Hymn', stanza 19.

1 But see! the Virgin blessed
Hath laid her Babe to rest.
Time is our tedious song should here have ending.
1629 'On the Morning of Christ's Nativity', 'The Hymn', stanza 27.

2 What needs my Shakespeare for his honoured bones
The labour of an age in pilèd stones,
Or that his hallowed relics should be hid
Under a star-y-pointing pyramid?
Dear son of memory, great heir of fame,
What need'st thou such weak witness of thy name?
Thou in our wonder and astonishment
Hast built thyself a livelong monument.
1630 'On Shakespeare'.

3 And so sepùlchered in such pomp dost lie,
That kings for such a tomb would wish to die.
1630 'On Shakespeare'.

4 Hence loathèd Melancholy,
Of Cerberus and blackest midnight born,
In Stygian cave forlorn
'Mongst horrid shapes, and shrieks, and sights unholy,
Find out some uncouth cell,
Where brooding Darkness spreads his jealous wings,
And the night-raven sings.
c.1631 L'Allegro, opening lines.

5 The frolic wind that breathes the spring,
Zephyr with Aurora playing,
As he met her once a-Maying,
There on beds of violets blue,
And fresh-blown roses washed in dew,
Filled her with a daughter fair,
So buxom, blithe, and debonair.
c.1631 L'Allegro, l.18–24. The 'daughter fair' is Euphrosyne, or
Mirth, one of the Three Graces.

6 Come, and trip it as ye go
On the light fantastic toe.
c.1631 L'Allegro, l.33–4.

7 While the cock with lively din
Scatters the rear of darkness thin,
And to the stack or the barn door,
Stoutly struts his dames before.

c.1631 L'Allegro, l.49–52.

8 Straight mine eye hath caught new pleasures
Whilst the landscape round it measures,
Russet lawns and fallows grey,
Where the nibbling flocks do stray,
Mountains on whose barren breast
The labouring clouds do often rest;
Meadows trim with daisies pied,
Shallow brooks, and rivers wide.
c.1631 L'Allegro, l.69–76.

9 Then to the spicy nut-brown ale.
c.1631 L'Allegro, l.100.

10 Towered cities pleased us then,
And the busy hum of men,
Where throngs of knights and barons bold
In weeds of peace high triumphs hold,
With store of ladies, whose bright eyes
Rain influence, and judge the prize
Of wit or arms, while both contend
To win her grace, whom all commend.
c.1631 L'Allegro, l.117–24.

11 Such sights as youthful poets dream
On summer eves by haunted stream.
c.1631 L'Allegro, l.129–30.

12 Hence vain deluding Joys,
The brood of Folly without father bred,
How little you bestead,
Or fill the fixèd mind with all your toys;
Dwell in some idle brain,
And fancies fond with gaudy shapes possess,
As thick and numberless
As the gay motes that people the sunbeams.
c.1631 Il Penseroso, opening lines.

13 But hail thou Goddess sage and holy,
Hail, divinest Melancholy,
Whose saintly visage is too bright
To hit the sense of human sight,
And therefore to our weaker view
O'erlaid with black, staid Wisdom's hue.
c.1631 Il Penseroso, l.11–16.

14 There held in holy passion still,
Forget thyself to marble.
c.1631 Il Penseroso, l.37–8.

15 Sweet bird that shunn'st the noise of folly,
Most musical, most melancholy!
c.1631 Of the nightingale. Il Penseroso, l.61–2.

16 And missing thee, I walk unseen
On the dry smooth-shaven green,
To behold the wandering moon,
Riding near her highest noon,
Like one that had been led astray
Through the heaven's wide pathless way;
And oft as if her head she bowed,
Stooping through a fleecy cloud.
c.1631 Il Penseroso, l.65–72.

17 Where glowing embers through the room
Teach light to counterfeit a gloom,
Far from all resort of mirth.
Save the cricket on the hearth.
c.1631 Il Penseroso, l.79–82.

18 Or bid the soul of Orpheus sing

Such notes as, warbled to the string,
Drew iron tears down Pluto's cheek,
And made Hell grant what Love did seek.
c.1631 *Il Penseroso*, l.105–8.

19 Where more is meant than meets the ear.
c.1631 *Il Penseroso*, l.120.

20 Till civil-suited Morn appear,
Not tricked and frounced as she was wont
With the Attic boy to hunt,
But kerchiefed in a comely cloud.
c.1631 *Il Penseroso*, l.122–5.

21 There in close covert by some brook,
Where no profaner eye may look,
Hide me from day's garish eye,
While the bee with honied thigh,
That at her flowery work doth sing,
And the waters murmuring
And such consort as they keep,
Entice the dewy-feathered Sleep.
c.1631 *Il Penseroso*, l.139–46.

22 But let my due feet never fail
To walk the studious cloister's pale,
And love the high embowèd roof,
With antic pillars massy proof,
And storied windows richly dight
Casting a dim religious light.
c.1631 *Il Penseroso*, l.155–60.

23 And may at last my weary age
Find out the peaceful hermitage,
The hairy gown and mossy cell,
Where I may sit and rightly spell
Of every star that heaven doth shew,
And every herb that sips the dew,
Till old experience to attain
To something like prophetic strain.
c.1631 *Il Penseroso*, l.167–74.

24 Such sweet compulsion doth in music lie.
1633 *Arcades*.

25 Before the starry threshold of Jove's court
My mansion is, where those immortal shapes
Of bright aerial spirits live inspher'd
In regions mild of calm and serene air,
Above the smoke and stir of this dim spot,
Which men call earth.
1634 *Comus, A Mask*, opening lines.

26 All other parts remaining as they were,
And they, so perfect in their misery,
Not once perceive their foul disfigurement,
But boast themselves more comely than before
And all their friends, and native home forget
To roll with pleasure in a sensual sty.
1634 Of Odysseus's men changed to beasts by Circe. *Comus, A Mask*, l.72–7.

27 The star that bids the shepherd fold,
Now the top of heav'n doth hold,
And the gilded car of day,
His glowing axle doth allay
In the steep Atlantic stream.
1634 *Comus, A Mask*, l.93–7.

28 What hath night to do with sleep?
1634 *Comus, A Mask*, l.122.

29 Come, knit hands, and beat the ground,
In a light fantastic round.
1634 *Comus, A Mask*, l.143–4.

30 Thus I hurl
My dazzling spells into the spongy air.
1634 *Comus, A Mask*, l.153–4.

31 A thousand fantasies
Begin to throng into my memory
Of calling shapes, and beckoning shadows dire,
And airy tongues, that syllable men's names
On sands, and shores, and desert wildernesses.
1634 *Comus, A Mask*, l.204–8.

32 These thoughts may startle well, but not astound
The virtuous mind, that ever walks attended
By a strong siding champion conscience.
1634 *Comus, A Mask*, l.209–11.

33 Sweet Echo, sweetest nymph, that liv'st unseen
Within thy airy shell
By slow meander's margent green,
And in the violet-embroidered vale.
1634 *Comus, A Mask*, l.230–3.

34 How sweetly did they float upon the wings
Of silence, through the empty-vaulted night
At every fall smoothing the raven down
Of darkness till it smil'd.
1634 *Comus, A Mask*, l.248–51.

35 Virtue could see to do what Virtue would
By her own radiant light, though sun and moon
Were in the flat sea sunk. And Wisdom's self
Oft seeks to sweet retired solitude,
Where with her best nurse contemplation
She plumes her feathers, and lets grow her wings
That in the various bustle of resort
Were all too ruffl'd, and sometimes impair'd.
He that has light within his own clear breast
May sit i' the centre, and enjoy bright day,
But he that hides a dark soul, and foul thoughts
Benighted walks under the midday sun;
Himself is his own dungeon.
1634 *Comus, A Mask*, l.372–83.

36 Yet where an equal poise of hope and fear
Does arbitrate the event, my nature is
That I incline to hope, rather than fear,
And gladly banish squint suspicion.
1634 *Comus, A Mask*, l.410–13.

37 Of dire chimeras and enchanted isle
And rifted rocks whose entrance leads to Hell,—
For such there be, but unbelief is blind.
1634 *Comus, A Mask*, l.515–17.

38 A pleasing fit of melancholy.
1634 *Comus, A Mask*, l.545.

39 And filled the air with barbarous dissonance.
1634 *Comus, A Mask*, l.550.

40 I was all ear,
And took in strains that might create a soul.
Under the ribs of Death.
1634 *Comus, A Mask*, l.560–2.

41 Thou canst not touch the freedom of my mind
With all thy charms, although this corporal rind
Thou hast immanacl'd, while heav'n sees good.
1634 *Comus, A Mask*, l.663–5.

42 The unexempt condition
By which all mortal frailty must subsist,
Refreshment after toil, ease after pain.
1634 *Comus, A Mask*, l.684–6.

43 But now my task is smoothly done,
I can fly, or I can run
Quickly to the green earth's end,
Where the bow'd welkin slow doth bend,
And from thence can soar as soon
To the corners of the Moon.
1634 *Comus, A Mask*, l.1011–16.

44 Mortals that would follow me,
Love virtue, she alone is free,
She can teach ye how to climb
Higher than the sphery chime;
Or if virtue feeble were,
Heav'n itself would stoop to her.
1634 *Comus, A Mask*, l.1017–22.

45 Yet once more, O ye laurels, and once more
Ye myrtles brown, with ivy never-sere
I come to pluck your berries harsh and crude,
And with forc'd fingers rude,
Shatter your leaves before the mellowing year.
Bitter constraint, and sad occasion dear,
Compels me to disturb your season due
For Lycidas is dead, dead ere his prime
Young Lycidas, and hath not left his peer.
1637 *Lycidas*, opening lines.

46 For we were nursed upon the self-same hill,
Fed the same flock; by fountain, shade, and rill.
1637 *Lycidas*, l.23–4.

47 But O the heavy change, now thou art gone,
Now thou art gone, and never must return!
Thee shepherd, thee the woods, and desert caves,
With wild thyme and the gadding vine o'ergrown,
And all their echoes mourn.
1637 *Lycidas*, l.37–41.

48 Where were ye Nymphs when the remorseless deep
Clos'd o'er the head of your lov'd Lycidas?
1637 *Lycidas*, l.50–1.

49 Alas! What boots it with uncessant care
To tend the homely slighted Shepherd's trade,
And strictly meditate the thankless muse;
Were it not better done as others use,
To sport with Amaryllis in the shade,
Or with the tangles of Neaera's hair?
Fame is the spur that the clear spirit doth raise
(That last infirmity of noble mind)
To scorn delights, and live laborious days;
But the fair guerdon when we hope to find,
And think to burst out into sudden blaze,
Comes the blind Fury with th'abhorred shears,
And slits the thin-spun life.
1637 *Lycidas*, l.64–76.

50 Fame is no plant that grows on mortal soil.
1637 *Lycidas*, l.78.

51 Blind mouths! that scarce themselves know how to hold
A sheep-hook.
1637 *Lycidas*, l.119–20.

52 They are sped;
And when they list, their lean and flashy songs

Grate on their scrannel Pipes of wretched straw,
The hungry sheep look up, and are not fed,
But swollen with wind, and the rank mist they draw,
Rot inwardly, and foul contagion spread,
Besides what the grim wolf with privy paw
Daily devours apace, and nothing said,
But that two-handed engine at the door,
Stands ready to smite once, and smite no more.
1637 *Lycidas*, l.122–31.

53 Ye valleys low where the mild whispers use,
Of shades and wanton winds, and gushing brooks,
On whose fresh lap the swart star sparely looks,
Throw hither all your quaint enameled eyes,
That on the green turf such the honeyed showers,
And purple all the ground with vernal flowers.
1637 *Lycidas*, l.136–41.

54 Bring the rathe primrose that forsaken dies,
The tufted crow-toe, and pale gessamine,
The white pink, and the pansy freaked with jet,
The glowing violet,
The musk-rose, and the well attir'd woodbine,
With cowslips wan that hang the pensive head,
And every flower that sad embroidery wears:
Bid amaranthus all his beauty shed,
And daffadillies fill their cups with tears,
To strew the laureate hearse where Lycid lies.
1637 *Lycidas*, l.142–51. rathe = early.

55 For to interpose a little ease,
Let our frail thoughts dally with false surmise.
1637 *Lycidas*, l.152–3.

56 Look homeward Angel, now, and melt with ruth.
1637 *Lycidas*, l.163. The phrase was used by Thomas Clayton Wolfe for his 1929 novel, *Look Homeward Angel*.

57 Weep no more, woeful shepherds, weep no more,
For Lycidas your sorrow is not dead,
Sunk though he be beneath the watery floor,
So sinks the day-star in the ocean bed,
And yet anon repairs his drooping head,
And tricks his beams, and with new spangled ore,
Flames in the forehead of the morning sky:
So Lycidas sunk low, but mounted high,
Through the dear might of Him that walked the waves.
1637 *Lycidas*, l.165–73.

58 There entertain him all the saints above,
In solemn troops, and sweet societies
That sing, and singing in their glory move,
And wipe the tears for ever from his eyes.
1637 *Lycidas*, l.178–81.

59 At last he rose, and twitched his mantle blue:
Tomorrow to fresh woods, and pastures new.
1637 *Lycidas*, l.192–3.

60 This manner of writing wherein knowing myself inferior
to myself… I have the use, as I may account it, but of my
left hand.
1642 Of his use of prose. *The Reason of Church Government*,
bk.2, introduction, 'Plans and Projects'.

61 Beholding the bright countenance of truth in the quiet
and still air of delightful studies.
1642 *The Reason of Church Government*, bk.2, introduction,
'Plans and Projects'.

62 As good almost kill a man as kill a good book: who kills a man kills a reasonable creature, God's image; but he who destroys a good book, kills reason itself, kills the image of God, as it were in the eye.

1644 *Areopagitica: a speech for the liberty of unlicensed printing.*

63 Promiscuous reading is necessary to the constituting of human nature. The attempt to keep out evil doctrine by licensing is like the exploit of that gallant man who thought to keep out the crows by shutting the park gate.

1644 *Areopagitica: a speech for the liberty of unlicensed printing.*

64 A good book is the precious life-blood of a master spirit, embalmed and treasured up on purpose to a life beyond life.

1644 *Areopagitica: a speech for the liberty of unlicensed printing.*

65 It was from out the rind of one apple tasted, that the knowledge of good and evil, as two twins cleaving together, leaped forth into the world.

1644 *Areopagitica: a speech for the liberty of unlicensed printing.*

66 Where there is much to learn, there of necessity will be much arguing, much writing, many opinions; for opinion in good men is but knowledge in the making.

1644 *Areopagitica: a speech for the liberty of unlicensed printing.*

67 As therefore the state of man now is, what wisdom can there be to choose, what continence to forbear, without the knowledge of good and evil?

1644 *Areopagitica: a speech for the liberty of unlicensed printing.*

68 Give me the liberty to know, to utter, and to argue freely according to conscience, above all liberties.

1644 *Areopagitica: a speech for the liberty of unlicensed printing.*

69 And though all the winds of doctrine were let loose to play upon the earth, so Truth be in the field, we do injuriously by licensing and prohibiting to misdoubt her strength. Let her and Falsehood grapple; who ever knew Truth put to the worse in a free and open encounter?

1644 *Areopagitica: a speech for the liberty of unlicensed printing.*

70 I cannot praise a fugitive and cloistered virtue, unexercised and unbreathed, that never sallies out and sees her adversary, but slinks out of the race where that immortal garland is to be run for, not without dust and heat. Assuredly we bring not innocence into the world, we bring impurity much rather; that which purifies us is trial, and trial is by what is contrary.

1644 *Areopagitica: a speech for the liberty of unlicensed printing.*

71 For who knows not that Truth is strong next to the Almighty? She needs no policies, nor stratagems, nor licensings to make her victorious.

1644 *Areopagitica: a speech for the liberty of unlicensed printing.*

72 That virtue therefore which is but a youngling in the contemplation of evil, and knows not the utmost that vice promises to her followers, and rejects it, is but a blank virtue, not a pure; her whiteness is but an excremental whiteness.

1644 *Areopagitica: a speech for the liberty of unlicensed printing.*

73 Since therefore the knowledge and survey of vice is in this world so necessary to the constituting of human virtue, and the scanning of error to the confirmation of truth, how can we more safely, and with less danger, scout into the regions of sin and falsity than by reading all manner of tractates and hearing all manner of reason? And this is the benefit which may be had of books promiscuously read.

1644 *Areopagitica: a speech for the liberty of unlicensed printing.*

74 When God gave [Adam] reason, he gave him freedom to choose, for reason is but choosing; he had been else a mere artificial Adam.

1644 *Areopagitica: a speech for the liberty of unlicensed printing.*

75 Wherefore did he [God] create passions within us, pleasures round about us, but that these rightly tempered are the very ingredients of virtue?

1644 *Areopagitica: a speech for the liberty of unlicensed printing.*

76 They are not skilful considerers of human things, who imagine to remove sin by removing the matter of sin.

1644 *Areopagitica: a speech for the liberty of unlicensed printing.*

77 We ourselves esteem not of that obedience, or love, or gift, which is of force: God therefore let him free, set before him a provoking object, ever almost in his eyes; herein consisted his merit, herein the right of his reward, the praise of his abstinence.

1644 *Areopagitica: a speech for the liberty of unlicensed printing.*

78 Though ye take from a covetous man all his treasure, he has yet one jewel left: ye cannot bereave him of his covetousness.

1644 *Areopagitica: a speech for the liberty of unlicensed printing.*

79 Truth indeed came once into the world with her divine Master, and was a perfect shape most glorious to look on: but…a wicked race of deceivers…took the virgin Truth, hewed her lovely form into a thousand pieces, and scattered them to the four winds. From that time ever since, the sad friends of Truth, such as durst appear, imitating the careful search that Isis made for the mangled body of Osiris, went up and down gathering up limb by limb, still as they could find them. We have not yet found them all…nor ever shall do, till her Master's second coming; he shall bring together every joint and member, and shall mould them into an immortal feature of loveliness and perfection.

1644 *Areopagitica: a speech for the liberty of unlicensed printing.*

80 Lords and Commons of England, consider what nation it is whereof ye are, and whereof ye are the governors: a nation not slow and dull, but of a quick, ingenious, and piercing spirit, acute to invent, subtle and sinewy to discourse, not beneath the reach of any point the highest that human capacity can soar to.

1644 *Areopagitica: a speech for the liberty of unlicensed printing.*

81 God is decreeing to begin some new and great period in his Church, even to the reforming of Reformation itself. What does he then but reveal Himself to his servants, and as his manner is, first to his Englishmen?

1644 *Areopagitica: a speech for the liberty of unlicensed printing.*

82 Methinks I see in my mind a noble and puissant nation rousing herself like a strong man after sleep, and shaking her invincible locks: methinks I see her as an eagle mewing her mighty youth, and kindling her undazzled eyes at the full midday beam; purging and unscaling her long-abused sight at the fountain itself of heavenly radiance; while the whole noise of timorous birds, with those also that love the twilight, flutter about, amazed at what she means.

1644 *Areopagitica: a speech for the liberty of unlicensed printing.*

83 I did but prompt the age to quit their clogs
By the known rules of ancient liberty,
When strait a barbarous noise environs me
Of owls and cuckoos, asses, apes and dogs.

c.1646 'On the Detraction Which Follow'd Upon My Writing Certain Treatises'.

84 None can love freedom heartily, but good men; the rest love not freedom, but licence.
1648–9 *The Tenure of Kings and Magistrates.*

85 No man who knows aught, can be so stupid to deny that all men naturally were born free.
1648–9 *The Tenure of Kings and Magistrates.*

86 The power of kings and magistrates is nothing else but what is only derivative; transformed and committed to them in trust from the people to the common good of them all, in whom the power yet remains fundamentally, and cannot be taken from them without a violation of their natural birthright.
1648–9 *The Tenure of Kings and Magistrates.*

87 Yet much remains
To conquer still; peace hath her victories
No less renowned then war, new foes arise
Threatening to bind our souls with secular chains:
Help us to save free conscience from the paw
Of hireling wolves whose gospel is their maw.
1652 'To the Lord General Cromwell'.

88 When I consider how my light is spent,
E're half my days, in this dark world and wide,
And that one talent which is death to hide,
Lodg'd with me useless, though my soul more bent
To serve therewith my Maker, and present
My true account, least he returning chide,
Doth God exact day-labour, light denied,
I fondly ask; But patience to prevent
That murmur, soon replies, God doth not need
Either man's work or his own gifts, who best
Bear his mild yoke, they serve him best, his state
Is kingly. Thousands at his bidding speed
And post o'er land and ocean without rest:
They also serve who only stand and wait.
c.1652 *Sonnets*, no.16, 'When I Consider'.

89 Methought I saw my late espoused Saint
Brought to me like Alcestis from the grave,
c.1658 *Sonnets*, no.19, 'Methought I Saw'.

90 But O as to embrace me she enclin'd
I wak'd, she fled, and day brought back my night.
c.1658 *Sonnets*, no.19, 'Methought I Saw'.

91 Of man's first disobedience, and the fruit
Of that forbidden tree, whose mortal taste
Brought death into the world, and all our woe,
With loss of Eden, till one greater Man
Restore us, and regain the blissful seat.
1665 *Paradise Lost* (published 1667), bk.1, opening lines.

92 Things unattempted yet in prose or rhyme.
1665 *Paradise Lost* (published 1667), bk.1, l.15.

93 And chiefly thou O spirit, that does prefer
Before all temples th'upright heart and pure,
Instruct me, for thou know'st; thou from the first
Wast present, and with mighty wings outspread
Dove-like sat'st brooding on the vast abyss
And mad'st it pregnant: what in me is dark
Illumine, what is low raise and support;
That to the highth of this great argument
I may assert Eternal Providence,
And justify the ways of God to men.

1665 *Paradise Lost* (published 1667), bk.1, l.16–25.

94 Who first seduced them to that foul revolt?
1665 *Paradise Lost* (published 1667), bk.1, l.33.

95 Him the Almighty Power
Hurled headlong flaming from th'ethereal sky
With hideous ruin and combustion down
To bottomless perdition, there to dwell
In adamantine chains and penal fire.
1665 *Paradise Lost* (published 1667), bk.1, l.44–8.

96 Now the thought
Both of lost happiness and lasting pain
Torments him.
1665 Of Satan. *Paradise Lost* (published 1667), bk.1, l.54–6.

97 A dungeon horrible, on all sides round
As one great furnace flamed; yet from those flames
No light, but rather darkness visible
Served only to discover sights of woe,
Regions of sorrow, doleful shades, where peace
And rest can never dwell, hope never comes
That comes to all.
1665 Of Hell. *Paradise Lost* (published 1667), bk.1, l.61–7.

98 O how fall'n! how changed
From him, who in the happy realms of light
Clothed with transcendent brightness didst outshine
Myriads though bright.
1665 Of Satan. *Paradise Lost* (published 1667), bk.1, l.84–7.

99 United thoughts and counsels, equal hope
And hazard in the glorious enterprise.
1665 *Paradise Lost* (published 1667), bk.1, l.88–9.

1 What though the field be lost?
All is not lost; the unconquerable will,
And study of revenge, immortal hate,
And courage never to submit or yield.
1665 Satan addressing the fallen angels. *Paradise Lost* (published 1667), bk.1, l.105–8.

2 Vaunting aloud, but racked with deep despair.
1665 *Paradise Lost* (published 1667), bk.1, l.126.

3 To be weak is miserable
Doing or suffering, but of this be sure,
To do aught good never will be our task,
But ever to do ill our sole delight.
1665 *Paradise Lost* (published 1667), bk.1, l.157–60.

4 If then his providence
Out of our evil seek to bring forth good,
Our labour must be to pervert that end,
And out of good still to find means of evil.
1665 *Paradise Lost* (published 1667), bk.1, l.162–5.

5 What reinforcement we may gain from hope;
If not, what resolution from despair.
1665 *Paradise Lost* (published 1667), bk.1, l.190–1.

6 Forthwith upright he rears from off the pool
His mighty stature; on each hand the flames
Driv'n backward slope their pointing spires, and rolled
In billows, leave i' th' midst a horrid vale.
1665 Of Satan. *Paradise Lost* (published 1667), bk.1, l.221.

7 The mind is its own place, and in itself
Can make a heav'n of hell, a hell of heav'n.
1665 *Paradise Lost* (published 1667), bk.1, l.254–5.

8 Better to reign in hell, than serve in heav'n.
1665 Satan. *Paradise Lost* (published 1667), bk.1, l.263.

9 For Spirits when they please
Can either sex assume, or both; so soft
And uncompounded is their essence pure,
Not tied or manacled with joint or limb,
Nor founded on the brittle strength of bones,
Like cumbrous flesh; but in what shape they choose
Dilated or condensed, bright or obscure,
Can execute their airy purposes,
And works of love or enmity fulfil.
1665 *Paradise Lost* (published 1667), bk.1, l.423–31.

10 And when night
Darkens the streets, then wander forth the sons
Of Belial, flown with insolence and wine.
1665 *Paradise Lost* (published 1667), bk.1, l.500–2.

11 With high words, that bore
Semblance of worth, not substance, gently raised
Their fainting courage, and dispelled their fears.
1665 *Paradise Lost* (published 1667), bk.1, l.528–30.

12 A shout that tore hell's concave, and beyond
Frighted the reign of Chaos and old Night.
1665 *Paradise Lost* (published 1667), bk.1, l.542–3.

13 For who can yet believe, though after loss,
That all these puissant legions, whose exile
Hath emptied heav'n, shall fail to reascend
Self-raised, and repossess their native seat?
1665 *Paradise Lost* (published 1667), bk.1, l.631–4.

14 Who overcomes
By force, hath overcome but half his foe.
1665 *Paradise Lost* (published 1667), bk.1, l.648–9.

15 War then, war
Open or understood must be resolved.
1665 Satan. *Paradise Lost* (published 1667), bk.1, l.661–2.

16 Let none admire
That riches grow in hell; that soil may best
Deserve the precious bane.
1665 *Paradise Lost* (published 1667), bk.1, l.690–2.

17 Pandemonium, the high capital
Of Satan and his peers.
1665 *Paradise Lost* (published 1667), bk.1, l.756–7.

18 Satan exalted sat, by merit raised
To that bad eminence; and from despair
Thus high uplifted beyond hope.
1665 *Paradise Lost* (published 1667), bk.2, l.5–7.

19 Where there is then no good
For which to strive, no strife can grow up there
From faction; for none sure will claim in hell
Precédence, none, whose portion is so small
Of present pain, that with ambitious mind
Will covet more.
1665 Satan. *Paradise Lost* (published 1667), bk.2, l.30–5.

20 His trust was with the eternal to be deemed
Equal in strength, and rather than be less
Cared not to be at all; with that care lost
Went all his fear.
1665 Of Moloch. *Paradise Lost* (published 1667), bk.2, l.46–9.

21 He seemed
For dignity composed and high exploit:
But all was false and hollow; though his tongue
Dropped manna, and could make the worse appear
The better reason.
1665 Of Belial. *Paradise Lost* (published 1667), bk.2, l.110–14.

22 To be no more; sad cure; for who would lose,
Though full of pain, this intellectual being,
Those thoughts that wander through eternity,
To perish rather, swallowed up and lost
In the wide womb of uncreated night,
Devoid of sense and motion?
1665 Belial. *Paradise Lost* (published 1667), bk.2, l.146–51.

23 Thus Belial with words clothed in reason's garb
Counselled ignoble ease, and peaceful sloth,
Not peace.
1665 *Paradise Lost* (published 1667), bk.2, l.226–8.

24 Our torments also may in length of time
Become our elements, these piercing fires
As soft as now severe, our temper changed
Into their temper.
1665 Mammon. *Paradise Lost* (published 1667), bk.2, l.274–7.

25 There is a place
(If ancient and prophetic fame in heav'n
Err not) another world, the happy seat
Of some new race called Man.
1665 Beelzebub. *Paradise Lost* (published 1667), bk.2, l.345–8.

26 This would surpass
Common revenge.
1665 Beelzebub speaking of the plan to tempt Man away from God. *Paradise Lost* (published 1667), bk.2, l.370–1.

27 When his darling sons
Hurled headlong to partake with us, shall curse
Their frail original, and faded bliss,
Faded so soon.
1665 Beelzebub. *Paradise Lost* (published 1667), bk.2, l.373–6.

28 Who shall tempt with wand'ring feet
The dark unbottomed infinite abyss
And through the palpable obscure find out
His uncouth way, or spread his aery flight
Upborne with indefatigable wings
Over the vast abrupt, ere he arrive
The happy isle.
1665 Beelzebub. *Paradise Lost* (published 1667), bk.2, l.404–10.

29 Long is the way
And hard, that out of hell leads up to light.
1665 *Paradise Lost* (published 1667), bk.2, l.432–3.

30 O shame to men! Devil with devil damned
Firm concord holds, men only disagree
Of creatures rational.
1665 *Paradise Lost* (published 1667), bk.2, l.496–8.

31 Meanwhile the Adversary of God and man,
Satan with thoughts inflamed of highest design,
Puts on swift wings, and towards the gates of hell
Explores his solitary flight.
1665 *Paradise Lost* (published 1667), bk.2, l.629–32.

32 Chaos umpire sits,
And by decision more embroils the fray
By which he reigns; next him high arbiter
Chance governs all.
1665 *Paradise Lost* (published 1667), bk.2, l.681–4.

33 Whence and what art thou, execrable shape?
1665 *Paradise Lost* (published 1667), bk.2, l.681.

34 A race of upstart creatures.
1665 Satan speaks to his daughter, Sin, of Man. *Paradise Lost* (published 1667), bk.2, l.834.

35 And fast by hanging in a golden chain

This pendent world.
1665 *Paradise Lost* (published 1667), bk.2, l.1051–2.

36 Hail holy Light, offspring of Heav'n first-born.
Bright effluence of bright essence increate.
1665 *Paradise Lost* (published 1667), bk.3, l.5–6.

37 Thee I revisit safe,
And feel thy sovran vital lamp; but thou
Revisit'st not these eyes, that roll in vain
To find thy piercing ray, and find no dawn;
So thick a drop serene hath quenched their orbs,
Or dim suffusion veiled.
1665 Of his blindness. *Paradise Lost* (published 1667), bk.3, l.22–7.

38 Thus with the year
Seasons return, but not to me returns
Day, or the sweet approach of ev'n or morn,
Or sight of vernal bloom, or summer's rose,
Or flocks, or herds, of human face divine;
But cloud instead, and ever-during dark
Surrounds me, from the cheerful ways of men
Cut off, and for the book of knowledge fair
Presented with a universal blank
Of nature's works to me expunged and razed,
And wisdom at one entrance quite shut out.
1665 *Paradise Lost* (published 1667), bk.3, l.40–50.

39 Our two first parents, yet the only two
Of mankind, in the happy garden placed,
Reaping immortal fruits of joy and love,
Uninterrupted joy, unrivalled love
In blissful solitude.
1665 *Paradise Lost* (published 1667), bk.3, l.65–9.

40 So bent he seems
On desperate revenge, that shall redound
Upon his own rebellious head.
1665 Of Satan. *Paradise Lost* (published 1667), bk.3, l.84–6.

41 Whose fault?
Whose but his own? Ingrate, he had of me
All he could have; I made him just and right,
Sufficient to have stood, though free to fall.
1665 God speaking of Satan. *Paradise Lost* (published 1667), bk.3, l.96–9.

42 Freely they stood who stood, and fell who fell.
1665 *Paradise Lost* (published 1667), bk.3, l.102.

43 I formed them free, and free they must remain,
Till they enthrall themselves
1665 *Paradise Lost* (published 1667), bk.3, l.124–5.

44 And I will place within them as a guide
My umpire conscience, whom if they will hear
Light after light well used they shall attain,
And to the end persisting, safe arrive.
1665 *Paradise Lost* (published 1667), bk.3, l.194–7.

45 Die he or justice must.
1665 *Paradise Lost* (published 1667), bk.3, l.210.

46 Behold me then, me for him, life for life
I offer, on me let thine anger fall;
Account me man; I for his sake will leave
Thy bosom, and this glory next to thee
Freely put off, and for him lastly die
Well pleased, on me let Death wreck all his rage.
1665 Christ speaking to God. *Paradise Lost* (published 1667), bk.3, l.236–241.

47 O thou
My sole complacence!
1665 God speaking to Christ. *Paradise Lost* (published 1667), bk.3, l.275–6.

48 So on this windy sea of land, the Fiend
Walked up and down alone bent on his prey.
1665 *Paradise Lost* (published 1667), bk.3, l.440–1.

49 Into a limbo large and broad, since called
The Paradise of Fools, to few unknown.
1665 *Paradise Lost* (published 1667), bk.3, l.495–6.

50 The pure marble air.
1665 *Paradise Lost* (published 1667), bk.3, l.564.

51 For neither man nor angel can discern
Hypocrisy, the only evil that walks
Invisible, except to God alone,
By his permissive will, through heav'n and earth.
1665 *Paradise Lost* (published 1667), bk.3, l.681–4.

52 Horror and doubt distract
His troubled thoughts, and from the bottom stir
The hell within him, for within him hell
He brings, and round about him, nor from hell
One step no more than from himself can fly.
1665 Of Satan. *Paradise Lost* (published 1667), bk.4, l.18–22.

53 Now conscience wakes despair
That slumbered, wakes the bitter memory
Of what he was, what is, and what must be
Worse; of worse deeds worse sufferings must ensue.
1665 Of Satan. *Paradise Lost* (published 1667), bk.4, l.23–6.

54 A grateful mind
By owing owes not, but still pays, at once
Indebted and discharged; what burden then?
1665 *Paradise Lost* (published 1667), bk.4, l.55–7.

55 Which way I fly is hell; myself am hell;
And in the lowest deep a lower deep
Still threat'ning to devour me opens wide,
To which the hell I suffer seems a heav'n.
1665 Satan. *Paradise Lost* (published 1667), bk.4, l.75–8.

56 The lower still I fall, only supreme
In misery; such joy ambition finds.
1665 Satan. *Paradise Lost* (published 1667), bk.4, l.91–2.

57 For never can true reconcilement grow
Where wounds of deadly hate have pierced so deep.
1665 Satan. *Paradise Lost* (published 1667), bk.4, l.98–9.

58 So clomb this first grand thief into God's fold:
So since into his church lewd hirelings climb.
Thence up he flew, and on the Tree of Life,
The middle tree and highest there that grew,
Sat like a cormorant.
1665 Of Satan. *Paradise Lost* (published 1667), bk.4, l.192–6.

59 Out of the fertile ground he caused to grow
All trees of noblest kind for sight, smell, taste;
And all amid them stood the Tree of Life,
High eminent, blooming ambrosial fruit
Of vegetable gold; and next to life
Our death the Tree of Knowledge grew fast by,
Knowledge of good bought dear by knowing ill.
1665 *Paradise Lost* (published 1667), bk.4, l.218–24.

60 Flowers of all hue, and without thorn the rose.
1665 *Paradise Lost* (published 1667), bk.4, l.256.

61 Two of far nobler shape erect and tall,

God-like erect, with native honor clad
In naked majesty seemed lords of all.
1665 Of Adam and Eve. *Paradise Lost* (published 1667), bk.4, l.288–90.

62 Though both
Not equal, as their sex not equal seemed;
For contemplation he and valour formed,
For softness she and sweet attractive grace,
He for God only, she for God in him.
1665 Of Adam and Eve. *Paradise Lost* (published 1667), bk.4, l.295–9.

63 Yielded with coy submission, modest pride,
And sweet reluctant amorous delay.
1665 Of Eve. *Paradise Lost* (published 1667), bk.4, l.310–11.

64 Ah gentle pair, ye little think how nigh
Your change approaches, when all these delights
Will vanish and deliver ye to woe,
More woe, the more your taste is now of joy.
1665 *Paradise Lost* (published 1667), bk.4, l.366–9.

65 Sole partner and sole part of all these joys.
1665 Adam to Eve. *Paradise Lost* (published 1667), bk.4, l.411.

66 These two
Emparadised in one another's arms
The happier Eden, shall enjoy their fill
Of bliss on bliss.
1665 Of Adam and Eve. *Paradise Lost* (published 1667), bk.4, l.505–8.

67 Man hath his daily work of body or mind
Appointed, which declares his dignity,
And the regard of Heav'n on all his ways.
1665 Adam to Eve. *Paradise Lost* (published 1667), bk.4, l.618–20.

68 God is thy law, thou mine: to know no more
Is woman's happiest knowledge and her praise.
With thee conversing I forget all time.
1665 Eve to Adam. *Paradise Lost* (published 1667), bk.4, l.637–9.

69 Millions of spiritual creatures walk the earth
Unseen, both when we wake, and when we sleep.
1665 *Paradise Lost* (published 1667), bk.4, l.677–8.

70 Iris all hues, roses, and jessamine
Reared high their flourished heads between, and wrought
Mosaic; underfoot the violet,
Crocus, and hyacinth with rich inlay
Broidered the ground, more coloured than with stone
Of costliest emblem: other creature here
Beast, bird, insect, or worm durst enter none;
Such was their awe of man.
1665 *Paradise Lost* (published 1667), bk.4, l.698–705.

71 Nor turned I ween
Adam from his fair spouse, nor Eve the rites
Mysterious of connubial love refused:
Whatever hypocrites austerely talk
Of purity and place and innocence,
Defaming as impure what God declares
Pure, and commands to some, leaves free to all.
1665 *Paradise Lost* (published 1667), bk.4, l.741–7.

72 Hail, wedded love, mysterious law, true source
Of human offspring, sole propriety
In Paradise of all things common else.
1665 *Paradise Lost* (published 1667), bk.4, l.750–2.

73 Him there they found
Squat like a toad, close at the ear of Eve.
1665 *Paradise Lost* (published 1667), bk.4, l.799–800.

74 When I am thy captive talk of chains,
Proud limitary cherub.
1665 *Paradise Lost* (published 1667), bk.4, l.970–1.

75 But wherefore thou alone? Wherefore with thee
Came not all hell broke loose?
1665 *Paradise Lost* (published 1667), bk.4, l.917–18.

76 My fairest, my espoused, my latest found,
Heav'n's last best gift, my ever new delight.
1665 Adam to Eve. *Paradise Lost* (published 1667), bk.5, l.18–19.

77 Best image of myself and dearer half.
1665 Adam to Eve. *Paradise Lost* (published 1667), bk.5, l.95.

78 Nor jealousy
Was understood, the injured lover's hell.
1665 *Paradise Lost* (published 1667), bk.5, l.449–50.

79 In contemplation of created things
By steps we may ascend to God.
1665 Adam to Raphael. *Paradise Lost* (published 1667), bk.5, l.511–12.

80 God made thee perfect, not immutable.
1665 Raphael to Adam. *Paradise Lost* (published 1667), bk.5, l.524.

81 Hear all ye angels, progeny of light,
Thrones, dominations, princedoms, virtues, powers.
1665 *Paradise Lost* (published 1667), bk.5, l.600–1.

82 All seemed well pleased, all seemed, but were not all.
1665 *Paradise Lost* (published 1667), bk.5, l.616.

83 Servant of God, well done, well hast thou fought
The better fight.
1665 God to his faithful angels. *Paradise Lost* (published 1667), bk.6, l.29–30.

84 Proud, art thou met?
1665 Abdiel to Satan. *Paradise Lost* (published 1667), bk.6, l.131.

85 This is servitude,
To serve th' unwise, or him who hath rebelled
Against his worthier, as thine now serve thee,
Thyself not free, but to thyself enthralled.
1665 Abdiel to Satan. *Paradise Lost* (published 1667), bk.6, l.178–81.

86 But pain is perfect misery, the worst
Of evils, and excessive, overturns
All patience.
1665 *Paradise Lost* (published 1667), bk.6, l.461–3.

87 On war and mutual slaughter bent.
1665 Of Mankind. *Paradise Lost* (published 1667), bk.6, l.506.

88 Headlong themselves they threw
Down from the verge of heaven, eternal wrath
Burnt after them to the bottomless pit.
1665 Pursued to the wall of Heaven by the Messiah, Satan and his rebelling angels fall to their punishment as the wall opens. *Paradise Lost* (published 1667), bk.6, l.864–6.

89 Standing on earth, not rapt above the pole,
More safe I sing with mortal voice, unchanged
To hoarse or mute, though fall'n on evil days,
On evil days though fallen, and evil tongues.
1665 *Paradise Lost* (published 1667), bk.7, l.23–6.

90 But knowledge is as food, and needs no less
Her temperance over appetite, to know

In measure what the mind may well contain,
Oppresses else with surfeit, and soon turns
Wisdom to folly, as nourishment to wind.
1665 *Paradise Lost* (published 1667), bk.7, l.126–30.

91 Necessity and chance
Approach not me, and what I will is fate.
1665 God. *Paradise Lost* (published 1667), bk.7, l.172–3.

92 He took the golden compasses, prepared
In God's eternal store, to circumscribe
This universe, and all created things:
One foot he centred, and the other turned
Round through the vast profundity obscure,
And said, 'Thus far extend, thus far thy bounds
This be thy just circumference, O world.'
1665 *Paradise Lost* (published 1667), bk.7, l.225–31.

93 And the earth self-balanced on her centre hung.
1665 *Paradise Lost* (published 1667), bk.7, l.242.

94 The great creator from his work returned
Magnificent, his six days' work, a world.
1665 *Paradise Lost* (published 1667), bk.7, l.567–8.

95 Witness this new-made world, another heav'n
From heaven gate not far, founded in view
On the clear hyaline, the glassy sea;
Of amplitude almost immense, with stars
Numerous, and every star perhaps a world
Of destined habitation.
1665 *Paradise Lost* (published 1667), bk.7, l.617–22.

96 O when meet now
Such pairs, in love and mutual honour joined?
1665 *Paradise Lost* (published 1667), bk.8, l.57–8.

97 He his fabric of the heavens
Hath left to their disputes, perhaps to move
His laughter at their quaint opinions wide
Hereafter, when they come to model heaven
And calculate the stars, how they will wield
The mighty frame, how build, unbuild, contrive
To save appearances, how gird the sphere
With centric and eccentric scribbled o'er,
Cycle and epicycle, orb in orb.
1665 *Paradise Lost* (published 1667), bk.8, l.76–84.

98 Heaven is for thee too high
To know what passes there; be lowly wise:
Think only what concerns thee and thy being.
Dream not of other worlds, what creatures there
Live, in what state, condition, or degree,
Contented that thus far hath been revealed
Not of earth only but of highest heav'n.
1665 Raphael to Adam. *Paradise Lost* (published 1667), bk.8, l.172–8.

99 For man to tell how human life began
Is hard; for who himself beginning knew?
1665 Adam to Raphael. *Paradise Lost* (published 1667), bk.8, l.250–1.

1 In solitude
What happiness, who can enjoy alone,
Or all enjoying, what contentment find?
1665 Adam. *Paradise Lost* (published 1667), bk.8, l.364–6.

2 Among unequals what society
Can sort, what harmony or true delight?
1665 Adam. *Paradise Lost* (published 1667), bk.8, l.383–4.

3 Yet when I approach

Her loveliness, so absolute she seems
And in herself complete, so well to know
Her own, that what she wills to do or say,
Seems wisest, virtuousest, discreetest, best.
1665 Adam speaking of Eve. *Paradise Lost* (published 1667), bk.8, l.546–50.

4 All higher knowledge in her presence falls
Degraded, wisdom in discourse with her
Loses discount'nanced, and like folly shows.
1665 Adam speaking of Eve. *Paradise Lost* (published 1667), bk.8, l.551–3.

5 Love refines
The thoughts, and heart enlarges, hath his seat
In reason, and is judicious, is the scale
By which to heav'nly love thou may'st ascend,
Not sunk in carnal pleasure, for which cause
Among the beasts no mate for thee was found.
1665 Raphael to Adam. *Paradise Lost* (published 1667), l.589–94.

6 My celestial patroness, who deigns
Her nightly visitation unimplored,
And dictates to me slumbering, or inspires
Easy my unpremeditated verse:
Since first this subject for heroic song
Pleased me long choosing, and beginning late.
1665 *Paradise Lost* (published 1667), bk.9, l.21–6.

7 And the more I see
Pleasures about me, so much more I feel
Torment within me.
1665 Satan. *Paradise Lost* (published 1667), bk.9, l.119–21.

8 This man of clay, son of despite.
1665 Satan speaking of Adam. *Paradise Lost* (published 1667), bk.9, l.176.

9 For nothing lovelier can be found
In woman, than to study household good,
And good works in her husband to promote.
1665 Adam to Eve. *Paradise Lost* (published 1667), bk.9, l.232–4.

10 For solitude sometimes is best society,
And short retirement urges sweet return.
1665 *Paradise Lost* (published 1667), bk.9, l.249–50.

11 That space the Evil One abstracted stood
From his own evil, and for the time remained
Stupidly good, of enmity disarmed,
Of guile, of hate, of envy, of revenge.
1665 Satan gazes upon Eve. *Paradise Lost* (published 1667), bk.9, l.463–6.

12 She fair, divinely fair, fit love for gods.
1665 Satan speaking of Eve. *Paradise Lost* (published 1667), bk.9, l.489.

13 Her rash hand in evil hour
Forth reaching to the fruit, she plucked, she ate:
Earth felt the wound, and nature from her seat
Sighing through all her works gave signs of woe,
That all was lost.
1665 *Paradise Lost* (published 1667), bk.9, l.781–5.

14 O fairest of creation, last and best
Of all God's works, creature in whom excelled
Whatever can to sight or thought be formed,
Holy, divine, good, amiable, or sweet!
How art thou lost, how on a sudden lost,
Defaced, deflow'red, and now to death devote?

1665 Adam to Eve. *Paradise Lost* (published 1667), bk.9, l.896–91.

15 Flesh of flesh,
Bone of my bone thou art, and from thy state
Mine never shall be parted, bliss or woe.
1665 Adam to Eve. *Paradise Lost* (published 1667), bk.9, l.914–16.

16 What thou art is mine;
Our state cannot be severed, we are one,
One flesh; to lose thee were to lose my self.
1665 Adam to Eve. *Paradise Lost* (published 1667), bk.9, l.957–9.

17 Linked in love so dear,
To undergo with me one guilt, one crime,
If any be, of tasting this fair fruit.
1665 Eve to Adam. *Paradise Lost* (published 1667), bk.9, l.970–2.

18 As with new wine intoxicated both
They swim in mirth, and fancy that they feel
Divinity within them breeding wings
Wherewith to scorn the earth.
1665 *Paradise Lost* (published 1667), bk.9, l.1007–10.

19 Thus they in mutual accusation spent
The fruitless hours, but neither self-condemning,
And of their vain contést appeared no end.
1665 *Paradise Lost* (published 1667), bk.9, l.1187–9.

20 Yet I shall temper so
Justice with mercy.
1665 *Paradise Lost* (published 1667), bk.10, l.77–8.

21 Love was not in their looks, either to God
Or to each other.
1665 *Paradise Lost* (published 1667), bk.10, l.111–12.

22 Adorned
She was indeed, and lovely to attract
Thy love, not thy subjection.
1665 Christ speaking to Adam of Eve. *Paradise Lost* (published 1667), bk.10, l.151–3.

23 Now possess,
As lords, a spacious world, to our native heaven
Little inferior, by my adventure hard
With peril great achieved.
1665 Satan, returning triumphantly from Earth to Hell after tempting Eve. *Paradise Lost* (published 1667), bk.10, l.466–9.

24 He hears
On all sides, from innumerable tongues
A dismal universal hiss, the sound
Of public scorn.
1665 Satan and the rebel angels are turned to snakes. *Paradise Lost* (published 1667), bk.10, l.506–9.

25 O fleeting joys
Of Paradise, dear bought with lasting woes!
1665 Adam's lament. *Paradise Lost* (published 1667), bk.10, l.741–2.

26 But say
That death be not one stroke, as I supposed,
Bereaving sense, but endless misery
From this day onward, which I feel begun
Both in me, and without me, and so last
To perpetuity; ay me, that fear
Comes thund'ring back with dreadful revolution
On my defenceless head; both Death and I
Am found eternal, and incorporate both,
Nor I on my part single, in me all

Posterity stands cursed: fair patrimony
That I must leave ye, sons; O were I able
To waste it all myself, and leave ye none!
1665 Adam muses on death. *Paradise Lost* (published 1667), bk.10, l.808–20.

27 O why did God,
Creator wise, that peopled highest heav'n
With Spirits masculine, create at last
This novelty on earth, this fair defect
Of nature, and not fill the world at once
With men as angels without feminine,
Or find some other way to generate
Mankind?
1665 Adam speaking of Eve. *Paradise Lost* (published 1667), bk.10, l.888–95.

28 Let us seek Death, or he not found, supply
With our own hands his office on ourselves;
Why stand we longer shivering under fears,
That show no end but death, and have the power,
Of many ways to die the shortest choosing,
Destruction with destruction to destroy.
1665 Eve. *Paradise Lost* (published 1667), bk.10, l.1001–6.

29 So send them forth, though sorrowing, yet in peace.
1665 God speaking to Michael of Adam and Eve. *Paradise Lost* (published 1667), bk.11, l.117.

30 Moping melancholy
And moon-struck madness.
Michael shows Adam a vision of what will happen before the Flood. *Paradise Lost* (published 1667), bk.11, l.485–6.

31 So may'st thou live, till like ripe fruit thou drop
Into thy mother's lap, or be with ease
Gathered, not harshly plucked, for death mature:
This is old age; but then thou must outlive
Thy youth, thy strength, thy beauty, which will change
To withered weak and grey.
1665 Michael to Adam. *Paradise Lost* (published 1667), bk.11, l.535–40.

32 Nor love thy life, nor hate; but what thou liv'st
Live well, how long or short permit to heaven.
1665 *Paradise Lost* (published 1667), bk.11, l.553–4.

33 Now I see
Peace to corrupt no less than war to waste.
1665 *Paradise Lost* (published 1667), bk.11, l.783–4.

34 O goodness infinite, goodness immense!
That all this good of evil shall produce,
And evil turn to good; more wonderful
Than that which by creation first brought forth
Light out of darkness!
1665 Adam to Michael. *Paradise Lost* (published 1667), bk.12, l.470–4.

35 This having learnt, thou hast attained the sum
Of wisdom; hope no higher, though all the stars
Thou knew'st by name, and all th'ethereal powers,
All secrets of the deep, all nature's works,
Or works of God in heav'n, air, earth, or sea,
And all the riches of this world enjoy'dst,
And all the rule, one empire; only add
Deeds to thy knowledge answerable, add faith,
Add virtue, patience, temperance, add love,
By name to come called charity, the soul
Of all the rest: then wilt thou not be loath
To leave this Paradise, but shalt possess

A paradise within thee, happier far.
1665 Michael to Adam. *Paradise Lost* (published 1667), bk.12, l.575–87.

36 Let us descend now therefore from this top
Of speculation.
1665 *Paradise Lost* (published 1667), bk.12, l.588–9.

37 Some natural tears they dropped, but wiped them soon;
The world was all before them, where to choose
Their place of rest, and Providence their guide:
They hand in hand with wand'ring steps and slow,
Through Eden took their solitary way.
1665 *Paradise Lost* (published 1667), bk.12, l.645–9.

38 For what can I increase
Or multiply, but curses on my head?
1665 Adam's lament. *Paradise Lost* (published 1667), bk.10, l.731–2.

39 Skill'd to retire, and in retiring draw
Hearts after them tangled in amorous nets.
1671 *Paradise Regained*, bk.2, l.161–2.

40 The childhood shows the man,
As morning shows the day. Be famous then
By wisdom; as thy empire must extend,
So let extend thy mind o'er all the world.
1671 *Paradise Regained*, bk.4, l.220–3.

41 The first and wisest of them all professed
To know this only, that he nothing knew.
1671 Of Socrates. *Paradise Regained*, bk.4, l.293–4.

42 Athens, the eye of Greece, mother of arts
And eloquence, native to famous wits
1671 *Paradise Regained*, bk.4, l.240–1.

43 Who reads
Incessantly, and to his reading brings not
A spirit and judgement equal or superior
(And what he brings, what needs he elsewhere seek?)
Uncertain and unsettled still remains,
Deep-versed in books and shallow in himself.
1671 *Paradise Regained*, bk.4, l.322–7.

44 But here I feel amends,
The breath of Heav'n fresh-blowing, pure and sweet,
With day-spring born; here leave me to respire.
1671 *Samson Agonistes*, l.9–11.

45 Ask for this great deliverer now, and find him
Eyeless in Gaza at the mill with slaves.
1671 *Samson Agonistes*, l.40–1.

46 O impotence of mind, in body strong!
But what is strength without a double share
Of wisdom, vast, unwieldy, burdensome,
Proudly secure, yet liable to fall
By weakest subtleties, not made to rule,
But to subserve where wisdom bears command.
1671 *Samson Agonistes*, l.52–7.

47 O loss of sight, of thee I most complain!
Blind among enemies, O worse than chains,
Dungeon, or beggary, or decrepit age!
Light the prime work of God to me is extinct,
And all her various objects of delight
Annull'd, which might in part my grief have eas'd,
Inferior to the vilest now become
Of man or worm; the vilest here excel me,
They creep, yet see, I dark in light expos'd
To daily fraud, contempt, abuse and wrong,

Within doors, or without, still as a fool,
In power of others, never in my own;
Scarce half I seem to live, dead more than half.
1671 *Samson Agonistes*, l.67–79.

48 If it be true
That light is in the soul,
She all in every part; why was the sight
To such a tender ball as th' eye confin'd?
1671 *Samson Agonistes*, l.91–4.

49 To live a life half dead, a living death.
1671 *Samson Agonistes*, l.100.

50 Thou art become (O worst imprisonment!)
The Dungeon of thy self.
1671 *Samson Agonistes*, l.155–6.

51 Salve to thy sores, apt words have power to suage
The tumours of a troubl'd mind,
And are as Balm to fester'd wounds.
1671 *Samson Agonistes*, l.184–6.

52 Just are the ways of God,
And justifiable to men;
Unless there be who think not God at all.
1671 *Samson Agonistes*, l.293–5.

53 So much I feel my genial spirits droop,
My hopes all flat, nature within me seems
In her functions weary of herself.
1671 *Samson Agonistes*, l.594–6.

54 My race of glory run, and race of shame,
And I shall shortly be with them that rest.
1671 *Samson Agonistes*, l.597–8.

55 God of our Fathers, what is man!
That thou towards him with hand so various,
Or might I say contrarious,
Temperst thy providence through his short course,
Not evenly, as thou rul'st
The angelic orders and inferior creatures mute,
Irrational and brute.
1671 *Samson Agonistes*, l.667–73.

56 That grounded maxim
So rife and celebrated in the mouths
Of wisest men; that to the public good
Private respects must yield.
1671 *Samson Agonistes*, l.865–8.

57 In argument with men a woman ever
Goes by the worse, whatever be her cause.
1671 *Samson Agonistes*, l.903–4.

58 At distance I forgive thee, go with that.
1671 *Samson Agonistes*, l.954.

59 Yet beauty, though injurious, hath strange power,
After offence returning, to regain
Love once possessed.
1671 *Samson Agonistes*, l.1003–5.

60 Love-quarrels oft in pleasing concord end.
1671 *Samson Agonistes*, l.1008.

61 Lords are lordliest in their wine.
1671 *Samson Agonistes*, l.1418.

62 Evil news rides post, while good news baits.
1671 *Samson Agonistes*, l.1538.

63 Death to life is crown or shame.
1671 *Samson Agonistes*, l.1579.

64 Not willingly, but tangl'd in the fold

Of dire necessity.
1671 *Samson Agonistes*, l.1665–6.

65 Nothing is here for tears, nothing to wail
Or knock the breast, no weakness, no contempt,
Dispraise, or blame, nothing but well and fair,
And what may quiet us in a death so noble.
1671 Of Samson's heroic death. *Samson Agonistes*, l.1721–4.

66 All is best, though we oft doubt,
What the unsearchable dispose
Of highest wisdom brings about,
And ever best found in the close.
1671 *Samson Agonistes*, l.1745–8.

67 Calm of mind, all passion spent.
1671 *Samson Agonistes*, l.1758.

Min, Anchee 1957–

Chinese writer who left China for America in 1984. Her autobiography *Red Azalea* (1993) is named after Madame Mao's propaganda film in which Min was an actress.

68 My parents lived like—as the neighbours described them—a pair of chopsticks, always in harmony.
1993 *Red Azalea*.

69 The Chairman looked dissatisfied lying on his death bed.
1993 Of Mao Zedong. *Red Azalea*.

Mingus, Charles 1922–79

US composer and bass player. He was one of the great idiosyncratic geniuses of modern jazz, and his musical legacy is only now being fully absorbed.

70 Today musicians listen to see who makes the most money on a style, and then they set to copying him. And they don't copy the ones that are beautiful, creative and good.
1977 Interview in Enstice and Rubin *Jazz Spoken Here* (1992).

Minot, Laurence d. c.1352

English poet.

71 War yit with the Skottes, for thai er ful of gile.
early to mid 14c 'Skottes out of Berwik', l.6.

Minow, Newton Norman 1926–

US lawyer, author and communications executive. Named Chair of the Federal Communications Commission (1961–3) by President Kennedy, he was noted for his controversial criticism of television broadcasting standards in the US. Since 1987 he has been director of the Annenberg Washington Program in Communications Policy Studies of Northwestern University in Washington.

72 When television is good, nothing is better. When it's bad, nothing is worse.
1961 Speech to the National Association of Broadcasters. Reported in the *New York Times*, 10 May.

73 You will observe a vast wasteland.
1961 Speech to the National Association of Broadcasters, inviting them to watch a full day of television. Reported in the *New York Times*, 10 May.

Minsky, Marvin Lee 1927–

US computer scientist and artificial intelligence researcher.

74 Logic doesn't apply to the real world.

1981 In Douglas R Hofstadter and Daniel C Dennett (eds) *The Mind's I: fantasies and reflections on self and soul.*

Mirabeau, Honoré Gabriel Riqueti, Comte de 1749–91

French revolutionary politician. After the publication of his *Essai sur le despotisme*, he was sentenced to death, but only served three years in prison. He espoused the Revolution, and died soon after he was elected President of the Assembly in 1791.

75 War is the national industry of Prussia.
1788 Attributed to Mirabeau by Albert Sorel (1842–1906), suggested by Mirabeau's introduction to *De la monarchie prussienne sous Frédéric le Grand*.

76 We will only leave our places by the force of the bayonet!
1789 Speech at the *Séance Royale*. Quoted in Webster *The French Revolution* (1919), p.50.

77 To administer is to govern; to govern is to reign. That is the problem.
1790 Memorandum, 3 Jul.

Miró, Joán 1893–1983

Spanish painter, graphic artist and designer.

78 I will break their guitar.
Of the Cubists and their reliance upon the still-life. Attributed in Saranne Alexandrian *Surrealist Art* (1970).

Mishan, E J 1917–

British economist.

79 If frequent teabreaks and other manifestations of disguised leisure are regarded as goods—and economics suggests that they be so regarded—their inclusion in any index of output per capita might go some way to enhance Britain's comparative performance.
Quoted in Alex Rubner *Three Sacred Cows of Economics* (1970), p.47.

Mishima, Yukio *pseudonym of* **Hiraoka Kimitake** 1925–70

Japanese writer of novels, plays and short stories. A keen advocate of the chivalrous ideals of Imperial Japan, he committed suicide by performing *seppuku* after a token effort at rallying his country to the right-wing nationalist traditions of pre-war Japan.

80 Teachers—a bunch of men all armed with the same information.
Acts of Worship, 'Cigarette' (translated by John Bester, 1989).

81 Held in the custody of childhood is a locked chest; the adolescent, by one means or another, tries to open it. the chest is opened: inside, there is nothing.
Acts of Worship, 'Cigarette' (translated by John Bester, 1989).

82 He'd been mistaken in thinking that if he killed himself the sordid bourgeois world would perish with him.
Acts of Worship, 'Raisin Bread' (translated by John Bester, 1989).

83 As he saw it, there was only one choice—to be strong and upright, or to commit suicide.
Acts of Worship, 'Sword' (translated by John Bester, 1989).

84 Human beings…they go on being born and dying, dying and being born. It's kind of boring, isn't it?
Acts of Worship, 'Sword' (translated by John Bester, 1989).

Mitchel, John 1815–75

Irish patriot. After starting the *United Irishman* (1848) he was tried for 'treason-felony' and transported, but in 1853 he escaped from Van Diemen's Land (Tasmania) to the USA. He returned to Ireland in 1874, and was elected to parliament but declared ineligible.

85 Surely, it is in youth man is most thoroughly depraved. Hell lies about us in our infancy. The youthful innocency sung by aged poets (who forget their first childhood) is nothing but ignorance of evil. As the child comes to know evil, he loves it.
1849 In the *Jail Journal*, 13 Apr.

Mitchell, Adrian 1932–

English writer. His poetry is populist and political in nature. He has also written novels, plays, and works for children.

86 Most people ignore most poetry because most poetry ignores most people.
1964 *Poems*, introduction.

87 The man who believes in giraffes would swallow anything.
1971 'Loose Leaf Poem'.

88 Poetry is an extra hand. It can caress or tickle. It can clench and fight.
1972 'Poetry Lives', in the *Sunday Times*, 13 Feb.

Mitchell, Austin 1934–

English Labour politician.

89 Welcome to Britain's New Political Order. No passion… No Right. No Left. Just multi-hued blancmange.
1999 In the *Observer*, 'Sayings of the Week', 11 Apr.

Mitchell, Joni (Roberta Joan) née *Anderson* 1943–

Canadian singer and songwriter. Her highly original and personal compositions made her a central figure in the folk movement of the 1960s. Her albums include *Ladies of the Canyon* (1970) and *Blue* (1971).

90 Woke up, it was a Chelsea morning, and the first thing that I knew
There was milk and toast and honey and a bowl of oranges, too.
And the sun poured in like butterscotch and stuck to all my senses.
1967 'Chelsea Morning'.

91 Don't it always seem to go
That you don't know what you've got
Till it's gone.
They paved paradise
And put up a parking lot.
1970 'Big Yellow Taxi'.

Mitchell, Margaret 1900–49

US writer. She worked as a journalist with the Atlanta *Constitution*. Her only novel, *Gone with the Wind* (written 1926–36, published 1936, Pulitzer Prize), rapidly became a bestseller and was made into a celebrated film in 1939.

92 I'm tired of everlastingly being unnatural and never doing anything I want to do…and I'm tired of pretending I don't know anything, so men can tell me things and feel important while they're doing it.

1936 Scarlett O'Hara. *Gone with the Wind*, ch.5.

93 Land is the only thing in the world worth working for, worth fighting for, worth dying for, because it's the only thing that lasts. It will come to you, this love of the land.
1939 *Gone with the Wind*.

94 Young misses whut eats heavy mos' gener'ly doan never ketch husbands.
1936 Mammy. *Gone with the Wind*, ch.5.

95 Until you've lost your reputation, you never realize what a burden it was or what freedom really is.
1936 Rhett Butler. *Gone with the Wind*, ch.9.

96 I'm going to live through this, and when it's over, I'm never going to be hungry again. No, nor any of my folks. If I have to steal or kill—as God is my witness, I'm never going to be hungry again.
1936 Scarlett O'Hara. *Gone with the Wind*, ch.25.

97 Fighting is like champagne. It goes to the heads of cowards as quickly as of heroes. Any fool can be brave on a battlefield when it's be brave or else be killed.
1936 Ashley Wilkes. *Gone with the Wind*, ch.31.

98 Southerners can never resist a losing cause.
1936 Rhett Butler. *Gone with the Wind*, ch.34.

99 Death and taxes and childbirth! There's never any convenient time for any of them!
1936 Scarlett O'Hara. *Gone with the Wind*, ch.38.

1 What is broken is broken, and I'd rather remember it as it was at its best than mend it and see broken places as long as I lived… I wish I could care what you do or where you go, but I can't. My dear, I don't give a damn.
1936 Rhett Butler's parting speech to Scarlett O'Hara. *Gone with the Wind*, ch.63; the more famous version of the final line from the film script by Sidney Howard (1939, spoken by Clark Gable) ran 'Frankly, my dear, I don't give a damn'.

2 Tomorrow, I'll think of some other way to get him back. After all, tomorrow is another day.
1936 Scarlett O'Hara's final words. *Gone with the Wind*, ch.63.

Mitchell, Warren 1926–

English actor.

3 You don't retire in this business. You just notice that the phone has not rung for ten years.
2000 In *The Guardian*, 31 Dec.

Mitford, Mary Russell 1787–1855

English novelist and dramatist, best known for her sketches of country manners, scenery and character that were collected as *Our Village* (1824–32). Other publications include *Recollections of a Literary Life* (1852).

4 To think of playing cricket for hard cash! Money and gentility would ruin any pastime under the sun.
1823 Letter to R B Haydon, 24 Aug.

5 Who would think that a little bit of leather, and two pieces of wood, had such a delightful and delighting power!
1824–32 *Our Village*.

Mitford, Nancy Freeman 1904–73

English writer. A daughter of the aristocracy, she achieved a considerable reputation for her witty novels.

6 Like all the very young we took it for granted that making

love is child's play.
1945 *The Pursuit of Love*, ch.3.

7 Aunt Sadie…so much disliked hearing about health that people often took her for a Christian Scientist, which, indeed, she might have become had she not disliked hearing about religion even more.
1945 *The Pursuit of Love*, ch.4.

8 I have only ever read one book in my life, and that is *White Fang*. It's so frightfully good I've never bothered to read another.
1945 *The Pursuit of Love*, ch.9.

9 Abroad is unutterably bloody and foreigners are fiends.
1945 Uncle Matthew. *The Pursuit of Love*, ch.15.

10 'Always be civil to the girls, you never know who they may marry' is an aphorism which has saved many an English spinster from being treated like an Indian widow.
1949 *Love in a Cold Climate*, pt.1, ch.2.

11 'Twenty three and a quarter minutes past,' Uncle Matthew was saying furiously, 'in precisely six and three-quarter minutes the damned fella will be late.'
1949 *Love in a Cold Climate*, pt.1, ch.13.

12 When the loo paper gets thicker and the writing paper thinner, it's always a bad sign, at home.
1949 *Love in a Cold Climate*, pt.2, ch.2.

13 An aristocracy in a republic is like a chicken whose head has been cut off: it may run about in a lively way, but in fact it is dead.
1956 *Noblesse Oblige*.

Mitsuharu, Kaneko 1895–1975

Japanese poet, noted for his unconventionality. He spent a number of years in Belgium and France and wrote a poem, 'Awa' ('Foam'), about Japanese atrocities in China.

14 The sky snivels green snot.
There is war.
c.1938 *Shijin* (Poet), 'Awa' (translated by A R Davies, 1988).

Mizner, Wilson 1876–1933

US dramatist and wit.

15 Be nice to people on your way up because you'll meet them on your way down.
Quoted in A Johnston *The Legendary Mizners* (1953).

16 Working for Warner Brothers was like fucking a porcupine—it's a hundred pricks against one.
Quoted in David Niven *Bring on the Empty Horses* (1975).

17 A trip through a sewer in a glass-bottomed boat.
1979 Of life in Hollywood. Quoted in Gary Herman *The Book of Hollywood Quotes* (1979).

Mo Yan *pseudonym of Guan Moye* 1956–

Chinese writer and the winner of nearly all the prestigious literary awards in China. He has written a number of novels. *Red Sorghum* (1993), his fourth novel, is set principally during the 1930s when Japanese forces occupied the country.

18 Words spoken on the road are heard by snakes in the grass.
1993 *Red Sorghum* (translated by Howard Goldblatt).

Mo, Timothy 1950–

British novelist. He was born in Hong Kong, and achieved prominence with *Sour Sweet*, set in the Chinese community in London.

19 The Chens had been living in the UK for four years, which was long enough to have lost their place in the society from which they had emigrated but not long enough to feel comfortable in the new.
1982 *Sour Sweet*, opening words.

20 It's all honourable enough in its way, but it creates societies which simply cannot sustain any kind of democratic structure. It always leads to totalitarian and corrupt tyrannies… There's no tradition of moral individual courage in Chinese culture.
1982 Of Chinese tradition. In *The Fiction Magazine*, vol.1, no.4.

21 The assaying of tea is an art and not a science. It is the man, and not his instruments, which is the most important. There can be no substitute for my experience and intuited knowledge.
1986 *An Insular Possession*, ch.4.

22 I see you belong to the category, old friend, which will have things in the round, which does love an end, causes, the balance sheet drawn and equalled. But, my dear Gid, the world is not like that—it *is* untidy, there are no reasons, the final sum never balances.
1986 *An Insular Possession*, ch.44.

23 There's no such thing as a hero—only ordinary people asked extraordinary things in terrible circumstances —and delivering.
1991 *The Redundancy of Courage*, ch.30.

Modersohn-Becker, Paula *née Becker* 1876–1907

German painter, a member of the Worpswede artists' colony near Bremen and an early Expressionist. In her later works naturalism gives way to simple forms and strong lyrical colour. She died soon after the birth of her first child.

24 In art one is usually totally alone with oneself.
1906 Diary entry, Paris, 18 Nov, quoted in Gillian Perry *Paula Modersohn-Becker* (1979).

Mola, Emilio 1887–1937

Spanish general, a nationalist leader during the Spanish Civil War.

25 *La quinta columna.*
The fifth column.
1936 Speech, Oct. Of the rebel sympathizers within Madrid who would help the four columns of nationalist rebels besieging it. Quoted in Hugh Thomas *The Spanish Civil War* (1961), ch.4, p.317.

Molière, Jean Baptiste Poquelin 1622–73

French actor and playwright who formed a theatrical company in 1643 and toured the provinces until 1658. He gained the patronage of the Duc d'Orléans and later of Louis XIV.

26 *On ne meurt qu'une fois, et c'est pour si longtemps!*
We only die once; and it's for such a long time!
1656 *Le dépit amoureux*, act 5, sc.3.

27 *Hors de Paris, il n'y a point de salut pour les honnêtes gens.*
Outside of Paris, there is no salvation for gentlemen.
1659 *Les précieuses ridicules*, sc.9.

28 *Les verrous et les grilles*
Ne font pas la vertu des femmes ni des filles.

Bolts and bars will not keep wives and daughters chaste.
1661 *L'École des maris*, act 1, sc.2.

29 *Le siècle s'encanaille furieusement.*
Our times have become vulgar.
1663 *La critique de l'École des femmes*, sc.6.

30 *Je voudrais bien savoir si la grande*
règle de toutes les règles n'est pas de plaire.
I shouldn't be surprised if the greatest
rule of all weren't to give pleasure.
1663 *La critique de l'École des femmes*, sc.6.

31 *Le Ciel défend, de vrai, certains contentements;*
Mais on trouve avec lui des accommodements.
True, heaven forbids us certain pleasures;
But we always find a way to arrange things.
1664 *Le Tartuffe*, act 4, sc.5.

32 *Le scandale du monde est ce qui fait l'offense,*
Et ce n'est pas pécher que pécher en silence.
A scandal is that which gives offence to the world.
To sin in private is not to sin at all.
1664 *Le Tartuffe*, act 4, sc.5.

33 *Qui vit sans tabac n'est pas digne de vivre.*
Anyone who lives without tobacco is not worthy of
living.
1665 *Dom Juan*, act 1, sc.1.

34 *La naissance n'est rien où la vertu n'est pas.*
Birth counts for little when virtue is lacking.
1665 *Dom Juan*, act 4, sc.4.

35 *L'ami du genre humain n'est point du tout mon fait.*
I have no use at all for the friend of mankind.
1666 *Le misanthrope*, act 1, sc.1.

36 *J'aime mieux un vice commode*
Qu'une fatigante vertu.
I prefer easygoing vice to tiresome virtue.
1668 *Amphitryon*, act 1, sc.4.

37 *Quand il y a à manger pour huit, il y en a bien pour dix.*
When there is enough food for eight, there is enough for
ten.
1668 *L'Avare*, act 3, sc.1.

38 *Il faut manger pour vivre, et non pas vivre pour manger.*
One should eat to live, not live to eat.
1668 *L'Avare*, act 3, sc.1.

39 *Ils commencent ici par faire pendre un*
homme, et puis ils lui font son procès.
Here they hang a men first, and try
him afterwards.
1669 In Paris. *Monsieur de Pourceaugnac*, act 3, sc.2.

40 *Par ma foi! il y a plus de quarante ans*
que je dis de la prose sans que j'en susse rien!
Good heavens! I've been speaking prose for
forty years without knowing it!
1670 *Le bourgeois gentilhomme*, act 2, sc.4.

41 *La grammaire qui sait régenter jusqu'aux rois.*
Even kings must bow to grammar.
1672 *Les femmes savantes*, act 2, sc.6.

42 *Je vis de bonne soupe, et non de beau langage.*
It's good food and not fine words that keeps me alive.
1672 *Les femmes savantes*, act 2, sc.7.

43 *Un sot savant est sot plus qu'un sot ignorant.*
A learned fool is more foolish than an ignorant fool.
1672 *Les femmes savantes*, act 4, sc.3.

44 *Presque tous les hommes meurent de leurs remèdes, et*
non de leurs maladies.
Almost all men die from their medicines and not from
their illnesses.
1673 *Le malade imaginaire*, act 3, sc.3.

45 We reason with one another; he prescribes the
remedies; I omit to take them and I recover.
On his relationship with his doctor, Mauvillan, in the presence of
Louis XI V. Quoted in Vincent Cronin *Louis XI V* (1964), p.291.

Moltke, Helmuth von, Count 1800–91

Prussian general. Chief of the General Staff of the Prussian
army 1858—88. He presided over successful wars with
Denmark (1863–4), Austria (1866) and France (1870–1).

46 Everlasting peace is a dream, and not even a pleasant
one; and war is a necessary part of God's arrangement
with the world… Without war the world would
deteriorate into materialism.
1880 Letter to Dr J K Bluntschi, 11 Dec, collected in *Helmuth von
Moltke as a Correspondent* (1893).

47 What our sword has won in half a year, our sword must
guard for half a century.
1891 *The Franco-Prussian War of 1870–71*.

Mondale, Walter F(rederick) 1928–

US Democratic politician and lawyer. He served under
President Carter as Vice-President (1977–81), and was the
Democratic nominee for President in 1984, when he lost to
Ronald Reagan. He was US Ambassador to Japan (1993–6).

48 I don't want to spend the next two years in Holiday Inns.
1976 On withdrawing from the presidential campaign.

49 In our system, at about 11.30pm on election night, they
just push you off the edge of the cliff—and that's it. You
might scream on the way down, but you're going to hit
the bottom, and you're not going to be in office.
1984 On losing to Ronald Reagan in the presidential elections,
in the *New York Times*, 4 Mar.

Mondrian, Piet 1872–1944

Dutch painter, one of the most important artists in the
development of abstract painting.

50 I hate everything approaching temperamental
inspiration, 'sacred fire' and all those attributes of genius
which serve only as cloaks for untidy minds.
Quoted in F Elgar *Mondrian* (1968).

51 Why should art continue to follow nature when every
other field has left nature behind?
Quoted in F Elgar *Mondrian* (1968).

52 The unconscious in us warns us that in art we have to
follow one particular path. And if we follow it, it is not the
sign of an unconscious act. On the contrary, it shows that
there is in our ordinary consciousness a greater
awareness of our unconsciousness.
Quoted in F Elgar *Mondrian* (1968).

Monet, Claude 1840–1926

French Impressionist painter. One of the creators of
Impressionism, it was his *Impression: soleil levant* (1872) that
gave the movement its name. He spent the last years of his life
as a recluse in Giverny.

53 When you go out to paint, try to forget what objects you have before you—a tree, a house, a field, or whatever. Merely think, here is a little square of blue, here an oblong of pink, here a streak of yellow, and paint it just as it looks to you, the exact colour and shape, until it gives your own naive impression of the scene before you.
Attributed, in reminiscences written in 1927 by the young American artist Lilla Cabot Perry.

54 It was as if a veil had been torn suddenly away; I had understood, I had grasped what painting could be.
After painting with the artist Boudin in the open air. Quoted in J Isaacson *Claude Monet* (1978).

Monod, Jacques 1910–76

French biologist and author. He proposed (1961) the concepts of messenger RNA. He shared the 1965 Nobel prize in physiology or medicine.

55 There are living systems; there is no 'living matter'.
1967 Lecture, College of France.

56 The scientific attitude implies…the postulate of objectivity—that is to say, the fundamental postulate that there is no plan; that there is no intention in the universe.
1970 *Le Hasard et la Necéssité*.

Monro, Harold Edward 1879–1932

English poet. He founded the influential *Poetry Review* in 1912. A *Collected Poems* appeared in 1933.

57 When the tea is brought at five o'clock,
And all the neat curtains are drawn with care,
The little black cat with bright green eyes
Is suddenly purring there.
1914 'Milk for the Cat'.

58 The white saucer like some full moon descends
At last from the clouds of the table above.
1914 'Milk for the Cat'.

Monroe, Marilyn *pseudonym of* **Norma Jean Baker** 1926–62

US film actress. Her sex appeal was exploited in films such as *How to Marry a Millionaire* and *Gentlemen Prefer Blondes* (both 1953), but she went on to light comedy (eg *Some Like It Hot*, 1959) and more serious roles such as *The Misfits* (1961), written by her third husband, Arthur Miller. Her suicide made her an icon, and a symbol of Hollywood's ruthlessness.

59 He's not a director, he's a dictator.
c.1959 On Billy Wilder, the director of *Some Like It Hot*, attributed.

60 He's the only person I know who's in worse shape than I am.
1961 On Montgomery Clift, her co-star in *The Misfits*.

Montagu, (Alexander) Victor Edward Paulet 1906–95

Conservative politician, private secretary to Stanley Baldwin (1932–4) and chairman of the Tory Reform Committee (1943–4). He succeeded as 10th Earl of Sandwich in 1962 but disclaimed his peerage for life the next year. His publications include *The Conservative Dilemma* (1970).

61 Lord Hailsham said the other day that the machinery of Government was creaking. My Lords, it is not even

moving sufficiently to emit a noise of any kind.
1963 House of Lords, 20 Apr, shortly before disclaiming his peerage.

Montagu, Ashley *originally* **Israel Ehrenberg** 1905–99

English-born US anthropologist, author of a number of scholarly and popular works. He has been closely associated with the view that cultural phenomena are not the result of genetics.

62 As the god of contemporary man's idolatry, science is a two-handed engine, and as such science is too important a human activity to leave to the scientists.
1964 Book review in the *New York Times*, 26 Apr.

Montagu, Lady Mary Wortley *née* **Pierrepoint** 1689–1762

English writer and socialite. She accompanied her ambassador husband to Constantinople (1716–18), writing there many entertaining letters. She introduced smallpox inoculation into England, and settled in Italy with her husband in 1739.

63 'Tis certain we have but very imperfect accounts of the manners and religion of these people; this part of the world being seldom visited, but by merchants, who mind little but their own affairs; or travellers, who make too short a stay to be able to report anything exactly of their own knowledge.
c.1716 Of Turkey. Collected in Lord Wharncliffe (ed) *The Letters and Works of Lady Mary Wortley Montagu* (1837).

64 Thus you see, Sir, that these people are not so unpolished as we represent them. 'Tis true, their magnificence is of a different taste from ours, and perhaps of a better. I am almost of opinion, they have a right notion of life. They consume it in music, gardens, wine, and delicate eating, while we are tormenting our brains with some new scheme of politics, or studying some science to which we can never attain, or, if we do, cannot persuade other people to set that value upon it we do ourselves… We die or grow old before we can reap the fruit of our labours. Considering what short-lived weak animals men are, is there any study so beneficial as the study of present pleasure?
c.1716 Collected in Lord Wharncliffe (ed) *The Letters and Works of Lady Mary Wortley Montagu* (1837).

65 I was here convinced of the truth of a reflection I had often made, that if it was the fashion to go naked, the face would be hardly observed.
c.1716 In a Turkish bath in Sofia. Collected in Lord Wharncliffe (ed) *The Letters and Works of Lady Mary Wortley Montagu* (1837).

66 If your daughters are inclined to love reading, do not check their inclination by hindering them of the diverting part of it. It is as necessary for the amusement of women as the reputation of men; but teach them not to expect any applause from it… Ignorance is as much the fountain of vice as idleness, and indeed generally produces it. People that do not read or work for a livelihood have many hours they know not how to employ, especially women, who commonly fall into vapours or something worse.
1750 Letter, Jan. Collected in R Halsband (ed) *Selected Letters of Lady Mary Wortley Montagu* (1970).

67 Their whole business abroad (as far as I can perceive) being to buy new clothes, in which they shine in some obscure coffee-house, where they are sure of meeting only one-another… I look upon them as the greatest blockheads.

1763 On those making the Grand Tour. Quoted in Eric Newby (ed) *A Book of Travellers' Tales* (1985).

Montague, C(harles) E(dward) 1867–1928

English novelist and essayist of Irish parentage. He wrote various novels, a collection of essays and many articles for the *Manchester Guardian* (1890–1925).

68 War hath no fury like a non-combatant.
1922 *Disenchantment*, ch.16.
➤ See Congreve 231:23.

69 I was born below par to the extent of two whiskies.
1923 'Fiery Particles'.

70 The Swiss are inspired hotel-keepers. Some centuries since, when the stranger strayed into one of their valleys, their simple forefathers would kill him and share out the little money he might have about him. Now they know better. They keep him alive and writing cheques.
1926 *The Right Place*.

Montaigne, Michel Eyquem de 1533–92

French essayist. He was a city counsellor of Bordeaux and later its Mayor. From 1571 he lived the life of a country gentleman and started composing his *Essais* (1580), a classic of French literature.

71 *Certes, c'est un sujet merveilleusement vain, divers et ondoyant, que l'homme.*
Man (in good earnest) is a marvellous vain, fickle, and unstable subject.
1580 *Essais*, bk.1, ch.1 (translated by Charles Cotton).

72 *Il faut estre tousjours boté et prest à partir.*
We should always be booted and spurred, and ready to go.
1580 *Essais*, bk.1, ch.20 (translated by Charles Cotton).

73 *Que la mort me trouve plantant mes choux, mais nonchalant d'elle, et encore plus de mon jardin imparfait.*
I would like death to come to me while I am planting cabbages, caring little for death and even less for the imperfection of my garden.
1580 *Essais*, bk.1, ch.20 (translated by Charles Cotton).

74 *Si on me presse de dire pourquoy je l'aymois, je sens que cela ne se peut exprimer, qu'en respondant: 'Parce que c'estoit luy; par ce que c'estoit moy.'*
If a man should importune me to give a reason why I loved him, I find it could no otherwise be expressed, than by making answer: because it was he, because it was I.
1580 *Essais*, bk.1, ch.28 (translated by Charles Cotton).

75 *Or la fin, ce crois-je, en est tout'une, d'en vivre plus à loisir et à son aise.*
Now the end, I take it, is all one, to live at more leisure and at one's ease.
1580 *Essais*, bk.1, ch.39 (translated by Charles Cotton).

76 *Il se faut reserver une arriere boutique toute nostre, toute franche, en laquelle nous establissons nostre vraye liberté et principale retraite et solitude.*
We must reserve a backshop, wholly our own and entirely free, wherein to settle our true liberty, our

principle solitude and retreat.
1580 *Essais*, bk.1, ch.39 (translated by Charles Cotton).

77 *La plus grande chose du monde, c'est de sçavoir estre à soy.*
The greatest thing in the world is for a man to know that he is his own.
1580 *Essais*, bk.1, ch.39 (translated by Charles Cotton).

78 *La gloire et le repos sont choses qui ne peuvent loger en mesme giste.*
Fame and tranquillity are two things that can't live under the same roof.
1580 *Essais*, bk.1, ch.39 (translated by Charles Cotton).

79 *Mon mestier et mon art, c'est vivre.*
My trade and art is to live.
1580 *Essais*, bk.2, ch.6 (translated by Charles Cotton).

80 *Quand je me jouë à ma chatte, qui sçait si elle passe son temps de moy plus que je ne fay d'elle?*
When I play with my cat, who knows whether I do not make her more sport than she makes me?
1580 *Essais*, bk.2, ch.12 (translated by Charles Cotton).

81 *L'homme est bien insensé. Il ne sçauroit forger un ciron, et forge des Dieux à douzaines.*
Man is quite insane. He wouldn't know how to make a maggot, and he makes Gods by the dozen.
1580 *Essais*, bk.2, ch.12 (translated by Charles Cotton).

82 *Nous veillons dormants, et veillants dormons.*
We wake sleeping, and sleep waking.
1580 *Essais*, bk.2, ch.12 (translated by Charles Cotton).

83 *Il n'y a point de fin en nos inquisitions. Nostre fin est en l'autre monde.*
There is no end to our researches; our end is in the other world.
1588 *Essays*, bk.3, ch.13 (translated by Donald M Frame).

84 *Nous sommes par tout vent.*
We are all wind throughout.
1588 *Essais*, bk.3, ch.13 (translated by Charles Cotton).

85 *Nostre grand et glorieux chef-d'œuvre, c'est vivre à propos.*
The great and glorious masterpiece of man is to know how to live to purpose.
1588 *Essais*, bk.3, ch.13 (translated by Charles Cotton).

Montcalm, Marquis de 1712–59

French Governor of Quebec, who unsuccessfully defended the city against General Wolfe's English troops in the Battle of the Plains of Abraham, 13 Sep 1759.

86 I am happy that I shall not live to see the surrender of Quebec.
1759 Spoken to his aides, 13 Sep. He died the following day. Quoted in Francis Parkman *Montcalm and Wolfe* (1884).

Monterroso, Augusto 1921–2003

Guatemalan writer who lived in exile in Mexico from 1944. His works are mainly collections of short stories in which paradox and a whimsical sense of humour are prominent.

87 *La Historia no se detiene nunca. Día y noche su marcha es incesante. Querer detenerla sería como querer detener la Geografía.*
History never stops. It progresses ceaselessly day and night. Trying to stop it is like trying to stop Geography.

1978 *Lo demás es silencio* ('The Rest is Silence'), 'Aforismos, dichos, etc'.

Montesquieu, Charles Louis de Secondat, Baron de la Brède et de 1689–1755

French philosopher and jurist, who turned from law to scientific research and literary work. His study of legal and social issues *De l'Esprit des lois* (1748, 'The Spirit of Laws') was very influential in 18c Europe.

88 *Si l'on vient à savoir mon nom, dès ce moment je me tais. Je connais une femme qui marche assez bien, mais qui boite dès qu'on la regarde.*
Once someone wants to know my name, I become quiet. I know a woman who walks rather well, but who limps once she sees someone watching her.
1721 *Lettres persanes*, introduction.

89 *Il n'y a jamais eu de royaume où il y ait eu tant de guerres civiles que dans celui du Christ.*
No kingdom has ever been so divided by civil wars as that of Christ.
1721 *Lettres persanes*, no.29.

90 *Il faut pleurer les hommes à leur naissance, et non pas à leur mort.*
A person should be mourned at his birth, not at his death.
1721 *Lettres persanes*, no.40.

91 *Si les triangles faisaient un dieu, ils lui donneraient trois côtés.*
If triangles had made a god, it would have three sides.
1721 *Lettres persanes*, no.59.

92 *Le droit des gens est naturellement fondé sur ce principe: que les diverses nations doivent se faire, dans la paix, le plus de bien, et, dans la guerre, le moins de mal qu'il est possible, sans nuire à leurs véritables intérêts.*
Law is naturally founded on this principle: that different nations should do, in peace and as far as best as they can in war, the least harm as possible, without harming their true interests.
1748 *De l'esprit des lois*, vol.1, ch.3.

93 *Le gouvernement est comme toutes les choses du monde; pour le conserver, il faut l'aimer.*
Government is like everything else in the world; to conserve it, we must love it.
1748 *De l'esprit des lois*, vol.4, ch.5.

94 *L'amour de la démocratie est celui de l'égalité.*
Love of democracy is love of equality.
1748 *De l'esprit des lois*, vol.5, ch.3.

95 *Les républiques finissent par le luxe; les monarchies, par la pauvreté.*
Republics end by wealth; monarchies end by poverty.
1748 *De l'esprit des lois*, vol.7, ch.4.

96 *La liberté est le droit de faire tout ce que les lois permettent.*
Freedom is the right to do anything the laws permit.
1748 *De l'esprit des lois*, vol.11, ch.3.

97 *Il en est de la luxure comme de l'avarice: elle augmente sa soif par l'acquisition des trésors.*
The same rule applies for lust, as for avarice: it increases its thirst by the acquisition of wealth.
1748 *De l'esprit des lois*, vol.16, ch.6.

98 *Le divorce a ordinairement une grande utilité politique; et quant à l'utilité civile, il est établi pour le mari et pour la femme, et n'est pas toujours favorable aux enfants.*
Divorce generally has a great political use; as for its civil use, it is established for the husband and wife and is not always favourable to the children.
1748 *De l'esprit des lois*, vol.16, ch.15.

99 *Les lois inutiles affaiblissent les lois nécessaires.*
Useless laws weaken the necessary ones.
1748 *De l'esprit des lois*, vol.29, ch.16.

Montgomery of Alamein, Bernard Law, 1st Viscount 1887–1976

British field marshal. He led the 8th Army in World War II, defeating Rommel at El Alamein (1942), and was Commander-in-Chief of Allied ground forces for the invasion of Normandy (1944), Chief of the Imperial General Staff (1946–8) and Supreme Commander of Nato forces in Europe (1951–8).

1 Rule 1, on page 1 of the book of war is: 'Do not march on Moscow'…[Rule 2] is: 'Do not go fighting with your land armies in China.'
1962 Speech in the House of Lords, 30 May.

Montgomery, L(ucy) M(aud) 1874–1942

Canadian novelist. Her first book was the phenomenally successful *Anne of Green Gables* (1908), the story of an orphan girl adopted in error for a boy by an elderly brother and sister. She followed it with several sequels.

2 The point of good writing is knowing when to stop.
1917 *Anne's House of Dreams*, ch.24.

Montrose, James Graham, 1st Marquis of 1612–50

Scottish soldier and poet, who, after first supporting the National Covenant in 1638, fought a brilliant campaign for Charles I during the Civil War from 1644 to 1645. Captured in 1650 after an abortive attempt to win Scotland for Charles II, he was hanged in Edinburgh.

3 My dear and only love, I pray
That little world of thee
Be governed by no other sway
Than purest monarchy.
c.1642 'My Dear and Only Love', stanza 1.

4 He either fears his fate too much,
Or his deserts are small,
That dares not put it to the touch,
To gain or lose it all.
c.1642 'My Dear and Only Love', stanza 2.

5 Let them bestow on every airth a limb,
Then open all my veins that I may swim
To thee, my Maker, in that crimson lake;
Then place my parboiled head upon a stake,
Scatter my ashes, strew them in the air—
Lord! since thou knowest where all these atoms are,
I'm hopeful thou'lt recover once my dust,
And confident thou'lt raise me with the just.
1650 'Lines Composed on the Eve of his Execution'.

Moodie, Susanna *née Strickland* 1803–85

English-born Canadian writer of fiction, non-fiction, poetry and letters. She reluctantly emigrated to Canada with her husband in 1832 and wrote for many magazines but is best remembered for *Roughing it in the Bush* (1852) and *Life in the*

Clearing, versus the Bush (1853).

6 Dear husband! I take shame to myself that my purpose was less firm, that my heart lingered so far behind yours in preparing for this great epoch in our lives; that like Lot's wife, I still turned and looked back, and clung with all my strength to the land I was leaving. It was not the hardships of an emigrant's life I dreaded. I could bear mere physical privations philosophically enough; it was the loss of society in which I had moved, the want of congenial minds, of persons engaged in congenial pursuits, that made me so reluctant to respond to my husband's call.
1852 *Roughing It in the Bush; or, A Life in Canada*, vol.1, ch.11, 'The Charivari'.

7 Speaking of the coldness of one particular day, a genuine brother Jonathan remarked, with charming simplicity, that it was thirty degrees below zero that morning, and it would have been much colder if the thermometer had been longer.
1852 'Brother Jonathan' refers to a typical Yankee. *Roughing It in the Bush; or, A Life in Canada*, vol.2, ch.9, 'The Fire'.

8 If these sketches should prove the means of deterring one family from sinking their property, and shipwrecking all their hopes, by going to reside in the backwoods of Canada, I shall consider myself amply repaid for revealing the secrets of the prison-house, and feel that I have not toiled and suffered in the wilderness in vain.
1852 *Roughing It in the Bush; or, A Life in Canada*, vol.2, ch.14, 'Adieu to the Woods'.

9 In most instances, emigration is a matter of necessity, not of choice.
1854 *Roughing It in the Bush; or, A Life in Canada*, introduction to the 3rd edition.

10 Will they ever forgive me for writing *Roughing It*? They know that it was the truth, but have I not been a mark for every vulgar editor of a village journal, throughout the length and breadth of the land to hurl a stone at, and point out as the enemy to Canada.
1856 Letter to her publisher, Richard Bentley, 19 Aug.

Moody, William Vaughn 1869–1910

US poet and playwright. He taught at the University of Chicago. His best-known prose play, *The Sabine Woman* (1906), was highly successful and focuses on the contrast between a puritanical woman and a free-thinking man. It was retitled *The Great Divide* (1909).

11 A man's a fool to look at things too near:
They look back, and begin to cut up queer.
1901 'The Menagerie'.

Moore, Brian 1921–99

Northern Irish-born writer, who emigrated to Canada in 1948, and also lived in California and New York. His first novel, *The Lonely Passion of Judith Hearne* (1955), was filmed in 1989. Later works include *Black Robe* (1985, filmed 1991), *Lies of Silence* (1990) and *The Statement* (1995).

12 He bathes daily in a running tap of words.
1987 Of a military colonel's desk work. *The Color of Blood*.

Moore, Charles W(illard) 1925–93

US architect, Professor of Architecture at UCLA, California

(1975–85). His writings include *The Place of Houses* (1974) and *The Poetics of Gardens* (1988).

13 You bind the goods and trappings of your life together with your dreams to make a place that is uniquely your own.
1974 *The Place of Houses*, introduction.

Moore, Clement 1779–1863

US writer and poet.

14 'Twas the night before Christmas, when all through the house
Not a creature was stirring, not even a mouse.
1822 *The Night Before Christmas*.

15 The stockings were hung by the chimney with care,
In hopes that St. Nicholas soon would be there;
The children were nestled all snug in their beds,
While visions of sugarplums danced in their heads.
1822 *The Night Before Christmas*.

16 The moon on the breast of the new-fallen snow,
Gave the lustre of midday to objects below,
When, what to my wondering eyes should appear,
But a miniature sleigh, and eight tiny reindeer.
1822 *The Night Before Christmas*.

17 More rapid than eagles his coursers they came,
And he whistled, and shouted, and called them by name;
'Now, *Dasher*! Now, *Dancer*! Now, *Prancer* and *Vixen*!
On, *Comet*! On, *Cupid*! On, *Donder* and *Blitzen*!
To the top of the porch! To the top of the wall!
Now dash away! Dash away! Dash away all!'
1822 *The Night Before Christmas*.

18 He was dressed all in fur, from his head to his foot,
And his clothes were all tarnished with ashes and soot;
A bundle of toys he had flung on his back,
And he looked like a pedlar just opening his pack.
1822 *The Night Before Christmas*.

19 He sprang to his sleigh, to his team gave a whistle,
And away they all flew like the down of a thistle.
But I heard him exclaim, ere he drove out of sight,
'Happy Christmas to all. And to all a good night.'
1822 *The Night Before Christmas*.

Moore, G(eorge) E(dward) 1873–1958

English Empiricist philosopher. He studied and taught at Cambridge, where he was Professor of Mental Philosophy and Logic (1925–39). His most famous and influential work was *Principia Ethica* (1903).

20 'Good', then, if we mean by it that quality which we assert to belong to a thing, when we say that the thing is good, is incapable of any definition, in the most important sense of the word.
1903 *Principia Ethica*, ch.1.

21 By far the most valuable things, which we know or can imagine, are certain states of consciousness, which may be roughly described as the pleasures of human intercourse and the enjoyment of beautiful objects.
1903 *Principia Ethica*, ch.6.

Moore, George 1852–1933

Irish novelist, poet and playwright. A co-founder of the Irish Literary Theatre with W B Yeats, he collaborated with Yeats on such poetic dramas as *The Bending of the Bough* (1900) and *Diarmuid and Grania* (1901).

22 A year passed; a year of art and dissipation—one part art, two parts dissipation. We mounted and descended at pleasure the rounds of society's ladder.
1870 *Confessions of a Young Man* (published 1888).

23 Acting is therefore the lowest of the arts, if it be an art at all.
1891 *Impressions and Opinions*, 'Mummer-Worship'.

Moore, Henry Spencer 1898–1986

English sculptor and graphic artist. He travelled widely in Europe and was an official war artist (1940–2). His sculptures, mainly semi-abstract figures and groups, are influenced by landscape forms and primitive art.

24 Sculpture in stone should look honestly like stone…to make it look like flesh and blood, hair and dimples is coming down to the level of the stage conjuror.
1930 In the *Architectural Association Journal*.

Moore, Jo

British political adviser.

25 It's now a very good day to get out anything we want to bury.
2001 E-mail sent on 11 Sep, after hijacked planes destroyed the World Trade Center in New York.

Moore, John 1729–1802

Scottish physician and writer. He travelled with Douglas, Duke of Hamilton (1772–8), writing accounts of these journeys, then settled in London. His novel *Zeluco* (1789) was the inspiration for Byron's *Childe Harold*.

26 There is no manner of doubt that a town surrounded by water is a very fine sight; but a town surrounded by land is much finer. Can there be any comparison in point of beauty, between the dull monotony of a watery surface, and the delightful variety of gardens, meadows, hills and woods ?
c.1780 *A View of Society and Manners in Italy.*

Moore, Lorrie 1957–

US writer. Her writings include short stories and novels, such as *Who Will Run the Frog Hospital?* (1994) and *Birds of America* (1998).

27 Literature…is lonely and waited for, brilliant and pure and frightened, a marriage of birds, a conversation of the blind.
1988 In the *New York Times*, 10 Jul.

Moore, Marianne Craig 1887–1972

US poet, whose crisp language, wit and idiosyncratic style established her as a leading literary figure. Her works include *Observations* (1924, rev 1925), *Collected Poems* (1951, Pulitzer Prize) and *Complete Poems* (1967, rev 1981).

28 It comes to this: of whatever sort it is,
it must be 'lit with piercing glances into the life of things';
it must acknowledge the spiritual forces which have made it.
1921 *Poems*, 'When I Buy Pictures'.

29 I, too, dislike it: there are things that are important beyond all this fiddle.

Reading it, however, with a perfect contempt for it, one discovers in
it, after all, a place for the genuine.
1921 *Poems*, 'Poetry'.

30 If 'compression is the first grace of style,' you have it.
1924 *Observations*, 'To A Snail'.

31 My father used to say,
'Superior people never make long visits,
have to be shown Longfellow's grave
or the glass flowers at Harvard.'
1924 *Observations*, 'Silence'.

32 Nor was he insincere in saying, 'Make my house your inn.'
Inns are not residencies.
1924 *Observations*, 'Silence'.

33 You are menaced by the goodness of your mechanics.
1937 To fellow-poet Elizabeth Bishop. Quoted in David Kalstone *Becoming a Poet* (1989), p.57.

34 A place as kind as it is green,
the greenest place I've never seen.
Every name is a tune.
1941 *What Are Years*, 'Spencer's Ireland'.

35 I do not write for money or fame… One writes because one has a burning desire to objectify what it is indispensible to one's happiness to express.
1956 Ewing Lecture, University of California, 3 Oct.

36 Omissions are not accidents.
1956 Ewing Lecture, University of California, 3 Oct.

37 O to be a dragon,
a symbol of the power of Heaven—of silkworm size or immense; at times invisible.
Felicitous phenomenon!
1959 *O To Be A Dragon*, 'O To Be A Dragon'.

38 A connoisseur of tame excitement.
1960 Self-description, in *Vogue*, 1 Aug.

39 Any writer overwhelmingly honest about pleasing himself is almost sure to please others.
1963 In *Vogue*, 15 Aug.

40 I am governed by the pull of the sentence as the pull of a fabric is governed by gravity.
Quoted in Louis Untermeyer 'Five Famous Poetesses', in *Ladies' Home Journal*, May 1964.

41 Subjects choose me… I lie in wait like a leopard on a branch-strained metaphor.
Quoted in Louis Untermeyer 'Five Famous Poetesses', in *Ladies' Home Journal*, May 1964.

42 Omissions are not accidents.
1967 Epigraph to *Complete Poems*.

43 To cite passages is to pull one quill from a porcupine.
Quoted in Patricia C Willis (ed) *The Complete Prose of Marianne Moore* (1986).

Moore, Michael 1954–

US film-maker and writer.

44 The things I believe in, I believe strongly enough in them and I think I'm right. When I'm wrong, then I change my mind and I'm right again.
2002 In a question and answer session at the National Film Theatre, London, 11 Nov.

45 We live in a time when we have fictitious election results that elect a fictitious president, a time where we have a man sending us to war for fictitious reasons. We are against this war, Mr Bush. Shame on you, Mr Bush. Shame on you.

2003 At the 76th Academy Awards, where he was awarded an Oscar for Best Documentary Director.

Moore, Sir Patrick 1923–

English astronomer, author and broadcaster. He began his popular television series, *The Sky at Night*, in 1957, and it has continued since that time.

46 The Moon is a splendid object in our skies, and we naturally tend to think of it as important.

1976 *Guide to the Moon.*

Moore, Thomas 1780–1852

Irish poet, songwriter and biographer. He wrote a number of patriotic songs and poems as well as lives of Sheridan, Byron (a close friend) and others. He also wrote satirical pieces and novels, including *The Fudge Family in Paris* (1818). He is remembered for *Lallah Rookh* (1817), a series of oriental tales in verse, and for the popular songs 'The Harp that once through Tara's Halls', 'The Minstrel-boy', and 'Tis the Last Rose of Summer'.

47 There is not in the wide world a valley so sweet
As that vale in whose bosom the bright waters meet;
Oh! the last rays of feeling and life must depart
Ere the bloom of that valley shall fade from my heart.

1807 *Irish Melodies*, 'The Meeting of the Waters'.

48 Let Erin remember the days of Old,
Ere her faithless sons betrayed her;
When Malachi wore the collar of gold
Which he won from her proud invader;
When her kings, with standards of green unfurled,
Led the Red-Branch Knights to danger;
Ere the emerald gem of the western world
Was set in the crown of a stranger.

1807 *Irish Melodies*, 'Let Erin Remember'.

49 The Minstrel-boy to the war is gone,
In the ranks of death you'll find him;
His father's sword he has girded on,
And his wild harp slung behind him.

1807 *Irish Melodies*,' The Minstrel-boy'.

50 'Tis the last rose of summer
Left blooming alone;
All her lovely companions
Are faded and gone.

1807 *Irish Melodies*,'' Tis the Last Rose of Summer'.

51 The harp that once through Tara's halls
The soul of music shed,
Now hangs as mute on Tara's walls
As if that soul were fled.

1807 *Irish Melodies*, 'The Harp that once through Tara's Halls'.

52 No, there's nothing half so sweet in life
As love's young dream.

1807 *Irish Melodies*, 'Love's Young Dream'.

53 Oh! ever thus, from childhood's hour,
I've seen my fondest hopes decay;
I never loved a tree or flower,
But 'twas the first to fade away.

I never nursed a dear gazelle,
To glad me with its soft black eye,
But when it came to know me well,
And love me, it was sure to die!

1817 *Lallah Rookh*, 'The Fire Worshippers'.

54 Yet, who can help loving the land that has taught us
Six hundred and eighty-five ways to dress eggs?

1818 *The Fudge Family in Paris*, letter 8.

Moorhouse, Geoffrey 1931–

English writer and traveller. He attempted to cross the Sahara from Mauretania to the Nile, but in March 1973, having travelled 2,000 miles (3,200km), 300 miles (480km) on foot after the last of his camels died, he reached Tamanrasset and gave up.

55 There was nothing but pain in the desert, for human beings and animals alike. Life was pain. Only in death was there relief.

1974 *The Fearful Void.*

Moran, Richard John McMoran Wilson, 2nd Baron 1924–

British diplomat and soldier. He filled a succession of diplomatic posts, including High Commissioner in Canada (1981–4). As John Wilson he wrote a Whitbread Award-winning biography of Sir Henry Campbell-Bannerman (1973).

56 Courage is a moral quality; it is not a chance gift of nature, like an aptitude for games. It is a cold choice between two alternatives; the fixed resolve not to quit, an act of renunciation that must be made not once but many times by the power of the will.

1945 *The Anatomy of Courage.*

More, Sir Thomas 1478–1534

English statesman, scholar and writer. Educated at Oxford in the new humanism, he was appointed Lord Chancellor by Henry VIII. He refused to take the oath of supremacy and was executed. His most famous work is *Utopia* (1516; translated into English 1556); other works include *History of King Richard III* (1513) and meditations in prison.

57 In the first place, most princes apply themselves to the arts of war, in which I have neither ability nor interest, instead of to the good arts of peace. They are generally more set on acquiring new kingdoms by hook or by crook than on governing well those that they already have.

1516 *Utopia* (English translation 1556), bk.1.

58 It is only natural, of course, that each man should think his own opinions best: the old crow loves his fledglings, and the ape his cubs.

1516 *Utopia* (English translation 1556), bk.1.

59 Such proud, obstinate, ridiculous judgements I have encountered many times, and once even in England.

1516 *Utopia* (English translation 1556), bk.1.

60 Severe and terrible punishments are enacted against theft, when it would be much better to enable every man to earn his own living, instead of being driven to the awful necessity of stealing and then dying for it.

1516 *Utopia* (English translation 1556), bk.1.

61 The law of Moses is harsh and severe, as for an enslaved and stubborn people, but it punishes theft with a fine,

not death. Let us not think that in his new law of mercy, where he treats us with the tenderness of a father, God has given us greater license to be cruel to one another.
1516 *Utopia* (English translation 1556), bk.1.

62 A king who wants to maintain an army can never have too much gold.
1516 *Utopia* (English translation 1556), bk.1.

63 A king has no dignity when he exercises authority over beggars, only when he rules over prosperous and happy subjects.
1516 *Utopia* (English translation 1556), bk.1.

64 The only real thing they accomplish that I can see is to make men feel a little more secure in their consciences about doing evil.
1516 Of preachers. *Utopia* (English translation 1556), bk.1.

65 Hardly any of the women, who are a full half of the population, work; or if they do, then as a rule their husbands lie snoring in bed.
1516 *Utopia* (English translation 1556), bk.2.

66 For where money is the standard of everything, many vain, superfluous trades are bound to be carried on simply to satisfy luxury and licentiousness.
1516 *Utopia* (English translation 1556), bk.2.

67 The chief aim of their constitution is that, whenever public needs permit, all citizens should be free, so far as possible, to withdraw their time and energy from the service of the body, and devote themselves to the freedom and culture of the mind. For that, they think, is the real happiness of life.
1516 *Utopia* (English translation 1556), bk.2.

68 They find pearls by the seashore, diamonds and rubies in certain cliffs, but never go out of set purpose to look for them. If they happen to find some, they polish them, and give them to the children who, when they are small, feel proud and pleased with such gaudy decorations. But after, when they grow a bit older, and notice that only babies like such toys, they lay them aside. Their parents don't have to say anything, they simply put these trifles away out of a shamefaced sense that they're no longer suitable, just as our children when they grow up put away their rattles, marbles and dolls.
1516 *Utopia* (English translation 1556), bk.2.

69 Thus they say that nature herself prescribes for us a joyous life, in other words, pleasure, as the goal of our actions; and living according to her prescriptions is to be defined as virtue.
1516 *Utopia* (English translation 1556), bk.2.

70 Two evils—greed and faction—are the destruction of all justice.
1516 *Utopia* (English translation 1556), bk.2.

71 Is not this house as nigh heaven as my own?
c.1534 Of the Tower of London. Attributed in William Roper *Life of Sir Thomas More* (ed E V Hitchcock, 1935).

72 I pray you, master Lieutenant, see me safe up, and my coming down let me shift for myself.
1535 On mounting the scaffold. Attributed in William Roper *Life of Sir Thomas More* (ed E V Hitchcock, 1935).

73 This hath not offended the king.
1535 Said on the scaffold as he drew his beard to one side. Attributed in William Roper *Life of Sir Thomas More* (ed E V Hitchcock, 1935).

Morell, Thomas 1703–84

English poet and librettist.

74 See, the conquering hero comes!
Sound the trumpets, beat the drums!
1747 *Judas Maccabeus*, 'A Chorus of Youths'.

Morey, Larry

US lyricist who frequently worked with Frank Churchill. Best known for contributing to *Snow White and the Seven Dwarfs* (1937) and *Bambi* (1941).

75 Heigh ho, heigh ho
It's off to work we go.
1937 First lines of the song 'Heigh-Ho' from the film *Snow White and the Seven Dwarfs*. Music by Frank Churchill.

76 Whistle While You Work.
1937 Title of song from the film *Snow White and the Seven Dwarfs*. Music by Frank Churchill.

Morgan, Edwin George 1920–

Scottish poet and critic, Professor Emeritus of English at Glasgow University. One of the most important Scottish writers, he is a skilled translator as well as an original poet.

77 Many things are unspoken
In the life of a man, and with a place
there is an unspoken love also
in undercurrents, drifting, waiting its time.
1968 'The Second Life'.

78 And later, wondering farmers as they passed would hear
beyond the lighted window in the autumn evening
two handsome yellow-bosomed basset-hounds
howling to a melodious basset-horn.
1968 'An Addition to the Family'.

79 Deplore what is to be deplored,
and then find out the rest.
1968 'King Billy'.

80 The man lies late since he has lost his job,
smokes on one elbow, letting his coughs fall
thinly into an air too poor to rob.
1973 'Glasgow Sonnets, I'.

81 No deliverer ever rose
from these stone tombs to get the hell they made
unmade.
1973 'Glasgow Sonnets, II'.

Morgan, Elaine 1920–

British science writer, journalist and playwright. She worked on the award-winning television screening of Vera Brittain's *Testament of Youth* (1980). Her controversial book *The Descent of Woman* (1972), which explores the origins of mankind, with special reference to women's evolution, was followed by *The Aquatic Ape* (1982).

82 It takes two to make a woman into a sex object.
1972 *The Descent of Woman*, ch.11.

Moritz, Karl Philipp 1756–93

German writer, an early Romantic. After travelling in England and Italy he wrote *Reisen eines Deutschen in England* (1783) and *Reisen eines Deutschen in Italien* (1792–3). His autobiographical novel *Anton Reise* (1785–90) influenced Goethe.

83 When you see how in this happy country the lowest and poorest member of society takes an interest in all public affairs; when you see how high and low, rich and poor, are all willing to declare their feelings and convictions; when you see how a carter, a common sailor, a beggar is still a man, nay, even more, an Englishman—then, believe me, you find yourself very differently affected from the experience you feel when staring at our soldiers drilling in Berlin.
1782 Letter to a friend after observing a London by-election.

Morley, Christopher Darlington 1890–1957

US writer and poet, founder and editor (1924–41) of the *Saturday Review*. His many novels include *Parnassus on Wheels* (1917).

84 Life is a foreign language: all men mispronounce it.
1925 *Thunder on the Left*, ch.14.

85 Dancing is a wonderful training for girls, it's the first way you learn to guess what a man is going to do before he does it.
1939 *Kitty Foyle*, ch.11.

86 When you sell a man a book, you don't sell him 12 ounces of paper and ink and glue—you sell him a whole new life.
Recalled on his death, 28 Mar 1957.

Morley, Robert 1908–92

English actor. A popular comic actor, he also made many film and television appearances, including *Beat the Devil* (1953), *Oscar Wilde* (1960) and *Who is Killing the Great Chefs of Europe?* (1978).

87 The French are a logical people, which is one reason the English dislike them so intensely. The other is that they own France, a country which we have always judged to be much too good for them.
1974 *A Musing Morley*, 'France and the French'.

88 It is a great help for a man to be in love with himself. For an actor, it is absolutely essential.
1979 In *Playboy*.

89 I started off in films as a king—a French king, admittedly, but nevertheless a king in *Marie Antoinette*—and stayed in that sort of income bracket.
Quoted in *The Best of Robert Morley* (1981).

90 Anyone who works is a fool. I don't work: I merely inflict myself on the public.
Attributed.

Morris, Desmond John 1928–

British ethologist and writer. His interest in primate behaviour led to his best-known work, the popular *The Naked Ape* (1967).

91 The Human Zoo.
1969 Title of book.

92 Clearly, then, the city is not a concrete jungle, it is a human zoo.
1969 *The Human Zoo*, introduction.

Morris, Jan formerly *James Morris* 1926–

English reporter and writer. As James Morris he wrote books and essays on travel. He accompanied the 1953 first ascent of Everest, covering it for *The Times*. As Jan Morris she has written a moving account of her sex change *Conundrum*

(1974), the *Pax Britannica* trilogy (1968–78) and other novels. She was made a CBE in 1999.

93 Venice will linger in your mind…and wherever you go in life you will feel somewhere over your shoulder, a pink, castellated, shimmering presence, the domes and riggings and crooked pinnacles of the Serenissima. There's romance for you! There's the lust and dark wine of Venice! No wonder George Eliot's husband fell into the Grand Canal.
1960 *Venice*.

94 The genius of Canada remains essentially a deflationary genius.
1976 'On the Confederation Special,' in *Travels*.

95 If I was an aspirant litterateur, I was also an aspirant anarchist. I have disliked Authority always, though sometimes seduced by its resplendence.
2003 *A Writer's World: Travels 1950–2000*, prologue.

Morris, John 1895–1980

English writer, traveller and academic. He travelled in Asia and Africa, and took part in two Everest expeditions. He taught at Keio University in Japan (1938–42) and later became Head of the Far Eastern Service then Controller of the Third Programme at the BBC (1952–8).

96 The Japanese…have a saying that there are two kinds of fool: those who have never climbed Mount Fuji, and those who have climbed it more than once.
1943 *Traveller from Tokyo*.

Morris, Sir Lewis 1833–1907

English versifier.

97 We hold a vaster Empire than has been.
'Song of Empire', written to celebrate Queen Victoria's Jubilee, 20 Jun. The words were printed on Canada's first commemorative postage stamp, 1898.

Morris, William 1834–96

English craftsman and poet, associated with the Pre-Raphaelite Brotherhood, a major figure in the Arts and Crafts Movement. He joined the Social Democratic Federation in 1883, and organized the Socialist League. In 1890 he set up the private Kelmscott Press.

98 The Socialist papers…came out full to the throat of well-printed matter…admirable and straightforward expositions of the doctrines and practice of Socialism, free from haste and spite and hard words…with a kind of May-day freshness amidst the worry and terror of the moment.
1890 *News from Nowhere*.

99 Between complete socialism and communism there is no difference whatever in my mind. Communism is in fact the completion of socialism; when that ceases to be militant and becomes triumphant, it will be communism.
1893 Addressing Hammersmith Socialist Society.

Morris, Wright Marion 1910–98

US writer. He wrote novels, short stories, memoirs and critical essays. He was an accomplished photographer, and published several books marrying text with photographs.

1 A Bill of Rites, A Bill of Wrongs, A Bill of Goods.
1968 Title of essay collection.

Morrison, R F

2 Just a wee deoch-an-doris,
Just a wee yin, that's a'.
Just a wee deoch-an-doris,
Afore we gang awa'.
There's a wee wifie waitin'
In a wee but-an-ben;
If ye can say 'It's a braw bricht moonlicht nicht',
Ye're a' richt, ye ken.
1911 'Just a Wee Deoch-an-Doris', chorus. The song was popularized by Sir Harry Lauder.

Morrison, Toni Chloe Anthony *née Wofford* 1931–

US novelist. Her novels have reflected black American experience and consciousness through a sophisticated literary sensibility. She was awarded the Nobel prize for literature in 1993.

3 We have to acknowledge that the thing we call 'literature' is more pluralistic now, just as society ought to be. The melting pot never worked.
1981 In *Newsweek*, 30 Mar.

4 How soon country people forget. When they fall in love with a city it is forever, and it is like forever… There, in a city, they are not so much new as themselves: their stronger, riskier selves.
1991 *Jazz*, ch.2.

5 In this country American means white. Everybody else has to hyphenate.
1992 In *The Guardian*, 29 Jan.

6 Slavery broke the world in half, it broke it in every way. It broke Europe. It made them into something else, it made them slave masters, it made them crazy. You can't do that for hundreds of years and it not take a toll. They had to dehumanize, not just the slaves but themselves.
Quoted in Paul Gilroy *Small Acts* (1993), 'Living memory: a meeting with Toni Morrison'.

7 I have always wanted to develop a way of writing that was irrevocably black. I don't have the resources of a musician but I thought that if it was truly black literature, it would not be black because I was, it would not even be black because of its subject matter. It would be something intrinsic, indigenous, something in the way it was put together—the sentences, the structure, texture and tone—so that anyone who read it would realize.
Quoted in Paul Gilroy *Small Acts* (1993), 'Living memory: a meeting with Toni Morrison'.

Morrissey *full name Steven Patrick Morrissey* 1959–

English singer and songwriter, former member of The Smiths.

8 Heaven Knows I'm Miserable Now.
1984 Song title.

9 No—he lives next door to me.
2002 When asked whether it was true that he lived next door to Johnny Depp. In the *Observer*, 15 Sep.

10 My best friend is myself… It's a lifelong relationship and divorce will never come into it.
2002 In the *Observer*, 15 Sep.

Morse, Samuel F(inley) B(reese) 1791–1872

US inventor and painter, who demonstrated (1844) the practicability of an electrical telegraph device to Congress. He had earlier trained as an artist.

11 Alas! My dear sir, the very name of *pictures* produces a sadness of heart I cannot describe. Painting has been a smiling mistress to many, but she has been a cruel jilt to me.
1849 Letter to his friend the writer James Fenimore Cooper, 20 Nov.

Mortimer, Sir John Clifford 1923–

English playwright, novelist and barrister. Called to the bar in 1948, he took part in several celebrated civil cases before achieving wider fame as a writer, notably as creator of the fictitious barrister Horace Rumpole. His other publications include volumes of autobiography, novels such as *Paradise Postponed* (1985) and *Summer's Lease* (1988) and several plays.

12 No brilliance is needed in the law. Nothing but common sense, and relatively clean finger nails.
1971 *A Voyage Round My Father*, act 1.

13 The law seems like a sort of maze through which a client must be led to safety, a collection of reefs, rocks, and underwater hazards through which he or she must be piloted.
1982 *Clinging to the Wreckage*, ch.7.

14 They do you a decent death in the hunting field.
1985 *Paradise Postponed*, ch.18.

15 The shelf life of the modern hardback writer is somewhere between the milk and the yoghurt.
1987 In the *Observer*, 28 Jun.

16 Life itself is a mystery which defies solution.
1990 In the *Sunday Times*, 1 Apr.

17 But plots come from—God knows where. They can't be summoned at will. They come reluctantly, unexpectedly, stealthily, when you have given up hope of them ever paying you a visit.
1993 'A Plot at Last', in Brown and Munro (eds) *Writers Writing* (1993).

Mortimer, (Charles) Raymond Bell 1895–1980

English literary and art critic.

18 People don't learn to enjoy pictures because they seldom look at them; and they seldom look at pictures because they have never learnt to enjoy them.
1976 *Try Anything Once*.

Morton, Jelly Roll (Ferdinand) 1890–1941

US jazz pianist. He was an important pioneer of the New Orleans jazz style, but was much given to making extravagant claims about his role in it.

19 It is evidently known, beyond contradiction, that New Orleans is the cradle of *jazz*, and I, myself, happened to be the creator in the year 1902… Jazz music is a style, not compositions; any kind of music may be played in *jazz*, if one has the knowledge.
1938 In *Downbeat*, Aug.

Morton, J(ohn Cameron Andrieu) B(ingham Michael) *pseudonym Beachcomber* 1893–1979

English writer. He wrote many books of humour, fantasy, satire and history, but is chiefly remembered for his humorous columns in the *Daily Express*, under the nom de plume 'Beachcomber'.

20 One disadvantage of being a hog is that at any moment some blundering fool may try to make a silk purse out of your wife's ear.
1931 *By the Way.*

21 Hush, hush!
Nobody cares!
Christopher Robin
Has
Fallen
Down
Stairs.
1931 *By the Way.*

22 The Doctor is said also to have invented an extraordinary weapon which will make war less brutal. It is described as a very powerful liquid which rots braces at a distance of a mile.
1936 'Bracerot'.

Morton, Rogers Clark Ballard 1914–1979

US former Republican politician. He was president of a flour manufacturing company and representative for Maryland in the 88th–92nd Congresses. He was Secretary of the Interior (1971–5) and a counsellor to the President on economic and domestic matters (1976–7).

23 I have no intention of rearranging the furniture on the deck of the Titanic.
1976 On declining to rescue President Ford's disastrous election campaign.

Morton, Thomas c.1764–1838

English playwright. He is usually remembered for his comedy *Speed the Plough* (1798).

24 What will Mrs Grundy say? What will Mrs Grundy think?
1798 *Speed the Plough.*

Moses, Anna Mary Robertson *known as 'Grandma Moses'* 1860–1961

US painter. The wife of a farmer in New York state, with no art training, she did not begin painting until in her 70s. Her primitive paintings are colourful, simple scenes of everyday rural life.

25 Paintin's not important. What's important is keepin' busy.
1954 In news summaries, 2 Jan.

Moses, Ed 1955–

US track athlete. He was unbeaten in any 400-metre hurdle race from August 1977 to June 1987, and was Olympic champion in 1976 and 1984 and four times world record holder.

26 There are three universal languages: love, music and sports.
2004 In the *Boston Herald*, 12 May.

Mosk, Stanley 1912–2001

US lawyer and Justice of State Supreme Court. He practised law in Los Angeles until 1939 and was Attorney General of California 1959–64. He was a Justice of the Supreme Court of California from 1964 until his death.

27 Little old ladies in tennis shoes.
Characterizing older, activist women. Quoted in William Safire *Safire's Political Dictionary* (1975).

Moss, Gary

US marketing coach, a former vice-president of marketing communications, Campbell Soup Co.

28 You can teach an elephant to dance, but the likelihood of its stepping on your toes is very high.
1993 On the decline of the advertising agencies' monopoly in marketing. In *Forbes*, 15 Mar.

Moss, Sir Stirling 1929–

English racing driver. Although he never won the World Championship, he became one of the most celebrated of all drivers, winning numerous Grand Prix races driving for a variety of teams. He retired in 1962 after a serious crash.

29 It is necessary to relax your muscles when you can. Relaxing your brain is fatal.
1955 In *Newsweek*, 16 May.

30 There are two things no man will admit he can't do well—drive and make love.
Quoted in Colin Jarman *The Guinness Dictionary of Sports Quotations* (1990).

Motherwell, Robert 1915–91

US painter and writer, an exponent of Abstract Realism. His works typically consist of large, amorphous blocks of strong colour, such as his most famous series, *Elegies to the Spanish Republic* (1975).

31 One of the most striking of abstract art's appearance is her nakedness, an art stripped bare.
1951 Paper given at a symposium, 5 Feb, at the Museum of Modern Art, New York, published in *What Abstract Art Means to Me: Bulletin of the Museum of Modern Art* (Spring 1951).

32 Every intelligent painter carries the whole culture of modern painting in his head…everything he paints is both an homage and a critique.
1977 In the *Los Angeles Times*, 31 Jul.

33 All my life I've been working on the work—every canvas a sentence or paragraph of it. Each picture is only an approximation of what I want.
Recalled on his death, 16 Jul 1991.

Motion, Andrew 1952–

English poet and biographer, Poet Laureate from 1999.

34 Earth's axle creeks; the year jolts on; the trees begin to slip their brittle leaves, their flakes of rust; and darkness takes the edge off daylight, not because it wants to—never that. Because it must.
1997 'Mythology', written for the funeral of Diana, Princess of Wales. Published in *Public Property* (2002).

35 O Jonny the power of your boot
And the accurate heart-stopping route
Of your goal as it ghosts
Through Australian posts
Is a triumph we gladly salute.
2004 'A Song for Jonny', written to commemorate England winning the rugby World Cup and the player Jonny Wilkinson.

Motson, John 1946–

English football commentator.

36 It's Arsenal 0 Everton 1 and the longer it stays like that the more you've got to fancy Everton.
Quoted in *Motson's National Obsession* (2004).

37 Nearly all the Brazilian supporters are wearing yellow shirts— it's a fabulous kaleidoscope of colour.
Quoted in *Motson's National Obsession* (2004).

38 For those of you watching in black and white, Spurs are in the all-yellow strip.
Quoted in *Motson's National Obsession* (2004).

Mountbatten of Burma, Louis Francis Albert Victor Nicholas, 1st Earl 1900–79

English admiral and statesman, chief of Combined Operations Command (1942) in World War II. As Supreme Commander, SE Asia, he received the Japanese surrender at Singapore, and in 1947 became last Viceroy of India. He returned to the Admiralty as First Sea Lord (1954) and Chief of the Defence Staff (1959). He retired in 1965 and in 1979 was assassinated by Irish Republican terrorists.

39 As a military man who has given half a century of active service, I say in all sincerity that the nuclear arms race has no military purpose. Wars cannot be fought with nuclear weapons; their existence only adds to our perils because of the illusions that they have generated. The world now stands on the brink of the final abyss. Let us all resolve to take all possible practicable steps to ensure that we do not, through our own folly, go over the edge.
1979 Speech at the Council of Europe in Strasbourg, 11 May.

Mowlam, Mo (Marjorie) 1949–

English Labour politician. She was Secretary of State for Northern Ireland from 1997 to 1999.

40 Ian Paisley said he pitied my husband having to put up with 'the sinner', which is what he often called me.
2000 In the *Sunday Times*, 16 Apr.

Moynihan, Daniel Patrick 1927–2003

US sociologist and diplomat, adviser to Presidents Kennedy, Johnson, Nixon and Ford. He was Ambassador to India (1973–5), US representative to the UN (1975–6), and subsequently a Senator (1976–2001). His writings include *Beyond the Melting Pot* (with Nathan Glazer, 1963).

41 We've come full circle but the best remains the heart of the city, the greatest center of the greatest city, our Acropolis, where our Christmas tree is lighted.
1991 On New York's Rockefeller Centre. In the *New York Times*, 15 Mar.

42 Things become complicated if there are enough people to complexify them.
1991 Of the 19,000-member congressional back-up staff. In the *New York Times*, 12 Nov.

43 They live off secrecy…[it] keep the mistakes secret.
1993 Of government intelligence agencies. *President Kennedy.*

44 The Lord looks after drunks and Americans.
1995 Of the avoidance of casualties in the Haitian intervention. In the *US News and World Report*, 9 Jan.

Mozart, (Johann Chrysostom) Wolfgang Amadeus 1756–91

Austrian composer. An infant prodigy, who suffered throughout his life from poverty and overwork, his many compositions include symphonies, concertos, string quintets, string quartets, numerous piano and violin sonatas, choral works and operas such as *The Marriage of Figaro* (1786), *Don Giovanni* (1787), *Così fan tutte* (1790) and *The Magic Flute* (1791).

45 It is much easier to play a thing quickly than to play it slowly.
1778 Letter.

46 Melody is the very essence of music. When I think of a good melodist I think of a fine race horse. A contrapuntist is only a post-horse.
1786 Letter to Michael Kelly.

Mugabe, Robert Gabriel 1924–

Zimbabwean politician. He co-founded ZANU (Zimbabwe African National Union, 1963), and on Zimbabwe's independence in 1980 became first Prime Minister (1980–7) and subsequently President (1987–).

47 Cricket? It civilises people and creates good gentlemen. I want everyone to play cricket in Zimbabwe. I want ours to be a nation of gentlemen.
Quoted in Helen Exley *Cricket Quotations* (1992).

Muggeridge, Malcolm 1903–90

English journalist. He was Editor of *Punch* from 1953 to 1957, and appeared frequently on television as reporter and interviewer. In his later years he became a Roman Catholic.

48 The orgasm has replaced the cross as the focus of longing and the image of fulfilment.
1966 *Tread Softly for You Tread on My Jokes.*

49 The media have, indeed, provided the Devil with perhaps the greatest opportunity accorded him since Adam and Eve were turned out of the Garden of Eden.
1976 *Christ and the Media*, introduction.

50 Future historians will surely see us as having created in the media a Frankenstein monster whom no one knows how to control or direct, and marvel that we should have so meekly subjected ourselves to its destructive and often malign influence.
1976 *Christ and the Media*, 'Lecture 1'.

51 It's very nearly impossible to tell the truth in television.
1976 *Christ and the Media*, 'Questions following the 3rd lecture'.

Muir, Edwin 1887–1959

Scottish writer and translator. He is best known as a poet, but also wrote literary and cultural criticism, and an autobiography.

52 The curse of Scottish literature is the lack of a whole language, which finally means the lack of a whole mind.
1936 *Scott and Scotland*, introduction.

53 The hills and towers
Stood otherwise than they should stand,
And without fear the lawless roads
Ran wrong throughout the land.
1937 *Journeys and Places*, 'Hölderlin's Journey', stanza 11.

54 There is a road that turning always
Cuts off the country of Again.

Archers stand there on every side
And as it runs time's deer is slain,
And lies where it has lain.
1937 'The Road'.

55 All through that summer at ease we lay,
And daily from the turret wall
We watched the mowers in the hay
And the enemy half a mile away.
They seemed no threat to us at all.
1946 *The Voyage*, 'The Castle', stanza 1.

56 It was not meant for human eyes,
That combat on the shabby patch
Of clods and trampled earth that lies
Somewhere beneath the sodden skies
For eye of toad or adder to catch.
1949 *The Labyrinth*, 'The Combat'.

57 Oh these deceits are strong almost as life.
Last night I dreamt I was in the labyrinth,
And woke far on. I did not know the place.
1949 *The Labyrinth*, 'The Labyrinth'.

58 We have seen
Good men made evil wrangling with the evil,
Straight minds grown crooked fighting crooked minds.
Our peace betrayed us; we betrayed our peace.
Look at it well. This was the good town once.
1949 *The Labyrinth*, 'The Good Town'.

59 Kindness and courage can repair time's faults,
And serving him breeds patience and courtesy
In us, light sojourners and passing subjects.
1949 *The Labyrinth*, 'The Good Town'.

60 The life of every man is an endlessly repeated
performance of the life of man.
1954 *An Autobiography*, ch.1.

61 Since then they have pulled our ploughs and borne our
loads.
But that free servitude still can pierce our hearts.
Our life is changed; their coming our beginning.
1956 *One Foot in Eden*, 'The Horses'.

62 Barely a twelvemonth after
The seven days war that put the world to sleep,
Late in the evening the strange horses came.
1956 *One Foot in Eden*, 'The Horses'.

63 One foot in Eden still, I stand
And look across the other land.
The world's great day is growing late,
Yet strange these fields that we have planted
So long with crops of love and hate.
1956 *One Foot in Eden*, 'One Foot in Eden'.

Muir, John 1838–1914

Scottish naturalist. He emigrated with his family to America as a boy, and became a champion of wilderness areas and the establishment of National Parks in the US. He is regarded as the father of the environmental movement.

64 The tendency nowadays to wander in wildernesses is delightful to see. Thousands of tired, nerve-shaken, over-civilized people are beginning to find out that going to the mountains is going home; that wildness is a necessity; and that mountain parks and reservations are useful not only as fountains of timber and irrigating rivers, but as fountains of life.

1901 *Our National Parks*, ch.1, 'The Wild Parks and Forest Reservations of the West'.

65 When we contemplate the whole globe as one great dewdrop, striped and dotted with continents and islands, flying through space with other stars all singing and shining together as one, the whole universe appears as an infinite storm of beauty.
Travels in Alaska, ch.1, 'The Puget Sound and British Columbia' (published 1915).

66 I have precious little sympathy for the selfish propriety of civilized man, and if a war of races should occur between the wild beasts and Lord Man, I would be tempted to sympathise with the bears.
A Thousand-Mile Walk to the Gulf, ch.5, 'Through Florida Swamps and Forests' (published 1916).

Muir, Willa (Wilhelmina) Johnstone *née* **Anderson** *also known as* **Agnes Neill Scott** 1890–1970

Scottish poet, novelist and translator, wife of the poet Edwin Muir whose unconventional religious beliefs forced her resignation from a teaching position in 1915. Her published works include many translations, several novels and a book of poetry.

67 Apparently the average man sees woman alternately as an inferior being and as an angel.
1925 *Women: An Inquiry*, pt.1, published as Hogarth Essay no.10 in *The Hogarth Essays* (Second Series, 1926).

68 A man can be a parent without knowing it: a woman cannot.
1925 *Women: An Inquiry*, pt.1, published as Hogarth Essay no.10 in *The Hogarth Essays* (Second Series, 1926).

Mullan, Peter 1960–

Scottish actor and director.

69 Worst script I've ever read.
2003 On *Braveheart*. In *The Herald*, 1 Feb.

70 There's no such thing as an actor giving positive criticism to a director. The minute you say 'Don't you think it would look nicer…', that director's going to hate your guts. Particularly if it's a good idea.
2003 In a question and answer session at the National Film Theatre, London, 4 Nov.

71 Nine out of ten delinquents are frustrated actors.
2003 In a question and answer session at the National Film Theatre, London, 4 Nov.

Muller, Herbert Joseph 1905–80

US writer.

72 Few have probably ever heard of Fra Luca Pacioli, the inventor of double-entry bookkeeping; but he has probably had much more influence on human life than has Dante or Michelangelo.
1957 *Uses of the Past*, ch.8.

Mulroney, (Martin) Brian 1939–

Canadian Conservative politician, Prime Minister (1984–93). His radical reforms included the Meech Lake Accords (which aimed at settling disputes between the provinces and the centre, but which later collapsed) and a free-trade agreement with the US.

73 In politics, madame, you need two things: friends, but

above all an enemy.
1990 Remark made to a journalist following the by-election victory of Liberal leader Jean Chrétien, 10 Dec, quoted two days later by Graham Fraser in *The Globe and Mail.*

Mumford, Lewis 1895–1990

US sociologist and author. A literary critic and journal editor, he began to write on architecture and urbanization in such works as *The Story of Utopias* (1922) and *The City in History* (1961), stressing the dehumanizing effects of technology.

74 Every generation revolts against its fathers and makes friends with its grandfathers.
1931 *The Brown Decades*, p.3.

75 However far modern science and technics have fallen short of their inherent possibilities, they have taught mankind at least one lesson: Nothing is impossible.
1934 *Technics and Civilization.*

76 The Fujiyama of Architecture…at once a lofty mountain and a national shrine.
1953 Of Frank Lloyd Wright. 'A Phoenix Too Infrequent', in the *New Yorker*, 28 Nov.

77 Our national flower is the concrete cloverleaf.
Collected in *Quote Magazine*, 8 Oct 1961.

78 The life-efficiency and adaptability of the computer must be questioned. Its judicious use depends upon the availability of its human employers quite literally to keep their own heads, not merely to scrutinize the programming but to reserve for themselves the right of ultimate decision. No automatic system can be intelligently run by automatons—or by people who dare not assert human intuition, human autonomy, human purpose.
1970 *The Myth of the Machine.*

79 As full of flavor as hickory smoke.
1994 Of geotechnic expert Benton MacKaye. In *Harvard University Magazine,* Jul.

Munch, Edvard 1863–1944

Norwegian painter and graphic artist.

80 One evening, I was walking along a path, the city was on one side and the fjord below. I felt tired and ill. I stopped and looked out over the fjord—the sun was setting, and the clouds turning blood red. I sensed a scream passing through nature; it seemed to me that I heard the scream. I painted this picture, painted the clouds as actual blood. The colour shrieked. This became The Scream.
1889 *Diary.*

Münch, Richard Friedrich 1945–

German sociologist, professor at the University of Bamberg.

81 Social life is mutual negotiation and society, social order, relies on this mutual negotiation between individuals; this represents both creed and particular reality in American society. In no other society is this creed and the corresponding reality as prominent as the United States.
1986 'The American Creed in Sociological Theory', in *Sociological Theory,* vol.4, issue 43.

Mundy, Peter c.1596–1667

English trader and seafarer. He was sent to France at the age of 12 to learn French. At 15 he went to sea and travelled continually thereafter. His journal was edited by the Hakluyt Society.

82 We all three got up on our elephant which brought us hither. For my own part I found [it] very uneasy riding, being badly seated and not accustomed (he had such a shuffling, jogging justling pace), sitting hindermost on the ridge of his monstrous massy chine bones, and nothing at all under me (nor they neither) that I wished myself on foot and would have let myself fall off but that it was somewhat too high. In fine, we alighted off from his back into the upper galleries of the house and saved the labour going upstairs.
c.1620 On riding on an elephant. *Travels* (pubished c.1650).

83 So that finding myself at present in or about one hundred and twenty degrees off east longitude from England, it bred in me a desire to proceed on the same easterly course till I had ended where I began, and so to have once made one circle round the globe of the earth, which would have been a voyage of voyages.
c.1640 Objections were raised and Mundy was unable to fulfil this aim. *Travels* (published c.1650).

Munro, Alice *née Laidlaw* 1931–

Canadian short-story writer; her first collection of short stories *Dance of the Happy Shades* (1968) won the Governor-General's Award, as did *Lives of Girls and Women* (1971).

84 Boys' hate was dangerous, it was keen and bright, a miraculous birthright, like Arthur's sword snatched out of the stone.
1971 *Lives of Girls and Women,* 'Changes and Ceremonies'.

85 I thought of my mother, who would publicly campaign for birth control but would never even think she needed to talk to me, so firmly was she convinced that sex was something no woman—no *intelligent* woman—would ever submit to unless she had to.
1971 *Lives of Girls and Women,* 'Baptizing'.

86 She had reached an age where she thought she could not stand to know any more…she pushed any discovery aside with embarassment.
1978 *Lives of Girls and Women,* 'Royal Beatings'.

87 Country manners. Even if somebody phones up to tell you your house is burning down, they ask first how you are.
1987 *The Progress of Love,* 'The Progress of Love'.

88 Hatred is always a sin, my mother told me. Remember that. One drop of hatred in your soul will spread and discolor everything like a drop of black ink in white milk. I was struck by that and meant to try it, but knew I shouldn't waste the milk.
1987 *The Progress of Love,* 'The Progress of Love'.

89 People live within winter in a way outsiders do not understand. They are watchful, provident, fatigued, exhilarated.
1987 *The Progress of Love,* 'Fits'.

90 Do such moments really mean, as they seem to, that we have a life of happiness with which we only occasionally, knowingly, intersect? Do they shed such light before and after that all that has happened in our lives—or that we've made to happen—can be dismissed?
1987 *The Progress of Love,* 'The Moon in the Orange Street Skating Rink'.

Münster, Count Georg 1794–1868

Hanoverian diplomat.

91 An intelligent Russian once remarked to me, 'Every country has its own Constitution. Ours is absolutism moderated by assassination.'
Political Sketches of the State of Europe 1814–1867

Murdoch, Dame (Jean) Iris 1919–99

Irish novelist and philosopher, of Anglo-Irish descent. Her novels, exploring human relationships with subtlety and humour, include *The Sea, The Sea* (1978) and *The Philosopher's Pupil* (1983).

92 All our failures are ultimately failures in love.
1958 *The Bell.*

93 Love is the extremely difficult realisation that something other than oneself is real. Love, and so art and morals, is the discovery of reality.
1959 'The Sublime and the Good'.

94 What can one do with the past?
Forgive it. Let it enter into you in peace.
1968 *The Nice and the Good.*

95 He was a sociologist; he had gotten into an intellectual muddle early on in life and never managed to get out.
1983 *The Philosopher's Pupil,* 'The Events in Our Town'.

Murdoch, (Keith) Rupert 1931–

Australian-born US newspaper publisher. He expanded his publishing empire first in Australia, then in Britain, buying the *News of the World* in 1969, *The Times* and the *Sunday Times* in 1981. He moved into the US market in 1976 and created a successful television network, the Fox Network. He became a US citizen in 1985.

96 I did not come all this way not to interfere.
c.1969 Quoted in S Somerfield *Banner Headlines* (1979). Somerfield was editor of the *News of the World* and complained that Murdoch, who had recently bought the paper, was interfering with his editorial role.

97 I have heard cynics who say he's a very political old monk shuffling around in Gucci shoes.
1999 On the Dalai Lama. In the *Daily Telegraph,* 7 Sep.

Murkowski, Frank H 1933–

US Governor of Alaska (2002–). Former Vice-Chair, US Senate Select Committee on Intelligence.

98 Low morale and high indigestion.
1991 Of the mood of the Senate confirming CIA Director Robert M Gates. In the *New York Times,* 12 Nov.

Murphy, Dervla 1931–

Irish writer and traveller. In 1963 she cycled to India, where she worked with Tibetan children.

99 On my tenth birthday a bicycle and an atlas coincided as presents and a few days later I decided to cycle to India.
1965 *Full Tilt: Ireland to India with a Bicycle.*

1 It is on occasions such as these that I thank God for my sanguine temperament, which refuses to allow me to believe in disaster until it is finally manifest.
1965 *Full Tilt: Ireland to India with a Bicycle.*

2 Each human spirit is immortal—for time cannot destroy

whatever element within us reverences the glory of a dawn in the mountains.
1968 *In Ethiopia with a Mule.*

3 Never before had I embarked on a journey that required courage.
1978 On embarking on travels and research into the problems of Northern Ireland. *A Place Apart.*

Murphy, Ian

Architect, lecturer at the University of Westminster.

4 The technology of decentralization can be the saviour or assassin of contemporary and future society. The role of architects may be uncertain, but the role of architecture is not. In order to look forward society may sometimes have to look back. This it should do in order to learn from previous mistakes and oversights and to preclude similar eventualities in the future. This does not imply historical dependency, as some would assert. The symbiosis of architecture and technology should prevail, engendered by honesty and integrity. The task will not be easy.
1993 'The impact of the environment: the shock of the new', in Ben Farmer and Hentie Louw (eds) *Companion to Contemporary Architectural Thought* (1993).

Murphy, Tom (Thomas) S 1925–

US media company executive, president (1964–72) and chair (1966–96) of ABC Inc.

5 If you hire mediocre people, they will hire mediocre people.
1991 In *Fortune,* 6 May.

Murray, Les(lie Allan) 1938–

Australian poet and writer whose exuberant verse reflects both his farming background and his preoccupation with language. His collections include *The Ilex Tree* (1965), *The Weatherboard Cathedral* (1969), *Subhuman Redneck Poems* (1996) and *Conscious and Verbal* (1999).

6 The houses there wear verandahs out of shyness.
1986 *Selected Poems,* 'Driving Through Sawmill Towns'.

7 If the cardinal points of costume
are Robes, Tato, Rig and Scunge,
where are shorts in this compass?

They are the never Robes
as other bareleg outfits have been:
the toga, the kilt, the lava-lava,
the Mahatma's cotton dhoti;

archbishops and field marshals
at their ceremonies never wear shorts.
The very word
means underpants in North America.
1986 *Selected Poems,* 'The Dream of Wearing Shorts Forever'.

8 A for adrenalin, the original A-bomb, fuel
and punishment of aspiration, the Enlightenment's
   air-burst
Back when God made me, I had no script. It was better.
For all the death, we also die unrehearsed.
In *Collected Poems* (1998).

Murray, Mike (Michael) c.1956–

US computer executive and philanthropist. Vice-President of Human Resources and Administration at Microsoft until 1999.

9 If Microsoft were a car it would have a large gas pedal and a small but workable brake. It would not have a rear-view mirror.
1994 In *Newsweek*, 11 Jul.

Murrow, Edward (Edgar) R(oscoe) 1908–65

US journalist and broadcaster. As CBS correspondent from Britain from 1937, he conveyed wartime spirit to the US. He became a producer of current affairs television programmes after the war, and his questioning of Joseph McCarthy contributed to the Senator's fall from grace.

10 He mobilized the English language and sent it into battle to steady his fellow countrymen and hearten those Europeans upon whom the long dark night of tyranny had descended.
1954 Of Churchill. Broadcast, 30 Nov, quoted in *In Search of Light* (1967).

11 The people you have seen have the strength to harvest your fruit and vegetables. They do not have the strength to influence legislation. Maybe you do.
1960 *Harvest of Shame*, CBS T V documentary on migrant labour, 25 Nov, concluding words.

12 The politician is trained in the art of inexactitude. His words tend to be blunt or rounded, because if they have a cutting edge they may later return to wound him.
Attributed.

Muschamp, Herbert

Architecture critic for the *New York Times*.

13 Red-and-gold disease…an itch, the theater a place to scratch it…a yearning for the wider world.
1995 In the *New York Times*, 30 Jul. The phrase 'red-and-gold disease' was coined by Lincoln Kirstein's mother when her son began haunting theatres.

Musgrove, F(rank)

English educationalist.

14 It is the business of education to eliminate the influence of parents on the life-chances of the young.
1966 *The Family, Education and Society*.

Mussolini, Benito *also called* Il Duce [the Leader] 1883–1945

Italian politician and Prime Minister (1922). By 1925 he had established himself as dictator. His declaration of war on Britain and France exposed Italy's military unpreparedness, and was followed by a series of defeats; his popularity waned, and he was overthrown and arrested (Jul 1943). Rescued by German paratroopers to head the puppet Italian Social Republic, in 1945 he was captured by the Italian Resistance and shot.

15 I could have transformed this grey assembly hall into an armed camp of Blackshirts, a bivouac for corpses. I could have nailed up the doors of Parliament.
1922 Inaugural speech to the Lower House as Prime Minister, 16 Nov.

16 If I advance, follow me. If I retreat, kill me. If I die, avenge me.
1926 Said to senior officials after an attempt on his life, 6 Apr.

17 Better one day as a lion than a hundred years as a sheep.
c.1930 Quoted in Denis Mack-Smith *Mussolini's Roman Empire* (1976), p.47.

18 War alone can carry to the maximum tension all human energies and imprint with the seal of nobility those people who have the courage to confront it; every other test is a mere substitute.
c.1930 Quoted in Denis Mack-Smith *Mussolini's Roman Empire* (1976), p.47.

19 Words are beautiful things, but muskets and machine guns are even more beautiful.
c.1932 Quoted in Denis Mack-Smith *Mussolini's Roman Empire* (1976).

20 A nation, to remain healthy, should make war every twenty-five years.
1934 Quoted in Denis Mack-Smith *Mussolini's Roman Empire* (1976), p.63.

21 War is to man as maternity to women.
1934 Speech, May. Quoted in Denis Mack-Smith *Mussolini's Roman Empire* (1976), p.54.

22 When the war in Spain is over I shall have to find something else: the Italian character has to be formed through fighting.
1936 Quoted in Thomas *The Spanish Civil War*, p.226.

23 Fascism accepts the individual only insofar as his interests coincide with the state's.
Quoted in the *Enciclopedia Italiana*.

Myers, Mike 1963–

US actor.

24 Party on, dude!
1992 As Wayne Campbell in *Wayne's World*.

25 Yeah, baby!
1997 As Austin Powers in *Austin Powers—International Man of Mystery*.

Myrdal, (Karl) Gunnar 1898–1987

Swedish economist. Professor of Economics, Stockholm University (1933–9, 1961–5). A prominent member of the 'Stockholm School' of macroeconomics of the 1930s. Swedish Minister for Trade and Commerce (1945–7) and Executive Secretary of the UN Economic Commerce (1947–57). In 1974 he was jointly awarded the Nobel prize for economics with Friedrich Hayek. His wife Alva was awarded the Nobel prize for peace in 1982 with Alfonso Garcia Robles.

26 Quantities defined in terms of measurements made at the end of the period in question are referred to as *ex post*; quantities defined in terms of action planned at the beginning of the period in question are referred to as *ex ante*.
1939 *Monetary Equilibrium*.

Nabokov, Vladimir 1899–1977

Russian-born US writer. He left Russia in 1917 and began writing in English in the 1940s. His most widely known novel is *Lolita* (1955). His work is multi-layered and highly literary.

27 There are aphorisms that, like airplanes, stay up only while they are in motion.
1937 *The Gift*, ch.1.

28 Poor Knight! he really had two periods, the first—a dull man writing broken English, the second—a broken man writing dull English.
1941 *The Real Life of Sebastian Knight*, ch.1.

29 The cradle rocks above an abyss, and common sense tells us that our existence is but a brief crack of light between two eternities of darkness.
1951 *Conclusive Evidence* (revised as *Speak, Memory*, 1966), ch.1.

30 Lolita, light of my life, fire of my loins. My sin, my soul. Lo-lee-ta: the tip of the tongue taking a trip of three steps down the palate to tap, at three, on the teeth. Lo. Lee. Ta.
1955 Humbert Humbert. *Lolita*, pt.1, ch.1.

31 You can always count on a murderer for a fancy prose style.
1955 Humbert Humbert. *Lolita*, ch.1.

32 The tiny madman in his padded cell.
1955 Humbert Humbert's description of an embryo. *Lolita*, ch.11.

33 Like so many ageing college people, Pnin had long ceased to notice the existence of students on campus.
1957 *Pnin*, ch.3, section 6.

34 As to the rest, I am no more guilty of imitating 'real life' than 'real life' is responsible for plagiarizing me.
1958 *Nabokov's Dozen*, bibliographical note.

35 Life is a great surprise. I do not see why death should not be an even greater one.
1962 *Pale Fire*.

36 Human life is but a series of footnotes to a vast, obscure unfinished masterpiece.
1962 *Pale Fire*, 'Commentary'.

37 Solitude is the playfield of Satan.
1962 *Pale Fire*, 'Commentary'.

38 I know more than I can express in words, and the little I can express would not have been expressed, had I not known more.
1964 Interview in *Playboy*, Jan.

39 A novelist is, like all mortals, more fully at home on the surface of the present than in the ooze of the past.
1964 Interview in *Playboy*, Jan.

40 A work of art has no importance whatever to society. It is only important to the individual, and only the individual reader is important to me.
1964 Interview in *Playboy*, Jan.

41 Style and structure are the essence of a book; great ideas are hogwash.
1967 Interview in the *Paris Review*, Summer.

42 Derivative writers seem versatile because they imitate many others, past and present. Artistic originality has only itself to copy.
1967 Interview in the *Paris Review*, Summer.

43 Satire is a lesson, parody is a game.
1967 Interview in *Wisconsin Studies in Contemporary Literature*, Spring.

44 Those Eggheads are terrible Philistines. A real good head is not oval but round.
1967 Interview in *Wisconsin Studies in Contemporary Literature*, Spring.

45 A good laugh is the best pesticide.
1968 Interview on BBC television. Reported in *The Listener*, 10 Oct.

46 I think like a genius, I write like a distinguished author, and I speak like a child.
1973 *Strong Opinions*, foreword.

47 Her exotic daydreams do not prevent her from being small-town bourgeois at heart, clinging to conventional ideas or committing this or that conventional violation of the conventional, adultery being a most conventional way to rise above the conventional.
'Madame Bovary'. Collected in *Lectures on Literature* (published 1980).

48 My answer to your question 'Does the writer have a social responsibility?' is NO. You owe me ten cents, sir.
Letter to an editor who had offered him $200 for 2,000 words. Quoted by Eleanor Blau in the *New York Times*, 24 Aug 1989.

Naipaul, Sir V(idiadhar) S(urajprasad) 1932–

Trinidadian writer. His works include *The Mystic Masseur* (1957, John Llewelyn Rhys Memorial Prize), *Miguel Street* (1959, Somerset Maugham Award), *A House for Mr. Biswas* (1961), *A Bend in the River* (1979, Booker Prize) and the autobiographical *Finding the Centre* (1984). He was awarded the Nobel prize for literature in 2001.

49 Worse, to have lived without even attempting to lay claim to one's portion of the earth; to have lived and died as one had been born, unnecessary and unaccommodated.
1961 *A House for Mr. Biswas*, prologue.

50 All that I know of our history and the history of the Indian Ocean I have got from books written by Europeans… Without Europeans, I feel, all our past would have been washed away, like the scuff marks of fishermen on the beach.
1979 *A Bend in the River*, ch.1, 'The Second Rebellion'.

51 I do not regard the knighthood as a social accomplishment.
1993 Quoted in 'Kingdom of Naipaul' by Zoë Heller in the *Independent on Sunday Review*, 28 Mar.

52 Take it on the chin and move on.
Attributed comment to Paul Theroux after their friendship ended. In *Sir Vidia's Shadow: A Friendship Across Five Continents* by Paul Theroux (1998).

Nairne, Caroline, Lady 1766–1845

Scottish songwriter, who collected traditional airs and wrote lyrics to them, often on Jacobite themes.

53 The laird o' Cockpen, he's proud an' he's great,
His mind is ta'en up wi' things o' the State.
'The Laird o' Cockpen', stanza 1.

54 I'm wearin' awa', John
Like snaw-wreaths in thaw, John,
I'm wearin' awa'
To the land o' the leal.
'The Land o' the Leal', stanza 1.

55 Bonnie Charlie's now awa,
Safely owre the friendly main;
Mony a heart will break in twa,
Should he ne'er come back again.

Will ye no come back again?
Will ye no come back again?
Better lo'ed ye canna be,
Will ye no come back again?
'Will Ye No Come Back Again?', stanza 1 and chorus.

Namath, Joe Willie (Joseph William)   1943–

US football player. Known as 'Broadway Joe', he was an
outstanding quarterback with Alabama University and, from
1965, the New York Jets. In 1969 he led the Jets to unexpected
victory in the Superbowl.

56 When you win, nothing hurts.
Quoted in Colin Jarman *The Guinness Dictionary of Sports
Quotations* (1990).

Napier, Sir Charles James   1782–1853

Scottish soldier, born in London. He served in Ireland, Portugal,
against the US and in 1841 was sent to India, where he broke the
power of the amirs at the Battle of Meeanee and became
Governor of Sind.

57 *Peccavi.*
I have sinned [Sind].
1843 Attributed encoded message, 24 Mar, sent after the Battle
of Hyderabad and the capture of Sind.

Napoleon I   1769–1821

French general and Emperor. Born in Corsica, he rose to
prominence during the French Revolution, and was appointed
to command the army of Italy in 1796. Campaigns in Egypt and
Austria followed, and his successes allowed him to lead a coup
against the government and become dictator. Although he was
exiled to Elba by the Allies in 1814, he returned in 1815, when he
was finally defeated at Waterloo and exiled to St Helena.

58 *Soldats, songez que, du haut de ces pyramides, quarante
siècles vous contemplent.*
Soldiers, think that, from the summit of these pyramids,
forty centuries look down upon you.
1798 Speech to the Army of Egypt, before the Battle of the
Pyramids, 21 Jul. Quoted in Gaspard Gourgaud *Mémoires* (1823),
vol.2, 'Egypte, Bataille des Pyramides'.

59 China? There lies a sleeping giant. Let him sleep! For
when he wakes he will move the world.
c.1800 Attributed.

60 Wisdom and policy dictate that we must do as destiny
demands and keep peace with the irresistible march of
events.
1808 Said to Alexander I of Russia, 2 Feb.

61 In war, three-quarters turns on moral considerations; the

balance of actual forces counts only for the remaining
quarter.
1808 Comment, 27 Apr. Quoted in *Observations sur les affaires
de l'Espagne, Saint Cloud*, in *Correspondance de Napoleon Ier*
(1858–69), vol.17.

62 France has more need of me than I have of France.
1813 Speech to Corps Législatif, Paris, 31 Dec.

63 How beautifully the English fight! But they must give
way.
1815 Attributed, at the Battle of Waterloo, 18 Jun.

64 The English conquered us; but they are far from being
our equals.
1815 Letter to Gaspar Gourgaud from St Helena, after the Battle
of Waterloo.

65 An army marches on its stomach.
1816 Attributed. Probably condensed from a long passage
dated 14 Nov in E A de Las Cases *Le Mémoriale de Sainte-Hélène*
(1823), vol.4.

66 In war, as in love, we must come into contact before we
can triumph.
Quoted in A G De Liancourt (ed) *Maximes de Napoleon* (1842).

67 William behaved like a bashful girl, who is afraid of her
lover's bad reputation and therefore avoids being alone
with him.
Of William I of Prussia, who invited other German Princes to
attend a meeting with Napoleon at Baden-Baden in June
originally intended to be a private discussion on the possibility
of a joint alliance with Russia. Quoted in A J P Taylor *Struggle for
Mastery in Europe 1848–1918* (1954), p.121.

68 England is a nation of shopkeepers.
Attributed while in exile on St Helena.

69 Power is my mistress. I have worked too hard in
conquering her to allow anyone to take her from me, or
even to covet her.
The Journal of Roederer.

70 Prussia was hatched from a cannon-ball.
Attributed.

Napoleon III   *until 1852* **Louis–Napoleon** *in full* **Charles Louis Napoleon Bonaparte**   1808–73

President of the Second French Republic (1848–52) and
Emperor of the French (1852–70). He encouraged economic
expansion and modernization, and presided over the Crimean
conflict (1854–6) and the ill-starred intervention in Mexico
(1861–7). After defeat by Prussia in 1870, the remainder of his
life was spent in exile in England.

71 For too long, society has resembled a pyramid that has
been turned upside down and made to rest on its
summit. I have replaced it on its base.
1852 Speech to the Legislative Assembly, 29 Mar.

72 We must not seek to fashion events, but let them happen
of their own accord.
1865 In conversation with Bismarck, Biarritz, 4 Oct.

73 When a man of my name is in power, he must do great
things.
Quoted in A J P Taylor *From Napoleon to the Second International*
(1993).

Narogin, Mudrooroo   *formerly* **Colin Jackson**   1938–

Australian writer and poet, who has piloted Aboriginal
literature courses at several Australian universities. His works
include *Dr. Wooreddy's Prescription for Enduring the Ending of*

the World (1983), the song cycle *Dalwurra: The Black Bittern* (1988), the anthology *Writing from the Fringe* (1990) and *The Promised Land* (2000).

74 The Aboriginal writer is a Janus-type figure with one face turned to the past and the other to the future while existing in a postmodern, multicultural Australia in which he or she must fight for cultural space.
1990 *Writing from the Fringe*, ch.1, 'Writing from the Fringe'.

Nash, (Frederic) Ogden 1902–71

US light versifier. His popular verse was published frequently in the *New Yorker* and helped establish its sophisticated tone. His collections include *Hard Lines* (1931) and *Boy is a Boy* (1960).

75 The cow is of the bovine ilk;
One end is moo, the other, milk.
1931 *Free Wheeling*, 'The Cow'.

76 The song of canaries
Never varies,
And when they're moulting
They're pretty revolting.
1931 *Free Wheeling*, 'The Canary'.

77 A bit of talcum
Is always walcum.
1931 *Free Wheeling*, 'The Baby'.

78 One would be in less danger
From the wiles of a stranger
If one's own kin and kith
Were more fun to be with.
1931 *Hard Lines*, 'Family Court'.

79 A girl whose cheeks are covered with paint
Has an advantage with me over one whose ain't.
1931 *Hard Lines*, 'Biological Reflection'.

80 Candy
Is dandy
But liquor
Is quicker.
1931 *Hard Lines*, 'Reflections on Ice-Breaking'.

81 The turtle lives 'twixt plated decks
Which practically conceal its sex.
I think it clever of the turtle
In such a fix to be so fertile.
1931 *Hard Lines*, 'Autres Bêtes, Autres Moeurs'.

82 It's better to be dead, or even perfectly well, than to suffer from the wrong affliction. The man who owns up to arthritis in a beri-beri year is as lonely as a woman in a last month's dress.
1933 'How's Your Sacro-iliac?', in the *Saturday Evening Post*, 14 Oct.

83 Any kiddie in school can love like a fool,
But hating, my boy, is an art.
1933 *Happy Days*, 'Plea for Less Malice Toward None'.

84 I think that I shall never see
A billboard lovely as a tree.
Perhaps, unless the billboards fall,
I'll never see a tree at all.
1933 *Happy Days*, 'Song of the Open Road'.
➤ See Kilmer 467:17.

85 Children aren't happy with nothing to ignore
And that's what parents were created for.
1933 *Happy Days*, 'The Parent'.

86 Home is heaven and orgies are vile,
But you *need* an orgy, once in a while.
1935 *The Primrose Path*, 'Home, 9944/100% Sweet Home'.

87 The camel has a single hump;
The dromedary, two;
Or else the other way around,
I'm never sure. Are you?
1936 *The Bad Parents' Garden of Verse*, 'The Camel'.

88 Let us pause to consider the English,
Who when they pause to consider themselves they get all reticently thrilled and tinglish,
Because every Englishman is convinced of one thing, viz.:
That to be an Englishman is to belong to the most exclusive club there is.
1938 *I'm a Stranger Here Myself*, 'England Expects'.

89 There was a young belle of old Natchez
Whose garments were always in patchez.
When comment arose
On the state of her clothes,
She drawled, When Ah itchez, Ah scratchez.
1938 *I'm a Stranger Here Myself*, 'Requiem'.

90 The trouble with a kitten is
THAT
Eventually it becomes a
CAT.
1940 *The Face Is Familiar*, 'The Kitten'.

91 One day he missed his loving bride.
She had, the guide informed him later,
Been eaten by an alligator.
Professor Twist could not but smile.
'You mean,' he said, 'a crocodile.'
1940 *The Face Is Familiar*, 'The Purist'.

92 Oh, what a tangled web do parents weave
When they think that their children are naïve.
1940 *The Face Is Familiar*, 'Baby, What Makes the Sky Blue'.

93 This infant whose middle
Is diapered still
Will want to marry
My daughter Jill.

Oh sweet be his slumber and moist his middle!
My dreams, I fear, are infanticiddle.
1940 *The Face Is Familiar*, 'Song to be Sung by the Father of Infant Female Children'.

94 Sure, deck your lower limbs in pants;
Yours are the limbs, my sweeting.
You look divine as you advance—
Have you seen yourself retreating?
1940 *The Face Is Familiar*, 'What's The Use'.

95 Life is not having been told that the man has just waxed the floor.
1942 *Good Intentions*, 'You and Me and P. B. Shelley'.

96 Beneath this slab
John Brown is stowed.
He watched the ads,
And not the road.
1942 *Good Intentions*, 'Lather As You Go'.

97 I have a bone to pick with Fate.
Come here and tell me, girlie,
Do you think my mind is maturing late,

Or simply rotted early?
1942 *Good Intentions*, 'Lines On Facing Forty'.

98 I test my bath before I sit,
And I'm always moved to wonderment
That what chills the finger not a bit
Is so frigid upon the fundament.
1942 *Good Intentions*, 'Samson Agonistes'.

99 Women would rather be right than be reasonable.
1942 *Good Intentions*, 'Frailty, Thy Name is a Misnomer'.

1 Parsley
Is gharsely.
1942 *Good Intentions*, 'Further Reflections on Parsley'.

2 God in His wisdom made the fly
And then forgot to tell us why.
1942 *Good Intentions*, 'The Fly'.

3 One thing that literature would be greatly the better for
Would be a more restricted employment by authors of
simile and metaphor.
1945 *Many Long Years Ago*, 'Very Like A Whale'.

4 He tells you when you've got on too much lipstick,
And helps you with your girdle when your hips stick.
1949 *Versus*, 'The Perfect Husband'.

5 All winter long,
I am one for whom the bell is tolling;
I can arouse no interest in basketball,
Indoor fly casting or bowling;
The sports pages are strictly no soap!
And until the cry Play Ball! I simply mope.
1957 Quoted in Colin Jarman *The Guinness Dictionary of Sports
Quotations* (1990).

6 It is a fact that a lady wants to be dressed exactly like
everybody else but she gets pretty upset if she sees
anybody else dressed exactly like her.
1964 *Marriage Lines*, 'Thoughts Thought on an Avenue'.

7 My verse represents a handle I can grasp in order not to
yield to the centrifugal forces which are trying to throw
me off the world.
Recalled on his death, 9 May 1971.

8 Basketball, a game which won't be fit for people until
they set the basket umbilicus-high and return the giraffes
to the zoo.
Quoted in Colin Jarman *The Guinness Dictionary of Sports
Quotations* (1990).

9 I eat my peas with honey;
I've done it all my life.
They do taste kinda funny,
but it keeps 'em on the knife.
Attributed.

Nashe, Thomas 1567–1601

English dramatist and satirist. His play *The Isle of Dogs* (1597,
now lost) was so scathing on the subject of state abuses that it
was suppressed, the theatre closed down and he himself
thrown into Fleet prison. *The Unfortunate Traveller* (1594) is a
picaresque tale, one of the earliest of its kind.

10 'New herrings, new!' we must cry, every time we make
ourselves public, or else we shall be christened with a
hundred new titles of idiotism.
1592 *Pierce Penniless, His Supplication to the Devil*, 'An Invective
Against Enemies of Poetry'.

11 Poetry is the honey of all flowers, the quintessence of all

sciences, the marrow of wit, and the very phrase of angels.
1592 *Pierce Penniless, His Supplication to the Devil*, 'An Invective
Against Enemies of Poetry'.

12 If I be evil intreated, or sent away with a flea in mine ear,
let him look that I will rail on him soundly; nor for an hour
or a day, whiles the injury is fresh in my memory; but in
some elaborate polished poem, which I will leave to the
world when I am dead, to be a living image to all ages of
his beggarly parsimony and ignoble illiberality.
1592 *Pierce Penniless, His Supplication to the Devil*, 'An Invective
Against Enemies of Poetry'.

13 I will confer with thee somewhat gravely, although thou
beest a goosecap and hast no judgement.
1592 *Strange News of the Intercepting Certain Letters*.

14 Immortal Spenser, no frailty hath thy fame but the
imputation of this idiot's friendship!
1592 *Strange News of the Intercepting Certain Letters*.

15 Spring, the sweet spring, is the year's pleasant king,
Then blooms each thing, then maids dance in a ring,
Cold doth not sting, the pretty birds do sing:
Cuckoo, jug-jug, pu-we, to-witta-woo!
1592 *Summer's Last Will and Testament*, 'Song'.

16 Fair summer droops, droop men and beasts therefore:
So fair a summer look for never more.
All good things vanish, less than in a day,
Peace, plenty, pleasure, suddenly decay.
Go not yet away, bright soul of the sad year;
The earth is hell when thou leav'st to appear.
1592 *Summer's Last Will and Testament*, 'Song'.

17 From winter, plague and pestilence, good lord, deliver us!
1592 *Summer's Last Will and Testament*.

18 Beauty is but a flower
Which wrinkles will devour;
Brightness falls from the air;
Queens have died young and fair;
Dust hath closèd Helen's eye.
I am sick, I must die.
Lord, have mercy on us!
1592 'A Litany in Time of Plague'.

19 He that is a traveller must have the back of an ass to bear
all, a tongue like the tail of a dog to flatter all, the mouth of
a hog to eat all what is set before him, the ear of a
merchant to hear all and say nothing; and if this be not
the highest step of thraldom, there is no liberty or
freedom.
1594 *The Unfortunate Traveller, or the Life of Jack Wilton*.

Nathan, George Jean 1882–1958

US theatre critic. He was co-editor of *The Smart Set* (1914–24)
and founded the *American Mercury* with H L Mencken in 1924.
Among the emerging playwrights to whom he gave support
was Eugene O'Neill.

20 The most loyal and faithful woman indulges her
imagination in a hypothetical liaison whenever she dons
a new street frock for the first time.
1921 *The Theatre, the Drama, the Girls*, 'Woman'.

21 The test of a real comedian is whether you laugh at him
before he opens his mouth.
Quoted in *American Mercury*, Sep 1929.

22 I always said that I'd like Barrymore's acting till the
cows came home. Well, ladies and gentlemen, last

night the cows came home.

1939 Review of John Barrymore's performance in *My Dear Children*.

23 Impersonal criticism…is like an impersonal fist fight or an impersonal marriage, and as successful.
Quoted in Charles Angoff (ed) *The World of George Jean Nathan* (1952).

24 The dramatic critic who is without prejudice is on the plane with the general who does not believe in taking human life.
Attributed.

Nation, Carry Amelia *née Moore* 1846–1911

US temperance agitator. She went on saloon-smashing expeditions with a hatchet and was frequently imprisoned for breach of the peace.

25 A woman is stripped of everything by them [saloons]. Her husband is torn from her; she is robbed of her sons, her home, her food, and her virtue; and then they strip her clothes off and hang her up bare in these dens of robbery and murder. Truly does the saloon make a woman bare of all things!
c.1893 Quoted in Carleton Beals *Cyclone Carry* (1962), ch.14.

Naughton, Bill 1910–92

Irish novelist and screenwriter. His screen credits include *Alfie* (1966), *The Family Way* (1966) and *Spring and Port Wine* (1970).

26 It seems to me if they ain't got you one way they got you another. So what's the answer? That's what I keep asking myself. What's it all about? Know what I mean?
1966 Line delivered by Michael Caine in *Alfie*.

Neale, J(ames) M(ason) 1818–66

English clergyman and hymn writer.

27 All glory, laud and honour
To Thee, Redeemer, King,
To whom the lips of children
Made sweet hosannas ring.
1851 'All Glory, Laud and Honour'.

28 Jerusalem the golden,
With milk and honey blessed,
Beneath thy contemplation
Sink heart and voice oppressed.
I know not, O I know not
What joys await us there,
What radiancy of glory,
What light beyond compare.
1858 'Jerusalem the Golden', translated from the original Latin of St Bernard of Cluny.

Nehru, Jawaharlal 1889–1964

Indian statesman, President of the Indian National Congress (1929) and India's first Prime Minister (1947–64). Neutral in the Cold War, he embarked on industrialization, reorganized the states linguistically and ended the dispute with Pakistan over Kashmir peacefully.

29 Stalin…that great lover of peace, a man of giant stature who moulded, as few other men have done, the destinies of his age… The occasion is not merely the passing away of a great figure but perhaps the ending of an historic era.
1953 Tribute, Indian Parliament, 9 Mar.

Neilson, John Shaw 1872–1942

Australian poet. His first work was published in the *Bulletin* and first collected in *Heart of Spring* (1919), followed by *Ballad and Lyrical Poems* (1923) and *New Poems* (1927). *Collected Poems* (1934) was followed by posthumous collections.

30 The young girl stood beside me. I
Saw not what her young eyes could see:
—A light, she said, not of the sky
Lives somewhere in the Orange Tree.
1923 *Ballad and Lyrical Poems*, 'The Orange Tree', stanza 1.

31 Here is the ecstasy
Of sun-fed wine and song:
Drink! it is melody
Under a kurrajong.
'Under a Kurrajong', stanza 1, in R H Croll (ed) *Collected Poems of John Shaw Neilson* (1934).

Nelson, Horatio, Viscount Nelson 1758–1805

English admiral. In 1794 he commanded at Bastia and Calvi, where he lost the sight of his right eye, and at Santa Cruz in 1796, where he lost his right arm. In 1798 he destroyed Napoleon's fleet in Aboukir Bay, and subsequently began an affair with Emma, Lady Hamilton. In 1805 he defeated the combined French and Spanish fleet at Trafalgar, but was mortally wounded.

32 A fleet of British ships of war are the best negotiators in Europe.
1801 Letter to Lady Hamilton, Mar, before the Battle of Copenhagen.

33 You know, Foley, I have only one eye—I have a right to be blind sometimes… I really do not see the signal.
1801 Said to Captain Foley during the Battle of Copenhagen, 2 Apr. Nelson disregarded the order of his superior, Admiral Hyde-Parker, to break off action and went on to win the engagement.

34 I wish to say Nelson confides that every man will do his duty.
1805 Instructions to the flag officer on HMS *Victory*, 21 Oct. The signal was amended to begin, 'England expects…'.

35 Kiss me, Hardy.
1805 Attributed, as he lay dying in the cockpit of the *Victory* during the Battle of Trafalgar, 21 Oct.

36 Thank God, I have done my duty.
1805 Last words at the Battle of Trafalgar, quoted in Robert Southey *Life of Nelson* (1813), ch.9.

Nemerov, Howard 1920–91

US poet, novelist and playwright. He was US Poet Laureate from 1988 to 1990, and won a National Book Award for his *Collected Poems* in 1977.

37 Children, to be illustrious is sad.
1958 *Mirrors and Windows*, 'The Statues in the Public Gardens'.

38 Till I, high in the tower of my time
Among familiar ruins, began to cry
For accident, sickness, justice, war and crime,
Because all died, because I had to die.
The snow fell, the trees stood, the promise kept,
And a child I slept.
1960 *New Poems*, 'The View from an Attic Window'.

39 For a Jewish Puritan of the middle class, the novel is serious, the novel is work, the novel is conscientious application—why, the novel is practically the retail business all over again.
1965 *Journal of the Fictive Life*, 'Reflexions of the Novelist Felix Ledger'.

40 I've never read a political poem that's accomplished anything. Poetry makes things happen, but rarely what the poet wants.
1988 In the *International Herald Tribune*, 14 Oct.
➤ *See Auden 40:2*.

Nero AD 37–68

Roman Emperor (AD 54–68). He was adopted by his stepfather Claudius and declared Emperor on Claudius's death. Ancient authors depict him as a debauched tyrant, and accuse him of starting the great fire of Rome in AD 64 (he blamed the Christians). A coup in AD 68 brought Galba to the throne, and Nero committed suicide.

41 *Qualis artifex pereo!*
Dead! And so great an artist!
Attributed words on the point of taking his life. Quoted in Suetonius *Nero*, 49.1 (translated by Robert Graves, 1957).

Neruda, Pablo *pseudonym of* Neftalí Ricardo Reyes Basoalto 1904–73

Chilean poet, essayist and diplomat, who travelled widely as a diplomat. His poetic themes range from subjective love to socially committed epic poems influenced by a communist ideology. He was awarded a Nobel prize in 1971.

42 *Sucede que me canso de mis pies y mis uñas*
y mi pelo y mi sombra.
Sucede que me canso de ser hombre.
I happen to be tired of my feet and my nails
and my hair and my shadow.
I happen to be tired of being a man.
1935 *Residencia en la tierra*, 'Walking Around' (translated as *Residence on Earth*, 1946).

43 *A nosotros nos enseñaron a respetar la iglesia,*
a no toser, a no escupir en el atrio,
a no lavar la ropa en el altar
y no es así: la vida rompe las religiones.
We were taught respect for the church,
no hawking and spitting on porticos,
don't soak your socks on the altar—
but things are different: life smashes religions.
1973 *La rosa separada*, 'Los hombres' (translated as *The Separate Rose*, 'The Men', 1985).

Nerval, Gérard de *pseudonym of* Gérard Labrunie 1808–55

French poet, novelist and author of critical essays, he was admired later by the Surrealists for his fantastic short tales.

44 *Philosophie! dont la lumière, comme celle des enfers de Milton, ne sert qu'à rendre les ténèbres visibles.*
Philosophy! In whose light, like that in Milton's hell, only serves to make the shadows visible.
1852 *Fragments*, 'Paradoxe et vérité'.

45 *Il n'y a qu'un seul vice dont on ne voie personne se vanter, c'est l'ingratitude.*
There is only one vice of which no one boasts—ingratitude.
1852 *Fragments*, 'Paradoxe et vérité'.

46 *La vie d'un poète est celle de tous.*
The life of the poet is the life of everyone.
1855 *Petits Châteaux de Bohême*, 'À un ami'.

Nervo, Amado *pseudonym of* Juan Crisóstomo Ruiz de Nervo 1870–1919

Mexican poet and diplomat. He abandoned the priesthood in 1888 to work as a journalist. He studied Buddhist philosophy in depth, and his introspective poetry is characterized by deep religious feeling and simple form.

47 *No te juzgues incompleto porque no responden a tus ternuras; el amor lleva en sí su propia plenitud.*
Siempre que haya un hueco en tu vida, llénalo de amor.
Don't judge yourself incomplete when your tenderness gets no response; love carries within itself its own plenitude.
Whenever there is a void in your life, fill it with love.
1918 *Plenitud*, 'Llénalo de amor' (translated as 'Fill It with love', 1928).

Nevelson, Louise 1900–88

Russian-born US sculptor. Her work incorporates pieces of wood, found objects, cast metal, and other materials, creating great mysterious walls or boxes of complex, abstract forms. Her autobiography, *Dawns and Dusks*, was published in 1976.

48 There's no denying that Caruso came with a voice…that Beethoven came with music in his soul, Picasso was drawing like an angel in the crib. You're born with it.
1976 *Dawns and Dusks*.

Neville, Katherine 1945–

US novelist.

49 'In Scotland,' Tavish muttered, picking up my bags, 'the *women* do the hod carrying while we blokes retire to the nearest pub—to deliberate upon the role of labour in society.'
1992 *A Calculated Risk*.

New York Times

First published 1851 as the *New-York Daily Times*.

50 Who owns history? The public servants who make it, or the people who hire them and to whom they are accountable?
1983 'Who Owns History?', editorial, 19 Nov.

51 Armed with a notebook, ingratiating grin and fine intelligence, he grew to be a most discerning witness of America's most distinctive rite, not just the election but the making of our presidents.
1986 Of journalist Theodore H White. 'Teddy White, the Maker of Epics', editorial, 17 May.

52 The best way to read [a poem] is off the top of your head, and out of the corner of your eye.
1987 *Noted With Pleasure*, in the *New York Times*, 16 Mar.

53 For Palestinians, PLO is a homeland of the mind.
1988 Editorial, 20 Mar.

54 Empty luggage may be easier to carry, but it's still empty.
1988 Of Michael S Dukakis's presidential campaign. 'The Painless Platform', editorial, 20 Jul.

55 Millions drew up before the international hearth of television.

1991 On international media coverage of the Allied deadline for Iraq's withdrawal from Kuwait. 'With Our Own Eyes', editorial, 24 Feb.

56 Lightning rods have had it better than Nancy Reagan.
1991 On the publication of Kitty Kelley's unauthorized biography *Nancy Reagan*. 'Scratching at the Teflon', editorial, 10 Apr.

57 Who is quickest on the drawl?
1992 On claims to Texas by both George Bush and rival presidential aspirant Ross Perot. Editorial, 9 Jun.

58 When it comes to the final judgements on political conduct, history is not merciful. It is just.
1994 'Justice and Mercy in Arkansas', editorial, 17 Dec.

Newman, Arnold 1918–

US photographer.

59 We don't take our pictures with cameras. We take them with our hearts, and we take them with our minds.
1992 In *Sunday Morning*, CBS T V, 2 Aug.

Newman, James R 1907–66

US mathematician and mathematical historian. He was the compiler of the magnum opus *The World of Mathematics* (1956).

60 There are two ways to teach mathematics. One is to take real pains toward creating understanding—visual aids, that sort of thing. The other is the old British style of teaching until you're blue in the face.
1956 Quoted in the *New York Times*, 30 Sep.

Newman, John Henry 1801–90

English theologian, active in Oxford in the Tractarian movement of the Church of England. He converted to the Roman Catholic faith in 1845 and was appointed Cardinal by Pope Leo XIII in 1879.

61 It is as absurd to argue men, as to torture them, into believing.
1831 'The Usurpations of Reason', collected in *Oxford University Sermons* (1843).

62 Lead, kindly Light, amid the encircling gloom,
Lead thou me on;
The night is dark, and I am far from home,
Lead thou me on.
Keep Thou my feet; I do not ask to see
The distant scene; one step enough for me.
1833 'Lead, kindly Light'.

63 May He support us all the day long, till the shades lengthen, and the evening comes, and the busy world is hushed, and the fever of life is over, and our work is done! Then in His mercy may He give us a safe lodging, and a holy rest, and peace at the last.
1834 'Wisdom and Innocence', collected in *Sermons Bearing on Subjects of the Day*.

64 *We can believe what we choose.* We are answerable for what we choose to believe.
1848 Letter to Mrs William Froude, 27 Jun.

65 It is very difficult to get up resentment towards persons whom one has never seen.
1864 *Apologia pro Vita Sua*, 'Mr Kingsley's Method of Disputation'.

66 Praise to the Holiest in the height,

And in the depth be praise;
In all His words most wonderful,
Most sure in all His ways.
1865 *The Dream of Gerontius*. In *The Month* (published in book form in 1866).

Newman, Peter C 1929–

Austrian-born Canadian author and political columnist.

67 And what I've learned is not to believe in magical leaders any more; that character and compassion are more important than ideology; and that even if it's absurd to think you can change things, it's even more absurd to think that it's foolish and unimportant to try.
1973 *Home Country: People, Places, and Power Politics*.

68 The rich don't have children; they have heirs.
1982 *The Establishment Man: A Portrait of Power*.

Newton, Sir Isaac 1642–1727

English mathematician and physicist, considered the greatest scientist of modern time. Newton was Professor of Mathematics (1669–1701) at Cambridge. Between 1664 and 1666 he discovered the law of gravitation, and began to develop differential calculus.

69 *Corpus omne perseverare in statu suo quiescendi vel movendi uniformiter in directum, nisi quatenus illud a viribus impressis cogitur statum suum mutare.*
Every body continues in its state of rest, or of uniform motion in a right line, unless it is compelled to change that state by forces impressed thereon.
1687 First Law of Motion. *Philosophiae Naturalis Principia Mathematica* (translated by Andrew Motte, 1729).

70 *Mutationem motus proportionalem esse vi motrici impressae et fieri secundum lineam rectam qua vis illa imprimitur.*
The alteration of motion is ever proportional to the motive force impressed; and is made in the direction of the right line in which that force is impressed.
1687 Second Law of Motion. *Philosophiae Naturalis Principia Mathematica* (translated by Andrew Motte, 1729).

71 We are to admit no more causes of natural things than such as are both true and sufficient to explain their appearances… Nature is pleased with simplicity, and affects not the pomp of the superfluous causes.
1687 Newton's First Rule of Reasoning in Philosophy. *Philosophiae Naturalis Principia Mathematica* (translated by Andrew Motte, 1729).

72 *Actioni contrarium semper et aequalem esse reactionem: sive corporum duorum actiones in se mutuo semper esse aequales et in partes contrarias dirigi.*
To every action there is always opposed an equal reaction: or, the mutual actions of two bodies upon each other are always equal, and directed to contrary parts.
1687 Third Law of Motion. *Philosophiae Naturalis Principia Mathematica* (translated by Andrew Motte, 1729).

73 Geometry is that part of universal mechanics which accurately proposes and demonstrates the art of measuring.
1687 *Philosophiae Naturalis Principia Mathematica* (translated by Andrew Motte, 1729).

74 I know not what I may appear to the world, but to myself I seem to have been only like a boy playing on the sea shore, and diverting myself in now and then finding a

smoother pebble or a prettier shell than ordinary, whilst the great ocean of truth lay all undiscovered before me.
Quoted in D Brewster (ed) *Memoirs of Newton* (1855), vol.2, ch.27.

75 In the absence of any other proof, the thumb alone would convince me of God's existence.
Attributed.

Newton, John 1725–1807

English divine and writer, who converted to Christianity in 1748 and became Curate of Olney, Buckinghamshire, in 1764.

76 Amazing grace! How sweet the sound
That saved a wretch like me!
I once was lost, but now am found,
Was blind, but now I see.
1779 *Olney Hymns*, 'Amazing Grace'.

77 Glorious things of thee are spoken,
Zion, city of our God!
1779 *Olney Hymns*, 'Glorious things of thee are spoken'.

78 How sweet the name of Jesus sounds
In a believer's ear!
1779 *Olney Hymns*, 'How sweet the name of Jesus sounds'.

Ngũgĩ wa Thiong'o *originally* **James Ngũgĩ** 1938–

Kenyan writer. His early works were written in English, but he now chooses to write solely in his native Gikuyu. Works include *Weep Not Child* (1964), *The River Between* (1965), *A Grain of Wheat* (1967) and *Matigari* (1987).

79 Today, children, I am going to tell you about the history of Mr. Blackman in three sentences. In the beginning he had the land and the mind and the soul together. On the second day, they took the body away to barter it for silver coins. On the third day, seeing that he was still fighting back, they brought priests and educators to bind his mind and soul so that these foreigners could more easily take his land and produce.
1977 *Petals of Blood*, ch.8.

80 He who produces should be able to control that which he produces.
1990 Quoted in Carol Sicherman *Ngũgĩ wa Thiong'o: The Making of a Rebel*, pt.1, ch.2, 'Ngũgĩ on Ngũgĩ' (by Ngũgĩ himself).

Nguyen, Xuan Oanh 1921–2003

Vietnamese economist who rose to become South Vietnam's acting Prime Minister briefly in 1964. After the country was reunited in 1975 he remained in limbo for ten years before his ideas for economic change were accepted. He is now regarded as the unofficial architect of Vietnam's economic reforms.

81 There is no such thing as communism versus capitalism. There are only degrees of communism and degrees of capitalism.
1995 In the *Eastern Express*, 17 May.

82 Patriotism in Vietnam took the communist road because it was the only one available. It had the appeal of a dream, a dream of social justice.
1995 In the *Eastern Express*, 17 May.

Nicholas I 1796–1855

Tsar of Russia (from 1825). During his reign, wars with Persia and Turkey increased Russia's territory. He died during the Crimean War, when Russia's attempts to absorb Turkey were resisted by Britain and France.

83 Russia has two generals in whom she can confide—Janvier and Février.
1855 Referring to the severe Russian winter climate. Quoted in *Punch*, 10 Mar.

Nicholas II 1868–1919

Last Emperor of Russia (1894–1917), whose reign was marked by alliance with France (1894), *entente* with Britain, disastrous war with Japan (1904–5) and the establishment of the Duma (1906). He fought against the Central Powers in 1915. Forced to abdicate at the Revolution, he was shot with his family by the Red Guards.

84 There are senseless dreams of the participation of local government representatives in the affairs of internal administration. I shall maintain the principle of autocracy just as firmly and unflinchingly as it was upheld by my own, ever to be remembered dead father.
1896 Declaration, 17 Jan.

Nichols, Grace 1950–

Guyanese poet, novelist and journalist, married to the poet John Agard; her publications include *Trust You, Wriggly!* (1981) and *The Poet Cat* (2000) for children, and the poetry sequences *i is a long memoried woman* (1983) (Commonwealth Poetry Prize) and *The Fat Black Woman's Poems* (1984).

85 I have crossed an ocean
I have lost my tongue
from the root of the old one
a new one has sprung
1983 *i is a long memoried woman*, epilogue.

86 IT'S BETTER TO DIE IN THE FLESH OF HOPE
THAN TO LIVE IN THE SLIMNESS OF DESPAIR.
1984 *The Fat Black Woman's Poems*, 'The Fat Black Woman's Motto on Her Bedroom Door'.

Nichols, Mike *originally* **Michael Peschowsky** 1931–

American stage and film director. He collected Tony Awards for the plays *Barefoot in the Park* (1963), *The Odd Couple* (1965) and *Plaza Suite* (1968). More recently he directed *Death and the Maiden* (New York, 1992) and the television adaptation of *Angels in America* (2003). His many films include *The Graduate* (1967, Academy Award), *Catch-22* (1969), *Silkwood* (1983), *Working Girl* (1988), *Postcards From The Edge* (1990) and *The Birdcage* (1995).

87 Style is beginning something in the manner which will make it necessary for things that happen later to happen.
1991 In *Film Comment*, May.

Nicholson, Bill 1919–2004

English footballer and manager. He played with Tottenham Hotspur, and as manager of the club achieved the double of the FA Cup and the League Championship (1961). He won two more FA Cup titles (1962 and 1967), the European Cup Winners' Cup (1963), two more League Championships (1971 and 1973) and the UEFA Cup (1972).

88 I prefer players not to be too good or clever at other things. It means they concentrate on football.
1973 Quoted in Peter Ball and Phil Shaw *The Book of Football Quotations* (1989).

Nicholson, Jack 1937–

US film actor. An office boy at MGM, he made his film debut in *Cry Baby Killer* (1958) and survived a decade of low-budget exploitation films before *Easy Rider* (1969) established his reputation. He has received twelve Academy Award nominations, winning three Oscars.

89 She's like a delicate fawn, crossed with a Buick.
  1984 Of actress Jessica Lange. In *Vanity Fair*, Oct.

Nicholson, Vivian 1936–

English housewife. In 1961 her husband Keith won £152,000 on the football pools, but the couple subsequently had difficulty coping with their fortune. Keith died in a car crash and Viv spent the money in just four years and turned to religion after several failed marriages and alcohol and drug abuse.

90 I want to spend, and spend, and spend!
  1961 Quoted in the *Daily Herald*, 28 Sep, when asked what her plans were on winning the pools. The words 'Spend, spend, spend!' were later used as the title of her autobiography and for a biographical television play by Jack Rosenthal in 1977.

Nicias c.470–413 BC

Athenian statesman and soldier, who negotiated a short-lived peace with Sparta (421 BC). He was a commander in the disastrous naval expedition against Sicily in 418 BC, and following a siege of Syracuse was captured and put to death.

91 For it is men that make a city, and not its walls, nor its ships empty of men.
  413 BC Speech to the defeated Athenian army. Quoted in Thucydides 7.77.

Nicklaus, Jack William *known as* 'the Golden Bear' 1940–

US golfer. He won the US Open Championship in 1962, the first of 20 major tournaments. He went into semi-retirement in 1986 and is now in demand as a golf course designer.

92 Golf is not and never has been a fair game.
  Quoted in Colin Jarman *The Guinness Dictionary of Sports Quotations* (1990).

93 I think I fail a bit less than everyone else.
  Quoted in Michael Hobbs *The Golf Quotation Book* (1992).

Nicolle, Charles Jules Henri 1866–1936

French physician and microbiologist, Director of the Pasteur Institute in Tunis, Tunisia and Professor of Bacteriology at the Collège de France. He was awarded a Nobel prize in 1928 for demonstrating the transmission of typhus by lice.

94 All method is imperfect. Error is all around it, and at the least opportunity invades it… But what can we do? There is no other way.
  1932 *Biologie de l'Invention*.

Nicolson, Sir Harold 1886–1968

English diplomat, author and critic, born in Tehran. A distinguished diplomat (1909–29), he turned to journalism and was a National Liberal MP (1935–45). He wrote works of literary criticism and literary and historical biography.

95 My first impression is of a slightly bearded spinster: my second is of Willie King made up like Philip II: my third of some thin little bird, peeking, crooked, reserved, violent and timid.
  1931 On meeting James Joyce. Diary entry, 30 Jul.

96 I feel pretty glum and devote myself to reviewing. There is Joyce's *Finnegans Wake*. I try very hard indeed to understand that book but fail completely. It is almost impossible to decipher, and when one or two lines of understanding emerge like telegraph poles above a flood, they are at once countered by other poles going in the opposite direction.
  1939 Diary entry, 29 Apr.

Niebuhr, Reinhold 1892–1971

US theologian, Professor at the Union Theological Seminary, New York.

97 All men who live with any degree of serenity live by some assurance of grace.
  1934 *Reflections on the End of Our Era*.

98 Perhaps the most sublime insights of the Jewish prophets and the Christian gospel is the knowledge that since perfection is love, the apprehension of perfection is at once the means of seeing one's imperfections and the consoling assurance of grace which makes this realization bearable. This ultimate paradox of high religion is not an invention of theologians or priests. It is constantly validated by the most searching experiences of life.
  1934 *Reflections on the End of an Era*.

99 The pretensions of final truth are always partly an effort to obscure a darkly felt consciousness of the limits of human knowledge.
  1941 *The Nature and Destiny of Man*, vol.1.

1 God, give us grace to accept with serenity the things that cannot be changed, courage to change the things that should be changed, and the wisdom to distinguish the one from the other.
  In Richard Wightman Fox *Reinhold Neibuhr* (1985), ch.12. Attributed to Neibuhr, but more probably 18c German.

Nielsen, Carl August 1865–1931

Danish composer, who experimented with polytonality and developed a characteristic contrapuntal style.

2 Music is life, and, like it, inextinguishable.
  1916 Symphony No. 4, motto.

Niemöller, Martin 1892–1984

German submarine commander, pastor and theologian, leader of Christian opposition to Nazism.

3 When Hitler attacked the Jews I was not a Jew, therefore, I was not concerned. And when Hitler attacked the Catholics, I was not a Catholic, and therefore, I was not concerned. And when Hitler attacked the unions and the industrialists, I was not a member of the unions and I was not concerned. Then, Hitler attacked me and the Protestant church—and there was nobody left to be concerned.
  1944 *Children of Light and Darkness*, foreword.

Nietzsche, Friedrich Wilhelm 1844–1900

German philosopher, scholar and writer. Professor of Classical Philology at the University of Basel (1868–78), he resigned in ill health. From 1872 he produced a stream of brilliant, unclassifiable works, rejecting Christianity for a new, heroic morality. In 1889 he had a complete mental and physical breakdown, from which he never recovered. His reputation suffered when his ideas were adopted in a distorted form by the Nazis, but he is now regarded as a major influence on 20c thought.

4 *Überzeugungen sind gefährlichere Feinde der Wahrheit als Lügen.*
Convictions are more dangerous enemies of truth than lies.
1878 *Menschliches, Allzumenschliches (Human, All Too Human)*, section 483 (translated by R J Hollingdale).

5 The press, the machine, the railway, the telegraph are premises whose thousand-year conclusion no one has yet dared to draw.
1880 *The Wanderer and His Shadow*, aphorism 278.

6 *Gott ist tot: aber so wie die Art der Menschen ist, wird es vielleicht noch Jahrtausende lang Höhlen geben, in denen man seinen Schatten zeigt.—Und wir—wir müssen auch noch seinen Schatten besiegen!*
God is dead; but given the way of men, there may still be caves for thousands of years in which his shadow will be shown.—And we—we still have to vanquish his shadow, too.
1882 *Die fröhliche Wissenschaft (The Gay Science)*, section 108 (translated by W Kaufmann). This is the first occurrence of the famous phrase, which appears elsewhere in Nietzsche's work.

7 *Moralität ist Herden-Instinkt im Einzelnen.*
Morality is herd instinct in the individual.
1882 *Die fröhliche Wissenschaft (The Gay Science)*, section 116 (translated by W Kaufmann).

8 *Und, alles in allem und großem: ich will irgendwann einmal nur noch ein Jasagender sein!*
And all in all and on the whole: some day I wish to be only a Yes-sayer.
1882 *Die fröhliche Wissenschaft (The Gay Science)*, section 276 (translated by W Kaufmann).

9 *Glaubt es mir!—das Geheimnis, um die größte Fruchtbarkeit und den größten Genuss vom Dasein einzuernten, heißt: gefährlich leben!*
For believe me: the secret for harvesting from existence the greatest fruitfulness and the greatest enjoyment is—to *live dangerously.*
1882 *Die fröhliche Wissenschaft (The Gay Science)*, section 283 (translated by W Kaufmann).

10 *Eins ist not.—Seinem Charakter 'Stil geben'.*
One thing is needful.—To 'give style' to one's character.
1882 *Die fröhliche Wissenschaft (The Gay Science)*, section 290 (translated by W Kaufmann).

11 *Ich lehre euch den Übermenschen. Der Mensch ist Etwas, das überwunden werden soll.*
I teach you the Superman. Man is something that should be surpassed.
1883–92 *Also sprach Zarathustra (Thus Spake Zarathustra)*, prologue, section 3 (translated by R J Hollingdale).

12 *Der Mensch ist ein Seil, geknüpft zwischen Tier und Übermensch,—ein Seil über einem Abgrunde.*
Man is a rope, fastened between animal and Superman—a rope over an abyss.
1883–92 *Also sprach Zarathustra (Thus Spake Zarathustra)*, prologue, section 4 (translated by R J Hollingdale).

13 *Was groß ist am Menschen, das ist, dass er eine Brücke und kein Zweck ist.*

What is great in man is that he is a bridge and not a goal.
1883–92 *Also sprach Zarathustra (Thus Spake Zarathustra)*, prologue, section 4 (translated by R J Hollingdale).

14 *Ich sage euch: man muss noch Chaos in sich haben, um einem tanzenden Stern gebären zu können.*
I tell you: one must have chaos in one, to give birth to a dancing star.
1883–92 *Also sprach Zarathustra (Thus Spake Zarathustra)*, prologue, section 5 (translated by R J Hollingdale).

15 *Du gehst zu Frauen? Vergiss die Peitsche nicht!*
You are going to women? Do not forget the whip!
1883–92 *Also sprach Zarathustra (Thus Spake Zarathustra)*, bk.1 (translated by R J Hollingdale).

16 Distrust all in whom the impulse to punish is powerful.
1883–92 *Also sprach Zarathustra (Thus Spake Zarathustra)* (translated by R J Hollingdale).

17 *Gesetzt, wir wollen Wahrheit: warum nicht lieber Unwahrheit? Und Ungewissheit? Selbst Unwissenheit?*
Granted we want truth: why not rather untruth? And uncertainty? Even ignorance?
1886 *Jenseits von Gut und Böse (Beyond Good and Evil)*, section 1 (translated by R J Hollingdale).

18 *Allmählich hat sich mir herausgestellt, was jede große Philosophie bisher war: nämlich das Selbstbekenntnis ihres Urhebers und eine Art ungewollter und unvermerkter mémoires.*
It has gradually become clear to me what every great philosophy has hitherto been: a confession on the part of its author and a kind of involuntary and unconscious memoir.
1886 *Jenseits von Gut und Böse (Beyond Good and Evil)*, section 6 (translated by R J Hollingdale).

19 *Sie schafft immer die Welt nach ihrem Bilde, sie kann nicht anders; Philosophie ist dieser tyrannische Treib selbst, der geistigste Wille zur Macht, zur 'Schaffung der Welt'.*
It [philosophy] always creates the world in its own image, it cannot do otherwise; philosophy is this tyrannical drive itself, the most spiritual will to power, to 'creation of the world'.
1886 *Jenseits von Gut und Böse (Beyond Good and Evil)*, section 9 (translated by R J Hollingdale).

20 *Alles, was tief ist, liebt die Maske.*
Everything profound loves the mask.
1886 *Jenseits von Gut und Böse (Beyond Good and Evil)*, section 40 (translated by R J Hollingdale).

21 The thought of suicide is a great source of comfort across many a bad night.
1886 *Jenseits von Gut und Böse (Beyond Good and Evil)*, section 157 (translated by R J Hollingdale).

22 *Das moralische Urteilen und Verurteilen ist die Lieblings-Rache der Geistig-Beschränkten an denen, die es weniger sind.*
Moral judgement and condemnation is the favourite form of revenge of the spiritually limited on those who are less so.
1886 *Jenseits von Gut und Böse (Beyond Good and Evil)*, section 219 (translated by R J Hollingdale).

23 *Durch schlechte Köchinnen—durch den vollkommenen Mangel an Vernunft in der Küche ist die Entwicklung des Menschen am längsten aufgehalten, am schlimmsten beeinträchtigt worden.*

Through bad female cooks—through the entire lack of reason in the kitchen—the development of mankind has been longest retarded and most interfered with.

1886 *Jenseits von Gut und Böse* (*Beyond Good and Evil*), section 234 (translated by Helen Zimmern, 1907).

24 *Herren-Moral und Sklaven-Moral.*
Master morality and slave morality.

1886 *Jenseits von Gut und Böse* (*Beyond Good and Evil*), section 260 (translated by R J Hollingdale).

25 Oh, how much is today hidden by science! Oh, how much it is expected to hide!

1887 *The Genealogy of Morals*, essay 3, 'What Do Ascetic Ideals Mean?'

26 *Hat je sich ein Weib, das sich gut bekleidet wusste, erkältet?*
Has a woman who knew she was well dressed ever caught a cold?

1889 *Die Götzen-Dämmerung* (*Twilight of the Idols*), 'Maxims and Arrows', no.25 (translated by R J Hollingdale).

27 Without music, life would be a mistake.

1889 *Die Götzen-Dämmerung* (*Twilight of the Idols*, translated by R J Hollingdale)

28 *Das, worin man die nationalen Unterschiede findet, ist viel mehr, als man bis jetzt eingesehen hat, nur der Unterschied verschiedener Kulturstufen und zum geringsten Teile etwas Bleibendes (und auch dies nicht in einem strengen Sinne).*
National differences consist, far more than has hitherto been observed, only in the differences of various grades of culture, and are only to a very small extent permanent (and not even that in a strict sense).

Nachgelassene Fragmente.

Nightingale, Benedict 1939–

British author and theatre critic. He has written for *The Times* since 1990.

29 He handles symbolism rather like an Olympic weight lifter, raising it with agonizing care, brandishing it with a tiny grunt of triumph, then dropping it with a terrible clang.

1984 Of playwright William Inge. In the *New York Times*, 28 Jul.

Nightingale, Florence 1820–1910

English nurse and hospital reformer during the Crimean War. She subsequently formed an institution for the training of nurses in London.

30 Why have women Passion, intellect, moral activity—these three—and a place in society where no one of the three can be exercised?

1852 'Cassandra' pt.1, part of an unpublished work *Suggestions for Thought to Searchers after Religious Truth* (revised and privately printed 1859). Published as an appendix in Ray Strachey *The Cause: A Short History of the Women's Movement in Great Britain* (1928).

31 Give us back our suffering, we cry to Heaven in our hearts—suffering rather than indifferentism; for out of nothing comes nothing… Better have pain than paralysis!

1852 'Cassandra' pt.1, part of an unpublished work *Suggestions for Thought to Searchers after Religious Truth* (revised and privately printed 1859). Published as an appendix in Ray Strachey *The Cause: A Short History of the Women's Movement in Great Britain* (1928).

32 Look at the poor lives we lead. It is a wonder that we are so good as we are, not that we are so bad.

1852 'Cassandra' pt.2, part of an unpublished work *Suggestions for Thought to Searchers after Religious Truth* (revised and privately printed 1859). Published as an appendix in Ray Strachey *The Cause: A Short History of the Women's Movement in Great Britain* (1928).

33 Marriage is the only chance (and it is but a chance) offered to women for escape from this death…and how eagerly and how ignorantly it is embraced.

1852 'Cassandra' pt.3, part of an unpublished work *Suggestions for Thought to Searchers after Religious Truth* (revised and privately printed 1859). Published as an appendix in Ray Strachey *The Cause: A Short History of the Women's Movement in Great Britain* (1928).

34 The next Christ will perhaps be a female Christ.

1852 'Cassandra' pt.4, part of an unpublished work *Suggestions for Thought to Searchers after Religious Truth* (revised and privately printed 1859). Published as an appendix in Ray Strachey *The Cause: A Short History of the Women's Movement in Great Britain* (1928).

35 No *man*, not even a doctor, ever gives any other definition of what a nurse should be than this—'devoted and obedient'. This definition would do just as well for a porter. It might even do for a horse. It would not do for a policeman.

1859 *Notes on Nursing.*

Nimitz, Admiral Chester (William) 1885–1966

US naval officer. He was Commander-in-Chief of the Pacific Fleet (1941–5), contributing significantly to the defeat of Japan. As fleet admiral he signed the Japanese surrender documents in Tokyo Bay (1945). He was chief of naval operations (1945–7).

36 A ship is always referred to as 'she' because it costs so much to keep her in paint and powder.

1959 In the *New York Times*, 24 May.

Nin, Anaïs 1903–77

US writer, born in Paris to parents of Spanish–Cuban descent. Her works explored sexuality and feminism with a frankness unusual in her era.

37 I stopped loving my father a long time ago. What remained was the slavery to a pattern.

1944 *Under a Glass Bell*, 'Birth'.

Nisbet, Robert 1913–96

US sociologist.

38 Countless works in the social sciences reveal the inability of their authors to bear in mind the crucial difference between what may properly be called the *logic of discovery* and the *logic of demonstration*. The second is properly subject to rules and prescriptions; the first isn't.

1976 *Sociology as an Art Form*, introduction.

39 With all allowance made for Marx's erudition and his historic impact upon the social sciences, especially sociology, it is as an art united with prophecy, virtually religious prophecy, that Marxism survives.

1976 *Sociology as an Art Form*, ch.5.

Niven, David *originally James David Graham Nevins*
1910–83

English actor. Signed by Samuel Goldwyn, he developed into a polished light comedian in films such as *The Charge of the Light Brigade* (1936), *The Dawn Patrol* (1938) and *Bachelor Mother* (1939). He won an Academy Award for *Separate Tables* (1958).

40 He passed rapidly through his marriages to Virginia Cherrill, Barbara Hutton and Betsy Drake and filled in the lonely gaps between them by falling in and out of love with most of his leading ladies, which, as his output of films was prodigious, underlined the excellence of his physical condition.
1975 Of Cary Grant. *Bring on the Empty Horses*.

Nixon, Pat 1912–93

Wife of President Richard M Nixon. She financed herself through college and taught typing until she married Nixon in 1940. She bore two daughters and was known for her gracious hospitality during her years in the White House. She was unswervingly loyal to her husband during and after his resignation in 1974.

41 The hearings are just like a snake about to devour people.
1973 On Watergate. Letter to a friend, quoted in Julie Nixon Eisenhower *Pat Nixon* (1986).

42 Dick, I don't know how you get up in the morning!
To her husband, who later wrote that he replied 'I do it to confound my enemies'. Quoted in Julie Nixon Eisenhower *Pat Nixon* (1986).

Nixon, Richard M(ilhous) 1913–94

US Republican politician and 37th President (1969–74). He resigned under threat of impeachment after the implication of leading members of his government in the Watergate affair. As President, he sought to end the Vietnam War and had diplomatic success with China and the USSR.

43 I don't believe that I ought to quit because I am not a quitter.
1952 National T V broadcast after allegations that he was financing his vice-presidential candidacy from a secret fund, Sep.

44 Tonight—to you, the great silent majority of my fellow Americans—I ask for your support.
1969 Appeal to the nation, 3 Nov, for support in the Vietnam War.

45 This is not an invasion of Vietnam.
1970 Television address to the nation announcing the invasion of Cambodia, 30 Apr.

46 I don't give a shit what happens. I want you all to stonewall…plead the Fifth Amendment, cover-up, or anything else. If that will save it, save the plan.
1973 From the White House tapes relating to the Watergate scandal, recorded Mar.

47 There will be no whitewash in the White House.
1973 Statement on the Watergate affair, 17 Apr.

48 In giving you these tapes, blemishes and all, I am placing my trust in the basic fairness of the American people.
1974 National address, 30 May, on relinquishing the Watergate tapes after the House Judiciary Committee warned him that refusal 'might constitute a ground for impeachment'.

49 Well, I screwed it up real good, didn't I?
1974 Comment to Chief of Staff Alexander M Haig and Press Secretary Ronald L Zeigler, 3 Aug, on beginning work on his

resignation address. Recalled in *RN: The Memoirs of Richard Nixon* (1978).

50 When the president does it, that means that it is not illegal… But I brought myself down. I gave them a sword and they stuck it in and twisted it with relish. And I guess that if I had been in their position, I'd have done the same thing.
1977 Interviewed by David Frost, May.

51 American people don't believe anything until they see it on television.
1994 In *Newsweek*, 2 May. He estimated that 80% of US citizens get their news from television.

Noble, Richard 1946–

English car racer. He established a new land-speed record of 1,019.467kmph (633.468mph) in 1983 in the specially built *Thrust 2*.

52 We did it for Britain and for the hell of it.
1983 After setting a new world land-speed record. Quoted in the *Sunday Times*, 'The Week in Words', 9 Oct.

Nofziger, Lyn (Franklin)

Press secretary and later Chief of the White House Office of Political Affairs in the Reagan administration.

53 Cashing in. That's what we all do. It's called experience.
1988 In *This Week*, 31 Jul.

Nolan, Sir Sidney Robert 1917–92

Australian painter. He made his name with a series of *Ned Kelly* paintings (begun 1946), followed by an 'explorer' series.

54 I wanted to know the true nature of the 'otherness' I had been born into. It was not a European thing. I wanted to paint the great purity and implacability of the landscape. I wanted a visual form of the 'otherness' of the thing not seen.
1971 Quoted in E Lynn *Sidney Nolan— Australia* (1979).

Noonan, Peggy 1950–

US writer. She was speechwriter for President Reagan (1984–9) and has since been a columnist for *Newsweek*, the *New York Times* and *Time* and contributing editor to the *Wall Street Journal*. She has written several books.

55 The battle for the mind of Ronald Reagan was like the trench warfare of World War I. Never have so many fought so hard for such barren terrain.
1990 *What I Saw at the Revolution*.

56 A speech is poetry: cadence, rhythm, imagery, sweep…and reminds us that words, like children, have the power to make dance the dullest beanbag of a heart.
1990 *What I Saw at the Revolution*.

Noonuccal, Oodgeroo *formerly Kath Walker née Kathleen Jean Mary Ruska* 1920–93

Australian poet and Aboriginal rights activist. Her works include *We Are Going* (1964), the first book by an Aboriginal writer to be published in English. She returned an MBE awarded to her in 1970, in protest at planned Australian bicentennial celebrations.

57 Do you know, Mr Menzies, that where I come from you

could be gaoled for supplying alcohol to an Aborigine?

1962 Remark to the then Prime Minister of Australia, Robert Menzies, when he offered her and other Aboriginal delegates a drink after a meeting. Quoted in Kathie Cochrane *Oodgeroo* (1994), pt.1, 'Protest'.

58 What can I tell you, son of mine?
I could tell you of heartbreak, hatred blind,
I could tell of crimes that shame mankind,
Of brutal wrong and deeds malign,
Of rape and murder, son of mine;
But I'll tell instead of brave and fine
When lives of black and white entwine,
And men in brotherhood combine—
This would I tell you, son of mine.

1964 *We Are Going*, 'Son of Mine'.

59 No more boomerang
No more spear;
Now all civilized—
Colour-bar and beer.

1970 *My People*, 'No More Boomerang'.

Norden, Denis 1922–

English broadcaster and humorist.

60 It's a funny kind of month, October. For the really keen cricket fan it's when you realise that your wife left you in May.

Quoted in *She* magazine, 1977.

Norman, Barry 1933–

English journalist and broadcaster. He made his name as an influential film critic through the television series that began with *Film '73* (1973–81, 1983–98).

61 The worst films were always bad but now they are bad in a more cynical way. They pander to an audience of 12–24 year olds, mostly male and mostly governed by raging testosterone. Dialogue is kept to a minimum because it holds up the action. Ditto characterisation and the building of it. As for wit, let's not bother with wit.

2002 *And Why Not?*.

Norman, Greg 1955–

Australian golfer. He won the Open championships in 1986 and 1993. The only player of modern times to have competed in a grand slam of playoffs, unfortunately he lost them all.

62 In the tournament of life, which is the biggest major, I have one of the best records ever.

2003 In *Golf Magazine*, Jul.

Norman, Major Mike

British marine. He was commanding officer of the 68 Royal marines who comprised the Falklands garrison at the time of the Argentinian invasion.

63 We've never surrendered before. It's not part of our training.

1982 Comment, Apr. Quoted in The Sunday Times Insight Team *The Falklands War* (1982), p.7.

Norris, Frank Benjamin Franklin 1870–1902

US novelist. He worked for the San Francisco *Chronicle* and while reporting became involved in the Jameson raid in South Africa. He was influenced by Zola and was one of the first US

naturalist writers. His novels include *McTeague* (1899) and *The Pit* (1903).

64 The kind of a man that *men* like—not women—is the kind of man that makes the best husband.

1903 *The Pit*, ch.2.

65 Here, of all her cities, throbbed the true life—the true power and spirit of America; gigantic, crude with the crudity of youth, disdaining rivalry; sane and healthy and vigorous; brutal in its ambition, arrogant in the new-found knowledge of its giant strength, prodigal of its wealth, infinite in its desires.

1903 Of Chicago. *The Pit*, ch.2.

North, Christopher *pseudonym of* John Wilson
1785–1854

Scottish critic and essayist, Professor of Moral Philosophy at Edinburgh University (1820–51), and regular contributor to *Blackwood's Magazine* under the pseudonym 'Christopher North'.

66 His Majesty's dominions, on which the sun never sets.

1829 'Noctes Ambrosianae', no.42, in *Blackwood's Magazine*, Apr.

67 Laws were made to be broken.

1830 'Noctes Ambrosianae', no.49, in *Blackwood's Magazine*, May.

68 It may be divided into three parts; in one you cannot hear, in another you cannot see, and in the third you can neither see nor hear. I remember once sitting alone in the third division—and never before or since have I had such a profound feeling of the power of solitude.

1832 Of the Theatre Royal, Glasgow. 'Noctes Ambrosianae', no.64, in *Blackwood's Magazine*, Nov.

69 Such accidents will happen in the best-regulated families.

1834 'Noctes Ambrosianae', no.67, in *Blackwood's Magazine*, Aug.

North, Oliver 1943–

US soldier, later columnist and broadcaster. He was a National Security official involved in the 1986 Iran–Contra scandal (the supporting of anti-government Contra rebels in Nicaragua with the proceeds of secret arms sales to Iran). Despite appeals to patriotism, he was convicted on three of twelve charges, which were later dropped on appeal.

70 I don't think there's another person in America that wants to tell this story as much as I do.

1986 Invoking the Fifth Amendment at the House Committee investigating arms sales to Iran, 10 Dec.

71 I thought using the Ayatollah's money to support the Nicaraguan resistance…was a neat idea.

1987 Testimony at the House Committee investigating arms sales to Iran, 8 Jul.

Novak, Michael 1933–

US critic, writer and philosopher.

72 Baseball is a Lockean game, a kind of contract theory in ritual form, a set of atomic individuals who assent to patterns of limited co-operation in their mutual interest.

1976 *The Joys of Sport*, pt.1.

Novalis *pseudonym of* **Friedrich von Hardenberg** 1772–1801

German poet, a leading early Romantic. The early death of the woman he loved left a lasting impression on him, and he wrote the prose lyrics of *Hymnen an die Nicht* (1800) in her memory. He died of tuberculosis.

73 *Der Tod ist das romantisierende Prinzip unsers Lebens. Der Tod ist—das Leben. Durch den Tod wird das Leben verstärkt.*
Death is the romantic principle of Life. Death is—life. Through death life is intensified.
1802 *Schriften, II, Fragmente.*

74 *Ein Charakter ist ein vollkommen gebildeter Willen.*
A character is a perfectly cultivated will.
1802 *Schriften, II, Fragmente.*

75 *Jeder Engländer ist eine Insel.*
Every Englishman is an island.
1802 *Schriften, II, Fragmente.*

76 *Mensch werden ist eine Kunst.*
To become human is art.
1802 *Schriften, II, Fragmente.*

Noyes, Alfred 1880–1958

English writer. He was best known for his florid poems, and especially his sea poems, but also wrote literary essays, plays and memoirs.

77 Go down to Kew in lilac-time (it isn't far from London!)
And you shall wander hand in hand with love in summer's wonderland.
1904 'The Barrel-Organ'.

78 The wind was a torrent of darkness among the gusty trees,
The moon was a ghostly galleon tossed upon cloudy seas,
The road was a ribbon of moonlight over the purple moor,
And the highwayman came riding—
Riding—riding—
The highwayman came riding, up to the old inn-door.
1907 'The Highwayman'.

79 Watch for me by moonlight;
I'll come to thee by moonlight, though hell should bar the way.
1907 'The Highwayman'.

Nozick, Robert 1938–2002

US philosopher, Professor at Harvard University.

80 The socialist society would have to forbid capitalist acts between consenting adults.
1974 *Anarchy, State, and Utopia*, p.163.

Nugent, Ted 1949–

US rock guitarist. His albums include *Free For All* (1976), *Cat Scratch Fever* (1977) and *Take No Prisoners* (2003).

81 If it's too loud, you're too old.
Quoted in David Pickering *Brewer's Twentieth-Century Music* (1994).

Nunn, Sir Trevor 1940–

English stage director. He was artistic director of the Royal Shakespeare Company (1968–86) and of the National Theatre (1997–2003).

82 The National [Theatre] is an organisation that benefits directly from taxpayers' money. I know of no edict that says that only those taxpayers with degrees in English literature pay for this place.
2001 In the *New Statesman*, 22 Oct.

Nuttgens, Patrick 1930–2004

British architect and educationalist. Director of Leeds Polytechnic (1969–86), his works include *The Landscape of Ideas* (1972) and *Understanding Modern Architecture* (1988).

83 In the final analysis, all architecture reveals the application of human ingenuity to the satisfaction of human needs. And among these needs are not only shelter, warmth and accommodation, but also the needs, felt at every moment in every part of the world in endlessly different ways, for something more profound, evocative and universal, for beauty, for permanence, for immortality.
1993 'The Nature of Architecture', in Ben Farmer and Hentie Louw (eds) *Companion to Contemporary Architectural Thought* (1993).

Nye, Joseph S, Jr 1937–

Professor of International Relations and Dean of the Kennedy School, Harvard. Formerly Assistant Secretary of Defense for International Security Affairs and Chair of the National Intelligence Council.

84 Not their style to say no. But when you listen…you don't hear yes.
1994 On asking for Saudi Arabia's help with the $500-million cost of US troop buildup in the Gulf. In the *New York Times*, 4 Nov.

Oakeshott, Michael Joseph 1901–90

English philosopher and political theorist, Professor of Political Science at the London School of Economics (1951–69). His key philosophical work was *Experience and its Modes* (1933), a broadly idealistic view which he developed in economic theory.

85 The politics of our society are a conversation in which past, present and future each has a voice; and though one or other of them may on occasion properly prevail none permanently dominates, and on this account we are free.
1962 *Rationalism in Politics.*

86 We consider ourselves to be free because no one in our society is allowed unlimited power—no leader, faction, party or 'class', no majority, no government, church, corporation, trade, or professional association or trade union. The secret of its freedom is that it is composed of a multitude of organisations in the constitution of the best of which is reproduced that diffusion of power

which is characteristic of the whole.
1962 *Rationalism in Politics.*

87 It is difficult to think of any circumstances where learning may be said to be impossible.
Quoted in R S Peters (ed) *The Concept of Education* (1966), ch.10, 'Learning and Teaching'.

88 Every human being is born an heir to an inheritance to which he can succeed only in a process of learning.
Quoted in R S Peters (ed) *The Concept of Education* (1966), ch.10, 'Learning and Teaching'.

Oakley, Charles Edward 1832–65

English clergyman and hymn writer.

89 Hills of the North, rejoice:
Rivers and mountain-spring,
Hark to the advent voice!
Valley and lowland, sing!
Though absent long, your Lord is nigh,
He judgement brings, and victory.
1870 Hymn.

Oates, Joyce Carol 1938–

US writer. She is best known as a novelist, but has also published several volumes of poetry, and essays, critical writings and journalism.

90 The worst cynicism: a belief in luck.
1970 *Do What You Will*, pt.2, ch.15.

91 Nothing is accidental in the universe—this is one of my Laws of Physics—except the entire universe itself, which is Pure Accident, pure divinity.
1970 *Do What You Will*, 'The Summing-Up: Meredith Dawe'.

92 Women Whose Lives Are Food, Men Whose Lives Are Money.
1978 Title of poetry collection.

93 I used to think getting old was about vanity—but actually it's about losing people you love.
1989 In *The Guardian*, 18 Aug.

94 Because It Is Bitter, And Because It Is My Heart.
1990 Title of novel.

95 For what *is* passes so swiftly and irrevocably into what *was*, no human claim can be of the least significance.
1994 *What I Lived For*, prologue, pt.1.

96 And Corky'd protested, You mean it isn't enough to be *right*?—they have to *like* me, too?
1994 *What I Lived For*, pt.1.

Oates, Lawrence Edward Grace 1880–1912

English explorer, one of the members of Captain Scott's ill-fated Antarctic expedition that set out for the South Pole in 1910.

97 I am just going outside and may be some time.
1912 Last words, Mar.
➤ *See Scott 722:82.*

O'Brien, (Donal) Conor (Dermod David Donat) Cruise 1917–

Irish historian, diplomat, critic and politician. He wrote *To Katanga and Back* (1962), an autobiographical narrative of the Congo crisis. He has also been a newspaper editor and written numerous books of biography, politics and history.

98 Irishness is not primarily a question of birth or blood or language: it is the condition of being involved in the Irish situation, and usually of being mauled by it. On that definition Swift is more Irish than Goldsmith or Sheridan, although by the usual tests they are Irish and he is pure English.
1959 Reviewing *The Oxford Book of Irish Verse* in the *New Statesman*, 17 Jan (written under the pseudonym Donat O'Donnell).

99 Of history and its consequences it may be said: 'Those who can, gloat; those who can't, brood.' Englishmen are born gloaters; Irishmen born brooders. There are, it is true, brooders who take to gloating, and they did much to build the Empire. Yet the brooder-gloater, such as the Irishman turned Englishman, is not, as a human type, altogether a success. He is a little too much on his guard, like an excessively assimilated Jew, or a son of Harlem who has decided to 'pass'. The past of the Irishman, the Jew, the Negro, is, psychologically, too explosive to be buried.
1962 *To Katanga and Back: a UN case history.*

1 In any case you Papists have no right to complain! If you won't have contraception how can you control the population without the assistance of Herod? You ought to be grateful.
1970 *King Herod Explains.*

2 We dislike the IRA, most of us, and fear it. We are a peaceful and democratic people. But our history, our idealistic pretensions and our fatal ambivalence have stuck us with an ideology that is warlike and anti-democratic, and calls increasingly for further human sacrifice.
1985 In the *New York Review of Books*, 29 Apr.

3 The United Nations cannot do anything, and never could. It is not an animate entity or agent. It is a place, a stage, a forum and a shrine…a place to which powerful people can repair when they are fearful about the course on which their own rhetoric seems to be propelling them.
1985 In *New Republic*, 4 Nov.

O'Brien, Edna 1932–

Irish novelist, short-story writer and playwright. Her works include *The Country Girls* (1960), *The Lonely Girl* (1962), *Girls in Their Married Bliss* (1964), *House of Splendid Isolation* (1994) and *Wild Decembers* (1999).

4 Ordinary life bypassed me, but I also bypassed it. It couldn't have been any other way. Conventional life and conventional people are not for me.
In Annalena Mc Afee (ed) *Lives and Works: Profiles of Leading Novelists, Poets and Playwrights* (2002).

O'Brien, Flann *pseudonym of* Brian O'Nolan *also known as* Myles na Gopaleen 1911–66

Irish writer who worked in the Irish Civil Service until 1953. In 1940 he began writing for *The Irish Times* under the pseudonym of Myles na Gopaleen and developed a reputation for being an eccentric and idiosyncratic columnist. He is best known for his novel, *At Swim-Two-Birds* (1939).

5 When things go wrong and will not come right,
Though you do the best you can,
When life looks black as the hour of night—

A PINT OF PLAIN IS YOUR ONLY MAN.
1939 *At Swim-Two-Birds*, ch.1, 'The Workman's Friend' (as Flann O'Brien).

6   There was a frightful, appalling row.
As a matter of fact the Pope told us all to go to hell. He threatened to silence Father Fahrt.
1961 *The Hard Life*.

7   And now the curse has come upon us, because I have personally met in the streets of Ireland persons who are clearly out of Synge's plays. They talk and dress like that, and damn the drink they'll swally but the mug of porter in the long nights after Samhain.
1968 *The Best of Myles*.

O'Brien, John J

Washington correspondent, Philadelphia *Inquirer*.

8   The only candidate who can whistle Dixie while humming the *Battle Hymn of the Republic*.
1976 Of President Johnson. Quoted in Harold Brayman (ed) *The President Speaks Off the Record* (1976).

O'Brien, (Angela Maxine) Margaret   1937–

US child actress, best known for her performance in *Meet Me in St Louis* (1944).

9   When I cry, shall I let the tears run all the way down my face or shall I stop them halfway down?
1944 Attributed remark to director Henry Koster when making *Music for Millions* (1944). Quoted by Larry Adler in *It Ain't Necessarily So* (1984).

O'Brien, Virginia

Manhattan office worker.

10 Crouch, swivel, tug, pull and plop.
1987 Advice on how to seat oneself at a picnic while wearing a mini-skirt. In the *New York Times*, 17 Jul.

O'Brien, William   1852–1928

Irish journalist and politician, born a Catholic but educated at a Protestant college. He founded the Land League journal *United Ireland* (1881) and became a Nationalist MP (1883–95, 1900–18).

11 What are we learning French or the piano for, I would like to know, if it is not to be sold to a man some day… We have to cringe, and manoeuvre, and grimace for a husband—a husband who may be deaf or have a hump if he is rich—a husband that may attack you in *delirium tremens* to-day if he makes a devout act of contrition for it to-morrow.
1890 *When We Were Boys*.

Ó Bruadair, Dáibhídh   c.1625–1698

Irish-Gaelic poet, who recorded the destruction of his culture. His patrons were exiled by wars and proscription, and he became a farm labourer.

12 I will sing no more songs: the pride of my country I sang
Through forty long years of good rhyme, without any avail;
And no one cared even as much as the half of a hang
For the song or the singer, so here is an end of the tale.
Adapted from the Irish by James Stephens.

O'Casey, Sean   1884–1964

Irish playwright. His early plays, including *Juno and the Paycock* (1924), deal with Dublin working-class life and were written for the Abbey Theatre. His later, more experimental, plays include *Cockadoodle Dandy* (1949).

13 Th' whole worl's in a state o' chassis!
1924 Boyle speaking. *Juno and the Paycock*, act 1.

14 JUNO: Sacred Heart o' Jesus, take away our hearts o' stone, and give us hearts o' flesh! Take away this murdherin' hate, an' give us Thine own eternal love!
1924 *Juno and the Paycock*, act 3.

15 She dhresses herself to keep him with her, but it's no use—afther a month or two, th' wondher of a woman wears off.
1926 *The Plough and the Stars*, act 1.

16 There's no reason to bring religion into it. I think we ought to have as great a regard for religion as we can, so as to keep it out of as many things as possible.
1926 *The Plough and the Stars*, act 1.

17 English literature's performing flea.
Of P G Wodehouse. In P G Wodehouse *Performing Flea* (1953).

Occam, William of   c.1285–c.1349

English philosopher, theologian and political writer. He was perhaps the most influential of later medieval philosophers.

18 *Entia non sunt multiplicanda praeter necessitatem.*
No more things should be presumed than is necessary.
This principle of intellectual economy, known as Occam's Razor, is not found in this form in his writings. Similar expressions can be found, eg *Pluralitas non est ponenda sine necessitate* ('Plurality should not be posited unnecessarily'), in *Scriptum in Librum Primum Sententiarum*.

O'Connell, Daniel   *known as* **the Liberator**   1775–1847

Irish Catholic political leader, able to take his Commons seat only after Catholic Emancipation (1829). He fought against tithes and in 1840 founded the Repeal Association, agitating to end the union with Britain. In 1844 he was imprisoned on a charge of sedition, and his influence subsequently waned.

19 Let us never tolerate the slightest inroad on the discipline of our holy Church. Let us never consent that she should be made the hireling of the Ministry. Our forefathers would have died—nay, perished in hopeless slavery—rather than consent to such degradation.
1814 Speech, Dublin, 23 Feb.

20 Not for all the universe contains would I, in the struggle for what I conceive to be my country's cause, consent to the effusion of a single drop of human blood, except my own.
1843 Speech, 18 Feb.

21 While I have a tongue I'll abuse you, you most inimitable periphery. Look at her, boys! there she stands—a convicted perpendicular in petticoats! There's contamination in her circumference, and she trembles with guilt down to the extremities of her corollaries. Ah! you're found out, you rectilineal antecedent, and equiangular old hag! 'Tis with you the devil will fly away, you porter-swiping similitude of the bisection of a vortex!
Winning thrust in a vituperation contest with Dublin's champion virago, Biddy Moriarty, reported by Daniel Owen-Madden in *Revelations of Ireland* (1877).

O'Connor, Edwin 1918–68

US novelist, originally a radio announcer and producer, best known for his novel *The Last Hurrah* (1956). *The Edge of Sadness* (1961) won a Pulitzer Prize.

22 The Last Hurrah.
1956 Title of novel, based on the career of politician James M Curley.

O'Connor, (Mary) Flannery 1925–64

US novelist and short-story writer. Her fiction, set in the Deep South, reflects a mordant sense of humour. Her works include two novels and two volumes of short stories.

23 I preach there are all kinds of truth, your truth and somebody else's. But behind all of them there is only one truth and that is that there's no truth.
1952 Hazel Motes. *Wise Blood*, ch.10.

24 While the South is hardly Christ-centred, it is most certainly Christ-haunted.
1960 'Some Aspects of the Grotesque in Southern Fiction'. Paper read at Wesleyan College, Fall.

25 There was a time when the average reader read a novel simply for the moral he could get out of it, and however naïve that may have been, it was a good deal less naïve than some of the limited objectives he has now.
1960 'Some Aspects of the Grotesque in Southern Fiction'. Paper read at Wesleyan College, Fall.

26 It's like building a nest. First she thinks about it, then she begins to gather the materials, then she begins to put it together.
On her mother's two-month process of making a fruit cake. Quoted in Sally Fitzgerald (ed) *The Habit of Being* (1979).

O'Connor, Frank *pseudonym of* *Michael O'Donovan* 1903–66

Irish writer, a member of the IRA in his teens and imprisoned after the War of Independence. His ideal medium was the short story, but he also wrote plays and literary criticism.

27 Every time I leave the old man I feel like a thousand dollars.
1948 Of Yeats. Quoted in Richard Ellmann *Yeats: the Man and the Masks* (1948).

O'Connor, Cardinal John Joseph 1920–2000

Catholic Archbishop of New York.

28 It is increasingly rare for many of us…to believe that people can be poor, but honest, poor but deserving of respect. Poverty is no longer blamed on anyone but the poor themselves. Contempt for the poor has become a virtue.
1994 In *Catholic New York*, quoted in the *New York Times*, 24 Nov.

Odets, Clifford 1906–63

US playwright and actor, an important figure in the US theatre of the 1930s.

29 Go out and fight so life shouldn't be printed on dollar bills.
1935 Jacob. *Awake and Sing*, act 1.

30 Music is the great cheer-up in the language of all countries.
1937 Mr Bonaparte. *Golden Boy*, act 1, sc.2.

O'Donnell, Kenneth P(hillip) 1924–77

Special Assistant to President Kennedy.

31 Mr President, the president is dead.
1963 To Lyndon B Johnson after the assassination of John F Kennedy, 22 Nov.

Oerter, Al(fred) 1936–

US athlete and discus-thrower. He won an unsurpassed four gold medals for the discus, at Melbourne (1956), Rome (1960), Tokyo (1964) and Mexico (1968).

32 I never had technique.
1978 In the *New York Times*, 16 May.

O'Faolain, Sean 1900–91

Irish writer and educator. He began writing in and translating from Gaelic. A successful novel, *A Nest of Simple Folk* (1933), was followed by biographies of Irish figures.

33 If we turn to early Irish literature, as we naturally may, to see what sort of people the Irish were in the infancy of the race, we find ourselves wandering in delighted bewilderment through a darkness shot with lightning and purple flame.
1947 *The Irish*.

34 He was like a man who takes a machine-gun to a shooting gallery. Everybody falls flat on his face, the proprietor at once takes to the hills, and when you cautiously peep up, you find that he has wrecked the place but got three perfect bull's-eyes.
On Frank O'Connor (pseudonym of Michael O'Donovan), attributed.

O'Flaherty, Liam 1897–1984

Irish Republican writer. He went to London in 1922 to become a writer, finding fame with his novel *The Informer* (1926). In addition to other novels, he wrote three volumes of autobiography (1930–4).

35 When the parish priest rebuked him for his celibacy, saying it would lead him into debauchery and sin, he said that a man who had to be muzzled by a wife as a protection against debauchery was not worthy of the joy of innocence. After that people began to treat him with priestly respect.
'The Mermaid'.

Ogden, Frank *also known as* *'Dr Tomorrow'* 1920–

Canadian futurist.

36 Although I am a futurist today, if I don't change tomorrow, I will be a historian.
1994 *Ogdenisms: The Frank Ogden Quote Book*.

37 As the planet globalizes, groups tribalize.
1994 *Ogdenisms: The Frank Ogden Quote Book*.

38 Holidays are the greatest learning experience unknown to man.
1994 *Ogdenisms: The Frank Ogden Quote Book*.

39 Technology breaks the laws and makes the laws.
1994 *Ogdenisms: The Frank Ogden Quote Book*.

40 My idea of long-range planning is lunch.
1994 *Ogdenisms: The Frank Ogden Quote Book*.

Ogilvy, David 1911–99

British-born US advertising executive, founder of Ogilvy and Mather.

41 It is the professional duty of the advertising agent to conceal his artifice. When Aeschines spoke, they said, 'How well he speaks', but when Demosthenes spoke, they said 'Let us march against Philip.'
1963 *Confessions of an Advertising Man*, ch.5.

42 The consumer isn't a moron. She's your wife.
1963 *Confessions of an Advertising Man*, ch.5.

Ogilvy, James, 1st Earl of Seafield 1644–1730

Scottish advocate, MP and political manager. He was one of the Scottish commissioners appointed to negotiate the Union of Parliaments.

43 There's ane end of ane auld sang.
1707 On signing the Treaty of Union between Scotland and England. Quoted in George Lockhart of Carnwath *Memoir of the Affairs of Scotland* (1714), vol.1.

O'Hagan, John *pseudonym* **Sliabh Cuilinn** 1822–90

Irish lawyer and poet.

44 My native heath is brown beneath,
My native waters blue;
But crimson red o'er both shall spread,
Ere I am false to you,
Dear land!
Ere I am false to you.
1845 'Dear Land' in *The Spirit of the Nation*.

O'Hanlon, Redmond 1947–

English naturalist, critic and traveller. With James Fenton, he made an expedition into the heart of Borneo in 1983 and wrote entertainingly about the land and its people.

45 The Iban, when they decide that something is really funny, and know that they are going to laugh for a long time, lie down first.
Dana, Leon and Inghai lay down.
1984 *Into the Heart of Borneo*.

O'Hara, Frank 1926–66

US poet and art critic. He published several volumes of poetry, which were closely linked to the New York environment in which he moved.

46 and I am sweating a lot by now and thinking of leaning on the john door in the 5 SPOT
while she whispered a song along the keyboard
to Mal Waldron and everyone and I stopped breathing
1964 Of Billie Holiday. *Lunch Poems*, 'The Day Lady Died'.

O'Hara, John Henry 1905–70

US novelist and short-story writer. His best-known works, several of which were successfully filmed, included *Appointment in Samarra* (1934), *Butterfield 8* (1935) and *Pal Joey* (1940).

47 George Gershwin died last week. I don't have to believe it if I don't want to.
1937 Quoted in Ian Crofton and Donald Fraser *A Dictionary of Musical Quotations* (1985).

48 But whats the use of being old if you cant be dumb?
1940 *Pal Joey*, ch.1.

49 I am making a little trip to N.Y. in the near future and we will have a little talk and you can explain your positon, altho the way I feel now if I saw you now your positon would be horizontle.
1940 *Pal Joey*, ch.2.

50 Illinois is a state of suspended animation and the people live in hibernation from Oct. to whenever it ever gets warmer.
1940 *Pal Joey*, ch.9.

O Henry *pseudonym of* **William Sydney Porter** 1862–1910

US writer. He is best known for his comic short stories.

51 Life is made up of sobs, sniffles, and smiles, with sniffles predominating.
1906 *The Four Million*, 'The Gift of the Magi'.

52 If men knew how women pass the time when they are alone, they'd never marry.
1906 *The Four Million*, 'Memoirs of a Yellow Dog'.

53 It was beautiful and simple as all truly great swindles are.
1908 *The Gentle Grafter*, 'The Octopus Marooned'.

54 Whenever he saw a dollar in another man's hands he took it as a personal grudge if he couldn't take it any other way.
1908 *The Gentle Grafter*, 'The Octopus Marooned'.

55 If ever there was an aviary overstocked with jays it is that Yaptown-on-the-Hudson, called New York.
1908 *The Gentle Grafter*, 'A Tempered Wind'.

56 A story with a moral appended is like the bite of a mosquito. It bores you, and then injects a stinging drop to irritate your conscience.
1910 *Strictly Business*, 'The Gold That Glittered'.

57 Turn up the lights; I don't want to go home in the dark.
Last words. Quoted in Charles Alphonso Smith *O. Henry* (1916), ch.9. The words are taken from the popular song by Harry Williams 'I'm afraid to come home in the dark' (1907).

58 A burglar who respects his art always takes his time before taking anything else.
Sixes and Sevens, 'Makes The Whole World Kin' (1911).

O'Keeffe, Georgia 1887–1986

US painter, a pioneer of abstract art (eg *Blue and Green Music*, 1919). She later moved towards a more figurative style, painting close-ups of parts of flowers and plants. Her works include *Black Iris* (New York, 1949).

59 Nobody sees a flower—really—it is so small—we haven't time—and to see takes time like to have a friend takes time… So I said to myself —I'll paint what I see—what the flower is to me, but I'll paint it big and they will be surprised into taking time to look at it—I will make even busy New Yorkers take time to see what I see of flowers.
Quoted in Goodrich and Bry *Georgia O'Keeffe* (1970).

60 The men liked to put me down as the best woman painter. I think I'm one of the best painters.
Quoted in W Chadwick *Women, Art and Society* (1990).

Okri, Ben 1959–

Nigerian writer, winner of the 1987 Commonwealth Prize for Africa for *Incidents at the Shrine* (1986) and the 1991 Booker Prize for *The Famished Road*. Other works include *Songs of Enchantment* (1993), *Dangerous Love* (1996) and *In Arcadia* (2002).

61 We feared the heartlessness of human beings, all of whom are born blind, few of whom ever learn to see.
1991 *The Famished Road*, ch.1.

Oldenburg, Claes Thure 1929–

Swedish-born US sculptor. From 1958 he was one of the pioneers of Pop Art. His works include giant hamburgers and other foodstuffs, the *Giant Clothespin* in Philadelphia (1975) and projects in Cologne, Eindhoven, Milan and London.

62 I am for an art that helps old ladies across the street… I am for Kool-art, 7-UP art, Pepsi-art, Sunshine art, 39 cents art, 15 cents art, Vatronol art, Dro-bomb art, Vam art, Menthol art, L & M art, Ex-lax art, Venida art, Heaven Hill art, Pamryl art, San-o-med art, Rx art, 9.99 art, Now art, New art, How art, Fire sale art, Last Chance art, Only art, Diamond art, Tomorrow art, Franks art, Ducks art, Meat-o-rama art.
1961 Written for an exhibition in New York, 1961, quoted in Arts Council of Great Britain *Oldenburg* (1970).

Oldman, Gary 1958–

English actor.

63 The industry has changed. Two years ago I could tell a company I've got Russell Crowe and that would get the film made. Now they'd ask 'And who's the girl?' Just one famous face isn't enough any more.
2004 In *Scotland on Sunday*, 30 May.

Oliphant, Margaret née *Wilson* 1828–97

Scottish novelist, essayist and critic. Widowed and debt-ridden at an early age with a large extended family dependent upon her, she was a prolific writer and maintained a long association with *Blackwood's Magazine* and *The Cornhill* as well as completing over 100 novels.

64 A woman who cannot be a governess or a novel-writer must fall back on that poor little needle, the primitive and original handicraft of femininity.
1858 'The Condition of Women', in *Blackwood's Magazine*, vol.83, Feb.

Oliver, Mary 1935–

US poet. Her work includes *American Primitive* (1983, Pulitzer Prize), *New and Selected Poems* (1992, National Book Award) and *The Leaf and the Cloud* (2000).

65 Poetry happens because of life. Poetry happens because of language. And poetry happens because of other poets.
1992 In the *New York Times*, 20 Nov.

Olivier, Laurence Kerr, Baron 1907–89

English actor, producer and director. A great Shakespearean actor, he also produced, directed and played in films of *Henry V* (1944), *Hamlet* (1948) and *Richard III* (1955). He campaigned for the foundation of the National Theatre.

66 Make up your mind dearheart. Do you want to be a great

actor or a household word?
c.1962 Comment to Richard Burton while filming *Cleopatra*. Burton replied 'Both'.

67 Acting is a masochistic form of exhibitionism. It is not quite the occupation of an adult.
1978 Quoted in *Time*, 3 Jul.

68 I'm not so artistic that I despise profit.
Attributed.

69 It looks like rows and rows of empty seats.
On being shown the view of the jungle enjoyed from Noël Coward's house on a Jamaican hillside. Attributed.

70 Shakespeare—the nearest thing in incarnation to the eye of God.
Quoted in *Kenneth Harris Talking To…*, 'Sir Laurence Olivier'.

71 What is the main problem of the actor? It is to keep the audience awake, and not let them go to sleep, then wake up and go home feeling they've wasted their money.
Attributed.

Ollivier, Émile 1825–1913

French politician, charged by Napoleon III to form a constitutional ministry. He rushed into war with Germany, was overthrown on 9 Aug 1870, and withdrew to Italy. He wrote numerous works, including *L'Empire libéral* (16 vols, 1894–1912), a defence of his policy.

72 One is never weaker than when one appears to have everybody's support.
1870 Letters.

Olsen, Tillie 1913–

US writer and feminist. She wrote proletarian fiction in the 1930s. In the 1960s she emerged as an advocate of feminism, and her work attracted wide attention for the first time. Her later work includes *Tell Me a Riddle* (1960).

73 Vinegar he poured on me all his life; I am well marinated; how can I be honey now?
1960 *Tell Me a Riddle*, section 1.

Olson, Charles 1910–70

US poet and literary theorist. He taught at Black Mountain College, North Carolina, where his ideas were influential on such poets as Robert Creeley and Robert Duncan. As a poet, he is best known for the sequence *The Maximus Poems* (1953).

74 I take SPACE to be the central fact to man born in America… I spell it large because it comes large here. Large and without mercy.
1947 *Call Me Ishmael*, section 1.

75 But that which matters, that which insists, that which will last,
that! o my people, where shall you find it, how, where, where shall you
listen
when all is become billboards, when, all, even silence, is spray-gunned?
1953 *The Maximus Poems*, 'I, Maximus of Gloucester, To You, 3'.

76 one loves only form,
and form only comes
into existence when
the thing is born.
1953 *The Maximus Poems*, 'I, Maximus of Gloucester, To You, 4'.

Olson, Elder James 1909–92

US poet and critic. In both his formal, cerebral poetry and criticism he adhered to the neo-Aristotelian principles espoused at the University of Chicago, where he taught.

77 We shall never know all about art or the values of art until all art is at an end; meanwhile artists will continue to instruct us.
Quoted in Elmer Borklund (ed) *Contemporary Literary Critics* (1977).

Onassis, Jacqueline Lee Kennedy née *Bouvier* 1929–94

Wife of President John F Kennedy. She supervised the restoration of the White House and wielded a powerful and widespread influence on fashion. After her husband's assassination she returned to private life, and in 1968 she married Aristotle Onassis, the Greek shipping magnate.

78 Put your brilliant mind to work for…dresses for public appearances…that I would wear if Jack were President of France.
1960 Letter to Oleg Cassini, 13 Dec. Quoted in Oleg Cassini *In My Fashion* (1987).

79 I felt like a moth hanging on the window pane.
1961 On her first night in the White House, in *Newsweek*, 1 Jan.

80 Lincoln's bedroom! And you see that great bed, it looks like a cathedral.
1961 On her first night in the White House, in *Newsweek*, 1 Jan.

81 You worked together for the finest things in the finest years… Later on when a series of disastrous Presidents and Prime Ministers…will have botched up everything—people will say 'Do you remember those days—how perfect they were?' The days of you and Jack.
1964 To Harold Macmillan, 31 Jan.

82 I cast only one vote—for Jack. It is a rare thing to be able to vote for one's husband for President and I didn't want to dilute it by voting for anyone else.
On the 1960 elections. Quoted in Arthur M Schlesinger Jr *A Thousand Days* (1965).

83 There'll never be another Camelot again.
On Frederick Lowe's lyrics from Alan Jay Lerner's *Camelot*, a title that became synonymous with the Kennedy administration—'Don't let it be forgot, that once there was a spot, for one brief shining moment that was known as Camelot.' Quoted in Theodore H White *In Search of History* (1978).

84 Uncle Cornpone and his Little Porkchop.
On the Johnsons. Quoted in *Newsweek*, 30 May 1994.

Ondaatje, (Philip) Michael 1943–

Sri Lankan-born Canadian poet and novelist. His poetry includes *Rat Jelly* (1973) and *Secular Love* (1987); other works include novels such as *Running in the Family* (1982), *The English Patient* (1992, Booker Prize) and *Anil's Ghost* (2000).

85 There was always, he thought, this pleasure ahead of him, an ace of joy up his sleeve so he could say you can do anything to me, take everything away, put me in prison, but I will know [her] when we are old.
1987 *In the Skin of a Lion*, 'Remorse'.

O'Neal, Shaquille 1972–

US basketball player. As centre for Orlando in 1995, he was the NBA leading scorer with 2,315 points from 79 games. He played for Orlando Magic from 1992 to 1996, when he joined the Los Angeles Lakers.

86 Nietzsche was so intelligent and advanced. And that's how I am. I'm the black, basketball-playing Nietzsche.
2003 On himself, having previously likened himself to Aristotle. In *Book*, Mar/Apr.

O'Neill, Eugene Gladstone 1888–1953

US playwright. His play *Beyond the Horizon* (1920) won a Pulitzer Prize, and he established his reputation with such serious-minded plays as *Mourning Becomes Electra* (1931), *The Iceman Cometh* (1946) and *Long Day's Journey into Night* (1956). He was awarded a Nobel prize in 1936.

87 The action of the play takes place on an island in the West Indies as not yet self-determined by White Mariners. The form of native government is, for the time being, an Empire.
1920 *The Emperor Jones*, scene direction.

88 For de little stealin' dey gits you in jail soon or late. For de big stealin' dey makes you Emperor and puts you in de Hall o' Fame when you croaks.
1921 Jones. *The Emperor Jones*, sc.1.

89 Life is for each man a solitary cell whose walls are mirrors.
1927 Lazarus. *Lazarus Laughed*, act 2, sc.1.

90 When men make gods, there is no God!
1927 Lazarus. *Lazarus Laughed*, act 2, sc.2.

91 Man's loneliness is but his fear of life!
1927 Lazarus. *Lazarus Laughed*, act 3, sc.2.

92 The old—like children—talk to themselves, for they have reached that hopeless wisdom of experience which knows that though one were to cry it in the streets to multitudes, or whisper it in the kiss to one's beloved, the only ears that can ever hear one's secrets are one's own!
1927 Tiberius. *Lazarus Laughed*, act 4, sc.1.

93 Life is perhaps most wisely regarded as a bad dream between two awakenings, and every day is a life in miniature.
1928 Chu-Yin. *Marco Millions*, act 2, sc.2.

94 The devil!…what beastly things our memories insist on cherishing!
1928 Marsden. *Strange Interlude*, pt.1, act 2.

95 Strange interlude! Yes, our lives are merely strange dark interludes in the electrical display of God the Father!
1928 Nina. *Strange Interlude*, pt.2, act 9.

96 Mourning Becomes Electra.
1931 Title of play.

97 The sea hates a coward!
1931 Bryant. *Mourning Becomes Electra*, pt.2, act 4.

98 EDMUND: (*sits down opposite his father—contemptuously*). Yes, facts don't mean a thing, do they? What you want to believe, that's the only truth! (*Derisively.*) Shakespeare was an Irish Catholic, for example.
TYRONE: (*stubbornly*). So he was. The proof is in his plays.
1939–41 *Long Day's Journey Into Night*, act 4 (published 1956).

99 Where do you get your taste in authors—That damned library of yours! (*He indicates the small bookcase at rear.*) Voltaire, Rousseau, Schopenhauer, Nietzsche, Ibsen! Atheists, fools, and madmen! And your poets! This Dowson, and this Baudelaire, and Swinburne and

Oscar Wilde, and Whitman and Poe! Whoremongers and degenerates! Pah! When I've three good sets of Shakespeare there (he nods at the large bookcase) you could read.
1939–41 Tyrone. *Long Day's Journey Into Night*, act 4 (published 1956).

1 A Long Day's Journey Into Night.
1939–41 Title of play (published 1956).

2 The Iceman Cometh.
1946 Title of play.

3 Little subconscious mind, say I each night, bring home the bacon.
Quoted in Kenneth Tynan *Tynan Right and Left* (1988). Tynan added the question, 'But how much of the bacon can we nowadays stomach?'

O'Neill, Martin 1952–

Northern Irish footballer and football manager.

4 I never try to make a right decision. I make a decision and then try to make it right.
2002 In *The Independent*, 20 Dec.

O'Neill, Molly

US writer, food columnist and restaurant critic.

5 Out of the kitchen, to stew is to fret, to worry, to agitate. In the kitchen, however, to stew is to have great expectations.
1994 In the *New York Times*, 30 Jan.

O'Neill, Thomas P known as 'Tip' 1912–94

US Congressman and Speaker of the House of Representatives.

6 Take advantage of the good cigars. You don't get much else in that job.
1977 Advice to Vice-President Walter P Mondale. Quoted in *Time*, 4 Jun 1984.

7 Ronald Reagan…wasn't without leadership ability, but he lacked most of the management skills that a President needs. But let me give him his due: he would have made a hell of a king.
1987 *Man of the House*.

8 You can teach an old dog new tricks—if the old dog wants to learn.
1989 On working with President Reagan. In NPR broadcast, 2 Jan.

9 Herbert Hoover with a smile, a cheerleader for selfishness.
On President Reagan. Recalled on O'Neill's death in the *New York Times*, 7 Jan 1994.

10 Keep your left hand high.
Recommending the boxer's defensive posture to President Carter. Recalled on O'Neill's death in the *New York Times*, 7 Jan 1994.

11 The Democratic Party has succeeded so well that many of its members are now Republicans.
Quoted in W AMU radio broadcast, Washington, 29 Mar 1995.

Onetti, Juan Carlos 1909–94

Uruguayan novelist. He moved to Buenos Aires in 1943 and later to Madrid, where he spent his final years. In many of his novels he sets the action in the mythical city of Santa María.

12 *Es asombroso ver en qué se puede convertir la revolución rusa a través del cerebro de un comerciante yanqui; basta ver las fotos de las revistas norteamericanas, nada más que las fotos porque no sé leerlas, para comprender que no hay pueblo más imbécil que ése sobre la tierra; no puede haberlo porque también la capacidad de estupidez es limitada en la raza humana.*
It's astonishing to see what the Russian Revolution can become thanks to the brain of a Yankee entrepreneur; you only have to see the photos in North American magazines, only the photos because I can't read them, to realize they're the most stupid people on earth; that's quite possible because even the human race has a limited potential for idiocy.
1939 *El pozo* (translated as *The Pit*, 1991).

Oppenheimer, J(ulius) Robert 1904–67

US physicist, lecturer at the University of California and the California Institute of Technology and from 1947 director of the Institute for Advanced Study at Princeton. He was director (1942–5) of the laboratory at Los Alamos, New Mexico, that designed and built the first atomic bomb.

13 When you see something that is technically sweet, you go ahead and do it and you argue about what to do about it only after you have had your technical success. That is the way it was with the atomic bomb.
1954 'In the Matter of J. Robert Oppenheimer', USAEC transcript of hearing before Personnel Security Board.

14 I remembered the line from the Hindu scripture, the *Bhagavad Gita*… 'I am become death, the destroyer of worlds.'
On the detonation of the first atomic bomb, 16 Jul 1945. Quoted in Len Giovanitti and Fred Freed *The Decision to Drop the Bomb* (1965).

15 Science has, as its whole purpose, the rendering of the physical world understandable and beautiful. Without this you have only tables and statistics.
1966 In *Look* magazine.

16 Science is not everything, but science is very beautiful.
1966 In *Look* magazine.

17 No man should escape our universities without knowing how little he knows.
1967 In *Partisan Review*, Summer issue.

18 The theory of our modern technic shows that nothing is as practical as the theory.
1977 In *Reflex*, Jul.

19 Those two scorpions in a bottle.
On the US and USSR in the early 1950s. Quoted in Anthony Cave Brown *Treason in the Blood* (1994).

O'Rahilly, Egan Gaelic name Aodhagán Ó Rathaille 1670–1726

Gaelic poet. Little is known of his life except that he lived and died in great poverty and was buried at Muckross Abbey. His *Vision* is regarded as one of the finest poems in Irish Gaelic.

20 For the future I cease, Death approaches with little delay,
Since the dragons of Laune and Lane and Lee are destroyed;
I'll follow the heroes far from the light of day,
The princes my ancestors followed before Christ died.
c.1729 Closing lines of his last known poem, translated

from the Irish by Owen Dudley Edwards.

21 That my old bitter heart was pierced in this black doom,
That foreign devils have made our land a tomb,
That the sun that was Munster's glory has gone down
Has made me a beggar before you, Valentine Brown.
'Valentine Brown', translated from the Irish by Michael
O'Donovan (pseudonym Frank O'Connor).

O'Rourke, P(atrick)](ake) 1947–

US writer and editor. He has written books and articles on government, politics, social mores and travel.

22 The best thing about the violence in Northern Ireland is that it's all so ancient and honorable… The Irish are in the same terrific position as the Shiites in Lebanon, the peasants in El Salvador, the blacks in America, the Jews in Palestine, the Palestinians in Israel (and everybody everywhere, if you read your history)—enough barbarism has been visited on the Irish to excuse all barbarities by the Irish barbarians.
1988 *Holidays in Hell.*

23 Communism doesn't really starve or execute that many people. Mostly it just bores them to death.
1988 *Holidays in Hell.*

24 Republicans are the party that says government doesn't work, and then they get elected and prove it.
1991 *Parliament of Whores.*

25 Sometimes it's hard to remember that bourgeois property is the real revolutionary force these days. All over the world we're bringing down dictatorships—or at least forcing them to go condo.
1992 *Give War a Chance.*

26 For reasons of high aesthetic principle, I do not write on a computer.
2003 In *Writers on Writing, Volume II: More Collected Essays from the New York Times.*

Orozco, José Clemente 1883–1949

Mexican painter, one of the three foremost artists in the revival of monumental fresco painting.

27 The highest, the most logical, the purest and strongest form of painting is the mural… It is, too, the most disinterested form, for it cannot be made a matter of private gain; it cannot be hidden away for the benefit of a certain privileged few. It is for the people. It is for ALL.
1929 *Creative Art.*

Ortega y Gasset, José 1883–1955

Spanish essayist and philosopher, Professor of Metaphysics at Madrid. He gained international fame with *The Revolt of the Masses* (1929), which argued in favour of an intellectual governing elite.

28 The man who discovers a new scientific truth has previously had to smash to atoms almost everything he had learnt, and arrives at the new truth with hands blood stained from the slaughter of a thousand platitudes.
1930 *The Revolt of the Masses.*

Orton, Joe originally *John Kingsley* 1933–67

English dramatist, known for his blackly comic, outrageous farces such as *Entertaining Mr Sloane* (1964). He was murdered by his lover, Kenneth Halliwell, who then committed suicide.

29 I'd the upbringing a nun would envy… Until I was fifteen I was more familiar with Africa than my own body.
1964 *Entertaining Mr Sloane,* act 1.

30 Every luxury was lavished on you — atheism, breast-feeding, circumcision.
1966 *Loot,* act 1.

31 Reading isn't an occupation we encourage among police officers. We try to keep the paperwork down to a minimum.
1966 *Loot,* act 2.

Orwell, George *pseudonym of* **Eric Arthur Blair** 1903–50

English novelist, essayist and journalist. He fought in the Spanish Civil War and during World War II worked for the BBC. He developed his own brand of socialism in *The Road to Wigan Pier* (1937) and other essays, but is best known for his satire of totalitarian ideology in *Animal Farm* (1945), and the prophetic novel, *Nineteen Eighty-Four* (1949).

32 While the journalist exists merely as the publicity agent of big business, a large circulation, got by fair means or foul, is a newspaper's one and only aim.
1928 In *G.K.'s Weekly,* 29 Dec.

33 He was an embittered atheist (the sort of atheist who does not so much disbelieve in God as personally dislike Him), and took a sort of pleasure in thinking that human affairs would never improve.
1933 *Down and Out in Paris and London,* ch.30.

34 Keep the Aspidistra Flying.
1936 Title of novel.

35 In the early morning the mill girls clumping down the cobbled street, all in clogs, making a curiously formidable sound, like an army hurrying into battle. I suppose this is the typical sound of Lancashire.
1936 Diary entry, 18 Feb. He used this as material for his book *The Road to Wigan Pier* (1937).

36 It is only because miners sweat their guts out that superior persons can remain superior.
1937 *The Road to Wigan Pier,* ch.2.

37 A thousand influences constantly press a working man into a *passive* role. He does not act, he is acted upon.
1937 *The Road to Wigan Pier,* ch.3.

38 A person of bourgeois origin goes through life with some expectation of getting what he wants, within reasonable limits. Hence the fact that in times of stress 'educated' people tend to come to the front.
1937 *The Road to Wigan Pier,* ch.3.

39 I sometimes think the price of liberty is not so much eternal vigilance as eternal dirt.
1937 *The Road to Wigan Pier,* ch.4.

40 In a Lancashire cotton-town you could probably go for months on end without once hearing an 'educated' accent, whereas there can hardly be a town in the South of England where you could throw a brick without hitting the niece of a bishop.
1937 *The Road to Wigan Pier,* ch.7.

41 As with the Christian religion, the worst advertisement for Socialism is its adherents.
1937 *The Road to Wigan Pier,* ch.11.

42 To the ordinary working man, the sort you would meet in any pub on Saturday night, Socialism does not mean

much more than better wages and shorter hours and nobody bossing you about.
1937 *The Road to Wigan Pier*, ch.11.

43 The underlying motive of many Socialists is, I believe, a hypertrophied sense of order…what they desire, basically, is to reduce the world to something resembling a chessboard.
1937 *The Road to Wigan Pier*, ch.11.

44 The high-water mark, so to speak, of Socialist literature is W.H. Auden, a sort of gutless Kipling.
1937 *The Road to Wigan Pier*, ch.11.

45 Cease to use your hands, and you have lopped off a huge chunk of your consciousness.
1937 *The Road to Wigan Pier*, ch.12.

46 It is usual to speak of the Fascist objective as the 'beehive state', which does a grave injustice to bees. A world of rabbits ruled by stoats would be nearer the mark.
1937 *The Road to Wigan Pier*, ch.12.

47 We of the sinking middle class…have nothing to lose but our aitches.
1937 *The Road to Wigan Pier*, ch.13.

48 The era of free speech is closing down. The freedom of the press in Britain was always something of a fake, because in the last resort, money controls opinion; still, so long as the legal right to say what you like exists, there are always loopholes for an unorthodox writer.
1938 In the *New Leader*, 24 Jun.

49 Roughly speaking it was the sensation of being *at the centre* of an explosion… I fancy you would feel much the same if you were struck by lightning. I knew immediately that I was hit, but because of that seeming bang and flash, I thought it was a rifle nearby that had gone off accidentally and shot me.
1938 Of his wounding during the Spanish Civil War. *Homage to Catalonia*, ch.12.

50 When you have had a glimpse of such a disaster as this…the result is not necessarily disillusionment and cynicism. Curiously enough, the whole experience has left me with not less but more belief in the decency of human beings.
1938 *Homage to Catalonia*, ch.14.

51 Down here it was still the England I had known in my childhood:…all sleeping the deep, deep sleep of England, from which I sometimes fear that we shall never wake till we are jerked out of it by the roar of bombs.
1938 *Homage to Catalonia*, ch.14.

52 I'm fat, but I'm thin inside. Has it ever struck you that there's a thin man inside every fat man, just as they say there's a statue inside every block of stone?
1939 *Coming Up For Air*, pt.1, ch.3.
➤ *See Connolly 233:82.*

53 Before the war, and especially before the Boer War, it was summer all the year round.
1939 *Coming Up For Air*, pt.2, ch.1.

54 If the war didn't happen to kill you it was bound to start you thinking. After that unspeakable idiotic mess you couldn't go on regarding society as something eternal and unquestionable, like a pyramid. You knew it was just a balls-up.
1939 *Coming Up For Air*, pt.2, ch.8.

55 Most revolutionaries are potential Tories, because they imagine that everything can be put right by altering the *shape* of society; once that change is effected, as it sometimes is, they see no need for any other.
1939 'Charles Dickens', collected in *Inside the Whale* (1940).

56 The novel is practically a Protestant form of art; it is the product of the free mind, of the autonomous individual.
1940 *Inside the Whale*, 'Inside The Whale'.

57 Contrary to popular belief, the past was not more eventful than the present. If it seems so it is because when you look backward things that happened years apart are telescoped together, and because very few of your memories come to you genuinely virgin.
1940 *Inside the Whale*, 'My Country Right or Left'.

58 As I write, highly civilized human beings are flying overhead, trying to kill me.
1941 *The Lion and the Unicorn: Socialism and the English Genius*, pt.1, 'England Your England'.

59 England is not the jewelled isle of Shakespeare's much-quoted passage, nor is it the inferno depicted by Dr Goebbels. More than either it resembles a family, a rather stuffy Victorian family, with not many black sheep in it but with all its cupboards bursting with skeletons.
1941 *The Lion and the Unicorn: Socialism and the English Genius*, pt.3, 'Shopkeeper at War'.

60 A family with the wrong members in control—that, perhaps, is as near as one can come to describing England in a phrase.
1941 *The Lion and the Unicorn: Socialism and the English Genius*, pt.3, 'The English Revolution'.

61 Probably the battle of Waterloo *was* won on the playing-fields of Eton, but the opening battles of all subsequent wars have been lost there. One of the dominant facts in English life during the past three-quarters of a century has been the decay of ability in the ruling class.
1941 *The Lion and the Unicorn: Socialism and the English Genius*, pt.4.

62 The great enemy of clear language is insincerity. When there is a gap between one's real and one's declared aims, one turns instinctively to long words and exhausted idioms—like cuttlefish squirting out ink.
1941 *The Lion and the Unicorn: Socialism and the English Genius*.

63 I believe that the BBC, in spite of the stupidity of its foreign propaganda and the unbearable voices of its announcers, is very truthful. It is generally regarded here as more reliable than the press.
1941 In the *Partisan Review*, 15 Apr. Reprinted in *Collected Essays, Journalism and Letters*, vol.2.

64 All propaganda is lies, even when one is telling the truth.
1942 Diary entry, 14 Mar.

65 Whatever is funny is subversive, every joke is ultimately a custard pie… A dirty joke is not, of course, a serious attack upon morality, but it is a sort of mental rebellion, a momentary wish that things were otherwise.
1942 'The Art of Donald McGill'.

66 On the whole, human beings want to be good, but not too good, and not all the time.
1942 'The Art of Donald McGill'.

67 Reminds me of nothing so much as a recently-dead fish before it has had time to stiffen.
1942 Of Clement Attlee. Diary entry, 19 May.

68 Any daily journalist will tell you that one of the most important secrets of his trade is the trick of making it appear that there is news when there is no news.
1944 In the *Tribune*, 21 Apr.

69 To blame someone like Northcliffe for making money in the quickest way is like blaming a skunk for stinking.
1944 In the *Tribune*, 21 Apr.

70 Cricket is a game full of forlorn hopes and sudden dramatic changes of fortune and its rules are so ill-defined that their interpretation is partly an ethical business.
1944 *Raffles and Miss Blandish.*

71 If liberty means anything at all, it means the right to tell people what they do not want to hear.
1945 Written for a rejected preface to *Animal Farm.*

72 Man is the only creature that consumes without producing.
1945 *Animal Farm*, ch.1.

73 Four legs good, two legs bad.
1945 *Animal Farm*, ch.3.

74 Napoleon had commanded that once a week there should be held something called a Spontaneous Demonstration.
1945 *Animal Farm*, ch.9.

75 All animals are equal but some animals are more equal than others.
1945 *Animal Farm*, ch.10.

76 The creatures outside looked from pig to man, and from man to pig, and from pig to man again; but already it was impossible to say which was which.
1945 *Animal Farm*, ch.10.

77 No modern Irish writer, even of the stature of Yeats or Joyce, is completely free from traces of nationalism.
1945 'Notes on Nationalism'.

78 In broadcasting your audience is conjectural, but it is an audience of *one.*
1945 'Poetry and the Microphone'.

79 Poetry on the air sounds like the Muses in striped trousers.
1945 'Poetry and the Microphone'.

80 To walk through the ruined cities of Germany is to feel actual doubt about the continuity of civilization.
1945 In the *Observer*, 8 Apr.

81 The books one reads in childhood, and perhaps most of all the bad and good bad books, create in one's mind a sort of false map of the world, a series of fabulous countries into which one can retreat at odd moments throughout the rest of life, and which in some cases can even survive a visit to the real countries which they are supposed to represent.
1946 'Riding Down from Bangor'.

82 Prolonged, indiscriminate reviewing of books involves constantly inventing reactions towards books about which one has no spontaneous feelings whatever.
1946 'Confessions of A Book Reviewer'.

83 The atom bombs are piling up in the factories, the police are prowling through the cities, the lies are streaming from the loudspeakers, but the earth is still going round the sun, and neither the dictators nor the bureaucrats, deeply as they disapprove of the process, are able to prevent it.

1946 'Some Thoughts on the Common Toad'.

84 To see what is in front of one's nose needs a constant struggle.
1946 'In Front of Your Nose'.

85 Good prose is like a window pane.
1946 'Why I Write'.

86 All writers are vain, selfish and lazy, and at the very bottom of their motives lies a mystery.
1946 'Why I Write'.

87 In our time, political speech and writing are largely the defence of the indefensible.
1946 'Politics and the English Language', collected in *Shooting an Elephant* (1950).

88 The inflated style is itself a kind of euphemism.
1946 'Politics and the English Language', collected in *Shooting an Elephant* (1950).

89 The great enemy of clear language is insincerity.
1946 'Politics and the English Language', collected in *Shooting an Elephant* (1950).

90 In prose, the worst thing one can do with words is surrender to them.
1946 'Politics and the English Language', collected in *Shooting an Elephant* (1950).

91 Political language...is designed to make lies sound truthful and murder respectable, and to give an appearance of solidity to pure wind.
1946 'Politics and the English Language', collected in *Shooting an Elephant* (1950).

92 The Catholic and the Communist are alike in assuming that an opponent cannot be both honest and intelligent.
1946 'The Prevention of Literature', in *Polemic*, Jan.

93 The controversy over freedom of speech and of the press is at the bottom a controversy over the desirability, or otherwise, of telling lies. What is really at issue is the right to report events truthfully, or as truthfully as is consistent with the ignorance, bias and self-deception from which every observer necessarily suffers.
1946 'The Prevention of Literature', in *Polemic*, Jan.

94 The friends of totalitarianism in this country tend to argue that since absolute truth is not attainable, a big lie is no worse than a little lie.
1946 'The Prevention of Literature', in *Polemic*, Jan.

95 Literature is doomed if liberty of thought perishes.
1946 'The Prevention of Literature', in *Polemic*, Jan.

96 The quickest way of ending a war is to lose it.
1946 'Second Thoughts on James Burnham', in *Polemic*, May.

97 It was a bright cold day in April, and the clocks were striking thirteen.
1949 *Nineteen Eighty-Four*, pt.1, ch.1.

98 On each landing, opposite the lift shaft, the poster with the enormous face gazed from the wall. It was one of those pictures which are so contrived that the eyes follow you about when you move. BIG BROTHER IS WATCHING YOU, the caption beneath it ran.
1949 *Nineteen Eighty-Four*, pt.1, ch.1.

99 War is peace. Freedom is slavery. Ignorance is strength.
1949 *Nineteen Eighty-Four*, pt.1, ch.1.

1 'Who controls the past,' ran the Party slogan, 'controls the future: who controls the present controls the past.'
1949 *Nineteen Eighty-Four*, pt.1, ch.3.

2 Freedom is the freedom to say that two plus two make four. If that is granted, all else follows.
1949 *Nineteen Eighty-Four*, pt.1, ch.7.

3 *Doublethink* means the power of holding two contradictory beliefs in one's mind simultaneously, and accepting both of them.
1949 *Nineteen Eighty-Four*, pt.2, ch.9.

4 If you want a picture of the future, imagine a boot stamping on a human face—for ever.
1949 *Nineteen Eighty-Four*, pt.3, ch.3.

5 Power is not a means, it is an end. One does not establish a dictatorship in order to safeguard a revolution; one makes the revolution in order to establish the dictatorship.
1949 *Nineteen Eighty-Four*, pt.3, ch.3.

6 Saints should always be judged guilty until they are proved innocent.
1949 'Reflections on Gandhi', collected in *Shooting an Elephant* (1950).

7 At 50, everyone has the face he deserves.
1949 Notebook entry, 17 Apr.

8 Serious sport has nothing to do with fair play. It is bound up with hatred, jealousy, boastfulness, disregard of all rules and sadistic pleasure in witnessing violence: in other words it is war minus the shooting…there are quite enough real causes of trouble already, and we need not add to them by encouraging young men to kick each other on the shins amid the roars of infuriated spectators.
1950 'The Sporting Spirit'.

9 One ought to be able to hold in one's head simultaneously the two facts that Dali is a good draughtsman and a disgusting human being. The one does not invalidate or, in a sense, affect the other.
Quoted in Michael Shelden *Orwell* (1991).

Osborne, Dorothy 1627–95
Wife of Sir William Temple, English diplomat and essay writer.

10 All letters, methinks, should be free and easy as one's discourse, not studied as an oration, nor made up of hard words like a charm.
1653 Letter to William Temple.

Osborne, John 1929–94
English playwright and actor. The success of *Look Back in Anger* (1956), with its anti-hero Jimmy Porter, marked a new departure in postwar English drama and identified the author as the most famous of the 'angry young men' of the 1950s. Later works included *The Entertainer* (1957), *Luther* (1961), *Inadmissible Evidence* (1964) and *A Patriot for Me* (1969).

11 She's so clumsy. I watch for her to do the same things every night. The way she jumps on the bed, as if she were stamping on someone's face, and draws the curtains back with a great clatter, in that casually destructive way of hers. It's like someone launching a battleship. Have you ever noticed how noisy women are? Have you? The way they kick the floor about, simply walking over it? Or have you watched them sitting at their dressing tables, dropping their weapons and banging down their bits of boxes and brushes and lipsticks?
1956 *Look Back in Anger*.

12 Don't clap too hard—it's a very old building.
1957 *The Entertainer*, 7.

13 There will be a quick rash of hairy American filth, but it shouldn't threaten the existence of decent, serious British filth.
1967 On the opening of the US musical *Hair*, in *Time* magazine.

Osler, Sir William 1849–1919
Canadian physician.

14 The greater the ignorance the greater the dogmatism.
1902 Quoted in *Montreal Medical Journal*, Sep.

15 The desire to take medicine is perhaps the greatest feature which distinguishes man from animals.
Quoted in H Cushing *Life of Sir William Osler* (1925), vol.1, ch.14.

16 One of the first duties of the physician is to educate the masses not to take medicine.
Collected in W B Bean (ed) *Sir William Osler: Aphorisms from His Bedside Teachings and Writings* (1950).

17 Failure to examine the throat is a glaring sin of omission, especially in children. One finger in the throat and one in the rectum makes a good diagnostician.
Collected in W B Bean (ed) *Sir William Osler: Aphorisms from His Bedside Teachings and Writings* (1950).

18 To talk of diseases is a sort of *Arabian Nights* entertainment.
Quoted in Oliver Sacks *The Man Who Mistook his Wife for a Hat*, epigraph (1985).

Otis, James 1725–83
American politician and patriot. As Advocate General he refused to assist royal revenue officers to search individual's homes and resigned to fight for popular rights. In 1769 he was beaten by revenue officers and received a head wound from which he never really recovered.

19 Taxation without representation is tyranny.
c.1761 His defence, which became a rallying call of the American Revolution.

O'Toole, Peter 1932–
Irish actor. His performance in *Lawrence of Arabia* (1962) made him an international film star, and he has since played a wide variety of roles.

20 I'm one of the younger oldies. I'm in the prime of senility.
2000 In *The Guardian*, 31 Dec.

Otway, Thomas 1652–85
English dramatist. Educated at Oxford. His first play was the tragedy *Alcibiades* (1675); in it his alleged lover, Elizabeth Barry, made her debut. His most famous play is *Venice Preserved, or a Plot Discovered* (1682).

21 Ere man's corruptions made him wretched, he
Was born most noble that was born most free;
Each of himself was lord; and unconfin'd
Obey'd the dictates of his godlike mind.
1676 *Don Carlos*, act 2.

22 You wags that judge by rote, and damn by rule.
1677 *Titus and Berenice*, prologue.

23 And for an apple damn'd mankind.
1680 *The Orphan*, act 3.

24 I may boldly speak

In right, though proud oppression will not hear me!
1682 *Venice Preserved, or a Plot Discovered*, act 1, sc.1.

25 May the hard hand of a vexatious need
Oppress and grind you; till at last you find
The curse of disobedience all your portion.
1682 *Venice Preserved, or a Plot Discovered*, act 1, sc.1.

26 Home I would go
But that my doors are hateful to my eyes,
Fill'd and damm'd up with gaping creditors,
Watchful as fowlers when their game will spring.
1682 *Venice Preserved, or a Plot Discovered*, act 1, sc.1.

27 I'm thinking…how that damn'd starving quality
Call'd honesty, got footing in the world.
1682 *Venice Preserved, or a Plot Discovered*, act 1, sc.1.

28 Honesty was a cheat invented first
To bind the hands of bold deserving rogues,
That fools and cowards might sit safe in power,
And lord it uncontroll'd above their betters.
1682 *Venice Preserved, or a Plot Discovered*, act 1, sc.1.

29 'Tis a ragged virtue.
1682 *Venice Preserved, or a Plot Discovered*, act 1, sc.1.

30 If love be treasure, we'll be wondrous rich.
1682 *Venice Preserved, or a Plot Discovered*, act 1, sc.1.

31 Is the world
Reform'd since our last meeting?
1682 *Venice Preserved, or a Plot Discovered*, act 1, sc.1.

32 No praying, it spoils Business,
1682 *Venice Preserved, or a Plot Discovered*, act 2, sc.1.

33 Give but an Englishman his whore and ease,
Beef and a sea-coal fire, he's yours forever.
1682 *Venice Preserved, or a Plot Discovered*, act 2, sc.3.

34 The poor sleep little.
1682 *Venice Preserved, or a Plot Discovered*, act 2, sc.3.

35 No, this vile world and I have long been jangling,
And cannot part on better terms than now,
When only men like thee are fit to live in't.
1682 *Venice Preserved, or a Plot Discovered*, act 4, sc.2.

Oud, J(acobus) J(ohannes) P(ieter) 1890–1963

Dutch architect, a pioneer of the modern architectural style based on simplified forms and pure planes.

36 If I was not optimistic, I would not be an architect.
Quoted in the *New York Times*, 4 Dec 1994.

Overbury, Sir Thomas 1581–1613

English poet and courtier.

37 He disdains all things above his reach, and preferreth all countries before his own.
1632 'An Affected Traveller', collected in *Miscellaneous Works*.

Overton, Robert fl.1642–68

English soldier. He fought for Parliament in the English Civil War and was made governor of Hull. He was imprisoned in 1656 for two years after he fought under Cromwell in Scotland and was suspected of planning an insurrection against the government. When Cromwell fell, Overton was released, but the doubts about him remained and his further support for a republic led to imprisonment for almost the rest of his life. The date and place of his death are unknown.

38 Whatever our forefathers were, or whatever they did or suffered, or were enforced to yield unto, we are the men of the present age, and ought to be absolutely free from all kinds of exorbitancies, molestations, or arbitrary power.
1646 Remonstrance to the House of Commons.

Ovid *full name* **Publius Ovidius Naso** 43 BC–AD 17

Roman poet, who trained for law but turned to poetry. His many works include the *Ars Amatoria*, the *Metamorphoses* and the *Fasti*. He was banished by Augustus in AD 8 to Tomi on the Black Sea, where he wrote the *Tristia*.

39 *Procul omen abesto!*
Far away be that fate!
Amores, bk.1, no.14, l.41.

40 *Iuppiter ex alto periuria ridet amantum.*
Jupiter from above laughs at lovers' perjuries.
Ars Amatoria, bk.1, l.633.

41 *Iam seges est ubi Troia fuit.*
Now there are cornfields where Troy once was.
Heroides, no.1, l.53.

42 *Chaos, rudis indigestaque moles.*
Chaos, a rough unordered mass.
Metamorphoses, bk.1, l.7.

43 *Medio tutissimus ibis.*
You will go most safely by the middle way.
Daedalus speaking to his son, Icarus. *Metamorphoses*, bk.2, l.137 (translated by Peter Green).

44 *Inopem me copia fecit.*
Plenty has made me poor.
Metamorphoses, bk.3, l.466.

45 *Video meliora, proboque;*
Deteriora sequor.
I see the better things, and approve; I follow the worse.
Metamorphoses, bk.7, l.20–1 (translated by Peter Green).

46 *Tempus edax rerum.*
Time the devourer of everything.
Metamorphoses, bk.15, l.234 (translated by Peter Green).

47 *Nec species sua cuique manet, rerumque novatrix*
ex aliis alias reddit natura figuras.
nec perit in toto quidquam, mihi crede, mundo,
sed variat faciemque novat, nascique vocatur
incipere esse aliud, quam quod fuit ante, morique,
desinere illud idem. cum sint huc forsitan illa,
haec translata illuc, summa tamen omnia constant.
No species remains constant: that great renovator of matter
Nature, endlessly fashions new forms from old: there's nothing
in the whole universe that perishes, believe me; rather
it renews and varies its substance. What we describe as birth
is no more than incipient change from a prior state, while dying
is merely to quit it. Though the parts may be transported
hither and thither, the sum of all matter is constant.
Metamorphoses, bk.15, l.252–8 (translated by Peter Green).

48 *Donec eris felix, multos numerabis amicos*
Tempora si fuerint nubila, solus eris.
So long as you are fortunate, you will count many

friends; if your life should become clouded, you will be alone.

Tristia, bk.1, no.9, l.5–6.

Owen, David Anthony Llewellyn Owen, Baron 1938–

English politician, one of the 'Gang of Four' who formed the Social Democratic Party (SDP) in 1981, becoming its leader in 1983. He resigned in 1987 rather than merge with the Liberal party, and led a minority, reconstituted SDP, dissolved in 1990. From 1992 to 1995 he was co-chairman (initially with Cyrus R Vance) of the international peace conference on the former Yugoslavia.

49 We are fed up with fudging and nudging, with mush and slush.

1980 Speech to Labour's national conference shortly before leaving the party to found the Social Democratic Party, Oct.

Owen, Robert 1771–1858

Welsh social reformer and philanthropist.

50 All the world is queer save thee and me, and even thou art a little queer.

Attributed. Said to his partner W Allen when they ended their business relationship.

Owen, Wilfred 1893–1918

English poet. Injured in the trenches in 1917, he met Siegfried Sassoon while recuperating in Edinburgh. He died in the last week of the war, and most of his poems were published posthumously. Their vivid and unsentimental realism is a powerful indictment of war, and they were memorably used by Benjamin Britten in his *War Requiem*, first performed in Coventry Cathedral (1962).

51 What passing-bells for these who die as cattle?
Only the monstrous anger of the guns.
Only the stuttering rifles' rapid rattle
Can patter out their hasty orisons.

1917 'Anthem for Doomed Youth'.

52 The pallor of girls' brows shall be their pall;
Their flowers the tenderness of patient minds,
And each slow dusk a drawing-down of blinds.

1917 'Anthem for Doomed Youth'.

53 Red lips are not so red
As the stained stones kissed by the English dead.

1917 'Greater Love'.

54 This book is not about heroes. English poetry is not yet fit to speak of them.

1918 *Poems* (published 1920), preface.

55 Above all, this book is not concerned with Poetry. The subject of it is War, and the pity of War. The Poetry is in the pity.

1918 *Poems* (published 1920), preface.

56 All the poet can do today is to warn.
That is why the true Poet must be truthful.

1918 *Poems* (published 1920), preface.

57 If you could hear, at every jolt, the blood
Come gargling from the froth-corrupted lungs,
Bitter as the cud
Of vile, incurable sores on innocent tongues,—
My friend, you would not tell with such high zest
To children ardent for some desperate glory

The old Lie: Dulce et decorum est
Pro patria mori.

1918 'Dulce et Decorum Est', collected in *Poems* (published 1920).

➤ *See Horace 413:23.*

58 It seemed that out of battle I escaped
Down some profound dull tunnel, long since scooped
Through granites which titanic wars had groined.

1918 'Strange Meeting', collected in *Poems* (published 1920).

59 And by his smile, I knew that sullen hall,
By his dead smile I knew we stood in Hell.

1918 'Strange Meeting', collected in *Poems* (published 1920).

60 'Strange friend,' I said, 'here is no cause to mourn.'
'None,' said the other, 'save the undone years,
The hopelessness. Whatever hope is yours
Was my life also; I went hunting wild
After the wildest beauty in the world.'

1918 'Strange Meeting', collected in *Poems* (published 1920).

61 I am the enemy you killed, my friend.

1918 'Strange Meeting', collected in *Poems* (published 1920).

62 Move him into the sun—
Gently its touch awoke him once,
At home, whispering of fields unsown.

1918 'Futility', collected in *Poems* (published 1920).

63 If anything might rouse him now
The kind old sun will know.

1918 'Futility', collected in *Poems* (published 1920).

64 Was it for this the clay grew tall?
—O what made fatuous sunbeams toil
To break earth's sleep at all?

1918 'Futility', collected in *Poems* (published 1920).

65 So secretly, like wrongs hushed-up, they went.

1918 'The Send-Off', collected in *Poems* (published 1920).

66 Whatever mourns when many leave these shores:
Whatever shares
The eternal reciprocity of tears.

1918 'Insensibility', collected in *Poems* (published 1920).

Owens, Jesse James Cleveland 1913–80

US athlete. The greatest sprinter of his generation, he won four gold medals at the Berlin Olympics in 1936, embarrassing the Nazi hosts, who had hoped to demonstrate the supremacy of Aryan athletes.

67 I let my feet spend as little time on the ground as possible. From the air, fast down, and from the ground, fast up.

Quoted in Colin Jarman *The Guinness Dictionary of Sports Quotations* (1990).

Ozick, Cynthia 1928–

US writer. She claimed to have begun her first novel, *Trust* (1966), an American writer and finished it six and a half years later a Jewish one. Other works include the short stories *The Shawl* (1989) and the novel *The Puttermesser Papers* (1997).

68 Yiddish is a household tongue, and God, like other members of the family, is sweetly informal in it.

1989 *Metaphor and Memory.*

Pacheco, José Emilio 1939–

Mexican poet, novelist, critic and translator. His poetry expresses his metaphysical concerns in brilliant images. The novel *Morirás lejos* (1967) documents the purges of Jews throughout history.

69 *Porque todo es irreal en este cuento. Nada sucedió como se indica. Hechos y sitios se deformaron por el empeño de tocar la verdad mediante una ficción, una mentira. Todo irreal, nada sucedió como aquí se refiere. Pero fue un pobre intento de contribuir a que el gran crimen nunca se repita.*
For everything in this story is unreal. Nothing happened the way it was suggested. Facts and places were distorted by that persistent desire to touch the truth by means of fiction, a lie. All of it is unreal; nothing happened the way it is told here. It was a poor attempt to help ensure that the great crime is never repeated.
1967 *Morirás lejos* (translated as *You Will Die in a Distant Land,* 1991).

Packard, David 1912–96

US businessman.

70 Flexitime is the essence of respect for and trust in people.
1995 *The HP Way.*

Packard, Vance 1914–96

US writer and journalist.

71 The Hidden Persuaders.
1957 Title of a book on advertising.

Packer, Herbert Leslie 1925–72

US Professor of Law, Stanford University (1959–72). He was admitted to the New York Bar in 1950, and later the Supreme Court. He practised law in Washington before teaching at Stanford.

72 Crime is a socio-political artifact, not a natural phenomenon. We can have as much or as little crime as we please, depending on what we choose to count as criminal.
1968 *The Limits of Criminal Sanction,* p.364.

Packer, Kerry 1937–

Australian media executive.

73 If a British guy saw someone at the wheel of a Rolls-Royce, he'd say 'come the revolution and we'll take that away from you, mate', where the American would say 'one day I'll have one of those, when I have worked hard enough'. It's unfortunate we Australians inherited the British mentality.
1977 In *The Guardian,* 1 Sep.

Packwood, Bob 1932–

US Republican Senator and lawyer. He was Senator for Oregon from 1969 until his resignation in 1995.

74 I am accused of kissing women…perhaps overeagerly kissing women. And that is the charge, not drugging, not robbing, kissing!
1995 Replying to charges of sexual misconduct, lobbying, and editing diaries subpoenaed by the Senate Ethics Committee. In the *New York Times,* 7 Sep.

75 More than Francis of Assisi…less than Wilt Chamberlain.
1995 Estimating the amount of controversial activity documented in his diaries. In the *New York Times,* 9 Sep.

Paderewski, Ignace Jan 1860–1941

Polish pianist, composer and statesman, director of the Warsaw Conservatory (from 1909). In 1919 he became premier of Poland. He retired from politics to return to his music, but in 1940 was elected President by Poland's provisional parliament in Paris.

76 If I don't practise for one day, I know it; if I don't practise for two days, the critics know it; if I don't practise for three days, the audience knows it.
Quoted in Nat Shapiro *An Encyclopedia of Quotations about Music* (1978).

Page, Geraldine 1924–87

US actress. She made her name with the lead role in Tennessee Williams's *Summer and Smoke* (1954).

77 Name me one character in literature or drama who can't be described as neurotic… We wouldn't want to know the people we get to see on the stage. How would you like to have Medea for dinner? Or Macbeth slurping your soup? Or Oedipus with his bloody, blinded eyes dripping all over your tablecloth?
Attributed.

Pagels, Heinz R(udolf) 1939–88

US theoretical physicist and social activist, the author of several works describing the complexities of modern physics for the public.

78 A good simulation, be it a religious myth or scientific theory, gives us a sense of mastery over experience. To represent something symbolically, as we do when we speak or write, is somehow to capture it, thus making it one's own. But with this appropriation comes the realization that we have denied the immediacy of reality and that in creating a substitute we have but spun another thread in the web of our grand illusion.
1988 *The Dreams of Reason.*

79 Science provides a vision of reality seen from the perspective of reason, a perspective that sees the vast order of the universe, living and non-living matter, as a material system governed by rules that can be known by the human mind. It is a powerful vision, formal and austere but strangely silent about many of the questions that deeply concern us. Science shows us what exists but not what to do about it.
1988 *The Dreams of Reason.*

Paglia, Camille 1947–

US writer, Professor of Humanities at the University of the Arts, Philadelphia. Her works include *Sexual Personae* (1990) and *Vamps and Tramps* (1994).

80 The historical repugnance to woman has a rational basis: disgust is reason's proper response to the grossness of procreative nature.
1990 *Sexual Personae: Art and Decadence from Nefertiti to Emily Dickinson*, ch.1, 'Sex and Violence, or Nature and Art'.

81 No woman has to prove herself a woman in the grim way a man has to prove himself a man. He must perform, or the show does not go on. Social convention is irrelevant. A flop is a flop.
1990 *Sexual Personae: Art and Decadence from Nefertiti to Emily Dickinson*, ch.1, 'Sex and Violence, or Nature and Art'.

82 Feminism has become a catch-all vegetable drawer where bunches of clingy sob sisters can store their moldy neuroses.
1992 'The Return of Carry Nation: Catharine Mackinnon and Andrea Dworkin', in *Playboy*, Oct. Collected in *Vamps and Tramps* (1994).

83 I like Hillary because she's kind of a bitch.
1993 In the *Sunday Times* magazine, 18 Apr. Collected as 'Kind of a Bitch: Why I Like Hillary Clinton' in *Vamps and Tramps* (1994).

Pagnol, Marcel 1895–1974

French dramatist and film director, best known for his popular trilogy about Marseilles, *Marius* (1929), *Fanny* (1931) and *César* (1936).

84 *Les coupables, il vaut mieux les choisir que les chercher.*
It's better to choose the culprits than to seek them out.
1928 *Topaze*, act 1.

85 *L'honneur, c'est comme les allumettes: ça ne sert qu'une fois.*
Honour is like a match, you can use it only once.
1929 *Marius*, act 4, sc.5.

86 One has to look out for engineers—they begin with sewing machines and end up with the atomic bomb.
1949 *Critique des critiques*, ch.3.

Paige, Satchel (Leroy Robert) 1906–82

US baseball player. One of the first blacks to play in the major leagues, he was a celebrated pitcher with the Cleveland Indians and the St Louis Browns.

87 1. Avoid fried meats which angry up the blood.
2. If your stomach disputes you, lie down and pacify it with cool thoughts.
3. Keep the juices flowing by jangling around gently as you move.
4. Go very light on vices such as carrying on in society. The social ramble ain't restful.
5. Avoid running at all times.
6. Don't look back. Something may be gaining on you.
1976 'Six Rules for a Happy Life', which he had inscribed on business cards, offered to fans seeking his autograph.

Paine, Thomas 1737–1809

English radical political writer. His *Common Sense* (1776) argued for complete American independence, and *The Rights of Man* (1791–2) supported the French Revolution. Arraigned for treason, he fled to Paris, and wrote *The Age of Reason* (1794) in favour of deism.

88 These are the times that try men's souls. The summer soldier and the sunshine patriot will, in this crisis, shrink from the service of his country; but he that stands it *now*, deserves the love and thanks of man and woman.
1776 *The Crisis*, introduction, Dec.

89 Not all the treasures of the world, so far as I believe, could have induced me to support an offensive war, for I think it murder; but if a thief breaks into my house, burns and destroys my property, and kills or threatens to kill me or those that are in it, and to '*bind me in all cases whatsoever*' to his absolute will, am I to suffer it?
1776 *The Crisis*, introduction, Dec.

90 Government, even in its best state, is but a necessary evil; in its worst state, an intolerable one. Government, like dress, is the badge of lost innocence; the palaces of kings are built upon the bowers of paradise.
1776 *Common Sense*, ch.1.

91 As to religion, I hold it to be the indispensable duty of government to protect all conscientious professors thereof, and I know of no other business which government hath to do therewith.
1776 *Common Sense*, ch.4.

92 Man is not the enemy of Man, but through the medium of a false system of government.
1791–2 *The Rights of Man*.

93 To establish any mode to abolish war, however advantageous it might be to nations, would be to take from such Government the most lucrative of its branches.
1791–2 *The Rights of Man*.

94 Persecution is not an original feature of *any* religion; but it is always the strongly marked feature of all law-religions, or religions established by law.
1791–2 *The Rights of Man*.

95 My country is the world, and my religion is to do good.
1791–2 *The Rights of Man*.

96 The final event to himself has been, that as he rose like a rocket, he fell like the stick.
1792 Of Edmund Burke. *Letters to the Addressers on the late Proclamation*.

97 It is a fraud of the Christian system to call the sciences human invention; it is only the application of them that is human. Every science has for its basis a system of principles as fixed and unalterable as those by which the universe is regulated and governed. Man cannot make principles, he can only discover them.
1794 *The Age of Reason*, pt.1.

98 It is necessary to the happiness of man that he be mentally faithful to himself. Infidelity does not consist in believing, or in disbelieving, it consists in professing to believe what one does not believe.
1794 *The Age of Reason*, pt.1.

99 One step above the sublime, makes the ridiculous; and one step above the ridiculous, makes the sublime again.
1795 *The Age of Reason*, pt.2.

Paisley, Bob 1919–96

English football manager. He succeeded Bill Shankly as manager of Liverpool in 1974 and led the team through a golden era of League success.

1 Yes, we've had bad times at Anfield; one year we came second.
Quoted in Peter Ball and Phil Shaw *The Book of Football Quotations* (1989).

Paisley, Ian 1926–

Northern Irish clergyman and politician, founder of the Free Presbyterian Church of Ulster. A vociferous opponent of Irish unification, he is the object of fanatical devotion from Ulster loyalists.

2 I would rather be British than just.
1971 In the *Sunday Times*, 12 Dec.

3 I will walk on no grave of Ulster's honoured dead to do a deal with the IRA or the British government.
1997 Speech at the annual conference of the Democratic Unionist Party. In *The Irish Times*, 'This Week They Said', 6 Dec.

4 The mother of all treachery.
1998 On the Good Friday agreement. In *The Times*, 16 Apr.

5 She has become a parrot.
1998 On the perceived readiness of the Queen to repeat the views of her Prime Minister. In the *Daily Telegraph*, 27 May.

Palacký, František 1798–1876

Czech historian and politician in Prague, and the founder of historiography in Bohemia. He served in the first Austrian Reichstag and campaigned for the formation of a separate Czech nation.

6 If the Austrian Empire did not exist, it would have to be created in the interest of Europe and of humanity.
Quoted in A J P Taylor *From Napoleon to the Second International* (1993), p.169.

Palafox, José de c.1776–1847

Spanish general in the Peninsular War, who defended Saragossa with an improvised garrison of civilians. Despite breaching the city wall, the French were unable to capture the city.

7 *Guerra a cuchillo.*
War to the knife.
1808 His reply to the French suggestion that he surrender during the siege of Saragossa, 4 Aug. The phrase was inscribed on survivors' medals.

Paley, Grace née *Goodside* 1922–

US writer and political activist. She is best known as a writer of short stories, often set in a Jewish milieu in New York, but she has also published poetry and collections of essays.

8 The Little Disturbances of Man.
1959 Title of story collection.

9 Enormous Changes at the Last Minute.
1974 Title of story collection.

10 Literature, fiction, poetry, whatever, makes justice in the world. That's why it almost always has to be on the side of the underdog.
1974 In *Ms* magazine.

11 All that is really necessary for survival of the fittest, it seems, is an interest in life, good, bad, or peculiar.
1976 In D L Fitzpatrick (ed) *Contemporary Novelists*.

12 No metaphor reinvents the job of the nurture of children except to muddy or mock.
1992 *Begin Again: New and Collected Poems*, 'Stanzas: Old Age

and the Conventions of Retirement Have Driven My Friends from the Work They Love'.

13 Poets!
Madness is a gift
god-given
(though not to me).
1992 *Begin Again: New and Collected Poems*, 'On the Bank Street Pier'.

14 It is the responsibility of society to let the poet be a poet
It is the responsibility of the poet to be a woman.
1992 *Begin Again: New and Collected Poems*, 'Responsibility'.

15 It is the responsibility of the poet to be lazy to hang out and prophesy.
1992 *Begin Again: New and Collected Poems*, 'Responsibility'.

Paley, William 1743–1805

English theologian, Archdeacon of Carlisle (1782) and Sub-Dean of Lincoln (1795). His most popular work was *Natural Theology, or Evidences of the Existence and Attributes of the Deity* (1802).

16 Suppose I had found a *watch* upon the ground, and it should be enquired how the watch happened to be in that place... The inference, we think, is inevitable; that the watch must have had a maker, that there must have existed, at some time and at some place or other, an artificer or artificers, who formed it for the purpose which we find it actually to answer; who comprehended its construction, and designed its use.
1802 *Natural Theology*, ch.1.

Palmer, Arnold 1929–

US golfer. Between 1958 and 1964 he won the US Masters four times, the British Open twice and the US Open once. He was twice captain of the US Ryder Cup team.

17 Winning isn't everything, but wanting to is.
Quoted in Colin Jarman *The Guinness Dictionary of Sports Quotations* (1990).

18 If Tiger Woods slamming his club into the ground is the biggest worry we have, our sport is in pretty good shape.
2000 Quoted in *Golf Digest*, Jan.

Palmerston, Henry John Temple, 3rd Viscount 1784–1865

English politician, Foreign Secretary (1830–41, 1846–51) and Prime Minister (1855–8, 1859–65). His abrasive, bullying approach to foreign affairs and propensity for brinkmanship made him unpopular with his colleagues and the public.

19 Half the wrong conclusions at which mankind arrive are reached by the abuse of metaphors, and by mistaking general resemblance or imaginary similarity for real identity.
1839 Letter to Henry Bulwer, 1 Sep.

20 Diplomats and protocols are very good things, but there are no better peace-keepers than well-appointed three-deckers.
c.1840 Quoted in Denis Judd *Palmerston* (1975). A three-decker is a warship.

21 We said to the Chinese, 'You have behaved very ill; we have had to teach you better manners; it has cost us something to do it, but we will send our bill in, and you must pay our charges.' That was done, and they have certainly profited by the lesson. They have become free traders too.

1847 On the Opium Wars of 1839–42. Election speech at Tiverton, Devon.

22 We have no eternal allies, and we have no perpetual enemies. Our interests are eternal, and it is our duty to follow them.

1848 Speech, House of Commons, 1 Mar.

23 Large republics seem to be essentially and inherently aggressive.

1848 Letter to the British Ambassador to Paris, 5 Mar.

24 I therefore fearlessly challenge the verdict which this house…is to give on the question now brought before it…whether, as the Roman, in days of old, held himself free from indignity, when he could say *Civis Romanus sum*; so also a British subject, in whatever land he may be, shall feel confident that the watchful eye and the strong arm of England will protect him against injustice and wrong.

1850 From his four-and-a-half hour Don Pacifico speech, Jun. Don Pacifico was a Portuguese Jew resident in Athens, born in Gibraltar and therefore a British subject. In support of his claims for compensation from the Greek government for damage done to his property by a mob, Palmerston sent the British fleet to blockade Piraeus and brought the two countries to the brink of war.

25 You may call it coalition, you may call it the accidental and fortuitous concurrence of atoms…but when gentlemen are in the habit of finding themselves in the same Lobby, it is not unnatural to suppose that they may, under certain circumstances, be ready to unite themselves together for the purpose of forming an Administration and becoming responsible for the opinions that they severally entertain.

1858 Speech on the rumoured Palmerston–Disraeli coalition, 5 Mar.

26 England is one of the greatest powers of the world. No event or series of events bearing on the balance of power, or on probabilities of peace or war, can be matters of indifference to her, and her right to have and to express opinions on matters thus bearing on her interests is unquestionable.

1859 Letter to Queen Victoria, 23 Aug.

Panama, Norman and Frank, Melvin 1914–2003, 1917–88

US screenwriters, who worked together on films such as *The Road to Utopia* (1945), *The Court Jester* (1955) and *Li'l Abner* (1959).

27 The pellet with the poison's in the chalice from the palace
The flagon with the dragon has the brew that is true.

1955 Lines delivered by Danny Kaye in *The Court Jester*.

Pangkor, Treaty of

The British signed a treaty (1874) with a claimant to the Perak Sultanate on the island of Pangkor, off the west coast of what is now peninsular Malaysia, and thereby formalized their economic and political interest in the region. It led to British control over the whole of the peninsula for the following 83 years.

28 A British officer to be called Resident who shall be

accredited to his Court and whose advice must be asked and acted upon on all questions other than those touching Malay religion and custom.

1874 Treaty, Nov.

Pankhurst, Christabel 1880–1958

English suffragette and religious writer. Co-founder with her mother Emmeline Pankhurst of the Women's Social and Political Union (1903), she studied law (LLB 1906) and applied to join Lincoln's Inn, but was rejected, as a woman.

29 How long you women have been trying for the vote. For my part, I mean to get it.

c.1890 Childhood remark, quoted by her mother, Emmeline Pankhurst, in *My Own Story* (1914), ch.2.

Pankhurst, Emmeline *née* **Goulden** 1858–1928

English suffragette, organizer of the Women's Social and Political Union. A militant campaigner, she was frequently imprisoned and undertook hunger strikes. During World War I she turned her attention to the industrial mobilization of women.

30 Women never took a single step forward without being pushed back first of all by their opponents.

1912 Speech, 14 Jan, during a tour of Canada.

31 There is something that Governments care for far more than human life, and that is the security of property. So it is through property that we shall strike the enemy… Be militant each in your own way… I incite this meeting to rebellion.

1912 Speech, Royal Albert Hall, 17 Oct.

32 Women had always fought for men, and for their children. Now they were ready to fight for their own human rights.

1914 *My Own Story*, ch.3.

33 What is the use of fighting for the vote if we do not have a country to vote in? With that patriotism that has nerved women to endure torture in prison for the national good, we ardently desire that our country shall be victorious.

1914 Declaring a truce on suffragette activities for the duration of World War I, 10 Aug.

34 There are women today who never thought to envy men their manhood, but who would, at least for this purpose, be glad to be men.

1914 Speech appealing for the right to fight, 30 Nov, at a meeting organized by the Women's Social and Political Union, in the Kingsway Hall, London.

Parens, Erik

US academic. He is Associate for Philosophical Studies at the Hastings Center, a bioethics research institute.

35 On Why Talking about Behavioral Genetics Is Important and Difficult.

2004 Subtitle of the Hastings Center Report 'Genetic Differences and Human Identities'.

Pareto, Vilfredo 1848–1923

French-born Swiss economist and sociologist.

36 All governments use force and all assert that they are founded on reason. In fact, whether universal suffrage prevails or not, it is always an oligarchy that governs, finding ways to give to 'the will of the people' the

expression which the few desire.
Quoted in Arthur Livingstone (ed) *The Mind and Society* (1935).

Parfitt, Harold Robert 1921–

US soldier. He served in Vietnam and advanced through the army grades to reach Major-General in 1971. He was decorated many times. He became governor of the Panama Canal Zone in 1975.

37 There will be no more tomorrows, only yesterdays, for the Canal Zone.
1979 On relinquishing authority as last governor of the Panama Canal Zone. Quoted in *Time*, 15 Oct.

Park, Mungo 1771–1806

Scottish explorer. He explored the Niger in 1796, then returned to Scotland and worked as a doctor, publishing *Travels in the Interior Districts of Africa* (1799), before leaving in 1805 for Africa again, sending back journals and letters.

38 I think it not unlikely but I shall be in England before you receive this—You may be sure that I feel happy at turning my face towards home. We this morning have done with all intercourse with the natives; and the sails are now hoisting for our departure for the coast.
1805 Last letter to his wife before leaving Sansanding on the River Niger. Collected in *Journal of a Mission to the Interior of Africa in the Year 1805* (published 1815). Park and his party reportedly drowned in the river when they were ambushed and their boat sank.

Parker, Charlie *known as* '*Bird*' 1920–55

US saxophonist, bandleader and composer, architect of the bebop style. Despite addiction to heroin and alcohol and recurring mental illness, he led jazz groups until his death. His works include 'Now's the Time' and 'Ornithology'.

39 It's just music. It's trying to play clean and looking for the pretty notes.
1949 On bebop. Quoted in Gary Giddins *Celebrating Bird* (1987), ch.1.

40 There is no boundary line to art. Music is your own experience, your thoughts, your wisdom. If you don't live it, it won't come out of your horn.
1950 Quoted in Ross Russell *Bird Lives!* (1972), pt.4, ch.22.

Parker, Dorothy *née Rothschild* 1893–1967

US writer and humorist, a central figure of the legendary Algonquin Hotel Round Table. She was an influential book and drama critic, contributing incisive and caustic reviews to the *New Yorker*. Her works include *Enough Rope* (1926) and *Here Lies* (1939).

41 Brevity is the soul of lingerie, as the Petticoat said to the Chemise.
1916 Caption for *Vogue*. Quoted in J Keats *You Might as Well Live* (1970).

42 Excuse My Dust.
1925 Suggested epitaph for herself. Quoted in Alexander Woollcott *While Rome Burns* (1934), 'Our Mrs Parker'. She also suggested 'This is on me' for her tombstone.

43 Lady, lady, should you meet
One whose ways are all discreet,
One who murmurs that his wife
Is the lodestar of his life,
One who keeps assuring you

That he never was untrue,
Never loved another one…
Lady, lady, better run!
1926 *Enough Rope*, 'Social Note'.

44 Where's the man could ease a heart
Like a satin gown?
1926 *Enough Rope*, 'The Satin Dress', stanza 1.

45 The affair between Margot Asquith and Margot Asquith will live as one of the prettiest love stories in all literature.
1927 Book review in the *New Yorker*, 22 Oct.

46 If, with the literate, I am
Impelled to try an epigram,
I never seek to take the credit;
We all assume that Oscar said it.
1928 *Sunset Gun*, 'Oscar Wilde'.

47 And it is that word 'hummy', my darlings, that marks the first place in 'The House at Pooh Corner' at which Tonstant Weader fwowed up.
1928 Book review in the *New Yorker*, 20 Oct.

48 More glutton than artist…he commences to chew up the scenery.
1930 Play review, alluding to an unidentified actor. This is said to have been the origin of the phrase 'chew up the scenery', used to describe an actor who is 'hamming it up'.

49 Now that you've got me right down to it, the only thing I didn't like about *The Barretts of Wimpole Street* was the play.
1931 Play review in the *New Yorker*.

50 *House Beautiful* is play lousy.
1933 Review in the *New Yorker*. Quoted in P Hartnoll *Plays and Players* (1984).

51 How did they know?
1933 Attributed response on hearing of the death of President Calvin Coolidge.

52 Katharine Hepburn runs the gamut of the emotions from A to B.
1933 Remark during the interval of *The Lake* on its Broadway première. Quoted in G Carey *Katharine Hepburn* (1983), ch.6.

53 That woman speaks eighteen languages, and can't say No in any of them.
Quoted in Alexander Woollcott *While Rome Burns* (1934), 'Our Mrs Parker'.

54 And there was that wholesale libel on a Yale prom. If all the girls attending it were laid end to end, Mrs Parker said, she wouldn't be at all surprised.
Quoted in Alexander Woollcott *While Rome Burns* (1934), 'Our Mrs Parker'.

55 Good work, Mary. We all knew you had it in you.
On the arrival of a baby. Quoted in Alexander Woollcott *While Rome Burns* (1934), 'Our Mrs Parker'.

56 Whose love is given over-well
Shall look on Helen's face in hell
Whilst they whose love is thin and wise
Shall see John Knox in Paradise.
1937 *Not So Deep as A Well*, 'Partial Comfort'.

57 Why is it no one ever sent me yet
One perfect limousine, do you suppose?
Ah no, it's always just my luck to get
One perfect rose.
1937 *Not So Deep as A Well*, 'One Perfect Rose'.

58 Four be the things I'd been better without:

Love, curiosity, freckles, and doubt.
1937 *Not So Deep as A Well*, 'Inventory'.

59 By the time you say you're his,
Shivering and sighing
And he vows his passion is
Infinite, undying—
Lady, make a note of this:
One of you is lying.
1937 *Not So Deep as A Well*, 'Unfortunate Coincidence'.

60 Oh, life is a glorious cycle of song,
A medley of extemporanea;
And love is a thing that can never go wrong;
And I am Marie of Roumania.
1937 *Not So Deep as A Well*, 'Comment'.

61 Drink and dance and laugh and lie,
Love, the reeling midnight through,
For tomorrow we shall die!
(But, alas, we never do).
1937 *Not So Deep as A Well*, 'The Flaw in Paganism'.
➤ See Bible 121:16.

62 He lies below, correct in cypress wood,
And entertains the most exclusive worms.
1937 *Not So Deep as A Well*, 'Tombstones in the Starlight'.

63 Men seldom make passes
At girls who wear glasses.
1937 *Not So Deep as A Well*, 'News Item'.

64 Scratch a lover, and find a foe.
1937 *Not So Deep as A Well*, 'Ballade of a Great Weariness'.

65 Razors pain you
Rivers are damp;
Acids stain you;
And drugs cause cramp.
Guns aren't lawful;
Nooses give;
Gas smells awful;
You might as well live.
1937 *Not So Deep as A Well*, 'Résumé'.

66 Sorrow is tranquillity remembered in emotion.
1939 *Here Lies*, 'Sentiment'.
➤ See Wordsworth 925:10.

67 And I'll stay off Verlaine, too; he was always chasing
Rimbauds.
1939 *Here Lies*, 'The Little Hours'.

68 You can always tell that the crash is coming when I start
getting tender about Our Dumb Friends. Three highballs
and I think I'm St Francis of Assisi.
1939 *Here Lies*, 'Just a Little One'.

69 There's a hell of a distance between wise-cracking and
wit. Wit has truth in it; wise-cracking is simply
callisthenics with words.
1956 In the *Paris Review*, Summer.

70 All those writers who write about their childhood!
Gentle God, if I wrote about mine you wouldn't sit in the
same room with me.
1956 In the *Paris Review*, Summer.

71 It serves me right for putting all my eggs in one bastard.
On her abortion. Quoted in J Keats *You Might as Well Live* (1970).

72 You can lead a horticulture, but you can't make her think.
Response to a challenge to use 'horticulture' in a sentence.
Quoted in J Keats *You Might as Well Live* (1970).

73 One more drink and I'd have been under the host.
Quoted in H Teichmann *George S Kaufman* (1972).

74 That should assure us of at least forty-five minutes of
undisturbed privacy.
Attributed, after pressing the button marked 'nurse' when her
secretary came to visit her in hospital. Quoted in Clifton
Fadiman *The Faber Book of Anecdotes* (1985).

75 Three be the things I shall never attain:
Envy, content, and sufficient champagne.
Quoted in Marion Meade *Dorothy Parker* (1988).

76 All writers are either 29 or Thomas Hardy.
On being asked Hemingway's age. Quoted in Marion Meade
Dorothy Parker (1988).

77 As American as a sawed-off shotgun.
Of Dashiell Hammett. Quoted in Marion Meade *Dorothy Parker*
(1988).

78 Upon my honour, I saw a Madonna
Standing in a niche
Above the door of the private whore
Of the world's worst son of a bitch.
Jotted into the visitor's book of William Randolph Hearst's house
at San Simeon after she had seen a Della Robbia Madonna over
the entrance to Marion Davies's bedroom. Quoted in R Hughes
Culture of Complaint (1994).

Parker, Hubert Lister 1900–72

English judge. He served as Lord Chief Justice of England.

79 A judge is not supposed to know anything about the
facts of life until they have been presented in evidence
and explained to him at least three times.
1961 Quoted in the *Observer*, 12 Mar.

Parker, John 1729–75

Commander of the Lexington militia company in the opening
engagement of the American Revolution.

80 Stand your ground. Don't fire unless fired upon, but if
they mean to have a war, let it begin here!
1775 Attributed command before the Battle of Lexington, 19 Apr.

Parker, Ross and Charles, Hugh 1914–74, 1907–95

British songwriters.

81 There'll always be an England
While there's a country lane,
Wherever there's a cottage small
Beside a field of grain.
1939 Song.

Parker, Stewart 1941–88

Northern Irish playwright. A lecturer at Cornell University, he
turned to full-time writing for the stage, TV and radio. His best-
known plays are *Spokesong* (1976) and *Pentecost* (1987).

82 The Kamikaze Ground Staff Re-union Dinner.
1979 Title of play.

Parkes, Sir Henry 1815–96

English-born Australian statesman, who emigrated to New
South Wales in 1839. A member of the colonial parliament in
1854, he held various offices, from 1872 was repeatedly Prime
Minister, and was identified with free trade.

83 Why should not the name of an Australian be equal to

that of a Briton…to that of a citizen of the proudest country under the sun? Make yourselves a united people, appear before the world as one, and the dream of going 'home' will die away.
1880 Speech to the Australian Federation Conference, Feb.

Parkinson, C(yril) Northcote 1909–93

English political scientist and Professor of History, best remembered for his seriocomic tilt at bureaucratic malpractices, *Parkinson's Law: the Pursuit of Progress* (1958).

84 Work expands so as to fill the time available for its completion.
1958 *Parkinson's Law: the Pursuit of Progress*, ch.1.

85 Time spent on any item of the agenda will be in inverse proportion to the sum involved.
1958 *Parkinson's Law: the Pursuit of Progress*, ch.3.

86 Men enter local politics solely as a result of being unhappily married.
1958 *Parkinson's Law: the Pursuit of Progress*, ch.10.

87 Expenditure rises to meet income.
1960 *The Law and the Profits*, ch.1.

Parkinson, Norman *originally* Ronald William Parkinson Smith 1913–90

English magazine photographer.

88 A photographer without a magazine behind him is like a farmer without fields.
1984 In the *New Yorker*, 10 Dec.

89 The camera can be the most deadly weapon since the assassin's bullet. Or it can be the lotion of the heart.
1984 In the *New Yorker*, 10 Dec.

Parks, Rosa Lee née McCauley 1913–

US civil rights protester.

90 All I was doing was trying to get home from work.
On refusing to give up her seat to a white man in Montgomery, Alabama, which led to the 1955 Montgomery bus boycott and in turn to a Supreme Court ruling that bus segregation was unconstitutional, and fuelled the civil rights movement. Quoted in *Time*, 15 Dec 1975.

Parnell, Charles Stewart 1846–91

Irish politician, elected President of the Irish National Land League (1878). In 1886 he allied with the Liberals in support of Gladstone's Home Rule bill, but was forced to retire as leader of the Irish Nationalists in 1890 in disgrace when cited as co-respondent in a divorce case.

91 When a man takes a farm from which another has been evicted, you must show him on the roadside when you meet him; you must show him in the streets of the town; you must show him in the fair and the market place; and even in the house of worship, by leaving him severely alone—by putting him into a moral Coventry, by isolating him from his kind as if he were a leper of old. You must show him your detestation of the crimes that he has committed.
1880 Speech that established the practice of boycotting, Ennis, 19 Sep.

92 And it is a good sign that this masquerading knight-errant, this pretended champion of the rights of every other nation except those of the Irish nation, should be obliged to throw off the mask today, and to stand revealed as the man who by his own utterances is prepared to carry fire and sword into your homesteads unless you humbly abase yourselves before him, and before the landlords of the country.
1881 Speech successfully inciting Gladstone to arrest him, 9 Oct.

93 No man has a right to fix the boundary of the march of a nation. No man has a right to say to his country, 'Thus far thou shalt go and no further.'
1885 Speech, Cork, 21 Jan.

Parra, Nicanor 1914–

Chilean physicist, poet and lecturer. He addresses common problems in a clear and direct language, with black humour and a highly ironic vision.

94 *Padre nuestro que estás en el cielo*
Lleno de toda clase de problemas
Con el ceño fruncido
Como si fueras un hombre vulgar y corriente
No pienses más en nosotros.
Our Father who art in Heaven
Full of all kinds of problems
Ceaselessly frowning
As if you were a simple man:
Stop thinking about us.
1969 *Obra gruesa*, 'Padre nuestro' ('Our Father').

Parr-Davies, Harry 1914–55

Welsh songwriter, best known for the songs he wrote for Gracie Fields. His credits include 'Sing As We Go' (1934), 'Queen of Hearts' (1936) and 'Shipyard Sally' (1939).

95 Wish me luck, as you wave me goodbye—
Cheerio, here I go, on my way.
1939 Sung by Gracie Fields in *Shipyard Sally*.

Parris, Matthew 1949–

British author, journalist and broadcaster, former Conservative MP (1979–86).

96 Wilde's captors were the police. But his persecutors were to be found on the letters page of the *Daily Telegraph*.
1993 In *The Times*, 7 Apr.

97 Being an MP feeds your vanity and starves your self-respect.
1994 In *The Times*, 9 Feb.

98 Bring on the fruitcakes, we want a fruitcake for an unlovable seat.
1997 On the day before the Kensington and Chelsea Conservatives chose Alan Clark as their parliamentary candidate. In the *Daily Mail*, 26 Jan.

Parry, Sir Charles Hubert Hastings 1848–1918

English composer. Director of the Royal College of Music from 1895, he composed the oratorios *Judith* (1888), *Job* (1892) and *King Saul* (1894); an opera, symphonies, quartets and cantatas. He also wrote various books on music.

99 Look out for this man's music; he has something to say and knows how to say it.
1899 After the première of Elgar's *Enigma Variations*. Quoted in Ian Crofton and Donald Fraser *A Dictionary of Musical Quotations* (1985).

Parsons, Talcott 1902–79

US sociologist and social theorist. A member of the faculty of Harvard University (1927–74), his chief works include *The Social System* (1951) and *Sociological Theory and Modern Society* (1967).

1 Science is intimately integrated with the whole social structure and cultural tradition. They mutually support one another—only in certain types of society can science flourish, and conversely without a continuous and healthy development and application of science such a society cannot function properly.
1951 *The Social System*, ch.8.

Parton, Dolly 1946–

US country singer, songwriter and actress.

2 Some people say that less is more. But I think more is more.
Attributed.

3 You'd be surprised how much it costs to look this cheap.
Attributed.

Parvin, Landon 1948–

US speechwriter. He was formerly speechwriter to President Reagan. He runs his own speechwriting and communications consultancy.

4 What you do is take the truth and just skew it a bit.
1991 On creating political wit for the Washington press's annual Gridiron dinners. In the *New York Times*, 29 Mar.

Pascal, Blaise 1623–62

French philosopher, mathematician and physicist, whose inventions included a calculating machine, barometer, hydraulic press and syringe, and who pioneered probability theory. An ascetic Christian and member of the Jansenist movement, he wrote much spiritual literature. Notes found after his death were published as *Pensées* in 1670.

5 *Il y a deux sortes d'esprits, l'un géométrique, et l'autre que l'on peut appeler de finesse. Le premier a des vues lentes, dures et inflexibles; mais le dernier a une souplesse de pensée.*
There are two kinds of mind, one mathematical, the other what one might call the intuitive. The first takes a slow, firm, inflexible view, but the latter has flexibility of thought.
c.1653 *Discours sur les passions de l'amour* (*Discourse on the Passions of Love*). This is usually attributed to Pascal.

6 *Dans une grande âme tout est grand.*
In a great soul everything is great.
c.1653 *Discours sur les passions de l'amour* (*Discourse on the Passions of Love*). This is usually attributed to Pascal.

7 *Quelque étendue d'esprit que l'on ait, l'on n'est capable que d'une grande passion.*
However vast a man's spirit, he is only capable of one great passion.
c.1653 *Discours sur les passions de l'amour* (*Discourse on the Passions of Love*). This is usually attributed to Pascal.

8 *La netteté de l'esprit cause aussi la netteté de la passion; c'est pourquoi un esprit grand et net aime avec ardeur, et il voit distinctement ce qu'il aime.*
Clarity of mind results in clarity of passion; that is why a great mind loves ardently and sees distinctly what it loves.

c.1653 *Discours sur les passions de l'amour* (*Discourse on the Passions of Love*). This is usually attributed to Pascal.

9 *L'on a beau se cacher à soi-même, l'on aime toujours.*
We vainly conceal from ourselves the fact that we are always in love.
c.1653 *Discours sur les passions de l'amour* (*Discourse on the Passions of Love*). This is usually attributed to Pascal.

10 *La vraie éloquence se moque de l'éloquence, la vraie morale se moque de la morale.*
True eloquence has no time for eloquence, true morality has no time for morality.
c.1654–1662 *Pensées*, no.4 (translated by A Krailsheimer).

11 *La dernière chose qu'on trouve en faisant un ouvrage, est de savoir celle qu'il faut mettre la première.*
The last thing one discovers in composing a work is what to put first.
c.1654–1662 *Pensées*, no.19 (translated by A Krailsheimer).

12 *Quand on voit le style naturel, on est tout étonné et ravi, car on s'attendait de voir un auteur, et on trouve un homme.*
When we see a natural style we are quite amazed and delighted, because we expected to see an author and find a man.
c.1654–1662 *Pensées*, no.29 (translated by A Krailsheimer).

13 *L'homme n'est qu'un sujet plein d'erreur, naturelle et ineffaçable sans la grâce.*
Man is nothing but a subject full of natural error that cannot be eradicated except through grace.
c.1654–1662 *Pensées*, no.83 (translated by A Krailsheimer).

14 *Condition de l'homme: inconstance, ennui, inquiétude.*
Man's condition. Inconstancy, boredom, anxiety.
c.1654–1662 *Pensées*, no.127 (translated by A Krailsheimer).

15 *Notre nature est dans le mouvement; le repos entier est la mort.*
Our nature consists in movement; absolute rest is death.
c.1654–1662 *Pensées*, no.129 (translated by A Krailsheimer).

16 *Tout le malheur des hommes vient d'une seule chose, qui est de ne savoir pas demeurer en repos, dans une chambre.*
The sole cause of man's unhappiness is that he does not know how to stay quietly in his room.
c.1654–1662 *Pensées*, no.139 (translated by A Krailsheimer).

17 *Le nez de Cléopâtre: s'il eût été plus court, toute la face de la terre aurait changé.*
Cleopatra's nose: if it had been shorter the whole face of the earth would have been different.
c.1654–1662 *Pensées*, no.162 (translated by A Krailsheimer).

18 *Le silence éternel de ces espaces infinis m'effraie.*
The eternal silence of these infinite spaces fills me with dread.
c.1654–1662 *Pensées*, no.206 (translated by A Krailsheimer).

19 *Combien de royaumes nous ignorent!*
How many kingdoms know nothing of us!
c.1654–1662 *Pensées*, no.207 (translated by A Krailsheimer).

20 *Le dernier acte est sanglant, quelque belle que soit la comédie en tout le reste; on jette enfin de la terre sur la tête, et en voilà pour jamais.*
The last act is bloody, however fine the rest of the play. They throw earth over your head and it is finished forever.
c.1654–1662 *Pensées*, no.210 (translated by A Krailsheimer).

21 *Pesons le gain et la perte, en prenant croix que Dieu est. Estimons ces deux cas: si vous gagnez, vous gagnez tout; si vous perdez, vous ne perdez rien. Gagez donc qu'il est, sans hésiter.*
Let us weigh up the gain and loss involved in calling heads that God exists. Let us assess the two cases: if you win you win everything, if you lose you lose nothing. Do not hesitate then; wager that he does exist.
c.1654–1662 *Pensées*, no.233 (translated by A Krailsheimer).

22 *Tout notre raisonnement se réduit à céder au sentiment.*
All our reasoning comes down to surrendering to feeling.
c.1654–1662 *Pensées*, no.274 (translated by A Krailsheimer).

23 *Le cœur a ses raisons, que la raison ne connaît point.*
The heart has its reasons of which reason knows nothing.
c.1654–1662 *Pensées*, no.277 (translated by A Krailsheimer).

24 *L'homme n'est qu'un roseau, le plus faible de la nature; mais c'est un roseau pensant.*
Man is only a reed, the weakest in nature, but he is a thinking reed.
c.1654–1662 *Pensées*, no.347 (translated by A Krailsheimer).

25 *Le moi est haïssable.*
The self is hateful.
c.1654–1662 *Pensées*, no.455 (translated by A Krailsheimer).

26 *À mesure qu'on a plus d'esprit, on trouve qu'il y a plus d'hommes originaux. Les gens du commun ne trouvent pas de différence entre les hommes.*
The more intelligent one is, the greater the differences one finds among men. Ordinary persons do not perceive differences among men.
c.1654–1662 *Pensées*, pt.1, no.7.

27 *Éloquence qui persuade par douceur, non par empire, en tyran, non en roi.*
Eloquence should persuade gently, not by force or like a tyrant or king.
c.1654–1662 *Pensées*, pt.1, no.15.

28 *Qu'est-ce que l'homme dans la nature? Un néant à l'égard de l'infini, un tout à l'égard du néant, un milieu entre rien et tout.*
What is man in nature? Nothing in comparison to the infinite, all in comparison to nothing, a mean between nothing and everything.
c.1654–1662 *Pensées*, pt.2, no.72.

29 *La chose la plus importante à toute la vie est le choix du métier: le hasard en dispose.*
The most important thing in life is to choose a profession: chance arranges for that.
c.1654–1662 *Pensées*, pt.2, no.97.

30 Knowledge of physical science will not console me for ignorance of morality in time of affliction, but knowledge of morality will always console me for ignorance of physical science.
c.1654–1662 *Pensées*, no.23.

31 *L'homme n'est ni ange ni bête, et le malheur veut que qui veut faire l'ange fait la bête.*
Man is neither angel nor beast. Unfortunately, he who wants to act the angel often acts the beast.
c.1654–1662 *Pensées*, pt.6, no.358.

32 *En un mot, l'homme connaît qu'il est misérable: il est donc misérable, puisqu'il l'est; mais il est bien grand,*

puisqu'il le connaît.
In one word, man knows that he is miserable and therefore he is miserable because he knows it; but he is also worthy, because he knows his condition.
c.1654–1662 *Pensées*, pt.6, no.416.

33 *Il n'y a que deux sortes d'hommes: les uns justes, qui se croient pécheurs; les autres pécheurs, qui se croient justes.*
There are only two types of people: the virtuous who believe themselves to be sinners and the sinners who believe themselves to be virtuous.
c.1654–1662 *Pensées*, pt.7, no.534.

34 *Il est non seulement impossible, mais inutile de connaître Dieu sans Jésus-Christ.*
It is not only impossible, but also useless to recognize God without Jesus.
c.1654–1662 *Pensées*, pt.7, no.549.

35 *Je ne crois que les histoires dont les témoins se feraient égorger.*
I only believe in histories told by witnesses who would have had their throats slit.
c.1654–1662 *Pensées*, pt.9, no.593.

36 *Le silence est la plus grande persécution: jamais les saints ne se sont tus.*
Silence is the greatest of all persecutions: no saint was ever silent.
c.1654–1662 *Pensées*, pt.14, no.920.

37 *Console-toi, tu ne me chercherais pas si tu ne m'avais trouvé.*
Comfort yourself. You would not seek me if you had not found me.
c.1654–1662 *Pensées*, pt.7, no.553 (translated by L Braunschvicg, 1909).

38 *Je n'ai fait plus longue que parce que je n'ai pas eu le loisir de la faire plus courte.*
I have made this letter longer than usual, only because I have not had the time to make it shorter.
1657 *Lettres provinciales*, letter 16.

39 FEU. *Dieu d'Abraham, Dieu d'Isaac, Dieu de Jacob, non des philosophes et savants. Certitude. Certitude. Sentiment. Joie. Paix.*
FIRE. God of Abraham, God of Isaac, God of Jacob, not of the philosophers and scholars. Certainty. Certainty. Feeling. Joy. Peace.
c.1662 Note found after his death on a parchment stitched to his coat.

Passell, Peter

US financial journalist, editor of the Milken Institute Review.

40 Six percent unemployment only looks good from the vantage point of the other 94 percent.
1994 In the *New York Times*, 31 Mar.

Pasternak, Boris   1890–1960

Russian poet and novelist. He was awarded a Nobel prize for literature in 1958, but refused it.

41 Yet the order of the acts is planned
And the end of the way inescapable.
I am alone; all drowns in the Pharisees' hypocrisy.
1958 *Doctor Zhivago.*

42 The whole wide world is a cathedral;
  I stand inside, the air is calm,
  And from afar at times there reaches
  My ear the echo of a psalm.
  1958 When It Clears Up (translated by Lydia Pasternak Slater).

Pasteur, Louis 1822–95

French chemist, the father of modern bacteriology. He promoted inoculation as a means of preventing diseases, and in 1888 he founded the Institut Pasteur and served as its first director.

43 *Dans les champs de l'observation le hasard ne favorise que les esprits préparés.*
  Where observation is concerned, chance favours only the prepared mind.
  1854 Speech at the inauguration of the Faculty of Science, University of Lille, 7 Dec.

44 Science proceeds by successive answers to questions more and more subtle, coming nearer and nearer to the very essence of phenomena.
  c.1856 Études sur la bière, ch.6 (translated by René Dubois).

45 *Il n'existe pas de sciences appliquées, mais seulement des applications de la science.*
  There are no such things as applied sciences, only applications of science.
  1872 Speech, Lyons, 11 Sep.

46 I am imbued with two deep impressions; the first, that science knows no country; the second, which seems to contradict the first, although it is really a direct consequence of it…that science is the highest personification of the nation. Science knows no country because knowledge belongs to humanity, and is the torch which illuminates the world. Science is the highest personification of the nation because that nation will remain the first which carries the furthest the works of thought and intelligence.
  1876 Toast at the banquet of the International Congress of Sericulture (translated by René Dubois).

47 Outside their laboratories, the physician and chemist are soldiers without arms on the field of battle.
  Some Reflections on Science in France, pt.1.

Patchen, Kenneth 1911–72

US author, playwright and poet. His many verse collections, illustrated by him, include *Before the Brave* (1936) and *Hallelujah Anyway* (1967), and his novels include *Memoirs of a Shy Pornographer* (1945).

48 For greatness is only the drayhorse that coaxes
  The built cart out; and where we go is reason.
  But genius is an enormous littleness, a trickling
  Of heart that covers alike the hare and the hunter.
  1939 First Will and Testament, 'The Character of Love Seen as a Search for the Lost'.

49 Dogs with broken legs are shot; men with broken souls write through the night.
  1941 The Journal of Albion Moonlight.

50 God must have loved the People in Power, for he made them so very like their own image of him.
  Quoted by Adrian Mitchell in *The Guardian*, 1 Feb 1972.

Pater, Walter 1839–94

English critic and essayist, whose highly polished prose style was very influential. He wrote many essays on Renaissance art, and won a wider audience with a romance, *Marius the Epicurean* (1885).

51 She is older than the rocks among which she sits; like the vampire, she has been dead many times, and learned the secrets of the grave.
  1873 Of the *Mona Lisa.* 'Leonardo da Vinci' in *Studies in the History of the Renaissance*.

52 All art constantly aspires towards the condition of music.
  1873 'The School of Giorgione' in *Studies in the History of the Renaissance*.

53 Of such wisdom, the poetic passion, the desire of beauty, the love of art for its own sake, has most. For art comes to you proposing frankly to give nothing but the highest quality to your moments as they pass, and simply for those moments' sake.
  1873 'Conclusion' in *Studies in the History of the Renaissance*.

Paterson, Banjo (Andrew Barton) 1864–1941

Australian poet and journalist. He worked on a station near Yass and later practised as a solicitor, contributing to the satirical weekly *Bulletin* as 'The Banjo'. His first collection of bush ballads, *The Man from Snowy River* (1895), gained him massive popularity.

54 Oh there once was a swagman camped in the billabongs,
  Under the shade of a Coolibah tree;
  And he sang as he looked at the old billy boiling,
  'Who'll come a-waltzing Matilda with me.'

  Who'll come a-waltzing Matilda, my darling,
  Who'll come a-waltzing Matilda with me.
  Waltzing Matilda and leading a water-bag,
  Who'll come a-waltzing Matilda with me.
  1885 'Waltzing Matilda', in the *Bulletin*, Apr.

55 I had written him a letter which I had, for want of better
  Knowledge, sent to where I met him, down the Lachlan, years ago.
  He was shearing when I knew him, so I sent the letter to him,
  Just 'on spec', addressed as follows: 'Clancy, of the Overflow'.
  And an answer came directed in a writing unexpected,
  (And I think the same was written with a thumbnail dipped in tar)
  'Twas his shearing mate who wrote it, and verbatim I will quote it:
  'Clancy's gone to Queensland droving, and we don't know where he are.'
  1895 'Clancy of the Overflow', first published in the *Bulletin*, collected in *The Man from Snowy River and Other Verses* (1895).

56 In all museums throughout the world one may see plaster casts of footprints of weird animals, footprints preserved for posterity, not because the animals were particularly good of their sort, but because they had the luck to walk on the lava while it was cooling. There is just a faint hope that something of the same sort may happen to us.
  Of Henry Lawson and himself writing in a new land. Quoted in Rosamund Campbell and Philippa Harvie *A Literary Heritage: 'Banjo' Paterson* (1988), introduction.

Patmore, Coventry Kersey Dighton 1823–96

English poet. He was associated with the Pre-Raphaelite brotherhood. His best work, *The Angel in the House* (4 vols. 1854–63), was a poetic treatment of married love which delighted a generation devoid of cynicism to whom he and his first wife, Emily, epitomized Victorian values.

57 Oh, wasteful woman, she who may
    On her sweet self set her own price,
    Knowing man cannot choose but pay,
    How has she cheapened paradise:
    How given for naught her priceless gift,
    How spoiled the bread and spilled the wine,
    Which, spent with due, respective thrift,
    Had made brutes men, and men divine.
    1854 *The Angel in the House*, bk.1, *The Betrothal*, canto 3, prelude 3, 'Unthrift'.

58 Love wakes men, once a lifetime each;
    They lift their heavy lids, and look;
    And, lo, what one sweet page can teach,
    They read with joy, then shut the book.
    1854 *The Angel in the House*, bk.1, *The Betrothal*, canto 8, prelude 2, 'The Revelation'.

59 'I saw you take his kiss!' ''Tis true.'
    'O modesty!' ''Twas strictly kept:
    He thought me asleep—at least, I knew
    He thought I thought he thought I slept.'
    1854 *The Angel in the House*, bk.2, *The Espousal*, canto 8, prelude 3, 'The Kiss'.

60 A woman is a foreign land.
    1854 *The Angel in the House*, bk.2, *The Espousal*, canto 9, prelude 2, 'The Foreign Land'.

61 It was not like your great and gracious ways!
    Do you, that have naught other to lament,
    Never, my love, repent.
    1877 *To the Unknown Eros*, bk.1, no.8, 'Departure'.

62 With all my will, but much against my heart,
    We two now part.
    1877 *To the Unknown Eros*, bk.1, no.16, 'A Farewell'.

63 'O say,
    Shall we no voluntary bars
    Set to our drift? I, Sister of the Stars,
    And Thou, my glorious, course-compelling Day!'
    1877 *To the Unknown Eros*, bk.2, no.2, 'The Contract'.

64 No writer, sacred or profane, ever uses the words 'he' or 'him' of the soul. It is always 'she' or 'her'; so universal is the intuitive knowledge that the soul, with regard to God who is her life, is feminine.
    1896 *The Rod, the Root, and the Flower*, 'Aurea Dicta', no.21.

65 Those who know God know that it is a quite a mistake to suppose that there are only five senses.
    1896 *The Rod, the Root, and the Flower*, 'Aurea Dicta', no.142.

66 May I know by love and speak by silence.
    1896 *The Rod, the Root, and the Flower*, 'Aphorisms and Extracts'.

67 He that but once too nearly hears
    The music of forfended spheres
    Is thenceforth lonely, and for all
    His days as one who treads the Wall
    Of China, and, on this hand, sees
    Cities and their civilities
    And, on the other, lions.
    1863 *The Victories of Love*, bk.1.

68 Some dish more sharply spiced than this
    Milk-soup men call domestic bliss.
    Olympus (published 1906).

Paton, Alan 1903–88

South African writer and educator. President of the South African Liberal Party (1953–60), he is best remembered for his novel *Cry, the Beloved Country* (1948), on racial divisions in South Africa.

69 Cry, the Beloved Country.
    1948 Title of book.

70 No second Johannesburg is needed upon the earth. One is enough.
    1948 *Cry, the Beloved Country*, bk.2, section 6.

St Patrick 5c AD

Bishop and Apostle of Ireland.

71 Christ for my guardianship today: against poison, against burning, against drowning, against wounding, that there may come to me a multitude of rewards;
    Christ with me,
    Christ before me,
    Christ behind me,
    Christ in me,
    Christ over me,
    Christ to right of me,
    Christ to left of me,
    Christ in lying down,
    Christ in sitting,
    Christ in rising up,
    Christ in the heart of every person who may think of me,
    Christ in the mouth of every person who may speak
      of me,
    Christ in every eye, which may look on me!
    Christ in every ear, which may hear me!
    St Patrick's Breastplate, traditionally attributed to the saint.

Patrick, John *pseudonym of* **John Patrick Goggan** 1905–95

US playwright and screenwriter. He received the Pulitzer Prize for the play *The Teahouse of the August Moon* (1953) and his screenplays include *Three Coins in the Fountain* (1954) and *Love is a Many Splendoured Thing* (1955).

72 Punctuality is the vice of virtuous women.
    1954 Line delivered by Clifton Webb in *Three Coins in the Fountain*.

Patton, George Smith *known as* **Old Blood and Guts**
1885–1945

US soldier, a daring and flamboyant commander in World War II. He led numerous expeditions, including the 3rd Army invasion of France, and was killed in a road accident in Germany soon after being appointed general.

73 The object of war is not to die for your country. The object of war is to make damn sure the other sonofabitch dies for *his*.
    Attributed.

Paul, Leslie 1905–85

Irish writer and poet.

74 Angry Young Man.
    1951 Title of book. Later associated with John Osborne.

Pauli, Wolfgang 1900–58

Austrian–Swiss theoretical physicist and Nobel prize winner (1945).

75 I don't mind your thinking slowly: I mind your publishing faster than you think.
Attributed.

Pauling, Linus Carl 1901–94

US chemist. He was Professor at the California Institute of Technology and won the Nobel prize for chemistry in 1954. He was awarded the Nobel peace prize in 1962.

76 Science is a search for truth—it is not a game in which one tries to best his opponent, to do harm to others.
1958 *No More War.*

Pavarotti, Luciano 1935–

Italian tenor.

77 If I could live my life over again there is one thing I would change. I would want to be able to eat less.
1997 In *The Times*, 8 Dec.

78 Horse riding is a perfect comparison with singing. You must know where the double fences are.
2002 In *The Guardian*, 7 Jan.

Pavlov, I(van) P(etrovich) 1849–1936

Russian physiologist and experimental psychologist, famed for his work on the physiology of the digestive system. He received the 1904 Nobel prize for physiology or medicine.

79 Learn the ABC of science before you try to ascend to its summit.
1936 *Bequest to the Academic Youth of Soviet Russia.*

Pavlov, Valentin Sergeyevich 1937–2003

Russian politician. He was Prime Minister from January 1991 until August of that year, when he was arrested as an accomplice in the failed coup d'état against Mikhail Gorbachev. He was granted amnesty by parliament in 1994.

80 Privatization must come after the liberalization of prices… How on earth can you privatize or denationalize anything if you have no means of assessing the value of assets before offering them on the market?
1991 Interview, *The Independent*, 18 Apr.

81 Civil war is impossible in the Soviet Union.
1991 Interview, *The Independent*, 18 Apr.

82 It is no use making revolutionary cavalry charges against the problems that we are facing.
1991 On Boris Yeltsin's proposals for economic republican autonomy. Interview, *The Independent*, 18 Apr.

Pavlova, Anna 1882–1931

Russian ballerina.

83 Although one may fail to find happiness in theatrical life, one never wishes to give it up after having once tasted its fruits. To enter the School of the Imperial Ballet is to enter a convent whence frivolity is banned, and where merciless discipline reigns.
Quoted in A H Franks (ed) *Pavlova: A Biography*, 'Pages of My Life' (1956).

Paxman, Jeremy 1950–

English journalist and broadcaster. He is perhaps best known as the presenter of such current affairs programmes as *Panorama* (1979–85), and *Newsnight* (1989–).

84 Did you threaten to overrule him?
1997 Question asked 14 times of Conservative politician Michael Howard, relating to the sacking of a prison governor by the director of the Prison Service, Derek Lewis. On BBC's *Newsnight*.

85 Once upon a time the English knew who they were.
1998 *The English: A Portrait of a People.*

86 Scots are Jocks, Welshmen Taffies, and Irishmen Paddies or Micks but…it is noticeable there is no similar designation for the English.
1998 *The English: A Portrait of a People.*

87 The more you look back into English history, the more you are forced to the conclusion that alongside civility and the deeply held convictions about individual rights, the English have a natural taste for disorder.
1998 *The English: A Portrait of a People.*

Paz, Octavio 1914–98

Mexican poet, writer and diplomat. He sided with the Republican cause during the Spanish Civil War. In Paris, he was strongly influenced by the Surrealist movement. He was awarded a Nobel prize in 1990.

88 *Amar es combatir, es abrir puertas,*
dejar de ser fantasma con un número
a perpetua cadena condenado
por un amo sin rostro.
To love is to battle, to open doors,
to cease to be a ghost with a number
forever in chains, forever condemned
by a faceless master.
1949 *Libertad bajo palabra*, 'Piedra de sol' (translated as 'The Sun Stone', 1963).

89 *Sin duda la cercanía de la muerte y la fraternidad de las armas producen, en todos los tiempos y en todos los países, una atmósfera propicia a lo extraordinario, a todo aquello que sobrepasa la condición humana y rompe el círculo de soledad que rodea a cada hombre.*
No doubt the nearness of death and the brotherhood of men-at-wars, at whatever time and in whatever country, always produce an atmosphere favorable to the extraordinary, to all that rises above the human condition and breaks the circle of solitude that surrounds each one of us.
1950 *El laberinto de la soledad*, pt.1 (translated as *The Labyrinth of Solitude*, 1961).

90 Technology is not an image of the world but a way of operating on reality. The nihilism of technology lies not only in the fact that it is the most perfect expression of the will to power…but also in the fact that it lacks meaning.
1967 *Alternating Current.*

Peace Pilgrim *real name* **Mildred Norman** c.1908–1981

US writer and mystic. From 1952 to 1981 she walked through North America, carrying only the bare minimum of necessities and teaching wherever she went; her intention was to stop walking only when there was total peace in the world.

91 I never give out my zodiac sign. Do you honestly think I can be pushed around by a planet? Good heavens, your divine nature is always free.
Quoted in Susan Hayward and Malcolm Cohen *The Bag of Jewels* (1988).

Peacock, Thomas Love 1785–1866

English novelist. He entered the service of the East India Company (1819–56) after producing three satirical romances, attacking common prejudices and affectations, and produced further works along similar lines.

92 Marriage may often be a stormy lake, but celibacy is almost always a muddy horsepond.
1817 *Melincourt*, ch.7.

93 Laughter is pleasant, but the exertion is too much for me.
1818 *Nightmare Abbey*, ch.5.

94 Sir, I have quarrelled with my wife; and a man who has quarrelled with his wife is absolved from all duty to his country.
1818 *Nightmare Abbey*, ch.11.

95 The mountain sheep are sweeter,
But the valley sheep are fatter;
We therefore deemed it meeter
To carry off the latter.
We made an expedition;
We met a host, and quelled it;
We forced a strong position,
And killed the men who held it.
1829 *The Misfortunes of Elphin*, 'The War-Song of Dinas Vawr'.

96 But though first love's impassioned blindness
Has passed away in colder light,
I still have thought of you with kindness,
And shall do, till our last goodnight.
The ever-rolling silent hours
Will bring a time we shall not know,
When our young days of gathering flowers
Will be an hundred years ago.
1860 'Love and Age'.

Pearson, Karl 1857–1936

English mathematician and Professor of Mathematics and Eugenics at University College London. Pearson is generally considered one of the founders of modern statistical theory.

97 When every fact, every present or past phenomenon of [the] universe, every phase of present or past life therein, has been examined, classified, and coordinated with the rest, then the mission of science will be completed. What is this but saying that the task of science can never end till man ceases to be, till history is no longer made, and development itself ceases?
1892 *The Grammar of Science*, pt.1, ch.5.

Pearson, Lester Bowles 1897–1972

Canadian politician, president of the UN General Assembly (1952–3). He won the Nobel peace prize (1957). Opposition leader from 1958, he was Prime Minister 1963–8.

98 The grim fact, however, is that we prepare for war like precocious giants and for peace like retarded pygmies.
1957 Acceptance speech on receiving the Nobel peace prize, 11 Dec.

99 Politics is the skilled use of blunt objects.

Quoted in Canadian Broadcasting Corporation tribute on his death, 1972.

Peary, Robert Edwin 1856–1920

US admiral and explorer. He made eight Arctic voyages by the Greenland coast. In 1906 he reached latitude 87° 6 mins N and on 6 Apr 1909 was the first to reach the North Pole.

1 I have got the North Pole out of my system after twenty-three years of effort, hard work, disappointments, hardships, privations, more or less suffering, and some risks… The work is the finish, the cap and climax of nearly four hundred years of effort, loss of life, and expenditure of fortunes by the civilized nations of the world, and it has been accomplished in a way that is thoroughly American. I am content.
1909 Diary entry, Apr. Quoted in *The North Pole* (published 1910).

2 In a march of only a few hours, I had passed from the western to the eastern hemisphere and had verified my position at the summit of the world. It was hard to realise that on the first miles of the brief march we had been travelling due north, while on the last few miles of the same march we had been travelling due south, although we had all the time been travelling precisely in the same direction.
1909 Description of crossing and then passing the Pole. *The North Pole* (published 1910).

Peck, M(organ) Scott 1936–

US writer and psychiatrist, author of the seminal self-help work *The Road Less Traveled* (1978). Later works, combining Christian teaching with psychiatric principles, include *The Different Drum* (1987).

3 Once we truly know that life is difficult—once we understand and accept it—then life is no longer difficult. Because once it is accepted, it no longer matters.
1978 *The Road Less Traveled*, ch.1.

4 The evil in this world is committed by the spiritual fat cats who think that they are without sin because they are unwilling to suffer the discomfort of significant self-examination.
1985 *What Return Can I Make?*

5 What being a Christian means, at the very least, is that whenever there is a decision to be made, which may be several times a day, an alternative should not be discarded simply because it is sacrificial.
1985 *What Return Can I Make?*

6 Simply seek happiness, and you are not likely to find it. Seek to create and love without regard to your happiness, and you will likely be happy much of the time.
1987 *The Different Drum*.

7 The healthy life is hardly one marked by an absence of crises. In fact, an individual's psychological health is distinguished by how early he or she can meet crisis.
1987 *The Different Drum*.

Peel, Sir Robert 1788–1850

English Tory statesman, Secretary for Ireland (1812–18), known as 'Orange Peel' for his strong anti-Catholic spirit. As Home Secretary (1822–7, 1828–30), he carried through the Catholic Emancipation Act (1829) and reorganized the London police force (the 'Peelers' or 'Bobbies'). As Prime Minister (1834–5, 1841–6), his decision to repeal the Corn Laws (1846) split his party, and precipitated his resignation, though he remained in Parliament as leader of the 'Peelites'.

8 If the spirit of the Reform Bill implies merely a careful review of institutions, civil and ecclesiastical, undertaken in a friendly temper, combining with the firm maintenance of established rights the correction of private abuses and the redress of real grievances, I can for myself and my colleagues undertake to act in such a spirit and with such intentions.
1834 *The Tamworth Manifesto.*

9 During my tenure of power, my earnest wish has been to impress the people of this country with a belief that the legislature was animated by a sincere desire to frame its legislation upon the principles of equity and justice… Deprive me of power tomorrow, but you can never deprive me of the consciousness that I have exercised the powers committed to me from no corrupt or interested motives, from no desire to gratify ambition, or to attain any personal object.
1846 On the repeal of the Corn Laws, House of Commons, 15 May.

10 It asks more steadiness, self-control, ay, and manly courage, than any other exercise. You must take as well as give—eye to eye, toe to toe, and arm to arm.
Of boxing. Quoted in John Boyle O'Reilly *Ethics of Boxing and Manly Sport* (1888).

Peele, George c.1556–1596

English dramatist and poet.

11 Fair and fair, and twice so fair,
As fair as any may be;
The fairest shepherd on our green,
A love for any lady.
1584 *The Arraignment of Paris*, act 1, sc.5.

12 What thing is love for (well I wot) love is a thing.
It is a prick, it is a sting,
It is a pretty, pretty thing;
It is a fire, it is a coal
Whose flame creeps in at every hole.
c.1591 *The Hunting of Cupid.*

Pei, I(eoh) M(ing) 1917–

Chinese-born US architect. He emigrated to the US in 1935 and was naturalized in 1954. A controversial and adventurous designer, his works include Mile High Center, Denver and the glass pyramid at the Louvre, Paris.

13 Let's do it right. This is for the ages.
1978 Quoted by J Carter Brown, Director, National Gallery of Art, Washington, in the *Washington Post*, 27 Aug 1995. On his design for the gallery's East Building which was soaring to an unbudgeted cost of $94.4m.

14 *Comment respecter la tradition, et innover en même temps? Quel pari difficile!*
How to respect tradition and to innovate at the same time? What a difficult challenge!
1989 *Les Grands desseins du Louvre* (with E J Biasini).

15 *L'architecture est le miroir même de la vie. Il n'est que de jeter les yeux sur des édifices pour sentir la présence du passé, l'esprit d'un lieu; ils sont le reflet de la société.*
Architecture is the very mirror of life. You only have to cast your eyes on buildings to feel the presence of the past, the spirit of a place; they are the reflection of society.
1989 *Les Grands desseins du Louvre* (with E J Biasini).

Pelé *pseudonym of* **Edson Arantes do Nascimento** 1940–

Brazilian footballer. He won World Cup medals with Brazil (1958 and 1970) and scored over 1,000 goals in first-class football.

16 A penalty is a cowardly way to score.
Quoted in Peter Ball and Phil Shaw *The Book of Football Quotations* (1989).

17 I was born for soccer, just as Beethoven was born for music.
Quoted in Colin Jarman *The Guinness Dictionary of Sports Quotations* (1990).

18 Football is like a religion to me. I worship the ball, and I treat it like a god. Too many players think of a football as something to kick. They should be taught to caress it and to treat it like a precious gem.
Quoted in David Pickering *The Cassell Soccer Companion* (1994).

Penecuik, Dr Alex 1652–1722

Scottish poet.

19 To curle on the ice, does greatly please,
Being a manly Scottish exercise;
It clears the Brains, stirs up the Native Heat,
And gives a gallant appetite for Meat.
1715 Quoted in Colin Jarman *The Guinness Dictionary of Sports Quotations* (1990).

Penfield, Wilder Graves 1891–1976

US-born Canadian neurosurgeon, who worked mainly at Montreal's Allan Memorial Institute, where he was first director (1934–60). He famously worked on the exposed brains of living human subjects, and on retirement turned to writing fiction and biography.

20 In all our studies of the brain, no mechanism has been discovered that can force the mind to think, or the individual to believe, anything. The mind continues free. That is a statement I have long considered. I have made every effort to disprove it, without success.
1970 *Second Thoughts: Science, the Arts, and the Spirit.*

Peniakoff, Vladimir 1897–1951

Belgian-born soldier and writer.

21 A message came on the wireless for me. It said: 'SPREAD ALARM AND DESPONDENCY'. So the time had come, I thought, Eighth Army was taking the offensive. The date was, I think, May 18th, 1942.
1950 *Popski's Private Army.*

Penn, William 1644–1718

English Quaker, imprisoned for his beliefs. In 1681, in settlement of Charles II's debt to his father, he was granted land in America, and founded the colony of Pennsylvania as a refuge for persecuted Quakers.

22 This day my country was confirmed to me under the great seal of England, with large powers and privileges, by the name of *Pennsylvania*; a name the king would give it in honor of my father.
1681 Letter to Robert Turner, 14 Mar.

23 Inquire often, but judge rarely, and thou wilt not often be mistaken.
1693 Some Fruits of Solitude.

People's Daily

The official daily newspaper of the Communist Party of China. Speaking for the Chinese government, in 1979 a series of articles denounced the Democracy Wall Movement. Changan Road in Beijing had been a centre for posters and news-sheets demanding democratic rights.

24 The imperialists brought the Chinese people cannons rather than flowers, death instead of 'human rights'… How can they be in a position to instruct us on 'civil rights'?
1979 People's Daily, 22 Mar.

Pepys, Samuel 1633–1703

English civil servant and diarist. He rose in the naval service to become Secretary to the Admiralty, 1672. His diary, covering the years 1660 to 1669, is an important historical and social document.

25 Boys do now cry 'Kiss my Parliament!' instead of 'Kiss my arse!' so great and general a contempt is the Rump come to among all men, good and bad.
1660 Diary entry, 7 Feb. The Rump Parliament was that which persisted after the fall of Richard Cromwell, and before the restoration of Charles II.

26 And so to bed.
1660 Diary entry, 20 Apr and passim.

27 A silk suit, which cost me much money, and I pray God to make me able to pay for it.
1660 Diary entry, 1 Jul.

28 I went out to Charing Cross to see Major-General Harrison hanged, drawn and quartered—which was done there—he looking as cheerfully as any man could do in that condition… Thus it was my chance to see the King beheaded at Whitehall and to see the first blood shed in revenge for the blood of the King at Charing Cross.
1660 Diary entry, 13 Oct.

29 A good honest and painful sermon.
1661 Diary entry, 17 Mar.

30 But methought it lessened my esteem of a king, that he should not be able to command the rain.
1662 Diary entry, 19 Jul.

31 I see it is impossible for the King to have things done as cheap as other men.
1662 Diary entry, 21 Jul.

32 To the King's Theatre, where we saw *Midsummer Night's Dream,* which I had never seen before, nor shall ever again, for it is the most insipid, ridiculous play that ever I ever saw in my life.
1662 Diary entry, 29 Sep.

33 But Lord! to see the absurd nature of Englishmen, that cannot forbear laughing and jeering at everything that looks strange.
1662 Diary entry, 27 Nov.

34 Then over the park (where I first in my life, it being a great frost, did see people sliding with their skates, which is a very pretty art).
1662 Diary entry, 1 Dec.

35 My wife, who, poor wretch, is troubled with her lonely life.
1662 Diary entry, 19 Dec.

36 After dinner to the Duke's house, and there saw *Twelfth Night* acted well, though it be but a silly play.
1663 Diary entry, 6 Jan.

37 Most of their discourse was about hunting, in a dialect I understand very little.
1663 Diary entry, 22 Nov.

38 To the Tennis Court, and there saw the King play at tennis and others; but to see how the King's play was extolled, without any cause at all, was a loathsome sight.
1664 Diary entry, 4 Jan.

39 Up, and by coach to Sir Ph. Warwickes, the street being full of footballs, it being a great frost.
1665 Diary entry, 3 Jan. Frost restricted the amount of horse traffic in the streets of London, making football a possibility.

40 This day, much against my will, I did in Drury Lane see two or three houses marked with a red cross upon the doors, and 'Lord have mercy upon us' writ there—which was a sad sight to me, being the first of that kind that to my remembrance I ever saw.
1665 Diary entry, 7 Jun. The houses were afflicted with bubonic plague, which lasted in London until the summer of 1666.

41 Up, all of us, and to Billiards.
1665 Diary entry, 17 Jul.

42 The people die so, that now it seems they are fain to carry the dead to be buried by daylight, the nights not sufficing to do it in. And my Lord Mayor commands people to be within at 9 at night, all (as they say) that the sick may have liberty to go abroad for ayre.
1665 Diary entry, 12 Aug.

43 And it is a wonder what will be the fashion after the plague is done as to periwigs, for nobody will dare to buy any haire for fear of the infection—that it had been cut off the heads of people dead of the plague.
1665 Diary entry, 3 Sep.

44 Strange to say what delight we married people have to see these poor fools decoyed into our condition.
1665 Diary entry, 25 Dec.

45 Music and women I cannot but give way to, whatever my business is.
1666 Diary entry, 9 Mar.

46 Poor people staying in their houses as long as till the very fire touched them, and then running into boats or clambering from one pair of stair by the waterside to another. And among other things, the poor pigeons I perceive were loath to leave their houses, but hovered about the windows and balconies till they were some of them burned, their wings, and fell down.
1666 Diary entry, 2 Sep. The Great Fire of London continued for four days, destroying four-fifths of the total area of the city.

47 A most horrid malicious bloody flame… It made me weep to see it.
1666 Observing the Great Fire of London. Diary entry, 2 Sep.

48 Hardly one lighter or boat in three that had the goods of a house in, but there was a pair of virginalls in it.
1666 Describing the chaos on the Thames as people attempted to rescue their possessions from the flames. Diary entry, 2 Sep.

49 But it is pretty to see what money will do.
1668 Diary entry, 21 Mar.

Percy, Walker 1916–90

US novelist. His best-known work of fiction is *The Moviegoer* (1961), but he wrote several novels, and volumes of collected essays and non-fiction.

50 As Einstein once said, ordinary life in an ordinary day in the modern world is a dreary business. I mean *dreary*. People will do anything just to escape this dreariness.
1977 Interview in *Esquire*, Dec.

51 Unlike God the artist does not start with nothing and make something of it. He starts with himself as nothing and makes something of the nothing with the things at hand.
1977 Interview in *Esquire*, Dec.

Perdue, Franklin P

US businessman, former chief executive of Perdue Farms Inc.

52 I hate pudgy poultry.
1987 In the *New Yorker*, 6 Jul.

Perelman, S(ydney) J(oseph) 1904–79

US humorist. He was a scriptwriter, and later one of the circle of wits who wrote for the *New Yorker*. He published a number of books.

53 I have Bright's disease and he has mine, sobbed the panting palooka.
1929 In *Judge*, 16 Nov. A palooka is US slang for a clumsy person, especially in sports.

54 Crazy Like a Fox.
1944 Title of book.

55 A feeling of emulsion swept over me.
1944 *Crazy Like a Fox*, 'The Love Decoy'.

56 He bit his lip in a manner which immediately awakened my maternal sympathy, and I helped him bite it.
1944 *Crazy Like a Fox*, 'The Love Decoy'.

57 I guess I'm just an old mad scientist at bottom. Give me an underground laboratory, half a dozen atomsmashers, and a beautiful girl in a diaphanous veil waiting to be turned into a chimpanzee, and I care not who writes the nation's laws.
1944 *Crazy Like a Fox*, 'Captain Future, Block That Kick'.

58 She had the rippling muscles of a panther, the solidity of a water buffalo, and the lazy insolence of a shoe salesman.
1944 *Crazy Like a Fox*, 'Kitchen Bouquet'.

59 For years I have let dentists ride roughshod over my teeth; I have been sawed, hacked, chopped, whittled, bewitched, bewildered, tattooed, and signed on again; but this is cuspid's last stand.
1944 *Crazy Like a Fox*, 'Nothing But the Tooth'.

60 You've got a sharp tongue in your head, Mr Essick. Look out it doesn't cut your throat.
1961 *The Rising Gorge*, 'All Out…'.

61 English life, while very pleasant, is rather bland. I expected kindness and gentility and I found it, but there is such a thing as too much couth.
1971 In the *Observer*, 24 Sep.

62 The dogs had eaten the upholstery of a Packard convertible that afternoon, and were consequently somewhat subdued.
1981 *The Last Laugh*, 'The Last Laugh'.

Peres, Shimon 1923–

Israeli statesman. In 1994 he shared the Nobel peace prize with Yasser Arafat and Yitzhak Rabin.

63 Television has made dictatorship impossible, but democracy unbearable.
1995 In the *Financial Times*, 31 Jan.

Pericles c.490–429 BC

Athenian statesman, who initiated democratic reforms and a great building programme (including the Parthenon). His famous *epitaphios* (Funerary Oration on the death of the first year of the Peloponnesian War) was reported by Thucydides. He died of the plague which struck Athens in 430 BC.

64 Famous men have the whole earth as their memorial.
Quoted in Thucydides *History of the Peloponnesian War*, 2.43 (translated by R Warner, 1961)

65 Your great glory is not to be inferior to what you have been given by nature, and the greatest glory of a woman is to be least talked about by men, whether they are praising or criticizing you.
Address to women in the Funerary Oration. Quoted in Thucydides *History of the Peloponnesian War*, 2.45.2 (translated by R Warner, 1961).

Perkins, Carl 1932–98

US songwriter and composer. A key figure of early rock 'n' roll, his guitar playing combined blues and country music.

66 Don't you step on my blue suede shoes.
1956 'Blue Suede Shoes'.

Perkins, Frances 1882–1965

US social reformer and politician. Educated at Mount Holyoke College, Massachusetts, she was the first woman to hold Cabinet rank in the US. She was appointed US Secretary of Labor (1933–45) in President Franklin D Roosevelt's Cabinet.

67 No one had any measure of its progress; no one had any plan for stopping it. Everyone tried to get out of its way.
On the depression of the 1930s which inspired her to set up the Social Security system. Recalled on her death, 14 May 1965.

Perry, Grayson 1960–

English potter who won the Turner Prize in 2003.

68 It's about time a transvestite potter won the Turner Prize.
2003 In his acceptance speech, referring to his habit of dressing as his alter ego, Claire.

Persius properly *Aulus Persius Flaccus* AD 34–62

Roman satirist and Stoic. Only one book of satires has survived.

69 *Quis leget haec?*
Who'll read that sort of thing?
Satirae, no.1, 1.2 (translated by W S Merwin, 1961).

Perth, James, 4th Earl of 1648–1716

Scottish Justice-General (1682) and Chancellor (1684). He was imprisoned in Stirling Castle (1688–96), after the fall of James II and VII, but then joined the exiled court of the King at St Germain, where he remained for the rest of his life. He was created Duke of Perth and Knight of the Garter.

70 I have been here a fortnight and I think I shall be here fifteen or twenty days longer, although I do not very

much like the place, for this puddling in a tub continually is no charm to me.
On Venice. Collected in *Letters to his sister the Countess of Erroll, and other members of his family.*

Pessoa, Fernando António Nogueira 1888–1935

Portuguese poet, an important figure in the Modernist movement.

71 *Sê plural como o universo!*
Be plural, like the universe!
Páginas Íntimas e de Auto-interpretação.

72 *Estrangeiro aqui como em toda a parte.*
I'm a stranger here, as I am everywhere.
1926 *Lisbon Revisited.*

73 *Não sou nada.*
Nunca serei nada.
Não posso querer ser nada.
À parte isso, tenho em mim todos os sonhos do mundo.
I am not nothing.
I will never be nothing.
I cannot ever want to be nothing.
Apart from that, I have in me all the dreams of the world.
1928 *Tabacaria* ('The Tobacconist's').

Pétain, (Henri) Philippe 1856–1951

French soldier and politician. In World War I his defence of Verdun (1916) made him a national hero, and he became Commander-in-Chief (1917) and Marshal of France (1918). When France collapsed in 1940, he negotiated the armistice with Germany and Italy, became chief of state, and collaborated with Germany in an attempt to keep France out of the war. He is regarded by some as a patriot, by others as a traitor.

74 They shall not pass.
This phrase came to symbolize the stubborn defence of Verdun against Ludendorf's siege, which cost 300,000 German and 400,000 French troops.
➥ *See Ibarruri Gomez 427:31.*

75 I was with you in the days of glory. At the head of the Government, I shall remain with you during the days of darkness. Stay by my side.
1940 Radio broadcast announcing his intention to seek an armistice, 20 Jun.

Peter, Laurence J 1919–90

Canadian academic and writer, professor at the University of South California.

76 In a hierarchy every employee tends to rise to his level of incompetence; the cream rises until it sours.
1969 *The Peter Principle*, ch.1 (with Raymond Hull).

77 Bureaucracy defends the status quo long past the time when the quo has lost its status.
1978 In the *San Francisco Chronicle*, 29 Jan.

Peters, Richard Stanley 1919–

English educationalist, Professor of the Philosophy of Education at the University of London Institute of Education (1962–82). He has written widely on education.

78 What matters is not what any individual thinks, but what is true. A teacher who does not equip his pupils with the

rudimentary tools to discover this is substituting indoctrination for teaching.
1966 *Ethics and Education.*

Petersen, Henry Edward 1921–

US Assistant Attorney General for Prosecutions. He went from clerk to chief of the organized crime and racketeering section of the FBI, Washington (1948–69).

79 What you have just said, Mr President, speaks very well of you as a man. It does not speak well of you as a president.
1973 On President Nixon's remark that he would need proof of the guilt of aides John Ehrichman and H R Hadelman on the Watergate break-in and cover-up before he could fire them. Quoted in Richard M Nixon *RN: The Memoirs of Richard Nixon* (1978).

Petersen, Wolfgang 1941–

German film director.

80 It has been condensed and moved around a bit. And we left out the gods.
2004 On how he adapted Homer to make the film *Troy.* Quoted in *The Scotsman*, 14 May.

Petrarch (Francesco Petrarca) 1304–74

Italian poet and classical scholar, responsible for the discovery of several works, including Cicero's letters and two of his orations, and a portion of Quintilian's *De Oratio.* In 1341 he was crowned Poet Laureate in Rome. Most famous for the lyrics of his *Canzionere,* he also composed prose treatises, historical works, and letters.

81 *Continue morimur, ego dum hec scribo, tu dum leges, alii dum audient dumque non audient, ego quoque dum hec leges moriar, tu moreris dum hec scribo, ambo morimur, omnes morimur, semper morimur.*
We are dying continuously: I while I write this, you while you read it, others while they hear or do not hear it. I will be dying as you read this, you will be dying as I write it. We are both dying, we are all dying, we are always dying.
c.1360 Letter to Philippe de Cabassoles.

Petronius Arbiter d. AD 66

Roman satirical writer, usually thought to be the Gaius Petronius whom Tacitus calls the 'arbiter elegantiae' at the court of Nero. His *Satyricon* wittily depicts the licentious life of the moneyed class of freedmen in southern Italy.

82 *Abiit ad plures.*
He has gone to the majority.
(ie He has died.) *Satyricon*, 42.

83 *Qualis dominus talis est servus.*
Like master like man.
Satyricon, 58.

Petty, Sir William 1623–87

English physician and pioneer economist. From humble beginnings he rose to become Professor of Anatomy at Oxford and of Music at Gresham's College, London. As Physician-General to Cromwell's army he acquired an immense fortune, and he was a founder of the Royal Society of London.

84 If a man bring to London an ounce of Silver out of the Earth in Peru in the same time that he can produce a

bushel of Corn, then one is the natural price of the other.
1662 *Treatise of Taxes.*

85 Labour is the Father and active principle of Wealth, as lands are the Mother.
1662 *Treatise of Taxes.*

86 Instead of using only comparative Words and intellectual Arguments, I have taken the course…to express myself in Terms of Number, Weight, or Measure; to use only Arguments of Sense, and to consider only such Causes, as have visible Foundations in Nature.
1690 *Political Arithmetick.*

Phelps, Edward John 1822–1900

US lawyer and diplomat.

87 The man who makes no mistakes does not usually make anything.
1889 In a speech given in London.

Philby, Kim 1912–88

British double-agent.

88 To betray, you must first belong.
1967 In the *Sunday Times*, 17 Dec.

Philip II 1527–98

King of Spain (1556–98), Naples and Sicily (1554–98) and Portugal (1580–98). He married Mary I in 1554, becoming joint sovereign of England until her death in 1558. A secular champion of the Counter-Reformation, he had more success against Turks than Protestant Dutch and English.

89 England's chief defence depends upon the navy being always ready to defend the realm against invasion.
c.1555 Submission to the Privy Council while King-Consort of England.

Philips, Ambrose c.1675–1749

English poet.

90 The flowers anew, returning seasons bring;
But beauty faded has no second spring.
1708 *The First Pastoral*, 'Lobbin'.

Philips, Katherine née *Fowler* 1632–64

English poet. Her reputation was greater during her brief life, when she was known as 'the Matchless Orinda', than after her death, but she proved a significant model to later female poets. Her poems were surreptitiously printed in 1664 and issued in 1667.

91 Thus our twin souls in one shall grow,
And teach the world new love,
Redeem the age and sex, and show
A flame fate dares not move:
And courting death to be our friend,
Our lives, together too, shall end.
1664 'To Mrs. M. A. at Parting'.

92 I did but see him, and he disappeared,
I did but touch the rosebud, and it fell;
A sorrow unforeseen and scarcely feared,
So ill can mortals their afflictions spell.
'On the Death of My First and Dearest Child, Hector Philips'. (Issued 1667).

Phillips, Arthur Angell 1900–85

Australian academic and literary critic. He wrote for the Melbourne literary journal *Meanjin* and much of his critical writing was collected as *Responses* (1971).

93 Cultural Cringe.
1950 On Australia's reliance on British cultural values. In *Meanjin*.

Phillips, Edward O 1931–

Canadian novelist.

94 To grow older is to realize the universe is Copernican, not Ptolemaic, and that self and the loved one do not form the epicentre of the solar system.
1990 *Sunday Best*.

Phillips, Wendell 1811–84

US abolitionist, born in Boston, Massachusetts. Called to the Bar in 1834, by 1837 he was chief orator of the anti-slavery party, associated with William Lloyd Garrison.

95 Some doubt the courage of the Negro. Go to Haiti and stand on those fifty thousand graves of the best soldiers France ever had, and ask them what they think of the Negro's sword.
1861 Address on Toussaint l'Ouverture, referring to the War of Haitian Independence, 1804.

Picasso, Pablo Ruiz y 1881–1973

Spanish painter, graphic artist, sculptor and ceramicist. The melancholy studies of his early 'blue period' (1902–4) gave way to a life-affirming 'pink period' (1904–6). In later works he moved towards Cubism, along with Georges Braque.

96 There is no abstract art. You must always start with something. Afterward you can remove all traces of reality.
1935 In an interview with Christian Zervos, editor of *Cahiers d'Art*, translated by Alfred H Barr Jr in his *Picasso: Fifty Years of His Art* (1946).

97 Art is not the application of a canon of beauty but what the instinct and the brain can conceive beyond any canon. When we love a woman we don't start measuring her limbs.
1935 In an interview with Christian Zervos, editor of *Cahiers d'Art*, translated by Alfred H Barr Jr in his *Picasso: Fifty Years of His Art* (1946).

98 No, painting is not done to decorate apartments. It is an instrument of war for attack and defense against the enemy.
1945 Responding to claims that his Communism was a mere caprice. Quoted in Alfred H Barr Jr *Picasso: Fifty Years of His Art* (1946).

99 I paint objects as I think them, not as I see them.
Quoted in John Golding *Cubism* (1959).

1 God is really only another artist. He invented the giraffe, the elephant, and the cat. He has no real style. He just goes on trying other things.
Quoted in F Gilot and C Lake *Life with Picasso* (1964), pt.1.

2 We all know that art is not truth. Art is a lie that makes us realize truth.
Quoted in Dore Ashton *Picasso on Art* (1972).

Pickens, T(homas) Boone, Jr 1928–

US oilman and hydrocarbon investor, a geologist with Phillips

Petroleum Co (1951–5) then founder and chair of Mesa Petroleum Co until 1996.

3 Work eight hours and sleep eight hours and make sure they are not the same.
   1992 In NPR broadcast, 28 May.

Pickford, Mary *originally* **Gladys Mary Smith** 1893–1979

US actress, born in Canada. Known as 'America's sweetheart', she played innocent heroines in a series of silent films (1909–29), and made her sound debut in 1929.

4 Adding sound to movies would be like putting lipstick on the Venus de Milo.
   Recalled on her death, 29 May 1979.

Pierce, C(harles) S(aunders) 1839–1914

US philosopher.

5 It is the man of science, eager to have his every opinion regenerated, his every idea rationalized, by drinking at the fountain of fact, and devoting all the energies of his life to the cult of truth, not as he understands it, but as he does not yet understand it, that ought properly to be called a philosopher.
   Selected Writings, 'Lessons on the History of Science'.

Piercy, Marge 1936–

US novelist and poet. Novels including *Woman on the Edge of Time* (1975) trace the emerging feminist consciousness of the post-1960s generation. Later works include the novel *Three Women* (1999) and the volume of poetry *Colors Passing Through Us* (2003).

6 Burning dinner is not incompetence but war.
   1983 *Stone, Paper, Knife*, 'What's that smell in the kitchen?'

7 Your anger was a climate I inhabited
   like a desert in a dry frigid weather
   of high thin air and ivory sun,
   sand dunes the wind lifted into stinging
   clouds that blinded and choked me
   where the only ice was in the blood.
   1983 *Stone, Paper, Knife*, 'The Weight'.

8 On this twelfth day of my diet
   I would rather die satiated
   than slim.
   1983 *Stone, Paper, Knife*, 'On Mental Corsets'.

9 Art is a game only if you play at it,
   a mirror that reflects from the inside out.
   1983 *Stone, Paper, Knife*, 'Stone, Paper, Knife'.

10 Hope sleeps in our bones like a bear
   waiting for spring to rise and walk.
   1983 *Stone, Paper, Knife*, 'Stone, Paper, Knife'.

Piero della Francesca c.1420–1492

Italian Renaissance painter.

11 Painting is nothing but a representation of surfaces and solids foreshortened or enlarged, and put on the plane of the picture in accordance with the fashion in which the real objects seen by the eye appear on this plane.
   c.1480–1490 *De Prospectiva Pingendi*.

Piggott, Lester Keith 1935–

English jockey. He became champion jockey 11 times, from 1948, and totalled 30 Classic winners, including nine Derbies.

12 People ask me why I ride with my bottom in the air. Well, I've got to put it somewhere.
   Quoted in Colin Jarman *The Guinness Dictionary of Sports Quotations* (1990).

13 When I won the Derby on Never Say Die I went home and cut the lawn. I haven't cut the lawn since.
   2004 In the *Observer*, 30 May.

Piglia, Ricardo 1941–

Argentinian novelist and critic.

14 *Sencillamente se me ocurre que la parodia se ha desplazado y hoy invade los gestos, las acciones. Donde antes había acontecimientos, experiencias, pasiones, hoy quedan sólo parodias. Eso trataba a veces de decirle a Marcelo en mis cartas: que la parodia ha sustitutido por completo a la historia.*
   It's simply that I believe that parody has been displaced and that it now invades all gestures and actions. Where there used to be events, experiences, passions, now there are nothing but parodies. This is what I tried to tell Marcelo so many times in my letters: that parody had completely replaced history.
   1980 *Respiración artificial*, pt.2, ch.4 (translated as *Artificial Respiration*, 1994).

Pigou, Arthur Cecil 1877–1959

English economist, a professor at Cambridge (1908–43).

15 If a man marries his housekeeper or his cook, the national dividend is diminished.
   1920 *Economics of Welfare*.

Pilger, John 1939–

Australian journalist, writer and film-maker highly regarded for his investigative work in Vietnam and Cambodia. His documentary films include *Year Zero—The Silent Death of Cambodia* (1979), *Death of a Nation* (1994), about the slaughter in East Timor, and *Breaking the Silence: Truth and Lies in the War on Terror* (2003).

16 I used to see Vietnam as a war rather than a country.
   1978 *Do you remember Vietnam?*

17 What Nixon and Kissinger began, Pol Pot completed.
   Collected in *Distant Voices* (1992).

Pindar c.522–440 BC

Greek lyric poet, born near Thebes in Boeotia.

18 Seek not, my soul, immortal life, but make the most of the resources that are within your reach.
   Pythia, 3.109.

Pinochet Ugarte, Augusto 1915–

Chilean soldier and dictator. He led the coup that overthrew the government of Salvador Allende (1973) and in 1980 enacted a constitution giving himself an eight-year presidential term (1981–9); he retained his military command until 1998, the year he was arrested in the UK at the request of Spain. General Pinochet was ruled unfit to face extradition, and in 2000 returned to Chile where attempts have been made to remove his immunity from prosecution.

19 I am not a dictator. It's just that I have a grumpy face.
   Attributed.

Pinter, Harold 1930–

English playwright, director and actor. Such early plays as *The Birthday Party* (1958) were dismissed as obscure, but after *The Caretaker* (1960) his work underwent a reappraisal and he was acknowledged as one of the most interesting playwrights of his generation. Subsequent works for the stage have included *The Homecoming* (1965) and *Celebration* (1999). He has also written numerous filmscripts, including *The Servant* (1963) and *The French Lieutenant's Woman* (1981).

20 If only I could get down to Sidcup! I've been waiting for the weather to break. He's got my papers, this man I left them with, it's got it all down there, I could prove everything.
   1960 *The Caretaker*, act 1.

21 The weasel under the cocktail cabinet.
   1962 His reply when asked what his plays were about. Quoted in J Russell Taylor *Anger and After*.

22 I no longer feel banished from myself.
   1995 On completing his first full-length play in 17 years. In *Newsweek*, 18 Sep.

Pirandello, Luigi 1867–1936

Italian playwright, novelist and short-story writer. His play *Right You Are (If You Think You Are)* (1917) was followed by such innovative works as *Six Characters in Search of an Author* (1921), *Enrico IV* (1922) and *Tonight We Improvise* (1929). He was awarded a Nobel prize in 1934.

23 Six Characters in Search of an Author.
   1921 Title of play (translated 1922).

24 Drama is action, sir, action and not confounded philosophy.
   1921 *Six Characters in Search of an Author* (translated 1922).

Pirsig, Robert M(aynard) 1928–

US writer. His most noted book is *Zen and the Art of Motorcycle Maintenance* (1974), a rumination on life and technology after a cross-country motorcycle trip.

25 The Buddha, the Godhead, resides quite as comfortably in the circuits of a digital computer or the gears of a cycle transmission as he does at the top of a mountain or in the petals of a flower.
   1974 *Zen and the Art of Motorcycle Maintenance*, pt.1, ch.1.

26 When people are fanatically dedicated to political or religious faiths or any other kind of dogmas or goals, it's always because these dogmas or goals are in doubt.
   1974 *Zen and the Art of Motorcycle Maintenance*, pt.2, ch.3.

27 Mental reflection is so much more interesting than TV it's a shame more people don't switch over to it. They probably think what they hear is unimportant but it never is.
   1974 *Zen and the Art of Motorcycle Maintenance*, pt.3, ch.17.

28 One thing about pioneers that you don't hear mentioned is that they are invariably, by their nature, mess-makers.
   1974 *Zen and the Art of Motorcycle Maintenance*, pt.3, ch.21.

29 One geometry can not be more true than another; it can only be more *convenient*. Geometry is not true, it is advantageous.
   1974 *Zen and the Art of Motorcycle Maintenance*, pt.3, ch.22.

30 Traditional scientific method has always been at the very *best*, 20-20 hindsight. It's good for seeing where you've been. It's good for testing the truth of what you think you know, but it can't tell you where you *ought* to go.
   1974 *Zen and the Art of Motorcycle Maintenance*, pt.3, ch.24.

31 That's the classical mind at work, runs fine inside but looks dingy on the surface.
   1974 *Zen and the Art of Motorcycle Maintenance*, pt.3, ch.26.

Pissarro, Camille 1830–1903

French Impressionist artist. Most of his works were painted in or around Paris.

32 But as I see it, the most corrupt art is the sentimental—the art of orange blossoms which make pale women swoon.
   1883 Letter to his son Lucien.

33 Watercolour is not especially difficult, but I must warn you to steer clear of those pretty English watercolourists, so skilful and alas so weak, and so often too truthful.
   1883 Letter to his son Lucien, Jul.

34 Draw more and more often—remember Degas.
   1883 Letter to his son Lucien, Oct.

35 Observe that it is a grave error to believe that all mediums of art are not closely tied to their time.
   1898 Letter to his son Lucien.

Pitt, William, 1st Earl of Chatham *known as* **the Elder** 1708–78

English statesman and orator. In 1756 he became Secretary of State, virtual Prime Minister. Forced to resign in 1757 by George II, he was recalled by public demand but resigned again in 1761 when his Cabinet refused to declare war on Spain. He formed a new ministry in 1766, but resigned in ill health (1768).

36 The atrocious crime of being a young man, which [Walpole] has, with such spirit and decency, charged upon me, I shall neither attempt to palliate nor deny; but content myself with wishing that I may be one of those whose follies cease with their youth, and not of those who continue ignorant in spite of their age and experience.
   1741 Speech to the House of Commons, 6 Mar.

37 It is now apparent that this great, this powerful, this formidable kingdom is considered only as a province of a despicable electorate.
   1742 Speech to the House of Commons, 10 Dec.

38 I know that I can save this country and that no one else can.
   1756 In conversation with one of his private secretaries, Nov.

39 I was called by my sovereign and by the voice of the people to assist the State when others had abdicated the service of it. That being so, no one can be surprised that I will go on no longer, since my advice is not taken. Being responsible, I will direct—and will be responsible for nothing that I do not direct.
   1761 On informing Cabinet of his resignation, 3 Oct.

40 I rejoice that America has resisted. Three millions of people, so dead to all the feelings of liberty, as voluntarily to submit to be slaves, would have been fit instruments to make slaves of the rest.

1766 Speech to the House of Commons, 14 Jan.

41 Where laws end, tyranny begins.
1770 Speech to the House of Lords, 2 Mar.

42 The spirit that now resists your taxation in America is…the same spirit that established the great fundamental, essential maxim of your liberties—that no subject of England shall be taxed but by his own consent. The glorious spirit of Whiggism animates three million in America, who prefer poverty with liberty to gilded chains and sordid affluence; and who will die in defence of their rights as men, as free men.
1775 Speech to the House of Lords, 20 Jan.

43 You cannot conquer America.
1777 Speech to the House of Lords, 18 Nov.

44 If I were an American, as I am an Englishman, while a foreign troop was landed in my country, I never would lay down my arms—never—never—never!
1777 Speech to the House of Lords, 18 Nov.

Pitt, William *known as* **the Younger** 1759–1806

English statesman and Prime Minister (1783–1801, 1804–6), son of William Pitt, the Elder. Elected MP in 1781, he became Chancellor in 1782 and Britain's youngest-ever Prime Minister in 1783. He resigned over the King's opposition to the union with Ireland in 1801 but returned in 1804 to lead a coalition of European powers against Napoleon.

45 I am sure that the immediate abolition of the slave trade is the first, the principal, the most indispensable act of policy, of duty and of justice the legislature of this country has to take, if it is indeed their wish to secure those important objects… For we continue to this hour a barbarous traffic in slaves, we continue it even yet, in spite of all our great and undeniable pretensions as civilisation.
1792 Speech to the House of Commons, 2 Apr. The House did not abolish slavery until 1806.

46 We must recollect…what it is we have at stake, what it is we have to contend for. It is for our property, it is for our liberty, it is for our independence, nay for our existence as a nation; it is for our character, it is for our very name as Englishmen, it is for everything dear and valuable to man on this side of the grave.
1803 Speech, 22 Jul, on the breaking of the Peace of Amiens and the resumption of the war with Napoleon. Quoted in *Speeches of the Rt. Hon. William Pitt* (1806), vol.4.

47 Amid the wreck and the misery of nations it is our just exaltation that we have continued superior to all that ambition or despotism could effect; and our still higher exaltation ought to be that we provide not only for our own safety but hold out a prospect for nations now bending under the yoke of tyranny of what the exertions of a free people can effect.
1804 Speech to the House of Commons, 25 Apr.

48 Roll up that map; it will not be wanted these ten years.
1805 Of a map of Europe. Remark on hearing of Napoleon's victory at Austerlitz, Dec. Quoted in Earl Stanhope *Life of the Rt. Hon. William Pitt*, vol.4 (1862), ch.43.

49 England has saved herself by her exertions, and will, as I trust, save Europe by her example.
1805 Replying to a toast in which he had been described as the saviour of his country in the wars with France. Quoted in R Coupland *War Speeches of William Pitt* (1915).

50 I think that I could eat one of Bellamy's veal pies.
1806 Attributed last words, 23 Jan.

Pittacus of Mytilene   650–570 BC

Greek ruler, one of the Seven Wise Men of Greece.

51 Know thine opportunity.
Attributed. Quoted in *Chambers Biographical Dictionary* (5th edn, 1990).

Pius II *real name* **Enea Silvio de Piccolomini**   1405–64

Italian-born churchman, Pope from 1458. After entering the service of Emperor Frederick II he took orders, becoming Bishop of Trieste and, on returning to Italy (1456), Cardinal then Pope. He tried unsuccessfully to organize a crusade against the Turks.

52 Of the two lights of Christendom, one has been extinguished.
1453 Attributed, on hearing of the fall of Constantinople to the Turks, 29 May.

53 Glorious deeds are not embraced by democracies, least of all by merchants, who, being by their nature intent on profit, loathe those splendid things that cannot be achieved without expense.
1584 *Commentaries*. Quoted in J H Plumb (ed) *The Horizon Book of the Renaissance* (1961, new edn by Penguin, 1982).

54 Nothing gives the Scots more pleasure than to hear the English abused.
1584 *Commentaries*. Quoted in J H Plumb (ed) *The Horizon Book of the Renaissance* (1961, new edn by Penguin, 1982).

Pius XII *real name* **Eugenio Pacelli**   1876–1958

Italian-born churchman, Pope from 1939.

55 Sport, rightly conceived, is an occupation carried out by the whole man. It renders the body a more perfect instrument of the soul and at the same time makes the soul itself a finer instrument of the whole man in seeking for Truth and in transmitting it to others. In this way it helps a man to reach that End to which all other ends are subordinate, the service and the greater glory of his Creator.
1945 Speech to the Central School of Sports of the USA, 29 Jul.

Pizzaro, Eddie

US stonecarver.

56 We're not all perfect, but we can do something perfect.
1990 On his work at New York's Cathedral of St John the Divine. Quoted in the *New York Times*, 14 Jul.

Planck, Max Karl Ernst   1858–1947

German physicist. He hypothesized that atoms emit and absorb energy only in discrete bundles called quanta and laid the foundations for quantum theory, the basis of contemporary theorizing in physics. He received the 1918 Nobel prize in physics for his work on radiation.

57 Science cannot exist without some small portion of metaphysics.
1931 *The Universe in the Light of Modern Physics*, ch.7.

58 Scientific discovery and scientific knowledge have been achieved only by those who have gone in pursuit of them without any practical purpose whatsoever in view.
1932 *Where is Science Going?* pt.4 (translated by James Murphy).

59 Science cannot solve the ultimate mystery of nature. And that is because, in the last analysis, we ourselves are part of nature and therefore part of the mystery that we are trying to solve.
1932 *Where is Science Going?* pt.4 (translated by James Murphy).

60 A new scientific truth does not triumph by convincing its opponents and making them see the light, but rather because its opponents eventually die, and a new generation grows up that is familiar with it.
A Scientific Autobiography and Other Papers (translated by Frank Gaynor, published 1949).

Plante, Jacques 1929–86

Canadian hockey player, a leading goalkeeper.

61 How would you like a job where, every time you make a mistake, a big red light goes on and 18,000 people boo?
Attributed. Quoted in John Robert Colombo (ed) *Colombo's All-Time Great Canadian Quotations* (1994).

Plath, Sylvia 1932–63

US poet who settled in England after her marriage to Ted Hughes. Her poetry and her only novel, *The Bell Jar* (1963), are deeply introspective. She committed suicide, and much of her work was published posthumously.

62 I am afraid of getting married. Spare me from cooking three meals a day—spare me from the relentless cage of routine and rote.
1949 Diary entry, 13 Nov. Collected in Aurelia Schober Plath (ed) *Letters Home by Sylvia Plath*, 'Diary Supplement' (1949).

63 I could never be a complete scholar or a complete housewife or a complete writer: I must combine a little of all, and thereby be imperfect in all.
1956 Letter to her mother, Aurelia Schober Plath, 25 Feb. Collected in Aurelia Schober Plath (ed) *Letters Home by Sylvia Plath* (1949).

64 Apparently, the most difficult feat for a Cambridge male is to accept a woman not merely as feeling, not merely as thinking, but as managing a complex, vital interweaving of both.
1956 Written while a student at Cambridge University, in *Isis*, 6 May.

65 Love set you going like a fat gold watch. The midwife slapped your footsoles, and your bald cry Took its place among the elements.
1961 'Morning Song', published posthumously by Ted Hughes (*Ariel*, 1965).

66 A sort of walking miracle, my skin Bright as a Nazi lampshade.
1962 'Lady Lazarus', published posthumously by Ted Hughes (*Ariel*, 1965).

67 Dying,
Is an art, like everything else.
I do it exceptionally well.
1962 'Lady Lazarus', published posthumously by Ted Hughes (*Ariel*, 1965).

68 Out of the ash
I rise with my red hair
And I eat men like air.
1962 'Lady Lazarus', published posthumously by Ted Hughes (*Ariel*, 1965).

69 Not God but a swastika
So black no sky could squeak through.

Every woman adores a Fascist,
The boot in the face, the brute
Brute heart of a brute like you.
1962 'Daddy', published posthumously by Ted Hughes (*Ariel*, 1965).

70 Daddy, daddy, you bastard, I'm through.
1962 'Daddy', published posthumously by Ted Hughes (*Ariel*, 1965).

71 Winter is for women—
The woman still at her knitting,
At the cradle of Spanish walnut,
Her body a bulb in the cold and too dumb to think.
1962 'Wintering', published posthumously by Ted Hughes (*Ariel*, 1965).

72 I saw my life branching out before me like the green fig-tree in the story.
From the tip of every branch, like a fat purple fig, a wonderful future beckoned and winked. One fig was a husband and a happy home and children, and another fig was a famous poet...I saw myself sitting in the crotch of this fig-tree, starving to death, just because I couldn't make up my mind which of the figs I would choose. I wanted each and every one of them, but choosing one meant losing all the rest, and, as I sat there, unable to decide, the figs began to wrinkle and go black, and, one by one, they plopped to the ground at my feet.
1963 *The Bell Jar*, ch.7.

73 If neurotic is wanting two mutually exclusive things at one and the same time, then I'm neurotic as hell. I'll be flying back and forth between one mutually exclusive thing and another for the rest of my days.
1963 *The Bell Jar*, ch.8.

Platini, Michel 1955–

French footballer. He scored a record 41 goals in 72 games for France (winning the European championship in 1984). He retired as a player in 1987 and was France's manager from then until 1992.

74 What Zidane does with a ball Maradona could do with an orange.
2000 In *The Independent*, 23 Dec.

Plato c.428–c.348 BC

Greek philosopher, a pupil of Socrates and the teacher of Aristotle. He wrote in the form of dialogues, often with Socrates as a leading character. Some 30 philosophical dialogues and some letters (not all considered genuine) have survived.

75 Let no one ignorant of mathematics enter here.
c.380 BC Inscription over the door of the Academy at Athens.

76 The wisest of you men is he who has realized, like Socrates, that in respect of wisdom he is really worthless.
Apology, 23b (translated by H Tredennick).

77 Socrates is guilty of corrupting the minds of the young, and of believing in deities of his own invention instead of the gods recognized by the state.
The formal indictment in Socrates' trial, quoted in the *Apology*, 24b (translated by H Tredennick).

78 For I spend all my time going about trying to persuade you, young and old, to make your first and chief concern

not for your bodies nor for your possessions, but for the highest welfare of your souls, proclaiming as I go, Wealth does not bring goodness, but goodness brings wealth and every other blessing, both to the individual and to the state.
Apology, 30b (translated by H Tredennick).

79 The unexamined life is not worth living.
Apology, 38a (translated by H Tredennick).

80 Now it is time that we were going, I to die and you to live, but which of us has the happier prospect is unknown to anyone but God.
Apology, 42a (translated by H Tredennick).

81 It is not living, but living well, which we ought to consider most important.
Crito, 48b (translated by H North Fowler, 1923).

82 Your country is more precious and more to be revered and is holier and in higher esteem among the gods and among men of understanding than your mother and your father and all your ancestors.
Crito, 51a–b (translated by H North Fowler, 1923).

83 Men of sound sense have Law for their god, but men without sense Pleasure.
Epistulae, 8. 354e (translated by R G Bury, 1925).

84 To do wrong is the greatest of evils.
Gorgias, 469b (translated by W D Woodhead). There is a similar remark in the *Crito*, 49b.

85 Much more wretched than lack of health in the body, it is to dwell with a soul that is not healthy, but corrupt.
Gorgias, 479b (translated by W R M Lamb, 1967).

86 No one can escape his destiny.
Gorgias, 512e (translated by W R M Lamb, 1967).

87 All the gold upon the earth and all the gold beneath it, does not compensate for lack of virtue.
Leges, 728a (translated by Trevor J Saunders, 1970).

88 Every unjust man is unjust against his will.
Leges, 731c (translated by Trevor J Saunders, 1970).

89 Is virtue something that can be taught?
Meno, 70a (translated by W K C Guthrie).

90 If we are ever to have pure knowledge of anything, we must get rid of the body and contemplate things by themselves with the soul by itself.
Phaedo, 66d (translated by H Tredennick).

91 One should die in silence.
Phaedo, 117e (translated by D Gallop, 1993).

92 Crito, we ought to offer a cock to Asclepius. See to it, and don't forget.
Phaedo, 118a (translated by H Tredennick).

93 For myself I am fairly certain that no wise man believes anyone sins willingly or willingly perpetrates any evil or base act.
Protagoras, 345e (translated by W K C Guthrie).

94 We must now examine whether just people also live better and are happier than unjust ones. I think it's clear already that this is so, but we must look into it further, since the argument concerns no ordinary topic, but the way we ought to live.
Republic, bk.1, 352d (translated by G M A Grube, revised by C D C Reeve).

95 Justice is superior to injustice.
Republic, bk.1, 367b (translated by P Shorey, 1953).

96 The most important stage of any enterprise is the beginning.
Republic, bk.2, 377b (translated by R Waterfield, 1993).

97 Justice is doing one's work and not meddling with what isn't one's own.
Republic, bk.4, 433a (translated by G M A Grube, revised by C D C Reeve).

98 Until philosophers rule as kings or those who are now called kings and leading men genuinely and adequately philosophize, that is, until political power and philosophy entirely coincide…cities will have no rest from evils, nor, I think, will the human race.
Republic, bk.5, 473c (translated by G M A Grube, revised by C D C Reeve).

99 Every soul pursues the good and does whatever it does for its sake.
Republic, bk.6, 505e (translated by G M A Grube, revised by C D C Reeve).

1 The power to learn is present in everyone's soul, and the instrument with which each learns is like an eye that cannot be turned around from darkness to light without turning the whole body.
Republic, bk.7, 518c (translated by G M A Grube, revised by C D C Reeve).

2 If the study of all these sciences which we have enumerated, should ever bring us to their mutual association and relationship, and teach us the nature of the ties which bind them together, I believe that the diligent treatment of them will forward the objects which we have in view, and that the labor, which otherwise would be fruitless, will be well bestowed.
Republic, bk.7, 531d (translated by G M A Grube, revised by C D C Reeve).

3 Extreme freedom can't be expected to lead to anything but a change to extreme slavery, whether for a private individual or for a city.
Republic, bk.8, 564a (translated by G M A Grube, revised by C D C Reeve).

4 God is a geometrician.
Quoted in Plutarch *Symposium*.

Plautus, Titus Maccius c.250–184 BC

Roman comic poet, who worked as a trader and craftsman before writing plays in middle life. He became the most important Latin adapter of the Greek New Comedy, which dealt with social life to the exclusion of politics. Only 21 of his comedies have survived.

5 *Lupus est homo homini, non homo, quom qualis sit non novit.*
A man is a wolf, and not a man, to another man, for as long as he doesn't know what he is like.
Asinaria, 495. The phrase is often rendered 'Homo homini lupus' ('Man is a wolf to another man').

Pliny *full name* **Gaius Plinius Secundus** *known as* **the Elder** AD 23–79

Roman statesman, scholar and writer. His only surviving work is his universal encyclopedia, *Historia Naturalis* (37 vols, AD 77). He was killed while observing the eruption of Vesuvius.

6 *Vulgoque veritas iam attributa vino est.*
And truth has come to be proverbially credited to wine.
AD 77 *Historia Naturalis*, bk.14, section 28 (translated by H

Rackham). The phrase is often rendered as 'in vino veritas'.

7 *Addito salis grano.*
With the addition of a pinch of salt.
AD 77 *Historia Naturalis*, bk.23, section 8. This is probably a version of a more ancient proverb, commonly rendered 'cum grano salis'.

Plomer, William 1903–73

South African-born British writer.

8 Out of that bungled, unwise war
An alp of unforgiveness grew.
1960 'The Boer War'.

9 On a sofa upholstered in panther skin
Mona did researches in original sin.
1960 'Mews Flat Mona'.

Plout, David

10 Deathbed utterances, like suicide notes, are a powerful coinage, stamped by an awareness that words can outlive us.
1990 In the *Wall Street Journal*, 26 Sep, reviewing J M Coetzee *Age of Iron* (1990).

Plutarch c.46–c.120 AD

Greek historian, biographer and philosopher. His extant writings include the essays in *Opera Moralia*, and the biographical *Bioi paralleloi* (*Parallel Lives*, translated into English by Thomas North in 1759), a major source for Shakespeare.

11 He who cheats with an oath acknowledges that he is afraid of his enemy, but that he thinks little of God.
Parallel Lives, 'Lysander', ch.8.

12 Though others before him had triumphed three times, Pompeius, by having gained his first triumph over Libya, his second over Europe, and this the last over Asia, seemed in a manner to have brought the whole world into his three triumphs.
Referring to Pompey's victories against the Marian party in Africa, in Spain, and against Mithridates in Asia Minor (c.62 BC).
Parallel Lives, 'Pompeius', ch.45.

Pobedonostsev, Constantin Petrovich 1827–1907

Russian jurist, tutor to Alexander III and Nicholas II. Initially a liberal, he became an uncompromising champion of autocracy and the supremacy of the Russian Orthodox Church, strongly opposed to westernization.

13 Parliaments are the great lie of our time.
Moskovskii Shornik.

Po Chü-I 772–846

Chinese poet and civil servant who rose to become the Governor of a number of different cities in China.

14 But now that age comes
A moment of joy is harder and harder to get.
812 'The Chrysanthemums in the Eastern Garden' (in *Chinese Poems*, translated by Arthur Waley, 1946).

15 Deeper and deeper, one's love of old friends;
Fewer and fewer, one's dealings with young men.
835 *Old Age*.

Poe, Edgar Allan 1809–49

US poet and short-story writer, a pioneer of the modern

detective story, whose poetry emphasizes the beauty of melancholy. He is best known for stories such as 'The Tell-Tale Heart' (1843) and his poem 'The Raven' (1845).

16 I know not how it was—but, with the first glimpse of the building, a sense of insufferable gloom pervaded my spirit… There was an iciness, a sinking, a sickening of the heart—an unredeemed dreariness of thought which no goading of the imagination could torture into aught of the sublime.
1839 'The Fall of the House of Usher', in the *Gentleman's Magazine*, Sep.

17 As the strong man exults in his physical ability, delighting in such exercises as call his muscles into action, so glories the analyst in that moral activity which *disentangles*.
1841 Of detective work. 'The Murders in the Rue Morgue', in the *Gentleman's Magazine*, Apr.

18 It will be found, in fact, that the ingenious are always fanciful, and the *truly* imaginative never otherwise than analytic.
1841 'The Murders in the Rue Morgue', in the *Gentleman's Magazine*, Apr.

19 And now was acknowledged the presence of the Red Death. He had come like a thief in the night. And one by one dropped the revellers in the blood-bedecked halls of their revel, and died each in the despairing posture of his fall.
1842 'The Masque of the Red Death', in the *Gentleman's Magazine*, May.

20 There is something in the unselfish and self-sacrificing love of a brute, which goes directly to the heart of him who has had frequent occasion to test the paltry friendship and gossamer fidelity of mere *Man*.
1843 'The Black Cat', in the *United States Saturday Post*, 19 Aug.

21 I have no faith in human perfectibility… Man is now only more active—not more happy—nor more wise, than he was 6,000 years ago.
1844 Letter to James Russell Lowell, 2 Jul.

22 On desperate seas long wont to roam,
Thy hyacinth hair, thy classic face,
Thy Naiad airs have brought me home
To the glory that was Greece,
And the grandeur that was Rome.
1845 'To Helen', stanza 2.

23 Yes, Heaven is thine; but this
Is a world of sweets and sours;
Our flowers are merely—flowers.
1845 'Israfel', stanza 7.

24 'Take thy beak from out my heart, and take thy form from off my door!'
Quoth the raven, 'Nevermore.'
1845 'The Raven', stanza 17. In *American Review*, Feb 1845.

25 The death… of a beautiful woman is, unquestionably, the most poetical topic in the world.
1846 'The Philosophy of Composition', in *Graham's Magazine*, Apr.

26 Mournful and Never-ending Remembrance.
1846 Of the significance of the bird in his poem 'The Raven'. 'The Philosophy of Composition', in *Graham's Magazine*, Apr.

27 To be *thoroughly* conversant with a Man's heart is to take our final lesson in the iron-clasped volume of despair.

1849 'Marginalia', in the *Southern Literary Messenger*, Jun.

28 The nose of a mob is its imagination. By this, at any time, it can be quietly led.

1849 'Marginalia', in the *Southern Literary Messenger*, Jul.

29 To vilify a great man is the readiest way in which a little man can himself attain greatness.

1849 *Marginalia 1844–49*.

30 Thank Heaven! the crisis—
The danger is past,
And the lingering illness
Is over at last—
And the fever called 'Living'
Is conquered at last.

1850 'For Annie'.

Poelzig, Hans 1869–1936

German Expressionist architect, Professor of Architecture at Breslau Academy of Arts (1900) and later director.

31 We cannot do without the past in solving the architectural problems of our own day.

1906 *Das Deutsche Kunstgewerbe 1906*.

Poincaré, (Jules) Henri 1854–1912

French mathematician and physicist. In his research in the theory of functions he contributed greatly to the field of mathematical physics.

32 If we ought not to fear mortal truth, still less should we dread scientific truth. In the first place it can not conflict with ethics… But if science is feared, it is above all because it can give no happiness… Man, then, can not be happy through science but today he can much less be happy without it.

1904 *The Value of Science*.

33 Science is facts. Just as houses are made of stones, so science is made of facts. But a pile of stones is not a house and a collection of facts is not necessarily a science.

1905 *Science and Hypothesis*, ch.9.

34 The scientist does not study nature because it is useful to do so. He studies it because he takes pleasure in it, and he takes pleasure in it because it is beautiful.

1909 *Science and Method*, vol.1, ch.1 (translated by Francis Maitland).

Poindexter, John Marlan 1936–

US naval officer and statesman, chief of naval operations in the 1970s. He became Reagan's National Security Adviser in 1985. He resigned (Nov 1986) after implication in the Irangate scandal, and was later convicted. His sentence was overturned by the Federal appeals court in 1991. He was head of the Pentagon's controversial Information Awareness Office until 2003.

35 I made a very deliberate decision not to ask the President, so that I could insulate him from the decision and provide some future deniability for him if it ever leaked out.

1987 On his action in diverting funds from arms sales at Iran–Contra hearings, 15 Jul.

Polanski, Roman 1933–

French–Polish film director, scriptwriter and actor, known for such films as *Rosemary's Baby* (1968).

36 The best films are the best because of no one but the director.

Quoted in Leslie Halliwell *Halliwell's Filmgoer's Book of Quotes* (1973).

Pollock, (Paul) Jackson 1912–56

US artist, best known for his technique of pouring or dripping paint on the canvas. A leader of 'action painting' and the Abstract Expressionist movement, his works include the enormous *One* and the monochrome *Echo and Blue Poles*.

37 On the floor I am more at ease, I feel nearer, more a part of the painting, since this way I can walk around it, work from the four sides and literally be 'in' the painting.

1947 Quoted in Italo Tomassoni *Pollock* (1968).

38 Abstract painting is abstract. It confronts you.

Quoted in Francis V O'Connor *Jackson Pollock* (1967).

Polo, Marco c.1254–1324

Venetian trader and traveller. In 1271–5 he accompanied his father and uncle to China and stayed on for 16 years, becoming the envoy of Kublai Khan. He returned to Venice in 1295 and, imprisoned by the Genoese, used his time to dictate his memoirs.

39 Now it came to pass…that the Tartars made them a King whose name was Chinghis Kaan [Genghis Khan]. He was a man of great worth, and of great ability, and valour. And as soon as the news that he had been chosen King was spread abroad through those countries, all the Tartars in the world came to him and owned him for their Lord.

c.1310 Quoted in Col. Henry Yule (ed and trans) *The Book of Ser Marco Polo, the Venetian, Concerning the Kingdoms and Marvels of the East* (1871), 2 vols.

40 I have not told even the half of the things that I have seen.

c.1320 On being accused of exaggeration in his accounts of China. Quoted in R H Poole and P Finch (eds) *Newnes Pictorial Knowledge* (1950), vol.2.

Pol Pot real name Saloth Sar 1925–98

Cambodian political and military leader whose Khmer Rouge army took over Cambodia in 1975. Prime Minister of Kampuchea (1976–8), he presided over the deaths of over a million people, by starvation or murder, before Vietnam liberated the country in Dec 1978.

41 We will burn the old grass and the new will grow.

c.1975 Quoted in John Pilger *Distant Voices* (1992), section 5.

42 If our people can build Angkor Wat they can do anything.

1979 Quoted by Dennis Bloodworth in the *Observer*, 20 Jan 1980.

Pol-Roger, Christian

US vintner.

43 Champagne! In victory, one deserves it; in defeat, one needs it.

1988 'Champagne, a Magnum Opus', in the *New York Times*, 31 Dec.

Pomfret, John 1667–1702

English clergyman and poet.

44 We live and learn, but not the wiser grow.

1700 'Reason'.

Pompadour, Madame de *full name* **Jeanne Antoinette Poisson, Marquise de Pompadour** 1721–64

French mistress of Louis XV. Installed at Versailles (1745), she assumed control of public affairs and swayed state policy, appointing her favourites. She was a lavish patron of the arts and literature.

45 The Duke takes a town in the same light-hearted way as he seduces a woman.
>**1756** Of Cardinal Duc de Richelieu, following his capture of the reputedly impregnable Fort St Phillip, Minorca, by taking his men up a cliff face to surprise the defenders. Quoted in Nancy Mitford *Madame de Pompadour* (1954), p.201.

46 *Après nous le déluge.*
After us the deluge.
>**1757** Quoted in Madame de Hausset *Mémoires* (1824).

Pompéia, Raul d'Avila 1863–95

Brazilian novelist, best known for *O Ateneu* (1888), the story of life in an oppressive boarding school. Unable to cope any longer with his emotional problems, he committed suicide at the age of 32.

47 *O tédio é a grande enfermidade da escola, o tédio corruptor que tanto se pode gerar da monotonia do trabalho como da ociosidade.*
Tedium is the worst disease in schools, the corrupting tedium that comes equally from monotony, work or leisure.
>**1888** *O Ateneu* ('The Atheneum'), ch.7.

Pompidou, Georges 1911–74

Second President (1969–74) of the Fifth French Republic. He served in the Resistance during World War II, and was a member of Charles de Gaulle's staff (1944–6) before taking control of the provisional government.

48 There are three roads to ruin—women, gambling and technicians. The most pleasant is women, the quickest is with gambling, but the surest is with technicians.
>**1968** In the *Sunday Telegraph*.

Pop, Iggy 1947–

US rock singer and songwriter.

49 What seems to pass for guitar more and more now is some wimp with a fuzz box. Somewhere around Hendrix, the line was crossed. Hendrix had both: he had the hands and he had the fuzz box. Now all they have is the fuzz box.
>**2004** In *Rolling Stone*, 15 Apr.

Pope, Alexander 1688–1744

English poet and essayist, crippled at 12 by a tubercular infection of the spine. His work, distinguished by its technical brilliance and skilful satire, includes *The Rape of the Lock* (1712, enlarged 1714), *The Dunciad* (1728, revised 1742) and *An Essay on Man* (1732–4).

50 Where'er you walk, cool gales shall fan the glade,
Trees where you sit, shall crowd into a shade:
Where'er you tread, the blushing flowers shall rise,
And all things flourish where you turn your eyes.
>**1709** *Pastorals*, 'Summer', l.73–6.

51 Some are bewildered in the maze of schools,
And some made coxcombs Nature meant but fools.
>**1711** *An Essay on Criticism*, l.26–7.

52 Some have at first for wits, then poets passed,
Turned critics next, and proved plain fools at last.
>**1711** *An Essay on Criticism*, l.36–7.

53 First follow Nature, and your judgement frame
By her just standard, which is still the same:
Unerring Nature, still divinely bright,
One clear, unchanged, and universal light,
Life, force and beauty must to all impart,
At once the source and end and test of art.
>**1711** *An Essay on Criticism*, l.68–73.

54 A little learning is a dangerous thing;
Drink deep, or taste not the Pierian spring:
There shallow draughts intoxicate the brain,
And drinking largely sobers us again.
>**1711** *An Essay on Criticism*, l.215–8.

55 Poets like painters, thus unskilled to trace
The naked nature and the living grace,
With gold and jewels cover ev'ry part,
And hide with ornaments their want of art.
True wit is Nature to advantage dressed,
What oft was thought, but ne'er so well expressed.
>**1711** *An Essay on Criticism*, l.293–8.

56 Expression is the dress of thought.
>**1711** *An Essay on Criticism*, l.318.

57 In Words, as Fashions, the same rule will hold;
Alike Fantastic, if too New, or Old;
Be not the *first* by whom the New are try'd,
Nor the *last* to lay the Old aside.
>**1711** *An Essay on Criticism*, l.333–6.

58 As some to church repair,
Not for the doctrine, but the music there.
>**1711** *An Essay on Criticism*, l.342–3.

59 True ease in writing comes from art, not chance,
As those move easiest who have learned to dance.
'Tis not enough no harshness gives offence,
The sound must seem an echo to the sense.
>**1711** *An Essay on Criticism*, l.362–5.

60 To err is human; to forgive, divine.
>**1711** *An Essay on Criticism*, l.525.

61 All seems infected that th'infected spy,
As all looks yellow to the jaundiced eye.
>**1711** *An Essay on Criticism*, l.558–9.

62 The bookful blockhead, ignorantly read,
With loads of learned lumbers in his head.
>**1711** *An Essay on Criticism*, l.612–3.

63 For fools rush in where angels fear to tread.
>**1711** *An Essay on Criticism*, l.625.

64 What dire offence from am'rous causes springs,
What mighty contests rise from trivial things.
>**1714** *The Rape of the Lock*, canto 1, l.1–2.

65 Now lap-dogs give themselves the rousing shake,
And sleepless lovers, just at twelve, awake.
>**1714** *The Rape of the Lock*, canto 1, l.15–16.

66 They shift the moving Toyshop of their heart.
>**1714** *The Rape of the Lock*, canto 1, l.100.

67 Bright as the sun, her eyes the gazers strike,
And, like the sun, they shine on all alike.
>**1714** *The Rape of the Lock*, canto 2, l.13–14.

68 If to her share some female errors fall,

Look on her face, and you'll forget 'em all.
1714 *The Rape of the Lock*, canto 2, l.17–18.

69 Belinda smiled, and all the world was gay.
1714 *The Rape of the Lock*, canto 2, l.52.

70 Whether the nymph shall break Diana's law,
Or some frail china jar receive a flaw,
Or stain her honour, or her new brocade,
Forget her pray'rs, or miss a masquerade.
1714 *The Rape of the Lock*, canto 2, l.105–8.

71 Here thou, great Anna! whom three realms obey,
Dost sometimes counsel take—and sometimes tea.
1714 *The Rape of the Lock*, canto 3, l.7–8.

72 At ev'ry word a reputation dies.
1714 *The Rape of the Lock*, canto 3, l.16.

73 The hungry judges soon the sentence sign,
And wretches hang that jury-men may dine.
1714 *The Rape of the Lock*, canto 3, l.21–2.

74 Let spades be trumps! she said, and trumps they were.
1714 *The Rape of the Lock*, canto 3, l.46.

75 Not louder shrieks to pitying heav'n are cast,
When husbands or when lapdogs breathe their last.
1714 *The Rape of the Lock*, canto 3, l.157–8.

76 Sir Plume, of amber snuff-box justly vain,
And the nice conduct of a clouded cane.
1714 *The Rape of the Lock*, canto 4, l.123–4.

77 Beauties in vain their pretty eyes may roll;
Charms strike the sight, but merit wins the soul.
1714 *The Rape of the Lock*, canto 5, l.33–4.

78 Happy the man, whose wish and care
A few paternal acres bound,
Content to breathe his native air,
In his own ground.
1717 'Ode on Solitude'.

79 Is there no bright reversion in the sky,
For those who greatly think or bravely die?
1717 *Elegy to the Memory of an Unfortunate Lady*, l.9–10.

80 On all the line a sudden vengeance waits,
And frequent hearses shall besiege your gates.
1717 *Elegy to the Memory of an Unfortunate Lady*, l.37–8.

81 By foreign hands thy dying eyes were closed,
By foreign hands thy decent limbs composed,
By foreign hands thy humble grave adorned,
By strangers honoured, and by strangers mourned.
1717 *Elegy to the Memory of an Unfortunate Lady*, l.51–4.

82 Oh happy state! when souls each other draw,
When love is liberty, and nature, law:
All then is full, possessing, and possessed,
No craving void left aching in the breast.
1717 'Eloisa to Abelard'.

83 No, make me mistress to the man I love;
If there be yet another name more free,
More fond than mistress, make me that to thee!
1717 'Eloisa to Abelard'.

84 Of all affliction taught a lover yet,
'Tis sure the hardest science to forget!
How shall I lose the sin, yet keep the sense,
And love th'offender, yet detest th'offence?
How the dear object from the crime remove,
Or how distinguish penitence from love?
1717 'Eloisa to Abelard'.

85 How happy is the blameless Vestal's lot!
The world forgetting, by the world forgot.
1717 'Eloisa to Abelard'.

86 And wine can of their wits the wise beguile,
Make the sage frolic, and the serious smile.
1726 *Odyssey*, bk.14, l.520–1.

87 Welcome the coming, speed the parting guest.
1726 *Odyssey*, bk. 15, l.83.

88 To endeavour to work upon the vulgar with fine sense, is like attempting to hew blocks with a razor.
1727 *Miscellanies*, 'Thoughts on Various Subjects', vol.2.

89 A man should never be ashamed to own he has been in the wrong, which is but saying, in other words, that he is wiser to-day than he was yesterday.
1727 *Miscellanies*, 'Thoughts on Various Subjects', vol.2.

90 It is with narrow-souled people as with narrow-necked bottles: the less they have in them, the more noise they make in pouring it out.
1727 *Miscellanies*, 'Thoughts on Various Subjects', vol.2.

91 When men grow virtuous in their old age, they only make a sacrifice to God of the devil's leavings.
1727 *Miscellanies*, 'Thoughts on Various Subjects', vol.2.

92 The most primitive men are the most credulous.
1727 *Miscellanies*, 'Thoughts on Various Subjects', vol.2.

93 Consult the genius of the place in all.
1731 *Epistles to Several Persons*, 'To Lord Burlington', l.57.

94 Still follow sense, of ev'ry art the soul,
Parts answering parts shall slide into a whole.
1731 *Epistles to Several Persons*, 'To Lord Burlington', l.65–6.

95 No pleasing Intricacies intervene,
No artful wildness to perplex the scene;
Grove nods at grove, each a mirror of the other.
The suff'ring eye inverted Nature sees,
Trees cut to Statues, Statues thick as trees,
With here a Fountain, never to be play'd,
And there a Summer-house, that knows no shade;
Here Amphitrite sails thro' myrtle bow'rs
There Gladiators fight, or die, in flow'rs
Un-water'd see the drooping sea-horse mourn,
And swallows roost in Nilus' dusty Urn.
1731 *Epistles to Several Persons*, 'To Lord Burlington', l.115–25.

96 To rest, the cushion and soft Dean invite,
Who never mentions Hell to ears polite.
1731 *Epistles to Several Persons*, 'To Lord Burlington', l.149–50.

97 Another age shall see the golden ear
Imbrown the slope, and nod on the parterre,
Deep harvests bury all his pride has planned,
And laughing Ceres re-assume the land.
1731 *Epistles to Several Persons*, 'To Lord Burlington', l.173–6.

98 'Tis use alone that sanctifies expense,
And splendour borrows all her rays from sense.
1731 *Epistles to Several Persons*, 'To Lord Burlington', l.179–80.

99 How often are we to die before we go quite off this stage? In every friend we lose a part of ourselves, and the best part.
1732 Letter to Swift, 5 Dec.

1 Who shall decide, when doctors disagree,
And soundest casuists doubt, like you and me?
1733 *Epistles to Several Persons*, 'To Lord Bathurst', l.1–2.

2 But thousands die, without or this or that,

Die, and endow a college, or a cat.
1733 *Epistles to Several Persons*, 'To Lord Bathurst', l.95–6.

3 The ruling passion be it what it will,
The ruling passion conquers reason still.
1733 *Epistles to Several Persons*, 'To Lord Bathurst', l.155–6.

4 Who sees pale Mammon pine amidst his store,
Sees but a backward steward for the poor;
This year a reservoir, to keep and spare,
The next a fountain, spouting through his heir,
In lavish streams to quench a country's thirst,
And men and dogs shall drink him 'till they burst.
1733 *Epistles to Several Persons*, 'To Lord Bathurst', l.173–8.

5 In the worst inn's worst room, with mat half-hung,
The floors of plaister, and the walls of dung,
On once a flock-bed, but repaired with straw,
With tape-tied curtains, never meant to draw,
The George and Garter dangling from that bed
Where tawdry yellow strove with dirty red,
Great Villiers lies.
1733 *Epistles to Several Persons*, 'To Lord Bathurst', l.229–35.

6 Awake, my St. John! leave all meaner things
To low ambition, and the pride of kings.
Let us (since Life can little more supply
Than just to look about us and to die)
Expatiate free o'er all this scene of man;
A mighty maze! but not without a plan.
1733 *An Essay on Man*, epistle 1, l.1–6.

7 Eye Nature's walks, shoot Folly as it flies,
And catch the Manners living as they rise.
Laugh where we must, be candid where we can;
But vindicate the ways of God to man.
1733 *An Essay on Man*, epistle 1, l.13–16.
➤ *See Milton 580:93.*

8 Observe how system into system runs,
What other planets circle other suns.
1733 *An Essay on Man*, epistle 1, l.25–6.

9 Who sees with equal eye, as God of all,
A hero perish, or a sparrow fall,
Atoms or systems into ruin hurled,
And now a bubble burst, and now a world.
1733 *An Essay on Man*, epistle 1, l.87–90.

10 Hope springs eternal in the human breast:
Man never Is, but always To be blest.
1733 *An Essay on Man*, epistle 1, l.95–6.

11 Lo! the poor Indian, whose untutored mind
Sees God in clouds, or hears him in the wind;
His soul proud Science never taught to stray
Far as the solar walk, or milky way;
Yet simple Nature to his hope has giv'n,
Behind the cloud-topped hill, an humbler heav'n.
1733 *An Essay on Man*, epistle 1, l.99–104.

12 Pride still is aiming at the blest abodes,
Men would be angels, angels would be gods.
1733 *An Essay on Man*, epistle 1, l.125–6.

13 The spider's touch, how exquisitely fine!
Feels at each thread, and lives along the line.
1733 *An Essay on Man*, epistle 1, l.217–8.

14 All are but parts of one stupendous whole,
Whose body, Nature is, and God the soul.
1733 *An Essay on Man*, epistle 1, l.267–8.

15 All nature is but art, unknown to thee;
All chance, direction, which thou canst not see;
All discord, harmony, not understood;
All partial evil, universal good:
And, spite of Pride, in erring Reason's spite,
One truth is clear, 'Whatever Is, is RIGHT.'
1733 *An Essay on Man*, epistle 1, l.289–94.

16 Know then thyself, presume not God to scan;
The proper study of mankind is man.
Placed on this isthmus of a middle state,
A being darkly wise, and rudely great:
With too much knowledge for the sceptic side,
With too much weakness for the stoic's pride,
He hangs between; in doubt to act or rest,
In doubt to deem himself a god, or beast;
In doubt his mind or body to prefer,
Born but to die, and reas'ning but to err;
Alike in ignorance, his reason such,
Whether he thinks too little, or too much.
1733 *An Essay on Man*, epistle 2, l.1–12.

17 Created half to rise, and half to fall;
Great lord of all things, yet a prey to all;
Sole judge of truth, in endless error hurled;
The glory, jest, and riddle of the world!
1733 *An Essay on Man*, epistle 2, l.15–18.

18 Vice is a monster of so frightful mien,
As, to be hated, needs but to be seen;
Yet seen too oft, familiar with her face,
We first endure, then pity, then embrace.
1733 *An Essay on Man*, epistle 2, l.217–19.

19 The learn'd is happy nature to explore,
The fool is happy that he knows no more.
1733 *An Essay on Man*, epistle 2, l.263–4.

20 For forms of government let fools contest;
Whate'er is best administered is best.
1733 *An Essay on Man*, epistle 3, l.303–4.

21 In faith and hope the world will disagree,
But all mankind's concern is charity.
1733 *An Essay on Man*, epistle 3, l.307–8.

22 Thus God and nature linked the gen'ral frame,
And bade self-love and social be the same.
1733 *An Essay on Man*, epistle 3, l.317–18.

23 Oh Happiness! our being's end and aim!
Good, pleasure, ease, content! whate'er thy name:
That something still which prompts th' eternal sigh,
For which we bear to live, or dare to die.
1734 *An Essay on Man*, epistle 4, l.1–4.

24 Order is Heaven's first law.
1733 *An Essay on Man*, epistle to 4, l.49.

25 A wit's a feather, and a chief a rod;
An honest man's the noblest work of God.
1734 *An Essay on Man*, epistle 4, l.247–8.

26 If parts allure thee, think how Bacon shined,
The wisest, brightest, meanest of mankind:
Or ravished with the whistling of a name,
See Cromwell, damned to everlasting fame!
1734 *An Essay on Man*, epistle 4, l.281–4.

27 Slave to no sect, who takes no private road,
But looks thro' Nature, up to Nature's God.
1734 *An Essay on Man*, epistle 4, l.331–2.

28 All our knowledge is, ourselves to know.
    1734 *An Essay on Man*, epistle 4, l.398.

29 Alas! in truth the man but changed his mind,
    Perhaps was sick, in love, or had not dined.
    1734 *Epistles to Several Persons*, 'To Lord Cobham', l.127–8.

30 'Tis from high life high characters are drawn;
    A saint in crape is twice a saint in lawn.
    1734 *Epistles to Several Persons*, 'To Lord Cobham', l.134–6.

31 Search then the Ruling Passion: There, alone,
    The wild are constant and the cunning known;
    The fool consistent, and the false sincere;
    Priests, princes, women, no dissemblers here.
    This clue once found, unravels all the rest.
    1734 *Epistles to Several Persons*, 'To Lord Cobham', l.174–8.

32 Odious! in woollen! 'twould a saint provoke!
    1734 *Epistles to Several Persons*, 'To Lord Cobham', l.246.

33 Shut, shut the door, good John! fatigued I said,
    Tie up the knocker; say I'm sick, I'm dead.
    The Dog-star rages!
    1735 'An Epistle to Dr Arbuthnot', l.1–3.

34 You think this cruel? take it for a rule,
    No creature smarts so little as a fool.
    Let peals of laughter, Codrus! round thee break,
    Thou unconcerned canst hear the mighty crack.
    Pit, box, and gallery in convulsions hurled,
    Thou stand'st unshook amidst a bursting world.
    1735 'An Epistle to Dr Arbuthnot', l.83–8.

35 Destroy his fib, or sophistry; in vain,
    The creature's at his dirty work again.
    1735 'An Epistle to Dr Arbuthnot', l.91–2.

36 Pretty! in amber to observe the forms
    Of hairs, or straws, or dirt, or grubs, or worms!
    The things, we know are neither rich nor rare,
    But wonder how the Devil they got there.
    1735 'An Epistle to Dr Arbuthnot', l.169–72.

37 And he, whose fustian's so sublimely bad,
    It is not poetry, but prose run mad.
    1735 'An Epistle to Dr Arbuthnot', l.187–8.

38 Damn with faint praise, assent with civil leer,
    And without sneering, teach the rest to sneer;
    Willing to wound, and yet afraid to strike,
    Just hint a fault, and hesitate dislike.
    1735 Of Addison. 'An Epistle to Dr Arbuthnot', l.201–4.

39 But still the great have kindness in reserve,
    He helped to bury whom he helped to starve.
    1735 Of a patron. 'An Epistle to Dr Arbuthnot', l.247–8.

40 Let Sporus tremble—'What? that thing of silk,
    Sporus, that mere white curd of ass's milk?
    Satire or sense, alas! can Sporus feel?
    Who breaks a butterfly upon a wheel?
    1735 Of Lord Hervey. 'An Epistle to Dr Arbuthnot', l.305–8.

41 And he himself one vile antithesis.
    1735 Of Lord Hervey. 'An Epistle to Dr Arbuthnot', l.325.

42 Unlearn'd, he knew no schoolman's subtle art,
    No language, but the language of the heart.
    1735 Of Pope's father. 'An Epistle to Dr Arbuthnot', l.398–9.

43 Most women have no characters at all.
    1735 *Epistles to Several Persons*, 'To a Lady', l.2.

44 A very heathen in the carnal part,
    Yet still a sad, good Christian at her heart.

45 Chaste to her husband, frank to all beside,
    A teeming mistress, but a barren bride.
    1735 *Epistles to Several Persons*, 'To a Lady', l.71–2.

46 'With every pleasing, every prudent part,
    Say, what can Cloe want?'—She wants a heart.
    1735 *Epistles to Several Persons*, 'To a Lady', l.159–60.

47 Virtue she finds too painful an endeavour,
    Content to dwell in decencies for ever.
    1735 *Epistles to Several Persons*, 'To a Lady', l.163–4.

48 In men, we various ruling passions find,
    In women, two almost divide the kind;
    Those, only fixed, they first or last obey
    The love of pleasure, and the love of sway.
    1735 *Epistles to Several Persons*, 'To a Lady', l.207–10.

49 Men, some to business, some to pleasure take;
    But every woman is at heart a rake:
    Men, some to quiet, some to public strife;
    But every lady would be Queen for life.
    1735 *Epistles to Several Persons*, 'To a Lady', l.215–8.

50 Still round and round the ghosts of Beauty glide,
    And haunt the places where their honour died.
    See how the world its veterans rewards!
    A youth of frolics, an old age of cards.
    1735 *Epistles to Several Persons*, 'To a Lady', l.241–4.

51 Woman's at best a contradiction still.
    1735 *Epistles to Several Persons*, 'To a Lady', l.270.

52 Who now reads Cowley? if he pleases yet,
    His moral pleases, not his pointed wit.
    1737 *Imitations of Horace*, bk.2, epistle 1, l.75–6.

53 The people's voice is odd,
    It is, and it is not, the voice of God.
    1737 *Imitations of Horace*, bk.2, epistle 1, l.89–90.

54 But those who cannot write, and those who can,
    All rhyme, and scrawl, and scribble, to a man.
    1737 *Imitations of Horace*, bk.2, epistle 1, l.187–8.

55 Ev'n copious Dryden, wanted, or forgot,
    The last and greatest art, the art to blot.
    1737 *Imitations of Horace*, bk.2, epistle 1, l.280–1.

56 There still remains, to mortify a wit,
    The many-headed monster of the pit.
    1737 *Imitations of Horace*, bk.2, epistle 1, l.304–5.

57 The more you drink, the more you crave.
    1737 *Imitations of Horace*, bk.2, espistle 2, l.212.

58 Not to go back, is somewhat to advance,
    And men must walk at least before they dance.
    1738 *Imitations of Horace*, bk.1, epistle 1, l.53–4.

59 Not to admire, is all the art I know,
    To make men happy, and to keep them so.
    1738 *Imitations of Horace*, bk.1, epistle 6, l.1–2.

60 The worst of madmen is a saint run mad.
    1738 *Imitations of Horace*, bk.1, epistle 6, l.27.

61 Ask you what provocation I have had?
    The strong antipathy of good to bad.
    1738 *Imitations of Horace*, epilogue to the satires, dialogue 2, l.197–8.

62 Yes, I am proud; I must be proud to see
    Men not afraid of God, afraid of me.
    1738 *Imitations of Horace*, epilogue to the satires, dialogue 2, l.208–9.

63 Teach me to feel another's woe;
  To hide the fault I see;
  That mercy I to others show,
  That mercy show to me.
  1738 *The Universal Prayer.*

64 Books and the Man I sing, the first who brings
  The Smithfield Muses to the Ear of Kings.
  Say great Patricians! (since your selves inspire
  These wond'rous works; so Jove and Fate require)
  Say from what cause, in vain decry'd and curst,
  Still Dunce the second reigns like Dunce the first?
  1742 *The Dunciad*, bk.1, l.1–6.

65 Poetic Justice, with her lifted scale,
  Where, in nice balance, truth with gold she weighs,
  And solid pudding against empty praise.
  1742 *The Dunciad*, bk.1, l.52–4.

66 Here gay Description Aegypt glads with showers;
  Or gives to Zembla fruits, to Barca flowers;
  Glitt'ring with ice here hoary hills are seen,
  There painted vallies of eternal green.
  1742 *The Dunciad*, bk.1, l.71–4.

67 While pensive poets painful vigils keep,
  Sleepless themselves, to give their readers sleep.
  1742 *The Dunciad*, bk.1, l.93–4.

68 In each she marks her image full exprest,
  But chief, in Tibbald's monster-breeding breast;
  Sees Gods with Daemons in strange league ingage,
  And earth, and heav'n, and hell her battles wage.
  1742 *The Dunciad*, bk.1, l.105–8.

69 Or where the pictures for the page atone,
  And Quarles is saved by beauties not his own.
  1742 *The Dunciad*, bk.1, l.139–40.

70 A brain of feathers, and a heart of lead.
  1742 *The Dunciad*, bk.2, l.44.

71 How little, mark! that portion of the ball,
  Where, faint at best, the beams of science fall.
  1742 *The Dunciad*, bk.3, l.83–4.

72 None need a guide, by sure attraction led,
  And strong impulsive gravity of head.
  1742 *The Dunciad*, bk.4, l.75–6.

73 A wit with dunces, and a dunce with wits.
  1742 *The Dunciad*, bk.4, l.90.

74 Leave not a foot of verse, a foot of stone,
  A Page, a Grave, that they can call their own;
  But spread, my sons, your glory thin or thick,
  On passive paper, or on solid brick.
  1742 *The Dunciad*, bk.4, l.127–30.

75 Whate'er the talents, or howe'er designed,
  We hang one jingling padlock on the mind.
  1742 *The Dunciad*, bk.4, l.161–2.

76 The Right Divine of Kings to govern wrong.
  1742 *The Dunciad*, bk.4, l.187.

77 How parts relate to parts, or they to whole,
  The body's harmony, the beaming soul.
  1742 *The Dunciad*, bk.4, l.235–6.

78 Isles of fragrance, lily-silver'd values.
  1742 *The Dunciad*, bk.4, l.303.

79 Love-whispering woods, and lute-resounding waves.
  1742 *The Dunciad*, bk.4, l.306.

80 —She marked thee there,

Stretched on the rack of a too easy chair,
  And heard thy everlasting yawn confess
  The pains and penalties of idleness.
  1742 *The Dunciad*, bk.4, l.341–4.

81 O! would the Sons of Men once think their Eyes
  And Reason giv'n them but to study Flies?
  See Nature in some partial narrow shape,
  And let the Author of the Whole escape.
  1742 *The Dunciad*, bk.4, l.453–6.

82 Religion blushing veils her sacred fires,
  And unawares Morality expires.
  1742 *The Dunciad*, bk.4, l.649–50.

83 Lo! thy dread empire, Chaos! is restored;
  Light dies before thy uncreating word:
  Thy hand, great Anarch! lets the curtain fall;
  And universal darkness buries all.
  1742 *The Dunciad*, bk.4, l.653–6.

84 I am his Highness' dog at Kew;
  Pray, tell me sir, whose dog are you?
  'Epigram Engraved on the Collar of a Dog which I gave to His Royal Highness'.

85 Here am I, dying of a hundred good symptoms.
  1744 His response to reassurance from his doctors that his health was showing signs of improvement. Quoted in Joseph Spence *Anecdotes by and about Alexander Pope* (1820).

Popova, Lyubov Sergeyevna 1889–1924

Russian painter and theatre and textile designer.

86 Texture is the content of painterly surfaces.
  Quoted in W Chadwick *Women, Art and Society* (1990).

Popper, Sir Karl Raimund 1902–94

Anglo-Austrian philosopher, professor (1949–69) at the London School of Economics. He expounded his political theory in *The Open Society and Its Enemies* (1945), and his philosophy of science in *The Logic of Scientific Discovery* (1934).

87 It must be possible for an empirical system to be refuted by experience.
  1934 *The Logic of Scientific Discovery.*

88 Every scientific statement must remain *tentative for ever.*
  1934 *The Logic of Scientific Discovery.*

89 In order that a new theory should constitute a discovery or step forward it should conflict with its predecessor …it should contradict its predecessor; it should overthrow it. In this sense, progress in science—or at least striking progress—is always revolutionary.
  1934 *The Logic of Scientific Discovery.*

90 It is not his possession of knowledge, of irrefutable truth, that makes the man of science, but his persistent and recklessly critical quest for truth.
  1934 *The Logic of Scientific Discovery.*

91 We may become the makers of our fate when we have ceased to pose as its prophets.
  1945 *The Open Society and Its Enemies*, introduction.

92 There is no history of mankind, there are only many histories of all kinds of aspects of human life. And one of these is the history of political power. This is elevated into the history of the world.
  1945 *The Open Society and Its Enemies*, vol.2, ch.25.

93 The belief that we can start with pure observations

alone, without anything in the nature of a theory, is absurd.
1953 *Conjectures and Refutations* (published 1963), ch.1.

94 Observation is always selective. It needs a chosen object, a definite task, an interest, a point of view, a problem.
1953 *Conjectures and Refutations* (published 1963), ch.1.

95 There is at least one philosophical problem in which all thinking men are interested. It is the problem of cosmology: *the problem of understanding the world—including ourselves, and our knowledge, as part of the world*. All science is cosmology, I believe, and for me the interest of philosophy, no less than that of science, lies solely in the contributions which it has made to it.
1959 *The Logic of Scientific Discovery* (1934), preface to 1959 edition.

96 In so far as a scientific statement speaks about reality, it must be falsifiable: and in so far as it is not falsifiable, it does not speak about reality.
1959 *The Logic of Scientific Discovery* (1934), appendix to 1959 edition.

97 What we should do, I suggest, is to give up the idea of ultimate sources of knowledge, and admit that all knowledge is human; that it is mixed with our errors, our prejudices, our dreams, and our hopes; that all we can do is to grope for truth even though it be beyond our reach.
1960 *Conjectures and Refutations* (published 1963), introduction.

98 The history of science, like the history of all human ideas, is a history of irresponsible dreams, of obstinacy, and of error. But science is one of the very few human activities—perhaps the only one—in which errors are systematically criticized and fairly often, in time, corrected. This is why we can say that, in science, we often learn from our mistakes, and why we can speak clearly and sensibly about making progress there.
1960 *Conjectures and Refutations* (published 1963), ch.10.

99 Science starts only with problems.
1960 *Conjectures and Refutations* (published 1963), ch.10.

1 For this, indeed, is the true source of our ignorance—the fact that our knowledge can only be finite, while our ignorance must necessarily be infinite.
1960 Lecture to the British Academy, 20 Jan.

2 Science may be described as the art of systematic over-simplification.
1982 Quoted in the *Observer*, 1 Aug.

Porter, Cole 1891–1964

US composer. He studied law at Harvard before turning to music, composing and writing lyrics for a string of successful stage and screen musicals including *Kiss Me Kate* (1948, filmed 1953), *High Society* (1956) and *Can-Can* (1953, filmed 1960).

3 I get no kick from champagne;
Mere alcohol doesn't thrill me at all.
So tell me why should it be true
That I get a kick out of you?
1934 'I Get a Kick Out of You', from the show *Anything Goes*.

4 In olden days a glimpse of stocking
Was looked on as something shocking.

But now, God knows,
Anything goes.
1934 'Anything Goes', from the show *Anything Goes*.

5 I'm a worthless check, a total wreck, a flop
But if baby I'm the bottom, you're the top.
1936 'You're the Top', from the show *Anything Goes*.

6 You're the top
You're the Louvr' Museum
You're a melody from a symphony by Strauss.
1936 'You're the Top', from the show *Anything Goes*.

7 My sole inspiration is a telephone call from a director.
1955 Interview, 8 Feb.

8 Who wants to be a millionaire?
And go to ev'ry swell affair?
1956 'Who Wants to Be a Millionaire', from the show *High Society*.

Porter, Katherine Anne 1890–1980

US novelist and short-story writer. Her works include the novella *Pale Horse, Pale Rider* (1939) and the long allegorical novel *The Ship of Fools* (1962).

9 Most people won't realize that writing is a craft. You have to take your apprenticeship in it like anything else.
1962 In the *Saturday Review*, 31 Mar.

10 The real sin against life is to abuse and destroy beauty, even one's own—even more, one's own, for that has been put in our care and we are responsible for its well-being.
1962 *Ship of Fools*, pt.3.

11 The pimple on the face of American literature.
On Truman Capote. Quoted in Gerald Clarke *Capote* (1988).

12 Oh, poor Pearl Buck! She has no more bounce than a boiled potato.
Quoted from the journals of Glenway Westcott, in Robert Phelps and Jerry Rosco (eds) *Continuous Lessons* (1990).

Porteus, Beilby 1731–1808

English prelate and poet.

13 One murder made a villain
Millions a hero.
1759 'Death'.

14 War its thousands slays, Peace its ten thousands.
1759 'Death'.

15 Teach him how to live,
And, oh! still harder lesson! how to die.
1759 'Death'.

Portillo, Michael 1953–

English Conservative politician. He was regarded as a potential future leader, but lost his seat in the 1997 general election. Victory in a 1999 by-election led to his return to the Commons.

16 A truly terrible night for the Conservatives.
1997 After losing Enfield South to Labour in the general election, 2 May. Quoted in Brian Cathcart *Were You Still Up for Portillo?*.

Pott, Frances 1832–1909

English cleric and translator.

17 The strife is o'er, the battle done;
Now is the Victor's triumph won;

O let the song of praise be sung;
Alleluia!
1861 Hymn, translated from the original Latin 'Finita iam sunt praelia'.

Potter, Beatrix 1866–1943

English author and illustrator of books for children, whose characters have become classics of children's literature.

18 Don't go into Mr McGregor's garden: your father had an accident there, he was put into a pie by Mr McGregor.
1902 *The Tale of Peter Rabbit*.

19 In the time of swords and periwigs and full-skirted coats with flowered lappets—when gentlemen wore ruffles, and gold-laced waistcoats of paduasoy and taffeta—there lived a tailor in Gloucester.
1903 *The Tailor of Gloucester*.

Potter, Henry Codman 1835–1908

US religious leader. For 15 years he was rector of Grace Church, New York City. He was elected Bishop Co-Adjutor of New York in 1883 and Bishop in 1887. He was known for his diplomacy and was outspoken on corruption.

20 If there be no nobility of descent in a nation, it is all the more indispensable that there should be nobility of ascent; a character in them that bear rule, so fine and high and pure, that as men come within the circle of its influence, they involuntarily pay homage to that which is the one pre-eminent distinction—the royalty of virtue.
1889 Washington centennial address, 30 Apr.

Potter, Stephen 1900–69

English humorous writer.

21 How to be one up—how to make the other man feel that something has gone wrong, however slightly.
1950 *Lifemanship*.

22 Each of us can, by ploy or gambit, most naturally gain the advantage.
1950 *Lifemanship*.

Pound, Ezra Loomis 1885–1972

US poet, a key figure in the Modernist movement, whose chief work was the massive poetic cycle *The Cantos* (collected 1970). He spent much of his life in Italy, and was committed to an asylum for a time after World War II, during which he espoused Fascist sympathies.

23 Bah! I have sung women in three cities,
But it is all the same;
And I will sing of the sun.
1908 *Personae*, 'Cino'.

24 No good poetry is written in a manner twenty years old, for to write in such a manner shows conclusively that the writer thinks from books, convention and cliché; and not from life.
1912 'Prolegomena', in *The Poetry Review*, Feb.

25 All great art is born of the metropolis.
1913 Letter to Harriet Monroe, 7 Nov.

26 Poetry must be *as well written as prose*.
1915 Letter to Harriet Monroe, Jan.

27 Winter is icummen in,
Lhude sing Goddamm,

Raineth drop and staineth slop,
And how the wind doth ramm!
Sing: Goddamm.
1916 *Lustra*, 'Ancient Music'.
➤ *See Anonymous 19:83*.

28 The apparition of these faces in the crowd;
Petals on a wet, black bough.
1916 *Lustra*, 'In a Station of the Metro'.

29 She is dying piece-meal
of a sort of emotional anaemia.
And round about there is a rabble
of the filthy, sturdy, unkillable infants
of the very poor.
1916 *Lustra*, 'The Garden'.

30 I make a pact with you, Walt Whitman—
I have detested you long enough.
I come to you as a grown child
Who has had a pig-headed father
I am old enough not to make friends.
1916 *Lustra*, 'A Pact'.

31 Poetry must be read as music and not as oratory.
1917 'Vers Libre and Arnold Dolmetsch', in *The Egoist*, Jul.

32 A chryselephantine poem of immeasurable length which will occupy me for the next four decades unless it becomes a bore.
1917 On beginning the poetic series *The Cantos*, which remained unfinished on his death.

33 A man of genius has a right to any mode of expression.
1918 Letter to J B Yeats, 4 Feb.

34 Of all those young women
Not one has enquired the cause of the world
Nor the modus of lunar eclipses
Nor whether there be any patch left of us
After we cross the infernal ripples.
1919 *Quia Pauper Amavi*, 'Homage to Sextus Propertius'.

35 For three years, out of key with his time,
He strove to resuscitate the dead art
Of poetry; to maintain 'the sublime'
In the old sense. Wrong from the start—

No, hardly, but seeing he had been born
In a half savage country, out of date.
1920 *Hugh Selwyn Mauberley*, pt.1.

36 His true Penelope was Flaubert,
He fished by obstinate isles;
Observed the elegance of Circe's hair
Rather than the mottoes on sundials.
1920 *Hugh Selwyn Mauberley*, pt.1.

37 Better mendacities
Than the classics in paraphrase!
1920 *Hugh Selwyn Mauberley*, pt.2.

38 Christ follows Dionysus
Phallic and ambrosial
Made way for macerations;
Caliban casts out Ariel.
1920 *Hugh Selwyn Mauberley*, pt.3.

39 Died some, *pro patria*,
non 'dulce' non 'et decor'…
walked eye-deep in hell
believing in old men's lies, then unbelieving
came home, home to a lie,

home to many deceits
home to old lies and new infamy;
usury age-old and age-thick
and liars in public places.
1920 *Hugh Selwyn Mauberley*, pt.4.

40 There died a myriad,
And of the best, among them,
For an old bitch gone in the teeth,
For a botched civilization.
1920 *Hugh Selwyn Mauberley*, pt.5.

41 And no one knows, at first sight, a masterpiece.
And give up verse, my boy.
There's nothing in it.
1920 *Hugh Selwyn Mauberley*, 'MR NIXON'.

42 I never mentioned a man but with the view
Of selling my own works.
The tip's a good one, as for literature
It gives no man a sinecure.
1920 *Hugh Selwyn Mauberley*, 'MR NIXON'.

43 The haven from sophistications and contentions
Leaks through its thatch;
He offers succulent cooking;
The door has a creaking latch.
1920 *Hugh Selwyn Mauberley*, pt.10.

44 The curse of me and my nation is that we always think
things can be bettered by immediate action of some
sort, *any* sort rather than no sort.
1920 Letter to James Joyce, 7–8 Jun.

45 And then went down to the ship,
Set keel to breakers, forth on the godly sea.
1925 *Draft of XVI Cantos*, no.1.

46 And even I can remember
A day when the historians left blanks in their writings,
I mean for things they didn't know.
1930 *Draft of XXX Cantos*, no.13.

47 Great literature is simply language charged with
meaning to the utmost possible degree.
1931 *How To Read*, pt.2.

48 Any general statement is like a cheque drawn on a bank.
Its value depends on what is there to meet it.
1934 *The ABC of Reading*, ch.1.

49 One of the pleasures of middle age is to *find out* that one
WAS right, and that one was much righter than one knew
at say 17 or 23.
1934 *The ABC of Reading*, ch.1.

50 Literature is news that STAYS news.
1934 *The ABC of Reading*, ch.2.

51 Real education must ultimately be limited to one who
INSISTS on knowing, the rest is mere sheep-herding.
1934 *The ABC of Reading*, ch.8.

52 The author's conviction on this day of New Year is that
music begins to atrophy when it departs too far from the
dance; that poetry begins to atrophy when it gets too far
from music . . .
1934 *The ABC of Reading*, 'Warning'.

53 To the beat of the measure
From star-up to the half-dark
From half-dark to half-dark
Unceasing the measure.
1934 *Eleven New Cantos*, no.34.

54 People find ideas a bore because they do not distinguish
between live ones and stuffed ones on a shelf.
1938 *Guide to Kulcher*, pt.1, section 1, ch.5.

55 Man is an over-complicated organism. If he is doomed
to extinction he will die out for want of simplicity.
1938 *Guide to Kulcher*, pt.3, section 5, ch.19.

56 Civilization itself is a certain sane balance of values.
1938 *Guide to Kulcher*, pt.3, section 5, ch.20.

57 Adolf Hitler was a Jeanne d'Arc, a saint. He was a martyr.
Like many martyrs, he held extreme views.
1945 In the *Philadelphia Record* and *Chicago Sun*, 9 May.

58 What thou lovest well remains,
The rest is dross
What thou lov'st well shall not be reft from thee
What thou lov'st well is thy true heritage.
1948 *The Pisan Cantos*, no.81.

59 The ant's a centaur in his dragon world.
Pull down thy vanity, it is not man
Made courage, or made order, or made grace.
1948 *The Pisan Cantos*, no.81.

60 Learn of the green world what can be thy place
In scaled invention or true artistry,
Pull down thy vanity,
Paquin pull down!
The green casque has outdone your elegance.
1948 *The Pisan Cantos*, no.81.

61 Thou art a beaten dog beneath the hail,
A swollen magpie in a fitful sun,
Half black half white
Nor knowst'ou wing from tail
Pull down thy vanity.
1948 *The Pisan Cantos*, no.81.

62 Tching prayed on the mountain and wrote MAKE IT NEW
on his bath tub.
Day by day make it new
cut underbrush,
pile the logs
keep it growing.
1954 *The Cantos*, no.53.

63 Artists are the antennae of the race, but the bullet-
headed many will never learn to trust their great artists.
1954 *Literary Essays*, 'Henry James'.

64 How did it go in the madhouse? Rather badly. But what
other place could one live in America?
1958 On his release after 13 years in St Elizabeth's Hospital,
Washington DC. Recalled on his death, 1 Nov 1972.

65 The worst mistake I made was that stupid, suburban
prejudice of anti-Semitism.
1968 Remark to Allen Ginsberg, 7 Jun. Quoted in H Carpenter
A Serious Character (1988), pt.5.

66 Art very possibly *ought* to be the supreme achievement,
the 'accomplished', but there is the other satisfactory
effect—that of a man hurling himself at an indomitable
chaos and yanking and hauling as much of it as possible
into some sort of order (or beauty) aware of it both as
chaos and as potential.
Quoted in H Kenner (ed) *The Pound Era* (1973).

67 A dirty book worth reading.
Of Henry Miller *Tropic of Cancer* (1934). Recalled on Miller's
death, 7 Jun 1980.

68 All America is an insane asylum.

Quoted in Patricia C Willis (ed) *The Complete Poems of Marianne Moore* (1986).

69 Some poems have form as a tree has form and some as water poured into a vase.
Quoted in Patricia C Willis (ed) *The Complete Poems of Marianne Moore* (1986).

70 The great writer is always the plodder.
Quoted in Patricia C Willis (ed) *The Complete Poems of Marianne Moore* (1986).

71 The true poet is most easily distinguished from the false when he trusts himself to the simplest expression and writes without adjectives.
Quoted in Patricia C Willis (ed) *The Complete Poems of Marianne Moore* (1986).

72 Use no word that under stress of emotion you could not actually say.
Quoted in Patricia C Willis (ed) *The Complete Poems of Marianne Moore* (1986).

73 Great poets seldom make bricks without straw. They pile up all the excellences they can beg, borrow, or steal from their predecessors and contemporaries and then set their own inimitable light atop the mountain.
Quoted in Patricia C Willis (ed) *The Complete Poems of Marianne Moore* (1986).

Pound, (Nathan) Roscoe 1870–1964

US jurist, Professor of Law at Harvard University.

74 Wealth, in a commercial age, is made up largely of promises.
1922 *An Introduction to the Philosophy of Law*, ch.6.

Poussin, Nicolas 1594–1665

French painter who spent most of his working life in Rome. The Classical tradition in French painting developed from his work.

75 The grand manner consists of four elements: subject or theme, concept, structure, and style. The first requirement, fundamental to all the others, is that the subject and the narrative be grandiose, such as battles, heroic actions, and religious themes.
Quoted in Giovanni Pietro Bellori *Lives of the Modern Painters* (1672).

Powell, Anthony Dymoke 1905–2000

English novelist. His major work is the sequence of twelve novels chronicling 20c English upper-middle-class life, collectively known as *A Dance to the Music of Time* (1951–75).

76 All the same, you know parents—especially step-parents—are sometimes a disappointment to their children. They don't fulfil the promise of their early years.
1952 *A Buyer's Market*, ch.2.

77 There is a strong disposition in youth, from which some individuals never escape, to suppose that everyone else is having a more enjoyable time than we are ourselves.
1952 *A Buyer's Market*, ch.4.

78 He fell in love with himself at first sight and it is a passion to which he has always remained faithful. Self-love seems so often unrequited.
1955 *The Acceptance World*, ch.1.

79 Dinner at the Huntercombes possessed 'only two dramatic features—the wine was a farce and the food a tragedy.'

1955 *The Acceptance World*, ch.4.

80 All men are brothers, but, thank God, they aren't all brothers-in-law.
1957 *At Lady Molly's*, ch.4.

81 Books Do Furnish a Room.
1971 Title of novel.

82 Growing old is like being increasingly penalised for a crime you haven't committed.
1973 *Temporary Kings*, ch.1.

83 People think that because a novel's invented, it isn't true. Exactly the reverse is the case.
1975 *Hearing Secret Harmonies*, ch.3.

84 One of the worst things about life is not how nasty the nasty people are. You know that already. It is how nasty the nice people can be.
1975 *Hearing Secret Harmonies*, ch.7.

85 In this country it is rare for anyone, let alone a publisher, to take writers seriously.
1979 In the *Daily Telegraph*, 8 Feb.

86 If you don't spend every morning of your life writing, it's awfully difficult to know what to do otherwise.
1984 In the *Observer*, 3 Apr.

Powell, Colin Luther 1937–

US army general. He fought in Vietnam, and became National Security Adviser to President Reagan (1987–9). He was appointed chairman of the Joint Chiefs of Staff (1989–93), and controlled US strategy during the Gulf War. In 2001 he was appointed Secretary of State by President George W Bush.

87 We have decapitated him from the dictatorship.
1988 On evicting from office Panama's General Manuel Noriega. Quoted in the *Washington Post*, 21 Dec.

88 The American people do not want their young dying for $1.50 a gallon oil.
1990 Urging caution against interfering with Iraq's invasion of oil-rich Kuwait in a White House meeting 2 Aug. Quoted in the *New York Times*, 23 Oct 1994.

89 First we're going to cut it off, and then we're going to kill it.
1991 On the opposition to Operation Desert Storm. In the *US News and World Report*, 4 Feb.

90 I remember the front door. I remember the auditorium. I remember the feeling that you can't make it. But you can.
1991 On revisiting the South Bronx high school from which he graduated in 1954. In the *New York Times*, 16 Apr.

91 I sleep like a baby too—every two hours I wake up screaming.
2003 On being reminded that George W Bush claims to sleep like a baby. In the *New Yorker*, 10 Feb.

Powell, (John) Enoch 1912–98

English Conservative and Ulster Unionist politician. Professor of Greek at Sydney University (1937–9), he was elected MP in 1950. Minister of Health (1960–3), he was dismissed from the shadow Cabinet in 1968 for his attitude to immigration. He was returned as an Ulster Unionist in 1974, but lost his seat in 1987. His books include *A Nation Not Afraid* (1965).

92 History is littered with the wars which everybody knew would never happen.
1967 Speech to Conservative Party conference, 19 Oct.

93 As I look ahead, I am filled with much foreboding. Like the Roman, I seem to see 'the River Tiber foaming with much blood'.
1968 Speech at Birmingham on racial tension in Britain, Apr.

94 I was born a Tory, am a Tory, and shall die a Tory. I never yet heard that it was any part of the faith of a Tory to take the institutions and liberties, the laws and customs that his country has evolved over the centuries, and merge them with those of eight other nations into a new-made artificial state—and what is more, to do so without the willing approbation and consent of the nation.
1974 Speech against Britain's entry into the Common Market, Shipley, 25 Feb.

95 All political lives, unless they are cut off in mid-stream at a happy juncture, end in failure, because that is the nature of politics and of human affairs.
1977 *Joseph Chamberlain.*

Powell, Michael 1905–90

English film-maker. He made various 'quota quickies' in the 1930s and then began a partnership with Emeric Pressburger. Known as 'the Archers', they collaborated on such films as *The Life and Death of Colonel Blimp* (1943*)*, *Black Narcissus* (1947) and *The Red Shoes* (1948).

96 What do they know of England, who only the West End know?
1950 Attributed comment in defence of *Gone to Earth.*
➤ See Kipling 471:99.

Powys, John Cowper 1872–1963

English novelist and essayist.

97 It is that cricket field that, in all the sharp and bitter moments of life as they come to me now, gives me a sense of wholesome proportion: 'At least I am not playing cricket!'
Quoted in Helen Exley *Cricket Quotations* (1992).

Prather, Hugh

US minister, counsellor and writer.

98 If the ocean was pure mind and I was a wave, I would be in terror if I tried to distinguish myself from the water that produced me. What is a wave without water, and what is a mind without God?
1982 *The Quiet Answer.*

99 Forgive and be happy. That is the ancient secret…the only wisdom ever to be attained.
1982 *The Quiet Answer.*

Pratt, Edwin John 1882–1964

Canadian poet. Born in Newfoundland, he obtained a PhD in divinity from the University of Toronto and became Professor of English there in 1919. He is best known for his documentary poetry, including *The Titanic* (1935), *Brébeuf and His Brethren* (1940) and *Towards the Last Spike* (1952).

1 It was the same world then as now—the same,
Except for little differences of speed
And power, and means to treat myopia
To show an axe-blade infinitely sharp
Splitting things infinitely small.
1952 *Towards the Last Spike.* The poet is speaking of the building of the Canadian National Railway, from coast to coast.

Prescott, John 1938–

English Labour politician, Deputy Prime Minister since 1997.

2 People like me were branded, pigeon-holed, a ceiling put on our ambitions.
1996 Speech at Oxford, 13 Jun. Quoted in *The Guardian*, 14 Jun.

3 Tony will go on and on and on.
2004 On Prime Minister Tony Blair. On BBC Radio 4's *Today* programme.

Presley, Elvis Aaron 1935–77

US singer and actor.

4 You ain't nothin' but a hound dog
cryin' all the time.
You ain't nothin' but a hound dog
cryin' all the time.
Well, you ain't never caught a rabbit
and you ain't no friend of mine.
1956 'Hound Dog' (written by Jerry Leiber and Mike Stoller).

5 Well since my baby left me
I found a new place to dwell
It's down at the end of lonely street
At Heartbreak Hotel.
1956 'Heartbreak Hotel' (with Mae Boren Axton and Tommy Durden).

6 I learned very early in life that: 'Without a song, the day would never end; without a song, a man ain't got no friend; without a song the road would never bend—without a song'. So I keep on singing. Goodnight. Thank you.
1971 Acceptance speech, Ten Outstanding Men of the Year Awards, 16 Jan.

7 I don't know anything about music—in my line you don't have to.
Quoted in David Pickering *Brewer's Twentieth Century Music* (1994).

Preston, James E 1933–

US businessman. He joined Avon Products in 1964 as a management trainee, becoming Chief Executive Officer (1988–98) and Chairman (1989–98).

8 A bad reputation is like a hangover. It takes a while to get rid of, and it makes everything else hurt.
1992 In *Fortune*, 10 Feb.

Previn, André (George) 1929–

German-born US conductor and composer. A US citizen from 1943, he conducted major orchestras around the world from 1967. His own compositions include musicals, film scores and orchestral works.

9 The basic difference between classical music and jazz is that in the former music is always greater than its performance—whereas the way jazz is performed is always more important than what is being played.
1967 Quoted in *The Times.*

Prévost, Abbé Antoine-François 1697–1763

French novelist, educated in the Jesuit tradition. He enlisted in the army before eventually deciding on a religious life after an unhappy love affair.

10 *Il ne reste donc que l'exemple qui puisse servir de règle à*

quantité de personnes dans l'exercice de la vertu.
Most people can learn only by example to be virtuous.
1731 *Histoire du chevalier Des Grieux et de Manon Lescaut*, Avis de l'auteur.

11 *Crois-tu qu'on puisse être bien tendre lorsqu'on manque de pain?*
Do you believe that a person can be truly affectionate when he is starving?
1731 *Histoire du chevalier Des Grieux et de Manon Lescaut*, ch.1.

12 *Il faut compter ses richesses par les moyens qu'on a de satisfaire ses désirs.*
We must count our riches by the means we have to satisfy our desires.
1731 *Histoire du chevalier Des Grieux et de Manon Lescaut*, ch.2.

Prial, Frank J

US writer and wine columnist for the *New York Times*.

13 Macaulay, Gibbon, Tolstoy, Francis Parkman and other immortals…never said anything in two pages that might possibly sound better in 10.
Quoted in the *New York Times*, 31 Mar 1990.

Price, Raymond

Nixon White House speechwriter.

14 The response is to the image, not to the man, since 99 percent of the voters have no contact with the man.
1967 Memo, 28 Nov. Quoted in the *New York Times*, 31 Oct 1993.

15 It's not what's *there* that counts, it's what's projected —and…it's not what *he* projects but rather what the voter receives… It's not the man we have to change, but rather the *received* impression.
1967 Memo, 28 Nov. Quoted in the *New York Times*, 31 Oct 1993.

Prichard, Katharine Susannah *married name* **Throssell**
1883–1969

Australian journalist, novelist and political activist. Western Australia is the background for her later novels including *Coonardoo* (1929).

16 Coonardoo they called it, the dark well, or the well in the shadows.
1929 *Coonardoo*, ch.1.

Priestley, J(ohn) B(oynton) 1894–1984

English writer, whose works include the novel *The Good Companions* (1929) and plays such as *Dangerous Corner* (1932). He achieved national renown as deliverer of radio 'postscripts' during World War II.

17 To say that these men paid their shillings to watch twenty-two hirelings kick a ball is merely to say that a violin is wood and catgut, that *Hamlet* is so much paper and ink. For a shilling the Bruddersford United AFC offered you Conflict and Art.
1929 *The Good Companions*, bk.1, ch.1.

18 The earth is nobler than the world we have put upon it.
1939 *Johnson Over Jordan*, act 3.

19 This little steamer, like all her brave and battered sisters, is immortal. She'll go sailing proudly down the years in the epic of Dunkirk. And our great-great-grand-children, when they learn how we began this war by snatching glory out of defeat, and then swept on to victory, may

also learn how the little holiday steamers made an excursion to hell and came back glorious.
1940 Radio broadcast, 5 Jun, quoted in *The Listener*, 13 Jun.

20 An Inspector Calls.
1947 Title of play.

21 The trouble is that we drink too much tea. I see in this the slow revenge of the Orient, which has diverted the Yellow River down our throats.
1949 In the *Observer*, 15 May.

22 Sometimes you might think that the machines we worship make all the chief appointments, promoting the human beings who seem closest to them.
1957 *Thoughts in the Wilderness*.

23 *Finnegans Wake* took him seventeen years to write, a length of time that suggests an elaborate hobby rather than a passionate desire to create something.
1960 Of James Joyce. *Literature and Western Man*.

24 He was a black Irish type, with centuries of rebelliousness behind him, and I decided to chance it.
1961 *Saturn Over the Water*.

25 I can't help feeling wary when I hear anything said about the masses. First you take their faces from 'em by calling 'em the masses and then you accuse 'em of not having any faces.
1961 *Saturn Over the Water*, ch.2.

26 It is hard to tell where the MCC ends and the Church of England begins.
1962 In the *New Statesman*, 20 Jul.

27 Some time ago, in an interview that turned towards the Theatre, I suggested that 'Pubic hair is not an adequate substitute for wit'. My point now is that depending upon shock tactics is easy, whereas writing a good play is difficult.
1974 *Outcries and Asides*, 'Danger of Shock Tactics'.

28 England is not ruined because sinewy brown men from a distant colony sometimes hit a ball further and oftener than our men do.
Quoted in Colin Jarman *The Guinness Dictionary of Sports Quotations* (1990).

Prince *in full* **Prince Roger Nelson** 1958–

US pop singer and composer. His works include the album *1999* (1982), and the film and album *Purple Rain* (1984).

29 Maybe at one time they could get Little Richard for a new car and a bucket of chicken. We don't roll like that no more.
2004 In *Rolling Stone*, 27 May.

Prior, Matthew 1664–1721

English poet and diplomat. His verse includes *The Hind and the Panther Transvers'd to the Story of the Country Mouse and the City Mouse* (with Charles Montagu, 1687, a satire on Dryden). He is remembered for his many witty, epigrammatic occasional verses.

30 They never taste who always drink;
They always talk who never think.
1697 'Upon this Passage in Scaligerana'.

31 Nobles and heralds, by your leave,
Here lies what once was Matthew Prior,
The son of Adam and of Eve,

Can Stuart or Nassaw go higher?
1702 'Epitaph'. In a later version 'Stuart' was changed to 'Bourbon'.

32 Be to her virtues very kind;
Be to her faults a little blind;
Let all her ways be unconfined;
And clap your padlock—on her mind.
1705 'An English Padlock'.

33 And of the pangs of absence to remove
By letters, soft interpreters of love.
1708 'Henry and Emma'.

34 But of good household features her person was made,
Nor by faction cry'd up nor of censure afraid,
And her beauty was rather for use than parade.
1708 'Jinny the Just' (first printed 1907). The title was given by A R Waller.

35 Cured yesterday of my disease,
I died last night of my physician.
1714 'The Remedy Worse than the Disease'.

36 Venus, take my votive glass;
Since I am not what I was,
What from this day I shall be
Venus never let me see.
1718 'The Lady Who Offered Her Looking-Glass to Venus'.

37 No, no; for my virginity,
When I lose that, says Rose, I'll die:
Behind the elms last night, cried Dick,
Rose, were you not extremely sick?
1718 'A True Maid'.

38 They walked and eat, good folks: What then?
Why then they walked and eat again:
They soundly slept the night away:
They did just nothing all the day.
1718 'An Epitaph', l.9–12.

39 Their beer was strong; their wine was port;
Their meal was large; their grace was short.
They gave the poor the remnant meat,
Just when it grew not fit to eat.
1718 'An Epitaph', l.29–32.

40 On his death bed poor Lubin lies:
His spouse is in despair.
With frequent sobs and mutual cries
They both express their care.

A different cause, says parson Sly,
The same effect may give:
Poor Lubin fears, that he shall die:
His wife, that he may live.
1718 'A Reasonable Affliction'.

41 What I speak, my fair Chloe, and what I write shows
The difference there is betwixt Nature and Art:
I court others in verse: but I love thee in prose:
And they have my whimsies, but thou hast my heart.
1718 'A Better Answer', stanza 4.

42 So when I am wearied with wandering all day;
To thee my delight in the evening I come:
No matter what beauties I saw in my way:
They were but my visits; but thou art my home.
1718 'A Better Answer', stanza 6.

43 And 'twould be a cruel thing,
When her black eyes have raised desire,

Should she not her bucket bring
And kindly help to quench the fire.
'Chloe Beauty Has and Wit'. (Date unknown. In *Matthew Prior: Literary Works*, edited by H B Wright and M K Spears, 2 vols, 1959.)

44 Rise not till noon, if life be but a dream,
As Greek and Roman poets have exprest:
Add good example to so grave a theme,
For he who sleeps the longest lives the best.
'Epigram'. (Date unknown. In *Matthew Prior: Literary Works*, edited by H B Wright and M K Spears, 2 vols, 1959.)

Pritchett, Sir V(ictor) S(awdon)   1900–97

English writer. He wrote novels and works of literary criticism and biography, but is best known for his short stories.

45 The principle of procrastinated rape is said to be the ruling one in all of the great best-sellers.
1946 *The Living Novel*, 'Clarissa'.

46 A touch of science, even bogus science, gives an edge to the superstitious tale.
1946 *The Living Novel*, 'An Irish Ghost'.

47 The detective novel is…the classic example of a specialized form of art removed from contact with the life it pretends to build on.
1951 In the *New Statesman*, 16 Jun.

48 He watched his restless hands, surprised they had remembered to come with him.
1951 *Mr Beluncle*, ch.15.

49 If evil does not exist, what is going to happen to literature?
1951 *Mr Beluncle*, ch.23.

50 Dickens was not the first or the last novelist to find virtue more difficult to portray than the wish for it.
1953 'Oliver Twist', collected in *Books in General* (1981).

51 It is well known that, when two or three authors meet, they at once start talking about money—like everyone else.
1978 In *The Author*, Spring.

52 What Chekhov saw in our failure to communicate was something positive and precious: the private silence in which we live, and which enables us to endure our own solitude.
1979 *The Myth Makers*, 'Chekhov'.

53 It is the role of the poet to look at what is happening in the world and to know that quite other things are happening.
1979 *The Myth Makers*, 'Pasternak'.

54 The poet is a master of the quotidian, of conveying a whole history in two or three lines that point to an exact past drama and intensify a future one.
1979 *The Myth Makers*, 'Borges'.

55 A short story is always a disclosure.
1981 *The Oxford Book of Short Stories* (edited by Pritchett), introduction.

56 'The firm'—a proud Victorian word. It evokes the lost sense of Victorian regard for the pride of people in their daily trade.
'Betjeman', in the *New Yorker*, 24 Jun.

Private Eye

British satirical magazine, founded 1962.

57 Kill An Argie—Win A Metro!

1982 Front page headline during the Falklands War, parodying the jingoism of tabloid coverage of the conflict.

Proctor, Adelaide Ann *pseudonym of* **Mary Berwick**
1825–64

English poet. She won renown with her *Legends and Lyrics* (1858–60), and her poem 'The Lost Chord' was set to music by Sir Arthur Sullivan.

58 Seated one day at the organ,
　　I was weary and ill at ease,
　　And my fingers wandered idly
　　Over the noisy keys;
　　I know not what I was playing,
　　Or what I was dreaming then,
　　But I struck one chord of music,
　　Like the sound of a great Amen.

1858 'The Lost Chord'.

Profumo, John Dennis 1915–

English Conservative politician, Secretary of State for War in 1960. He resigned in 1963 during the 'Profumo Affair', admitting that he had deceived the House over the nature of his relationship with Christine Keeler, who was at the time also involved with a Russian diplomat. He turned to charitable service, and was awarded the CBE in 1975.

59 There was no impropriety whatsoever in my acquaintanceship with Miss Keeler… I shall not hesitate to issue writs for libel and slander if scandalous allegations are made or repeated outside the House.

1963 House of Commons, Mar.

Prokofiev, Sergei Sergeyevich 1891–1953

Russian composer, who lived in exile in the West (1918–36). His works include the *Classical Symphony* (1917), the opera *The Love for Three Oranges* (1919), the ballets *The Prodigal Son* (1928) and *Romeo and Juliet* (1936), *Peter and the Wolf* (1936) and the opera *War and Peace* (1943).

60 Bach on the wrong notes.

Of the music of Stravinsky. Quoted in V Seroff *Sergei Prokofiev* (1968).

Propertius, Sextus 1c BC

Roman poet.

61 *Navita de ventis, de tauris narrat arator,*
　　Enumerat miles vulnera, pastor oves.
　　The sailor tells stories of the winds, the ploughman of bulls; the soldier lists his wounds, the shepherd his sheep.

Elegies, bk.2, no.1, l.43–4.

62 *Cedite Romani scriptores, cedite Grai!*
　　Nescioquid maius nascitur Iliade.
　　Make way, Roman writers, make way, Greeks! Something greater than the *Iliad* is born.

Of Virgil's *Aeneid*. *Elegies*, bk.2, no.34, l.65–6.

Protagoras c.490–c.420 BC

Greek Sophist and teacher, the first and most famous of the Sophists who, for a fee, offered professional training in public life and other skills. His works survive only as fragments in other writers (notably Plato).

63 Man is the measure of all things, of the existence of the things that are, and the non-existence of the things that are not.

Fragment quoted in Plato *Theaetetus*, 152a (translated by H North Fowler, 1977).

64 He said that there is no art without practice, and no practice without art.

Fragment quoted in H Diels and W Kranz (eds) *Die Fragmente der Vorsokratiker*, vol.2 (1952), 268, no.10.

65 Concerning the gods I am not in a position to know either that they are or that they are not, or what they are like in appearance; for there are many things that are preventing knowledge, the obscurity of the matter and the brevity of human life.

Quoted in G B Kerferd *The Sophistic Movement* (1981), ch.13.

Proudhon, Pierre Joseph 1809–65

French socialist and political theorist, the founder of French radicalism. His works include the great *Système des contradictions économiques* (1846, *System of Economic Contradictions*). Imprisoned for three years in 1849 and again in 1858, he spent the time writing further works arguing for liberty, equality and justice.

66 *La propriété, c'est le vol.*
　　Property is theft.

1840 *Qu'est-ce que la propriété?*.

67 Universal suffrage is counter-revolution.

On Europe after the 1848 revolution. Quoted in A J P Taylor *From Napoleon to the Second International* (1993).

Proulx, Annie 1935–

US author whose works include *The Shipping News* (1993), which won a number of awards including the Pulitzer Prize (1994).

68 If you get the landscape right, the characters will step out of it, and they'll be in the right place.

1993 *Time*, 29 Nov.

69 At thirty-six, bereft, brimming with grief and thwarted love, Quoyle steered away to Newfoundland, the rock that had generated his ancestors, a place he had never been nor thought to go.

1993 *The Shipping News*, ch.1.

Proust, Marcel 1871–1922

French novelist who withdrew (c.1905) from society because of asthma, the death of his parents and disillusionment with the world. He introduced psychological analysis into fiction, notably in his 13-volume novel sequence *À la recherche du temps perdu* (1913–27).

70 *Il vaut mieux rêver sa vie que la vivre, encore que la vivre ce soit encore la rêver.*
　　It's better to dream your life than to live it, and even though you live it, you will still dream it.

1896 *Les Plaisirs et les jours*.

71 *Le bonheur est dans l'amour un état anormal.*
　　In love, happiness is abnormal.

1919 *À la recherche du temps perdu*, 'À l'ombre des jeunes filles en fleurs'.

72 *Nous sommes tous obligés, pour rendre la réalité supportable, d'entretenir en nous quelques petites folies.*
　　We must all indulge in a few follies if we are to make reality bearable.

1919 *À la recherche du temps perdu*,'À l'ombre des jeunes filles en fleurs'.

73 *L'adolescence est le seul temps où l'on ait appris quelque chose.*
Adolescence is the only time when we can learn something.
1919 *À la recherche du temps perdu*,'À l'ombre des jeunes filles en fleurs'.

74 *On devient moral dès qu'on est malheureux.*
We become moral once we are miserable.
1919 *À la recherche du temps perdu*,'À l'ombre des jeunes filles en fleurs'.

75 *On ne reçoit pas la sagesse, il faut la découvrir soi-même, après un trajet que personne ne peut faire pour nous, ne peut nous épargner.*
We do not receive wisdom.We must discover it ourselves after experiences which no one else can have for us and from which no one else can spare us.
1919 *À la recherche du temps perdu*,'À l'ombre des jeunes filles en fleurs'.

76 *Il n'y avait pas d'anormaux quand l'homosexualité était la norme.*
There was nothing abnormal about it when homosexuality was the norm.
1921 *À la recherche du temps perdu*,'Sodome et Gomorrhe'.

77 *La médecine a fait quelques petits progrès dans ses connaissances depuis Molière, mais aucun dans son vocabulaire.*
Medicine has made a few, small advances in knowledge since Molière, but none in its vocabulary.
1921 *À la recherche du temps perdu*,'Sodome et Gomorrhe'.

78 Neurosis has an absolute genius for malingering. There is no illness which it cannot counterfeit perfectly.
1922 *Sodom and Gomorrah.*

79 *L'amour, c'est l'espace et le temps rendus sensibles au cœur.*
Love is space and time made tender to the heart.
1923 *À la recherche du temps perdu*,'La Prisonnière'.

80 *La possession de ce qu'on aime est une joie plus grande encore que l'amour.*
Possessing what one loves is an even greater joy than love itself.
1923 *À la recherche du temps perdu*,'La Prisonnière'.

81 *On a dit que la beauté est une promesse de bonheur. Inversement, la possibilité du plaisir peut être un commencement de beauté.*
It has been said that beauty is a guarantee of happiness. Conversely, the possibility of pleasure can be the beginning of beauty.
1923 *À la recherche du temps perdu*,'La Prisonnière'.

82 *L'adultère introduit l'esprit dans la lettre que bien souvent le mariage eût laissée morte.*
Adultery breathes new life into marriages which have been left for dead.
1923 *À la recherche du temps perdu*,'La Prisonnière'.

83 *L'idée qu'on mourra est plus cruelle que mourir, mais moins que l'idée qu'un autre est mort.*
The idea of dying is worse than dying itself, but less cruel than the idea that another has died.
1923 *À la recherche du temps perdu*,'La Prisonnière'.

84 [Music] a pederast might hum when raping a choirboy.

Of Fauré's *Romances sans paroles*. Quoted in *Musical Quarterly*, 1924.

85 *Laissons les jolies femmes aux hommes sans imagination.*
Leave the pretty women for the men without imagination.
1925 *À la recherche du temps perdu*,'Albertine disparue'.

86 *Le mensonge est essentiel à l'humanité. Il y joue peut-être un aussi grand rôle que la recherche du plaisir, et d'ailleurs est commandé par cette recherche.*
Lies are essential to humanity. They play perhaps as great a role as the pursuit of pleasure, and are indeed controlled by this pursuit.
1925 *À la recherche du temps perdu*,'Albertine disparue'.

87 *Si notre vie est vagabonde, notre mémoire est sédentaire.*
Even though our lives wander, our memories remain in one place.
1927 *À la recherche du temps perdu*,'LeTemps retrouvé'.

88 *Le temps qui change les êtres ne modifie pas l'image que nous avons gardée d'eux.*
Although time changes people, it cannot change the image we have already made of them.
1927 *À la recherche du temps perdu*,'LeTemps retrouvé'.

89 *Le bonheur est salutaire pour les corps, mais c'est le chagrin qui développe les forces de l'esprit.*
Happiness is healthy for the body, but it is sorrow which enhances the forces of the mind.
1927 *À la recherche du temps perdu*,'LeTemps retrouvé'.

90 *Le style, pour l'écrivain aussi bien que pour le peintre, est une question non de technique mais de vision.*
For the writer as well as for the painter, style is not a question of technique, but of vision.
1927 *À la recherche du temps perdu*,'LeTemps retrouvé'.

91 *Pour écrire ce livre essentiel, le seul livre vrai, un grand écrivain n'a pas, dans le sens courant, à l'inventer puisqu'il existe déjà en chacun de nous, mais à le traduire.*
To write the essential book, the only true book, a great writer does not need to invent because the book already exists inside each one of us and merely needs translation.
1927 *À la recherche du temps perdu*,'LeTemps retrouvé'.

92 *En réalité, chaque lecteur est, quand il lit, le propre lecteur de soi-même. L'ouvrage de l'écrivain n'est qu'une espèce d'instrument optique qu'il offre au lecteur afin de lui permettre de discerner ce que, sans ce livre, il n'eût peut-être pas vu en soi-même.*
In reality, each reader reads only what is already within himself. The book is only a kind of optical instrument which the writer offers to the reader to enable him to discover in himself what he could not have found but for the aid of the book.
1927 *À la recherche du temps perdu*,'LeTemps retrouvé'.

Prout, Father

➤ *See Mahony, Francis Sylvester*

Prynne, William 1600–69

English Puritan. An opponent of the theatre, he was imprisoned for publishing *Histrio Mastix: The Players' Scourge, or Actors' Tragedie* (1633), with its criticism of Charles I's queen Henrietta

Maria. His ears were cut off as a punishment in 1634 and he was imprisoned again in 1650 for refusing to pay taxes.

93 Stage-plays…are sinfull, heathenish, lewd, ungodly Spectacles and most pernicious Corruptions, condemned in all ages as intolerable Mischiefes to Churches, to Republickes, to the manners, mindes and soules of men. And that the Profession of Play-poets, of Stage-players; together with the penning, acting and frequenting of Stage-plays are unlawfull, infamous and misbeseeming Christians.

1633 *Histrio Mastix: The Players' Scourge, or Actors' Tragedie.*

Pryor, Richard 1940–

US comedian.

94 Two things people throughout history have had in common are hatred and humour. I am proud that I have been able to use humour to lessen people's hatred.

2004 In *The Scotsman*, 5 Jun.

Publilius Syrus 1c BC

Writer of Latin mimes.

95 *Formosa facies muta commendatio est.*
A beautiful face is a dumb commendation.
Sententiae.

96 *Inopi beneficium bis dat qui dat celeriter.*
He who gives quickly gives the poor man twice as much.
Sententiae.

Puccini, Giacomo Antonio Domenico Michele Secondo Maria 1858–1924

Italian composer, best known for his operas *La Bohème* (1896), *Tosca* (1900) and *Madama Butterfly* (1900). His last opera, *Turandot*, was unfinished.

97 Who sent you to me—God?

To Caruso, who was auditioning for him. Quoted in Derek Watson *Music Quotations* (1991).

Puckett, B Earl

US businessman, President of Allied Stores Corp.

98 It is our job to make women unhappy with what they have.

Recalled on his death, in *Newsweek*, 23 Feb 1976.

Pudney, John Sleigh 1909–77

British poet, journalist and novelist. He is best known for his poem 'For Johnny' (1941) and his novel *The Net* (1952).

99 Do not despair
For Johnny Head-in-Air
He sleeps as sound
As Johnny Underground.

1941 'For Johnny', spoken by Sir Michael Redgrave at the end of the film *The Way to the Stars* (1945).

Puig, Manuel 1932–90

Argentinian novelist. He studied cinema in Rome and spent several years in New York. His novels, which often exploit society's popular icons, include *El beso de la mujer araña* (1976), adapted for stage, screen and Broadway musical.

1 *Porque, sí, fuera de la celda están nuestros opresores,*

pero adentro no. Aquí nadie oprime a nadie. Lo único que hay, de perturbador, para mi mente…cansada, o condicionada o deformada…es que alguien me quiere tratar bien, sin pedir nada a cambio.
Because, well, outside of this cell we may have our oppressors, yes, but not inside. Here no one oppresses the other. The only thing that seems to disturb me… because I'm exhausted, or conditioned, or perverted…is that someone wants to be nice to me, without asking anything back for it.

1976 *El beso de la mujer araña*, ch.11 (translated as *Kiss of the Spider Woman*, 1978).

Pulitzer, Joseph 1847–1911

Hungarian-born US newspaper proprietor. He emigrated to the US in 1864, became a reporter and began to acquire and revitalize old newspapers, notably the New York *World*. He established the annual Pulitzer prizes.

2 I want to talk to a nation, not to a select committee.

1909 In *Pearson's Magazine*, Mar.

3 We are a democracy, and there is only one way to get a democracy on its feet in the matter of its individual, its social, its municipal, its State, its National conduct, and that is by keeping the public informed about what is going on. There is not a crime, there is not a dodge, there is not a trick, there is not a swindle, there is not a vice which does not live by secrecy. Get these things out in the open, describe them, attack them, ridicule them in the press, and sooner or later public opinion will sweep them away.

c.1910 Quoted in Alleyne Ireland *An Adventure with a Genius*, ch.4.

4 What a newspaper needs in its news, in its headlines, and on its editorial page is terseness, humor, descriptive power, satire, originality, good literary style, clever condensation and accuracy, accuracy, accuracy.

c.1910 Quoted in Alleyne Ireland *An Adventure with a Genius*, ch.4.

Punch

British humorous weekly periodical, founded 1841.

5 Advice to persons about to marry—don't.
1845

6 You pays your money and you takes your choice.
1846

7 Let us be a nation of shopkeepers as much as we please, but there is no necessity that we should become a nation of advertisers.

1848 Quoted in David Ogilvy *Confessions of an Advertising Man* (1963), ch.2.

➤ See Smith 798:50.

8 Never do today what you can put off till tomorrow.
1849

9 Nothink for nothink 'ere, and precious little for sixpence.
1869

10 Sure, the next train has gone ten minutes ago.
1871

11 Go directly—see what she's doing, and tell her she mustn't.
1872

12 There was one poor tiger that hadn't *got* a Christian.
1875

13 I am not hungry; but thank goodness, I am greedy.
1878

14 Nearly all our best men are dead! Carlyle, Tennyson, Browning, George Eliot!—I'm not feeling very well myself.
1891

15 Botticelli isn't a wine, you Juggins! Botticelli's a *cheese!*
1891

16 Sometimes I sits and thinks, and then again I just sits.
1906

Purdy, Al 1918–2000

Canadian poet. Born in rural Ontario, he settled there again after some years away. He published nearly 30 volumes of poetry, including *The Cariboo Horses* (1965), *The Stone Bird* (1981) and *To Paris Never Again: New Poems* (1997).

17 Uneasily the leaves fall at this season,
forgetting what to do or where to go;
the red amnesiacs of autumn
drifting thru the graveyard forest.

What they have forgotten they have forgotten:
what they meant to do instead of fall
is not in earth or time recoverable—
the fossils of intention, the shapes of rot.
1962 *Poems for All the Annettes*, 'Pause' (revised 1968).

18 This is the country of defeat.
1965 *The Cariboo Horses*, 'The Country North of Belleville' (revised 1972).

19 They had their being once
and left a place to stand on.
1968 *Poems for All the Annettes*, 'Roblin Mills' (revised 1972).

Pushkin, Aleksandr Sergeyevich 1799–1837

Russian poet and writer. He is best known for the novel in verse *Eugene Onegin* (1833) and the tragic drama *Boris Godunov* (1825). He also wrote ballads and prose pieces. He was killed in a duel with his brother-in-law.

20 Moscow…what surge that sound can start
In every Russian's inmost heart!
1833 *Eugene Onegin*, ch.7, stanza 36 (translated by Adrian Room, 1995).

Putnam, Israel 1718–90

American general in the American Revolution.

21 Men, you are all marksmen—don't one of you fire until you see the white of their eyes.
1775 Order before the Battle of Bunker Hill. Quoted in R Frothingham *History of the Siege of Boston* (1873), ch.5.

Pu Yi 1906–67

Chinese puppet emperor. He was proclaimed Emperor at the age of two, but after the Chinese Revolution (1911) he was given a pension and a summer palace. He eventually became a private citizen. The story of his life was made into a film, *The Last Emperor*, in 1988.

22 For the past 40 years I had never folded my own quilt, made my own bed, or poured out my own washing. I had never even washed my own feet or tied my shoes.
1964 *From Emperor to Citizen: The Autobiography of Aisin-Gioro Pu Yi* (translated by W J F Jenner).

Puzo, Mario 1920–99

US novelist. His breakthrough as a writer came with his novel about the Mafia, *The Godfather* (1969). It became a bestseller and the basis of a trilogy of films directed by Francis Ford Coppola.

23 I'll make him an offer he can't refuse.
1969 *The Godfather*, bk.1, ch.1.

24 A lawyer with a briefcase can steal more than a hundred men with guns.
1969 *The Godfather*, bk.1, ch.1.

25 Like many businessmen of genius he learned that free competition was wasteful, monopoly efficient. And so he simply set about achieving that efficient monopoly.
1969 *The Godfather*, bk.3, ch.14.

26 Show me a gambler and I'll show you a loser, show me a hero, and I'll show you a corpse.
1978 *Fools Die*, ch.2.

27 Our own death wish is our only real tragedy.
1978 *Fools Die*, ch.55.

28 No, I never heard nothing about it, but when they name any disease after two guys, it's got to be terrible!
On Guillain-Barré syndrome. Quoted in Heller and Vogel *No Laughing Matter* (1986).

Pyke, Magnus 1908–92

British scientist and broadcaster.

29 Once a man or woman begins to take a serious interest in the way the universe works—that is to say in science—there is no telling what may turn up.
1976 *Butter Side Up*.

Pyrrhus of Epirus 319–272 BC

Greek king, renowned for his wars against the Romans. From 281 BC he fought Rome on behalf of the Tarentines and won battles in 280 BC and 279 BC, but with very high casualties (hence the expression a 'Pyrrhic victory'). He was killed in a street fight in Argos during a war with the Macedonians.

30 One more such victory, and we are lost!
279 BC After defeating the Romans at Asculum. Quoted in Plutarch *Regum et imperatorum apophthegmata*, 184c.

Pythagoras 6c BC

Greek philosopher and mathematician. He founded a school in Crotona but was persecuted there and settled in Lucania. He taught an abstemious way of life and a doctrine of transmigration, but is best remembered for his mathematical work.

31 There is geometry in the humming of the strings. There is music in the spacings of the spheres.
Quoted in Aristotle *Metaphysics*.

Qaboos, Bin Said 1940–

Sultan of Oman. On the deposition of his father in 1970 he became Oman's ruler. He is also Prime Minister and Minister of Foreign Affairs, Defence and Finance.

32 Don't wait for schools to be built. Teach the children under the nearest tree.
> **1995** Quoted by Rosalind Miles in 'An Oxonian in Oman', in *Oxford Today*, vol.7, no.2, Hilary Issue, 1995.

Qian, Zhang

33 They gave us our rice bowl and we don't want it broken.
> **1993** On the need to avoid offending the government that permitted broadcasts by Shanghai's Radio Orient. In the *New York Times*, 26 Apr.

Quant, Mary 1934–

English fashion designer. She opened a small boutique, Bazaar, in Chelsea in 1955. In the 1960s she became one of the best-known designers of the 'swinging Britain' era when the simplicity of her designs, especially the mini-skirt, and the originality of her colours attracted international attention.

34 A fashionable woman wears clothes; the clothes don't wear her.
> **1966** *Quant by Quant.*

35 Fashion should be a game.
> **1966** *Quant by Quant.*

36 A woman is as young as her knee.
> Attributed.

Quarles, Francis 1592–1644

English religious poet. His best-known works are *Emblems* (1635), a series of symbolic pictures with verse commentary, and a book of aphorisms, *Enchyridion* (1640).

37 My soul; sit thou a patient looker-on;
Judge not the play before the play is done:
Her plot hath many changes, every day
Speaks a new scene; the last act crowns the play.
> **1630** *Epigram, Respice Finem.*

Quayle, Dan (James Danforth) 1947–

US politician. He became a member of Congress (1977–81) and the Senate (1981–8) and served as Vice-President under George Bush (1988–92).

38 It doesn't help…when primetime TV has a character… bearing a child alone…just another lifestyle choice.
> **1992** Criticism of Murphy Brown, played by Candice Bergen. In the *Washington Post*, 21 May. The comment set off a great controversy about single mothers and freedom of choice.
> ➤ *See Bentsen 78:84.*

Quennell, Sir Peter Courtney 1905–93

English biographer, Professor of English at Tokyo (1930). He wrote travel books, verse and novels, but is best known for his biographies of literary figures.

39 Every occupation, unless it employs the whole mind and satisfies the human creative instinct, is to some extent absurd; and about the advertising business what I chiefly disliked was not so much the work I did as its general atmosphere of unreality. We dealt in fairy-gold—in fugitive dreams and illusions.
> **1977** *The Marble Foot: an Autobiography, 1905–1938*, p.227.

Quiller-Couch, Sir Arthur Thomas *known as* 'Q' 1863–1944

English writer and critic. His prominence as a critic dates from 1900, when he edited the *Oxford Book of English Verse*. He also wrote novels, short stories, children's books and poetry.

40 He that loves but half of Earth
Loves but half enough for me.
> **1896** 'The Comrade'.

41 Not as we wanted it,
But as God granted it.
> **1896** 'To Bearers'.

42 O the Harbour of Fowey
Is a beautiful spot,
And it's there I enjowey
To sail in a yot;
Or to race in a yacht
Round a mark or a buoy—
Such a beautiful spacht
Is the Harbour of Fuoy!
> **1899** *A Fowey Garland*, 'The Harbour of Fowey'.

43 The best is the best, though a hundred judges have declared it so.
> **1900** *The Oxford Book of English Verse*, preface.

44 Our fathers have, in process of centuries, provided this realm, its colonies and wide dependencies, with a speech as malleable and pliant as Attic, dignified as Latin, masculine, yet free of Teutonic guttural, capable of being precise as French, dulcet as Italian, sonorous as Spanish, and captaining all these excellences to its service.
> **1900** *The Oxford Book of English Verse*, preface.

45 Literature is not an abstract science, to which exact definitions can be applied. It is an Art rather, the success of which depends on personal persuasiveness, on the author's skill to give as on ours to receive.
> **1913** Inaugural lecture as Professor of English at Cambridge University.

46 Gilbert had a baddish streak or two in him; and one in particular which was not only baddish but so thoroughly caddish that no critic can ignore or, in my view, extenuate it. The man, to summarize, was essentially cruel, and delighted in cruelty.
> **1929** Of W S Gilbert. *Studies in Literature*, 3rd series, 'Lecture on W.S. Gilbert', no.4.

47 There was an old man of St Omer
Who objected, 'This town's a misnomer;
You've no right to translate
And beatificate
A simple digamma in Homer.'
> **1941** 'A Limerick', in *Chanticlere*, Michaelmas Term.

48 Swinburne is just emptiness to me as he gets older, and the more maddening as he goes on exploiting a heavenly gift. I wish he had just shut up, like Coleridge, and left us surmising wonders.

Quoted in A L Rowse *Quiller-Couch: a Portrait of 'Q'* (1988).

Quin, James 1693–1766

English actor. A performer in the tradition of heroic tragedy, whose most acclaimed roles included Falstaff, he outlived the popularity of the bombastic declamatory style of which he was the master but steadfastly refused to change with the times. He was also noted for his fiery temper.

49 If the young fellow is right, I and the rest of the players have been all wrong.

c.1741 Of David Garrick and his revolutionary, more naturalistic acting style. Attributed.

Quindlen, Anna 1953–

US journalist and author. She worked as a reporter for the *New York Times* (1977–81) and is now a syndicated columnist. She won the Pulitzer Prize for Commentary in 1992 and was named Woman of the Year for 1991 by *Glamour* magazine.

50 The purse is the mirror of the soul.

1987 In the *New York Times*, 16 Dec.

Quine, Willard Van Orman 1908–2000

US philosopher and logician, Professor of Philosophy at Harvard (1948–78). He wrote many works on logic and language, including *Two Dogmas of Empiricism* (1951), *Word and Object* (1960) and *From Stimulus to Science* (1995).

51 To define an expression is, paradoxically speaking, to explain how to get along without it. To define is to eliminate.

1987 *Quiddities*, 'Definition'.

52 We can applaud the state lottery as a public subsidy of intelligence, for it yields public income that is calculated to lighten the tax burden of us prudent abstainers at the expense of the benighted masses of wishful thinkers.

1987 *Quiddities*, 'Gambling'.

Quinet, Edgar 1803–75

French writer and politician.

53 *La famille des Bourbons est un poignard que l'étranger en 1814 a laissé dans le cœur de la France: changez le manche comme il vous plaira, dorez la lame si vous voulez, le poignard reste poignard.*

The Bourbon family is a dagger which the foreigner left in the heart of France in 1814: change the haft if you please, gild the blade if you will, the dagger remains a dagger.

1877 *Œuvres*, vol.3, p.267.

Quinn, Jane Bryant 1939–

US journalist, broadcaster and financial pundit. Her works include *Everyone's Money Book* (1979) and *Making the Most of Your Money* (1991).

54 Half of them don't know what's going to happen tomorrow and the other half don't know they don't know.

1994 Of stock market players. On CNN TV, 4 Apr.

Quintilian *properly* Marcus Fabius Quintilianus

c.35–c.100 AD

Roman rhetorician born in Spain. He studied oratory at Rome

and settled there as an advocate and teacher of rhetoric. His pupils included Pliny the Younger. His reputation rests on his *Institutio Oratoria* ('Education of an Orator').

55 *Mendaces memorem esse oportere.*

Liars need to have good memories.

Institutio Oratoria, 4.2.9.1 (translated by H E Butler, 1968).

56 *Scribitur ad narrandum, non ad probandum.*

It is written for the purpose of narrative, not of proof.

Of history. *Institutio Oratoria*, 10.1.31 (translated by H E Butler, 1968).

Quiroga, Horacio 1878–1937

Uruguayan short-story writer, who spent most of his life in the Argentinian province of Misiones, where most of his stories, generally dealing with morbid themes, are set. He committed suicide in a charity hospital.

57 *Se comprende muy bien que el advenimiento del cinematógrafo haya sido para mí el comienzo de un nueva era, por la cual cuento las noches sucesivas en que he salido mareado y pálido del cine, porque he dejado mi corazón…en la pantalla que impregnó por tres cuartos de hora el encanto de Brownie Vernon.*

It is easy to understand that, for me, cinema was the beginning of a new era which marked my nights, one after the other, as I left the theatre, dizzy and pale after leaving my heart on the screen…on that screen that for forty-five minutes was impregnated by Brownie Vernon's charm.

1921 *Anaconda*, 'Miss Dorothy Phillips, mi esposa' ('Miss Dorothy Phillips, My Wife').

Raban, Jonathan 1942–

English writer. He has written novels and literary criticism, but is best known for his travel books. He now lives in the US.

58 The Falklands held a mirror up to our own islands, and it reflected, in brilliantly sharp focus, all our injured belittlement, our sense of being beleaguered, neglected and misunderstood.

1986 *Coasting*, ch.3.

59 If we live inside a bad joke, it is up to us to learn, at best and worst, to tell it well.

1986 *Coasting*, ch.6.

60 Good travel books are novels at heart.

Recalled by Christopher Lehmann-Haupt in the *New York Times*, 26 Jan 1987, reviewing Raban's novel *Coasting* (1986).

61 The mythical America…—that marvellous, heroic, sentimental land—was an object of faith. It challenged you to make the believer's leap over the rude facts at your feet.

1990 *Hunting Mister Heartbreak*, ch.2.

Rabelais, François c.1494–c.1553

French humanist and satirist, who began his career as a

Franciscan monk. He studied Greek and Latin as well as medicine, law and philology, and wrote two novels under the pseudonym Alcofribas Nasier.

62 *Science sans conscience n'est que ruine de l'âme.*
Science without conscience is the soul's perdition.
1532 *Pantagruel*, bk.2, ch.8.

63 *Il avait soixante et trois manières d'en trouver toujours à son besoin, dont la plus honorable et la plus commune était par façon de larcin furtivement fait.*
He had sixty-three ways to find the money when he needed it, the most honourable and most ordinary of which was to steal secretively.
1532 *Pantagruel*, bk.2, ch.16.

64 *Mieux est de ris que de larmes écrire*
Pour ce que rire est le propre de l'homme.
It is better to write of laughter than of tears
For laughter is the basis of humankind.
1534 *Gargantua*, Aux lecteurs.

65 *L'odeur du vin, ô combien plus est friand, riant, priant, plus céleste et délicieux que d'huile!*
The odour of wine, oh how much sweeter, more cheerful, pleasing, heavenly and delicious it is than oil!
1534 *Gargantua*, Prologue de l'auteur.

66 *Rompre l'os et sucer la substantifique moelle.*
Break the bone and suck out the very substance.
1534 *Gargantua*, Prologue de l'auteur.

67 *L'appétit vient en mangeant.*
Appetite comes with eating.
1534 *Gargantua*, bk.1, ch.5.

68 *Du cheval donné toujours regardait en la gueule.*
Always look a gift horse in the mouth.
1534 *Gargantua*, bk.1, ch.11.

69 *Lever matin n'est point bonheur;*
Boire matin est le meilleur.
Getting up in the morning does not make you happy;
Drinking in the morning is the best.
1534 *Gargantua*, bk.1, ch.22.

70 *Nature n'endure mutations soudaines sans grande violence.*
Nature does not endure sudden changes without great violence.
1534 *Gargantua*, bk.1, ch.23.

71 *Thésauriser est fait de vilain.*
To hoard is a villainous act.
1534 *Gargantua*, bk.1, ch.33.

72 *Jamais je ne m'assujettis aux heures: les heures sont faites pour l'homme, et non l'homme pour les heures.*
I never subject myself to hours: hours are made for men; men are not made for hours.
1534 *Gargantua*, bk.1, ch.41.

73 *En leur règle n'était que cette clause: FAIS CE QUE VOUDRAS.*
In their laws there was but this one clause: DO WHAT YOU WISH.
1534 *Gargantua*, bk.1, ch.57.

74 *Un fol enseigne bien un sage.*
A fool has a lot to teach a wise man.
1546 *Tiers Livre*, pt.37.

75 *O que trois et quatre fois heureux sont ceux qui plantent choux!*
Oh, those who plant cabbages are three and four times happier than the rest of us!
1548 *Quart Livre*, pt.18.

76 *Pantagruélisme…est certaine gaieté d'esprit confite en mépris des choses fortuites.*
Pantagruelism is a certain liveliness of mind made in contempt of chance happenings.
1552 *Quart Livre*, Prologue de l'auteur.

77 *Ignorance est mère de tous les maux.*
Ignorance is the mother of all evils.
1564 *Cinquième Livre*, pt.7.

78 Abandon yourself to Nature's truths, and let nothing in this world be unknown to you.
Quoted in J H Plumb (ed) *The Horizon Book of the Renaissance* (1961).

Rabi, Isidor Isaac 1898–1988

US physicist, born in Austria. He taught physics at Columbia from 1929 and served as an adviser to the US Atomic Energy Commission. Rabi won the 1944 Nobel prize in physics for his discovery and measurement of the radio-frequency spectra of atomic nuclei.

79 It is only in science, I find, that we can get outside ourselves. It's realistic, and to a great degree verifiable, and it has this tremendous stage on which it plays. I have the same feeling—to a certain degree—about some religious expressions…but only to a certain degree. For me, the proper study of mankind is science, which also means that the proper study of mankind is man.
Quoted in Jeremy Bernstein *Experiencing Science* (1978).

Rabin, Yitzhak 1922–95

Israeli soldier and statesman. He was awarded the Nobel peace prize jointly with Shimon Peres and Yasser Arafat in 1994.

80 We say to you today in a loud and a clear voice: enough of blood and tears. Enough.
1993 To the Palestinians. Speech in Washington, 13 Sep.

Rachmaninov, Sergei Vasilevich 1873–1943

Russian composer and pianist, who settled in the US in 1918, best known for his piano music. His style epitomizes the lush romanticism of the later 19c, still apparent in his last major composition, *Rhapsody on a Theme of Paganini* (1934).

81 My dear hands. Farewell, my poor hands.
On being told that he was dying of cancer. Quoted in H Schonberg *The Great Pianists* (1964).

Racine, Jean 1639–99

French court dramatist who studied at Port Royal and went on to write many of his dramatic works for performance there.

82 *Ah! je l'ai trop aimé pour ne le point haïr!*
Oh! I loved him too much not to hate him now!
1667 *Andromaque*, act 2, sc.1.

83 *Les témoins sont fort chers, et n'en a pas qui veut.*
Witnesses are expensive and not everyone can afford them.
1668 *Les Plaideurs*, act 3, sc.3.

84 *J'aimais jusqu'à ses pleurs que je faisais couler.*
I loved even the tears which I made her cry.
1669 *Britannicus*, act 2, sc.2.

85 *J'embrasse mon rival, mais c'est pour l'étouffer.*
If I embrace my rival, it is to strangle him.
1669 *Britannicus*, act 4, sc.3.

86 *Ainsi que la vertu, le crime a ses degrés.*
Crime, like virtue, has its degrees.
1677 *Phèdre*, act 4, sc.2.

87 *Pensez-vous être saint et juste impunément?*
You think you can be holy and righteous with impunity?
1691 *Athalie*, act 1, sc.1.

Radisson, Pierre-Esprit 1636–1710

French traveller, explorer of New France (Canada).

88 We were Caesars, there being nobody to contradict us.
Attributed boast of the *coureur de bois* in the Canadian North West. Quoted in Arthur T Adams (ed) *The Explorations of Pierre-Esprit Radisson* (1961).

Rado, James 1939–

US composer and librettist.

89 This is the dawning of the age of Aquarius.
1968 *Hair*, 'Aquarius' (music by Galt MacDermot).

Rae, John 1931–

English writer.

90 War is, after all, the universal perversion.
1960 *The Custard Boys*, ch.13.

Rahner, Karl 1904–84

German Jesuit priest, who taught at Innsbruck and Munich and who was widely recognized as a leading Roman Catholic theologian.

91 But there is yet another form of this hidden heresy, and, paradoxically, it can affect those who are proudest of their long-standing and unimpeachable orthodoxy; heresy in the form of indifference.
1963 'Natur und Gnade' in *Fragen der Theologie Heute* (translated by Dinah Wharton as *Nature and Grace*, 1963).

Rainborowe, Thomas 1598–1648

English soldier.

92 The poorest He that is in England hath a life to live as well as the greatest He, and therefore, truly Sirs, I think that every man that is to live under a Government ought first, by his own consent, to put himself under that Government.
1647 Said to Cromwell during the Army Debates, Putney, 29 Oct.

Raine, Craig Anthony 1944–

English poet and critic. His collections include *A Martian Sends a Postcard Home* (1979) and *Collected Poems 1978–1999* (1999).

93 We live in the great indoors:
the vacuum cleaner grazes
over the carpet, lowing,
its udder a swollen wobble.
1978 'An Inquiry into Two Inches of Ivory'.
➤ *See Austen 43:88.*

94 Caxtons are mechanical birds with many wings
and some are treasured for their markings.
1979 'A Martian Sends a Postcard Home'.

95 But time is tied to the wrist

or kept in a box, ticking with impatience.
1979 'A Martian Sends a Postcard Home'.

96 The mind is a museum
to be looted at night.
1984 'The Grey Boy'.

Raine, Kathleen Jessie 1908–2003

English poet and critic. Her poetry reflects a mystical, visionary appreciation of nature, and she was a sympathetic critic of symbolists such as Blake, Hopkins and Yeats.

97 Nowadays harmony comes almost as a shock.
Letter to Arthur Bliss.

Raleigh, Sir Walter 1552–1618

English courtier, navigator and poet. His writings include lyric poems, *The Discovery of Guyana* (1596) and an unfinished *History of the World* (1614). Implicated in a plot to overthrow Queen Elizabeth, his death sentence was suspended until 1618, when he was beheaded.

98 If all the world and love were young,
And truth in every shepherd's tongue
These pretty pleasures might me move
To live with thee and be thy love.
c.1592 'The Nymph's Reply to the Shepherd', a response to Marlowe's 'The Passionate Shepherd to His Love', attributed to Raleigh.
➤ *See Marlowe 553:17.*

99 Give me my scallop-shell of quiet,
My staff of faith to walk upon,
My scrip of joy, immortal diet,
My bottle of salvation,
My gown of glory, hope's true gage,
And thus I'll take my pilgrimage.
1604 *The Passionate Man's Pilgrimage.*

1 What is our life? a play of passion;
Our mirth the music of division;
Our mothers' wombs the tiring-houses be
Where we are dressed for this short comedy.
Heaven the judicious sharp spectator is,
That sits and marks still who doth act amiss;
Our graves that hide us from the searching sun
Are like drawn curtains when the play is done.
Thus march we, playing, to our latest rest,
Only we die in earnest—that's no jest.
1612 'On the Life of Man'.

2 I shall never be persuaded that God hath shut up all light of learning within the lantern of Aristotle's brain.
1614 *The History of the World.*

3 Even such is Time, which takes in trust
Our youth, our joys, and all we have,
And pays us but with age and dust,
Who in the dark and silent grave
When we have wandered all our ways
Shuts up the story of our days,
And from which earth, and grave, and dust
The Lord shall raise me up, I trust.
1618 'The Author's Epitaph, Made by Himself'. Poem written the night before his death.

Rambert, Dame Marie 1888–1982

Polish-born British ballet dancer and teacher.

4 One is often asked whether his jump was really as high as it is always described. To that I answer: 'I don't know how far from the ground it was, but I know it was near the stars.' Who would watch the floor when he danced?
1960 On Vaslav Nijinsky. *Quicksilver.*

Ramón y Cajal, Santiago 1852–1934

Spanish physician and histologist. He made use of the specialized histological staining techniques of Camillo Golgi, and the two men shared the 1906 Nobel prize for physiology or medicine.

5 In my systematic explorations through the realms of microscopic anatomy, there came the turn of the nervous system, that masterpiece of life.
1937 *Recollections of My Life.*

Ramos, Graciliano 1892–1953

Brazilian novelist. In 1936 he was arrested and imprisoned, and on his release settled in Rio de Janeiro. His work explores the lives of characters shaped by the rural misery of north-east Brazil.

6 *Sempre que os homens sabidos lhe diziam palavras difíceis, ele saía logrado. Sobressaltava-se escutando-as. Evidentemente só serviam para encobrir ladroeiras. Mas eram bonitas.*
Whenever men with book learning used big words in dealing with him, he came out the loser. It startled him just to hear those words. Obviously they were just a cover for robbery. But they sounded nice.
1938 *Vidas secas* (translated as *Barren Lives,* 1965), 'Contas'.

Ramsey, Sir Alf(red) 1922–99

English footballer and manager. A player with Southampton and Tottenham Hotspur, he managed Ipswich Town in the early 1960s and went on to manage the England side that won the World Cup in 1966.

7 I feel like jumping over the moon.
1962 Quoted in Nigel Rees *Dictionary of Popular Phrases* (1990). This is one of the earliest records of the phrase 'over the moon' being used in the context of football.

8 Listen to them moan, but those people will be going mad if we beat West Germany by a goal in the World Cup Final.
1966 Of press criticism after England lost against West Germany in February, several months before England won the World Cup. Quoted in Bryon Butler *The Official History of the Football Association* (1986).

9 You've beaten them once. Now go out and bloody beat them again.
1966 Addressing his players when the World Cup final went into extra time.

Rand, Ayn 1905–82

Russian-born US novelist, screenwriter and ardent propagandist for her philosophy of self-interest against the altruistic tendencies of the welfare state. Her novels include *The Fountainhead* (1943) and *Atlas Shrugged* (1957).

10 The entire history of science is a progression of exploded fallacies, not of achievements.
1957 *Atlas Shrugged.*

Randall, Clarence Beldan 1891–1967

US businessman, Chief Executive Officer of Inland Steel. He wrote several books on business.

11 Every man who has lived his life to the full, should, by the time his senior years are reached, have established a reserve inventory of unfinished thinking.
1963 *Sixty-Five Plus.*

12 The leader must know, must know that he knows and must be able to make it abundantly clear to those about him that he knows.
1964 *Making Good in Management.*

Randall, Dudley 1914–2000

US poet and librarian. He established the Broadside Press, which prints the work of black US poets, including his own books.

13 Musing on roses and revolutions,
I saw night close down on the earth like a great dark wing.
1968 *Cities Burning,* 'Roses and Revolutions'.

14 I saw dawn upon them like the sun a vision
of a time when all men walk proudly through the earth
and the bombs and missiles lie at the bottom of the ocean
like the bones of dinosaurs buried under the shale of eras.
1968 *Cities Burning,* 'Roses and Revolutions'.

15 Then washed in the brightness of this vision,
I saw how in its radiance would grow and be nourished and suddenly
burst into terrible and splendid bloom
the blood-red flower of revolution.
1968 *Cities Burning,* 'Roses and Revolutions'.

Ranjitsinhji, Prince 1872–1933

Indian nobleman and England cricketer. A star batsman with Sussex and England, he succeeded as Jam Sahib of Nawanagar in 1906 (Maharaja in 1918), and did much to modernize and improve conditions in his home state.

16 He turned the old one-stringed instrument into a many-chorded lyre… W.G. discovered batting; he turned its many narrow straight channels into one great winding river.
1897 Of W G Grace. *The Jubilee Book of Cricket.*

17 Find out where the ball is, get there; hit it.
Explaining his tactics as a batsman. Quoted in Colin Jarman *The Guinness Dictionary of Sports Quotations* (1990).

Rankin, Ian 1960–

Scottish author, known for his detective novels featuring Inspector Rebus.

18 It was one of those cool, crepuscular days that could have belonged to any of at least three Scottish seasons, a sky like slate roofing and a wind that Rebus's father would have called 'snell'.
2001 *The Falls.*

Rankin, Jeanette 1880–1973

US pacifist and politician, the first woman in Congress. She voted against US entry into both World Wars and demonstrated against the war in Vietnam.

19 As a woman I can't go to war, and I refuse to send anyone else.
Quoted in Hannah Josephson *Lady in Congress* (1974).

20 You can no more win a war than you can win an earthquake.
Quoted in Hannah Josephson *Lady in Congress* (1974).

Ransom, John Crowe 1888–1974

US poet and critic. He was an influential figure in the rise of the New Criticism movement in the US, and an important Southern poet.

21 Here lies a lady of beauty and high degree.
Of chills and fever she died, of fever and chills,
The delight of her husband, her aunts, an infant of three,
And of medicos marvelling sweetly on her ills.
1924 *Chills and Fever*, 'Here Lies a Lady'.

22 The little cousin is dead, by foul subtraction,
A green bough from Virginia's aged tree.
1924 *Chills and Fever*, 'Dead Boy'.

23 Tawny are the leaves turned but they still hold,
And it is harvest; what shall this land produce?
A meagre hill of kernels, a runnel of juice;
Declension looks from our land, it is old.
Therefore let us assemble, dry, gray, spare,
And mild as yellow air.
1924 *Chills and Fever*, 'Antique Harvesters'.

24 The curse of hell upon the sleek upstart
That got the Captain finally on his back
And took the red red vitals of his heart
And made the kites to whet their beaks clack clack.
1924 *Chills and Fever*, 'Captain Carpenter'.

25 Two evils, monstrous either one apart,
Possessed me, and were long and loath at going:
A cry of Absence, Absence, in the heart,
And in the wood the furious winter blowing.
1924 *Chills and Fever*, 'Winter Remembered'.

26 And if no Lethe flows beneath your casement,
And when ten years have not brought full effacement,
Philosophy was wrong, and you may meet.
1924 *Grace after Meat*, 'Parting at Dawn'.

27 Old Hodge stays not his hand, but whips to kennel
The renegade. God's peace betide the souls
Of the pure in heart. But in the box that fennel
Grows around, are two red eyes that stare like coals.
1927 *Two Gentlemen in Bonds*, 'Dog'.

28 God have mercy on the sinner
Who must write with no dinner,
No gravy and no grub,
No pewter and no pub,
No belly and no bowels,
Only consonants and vowels.
1955 *Poems and Essays*, 'Survey of Literature'.

Raphael, Frederic 1931–

British novelist and screenwriter.

29 City of perspiring dreams.
1976 Of Cambridge. *The Glittering Prizes*, ch.3.

Rapoport, Anatol 1911–

Russian-born Canadian mathematician, social philosopher and peace advocate.

30 Cooperate on move one; thereafter, do whatever the other player did the previous move.
The two commands for his computer program, Tit for Tat, designed at the University of Toronto. It outperformed all other programs at an international computer tournament in 1979, and it continues to excel in tournaments. The program initiates reciprocal cooperation yet responds in kind to provocation.

Rattigan, Sir Terence 1911–77

English playwright.

31 When you're between any sort of devil and the deep blue sea, the deep blue sea sometimes looks very inviting.
1952 *The Deep Blue Sea*.

32 You can be in the Horseguards and still be common, dear.
1954 *Separate Tables*.

Rauschenberg, Robert 1925–

US artist, whose paintings and collages incorporate images and objects from everyday life. *Gloria* (1956) is a typical example of his 'combines', or collages.

33 I don't like masterpieces having one-night stands in collectors' homes between auctions.
1989 On quick-turnover profits on his work. In the *New York Times*, 10 May.

34 Most artists try to break your heart, or they accidentally break their own hearts. But I find the quietness in the ordinary much more satisfying.
2004 In the *New York Times*, 15 Feb.

35 They block the view.
2004 When asked what he had against mountains. In the *New York Times*, 15 Feb.

Ravel, (Joseph) Maurice 1875–1937

French composer. A pupil of Fauré, his innovative early compositions include *Schéhérazade* and the *Pavane pour une infante défunte* (both 1899). Other notable works include the ballet *Daphnis et Chloé* (1912), and *Boléro* (1928).

36 I've still so much music in my head. I have said nothing. I have so much more to say.
1937 Spoken on his deathbed. Quoted in Jourdan-Morhange *Ravel et nous* (1945).

37 A piece for orchestra without music.
Of his *Boléro*. Quoted in R Nichols *Ravel* (1977).

Ravitch, Diane Silvers 1938–

US historian, writer and Research Professor of Education at New York University. She was a member of the US Department of Education from 1991 to 1993.

38 The person who knows 'how' will always have a job. The person who knows 'why' will always be his boss.
1985 Speech at Reed College commencement. Reported in *Time*, 17 Jun.

Rawnsley, Andrew 1962–

English author, broadcaster and journalist.

39 The Millennium Dome was intended to be New Labour's Xanadu and Tony Blair its Kubla Khan.
2000 *Servants of the People: The Inside Story of New Labour.*

Ray, Dixy Lee   1914–94

US politician and administrator.

40 The general public has long been divided into two parts: those who think that science can do anything, and those who are afraid that it will.
1973 In *New Scientist*, 5 Jul.

Ray, James Earl   1928–98

US assassin of Martin Luther King. He was imprisoned in 1960 for armed robbery but escaped in 1967 and shot King. He was apprehended in London and sentenced in Memphis to 99 years.

41 I was in Tennessee 24 hours and got 99 years.
1988 On beginning the 20th year of his prison sentence for the assassination of Martin Luther King. In *Life*, March.

Rayburn, Sam(uel Taliaferro)   1882–1961

US politician. A Democrat, he represented Texas (1913–61) and was Speaker of the House for a record 17 terms between 1940 and 1961. He was a supporter of Roosevelt's New Deal.

42 I like to make running water walk.
Quoted in Valton J Young *The Speaker's Agent* (1956).

43 These…society women never serve chilli.
His reason for not attending parties. Quoted in David Brinkley *Washington Goes to War* (1988).

44 Go along and get along.
On politics as a process of accommodation, recalled by former Speaker Gerald R Ford in the *Washington Times*, 24 May 1995.

Read, Sir Herbert Edward   1893–1968

English poet and art critic. Editor of the *Burlington Magazine* (1933–9) and Professor of Fine Art at Edinburgh (1931–3), he wrote works on art criticism and *Naked Warriors* (1919), a poetry collection inspired by his war experiences.

45 I saw him stab
And stab again
A well-killed Boche.
1919 *Naked Warriors*, 'The Scene of War, 4. The Happy Warrior'.

46 This is the happy warrior,
This is he.
1919 *Naked Warriors*, 'The Scene of War, 4. The Happy Warrior'.

47 It is defiant—the desperate act of men too profoundly convinced of the rottenness of our civilization to want to save a shred of its respectability.
1936 Catalogue of the International Surrealist Exhibition, New Burlington Galleries, London, Jun/Jul, introduction.

48 But one thing we learned: there is no glory in the deed
Until the soldier wears a badge of tarnished braid.
1948 'To a Conscript of 1940'.

49 It will be a gay world. There will be lights everywhere except in the minds of men, and the fall of the last civilization will not be heard above the din.
1964 Quoted in Hoggart and Johnston, *An Idea of Europe* (1987), 'Pyramids and Planes'.

Reade, Charles   1814–84

English novelist and playwright.

50 Take courage, my friend, the devil is dead!
1861 *The Cloister and the Hearth.*

Reagan, Nancy   1923–

US actress and First Lady, second wife of US President Ronald Reagan.

51 If the President has a bully pulpit, then the First Lady has a white glove pulpit…more refined, restricted, ceremonial, but it's a pulpit all the same.
1988 In the *New York Times*, 10 Mar.

52 I'm more aware if somebody is trying to end-run him…it just never occurs to him.
1988 On protecting her husband. In *Time*, 28 Nov.

53 For eight years I was sleeping with the President, and if that doesn't give you special access, I don't know what does!
1989 *My Turn* (with William Novack).

Reagan, Ronald Wilson   1911–2004

US Republican politician, 40th President (1981–9), a radio sports announcer and film star. A Democrat turned Republican, he won nomination in 1980, defeating Carter to become President. He introduced economic reform, took a strong anti-communist stand and introduced the Strategic Defence Initiative ('Star Wars'). In 1981 he was wounded in an assassination attempt. Re-elected in 1984, he achieved a major arms-reduction accord with Gorbachev. His reputation was tarnished by the Iran–Contra affair.

54 To sit back hoping that some day, some way, someone will make things right is to go on feeding the crocodile, hoping that he will eat you last—but eat you he will.
1974 CBS News, 7 Nov.

55 Recession is when your neighbour loses his job. Depression is when you lose yours.
1980 Election campaign speech, Jersey City, 1 Sep.
➤ *See Truman 868:38.*

56 I can tell a lot about a fellow's character by the way that he eats jelly beans.
1981 In the *Daily Mail*, Jan.

57 Honey, I forgot to duck.
1981 Said to his wife, Nancy, after being shot by John R Hinckley, Jr, 30 Mar.
➤ *See Dempsey 261:86.*

58 Who's minding the store?
1981 After he was shot by John R Hinckley, Jr, 30 Mar.

59 This is not the end of anything. This is the beginning of everything.
1984 On his re-election. In *Time*, Nov.

60 We are not going to tolerate these attacks from outlaw states, run by the strangest collection of misfits, looney tunes and squalid criminals since the advent of the Third Reich.
1985 Speech after terrorist attacks by Shi'ite Muslims, Jul.

61 We must say something but not much because I'm being held out to dry.
1986 Comment at a meeting with National Security Council advisers, 10 Nov. Quoted by Theodore Draper *A Very Thin Line* (1991).

62 We make history and changing it is within our power.
1987 On welcoming Soviet premier Mikhail S Gorbachev to the White House, 8 Dec.

63 We don't know where that money came from and we don't know who had it and we don't know where it went.
1988 Of the Iran–Contra funding. In the *New York Times*, 17 Mar.

64 I paid for this microphone.
1988 To a New Hampshire moderator who tried to keep President Reagan from speaking on behalf of other candidates. Reported in *Congressional Quarterly*, 23 May.

65 There is our little bungalow down there.
1989 On viewing the White House from a helicopter the day he left office. Quoted in the *Washington Post*, 22 Apr 1991.

66 Washington is a sieve…it was virtually impossible to find out who was doing the leaking and shut them up.
1990 Deposition on the Iran–Contra arms sales. In the *New York Times*, 23 Feb.

67 Politics is just like show business…a hell of an opening, you coast for a while, you have a hell of a closing.
1995 In the *New York Times*, 23 Apr.

68 When men fail to drive toward a goal or purpose, but only drift, the drift is always towards barbarism.
Quoted in Edmund Morris *Dutch: A Memoir of Ronald Reagan* (1999).

Reardon, Ray 1932–

Welsh snooker player. He was world champion in 1970, 1973, 1976 and 1978.

69 I cannot remember anyone ever asking 'Who came second?' Can you?
Quoted in Colin Jarman *The Guinness Dictionary of Sports Quotations* (1990).

70 If I had to make the choice between staying married and playing snooker, snooker would win.
Quoted in Colin Jarman *The Guinness Dictionary of Sports Quotations* (1990).

Red Cloud *original name* **Mahpiua Luta** 1822–1909

Oglala Sioux chief who led the Indian war against the Americans.

71 You have heard the sound of the white soldier's axe on the Little Piney. His presence here is…an insult to the spirits of our ancestors. Are we to give up their sacred graves to be ploughed for corn? Dakotas, I am for war.
1866 Speech before war council at Fort Laramie, Wyoming.

Redmond, John Edward 1856–1918

Irish politician. A champion of Home Rule, he was Chairman of the Nationalist Party in 1900. He declined a seat in Asquith's coalition ministry (1915), but supported World War I, deplored the Irish rebellion, and opposed Sinn Féin.

72 The government may tomorrow withdraw every one of their troops from Ireland. Ireland will be defended by her armed sons from foreign invasion, and for that purpose the armed Catholics in the south will be only too glad to join arms with the armed Protestant Ulsterman. Is it too much to hope that out of this situation a result may spring that will be good not merely for the Empire but for the future welfare and integrity of the Irish nation?
1914 Speech, House of Commons, 3 Aug.

Redon, Odilon 1840–1916

French Symbolist painter and graphic artist, also well known for his work in pastel.

73 What distinguishes the artist from the dilettante? Only the pain that the artist feels. The dilettante looks only for pleasure in art.
c.1871 Journal entry, quoted in *Portfolio*, no.8, Spring 1964 (translated by Richard Howard).

74 All my originality consists…in giving life in human fashion to beings which are impossible according to the laws of possibility.
Quoted in Edward Lucie-Smith *Symbolist Art* (1972).

75 I am repelled by those who voice the word 'nature', without having any trace of it in their hearts.
Quoted in Edward Lucie-Smith *Symbolist Art* (1972).

Redtenbacher, Ferdinand 1818–83

German engineer, Professor of Mechanical Engineering and author on the construction of machinery.

76 Thanks to his bodily form and thanks to his mind, [man] is a universal machine, capable of an infinite diversity of movement.
1840 *Resultate fur den Maschinenbau* (published 1848).

Reed, Henry 1914–86

English poet and dramatist. He is best known for his war poems and for his radio plays, notably *The Private Life of Hilda Tablet* (1954). 'Chard Whitlow' (1946) is a parody of T S Eliot's 'Burnt Norton'.

77 Today we have naming of parts. Yesterday,
We had daily cleaning. And tomorrow morning,
We shall have what to do after firing. But today,
Today we have naming of parts. Japonica
Glistens like coral in all of the neighbouring gardens
And today we have naming of parts.
1946 *Lessons of the War*, pt.1, 'Naming of Parts'.

78 We can slide it
Rapidly backwards and forwards: we call this
Easing the spring. And rapidly backwards and forwards
The early bees are assaulting and fumbling the flowers:
They call it easing the Spring.
1946 *Lessons of the War*, pt.1, 'Naming of Parts'.

79 There may be dead ground in between; and I may not have got
The knack of judging a distance; I will only venture
A guess that perhaps between me and the apparent lovers,
(Who, incidentally, appear by now to have finished,)
At seven o'clock from the houses, is roughly a distance
Of about one year and a half.
1946 *Lessons of the War*, pt.2, 'Judging Distances'.

80 As we get older we do not get any younger.
Seasons return, and today I am fifty-five,
And this time last year I was fifty-four,
And this time next year I shall be sixty-two.
1946 'Chard Whitlow (Mr Eliot's Sunday Evening Postscript)', a parody of T S Eliot's style.

81 It is, we believe,
Idle to hope that the simple stirrup-pump
Can extinguish hell.
1946 'Chard Whitlow (Mr Eliot's Sunday Evening Postscript)'.

82 Modest? My word, no… He was an all-the-lights-on man.
1953 *A Very Great Man Indeed*, radio play.

83 And the sooner the tea's out of the way, the sooner we can get out the gin, eh?

1954 *The Private Life of Hilda Tablet*, radio play.

84 In a civil war, a general must know—and I'm afraid it's a thing rather of instinct than of practice—he must know exactly when to move over to the other side.

1959 *Not a Drum Was Heard: The War Memoirs of General Gland*, unpublished radio play.

Reed, Ishmael Scott   1938–.

US novelist, poet and publisher. He founded the experimental literary magazine *East Village Other* in New York. His works include the novels *The Free-Lance Pallbearers* (1967) and *Mumbo Jumbo* (1972).

85 When State Magic fails unofficial magic becomes stronger.

1968 *Yellow Back Radio Broke Down*, 'II. The Loop Garou Kid Comes Back Mad'.

86 Hoo-doo, which in America flowered in New Orleans, was an unorganized religion without ego-games or death worship.

1968 *Yellow Back Radio Broke Down*, 'V. A Jigsaw of a Last Minute Rescue'.

Reed, John   1887–1920

US writer and journalist. He is best known as a war correspondent in Mexico and Europe, and for his reports from Russia in the wake of the revolution.

87 Ten Days That Shook the World.

1919 Title of book.

88 In the relations of a weak Government and a rebellious people there comes a time when every act of the authorities exasperates the masses, and every refusal to act excites their contempt.

1919 *Ten Days That Shook the World*, ch.3.

Rees-Mogg, William Rees-Mogg, Baron   1928–

English journalist. He joined the *Financial Times* (1952) and the *Sunday Times* (1960), becoming deputy editor (1964). He was editor of *The Times* (1967–81) and headed the Broadcasting Standards Council (1988–93).

89 Information, free from interest or prejudice, free from the vanity of the writer or the influence of a Government, is as necessary to the human mind as pure air and water to the human body.

1970 *Christian Science Monitor*, 22 Sep.

Reeve, Christopher   1952–2004

US actor, best known for his role as the superhero in *Superman* (1978) and subsequent films. Paralysed in a horse-riding accident, he became a spokesperson for medical research into treatments and cures for spinal injuries.

90 Every scientist should remove the word 'impossible' from their lexicon.

2004 In the *Observer*, 15 Feb.

Regan, Donald Thomas   1918–2003

US financier, writer and lecturer. He was chair of Merrill Lynch & Co Inc (1973–81), secretary to the US Treasury Department (1981–85) and White House Chief of Staff (1985–87) for President Reagan. Following the Tower Commission Report on the Iran–Contra affair, he was forced to resign.

91 The buck doesn't even *pause* here.

1987 Of his job. In the *New York Times*, 31 Jul.

➤ See Truman 869:45.

92 I thought I was Chief of Staff to the President, not to his wife.

1988 On submitting his resignation. *For the Record*.

93 Mistaken in its assumptions, defective in its evidence and wrong in its conclusions.

1988 Of the congressional report faulting him on lack of direction and public disclosure of Iran–Contra arms sales. *For the Record*.

Reger, Max   1873–1916

German composer. He was Director of Music (1907) and professor (1908) at Leipzig University. His work includes organ music, piano concertos, choral works and songs.

94 *Ich sitze in dem kleinsten Zimmer in meinem Hause. Ich habe Ihre Kritik vor mir. Im nächsten Augenblick wird sie hinter mir sein.*

I am sitting in the smallest room of my house. I have your review before me. In a moment it will be behind me.

1906 Written in response to an unfavourable review by Rudolf Louis. Quoted in Nicolas Slonimsky *Lexicon of Musical Invective* (2nd edn, 1969), p.139.

Reid, Alastair   1926–

Scottish-born poet, essayist and translator of Spanish and Latin American literature. After serving in the Navy in World War II, he became a professional itinerant, his only permanent address the *New Yorker*. His witty poetry collections include *Weathering* (1978).

95 The point is the seeing—the grace
 beyond recognition, the ways
 of the bird rising, unnamed, unknown,
 beyond the range of language, beyond its noun.
 Eyes open on growing, flying, happening,
 and go on opening. Manifold, the world
 dawns on unrecognizing, realizing eyes.
 Amazement is the thing.
 Not love, but the astonishment of loving.

1978 *Weathering*, 'Growing, Flying, Happening'.

Reid, Thomas Mayne   1818–83

Irish writer of boys' stories. After work as a journalist and soldier in the Mexican War of 1847, he won a wide readership with a string of adventure tales, which included such titles as *The Rifle Rangers* (1850), *War Trail* (1857) and *Boy Tar* (1859).

96 Praise the sports of the land
 And water, each one—
 The bath by the beach, or the yacht on the sea—
 But of all the sweet pleasures
 Known under the sun;
 A good game of Croquet's the sweetest to me.

1863 Quoted in Colin Jarman *The Guinness Dictionary of Sports Quotations* (1990).

Remarque, Erich Maria   1898–1970

German-born US novelist, who served in World War I. His novels were banned by the Nazis in 1933, and he emigrated to the US in 1939.

97 *ImWesten nichts Neues.*
All Quiet on the Western Front.
1929 Title of novel.

Renan, (Joseph) Ernest 1823–92

French philologist and historian, whose studies led him to abandon traditional faith. His works include *Histoire général des langues sémitiques* (1854), *Études d'histoire religieuse* (1856) and the controversial *Vie de Jésus* (1863), the first of a series on the history of Christianity.

98 War is a condition of progress; the whip-cut that prevents a country from going to sleep and forces satisfied mediocrity to shake off its apathy.
1871 *La Réforme intellectuelle et morale.*

Reno, Janet 1938–

US politician and lawyer. She was State Attorney in Florida (1978–93) and subsequently US Attorney-General in the Clinton administration (1993–2001).

99 I'm just an awkward old maid with a very great affection for men.
1993 Denying rumours that she was a lesbian. In the *Washington Times*, 22 Feb.

1 Nothing can make me madder than lawyers who don't care about others.
1993 Address to the American Bar Association. In the *New York Times*, 9 Aug.

2 Vengeance is a personal reaction. But not one that government can indulge in.
1994 Opposing the death penalty. In the *New York Times*, 15 May.

3 I made the decision long ago that to be afraid would be to diminish my life.
1995 Interview in NPR broadcast, 18 Jul.

Renoir, Jean 1894–1979

French film director, son of Pierre Auguste Renoir. His *La Grande Illusion* (1937) and *La Bête humaine* (1939) are among the masterpieces of the cinema.

4 A director makes only one film in his life. Then he breaks it into pieces and makes it again.
Quoted in Leslie Halliwell *Halliwell's Filmgoer's Companion* (1993).

5 Goodbye Mr Zanuck. It certainly has been a pleasure working for 16th Century Fox.
On leaving Hollywood. Attributed.

Renoir, Pierre Auguste 1841–1919

French Impressionist painter, born in Limoges. He exhibited with the Impressionists, and his *Moulin de la Galette* (1876) with sunlight filtering through leaves epitomizes his colourful, happy art. His visit to Italy in 1880 was followed by a series of *Bathers* (1884–7) in a more cold and classical style. He then returned to reds, orange and gold to portray nudes in sunlight, a style which he continued to develop until his death. His works include *The Umbrellas* (c.1883) and *The Judgement of Paris* (c.1914).

6 There is something in painting which cannot be explained, and that something is essential. You come to nature with your theories, and nature knocks them all flat.
c.1915 Quoted in Ambroise Vollard *Renoir, an Intimate Record* (1930).

7 I have a horror of the word 'flesh', which has become so shopworn. Why not 'meat' while they're about it? What I like is skin, a young girl's skin that is pink and shows that she has a good circulation.
Quoted in Jean Renoir *Renoir, My Father* (translated by R and D Weaver, 1962).

8 The only reward one should offer an artist is to buy his work.
From Renoir's notebook, quoted in L Nochlin *Impressionism and Post-Impressionism 1874– 1904* (1966).

9 It is impossible to repeat in one period what was done in another. The point of view is not the same, any more than are the tools, the ideals, the needs, or the painters' techniques.
From Renoir's notebook, quoted in L Nochlin *Impressionism and Post-Impressionism 1874– 1904* (1966).

10 They were madmen, but they had in them that little flame which never dies.
On the Communards. Quoted in A J P Taylor *From Napoleon to the Second International* (1993).

11 Why shouldn't art be pretty? There are enough unpleasant things in the world.
Quoted in Ian Chilvers and Harold Osborne (eds) *The Oxford Dictionary of Art* (1994).

Repplier, Agnes 1858–1950

US writer and social critic.

12 Science may carry us to Mars, but it will leave the Earth peopled as ever by the inept.
1936 *In Pursuit of Laughter.*

Reston, James B(arrett) 1909–95

Scottish-born US journalist and author. He enjoyed a distinguished career with the *New York Times* and his national news reporting in World War II was recognized in a Pulitzer Prize (1945) and in his promotion to Chief of the Washington Bureau (1953–1964). He won a second Pulitzer Prize in 1957. He was vice-president of the *New York Times* (1969–74) and internationally respected for his political analysis.

13 Smarter than most of his colleagues in the Truman cabinet, but not smart enough to hide it.
1991 Of Secretary of State Dean Acheson. *Deadline.*

14 A little shorter than the Washington monument, erect, elegant, dogmatic, and ironically witty.
1991 Of Secretary of State Dean Acheson. *Deadline.*

15 He could strut sitting down.
1991 Of Senator Arthur Vandenberg. *Deadline.*

16 They were always…getting more credit than they deserved, more sorrow than they could bear, climbing into jobs before they were ready and failing just when they were succeeding.
1991 Of John F, Robert F and Edward M Kennedy. *Deadline.*

17 He not only knew a lot about foreign affairs, he *was* a foreign affair.
1991 Of former Secretary of State Henry A Kissinger. *Deadline.*

18 The American people…were like him: cheerful, optimistic, patriotic, inconsistent, and casually inattentive.
1991 Of President Ronald Reagan. *Deadline.*

Revlon, Charles Haskell 1906–75

US cosmetics salesman, founder with his brother Joseph and chemist Charles Lachman of Revlon Inc (1932). His success was due to initiatives such as giving exotic names to colours and also to intimidation and attacks on competitors.

19 I don't meet competition. I crush it.
  1958 In *Time*, 16 Jun.

20 In the factory, we make cosmetics; in the store we sell hope.
  Quoted in Andrew P Tobias *Fire and Ice* (1976), ch.8.

Reyes, Alfonso 1889–1959

Mexican poet, novelist, essayist, critic, educator and diplomat. His classical background and humanistic approach lend his writings a distinctive elegance.

21 *El orbe hispano nunca se vino abajo, ni siquiera a la caída del imperio español, sino que se ha multiplicado en numerosas facetas de ensanches todavía insospechados… No somos pueblos en estado de candor, que se deslumbren fácilmente con los instrumentos externos de que se acompaña la cultura, sino pueblos que heredan una vieja civilización y exigen la excelencia misma de la cultura.*
  The Hispanic world never crumbled, not even after the Spanish Empire fell, but instead has multiplied itself in broad ways that are still largely unknown… Our people are not naive and are not blinded by the external tools that go together with culture; we are rather the inheritors of an old civilization, and we demand the excellence proper to culture itself.
  1941 *Páginas escogidas*, 'Valor de la literatura hispanoamericana' (translated as 'The Value of Hispanic American Literature').

Reynolds, Sir Joshua 1723–92

English painter, writer on art and the first President of the Royal Academy. He is one of the most important figures in the history of English painting.

22 A mere copier of nature never produces anything great.
  1770 *Discourses on Art*, no.3, 14 Dec.

Rhodes, Cecil John 1853–1902

South African statesman. He entered the Cape House of Assembly, where he secured the charter for the British South Africa Company (1889), whose territory was later named Rhodesia. Prime Minister of Cape Colony (1890–6), he resigned after the Jameson raid (when the Boers defeated Dr Jameson's attempt to reach Johannesburg). During the Boer War of 1899–1902 he organized the defences of Kimberley.

23 Remember that you are an Englishman, and have consequently won first prize in the lottery of life.
  Quoted in Peter Ustinov *Dear Me* (1977). This has also been attributed to Lord Milner.

Rhys, Jean *pseudonym of Ellen Gwendolen Rees Williams* 1894–1979

British novelist, born in the West Indies, of Welsh and Creole descent. Of her novels and short stories *Wide Sargasso Sea* (1966), redefining Charlotte Brontë's first Mrs Rochester, is the best known.

24 The perpetual hunger to be beautiful and that thirst to be loved which is the real curse of Eve.
  1927 *The Left Bank*, 'Illusion'.

25 I wanted to be black. I always wanted to be black… Being black is warm and gay, being white is cold and sad.
  1934 *Voyage in the Dark*, ch.1.

26 It's funny when you feel as if you don't want anything more in your life except to sleep, or else to lie without moving. That's when you can hear time sliding past you, like water running.
  1934 *Voyage in the Dark*, ch.2.

27 Cold—cold as truth, cold as life. No, nothing can be as cold as life.
  1934 *Voyage in the Dark*, ch.3.

28 The feeling of Sunday is the same everywhere, heavy, melancholy, standing still. Like when they say 'As it was in the beginning, is now, and ever shall be, world without end'.
  1934 *Voyage in the Dark*, ch.4, pt.1.

29 We will watch the sun set again—many times, and perhaps we'll see the Emerald Drop, the green flash that brings good fortune.
  1966 *Wide Sargasso Sea*, pt.2.

30 There is no looking-glass here and I don't know what I am like now. I remember watching myself brush my hair and how my eyes looked back at me. The girl I saw was myself and yet not quite myself. Long ago when I was a child and very lonely I tried to kiss her. But the glass was between us—hard, cold and misted over with my breath. Now they have taken everything away. What am I doing in this place and who am I?
  1966 The consciousness of Antoinette Mason/Bertha Rochester at a point of intersection with the text of *Jane Eyre*. *Wide Sargasso Sea*, pt.3.

Ricardo, David 1772–1823

English political economist. He set up in business as a young man, and in 1817 produced his chief work, *Principles of Political Economy and Taxation*. In 1819 he became an MP, and was influential in the free-trade movement.

31 It is not to be understood that the natural price of labour, estimated even in food and necessaries, is absolutely fixed and constant. It varies at different times in the same country and very materially differs in different countries. It essentially depends on the habits and customs of the people.
  1817 *Principles of Political Economy and Taxation*.

32 In every case, agricultural as well as manufacturing profits are lowered by a rise in the price of raw produce, if it be accompanied by a rise of wages. The natural tendency of profits is to fall; for in the progress of society and wealth, the additional quantity of food required is obtained by the sacrifice of more and more labour.
  1817 *Principles of Political Economy and Taxation*.

33 Like all other contracts, wages should be left to the fair and free competition of the market, and should never be controlled by the interference of the legislature.
  1817 *Principles of Political Economy and Taxation*.

34 Possessing utility, commodities derive their exchangeable value from two sources: from their scarcity and from the labour required to obtain them. By far the greatest part of those goods which are the

objects of desire, are procured by labour.
1817 *Principles of Political Economy and Taxation.*

35 The interest of the landlord is always opposed to the interests of every other class in the community.
1817 *Principles of Political Economy and Taxation.*

36 The natural price of labour is that price which is necessary to enable the labourers, one with another, to subsist and to perpetuate their race, without either increase or diminution.
1817 *Principles of Political Economy and Taxation.*

Rice, Grantland 1880–1954

US sportswriter and poet. He is remembered for his colourful reporting style and popular verse.

37 For when the One Great Scorer comes
To write against your name,
He marks—not that you won or lost—
But how you played the game.
1941 *Only the Brave*, 'Alumnus Football'.

38 All wars are planned by old men
In council rooms apart.
1955 *The Final Answer*, 'The Two Sides of War'.

39 Play ball! Means something more than runs
Or pitches thudding into gloves!
Remember through the summer suns
This is the game your country loves.
Quoted in Colin Jarman *The Guinness Dictionary of Sports Quotations* (1990).

Rice-Davies, Mandy 1944–

Welsh model and show girl.

40 He would, wouldn't he?
1963 On hearing that during the trial of Stephen Ward, Lord Astor had denied her allegations of orgies at his house parties at Cliveden, 29 Jun.

Rich, Adrienne Cecile 1929–

US poet. She is one of the most prominent feminist poets of her generation. Her best-known work includes *Diving into the Wreck* (1973).

41 Weather abroad
And weather in the heart alike come on
Regardless of prediction.
1951 *A Change of World*, 'Storm Warnings'.

42 Love only what you do,
And not what you have done.
1955 *The Diamond Cutters and Other Poems*, 'The Diamond Cutters'.

43 Your mind now, moldering like wedding-cake,
heavy with useless experience, rich
with suspicion, rumour, fantasy,
crumbling to pieces under the knife-edge
of mere fact. In the prime of your life.
1963 *Snapshots of a Daughter-in-Law*, 'Snapshots of a Daughter-in-Law, 1'.

44 Only
a fact could be so dreamlike.
1966 *Necessities of Life*, 'Like This Together'.

45 Only where there is language is there world.
1969 *Leaflets*, 'The Demon Lover'.

46 All wars are useless to the dead.
1969 *Leaflets*, 'Implosions'.

47 I am an instrument in the shape
of a woman trying to translate pulsations
into images for the relief of the body
and the reconstruction of the mind.
1971 *The Will to Change*, 'Planetarium'.

48 It's exhilarating to be alive in a time of awakening consciousness; it can also be confusing, disorienting, and painful.
1971 Talk delivered to Forum on 'The Woman Writer in the Twentieth Century'. Collected as 'When We Dead Awaken: Writing as Re-Vision', in *College English*, Oct 1972.

49 the thing I came for:
the wreck and not the story of the wreck
the thing itself and not the myth.
1973 *Diving into the Wreck*, 'Diving into the Wreck'.

50 When did we begin to dress ourselves?
1973 *Diving into the Wreck*, 'Blood-Sister'.

51 Any woman's death diminishes me.
1974 *Poems: Selected and New*, 'From an Old House in America, 16'.
➤ See Donne 281:85.

52 Without contemplating last and late
the true nature of poetry. The drive
to connect. The dream of a common language.
1978 *The Dream of a Common Language*, 'Origins and History of Consciousness'.

53 Since we're not young, weeks have to do time for years
of missing each other. Yet only this odd warp in time tells
me we're not young.
1978 *The Dream of a Common Language*, 'Twenty-One Love Poems, III'.

54 Anger and tenderness: my selves.
And now I can believe they breathe in me
as angels, not polarities.
1981 *A Wild Patience Has Taken Me This Far*, 'Integrity'.

55 I refuse to become a seeker for cures.
Everything that has ever
helped me has come through what already
lay stored in me.
1986 *Your Native Land, Your Life*, 'Sources, II'.

56 This is the day of atonement; but do my people forgive me?
If a cloud knew loneliness and fear, I would be that cloud.
1986 *Your Native Land, Your Life*, 'Yom Kippur, 1984'.

57 Experience is always larger than language.
1991 Interview in the *American Poetry Review*, Jan–Feb.

Richard I known as 'the Lionheart' 1157–99

King of England (from 1189). He led the Crusaders in 1190 and after concluding a peace sailed for home (1191), but was captured by Leopold, Duke of Austria and handed over to Emperor Henry VI. Ransomed in 1194, he went to France where he warred against Philip II until he was killed in the siege of Chalus.

58 *Si inuenissem emptorum, Londoniam uendidissem.*
If I could have found a buyer I would have sold London itself.
1190 Of his fundraising for the Crusade to Palestine. Quoted in Richard of Devizes *Chronicle of Richard of Devizes of the Time of King Richard I* (c.1192).

Richard of Devizes fl.c.1190

English Benedictine monk and chronicler.

59 *Si nolueris habitare cum turpidis, non habitatis Londonie.*

If you do not want to live among wicked people, do not live in London.

c.1192 *Chronicle of Richard of Devizes of the Time of King Richard I.*

Richards, Ann 1933–

US Democratic politician. State Treasurer of Texas from 1982 to 1990, she then became Governor of Texas (1991–5).

60 You can put lipstick on a hog, and it's still a pig.

1992 On Republicans' attempts to enhance their candidates. In *Sunday Morning*, CBS TV broadcast, 25 Oct.

Richards, Sir Gordon 1904–86

English jockey. In 34 seasons (1921–54) he was champion jockey 26 times, and rode 4,870 winners. In 1953 he won his first Derby, on Pinza, and also received a knighthood.

61 Mother always told me my day was coming, but I never realized I'd end up being the shortest knight of the year.

1953 Quoted in Colin Jarman *The Guinness Dictionary of Sports Quotations* (1990).

Richards, I(vor) A(rmstrong) 1893–1979

English scholar and literary critic. He was the initiator of the influential 'New Criticism' school of textual criticism at Cambridge University in the 1920s.

62 To be forced by desire into any unwarrantable belief is a calamity.

1924 *Principles of Literary Criticism.*

63 Poetry…is capable of saving us; it is a perfectly possible means of overcoming chaos.

1926 *Science and Poetry*, ch. 7.

Richardson, Henry Handel *pen-name of* *Ethel Florence Lindesay Robertson* née *Richardson* 1870–1946

Australian novelist, who settled in England in 1904. Her first novel was *Maurice Guest* (1908) but she made her name with a trilogy set in Australia, *The Fortunes of Richard Mahoney* (1917–29). She was nominated for the Nobel prize in 1932.

64 You're blessed with a woman's brain: vague, slippery, inexact, interested only in the personal aspect of a thing.

1910 *The Getting of Wisdom*, ch.9.

Richardson, Tony (Cecil Antonio) 1928–91

British film and stage director. He made a number of highly acclaimed films at the beginning of the 1960s including *The Entertainer* (1960), *A Taste of Honey* (1961) and *Tom Jones* (1963), which won an Academy Award.

65 People in this country haven't got the cinema in their blood—the real creative talent has been drained off into theatre.

1961 On Britain. Quoted in the *Monthly Film Bulletin*, Apr 1993.

Richelieu, Armand Jean du Plessis, Duc de *known as* *Cardinal Richelieu* 1585–1642

French statesman. A protégé of the regent Marie de Médicis, he became Minister of State (1624), and as Chief Minister to Louis

XIV (1624–42) was effective ruler of France. He succeeded in destroying Huguenot power, securing universal obedience to the Bourbon monarchy, checking Habsburg power and enhancing France's international prestige, but his ruthless severity, his intrigues and his high taxes earned him the hatred of many.

66 Not least among the qualities in a great King is a capacity to permit his Ministers to serve him.

1688 *Testament Politique.*

67 Secrecy is the first essential in the affairs of State.

1688 *Testament Politique.*

68 When people are too comfortable, it is not possible to restrain them within the bounds of their duty… They may be compared to mules who, being accustomed to burdens, are spoilt by rest rather than labour.

1688 *Testament Politique.*

69 Wounds inflicted by the sword heal more easily than those inflicted by the tongue.

1688 *Testament Politique.*

Richler, Mordecai 1931–2001

Canadian novelist, journalist and essayist. His greatest works, including *The Apprenticeship of Duddy Kravitz* (1959), *St Urbain's Horseman* (1971) and *Joshua Then and Now* (1980), are darkly comic novels about the working-class Jewish community in Montreal in which he grew up.

70 Thousands of miles of wheat, indifference, and self-apology.

1971 Of Canada. *St Urbain's Horseman*, ch.1.

71 Tomorrow country then, tomorrow country now.

1971 Of Canada. *St Urbain's Horseman*, ch.1.

72 Even in Paris, I remained a Canadian. I puffed hashish, but I didn't inhale.

1971 *St Urbain's Horseman*, ch.2. The last phrase was later popularized by Bill Clinton, responding to claims that he had taken drugs as a student.

73 The Canadian kid who wants to grow up to be Prime Minister isn't thinking big, he is setting a limit to his ambitions rather early.

Quoted in *Time* (Canadian edition), 31 May 1971.

Rickword, Edgell 1898–1982

English poet and critic. His early work was influenced by Sassoon. He edited *Left Review* in the 1930s.

74 The oldest griefs of summer seem less sad
than drone of mowers on suburban lawns
and girls' thin laughter, to the ears that hear
the soft rain falling of the failing stars.

1921 'Regret for the Passing of the Entire Scheme of Things'.

75 My soul's a trampled duelling ground where Sade,
the gallant marquis, fences for his life
against the invulnerable retrograde
Masoch, his shade, more constant than a wife.

1928 'Chronique Scandaleuse'.

76 Why stir the wasps that rim Fame's luscious pot?
Love costs us nothing, satire costs a lot!

1931 'The Contemporary Muse'.

Ridge, W(illiam) Pett 1857–1930

English novelist. He was a prolific writer, publishing over 60 books in total.

77 He took her up in his arms in the way of a bachelor who has had amateur experience of the carrying of nieces.
1902 *Lost Property*, pt.1, ch.8.

78 Ballard admitted he was no hand at giving descriptions; the man was apparently a gentleman and the woman— well, not exactly a lady, although she had a very fine flow of language.
1905 *Mrs Galer's Business*, ch.6.

79 Gertie recommended her to adopt the habit of not magnifying grievances; if you wanted to view trouble, you could take opera-glasses, but you should be careful to hold them the wrong way round.
1912 *Love at Paddington Green*, ch.4.

80 'How did you think I managed at dinner, Clarence?'
'Capitally!'
'I had a knife and two forks left at the end,' she said regretfully.
1912 *Love at Paddington Green*, ch.6.

Riding, Laura née *Reichenthal* 1901–91

US poet and fiction writer. She was first published by Leonard and Virginia Woolf's Hogarth Press, and is more admired as a poet than for her polemical prose writings.

81 Art, whose honesty must work through artifice, cannot avoid cheating truth.
1975 *Selected Poems: In Five Sets*, preface.

Rifkind, Simon Hirsch 1901–95

US judge. He was a partner in his legal firm and an adviser to General Eisenhower on Jewish matters in the American occupied zone (1945).

82 Impartiality is an acquired taste, like olives. You have to be habituated to it.
1979 In *Time*, 20 Aug.

Rilke, Rainer Maria 1875–1926

German poet who travelled widely and lived throughout Europe.

83 *Ach, aber mit Versen ist so wenig getan, wenn man sie früh schreibt. Man sollte warten damit und Sinn und Süßigkeit sammeln ein ganzes Leben lang und ein langes womöglich, und dann, ganz zum Schluss, vielleicht könnte man dann zehn Zeilen schreiben, die gut sind.*
Ah, poems amount to so little when you write them too early in your life. You ought to wait and gather sense and sweetness for a whole lifetime, and a long one if possible, and then, at the very end, you might perhaps be able to write ten good lines.
1910 *Die Aufzeichnungen des Malte Laurids Brigge* (translated by Stephen Mitchell in *The Selected Poetry of Rainer Maria Rilke*, 1989).

84 *Ich habe um meine Kindheit gebeten, und sie ist wiedergekommen, und ich fühle, dass sie immer noch so schwer ist wie damals, und dass es nichts genützt hat, älter zu werden.*
I prayed to rediscover my childhood, and it has come back, and I feel that it is just as difficult as it used to be, and that growing older has served no purpose at all.
1910 *Die Aufzeichnungen des Malte Laurids Brigge* (translated by Stephen Mitchell in *The Selected Poetry of Rainer Maria Rilke*, 1989).

85 *Und das Totsein ist mühsam und voller Nachholn, dass man allmählich ein wenig Ewigkeit spürt.*
And being dead is hard work and full of retrieval before one can gradually feel a trace of eternity.
1923 *Duinieser Elegien*, no.1 (translated by Stephen Mitchell in *The Selected Poetry of Rainer Maria Rilke*, 1989).

86 *Siehe, wir lieben nicht, wie die Blumen, aus einem einzigen Jahr; uns steigt, wo wir lieben, unvordenklicher Saft in die Arme.*
No, we don't accomplish our love in a single year as the flowers do; an immemorial sap flows up through our arms when we love.
1923 *Duinieser Elegien*, no.3 (translated by Stephen Mitchell in *The Selected Poetry of Rainer Maria Rilke*, 1989).

87 *Wer zeigt ein Kind, so wie es steht? Wer stellt es ins Gestirn und gibt das Maß des Abstands ihm in die Hand?*
Who shows a child as he really is? Who sets him in his constellation and puts the measuring-rod of distance in his hand?
1923 *Duinieser Elegien*, no.4 (translated by Stephen Mitchell in *The Selected Poetry of Rainer Maria Rilke*, 1989).

Rimbaud, (Jean Nicolas) Arthur 1854–91

French poet who wrote his entire work before the age of 20. His relationship with poet Paul Verlaine was notorious. He eventually became an arms trader in Abyssinia.

88 *Et j'ai vu quelquefois ce que l'homme a cru voir.*
I've sometimes seen what other men have only dreamed of seeing.
1871 *Poésies*, 'Le Bateau ivre'.

89 *Je regrette l'Europe aux anciens parapets!*
I long for Europe of the ancient parapets!
1871 *Poésies*, 'Le Bateau ivre'.

90 *Ô mes petites amoureuses, Que je vous hais!*
Oh my little mistresses, How I hate you!
1871 *Poésies*, 'Mes petites amoureuses'.

91 *On n'est pas sérieux, quand on a dix-sept ans.*
When you are seventeen, you are not serious.
1871 *Poésies*, 'Roman', no.1.

92 *Le poète est vraiment voleur de feu.*
The poet is the true fire-stealer.
1871 Letter to Paul Demeny, 15 May.

93 *La Poésie ne rythmera plus l'action; elle sera en avant.*
Poetry will no longer keep step with the action; it will be ahead of it.
1871 Letter to Paul Demeny, 15 May.

94 *Elle est retrouvée. Quoi?—L'Éternité. C'est la mer allée Avec le soleil.*
It has been recovered. What?—Eternity. It is the sea escaping With the sun.
1872 *Derniers vers, Fêtes de la patience*, 'L'Éternité'.

95 *J'ai fait la magique étude*

Du Bonheur, que nul n'élude.
I studied the magic lore of Happiness
Which no one can escape.
1872 *Derniers vers, Fêtes de la faim,*'Ô saisons, ō châteaux!'.

96 *Un soir, j'ai assis la Beauté sur mes genoux.—Et je l'ai trouvée amère.—Et je l'ai injuriée.*
One evening, I sat Beauty on my knees.—And I found her bitter.—And I hurt her.
1873 *Une saison en enfer,*'Jadis, si je me souviens bien'.

97 *Je me crois en enfer, donc j'y suis.*
I believe myself to be in hell; therefore I am.
1873 *Une saison en enfer,*'Mauvais sang'.

98 *Le Bonheur était ma fatalité, mon remords, mon ver: ma vie serait toujours trop immense pour être dévouée à la force et à la beauté.*
Happiness was my fate, my remorse, my worm: my life would always be too large to be dedicated to force and to beauty.
1873 *Une saison en enfer, Délires,* no.2,'Alchimie du verbe'.

Rimsky-Korsakov, Nikolai Andreievich 1844–1908

Russian composer. He established his reputation with three great orchestral masterpieces (1887–8), *Capriccio Espagnol*, *Easter Festival* and *Scheherazade*. He then turned to opera, producing *The Snow Maiden* (1882), *Legend of Tsar Saltan* (1900), *The Invisible City of Kitesh* (1906) and *The Golden Cockerel* (1906).

99 I have already heard it. I had better not go: I will start to get accustomed to it and finally like it.
Of the music of Debussy, when invited to a concert where it was to be performed. Quoted in Igor Stravinsky *Chronicles of My Life* (1936).

Riva, Maria 1924–

Daughter and biographer of Marlene Dietrich.

1 They filled our hall like a monogrammed Stonehenge.
1992 Of the six closet-size wardrobe trunks used by her mother. *Marlene Dietrich.*

Rivera, Diego 1886–1957

Mexican painter, one of the three foremost artists in the revival of monumental fresco painting.

2 The subject is to the painter what the rails are to a locomotive. He cannot do without it.
1929 *Creative Art.*

Rivera, José Eustasio 1889–1928

Colombian lawyer, poet and novelist. A journey through the Amazon jungle with a commission to settle the boundary dispute between Colombia and Venezuela inspired him to write the magnificently descriptive novel *La vorágine* (1924).

3 *Antes que me hubiera apasionado por mujer alguna, jugué mi corazón al azar y me lo ganó la violencia.*
Before I felt passion for any woman, I gambled my heart and lost it to violence.
1924 *La vorágine,* pt.1 (translated as *The Vortex,* 1935).

Rivers, Joan *pseudonym of* *Joan Alexandra Molinsky* 1933–

US comedienne and writer. An acid-tongued stand-up comedienne in the 1960s, she went on to host television shows, as well as directing and appearing in films, recording an album and publishing books.

4 I'm Jewish. I don't work out. If God had wanted us to bend over he'd've put diamonds on the floor.
Quoted in Colin Jarman *The Guinness Dictionary of Sports Quotations* (1990).

Robb, Charles S(pittal) 1939–

US lawyer, Senator for Virginia (1989–2001).

5 The threat to morale comes not from the orientation of a few, but from the closed minds of the many.
1993 On gays in the military. In the *New York Times,* 5 Feb.

Robbe-Grillet, Alain 1922–

French novelist, scriptwriter and film director, whose repetitive style blurs the standard narrative distinctions in writing.

6 *On n'échappe pas à son sort.*
One cannot escape destiny.
1953 *Les Gommes.*

7 *Deux mètres—ou un peu plus—séparent donc l'homme de la femme.*
Two metres, or a little more, separates a man from a woman.
1955 *Le Voyeur.*

8 *Le lecteur, lui non plus, ne voit pas les choses du dehors. Il est dans le labyrinthe aussi.*
The reader [as well as the main character] does not view the work from outside. He too is in the labyrinth.
1959 *Dans le labyrinthe.*

9 *Et une fois de plus je m'avançais le long de ces mêmes couloirs, marchant depuis des jours, depuis des mois, depuis des années, à votre rencontre.*
And one more time, I advanced along these same hallways, walking for *days,* for *months,* for *years,* to meet you.
1961 *L'Année dernière à Marienbad.*

10 *Car loin de le [le lecteur] négliger, l'auteur aujourd'hui proclame l'absolu besoin qu'il a de son concours actif, conscient, créateur. Ce qu'il lui demande, ce n'est plus de recevoir tout fait un monde achevé, plein, clos sur lui-même, c'est au contraire de participer à une création, d'inventer à son tour l'œuvre—et le monde—et d'apprendre ainsi à inventer sa propre vie.*
Far from neglecting him [the reader], the author today proclaims the absolute necessity of the reader's active, conscious and creative assistance. What he demands of the reader is no longer to receive a ready-made world, complete, full, closed in upon itself. On the contrary, the reader is asked to participate in the creation, to invent for himself a work—and the world—and to understand thus how to invent his own life.
1963 *Pour un nouveau roman.*

11 *L'amour est un jeu, la poésie est un jeu, la vie doit devenir un jeu (c'est le seul espoir de nos luttes politiques) et 'la révolution elle-même est un jeu', comme disaient les plus conscients des révolutionnaires de mai.*
Love is a game, poetry is a game, life should become a game (it's the only hope for our political struggles) and 'the revolution itself is a game', as the most aware of the May revolutionaries said.
1970 *Projet pour une révolution à New York.*

12 *Première approximation: j'écris pour détruire, en les décrivant avec précision, des monstres nocturnes qui menacent d'envahir ma vie éveillée.*
First general point: I write to destroy, by describing exactly the nocturnal monsters that threaten to invade my waking life.
1984 *Le Miroir qui revient.*

Robbins, Colonel

US Red Cross representative at Petrograd.

13 A four-kind son-of-a-bitch, but the greatest Jew since Jesus Christ.
Of Leon Trotsky. Quoted by A J P Taylor in the *New Statesman and Nation*, 20 Feb 1954.

Robbins, Lionel Charles, Baron Robbins of Clare Market 1898–1984

English economist, Professor at the London School of Economics and later chairman of the *Financial Times*.

14 Economics is the science which studies human behaviour as a relationship between scarce resources and ends which have alternative uses… It does not attempt to pick out certain *kinds* of behaviour, but focuses attention on a particular *aspect* of behaviour, the form imposed by the influence of scarcity.
1932 *An Essay on the Nature and Significance of Economic Science*, p.16–17.

Robbins, Tim 1958–

US actor and director, whose acting credits include *Jacob's Ladder* (1990), *The Player* (1992) and *The Shawshank Redemption* (1994).

15 As we applaud the hard-edged realism of the opening battle scene of *Saving Private Ryan*, we cringe at the thought of seeing the same on the nightly news. We are told it would be pornographic.
2003 Speech to the National Press Club, Washington DC, 15 Apr.

16 I had been unaware that baseball was a Republican sport.
2003 In a letter to Dale Petroskey, president of the National Baseball Hall of Fame, after his appearance there was cancelled when he criticized President George W Bush, Apr.

Robert of Clari fl.c.1216

Picard knight.

17 When they were on that sea and had spread their sails and had their banners set high on the poops of the ships and their ensigns, it seemed indeed as if the sea were all a-tremble and all on fire with the ships they were sailing and the great joy they were making.
1203 Describing the Venetian fleet setting out. *The Conquest of Constantinople* (translated by E H McNeal, 1936), p.42–3.

Roberts, Sir Charles George Douglas 1860–1943

Canadian poet, naturalist, novelist and short-story writer. His first book of poems, *Orion, and Other Poems* (1880), inspired the group later known as 'The Confederation Poets'. In 1892 he published his first animal story, of which there would eventually be about 20 collected volumes. Roberts also translated French–Canadian literature into English.

18 This is the voice of high midsummer's heat.

The rasping vibrant clamour soars and shrills
O'er all the meadowy range of shadeless hills,
As if a host of giant cicadae beat
The cymbals of their wings with tireless feet,
Or brazen grasshoppers with triumphing note
From the long swath proclaimed the fate that smote
The clover and timothy-tops and meadowsweet.
1893 'The Mowing'.

19 When Winter scourged the meadow and the hill
And in the withered leafage worked his will,
Then water shrank, and shuddered, and stood still,—
Then built himself a magic house of glass,
Irised with memories of flowers and grass,
Wherein to sit and watch the fury pass.
1898 'Ice'.

20 And I turned and fled, like a soul pursued,
From the white, inviolate solitude.
1901 'The Skater'.

Robertson (of Port Ellen), George Islay Macneill Robertson, Baron 1946–

Scottish Labour politician, Secretary-General of NATO since 1999.

21 Serbs out, Nato in, refugees back.
1999 Summing up the Nato objective in Kosovo, 7 Jun.

Robeson, Paul 1898–1976

US singer, actor and civil rights activist.

22 My father was a slave, and my people died to build this country, and I am going to stay here and have a piece of it, just like you.
1956 Statement to the House of Representatives Committee on Un-American Activities.

Robin, Leo 1899–1985

US lyricist best known for his collaboration with composer Ralph Rainger between 1932 and 1942. After Rainger's death he wrote with various other composers.

23 Thanks for the Memory.
1937 Title of song, which became Bob Hope's signature tune. Music by Ralph Rainger.

Robinson, (Edward) Austin George 1897–1993

English economist, professor at Cambridge University.

24 All industrial efficiency consists in trying to do with eight men what we have hitherto been doing with ten men. It consists in creating unemployment.
1931 *The Structure of Competitive Industry*.

Robinson, Casey 1903–79

US screenwriter. His credits include *Captain Blood* (1935), *Now, Voyager* (1942) and *The Snows of Kilimanjaro* (1952).

25 Don't let's ask for the moon. We have the stars.
1942 Line delivered by Bette Davis to Paul Henreid in *Now, Voyager*.

26 Where's the rest of me?
1942 Line delivered by Ronald Reagan on discovering his legs have been amputated in *King's Row*.

Robinson, Edward G *pseudonym of* *Emanuel Goldenberg* 1893–1973

Hungarian-born US actor, whose portrayal of a vicious gangster in *Little Caesar* (1930) brought him stardom. Other films include *The Whole Town's Talking* (1935), *Double Indemnity* (1944) and *Key Largo* (1948).

27 Mother of Mercy, is this the end of Rico?
> **1930** Line delivered by him in *Little Caesar* (screenplay by Francis Faragoh and Robert E Lee).

Robinson, Edwin Arlington 1869–1935

US poet. He created a fictional New England village, Tilbury Town, in which his best poetry is set. He won three Pulitzer Prizes (1922, 1925 and 1928).

28 In fine, we thought that he was everything
To make us wish that we were in his place.

So on we worked, and waited for the light,
And went without meat, and cursed the bread;
And Richard Cory, one calm summer night,
Went home and put a bullet through his head.
> **1897** *The Children of the Night*, 'Richard Cory'.

29 Friends
To borrow my books and set wet glasses on
them.
> **1902** *Captain Craig*, 'Captain Craig', pt.2.

30 Miniver Cheevy, child of scorn,
Grew lean while he assailed the seasons;
He wept that he was ever born,
And he had reasons.
> **1910** *The Town down the River*, 'Miniver Cheevy'.

31 Miniver loved the Medici,
Albeit he had never seen one;
He would have sinned incessantly
Could he have been one.
> **1910** *The Town down the River*, 'Miniver Cheevy'.

32 Miniver Cheevy, born too late,
Scratched his head and kept on thinking;
Miniver coughed, and called it fate,
And kept on drinking.
> **1910** *The Town down the River*, 'Miniver Cheevy'.

33 The world is…a kind of kindergarten, where millions of bewildered infants are trying to spell God with the wrong blocks.
> **1917** *Literature in the Making*.

34 I shall have more to say when I am dead.
> **1920** *The Three Taverns*, 'John Brown'.

35 Below him, in the town among the trees,
Where friends of other days had honored him,
A phantom salutation of the dead
Rang thinly till old Eben's eyes were dim.
> **1921** *Avon's Harvest*, 'Mr Flood's Party'.

36 The Man Who Died Twice.
> **1924** Title of book.

37 Joy shivers in the corner where she knits
And Conscience always has the rocking-chair,
Cheerful as when she tortured into fits
The first cat that was ever killed by Care.
> **1925** *Dionysus in Doubt*, 'New England'.

Robinson, Joan Violet *née* *Maurice* 1903–83

English economist, a leader of the Cambridge school which developed macroeconomic theories of growth and distribution based on the work of Keynes. Her works include *The Economics of Imperfect Competition* (1933) and *Economic Heresies* (1971).

38 The typical entrepreneur is no longer the bold and tireless man of Marshall, or the sly and rapacious Moneybags of Marx, but a mass of inert shareholders, indistinguishable from *rentiers*, who employ salaried managers to run their concerns.
> **1947** *An Essay on Marxian Economics*.

39 The purpose of studying economics is not to acquire a set of ready-made answers to economic questions, but to learn how to avoid being deceived by economists.
> **1955** Quoted in *Contributions to Modern Economics* (1978), p.75.

40 It is impossible to understand the economic system in which we are living if we try to interpret it as a rational scheme. It has to be understood as an awkward phase in a continuing process of historical development.
> **1966** *Economics: an Awkward Corner*.

41 Hitler had already found out how to cure unemployment before Keynes had finished explaining why it occurred.
> **1971** Collected in *Contributions to Modern Economics* (1978), p.10.

Robinson, John Arthur Thomas 1919–83

English churchman and radical theologian, Bishop of Woolwich, latterly Dean of Clare College, Cambridge.

42 Jesus never claims to be God, personally, yet he always claims to bring God, completely.
> **1963** *Honest to God*.

Robinson, Mary 1944–

Irish Labour politician, President (1990–7) and UN High Commissioner for Human Rights (1997–2002).

43 Instead of rocking the cradle, they rocked the system.
> **1990** Paying tribute to Irish women, in her victory speech. Quoted in *The Times*, 10 Nov.

Robson, Sir Bobby 1933–

English footballer and football manager. He has been manager of Ipswich Town (1969–82), England (1982–90) and Newcastle United (1999–2004).

44 I'd have given my right arm to be a pianist.
> **2000** On what he would have done if he were not a football manager. In *The Times*, 26 Dec.

Roche, Sir Boyle 1743–1807

Irish politician. He joined the British army and fought in the war in America. On returning to Ireland he entered parliament in 1776 and remained an MP until the Act of Union (1800). He opposed Catholic emancipation and supported the Union. He was granted a pension for his constant support of the government.

45 Mr Speaker, I think the noble young man has no business to make any apology. He is a gentleman, and none such should be asked to make an *apology*, because no *gentleman* could mean to *give offence*.
> **c.1796** Debate on motion to expel Lord Edward Fitzgerald from Irish House of Commons, quoted in Sir Jonah Barrington

Personal Sketches and Recollections of his own Times (1827).

46 Sir, there is no Levitical degrees between nations, and on this occasion I can see neither sin nor shame in *marrying our own sister.*

c.1800 Debate on the Act of Union between Great Britain and Ireland, Irish House of Commons, quoted in Sir Jonah Barrington *Personal Sketches and Recollections of his own Times* (1827).

47 What, Mr Speaker! and so we are to beggar ourselves for fear of vexing posterity! Now, I would ask the honourable gentleman, and *still more* honourable House, why should we put ourselves out of our way to do anything for *posterity*; for what has *posterity* done for *us?*

Debate in Irish House of Commons, quoted in Sir Jonah Barrington *Personal Sketches and Recollections of his own Times* (1827).

➤ *See Addison 7:40.*

48 The best way to *avoid* danger is to *meet it plump.*

Quoted in Sir Jonah Barrington *Personal Sketches and Recollections of his own Times* (1827).

Rochester, John Wilmot, 2nd Earl of   1647–80

English courtier and lyric poet. He is noted for his entertaining letters, for satires, including 'A Satyr Against Mankind' (1674), and for his verses and songs, many of which are sexually frank or defamatory.

49 I hold you six to four I love you with all my heart, if I would bet with other people I'm sure I could get ten to one.

c.1667 Letter from Newmarket to his wife. In *The Letters of John Wilmot, Earl of Rochester*, edited by Jeremy Treglown (1980).

50 Naked she lay, clasped in my longing arms,
I filled with love, and she all over charms,
Both equally inspired with eager fire,
Melting through kindness, flaming in desire;
With arms, legs, lips, close clinging to embrace.

c.1672 'The Imperfect Enjoyment', l.1–6 (published 1680).

51 'Is there no more?'
She cries. 'All this to love, and rapture's due,
Must we not pay a debt to pleasure too?'

c.1672 'The Imperfect Enjoyment', l.22–4 (published 1680).

52 Restless, he rolls about from whore to whore,
A merry Monarch, scandalous and poor.

1673 Of Charles II. 'I' th' Isle of Britain', l.14–15. The poem resulted in a brief period of exile for Rochester.

53 Great Negative, how vainly would the wise
Enquire, define, distinguish, teach, devise,
Didst thou not stand to point their blind Philosophies.

c.1673 'Upon Nothing', stanza 10 (published 1679).

54 French truth, Dutch prowess, British policy,
Hibernian learning, Scotch civility,
Spaniards' dispatch, Danes' wit, are mainly seen in thee.

c.1673 'Upon Nothing', stanza 16 (published 1679).

55 Were I (who to my loss already am
One of those strange prodigious creatures, Man)
A spirit, free to choose for my own share
What case of flesh and blood I'd choose to wear,
I'd be a dog, a monkey, or a bear.

1674 'A Satyr Against Mankind', l.1–5 (published 1679).

56 Reason, an ignis fatuus in the mind,

Which leaving light of nature, sense behind,
Pathless and dangerous wandering ways it takes,
Through error's fenny bogs and thorny brakes;
Whilst the misguided follower climbs, with pain,
Mountains of whimsy heaped in his own brain.

1674 'A Satyr Against Mankind', l.12–17 (published 1679).

57 Then old age and experience, hand in hand,
Lead him to death, and make him understand,
After a search so painful and so long,
That all his life he has been in the wrong.
Huddled in dirt, the reasoning engine lies,
Who was so proud, so witty, and so wise.

1674 'A Satyr Against Mankind', l.25–30 (published 1679).

58 Birds feed on birds, beasts on each other prey,
But savage man alone does man betray.

1674 'A Satyr Against Mankind', l.129–30 (published 1679).

59 That cordial drop heaven in our cup has thrown
To make the nauseous draught of life go down.

c.1674 Of love. 'A Letter from Artemisia in the Town to Chloe in the Country', l.44–5 (published 1679).

60 What vain, unnecessary things are men,
How well we do without 'em!

c.1674–1675 'Fragment of a Satire on Men', l.1–2 (published in full 1953).

61 Dear Madam, You are stark mad, and therefore the fitter for me to love; and that is the reason I think I can never leave to be Your humble servant.

c.1675 Letter to his mistress, the actress Elizabeth Barry. In *The Letters of John Wilmot, Earl of Rochester*, edited by Jeremy Treglown (1980).

62 To pick out the wildest and most fantastical odd man alive, and to place your kindness there, is an act so brave and daring as will show the greatness of your spirit and distinguish you in love, as you are in all things else, from womankind.

c.1675 Letter to his mistress, the actress Elizabeth Barry. In *The Letters of John Wilmot, Earl of Rochester*, edited by Jeremy Treglown (1980).

63 They who would be great in our little government seem as ridiculous to me as schoolboys who…climb a crab-tree, venturing their necks for fruit which solid pigs would disdain if they were not starving.

c.1676 Letter to Henry Savile. In *The Letters of John Wilmot, Earl of Rochester*, edited by Jeremy Treglown (1980).

64 He is a rarity which I cannot but be fond of, as one would be of a hog that could fiddle, or a singing owl.

c.1676 Of Dryden. Letter to Henry Savile. In *The Letters of John Wilmot, Earl of Rochester*, edited by Jeremy Treglown (1980).

65 Son of a whore, God damn you! can you tell
A Peerless Peer the readiest way to Hell?

c.1676 'To the Post-Boy', l.1–2 (published 1926). The postboy's answer is 'The readiest way, my lord, is by Rochester'.

66 My most neglected wife, till you are a much respected widow, I find you will scarce be a contented woman, and to say no more than the plain truth, I do endeavour so fairly to do you that last good service.

c.1677 Letter to his wife, 20 Nov. In *The Letters of John Wilmot, Earl of Rochester*, edited by Jeremy Treglown (1980).

67 There can be no danger in sweetness and youth
Where love is secured by good nature and truth,
On her beauty I'll gaze, and of pleasure complain,
While every kind look adds a link to my chain.

'The Submission', l.13–16 (published 1680).

68 Farewell Woman, I intend,
Henceforth, every night to sit,
With my lewd well natured friend,
Drinking, to engender wit.
'Love a Woman!', l.9–12 (published 1680).

69 Since 'tis nature's law to change,
Constancy alone is strange.
'A Dialogue between Strephon and Daphne', l.31–2 (published 1691).

70 An age in her embraces passed,
Would seem a winter's day;
Where life and light, with envious haste,
Are torn and snatched away.

But, oh how slowly minutes roll,
When absent from her eyes
That feed my love, which is my soul,
It languishes and dies.
'The Mistress', l.1–8 (published 1691).

71 Ancient Person, for whom I
All the flattering youth defy;
Long be it ere thou grow old,
Aching, shaking, crazy, cold;
But still continue as thou art,
Ancient person of my heart.
'A Song of a Young Lady to Her Ancient Lover', stanza 1 (published 1691).

72 God bless our good and gracious King
Whose promise none relies on,
Who never said a foolish thing
Nor ever did a wise one.
Of Charles II (published 1707). The verse was later changed to an epitaph ('Here lies a great and mighty king…').

Rockefeller, David 1915–

US banker and philanthropist, born into the wealthy Rockefeller dynasty, Chairman and Chief Executive Officer of the Chase Manhattan Bank (1969–81).

73 One thing this family does not need to do is make itself resented by thousands more people.
Explaining his reluctance to join the management of the Chase Manhattan Bank. Quoted in Peter Collier and David Horowitz *The Rockefellers* (1976).

74 I was born into wealth and there was nothing I could do about it. It was there like food or air.
1990 In *Merchants and Masterpieces*, WETA TV broadcast, 31 Dec.

Rockefeller, John D(avison) 1839–1937

US industrialist and philanthropist. In 1875 he founded with his brother William the Standard Oil Company, securing control of US oil trade. After 1897 he devoted himself to philanthropy, and in 1913 established the Rockefeller Foundation 'to promote the wellbeing of mankind'.

75 The growth of a large business is merely a survival of the fittest… The American Beauty rose can be produced in the splendor and fragrance which bring cheer to its beholder only by sacrificing the early buds which grow up around it.
Quoted in W J Ghent *Our Benevolent Feudalism* (1902).

Rockefeller, John D(avison), Jr 1874–1960

US business and oil magnate. He took over his father's business empire in 1911 and continued the Rockefeller philanthropic tradition. He founded the Rockefeller Center, New York (1931, completed 1939).

76 The secretaries here have an advantage I never had. They can prove to themselves their commercial worth.
1950 Speech to the New York Chamber of Commerce, 6 Apr. Quoted in Peter Collier and David Horowitz *The Rockefellers* (1976).

77 The rendering of useful service is the common duty of mankind, and…only in the purifying fire of sacrifice is the dross of selfishness consumed and the greatness of the human soul set free.
Credo engraved in Rockefeller Center Plaza, New York.

Rockefeller, John D(avison), III 1906–78

US businessman and art collector, Governor of West Virginia.

78 If my name were John D Smith IV I wouldn't have been elected to anything.
1970 On becoming West Virginia's Secretary of State (before moving on to be Governor). In the *New York Times*, 4 Oct.

79 It's like orchestrating a symphony of unhappiness.
1971 On the necessity of compromise in health-care financing. In the *Washington Post*, 1 Jul.

Rockefeller, Laurance S 1910–2004

US businessman, son of John D Rockefeller, Jr. He has been involved with a variety of conservation and environmental organizations.

80 Lyndon gave me that instead of the Hawaii air route.
Of the Medal of Freedom which he received from President Johnson after Eastern Airlines failed to receive permission to fly a coveted route. Quoted in Peter Collier and David Horowitz *The Rockefellers* (1978).

Rockefeller, Nelson A(ldrich) 1908–79

US Republican politician. Director of the Rockefeller Center (1931–58), he became Governor of New York State (1958–73) and Vice-President (1974–7) under Ford, after failing to win the presidential nomination.

81 If there is anything more satisfying than dedicating a new building, it is dedicating eight new buildings.
1970 On Albany's Government Mall. In the *New York Times*, 13 Mar.

82 When you think of what I had, what else was there to aspire to?
Of his lifelong ambition to be US President. Quoted in Michael Kramer and Sam Roberts *I Never Wanted to be Vice President of Anything* (1976).

Rockefeller, Winthrop 1912–73

US businessman and politician, son of John D Rockefeller Jr, who ran a farm in Arkansas on experimental principles. He served as Republican Governor of Arkansas (1967–70).

83 In them one can see the spontaneous—and often aesthetic—expression of a people reflected, not in a gilt-framed drawing room mirror, but in an honest glass held up to the face of a nation.
1962 On an exhibition of American folk art at the US Embassy, London. In news summaries, 31 Jan.

84 In the springtime of America's cultural life, its itinerant folk artists took to the road to record the life and times of a people. Perhaps never again will we have an artistic record created in such direct and unassuming terms.
   1962 On an exhibition of American folk art at the US Embassy, London. In news summaries, 31 Jan.

Rockne, Knute Kenneth 1888–1931

Norwegian-born US football coach. Coach for the University of Notre Dame team after World War I, he dominated US college football until his death in an air crash.

85 When the going gets tough, the tough get going.
   His catchphrase, later adopted by John F Kennedy.

Rockwell, Norman 1894–1978

US popular illustrator, best known for his *Saturday Evening Post* covers. His style is typically anecdotal, idealized scenes of everyday American small-town life.

86 If the public dislikes one of my *Post* covers, I can't help disliking it myself.
   Quoted in the *New York Times*, 28 Sep 1986.

Rodchenko, Alexander 1891–1956

Russian artist who was a leader of the Russian Constructivist painters before he took up photography in 1922 and became active in the field of typography and photographic journalism.

87 Tell me, frankly, what ought to remain of Lenin:
   an art bronze,
   oil portraits,
   etchings,
   watercolours,
   his secretary's diary, his friends' memoirs—
   or
   a file of photographs taken of him at work and rest, archives of his books, writing pads, notebooks, shorthand reports, films, phonograph records?
   I don't think there's any choice.
   Art has no place in modern life… Every cultured modern man must wage war against art, as against opium.

   Photograph and be photographed!
   Quoted in Robert Hughes *The Shock of the New* (1980).

Roddenberry, Gene 1921–91

US scriptwriter, producer and director. A former air force pilot, he made his name as the creator of the popular *Star Trek* television series.

88 Space—the final frontier.
   1966 Introductory voiceover to *Star Trek*.

89 To boldly go where no man has gone before.
   1966 The mission of the starship *Enterprise*. Introductory voiceover to *Star Trek*.

90 Beam us up, Mr Scott.
   1966 *Star Trek*, 'Gamesters of Triskelion'. The phrase is often misquoted as 'Beam me up, Scotty'.

Roddick, Anita 1942–

English retail entrepreneur, founder (in 1976) of the Body Shop.

91 I think that business practices would improve immeasurably if they were guided by 'feminine'

principles—qualities like love and care and intuition.
   1991 *Body and Soul*.

Rodgers, Richard and Hart, Lorenz 1902–79; 1896–1943

US composer and songwriter partnership. They wrote a series of popular musicals including *Pal Joey* (1940).

92 Sigmund Freud has often stated
   Dreams and drives are all related.
   Zip, I am such a scholar!
   1940 'Zip', in *Pal Joey*.

Rodgers, T J

US businessman. He is founder, president and chief executive officer of Cypress Semiconductor Corporation.

93 Most entrepreneurs who have the guts to take on a big challenge are a lot like Babe Ruth—they set records for both home runs and strike outs.
   1993 Letter about Steven Jobs of Next in the *San Francisco Chronicle*, 6 Dec.

Rodó, José Enrique 1872–1917

Uruguayan essayist and philosopher, a leading stylist and thinker of the Modernist group. His most famous work, *Ariel*, admonishes the youth of South America to cultivate spiritual (Ariel) rather than material (Caliban) values.

94 *La visión de una América deslatinizada por propia voluntad, sin la extorsión de la conquista, y regenerada luego a imagen y semejanza del arquetipo del Norte, flota ya sobre los sueños de muchos sinceros interesados por nuestro porvenir… Tenemos nuestra nordomanía. Es necesario oponerle los límites que la razón y el sentimiento señalan.*
   The vision of an America de-Latinized of its own will, without threat of conquest, and reconstituted in the image and likeness of the North, now looms in the nightmares of many who are genuinely concerned about our future… We have our *USA-mania*. It must be limited by the boundaries our reason and sentiment jointly dictate.
   1900 *Ariel* (translated 1922), pt.5.

Rodriguez, Richard 1944–

US writer and journalist.

95 The genius of American culture and its integrity comes from fidelity to the light. Plain as day, we say. Happy as the day is long. Early to bed, early to rise. American virtues are daylight virtues: honesty, integrity, plain speech. We say yes when we mean yes and no when we mean no, and all else comes from the evil one. America presumes innocence and even the right to happiness.
   1990 *Frontiers*, 'Night and Day'.

96 In the modern city, it takes on the status of a cathedral, our Chartres, our Notre Dame, our marble museum of the soul.
   1995 On San Francisco's new Museum of Modern Art. In the *MacNeil-Lehrer Report*, 27 Feb.

Rodriguez, Sue 1950–94

Canadian campaigner for euthanasia, who suffered from ALS (amyotrophic lateral sclerosis, or Lou Gehrig's disease, a progressive and terminal illness).

97 I want to ask you gentlemen, if I cannot give consent to my own death, then whose body is this? Who owns my life?

> **1992** Videotaped presentation to the Justice Committee of the House of Commons, Ottawa, Nov. Reported by Deborah Wilson in *The Globe and Mail*, 5 Dec. The Supreme Court of Canada denied Rodriguez's request for a physician-assisted death.

Roethke, Theodore 1908–63

US poet. Professor of English at the University of Washington from 1948, he won a Pulitzer Prize for his collection *The Waking* (1953).

98 I have known the inexorable sadness of pencils,
Neat in their boxes, dolor of pad and paper-weight,
All the misery of manila folders and mucilage,
Desolation in immaculate public places.

> **1948** *The Lost Son*, 'Dolor'.

99 And I have seen dust from the walls of institutions,
Finer than flour, alive, more dangerous than silica,
Sift, almost invisible, through long afternoons of tedium.

> **1948** *The Lost Son*, 'Dolor'.

1 To know that light falls and fills, often without our knowing,
As an opaque vase fills to the brim from quick pouring,
Fills and trembles at the edge yet does not flow over,
Still holding and feeding the stem of the contained flower.

> **1948** *The Lost Son*, 'The Shape of Fire'.

2 And what a congress of stinks!—
Roots ripe as old bait,
Pulpy stems, rank, silo-rich,
Leaf-mold, manure, lime, piled against slippery planks.
Nothing would give up life:
Even the dirt kept breathing a small breath.

> **1948** *The Lost Son*, 'Root Cellar'.

3 I wake to sleep, and take my waking slow.
I feel my fate in what I cannot fear.
I learn by going where I have to go.

> **1953** *The Waking*, 'The Waking'.

4 Over this damp grave I speak the words of my love;
I, with no rights in this matter,
Neither father nor lover.

> **1953** Poem addressed to a dead student. *The Waking*, 'Elegy for Jane'.

5 Of her choice virtues only gods should speak,
Or English poets who grew up on Greek
(I'd have them sing in chorus, cheek to cheek).

> **1958** *Words for the Wind*, 'I Knew a Woman'.

6 What's freedom for? To know eternity.
I swear she cast a shadow white as stone.
But who would count eternity in days?
These old bones live to learn her wanton ways:
(I measure time by how a body sways).

> **1958** *Words for the Wind*, 'I Knew a Woman'.

7 In a dark time the eye begins to see.

> **1963** *Sequence, Sometimes Metaphysical*, 'In a Dark Time'.

8 The self persists like a dying star,
In sleep, afraid.

> **1964** *The Far Field*, 'Meditation at Oyster River'.

Rogers, Carl Ransom 1902–87

US psychologist and pioneer of client-centred counselling. His *Client-Centred Therapy* (1951) and *On Becoming a Person* (1961) emphasized the value of genuine empathy with the patient.

9 Unconditional positive regard.

> **c.1950** The slogan of the Rogerian counselling movement.

Rogers, Richard George Rogers, Baron 1933–

English architect, concerned with advancing technology in architecture and pushing the limits of design. His works include the Beaubourg or Pompidou Centre, Paris (1971–9, with Renzo Piano), Lloyds Building, London (1979–85), the Millennium Dome (1999) and the National Assembly for Wales (1999).

10 'Form follows profit' is the aesthetic principle of our times. Thus, design skill is measured today by the architect's ability to build the largest possible enclosure for the smallest investment in the quickest time.

> **1990** 22nd annual Walter Neurath lecture. Collected in *Architecture: a Modern View*.

11 Architects cannot work in a vacuum; unlike other artists they are totally dependent on a site, a brief and finance.

> **1990** 22nd annual Walter Neurath lecture. Collected in *Architecture: a Modern View*.

12 The problem is not style but quality, not aesthetics but ethics.

> **1990** 22nd annual Walter Neurath lecture. Collected in *Architecture: a Modern View*.

Rogers, Will 1879–1935

US actor, rancher and humorist. Best known for his ready wisecracks, he had a syndicated column, and wrote a number of books, including a posthumously compiled *Autobiography*.

13 Will you please tell me what you do with all the vice presidents a bank has?… The United States is the biggest business institution in the world and they only have one vice president and nobody has ever found anything for him to do.

> **1922** Speech, International Bankers' Association.

14 Well, all I know is what I read in the papers.

> **1923** In the *New York Times*, 30 Sep.

15 You know everybody is ignorant, only on different subjects.

> **1924** In the *New York Times*, 31 Aug.

16 The more you read and observe about this Politics thing, you got to admit that each party is worse than the other. The one that's out always looks the best.

> **1924** *The Illiterate Digest*, 'Breaking into the Writing Game'.

17 Everything is funny as long as it is happening to Somebody Else.

> **1924** *The Illiterate Digest*, 'Warning to Jokers: Lay Off the Prince'.

18 The Income Tax return has made more Liars out of the American people than Golf has. Even when you make one out on the level, you don't know when it's through if you are a Crook or a Martyr.

> **1924** *The Illiterate Digest*, 'Helping the Girls with Their Income Taxes'.

19 I bet you if I had met him and had a chat with him, I would have found him a very interesting and human fellow, for I never yet met a man that I didn't like.

> **1926** On Trotsky. In the *Saturday Evening Post*, 6 Nov.

20 Communism is like prohibition, it's a good idea but it won't work.
1927 Syndicated column, Nov. Collected in *The Weekly Articles*, vol. 3 (1981).

21 You can't say civilization don't advance, however, for in every war they kill you in a new way.
1929 In the *New York Times*, 23 Dec.

22 Half our life is spent trying to find something to do with the time we have rushed through life trying to save.
1930 In the *New York Times*, 29 Apr.

23 The United States is the only country ever to go to the poorhouse in an automobile.
c.1930 Attributed.

24 I was born because it was a habit in those days, people didn't know anything else.
The Autobiography of Will Rogers (published 1949), ch.1.

25 There is only one thing that can kill the Movies, and that is education.
The Autobiography of Will Rogers (published 1949), ch.6.

26 When a man goes in for politics over here, he has no time to labour, and any man that labours has no time to fool with politics. Over there, politics is an obligation; over here it's a business.
On Britain electing a Labour government. *The Autobiography of Will Rogers* (published 1949), ch.14.

27 It's great to be great but it's greater to be human.
The Autobiography of Will Rogers (published 1949), ch.15.

28 Being a hero is about the shortest-lived profession on earth.
Quoted in 'A Rogers Thesaurus' in *The Saturday Review*, 25 Aug 1962. Another form of the quote appeared in a syndicated newspaper article, 15 Feb 1925: 'Heroing is one of the shortest-lived professions there is'.

29 I don't make jokes—I just watch the government and report the facts.
Quoted in 'A Rogers Thesaurus' in *The Saturday Review*, 25 Aug 1962.

30 I guess there is nothing that will get your mind off everything like golf. I have never been depressed enough to take up the game but they say you get so sore at yourself you forget to hate your enemies.
Quoted in Michael Hobbs *The Golf Quotation Book* (1992).

Rogers, William Pierce 1913–2001

US lawyer and government official. As Deputy Attorney General (1953–7) he supported the 1957 Civil Rights Act, becoming Attorney General (1957–61). As Secretary of State (1969–73) he brought about a Middle East ceasefire.

31 Making foreign policy is like pornographic movies…more fun doing it than watching it.
1982 On becoming Under-Secretary of State for Economic Affairs, 7 Jun.

Rolleston, Humphrey 1862–1944

English physician.

32 Medicine is a noble profession but a damn bad business.
1944 Quoted in *Who Said What When* (1988).

Rollins, Sonny (Theodore Walter) 1930–

US jazz saxophonist. He is a leading figure in the development of jazz in the post-bebop era.

33 America is deeply rooted in Negro culture: its colloquialisms, its humour, its music. How ironic that the Negro, who more than any other people can claim America's culture as his own, is being persecuted and repressed, that the Negro, who has exemplified the humanities in his very existence, is being rewarded with inhumanity.
1958 Statement on sleeve of *Freedom Suite*.

Romani, Felice 1788–1865

Italian librettist, poet, essayist and critic. He provided libretti for more than 100 composers, striking a balance between Classicism and Romanticism. He is best known for his collaborations with Donizetti and Bellini.

34 *Casta Diva.*
Chaste goddess.
1831 Norma's aria. *Norma*, act 1 (music by Bellini, published 1832).

35 *Una furtiva lagrima.*
A furtive tear.
1832 Nemorino's aria. *L'Elisir d'Amore*, act 2 (music by Donizetti).

Romney, George W 1907–95

US politician. He was Governor of Michigan (1963–9) and member of the Nixon administration (1969–73).

36 I didn't say I didn't say it. I said I didn't say I said it. I want to make that very clear.
1967 Clarifying his policy. In the *National Review*, 12 Dec.

Roosevelt, (Anna) Eleanor 1884–1962

US humanitarian and diplomat, wife and adviser of Franklin D Roosevelt. After his death she was US delegate to the UN (1945–53, 1961), chair of the Human Rights Commission (1946–51) and US representative to the General Assembly (1946–52).

37 You always admire what you don't really understand.
1956 In *Meet the Press*, NBC TV broadcast, 16 Sep.

38 She can talk beautifully about democracy but doesn't know how to live democracy.
Of Madame Chiang Kai-shek. Recalled on Mrs Roosevelt's death, 7 Nov 1962.

39 Where, after all, do human rights begin? They begin in small places, close to home—so close and so small that they cannot be seen on any map of the world.
1965 Quoted in the *New York Times*, 26 Dec.

40 A woman is like a tea bag; when she is in hot water she just gets stronger.
Quoted by Hillary Rodham Clinton in the *Wall Street Journal*, 30 Sep 1994.

Roosevelt, Franklin D(elano) 1882–1945

US Democratic statesman, 32nd President (1933–45) despite being stricken with polio in 1921. He introduced a 'New Deal' for national recovery (1933), and was re-elected three times. He entered World War II after Pearl Harbor (1941), meeting Churchill and Stalin at Teheran (1943) and Yalta (1945), but died just before the German surrender.

41 I pledge you, I pledge myself, to a New Deal for the American people.
1932 Speech accepting the Democratic Convention's

presidential nomination, Chicago, 2 Jul.

42 In the field of world policy, I would dedicate this nation to the policy of the good neighbour.
1933 Inaugural address, 4 Mar.

43 Let me assert my belief that the only thing that we have to fear is fear itself—nameless, unreasoning, unjustified terror that paralyses needed efforts to convert retreat into advance.
1933 Inaugural address, 4 Mar.

44 Better the occasional faults of a Government that lives in a spirit of charity than the consistent omissions of a Government frozen in the ice of its own indifference.
1936 Renomination acceptance speech, Philadelphia, 27 Jun.

45 I have seen war… I hate war.
1936 Speech at Chantauqua, New York, 14 Aug.

46 When peace has been broken anywhere, the peace of all countries is in danger.
1939 Radio broadcast, 3 Sep.

47 A conservative is a man with two perfectly good legs who has never learned to walk forwards. A reactionary is a somnambulist walking backwards. A radical is a man with both feet planted firmly in the air.
1939 Radio broadcast, Oct.

48 I have said this before, but I shall say it again and again and again: Your boys are not going to be sent into any foreign wars.
1940 Speech in Boston, 30 Oct.

49 We have the men—the skill—the wealth—and above all, the will… We must be the great arsenal of democracy.
1940 'Fireside chat' radio broadcast, 29 Dec.

50 In the future days, which we seek to make secure, we look forward to a world founded upon four essential freedoms. The first is freedom of speech and expression, everywhere in the world. The second is the freedom of every person to worship God in his own way, everywhere in the world. The third is freedom from want… The fourth is freedom from fear.
1941 Third inaugural address, 6 Jan.

51 Yesterday, December 7, 1941—a date which will live in infamy—the United States of America was suddenly and deliberately attacked by naval and air forces of the Empire of Japan.
1941 Address to Congress, 8 Dec, following the Japanese attack on Pearl Harbor.

Roosevelt, Theodore 1858–1919

US Republican statesman and 26th President (1901–9). Elected Vice-President in 1900, he became President on McKinley's assassination and was re-elected in 1904. His expansionist policies included a strong navy, the regulation of trusts and monopolies, and his 'Square Deal' policy for social reform.

52 There is a homely adage that runs, 'Speak softly and carry a big stick, and you will go far.' If the American nation will speak softly and yet build, and keep at a pitch of the highest training, the Monroe Doctrine will go far.
1901 Vice-presidential speech, Sep.

53 In the western hemisphere, the adherence of the United States to the Monroe Doctrine may force the United States, however reluctantly, in flagrant cases of

wrongdoing or impotence, to the exercise of an international police power.
1904 Message to Congress, 6 Dec.

54 The men with the muck-rakes are often indispensable to the well-being of society, but only if they know when to stop raking the muck.
1906 House of Representatives, 14 Apr.

55 I stand for the square deal… not merely for fair play under the present rules of the game, but for having those rules changed, so as to work for a more substantial equality of opportunity and of reward for equally good service.
1910 Speech, Osawatomie, 31 Aug.

56 Do not hit at all if it can be avoided, but never hit softly.
1913 *Theodore Roosevelt: an Autobiography.*

57 Practical efficiency is common, and lofty idealism is not uncommon; it is the combination that is necessary, and that combination is rare.
1913 *Theodore Roosevelt: an Autobiography.*

58 There is no reason why people should not call themselves Cubists, or Octagonists, or Parallelopipedonists, or Knights of the Isosceles Triangle, or Brothers of the Cosine, if they so desire; as expressing anything serious and permanent, one term is as fatuous as another.
1913 His opinion on the *International Exhibition of Modern Art* in New York, popularly known as *The Armoury Show*. 'A Layman's Views of an Art Exhibition', in *The Outlook* (9 Mar).

59 We are fighting in the quarrel of civilization against barbarism, of liberty against tyranny. Germany has become a menace to the whole world. She is the most dangerous enemy of liberty now existing.
1917 Speech at Oyster Bay, Long Island, Apr.

60 We have room in this country but for one flag, the Stars and Stripes. We have room for but one loyalty, loyalty to the United States. We have room for but one language, the English language.
1919 Message to the American Defense Society two days before his death, 3 Jan.

Rosebery, Archibald Philip Primrose, 5th Earl of 1847–1929

English statesman, Foreign Secretary (1886, 1892–4) under Gladstone, whom he succeeded as Prime Minister for a brief period in 1894 before the Liberals lost the election of 1895. He was noted for his racehorse stables, and as a biographer of British statesmen.

61 It is beginning to be hinted that we are a nation of amateurs.
1900 Rectorial address, Glasgow University, 16 Nov.

62 For the present at any rate, I must proceed alone. I must plough my own furrow alone—but before I get to the end of that furrow, it is possible that I may not find myself alone.
1901 On breaking from the Liberal Party, Jul.

Rosenberg, Harold 1906–78

US critic of the modern movement in painting and literature.

63 At a certain moment the canvas began to appear to one American painter after another as an arena in which to act—rather than as a space in which to reproduce,

re-design, analyze or 'express' an object, actual or imagined. What was to go on the canvas was not a picture but an event.
1952 'The American Action Painters', in *Art News*, no.51, Dec.

64 A painting that is an act is inseparable from the biography of the artist.
1952 'The American Action Painters', in *Art News*, no.51, Dec.

65 Everyone knows that the label Modern Art no longer has any relation to the words that compose it. To be Modern Art a work need not be either modern nor art; it need not even be a work. A three-thousand-year-old mask from the South Pacific qualifies as Modern and a piece of wood found on a beach becomes Art.
1952 'The American Action Painters', in *Art News*, no.51, Dec.

66 As we have seen Modern Art does not have to be actually new; it only has to be new to somebody—to the last lady who found out about the driftwood.
1952 'The American Action Painters', in *Art News*, no.51, Dec.

Rosenberg, Isaac 1890–1918

English poet and artist. He published two volumes of poems before being killed in action in France. A third appeared posthumously, and his *Collected Works* (1937, rev edn 1973) revived his reputation.

67 The darkness crumbles away—
It is the same old druid Time as ever.
1916 'Break of Day in the Trenches'.

68 Droll rat, they would shoot you if they knew
Your cosmopolitan sympathies.
1916 'And God Knows What Antipathies'.

69 Earth has waited for them,
All the time of their growth
Fretting for their decay:
Now she has them at last.
1917 'Dead Man's Dump'.

70 Death could drop from the dark
As easily as song.
1917 'Returning, We Hear the Larks'.

Rosenblum, Robert 1927–

US art historian. His works include *Cubism and Twentieth Century Art* (1960) and *Andy Warhol: Portrait of the 70s* (1981).

71 She transformed junkyards of secular carpentry into almost sacred altarpieces.
1988 On sculptor Louise Nevelson. In *Time*, 26 Dec.

Ross, Edward Alsworth 1866–1951

US sociologist, Professor at the University of Wisconsin.

72 A society…which is riven by a dozen oppositions along lines running in every direction, may actually be in less danger of being torn with violence or falling to pieces than one split along just one line. For each new cleavage contributes to narrow the cross clefts, so that one might say that society is *sewn together* by its internal conflicts.
1920 *The Principles of Sociology*.

Rossetti, Christina Georgina 1830–94

English poet and sister of Dante Gabriel Rossetti. She helped found with her brother the Pre-Raphaelite Brotherhood. A devout Christian, her poetry has a melancholic and religiously intense quality.

73 Because the birthday of my life
Is come, my love is come to me.
1862 *Goblin Market and Other Poems*, 'A Birthday'.

74 Come to me in the silence of the night;
Come in the speaking silence of a dream;
Come with soft rounded cheeks and eyes as bright
As sunlight on a stream;
Come back in tears,
O memory, hope, love of finished years.
1862 *Goblin Market and Other Poems*, 'Echo'.

75 For there is no friend like a sister
In calm or stormy weather;
To cheer one on the tedious way,
To fetch one if one goes astray,
To lift one if one totters down,
To strengthen whilst one stands.
1862 *Goblin Market and Other Poems*, 'Goblin Market'.

76 The hope I dreamed of was a dream,
Was but a dream; and now I wake,
Exceeding comfortless, and worn, and old,
For a dream's sake.
1862 *Goblin Market and Other Poems*, 'Mirage'.

77 Oh roses for the flush of youth,
And laurel for the perfect prime;
But pluck an ivy branch for me
Grown old before my time.
1862 *Goblin Market and Other Poems*, 'Oh Roses for the Flush of Youth'.

78 Remember me when I am gone away,
Gone far away into the silent land.
1862 *Goblin Market and Other Poems*, 'Remember'.

79 Better by far you should forget and smile
Than that you should remember and be sad.
1862 *Goblin Market and Other Poems*, 'Remember'.

80 O Earth, lie heavily upon her eyes;
Seal her sweet eyes weary of watching, Earth.
1862 *Goblin Market and Other Poems*, 'Rest'.

81 Silence more musical than any song.
1862 *Goblin Market and Other Poems*, 'Rest'.

82 Does the road wind up-hill all the way?
Yes, to the very end.
Will the day's journey take the whole long day?
From morn to night, my friend.
1862 *Goblin Market and Other Poems*, 'Up-Hill'.

83 When I am dead, my dearest,
Sing no sad songs for me;
Plant thou no roses at my head,
Nor shady cypress tree:
Be the green grass above me
With showers and dewdrops wet;
And if thou wilt, remember,
And if thou wilt, forget.
1862 *Goblin Market and Other Poems*, 'When I Am dead'.

84 In the bleak mid-winter
Frosty wind made moan,
Earth stood hard as iron,
Water like a stone;
Snow had fallen, snow on snow,
Snow on snow,

In the bleak mid-winter,
Long ago.
1875 'Mid-Winter'.

85 Love came down at Christmas,
Love all lovely, Love Divine;
Love was born at Christmas,
Star and angels gave the sign.
1893 *Verses*, 'Love Came Down at Christmas'.

Rossetti, Dante Gabriel 1828–82

English painter and poet, who with his sister Christina Rossetti,
Millais and Holman Hunt, founded the Pre-Raphaelite
Brotherhood. His poetic works include *Poems* (1870) and
Ballads and Sonnets (1881).

86 The blessed damozel leaned out
From the gold bar of Heaven;
Her eyes were deeper than the depth
Of waters stilled at even;
She had three lilies in her hand,
And the stars in her hair were seven.
1870 *Poems*, 'The Blessed Damozel', stanza 1.

87 Her hair that lay along her back
Was yellow like ripe corn.
1870 *Poems*, 'The Blessed Damozel', stanza 2.

88 As low as where this earth
Spins like a fretful midge.
1870 *Poems*, 'The Blessed Damozel', stanza 6.

89 And the souls mounting up to God
Went by her like thin flames.
1870 *Poems*, 'The Blessed Damozel', stanza 7.

90 'We two,' she said, 'will seek the groves
Where the lady Mary is,
With her five handmaidens, whose names
Are five sweet symphonies,
Cecily, Gertrude, Magdalen,
Margaret and Rosalys.'
1870 *Poems*, 'The Blessed Damozel', stanza 18.

91 I have been here before,
But when or how I cannot tell:
I know the grass beyond the door,
The sweet keen smell,
The sighing sound, the lights around the shore.
1870 *Poems*, 'Sudden Light'.

92 A sonnet is a moment's monument,—
Memorial from the Soul's eternity
To one dead deathless hour.
1881 *The House of Life*, introduction.

93 'Tis visible silence, still as the hour-glass.
1881 *The House of Life*, 'Silent Noon', pt.1.

94 Deep in the sun-searched growths the dragon-fly
Hangs like a blue thread loosened from the sky:—
So this winged hour is dropt to us from above.
Oh! clasp we to our hearts, for deathless dower,
This close-companioned inarticulate hour
When twofold silence was the song of love.
1881 *The House of Life*, 'Silent Noon', pt.1.

95 Lo! as that youth's eyes burned at thine, so went
Thy spell through him, and left his straight neck bent
And round his heart one strangling golden hair.
1881 *The House of Life*, 'Body's Beauty', pt.2.

96 They die not,—for their life was death,—but
cease;
And round their narrow lips the mould falls close.
1881 *The House of Life*, 'The Choice', pt.1.

97 I do not see them here; but after death
God knows I know the faces I shall see,
Each one a murdered self, with low last breath.
'I am thyself,—what hast thou done to me?'
'And I—and I—thyself,' (lo! each one saith,)
'And thou thyself to all eternity!'
1881 *The House of Life*, 'Lost Days', pt.2.

98 Give honour unto Luke Evangelist;
For he it was (the aged legends say)
Who first taught Art to fold her hands and pray.
1881 *The House of Life*, 'Old and New Art', pt.2.

99 When vain desire at last and vain regret
Go hand in hand to death, and all is vain,
What shall assuage the unforgotten pain
And teach the unforgetful to forget?
1881 *The House of Life*, 'The One Hope', pt.2.

1 Look in my face; my name is Might-have-been;
I am also called No-more, Too-late, Farewell.
1881 *The House of Life*, 'A Superscription', pt.2.

2 Sleepless with cold commemorative eyes.
1881 *The House of Life*, 'A Superscription', pt.2.

3 Unto the man of yearning thought
And aspiration, to do nought
Is in itself almost an act.
1881 *Ballads and Sonnets*, 'Soothsay', stanza 10.

Rossini, Gioacchino Antonio 1792–1868

Italian composer. His early operas including *La Scala de seta*
(1812) and *L'Italiana in Algeri* (1813) were followed by his
masterpiece, *Il Barbiere de Seviglia* (1816). His later works,
mostly written in Paris, include *La Gazza Ladra* (1817),
Semiramide (1823) and *Guillaume Tell* (1829).

4 I was born for *opera buffa*, as well Thou knowest. Little
skill, a little heart, and that is all. So be Thou blessed and
admit me to Paradise.
1863 Manuscript inscription on the score of his 'Petite Messe
Solennelle'.

5 Monsieur Wagner has good moments, but awful
quarters of an hour!
1867 Quoted in Emile Naumann *Italienische Tondichter* (1883).

Rosso, Medardo 1858–1928

Italian sculptor. Sometimes known as the 'Impressionist'
sculptor, he was a major influence on the Italian Futurists.

6 When I make a portrait, I cannot limit it to the lines of the
head, for that head belongs to a body, it exists in a setting
which influences it, it is part of a totality that I cannot
suppress. The impression you produce upon me is not
the same if I catch sight of you alone in a garden or if I see
you in the midst of a group of other people, in a living
room or on the street.
Quoted in Edmond Claris *De l'impressionisme en sculpture*,
'Medardo Rosso' (1902).

7 One does not walk around a statue any more than one
walks around a painting, because one does not walk
around a figure to receive an impression from it. Nothing
is material in space.

Quoted in Edmond Claris *De l'impressionisme en sculpture*, 'Medardo Rosso' (1902).

Rostand, Jean 1894–1977

French biologist and writer.

8 A body of work such as Pasteur's is inconceivable in our time: no man would be given a chance to create a whole science. Nowadays a path is scarcely opened up when the crowd begins to pour in.
1939 'Pensées d'un Biologiste', collected in *The Substance of Man* (translated by Irma Brandeis, 1962).

9 Nothing leads the scientist so astray as a premature truth.
1939 'Pensées d'un Biologiste', collected in *The Substance of Man* (translated by Irma Brandeis, 1962).

Rosten, Leo Calvin 1908–97

US writer, humorist and anthologist. He is best known for his humorous compendium *The Joys of Yiddish* (1968), but has also written novels and stage plays (some as Leonard Ross).

10 The only thing I can say about W C Fields, whom I have admired since the day he advanced upon Baby LeRoy with an ice pick, is this: any man who hates dogs and babies can't be all bad.
1939 Speech at a Hollywood dinner in honour of W C Fields, 16 Feb.

11 The only reason for being a professional writer is that you just can't help it.
In D L Kirkpatrick (ed) *Contemporary Novelists* (1976).

Roth, Guenther 1931–

German-born US sociologist, Professor of Sociology at Columbia University.

12 My draft-dodging father proved that in the struggle for survival the fittest are most likely to get killed off.
'Partisanship and Scholarship', collected in Bennett Berger (ed) *Authors of Their Own Lives* (1990).

Roth, Henry 1906–95

US novelist. His novel of Jewish life in New York, *Call It Sleep* (1934), was rediscovered on its paperback publication in 1962. Apart from the shorter writings collected in *Shifting Landscape* (1987), he did not publish another until the first part of a massive six-book project, *Mercy of a Rude Stream* (1994).

13 The mind shuttles and reminds: we go this way only once; and shuttles again and rejoins: once is enough.
1960 'The Dun Dakotas', in *Commentary*, 30 Aug.

14 Detach the writer from the milieu where he has experienced his greatest sense of belonging, and you have created a discontinuity within his personality, a short circuit in his identity. The result is his originality, his creativity comes to an end. He becomes the one-book novelist or the one-trilogy writer.
1987 'The Eternal Plebeian and Other Matters', in *Shifting Landscape*.

Roth, Philip Milton 1933–

US novelist. His *succès de scandale*, *Portnoy's Complaint* (1969), was followed by a series of highly literary novels featuring his fictional alter ego, Nathan Zuckerman, all dealing with questions of Jewish identity.

15 Since I was a little girl I always wanted to be Very Decent to People. Other little girls wanted to be nurses and pianists. They were less dissembling.
1962 *Letting Go*, pt.1, ch.1.

16 It's the little questions from women about tappets that finally push men over the edge.
1962 *Letting Go*, pt.1, ch.1.

17 It's a family joke that when I was a tiny child I turned from the window out of which I was watching a snowstorm, and hopefully asked, 'Momma, do we believe in winter?'
1969 *Portnoy's Complaint*, 'The Most Unforgettable Character I've Ever Met'.

18 A Jewish man with parents alive is a fifteen-year-old boy, and will remain a fifteen-year-old boy until *they die*!
1969 *Portnoy's Complaint*, 'Cunt Crazy'.

19 Doctor, doctor, what do you say, LET'S PUT THE ID BACK IN YID!
1969 *Portnoy's Complaint*, 'Cunt Crazy'.

20 Know that famous proverb? When the prick stands up, the brains get buried in the ground!
1969 *Portnoy's Complaint*, 'Cunt Crazy'.

21 My Life as a Man.
1974 Title of novel.

22 Satire is moral outrage transformed into comic art.
1975 *Reading Myself and Others*, 'On *Our Gang*'.

23 The road to hell is paved with works-in-progress.
1979 In the *New York Times Book Review*, 15 Jul.

24 In America everything goes and nothing matters, while in Europe nothing goes and everything matters.
1983 Interview in *Time*, Nov.

25 In Israel it's enough to live—you don't have to do anything else and you go to bed exhausted. Have you ever noticed that Jews shout? Even one ear is more than you need.
1987 *The Counterlife*, ch.2.

26 What makes you a normal Jew, Nathan, is how you are riveted by Jewish abnormality.
1987 *The Counterlife*, ch.2.

27 Is an intelligent human being likely to be much more than a large-scale manufacturer of misunderstanding?
1987 *The Counterlife*, ch.5.

28 For me, as for most novelists, every genuine imaginative event begins down there, with the facts, with the specific, and not with the philosophical, the ideological, or the abstract.
1988 *The Facts: A Novelist's Autobiography*, 'Dear Zuckerman'.

29 In our lore, the Jewish family was an inviolate haven against every form of menace, from personal isolation to gentile hostility. Regardless of internal friction and strife, it was assumed to be an indissoluble consolidation… Family indivisibility, the first commandment.
1988 *The Facts: A Novelist's Autobiography*, 'Dear Zuckerman'.

30 I write fiction and I'm told it's autobiography, I write autobiography and I'm told it's fiction, so since I'm so dim and they're so smart, let *them* decide what it is or it isn't.
1990 Of critics. *Deception*, 'Philip'.

31 It was the summer when a president's penis was on everyone's mind, and life, in all its shameless impurity,

once again confounded America.
2001 *The Human Stain.*

32 I want to make it clear that it wasn't impotence that led me in to a reclusive existence.
2001 *The Human Stain.*

Roth, William V, Jr 1921–

US senator. A member of Congress for Delaware (1967–71), he became a Senator (1971–) and a member of the finance government affairs committee.

33 If only trimmed, it inevitably creeps back…thicker and more deeply rooted than before.
1995 Of bureaucracy, compared to crab grass. In the *Washington Times*, 19 May.

Rothko, Mark *originally* ***Marcus Rothkovitch*** 1903–70

Latvian-born painter, who emigrated to the US as a child. A largely self-taught artist, he moved from Surrealism to a distinctively meditative form of Abstract Expressionism, filling large canvases with blocks of pure colour.

34 I am not interested in relationships of color or form or anything else… I am interested only in expressing the basic human emotions—tragedy, ecstasy, doom, and so on—and the fact that lots of people break down and cry when confronted with my pictures shows that I communicate with those basic human emotions. The people who weep before my pictures are having the same religious experience I had when I painted them. And if you, as you say, are moved only by their color relationships, then you miss the point!
Quoted in R Rosenblum *Modern Painting and the Northern Romantic Tradition* (1975).

Rothwell, Talbot 1916–74

British screenwriter who wrote for film and television, best known for his contribution to many of the *Carry On…* films.

35 Infamy! Infamy! They've all got it in for me!
1964 Line delivered by Kenneth Williams as Julius Caesar in *Carry On Cleo.*

36 The eunuchs are on strike. They are complaining about loss of assets.
1964 *Carry On Cleo.*

Rotten, Johnny *stage name of* ***John Lydon*** 1956–

English punk singer, member of The Sex Pistols.

37 Ever get the feeling you've been cheated?
1978 Having walked offstage at the Winterland Ballroom during The Sex Pistols tour of the US, 14 Jan.

Rouault, Georges Henri 1871–1958

French painter and engraver. Apprenticed to a stained-glass designer in his youth, he retained the characteristic glowing colour outlined in black in his later work. He joined the Fauves c.1904. His works include the large religious engravings *Miserere* and *Guerre.*

38 Decorative art does not exist—only art, intimate, heroic, or epic.
1937 *La Renaissance.*

Rous, Sir Stanley 1895–1986

English football administrator. A former player and referee, he became Secretary of the Football Association in 1934 and President of FIFA in 1961. His codification of the rules of football into 17 laws is still followed today.

39 If this can be termed the century of the common man, then soccer, of all sports, is surely his game… In a world haunted by the hydrogen and napalm bomb, the football field is a place where sanity and hope are still left unmolested.
1952 Quoted in Bryon Butler *The Official History of the Football Association* (1986).

Rousseau, Jean Jacques 1712–78

French political philosopher, educationalist and writer. The father of French Romanticism, he wrote in many different genres. He is best known for his novel *Julie, ou la Nouvelle Héloïse* (1761), his autobiography, his posthumously published *Confessions*, and for *Du contrat social* (*The Social Contract*, 1762).

40 *Le premier qui, ayant enclos un terrain, s'avisa de dire: 'Ceci est à moi' et trouva des gens assez simples pour le croire, fut le vrai fondateur de la société civile.*
The first person who fenced in a piece of land, ventured to say: 'This is mine,' and found others simple enough to believe him, was the true founder of civil society.
1755 *Discours sur l'origine et les fondements de l'inégalité parmi les hommes*, ch.1.

41 *L'homme est né libre, et partout il est dans les fers.*
Man is born free, yet everywhere he is in chains.
1762 *Du contrat social* (*The Social Contract*), bk.1, ch.1 (translated by M Cranston).

42 *La force a fait les premiers esclaves, leur lâcheté les a perpétués.*
Force made the first slaves; their cowardice perpetuated slavery.
1762 *Du contrat social* (*The Social Contract*), bk.1, ch.2 (translated by M Cranston).

43 *Si l'on recherche en quoi consiste précisément le plus grand bien de tous, qui doit être le fin de tout système de législation, on trouvera qu'il se réduit à ces deux objets principaux, la liberté et l'égalité.*
If we enquire wherein lies precisely the greatest good of all, which ought to be the goal of every system of law, we shall find that it comes down to two main objects, freedom and equality.
1762 *Du contrat social* (*The Social Contract*), bk.2, ch.11 (translated by M Cranston).

44 *L'éducation de l'homme commence à sa naissance; avant de parler, avant que d'entendre, il s'instruit déjà.*
A man's education begins when he is born; before speaking, before understanding, he is already teaching himself.
1762 *Émile ou de l'éducation*, pt.1.

45 *J'aime mieux être homme à paradoxes qu'homme à préjugés.*
I would rather be a man of paradoxes than of prejudices.
1762 *Émile ou de l'éducation*, pt.2.

46 *C'est dans le cœur de l'homme qu'est la vie du spectacle de la nature; pour le voir, il faut le sentir.*
The spectacle of nature is in the heart of a man; to see it, he must feel it.
1762 *Émile ou de l'éducation*, pt.3.

47 *L'homme dit ce qu'il sait, la femme dit ce qui plaît.*

A man says what he knows, a woman says what pleases.
1762 *Émile ou de l'éducation*, pt.5.

48 War, then, is not a relationship between man and man, but between State and State, in which private persons are only enemies accidentally.
Quoted in A J P Taylor *From the Boer War to the Cold War: Essays on Twentieth-Century Europe* (1995), 'War and Peace', p.15.

Rowbotham, Sheila 1943–

English social historian and feminist. Together with Segel and Wainwright, she wrote the controversial *Beyond the Fragments: Feminism and the Making of Socialism* (1979). She has also written *Women, Resistance and Revolution* (1972) and *Women Resist Globalization: Mobilizing for Livelihood and Rights* (2001).

49 There is no 'beginning' of feminism in the sense that there is no beginning to defiance in women.
1972 *Women, Resistance and Revolution*, ch.1.

Rowland, Helen 1876–1950

US journalist, writer and humorist.

50 When you see what some girls marry, you realize how they must hate to work for a living.
1909 *Reflections of a Bachelor Girl*.

51 Never trust a husband too far, or a bachelor too near.
1915 *The Rubaiyat of a Bachelor*.

52 A husband is what is left of the lover after the nerve has been extracted.
1922 *A Guide to Men*.

53 The follies which a man regrets most in his life are those which he didn't commit when he had the opportunity.
1922 *A Guide to Men*.

Rowling, J K 1965–

English author whose first children's book, *Harry Potter and the Philosopher's Stone* (1997, published in the US as *Harry Potter and the Sorcerer's Stone*, 1998), set in the Hogwarts School of Witchcraft and Wizardry, was an immediate success, and was followed by equally successful sequels.

54 Before we begin our banquet, I would like to say a few words. And here they are: Nitwit! Blubber! Oddment! Tweak!
1997 *Harry Potter and the Philosopher's Stone* (published in the US as *Harry Potter and the Sorcerer's Stone*, 1998), ch.7.

55 Harry Potter was a highly unusual boy in many ways. For one thing, he hated the summer holidays more than any other time of year. For another, he really wanted to do his homework, but was forced to do it in secret, in the dead of night. And he also happened to be a wizard.
1999 *Harry Potter and the Prisoner of Azkaban*, opening lines.

Roy, Arundhati 1960–

Indian author and environmental activist. Her first novel, *The God of Small Things* (1997), won the Booker Prize.

56 The whole of contemporary history, the World Wars, the War of Dreams, the Man on the Moon, science, literature, philosophy, the pursuit of knowledge—was no more than a blink of the Earth Woman's eye.
1997 *The God of Small Things*.

Roy, Gabrielle 1909–83

Canadian novelist and memoirist.

57 Every writer must eventually write his Ninth Symphony or give in to despair.
1973 Letter, 1 Aug, quoted in Joan Hind-Smith *Three Voices* (1975).

Royden, (Agnes) Maude 1876–1956

English social worker and preacher who took a religious and moral approach to women's suffrage.

58 The Church of England should no longer be satisfied to represent only the Conservative Party at prayer.
1917 Address to the Life and Liberty Movement, London, 16 Jul.

Rubenstein, Helena 1870–1965

Polish cosmetics businesswoman. She developed and sold the first tinted foundation and face powder when she moved to New York in World War I and pioneered the use of silk in cosmetics. She used methods of mass production and marketing to attract customers who were intimidated by the cosmetics of her biggest rival—Elizabeth Arden.

59 Some women won't buy anything unless they can pay a lot.
1965 In *Time*, 9 Apr.

Ruckelshaus, William D(oyle) 1932–

US government administrator, lawyer and businessman. He served Indiana in the House of Representatives (1967–9) as majority leader and was administrator of the new Environmental Protection Agency, Washington (1970–3, 1983–5).

60 Everybody wants you to pick it up, and nobody wants you to put it down.
1988 Articulating 'the First Law of Garbage'. In *Fortune*, 21 Nov.

Rudofsky, Bernard 1905–88

Austrian-born architect, engineer and critic. He studied in Vienna, but worked in New York.

61 For it seems that long before the first enterprising man bent some twigs into a leaky roof, many animals were already accomplished builders.
1964 *Architecture without Architects*.

62 There is much to learn from architecture before it became an expert's art.
1964 *Architecture without Architects*.

Ruether, Rosemary Radford 1936–

US theologian, leading Roman Catholic exponent of feminist and liberation theology.

63 Indeed, if one can say that Christ comes to the oppressed and the oppressed especially hear him, then it is women within these marginal groups who are often seen both as the oppressed of the oppressed and also as those particularly receptive to the gospel.
1981 *To Change the World: Christology and Cultural Criticism*.

Ruiz, Juan c.1290–c.1350

Spanish poet, arch-priest of Hita. He was a vagabond for several years before entering the Church. In 1337 he was imprisoned for 13 years by the Archbishop of Toledo, Don Gil de Ardonoz.

64 *El amor siempre fabla mentiroso.*
Love is always a liar.
c.1330 *Libro de Buen Amor,* stanza 161.

65 *Por las verdades se pierden los amigos,*
e per las non dezir se fazen desamigos.
Telling the truth loses you friends;
not telling it gains you enemies.
c.1330 *Libro de Buen Amor,* stanza 165.

Rulfo, Juan 1918–86

Mexican writer. He grew up in the rural countryside that provides the setting for his two masterpieces, the short story collection *El llano en llamas* (1953) and the novel *Pedro Páramo* (1955). Although his writing output is slim, it has been enormously influential.

66 *Sólo yo entiendo lo lejos que está el cielo de nosotros; pero conozco cómo acortar las veredas. Todo consiste en morir, Dios mediante, cuando uno quiera y no cuando Él lo disponga. O, si tú quieres, forzarlo a disponer antes de tiempo.*
I know how far away Heaven is, all right, but I know the shortcuts. You just die, God willing, when you want to, not when He arranges it. Or if you want you can make Him arrange it earlier.
1955 *Pedro Páramo* (translated 1959).

Rumsfeld, Donald 1932–

US politician. He was US ambassador to NATO (1973–4), White House Chief of Staff (1974–5) and Secretary of Defense (1975–7), and in 2001 was appointed Secretary of Defense for a second time by George W Bush.

67 You're thinking of Europe as Germany and France. I don't. I think that's old Europe.
2003 Responding to questions about European hostility to military intervention in Iraq, 22 Jan.

68 They seem to be a country that disagrees with a lot of other countries.
2003 Discussing the French standpoint on Iraq. In *Time,* 17 Feb.

69 Answering the question as to whether we are winning— that is a very difficult one.
2004 Television interview, 27 Jun.

70 We don't seek empires. We're not imperialistic.
Quoted in Niall Ferguson *Colossus: The Rise and Fall of the American Empire* (2004).

Runcie, Robert Alexander Kennedy Runcie, Baron 1921–2000

English Anglican prelate and Archbishop of Canterbury (1980–91). His career was marked by a papal visit to Canterbury, controversies over homosexuality and women in the Church, the Falklands War, and his envoy Terry Waite's captivity in Beirut (1987–91).

71 Royalty puts a human face on the operations of government.
1980 Sermon at a service to mark the Queen Mother's 80th birthday, St Paul's Cathedral, 15 Jul.

72 Those who dare to interpret God's will must never claim Him as an asset for one nation or group rather than another. War springs from the love and loyalty that should be offered to God being applied to some God substitute—one of the most dangerous being nationalism.

1982 Sermon at Thanksgiving Service after the Falklands War, St Paul's Cathedral, 26 Jul.

Runciman, Sir Steven 1903–2000

English historian of the Crusades. His works include *The Fall of Constantinople, 1453* (1965) and *Byzantine Style and Civilization* (1975).

73 The triumphs of the Crusades were the triumphs of faith. But faith without wisdom is a dangerous thing.
1954 *A History of the Crusades,* vol.3.

Runge, Philipp Otto 1777–1810

German painter and draughtsman, a member of the German Romantic movement.

74 Art of all periods teaches us that humanity changes, and that a period, once past, never returns.
1802 Letter, Feb. Quoted in L Eitner *Neoclassicism and Romanticism 1750–1850* (1964).

75 But could we not reach the point of highest perfection in a new kind of art, in this art of landscape, and perhaps reach a higher beauty than existed before?
1802 Letter, quoted in L Eitner *Neoclassicism and Romanticism 1750–1850* (1964).

76 Colour is the ultimate in art. It is still and will always remain a mystery to us, we can only apprehend it intuitively in flowers.
1802 Letter, quoted in L Eitner *Neoclassicism and Romanticism 1750–1850* (1964).

77 We must become children again if we wish to achieve the best.
1802 Letter, quoted in R Rosenblum *Modern Painting and the Northern Romantic Tradition* (1975).

Runyon, (Alfred) Damon 1884–1946

US journalist, sportswriter and humorist. He is remembered for the colourful argot of his New York stories, which have been gathered in several collections, and provided the basis of the musical *Guys and Dolls* (1931).

78 'My boy,' he says, 'always try to rub up against money, for if you rub up against money long enough, some of it may rub off on you.'
1931 *Guys and Dolls,* 'A Very Honourable Guy'.

79 'You are snatching a hard guy when you snatch Bookie Bob. A very hard guy, indeed. In fact,' I say, 'I hear the softest thing about him is his front teeth.'
1933 *Blue Plate Special,* 'Snatching of Bookie Bob'.

80 Any time you see him he is generally by himself because being by himself is not apt to cost him anything.
1933 *Blue Plate Special,* 'Little Miss Marker'.

81 The best thing to do right now is to throw a feed into her as the chances are that her stomach thinks her throat is cut.
1933 *Blue Plate Special,* 'Little Miss Marker'.

82 'In fact,' Sam the Gonoph says, 'I long ago come to the conclusion that all life is 6 to 5 against.'
1935 *Money from Home,* 'A Nice Price'.

83 I do not approve of guys using false pretences on dolls, except, of course, when nothing else will do.
1935 *Money from Home,* 'It Comes Up Mud'.

84 He is without strict doubt a Hoorah Henry, and he is

generally figured as nothing but a lob as far as doing anything useful in this world is concerned.
1935 *Money from Home*, 'Tight Shoes'.

85 I always claim the mission workers came out too early to catch any sinners on this part of Broadway. At such an hour the sinners are still in bed resting up from their sinning of the night before, so they will be in good shape for more sinning a little later on.
1944 *Runyon à la Carte*, 'The Idyll of Miss Sarah Brown'.

86 You can keep the things of bronze and stone and give me one man to remember me just once a year.
1946 Last words.

Rushdie, (Ahmed) Salman 1947–

British novelist, born in Bombay. His works include *Midnight's Children* (1981, Booker Prize), *The Moor's Last Sigh* (1995) and *Fury* (2001). His novel *The Satanic Verses* (1988) provoked Iran's Ayatollah Khomeini to issue a fatwa against him (1989) forcing Rushdie to live in hiding for several years.

87 Most of what matters in your life takes place in your absence.
1981 *Midnight's Children*, 'Alpha and Omega', bk.2.

88 A poet's work… To name the unnamable, to point at frauds, to take sides, start arguments, shape the world and stop it from going to sleep.
1988 *The Satanic Verses*, pt.2.

89 To burn a book is not to destroy it. One minute of darkness will not make us blind.
1989 Book review in the *Weekend Guardian*, 14–15 Oct.

90 No story comes from nowhere; new stories are born from old—it is the new combinations that make them new.
1990 *Haroun and the Sea of Stories*.

91 Books have to teach their readers how to read them.
1995 Quoted in the *Observer Review*, 16 Apr.

92 We are the lethal voyeurs.
1997 Reflecting on the death of Diana, Princess of Wales.

93 I know of very few great film-makers who might have been good novelists—Satyajit Ray, Ingmar Bergman, Woody Allen, Jean Renoir, and that's about it.
2002 *Step Across This Line: Collected Non-Fiction 1992–2002*.

94 [Charlton] Heston thinks America should arm its teachers; he seems to believe that schools would be safer if staff had the power to gun down children in their charge.
2002 *Step Across This Line: Collected Non-Fiction 1992–2002*.

95 I knew a man whose thing it was to wreck the toilets in office buildings and write a slogan on the ruined walls: 'If the cistern cannot be changed it must be destroyed.' I'm beginning to understand how he felt.
2002 *Step Across This Line: Collected Non-Fiction 1992–2002*.

Rushworth, John c.1612–1690

English historian, whose *Historical Collections of Private Passages of State* (8 vols, 1659–1701) cover the period 1618–48. Clerk-assistant to the House of Commons in the Long Parliament (1640), and a parliamentary secretary, in 1684 he was imprisoned for debt.

96 His Majesty entered the House, and as he passed up towards the Chair, he cast his eye on the right hand near the Bar of the House where Mr Pym used to sit; but His Majesty, not seeing him there (knowing him well) went up to the Chair and said, 'By your leave, Mr Speaker, I must borrow your chair a little.'
1642 His account of the attempt made by Charles I to arrest five Members of Parliament on 4 Jan.

Rusk, (David) Dean 1909–94

US politician. As Secretary of State under Kennedy and Johnson (1961–9), he played a major role in the Cuban Missile Crisis of 1962.

97 We were eyeball to eyeball and the other fellow just blinked.
1962 Recalling his words on the retreat of Soviet ships during the Cuban Missile Crisis. In the *Saturday Evening Post*, 8 Dec.

98 Communications today puts a special emphasis on what happens next, for an able, sophisticated and competitive press knows that what happens today is no longer news—it is what is going to happen tomorrow that is the object of interest and concern.
1963 At *Time*'s 40th anniversary dinner, 17 May.

99 We looked into the mouth of the cannon, the Russians flinched.
Of the Cuban Missile Crisis. Quoted in Robert F Kennedy *Thirteen Days* (1969).

Ruskin, John 1819–1900

English author, the major art critic and social philosopher of his day, champion of Turner and the pre-Raphaelites and an opponent of Utilitarianism. His most famous works are *Modern Painters* (1843–60) and *Seven Lamps of Architecture* (1849).

1 I believe the right question to ask, respecting all ornament, is simply this: Was it done with enjoyment— was the carver happy while he was about it?
1849 *Seven Lamps of Architecture*, 'The Lamp of Life', sect.24.

2 Better the rudest work that tells a story or records a fact, than the richest without meaning.
1849 *Seven Lamps of Architecture*, 'The Lamp of Memory', sect.7.

3 When we build, let us think that we build for ever.
1849 *Seven Lamps of Architecture*, 'The Lamp of Memory', sect.10.

4 Remember that the most beautiful things in the world are the most useless; peacocks and lilies for instance.
1851–3 *The Stones of Venice*, vol.i, ch.2.

5 But for me, the Alps and their people were alike beautiful in their snow, and their humanity; and I wanted, neither for them nor myself, sight of any thrones in heaven but the rocks, or of any spirits in heaven but the clouds.
1851–3 *The Stones of Venice*, vol.i, ch.2.

6 The purest and most thoughtful minds are those which love colour the most.
1851–3 *The Stones of Venice*, vol.ii, ch.5.

7 All things are literally better, lovelier, more beloved for the imperfections which have been divinely appointed.
1851–3 *The Stones of Venice*, vol.ii, ch.6.

8 No person who is not a great sculptor or painter can be an architect. If he is not a sculptor or painter, he can only be a *builder*.
1854 *Lectures on Architecture and Painting*.

9 What is poetry?… The suggestion, by the imagination, of noble grounds for the noble emotions.

1856 *Modern Painters*, vol.3, pt.4, ch.1.

10 All violent feelings…produce in us a falseness in all our impressions of external things, which I would generally characterize as the 'Pathetic Fallacy'.
1856 *Modern Painters*, vol.3, pt.4, ch.12.

11 Mountains are the beginning and the end of all natural scenery.
1856 *Modern Painters*, vol.4, pt.5, ch.20.

12 Fine art is that in which the hand, the head, and the heart of man go together.
1859 *The Two Paths*, lecture 2.

13 Not only is there but one way of *doing* things rightly, but there is only one way of *seeing* them, and that is, seeing the whole of them.
1859 *The Two Paths*, lecture 2.

14 Nobody cares much at heart about Titian; only there is a strange undercurrent of everlasting murmur about his name, which means the deep consent of all great men that he is greater than they.
1859 *The Two Paths*, lecture 2.

15 It ought to be quite as natural and straightforward a matter for a labourer to take his pension from his parish, because he has deserved well of his parish, as for a man in higher rank to take his pension from his country, because he has deserved well of his country.
1862 *Unto this Last*, preface.

16 The force of the guinea you have in your pocket depends wholly on the default of a guinea in your neighbour's pocket. If he did not want it, it would be of no use to you.
1862 *Unto this Last*, essay 2.

17 Political economy (the economy of a State, or of citizens) consists simply in the production, preservation, and distribution, at fittest time and place, of useful or pleasurable things.
1862 *Unto this Last*, essay 2.

18 Soldiers of the ploughshare as well as soldiers of the sword.
1862 *Unto this Last*, essay 3.

19 Government and co-operation are in all things the laws of life; anarchy and competition the laws of death.
1862 *Unto this Last*, essay 3.

20 Whereas it has long been known and declared that the poor have no right to the property of the rich, I wish it also to be known and declared that the rich have no right to the property of the poor.
1862 *Unto this Last*, essay 3.

21 There is no wealth but life.
1862 *Unto this Last*, essay 4.

22 All books are divided into two classes, the books of the hour, and the books of all time.
1865 *Sesame and Lilies*, 'Of Kings' Treasures'.

23 Be sure that you go to the author to get at his meaning, not to find yours.
1865 *Sesame and Lilies*, 'Of Kings' Treasures'.

24 Which of us…is to do the hard and dirty work for the rest—and for what pay? Who is to do the pleasant and clean work, and for what pay?
1865 *Sesame and Lilies*, 'Of Kings' Treasures'.

25 You hear of me, among others, as a respectable architectural man-milliner; and you send for me, that I may tell you the leading fashion.
1866 *The Crown of Wild Olive*, 'Traffic', lecture 2.

26 Labour without joy is base. Labour without sorrow is base. Sorrow without labour is base. Joy without labour is base.
1867 *Time and Tide*, letter 5.

27 Your honesty is *not* to be based either on religion or policy. Both your religion and policy must be based on *it*.
1867 *Time and Tide*, letter 8.

28 The first duty of a state is to see that every child born therein shall be well housed, clothed, fed and educated, till it attain years of discretion.
1867 *Time and Tide*, letter 13.

29 Life without industry is guilt, and industry without art is brutality.
1870 *Lectures on Art*, 'The Relation of Art to Morals', lecture 3, section 95.

30 Engraving then, is, in brief terms, the Art of Scratch.
1870–85 *Ariadne Florentina*, lecture 1.

31 Thackeray settled like a meat-fly on whatever one had got for dinner, and made one sick of it.
1873 *Fors Clavigera* (published 1871–84), letter no.31, 1 Jul.

32 English artists are usually entirely ruined by residence in Italy.
1873 *Modern Painters*, vol.1, pt.1, 'Of General Principles'.

33 The greatest thing a human soul ever does in this world is to *see* something, and tell what it *saw* in a plain way. Hundreds of people can talk for one who can think, but thousands can think for one who can see. To see clearly is poetry, prophecy, and religion, all in one.
1873 *Modern Painters*, vol.3, pt.4, ch.16.

34 I have seen, and heard, much of Cockney impudence before now; but never expected to hear a coxcomb ask two hundred guineas for flinging a pot of paint in the public's face.
1877 On Whistler's *Nocturne in Black and Gold*. *Fors Clavigera* (published 1871–84), letter no.79, 18 Jun.

35 Men don't and can't live by exchanging articles, but by producing them. They don't live by trade, but by work. Give up that foolish and vain title of Trades Unions; and take that of Labourers' Unions.
1880 Open letter to English Trades Unions, 29 Sep.

36 Beethoven always sounds to me like the upsetting of a bag of nails, with here and there an also dropped hammer.
1881 Letter.

37 Of all the affected, sapless, soulless, beginningless, endless, topless, bottomless, topsiturviest, scrannel-pipiest, tongs and boniest doggerel of sounds I ever endured the deadliest of, that eternity of nothing was the deadliest.
1882 Of Wagner's *Die Meistersinger*. Letter to Mrs Burne-Jones, 30 Jun.

38 There was a rocky valley between Buxton and Bakewell…divine as the vale of Tempe; you might have seen the gods there morning and evening—Apollo and the sweet Muses of the Light… You enterprised a railroad…you blasted its rocks away… And, now, every fool in Buxton can be at Bakewell in half-an-hour, and every fool in Bakewell at Buxton.
1886–8 *Praeterita*, vol.3, pt.4, 'Joanna's Cave', note.

Russell, Bertrand Arthur William Russell, 3rd Earl
1872–1970

English philosopher and mathematician, a controversial public figure ('an enemy of religion and morality') who produced a stream of popular and provocative works on social, moral and religious issues. After 1949 he championed nuclear disarmament, and engaged in correspondence with several world leaders. He won the Nobel prize for literature in 1950.

39 Mathematics possesses not only truth, but supreme beauty—a beauty cold and austere, like that of sculpture.
1903 *The Principles of Mathematics.*

40 Philosophy, if it cannot *answer* so many questions as we could wish, has at least the power of *asking* questions which increase the interest of the world, and show the strangeness and wonder lying just below the surface even in the commonest things of daily life.
1912 *The Problems of Philosophy*, ch.1.

41 The essential characteristic of philosophy, which makes it a study distinct from science, is *criticism*. It examines critically the principles employed in science and in daily life; it searches out any inconsistencies there may be in these principles, and it only accepts them when, as the result of a critical inquiry, there is no reason for rejecting them.
1912 *The Problems of Philosophy*, ch.14.

42 Philosophy is to be studied, not for the sake of any definite answers to its questions, since no definite answers can, as a rule, be known to be true, but rather for the sake of the questions themselves; because these questions enlarge our conception of what is possible, enrich our intellectual imagination, and diminish the dogmatic assurance which closes the mind against speculation; but above all because, through the greatness of the universe which philosophy contemplates, the mind also is rendered great, and becomes capable of that union with the universe which constitutes its highest good.
1912 *The Problems of Philosophy*, ch.14.

43 Every proposition which we can understand must be composed wholly of constituents with which we are acquainted.
1917 *A Free Man's Worship*, 'Knowledge by Acquaintance and Knowledge by Description'.

44 The true spirit of delight, the exaltation, the sense of being more than man, which is the touchstone of the highest excellence, is to be found in mathematics as surely as in poetry.
1917 *Mysticism and Logic.*

45 The typical Westerner wishes to be the cause of as many changes as possible in his environment; the typical Chinese wishes to enjoy as much and as delicately as possible.
1922 *The Problems of China.*

46 In science men have discovered an activity of the very highest value in which they are no longer, as in art, dependent for progress upon the appearance of continually greater genius, for in science the successors stand upon the shoulders of their predecessors; where one man of supreme genius has invented a method, a

thousand lesser men can apply it.
1923 *A Free Man's Worship and Other Essays.*

47 Machines are worshipped because they are beautiful, and valued because they confer power; they are hated because they are hideous, and loathed because they impose slavery.
1928 *Sceptical Essays.*

48 The scientific attitude of mind involves a sweeping away of all other desires in the interest of the desire to know.
1930 Interview in the *New Statesman*, 24 May.

49 It is, of course, clear that a country with a large foreign population must endeavour, through its schools, to assimilate the children of immigrants… It is, however, unfortunate that a large part of this process should be effected by means of a somewhat blatant nationalism.
1935 *In Praise of Idleness*, 'Modern Homogeneity'.

50 No rules, however wise, are a substitute for affection and tact.
1935 *In Praise of Idleness*, 'Education and Discipline'.

51 I think modern educational theorists are inclined to attach too much importance to the negative virtue of not interfering with children, and too little to the positive merit of enjoying their company.
1935 *In Praise of Idleness*, 'Education and Discipline'.

52 Two men who differ as to the ends of life cannot hope to agree about education.
1935 *In Praise of Idleness*, 'Education and Discipline'.

53 Can a society in which thought and technique are scientific persist for a long period, as, for example, ancient Egypt persisted, or does it necessarily contain within itself forces which must bring either decay or explosion?
1949 'Can a Scientific Community Be Stable?', Lloyd Roberts lecture to the Royal Society of Medicine, 29 Nov.

54 There is only one constant preoccupation: I have throughout been anxious to discover how much we can be said to know and with what degree of certainty or doubtfulness.
1959 *My Philosophical Development*, ch.1.

55 I do not think it possible to get anywhere if we start from scepticism. We must start from a broad acceptance of whatever seems to be knowledge and is not rejected for some specific reason.
1959 *My Philosophical Development*, ch.16.

56 Ever since I was engaged on *Principia Mathematica*, I have had a certain method of which at first I was scarcely conscious, but which has gradually become more explicit in my thinking. The method consists in an attempt to build a bridge between the world of sense and the world of science.
1959 *My Philosophical Development*, ch.16.

57 This idea of weapons of mass extermination is utterly horrible, and is something that no one with a spark of humanity can tolerate. I will not pretend to obey a Government that is organizing a mass massacre of mankind.
1961 Speech urging civil disobedience in support of nuclear disarmament, Birmingham, 15 Apr.

58 Obscenity is what happens to shock some elderly and ignorant magistrate.
1961 Quoted in *Look* magazine.

59 I've got a one-dimensional mind.

Quoted in R Crawshay-Williams *Russell Remembered* (1970), ch.2.

Russell, Dora 1894–1986

English feminist and pacifist, second wife of Bertrand Russell. In her many works she advocated sexual freedom and birth control.

60 We want better reasons for having children than not knowing how to prevent them.

1925 *Hypatia: or Women and Knowledge*, ch.4.

Russell, George William *pseudonym* Æ 1867–1935

Irish poet, painter, writer and economist. He met Yeats in Dublin and turned from his art studies to theosophy. His first book *Homeward: Songs by the Way* (1894) established his role in the Irish literary renaissance. He edited the *Irish Homestead* (1906–23) and subsequently the *Irish Statesman* (1923–30).

61 As Michael read the Gaelic scroll
   It seemed the story of the soul;
   And those who wrought, lest there should fail
   From earth the legend of the Gael,
   Seemed warriors of Eternal Mind
   Still holding in a world gone blind,
   From which belief and hope had gone,
   The lovely magic of its dawn.

1922 *The Interpreters*, 'Michael'.

62 In ancient shadows and twilights
   Where childhood had strayed,
   The world's great sorrows were born
   And its heroes were made.
   In the lost boyhood of Judas,
   Christ was betrayed.

1930 *Enchantment and Other Poems*, 'Germinal'.

63 No blazoned banner we unfold—
   One charge alone we give to youth,
   Against the sceptred myth to hold,
   The golden heresy of truth.

'On Behalf of Some Irishmen not Followers of Tradition'.

Russell, John Russell, 1st Earl 1792–1878

English Whig politician, proposer of the first Reform Bill (1832) and Prime Minister (1846–52, 1865–6).

64 If peace cannot be maintained with honour, it is no longer peace.

1853 Speech, Greenock, 19 Sep.

➤ *See Cecil 202:26, Chamberlain 204:63, Disraeli 277:85.*

Russell, John 1919–

English-born US art critic. He was art critic for the *Sunday Times* (1949–74) and the *New York Times* (1974–2001). His many books include *The Meanings of Modern Art* (1981) and *Matisse: Father and Son* (1999).

65 It was not in Dalí's nature to play Gilbert to someone else's Sullivan.

1989 On Salvador Dalí's death. In the *New York Times*, 24 Jan.

66 When Dalí hallucinated…the whole world hallucinated with him.

1989 On Salvador Dalí's death. In the *New York Times*, 24 Jan.

Russell, Mary Annette Russell, Countess *née* Beauchamp *pseudonym* Elizabeth 1866–1941

New Zealand-born writer, cousin of Katherine Mansfield. She came to Britain in 1871 and in 1891 married Count Von Arnim and moved to Germany, where she wrote her best-known novel, *Elizabeth and her German Garden* (1898). After his death in 1910 she married Francis, 2nd Earl Russell, brother of Bertrand (1916, separated 1919). In later life she spent much time in the US, where she enjoyed considerable popularity.

67 Far from being half a woman, a widow is the only complete example of her sex. In fact, the finished article.

1936 *All the Dogs of My Life*, pt.2, dog 9, 'Coco'.

Russell, Rosalind 1911–76

US actress. A graduate, she started her acting career in summer stock. After a contract with MGM, she formed the production company Independent Artists with her husband in 1947 and appeared in 51 films. She starred in the Broadway shows *Wonderful Town* (1953) and *Auntie Mame* (1956).

68 Flops are a part of life's menu, and I've never been a girl to miss out on any of the courses.

1957 In the *New York Herald Tribune*, 11 Apr.

Russell, Sir William Howard 1820–1907

Irish-born British war correspondent. He joined *The Times* in 1843, and wrote despatches from the Crimean War (1854–5) which swayed British public opinion against the conflict. He subsequently wrote from the Indian Mutiny (1858), the American Civil War (1861) and the Austro-Prussian War (1866).

69 They dashed on towards that thin red line tipped with steel.

1877 Of the Russians charging the British at the Battle of Balaclava, 14 Nov 1854. *The British Expedition to the Crimea*.

Russell, Willy (William) 1947–

English playwright, best known for *Educating Rita* (1979) and *Shirley Valentine* (1986).

70 Of course I'm drunk—you don't really expect me to teach this stuff when I'm sober.

1979 *Educating Rita*.

Rutherford, Ernest, Baron Rutherford of Nelson 1871–1937

New Zealand-born English physicist, who taught at McGill, Montreal and the University of Manchester (1907–19). In 1919 he became director of the Cavendish Laboratory, Cambridge. Rutherford researched radiation and received the 1908 Nobel prize in chemistry.

71 All science is either physics or stamp collecting.

Quoted in J B Birks *Rutherford at Manchester* (1962).

72 We haven't got the money, so we've got to think.

Quoted in *Bulletin of the Institute of Physics*, vol.13, 1962.

Ryan, Desmond 1893–1964

Irish journalist. He fought at the GPO in the 1916 Rising and became a journalist on his release from internment. His books include *The Man Called Pearse* (1919), *The Phoenix Flame* (1937) and *The Rising* (1949).

73 The triumph of failure.

1949 Of the Irish uprising of 1916. *The Rising*, closing words.

Rybczynski, Witold Marian 1943–

Scottish-born Canadian architect and writer, professor at the University of Pennsylvania. His works include *Home: A Short History of an Idea* (1986) and *The Look of Architecture* (2001).

74 The most beautiful house in the world is the one that you build for yourself.
Quoted by Pamela Young in *Maclean's*, 19 Jun 1989.

75 It is truly a place for self-presentation—of oneself, to oneself. A fitting sign of the self-absorbed 1980s.
1992 On the increasing luxuriousness of bathrooms. *Looking Around*.

Ryder, Albert Pinkham 1847–1917

US painter, whose works are characterized by dreamlike figures and landscapes, evoking a romantic, lonely mood, such as *Toilers of the Sea*. His experimental technique of loading paint on the canvas caused many works to deteriorate. He became misanthropic in later life.

76 The artist needs but a roof, a crust of bread, and his easel, and all the rest God gives him in abundance. He must live to paint and not paint to live.
Quoted in Sherman *Albert Pinkham Ryder* (1920).

77 The artist should fear to become the slave of detail. He should strive to express his thought and not the surface of it. What avails a storm cloud accurate in form and colour if the storm is not therein?
Quoted in Goodrich *Albert Pinkham Ryder* (1959).

Ryle, Gilbert 1900–76

English philosopher and Professor of Philosophy at Oxford. His most famous work was *The Concept of Mind* (1949) in which he denounced Cartesian ideas of mind.

78 The dogma of the Ghost in the Machine.
1949 *The Concept of Mind*.

79 The sorts of things that I can find out about myself are the same as the sorts of things that I can find out about other people and the methods of finding them out are much the same.
1949 *The Concept of Mind*.

80 As every teacher, like every drill-sergeant or animal trainer, knows in his practice, teaching and training have virtually not yet begun, so long as the pupil is too young, too stupid, too scared or too sulky to respond—and to respond is not just to yield. Where there is a modicum of alacrity, interest or anyhow docility in the pupil, where he tries, however faintheartedly, to get things right rather than awkward, where, even, he registers even a slight contempt for the poor performances of others, of chagrin at his own, pleasure at his own successes and envy of those of others, then he is, in however slight a degree, co-operating and so self-moving.
Quoted in R S Peters (ed) *The Concept of Education* (1966), ch.7.

S

Saarinen, Aline Bernstein née *Loucheim* 1914–72

US art critic. In 1955 she married the architect Eero Saarinen, who was one of the leaders of a trend in experimentation in American architecture in the 1950s.

81 He meant to gather for America an undreamed-of collection of art so great and complete that a trip to Europe would be superfluous.
1991 On the philanthropist and collector John Pierpont Morgan. In *Antiques*, Oct.

Sábato, Ernesto 1911–

Argentinian novelist, journalist and essayist. Trained in physics, he increasingly devoted himself to literature. *El túnel* (1948) is a typical existential novel that confronts the problem of the condition of human life.

82 *Había un solo túnel, oscuro y solitario: el mío, el túnel en que había transcurrido mi infancia, mi juventud, toda mi vida… Y entonces, mientras yo avanzaba siempre por mi pasadizo, ella vivía afuera su vida normal, la vida agitada que llevan esas gentes que viven afuera.*
There was only one tunnel, dark and solitary: mine, the tunnel in which I had spent my childhood, my youth, my entire life… And then, while I kept moving through my passageway, she lived her normal life outside, the exciting life of people who live outside.
1948 *El túnel*, ch.36 (translated as *The Outsider*, 1950).

Sachar, Abram Leon 1899–1993

US educator, president of Brandeis University, Massachusetts (1948–68), chancellor there (1968–82, emeritus from 1982). His works include *A History of the Jews* (1929) and *The Redemption of the Unwanted* (1983).

83 A university where, at last, the Jews are hosts, and not guests as we have always been before.
1956 Of Brandeis University, on its 10th anniversary. Speech, 19 Nov.

Sacks, Jonathan 1948–

English rabbi, Chief Rabbi of Great Britain since 1991.

84 Religious law is like the grammar of language. Any language is governed by such rules; otherwise it ceases to be a language. But within them, you can say many different sentences and write many different books.
1994 In *The Independent*, 30 Jun.

85 After the destruction of the Second Temple Jews lived by an ancient and fundamental insight, that God does not live in buildings but in the human heart.
1995 *Community of Faith*.

Sacks, Oliver Wolf 1933–

English-born US neurologist and writer.

86 The Man Who Mistook His Wife for a Hat.
1985 Title of book.

Sackville-West, Vita (Victoria Mary) 1892–1962

English novelist. The daughter of the 3rd Baron Sackville, she married the diplomat Harold Nicolson. She wrote novels, poetry and memoirs, and a regular gardening column for the *Observer*.

87 Forget not bees in winter, though they sleep,
　　For winter's big with summer in her womb.
1926 *The Land*, 'Spring'.

88 All craftsmen share a knowledge.
　　They have held
　　Reality down fluttering to a bench.
1926 *The Land*, 'Summer'.

89 The country habit has me by the heart,
　　For he's bewitched for ever who has seen,
　　Not with his eyes but with his vision, Spring
　　Flow down the woods and stipple leaves with sun.
1926 *The Land*, 'Winter'.

90 The greater cats with golden eyes
　　Stare out between the bars.
　　Deserts are there, and different skies,
　　And night with different stars.
1929 'The Greater Cats with Golden Eyes'.

91 I have come to the conclusion, after many years of sometimes sad experience, that you cannot come to any conclusion at all.
1953 'In Your Garden Again'.

Sadat, Anwar el- 1918–81

Egyptian soldier and politician, jointly awarded the Nobel peace prize with Menachem Begin in 1978.

92 Peace is much more precious than a piece of land.
1978 *In Search of Identity*.

Sade, Donatien Alphonse François, Marquis de 1740–1814

French libertine who expressed his critique of society and the Enlightenment through his controversial behaviour. He spent most of his adult life in the prisons of Vincennes, was released during the Revolution, and eventually died in confinement.

93 *La cruauté, bien loin d'être un vice, est le premier sentiment qu'imprime en nous la nature; l'enfant brise son hochet, mord le téton de sa nourrice, étrangle son oiseau, bien avant que d'avoir l'âge de raison.*
　　Far from being a vice, cruelty is the primary feeling that nature imprints in us. The infant breaks its rattle, bites its nurse's nipple, and strangles a bird, well before reaching the age of reason.
1795 *La Philosophie dans le boudoir*.

94 *Quand l'athéisme voudra des martyrs, qu'il le dise et mon sang est tout prêt.*
　　When atheism wants martyrs, let it say so and my blood will be ready.
1797 *La Nouvelle Justine*.

Safer, Morley 1931–

Canadian-born journalist and broadcaster, who moved to the US in 1964. His distinguished career includes work for Reuters,

London (1955), the BBC (1961) and CBS, as Vietnam correspondent (1964–71) and as co-host of *60 Minutes* news (1970–). He has seven Emmy and several Peabody awards.

95 BBC Radio is a never-never land of broadcasting, a safe haven from commercial considerations, a honey pot for every scholar and every hare-brained nut to stick a finger into.
1985 In *60 Minutes*, CBS TV broadcast, 15 Sep.

Safire, William 1929–

US journalist and author. A correspondent for radio and TV, he ran his own public relations company before President Nixon made him a special assistant (1969–73). A Pulitzer Prize winner for distinguished commentary (1978), he is a columnist for the *New York Times* (1973–).

96 The new, old, and constantly changing language of politics is a lexicon of conflict and drama…ridicule and reproach…pleading and persuasion.
1968 *Safire's Political Dictionary*, introduction.

97 Color and bite permeate a language designed to rally many men, to destroy some, and to change the minds of others.
1968 *Safire's Political Dictionary*, introduction.

98 Cover your ass—the bureaucrat's method of protecting his posterior from posterity.
1968 *Safire's Political Dictionary*, introduction.

99 A man who lies, thinking it is the truth, is an honest man, and a man who tells the truth, believing it to be a lie, is a liar.
1975 *After the Fall*, referring to Watergate and the resignation of Richard M Nixon.

1 President Reagan is a rhetorical roundheels, as befits a politician seeking empathy with his audience.
1990 *Language Maven Strikes Again*.

2 The remarkable legion of the unremarked, whose individual opinions are not colorful or different enough to make news, but whose collective opinion, when crystallized, can make history.
1993 Of the so-called 'silent majority'. *Safire's New Political Dictionary*.

3 I was egregiously wrong.
1995 Of serving as a speech-writer for President Nixon. In *USA Today*, 30 Aug.

Sagan, Carl Edward 1934–96

US astronomer and popularizer of science. He has advised NASA on interplanetary probes, was president of the Planetary Society (1979–96) and was a strong proponent of SETI, the search for extraterrestrial intelligence.

4 There is a lurking fear that some things are not meant 'to be known', that some inquiries are too dangerous for human beings to make.
1979 *Broca's Brain*.

5 Science is a way of thinking much more than it is a body of knowledge.
1979 'Can We Know the Universe? Reflections on a Grain of Salt'.

6 Sceptical scrutiny is the means, in both science and religion, by which deep thoughts can be winnowed from deep nonsense.
1980 Interview in *The Times*, 20 Oct.

Sagan, Françoise 1935–

French novelist.

7 Art must take reality by surprise.
1958 *Writers at Work*.

8 To jealousy, nothing is more frightful than laughter.
1965 *La Chamade*, ch.9.

Sage, Lorna 1943–2001

British literary critic and author.

9 The night I finished *Dracula* was a lot more exciting than Saturday night at the Regal.
2000 *Bad Blood*.

Saifoutdinov, Anvar

10 Life is not easy. I paint the memory of happiness.
Quoted by M S Mason in *Christian Science Monitor*, 19 Nov 1992.

Saint-Exupéry, Antoine de 1900–44

French author and aviator. A commercial and wartime pilot, his works include *Vol de nuit* (1931) and the children's fable *Le Petit Prince* (1943). He was declared missing after a flight to North Africa in 1944.

11 *Il n'y a pas de fatalité extérieure. Mais il y a une fatalité intérieure.*
There is no exterior fatality, only an interior one.
1931 *Vol de nuit*.

12 *L'expérience nous montre qu'aimer ce n'est point nous regarder l'un l'autre mais regarder ensemble dans la même direction.*
Life has taught us that love does not consist in gazing at each other but in looking together in the same direction.
1939 *Terre des hommes*.

13 *Quand une femme me paraît belle, je n'ai rien à en dire. Je la vois sourire, tout simplement. Les intellectuels démontent le visage, pour l'expliquer par les morceaux, mais ils ne voient plus le sourire.*
When I find a woman attractive, I have nothing at all to say. I simply watch her smile. Intellectuals take apart her face in order to explain it bit by bit, but they no longer see the smile.
1942 *Pilote de guerre*.

14 *Je combattrai pour l'Homme. Contre ses ennemis. Mais aussi contre moi-même.*
I shall fight for mankind. Against his enemies. But also against myself.
1942 *Pilote de guerre*.

15 *Les grandes personnes ne comprennent jamais rien toutes seules, et c'est fatigant, pour les enfants, de toujours et toujours leur donner des explications.*
Adults never understand anything for themselves, and it is tiresome for children to be always and forever explaining things to them.
1943 *Le Petit Prince*.

16 *On est un peu seul dans le désert.*
—On est seul aussi chez les hommes.
One is a little bit alone in the desert.
One is also alone among others.
1943 *Le Petit Prince*.

17 *On ne voit bien qu'avec le cœur. L'essentiel est invisible pour les yeux.*
Only with the heart can a person see rightly; what is essential is invisible to the eye.
1943 *Le Petit Prince*.

18 *Un sourire est souvent l'essentiel. On est payé par un sourire. On est récompensé par un sourire. On est animé par un sourire. Et la qualité d'un sourire peut faire que l'on meure.*
A smile is often the key thing. One is paid with a smile. One is rewarded with a smile. One is brightened by a smile. And the quality of a smile can make one die.
1943 *Lettre à un otage*.

19 *La vie crée l'ordre, mais l'ordre ne crée pas la vie.*
Life creates order, but order does not create life.
1943 *Lettre à un otage*.

20 *Je suis triste pour ma génération qui est vide de toute substance humaine.*
I am sad for my generation which is empty of all human substance.
1944 *Lettre au général*, no.10. Published 10 Apr 1948 in *Le Figaro littéraire*.

21 *J'aime l'homme délivré par sa religion et vivifié par les dieux que je fonde en lui.*
I admire the person freed from his religion and inspired by the gods inside of himself.
Citadelle (published 1948).

22 *L'homme, c'est ce qui est, non point ce qui s'exprime.*
Man is who he is, not how he expresses himself.
Citadelle (published 1948).

23 *Car l'homme, je te le dis, cherche sa propre destinée et non pas son bonheur.*
Because man, I tell you, is looking for his own destiny, not his own happiness.
Citadelle (published 1948).

24 *Prendre conscience, disait ailleurs mon père, c'est d'abord acquérir un style.*
To become conscious, as my father said, one must first acquire a style.
Citadelle (published 1948).

25 *Quiconque craint la contradiction et demeure logique tue en lui la vie.*
Whoever fears contradiction and remains logical kills life within himself.
Carnets (published 1953).

26 *La vérité, pour l'homme, c'est ce qui fait de lui un homme.*
Truth, for a human, is what makes him or her a human being.
Un Sens à la vie (unedited texts collected by Claude Reynal, published 1956).

Saint Laurent, Louis 1882–1973

Canadian politician, Prime Minister (1948–57). He was fluently bilingual, having a French father and an English mother.

27 I didn't know at first that there were two languages in Canada. I just thought that there was one way to speak to my father and another to talk to my mother.
Attributed. Quoted in Dale C Thomson *Louis St. Laurent* (1967).

28 Socialists are Liberals in a hurry.
Attributed. Quoted in Dale C Thomson *Louis St. Laurent* (1967).

Saint-Saëns, (Charles) Camille 1835–1921

French composer, music critic, pianist and organist. Founder of the Société Nationale de Musique in 1871, he composed widely and prolifically.

29 There are two kinds: one takes the music too fast, and the other too slow. There is no third!
Of conductors. Quoted in SirThomas Beecham *A Mingled Chime* (1944).

Saki *pseudonym of* Hector Hugh Munro 1870–1916

British novelist and short-story writer. His short stories are humorous, macabre, and filled with eccentric wit. He was a gifted satirist of the Edwardian world. His collections include *Reginald* (1904) and *The Chronicles of Clovis* (1911). He was killed in World War I.

30 I always say beauty is only sin deep.
1904 *Reginald*, 'Reginald's ChoirTreat'.

31 People can say what they like about the decay of Christianity; the religious system that produced green Chartreuse can never really die.
1904 *Reginald*, 'Reginald on Christmas Presents'.

32 Her frocks are built in Paris, but she wears them with a strong English accent.
1904 *Reginald*, 'Reginald onWorries'.

33 The young have aspirations that never come to pass, the old have reminiscences of what never happened.
1904 *Reginald*, 'Reginald at the Carlton'.

34 There may have been disillusionments in the lives of the medieval saints, but they would scarcely have been better pleased if they could have foreseen that their names would be associated nowadays chiefly with racehorses and the cheaper clarets.
1904 *Reginald*, 'Reginald at the Carlton'.

35 The cook was a good cook, as cooks go; and as good cooks go, she went.
1904 *Reginald*, 'Reginald on Besetting Sins'.

36 But, good gracious, you've got to educate him first. You can't expect a boy to be vicious till he's been to a good school.
1910 *Reginald in Russia*, 'The Baker's Dozen'.

37 'Is your maid called Florence?' 'Her name is Florinda.' 'What an extraordinary name to give a maid!' 'I did not give it to her; she arrived in my service already christened'. 'What I mean is,' said Mrs Riversedge, 'that when I get maids with unsuitable names I call them Jane; they soon get used to it.' 'An excellent plan,' said the aunt of Clovis coldly; 'unfortunately I have got used to being called Jane myself. It happens to be my name.'
1911 *The Chronicles of Clovis*, 'The Secret Sin of Septimus Brope'.

38 The censorious said that she slept in a hammock and understood Yeats's poems, but her family denied both stories.
1911 *The Chronicles of Clovis*, 'The Jesting of Arlington Stringham'.

39 The people of Crete unfortunately make more history than they can consume locally.
1911 *The Chronicles of Clovis*, 'The Jesting of Arlington Stringham'.

40 You needn't tell me that a man who doesn't love oysters and asparagus and good wines has got a soul, or a stomach either. He's simply got the instinct for being unhappy highly developed.
1911 *The Chronicles of Clovis*, 'The Match-Maker'.

41 His socks compelled one's attention without losing one's respect.
1911 *The Chronicles of Clovis*, 'Ministers of Grace'.

42 There's nothing in Christianity or Buddhism that quite matches the sympathetic unselfishness of an oyster.
1911 *The Chronicles of Clovis*, 'The Match-Maker'.

43 All decent people live beyond their incomes nowadays, and those who aren't respectable live beyond other peoples'. A few gifted individuals manage to do both.
1911 *The Chronicles of Clovis*, 'The Match-Maker'.

44 One of the great advantages of Ireland as a place of residence is that a large number of excellent people never go there.
1914 Ludovic. *The Watched Pot, orThe Mistress of Briony.*

45 'But why should you want to shield him?' cried Egbert; 'the man is a common murderer.'
'A common murderer, possibly, but a very uncommon cook.'
1914 *Beasts and Super-Beasts*, 'The Blind Spot'.

46 'Waldo is one of those people who would be enormously improved by death,' said Clovis.
1914 *Beasts and Super-Beasts*, 'The Feast of Nemesis'.

47 'I believe I take precedence,' he said coldly; 'you are merely the Club Bore: I am the Club Liar.'
1914 *Beasts and Super-Beasts*, 'A Defensive Diamond'.

48 I should be the last person to say anything against temptation, naturally, but we have a proverb down here 'in baiting a mouse-trap with cheese, always leave room for the mouse.'
The Square Egg, 'The Infernal Parliament' (published 1924).

49 A little inaccuracy sometimes saves tons of explanation.
The Square Egg, 'Clovis on the Alleged Romance of Business' (published 1924).

Sala, George Augustus Henry 1828–95

English journalist, book illustrator and novelist, born in London of Italian ancestry. He was in the US during the Civil War, in Italy with Garibaldi, in France in 1870–71, in Russia in 1876 and in Australia in 1885.

50 The foaminess of the Falls, together with the tinge of tawny yellow in the troubled waters, only reminded me of so much unattainable soda and sherry, and made me feel thirstier than ever.
1865 On seeing Niagara Falls for the first time. *My Diary in America in the Midst of War.*

Salinger, J(erome) D(avid) 1919–

US novelist. His novel *The Catcher in the Rye* (1951) is one of the most widely read novels of the era. He has published little since, and lives as a recluse in New Hampshire.

51 If you really want to hear about it, the first thing you'll probably want to know is where I was born, and what my lousy childhood was like, and how my parents were occupied and all before they had me, and all that David Copperfield kind of crap, but I don't feel like going into it.
1951 *The Catcher in the Rye*, ch.1.

52 What really knocks me out is a book that, when you're all

done reading it, you wish the author that wrote it was a terrific friend of yours and you could call him up on the phone whenever you felt like it.
1951 *The Catcher in the Rye*, ch.3.

53 Sex is something I really don't understand too hot. You never know *where* the hell you are. I keep making up these sex rules for myself, and then I break them right away.
1951 *The Catcher in the Rye*, ch.9.

54 That's the thing about girls. Every time they do something pretty, even if they're not much to look at, or even if they're sort of stupid, you fall half in love with them, and then you never know *where* you are.
1951 *The Catcher in the Rye*, ch.10.

55 He looked like the kind of guy that wouldn't talk to you much unless he wanted something off you. He had a lousy personality.
1951 *The Catcher in the Rye*, ch.11.

56 The thing is it's really hard to be room-mates with people if your suitcases are much better than theirs—if yours are really good and theirs aren't. You think if they're intelligent and all, the other person, and have a good sense of humour, that they don't give a damn whose suitcases are better, but they do.
1951 *The Catcher in the Rye*, ch.15.

57 The trouble with me is, I always have to read that stuff by myself. If an actor reads it out, I hardly listen. I keep worrying about whether he's going to do something phoney every minute.
1951 Of Hamlet. *The Catcher in the Rye*, ch.16.

58 Take most people, they're crazy about cars… I'd rather have a goddam horse. A horse is at least *human*, for God's sake.
1951 *The Catcher in the Rye*, ch.17.

59 The trouble with girls is, if they like a boy, no matter how big a bastard he is, they'll say he has an inferiority complex, and if they don't like him, no matter how nice a guy he is, or how big an inferiority complex he has, they'll say he's conceited. Even smart girls do it.
1951 *The Catcher in the Rye*, ch.18.

60 Sally said I was a sacrilegious atheist. I probably am. The thing that Jesus *really* would've liked would be the guy that plays the kettle drums in the orchestra.
1951 *The Catcher in the Rye*, ch.18.

61 Anyway, I keep picturing all these little kids playing some game in this big field of rye and all. Thousands of little kids, and nobody's around—nobody big, I mean—except me. And I'm standing on the edge of some crazy cliff. What I have to do, I have to catch everybody if they start to go over the cliff—I mean if they're running and they don't look where they're going I have to come out from somewhere and catch them. That's all I'd do all day. I'd just be the catcher in the rye and all. I know it's crazy, but that's the only thing I'd really like to be.
1951 *The Catcher in the Rye*, ch.22.

62 Never tell anyone anything. If you do you start missing everyone.
1951 *The Catcher in the Rye*, last words.

63 For Esmé—with Love and Squalor.
1953 Title of story.

64 Poetry, surely, is a crisis, perhaps the only actionable one we can call our own.
1959 'Seymour: An Introduction'.

65 A confessional passage has probably never been written that didn't stink a little bit of the writer's pride in having given up his pride.
1959 'Seymour: An Introduction'.

66 One of the reasons that I quit going to the theatre when I was about twenty was that I resented like hell filing out of the theatre because some playwright was forever slamming down his silly curtain.
1959 'Seymour: An Introduction'.

Salisbury, Robert Arthur Talbot Gascoyne Cecil, 3rd Marquis of 1830–1903

English Conservative statesman. He succeeded Disraeli as Leader of the Opposition, and was subsequently Prime Minister (1885–6, 1886–92, 1895–1902), as well as holding other posts. He was head of government during the Boer War (1889–1902).

67 Horny-handed sons of toil.
1873 In the *Quarterly Review*, Oct.

68 No lesson seems to be so deeply inculcated by the experience of life as that you should never trust experts. If you believe the doctors, nothing is wholesome: if you believe the theologians, nothing is innocent: if you believe the soldiers, nothing is safe. They all require to have their strong wine diluted by a very large admixture of insipid common sense.
1877 Letter to Lord Lytton, 15 Jun. Quoted in Lady Gwendolen Cecil *Life of Robert, Marquis of Salisbury* (1921–32), vol.2, ch.4.

69 We are part of the community of Europe and we must do our duty as such.
1888 Speech at Caernarvon, 10 Apr. In *The Times*, 11 Apr.

70 By office boys for office boys.
Of the *Daily Mail*. The phrase recalls Thackeray's Pendennis who started a newspaper 'by gentlemen for gentlemen'. Quoted in S J Taylor *The Great Outsiders: Northcliffe, Rothermere and the Daily Mail* (1966), ch.2.

Sallust *in full* Gaius Sallustius Crispus 86–34 BC

Roman historian and politician. As Governor of Numidia he enriched himself enormously. He wrote *Bellum Catilinae*, *Bellum Iugurthinum* and *Historiarum libri quinque*, of which only fragments survive.

71 *Alieni appetens, sui profusus.*
Greedy for the belongings of others, extravagant with his own.
Bellum Catilinae, 5.

72 *Esse quam videri bonus malebat.*
He preferred to be good, rather than seem good.
Of Cato. *Bellum Catilinae*, 54.

73 *Punica fide.*
With Punic faith.
Used ironically (meaning treacherously) of the Numidian Bocchus, a double agent between Iugurtha and Sulla. *Bellum Iugurthinum*, 108.3.

Salter, Sir (James) Arthur, 1st Baron Salter 1881–1975

English economist and international civil servant.

74 The normal economic system works itself.

Quoted in Ronald H Coase *Essays on Economics and Economists* (1994), p.6.

Salvianus c.400–c.470 AD

Christian writer from Gaul. His surviving works include nine epistles, *Ad Ecclesiam* and the unfinished *De Gubernatione Dei*. He urged that all estates be bequeathed to the poor, and denounced inherited wealth.

75 *Quot curiales, tot tyranni.*
As many councillors, so many tyrants.
De Gubernatione Dei, 5.18.27.

Sampson, Anthony (Terrell Seward) 1926–

English journalist and writer. His most influential book was *The Anatomy of Britain* (1962), which was followed by other titles on the same theme. He was a staff member of the *Observer* (1955–66).

76 In America journalism is apt to be regarded as an extension of history: in Britain, as an extension of conversation.
1965 *The Anatomy of Britain Today*, ch.9.

Samuel, Herbert Louis, 1st Viscount Samuel 1870–1963

English Liberal statesman and philosophical writer, Home Secretary (1916, 1931–2) and High Commissioner for Palestine (1920–5). His philosophical works include *Practical Ethics* (1935), *Belief and Action* (1937) and *In Search of Reality* (1957).

77 The House of Lords must be the only institution in the world that is kept efficient by the persistent absenteeism of its members.
1948 In *American News Review*, 5 Feb.

78 Hansard is history's ear, already listening.
1949 House of Lords, Dec.

Samuelson, Paul Anthony 1915–

US economist and journalist, professor at Massachusetts Institute of Technology (1940–85). His works include *Foundations of Economic Analysis* (1947) and the classic *Economics* (1948). He won the Nobel prize for economics in 1970.

79 The consumer, so it is said, is the king…each is a voter who uses his money as votes to get the things done that he wants done.
1948 *Economics*.

80 Commentators quote economic studies alleging that market downturns predicted four out of the last five recessions. That is an understatement. Wall Street indexes predicted nine out of the last five recessions!
1966 Quoted in *The Samuelson Sampler* (1973).

Samuelson, Sir Sydney 1925–

British film commissioner. He started in the film industry in 1939 and worked as a cinema projectionist, editor and cameraman. He founded Samuelson Film Service and in 1991 was appointed the first British Film Commissioner.

81 We welcome all enquiries about the UK climate—after all, we have more weather available in this country than anywhere else.
1994 *Check Book*.

Sand, George *pseudonym of* Amandine Aurore Lucille Dupin, Baronne Dudevant 1804–76

French novelist, the illegitimate daughter of Marshal de Saxe, known for her scandalous bohemian lifestyle and her liaisons with Musset and Chopin, and later with prominent politicians.

82 *L'amour, heurtant son front aveugle à tous les obstacles de la civilisation.*
Love, knocking its blind forehead against all of civilization's obstacles.
1832 *Indiana*, preface.

83 *En France particulièrement, les mots ont plus d'empire que les idées.*
In France particularly, words reign over ideas.
1832 *Indiana*, pt.1, ch.2.

84 *L'homme qui a un peu usé ses émotions est plus pressé de plaire que d'aimer.*
The person who has used his emotions even a little is more anxious to please than to love.
1832 *Indiana*, pt.1, ch.5.

85 *La société ne doit rien exiger de celui qui n'attend rien d'elle.*
Society should not ask anything of the person who expects nothing from society.
1832 *Indiana*, conclusion.

86 *Nous ne pouvons arracher une seule page de notre vie, mais nous pouvons jeter le livre au feu.*
We cannot tear out a single page from our life, but we can throw the entire book in the fire.
1832 *Mauprat*.

87 *Nulle créature humaine ne peut commander à l'amour.*
No human being can give orders to love.
1833 *Jacques*.

88 *Le vrai est trop simple, il faut y arriver toujours par le compliqué.*
Truth is too simple; it must always be arrived at in a complicated manner.
1867 Letter to Armand Barbès, May.

89 *L'art pour l'art est un vain mot. L'art pour le vrai, l'art pour le beau et le bon, voilà la religion que je cherche.*
Art for art's sake is an empty phrase. Art for the sake of the true, art for the sake of the good and the beautiful, that is the faith I search for.
1872 Letter to Alexandre Saint-Jean.

Sandburg, Carl 1878–1967

US poet, originally a journalist in Chicago. His volumes of poetry, celebrating US life in free verse, include *Chicago Poems* (1916) and *Good Morning, America* (1928). He also published a collection of folk-songs, *The American Songbag* (1927), and a *Life of Abraham Lincoln* (6 vols, 1926–39, Pulitzer Prize). He was awarded another Pulitzer Prize for his *Complete Poems* (1950).

90 The ache to utter and see in word
The silhouette of a brooding soul.
1904 Describing the poet's motivation. *In Reckless Ecstasy*.

91 Hog Butcher for the World,
Tool Maker, Stacker of Wheat,
Player with Railroads and the Nation's Freight Handler;
Stormy, husky, brawling,
City of the Big Shoulders.
1916 *Chicago Poems*, 'Chicago'.

92 The fog comes
    on little cat feet.

It sits looking
over harbor and city
on silent haunches
and then moves on.
1916 *Chicago Poems*, 'Fog'.

93 (All the coaches shall be scrap and rust and all the men
    and women
laughing in the diners and sleepers shall pass to ashes.)
I ask a man in the smoker where he is going and he
    answers: 'Omaha'.
1916 *Chicago Poems*, 'Limited'.

94 I tell you the past is a bucket of ashes.
1918 *Cornhuskers*, 'Prairie'.

95 When Abraham Lincoln was shovelled into the tombs,
he forgot the copperheads and the assassin…
in the dust, in the cool tombs.
1918 *Cornhuskers*, 'Cool Tombs'.

96 Pile the bodies high at Austerlitz and Waterloo.
Shovel them under and let me work—
I am the grass; I cover all.
1918 *Cornhuskers*, 'Grass'.

97 Why is there always a secret singing
When a lawyer cashes in?
Why does a hearse horse snicker
Hauling a lawyer away?
1920 *Smoke and Steel*, 'The Lawyers Know Too Much'.

98 Look how you use proud words,
When you let proud words go, it is not easy to call them
    back,
They wear long boots, hard boots; they walk off proud;
    they can't hear you calling—
look out how you use proud words.
1922 *Slabs of the Sunburnt West*, 'Primer Lesson'.

99 Poetry is the opening and closing of a door, leaving
those who look through to guess about what is seen
during a moment.
1923 'Poetry Considered', in the *Atlantic Monthly*, Mar.

1 Poetry is the achievement of the synthesis of hyacinths
and biscuits.
1923 'Poetry Considered', in the *Atlantic Monthly*, Mar.

2 The people will live on.
The learning and blundering will live on.
They will be tricked and sold and again sold
And go back to the nourishing earth for rootholds.
1936 *The People, Yes*.

3 I never made a mistake in grammar but once
in my life and as soon as I done it I seen it.
1936 *The People, Yes*.

4 'Would you just as soon get off the earth?'
holding ourselves aloof in pride of distinction
saying to ourselves this costs us nothing
as though hate has no cost
as though hate ever grew anything worth growing.
1936 On 'the red men'. *The People, Yes*.

5 or we may hold them in respect and affection
as fellow creepers on a commodious planet
saying, 'Yes you too you too are people'.
1936 On 'the red men'. *The People, Yes*.

6 Sometime they'll give a war and nobody will come.
1936 *The People, Yes*

7 The people know what the land knows.
1936 *The People, Yes*.

8 I am still studying verbs and the mystery of how they
connect nouns. I am more suspicious of adjectives than
at any other time in all my born days.
c.1940 On receiving nearly a dozen honorary doctorates for his
biography of Lincoln. Quoted in *The Complete Poems of Carl
Sandburg* (1986), 'Notes for a Preface'.

9 A baby is God's opinion that life should go on.
1948 *Remembrance Rock*, ch.2.

10 Slang is a language that rolls up its sleeves, spits on its
hands and goes to work.
1959 In the *New York Times*, 13 Feb.

11 In these times you have to be an optimist to open your
eyes when you wake in the morning.
1960 In the *New York Post*, 9 Sep.

12 The simple dignity of a child drinking a bowl of milk
embodies the fascination of an ancient rite.
Quoted in *Personalia, the Complete Poems of Carl Sandburg*
(1970).

13 In the spacious highways of books major or minor, each
poet is allowed the stride that will get him where he
wants to go if, God help him, he can hit that stride and
keep it.
Quoted in *The Complete Poems of Carl Sandburg* (1986), 'Notes for
a Preface'.

14 The more rhyme there is in poetry the more danger of its
tricking the writer into something other than the urge in
the beginning.
Quoted in *The Complete Poems of Carl Sandburg* (1986), 'Notes for
a Preface'.

15 There is a formal poetry perfect only in form…the
number of syllables, the designated and required
stresses of accent, the rhymes if wanted—they come off
with the skill of a solved crossword puzzle.
Quoted in *The Complete Poems of Carl Sandburg* (1986), 'Notes for
a Preface'.

Sanders, George 1906–72

British actor who became renowned for playing cads and
sophisticated villains. Among his many roles, his parts in
Rebecca (1940), *The Moon and Sixpence* (1942), *The Picture of
Dorian Gray* (1944), *All About Eve* (1950) and *A Shot in the Dark*
(1964) were particularly notable.

16 Dear World, I am leaving because I am bored. I feel I have
lived long enough. I am leaving you with your worries in
this sweet cesspool. Good luck.
1972 His suicide note.

Sandys, George 1578–1644

English translator and traveller, youngest son of the Archbishop
of York. He published a verse translation of Ovid's
Metamorphoses, written while treasurer to the colony in
Virginia. He also wrote poetic versions of the *Psalms* (1636)
and the *Song of Solomon* (1641).

17 Men ignorant of letters, studious for their bellies, and
ignominiously lazy.
1610 On the monks of Patmos. *Relation of a Journey Begun An.
Dom. 1610*.

Santayana, George originally *Jorge Agustín Nicolás Ruiz de Santayana* 1863–1952

Spanish–US philosopher, poet and novelist, Professor of Philosophy at Harvard (1907–12). His writing career began as a poet with *Sonnets and Other Verses* (1894), but he later became known as a philosopher and stylist, in such works as *The Life of Reason* (5 vols, 1905–6), *Realms of Being* (4 vols, 1927–40), and his novel *The Last Puritan* (1935). He moved to Europe in 1912, stayed at Oxford during World War I, then settled in Rome.

18 Fashion is something barbarous, for it produces innovation without reason and imitation without benefit.
1905–6 *The Life of Reason*,'Reason in Religion'.

19 Those who cannot remember the past are condemned to repeat it.
1905–6 *The Life of Reason.*

20 For an idea ever to be fashionable is ominous, since it must afterwards be always old-fashioned.
1913 *Winds of Doctrine*,'Modernism and Christianity'.

21 Philosophy to him was rather like a maze in which he happened to find himself wandering, and what he was looking for was the way out.
1920 Of William James. *Character and Opinion in the United States.*

22 The empiricist…thinks he believes only what he sees, but he is much better at believing than at seeing.
1955 *Scepticism and Animal Faith.*

23 Art is dedicated echo.
Quoted in John Gassner and SidneyThomas (eds) *The Nature of Art* (1964).

24 Nothing is so poor and melancholy as an art that is interested in itself and not in its subject.
Quoted in John Gassner and SidneyThomas (eds) *The Nature of Art* (1964).

25 A building without ornamentation is like a heaven without stars.
Quoted in the *Christian Science Monitor*, 14 Dec 1990.

26 Pure poetry is pure experiment…memorable nonsense.
Quoted in Helen Gardner (ed) *The New Oxford Book of English Verse* (1991).

Sappho 7c BC

Greek lyric poetess, born on Lesbos. Most of her surviving poems are from papyrus fragments discovered in recent times.

27 He looks to me to be in heaven, that man who sits across from you and listens near you to your soft speaking, your laughing lovely: that, I vow, makes the heart leap in my breast; for watching you a moment, speech fails me, my tongue is paralysed, at once a light fire runs beneath my skin, my eyes are blinded, and my ears drumming, the sweat pours down me, and I shake all over, sallower than grass: I feel as if I'm not far off dying.
D L Page (ed) *Lyrica Graeca Selecta* (1968), no.199 (translated by M L West).

28 Just as the sweet-apple reddens on the high branch, high on the highest, and the apple-pickers missed it, or rather did not miss it out, but could not reach it.
Of a girl before her marriage. D L Page (ed) *Lyrica Graeca Selecta* (1968), no.224.

Sarduy, Severo 1937–93

Cuban novelist and essayist. He left his country for Paris in 1960. A practitioner and a theoretician of so-called neo-Baroque, he used in his novels a variety of experimental techniques, satire, parody and a carnivalistic approach.

29 *¡Ah sí, ponerse a escribir otra vez, qué vomitivo! ¡Como si todo esto sirviera para algo, como si todo esto fuera a entrar en alguna cabezota, a entretener a alguno de los lectores babosos, ovillados en sus poltronas, frente al sopón soporífero de cada día!*
Ah yes, going back to writing, how disgusting! As if all this had some purpose, as if all this would penetrate some thick skull, amuse some drivelling reader curled up in his armchair before the soporific stew of every day!
1967 *De donde son los cantantes* (translated as *From Cuba with a Song*, 1972),'La Dolores Rondón'.

Sargent, John Singer 1856–1925

US painter.

30 Every time I paint a portrait I lose a friend.
Attributed.

Sargent, Sir (Harold) Malcolm Watts 1895–1967

English conductor. Originally trained as an organist, he was conductor of the Royal Choral Society from 1928, was in charge of the Liverpool Philharmonic Orchestra (1942–48) and led the BBC Symphony Orchestra (1950–57).

31 Just a little more reverence, please, and not so much astonishment.
Attributed, admonishing a choir singing Handel's 'For Unto Us a Child is Born'.

Sarnoff, David 1891–1971

Russian-born US radio and television pioneer. He began with the Marconi Wireless Co, covering the Titanic disaster (1912), and became president (1930) and chairman of the board (1947) of the Radio Corporation of America, a key figure in the development of television.

32 Seldom is it given to one generation to have such an opportunity to rise again, but now before you is that opportunity in television—a larger, richer, broader opportunity than ever existed in radio.
c.1948 Speech to NBC station affiliates. Recalled on his death, 12 Dec 1971.

33 Competition brings out the best in products and the worst in people.
Attributed.

Saroyan, William 1908–81

US playwright and novelist. He was awarded the Pulitzer Prize in 1939 for his best-known play, *The Time of Your Life*.

34 The Daring Young Man on the Flying Trapeze.
1934 Title of story collection.

35 The events of life have never fallen into the form of the short story or the form of the poem, or into any other form. Your own consciousness is the only form you need.
1934 *The Daring Young Man on the Flying Trapeze*,'A Cold Day'.

36 Now what?
1981 Last words.

Sarraute, Nathalie 1902–99

French novelist and literary critic.

37 *Le mot 'psychologie' est un de ceux qu'aucun auteur d'aujourd'hui ne peut entendre prononcer à son sujet sans baisser les yeux et rougir.*
The word 'psychology' is one that no author today can hear said about her work without lowering her eyes and blushing.
1956 *L'Ère du soupçon.*

38 *Vous savez qu'on doit se sentir heureux. Tous les vrais écrivains ont éprouvé ce sentiment. Quand on ne l'éprouve pas, je suis obligé de vous en avertir, c'est mauvais signe.*
You know that one should feel happy. All the true writers have experienced this feeling. When one does not experience it, I am obliged to tell you that it is a bad sign.
1968 *Entre la vie et la mort.*

39 *Chacun peut éprouver en soi ce double mouvement: désir de s'intégrer à la société, besoin de se réaliser par soi-même en dehors d'elle.*
We all have this double impulse within ourselves: the desire to integrate into society, and the need to fulfil ourselves outside of it, through our own efforts.
La Quinzaine littéraire, 50.

Sarton, George A 1884–1956

US academic and historian of science.

40 Definition—Science is systematized positive knowledge, what has been taken as such in different ages and in different places. Theorem—The acquisition and systematization of positive knowledge are the only human activities which are truly cumulative and progressive. Corollary—The history of science is the only history which can illustrate the progress of mankind. In fact, progress has no definite and unquestionable meaning in other fields than the field of science.
1957 *The Study of the History of Science.*

Sarton, May 1912–95

US poet and novelist. Her poetry collections include *Inner Landscape* (1939), *The Land of Silence* (1953) and *The Silence Now* (1988), and she wrote other works such as *Mrs Stevens Hears the Mermaids Singing* (1965).

41 The poet must be free to love or hate as the spirit moves him, free to change, free to be a chameleon, free to be an *enfant terrible*. He must above all never worry about his effect on other people. Power requires that one do just that all the time. Power requires that the inner person never be unmasked. No, we poets have to go naked. And since this is so, it is better that we stay private people; a naked public person would be rather ridiculous, what?
1965 Hilary Stevens. *Mrs Stevens Hears the Mermaids Singing*, pt.2.

42 I write poems, have always written them, to transcend the painfully personal and reach the universal.
Quoted in *Encore: A Journal of the 80th Year* (1993).

43 When you're a poet, you're a poet first. When it comes, it's like an angel.
Quoted by Mel Gussow in her obituary, in the *New York Times*, 18 Jul 1995.

Sartre, Jean-Paul 1905–80

French existentialist philosopher and writer, a prominent intellectual and friend of Simone de Beauvoir. His works include the trilogy *Les Chemins de la liberté* (1945–9, *The Roads to Freedom*) and many plays. His philosophy is presented in *L'Être et le néant* (1943, *Being and Nothingness*). In 1964 he published his autobiography *Les Mots* (*Words*), and was awarded (but declined) the Nobel prize for literature.

44 *Trois heures, c'est toujours trop tard ou trop tôt pour tout ce qu'on veut faire.*
Three o'clock is always either too late or too early for anything one might want to do.
1938 *La Nausée,* 'Vendredi'.

45 *L'homme est une passion inutile.*
Man is a useless passion.
1943 *L'Être et le néant* (*Being and Nothingness*, 1957) pt.4, ch.2, section 3 (translated by Hazel Barnes).

46 *L'Enfer, c'est les Autres.*
Hell is other people.
1945 *Huis clos.*

47 *Est-ce qu'au fond, ce qui fait peur, dans la doctrine que je vais essayer de vous exposer, ce n'est pas le fait qu'elle laisse une possibilité de choix à l'homme?*
For at bottom, what is alarming in the doctrine that I am about to try to explain to you is—is it not?—that it confronts man with a possibility of choice.
1946 *L'Existentialisme est un humanisme* (*Existentialism and Humanism*, 1948) (translated by Philip Mairet).

48 *Ce qu'ils ont en commun, c'est simplement le fait qu'ils estiment que l'existence précède l'essence, ou, si vous voulez, qu'il faut partir de la subjectivité.*
What [existentialists] have in common is simply the fact that they believe that *existence* comes before *essence*—or, if you will, that we must begin from the subjective.
1946 *L'Existentialisme est un humanisme* (*Existentialism and Humanism*, 1948) (translated by Philip Mairet).

49 *Qu'est-ce que signifie que l'existence précède l'essence? Cela signifie que l'homme existe d'abord, se rencontre, surgit dans le monde, et qu'il se définit après.*
What do we mean by saying that existence precedes essence? We mean that man first of all exists, encounters himself, surges up in the world—and defines himself afterwards.
1946 *L'Existentialisme est un humanisme* (*Existentialism and Humanism*, 1948) (translated by Philip Mairet).

50 *L'homme n'est rien d'autre que ce qu'il se fait. Tel est le premier principe de l'existentialisme.*
Man is nothing else but that which he makes of himself. That is the first principle of existentialism.
1946 *L'Existentialisme est un humanisme* (*Existentialism and Humanism*, 1948) (translated by Philip Mairet).

51 *L'homme est condamné à être libre.*
Man is condemned to be free.
1946 *L'Existentialisme est un humanisme* (*Existentialism and Humanism*, 1948) (translated by Philip Mairet).

52 *Un homme n'est rien d'autre qu'une série d'entreprises.*
A man is no other than a series of undertakings.
1946 *L'Existentialisme est un humanisme* (*Existentialism and Humanism*, 1948) (translated by Philip Mairet).

53 *Il n'y a pas d'autre univers qu'un univers humain, l'univers de la subjectivité humaine.*

There is no other universe except the human universe, the universe of human subjectivity.
1946 *L'Existentialisme est un humanisme* (*Existentialism and Humanism*, 1948) (translated by Philip Mairet).

54 *Vous êtes libre, choisissez, c'est-à-dire, inventez. Aucune morale générale ne peut vous indiquer ce qu'il y a à faire.*
You are free, therefore choose—that is to say, invent. No rule of general morality can show you what you ought to do.
1946 *L'Existentialisme est un humanisme* (*Existentialism and Humanism*, 1948) (translated by Philip Mairet).

55 The status of 'native' is a nervous condition introduced and maintained by the settler among colonized people *with their consent*.
1961 Preface to Franz Fanon *Les Damnés de la terre* (*The Wretched of the Earth*, 1967, translated by Constance Farrington). Tsitsi Dangarembga uses this sentence to supply both epigraph and title of her 1988 novel *Nervous Conditions*.

Sassoon, Siegfried Louvain 1886–1967

English poet and novelist. He established his reputation as a war poet while serving in World War I. He wrote a semi-autobiographical trilogy, *The Memoirs of George Sherston* (1928–36), and several volumes of actual memoirs.

56 I am making this statement as an act of wilful defiance of military authority, because I believe that the War is being deliberately prolonged by those who have the power to end it.
1917 'A Soldier's Declaration'. Statement sent to his commanding officer which was read out in the House of Commons and printed in *The Times*.

57 I'd like to see a Tank come down the stalls,
Lurching to rag-time tunes, or 'Home sweet Home',—
And there'd be no more jokes in Music-halls
To mock the riddled corpses round Bapaume.
1917 'Blighters'.

58 How right it seemed that he should reach the span
Of comfortable years allowed to man!
Splendid to eat and sleep and choose a wife,
Safe with his wound, a citizen of life.
He hobbled blithely through the garden gate,
And thought: 'Thank God they had to amputate!'
1917 'The One-Legged Man'.

59 We'd gained our first objective hours before
While dawn broke like a face with blinking eyes,
Pallid, unshaved and thirsty, blind with smoke.
1918 'Counter-Attack'.

60 Soldiers are citizens of death's grey land,
—Drawing no dividend from time's to-morrows.
In the great hour of destiny they stand,
—Each with his feuds, and jealousies, and sorrows.
Soldiers are sworn to action; they must win
—Some flaming, fatal climax with their lives.
Soldiers are dreamers; when the guns begin
—They think of firelit homes, clean beds and wives.
1918 'Dreamers'.

61 If I were fierce and bald and short of breath
I'd live with scarlet Majors at the Base,
And speed glum heroes up the line to death.
1918 'Base Details'.

62 And when war is done and youth stone dead

I'd toddle safely home and die—in bed.
1918 'Base Details'.

63 'Good-morning; good-morning!' the General said
When we met him last week on our way to the line.
Now the soldiers he smiled at are most of 'em dead,
And we're cursing his staff for incompetent swine.
'He's a cheery old card,' grunted Harry to Jack
As they slogged up to Arras with rifle and pack.

But he did for them both by his plan of attack.
1918 'The General'.

64 Does it matter?—losing your sight?…
There's such splendid work for the blind;
And people will always be kind
As you sit on the terrace remembering
And turning your face to the light.
1918 'Does It Matter'.

65 From you, Beethoven, Bach, Mozart,
The substance of my dreams took fire.
You built cathedrals in my heart,
And lit my pinnacled desire.
1918 'Dead Musicians'.

66 You have no part with lads who fought
And laughed and suffered at my side.
Your fugues and symphonies have brought
No memory of my friends who died.
1918 'Dead Musicians'.

67 Why do you lie with your legs ungainly huddled,
And one arm bent across your sullen cold
Exhausted face?
1918 'The Dug-Out'.

68 You are too young to fall asleep for ever;
And when you sleep you remind me of the dead.
1918 'The Dug-Out'.

69 Everyone suddenly burst out singing;
And I was filled with such delight
As prisoned birds must find in freedom,
1919 'Everyone Sang'.

70 But the past is just the same,—and
War's a bloody game.
1919 'Aftermath'.

71 When all is said and done, leading a good life is more important than keeping a good diary.
1923 Diary entry, 8 Jul.

72 In me the tiger sniffs the rose.
1928 *The Heart's Journey*, pt.7, 'In me, past, present, future meet'.

73 And what is time but shadows that were cast
By these storm-sculptured stones while centuries fled?
The stones remain; their stillness can outlast
The skies of history hurrying overhead.
1928 *The Heart's Journey*, pt.9, 'What is Stonehenge? It is the roofless past'.

74 *Alone*… The word is life endured and known.
It is the stillness where our spirits walk
And all but inmost faith is overthrown.
1928 *The Heart's Journey*, pt.11, '"When I'm alone"—the words tripped off his tongue'.

75 They have spoken lightly of my deathless friends,
(Lamps for my gloom, hands guiding where I stumble,)
Quoting, for shallow conversational ends,

What Shelley shrilled, what Blake once wildly
  muttered…
How can they use such names and be not humble?
1928 *The Heart's Journey*, pt.15, 'Grandeur of Ghosts'.

76 Who will remember, passing through this Gate,
The unheroic Dead who fed the guns?
Who shall absolve the foulness of their fate,—
Those doomed, conscripted, unvictorious ones?
1928 *The Heart's Journey*, pt.21, 'On Passing the New Menin Gate'.

77 Here Vaughan lies dead, whose name flows on for ever
Through pastures of the spirit washed with dew
And starlit with eternities unknown.
1928 *The Heart's Journey*, pt.23, 'At the Grave of Henry Vaughan'.

78 The skull that housed white angels and had vision
Of daybreak through the gateways of the mind.
1928 *The Heart's Journey*, pt.23, 'At the Grave of Henry Vaughan'.

79 A man may be born a poet, but he has to make himself an
artist as well.
1939 *On Poetry*.

Satie, Erik Alfred Leslie 1866–1925

French composer. A pupil of Vincent d'Indy and Albert Roussel,
he wrote ballets, lyric dramas and numerous whimsical pieces
in which he rebelled against Wagnerism and orthodoxy in
general. His music had some influence on Debussy, Ravel and
others.

80 Before I compose a piece, I walk round it several times,
accompanied by myself.
Quoted in *Bulletin des éditions musicales* (1913).

81 To be played with both hands in the pocket.
Instruction on one of his piano compositions. Quoted in Oscar
Levant *The Unimportance of Being Oscar* (1968).

82 It is not enough to refuse the Legion d'Honneur. One
should never have deserved it.
Of Maurice Ravel, who had declined the honour. Quoted by
Alister Kershaw in *The Australian*, 1991.

Sayers, Dorothy L(eigh) 1893–1957

English detective-story writer. Her hero, Lord Peter Wimsey, is
one of the most popular of the great detectives, and her books
are distinguished by realistically created settings as well as
stylish wit. She also wrote plays and poems.

83 I admit it is more fun to punt than to be punted, and that a
desire to have all the fun is nine-tenths of the law of
chivalry.
1935 *Gaudy Night*, ch.14.

84 I can't see that she could have found anything nastier to
say if she'd thought it out with both hands for a fortnight.
1937 'Prothalamion'.

85 Plain lies are dangerous.
1937 'The Psychology of Advertising', in *The Spectator*, 19 Nov.

86 Those who prefer their English sloppy have only
themselves to thank if the advertisement writer uses his
mastery of vocabulary and syntax to mislead their weak
minds.
1937 'The Psychology of Advertising', in *The Spectator*, 19 Nov.

87 The moral of all this…is that we have the kind of
advertising we deserve.
1937 'The Psychology of Advertising', in *The Spectator*, 19 Nov.

88 As I grow older and older,

And totter towards the tomb,
I find that I care less and less
Who goes to bed with whom.
'That's Why I Never Read Modern Novels', collected in Janet
Hitchman *Such a Strange Lady* (1975), ch.12.

Scargill, Arthur 1938–

English trade union leader, president of the National Union of
Mineworkers (1981–2002). A powerful orator, his strong
defence of miners and his socialist politics led to conflict with
government, particularly in the miners' strike of 1984–5. He
started a new socialist party in 1996.

89 My father still reads the dictionary every day. He says
that your life depends on your power to master words.
1982 In the *Sunday Times*, 10 Jan.

90 I speak of that most dangerous duo—President Ray-Gun
and the plutonium blonde, Margaret Thatcher.
1984 Quoted in *Time*, 3 Dec.

91 I wouldn't vote for Ken Livingstone if he were running for
mayor of Toytown.
2000 In *The Guardian*, 3 May.

Scève, Maurice c.1510–c.1564

French poet of the École Lyonnaise. His most famous collection
of poems, *Délie, objet de plus haute vertu* (1544), is a meditation
on love.

92 *Car loi d'Amour est de l'un captiver,*
L'autre donner d'heureuse liberté.
The law of love is to captivate one,
And to give another joyous freedom.
1544 *Délie*, no.40.

93 *En toi je vis, où que tu sois absente;*
En moi je meurs, où que je sois présent.
Tant loin sois-tu, toujours tu es présente;
Pour près que sois, encore suis-je absent.
I live in you, wherever you are, when you are absent;
I die in myself wherever I am.
No matter how far away you are, you are always present;
And no matter how near you are, I am always absent.
1544 *Délie*, no.144.

94 *Tu es le Corps, Dame, et je suis ton ombre.*
You are the body, lady, and I am your shadow.
1544 *Délie*, no.376.

Schacht, Hjalmar Horace Greely 1877–1970

German financier. As president of the Reichsbank (1923) he
ended inflation, and recalled by the Nazis from resignation in
1933, he restored the German trade balance by unorthodox
methods. Dismissed after disagreement with Hitler, he was
later acquitted at Nuremberg of crimes against humanity.

95 I wouldn't believe that Hitler was dead, even if he told
me himself.
1945 Attributed remark, 8 May.

Schaw, Janet b.c.1730

Scottish traveller. She was distantly related to Sir Walter Scott
and was well educated, but little is known of her other than
what is told in her *Journal of a Lady of Quality*, an account of
her travels in the West Indies in 1774–6.

96 At last America is in my view; a dreary waste of white
barren sand, and melancholy, nodding pines. In the

course of many miles, no cheerful cottage has blest my eyes. All seems dreary, savage and desert; and was it for this such sums of money, such streams of British blood have been lavished away? Oh, thou dear land, how dearly hast thou purchased this habitation for bears and wolves. Dearly has it been purchased, and at a price far dearer still it will be kept. My heart dies within me, while I view it.

c.1776 On her first sight of the country around Cape Fear. *Journal of a Lady of Quality; Being the Narrative of a Journey from Scotland to the West Indies, North Carolina, and Portugal, in the years 1774 to 1776.*

Scheckter, Jody 1950–

South African Formula One driver.

97 Fewer girls, more technology.

1997 On how Formula One had changed since he won the world championship in 1979. In *The Times*, 29 Dec.

Schiaparelli, Elsa 1890–1973

Italian fashion designer who opened one of the first couture boutiques in Paris in 1935. She was known for introducing the colour 'shocking pink' into the fashion world.

98 So fashion is born by small facts, trends, or even politics, never by trying to make little pleats and furbelows, by trinkets, by clothes easy to copy, or by the shortening or lengthening of a skirt.

1954 *A Shocking Life*, ch.9.

99 A good cook is like a sorceress who dispenses happiness.

1954 *A Shocking Life*, ch.21.

Schiller, Friedrich 1759–1805

German poet and playwright who was briefly a surgeon before turning his attention to writing and travelling.

1 *In seinen Göttern malt sich der Mensch.*
Humankind is reflected in its gods.

1789 *Was heißt und zu welchem Ende studiert man Universalgeschichte?*

2 *Alle anderen Dinge müssen; der Mensch ist das Wesen, welches will.*
All other things must; man is the being who wills.

1794 *Über das Erhabene.*

3 *Man kann den Menschen nicht verwehren, Zu denken, was sie wollen.*
One cannot prevent people from thinking what they please.

1800 *Maria Stuart*, act 1, sc.8.

4 *Was man scheint, Hat jedermann zum Richter; was man ist, hat keine.*
What we appear to be is subject to the judgement Of all mankind, and what we truly are, of no one.

1800 *Maria Stuart*, act 2, sc.5.

5 *Was man nicht aufgibt, hat man nie verloren.*
What is not abandoned is never completely lost.

1800 *Maria Stuart*, act 2, sc.5.

6 *Das Leben ist Nur ein Moment, der Tod ist auch nur einer.*
Life is but a moment. Death is but a moment, too.

1800 *Maria Stuart*, act 3, sc.6.

7 *Den stolzen Sieger stürzt sein eignes Glück.*
The victor is often vanquished by his own success.

1801 *Die Jungfrau von Orléans*, act 1, sc.5.

8 *Mehr als das Leben lieb' ich meine Freiheit.*
More than life, I cherish freedom.

1801 *Die Jungfrau von Orléans*, act 2, sc.2.

9 *Mitt der Dummheit kämpfen Götter selbst vergebens.*
Even the gods themselves struggle in vain against stupidity.

1801 *Die Jungfrau von Orléans*, act 3, sc.6.

Schlesinger, Arthur Meier 1888–1965

US historian. His works include *New Viewpoints in American History* (1922) and a *History of American Life* (13 vols, 1928–43).

10 The military struggle may frankly be regarded for what it actually was, namely a war for independence, an armed attempt to impose the views of the revolutionists on the British government and large sections of the colonial population at whatever cost to freedom of opinion or the sanctity of life and property.

1919 'The American Revolution Reconsidered', in *Political Science Quarterly*, Mar.

Schlesinger, Arthur M(eier), Jr 1917–

US historian and special assistant to President Kennedy (1961–3). His works include the Pulitzer prize-winning *The Age of Jackson* (1945) and *A Thousand Days: John F Kennedy in the White House* (1965). He became president of the American Institute of Arts and Letters (1981).

11 He read partly for information, partly for comparison, partly for insight, partly for the sheer joy of felicitous statement. He delighted particularly in quotations which distilled the essence of an argument.

1965 Of John F Kennedy. *A Thousand Days*.

12 Ceremony, circus, farce, melodrama, tragedy…nothing else offers all at once the whirl, the excitement, the gaiety, the intrigue and the anguish.

1965 On national political conventions. *A Thousand Days*.

13 At the time it is all a confusion; in retrospect…all a blur.

1965 On national political conventions. *A Thousand Days*.

14 The things people had once held against her… unconventional beauty…un-American elegance, the taste for French clothes and French food—were suddenly no longer liabilities but assets.

1965 On Jacqueline Kennedy's post-election image. *A Thousand Days*.

15 Television has spread the habit of instant reaction and has stimulated the hope of instant results.

1970 In *Newsweek*, 6 Jul.

Schlesinger, James 1932–

16 The notion of a defence that will protect American cities is one that will not be achieved, but it is that goal that supplies the political magic in the President's vision.

1987 Senate Foreign Relations Committee, 6 Feb.

Schmitt, Wolfgang Rudolph 1944–

German-born US businessman. He joined houseware manufacturers Rubbermaid Inc in 1966, becoming president in 1991.

17 Innovation most of the time is simply taking A, B, C and D, which already exist, and putting them together in a form called E.
1994 In *Fortune*, 14 Nov.

Schnabel, Artur 1882–1951

Austrian pianist and composer. He studied under Leschetizsky and made his debut at the age of eight. Subsequently he toured throughout Europe and the US, where he settled in 1939. He was an authoritative player of a small range of German classics—notably Beethoven, Mozart and Schubert.

18 The notes I handle no better than many pianists. But the pauses between the notes—ah, that is where the art resides.
1958 In the *Chicago Daily News*, 11 Jun.

19 Applause is a receipt, not a bill.
Explaining why he did not play encores. Quoted in I Kolodin *The Musical Life* (1958).

20 I know two kinds of audience only—one coughing and one not coughing.
1961 *My Life and Music*.

21 I don't think there was ever a piece of music that changed a man's decision on how to vote.
1961 *My Life and Music*.

22 When a piece gets difficult make faces.
Quoted in Oscar Levant *The Unimportance of Being Oscar* (1968).

23 The sonatas of Mozart are unique; they are too easy for children, and too difficult for artists.
Quoted in Nat Shapiro *An Encyclopedia of Quotations about Music* (1978).

Schoenbaum, Thomas J

Professor of Political Science, University of Georgia.

24 [He] made himself the rock against which crashed the successive waves of dissent.
1988 Of Secretary of State Dean Rusk during the Vietnam War. *Waging Peace and War*.

Schoenberg, Arnold Franz Walter 1874–1951

Austrian composer, conductor and teacher. A self-taught pioneer of atonality, his works include the tone poem *Pelleas und Melisande* (1903), the song cycle *Pierrot Lunaire* (1912), operas, chamber music and other choral and orchestral pieces. He lived in the US from 1933.

25 Harmony! Harmony!
1951 Attributed last words.

26 My music is not modern, it is merely badly played.
Quoted in C Rosen *Schoenberg* (1976).

27 If it is art it is not for all, and if it is for all it is not art.
Quoted in Ian Crofton and Donald Fraser *A Dictionary of Musical Quotations* (1985).

Schopenhauer, Arthur 1788–1860

German philosopher, whose work is often characterized as a systematic philosophical pessimism. His major work was *Die Welt als Wille und Vorstellung* (*The World as Will and Representation*), published in 1819. A second enlarged edition followed in 1844.

28 *Alle Befriedigung, oder was man gemeinhin Glück nennt, ist eigentlich und wesentlich immer nur negativ und durchaus nie positiv.*
All satisfaction, or what is commonly called happiness, is really and essentially always *negative* only, and never positive.
1819 *Die Welt als Wille und Vorstellung* (*The World as Will and Representation*), vol.1, bk.4, ch.58 (translated by E F J Payne).

29 *Wir tappen im Labyrinth unsers Lebenswandels und im Dunkel unserer Forschungen umher: helle Augenblicke erleuchten dabei wie Blitze unsern Weg.*
We grope about in the labyrinth of our life and in the obscurity of our investigations; bright moments illuminate our path like flashes of lightning.
1844 *Die Welt als Wille und Vorstellung* (*The World as Will and Representation*), vol.2, ch.15 (translated by E F J Payne).

30 *Das Ganze der Erfahrung gleicht einer Geheimschrift und die Philosophie der Entzifferung derselben.*
The whole of experience is like a cryptograph, and philosophy is like the deciphering of it.
1844 *Die Welt als Wille und Vorstellung* (*The World as Will and Representation*), vol.2, ch.17 (translated by E F J Payne).

31 *Ist es an und für sich absurd, das Nichtsein für ein Übel zu halten; da jedes Übel wie jedes Gut das Dasein zur Voraussetzung hat, ja sogar das Bewusstsein.*
It is in and by itself absurd to regard non-existence as an evil; for every evil, like every good, presupposes existence, indeed even consciousness.
1844 *Die Welt als Wille und Vorstellung* (*The World as Will and Representation*), vol.2, ch.41 (translated by E F J Payne).

32 *Unsterblichkeit der Individualität verlangen heißt eigentlich einen Irrtum ins Unendliche perpetuieren wollen. Denn im Grunde ist doch jede Individualität nur ein spezieller Irrtum, Fehltritt, etwas, das besser nicht wäre, ja wovon uns zurückzubringen der eigentliche Zweck des Lebens ist.*
To desire immortality for the individual is really the same as wanting to perpetuate an error for ever; for at bottom every individuality is really only a special error, a false step, something that it would be better should not be, in fact something from which it is the real purpose of life to bring us back.
1844 *Die Welt als Wille und Vorstellung* (*The World as Will and Representation*), vol.2, ch.41 (translated by E F J Payne).

33 *Alle Verliebtheit [...] wurzelt allein im Geschlechtstriebe.*
All amorousness [...] is rooted in the sexual impulse alone.
1844 *Die Welt als Wille und Vorstellung* (*The World as Will and Representation*), vol.2, ch.44 (translated by E F J Payne).

34 *Was man auch sagen mag, der glücklichste Augenblick des Glücklichen ist doch der seines Einschlafens wie der unglücklichste des Unglücklichen der seines Erwachens.*
Whatever we may say, the happiest moment of the happy man is that of his falling asleep, just as the unhappiest moment of the unhappy man is that of his awakening.
1844 *Die Welt als Wille und Vorstellung* (*The World as Will and Representation*), vol.2, ch.46 (translated by E F J Payne).

35 *Es gibt nur einen Irrtum, und es ist der, dass wir dasind, um glücklich zu sein.*
There is only one inborn error, and that is the notion that we exist in order to be happy.
1844 *Die Welt als Wille und Vorstellung* (*The World as Will and Representation*), vol.2, ch.49 (translated by E F J Payne).

36 *Die Szenen unsers Lebens gleichen den Bildern in großer Mosaik, welche in der Nähe keine Wirkung tun, sondern von denen man fern stehn muss, um sie schön zu finden.*
The scenes of our life resemble pictures in rough mosaic; they are ineffective from close up, and have to be viewed from a distance if they are to seem beautiful.
1851 *Parerga und Paralipomena*, ch.11 (translated by R J Hollingdale).

37 *Jede Trennung gibt einen Vorgeschmack des Todes—und jedes Wiedersehen einen Vorgeschmack der Auferstehung.*
Every parting is a foretaste of death, and every reunion a foretaste of resurrection.
1851 *Parerga und Paralipomena*, ch.26 (translated by R J Hollingdale).

Schreiner, Olive Emily Albertina *pseudonym* Ralph Iron 1855–1920

South African feminist, novelist and polemicist. Educated at home against a strict religious background, she is best known for her semi-autobiographical novel, *The Story of an African Farm* (1883), which rejects the spiritual aridity of colonial life and loveless marriage.

38 This pretty ring… I will give it to the first man who tells me he would like to be a woman. It is delightful to be a woman; but every man thanks the Lord devoutly that he isn't one.
1883 *The Story of an African Farm*, ch.17, 'Lyndall'.

39 We are cursed, Waldo, born cursed from the time our mothers bring us into the world till the shrouds are put on us.
1883 Lyndall. *The Story of an African Farm*, ch.17, 'Lyndall'.

40 We sit…and look out at the boys in their happy play…we kneel still with one little cheek wistfully pressed against the pane…and we go and stand before the glass. We see the complexion we were not to spoil, and the white frock… Then the curse begins to act upon us. It finishes its work when we are grown women, who no more look out wistfully at a more healthy life; we are contented. We fit our sphere as a Chinese woman's foot fits her shoe, exactly, as though God made both—and yet he knows nothing of either.
1883 Lyndall. *The Story of an African Farm*, ch.17, 'Lyndall'.

41 Men are like the earth and we are the moon; we turn always one side to them, and they think there is no other, because they don't see it—but there is.
1883 Lyndall. *The Story of an African Farm*, ch.17, 'Lyndall'.

42 Give us labour and the training which fits for labour! We demand this, not for ourselves alone, but for the race.
1911 *Women and Labour*, ch.1.

43 With each generation the entire race passes through the body of its womanhood as through a mould, reappearing with the indelible marks of that mould upon it, that as the *os cervix* of woman, through which the head of the human infant passes at birth, forms a ring, determining for ever the size at birth of the human head…so exactly the intellectual capacity, the physical vigour, the emotional depth of woman, forms also an untranscendable circle, circumscribing with each successive generation the limits of expansion of the human race.
1911 *Women and Labour*, ch.3.

Schroeder, Patricia Scott 1940–

US Congresswoman and lawyer. She practised law in Denver and then became a faculty member of the University of Colorado (1969–72), before being elected to Congress (1972–96).

44 I was cooking breakfast this morning for my kids and I thought, 'He's just like Teflon. Nothing sticks to him.'
1984 Of President Ronald Reagan. In the *Boston Globe*, 24 Oct.

45 Washington is awash in post-war testosterone.
1991 On her decision not to seek presidential nomination in the wake of victory in the Gulf War. In the *New York Times*, 30 Jun.

Schulberg, Budd Wilson 1914–

US novelist and scritpwriter. He is best known for his screenplay for the film *On the Waterfront* (1954).

46 What Makes Sammy Run?
1941 Title of novel.

47 You don't understand. I could have had class. I could have been a contender. I could have been somebody—instead of a bum, which is what I am, let's face it.
1954 Lines spoken by Marlon Brando. *On the Waterfront*.

Schultz, Howard 1952–

US businessman.

48 Retail is detail.
1994 On building Starbucks, the largest US coffee-bar chain and mail-order business. In the *New York Times*, 14 Dec.

Schulz, Charles Monroe 1922–2000

US cartoonist. He created the syndicated comic strip *Peanuts* (1950), internationally loved for its characters of Charlie Brown, Snoopy, Lucy, Linus, Schroeder, Peppermint Patty, Pigpen, Marcie and the bird Woodstock.

49 Jogging is very beneficial. It's very good for your legs and your feet. It's also very good for the ground. It makes it feel needed.
Quoted in Colin Jarman *The Guinness Dictionary of Sports Quotations* (1990).

Schumacher, E(rnst) F(riedrich) 1911–77

British economist and public servant, member of the Control Commission in Germany (1946–50) and economist of the National Coal Board (1950–70).

50 Small Is Beautiful: a Study of Economics as if People Mattered.
1973 Title of book.

51 I have no doubt that it is possible to give a new direction to technological development, a direction that shall lead it back to the real needs of man, and that also means: to the actual size of man. Man is small, and, therefore, small is beautiful. To go for giantism is to go for self-destruction.
1973 *Small Is Beautiful*.

Schumacher, Michael 1969–

German Formula One driver, winner of the world championship in 1994 and 1995, and 2000–4.

52 To control 800 horse power relying just on arm muscles and foot sensitivity can turn out to be a dangerous exercise.
2003 In the *Observer*, 2 Mar.

Schumpeter, Joseph Alois 1883–1950

Austrian-born US economist, who emigrated to the US in 1932 and later became professor at Harvard. He emphasized the importance of the entrepreneur in the business cycle and traced the economic history of capitalism.

53 When I was a young man, I wanted to be three things: I wanted to be the world's greatest horseman, the world's greatest economist, and the world's greatest lover. Unfortunately I never became the world's greatest horseman.
1940s Attributed, Harvard oral tradition.

54 The cold metal of economic theory is in Marx's pages immersed in such a wealth of steaming phrases as to acquire a temperature not naturally its own.
1942 *Capitalism, Socialism, and Democracy*, p.21.

55 Can capitalism survive? No, I do not think it can.
1942 *Capitalism, Socialism, and Democracy*, p.61.

56 Queen Elizabeth owned silk stockings. The capitalist achievement does not typically consist in providing more silk stockings for queens but in bringing them within the reach of factory girls in return for steadily decreasing amount of effort.
1942 *Capitalism, Socialism, and Democracy*, p.67.

57 The question that is so clearly in many potential parents' minds: 'Why should we stunt our ambitions and impoverish our lives in order to be insulted and looked down upon in our old age?'
1942 *Capitalism, Socialism, and Democracy*, ch. 14.

58 Bureaucracy is not an obstacle to democracy but an inevitable complement to it.
1942 *Capitalism, Socialism, and Democracy*, ch. 18.

Schwartz, Eugene M

US art collector, known for amassing one of the nation's leading collections of contemporary art and giving it away with almost as much zeal.

59 Collecting is the only socially commendable form of greed.
1995 In the *New York Times*, 7 Sep.

Schwartz, Sanford

US writer.

60 Dalí's importance for the Surrealists at that time, and for art historians now, is that he found a way to put Freud on canvas.
1994 In the *New Republic*, 17 Oct.

Schwarzenegger, Arnold 1947–

Austrian-born US actor and politician. He began as a body builder, winning the Mr Universe title, and became a Hollywood star in adventure films such as *The Terminator* (1984) and *True Lies* (1994). He was elected Republican Governor of California in 2003.

61 Posing is a performing art.
Quoted in *The Guardian*, 1975.

62 I'll be back.
1984 *The Terminator*.

63 Hasta la vista, baby.
1991 *Terminator 2: Judgment Day*.

64 I am humbled, I am honoured and I am moved beyond words to be your governor.
2003 On being sworn in as Governor of California, 17 Nov.

Schwarzkopf, H Norman 1934–

US army general. He served in the Vietnam War and as deputy commander in Grenada (1983), and in 1991 commanded allied troops in the Gulf War. He retired the following year.

65 We are not going after Saddam Hussein. If I can eliminate his ability to communicate with his forces, I would be entirely satisfied with that result.
1991 Press briefing on the start of the Gulf War, 15 Jan.

66 I don't consider myself dovish and I certainly don't consider myself hawkish. Maybe I would describe myself as owlish—that is wise enough to understand that you want to do everything possible to avoid war.
1991 In the *New York Times*, 28 Jan.

67 I asked you to be the thunder and lightning of Desert Storm. You were all of that and more.
1991 Message to US units on the cease-fire that ended the Gulf War.

68 Seven months ago I could give a single command and 541,000 people would immediately obey it. Today I can't get a plumber to come to my house.
1991 In *Newsweek*, 11 Nov.

Schweikart, Russell 1935–

US astronaut.

69 The most beautiful sight in orbit…is a urine dump at sunset, because as the stuff comes out and as it hits the exit nozzle it instantly flashes into ten million little ice crystals which go out almost in a hemisphere… It's really a spectacular sight.
1981 *The Next Whole Earth Catalog*.

Schweitzer, Albert 1875–1965

German medical missionary, theologian, musician and philosopher. In 1896 he vowed to live for science and art until he was 30, and then devote his life to serving humanity. He became principal of a theological college (1903) and wrote *Von Reimarus zu Wrede* (1906, *The Quest for the Historical Jesus*) and major works on St Paul. Despite his international reputation in music and theology, he turned to medicine in 1905, and with his wife set up a hospital in French Equatorial Africa. He was awarded the Nobel peace prize in 1952.

70 He comes to us as One unknown, without a name, as of old, by the lakeside, He came to those who knew Him not. He speaks to us the same word: 'Follow thou me!' and sets us to the tasks which He has to fulfil for our time. He commands. And to those who obey Him, whether they be wise or simple, He will reveal Himself in the toils, the conflicts, the sufferings which they shall pass through in His fellowship, and, as an ineffable mystery, they shall learn in their own experience who He is.
1906 *Von Reimarus zu Wrede* (translated by W Montgomery as *The Quest for the Historical Jesus*, 1910).

71 An optimist is a person who sees a green light everywhere, while the pessimist sees only the red stoplight. The truly wise person is colour-blind.
1965 Quoted in CBS News tribute, 14 Jan.

Scorsese, Martin 1942–

US film director. With films such as *Taxi Driver* (1976) and *Raging Bull* (1980), he established himself as one of the foremost directors of his generation.

72 I always tell the younger film-makers and students: Do it like the painters used to… Study the old masters. Enrich your palette. Expand the canvas. There's always so much more to learn.
1997 *Scorsese: A Personal Journey Through American Movies.*

73 Cinema is a matter of what's in the frame and what's out.
1997 *Scorsese: A Personal Journey Through American Movies.*

Scott, C(harles) P(restwich) 1846–1932

English newspaper editor and Liberal MP (1895–1906). At the age of 26 he became editor of the *Manchester Guardian*, and made it a serious liberal rival of *The Times* by a highly independent and often controversial editorial policy and high literary standards.

74 The newspaper is of necessity something of a monopoly, and its first duty is to shun the temptations of a monopoly. Its primary office is the gathering of News. At the peril of its soul it must see that the supply is not tainted. Neither in what it gives, nor in what it does not give, nor in the mode of presentation, must the unclouded face of Truth suffer wrong. Comment is free, but facts are sacred.
1921 Of the newspaper industry. In the *Manchester Guardian*, special centenary issue, 6 May.

75 One of the virtues, perhaps almost the chief virtue, of a newspaper is its independence. Whatever its position or character, at least it should have a soul of its own.
1921 In the *Manchester Guardian*, special centenary issue, 6 May.

Scott, Duncan Campell 1862–1947

Canadian poet. One of the 'Confederation Poets', he also wrote short stories, biographies and a play.

76 How strange the stars have grown;
The presage of extinction glows on their crests
And they are beautied with impermanence.
1916 'The Height of Land'.

Scott, F(rancis) R(eginald) 1899–1985

Canadian poet. A lawyer, professor and politician (a founder of the Canadian social democratic party, the Co-operative Commonwealth Federation), he established several important literary reviews. His collected poems were published in 1981.

77 I have sat by night beside a cold lake
And touched things smoother than moonlight on still water,
But the moon on this cloud sea is not human,
And here is no shore, no intimacy,
Only the start of space, the road to suns.
1945 'Trans Canada'.

78 Hidden in wonder and snow, or sudden with summer,
This land stares at the sun in a huge silence
Endlessly repeating something we cannot hear.
Inarticulate, arctic,
Not written on by history, empty as paper,
It leans away from the world with songs in its lakes
Older than love, and lost in the miles.
1954 Of Canada. 'Laurentian Shield'.

79 Newspapers are born free and everywhere are in chains.
1973 Aphorism, collected in John Robert Colombo (ed) *Colombo's Canadian Quotations* (1974).
➤ *See Rousseau 700:41.*

Scott, Robert Falcon 1868–1912

English Antarctic explorer. In 1900–4 he commanded the National Antarctic Expedition to the Ross Sea. On his second expedition he reached the South Pole (Jan 1912), only to discover that Amundsen had beaten him by a month. He and his party died on the way back; their bodies and diaries were found by a search party eight months later.

80 Great God! This is an awful place and terrible enough for us to have laboured to it without the reward of priority.
1912 Journal entry, 18 Jan. *Scott's Last Expedition: The Personal Journals of Captain R F Scott, CVO, RN, on His Journey to the South Pole* (published 1923).

81 Had we lived, I should have had a tale to tell of the hardihood, endurance, and courage of my companions which would have stirred the heart of every Englishman. These rough notes and our dead bodies must tell the tale.
1912 Message to the public. Quoted in *The Times*, 11 Feb 1913.

82 It seems a pity but I do not think I can write more. For God's sake look after our people.
1912 Last entry in journal, 29 Mar. In *Scott's Last Expedition: The Personal Journals of Captain R F Scott, CVO, RN, on His Journey to the South Pole* (published 1923).

Scott, Rose 1847–1925

Australian feminist.

83 Life is too short to waste on the admiration of one man.
Her habitual response to offers of marriage. Quoted in Jennifer Uglow (ed) *The Macmillan Dictionary of Women's Biography* (2nd edn, 1989).

Scott, Sir Walter 1771–1832

Scottish novelist and poet. He studied law and became an advocate and later a sheriff, but achieved worldwide fame as a writer of epic poetry and as the author of the *Waverley Novels*, promoting a fundamentally romantic image of history and in particular of Scotland's past.

84 The way was long, the wind was cold,
The Minstrel was infirm and old;
His withered cheek, and tresses grey,
Seemed to have known a better day;
The harp, his sole remaining joy,
Was carried by an orphan boy,
The last of all the Bards was he,
Who sung of Border chivalry.
1805 *The Lay of the Last Minstrel*, introduction.

85 He poured, to lord and lady gay,
The unpremeditated lay.
1805 *The Lay of the Last Minstrel*, introduction.

86 And said I that my limbs were old,
And said I that my blood was cold,
And that my kindly fire was fled,
And my poor withered heart was dead,
And that I might not sing of Love?
1805 *The Lay of the Last Minstrel*, canto 1, stanza 1.

87 If thou would'st view fair Melrose aright,
Go visit it by the pale moonlight.
1805 *The Lay of the Last Minstrel*, canto 2, stanza 1.

88 The woodland brook he bounding crossed,
And laughed, and shouted, 'Lost! lost! lost!'
1805 *The Lay of the Last Minstrel*, canto 3, stanza 13.

89 The Harper smiled, well pleased; for ne'er
Was flattery lost on poet's ear:
A simple race! they waste their toil
For the vain tribute of a smile.
1805 *The Lay of the Last Minstrel*, canto 4, conclusion.

90 Call it not vain:—they do not err
Who say, that when the Poet dies,
Mute Nature mourns her worshipper,
And celebrates his obsequies.
1805 *The Lay of the Last Minstrel*, canto 5, stanza 1.

91 Breathes there the man, with soul so dead,
Who never to himself hath said,
This is my own, my native land!
Whose heart hath ne'er within him burned,
As home his footsteps he hath turned
From wandering on a foreign strand!
1805 *The Lay of the Last Minstrel*, canto 6, stanza 1.

92 O Caledonia! stern and wild,
Meet nurse for a poetic child!
Land of brown heath and shaggy wood,
Land of the mountain and the flood.
Land of my sires! what mortal hand
Can e'er untie the filial band
That knits me to thy rugged strand!
1805 *The Lay of the Last Minstrel*, canto 6, stanza 2.

93 November's sky is chill and drear,
November's leaf is red and sear.
1808 *Marmion*, canto 1, introduction.

94 And come he slow, or come he fast,
It is but Death who comes at last.
1808 *Marmion*, canto 2, stanza 30.

95 Still is thy name in high account,
And still thy verse has charms,
Sir David Lindesay of the Mount,
Lord Lion King-at-arms!
1808 *Marmion*, canto 4, stanza 7.

96 O, young Lochinvar is come out of the west,
Through all the wide Border his steed was the best;
And save his good broadsword he weapon had none,
He rode all unarmed, and he rode all alone.
So faithful in love, and so dauntless in war,
There never was knight like the young Lochinvar.
1808 *Marmion*, canto 5, stanza 12, 'Lochinvar'.

97 Heap on more wood!—the wind is chill;
But let it whistle as it will,
We'll keep our Christmas merry still.
1808 *Marmion*, canto 6, introduction.

98 And dar'st thou then
To beard the lion in his den,
The Douglas in his hall?
1808 *Marmion*, canto 6, stanza 14.

99 Oh what a tangled web we weave,
When first we practise to deceive!
1808 *Marmion*, canto 6, stanza 17.

1 O Woman! in our hours of ease,
Uncertain, coy, and hard to please,
And variable as the shade

By the light quivering aspen made;
When pain and anguish wring the brow,
A ministering angel thou!
1808 *Marmion*, canto 6, stanza 30.

2 The stubborn spearmen still made good
Their dark impenetrable wood,
Each stepping where his comrade stood
The instant that he fell.
1808 *Marmion*, canto 6, stanza 34.

3 Still from the sire the son shall hear
Of the stern strife, and carnage drear,
Of Flodden's fatal field,
Where shivered was fair Scotland's spear,
And broken was her shield!
1808 *Marmion*, canto 6, stanza 34.

4 The stag at eve had drunk his fill,
Where danced the moon on Monan's rill.
1810 *The Lady of the Lake*, canto 1, stanza 1.

5 Hail to the Chief who in honour advances!
Honoured and bless'd be the evergreen Pine!
1810 *The Lady of the Lake*, canto 2, stanza 19, 'Boat Song'.

6 Time rolls his ceaseless course.
1810 *The Lady of the Lake*, canto 3, stanza 1.

7 He is gone on the mountain,
He is lost to the forest,
Like a summer-dried fountain,
When our need was the sorest.
1810 *The Lady of the Lake*, canto 3, stanza 16, 'Coronach'.

8 Like the dew on the mountain,
Like the foam on the river,
Like the bubble on the fountain,
Thou art gone, and for ever!
1810 *The Lady of the Lake*, canto 3, stanza 16, 'Coronach'.

9 Merry it is in the good greenwood,
When the mavis and merle are singing,
When the deer sweeps by, and the hounds are in cry,
And the hunter's horn is ringing.
1810 *The Lady of the Lake*, canto 4, stanza 12, 'Alice Brand'.

10 O, Brignal banks are wild and fair,
And Greta woods are green
And you may gather garlands there
Would grace a summer queen.
1813 *Rokeby*, canto 3, stanza 16.

11 A weary lot is thine, fair maid,
A weary lot is thine!
To pull the thorn thy brow to braid,
And press the rue for wine!
1813 *Rokeby*, canto 3, stanza 28, 'Song'.

12 Look back, and smile at perils past!
1813 *The Bridal of Triermain*, introduction.

13 He that steals a cow from a poor widow, or a stirk from a cottar, is a thief; he that lifts a drove from a Sassenach laird, is a gentleman-drover. And, besides, to take a tree from the forest, a salmon from the river, a deer from the hill, or a cow from a Lowland strath, is what no Highlander need ever think shame upon.
1814 Evan Dhu Maccombich to Edward Waverley. *Waverley*, ch.18.

14 I am heartily glad you continued to like Waverley to the end—the hero is a sneaking piece of imbecility and if he had married Flora she would have set him up upon the

chimney-piece as Count Boralaski's wife used to do with him.
1814 Letter to John Morritt, 28 Jul. Joseph Borowlaski was a Polish dwarf known as 'The Little Count' who left France at the Revolution and exhibited himself at fairs throughout Britain.

15 Then strip lads, and to it, though sharp be the weather,
And if, by mischance, you should happen to fall,
There are worse things in life than a tumble on the heather
And life is itself a game of football.
1815 On a match between the Scottish teams Ettrick and Selkirk, published in the *Edinburgh Journal*.

16 But ruffian stern, and soldier good,
The noble and the slave,
From various cause the same wild road,
On the same bloody morning, trode,
To that dark inn—the Grave!
1815 *The Lord of the Isles*, canto 6, stanza 26.

17 Pro-di-gi-ous!
1815 Dominie Sampson. *Guy Mannering*, ch.8.

18 'That sounds like nonsense, my dear.'
'Maybe so, my dear; but it may be very good law for all that.'
1815 Mrs and Mr Bertram in conversation. *Guy Mannering*, ch.9.

19 Gin by pailfuls, wine in rivers,
Dash the window-glass to shivers!
For three wild lads were we, brave boys,
And three wild lads were we;
Thou on the land, and I on the sand,
And Jack on the gallows-tree!
1815 *Guy Mannering*, ch.34.

20 The frolicsome company had begun to practise the ancient and now forgotten pastime of *High Jinks*.
1815 *Guy Mannering*, ch.36.

21 'Why weep ye by the tide, ladie?
Why weep ye by the tide?
I'll wed ye to my youngest son,
And ye sall be his bride:
And ye sall be his bride, ladie,
Sae comely to be seen'—
But aye she loot the tears down fa'
For Jock of Hazeldean.
1816 'Jock of Hazeldean', stanza 1.

22 'A chain of gold ye sall not lack,
Nor braid to bind your hair;
Nor mettled hound, nor managed hawk,
Nor palfrey fresh and fair.'
1816 'Jock of Hazeldean', stanza 3.

23 They sought her baith by bower and ha';
The ladie was not seen!
She's o'er the Border and awa'
Wi' Jock of Hazeldean.
1816 'Jock of Hazeldean', stanza 4.

24 Prætorian here, prætorian there, I mind the bigging o't.
1816 Edie Ochiltree to Jonathan Oldbuck. *The Antiquary*, ch.4.

25 It's no fish ye're buying—it's men's lives.
1816 Maggie Mucklebackit to Oldbuck. *The Antiquary*, ch.11.

26 It's weel wi' you gentles, that can sit in the house wi' handkerchers at your een when ye lose a friend; but the like o' us maun to our wark again, if our hearts were beating as hard as my hammer.

1816 Saunders Mucklebackit to Oldbuck. *The Antiquary*, ch.34.

27 He that is without name, without friends, without coin, without country, is still at least a man; and he that has all these is no more.
1817 Rob Roy to Francis Osbaldistone. *Rob Roy*, ch.21.

28 Come fill up my cup, come fill up my cann,
Come saddle my horses, and call up my man;
Come open your gates, and let me gae free,
I daurna stay langer in Bonny Dundee!
1817 *Rob Roy*, ch.23.

29 If your honour disna ken when ye hae a gude servant, I ken when I hae a gude master, and the deil be in my feet gin I leave ye.
1817 Andrew Fairservice to Francis Osbaldistone. *Rob Roy*, ch. 24.

30 It's ill taking the breeks aff a Hielandman.
1817 Andrew Fairservice to Bailie Nicol Jarvie. *Rob Roy*, ch.27.

31 There's a gude time coming.
1817 Rob Roy to the Duke. *Rob Roy*, ch.32.

32 Speak out, sir, and do not Maister or Campbell me—my foot is on my native heath, and my name is MacGregor!
1817 Rob Roy to Francis Osbaldistone. *Rob Roy*, ch.34.

33 Ye ken weel eneugh that women and gear are at the bottom of a' the mischief in this warld.
1817 Rob Roy to Francis Osbaldistone. *Rob Roy*, ch.35.

34 The hour's come, but not the man.
1818 *The Heart of Midlothian*, ch.4, motto.

35 'I dinna ken muckle about the law,' answered Mrs Howden; 'but I ken, when we had a king, and a chancellor, and parliament-men o' our ain, we could aye peeble them wi' stanes when they werena gude bairns—But naebody's nails can reach the length o' Lunnon.'
1818 *The Heart of Midlothian*, ch.4.

36 Jock, when ye hae naething else to do, ye may be aye sticking in a tree; it will be growing, Jock, when ye're sleeping.
1818 The Laird of Dumbiedikes to his son. *The Heart of Midlothian*, ch.8.

37 Never mind my grace, lassie; just speak out a plain tale, and show you have a Scotch tongue in your head.
1818 The Duke of Argyle to Jeanie Deans. *The Heart of Midlothian*, ch.35.

38 Dinna be chappit back or cast down wi' the first rough answer.
1818 Jeanie Deans to the Duke of Argyle. *The Heart of Midlothian*, ch.35.

39 Proud Maisie is in the wood,
Walking so early;
Sweet Robin sits on the bush,
Singing so rarely.
1818 *The Heart of Midlothian*, ch.40 (Madge Wildfire's song).

40 Look not thou on beauty's charming,—
Sit thou still when kings are arming.—
Taste not when the wine-cup glistens,—
Speak not when the people listens,—
Stop thine ear against the singer,—
From the red gold keep thy finger,—
Vacant heart, and hand, and eye,—
Easy live and quiet die.
1819 *The Bride of Lammermoor*, ch.3 (Lucy Ashton's song).

41 But no one shall find me rowing against the stream. I care not who knows it—I write for the general amusement.
1822 *The Fortunes of Nigel*, introductory epistle.

42 For a con-si-de-ra-tion.
1822 Trapbois. *The Fortunes of Nigel*, ch.22.

43 O Geordie, Jingling Geordie, it was grand to hear Baby Charles laying down the guilt of dissimulation and Steemie lecturing on the turpitude of incontinence.
1822 *The Fortunes of Nigel*, ch.31.

44 Carle, now the King's come!
Carle, now the King's come!
Thou shalt dance, and I will sing,
Carle, now the King's come!
1822 'Carle, Now the King's Come', written in celebration of George IV's visit to Edinburgh.

45 Ah! County Guy, the hour is nigh,
The sun has left the lea,
The orange flower perfumes the bower,
The breeze is on the sea.
1823 *Quentin Durward*, ch.4.

46 Fair, fat, and forty.
1823 *St Ronan's Well*, ch.7.

47 It's ill speaking between a fou man and a fasting.
1824 *Redgauntlet*, letter 11, 'Wandering Willie's Tale'.

48 The ae half of the warld thinks the tither daft.
1824 Peter Peebles to Justice Foxley. *Redgauntlet*, ch.7.

49 'Then, gentlemen,' said Redgauntlet, clasping his hands together as the words burst from him, 'the cause is lost for ever!'
1824 *Redgauntlet*, ch.23.

50 Widowed wife, and married maid,
Betrothed, betrayer, and betrayed!
1825 *The Betrothal*, ch.15.

51 Came through cold roads to as cold news.
1826 *Journal*, 16 Jan, referring to the financial collapse of his publisher, Constable, which led directly to Scott's own bankruptcy.

52 We had better remain in union with England, even at the risk of becoming a subordinate species of Northumberland, as far as national consequence is concerned, than remedy ourselves by even hinting the possibility of a rupture. But there is no harm in wishing Scotland to have just so much ill-nature, according to her own proverb, as may keep her good-nature from being abused.
1826 *Letters of Malachi Malagrowther on the Proposed Change of Currency*, letter 1.

53 If I can but get the sulky Scottish spirit set up, the devil won't turn them.
1826 *Journal*, 25 Feb.

54 The Big Bow-wow strain I can do myself like any now going; but the exquisite touch, which renders ordinary commonplace things and characters interesting, from the truth of description and the sentiment, is denied to me.
1826 On Jane Austen. *Journal*, 14 Mar.

55 But if you *unscotch* us you will find us damned mischievous Englishmen.
1826 Letter to J W Croker, 19 Mar.

56 I would like to be there, were it but to see how the cat jumps. One knows nothing of the world, if you are absent from it so long as I have been.
1826 *Journal*, 7 Oct, expressing frustration and wonder at the machinations of London bureaucracy which prevented him accessing government papers for his *Life of Napoleon*.

57 Long life to thy fame and peace to thy soul, Rob Burns! When I want to express a sentiment which I feel strongly, I find the phrase in Shakespeare—or thee. The blockheads talk of my being like Shakespeare—not fit to tie his brogues.
1826 *Journal*, 11 Dec.

58 To the Lords of convention 'twas Claver'se who spoke, 'Ere the King's crown shall fall there are crowns to be broke;
So let each Cavalier who loves honour and me, Come follow the bonnet of Bonny Dundee.'
1830 *The Doom of Devorgoil*, act 2, sc.2, 'Bonny Dundee', stanza 1.

59 No repose for Sir Walter but in the grave. Friends, don't let me expose myself—get me to bed—that's the only place.
1832 Quoted in John G Lockhart *Memoirs of the Life of Sir Walter Scott, Bart.* (1837–8). Scott had fallen asleep in his bath-chair while trying to write a few words.

60 Be a good man—be virtuous—be religious—be a good man. Nothing else will give you any comfort when you come to lie here.
1832 Last words, addressed to Lockhart, quoted in John G Lockhart *Memoirs of the Life of Sir Walter Scott, Bart.* (1837–8). Scott concluded by saying 'God bless you all.'

Scottish Metrical Psalms

61 The Lord's my shepherd, I'll not want.
He makes me down to lie
In pastures green: he leadeth me
the quiet waters by.
My soul he doth restore again:
and me to walk doth make
Within the paths of righteousness,
ev'n for his own name's sake.

Yea, though I walk in death's dark vale,
yet will I fear no ill:
For thou art with me; and thy rod
and staff me comfort still.
1650 Translation of Psalm 23:1–4.

62 God is our refuge and our strength,
in straits a present aid;
Therefore, although the earth remove,
we will not be afraid.
1650 Psalm 46:1–2.

63 How lovely is thy dwelling-place
O Lord of hosts, to me!
The tabernacles of thy grace
how pleasant, Lord, they be!
1650 Psalm 84:1.

64 All people that on earth do dwell,
Sing to the Lord with cheerful voice.
Him serve with mirth, his praise forth tell,
Come ye before him and rejoice.
Know that the Lord is God indeed;
Without our aid he did us make:

We are his folk, he doth us feed,
And for his sheep he doth us take.
1650 Psalm 100:1–3.

65 I to the hills will lift mine eyes,
from whence doth come mine aid.
My safety cometh from the Lord,
Who heav'n and earth hath made.
1650 Psalm 121:1–2.

Scribner, Charles, Jr 1921–95

US publisher, chairman of Charles Scribner's Sons (1977–8) and Scribner Book Companies from 1978. His autobiography is *In the Company of Writers: Life in Publishing* (1991).

66 Nowadays a sales conference resembles a Passion play: everybody is invited to participate and marvel at the drama.
1991 *In the Company of Writers: A Life in Publishing.*

Seaborg, Glenn 1912–99

US atomic scientist. His principal work was with Enrico Fermi's team, which achieved the first chain reaction in uranium-235 in 1942. He shared the 1951 Nobel prize for chemistry.

67 People must understand that science is inherently neither a potential for good nor for evil. It is a potential to be harnessed by man to do his bidding.
1964 Interview, 29 Sep.

Seacole, Mary c.1805–1884

Jamaican nurse and adventurer.

68 I wonder if the people of other countries are as fond of carrying with them everywhere their home habits as the English. I think not.
1857 *Wonderful Adventures of Mrs Seacole in Many Lands.*

Seaton, George *pseudonym of George Stenius* 1911–79

US screenwriter and director. He won Academy Awards for both *Miracle on 34th Street* (1947) and *The Country Girl* (1954).

69 For those who believe in God no explanation is necessary. For those who do not believe in God no explanation is possible.
1943 Prologue to *The Song of Bernadette.*

Seeger, Alan 1888–1916

US poet. He settled in Paris, and enlisted in the French Foreign Legion when World War I broke out. He was killed at the Battle of the Somme.

70 I have a rendezvous with Death
At some disputed barricade,
When Spring comes round with rustling shade
And apple blossoms fill the air.
I have a rendezvous with Death
When Spring brings back blue days and fair.
1916 'I Have a Rendezvous with Death', in the *North American Review*, Oct.

Seeger, Pete 1919–

US folk singer and songwriter.

71 Where have all the flowers gone?
1961 Title of song.

Seeley, Sir John Robert 1834–95

English historian, Professor of Modern History at Cambridge (1869). His *Ecce Homo* (1865), a popular life of Christ, caused much controversy. Other works include the authoritative *Life and Times of Stein* (1874), *Natural Religion* (1882) and *The Expansion of England* (1883).

72 We [the English] seem to have conquered and peopled half the world in a fit of absence of mind.
1883 *The Expansion of England.*

Segal, Erich 1937–

US novelist. He is known for the popular success of *Love Story*, which was both a bestselling novel and a major film.

73 Love means not ever having to say you're sorry.
1970 *Love Story*, ch.13.

Segovia, Andrés 1893–1987

Spanish guitarist. Influenced by the Spanish nationalist composers, he evolved a revolutionary guitar technique permitting the performance of a wide range of music, and many composers wrote works for him.

74 Electric guitars are an abomination, whoever heard of an electric violin? An electric cello? Or for that matter an electric singer?
Quoted in Rick Friedman *The Beatles: Words without Music* (1968).

Seibel, Cathy

Assistant US Attorney.

75 Just because you're rich doesn't mean you're not cheap.
1989 On the prosecution of hotel owner Leona Helmsley. In the *New York Times*, 24 Aug.

Seinfeld, Jerry 1954–

US comedian.

76 Everybody lies about sex. People lie during sex. If it weren't for lies, there'd be no sex.
1998 In the *New York Times*, 18 Dec.

Selden, John 1584–1654

English jurist, historian and antiquary. A member of the Long Parliament in 1640, he withdrew from politics after the execution of Charles I, of which he disapproved. His many writings on constitutional matters included *Titles of Honour* (1614), *Analecton Britannicon* (1615) and *History of Tithes* (1618). The most notable of his many tracts and treatises was the posthumous *Table Talk* (published 1689).

77 Every law is a contract between the king and the people and therefore to be kept.
Table Talk (published 1689).

78 Ignorance of the law excuses no man; not that all men know the law, but because 'tis an excuse every man will plead, and no man can tell how to confute him.
Table Talk (published 1689).

79 Those that govern most make least noise.
Table Talk (published 1689).

Self, Will 1961–

English novelist, columnist and critic. He was a cartoonist with the *New Statesman*, but turned to writing fiction. He was awarded the Geoffrey Faber Memorial Award in 1992.

80 No one ever complains if a great artist says that he was driven to create a masterpiece by a hunger for recognition and money. But a scientist? Well, he is meant to be disinterested, pure, his ambition merely to descry the cement of the universe. He isn't meant to use it to start laying his own patio.
  1991 *The Quantity Theory of Insanity and Five Supporting Propositions*, 'The Quantity Theory of Insanity'.

81 I think in retrospect that all those 'alternative' modes of living were little more than exercises in arrested development.
  1991 *The Quantity Theory of Insanity and Five Supporting Propositions*, 'The Quantity Theory of Insanity'.

82 I make no apology for preoccupying myself with architecture, television, conceptual art, restaurants and Jane Asher's cakes.
  2001 *Feeding Frenzy*.

Sellar, W(alter) C(arruthers) and Yeatman, R(obert) J(ulian) 1898–1951, 1897–1968

British humorous writers.

83 [Gladstone] spent his declining years trying to guess the answer to the Irish Question. Unfortunately, whenever he was getting warm, the Irish secretly changed the question.
  1930 *1066 and All That*.

84 The National Debt is a very Good Thing, and it would be dangerous to pay it off for fear of Political Economy.
  1930 *1066 and All That*.

Sellers, Peter 1925–80

English actor and comedian. He came to prominence in the *Goon Show* on radio, but is perhaps best remembered as the incompetent French detective Inspector Clouseau in a series of films that began with *The Pink Panther* (1963).

85 If you ask me to play myself, I will not know what to do. I do not know who or what I am.
  Attributed.

Selye, Hans 1907–83

Austrian-born Canadian endocrinologist, founder of Montreal's Institute of Experimental Medicine.

86 Stress is the state manifested by a specific syndrome which consists of all the nonspecifically inducted changes within a biologic system.
  1956 *The Stress of Life*.

Selznick, David O(liver) 1902–65

US cinema mogul. He founded his own company in 1936, producing the screen adaptation of *Gone with the Wind* in 1939. Other successes include *Rebecca* (1940), *Duel in the Sun* (1946) and *A Farewell to Arms* (1957).

87 This is the story of the unconquerable fortress—the American home.
  1944 *Since You Went Away*, opening line.

88 If they will only do their job…that is all that they are being overpaid for.
  Of his stars, while filming *The Garden of Allah*. Quoted in Maria Riva *Marlene Dietrich* (1992).

Seneca full name Lucius Annaeus Seneca called the Younger c.4 BC–65 AD

Roman Stoic philosopher, statesman and tragedian, son of the orator Seneca the Elder. He tutored Nero and for a time enjoyed considerable political influence, but he lost favour and was forced to commit suicide. His works include the *Epistulae morales ad Lucilium*, the *Apocolocyntosis divi Claudii* (literally 'The Pumpkinification of the Divine Claudius'), and several tragedies.

89 *Utrumque enim vitium est, et omnibus credere et nulli.*
  It is equally unsound to trust everyone and to trust no one.
  Epistulae, 3.4.

90 *Longum iter est per praecepta, breve et efficax per exempla.*
  The way is long if one follows precepts, but short and helpful, if one follows patterns.
  Epistulae, 6.5 (translated by R M Gummere).

91 *Homines dum docent discunt.*
  Men learn while they teach.
  Epistulae 7.8 (translated by R M Gummere).

92 *Vitae, non scholae discimus.*
  It is for life, not for school that we learn.
  Oral tradition based on Seneca's conclusion of a letter to Lucilius which says the opposite: 'Non vitae, sed scholae discimus', *Epistulae*, 106.12.

93 *Qui timide rogat, docet negare.*
  Who makes timid requests, invites denial.
  Phaedra, 593–4 (translated by F J Miller).

Senghor, Léopold Sédar 1906–2001

Senegalese poet who explored the theme of black African culture.

94 *J'ai choisi mon peuple noir peinant, mon peuple paysan, toute la race paysanne, par le monde.*
  I chose my black people struggling, my country people, all country people, in the world.
  1945 *Chants d'ombre*, 'Que m'accompagnent kára et balafong, 3'.

95 *Seul le rythme provoque le court-circuit poétique et transmue le cuivre en or, la parole en verbe.*
  Only rhythm brings about a poetic short-circuit and transforms the copper into gold, the words into life.
  1956 *Éthiopiques*, postface.

96 *Au contraire de l'Européen classique, le Négro-Africain ne se distingue pas de l'objet, il ne le tient pas à distance, il ne le regarde pas, il ne l'analyse pas… Il le touche, il le palpe, il le sent.*
  Unlike the classical European, the Black-African does not distinguish himself from an object. He does not hold it at a distance, he does not look at it, he does not examine it… He touches it, he fingers it, he *feels* it.
  1960 Au Congrès de l'Union nationale de la Jeunesse du Mali, Dakar.

97 *Danser, c'est découvrir et recréer, surtout lorsque la danse est danse d'amour. C'est, en tout cas, le meilleur mode de connaissance.*
  To dance is to discover and to recreate, above all when the dance is the dance of love. It is the best mode of knowledge.
  1960 Au Congrès de l'Union nationale de la Jeunesse du Mali, Dakar.

Senior, Nassau William 1790–1864

English economist. He stressed the importance of the last hour's work in the cotton factories and opposed the trade unions. His works include *On the Cost of Obtaining Money* (1830), *An Outline of the Science of Political Economy* (1836) and *Value of Money* (1840).

98 This barbarous feeling of nationality…has become the curse of Europe.
1850 *Diary*, 20 May.

Senna, Ayrton 1960–94

Brazilian Formula One driver. World champion in 1988, 1990, and 1991, he died after crashing during the San Marino Grand Prix.

99 To survive in grand prix racing, you need to be afraid. Fear is an important feeling. It helps you to race longer and live longer.
1994 In *The Times*, 3 May.
➤ See Berger 79:93.

Service, Robert William 1874–1958

English-born poet. He emigrated to Canada, and became famous for his popular ballads of life in the Canadian wilderness, which earned him the nickname 'The Canadian Kipling'. He also wrote several novels.

1 This is the law of the Yukon, that only the Strong shall thrive;
That surely the Weak shall perish, and only the Fit survive.
1907 *Songs of a Sourdough*, 'The Law of the Yukon'.

2 A promise made is a debt unpaid, and the trail has its own stern code.
1907 *Songs of a Sourdough*, 'The Cremation of Sam McGhee'.

3 Back of the bar, in a solo game, sat dangerous Dan McGrew,
And watching his luck was his light-o'-love, the lady that's known as Lou.
1907 *Songs of a Sourdough*, 'The Shooting of Dan McGrew'.

4 Ah! The clock is always slow;
It is later than you think.
1921 *Ballads of a Bohemian*, 'It Is Later Than You Think'.

5 When we, the Workers, all demand: What are WE fighting for?
Then we'll end that stupid crime, that devil's madness—War.
1921 *Ballads of a Bohemian*, 'Michael'.

Seuss, Dr *pseudonym of* *Theodor Seuss Geisel* 1904–91

US children's author and illustrator, remembered for his 'Beginner Books', intended to help teach reading, starting with *The Cat in the Hat* (1957).

6 We looked!
Then we saw him step in on the mat!
We looked!
And we saw him!
The Cat in the Hat!
1957 *The Cat in the Hat*.

7 You will see something new.
Two things. And I call them
Thing One and Thing Two.
1957 *The Cat in the Hat*.

8 Do you like green eggs and ham?
1960 *Green Eggs and Ham*.

Sévigné, Marie de Rabutin-Chantal, Marquise de 1626–96

French writer famed for her letters which recounted daily life at court and in her family. They were collected by her daughter and published in 1725.

9 *La grande amitié n'est jamais tranquille.*
Great friendship is never peaceful.
1671 Letter to Mme de Grignan, 16 Sep.

10 *Le temps vole et m'emporte malgré moi; j'ai beau vouloir le retenir, c'est lui qui m'entraîne; et cette pensée me fait grande peur: vous devinez à peu près pourquoi.*
Time flies and takes me with it despite my efforts; I'd like to hold it back, but it keeps dragging me along and this thought frightens me greatly: you can perhaps guess why.
1691 Letter to the Comte de Bussy-Rabutin, 12 Jul.

Sexton, Anne *née* *Harvey* 1928–74

US poet, lecturer, and writer of children's books. Her works include *To Bedlam and Part Way Back* (1962), *All My Pretty Ones* (1962), *Live or Die* (1966), for which she won a Pulitzer Prize (1967), and *The Death Notebooks* (1974). She committed suicide.

11 Go child, who is my sin and nothing more.
1962 *To Bedlam and Part Way Back*, 'Unknown Child in the Maternity Ward'.

12 Now I fold you down, my drunkard, my navigator, my first lost keeper, to love or look at later.
1962 On photographs of her dead father. *All My Pretty Ones*, 'All My Pretty Ones'.

13 Whether you are pretty or not, I outlive you, bend down my strange face to yours and forgive you.
1962 *All My Pretty Ones*, 'All My Pretty Ones'.

14 In a dream you are never eighty.
1962 *All My Pretty Ones*, 'Old'.

15 But suicides have a special language.
Like carpenters they want to know *which tools*.
They never ask *why* build.
1964 'Wanting To Die', dated 3 Feb. Collected in *Live or Die* (1966).

16 I was tired of being a woman, tired of the spoons and the pots, tired of my mouth and my breasts tired of the cosmetics and the silks…
I was tired of the gender of things.
1966 *Live or Die*, 'Consorting with Angels'.

17 The sea is mother-death and she is a mighty female, the one who wins, the one who sucks us all up.
1971 Journal entry, 19 Nov, in *The Poet's Story*, 'A Small Journal'.

18 It doesn't matter who my father was; it matters who I remember he was.
1972 Journal entry, 1 Jan, in *The Poet's Story*, 'A Small Journal'.

19 The Awful Rowing Toward God.
1975 Title of book.

20 God owns heaven
but He craves the earth.
1975 *The Awful Rowing Toward God*, 'The Earth'.

Shaffer, Peter 1926–

English dramatist. His best-known plays include *Equus* (1973) and *Amadeus* (1979).

21 All my wife has ever taken from the Mediterranean—from that whole vast intuitive culture—are four bottles of Chianti to make into lamps.
1973 *Equus*, act 1, sc.18.

22 We keep saying old people are square. Then when they aren't—we don't like it!
1973 *Equus*, act 2, sc.31.

Shakespeare, William 1564–1616

English poet, playwright and actor. He lived in Stratford-upon-Avon, the home of his wife and children, and in London, where he worked in the theatre, becoming England's greatest playwright. His influence on literature and language throughout the world has been immense. The dates of composition of many of the plays are uncertain. Line numbers conform to *The Oxford Shakespeare* (Oxford University Press, 1988).

23 Home-keeping youth have ever homely wits.
1590–1 Valentine. *The Two Gentlemen of Verona*, act 1, sc.1, l.2.

24 He was more than over-shoes in love.
1590–1 Proteus, of Lysander. *The Two Gentlemen of Verona*, act 1, sc.1, l.24.

25 I have no other but a woman's reason:
I think him so because I think him so.
1590–1 Lucetta, explaining her preference for Proteus. *The Two Gentlemen of Verona*, act 1, sc.2, l.23–4.

26 O, how this spring of love resembleth
The uncertain glory of an April day,
Which now shows all the beauty of the sun,
And by and by a cloud takes all away.
1590–1 Proteus. *The Two Gentlemen of Verona*, act 1, sc.3, l.84–7.

27 I was in love with my bed.
1590–1 Speed. *The Two Gentlemen of Verona*, act 2, sc.1, l.76.

28 What, gone without a word?
Ay, so true love should do. It cannot speak,
For truth hath better deeds than words to grace it.
1590–1 Proteus. *The Two Gentlemen of Verona*, act 2, sc.2, l.16–18.

29 A fine volley of words, gentlemen, and quickly shot off.
1590–1 Silvia to Thurio and Valentine. *The Two Gentlemen of Verona*, act 2, sc.4, l.32.

30 When I was sick, you gave me bitter pills,
And I must minister the like to you.
1590–1 Proteus to Valentine. *The Two Gentlemen of Verona*, act 2, sc.4, l.147–8.

31 For love, thou know'st, is full of jealousy.
1590–1 Valentine. *The Two Gentlemen of Verona*, act 2, sc.4, l.175.

32 As one nail by strength drives out another,
So the remembrance of my former love
Is by a newer object quite forgotten.
1590–1 Proteus. *The Two Gentlemen of Verona*, act 2, sc.4, l.191–3.

33 Didst thou but know the inly touch of love
Thou wouldst as soon go kindle fire with snow
As seek to quench the fire of love with words
1590–1 Julia to Lucetta. *The Two Gentlemen of Verona*, act 2, sc.7, l.18–20.

34 Win her with gifts if she respects not words.
Dumb jewels often in their silent kind

More than quick words do move a woman's mind.
1590–1 Valentine to Duke. *The Two Gentlemen of Verona*, act 3, sc.1, l.89–91.

35 Love is like a child
That longs for everything that he can come by.
1590–1 Duke to Valentine. *The Two Gentlemen of Verona*, act 3, sc.1, l.124–5.

36 Except I be by Silvia in the night
There is no music in the nightingale.
Unless I look on Silvia in the day
There is no day for me to look upon.
1590–1 Valentine. *The Two Gentlemen of Verona*, act 3, sc.1, l.178–81.

37 Slander Valentine
With falsehood, cowardice, and poor descent,
Three things that women highly hold in hate.
1590–1 Proteus to Duke. *The Two Gentlemen of Verona*, act 3, sc.2, l.31–3.

38 You must lay lime to tangle her desires
By wailful sonnets.
1590–1 Proteus to Thurio. *The Two Gentlemen of Verona*, act 3, sc.2, l.68–9.

39 Who is Silvia? What is she,
That all our swains commend her?
1590–1 Song. *The Two Gentlemen of Verona*, act 4, sc.2, l.38–9.

40 How use doth breed a habit in a man!
1590–1 Valentine. *The Two Gentlemen of Verona*, act 5, sc.4, l.1.

41 O heaven, were man
But constant, he were perfect!
1590–1 Proteus. *The Two Gentlemen of Verona*, act 5, sc.4, l.109–10.

42 My thoughts are whirlèd like a potter's wheel;
I know not where I am, nor what I do.
1592 Talbot. *Henry VI Part One*, act 1, sc.7, l.19–20.

43 I have heard it said, 'Unbidden guests
Are often welcomest when they are gone'.
1592 Bedford. *Henry VI Part One*, act 2, sc.2, l.55–6.

44 Faith, I have been a truant in the law,
And never yet could frame my will to it,
And therefore frame the law unto my will.
1592 Suffolk. *Henry VI Part One*, act 2, sc.4, l.7–9.

45 We will bestow you in some better place,
Fitter for sickness and for crazy age.
1592 Talbot to Bedford. *Henry VI Part One*, act 3, sc.5, l.47–8.

46 I owe him little duty and less love.
1592 Somerset, of York. *Henry VI Part One*, act 4, sc.4, l.34.

47 Beauty's princely majesty is such,
Confounds the tongue, and makes the senses rough.
1592 Suffolk. *Henry VI Part One*, act 5, sc.5, l.26–7.

48 She's beautiful, and therefore to be wooed;
She is a woman, therefore to be won.
1592 Suffolk, of Margaret. *Henry VI Part One*, act 5, sc.5, l.34–5.

49 To be a queen in bondage is more vile
Than is a slave in base servility,
For princes should be free.
1592 Margaret. *Henry VI Part One*, act 5, sc.5, l.68–70.

50 Marriage is a matter of more worth
Than to be dealt in by attorneyship.
1592 Suffolk. *Henry VI Part One*, act 5, sc.7, l.55–6.

51 O Lord that lends me life,

Lend me a heart replete with thankfulness.
1592 Henry of Queen Margaret. *Henry VI Part Two*, act 1, sc.1, l.19–20.

52 All his mind is bent to holiness,
To number Ave-Maries on his beads.
1592 Queen Margaret of Henry. *Henry VI Part Two*, act 1, sc.3, l.58–9.

53 Could I come near your beauty with my nails,
I'd set my ten commandments in your face.
1592 Duchess to Queen Margaret. *Henry VI Part Two*, act 1, sc.3, l.144–5.

54 How irksome is this music to my heart!
When such strings jar, what hope of harmony?
1592 Henry. *Henry VI Part Two*, act 2, sc.1, l.59–60.

55 God shall be my hope,
My stay, my guide, and lantern to my feet.
1592 Henry. *Henry VI Part Two*, act 2, sc.3, l.24–5.

56 Smooth runs the water where the brook is deep,
And in his simple show he harbours treason.
1592 Suffolk to Henry. *Henry VI Part Two*, act 3, sc.1, l.53–4.

57 The fox barks not when he would steal the lamb.
1592 Suffolk. *Henry VI Part Two*, act 3, sc.1, l.55.

58 The commons, like an angry hive of bees
That want their leader, scatter up and down
And care not who they sting.
1592 Warwick to Henry. *Henry VI Part Two*, act 3, sc.2, l.125–7.

59 What stronger breastplate than a heart untainted?
Thrice is he armed that hath his quarrel just;
And he but naked, though locked up in steel,
Whose conscience with injustice is corrupted.
1592 Henry. *Henry VI Part Two*, act 3, sc.2, l.232–5.

60 Forbear to judge, for we are sinners all.
1592 Henry. *Henry VI Part Two*, act 3, sc.3, l.31.

61 The gaudy, babbling, and remorseful day
Is crept into the bosom of the sea.
1592 Captain. *Henry VI Part Two*, act 4, sc.1, l.1–2.

62 I say it was never merry world in England since
gentlemen came up.
1592 Second rebel. *Henry VI Part Two*, act 4, sc.2, l.9–10.

63 There shall be in England seven halfpenny loaves sold
for a penny, the three-hooped pot shall have ten hoops,
and I will make it felony to drink small beer.
1592 Cade. *Henry VI Part Two*, act 4, sc.2, l.67–9.

64 The first thing we do let's kill all the lawyers.
1592 The Butcher. *Henry VI Part Two*, act 4, sc.2, l.78.

65 And Adam was a gardener.
1592 Cade. *Henry VI Part Two*, act 4, sc.2, l.133.

66 Thou hast most traitorously corrupted the youth of the
realm in erecting a grammar school; and, whereas
before, our forefathers had no other books but the score
and the tally, thou hast caused printing to be used and,
contrary to the King his crown and dignity, thou hast
built a paper-mill. It will be proved to thy face that thou
hast men about thee that usually talk of a noun and a verb
and such abominable words as no Christian ear can
endure to hear.
1592 Cade. *Henry VI Part Two*, act 4, sc.7, l.30–8.

67 Ignorance is the curse of God,
Knowledge the wing wherewith we fly to heaven.
1592 Saye. *Henry VI Part Two*, act 4, sc.7, l.72–3.

68 It is great sin to swear unto a sin,
But greater sin to keep a sinful oath.
1592 Salisbury to Henry. *Henry VI Part Two*, act 5, sc.1, l.180–1.

69 Farewell, faint-hearted and degenerate king,
In whose cold blood no spark of honour bides.
1592 Westmorland to Henry. *Henry VI Part Three*, act 1, sc.1, l.184–5.

70 O tiger's heart wrapped in a woman's hide!
1592 York to Margaret. *Henry VI Part Three*, act 1, sc.4, l.138.

71 Women are soft, mild, pitiful and flexible—
Thou stern, obdurate, flinty, rough, remorseless.
1592 York to Margaret. *Henry VI Part Three*, act 1, sc.4, l.142–3.

72 Many strokes, though with a little axe,
Hews down and fells the hardest-timbered oak.
1592 Messenger to Richard telling of his father York's death.
Henry VI Part Three, act 2, sc.1, l.54–5.

73 To weep is to make less the depth of grief;
Tears, then, for babes—blows and revenge for me!
1592 Richard. *Henry VI Part Three*, act 2, sc.1, l.85–6.

74 This battle fares like to the morning's war,
When dying clouds contend with growing light,
What time the shepherd, blowing of his nails,
Can neither call it perfect day nor night.
1592 Henry. *Henry VI Part Three*, act 2, sc.5, l.1–4.

75 O God! Methinks it were a happy life
To be no better than a homely swain.
To sit upon a hill, as I do now;
To carve out dials quaintly, point by point.
1592 Henry. *Henry VI Part Three*, act 2, sc.5, l.21–4.

76 Thereby to see the minutes how they run:
How many makes the hour full complete,
How many hours brings about the day,
How many days will finish up the year,
How many years a mortal man may live.
1592 Henry. *Henry VI Part Three*, act 2, sc.5, l.25–9.

77 Gives not the hawthorn bush a sweeter shade
To shepherds looking on their seely sheep
Than doth a rich embroidered canopy
To kings that fear their subjects' treachery?
1592 Henry. *Henry VI Part Three*, act 2, sc.5, l.42–5.

78 The common people swarm like summer flies.
1592 Clifford. *Henry VI Part Three*, act 2, sc.6, l.8.

79 I know I am too mean to be your queen,
And yet too good to be your concubine.
1592 Lady Gray to Edward. *Henry VI Part Three*, act 3, sc.2, l.97–8.

80 Hasty marriage seldom proveth well.
1592 Richard of Gloucester. *Henry VI Part Three*, act 4, sc.1, l.18.

81 What fates impose, that men must needs abide.
It boots not to resist both wind and tide.
1592 Edward. *Henry VI Part Three*, act 4, sc.4, l.31–2.

82 Fearless minds climb soonest unto crowns.
1592 Richard of Gloucester. *Henry VI Part Three*, act 4, sc.8, l.62.

83 My pity hath been balm to heal their wounds.
1592 Henry. *Henry VI Part Three*, act 4, sc.10, l.9.

84 Lo now my glory smeared in dust and blood.
My parks, my walks, my manors that I had,
Even now forsake me, and of all my lands
Is nothing left me but my body's length.
1592 Warwick wounded and dying. *Henry VI Part Three*, act 5, sc.2, l.23–6.

85 Why, courage, then—what cannot be avoided
'Twere childish weakness to lament or fear.
1592 Margaret. *Henry VI Part Three*, act 5, sc.4, l.37–8.

86 Down, down to hell; and say I sent thee thither!
1592 Richard of Gloucester to Henry. *Henry VI Part Three*, act 5, sc.6, l.67.

87 Since the heavens have shaped my body so,
Let hell make crooked my mind to answer it.
I had no father, I am like no father;
I have no brother, I am like no brother;
And this word, 'love', which greybeards call divine,
Be resident in men like one another
And not in me—I am myself alone.
1592 Richard of Gloucester. *Henry VI Part Three*, act 5, sc.6, l.78–84.

88 Wilt thou draw near the nature of the gods?
Draw near them then in being merciful.
1592 Tamora to Titus. *Titus Andronicus*, act 1, sc.1, l.117–18.

89 Give me a staff of honour for mine age,
But not a sceptre to control the world.
1592 Titus. *Titus Andronicus*, act 1, sc.1, l.198–9.

90 Vengeance is in my heart, death in my hand,
Blood and revenge are hammering in my head.
1592 Aaron to Tamora. *Titus Andronicus*, act 2, sc.3, l.38–9.

91 Dost thou not perceive
That Rome is but a wilderness of tigers?
1592 Titus to Lucius. *Titus Andronicus*, act 3, sc.1, l.52–3.

92 To weep with them that weep doth ease some deal,
But sorrow flouted at is double death.
1592 Marcus. *Titus Andronicus*, act 3, sc.1, l.243–4.

93 My heart, all mad with misery,
Beats in the hollow prison of my flesh.
1592 Titus. *Titus Andronicus*, act 3, sc.2, l.9–10.

94 I'll to thy closet and go read with thee
Sad stories chancèd in the times of old.
1592 Titus to Lavinia. *Titus Andronicus*, act 3, sc.2, l.81–2.

95 I have heard my grandsire say full oft
Extremity of griefs would make men mad.
1592 Young Lucius. *Titus Andronicus*, act 4, sc.1, l.18–19.

96 The eagle suffers little birds to sing,
And is not careful what they mean thereby,
Knowing that with the shadow of his wings
He can at pleasure stint their melody.
1592 Tamora to Saturninus. *Titus Andronicus*, act 4, sc.4, l.83–6.

97 If one good deed in all my life I did
I do repent it from my very soul.
1592 Aaron. *Titus Andronicus*, act 5, sc.3, l.188–9.

98 Now is the winter of our discontent
Made glorious summer by this son of York.
1592–3 Richard. *Richard III*, act 1, sc.1, l.1–2.

99 Grim-visaged war hath smoothed his wrinkled front,
And now—instead of mounting barbèd steeds
To fright the souls of fearful adversaries—
He capers nimbly in a lady's chamber
To the lascivious pleasing of a lute.
But I, that am not shaped for sportive tricks
Nor made to court an amorous looking-glass.
1592–3 Richard. *Richard III*, act 1, sc.1, l.9–15.

1 Cheated of feature by dissembling nature,
Deformed, unfinished, sent before my time
Into this breathing world scarce half made up.
1592–3 Richard. *Richard III*, act 1, sc.1, l.19–21.

2 I in this weak piping time of peace
Have no delight to pass away the time,
Unless to spy my shadow in the sun
And descant on mine own deformity.
1592–3 Richard. *Richard III*, act 1, sc.1, l.24–7.

3 Teach not thy lip such scorn, for it was made
For kissing, lady, not for such contempt.
1592–3 Richard to Lady Anne. *Richard III*, act 1, sc.2, l.159–60.

4 Was ever woman in this humour wooed?
Was ever woman in this humour won?
1592–3 Richard. *Richard III*, act 1, sc.2, l.215–16.

5 Were you snarling all before I came,
Ready to catch each other by the throat,
And turn you all your hatred now on me?
1592–3 Margaret. *Richard III*, act 1, sc.3, l.185–7.

6 They that stand high have many blasts to shake them,
And if they fall they dash themselves to pieces.
1592–3 Margaret. *Richard III*, act 1, sc.3, l.257–8.

7 And thus I clothe my naked villainy
With odd old ends, stol'n forth of Holy Writ,
And seem a saint when most I play the devil.
1592–3 Richard. *Richard III*, act 1, sc.3, l.334–6.

8 O Lord! Methought what pain it was to drown,
What dreadful noise of waters in my ears,
What sights of ugly death within my eyes.
Methoughts I saw a thousand fearful wrecks,
Ten thousand men that fishes gnawed upon,
Wedges of gold, great ouches, heaps of pearl,
Inestimable stones, unvalued jewels,
All scattered in the bottom of the sea.
1592–3 Clarence, shortly before he is murdered. *Richard III*, act 1, sc.4, l.21–8.

9 Woe to that land that's governed by a child.
1592–3 Third Citizen. *Richard III*, act 2, sc.3, l.11.

10 So wise so young, they say, do never live long.
1592–3 Richard, aside. *Richard III*, act 3, sc.1, l.79.

11 Talk'st thou to me of 'ifs'? Thou art a traitor.—
Off with his head.
1592–3 Richard. *Richard III*, act 3, sc.4, l.75–6.

12 I am not in the giving vein today.
1592–3 Richard. *Richard III*, act 4, sc.2, l.119.

13 Thou cam'st on earth to make the earth my hell.
1592–3 Duchess of York to Richard. *Richard III*, act 4, sc.4, l.167.

14 True hope is swift, and flies with swallows' wings.
1592–3 Henry, Earl of Richmond. *Richard III*, act 5, sc.2, l.23.

15 The King's name is a tower of strength.
1592–3 Richard. *Richard III*, act 5, sc.3, l.12.

16 Give me another horse! Bind up my wounds!
Have mercy, Jesu!—Soft, I did but dream.
O coward conscience, how dost thou afflict me?
1592–3 Richard. *Richard III*, act 5, sc.5, l.131–3.

17 Richard loves Richard; that is, I am I.
1592–3 Richard. *Richard III*, act 5, sc.5, l.137.

18 My conscience hath a thousand several tongues,
And every tongue brings in a several tale,
And every tale condemns me for a villain.
1592–3 Richard. *Richard III*, act 5, sc.5, l.147–9.

19 There is no creature loves me,

And if I die no soul will pity me.
Nay, wherefore should they?—Since that I myself
Find in myself no pity to myself.
1592–3 Richard. *Richard III*, act 5, sc.5, l.154–7.

20 Methought the souls of all that I had murdered
Came to my tent, and every one did threat
Tomorrow's vengeance on the head of Richard.
1592–3 Richard on the eve of the Battle of Bosworth. *Richard III*, act 5, sc.5, l.158–60.

21 Conscience is but a word that cowards use,
Devised at first to keep the strong in awe.
Our strong arms be our conscience; swords, our law.
March on, join bravely! Let us to't, pell mell—
If not to heaven, then hand in hand to hell.
1592–3 Richard. *Richard III*, act 5, sc.6, l.39–43.

22 A thousand hearts are great within my bosom.
Advance our standards! Set upon the foes!
Our ancient word of courage, fair Saint George,
Inspire us with the spleen of fiery dragons.
Upon them! Victory sits on our helms!
1592–3 Richard. *Richard III*, act 5, sc.6, l.77–81.

23 A horse! A horse! My kingdom for a horse!
1592–3 Richard. *Richard III*, act 5, sc.7, l.7.

24 Slave, I have set my life upon a cast,
And I will stand the hazard of the die.
1592–3 Richard. *Richard III*, act 5, sc.7, l.9–10.

25 Frame your mind to mirth and merriment,
Which bars a thousand harms, and lengthens life.
1593 Messenger to Sly. *The Taming of the Shrew*, Induction 2, l.131–2.

26 Think'st thou, Hortensio, though her father be very rich,
any man is so very a fool to be married to hell?
1593 Gremio. *The Taming of the Shrew*, act 1, sc.1, l.122–4.

27 There's small choice in rotten apples.
1593 Hortensio to Gremio. *The Taming of the Shrew*, act 1, sc.1, l.133–4.

28 I come to wive it wealthily in Padua;
If wealthily, then happily in Padua.
1593 Petruccio to Hortensio. *The Taming of the Shrew*, act 1, sc.2, l.74–5.

29 O this learning, what a thing it is!
1593 Gremio. *The Taming of the Shrew*, act 1, sc.2, l.157.

30 She is your treasure, she must have a husband.
I must dance barefoot on her wedding day,
And for your love to her lead apes in hell.
1593 Katherine. *The Taming of the Shrew*, act 2, sc.1, l.32–4.

31 I am rough, and woo not like a babe.
1593 Petruccio. *The Taming of the Shrew*, act 2, sc.1, l.137.

32 Good morrow, Kate, for that's your name, I hear.
1593 Petruccio. *The Taming of the Shrew*, act 2, sc.1, l.182.

33 You are called plain Kate,
And bonny Kate, and sometimes Kate the curst,
But Kate, the prettiest Kate in Christendom,
Kate of Kate Hall, my super-dainty Kate.
1593 Petruccio. *The Taming of the Shrew*, act 2, sc.1, l.185–8.

34 Your father hath consented
That you shall be my wife, your dowry 'greed on,
And will you, nill you, I will marry you.
1593 Petruccio to Kate. *The Taming of the Shrew*, act 2, sc.1, l.263–5.

35 We will have rings, and things, and fine array;
And kiss me, Kate. We will be married o' Sunday.
1593 Petruccio. *The Taming of the Shrew*, act 2, sc.1, l.319–20.

36 Preposterous ass, that never read so far
To know the cause why music was ordained!
Was it not to refresh the mind of man
After his studies or his usual pain?
1593 Lucentio to Hortensio. *The Taming of the Shrew*, act 3, sc.1, l.9–12.

37 Old fashions please me best. I am not so nice
To change true rules for odd inventions.
1593 Bianca to Hortensio. *The Taming of the Shrew*, act 3, sc.1, l.78–9.

38 Go, girl. I cannot blame thee now to weep.
For such an injury would vex a very saint.
1593 Baptista. *The Taming of the Shrew*, act 3, sc.2, l.27–8.

39 To me she's married, not unto my clothes.
1593 Petruccio. *The Taming of the Shrew*, act 3, sc.2, l.117.

40 He took the bride about the neck
And kissed her lips with such a clamorous smack
That at the parting all the church did echo.
1593 Gremio, of Petruccio. *The Taming of the Shrew*, act 3, sc.3, l.50–2.

41 This is a way to kill a wife with kindness.
1593 Petruccio. *The Taming of the Shrew*, act 4, sc.1, l.194.

42 How say you to a fat tripe finely broiled?
1593 Grumio to Katherine. *The Taming of the Shrew*, act 4, sc.3, l.20.

43 What, is the jay more precious than the lark
Because his feathers are more beautiful?
Or is the adder better than the eel
Because his painted skin contents the eye?
1593 Petruccio to Kate. *The Taming of the Shrew*, act 4, sc.3, l.173–6.

44 Your plainness and your shortness please me well.
1593 Baptista to Pedant. *The Taming of the Shrew*, act 4, sc.4, l.38.

45 Then God be blessed, it is the blessèd sun,
But sun it is not when you say it is not,
And the moon changes even as your mind.
What you will have it named, even that it is,
And so it shall be still for Katherine.
1593 Katherine. *The Taming of the Shrew*, act 4, sc.6, l.19–23.

46 Thy husband is thy lord, thy life, thy keeper,
Thy head, thy sovereign.
1593 Katherine. *The Taming of the Shrew*, act 5, sc.2, l.151–2.

47 I am ashamed that women are so simple
To offer war where they should kneel for peace.
1593 Katherine. *The Taming of the Shrew*, act 5, sc.2, l.166–7.

48 Come on, and kiss me, Kate.
1593 Katherine. *The Taming of the Shrew*, act 5, sc.2, l.185.

49 Hunting he loved, but love he laughed to scorn.
1593 *Venus and Adonis*, stanza 1, l.4.

50 Make use of time; let not advantage slip.
Beauty within itself should not be wasted.
Fair flowers that are not gathered in their prime
Rot, and consume themselves in little time.
1593 *Venus and Adonis*, stanza 22, l.129–32.

51 Bid me discourse, I will enchant thine ear.
1593 *Venus and Adonis*, stanza 25, l.145.

52 Love is a spirit all compact of fire,

Not gross to sink, but light, and will aspire.
1593 *Venus and Adonis*, stanza 25, l.149–50.

53 Affection is a coal that must be cooled;
Else, suffered, it will set the heart on fire.
1593 *Venus and Adonis*, stanza 65, l.387–8.

54 Dismiss your vows, your feignèd tears, your flatt'ry;
For where a heart is hard they make no batt'ry.
1593 *Venus and Adonis*, stanza 71, l.425–6.

55 Melodious discord, heavenly tune harsh sounding,
Ear's deep-sweet music, and heart's deep-sore
wounding.
1593 *Venus and Adonis*, stanza 72, l.431–2.

56 Love comforteth, like sunshine after rain.
1593 *Venus and Adonis*, stanza 134, l.799.

57 Their copious stories, oftentimes begun,
End without audience, and are never done.
1593 *Venus and Adonis*, stanza 141, l.845–6.

58 I to the world am like a drop of water
That in the ocean seeks another drop.
1594 Antipholus of Syracuse. *The Comedy of Errors*, act 1, sc.2,
l.35–6.

59 They say this town is full of cozenage,
As nimble jugglers that deceive the eye,
Dark-working sorcerers that change the mind,
Soul-killing witches that deform the body.
1594 Antipholus of Syracuse. *The Comedy of Errors*, act 1, sc.2,
l.97–100.

60 Am I so round with you as you with me,
That like a football you do spurn me thus?
You spurn me hence, and he will spurn me hither.
If I last in this service, you must case me in leather.
1594 Dromio of Ephesus. *The Comedy of Errors*, act 2, sc.1, l.81–4.

61 They brought one Pinch, a hungry lean-faced villain,
A mere anatomy, a mountebank,
A threadbare juggler, and a fortune-teller,
A needy, hollow-eyed, sharp-looking wretch,
A living dead man.
1594 Antipholus of Ephesus. *The Comedy of Errors*, act 5, sc.1,
l.238–42.

62 Respect and reason wait on wrinkled age!
1594 *The Rape of Lucrece*, stanza 39, l.275.

63 Thy beauty hath ensnared thee to this night.
1594 *The Rape of Lucrece*, stanza 70, l.485.

64 To show the beldame daughters of her daughter,
To make the child a man, the man a child,
To slay the tiger that doth live by slaughter,
To tame the unicorn and lion wild,
To mock the subtle in themselves beguiled,
To cheer the ploughman with increasing crops,
And waste huge stones with little water drops.
1594 *The Rape of Lucrece*, stanza 137, l.953–9.

65 Like an unpractised swimmer plunging still,
With too much labour drowns for want of skill.
1594 *The Rape of Lucrece*, stanza 157, l.1098–9.

66 It cannot be, I find,
But such a face should bear a wicked mind.
1594 *The Rape of Lucrece*, stanza 220, l.1539–40.

67 Let fame, that all hunt after in their lives,
Live registered upon our brazen tombs,
And then grace us in the disgrace of death

When, spite of cormorant devouring time,
Th'endeavour of this present breath may buy
That honour which shall bate his scythe's keen edge
And make us heirs of all eternity.
1594–5 King. *Love's Labour's Lost*, act 1, sc.1, l.1–7.

68 Study is like the heavens' glorious sun,
That will not be deep searched with saucy looks.
1594–5 Biron. *Love's Labour's Lost*, act 1, sc.1, l.84–5.

69 Small have continual plodders ever won,
Save base authority from others' books.
1594–5 Biron to King. *Love's Labour's Lost*, act 1, sc.1, l.86–7.

70 How well he's read, to reason against reading!
1594–5 King. *Love's Labour's Lost*, act 1, sc.1, l.94.

71 At Christmas I no more desire a rose
Than wish a snow in May's new-fangled shows.
1594–5 Biron. *Love's Labour's Lost*, act 1, sc.1, l.105–6.

72 Necessity will make us all forsworn.
1594–5 Biron. *Love's Labour's Lost*, act 1, sc.1, l.147.

73 A man in all the world's new fashion planted,
That hath a mint of phrases in his brain.
One who the music of his own vain tongue
Doth ravish like enchanting harmony.
1594–5 King, of Armado. *Love's Labour's Lost*, act 1, sc.1, l.162–5.

74 A child of our grandmother Eve, a female, or, for thy more
sweet understanding, a woman.
1594–5 Armado's letter. *Love's Labour's Lost*, act 1, sc.1, l.255.

75 Assist me, some extemporal god of rhyme, for I am sure I
shall turn sonnet. Devise wit, write pen, for I am for
whole volumes, in folio.
1594–5 Armado. *Love's Labour's Lost*, act 1, sc.2, l.174–6.

76 This wimpled, whining, purblind, wayward boy,
This Signor Junior, giant dwarf, Dan Cupid,
Regent of love-rhymes, lord of folded arms,
Th'anointed sovereign of sighs and groans,
Liege of all loiterers and malcontents,
Dread prince of plackets, king of codpieces,
Sole imperator and great general
Of trotting paritors—O my little heart!
1594–5 Biron. *Love's Labour's Lost*, act 3, sc.1, l.174–81.

77 A giving hand, though foul, shall have fair praise.
1594–5 Princess. *Love's Labour's Lost*, act 4, sc.1, l.23.

78 O thou monster ignorance, how deformed dost thou
look!
1594–5 Holofernes, to Dull. *Love's Labour's Lost*, act 4, sc.2, l.23.

79 He hath never fed of the dainties that are bred in a book.
He hath not eat paper, as it were, he hath not drunk ink.
1594–5 Nathaniel, of Dull. *Love's Labour's Lost*, act 4, sc.2, l.24–5.

80 The elegancy, facility, and golden cadence of poesy.
1594–5 Holofernes. *Love's Labour's Lost*, act 4, sc.2, l.123.

81 By heaven, I do love; and it hath taught me to rhyme, and
to be melancholy.
1594–5 Biron. *Love's Labour's Lost*, act 4, sc.3, l.11.

82 What fool is not so wise
To lose an oath to win a paradise?
1594–5 Longueville. *Love's Labour's Lost*, act 4, sc.3, l.69–70.

83 Love's feeling is more soft and sensible
Than are the tender horns of cockled snails.
1594–5 Biron. *Love's Labour's Lost*, act 4, sc.3, l.313–14.

84 And when love speaks, the voice of all the gods
Make heaven drowsy with the harmony.

1594–5 Biron. *Love's Labour's Lost*, act 4, sc.3, l.320–1.

85 Never durst poet touch a pen to write
Until his ink were tempered with love's sighs.
1594–5 Biron. *Love's Labour's Lost*, act 4, sc.3, l.322–3.

86 From women's eyes this doctrine I derive.
They sparkle still the right Promethean fire.
They are the books, the arts, the academes
That show, contain, and nourish all the world,
Else none at all in aught proves excellent.
1594–5 Biron. *Love's Labour's Lost*, act 4, sc.3, l.326–30.

87 He draweth out the thread of his verbosity finer than the
staple of his argument.
1594–5 Holofernes, of Armado. *Love's Labour's Lost*, act 5, sc.1,
l.16.

88 O, they have lived long in the alms-basket of words.
I marvel thy master hath not eaten thee for a word,
for thou art not so long by the head as
honorificabilitudinitatibus. Thou art easier swallowed
than a flapdragon.
1594–5 Costard. *Love's Labour's Lost*, act 5, sc.1, l.38–42.

89 A light heart lives long.
1594–5 Catherine. *Love's Labour's Lost*, act 5, sc.2, l.18.

90 There's no such sport as sport by sport o'erthrown.
1594–5 Princess. *Love's Labour's Lost*, act 5, sc.2, l.152.

91 Taffeta phrases, silken terms precise,
Three-piled hyperboles, spruce affectation,
Figures pedantical—these summer flies
Have blown me full of maggot ostentation.
1594–5 Biron. *Love's Labour's Lost*, act 5, sc.2, l.406–10.

92 Mirth cannot move a soul in agony.
1594–5 Biron. *Love's Labour's Lost*, act 5, sc.2, l.843.

93 A jest's prosperity lies in the ear
Of him that hears it, never in the tongue
Of him that makes it.
1594–5 Rosaline. *Love's Labour's Lost*, act 5, sc.2, l.847–9.

94 When icicles hang by the wall,
And Dick the shepherd blows his nail,
And Tom bears logs into the hall,
And milk comes frozen home in pail;
When blood is nipped, and ways be foul,
Then nightly sings the staring owl;
Tu-whit, tu-whoo!—a merry note,
While greasy Joan doth keel the pot.
1594–5 Winter's song. *Love's Labour's Lost*, act 5, sc.2, l.897–904.

95 When all aloud the wind doth blow,
And coughing drowns the parson's saw,
And birds sit brooding in the snow,
And Marian's nose looks red and raw;
When roasted crabs hiss in the bowl.
1594–5 Winter's song. *Love's Labour's Lost*, act 5, sc.2, l.905–9.

96 Our doctors say this is no time to bleed.
1595 Richard. *Richard II*, act 1, sc.1, l.157.

97 I am disgraced, impeached, and baffled here,
Pierced to the soul with slander's venomed spear.
1595 Mowbray to Richard. *Richard II*, act 1, sc.1, l.170–1.

98 Lions make leopards tame.
1595 Richard. *Richard II*, act 1, sc.1, l.174.

99 The purest treasure mortal times afford
Is spotless reputation; that away,
Men are but gilded loam, or painted clay.

A jewel in a ten-times barred-up chest
Is a bold spirit in a loyal breast.
Mine honour is my life. Both grow in one.
Take honour from me, and my life is done.
1595 Mowbray to Richard. *Richard II*, act 1, sc.1, l.177–83.

1 As gentle and as jocund as to jest
Go I to fight. Truth hath a quiet breast.
1595 Mowbray. *Richard II*, act 1, sc.3, l.95–6.

2 This must my comfort be:
That sun that warms you here shall shine on me.
1595 Bolingbroke to Richard. *Richard II*, act 1, sc.3, l.138–9.

3 How long a time lies in one little word!
Four lagging winters and four wanton springs
End in a word: such is the breath of kings.
1595 Bolingbroke. *Richard II*, act 1, sc.3, l.206–8.

4 O, who can hold a fire in his hand
By thinking on the frosty Caucasus,
Or cloy the hungry edge of appetite
By bare imagination of a feast,
Or wallow naked in December snow
By thinking on fantastic summer's heat?
1595 Bolingbroke. *Richard II*, act 1, sc.3, l.257–62.

5 Methinks I am a prophet new-inspired,
And thus, expiring, do foretell of him.
His rash, fierce blaze of riot cannot last,
For violent fires soon burn out themselves.
1595 John of Gaunt, to Richard. *Richard II*, act 2, sc.1, l.31–4.

6 Small showers last long, but sudden storms are short.
1595 John of Gaunt. *Richard II*, act 2, sc.1, l.35.

7 With eager feeding food doth choke the feeder.
1595 John of Gaunt. *Richard II*, act 2, sc.1, l.37.

8 This royal throne of kings, this sceptred isle,
This earth of majesty, this seat of Mars,
This other Eden, demi-paradise,
This fortress built by nature for herself
Against infection and the hand of war,
This happy breed of men, this little world,
This precious stone set in the silver sea,
Which serves it in the office of a wall,
Or as a moat defensive to a house
Against the envy of less happier lands;
This blessèd plot, this earth, this realm, this England.
1595 John of Gaunt. *Richard II*, act 2, sc.1, l.40–50.

9 England that was wont to conquer others
Hath made a shameful conquest of itself.
1595 John of Gaunt. *Richard II*, act 2, sc.1, l.65–6.

10 Each substance of a grief hath twenty shadows,
Which shows like grief itself.
1595 Bushy. *Richard II*, act 2, sc.2, l.14–15.

11 Comfort's in heaven, and we are on the earth,
Where nothing lives but crosses, cares, and griefs.
1595 York. *Richard II*, act 2, sc.2, l.78–9.

12 Hope to joy is little less in joy
Than hope enjoyed.
1595 Northumberland. *Richard II*, act 2, sc.3, l.15–16.

13 I count myself in nothing else so happy
As in a soul rememb'ring my good friends.
1595 Bolingboke. *Richard II*, act 2, sc.3, l.46–7.

14 Things past redress are now with me past care.
1595 York. *Richard II*, act 2, sc.3, l.170.

15 Not all the water in the rough rude sea
Can wash the balm from an anointed king.
1595 Richard. *Richard II*, act 3, sc.2, l.50–1.

16 O, call back yesterday, bid time return,
And thou shalt have twelve thousand fighting men.
Today, today, unhappy day too late.
1595 Salisbury. *Richard II*, act 3, sc.2, l.65–7.

17 Time hath set a blot upon my pride.
1595 Richard. *Richard II*, act 3, sc.2, l.77.

18 Cry woe, destruction, ruin, loss, decay;
The worst is death, and death will have his day.
1595 Richard. *Richard II*, act 3, sc.2, l.98–9.

19 And nothing can we call our own but death,
And that small model of the barren earth
Which serves as paste and cover to our bones.
1595 Richard. *Richard II*, act 3, sc.2, l.148–50.

20 For God's sake, let us sit upon the ground,
And tell sad stories of the death of kings—
How some have been deposed, some slain in war,
Some haunted by the ghosts they have deposed,
Some poisoned by their wives, some sleeping killed,
All murdered. For within the hollow crown
That rounds the mortal temples of a king
Keeps Death his court; and there the antic sits,
Scoffing his state and grinning at his pomp,
Allowing him a breath, a little scene,
To monarchize, be feared, and kill with looks,
Infusing him with self and vain conceit,
As if this flesh which walls about our life
Were brass impregnable; and humoured thus,
Comes at the last, and with a little pin
Bores through his castle wall; and farewell, king.
1595 Richard. *Richard II*, act 3, sc.2, l.151–166.

21 O, that I were as great
As is my grief, or lesser than my name,
Or that I could forget what I have been,
Or not remember what I must be now!
1595 Richard. *Richard II*, act 3, sc.3, l.135–8.

22 What must the King do now? Must he submit?
The King shall do it. Must he be deposed?
The King shall be contented. Must he lose
The name of King? A God's name, let it go.
I'll give my jewels for a set of beads,
My gorgeous palace for a hermitage,
My gay apparel for an almsman's gown,
My figured goblets for a dish of wood,
My sceptre for a palmer's walking staff,
My subjects for a pair of carvèd saints,
And my large kingdom for a little grave.
1595 Richard. *Richard II*, act 3, sc.3, l.142–52.

23 Alack, why am I sent for to a king
Before I have shook off the regal thoughts
Wherewith I reigned? I hardly yet have learned
To insinuate, flatter, bow, and bend my knee.
Give sorrow leave awhile to tutor me
To this submission. Yet I well remember
The favours of these men. Were they not mine?
Did they not sometime cry 'All hail!' to me?
So Judas did to Christ. But He in twelve
Found the truth in all but one; I, in twelve thousand,
  none.

God save the King! Will no man say 'Amen'?
Am I both the priest and clerk? Well then, Amen.
1595 Richard. *Richard II*, act 4, sc.1, l.153–164.

24 You may my glories and my state depose,
But not my griefs; still am I king of those.
1595 Richard. *Richard II*, act 4, sc.1, l.182–3.

25 Mine eyes are full of tears; I cannot see.
And yet salt water blinds them not so much
But they can see a sort of traitors here.
Nay, if I turn mine eyes upon myself
I find myself a traitor with the rest.
1595 Richard. *Richard II*, act 4, sc.1, l.234–8.

26 I am sworn brother, sweet,
To grim necessity, and he and I
Will keep a league till death.
1595 Richard. *Richard II*, act 5, sc.1, l.20–1.

27 The love of wicked friends converts to fear;
That fear to hate.
1595 Richard. *Richard II*, act 5, sc.1, l.66–7.

28 Had not God, for some strong purpose steeled
The hearts of men, they must perforce have melted.
1595 York. *Richard II*, act 5, sc.2, l.34–5.

29 Say 'Pardon', king. Let pity teach thee how.
The word is short, but not so short as sweet;
No word like 'Pardon' for kings' mouths so meet.
1595 Duchess of York. *Richard II*, act 5, sc.3, l.115–16.

30 Thoughts tending to ambition, they do plot
Unlikely wonders: how these vain weak nails
May tear a passage through the flinty ribs
Of this hard world.
1595 Richard. *Richard II*, act 5, sc.5, l.18–21.

31 How sour sweet music is
When time is broke and no proportion kept.
So is it in the music of men's lives.
1595 Richard. *Richard II*, act 5, sc.5, l.42–4.

32 Mount, mount, my soul; thy seat is up on high,
Whilst my gross flesh sinks downward, here to die.
1595 Richard. *Richard II*, act 5, sc.5, l.111–12.

33 From forth the fatal loins of these two foes
A pair of star-crossed lovers take their life.
1595 Chorus. *Romeo and Juliet*, Prologue, l.5–6.

34 Alas that love, so gentle in his view,
Should be so tyrannous and rough in proof.
1595 Benvolio to Romeo. *Romeo and Juliet*, act 1, sc.1, l.166–7.

35 'Tis not hard, I think,
For men so old as we to keep the peace.
1595 Capulet. *Romeo and Juliet*, act 1, sc.2, l.2–3.

36 Such comfort as do lusty young men feel
When well-apparell'd April on the heel
Of limping winter treads.
1595 Capulet. *Romeo and Juliet*, act 1, sc.2, l.24–6.

37 Is love a tender thing? It is too rough,
Too rude, too boist'rous, and it pricks like thorn.
1595 Romeo. *Romeo and Juliet*, act 1, sc.4, l.25–6.

38 She is the fairies' midwife, and she comes
In shape no bigger than an agate stone
On the forefinger of an alderman,
Drawn with a team of little atomi
Athwart man's noses as they lie asleep.
1595 Mercutio. *Romeo and Juliet*, act 1, sc.4, l.55–9.

39 Her chariot is an empty hazelnut
Made by the joiner squirrel or old grub,
Time out o' mind the fairies' coachmakers.
And in this state she gallops night by night
Through lovers' brains, and then they dream of love.
1595 Mercutio. *Romeo and Juliet*, act 1, sc.4, 1.68–72.

40 I talk of dreams,
Which are the children of an idle brain,
Begot of nothing but vain fantasy.
1595 Mercutio. *Romeo and Juliet*, act 1, sc.4, 1.96–8.

41 You and I are past our dancing days.
1595 Capulet to his cousin. *Romeo and Juliet*, act 1, sc.5, 1.31.

42 O, she doth teach the torches to burn bright!
It seems she hangs upon the cheek of night
As a rich jewel in an Ethiope's ear—
Beauty too rich for use, for earth too dear.
1595 Romeo of Juliet. *Romeo and Juliet*, act 1, sc.5, 1.43–6.

43 Did my heart love till now? Forswear it, sight,
For I ne'er saw true beauty till this night.
1595 Mercutio. *Romeo and Juliet*, act 1, sc.5, 1.51–2.

44 My only love sprung from my only hate!
Too early seen unknown, and known too late!
1595 Juliet. *Romeo and Juliet*, act 1, sc.5, 1.137–8.

45 He jests at scars that never felt a wound.
But soft, what light through yonder window breaks?
It is the east, and Juliet is the sun.
1595 Romeo. *Romeo and Juliet*, act 2, sc.1, 1.43–5.

46 O, speak again, bright angel; for thou art
As glorious to this night, being o'er my head,
As is a wingèd messenger of heaven.
1595 Romeo of Juliet. *Romeo and Juliet*, act 2, sc.1, 1.68–70.

47 O Romeo, Romeo, wherefore art thou Romeo?
Deny thy father and refuse thy name,
Or if thou will not, be but sworn my love,
And I'll no longer be a Capulet.
1595 Juliet. *Romeo and Juliet*, act 2, sc.1, 1.75–8.

48 What's in a name? That which we call a rose
By any other word would smell as sweet.
1595 Juliet. *Romeo and Juliet*, act 2, sc.1, 1.85–6.

49 Call me but love and I'll be new baptized.
Henceforth I never will be Romeo.
1595 Romeo. *Romeo and Juliet*, act 2, sc.1, 1.93–4.

50 If thou think'st I am too quickly won,
I'll frown and be perverse and say thee nay,
So thou wilt woo.
1595 Juliet. *Romeo and Juliet*, act 2, sc.1, 1.137–9.

51 O swear not by the moon, th'inconstant moon
That monthly changes in her circled orb,
Lest that thy love prove likewise variable.
1595 Juliet. *Romeo and Juliet*, act 2, sc.1, 1.151–3.

52 My bounty is as boundless as the sea,
My love as deep. The more I give to thee
The more I have, for both are infinite.
1595 Juliet. *Romeo and Juliet*, act 2, sc.1, 1.175–7.

53 Parting is such sweet sorrow
That I shall say good-night till it be morrow.
1595 Juliet. *Romeo and Juliet*, act 2, sc.1, 1.229–30.

54 Sleep dwell upon thine eyes, peace in thy breast.
1595 Romeo. *Romeo and Juliet*, act 2, sc.1, 1.231.

55 O mickle is the powerful grace that lies

In plants, herbs, stones, and their true qualities,
For nought so vile that on the earth doth live
But to the earth some special good doth give.
1595 Friar Laurence. *Romeo and Juliet*, act 2, sc.2, 1.15–18.

56 Virtue itself turns vice, being misapplied,
And vice sometime's by action dignified.
1595 Friar Laurence. *Romeo and Juliet*, act 2, sc.2, 1.21–2.

57 Care keeps his watch in every old man's eye.
1595 Friar Laurence to Romeo. *Romeo and Juliet*, act 2, sc.2, 1.35.

58 Wisely and slow. They stumble that run fast.
1595 Friar Laurence to Romeo. *Romeo and Juliet*, act 2, sc.2, 1.94.

59 A gentleman, Nurse, that loves to hear himself talk, and
will speak more in a minute than he will stand to in a
month.
1595 Romeo. *Romeo and Juliet*, act 2, sc.3, 1.138–9.

60 These violent delights have violent ends.
1595 Friar Laurence. *Romeo and Juliet*, act 2, sc.5, 1.9.

61 Thy head is as full of quarrels as an egg is full of meat.
1595 Mercutio to Benvolio. *Romeo and Juliet*, act 3, sc.1, 1.20.

62 A plague o' both your houses.
They have made worms' meat of me.
1595 Mercutio, dying stabbed by Tybalt. *Romeo and Juliet*, act 3,
sc.1, 1.106–7.

63 Come, civil night,
Thou sober-suited matron all in black.
1595 Juliet. *Romeo and Juliet*, act 3, sc.2, 1.10–11.

64 So tedious is this day
As is the night before some festival
To an impatient child that hath new robes
And may not wear them.
1595 Juliet. *Romeo and Juliet*, act 3, sc.2, 1.28–31.

65 Steal immortal blessing from her lips.
1595 Romeo. *Romeo and Juliet*, act 3, sc.3, 1.37.

66 Hang up philosophy!
Unless philosophy can make a Juliet.
1595 Romeo. *Romeo and Juliet*, act 3, sc.3, 1.57–8.

67 A joy past joy calls out on me.
1595 Romeo. *Romeo and Juliet*, act 3, sc.3, 1.172.

68 It was the nightingale, and not the lark,
That pierced the fear-full hollow of thine ear.
Nightly she sings on yon pom'granate tree.
1595 Juliet to Romeo. *Romeo and Juliet*, act 3, sc.5, 1.2–4.

69 Night's candles are burnt out, and jocund day
Stands tiptoe on the misty mountaintops.
I must be gone and live, or stay and die.
1595 Romeo to Juliet. *Romeo and Juliet*, act 3, sc.5, 1.9–11.

70 O, fortune, fortune, all men call thee fickle.
1595 Juliet. *Romeo and Juliet*, act 3, sc.5, 1.60.

71 Mistress minion, you,
Thank me no thankings, nor proud me no prouds,
But fettle your fine joints 'gainst Thursday next
To go with Paris to Saint Peter's Church,
Or I will drag thee on a hurdle thither.
Out, you green-sickness carrion! Out, you baggage,
You tallow-face!
1595 Capulet, to Juliet, ordering her marriage to Paris. *Romeo
and Juliet*, act 3, sc.5, 1.151–7.

72 Is there no pity sitting in the clouds,
That sees into the bottom of my grief?
1595 Juliet. *Romeo and Juliet*, act 3, sc.5, 1.196–7.

73 I think it best you married with the County.
O, he's a lovely gentleman!
Romeo's a dishclout to him.
1595 Nurse to Juliet. *Romeo and Juliet*, act 3, sc.5, 1.217–19.

74 'Tis an ill cook that cannot lick his own fingers.
1595 Servingman to Capulet. *Romeo and Juliet*, act 4, sc.2, 1.6.

75 I have a faint cold fear thrills through my veins
That almost freezes up the heat of life.
1595 Juliet. *Romeo and Juliet*, act 4, sc.3, 1.15–16.

76 Out, alas, she's cold.
Her blood is settled, and her joints are stiff.
Life and these lips have long been separated.
Death lies on her like an untimely frost
Upon the sweetest flower of all the field.
1595 Capulet, of Juliet, as she feigns death. *Romeo and Juliet*,
act 4, sc.4, 1.52–6.

77 She's not well married that lives married long,
But she's best married that dies married young.
1595 Friar Laurence. *Romeo and Juliet*, act 4, sc.4, 1.104–5.

78 I dreamt my lady came and found me dead—
Strange dream, that gives a dead man leave to think!—
And breathed such life with kisses in my lips
That I revived and was an emperor.
1595 Romeo. *Romeo and Juliet*, act 5, sc.1, 1.6–9.

79 Art thou so bare and full of wretchedness,
And fear'st to die? Famine is in thy cheeks,
Need and oppression starveth in thy eyes,
Contempt and beggary hangs upon thy back.
The world is not thy friend, nor the world's law.
1595 Romeo to Apothecary. *Romeo and Juliet*, act 5, sc.1, 1.68–72.

80 Give me thy hand,
One writ with me in sour misfortune's book.
1595 Romeo to Paris, whom he has just killed. *Romeo and Juliet*,
act 5, sc.3, 1.81–2.

81 Here, here will I remain
With worms that are thy chambermaids. O, here
Will I set up my everlasting rest,
And shake the yoke of inauspicious stars
From this world-wearied flesh.
1595 Romeo. *Romeo and Juliet*, act 5, sc.3, 1.108–12.

82 Never was a story of more woe
Than this of Juliet and her Romeo.
1595 Prince. *Romeo and Juliet*, act 5, sc.3, 1.308–9.

83 To you your father should be as a god.
1595 Theseus to Hermia. *A Midsummer Night's Dream*, act 1, sc.1,
1.47.

84 The course of true love never did run smooth.
1595 Lysander to Hermia. *A Midsummer Night's Dream*, act 1,
sc.1, 1.134.

85 Your eyes are lodestars, and your tongue's sweet air
More tuneable than lark to shepherd's ear
When wheat is green, when hawthorn buds appear.
1595 Helena. *A Midsummer Night's Dream*, act 1, sc.1, 1.183–5.

86 Love looks not with the eyes, but with the mind,
And therefore is winged Cupid painted blind.
1595 Helena. *A Midsummer Night's Dream*, act 1, sc.1, 1.234–5.

87 Marry, our play is The Most Lamentable Comedy and
Most Cruel Death of Pyramus and Thisbe.
1595 Quince. *A Midsummer Night's Dream*, act 1, sc.2, 1.11–12.

88 That will ask some tears in the true performing of it. If I do

it, let the audience look to their eyes. I will move stones.
1595 Bottom. *A Midsummer Night's Dream*, act 1, sc.2, 1.21–3.

89 Nay, faith, let not me play a woman. I have a beard
coming.
1595 Flute, on his reluctance to act the role of Thisbe. *A
Midsummer Night's Dream*, act 1, sc.2, 1.43–4.

90 SNUG: Have you the lion's part written? Pray you, if it be,
give it me; for I am slow of study.
QUINCE: You may do it extempore, for it is nothing but
roaring.
BOTTOM: Let me play the lion too. I will roar that I will do
any man's heart good to hear me. I will roar that I will
make the Duke say 'Let him roar again; let him roar again'.
1595 *A Midsummer Night's Dream*, act 1, sc.2, 1.62–69.

91 I will roar you as gently as any sucking dove. I will roar
you an 'twere any nightingale.
1595 Bottom. *A Midsummer Night's Dream*, act 1, sc.2, 1.77–8.

92 Over hill, over dale,
Thorough bush, thorough brier,
Over park, over pale,
Thorough flood, thorough fire:
I do wander everywhere
Swifter than the moon's sphere,
And I serve the Fairy Queen
To dew her orbs upon the green.
The cowslips tall her pensioners be.
In their gold coats spots you see;
Those be rubies, fairy favours;
In those freckles live their savours.
I must go seek some dewdrops here,
And hang a pearl in every cowslip's ear.
1595 Fairy. *A Midsummer Night's Dream*, act 2, sc.1, 1.2–15.

93 Ill met by moonlight, proud Titania.
1595 Oberon. *A Midsummer Night's Dream*, act 2, sc.1, 1.60.

94 Yet marked I where the bolt of Cupid fell.
It fell upon a little western flower—
Before, milk-white; now, purple with love's wound—
And maidens call it love-in-idleness.
1595 Oberon. *A Midsummer Night's Dream*, act 2, sc.1, 1.165–8.

95 I'll put a girdle round about the earth
In forty minutes.
1595 Robin Goodfellow. *A Midsummer Night's Dream*, act 2, sc.1,
1.175–6.

96 We cannot fight for love as men may do;
We should be woo'd, and were not made to woo.
1595 Helena. *A Midsummer Night's Dream*, act 2, sc.1, 1.241–2.

97 I know a bank where the wild thyme blows,
Where oxlips and the nodding violet grows,
Quite overcanopied with luscious woodbine,
With sweet musk-roses, and with eglantine.
1595 Oberon. *A Midsummer Night's Dream*, act 2, sc.1, 1.249–52.

98 You spotted snakes with double tongue,
Thorny hedgehogs, be not seen;
Newts and blindworms, do no wrong;
Come not near our Fairy Queen.
1595 First Fairy. *A Midsummer Night's Dream*, act 2, sc.2, 1.9–12.

99 A surfeit of the sweetest things
The deepest loathing to the stomach brings.
1595 Lysander. *A Midsummer Night's Dream*, act 2, sc.2, 1.143–4.

1 A lion among ladies is a most dreadful thing.
1595 Bottom. *A Midsummer Night's Dream*, act 3, sc.1, 1.28.

2 FLUTE: (as Thisbe)
Most radiant Pyramus, most lily-white of hue,
Of colour like the red rose on triumphant brier;
Most bristly juvenile, and eke most lovely Jew,
As true as truest horse that yet would never tire:
I'll meet thee, Pyramus, at Ninny's tomb.
QUINCE: Ninus' tomb, man!
1595 *A Midsummer Night's Dream*, act 3, sc.1, l.87–92.

3 What angel wakes me from my flow'ry bed?
1595 Titania, of Bottom. *A Midsummer Night's Dream*, act 3, sc.1, l.122.

4 I pray thee, gentle mortal, sing again.
Mine ear is much enamoured of thy note;
So is mine eye enthrallèd to thy shape;
And thy fair virtue's force perforce doth move me
On the first view to say, to swear, I love thee.
1595 Titania. *A Midsummer Night's Dream*, act 3, sc.1, l.130–4.

5 I go, I go—look how I go,
Swifter than arrow from the Tartar's bow.
1595 Robin Goodfellow to Oberon. *A Midsummer Night's Dream*, act 3, sc.2, l.100–1.

6 Lord, what fools these mortals be!
1595 Robin Goodfellow. *A Midsummer Night's Dream*, act 3, sc.2, l.115.

7 Sleep, that sometimes shuts up sorrow's eye,
Steal me a while from mine own company.
1595 Helena. *A Midsummer Night's Dream*, act 3, sc.3, l.23–4.

8 I must to the barber's, monsieur, for methinks I am
marvellous hairy about the face; and I am such a tender
ass, if my hair do but tickle me I must scratch.
1595 Bottom. *A Midsummer Night's Dream*, act 4, sc.1, l.23–6.

9 Methinks I have a great desire to a bottle of hay. Good
hay, sweet hay, hath no fellow.
1595 Bottom. *A Midsummer Night's Dream*, act 4, sc.1, l.32–3.

10 My Oberon, what visions have I seen!
Methought I was enamoured of an ass.
1595 Titania. *A Midsummer Night's Dream*, act 4, sc.1, l.75–6.

11 I have had a dream past the wit of man to say what dream
it was.
1595 Bottom. *A Midsummer Night's Dream*, act 4, sc.1, l.202–3.

12 Lovers and madmen have such seething brains,
Such shaping fantasies, that apprehend
More than cool reason ever comprehends.
1595 Theseus. *A Midsummer Night's Dream*, act 5, sc.1, l.4–6.

13 The lunatic, the lover, and the poet
Are of imagination all compact.
One sees more devils than vast hell can hold:
That is the madman. The lover, all as frantic,
Sees Helen's beauty in a brow of Egypt.
The poet's eye , in a fine frenzy rolling,
Doth glance from heaven to earth, from earth to heaven,
And as imagination bodies forth
The forms of things unknown, the poet's pen
Turns them to shapes, and gives to airy nothing
A local habitation and a name.
Such tricks hath strong imagination
That if it would but apprehend some joy
It comprehends some bringer of that joy;
Or in the night, imagining some fear,
How easy is a bush supposed a bear!
1595 Theseus. *A Midsummer Night's Dream*, act 5, sc.1, l.7–22.

14 [LYSANDER] (reads)
'A tedious 'brief' scene of young Pyramus
And his love Thisbe: very tragical mirth.'
THESEUS:
'Merry' and 'tragical'? 'Tedious' and 'brief'?—
That is, hot ice and wondrous strange black snow.
1595 *A Midsummer Night's Dream*, act 5, sc.1, l.56–9.

15 A play there is, my lord, some ten words long,
Which is as brief as I have known a play;
But by ten words, my lord, it is too long.
1595 [Egeus]. *A Midsummer Night's Dream*, act 5, sc.1, l.61–3.

16 Anon comes Pyramus, sweet youth and tall,
And finds his trusty Thisbe's mantle slain;
Whereat with blade—with bloody, blameful blade—
He bravely broached his boiling bloody breast;
And Thisbe, tarrying in mulberry shade,
His dagger drew and died.
1595 Quince's prologue to Pyramus and Thisbe. *A Midsummer Night's Dream*, act 5, sc.1, l.143–8.

17 O dainty duck, O dear!
Thy mantle good,
What, stained with blood?
Approach, ye furies fell.
O fates, come, come,
Cut the thread and thrum,
Quail, crush, conclude, and quell.
1595 Bottom (as Pyramus). *A Midsummer Night's Dream*, act 5, sc.1, l.276–82.

18 His eyes were green as leeks.
1595 Flute (as Thisbe). *A Midsummer Night's Dream*, act 5, sc.1, l.330.

19 If we shadows have offended,
Think but this, and all is mended:
That you have but slumbered here,
While these visions did appear.
1595 Robin Goodfellow. *A Midsummer Night's Dream*, act 5, sc.2, l.1–4.

20 By how much unexpected, by so much
We must awake endeavour for defence,
For courage mounteth with occasion.
1596 Duke of Austria. *King John*, act 2, sc.1, l.80–2.

21 Well, whiles I am a beggar I will rail,
And say there is no sin but to be rich,
And being rich, my virtue then shall be
To say there is no vice but beggary.
Since kings break faith upon commodity,
Gain, be my lord, for I will worship thee.
1596 Bastard. *King John*, act 2, sc.1, l.594–9.

22 I will instruct my sorrows to be proud,
For grief is proud and makes his owner stoop.
1596 Constance. *King John*, act 2, sc.2, l.68–9.

23 My grief's so great
That no supporter but the huge firm earth
Can hold it up. Here I and sorrows sit.
1596 Constance. *King John*, act 2, sc.2, l.71–3.

24 Bell, book, and candle shall not drive me back
When gold and silver becks me to come on.
1596 Bastard. *King John*, act 3, sc.3, l.12–13.

25 Grief fills the room up of my absent child,
Lies in his bed, walks up and down with me.

1596 Constance. *King John*, act 3, sc.4, l.93–4.

26 Life is as tedious as a twice-told tale
Vexing the dull ear of a drowsy man.
1596 Louis the Dauphin. *King John*, act 3, sc.4, l.108–9.

27 When Fortune means to men most good,
She looks upon them with a threat'ning eye.
1596 Pandolf. *King John*, act 3, sc.4, l.119–20.

28 He that stands upon a slipp'ry place
Makes nice of no vile hold to stay him up.
1596 Pandolf. *King John*, act 3, sc.4, l.137–8.

29 Strong reasons make strange actions.
1596 Louis the Dauphin. *King John*, act 3, sc.4, l.182.

30 To gild refinèd gold, to paint the lily,
To throw a perfume on the violet,
To smooth the ice, or add another hue
Unto the rainbow, or with taper-light
To seek the beauteous eye of heaven to garnish,
Is wasteful and ridiculous excess.
1596 Salisbury. *King John*, act 4, sc.2, l.11–16.

31 The rich advantage of good exercise?
1596 Pembroke. *King John*, act 4, sc.2, l.60.

32 Think you I bear the shears of destiny?
Have I commandment on the pulse of life?
1596 John. *King John*, act 4, sc.2, l.91–2.

33 Entreat the north
To make his bleak winds kiss my parchèd lips,
And comfort me with cold. I do not ask you much;
I beg cold comfort.
1596 John to Prince Henry. *King John*, act 5, sc.7, l.39–42.

34 This England never did, nor never shall,
Lie at the proud foot of a conqueror.
1596 Bastard. *King John*, act 5, sc.7, l.112–3.

35 Now, by two-headed Janus,
Nature hath framed strange fellows in her time:
Some that will evermore peep through their eyes
And laugh like parrots at a bagpiper.
1596–7 Solanio. *The Merchant of Venice*, act 1, sc.1, l.50–3.

36 I hold the world but as the world, Graziano;
A stage where every man must play a part,
And mine a sad one.
1596–7 Antonio. *The Merchant of Venice*, act 1, sc.1, l.77–9.

37 Let me play the fool.
With mirth and laughter let old wrinkles come.
1596–7 Graziano to Antonio. *The Merchant of Venice*, act 1, sc.1, l.79–80.

38 O my Antonio, I do know of these
That therefore only are reputed wise
For saying nothing.
1596–7 Graziano. *The Merchant of Venice*, act 1, sc.1, l.95–7.

39 Fish not with this melancholy bait
For this fool gudgeon, this opinion.
1596–7 Graziano. *The Merchant of Venice*, act 1, sc.1, l.101–2.

40 For silence is only commendable
In a neat's tongue dried and a maid not vendible.
1596–7 Graziano. *The Merchant of Venice*, act 1, sc.1, l.111–2.

41 Graziano speaks an infinite deal of nothing, more than
any man in all Venice. His reasons are as two grains of
wheat hid in two bushels of chaff: you shall seek all day
ere you find them, and when you have them they are not
worth the search.

1596–7 Bassanio to Antonio. *The Merchant of Venice*, act 1, sc.1, l.114–18.

42 They are as sick that surfeit with too much as they that
starve with nothing.
1596–7 Nerissa. *The Merchant of Venice*, act 1, sc.2, l.5–6.

43 I can easier teach twenty what were good to be done
than to be one of the twenty to follow mine own
teaching.
1596–7 Portia. *The Merchant of Venice*, act 1, sc.2, l.15–17.

44 The brain may devise laws for the blood, but a hot
temper leaps o'er a cold decree.
1596–7 Portia. *The Merchant of Venice*, act 1, sc.2, l.17–18.

45 He doth nothing but talk of his horse.
1596–7 Portia. *The Merchant of Venice*, act 1, sc.2, l.39–40.

46 I fear he will prove the weeping philosopher when he
grows old, being so full of unmannerly sadness in his
youth.
1596–7 Portia, of her suitor the County Palatine. *The Merchant of
Venice*, act 1, sc.2, l.47–9.

47 God made him, and therefore let him pass for a man.
1596–7 Portia, of her suitor M. le Bon. *The Merchant of Venice*,
act 1, sc.2, l.54–5.

48 I will do anything, Nerissa, ere I will be married to a
sponge.
1596–7 Portia. *The Merchant of Venice*, act 1, sc.2, l.95–6.

49 There is not one among them but I dote on his very
absence, and I pray God grant them a fair departure.
1596–7 Portia, of the suitors. *The Merchant of Venice*, act 1, sc.2,
l.106–8.

50 Yes, to smell pork, to eat of the habitation which your
prophet the Nazarite conjured the devil into! I will buy
with you, sell with you, talk with you, walk with you, and
so following, but I will not eat with you, drink with you,
nor pray with you.
1596–7 Shylock, invited to dine with Bassanio. *The Merchant of
Venice*, act 1, sc.3, l.31–5.

51 How like a fawning publican he looks.
I hate him for he is a Christian.
1596–7 Shylock, of Antonio. *The Merchant of Venice*, act 1, sc.3,
l.39–40.

52 The devil can cite Scripture for his purpose.
An evil soul producing holy witness
Is like a villain with a smiling cheek,
A goodly apple rotten at the heart.
O, what a goodly outside falsehood hath!
1596–7 Antonio. *The Merchant of Venice*, act 1, sc.3, l.97–101.

53 Signor Antonio, many a time and oft
In the Rialto you have rated me
About my moneys and my usances.
Still have I borne it with a patient shrug,
For suff'rance is the badge of all our tribe.
1596–7 Shylock. *The Merchant of Venice*, act 1, sc.3, l.105–109.

54 If thou wilt lend this money, lend it not
As to thy friends; for when did friendship take
A breed for barren metal of his friend?
1596–7 Antonio to Shylock. *The Merchant of Venice*, act 1, sc.3,
l.130–3.

55 I like not fair terms and a villain's mind.
1596–7 Bassanio. *The Merchant of Venice*, act 1, sc.3, l.178.

56 It is a wise father that knows his own child.
1596–7 Lancelot. *The Merchant of Venice*, act 2, sc.2, l.72–3.

57 I'll take my leave of the Jew in the twinkling.
1596–7 Lancelot to Gobbo. *The Merchant of Venice*, act 2, sc.2, l.161–2.

58 Alack, what heinous sin is it in me
To be ashamed to be my father's child!
But though I am a daughter to his blood,
I am not to his manners.
1596–7 Jessica. *The Merchant of Venice*, act 2, sc.3, l.16–19.

59 Then it was not for nothing that my nose fell a-bleeding
on Black Monday.
1596–7 Lancelot. *The Merchant of Venice*, act 2, sc.5, l.23–5.

60 There is some ill a-brewing towards my rest,
For I did dream of money-bags tonight.
1596–7 Shylock. *The Merchant of Venice*, act 2, sc.5, l.17–18.

61 But love is blind, and lovers cannot see
The pretty follies that themselves commit.
1596–7 Jessica. *The Merchant of Venice*, act 2, sc.6, l.36.

62 I will not choose what many men desire,
Because I will not jump with common spirits
And rank me with the barbarous multitudes.
1596–7 Aragon. *The Merchant of Venice*, act 2, sc.9, l.30–2.

63 O, that estates, degrees, and offices
Were not derived corruptly, and that clear honour
Were purchased by the merit of the wearer!
1596–7 Aragon. *The Merchant of Venice*, act 2, sc.9, l.40–2.

64 The ancient saying is no heresy;
Hanging and wiving goes by destiny.
1596–7 Nerissa. *The Merchant of Venice*, act 2, sc.9, l.81–2.

65 A day in April never came so sweet,
To show how costly summer was at hand.
1596–7 Messenger, of Bassanio's arrival. *The Merchant of Venice*, act 2, sc.9, l.92.

66 The bird was fledged; and then it is the complexion of
them all to leave the dam.
1596–7 Solanio, of Jessica. *The Merchant of Venice*, act 3, sc.1, l.27.

67 Let him look to his bond.
1596–7 Shylock, of Antonio. *The Merchant of Venice*, act 3, sc.1, l.45–6.

68 Hath not a Jew eyes? Hath not a Jew hands, organs,
dimensions, senses, affections, passions; fed with the
same food, hurt with the same weapons, subject to the
same diseases, healed by the same means, warmed and
cooled by the same winter and summer as a Christian is?
If you prick us do we not bleed? If you tickle us do we not
laugh? If you poison us do we not die? And if you wrong
us shall we not revenge? If we are like you in the rest, we
will resemble you in that.
1596–7 Shylock. *The Merchant of Venice*, act 3, sc.1, l.54–63.

69 Let music sound while he doth make his choice.
Then if he lose he makes a swanlike end,
Fading in music.
1596–7 Portia to Bassanio. *The Merchant of Venice*, act 3, sc.2, l.43–5.

70 There is no vice so simple but assumes
Some mark of virtue on his outward parts.
1596–7 Bassiano, aside. *The Merchant of Venice*, act 3, sc.2, l.81–2.

71 Look on beauty
And you shall see 'tis purchased by the weight,
Which therein works a miracle in nature,
Making them lightest that wear most of it.

72 Thou gaudy gold,
Hard food for Midas, I will none of thee.
1596–7 Bassiano, aloud. *The Merchant of Venice*, act 3, sc.2, l.101–2.

73 An unlessoned girl, unschooled, unpractisèd,
Happy in this, she is not yet so old
But she may learn.
1596–7 Portia, of herself. *The Merchant of Venice*, act 3, sc.2, l.159–61.

74 Madam, you have bereft me of all words.
Only my blood speaks to you in my veins.
1596–7 Bassanio to Portia. *The Merchant of Venice*, act 3, sc.2, l.175–6.

75 Here are a few of the unpleasant'st words
That ever blotted paper.
1596–7 Bassanio, reading of Antonio's misfortunes. *The Merchant of Venice*, act 3, sc.2, l.249–50.

76 Let it serve for table-talk.
Then, howsome'er thou speak'st, 'mong other things
I shall digest it.
1596–7 Lorenzo. *The Merchant of Venice*, act 3, sc.5, l.83–5.

77 Some men there are love not a gaping pig,
Some that are mad if they behold a cat,
And others when the bagpipe sings i'th' nose
Cannot contain their urine.
1596–7 Shylock. *The Merchant of Venice*, act 4, sc.1, l.46–49.

78 We turned o'er many books together.
1596–7 Bellario's letter of recommendation for Portia (as Balthasar). *The Merchant of Venice*, act 4, sc.1, l.154–5.

79 The quality of mercy is not strained.
It droppeth as the gentle rain from heaven
Upon the place beneath. It is twice blest:
It blesseth him that gives, and him that takes.
1596–7 Portia. *The Merchant of Venice*, act 4, sc.1, l.181–4.

80 It is enthronèd in the hearts of kings;
It is an attribute to God himself,
And earthly power doth then show likest God's
When mercy seasons justice.
1596–7 Portia. *The Merchant of Venice*, act 4, sc.1, l.190–4.

81 A Daniel come to judgement, yea, a Daniel!
O wise young judge, how I do honour thee!
1596–7 Shylock, of the disguised Portia. *The Merchant of Venice*, act 4, sc.1, l.220–1.

82 Antonio, I am married to a wife
Which is as dear to me as life itself,
But life itself, my wife, and all the world
Are not with me esteemed above thy life.
I would lose all, ay, sacrifice them all
Here to this devil, to deliver you.
1596–7 Bassanio. *The Merchant of Venice*, act 4, sc.1, l.279–84.

83 Take thou thy pound of flesh.
1596–7 Portia to Shylock. *The Merchant of Venice*, act 4, sc.1, l.305.

84 Nay, take my life and all, pardon not that.
You take my house when you do take the prop
That doth sustain my house; you take my life
When do you take the means whereby I live.
1596–7 Shylock to the Duke. *The Merchant of Venice*, act 4, sc.1, l.371–4.

85 How sweet the moonlight sleeps upon this bank!

Here will we sit, and let the sounds of music
Creep in our ears.
1596–7 Lorenzo to Jessica. *The Merchant of Venice*, act 5, sc.1,
l.54–6.

86 Look how the floor of heaven
Is thick inlaid with patens of bright gold.
There's not the smallest orb which thou behold'st
But in his motion like an angel sings.
1596–7 Lorenzo to Jessica. *The Merchant of Venice*, act 5, sc.1,
l.58–61.

87 I am never merry when I hear sweet music.
1596–7 Jessica. *The Merchant of Venice*, act 5, sc.1, l.69.

88 The man that hath no music in himself,
Nor is not moved with concord of sweet sounds,
Is fit for treasons, stratagems, and spoils.
1596–7 Lorenzo. *The Merchant of Venice*, act 5, sc.1, l.83–5.

89 How far that little candle throws his beams—
So shines a good deed in a naughty world.
1596–7 Portia. *The Merchant of Venice*, act 5, sc.1, l.90–1.

90 A substitute shines brightly as a king
Until a king be by.
1596–7 Portia. *The Merchant of Venice*, act 5, sc.1, l.94–5.

91 The crow doth sing as sweetly as the lark
When neither is attended.
1596–7 Portia. *The Merchant of Venice*, act 5, sc.1, l.102–3.

92 A light wife doth make a heavy husband.
1596–7 Portia. *The Merchant of Venice*, act 5, sc.1, l.130.

93 O, that it could be proved
That some night-tripping fairy had exchanged
In cradle clothes our children where they lay.
1596–7 King Henry of his son, Harry, and Northumberland's son,
Hotspur. *Henry IV Part One*, act 1, sc.1, l.85–7.

94 What a devil hast thou to do with the time of the day?
Unless hours were cups of sack, and minutes capons,
and clocks the tongues of bawds, and dials the signs of
leaping-houses, and the blessed sun himself a fair hot
wench in flame-coloured taffeta, I see no reason why
thou shouldst be so superfluous to demand the time of
the day.
1596–7 Prince Harry to Falstaff. *Henry IV Part One*, act 1, sc.2,
l.6–12.

95 How now, how now, mad wag? What, in thy quips and
thy quiddities? What a plague have I to do with a buff
jerkin?
1596–7 Falstaff to Prince Harry. *Henry IV Part One*, act 1, sc.2,
l.44–6.

96 I would to God thou and I knew where a commodity of
good names were to be bought.
1596–7 Falstaff. *Henry IV Part One*, act 1, sc.2, l.82–3.

97 'Tis my vocation, Hal. 'Tis no sin for a man to labour in his
vocation.
1596–7 Falstaff, of stealing. *Henry IV Part One*, act 1, sc.2, l.104–5.

98 What says Monsieur Remorse? What says Sir John, sack-
and-sugar Jack? How agrees the devil and thee about
thy soul, that thou soldest him on Good Friday last, for a
cup of Madeira and a cold capon's leg?
1596–7 Poins to Falstaff. *Henry IV Part One*, act 1, sc.2,
l.111–15.

99 He was never yet a breaker of proverbs: he will give the
devil his due.
1596–7 Prince Harry. *Henry IV Part One*, act 1, sc.2, l.117–8.

1 He made me mad
To see him shine so brisk, and smell so sweet,
And talk so like a waiting gentlewoman
Of guns, and drums, and wounds, God save the mark!
And telling me the soverign'st thing on earth
Was parmacity for an inward bruise,
And that it was great pity, so it was,
This villainous saltpetre should be digged
Out of the bowels of the harmless earth,
Which many a good tall fellow had destroyed
So cowardly, and but for these vile guns
He would himself have been a soldier.
1596–7 Hotspur. *Henry IV Part One*, act 1, sc.3, l.52–63.

2 To put down Richard, that sweet lovely rose,
And plant this thorn, this canker, Bolingbroke?
1596–7 Hotspur. *Henry IV Part One*, act 1, sc.3, l.173–4.

3 If he fall in, good night, or sink or swim.
1596–7 Hotspur. *Henry IV Part One*, act 1, sc.3, l.192.

4 —O, the blood more stirs
To rouse a lion than to start a hare!
1596–7 Hotspur. *Henry IV Part One*, act 1, sc.3, l.195–6.

5 By heaven, methinks it were an easy leap
To pluck bright honour from the pale-faced moon,
Or dive into the bottom of the deep,
Where fathom-line could never touch the ground,
And pluck up drownèd honour by the locks.
1596–7 Hotspur. *Henry IV Part One*, act 1, sc.3, l.199–203.

6 I am joined with no foot-landrakers, no longstaff
sixpenny strikers, none of these mad mustachio purple-
hued maltworms, but with nobility and tranquillity,
burgomasters and great 'oyez'-ers; such as can hold in,
such as will strike sooner than speak, and speak sooner
than drink, and drink sooner than pray.
1596–7 Gadshill. *Henry IV Part One*, act 2, sc.1, l.73–8.

7 I am bewitched with the rogue's company. If the rascal
have not given me medicines to make me love him, I'll be
hanged.
1596–7 Falstaff, of Prince Harry. *Henry IV Part One*, act 2, sc.2,
l.17–20.

8 A plague upon't when thieves cannot be true one to
another.
1596–7 Falstaff. *Henry IV Part One*, act 2, sc.2, l.27–8.

9 Hang thyself in thine own heir-apparent garters!
1596–7 Falstaff to Prince Harry. *Henry IV Part One*, act 2, sc.2,
l.43.

10 Out of this nettle danger we pluck this flower safety.
1596–7 Hotspur. *Henry IV Part One*, act 2, sc.4, l.9–10.

11 Constant you are,
But yet a woman; and for secrecy
No lady closer, for I well believe
Thou wilt not utter what thou dost not know.
1596–7 Hotspur to Kate. *Henry IV Part One*, act 2, sc.4, l.105–8.

12 I am not yet of Percy's mind, the Hotspur of the North
—he that kills me some six or seven dozen of Scots at a
breakfast, washes his hands, and says to his wife, 'Fie
upon this quiet life! I want work.'
1596–7 Prince Harry. *Henry IV Part One*, act 2, sc.5, l.102–6.

13 There lives not three good men unhanged in England,
and one of them is fat and grows old.
1596–7 Falstaff, of himself. *Henry IV Part One*, act 2, sc.5, l.130–1.

14 Give you a reason on compulsion? If reasons were as

plentiful as blackberries, I would give no man a reason upon compulsion.
1596–7 Falstaff. *Henry IV Part One*, act 2, sc.5, l.242–4.

15 PRINCE HARRY: This sanguine coward, this bed-presser, this horse-backbreaker, this huge hill of flesh—
SIR JOHN: 'Sblood, you starveling, you elf-skin, you dried neat's tongue, you bull's pizzle, you stock-fish—O, for breath to utter what is like thee!—you tailor's yard, you sheath, you bow-case, you vile standing tuck.
1596–7 *Henry IV Part One*, act 2, sc.5, l.245–52.

16 SIR JOHN: Sweet Jack Oldcastle, kind Jack Oldcastle, true Jack Oldcastle, valiant Jack Oldcastle, and therefore more valiant being, as he is, old Jack Oldcastle Banish not him thy Harry's company, Banish not him thy Harry's company. Banish plump Jack, and banish all the world.
PRINCE HARRY: I do; I will.
1596–7 Falstaff. *Henry IV Part One*, act 2, sc.5, l.480–6.

17 I can teach thee, coz, to shame the devil, By telling truth: 'Tell truth, and shame the devil'.
1596–7 Hotspur to Glyndwr. *Henry IV Part One*, act 3, sc.1, l.55–6.

18 Mincing poetry.
'Tis like the forced gait of a shuffling nag.
1596–7 Hotspur. *Henry IV Part One*, act 3, sc.1, l.130–1.

19 I understand thy kisses, and thou mine,
And that's a feeling disputation.
1596–7 Mortimer to his wife. *Henry IV Part One*, act 3, sc.1, l.200–1.

20 Now I perceive the devil understands Welsh;
And 'tis no marvel, he is so humorous.
1596–7 Hotspur. *Henry IV Part One*, act 3, sc.1, l.226–7.

21 Swear me, Kate, like a lady as thou art,
A good mouth-filling oath.
1596–7 Hotspur. *Henry IV Part One*, act 3, sc.1, l.249–50.

22 Do thou amend thy face, and I'll amend my life.
1596–7 Falstaff to Bardolph. *Henry IV Part One*, act 3, sc.3, l.23.

23 Thou knowest in the state of innocency Adam fell, and what should poor Jack Oldcastle do in the days of villainy? Thou seest I have more flesh than another man, and therefore more frailty.
1596–7 Falstaff. *Henry IV Part One*, act 3, sc.3, l.165–7.

24 I am as vigilant as a cat to steal cream.
1596–7 Falstaff. *Henry IV Part One*, act 4, sc.2, l.58–9.

25 Rebellion lay in his way, and he found it.
1596–7 Falstaff, of Worcester. *Henry IV Part One*, act 5, sc.1, l.28.

26 I would 'twere bed-time, Hal, and all well.
1596–7 Falstaff. *Henry IV Part One*, act 5, sc.1, l.125.

27 Honour pricks me on. Yea, but how if honour prick me off when I come on? How then?
1596–7 Falstaff. *Henry IV Part One*, act 5, sc.1, l.129–131.

28 What is honour? A word.
1596–7 Flastaff. *Henry IV Part One*, act 5, sc.1, l.133–4.

29 Who hath it [honour]? He that died o' Wednesday.
1596–7 Falstaff. *Henry IV Part One*, act 5, sc.1, l.135–6.

30 Treason is but trusted like the fox,
Who, ne'er so tame, so cherished and locked up,
Will have a wild trick of his ancestors.
1596–7 Worcester. *Henry IV Part One*, act 5, sc.2, l.9–11.

31 O gentlemen, the time of life is short.
To spend that shortness basely were too long

If life did ride upon a dial's point,
Still ending at the arrival of an hour.
1596–7 Hotspur. *Henry IV Part One*, act 5, sc.2, l.81–4.

32 Sound all the lofty instruments of war,
And by that music let us all embrace,
For, heaven to earth, some of us never shall
A second time do such a courtesy.
1596–7 Hotspur. *Henry IV Part One*, act 5, sc.2, l.97–100.

33 I am as hot as molten lead, and as heavy too.
1596–7 Falstaff. *Henry IV Part One*, act 5, sc.3, l.33–4.

34 Time, that takes survey of all the world,
Must have a stop.
1596–7 Hotspur. *Henry IV Part One*, act 5, sc.4, l.81–2.

35 Fare thee well, great heart.
Ill-weaved ambition, how much art thou shrunk!
When that this body did contain a spirit,
A kingdom for it was too small a bound,
But now two paces of the vilest earth
Is room enough.
1596–7 Prince Harry, of Hotspur. *Henry IV Part One*, act 5, sc.4, l.86–91.

36 The better part of valour is discretion, in the which better part I have saved my life.
1596–7 Falstaff. *Henry IV Part One*, act 5, sc.4, l.118–20.

37 In poison there is physic; and these news,
Having been well, that would have made me sick,
Being sick, have in some measure made me well.
1597–8 Northumberland. *Henry IV Part Two*, act 1, sc.1, l.137–9.

38 I am not only witty in myself, but the cause that wit is in other men.
1597–8 Falstaff. *Henry IV Part Two*, act 1, sc.2, l.9–10.

39 Your lordship, though not clean past your youth, hath yet some smack of age in you, some relish of the saltness of time.
1597–8 Falstaff, of the Lord Justice. *Henry IV Part Two*, act 1, sc.2, l.98–9.

40 I am as poor as Job, my lord, but not so patient.
1597–8 Falstaff. *Henry IV Part Two*, act 1, sc.2, l.128.

41 If it be a hot day and I brandish anything but my bottle, would I might never spit white again.
1597–8 Falstaff. *Henry IV Part Two*, act 1, sc.2, l.211–13.

42 It was alway yet the trick of our English nation, if they have a good thing, to make it too common.
1597–8 Falstaff. *Henry IV Part Two*, act 1, sc.2, l.215–17.

43 I can get no remedy against this consumption of the purse. Borrowing only lingers and lingers it out, but the disease is incurable.
1597–8 Falstaff. *Henry IV Part Two*, act 1, sc.2, l.237–9.

44 [He] lined himself with hope,
Eating the air on promise of supply.
1597–8 Lord Bardolph, of Hotspur. *Henry IV Part Two*, act 1, sc.3, l.27–8.

45 Away, you scullion, you rampallion, you fustilarian! I'll tickle your catastrophe!
1597–8 Page to Mistress Quickly. *Henry IV Part Two*, act 2, sc.1, l.61–2.

46 He hath eaten me out of house and home.
1597–8 Mistress Quickly, of Falstaff. *Henry IV Part Two*, act 2, sc.1, l.75–6.

47 Thus we play the fools with the time, and the spirits of

the wise sit in the clouds and mock us.
1597–8 Prince Harry. *Henry IV Part Two*, act 2, sc.2, l.133–5.

48 He was indeed the glass
Wherein the noble youth did dress themselves.
1597–8 Lady Percy, of Hotspur. *Henry IV Part Two*, act 2, sc.3, l.21–2.

49 Shall pack-horses
And hollow pampered jades of Asia,
Which cannot go but thirty mile a day,
Compare with Caesars and with cannibals,
And Trojan Greeks?
Nay, rather damn them with King Cerberus,
And let the welkin roar.
1597–8 Pistol. *Henry IV Part Two*, act 2, sc.4, l.160–6.

50 Thou whoreson little tidy Bartholomew boar-pig, when wilt thou leave fighting o'days, and foining o'nights, and begin to patch up thine old body for heaven?
1597–8 Doll Tearsheet, of Falstaff. *Henry IV Part Two*, act 2, sc.4, l.232–5.

51 Is it not strange that desire should so many years outlive performance?
1597–8 Poins. *Henry IV Part Two*, act 2, sc.4, l.262–3.

52 O sleep, O gentle sleep,
Nature's soft nurse, how have I frighted thee,
That thou no more wilt weigh my eyelids down.
1597–8 King Henry. *Henry IV Part Two*, act 3, sc.1, l.5–7.

53 Canst thou, O partial sleep, give thy repose
To the wet sea-boy in an hour so rude,
And in the calmest and most stillest night,
With all appliances and means to boot,
Deny it to a king? Then happy low, lie down.
Uneasy lies the head that wears a crown.
1597–8 King Henry. *Henry IV Part Two*, act 3, sc.1, l.25–31.

54 Death, as the Psalmist saith, is certain to all: all shall die.
How a good yoke of bullocks at Stamford fair?
1597–8 Shallow. *Henry IV Part Two*, act 3, sc.2, l.35–6.

55 We have heard the chimes at midnight, Master Shallow.
1597–8 Falstaff. *Henry IV Part Two*, act 3, sc.2, l.211.

56 A man can die but once. We owe God a death.
1597–8 Feeble. *Henry IV Part Two*, act 3, sc.2, l.233–4.

57 Lord, Lord, how subject we old men are to this vice of lying!
1597–8 Falstaff. *Henry IV Part Two*, act 3, sc.2, l.298–9.

58 When a was naked, he was for all the world like a forked radish, with a head fantastically carved upon it with a knife.
1597–8 Falstaff, of Shallow. *Henry IV Part Two*, act 3, sc.2, l.305–7.

59 An iron man,
Cheering a rout of rebels with your drum,
Turning the word to sword, and life to death.
1597–8 Prince John. *Henry IV Part Two*, act 4, sc.1, l.234–6.

60 Sudden sorrow
Serves to say thus: some good thing comes tomorrow.
1597–8 Westmorland. *Henry IV Part Two*, act 4, sc.1, l.309–10.

61 A peace is of the nature of a conquest,
For then both parties nobly are subdued,
And neither party loser.
1597–8 Archbishop of York. *Henry IV Part Two*, act 4, sc.1, l.315–17.

62 He saw me, and yielded, that I may justly say, with the

hook-nosed fellow of Rome, 'I came, saw, and overcame'.
1597–8 Falstaff. *Henry IV Part Two*, act 4, sc.2, l.39–41.

63 A man cannot make him laugh. But that's no marvel; he drinks no wine.
1597–8 Falstaff. *Henry IV Part Two*, act 4, sc.2, l.85–6.

64 Will fortune never come with both hands full,
But write her fair words still in foulest letters?
1597–8 Henry, receiving good news when ill. *Henry IV Part Two*, act 4, sc.3, l.103–4.

65 How quickly nature falls into revolt
When gold becomes her object!
1597–8 King Henry, of his son Harry. *Henry IV Part Two*, act 4, sc.3, l.195–6.

66 Revel the night, rob, murder, and commit
The oldest sins the newest kind of ways?
1597–8 King Henry to Harry. *Henry IV Part Two*, act 4, sc.3, l.254–5.

67 I know thee not, old man. Fall to thy prayers.
How ill white hairs becomes a fool and jester!
1597–8 The newly-crowned King Harry, rejecting Falstaff. *Henry IV Part Two*, act 5, sc.5, l.47–8.

68 Here will be an old abusing of God's patience and the King's English.
1597–8 Mistress Quickly. *The Merry Wives of Windsor*, act 1, sc.4, l.4–5.

69 His worst fault is that he is given to prayer; he is something peevish that way.
1597–8 Mistress Quickly. *The Merry Wives of Windsor*, act 1, sc.4, l.11–12.

70 Why, then the world's mine oyster, which I with sword will open.
1597–8 Pistol. *The Merry Wives of Windsor*, act 2, sc.2, l.4–5.

71 Thinkst thou I'll endanger my soul gratis?
1597–8 Falstaff. *The Merry Wives of Windsor*, act 2, sc.2, l.16–17.

72 If money go before, all ways do lie open.
1597–8 Ford (as Brooke). *The Merry Wives of Windsor*, act 2, sc.2, l.164–5.

73 Money is a good soldier, sir, and will go on.
1597–8 Falstaff. *The Merry Wives of Windsor*, act 2, sc.2, l.166.

74 There is money. Spend it, spend it; spend more.
1597–8 Ford (as Brooke). *The Merry Wives of Windsor*, act 2, sc.2, l.223–4.

75 I cannot tell what the dickens his name is.
1597–8 Mistress Page. *The Merry Wives of Windsor*, act 3, sc.2, l.16.

76 He capers, he dances, he has eyes of youth; he writes verses, he speaks holiday, he smells April and May. He will carry't, he will carry't; 'tis in his buttons he will carry't.
1597–8 Host, of Master Feuton. *The Merry Wives of Windsor*, act 3, sc.2, l.61–4.

77 O, what a world of vile ill-favoured faults
Looks handsome in three hundred pounds a year!
1597–8 Anne. *The Merry Wives of Windsor*, act 3, sc.4, l.31–2.

78 A woman would run through fire and water for such a kind heart.
1597–8 Mistress Quickly. *The Merry Wives of Windsor*, act 3, sc.4, l.101–2.

79 Have I lived to be carried in a basket like a barrow of butcher's offal, and to be thrown in the Thames? Well, if I be served such another trick, I'll have my brains ta'en out

and buttered, and give them to a dog for a New Year's gift. 'Sblood, the rogues slighted me into the river with as little remorse as they would have drowned a blind bitch's puppies, fifteen i'th' litter! And you may know by my size that I have a kind of alacrity in sinking.
1597–8 Falstaff. *The Merry Wives of Windsor*, act 3, sc.5, l.4–12.

80 They say there is divinity in odd numbers, either in nativity, chance, or death.
1597–8 Falstaff. *The Merry Wives of Windsor*, act 5, sc.1, l.3–4.

81 Let the sky rain potatoes, let it thunder to the tune of 'Greensleeves'.
1597–8 Falstaff. *The Merry Wives of Windsor*, act 5, sc.5, l.17–18.

82 A victory is twice itself when the achiever brings home full numbers.
1598 Leonato. *Much Ado About Nothing*, act 1, sc.1, l.8–9.

83 How much better is it to weep at joy than to joy at weeping!
1598 Leonato. *Much Ado About Nothing*, act 1, sc.1, l.27–8.

84 He wears his faith but as the fashion of his hat, it ever changes with the next block.
1598 Beatrice, of Benedick. *Much Ado About Nothing*, act 1, sc.1, l.71–3.

85 He is sooner caught than the pestilence.
1598 Beatrice, of Claudio. *Much Ado About Nothing*, act 1, sc.1, l.82.

86 I wonder that you will still be talking, Signor Benedick. Nobody marks you.
1598 Beatrice. *Much Ado About Nothing*, act 1, sc.1, l.110–11.

87 What, my dear Lady Disdain! Are you yet living?
1598 Benedick to Beatrice. *Much Ado About Nothing*, act 1, sc.1, l.112–13.

88 I had rather hear my dog bark at a crow than a man swear he loves me.
1598 Beatrice. *Much Ado About Nothing*, act 1, sc.1, l.125–6.

89 Were she other than she is she were unhandsome, and being no other but as she is, I do not like her.
1598 Benedick, of Hero. *Much Ado About Nothing*, act 1, sc.1, l.166–7.

90 If he send me no husband, for the which blessing I am at him upon my knees every morning and evening. Lord, I could not endure a husband with a beard on his face. I had rather lie in the woollen.
1598 Beatrice. *Much Ado About Nothing*, act 2, sc.1, l.24–7.

91 He shows me where the bachelors sit, and there live we as merry as the day is long.
1598 Beatrice, of St Peter. *Much Ado About Nothing*, act 2, sc.1, l.42–4.

92 I have a good eye, uncle. I can see a church by daylight.
1598 Beatrice to Leonato. *Much Ado About Nothing*, act 2, sc.1, l.74–5.

93 Beauty is a witch
Against whose charms faith melteth into blood.
1598 Claudio. *Much Ado About Nothing*, act 2, sc.1, l.169–70.

94 She speaks poniards, and every word stabs. If her breath were as terrible as her terminations, there were no living near her, she would infect to the North Star.
1598 Benedick, of Beatrice. *Much Ado About Nothing*, act 2, sc.1, l.231–4.

95 Will your grace command me any service to the world's end? I will go on the slightest errand now to the Antipodes that you can devise to send me on. I will fetch you a tooth-picker now from the furthest inch of Asia,

bring you the length of Prester John's foot, fetch you a hair off the Great Cham's beard, do you any embassage to the pigmies, rather than hold three words' conference with this harpy.
1598 Benedick, of Beatrice. *Much Ado About Nothing*, act 2, sc.1, l.246–53.

96 O God, sir, here's a dish I love not. I cannot endure my Lady Tongue.
1598 Benedick, of Beatrice. *Much Ado About Nothing*, act 2, sc.1, l.256–7.

97 Silence is the perfectest herald of joy. I were but little happy if I could say how much.
1598 Claudio. *Much Ado About Nothing*, act 2, sc.1, l.287–8.

98 Your silence most offends me, and to be merry best becomes you; for out o' question, you were born in a merry hour.
1598 Don Pedro to Beatrice. *Much Ado About Nothing*, act 2, sc.1, l.310–12.

99 But then there was a star danced, and under that was I born.
1598 Beatrice. *Much Ado About Nothing*, act 2, sc.1, l.313–14.

1 There's little of the melancholy element in her, my lord. She is never sad but when she sleeps, and not ever sad then; for I have heard my daughter say she hath often dreamt of unhappiness and waked herself with laughing.
1598 Leonato, of Beatrice. *Much Ado About Nothing*, act 2, sc.1, l.321–5.

2 If they were but a week married they would talk themselves mad.
1598 Leonato, of Beatrice and Benedick. *Much Ado About Nothing*, act 2, sc.1, l.330–1.

3 Time goes on crutches till love have all his rites.
1598 Claudio. *Much Ado About Nothing*, act 2, sc.1, l.334–5.

4 He was wont to speak plain and to the purpose, like an honest man and a soldier, and now is he turned orthography. His words are a very fantastical banquet, just so many strange dishes.
1598 Benedick, of Claudio. *Much Ado About Nothing*, act 2, sc.3, l.18–21.

5 Is it not strange that sheep's guts should hale souls out of men's bodies?
1598 Benedick. *Much Ado About Nothing*, act 2, sc.3, l.57–9.

6 Sigh no more, ladies, sigh no more.
Men were deceivers ever,
One foot in sea, and one on shore,
To one thing constant never.
1598 Balthasar's song. *Much Ado About Nothing*, act 2, sc.3, l.61–4.

7 He doth indeed show some sparks that are like wit.
1598 Don Pedro, of Benedick. *Much Ado About Nothing*, act 2, sc.3, l.178–9.

8 I will be horribly in love with her.
1598 Benedick, of Beatrice, having been tricked into thinking she secretly loves him. *Much Ado About Nothing*, act 2, sc.3, l.222–3.

9 Look where Beatrice like a lapwing runs
Close by the ground to hear our conference.
1598 Hero to Ursula. *Much Ado About Nothing*, act 3, sc.1, l.24–5.

10 From the crown of his head to the sole of his foot he is all mirth.
1598 Don Pedro, of Benedick. *Much Ado About Nothing*, act 3, sc.2, l.7–9.

11 He hath twice or thrice cut Cupid's bow-string, and the little hangman dare not shoot at him. He hath a heart as sound as a bell, and his tongue is the clapper, for what his heart thinks his tongue speaks.
1598 Don Pedro, of Benedick. *Much Ado About Nothing*, act 3, sc.2, l.9–13.

12 Everyone can master a grief but he that has it.
1598 Benedick. *Much Ado About Nothing*, act 3, sc.2, l.26–7.

13 The barber's man hath been seen with him, and the old ornament of his cheek hath already stuffed tennis balls.
1598 Claudio, of Benedick. *Much Ado About Nothing*, act 3, sc.2, l.41–3.

14 Seest thou not, I say, what a deformed thief this fashion is, how giddily a turns about all the hot-bloods between fourteen and five-and-thirty…?
1598 Borachio to Conrad. *Much Ado About Nothing*, act 3, sc.3, l.126–9.

15 The fashion wears out more apparel than the man.
1598 Conrad to Borachio. *Much Ado About Nothing*, act 3, sc.3, l.134–5.

16 Comparisons are odorous.
1598 Dogberry to Verges. *Much Ado About Nothing*, act 3, sc.5, l.15.

17 As they say, when the age is in, the wit is out.
1598 Dogberry. *Much Ado About Nothing*, act 3, sc.5, l.32–3.

18 Well, God's a good man. An two men ride of a horse, one must ride behind.
1598 Dogberry to Verges. *Much Ado About Nothing*, act 3, sc.5, l.35–6.

19 O, what authority and show of truth
Can cunning sin cover itself withal!
1598 Claudio, of Hero. *Much Ado About Nothing*, act 4, sc.1, l.35–6.

20 'Tis all men's office to speak patience
To those that wring under the load of sorrow.
1598 Leonato. *Much Ado About Nothing*, act 5, sc.1, l.27–8.

21 There was never yet philosopher
That could endure the toothache patiently.
1598 Leonato. *Much Ado About Nothing*, act 5, sc.1, l.35–6.

22 Though care killed a cat, thou hast mettle enough in thee to kill care.
1598 Claudio, of Benedick. *Much Ado About Nothing*, act 5, sc.1, l.133–4.

23 Marry, sir, they have committed false report, moreover they have spoken untruths, secondarily they are slanders, sixth and lastly they have belied a lady, thirdly they have verified unjust things, and to conclude, they are lying knaves!
1598 Dogberry to Don Pedro. *Much Ado About Nothing*, act 5, sc.1, l.208–12.

24 I can find out no rhyme to 'lady' but 'baby', an innocent rhyme; for 'scorn' 'horn', a hard rhyme; for 'school' 'fool', a babbling rhyme. Very ominous endings. No, I was not born under a rhyming planet, nor I cannot woo in festival terms.
1598 Benedick. *Much Ado About Nothing*, act 5, sc.2, l.35–9.

25 If a man do not erect in this age his own tomb ere he dies, he shall live no longer in monument than the bell rings and the widow weeps.
1598 Benedick. *Much Ado About Nothing*, act 5, sc.2, l.69–72.

26 Good morrow, Benedick. Why, what's the matter

That you have such a February face,
So full of frost, of storm and cloudiness?
1598 Don Pedro. *Much Ado About Nothing*, act 5, sc.4, l.40–2.

27 Let's have a dance ere we are married, that we may lighten our own hearts and our wives' heels.
1598 Benedick. *Much Ado About Nothing*, act 5, sc.4, l.116–18.

28 Prince, thou art sad, get thee a wife, get thee a wife.
1598 Benedick to Don Pedro. *Much Ado About Nothing*, act 5, sc.4, l.121–2.

29 O for a muse of fire, that would ascend
The brightest heaven of invention.
1598–9 Chorus. *Henry V*, prologue to act 1, l.1–2.

30 When we have matched our rackets to these balls,
We will in France, by God's grace, play a set
Shall strike his father's crown into the hazard.
1598–9 King Harry, on the gift of tennis balls from the Dauphin. *Henry V*, act 1, sc.2, l.261–3.

31 'Tis ever common
That men are merriest when they are from home.
1598–9 King Harry. *Henry V*, act 1, sc.2, l.271–2.

32 Now all the youth of England are on fire,
And silken dalliance in the wardrobe lies.
1598–9 Chorus. *Henry V*, prologue to act 2, l.1–2.

33 O England! model to thy inward greatness,
Like little body with a mighty heart,
What might'st thou do, that honour would thee do,
Were all thy children kind and natural.
1598–9 Chorus. *Henry V*, prologue to act 2, l.16–19.

34 Though Patience be a tired mare, yet she will plod.
1598–9 Nim. *Henry V*, act 2, sc.1, l.22–3.

35 Treason and murder ever kept together,
As two yoke-devils sworn to either's purpose.
1598–9 King Harry. *Henry V*, act 2, sc.2, l.102–3.

36 I saw him fumble with the sheets, and play with flowers, and smile upon his finger's end.
1598–9 Hostess, describing Falstaff's death. *Henry V*, act 2, sc.3, l.13–15.

37 NIM: They say he cried out of sack.
HOSTESS: Ay, that a did.
BARDOLPH: And of women.
HOSTESS: Nay, that a did not.
BOY: Yes, that a did, and said they were devils incarnate.
HOSTESS: A could never abide carnation, 'twas a colour he never liked.
1598–9 Of Falstaff's death. *Henry V*, act 2, sc.3, l.26–32.

38 Look to my chattels and my movables.
Let senses rule. The word is 'Pitch and pay'.
Trust none, for oaths are straws, men's faiths are wafer-cakes,
And Holdfast is the only dog, my duck.
1598–9 Pistol to Nim. *Henry V*, act 2, sc.3, l.45–8.

39 Let us do it with no show of fear,
No, with no more than if we heard that England
Were busied with a Whitsun morris dance.
For, my good liege, she is so idly kinged,
Her sceptre so fantastically borne
By a vain, giddy, shallow, humorous youth,
That fear attends her not
1598–9 Dauphin, to King Charles. *Henry V*, act 2, sc.4, l.23–9.

40 In cases of defence 'tis best to weigh
The enemy more mighty than he seems.

1598–9 Dauphin. *Henry V*, act 2, sc.4, l.43–4.

41 Self-love, my liege, is not so vile a sin
As self-neglecting.
1598–9 Dauphin, to King Charles. *Henry V*, act 2, sc.4, l.73–4.

42 Once more unto the breach, dear friends, once more,
Or close the wall up with our English dead.
In peace there's nothing so becomes a man
As modest stillness and humility.
But when the blast of war blows in our ears,
Then imitate the action of the tiger.
Stiffen the sinews, conjure up the blood,
Disguise fair nature with hard-favoured rage.
1598–9 King Harry rallying his men at the siege of Harfleur. *Henry V*, act 3, sc.1, l.1–8.

43 I see you stand like greyhounds in the slips,
Straining upon the start. The game's afoot.
1598–9 King Harry rallying his men at the siege of Harfleur. *Henry V*, act 3, sc.1, l.31–2.

44 Cry, 'God for Harry! England and Saint George!'
1598–9 King Harry rallying his men at the siege of Harfleur. *Henry V*, act 3, sc.1, l.34.

45 FLUELLEN: Captain Macmorris, I think, look you, under your correction, there is not many of your nation— MACMORRIS: Of my nation? What ish my nation? Ish a villain and a bastard and a knave and a rascal? What ish my nation? Who talks of my nation?
1598–9 *Henry V*, act 3, sc.3, l.64–8.

46 From camp to camp through the foul womb of night
The hum of either army stilly sounds.
1598–9 Chorus. *Henry V*, prologue to act 4, l.4–5.

47 A little touch of Harry in the night.
1598–9 Chorus. *Henry V*, prologue to act 4, l.47.

48 There is some soul of goodness in things evil,
Would men observingly distil it out.
1598–9 King Harry. *Henry V*, act 4, sc.1, l.4–5.

49 The King's a bawcock and a heart-of-gold,
A lad of life, an imp of fame,
Of parents good, of fist most valiant.
I kiss his dirty shoe, and from my heartstring
I love the lovely bully.
1598–9 Pistol to King Harry, disguised. *Henry V*, act 4, sc.1, l.45–9.

50 Every subject's duty is the King's, but every subject's soul is his own.
1598–9 King Harry. *Henry V*, act 4, sc.1, l.175–6.

51 Be friends, you English fools, be friends. We have French quarrels enough, if you could tell how to reckon.
1598–9 Bates. *Henry V*, act 4, sc.1, l.220–1.

52 Upon the King.
'Let us, our lives, our souls, our debts, our care-full wives,
Our children, and our sins, lay on the King.'
1598–9 King Harry. *Henry V*, act 4, sc.1, l.227–9.

53 O God of battles, steel my soldiers' hearts.
1598–9 King Harry, before Agincourt. *Henry V*, act 4, sc.1, l.286.

54 O that we now had here
But one ten thousand of those men in England
That do no work today.
1598–9 Warwick, before Agincourt. *Henry V*, act 4, sc.3, l.16–18.

55 If it be a sin to covet honour
I am the most offending soul alive.
1598–9 King Harry. *Henry V*, act 4, sc.3, l.28–9.

56 He which hath no stomach to this fight,
Let him depart.
1598–9 King Harry, before Agincourt. *Henry V*, act 4, sc.3, l.35.

57 He that shall see this day and live t'old age,
Will yearly on the vigil feast his neighbours
And say, 'Tomorrow is Saint Crispian.'
1598–9 King Harry, before Agincourt. *Henry V*, act 4, sc.3, l.44–6.

58 Then will he strip his sleeve and show his scars
And say, 'These wounds I had on Crispin's day.'
Old men forget; yet all shall be forgot,
But he'll remember.
1598–9 King Harry, before Agincourt. *Henry V*, act 4, sc.3, l.47–50.

59 Then shall our names,
Familiar in his mouth as household words…
Be in their flowing cups freshly remembered.
1598–9 King Harry, before Agincourt. *Henry V*, act 4, sc.3, l.51–5.

60 This story shall the good man teach his son,
And Crispin Crispian shall ne'er go by
From this day to the ending of the world
But we in it shall be rememberèd,
We few, we happy few, we band of brothers.
1598–9 King Harry, before Agincourt. *Henry V*, act 4, sc.3, l.56–60.

61 He today that sheds his blood with me
Shall be my brother; be he ne'er so vile.
1598–9 King Harry, before Agincourt. *Henry V*, act 4, sc.3, l.61–2.

62 And gentlemen in England now abed
Shall think themselves accursed they were not here,
And hold their manhoods cheap whiles any speaks
That fought with us upon Saint Crispin's day.
1598–9 King Harry, before Agincourt. *Henry V*, act 4, sc.3, l.64–7.

63 Let life be short, else shame will be too long.
1598–9 Bourbon, returning to the battle. *Henry V*, act 4, sc.5, l.19.

64 There is occasions and causes why and wherefore in all things.
1598–9 Fluellen. *Henry V*, act 5, sc.1, l.3–4.

65 Not for Cadwallader and all his goats.
1598–9 Pistol, refusing to eat leeks. *Henry V*, act 5, sc.1, l.27.

66 An angel is like you, Kate, and you are like an angel.
1598–9 King Harry, wooing Catherine. *Henry V*, act 5, sc.2, l.109–10.

67 Thou wouldst find me such a plain king that thou wouldst think I had sold my farm to buy my crown.
1598–9 King Harry, wooing Catherine. *Henry V*, act 5, sc.2, l.125–7.

68 You have witchcraft in your lips, Kate. There is more eloquence in a sugar touch of them than in the tongues of the French Council.
1598–9 King Harry, wooing Catherine. *Henry V*, act 5, sc.2, l.274–6.

69 God, the best maker of all marriages,
Combine your hearts in one, your realms in one.
1598–9 Queen Isabel, on the marriage of King Harry and Catherine. *Henry V*, act 5, sc.2, l.354–5.

70 Hence, home, you idle creatures, get you home!
1599 Flavius. *Julius Caesar*, act 1, sc.1, l.1.

71 You blocks, you stones, you worse than senseless things!
O, you hard hearts, you cruel men of Rome,
Knew you not Pompey?
1599 Murellus, to the citizens of Rome. *Julius Caesar*, act 1, sc.1, l.34–7.

72 Beware the ides of March.
1599 Soothsayer to Caesar. *Julius Caesar*, act 1, sc.2, l.19.

73 Poor Brutus, with himself at war,
Forgets the shows of love to other men.
1599 Brutus. *Julius Caesar*, act 1, sc.2, l.48–9.

74 Set honour in one eye and death i' the other,
And I will look on both indifferently.
1599 Brutus. *Julius Caesar*, act 1, sc.2, l.88–9.

75 I cannot tell what you and other men
Think of this life; but for my single self,
I had as lief not be, as live to be
In awe of such a thing as I myself.
I was born free as Caesar, so were you.
1599 Cassius to Brutus. *Julius Caesar*, act 1, sc.2, l.95–9.

76 He doth bestride the narrow world
Like a Colossus, and we petty men
Walk under his huge legs, and peep about
To find ourselves dishonourable graves.
Men at sometime were masters of their fates.
The fault, dear Brutus, is not in our stars,
But in ourselves, that we are underlings.
1599 Cassius, of Caesar. *Julius Caesar*, act 1, sc.2, l.136–42.

77 Brutus and Caesar: what should be in that 'Caesar'?
Why should that name be sounded more than
yours?
Write them together: yours is as fair a name.
Sound them: it doth become the mouth as well.
Weigh them: it is as heavy. Conjure with 'em:
'Brutus' will start a spirit as soon as 'Caesar'.
1599 Cassius to Brutus. *Julius Caesar*, act 1, sc.2, l.143–8.

78 Upon what meat doth this our Caesar feed
That he is grown so great?
1599 Cassius to Brutus. *Julius Caesar*, act 1, sc.2, l.150–1.

79 Let me have men about me that are fat;
Sleek-headed men, and such as sleep o'nights;
Yond Cassius has a lean and hungry look;
He thinks too much: such men are dangerous.
1599 Caesar. *Julius Caesar*, act 1, sc.2, l.193–6.

80 Seldom he smiles, and smiles in such a sort
As if he mocked himself.
1599 Caesar, of Cassius. *Julius Caesar*, act 1, sc.2, l.206–7.

81 Cassius from bondage will deliver Cassius.
Therein, ye gods, you make the weak most strong;
Therein, ye gods, you tyrants do defeat.
Nor stony tower, nor walls of beaten brass,
Nor airless dungeon, nor strong links of iron,
Can be retentive to the strength of spirit;
But life, being weary of these worldly bars,
Never lacks power to dismiss itself.
1599 Cassius. *Julius Caesar*, act 1, sc.3, l.89–96.

82 It is the bright day that brings forth the adder,
And that craves wary walking.
1599 Brutus. *Julius Caesar*, act 2, sc.1, l.14–15.

83 Between the acting of a dreadful thing
And the first motion, all the interim is
Like a phantasma or a hideous dream.
1599 Brutus. *Julius Caesar*, act 2, sc.1, l.63–5.

84 Let's carve him as a dish fit for the gods,
Not hew him as a carcass fit for hounds.
1599 Brutus, of Caesar. *Julius Caesar*, act 2, sc.1, l.173–4.

85 Am I your self
But as it were in sort or limitation?
To keep with you at meals, comfort your bed,
And talk to you sometimes? Dwell I but in the suburbs
Of your good pleasure? If it be no more,
Portia is Brutus' harlot, not his wife.
1599 Portia. *Julius Caesar*, act 2, sc.1, l.281–6.

86 You are my true and honourable wife,
As dear to me as are the ruddy drops
That visit my sad heart.
1599 Brutus to Portia. *Julius Caesar*, act 2, sc.1, l.287–9.

87 When beggars die there are no comets seen;
The heavens themselves blaze forth the death of
princes.
1599 Calpurnia. *Julius Caesar*, act 2, sc.2, l.30–1.

88 Cowards die many times before their deaths;
The valiant never taste of death but once.
1599 Caesar. *Julius Caesar*, act 2, sc.2, l.32–3.

89 Of all the wonders that I yet have heard,
It seems to me most strange that men should fear,
Seeing that death, a necessary end,
Will come when it will come.
1599 Caesar. *Julius Caesar*, act 2, sc.2, l.34–7.

90 Danger knows full well
That Caesar is more dangerous than he.
1599 Caesar. *Julius Caesar*, act 2, sc.2, l.44–5.

91 The cause is in my will; I will not come.
1599 Caesar. *Julius Caesar*, act 2, sc.2, l.71.

92 Ay me! How weak a thing
The heart of woman is!
1599 Portia. *Julius Caesar*, act 2, sc.4, l.41–2.

93 I could be well moved if I were as you.
If I could pray to move, prayers would move me.
But I am constant as the Northern star,
Of whose true fixed and resting quality
There is no fellow in the firmament.
The skies are painted with unnumbered sparks;
They are all fire, and every one doth shine;
But there's but one in all doth hold his place.
So in the world: 'tis furnished well with men,
And men are flesh and blood, and apprehensive;
Yet in the number I do know but one
That unassailable holds on his rank,
Unshaked of motion; and that I am he
Let me a little show it even in this—
That I was constant Cimber should be banished,
And constant do remain to keep him so.
1599 Caesar. *Julius Caesar*, act 3, sc.1, l.58–73.

94 Et tu, Bruté?—Then fall Caesar.
1599 *Julius Caesar*, act 3, sc.1, l.76.

95 Ambition's debt is paid.
1599 Brutus, after he has killed Caesar. *Julius Caesar*, act 3, sc.1, l.82.

96 Fates, we will know your pleasures.
That we shall die, we know; 'tis but the time
And drawing days out that men stand upon.
1599 Brutus. *Julius Caesar*, act 3, sc.1, l.99–101.

97 He that cuts off twenty years of life
Cuts off so many years of fearing death.
1599 Casca. *Julius Caesar*, act 3, sc.1, l.102–3.

98 How many ages hence
   Shall this our lofty scene be acted over,
   In states unborn and accents yet unknown!
   1599 Cassius, of the murder of Caesar. *Julius Caesar*, act 3, sc.1,
   l.112–14.

99 O mighty Caesar! Dost thou lie so low?
   Are all thy conquests, glories, triumphs, spoils,
   Shrunk to this little measure?
   1599 Antony. *Julius Caesar*, act 3, sc.1, l.149–51.

1 O pardon me, thou bleeding piece of earth,
   That I am meek and gentle with these butchers.
   1599 Antony. *Julius Caesar*, act 3, sc.1, l.257–8.

2 Caesar's spirit, ranging for revenge,
   With Ate by his side come hot from hell,
   Shall in these confines with a monarch's voice
   Cry 'havoc!', and let slip the dogs of war,
   That this foul deed shall smell above the earth
   With carrion men, groaning for burial.
   1599 Antony. *Julius Caesar*, act 3, sc.1, l.273–8.

3 This is my answer: not that I loved Caesar less, but that I
   loved Rome more.
   1599 Brutus, explaining his reasons for killing Caesar. *Julius
   Caesar*, act 3, sc.2, l.20–1.

4 As Caesar loved me, I weep for him. As he was fortunate,
   I rejoice at it. As he was valiant, I honour him. But as he
   was ambitious, I slew him.
   1599 Brutus. *Julius Caesar*, act 3, sc.2, l.24–7.

5 Friends, Romans, countrymen, lend me your ears.
   I come to bury Caesar, not to praise him.
   The evil that men do lives after them;
   The good is oft interrèd with their bones.
   So let it be with Caesar. The noble Brutus
   Hath told you Caesar was ambitious.
   If it were so, it was a grievous fault,
   And grievously hath Caesar answered it.
   Here, under leave of Brutus and the rest—
   For Brutus is an honourable man,
   So are they all, all honourable men—
   Come I to speak in Caesar's funeral.
   He was my friend, faithful and just to me.
   1599 Antony. *Julius Caesar*, act 3, sc.2, l.74–86.

6 When that the poor have cried, Caesar hath wept.
   Ambition should be made of sterner stuff.
   1599 Antony. *Julius Caesar*, act 3, sc.2, l.92–3.

7 O judgement! thou art fled to brutish beasts,
   And men have lost their reason!
   1599 Antony. *Julius Caesar*, act 3, sc.2, l.105–6.

8 Bear with me.
   My heart is in the coffin there with Caesar,
   And I must pause till it come back to me.
   1599 Antony. *Julius Caesar*, act 3, sc.2, l.106–8.

9 But yesterday the word of Caesar might
   Have stood against the world. Now lies he there,
   And none so poor to do him reverence.
   1599 Antony. *Julius Caesar*, act 3, sc.2, l.119–21.

10 If you have tears, prepare to shed them now.
   1599 Antony. *Julius Caesar*, act 3, sc.2, l.167.

11 This was the most unkindest cut of all.
   For when the noble Caesar saw him stab,
   Ingratitude, more strong than traitors' arms,
   Quite vanquished him.

1599 Antony of Brutus. *Julius Caesar*, act 3, sc.2, l.181–4.

12 O now you weep, and I perceive you feel
   The dint of pity. These are gracious drops.
   1599 Antony to the crowd. *Julius Caesar*, act 3, sc.2, l.191–2.

13 I am no orator as Brutus is,
   But, as you know me all, a plain blunt man.
   1599 Antony. *Julius Caesar*, act 3, sc.2, l.212–13.

14 Fortune is merry,
   And in this mood will give us anything.
   1599 Antony. *Julius Caesar*, act 3, sc.2, l.259–60.

15 Good reasons must of force give place to better.
   1599 Brutus. *Julius Caesar*, act 4, sc.2, l.255.

16 There is a tide in the affairs of men
   Which, taken at the flood, leads on to fortune;
   Omitted, all the voyage of their life
   Is bound in shallows and in miseries.
   1599 Brutus. *Julius Caesar*, act 4, sc.2, l.270–3.

17 We'll along ourselves, and meet them at Philippi.
   1599 Cassius. *Julius Caesar*, act 4, sc.2, l.277.

18 I should not urge thy duty past thy might.
   1599 Brutus to Lucius. *Julius Caesar*, act 4, sc.2, l.312.

19 Good words are better than bad strokes.
   1599 Brutus to Octavius. *Julius Caesar*, act 5, sc.1, l.29.

20 Blow wind, swell billow, and swim bark.
   The storm is up, and all is on the hazard.
   1599 Cassius, at Philippi. *Julius Caesar*, act 5, sc.1, l.67–8.

21 Since the affairs of men rest still incertain,
   Let's reason with the worst that may befall.
   1599 Cassius to Brutus. *Julius Caesar*, act 5, sc.1, l.95–6.

22 O that a man might know
   The end of this day's business ere it come!
   But it sufficeth that the day will end,
   And then the end is known.
   1599 Brutus. *Julius Caesar*, act 5, sc.1, l.123–6.

23 I prithee, Strato, stay thou by thy lord.
   Thou art a fellow of a good respect.
   Thy life hath had some smatch of honour in it.
   Hold then my sword, and turn away thy face
   While I do run upon it.
   1599 Brutus, killing himself. *Julius Caesar*, act 5, sc.5, l.44–8.

24 Caesar, now be still,
   I killed not thee with half so good a will.
   1599 Brutus, killing himself. *Julius Caesar*, act 5, sc. 5, l.50–1.

25 This was the noblest Roman of them all.
   All the conspirators save only he
   Did that they did in envy of great Caesar.
   He only in a general honest thought
   And common good to all made one of them.
   His life was gentle, and the elements
   So mixed in him that nature might stand up
   And say to all the world 'This was a man'.
   1599 Antony, of Brutus. *Julius Caesar*, act 5, sc.5, l.67–74.

26 Let us sit and mock the good housewife Fortune from
   her wheel, that her gifts may henceforth be bestowed
   equally.
   1599–1600 Celia to Rosalind. *As You Like It*, act 1, sc.2, l.30–2.

27 Where is this young gallant that is so desirous to lie with
   his mother earth?
   1599–1600 Charles to Orlando. *As You Like It*, act 1, sc.2, l.188–9.

28 My pride fell with my fortunes.

1599–1600 Rosalind. *As You Like It*, act 1, sc.2, l.241.

29 Fare you well.
Hereafter, in a better world than this,
I shall desire more love and knowledge of you.
1599–1600 Le Beau to Orlando. *As You Like It*, act 1, sc.2, l.273–4.

30 Thy words are too precious to be cast away upon curs.
Throw some of them at me.
1599–1600 Celia to Rosalind. *As You Like It*, act 1, sc.3, l.4–6.

31 Thou art thy father's daughter—there's enough.
1599–1600 Duke Frederick to Rosalind, explaining why he does not trust her. *As You Like It*, act 1, sc.3, l.57.

32 What danger will it be to us,
Maids as we are, to travel forth so far!
Beauty provoketh thieves sooner than gold.
1599–1600 Rosalind to Celia. *As You Like It*, act 1, sc.3, l.107–9.

33 Sweet are the uses of adversity
Which, like the toad, ugly and venomous,
Wears yet a precious jewel in his head.
1599–1600 Duke Senior. *As You Like It*, act 2, sc.1, l.12–14.

34 And this our life, exempt from public haunt,
Finds tongues in trees, books in the running brooks,
Sermons in stones, and good in everything.
1599–1600 Duke Senior. *As You Like It*, act 2, sc.1, l.15–17.

35 Sweep on, you fat and greasy citizens.
1599–1600 First Lord, quoting Jaques. *As You Like It*, act 2, sc.1, l.55.

36 I love to cope him in these sullen fits,
For then he's full of matter.
1599–1600 Duke Senior, of Jaques. *As You Like It*, act 2, sc.1, l.67–8.

37 Unregarded age in corners thrown.
1599–1600 Adam. *As You Like It*, act 2, sc.3, l.43.

38 He that doth the ravens feed,
Yea providently caters for the sparrow,
Be comfort to my age.
1599–1600 Adam to Orlando. *As You Like It*, act 2, sc.3, l.44–6.

39 Though I look old, yet I am strong and lusty,
For in my youth I never did apply
Hot and rebellious liquors in my blood,
Nor did not with unbashful forehead woo
The means of weakness and debility.
Therefore my age is as a lusty winter.
1599–1600 Adam to Orlando. *As You Like It*, act 2, sc.3, l.48–53.

40 Thou art not for the fashion of these times,
Where none will sweat but for promotion.
1599–1600 Orlando, of Adam. *As You Like It*, act 2, sc.3, l.60–1.

41 I think you have no money in your purse.
1599–1600 Touchstone to Celia. *As You Like It*, act 2, sc.4, l.12.

42 Now I am in Ardenne; the more fool I. When I was at home I was in a better place; but travellers must be content.
1599–1600 Touchstone. *As You Like It*, act 2, sc.4, l.14–15.

43 Under the greenwood tree
Who loves to lie with me,
And turn his merry note
Unto the sweet bird's throat.
1599–1600 Amiens's song. *As You Like It*, act 2, sc.5, l.1–4.

44 I can suck melancholy out of a song as a weasel sucks eggs.
1599–1600 Jaques. *As You Like It*, act 2, sc.5, l.11–12.

45 I'll go sleep if I can. If I cannot, I'll rail against all the firstborn of Egypt.
1599–1600 Jaques. *As You Like It*, act 2, sc.5, l.57–8.

46 A fool, a fool, I met a fool i'th' forest,
A motley fool—a miserable world!—
As I do live by food, I met a fool,
Who laid him down and basked him in the sun,
And railed on Lady Fortune in good terms,
In good set terms, and yet a motley fool.
1599–1600 Jaques. *As You Like It*, act 2, sc.7, l.12–17.

47 'Thus we may see', quoth he, 'how the world wags.
'Tis but an hour ago since it was nine,
And after one hour more 'twill be eleven.
And so from hour to hour we ripe and ripe,
And then from hour to hour we rot and rot;
And thereby hangs a tale.'
1599–1600 Jaques, quoting Touchstone. *As You Like It*, act 2, sc.7, l.23–8.

48 All the world's a stage,
And all the men and women merely players.
They have their exits and their entrances,
And one man in his time plays many parts.
1599–1600 Jaques. *As You Like It*, act 2, sc.7, l.139–42.

49 The whining schoolboy with his satchel
And shining morning face.
1599–1600 Jaques. *As You Like It*, act 2, sc.7, l.145–6.

50 Jealous in honour, sudden, and quick in quarrel,
Seeking the bubble reputation
Even in the cannon's mouth.
1599–1600 Jaques, of the soldier. *As You Like It*, act 2, sc.7, l.151–3.

51 Second childishness and mere oblivion,
Sans teeth, sans eyes, sans taste, sans everything.
1599–1600 Jaques, of old age. *As You Like It*, act 2, sc.7, l.165–6.

52 Blow, blow, thou winter wind,
Thou art not so unkind
As man's ingratitude.
1599–1600 Amiens singing. *As You Like It*, act 2, sc.7, l.175–7.

53 Most friendship is feigning, most loving, mere folly.
1599–1600 Amiens. *As You Like It*, act 2, sc.7, l.182.

54 These trees shall be my books
And in their barks my thoughts I'll character.
1599–1600 Orlando. *As You Like It*, act 3, sc.2, l.5–6.

55 Run, run, Orlando; carve on every tree
The fair, the chaste, and unexpressive she.
1599–1600 Orlando. *As You Like It*, act 3, sc.2, l.9–10.

56 Hast any philosophy in thee, shepherd?
1599–1600 Touchstone to Corin. *As You Like It*, act 3, sc.2, l.21–2.

57 I earn that I eat, get that I wear; owe no man hate, envy no man's happiness.
1599–1600 Corin. *As You Like It*, act 3, sc.2, l.71–2.

58 This is the very false gallop of verses.
1599–1600 Touchstone, of Orlando's poem. *As You Like It*, act 3, sc.2, l.111.

59 I was never so berhymed since Pythagoras' time that I was an Irish rat, which I can hardly remember.
1599–1600 Rosalind. *As You Like It*, act 3, sc.2, l.172–4.

60 O wonderful, wonderful, and most wonderful-wonderful, and yet again wonderful, and after that out of all whooping!

1599–1600 Celia, on the arrival of Orlando. *As You Like It*, act 3, sc.2, l.187–9.

61 Do you not know that I am a woman? When I think, I must speak.
   1599–1600 Rosalind to Celia. *As You Like It*, act 3, sc.2, l.244–5.

62 I do desire we may be better strangers.
   1599–1600 Orlando to Jaques. *As You Like It*, act 3, sc.2, l.253.

63 Time travels in divers paces with divers persons.
   1599–1600 Rosalind. *As You Like It*, act 3, sc.2, l.301–2.

64 Love is merely a madness, and, I tell you, deserves as well a dark house and a whip as madmen do.
   1599–1600 Rosalind to Orlando. *As You Like It*, act 3, sc.2, l.386–8.

65 I would the gods had made thee poetical.
   1599–1600 Touchstone to Audrey. *As You Like It*, act 3, sc.3, l.12–13.

66 The truest poetry is the most feigning.
   1599–1600 Touchstone to Audrey. *As You Like It*, act 3, sc.3, l.16–17.

67 Honesty coupled to beauty is to have honey a sauce to sugar.
   1599–1600 Touchstone to Audrey. *As You Like It*, act 3, sc.3, l.26–7.

68 His kissing is as full of sanctity as the touch of holy bread.
   1599–1600 Rosalind. *As You Like It*, act 3, sc.4, l.12–13.

69 Mistress, know yourself; down on your knees
   And thank heaven, fasting, for a good man's love.
   1599–1600 Rosalind, in disguise, to Phoebe. *As You Like It*, act 3, sc.5, l.58–9.

70 I pray you do not fall in love with me,
   For I am falser than vows made in wine.
   Besides, I like you not.
   1599–1600 Rosalind, in disguise, to Phoebe. *As You Like It*, act 3, sc.5, l.73–5.

71 Dead shepherd, now I find thy saw of might:
   'Who ever loved that loved not at first sight?'
   1599–1600 Phoebe, in love with Rosalind (disguised as a young man). *As You Like It*, act 3, sc.5, l.82–3.

72 It is a melancholy of mine own, compounded of many simples, extracted from many objects, and indeed the sundry contemplation of my travels.
   1599–1600 Jaques. *As You Like It*, act 4, sc.1, l.15–17.

73 A traveller! By my faith, you have great reason to be sad. I fear you have sold your own lands to see other men's.
   1599–1600 Rosalind to Jaques. *As You Like It*, act 4, sc.1, l.20–2.

74 I had rather have a fool to make me merry than experience to make me sad—and to travel for it too!
   1599–1600 Rosalind to Jaques. *As You Like It*, act 4, sc.1, l.25–7.

75 JAQUES: Nay then, God b'wi'you an you talk in blank verse.
   ROSALIND: Farewell, Monsieur Traveller. Look you lisp, and wear strange suits; disable all the benefits of your own country; be out of love with your nativity, and almost chide God for making you that countenance you are, or I will scarce think you have swam in a gondola.
   1599–1600 *As You Like It*, act 4, sc.1, l.29–36.

76 Come, woo me, woo me, for now I am in a holiday humour, and like enough to consent.
   1599–1600 Rosalind, in disguise, to Orlando. *As You Like It*, act 4, sc.1, l.64–5.

77 Men have died from time to time, and worms have eaten

them, but not for love.
   1599–1600 Rosalind, in disguise, to Orlando. *As You Like It*, act 4, sc.1, l.99–101.

78 Can one desire too much of a good thing?
   1599–1600 Rosalind, in disguise, to Orlando. *As You Like It*, act 4, sc.1, l.115–16.

79 Men are April when they woo, December when they wed. Maids are May when they are maids, but the sky changes when they are wives.
   1599–1600 Rosalind, in disguise, to Orlando. *As You Like It*, act 4, sc.1, l.139–41.

80 Make the doors upon a woman's wit, and it will out at the casement. Shut that, and 'twill out at the key-hole. Stop that, 'twill fly with the smoke out at the chimney.
   1599–1600 Rosalind, in disguise, to Orlando. *As You Like It*, act 4, sc.1, l.153–4.

81 'Tis no matter how it be in tune, so it make noise enough.
   1599–1600 Jaques. *As You Like It*, act 4, sc.2, l.8–9.

82 The horn, the horn, the lusty horn
   Is not a thing to laugh to scorn.
   1599–1600 Lords, singing. *As You Like It*, act 4, sc.2, l.18–19.

83 I do now remember a saying: 'The fool doth think he is wise, but the wise man knows himself to be a fool.'
   1599–1600 Touchstone to William. *As You Like It*, act 5, sc.1, l.29–31.

84 To wit, I kill thee, make thee away, translate thy life into death, thy liberty into bondage. I will deal in poison with thee, or in bastinado, or in steel. I will bandy with thee in faction, I will o'errun thee with policy. I will kill thee a hundred and fifty ways. Therefore tremble, and depart.
   1599–1600 Touchstone. *As You Like It*, act 5, sc.1, l.51–6.

85 [They] no sooner looked but they loved; no sooner loved but they sighed; no sooner sighed but they asked one another the reason; no sooner knew the reason but they sought the remedy.
   1599–1600 Rosalind, of Celia and Oliver. *As You Like It*, act 5, sc.2, l.32–5.

86 How bitter a thing it is to look into happiness through another man's eyes.
   1599–1600 Orlando. *As You Like It*, act 5, sc.2, l.41–2.

87 I can live no longer by thinking.
   1599–1600 Orlando. *As You Like It*, act 5, sc.2, l.48.

88 It was a lover and his lass,
   With a hey, and a ho, and a hey-nonny-no,
   That o'er the green cornfield did pass
   In spring-time, the only pretty ring-time,
   When birds do sing, hey ding-a-ding ding,
   Sweet lovers love the spring.
   1599–1600 Pages' song. *As You Like It*, act 5, sc.3, l.15–20.

89 A poor virgin, sir, an ill-favoured thing, sir, but mine own.
   1599–1600 Touchstone, of Audrey. *As You Like It*, act 5, sc.4, l.57–8.

90 I durst go no further than the Lie Circumstantial, nor he durst not give me the Lie Direct; and so we measured swords, and parted.
   1599–1600 Touchstone. *As You Like It*, act 5, sc.4, l.83–5.

91 O sir, we quarrel in print, by the book, as you have books for good manners. I will name you the degrees. The first, the Retort Courteous; the second, the Quip Modest; the third, the Reply Churlish; the fourth, the Reproof Valiant; the fifth, the Countercheck Quarrelsome; the sixth, the

Lie with Circumstance; the seventh, the Lie Direct.
1599–1600 Touchstone. *As You Like It*, act 5, sc.4, l.88–94.

92 Your 'if' is the only peacemaker; much virtue in 'if'.
1599–1600 Touchstone. *As You Like It*, act 5, sc.4, l.100–1.

93 He uses his folly like a stalking-horse, and under the presentation of that he shoots his wit.
1599–1600 Duke Senior, of Touchstone. *As You Like It*, act 5, sc.4, l.104–5.

94 If it be true that good wine needs no bush, 'tis true that a good play needs no epilogue.
1599–1600 Rosalind. *As You Like It*, epilogue.

95 For this relief much thanks. 'Tis bitter cold, And I am sick at heart.
1600–1 Francisco. *Hamlet*, act 1, sc.1, l.6–7.

96 Thus twice before, and just at this dead hour, With martial stalk hath he gone by our watch.
1600–1 Marcellus, of the ghost of Hamlet's father. *Hamlet*, act 1, sc.1, l.64–5.

97 And then it started like a guilty thing Upon a fearful summons.
1600–1 Horatio, of the ghost. *Hamlet*, act 1, sc.1, l.129–30.

98 The head is not more native to the heart, The hand more instrumental to the mouth, Than is the throne of Denmark to thy father.
1600–1 Claudius to Laertes. *Hamlet*, act 1, sc.2, l.47–9.

99 A little more than kin and less than kind.
1600–1 Hamlet, of Claudius. *Hamlet*, act 1, sc.2, l.65.

1 I am too much i' th' sun.
1600–1 Hamlet. *Hamlet*, act 1, sc.2, l.67.

2 Good Hamlet, cast thy nightly colour off, And let thine eye look like a friend on Denmark. Do not for ever with thy vailèd lids Seek for thy noble father in the dust.
1600–1 Gertrude. *Hamlet*, act 1, sc.2, l.68–71.

3 Seems, madam? Nay, it *is*. I know not 'seems'.
1600–1 Hamlet to Gertrude. *Hamlet*, act 1,sc.2, l.76.

4 But I have that within which passeth show— These but the trappings and the suits of woe.
1600–1 Hamlet to Gertrude. *Hamlet*, act 1, sc.2, l.85–6.

5 O that this too too solid flesh would melt, Thaw, and resolve itself into a dew, Or that the Everlasting had not fixed His canon 'gainst self-slaughter!
1600–1 Hamlet. *Hamlet*, act 1, sc.2, l.129–32.

6 How weary, stale, flat, and unprofitable Seem to me all the uses of this world!
1600–1 Hamlet. *Hamlet*, act 1, sc.2, l.133–4.

7 So loving to my mother That he might not beteem the winds of heaven Visit her face too roughly!
1600–1 Hamlet, of his father. *Hamlet*, act 1, sc.2, l.140–3.

8 Frailty, thy name is woman.
1600–1 Hamlet, of Gertrude. *Hamlet*, act 1, sc.2, l.146.

9 We'll teach you to drink deep ere you depart.
1600–1 Hamlet to Horatio. *Hamlet*, act 1, sc.2, l.174.

10 Thrift, thrift, Horatio. The funeral baked meats Did coldly furnish forth the marriage tables.
1600–1 Hamlet to Horatio, on the reason for his mother's swift marriage to Claudius. *Hamlet*, act 1, sc.2, l.179–80.

11 A was a man. Take him for all in all,

I shall not look upon his like again.
1600–1 Hamlet, of his father. *Hamlet*, act 1, sc.2, l.186–7.

12 A countenance more In sorrow than in anger.
1600–1 Horatio, of Hamlet's father's ghost. *Hamlet*, act 1, sc.2, l.228–9.

13 I doubt some foul play. Would the night were come. Till then, sit still, my soul. Foul deeds will rise, Though all the earth o'erwhelm them, to men's eyes.
1600–1 Hamlet. *Hamlet*, act 1, sc.2, l.255–7.

14 And keep within the rear of your affection, Out of the shot and danger of desire.
1600–1 Laertes to Ophelia. *Hamlet*, act 1, sc.3, l.34–5.

15 The chariest maid is prodigal enough If she unmask her beauty to the moon.
1600–1 Laertes to Ophelia. *Hamlet*, act 1, sc.3, l.36–7.

16 Do not, as some ungracious pastors do, Show me the steep and thorny way to heaven, Whilst, like a puffed and reckless libertine Himself the primrose path of dalliance treads.
1600–1 Ophelia to Laertes. *Hamlet*, act 1, sc.3, l.47–50.

17 The friends thou hast, and their adoption tried, Grapple them to thy soul with hoops of steel.
1600–1 Polonius to Laertes. *Hamlet*, act 1, sc.3, l.62–3.

18 Beware Of entrance to a quarrel, but being in, Bear't that th' opposèd may beware of thee.
1600–1 Polonius to Laertes. *Hamlet*, act 1, sc.3, l.65–7.

19 Give every man thine ear but few thy voice. Take each man's censure, but reserve thy judgement.
1600–1 Polonius to Laertes. *Hamlet*, act 1, sc.3, l.68–9.

20 Costly thy habit as thy purse can buy, But not expressed in fancy; rich not gaudy; For the apparel oft proclaims the man.
1600–1 Polonius to Laertes. *Hamlet*, act 1, sc.3, l.70–2.

21 Neither a borrower nor a lender be.
1600–1 Polonius to Laertes. *Hamlet*, act 1, sc.3, l.75.

22 This above all—to thine own self be true, And it must follow, as the night the day, Thou canst not then be false to any man.
1600–1 Polonius to Laertes. *Hamlet*, act 1, sc.3, l.78–80.

23 Ay, springes to catch woodcocks. I do know When the blood burns how prodigal the soul Lends the tongue vows.
1600–1 Polonius. *Hamlet*, act 1, sc.3, l.115–7.

24 And to my mind, though I am native here And to the manner born, it is a custom More honoured in the breach than the observance.
1600–1 Hamlet. *Hamlet*, act 1, sc.4, l.16–18.

25 Be thou a spirit of health or goblin damned, Bring with thee airs from heaven or blasts from hell, Be thy intents wicked or charitable, Thou com'st in such a questionable shape That I will speak to thee.
1600–1 Hamlet to the ghost. *Hamlet*, act 1, sc.4, l.21–5.

26 I do not set my life at a pin's fee, And for my soul, what can it do to that, Being a thing immortal as itself?
1600–1 Hamlet. *Hamlet*, act 1, sc.4, l.46–8.

27 Something is rotten in the state of Denmark.

1600–1 Marcellus. *Hamlet*, act 1, sc.4, l.67.

28 I could a tale unfold whose lightest word
Would harrow up thy soul, freeze thy young blood,
Make thy two eyes like stars start from their spheres,
Thy knotty and combinèd locks to part,
And each particular hair to stand on end
Like quills upon the fretful porcupine.
1600–1 Ghost to Hamlet. *Hamlet*, act 1, sc.5, l.15–20.

29 Murder most foul, as in the best it is,
But this most foul, strange, and unnatural.
1600–1 Ghost to Hamlet. *Hamlet*, act 1, sc.5, l.27–8.

30 O my prophetic soul! Mine uncle?
1600–1 Hamlet to the ghost. *Hamlet*, act 1, sc.5, l.41.

31 [My] love was of that dignity
That it went hand-in-hand even with the vow
I made to her in marriage.
1600–1 Ghost, of Gertrude. *Hamlet*, act 1, sc.5, l.48–50.

32 In the porches of mine ears.
1600–1 Ghost. *Hamlet*, act 1, sc.5, l.63.

33 Let not the royal bed of Denmark be
A couch for luxury and damnèd incest.
1600–1 Ghost to Hamlet. *Hamlet*, act 1, sc.5, l.82–4.

34 O all you host of heaven! O earth! What else?
And shall I couple hell? O fie! Hold, hold, my heart,
And you, my sinews, grow not instant old,
But bear me stiffly up. Remember thee?
Ay, thou poor ghost, while memory holds a seat
In this distracted globe.
1600–1 Hamlet. *Hamlet*, act 1, sc.5, l.92–7.

35 My tables—meet it is I set it down
That one may smile and smile and be a villain.
1600–1 Hamlet. *Hamlet*, act 1, sc.5, l.108–9.

36 There's ne'er a villain dwelling in all Denmark
But he's an arrant knave.
1600–1 Hamlet. *Hamlet*, act 1, sc.5, l.127–8.

37 Well said, old mole. Canst work i'th' earth so fast?
1600–1 Hamlet. *Hamlet*, act 1, sc.5, l.164.

38 There are more things in heaven and earth, Horatio,
Than are dreamt of in our philosophy.
1600–1 Hamlet. *Hamlet*, act 1, sc.5, l.168–9.

39 The time is out of joint. O cursèd spite
That ever I was born to set it right!
1600–1 Hamlet. *Hamlet*, act 1, sc.5, l.189–90.

40 Lord Hamlet, with his doublet all unbraced,
No hat upon his head, his stockings fouled,
Ungartered, and down-gyvèd to his ankle.
1600–1 Ophelia. *Hamlet*, act 2, sc.1, l.79–81.

41 This is the very ecstasy of love,
Whose violent property fordoes itself
And leads the will to desperate undertakings.
1600–1 Polonius, of Hamlet. *Hamlet*, act 2, sc.1, l.103–5.

42 Brevity is the soul of wit.
1600–1 Polonius. *Hamlet*, act 2, sc.2, l.91.

43 More matter with less art.
1600–1 Gertrude to Polonius, urging him to speak more plainly. *Hamlet*, act 2, sc.2, l.96.

44 'To the celestial and my soul's idol, the most beautified Ophelia'—that's an ill phrase, a vile phrase, 'beautified' is a vile phrase.
1600–1 Polonius to Gertrude, quoting Hamlet's letter to Ophelia.

Hamlet, act 2, sc.2, l.110–12.

45 Doubt thou the stars are fire,
Doubt that the sun doth move,
Doubt truth to be a liar,
But never doubt I love.
1600–1 Polonius to Gertrude, quoting Hamlet's letter to Ophelia. *Hamlet*, act 2, sc.2, l.116–19.

46 If circumstances lead me I will find
Where truth is hid, though it were hid indeed
Within the centre.
1600–1 Polonius, of Hamlet's madness. *Hamlet*, act 2, sc.2, l.159–61.

47 To be honest, as this world goes, is to be one man picked out of ten thousand.
1600–1 Hamlet to Polonius. *Hamlet*, act 2, sc.2, l.180–1.

48 POLONIUS: What do you read, my lord?
HAMLET: Words, words, words.
1600–1 *Hamlet*, act 2, sc.2, l.193–5.

49 Though this be madness, yet there is method in't.
1600–1 Polonius (aside), of Hamlet. *Hamlet*, act 2, sc.2, l.207–8.

50 POLONIUS: My lord, I will take my leave of you.
HAMLET: You cannot, sir, take from me anything that I will more willingly part withal—except my life, my life, my life.
1600–1 *Hamlet*, act 2, sc.2, l.215–19.

51 [We are] happy in that we are not over-happy,
On Fortune's cap we are not the very button.
1600–1 Guildenstern to Hamlet. *Hamlet*, act 2, sc.2, l.230–1.

52 HAMLET: What's the news?
ROSENCRANTZ: None, my lord, but that the world's grown honest.
HAMLET: Then is doomsday near.
1600–1 *Hamlet*, act 2, sc.2, l.238–41.

53 There is nothing either good or bad, but thinking makes it so.
1600–1 Hamlet. *Hamlet*, act 2, sc.2, l.251–2.

54 I could be bounded in a nutshell and count myself a king of infinite space, were it not that I have bad dreams.
1600–1 Hamlet. *Hamlet*, act 2, sc.2, l.256–8.

55 I hold ambition of so airy and light a quality that it is but a shadow's shadow.
1600–1 Rosencrantz. *Hamlet*, act 2, sc.2, l.263–4.

56 I have of late—but wherefore I know not—lost all my mirth, forgone all custom of exercise; and indeed it goes so heavily with my disposition that this goodly frame, the earth, seems to me a sterile promontory. This most excellent canopy the air, look you, this brave o'erhanging, this majestical roof fretted with golden fire—why, it appears no other thing to me than a foul and pestilent congregation of vapours.
1600–1 Hamlet. *Hamlet*, act 2, sc.2, l.296–304.

57 What a piece of work is a man! How noble in reason, how infinite in faculty, in form and moving how express and admirable, in action how like an angel, in apprehension how like a god—the beauty of the world, the paragon of animals! And yet to me what is this quintessence of dust?
1600–1 Hamlet. *Hamlet*, act 2, sc.2, l.305–10.

58 Man delights not me—no, nor woman neither.
1600–1 Hamlet. *Hamlet*, act 2, sc.2, l.310–11.

59 If you delight not in man what lenten entertainment the players shall receive from you.
1600–1 Rosencrantz. *Hamlet*, act 2, sc.2, l.317–19.

60 There is something in this more than natural, if philosophy could find it out.
1600–1 Hamlet. *Hamlet*, act 2, sc.2, l.367–9.

61 I am but mad north-north-west; when the wind is southerly, I know a hawk from a handsaw.
1600–1 Hamlet to Guildenstern. *Hamlet*, act 2, sc.2, l.380–1.

62 The best actors in the world, either for tragedy, comedy, history, pastoral, pastoral-comical, historical-pastoral, tragical-historical, tragical-comical-historical-pastoral, scene individable, or poem unlimited.
1600–1 Polonius. *Hamlet*, act 2, sc.2, l.398–401.

63 Thy face is valanced since I saw thee last. Com'st thou to beard me in Denmark?
1600–1 Hamlet to one of the players. *Hamlet*, act 2, sc.2, l.426–7.

64 The play, I remember, pleased not the million. 'Twas caviare to the general.
1600–1 Hamlet to one of the players. *Hamlet*, act 2, sc.2, l.438–40.

65 Will you see the players well bestowed? Do ye hear? —let them be well used, for they are the abstracts and brief chronicles of the time.
1600–1 Hamlet to Polonius. *Hamlet*, act 2, sc.2, l.524–7.

66 Use every man after his desert, and who should scape whipping?
1600–1 Hamlet to Polonius. *Hamlet*, act 2, sc.2, l.532–3.

67 O, what a rogue and peasant slave am I!
Is it not monstrous that this player here,
But in a fiction, in a dream of passion,
Could force his soul so to his whole conceit
That from her working all his visage wanned,
Tears in his eyes, distraction in 's aspect,
A broken voice, and his whole function suiting
With forms to his conceit? And all for nothing.
For Hecuba!
What's Hecuba to him, or he to Hecuba,
That he should weep for her?
1600–1 Hamlet. *Hamlet*, act 2, sc.2, l.552–62.

68 But I am pigeon-livered and lack gall
To make oppression bitter
1600–1 Hamlet. *Hamlet*, act 2, sc.2, l.579–80.

69 Why, what an ass am I? Ay, sure, this is most brave,
That I, the son of the dear murderèd,
Prompted to my revenge by heaven and hell,
Must, like a whore, unpack my heart with words.
1600–1 Hamlet. *Hamlet*, act 2, sc.2, l.585–8.

70 Murder, though it have no tongue, will speak
With most miraculous organ.
1600–1 Hamlet. *Hamlet*, act 2, sc.2, l.595–6.

71 The spirit I have seen
May be the devil, and the devil hath power
T'assume a pleasing shape.
1600–1 Hamlet. *Hamlet*, act 2, sc.2, l.600–2.

72 The play's the thing
Wherein I'll catch the conscience of the King.
1600–1 Hamlet. *Hamlet*, act 2, sc.2, l.606–7.

73 The harlot's cheek, beautied with plast'ring art,
Is not more ugly to the thing that helps it

Than is my deed to my most painted word.
1600–1 Claudius. *Hamlet*, act 3, sc.1, l.53–5.

74 To be, or not to be; that is the question:
Whether 'tis nobler in the mind to suffer
The slings and arrows of outrageous fortune,
Or to take arms against a sea of troubles,
And, by opposing, end them. To die, to sleep—
No more, and by a sleep to say we end
The heartache and the thousand natural shocks
That flesh is heir to—'tis a consummation
Devoutly to be wished. To die, to sleep.
To sleep, perchance to dream. Ay, there's the rub,
For in that sleep of death what dreams may come
When we have shuffled off this mortal coil
Must give us pause. There's the respect
That makes calamity of so long life,
For who would bear the whips and scorns of time,
Th'oppressor's wrong, the proud man's contumely,
The pangs of disprized love, the law's delay,
The insolence of office, and the spurns
That patient merit of th'unworthy takes,
When he himself might his quietus make
With a bare bodkin? Who would these fardels bear,
To grunt and sweat under a weary life,
But that the dread of something after death,
The undiscovered country from whose bourn
No traveller returns, puzzles the will,
And makes us rather bear those ills we have
Than fly to others that we know not of?
Thus conscience does make cowards of us all,
And thus the native hue of resolution
Is sicklied o'er with the pale cast of thought,
And enterprises of great pith and moment
With this regard their currents turn awry,
And lose the name of action.
1600–1 Hamlet. *Hamlet*, act 3, sc.1, l.58–90.

75 To the noble mind
Rich gifts wax poor when givers prove unkind.
1600–1 Ophelia to Hamlet. *Hamlet*, act 3, sc.1, l.102–4.

76 The power of beauty will sooner transform honesty from what it is to a bawd than the force of honesty can translate beauty into his likeness.
1600–1 Hamlet to Ophelia. *Hamlet*, act 3, sc.1, l.113–15.

77 Get thee to a nunnery. Why wouldst thou be a breeder of sinners?
1600–1 Hamlet to Ophelia. *Hamlet*, act 3, sc.1, l.123–4.

78 I am very proud, revengeful, ambitious, with more offences at my beck than I have thoughts to put them in, imagination to give them shape, or time to act them in.
1600–1 Hamlet. *Hamlet*, act 3, sc.1, l.126–9.

79 What should such fellows as I do crawling between heaven and earth?
1600–1 Hamlet. *Hamlet*, act 3, sc.1, l.129–31.

80 Let the doors be shut upon him, that he may play the fool nowhere but in's own house.
1600–1 Hamlet, of Polonius. *Hamlet*, act 3, sc.1, l.134–5.

81 God has given you one face, and you make yourselves another.
1600–1 Hamlet, of women. *Hamlet*, act 3, sc.1, l.145–7.

82 I say we will have no more marriages; those that are married already—all but one—shall live. The rest shall

keep as they are.
1600–1 Hamlet to Ophelia. *Hamlet*, act 3, sc.1, l.150–2.

83 O what a noble mind is here o'erthrown!
1600–1 Ophelia, of Hamlet. *Hamlet*, act 3, sc.1, l.153.

84 Madness in great ones must not unwatched go.
1600–1 Claudius, of Hamlet. *Hamlet*, act 3, sc.1, l.191.

85 Speak the speech, I pray you, as I pronounced it to you
—trippingly on the tongue; but if you mouth it, as many
of your players do, I had as lief the town-crier had spoke
my lines.
1600–1 Hamlet to the players. *Hamlet*, act 3, sc.2, l.1–4.

86 Hold as 'twere the mirror up to nature, to show virtue her
own feature, scorn her own image.
1600–1 Hamlet to the players. *Hamlet*, act 3, sc.2, l.22–3.

87 Let those that play your clowns speak no more than is set
down for them.
1600–1 Hamlet to the players. *Hamlet*, act 3, sc.2, l.38–9.

88 A man that Fortune's buffets and rewards
Hath ta'en with equal thanks.
1600–1 Hamlet, of Horatio. *Hamlet*, act 3, sc.2, l.65–6.

89 Give me that man
That is not passion's slave, and I will wear him
In my heart's core.
1600–1 Hamlet. *Hamlet*, act 3, sc.2, l.69–71.

90 OPHELIA: 'Tis brief, my lord.
HAMLET: As woman's love.
1600–1 *Hamlet*, act 3, sc.2, l.146–7.

91 Our wills and fates do so contrary run
That our devices still are overthrown.
1600–1 Player King. *Hamlet*, act 3, sc.2, l.202–3.

92 The lady protests too much, methinks.
1600–1 Gertrude to Hamlet, of the Player Queen. *Hamlet*, act 3,
sc.2, l.219.

93 No, no, they do but jest, poison in jest.
1600–1 Hamlet, of the play. *Hamlet*, act 3, sc.2, l.224.

94 KING CLAUDIUS: What do you call the play?
HAMLET: The Mousetrap.
1600–1 *Hamlet*, act 3, sc.2, l.225–6.

95 Let the galled jade wince, our withers are unwrung
1600–1 Hamlet, of the play. *Hamlet*, act 3, sc.2, l.231.

96 'Sblood, do you think I am easier to be played on than a
pipe?
1600–1 Hamlet to Guildenstern. *Hamlet*, act 3, sc.2, l.357–8.

97 'Tis now the very witching time of night,
When churchyards yawn and hell itself breathes out
Contagion to this world.
1600–1 Hamlet. *Hamlet*, act 3, sc.2, l.377–9.

98 I will speak daggers to her, but use none;
My tongue and soul in this be hypocrites.
1600–1 Hamlet, of Gertrude. *Hamlet*, act 3, sc.2, l.385–6.

99 O, my offence is rank! It smells to heaven.
1600–1 Claudius. *Hamlet*, act 3, sc.3, l.36.

1 Try what repentance can. What can it not?
Yet what can it when one cannot repent?
1600–1 Claudius. *Hamlet*, act 3, sc.3, l.65–6.

2 O limèd soul that, struggling to be free,
Art more engaged! Help, angels! make assay.
1600–1 Claudius. *Hamlet*, act 3, sc.3, l.68–9.

3 My words fly up, my thoughts remain below.

Words without thoughts never to heaven go.
1600–1 Claudius. *Hamlet*, act 3, sc.3, l.97–8.

4 You shall not budge.
You go not till I set you up a glass
Where you may see the inmost part of you.
1600–1 Hamlet to Gertrude. *Hamlet*, act 3, sc.4, l.18–20.

5 How now, a rat? Dead for a ducat, dead.
1600–1 Hamlet, hearing Polonius behind the arras. *Hamlet*,
act 3, sc.4, l.23.

6 A bloody deed—almost as bad, good-mother,
As kill a king and marry with his brother.
1600–1 Hamlet. *Hamlet*, act 3, sc.4, l.27–8.

7 Thou wretched, rash, intruding fool, farewell.
I took thee for thy better.
1600–1 Hamlet to Polonius, whom Hamlet has just stabbed.
Hamlet, act 3, sc.4, l.29–31.

8 You cannot call it love, for at your age
The heyday in the blood is tame.
1600–1 Hamlet to Gertrude. *Hamlet*, act 3, sc.4, l.67–8.

9 To flaming youth let virtue be as wax
And melt in her own fire.
1600–1 Hamlet to Gertrude. *Hamlet*, act 3, sc.4, l.74–5.

10 Nay, but to live
In the rank sweat of an enseamèd bed,
Stewed in corruption, honeying and making love
Over the nasty sty.
1600–1 Hamlet to Gertrude. *Hamlet*, act 3, sc.4, l.81–4.

11 Confess yourself to heaven;
Repent what's past, avoid what is to come.
1600–1 Hamlet to Gertrude. *Hamlet*, act 3, sc.4, l.140–1.

12 In the fatness of these pursy times
Virtue itself of vice must pardon beg.
1600–1 Hamlet to Gertrude. *Hamlet*, act 3, sc.4, l.144–5.

13 Assume a virtue if you have it not.
1600–1 Hamlet to Gertrude. *Hamlet*, act 3, sc.4, l.151.

14 I'll lug the guts into the neighbour room.
1600–1 Hamlet, of Polonius, whom he has killed. *Hamlet*, act 3,
sc.4, l.186.

15 A man may fish with the worm that hath eat of a king, and
eat of the fish that hath fed of that worm.
1600–1 Hamlet to Claudius. *Hamlet*, act 4, sc.3, l.27–8.

16 He is dead and gone, lady,
He is dead and gone.
At his head a grass-green turf,
At his heels a stone.
1600–1 Ophelia, singing. *Hamlet*, act 4, sc.5, l.29–32.

17 We know what we are, but know not what we may be.
1600–1 Ophelia. *Hamlet*, act 4, sc.5, l.42–3.

18 Good night, ladies, good night, sweet ladies, good night,
good night.
1600–1 Ophelia. *Hamlet*, act 4, sc.5, l.71–2.

19 When sorrows come they come not single spies,
But in battalions.
1600–1 Claudius to Gertrude. *Hamlet*, act 4, sc.5, l.76–7.

20 The people muddied,
Thick and unwholesome in their thoughts and whispers.
1600–1 Claudius to Gertrude. *Hamlet*, act 4, sc.5, l.78–9.

21 There's such divinity doth hedge a king
That treason can but peep to what it would.
1600–1 Claudius to Gertrude. *Hamlet*, act 4, sc.5, l.122–3.

22 O, how the wheel becomes it!
1600–1 Ophelia. *Hamlet*, act 4, sc.5, l.172.

23 There's rosemary, that's for remembrance. Pray, love, remember. And there is pansies; that's for thoughts.
1600–1 Ophelia. *Hamlet*, act 4, sc.5, l.175–7.

24 Where th'offence is, let the great axe fall.
1600–1 Claudius. *Hamlet*, act 4, sc.5, l.216.

25 There is a willow grows aslant a brook
That shows his hoar leaves in the glassy stream.
Therewith fantastic garlands did she make
Of crow-flowers, nettles, daisies, and long purples,
That liberal shepherds give a grosser name,
But our cold maids do dead men's fingers call them.
1600–1 Gertrude, describing the scene of Ophelia's death. *Hamlet*, act 4, sc.7, l.138–42.

26 Her garments, heavy with their drink,
Pulled the poor wretch from her melodious lay
To muddy death.
1600–1 Gertrude, describing how Ophelia drowned. *Hamlet*, act 4, sc.7, l.153–5.

27 Too much of water hast thou, poor Ophelia,
And therefore I forbid my tears.
1600–1 Laertes. *Hamlet*, act 4, sc.7, l.158–9.

28 There is no ancient gentlemen but gardeners, ditchers, and gravemakers; they hold up Adam's profession.
1600–1 First Clown. *Hamlet*, act 5, sc.1, l.29–31.

29 This might be the pate of a politician which this ass o'er-offices, one that would circumvent God, might it not?
1600–1 Hamlet to Horatio. *Hamlet*, act 5, sc.1, l.77–9.

30 HAMLET: Ay, marry, why was he [Hamlet] sent into England?
FIRST CLOWN: Why, because a was mad. A shall recover his wits there; or if a do not, 'tis no great matter there.
HAMLET: Why?
FIRST CLOWN: 'Twill not be seen in him there. There the men are as mad as he.
1600–1 *Hamlet*, act 5, sc.1, l.146–152.

31 Alas, poor Yorick. I knew him, Horatio—a fellow of infinite jest, of most excellent fancy. He hath borne me on his back a thousand times; and now, how abhorred my imagination is! My gorge rises at it.
1600–1 Hamlet, of Yorick's skull. *Hamlet*, act 5, sc.1, l.180–4.

32 HAMLET: Dost thou think Alexander looked o' this fashion i'th' earth?
HORATIO: E'en so.
HAMLET: And smelt so? Pah!
1600–1 *Hamlet*, act 5, sc.1, l.193–6.

33 Imperial Caesar, dead and turned to clay,
Might stop a hole to keep the wind away.
1600–1 Hamlet. *Hamlet*, act 5, sc.1, l.208–9.

34 Hold off the earth a while,
Till I have caught her once more in mine arms.
1600–1 Laertes, of Ophelia, at her burial. *Hamlet*, act 5, sc.1, l.245–6.

35 For though I am not splenative and rash,
Yet have I something in me dangerous,
Which let thy wiseness fear.
1600–1 Hamlet to Laertes. *Hamlet*, act 5, sc.1, l.258–9.

36 Let Hercules himself do what he may,
The cat will mew, and dog will have his day.

37 There's a divinity that shapes our ends,
Rough-hew them how we will.
1600–1 Hamlet to Horatio. *Hamlet*, act 5, sc.2, l.10–11.

38 The bravery of his grief did put me
Into a tow'ring passion.
1600–1 Hamlet, of Laertes. *Hamlet*, act 5, sc.2, l.80–1.

39 A hit, a very palpable hit.
1600–1 Osric. *Hamlet*, act 5, sc.2, l.232.

40 I am more an antique Roman than a Dane.
Here's yet some liquor left.
1600–1 Horatio, intending to drink from the poisoned chalice. *Hamlet*, act 5, sc.2, l.294–5.

41 Absent thee from felicity a while,
And in this harsh world draw thy breath in pain
To tell my story.
1600–1 Hamlet to Horatio. *Hamlet*, act 5, sc.2, l.299–301.

42 O, I die, Horatio!
The potent poison quite o'ercrows my spirit.
1600–1 Hamlet. *Hamlet*, act 5, sc.2, l.304–5.

43 The rest is silence.
1600–1 Hamlet's last words. *Hamlet*, act 5, sc.2, l.310.

44 Good night, sweet prince,
And flights of angels sing thee to thy rest.
1600–1 Horatio. *Hamlet*, act 5, sc.2, l.312–13.

45 If music be the food of love, play on,
Give me excess of it that, surfeiting,
The appetite may sicken and so die.
That strain again, it had a dying fall.
O, it came o'er my ear like the sweet sound
That breathes upon a bank of violets,
Stealing and giving odour. Enough, no more,
'Tis not so sweet now as it was before.
1601 Orsino. *Twelfth Night*, act 1, sc.1, l.1–8.

46 O spirit of love, how quick and fresh art thou
That, notwithstanding thy capacity
Receiveth as the sea, naught enters there,
Of what validity and pitch so e'er,
But falls into abatement and low price
Even in a minute! So full of shapes is fancy
That it alone is high fantastical.
1601 Orsino. *Twelfth Night*, act 1, sc.1, l.9–15.

47 O, when mine eyes did see Olivia first
Methought she purged the air of pestilence;
That instant was I turned into a hart,
And my desires, like fell and cruel hounds,
E'er since pursue me.
1601 Orsino. *Twelfth Night*, act 1, sc.1, l.18–22.

48 He plays o'th' viol-de-gamboys, and speaks three or four languages word for word without book, and hath all the good gifts of nature.
1601 Sir Toby, of Sir Andrew. *Twelfth Night*, act 1, sc.3, l.23–6.

49 He's a great quarreller, and but that he hath the gift of a coward to allay the gust he hath in quarrelling, 'tis thought among the prudent he would quickly have the gift of a grave.
1601 Maria, of Sir Andrew. *Twelfth Night*, act 1, sc.3, l.28–31.

50 I'll drink to her as long as there is a passage in my throat and drink in Illyria.
1601 Sir Toby. *Twelfth Night*, act 1, sc.3, l.36–8.

51 I am a great eater of beef, and I believe that does harm to my wit.
1601 Sir Andrew. *Twelfth Night*, act 1, sc.3, l.83–4.

52 I have unclasped
To thee the book even of my secret soul.
1601 Orsino to Viola, disguised as Cesario. *Twelfth Night*, act 1, sc.4, l.13–14.

53 Many a good hanging prevents a bad marriage.
1601 Orsino. *Twelfth Night*, act 1, sc.5, l.18.

54 'Better a witty fool than a foolish wit.'
1601 Feste. *Twelfth Night*, act 1, sc.5, l.32–3.

55 Virtue that transgresses is but patched with sin.
1601 Feste. *Twelfth Night*, act 1, sc.5, l.44–5.

56 (*He belches*) A plague o' these pickle herring!
1601 Sir Toby. *Twelfth Night*, act 1, sc.5, l.116–17.

57 I would be loath to cast away my speech, for besides that it is excellently well penned, I have taken great pains to con it.
1601 Viola, in disguise, to Olivia. *Twelfth Night*, act 1, sc.5, l.165–7.

58 O sir, I will not be so hard-hearted. I will give out divers schedules of my beauty. It shall be inventoried and every particle and utensil labelled to my will, as *item*, two lips, indifferent red; *item*, two grey eyes, with lids to them; *item*, one neck, one chin, and so forth. Were you sent hither to praise me?
1601 Olivia to Viola (disguised as a young man). *Twelfth Night*, act 1, sc.5, l.233–8.

59 Make me a willow cabin at your gate
And call upon my soul within the house,
Write loyal cantons of contemnèd love,
And sing them loud even in the dead of night;
Halloo your name to the reverberate hills,
And make the babbling gossip of the air
Cry out 'Olivia!' O, you should not rest
Between the elements of air and earth
But you should pity me.
1601 Viola, describing how she would woo Olivia, were she in love with her. *Twelfth Night*, act 1, sc.5, l.258–65.

60 O mistress mine, where are you roaming?
O stay and hear, your true love's coming,
That can sing both high and low.
Trip no further, pretty sweeting.
Journeys end in lovers meeting,
Every wise man's son doth know.
1601 Feste's song. *Twelfth Night*, act 2, sc.3, l.38–43.

61 What is love? 'Tis not hereafter,
Present mirth hath present laughter.
What's to come is still unsure.
In delay there lies no plenty,
Then come kiss me, sweet and twenty.
Youth's a stuff will not endure.
1601 Feste's song. *Twelfth Night*, act 2, sc.3, l.46–51.

62 Is there no respect of place, persons, nor time in you?
1601 Malvolio to Feste, Sir Andrew and Sir Toby. *Twelfth Night*, act 2, sc.3, l.88–9.

63 Dost thou think because thou art virtuous there shall be no more cakes and ale?
1601 Sir Toby to Feste. *Twelfth Night*, act 2, sc.3, l.110–11.

64 Let still the woman take
An elder than herself. So wears she to him;
So sways she level in her husband's heart.
1601 Orsino. *Twelfth Night*, act 2, sc.4, l.28–30.

65 Then let thy love be younger than thyself,
Or thy affection cannot hold the bent;
For women are as roses, whose fair flower
Being once displayed, doth fall that very hour.
1601 Orsino. *Twelfth Night*, act 2, sc.4, l.35–8.

66 Now the melancholy god protect thee, and the tailor make thy doublet of changeable taffeta, for thy mind is a very opal.
1601 Feste to Orsino. *Twelfth Night*, act 2, sc.4, l.72–4.

67 My father had a daughter loved a man
As it might be, perhaps, were I a woman
I should your lordship.
1601 Viola, in disguise, to Orsino. *Twelfth Night*, act 2, sc.4, l.107–9.

68 She never told her love,
But let concealment, like a worm i' th' bud,
Feed on her damask cheek.
1601 Viola, in disguise, to Orsino. *Twelfth Night*, act 2, sc.4, l.110–12.

69 With a green and yellow melancholy
She sat like patience on a monument,
Smiling at grief.
1601 Viola, in disguise, to Orsino. *Twelfth Night*, act 2, sc.4, l.113–15.

70 By my life, this is my lady's hand. These be her very c's, her u's, and her t's, and thus makes she her great P's. It is in contempt of question her hand.
1601 Malvolio. *Twelfth Night*, act 2, sc.5, l.84–7.

71 Be not afraid of greatness. Some are born great, some achieve greatness, and some have greatness thrust upon 'em.
1601 Malvolio. *Twelfth Night*, act 2, sc.5, l.139–41.

72 He will come to her in yellow stockings, and 'tis a colour she abhors, and cross-gartered, a fashion she detests.
1601 Maria, of Malvolio. *Twelfth Night*, act 2, sc.5, l.192–4.

73 Fools are as like husbands as pilchards are to herrings—the husband's the bigger.
1601 Feste to Viola. *Twelfth Night*, act 3, sc.1, l.32–4.

74 Now Jove in his next commodity of hair send thee a beard.
1601 Feste to Viola. *Twelfth Night*, act 3, sc.1, l.43–4.

75 Most excellent accomplished lady, the heavens rain odours on you.
1601 Viola to Olivia. *Twelfth Night*, act 3, sc.1, l.83–4.

76 O world, how apt the poor are to be proud!
1601 Olivia. *Twelfth Night*, act 3, sc.1, l.126.

77 Then westward ho!
1601 Viola. *Twelfth Night*, act 3, sc.1, l.133.

78 O, what a deal of scorn looks beautiful
In the contempt and anger of his lip!
1601 Olivia, of Viola (as Cesario). *Twelfth Night*, act 3, sc.1, l.143–4.

79 Love sought is good, but given unsought, is better.
1601 Olivia. *Twelfth Night*, act 3, sc.1, l.154.

80 You are now sailed into the north of my lady's opinion, where you will hang like an icicle on a Dutchman's beard unless you do redeem it by some laudable attempt either of valour or policy.
1601 Fabian, of Sir Toby. *Twelfth Night*, act 3, sc.2, l.24–8.

81 There is no love-broker in the world can more prevail in man's commendation with woman than report of valour.
1601 Sir Toby to Sir Andrew. *Twelfth Night*, act 3, sc.2, l.34–6.

82 For Andrew, if he were opened and you find so much blood in his liver as will clog the foot of a flea, I'll eat the rest of th'anatomy.
1601 Sir Toby. *Twelfth Night*, act 3, sc.2, l.58–60.

83 Why, this is very midsummer madness.
1601 Olivia, of Malvolio. *Twelfth Night*, act 3, sc.4, l.54.

84 If this were played upon a stage now, I could condemn it as an improbable fiction.
1601 Fabian. *Twelfth Night*, act 3, sc.4, l.125–6.

85 Still you keep o' th' windy side of the law.
1601 Fabian. *Twelfth Night*, act 3, sc.4, l.162.

86 A terrible oath, with a swaggering accent sharply twanged off, gives manhood more approbation than ever proof itself would have earned him.
1601 Sir Toby to Sir Andrew. *Twelfth Night*, act 3, sc.4, l.176–8.

87 I am sure no man hath any quarrel to me. My remembrance is very free and clear from any image of offence done to any man.
1601 Viola (as Cesario) to Sir Toby. *Twelfth Night*, act 3, sc.4, l.221–3.

88 In nature there's no blemish but the mind.
None can be called deformed but the unkind.
1601 Antonio. *Twelfth Night*, act 3, sc.4, l.359–60.

89 There is no darkness but ignorance.
1601 Feste to Malvolio. *Twelfth Night*, act 4, sc.2, l.43–4.

90 Thus the whirligig of time brings in his revenges.
1601 Feste. *Twelfth Night*, act 5, sc.1, l.373.

91 I'll be revenged on the whole pack of you.
1601 Malvolio. *Twelfth Night*, act 5, sc.1, l.374.

92 When that I was and a little tiny boy,
With hey, ho, the wind and the rain,
A foolish thing was but a toy,
For the rain it raineth every day.
1601 Feste. *Twelfth Night*, act 5, sc.1, l.385–8.

93 Then everything includes itself in power,
Power into will, will into appetite;
And appetite, an universal wolf.
1602 Ulysses. *Troilus and Cressida*, act 1, sc.3, l.119–21.

94 The general's disdained
By him one step below; he, by the next;
That next, by him beneath. So every step,
Exampled by the first pace that is sick
Of his superior, grows to an envious fever
Of pale and bloodless emulation.
1602 Ulysses. *Troilus and Cressida*, act 1, sc.3, l.129–134.

95 The nature of the sickness found, Ulysses,
What is the remedy?
1602 Agamemnon. *Troilus and Cressida*, act 1, sc.3, l.140–1.

96 In such indices, although small pricks
To their subsequent volumes, there is seen
The baby figure of the giant mass
Of things to come at large.
1602 Nestor. *Troilus and Cressida*, act 1, sc.3, l.337–40.

97 The common curse of mankind, folly and ignorance, be thine.
1602 Thersites. *Troilus and Cressida*, act 2, sc.3, l.26–7.

98 He that is proud eats up himself. Pride is his own glass, his own trumpet, his own chronicle.
1602 Agamemnon. *Troilus and Cressida*, act 2, sc.3, l.153–5.

99 To make a sweet lady sad is a sour offence.
1602 Helen to Pandarus. *Troilus and Cressida*, act 3, sc.1, l.71.

1 I am giddy. Expectation whirls me round.
Th'imaginary relish is so sweet
That it enchants my sense.
1602 Troilus, on the prospect of an assignation with Cressida. *Troilus and Cressida*, act 3, sc.2, l.16–18.

2 Words pay no debts.
1602 Pandarus to Troilus. *Troilus and Cressida*, act 3, sc.2, l.54.

3 This is the monstruosity in love, lady—that the will is infinite and the execution confined; that the desire is boundless and the act a slave to limit.
1602 Troilus to Cressida. *Troilus and Cressida*, act 3, sc.2, l.77–80.

4 Some men creep in skittish Fortune's hall
Whiles others play the idiots in her eyes.
1602 Ulysses. *Troilus and Cressida*, act 3, sc.3, l.129–30.

5 Time hath, my lord,
A wallet at his back, wherein he puts
Alms for oblivion.
1602 Ulysses to Achilles. *Troilus and Cressida*, act 3, sc.3, l.139–41.

6 Perseverance, dear my lord,
Keeps honour bright. To have done is to hang
Quite out of fashion, like a rusty mail
In monumental mock'ry.
1602 Ulysses. *Troilus and Cressida*, act 3, sc.3, l.144–7.

7 One touch of nature makes the whole world kin.
1602 Ulysses to Achilles. *Troilus and Cressida*, act 3, sc.3, l.169.

8 I see my reputation is at stake.
My fame is shrewdly gored.
1602 Achilles. *Troilus and Cressida*, act 3, sc.3, l.220–1.

9 The busy day,
Waked by the lark, hath roused the ribald crows,
And dreaming night will hide our joys no longer.
1602 Troilus to Cressida. *Troilus and Cressida*, act 4, sc.2, l.10–11.

10 The kiss you take is better than you give.
1602 Cressida to Menelaus. *Troilus and Cressida*, act 4, sc.6, l. 39.

11 With too much blood and too little brain these two may run mad.
1602 Thersites, of Achilles and Patroclus. *Troilus and Cressida*, act 5, sc.1, l.45–7.

12 Lechery, lechery, still wars and lechery! Nothing else holds fashion.
1602 Thersites. *Troilus and Cressida*, act 5, sc.2, l.197–8.

13 Words, words, mere words, no matter from the heart.
1602 Troilus, on his letter from Cressida. *Troilus and Cressida*, act 5, sc.3, l.111.

14 Scare Troy out of itself. But march away.
1602 Troilus. *Troilus and Cressida*, act 5, sc.11, l.21.

15 Heaven doth with us as we with torches do,
Not light them for themselves.
1603 Duke. *Measure for Measure*, act 1, sc.1, l.32–3.

16 I had as lief have the foppery of freedom as the morality of imprisonment.
1603 Lucio to Claudio. *Measure for Measure*, act 1, sc.2, l.125–6.

17 Our doubts are traitors,
And makes us lose the good we oft might win,
By fearing to attempt.

1603 Lucio to Isabella. *Measure for Measure*, act 1, sc.4, l.77–9.

18 We must not make a scarecrow of the law,
Setting it up to fear the birds of prey,
And let it keep one shape till custom make it
Their perch, and not their terror.
1603 Angelo. *Measure for Measure*, act 2, sc.1, l.1–4.

19 'Tis one thing to be tempted, Escalus,
Another thing to fall.
1603 Angelo. *Measure for Measure*, act 2, sc.1, l.17–18.

20 I not deny
The jury passing on the prisoner's life
May in the sworn twelve have a thief or two
Guiltier than him they try.
1603 Angelo. *Measure for Measure*, act 2, sc.1, l.18–21.

21 The jewel that we find, we stoop and take't
Because we see it, but what we do not see
We tread upon.
1603 Angelo. *Measure for Measure*, act 2, sc.1, l.24–26.

22 Some rise by sin, and some by virtue fall.
1603 Escalus. *Measure for Measure*, act 2, sc.1, l.38.

23 The law hath not been dead, though it hath slept.
1603 Angelo to Isabella. *Measure for Measure*, act 2, sc.2, l.92.

24 ISABELLA: Yet show some pity,
ANGELO: I show it most of all when I show justice,
For then I pity those I do not know.
1603 *Measure for Measure*, act 2, sc.2, l.101–3.

25 O, it is excellent
To have a giant's strength, but it is tyrannous
To use it like a giant.
1603 Isabella to Angelo. *Measure for Measure*, act 2, sc.2, l.109–11.

26 But man, proud man,
Dressed in a little brief authority,
Most ignorant of what he's most assured,
His glassy essence, like an angry ape
Plays such fantastic tricks before high heaven
As makes the angels weep.
1603 Isabella to Angelo. *Measure for Measure*, act 2, sc.2, l.120–5.

27 Great men may jest with saints; 'tis wit in them,
But in the less, foul profanation.
1603 Isabella to Angelo. *Measure for Measure*, act 2, sc.2, l.130–1.

28 Thieves for their robbery have authority,
When judges steal themselves.
1603 Angelo. *Measure for Measure*, act 2, sc.2, l.181–2.

29 When men were fond, I smiled, and wondered how.
1603 Angelo. *Measure for Measure*, act 2, sc.2, l.191–2.

30 When I would pray and think, I think and pray
To several subjects; heaven hath my empty words,
Whilst my invention, hearing not my tongue,
Anchors on Isabel.
1603 Angelo. *Measure for Measure*, act 2, sc.4, l.1–4.

31 The miserable have no other medicine
But only hope.
1603 Claudio to the Duke. *Measure for Measure*, act 3, sc.1, l.2–3.

32 Reason thus with life
If I do lose thee, I do lose a thing
That none but fools would keep.
1603 Duke to Claudio. *Measure for Measure*, act 3, sc.1, l.6–8.

33 If thou art rich, thou'rt poor,
For like an ass whose back with ingots bows,

Thou bear'st thy heavy riches but a journey,
And death unloads thee.
1603 Duke to Claudio. *Measure for Measure*, act 3, sc.1, l.25–8.

34 The sense of death is most in apprehension,
And the poor beetle that we tread upon
In corporal sufferance finds a pang as great
As when a giant dies.
1603 Isabella to Claudio. *Measure for Measure*, act 3, sc.1, l.76–9.

35 If I must die,
I will encounter darkness as a bride,
And hug it in mine arms.
1603 Claudio to Isabella. *Measure for Measure*, act 3, sc.1, l.81–3.

36 Sure it is no sin,
Or of the deadly seven it is the least.
1603 Claudio to Isabella, of fornication. *Measure for Measure*, act 3, sc.1, l.109–10.

37 Ay, but to die, and go we know not where;
To lie in cold obstruction, and to rot.
1603 Claudio. *Measure for Measure*, act 3, sc.1, l.118–19.

38 The weariest and most loathèd worldly life
That age, ache, penury, and imprisonment
Can lay on nature is a paradise
To what we fear of death.
1603 Claudio to Isabella. *Measure for Measure*, act 3, sc.1, l.129–32.

39 Virtue is bold, and goodness never fearful.
1603 Duke to Isabella. *Measure for Measure*, act 3, sc.1, l.210.

40 Take, O take thy lips away
That so sweetly were forsworn.
1603 Boy, singing. *Measure for Measure*, act 4, sc.1, l.1–2.

41 Music oft hath such a charm
To make bad good, and good provoke to harm.
1603 Duke. *Measure for Measure*, act 4, sc.1, l.14–15.

42 You weigh equally; a feather will turn the scale.
1603 Provost to Abhorson. *Measure for Measure*, act 4, sc.2, l.28–29.

43 Every true man's apparel fits your thief.
1603 Abhorson. *Measure for Measure*, act 4, sc.2, l.41.

44 Drunk many times a day, if not many days entirely drunk.
1603 Provost, of Barnardine. *Measure for Measure*, act 4, sc.2, l.151–2.

45 Death's a great disguiser.
1603 Duke to Provost. *Measure for Measure*, act 4, sc.2, l.175.

46 If she be mad, as I believe no other,
Her madness hath the oddest frame of sense.
1603 Duke to Isabella. *Measure for Measure*, act 5, sc.1, l.60–1.

47 Haste still pays haste, and leisure answers leisure;
Like doth quit like, and measure still for measure.
1603 Duke. *Measure for Measure*, act 5, sc.1, 407–8.

48 They say best men are moulded out of faults,
And, for the most, become much more the better
For being a little bad. So may my husband.
1603 Mariana, of Angelo. *Measure for Measure*, act 5, sc.1, l.436–8.

49 In following him I follow myself.
1603–4 Iago, of Othello. *Othello*, act 1, sc.1, l.58.

50 For when my outward action doth demonstrate
The native act and figure of my heart
In compliment extern, 'tis not long after
But I will wear my heart upon my sleeve

For daws to peck at. I am not what I am.
1603–4 Iago. *Othello*, act 1, sc.1, l.60–5.

51 Though he in a fertile climate dwell,
Plague him with flies.
1603–4 Iago, of Brabanzio. *Othello*, act 1, sc.1, l.70–1.

52 Even now, now, very now, an old black ram
Is tupping your white ewe.
1603–4 Iago to Brabanzio. *Othello*, act 1, sc.1, l.88–89.

53 I am one, sir, that comes to tell you your daughter and
the Moor are now making the beast with the two
backs.
1603–4 Iago to Brabanzio. *Othello*, act 1, sc.1, l.117–9.

54 Though in the trade of war I have slain men,
Yet do I hold it very stuff o'th' conscience
To do no contrived murder. I lack iniquity,
Sometime, to do me service. Nine or ten times
I had thought to've yerked him here, under the ribs.
1603–4 Iago. *Othello*, act 1, sc.2, l.1–5.

55 But that I love the gentle Desdemona
I would not my unhousèd free condition
Put into circumscription and confine
For the seas' worth.
1603–4 Othello. *Othello*, act 1, sc.2, l.25–8.

56 Whether a maid so tender, fair, and happy,
So opposite to marriage that she shunned
The wealthy curlèd darlings of our nation,
Would ever have, t'incur a general mock,
Run from her guardage to the sooty bosom
Of such a thing as thou.
1603–4 Brabanzio to Othello. *Othello*, act 1, sc.2, l.67–72.

57 My particular grief
Is of so floodgate and o'erbearing nature
That it engluts and swallows other sorrows,
And it is still itself.
1603–4 Brabanzio, learning of Desdemona's marriage. *Othello*,
act 1, sc.3, l.55–8.

58 For nature so preposterously to err,
Being not deficient, blind, or lame of sense,
Sans witchcraft could not.
1603–4 Brabanzio, of Desdemona's marriage. *Othello*, act 1, sc.3,
l.62–4.

59 Rude am I in my speech,
And little blessed with the soft phrase of peace.
1603–4 Othello. *Othello*, act 1, sc.3, l.81–2.

60 A maiden never bold,
Of spirit so still and quiet that her motion
Blushed at herself—and she in spite of nature,
Of years, of country, credit, everything,
To fall in love with what she feared to look on!
It is a judgement maimed and most imperfect
That will confess perfection so could err
Against all rules of nature.
1603–4 Brabanzio of Desdemona. *Othello*, act 1, sc.3, l.94–100.

61 The Anthropophagi, and men whose heads
Do grow beneath their shoulders.
1603–4 Othello. *Othello*, act 1, sc.3, l.143–4.

62 She gave me for my pains a world of kisses.
She swore in faith 'twas strange, 'twas passing strange,
'Twas pitiful, 'twas wonderous pitiful.
She wished she had not heard it, yet she wished
That heaven had made her such a man.

1603–4 Othello, of his courtship of Desdemona. *Othello*, act 1,
sc.3, l.158–162.

63 She loved me for the dangers I had passed,
And I loved her that she did pity them.
1603–4 Othello, of Desdemona. *Othello*, act 1, sc.3, l.166–7.

64 My noble father,
I do perceive here a divided duty.
1603–4 Desdemona. *Othello*, act 1, sc.3, l.179–80.

65 For your sake, jewel,
I am glad at soul I have no other child,
For thy escape would teach me tyranny,
To hang clogs on 'em.
1603–4 Brabanzio to Desdemona. *Othello*, act 1, sc.3, l.194–7.

66 When remedies are past, the griefs are ended
By seeing the worst which late on hopes depended.
To mourn a mischief that is past and gone
Is the next way to draw new mischief on.
1603–4 Duke to Brabanzio. *Othello*, act 1, sc.3, l.201–4.

67 The robbed that smiles steals something from the thief;
He robs himself that spends a bootless grief.
1603–4 Duke. *Othello*, act 1, sc.3, l.207–8.

68 But words are words. I never yet did hear
That the bruised heart was piercèd through the ear.
1603–4 Brabanzio. *Othello*, act 1, sc.3, l.217–8.

69 I never found man that knew how to love himself. Ere I
would say I would drown myself for the love of a guinea-
hen, I would change my humanity with a baboon.
1603–4 Iago to Roderigo. *Othello*, act 1, sc.3, l.313–6.

70 Virtue? A fig! 'Tis in ourselves that we are thus or thus.
Our bodies are our gardens, to the which our wills are
gardeners.
1603–4 Iago to Roderigo. *Othello*, act 1, sc.3, l.319–21.

71 Make all the money thou canst. If sanctimony and a frail
vow betwixt an erring barbarian and a super-subtle
Venetian be not too hard for my wits and all the tribes of
hell, thou shalt enjoy her.
1603–4 Iago to Roderigo. *Othello*, act 1, sc.3, l.352–6.

72 The Moor is of a free and open nature,
That thinks men honest that but seem to be so,
And will as tenderly be led by th' nose
As asses are.
I ha't. It is ingendered. Hell and night
Must bring this monstrous birth to the world's light.
1603–4 Iago. *Othello*, act 1, sc.3, l.391–6.

73 You are pictures out of doors,
Bells in your parlours; wildcats in your kitchens,
Saints in your injuries; devils being offended,
Players in your housewifery, and hussies in your beds.
1603–4 Iago of women. *Othello*, act 2, sc.1, l.112–15.

74 With as little web as this will I ensnare as great a fly as
Cassio.
1603–4 Iago (aside). *Othello*, act 2, sc.1, l.171–2.

75 If it were now to die
'Twere now to be most happy, for I fear
My soul hath her content so absolute
That not another comfort like to this
Succeeds in unknown fate.
1603–4 Othello to Desdemona. *Othello*, act 2, sc.1, l.190–4.

76 The heavens forbid
But that our loves and comforts should increase

Even as our days do grow.
1603–4 Desdemona to Othello. *Othello*, act 2, sc.1, l.194–6.

77 [I'll] make the Moor thank me, love me, and reward me
For making him egregiously an ass.
1603–4 Iago. *Othello*, act 2, sc.1, l.307–8.

78 Reputation, reputation, reputation! O—I ha' lost my
reputation, I ha' lost the immortal part of myself, and
what remains is bestial.
1603–4 Cassio to Iago. *Othello*, act 2, sc.3, l.256–8.

79 Reputation is an idle and most false imposition, oft got
without merit and lost without deserving.
1603–4 Iago to Cassio. *Othello*, act 2, sc.3, l.262–4.

80 O God, that men should put an enemy in their mouths to
steal away their brains!
1603–4 Cassio, of wine. *Othello*, act 2, sc.3, l.283–5.

81 So will I turn her virtue into pitch,
And out of her own goodness make the net
That shall enmesh them all.
1603–4 Iago. *Othello*, act 2, sc.3, l.351–3.

82 How poor are they that ha' not patience!
What wound did ever heal but by degrees?
1603–4 Iago to Roderigo. *Othello*, act 2, sc.3, l.360–1.

83 Excellent wretch! Perdition catch my soul
But I do love thee, and when I love thee not,
Chaos is come again.
1603–4 Othello, of Desdemona. *Othello*, act 3, sc.3, l.91–3.

84 I know thou'rt full of love and honesty,
And weigh'st thy words before thou giv'st them
breath.
1603–4 Othello to Iago. *Othello*, act 3, sc.3, l.123–4.

85 Good name in man and woman, dear my lord,
Is the immediate jewel of their souls.
Who steals my purse steals trash; 'tis something,
nothing;
'Twas mine, 'tis his, and has been slave to thousands.
But he that filches from me my good name
Robs me of that which not enriches him
And makes me poor indeed.
1603–4 Iago to Othello. *Othello*, act 3, sc.3, l.160–6.

86 O, beware, my lord, of jealousy,
It is the green-eyed monster which doth mock
The meat it feeds on.
1603–4 Iago to Othello. *Othello*, act 3, sc.3, l.169–71.

87 Poor and content is rich, and rich enough,
But riches fineless is as poor as winter
To him that ever fears he shall be poor.
1603–4 Iago to Othello. *Othello*, act 3, sc.3, l.176–8.

88 I humbly do beseech you of your pardon
For too much loving you.
1603–4 Iago to Othello. *Othello*, act 3, sc.3, l.216–7.

89 If I do prove her haggard,
Though that her jesses were my dear heart-strings
I'd whistle her off and let her down the wind
To prey at fortune.
1603–4 Othello. *Othello*, act 3, sc.3, l.264–7.

90 If she be false, O then heaven mocks itself!
I'll not believe't.
1603–4 Othello, of Desdemona. *Othello*, act 3, sc.3, l.282–3.

91 Trifles light as air
Are to the jealous confirmations strong

As proofs of holy writ.
1603–4 Iago. *Othello*, act 3, sc.3, l.326–8.

92 Not poppy nor mandragora
Nor all the drowsy syrups of the world
Shall ever medicine thee to that sweet sleep
Which thou owedst yesterday.
1603–4 Iago, of Othello. *Othello*, act 3, sc.3, l.334–7.

93 He that is robbed, not wanting what is stol'n,
Let him not know't and he's not robbed at all.
1603–4 Othello to Iago. *Othello*, act 3, sc.3, l.347–8.

94 I had been happy if the general camp,
Pioneers and all, had tasted her sweet body,
So I had nothing known. O, now for ever
Farewell the tranquil mind, farewell content,
Farewell the plumèd troops and the big wars
That makes ambition virtue! O, farwell,
Farewell the neighing steed and the shrill trump,
The spirit-stirring drum, th'ear-piercing fife,
The royal banner, and all quality,
Pride, pomp, and circumstance of glorious war!
And O, you mortal engines whose rude throats
Th'immortal Jove's dread clamours counterfeit,
Farewell! Othello's occupation's gone.
1603–4 Othello. *Othello*, act 3, sc.3, l.350–62.

95 But this denoted a foregone conclusion.
1603–4 Othello. *Othello*, act 3, sc.3, l.433.

96 My bloody thoughts with violent pace
Shall ne'er look back, ne'er ebb to humble love,
Till that a capable and wide revenge
Swallow them up.
1603–4 Othello to Iago. *Othello*, act 3, sc.3, l.460–3.

97 Jealous souls will not be answered so.
They are not ever jealous for the cause,
But jealous for they're jealous. It is a monster
Begot upon itself, born on itself.
1603–4 Emilia to Desdemona. *Othello*, act 3, sc.4, l.156–9.

98 But yet the pity of it, Iago. O, Iago, the pity of it, Iago!
1603–4 Othello. *Othello*, act 4, sc.1, l.191–2.

99 Do it not with poison. Strangle her in her bed.
1603–4 Iago to Othello. *Othello*, act 4, sc.1, l.202–3.

1 Is this the noble Moor whom our full senate
Call all-in-all sufficient? Is this the nature
Whom passion could not shake, whose solid virtue
The shot of accident nor dart of chance
Could neither graze nor pierce?
1603–4 Lodovico. *Othello*, act 4, sc.1, l.266–70.

2 O thou weed,
Who art so lovely fair, and smell'st so sweet,
That the sense aches at thee—would thou hadst ne'er
been born!
1603–4 Othello, of Desdemona. *Othello*, act 4, sc.2, l.69–72.

3 I cry you mercy then.
I took you for that cunning whore of Venice
That married with Othello.
1603–4 Othello to Desdemona. *Othello*, act 4, sc.2, l.93–4.

4 I will be hanged, if some eternal villain,
Some busy and insinuating rogue,
Some cogging, cozening slave, to get some office,
Have not devised this slander.
1603–4 Emilia. *Othello*, act 4, sc.2, l.134–7.

5 Mine eyes do itch. Doth that bode weeping?
   1603–4 Desdemona to Emilia. *Othello*, act 4, sc.3, l.56–7.

6 Let husbands know
   Their wives have sense like them. They see, and smell,
   And have their palates both for sweet and sour,
   As husbands have.
   1603–4 Emilia to Desdemona. *Othello*, act 4, sc.3, l.92–5.

7 It is the cause, it is the cause, my soul.
   Let me not name it to you, you chaste stars.
   It is the cause. Yet I'll not shed her blood,
   Nor scar that whiter skin of hers than snow,
   And smooth as monumental alabaster.
   Yet she must die, else she'll betray more men.
   Put out the light, and then put out the light.
   1603–4 Othello. *Othello*, act 5, sc.2, l.1–7.

8 When I have plucked thy rose
   I cannot give it vital growth again.
   It needs must wither. I'll smell thee on the tree.
   1603–4 Othello. *Othello*, act 5, sc.2, l.13–15.

9 Had all his hairs been lives, my great revenge
   Had stomach for 'em all.
   1603–4 Othello, of Cassio. *Othello*, act 5, sc.2, l.81–2.

10 Kill me tomorrow; let me live tonight.
   1603–4 Desdemona to Othello. *Othello*, act 5, sc.2, l.87.

11 It is the very error of the moon,
   She comes more nearer earth than she was wont,
   And makes men mad.
   1603–4 Othello. *Othello*, act 5, sc.2, l.118–20.

12 Not Cassio killed? Then murder's out of tune,
   And sweet revenge grows harsh.
   1603–4 Othello. *Othello*, act 5, sc.2, l.124–5.

13 She's like a liar gone to burning hell.
   'Twas I that killed her.
   1603–4 Othello. *Othello*, act 5, sc.2, l.138–9.

14 May his pernicious soul
   Rot half a grain a day.
   1603–4 Emilia, of Iago. *Othello*, act 5, sc.2, l.162–3.

15 Thou hast not half that power to do me harm
   As I have to be hurt. O gull, O dolt,
   As ignorant as dirt!
   1603–4 Emilia to Othello. *Othello*, act 5, sc.2, l.169–71.

16 Here is my journey's end, here is my butt
   And very sea-mark of my utmost sail.
   1603–4 Othello. *Othello*, act 5, sc.2, l.274–5.

17 O ill-starred wench,
   Pale as thy smock! When we shall meet at count
   This look of thine will hurl my soul from heaven,
   And fiends will snatch at it.
   1603–4 Othello, of Desdemona. *Othello*, act 5, sc.2, l.279–2.

18 Demand me nothing. What you know, you know.
   From this time forth I never will speak word.
   1603–4 Iago to Othello. *Othello*, act 5, sc.2, l.309–10.

19 I pray you, in your letters,
   When you shall these unlucky deeds relate,
   Speak of me as I am. Nothing extenuate,
   Nor set down aught in malice. Then must you speak
   Of one that loved not wisely but too well,
   Of one not easily jealous but, being wrought,
   Perplexed in the extreme; of one whose hand,
   Like the base Indian, threw a pearl away

Richer than all his tribe; of one whose subdued eyes,
Albeit unusèd to the melting mood,
Drops tears as fast as the Arabian trees
Their medicinable gum. Set you down this,
And say besides that in Aleppo once,
Where a malignant and a turbaned Turk
Beat a Venetian and traduced the state,
I took by th' throat the circumcisèd dog
And smote him thus.
   1603–4 Othello's speech as he stabs himself. *Othello*, act 5, sc.2, l.349–65.

20 I kiss thee ere I killed thee. No way but this:
   Killing myself, to die upon a kiss.
   1603–4 Othello. *Othello*, act 5, sc.2, l.368–9.

21 Be checked for silence,
   But never taxed for speech.
   1604–5 Countess to Bertram. *All's Well That Ends Well*, act 1, sc.1, l.64–5.

22 'Twere all one
   That I should love a bright particular star
   And think to wed it, he is so above me.
   1604–5 Helen, of Bertram. *All's Well That Ends Well*, act 1, sc.1, l.84–6.

23 The hind that would be mated by the lion
   Must die for love.
   1604–5 Helen, of Bertram. *All's Well That Ends Well*, act 1, sc.1, l.90–1.

24 Virginity is peevish, proud, idle, made of self-love
   —which is the most inhibited sin in the canon. Keep it
   not.
   1604–5 Paroles to Helen. *All's Well That Ends Well*, act 1, sc.1, l.141–3.

25 Get thee a good husband, and use him as he uses thee.
   1604–5 Paroles to Helen. *All's Well That Ends Well*, act 1, sc.1, l.209–10.

26 Our remedies oft in ourselves do lie
   Which we ascribe to heaven.
   1604–5 Helen. *All's Well That Ends Well*, act 1, sc.1, l.212.

27 Though honesty be no puritan, yet it will do no hurt.
   1604–5 Lavatch. *All's Well That Ends Well*, act 1, sc.3, l.91–2.

28 He and his physicians
   Are of a mind: he, that they cannot help him;
   They, that they cannot help.
   1604–5 Countess, of the King. *All's Well That Ends Well*, act 1, sc.3, l.235–7.

29 They say miracles are past, and we have our
   philosophical persons to make modern and familiar
   things supernatural and causeless. Hence it is that we
   make trifles of terrors, ensconcing ourselves into
   seeming knowledge when we should submit ourselves
   to an unknown fear.
   1604–5 Lafeu. *All's Well That Ends Well*, act 2, sc.3, l.1–6.

30 Why, these balls bound, there's noise in it. 'Tis hard:
   A young man married is a man that's marred.
   1604–5 Paroles. *All's Well That Ends Well*, act 2, sc.3, l.294–5.

31 The soul of this man is his clothes.
   1604–5 Lafeu. *All's Well That Ends Well*, act 2, sc.5, l.43.

32 No legacy is so rich as honesty.
   1604–5 Mariana to Diana. *All's Well That Ends Well*, act 3, sc.5, l.12–13.

33 'Tis not the many oaths that make the truth,

But the plain single vow that is vowèd true.
1604–5 Diana. *All's Well That Ends Well*, act 4, sc.2, l.22–3.

34 My chastity's the jewel of our house,
Bequeathèd down from many ancestors,
Which were the greatest obloquy i' th' world
In me to lose.
1604–5 Diana. *All's Well That Ends Well*, act 4, sc.2, l.47–50.

35 A heaven on earth I have won by wooing thee.
1604–5 Bertram to Diana. *All's Well That Ends Well*, act 4, sc.2, l.67.

36 The web of our life is of mingled yarn, good and ill together.
1604–5 First Lord Dumaine. *All's Well That Ends Well*, act 4, sc.3, l.74–5.

37 Drunkenness is his best virtue, for he will be swine-drunk, and in his sleep he does little harm, save to his bedclothes.
1604–5 Paroles, of the Duke. *All's Well That Ends Well*, act 4, sc.3, l.257–9.

38 'Twas a good lady, 'twas a good lady. We may pick a thousand salads ere we light on such another herb.
1604–5 Lafeu, of Helen. *All's Well That Ends Well*, act 4, sc.5, l.13–15.

39 I am for the house with the narrow gate, which I take to be too little for pomp to enter. Some that humble themselves may, but the many will be too chill and tender, and they'll be for the flow'ry way that leads to the broad gate and the great fire.
1604–5 Lavatch to Lafeu. *All's Well That Ends Well*, act 4, sc.5, l.50–5.

40 Praising what is lost
Makes the remembrance dear.
1604–5 King. *All's Well That Ends Well*, act 5, sc.3, l.19–20.

41 Th'inaudible and noiseless foot of time.
1604–5 King. *All's Well That Ends Well*, act 5, sc.3, l.42.

42 I wonder men dare trust themselves with men.
1605 Apemantus. *Timon of Athens*, act 1, sc.2, l.42.

43 Grant I may never prove so fond
To trust man on his oath or bond.
1605 Apemantus' grace. *Timon of Athens*, act 1, sc.2, l.63–4.

44 Men shut their doors against a setting sun.
1605 Apemantus. *Timon of Athens*, act 1, sc.2, l.141.

45 Every man has his fault, and honesty is his.
1605 Lucullus, of Timon. *Timon of Athens*, act 3, sc.1, l.27–8.

46 Men must learn now with pity to dispense,
For policy sits above conscience.
1605 First Stranger. *Timon of Athens*, act 3, sc.2, l.87–8.

47 Nothing emboldens sin so much as mercy.
1605 First Senator. *Timon of Athens*, act 3, sc.6, l.3.

48 This yellow slave
Will knit and break religions, bless th'accursed.
1605 Timon, of gold. *Timon of Athens*, act 4, sc.3, l.34–5.

49 Thanks I must you con
That you are thieves professed, that you work not
In holier shapes; for there is boundless theft
In limited professions.
1605 Timon to thieves. *Timon of Athens*, act 4, sc.3, l.426–30.

50 Trust not the physician;
His antidotes are poison, and he slays
More than you rob.
1605 Timon to thieves. *Timon of Athens*, act 4, sc.3, l.433–5.

51 Rich men deal gifts,
Expecting in return twenty for one?
1605 Timon to Flavius. *Timon of Athens*, act 4, sc.3, l.510–11.

52 I cannot heave
My heart into my mouth. I love your majesty
According to my bond, nor more nor less.
1605–6 Cordelia to Lear. *King Lear*, act 1, sc.1, l.91–3.

53 Thy youngest daughter does not love thee least,
Nor are those empty-hearted whose low sounds
Reverb no hollowness.
1605–6 Kent to Lear. *King Lear*, act 1, sc.1, l.152–4.

54 If for I want that glib and oily art
To speak and purpose not—since what I well intend,
I'll do't before I speak—that you make known
It is no vicious blot, murder, or foulness,
No unchaste action or dishonoured step
That hath deprived me of your grace and favour,
But even the want of that for which I am richer—
A still-soliciting eye, and such a tongue
That I am glad I have not, though not to have it
Hath lost me in your liking.
1605–6 Cordelia to Lear. *King Lear*, act 1, sc.1, l.224–33.

55 Time shall unfold what pleated cunning hides.
1605–6 Cordelia. *King Lear*, act 1, sc.1, l.280.

56 Fine word, 'legitimate'.
Well, my legitimate, if this letter speed
And my invention thrive, Edmond the base
Shall to th' legitimate. I grow, I prosper.
Now gods, stand up for bastards!
1605–6 Edmond. *King Lear*, act 1, sc.2, l.18–22.

57 We make guilty of our disasters the sun, the moon, and stars, as if we were villains on necessity, fools by heavenly compulsion, knaves, thieves, and treachers by spherical predominance, drunkards, liars, and adulterers by an enforced obedience of planetary influence, and all that we are evil in by a divine thrusting on. An admirable evasion of whore-master man, to lay his goatish disposition on the charge of a star!
1605–6 Edmond. *King Lear*, act 1, sc.2, l.118–26.

58 You base football player.
1605–6 Kent to Oswald. *King Lear*, act 1, sc.4, l.84–5.

59 Have more than thou showest,
Speak less than thou knowest,
Lend less than thou owest.
1605–6 Fool to Kent. *King Lear*, act 1, sc.4, l.117–19.

60 The hedge-sparrow fed the cuckoo so long
That it's had it head bit off by it young.
1605–6 Fool, singing to Lear. *King Lear*, act 1, sc.4, l.198–9.

61 As you are old and reverend, should be wise.
1605–6 Goneril to Lear. *King Lear*, act 1, sc.4, l.218.

62 Ingratitude, thou marble-hearted fiend,
More hideous when thou show'st thee in a child
Than the sea-monster.
1605–6 Lear. *King Lear*, act 1, sc.4, l.237–9.

63 How sharper than a serpent's tooth it is
To have a thankless child.
1605–6 Lear. *King Lear*, act 1, sc.4, l.268–9.

64 O, let me not be mad, not mad, sweet heaven!
Keep me in temper. I would not be mad!
1605–6 Lear. *King Lear*, act 1, sc.5, l.45–6.

65 Thou whoreson Z, thou unnecessary letter.
1605–6 Kent. *King Lear*, act 2, sc.2, l.63.

66 I have seen better faces in my time
Than stands on any shoulder that I see
Before me at this instant.
1605–6 Kent. *King Lear*, act 2, sc.2, l.91–3.

67 A good man's fortune may grow out at heels.
1605–6 Kent. *King Lear*, act 2, sc.2, l.148.

68 All the stored vengeances of heaven fall
On her ingrateful top!
1605–6 Lear to Regan. *King Lear*, act 2, sc.2, l.334–5.

69 Return to her, and fifty men dismissed?
No, rather I abjure all roofs, and choose
To be a comrade with the wolf and owl,
To wage against the enmity o'th' air,
Necessity's sharp pinch!
1605–6 Lear, of Goneril. *King Lear*, act 2, sc.2, l.380–4.

70 Touch me with noble anger,
And let not women's weapons, water-drops,
Stain my man's cheeks. No, you unnatural hags,
I will have such revenges on you both
That all the world shall—I will do such things—
What they are, yet I know not; but they shall be
The terrors of the earth. You think I'll weep.
No, I'll not weep. I have full cause of weeping,
But this heart shall break into a hundred thousand flaws
Or ere I'll weep.—O Fool, I shall go mad!
1605–6 Lear. *King Lear*, act 2, sc.2, l.450–9.

71 Blow, winds, and crack your cheeks! Rage, blow,
You cataracts and hurricanoes, spout
Till you have drenched our steeples, drowned the cocks!
1605–6 Lear. *King Lear*, act 3, sc.2, l.1–3.

72 Thou all-shaking thunder,
Strike flat the thick rotundity o' th' world.
1605–6 Lear. *King Lear*, act 3, sc.2, l.6–7.

73 There was never yet fair woman, but she made mouths in
a glass.
1605–6 Fool. *King Lear*, act 3, sc.2, l.35–6.

74 I am a man
More sinned against than sinning.
1605–6 Lear to Kent. *King Lear*, act 3, sc.2, l.59–60.

75 How dost, my boy? Art cold?
I am cold myself.—Where is this straw, my fellow?
The art of our necessities is strange,
And can make vile things precious.
1605–6 Lear to Fool. *King Lear*, act 3, sc.2, l.68–71.

76 He that has and a little tiny wit,
With heigh-ho, the wind and the rain,
Must make content with his fortunes fit,
Though the rain it raineth every day.
1605–6 Fool. *King Lear*, act 3, sc.2, l.74–7.

77 O, that way madness lies.
1605–6 Lear. *King Lear*, act 3, sc.4, l.21.

78 Poor naked wretches, wheresoe'er you are,
That bide the pelting of this pitiless storm,
How shall your houseless heads and unfed sides,
Your looped and windowed raggedness, defend you
From seasons such as these?
1605–6 Lear. *King Lear*, act 3, sc.4, l.28–32.

79 Child Roland to the dark tower came,

His word was still 'Fie, fo, and fum;
I smell the blood of a British man.'
1605–6 Edgar. *King Lear*, act 3, sc.4, l.170–2.

80 Let them anatomize Regan; see what breeds about her
heart. Is there any cause in nature that makes these hard-
hearts?
1605–6 Lear. *King Lear*, act 3, sc.6, l.34–6.

81 Out, vile jelly!
Where is thy lustre now?
1605–6 Cornwall, pulling out Gloucester's other eye. *King Lear*,
act 3, sc.7, l.81–2.

82 Turn out that eyeless villain. Throw this slave
Upon the dunghill.
1605–6 Cornwall to his servants. *King Lear*, act 3, sc.7, l.94–5.

83 The worst is not
So long as we can say 'This is the worst'.
1605–6 Edgar. *King Lear*, act 4, sc.1, 27–8.

84 As flies to wanton boys are we to th' gods;
They kill us for their sport.
1605–6 Gloucester. *King Lear*, act 4, sc.1, l.37–8.

85 GONERIL: I have been worth the whistling.
ALBANY: O Goneril,
You are not worth the dust which the rude wind
Blows in your face.
1605–6 *King Lear*, act 4, sc.2, l.29–32.

86 Alack, 'tis he! Why, he was met even now,
As mad as the vexed sea, singing aloud,
Crowned with rank fumitor and furrow-weeds,
With burdocks, hemlock, nettles, cuckoo-flowers,
Darnel, and all the idle weeds that grow
In our sustaining corn.
1605–6 Cordelia, of Lear. *King Lear*, act 4, sc.3, l.1–6.

87 GLOUCESTER: The trick of that voice I do well remember.
Is't not the King?
LEAR: Ay, every inch a king.
1605–6 *King Lear*, act 4, sc.5, l.106–7.

88 When I do stare, see how the subject quakes!
I pardon that man's life. What was thy cause?
Adultery? Thou shalt not die. Die for adultery!
No, the wren goes to't, and the small gilded fly
Does lecher in my sight. Let copulation thrive.
1605–6 Lear. *King Lear*, act 4, sc.5, l.108–12.

89 Down from the waist
They're centaurs, though women all above.
But to the girdle do the gods inherit;
Beneath is all the fiend's. There's hell, there's darkness,
there is the sulphurous pit, burning, scalding stench,
consumption. Fie, fie, fie; pah, pah! Give me an ounce of
civet, good apothecary, sweeten my imagination.
1605–6 Lear. *King Lear*, act 4, sc.5, l.121–7.

90 O ruined piece of nature! This great world
Shall so wear out to naught. Dost thou know me?
1605–6 Gloucester to Lear. *King Lear*, act 4, sc.5, l.130–1.

91 Hark in thine ear. Change places, and handy-dandy,
which is the justice, which is the thief?
1605–6 Lear. *King Lear*, act 4, sc.5, l.148–50.

92 A dog's obeyed in office.
Thou rascal beadle, hold thy bloody hand.
Why dost thou lash that whore? Strip thy own back.
Thou hotly lusts to use her in that kind

For which thou whip'st her.
1605–6 Lear. *King Lear*, act 4, sc.5, l.154–9.

93 Get thee glass eyes,
And, like a scurvy politician, seem
To see the things thou dost not.
1605–6 Lear. *King Lear*, act 4, sc.5, l.166–8.

94 When we are born, we cry that we are come
To this great stage of fools.
1605–6 Lear to Gloucester. *King Lear*, act 4, sc.5, l.178–9.

95 I know thee well—a serviceable villain.
1605–6 Edgar, of Oswald. *King Lear*, act 4, sc.5, l.250.

96 Mine enemy's dog though he had bit me, should have
   stood
That night against my fire.
1605–6 Cordelia. *King Lear*, act 4, sc.6, l.30–1.

97 You do me wrong to take me out o'th' grave.
Thou art a soul in bliss, but I am bound
Upon a wheel of fire, that mine own tears
Do scald like molten lead.
1605–6 Lear to Cordelia. *King Lear*, act 4, sc.6, l.38–41.

98 Pray do not mock.
I am a very foolish, fond old man,
Fourscore and upward,
Not an hour more nor less; and to deal plainly,
I fear I am not in my perfect mind.
1605–6 Lear to Cordelia. *King Lear*, act 4, sc.6, l.52–6.

99 Men must endure
Their going hence even as their coming hither.
Ripeness is all.
1605–6 Edgar. *King Lear*, act 5, sc.2, l.9–11.

1 [We'll] take upon 's the mystery of things
As if we were God's spies.
1605–6 Lear to Cordelia. *King Lear*, act 5, sc.3, l.16–17.

2 The gods are just, and of our pleasant vices
Make instruments to plague us.
1605–6 Edgar to Edmond. *King Lear*, act 5, sc.3, l.161–2.

3 The wheel is come full circle. I am here.
1605–6 Edmond to Edgar. *King Lear*, act 5, sc.3, l.165.

4 His flawed heart—
Alack, too weak the conflict to support—
'Twixt two extremes of passion, joy and grief,
Burst smilingly.
1605–6 Edgar, of Gloucester. *King Lear*, act 5, sc.3, l.188–91.

5 Howl, howl, howl, howl! O, you are men of stones.
Had I your tongues and eyes, I'd use them so
That heaven's vault should crack.
1605–6 Lear, grief-stricken at the death of Cordelia. *King Lear*, act 5, sc.3, l.232–4.

6 Her voice was ever soft,
Gentle, and low, an excellent thing in woman.
1605–6 Lear, of Cordelia. *King Lear*, act 5, sc.3, l.247–8.

7 Why should you a dog, a horse, a rat have life,
And thou no breath at all? Thou'lt come no more.
Never, never, never, never, never.
Pray you, undo this button.
1605–6 Edgar. *King Lear*, act 5, sc.3, l.282–5.

8 The weight of this sad time we must obey,
Speak what we feel, not what we ought to say.
The oldest hath borne most. We that are young
Shall never see so much, nor live so long.
1605–6 Edgar. *King Lear*, act 5, sc.3, l.299–302.

9 His captain's heart,
Which in the scuffles of great fights hath burst
The buckles on his breast.
1606 Philo, of Antony. *Antony and Cleopatra*, act 1, sc.1, l.6–8.

10 The triple pillar of the world transformed
Into a strumpet's fool. Behold and see.
1606 Philo, of Antony. *Antony and Cleopatra*, act 1, sc.1, l.12–13.

11 There's beggary in the love that can be reckoned.
1606 Antony to Cleopatra. *Antony and Cleopatra*, act 1, sc.1, l.15.

12 Let Rome in Tiber melt, and the wide arch
Of the ranged empire fall.
1606 Antony to Cleopatra. *Antony and Cleopatra*, act 1, sc.1, l.35–6.

13 In nature's infinite book of secrecy
A little I can read.
1606 Soothsayer. *Antony and Cleopatra*, act 1, sc.2, l.9–10.

14 I love long life better than figs.
1606 Charmian. *Antony and Cleopatra*, act 1, sc.2, l.28.

15 The tears live in an onion that should water this sorrow.
1606 Enobarbus, of the death of Fulvia. *Antony and Cleopatra*, act 1, sc.2, l.161–2.

16 In time we hate that which we often fear.
1606 Charmian. *Antony and Cleopatra*, act 1, sc.3, l.12.

17 Eternity was in our lips and eyes,
Bliss in our brow's bent; none our parts so poor
But was a race of heaven.
1606 Cleopatra to Antony. *Antony and Cleopatra*, act 1, sc.3, l.35–7.

18 The strong necessity of time commands
Our services a while, but my full heart
Remains in use with you.
1606 Antony to Cleopatra. *Antony and Cleopatra*, act 1, sc.3, l.42–4.

19 Age from folly could not give me freedom.
1606 Cleopatra. *Antony and Cleopatra*, act 1, sc.3, l.57.

20 Sir, you and I must part; but that's not it.
Sir, you and I have loved; but there's not it;
That you know well. Something it is I would—
O, my oblivion is a very Antony,
And I am all forgotten.
1606 Cleopatra to Antony. *Antony and Cleopatra*, act 1, sc.3, l.88–92.

21 Now I feed myself
With most delicious poison.
1606 Cleopatra, thinking of Antony. *Antony and Cleopatra*, act 1, sc.5, l.26–7.

22 My salad days,
When I was green in judgement.
1606 Cleopatra. *Antony and Cleopatra*, act 1, sc.5, l.72–3.

23 The barge she sat in, like a burnished throne
Burned on the water. The poop was beaten gold;
Purple the sails, and so perfumèd that
The winds were love-sick with them. The oars were
   silver,
Which to the tune of flutes kept stroke, and made
The water which they beat to follow faster,
As amorous of their strokes. For her own person,
It beggared all description.
1606 Enobarbus, of Cleopatra. *Antony and Cleopatra*, act 2, sc.2, l.198–205.

24 Antony,
Enthroned i'th' market-place, did sit alone,
Whistling to th'air, which but for vacancy
Had gone to gaze on Cleopatra too,
And made a gap in nature.
1606 Enobarbus. *Antony and Cleopatra*, act 2, sc.2, l.221–5.

25 I saw her once
Hop forty paces through the public street,
And having lost her breath, she spoke and panted,
That she did make defect perfection.
1606 Enobarbus, of Cleopatra. *Antony and Cleopatra*, act 2, sc.2, l.235–8.

26 Age cannot wither her, nor custom stale
Her infinite variety.
1606 Enobarbus, of Cleopatra. *Antony and Cleopatra*, act 2, sc.2, l.241–2.

27 If thou dost play with him at any game
Thou art sure to lose; and of that natural luck
He beats thee 'gainst the odds.
1606 Soothsayer. *Antony and Cleopatra*, act 2, sc.3, l.23–5.

28 Give me some music—music, moody food
Of us that trade in love.
1606 Cleopatra. *Antony and Cleopatra*, act 2, sc.5, l.1–2.

29 Let it alone. Let's to billiards.
1606 Cleopatra. *Antony and Cleopatra*, act 2, sc.5, l.3.

30 I laughed him out of patience, and that night
I laughed him into patience, and next morn,
Ere the ninth hour, I drunk him to his bed.
1606 Cleopatra, of Antony. *Antony and Cleopatra*, act 2, sc.5, l.19–21.

31 There is gold, and here
My bluest veins to kiss—a hand that kings
Have lipped, and trembled kissing.
1606 Cleopatra to a messenger bringing news of Antony. *Antony and Cleopatra*, act 2, sc.5, l.28–30.

32 I will praise any man that will praise me.
1606 Enobarbus. *Antony and Cleopatra*, act 2, sc.6, l.90.

33 If I lose mine honour,
I lose myself.
1606 Antony to Octavia. *Antony and Cleopatra*, act 3, sc.4, l.22–3.

34 We have kissed away
Kingdoms and provinces.
1606 Scarus. *Antony and Cleopatra*, act 3, sc.10, l.7–8.

35 I have offended reputation;
A most unnoble swerving.
1606 Antony. *Antony and Cleopatra*, act 3, sc.11, l.48–9.

36 Thou knew'st too well
My heart was to thy rudder tied by th'strings,
And thou should'st tow me after.
1606 Antony. *Antony and Cleopatra*, act 3, sc.11, l.56–8.

37 Fortune knows
We scorn her most when most she offers blows.
1606 Antony. *Antony and Cleopatra*, act 3, sc.11, l.74–5.

38 He wears the rose
Of youth upon him.
1606 Antony, of Caesar. *Antony and Cleopatra*, act 3, sc.13, l.19–20.

39 I dare him therefore
To lay his gay caparisons apart
And answer me declined, sword against sword,

Ourselves alone.
1606 Antony's message to Caesar. *Antony and Cleopatra*, act 3, sc.13, l.24–7.

40 Let's have one other gaudy night. Call to me
All my sad captains. Fill our bowls once more.
Let's mock the midnight bell.
1606 Antony. *Antony and Cleopatra*, act 3, sc.13, l.185–7.

41 Never anger
Made good guard for itself.
1606 Maecenas. *Antony and Cleopatra*, act 4, sc.1, l.9–10.

42 To business that we love we rise betime,
And go to't with delight.
1606 Antony. *Antony and Cleopatra*, act 4, sc.4, l.20–1.

43 O sovereign mistress of true melancholy,
The poisonous damp of night disponge upon me,
That life, a very rebel to my will,
May hang no longer on me.
1606 Enobarbus. *Antony and Cleopatra*, act 4, sc.10, l.11–14.

44 There is left us
Ourselves to end ourselves.
1606 Antony to Eros. *Antony and Cleopatra*, act 4, sc.15, l.21–2.

45 All strange and terrible events are welcome,
But comforts we despise.
1606 Cleopatra. *Antony and Cleopatra*, act 4, sc.16, l.3–4.

46 Is it sin
To rush into the secret house of death
Ere death dare come to us?
1606 Cleopatra. *Antony and Cleopatra*, act 4, sc.16, l.82–4.

47 But I will be
A bridegroom in my death, and run into't
As to a lover's bed.
1606 Antony. *Antony and Cleopatra*, act 4, sc.15, l.99–101.

48 Let him that loves me strike me dead.
1606 Antony. *Antony and Cleopatra*, act 4, sc.15, l.108.

49 So it should be,
That none but Antony should conquer Antony.
1606 Cleopatra. *Antony and Cleopatra*, act 4, sc.16, l.16–17.

50 Of many thousand kisses the poor last
I lay upon thy lips.
1606 Antony to Cleopatra. *Antony and Cleopatra*, act 4, sc.16, l.21–2.

51 Shall I abide
In this dull world, which in thy absence is
No better than a sty?
1606 Cleopatra to Antony. *Antony and Cleopatra*, act 4, sc.16, l.62–4.

52 There is nothing left remarkable
Beneath the visiting moon.
1606 Cleopatra, of the death of Antony. *Antony and Cleopatra*, act 4, sc.16, l.69–70.

53 What's brave, what's noble,
Let's do it after the high Roman fashion,
And make death proud to take us.
1606 Cleopatra. *Antony and Cleopatra*, act 4, sc.16, l.88–90.

54 It is great
To do that thing that ends all other deeds.
1606 Cleopatra. *Antony and Cleopatra*, act 5, sc.2, l.4–5.

55 I dreamt there was an Emperor Antony,
O, such another sleep, that I might see

But such another man!
1606 Cleopatra. *Antony and Cleopatra*, act 5, sc.2, l.75–7.

56 His legs bestrid the ocean; his reared arm
Crested the world.
1606 Cleopatra, of Antony. *Antony and Cleopatra*, act 5, sc.2,
l.81–2.

57 The bright day is done,
And we are for the dark.
1606 Iras. *Antony and Cleopatra*, act 5, sc.2, l.189–90.

58 Hast thou the pretty worm
Of Nilus there, that kills and pains not?
1606 Cleopatra. *Antony and Cleopatra*, act 5, sc.2, l.238–9.

59 His biting is immortal; those that do die of it do seldom
or ever recover.
1606 Clown. *Antony and Cleopatra*, act 5, sc.2, l.241–3.

60 Give me my robe. Put on my crown. I have
Immortal longings in me.
1606 Cleopatra. *Antony and Cleopatra*, act 5, sc.2, l.275–6.

61 Husband, I come.
Now to that name my courage prove my title.
1606 Cleopatra. *Antony and Cleopatra*, act 5, sc.2, l.282–3.

62 If thou and nature can so gently part,
The stroke of death is as a lover's pinch,
Which hurts and is desired. Dost thou lie still?
If thus thou vanishest, thou tell'st the world
It is not worth leave-taking.
1606 Cleopatra. *Antony and Cleopatra*, act 5, sc.2, l.289–93.

63 A lass unparalleled. Downy windows, close,
And golden Phoebus never be beheld
Of eyes again so royal.
1606 Charmian. *Antony and Cleopatra*, act 5, sc.2, l.310–12.

64 When shall we three meet again?
In thunder, lightning, or in rain?
1606 First Witch. *Macbeth*, act 1, sc.1, l.1–2.

65 Fair is foul, and foul is fair,
Hover through the fog and filthy air.
1606 Witches. *Macbeth*, act 1, sc.1, l.10–11.

66 Fortune on his damnèd quarry smiling
Showed like a rebel's whore.
1606 Captain. *Macbeth*, act 1, sc.2, l.14–15.

67 A sailor's wife had chestnuts in her lap,
And munched, and munched, and munched. 'Give me,'
  quoth I.
'Aroint thee, witch,' the rump-fed runnion cries.
Her husband's to Aleppo gone, master o'th' Tiger.
But in a sieve I'll thither sail,
And like a rat without a tail
I'll do, I'll do, and I'll do.
1606 First Witch. *Macbeth*, act 1, sc.3, l.3–9.

68 I'll drain him dry as hay.
Sleep shall neither night nor day
Hang upon his penthouse lid.
He shall live a man forbid.
Weary sennights nine times nine
Shall he dwindle, peak, and pine.
Though his barque cannot be lost,
Yet it shall be tempest-tossed.
1606 First Witch. *Macbeth*, act 1, sc.3, l.17–23.

69 The weird sisters hand in hand,
Posters of the sea and land,

Thus do go about, about.
1606 Witches. *Macbeth*, act 1, sc.3, l.30–2.

70 So foul and fair a day I have not seen.
1606 Macbeth. *Macbeth*, act 1, sc.3, l.36.

71 Live you, or are you aught
That man may question? You seem to understand me
By each at once her choppy finger laying
Upon her skinny lips. You should be women,
And yet your beards forbid me to interpret
That you are so.
1606 Banquo. *Macbeth*, act 1, sc.3, l.40–4.

72 If you can look into the seeds of time
And say which grain will grow and which will not,
Speak then to me.
1606 Banquo to the witches. *Macbeth*, act 1, sc.3, l.56–9.

73 To be king
Stands not within the prospect of belief.
1606 Macbeth to the witches. *Macbeth*, act 1, sc.3, l.71–2.

74 The earth hath bubbles, as the water has,
And these are of them.
1606 Banquo, of the witches. *Macbeth*, act 1, sc.3, l.77–8.

75 What, can the devil speak true?
1606 Banquo, hearing that the first of the witches' predictions
has come true. *Macbeth*, act 1, sc.3, l.105.

76 The Thane of Cawdor lives. Why do you dress me
In borrowed robes?
1606 Macbeth. *Macbeth*, act 1, sc.3, l.106–7.

77 Come what come may,
Time and the hour runs through the roughest day.
1606 Macbeth. *Macbeth*, act 1, sc.3, l.145–6.

78 Nothing in his life
Became him like the leaving of it. He died
As one that had been studied in his death
To throw away the dearest thing he owed
As 'twere a careless trifle.
1606 Malcolm, of Cawdor. *Macbeth*, act 1, sc.4, l.7–11.

79 There's no art
To find the mind's construction in the face.
He was a gentleman on whom I built
An absolute trust.
1606 King Duncan, of Cawdor. *Macbeth*, act 1, sc.4, l.11–14.

80 Yet do I fear thy nature;
It is too full o'th' milk of human kindness
To catch the nearest way.
1606 Lady Macbeth, of Macbeth. *Macbeth*, act 1, sc.5, l.15–17.

81 Thou wouldst be great,
Art not without ambition, but without
The illness should attend it.
1606 Lady Macbeth, of Macbeth. *Macbeth*, act 1, sc.5, l.17–19.

82 Come, you spirits
That tend on mortal thoughts, unsex me here,
And fill me from the crown to the toe top-full
Of direst cruelty.
1606 Lady Macbeth. *Macbeth*, act 1, sc.5, l.39–42.

83 Your face, my thane, is as a book where men
May read strange matters.
1606 Lady Macbeth to Macbeth. *Macbeth*, act 1, sc.5, l.61–2.

84 Bear welcome in your eye,
Your hand, your tongue; look like the innocent flower,
But be the serpent under 't.

1606 Lady Macbeth to Macbeth. *Macbeth*, act 1, sc.5, l.63–5.

85 KING DUNCAN: This castle hath a pleasant seat. The air
Nimbly and sweetly recommends itself
Unto our gentle senses.
BANQUO: This guest of summer,
The temple-haunting marlet, does approve
By his loved mansionry that the heavens' breath
Smells wooingly here. No jutty, frieze,
Buttress, nor coign of vantage but this bird
Hath made his pedant bed and procreant cradle;
Where they most breed and haunt I have observed
The air is delicate.
1606 *Macbeth*, act 1, sc.6, l.1–10.

86 If it were done when 'tis done, then 'twere well
It were done quickly. If th'assassination
Could trammel up the consequence, and catch
With his surcease success: that but this blow
Might be the be-all and the end-all, here,
But here upon this bank and shoal of time,
We'd jump the life to come. But in these cases
We still have judgement here, that we but teach
Bloody instructions which, being taught, return
To plague th'inventor.
1606 Macbeth, on the prospect of murdering Duncan. *Macbeth*, act 1, sc.7, l.1–10.

87 Besides, this Duncan
Hath borne his faculties so meek, hath been
So clear in his great office, that his virtues
Will plead like angels, trumpet-tongued against
The deep damnation of his taking-off,
And pity, like a naked new-born babe,
Striding the blast, or heaven's cherubin, horsed
Upon the sightless couriers of the air,
Shall blow the horrid deed in every eye
That tears shall drown the wind. I have no spur
To prick the sides of my intent, but only
Vaulting ambition which o'erleaps itself
And falls on th'other.
1606 Macbeth. *Macbeth*, act 1, sc.7, l.16–29.

88 Wouldst thou have that
Which thou esteem'st the ornament of life,
And live a coward in thine own esteem,
Letting 'I dare not' wait upon 'I would',
Like the poor cat i'th' adage?
1606 Lady Macbeth to Macbeth. *Macbeth*, act 1, sc.7, l.41–45.

89 I dare do all that may become a man;
Who dares do more is none.
1606 Macbeth to Lady Macbeth. *Macbeth*, act 1, sc.7, l.46–7.

90 Screw your courage to the sticking-place
And we'll not fail.
1606 Lady Macbeth to Macbeth. *Macbeth*, act 1, sc.7, l.60–1.

91 Bring forth men-children only,
For thy undaunted mettle should compose
Nothing but males.
1606 Macbeth to Lady Macbeth. *Macbeth*, act 1, sc.7, l.72–4.

92 Away, and mock the time with fairest show.
False face must hide what the false heart doth know.
1606 Macbeth. *Macbeth*, act 1, sc.7, l.81–2.

93 There's husbandry in heaven,
Their candles are all out.
1606 Banquo. *Macbeth*, act 2, sc.1, l.4–5.

94 Is this a dagger which I see before me,
The handle toward my hand? Come, let me clutch thee.
I have thee not, and yet I see thee still.
1606 Macbeth. *Macbeth*, act 2, sc.1, l.33–5.

95 Mine eyes are made the fool o'th' other senses,
Or else worth all the rest.
1606 Macbeth. *Macbeth*, act 2, sc.1, l.44–5.

96 Whiles I threat, he lives.
Words to the heat of deeds too cold breath gives.
I go, and it is done. The bell invites me.
Hear it not, Duncan; for it is a knell
That summons thee to heaven or to hell.
1606 Macbeth, steeling himself to murder Duncan. *Macbeth*, act 2, sc.1, l.60–4.

97 That which hath made them drunk hath made me bold.
What hath quenched them hath given me fire.
1606 Lady Macbeth. *Macbeth*, act 2, sc.2, l.1–2.

98 Th'attempt and not the deed
Confounds us.
1606 Lady Macbeth. *Macbeth*, act 2, sc.2, l.10–11.

99 I laid their daggers ready;
He could not miss 'em. Had he not resembled
My father as he slept, I had done't.
1606 Lady Macbeth, of Duncan. *Macbeth*, act 2, sc.2, l.11–13.

1 I had most need of blessing, and 'Amen'
Stuck in my throat.
1606 Macbeth. *Macbeth*, act 2, sc.2, l.30–1.

2 Methought I heard a voice cry 'Sleep no more,
Macbeth does murder sleep'—the innocent sleep,
Sleep that knits up the ravelled sleave of care.
1606 Macbeth. *Macbeth*, act 2, sc.2, l.33–5.

3 Still it cried 'Sleep no more' to all the house,
'Glamis hath murdered sleep, and therefore Cawdor
Shall sleep no more, Macbeth shall sleep no more.'
1606 Macbeth. *Macbeth*, act 2, sc.2, l.39–41.

4 Infirm of purpose!
Give me the daggers. The sleeping and the dead
Are but as pictures. 'Tis the eye of childhood
That fears a painted devil.
1606 Lady Macbeth. *Macbeth*, act 2, sc.2, l.50–4.

5 Will all great Neptune's ocean wash this blood
Clean from my hand? No, this my hand will rather
The multitudinous seas incarnadine,
Making the green one red.
1606 Macbeth. *Macbeth*, act 2, sc.2, l.58–61.

6 A little water clears us of this deed.
1606 Lady Macbeth. *Macbeth*, act 2, sc.2, l.65.

7 But this place is too cold for hell. I'll devil-porter it no
further. I had thought to have let in some of all
professions that go the primrose way to th'everlasting
bonfire.
1606 Porter. *Macbeth*, act 2, sc.3, l.15–18.

8 The labour we delight in physics pain.
1606 Macbeth. *Macbeth*, act 2, sc.3, l.49.

9 Confusion now hath made his masterpiece.
Most sacreligious murder hath broke ope
The Lord's anointed temple and stole thence
The life o'th' building.
1606 Macduff, announcing Duncan's murder. *Macbeth*, act 2, sc.3, l.65–8.

10 There's daggers in men's smiles.
1606 Donalbain. *Macbeth*, act 2, sc.3, l.139.

11 Go not my horse the better,
I must become a borrower of the night
For dark hour or twain.
1606 Banquo. *Macbeth*, act 3, sc.1, l.26–8.

12 I could
With barefaced power sweep him from my sight.
1606 Macbeth, of Banquo. *Macbeth*, act 3, sc.1, l.119–20.

13 Things without all remedy
Should be without regard. What's done is done.
1606 Lady Macbeth. *Macbeth*, act 3, sc.2, l.13–14.

14 Duncan is in his grave.
After life's fitful fever he sleeps well.
Treason has done his worst.
1606 Macbeth. *Macbeth*, act 3, sc.2, l.24–5.

15 Come, seeling night,
Scarf up the tender eye of pitiful day.
1606 Macbeth. *Macbeth*, act 3, sc.2, l.47–8.

16 Light thickens, and the crow
Makes wing to th' rooky wood.
Good things of day begin to droop and drowse,
Whiles night's black agents to their preys do rouse.
1606 Macbeth. *Macbeth*, act 3, sc.2, l.51–4.

17 Thou canst not say I did it. Never shake
Thy gory locks at me.
1606 Macbeth to Banquo's ghost. *Macbeth*, act 3, sc.4, l.49–50.

18 You make me strange
Even to the disposition that I owe,
When now I think you can behold such sights
And keep the natural ruby of your cheeks,
When mine is blanched with fear.
1606 Macbeth to Lady Macbeth. *Macbeth*, act 3, sc.4, l.111–15.

19 I am in blood
Stepped in so far that, should I wade no more,
Returning were as tedious as go o'er.
1606 Macbeth. *Macbeth*, act 3, sc.4, l.135–7.

20 Double, double, toil and trouble,
Fire burn, and cauldron bubble.
1606 Witches. *Macbeth*, act 4, sc.1, l.10–11.

21 By the pricking of my thumbs,
Something wicked this way comes.
1606 Second witch. *Macbeth*, act 4, sc.1, l.61–2.

22 MACBETH: How now, you secret, black, and midnight hags,
What is't you do?
WITCHES: A deed without a name.
1606 *Macbeth*, act 4, sc.1, l.63–5.

23 Be bloody, bold, and resolute. Laugh to scorn
The power of man, for none of woman born
Shall harm Macbeth.
1606 Second apparition to Macbeth. *Macbeth*, act 4, sc.1, l.95–7.

24 Macbeth shall never vanquished be until
Great Birnam Wood to high Dunsinane Hill
Shall come against him.
1606 Third Apparition. *Macbeth*, act 4, sc.1, l.108–10.

25 No boasting like a fool;
This deed I'll do before this purpose cool.
1606 Macbeth, intending to murder Macduff's family.
Macbeth, act 4, sc.1, l.169–70.

26 Our fears do make us traitors.
1606 Lady Macduff. *Macbeth*, act 4, sc.2, l.4.

27 He loves us not,
He wants the natural touch.
1606 Lady Macduff, of Macduff. *Macbeth*, act 4, sc.2, l.8–9.

28 Each new morn
New widows howl, new orphans cry, new sorrows
Strike heaven on the face.
1606 Macduff. *Macbeth*, act 4, sc.3, l.4–6.

29 MACDUFF: Stands Scotland where it did?
ROSS: Alas, poor country,
Almost afraid to know itself.
1606 *Macbeth*, act 4, sc.3, l.165–6.

30 MACDUFF: He has no children. All my pretty ones?
Did you say all? O hell-kite! All?
What, all my pretty chickens and their dam
At one fell swoop?
MALCOLM: Dispute it like a man.
MACDUFF: I shall do so,
But I must also feel it as a man.
I cannot but remember such things were
That were most precious to me. Did heaven look on
And would not take their part?
1606 Macduff, of his murdered wife and children. *Macbeth*, act 4, sc.3, l.217–26.

31 The night is long that never finds the day.
1606 Malcolm. *Macbeth*, act 4, sc.3, l.242.

32 It is an accustomed action with her, to seem thus
washing her hands. I have known her continue in this a
quarter of an hour.
1606 Gentlewoman, of Lady Macbeth. *Macbeth*, act 5, sc.1, l.27–9.

33 Out, damned spot; out, I say. One, two,—why, then 'tis
time to do't. Hell is murky. Fie, my lord, fie, a soldier and
afeard? What need we fear who knows it when none
can call our power to account? Yet who would have
thought the old man to have had so much blood in him?
1606 Lady Macbeth, sleepwalking, of the murdered Duncan.
Macbeth, act 5, sc.1, l.33–8.

34 The Thane of Fife had a wife. Where is
she now? What, will these hands ne'er be clean?
1606 Lady Macbeth. *Macbeth*, act 5, sc.1, l.40–1.

35 Now does he feel
His secret murders sticking on his hands.
Now minutely revolts upbraid his faith-breach.
Those he commands move only in command,
Nothing in love. Now does he feel his title
Hang loose about him, like a giant's robe
Upon a dwarfish thief.
1606 Angus, of Macbeth. *Macbeth*, act 5, sc.2, l.16–22.

36 The devil damn thee black, thou cream-faced loon!
1606 Macbeth to his servant. *Macbeth*, act 5, sc.3, l.11.

37 I have lived long enough. My way of life
Is fall'n into the sere, the yellow leaf,
And that which should accompany old age,
As honour, love, obedience, troops of friends,
I must not look to have.
1606 Macbeth. *Macbeth*, act 5, sc.3, l.24–8.

38 Canst thou not minister to a mind diseased,
Pluck from the memory a rooted sorrow,
Raze out the written troubles of the brain,

And with some sweet oblivious antidote
Cleanse the fraught bosom?
1606 Macbeth to the doctor, of Lady Macbeth. *Macbeth*, act 5, sc.3, l.42–5.

39 Throw physic to the dogs; I'll none of it.
1606 Macbeth. *Macbeth*, act 5, sc.3, l.49.

40 What rhubarb, cyme, or what purgative drug
Would scour these English hence?
1606 Macbeth to the doctor. *Macbeth*, act 5, sc.3, l.57–8.

41 I have supped full with horrors.
Direness, familiar to my slaughterhouse thoughts,
Cannot once start me.
1606 Macbeth. *Macbeth*, act 5, sc.5, l.13–14.

42 She should have died hereafter.
There would have been a time for such a word.
Tomorrow, and tomorrow, and tomorrow
Creeps in this petty pace from day to day
To the last syllable of recorded time,
And all our yesterdays have lighted fools
The way to dusty death. Out, out, brief candle.
Life's but a walking shadow, a poor player
That struts and frets his hour upon the stage,
And then is heard no more. It is a tale
Told by an idiot, full of sound and fury,
Signifying nothing.
1606 Macbeth, hearing of Lady Macbeth's death. *Macbeth*, act 5, sc.5, l.16–27.

43 They have tied me to a stake. I cannot fly,
But bear-like I must fight the course.
1606 Macbeth. *Macbeth*, act 5, sc.7, l.1–2.

44 YOUNG SIWARD: What is thy name?
MACBETH: Thou'lt be afraid to hear it.
YOUNG SIWARD: No, though thou call'st thyself a hotter name
Than any in hell.
MACBETH: My name's Macbeth.
1606 *Macbeth*, act 5, sc.7, l.5–8.

45 Macduff was from his mother's womb
Untimely ripped.
1606 Macduff. *Macbeth*, act 5, sc.10, l.15–16.

46 Lay on, Macduff,
And damned be him that first cries 'Hold, enough!'
1606 Macbeth. *Macbeth*, act 5, sc.10, l.33–4.

47 Your cause of sorrow
Must not be measured by his worth, for then
It hath no end.
1606 Ross to Siward. *Macbeth*, act 5, sc.11, l.10–12.

48 Kings are earth's gods; in vice their law's their will,
And if Jove stray, who dares say Jove doth ill?
1607 Pericles. *Pericles*, sc.1, l.146–7.

49 They do abuse the King that flatter him,
For flatt'ry is the bellows blows up sin.
1607 Helicanus. *Pericles*, sc.2, l.43–4.

50 'Tis time to fear when tyrants seems to kiss.
1607 Pericles. *Pericles*, sc.2, l.84.

51 We'll mingle our bloods together in the earth
From whence we had our being and our birth.
1607 Helicanus to Pericles. *Pericles*, sc.2, l.118–9.

52 I'll take thy word for faith, not ask thine oath;
Who shuns not to break one will sure crack both.
1607 Pericles to Helicanus. *Pericles*, sc.2, l.125–6.

53 Shall we rest us here
And, by relating tales of others' griefs,
See if 'twill teach us to forget our own?
1607 Cleon to Dioniza. *Pericles*, sc.4, l.1–3.

54 One sorrow never comes but brings an heir
That may succeed as his inheritor.
1607 Cleon. *Pericles*, sc.4, l.62–3.

55 He's a very dog to the commonalty.
1608 Fourth citizen. *Coriolanus*, act 1, sc.1, l.27.

56 What's the matter, you dissentious rogues,
That, rubbing the poor itch of your opinion,
Make yourselves scabs?
1608 Martius. *Coriolanus*, act 1, sc.1, l.162–4.

57 They threw their caps
As they would hang them on the horns o'th' moon.
1608 Martius. *Coriolanus*, act 1, sc.1, l.210–11.

58 Nature teaches beasts to know their friends.
1608 Sicinius. *Coriolanus*, act 2, sc.1, l.6.

59 [I am] one that loves a cup of hot wine with not a drop of allaying Tiber in't.
1608 Menenius. *Coriolanus*, act 2, sc.1, l.47–8.

60 What I think, I utter, and spend my malice in my breath.
1608 Menenius. *Coriolanus*, act 2, sc.1, l.52–3.

61 That's a brave fellow, but he's vengeance proud and loves not the common people.
1608 First Officer, of Coriolanus. *Coriolanus*, act 2, sc.2, l.5–6.

62 He seeks their hate with greater devotion than they can render it him.
1608 First Officer, of Coriolanus. *Coriolanus*, act 2, sc.2, l.18–19.

63 Ingratitude is monstrous, and for the multitude to be ingrateful were to make a monster of the multitude.
1608 Third Citizen. *Coriolanus*, act 2, sc.3, l.9–10.

64 'Shall remain'?
Hear you this Triton of the minnows? Mark you
His absolute 'shall'?
1608 Coriolanus. *Coriolanus*, act 3, sc.1, l.91–3.

65 On both sides more respect.
1608 Menenius. *Coriolanus*, act 3, sc.1, l.183.

66 You common cry of curs, whose breath I hate
As reek o'th' rotten fens, whose loves I prize
As the dead carcasses of unburied men
That do corrupt my air: I banish you.
1608 Coriolanus to the citizens. *Coriolanus*, act 3, sc.3, l.124–7.

67 Now we have shown our power,
Let us seem humbler after it is done.
1608 Brutus. *Coriolanus*, act 4, sc.2, l.3–4.

68 Anger's my meat, I sup upon myself,
And so shall starve with feeding.
1608 Volumnia. *Coriolanus*, act 4, sc.2, l.53–4.

69 He'll shake your Rome about your ears.
1608 Cominius. *Coriolanus*, act 4, sc.6, l.103.

70 Like a dull actor now
I have forgot my part, and I am out
Even to a full disgrace.
1608 Coriolanus. *Coriolanus*, act 5, sc.3, l.40–2.

71 O, a kiss
Long as my exile, sweet as my revenge!
1608 Coriolanus to Virgilia. *Coriolanus*, act 5, sc.3, l.44–5.

72 O mother, mother!
What have you done? Behold, the heavens do ope,
The gods look down, and this unnatural scene
Thay laugh at.
1608 Coriolanus. *Coriolanus*, act 5, sc.3, l.183–6.

73 Cut me to pieces, Volsces. Men and lads,
Stain all your edges on me. 'Boy'! False hound,
If you have writ your annals true, 'tis there
That, like an eagle in a dove-cot, I
Fluttered your Volscians in Corioles.
Alone I did it. 'Boy'!
1608 Coriolanus. *Coriolanus*, act 5, sc.6, l.112–7.

74 We were, fair Queen,
Two lads that thought there was no more behind
But such a day tomorrow as today,
And to be boy eternal.
1609 Polixenes to Hermione. *The Winter's Tale*, act 1, sc.2, l.63–6.

75 One good deed dying tongueless
Slaughters a thousand waiting upon that.
1609 Hermione. *The Winter's Tale*, act 1, sc.2, l.94–5.

76 He makes a July's day as short as December.
1609 Polixenes, of Mamillius. *The Winter's Tale*, act 1, sc.2, l.170.

77 Should all despair
That have revolted wives, the tenth of mankind
Would hang themselves.
1609 Leontes. *The Winter's Tale*, act 1, sc.2, l.199–201.

78 I saw his heart in's face.
1609 Polixenes, of Leontes. *The Winter's Tale*, act 1, sc.2, l.447.

79 A sad tale's best for winter.
1609 Mamillius. *The Winter's Tale*, act 2, sc.1, l.27.

80 It is an heretic that makes the fire,
Not she which burns in't.
1609 Paulina. *The Winter's Tale*, act 2, sc.3, l.115–6.

81 *Exit, pursued by a bear.*
1609 Stage Direction. *The Winter's Tale*, act 3, sc.3, l.57.

82 A snapper-up of unconsidered trifles.
1609 Autolycus, of himself. *The Winter's Tale*, act 4, sc.3, l.25–6.

83 Jog on, jog on, the footpath way,
And merrily hent the stile-a.
A merry heart goes all the day,
Your sad tires in a mile-a.
1609 Autolycus, singing. *The Winter's Tale*, act 4, sc.3, l.123–6.

84 Let's be red with mirth.
1609 Florizel. *The Winter's Tale*, act 4, sc.4, l.54.

85 Blasts of January
Would blow you through and through.
1609 Perdita, of Camillo. *The Winter's Tale*, act 4, sc.4, l.111–12.

86 Daffodils,
That come before the swallow dares, and take
The winds of March with beauty.
1609 Perdita. *The Winter's Tale*, act 4, sc.4, l.118–20.

87 When you speak, sweet,
I'd have you do it ever; when you sing,
I'd have you buy and sell so, so give alms,
Pray so; and for the ord'ring your affairs,
To sing them too. When you do dance, I wish you
A wave o'th' sea, that you might ever do
Nothing but that, move still, still so,
And own no other function. Each your doing,
So singular in each particular,

88 Good sooth, she is
The queen of curds and cream.
1609 Camillo, of Perdita. *The Winter's Tale*, act 4, sc.4, l.160–1.

89 Garlic to mend her kissing with!
1609 Dorcas, of Mopsa. *The Winter's Tale*, act 4, sc.4, l.162–3.

90 He says he loves my daughter:
I think, so too, for never gazed the moon
Upon the water as he'll stand and read,
As 'twere, my daughter's eyes.
1609 Old Shepherd. *The Winter's Tale*, act 4, sc.4, l.172–5.

91 He has the prettiest love songs for maids, so without
bawdry, which is strange, with such delicate burdens of
dildos and fadings, 'Jump her, and thump her'; and where
some stretch-mouthed rascal would, as it were, mean
mischief and break a foul gap into the matter, he makes
the maid to answer, 'Whoop, do me no harm, good
man!'
1609 Servant. *The Winter's Tale*, act 4, sc.4, l.193–200.

92 Lawn as white as driven snow.
1609 Autolycus. *The Winter's Tale*, act 4, sc.4, l.219.

93 If I were not in love with Mopsa thou shouldst take no
money of me, but being enthralled as I am, it will also be
the bondage of certain ribbons and gloves.
1609 Clown to Autolycus (in disguise). *The Winter's Tale*, act 4,
sc.4, l.231–3.

94 I love a ballad in print, alife, for then we are sure they are
true.
1609 Mopsa to Autolycus (in disguise). *The Winter's Tale*, act 4,
sc.4, l.258–9.

95 Though I am not naturally honest, I am so sometimes by
chance.
1609 Autolycus. *The Winter's Tale*, act 4, sc.4, l.712–13.

96 Stars, stars,
And all eyes else, dead coals!
1609 Leontes. *The Winter's Tale*, act 5, sc.1, l.67–8.

97 Women will love her that she is a woman
More worth than any man; men, that she is
The rarest of all women.
1609 Servant, of Perdita. *The Winter's Tale*, act 5, sc.1, l.110–12

98 My lord, your sorrow was too sore laid on,
Which sixteen winters cannot blow away,
So many summers dry. Scarce any joy
Did ever so long live.
1609 Camillo to Leontes. *The Winter's Tale*, act 5, sc.3, l.49–52.

99 O, she's warm!
If this be magic, let it be an art
Lawful as eating.
1609 Leontes, of the now animated statue of Hermione. *The
Winter's Tale*, act 5, sc.3, l.109–11.

1 Thou art thy mother's glass, and she in thee
Calls back the lovely April of her prime.
1609 *Sonnets*, sonnet 3.

2 Music to hear, why hear'st thou music sadly?
Sweets with sweets war not, joy delights in joy.
Why lov'st thou that which thou receiv'st not gladly?
1609 *Sonnets*, sonnet 8.

3 For thou art so possessed with murd'rous hate

That 'gainst thyself thou stick'st not to conspire.
1609 *Sonnets*, sonnet 10.

4 If I could write the beauty of your eyes
And in fresh numbers number all your graces,
The age to come would say 'This poet lies;
Such heavenly touches ne'er touched earthly faces.'
1609 *Sonnets*, sonnet 17.

5 Shall I compare thee to a summer's day?
Thou art more lovely and more temperate.
Rough winds do shake the darling buds of May,
And summer's lease hath all too short a date.
Sometime too hot the eye of heaven shines,
And often is his gold complexion dimmed,
And every fair from fair sometime declines,
By chance or nature's changing course untrimmed;
But thy eternal summer shall not fade
Nor lose possession of that fair thou ow'st,
Nor shall death brag thou wander'st in his shade
When in eternal lines to time thou grow'st.
So long as men can breathe or eyes can see,
So long lives this, and this gives life to thee.
1609 *Sonnets*, sonnet 18.

6 Yet do thy worst, old time; despite thy wrong
My love shall in my verse ever live young.
1609 *Sonnets*, sonnet 19.

7 A woman's face with nature's own hand painted
Hast thou, the master-mistress of my passion.
1609 *Sonnets*, sonnet 20.

8 My glass shall not persuade me I am old
So long as youth and thou are of one date;
But when in thee time's furrows I behold,
Then look I death my days should expiate.
1609 *Sonnets*, sonnet 22.

9 Presume not on thy heart when mine is slain:
Thou gav'st me thine not to give back again.
1609 *Sonnets*, sonnet 22.

10 O let my books be then the eloquence
And dumb presagers of my speaking breast,
Who plead for love, and look for recompense
More than that tongue that more hath more expressed.
O learn to read what silent love hath writ;
To hear with eyes belongs to love's fine wit.
1609 *Sonnets*, sonnet 23.

11 Now see what good turns eyes for eyes have done:
Mine eyes have drawn thy shape, and thine for me
Are windows to my breast, wherethrough the sun
Delights to peep, to gaze therein on thee.
Yet eyes this cunning want to grace their art:
They draw but what they see, know not the heart.
1609 *Sonnets*, sonnet 24.

12 The painful warrior famousèd for might,
After a thousand victories once foiled
Is from the book of honour razèd quite,
And all the rest forgot for which he toiled.
1609 *Sonnets*, sonnet 25.

13 Weary with toil I haste me to my bed,
The dear repose for limbs with travel tired;
But then begins a journey in my head
To work my mind when body's work's expired.
1609 *Sonnets*, sonnet 27.

14 When, in disgrace with fortune and men's eyes,

I all alone beweep my outcast state,
And trouble deaf heaven with my bootless cries,
And look upon myself and curse my fate,
Wishing me like to one more rich hope,
Featured like him, like him with friends possessed,
Desiring this man's art and that man's scope,
With what I most enjoy contented least:
Yet in these thoughts myself almost despising,
Haply I think on thee, and then my state,
Like to the lark at break of day arising
From sullen earth, sings hymns at heaven's gate;
For thy sweet love remembered such wealth brings
That then I scorn to change my state with kings'.
1609 *Sonnets*, sonnet 29.

15 When to the sessions of sweet silent thought
I summon up remembrance of things past,
I sigh the lack of many a thing I sought,
And with old woes new wail my dear time's waste.
Then can I drown an eye unused to flow
For precious friends hid in death's dateless night,
And weep afresh love's long-since-cancelled woe,
And moan th'expense of many a vanished sight.
Then can I grieve at grievances foregone,
And heavily from woe to woe tell o'er
The sad account of fore-bemoanèd moan,
Which I new pay as if not paid before.
But if the while I think on thee, dear friend,
All losses are restored, and sorrows end.
1609 *Sonnets*, sonnet 30.

16 Full many a glorious morning have I seen
Flatter the mountain tops with sovereign eye,
Kissing with golden face the meadows green.
1609 *Sonnets*, sonnet 33.

17 As a decrepit father takes delight
To see his active child do deeds of youth,
So I, made lame by fortune's dearest spite,
Take all my comfort of thy worth and truth.
1609 *Sonnets*, sonnet 37.

18 All days are nights to see till I see thee,
And nights bright days when dreams do show thee me.
1609 *Sonnets*, sonnet 43.

19 O how much more doth beauty beauteous seem
By that sweet ornament which truth doth give!
1609 *Sonnets*, sonnet 54.

20 The rose looks fair, but fairer we it deem
For that sweet odour which doth in it live.
1609 *Sonnets*, sonnet 54.

21 Not marble nor the gilded monuments
Of princes shall outlive this powerful rhyme,
But you shall shine more bright in these contents
Than unswept stone besmeared with sluttish time.
1609 *Sonnets*, sonnet 55.

22 So, till the judgement that yourself arise,
You live in this, and dwell in lovers' eyes.
1609 *Sonnets*, sonnet 55.

23 Being your slave, what should I do but tend
Upon the hours and times of your desire?
I have no precious time at all to spend,
Nor services to do, till you require;
Nor dare I chide the world-without-end hour
Whilst I, my sovereign, watch the clock for you,

Nor think the bitterness of absence sour
When you have bid your servant once adieu.
Nor dare I question with my jealous thought
Where you may be, or your affairs suppose,
But like a sad slave stay and think of naught
Save, where you are, how happy you make those.
So true a fool is love that in your will,
Though you do anything, he thinks no ill.
1609 *Sonnets*, sonnet 57.

24 Like as the waves make towards the pebbled shore,
So do our minutes hasten to their end.
1609 *Sonnets*, sonnet 60.

25 Since brass, nor stone, nor earth, nor boundless sea,
But sad mortality o'ersways their power,
How with this rage shall beauty hold a plea,
Whose action is no stronger than a flower?
O how shall summer's honey breath hold out
Against the wrackful siege of battering days
When rocks impregnable are not so stout,
Nor gates of steel so strong, but time decays?
O fearful meditation! where, alack,
Shall time's best jewel from time's chest lie hid,
Or what strong hand can hold his swift foot back,
Or who his spoil of beauty can forbid?
O none, unless this miracle have might:
That is black ink my love may still shine bright.
1609 *Sonnets*, sonnet 65.

26 Right perfection wrongfully disgraced.
1609 *Sonnets*, sonnet 66.

27 Simple truth miscalled simplicity.
1609 *Sonnets*, sonnet 66.

28 They look into the beauty of thy mind,
And that in guess they measure by thy deeds.
1609 *Sonnets*, sonnet 69.

29 No longer mourn for me when I am dead
Than you shall hear the surly sullen bell
Give warning to the world that I am fled
From this vile world with vilest worms to dwell.
Nay, if you read this line, remember not
The hand that writ it; for I love you so
That I in your sweet thoughts would be forgot
If thinking on me then should make you woe.
O, if, I say, you look upon this verse
When I perhaps compounded am with clay,
Do not so much as my poor name rehearse,
But let your love even with my life decay,
Lest the wise world should look into your moan
And mock you with me after I am gone.
1609 *Sonnets*, sonnet 71.

30 That time of year thou mayst in me behold
When yellow leaves, or none, or few, do hang
Upon those boughs which shake against the cold,
Bare ruined choirs where late the sweet birds sang.
In me thou seest the twilight of such day
As after sunset fadeth in the west,
Which by and by black night doth take away,
Death's second self. that seals up all in rest.
1609 *Sonnets*, sonnet 73.

31 O know, sweet love, I always write of you,
And you and love are still my argument.
1609 *Sonnets*, sonnet 76.

32 For as the sun is daily new and old,
So is my love, still telling what is told.
1609 *Sonnets*, sonnet 76.

33 Thy glass will show thee how thy beauties wear,
Thy dial how thy precious minutes waste,
The vacant leaves thy mind's imprint will bear,
And of this book this learning mayst thou taste:
The wrinkles which thy glass will truly show
Of mouthèd graves will give thee memory;
Thou by thy dial's shady stealth mayst know
Time's thievish progress to eternity.
1609 *Sonnets*, sonnet 77.

34 Who is it that says most which can say more
Than this rich praise: that you alone are you.
1609 *Sonnets*, sonnet 84.

35 Farewell—thou art too dear for my possessing,
And like enough thou know'st thy estimate.
The charter of thy worth gives thee releasing;
My bonds in thee are all determinate.
For how do I hold thee but by thy granting,
And for that riches where is my deserving?
The cause of this fair gift in me is wanting,
And so my patent back again is swerving.
Thyself thou gav'st, thy own worth then not
   knowing,
Or me to whom thou gav'st it else mistaking;
So thy great gift, upon misprision growing,
Comes home again, on better judgement making.
Thus have I had thee as a dream doth flatter:
In sleep a king, but waking no such matter.
1609 *Sonnets*, sonnet 87.

36 So shall I live supposing thou art true
Like a deceived husband; so love's face
May still seem love to me, though altered new.
1609 *Sonnets*, sonnet 93.

37 They that have power to hurt and will do none,
That do not do the thing they most do show,
Who moving others are themselves as stone,
Unmovèd, cold, and to temptation slow—
They rightly do inherit heaven's graces,
And husband nature's riches from expense;
They are the lords and owners of their faces,
Others but stewards of their excellence.
1609 *Sonnets*, sonnet 94.

38 For sweetest things turn sourest by their deeds:
Lilies that fester smell far worse than weeds.
1609 *Sonnets*, sonnet 94.

39 How like a winter hath my absence been
From thee, the pleasure of the fleeting year!
What freezings have I felt, what dark days seen.
What old December's bareness everywhere.
1609 *Sonnets*, sonnet 97.

40 From you have I been absent in the spring
When proud-pied April, dressed in all his trim,
Hath put a spirit of youth in everything.
1609 *Sonnets*, sonnet 98.

41 Nor did I wonder at the lily's white,
Nor praise the deep vermilion in the rose.
1609 *Sonnets*, sonnet 98.

42 To me, fair friend, you never can be old;
For as you were when first your eye I eyed,

Such seems your beauty still.
1609 *Sonnets*, sonnet 104.

43 Kind is my love today, tomorrow kind,
Still constant in a wondrous excellence.
1609 *Sonnets*, sonnet 105.

44 Not mine own fears nor the prophetic soul
Of the wide world dreaming on things to come
Can yet the lease of my true love control,
Supposed as forfeit to a confined doom.
1609 *Sonnets*, sonnet 107.

45 What's in the brain that ink may character
Which hath not figured to thee my true spirit?
What's new to speak, what now to register,
That may express my love or thy dear merit?
Nothing, sweet boy; but yet like prayers divine
I must each day say o'er the very same,
Counting no old thing old, thou mine, I thine,
Even as when first I hallowed thy fair name.
1609 *Sonnets*, sonnet 108.

46 O never say that I was false of heart,
Though absence seemed my flame to qualify.
1609 *Sonnets*, sonnet 109.

47 Then give me welcome, next my heaven the best,
Even to thy pure and most loving breast.
1609 *Sonnets*, sonnet 110.

48 Let me not to the marriage of true minds
Admit impediments. Love is not love
Which alters when it alteration finds,
Or bends with the remover to remove.
O no, it is an ever fixèd mark
That looks on tempests and is never shaken;
It is the star to every wand'ring barque,
Whose worth's unknown although his height be
  taken.
Love's not time's fool, though rosy lips and cheeks
Within his bending sickle's compass come;
Love alters not with his brief hours and weeks,
But bears it out even to the edge of doom.
If this be error and upon me proved,
I never writ, nor no man ever loved.
1609 *Sonnets*, sonnet 116.

49 What potions have I drunk of siren tears
Distilled from limbecks foul as hell within,
Applying fears to hopes and hopes to fears,
Still losing when I saw myself to win!
1609 *Sonnets*, sonnet 119.

50 For if you were by my unkindness shaken,
As I by yours, you've passed a hell of time.
1609 *Sonnets*, sonnet 120.

51 My mistress' eyes are nothing like the sun;
Coral is far more red than her lips' red.
If snow be white, why then her breasts are dun;
If hairs be wires, black wires grow on her head.
I have seen roses damasked, red and white,
But no such roses see I in her cheeks;
And in some perfumes is there more delight
Than the breath that from my mistress reeks.
I love to hear her speak, yet well I know
That music hath a far more pleasing sound.
I grant I never saw a goddess go:
My mistress when she walks treads on the ground.

And yet, by heaven, I think my love as rare
As any she belied with false compare.
1609 *Sonnets*, sonnet 130.

52 Whoever hath her wish, thou hast thy Will,
And Will to boot, and Will in overplus.
1609 *Sonnets*, sonnet 135.

53 So thou, being rich in Will, add to thy Will
One will of mine to make thy large Will more.
Let no unkind no fair beseechers kill;
Think all but one, and me in that one Will.
1609 *Sonnets*, sonnet 135.

54 When my love swears that she is made of truth
I do believe her though I know she lies.
1609 *Sonnets*, sonnet 138.

55 Two loves I have, of comfort and despair,
Which like two spirits do suggest me still.
The better angel is a man right fair,
The worser spirit a woman coloured ill.
1609 *Sonnets*, sonnet 144.

56 My love is as a fever, longing still
For that which longer nurseth the disease,
Feeding on that which doth preserve the ill,
Th'uncertain sickly appetite to please.
My reason, the physician to my love,
Angry that his prescriptions are not kept,
Hath left me, and I desperate now approve
Desire is death, which physic did except.
Past cure I am, now reason is past care,
And frantic mad with evermore unrest.
My thoughts and my discourse as madmen's are,
At random from the truth vainly expressed;
For I have sworn thee fair, and thought thee bright,
Who art as black as hell, as dark as night.
1609 *Sonnets*, sonnet 147.

57 Was there ever man had such luck? When I kissed the
jack upon an upcast to be hit away! I had a hundred
pound on't, and then a whoreson jackanapes must take
me up for swearing.
1610 Cloten. *Cymbeline*, act 2, sc.1, l.1–4.

58 When a gentleman is disposed to swear it is not for any
standers-by to curtail his oaths.
1610 Cloten. *Cymbeline*, act 2, sc.1, l.10–11.

59 On her left breast
A mole, cinque-spotted, like the crimson drops
I'th' bottom of a cowslip.
1610 Giacomo, of Innogen. *Cymbeline*, act 2, sc.2, l.37–9.

60 I am advised to give her music o' mornings; they say it
will penetrate.
1610 Cloten, of Innogen. *Cymbeline*, act 2, sc.3, l.11–12.

61 Hark, hark, the lark at heaven gate sings,
And Phoebus gins arise.
1610 Musician, singing. *Cymbeline*, act 2, sc.3, l.19–20.

62 Is there no way for men to be, but women
Must be half-workers? We are bastards all.
1610 Posthumus. *Cymbeline*, act 2, sc.5, l.1–2.

63 I thought her
As chaste as unsunned snow.
1610 Posthumus, of Innogen. *Cymbeline*, act 2, sc.5, l.12–13.

64 I am stale, a garment out of fashion.
1610 Innogen. *Cymbeline*, act 3, sc.4, l.51.

65 Against self-slaughter
There is a prohibition so divine
That cravens my weak hand.
1610 Innogen. *Cymbeline*, act 3, sc.4, l.76–8.

66 Thus may poor fools
Believe false teachers.
1610 Innogen. *Cymbeline*, act 3, sc.4, l.84–5.

67 Though those that are betrayed
Do feel the treason sharply, yet the traitor
Stands in worse case of woe.
1610 Innogen. *Cymbeline*, act 3, sc.4, l.85–7.

68 Hath Britain all the sun that shines? Day, night,
Are they not but in Britain? I'th' world's volume
Our Britain seems as of it but not in't,
In a great pool a swan's nest.
1610 Innogen to Pisanio. *Cymbeline*, act 3, sc.4, l.137–40.

69 Thou art all the comfort
The gods will diet me with.
1610 Innogen to Pisanio. *Cymbeline*, act 3, sc.4, l.180–1.

70 Weariness
Can snore upon the flint when resty sloth
Finds the down pillow hard.
1610 Belarius. *Cymbeline*, act 3, sc.6, l.33–5.

71 By Jupiter, an angel—or, if not,
An earthly paragon.
1610 Belarius, of Innogen in disguise. *Cymbeline*, act 3, sc.6, l.42–3.

72 All gold and silver rather turn to dirt.
1610 Arviragus. *Cymbeline*, act 3, sc.6, l.52.

73 Society is no comfort
To one not sociable.
1610 Innogen. *Cymbeline*, act 4, sc.2, l.12–13.

74 Fear no more the heat o'th' sun,
Nor the furious winter's rages.
Thou thy worldly task hast done,
Home art gone and ta'en thy wages.
Golden lads and girls all must,
As chimney-sweepers, come to dust.
1610 Guiderius. *Cymbeline*, act 4, sc.2, l.259–64.

75 By medicine life may be prolonged, yet death
Will seize the doctor too.
1610 Cymbeline. *Cymbeline*, act 5, sc.6, l.29–30.

76 The power that I have on you is to spare you.
1610 Posthumus to Giacomo. *Cymbeline*, act 5, sc.6, l.419.

77 What seest thou else
In the dark backward and abyss of time?
1611 Prospero to Miranda. *The Tempest*, act 1, sc.2, l.49–50.

78 I find my zenith doth depend upon
A most auspicious star, whose influence
If now I court not, but omit, my fortunes
Will ever after droop.
1611 Prospero to Miranda. *The Tempest*, act 1, sc.2, l.182–5.

79 Thou art inclined to sleep; 'tis a good dullness,
And give it way. I know thou canst not choose.
1611 Prospero to Miranda. *The Tempest*, act 1, sc.2, l.186–7.

80 You taught me language, and my profit on't
Is I know how to curse.
1611 Caliban to Miranda. *The Tempest*, act 1, sc.2, l.365–6.

81 Come unto these yellow sands,
And then take hands.
1611 Ariel, singing. *The Tempest*, act 1, sc.2, l.377–8.

82 This music crept by me upon the waters,
Allaying both their fury and my passion
With its sweet air.
1611 Ferdinand. *The Tempest*, act 1, sc.2, l.394–6.

83 Full fathom five thy father lies.
Of his bones are coral made.
1611 Ariel. *The Tempest*, act 1, sc.2, l.399–400.

84 Nothing of him that doth fade
But doth suffer a sea-change
Into something rich and strange.
1611 Ariel. *The Tempest*, act 1, sc.2, l.402–4.

85 He receives comfort like cold porridge.
1611 Sebastian, of Alonso. *The Tempest*, act 2, sc.1, l.11.

86 Look, he's winding up the watch of his wit.
By and by it will strike.
1611 Sebastian, of Gonzalo. *The Tempest*, act 2, sc.1, l.13–14.

87 Misery acquaints a man with strange bedfellows.
1611 Trinculo, of Caliban. *The Tempest*, act 2, sc.2, l.39.

88 'Ban, 'ban, Cacaliban
Has a new master.—Get a new man!
1611 Caliban. *The Tempest*, act 2, sc.2, l.183–4.

89 FERDINAND: I do beseech you,
Chiefly that I might set it in my prayers,
What is your name?
MIRANDA: Miranda. O my father,
I have broke your hest to say so!
FERDINAND: Admired Miranda!
Indeed the top of admiration, worth
What's dearest to the world.
1611 *The Tempest*, act 3, sc.1, l.36–9.
Shakespeare invented the name Miranda, taking it from the Latin word meaning 'worthy to be admired'.

90 Remember
First to possess his books, for without them
He's but a sot as I am, nor hath not
One spirit to command—they all do hate him
As rootedly as I. Burn but his books.
1611 Caliban, of Prospero. *The Tempest*, act 3, sc.2, l.92–6.

91 He that dies pays all debts.
1611 Stefano. *The Tempest*, act 3, sc.2, l.134.

92 The isle is full of noises,
Sound, and sweet airs, that give delight and hurt not.
1611 Caliban. *The Tempest*, act 3, sc.2, l.138–9.

93 Thou shalt find that she will outstrip all praise,
And make it halt behind her.
1611 Prospero, of Miranda. *The Tempest*, act 4, sc.1, l.10–11.

94 The cloud-capped towers, the gorgeous palaces,
The solemn temples, the great globe itself,
Yea, all which it inherit, shall dissolve;
And, like this insubstantial pageant faded,
Leave not a rack behind.
1611 Prospero. *The Tempest*, act 4, sc.1, l.152–6.

95 We are such stuff
As dreams are made on, and our little life
Is rounded with a sleep.
1611 Prospero. *The Tempest*, act 4, sc.1, l.156–8.

96 They were red-hot with drinking;
So full of valour that they smote the air
For breathing in their faces.
1611 Ariel. *The Tempest*, act 4, sc.1, l.171–3.

97 This rough magic
I here abjure.
1611 Prospero. *The Tempest*, act 5, sc.1, l.50–1.

98 I'll break my staff,
Bury it certain fathoms in the earth,
And deeper than did ever plummet sound
I'll drown my book.
1611 Prospero. *The Tempest*, act 5, sc.1, l.54–7.

99 Where the bee sucks, there suck I:
In a cowslip's bell I lie;
There I couch when owls do cry.
On the bat's back I do fly
After summer merrily.
Merrily, merrily shall I live now
Under the blossom that hangs on the bough.
1611 Ariel's song. *The Tempest*, act 5, sc.1, l.88–94.

1 How beauteous mankind is! O brave new world
That hath such people in't!
1611 Miranda. *The Tempest*, act 5, sc.1, l.186–7.

2 What a thrice-double ass
Was I to take this drunkard for a god,
And worship this dull fool!
1611 Caliban. *The Tempest*, act 5, sc.1, l.299–301.

3 Now my charms are all o'erthrown,
And what strength I have's mine own.
1611 Prospero. *The Tempest*, epilogue, l.1–2.

4 Heat not a furnace for your foe so hot
That it do singe yourself.
1613 Norfolk. *Henry VIII*, act 1, sc.1, l.140–1.

5 Travelled gallants
That fill the court with quarrels, talk, and tailors.
1613 Lovell. *Henry VIII*, act 1, sc.3, l.19–20.

6 Good company, good wine, good welcome
Can make good people.
1613 Guildford. *Henry VIII*, act 1, sc.4, l.6–7.

7 Two women placed together makes cold weather.
1613 Lord Chamberlain. *Henry VIII*, act 1, sc.4, l.22.

8 If I chance to talk a little wild, forgive me.
I had it from my father.
1613 Sands. *Henry VIII*, act 1, sc.4, l.26–7.

9 Those you make friends
And give your hearts to, when they once perceive
The least rub in your fortunes, fall away
Like water from ye.
1613 Buckingham. *Henry VIII*, act 2, sc.1, l.128–31.

10 I would not be a queen
For all the world.
1613 Anne Boleyn. *Henry VIII*, act 2, sc.3, l.45–6.

11 You have many enemies that know not
Why they are so, but, like to village curs,
Bark when their fellows do.
1613 Henry to Wolsey. *Henry VIII*, act 2, sc.4, l.155–7.

12 Orpheus with his lute made trees,
And the mountain tops that freeze,
Bow themselves when he did sing.
1613 Gentlewoman, singing. *Henry VIII*, act 3, sc.1, l.3–5.

13 Everything that heard him play,
Even the billows of the sea,
Hung their heads, and then lay by.
In sweet music is such art,

Killing care and grief of heart
Fall asleep, or hearing, die.
1613 Gentlewoman, singing. *Henry VIII*, act 3, sc.1, l.9–14.

14 Methought
I stood not in the smile of heaven.
1613 Henry. *Henry VIII*, act 2, sc.4, l.183–4.

15 In sweet music is such art,
Killing care and grief of heart
Fall asleep, or hearing die.
1613 Gentlewoman. *Henry VIII*, act 3, sc.1, l.13–15.

16 Yet I know her for
A spleeny Lutheran, and not wholesome to
Our cause.
1613 Cardinal Wolsey, of Anne Boleyn. *Henry VIII*, act 3, sc.2, l.99–101.

17 Nature does require
Her times of preservation.
1613 Wolsey to Henry. *Henry VIII*, act 3, sc.2, l.147–8.

18 I have touched the highest point of all my greatness,
And from that full meridian of my glory
I haste now to my setting.
1613 Wolsey. *Henry VIII*, act 3, sc.2, l.224–6.

19 I feel within me
A peace above all earthly dignities,
A still and quiet conscience.
1613 Wolsey. *Henry VIII*, act 3, sc.2, l.379–81.

20 This is the state of man. He puts forth
The tender leaves of hopes; tomorrow blossoms,
And bears his blushing honours thick upon him;
The third day comes a frost, a killing frost,
And when he thinks, good easy man, full surely
His greatness is a-ripening, nips his root,
And then he falls, as I do.
1613 Wolsey. *Henry VIII*, act 3, sc.2, l.353–9.

21 Had I but served my God with half the zeal
I served my King, He would not in mine age
Have left me naked to mine enemies.
1613 Wolsey. *Henry VIII*, act 3, sc.2, l.456–8.

22 Still in thy right hand carry gentle peace
To silence envious tongues.
1613 Wolsey. *Henry VIII*, act 3, sc.2, l.446–7.

23 An old man broken with the storms of state
Is come to lay his weary bones among ye.
Give him a little earth, for charity.
1613 Griffith, recalling Wolsey. *Henry VIII*, act 4, sc.2, l.21–3.

24 Men's evil manners live in brass, their virtues
We write in water.
1613 Griffith. *Henry VIII*, act 4, sc.2, l.45–6.

25 That comfort comes too late,
'Tis like a pardon after execution.
1613 Katherine. *Henry VIII*, act 4, sc.2, l.121–2.

26 Good grows with her.
In her days every man shall eat in safety
Under his own vine what he plants, and sing
The merry songs of peace to all his neighbours.
1613 Cranmer, of Elizabeth. *Henry VIII*, act 5, sc.4, l.32–5.

Shange, Ntozake *originally Paulette Williams* 1948–

Black US writer, who adopted a Zulu name for political reasons.
She has written mainly for the stage, often adopting a multi-
media approach combining poetry, dance and music.

27 For coloured girls who have considered suicide / when the rainbow is enuf.
1975 Title of 'choreo-poem'.

Shankly, Bill (William) 1913–81

Scottish footballer and manager. A player with Preston North End and Scotland, he established a reputation as one of the finest managers of his generation through his management of Liverpool in the 1960s and was widely known for his grim determination and biting wit.

28 Some people think football is a matter of life and death. I don't like that attitude. I can assure them it is much more serious than that.
Quoted in the *Sunday Times*, 4 Oct 1981.

29 I don't drop players, I make changes.
Quoted in Peter Ball and Phil Shaw *The Book of Football Quotations* (1990).

30 If Everton were playing down at the bottom of my garden, I'd draw the curtains.
Quoted in Colin Jarman *The Guinness Dictionary of Sports Quotations* (1990).

31 If you're in the penalty area and aren't sure what to do with the ball, just stick it in the net, and we'll discuss your options afterwards.
Quoted in Colin Jarman *The Guinness Dictionary of Sports Quotations* (1990).

32 Of course I didn't take my wife to see Rochdale as an anniversary present. It was her birthday. Would I have got married during the football season? And anyway it wasn't Rochdale, it was Rochdale reserves.
Quoted in Peter Ball and Phil Shaw *The Book of Football Quotations* (1990).

33 This town has two great teams—Liverpool and Liverpool reserves.
Deliberately ignoring rival team Everton. Quoted in Colin Jarman *The Guiness Dictionary of Sports Quotations* (1990).

34 We murdered them 0–0.
Quoted in Colin Jarman *The Guiness Dictionary of Sports Quotations* (1990).

35 Me having no education, I had to use my brains.
Quoted in David Pickering *The Cassell Soccer Companion* (1994)

Shapin, Steven 1955–

US sociologist

36 The very power of science to hold knowledge as collective knowledge is founded upon a degree and a quality of trust which are arguably unparalleled elsewhere in our culture… Scientists know so much about the natural world by knowing so much about whom they can trust.
1994 *A Social History of Truth*.

Sharansky, Natan Anatoly Borisovich 1948–

Ukrainian-born Soviet dissident, human rights activist and politician. He was imprisoned (1977–86) by the Soviet government. As a Jew, he applied for emigration rights to Israel in 1975, but was harassed by the KGB and discharged from his job. He was arrested in 1977 and accused of treason and espionage. On his release from prison he was allowed to go to Israel, where he became a politician.

37 All the resources of a superpower cannot isolate a man who hears the voice of freedom; a voice that I heard from the very chamber of my soul.
1986 Speech, New York, 11 May, shortly after his release following nine years in a Soviet labour colony.

Sharp, William *pseudonym Fiona Macleod* 1855–1905

Scottish writer and traveller. He published poetry and literary criticism, but he is best known as the author of a series of neo-Celtic romantic tales written under the pseudonym he systematically refused to acknowledge.

38 My heart is a lonely hunter that hunts on a lonely hill.
1896 'The Lonely Hunter', stanza 6. Carson McCullers adapted the phrase as the title of a 1940 novel, *The Heart Is a Lonely Hunter*.

Sharpe, Tom (Thomas Ridley) 1928–

English novelist. His early works were plays written in South Africa. He returned to England in 1961, and became known for the vigorous satire of his comic novels.

39 The South African police would leave no stone unturned to see that nothing disturbed the even terror of their lives.
1973 *Indecent Exposure*, ch.1.

40 Skullion had little use for contraceptives at the best of times. Unnatural, he called them, and placed them in the lower social category of things along with elastic-sided boots and made-up bow ties. Not the sort of attire for a gentleman.
1974 *Porterhouse Blue*, ch.9.

41 And besides, Mrs Forthby in the flesh was a different kettle of fish to Mrs Forthby in his fantasies. In the latter she had a multitude of perverse inclinations, which corresponded exactly with his own unfortunate requirements, while possessing a discretion that would have done credit to a Trappist nun. In the flesh she was disappointingly different.
1975 *Blott on the Landscape*, ch.3.

42 In the lotus position at her yoga class she managed to exude energy, and her attempts at Transcendental Meditation had been likened to a pressure-cooker on simmer.
1976 *Wilt*, ch.1.

43 God, in his view, had created a perfect world if the book of Genesis was to be believed and it had been going downhill ever since.
1976 *Wilt*, ch.17.

44 All you had to do was tell people what they wanted to hear and they would believe you no matter how implausible your story might be.
1976 *Wilt*, ch.18.

45 The Rev St John Froude put the phone down thoughtfully. The notion that he was sharing the house with a disembodied and recently murdered woman was not one that he had wanted to put to his caller. His reputation for eccentricity was already sufficiently widespread without adding to it.
1976 *Wilt*, ch.19.

46 If any writer thinks the world is full of middle-class people of nice sensibilities, then he is out of his mind.
1985 In the *Observer*, 3 Feb.

Shaw, George Bernard 1856–1950

Anglo-Irish dramatist and socialist. He moved to London in 1876 and in 1882 joined the Fabian Society. He wrote over 40 plays including *Arms and the Man* (1894, published 1898), *Candida* (1895), *Man and Superman* (1903), *Pygmalion* (1913), *Saint Joan* (1923, published 1924) and *The Apple Cart* (1929). He was also a lifelong advocate of vegetarianism, and a passionate supporter of spelling reform. In 1935 he was awarded the Nobel prize for literature.

47 Money is indeed the most important thing in the world: and all sound and successful personal and national morality should have this fact for its basis.
1880 *The Irrational Knot*, preface.

48 Reminiscences make one feel so deliciously aged and sad.
1880 *The Irrational Knot*, ch.14.

49 A man who has no office to go to—I don't care who he is—is a trial of which you can have no conception.
1880 *The Irrational Knot*, ch.18.

50 'Do you know what a pessimist is?'
'A man who thinks everybody is as nasty as himself, and hates them for it.'
1887 *An Unsocial Socialist*, ch.5.

51 Don't ask me for promises until I know what I am promising.
1894 Catherine to Raina. *Arms and the Man*, act 1.

52 You can always tell an old soldier by the inside of his holsters and cartridge boxes. The young ones carry pistols and cartridges; the old ones, grub.
1894 The Man to Raina. *Arms and the Man*, act 1.

53 Oh, you are a very poor soldier—a chocolate cream soldier!
1894 Raina to The Man. *Arms and the Man*, act 1.

54 You're not a man, you're a machine.
1894 Sergius to Bluntschli. *Arms and the Man*, act 3.

55 We have no more right to consume happiness without producing it than to consume wealth without producing it.
1895 Morell to Lexy. *Candida*, act 1.

56 Do you think that the things people make fools of themselves about are any less real and true than the things they behave sensibly about? They are more true: they are the only things that are true.
1895 Marchbanks to Morell. *Candida*, act 1.

57 It is easy—terribly easy—to shake a man's faith in himself. To take advantage of that to break a man's spirit is devil's work.
1895 Morell to Marchbanks. *Candida*, act 1.

58 Wicked people means people who have no love: therefore they have no shame. They have the power to ask for love because they don't need it: they have the power to offer it because they have none to give. But we, who have love, and long to mingle it with the love of others: we cannot utter a word. You find that, don't you?
1895 Marchbanks to Proserpine. *Candida*, act 2.

59 I'm only a beer teetotaller, not a champagne teetotaller.
1895 Proserpine. *Candida*, act 3.

60 I no longer desire happiness: life is nobler than that.
1895 Marchbanks. *Candida*, act 3.

61 We're from Madeira, but perfectly respectable, so far.
1896 Philip Clandon to Valentine. *You Never Can Tell*, act 1.

62 We don't bother much about dress and manners in England, because, as a nation, we don't dress well and we've no manners.
1896 Valentine to Dolly and Philip Clandon. *You Never Can Tell*, act 1.

63 The great advantage of a hotel is that it's a refuge from home life.
1896 Waiter. *You Never Can Tell*, act 2.

64 Well, sir, you never can tell. That's a principle in life with me, sir, if you'll excuse my having such a thing, sir.
1896 Waiter to Fergus Crampton. *You Never Can Tell*, act 2.

65 There is nothing so bad or so good that you will not find Englishmen doing it; but you will never find an Englishman in the wrong. He does everything on principle. He fights you on patriotic principles; he robs you on business principles; he enslaves you on imperial principles; he bullies you on manly principles; he supports his king on loyal principles and cuts off his head on republican principles.
1897 *The Man of Destiny*.

66 The worst sin towards our fellow creatures is not to hate them, but to be indifferent to them: that's the essence of inhumanity.
1897 Pastor Anderson to Judith Anderson. *The Devil's Disciple*, act 2.

67 Martyrdom…the only way in which a man can become famous without ability.
1897 *The Devil's Disciple*, act 3.

68 I never expect a soldier to think, sir.
1897 Richard Dudgeon to Major Swindon. *The Devil's Disciple*, act 3.

69 'I can't believe it! What will History say?'
'History, sir, will tell lies as usual.'
1897 Major Swindon and Gen Burgoyne. *The Devil's Disciple*, act 3.

70 Your friend the British soldier can stand up to anything except the British War Office.
1897 Gen Burgoyne to Major Swindon. *The Devil's Disciple*, act 3.

71 Brains are not everything.
1898 Rev Samuel Gardner. *Mrs Warren's Profession*, act 1.

72 If there is anything I hate in a woman, it's want of character.
1898 Mrs Warren. *Mrs Warren's Profession*, act 2.

73 The only way for a woman to provide for herself decently is for her to be good to some man that can afford to be good to her.
1898 Mrs Warren to Vivie Warren. *Mrs Warren's Profession*, act 2.

74 There are no secrets better kept than the secrets everybody guesses.
1898 Sir George Crofts. *Mrs Warren's Profession*, act 3.

75 'Damn you!'
'You need not. I feel among the damned already.'
1898 Sir George Crofts and Vivie Warren. *Mrs Warren's Profession*, act 3.

76 Miss Warren is a great devotee of the Gospel of Getting On.
1898 Praed. *Mrs Warren's Profession*, act 4.

77 He is a barbarian, and thinks that the customs of his tribe

and island are the laws of nature.
1899 Of the Briton. Caesar to Theodotus. *Caesar and Cleopatra*, act 2.

78 When a stupid man is doing something he is ashamed of, he always declares that it is his duty.
1899 Apollodorus. *Caesar and Cleopatra*, act 3.

79 A man of great common sense and good taste, meaning thereby a man without originality or moral courage.
1899 Of Caesar. *Caesar and Cleopatra*, notes.

80 But a lifetime of happiness! No man alive could bear it: it would be hell on earth.
1903 John Tanner. *Man and Superman*, act 1.

81 I am proud of your contempt for my character and opinions, sir.
1903 Roebuck Ramsden to John Tanner. *Man and Superman*, act 1.

82 The more things a man is ashamed of, the more respectable he is.
1903 John Tanner. *Man and Superman*, act 1.

83 Vitality in a woman is a blind fury of creation.
1903 John Tanner to Octavius Robinson. *Man and Superman*, act 1.

84 Of all human struggles there is none so treacherous and remorseless as the struggle between the artist man and the mother woman.
1903 John Tanner. *Man and Superman*, act 1.

85 A sensitive boy's humiliations may be very good fun for ordinary thick-skinned grown-ups; but to the boy himself they are so acute, so ignominious, that he cannot confess them—cannot but deny them passionately.
1903 John Tanner. *Man and Superman*, act 1.

86 There is no love sincerer than the love of food.
1903 John Tanner to Octavius Robinson. *Man and Superman*, act 1.

87 That damnable woman's trick of heaping obligations on a man, of placing yourself so entirely and helplessly at his mercy that at last he dare not take a step without running to you for leave. I know a poor wretch whose one desire in life is to run away from his wife. She prevents him by threatening to throw herself in front of the engine of the train he leaves her in. That is what all women do. If we try to go where you do not want us to go there is no law to prevent us; but when we take the first step your breasts are under our foot as it descends: your bodies are under our wheels as we start. No woman shall ever enslave me in that way.
1903 John Tanner to Ann Whitefield. *Man and Superman*, act 1.

88 You think that you are Ann's suitor; that you are the pursuer and she the pursued… Fool: it is you who are pursued, the marked down quarry, the destined prey.
1903 John Tanner to Octavius Robinson. *Man and Superman*, act 2.

89 'I am a brigand: I live by robbing the rich.'
'I am a gentleman: I live by robbing the poor.'
1903 Mendoza and John Tanner. *Man and Superman*, act 3.

90 Hell is full of musical amateurs: music is the brandy of the damned.
1903 Don Juan to the Devil. *Man and Superman*, act 3.

91 Englishmen never will be slaves: they are free to do whatever the Government and public allow them to do.
1903 The Devil to Ann Whitefield. *Man and Superman*, act 3.

92 An Englishman thinks he is moral when he is only uncomfortable.
1903 The Devil. *Man and Superman*, act 3.

93 In the arts of life man invents nothing; but in the arts of death he outdoes Nature herself, and produces by chemistry and machinery all the slaughter of plague, pestilence and famine.
1903 The Devil to Don Juan. *Man and Superman*, act 3.

94 In the arts of peace Man is a bungler.
1903 The Devil to Don Juan. *Man and Superman*, act 3.

95 As an old soldier I admit the cowardice: it's as universal as sea sickness, and matters just as little.
1903 The Statue. *Man and Superman*, act 3.

96 Sexually, Woman is Nature's contrivance for perpetuating its highest achievement.
1903 Don Juan to Ana. *Man and Superman*, act 3.

97 When the military man approaches, the world locks up its spoons and packs off its womankind.
1903 Don Juan. *Man and Superman*, act 3.

98 What is virtue but the Trade Unionism of the married?
1903 Don Juan to Ann Whitefield. *Man and Superman*, act 3.

99 Marriage is the most licentious of human institutions.
1903 Don Juan. *Man and Superman*, act 3.

1 Those who talk most about the blessings of marriage and the constancy of its vows are the very people who declare that if the claim were broken and the prisoners were left free to choose, the whole social fabric would fly asunder. You can't have the argument both ways. If the prisoner is happy, why lock him in? If he is not, why pretend that he is?
1903 Don Juan to Ann Whitefield. *Man and Superman*, act 3.

2 Beauty is all very well at first sight; but who ever looks at it when it has been in the house three days?
1903 Ann Whitefield. *Man and Superman*, act 4.

3 Revolutions have never lightened the burden of tyranny: they have only shifted it to another shoulder.
1903 *Man and Superman*, 'The Revolutionist's Handbook and Pocket Companion, by John Tanner', foreword.

4 The art of government is the organization of idolatry.
1903 *Man and Superman*, 'Maxims for Revolutionists: Idolatry'.

5 Democracy substitutes election by the incompetent many for appointment by the corrupt few.
1903 *Man and Superman*, 'Maxims for Revolutionists: Democracy'.

6 Liberty means responsibility. That is why most men dread it.
1903 *Man and Superman*, 'Maxims for Revolutionists: Liberty and Equality'.

7 He who can, does. He who cannot, teaches.
1903 *Man and Superman*, 'Maxims for Revolutionists: Education'.

8 Marriage is popular because it combines the maximum of temptation with the maximum of opportunity.
1903 *Man and Superman*, 'Maxims for Revolutionists: Marriage'.

9 Titles distinguish the mediocre, embarrass the superior, and are disgraced by the inferior.
1903 *Man and Superman*, 'Maxims for Revolutionists: Titles'.

10 When domestic servants are treated as human beings it is not worth while to keep them.
1903 *Man and Superman*, 'Maxims for Revolutionists: Servants'.

11 If you strike a child take care that you strike it in anger, even at the risk of maiming it for life. A blow in cold blood neither can nor should be forgiven.

1903 *Man and Superman*, 'Maxims for Revolutionists: How to Beat Children'.

12 Beware of the man whose God is in the skies.

1903 *Man and Superman*, 'Maxims for Revolutionists: Religion'.

13 The most intolerable pain is produced by prolonging the keenest pleasure.

1903 *Man and Superman*, 'Maxims for Revolutionists: Beauty and Happiness'.

14 Economy is the art of making the most of life.

1903 *Man and Superman*, 'Maxims for Revolutionists: Virtues and Vices'.

15 Self-denial is not a virtue: it is only the effect of prudence on rascality.

1903 *Man and Superman*, 'Maxims for Revolutionists: Virtues and Vices'.

16 A moderately honest man with a moderately faithful wife, moderate drinkers both, in a moderately healthy house: that is the true middle-class unit.

1903 *Man and Superman*, 'Maxims for Revolutionists: Moderation'.

17 The reasonable man adapts himself to the world: the unreasonable one persists in trying to adapt the world to himself. Therefore all progress depends on the unreasonable man.

1903 *Man and Superman*, 'Maxims for Revolutionists: Reason'.

18 The man who listens to Reason is lost: Reason enslaves all whose minds are not strong enough to master her.

1903 *Man and Superman*, 'Maxims for Revolutionists: Reason'.

19 Decency is Indecency's conspiracy of silence.

1903 *Man and Superman*, 'Maxims for Revolutionists: Decency'.

20 Life levels all men: death reveals the eminent.

1903 *Man and Superman*, 'Maxims for Revolutionists: Fame'.

21 Home is the girl's prison and the woman's workhouse.

1903 *Man and Superman*, 'Maxims for Revolutionists: Women in the Home'.

22 Every man over forty is a scoundrel.

1903 *Man and Superman*, 'Maxims for Revolutionists: Stray Sayings'.

23 Youth, which is forgiven everything, forgives itself nothing: age, which forgives itself everything, is forgiven nothing.

1903 *Man and Superman*, 'Maxims for Revolutionists: Stray Sayings'.

24 Take care to get what you like or you will be forced to like what you get.

1903 *Man and Superman*, 'Maxims for Revolutionists: Stray Sayings'.

25 Beware of the man who does not return your blow: he neither forgives you nor allows you to forgive yourself.

1903 *Man and Superman*, 'Maxims for Revolutionists: Stray Sayings'.

26 Self-sacrifice enables us to sacrifice other people without blushing.

1903 *Man and Superman*, 'Maxims for Revolutionists: Self-Sacrifice'.

27 Do not do unto others as you would they should do to you. Their tastes may not be the same.

1903 *Man and Superman*, 'Maxims for Revolutionists: The Golden Rule'.

28 The golden rule is that there are no golden rules.

1903 *Man and Superman*, 'Maxims for Revolutionists: The Golden Rule'.

29 When a man wants to murder a tiger he calls it sport; when a tiger wants to murder him he calls it ferocity.

1903 *Man and Superman*, 'Maxims for Revolutionists: Crime and Punishment'.

30 An Irishman's imagination never lets him alone, never convinces him, never satisfies him; but it makes him that he can't face reality nor deal with it nor handle it nor conquer it: he can only sneer at them that do, and be 'agreeable to strangers', like a good-for-nothing woman on the streets.

1904 Larry Doyle to Tom Broadbent. *John Bull's Other Island*, act 1.

31 An Irishman's heart is nothing but his imagination.

1904 Larry Doyle to Tom Broadbent. *John Bull's Other Island*, act 1.

32 The poor silly-clever Irishman takes off his hat to God's Englishman.

1904 Larry Doyle. *John Bull's Other Island*, act 1.

33 My way of joking is to tell the truth. It's the funniest joke in the world.

1904 Peter Keegan to Nora Reilly. *John Bull's Other Island*, act 2.

34 I am sincere; and my intentions are perfectly honourable. I think you will accept the fact that I'm an Englishman as a guarantee that I am not a man to act hastily or romantically.

1904 Tom Broadbent to Nora Reilly. *John Bull's Other Island*, act 2.

35 You jast keep your air on and listen to me. You Awrish people are too well off: thet's wots the matter with you.

1904 Hodson to Matthew Haffigan. *John Bull's Other Island*, act 3.

36 There are only two qualities in the world: efficiency and inefficiency, and only two sorts of people: the efficient and the inefficient.

1904 Tom Broadbent. *John Bull's Other Island*, act 4.

37 In my dreams is a country where the State is the Church and the Church the people: three in one and one in three. It is a commonwealth in which work is play and play is life: three in one and one in three. It is a temple in which the priest is the worshipper and the worshipper the worshipped: three in one and one in three. It is a godhead in which all life is human and all humanity divine: three in one and one in three. It is, in short, the dream of a madman.

1904 Of Heaven, Keegan speaking. *John Bull's Other Island*, act 4.

38 The greatest of evils and the worst of crimes is poverty…our first duty—a duty to which every other consideration should be sacrificed—is not to be poor.

1905 *Major Barbara*, preface.

39 Nobody can say a word against Greek: it stamps a man at once as an educated gentleman.

1905 Lady Britomart Undershaft to Stephen. *Major Barbara*, act 1.

40 I am a Millionaire. That is my religion.

1905 Undershaft to Barbara Undershaft. *Major Barbara*, act 2.

41 I can't talk religion to a man with bodily hunger in his eyes.
1905 Barbara Undershaft. *Major Barbara*, act 2.

42 Alcohol is a very necessary article... It makes life bearable to millions of people who could not endure their existence if they were quite sober. It enables Parliament to do things at eleven at night that no sane person would do at eleven in the morning.
1905 Undershaft to Barbara Undershaft. *Major Barbara*, act 2.

43 It's nao good: you cawnt get rahnd me nah. Aw downt blieve in it; and Awve seen tody that Aw was rawt. Sao long, aol soupkitchener! Ta, ta, Mijor Earl's Grendorter! Wot prawce selvytion nah? Snobby Prawce! Ha! ha!
1905 Bill Walker to Barbara Undershaft. *Major Barbara*, act 2.

44 He knows nothing; and he thinks he knows everything. That points clearly to a political career.
1905 Undershaft speaking of Stephen. *Major Barbara*, act 3.

45 Like all young men, you greatly exaggerate the difference between one young woman and another.
1905 Undershaft about Adolphus Cusins. *Major Barbara*, act 3.

46 Fashions, after all, are only induced epidemics.
1906 *The Doctor's Dilemma*, 'Preface on Doctors: Fashions and Epidemics'.

47 Science becomes dangerous only when it imagines that it has reached its goal.
1906 *The Doctor's Dilemma*, preface, 'The Latest Theories'.

48 There is at bottom only one genuinely scientific treatment for all diseases, and that is to stimulate the phagocytes.
1906 BB (Sir Ralph Bloomfield Bonington). *The Doctor's Dilemma*, act 1.

49 All professions are conspiracies against the laity.
1906 Sir Patrick Cullen. *The Doctor's Dilemma*, act 1.

50 A man's behaviour may be quite harmless and even beneficial, when he is morally behaving like a scoundrel. And he may do great harm when he is morally acting on the highest principles.
1906 BB. *The Doctor's Dilemma*, act 3.

51 The criminal law is no use to decent people.
1906 Sir Patrick. *The Doctor's Dilemma*, act 3.

52 There's almost as many different sorts of marriage as there's different sorts of people. There's the young things that marry for love, not knowing what they're doing, and the old things that marry for money and comfort and companionship. There's the people that marry for children. There's the people that don't intend to have children and that aren't fit to have them. There's the people that marry because they're so much run after by the other sex that they have to put a stop to it somehow. There's the people that want to try a new experience, and the people that want to have done with experiences.
1908 Bill Collins. *Getting Married*.

53 Home life as we understand it is no more natural to us than a cage is natural to a cockatoo.
1908 *Getting Married*, preface, 'Hearth and Home'.

54 The one point on which all women are in furious secret rebellion against the existing law is the saddling of the right to a child with the obligation to become the servant of a man.
1908 *Getting Married*, preface, 'The Right to Motherhood'.

55 Physically there is nothing to distinguish human society from the farmyard except that children are more troublesome and costly than chickens and calves, and that men and women are not so completely enslaved as farm stock.
1908 *Getting Married*, preface, 'The Personal Sentimental Basis of Monogamy'.

56 You see, family life is all the life she knows: she's like a bird born in a cage, that would die if you let it loose in the woods.
1908 Bill Collins about his wife. *Getting Married*.

57 A man is like a phonograph with half-a-dozen records. You soon get tired of them all; and yet you have to sit at table whilst he reels them off to every new visitor. In the end you have to be content with his common humanity.
1908 The Bishop of Chelsea. *Getting Married*.

58 I am a snob, not only in fact, but on principle.
1908 St John Hotchkiss. *Getting Married*.

59 Optimistic lies have such immense therapeutic value that a doctor who cannot tell them convincingly has mistaken his profession.
1910 *Misalliance*, preface.

60 Anybody on for a game of tennis?
1910 *Misalliance*. This may be the origin of 'Anyone for tennis?', as used in archetypal theatrical drawing-room comedies.

61 The English have no respect for their language, and will not teach their children to speak it. They spell it so abominably that no man can teach himself what it sounds like. It is impossible for an Englishman to open his mouth without making some other Englishman hate or despise him.
1913 *Pygmalion*, Preface.

62 He's a gentleman: look at his boots.
1913 Bystander. *Pygmalion*, act 1.

63 I don't want to talk grammar, I want to talk like a lady.
1913 Eliza Doolittle. *Pygmalion*, act 2.

64 Have you ever met a man of good character where women are concerned?
1913 Higgins to Pickering. *Pygmalion*, act 2.

65 'Have you no morals, man?'
'Can't afford them, Governor.'
1913 Col Pickering and Alfred Doolittle. *Pygmalion*, act 2.

66 I'm one of the undeserving poor...up agen middle-class morality all the time... What is middle-class morality? Just an excuse for never giving me anything.
1913 Alfred Doolittle. *Pygmalion*, act 2.

67 Gin was mother's milk to her.
1913 Eliza, speaking of her Aunt. *Pygmalion*, act 3.

68 Walk! Not bloody likely. I am going in a taxi.
1913 Eliza to Freddy. *Pygmalion*, act 3.

69 The secret of being miserable is to have leisure to bother about whether you are happy or not. The cure for it is occupation.
1914 *Parents and Children*.

70 A perpetual holiday is a good working definition of hell.
1914 *Parents and Children*.

71 I am a woman of the world, Hector; and I can assure you that if you will only take the trouble always to do the perfectly correct thing, and to say the perfectly correct thing, you can do just what you like.

1919 Lady Utterword to Hector Hushabye. *Heartbreak House*, act 1.

72 It's prudent to gain the whole world and lose your own soul. But don't forget that your soul sticks to you if you stick to it; but the world has a way of slipping through your fingers.
1919 Captain Shotover. *Heartbreak House*, act 2.

73 There are only two classes in good society in England: the equestrian classes and the neurotic classes.
1919 Lady Utterword. *Heartbreak House*, act 3.

74 Go anywhere in England where there are natural, wholesome, contented, and really nice English people; and what do you always find? That the stables are the real centre of the household.
1919 Lady Utterword. *Heartbreak House*, act 3.

75 This souls' prison we call England.
1919 Hector Hushabye. *Heartbreak House*, act 3.

76 The captain is in his bunk, drinking bottled ditch-water; and the crew is gambling in the forecastle. She will strike and sink and split. Do you think the laws of God will be suspended in favour of England because you were born in it?
1919 Captain Shotover. *Heartbreak House*, act 3.

77 Everyone can see that the people who hunt are the right people and the people who don't are the wrong ones.
1919 Lady Usherword to Mrs Hushabye. *Heartbreak House*, act 3.

78 All great truths begin as blasphemies.
1919 *Annajanska*.

79 I enjoy convalescence. It is the part that makes illness worth while.
1921 *Back to Methuselah*.

80 Silence is the most perfect expression of scorn.
1921 *Back to Methuselah*.

81 If ever I utter an oath again may my soul be blasted to eternal damnation!
1923 Captain La Hire. *Saint Joan*, sc.2.

82 No Englishman is ever fairly beaten.
1923 The Chaplain. *Saint Joan*, sc.4.

83 How can what an Englishman believes be heresy? It is a contradiction in terms.
1923 The Chaplain to Peter Cauchon. *Saint Joan*, sc.4.

84 Some men are born kings; and some are born statesmen. The two are seldom the same.
1923 Peter Cauchon. *Saint Joan*, sc.4.

85 Must then a Christ perish in torment in every age to save those that have no imagination?
1923 *Saint Joan*, epilogue.

86 Idiots are always in favour of inequality of income (their only chance of eminence), and the really great in favour of equality.
1928 *The Intelligent Woman's Guide to Socialism and Capitalism*.

87 Many men would hardly miss their heads, there is so little in them.
1929 King Magnus. *The Apple Cart*, act 1.

88 One man that has a mind and knows it can always beat ten men who haven't and don't.
1929 Joe Proteus. *The Apple Cart*, act 1.

89 As interesting as a wall can be.
c.1930 Asked what he thought of the Great Wall after his flight

over China. Quoted in Hesketh Pearson *Bernard Shaw: His Life and Personality* (1961).

90 The fact is, there are no rules and there never were any rules, and there never will be any rules of musical composition except rules of thumb; and thumbs vary in length, like ears.
1931 *Music in London, 1890–1894*.

91 [The Red Flag] is the funeral march of a fried eel.
Quoted by Winston Churchill in *Great Contemporaries* (1937).

92 A perpendicular expression of a horizontal desire.
Of dancing. Quoted in the *New Statesman*, 23 Mar 1962.

93 That's the difference between us. You talk of art Mr Goldwyn, I think of money.
To Samuel Goldwyn. Quoted in David Niven *Bring on the Empty Horses* (1975).

94 Baseball has the great advantage over cricket of being sooner ended. It combines the best features of that primitive form of cricket known as Tip-and-Run with those of lawn tennis, Puss-in-the-corner and Handel's Messiah.
Quoted in Colin Jarman *The Guinness Dictionary of Sports Quotations* (1990).

95 No sportsman wants to kill a fox or the pheasant as I want to kill him when I see him doing it.
Quoted in Colin Jarman *The Guinness Dictionary of Sports Quotations* (1990).

96 There is no reason why the infield should not try to put the batter off his stride at the critical moment, by neatly-timed disparagements of his wife's fidelity and his mother's respectability.
Alluding to baseball. Quoted in Colin Jarman *The Guinness Dictionary of Sports Quotations* (1990).

97 Who is this 'Babe' Ruth? And what does she do?
Of the legendary baseball star 'Babe' Ruth. Quoted in Colin Jarman *The Guinness Dictionary of Sports Quotations* (1990).

98 England and America are two countries divided by a common language.
Attributed.

99 If all the economists in the world were laid end to end, they would not reach a conclusion.
Attributed.

1 To begin with, I was born with an unreasonably large stock of relations, who have increased and multiplied ever since. My aunts and uncles were legion, and my cousins as the sands of the sea without number. Consequently, even a low death-rate meant, in the course of mere natural decay, a tolerably steady supply of funerals for a by no means affectionate but exceedingly clannish family to go to. Add to this that the town we lived in, being divided in religious opinion, buried its dead in two great cemeteries, each of which was held by the opposite faction to be the ante-chamber of perdition, and by its own patrons to be the gate of paradise.
'Music in London'.

2 You see things, and you say, 'Why?' But I dream things that never were; and I say 'Why not?'
The Serpent

3 [Lord Rosebery] was a man who never missed an occasion to let slip an opportunity.
Quoted by Winston Churchill in *Great Contemporaries* (1937).

Shawcross, Sir Hartley William, Baron Shawcross
1902–2003

English jurist, Attorney General (1945–51) and President of the Board of Trade (1951). He established his reputation as chief British prosecutor at the Nuremberg Trials (1945–6), and as prosecutor in the Fuchs atom spy case (1950). He was made a life peer in 1959.

4 We are the masters at the moment, and not only at the moment, but for a very long time to come.
1946 Alluding to Labour's victory in the general election, House of Commons, 2 Apr.

5 The so-called new morality is too often the old immorality condoned.
1963 In the *Observer*, 17 Jul.

Shawcross, William   1946–

English journalist whose book *Sideshow* (1979) detailed US involvement in Cambodia up to 1975.

6 Cambodia was not a mistake; it was a crime. The world is diminished by the experience.
1979 *Sideshow*, afterword.

Sheehy-Skeffington, Francis   1878–1916

Irish pacifist and feminist.

7 A crank is a small engine that causes revolutions.
On being described as a crank, quoted by his son Owen.

Sheen, Fulton John   1895–1979

US Roman Catholic prelate, who argued strenuously against Communism and birth control.

8 Our Lord…said that if men withheld their praise of him, 'the very stones would cry out', which they did as, later, they burst into Gothic cathedrals.
1962 *These Are the Sacraments.*

Shelley, Mary Godwin   1797–1851

English novelist, who married Percy Bysshe Shelley (1816). Her most famous work is *Frankenstein* (1818), written when she was only 19. After her husband's death she wrote *Valperga* (1823), *The Last Man* (1826), *Perkin Warbeck* (1830), *Lodore* (1835) and *Falkner* (1837) and edited her husband's works.

9 You seek for knowledge and wisdom as I once did; and I ardently hope that the gratification of your wishes may not be a serpent to sting you, as mine has been.
1818 *Frankenstein*, letter 4.

10 I was their plaything and their idol, and something better—their child.
1818 Frankenstein, speaking of his parents. *Frankenstein*, ch.1.

11 So much has been done, exclaimed the soul of Frankenstein—more, far more, will I achieve; treading the steps already marked, I will pioneer a new way, explore unknown powers, and unfold to the world the deepest mysteries of creation.
1818 *Frankenstein*, ch.3.

12 All men hate the wretched; how, then, must I be hated, who am miserable beyond all living things! Yet you, my creator, detest and spurn me, thy creature, to whom thou art bound by ties only dissoluble by the annihilation of one of us.
1818 Frankenstein's monster. *Frankenstein*, ch.10.

13 Everywhere I see bliss, from which I alone am irrevocably excluded.
1818 Frankenstein's monster. *Frankenstein*, ch.10.

Shelley, Percy Bysshe   1792–1822

English lyric poet, who eloped with and later married Mary Godwin. He was a leading light of the Romantic movement and a lifelong atheist. His early poems include *Queen Mab* (1813). He later wrote tragedies such as *The Cenci* (1818), lyrical poems such as 'Ode to the West Wind' (1819) and lyric dramas such as *Prometheus Unbound* (1820).

14 The discussion of any subject is a right that you have brought into the world with your heart and tongue. Resign your heart's blood before you part with this inestimable privilege of man.
1812 *An Address to the Irish People.*

15 Titles are tinsel, power a corrupter, glory a bubble, and excessive wealth a libel on its possessor.
1812 *Declaration of Rights*, article 27.

16 That sweet bondage which is freedom's self.
1813 *Queen Mab*, canto 9.

17 There is no disease, bodily or mental, which adoption of vegetable diet and pure water has not infallibly mitigated, wherever the experiment has been fairly tried.
1813 'A Vindication of Natural Diet'.

18 Mont Blanc yet gleams on high: the power is there,
The still and solemn power of many sights
And many sounds, and much of life and death.
In the long glare of day, the snows descend
Upon that Mountain; none beholds them there,
Nor when the flakes burn in the sinking sun,
Or the sunbeams dart through them.
1816 'Mont Blanc'.

19 The awful shadow of some unseen Power
Floats though unseen among us,—visiting
This various world with as inconstant wing
As summer winds that creep from flower to flower.
1816 'Hymn to Intellectual Beauty'.

20 While yet a boy I sought for ghosts, and sped
Through many a listening chamber, cave and ruin,
And starlight wood, with fearful steps pursuing
Hopes of high talks with the departed dead.
1816 'Hymn to Intellectual Beauty'.

21 The day becomes more solemn and serene
When noon is past—there is a harmony
In autumn, and a lustre in its sky,
Which through the summer is not heard or seen,
As if it could not be, as if it had not been!
1816 'Hymn to Intellectual Beauty'.

22 Nought may endure but Mutability.
1816 'Mutability'.

23 In honoured poverty thy voice did weave
Songs concentrate to truth and liberty,—
Deserting these, thou leavest me to grieve,
Thus having been, that thou shouldst cease to be.
1816 'To Wordsworth'.

24 I love all waste
And solitary places; where we taste
The pleasure of believing what we see
Is boundless, as we wish our souls to be.
1818 'Julian and Maddalo', l.14–16.

25 Thou Paradise of exiles, Italy!
   1818 'Julian and Maddalo', l.57.

26 Me—who am as a nerve o'er which do creep
   The else unfelt oppressions of this earth.
   1818 'Julian and Maddalo', l.449–50.

27 Most wretched men
   Are cradled into poetry by wrong:
   They learn in suffering what they teach in song.
   1818 'Julian and Maddalo', l.544–7.

28 Beneath is spread like a green sea
   The waveless plain of Lombardy,
   Bounded by the vaporous air,
   Islanded by cities fair;
   Underneath Day's azure eyes,
   Ocean's nursling, Venice lies,—
   A peopled labyrinth of walls,
   Amphitrite's destined halls.
   1818 'Lines written amongst the Euganean Hills', l.90–7.

29 Sun-girt city, thou hast been
   Ocean's child, and then his queen;
   Now is come a darker day,
   And thou soon must be his prey.
   1818 'Lines written amongst the Euganean Hills', l.115–18.

30 The City's voice itself is soft like Solitude's.
   1818 'Stanzas Written in Dejection, near Naples'.

31 I see the waves upon the shore,
   Like light dissolved in star-showers, thrown.
   1818 'Stanzas Written in Dejection, near Naples'.

32 Alas! I have nor hope nor health,
   Nor peace within nor calm around,
   Nor that content surpassing wealth
   The sage in meditation found.
   1818 'Stanzas Written in Dejection, near Naples'.

33 With hue like that when some great painter dips
   His pencil in the gloom of earthquake and eclipse.
   1818 'The Revolt of Islam'.

34 An old, mad, blind, despised, and dying king.
   1819 'England in 1819' (published in 1839).

35 His big tears, for he wept well,
   Turned to mill-stones as they fell.
   And the little children, who
   Round his feet played to and fro,
   Thinking every tear a gem,
   Had their brains knocked out by them.
   1819 Of Fraud (ie, Lord Eldon). 'The Mask of Anarchy'.

36 I met Murder on the way—
   He had a mask like Castlereagh.
   1819 'The Mask of Anarchy', alluding to English foreign
   secretary Viscount Castlereagh, who was held responsible for
   the Peterloo Massacre in 1819.

37 On his brow this mark I saw—
   'I AM GOD, AND KING, AND LAW!'
   1819 'The Mask of Anarchy'.

38 Rise like Lions after slumber
   In unvanquishable number—
   Shake your chains to earth like dew
   Which in sleep has fallen on you—
   Ye are many—they are few.
   1819 'The Mask of Anarchy'.

39 I wield the flail of the lashing hail,

And whiten the green plains under,
And then again I dissolve it in rain,
And laugh as I pass in thunder.
   1819 'The Cloud'.

40 That orbèd maiden, with white fire laden,
   Whom mortals call the Moon.
   1819 'The Cloud'.

41 I am the daughter of Earth and Water,
   And the nursling of the Sky;
   I pass through the pores of the ocean and shores;
   I change, but I cannot die,
   For after the rain when with never a stain
   The pavilion of Heaven is bare,
   And the winds and sunbeams with their convex gleams
   Build up the blue dome of air,
   I silently laugh at my own cenotaph,
   And out of the caverns of rain,
   Like a child from the womb, like a ghost from the tomb,
   I arise and unbuild it again.
   1819 'The Cloud'.

42 The fountains mingle with the river,
   And the rivers with the ocean;
   The winds of heaven mix for ever
   With a sweet emotion;
   Nothing in the world is single;
   All things, by a law divine,
   In one spirit meet and mingle.
   Why not I with thine?
   1819 'Love and Philosophy'.

43 O wild West Wind, thou breath of Autumn's being,
   Thou, from whose unseen presence the leaves dead
   Are driven, like ghosts from an enchanter fleeing.
   1819 'Ode to the West Wind', l.1–3.

44 Wild Spirit, which art moving everywhere;
   Destroyer and preserver; hear, oh, hear!
   1819 'Ode to the West Wind', l.13–4.

45 Thou who didst waken from his summer dreams
   The blue Mediterranean, where he lay,
   Lulled by the coil of his crystalline streams

   Beside a pumice isle in Baiae's bay,
   And saw in sleep old palaces and towers
   Quivering within the wave's intenser day,

   All overgrown with azure moss and flowers
   So sweet, the sense faints picturing them.
   1819 'Ode to the West Wind', l.29–36.

46 Oh, lift me as a wave, a leaf, a cloud!
   I fall upon the thorns of life! I bleed!
   1819 'Ode to the West Wind', l.53–4.

47 Make me thy lyre, even as the forest is:
   What if my leaves are falling like its own!
   The tumult of thy mighty harmonies
   Will take from both a deep, autumnal tone,
   Sweet though in sadness.
   1819 'Ode to the West Wind', l.57–61.

48 And, by the incarnation of this verse,
   Scatter, as from an unextinguished hearth
   Ashes and sparks, my words among mankind!
   Be through my lips to unawakened earth

The trumpet of a prophecy! O, Wind,
If Winter comes, can Spring be far behind?
1819 'Ode to the West Wind', l.65–70.

49 I met a traveller from an antique land
Who said: Two vast and trunkless legs of stone
Stand in the desert.
1819 'Ozymandias'.

50 'My name is Ozymandias, king of kings:
Look on my works, ye Mighty, and despair!'
Nothing beside remains. Round the decay
Of that colossal wreck, boundless and bare
The lone and level sands stretch far away.
1819 'Ozymandias'.

51 Hell is a city much like London—
A populous and smoky city.
1819 'Peter Bell the Third' pt.3, stanza 1.

52 But from the first 'twas Peter's drift
To be a kind of moral eunuch,
He touched the hem of Nature's shift,
Felt faint—and never dared uplift
The closest, all-concealing tunic.
1819 'Peter Bell the Third', pt.4, stanza 11.

53 Men of England, wherefore plough
For the lords who lay you low?
1819 'Song to the Men of England'.

54 Hail to thee, blithe Spirit!
Bird thou never wert,
That from Heaven, or near it,
Pourest thy full heart
In profuse strains of unpremeditated art.
1820 'To a Skylark', stanza 1.

55 Higher still and higher
From the earth thou springest
Like a cloud of fire;
The blue deep thou wingest
And singing still dost soar, and soaring ever singest.
1820 'To a Skylark', stanza 2.

56 In the golden lightning
Of the sunken sun
O'er which clouds are brightening,
Thou dost float and run
Like an unbodied joy whose race is just begun.
1820 'To a Skylark', stanza 3.

57 Keen as are the arrows
Of that silver sphere,
Whose intense lamp narrows
In the white dawn clear
Until we hardly see, we feel that it is there.
1820 'To a Skylark', stanza 5.

58 Like a Poet hidden
In the light of thought,
Singing hymns unbidden,
Till the world is wrought
To sympathy with hopes and fears it heeded not.
1820 'To a Skylark', stanza 8.

59 What objects are the fountains
Of thy happy strain?
What fields, or waves, or mountains?
What shapes of sky or plain?
What love of thine own kind? What ignorance of pain?
1820 'To a Skylark', stanza 15.

60 With thy clear keen joyance
Languor cannot be:
Shadow of annoyance
Never came near thee:
Thou lovest—but ne'er knew love's sad satiety.
1820 'To a Skylark', stanza 16.

61 We look before and after,
And pine for what is not:
Our sincerest laughter
With some pain is fraught:
Our sweetest songs are those that tell of saddest
thought.
1820 'To a Skylark', stanza 18.

62 Better than all measures
Of delightful sound,
Better than all treasures
That in books are found,
Thy skill to poet were, thou scorner of the ground!
1820 'To a Skylark', stanza 21.

63 Teach me half the gladness
That thy brain must know,
Such harmonious madness
From my lips would flow
The world should listen then—as I am listening now.
1820 'To a Skylark', stanza 21.

64 Chameleons feed on light and air:
Poet's food is love and game.
1820 'An Exhortation'.

65 London, that great sea, whose ebb and flow
At once is deaf and loud, and on the shore
Vomits its wrecks, and still howls on for more.
1820 'Letter to Maria Gisborne', l.193–5.

66 You will see Coleridge—he who sits obscure
In the exceeding lustre and the pure
Intense irradiation of a mind,
Which, through its own internal lighting blind,
Flags wearily through darkness and despair—
A cloud-encircled meteor of the air,
A hooded eagle among blinking owls—
You will see Hunt—one of those happy souls
Which are the salt of the earth, and without whom
This world would smell like what it is—a tomb.
1820 'Letter to Maria Gisborne' l.202–11.

67 Have you not heard
When a man marries, dies, or turns Hindoo,
His best friends hear no more of him?
1820 'Letter to Maria Gisborne' l.235–7.

68 His fine wit
Makes such a wound, the knife is lost in it.
1820 Of Thomas Love Peacock. 'Letter to Maria Gisborne',
l.240–1.

69 Ere Babylon was dust,
The Magus Zoroaster, my dead child,
Met his own image walking in the garden,
That apparition, sole of men, he saw.
1820 *Prometheus Unbound*, act 1, l.191–4.

70 Cruel he looks, but calm and strong,
Like one who does, not suffers wrong.
1820 *Prometheus Unbound*, act 1, l.238–9.

71 It doth repent me: words are quick and vain:
Grief for a while is blind, and so was mine.

I wish no living thing to suffer pain.
1820 *Prometheus Unbound*, act 1, l.303–5.

72 Kingly conclaves stern and cold,
Where blood with guilt is bought and sold.
1820 *Prometheus Unbound* act 1, l.530–1.

73 The good want power, but to weep barren tears.
The powerful goodness want: worse need for them.
The wise want love; and those who love want wisdom.
1820 *Prometheus Unbound* act 1, l.625–7.

74 Peace is in the grave.
The grave hides all things beautiful and good:
I am a God and cannot find it there.
1820 *Prometheus Unbound* act 1, l.638–40.

75 The dust of creeds outworn.
1820 *Prometheus Unbound* act 1, l.697.

76 On a poet's lips I slept
Dreaming like a love-adept
In the sound his breathing kept.
1820 *Prometheus Unbound*, act 1, l.737–9.

77 To be
Omnipotent but friendless is to reign.
1820 *Prometheus Unbound*, act 2, sc.4, l.47–8.

78 He gave man speech, and speech created thought,
Which is the measure of the universe.
1820 *Prometheus Unbound*, act 2, sc.4, l.72–3.

79 Fate, Time, Occasion, Chance, and Change? To these
All things are subject but eternal love.
1820 *Prometheus Unbound*, act 2, sc.4, l.119–20.

80 My soul is an enchanted boat,
Which, like a sleeping swan, doth float
Upon the silver waves of thy sweet singing.
1820 *Prometheus Unbound*, act 2, sc.5, l.72–4.

81 The loathsome mask has fallen, the man remains
Sceptreless, free, uncircumscribed, but man
Equal, unclassed, tribeless, and nationless,
Exempt from awe, worship, degree, the king
Over himself; just, gentle, wise: but man
Passionless?—no, yet free from guilt or pain,
Which were, for his will made or suffered them,
Nor yet exempt, though ruling them like slaves,
From chance, and death, and mutability,
The clogs of that which else might oversoar
The loftiest star of unascended heaven,
Pinnacled dim in the intense inane.
1820 *Prometheus Unbound*, act 3, sc.4, l.193–204.

82 A traveller from the cradle to the grave
Through the dim night of this immortal day.
1820 *Prometheus Unbound*, act 4, l.551–2.

83 To suffer woes which Hope thinks infinite;
To forgive wrongs darker than death or night;
To defy Power, which seems omnipotent:
To love, and bear; to hope till Hope creates
From its own wreck the thing it contemplates;
Neither to change, nor falter, nor repent;
This, like thy glory, Titan, is to be
Good, great and joyous, beautiful and free;
This is alone Life, Joy, Empire and Victory.
1820 *Prometheus Unbound*, act 4, l.570–8.

84 A Sensitive Plant in a garden grew.
1820 'The Sensitive Plant', pt.1, l.1.

85 And the rose like a nymph to the bath addressed,
Which unveiled the depth of her glowing breast,
Till, fold after fold, to the fainting air
The soul of her beauty and love lay bare.
1820 'The Sensitive Plant', pt.1, l.29–32.

86 And the jessamine faint, and the sweet tuberose,
The sweetest flower for scent that blows.
1820 'The Sensitive Plant', pt.1, l.37–8.

87 A lovely lady, garmented in light
From her own beauty.
1820 'The Witch of Atlas', stanza 5.

88 For she was beautiful—her beauty made
The bright world dim, and everything beside
Seemed like the fleeting image of a shade.
1820 'The Witch of Atlas', stanza 12.

89 The cemetery is an open space among the ruins,
covered in winter with violets and daisies. It might make
one in love with death, to think that one should be
buried in so sweet a place.
1821 *Adonais*, preface.

90 I weep for Adonais—he is dead!
O, weep for Adonais! though our tears
Thaw not the frost which binds so dear a head!
1821 *Adonais*, stanza 1.

91 He died,
Who was the Sire of an immortal strain,
Blind, old and lonely.
1821 *Adonais*, stanza 4.

92 To that high Capital, where kingly Death
Keeps his pale court in beauty and decay,
He came.
1821 *Adonais*, stanza 7.

93 The quick Dreams,
The passion-winged Ministers of thought.
1821 *Adonais*, stanza 9.

94 Lost Angel of a ruined Paradise!
She knew not 'twas her own; as with no stain
She faded, like a cloud which had outwept its rain.
1821 *Adonais*, stanza 10.

95 Ah, woe is me! Winter is come and gone,
But grief returns with the revolving year.
1821 *Adonais*, stanza 18.

96 From the great morning of the world when first
God dawned on Chaos.
1821 *Adonais*, stanza 19.

97 Alas! that all we loved of him should be,
But for our grief, as if it had not been,
And grief itself be mortal!
1821 *Adonais*, stanza 21.

98 Whence are we, and why are we? Of what scene
The actors or spectators?
1821 *Adonais*, stanza 21.

99 A pard-like Spirit, beautiful and swift—
A love in desolation masked;—a Power
Girt round with weakness;—it can scarce uplift
The weight of the superincumbent hour;
It is a dying lamp, a falling shower,
A breaking billow;—even whilst we speak
Is it not broken?
1821 *Adonais*, stanza 32.

1 Our Adonais has drunk poison—oh!
What deaf and viperous murderer could crown
Life's early cup with such a draught of woe?
1821 *Adonais*, stanza 36.

2 He wakes or sleeps with the enduring dead;
Thou canst not soar where he is sitting now—
Dust to the dust! but the pure spirit shall flow
Back to the burning fountain whence it came,
A portion of the Eternal.
1821 *Adonais*, stanza 38.

3 He hath awakened from the dream of life—
'Tis we, who lost in stormy visions, keep
With phantoms an unprofitable strife,
And in mad trance, strike with our spirit's knife
Invulnerable nothings.
1821 *Adonais*, stanza 39.

4 He has out-soared the shadow of our night;
Envy and calumny and hate and pain,
And that unrest which men miscall delight,
Can touch him not and torture not again;
From the contagion of the world's slow stain
He is secure, and now can never mourn
A heart grown cold, a head grown grey in vain.
1821 *Adonais*, stanza 40.

5 He lives, he wakes,—'tis Death is dead, not he.
1821 *Adonais*, stanza 41.

6 He is a portion of the loveliness
Which once he made more lovely.
1821 *Adonais*, stanza 43.

7 The One remains, the many change and pass;
Heaven's light forever shines, Earth's shadows fly:
Life, like a dome of many-coloured glass,
Stains the white radiance of Eternity,
Until Death tramples it to fragments.
1821 *Adonais*, stanza 52.

8 I never was attached to that great sect,
Whose doctrine is that each one should select
Out of the crowd a mistress or a friend,
And all the rest, though fair and wise, commend
To cold oblivion.
1821 'Epipsychidion', l.149–53.

9 The beaten road
Which those poor slaves with weary footsteps tread,
Who travel to their home among the dead
By the broad highway of the world, and so
With one chained friend, perhaps a jealous foe,
The dreariest and the longest journey go.
1821 'Epipsychidion', l.154–9.

10 True Love in this differs from gold and clay,
That to divide is not to take away.
1821 'Epipsychidion', l.160–1.

11 An isle under Ionian skies
Beautiful as a wreck of Paradise.
1821 'Epipsychidion', l.422–3.

12 I pant, I sink, I tremble, I expire!
1821 'Epipsychidion', l.591.

13 The vanity of translation; it were as wise to cast a violet
into a crucible that you might discover the formal
principle of its colour and odour, as seek to transfuse
from one language to another the creations of a poet.

The plant must spring again from its seed, or it will bear
no flower.
1821 *A Defence of Poetry.*

14 The great instrument of moral good is the imagination;
and poetry administers to the effect by acting on the
cause.
1821 *A Defence of Poetry.*

15 A single word even may be a spark of inextinguishable
thought.
1821 *A Defence of Poetry.*

16 Poetry is a record of the best and happiest moments of
the happiest and best minds.
1821 *A Defence of Poetry.*

17 Poets are the hierophants of an unapprehended
inspiration; the mirrors of the gigantic shadows which
futurity casts upon the present; the words which express
what they understand not; the trumpets which sing to
battle, and feel not what they inspire; the influence
which is moved not, but moves. Poets are the
unacknowledged legislators of the world.
1821 *A Defence of Poetry.*

18 Death will come when thou art dead,
Soon, too soon—
Sleep will come when thou art fled;
Of neither would I ask the boon
I ask of thee, belovèd Night—
Swift be thine approaching flight,
Come soon, soon!
1821 'To Night'.

19 Life may change, but it may fly not,
Hope may vanish, but can die not;
Truth be veiled, but still it burneth;
Love repulsed,—but it returneth!
1822 'Hellas', l.34–7.

20 Let there be light! Said Liberty,
And like sunrise from the sea,
Athens arose!
1822 'Hellas', l.682–4.

21 The world's great age begins anew,
The golden years return,
The earth doth like a snake renew
Her winter weeds outworn;
Heaven smiles, and faiths and empires gleam,
Like wrecks of a dissolving dream.
1822 'Hellas', l.1060–5.

22 O cease! must hate and death return,
Cease! must men kill and die?
Cease! drain not to its dregs the urn
Of bitter prophecy.
The world is weary of the past,
Oh, might it die or rest at last!
1822 'Hellas', l.1096–101.

23 I dreamed that, as I wandered by the way,
Bare Winter suddenly was changed to Spring,
And gentle odours led my steps astray,
Mixed with a sound of water's murmuring
Along a shelving bank of turf, which lay
Under a copse, and hardly dared to fling
Its green arms round the bosom of the stream,
But kissed it and then fled, as thou mightst in dream.
1822 'The Question', stanza 1.

24 Daisies, those pearled Arcturi of the earth,
The constellated flower that never sets.
1822 'The Question', stanza 2.

25 And in the warm hedge grew lush eglantine,
Green cowbind and the moonlight-coloured may.
1822 'The Question', stanza 3.

26 Less oft peace in Shelley's mind,
Than calm in waters seen.
1822 'To Jane: The Recollection'.

27 Music when soft voices die,
Vibrates in the memory—
Odours, when sweet violets sicken,
Live within the sense they quicken.
'To—: Music when soft voices die' (published 1824).

28 I pursued a maiden and clasped a reed:
Gods and men, we are all deluded thus!
It breaks in our bosom and then we bleed.
'Hymn of Pan' (published 1824).

29 Swiftly walk o'er the western wave,
Spirit of Night!
Out of the misty eastern cave,
Where, all the long and lone daylight,
Thou wovest dreams of joy and fear,
Which make thee terrible and dear,
Swift be thy flight!
'To Night' (published 1824).

30 Art thou pale for weariness
Of climbing heaven, and gazing on the earth,
Wandering companionless
Among the stars that have a different birth,—
And ever-changing, like a joyless eye
That finds no object worth its constancy?
'To the Moon' (published 1824).

31 And like a dying lady, lean and pale,
Who totters forth, wrapped in a gauzy veil.
'The Waning Moon' (published 1824).

Sheridan, Philip Henry 1831–88

American Union cavalry commander in the Civil War and the American-Indian wars.

32 The only good Indian is a dead Indian.
1869 Attributed comment at Fort Cobb, Jan.

33 We took away their country and their means of support, broke up their mode of living, their habits of life, introduced disease and decay among them and it was for this and against this they made war. Could anyone expect less?
c.1870 Quoted in Thomas C Leonard *Above the Battle* (1978).

Sheridan, Richard Brinsley 1751–1816

Irish dramatist. His major plays, *The Rivals*, *The Duenna*, and *The Critic*, were produced between 1775 and 1779. He became an MP and in 1782 under-secretary for foreign affairs, a renowned orator. He lost his seat in 1812.

34 Promise to forget this fellow—to illiterate him, I say, quite from your memory.
1775 Mrs Malaprop to Lydia. *The Rivals*, act 1, sc.2.

35 What business have you, miss, with preference and aversion?…You ought to know, that as both always wear off, 'tis safest in matrimony to begin with a little aversion.

36 Madam, a circulating library in a town is as an evergreen tree of diabolical knowledge!… Depend upon it, Mrs Malaprop, that they who are so fond of handling the leaves, will long for the fruit at last.
1775 Sir Anthony Absolute. *The Rivals*, act 1, sc.2.

37 I'll make my old clothes know who's master. I shall straightaway cashier the hunting-frock, and render my leather breeches incapable. My hair has been in training some time.
1775 Bob Acres. *The Rivals*, act 2, sc.1.

38 Though one eye may be very agreeable, yet as the prejudice has always run in favour of two, I would not wish to affect a singularity in that article.
1775 Jack Absolute. *The Rivals*, act 3, sc.1.

39 He is the very pine-apple of politeness.
1775 Mrs Malaprop of Jack Absolute. *The Rivals*, act 3, sc.3.

40 Sure, if I reprehend anything in this world it is the use of my oracular tongue, and a nice derangement of epitaphs.
1775 Mrs Malaprop. *The Rivals*, act 3, sc.3.

41 She's as headstrong as an allegory on the banks of the Nile.
1775 Mrs Malaprop of Lydia Languish. *The Rivals*, act 3, sc.3.

42 That's too civil by half.
1775 Bob Acres to Sir Lucius O' Trigger. *The Rivals*, act 3, sc.4.

43 Pray, sir, be easy; the quarrel is a very pretty quarrel as it stands; we should only spoil it by trying to explain it.
1775 Sir Lucius O'Trigger to Jack Absolute. *The Rivals*, act 4, sc.3.

44 [To] have an unmannerly fat clerk ask the consent of every butcher in the parish to join John Absolute and Lydia Languish, spinster. Oh that I should live to hear myself called spinster!
1775 Lydia Languish, who had hoped for a romantic elopement. *The Rivals*, act 5, sc.1.

45 Oh, poor Dolly! I never shall see her like again; such an arm for a bandage—veins that seemed to invite the lancet.
1775 Dr Rosy. *St Patrick's Day*, act 1, sc.1.

46 A bumper of good liquor,
Will end a contest quicker
Than justice, judge or vicar.
1775 *The Duenna*, act 2, sc.3.

47 Conscience has no more to do with gallantry than it has with politics.
1775 Isaac to Don Antonio. *The Duenna*, act 2, sc.4.

48 BERINTHIA: Your lordship, I suppose, is fond of music?
LORD FOP: Oh, passionately, on Tuesdays and Saturdays.
1777 *A Trip to Scarborough*, act 2, sc.1.

49 Ah, Amanda, it's a delicious thing to be a young widow!
1777 *A Trip to Scarborough*, act 2, sc.1.

50 Alas! the devil's sooner raised than laid.
So strong, so swift, the monster there's no gagging:
Cut Scandal's head off, still the tongue is wagging.
1777 *The School for Scandal*, prologue.

51 I think you will like them, when you shall see them on a beautiful quarto page, where a neat rivulet of text shall meander through a meadow of margin.
1777 Sir Benjamin Backbite, of his love elegies to Maria. *The School for Scandal*, act 1, sc.1.

1775 Mrs Malaprop to Lydia. *The Rivals*, act 1, sc.2.

52 I'm called away by particular business. But I leave my character behind me.
1777 Sir Peter Teazle, leaving a gathering of gossips. *The School for Scandal*, act 2, sc.2.

53 I hate to see prudence clinging to the green suckers of youth; 'tis like ivy round a sapling, and spoils the growth of the tree.
1777 Sir Oliver Surface. *The School for Scandal*, act 2, sc.3.

54 Here's to the maiden of bashful fifteen;
Here's to the widow of fifty;
Here's to the flaunting extravagant quean;
And here's to the housewife that's thrifty.
Chorus. Let the toast pass,
          Drink to the lass—
I'll warrant she'll prove an excuse for a glass!
1777 Song. *The School for Scandal*, act 3, sc.3.

55 Wine does but draw forth a man's natural qualities.
1777 Charles Surface. *The School for Scandal*, act 3, sc.3.

56 When a scandalous story is believed against one, there is certainly no comfort like the conscience of having deserved it.
1777 Joseph Surface. *The School for Scandal*, act 4, sc.3.

57 There needs no small degree of address to gain the reputation of benevolence without incurring the expense.
1777 Joseph Surface. *The School for Scandal*, act 5, sc.1.

58 The *newspapers! Sir, they are the most villainous—licentious—abominable—infernal—Not that I ever read them—No—I make it a rule never to look into a newspaper.*
1779 *The Critic*, act 1, sc.1.

59 If there is anything to one's praise, it is a foolish vanity to be gratified at it; and, if it is abuse—why one is always sure to hear of it from one damned good-natured friend or other!
1779 Sir Fretful Plagiary, of newspaper criticism. *The Critic*, act 1, sc.1.

60 Mr Dangle, here are two very civil gentlemen trying to make themselves understood, and I don't know which is the interpreter.
1779 Mrs Dangle. *The Critic*, act 1, sc.2.

61 Puffing is of various sorts; the principal are, the puff direct, the puff preliminary, the puff collateral, the puff collusive, and the puff oblique, or puff by implication.
1779 Mr Puff. *The Critic*, act 1, sc.2.

62 The number of those who undergo the fatigue of judging for themselves is very small indeed.
1779 Mr Puff. *The Critic*, act 1, sc.2.

63 The puff collusive is the newest of any; for it acts in the disguise of determined hostility. It is much used by bold booksellers and enterprising poets.
1779 Mr Puff. *The Critic*, act 1, sc.2.

64 No scandal about Queen Elizabeth, I hope?
1779 Mr Sneer, of Mr Puff's tragedy 'The Spanish Armada'. *The Critic*, act 2, sc.1.

65 I open with a clock striking, to beget an awful attention in the audience: it also marks the time, which is four o'clock in the morning, and saves a description of the rising sun, and a great deal about gilding the eastern hemisphere.
1779 Mr Puff, of his tragedy 'The Spanish Armada'. *The Critic*, act 2, sc.2.

66 BEEFEATER: [a character in Mr Puff's play within a play, 'The Spanish Armanda'] Perdition catch my soul but I do love thee.
SNEER: Haven't I heard that line before?
PUFF: No, I fancy not.—Where pray?
DANGLE: Yes, I think there is something like it in *Othello*.
PUFF: Gad! now you put me in mind on't, I believe there is—but that's of no consequence; all that can be said is, that two people happened to hit upon the same thought—and Shakespeare made use of it first, that's all.
1779 *The Critic*, act 3, sc.1.

67 When a heroine goes mad, she always goes into white satin.
1779 Mr Puff. *The Critic*, act 3, sc.1.

68 An oyster may be crossed in love!
1779 Tilburnia's 'mad' speech from 'The Spanish Armada'. *The Critic*, act 3, sc.1.

69 Give me the liberty of the Press, and I will give the Minister a venal House of Peers, I will give him a corrupt and servile House of Commons…armed with the liberty of the Press, I will go forth to meet him undismayed.
1810 Speech, House of Commons.

Sherman, Richard M and Robert B   1928–, 1925–

US song-writing brothers, who wrote songs for Disney films from 1959 and also complete scores for musicals. Among their best-known films are *Mary Poppins* (1964) and *Chitty Chitty Bang Bang* (1968).

70 Supercalifragilisticexpialidocious.
1964 Title of song from *Mary Poppins*.

71 Protocoligorically Correct.
1976 Title of song from *The Slipper and the Rose*.

Sherman, William Tecumseh   1820–91

US general. He was Union commander during the American Civil War, when he captured Atlanta in 1864 and divided Confederate forces by his 'march to the sea', hastening the surrender of the South.

72 There is many a boy here today who looks on war as all glory, but, boys, it is all hell.
1880 Speech at Columbus, Ohio, 11 Aug. Quoted in Lloyd Lewis Sherman *Fighting Prophet* (1932).

Sherriff, R(obert) C(edric)   1896–1975

British playwright, novelist and screenwriter. He achieved an international reputation with his first play *Journey's End* (1929). He also wrote screenplays for films such as *The Invisible Man* (1933), *Goodbye Mr Chips* (1939) and *The Odd Man Out* (1947).

73 Even the moon is frightened of me, frightened to death! The whole world is frightened to death!
1933 Line delivered by Claude Rains in *The Invisible Man* (with Philip Wylie).

Shevardnadze, Eduard Ambrosievich   1928–

Georgian-born Soviet politician. In 1978 he was inducted into the Politburo and was appointed Foreign Minister in 1985. He rapidly overhauled the Soviet foreign policy machine for a new era of détente. In 1992 he returned to Georgia, where he became Chairman of the Supreme Council and Head of State (1992–95) then President (1995–).

74 Democrats are fleeing in all directions. Reformers are going into hiding. A dictatorship is beginning, and no one knows what shape it will take or who will come to power.

1990 On the increasing disarray in the USSR caused by failing Soviet reforms, rivalry between the Gorbachev and Yeltsin factions and unrest in the Baltic states, in the *Sunday Times*, 23 Dec.

Shinwell, Emanuel Shinwell, Baron 1884–1986

English Labour politician. A 'street-corner' socialist in Glasgow, he became Secretary of State for War (1947) and Minister of Defence (1950–1). Known for his belligerence, he mellowed into a backbench 'elder statesman'. He wrote several autobiographical works.

75 We know that you, the organized workers of the country, are our friends… As for the rest, they do not matter a tinker's curse.

1947 Trade union conference, 7 May.

Shipton, Eric Earle 1908–77

British mountaineer, explorer and writer. The foremost mountain explorer of his generation, he facilitated the successful ascent of Everest in 1953. He wrote seven books, including an autobiography, *That Untravelled World* (1969).

76 I have never been able to decide whether, in mountain exploration, it is the prospect of tackling an unsolved problem, or the performance of the task itself, or the retrospective enjoyment of successful effort, which affords the greatest amount of pleasure.

1936 *Nanda Devi.*

77 Whatever may have been my enthusiasm or impatience to be up and doing on the night before, the hour for getting up always finds me with no other ambition in the world than to be permitted to lie where I am and sleep, sleep, sleep. Not so Tilman. I have never met anyone with such a complete disregard for the sublime comforts of the early morning bed. However monstrously early we might decide, the night before, to get up, he was about at least half an hour before the time. He was generally very good about it, and used to sit placidly smoking his pipe over the fire.

1936 On climbing with H W (Bill) Tilman. *Nanda Devi.*

78 We were now actually in the inner sanctuary of the Nanda Devi Basin, and at each step I experienced that subtle thrill which anyone of imagination must feel when treading hitherto unexplored country… My most blissful dream as a child was to be in some such valley, free to wander where I liked, and discover for myself some hitherto unrevealed glory of Nature. Now the reality was no less wonderful than that half-forgotten dream; and of how many childish fancies can that be said, in this age of disillusionment ?

1936 *Nanda Devi.*

Shirley, James 1596–1666

English dramatist. Educated at Oxford and Cambridge, he took holy orders but renounced them upon conversion to Catholicism. He died in the Great Fire of London. He wrote plays and masques, including the comedies *Hyde Park* (1634) and *The Lady of Pleasure* (1635), the tragedy *The Cardinal* (1641), and the masque *The Contention of Ajax and Ulysses* (1659).

79 How little room
Do we take up in death, that, living know
No bounds?

1626 *The Wedding*, act 4, sc.4.

80 'Tis no shame for men
Of his high birth to love a wench; his honour
May privilege more sins. Next to a woman,
He loves a running-horse.

1634 *Hyde Park*, act 1, sc.1.

81 RIDER: …we can be but
What we are.
VENTURE: A pair of credulous fools.

1634 *Hyde Park*, act 1, sc.1.

82 I presume you're mortal, and may err.

1635 *The Lady of Pleasure*, act 2, sc.2.

83 The glories of our blood and state
Are shadows, not substantial things;
There is no armour against fate;
Death lays his icy hand on kings:
Scepter and crown
Must tumble down,
And in the dust be equal made
With the poor crooked scythe and spade.

1659 *The Contention of Ajax and Ulysses*, act 1, sc.3.

Shultz, George P(ratt) 1920–

US Former Secretary of State. A Professor of Chicago University's graduate business school (1957–68), he was US Secretary of Labor (1969–70), then assistant to President Nixon (1972–4). He was Secretary of State to President Reagan (1982–89). A fellow of the Hoover Institution, Stanford University (1989–) he is a distinguished author and was awarded the Seoul Peace Prize (1992).

84 He made a combative apology.

1987 On the ability of Elliott Abrams, Assistant Secretary for Inter-American Affairs, to acknowledge a sensitive question without giving a definite reply. In the *New York Times*, 25 Jul.

85 Gardening…is one of the most underrated aspects of diplomacy.

1993 On the need to meet people 'on their own turf'. *Turmoil and Triumph.*

86 Washington is a resigning town. Nothing else holds the special excitement of a rumored resignation.

1993 *Turmoil and Triumph.*

87 The way to keep weeds from overwhelming you is to deal with them constantly and in their early stages.

1993 *Turmoil and Triumph.*

88 The Soviet game is chess…ours is poker. We will have to play a creative mixture of both games.

1993 Comment to President Reagan. Recalled in *Turmoil and Triumph.*

89 Better to use force when you *should* rather than when you *must*.

1993 On Soviet alarm at the prospect of US science 'turned on' and venturing into the realm of space defence. *Turmoil and Triumph.*

90 Agreement reached by the negotiators…usually starts to collapse in the hands of those who implement it, no matter how carefully cleared at the top.

1993 On negotiating the release of Russian political prisoners. *Turmoil and Triumph.*

91 The decision makers face each other. No safety screen stands between the issues and the highest authorities.
1993 Of summit meetings, particularly that between the US and the Soviets at Reykjavik, Iceland, 9–12 Oct 1986. *Turmoil and Triumph.*

92 A 'staffocracy' has been created.
1993 On the National Security Council. *Turmoil and Triumph.*

93 You can't figure him out like a fact, because to Reagan the main fact was a vision… He came from the heartland of the country, where people could be down-to-earth yet feel that the sky is the limit—not ashamed of, or cynical about, the American dream.
1993 Of Ronald Reagan. *Turmoil and Triumph.*

Shute, Nevil *originally* **Nevil Shute Norway** 1899–1960

English writer. An aeronautical engineer, he began to write novels in 1926 and after World War II emigrated to Australia, the setting for most of his later books, notably *A Town Like Alice* (1949) and *On the Beach* (1957).

94 A Town Like Alice
1949 Title of book.

Sidgwick, Henry 1838–1900

British economist, Professor at Cambridge.

95 We cannot not say how much wealth there is in a country till we know how it is shared among its inhabitants.
1883 *Principles of Political Economy.*

Sidmouth, Henry Addington, 1st Viscount 1757–1844

English statesman and Tory Prime Minister (1801–4) after the resignation of William Pitt the Younger. As Home Secretary (1812–21) he had to deal with the Luddite riots and the 'Peterloo Massacre' in Manchester (1819).

96 I hate liberality. Nine times out of ten it is cowardice—and the tenth time, lack of principle.
Attributed.

Sidney, Algernon 1622–83

English Whig politician. He fought for the Parliamentary army in the English Civil War and in 1645 entered Parliament, but he resented Cromwell's assumption of power, and retired to Penshurst (1653–9). In exile after the Restoration, in 1677 he was pardoned and returned, but was implicated in the Rye House Plot (1683) and beheaded.

97 Liars ought to have good memories.
Discourses Concerning Government (published 1689).

Sidney, Sir Philip 1554–86

English poet and patron. Educated at Oxford, he travelled widely; in 1585 he was made Governor of Flushing. He died after being wounded in the battle of Zutphen. His sonnet sequence *Astrophel and Stella* (published 1591) was an early example of the genre in English, as was his prose romance *The Arcadia* (*The Old Arcadia*, as it is called, was not published during Sidney's lifetime; a revised version, *The New Arcadia*, was first published in 1590); his *Defence of Poetry* (published 1595) was the first English essay on literary criticism.

98 I readily admit that I am often more serious than I should be at my age or in my present circumstances, yet I know from experience that I am never less given to melancholy than when I am keenly applying the feeble powers of my mind to some arduous and difficult matter.
1574 Letter to Hubert Languet, 4 Feb.

99 O wretched state of man in self-division!
1581 *The Old Arcadia,* 'First Eclogues'.

1 She was stricken with most obstinate love to a young man.
1581 *The Old Arcadia,* 'First Eclogues'.

2 What allurements she used indifferently were long to tell.
1581 *The Old Arcadia,* 'Second Eclogues'.

3 What be the fruits of speaking art? What grows by the words?
1581 *The Old Arcadia,* 'Second Eclogues'.

4 My true love hath my heart and I have his,
By just exchange one for the other giv'n;
I hold his dear, and mine he cannot miss,
There never was a better bargain driv'n.
1581 *The Old Arcadia,* 'Third Eclogues'.

5 O sweet, on a wretch wilt thou be revenged?
Shall such high planets tend to the loss of a worm?
1581 *The Old Arcadia,* 'Fourth Eclogues'.

6 A lamentable tune is the sweetest music to a woeful mind.
1590 *Arcadia,* pt.2.

7 Loving in truth, and vain in verse my love to show,
That she (dear she) might take some pleasure of my pain,
Pleasure might cause her read, reading might make her know;
Knowledge might pity win, and pity grace obtain.
1591 *Astrophel and Stella,* sonnet 1.

8 But words came halting forth, wanting Invention's stay;
Invention, Nature's child, fled step-dame Study's blows…
Biting my truant pen, beating myself for spite,
'Fool,' said my muse to me; 'look in thy heart, and write.'
1591 *Astrophel and Stella,* sonnet 1.

9 Your rhubarb words.
1591 *Astrophel and Stella,* sonnet 14.

10 Come sleep, O sleep, the certain knot of peace,
The baiting place of wit, the balm of woe,
The poor man's wealth, the prisoner's release,
The indifferent judge between the high and low.
1591 *Astrophel and Stella,* sonnet 39.

11 That sweet enemy, France.
1591 *Astrophel and Stella,* sonnet 41.

12 Hope, art thou true, or dost thou flatter me?
1591 *Astrophel and Stella,* sonnet 67.

13 Oh heav'nly fool, thy most kiss-worthy face
Anger invests with such a lovely grace
That Anger's self I needs must kiss again.
1591 *Astrophel and Stella,* sonnet 73.

14 I am no pick-purse of another's wit.
1591 *Astrophel and Stella,* sonnet 74.

15 Stella, think not that I by verse seek fame;
Who seek, who hope, who love, who live, but thee:
Thine eyes my pride, thy lips my history;
If thou praise not, all other praise is shame.
1591 *Astrophel and Stella,* sonnet 90.

16 I have just cause to make a pitiful defence of poor poetry, which from almost the highest estimation of learning is

fallen to be the laughing stock of children.
1595 *The Defence of Poetry.*

17 And truly, even Plato, whosoever well considereth shall find that in the body of his work, though the inside and strength were philosophy, the skin as it were and beauty depended most on poetry.
1595 *The Defence of Poetry.*

18 [Nature's] world is brazen, the poets only deliver a golden.
1595 *The Defence of Poetry.*

19 Poetry therefore, is an art of imitation… A speaking picture, with this end: to teach and delight.
1595 *The Defence of Poetry.*

20 With a tale forsooth he cometh unto you, with a tale which holdeth children from play, and old men from the chimney corner.
1595 Of the poet. *The Defence of Poetry.*

21 Comedy is an imitation of the common errors of our life, which he representeth in the most ridiculous and scornful sort that may be, so as it is impossible that any beholder can be content to be such a one.
1595 *The Defence of Poetry.*

22 I…am admitted into the company of paper-blurrers.
1595 *The Defence of Poetry.*

23 [This] much curse I must send you, in the behalf of all poets, that while you live, you live in love, and never get favour for lacking skill of a sonnet, and, when you die, your memory die from the earth for want of an epigraph.
1595 *The Defence of Poetry.*

Siegel, Jerome 1914–92

US writer, co-creator of Superman.

24 I'm lying in bed counting sheep when all of a sudden it hits me…a character like Samson, Hercules and all the strong men I heard tell of rolled into one. Only more so.
Recalling the inspiration behind Superman, created 1938. Quoted in *Time*, 14 Mar 1988.

25 Faster than a speeding bullet! More powerful than a locomotive! Able to leap tall buildings in a single bound!
Introduction for the Superman radio serial. Quoted in *Time*, 14 Mar 1988.

Sièyes, Emmanuel Joseph, Comte also called *Abbé Sièyes* 1748–1836

French cleric and political theorist. His pamphlet, *Qu'est-ce que le tiers-état?* ('What is the Third Estate?', 1789) was very popular with the bourgeoisie. He helped organize the revolution of 18th Brumaire (in which Napoleon overthrew the Directory, 1799). Exiled at the Restoration (1815), he returned after the July Revolution (1830).

26 Who will dare deny that the Third Estate contains within itself all that is needed to constitute a nation?… What would the Third Estate be without the privileged classes? It would be a whole in itself, and a prosperous one. Nothing can be done without it, and everything would be done far better without the others.
1789 *Qu'est-ce que le tiers-état?*

Sigismund 1368–1437

Holy Roman Emperor from 1433. He became King of Hungary in 1387 and as Emperor presided over the Council of Constance, which ended the Great Schism (1414–18).

27 Only do always in health what you have often promised to do when you are sick.
His advice for a happy life, quoted in Clifton Fadiman *Faber Book of Anecdotes* (1985).

Sigourney, Lydia Howard née *Huntley* 1791–1865

American poet. Her pious, sentimental poetry made her the most popular woman poet of her generation. She was an important campaigner in the cause of higher education for women. Her collections include *Moral Pieces in Prose and Verse* (1815)

28 Ye say, they all have passed away,
That noble race and brave,
That their light canoes have vanished
From off the crested wave;
That 'mid the forests where they roamed
There rings no hunter's shout;
But their name is on your waters,
Ye may not wash it out.
1848 *Select Poems*, 'Indian Names'.

Sihanouk, Prince Norodom 1922–

Cambodian politician who as Prime Minister tried but failed to keep his country out of the Vietnam War. He was deposed in 1970 by a military coup but returned in 1993 and was elected king. He attacked the intensive US bombing of his country.

29 What is the difference between burning and gassing people in ovens and doing it to a whole nation out in the open?
1973 Of the US bombing of Cambodia. *My War with the CIA* (with W Burchett).

30 The humble people of Cambodia are the most wonderful in the world. Their great misfortune is that they always have terrible leaders who make them suffer. I am not sure I was much better myself, but perhaps I was the least bad.
1978 In an interview with William Shawcross, author of *Sideshow* (1979).

Sikorski, Gerry 1948–

US politician.

31 Like a toothless terrier on Valium.
1987 On the workings of the Office of Government Ethics. In the *New York Times*, 8 Jul.

Sikorsky, Igor Ivan 1889–1972

Russian-born US aeronautical engineer. He built and flew the first four-engined aeroplane (1913), then founded the Sikorsky Aero Engineering Corporation in the USA (1923). He built several flying boats, and in 1939 produced the first successful helicopter.

32 The work of the individual still remains the spark that moves mankind ahead, even more than teamwork.
Quoted in his *New York Times* obituary, 27 Oct 1972.

Sillitoe, Alan 1928–

English novelist. Several of his novels set in the north of England have been adapted as successful films, notably *Saturday Night and Sunday Morning* (1960).

33 The Loneliness of the Long Distance Runner.
1962 Title of book.

Silva, José Asunción 1865–96

Colombian poet whose life was marked by financial reverses, the death of loved ones, and the loss of his manuscripts in a shipwreck. His poetry is characteristically melancholy, and after only ten years of writing he committed suicide.

34 *Y si evitas la sífilis, siguiendo*
la sabia profilaxia,
al llegar los cuarenta irás sintiendo
un principio de ataxia.
And if you manage to avoid syphilis
by following a wise course of prophylaxis,
when you turn forty you will feel
the beginnings of ataxia.
1908 *Gotas amargas*, 'Filosofías' ('Philosophies').

Silvers, Phil *originally* **Philip Silver** 1912–85

US comic actor. His success in films and on Broadway led to the *Phil Silvers Show* (1955–9) on television, where he introduced the character of Sergeant Bilko. He won three Emmy awards during his career, and a Tony Award for his performance in *A Funny Thing Happened on the Way to the Forum* (1972).

35 Be funny on a golf course? Do I kid my best friend's mother about her heart condition?
Quoted in Michael Hobbs *The Golf Quotation Book* (1992).

Simon, Caroline K(lein) d.1993

Judge, NY State Court of Claims.

36 Look like a girl, act like a lady, think like a man and work like a dog.
Comment the year after her candidacy for Postmaster General was barred by federal officials who claimed the job was unsuited to a woman. Recalled on her death, in the *New York Times*, 30 Jul 1993.

Simon, Herbert A 1916–2001

US psychologist and economist; awarded a Nobel prize in economics (1978).

37 It is a fatal defect of current principles of administration that, like proverbs, they occur in pairs. For almost every principle one can find an equally plausible and acceptable contradictory principle. Although the two principles of the pair will lead to exactly opposite recommendations, there is nothing in the theory to indicate which is the appropriate one to apply.
1945 *Administrative Behavior.*

Simon (of Stackpole Elidor), John Allsebrook Simon, 1st Viscount 1873–1954

English Liberal politician and lawyer. Attorney-General (1913–15) and Home Secretary (1915–16), he resigned from the Cabinet over conscription. Deserting the Liberals to form the Liberal National Party, he supported Ramsay MacDonald's coalition governments and became Foreign Secretary (1931–5), Home Secretary (1935–7), Chancellor of the Exchequer (1937–40) and Lord Chancellor (1940–5).

38 If Joan of Arc had been born in Austria and worn a moustache, she might have conveyed much the same impression.
1935 Letter to George V, referring to his first meeting with Adolf Hitler, 27 Mar.

Simon, (Marvin) Neil 1927–

US playwright. His plays and musicals include *Barefoot in the Park* (1963), *The Odd Couple* (1965) and the semi-autobiographical trilogy *Brighton Beach Memoirs* (1983), *Biloxi Blues* (1984) and *Broadway Bound* (1986). More recent works include *Lost in Yonkers* (1991), which won him a Pulitzer Prize and a Tony Award, and *London Suite* (1995).

39 I've already had medical attention—a dog licked me when I was on the ground.
1982 *Only When I Laugh.*

40 I would have been disappointed if I hung up my pen without ever getting one…[and] now I hope to get one every 30 years like clockwork.
1991 On receiving the Pulitzer Prize for *Lost in Yonkers*. In the *Washington Post*, 10 Apr.

Simone, Nina *pseudonym of* **Eunice Waymon** 1933–2003

US singer and pianist. She was a gifted classical pianist as a teenager, but her career was blocked by the racial prejudice of the time, and she went on to become a cult figure in jazz, gospel and soul music.

41 It wasn't a matter of becoming interested in music; music is a gift and a burden I've had since I can remember who I was. I was born into music. The decision was how to make the best use of it.
Quoted in Art Taylor *Notes and Tones* (1977), 'Nina Simone'.

Simonides of Ceos c.556–468 BC

Greek lyric poet. His poetry survives only in fragments, but he is known to have written epitaphs for Greeks who fell in the Persian Wars, and in 489 BC he beat Aeschylus in a competition for the best elegy on those who fell at Marathon.

42 Go, stranger, and tell the Spartans that here we lie, obedient to their commands.
c.480 BC Epitaph for the Spartan army dead after the Battle of Thermopylae. Quoted in Herodotus *Histories*, bk.7, ch.228.

43 Man's strength is but little, and futile his concerns.
Lyrica Graeca Selecta, (ed. D L Page), no.354.

Simons, Henry C 1899–1946

US economist, Professor at the University of Chicago.

44 Monopoly power must be abused. It has no use save abuse.
1944 *Economic Policy for a Free Society*, p.129.

Simple, Peter *pseudonym of* **Michael Wharton** 1913–

45 Rentacrowd Ltd—the enterprising firm that supplies crowds for all occasions, and has done so much to keep progressive causes in the public eye.
1962 In the *Daily Telegraph*.

Simpson, Alan (Kooi) 1931–

US Senator and lawyer. He was a member of Wyoming's House of Representatives (1964–77) and acted as a majority whip (1973–5) and floor leader (1975–7). He became a member of the US Senate for Wyoming in 1978.

46 Like giving dry birth to a porcupine.
1989 On the passage of immigration reform bill. In the *Washingtonian*, Mar.

47 I come from a state where gun control is just how

steady you hold your weapon.
1991 In *Fortune*, 30 Dec.

Simpson, Kirke L 1881–1972

US journalist. He was awarded a Pulitzer Prize in 1921 for his article on the Unknown Soldier.

48 Chosen by a group of men in a smoke-filled room.
Of Warren G Harding, presidential candidate. Recalled on Simpson's death in the *New York Times*, 17 Jun 1972. The 'smoke-filled room' became a common phrase in presidential nomination.

Simpson, O J (Orenthal James) 1947–

US former professional football player, actor and sports commentator. He joined the Buffalo Bills professionally in 1969, and retired in 1979 to become an actor and broadcaster. He was charged with the murders of his estranged wife Nicole and Ronald Goodman, but was acquitted in 1995.

49 Absolutely 100 per cent not guilty.
1994 Plea on arraignment for the murder of his estranged wife. Reported in the *New York Times*, 23 Jul. Simpson was later found not guilty.

Simpson, Tom 1938–67

English cyclist. In 1962 he became the first Briton ever to wear the leader's yellow jersey in the Tour de France. He died from heart failure during the Tour de France.

50 Put me back on my bike.
1967 Last words.

Sinatra, Frank (Francis Albert) 1915–98

US singer and actor. He began with the Tommy Dorsey orchestra (1940–2), and starred on radio and in films (eg *Anchors Aweigh*, 1945). His recordings (1956–65) include *Songs For Swinging Lovers*, *Come Fly With Me*, and *That's Life*. His highly publicized and controversial personal life included four marriages (amongst them, to Ava Gardner and Mia Farrow).

51 My greatest teacher was not a vocal coach, not the work of other singers, but the way Tommy Dorsey breathed and phrased on the trombone.
Foreword to George T Simon *The Big Bands* (1967).

Singer, Isaac Bashevis 1904–91

US Yiddish writer of novels and short stories. Awarded the Nobel prize for literature (1978).

52 Children…have no use for psychology.
1978 Speech on receiving his Nobel prize.

Singh, Vijay 1963–

Fijian golfer whose wins include the US Masters in 2000 and US Open in 2004.

53 Golf is to Fiji what cricket is to America.
2000 In *The Independent*, 23 Dec.

Sisco, Joseph John 1919–

US diplomat and businessman. He set up his own management consultancy, and also acted as a consultant and adviser to the UN.

54 Welcome to shuttle diplomacy!
1995 Comment to reporters Marvin Kalb and Ted Koppel on Henry A Kissinger's first trip to the Middle East after the Yom Kippur War. Reported in the *New York Times*, 29 Oct.

Sisson, C(harles) H(erbert) 1914–2003

English poet and critic. One of the leading poets of the period, he also wrote novels and an autobiography.

55 Here lies a civil servant. He was civil
To everyone, and servant to the devil.
1961 'Civil Servant'.

Sitting Bull *real name Tatanka Iyotake* 1834–90

Chief of the Dakota Sioux, who led the defeat of Custer at Little Big Horn, 1876. He later featured in Buffalo Bill Cody's Wild West Show, 1885, but was killed evading arrest during the 'ghost dance' uprising of 1890.

56 When I was a boy the Sioux owned the world; the sun rose and set on their land; they sent ten thousand men to battle. Where are the warriors today? Who slew them? Where are our lands? Who owns them?… What law have I broken? Is it wrong for me to love my own? Is it wicked for me because my skin is red? Because I am a Sioux; because I was born where my father lived; because I would die for my country?
c.1866 Quoted in T C McLuhan *Touch the Earth* (1973).

Sitwell, Dame Edith Louisa 1887–1964

English poet and essayist, sister of Osbert and Sacheverell Sitwell. Her poems were designed to shock her audiences and revitalize English poetry. Her numerous prose works reflect her interest in English history. Her books include *Façade* (1923, set to music by Walton), *English Eccentrics* (1933), and *Fanfare of Elizabeth* (1946).

57 Lady Venus on the settee of the horsehair sea!
1923 *Façade*, 'Hornpipe'.

58 This minx, of course,
Is as sharp as any lynx and blacker—deeper than the drinks and quite as
Hot as any hottentot, without remorse!
1923 *Façade*, 'Hornpipe'.

59 An admiral red, whose only notion,
(A butterfly poised on a pigtailed ocean)
Is of the peruked sea whose swell
Breaks on the flowerless rocks of Hell.
1923 *Façade*, 'En Famille'.

60 The Admiral said, 'You could never call—
I assure you it would not do at all!
She gets down from the table without saying 'please',
Forgets her prayers and to cross her T's,
In short, her scandalous reputation
Has shocked the whole of the Hellish nation'.
1923 *Façade*, 'En Famille'.

61 Those trains will run over their tails, if they can,
Snorting and sporting like porpoises. Flee
The burly, the whirligig wheels of the train,
As round as the world and as large again.
1923 *Façade*, 'Mariner Man'.

62 The light is braying like an ass.
1923 *Façade*, 'Long Steel Grass'.

63 Through gilded trellises
Of the heat, spangles
Pelt down through the tangles
Of bell-flowers.

1923 *Façade*, 'Through Gilded Trellises'.

64 But a word stung him like a mosquito…
For what they hear, they repeat!
1923 *Façade*, 'Tango-Pasodoble'.

65 In a room of the palace
Black Mrs Behemoth
Gave way to wrath
And the wildest malice.
1923 *Façade*, 'Black Mrs Behemoth'.

66 Where the satyrs are chattering, nymphs with their
flattering
Glimpse of the forest enhance
All the beauty of marrow and cucumber narrow
And Ceres will join in the dance.
1923 *Façade*, 'Tarantella'.

67 That hobnailed goblin, the bob-tailed Hob,
said, 'It is time I began to rob'.
1923 *Façade*, 'Country Dance'.

68 And shade is on the brightest wing,
And dust forbids the birds to sing.
1923 *Façade*, 'Popular Song'.

69 Came the great Popinjay
Smelling his nosegay:
In cage like grots
The birds sing gavottes.
1923 *Façade*, 'Came the Great Popinjay'.

70 Jane, Jane,
Tall as a crane,
The morning light creaks down again.
1923 *Façade*, 'Aubade'.

71 The fire was furry as a bear.
1923 *Façade*, 'Dark Song'.

72 Daisy and Lily,
Lazy and silly,
Walk by the shore of the wan grass sea,—
Talking once more 'neath a swan-bosomed tree.
1923 *Façade* 'Valse'.

73 Still falls the Rain—
Dark as the world of man, black as our loss—
Blind as the nineteen hundred and forty nails
Upon the cross.
1942 'The Raids, 1940. Night and Dawn'.

74 The Englishwoman's clothes, too, have improved out of
all knowledge…no longer are our hats, as in Victorian
days, a kind of Pageant of Empire, whereon the products
of all the colonies battle for precedence.
1942 *English Women*.

75 I have often wished I had time to cultivate modesty… But
I am too busy thinking about myself.
1950 In the *Observer*, 30 Apr.

76 I enjoyed talking to her, but thought *nothing* of her
writing. I considered her 'a beautiful little knitter'.
1955 Of Virginia Woolf. Letter to Geoffrey Singleton, 11 Jul.

77 Mr Lewis's pictures appeared, as a very great painter said
to me, to have been painted by a mailed fist in a cotton
glove.
1965 On Wyndham Lewis. *Taken Care Of*, ch.11.

78 I wish the Government would put a tax on pianos for the
incompetent.
Collected in *Letters, 1916–1964* (1970).

Sitwell, Sir (Francis) Osbert 1892–1969

English writer. He was the brother of Edith and Sacheverell
Sitwell, and a friend of Eliot, Pound and Wyndham Lewis,
whose radical aesthetic he shared.

79 The British Bourgeosie
Is not born
And does not die,
But, if it is ill,
It has a frightened look in its eyes.
1921 *At the House of Mrs Kinfoot*.

80 But what is Dust,
Save Time's most lethal weapon,
Her faithful ally and our sneaking foe?
1927 'Mrs Southern's Enemy'.

81 *Educated: during the holidays from Eton.*
1929 From his entry in *Who's Who*.

82 Now the nimble fingers are no more nimble,
And the silver thimble lies cold and tarnished black.
1931 'Mrs Mew's Windowbox'.

83 But he was never, well,
What I call
A Sportsman:
For forty days
He went out into the desert
—And never shot anything.
1931 Of Jesus Christ. 'Old Fashioned Sportsmen'.

84 The artist, like the idiot or clown, sits on the edge of the
world, and a push may send him over it.
1946 *The Scarlet Tree*, bk.4, ch.2.

85 A word is the carving and colouring of a thought, and
gives it permanence.
1949 *Laughter in the Next Room*, ch.7.

86 In reality, killing time
Is only the name for another of the multifarious ways
By which Time kills us.
1958 'Milordo Inglese'.

87 Hunting the author, painter and musician is a traditional
and popular sport. In this country poet-baiting at an
early stage assumed the place of bull-baiting.
1963 'What It Feels Like to be an Author'.

Sixtus V *originally Felice Peretti* 1521–90

Franciscan preacher and a professor of theology, created
cardinal in 1570. Elected Pope in 1585, because of his
presumed feebleness, he implemented vigorous moral, legal
and financial reforms.

88 Just see how well she governs! She is only a woman, only
the mistress of half an island, and yet she makes herself
feared by Spain, by France, by the Empire, by all!
1588 Of Elizabeth I. Quoted in L von Pastor *The History of the
Popes* (edited by Kerr R F, 1932), vol.22, p.34.

Skelton, John c.1460–1529

English poet. Educated at Oxford and Cambridge, he was tutor
to Prince Henry (later Henry VIII). He began his poetic career
with translations and elegies, but turned to writing satirical
vernacular poetry, including *Colin Clout* (1521) and *Why Come
Ye Not to Court?* (1521), both of which were attacks on Cardinal
Wolsey.

89 The sovereign'st thing that any man may have

Is little to say, and much to hear and see.
1499 *The Bouge of Court*, l. 211.

90 With Mannerly Margery milk and ale.
1523 'Mannerly Margery Milk and Ale'.

91 Far may be sought
Erst that ye can find
So courteous, so kind,
As Merry Margaret,
This midsummer flower,
Gentle as falcon
Or hawk of the tower.
1523 *The Garland of Laurel*, 'To Mistress Margaret Hussey'.

92 With lullay, lullay, like a child,
Thou sleepest too long, thou art beguiled.
1527 'Lullay, Lullay, Like a Child'.

93 What dreamest thou, drunkard, drowsy pate?
Thy lust and liking is from thee gone.
Thou blinkard blowboll, thou wakest too late.
1527 'Lullay, Lullay, Like a Child'.

Skelton, (Archibald) Noel 1880–1935

Scottish-born politician and lawyer. He was MP for Perth (1922–3 and 1924–31) and Parliamentary Under-Secretary in the Scottish Office (1931–5).

94 To state as clearly as may be what means lie ready to develop a property-owning democracy, to bring the industrial and economic status of the wage-earner abreast of his political and educational status, to make democracy stable and four-square.
1923 In *The Spectator*, 19 May.

Skelton, Red (Richard) 1913–97

US comedian. A star of radio and television, he also made a few films in the 1940s, among them *Whistling in the Dark* (1941) and *DuBarry Was a Lady* (1943).

95 Exercise? I get it on the golf course. When I see my friends collapse, I run for the paramedics.
Attributed.

Skelton, Robin 1925–97

English-born Canadian poet and aphorist.

96 When someone says, 'It is good business', you may be sure it is bad morality.
1991 *A Devious Dictionary*.

97 Some part of us still believes that men should kill.
1991 *A Devious Dictionary*.

98 Death is the only mystery we all solve.
1991 *A Devious Dictionary*.

99 Never believe what you cannot doubt.
1991 *A Devious Dictionary*.

1 Headlines pass; breadlines continue.
1991 *A Devious Dictionary*.

2 Anything said off the cuff has usually been written on it first.
1991 *A Devious Dictionary*.

3 It requires less skill to love than to be loved.
1991 *A Devious Dictionary*.

4 When one hears of progress one should ask for whom.
1991 *A Devious Dictionary*.

5 Procrustes was an editor.
1991 *A Devious Dictionary*.

6 Kneel to nobody; bow to everyone.
1991 *A Devious Dictionary*.

7 Those who have the habit of revelation lose the habit of thought.
1991 *A Devious Dictionary*.

8 More dreams are destroyed in bed than are ever found there.
1991 *A Devious Dictionary*.

Skinner, B(urrhus) F(rederic) 1904–90

US psychologist and social philosopher, developer and exponent of behaviourism, which views human behaviour and learning as physiological responses. His works include *Walden Two* (1961) and *The Technology of Teaching* (1968).

9 Education is what survives when what has been learnt has been forgotten.
1964 In *New Scientist*, 21 May.

10 The real problem is not whether machines think but whether men do.
1969 *Contingencies of Reinforcement*, ch.9.

Skinner, Cornelia Otis 1902–79

US actress, singer and writer.

11 It's as though some poor devil were to set out for a large dinner party with the knowledge that the following morning he would be hearing exactly what each of the other guests thought of him.
1959 Of opening night reviews. *The Ape In Me*.

12 There are compensations for growing older. One is the realization that to be sporting isn't at all necessary. It is a great relief to reach this stage of wisdom.
Attributed.

Skinner, John 1721–1807

Jacobite songwriter and Episcopalian minister in Aberdeenshire, whose 'Tullochgorum' was described by Robert Burns as 'the best Scotch song ever Scotland saw'.

13 Come, gie's a sang, Montgomery cry'd,
And lay your disputes a'aside;
What signifies't for folks to chide
For what's been done before them?
Let Whig and Tory a'agree,
Whig and Tory, Whig and Tory,
Whig and Tory a'agree
To drop their whigmigmorum;
Let Whig and Tory a'agree
To spend this night wi' mirth and glee,
And cheerfu' sing, alang wi' me,
The Reel o' Tullochgorum.
'Tullochgorum', stanza 1.

Skirving, Adam 1719–1803

Scottish composer of Jacobite songs.

14 Hey, Johnnie Cope, are ye wauking yet?
Or are your drums a-beating yet?
If ye were wauking I wad wait
To gang to the coals i' the morning.
1745 'Johnnie Cope', chorus (commemorating the Battle of

Prestonpans and General Cope's flight to Newcastle).

Slessor, Kenneth Adolf 1901–71

Australian poet and journalist. In 1924 he published *Thief of the Moon* and in 1926 *Earth-Visitors*. *Darlinghurst Nights and Morning Glories* (1933) celebrates 'The Cross', the bohemian district of Sydney where he lived for most of his life. His verse was collected in *One Hundred Poems: 1919–1939* (1944, reissued as *Poems*, 1957), and his prose in *Bread and Wine* (1970).

15 Time that is moved by little fidget wheels
Is not my Time, the flood that does not flow.
Between the double and the single bell
Of a ship's hour, between a round of bells
From the dark warship riding there below,
I have lived many lives, and this one life
Of Joe, long dead, who lives between five bells.
1939 *Five Bells*, title poem. The poem was written as an elegy for Joe Lynch, a friend who fell overboard from a Sydney ferry.

Slezak, Leo 1873–1946

Czech tenor. Tall and commanding, he was internationally famous as an interpreter of the heroes of Wagnerian opera.

16 *Wann geht der nächste Schwan?*
What time's the next swan?
1900 When the swan-boat failed to arrive to take him off in Wagner's *Lohengrin*. Quoted in Hugh Vickers *Great Operatic Disasters* (1979).

Sloan, John French 1871–1951

US painter of the Ashcan school, painting everyday subjects, particularly street life in New York City. His works include *Sunday, Women Drying Their Hair* (1912) and *Backyards, Greenwich Village* (1914).

17 Facility is a dangerous thing. Where there is too much technical ease the brain stops criticising. Don't let the hand fall into a smart way of putting the mind to sleep.
1939 *Gist of Art*.

18 Artists are the only people in the world who really live. The others have to hope for heaven.
Recalled on his death, 7 Sep 1951, and quoted in the *Smithsonian*, Apr 1988.

Slovo, Gillian 1952–

South African writer.

19 In most families it is the children who leave home. In mine it was the parents.
1997 Both her parents, Joe Slovo and Ruth First, were anti-apartheid activists. In *Every Secret Thing*.

Small, Albion W 1854–1926

US sociologist; first head of the first department of sociology in the US, at the University of Chicago.

20 Sociology was born of the modern ardor to improve society.
1894 *An Introduction to the Study of Society* (with George E Vincent, 1894).

21 The social problem of the twentieth century is whether civilized nations can restore themselves to sanity after their nineteenth-century aberrations of individualism and capitalism.

1914 'A Vision of Social Efficiency', in the *American Journal of Sociology*, Jan.

Smart, Christopher 1722–71

English poet. He made a precarious living as a writer, helped by Dr Johnson and others, but suffered from bouts of insanity. His poetry includes *The Hilliad* (1753, a satire on doctors modelled on *The Dunciad*) and the structurally complex *A Song To David* (1763). During one of his confinements in a private madhouse he wrote the extraordinary and highly allusive *Jubilate Agno* (1758–63, first published as *Rejoice in the Lamb* 1939, edited by W F Stead).

22 Night, with all her negro train,
Took possession of the plain;
In an hearse she rode reclined,
Drawn by screech-owls slow and blind:
Close to her, with printless feet,
Crept Stillness, in a winding sheet.
1748 'A Night-Piece; or, Modern Philosophy', stanza 2. In the *London Magazine*, no.14, Dec. Collected in *Poems on Several Occasions* (1752).

23 Let Eli rejoice with Leucon—he is an honest fellow, which is a rarity.
For I have seen the White Raven and Thomas Hall of Willingham and am myself a greater curiosity than both.
Let Jemuel rejoice with Charadrius, who is from the HEIGHT and the sight of him is good for the jaundice.
For I look up to heaven which is my prospect to escape envy by surmounting it.
1758–63 *Jubilate Agno*, fragment B, stanzas 25–6 (first published 1939). Both the white raven and Thomas Hall, a giant of four feet at the age of three, were curiosities exhibited in the 1740s.

24 For every word has its marrow in the English tongue for order and for delight.
For the dissyllables such as able table &c are the fiddle rhymes.
For all dissyllables and some trissyllables are fiddle rhymes.
For the relations of words are in pairs first.
For the relations of words are sometimes in oppositions.
For the relations of words are according to their distances from the pair.
1758–63 *Jubilate Agno*, fragment B, l.595–600. (First published 1939.)

25 For I will consider my cat Jeoffry.
For he is the servant of the Living God duly and daily serving him.
For at the first glance of the glory of God in the East he worships in his way.
1758–63 Of his cat Jeoffry. *Jubilate Agno*, fragment B, l.695–7. (First published 1939.)

26 For he counteracts the powers of darkness by his electrical skin and glaring eyes.
For he counteracts the Devil, who is death, by brisking about the life.
For in his morning orisons he loves the sun and the sun loves him.
For he is of the tribe of Tiger.
1758–63 Of his cat Jeoffry. *Jubilate Agno*, fragment B, l.719–22. (First published 1939.)

27 For ADORATION seasons change,
And order, truth, and beauty range,
Adjust, attract, and fill:

The grass the polyanthus cheques;
And polished porphyry reflects,
By the descending rill.
1763 *A Song to David*, stanza 52.

28 Strong is the lion—like a coal
His eye-ball—like a bastion's mole
His chest against the foes:
Strong, the gier-eagle on his sail,
Strong against tide, th'enormous whale
Emerges as he goes.
1763 *A Song to David*, stanza 76.

29 Beauteous the fleet before the gale;
Beauteous the multitudes in mail,
Rank'd arms and crested heads:
Beauteous the garden's umbrage mild,
Walk, water, meditated wild,
And all the bloomy beds.
1763 *A Song to David*, stanza 78.

30 Glorious the northern lights astream;
Glorious the song, when God's the theme;
Glorious the thunder's roar:
Glorious hosanna from the den;
Glorious the catholic amen;
Glorious the martyr's gore.
1763 *A Song to David*, stanza 85.

31 Lo, thro' her works gay nature grieves
How brief she is and frail,
As ever o'er the falling leaves
Autumnal winds prevail.
Yet still the philosophic mind
Consolatory food can find,
And hope her anchorage maintain:
We never are deserted quite;
'Tis by succession of delight
That love supports his reign.
1764 *Ode to the Earl of Northumberland, with Some Other Pieces*,
'On a Bed of Guernsey Lilies: written in September 1763',
stanza 2.

Smiles, Samuel 1812–1904

Scottish writer and social reformer who settled as a surgeon in
Leeds, and published works encouraging self-improvement
such as *Self-Help* (1859), *Character* (1871), *Thrift* (1875) and *Duty*
(1880).

32 The spirit of self-help is the root of all genuine growth in
the individual.
1859 *Self-Help*, ch.1.

33 The shortest way to do many things is to do only one
thing at once.
1859 *Self-Help*, ch.9.

34 The healthy spirit of self-help created among working
people would, more than any other measure, serve to
raise them as a class; and this, not by pulling down
others, but by levelling them up to a higher and still
advancing standard of religion, intelligence, and
virtue.
1859 *Self-Help*, ch.10.

35 We often discover what *will* do, by finding out what will
not do; and probably he who never made a mistake
never made a discovery.
1859 *Self-Help*, ch.11.

Smith, A J M 1902–80

Canadian-born US poet and anthologist.

36 McLuhan put a telescope to his ear;
What a lovely smell, he said, we have here.
1967 *Poems*, 'The Taste of Space'. When McLuhan first heard this
couplet, his response was 'Synaesthesia!'

Smith, Adam 1723–90

Scottish economist and philosopher. His *Inquiry into the Nature
and Causes of the Wealth of Nations* (1776), the first major work of
political economy, examined in detail the consequences of
economic freedom—division of labour, the function of
markets and the international implications of a *laissez-faire*
economy. He was Professor of Moral Philosophy at the
University of Glasgow.

37 In ease of body, peace of mind, all the different ranks of
life are nearly upon a level and the beggar who suns
himself by the side of the highway, possesses that
security which kings are fighting for.
1759 *The Theory of Moral Sentiments.*

38 The greatest improvement in the productive powers of
labour, and the greater part of the skill, dexterity and
judgement with which it is any where directed, as
applied, seem to have been the effects of the division of
labour.
1776 *An Inquiry into the Nature and Causes of the Wealth of
Nations*, bk.1, ch.1.

39 It is not from the benevolence of the butcher, the brewer,
or the baker, that we expect our dinner, but from their
regard to their own interest.
1776 *An Inquiry into the Nature and Causes of the Wealth of
Nations*, bk.1, ch.2.

40 The difference between the most dissimilar characters,
between a philosopher and a common street porter,
seems to arise not so much from nature, as from habit,
custom and education
1776 *An Inquiry into the Nature and Causes of the Wealth of
Nations*, bk.1, ch.2.

41 The word VALUE, it is to be observed, has two different
meanings, and sometimes the utility of some particular
object, and sometimes the power of purchasing other
goods which the possession of that object conveys. This
one may be called 'value in use'; the other, 'value in
exchange'. The things which have the greatest value in
use have frequently little or no value in exchange; and on
the contrary, those which have the greatest value in
exchange have frequently little or no value in use.
Nothing is more useful than water: but it will purchase
scarce any thing; scarce any thing can be had in
exchange for it. A diamond, on the contrary, has scarce
any value in use; but a very great quantity of other goods
may frequently be had in exchange for it.
1776 *An Inquiry into the Nature and Causes of the Wealth of
Nations*, bk.1, ch.4.

42 The real price of every thing, what every thing really costs
to the man who wants to acquire it, is the toil and trouble
of acquiring it. Labour was the first price, the original
purchase money that was paid for all things.
1776 *An Inquiry into the Nature and Causes of the Wealth of
Nations*, bk.1, ch.5.

43 The common wages of labour depends every where

upon the contract usually made between those two parties whose interests are by no means the same…Masters are always and every where in a sort of tacit, but constant and uniform combination, not to raise the wages of labour above their actual rate.
1776 *An Inquiry into the Nature and Causes of the Wealth of Nations*, bk.1, ch.8.

44 People of the same trade seldom meet together, even for merriment and diversion, but the conversation ends in a conspiracy against the public, or in some contrivance to raise prices.
1776 *An Inquiry into the Nature and Causes of the Wealth of Nations*, bk.1, ch.10, pt.2.

45 The rate of profit does not, like rent and wages, rise with the prosperity, and fall with the declension, of the society. On the contrary, it is naturally low in rich, and high in poor countries, and it is always highest in the countries which are going fastest to ruin.
1776 *An Inquiry into the Nature and Causes of the Wealth of Nations*, bk.1, ch.11, conclusion.

46 Capitals are increased by parsimony, and diminished by prodigality and misconduct. By what a frugal man annually saves he not only affords maintenance to an additional number of productive hands…but…he establishes as it were a perpetual fund for the maintenance of an equal number in all times to come.
1776 *An Inquiry into the Nature and Causes of the Wealth of Nations*, bk.2, ch.3.

47 The principle which prompts to save is the desire of bettering our condition—a desire which…comes with us from the womb and never leaves us till we go into the grave.
1776 *An Inquiry into the Nature and Causes of the Wealth of Nations*, bk.2, ch.3.

48 It is the maxim of every prudent master of a family never to attempt to make at home what it will cost him more to make than to buy. The taylor does not attempt to make his own shoe… All of them find it for their interest to employ their whole industry in a way in which they have some advantage over their neighbours and to purchase with a part of its produce…whatever else they have occasion for… What is prudence in the conduct of every private family, can scarce be folly in that of a great kingdom… Would it be a reasonable law to prohibit the importation of all foreign wines, merely to encourage the making of claret and burgundy in Scotland?
1776 *An Inquiry into the Nature and Causes of the Wealth of Nations*, bk.4, ch.2.

49 Every individual…intends only his own gain, and he is in this as in many other cases led by an invisible hand to promote an end which was no part of his intention… By pursuing his own interest he frequently promotes that of the society more effectually than when he really intends to promote it. I have never known much good done by those who affected to trade for the publick good.
1776 *An Inquiry into the Nature and Causes of the Wealth of Nations*, bk.4, ch.3.

50 To found a great Empire for the sole purpose of raising up a people of customers, may at first sight appear a project fit only for a nation of shopkeepers. It is, however, a project altogether unfit for a nation of shopkeepers; but

extremely fit for a nation that is governed by shopkeepers.
1776 *An Inquiry into the Nature and Causes of the Wealth of Nations*, bk.4, ch.7, pt.3.
➤ See Napoleon 607:68, Punch 672:7, Stoppard 825:66.

51 Consumption is the sole end and purpose of all production.
1776 *An Inquiry into the Nature and Causes of the Wealth of Nations*, bk.4, ch.8.

52 The man whose life is spent in performing a few simple operations of which the effects too are, perhaps, always the same or very nearly the same, has no occasion to exert his understanding, or to exercise his invention. He generally becomes as stupid and ignorant as it is possible for a human creature to become.
1776 *An Inquiry into the Nature and Causes of the Wealth of Nations*, bk.5, ch.1, pt.3, article 2.

53 Science is the great antidote to the poison of enthusiasm and superstition.
1776 *An Inquiry into the Nature and Causes of the Wealth of Nations*, bk.5, ch.1, pt.3, article 3.

54 There is no art which one government sooner learns of another than that of draining money from the pockets of the people.
1776 *An Inquiry into the Nature and Causes of the Wealth of Nations*, bk.5, ch.2.

Smith, Al(fred) Emmanuel 1873–1944

US Democrat politician, who rose from newsboy to be Governor of New York State (1919–20, 1923–8). He was defeated as Democratic candidate for the Presidency in 1928.

55 Nobody shoots Santa Claus.
1936 Denouncing criticisms of the US aid programme.

56 No matter how thin you slice it, it's still baloney.
1936 Election campaign speech, October.

Smith, Alexander McCall 1949–

Scottish Professor of Medical Law and author of numerous works of fiction and non-fiction.

57 The No.1 Ladies' Detective Agency.
1998 Novel title.

Smith, Arthur 1954–

English comedian and broadcaster.

58 On paper, England are a good cricket team. The trouble is they play on grass.
Attributed.

Smith, Sir Cyril 1928–

English Liberal politician, who founded a spring manufacturing company before his election to Parliament in 1972. A popular MP, of unusually large physical dimensions, he was knighted in 1988.

59 If the fence is strong enough, I'll sit on it.
1974 In the *Observer*, 15 Sep.

Smith, Dodie 1896–1990

English playwright, novelist and theatre producer, whose works include the highly popular children's book *The Hundred and One Dalmatians* (1956).

60 The family—that dear octopus from whose tentacles we never quite escape.
1938 *Dear Octopus*.

Smith, Godfrey 1926–

English writer and columnist. He was Associate Editor of the *Sunday Times* from 1972 to 1991 and has written novels and books about English social life and customs. He has also compiled anthologies.

61 A scoop of pure honey set in a green bowl.
1984 Of Bath. *The English Companion*.

62 Try as one may to stress the cultural and historical role of the place…it still conveys one overwhelmingly powerful image to your average Englishman: the dirty weekend.
1984 Of Brighton. *The English Companion*.

Smith, Iain Crichton *Gaelic name* **Blain Mac A'Ghobhainn** 1928–98

Scottish poet and novelist, who wrote in both English and Gaelic. His novels include *Consider the Lilies* (1968). His *Collected Poems* were published in 1992.

63 Here they have no time for the fine graces
of poetry, unless it freely grows
in deep compulsion, like water in the well,
woven into the texture of the soil
in a strong pattern.
1955 'Poem of Lewis'.

64 And she, being old, fed from a mashed plate
as an old mare might droop across a fence
to the dull pastures of her ignorance.
Her husband held her upright while he prayed

to God who is all-forgiving to send down
some angel somewhere who might land perhaps
in his foreign wings among the gradual crops.
She munched, half dead, blindly searching the spoon.
1961 *Thistles and Roses*, 'Old Woman', stanzas 1–2.

65 This is the land God gave to Andy Stewart—we have our inheritance.
There shall be no ardour, there shall be indifference.
There shall not be excellence, there shall be the average.
We shall be the intrepid hunters of golf balls.
1969 'The White Air of March'.

66 I tremble in this factory of books.
What love he must have lost to write so much.
1985 After seeing an exhibit of Sir Walter Scott's manuscripts. 'At the Scott Exhibition, Edinburgh Festival', collected in *Selected Poems* (1985).

Smith, Iain Duncan 1954–

English Conservative politician, leader of the Conservative Party from 2001 to 2003.

67 The quiet man is here to stay, and he's turning up the volume!
2003 At the Conservative Party Conference, Oct.

Smith, Ian Douglas 1919–

Zimbabwean (Rhodesian) politician, a founder of the pro-independence Rhodesian Front. Prime Minister from 1964, he unilaterally declared independence in 1965. Britain applied sanctions, and in 1979 majority rule was granted. He was suspended from government (1987) for South African links.

68 We have the happiest Africans in the world.
1971 In the *Observer*, 28 Nov.

69 Let me say it again, I don't believe in black majority rule ever in Rhodesia. Not in a thousand years.
1976 Radio broadcast, 20 Mar.

Smith, John 1938–94

Scottish politician. He was called to the Bar in 1967, and made a QC in 1983. He became MP for Lanarkshire North in 1970, and for Monklands East in 1983. He served as a cabinet minister under Harold Wilson and James Callaghan, and in the shadow cabinet (1972–92). He succeeded Neil Kinnock as leader of the Labour Party in 1992.

70 The settled will of the Scottish people.
1994 Of the creation of a Scottish parliament, in a speech at the Scottish Labour Conference, 11 Mar.

71 We will do our best to reward your faith in us, but please give us the opportunity to serve our country, that is all we ask.
1994 Address to a European Gala Dinner, 11 May. They were his final public words; he died the next morning of a heart attack.

Smith, Logan Pearsall 1865–1946

US-born British writer, who took British nationality in 1913. He is best known for his polished essays and aphorisms, gathered in books such as *Afterthoughts* (1931); he also wrote criticism and short stories.

72 The denunciation of the young is a necessary part of the hygiene of older people, and greatly assists the circulation of their blood.
1931 *Afterthoughts*, 'Age and Death'.

73 There are two things to aim at in life: first, to get what you want; and, after that, to enjoy it. Only the wisest of mankind achieve the second.
1931 *Afterthoughts*, 'Life and Human Nature'.

74 How awful to reflect that what people say of us is true!
1931 *Afterthoughts*, 'Life and Human Nature'.

75 There are few sorrows, however poignant, in which a good income is of no avail.
1931 *Afterthoughts*, 'Life and Human Nature'.

76 An improper mind is a perpetual feast.
1931 *Afterthoughts*, 'Life and Human Nature'.

77 There is more felicity on the far side of baldness than young men can possibly imagine.
1931 *Afterthoughts*, 'Age and Death'.

78 What music is more enchanting than the voices of young people, when you can't hear what they say?
1931 *Afterthoughts*, 'Age and Death'.

79 Most people sell their souls, and live with a good conscience on the proceeds.
1931 *Afterthoughts*, 'Other People'.

80 A friend who loved perfection would be the perfect friend, did not that love shut his door on me.
1931 *Afterthoughts*, 'Other People'.

81 All Reformers, however strict their social conscience, live in houses just as big as they can pay for.
1931 *Afterthoughts*, 'Other People'.

82 When they come downstairs from their Ivory Towers,

Idealists are very apt to walk straight into the gutter.
1931 *Afterthoughts*, 'Other People'.

83 Married women are kept women, and they are beginning to find it out.
1931 *Afterthoughts*, 'Other People'.

84 A best-seller is the gilded tomb of a mediocre talent.
1931 *Afterthoughts*, 'Art and Letters'.

85 People say that life is the thing, but I prefer reading.
1931 *Afterthoughts*, 'Myself'.

86 Thank heavens, the sun has gone in, and I don't have to go out and enjoy it.
1931 *Afterthoughts*, 'Myself'.

87 What I like in a good author is not what he says, but what he whispers.
1933 *All Trivia*, 'Afterthoughts'.

Smith, Margaret Chase 1897–1995

US Senator. Elected to the US Senate in 1948, she served four terms and continued to be politically active afterwards. She supported the draft for women, was a teacher and a syndicated columnist. She held 95 honorary degrees from various universities and colleges.

88 The greatest deliberative body in the world…has too often been debased to the level of a forum of hate and character assassination sheltered by the shield of congressional immunity.
1950 'Declaration of Conscience' address to the Senate, 1 Jun, denouncing accusations by Senator Joseph R McCarthy.

Smith, Patti 1946–

US singer, songwriter, poet and political activist.

89 Everybody's got to reclaim these things—poetry, rock'n'roll, political activism—and it's got to be done over and over again. It's like eating: you can't say, 'Oh, I ate yesterday'. You have to eat again.
2004 In *Rolling Stone*, 27 May.

Smith, Red 1905–82

US sportswriter.

90 It was an ideal day for football—too cold for the spectators and too cold for the players.
1963 Reporting on a match between the Chicago Bears and the New York Giants.

Smith, Samuel Francis 1808–95

US clergyman and poet.

91 My country, 'tis of thee,
Sweet land of liberty,
Of thee I sing:
Land where my fathers died,
Land of the pilgrims' pride,
From every mountain-side
Let the freedom ring.
1831 'America'.

Smith, Stevie (Florence Margaret) 1902–71

English poet and novelist. She lived most of her life with her aunt in a London suburb, and much of her work reflected that setting. Loneliness is a persistent theme, but she was also adept at dealing wittily with serious matters.

92 If you cannot have your dear husband for a comfort and a delight, for a breadwinner and a crosspatch, for a sofa, chair or a hot-water bottle, one can use him as a Cross to be Borne.
1936 *Novel On Yellow Paper*.

93 A Good Time was Had By All.
1937 Title of poetry collection.

94 This Englishwoman is so refined
She has no bosom and no behind.
1937 *A Good Time was Had By All*, 'This Englishwoman'.

95 Here is all straight and narrow as a tomb
Oh shut me not within a little room.
1950 *Harold's Leap*, 'The Commuted Sentence'.

96 Let all the little poets be gathered together in classes
And let prizes be given to them by the Prize Asses.
1950 *Harold's Leap*, 'To School!'

97 Oh, no, no, no, it was too cold always
(Still the dead one lay moaning)
I was much too far out all my life
And not waving but drowning.
1957 *Not Waving but Drowning*, 'Not Waving but Drowning'.

98 People who are always praising the past
And especially the times of faith as best
Ought to go and live in the Middle Ages
And be burnt at the stake as witches and sages.
1957 *Not Waving but Drowning*, 'The Past'.

99 Shall I tell you the signs of a New Age coming?
It is a sound of drubbing and sobbing
Of people crying, We are old, we are old
And the sun is going down and becoming cold.
1957 *Not Waving but Drowning*, 'The New Age'.

1 Why does my Muse only speak when she is unhappy?
She does not, I only listen when I am unhappy
When I am happy I live and despise writing
For my Muse this cannot but be dispiriting.
1962 *Selected Poems*, 'My Muse'.

2 I long for the Person from Porlock
To bring my thoughts to an end.
I am growing impatient to see him
I think of him as a friend.
1962 *Selected Poems*, 'Thoughts About the Person from Porlock' (a reference to the 'person from Porlock' mentioned in Coleridge's preliminary note to 'Kubla Khan').

3 Private Means is dead
God rest his soul, officers and fellow-rankers said.
1962 *Selected Poems*, 'Private Means is Dead'.

4 'This night shall thy soul be required of thee.'
My soul is never required of *me*
It always has to be somebody else of course.
Will my soul be required of me tonight perhaps?
1972 *Scorpion*, 'Scorpion'.
➤ See Bible 115:42.

5 Scorpion so wishes to be gone.
1972 *Scorpion*, 'Scorpion'.

6 Oh I am a cat that likes to
Gallop about doing good.
1972 *Scorpion*, 'The Galloping Cat'.

Smith, Rev Sydney 1771–1845

English journalist, clergymen and preacher and lecturer on moral philosophy, also one of the founders of the *Edinburgh*

Review. He wrote letters and pamphlets in favour of Catholic emancipation, the ballot, the abolition of prison abuses and other causes, and is best known as a conversationalist and wit.

7 The moment that the very name of Ireland is mentioned, the English seem to bid adieu to common feeling, common prudence, and common sense, and to act with the barbarity of tyrants and the fatuity of idiots.
1807–8 *Peter Plymley's Letters.*

8 I look upon Switzerland as an inferior sort of Scotland.
1815 Letter to Lord Holland, [August]. In *The Letters of Sydney Smith* edited by Nowell C Smith (1953), vol. 1.

9 What two ideas are more inseparable than Beer and Britannia.
1823 In the *Edinburgh Review*, quoted in H Pearson *The Smith of Smiths* (1934), ch.11.

10 Alas, alas, how easily a priest begets children and with what difficulty he provides for them; a priest I mean who is extravagant enough to keep a conscience; a point wherein our profession commits (I must say) little excess.
1825 Letter to Lord Holland, 14 Jul. In *The Letters of Sydney Smith* edited by Nowell C Smith (1953), vol. 1.

11 He who drinks a tumbler of London Water has literally in his stomach more animated beings than there are men, Women and Children on the face of the globe.
1834 Letter to Lady Grey, 19 Nov.

12 No furniture so charming as books.
Quoted in Lady Holland *Memoir* (1855), vol 1, ch. 9.

13 Take short views, hope for the best, and trust in God.
Quoted in Lady Holland *Memoir* (1855), vol 1, ch. 6.

14 That knuckle-end of England—that land of Calvin, oat-cakes and sulphur.
Quoted in Lady Holland *Memoir* (1855), vol 1, ch. 2.

15 I heard him [Jeffrey] speak disrespectfully of the Equator!
Quoted in Lady Holland *Memoir* (1855), vol.1, ch.2.

16 As the French say, there are three sexes—men, women, and clergymen.
Quoted in Lady Holland *Memoir* (1855), vol.1, ch.9.

17 He is like a book in breeches.
Of Lord Macaulay. Quoted in Lady Holland *Memoir* (1855), vol.1, ch.11.

18 He has occasional flashes of silence that make his conversation perfectly delightful.
Of Lord Macaulay. Quoted in Lady Holland *Memoir* (1855), vol.1, ch.11.

19 My definition of marriage… It resembles a pair of shears, so joined that they cannot be separated; often moving in opposite directions, yet always punishing anyone who comes between them.
Quoted in Lady Holland *Memoir* (1855), vol.1, ch.11.

20 Let onion atoms lurk within the bowl,
And, half-suspected, animate the whole.
'Receipt for a Salad', quoted in Lady Holland *Memoir* (1855), vol.1, ch.11.

21 Serenely full, the epicure would say,
'Fate cannot harm me, I have dined today.'
'Receipt for a Salad', concluding lines, quoted in Lady Holland *Memoir*, (1855), vol.1, ch.11.

22 My idea of heaven is, eating *paté de foie gras* to the sound of trumpets.
Quoted in H Pearson *The Smith of Smiths*, (1934), ch.10.

23 What a pity it is we have no amusements in England but vice and religion!
Quoted in H Pearson *The Smith of Smiths*, (1934), ch.10.

24 I am just going to pray for you at St Paul's, but with no very lively hope of success.
Quoted in H Pearson *The Smith of Smiths*, (1934), ch.10.

Smith, Sydney Goodsir 1915–75

New Zealand-born Scottish poet and critic, who played an important part in the 20c revival of poetry in the Scots language. His first volume, *Skail Wind* (1941), was followed by several others. He also edited works on Scottish literature.

25 This rortie wretched city
Sair come down frae its auld hiechts
—The hauf o't smug, complacent,
Lost til all pride of race or spirit,
The tither wild and rouch as ever
In its secret hairt
But lost alsweill, the smeddum tane,
The man o'independent mind has cap in hand the day
—Sits on its craggy spine
And drees the wind and rain
That nourished all its genius
—Weary wi centuries
This empty capital snorts like a great beast
Caged in its sleep, dreaming of freedom.
1954 Of Edinburgh. 'Kynd Kittock's Land' (Kynd Kittock is a character in the poetry of the 16c Scottish poet William Dunbar.) rortie=splendid, smeddum=spirit, drees=endures.

Smith, Walter Chalmers 1824–1908

Scottish clergyman and poet.

26 Immortal, invisible, God only wise,
In light inaccessible hid from our eyes,
Most blessèd, most glorious, the Ancient of Days,
Almighty, victorious, Thy great name we praise.
1867 'Immortal, Invisible', hymn.

Smollett, Tobias George 1721–71

Scottish novelist. He wrote a history of England and from 1753 edited the *Critical Review*, which led to his being imprisoned for libel in 1760. His unfavourable account of his travels in France and Italy, which he was ordered to visit for the sake of his health, earned him Sterne's designation as 'Smelfungus'. His novel *Humphrey Clinker* (1771) remains popular.

27 I think for my part one half of the nation is mad—and the other not very sound.
1762 *The Adventures of Sir Launcelot Greaves*, ch.6.

28 They have no education, no taste for reading, no housewifery, nor, indeed, any earthly occupation but that of dressing their hair, and adorning their bodies. They hate walking, and would never go abroad, if they were not stimulated by the vanity of being seen… Nothing can be more parsimonious than the economy of these people. They live upon soup and bouille, fish and salad.
1766 Of the nobility of Boulogne. *Travels through France and Italy.*

29 The capital is become an overgrown monster; which, like a dropsical head, will in time leave the body and extremities without nourishment and support.
1771 Of London. Letter from Matthew Bramble, 29 May, *Humphrey Clinker*, vol.1.

30 I am pent up in frowzy lodgings, where there is not room enough to swing a cat.

1771 Letter from Matthew Bramble, 8 Jun, *Humphrey Clinker*, vol.1.

Smuts, Jan Christian 1870–1950

South African general and statesman, Prime Minister (1919–24). A significant figure at Versailles, he was instrumental in the founding of the League of Nations. As Minister of Justice under Hertzog, his coalition with the Nationalists in 1934 produced the United Party, and he became Premier again (1939–48).

31 Perhaps it is God's will to lead the people of South Africa through defeat and humiliation to a better future and a brighter day.

1902 Speech at the Vereeniging peace talks, 31 May.

32 What was everybody's business in the end proved to be nobody's business. Each one looked to the other to take the lead, and the aggressors got away with it.

1943 Explaining the failure of the League of Nations to the Empire Parliamentary Association, London, 25 Nov.

Snagge, John 1904–96

English radio commentator.

33 I can't tell who's leading—it's either Oxford or Cambridge.

1949 Radio commentary on the Boat Race, when the engine of Snagge's launch broke down. Quoted in C Dodd *Oxford and Cambridge Boat Race* (1983), ch.14.

Snow, Carmel 1887–1961

Irish-born US journalist. She was fashion editor (1932–35) and then editor-in-chief (1935–57) of *Harper's Bazaar*.

34 Elegance is good taste *plus* a dash of daring.

1962 *The World of Carmel Snow.*

Snow, C(harles) P(ercy), 1st Baron 1905–80

English novelist and physicist. His works include a cycle of novels portraying English life from 1920, including *Strangers and Brothers* (1940), *The Masters* (1951), *The New Men* (1954) and *Corridors of Power* (1964). In his controversial *Two Cultures* (Rede lecture, 1959) he discussed the need for closer contact of science and literature.

35 Drinking the best tea in the world in an empty cricket ground—that, I think, is the final pleasure left to man.

1932 Quoted in Colin Jarman *The Guinness Dictionary of Sports Quotations* (1990).

36 The official world, the corridors of power, the dilemmas of conscience and egotism—she disliked them all.

1956 *Homecomings*, ch.22. This phrase was later used as the title of his 1964 novel, *Corridors of Power.*

37 A good many times I have been present at gatherings of people who…are thought highly educated and who have…been expressing their incredulity at the illiteracy of scientists. Once or twice I have been provoked and have asked the company how many of them could describe the Second Law of Thermodynamics. The response was cold: it was also negative.

1959 *The Two Cultures*, Rede Lecture, ch.1.

38 I believe the intellectual life of the whole of western society is increasingly being split into two polar groups… Literary intellectuals at one pole—at the other scientists, and as the most representative, the physical scientists. Between the two a gulf of mutual incomprehension.

1959 *The Two Cultures*, Rede Lecture.

39 'I grant you that he's not two-faced,' I said. 'But what's the use of that when the one face he has got is so peculiarly unpleasant?'

1960 *The Affair*, ch.4.

40 Technology…is a queer thing. It brings you great gifts with one hand, and it stabs you in the back with the other.

1971 In the *New York Times*, 15 Mar.

41 There have been many crimes committed in the name of duty and obedience—many more than in the name of dissent.

1971 'Testimony of Four Peers', in *Esquire*, Dec.

42 Writers are much more esteemed in Russia, they play a much larger part in society than they do in the West. The advantage of not being free is that people listen to you.

1971 Interview on Radio Moscow.

43 In not much over a generation, physicists have changed our world.

1981 *The Physicists* (published posthumously).

44 There are no secrets in science.

1981 *The Physicists* (published posthumously).

Snow, Clyde Collins 1928–

Forensic anthropologist.

45 The ground is like a beautiful woman. If you treat her gently, she'll tell you all her secrets.

1991 On exploring the massacre of thousands of Mayan Indians in Guatemala in the early 1980s. In the *Washington Post*, 18 Dec.

Snowden, Philip Snowden, 1st Viscount 1864–1937

English Labour statesman, crippled in a cycling accident. A socialist MP from 1906, he opposed conscription and as Chancellor of the Exchequer from 1924 aggravated the financial crises. A free trader, he resigned in 1932, and wrote an *Autobiography* (1934).

46 The Labour Party's election programme…is the most fantastic and impracticable programme ever put before the electors. This is not socialism. It is bolshevism run mad.

1931 Radio broadcast, 17 Oct.

Snyder, Gary Sherman 1930–

US poet. The 'Japhy Ryder' of Kerouac's *The Dharma Bums*, his writings reflect an almost sacramental vision of man's relationship to his natural environment.

47 I cannot remember things I once read
A few friends, but they are in cities.
Drinking cold snow-water from a tin cup
Looking down for miles
Through high still air.

1959 *Riprap*, 'Mid-August at Sourdough Mountain Lookout'.

48 A clear, attentive mind
Has no meaning but that
Which sees is truly seen.

1959 *Riprap*, 'Piute Creek'.

49 In ten thousand years the Sierras
Will be dry and dead, home of the scorpion.
Ice-scratched slabs and bent trees.
No paradise, no fall,
Only the weathering land
The wheeling sky,
Man, with his Satan
Scouring the chaos of the mind.
Oh Hell!
1959 *Riprap*, 'Milton By Firelight (Piute Creek, August 1955)'.

50 After weeks of watching the roof leak
I fixed it tonight
by moving a single board.
1968 *The Back Country*, 'Hitch Haiku'.

51 Down for a new radio, to Ross Lake, and back up. Three
days walking. Strange how unmoved this place leaves
one;
neither articulate or worshipful; rather the pressing
need to look
within and adjust the mechanism of perception.
1969 *Earth House Hold*, 'Lookout's Journal, Crater Shan 28 July'.

52 Beware of anything that promises freedom or
enlightenment—traps for eager and clever fools—a dog
has a keener nose—every creature in a cave can justify
himself. Three-fourths of philosophy and literature is the
talk of people trying to convince themselves that they
really like the cage they were tricked into entering.
1969 *Earth House Hold*, 'Japan First Time Around, 24: X'.

53 I recalled when I worked in the woods
and the bars of Madras, Oregon.
That short-haired joy and roughness—
America—your stupidity.
I could almost love you again.
1974 *Turtle Island*, 'I Went Into The Maverick Bar'.

Socrates   469–399 BC

Greek philosopher. Our knowledge of his life and teaching
derives mainly from the work of his pupil Plato, in dialogues
including the *Republic*, and the *Apology, Crito* and *Phaedo*,
which describe Socrates' trial for 'corrupting the young' and his
death by drinking hemlock.

54 I am so far like the midwife that I cannot myself give birth
to wisdom, and the common reproach is true, that,
though I question others, I can myself bring nothing to
light because there is no wisdom in me.
Quoted in Plato *Theaetetus*, 150c (translated by F M Cornford).

55 This sense of wonder is the mark of the philosopher.
Philosophy indeed has no other origin.
Quoted in Plato *Theaetetus*, 150c (translated by F M Cornford).

56 How many things I can do without!
On viewing goods for sale. Quoted in Diogenes Laertius *Vitae
Philosophorum*, 2.25 (translated by R D Hicks, 1950).

57 The unexamined life is not worth living.
Quoted in Plato *Apology*, 38a.

58 There is only one good, knowledge, and only one evil,
ignorance.
Quoted in Diogenes Laertius *Vitae Philosophorum*, 2.31
(translated by R D Hicks, 1950).

Solon   c.640–c.559 BC

Athenian lawgiver and poet. Archon in 594 BC (or 591 BC), he
reformed the constitution, abolishing debt-slavery and
admitting a fourth class to the Assembly. After 10 years of
voluntary exile he returned to Athens in 580 BC

59 As I grow older, I constantly learn more.
Quoted in Bergk (ed) *Poetae Lyrici Graeci*, 'Solon', no.18.

Solow, Robert M   1924–

US economist, winner of the Nobel prize (1987).

60 Thinking precisely and systematically about something
as complex and irregular as a modern economy is very
difficult, maybe impossible.
1984 In the *New York Times Book Review*, 30 Dec.

61 Merely to adopt the more powerful assumption is no
more than to assume the more powerful conclusion.
1994 In the *Journal of Economic Perspectives*, 8:53.

Solzhenitsyn, Aleksandr Isayevich   1918–

Russian writer, a labour camp prisoner (1945–53). His *One Day
in the Life of Ivan Denisovich* (1962) was widely acclaimed, but
his subsequent denunciation of Soviet censorship led to the
banning of his novels *Cancer Ward* (1968) and *The First Circle*
(1968). He was awarded the Nobel prize for literature in 1970
(received 1974). After *The Gulag Archipelago* (3 vols, 1973–6),
an account of the Stalinist terror, he was exiled (1974). His
citizenship was restored in 1990, and the treason charges
against him dropped in 1991. In 1994 he returned to Russia.

62 You only have power over people so long as you do not
take everything away from them. But when you have
robbed man of everything, he is no longer in your
pocket—he is free.
1968 *The First Circle*.

63 In our country the lie has become not just a moral
category but a pillar of the State.
1974 Quoted in the *Observer*, 29 Dec.

64 For us in Russia, communism is a dead dog, while, for
many people in the West, it is still a living lion.
1979 In the *Listener*, 15 Feb.

Somerville, Edith (Anna Oenone) and Martin, Violet
Florence *née Ross who wrote under the pseudonym
Martin Ross* 1858–1949; 1862–1915

Irish cousins who first met in 1886. They formed a lasting
successful literary partnership and are both known for a series
of novels that makes fun of the Irish.

65 'May the divil choke ye!' says he, pleasant enough, but I
knew by the blush he had he was vexed.
1898 *Some Experiences of an Irish R.M.*, 'Lisheen Races, Second-
Hand'.

66 'I call it a criminal thing in any one's great-great-
grandfather to rear up a preposterous troop of sons and
plant them all out in his own country', Lady Knox said to
me with apparent irrelevance. 'I detest collaterals. Blood
may be thicker than water, but it is also a great deal
nastier.'
1898 *Some Experiences of an Irish R.M.*, 'Philippa's Fox-Hunt'.

67 Every known class of refusal was successfully exhibited.
One horse endeavoured to climb the rails into the Grand
Stand; another, having stopped dead at the critical point,
swung round, and returned in consternation to the
starting-point, with his rider hanging like a locket around
his neck. Another, dowered with a sense of humour

unusual among horses, stepped delicately over the furze-bushes, and, amidst rounds of applause, walked through the lime with a stoic calm.
1908 *Further Experiences of an Irish R.M.*,'A Royal Command'.

Somoza, (García) Anastasio 1925–80

Nicaraguan dictator, educated in the US. As Chief of the National Guard he established himself in supreme power in the early 1930s, and retained it until assassinated, when the rule passed to his sons.

68 You won the elections. But I won the count.
1977 In *The Guardian*, 17 Jun.

Sontag, Susan 1933–

US writer and critic. Although she emerged first as an experimental fiction writer her main impact has been as a critic.Her essays in leading journals were expanded into books including *On Photography* (1976) and *Illness As Metaphor* (1978). Later publications include the novels *The Volcano Lover* (1992) and *In America* (2000), and a play, *Alice in Bed* (1993).

69 Ambition if it feeds at all, does so on the ambition of others.
1963 *The Benefactor*, ch.1.

70 Interpretation is the revenge of the intellect upon art.
1964 In *The Evergreen Review*, Dec.

71 Perversity is the muse of modern literature.
1966 *Against Interpretation*,'Camus' Notebooks'.

72 What pornography is really about, ultimately, isn't sex but death.
1967 In *Partisan Review*, Spring.

73 The white race *is* the cancer of human history, it is the white race, and it alone—its ideologies and inventions—which eradicates autonomous civilizations wherever it spreads, which has upset the ecological balance of the planet, which now threatens the very existence of life itself.
1967 In *Partisan Review*,Winter.

74 The camera makes everyone a tourist in other people's reality, and eventually in one's own.
1974 In the *New York Review of Books*, 18 Apr. Later published in book form as *On Photography* (1976).

75 When we're afraid we shoot. But when we're nostalgic we take pictures.
1974 In the *New York Review of Books*, 18 Apr.

76 The most interesting ideas are heresies.
1975 Interview in *Salmagundi*, Fall–Winter.

77 Illness is the night-side of life, a more onerous citizenship. Everyone who is born holds dual citizenship, in the kingdom of the well and in the kingdom of the sick. Although we all prefer to use only the good passport, sooner or later each of us is obliged, at least for a spell, to identify ourselves as citizens of that other place.
1978 In the *New York Review of Books*, 26 Jan.

78 It seems the very model of all the catastrophes privileged populations feel await them.
1989 Of AIDS. *AIDS and Its Metaphors*, ch.8.

79 I envy paranoids; they actually feel people are paying attention to them.
1992 In *Time Out*, 19 Aug.

80 In the matter of courage (a morally neutral virtue): whatever may be said of the perpetrators of Tuesday's slaughter, they were not cowards.
2001 Reflecting on the 11 Sep terrorist attacks in New York. In the *New Yorker*, 24 Sep.

Sophocles c.496–405 BC

Athenian playwright. He wrote well over 100 plays, of which seven tragedies have survived, including *Oedipus Tyrannus*.

81 Woman, silence makes a woman beautiful.
Ajax, 293 (translated by H Lloyd-Jones, 1994).

82 Hope has often caused the love of gain to ruin men.
Antigone, 222 (translated by H Lloyd-Jones, 1994).

83 Many things are formidable, and none more formidable than man.
Antigone, 332–3 (translated by H Lloyd-Jones, 1994).

84 One must obey the man whom the city sets up in power in small things and in justice and in its opposite.
Creon speaking. *Antigone*, 666–7 (translated by H Lloyd-Jones, 1994).

85 You see how when rivers are swollen in winter those trees that yield to the flood retain their branches, but those that offer resistance perish, trunk and all.
Haemon speaking. *Antigone*, 712–14 (translated by H Lloyd-Jones, 1994).

86 Love invincible in battle.
Antigone, 781–90 (translated by H Lloyd-Jones, 1994).

87 Remember there is no success without hard work.
Electra, 945 (translated by H Lloyd-Jones, 1994).

88 When I do not understand, I like to say nothing.
Oedipus Tyrannus, 569 (translated by H Lloyd-Jones, 1994).

89 It is best to live anyhow, as one may; do not be afraid of marriage with your mother! Many have lain with their mothers in dreams too. It is he to whom such things are nothing who puts up with life best.
Jocasta to Oedipus, her son and husband, before they both discover the truth of the prophecy. *Oedipus Tyrannus*, 979–83 (translated by H Lloyd-Jones, 1994).

Sorley, Charles Hamilton 1895–1915

Scottish poet, killed in action during World War I.

90 When you see millions of the mouthless dead
Across your dreams in pale battalions go,
Say not soft things as other men have said,
That you'll remember. For you need not so.
Give them not praise. For, deaf, how should they know
It is not curses heaped on each gashed head?
Marlborough and Other Poems,'A Sonnet' (published 1916).

Soule, John Babsone Lane 1815–91

91 Go West, young man, go West!
Terre Haute Express.

Sousa, John Philip 1854–1932

US composer and bandmaster. He became conductor of the United States Marine Band in 1880 and formed his own band, which built up an international reputation, 12 years later. As well as more than a hundred popular marches, he composed 10 comic operas.

92 Jazz will endure just as long as people hear it

through their feet instead of their brains.
c.1920 Attributed.

Soutar, William 1898–1943

Scottish poet and diarist, who was confined to bed for the last 13 years of his life with a form of spondylitis. His poems in Scots for adults and children were praised by Hugh MacDiarmid and others.

93 O luely, luely cam she in
And luely she lat doun:
I kent her be her caller lips
And her breists sae sma' an' roun'.

A' thru the nicht we spak nae word
Nor sinder'd bane frae bane:
A' thru the nicht I heard her hert
Gang soundin' wi' my ain.
1932 'TheTryst', stanzas 1–2.

94 Sae luely, luely, cam she in
Sae luely was she gaen
And wi' her a' my simmer days
Like they had never been.
1932 'TheTryst', stanza 4.

Southey, Robert 1774–1843

English poet and writer and friend of Wordsworth. His epics include *Thalaba* (1801) and *Madoc* (1805). His shorter poems are 'The Battle of Blenheim' and 'The Inchcape Rock'. He also wrote a *Life of Nelson* (1813), and became Poet Laureate in 1813.

95 She has made me in love with a cold climate, and frost and snow, with a northern moonlight.
1797 On Mary Wollstonecraft. Letter to his brotherThomas Southey, 28 Apr.

96 You are old, Father William, the young man cried,
The few locks which are left you are grey;
You are hale, Father William, a hearty old man,
Now tell me the reason, I pray.
1799 'The Old Man's Comforts'.
➤ See Carroll 194:67.

97 In the days of my youth I remembered my God!
And He hath not forgotten my age.
1799 'The Old Man's Comforts'.

98 It was a summer evening,
Old Kasper's work was done,
And he before his cottage door
Was sitting in the sun,
And by him sported on the green
His little grandchild Wilhelmine.
1800 'The Battle of Blenheim'.

99 Now tell us all about the war,
And what they fought each other for.
1800 'The Battle of Blenheim'.

1 'And everybody praised the Duke,
Who this great fight did win.'
'But what good came of it at last?'
Quoth little Peterkin.
'Why that I cannot tell,' said he,
'But 'twas a famous victory.'
1800 'The Battle of Blenheim'.

2 Blue, darkly, deeply, beautifully blue.
1805 *Madoc*, 'Lincoya', pt.1, canto 5, 1.102.

3 We wage no war with women nor with priests.
1805 *Madoc*, 'The Excommunication', pt.1, canto 15, 1.65.

4 Curses are like young chickens, they always come home to roost.
1810 *The Curse of Kehama*, motto.

5 Thou has been called, O Sleep! the friend of Woe,
But 'tis the happy who have called thee so.
1810 *The Curse of Kehama*, canto 15, stanza 12.

6 Your true lover of literature is never fastidious.
1812 *The Doctor*, ch.12.

7 Show me a man who cares no more for one place than another, and I will show you in that same person one who loves nothing but himself. Beware of those who are homeless by choice.
1812 *The Doctor*, ch.34.

8 Live as long as you may, the first twenty years are the longest half of your life.
1812 *The Doctor*, ch.130.

9 The death of Nelson was felt in England as something more than a public calamity; men started at the intelligence, and turned pale, as if they had heard of the loss of a dear friend.
1813 *The Life of Nelson*, ch.9.

10 My name is Death: the last best friend am I.
1816 'The Lay of the Laureate', stanza 87.

11 The arts babblative and scribblative.
1829 *Colloquies on the Progress and Prospects of Society*, no.10, pt.2.

12 The march of intellect.
1829 *Colloquies on the Progress and Prospects of Society*, no.14.

Soyinka, Wole *pseudonym of* **Akinwande Oluwole Soyinka** 1934–

Nigerian dramatist, poet and novelist. He was held as a political prisoner for two years (1967–9). His writing is concerned with the tension between old and new in modern Africa, and includes his first novel, *The Interpreters* (1964), the poetic collection *A Shuttle in the Crypt* (1972), the mostly prose 'prison notes', *The Man Died* (1973) and the play *The Beatification of Area Boy* (1995). He was awarded the Nobel prize for literature in 1986.

13 But the skin of progress
Masks, unknown, the spotted wolf of sameness.
1959 *The Lion and theJewel* (published 1962), 'Night'.

14 Americans expect to be loved.
1964 *The Interpreters*.

Spacey, Kevin 1959–

US actor. His film appearances include *Glengarry Glen Ross* (1992), *The Usual Suspects* (1995), *LA Confidential* (1997), *American Beauty* (1999) and *The Shipping News* (2001).

15 The less you know about me the easier it is to convince you that I'm the character on screen.
2004 In *The Scotsman*, 20 Apr.

Spark, Dame Muriel Sarah *née* **Camberg** 1918–

Scottish novelist, poet, playwright and writer of short stories. Her many works include biographical studies on Mary Wollstonecraft Shelley (1951) and Emily Brontë (1953) and her best-known novel, *The Prime of Miss Jean Brodie* (1961). She converted to Catholicism in 1954 and lives in Italy.

16 The one certain way for a woman to hold a man is to leave him for religion.
1957 *The Comforters*, ch.1.

17 Parents learn a lot from their children about coping with life.
1957 *The Comforters*, ch.6.

18 Selwyn MacGregor, the nicest boy who ever committed the sin of whisky.
1958 *The Go-Away Bird*, 'A Sad Tale's Best for Winter'.

19 She doesn't have anything to do with youth clubs. There are classes within classes in Peckham.
1960 *The Ballad of Peckham Rye*, ch.3.

20 A short neck denotes a good mind… You see, the messages go quicker to the brain because they've shorter to go.
1960 *The Ballad of Peckham Rye*, ch.7.

21 I am putting old heads on your young shoulders…all my pupils are the crème de la crème.
1961 *The Prime of Miss Jean Brodie*, ch.1.

22 One's prime is elusive. You little girls, when you grow up, must be on the alert to recognise your prime at whatever time of your life it may occur. You must live it to the full.
1961 *The Prime of Miss Jean Brodie*, ch.1.

23 Give me a girl at an impressionable age, and she is mine for life.
1961 *The Prime of Miss Jean Brodie*, ch.1.

24 'Whoever has opened the window has opened it too wide,' said Miss Brodie. 'Six inches is perfectly adequate. More is vulgar.'
1961 *The Prime of Miss Jean Brodie*, ch.3.

25 All the nice people were poor; at least, that was a general axiom, the best of the rich being poor in spirit.
1963 *The Girls of Slender Means*, ch.1.

26 A nice girl should only fall in love once in her life.
1963 *The Girls of Slender Means*, ch.2.

27 Every communist has a fascist frown, every fascist a communist smile.
1963 *The Girls of Slender Means*.

28 Well, it's about everything in particular, isn't it?
1988 Of Proust. *A Far Cry from Kensington*, ch.6.

29 Beware of men bearing flowers.
Her personal motto, quoted by John Cornwell in the *Sunday Times*, 15 May 1994.

30 Writing a novel you have to be quite aware that what you are writing is not all true. Such a character did not cross the road at such a time; this is not true.
In John Tusa *On Creativity: Interviews Explaining the Process* (2003).

31 I believe I have liberated the novel in many ways, showing how anything whatsoever can be narrated, including sheer damn cheek. I think I have opened doors and windows in the mind, and challenged fears—especially the most inhibiting fears about what a novel should be.
2004 In the *Sunday Herald*, 22 Feb.

32 The dedication of an artist involves willing oblivion to everybody else while the art is being practised, and for the hours ambiguous to it.
2004 *The Finishing School*.

33 Most marriages, where both or one is an artist, are

rickety.—Most marriages of this kind comprise one failed artist.
2004 *The Finishing School*.

Sparshott, Francis 1926–

Canadian philosopher and professor.

34 For every philosopher, in every age, the first question must be: Just what is philosophy?
1972 *Looking for Philosophy*, 'Speculation and Reflection'.

Speke, John Hanning 1827–64

English explorer. In 1854, with Richard Burton, he searched for the equatorial lakes of Africa. While travelling alone he discovered Victoria Nyanza, source of the Nile, and in 1860 tracked the Nile flowing out of it. His findings were controversial, and on the day he was to meet with Burton to discuss them he was killed by a shot from his own rifle.

35 The expedition had now performed its functions. I saw that old father Nile without any doubt rises in the Victoria Nyanza, and as I had foretold, that lake is the great source of the holy river which cradled the first expounder of our religious belief.
1863 *Journal of the Discovery of the Source of the Nile*.

36 As fattening is the first duty of fashionable female life, it must be duly enforced by the rod if necessary. I got up a bit of flirtation with missy, and induced her to rise and shake hands with me. Her face was lovely, but her body was as round as a ball.
1863 In Karagwe, west of Lake Victoria, among the Galla people. *Journal of the Discovery of the Source of the Nile*.

Spencer, Charles, Earl 1964–

English writer and broadcaster.

37 I pledge that we, your blood family, will do all we can to continue the imaginative way in which you were steering these two exceptional young men [the princes, William and Harry] so that their souls are not simply immersed by duty and tradition, but can sing openly as you planned.
1997 Oration at the funeral of his sister, Diana, Princess of Wales, 6 Sep.

Spencer, Herbert 1820–1903

English philosopher. He expounded his evolutionary theories in *Principles of Psychology* (1855), and was a leading advocate of 'Social Darwinism'. Other works included *Social Statics* (1851), *System of Synthetic Philosophy* (1862–93) and an *Autobiography* (1904).

38 No one can be perfectly free until all are free; no one can be perfectly moral till all are moral; no one can be perfectly happy till all are happy.
1851 *Social Statics*, pt.4, ch.30, section 16.

39 Science is organized knowledge.
1861 *Education*, ch. 2.

40 The preservation of health is a *duty*. Few seem conscious that there is such a thing as physical morality.
1861 *Education*, ch.4.

41 It cannot but happen…that those will survive whose functions happen to be most nearly in equilibrium with the modified aggregate of external forces… This survival of the fittest implies multiplication of the fittest.
1865 *Principles of Biology*, pt.3, ch.12, sect.164.

42 How often misused words generate misleading
thoughts.
1879 *Principles of Ethics*, bk.1, pt.2, ch.8, sect.152.

43 The liberty that the citizen enjoys is to be measured not
by the governmental machinery that he lives under,
whether representative or otherwise, but by the paucity
of restraints that it imposes upon him.
1884 *The Man Versus the State.*

44 The Republican form of government is the highest form
of government; but because of this, it requires the
highest type of human nature—a type nowhere at
present existing.
'The Americans', collected in *Essays* (1891).

45 It was remarked to me by the late Mr Charles
Roupell…that to play billiards well was a sign of an ill-
spent youth.
Quoted in Duncan *Life and Letters of Spencer*, ch.20. Robert
Louis Stevenson has also been credited with this observation.

Spender, Sir Stephen Harold 1909–95

English poet and critic. A liberal idealist, he served in the
Spanish Civil War, and was a fireman in London during the
Blitz. He co-edited *Horizon* (with Cyril Connolly) and later
Encounter, and published several volumes of poetry and
criticism, as well as journals and memoirs.

46 I think continually of those who were truly great.
1933 'I Think Continually of Those'.

47 The names of those who in their lives fought for life,
Who wore at their hearts the fire's centre.
Born of the sun they travelled a short while towards
the sun,
And left the vivid air signed with their honour.
1933 'I Think Continually of Those'.

48 What I had not foreseen
Was the gradual day
Weakening the will
Leaking the brightness away
1933 'What I Expected, Was'.

49 For I had expected always
Some brightness to hold in trust,
Some final innocence
To save from dust
1933 'What I Expected, Was'.

50 They lounge at corners of the street
And greet friends with a shrug of shoulder
And turn their pockets out,
The cynical gestures of the poor.
1933 'Moving Through the Silent Crowd'.

51 Never being, but always at the edge of Being.
1933 'Never Being'.

52 My parents kept me from children who were rough
Who threw words like stones and who wore torn clothes
1933 'My Parents Kept Me from Children Who Were Rough'.

53 Who live under the shadow of war,
What can I do that matters?
1933 'Who Live Under the Shadow'.

54 After the first powerful plain manifesto
The black statement of pistons, without more fuss,
But gliding like a queen, she leaves the station.
1933 'The Express'.

55 Pylons, those pillars
Bare like nude, giant girls that have no secret.
1933 'Pylons'.

56 Different living is not living in different places
But creating in the mind a map.
1933 'Different Living'.

57 Consider: only one bullet in ten thousand kills a man.
Ask: was so much expenditure justified
On the death of one so young and so silly
Stretched under the olive trees, Oh, world, Oh, death?
1939 'Regum Ultimo Ratio'.

58 Their collected
Hearts wound up with love, like little watch springs.
1939 'The Past Values'.

59 The light in the window seemed perpetual
Where you stayed in the high room for me
1942 'The Room Above The Square'.

60 The poet shares with other artists the faculty of seeing
things as though for the first time.
1942 *Life and the Poet.*

61 Poetry cannot take sides except with life.
1942 *Life and the Poet.*

62 My uncle was famous for his balanced point of view. At
the time of which I am writing (when he was nearly
seventy) it had become so balanced, that the act of
balancing seemed rather automatic. One had only to
offer him an opinion for him to balance it with a counter-
opinion of exactly the same weight, as a grocer puts a
pound weight against a pound of sugar.
1951 *World within World*, p.77.

63 My brothers and sister and I were brought up in an
atmosphere which I would describe as 'Puritan
decadence'. Puritanism names the behaviour which is
condemned; Puritan decadence regards the name itself
as indecent, and pretends that the object behind that
name does not exist until it is named.
1951 *World within World*, p.314–15.

64 People sometimes divide others into those you laugh at
and those you laugh with. The young Auden was
someone you could laugh-at-with.
1973 Address at Auden's Memorial Service, Oxford, 27 Oct.

65 But reading is not idleness…it is the passive, receptive
side of civilization without which the active and creative
world would be meaningless. It is the immortal spirit of
the dead realised within the bodies of the living. It is
sacramental.
1980 Journal entry, 4 Jan.

66 We were obsessed by the feeling that this was the
supreme cause of our time. The cause of poets and of
writers. The cause of freedom. And that unless the cause
of anti-Fascism was won, unless Fascism was defeated,
we would be unable to exist as writers.
1982 Speaking on the ITV series *The Spanish Civil War*, no.3,
'Battleground for idealists'.

Spenser, Edmund c.1552–1599

English poet. Educated at Cambridge, he held positions in
government, including secretary to the lord deputy in Ireland
during a period of rebellion, for most of his life, although he
died in poverty. His epic Protestant romance, *The Faerie Queen*,
was published in two instalments, Books I–III (1590) and Books

IV–VI (1596). Other works include *The Shepherd's Calendar* (1579), *Colin Clout's Come Home Again* (1595), *Amoretti* and *Epithalamion* (1595), and *Four Hymns* (1596).

67 Go little book, thy self present,
As child whose parent is unkent:
To him that is the president
Of noblesse and of chivalry,
And if that Envy bark at thee,
As sure it will, for succour flee.
1579 *The Shepherd's Calendar*, 'To His Book'.

68 Bring hither the pink and purple columbine,
With gillyflowers:
Bring coronation, and sops in wine,
Worn of paramours.
Strew me the ground with daffadowndillies,
And cowslips, and kingcups, and loved lilies.
1579 *The Shepherd's Calendar*, 'April', l.136–41.

69 And he that strives to touch the stars,
Oft stumbles at a straw.
1579 *The Shepherd's Calendar*, 'July', l.99–100.

70 Uncouth unkist, said the old famous poet Chaucer.
1579 *The Shepherd's Calendar*, 'Letter to Gabriel Harvey'.

71 So now they have made our English tongue a gallimaufry
or hodgepodge of all other speeches.
1579 *The Shepherd's Calendar*, 'Letter to Gabriel Harvey'.

72 A gentle knight was pricking on the plain.
1590 *The Faerie Queen*, bk.1, canto 1, stanza 1.

73 The sailing pine, the cedar proud and tall,
The vine-prop elm, the poplar never dry,
The builder oak, sole king of forests all,
The aspen good for staves, the cypress funeral.

The laurel, meed of mighty conquerors
And poets sage, the fir that weepeth still,
The willow worn of forlorn paramours,
The ewe obedient to the benders will,
The birch for shafts, the sallow for the mill,
The myrrh sweet bleeding in the bitter wound,
The warlike beech, the ash for nothing ill,
The fruitful olive, and the platan round,
The carver holme, the maple seldom inward sound.
1590 *The Faerie Queen*, bk.1, canto 1, stanzas 8–9.
plantan=plane tree; holme=holly.

74 Oft fire is without smoke.
1590 *The Faerie Queen*, bk.1, canto 1, stanza 12.

75 A stately palace built of squarèd brick,
Which cunningly was without mortar laid,
Whose walls were high, but nothing strong, nor thick,
And golden foil all over them displayed,
That purest sky with brightness they dismayed.
1590 Of the palace of pride. *The Faerie Queen*, bk.1, canto 4,
stanza 4.

76 And by his side rode loathsome Gluttony,
Deformèd creature, on a filthy swine.
1590 *The Faerie Queen*, bk.1, canto 4, stanza 21.

77 Fretting grief the enemy of life.
1590 *The Faerie Queen*, bk.1, canto 4, stanza 35.

78 But who can turn the stream of destiny,
Or break the chain of strong necessity?
1590 Night argues against the necessity of faith. *The Faerie
Queen*, bk.1, canto 5, stanza 25.

79 What worlds delight, or joy of living speech
Can heart, so plunged in sea of sorrows deep,
And heapèd with so huge misfortunes, reach?
The careful cold beginneth for to creep,
And in my heart his iron arrow steep,
Soon as I think upon my bitter bale.
1590 *The Faerie Queen*, bk.1, canto 7, stanza 39.

80 Still as he fled, his eye was backward cast,
As if his fear still followed him behind.
1590 *The Faerie Queen*, bk.1, canto 9, stanza 21.

81 Sleep after toil, port after stormy seas,
Ease after war, death after life does greatly please.
1590 *The Faerie Queen*, bk.1, canto 9, stanza 40.

82 Where justice grows, there grows eke greater grace.
1590 *The Faerie Queen*, bk.1, canto 9, stanza 53

83 His iron coat all overgrown with rust,
Was underneath envelopèd with gold,
Whose glistering gloss darkened with filthy dust,
Well yet appearèd, to have been of old
A work of rich entail, and curious mold,
Woven with antics and wild imagery.
1590 Of Mammon. *The Faerie Queen*, bk.2, canto 7, stanza 4.

84 And all for love, and nothing for reward.
1590 *The Faerie Queen*, bk.2, canto 8 stanza 2.

85 Of all God's works, which do this world adorn,
There is no one more fair and excellent,
Then is mans body both for power and form,
Whiles it is kept in sober government.
1590 *The Faerie Queen*, bk.2, canto 9, stanza 1.

86 So passeth, in the passing of a day,
Of mortal life the leaf, the bud, the flower,
No more doth flourish after first decay,
That erst was sought to deck both bed and bower,
Of many a lady, and many a paramour:
Gather therefore the rose, whilst yet is prime,
For soon comes age, that will her pride deflower:
Gather the rose of love, whilst yet is time,
Whilst loving thou mayst lovèd be with equal crime.
1590 *The Faerie Queen*, bk.2, canto 12, stanza 75.

87 Nought so of love this looser dame did skill,
But as a coal to kindle fleshly flame,
Giving the bridle to her wanton will,
And treading underfoot her honest name.
1590 Of Malecasta. *The Faerie Queen*, bk.3, canto 1, stanza 50.

88 But as it falleth, in the gentlest hearts
Imperious love hath highest set his throne,
And tyrannizeth in the bitter smarts
Of them, that to him buxom are and prone.
1590 *The Faerie Queen*, bk.3, canto 2, stanza 23.
buxom = 'yielding'.

89 Most sacred fire, that burnest mightily
In living breasts, ykindled first above,
Amongst th'eternal spheres and lamping sky,
And thence poured into men, which men call Love.
1590 *The Faerie Queen*, bk.3, canto 3, stanza 1.

90 Where is the antique glory now become,
What whilom wont in women to appear?
Where be the brave achievements doen by some?
Where be the battles, where the shield and spear,
And all the conquests, which them high did rear,
That matter made for famous poet's verse,

And boastful men so oft abashed to hear?
Bene they all dead, and laid in doleful hearse?
Or doen they only sleep, and shall again reverse?
1590 *The Faerie Queen*, bk.3, canto 4, stanza 1.

91 But ah, who can deceive his destiny,
Or ween by warning to avoid his fate?
1590 *The Faerie Queen*, bk.3, canto 4, stanza 27.

92 There is continual spring, and harvest there
Continual, both meeting at one time:
For both the boughs do laughing blossoms bear,
And with fresh colours deck the wanton prime,
And eke attonce the heavy trees they climb,
Which seem to labour under their fruits load:
The whiles the joyous birds make their pastime
Amongst the shady leaves, their sweet above,
And their true loves without suspicion tell abroad.
1590 Of the Garden of Adonis. *The Faerie Queen*, bk.3, canto 6, stanza 42.

93 Yet never can he die, but dying lives,
And doth himself with sorrow new sustain,
That death and life attonce unto him gives,
And painful pleasure turns to pleasing pain.
1590 *The Faerie Queen*, bk.3, canto 10, stanza 60.

94 And as she looked about, she did behold,
How over that same door was likewise writ,
Be bold, be bold, and everywhere Be bold…
At last she spied at that room's upper end
Another iron door, on which was writ
Be not too bold.
1590 *The Faerie Queen*, bk.3, canto 11, stanza 54.

95 Of such deep learning little had he need,
Ne yet of Latin, ne of Greek that breed
Doubts 'mongst divines, and difference of texts,
From when arise diversity of sects,
And hateful heresies.
1591 *Prosopopoia*, l.385–9.

96 Most glorious Lord of Life! that, on this day,
Didst make Thy triumph over death and sin;
And having harrowed hell, didst bring away
Captivity thence captive, us to win:
1595 *Amoretti*, sonnet 68.

97 But when I plead, she bids me play my part,
And when I weep, she says tears are but water:
And when I sigh, she says I know the art,
And when I wail, she turns herself to laughter.
1595 *Amoretti*, sonnet 18.

98 The merry cuckoo, messenger of Spring,
His trumpet shrill hath thrice already sounded.
1595 *Amoretti*, sonnet 19.

99 Most glorious Lord of Life! that, on this day,
Didst make Thy triumph over death and sin;
And having harrowed hell, didst bring away
Captivity thence captive, us to win:
1595 *Amoretti*, sonnet 68.

1 One day I wrote her name upon the strand,
But came the waves and washèd it away;
Again I wrote it with a second hand,
But came the tide, and made my pains his prey.
'Vain man,' said she, 'that doest in vain assay
A mortal thing so to immortalise,
For I my self shall like to this decay,

And eke my name be wipèd out likewise.'
'Not so,' quod I, 'let baser things devise
To die in dust, but you shall live by fame:
My verse your virtues rare shall eternise,
And in the heavens write your glorious name.
Where when as death shall all the world subdue,
Our love shall live, and later life renew.'
1595 *Amoretti*, sonnet 75.

2 In youth, before I waxèd old,
The blind boy, Venus' baby,
For want of cunning made me bold,
In bitter hive to grope for honey.
1595 *Amoretti*, 'Anacreontics', no.1.

3 Open the temple gates unto my love,
Open them wide that she may enter in.
1595 *Epithalamion*, section 12.

4 Pour out the wine without restraint or stay,
Pour not by cups, but by the belly full,
Pour out to all that will,
And sprinkle all the posts and walls with wine,
That they may sweat, and drunken be withal.
1595 *Epithalamion*, section 14.

5 Ah when will this long weary day have end,
And lend me leave to come unto my love?
How slowly do the hours their numbers spend!
How slowly does sad Time his feathers move!
1595 *Epithalamion*, section 16.

6 Dan Chaucer, well of English undefiled,
On Fame's eternal beadroll worthy to be filed.
1596 *The Faerie Queen*, bk.4, canto 2, stanza 32.

7 O sacred hunger of ambitious minds.
1596 *The Faerie Queen*, bk.5, canto 12, stanza 1.

8 A monster, which the Blatant beast men call,
A dreadful fiend of gods and men ydrad.
1596 *The Faerie Queen*, bk.5, canto 12, stanza 37.

9 Me seems the world is run quite out of square,
And being once amiss grows daily worse and worse.
1596 *The Faerie Queen*, bk.5, proem, stanza 1.

10 For that which all men then did virtue call,
Is now called vice; and that which vice was hight,
Is now hight virtue, and so used of all:
Right now is wrong, and wrong that was is right,
1596 *The Faerie Queen*, bk.5, proem, stanza 4.

11 Yet is that glass so gay, that it can blind
The wisest sight, to think gold that is brass.
1596 Of the mirror of fashion. *The Faerie Queen*, bk.6, proem, stanza 5.

12 The gentle mind by gentle deeds is known.
For a man by nothing is so well bewrayed,
As by his manners.
1596 *The Faerie Queen*, bk.6, canto 3, stanza 1.

13 Sweet Thames, run softly, till I end my song.
1596 *Prothalamion*, l.1.

14 What man that sees the ever-whirling wheel
Of Change, the which all mortal things doth sway,
But that thereby doth find, and plainly feel,
How mutability in them doth play
Her cruel sports, to many men's decay?
1609 *The Faerie Queen*, 'Mutability', canto 6, stanza 1.

15 First, sturdy March with brows full sternly bent,

And armèd strongly, rode upon a ram,
The same which over Hellespontus swam:
Yet in his hand a spade he also hent,
And in a bag all sorts of seeds ysame,
Which on the earth he strowèd as he went,
And filled her womb with fruitful hope of nourishment.
1609 *The Faerie Queen*,'Mutability', canto 7, stanza 32.
hent = grasped; ysame = together.

16 Jolly June, arrayed
All in green leaves, as he a Player were.
1609 *The Faerie Queen*,'Mutability', canto 7, stanza 35.

17 Next was November, he full gross and fat,
As fed with lard, and that right well might seem;
For, he had been a fatting hogs of late.
1609 *The Faerie Queen*,'Mutability', canto 7, stanza 40.

18 I was promised on a time,
To have reason for my rhyme;
From that time unto this season,
I received nor rhyme nor reason.
'Lines on his Pension.' Attributed.

Spielberg, Steven 1947–

US film-maker. His many films include *Jaws* (1975), *Close Encounters of the Third Kind* (1977), *The Color Purple* (1985), *Schindler's List* (1993), *Men in Black* (1997) and *Saving Private Ryan* (1998).

19 I hope we're such a communal society that we'll always insist on sharing an adventure in the dark with strangers, no matter what the platform hardware. That's my wish and dream—that we never give up the communal experience. It started a long time ago with cave paintings and I hope it doesn't go away.
2002 On whether cinema has a future. Quoted on www.filmmonthly.com, 12 Dec.

20 Technology can be our best friend, and technology can also be the biggest party pooper of our lives. It interrupts our own story, interrupts our ability to have a thought or a daydream, to imagine something wonderful because we're too busy bridging the walk from the cafeteria back to the office on the cell phone.
2002 In *Wired*, Jun.

Spillane, Mickey *properly* Frank Morrison Spillane 1918–

US popular novelist. He wrote for pulp magazines to pay for his education, and produced his first novel *I, the Jury* in 1947. His private detective character Mike Hammer inspired many films and a television series.

21 There are more salted peanuts consumed than caviar.
Defending his low-brow fiction. Quoted in Neil J Jones (ed) *A Book of Days for the Literary Year* (1984).

Spinoza, Baruch *also known as* Benedict de Spinoza 1632–77

Dutch philosopher, of Jewish descent. The *Tractatus Theologico-Politicus* was published in 1670, and the more famous *Ethics* in 1677. His pantheistic monism led to accusations of atheism but was influential in the development of metaphysics.

22 *Sedulo curavi, humanas actiones non ridere, non lugare, neque detestari, sed intelligere.*
I have striven not to laugh at human actions, not to weep

at them, nor to hate them, but to understand them.
1670 *Tractatus Theologico-Politicus*, bk.1, pt.4.

23 *Quicquid est, in Deo est, et nihil sine Deo esse necque concipi potest.*
Whatever is, is in God, and nothing can exist or be conceived without God.
1677 *Ethics*, bk.1, prop.15.

24 *In rerum natura nullum datur contingens; sed omnia ex necessitate divinae naturae determinata sunt ad certo modo existandum et operandum.*
In the nature of things nothing contingent is granted, but all things are determined by the necessity of divine nature for existing and working in a certain way.
1677 *Ethics*, bk.1, prop.29.

25 *Nempe falluntur homines, quod se liberos esse putant; quae opinio in hoc solo consistit, quod suarum actionum sint conscii, et ignari causarum, a quibus determinantur. Haec ergo est eorum libertatis idea, quod suarum actionum nullam cognoscant causam.*
Men are mistaken in thinking themselves free; and this opinion consists of this alone, that they are conscious of their actions and ignorant of the causes by which they are determined. This, therefore, is their idea of liberty, that they should know no cause of their actions.
1677 *Ethics*, bk.2, prop.35, note.

26 *Veritas norma sua est.*
Truth is its own standard.
1677 *Ethics*, bk.2, prop.43, note.

27 *De natura Rationis est, res sub quadam aeternitatis specie percipere.*
It is the nature of reason to perceive things under a certain species of eternity.
1677 *Ethics*, bk.2, prop.44, corollary 2.

28 *Unaquaeque res, quantum in se est, in suo esse perseverare conatur.*
Everything in so far as it is in itself endeavours to persist in its own being.
1677 *Ethics*, bk.3, prop.6.

29 *Nihil nos conari, velle, appetere, neque cupere, quia id bonum esse judicamus; sed contra, nos propterea aliquid bonum esse judicare, quia id conamur, volumus, appetimus, atque cupimus.*
We endeavour, wish, desire, or long for nothing because we deem it good; but on the other hand, we deem a thing good because we endeavour, wish for, desire, or long for it.
1677 *Ethics*, bk.3, prop.9, note.

30 *Nempe Amor nihil aliud est, quam Laeititia concomitante idea causae externae; et Odium nihil aliud est, quam Tristitia concomitante idea causae externae.*
Love is nothing else than pleasure accompanied by the idea of an external cause; and hate pain accompanied by the idea of an external cause.
1677 *Ethics*, bk.3, prop.13, note.

31 *Ex virtute absoluto agere nihil aliud in nobis est, quam ex ductu Rationis agere, vivere, suum esse conservare (haec tria idem significant) ex fundamento proprium utile quaerendi.*
To act absolutely according to virtue is nothing else in us than to act under the guidance of reason, to live so, and to preserve one's being (these three have the same

meaning) on the basis of seeking what is useful to oneself.
1677 *Ethics*, bk.4, prop.24.

32 *Summum Mentis bonum est Dei cognitio, et summa Mentis virtus Deum cognoscere.*
The greatest good of the mind is the knowledge of God, and the greatest virtue of the mind is to know God.
1677 *Ethics*, bk.4, prop.28.

33 *Homo liber de nulla re minus quam de morte cogitat; et ejus sapienta non mortis, sed vitae meditatio est.*
A free man thinks of nothing less than of death, and his wisdom is a meditation not of death but of life.
1677 *Ethics*, bk.4, prop.67.

34 *In vita itaque apprime utile est, intellectum seu Rationem, quantum possumus, perficere, et in hoc uno summa hominis felicitas seu beatitudo consistit; quippe beatitudo nihil aliud est, quam ipsa animi acquiescentia quae ex Dei intuitiva cognitione oritur.*
It is therefore extrememly useful in life to perfect as much as we can the intellect or reason, and of this alone does the greatest happiness or blessedness of man exist: for blessedness is nothing else than satisfaction of mind which arises from the intuitive knowledge of God.
1677 *Ethics*, bk.4, appendix.

35 *Ex tertio cognitionis genere oritur necessario Amor Dei intellectualis.*
From the third kind of knowledge [intuition] arises necessarily the intellectual love of God.
1677 *Ethics*, bk.5, prop.32, corollary.

36 *Per Deum intelligo ens absolute infinitum, hoc est, substantiam constantem infinitis attributis, quorum unumquodque aeternam et infinitam essentiam exprimit.*
By God I mean a being absolutely infinite—that is, a substance consisting in infinite attributes, of which each expresses eternal and infinite essentiality.
1677 *Ethics*.

Spock, Dr Benjamin McLane 1903–98

US paediatrician. His *Common Sense Book of Baby and Child Care* (1946) sold over 30 million copies, transforming childcare. He gave up psychiatry to devote himself to pacifism, and ran for the presidency in 1972.

37 You know more than you think you do.
1946 *The Common Sense Book of Baby and Child Care*, opening words.

38 To win in Vietnam, we will have to exterminate a nation.
1968 *Dr Spock on Vietnam*, ch.7.

Spring-Rice, Sir Cecil Arthur 1858–1918

English diplomat.

39 I vow to thee, my country—all earthly things above—
Entire and whole and perfect, the service of my love.
1918 *I Vow To Thee, My Country*.

Springsteen, Bruce 1949–

US rock singer and guitarist. His albums include *Born To Run* (1975) and *Born In The USA* (1984).

40 We gotta get out while we're young
'Cause tramps like us, baby, we were born to run.
1975 'Born to Run'.

Spurgeon, Charles Haddon 1834–92

English Baptist preacher, famous for his eloquent sermons. A strong Calvinist, he left the Evangelical Alliance (1864) and Baptist Union (1887) over doctrinal differences and a concern for orthodoxy.

41 If you want truth to go round the world you must hire an express train to pull it; but if you want a lie to go round the world, it will fly: it is as light as a feather, and a breath will carry it. It is well said in the old proverb, 'a lie will go round the world while truth is pulling its boots on'.
Collected in *Gems from Spurgeon* (1859).

Squire, Sir J(ohn) C(ollings) 1884–1958

English poet and editor. He was an influential anti-modernist figure in the 1920s, with a gift for amusing parody.

42 It did not last: the Devil howling 'Ho!
Let Einstein be!' restored the status quo.
1926 'In Continuation of Pope on Newton'.

43 But I'm not so think as you drunk I am.
1931 'Ballade of Soporific Absorption'.

Staël, Germaine Necker, Baronne de 1766–1817

French author of important critical, political and philosophical essays as well as novels and plays seen as precursors of Romanticism. She was an opponent of Napoleon.

44 *L'amour est l'histoire de la vie des femmes, c'est un épisode dans celle des hommes.*
Love is the story of a woman's life, but only an episode in the life of a man.
1796 *De l'influence des passions sur le bonheur des individus et des nations*.

45 *La force de l'esprit ne se développe toute entière qu'en attaquant la puissance.*
The mind fully develops its faculties when it attacks power.
1800 *De la littérature considerérée dans ses rapports avec les institutions sociales*.

46 *En cherchant la gloire, j'ai toujours espéré qu'elle me ferait aimer.*
I have pursued fame always in the hope of winning her love.
1807 *Corinne ou de l'Italie*.

47 *Quand une fois on a tourné l'enthousiasme en ridicule, on a tout défait, excepté l'argent et le pouvoir.*
Once we have made enthusiasm ridiculous, there is nothing left but money and power.
1807 *Corinne ou de l'Italie*.

48 *Les païens ont divinisé la vie, et les chrétiens ont divinisé la mort.*
Pagans deified life and Christians deified death.
1807 *Corinne ou de l'Italie*.

49 *On dirait que l'âme des justes donne, comme les fleurs, plus de parfums vers le soir.*
It seems that the soul of the just gives off, like flowers, a stronger scent towards evening.
1807 *Corinne ou de l'Italie*.

50 *On cesse de s'aimer si quelqu'un ne nous aime.*
We stop loving ourselves when no one loves us.
1810 *De l'Allemagne*.

51 *La première condition pour écrire, c'est une manière de sentir vive et forte.*

The primary requirement for a writer is to feel keenly and strongly.

1810 *De l'Allemagne.*

52 *En France, on étudie les hommes; en Allemagne, les livres.*

In France, they study men; in Germany, books.

1810 *De l'Allemagne.*

53 *La poésie est le langage naturel de tous les cultes.*

Poetry is the natural language of all religions.

1810 *De l'Allemagne.*

54 *Le sentiment de l'infini est le véritable attribut de l'âme.*

To feel the infinite is the true attribute of the soul.

1810 *De l'Allemagne.*

Stalin, Joseph *originally* Iosif Vissarionovich Dzhugashvili
1879–1953

Soviet leader. Appointed General Secretary to the Communist Party Central Committee (1922), enabling him to take power after Lenin's death in 1924. His collectivization was responsible for millions of deaths, as were his political purges (1934–38). Although he signed a non-aggression pact with Hitler (1939), he declared war, joining the Allies, when Hitler threatened the Soviet Union in 1941.

55 In the name of the Constitution, Cromwell took up arms, executed the king, dissolved Parliament, imprisoned some, and beheaded others.

1934 In conversation with H G Wells, Moscow.

56 To attempt to export revolution is nonsense.

1936 Said to Roy Howard, US newspaper proprietor, 1 Mar.

57 History shows that there are no invincible armies.

1941 Radio broadcast, 3 Jul, announcing the declaration of war against Germany, three weeks before Hitler invaded.

58 Communism fits Germany as a saddle fits a cow.

1944 In conversation with the Polish politician, Stanislaw Mikolajcik, Aug.

Stallone, Sylvester 1946–

US actor and film director, best known for his roles in action films such as *Rocky* (1976) and *Rambo* (1985) and their sequels.

59 Playing polo is like trying to play golf during an earthquake.

1990 Quoted in Colin Jarman *The Guinness Dictionary of Sports Quotations* (1990).

Stamp, Sir Josiah Charles, Baron Stamp of Shortlands 1880–1941

British economist and statistician, who published early estimates of the British national income.

60 The first argument that is brought against every new proposal departing from conventional lines is nearly always that it is impracticable.

1921 *Fundamental Principles of Taxation*, p.95.

Stanley, Sir Henry Morton *originally* John Rowlands
1841–1904

Welsh-born US explorer and journalist. He fought on both sides in the American Civil War and then, as a journalist, was commissioned by the *New York Herald* to lead an expedition in search of Dr David Livingstone, who was rumoured to have died while exploring rivers in Central Africa. On one of the three subsequent expeditions he travelled the length of the Congo.

61 I would have run to him, only I was a coward in the presence of such a mob—would have embraced him, only, he being an Englishman, I did not know how he would receive me; so I did what cowardice and false pride suggested was the best thing—walked deliberately to him, took off my hat, and said: 'Dr Livingstone, I presume?'
'Yes,' said he, with a kind smile, lifting his cap slightly.
I replace my hat on my head, and he puts on his cap, and we both grasp hands, and I then say aloud: 'I thank God, Doctor, I have been permitted to see you.'
He answered, 'I feel thankful that I am here to welcome you.'

1872 *How I Found Livingstone in Central Africa.*

Stanton, Elizabeth *née* Cady 1815–1902

US reformer and suffragette; organizer of the first Women's Rights Convention, Seneca Falls, US (1848). She is remembered chiefly as co-author of *The History of Woman Suffrage* (1881–6) and she also wrote *The Women's Bible* (1895).

62 We hold these truths to be self-evident: that all men and women are created equal; that they are endowed by their Creator with certain inalienable rights; that among these are life, liberty, and the pursuit of happiness.

1848 'Declaration of Sentiments', Seneca Falls Women's Rights Convention, 19–20 Jul. This is modelled on the American Declaration of Independence of 4 Jul 1776.

63 Quite as many false ideas prevail as to woman's true position in the home as to her status elsewhere. Womanhood is the great fact in her life; wifehood and motherhood are but incidental relations.

1881 *The History of Woman Suffrage 1848–61*, vol.1, introduction.

64 Men are the Brahmin, women the Pariahs, under our existing civilization.

1881 *The History of Woman Suffrage 1848–61*, vol.1, ch.1, 'Preceding Causes'.

65 Although woman has performed much of the labor of the world, her industry and economy have been the very means of increasing her degradation.

1881 *The History of Woman Suffrage 1848–61*, vol.1, ch.1, 'Preceding Causes'.

66 As to woman's subjection…it is important to note that equal dominion is given to woman over every living thing, but not one word is said giving man dominion over woman.

1895 *The Woman's Bible*, pt.1, ch.1, 'Comments on Genesis'.

67 The Old Testament makes woman a mere after-thought in creation; the author of evil; cursed in her maternity; a subject in marriage; and all female life, animal and human, unclean.

1898 *The Woman's Bible*, pt.2, preface.

68 'Self-development is a higher duty than self-sacrifice', should be a woman's motto henceforward.

1898 *The Woman's Bible*, pt.2, 'Comments on Mark'.

Stanwyck, Barbara *originally* Ruby Stevens 1907–90

American film, television and radio actress. She was a dancer in the Ziegfeld Follies at the age of 13 and went on to play gutsy, pioneering women in westerns such as *Annie Oakley* (1935), as well as sultry femmes fatales in films noirs, including *Double*

Indemnity (1944). She became a successful radio star in the 1960s.

69 To eat, to survive and to have a good coat.

> **1987** Her three goals in life, recalled on receiving the American Film Institute Life Achievement Award. Reported in the *New York Times*, 11 Apr.

Stapledon, Olaf 1886–1950

English writer and social philosopher. He used science fiction as a means of embodying his social theories.

70 That strange blend of the commercial traveller, the missionary, and the barbarian conqueror, which was the American abroad.

> **1930** *Last and First Men*, ch.3.

Stark, Dame Freya Madeleine 1893–1993

English writer and traveller, born in Paris. She studied Arabic and made her first journey to the Middle East in 1928, after which she travelled extensively in Europe, the Middle East and Asia, writing over 30 books.

71 The great and almost only comfort about being a woman is that one can always pretend to be more stupid than one is and no one is surprised.

> **1934** *The Valley of the Assassins*.

72 I came to the conclusion that some more ascetic reason than mere enjoyment should be found if one wishes to travel in peace: to do things for fun smacks of levity, immorality almost, in our utilitarian world. And though personally I think the world is wrong, and I know in my heart of hearts that it is a most excellent reason to do things merely because one likes the doing of them, I would advise all those who wish to see unwrinkled brows in passport offices to start out ready labelled as entomologists, anthropologists, or whatever other -ology they think suitable and propitious.

> **1936** *The Valleys of the Assassins and other Persian Travels*.

73 The true call of the desert, of the mountains, or the sea, is their silence—free of the networks of dead speech.

> **1948** *Perseus in the Wind*.

74 This is the prospect from the watershed, and when the traveller reaches it, it is a good thing to take an hour's leisure and look out on the visible portions of the journey, since never in one's life can one see the same view twice.

> **1948** *Perseus in the Wind*.

75 The *inscrutability* of the East is, indeed, I believe a myth… The ordinary inhabitant is incomprehensible merely to people who never trouble to have anything much to do with them.

> **1963** *The Journey's Echo*.

Stark, John 1728–1822

American revolutionary commander. He saw service in the French and Indian war (1754–9), and at Bunker Hill (1775) and Bennington (1777) during the American Revolution.

76 We beat them today or Molly Stark's a widow.

> **1777** Speech before the Battle of Bennington, 16 Aug. Quoted in *Cyclopaedia of American Biography*, vol.5.

Starr, Roger

77 A busy man who can keep up a daily journal resembles a

person preparing for bed with the shades up… When such a man publishes parts of his journal, the reader must conclude he always knew the lights were on.

> **1989** On George F Kennan *Sketches From a Life* (1989). In the *Washington Post*, 8 May.

Steacie, E W 1900–62

Canadian government official, President of the National Research Council of Canada (1952).

78 The academic atmosphere, produced mainly by the humanities, is the only atmosphere in which pure science can flourish.

> **1956** Collected in J D Babbitt (ed) *Science in Canada: Selections from the Speeches of E. W. Steacie* (1965).

79 An efficient organization is one in which the accounting department knows the exact cost of every useless administrative procedure which they themselves have initiated.

> Quoted by J D Babbitt in his introduction to Steacie's *Science in Canada* (published posthumously, 1965).

Stead, William Thomas 1849–1912

English journalist and reformer. Editor of the *Pall Mall Gazette* (1883–90). He drowned in the *Titanic* disaster.

80 The Press is at once the eye and the ear and the tongue of the people. It is the visible speech, if not the voice, of the democracy. It is the phonograph of the world.

> **1886** 'Government by Journalism', in the *Contemporary Review*, May. Collected in *A Journalist on Journalism* (1892).

81 He may be more potent than any other man. The damnable iteration day after day of earnest conviction wears like the dropping of the water upon the stone.

> **1886** Of the journalist. 'Government by journalism', in the *Contemporary Review*, May. Collected in *A Journalist on Journalism* (1892).

82 An editor is the uncrowned king of an educated democracy.

> **1886** 'Government by Journalism', in the *Contemporary Review*, May. Collected in *A Journalist on Journalism* (1892).

83 The duty of a journalist is the duty of a watchman.

> **1886** 'Government by Journalism', in the *Contemporary Review*, May. Collected in *A Journalist on Journalism* (1892).

84 It is the great inspector, with a myriad eyes, who never sleeps, and whose daily reports are submitted, not to a functionary or department, but to the whole people.

> **1886** Of a newspaper. 'Government by Journalism', in the *Contemporary Review*, May. Collected in *A Journalist on Journalism* (1892).

85 What a marvellous opportunity for attacking the devil!

> Letter of appointment to the *Northern Echo*, quoted by Harold Evans in his preface to Ray Boston *The Essential Fleet Street* (1990).

Steel, David Martin Scott Steel, Baron 1938–

Scottish Liberal politician. He sponsored a controversial bill to reform abortion laws (1966–7), and was active in the anti-apartheid movement. The last Liberal leader (1976–88), he led the Liberals into an Alliance with the Social Democrats (1981) and later negotiated their merger. From 1999 to 2003 he was the Presiding Officer of the Scottish Parliament.

86 I have the good fortune to be the first Liberal for over half a century who is able to say to you at the end of our

annual Assembly, go back to your constituencies and prepare for government.
1981 Speech at party conference, 18 Sep.

87 [Margaret Thatcher] has turned the British bulldog into a Reagan poodle.
1986 In *Time*, 28 Apr.

88 I trust that the Duke of Edinburgh will not disagree that this ancient capital whose name he bears, with its legal and ecclesiastical headquarters and its worldwide reputation for quality education and financial management has nonetheless until now seemed like a body with its heart missing.
1999 At the opening of the Scottish Parliament, 12 May.

Steele, Sir Richard 1672–1729

Irish essayist, dramatist and politician. His plays include *The Funeral* (1701). He founded the *Tatler* (1709–11), a periodical published three times a week, on which he was joined by Joseph Addison. Together they founded the *Spectator*, a daily which ran from 1711 to 1712 under their joint editorship.

89 Dear Prue,
If a servant I sent last night got to Hampton-court, you received 29 walnuts and a letter from me. I inclose the Gazette; and am, with all my soul,
Your passionate lover, and faithful husband,
RICH. STEELE
1708 Letter, 20 Sep (published 1787).

90 I am, dear Prue, a little in drink, but at all times your faithful husband,
RICH. STEELE
1708 Letter, 27 Sep (published 1787).

91 It is to be noted that when any part of this paper appears dull there is a design in it.
1709 In the *Tatler*, no.38, 7 Jul.

92 To love her is a liberal education.
1709 Of Lady Elizabeth Hastings *Tatler*, no.49, 2 Aug.

93 Every man is the maker of his own fortune
1709 In the *Tatler*, no.52, 9 Aug.

94 It gave me a great notion of the credit of our present government and administration, to find people press as eagerly to pay money as they would to receive it; and, at the same time, a due respect for that body of men who have found out so pleasing an expedient for carrying on the common cause, that they have turned a tax into a diversion.
1710 On the first state lottery of 1710. In the *Tatler*, no.124, 24 Jan.

95 Reading is to the mind what exercise is to the body.
1710 In the *Tatler*, no.147, 18 Mar. Also attributed to Addison.

96 Let your precept be, Be Easy.
1710 In the *Tatler*, no.196, 11 Jul.

97 I was undone by my Auxiliary; when I had once called him in, I could not subsist without Dependance on him.
1711 Of Addison's contribution to the *Tatler*. Preface to vol.4 of the collected edition.

98 I have heard Will Honeycomb say, A Woman seldom Writes her Mind but in her Postscript.
1711 In the *Spectator*, no.79, 30 May.

99 We were in some little time fixed in our seats, and sat with that dislike which people not too good-natured usually conceive of each other at first sight.

1711 Embarking on a coach journey. In the *Spectator*, no.132, 1 Aug.

1 I am confident that no boy, who will not be allured to letters without blows, will ever be brought to anything with them.
1711 On flogging in schools. In the *Spectator*, no.157, 30 Aug.

2 Those grave fellows are my aversion who sift everything with the utmost nicety, and find the malignity of a lie in a piece of humour, pushed a little beyond exact truth.
1713 In the *Guardian*, no.42, 29 Apr.

Stefansson, Vilhjalmur 1879–1962

Canadian Arctic explorer and author.

3 There are two kinds of Arctic problems, the imaginary and the real. Of the two, the imaginary are the most real.
1945 *The Arctic in Fact and Fable*.

4 What is the difference between unethical and ethical advertising? Unethical advertising uses falsehoods to deceive the public; ethical advertising uses truth to deceive the public.
Discovery (published 1964).

5 A land may be said to be discovered the first time a European, presumably an Englishman, sets foot on it.
Discovery (published 1964).

Steffens, (Joseph) Lincoln 1866–1936

US journalist. While editor of *McClure's Magazine* (1902–6), his revision of an article on city corruption led to a series published as *The Shame of the Cities* (1904), a key work in urban reform. His *Struggle for Self-Government* (1906) analysed corruption and reform at state level.

6 I have seen the future and it works.
1919 On his visit to post-Revolutionary Russia, in *Autobiography* (2 vols, 1931).
➤ *See Toynbee 864:30.*

Stegner, Wallace Earle 1909–93

US novelist. Professor of English at Stanford University.

7 A political animal can be defined as a body that will go on circulating a petition even with its heart cut out.
1954 *Beyond the Hundredth Meridian*.

8 If you're going to get old, you might as well get as old as you can get.
1989 On his 80th birthday. Reported in the *San Francisco Chronicle*, 6 Mar.

Steichen, Edward Jean 1879–1973

Belgian-born US photographer, credited with developing photography as an art form. He also pioneered aerial and naval photography during World Wars I and II.

9 Photography was conceived as a mirror of the universal elements and emotions of the everydayness of life—as a mirror of the essential oneness of mankind throughout the world.
Quoted in *Dialogue*, May 1989.

Stein, Gertrude 1874–1946

US writer, influential in the development of Modernism. She settled in Paris in 1903, where with her friend Alice B Toklas she dominated expatriate life. Her less experimental works include *The Autobiography of Alice B. Toklas* (1933) and *Everybody's Autobiography* (1937).

10 You are so afraid of losing your moral sense that you are not willing to take it through anything more dangerous than a mud-puddle.
1903 'Q.E.D.', bk.1. Collected in *Fernhurst, Q.E.D., and Other Early Writings* (1971).

11 Rose is a rose is a rose is a rose, is a rose.
1914 *Tender Buttons*, 'Sacred Emily'.

12 You are all a lost generation.
Quoted as epigraph in Ernest Hemingway *The Sun Also Rises* (1926).

13 He had added to his stories a little story of meditations and in these he said that The Enormous Room was the greatest book he had ever read. It was then that Gertrude Stein said, Hemingway, remarks are not literature.
1933 *The Autobiography of Alice B. Toklas*, ch.7.

14 Pigeons on the grass alas.
1934 *Four Saints in Three Acts*, act 3, sc.2.

15 Disillusionment in living is the finding out nobody agrees with you . . . Complete disillusionment is when you realise that no one can for they can't change.
1934 *The Making of Americans*, ch.5.

16 In the United States there is more space where nobody is than where anybody is. That is what makes America what it is.
1936 *The Geographical History of America*.

17 Native always means people who belong somewhere else, because they had once belonged somewhere. That shows that the white race does not really think they belong anywhere because they think of everybody else as native.
1937 *Everybody's Autobiography*, ch.1.

18 Anything scares me, anything scares anyone but really after all considering how dangerous everything is nothing is really very frightening.
1937 *Everybody's Autobiography*, ch.2.

19 It takes a lot of time to be a genius, you have to sit around so much doing nothing, really doing nothing.
1937 *Everybody's Autobiography*, ch.2.

20 What was the use of my having come from Oakland it was not natural to have come from there yes write about it if I like or anything if I like but not there, there is no there there.
1937 *Everybody's Autobiography*, ch.4.

21 Two things are always the same the dance and war.
1937 *Everybody's Autobiography*, ch.5.

22 Everybody gets so much information all day long that they lose their common sense.
1959 'Reflection on the Atomic Bomb', collected in Robert A Goodwin (ed) *Readings in World Politics* (1959).

23 Nature is commonplace. Imitation is more interesting.
Quoted in Sir Charles Spencer Chaplin *My Autobiography* (1964).

24 You should only read what is truly good or what is frankly bad.
Quoted in Ernest Hemingway *A Moveable Feast* (1964), ch.3.

25 Anyone who marries three girls from St Louis hasn't learned much.
Of Ernest Hemingway. Quoted in R Mellow *Charmed Circle* (1974), ch.16.

26 Just before she died she asked, 'What is the answer?' No answer came. She laughed and said, 'In that case what is the question?' Then she died.
Last words, as quoted in D Sutherland *Gertrude Stein* (1951), ch.6.

27 She said he was a village explainer, excellent if you were a village, but if you were not, not.
Of Ezra Pound. Quoted in J Hobhouse *Everyone Who Was Anybody* (1975), ch.6.

Stein, Herbert 1916–99

US economist, member of the Council of Economic Advisers under Nixon, Ford and Reagan.

28 *Consumer*: A person who is capable of choosing a president but incapable of choosing a bicycle without help from a government agency.
1979 *Washington Bedtime Stories*.

29 Whatever may be the distribution of uncertainty among economists, the public only gets to hear from those who have certain opinions.
1979 *Washington Bedtime Stories*.

30 A few weeks ago I had a revelation and told my secretary that I could give him a synthesis of forty-six years of living with economic policy. It is: 'Economic policy is random with respect to the performance of the American economy, but, thank God, there isn't much of it.'
1979 *Washington Bedtime Stories*.

Steinbeck, John Ernest 1902–68

US novelist. His works include *Of Mice and Men* (1937), *The Grapes of Wrath* (1939) and *East of Eden* (1952). He received the Nobel prize for literature in 1962.

31 Man, unlike any other thing organic or inorganic in the universe, grows beyond his work, walks up the stairs of his concepts, emerges ahead of his accomplishments.
1939 *The Grapes of Wrath*, ch.14.

32 I know this—a man got to do what he got to do.
1939 *The Grapes of Wrath*, ch.18.

33 Okie use' ta mean you was from Oklahoma. Now it means you're a dirty son-of-a-bitch. Okie means you're scum. Don' mean nothing itself, it's the way they say it.
1939 *The Grapes of Wrath*, ch.18.

34 Well, maybe like Casy says, a fellow ain't got a soul of his own, but on'y a piece of a big one—an then—… Then it don' matter. Then I'll be all aroun' in the dark. I'll be everywhere—wherever you look. Wherever they's a fight so hungry people can eat, I'll be there. Wherever they's a cop beatin' up a guy, I'll be there. If Casy knowed, why, I'll be in the way guys yell when they're mad an'—I'll be in the way kids laugh when they're hungry an' they know supper's ready. An' when our folks eat the stuff they raise an' live in the houses they build—why, I'll be there. See?
1939 *The Grapes of Wrath*, ch.28.

35 All Americans believe that they are born fishermen. For a man to admit a distaste for fishing would be like denouncing mother-love or hating moonlight.
1954 Quoted in Colin Jarman *The Guinness Dictionary of Sports Quotations* (1990).

36 Unless the bastards have the courage to give you unqualified praise, I say ignore them.

1958 Of critics. Quoted in J K Galbraith *The Affluent Society* (1977), introduction.

37 I pulled to the side of the street and got out my book of road maps. But to find where you are going, you must know where you are, and I didn't.
1962 *Travels With Charley In Search of America.*

38 A journey is like a marriage. The certain way to be wrong is to think you control it.
1962 *Travels With Charley In Search of America*, pt.1.

39 It is the nature of a man as he grows older, a small bridge in time, to protest against change, particularly change for the better.
1962 *Travels With Charley In Search of America*, pt.2.

40 The profession of book writing makes horse racing seem like a solid, stable business.
1962 In *Newsweek*, 24 Dec.

41 A good writer always works at the impossible.
Recalled on his death, 20 Dec 1968.

Steinem, Gloria 1934–

US feminist and writer. She emerged as a leading figure in the women's movement in the 1960s, and as a campaigner against the Vietnam War and racism. She co-founded the Women's Action Alliance (1970) and *Ms* magazine (1971).

42 A woman needs a man like a fish needs a bicycle.
c.1970 Attributed, in various forms.

43 This is what forty looks like. We've been lying so long who would know?
c.1974 Response when complimented by a reporter on not looking forty years old, quoted by Lisa Jardine in 'Still Angry After All These Years', in the *Sunday Times*, 15 May 1994.

44 What would happen if…men could menstruate and women could not? Clearly, menstruation would become an enviable, boast-worthy, masculine event: Men would brag about how long and how much. Young boys would talk about it as the envied beginning of manhood… Generals, right-wing politicians, and religious fundamentalists would cite …'mens'-truation' as proof that only men could serve God and country in combat… If men could menstruate, the power justifications would go on and on. If we let them.
1978 'If Men could Menstruate', collected in *Outrageous Acts and Everyday Rebellions* (1983).

45 I've finally figured out why soap operas are, and logically should be, so popular with generations of housebound women. *They are the only place in our culture where grown-up men take seriously all the things that grown-up women have to deal with all day long.*
1980 'Night Thoughts of a Media Watcher', collected in *Outrageous Acts and Everyday Rebellions* (1983).

Steiner, George 1929–

French-born US literary critic and scholar.

46 Where God's presence is no longer a tenable proposition and where his absence is no longer a felt, indeed overwhelming weight, certain dimensions of thought and creativity are no longer attainable.
1989 *Real Presences.*

Steinmetz, Charles Proteus 1865–1923

German-born US electrical engineer and inventor, whose most notable work was the development of alternating current.

47 In the realm of science, all attempts to find any evidence of supernatural beings, of metaphysical concepts, as God, immortality, infinity, etc have thus far failed, and if we are honest, we must confess that in science there exists no God, no immortality, no soul or mind, as distinct from the body.
1941 In the *American Freeman*, Jul.

Steloff, Frances 1887–1989

US bookseller. She worked at Loeser's Department Store, New York City, then at Bretanos where she ran the drama department (1917–19). She founded Gotham Book Mart, New York City, in 1920.

48 Wise men fish here.
Sign for Gotham Book Mart. Quoted in the *New York Times*, 30 Dec 1987.

Stendhal *pseudonym of* *Henri Beyle* 1783–1842

French writer who lived many years in Italy, he wrote novels and treatises on literature. He held a modernist concept of Romanticism and was opposed to those who sought literary models from the past.

49 *L'esprit et le génie perdent vingt-cinq pour cent de leur valeur, en débarquant en Angleterre.*
The mind and genius lose twenty-five percent of their value on entry into England.
1830 *Le Rouge et le noir*, bk.2, ch.7.

50 *La politique au milieu des intérêts d'imagination, c'est un coup de pistolet au milieu d'un concert.*
Politics mixed with the imagination is like a shot fired in the middle of a concert.
1830 *Le Rouge et le noir*, bk.2, ch.22.

51 *Grand Dieu! Pourquoi suis-je moi?*
Great God! Why am I me?
1830 *Le Rouge et le noir*, bk.2, ch.28.

52 *Le pire des malheurs en prison, pensa-t-il, c'est de ne pouvoir fermer sa porte.*
The worst of prison life, he thought, was not being able to close his door.
1830 *Le Rouge et le noir*, bk.2, ch.44.

53 *Les gens qu'on honore ne sont que des fripons qui ont eu le bonheur de n'être pas pris en flagrant délit.*
Respected people are only rascals who have had the good fortune not to be caught in the act.
1830 *Le Rouge et le noir*, bk.2, ch.44.

Stengel, Casey (Charles Dillon) 1890–1975

US baseball player and manager. An outfielder with the Brooklyn Dodgers and other teams, he became manager of the New York Yankees (1949–62), leading them to seven World Series victories, and of the New York Mets (1962–5).

54 The secret of managing a ball club is to keep the five guys who hate you away from the five who are undecided.
Quoted in Colin Jarman *The Guinness Dictionary of Sports Quotations* (1990).

55 There's three things you can do in a baseball game – you can win, you can lose, or it can rain.
Quoted in Colin Jarman *The Guinness Dictionary of Sports Quotations* (1990).

56 Without losers, where would the winners be?

> Quoted in Colin Jarman *The Guinness Dictionary of Sports Quotations* (1990).

57 Not bad. Most people my age are dead. You could look it up.

> Attributed, when asked how he was. 'You could look it up' was one of his catchphrases.

Stephen, J(ames) K(enneth) 1859–92

English lawyer and journalist, a cousin of Virginia Woolf. He began a weekly paper, *The Reflector* in 1888 and was a successful parodist and light versifier.

58 Two voices are there: one is of the deep;
It learns the storm-clouds thundrous melody,
Now roars, now murmurs with the changing sea,
Now bird-like pipes, now closes soft in sleep:
And one is of an old half-witted sheep
Which bleats articulate monotony,
And indicates that two and one are three,
That grass is green, lakes damp, and mountains steep
And, Wordsworth, both are thine.

> **1896** *Lapsus Calami*, 'A Sonnet'.

59 Will there never come a season
Which shall rid us of the curse
Of a prose which knows no reason
And an unmelodious verse…
When there stands a muzzled stripling,
Mute, beside a muzzled bore:
When the Rudyards cease from kipling
And the Haggards Ride no more.

> 'To R K'.

Stephenson, Bette 1924–

Former President of the Canadian Medical Association and Ontario Minister of Health.

60 Men are very fragile creatures. Their psyches are so closely tied to their epididymis.

> **1975** Interviewed by Christina McCall Newman in *The Globe and Mail*, 12 Jul. The epididymis is the tube carrying sperm out from the testicle.

Sterling, Bruce 1954–

US science fiction writer.

61 Unfortunately, computers are…stupid. Unlike human beings, computers possess the truly profound stupidity of the inanimate.

> **1992** *The Hacker Crackdown: law and disorder on the electronic frontier*.

62 It's a truism in technological development that no silver lining comes without its cloud.

> **1993** Opening statement to the House Subcommittee on Telecommunications and Finance, Washington DC, 29 Apr.

63 Cyberspace is the funhouse mirror of our own society.

> **1993** National Academy of Sciences Convocation on Technology and Education, Washington DC, 10 May.

Sterling, Rod

64 Every writer is a frustrated actor who recites his lines in the hidden auditorium of his skull.

> **1957** In *Vogue*, 1 Apr.

Stern, Robert A(rthur) M(orton) 1939–

US architect and writer, author of *New Directions in American Architecture* (1969, revised 1977) and *The House that Bob Built* (1991).

65 The dialogue between client and architect is about as intimate as any conversation you can have because, when you're talking about building a house, you're talking about dreams.

> **1985** 'The Trend-Setting Traditionalism of Architecture', in the *New York Times*, 13 Jan.

66 Our greatest responsibility is not to be pencils of the past.

> **1985** 'The Trend-Setting Traditionalism of Architecture', in the *New York Times*, 13 Jan.

Sterne, Laurence 1713–68

Irish novelist. He extended the scope of the novel with his major work *Tristram Shandy* (1759–67). As his health failed, he spent much of his time in France and Italy and published *A Sentimental Journey through France and Italy* in 1768.

67 I wish either my father or my mother, or indeed both of them, as they were in duty both equally bound to it, had minded what they were about when they begot me.

> **1759–67** *Tristram Shandy*, bk.1, ch.1.

68 'Pray, my dear,' quoth my mother, 'have you not forgot to wind up the clock?'—'Good G—?' cried my father, making an exclamation, but taking care to moderate his voice at the same time,—'Did ever woman, since the creation of the world, interrupt a man with such a silly question?'

> **1759—67** *Tristram Shandy*, bk.1, ch.6.

69 As we jog on, either laugh with me, or at me, or in short do anything,—only keep your temper.

> **1759–67** Tristram to reader. *Tristram Shandy*, bk.1, ch.6.

70 Have not the wisest of men in all ages, not excepting Solomon himself,—have they not had their Hobby-Horses…and so long as a man rides his Hobby-Horse peaceably and quietly along the King's highway, and neither compels you or me to get up behind him,—pray, Sir, what have either you or I to do with it?

> **1759–67** *Tristram Shandy*, bk.1, ch.7.

71 He was in a few hours of giving his enemies the slip for ever.

> **1759–67** Of Eugenis. *Tristram Shandy*, bk.1, ch.12.

72 'Tis known by the name of perseverance in a good cause,—and of obstinacy in a bad one.

> **1759–67** Toby. *Tristram Shandy*, bk.1, ch.17.

73 What is the character of a family to an hypothesis? my father would reply.

> **1759–67** *Tristram Shandy*, bk.1, ch.21.

74 My uncle Toby would never offer to answer this by any other kind of argument, than that of whistling half a dozen bars of Lillabullero.

> **1759–67** *Tristram Shandy*, bk.1, ch.21.

75 Digressions, incontestably, are the sunshine;—they are the life, the soul of reading;—take them out of this book for instance,—you might as well take the book along with them.

> **1759–67** *Tristram Shandy*, bk.1, ch.22.

76 I should have no objection to this method, but that I think

it must smell too strong of the lamp.
1759–67 Toby. *Tristram Shandy*, bk.1, ch.23.

77 Writing, when properly managed (as you may be sure I think mine is) is but a different name for conversation.
1759–67 *Tristram Shandy*, bk.2, ch.11.

78 'I'll not hurt thee,' says my uncle Toby, rising from his chair, and going across the room, with the fly in his hand, 'I'll not hurt a hair of thy head:—Go,' says he, lifting up the sash, and opening his hand as he spoke, to let it escape;—'go, poor devil, get thee gone, why should I hurt thee?—This world surely is wide enough to hold both thee and me.'
1759–67 *Tristram Shandy*, bk.2, ch.12.

79 Whenever a man talks loudly against religion,—always suspect that it is not his reason, but his passions which have got the better of his creed.
1759–67 Trim. *Tristram Shandy*, bk.2, ch.17.

80 It is the nature of an hypothesis, when once a man has conceived it, that it assimilates everything to itself, as proper nourishment; and, from the first moment of your begetting it, it generally grows the stronger by every thing you see, hear, read, or understand.
1759–67 *Tristram Shandy*, bk.2, ch.19.

81 'Our armies swore terribly in Flanders,' cried my uncle Toby,—'but nothing to this.'
1759–67 *Tristram Shandy*, bk.3, ch.11.

82 The corregiescity of Corregio.
1759–67 *Tristram Shandy*, bk.3, ch.12.

83 Of all the cants which are canted in this canting world,—though the cant of hypocrites may be the worst,—the cant of criticism is the most tormenting.
1759–67 *Tristram Shandy*, bk.3, ch.12.

84 Is this a fit time, said my father to himself, to talk of Pensions and Grenadiers?
1759–67 *Tristram Shandy*, bk.4, ch.5.

85 True *Shandeism*, think what you will against it, opens the heart and lungs, and like all those affections which partake of its nature, it forces the blood and other vital fluids of the body to run freely through its channels, and makes the wheel of life run long and cheerfully round.
1759–67 *Tristram Shandy*, bk.4, ch.32.

86 'There is no terror, brother Toby, in its looks, but what it borrows from groans and convulsions—and the blowing of noses, and the wiping away of tears with the bottoms of curtains, in a dying man's room—Strip it of these, what is it?'—'Tis better in battle than in bed,' said my uncle Toby.
1759–67 Of death. *Tristram Shandy*, bk.5, ch.3.

87 There is a North-west passage to the intellectual World.
1759–67 *Tristram Shandy*, bk.5, ch.42.

88 To say a man is fallen in love,—or that he is deeply in love,—or up to the ears in love,—and sometimes even over head and ears in it,—carries an idiomatical kind of implication, that love is a thing below a man:—this is recurring again to Plato's opinion, which, with all his divinityship,—I hold to be damnable and heretical:—and so much for that. Let love therefore be what it will,—my uncle Toby fell into it.
1759–67 *Tristram Shandy*, bk.6, ch.37.

89 My brother Toby, quoth she, is going to be married to Mrs

Wadman. Then he will never, quoth my father, lie *diagonally* in his bed again as long as he lives.
1759–67 *Tristram Shandy*, bk.6, ch.39.

90 Now hang it! quoth I, as I look'd towards the French coast—a man should know something of his own country too, before he goes abroad.
1759–67 Tristram. *Tristram Shandy*, bk.7, ch.2.

91 And who are you? Said he.—Don't puzzle me, said I.
1759–67 Tristram to the commissary. *Tristram Shandy*, bk.7, ch.33.

92 'A soldier,' cried my uncle Toby, interrupting the corporal, 'is no more exempt from saying a foolish thing, Trim, than a man of letters.'—'But not so often, an' please your honour,' replied the corporal.
1759–67 *Tristram Shandy*, bk.8, ch.19.

93 Everything presses on—whilst thou art twisting that lock,—see! It grows grey; and every time I kiss thy hand to bid adieu, and every absence which follows it, are preludes to that eternal separation which we are shortly to make.
1759–67 Tristram to Jenny. *Tristram Shandy*, bk.9, ch.8.

94 '—d!' said my mother, 'what is all this story about?'—'A Cock and a Bull,' said Yorick.
1759–67 *Tristram Shandy*, bk.9, ch.33.

95 A man cannot dress, but his ideas get cloath'd at the same time.
1759–67 *Tristram Shandy*, bk.9, ch.13.

96 This sad vicissitude of things.
1767 *Sermons*, 'The Character of Shimei', no.16.

97 They order, said I, this matter better in France.
1768 *A Sentimental Journey*, opening words.

98 As an Englishman does not travel to see Englishmen, I retired to my room.
1768 *A Sentimental Journey*, 'Preface. In the Desobligeant'.

99 I pity the man who can travel from Dan to Beersheba, and cry, 'tis all barren.
1768 *A Sentimental Journey*, 'In the Street. Calais'.

1 I had had an affair with the moon, in which there was neither sin nor shame.
1768 *A Sentimental Journey*, 'The Monk, Calais'.

2 If ever I do a mean action, it must be in some interval betwixt one passion and another.
1768 *A Sentimental Journey*, 'Montriul'.

3 Vive l'amour! Et vive la bagatelle!
1768 *A Sentimental Journey*, 'The Latter'.

4 Hail, ye small sweet courtesies of life.
1768 *A Sentimental Journey*, 'The Pulse, Paris'.

5 There are worse occupations in this world than feeling a woman's pulse.
1768 *A Sentimental Journey*, 'The Pulse, Paris'.

6 God tempers the wind, said Maria, to the shorn lamb.
1768 *A Sentimental Journey*, 'Maria'. This is an allusion to an old French proverb.

7 Dear sensibility! Source inexhausted of all that's precious in our joys, or costly in our sorrows!
1768 *A Sentimental Journey*, 'The Bourbonnois'.

Steuart (later Denham), Sir James 1712–80

Scottish advocate and economist. A fervent Jacobite who was a member of the Council of Prince Charles Edward Stuart in 1745 and subsequently in exile until 1763, travelling extensively on the Continent and studying political economy. His *Principles of Political Oeconomy* (1767) was soon eclipsed by the *Wealth of Nations* of Adam Smith.

8 To preserve a trading state from decline, the greatest care must be taken, to support a perfect balance between the hands employed in work and the demand for their labour.
1767 *Inquiry into the Principles of Political Oeconomy.*

9 It is the business of a statesman to judge of the expediency of different schemes of economy, and by degrees to model the minds of his subjects so as to induce them from the allurement of private interest to concur in the execution of his plan.
1767 *Inquiry into the Principles of Political Oeconomy.*

Stevens, Brooks 1911–95

US industrial designer.

10 Our whole economy is based on planned obsolescence… We make good products, we induce people to buy them, and then the next year we deliberately introduce something that will make these products old-fashioned, out of date, obsolete.
Quoted in Vance Packard *The Waste Makers* (1960), ch.6. This is thought to be the first use of the phrase 'planned obsolescence'.

Stevens, Roger Lacey 1910–98

US theatrical producer. He worked as a real estate broker (1934–60) but was increasingly involved as a producer in over 200 theatrical productions. He was Chair of the National Council on the Arts (1965–9), and a member of the President's Committee on Arts and Humanities.

11 Whenever I think, I make a mistake.
1955 In 'How Businessmen Make Decisions', *Fortune*, Aug.

Stevens, Wallace 1879–1955

US poet. He began as a journalist and lawyer, then joined an insurance company. *Harmonium*, his first collection of philosophical verse, appeared in 1923. Further works include *The Man with the Blue Guitar* (1937) and *Collected Poems* (1954, winner of a Pulitzer Prize).

12 I placed a jar in Tennessee,
And round it was, upon a hill.
It made the slovenly wilderness
Surround that hill.
1923 *Harmonium*, 'Anecdote of the Jar'.

13 Poetry is the supreme fiction, madame.
Take the moral law and make a nave of it
And from the nave build haunted heaven.
1923 *Harmonium*, 'A High-Toned Old Christian Woman'.

14 Call the roller of big cigars,
The muscular one, and bid him whip
In kitchen cups of concupiscent curds.
1923 *Harmonium*, 'The Emperor of Ice-Cream'.

15 The only emperor is the emperor of ice-cream.
1923 *Harmonium*, 'The Emperor of Ice-Cream'.

16 I shall whisper
Heavenly labials in a world of gutterals.
It will undo him.
1923 *Harmonium*, 'The Plot Against the Giant'.

17 Complacencies of the peignoir, and late

Coffee and oranges in a sunny chair,
And the green freedom of a cockatoo
Upon a rug mingle to dissipate
The holy hush of ancient sacrifice.
1923 *Harmonium*, 'Sunday Morning', pt.1.

18 What is divinity if it can come
Only in silent shadows and in dreams?
1923 *Harmonium*, 'Sunday Morning', pt.2.

19 And, in the isolation of the sky,
At evening, casual flocks of pigeons make
Ambiguous undulations as they sink,
Downward to darkness, on extended wings.
1923 *Harmonium*, 'Sunday Morning', pt.8.

20 Chieftain Iffucan of Azcan in caftan
Of tan with henna hackles, halt!
1923 *Harmonium*, 'Bantams in Pine-Woods'.

21 Just as my fingers on these keys
Make music, so the self-same sounds
On my spirit make a music, too.

Music is feeling, then, not a sound;
And thus it is that what I feel,
Here in this room, desiring you,

Thinking of your blue-shadowed silk,
Is music.
1923 *Harmonium*, 'Peter Quince at the Clavier', pt.1.

22 I do not know which to prefer,
The beauty of inflections
Or the beauty of innuendoes,
The blackbird whistling
or just after.
1923 *Harmonium*, 'Thirteen Ways of Looking At A Blackbird', pt.5.

23 I know noble accents
And lucid, inescapable rhythms;
But I know, too,
That the blackbird is involved
In what I know.
1923 *Harmonium*, 'Thirteen Ways of Looking At A Blackbird', pt.8.

24 What counted was the mythology of self,
Blotched out beyond unblotching.
1923 *Harmonium*, 'The Comedian as the Letter C', pt.1.

25 Like a dull scholar, I behold, in love,
An ancient aspect touching a new mind.
It comes, it blooms, it bears its fruit and dies.
This trivial trope reveals a way of truth.
Our bloom is gone. We are the fruit thereof.
1923 *Harmonium*, 'Le Monocle de Mon Oncle', pt.8.

26 Only, here and there, an old sailor,
Drunk and asleep in his boots,
Catches tigers
In red weather.
1923 *Harmonium*, 'Disillusionment of Ten O'Clock'.

27 It was her voice that made
The sky acutest at its vanishing.
She measured to the hour its solitude.
She was the single artificer of the world
In which she sang.
1935 *Ideas of Order*, 'The Idea of Order at Key West'.

28 They said, 'You have a blue guitar,
You do not play things as they are.'

The man replied, 'Things as they are
Are changed upon a blue guitar.'
1937 *The Man with the Blue Guitar and Other Poems*, title poem.

29 It has to be living, to learn the speech of the place,
It has to face the man of the time.
1942 *Parts of a World*, 'Of Modern Poetry'.

30 The first idea was not our own.
1942 *Notes Toward A Supreme Fiction*, 'It Must Be Abstract'.

31 There was a muddy centre before we breathed
There was a myth before the myth began,
Venerable and articulate and complete.
1942 *Notes Toward A Supreme Fiction*, 'It Must Be Abstract'.

32 They will get it straight one day at the Sorbonne.
We shall return at twilight from the lecture
Pleased that the irrational is rational.
1942 *Notes Toward A Supreme Fiction*, 'It Must Give Pleasure'.

33 Not evocations but last choirs, last sounds,
With nothing else compounded, carried full,
Pure rhetoric of a language without words.
1947 *Transport to Summer*, 'Credences of Summer'.

34 Sentimentality is a failure of feeling.
1957 *Opus Posthumous*, Aphorisms, 'Adagia'.

35 Poetry is a means of redemption.
1957 *Opus Posthumous*, Aphorisms, 'Adagia'.

36 Literature is based not on life but on propositions about
life, of which this is one.
1957 *Opus Posthumous*, Aphorisms, 'Adagia'.

37 Poetry must resist the intelligence almost successfully.
1957 *Opus Posthumous*, Aphorisms, 'Adagia'.

38 All poetry is experimental poetry.
1957 *Opus Posthumous*, Aphorisms, 'Adagia'.

39 Ethics are no more a part of poetry than they are of
painting.
1957 *Opus Posthumous*, Aphorisms, 'Adagia'.

40 The poet makes silk dresses out of worms.
1957 *Opus Posthumous*, Aphorisms, 'Adagia'.

41 After one has abandoned a belief in God, poetry is the
essence which takes its place as life's redemption.
1957 *Opus Posthumous*, Aphorisms, 'Adagia'.

42 Authors are actors, books are theatres.
1957 *Opus Posthumous*, Aphorisms, 'Adagia'.

43 The poet represents the mind in the act of defending us
against itself.
1957 *Opus Posthumous*, Aphorisms, 'Adagia'.

44 Poetry is a rich, full-blooded whistle, cracked ice
crunching in pails, the night that numbers the leaf, the
duet of two nightingales, the sweet pea, that has run
wild, Creation's tears in shoulder blades.
Quoted in *Life*, 13 Jun 1960.

45 Money is a kind of poetry.
Quoted in *Harper's*, Oct 1985.

46 Words of the world are the life of the world.
Quoted in Brendan Gill *A New York Life* (1990).

47 Poetry is the supreme fiction, madame.
Quoted in Helen Gardner (ed) *The New Oxford Book of English
Verse* (1991).

Stevenson, Adlai E(wing) 1900–65

US Democratic politician, Governor of Illinois (1948). He helped

to found the United Nations (1946), stood twice against
Eisenhower as presidential candidate (1952, 1956), and was
the US Delegate to the UN (1961–5).

48 A lie is an abomination unto the Lord, and a very present
help when in trouble.
1951 Speech, Washington, Jan.

49 It is often easier to fight for principles than to live up to
them.
1952 Speech, New York, 27 Aug.

50 If Republicans will stop telling lies about the United
States, we will stop telling the truth about them.
1952 Speech at Bakersfield, California. Quoted in *Time*, 10 Sep.

51 Looking back, I am content. Win or lose I have told you
the truth as I see it. I have said what I meant and meant
what I said.
1952 Concluding his campaign. Reported in *Time*, 10 Sep.

52 Man has wrested from nature the power to make the
world a desert or to make the deserts bloom. There is no
evil in the atom—only in men's souls.
1952 Speech, Connecticut, 18 Sep.

53 When political ammunition runs low, inevitably the rusty
artillery of abuse is wheeled into action.
1952 Speech, New York, 22 Sep.

54 My definition of a free society is a society in which it is
safe to be unpopular.
1952 Speech, Detroit, Oct.

55 Eggheads of the world unite; you have nothing to lose
but your yolks.
1952 Presidential election campaign speech.

56 Via ovum cranium difficilis est. The way of the egghead is
hard.
1954 Reply to charges that he was too intellectual. Lecture at
Harvard, 17 Mar.

57 Shouting is not a substitute for thinking and reason is not
the subversion but the salvation of freedom.
1954 Lecture at Harvard, 17 Mar.

58 Technology, while adding daily to our physical ease,
throws daily another loop of fine wire around our souls.
It contributes hugely to our mobility, which we must not
confuse with freedom. The extensions of our senses,
which we find so fascinating, are not adding to the
discrimination of our minds, since we need increasingly
to take the reading of a needle on a dial to discover
whether we think something is good or bad, or right or
wrong.
1955 'My Faith in Democratic Capitalism', in *Fortune*, Oct.

59 You will find that the truth is often unpopular and the
contest between agreeable fancy and disagreeable fact
is unequal. For, in the vernacular, we Americans are
suckers for good news.
1958 Speech, Michigan, 8 Jun.

60 Freedom is not an ideal; it is not even a protection, if it
means nothing more than the freedom to stagnate.
1960 *Putting First Things First*.

61 We have confused the free with the free and easy.
1960 *Putting First Things First*.

62 The Republican Party needs to be dragged kicking and
screaming into the 20th century.
Quoted in Kenneth Tynan *Curtains* (1961).

63 It will be helpful in our mutual objective to allow every

man in America to look his neighbour in the face and see a man—not a colour.
1964 In the *New York Times*, 22 Jun.

64 He who slings mud generally loses ground.
Recalled on his death, 14 Jul 1965.

65 You can't teach an underdog new tricks.
On presidential hopeful Estes Kefauver's replay of his anti-bossism theme. Quoted in *Newsweek*, 1 Nov 1971.

66 The best politics is good government.
Quoted by New York Governor Mario Cuomo in the *New York Times*, 26 Aug 1990.

67 A politician is a statesman who approaches every question with an open mouth.
Attributed.

68 He is the kind of politician who would cut down a redwood tree and then mount the stump to make a speech for conservation.
On Richard M Nixon. Attributed.

69 In America, any boy may become president. I suppose that's just one of the risks that he takes.
Attributed.

Stevenson, Robert Louis 1850–94

Scottish author. He wrote travel sketches, essays, short stories, serials and romantic thrillers, including *Treasure Island* (1883), *The Strange Case of Dr Jekyll and Mr Hyde* (1886) and *Kidnapped* (1886). In his early years he toured Belgium and northern France by canoe and the Cévennes by donkey, described in *Travels with a Donkey in the Cévennes* (1879). He struggled for many years against tuberculosis and spent the last five years of his life living on his estate in Samoa.

70 For will anyone dare to tell me that business is more entertaining than fooling among boats? He must have never seen a boat, or never seen an office, who says so. And for certain the one is a great deal better for the health.
1878 *An Inland Voyage*, 'The Royal Sport Nautique'.

71 Respectability is a very good thing in its way, but it does not rise superior to all considerations. I would not for a moment venture to hint that it was a matter of taste; but I think I will go as far as this: that if a position is admittedly unkind, uncomfortable, unnecessary, and superfluously useless, although it were as respectable as the Church of England, the sooner a man is out of it, the better for himself, and all concerned.
1878 *An Inland Voyage*, 'At Maubeuge'.

72 The gauger walked with willing foot,
And aye the gauger played the flute;
And what should Master Gauger play
But *Over the hills and far away?*
1878 'A Song of the Road', stanza 1 (dated 'Forest of Montargis, 1878'), collected in *Underwoods* (1887), bk.1, no.2.

73 If a man knows he will sooner or later be robbed upon a journey, he will have a bottle of the best in every inn, and look upon all his extravagances as so much gained upon the thieves.
1878 *An Inland Voyage*, 'The Oise in Flood'.

74 The most patient people grow weary at last with being continually wetted with rain; except, of course, in the Scottish Highlands, where there are not enough fine intervals to point the difference.
1878 *An Inland Voyage*, 'Down the Oise: to Compiègne'.

75 For my part, I travel not to go anywhere, but to go. I travel for travel's sake. The great affair is to move.
1879 *Travels with a Donkey*, 'Cheylard and Luc'.

76 I opened a tin of Bologna sausage and broke a cake of chocolate, and that was all I had to eat. It may sound offensive, but I ate them together, bite by bite, by way of bread and meat. All I had to wash down this revolting mixture was neat brandy; a revolting beverage in itself. But I was rare and hungry; ate well, and smoked one of the best cigarettes in my experience. Then I put a stone in my straw hat, pulled the flap of my fur cap over my neck and eyes, put my revolver ready to hand, and snuggled well down among the sheepskins.
1879 *Travels with a Donkey*.

77 I own I like definite form in what my eyes are to rest upon; and if landscapes were sold, like the sheets of characters of my boyhood, one penny plain and twopence coloured, I should go the length of twopence every day of my life.
1879 *Travels with a Donkey*, 'Father Apollinaris'.

78 To live out of doors with the woman a man loves is of all lives the most complete and free.
1879 *Travels with a Donkey*, 'A Night Among the Pines'.

79 The fact is, we are much more afraid of life than our ancestors, and cannot find it in our hearts either to marry or not to marry. Marriage is terrifying, but so is a cold and forlorn old age.
1881 *Virginibus Puerisque*, 'Virginibus Puerisque', pt.1.

80 In marriage, a man becomes slack and selfish, and undergoes a fatty degeneration of his moral being.
1881 *Virginibus Puerisque*, 'Virginibus Puerisque', pt.1.

81 I see women marry indiscriminately with staring burgesses and ferret-faced, white-eyed boys, and men dwell in contentment with noisy scullions, or taking into their lives acidulous vestals.
1881 *Virginibus Puerisque*, 'Virginibus Puerisque', pt.1.

82 And you have only to look these happy couples in the face, to see they have never been in love, or in hate, or in any other high passion all their days.
1881 *Virginibus Puerisque*, 'Virginibus Puerisque', pt.1.

83 Even if we take marriage at its lowest, even if we regard it as no more than a sort of friendship recognised by the police.
1881 *Virginibus Puerisque*, 'Virginibus Puerisque', pt.1.

84 Lastly (and this is, perhaps, the golden rule) no woman should marry a teetotaller, or a man who does not smoke.
1881 *Virginibus Puerisque*, 'Virginibus Puerisque', pt.1.

85 Marriage is a step so grave and decisive that it attracts light-headed, variable men by its very awfulness.
1881 *Virginibus Puerisque*, 'Virginibus Puerisque', pt.1.

86 Marriage is like life in this—that it is a field of battle, and not a bed of roses.
1881 *Virginibus Puerisque*, 'Virginibus Puerisque', pt.1.

87 Times are changed with him who marries; there are no more by-path meadows, where you may innocently linger, but the road lies long and straight and dusty to the grave. Idleness, which is often becoming and even wise in the bachelor, begins to wear a different aspect when

you have a wife to support.
1881 *Virginibus Puerisque*, 'Virginibus Puerisque', pt.2.

88 To marry is to domesticate the Recording Angel. Once you are married, there is nothing left for you, not even suicide, but to be good.
1881 *Virginibus Puerisque*, 'Virginibus Puerisque', pt.2.

89 Man is a creature who lives not upon bread alone, but principally by catchwords.
1881 *Virginibus Puerisque*, 'Virginibus Puerisque', pt.2.

90 The cruellest lies are often told in silence.
1881 *Virginibus Puerisque*, 'Truth of Intercourse'.

91 Most of our pocket wisdom is conceived for the use of mediocre people, to discourage them from ambitious attempts, and generally console them in their mediocrity.
1881 *Virginibus Puerisque*, 'Crabbed Age and Youth'.

92 Old and young, we are all on our last cruise.
1881 *Virginibus Puerisque*, 'Crabbed Age and Youth'.

93 It is better to be a fool than to be dead.
1881 *Virginibus Puerisque*, 'Crabbed Age and Youth'.

94 For God's sake give me the young man who has brains enough to make a fool of himself!
1881 *Virginibus Puerisque*, 'Crabbed Age and Youth'.

95 To travel hopefully is a better thing than to arrive, and the true success is to labour.
1881 *Virginibus Puerisque*, 'El Dorado'.

96 Books are good enough in their own way, but they are a mighty bloodless substitute for life.
1881 *Virginibus Puerisque*, 'An Apology for Idlers'.

97 Extreme *busyness*, whether at school or college, kirk or market, is a symptom of a deficient vitality; and a faculty for idleness implies a catholic appetite and a strong sense of personal identity.
1881 *Virginibus Puerisque*, 'An Apology for Idlers'.

98 There is no duty we so much underrate as the duty of being happy.
1881 *Virginibus Puerisque*, 'An Apology for Idlers'.

99 We live the time that a match flickers; we pop the cork of a ginger-beer bottle, and the earthquake swallows us on the instant. Is it not odd, is it not incongruous, is it not, in the highest sense of human speech, incredible, that we should think so highly of the ginger-beer, and regard so little the devouring earthquake?
1881 *Virginibus Puerisque*, 'Aes Triplex'.

1 Think of the heroism of Johnson, think of that superb indifference to mortal limitation that set him upon his dictionary, and carried him through triumphantly until the end! Who, if he were wisely considerate of things at large, would ever embark upon any work much more considerable than a halfpenny post-card? Who would project a serial novel, after Thackeray and Dickens had each fallen in mid-course? Who would find heart enough to begin to live, if he dallied with the consideration of death?
1881 *Virginibus Puerisque*, 'Aes Triplex'.

2 Even if the doctor does not give you a year, even if he hesitates about a month, make one brave push and see what can be accomplished in a week.
1881 *Virginibus Puerisque*, 'Aes Triplex'.

3 Though we are mighty fine fellows nowadays, we cannot write like Hazlitt.
1881 *Virginibus Puerisque*, 'Walking Tours'.

4 We are in such haste to be doing, to be writing, to be gathering gear, to make our voice audible a moment in the derisive silence of eternity, that we forget that one thing, of which these are but the parts—namely, to live.
1881 *Virginibus Puerisque*, 'Walking Tours'.

5 It seems he had no design except to appear respectable, and here he keeps a private book to prove that he was not.
1882 Of Samuel Pepys and his *Diary*. *Familiar Studies of Men and Books*.

6 Politics is perhaps the only profession for which no preparation is thought necessary.
1882 *Familiar Studies of Men and Books*, 'Yoshida-Torajiro'.

7 Fifteen men on a dead man's chest—
Yo-ho-ho, and a bottle of rum!
Drink and the devil had done for the rest—
Yo-ho-ho, and a bottle of rum!
1883 *Treasure Island*, ch.1, 'The Old Sea-Dog at the 'Admiral Benbow''.

8 Pieces of eight!
1883 *Treasure Island*, ch.10, 'The Voyage'.

9 You mightn't happen to have a piece of cheese about you, now? No? Well, many's the long night I've dreamed of cheese—toasted, mostly—and woke up again, and here I were.
1883 Ben Gunn to Jim Hawkins. *Treasure Island*, ch.15, 'The Man of the Island'.

10 Under the wide and starry sky,
Dig the grave and let me lie.
Glad did I live and gladly die,
And I laid me down with a will.

This be the verse you grave for me:
Here he lies where he longed to be,
Home is the sailor, home from sea,
And the hunter home from the hill.
1884 'Requiem' (dated 'Hyères, May 1884'), collected in *Underwoods* (1887), bk.1, no.21.

11 In winter I get up at night
And dress by yellow candle-light.
In summer, quite the other way,
I have to go to bed by day.

I have to go to bed and see
The birds still hopping on the tree,
Or hear the grown-up people's feet
Still going past me in the street.
1885 *A Child's Garden of Verses*, no.1, 'Bed in Summer', stanzas 1–2.

12 A child should always say what's true,
And speak when he is spoken to,
And behave mannerly at table:
At least as far as he is able.
1885 *A Child's Garden of Verses*, no.5, 'Whole Duty of Children'.

13 Whenever the moon and stars are set,
Whenever the wind is high,
All night long in the dark and wet,
A man goes riding by.
Late in the night when the fires are out,
Why does he gallop and gallop about?
1885 *A Child's Garden of Verses*, no.9, 'Windy Nights', stanza 1.

14 When I am grown to man's estate
I shall be very proud and great,
And tell the other girls and boys
Not to meddle with my toys.
1885 *A Child's Garden of Verses*, no.12, 'Looking Forward'.

15 Whenever Auntie moves around,
Her dresses make a curious sound;
They trail behind her up the floor,
And trundle after through the door.
1885 *A Child's Garden of Verses*, no.15, 'Auntie's Skirts'.

16 When I was sick and lay a-bed,
I had two pillows at my head,
And all my toys beside me lay
To keep me happy all the day.
1885 *A Child's Garden of Verses*, no.16, 'The Land of Counterpane',
stanza 1.

17 I have a little shadow that goes in and out with me,
And what can be the use of him is more than I can see.
1885 *A Child's Garden of Verses*, no.18, 'My Shadow', stanza 1.

18 The world is so full of a number of things,
I'm sure we should all be as happy as kings.
1885 *A Child's Garden of Verses*, no.24, 'Happy Thought'.

19 Children, you are very little,
And your bones are very brittle;
If you would grow great and stately,
You must try to walk sedately.
1885 *A Child's Garden of Verses*, no.27, 'Good and Bad Children',
stanza 1.

20 My tea is nearly ready and the sun has left the sky;
It's time to take the window to see Leerie going by;
For every night at tea-time and before you take your seat,
With lantern and with ladder he comes posting up the
street.
1885 *A Child's Garden of Verses*, no.30, 'The Lamplighter',
stanza 1.

21 Must we to bed indeed? Well then,
Let us arise and go like men,
And face with an undaunted tread
The long black passage up to bed.
1885 *A Child's Garden of Verses*, XLI, 'North-West Passage', pt.1,
'Good Night', stanza 3.

22 In the Land of Nod at last.
1885 *A Child's Garden of Verses*, XLI, 'North-West Passage', pt.3, 'In
Port', stanza 3.

23 Am I no a bonny fighter?
1886 Alan Breck to David Balfour. *Kidnapped*, ch.10.

24 Even though his tongue acquire the Southern knack, he
will still have a strong Scots accent of the mind.
1887 *Memories and Portraits*, ch.1, 'The Foreigner at Home'.

25 I have thus played the sedulous ape to Hazlitt, to Lamb,
to Wordsworth, to Sir Thomas Browne, to Defoe, to
Hawthorne, to Montaigne, to Baudelaire and to
Obermann.
1887 *Memories and Portraits*, ch.4, 'A College Magazine'.

26 Every one lives by selling something, whatever be his
right to it.
1888 'Beggars', originally published in *Scribner's Magazine*.

27 Here lies one who meant well, tried a little, failed
much:—surely that may be his epitaph, of which he
need not be ashamed.
1892 *Across the Plains*, 'A Christmas Sermon', pt.4.

28 The bright face of danger.
1892 *Across the Plains*, 'The Lantern-Bearers', pt.4.

29 Life is not all Beer and Skittles. The inherent tragedy of
things works itself out from white to black and blacker,
and the poor things of a day look ruefully on. Does it
shake my cast-iron faith? I cannot say it does. I believe in
an ultimate decency of things: ay, and if I woke in hell,
should still believe it!
1893 Letter to Sidney Colvin, 23 Aug.

30 Give to me the life I love,
Let the lave go by me,
Give the jolly heaven above
And the byway nigh me.
Bed in the bush with the stars to see,
Bread I dip in the river—
There's the life for a man like me,
There's the life for ever.
1894 *Songs of Travel* (published 1896), no.1, 'The Vagabond',
stanza 1.

31 Wealth I ask not, hope nor love,
Nor a friend to know me.
All I ask, the heaven above,
And the road below me.
1894 *Songs of Travel* (published 1896), no.1, 'The Vagabond',
stanza 4.

32 I will make you brooches and toys for your delight
Of bird-song at morning and star-shine at night.
I will make a palace fit for you and me
Of green days in forests and blue days at sea.
I will make my kitchen, and you shall keep your room,
Where white flows the river and bright blows the
broom,
And you shall wash your linen and keep your body white
In rainfall at morning and dewfall at night.
1894 *Songs of Travel* (published 1896), no.11, stanza 1.

33 In the highlands, in the country places,
Where the old plain men have rosy faces,
And the young fair maidens
Quiet eyes.
1894 *Songs of Travel* (published 1896), no.16.

34 Trusty, dusky, vivid, true,
With eyes of gold and bramble-dew,
Steel-true and blade-straight,
The great artificer
Made my mate.
1894 *Songs of Travel* (published 1896), 'My Wife'.

35 Blows the wind to-day, and the sun and the rain are
flying,
Blows the wind on the moors to-day and now,
Where about the graves of the martyrs the whaups are
crying,
My heart remembers how!
1894 *Songs of Travel* (published 1896), no.45, 'To S.R. Crockett (in
reply to a dedication)', stanza 1.

36 Be it granted to me to behold you again in dying,
Hills of home! and to hear again the call;
Hear about the graves of the martyrs the peewees
crying,
And hear no more at all.
1894 *Songs of Travel* (published 1896), no.45, 'To S.R. Crockett (in
reply to a dedication)', stanza 3.

37 And all that I could think of, in the darkness and the cold,

Was just that I was leaving home and my folks were
growing old.
1894 'Christmas at Sea', stanza 11.

38 I saw rain falling and the rainbow drawn
On Lammermuir. Hearkening I heard again
In my precipitous city beaten bells
Winnow the keen sea wind. And here afar,
Intent on my own race and place, I wrote.
1894 *Weir of Hermiston* (published 1896), Dedication 'To My
Wife'.

39 It seemed unprovoked, a wilful convulsion of brute
nature…
1894 *Weir of Hermiston* (published 1896), ch.9, 'At the Weaver's
Stone'. These are the last words of the unfinished novel, dictated
by Stevenson on the morning of his death from a blood-clot on
the brain.

40 The *bourgeoisie's* weapon is starvation. If as a writer or
artist you run counter to their narrow notions they
simply and silently withdraw your means of subsistence.
I sometimes wonder how many people of talent are
executed in this way every year.
Quoted by Lloyd Osbourne in 'The Death of Stevenson', preface
to Tusitala edition of *Weir of Hermiston* (published 1924).

41 The saddest object in civilization, and to my mind the
greatest confession of its failure, is the man who can
work, who wants work, and who is not allowed to work.
Quoted by Lloyd Osbourne in 'The Death of Stevenson', preface
to Tusitala edition of *Weir of Hermiston* (published 1924).

Stewart, John Innes Mackintosh 1906–94

Scots-born academic, author and critic, Chair of Literature at
Adelaide University (1935–45). His sequence of novels on life
at Oxford, *A Staircase in Surrey*, began in 1974 with *The Gaudy*.
As 'Michael Innes' he wrote erudite detective novels.

42 I am most grateful to the CLF [Commonwealth Literary
Fund] for providing the funds to give these lectures in
Australian literature, but unfortunately they have
neglected to provide any literature. I will lecture
therefore on D H Lawrence's 'Kangaroo'.
1940 Quoted in the *London Magazine*, Nov 1985.

43 On the platform stood a policeman of normal
proportions, and instead of a revolver and a truncheon
he carried a copy of *Ben Hur* translated into Irish, which
he was evidently studying for an examination important
to his professional advancement. Mr Thewless realised
that the imperial might of Great Britain lay behind him
and that in front was the philosophic republic of Mr de
Valera.
1949 *The Journeying Boy.*

44 'In about half a mile you cross the river by an Irish
bridge—'
'Whatever is that?'
'It's just a bridge, but built under the water instead of over
it.'
'Extremely sensible.'
1969 *A Family Affair.*

Stigler, George Joseph 1911–91

US economist, University of Chicago; awarded a Nobel prize
(1982).

45 The branch of economics dealing with how to enrich

a new nation ('economic development' was the title)
was actually forbidden by the courts, on the grounds
that no university could pay for the damage its teachers
did.
1973 'The History of Truth in Teaching', in *The Intellectual and the
Marketplace* (1984).

Still, Bayrd 1906–92

US historian and archivist.

46 The tombstone of capitalism…with windows.
1956 Of the Rockefeller Center. *Mirror for Gotham.*

Stilwell, General Joseph 1883–1946

US general, commander in the Far East during World War II, who
led the successful attack against the Japanese in Myanmar
(1943–4). His acerbic manner earned him the nickname of
'Vinegar Joe'.

47 This little book contains none of your damn business.
Note on flyleaf of 1906 diary. Quoted in Barbara Tuchman
General Stilwell and the American Experience in China (1970).

Stinchcombe, Arthur S 1933–

US sociologist, University of Chicago.

48 The question of how to apply social theory to historical
materials, as it is usually posed, is ridiculous. One does
not apply theory to history; rather one uses history to
develop theory.
1978 *Theoretical Methods in Social History*, p.1.

Sting originally *Gordon Matthew Sumner* 1951–

English singer-songwriter and actor, also known as a
campaigner to save Brazilian rainforests.

49 If I were a Brazilian without land or money or the means
to feed my children, I would be burning the rainforest
too.
1989 In the *International Herald Tribune*, 14 Apr.

Stipe, Michael 1960–

US singer and songwriter, member of the band REM.

50 Everybody hurts sometimes
Everybody cries
1992 'Everybody Hurts' (co-written by members of REM).

51 We don't get groupies. We get teenagers who want to
read us their poetry.
1994 In *Q*, 1 Sep.

52 There is always something of the writer in the work but I
don't think Melville had to be swallowed by a whale to
write a great novel. If I had lived the lives of all the
characters of the songs I've written, that would truly be
an extraordinary story.
2001 In the *Daily Telegraph*, 20 Oct.

Stockwood, (Arthur) Mervyn 1913–95

English cleric. As Bishop of Southwark (1959–80) he was
renowned for his liberal writings on the uniformity of faith and
the communality of belief.

53 A psychiatrist is a man who goes to the Folies-Bergère
and looks at the audience.
1961 In the *Observer*, 15 Oct.

Stoker, Bram 1847–1912

Irish writer best remembered for the classic vampire story *Dracula* (1897).

54 The mouth, so far as I could see it under the heavy moustache, was fixed and rather cruel-looking, with peculiarly sharp white teeth; these protuded over the lips, whose remarkable ruddiness showed astonishing vitality in a man of his years.
    1897 Describing Count Dracula. *Dracula*, ch.2.

Stokowski, Leopold *pseudonym of* **Antoni Stanislaw Boleslawowich** 1882–1977

US conductor of Polish origin. He built up an international reputation as conductor of the Philadelphia Symphony Orchestra (1912–36), the New York Philharmonic (1946–50) and the Houston Symphony Orchestra (1955–60). He also worked in films and founded the American Symphony Orchestra in New York in 1962.

55 Musicians paint their pictures on silence—we provide the music, and you provide the silence.
    Addressing an audience at Carnegie Hall. Quoted in Derek Watson *Music Quotations* (1991).

Stone, Robert Anthony 1937–

US novelist and screenwriter. His best-known book is the novel *Dog Soldiers* (1974).

56 People are getting to be a disgrace to the planet.
    1982 *A Flag for Sunrise*, ch.6.

Stone, Samuel John 1839–1900

English cleric and hymnwriter

57 The Church's one foundation
Is Jesus Christ, her Lord;
She is his new creation
By water and the word;
From heaven he came and sought her
To be his holy bride,
With his own blood he bought her.
And for her life he died.
    1866 *Lyra fidelium*.

Stopes, Marie 1880–1958

British birth-control pioneer and palaeobotanist.

58 An impersonal and scientific knowledge of the structure of our bodies is the surest safeguard against prurient curiosity and lascivious gloating.
    1918 *Married Love*, ch.5.

59 Each coming together of a man and wife, even if they have been mated for many years, should be a fresh adventure; each winning should necessitate a fresh wooing.
    1918 *Married Love*, ch.10.

Stoppard, Sir Tom *originally* **Tom Straussler** 1937–

Czech-born British dramatist. After writing for radio, he made his name with *Rosencrantz and Guildenstern are Dead* (1967) at the Edinburgh Festival. Other plays include the philosophical satire *Jumpers* (1972), *Travesties* (1974) and *Arcadia* (1993). He shared an Academy Award with Marc Norman for the screenplay of *Shakespeare in Love* (1998).

60 The House of Lords, an illusion to which I have never been able to subscribe—responsibility without power, the prerogative of the eunuch throughout the ages.
    1966 *Lord Malquist and Mr Moon*, pt.6.
    ➤ *See Baldwin 54:46.*

61 To sum up: your father, whom you love, dies, you are his heir, you come back to find that hardly was the corpse cold before his younger brother popped on to his throne and into his sheets, thereby offending both legal and natural practice. Now why exactly are you behaving in this extraordinary manner.
    1967 To Hamlet. *Rosecrantz and Guildenstern are Dead*, act 1.

62 Sometimes I dream of revolution, a bloody *coup d'état* by the second rank—troupes of actors slaughtered by their understudies, magicians sawn in half by indefatigably smiling glamour girls, cricket teams wiped out by marauding bands of twelfth men.
    1968 *The Real Inspector Hound*.

63 It's not the voting that's democracy; it's the counting.
    1972 *Jumpers*.

64 War is capitalism with the gloves off.
    1974 *Travesties*.

65 I learned three things in Zurich during the war… Firstly you're either a revolutionary or you're not, and if you're not you might as well be an artist as anything else. Secondly, if you can't be an artist, you might as well be a revolutionary… I forget the third thing.
    1974 *Travesties*, final lines.

66 Maybe Napoleon was wrong when he said we were a nation of shopkeepers… Today England looked like a nation of goalkeepers.
    1977 *Professional Foul*.
    ➤ *See Napoleon 607:68.*

67 Ambushing the audience is what theatre is all about.
    1984 In *Newsweek*, 16 Jan.

68 I don't think I can be expected to take seriously a game which takes less than three days to reach its conclusion.
    1984 Of baseball. In *The Guardian*, 24 Dec.

69 We're better at predicting events at the edge of the galaxy or inside the nucleus of an atom than whether it'll rain on auntie's garden party three Sundays from now.
    1993 *Arcadia*.

Storr, Robert 1949–

US art administrator, curator of painting and sculpture at the Museum of Modern Art. His writings include *Philip Guston* (1986).

70 It's a letting go of distances.
    1995 On the necessity of establishing an intimacy and trust between artist and sitter. In the *New York Times*, 1 Jan.

Stowe, Harriet (Elizabeth) *née* **Beecher** 1811–96

US novelist. Her novel *Uncle Tom's Cabin* (1852) was written in anger after the passage of the Fugitive Slave Law. She caused a furore with *Lady Byron Vindicated* (1870) in which she accused Byron of having an incestuous relationship with his sister.

71 What makes saintliness in my view, as distinguished from ordinary goodness, is a certain quality of magnanimity and greatness of soul that brings life within the circle of the heroic.

1846 'The Cathedral', in the *Atlantic Monthly*, Dec.

72 So long as the law considers all these human beings, with beating hearts and living affections, only as so many *things* belonging to the master—so long as the failure, or misfortune, or imprudence, or death of the kindest owner, may cause them any day to exchange a life of kind protection and indulgence for one of hopeless misery and toil—so long is it impossible to make anything beautiful or desirable in the best-regulated administration of slavery.
1852 *Uncle Tom's Cabin*, ch.1.

73 I've got just as much conscience as any man in business can afford to keep,—just a little, you know, to swear by, as 't were.
1852 *Uncle Tom's Cabin*, ch.1.

74 'Do you know who made you?'
'Nobody, as I knows on,' said the child…I 'spect I grow'd. Don't think nobody never made me.'
1852 *Uncle Tom's Cabin*, ch.20. The child is Topsy.

75 Whipping and abuse are like laudanum; you have to double the dose as the sensibilities decline.
1852 *Uncle Tom's Cabin*, ch.20.

76 The longest day must have its close,—the gloomiest night will wear on to a morning. An eternal, inexorable lapse of moments is ever hurrying the day of the evil to an eternal night, and the night of the just to an eternal day.
1852 *Uncle Tom's Cabin*, ch.40.

77 The bitterest tears shed over graves are for words left unsaid and deeds left undone.
1865 *Little Foxes*, ch.3.

78 The obstinacy of cleverness and reason is nothing to the obstinacy of folly and inanity.
1865 *Little Foxes*, ch.4.

Strachey, (Evelyn) John 1901–63

British writer and political leader.

79 If socialists lose sight of the central importance of social ownership of the means of production, they will cease, in a very real sense, to be socialists at all: they will subside into the role of well-intentioned, amiable, rootless, drifting social reformers.
1956 *Contemporary Capitalism*.

Strachey, (Giles) Lytton 1880–1932

English writer. He is best known for his biographies, especially *Eminent Victorians* (1918), which challenged established concepts of the Victorian age.

80 The history of the Victorian age will never be written: we know too much about it. For ignorance is the first requisite of the historian—ignorance, which simplifies and clarifies, which selects and omits, with a placid perfection unattainable by the highest art.
1918 *Eminent Victorians*, preface.

81 The time was out of joint, and he was only too delighted to have been born to set it right.
1918 Of Hurrell Froude. *Eminent Victorians*, 'Cardinal Manning'.

82 'Before she came,' said a soldier, 'there was cussin' and swearin', but after that it was 'oly as a church.' The most cherished privilege of the fighting man was abandoned for the sake of Miss Nightingale.

1918 *Eminent Victorians*, 'Florence Nightingale'.

83 Yet her conception of God was certainly not orthodox. She felt towards Him as she might have felt towards a glorified sanitary engineer; and in some of her speculations she seems hardly to distinguish between the Deity and the Drains.
1918 *Eminent Victorians*, 'Florence Nightingale'.

84 His legs, perhaps, were shorter than they should have been.
1918 *Eminent Victorians*, 'Dr Arnold'.

85 Johnson's aesthetic judgements are almost invariably subtle, or solid, or bold; they have always some good quality to recommend them—except one: they are never right.
1922 On Samuel Johnson. *Books and Characters*, 'Lives of the Poets'.

86 Asked by the chairman the usual question: 'I understand, Mr Strachey, that you have a conscientious objection to war?' he replied (in his curious falsetto voice), 'Oh no, not at all, only to *this* war.' Better than this was his reply to the chairman's other stock question, which had previously never failed to embarrass the claimant. 'Tell me, Mr Strachey, what would you do if you saw a German soldier trying to violate your sister?' With an air of noble virtue: 'I would try to get between them.'
On his appearance before a military tribunal, in Robert Graves *Goodbye To All That* (1929), ch.23.

87 If this is dying, then I don't think much of it.
1932 Last words, attributed.

Strafford, Thomas Wentworth, 1st Earl of 1593–1641

English statesman. As Lord Deputy of Ireland from 1632 he imposed firm rule, and in 1639 became the King's principal adviser. After failing to suppress the rebellion in Scotland (1639–40), he was impeached by the Long Parliament and executed despite a famous defence.

88 Divide not between Protestant and Papist. Divide not nationally, betwixt English and Irish. The King makes no distinction betwixt you.
1634 To the Irish Parliament, 15 Jul.

89 I would desire that every man would lay his hand on his heart, and consider seriously whether the beginnings of the people's happiness should be written in letters of blood.
1641 At his execution on Tower Hill, 12 May.

Stravinsky, Igor Fedorovich 1882–1971

Russian composer, who achieved fame with his ballet *The Firebird* (1910). Other ballets include *Petrushka* (1911) and the innovative *Rite of Spring* (1913). Among his significant later works are *The Soldier's Tale* (1918), *Orpheus* (1948, using the 12-tone system), *Oedipus Rex* (1927) and the opera *The Rake's Progress* (1951). He lived in France from 1934 and finally settled in the US (1945).

90 My music is best understood by children and animals.
1961 In the *Observer*, 8 Oct.

91 The most perfect of Swiss clockmakers.
Of Ravel. Quoted in R Nichols *Ravel* (1977).

Streeton, Sir Arthur Ernest 1867–1943

Australian landscape painter, one of the founders of the

influential Heidelberg School and a contributor to the *9x5 Impression Exhibition* (1889), Australia's first Impressionist exhibition. He was official war artist in France in World War I.

92 Nature's scheme of colour in Australia is gold and blue.
    Quoted in William Moore *The Story of Australian Art* (1934), vol. 1.

Streisand, Barbra 1942–

US actress, director and bestselling singer.

93 We elected a President, not a Pope.
    1998 Referring to Bill Clinton. To journalists at the White House, 5 Feb.

Strindberg, August 1849–1912

Swedish dramatist and novelist, regarded as Sweden's greatest modern writer.

94 Family!… the home of all social evil, a charitable institution for comfortable women, an anchorage for house-fathers, and a hell for children.
    1886 *The Son of a Servant.*

Strong, L(eonard) A(lfred) G(eorge) 1896–1958

English novelist and poet.

95 Have I a wife? Bedam I have! But we was badly mated.
    I hit her a great clout one night And now we're separated.
    And mornin's going to me work I meets her on the quay:
    'Good mornin' to you, ma'am!' says I, 'To hell with ye!' says she.
    1921 *Dublin Days*, 'The Brewer's Man'.

Stuart, Francis 1902–2000

Australian-born Irish novelist and poet. He was interned by the Free State government as an Irish republican (1922–3), and by the Germans during World War II after he taught at Berlin University. He later lived and wrote in Paris, London and Ireland.

96 Those are old patterns, faded and bleached in the glare of the pressing present moments in the story.
    'Jacob: An Episode from a Theme Based upon the Biblical Story of Jacob, Laban and Two Daughters'.

Stuart, John McDouall 1815–66

Scottish-born explorer, who emigrated to Australia aged 25. He led six expeditions from Adelaide (1858–62), becoming in 1860 the first European to reach the centre of the continent and in 1862 the first to cross Australia from south to north. His health was wrecked by his adventures.

97 To-day I find from my observations of the sun…that I am now camped in the centre of Australia. I have marked a tree and planted the British flag there. There is a high mount about two miles and a half to the north-north-east. I wish it had been in the centre; but on it to-morrow I will raise a cone of stones, and plant the flag there, and name it 'Central Mount Stuart'.
    1860 Journal entry, 22 Apr. On reaching the centre of Australia, at Small Gum Creek. Collected in W. Hardman (ed) *Journals of John McDou'all Stuart during the Years 1858, 1859, 1860, 1861 and 1862*.

98 If this country is settled, it will be one of the finest Colonies under the Crown, suitable for the growth of any and everything.
    1862 On reaching the sea at the Gulf of Carpentaria. Journal entry, Jul.

Stuart, Mary *known as* **Mary, Queen of Scots** 1542–87

Daughter of James V of Scotland, she married the Dauphin of France in 1558. During her stormy rule, she attempted to support Roman Catholicism in Reformation Scotland, was deposed and fled to England, eventually being imprisoned and executed for treason against her cousin, Queen Elizabeth I of England.

99 *O Domine Deus! speravi in Te;*
    O care mi Jesu! nunc libera me;
    In dura catena, in misera poena,
    Desidero Te,
    Languendo, gemendo, et genu flectendo
    Adoro, imploro, ut liberes me!
    O Lord my God, I hope in thee;
    My dear Lord Jesus, set me free;
    In chains, in pains
    On bended knee
    I adore thee, implore thee
    To set me free.
    1587 Poem composed just before her execution (translated by E Milner-White and G W Briggs, 1941).

Stubbes, Philip 1543–93

English Puritan pamphleteer. His *Anatomie of Abuses in the Realme of England* (1583) was a vehement denunciation of the luxury of the times.

1 Lord, remove these exercises from the Sabbath. Any exercise which withdraweth from godliness either upon the Sabbath or on any other day, is wicked and to be forbidden.
    1583 *Anatomie of Abuses in the Realme of England.*

2 For as concerning football playing, I protest unto you it may be rather called a friendly kind of fight than a play or recreation, a bloody or murmuring practice than a fellowly sport or pastime.
    1583 *Anatomie of Abuses in the Realme of England.*

3 Football causeth fighting, brawling, contention, quarrel-picking, murder, homicide, and a great effusion of blood, as daily experiences teaches.
    1583 *Anatomie of Abuses in the Realme of England.*

Studdert Kennedy, G(eoffrey) A(nketell) *known as* **'Woodbine Willie'** 1883–1929

Army chaplain, theologian and poet of World War I.

4 Waste of Blood, and waste of Tears,
    Waste of youth's most precious years,
    Waste of ways the saints have trod,
    Waste of Glory, waste of God,
    War!
    1919 *More Rough Rhymes of a Padre*, 'Waste'.

5 When Jesus came to Birmingham they simply passed Him by,
    They never hurt a hair of him, they only let Him die.
    For men had grown more tender and they would not give Him pain,
    They only just passed down the street, and left Him in the rain.
    1921 *Peace Rhymes of a Padre*, 'Indifference'.

Su Wu fl. c.100 BC

Chinese general whose poem *To his Wife* expresses his dismay at their forced parting when he was called to battle.

6 With all your might enjoy the spring flowers,
But do not forget the time of our love and pride
c.100 BC *To his Wife* (translated by Arthur Waley).

Suckling, Sir John 1609–41

English poet and playwright. His father was Secretary of State, and he served as ambassador, but upon his inheritance devoted himself to extravagance and court life. Works include the plays *Aglaura* (1638) and *The Goblins* (by 1641), the mock-ballad *The Wits* (1637) and shorter lyrics. By 1641 he had fled to France, where Aubrey says he committed suicide.

7 Why so pale and wan, fond lover?
Prithee, why so pale?
Will, when looking well can't move her,
Looking ill prevail?
1637 *Aglaura*, act 4, sc.1, 'Song'.

8 'Tis love in love that makes the sport.
c.1638 Sonnet no.2.

9 'Tis not the meat; but 'tis the appetite
Makes eating a delight.
c.1638 Sonnet no.2.

10 Women enjoyed (whatsoe'er before they've been)
Are like romances read, or sights once seen:
Fruition's dull, and spoils the play much more
Than if one read or knew the plot before;
'Tis expectation makes a blessing dear;
It were not heaven, if we knew what it were.
1646 'Against Fruition'.

11 The maid (and thereby hangs a tale)
For such a maid no Whitson-ale
Could ever yet produce:
No grape that's kindly ripe, could be
So round, so plump, so soft as she,
Nor half so full of juice.
1646 'Ballad: Upon a Wedding'.

12 Love is the fart
Of every heart:
It pains a man when 'tis kept close,
And others doth offend, when 'tis let loose.
1646 'Love's Offence'.

13 Out upon it! I have loved
Three whole days together;
And am like to love three more,
If it prove fair weather.
1656 'Out Upon It!'

Sullivan, Andrew 1963–

English journalist and writer, based in the US.

14 From the moment she danced with John Travolta, she became an honorary American.
1997 On Diana, Princess of Wales. In the *Sunday Times*, 7 Sep.

Sullivan, Anne 1866–1936

US educator, best known as the teacher of Helen Keller, whom she taught using the manual alphabet and touch-teaching.

15 Language grows out of life, out of its needs and experiences.
1894 Speech to the American Association to Promote the Teaching of Speech to the Deaf, Jul.

16 *Language* and *knowledge* are indissolubly connected; they are interdependent. Good work in language presupposes and depends on a real knowledge of things.
1894 Speech to the American Association to Promote the Teaching of Speech to the Deaf, Jul.

Sullivan, Timothy Daniel 1827–1914

17 High upon the gallows tree
Swung the noble-hearted three
By the vengeful tyrant stricken in their bloom;
But they met him face to face
With the courage of their race,
And they went with souls undaunted to their doom.
'God save Ireland!' said the heroes;
'God save Ireland', say they all:
Whether on the scaffold high
Or the battlefield we die,
Oh, what matter when for Erin dear we fall.
1867 'God Save Ireland'.

Sumner, William Graham 1840–1910

US sociologist, formerly an Episcopal rector, Professor of Political and Social Science at Yale University. He was a disciple of Herbert Spencer, and a strong believer in laissez-faire and free economy.

18 It would be hard to find a single instance of a direct assault by positive effort upon poverty, vice, and misery which has not either failed or, if it has not failed directly and entirely, has not entailed other evils greater than the one which it removed.
1881 'Sociology', collected in *War and Other Essays* (1911).

19 The law of the survival of the fittest was not made by man and cannot be abrogated by man. We can only by interfering with it, produce the survival of the unfittest.
1881 'Sociology', collected in *War and Other Essays* (1911).

20 Society needs first of all to be free from meddlers—that is, to be let alone.
Attributed.

The Sun

British tabloid newspaper.

21 GOTCHA!
1982 Headline, 4 May, reporting the sinking of the Argentinian battleship *General Belgrano* by the British nuclear submarine *HMS Conqueror*. It was withdrawn after the first edition.

22 UP YOURS DELORS
1990 Headline, 1 Nov, supporting Margaret Thatcher's speech in defiance of European Commission president Jacques Delors' wish for Britain to adopt the Ecu.

23 IT'S THE SUN WOT WON IT
1992 Headline, 11 Apr, after the general election victory by the Conservatives.

Sun Tzu c.500–c.320 BC

Name used by the Chinese authors of the *Art of War*. The core text was probably written by one person, perhaps a feudal warrior, but the exact date is unknown. It includes many commentaries by later Chinese philosophers.

24 The art of war is of vital importance to the state.
c.500–320 BC *The Art of War*, ch.1, 'Laying Plans', section 1 (translated by James Clavell, 1981).

25 All warfare is based on deception.
c.**500–320 BC** *The Art of War*, ch.1, 'Laying Plans', section 18 (translated by James Clavell, 1981).

26 There is no instance of a country having benefitted from prolonged warfare.
c.**500–320 BC** *The Art of War*, ch.2, 'Waging War', section 6 (translated by James Clavell, 1981).

27 Know the enemy and know yourself; in a hundred battles, you will never be defeated.
c.**500 BC** *Art of War*, ch.3 (translated by Yuan Shibang, 1987).

28 A victorious general is able to make his soldiers fight with the effect of pent-up waters which, suddenly released, plunge into a bottomless abyss.
c.**500 BC** *Art of War*, ch.4 (translated by Yuan Shibang, 1987).

29 The business of a general is to kick away the ladder behind soldiers when they have climbed up a height.
c.**500 BC** *Art of War*, ch.10 (translated by Yuan Shibang, 1987).

30 The general who advances without coveting fame and retreats without fearing disgrace, whose only thought is to protect the country and do good service to his sovereign, is the jewel of the kingdom.
c.**500–320 BC** *The Art of War*, ch.10, 'Terrain', section 24 (translated by James Clavell, 1981).

31 There is no place where espionage is not possible.
c.**500 BC** *Art of War*, ch.13 (translated by Yuan Shibang, 1987).

Sun Yat-Sen *or Sun Yixian* 1867–1925

Chinese non-Communist revolutionary, regarded as the father of the Chinese Republic. Founder and early leader of China's Nationalist Party, he founded the Society for the Revival of China, but was kidnapped by the Chinese legation in London. After his release he organized risings in South China. The assassination of his follower, Sung Chiao-Jen, led to civil war (1913), and he set up a separate government at Guangzhou (Canton).

32 Modern European culture is nothing but a culture of natural sciences.
1924 Speech, Nov, calling for a union of Japan and China to liberate Asia from European influence. Quoted in John Wu *Sun Yat-Sen: The Man and His Ideas* (1971).

33 The foundation of the government of a nation must be built upon the rights of the people, but the administration must be entrusted to experts. We must not look upon those experts as stately and grand presidents and ministers, but simply as our chauffeurs, guards at the gate, cooks, physicians, carpenters, or tailors.
1927 *The Three Principles of the People*.

Surrey, Henry Howard, Earl of c.1517–1547

English poet; of royal blood, he served Henry VIII at court and in France. In the turmoil over the succession, he became the target of the rival Seymour family, and was arrested and executed on trumped-up charges. He, with Wyatt, introduced the sonnet to England. *Tottel's Miscellany* (1557) contained forty of his poems.

34 Love, that doth reign and live within my thought,
And built his seat within my captive breast,
Clad in the arms wherein with me he fought,
Oft in my face he doth his banner rest.
1557 'Love, that doth reign'.

35 Alas! so all things now do hold their peace,
Heaven and earth disturbed in no thing…

Calm is the sea, the waves work less and less;
So am not I whom love, alas, doth wring,
Bringing before my face the great increase
Of my desires, whereat I weep and sing,
In joy and woe, as in a doubtful ease.
For my sweet thoughts sometime do pleasure bring,
But by and by the cause of my disease
Gives me a pang that inwardly doth sting,
When that I think what grief it is again
To live and lack the thing should rid my pain.
1557 'Alas! so all things now do hold their peace'.

36 Wyatt resteth here, that quick could never rest;
Whose heavenly gifts increased by disdain,
And virtue sank the deeper in his breast;
Such profit he of envy could obtain.
1557 'Wyatt resteth here'.

37 So cruel prison how could betide, alas,
As proud Windsor? Where I in lust and joy
With a king's son my childish years did pass
In greater feast than Priam's sons of Troy.
1557 'So cruel prison'.

38 London, hast thou accused me
Of breach of laws, the root of strife?
Within whose breast did boil to see,
So fervent hot, thy dissolute life,
That even the hate of sins that grow
Within thy wicked walls so rife,
For to break forth did convert so
That terror could it not repress.
1557 'London, hast thou accused me'.

39 O happy dames, that may embrace
The fruit of your delight,
Help to bewail the woeful case
And eke the heavy plight
Of me, that wonted to rejoice
The fortune of my pleasant choice.
Good ladies, help to fill my mourning voice.
1557 'O happy dames'.

40 Set me whereas the sun doth parch the green,
Or where his beams may not dissolve the ice,
In temperate heat, where he is felt and seen,
With proud people, in presence sad and wise;
Set me in base, or yet in high degree,
In the long night, or in the shortest day,
In clear weather, or where mists thickest be,
In lusty youth, or when my hairs be grey…
Yours will I be, and with that only thought
Comfort myself when that my hap is nought.
'Set me whereas the sun doth parch the green'.

Surtees, Robert Smith 1803–64

English journalist and novelist. Founder of the *New Sporting Magazine* in 1831, he introduced the popular Cockney character John Jorrocks. Later works include *Jorrocks' Jaunts and Jollities* (1838) and *Hillingdon Hall* (1845).

41 The horse loves the hound, and I loves both.
Quoted in Colin Jarman *The Guinness Dictionary of Sports Quotations* (1990).

42 There is no secret so close as that between a rider and his horse.
Attributed.

Sutherland, Arthur Jr 1902–73

US lawyer, Professor of Law at Harvard University.

43 One can scarcely imagine a speaker at a meeting of a county medical society discussing the possible elimination of some disease by public health measures, and then qualifying his observations by the statement that many practitioners make a living out of treating the disease in question; and that unless the physicians are vigilant to prevent the adoption of such measures, this source of business will be taken from them. Yet speakers at bar association meetings are frequently heard to make similar observations about the effect of proposed reforms.
1938 'A New Society and an Old Calling,' in the *Cornell Law Quarterly.*

Swanson, Gloria *originally* *Gloria May Josephine Svensson* 1897–1983

US film actress. She rose from an extra in silent films in 1915 to leading roles as a chic sophisticate in the front line of the battle of the sexes, under the direction of Cecil B de Mille in the 1920s.

44 Arriving Monday… Arrange ovation.
Transatlantic cable to Adolf Zukor. Quoted in the *New Yorker*, 21 Mar 1994.

Sweetenham, Bill 1950–

Australian swimming coach.

45 The Romans conquered the world not because they held committees but because they killed the opposition. That's where I'm coming from.
2003 In *The Independent*, 29 Dec.

Sweezy, Paul Malor 1910–2004

Independent US Marxist economist, founder of the *Monthly Review* (1949).

46 Capitalism only works well when it has a strong opposition, because that forces it to be more egalitarian than it wants to be.
1992 Interview in *The Progressive*, May.

Swettenham, Sir Frank Athelstane 1850–1946

English colonial administrator, serving as the British Resident in Selangor and Perak before being appointed the Resident General in the Federated Malay States (1896–1901)

47 The Malay Peninsula, with the climate of a perpetual Turkish bath.
1906 *British Malaya.*

Swift, Graham 1949–

English writer. He has written several novels including *Waterland* (1983), which was shortlisted for the Booker Prize, and *Last Orders*, which won the Booker Prize in 1996.

48 Life is one-tenth Here and Now, nine-tenths a history lesson. For most of the time the Here and Now is neither now nor here.
1983 *Waterland*, ch.8.

49 People die when curiosity goes. People have to find out, people have to know. How can there be any true revolution till we know what we're made of?
1983 *Waterland*, ch.27.

Swift, Jonathan 1667–1745

Anglo-Irish poet, novelist, essayist, pamphleteer and letter writer. Born in Ireland, he became a satirist in London but returned to Dublin to become Dean of St Patrick's. His works, characterized by biting wit, include *Gulliver's Travels* (1726), a satire on religious dissension, *A Tale of a Tub* (1704), *A Modest Proposal* (1729) and *Drapier's Letters* (1724), in which he campaigned for Irish liberty.

50 Th' artillery of words.
1692 'My Lady's Lamentation'.

51 Philosophy! the lumber of the schools.
1692 'Ode to Dr William Sancroft'.

52 Satire is a sort of glass, wherein beholders do generally discover everybody's face but their own.
1704 *The Battle of the Books*, preface.

53 Instead of dirt and poison we have rather chosen to fill our hives with honey and wax; thus furnishing mankind with the two noblest of things, which are sweetness and light.
1704 *The Battle of the Books.*

54 Books, like men their authors, have no more than one way of coming into the world, but there are ten thousand to go out of it, and return no more.
1704 *A Tale of a Tub*, 'Epistle Dedicatory'.

55 Satire, being levelled at all, is never resented for an offence by any.
1704 *A Tale of a Tub*, 'Author's Preface'.

56 What though his head be empty, provided his commonplace book be full.
1704 *A Tale of a Tub*, 'Digression in praise of digression', ch.7.

57 Last week I saw a woman flayed, and you will hardly believe, how much it altered her person for the worse.
1704 *A Tale of a Tub*, ch.9.

58 Laws are like cobwebs, which may catch small flies, but let wasps and hornets break through.
1709 *A Critical Essay upon the Faculties of the Mind.*

59 There is nothing in this world constant, but inconstancy.
1709 *A Critical Essay upon the Faculties of the Mind.*

60 Surely mortal man is a broomstick!
1710 *A Meditation upon a Broomstick.*

61 We are so fond of one another, because our ailments are the same.
1711 *Journal to Stella*, 1 Feb.

62 Will she pass in a crowd? Will she make a figure in a country church?
1711 *Journal to Stella*, 9 Feb.

63 I love good creditable acquaintance; I love to be the worst of the company.
1711 *Journal to Stella*, 17 May.

64 He was a fiddler, and consequently a rogue.
1711 *Journal to Stella*, 25 July.

65 He showed me his bill of fare to tempt me to dine with him; poh, said I, I value not your bill of fare, give me your bill of company.
1711 *Journal to Stella*, 2 Sep.

66 We have just enough religion to make us hate, but not enough to make us love one another.
1711 *Thoughts on Various Subjects.*

67 When a true genius appears in the world, you may know

him by this sign, that the dunces are all in confederacy against him.
1711 *Thoughts on Various Subjects.*

68 What they do in heaven we are ignorant of: what they do *not* we are told expressly, that they neither marry, nor are given in marriage.
1711 *Thoughts on Various Subjects.*

69 The stoical scheme of supplying our wants, by lopping off our desires, is like cutting off our feet when we want shoes.
1711 *Thoughts on Various Subjects.*

70 The reason why so few marriages are happy, is, because young ladies spend their time in making nets, not in making cages.
1711 *Thoughts on Various Subjects.*

71 We were to do more business after dinner, but after dinner is after dinner—an old saying and a true, 'much drinking, little thinking'.
1712 *Journal to Stella*, 26 Feb.

72 Proper words in proper places, make the true definition of style.
1720 *Letter to a Young Gentleman lately entered into Holy Orders.*

73 Indeed the arguments on both sides were invincible; for in reason, all government without the consent of the governed is the very definition of slavery; but in fact eleven men well armed will certainly subdue one single man in his shirt.
1724 *Fourth letter to…Ireland*, written under the pseudonym of 'M B Drapier'.

74 I have heard of a man who had a mind to sell his house, and therefore carried a piece of brick in his pocket, which he shewed as a pattern to encourage purchasers.
1724 *Drapier's Letters*, no.2.

75 In Church your grandsire cut his throat;
To do the job too long he tarried,
He should have had my hearty vote,
To cut his throat before he married.
1724 'Verses on the Upright Judge'.

76 'Libertas et natale solum':
Fine words! I wonder where you stole 'em.
1724 'Whitshed's motto on his Coach'.

77 He is taller by almost the breadth of my nail than any of his court, which alone is enough to strike an awe into the beholders.
1726 Of the Emperor. *Gulliver's Travels*, 'A Voyage to Lilliput', ch.2.

78 It is alleged indeed, that the high heels are most agreeable to our ancient constitution: but however this be, his Majesty hath determined to make use of only low heels in the administration of the government.
1726 *Gulliver's Travels*, 'A Voyage to Lilliput', ch.4.

79 I cannot but conclude the bulk of your natives to be the most pernicious race of little odious vermin that nature ever suffered to crawl upon the surface of the earth.
1726 *Gulliver's Travels*, 'A Voyage to Brobdingnag', ch.6.

80 And he gave it for his opinion, that whoever could make two ears of corn or two blades of grass to grow upon a spot of ground where only one grew before, would deserve better of mankind, and do more essential service to his country than the whole race of politicians put together.
1726 *Gulliver's Travels*, 'A Voyage to Brobdingnag', ch.7.

81 He had been eight years upon a project for extracting sun-beams out of cucumbers, which were to be put into vials hermetically sealed, and let out to warm the air in raw inclement summers.
1726 *Gulliver's Travels*, 'A Voyage to Laputa, etc.' ch.5.

82 These unhappy people were proposing schemes for persuading monarchs to choose favourites upon the score of their wisdom, capacity and virtue; of teaching ministers to consult the public good; of rewarding merit, great abilities and eminent services; of instructing princes to know their true interest by placing it on the same foundation with that of their people: of choosing for employment persons qualified to exercise them; with many other wild impossible chimeras, that never entered before into the heart of man to conceive, and confirmed in me the old observation, that there is nothing so extravagant and irrational which some philosophers have not maintained for truth.
1726 *Gulliver's Travels*, 'A Voyage to Laputa, etc.' ch.6.

83 He replied that I must needs be mistaken, or that I *said the thing which was not*. (For they have no word in their language to express lying or falsehood.)
1726 *Gulliver's Travels*, 'A Voyage to the Houyhnhnms', ch.3.

84 I told him…that we ate when we were not hungry, and drank without the provocation of thirst.
1726 *Gulliver's Travels*, 'A Voyage to the Houyhnhnms', ch.6.

85 Few are qualified to shine in company; but it is in most men's power to be agreeable.
1727 *Thoughts on Various Subjects* (enlarged edn).

86 Every man desires to live long; but no man would be old.
1727 *Thoughts on Various Subjects* (enlarged edn).

87 A nice man is a man of nasty ideas.
1727 *Thoughts on Various Subjects* (enlarged edn).

88 Old men and comets have been reverenced for the same reason; their long beards, and pretences to foretell events.
1727 *Thoughts on Various Subjects* (enlarged edn).

89 How haughtily he lifts his nose,
To tell what every schoolboy knows.
1727 'The Journal', l.81–2.

90 Walls have tongues, and hedges ears.
1727 'A Pastoral Dialogue between Richmond Lodge and Marble Hill', l.8.

91 Hail fellow, well met,
All dirty and wet:
Find out, if you can,
Who's master, who's man.
1728 'My Lady's Lamentation', l.171.

92 These *Mothers*, instead of being able to work for their honest livelihood, are forced to beg Sustenance for their *helpless Infants*; who, as they grow up either turn *Thieves* for want of Work; or leave their dear native country, to fight for the *Pretender* in Spain; or sell themselves to the *Barbadoes*.
1729 *A Modest Proposal for Preventing the Children of Ireland from being a Burden to their Parents or Country.*

93 I have been assured by a very knowing American of my Acquaintance in London; that a young healthy Child, well nursed, is, at a Year old, a most delicious, nourishing, and wholesome Food; whether Stewed, Roasted, Baked, or Boiled; and, I make no doubt, that it will equally serve

in a Fricassee, or a Ragout.
1729 *A Modest Proposal for Preventing the Children of Ireland from being a Burden to their Parents or Country.*

94 A Child will make two Dishes at an Entertainment for Friends; and when the Family dines alone, the fore or hind Quarter will make a reasonable Dish; and seasoned with a little Pepper or Salt, will be very good Boiled on the fourth Day, especially in Winter.
1729 *A Modest Proposal for Preventing the Children of Ireland from being a Burden to their Parents or Country.*

95 Say, Britain, could you ever boast,—
Three poets in an age at most?
Our chilling climate hardly bears
A sprig of bays in fifty years.
1733 'On Poetry', l.5–8.

96 Then, rising with Aurora's light,
The Muse invoked, sit down to write;
Blot out, correct, insert, refine,
Enlarge, diminish, interline.
1733 'On Poetry', l.85–8.

97 As learned commentators view
In Homer than Homer knew.
1733 'On Poetry', l.103–4.

98 So geographers, in Afric-maps,
With savage-pictures fill their gaps;
And o'er unhabitable downs
Place elephants for want of towns.
1733 'On Poetry', l.177–80.

99 He gives direction to the town,
To cry it up, or run it down.
1733 'On Poetry', l.269–70.

1 Hobbes clearly proves, that every creature
Lives in a state of war by nature.
1733 'On Poetry', l.319–20.

2 So, naturalists observe, a flea
Hath smaller fleas on him prey;
And these have smaller fleas to bite 'em,
And so proceed *ad infinitum*.
Thus every poet, in his kind,
Is bit by him that comes behind.
1733 'On Poetry', l.337–42.

3 I mean, you lie—under a mistake.
1738 *Polite Conversation*, dialogue 1.

4 I think she was cut out for a Gentlewoman, but she was spoiled in the making. She wears her clothes as if they were thrown on with a pitchfork; and, for the fashion, I believe they were made in the days of Queen Bess.
1738 *Polite Conversation*, dialogue 1.

5 The more careless, the more modish.
1738 *Polite Conversation*, dialogue 1.

6 I won't quarrel with my Bread and Butter.
1738 *Polite Conversation*, dialogue 1.

7 He was a bold Man that first ate an Oyster.
1738 *Polite Conversation*, dialogue 2.

8 Faith, that's as well said, as if I had said it myself.
1738 *Polite Conversation*, dialogue 2.

9 I always love to begin a journey on Sundays, because I shall have the prayers of the church, to preserve all that travel by land, or by water.
1738 *Polite Conversation*, dialogue 2.

10 Lord, I wonder what fool it was that first invented kissing!
1738 *Polite Conversation*, dialogue 2.

11 Promises and pie-crust are made to be broken.
1738 *Polite Conversation*.

12 Be she barren, be she old,
Be she slut, or be she scold,
Eat my oysters, and lie near her,
She'll be fruitful, never fear her.
1746 'Verses Made for the Women Who Cry Oysters'.

13 I never saw, heard, nor read, that the clergy were beloved in any nation where Christianity was the religion of the country. Nothing can render them popular, but some degree of persecution.
1765 *Thoughts on Religion*.

14 I must complain the cards are ill shuffled till I have a good hand.
Quoted in Colin Jarman *The Guinness Dictionary of Sports Quotations* (1990).

Swinburne, Algernon Charles 1837–1909

English playwright and poet. He made his name with *Poems and Ballads* (1866). Later works include *A Song of Italy* (1867), *Erechtus* (1876) and *Tristam of Lyonesse* (1882).

15 Swallow, my sister, O sister swallow,
How can thine heart be full of the spring?
A thousand summers are over and dead.
What hast thou found in the spring to follow?
What hast thou found in thine heart to sing?
What wilt thou do when the summer is shed?
1864 'Itylus'.

16 Till life and death remember,
Till thou remember and I forget.
1864 'Itylus'.

17 Maiden, and mistress of the months and stars
Now folded in the flowerless fields of heaven.
1865 *Atlanta in Calydon*, l.1

18 When the hounds of spring are on winter's traces,
The mother of months in meadow or plain
Fills the shadows and windy places
With lisp of leaves and ripple of rain;
And the brown bright nightingale amorous
Is half assured for Itylus,
For the Thracian ships and the foreign faces,
The tongueless vigil and all the pain.
1865 *Atlanta in Calydon*, chorus, 'When the hounds of spring'.

19 For winter's rains and ruins are over,
And all the season of snows and sins;
The days dividing lover and lover,
The light that loses, the night that wins;
And time remembered is grief forgotten,
And frosts are slain and flowers begotten,
And in green underwood and cover
Blossom by blossom the spring begins.
1865 *Atlanta in Calydon*, chorus, 'When the hounds of spring'.

20 And soft as lips that laugh and hide
The laughing leaves of the tree divide,
And screen from seeing and leave in sight
The god pursuing, the maiden hid.
1865 *Atlanta in Calydon*, chorus 'When the hounds of spring'.

21 Before the beginning of years
There came to the making of man

Time with a gift of tears,
Grief with a glass that ran.
1865 *Atlanta in Calydon*, chorus, 'Before the beginning of years'.

22 Strength without hands to smite,
Love that endures for a breath;
Night, the shadow of light,
And Life, the shadow of death.
1865 *Atlanta in Calydon*, chorus, 'Before the beginning of years'.

23 For words divide and rend;
But silence is most noble till the end.
1865 *Atlanta in Calydon*, chorus, 'Who hath given man speech'.

24 Ah, yet would God this flesh of mine might be
Where air might wash and long leaves cover me;
Where tides of grass break into foam of flowers,
Or where the wind's feet shine along the sea.
1866 'Laus Veneris'.

25 Superflux of pain.
1866 *Poems and Ballads*, 'Anactoria'

26 We shift and bedeck and bedrape us,
Thou art noble and nude and antique.
1866 *Poems and Ballads*, 'Dolores', stanza 7.

27 Change in a trice
The lilies and languors of virtue
For the raptures and roses of vice.
1866 *Poems and Ballads*, 'Dolores', stanza 9.

28 O splendid and sterile Dolores,
Our Lady of Pain.
1866 *Poems and Ballads*, 'Dolores', stanza 9.

29 Ah beautiful passionate body
That never has ached with a heart!
1866 *Poems and Ballads*, 'Dolores', stanza 11.

30 For the crown of our life as it closes
Is darkness, the fruit thereof dust;
No thorns go as deep as a rose's,
And love is more cruel than lust.
Time turns the old days to derision,
Our loves into corpses or wives;
And marriage and death and division
Make barren our lives.
1866 *Poems and Ballads*, 'Dolores', stanza 20.

31 I shall remember while the light lives yet
And in the night time I shall not forget.
1866 *Poems and Ballads*, 'Erotion'.

32 Pale, beyond porch and portal,
Crowned with calm leaves, she stands
Who gathers all things mortal
With cold immortal hands.
1866 *Poems and Ballads*, 'The Garden of Proserpine'.

33 Here, where the world is quiet,
Here, where all trouble seems
Dead winds' and spent waves' riot
In doubtful dreams of dreams.
1866 *Poems and Ballads*, 'The Garden of Proserpine'.

34 Yea, is not even Apollo, with hair and harpstring of gold,
A bitter God to follow, a beautiful God to behold?
1866 *Poems and Ballads*, 'Hymn to Proserpine'.

35 Thou hast conquered, O pale Galilean; the world has
grown grey from Thy breath;
We have drunken of things Lethean, and fed on the
fullness of death.

1866 *Poems and Ballads*, 'Hymn to Proserpine'.

36 Though these that were Gods are dead, and thou being
dead art God,
Though before thee the throned Cytherean be fallen,
and hidden her head,
Yet thy kingdom shall pass, Galilean, thy dead shall go
down to thee dead.
1866 *Poems and Ballads*, 'Hymn to Proserpine'.

37 I remember the way we parted,
The day and the way we met;
You hoped we were both broken-hearted,
And knew we should both forget.
1866 *Poems and Ballads*, 'An Interlude'.

38 And the best and the worst of this is
That neither is most to blame
If you have forgotten my kisses
And I have forgotten your name.
1866 *Poems and Ballads*, 'An Interlude'.

39 If love were what the rose is,
And I were like the leaf,
Our lives would grow together
In sad or singing weather,
Blown fields or flowered closes,
Green pleasure or grey grief.
1866 *Poems and Ballads*, 'A Match'.

40 I will go back to the great sweet mother,
Mother and lover of men, the sea.
I will go down to her, I and no other,
Close with her, kiss her and mix her with me.
1866 *Poems and Ballads*, 'The Triumph of Time'.

41 I shall sleep, and move with the moving ships,
Change as the winds change, veer in the tide.
1866 *Poems and Ballads*, 'The Triumph of Time'.

42 There lived a singer in France of old
By the tideless dolorous midland sea.
In a land of sand and ruin and gold
There shone one woman, and none but she.
1866 *Poems and Ballads*, 'The Triumph of Time'.

43 O slain and spent and sacrificed
People, the grey-grown speechless Christ.
1871 *Songs before Sunrise*, 'Before a Crucifix'.

44 But God, if a God there be, is the substance of men
which is man.
1871 *Songs before Sunrise*, 'Hymn of Man'.

45 Glory to Man in the highest! for Man is the master of
things.
1871 *Songs before Sunrise*, 'Hymn of Man'.

46 There was a poor poet named Clough,
Whom his friends all united to puff,
But the public, though dull,
Had not such a skull
As belonged to believers in Clough.
1875 *Essays and Studies*, 'Matthew Arnold'.

47 For a day and a night Love sang to us, played with us,
Folded us round from the dark and the light;
And our hearts were fulfilled with the music he made
with us,
Made with our hands and our lips while he stayed
with us,
Stayed in mid passage his pinions from flight
For a day and a night.

1878 *Poems and Ballads* (2nd edn), 'At Parting'.

48 The deep division of prodigious breasts,
The solemn slope of mighty limbs asleep.
1878 *Poems and Ballads* (2nd edn), 'Ave Atque Vale', stanza 6.

49 Sleep; and if life was bitter to thee, pardon,
If sweet, give thanks; thou hast no more to live;
And to give thanks is good, and to forgive.
1878 *Poems and Ballads* (2nd edn), 'Ave Atque Vale', stanza 17.

50 Villon, our sad bad glad mad brother's name.
1878 *Poems and Ballads* (2nd edn), 'Ballad of François Villon'.

51 In a coign of the cliff between lowland and highland,
At the sea-down's edge between windward and lee,
Walled round with rocks as an inland island,
The ghost of a garden fronts the sea.
1878 *Poems and Ballads* (2nd edn), 'A Forsaken Garden'.

52 As a god self-slain on his own strange altar,
Death lies dead.
1878 *Poems and Ballads* (2nd edn), 'A Forsaken Garden'.

53 Fiddle, we know, is diddle: and diddle, we take it, is
dee.
1880 *The Heptalogia*, 'The Higher Pantheism in a Nutshell'.

Symington, Stuart   1901–88

US Senator. In 1939 he became President and Chairman of the Emerson Electric Manufacturing Company. He was the first Secretary of the Air Force (1945–48) and was elected Senator for Missouri in 1952.

54 I found out that he was a bachelor, as was his father
before him.
1960 On hiring a speechwriter. Address to Washington's Gridiron Club, 12 Mar, quoted in Harold Brayman *The President Speaks-off-the-Record* (1976).

Synge, John Millington   1871–1909

Irish dramatist. On the advice of W B Yeats he travelled to the Aran Islands and there found materials for his plays which include *Riders to the Sea* (1904) and his masterpiece, *The Playboy of the Western World* (1907), which caused riots when it was first staged in Dublin.

55 No man at all can be living for ever, and we must be
satisfied.
1904 *Riders to the Sea*.

56 They're all gone now, and there isn't anything more the
sea can do to me.
1904 Maurya speaking. *Riders to the Sea*.

57 Well, if the worst comes in the end of all, it'll be great
game to see if there's none to pity him but a widow
woman, the like of me, has buried her children and
destroyed her man.
1907 Widow Quin. *The Playboy of the Western World*, act 2.

58 Drink a health to the wonders of the western world, the
pirates, preachers, poteen-makers, with the jobbing
jockies; parching peelers, and the juries fill their
stomachs selling judgments of the English law.
1907 *The Playboy of the Western World*, act 2.

59 I'll say, a strange man is a marvel, with his mighty talk; but
what's a squabble in your back-yard, and the blow of a
loy, have taught me that there's a great gap between a
gallous story and a dirty deed.
1907 Pegeen Mike. *The Playboy of the Western World*, act 3.

60 Oh my grief, I've lost him surely. I've lost the only
Playboy of the Western World.
1907 Pegeen Mike. *The Playboy of the Western World*, act 3, closing words.

Szasz, Thomas Stephen   1920–

Hungarian-born US psychiatrist. His books argue that disease is physical, hence mental illness is a myth, that the individual should be allowed complete freedom within the law, and all psychiatric therapy should be contractual.

61 Formerly, when religion was strong and science weak,
men mistook magic for medicine, now, when science is
strong and religion weak, men mistake medicine for
magic.
1974 *The Second Sin*.

62 Men are rewarded and punished not for what they do,
but rather for how their acts are defined. This is why men
are more interested in better justifying themselves than
in better behaving themselves.
1974 *The Second Sin*.

63 Psychiatrists classify a person as neurotic if he suffers
from his problems in living, and a psychotic if he makes
others suffer.
1974 *The Second Sin*.

Szent-Györgyi, Albert von Nagyrapolt   1893–1986

Hungarian-born US biochemist, authority on the processes of biological combustion. He was educated at the universities of Budapest and Cambridge. In 1947, he migrated to the US to join the Marine Biological Laboratories, Massachusetts. He was awarded the 1937 Nobel prize in physiology or medicine.

64 Discovery consists of seeing what everybody has seen
and thinking what nobody has thought.
Quoted in Irving Good (ed) *The Scientist Speculates* (1962).

65 Knowledge is a sacred cow, and my problem will
be how we can milk her while keeping clear of her
horns.
1964 In *Science*, vol.146.

Szilard, Leo   1898–1964

Hungarian-born US nuclear physicist, who contributed to the development of controlled nuclear fission. He left the University of Berlin with the advent of Hitler, jointing Columbia University in 1938. He urged Albert Einstein to write to President Roosevelt warning of the possible military use of atomic energy by the Nazis.

66 We turned the switch, saw the flashes, watched for
ten minutes, then switched everything off and went
home. That night I knew the world was headed for
sorrow.
1939 After an early experiment at Columbia University which proved the possibility of splitting the atom. Quoted in James B Simpson *Simpson's Contemporary Quotations* (1988).

67 Don't lie if you don't have to.
1972 In *Science*, vol.176, p.966.

Taaffe, Eduard Franz Josef, Graf von 1833–95

Austrian statesman, Minister of the Interior (1867) and Chief Minister (1869–70, 1879–93).

68 As a Minister, it is my policy to keep all the nationalities within the Habsburg monarchy in a balanced state of well-modulated dissatisfaction.
1881 Letters.

Tacitus, Cornelius *full name* Publius or Gaius Cornelius Tacitus AD 55–c.120

Roman historian and orator, who lived under Domitian, Nerva, Trajan and Hadrian. He wrote a biography of his father-in-law Agricola. His major historical works are the *Historiae* (Histories), of which only the first four books survive whole, and the *Annales* (Annals), of which only eight books survive.

69 *Solitudinem faciunt pacem appellant.*
They make a wilderness and they call it peace.
Speech of the British chieftain Calgacus, before the battle of Mons Graupius, referring to the Romans. *Agricola*, ch.30.

70 *Proprium humani ingenii est odisse quem laeseris.*
It is part of human nature to hate a man you have hurt.
Agricola, ch.42.

71 *Perdomita Britannia et statim omissa.*
Britain was conquered and immediately lost.
Referring to Agricola's conquest of Britain, and the loss of much of it under Domitian. *Histories*, bk.1, ch.2.

72 *Deos fortioribus adesse.*
The gods support those who are stronger.
Histories, bk.4, ch.17.

73 *Miseram pacem vel bello bene mutari.*
Even war is preferable to a shameful peace.
Annals, bk.3, ch.44.

74 *Auctor nominis eius Christus, Tiberio imperitante, per procuratorem Pontium Pilatum, supplicio affectus erat.*
Christ, the leader of the sect, had been put to death by the procurator Pontius Pilate in the reign of Tiberius.
Annals, bk.15, ch.44.

75 *Elegantiae arbiter.*
The arbiter of taste.
Of Petronius. *Annals*, bk.16, ch.18.

Taft, Robert A(lphonso) 1889–1953

US politician. Son of US President William Howard Taft, he entered the Senate in 1932 and was a prominent isolationist. He co-sponsored the Taft-Hartley Act (1947), which acted against the 'closed shop' power of trade unions. He failed three times (1940, 1948, 1952) to gain the Republican nomination for the US presidency.

76 Lending arms is like lending chewing gum. You don't get it back.
On the lend-lease agreement. Quoted in David Brinkley *Washington Goes to War* (1988).

Taft, William Howard 1857–1930

US Republican politician and 27th US President. Secretary of War (1904–8) and provisional governor of Cuba (1906), he became President in 1909 and remained in the post until 1913, when he was defeated by Woodrow Wilson. Subsequently he became US Chief Justice (1921).

77 There are a great many people who are in favor of conservation no matter what it means.
Quoted in J W Milliman *Land Economics* (1962).

78 Golf is in the interest of good health and good manners. It promotes self-restraint and affords a chance to play the man and act the gentleman.
Quoted in Michael Hobbs *The Golf Quotation Book* (1992).

Takuboku, Ishikawa 1886–1902

Japanese poet whose first book of poems, *Akogare* (Longing), was published in 1905. Five years later, a second collection, *Ichiaku no Suna* (A Handful of Dust), broke new ground by writing about aspects of everyday life.

79 There are some lives duller
Than dusty glass
1910 *Ichiaku no Suna* (translated by Sakanishi Shio).

80 Like a stone
That rolls down a hill,
I have come to this day.
1910 *Ichiaku no Suna* (translated by Sakanishi Shio).

Talbot, Godfrey Walker 1908–2000

English broadcaster and writer. He was the BBC's war correspondent in World War II and their court correspondent from 1948 to 1969. He wrote articles on the Royal Family and an autobiography, *Ten Seconds from Now* (1973).

81 A man who, until he made the journey from London, thought that woad began at Watford.
1973 *Ten Seconds from Now*, ch.3. An early reference to the 'north of Watford' concept, in which Watford is regarded as the limit of 'civilization' northwards from London.

Talese, Gay 1932–

US writer and journalist. His works include *New York: A Serendipiter's Journey* (1961), *Fame and Obscurity* (1970) and *Unto the Sons* (1992).

82 New glass skyscrapers stand shoulder to shoulder, reflecting one another narcissistically.
1965 In the *New York Times*, 23 Jun.

Talleyrand-Périgord, Charles-Maurice de, Prince of Benevento 1754–1838

French statesman, President of the Assembly (1790). He lived in exile until the fall of Robespierre. As Foreign Minister under the Directory (1797–1807) he helped consolidate Napoleon's position, but alarmed by his ambitions resigned in 1807 to become leader of the anti-Napoleonic faction. Foreign Minister under Louis XVIII, he represented France at the Congress of Vienna (1814–15). He was Louis Philippe's chief adviser at the July Revolution, and Ambassador to England (1830–4).

83 *Ils n'ont rien appris, ni rien oublié.*
They have learned nothing, and forgotten nothing.
Attributed.

84 *Voilà le commencement de la fin.*

This is the beginning of the end.
Attributed.

85 The allies are too frightened to fight each other, too stupid too agree.
1814 Congress of Vienna, Nov.

Tally, Ted 1952–

US screenwriter, best known for *The Silence of the Lambs* (1991) for which he won an Academy Award for Best Adapted Screenplay.

86 A census taker once tried to test me, I ate his liver with some fava beans and a nice Chianti.
1991 Anthony Hopkins as Dr Hannibal Lecter ('Hannibal the Cannibal') in *The Silence of the Lambs*.

87 I do wish we could chat longer but I'm having an old friend for dinner.
1991 Anthony Hopkins as Dr Hannibal Lecter ('Hannibal the Cannibal') in *The Silence of the Lambs*.

Talma, François-Joseph 1763–1826

French actor-manager. He established his reputation as a powerful tragedian in the central role of Chénier's *Charles IX* in 1789, which caused a sensation; subsequently he formed his own company and staged admired productions of Corneille, Shakespeare and others. As head of the French national theatre under Napoleon he introduced various important reforms.

88 *Voltaire! Comme Voltaire, toujours comme Voltaire.*
Voltaire! Like Voltaire, always like Voltaire.
1826 Last words.

Tanaka, Kakuei 1918–93

Japanese politician who rose through the ranks of the Liberal Democratic party to become Prime Minister. Arrested in 1976 for bribery, he resigned the premiership, although he remained influential.

89 The politics of numbers.
1983 Describing democracy, in an interview with the *Nihon Keizai Shimbun*, 25 Jan.

90 Why should not a large shareholder sometimes name the president?
1983 Responding to criticism that candidates for the premiership must win his approval. Quoted in the *Financial Times*, 11 Oct.

Tannahill, Robert 1774–1810

Scottish poet and songwriter, born in Paisley, the son of a weaver.

91 The sun has gane down o'er the lofty Benlomond,
And left the red clouds to preside o'er the scene,
While lanely I stray, in the calm simmer gloamin',
To muse on sweet Jessie, the flower o' Dunblane.
How sweet is the brier wi' its saft faulding blossom,
And sweet is the birk, wi' its mantle o' green;
Yet sweeter, and fairer, and dear to this bosom,
Is lovely young Jessie, the flower o' Dunblane.
1807 'Jessie, the Flower o' Dunblane', stanza 1.

T'ao Ch'ien AD 372–427

Chinese poet about whom little is known.

92 I beg you listen to this advice—

When you get wine, be sure to drink it.
c.400 AD Collected in *Substance, Shadow and Spirit*, translated by Arthur Waley.

Tarantino, Quentin 1963–

US director and screenwriter, known for the brutality and violent escapism of his films. One of his many scripts was made into his debut film as director, *Reservoir Dogs* (1993). In 1994 his second film, *Pulp Fiction*, won the Palme d'Or at the Cannes Film Festival. Later films include *Jackie Brown* (1997).

93 Violence in real life is terrible; violence in movies can be cool. It's just another colour to work with.
1994 In the *Observer*, 'Sayings of the Week', 16 Oct.

94 Violence is fun, man.
2004 In *The Times*, 17 May.

Tarkington, (Newton) Booth 1869–1946

US novelist, best known for his Penrod books, *Penrod* (1914) and *Seventeen* (1916). His novel *The Magnificent Ambersons* (1918) won the Pulitzer Prize and was made into a successful film by Orson Welles.

95 There are two things that will be believed of any man whatsoever, and one of them is that he has taken to drink.
1914 *Penrod*, ch.10.

96 The Magnificent Ambersons.
1918 Title of novel.

97 An ideal wife is any woman who has an ideal husband.
1924 *Looking Forward And Others*, 'The Hopeful Pessimist'.

Tarrant, Chris 1946–

English radio and television presenter.

98 Is that your final answer?
Catchphrase on the television show *Who Wants To Be A Millionaire?*.

Tartt, Donna 1963–

US author. She achieved widespread succes with her first novel, *The Secret History* (1992). Her second novel, *The Little Friend* (2002), appeared a decade later.

99 The snow in the mountains was melting and Bunny had been dead for several weeks before we came to understand the gravity of our situation.
1992 *The Secret History*.

1 I'd love to write a book a year, but I don't think I'd have any fans.
2002 In the *Sunday Times*, 2 Jun.

2 Birds—birds, everywhere, great black cawing explosions of them, like radioactive fall-out, like shrapnel.
2002 *The Little Friend*.

Tate, (John Orley) Allen 1899–1979

US poet, critic and biographer. He was the editor of the influential *Sewanee Review* (1944–7). His own poetry was strongly influenced by T S Eliot.

3 Row upon row with strict impunity
The headstones yield their names to the element.
1948 *Poems 1922–1947*, 'Ode to the Confederate Dead'.

4 Autumn is desolation in the plot
Of a thousand acres, where these memories grow
From the inexhaustible bodies that are not
Dead, but feed the grass, row after rich row.
1948 *Poems 1922–1947*, 'Ode to the Confederate Dead'.

5 The brute curiosity of an angel's stare
Turn you like them to stone.
1948 *Poems 1922–1947*, 'Ode to the Confederate Dead'.

6 I've heard the wolves scuffle, and said: So this
Is man; so—what better conclusion is there—
The day will not follow night, and the heart
Of man has a little dignity, but less patience
Than a wolf's, and a duller sense that cannot
Smell its own mortality.
1948 *Poems 1922–1947*, 'The Wolves'.

Tate, Greg

US writer and music critic.

7 Commodity fetishism is the true God of this nation.
1992 In *Vibe*, reported in *USA Today*, 14 Sep.

Tawney, R(ichard) H(enry) 1880–1962

British economic historian, active in the Workers' Educational Association at Rochdale, Lancashire, and its President (1928–44). He was Professor of Economic History at London (1931–49) and wrote a number of studies in English economic history.

8 The instinct of mankind warns it against accepting at their face value spiritual demands that cannot satisfy themselves by practical achievements. The road along which the organized workers, like any other class, must climb to power starts from the provision of a more effective economic service than their masters, as their grip upon industry becomes increasingly vacillating and uncertain, are able to supply.
1926 *The Acquisitive Society*.

9 As long as men are men, a poor society cannot be too poor to find a right order of life; nor a rich society too rich to have need to seek it.
1926 *The Acquisitive Society*.

Taylor, A(lan) J(ohn) P(ercivale) 1906–90

English historian, whose major work was *The Struggle for Mastery in Europe 1848–1918* (1954). His controversial revisionist *Origins of the Second World War* (1961) argued against a grand design. Other works include *English History 1914–1945* (1965), *The Trouble Makers* (1957), on critics of British foreign policy, and *A Personal History* (1983).

10 Crimea: The War That Would Not Boil.
1952 *Rumours of Wars*, ch.6, chapter title.

11 Human blunders usually do more to shape history than human wickedness.
1961 *The Origins of the Second World War*.

12 The First World War had begun—imposed on the statesmen of Europe by railway timetables. It was an unexpected climax to the railway age.
1963 *The First World War*, ch.1.

13 Like most of those who study history, Napoleon learned from the mistakes of the past how to make new ones.
1963 BBC radio broadcast, 6 Jun.

14 History gets thicker and thicker as it approaches recent times.
1965 *English History 1914–1945*.

Taylor, Dwight 1902–86

US screenwriter. Best known for his screenplays for two of the Fred Astaire/Ginger Rogers musicals *Top Hat* (1935) and *Follow the Fleet* (1936).

15 Are you sure you didn't forget yourself in the park?
Positive. If I ever forget myself with that girl I'd remember it.
1935 Dialogue between Edward Everett Horton and Fred Astaire in *Top Hat* (with Allan Scott).

Taylor, Elizabeth Rosemond 1932–

English-born US film actress. She graduated from child star to screen goddess in films such as *A Place in the Sun* (1951), *Raintree County* (1957), *Butterfield 8* (1960), *Cleopatra* (1962) and *Who's Afraid of Virginia Woolf?* (1966). She has had seven husbands, most famously Richard Burton, whom she married twice.

16 It will be fun to be the first Jewish Queen of Egypt.
c.1962 On taking the title role in *Cleopatra*. Attributed.

17 If someone was stupid enough to offer me a million dollars to make a picture—I was certainly not dumb enough to turn it down.
Quoted in David Niven *The Moon's a Balloon* (1975).

18 Success is a great deodorant.
1977 ABC TV broadcast, 6 Apr.

19 You help them get elected, and then the Senate becomes the wife, the mistress. That was one lady I couldn't begin to fight. She was too tough.
1987 After her marriage to Senator John Warner. In *Cosmopolitan*, Sep.

20 Some of my best leading men have been horses and dogs.
Attributed.

Taylor, Graham 1944–

English football manager. Manager of Aston Villa and other sides, he succeeded Bobby Robson as manager of England in 1990 but resigned three years later after England failed to qualify for the 1994 World Cup.

21 Agents do nothing for the good of football. I'd like to see them lined up against a wall and machine-gunned …some accountants and solicitors with them.
1983 Quoted in Peter Ball and Phil Shaw *The Book of Football Quotations* (1989).

22 Do I not like that!
1993 During England defeat to Norway, recorded in television documentary.

Taylor, Jeremy 1613–67

English divine, whose sermons and devotional writings are masterpieces and considered to be of sacred eloquence.

23 Faith gives new light to the soul, but it does not put our eyes out; and what God hath given us in our nature could never be intended as a snare to Religion, or engage us to believe a lie.
1660 *The Worthy Communicant*.

Taylor, John Vincent

24 The Holy Spirit is the invisible third party who stands between me and the other, making us mutually aware.
1972 *The Go-Between God.*

25 [God's] changelessness means that he cannot cease to be what he is, but it does not preclude his doing some new thing to express what he is.
1992 *The Christlike God.*

Taylor, Maxwell Davenport 1901–87

US soldier, air commander in World War II and superintendent of West Point (1945–9). After commanding in Korea and the Far East, he was appointed army chief of staff (1955–9) but resigned when his proposals for army reorganization were disregarded. He was instrumental in securing US support for the war in Vietnam.

26 They didn't know how it ran, where you put in the gas, where you put in the oil, where you turn the throttle.
On the Kennedy White House and the botched invasion of Cuba's Bay of Pigs. Quoted in Ralph G Martin *A Hero for Our Time* (1983).

Teal, Clare

English jazz singer.

27 Jazz is a small word for a vast sound.
2002 In *The Guardian*, 29 Dec.

Tebbit, Norman (Beresford) Tebbit, Baron 1931–

English Conservative politician, Employment Secretary (1981–3) and Secretary for Trade and Industry (1983–5). In 1984 he and his wife were injured by an IRA bomb in Brighton. In 1985 he became Chairman of the Party, but after 1987 he returned to the backbenches until his retirement in 1992.

28 He didn't riot. He got on his bike and looked for work, and he kept looking till he found it.
1981 Speaking of his father after criticism of high unemployment under the Conservative Government, party conference, 15 Oct.

29 The cricket test—which side do they cheer for?
1990 On the loyalties of immigrants in Britain. In the *Los Angeles Times*, Apr.

Te Kanawa, Dame Kiri 1944–

New Zealand soprano.

30 When men reach about the age of 50 they tend to digress and don't want to do anything. You can't inspire them to do anything—they almost go to sleep in their bodies.
2001 In *The Mail on Sunday*, 25 Nov.

Teller, Edward 1908–2003

Hungarian-born US physicist, called the father of the hydrogen bomb. He was born in Budapest, and educated in Germany. In 1941 he became a US citizen and joined the US atomic bomb development project known as the Manhattan Project.

31 If there ever was a misnomer, it is 'exact science'. Science has always been full of mistakes; they require a genius to correct them. Of course, we do not see our own mistakes.
1991 *Conversations on the Dark Secrets of Physics.*

Temple, William 1881–1944

English prelate. Headmaster of Repton School (1910–14), he became a bishop in 1921, Archbishop of York in 1919, and succeeded as Archbishop of Canterbury in 1942. He was an outspoken advocate of social reform.

32 Personally, I have always looked upon cricket as organized loafing.
c.1914 Address to parents of pupils at Repton School, Derbyshire.

33 Christianity is the most materialist of all great religions.
1939 *Readings in St John's Gospel*, vol.1.

34 I believe in the Church, one Holy Catholic and Apostolic Church; and nowhere does it exist.
Attributed.

Templeton, Charles 1915–2001

Canadian media personality and author.

35 You are born with two things: existence and opportunity, and these are the raw materials out of which you can make a successful life.
1989 *Succeeding.*

Tennyson, Alfred, 1st Baron *also called* **Alfred, Lord Tennyson** 1809–92

English lyric poet, a master of rhythm, mood and imagery. He became Poet Laureate in 1850. Among the finest poems are *Morte d'Arthur* (1842), the elegiac *In Memoriam* (1850) and *The Idylls of the King* (1859).

36 Below the thunders of the upper deep;
Far, far beneath in the abysmal sea,
His ancient, dreamless, uninvaded sleep
The Kraken sleepeth.
1830 *Poems, Chiefly Lyrical*, 'The Kraken', l.1–4.

37 There hath he lain for ages and will lie
Battening upon huge seaworms in his sleep
Until the latter fire shall heat the deep.
1830 *Poems, Chiefly Lyrical*, 'The Kraken', l.11–13.

38 Vex not thou the poet's mind
With thy shallow wit:
Vex not thou the poet's mind;
For thou canst not fathom it.
1830 *Poems, Chiefly Lyrical*, 'The Poet's Mind', l.1–4.

39 Airy, fairy Lilian.
1830 *Poems*, 'Lilian', l.1.

40 A daughter of the gods, divinely tall,
And most divinely fair.
1832 *Poems*, 'A Dream of Fair Women', l.87–8.

41 O Love, O fire! once he drew
With one long kiss my whole soul through
My lips, as sunlight drinketh dew.
1832 *Poems*, 'Fatima', stanza 3.

42 On either side the river lie
Long fields of barley and of rye,
That clothe the wold and meet the sky;
And through the field the road runs by
To many-towered Camelot.
1832 *Poems*, 'The Lady of Shalott' (revised 1842), pt.1, l.1–5.

43 Willows whiten, aspens quiver,
Little breezes dusk and shiver.
1832 *Poems*, 'The Lady of Shalott' (revised 1842), pt.1, l.10–11.

44 Four grey walls, and four grey towers,
Overlook a space of flowers,
And the silent isle imbowers
The Lady of Shalott.
1832 *Poems*, 'The Lady of Shalott' (revised 1842), pt.1, l.15–18.

45 Only reapers, reaping early
In among the bearded barley,
Hear a song that echoes cheerly
From the river winding clearly,
Down to towered Camelot.
1832 *Poems*, 'The Lady of Shalott' (revised 1842), pt.1, l.28–32.

46 And moving through a mirror clear
That hangs before her all the year,
Shadows of the world appear.
1832 *Poems*, 'The Lady of Shalott' (revised 1842), pt.2, l.46–8.

47 Or when the moon was overhead,
Came two young lovers lately wed;
'I am half sick of shadows,' said
The Lady of Shalott.
1832 *Poems*, 'The Lady of Shalott' (revised 1842), pt.2, l.69–72.

48 A bow-shot from her bower-eaves,
He rode between the barley-sheaves,
The sun came dazzling through the leaves,
And flamed upon the brazen greaves
Of bold Sir Lancelot.
A red-cross knight forever kneeled
To a lady in his shield,
That sparkled on the yellow field,
Beside remote Shalott.
1832 *Poems*, 'The Lady of Shalott' (revised 1842), pt.3, l.73–81.

49 All in the blue unclouded weather
Thick-jewelled shone the saddle leather,
The helmet and the helmet-feather
Burned like one burning flame together,
As he rode down to Camelot.
1832 *Poems*, 'The Lady of Shalott' (revised 1842), pt.3, l.91–5.

50 She left the web, she left the loom,
She made three paces through the room,
She saw the water-lily bloom,
She saw the helmet and the plume,
She looked down to Camelot.
Out flew the web and floated wide;
The mirror cracked from side to side;
'The curse is come upon me', cried
The Lady of Shalott.
1832 *Poems*, 'The Lady of Shalott' (revised 1842), pt.3, l.109–17.

51 Down she came and found a boat
Beneath a willow left afloat,
And round about the prow she wrote
The Lady of Shalott.
1832 *Poems*, 'The Lady of Shalott' (revised 1842), pt.4, l.123–6.

52 But Lancelot mused a little space;
He said, 'She has a lovely face;
God in his mercy lend her grace,
The Lady of Shalott.'
1832 *Poems*, 'The Lady of Shalott' (revised 1842), pt.4, l.168–71.

53 'Courage!' he said, and pointed toward the land,
'This mounting wave will roll us shoreward soon.'
In the afternoon they came unto a land
In which it seemèd always afternoon.
All round the coast the languid air did swoon,

Breathing like one that hath a weary dream.
1832 *Poems*, 'The Lotos–Eaters', l.1–6.

54 There is sweet music here that softer falls
Than petals from blown roses on the grass,
Or night dews on still waters between walls
Of shadowy granite, in a gleaming pass;
Music that gentlier on the spirit lies,
Than tired eyelids upon tired eyes.
1832 *Poems*, 'The Lotos–Eaters', Choric Song, stanza 1, l.46–51.

55 There is no joy but calm!
1832 *Poems*, 'The Lotos–Eaters', Choric Song, stanza 2, l.68.

56 Death is the end of life; ah, why
Should life all labour be?
1832 *Poems* 'The Lotos–Eaters', Choric Song, stanza 4, l.86–87.

57 Live and lie reclined
On the hills like Gods together, careless of mankind.
For they lie beside their nectar, and the bolts are hurled
Far below them in the valleys, and the clouds are lightly
curled
Round their golden houses, girdled with the gleaming
world.
1832 *Poems*, 'The Lotos–Eaters', Choric Song, stanza 8, l.154–8.

58 Surely, surely, slumber is more sweet than toil, the shore
Than labour in the deep mid-ocean, wind and wave and
oar;
Oh rest ye, brother mariners, we will not wander more.
1832 *Poems*, 'The Lotos–Easters', Choric Song, stanza 8, l.171–3.

59 I built my soul a lordly pleasure-house,
Wherein at ease for aye to dwell.
1832 *Poems*, 'The Palace of Art', stanza 1, l.1–2.

60 And 'while the world runs round and round,' I said,
'Reign thou apart, a quiet king,
Still as, while Saturn whirls, his steadfast shade
Sleeps on his luminous ring.'
1832 *Poems*, 'The Palace of Art', stanza 4, l.13–16.

61 An English home—grey twilight poured
On dewy pasture, dewy trees,
Softer than sleep—all things in order stored,
A haunt of ancient Peace.
1832 *Poems*, 'The Palace of Art', stanza 22, l.85–8.

62 It little profits that an idle king
By this still hearth, among these barren crags,
Matched with an agèd wife, I mete and dole
Unequal laws unto a savage race,
That hoard, and sleep, and feed, and know not me.
1833 *Poems*, 'Ulysses' (published 1842), l.1–5.

63 I cannot rest from travel: I will drink
Life to the lees: all times I have enjoyed
Greatly, have suffered greatly, both with those
That loved me, and alone; on shore, and when
Through scudding drifts the rainy Hyades
Vext the dim sea: I am become a name;
For always roaming with a hungry heart
Much have I seen and known; cities of men
And manners, climates, council, governments,
Myself not least, but honoured of them all;
And drunk delight of battle with my peers,
Far on the ringing plains of windy Troy.
I am part of all that I have met;
Yet all experience is an arch wherethrough
Gleams that untravelled world, whose margin fades

For ever and for ever when I move.
How dull it is to pause, to make an end,
To rust unburnished, not to shine in use!
As though to breathe were life.
1833 *Poems*, 'Ulysses' (published 1842), l.6–24.

64 This grey spirit yearning in desire
To follow knowledge like a sinking star,
Beyond the utmost bound of human thought.
1833 *Poems*, 'Ulysses' (published 1842), l.30–2.

65 This is my son, mine own Telemachus.
1833 *Poems*, 'Ulysses' (published 1842), l.33.

66 There lies the port; the vessel, puffs her sail:
There gloom the dark broad seas. My mariners,
Souls that have toiled, and wrought, and thought with
  me—
That ever with a frolic welcome took
The thunder and the sunshine, and opposed
Free hearts, free foreheads—you and I are old:
Old age hath yet his honour and his toil;
Death closes all: but something ere the end,
Some work of noble note, may yet be done,
Not unbecoming men that strove with gods.
The lights begin to twinkle from the rocks:
The long day wanes: the slow moon climbs: the deep
Moans round with many voices. Come, my friends,
'Tis not too late to seek a newer world.
Push off, and sitting well in order smite
The sounding furrows: for my purpose holds
To sail beyond the sunset, and the baths
Of all the western stars, until I die.
It may be that the gulfs will wash us down:
It may be we shall touch the Happy Isles,
And see the great Achilles, whom we knew.
Though much is taken, much abides: and though
We are not now that strength which in old days
Moved earth and hearth: that which we are, we are:
One equal temper of heroic hearts,
Made weak by time and fate, but strong in will
To strive, to seek, to find, and not to yield.
1833 *Poems*, 'Ulysses' (published 1842), l.44–70.

67 Break, break, break,
On thy cold grey stones, O Sea!
And I would that my tongue could utter
The thoughts that arise in me.
1842 *Poems*, 'Break, Break, Break', stanza 1.

68 And the stately ships go on
To their haven under the hill;
But O for the touch of a vanished hand,
And the sound of a voice that is still!
1842 *Poems*, 'Break, Break, Break', stanza 3.

69 'Tis not your work, but Love's. Love, unperceived,
A more ideal Artist he than all,
Came, drew your pencil from you, made those eyes
Darker than the darkest pansies, and that hair
More black than ashbuds in the front of March.
1842 *Poems*, 'The Gardener's Daughter', l.24–8.

70 A sight to make an old man young.
1842 *Poems*, 'The Gardener's Daughter', l.140.

71 Then she rode forth, clothed on with chastity.
1842 *Poems*, 'Godiva', l.53.

72 With twelve great shocks of sound, the shameless noon

Was clashed and hammered from a hundred towers.
1842 *Poems*, 'Godiva', l.74–5.

73 At me you smiled, but unbeguiled
I saw the snare, and I retired:
The daughter of a hundred Earls,
You are not one to be desired.
1842 *Poems*, 'Lady Clara Vere de Vere', stanza 1, l.5–8.

74 From yon blue heavens above us bent
The gardener Adam and his wife
Smile at the claims of long descent.
Howe'er it be, it seems to me,
'Tis only noble to be good.
Kind hearts are more than coronets,
And simple faith than Norman blood.
1842 *Poems*, 'Lady Clara Vere de Vere', stanza 7, l.50–6.

75 In the Spring a fuller crimson comes upon the robin's
  breast;
In the Spring the wanton lapwing gets himself another
  crest
In the Spring a livelier iris changes on the burnished
  dove;
In the Spring a young man's fancy lightly turns to
  thoughts of love.
1842 *Poems*, 'Locksley Hall', l.17–20.

76 And our spirits rushed together at the touching of the lips.
1842 *Poems*, 'Locksley Hall', l.38.

77 He will hold thee, when his passion shall have spent its
  novel force,
Something better than his dog, a little dearer than his
  horse.
1842 *Poems*, 'Locksley Hall', l.49–50.

78 This is truth the poet sings,
That a sorrow's crown of sorrow is remembering happier
  things.
1842 *Poems*, 'Locksley Hall' l.75–6.

79 Like a dog, he hunts in dreams.
1842 *Poems*, 'Locksley Hall', l.79.

80 But the jingling of the guinea helps the hurt that Honour
  feels.
1842 *Poems*, 'Locksley Hall', l.105.

81 Men, my brothers, men the workers, ever reaping
  something new:
That which they have done but earnest of the things that
  they shall do:

For I dipped into the future, far as human eye could see,
Saw the vision of the world, and all the wonder that
  would be;

Saw the heaven fill with commerce, argosies of magic
  sails,
Pilots of the purple twilight, dropping down with costly
  bales;

Heard the heavens fill with shouting, and there rained a
  ghastly dew
From the nations' airy navies grappling in the central
  blue;

Far along the world-wide whisper of the south-wind
  rushing warm,

With the standards of the peoples plunging through the thunder-storm;

Till the war-drum throbbed no longer, and the battle-flags were furled
In the Parliament of man, the Federation of the world.
1842 *Poems*, 'Locksley Hall', l.117–28.

82 Science moves, but slowly slowly, creeping on from point to point.
1842 *Poems*, 'Locksley Hall', l.134.

83 Yet I doubt not through the ages one increasing purpose runs,
And the thoughts of men are widened with the process of the suns.
1842 *Poems*, 'Locksley Hall', l.137–8.

84 Knowledge comes, but wisdom lingers, and I linger on the shore,
And the individual withers, and the world is more and more.
1842 *Poems*, 'Locksley Hall', l.141–2.

85 I will take some savage woman, she shall rear my dusky race.
1842 *Poems*, 'Locksley Hall', l.168.

86 I the heir of all the ages, in the foremost files of time.
1842 *Poems*, 'Locksley Hall', l.178.

87 Forward, forward let us range,
Let the great world spin for ever down the ringing grooves of change.
1842 *Poems*, 'Locksley Hall', l.181–2.

88 Better fifty years of Europe than a cycle of Cathay.
1842 *Poems*,' Locksley Hall', l.184.

89 This truth within thy mind rehearse,
That in a boundless universe
Is boundless better, boundless worse.
1842 *Poems*, 'The Two Voices', stanza 9, l.25–7.

90 No life that breathes with human breath
Has ever truly longed for death.
1842 *Poems*, 'The Two Voices', stanza 132, l.395–6.

91 Fill the cup, and fill the can:
Have a rouse before the morn:
Every moment dies a man,
Every moment one is born.
1842 *Poems*, 'The Vision of Sin', pt.4, stanza 9, l.95–8.

92 I grow in worth, and wit, and sense,
Unboding critic-pen,
Or that eternal want of pence,
Which vexes public men.
1842 *Poems*, 'Will Waterproof's Lyrical Monologue', stanza 6, l.41–4.

93 A land of settled government,
A land of just and old renown,
Where Freedom slowly broadens down
From precedent to precedent.
1842 *Poems*, 'You ask me, why, though ill at ease', stanza 3, l.9–12.

94 But we grow old, Ah! when shall all men's good
Be each man's rule, and universal peace
Lie like a shaft of light across the land,
And like a lane of beams athwart the sea,
Through all the circle of the golden year.
1846 'The Golden Year', l.47–51.

95 With prudes for proctors, dowagers for deans,
And sweet girl-graduates in their golden hair.
1847 *The Princess*, 'Prologue', l.141–2.

96 A classic lecture, rich in sentiment,
With scraps of thundrous Epic lilted out
By violet-hooded Doctors, elegies
And quoted odes, and jewels five-words-long,
That on the stretched forefinger of all Time
Sparkle for ever.
1847 *The Princess*, pt.2, l.352–7.

97 Man is the hunter; woman is his game:
The sleek and shining creatures of the chase,
We hunt them for the beauty of their skins;
They love us for it, and we ride them down.
1847 *The Princess*, pt.5, l.147–50.

98 The woman is so hard
Upon the woman.
1847 *The Princess*, pt.6, l.205–6.

99 No little lily-handed baronet he,
A great broad-shouldered genial Englishman,
A lord of fat prize-oxen and of sheep,
A raiser of huge melons and of pine,
A patron of some thirty charities,
A pamphleteer on guano and on grain.
1847 *The Princess*, 'Conclusion', l.84–9.

1 And blessings on the falling out
That all the more endears,
When we fall out with those we love
And kiss again with tears!
1850 *The Princess*, pt.2, added song, l.6–9.

2 Sweet and low, sweet and low,
Wind of the western sea,
Low, low, breathe and blow,
Wind of the western sea!
Over the rolling waters go,
Come from the dying moon, and blow,
Blow him again to me;
While my little one, while my pretty one, sleeps.

Sleep and rest, sleep and rest,
Father will come to thee soon;
Rest, rest, on mother's breast,
Father will come to thee soon;
Father will come to his babe in the nest,
Silver sails all out of the west
Under the silver moon:
Sleep, my little one, sleep, my pretty one, sleep.
1850 *The Princess*, pt.3, added song, stanzas 1–2.

3 The splendour falls on castle walls
And snowy summits old in story:
The long light shakes across the lakes,
And the wild cataract leaps in glory.
Blow, bugle, blow, set the wild echoes flying,
Blow, bugle; answer, echoes, dying, dying, dying.
1850 *The Princess*, pt.4, added song, stanza 1.

4 O hark, O hear! how thin and clear
And thinner, clearer, farther going!
O sweet and far from cliff and scar
The horns of Elfland faintly blowing!
Blow, let us hear the purple glens replying:

Blow, bugle; answer, echoes, dying, dying, dying.
1850 *The Princess*, pt.4, added song, stanza 2.

5   O love, they die in yon rich sky,
They faint on hill or field or river:
Our echoes roll from soul to soul,
And grow for ever and for ever.
1850 *The Princess*, pt.4, added song, stanza 3.

6   Tears, idle tears, I know not what they mean,
Tears from the depth of some divine despair
Rise in the heart, and gather to the eyes,
In looking on the happy autumn-fields,
And thinking of the days that are no more.
1850 *The Princess*, pt.4, added song, stanza 1.

7   So sad, so fresh, the days that are no more.
1850 *The Princess*, pt.4, added song, stanza 2.

8   Ah, sad and strange as in dark summer dawns
The earliest pipe of half-awakened birds
To dying ears, when unto dying eyes
The casement slowly grows a glimmering square;
So sad, so strange, the days that are no more.

Dear as remembered kisses after death,
And sweet as those by hopeless fancy feigned
On lips that are for others; deep as love,
Deep as first love, and wild with all regret;
O Death in Life, the days that are no more.
1850 *The Princess*, pt.4, added song, stanzas 3–4.

9   O Swallow, Swallow, flying, flying South,
Fly to her, and fall upon her gilded eaves,
And tell her, tell her, what I tell to thee.
O tell her, Swallow, thou that knowest each,
That bright and fierce and fickle is the South,
And dark and true and tender is the North.
1850 *The Princess*, pt.4, added song, stanzas 1–2.

10 O tell her, Swallow that thy brood is flown:
Say to her, I do but wanton in the South,
But in the North long since my nest is made.
1850 *The Princess*, pt.4, added song, stanza 6.

11 Home they brought her warrior dead.
She nor swooned, nor uttered cry:
All her maidens, watching said,
'She must weep or she will die.'
1850 *The Princess*, pt.6, added song, stanza 1.

12 Rose a nurse of ninety years,
Set his child upon her knee—
Like summer tempest came her tears—
'Sweet my child, I live for thee.'
1850 *The Princess*, pt.6, added song, stanza 4.

13 Ask me no more: what answer should I give?
I love not hollow cheek or faded eye:
Yet, O my friend, I will not have thee die!
Ask me no more, lest I should bid thee live.
1850 *The Princess*, pt.7, added song, stanza 2.

14 Now sleeps the crimson petal, now the white;
Nor waves the cypress in the palace walk;
Nor winks the gold fin in the porphyry font:
The fire-fly wakens: waken thou, with me.

Now droops the milk-white peacock like a ghost,
And like a ghost she glimmers on to me.
Now lies the Earth all Danaë to the stars,

And all thy heart lies open unto me.

Now slides the silent meteor on, and leaves
A shining furrow, as thy thoughts in me.

Now folds the lily all her sweetness up,
And slips into the bosom of the lake:
So fold thyself, my dearest, thou, and slip
Into my bosom and be lost in me.
1850 *The Princess*, pt.7, added song, complete.

15 Come down, O maid, from yonder mountain height:
What pleasure lives in height?
1850 *The Princess*, pt.7, added song, l.1–2.

16 For love is of the valley, come thou down
And find him; by the happy threshold, he,
Or hand in hand with Plenty in the maize,
Or red with spirited purple of the vats,
Or foxlike in the vine; nor cares to walk
With Death and Morning on the silver horns.
1850 *The Princess*, pt.7, added song, l.184–9.

17 Sweet is every sound,
Sweeter thy voice, but every sound is sweet;
Myriads of rivulets hurrying through the lawn,
The moan of doves in immemorial elms,
With murmuring of innumerable bees.
1850 *The Princess*, pt.7, added song, l.203–7.

18 Come not, when I am dead,
To drop thy foolish tears upon my grave,
To trample round my fallen head,
And vex the unhappy dust thou wouldst not save.
There let the wind sweep and the plover cry;
But thou, go by.

Child, if it were thine error or thy crime
I care no longer, being all unblest;
Wed whom thou wilt, but I am sick of Time,
And I desire to rest.
Pass on, weak heart, and leave me where I lie:
Go by, go by.
1850 'Come not, when I am dead', complete poem.

19 Strong Son of God, immortal Love,
Whom we, that have not seen thy face,
By faith, and faith alone, embrace,
Believing where we cannot prove.
1850 *In Memoriam A.H.H.*, prologue, l.1–4.

20 Thou madest man, he knows not why,
He thinks he was not made to die;
And thou hast made him: thou art just.
1850 *In Memoriam A.H.H.*, prologue, l.10–12.

21 Our little systems have their day;
They have their day and cease to be;
They are but broken lights of thee,
And thou, O Lord, art more than they.
1850 *In Memoriam A.H.H.*, prologue, l.17–20.

22 Let knowledge grow from more to more,
But more of reverence in us dwell;
That mind and soul, according well,
May make one music as before.
1850 *In Memoriam A.H.H.*, prologue, l.25–8.

23 I sometimes hold it half a sin
To put in words the grief I feel;

For words, like Nature, half reveal
And half conceal the Soul within.

But, for the unquiet heart and brain,
A use in measured language lies;
The sad mechanic exercise,
Like dull narcotics, numbing pain.
1850 *In Memoriam A.H.H.*, canto 5, l.1–8.

24 And common is the commonplace,
And vacant chaff well meant for grain.
1850 *In Memoriam A.H.H.*, canto 6, l.3–4.

25 Never morning wore
To evening, but some heart did break.
1850 *In Memoriam A.H.H.*, canto 6, l.7–8.

26 His heavy-shotted hammock-shroud
Drops in his vast and wandering grave.
1850 *In Memoriam A.H.H.*, canto 6, l.15–16.

27 Dark house, by which once more I stand
Here in the long unlovely street,
Doors, where my heart was used to beat
So quickly, waiting for a hand.
1850 *In Memoriam A.H.H.*, canto 7, l.1–4.

28 And ghastly through the drizzling rain
On the bald street breaks the blank day.
1850 *In Memoriam A.H.H.*, canto 7, l.11–12.

29 The last red leaf is whirled away,
The rooks are blown about the skies.
1850 *In Memoriam A.H.H.*, canto 15, l.3–4.

30 There twice a day the Severn fills;
The salt sea-water passes by,
And hushes half the babbling Wye,
And makes a silence in the hills.
1850 *In Memoriam A.H.H.*, canto 19, l.5–8.

31 The Shadow cloaked from head to foot,
Who keeps the keys of all the creeds.
1850 *In Memoriam A.H.H.*, canto 23, l.4–5.

32 And Thought leapt out to wed with Thought
Ere Thought could wed itself with Speech.
1850 *In Memoriam A.H.H.*, canto 23, l.15–16.

33 I envy not in any moods
The captive void of noble rage,
The linnet born within the cage,
That never knew the summer woods.
1850 *In Memoriam A.H.H.*, canto 27, l.1–4.

34 I hold it true, whate'er befall;
I feel it, when I sorrow most;
'Tis better to have loved and lost
Than never to have loved at all.
1850 *In Memoriam A.H.H.*, canto 27, l.13–16.

35 A solemn gladness even crowned
The purple brows of Olivet.
1850 *In Memoriam A.H.H.*, canto 31, l.11–12.

36 Who trusted God was love indeed
And love Creation's final law—
Though Nature, red in tooth and claw
With ravine, shrieked against his creed.
1850 *In Memoriam A.H.H.*, canto 31.

37 Her eyes are homes of silent prayer.
1850 *In Memoriam A.H.H.*, canto 32, l.1.

38 Short swallow-flights of song, that dip

Their wings in tears, and skim away.
1850 *In Memoriam A.H.H.*, canto 48, l.15–16.

39 Be near me when my light is low,
When the blood creeps, and the nerves prick
And tingle; and the heart is sick,
And all the wheels of Being slow.

Be near me when the sensuous frame
Is racked with pains that conquer trust;
And Time, a maniac scattering dust,
And Life, a Fury slinging flame.
1850 *In Memoriam A.H.H.*, canto 50, l.1–8.

40 Oh yet we trust that somehow good
Will be the final goal of ill.
1850 *In Memoriam A.H.H.*, canto 54, l.1–2.

41 That nothing walks with aimless feet;
That not one life shall be destroyed,
Or cast as rubbish to the void,
When God hath made the pile complete.
1850 *In Memoriam A.H.H.*, canto 54, l.5–8.

42 Behold, we know not anything;
I can but trust that good shall fall
At last—far off—at last, to all,
And every winter change to spring.

So runs my dream: but what am I?
An infant crying in the night:
An infant crying for the light:
And with no language but a cry.
1850 *In Memoriam A.H.H.*, canto 54, l.13–20.

43 So careful of the type she seems,
So careless of the single life.
1850 Of Nature. *In Memoriam A.H.H.*, canto 55, l.7–8.

44 The great world's altar-stairs
That slope through darkness up to God.
1850 *In Memoriam A.H.H.*, canto 55, l.15–16.

45 Man, her last work, who seemed so fair,
Such splendid purpose in his eyes,
Who rolled the psalm to wintry skies,
Who built him fanes of fruitless prayer,
Who trusted God was love indeed
And love Creation's final law—
Though Nature, red in tooth and claw
With ravine, shrieked against his creed.
1850 *In Memoriam A.H.H.*, canto 56, l.9–16.

46 Peace; come away: the song of woe
Is after all an earthly song:
Peace; come away: we do him wrong
To sing so wildly: let us go.
1850 *In Memoriam A.H.H.*, canto 57, l.1–4.

47 O Sorrow, wilt thou live with me
No casual mistress, but a wife.
1850 *In Memoriam A.H.H.*, canto 59, l.1–2.

48 Dost thou look back on what hath been,
As some divinely gifted man,
Whose life in low estate began
And on a simple village green;

Who breaks his birth's invidious bar,
And grasps the skirts of happy chance,
And breasts the blows of circumstance,

And grapples with his evil star.
1850 *In Memoriam A.H.H.*, canto 64, l.1–8.

49 So many worlds, so much to do,
So little done, such things to be.
1850 *In Memoriam A.H.H.*, canto 73, l.1–2.

50 Death has made
His darkness beautiful with thee.
1850 *In Memoriam A.H.H.*, canto 74, l.11–12.

51 And round thee with the breeze of song
To stir a little dust of praise.
1850 *In Memoriam A.H.H.*, canto 75, l.11–12.

52 O last regret, regret can die!
1850 *In Memoriam A.H.H.*, canto 78, l.17.

53 Laburnums, dropping-wells of fire.
1850 *In Memoriam A.H.H.*, canto 83, l.12.

54 God's finger touched him, and he slept.
1850 *In Memoriam A.H.H.*, canto 85, l.20.

55 He brought an eye for all he saw;
He mixed in all our simple sports;
They pleased him, fresh from brawling courts
And dusty purlieus of the law.
1850 *In Memoriam A.H.H.*, canto 89, l.9–12.

56 You tell me, doubt is Devil-born.
1850 *In Memoriam A.H.H.*, canto 96, l.4.

57 There lives more faith in honest doubt,
Believe me, than in half the creeds.
1850 *In Memoriam A.H.H.*, canto 96, l.11–12.

58 Their meetings made December June,
Their every parting was to die.
1850 *In Memoriam A.H.H.*, canto 97, l.11–12.

59 He seems so near and yet so far.
1850 *In Memoriam A.H.H.*, canto 97, l.23.

60 Ring out, wild bells, to the wild sky,
The flying cloud, the frosty light:
The year is dying in the night;
Ring out, wild bells, and let him die.

Ring out the old, ring in the new,
Ring, happy bells, across the snow:
The year is going, let him go;
Ring out the false, ring in the true.
1850 *In Memoriam A.H.H.*, canto 106, l.1–8.

61 Ring out the want, the care, the sin,
The faithless coldness of the times;
Ring out, ring out my mournful rhymes,
But ring the fuller minstrel in.

Ring out false pride in place and blood,
The civic slander and the spite;
Ring in the love of truth and right,
Ring in the common love of good.

Ring out old shapes of foul disease;
Ring out the narrowing lust of gold;
Ring out the thousand wars of old,
Ring in the thousand years of peace.

Ring in the valiant man and free,
The larger heart, the kindlier hand;
Ring out the darkness of the land;

Ring in the Christ that is to be.
1850 *In Memoriam A.H.H.*, canto 106, l.17–32.

62 Not the schoolboy heat,
The blind hysterics of the Celt.
1850 *In Memoriam A.H.H.*, canto 109, l.15–16.

63 Now fades the last streak of snow,
Now burgeons every maze of quick
About the flowering squares, and thick
By ashen roots the violets blow.
1850 *In Memoriam A.H.H.*, canto 115, l.1–4.

64 And drowned in yonder living blue
The lark become a sightless song.
1850 *In Memoriam A.H.H.*, canto 115, l.7–8.

65 There, where the long street roars, hath been
The stillness of the central sea.
1850 *In Memoriam A.H.H.*, canto 123, l.3–4.

66 And thou art worthy; full of power;
As gentle; liberal-minded, great,
Consistent; wearing all that weight
Of learning lightly like a flower.
1850 *In Memoriam A.H.H.*, epilogue, l.37–40.

67 One God, one law, one element,
And one far-off divine event,
To which the whole creation moves.
1850 *In Memoriam A.H.H.*, epilogue, l.142–4.

68 He clasps the crag with crooked hands;
Close to the sun in lonely lands,
Ringed with the azure world, he stands.

The wrinkled sea beneath him crawls;
He watches from his mountain walls,
And like a thunderbolt he falls.
1851 'The Eagle', complete poem.

69 Gigantic daughter of the West,
We drink to thee across the flood,
We know thee most, we love thee best,
For art thou not of British blood?
1852 'Hands all Round', stanza 4, l.37–40.

70 The last great Englishman is low.
1852 'Ode on the Death of the Duke of Wellington', stanza 3, l.18.

71 O good grey head which all men knew!
1852 'Ode on the Death of the Duke of Wellington', stanza 4, l.35.

72 O fall'n at length that tower of strength
Which stood four-square to all the winds that blew!
1852 'Ode on the Death of the Duke of Wellington', stanza 4, l.38–9.

73 That world-earthquake, Waterloo!
1852 'Ode on the Death of the Duke of Wellington', stanza 6, l.133.

74 Who never sold the truth to serve the hour,
Nor paltered with Eternal God of power.
1852 'Ode on the Death of the Duke of Wellington', stanza 7, l.179–80.

75 Half a league, half a league,
Half a league onward,
All in the valley of Death
Rode the six hundred.
1854 'The Charge of the Light Brigade', l.1–4.

76 'Forward, the Light Brigade!'
Was there a man dismayed?
Not though the soldier knew

Some one had blundered:
Their's not to make reply,
Their's not to reason why,
Their's but to do and die:
Into the valley of Death
Rode the six hundred.

Cannon to right of them,
Cannon to left of them,
Cannon in front of them
Volleyed and thundered.
1854 'The Charge of the Light Brigade', l.9–21.

77 Into the jaws of Death,
Into the mouth of Hell
Rode the six hundred.
1854 'The Charge of the Light Brigade', l.24–6.

78 Faultily faultless, icily regular, splendidly null,
Dead perfection, no more.
1855 *Maud*, pt.1, sect.2, l.82–3.

79 The passionate heart of the poet is whirled into folly and
vice.
1855 *Maud*, pt.1, sect.4, stanza 7, l.139.

80 And most of all would I flee from the cruel madness of
love,
The honey of poison-flowers and all the measureless ill.
1855 *Maud*, pt.1, sect.4, stanza 10, l.156–7.

81 That jewelled mass of millinery,
That oiled and curled Assyrian Bull.
1855 *Maud*, pt.1, sect.6, stanza 6, l.232–3.

82 She came to the village church,
And sat by a pillar alone;
An angel watching an urn
Wept over her, carved in stone.
1855 *Maud*, pt.1, sect.8, l.301–4.

83 I heard no longer
The snowy-banded, dilettante,
Delicate-handed priest intone.
1855 *Maud*, pt.1, sect.8, l.309–11.

84 Ah God, for a man with heart, head, hand,
Like some of the simple great ones gone
For ever and ever by,
One still strong man in a blatant land,
Whatever they call him, what care I,
Aristocrat, democrat, autocrat—one
Who can rule and dare not lie.
1855 *Maud*, pt.1, sect.10, stanza 5, l.389–95.

85 And ah for a man to arise in me
That the man I am may cease to be!.
1855 *Maud*, pt.1, sect.10, stanza 6, l.396–7.

86 I kissed her slender hand,
She took the kiss sedately;
Maud is not seventeen,
But she is tall and stately.
1855 *Maud*, pt.1, sect.12, stanza 4, l.424–7.

87 Gorgonised me from head to foot
With a stony British stare.
1855 *Maud*, pt.1, sect.13, stanza 2, l.464–5.

88 A livelier emerald twinkles in the grass,
A purer sapphire melts into the sea.
1855 *Maud*, pt.1, sect.18, stanza 6, l.649–50.

89 Come into the garden, Maud,
For the black bat, night, has flown,
Come into the garden, Maud,
I am here at the gate alone;
And the woodbine spices are wafted abroad,
And the musk of the rose is blown.

For a breeze of morning moves,
And the planet of Love is on high,
Beginning to faint in the light that she loves
On a bed of daffodil sky.
1855 *Maud*, pt.1, sect.22, stanza 1, l.850–9.

90 All night has the casement jessamine stirred
To the dancers dancing in tune;
Till a silence fell with the waking bird,
And a hush with the setting moon.
1855 *Maud*, pt.1, sect.22, stanza 3, l.864–7.

91 Queen rose of the rosebud garden of girls.
1855 *Maud*, pt.1, sect.22, stanza 9, l.902.

92 There has fallen a splendid tear
From the passion-flower at the gate.
She is coming, my dove, my dear;
She is coming, my life, my fate;
The red rose cries, 'She is near, she is near;'
And the white rose weeps, 'She is late;'
The larkspur listens, 'I hear, I hear;'
And the lily whispers, 'I wait.'

She is coming, my own, my sweet;
Were it ever so airy a tread,
My heart would hear her and beat,
Were it earth in an earthy bed;
My dust would hear her and beat,
Had I lain for a century dead;
Would start and tremble under her feet,
And blossom in purple and red.
1855 *Maud*, pt.1, sect.22, stanzas 10–11, l. 908–23.

93 O that 'twere possible
After long grief and pain
To find the arms of my true love
Round me once again!
1855 *Maud*, pt.2, sect.4, stanza 1, l.141–4.

94 Dead, long dead,
Long dead!
And my heart is a handful of dust,
And the wheels go over my head.
1855 *Maud*, pt.2, sect.5, stanza 1, l.239–42.

95 But the churchmen fain would kill their church,
As the churches have killed their Christ.
1855 *Maud*, pt.2, sect.5, stanza 2, l.266–7.

96 O me, why have they not buried me deep enough?
Is it kind to have made me a grave so rough,
Me, that was never a quiet sleeper?
1855 *Maud*, pt.2, sect. 5, stanza 11, l.334–6.

97 My life has crept so long on a broken wing
Through cells of madness, haunts of horror and fear,
That I come to be grateful at last for a little thing.
1855 *Maud*, pt.2, sect.6, stanza 1, l.1–3.

98 When the face of night is fair on the dewy downs,
And the shining daffodil dies.
1855 *Maud*, pt.3, sect.6, stanza 1, l.5–6.

99 And now by the side of the Black and the Baltic deep,
  And deathful-grinning mouths of the fortress, flames
  The blood-red blossom of war with a heart of fire.
  1855 *Maud*, pt.3, sect.6, stanza 4, l.51–3.

1 It is better to fight for the good, than to rail at the ill;
  I have felt with my native land, I am one with my kind,
  I embrace the purpose of God, and the doom assigned.
  1855 *Maud*, pt.3, sect.6, stanza 5, l.57–9.

2 I come from haunts of coot and hern,
  I make a sudden sally
  And sparkle out among the fern,
  To bicker down a valley.
  1855 'The Brook', l.23–6.

3 For men may come and men may go,
  But I go on for ever.
  1855 'The Brook', l.33–4.

4 That a lie which is all a lie may be met and fought with
    outright,
  But a lie which is part a truth is a harder matter to fight.
  1859 'The Grandmother', stanza 8, l.31–2.

5 Wearing the white flower of a blameless life,
  Before a thousand peering littlenesses,
  In that fierce light which beats upon a throne,
  And blackens every blot.
  1859 *Idylls of the King*, dedication, l.24–7.

6 For man is man and master of his fate.
  1859 *Idylls of the King*, 'The Marriage of Geraint', l.355.

7 Our hoard is little, but our hearts are great.
  1859 *Idylls of the King*, 'The Marriage of Geraint', l.374.

8 They take the rustic murmur of their bourg
  For the great wave that echoes round the world.
  1859 *Idylls of the King*, 'The Marriage of Geraint', l.419–20.

9 It is little rift within the lute,
  That by and by will make the music mute,
  And ever widening slowly silence all.
  1859 *Idylls of the King*, 'Merlin and Vivien', l.388–90.

10 And trust me not at all or all in all.
  1859 *Idylls of the King*, 'Merlin and Vivien', l.396.

11 Man dreams of fame while woman wakes to love.
  1859 *Idylls of the King*, 'Merlin and Vivien', l.458.

12 With this for motto, 'Rather use than fame'.
  1859 *Idylls of the King*, 'Merlin and Vivien', l.478.

13 Where blind and naked Ignorance
  Delivers brawling judgements, unashamed,
  On all things all day long.
  1859 *Idylls of the King*, 'Merlin and Vivien', l.662–4.

14 But every page having an ample marge,
  And every marge enclosing in the midst
  A square of text that looks a little blot.
  1859 *Idylls of the King*, 'Merlin and Vivien', l.667–9.

15 Elaine the fair, Elaine the loveable,
  Elaine the lily maid of Astolat.
  1859 *Idylls of the King*, 'Lancelot and Elaine'.

16 He is all fault who hath no fault at all:
  For who loves me must have a touch of earth.
  1859 *Idylls of the King*, 'Lancelot and Elaine', l.132–3.

17 In me there dwells
  No greatness, save it be some far-off touch
  Of greatness to know well I am not great.
  1859 *Idylls of the King*, 'Lancelot and Elaine', l.447–9.

18 I know not if I know what true love is,
  But if I know, then, if I love not him,
  I know there is none other I can love.
  1859 *Idylls of the King*, 'Lancelot and Elaine', l.672–4.

19 The shackles of an old love straitened him,
  His honour rooted in dishonour stood,
  And faith unfaithful kept him falsely true.
  1859 *Idylls of the King*, 'Lancelot and Elaine', l.870–2.

20 —Never yet
  Was noble man but made ignoble talk.
  He makes no friend who never made a foe.
  1859 *Idylls of the King*, 'Lancelot and Elaine', l.1081–2.

21 To reverence the King, as if he were
  Their conscience, and their conscience as their King,
  To break the heathen and uphold the Christ,
  To ride abroad redressing human wrongs,
  To speak no slander, no, nor listen to it,
  To honour his own words as if his God's.
  1859 *Idylls of the King*, 'Guinevere', l.465–70.

22 To love one maiden only, cleave to her,
  And worship her by years of noble deeds,
  Until they won her; for indeed I knew
  Of no more subtle master under heaven
  Than is the maiden passion for a maid,
  Not only to keep down the base in man,
  But teach high thought, and aimable words
  And courtliness, and the desire of fame,
  And love of truth, and all that makes man.
  1859 *Idylls of the King*, 'Guinevere', l.472–80.

23 I thought I could not breathe in that fine air
  That pure severity of perfect light—
  I yearned for warmth and colour which I found
  In Lancelot.
  1859 *Idylls of the King*, 'Guinevere', l.640–3.

24 It was my duty to have loved the highest;
  It surely was my profit had I known:
  It would have been my pleasure had I seen.
  We needs must love the highest when we see it,
  Not Lancelot, nor another.
  1859 *Idylls of the King*, 'Guinevere', l.652–6.

25 The woods decay, the woods decay and fall,
  The vapours weep their burthen to the ground,
  Man comes and tills the field and lies beneath,
  And after many a summer dies the swan.
  Me only cruel immortality
  Consumes: I wither slowly in thine arms,
  Here at the quiet limit of the world.
  1860 'Tithonus' (revised 1864), l.1–7.

26 Why wilt thou ever scare me with thy tears,
  And make me tremble lest a saying learnt,
  In days far-off, on that dark earth, be true?
  'The gods themselves cannot recall their gifts.'
  1860 'Tithonus' (revised 1864), l.46–9.

27 Of happy men that have the power to die,
  And grassy barrows of the happier dead.
  1860 'Tithonus' (revised 1864), l.70–1.

28 O mighty-mouthed inventor of harmonies,
  O skilled to sing of Time or Eternity,
  God-gifted organ-voice of England,
  Milton, a name to resound for ages.
  1863 'Milton: Alcaics', l.1–4.

29 All that bowery loneliness,
The brooks of Eden mazily murmuring.
1863 'Milton: Alcaics', l.9–10.

30 O you chorus of indolent reviewers.
1863 'Milton: Hendecasyllabics', l.1.

31 And when they buried him the little port
Had seldom seen a costlier funeral.
1864 'Enoch Arden', closing words.

32 The voice of the dead was a living voice to me.
1864 'In the Valley of Cauteretz', l.10.

33 I saw the flaring atom-streams
And torrents of her myriad universe,
Ruining along the illimitable inane
Fly on to clash together again, and make
Another and another frame of things
For ever.
1868 'Lucretius', l.38–40.

34 Nor at all can tell
Whether I mean this day to end myself,
Or lend an ear to Plato where he says,
That men like soldiers may not quit the post
Allotted by the Gods.
1868 'Lucretius', l.145–9.

35 Passionless bride, divine Tranquillity,
Yearned after by the wisest of the wise,
Who fail to find thee, being as thou art
Without one pleasure and without one pain.
1868 'Lucretius', l.265–8.

36 Speak to Him thou for He hears, and Spirit with Spirit
can meet—
Closer is He than breathing, and nearer than hands and
feet.
1869 'The Higher Pantheism', l.11–12.

37 Man's word is God in man.
1869 *Idylls of the King*, 'The Coming of Arthur', l.132.

38 Clothed in white samite, mystic, wonderful.
1869 *Idylls of the King*, 'The Coming of Arthur', l.284.

39 Rain, rain, and sun! a rainbow in the sky!
A young man will be wiser by and by;
An old man's wit may wander ere he die.
1869 *Idylls of the King*, 'The Coming of Arthur', l.402–4.

40 From the great deep to the great deep he goes.
1869 *Idylls of the King*, 'The Coming of Arthur', l.410.

41 Blow trumpet, for the world is white with May.
1869 *Idylls of the King*, 'The Coming of Arthur', l.481.

42 For good ye are and bad, and like to coins,
Some true, some light, but every one of you
Stamped with the image of the King.
1869 *Idylls of the King*, 'The Holy Grail', l.25–7.

43 I will be deafer than the blue-eyed cat,
And thrice as blind as any noonday owl,
To holy virgins in their ecstasies.
1869 *Idylls of the King*, 'The Holy Grail', l.862–4.

44 I found Him in the shining of the stars,
I marked Him in the flowering of His fields,
But in His ways with men I find Him not.
1869 *Idylls of the King*, 'The Passing of Arthur', l.9–11.

45 So all day long the noise of battle rolled
Among the mountains by the winter sea.
1869 *Idylls of the King*, 'The Passing of Arthur', l.170–1.

46 On one side lay the Ocean, and on one
Lay a great water, and the moon was full.
1869 *Idylls of the King*, 'The Passing of Arthur', l.179–80.

47 Authority forgets a dying king.
1869 *Idylls of the King*, 'The Passing of Arthur', l.289.

48 Clothed with his breath, and looking, as he walked,
Larger than human on the frozen hills.
He heard the deep behind him, and a cry
Before.
1869 *Idylls of the King*, 'The Passing of Arthur', l.350–3.

49 And the days darken round me, and the years,
Among new men, strange faces, other minds.
1869 *Idylls of the King*, 'The Passing of Arthur', l.405–6.

50 The old order changeth, yielding place to new,
And God fulfils himself in many ways,
Lest one good custom should corrupt the world.
1869 *Idylls of the King*, 'The Passing of Arthur', l.408–10.

51 If thou shouldst never see my face again,
Pray for my soul. More things are wrought by prayer
Than this world dreams of. Wherefore, let thy voice
Rise like a fountain for me night and day.
For what are men better than sheep or goats
That nourish a blind life within the brain,
If, knowing God, they lift not hands of prayer
Both for themselves and those who call them friend?
For so the whole round earth is every way
Bound by gold chains about the feet of God.
1869 *Idylls of the King*, 'The Passing of Arthur', l.414–23.

52 I am going a long way
With these thou se'st—if indeed I go
(For all my mind is clouded with a doubt)—
To the island-valley of Avilion;
Where falls not hail, or rain, or any snow,
Nor ever wind blows loudly; but it lies
Deep-meadowed, happy, fair with orchard lawns
And bowery hollows crowed with summer sea,
Where I will heal me of my grievous wound.
1869 *Idylls of the King*, 'The Passing of Arthur', l.424–32.

53 Like some full-breasted swan
That, fluting a wild carol ere her death,
Ruffles her pure cold plume, and takes the flood
With swarthy webs.
1869 *Idylls of the King*, 'The Passing of Arthur', l.434–7.

54 But I knaw'd a Quaäker feller as often 'as towd ma this:
'Doänt thou marry for munny, but goä wheer munny is!'
1869 'Northern Farmer. New Style', stanza 5.

55 Taäke my word for it, Sammy, the poor in a loomp is bad.
1869 'Northern Farmer. New Style', stanza 12.

56 The dirty nurse, Experience, in her kind
Hath fouled me.
1871 *Idylls of the King*, 'The Last Tournament', l.317–18.

57 The greater man, the greater courtesy.
1871 *Idylls of the King*, 'The Last Tournament', l.628.

58 Live pure, speak true, right wrong, follow the King—
Else, wherefore born?
1872 *Idylls of the King*, 'Gareth and Lynette', l.117–18.

59 The city is built
To music, therefore never built at all,
And therefore built for ever.
1872 *Idylls of the King*, 'Gareth and Lynette', l.272–4.

60 At Flores in the Azores Sir Richard Grenville lay,
And a pinnace, like a fluttered bird, came flying from far
  away:
'Spanish ships of war at sea! We have sighted fifty-three!'
Then sware Lord Thomas Howard: ''Fore God I am no
  coward;
But I cannot meet them here, for my ships are out of gear,
And the half my men are sick. I must fly, but follow quick.
We are six ships of the line; can we fight with fifty-three?'

Then spake Sir Richard Grenville: 'I know you are no
  coward;
You fly them for a moment to fight with them again.
But I've ninety men and more that are lying sick ashore.
I should count myself the coward if I left them, my Lord
  Howard,
To these Inquisition dogs and the devildoms of Spain.'

So Lord Howard passed away with five ships of war that
  day,
Till he melted like a cloud in the silent summer heaven.
    1878 'The Revenge', stanzas 1–3, l.1–14.

61 And Sir Richard said again: 'We be all good English men.
Let us bang these dogs of Seville, the children of the devil,
For I never turned my back upon Don or devil yet.'
    1878 'The Revenge', stanza 4, l.29–31.

62 And the sun went down, and the stars came out far over
  the summer sea,
But never a moment ceased the fight of the one and the
  fifty-three.
    1878 'The Revenge', stanza 9, l.56–7.

63 'Sink me the ship, Master Gunner—sink her, split her in
  twain!
Fall into the hands of God, not into the hands of Spain!'

And the gunner said 'Ay, ay,' but the seamen made reply:
'We have children we have wives,
And the Lord hath spared our lives.'
    1878 'The Revenge', stanzas 11–12, l.89–93.

64 And they praised him to his face with their courtly
  foreign grace;
But he rose upon their decks, and he cried:
'I have fought for Queen and Faith like a valiant man and
  true;
I have only done my duty as a man is bound to do:
With a joyful spirit I Sir Richard Grenville die!'
And he fell upon their decks, and he died.
    1878 'The Revenge', stanza 13, l.99–104.

65 And little Revenge herself went down by the island crags
To be lost evermore in the main.
    1878 'The Revenge', stanza 14, l.118–19.

66 That man's the true Conservative
Who lops the mouldered branch away.
    1882 'Hands All Round', l.7–8.

67 Pray God our greatness may not fail
Through craven fears of being great.
    1882 'Hands All Round', l.31–2.

68 For nothing worthy proving can be proven,
Nor yet disproven: wherefore thou be wise,
Cleave ever to the sunnier side of doubt.
    1885 'The Ancient Sage', l.66–8.

69 France had shown a light to all men, preached a Gospel,
  all men's good;
Celtic Demos rose a Demon, shriek'd and slaked the
  light with blood.
    1886 'Locksley Hall Sixty Years After', l.89–90.

70 Twilight and evening bell,
And after that the dark!
And may there be no sadness of farewell,
When I embark;

For though from out our bourne of Time and Place
The flood may bear me far,
I hope to see my Pilot face to face
When I have crossed the bar.
    1889 'Crossing the Bar', l.9–16. This was Tennyson's last
    poem.

71 The mellow lin-lan-lone of evening bells.
    1889 'Far-Far-Away', l.5.

72 Launch your vessel,
And crowd your canvas,
And, ere it vanishes
Over the margin,
After it, follow it,
Follow The Gleam.
    1889 'Merlin and The Gleam', stanza 9, l.126–31.

73 What is it all but a trouble of ants in the gleam of a million
  million of suns?
    1889 'Vastness', stanza 2, l.4.

74 A louse in the locks of literature.
    Of Churton Collins. Quoted in Evan Charteris *Life and Letters of
    Sir Edmund Gosse* (1931), ch.14.

Tenzing Norgay *known as* **Sherpa Tenzing** 1914–86

Nepalese mountaineer. He took part in several Himalayan
expeditions before accompanying Edmund Hillary to the
summit of Everest in 1953. Subsequently he became head of
the Institute of Mountaineering in Darjeeling and President of
the Sherpa Association.

75 We done the bugger!
    1953 On reaching the summit of Everest, 29 May.

Terence *full name* **Publius Terentius Afer** 185–159 BC

Roman comic dramatist. A freed slave, he enjoyed his first
success with *Andria* ('The Andrian Girl', 166 BC). His six
surviving comedies are Greek in origin and scene, and four
are directly based on Menander. Many of his conventions were
later used by European dramatists.

76 *Homo sum: nihil humani a me alienum puto.*
I am a man, I regard nothing that is human alien to me.
    163 BC *Heauton timorumenos*, 77.

77 *Fortis fortuna adiuvat.*
Fortune favours the brave.
    161 BC *Phormio*, 203.

78 *Nil est dictu facilius.*
Nothing is easier to say.
    161 BC *Phormio*, 300.

79 *Quot homines tot sententiae: suo quoique mos.*
There are as many opinions as there are people: each has
his own view.
    161 BC *Phormio*, 454.

Terentianus Maurus 2/3c BC

Latin grammarian from north Africa. He is remembered for his didactic poem *De litteris syllabis et metris*.

80 *Pro captu lectoris habent sua fata libelli.*
Depending on the reception of the reader, books have their own fate.
De litteris syllabis et metris, 1286. The phrase is often incorrectly attributed to Horace.

Terry, Quinlan 1937–

English architect.

81 An architect is only really a glorified tailor and if people want a suit—as long as they don't ask for three sleeves or something—it's do-able.
2004 In the *Observer*, 7 Mar.

Tertullian *full name* *Quintus Septimius Florens Tertullianus* c.160–c.220 AD

Christian theologian, a lawyer in Rome until he converted in c.196 AD, an opponent of worldliness in the Church and leader of the Montanist sect (c.207 AD). His most famous work is *Apologeticus* (c. 197 AD), an impassioned defence of Christianity against pagan charges of immorality, economic worthlessness and political subversion.

82 *Plures efficimus quoties metimur a vobis, semen est sanguis Christianorum.*
As often as we are mown down by you, the more we grow in numbers; the blood of the Christians is the seed.
Apologeticus, ch.50, section 13. The phrase is often quoted as 'The blood of the martyrs is the seed of the church.'

83 *Certum est quia impossibile est.*
It is certain because it is impossible.
De Carne Christi, ch.5. The phrase is commonly rendered 'It is so extraordinary that it must be true.'

Tessimond, A(rthur) S(eymour) J(ohn) 1902–62

84 Cats, no less liquid than their shadows,
Offer no angles to the wind.
They slip, diminished, neat, through loopholes
Less than themselves.
'Cats', pt.2.

Thackeray, William Makepeace 1811–63

English novelist. He earned his living from journalism, working for *Punch* from 1842–54. He provided a complex view of the changing nature of English society with its mingling of rich parvenus and decadent upper class. His best-known novels include *Vanity Fair* (1847–8) and *Henry Esmond* (1852).

85 'A chilli,' said Rebecca, gasping, 'Oh, yes!' She thought a chilli was something cool, as its name imported, and was served with some. 'How fresh and green they look,' she said, and put one into her mouth. It was hotter than the curry; flesh and blood could bear it no longer. She laid down her fork. 'Water, for Heaven's sake, water!' she cried.
1847–8 *Vanity Fair*, ch.3

86 A woman with fair opportunities and without a positive hump, may marry whom she likes.
1847–8 Rebecca Sharp. *Vanity Fair*, ch.4.

87 Whenever he met a great man he grovelled before him,

and my-lorded him as only a free-born Briton can do.
1847–8 Of Old Osbourne. *Vanity Fair*, ch.13.

88 If a man's character is to be abused, say what you will, there's nobody like a relation to do the business.
1847–8 Miss Crawley. *Vanity Fair*, ch.19.

89 Them's my sentiments!
1847–8 Fred Bullock. *Vanity Fair*, ch.21.

90 Darkness came down on the field and city: and Amelia was praying for George, who was lying on his face, dead, with a bullet through his heart.
1847–8 *Vanity Fair*, ch.32.

91 Nothing like blood, sir, in hosses, dawgs, and men.
1847–8 James Crawley. *Vanity Fair*, ch.35.

92 How to Live Well on Nothing a Year.
1847–8 *Vanity Fair*, ch.36, title of chapter.

93 I think I could be a good woman if I had five thousand a year.
1847–8 *Vanity Fair*, ch.36.

94 Ah! Vanitas Vanitatum! Which of us is happy in this world? Which of us has his desire? or, having it, is satisfied?—Come, children, let us shut up the box and the puppets, for our play is played out.
1847–8 Concluding words. *Vanity Fair*, ch.67.

95 He who meanly admires mean things is a Snob.
1848 *The Book of Snobs*, ch.2.

96 Yes, I am a fatal man, Madame Fribsbi. To inspire hopeless passion is my destiny.
1848–50 Mirobolant. *Pendennis*, ch.23.

97 Remember, it is as easy to marry a rich woman as a poor woman.
1848–50 *Pendennis*, ch.28.

98 The Pall Mall Gazette is written by gentlemen for gentlemen.
1848–50 *Pendennis*, ch.32.

99 For a slashing article, sir, there's nobody like the Capting.
1848–50 Mr Bungay. *Pendennis*, ch.32.

1 'Tis not the dying for a faith that's so hard, Master Harry—every man of every nation has done that—'tis the living up to it that is difficult.
1852 *The History of Henry Esmond*, bk.1, ch.6.

2 'Tis strange what a man may do, and a woman yet think him an angel.
1852 *The History of Henry Esmond*, bk.1, ch.7.

3 What money is better bestowed than that of a schoolboy's tip?
1853–5 *The Newcomes*, vol.1, ch.16.

4 He lifted up his head a little, and quickly said, 'Adsum!' and fell back… He, whose heart was as that of a little child, had answered to his name, and stood in the presence of The Master.
1853–5 *The Newcomes*, vol.1, ch.80.

5 Werther had a love for Charlotte
Such as words could never utter;
Would you know how first he met her?
She was cutting bread and butter.
1855 'Sorrows of Werther'.

6 Business first; pleasure afterwards
1855 *The Rose and the Ring*, ch.1.

Tharp, Twyla 1941–

US dancer and choreographer.

7 The notion of doing something impossibly new usually turns out to be an illusion.
1995 In *The Independent*, 8 Dec.

Thatcher, Margaret Hilda Thatcher, Baroness 1925–

English Conservative politician and Prime Minister (1979–90). A research chemist, she entered Parliament (1959) and was Minister of Education (1970–4), becoming party leader in 1975. As premier she instituted privatization of nationalized industries and utilities. She resigned (Nov 1990) after a leadership challenge following controversy over economic union with Europe.

8 No woman in my time will be Prime Minister or Chancellor of the Exchequer or Foreign Secretary—not the top jobs. Anyway, I would not want to be Prime Minister; you have to give yourself 100 per cent.
1969 On her appointment as a junior Education Minister, in the *Sunday Telegraph*, 26 Oct.

9 I owe nothing to Women's Lib.
1974 Quoted in the *Observer*, 1 Dec.

10 In politics, if you want anything said, ask a man. If you want anything done, ask a woman.
1975 *People*, 15 Sep.

11 Let our children grow tall, and some taller than others if they have it in them to do so.
1975 Speech, Oct.

12 I stand before you tonight in my green chiffon evening gown, my face softly made up, my fair hair gently waved…the Iron Lady of the Western World? Me? A Cold War warrior? Well, yes—if that is how they wish to interpret my defence of values and freedoms fundamental to our way of life.
1976 Speech, Dorking. Alluding to the title bestowed upon her by the Soviet defence journal, in *Red Star*, 31 Jan.

13 We want a society in which we are free to make choices, to make mistakes, to be generous and compassionate. That is what we mean by a moral society—not a society in which the State is responsible for everything, and no one is responsible for the State.
1977 Speech, Zurich University, 14 Mar.

14 Let us make this country safe to work in. Let us make this a country safe to walk in. Let us make it a country safe to grow up in. Let us make it a country safe to grow old in.
1979 General election party broadcast, 30 Apr.

15 Unless we change our ways and our direction, our greatness as a nation will soon be a footnote in the history books, a distant memory of an offshore island, lost in the mist of time like Camelot, remembered kindly for its noble past.
1979 General election campaign speech, Bolton, 2 May.

16 Where there is discord, may we bring harmony. Where there is error, may we bring truth. Where there is doubt, may we bring faith. Where there is despair, may we bring hope.
1979 Said on entering No.10 Downing Street for the first time as Prime Minister; 4 May. A misquotation of St Francis of Assisi.
➤ *See St Francis 334:98.*

17 Any woman who understands the problems of running a home will be nearer to understanding the problems of running a country.
1979 Interviewed by the *Observer* four days after becoming Britain's first woman Prime Minister, 8 May.

18 Pennies don't fall from heaven. They have to be earned here on earth.
1979 Quoted in the *Observer*, 'Sayings of the Week', 18 Nov.
➤ *See Burke 169:53.*

19 There is no easy popularity, in that I believe that people accept that there is no alternative.
1980 On her Government's stringent economic policies. Speech at the Conservative Women's Conference, 21 May.

20 To those who wait with bated breath for that favourite media catchphrase, the U-turn, I have only this to say. You turn if you want to. The lady's not for turning.
1980 Address to the Conservative Party Conference.
➤ *See Fry 340:25.*

21 It is exciting to have a real crisis on your hands, when you have spent half your political life dealing with humdrum issues like the environment.
1982 Of the Falklands conflict. Speech to the Scottish Conservative Party Conference, 14 May.

22 This is the day that I was meant not to see.
1984 On attending church the Sunday after she had narrowly escaped being killed in the IRA bomb explosion at the Grand Hotel, Brighton, Oct.

23 I like Mr Gorbachev. We can do business together.
1984 Said on her first meeting with him, before he became premier, 17 Dec.

24 Democracies must try to find ways to starve the terrorist and the hijackers of the oxygen of publicity on which they depend.
1985 Speech to the American Bar Association meeting in London, referring in particular to increasing British press coverage of IRA terrorist activities, 15 Jul.

25 I always cheer up immensely if an attack is particularly wounding because…it means that they have not a single political argument left.
1986 In the *Daily Telegraph*, 21 Mar.

26 If you want to cut your own throat, don't come to me for a bandage.
1986 Comment to Robert Mugabe, Prime Minister of Zimbabwe, when he pressed for sanctions against South Africa. Quoted in *Time*, 7 Jul.

27 To wear your heart on your sleeve isn't a very good plan. You should wear it inside, where it functions best.
1987 Interview, ABC TV, 18 Mar.

28 There is no such thing as society. There are individual men and women, and there are families.
1987 In *Woman's Own*, 31 Oct.

29 I don't mind how much my Ministers talk—as long as they do what I say.
1987 In *The Times*.

30 If one leads a country such as Britain—a strong country that has taken a lead in world affairs in good times and bad, that is always reliable, then you must have a touch of iron about you.
1987 In *The Times*.

31 We have become a grandmother.
1989 *The Times*, 4 Mar.

32 I seem to smell the stench of appeasement in the air.

1990 Describing the western attitude to the Gulf crisis. In *The Independent*, 31 Oct.

33 After three general election victories, leading the only party with clear policies, resolutely carried out, I intend to continue.
1990 On Michael Heseltine's challenge for the leadership of the Conservative Party, in the *Sunday Times*, 18 Nov.

34 I shall fight. I will fight on.
1990 To reporters, on learning that she had not won the necessary majority to secure her re-election as party leader, two days before announcing her decision to step down, 21 Nov.

35 There is no way in which one can buck the market.
1990 Speech to the Commons on 10 Mar, before the Budget, complaining about what she called 'excessive' intervention in the exchange markets which would lead to inflation.

36 If you are guided by opinion polls, you are not practising leadership—you are practising followship.
1991 US TV interview, 5 Mar.

37 Marxism is at the root of debunking journalism.
Quoted in John Birt *The Harder Path* (2002).

38 Is he one of us?
Attributed comment on considering a candidate for office in her new Government.

Theophilus c.10c

Greek writer and courtier. His *Diversarum Artium Schedula* was the most important art book of the Middle Ages, describing the methods of ecclesiastical art of his time.

39 All arts are taught by degrees. The first process in art of the painter is the composition of colours. Let your mind be afterwards applied to the study of the mixtures.
An Essay Upon Various Arts (translated by Robert Hendrie, 1847), bk.1, preface.

Theophrastus c.372–286 BC

Greek philosopher. A student of Aristotle, he succeeded him as head of the Lyceum from 322. Most of his prolific output is lost; among the writings that survive is a volume of *Characters*, containing 30 sketches of different moral types, which has been widely translated and imitated.

40 The sound of the flute will cure epilepsy and sciatic gout.
Quoted in David Pickering *Brewer's Twentieth-Century Music* (1994).

Theresa (of Calcutta), Mother originally *Agnes Gonxha Bojaxhiu* 1910–97

Roman Catholic nun, born in Yugoslavia. She went to India in 1928 and in 1948 left a convent school to work in the slums. She founded the Missionaries of Charity sisterhood (1950) and a House for the Dying (1952), and in 1957 began work with lepers and in disaster areas of the world. She was awarded the Pope John XXIII Peace Prize in 1971, and the Nobel peace prize in 1979.

41 The biggest disease today is not leprosy or tuberculosis, but rather the feeling of being unwanted.
Quoted in the *Observer*, 3 Oct 1971.

42 To keep a lamp burning, we have to keep putting oil in it.
1975 In *Time*, 29 Dec.

43 There should be less talk; a preaching point is not a meeting point. What do you do then? Take a broom and clean someone's house. That says enough.
1975 *A Gift for God*, 'Carriers of Christ's Love'.

44 We need to find God, and he cannot be found in noise and restlessness. God is the friend of silence. See how nature—trees, flowers, grass—grows in silence; see the stars, the moon and the sun, how they move in silence… We need silence to be able to touch souls.
1975 *A Gift for God*, 'Willing Slaves to the Will of God'.

Theroux, Paul Edward 1941–

US novelist and travel writer. His best-known novel is *The Mosquito Coast* (1982), but he is particularly regarded for his travel writings, notably those concerned with epic rail journeys.

45 Extensive travelling induces a feeling of encapsulation, and travel, so broadening at first, contracts the mind.
1975 *The Great Railway Bazaar*, ch.21.

46 Nothing happens in Burma, but then nothing is expected to happen.
1975 *The Great Railway Bazaar*, ch.23.

47 I went to Vietnam to take the train: people have done stranger things in that country.
1975 *The Great Railway Bazaar*, ch.24.

48 The Japanese have perfected good manners and made them indistinguishable from rudeness.
1975 *The Great Railway Bazaar*, ch.28.

49 Like a lower form of life, like the cross-eyed planarian or squashed amoeba, the sort of creature that can't die even when it is cut to pieces.
1975 Of Laos. *The Great Railway Bazaar*.

50 In Turkey it was always 1952, in Malaysia 1937; Afghanistan was 1910 and Bolivia 1949. It is twenty years ago in the Soviet Union, ten in Norway, five in France. It is always last year in Australia and next week in Japan.
1983 *The Kingdom By The Sea*, ch.1.

Thesiger, Sir Wilfred Patrick 1910–2003

English explorer. He twice crossed the Empty Quarter (Rub'al Khali) between 1946 and 1949 and wrote sensitively about the Bedu and their changing way of life.

51 For me, exploration was a personal venture. I did not go to the Arabian desert to collect plants nor to make a map; such things were incidental. At heart I knew that to write or even to talk of my travels was to tarnish the achievement. I went there to find peace in the hardship of desert travel and the company of desert people. I set myself a goal on these journeys, and, although the goal itself was unimportant, its attainment had to be worth every effort and sacrifice.
1959 *Arabian Sands*.

Thiers, (Louis) Adolphe 1797–1877

French statesman, twice Prime Minister (1836, 1839). He supported Napoleon in 1848, but was banished in the *coup d'état* of 1851 and re-entered the Chamber in 1863 as a critic. After the collapse of the Second Empire he suppressed the Paris Commune and became first President of the Third Republic (1871–3). Defeated by monarchists, he resigned in 1873. He wrote *L'histoire du consulat et de l'empire* ('History of the Consulate and the Empire', 20 vols, 1845–62).

52 The Republic will be conservative, or it will be nothing.
1872 Presidential address to the French National Assembly, Nov.

Thomas, (Walter) Brandon 1857–1914

English playwright, actor and songwriter. He is usually remembered for his classic farce, *Charley's Aunt* (1892).

53 Where the nuts come from.
1892 Of Brazil. *Charley's Aunt.*

Thomas, D(onald) M(itchell) 1935–

English writer. He made his initial reputation as a poet, but became better known as the author of the novel *The White Hotel* (1981).

54 Freud becomes one of the dramatis personae, in fact, as discoverer of the great and beautiful modern myth of psychoanalysis. By myth, I mean a poetic, dramatic expression of a hidden truth; and in placing this emphasis, I do not intend to put into question the scientific validity of psychoanalysis.
1981 *The White Hotel*, author's note.

55 She was cut off from the past and therefore did not live in the present. But suddenly, as she stood close against a pine tree and breathed in its sharp, bitter scent, a clear space opened to her childhood, as though a wind had sprung from the sea, clearing a mist. It was not a memory from the past, it was the past itself, as alive, as real; and she knew that she and the child of forty years ago were the same person.
1981 *The White Hotel*, ch.4.

56 The soul of man is a far country, which cannot be approached or explored. Most of the dead were poor and illiterate. But every single one of them had dreamed dreams, seen visions and had amazing experiences, even the babes in arms (perhaps especially the babes in arms).
1981 *The White Hotel*, ch.5.

Thomas, Dylan Marlais 1914–53

Welsh poet. The son of a schoolmaster, he worked as a journalist for a time. He also wrote short stories and novels, and later turned to drama, notably the celebrated radio play *Under Milk Wood* (published 1954). His tempestuous lifestyle culminated in his death from alcohol abuse on a lecture tour of the US.

57 The force that through the green fuse drives the flower
Drives my green age; that blasts the roots of trees
Is my destroyer.
And I am dumb to tell the crooked rose
My youth is bent by the same wintry fever.
1934 'The Force That Through the Green Fuse Drives the Flower'.

58 Light breaks where no sun shines;
Where no sea runs, the waters of the heart
Push in their tides.
1934 'Light Breaks Where No Sun Shines'.

59 Man be my metaphor.
1934 'If I Were Tickled by The Rub of Love'.

60 I am getting more obscure day by day.
1934 Letter to Pamela Hansford Johnson, 9 May.

61 Though they go mad they shall be sane
Though they sink through the sea they shall rise again;
Though lovers be lost love shall not;
And death shall have no dominion.
1936 'And Death Shall Have No Dominion'.

62 The hand that signed the paper felled a city;

Five sovereign fingers taxed the breath,
Doubled the globe of dead and halved a country;
These five kings did a king to death.
1936 'The Hand That Signed the Paper Felled a City'.

63 The hand that signed the treaty bred a fever,
And famine grew, and locusts came;
Great is the hand that holds dominion over
Man by a scribbled name.
1936 'The Hand That Signed the Paper Felled a City'.

64 What is the metre of the dictionary?
1936 'Altarwise by Owl-light'.

65 Shall gods be said to thump the clouds
When clouds are cursed by thunder?
1936 'Shall Gods be Said to Thump the Clouds'.

66 I hold a beast, an angel and a madman within me, and my enquiry is as to their working, and my problem is their subjugation and victory, downthrow and upheaval, and my effort is their self expression.
1938 Letter to Henry Treece.

67 Her fist of a face died clenched on a round pain;
And sculptured Ann is seventy years of stone.
1939 'After the Funeral'.

68 I don't think it does any harm to the artist to be lonely as an artist.
1939 Letter to Pennar Davies.

69 Portrait of the Artist as a Young Dog.
1940 Title of book.

70 And the wild boys innocent as strawberries.
1946 'The Hunchback in the Park'.

71 Now as I was young and easy under the apple boughs
About the lilting house and happy as the grass was green.
1946 'Fern Hill'.

72 Oh as I was young and easy in the mercy of his means,
Time held me green and dying
Though I sang in my chains like the sea.
1946 'Fern Hill'.

73 After the first death, there is no other.
1946 'A Refusal to Mourn the Death, By Fire, of a Child in London'.

74 It was my thirtieth year to heaven
Woke to my hearing from harbour and neighbour wood
And the mussel pooled and the heron
Priested shore.
1946 'Poem in October'.

75 Pale rain over the dwindling harbour
And over the sea wet church the size of a snail
With its horns through mist and the castle
Brown as owls.
1946 'Poem in October'.

76 And I rose
In rainy autumn
And walked abroad in the shower of all my days.
1946 'Poem in October'.

77 I hear John Arlott's voice every weekend, describing cricket matches. He sounds like Uncle Tom Cobleigh reading Neville Cardus to the Indians.
1947 Letter to Margaret Taylor, 11 Jul.

78 The joy and function of poetry is, and was, the celebration of man, which is also the celebration of God.
1951 Letter to a student.

79 If you want a definition of poetry, say: 'Poetry is what makes me laugh or cry or yawn, what makes my toenails twinkle, what makes me want to do this or that or nothing' and let it go at that.
1951 Letter to a student.

80 I fell in love—that is the only expression I can think of—at once, and am still at the mercy of words, though sometimes now, knowing a little of their behaviour very well, I think I can influence them slightly and have even learned to beat them now and gain, which they appear to enjoy.
1951 Letter to a student.

81 Do not go gentle into that good night,
Old age should burn and rave at close of day;
Rage, rage against the dying of the light.
1952 'Do Not Go Gentle Into That Good Night'.

82 These poems, with all their crudities, doubts, and confusions, are written for the love of Man, and in praise of God, and I'd be a damn' fool if they weren't.
1952 Collected Poems, author's note.

83 The land of my fathers. My fathers can have it.
1953 Of Wales. In Adam, Dec.

84 I've had eighteen straight whiskies. I think that's the record.
1953 Attributed, supposedly said before lapsing into his final coma.

85 To begin at the beginning: It is spring, moonless night in the small town, starless and bible-black, the cobblestreets silent and the hunched, courters'-and-rabbits' wood limping invisible down to the sloeblack, slow, black, crowblack, fishingboat-bobbing sea.
1954 Under Milk Wood, opening words.

86 Oh I'm a martyr to music.
1954 Under Milk Wood.

87 The boys are dreaming wicked or of the bucking ranches of the night and the jolly-rogered sea.
1954 Under Milk Wood.

88 And before you let the sun in, mind it wipes its shoes.
1954 Under Milk Wood.

89 Alone until she dies, Bessie Bighead, hired help, born in the workhouse, smelling of the cowshed, snores bass and gruff on a couch of straw in a loft in Salt Lake Farm and picks a posy of daisies in Sunday Meadow to put on the grave of Gomer Owen who kissed her once by the pig-sty when she wasn't looking and never kissed her again although she was looking all the time.
1954 Under Milk Wood.

90 Straightfaced in his cunning sleep he pulls the legs of his dreams.
1954 Under Milk Wood.

91 Nothing grows in our garden, only washing. And babies. And where's their fathers live, my love? Over the hills and far away.
1954 Under Milk Wood.

92 You're thinking, you're no better than you should be, Polly, and that's good enough for me. Oh, isn't life a terrible thing, thank God?
1954 Under Milk Wood.

93 Hullo, Polly, my love, can you hear the dumb goose-hiss of the wives as they huddle and peck or flounce at a waddle away? Who cuddled you when? Which of their gandering hubbies moaned in Milk Wood for your naughty mothering arms and body like a wardrobe, love?
1954 Under Milk Wood.

94 The sun hums down through the cotton flowers of her dress into the bell of her heart and buzzes in the honey there and couches and kisses, lazy-loving and boozed, in her red-berried breast.
1954 Under Milk Wood.

95 Alone in the hissing laboratory of his wishes, Mr Pugh minces among bad vats and jeroboams, tiptoes through spinneys of murdering herbs, agony dancing in his crucibles, and mixes especially for Mrs Pugh a venomous porridge unknown to toxicologists which will scald and viper through her until her ears fall off like figs, her toes grow big and black as balloons, and steam comes screaming out of her navel.
1954 Under Milk Wood.

96 You just wait. I'll sin until I blow up!
1954 Under Milk Wood.

97 Too many of the artists of Wales spend too much time talking about the position of the artists of Wales. There is only one position for an artist anywhere: and that is, upright.
1954 Quite Early One Morning, 'Wales and the Artist'.

98 The best poem is that whose worked-upon unmagical passages come closest, in texture and intensity, to those moments of magical accident.
1954 Quite Early One Morning, 'On Poetry'.

99 A good poem is a contribution to reality. The world is never the same once a good poem has been added to it.
1954 Quite Early One Morning, 'On Poetry'.

1 One Christmas was much like another… I can never remember whether it snowed for six days and six nights when I was twelve or whether it snowed for twelve days and twelve nights when I was six.
1954 A Child's Christmas in Wales.

2 Years and years ago, when I was a boy, when there were wolves in Wales, and birds the colour of red-flannel petticoats whisked past the harp-shaped hills, when we sang and wallowed all night and day in caves that smelt like Sunday afternoons in damp front farmhouse parlours, and we chased, with the jawbones of deacons, the English and the bears, before the motor car, before the wheel, before the duchess-faced horse, when we rode the daft and happy hills bareback, it snowed and it snowed.
1954 A Child's Christmas in Wales.

Thomas, (Philip) Edward 1878–1917

English nature writer and poet. His poetry was all written during World War I, in which he was killed in action at Arras. Very few poems were published in his lifetime, but posthumous collections established his reputation as a great nature poet.

3 A merely great intellect can produce great prose, but not poetry, not one line.
1908 Letter to Gordon Bottomley, 26 Feb.

4 When Gods were young
This wind was old.
1914 'The Mountain Chapel'.

5 The Past is a strange land, most strange.
1915 'Parting'.

6 Yes; I remember Adlestrop—
The name, because one afternoon
Of heat the express-train drew up there
Unwontedly. It was late June.
1915 'Adlestrop'.

7 And for that minute a blackbird sang
Close by, and round him, mistier,
Farther and farther, all the birds
Of Oxfordshire and Gloucestershire.
1915 'Adlestrop'.

8 The men, the music piercing that solitude
And silence, told me truths I had not dreamed,
And have forgotten since their beauty passed.
1915 'Tears'.

9 The last light has gone out of the world, except
This moonlight lying on the grass like frost
Beyond the brink of the tall elm's shadow.
1915 'Liberty'.

10 This is no case of petty right or wrong
That politicians or philosophers
Can judge. I hate not Germans, nor grow hot
With love of Englishmen, to please newspapers.
1915 'This Is No Case of Petty Right Or Wrong'.

11 The dark-lit stream has drowned the Future and the Past.
1915 'The Bridge'.

12 The new moon hangs like an ivory bugle
In the naked frosty blue.
1915 'The Penny Whistle'.

13 It is a fine world and I wish I knew how to make £200 a
year in it.
1915 Letter to Gordon Bottomley, 16 Jun.

14 The past is the only dead thing that smells sweet,
The only sweet thing that is not also fleet.
1916 'Early One Morning'.

15 For the life in them he loved most living things,
But a tree chiefly.
1916 'Bob's Lane'.

16 That girl's clear eyes utterly concealed all
Except that there was something to reveal.
1916 'That Girl's Clear Eyes'.

17 I have come to the borders of sleep,
The unfathomable deep
Forest, where all must lose
Their way, however straight
Or winding, soon or late;
They cannot choose.
1916 'Lights Out'.

18 As well as any bloom upon a flower
I like the dust on the nettles, never lost
Except to prove the sweetness of a shower.
1916 'Tall Nettles'.

19 Now all the roads lead to France
And heavy is the tread
Of the living: but the dead
Returning lightly dance.
1916 'Roads'.

20 Out in the dark over the snow
The fallow fawns invisible go

With the fallow doe;
And the winds blow
Fast as the stars are slow.
1916 'Out in the Dark'.

21 The sorrow of true love is a great sorrow
And true love parting blackens a bright morrow.
1917 'Last Poem'.

Thomas, Sir George   1881–1972

English badminton administrator, founder and first president of
the International Badminton Federation.

22 The art of badminton is to deceive.
Quoted in *The Guinness Book of Badminton* (1983).

Thomas, John Parnell   1895–1970

US congressman. He was an insurance broker before entering
Congress (1937–49). He served as Chairman of the Committee
on Un-American Activities.

23 Are you now, or have you ever been, a member of the
Communist Party?
1947–57 Stock question to those called before the House of
Representatives Committee on Un-American Activities.

Thomas, Michael M   1936–

US novelist.

24 Bankers' genes were Wall St. genes, especially in the big
cities. If the banks were conservative just now [1955], it
was because bankers still awoke in the middle of the
night, trembling and sweaty with thoughts of the Crash.
But in time a new generation would take over: ambitious,
overcompetitive young men to whom 1929 would be
merely a date on a page; such men would sever the roots
of memory as if with an ax, not realizing that those
tendrils were also the rudder cables.
1987 *The Ropespinner Conspiracy*.

Thomas, R(onald) S(tuart)   1913–2000

Welsh poet and priest. His poetry characteristically deals with
the themes of nature, religion and his love of Wales.

25 We were a people taut for war; the hills
Were no harder, the thin grass
Clothed them more warmly than the coarse
Shirts our small bones.
1952 'Welsh History'.

26 An impotent people,
Sick with inbreeding.
Worrying the carcase of an old song.
1952 'Welsh Landscape'.

27 We will listen to the wind's text
Blown through the roof, or the thrush's song
In the thick bush that proved him wrong,
Wrong from the start, for nature's truth
Is primary and her changing seasons
Correct out of a vaster reason
The vague errors of the flesh.
1953 'The Minister'.

28 For the first twenty years you are still growing,
Bodily that is; as a poet, of course,
You are not born yet. It's the next ten
You cut your teeth on to emerge smirking

For your brash courtship of the muse.
1963 'To A Young Poet'.

29 Prompt me, God,
But not yet. When I speak
Though it be you who speak
Through me, something is lost.
The meaning is the waiting.
1968 'Kneeling'.

30 The poem in the rock and
The poem in the mind
Are not one.
It was in dying
I tried to make them so.
1972 'The Epitaph'.

31 Among the forests
Of metal the one human
Sound was the lament of
The poets for deciduous language.
1972 'Postscript'.

32 Life is not hurrying
on to a receding future, nor hankering after
an imagined past. It is the turning
aside like Moses to the miracle
of the lit bush, to a brightness
that seemed as transitory as your youth
once, but is the eternity that awaits you.
1976 *Laboratories of the Spirit*, 'The Bright Field'.

33 We are beginning to see
now it is matter is the scaffolding
of spirit; that the poet emerges
from morphemes and phonemes; that
as form in sculpture is the prisoner
of the hard rock, so in everyday life
it is the plain facts and natural happenings
that conceal God and reveal him to us
little by little under the mind's tooling.
1978 *Frequencies*, 'Emerging'.

Thompson, E P 1924–93

British historian.

34 This going into Europe will not turn out to be the thrilling
mutual exchange supposed. It is more like nine middle-
aged couples with failing marriages meeting in a
darkened bedroom in a Brussels hotel for a group grope.
1975 On Britain's entry into the EEC, in the *Sunday Times*, 27 Apr.

Thompson, Francis 1859–1907

English poet. His poems, mainly religious in theme and
collected in such publications as *Poems* (1893) and *Sister
Songs* (1895), include the well-known 'The Hound of Heaven'.

35 The fairest things have fleetest end,
Their scent survives their close:
But the rose's scent is bitterness
To him that loved the rose.
'Daisy' (published 1890).

36 I fled Him, down the nights and down the days;
I fled Him, down the arches of the years;
I fled Him, down the labyrinthine ways
Of my own mind; and in the midst of tears
I hid from Him, and under running laughter.
1893 *Poems*, 'The Hound of Heaven'.

37 I said to Dawn: Be sudden—to Eve: Be soon.
1893 *Poems*, 'The Hound of Heaven'.

38 O world invisible, we view thee,
O world intangible, we touch thee,
O world unknowable, we know thee,
Inapprehensible, we clutch thee!
1897 'In No Strange Land'.

39 It is little I repair to the matches of the Southron folk,
Though my own red roses there may blow;
It is little I repair to the matches of the Southron folk,
Though the red roses crest the caps, I know.
For the field is full of shades as I near the shadowy coast,
And a ghostly batsman plays to the bowling of a ghost,
And I look through my tears on a soundless-clapping
host
As the run-stealers flicker to and fro,
To and fro:—
O my Hornby and my Barlow long ago!
1907 'At Lord's', poem dedicated to friends to explain why he
could not attend a match at Lord's at their invitation for fear of
the sadness it would cause him, remembering the long-dead
friends who had played there (for Lancashire) back in 1878.

40 There is no expeditious road
To pack and label men for God,
And save them by the barrel-load,
Some may perchance, with strange surprise,
Have blundered into Paradise.
1913 'A Judgment in Heaven', epilogue.

41 Wake! for the Ruddy Ball has taken flight
That scatters the slow Wicket of the Night;
And the swift Batsman of the Dawn has driven
Against the Star-spiked Rails a fiery smite.
'Wake! for the Ruddy Ball has Taken Flight', parody of Edward
Fitzgerald, quoted in J C Squire *Apes and Parrots* (1929).
➤ *See Fitzgerald 324:82.*

Thompson, Hunter S(tockton) 1939–

US writer, inventor of a semi-fictionalized participatory
journalism he dubbed 'gonzo'. His work for *Rolling Stone*
magazine made him a cult figure. He sometimes writes as
'Raoul Duke'.

42 Weird heroes and mould-breaking champions exist as
living proof to those who need it that the tyranny of 'the
rat race' is not yet final.
1969 'Those Daring Young Men In Their Flying Machines…Ain't
What They Used To Be!', in *Pageant*, Sep.

43 History is hard to know…but…it seems entirely
reasonable to think that every now and then the energy
of a whole generation comes to a head in a long fine
flash, for reasons that nobody really understands at the
time—and which never explain, in retrospect, what
actually happened.
1971 *Fear and Loathing in Las Vegas*, ch.8.

44 Absolute truth is a very rare and dangerous commodity
in the context of professional journalism.
1973 'Fear and Loathing at the Superbowl', in *Rolling Stone*,
15 Feb.

45 In a nation ruled by swine, all pigs are upwardly-
mobile—and the rest of us are fucked until we can put
our acts together: not necessarily to win, but mainly to
keep from losing completely. We owe that to ourselves
and our crippled self-image as something better than a

nation of panicked sheep.

1979 *The Great Shark Hunt*, 'Jacket Copy for *Fear and Loathing in Las Vegas*'.

46 Going to trial with a lawyer who considers your whole life-style a Crime in Progress is not a happy prospect.

1990 Letter to *The Champion*, a legal journal, Jul.

Thompson, James R 1936–

US lawyer and politician, Republican governor of Illinois (1977–91).

47 It is not so much who you elect, it's who you throw out.

1981 On the campaign to clean up government. In the *Chicago Tribune*, 26 Jul.

Thompson, Robert 1914–97

Canadian politician, leader of the Social Credit Party of Canada (1961–7) and renowned malapropist.

48 The Americans are our best friends, whether we like it or not.

Oft-quoted remark recalled by Peter C Newman in *Home Country* (1973).

Thompson, Tommy

Canadian public official, Parks Commissioner, Metropolitan Toronto.

49 Please Walk on the Grass

1960 Message on a sign erected in Toronto's Edwards Gardens, which attracted national and then international attention for its 'hands-on' approach to public parks.

Thomson, David 1914–88

Scottish writer. His often autobiographical books include *Woodbrook* and *Nairn in Darkness and Light*.

50 The vice of meanness, condemned in every other country, is in Scotland translated into a virtue called 'thrift'.

1987 *Nairn in Darkness and Light*.

51 Even stroking a cat may be regarded by strict Presbyterians as a carnal sin.

1987 *Nairn in Darkness and Light*.

Thomson, James 1700–48

Scottish poet. He studied for the ministry but moved to London to become a writer. His chief works were *The Castle of Indolence* (1748) and *The Seasons*, an early nature poem extensively revised between 1730 and 1746.

52 When Britain first, at heaven's command,
Arose from out the azure main,
This was the charter of the land,
And guardian angels sung this strain:
'Rule, Britannia, rule the waves;
Britons never will be slaves.'

1740 *Alfred: a Masque*, act 2, sc.5.

53 Delightful task! to rear the tender thought,
To teach the young idea how to shoot.

1746 *The Seasons*, 'Spring', l.1152–3.

54 An elegant sufficiency, content,
Retirement, rural quiet, friendship, books,
Ease and alternate labour, useful life,
Progressive virtue, and approving Heaven!

1746 *The Seasons*, 'Spring', l.1161–4.

55 Or sighed and looked unutterable things.

1746 *The Seasons*, 'Summer', l.188.

56 Poor is the triumph o'er the timid hare!

1746 *The Seasons*, 'Autumn', l.401.

57 Welcome, kindred glooms!
Congenial horrors, hail!

1746 *The Seasons*, 'Winter', l.5–6.

58 There studious let me sit,
And hold high converse with the mighty dead.

1746 *The Seasons*, 'Winter', l.431–2.

59 A little round, fat, oily man of God,
Was one I chiefly marked among the fry:
He had a roguish twinkle in his eye.

1748 *The Castle of Indolence*, canto 1, stanza 69.

Thomson, James *pseudonym* '*BV*', *Bysshe Vanolis* 1834–82

Scottish poet born in Port Glasgow. He trained as an army schoolmaster but was dismissed from army service in 1862 for alcoholism. He worked in London as a poet, journalist and critic, and published his greatest work *The City of Dreadful Night* in 1874.

60 As we rush, as we rush in the train,
The trees and the houses go wheeling back,
But the starry heavens above that plain
Come flying on our track.

1863–5 'Sunday at Hampstead', stanza 10.

61 The City is of Night, but not of Sleep;
There sweet Sleep is not for the weary brain;
The pitiless hours like years and ages creep,
A night seems termless hell.

1874 *The City of Dreadful Night*, pt.1.

62 The City is of Night; perchance of Death,
But certainly of Night.

1874 *The City of Dreadful Night*, pt.1.

63 As I came through the desert thus it was,
As I came through the desert: All was black,
In heaven no single star, on earth no track;
A brooding hush without a stir or note;
The air so thick it clotted in my throat.

1874 *The City of Dreadful Night*, pt.4.

64 Yet I strode on austere;
No hope could have no fear.

1874 *The City of Dreadful Night*, pt.4.

Thomson, Roy Herbert, 1st Baron Thomson of Fleet 1894–1976

Canadian-born British newspaper and television magnate. After setting up his first radio station in 1931 and buying many Canadian and US newspapers, he settled in Edinburgh on acquiring *The Scotsman* (1952), and bought the Kemsley newspapers (1959) and *The Times* (1966).

65 A TV licence is a licence to print money.

1957 On being awarded the licence to operate Scottish Television Ltd, 19 Jun. Recalled in his memoirs *After I Was Sixty* (1975).

Thomson, Virgil 1896–1989

US composer and critic. His work, notable for its simplicity of style, includes the operas *Four Saints in Three Acts* (1934) and *The Mother of Us All* (1947) in addition to symphonies, ballets, choral, chamber and film music. He was music critic of the *New York Herald* (1940–54).

66 A libretto that should never have been accepted on a subject that should never have been chosen by a man who should never have attempted it.
   1935 Of Gershwin's *Porgy and Bess*. *Modern Music*.

67 The way to write American music is simple. All you have to do is be an American and then write any kind of music you wish.
   Quoted in Machlis *Introduction to Contemporary Music* (1963).

Thoreau, Henry David 1817–62

US essayist and poet, known as 'the hermit of Walden'. In 1839 he began his nature studies, and lived as a hermit (1845–7). His works include *Walden, or Life in the Woods* (1854) and his nature observations, beginning with *Early Spring in Massachusetts* (1881). His essay *Civil Disobedience* (1849) was provoked by his opposition to the Mexican war.

68 We seem but to linger in manhood to tell the dreams of our childhood, and they vanish out of memory ere we learn the language.
   1841 Journal entry, 19 Feb.

69 Being is the great explainer.
   1841 Journal entry, 26 Feb.

70 Men reverence one another, not yet God.
   1849 *A Week on the Concord and Merrimack Rivers*, 'Sunday'.

71 Under a government which imprisons any unjustly, the true place for a just man is also a prison.
   1849 *Civil Disobedience*.

72 Read the best books first, or you may not have a chance to read them at all.
   1849 *A Week on the Concord and Merrimack Rivers*, 'Sunday'.

73 The lawyer's truth is not Truth, but consistency or a consistent expediency.
   1849 *Civil Disobedience*.

74 It takes two to speak the truth,—one to speak, and another to hear.
   1849 *A Week on the Concord and Merrimack Rivers*, 'Wednesday'.

75 A truly good book is something as wildly natural and primitive, mysterious and marvelous, ambrosial and fertile, as a fungus or a lichen.
   1850 Journal entry, 16 Nov. In Bradford Torrey and F H Allen (eds) *The Journals of Henry David Thoreau* (1906).

76 Some circumstantial evidence is very strong, as when you find a trout in the milk.
   1850 Journal entry, 11 Nov.

77 How many a man has dated a new era in his life from the reading of a book!… The at present unutterable things we may find somewhere uttered.
   1854 *Walden, or Life in the Woods*, 'Reading'.

78 If we knew all the laws of Nature, we should need only one fact, or the description of one actual phenomenon, to infer all the particular results at that point. Now we know only a few laws, and our result is vitiated, not, of course, by any confusion or irregularity in Nature, but by our ignorance of essential elements in the calculation. Our notions of law and harmony are commonly confined to those instances which we detect; but the harmony which results from a far greater number of seemingly conflicting, but really concurring, laws, which

we have not detected, is still more wonderful. The particular laws are as our points of view, as, to the traveler, a mountain outline varies with every step, and it has an infinite number of profiles, though absolutely but one form. Even when cleft or bored through it is not comprehended in its entireness.
   1854 *Walden, or Life in the Woods*, 'The Pond in Winter'.

79 Every man is the builder of a temple, called his body, to the god he worships, after a style purely his own, nor can he get off by hammering marble instead. We are all sculptors and painters, and our material is our own flesh and blood and bones.
   1854 *Walden, or Life in the Woods*, 'Higher Laws'.

80 It is a part of the destiny of the human race, in its gradual improvement, to leave off eating animals, as surely as the savage tribes have left off eating each other when they come in contact with the more civilized.
   1854 *Walden, or Life in the Woods*, 'Higher Laws'.

81 We can never have enough of nature. . . . We need to witness our own limits transgressed, and some life pasturing freely where we never wander.
   1854 *Walden, or Life in the Woods*, 'Spring'.

82 There is no odor so bad as that which arises from goodness tainted.
   1854 *Walden, or Life in the Woods*, 'Economy'.

83 The mass of men lead lives of quiet desperation.
   1854 *Walden, or Life in the Woods*, 'Economy'.

84 Our inventions are wont to be pretty toys, which distract our attention from serious things. They are but improved means to an unimproved end.
   1854 *Walden, or Life in the Woods*, 'Economy'.

85 Men have become the tools of their tools.
   1854 *Walden, or Life in the Woods*, 'Economy'.

86 I have yet to hear the first syllable of valuable or even earnest advice from my seniors.
   1854 *Walden, or, Life in the Woods*, 'Economy'.

87 As for Doing-good, that is one of the professions which are full.
   1854 *Walden, or Life in the Woods*, 'Economy'.

88 I say, beware of all enterprises that require new clothes, and not rather a new wearer of clothes.
   1854 *Walden, or Life in the Woods*, 'Economy'.

89 Every generation laughs at the old fashions, but follows religiously the new.
   1854 *Walden, or Life in the Woods*, 'Economy'.

90 As long as possible live free and uncommitted. It makes but little difference whether you are committed to a farm or the county jail.
   1854 *Walden, or Life in the Woods*, 'Where I Lived, and What I Lived For'.

91 I went to the woods because I wished to live deliberately, to front only the essential facts of life, and see if I could not learn what it had to teach, and not, when I came to die, discover that I had not lived.
   1854 *Walden, or Life in the Woods*, 'Where I Lived, and What I Lived For'.

92 Our life is frittered away by detail.
   1854 *Walden, or Life in the Woods*, 'Where I Lived, and What I Lived For'.

93 We do not ride on the railroad; it rides upon us.

1854 *Walden, or Life in the Woods*, 'Where I Lived and What I Lived For'.

94 Will you be a reader, a student merely, or a seer? Read your fate, see what is before you, and walk on into futurity.
1854 *Walden, or Life in the Woods*, 'Sounds'.

95 I never found the companion that was so companionable as solitude.
1854 *Walden, or Life in the Woods*, 'Solitude'.

96 I was determined to know beans.
1854 *Walden, or Life in the Woods*, 'The Bean-Field'.

97 If a man does not keep pace with his companions, perhaps it is because he hears a different drummer.
1854 *Walden, or Life in the Woods*, 'Conclusion'.

98 Why level downward to our dullest perception always, and praise that as common sense?
1854 *Walden, or Life in the Woods*, 'Conclusion'.

99 As for style of writing—if one has anything to say, it drops from him simply and directly, as a stone falls to the ground.
1857 Letter to Daniel Ricketson, 18 Aug.

1 I fear that I have not got much to say about Canada, not having seen much; what I got by going to Canada was a cold.
1866 *A Yankee in Canada*.

2 A gun gives you the body, not the bird.
Quoted in Colin Jarman *The Guinness Dictionary of Sports Quotations* (1990).

Thorndike, Dame (Agnes) Sybil 1882–1976

English actress. She made her stage debut in 1904 and went on to distinguish herself in both modern and classical tragedies. Her most famous roles included Medea, George Bernard Shaw's St Joan and Shakespeare's Volumnia. She was married to the actor and director Sir Lewis Casson.

3 You're never too old to play Saint Joan; you're only too young.
Quoted in *Julie Harris Talks to Young Actors* (1971).

Thorne, James 1815–81

English antiquary. He contributed topographical articles to many publications and spent many years researching material for his *Handbook to the Environs of London* (1876), in which he combines factual knowledge with entertaining passages on places and personalities of local interest.

4 An unenviable reputation for dirt and ill odours.
1876 Of Brentford, Middlesex, now in Greater London. *Handbook to the Environs of London*.

5 A town of narrow streets, old houses, shops curiously low, with little in it to interest any one.
1876 Of Hatfield, Hertfordshire. *Handbook to the Environs of London*.

6 A waste of modern tenements, mean, monotonous, and wearisome.
1876 On Penge, Surrey, now in Greater London. *Handbook to the Environs of London*.

7 A populous railway town of hideous brick shops and habitations.
1876 Of Redhill, Surrey. *Handbook to the Environs of London*.

8 Twickenham is one of those happy places which is not burdened with a history.
1876 *Handbook to the Environs of London*.

Thorneycroft, Lord (George Edward) Peter 1909–94

English politician. He entered the House of Commons in 1938, and was President of the Board of Trade (1951–7). Appointed Chancellor of the Exchequer in 1957, he resigned a year later, in disagreement with the government's financial policy, and lost his seat in 1966. He was created a life peer in 1967, and was Chairman of the Conservative Party (1975–81).

9 The choice in politics isn't usually between black and white. It is between two horrible shades of grey.
1979 In the *Sunday Telegraph*, 11 Feb.

10 Some men go through life absolutely miserable because, despite the most enormous achievements, they just didn't do one thing—like the architect who didn't build St Paul's. I didn't quite build St Paul's, but I stood on more mountain tops than possibly I deserved.
1979 In the *Sunday Telegraph*, 11 Feb.

Thornton, Sir Henry 1871–1933

Canadian pioneer of public broadcasting.

11 It is essential that broadcasting be surrounded with such safeguards as will prevent the air becoming what might be described as an atmospheric billboard.
1926 Address to the Advertising Clubs of the World, Philadelphia, 21 Jun. Quoted in E Austin Weir *The Struggle for National Broadcasting in Canada* (1965).

Thorpe, (John) Jeremy 1929–

English politician. Leader of the Liberal Party from 1967, he resigned in 1976 following allegations concerning a previous homosexual relationship with a Mr Norman Scott and was later acquitted of charges of conspiracy and incitement to murder Mr Scott.

12 Greater love hath no man than this, that he lay down his friends for his life.
1962 On Harold Macmillan's sacking of several Cabinet members, House of Commons.

13 Looking around the House, one realizes that we are all minorities now.
1974 On the absence of a clear party majority, House of Commons, 6 Mar.
➤ *See Shawcross 782:4*.

Thrasymachus 5c BC

Greek sophist and rhetorician from Chalcedon in Bithynia, he figures in Plato's *Republic* defending the proposition that might is right.

14 Morality is nothing other than the advantage of the stronger party.
Quoted in Plato *Republic*, 338b (translated by Robin Waterfield, 1993).

Thubron, Colin Gerald Dryden 1939–

English travel writer, novelist and film-maker.

15 Around me, around them [the dissidents], the total, all-eclipsing Soviet world, which renders any other world powerless and far away, had become profoundly, morally hostile.
1983 *Among the Russians* (published in the US as *Where the Nights are Longest*).

Thucydides   c.460–c.400 BC

Athenian politician and historian. As a naval commander in the Peloponnesian war he failed to relieve the Amphipolis in 424, and was exiled from Athens. He began a *History of the Peloponnesian War*, but died before its completion.

16 *Ktema es aei.*
   A possession intended to last for ever.
   Of his *History of the Peloponnesian War*, 1.22.4.

Thurber, James Grover   1894–1961

US humorist and cartoonist. In 1927 he was appointed managing editor of the *New Yorker* where he published many sketches and cartoons. Collections of his work include *Men Women and Dogs* (1943). His best-known short story is *The Secret Life of Walter Mitty* (1939) which was later filmed (1946).

17 It takes that *je ne sais quoi* which we call sophistication for a woman to be magnificent in a drawing-room when her faculties have departed but she herself has not yet gone home.
   1930 In the *New Yorker*, 2 Aug.

18 All right, have it your own way—you heard a seal bark!
   1932 Cartoon caption, in the *New Yorker*, 30 Jan.

19 That's my first wife up there and this is the *present* Mrs Harris.
   1933 Cartoon caption, in the *New Yorker*, 16 Mar.

20 I myself have accomplished nothing of excellence except a remarkable and, to some of my friends, unaccountable expertness in hitting empty ginger ale bottles with small rocks at a distance of thirty paces.
   1933 *My Life and Hard Times*, preface.

21 They lead, as a matter of fact, an existence of jumpiness and apprehension. They sit on the edge of the chair of Literature. In the house of Life they have the feeling that they have never taken off their overcoats.
   1933 On humorists. *My Life and Hard Times*, preface.

22 I suppose that the high-water mark of my youth in Colombus, Ohio, was the night the bed fell on my father.
   1933 *My Life and Hard Times*, ch.1.

23 Her own mother lived the latter years of her life in the horrible suspicion that electricity was dripping invisibly all over the house.
   1933 *My Life and Hard Times*, ch.2.

24 The war between men and women.
   1934 Title of series of cartoons in the *New Yorker*, 20 Jan.–28 Apr.

25 The Middle-Aged Man on the Flying Trapeze.
   1935 Title of book.

26 It's a naïve domestic Burgundy without any breeding, but I think you'll be amused by its presumption.
   1937 Cartoon caption, in the *New Yorker*, 27 Mar.

27 Well, if I called the wrong number, why did you answer the phone?
   1937 Cartoon caption, in the *New Yorker*, 5 Jun.

28 There is no safety in numbers, or in anything else.
   1939 'The Fairly Intelligent Fly', in the *New Yorker*, 4 Feb.

29 Early to rise and early to bed makes a male healthy and wealthy and dead.
   1939 'The Shrike and the Chipmunks', in the *New Yorker*, 18 Feb.

30 It's our *own* story *exactly*! He bold as a hawk, she soft as the dawn.
   1939 Cartoon caption, in the *New Yorker*, 28 Feb.

31 Then, with that faint fleeting smile playing about his lips, he faced the firing squad; erect and motionless, proud and disdainful, Walter Mitty, the undefeated, inscrutable to the last.
   1939 'The Secret Life of Walter Mitty', in the *New Yorker*, 18 Mar.

32 You might as well fall flat on your face as lean over too far backward.
   1939 'The Bear Who Let It Alone', in the *New Yorker*, 29 Apr.

33 You can fool too many of the people too much of the time.
   1939 'The Owl Who Was God', in the *New Yorker*, 29 Apr.
   ➤ *See Lincoln 510:35.*

34 Art—the one achievement of Man which has made the long trip from all fours seem well advised.
   1939 In *Forum and Century* magazine, Jun.

35 It is better to have loafed and lost than never to have loafed at all.
   1940 *Fables for Our Time*, 'The Courtship of Arthur and Al'.

36 No oyster ever profited from its pearl.
   1940 *Fables for Our Time*, 'The Philosopher and the Oyster'.

37 My World—And Welcome To It.
   1942 Title of book.

38 If he knew where he was going, it is not apparent from this distance. He fell down a great deal during this period, because of a trick he had of walking into himself.
   1945 Of his young self. *The Thurber Carnival*, preface.

39 I suppose that even the most pleasurable of imaginable occupations, that of batting baseballs through the windows of the RCA Building, would pall a little as the days ran on.
   1945 *The Thurber Carnival*, 'Memoirs of a Drudge'.

40 He who hesitates is sometimes saved.
   1945 *The Thurber Carnival*, 'The Glass in the Field'.

41 She developed a persistent troubled frown which gave her the expression of someone who is trying to repair a watch with his gloves on.
   1948 *The Beast In Me and Other Animals*, 'Look Homeward, Jeannie'.

42 'We all have flaws,' he said, 'and mine is being wicked.'
   1950 *The 13 Clocks*, ch.8.

43 'For God, for Country and for Yale', the outstanding single anti-climax in the English language.
   1951 In *Time*, 11 Jun.

44 The theater is the primary evidence of a nation's culture.
   1952 In the *New York Times*, 27 Jul.

45 Try to imagine a famous witty saying that is not immediately clear.
   1954 Letter to Malcolm Cowley, 11 Mar.

46 With sixty staring me in the face, I have developed inflammation of the sentence structure and definite hardening of the paragraphs.
   1955 In the *New York Post*, 30 Jun.

47 Seeing is deceiving. It's eating that's believing.
   1956 *Further Fables for Our Time*.

48 'I think this calls for a drink' has long been one of our national slogans.
   1957 *Alarms and Diversions*, 'Merry Christmas'.

49 'Poe,' I said, 'was perhaps the first great nonstop literary drinker of the American nineteenth century. He made the indulgences of Coleridge and De Quincey seem like a bit of mischief in the kitchen with the cooking sherry.

1957 *Alarms and Diversions*, 'The Moribundant Life, or, Grow Old Along with Whom?'.

50 I was seized by the stern hand of Compulsion, that dark, unseasonable Urge that impels women to clean house in the middle of the night.
1957 *Alarms and Diversions*, 'There's A Time For Flags'.

51 The laughter of man is more terrible than his tears, and takes more forms—hollow, heartless, mirthless, maniacal.
1958 In the *New York Times Magazine*, 7 Dec.

52 The power that created the poodle, the platypus and people has an integrated sense of both comedy and tragedy.
1959 Letter to Frances Glennon, Jun.

53 'Humour,' he said, 'is emotional chaos remembered in tranquillity.'
1960 In the *New York Post*, 29 Feb.
➤ *See* Wordsworth 925:10.

54 Ours is a precarious language, as every writer knows, in which the merest shadow line often separates affirmation from negation, sense from nonsense, and one sex from another.
1961 Of English. *Lanterns and Lances*, 'Such a Phrase as Drifts Through Dreams'.

55 Writers of comedy have outlook, whereas writers of tragedy have, according to them, insight.
1961 *Lanterns and Lances*, 'The Case for Comedy'.

56 The only rules comedy can tolerate are those of taste, and the only limitations those of libel.
1961 *Lanterns and Lances*, 'The Duchess and the Bugs'.

57 God bless… God damn!
1961 Last words.

58 I have the reputation of having read all of Henry James, which would argue a misspent youth *and* middle age.
Recalled on his death, 2 Nov 1961.

59 Word has somehow got around that the split infinitive is always wrong. That is of a piece with the outworn notion that it is always wrong to strike a lady.
Recalled on his death, 2 Nov 1961.

60 Unless [artists] can remember what it was to be a little boy, they are only half complete as artist and as man.
Quoted in Helen Thurber and Edward Weeks (eds) *Selected Letters of James Thurber* (1981).

61 Laughter need not be cut out of anything, since it improves everything.
Quoted in Helen Thurber and Edward Weeks (eds) *Selected Letters of James Thurber* (1981).

62 There is something about a poet which leads us to believe that he died, in many cases, as long as 20 years before his birth.
Quoted in Helen Thurber and Edward Weeks (eds) *Selected Letters of James Thurber* (1981).

63 Some American writers who have known each other for years have never met in the daytime or when both were sober.
Quoted in Neil T Jones (ed) *A Book of Days for the Literary Year* (1984).

64 It had only one fault. It was kind of lousy.
Of a play he had recently seen. Attributed.

Thurow, Lester C(arl) 1938–

US economist, professor at Massachusetts Institute of Technology.

65 America no longer lives behind its great wall. Economically, Genghis Khan has arrived.
1992 *Head to Head*.

Tilden, Bill (William Tatem II) 1893–1953

US tennis player. One of the greatest players of his time, he was Wimbledon singles champion three times (1920, 1921, 1930) and doubles champion (1927). He was also six times US singles champion and four times doubles champion in the 1920s.

66 Never change a winning game: always change a losing one.
Quoted in Colin Jarman *The Guinness Dictionary of Sports Quotations* (1990).

Tillich, Paul Johannes 1886–1965

German pastor, theologian and philosopher. Dismissed from his professorship by Nazis in 1933, he left to teach in the US. His theories blend philosophical and psychoanalytical elements with the theological.

67 Neurosis is the way of avoiding non-being by avoiding being.
1952 *The Courage to Be*.

68 Faith comprises both itself and doubt of itself.
1955 *Biblical Religion and the Search for Ultimate Reality*.

69 Faith is the state of being ultimately concerned.
1957 *Dynamics of Faith*.

70 I had the honor to be the first non-Jewish professor dismissed from a German university.
Recalled on his death, 22 Oct 1965.

Tilman, Bill (Harold William) 1898–1977

English mountaineer, explorer and sailor. He went to Kenya as a planter and there met Eric Shipton, with whom he made many notable explorations and climbs. After serving in World War II he took up sailing in remote areas such as Patagonia, the Arctic and the Antarctic. He disappeared on a voyage to the South Shetland Islands in 1977.

71 We live and learn, and big mountains are stern teachers.
1949 *Two Mountains and a River*.

Time

US news periodical.

72 The old man puffed into sight like a venerable battlewagon pressing up over the horizon. First a smudge of smoke, then the long cigar, then the familiar, stoop-shouldered hulk that a generation has come to know as the silhouette of greatness.
1952 Of Winston Churchill disembarking from the *Queen Mary*. 14 Jan.

73 The mighty US suddenly seemed as impotent as a beached whale.
1968 On the fall of 28 of South Vietnam's 44 provincial capitals. 15 Feb.

74 His career was a text book example of the rise of a patrician in the snug embrace of the American establishment.
1971 Of Dean Acheson. 25 Oct.

75 The rescuers had to rescue themselves.
1980 On the ill-fated helicopter attempt to free the hostages held in Iran. 5 May.

The Times

British newspaper, founded as the *Daily Universal Register* on 1 Jan 1785. It changed its name to *The Times* on 1 Jan 1788.

76 Of all journals, and of all writers, those will obtain the largest measure of public support who have told the truth most constantly and most fearlessly.
1852 Leading article, 6 Feb.

77 The first duty of the press is to obtain the earliest and most correct intelligence of the events of the time, and by disclosing them, to make them the common property of the nation.
1852 Leading article, 6 Feb.

Tintoretto *real name* **Jacopo Robusti** 1518–94

Venetian painter.

78 In judging paintings, you should consider whether the first impression pleases the eye and whether the artist has followed the rules; as for the rest, everyone makes some mistakes.
Quoted in Carlo Ridolfi *Life of Tintoretto* (1642).

Tobin, James 1918–2002

US economist, winner of the Nobel prize in economics (1981) and a professor at Yale University.

79 Why do so many talented economic theorists believe and teach elegant fantasies so obviously refutable by plainly evident facts?
1992 'An Old Keynesian Counterattacks', in the *Eastern Economic Journal*, Fall issue.

Tocqueville, Alexis Charles Henri Clérel de 1805–59

French historian and politician, Minister of Foreign Affairs for a few months in 1849. His major works are *De la Démocratie en Amérique* (1835–40, *Democracy in America*) and *L'Ancien Régime et la Révolution* (1856, *The Old Regime and the Revolution*).

80 Why, as civilization spreads, do outstanding men become fewer? Why, when attainments are the lot of all, do great intellectual talents become rarer? Why, when there are no longer lower classes, are there no longer upper classes? Why, when knowledge of how to rule reaches the masses, is there a lack of great abilities in the direction of society? America clearly poses these questions. But who can answer them?
1831 Translated by George Lawrence. Quoted in J P Mayer (ed) *Journey to America* (1960).

81 From this foul drain the greatest stream of human industry flows out to fertilize the whole world. From this filthy sewer pure gold flows. Here humanity attains its most complete development and its most brutish, here civilization works its miracles and civilized man is turned almost into a savage.
1835 Of Manchester. Journal entry, 2 Jul. *Journeys to England and Ireland* (translated by George Lawrence and J P Mayer, 1958).

82 *En matière de presse, il n'y a donc réellement pas de milieu entre la servitude et la licence. Pour recueillir les biens inestimables qu'assure la liberté de la presse, il faut savoir se soumettre aux maux inévitables qu'elle fait naître.*
As for the press, there is no middle way between servitude and extreme licence. In order to enjoy the invaluable benefits ensured by freedom of the press, it is necessary to submit to the inevitable evils that it engenders.
1835–40 *De la Démocratie en Amérique* (*Democracy in America*), vol.1, pt.2, ch.3.

83 *C'est un axiome de la science politique aux États-Unis, que le seul moyen de neutraliser les effets des journaux est d'en multiplier le nombre.*
It is an axiom of politics in the United States, that the only means of neutralising the effects of newspapers is to increase their number.
1835–40 *De la Démocratie en Amérique* (*Democracy in America*), vol.1, pt.2, ch.3.

84 *La presse exerce encore un immense pouvoir en Amérique. Elle fait circuler la vie politique dans toutes les portions de ce vaste territoire. C'est elle dont l'œil toujours ouvert met sans cesse à nu les secrets ressorts de la politique, et force les hommes publics à venir tour à tour comparaître devant le tribunal de l'opinion. C'est elle qui rallie les intérêts autour de certaines doctrines et formule le symbole des partis; c'est par elle que ceux-ci se parlent sans se voir, s'entendent sans être mis en contact.*
The press has enormous power in America. It is the press that circulates political life through all parts of this vast territory. Its eye is always open, and making known the secret springs of politics, thus forcing public men to appear before the tribunal of public opinion. It is the press which rallies the interests of the community round certain principles and forms the creed of different parties. Through the press these parties can speak to each other without seeing each other, can listen without meeting.
1835–40 *De la Démocratie en Amérique* (*Democracy in America*), vol.1, pt.2, ch.3.

85 *Le journal représente l'association; l'on peut dire qu'il parle à chacun de ses lecteurs au nom de tous les autres, et il les entraîne d'autant plus aisément qu'ils sont individuellement plus faibles. L'empire des journaux doit donc croître à mesure que les hommes s'égalisent.*
A newspaper represents an association; one might say that it addresses each of its readers in the name of all the others, and influences them in proportion to their individual weakness. The power of newspapers should therefore increase as men become more equal.
1835–40 *De la Démocratie en Amérique* (*Democracy in America*), vol.2, pt.2, ch.6.

86 *Il n'y a qu'un journal qui puisse venir déposer au même moment dans mille esprits la même pensée.*
Only a newspaper can place at the same time in a thousand minds the same thought.
1835–40 *De la Démocratie en Amérique* (*Democracy in America*), vol.2, pt.2, ch.6.

87 *Un journal est un conseiller qu'on n'a pas besoin d'aller chercher, mais qui se présente de lui-même et qui vous parle tous les jours et brièvement de l'affaire commune, sans vous déranger de vos affaires particulières.*
A newspaper is an adviser whom one does not need to

seek out, but one who comes of his own accord and speaks to you every day, briefly, of public affairs, without disturbing you from your own.
1835–40 *De la Démocratie en Amérique* (*Democracy in America*), vol.2, pt.2, ch.6.

88 *Ce serait diminuer leur importance que de croire qu'ils ne servent qu'à garantir la liberté; ils maintiennent la civilisation.*
It would diminish the importance [of newspapers] to believe that they only serve to guarantee freedom; they maintain civilization.
1835–40 *De la Démocratie en Amérique* (*Democracy in America*), vol.2, pt.2, ch.6.

Todd, Mike 1907–58

89 No gals, no gags, no chance.
1943 On attending rehearsals for *Oklahoma!* Quoted in the *US News and World Report*, 12 Apr 1993, on the 50th anniversary of the musical that ran six years, won a Pulitzer Prize, and was to have 750 revivals in 1993.

Todd, Ron(ald) 1927–

English trade union leader, a member of the Transport and General Workers' Union. He became General-Secretary in 1985, with strong left-wing support.

90 You don't have power if you surrender all your principles—you have office.
1988 Speech, London, Jun.

Toffler, Alvin 1928–

US writer and journalist, one of the most successful trend-spotters of the age. Toffler coined the phrase 'future shock' and convinced a sizable number of the reading public and policy administrators that what ailed them was the fact that everything was changing so fast.

91 'Future shock'…the shattering stress and disorientation that we induce in individuals by subjecting them to too much change in too short a time.
1970 *Future Shock*.

92 That great, growing engine of change—technology.
1970 *Future Shock*.

93 Technology feeds on itself. Technology makes more technology possible.
1970 *Future Shock*.

Tojo, Hideki 1885–1948

Japanese soldier who rose to become Minister of War (1940–1) and from 1941 premier and dictator of Japan. He was sentenced to death in 1948.

94 This is farewell.
I shall wait beneath the moss
Until the flowers are fragrant
In this island country of Japan.
1948 His final statement before execution, 23 Dec. Quoted in R J C Butow *Tojo and the Coming War* (1961).

Tolkien, J(ohn) R(onald) R(euel) 1892–1973

English writer and philologist. He was born in South Africa, educated in England, and he taught at Oxford. He wrote scholarly books, but is famous for his hugely popular fantasy novels *The Hobbit* (1937) and *The Lord of the Rings* trilogy (1954–6).

95 In a hole in the ground there lived a hobbit. Not a nasty, dirty, wet hole, filled with the ends of worms and an oozy smell, nor yet a dry, bare, sandy hole with nothing in it to sit down on or to eat: it was a hobbit-hole, and that means comfort.
1937 *The Hobbit*, ch.1.

96 My political opinions lean more and more to anarchy (philosophically understood, meaning abolition of control not whiskered men with bombs)… The most improper job of any man is bossing other men.
1943 Letter to Christopher Tolkien, 29 Apr.

97 There is only one bright spot and that is the growing habit of disgruntled men of dynamiting factories and power stations. I hope that, encouraged now as patriotism, it may remain a habit! But it won't do any good, if it is not universal.
1943 Letter to Christopher Tolkien, 29 Apr.

98 One Ring to rule them all, One Ring to find them, One Ring to bring them all and in the darkness bind them.
In the Land of Mordor where the Shadows lie.
1954 *The Fellowship of the Ring*, epigraph and passim.

99 But I cordially dislike allegory in all its manifestations, and always have done so since I grew old and wary enough to detect its presence. I much prefer history, true or feigned, with its varied applicability to the thought and experience of readers.
1954 *The Fellowship of the Ring*, foreword.

1 Hobbits are an unobtrusive but very ancient people, more numerous formerly than they are today; for they love peace and quiet and good tilled earth: a well-ordered and well-farmed countryside was their favourite haunt… Even in ancient days they were, as a rule, shy of 'the Big Folk', as they call us, and now they avoid us with dismay and are becoming hard to find.
1954 *The Fellowship of the Ring*, prologue.

2 Do not meddle in the affairs of Wizards, for they are subtle and quick to anger.
1954 Gandalf. *The Fellowship of the Ring*, bk.1, ch.3.

3 Where iss it, where iss it: my Precious, my Precious? It's ours, it is, and we wants it.
1955 Gollum. *The Two Towers*, ch.1.

Tolstoy, Leo Nikolayevich 1828–1910

Russian novelist, social philosopher, social critic and sometime mystic. His best-known works are *War and Peace* (1868–9) and *Anna Karenina* (1875–7).

4 Our body is a machine for living. It is organized for that, it is its nature. Let life go on in it unhindered and let it defend itself, it will do more than if you paralyse it by encumbering it with remedies.
1869 *War and Peace*, bk.10, ch.29.

5 All happy families resemble each other; each unhappy family is unhappy in its own way.
1874 *Anna Karenina*, opening words.

6 I sit on a man's back, choking him and making him carry me, and yet assure myself and others that I am very sorry for him and wish to ease his lot by all possible means—except by getting off his back.
1886 *What Then Must We Do?*, ch.16 (translated by Maude).

7 What is called science today consists of a haphazard heap of information, united by nothing, often utterly unnecessary, and not only failing to present one unquestionable truth, but as often as not containing the grossest errors today put forward as truths, and tomorrow overthrown.
1898 *What is Art?* (translated by V Tchertkoff).

8 I am convinced that the history of so-called scientific work in our famous centers of European civilization will, in a couple of hundred years, represent an inexhaustible source of laughter and sorrow for future generations. The learned men of the small western part of our European continent lived for several centuries under the illusion that the eternal blessed life was the West's future. They were interested in the problem of when and where this blessed life would come. But they never thought of how they were going to make their life better.
1898 *What is Art?* (translated by V Tchertkoff).

Tomé Pires c.1480–1525

Portuguese scholar and diplomat who came to Malacca in 1512, shortly after his country's conquest of the region. Portuguese control of new sea routes meant that valuable spices no longer needed to travel via Venice to reach Europe.

9 Whoever is Lord of Malacca has his hand on the throat of Venice.
1512–15 *The Suma Oriental of Tomé Pires* (translated by Armando Cortasao, 1944).

Tomlinson, (Alfred) Charles 1927–

English poet and critic. Emeritus Professor of English, University of Bristol. His publications include *Poems* (1964) and *The Flood* (1981).

10 Everything we see
Teaches the time that we are living in.
1984 'Poem for My Father'.

Tomlinson, H(enry) M(ajor) 1873–1958

English writer. He wrote novels, travel books, memoirs and a biography of Norman Douglas.

11 I will never believe again that the sea was ever loved by anyone whose life was married to it.
1912 *The Sea and the Jungle*, ch.1.

Toole, John Kennedy 1937–69

US novelist. He published nothing in his lifetime, and committed suicide. His novel *A Confederacy of Dunces* was published to great acclaim in 1980, and *The Neon Bible* in 1989.

12 Her logic was a combination of half-truths and clichés, her worldview a compound of misconceptions deriving from a history of our nation as written from the perspective of a subway tunnel.
A Confederacy of Dunces (published 1980), ch.5, pt.3.

13 The human desire for food and sex is relatively equal. If there are armed rapes why should there not be armed hot dog thefts?
A Confederacy of Dunces (published 1980), ch.7, pt.1.

14 You can always tell employees of the government by the total vacancy which occupies the space where most other people have faces.
A Confederacy of Dunces (published 1980), ch.9, pt.1.

Toplady, Augustus Montague 1740–78

English clergyman and hymn writer.

15 Rock of Ages, cleft for me,
Let me hide myself in Thee,
Let the water and the blood,
From thy riven side which flowed,
Be of sin the double cure,
Cleanse me from its guilt and power.
1776 Hymn.

Torrance, Sam 1953–

Scottish golfer, captain of the successful European Ryder Cup team in 2002.

16 I just led them to the water—and they drank copiously.
2002 On his victorious European Ryder Cup team. In *The Times*, 28 Dec.

Toscanini, Arturo 1867–1957

Italian conductor. He made his debut at La Scala in 1898 and remained there until 1908, returning between 1920 and 1929. He conducted many major orchestras, and created the National Broadcasting Orchestra of America (1937–53). He had a reputation as a tyrannical perfectionist.

17 God tells me how he wants this music played—and you get in his way.
1930 Berating players in his orchestra. Quoted in Howard Tubman *Etude*.

18 After I die I am coming back to earth as the doorkeeper of a bordello. And I won't let a one of you in.
To an uncooperative orchestra. Quoted in Norman Lebrecht *Discord* (1982).

Towne, Robert 1936–

US screenwriter. His credits include *The Tomb of Ligeia* (1964), *Chinatown* (1974), *Greystoke: the Legend of Tarzan* (1984), *Mission: Impossible* (1996) and *Mission: Impossible II* (2000).

19 Why are you doing it? What can you buy that you can't already afford?
The future, Mr Gittes, the future.
1974 *Chinatown*.

20 Forget it, Jake, it's Chinatown.
1974 *Chinatown*, closing line.

Townsend, Sue 1945–

English writer. She has written novels and plays, but is best known for her 'Adrian Mole' books.

21 The Secret Diary of Adrian Mole Aged 13¾.
1982 Title of book.

22 I have decided to be a poet. My father said there isn't a suitable career structure for poets and no pensions and other boring things, but I am quite decided.
1982 *The Secret Diary of Adrian Mole Aged 13¾*, 'Monday, May 25th'.

23 I think it's essential for comic writers to have a hate figure, a despot, a regime to react against, and I think Thatcher was perfect for me, I loathed everything she stood for.
2002 In the *Observer*, 24 Mar.

Townshend, Pete 1945–

British rock musician.

24 Hope I die before I get old.
  1966 'My Generation'.

Toynbee, Arnold 1852–83

English economic historian and social reformer, best known as the author of *The Industrial Revolution in England* (1884). Toynbee Hall, Whitechapel was founded in his memory in 1885.

25 The Industrial Revolution.
  1880–1 Title of Oxford lectures, published posthumously in 1884. The phrase passed into common usage.

Toynbee, Arnold Joseph 1889–1975

English historian, nephew of Arnold Toynbee. His greatest work is *A Study of History*, published in 10 volumes (1934–54).

26 No annihilation without representation.
  1947 Advocating greater British representation at the United Nations.
  ➤ See Otis 630:19.

27 America is a large, friendly dog in a very small room. Every time it wags its tail, it knocks over a chair.
  1949 Letter, 26 Oct.

28 Civilisation is a movement and not a condition; a voyage and not a harbour.
  Quoted in *Reader's Digest*, Oct 1958.

29 Angkor is perhaps the greatest of Man's essays in rectangular architecture that has yet been brought to life.
  1958 *East to West*.

Toynbee, (Theodore) Philip 1916–81

English novelist and journalist, son of the historian Arnold Joseph Toynbee. An experimental writer, his semi-autobiographical *Pantaloon* sequence is particularly innovative.

30 I have seen the future and it does not work.
  1974 Of the USA. In the *Observer*, 27 Jan.
  ➤ See Steffens 814:6.

31 He was the type of man who was always trying to live beyond his moral means.
  1975 Of J Middleton Murry. In the *Observer*, 12 Jan.

32 The basic command of religion is not 'do this!' or 'do not do that!' but simply 'look!'
  1978 Journal entry, 15 Feb. Collected in *Part of a Journey* (1981).

33 The primary duty of a serious biographer is to illuminate his subject's life work, not to play the spy in his bedroom.
  1979 Book review in the *Observer*, 18 Mar.

Toynbee, Polly 1946–

English journalist, columnist at *The Guardian* (1977–88, 1998–).

34 I hate to join the chortling ranks of [Millennium] Dome rubbishers in the right-wing press…but, alas, I have to admit the Dome is a lemon.
  2000 In *The Guardian*, 5 Jan.

Traherne, Thomas c.1636–1674

English poet and mystic. Educated at Oxford, he took holy orders and in 1667 became Chaplain to the Lord Keeper of the Great Seal. He wrote religious prose, including *Roman Forgeries* (1673), *Christian Ethics* (1675) and *Centuries of Religious Meditations* (published 1908); his poetry was not published until 1903.

35 In unexperienc'd Infancy
  Many a sweet mistake doth lie.
  'Shadows in the Water' (published 1903).

36 Some unknown joys there be
  Laid up in store for me.
  'Shadows in the Water' (published 1903).

37 Sleep is cousin-german unto death:
  Sleep and death differ, no more, than a carcass
  And a skeleton.
  'A Serious and a Curious Night-Meditation' (published 1903).

38 A Stranger here
  Strange things doth meet, strange glories see;
  Strange Treasures lodg'd in this fair world appear,
  Strange all, and New to me,
  But that they mine should be, who nothing was,
  That Strangest is of all, yet brought to pass.
  The Salutation (published 1903).

39 You never enjoy the world aright, till the sea itself floweth in your veins, till you are clothed with the heavens, and crowned with the stars: and perceive yourself to be the sole heir of the whole world.
  Centuries of Meditations, 'First Century', section 29 (published 1908).

Travers, Ben 1886–1980

English dramatist and screenwriter.

40 The really great batsmen fall into two categories. One comes to the wicket saying to the bowlers 'I am going to slaughter you'. The other comes to the wicket saying 'You can't get me out'.
  1981 *94 Declared Cricket Reminiscences*.

Travers, P(amela) L(yndon) 1906–96

British writer. She worked as a journalist, actress and dancer, and for the British Ministry of Information in the US during World War II. *Mary Poppins* was published in 1934; subsequent titles include *Mary Poppins Comes Back* (1935), *Mary Poppins Opens the Door* (1943) and *Mary Poppins in the Park* (1952).

41 'Now,' she said, 'spit-spot into bed.'
  1934 *Mary Poppins*, ch.1.

42 From the [empty] carpet-bag she took out seven flannel night-gowns, four cotton ones, a pair of boots, a set of dominoes, two bathing-caps and a postcard album. Last of all came a folding camp-bedstead with blankets and eiderdown complete.
  1934 *Mary Poppins*, ch.1.

43 Mary Poppins looked down at her feet and rubbed the toe of one shoe along the pavement two or three times. Then she smiled at the shoe in such a way that the shoe knew quite well that the smile wasn't meant for it.
  1934 *Mary Poppins*, ch.2.

44 'Don't you know,' she said pityingly, 'that everybody's got a Fairyland of their own?'
  1934 *Mary Poppins*, ch.2.

45 If I laugh on that particular day I become so filled with Laughing Gas that I simply can't keep on the ground. Even if I smile it happens. The first funny thought, and I'm up like a balloon. And until I can think of something serious I can't get down again.
  1934 Mr Wigg, Mary Poppins's uncle. The 'particular day' is when his birthday falls on a Friday. *Mary Poppins*, ch.3.

46 Oh, my Gracious, Glorious, Galumphing Goodness!
  1934 Mr Wigg. *Mary Poppins*, ch.3.

47 The Red Cow was very respectable, she always behaved like a perfect lady and she knew What was What. To her a thing was either black or white—there was no question of it being grey or perhaps pink. People were good or they were bad—there was nothing in between. Dandelions were either sweet or sour—there were never any moderately nice ones.
  1934 *Mary Poppins*, ch.5.

48 He could smell her crackling white apron and the faint flavour of toast that always hung about her so deliciously.
  1934 Michael's impressions of Mary Poppins. *Mary Poppins*, ch.6.

49 Feed the Birds, Tuppence a Bag! Feed the Birds, Tuppence a Bag!
  1934 *Mary Poppins*, ch.7.

50 Trouble trouble and it will trouble you!
  1934 Mary Poppins. *Mary Poppins*, ch.12.

Tree, Sir Herbert (Draper) Beerbohm 1852–1917

English actor-manager. He played a wide range of roles, of which the most successful included Svengali in George du Maurier's *Trilby*, Higgins in George Bernard Shaw's *Pygmalion* and Charles Dickens's Fagin. He assumed the management of the Comedy Theatre in London in 1887 and then spent a prosperous 10 years as manager of the Haymarket before opening Her Majesty's in 1897. He was also the founder of the Royal Academy of Dramatic Art (1904).

51 Ladies, just a little more virginity, if you don't mind.
  To actresses playing the roles of ladies-in-waiting. Quoted in Alexander Woollcott *Shouts and Murmurs* (1923), 'Capsule Criticism'.

52 He is an old bore. Even the grave yawns for him.
  Of Israel Zangill. Quoted in Hesketh Pearson *Beerbohm* (1956).

53 It is difficult to live up to one's poster… When I pass my name in large letters I blush, but at the same time instinctively raise my hat.
  Quoted in Hesketh Pearson *Beerbohm* (1956).

54 The national sport of England is obstacle-racing. People fill their rooms with useless and cumbersome furniture, and spend the rest of their lives trying to dodge it.
  Quoted in Hesketh Pearson *Beerbohm* (1956).

Treitschke, Georg Friedrich 1776–1842

German librettist and translator best known for revising the libretto for the final version (1814) of Beethoven's opera *Fidelio* from earlier versions by Stefan von Breuning (1806) and Joseph Sonnleithner (1805).

55 *Abscheulicher!*
  Perfidious wretch!
  1814 Leonora's recitative and aria. *Fidelio*, act 1.

56 *O welche Lust!*
  Oh what delight!
  1814 The prisoners' chorus. *Fidelio*, act 1.

Trevelyan, George Macaulay 1876–1962

English historian. After serving in World War I, he became Professor of Modern History at Cambridge (1927–40). A pioneer social historian, he wrote *English Social History* (1944) —a companion volume to his *History of England* (1926).

57 Disinterested intellectual curiosity is the life-blood of real civilisation.
  1944 *English Social History*.

58 Village cricket spread fast through the land. In those days, before it became scientific, cricket was the best game in the world to watch—each ball a potential crisis.
  Quoted in Helen Exley *Cricket Quotations* (1992).

Trevelyan, John 1904–85

British executive. He was secretary of the British Board of Film Censors between 1958 and 1970.

59 Censors are paid to have dirty minds.
  1970 Attributed.

Trevino, Lee Buck 1939–

US golfer. He won his first US Open in 1968 and in 1971 established a record by winning three Open titles (the US, Canadian and British) in the same year, retaining his British title the following year.

60 I'm not saying my golf game went bad, but if I grew tomatoes they'd come up sliced.
  Quoted in *Scholastic Coach*, 'Coaches' Corner', Dec 1982.

61 If my IQ had been two points lower, I'd have been a plant somewhere.
  Quoted in Colin Jarman *The Guinness Dictionary of Sports Quotations* (1990).

62 I'm hitting the driver so good, I gotta dial the operator for long distance after I hit it.
  Attributed.

Trevor-Roper, Hugh Redwald, Baron Dacre of Glanton 1914–2003

English historian, known for his vivid reconstruction of *The Last Days of Hitler* (1947). He was Professor at Oxford (1957–80) and Master of Peterhouse, Cambridge (1980–7).

63 Any society, so long as it is, or feels itself to be, a working society, tends to invest in itself: a military society tends to become more military, a bureaucratic society more bureaucratic, a commercial society more commercial, as the status and profits of war or office or commerce are enhanced by success, and institutions are framed to forward it. Therefore, when such a society is hit by a general crisis, it finds itself partly paralyzed by the structural weight of increased social investment. The dominant military or official or commercial classes cannot easily change their orientation: and their social dominance, and the institutions through which it is exercised, prevent other classes from securing power or changing policy.
  1965 *The Rise of Christian Europe*.

Trillin, Calvin Marshall 1935–

US journalist and author.

64 A shelf life somewhere between butter and yoghurt.
  1987 On the plethora of new book titles. In the *New York Times*, 14 Jun.

65 Math was my worst subject because I could never persuade the teacher that my answers were meant ironically.
  1990 In the *New York Times*, 7 Oct.

Trilling, Lionel 1905–75

US literary critic whose works, such as *The Liberal Imagination* (1950) and *Beyond Culture* (1965), gained him a reputation for scholarly and astute social comment. He also wrote a novel, *The Middle of the Journey* (1947).

66 Literature is the human activity that takes the fullest and most precise account of variousness, possibility, complexity, and difficulty.
1950 *The Liberal Imagination*, preface.

67 We are all ill: but even a universal sickness implies an idea of health.
1950 *The Liberal Imagination*, 'Art and Neurosis'.

68 We who are liberal and progressive know that the poor are our equals in every sense except that of being equal to us.
1950 *The Liberal Imagination*, 'Princess Casamassima'.

69 It would seem that Americans have a kind of resistance to looking closely at society.
1950 *The Liberal Imagination*, 'Manners, Morals and the Novel'.

70 The poet…may be used as a barometer, but let us not forget that he is also part of the weather.
1950 *The Liberal Imagination*.

71 The function of literature through all its mutations, has been to make us aware of the particularity of selves, and the high authority of the self in its quarrel with its society and its culture. Literature is in that sense subversive.
1965 *Beyond Culture*, introduction.

Trinder, Tommy 1909–89

English comedian and actor, whose famous catchphrase was 'You lucky people'.

72 Overpaid, overfed, oversexed, and over here.
Of US troops stationed in Britain during World War II. This phrase is associated with Trinder, but was probably not his invention.

Trollope, Anthony 1815–82

English novelist. He is best known for his two novel sequences, the Barchester novels and the 'Palliser' novels, both of which chronicle the life of a region and are distinguished by their slow pace and quiet comedy. His novels include *Barchester Towers* (1857) and *Can You Forgive Her?* (1864).

73 The tenth Muse, who now governs the periodical press.
1855 *The Warden*, ch.14.

74 She was rich in apparel, but not bedizened with finery… She well knew the great architectural secret of decorating her constructions, and never descended to construct a decoration.
1857 Of Mrs Stanhope. *Barchester Towers*, ch.9.

75 There is no road to wealth so easy and respectable as that of matrimony.
1858 *Doctor Thorne*, ch.16.

76 Let no man boast himself that he has got through the perils of winter till at least the seventh of May.
1858 *Doctor Thorne*, ch.47.

77 Those who have courage to love should have courage to suffer.
1859 *The Bertrams*, ch.27.

78 For the most of us, if we do not talk of ourselves, or at any rate of the individual circles of which we are the centres, we can talk of nothing. I cannot hold with those who wish to put down the insignificant chatter of the world.
1861 *Framley Parsonage*, ch.10.

79 We cannot bring ourselves to believe it possible that a foreigner should in any respect be wiser than ourselves. If any such point out to us our follies, we at once claim those follies as the special evidence of our wisdom.
1862 Stavely. *Orley Farm*, ch.18.

80 It is because we put up with bad things that hotel-keepers continue to give them to us.
1862 Stavely. *Orley Farm*, ch.18.

81 As for conceit, what man will do any good who is not conceited? Nobody holds a good opinion of a man who has a low opinion of himself.
1862 *Orley Farm*, ch.22.

82 Mr Palliser was one of those politicians in possessing whom England has perhaps more reason to be proud than of any other of her resources, and who, as a body, give to her that exquisite combination of conservatism and progress which is her present strength and best security for the future.
1864 *Can You Forgive Her?*, ch.24.

83 To think of one's absent love is very sweet; but it becomes monotonous… I doubt whether any girl would be satisfied with her lover's mind if she knew the whole of it.
1864 *The Small House at Allington*, ch.4.

84 Why is it that girls so constantly do this, so frequently ask men who have loved them to be present at their marriages with other men? There is no triumph in it. It is done in sheer kindness and affection. They intend to offer something which shall soften and not aggravate the sorrow that they have caused… I fully appreciate the intention, but in honest truth, I doubt the eligibility of the proffered entertainment.
1864 John Eames. *The Small House at Allington*, ch.9.

85 It may almost be a question whether such wisdom as many of us have in our mature years has not come from the dying out of the power of temptation, rather than as the results of thought and resolution.
1864 *The Small House at Allington*, ch.14.

86 Never think that you're not good enough yourself. A man should never think that. My belief is that in life people will take you much at your own reckoning.
1864 Lord De Guest to Johnny. *The Small House at Allington*, ch.32.

87 With many women I doubt whether there be any more effectual way of touching their hearts than ill-using them and then confessing it. If you wish to get the sweetest fragrance from the herb at your feet, tread on it and bruise it.
1865 *Miss Mackenzie*, ch.10.

88 It was manifest to me that there was something in the Roman Catholic religion which made the priests very dear to the people; for I doubt whether in any village in England, had such an accident happened to the rector, all the people would have roused themselves at midnight to wreak their vengeance on the assailant.
1866 *Argosy*, 'Father Giles of Ballymoy', May.

89 How I did respect you when you dared to speak the truth to me! Men don't know women, or they would be harder to them.
1867 *The Claverings*, ch.15.

90 She understood how much louder a cock can crow in its own farmyard then elsewhere.
1867 *The Last Chronicle of Barset*, ch.17.

91 It's dogged as does it. It ain't thinking about it.
1867 *The Last Chronicle of Barset*, ch.61, 'Giles Hoggett'.

92 They who do not understand that a man may be brought to hope that which of all things is the most grievous to him, have not observed with sufficient closeness the perversity of the human mind.
1869 Of Trevelyan's paranoia about his wife's fidelity. *He Knew He Was Right*, ch.38.

93 A faineant government is not the worst government that England can have. It has been the great fault of our politicians that they have all wanted to do something.
1869 *Phineas Finn*, ch.13.

94 Mr Turnball had predicted evil consequences…and was now doing the best in his power to bring about the verification of his own prophecies.
1869 *Phineas Finn*, ch.25.

95 Perhaps there is no position more perilous to a man's honesty than that…of knowing himself to be quite loved by a girl whom he almost loves himself.
1869 *Phineas Finn*, ch.50.

96 She knew how to allure by denying, and to make the gift rich by delaying it.
1869 *Phineas Finn*, ch.57.

97 We cannot have heroes to dine with us. There are none. And were those heroes to be had, we should not like them…the persons whom you cannot care for in a novel, because they are so bad, are the very same that you so dearly love in your life, because they are so good.
1873 Of Frank Greystock. *The Eustace Diamonds*, ch.35.

98 What man thinks of changing himself so as to suit his wife? And yet men expect that women shall put on altogether new characters when they are married, and girls think that they can do so.
1874 Lady Chiltern to Mr Maule. *Phineas Redux*, ch.3.

99 It is the necessary nature of a political in this country to avoid, as long as it can be avoided, the consideration of any question which involves a great change… The best carriage horses are those which can most steadily hold back against the coach as it trundles down the hill.
1874 *Phineas Redux*, ch.4.

1 Is it not singular how some men continue to obtain the reputation of popular authorship without adding a word to the literature of their country worthy of note?… To puff and to get one's self puffed have become different branches of a new profession.
1875 *The Way We Live Now*, ch.1.

2 Love is like any other luxury. You have no right to it unless you can afford it.
1875 *The Way We Live Now*, ch.84.

3 Equality would be a heaven, if we could attain it.
1876 Prime Minister to Phineas. *The Prime Minister*, ch.68.

4 I hold that gentleman to be the best dressed whose dress no one observes.
1879 *Thackeray*, ch.9.

5 A man's mind will very generally refuse to make itself up until it be driven and compelled by emergency.
1881 Houston. *Ayala's Angel*, ch.41.

6 He must have known me had he seen me as he was wont to see me, for he was in the habit of flogging me constantly. Perhaps he did not recognize me by my face.
1883 *Autobiography*, ch.1.

7 She was neither clear-sighted nor accurate; and in her attempts to describe morals, manners, and even facts, was unable to avoid the pitfalls of exaggeration.
1883 Of his mother, Frances Trollope, author of *The Domestic Manners of the Americans*. *Autobiography*, ch.2.

8 Take away from English authors their copyrights, and you would very soon take away from England her authors.
1883 *Autobiography*, ch.6.

9 It is admitted that a novel can hardly be made interesting or successful without love… It is necessary because the passion is one which interests or has interested all. Everyone feels it, has felt it, or expects to feel it.
1883 *Autobiography*, ch.12.

10 Three hours a day will produce as much as a man ought to write.
1883 *Autobiography*, ch.15.

11 I think that Plantagenet Palliser, Duke of Omnium, is a perfect gentleman. If he be not, then I am unable to describe a gentleman.
1883 *Autobiography*, ch.20.

Trollope, Joanna 1943–

English writer. She is best known for her novels set in rural English communities, but also writes historical fiction and, under the name Caroline Harvey, romances.

12 Contentment and fulfilment don't make for very good fiction.
1994 In *The Times*, 25 Jun.

Trotsky, Leon *originally* **Lev Davidovich Bronstein** 1879–1940

Russian Jewish revolutionary, born in Ukraine. Already a noted revolutionary, he played a major role in the October Revolution (1917), and created the Red Army. After Lenin's death (1924) his influence began to decline and under Stalin he was expelled from the Soviet Union (1929) and sentenced to death (1937). He was assassinated in Mexico by one of Stalin's agents.

13 You have played out your role. Go where you belong: to the dustheap of history.
1917 To the Mensheviks, at the first Congress of Soviets following the October Revolution. Quoted in A J P Taylor *From the Boer War to the Cold War: Essays on Twentieth-Century Europe* (1995), p.271.

14 A cossack's whip wrapped in the parchment of a constitution.
1905 On the October Manifesto, a package of limited constitutional reforms conceded by the Tzarist government following the strikes and civil unrest of early October 1905. Quoted in Lionel Kochan *Russia in Revolution* (1967).

15 The Soviet Republic needs an army that will be able to fight and conquer.
1918 Speech to the Moscow Soviet of Workers', Soldiers' and Peasants' Deputies, 19 Mar.

16 It was the supreme expression of the mediocrity of the apparatus that Stalin himself rose to his position.
1930 *My Life*, p.501.

17 Civilization has made the peasantry its pack animal. The bourgeoisie in the long run only changed the form of the pack.

1934 *History of the Russian Revolution* (translated by Max Eastman, 1934), vol.3, pt.3.

18 Old age is the most unexpected of all things that happens to a man.

1935 *Diary in Exile.*

19 In a country that is economically backward, the proletariat can take power earlier than in countries where capitalism is advanced.

1931 *The Permanent Revolution.*

20 Marxism is, above all, a method of analysis.

1931 *The Permanent Revolution.*

21 The end may justify the means, as long as there is something that justifies the end.

Attributed.

Trudeau, Pierre Elliott 1919–2000

Canadian politician. As Minister of Justice and Attorney-General (1967) he opposed the separation of Quebec from Canada. He became Liberal Prime Minister (1968–79, 1980–4), urging independence from US influence and home economic control. He proposed a new constitution for complete Canadian independence, secured Apr 1982.

22 The state has no place in the bedrooms of the nation.

1967 Of the liberalization of the Criminal Code. Interview in Ottawa, 22 Dec. The remark is based on similar words written by the journalist Martin O'Malley in an unsigned editorial in the *Globe and Mail*, 12 Dec 1967.

23 Living next to you is like sleeping with an elephant. No matter how friendly and even-tempered the beast, one is affected by every twitch and grunt.

1969 Of the US. Speech, National Press Club, Washington DC, 25 Mar. Quoted in Lawrence Martin *The Presidents and the Prime Ministers* (1982).

24 Fuddle-duddle.

1971 Neologism coined by Trudeau when accused of uttering a 'four-letter word' in the House of Commons, Ottawa, 16 Feb. 'No, it was fuddle-duddle,' replied Trudeau. The reply led an opposition Member of Parliament to observe, 'Mr. Trudeau wants to be obscene but not heard.'

Trueman, Fred (Frederick Sewards) 1931–

English cricketer, a notoriously fast bowler. He played for Yorkshire (1949–68) and made 67 Test appearances for England (1952–65). He took a record 307 Test wickets.

25 If there is any game in the world that attracts the half-baked theorist more than cricket I have yet to hear of it.

1964 *Freddie Trueman's Book of Cricket.*

26 The difference between a fast bowler and a good fast bowler is not extra muscle but extra brains.

1964 *Freddie Trueman's Book of Cricket.*

27 We didn't have metaphors in my day. We didn't beat about the bush.

1996 Quoted in the *Sunday Times*, 22 Dec.

Truman, Harry S 1884–1972

US Democratic statesman, 33rd President (1945–53), responsible for the first atom bombing on Japan, the postwar loan to Britain, the establishment of NATO (1949) and the sending of US troops to South Korea (1950). He gave military and economic aid to countries threatened by communist interference, and introduced a 'Fair Deal' of economic reform at home.

28 When I first came to Washington, for the first six months I wondered how the hell I ever got here. For the next six months, I wondered how the hell the rest of them ever got here.

1940 Speech, Apr.

29 Every segment of our population, and every individual, has a right to expect from his Government a Fair Deal.

1945 Speech to Congress, 6 Sep.

30 If you think somebody is telling a big lie about you, the only way to answer is with the whole truth.

1950 On Senator Joseph R McCarthy. Quoted in John Hersey *Aspects of the Presidency* (1980).

31 The only thing you have to worry about is bad luck. I never had bad luck.

1950 After an assassination attempt, 1 Nov.

32 If you can't stand the heat you better get out of the kitchen.

1952 Address to the Aero Club of Washington, 27 Dec, quoting a colleague from his days as a county judge.

33 Why, this fellow doesn't know any more about politics than a pig on Sunday.

1952 Of presidential hopeful Eisenhower. Quoted in Richard M Nixon *RN: Memoirs of Richard Nixon* (1978).

34 In 1945 we did much more than draft an international agreement among 50 nations. We set down on paper the only principles that will enable civilized human life to continue to survive on this globe.

1955 On the 10th anniversary of the United Nations, 24 Jun.

35 Party platforms are contracts with the people.

1956 *Memoirs: Years of Trial and Hope.*

36 I never give them hell. I just tell the truth and they think it is hell.

1956 Interview, in *Look*, 3 Apr.

37 A politician is a man who understands government, and it takes a politician to run a Government. A statesman is a politician who has been dead 10 or 15 years.

1958 New York World Telegram, 12 Apr.

38 It's a recession when your neighbour loses his job; it's a depression when you lose yours.

1958 In the *Observer*, 13 Apr.

➤ *See Reagan 680:55.*

39 Too many…pass judgement on wartime decisions in the luxury of a peacetime environment.

1963 Reply to a Boston University official who had criticized Truman's use of the atomic bomb. Truman Library archives, 23 Sep.

40 The President hears a hundred voices telling him that he is the greatest man in the world. He must listen carefully indeed to hear the one voice that tells him he is not.

1964 In *This Week*, 5 Apr.

41 Being criticized…he never did get it through his head that that's what politics is all about.

Of President Eisenhower. Quoted in Merle Miller (ed) *Plain Speaking* (1974).

42 Can't somebody bring me a one-handed economist?

Recalled on the death of his economic adviser Edwin Nourse, 9 Apr 1974. Nourse had been fond of saying 'on one hand…but on the other'.

43 I told him to fire away. He did and it is dynamite.
On asking Joseph Stalin for the Soviet agenda at the Potsdam Conference. Quoted in the *New York Times*, 2 Jun 1980.

44 Being president is like riding a tiger…keep on riding or be swallowed.
Quoted in the *New York Times*, 28 Dec 1984.

45 The buck stops here.
Motto displayed on a sign on his desk. Quoted in William Safire *Safire's New Political Dictionary* (1993).

46 I don't much care for your law, but, by golly, this bourbon is good.
To US Supreme Court Justice William O Douglas. Attributed.

Trump, Donald 1946–

US businessman, renowned for his flamboyant and initially successful dealings in real estate. His best-known developments include Trump Tower, New York City, and Trump Castle, Trump Plaza and the Taj Mahal casino in Atlantic City.

47 I like thinking big. If you're going to be thinking anyway, you might as well think big.
1989 In *Time*, 16 Jan.

48 A gambler is someone who plays slot machines. I prefer to own slot machines.
1990 On the opening of his Atlanta City Taj Mahal casino. In *Time*, 9 Apr.

49 See that gold Cadillac down the street? That's the color I want those handrails. Gold. Cadillac Gold. Not yellow like a daisy.
Of the handrails in Manhattan's Trump Tower. Quoted by Paul Trachtman in the *Smithsonian*, Mar 1995, reviewing Alexander Theroux *The Primary Colors*.

Truss, Lynne

English writer and broadcaster.

50 The Zero Tolerance Approach to Punctuation.
2003 Subtitle of *Eats, Shoots & Leaves*.

Truth, Sojourner née *Isabella* c.1797–1883

American abolitionist. Born a slave, she gained her freedom and later became an ardent evangelist. In 1843 she changed her name to Sojourner Truth and campaigned against slavery and for woman suffrage.

51 Well, chilern, whar dar is so much racket dar must be something out o' kilter. I tink dat 'twixt de niggers of de Souf and de women at de Norf all a talkin' 'bout rights, de white men will be in a fix pretty soon.
1851 Women's Rights Convention, Akron, Ohio. Quoted in *Narrative of Sojourner Truth* (1875), pt.2, 'Book of Life'.

52 Look at me! Look at my arm!… I have plowed, and planted, and gathered into barns, and no man could head me—and ar'n't I a woman? I could work as much and eat as much as a man (when I could get it), and bear de lash as well—and ar'n't I a woman? I have borne thirteen chilern and seen 'em mos' all sold off into slavery, and when I cried out with a mother's grief, none but Jesus heard—and ar'n't I a woman?
1851 Women's Rights Convention, Akron, Ohio. Quoted in *Narrative of Sojourner Truth* (1875), pt.2, 'Book of Life'.

Ts'ao Sung c.830–910

Chinese poet from Anhui about whom very little is known. He was in his seventies before finally passing a set of literary examinations.

53 I charge thee, sir, not to talk of high honours, A single general achieves fame on the rotting bones of ten thousand.
c.879 'Written in the year Chi hai (879)', collected in *A Book of Chinese Verse* (translated by N L Smith and R H Kotewall).

Tsongas, Paul Efthemios 1941–97

US politician, Senator from Massachusetts and a candidate for Democratic presidential nomination.

54 We are becoming an economic colony. America is up for sale. One percent of Japan's manufacturing base is foreign-owned; 2 per cent of Germany's is; 3 per cent of France's. Ours is 18 per cent and growing rapidly.
1992 Quoted in the *Los Angeles Times*, 17 Mar.

55 You cannot be pro-jobs and anti-government at the same time. You cannot love employees and despise employers. You cannot redistribute wealth that you never created. No goose, no golden egg.
1992 Quoted in the *Los Angeles Times*, 19 Feb.

Tu Fu 712–70

Chinese poet who never achieved a settled existence and is known to have spent a large part of his life travelling in a state of hardship.

56 Sundered by peaks unscalable, Tomorrow shall we strangers be.
c.750 'Visiting an Old Friend', collected in *A Golden Treasury of Chinese Poetry* (translated by John Turner, 1967).

Tuchman, Barbara W(ertheim) 1912–89

US historian, best known for *The Guns of August* (1962, Pulitzer Prize), tracing the origins of World War I, and *Stilwell and the American Experience in China* (1970, Pulitzer Prize). Other works include *A Distant Mirror* (1978).

57 Dead battles, like dead generals, hold the military mind in their dead grip.
1962 *The Guns of August*, ch.2.

58 No more distressing moment can ever face a British Government than that which requires it to come to a hard and fast and specific decision.
1962 *The Guns of August*, ch.9.

59 Reasonable orders are easy enough to obey; it is capricious, bureaucratic or plain idiotic demands that form the habit of discipline.
1970 *Stilwell and the American Experience in China*, pt.1, ch.1.

60 Most people are relieved to find a superior on whose judgment they can rest. That, indeed, is the difference between most people and Generals.
1972 Address at US Army War College, Apr. Collected in *Practising History* (1981).

61 To a historian libraries are food, shelter, and even muse.
1981 *Practising History*, 'The Houses of Research'.

Tucker, Sophie pseudonym of *Sophia Abuza* 1884–1966

US jazz singer, born in Russia. A legendary star of cabaret and vaudeville in the 1920s, she included among her biggest hits such songs as 'Some of These Days' (1926) and 'My Yiddische Momma' (1928). She led her own band in the 1930s and made several appearances on Broadway and in musical films.

62 I've been rich and I've been poor. Believe me, honey, rich is better.
1945 *Some of These Days*.

63 The Last of the Red-Hot Mamas.
Title of song, adopted by Tucker as her nickname.

Turgenev, Ivan 1818–83

Russian novelist. His best-known work is the novel *Fathers and Sons* (1862).

64 Nature is not a temple, but a workshop, and man's the workman in it.
1862 *Fathers and Sons* (translated by Rosemary Edmonds), ch.9.

65 I share no one's ideas. I have my own.
1862 *Fathers and Sons* (translated by Rosemary Edmonds), ch.13.

66 Whatever a man prays for, he prays for a miracle. Every prayer reduces itself to this: Great God, grant that twice two be not four.
1881 *Poems in Prose*, 'Prayer'.

Turner, Bruce 1922–93

British jazz saxophonist. He played in the Humphrey Lyttelton Band for many years, as well as leading his own groups.

67 Jazz musicians are not demigods. They are warm, vulnerable human beings with a desperate need to go on paying the rent.
1984 *Hot Air, Cool Music*, ch.10.

Turner, Joseph Mallard William 1775–1851

English painter, one of Britian's most important 19c artists.

68 This is the end of Art. I am glad I have had my day.
Attributed, on first seeing a daguerrotype. Quoted in J G Links *Canaletto and his Patrons* (1977).

Tutu, Desmond Mpilo 1931–

Black South African prelate, the first black Bishop of Johannesburg (1984) and Archbishop of Cape Town (1986). A fierce critic of apartheid, advocating international sanctions, he also condemned the use of violence, seeking instead a negotiated solution. He was awarded the Nobel peace prize in 1984.

69 Be nice to whites. They need you to rediscover their humanity.
1984 In the *New York Times*, 19 Oct.

70 I am not interested in picking up crumbs of compassion thrown from the table of someone who considers himself to be my master. I want the full menu of rights.
1985 NBC News, 9 Jan.

71 We don't want apartheid liberalized. We want it dismantled. You can't improve something that is intrinsically evil.
1985 Speech, Mar.

72 I have struggled against tyranny. I didn't do that in order to substitute one tyranny with another.
1998 In *The Irish Times*, 'This Week They Said', 31 Oct.

Twain, Mark *pseudonym of* Samuel Langhorne Clemens 1835–1910

US writer. He worked as a steamboat pilot and took his pen-name from a term used for measuring the depth of the Mississippi. His novel *Huckleberry Finn* (1884) is a classic. His work ranges from the lightly comic *The Innocents Abroad* (1869) to the darkly pessimistic *What is Man?* (1906).

73 No woman can look as well out of the fashion as in it.
1867 Letter, 16 Apr, quoted in Franklin Walker and G Ezra Dane (eds) *Mark Twain's Travels with Mr. Brown* (1940), letter 14.

74 I must have a prodigious quantity of mind; it takes me as much as a week to make it up.
1869 *The Innocents Abroad*, ch.7.

75 They spell it Vinci and pronounce it Vinchy; foreigners always spell better than they pronounce.
1869 *The Innocents Abroad*, ch.19.

76 The French are polite, but it is often mere ceremonious politeness. A Russian imbues his polite things with a heartiness that compels belief in their sincerity.
1869 *The Innocents Abroad*.

77 Lump the whole thing! Say that the Creator made Italy from designs by Michael Angelo!
1869 *The Innocents Abroad*.

78 Travel is fatal to prejudice.
1869 *The Innocents Abroad*, conclusion.

79 Soap and education are not as sudden as a massacre, but they are more deadly in the long run.
1872 *A Curious Dream*, 'Facts Concerning the Recent Resignation'.

80 Nothing helps scenery like ham and eggs.
1872 *Roughing It*, ch.17.

81 Well-a-well, man that is born of woman is of few days and full of trouble, as the Scripture says.
1876 Aunt Polly. *The Adventures of Tom Sawyer*, ch.1.

82 I reckon you're a kind of singed cat, as the saying is—better'n you look.
1876 Aunt Polly to Tom. *The Adventures of Tom Sawyer*, ch.1.

83 He was not the Model Boy of the village. He knew the model boy very well though—and loathed him.
1876 *The Adventures of Tom Sawyer*, ch.1.

84 Tom turned in without the added vexation of prayers.
1876 *The Adventures of Tom Sawyer*, ch.3.

85 He held curls to be effeminate, and his own filled his life with bitterness.
1876 *The Adventures of Tom Sawyer*, ch.4.

86 Often, the less there is to justify a traditional custom, the harder it is to get rid of it.
1876 *The Adventures of Tom Sawyer*, ch.5.

87 Church ain't shucks to a circus.
1876 *The Adventures of Tom Sawyer*, ch.7.

88 So they inwardly resolved that so long as they remained in the business, their piracies should not again be sullied with the crime of stealing.
1876 *The Adventures of Tom Sawyer*, ch.13.

89 There comes a time in every rightly constructed boy's life when he has a raging desire to go somewhere and dig for hidden treasure.
1876 *The Adventures of Tom Sawyer*, ch.25.

90 The cross of the Legion of Honour has been conferred upon me. However, few escape that distinction.
1880 *A Tramp Abroad*, ch.8.

91 An Irishman is lined with copper, and the beer corrodes it.

But whiskey polishes the copper and is the saving of him.
1883 *Life on the Mississippi*, ch.23.

92 In the South, the war is what AD is elsewhere: they date from it.
1883 Of the American Civil War. *Life on the Mississippi*, ch.45.

93 Persons attempting to find a motive in this narrative will be prosecuted; persons attempting to find a moral in it will be banished; persons attempting to find a plot in it will be shot.
1884 *The Adventures of Huckleberry Finn*, 'Notice'.

94 She allowed she would sivilize me.
1884 *The Adventures of Huckleberry Finn*, ch.1.

95 If you are with the quality, or at a funeral, or trying to go to sleep when you ain't sleepy…why you itch all over in upward of a thousand places.
1884 *The Adventures of Huckleberry Finn*, ch.2.

96 You think you're a good deal of a big-bug, *don't* you.
1884 Huck's Pap to Huck. *The Adventures of Huckleberry Finn*, ch.5.

97 [He] reckoned a body could reform the old man with a shotgun, maybe, but he didn't know no other way.
1884 Judge Thatcher's opinion of Pap. *The Adventures of Huckleberry Finn*, ch.5.

98 Pap warn't in a good humor—so he was his natural self.
1884 *The Adventures of Huckleberry Finn*, ch.6.

99 A body would 'a thought he was Adam—he was just all mud.
1884 *The Adventures of Huckleberry Finn*, ch.6.

1 After supper Pap took the jug, and said he had enough whisky there for two drunks and one delirium tremens.
1884 *The Adventures of Huckleberry Finn*, ch.6.

2 How slow and still the time did drag along.
1884 *The Adventures of Huckleberry Finn*, ch.6.

3 I's rich now, come to look at it. I owns myself, en I's wuth eight hund'd dollars.
1884 Jim. *The Adventures of Huckleberry Finn*, ch.8.

4 But it warn't no time to be sentimentering.
1884 *The Adventures of Huckleberry Finn*, ch.13.

5 It was fifteen minutes before I could work myself up to go and humble myself to a nigger—but I done it, and I warn't ever sorry for it afterwards, neither. I didn't do him no more mean tricks, and I wouldn' done that one if I'd a knowed it would make him feel that way.
1884 Huck, of Jim. *The Adventures of Huckleberry Finn*, ch.15.

6 Jim said it made him all over trembly and feverish to be so close to freedom.
1884 *The Adventures of Huckleberry Finn*, ch.16.

7 To be, or not to be; that is the bare bodkin
That makes calamity of so long life;
For who would fardels bear, till Birnam Wood do come
  to Dunsinane,
But that the fear of something after death
Murders the innocent sleep,
Great nature's second course,
And makes us rather sling the arrows of outrageous
  fortune
Than fly to others that we know not of.
There's the respect must give us pause:
Wake Duncan with thy knocking! I would thou couldst;
For who would bear the whips and scorns of time,

The oppressor's wrong, the proud man's contumely,
The law's delay, and the quietus which his pangs might
  take,
In the dead waste and middle of the night, when
Churchyards yawn
In customary suits of solemn black,
But that the undiscovered country from whose bourne
  no traveler returns,
Breathes forth contagion on the world,
And thus the native hue of resolution, like the poor cat i'
  the adage,
Is sicklied o'er with care,
And all the clouds that lowered o'er our housetops,
With this regard their currents turn awry,
And lose the name of action.
'Tis a consummation devoutly to be wished.
But soft you, the fair Ophelia:
Ope not thy ponderous and marble jaws,
But get thee to a nunnery—go!
1884 The Duke's version of Hamlet's soliloquy, combining elements of other speeches by Hamlet and pieces of *Macbeth*. *The Adventures of Huckleberry Finn*, ch.21.
➤ *See Shakespeare 753:74.*

8 All kings is mostly rapscallions.
1884 *The Adventures of Huckleberry Finn*, ch.22.

9 Hain't we got all the fools in town on our side? And ain't that a big enough majority in any town?
1884 *The Adventures of Huckleberry Finn*, ch.26.

10 It don't make no difference whether you do right or wrong, a person's conscience ain't got no sense, and just goes for him *anyway*. If I had a yaller dog that didn't know no more than a person's conscience does I would poison him. It takes up more room than all the rest of a person's insides, and yet ain't no good, nohow. Tom Sawyer he says the same.
1884 *The Adventures of Huckleberry Finn*, ch.33.

11 But that's always the way; it don't make no difference whether you do right or wrong, a person's conscience ain't got no sense, and just goes for him *anyway*.
1884 Huck. *The Adventures of Huckleberry Finn*, ch.33.

12 But I reckon I got to light out for the territory ahead of the rest, because Aunt Sally she's going to adopt me and sivilize me, and I can't stand it. I been there before.
1884 Huck. *The Adventures of Huckleberry Finn*, closing words.

13 The boy's mouth is a trifle more Irishy than is necessary.
1884 Letter to his publishers.

14 An experienced, industrious, ambitious, and often quite picturesque liar.
1885 'The Private History of a Campaign That Failed'.

15 Many a small thing has been made large by the right kind of advertising.
1889 *A Connecticut Yankee in King Arthur's Court*, ch.22.

16 The master minds of all nations, in all ages, have sprung in affluent multitude from the mass of the nation, and from the mass of the nation only—not from its privileged classes.
1889 *A Connecticut Yankee in King Arthur's Court*, ch.25.

17 If you pick up a starving dog and make him prosperous, he will not bite you. This is the principal difference between a dog and a man.
1894 *Pudd'nhead Wilson*, ch.16.

18 Few things are harder to put up with than the annoyance of a good example.
1894 *Pudd'nhead Wilson*, ch.19.

19 Familiarity breeds contempt—and children.
c.1894 Quoted in Albert Bigelow Paine (ed) *Mark Twain's Notebook* (1935).

20 What marriage is to morality, a properly conducted licensed liquor traffic is to sobriety.
1895 Quoted in Albert Bigelow Paine (ed) *Mark Twain's Notebook* (1935), ch.23.

21 When in doubt, tell the truth.
1897 *Following the Equator*, ch.2.

22 I admire him, I frankly confess it; and when his time is come I shall buy a piece of the rope for a keepsake.
1897 Of Cecil Rhodes. *Following the Equator*, ch.2.

23 Man is the Only Animal that Blushes. Or needs to.
1897 *Following the Equator*, ch.27.

24 When people do not respect us we are sharply offended; yet deep down in his private heart no man much respects himself.
1897 *Following the Equator*, ch.29.

25 The man with a new idea is a crank until the idea succeeds.
1897 *Following the Equator*, ch.32.

26 There are several good protections against temptation but the surest is cowardice.
1897 *Following the Equator*, ch.36.

27 It takes your enemy and your friend, working together, to hurt you to the heart; the one to slander you and the other to get the news to you.
1897 *Following the Equator*, ch.45.

28 Human nature is the same everywhere; it deifies success, it has nothing but scorn for defeat.
1897 *Joan of Arc*, bk.1, ch.8.

29 Education consists mainly in what we have unlearned.
c.1897 Quoted in Albert Bigelow Paine (ed) *Mark Twain's Notebook* (1935).

30 There are many scapegoats for our blunders, but the most popular one is Providence.
c.1897 Quoted in Albert Bigelow Paine (ed) *Mark Twain's Notebook* (1935).

31 The report of my death was an exaggeration.
1897 In the *New York Journal*, 2 Jun. This was the substance of Twain's cable to the Associated Press in response to the news item that he had died.

32 I am a democrat only on principle, not by instinct—nobody is *that*. Doubtless some people *say* they are, but this world is grievously given to lying.
1898 *Notebook*, ch.31, Feb–Mar.

33 A classic…something that everybody wants to have read and nobody wants to read.
1900 Speech on 'The Disappearance of Literature' at the Nineteenth Century Club, 20 Nov. Quoted in Albert Bigelow Paine (ed) *Mark Twain's Speeches* (1910).

34 Always do right. This will gratify some people, and astonish the rest.
1901 Speech, Brooklyn, 16 Feb.

35 The man who is a pessimist before 48 knows too much; if he is an optimist after it, he knows too little.
1902 Notebook, ch.33, Dec.
➤ See also Willkie 914:67.

36 Of the delights of this world man cares most for sexual intercourse. He will go any length for it—risk fortune, character, reputation, life itself.
c.1906 Quoted in Albert Bigelow Paine (ed) *Mark Twain's Notebook* (1935).

37 Scientists have odious manners, except when you prop up their theory; then you can borrow money off them.
The Bee (published 1917).

38 I have been told that Wagner's music is better than it sounds.
Autobiography (published in 1924).

39 I have never taken any exercise, except sleeping and resting, and I never intend to take any. Exercise is loathsome.
Quoted in Colin Jarman *The Guinness Dictionary of Sports Quotations* (1990).

40 Golf is a good walk spoiled.
Attributed.

41 I don't know anything that mars good literature so completely as too much truth.
'The Savage Club Dinner'. Quoted in Albert Bigelow Paine (ed) *Mark Twain's Speeches* (1923).

42 A habit cannot be tossed out of the window, it must be coaxed down the stairs one step at a time.
Attributed.

Tynan, Kenneth 1927–80

English theatre critic. Writing for the *Observer* and for the *New Yorker*, he argued strongly for the foundation of the National Theatre and lent his support to many talented radical playwrights. He was also the moving force behind the stylish erotic revue *Oh, Calcutta!* (1969).

43 There was a heated division of opinion in the lobbies during the interval but a small conservative majority took the view that it might be as well to remain in the theatre.
1953 Reviewing the play *The Glorious Days*.

44 A good many inconveniences attend play-going in any large city, but the greatest of them is usually the play itself.
1957 In the *New York Herald Tribune*.

45 A novel is a static thing that one moves through; a play is a dynamic thing that moves past one.
1961 *Curtains*.

46 Forty years ago he was Slightly in *Peter Pan*, and you might say that he has been wholly in *Peter Pan* ever since.
1961 Of Noël Coward. *Curtains*.

47 A critic is a man who knows the way but can't drive the car.
1966 In the *New York Times Magazine*, 9 Jan.

48 A good drama critic is one who perceives what is happening in the theatre of his time. A great drama critic also perceives what is *not* happening.
1967 *Tynan Right and Left*, foreword.

49 I doubt if I could love anyone who did not wish to see *Look Back in Anger*.
1956 In the *Observer*, 13 May.

50 A useful word previously unknown to me: 'ergophobia',

meaning 'fear or hatred of work'. At last I can define myself in one word.
The Diaries of Kenneth Tynan (2001), entry for 26 Oct 1975.

51 Dichotomy = operation performed on lesbians to make them normal.
The Diaries of Kenneth Tynan (2001), entry for 11 Oct 1977.

Tyson, Don(ald) John   1930–

US businessman, chairman and chief executive officer of Tyson Foods Inc, Arkansas.

52 If you can take $20,000 in one-hundred-dollar bills and walk up on a windy hill and tear them up and watch them blow away, and it doesn't bother you, then you should go into the commodities market.
1994 In the *New Yorker*, 30 May.

Tyson, Mike   1966–

US boxer.

53 Everybody in America is so money-hungry. It's like a rat race and even when you win you're still a freaking rat.
2000 In *The Times*, Dec 26.

54 I'm not Mother Teresa. I'm not Charles Manson either.
2002 In *The Independent*, 20 Dec.

55 My main objective is to be professional, but to kill him.
2002 On Lennox Lewis. In *The Independent*, 20 Dec.

Tzara, Tristan *pseudonym of* **Samy Rosenstock**   1896–1963

Romanian-born poet, essayist and editor in Paris, a leader of the Dadaist movement.

56 *La mort serait un beau long voyage et les vacances illimitées de la chair des structures et des os.*
Death should be a long, beautiful voyage and limitless vacations of the flesh.
1923 *De nos oiseaux*, 'La mort de Guillaume Apollinaire'.

57 *Dada ne signifie rien.*
Dada means nothing.
1924 *Sept manifestes Dada*, 'Manifeste Dada 1918'.

58 *Liberté:* DADA DADA DADA, *hurlement de couleurs crispées, entrelacements des contraires et de toutes les contradictions, des grotesques, des inconséquences:* LA VIE.
Freedom: DADA DADA DADA, a howl of unnerving colours, intertwinings of contrarities and contradictions, of the grotesque, of inconsistencies: LIFE.
1924 *Sept manifestes Dada*, 'Manifeste Dada 1918'.

59 All pictorial or plastic art is useless; art should be a monster which casts servile minds into terror.
Quoted in Saranne Alexandrian *Surrealist Art* (1970).

60 Dada began not as an art form but as a disgust.
Quoted in Saranne Alexandrian *Surrealist Art* (1970).

Uccello, Paolo   1397–1475

Florentine painter. One of the first Italian painters of the Renaissance to explore the use of perspective.

61 O what a lovely thing this perspective is!
Attributed in Giorgio Vasari *Lives of the Artists* (1568, translated by George Bull, 1965).

Umaseo, Tadao   c.1950–

Japanese intellectual who has written about and commented on his country's social and political traditions.

62 In terms of communication, Japan is like the black hole of the universe. It receives signals but does not emit them.
Quoted in David Halberstam *The Reckoning* (1986).

Unamuno, Miguel de   1864–1936

Spanish fatalist philosopher and writer. Rector at the University of Salamanca, he first supported and then denounced Franco and subsequently died at the hands of the Fascists.

63 *La vida es duda, y la fe sin la duda es solo muerte.*
Life is doubt, and faith without doubt is nothing but death.
1907 *Poesías*, 'Salmo II'.

64 It is not usually our ideas that make us optimistic or pessimistic, but it is our optimism or pessimism of physiological or pathological origin that makes our ideas.
1913 *The Tragic Sense of Life*.

65 Science is a cemetery of dead ideas.
1913 *The Tragic Sense of Life* (translated by P Smith, 1953).

66 True science teaches, above all, to doubt and to be ignorant.
1913 *The Tragic Sense of Life* (translated by P Smith, 1953).

67 Science robs men of wisdom and usually converts them into phantom beings loaded up with facts.
Collected in *Essays and Soliloquies* (translated by J E Crawford Flitch, 1925).

Unesco Constitution

An organization founded (in 1946) to promote collaboration among nations through education, science and culture.

68 Since wars begin in the minds of men, it is in the minds of men that the defences of peace must be constructed.
1945 Signed 16 Nov. The Unesco Constitution came into force 4 Nov 1946.

United Nations Charter

Drafted during World War II by the US, UK and USSR. Key figures included John Foster Dulles, Ralph Bunche and Field Marshal Jan Smuts.

69 We the Peoples of the United Nations, determined to save succeeding generations from the scourge of war, which twice in our lifetime has brought untold sorrow to

mankind, and to reaffirm faith in fundamental human rights, in the dignity and worth of the human person, in the equal rights of men and women and of nations large and small, and to establish conditions under which justice and respect for the obligations arising from treaties and other sources of international law can be maintained, and to promote social progress and better standards of life in larger freedom, and for these ends, to practice tolerance and live together in peace with one another as good neighbours, and to unite our strength to maintain international peace and security, and to ensure by the acceptance of principles and the institution of methods, that armed force shall not be used, save in the common interest, and to employ international machinery for the promotion of the economic and social advancement of all peoples, have resolved to combine our efforts to accomplish these aims.
1945 26 Jun.

Unseld, Siegfried   1924–2002

German publisher, head of Suhrkamp Verlag (Frankfurt).

70 One of the signs of Napoleon's greatness—according to a sociologist who recently wrote to our publishing house—is that he once had a publisher shot.
1978 *The Author and his Publisher* (translated by H and H Hannum, 1980), p.1.

Untermeyer, Louis   1885–1977

US writer and editor, best known as the editor of anthologies such as *Modern American Poetry* (1919), which introduced some important new voices, and *Treasury of Great Poems* (1955).

71 Every poet knows the pun is Pierian, that it springs from the same soil as the Muse…a matching and shifting of vowels and consonants, an adroit assonance sometimes derided as jackassonance.
1965 *Bygones*.

Updike, John Hoyer   1932–

US novelist, poet and critic. He is best known for his novels, notably the 'Rabbit' series, but has also written poetry, short stories, criticism and *Self-Consciousness* (1989), a volume of memoirs.

72 Everybody who tells you how to act has whisky on their breath.
1960 *Rabbit, Run*.

73 The difficulty with humorists is that they will mix what they believe with what they don't; whichever seems likelier to win an effect.
1960 *Rabbit, Run*.

74 Many-maned scud-thumper, tub
of male whales, maker of worn wood, shrub-
ruster, sky-mocker, rave!
portly pusher of waves, wind-slave.
1960 *Telephone Poles and Other Poems*, 'Winter Ocean'.

75 School is where you go between when your parents can't take you and industry can't take you.
1963 *The Centaur*, ch.4.

76 One out of three hundred and twelve Americans is a bore, for instance, and a healthy male adult bore consumes each year one and a half times his own weight in other people's patience.

1965 *Assorted Prose*, 'Confessions of a Wild Bore'.

77 The first breath of adultery is the freest; after it, constraints aping marriage develop.
1968 *Couples*, ch.2.

78 Sex is like money; only too much is enough.
1968 *Couples*, ch.5.

79 Facts are generally overesteemed. For most practical purposes, a thing is what men think it is. When they judged the earth flat, it was flat. As long as men thought slavery tolerable, it was tolerable. We live down here among shadows, shadows among shadows.
1974 Buchanan. *Buchanan Dying*, act 1.

80 To be President of the United States, sir, is to act as advocate for the blind, venomous, and ungrateful client; still, one must make the best of the case, for the purposes of Providence.
1974 Polk. *Buchanan Dying*, act 2.

81 In general the churches…bore for me the same relation to God that billboards did to Coca-Cola: they promoted thirst without quenching it.
1975 *A Month of Sundays*, ch.2.

82 Americans have been conditioned to respect newness, whatever it costs them.
1975 *A Month of Sundays*, ch.18.

83 One of the last…of the great narrating English virgins.
Of Mildred Lathbury, protagonist of Barbara Pym's *Excellent Women* (1978). Attributed.

84 America is a vast conspiracy to make you happy.
1980 *Problems*, 'How to Love America and Leave It at the Same Time'.

85 Writing criticism is to writing fiction and poetry as hugging the shore is to sailing in the open sea.
1984 *Hugging The Shore*, foreword.

86 Why does one never hear of government funding for the preservation and encouragement of comic strips, girlie magazines and TV soap operas? Because these genres still hold the audience they were created to amuse and instruct.
1985 In the *New York Review of Books*, 18 Jul.

87 There's a crystallization that goes on in a poem which the young man can bring off, but which the middle-aged man can't.
1986 In the *New York Times*, 24 Mar.

88 How circumstantial reality is! Facts are like individual letters, with their spikes and loops and thorns, that make up words: eventually they hurt our eyes, and we long to take a bath, to rake the lawn, to look at the sea.
1989 *Self-Consciousness*, I. 'A Soft Spring Night in Shillington'.

89 A writer's self-consciousness, for which he is much scorned, is really a mode of interestedness, that inevitably turns outward.
1989 *Self-Consciousness*, I. 'A Soft Spring Night in Shillington'.

90 The essential self is innocent, and when it tastes its own innocence knows that it lives forever.
1989 *Self-Consciousness*, I. 'A Soft Spring Night in Shillington'.

91 The throat: how strange, that there is not more erotic emphasis upon it. For here, through this compound pulsing pillar, our life makes its leap into spirit, and in the other direction gulps down what it needs of the material world.

92 The great temple of fiction has no well-marked front portal; most devotees arrive through a side door, and not dressed for worship.
1989 *Self-Consciousness*, III. 'Getting The Words Out'.

93 In fact we do not try to picture the afterlife, nor is it our selves in our nervous tics and optical flecks that we wish to perpetuate; it is the self as the window on the world that we can't bear to think of shutting.
1989 *Self-Consciousness*, VI. 'On Being A Self Forever'.

94 Not only are selves conditional but they die. Each day, we wake slightly altered, and the person we were yesterday is dead.
1989 *Self-Consciousness*, VI. 'On Being A Self Forever'.

95 So writing is my sole remaining vice. It is an addiction, an illusory release, a presumptuous taming of reality, a way of expressing lightly the unbearable.
1989 *Self-Consciousness*, VI. 'On Being A Self Forever'.

96 Now that I am sixty, I see why the idea of elder wisdom has passed from currency.
1992 In the *New Yorker*, Nov.

97 [There is] an undercurrent of emotion bred of the deep acquaintance that can take a landscape and its inhabitants to be a vocabulary, a set of wordless symbols effortlessly shared.
1995 On the artist Edward Hopper. In the *Washington Post*, 25 Jun.

98 The United States, democratic and various though it is, is not an easy country for a fiction-writer to enter: the slot between the fantastic and the drab seems too narrow.
1995 *Rabbit Angstrom: The Four Novels*, introduction.

99 Clarence's mind was like a many-legged, wingless insect that had long and tediously been struggling to climb up the walls of a slick-walled porcelain basin; and now a sudden impatient wash of water swept it down the drain.
1996 *In the Beauty of the Lilies*.

1 But when has happiness ever been the subject of fiction? The pursuit of it is just that—a pursuit.
2003 *The Early Stories: 1953–1975*, foreword.

Urey, Harold Clayton 1893–1981

US chemist and discoverer of deuterium, or heavy hydrogen. He taught at the Universities of Montana, John Hopkins, Columbia, Chicago and Oxford, and was awarded the 1934 Nobel prize in chemistry.

2 I thought it might have a practical use in something like neon signs.
c.1934 Recalling his 1932 discovery of heavy water which proved critical to the development of the atomic bomb.

Ustinov, Sir Peter Alexander 1921–2004

English actor, playwright and director, of Russian descent. He appeared in a wide range of European works, including both comedies and tragedies, and also enjoyed success in plays of his own, among them *The Love of Four Colonels* (1951), *Romanoff and Juliet* (1956) and *Beethoven's Tenth* (1983). His talent as a witty raconteur and his many film appearances also contributed to his international reputation.

3 Critics search for ages for the wrong word, which, to give them credit, they eventually find.
1952 BBC radio broadcast, Feb.

4 A diplomat these days is nothing but a head waiter who's allowed to sit down occasionally.
1956 *Romanoff and Juliet*.

5 Would it have helped Ben Hur if Christ had not been crucified?
1962 Comment when the financiers of his *Billy Budd* expressed their preference for a happy ending. Recalled in his autobiography *Dear Me* (1977).

6 Thanks to the movies, gunfire has always sounded unreal to me, even when being fired at.
1977 *Dear Me*.

7 There is always something engagingly lunatic about Ralph, a Quixotic quality, although his windmills are ditches and his faithful nag a powerful motor-cycle.
1977 Of Sir Ralph Richardson. *Dear Me*.

8 Toronto is a kind of New York operated by the Swiss.
Quoted by John Bentley Mays in the *Globe and Mail*, 1 Aug 1987.

9 I was relieved to hear that your welcome was not excessive.
To the audience, opening a one-man show at the Curran Theater. Quoted in the *San Francisco Chronicle*, 25 Apr 1991.

Uttley, Alison 1884–1976

English writer. She is remembered for her books for children, notably the 'Little Grey Rabbit' series (1929 onwards).

10 For a long time we dreamed of a real leather ball, and at last my brother had one for his birthday. The feel of the leather, the stitching round it, the faint gold letters stamped upon it, the touch of the seam, the smell of it, all affected me so deeply that I still have that ache of beauty when I hold a cricket ball.
1948 *Carts and Candlesticks*.

Vachell, Horace Annesley 1861–1955

British writer.

11 In nature there are no rewards or punishments; there are only consequences.
1906 *The Face of Clay*.

Valenzuela, Luisa 1940–

Argentinian fiction writer.

12 *Siendo el esperar sentada la forma más muerta de la espera muerta, siendo el esperar la forma menos estimulante de muerte.*
To wait, seated in a chair, is the deadest form of dead anticipation, and waiting the most uninspired form of death.
1982 *Cambio de armas*, 'Ceremonias de rechazo' (translated as *Other Weapons*, 'Rituals of Rejection', 1985).

Valéry, Paul 1871–1945

French poet, writer and critic, considered one of the great

modern philosophical writers in French verse. He wrote widely on philosophical issues and on the metaphysics of life.

13 *Un poème n'est jamais achevé—c'est toujours un accident qui le termine, c'est-à-dire qui le donne au public.*
A poem is never finished; it is always an accident that puts a stop to it, that gives it to the public.
1930 *Littérature.*

14 *Il faut n'appeler Science que l'ensemble des recettes qui réussissent toujours.—Tout le reste est littérature.*
Science means simply the aggregate of all the recipes that are always successful. All the rest is literature.
1932 *Moralités.*

15 *Dieu créa l'homme, et ne le trouvant pas assez seul, il lui donne une compagne pour lui faire mieux sentir sa solitude.*
God created man and, finding him not sufficiently alone, gave him a companion to make him feel his solitude more keenly.
1941 *Tel Quel 1*, 'Moralités'.

16 *La politique est l'art d'empêcher les gens de se mêler de ce qui les regarde.*
Politics is the art of preventing people from taking part in affairs which concern them.
1943 *Tel Quel 2*, 'Rhumbs'.

Valle y Caviedes, Juan del   c.1652–?1695

Peruvian poet born in a small town in Andalusia, Spain. He lived most of his life in Lima. Little is known of his life. His collection *Diente del Parnaso* (1689) is an earthy satire of the medical profession.

17 *Y así, enfermos, ojo alerta,*
y a ningún médico admitan;
mueran de gorra, sin dar
un real a la medicina.
Be careful then, patients,
and don't accept any doctor;
die for free and do not give
a single coin to medicine.
1689 *Diente del Parnaso* ('Parnassus' Tooth'), 'Prólogo al que leyere este tratado'.

Vallejo, César Abraham   1892–1938

Peruvian poet. A first-hand witness to poverty and the injustices done to the indigenous peoples, after the publication of his collection *Trilce* (1922), he left Peru (1923) and spent the rest of his life in France and Spain living in precarious circumstances and without publishing a single poem. He also wrote novels and non-fiction.

18 *Yo nací un día*
que Dios estuvo enfermo.
I was born on a day
God was sick.
1918 *Los heraldos negros* (translated as *The Black Heralds*, 1990), 'Espergesia'.

19 *Absurdo, sólo tú eres puro.*
Absurdo, este exceso sólo ante ti se
suda de dorado placer.
Absurdity, only you are pure.
Absurdity, only before you
is this excess sweated out of golden pleasure.

1922 *Trilce* (translated 1973), no.73.

20 *Me moriré en París con aguacero,*
un día del cual tengo ya el recuerdo.
Me moriré en París—y no me corro—
tal vez un jueves, como es hoy, de otoño.
I will die in Paris with a sudden shower,
a day I can already remember.
I will die in Paris—and I don't budge—
maybe a Thursday, like today is, in autumn.
1939 *Poemas humanos*, 'Piedra negra sobre una piedra blanca' (translated as 'Black Stone on a White Stone', 1968).

Vance, Paul and Pockriss, Lee

US songwriters who have composed many popular songs, including 'Catch a Falling Star' which was made popular by Perry Como.

21 Itsy Bitsy Teenie Weenie Yellow Polkadot Bikini.
1960 Title of song.

van den Berghe, Pierre L   1933–

US sociologist, Emeritus Professor at the University of Washington.

22 I suffer the anthropological malady diagnosed by Lévi-Strauss in *Tristes tropiques*: I find it much more difficult to suspend value judgments about the society in which I normally reside than I do abroad. It takes physical and cultural distance to gain moral detachment and political noncommitment. Relativism implies a solid measure of indifference.
'From the Popocatepetl to the Limpopo', collected in Bennett Berger (ed) *Authors of their Own Lives* (1990).

23 Sociology seems to have missed every intellectually promising boat in the last half century.
'From the Popocatepetl to the Limpopo', collected in Bennett Berger (ed) *Authors of their Own Lives* (1990).

Vanderbilt, Amy   1908–74

US hostess and writer, an authority on social etiquette.

24 Breakfast is the one meal at which it is perfectly good manners to read the paper.
1954 *Amy Vanderbilt's Complete Book of Etiquette.*

van der Post, Sir Laurens   1906–96

South African soldier, explorer, writer and philosopher.

25 Human beings are perhaps never more frightened than when they are convinced beyond doubt that they are right.
1958 *Lost World of the Kalahari.*

van de Wetering, Janwillem   1931–

Dutch murder-mystery writer.

26 The desire to make money is a symptom of all sorts of emotional disturbances—greed is only one of them.
1988 *The Maine Massacre.*

Van Druten, John William   1901–57

US playwright of Dutch extraction, who was born in London. His mainly light comic plays include *Old Acquaintance* (1940), *Bell, Book and Candle* (1950) and *I Am a Camera* (1951), a stage adaptation of Isherwood's Berlin stories.

27 If I were a woman I'd wear coffee as a perfume.
Quoted in *Think*, Feb 1963.

van Gogh, Vincent 1853–90

Dutch Post-Impressionist painter. He was an evangelistic preacher in Le Borinage (1878–80) and after studying in Paris he settled in Arles (1888), where the light and colour transformed his art. He became increasingly mentally disturbed, and finally shot himself.

28 There is no blue without yellow and without orange.
1888 Letter to Émile Bernard, Jun.

29 I have a terrible lucidity at moments when nature is so beautiful. I am not conscious of myself any more, and the pictures come to me as if in a dream.
1888 Letter to his brother Theo, c.27 Sep.

30 It is no more easy to make a good picture than it is to find a diamond or a pearl. It means trouble and you risk your life for it.
1888 From a letter to his brother Theo, early Oct.

31 I cannot help it that my paintings do not sell. The time will come when people will see that they are worth more than the price of the paint.
1888 Letter to his brother Theo, 24 Oct.

Van Hooijdonk, Pierre 1969–

Dutch footballer.

32 £7,000 a week would be fine for the homeless. But not for me.
1997 Rejecting a new wage deal at Celtic Football Club. Quoted in the *Observer*, 6 Jun 2004.

Van Horne, Harriet 1920–

US journalist.

33 Cooking is like love. It should be entered into with abandon or not at all.
1956 *Vogue*, Oct.

34 After nightfall, I wouldn't leave a burning building without an escort.
1969 On muggings in Manhattan. In the *Washington Post*, 26 Feb.

Varèse, Edgar 1883–1965

US composer of Italo-French parentage. He settled in New York in 1919 and founded the New Symphony Orchestra to further the cause of modern music. In 1921 he founded the international Composers' Guild, which has become the leading organ of progressive musicians. His work is almost entirely orchestral, examples including the largely abstract *Hyperprism* (1923) and *Ionisation* (1931).

35 There is no avant-garde: only some people a bit behind.
Attributed.

Vargas Llosa, Mario 1936–

Peruvian writer, who spent his early life in Bolivia and moved to Paris in 1959, living in several European cities. He was a defeated candidate for the Peruvian presidency (1990), having declined an offer of the premiership in 1984, and remains active and often controversial in literary and political matters.

36 *Por qué esos personajes que se servían de la literatura como adorno o pretexto iban a ser más escritores que Pedro Camacho, quien sólo vivía para escribir? Porque*

ellos habían leído (o, al menos, sabían que deberían haber leído) a Proust, a Faulker, a Joyce, y Pedro Camacho era poco más que un analfabeto?
Why should those persons who used literature as an ornament or pretext have any more right to be considered real writers than Pedro Camacho, who lived *only* to write? Because they had read (or at least knew that they should have read) Proust, Faulkner, Joyce, while Pedro Camacho was very nearly illiterate?
1977 *La tía Julia y el escribidor* (translated as *Aunt Julia and the Scriptwriter*, 1982), ch.11.

Vasari, Giorgio 1511–74

Italian painter, architect and author of the first biography of the Italian Renaissance artists.

37 According to Pliny, painting was brought to Egypt by Gyges of Lydia; for he says that Gyges once saw his own shadow cast by the light of a fire and instantly drew his own outline on the wall with a piece of charcoal.
1568 *Lives of the Artists* (translated by George Bull, 1965).

38 [Michelangelo] Buonarotti commended it [Titian's painting] highly, saying that his colouring and his style pleased him very much but that it was a shame that in Venice they did not learn to draw well from the beginning.
1568 *Lives of the Artists* (translated by George Bull, 1965).

Vasconcelos, José 1882–1959

Mexican educator, politician, essayist and philosopher, Minister of Education (1920–4). His political activism led to exile on several occasions. His works call for the incorporation of native culture into Mexican life to transcend the limitations of Western culture.

39 *La América Latina debe lo que es al europeo blanco y no va a renegar de él…Sin embargo, aceptamos los ideales superiores del blanco, pero no su arrogancia.*
Latin America owes its being to the European, and should not deny it…but, while accepting the white man's superior ideals, we do not accept his arrogance.
1925 *La raza cósmica* (translated as *The Cosmic Race*, 1979), pt.1, ch.2.

Vaughan Williams, Ralph 1872–1958

British composer. He established his reputation with the choral *Sea Symphony* (1910) and promoted the English folksong movement. His works include *Fantasia on a Theme of Tallis* (1909), for strings, the *Pastoral Symphony* (1922), the opera *The Pilgrim's Progress* (1948–9) and many choral works.

40 Misbegotten abortions.
1930 Of critics. Letter to Holst.

41 I don't know whether I like it, but it's what I meant.
Of his Fourth Symphony. Quoted in Ian Crofton and Donald Fraser *A Dictionary of Musical Quotations* (1985).

42 It takes perhaps a thousand poor musicians to produce one virtuoso.
1954 In *The New York Times*, 5 Dec.

Vaughan, Henry 1622–95

Welsh religious poet. Educated at Oxford, he later practised as a physician. His verse publications include *Silex Scintillans* (1650, enlarged 1655) and *Olor Iscansus* (1651); prose meditations include *The Mount of Olives* (1652) and *Flores Solitudinis* (1652).

43 The skin and shell of things
Though fair
are not
Thy wish nor prayer
but got
My meer despair
of wings.
1650 *Silex Scintillans*, 'The Search'.

44 Happy those early days when I
Shined in my Angel-infancy.
Before I understood this place
Appointed for my second race,
Or taught my soul to fancy aught
But a white, celestial thought;
When yet I had not walked above
A mile or two from my first love,
And looking back (at that short space)
Could see a glimpse of His bright face.
When on some gilded cloud or flower
My gazing soul would dwell an hour
And in those weaker glories spy
Some shadows of eternity.
1650 *Silex Scintillans*, 'The Retreat'.

45 Before I taught my tongue to wound
My conscience with a sinful sound,
Or had the black art to dispense
A several sin to every sense,
But felt through all this fleshly dress
Bright shoots of everlastingness.
1650 *Silex Scintillans*, 'The Retreat'.

46 Some men a forward motion love,
But I by backward steps would move,
And when this dust falls to the urn
In that state I came, return.
1650 *Silex Scintillans*, 'The Retreat'.

47 My soul, there is a country
Far beyond the stars,
Where stands a wingèd sentry
All skilful in the wars;
1650 *Silex Scintillans*, 'Peace'.

48 King of comforts, King of life,
Thou hast cheered me,
And when fears and doubts were rife,
Thou hast cleared me.

Not a hook in all my breast
But thou fill'st it,
Not a thought in all my rest
But thou kill'st it.

Wherefore with my utmost strength
I will praise thee,
And as thou giv'st line, and length,
I will raise thee.
1650 *Silex Scintillans*, 'Praise'.

49 I saw Eternity the other night
Like a great ring of pure and endless light,
All calm, as it was bright,
And round beneath it, Time in hours, days, years

Driven by the spheres
Like a vast shadow moved.
1650 *Silex Scintillans*, 'The World'.

50 Man is the shuttle, to whose winding quest
And passage through these looms
God ordered motion, but ordained no rest.
1650 *Silex Scintillans*, 'Man'.

51 They are all gone into the world of light,
And I alone sit lingering here;
Their very memory is fair and bright,
And my sad thoughts doth clear.
1650 *Silex Scintillans*, 'They Are All Gone'.

52 I played with fire, did counsel spurn,
Made life my common stake;
But never thought that fire would burn,
O that a soul could ache.
1650 *Silex Scintillans*, 'The Garland'.

Vaz de Caminha, Pero   late 15c–early 16c

Portuguese historian, who came to the New World only eight years after Columbus. His account avoids the prevalent hyperbole, striving instead to give a realistic picture of the native peoples.

53 *Esta gente é boa e de boa simplicidade. E imprimir-se-á ligeiramente neles cualquer cunho, que les quiserem dar. E logo lhes, Nosso Senhor, deu bons corpos e bons rostos, como a bons homens, e Ele que nos por aqui trouxe, creio que não foi sem causa. E portanto, Vossa Alteza, pois tanto deseja acrescentar na santa fé católica, deve entender em sua salvação.*
These people are good and simple. You can stamp on them any design that you wish to give them. And Our Lord gave them good bodies and good faces, and I think that it was his plan that we arrive here. Therefore, Your Majesty, since you wish so much to increase Catholic faith, you must provide for their salvation.
Carta (published 1817).

Veblen, Thorstein   1857–1929

US economist and social critic. He attacked commercial values in his best-known work, *Theory of the Leisure Class* (1899). He was instrumental in breaking the hold of neo-classical economic theory and became a leader in the institutional school of economics.

54 The corset is…a mutilation, undergone for the purpose of lowering the subject's vitality and rendering her permanently and obviously unfit for work.
1899 *Theory of the Leisure Class*.

55 When seen in the perspective of half-a-dozen years or more, the best of our fashions strike us as grotesque, if not unsightly.
1899 *Theory of the Leisure Class*.

56 Conspicuous consumption of valuable goods is a means of reputability to the gentleman of leisure.
1899 *Theory of the Leisure Class*.

Vega Carpio, Lope Félix de   1562–1635

Spanish playwright and poet. His prolific output included some 1,800 plays, of which around 600 survive. He served with the Spanish Armada in 1588 and was ordained as a priest in 1614, though he continued to enjoy numerous love affairs.

57 All right, then, I'll say it: Dante makes me sick.
　　1635 Last words.

Vegetius *full name Flavius Vegetius Renatus*
fl.c.385–400 AD

Roman military writer under Theodosius I, the Great. After AD 375 he produced the *Epitoma Rei Militaris*, mainly extracted from other authors, which was a supreme authority on warfare during the Middle Ages.

58 *Qui desiderat pacem, praeparat bellum.*
　　Let him who desires peace prepare for war.
　　c.380 AD *Epitoma Rei Miltaris*, no.3, prologue. This became familiar in the Middle Ages as *Si vis pacem para bellum* (If you want peace, prepare for war).

Venables, Terry 1943–

English footballer and manager. He was dismissed as manager of Tottenham Hotspur in 1993, but appointed manager of England a year later. He resigned after the 1996 European championships.

59 I had mixed feelings—like watching your mother-in-law drive over a cliff in your car.
　　1992 Of Paul Gascoigne's move from Tottenham Hotspur to the Italian club Lazio. Quoted in David Pickering *The Cassell Soccer Companion* (1994).

60 Never's a hard call, isn't it? Never-ish.
　　2000 On whether he would ever manage England again. In *The Times*, 26 Dec.

61 If you can't stand the heat in the dressing room, get out of the kitchen.
　　Attributed.
　　➤ *Truman 868:32.*

Venturi, Robert Charles 1925–

US architect, renowned for his eclectic and sometimes humorous designs, a key figure of the postmodernist school.

62 [It is] drawing a moustache on a madonna.
　　1977 On designing an addition to Oberlin College's 1917 Allen Memorial Art Museum. In the *New York Times*, 30 Jan.

Vergniaud, Pierre Victurnien 1753–93

French revolutionary politician, leader of the Girondists. When the Girondists clashed with the Montagnards, who wished to retain dictatorial power, he and his party were arrested and guillotined.

63 *Il a été permis de craindre que la Révolution, comme Saturne, dévorât successivement tous ses enfants.*
　　There is reason to fear that the Revolution may, like Saturn, devour each of her children one by one.
　　1793 Spoken at his trial, Oct.

Verlaine, Paul 1844–96

French poet who befriended and promoted the poetry of Arthur Rimbaud with whom he had a volatile relationship.

64 *Les sanglots longs*
　　Des violons
　　De l'automne
　　Blessent mon cœur
　　D'une langueur
　　Monotone.
　　Slow sobs

　　Of the violins
　　Of autumn
　　Wound my heart
　　With a monotonous languor.
　　1866 *Poèmes saturniens, Paysages tristes, V:* 'Chansons d'Automne'.

65 *Un vaste et tendre*
　　Apaisement
　　Semble descendre
　　Du firmament . . .
　　C'est l'heure exquise.
　　A vast and tender
　　Calm
　　Seems to descend
　　From the heavens . . .
　　This is the exquisite hour.
　　1866 *Poèmes saturniens,* 'La Bonne Chanson, no.6'.

66 *Il pleure dans mon cœur*
　　Comme il pleut sur la ville.
　　The tears fall in my heart
　　As the rain over the town.
　　1874 *Romances sans paroles,* 'Ariettes oubliées, no.3'.

67 *Voici des fruits, des fleurs, des feuilles et des branches*
　　Et puis voici mon cœur qui ne bat que pour vous.
　　Here are fruits, flowers, leaves and branches
　　And here also is my heart which beats only for you.
　　1874 *Romances sans paroles,* 'Aquarelles, Green'.

68 *Pas la Couleur, rien que la Nuance!*
　　No colour, only nuance!
　　1884 *Jadis et naguère,* 'Art poétique'.

69 *Prends l'éloquence et tords-lui son cou!*
　　Take eloquence and break its neck!
　　1884 *Jadis et naguère,* 'Art poétique'.

70 *Que ton vers soit la bonne aventure*
　　Éparse au vent crispé du matin
　　Qui va fleurant la menthe et le thym.
　　Et tout le reste est littérature.
　　May your verse be a glorious adventure
　　Strewn by the crisp morning air
　　Which helps the mint and the thyme grow.
　　Everything else is mere literature.
　　1884 *Jadis et naguère,* 'Art poétique'.

Verne, Jules 1828–1905

French novelist. His best-known works include *A Journey to the Centre of the Earth* (1864), *Twenty Thousand Leagues Under the Sea* (1869) and *Around the World in Eighty Days* (1873).

71 An Englishman does not joke about such an important matter as a bet.
　　1873 *Around the World in Eighty Days.*

Vespasian *full name Titus Flavius Vespasianus* AD 9–79

Roman Emperor, commander of the legions in the East when Nero was deposed. He was proclaimed emperor by his troops in Alexandria, and after defeating his rival Vitellius (AD 69) reached Rome and restored order. He began an ambitious building programme, including the Colosseum, and extended and consolidated the Empire.

72 *Pecunia non olet.*
　　Money does not smell.
　　Attributed. His son Titus had objected to a tax on the contents of

the city's urinals (used by fullers). Vespasian held a coin to Titus's nose, asking him whether it smelled. When Titus said no he replied 'Atqui e lotio est' ('And yet, it comes from urine'). Quoted in Suetonius *Vespasian*, 23.

73 *Vae, puto deus fio.*

Dear me, I must be turning into a god.

AD 79 Attributed last words. Quoted in Suetonius *Vespasian*, 23 (translated by Robert Graves, 1967).

Vettriano, Jack 1953–

Scottish artist whose works have proved particularly popular as prints and posters.

74 Rather the poster on the student's wall than the original unseen on a shelf in a big gallery storeroom.

2004 In *The Times*, 13 Mar.

Vian, Boris 1920–59

French novelist associated with the Surrealist movement.

75 *Les gens ne changent pas. Ce sont les choses qui changent.*

People do not change. Things change.

1947 *L'Écume des jours.*

76 *Les masses ont tort et les individus toujours raison.*

The masses are wrong; individuals are always right.

1947 *L'Écume des jours.*

77 *Mais enfin, bande de critiques, les livres que vous ne comprenez pas ne vaudraient-ils pas au moins que vous les signaliez?*

For heaven's sake, gang of critics, don't the books which you do not understand at least deserve recognition?

1948 In *La Seine*, 19 Apr.

78 *Rien n'est plus parfait, plus achevé qu'un cadavre.*

Nothing is more perfect, more complete than a corpse.

1950 *L'Herbe rouge.*

79 *Savoir qu'il existe des passions et ne pas le ressentir, c'est affreux.*

To know that there are passions and to not feel any, that is horrible.

1950 *L'Herbe rouge.*

80 *Les femmes et les hommes ne vivent pas sur le même plan.*

Women and men do not live according to the same design.

1953 *L'Arrache-cœur.*

81 *Un poète*

C'est un être unique

À des tas d'exemplaires

Qui ne pense qu'en vers

Et n'écrit qu'en musique

Sur des sujets divers

Des rouges ou des verts

Mais toujours magnifiques.

A poet

Is a unique being

From an exemplary multitude

Who only thinks in verse

And only writes in music

On diverse subjects

Reds and greens

But always magnificently.

1962 *Je voudrais pas crever.*

Vicious, Sid *pseudonym of* John Simon Ritchie 1957–79

British rock bassist. He played with the notorious punk rock group The Sex Pistols in the 1970s, and died of a drug overdose while awaiting trial for the murder of his girlfriend, Nancy Spungen, in the US.

82 You just pick a chord, go twang, and you've got music.

1976 In *The Sun*.

Victoria *in full* Alexandrina Victoria 1819–1901

Queen of Great Britain (1837–1901). She married Prince Albert of Saxe-Coburg and Gotha (1840), and bore him nine children. After his death (1861) she neglected her duties, but her recognition as Empress of India (1876) and the celebratory Golden (1887) and Diamond (1897) Jubilees restored her prestige. She had strong preferences for certain Prime Ministers (eg Melbourne and Disraeli) over others (notably Peel and Gladstone).

83 This mad, wicked folly of 'Women's Rights' with all its attendant horrors, on which her poor sex is bent, forgetting every sense of womanly feeling and propriety. Lady Amberley ought to get a good whipping.

1870 Letter to Sir Theodore Martin, 29 Mar. The feminist Lady Amberley was Bertrand Russell's mother.

84 Oh, if the Queen were a man, she would like to go and give those Russians, whose word one cannot believe, such a beating! We shall never be friends again till we have it out.

1878 Letter to Lord Beaconsfield, 10 Jan.

85 Please understand that there is no one depressed in this house. We are not interested in the possibilities of defeat; they do not exist.

1899 On the 2nd Boer War. Comment to the Prime Minister, Arthur Balfour, Dec. Quoted in Lady Gwendolen Cecil *Life of Robert, Marquis of Salisbury* (1931), vol.3, ch.6.

86 A strange, horrible business, but I suppose good enough for Shakespeare's day.

Attributed comment after watching a performance of *King Lear*.

87 He speaks to Me as if I were a public meeting.

Of Gladstone. Attributed in G W E Russell *Collections and Recollections*.

88 We are not amused.

Attributed.

Vidal, Gore *originally* Eugene Luther Vidal, Jr 1925–

US writer and polemicist. He ran for congress in 1960 and spent some time as a TV commentator. His novels include the satirical comedies *Myra Breckenridge* (1968) and *Duluth* (1983), and the historical trilogy *Burr* (1974), *1876* (1976) and *Lincoln* (1984). He published his memoirs, *Palimpsest*, in 1995.

89 A talent for drama is not a talent for writing, but is an ability to articulate human relationships.

1956 In the *New York Times*, 17 Jun.

90 I'm all for bringing back the birch. But only between consenting adults.

1966 Interview on *The Frost Programme*.

91 It is the spirit of the age to believe that any fact, no matter how suspect, is superior to any imaginative exercise, no matter how true.

1967 'French Letters: Theories of the New Novel', in *Encounter*, Dec.

92 Astronauts! Rotarians in space!

1968 *Myra Breckenridge*.

93 There is something about a bureaucrat that does not like a poem.
1968 *Sex, Death and Money*, preface.
➤ *See Frost 338:84.*

94 People who obtain power do so because it delights them for its own sake and for no other reason.
1970 In *Esquire*, Sep.

95 From primeval ooze to the stars, we killed anything that stood in our way, including each other.
1970 On the human race. In *Esquire*, Sep.

96 Whenever a friend succeeds, a little something in me dies.
1973 In the *Sunday Times Magazine*, 16 Sep.

97 It is not enough to succeed. Others must fail.
Quoted in G Irvine *Antipanegyric for Tom Driberg* (1976).

98 A triumph of the embalmer's art.
1981 Of Ronald Reagan. Quoted in the *Observer*, 26 Apr.

99 But to ignore the absence of evidence is the basis of true faith.
1981 'Pink Triangle and Yellow Star', in the *Nation*, 14 Nov.

1 For certain people, after fifty, litigation takes the place of sex.
1981 Quoted in the *Evening Standard*.

2 Democracy is supposed to give you the feeling of choice, like Painkiller X and Painkiller Y. But they're both just aspirin.
1982 Interview in the *Observer*, 7 Feb.

3 It's a country evenly divided between conservatives and reactionaries.
1984 Of the US. In the *Observer*, 16 Sep.

4 American men do not read novels because they feel guilty when they read books which do not have facts in them.
1984 In *Saturday Review*, 18 Jun.

5 The century that began with a golden age in all the arts (or at least the golden twilight of one) is ending not so much without art as without the idea of art.
Introduction to Logan Pearsall Smith *All Trivia* (1984).

6 Fifty per cent of them won't vote and the other half doesn't read newspapers. I hope it's the same.
1991 In *Emmy*, May.

7 When it comes to getting things wrong, the English are born masters.
1991 'Reflections on Glory Reflected and Otherwise', in the *Threepenny Review*, Spring.

8 Meanwhile, let us give Clinton his due. Lincoln to one side, he does better funerals than any American president in an increasingly murderous history.
1997 *Virgin Islands: Essays 1992–1997*.

9 We are, said President Clinton, the one indispensable—or was it indisposable?—nation.
1997 *Virgin Islands: Essays 1992–1997*.

10 There are as many good writers as ever there were. The problem is that there are so few good readers.
2003 Quoted in *Writers on Writing, Volume II: More Collected Essays from the New York Times*.

Vidor, King Wallis 1894–1982

US film director, born in Galveston, Texas. In Hollywood from 1915, he worked as a writer and extra before moving into directing. His many films include *The Big Parade* (1925), *The Crowd* (1928), *Our Daily Bread* (1934) and *The Fountainhead* (1949).

11 The crowd laughs with you always but it will cry with you for only a day.
1929 *The Crowd* (with John V A Weaver and Harry Behn).

Vieira, Antônio 1608–97

Jesuit missionary, orator, diplomat and writer, condemned by the Inquisition and briefly imprisoned. His sermons, letters and state papers are a valuable index to the climate of opinion in 17c Brazil and Portugal.

12 *Que coisa é a formosura, senão uma caveira bem vestida, a que a menor enfermidade tira a cor, e antes de a morte a despir de todo, os anos lhe vão mortificando a graça daquela exterior e aparente superfície, de tal sorte, que, se os olhos pudessem penetrar o interior dela, o não poderiam ver sem horror?*
What is beauty, but a well-dressed skull that loses colour with the slightest illness, and, before death robs it of everything, the grace of its external and apparent surface is mortified by the years in such a way that, if eyes could penetrate within beauty, they could watch it only full of horror?
c.1666 *Sermões*, 'Sermão do demónio mudo' ('Sermon of the Silent Devil').

Villon, François b.1431

French poet, member of the criminal organization 'The Brotherhood of the Cocquille'. Several times sentenced to death for various crimes, he was repeatedly pardoned. In 1463 he received his final death sentence, but this was commuted to banishment.

13 *Mais où sont les neiges d'antan?*
But where are last year's snows?
1461 'Ballade des Dames du Temps Jadis', refrain.

St Vincent of Lérins *known as* **Vincentius Lerinensis** d.c.450 AD

A native of Gaul, and monk on the island of Lerna (Lérins).

14 *Quod ubique, quod semper, quod ab omnibus creditum est.*
What is everywhere, what is always, what is by all people believed.
Commonitorium Primum, section 2 (translated by Heurtley, 1895).

Viner, Jacob 1892–1970

US economist, a professor at the University of Chicago and Princeton University.

15 The classical economists were not wholly free from error, for they were only mortals, even if of a superior species.
1930 *The Long View and the Short*.

Virgil *full name* **Publius Vergilius Maro** 70–19 BC

Roman poet, under the patronage of Maecenas and Augustus. He published the *Eclogues*, a collection of pastorals, in 37 BC, and the *Georgics* (a didactic poem on husbandry in four books) in 30 BC. The *Aeneid*, a national epic based on the legendary founder of the Roman nation, was published posthumously.

16 *Arma virumque cano, Troiae qui primus ab oris*
Italiam fato profugus Laviniaque venit
Litora.
This is a tale of arms and of a man. Fated to be an exile, he
was the first to sail from the land of Troy and reach Italy, at
its Lavinian shore.
Aeneid, opening lines (translated by W F Jackson Knight).

17 *Non ignara mali, miseris succurrere disco.*
No stranger to trouble myself, I am learning to help those
who are in distress.
Dido, queen of Carthage. *Aeneid*, bk.1, l.630.

18 *Conticuere omnes intentique ora tenebant*
Inde toro pater Aeneas sic orsus ab alto.
They fell silent, every one, and each face was turned
intently towards him. From high on the dais Aeneas,
Troy's Chieftain, began to speak.
Aeneid, bk.2, l.1–2 (translated by W F Jackson Knight).

19 *Quidquid id est, timeo Danaos et dona ferentis.*
Whatever it may be, I fear the Greeks, even when
bearing gifts.
Spoken by Laocoon, a Trojan prince and priest of Apollo,
warning the city against the wooden horse left by the Greeks.
Aeneid, bk.2, l.49.

20 *Una salus victis nullam sperare salutem.*
Nothing can save the conquered but the knowledge that
they cannot now be saved.
Aeneid, bk.2, l.354 (translated by W F Jackson Knight).

21 *Dis aliter visum.*
The gods thought otherwise.
Aeneid, bk.2, l.428.

22 *Fama, malum qua non aliud velocius ullum.*
Rumour is of all pests the swiftest.
Aeneid, bk.4, l.174 (translated by W F Jackson Knight).

23 *Quis fallere possit amantem?*
Who can deceive a lover?
Aeneid, bk.4, l.296.

24 *Varium et mutabile semper*
femina.
Women were ever things of many changing moods.
Aeneid, bk.4, l.569–70 (translated by W F Jackson Knight).

25 *Audentis Fortuna iuvat!*
Fortune helps those who dare.
Aeneid, bk.10, l.284. The phrase is often rendered as 'Fortune
favours the brave'.

26 *Experto credite.*
Believe one who has experienced it.
Aeneid, bk.11, l.283.

27 *Latet anguis in herba.*
A snake lurks in the grass.
Eclogues, 3.93.

28 *Sicelides Musae, paulo maiora canamus.*
Non omnis arbusta iuvant humilesque myricae.
Sicilian Muses, let us sing a somewhat loftier strain. Not
all do orchards please and the lowly tamarisks.
Eclogues, 4.1–2 (translated by H Rushton Fairclough).

29 *Non omnia possumus omnes.*
We cannot all do everything.
Eclogues, 8.63 (translated by H Rushton Fairclough).

30 *Omnia vincit amor.*
Love conquers all things.
Eclogues, 10.69.

31 *Labor omnia vicit*
improbus et duris urgens in rebus egestas.
Toil conquered the world, unrelenting toil, and want that
pinches when life is hard.
Georgics, 1.145–6 (translated by H Rushton Fairclough).

32 *Felix qui potuit rerum cognoscere causas.*
Blessed is he who has been able to win knowledge of the
causes of things.
Georgics, 2.490 (translated by H Rushton Fairclough).

33 *Mantua me genuit, Calabri rapuere, tenet nunc*
Parthenope; cecini pascua rura duces.
Mantua brought me life, Calabria death; now Naples
holds me: I sang of flocks and farms and heroes.
19 BC Epitaph on his tomb near Naples, supposedly dictated on
his deathbed. Quoted in Donatus *Vita Vergilii*, 'Life of Virgil'.

Vitruvius *full name* **Marcus Vitruvius Pollio** c.70 BC–25 BC

Roman architect and engineer whose ten books on
architecture, *De Architectura*, are the oldest surviving work on
the subject.

34 Neither talent without instruction, nor instruction
without talent can produce the perfect craftsman.
c.25 BC *On Architecture*.

Vlaminck, Maurice de 1876–1958

French painter, graphic artist and writer.

35 Good painting is like good cooking: it can be tasted, but
not explained.
Attributed.

Voltaire *pseudonym of* **François Marie Arouet** 1694–1778

French philosopher. He was imprisoned for lampooning the
Duc d'Orleans, 1717–18, and later went into exile in England,
1726–9. He returned to France, but moved to Berlin in 1750 to
the court of Frederick the Great. His works include *Œdipe*
(1718), *Candide* (1759) and the *Dictionnaire philosophique*
(1764).

36 *Le superflu, chose très nécessaire.*
The superfluous, a very necessary thing.
1736 *Le Mondain*.

37 *Dans ce pays-ci il est bon de tuer de temps en temps un*
amiral pour encourager les autres.
In this country it is considered a good thing to kill an
admiral from time to time, to encourage the others.
1759 Of England. Reference to the execution of Admiral Byng
following his failure to engage the French at Menorca, 1757.
Candide, ch.23.

38 *Tout est pour le mieux dans le meilleur des mondes*
possibles.
All is for the best in the best of all possible worlds.
1759 *Candide*, ch.30.

39 *Cela est bien dit, répondit Candide, mais il faut cultiver*
notre jardin.
'Well said', Candide replied, 'but we must cultivate our
own garden.'
1759 *Candide*, ch.30.

40 I am the best-tempered man there ever was, yet I have
killed three men, and two of them were priests!
1759 *Candide*, ch.15.

41 You know that these two nations have been at war over a
few acres of snow near Canada, and that they are

spending on this fine struggle more than Canada itself is worth.
1759 Of the French and English struggle in Quebec. *Candide*, ch.23.

42 Men will always be mad, and those who think they can cure them are the maddest of all.
1762 Letter.

43 *La superstition met le monde entier en flammes; la philosophie les éteint.*
Superstition sets the whole world in flames; philosophy puts out the fire.
1764 *Dictionnaire philosophique*, 'Superstition'.

44 *En effet, l'histoire n'est que le tableau des crimes et des malheurs.*
In fact, history is nothing but a tableau of crimes and misfortunes.
1767 *L'Ingénu*, ch.10.

45 *Ce corps qui s'appelait et qui s'appelle encore le saint empire romain n'était en aucune manière ni saint, ni romain, ni empire.*
This state which was called and is still called the Holy Roman Empire, was not in any way holy, or Roman or an Empire.
1769 *Essai sur Les Moeurs et l'Ésprit des Nations*.

46 *La foi consiste à croire ce que la raison ne croit pas... Il ne suffit pas qu'une chose soit possible pour la croire.*
Faith consists in believing what reason cannot...In order to believe something, it is not enough that it should be possible.
1770 *Questions sur l'Encyclopédie*.

47 *Le mieux est l'ennemi du bien.*
The best is the enemy of the good.
1772 *Contes*, 'La Bégueule', l.2. He is quoting an Italian proverb, *Il meglio è l'inimico del bene*.

48 This enormous dunghill.
1776 Of the works of William Shakespeare. Letter to d'Argental, 19 Jul.

49 *On doit des égards aux vivants; on ne doit aux morts que la vérité.*
We should be considerate to the living; to the dead we owe only the truth.
'Première Lettre sur Œdipe'. In *Œuvres*, vol.1 (published 1785).

50 *Dieu n'est pas pour les gros bataillons, mais pour ceux qui tirent le mieux.*
God is on the side not of the big battalions, but of the best shots.
In *Voltaire's Notebooks*, edited by Th. Besterman (1952).

51 *Il faut, dans le gouvernement, des bergers et des bouchers.*
Governments need both shepherds and butchers.
In *Voltaire's Notebooks*, edited by Th. Besterman (1952).

52 One goes to see a tragedy to be moved, to the opera one goes either for want of any other interest or to facilitate digestion.
Quoted in J Wechsberg *The Opera* (1972).

53 *Si Dieu n'existait pas, il faudrait l'inventer.*
If God did not exist, it would be necessary to invent him.
Epîtres, 'À l'Auteur du Livre desTrois Imposteurs'.

54 The art of medicine consists of amusing the patient while Nature cures the disease.
Attributed.

55 I disapprove of what you say, but I will defend to the death your right to say it.
Attributed.

Vonnegut, Kurt, Jr 1922–

US novelist. *Player Piano* (1952) was his first novel and there were another three before *Slaughterhouse-Five* (1969), the central event of which is the destruction of Dresden during World War II, an event witnessed by the author as a prisoner-of-war.

56 The British had no way of knowing it, but the candles and the soap were made from the fat of rendered Jews and Gypsies and fairies and communists, and other enemies of the state. So it goes.
1969 *Slaughterhouse-Five*, ch.5.

57 Their only English-speaking guard told them to memorize their simple address, in case they got lost in the city. Their address was this: 'Schlachthof-fünf'. *Schlachthof* meant *slaughterhouse*. *Fünf* was good old *five*.
1969 *Slaughterhouse-Five*, ch.6.

Vorster, John originally *Balthazar Johannes Vorster* 1915–83

South African Nationalist politician, an extreme Afrikaner. As Prime Minister (1966–78) he maintained a policy of apartheid and protected white interests. In 1978 he became President, but resigned over a financial scandal.

58 As far as criticism is concerned, we don't resent that unless it is absolutely biased—as it is in most cases.
1969 In the *Observer*, 9 Nov.

Vreeland, Diana originally *Diana Dalziel* 1906?–1989

US journalist, editor of *Vogue*. Born in Paris, she married Thomas Vreeland in 1924 in NewYork and joinedVogue as editor-in-chief in 1962. She transformed the high-fashion magazine into a society journal. She also acted as consultant to the costume institute at the Metropolitan Museum of Art.

59 A little bad taste is like a splash of paprika.We all need a splash of bad taste—it's hearty, it's healthy, it's physical.
1984 *D.V.* (her autobiography, edited by George Plimpton and Christopher Hemphill).

60 The biggest thing since the atom bomb.
1990 On the bikini. In her obituary in the *NewYork Times*, 1 Apr.

61 People who eat white bread have no dreams.
Quoted in AnnetteTapert and Diana Edkins *The Power of Style* (1994).

Vukovich, Bill 1918–55

US motor-racing driver. He won the Indianapolis 500 in 1953 and 1954 but was killed in the race while in the lead the following year.

62 There's no secret. You just press the accelerator to the floor and steer left.
1954 Of his tactics in the Indianapolis 500. Quoted in Colin Jarman *The Guinness Dictionary of Sports Quotations* (1990).

Waddington, Miriam 1917–2004

Canadian poet and critic. Of Russian-Jewish origin, she was a social worker in Montreal and taught at York University, Toronto. Her works include poetry such as *The Glass Trumpet* (1966), *The Price of Gold* (1976) and *The Visitants* (1981), and short stories and essays.

63 Keep bees and
grow asparagus,
watch the tides
and listen to the
wind instead of
the politicians
make up your own
stories and believe
them if you want to
live the good life.
1972 *Driving Home: Poems New and Selected*, 'Advice to the Young'.

Wagner, Otto 1841–1918

Austrian architect and teacher, considered the founder of the modern movement.

64 The whole basis of the views of architecture prevailing today must be displaced by the recognition that the only possible point of departure for our artistic creation is modern life.
1895 *Modern Architecture* (1895), preface.

Wagner, Robert Ferdinand, Jr 1944–93

US former deputy mayor of New York City.

65 When in danger, ponder. When in trouble, delegate. And when in doubt, mumble.
1991 In the *New York Times*, 17 Feb.

Wain, John Barrington 1925–94

English writer. He is known primarily as a critic and novelist, but he also wrote poetry, plays and a biography of Samuel Johnson.

66 Poetry is to prose as dancing is to walking.
1976 BBC radio broadcast, 13 Jan.

Waite, Terry (Terence Hardy) 1939–

English religious adviser, envoy of Archbishop of Canterbury Robert Runcie from 1980. On 20 Jan 1987, while making inquiries in Beirut about European hostages, he was kidnapped. Following worldwide efforts to secure his release and that of his fellow hostages, 1,763 days later he was freed.

67 Politics come from man. Mercy, compassion, and justice come from God.
1985 In the *Observer*, 13 Jan.

68 Freeing hostages is like putting up a stage set—which you do with the captors, agreeing on each piece as you slowly put it together. Then you leave an exit through which both the captor and the captive can walk with sincerity and dignity.
1986 Interviewed on ABC news, 3 Nov.

Waits, Tom 1949–

US singer, songwriter, musician and actor. His albums include *Heartattack and Vine* (1980), *Swordfishtrombones* (1983) and *Mule Variations* (1999).

69 There's a lot of intelligence in the hands. When you pick up a shovel, the hands know what to do. The same thing's true of sitting at the piano.
1999 In the *Dallas Observer*, 6 May.

Walcott, Derek Alton 1930–

West Indian poet and dramatist. He founded the Trinidad Theatre Workshop in 1959 and is Visiting Professor of English at Boston University. His poetry includes *In A Green Night* (1962), *Castaway* (1965), *The Gulf* (1969) and *Collected Poems* (1986). He was awarded the Nobel prize for literature in 1992.

70 I who have cursed
The drunken officer of British rule, how choose
Between this Africa and the English tongue I love?
Betray them both, or give back what they give?
How can I face such slaughter and be cool?
How can I turn from Africa and live?
1962 *In a Green Night*, 'A Far Cry from Africa'.

71 I'm just a red nigger who love the sea,
I had a sound colonial education,
I have Dutch, nigger, and English in me,
and either I'm nobody or I'm a nation.
1980 *The Star-Apple Kingdom*, 'The Schooner *Flight*', pt.1.

72 Who knows
who his grandfather is, much less his name?
1980 *The Star-Apple Kingdom*, 'The Schooner *Flight*', pt.5.

73 But we live like our names and you would have to be colonial to know the difference,
to know the pain of history words contain.
1980 *The Star-Apple Kingdom*, 'The Schooner *Flight*', pt.6.

74 I see these islands and I feel to bawl,
'area of darkness' with V.S. Nightfall.
1982 *The Fortunate Traveller*, 'The Spoiler's Return'.

75 The English language is nobody's special property. It is the property of the imagination: it is the property of the language itself.
Interviewed in George Plimpton (ed) *Writers at Work* (8th series, 1988).

76 every 'I'
is a fiction finally.
1990 *Omeros*, bk.1, ch.5, section 2.

77 Time is the metre, memory the only plot.
1990 *Omeros*, bk.2, ch.24, section 2.

78 'We were the colour of shadows when we came down with tinkling leg-irons to join the chains of the sea, for the silver coins multiplying on the sold horizon.'
1990 *Omeros*, bk.3, ch.28, section 1.

79 The worst crime is to leave a man's hands empty.
Men are born makers, with that primal simplicity
in every maker since Adam.
1990 *Omeros*, bk.3, ch.28, section 2.

80 Art is History's nostalgia, it prefers a thatched roof to a concrete factory, and the huge church above a bleached village.
1990 *Omeros*, bk.6, ch.45, section 2.

81 Poetry…is perfection's sweat but most seen as fresh as the raindrops on a statue's brow.
1992 In the *New York Times*, 8 Dec.

82 The fate of poetry is to fall in love with the world, in spite of History.
1992 In the *New York Times*, 8 Dec.

83 The process of poetry is one of excavation and of self-discovery.
1992 In the *New York Times*, 8 Dec.

84 V S Nightfall.
Nickname for V S Naipaul. Attributed to Derek Walcott by Paul Theroux, in *Sir Vidia's Shadow: A Friendship Across Five Continents* (1998).

Wald, George 1906–97

US biochemist and member of the faculty at Harvard University. He shared the 1967 Nobel prize in physiology or medicine and became known widely for his view opposing the War in Vietnam.

85 We are the products of editing, rather than of authorship.
1975 'The Origin of Optical Activity', in *Annals of the New York Academy of Sciences*, vol.69.

Wald, Jerry 1911–62

US writer and producer. His films include *Mildred Pierce* (1945), *Johnny Belinda* (1948) and *The Glass Menagerie* (1950).

86 He used to be a big shot.
1939 The words of Panama Smith (Gladys George) as Eddie Bartlett (James Cagney) dies on the steps of the church in *The Roaring Twenties*. With Richard Macauley and Robert Rossen.

Waldron, Hicks

Chair, Boardroom Consultants Inc.

87 People do what you pay them to do, not what you ask them to do.
1991 In the *Wall Street Journal*, 17 Apr.

Walesa, Lech 1943–

Polish trade unionist, politician and President. A former shipyard worker, he became leader of the independent trade union, Solidarity, which openly challenged the government's policies, and was imprisoned under martial law (1981). Released in 1982, he was awarded the Nobel peace prize in 1983. He was President from 1990 to 1995.

88 He who once became aware of the power of Solidarity and who breathed the air of freedom will not be crushed.
1983 Nobel peace prize lecture, read on his behalf, 11 Dec.

89 The English are all right. They're quiet, they're slow, they count things carefully, they hesitate—and I'm switching to their track.
1991 In *The Times*, 17 Apr, on the eve of his state visit to London.

90 The Soviet Union remains a superpower in the military and nuclear sense—only its economy is in difficulty. People want me to lead the troops out or to chuck them over the border, but I have neither the strength nor the will to do it.
1991 In *The Times*, 17 Apr.

Waley, Arthur David 1889–1966

English poet and Sinologist. He was a distinguished translator of Chinese and Japanese literature.

91 It is not difficult to censor foreign news.
What is difficult today is to censor one's own thoughts,—
To sit by and see the blind man
On the sightless horse, riding into the bottomless abyss.
1940 'Censorship'.

Walken, Christopher 1943–

US actor. His numerous films include *The Deer Hunter* (1978), *A View to a Kill* (1985), *True Romance* (1993) and *Sleepy Hollow* (1999).

92 I'm better off not socialising. I make a better impression if I'm not around.
2004 In *The Scotsman*, 12 Jun.

Walker, Alice Malsenior 1944–

US writer. She has written poetry and non-fiction, and established her reputation with her novels, notably *The Color Purple* (1983, filmed 1985).

93 The gift of loneliness is sometimes a radical vision of society or one's people that has not previously been taken into account.
1973 Interview in J O'Brien (ed) *Interviews with Black Writers*.

94 It is healthier, in any case, to write for the adults one's children will become than for the children one's 'mature' critics often are.
1976 'A Writer Because of, Not in Spite of, Her Children', in *Ms.*, Jan.

95 Writing saved me from the sin and inconvenience of violence.
1979 'One Child of One's Own', in *Ms.*, Aug.

96 The good news may be that Nature is phasing out the white man, but the bad news is that's who She thinks we all are.
1982 'Nuclear Madness: What You Can Do', in *Black Scholar*, Spring.

97 Anybody can observe the Sabbath, but making it holy surely takes the rest of the week.
1983 *In Search of Our Mothers' Gardens*, 'To the Editors of *Ms.* Magazine'.

98 The trouble with our people is as soon as they got out of slavery they didn't want to give the white man nothing else. But the fact is, you got to give 'em something. Either your money, your land, your woman or your ass.
1985 Pa. *The Color Purple*.

99 She say, Celie, tell the truth, have you ever found God in church? I never did. I just found a bunch of folks hoping for him to show. Any God I ever felt in church I brought in with me. And I think all the other folks did too. They come to church to *share* God, not find God.
1985 Shug. *The Color Purple*.

1 There are those who believe Black people possess the secret of joy and that it is this which will sustain them through any spiritual or moral or physical devastation.
1992 *Possessing the Secret of Joy*, epigraph.

Wall Street Journal

Leading US financial newspaper.

2   God is registered to vote for Hollywood as a Republican.
     However, Jesus Christ is a Democrat from Santa Monica.
     1995 'God Lives in Hollywood', editorial on California's voter
     registration lists, 12 Jul.

Wall, Mervyn   1908–97

Irish writer.

3   The Bishop gave vent to a long-drawn sigh.
     'Did it ever occur to you to wonder why God created
     women?' he asked. 'It's the one thing that tempts me at
     times to doubt His infinite goodness and wisdom.'
     1946 *The Unfortunate Fursey.*

4   The odour of sanctity was clearly discernible from his
     breath and person.
     1946 *The Unfortunate Fursey.*

5   'Did you ever hear the like?' said the Devil, and a hard
     note crept into his voice. 'If there's one thing I can't stand',
     he said, 'it's superstition.'
     1946 *The Unfortunate Fursey.*

Wallace, George Corley   1919–98

US Democratic lawyer and politician, opponent of the civil
rights movement and Governor of Alabama (1963–7, 1971–4,
1975–8 and 1983–7). A presidential bid ended with an assassination attempt, on 15 May 1972, which left him paralyzed.

6   Segregation now, segregation tomorrow, and
     segregation for ever.
     1963 Inaugural speech as Governor of Alabama, 19 Feb.

7   I've climbed my last political mountain.
     1972 On retiring after being crippled in an assassination
     attempt. Quoted in the *New York Times*, 3 Apr 1986.

8   A great deal has been lost and a great deal gained…may
     your message be heard…your lessons never be
     forgotten.
     1995 Reversing the 'segregation for ever' stance of 1963. In news
     reports, 11 Mar.

Wallace, Henry Agard   1888–1965

US agriculturist and statesman, editor of *Wallace's Farmer*
(1933–40) until nominated Vice-President to Roosevelt.
Chairman of the Board of Economic Welfare (1941–5) and
Secretary of Commerce (1945–6), he stood unsuccessfully as
President in 1948.

9   The century on which we are entering, the century that
     will come out of this war, can be and must be the century
     of the common man.
     1942 Speech, New York, 8 May.

Wallace, William Ross   1819–81

US poet. Only a few of his poems, mostly militant patriotic
songs, have survived as anthology works. He practised as a
lawyer in New York from 1841 until his death and was a
contributor to Harper's magazine. Stimulated by the American
Civil War, he wrote *Sword of Bunker Hill* (1861) and *The Liberty
Bell* (1862).

10   The hand that rocks the cradle
     Is the hand that rules the world.
     c.1865 *John o' London's Treasure Trove.*

Wallach, Eli   1915–

US actor. A star of both stage and screen, he appeared in such
films as *The Moonspinners* (1964), *The Tiger Makes Out* (1967)
and *The Sentinel* (1977). On the stage he has won particular
acclaim in plays by Tennessee Williams and others.

11   There's something about a crowd like that that brings a
     lump to my wallet.
     1964 Observing the crowds that were gathering at the box office
     to see the highly successful Broadway show *Luv.* Attributed.

Waller, Edmund   1606–87

English poet and politician. Educated at Cambridge, he went on
to be an MP; his involvement in a plot against Parliament during
the Civil War led to his banishment in 1643. His collected poems
were published in 1645.

12   Go, lovely rose,
     Tell her that wastes her time and me,
     That now she knows,
     When I resemble her to thee,
     How sweet and fair she seems to be.
     1645 'Go, lovely rose'.

13   Small is the worth
     Of beauty from the light retir'd;
     Bid her come forth,
     Suffer her self to be desir'd,
     And not blush to be admir'd.
     1645 'Go, lovely rose'.

14   Phillis, why shou'd we delay
     Pleasures shorter than the day?
     1645 'To Phillis'.

15   Since thou wouldst needs, bewitched with some ill
       charms,
     Be buried in those monumental arms:
     As we can wish, is, may that earth lie light
     Upon thy tender limbs, and so good night.
     1645 'To One Married to an Old Man'.

16   Poets may boast (as safely-vain)
     Their work shall with the world remain:
     Both bound together, live, or die,
     The verses and the prophecy.

     But who can hope his lines shou'd long
     Last, in a daily changing tongue?
     While they are new, envy prevails,
     And as that dies, our language fails.
     1645 'Of English Verse'.

17   We write in sand, our language grows,
     And like our tide ours overflows.
     1645 'Of English Verse'.

18   Verse thus design'd has no ill fate,
     If it arrive but at the date
     Of fading beauty, if it prove
     But as long-liv'd as present love.
     1645 'Of English Verse'.

Waller, Fats (Thomas Wright)   1904–43

US jazz pianist, composer and entertainer. A professional
musician at 15, he began his recording career in 1922. Among
the jazz standards he wrote were 'Ain't Misbehavin'' and
'Honeysuckle Rose'.

19 Madam, if you don't know by now, don't mess with it!

When asked what jazz was. Quoted in Marshall Stearns *The Story of Jazz* (1956).

➤ *See* Armstrong 30:75.

Wallis, Hal 1898–1986

US producer. He worked in Hollywood for many years and then became an independent producer.

20 Louis, I think this is the beginning of a beautiful friendship.

1942 Closing words of *Casablanca*, one of his contributions to a script largely written by the Epstein twins and Howard Koch.

Walpole, Horace, 4th Earl of Orford 1717–97

English writer and politician. Architectural pursuits, correspondence, writing, visits to Paris, his house, Strawberry Hill, and the establishment of a private press were the main occupations of his life. He exchanged more than 1600 letters with Mme du Deffand between 1769 and 1797 and corresponded also with Sir Horace Mann and the Countess of Upper Ossory.

21 We were eight days in coming hither from Lyons; the four last in crossing the Alps. Such uncouth rocks, and such uncomely inhabitants!

1739 Letter to Richard West. Collected in P Cunningham (ed) *The Letters of Horace Walpole, Fourth Earl of Orford* (1857–9).

22 I am very glad that I see Rome while it yet exists; before a great number of years are elapsed, I question whether it will be worth seeing. Between the ignorance and poverty of the present Romans, every thing is neglected and falling to decay.

1740 Letter. Collected in P Cunningham (ed) *The Letters of Horace Walpole, Fourth Earl of Orford* (1857–9).

23 It is a little plaything-house that I got out of Mrs Chevenix's shop, and it is the prettiest bauble you ever saw. It is set in enamelled meadows with filigree hedges…barges as solemn as Barons of the Exchequer move under my window… Thank God! the Thames is between me and the Duchess of Queensberry.

1747 Of Strawberry Hill, the first 'Gothic' cottage, a showplace in its day. Letter to Henry Seymour Conway, 8 Jun. In W S Lewis (ed) *Selected Letters of Horace Walpole* (1973). Mrs Chevenix kept a well-known toy-shop.

24 Every drop of ink in my pen ran cold.

1752 Letter to George Montague, 30 Jul. In *The Correspondence of Horace Walpole* (Yale edition, 1937–8).

25 One of the greatest geniuses that ever existed, Shakespeare, undoubtedly wanted taste.

1764 Letter to Christopher Wren, 9 Aug. In *The Correspondence of Horace Walpole* (Yale edition, 1937–8).

26 It is charming to totter into vogue.

1765 Letter to George Selwyn, 2 Dec. In *The Correspondence of Horace Walpole* (Yale edition, 1937–8).

27 Wondrously clean, but as evidently an actor as Garrick.

1766 Of the Methodist preacher John Wesley. Letter to John Chute, 10 Oct. In William Hadley (ed) *The Letters of Horace Walpole* (1926).

28 It was easier to conquer it than to know what to do with it.

1772 Of the Orient. Letter to Sir Horace Mann, 27 Mar. In *The Correspondence of Horace Walpole* (Yale edition, 1937–8).

29 The way to ensure summer in England is to have it framed and glazed in a comfortable room.

1774 Letter to William Cole, 28 May. In *The Correspondence of Horace Walpole* (Yale edition, 1937–8).

30 By the waters of Babylon we sit down and weep, when we think of thee, O America!

1775 Letter to William Mason, 12 Jun. In *The Correspondence of Horace Walpole* (Yale edition, 1937–8).

31 The world is a comedy to those that think, a tragedy to those that feel.

1776 Letter to Lady Ossory, 11 Dec. In W S Lewis (ed) *Selected Letters of Horace Walpole* (1973).

32 Your daughters, I hope, will be married to Americans, and not in this dirty, despicable little island.

1777 Letter to Lady Ossory, 11 Dec. In W S Lewis (ed) *Selected Letters of Horace Walpole* (1973).

33 When will the world know that peace and propagation are the two most delightful things in it?

1778 Letter to Sir Horace Mann, 7 Jul. In *The Correspondence of Horace Walpole* (Yale edition, 1937–8).

34 It is the story of a mountebank and his zany.

1785 Of Boswell's account of his *Tour of the Hebrides* with Dr Johnson. Letter to Henry Conway, 6 Oct. In *The Correspondence of Horace Walpole* (Yale edition, 1937–8).

35 All the sensible Tories that I ever knew were either Jacobites or became Whigs; those that remained Tories remained fools.

Memoirs of the Reign of King George III (published 1845).

36 Virtue knows to a farthing what it has lost by not being vice.

Quoted in L Kronenberger *The Extraordinary Mr Wilkes* (1973).

37 A fertile pedant.

Of Margaret Cavendish, Duchess of Newcastle. Quoted in Nicholas T Parsons *The Joy of Bad Verse* (1988).

Walpole, Sir Robert, 1st Earl of Orford 1676–1745

English statesman and leading minister of George I and II. Elected as a Whig MP in 1701, he became Secretary for War (1708), Treasurer of the Navy (1710) and Chancellor of the Exchequer (1715). Recognized as England's first Prime Minister from 1721, he resigned in 1742, when a war he had opposed broke out.

38 Madam, there are fifty thousand men slain this year in Europe, and not one an Englishman.

1734 To Queen Caroline, on avoiding British participation in the War of the Polish Succession. Quoted in John Hervey *Memoirs 1734–43* (1848), vol.1.

39 They may ring their bells now; before long they will be wringing their hands.

1739 Remark on hearing church bells celebrating the declaration of war against Spain, 19 Oct.

40 I have lived long enough in the world to know that the safety of a Minister lies in his having the approbation of this House. Former Ministers neglected that and therefore they fell; I have always made it my first study to obtain it, and therefore I hope to stand.

1739 Speech, House of Commons, 21 Nov.

41 Patriots spring up like mushrooms. I could raise 50 of them within the four and twenty hours. I have raised many of them in one night. It is but refusing to gratify an immeasurable or insolent demand, and up starts a patriot.

1741 Speech, House of Commons, 13 Feb.

42 All those men have their price.

Quoted in William Coxe *Memoirs of Sir Robert Walpole* (1798).

Walters, Julie 1950–

English actress. On television she has appeared in both comedy and drama, and her films include *Educating Rita* (1983) and *Billy Elliot* (2000).

43 There's something great about going through the menopause and being in your 50s. You trade in that youthful thing, where everything is brand new. You swap it hopefully for some kind of wisdom; all the stuff you've learned. And I think HRT and plastic surgery kind of stopped that.

2003 In *The Guardian*, 1 Sep.

Walther Von der Vogelweide c.1170–1230

German poet. One of the most celebrated poets of his time, he found particular favour at the Austrian court, and was awarded a small estate by Emperor Frederick II.

44 *Jâ leider desn mac nicht gesîn,*
Das guot und wertlich êre
Und gotes hulde mêre
Zesamene in ein herze komen.
It is sadly impossible
For wealth and a good name,
along with God's favour,
to be united in one heart.

c.1195 'Ich sass ûf eime steine', l.16–19.

Walton, Izaak 1593–1683

English writer. He is remembered for *The Compleat Angler* (1653), which discusses the business of fishing and is interspersed with scraps of dialogue, moral reflections, quaint old verses, songs and sayings, and idyllic glimpses of country life.

45 But God, who is able to prevail, wrestled with him, as the Angel did with Jacob, and marked him; marked him for his own.

1653 Of Donne. *Life of John Donne*.

46 Angling may be said to be so like mathematics, that it can never be fully learnt.

1653 *The Compleat Angler*, 'Epistle to the Reader'.

47 I shall stay [the reader] no longer than to wish him a rainy day to read this…discourse; and that if he be an honest angler, the east wind may never blow when he goes a-fishing.

1653 *The Compleat Angler*, 'Epistle to the Reader'.

48 Angling is somewhat like poetry, men are to be born so: I mean with inclination to it.

1653 *The Compleat Angler*, pt.1, ch.1.

49 Sir Henry Wotton…was also a most dear lover, and a frequent practiser of the art of angling; of which he would say, 'it was an employment for his idle time…a rest to his mind, a cheerer of his spirits, a diverter of sadness, a calmer of unquiet thoughts, a moderator of passions, a procurer of contentedness; and that it begat habits of peace and patience in those that professed and practised it.'

1653 *The Compleat Angler*, pt.1, ch.1.

50 An excellent angler, and now with God.

1653 Of Sir George Hastings, *The Compleat Angler*, pt.1, ch.4.

51 She and I both love all anglers, they be such honest, civil quiet men.

1653 The milkwoman. *The Compleat Angler*, pt.1, ch.4.

52 No life, my honest scholar, no life so happy and so pleasant as the life of a well-governed angler; for when the lawyer is swallowed up with business, and the statesman is preventing or contriving plots, then we sit on cowslip-banks, hear the birds sing, and possess ourselves in as much quietness as these silver streams, which we now see glide so quietly by us.

1653 *The Compleat Angler*, pt.1, ch.5.

53 He would often say, Religion does not banish mirth, but only moderates and sets rules to it.

1670 Of George Herbert. *Life of George Herbert*.

Walton, Sir William Turner 1902–83

British composer. His works include *Façade* (1923), designed to accompany verses by Edith Sitwell, the *Sinfonia Concertante* (1927), the biblical cantata *Belshazzar's Feast* (1931), the opera *Troilus and Cressida* (1954) and much incidental music for films.

54 I seriously advise all sensitive composers to die at the age of thirty-seven. I know I've gone through the first halcyon period, and am just about ripe for my critical damnation.

1939 Letter.

Wang Xizhe 1956–

Chinese dissident, released from prison in 1993 after 12 years for his role in the Democracy Wall Movement.

55 You may keep me under surveillance until the year 2000, but will you even be able to hold on to power until then?

1995 Quoted in the *Eastern Express*, 10 May.

Ward, Artemus *pseudonym of* *Charles Farrar Browne* 1834–67

US humorist. In 1857 he began to publish letters from 'Artemus Ward' in the Cleveland *Plain Dealer*. His backwoods humour was an immediate success, and Lincoln interrupted a Cabinet meeting to read from him. In 1866 he moved to England where he worked for *Punch* and became a popular lecturer.

56 Traters…are a unfortunate class of people. If they wasn't they wouldn't be traters. They conspire to bust up a country—they fail, and they're traters. They bust her, and they become statesmen and heroes.

1867 *Artemus Ward in London and Other Papers*, 'The Tower of London'.

57 Let us all be happy, and live within our means, even if we have to borrow the money to do it with.

1867 *Artemus Ward in London, and Other Papers*, 'Science and Natural History'.

58 I am happiest when I am idle.

I could live for months without performing any kind of labour, and at the expiration of that time I should feel fresh and vigorous enough to go right on in the same way for numerous more months.

1867 *Artemus Ward in London, and Other Papers*, 'Pyrotechny', 3.

59 Why care for grammar as long as we are good?

1867 *Artemus Ward in London, and Other Papers*, 'Pyrotechny', 5.

60 He [Brigham Young] is dreadfully married. He's the most married man I ever saw in my life.

1869 *Artemus Ward's Lecture*, 'Brigham Young's Palace'.

61 'Why is this thus? What is the reason of this thusness?'
1869 *Artemus Ward's Lecture*, 'Heber C. Kimball's Harem'

Warhol, Andy 1928–87

US graphic artist, painter and film-maker. He was one of the most controversial figures in American Pop Art.

62 If you want to know all about Andy Warhol, just look at the surface of my paintings and films and me, there I am. There's nothing behind it!
1967 Quoted in Gretchen Berg 'Andy: My True Story', in the *LA Free Press*, 17 Mar.

63 In the future everybody will be world famous for fifteen minutes.
Quoted in Andy Warhol, Kasper König, Pontus Hultén and Olle Granath (eds) *Andy Warhol* (1968).

64 The Pop artists did images that anybody walking down Broadway could recognize in a split second—comics, picnic tables, men's trousers, celebrities, shower curtains, refrigerators, Coke bottles—all the great modern things that the Abstract Expressionists tried so hard not to notice at all.
Quoted in Andy Warhol and Pat Hackett *POPism: The Warhol '60s* (1980).

65 When you think about it, department stores are kind of like museums.
1985 *America*.

Warner, Marina Sarah 1946–

British writer and literary and social critic. Her works include *Alone of All Her Sex* (1976) and *From the Beast to the Blonde* (1994), and novels such as *Indigo* (1992). In 1994 she delivered the Reith Lectures, later published as *Managing Monsters* (1994).

66 Although Mary cannot be a model for the New Woman, a goddess is better than no goddess at all, for the sombre-suited masculine world of the Protestant religion is altogether too much like a gentlemen's club to which the ladies are only admitted on special days.
1976 *Alone of All Her Sex: the Myth and Cult of the Virgin Mary*, epilogue.

Warner, Sir Pelham Plum 1873–1963

English cricketer, born in Trinidad. He played for Middlesex and captained England on tours of Australia and South Africa. He was secretary (1939–45) and president (1950) of the MCC and was knighted in 1937.

67 Cricket is the greatest game that the wit of man has yet devised.
Quoted in Colin Jarman *The Guinness Dictionary of Sports Quotations* (1990).

Warren, Earl 1891–1974

US politician and judge. As chief justice of the US Supreme Court (1943–53) he was a liberalizing influence, ending segregation in schools and protecting accused persons from police abuses. He headed the Commission into the assassination of John F Kennedy (1963–4).

68 We conclude that in the field of public education the doctrine of 'separate but equal' has no place.
1954 Ruling to declare segregated schools unconstitutional, 17 May.

69 The freedom to marry has long been recognized as one of the vital personal rights essential to the orderly pursuit of happiness by free men.
1957 2 Jun. Unanimous ruling against a Virginian law forbidding intermarriage of blacks and whites.

70 I always turn to the sports section first. The sports page records people's accomplishments; the front page has nothing but man's failures.
1968 In *Sports Illustrated*, 'Scorecard', 22 Jul.

Warren, Harry *pseudonym of* Salvatore Guaragno 1893–1981

US songwriter, born in Brooklyn. During the 1930s, he collaborated with Al Dubin on several Busby Berkeley movies. During the war years he worked with Mark Gordon for Fox and then also for MGM.

71 Walk two Oscars behind me.
1975 Comment to Harold Arlen on winning a second Oscar for *On the Atchison, Topeka and the Santa Fe*. Quoted in Tony Thomas *Harry Warren*.

Warren, Robert Penn 1905–89

US writer, Professor of English at Louisiana, Minnesota and Yale. He established an international reputation with his novel *All the King's Men* (1943, filmed 1949), and wrote several other novels, short stories and volumes of poetry.

72 The poem…is a little myth of man's capacity of making life meaningful. And in the end, the poem is not a thing we see—it is, rather, a light by which we may see—and what we see is life.
1958 In the *Saturday Review*, 22 Mar.

73 The urge to write poetry is like having an itch. When the itch becomes annoying enough, you scratch it.
1969 In the *New York Times*, 16 Dec.

74 How do poems grow? They grow out of your life.
1985 In the *New York Times*, 12 May.

75 What is a poem but a hazardous attempt at self-understanding? It is the deepest part of autobiography.
1985 In the *New York Times*, 12 May.

76 I don't expect you'll hear me writing any poems to the greater glory of Ronald and Nancy Reagan.
1986 On being appointed the first US Poet Laureate. In the *Washington Post*, 27 Feb.

77 He woke me from the torpor of the accustomed.
On familiar scenes more fully realized through Walker Evans's realistic photographs. Quoted in Belinda Rathbone *Walker Evans* (1995).

Washington, Booker Taliaferro 1856–1915

African-American educationalist, born a slave in Virginia. He became principal of the Tuskegee Institute in Alabama in 1881 and was a moderate in the negro movement. His autobiography, *Up from Slavery*, was published in 1901.

78 No race can prosper until it learns that there is as much dignity in tilling a field as in writing a poem. It is at the bottom of life we must begin, and not at the top.
1895 'The Atlanta Exposition Address', in *Up from Slavery* (1901), ch.14.

79 In all things that are purely social we can be as separate as the fingers, yet one as the hand in all things essential to mutual progress.

1895 'The Atlanta Exposition Address,' in *Up from Slavery* (1901), ch.14.

Washington, George 1732–99

American soldier and statesman, first President. As commander of American forces in the War of Independence he displayed great powers of leadership, suffering defeats at Brandywine and Germantown, but holding his army together through the winter of 1777–8 at Valley Forge. After the alliance with France (1778), he forced the surrender of Cornwallis (1781) then retired to Mount Vernon, and sought strong constitutional government. In 1787 he presided over the Constitutional Convention and became President, eventually joining the Federalist Party, and retired in 1797.

80 Father, I cannot tell a lie. I did it with my little hatchet.
In childhood, on admitting to vandalizing a cherry tree, attributed by Mason Locke Weems (Parson Weems) in his *Life and Memorable Actions of George Washington* (5th edn, c.1810). Weems claimed to have heard the tale from an elderly lady, a distant relation of Washington's, 20 years earlier.

81 When we assumed the soldier, we did not lay aside the citizen.
1775 Address to the New York legislature, 26 Jun.

82 I can answer for but three things: a firm belief in the justice of our cause, close attention in the prosecution of it, and the strictest integrity.
1775 On being elected Commander of the Unionist Army, 19 Jun.

83 The time is now near at hand which must probably determine whether Americans are to be freemen or slaves… The fate of unborn millions will now depend, under God, on the courage and conduct of this army. Our cruel and unrelenting enemy leaves us only the choice of brave resistance or abject submission. We have, therefore, to resolve to conquer or die.
1776 General orders, 2 Jul. Quoted in J C Fitzpatrick (ed) *Writings of George Washington* (1932), vol.5.

84 An old-fashioned Virginia fox hunt, gentlemen.
1777 Comment on the skirmish at Princeton, 3 Jan. Attributed.

85 The preservation of the sacred fire of liberty, and the destiny of the republican model of government, are justly considered as deeply, perhaps as finally staked, on the experiment entrusted to the hands of the American people.
1789 Inaugural address, 30 Apr.

86 To be prepared for war is one of the most effective means of preserving peace.
1790 First Annual Address, 8 Jan.

87 It is our true policy to steer clear of permanent alliance with any portion of the foreign world.
1796 Farewell address to the union, 17 Sep.

Washington Post

US newspaper.

88 The Closest of Strangers.
1994 Headline, 9 Jan, on the sharing of Nobel peace prize by South Africa's F W de Klerk and Nelson Mandela.

Washington Times

US newspaper.

89 Cool is Hot.
1988 Headline, 9 May, on Massachusetts Governor Michael Dukakis's low-key campaign for Democratic presidential nomination.

90 There's no crime like the present.
1995 In the week in which three persons jumped the White House fence, 25 May.

Waterhouse, Keith Spencer 1929–

English novelist, dramatist, humorist and journalist. His whimsical novel *Billy Liar* (1959) was adapted for the stage the next year and filmed in 1963, and he continued writing mordantly humorous novels, such as *Jubb* (1963) and *Office Life* (1978). Later works include *Unsweet Charity* (1992), a novel, and two volumes of autobiography, *City Lights* (1994) and *Streets Ahead* (1995).

91 Lying in bed, I abandoned the facts again and was back in Ambrosia.
1959 *Billy Liar*, opening sentence.

92 I cannot bring myself to vote for a woman who has been voice-trained to speak to me as though my dog has just died.
1978 On Margaret Thatcher, attributed.

93 The 50s face was angry, the 60s face was well-fed, the 70s face was foxy. Perhaps it was the right expression: there was a lot to be wary about.
1979 In the *Observer Magazine*, 30 Dec.

94 Why should it take three times longer to elect a Mayor for London as it does to set up an entire Scottish Parliament?
1999 In the *Observer*, 'They Said What…?', 24 Oct.

Waterman, Pete 1947–

English pop record producer, one of the founder members of Stock Aitken and Waterman (1984–93).

95 I wish there was a formula. I'd be billionaire instead of a millionaire.
2003 On making hit records. In *Varsity*, 28 Nov.

Watson, James D(ewey) 1928–

US biochemist who with Francis Crick helped to determine the structure of the nucleic acid known as DNA. Crick, Maurice Wilkins and Watson shared the 1962 Nobel prize in physiology or medicine. Watson wrote *The Double Helix* (1968), the story of the discovery of the structure of DNA.

96 We wish to suggest a structure for the salt of deoxyribose nucleic acid (DNA).
1953 First sentence of the paper describing the structure of DNA, with Francis Crick. *Nature*, 25 Apr.

97 [Science] seldom proceeds in the straightforward logical manner imagined by outsiders. Instead, its steps forward…are often very human events in which personalities and cultural traditions play major roles.
1968 *The Double Helix*.

Watson, Thomas John 1874–1956

US businessman and computing pioneer, president of IBM.

98 I think there is a world market for about five computers.
1943 Quoted in Christopher Cerf and Victor Navasky *The Experts Speak* (1984).

Watson, Thomas John, Jr   1914–93

US businessman, president (1952–61), chairman (1961–71) and chairman of the executive board (1972–9) at IBM. He also served as Ambassador to the USSR (1979–81).

99 Solve it quickly, solve it right or wrong.
   1977 His advice on dealing with problems. In *Fortune*.

Watson, William   c.1559–1603

English Catholic conspirator and secular priest.

1 *Fiat justitia et ruant coeli.*
   Let justice be done, though the heavens may fall.
   1602 *A Decacordon of Ten Quodlibeticall Questions Concerning Religion and State.* This was an influential reworking of Ferdinand I's motto.
   ➤ *See Ferdinand I 320:1.*

Watt, James   1736–1819

Scottish inventor and mechanical engineer, best remembered for his refinements to the steam engine.

2 That vessel in which the powers of steam are to be employed to work the engine, which is called the Cylinder in common fire engines, and which I call the Steam Vessel, must, during the whole time the engine is at work, be kept as hot as the steam that enters it; first, by enclosing it in a case of wood, or any other materials that transmit heat slowly; secondly, by surrounding it with steam or other heated bodies; and thirdly, by suffering neither water nor any other substance colder than steam to enter and touch it during that time.
   1769 Specification of patent, 5 Jan, for a new method of lessening the consumption of steam and fuel in fire engines.

Watts, Isaac   1674–1748

English independent preacher and hymn writer.

3 When I survey the wondrous cross
   On which the prince of glory died,
   My richest gain I count but loss,
   And pour contempt on all my pride.
   1707 *Hymns and Spiritual Songs,* 'Crucifixion to the World, by the Cross of Christ'.

4 Jesus shall reign where'er the sun
   Does his successive journeys run;
   His kingdom stretch from shore to shore,
   Till moons shall wax and wane no more.
   1719 *The Psalms of David Imitated*, Psalm 72.

5 Our God, our help in ages past
   Our hope for years to come,
   Our shelter from the stormy blast
   And our eternal home.
   1719 *The Psalms of David Imitated*, Psalm 90 (in 1738 John Wesley substituted 'O God' for 'Our God').

Waugh, Auberon Alexander   1939–2001

English writer and editor, the eldest son of Evelyn Waugh. He was a journalist and novelist, and the editor of the *Literary Review*.

6 I will endeavour to put the word sex in capital letters on the cover of every issue of the *Literary Review* under my editorship, regardless of its actual contents… My purpose is simply to embolden booksellers.
   1986 In the *Daily Telegraph*, 9 May.

7 It was inevitable that as soon as we had enjoyed a few days of reasonable summer weather, the country would suffer an acute water shortage. It can rain for 100 days, but if the sun shines on the 101st there will be hosepipe restrictions on the 102nd.
   1997 *Way of the World: The Forgotten Years: 1995–6.*

8 Those who argue that the free supply of heroin to elderly addicts in Denmark would help to cut the crime rate—nine out of 10 burglaries are thought to be drug-related—ignore an important question. How many Copenhagen burglaries are committed by the elderly?
   1997 *Way of the World: The Forgotten Years: 1995–6.*

Waugh, Evelyn Arthur St John   1903–66

English novelist. He enjoyed great success with his first novel, *Decline and Fall* (1928), the first of a series of barbed satirical novels which included *Vile Bodies* (1930) and *Scoop* (1938). Preoccupied with the decline of English civilization, his works include *Brideshead Revisited* (1945) and the *Sword of Honour* trilogy (1952–61). A supreme stylist, and considered one of the great comic novelists, he also wrote travel books and biographies.

9 I expect you'll be becoming a schoolmaster, sir. That's what most of the gentlemen does, sir, that gets sent down for indecent behaviour.
   1928 *Decline and Fall*, Prelude.

10 'We class schools, you see, into four grades: Leading School, First-rate School, Good School, and School. Frankly,' said Mr Levy, 'School is pretty bad.'
   1928 *Decline and Fall*, pt.1, ch.1.

11 That's the public-school system all over. They may kick you out but they never let you down.
   1928 *Decline and Fall*, pt.1, ch.3.

12 You can't get into the soup in Ireland, do what you like.
   1928 *Decline and Fall*, pt.1, ch.3.

13 Meanwhile, you will write an essay on 'self-indulgence'. There will be a prize of half a crown for the longest essay, irrespective of any possible merit.
   1928 *Decline and Fall*, pt.1, ch.5.

14 For generations the British bourgeoisie have spoken of themselves as gentlemen, and by that they have meant, among other things, a self-respecting scorn of irregular perquisites. It is the quality that distinguishes the gentleman from both the artist and the aristocrat.
   1928 *Decline and Fall*, pt.1, ch.6.

15 There aren't many left like him nowadays, what with education and whisky the price it is.
   1928 *Decline and Fall*, pt.1, ch.7.

16 'I often think,' he continued, 'that we can trace almost all the disasters of English history to the influence of Wales!'
   1928 *Decline and Fall*, pt.1, ch.8.

17 I have noticed again and again since I have been in the Church that lay interest in ecclesiastical matters is often a prelude to insanity.
   1928 *Decline and Fall*, pt.1, ch.8.

18 I have often observed in women of her type a tendency to regard all athletics as inferior forms of fox-hunting.
   1928 *Decline and Fall*, pt.1, ch.10.

19 I'm one of the blind alleys off the main road of procreation.
1928 *Decline and Fall*, pt.1, ch.12.

20 I haven't been to sleep for over a year. That's why I go to bed early. One needs more rest if one doesn't sleep.
1928 *Decline and Fall*, pt.2, ch.3.

21 There is a species of person called a 'Modern Churchman' who draws the full salary of a beneficed clergyman and need not commit himself to any religious belief.
1928 *Decline and Fall*, pt.2, ch.4.

22 Instead of this absurd division into sexes, they ought to class people as static and dynamic.
1928 *Decline and Fall*, pt.2, ch.7.

23 I came to the conclusion many years ago that almost all crime is due to the repressed desire for aesthetic expression.
1928 *Decline and Fall*, pt.3, ch.1.

24 Anyone who has been to an English public school will always feel comparatively at home in prison. It is the people brought up in the gay intimacy of the slums, Paul learned, who find prison so soul-destroying.
1928 *Decline and Fall*, pt.3, ch.4.

25 Creative Endeavour lost her wings, Mrs Ape.
1930 *Vile Bodies*, ch.1.

26 Particularly against books the Home Secretary is. If we can't stamp out literature in the country, we can at least stop it being brought in from outside.
1930 *Vile Bodies*, ch.2.

27 When the war broke out she took down the signed photograph of the Kaiser and, with some solemnity, hung it in the men-servants' lavatory; it was her one combative action.
1930 *Vile Bodies*, ch.3.

28 All this fuss about sleeping together. For physical pleasure I'd sooner go to my dentist any day.
1930 *Vile Bodies*, ch.6.

29 'The Beast stands for strong mutually antagonistic governments everywhere,' he said. 'Self-sufficiency at home, self-assertion abroad.'
1938 *Scoop*, bk.1, ch.1.

30 Mr Salter's side of the conversation was limited to expressions of assent. When Lord Copper was right, he said, 'Definitely, Lord Copper'; when he was wrong, 'Up to a point.'
1938 *Scoop*, bk.1, ch.1.

31 'He's supposed to have a particularly high-class style: "Feather footed through the plashy fen passes the questing vole"...would that be it?' 'Yes,' said the Managing Editor. 'That must be good style.'
1938 *Scoop*, bk.1, ch.1.

32 News is what a chap who doesn't care much about anything wants to read. And it's only news until he's read it. After that it's dead.
1938 *Scoop*, bk.1, ch.5.

33 'I will not stand for being called a woman in my own house,' she said.
1938 *Scoop*, bk.2, ch.1.

34 Other nations use 'force'; we Britons alone use 'might'.
1938 *Scoop*, bk.2, ch.5.

35 Lady Peabury was in the morning room reading a novel;

early training gave a guilty spice to this recreation, for she had been brought up to believe that to read a novel before luncheon was one of the gravest sins it was possible for a gentlewoman to commit.
1939 'An Englishman's Home'.

36 Like German opera, too long and too loud.
1941 Of warfare. Attributed.

37 I do not think I shall ever forget the sight of Etna at sunset... Nothing I have ever seen in Art or Nature was quite so revolting.
1946 *Labels*.

38 The historic destiny of the Irish is being fulfilled on the other side of the Atlantic, where they have settled in their millions, bringing with them all their ancient grudges and the melancholy of the bogs, but also their hard, ancient wisdom. They alone of the newcomers are never for a moment taken in by the multifarious frauds of modernity. They have been changed from peasants and soldiers into townsmen. They have learned some of the superficial habits of 'good citizenship', but at heart they remain the same adroit and joyless race that broke the hearts of all who ever tried to help them.
1947 'The American Epoch in the Catholic Church'.

39 You never find an Englishman among the under-dogs—except in England, of course.
1948 *The Loved One*, ch.1.

40 In the dying world I come from, quotation is a national vice. No one would think of making an after-dinner speech without the help of poetry. It used to be classics, now it's lyric verse.
1948 *The Loved One*, ch.9.

41 Words should be an intense pleasure, just as leather should be to a shoemaker.
1950 In the *New York Times*, 19 Nov.

42 Most writers in the course of their careers become thick-skinned and learn to accept vituperation, which in any other profession would be unimaginably offensive, as a healthy counterpoise to unintelligent praise.
1952 In the *New York Times Magazine*, 30 Nov.

43 He sat at the cocktail bar... It wore the air of a fashion magazine, once stiff and shiny, which too many people had handled.
1955 *Officers and Gentlemen*, bk.1, ch.8.

44 Enclosing every thin man, there's a fat man demanding elbow room.
1955 *Officers and Gentlemen*, interlude.
➤ See Connolly 233:82, Orwell 628:52.

45 He did not, even in his extremity, quite abandon his faith in the magic of official forms. In bumf lay salvation.
1955 *Officers and Gentlemen*, bk.2, ch.5.

46 We are all American at puberty; we die French.
1961 Diary note, 18 Jul.

47 Most of the world's troubles seem to come from people who are too busy. If only politicians and scientists were lazier, how much happier we should all be.
1962 *Seven Deadly Sins*.

48 Punctuality is the virtue of the bored.
1962 Diary note, 26 Mar.

49 Manners are especially the need of the plain. The pretty can get away with anything.

1962 In the *Observer*, 15 Apr.

50 One can write, think and pray exclusively of others;
dreams are all egocentric.
1962 Diary entry, 5 Oct.

51 One forgets words as one forgets names. One's
vocabulary needs constant fertilizing or it will die.
1962 Diary entry, 25 Dec.

52 All fictional characters are flat.
1963 'The Art of Fiction XXX: Evelyn Waugh', in *The Paris Review*,
no.8, Summer/Fall.

53 No writer before the middle of the 19th century wrote
about the working classes other than as grotesques or as
pastoral decorations. Then when they were given the
vote certain writers started to suck up to them.
1963 'The Art of Fiction XXX: Evelyn Waugh', in *The Paris Review*,
no.8, Summer/Fall.

54 Only when one has lost all curiosity has one reached the
age to write an autobiography.
1964 *A Little Learning*, opening words.

55 With a thorough knowledge of the Bible, Shakespeare
and Wisden, you cannot go far wrong.
1964 *A Little Learning*.

56 Randolph Churchill went into hospital…to have a lung
removed. It was announced that the trouble was not
'malignant'. Seeing Ed Stanley in White's, on my way to
Rome, I remarked that it was a typical triumph of modern
science to find the only part of Randolph that was not
malignant and remove it.
1964 Diary note, Mar.

57 To watch him fumbling with our rich and delicate English
language is like seeing a Sèvres vase in the hands of a
chimpanzee.
Of Sir Stephen Spender. Quoted by Eric Pace in Spender's
obituary in the *New York Times*, 18 Jul 1995.

Wavell, Archibald Percival, 1st Earl 1883–1950

British field-marshal. He held the Middle East Command from
1939 and was Viceroy of India 1943–7. His *Generals and
Generalship* (1941) served as a combat handbook to his most
formidable opponent, Erwin Rommel.

58 For sheer courage and endurance, physical and mental,
the two men stand together as examples of what
toughness the body will find, if the spirit within it is
tough; and as very worthy representatives of our
national capacity for individual enterprise, which it is
hoped even the modern craze for regulating every detail
of our lives will never stifle.
1948 Of F Spencer Chapman and T E Lawrence. Quoted in
foreword to F Spencer Chapman *The Jungle is Neutral* (1950).

59 The story of Colonel Chapman's adventures is typical of
the British way of war, and therefore begins with a
complete lack of preparation.
1948 Quoted in foreword to F Spencer Chapman *The Jungle is
Neutral* (1950).

Waxman, Howard

Editor of the *Ice Cream Reporter*.

60 The relation between the human tongue, the human
psyche and butterfat is not very complex. The first two
love the third.
1992 In *Newsweek*, 30 Nov.

Weatherill, (Bruce) Bernard Weatherill, Baron 1920–

English politician, chair of the Ways and Means Committee
(1979–1983) and Speaker of the House of Commons
(1987–1992). He oversaw with enthusiasm the televising of
parliamentary proceedings.

61 Mine is one of the jobs that, if you want it, you will never
get it—and if you're seen to want it you will certainly
never get it.
1991 In *The House Magazine*, Jan.

Webb, (Martha) Beatrice *née Potter* 1858–1943

English social reformer, social historian, and economist. She
wrote many studies with her husband, Sidney Webb.

62 His sensuality has all drifted into sexual vanity, delight for
being the candle to the moths, with a dash of intellectual
curiosity to give flavour to his tickled vanity… His
incompleteness as a thinker, his shallow and vulgar view
of many human relationships—the lack of a sterner kind
of humour which would show him the dreariness of his
farce and the total absence of proportion and
inadequateness in some of his ideas—all these defects
came largely from the flippant and worthless self-
complacency brought about by the worship of rather
second-rate women.
1897 Of George Bernard Shaw. Diary entry, 8 May.

63 All along the line, physically, mentally, morally, alcohol is
a weakening and deadening force, and it is worth a great
deal to save women and girls from its influence.
1917 *Health of Working Girls*, ch.10.

Webb, Phyllis 1927–

Canadian poet, university teacher and broadcaster. Her poetry
includes *The Sea is Also a Garden* (1962), *Naked Poems* (1965)
and *Wilson's Bowl* (1980); she has also published a collection
of her essays.

64 Some people swim lakes, others climb flagpoles,
some join monasteries, but we, my friends,
who have considered suicide take our daily walk
with death and are not lonely.
In the end it brings more honesty and care
than all the democratic parliaments of tricks.
1956 *Even Your Right Eye*, 'To Friends Who Have Also Considered
Suicide'.

Webb, Sidney James 1859–1947

English social reformer, historian and economist. A lawyer and
Fabian, he wrote many powerful tracts and in 1892 married
fellow socialist Beatrice Potter. They wrote a classic *History of
Trade Unionism* (1894) and *English Local Government* (1906–29,
9 vols), and began the *New Statesman* (1913). He became
President of the Board of Trade (1924), Dominions and Colonial
Secretary (1929–30) and Colonial Secretary (1930–1).

65 No philosopher now looks for anything but the gradual
evolution of the new order from the old… History shows
us no example of the sudden substitutions of Utopian
and revolutionary romance.
1889 *Fabian Essays*.

66 How anyone can fear that the British electorate,
whatever mistakes it can make or may condone, can ever
go too far or too fast is incomprehensible… The Labour
Party, when in due course it comes to be entrusted with

power, will naturally not want to do everything at once. Once we face the necessity of putting our principles into execution from one end of the kingdom to the other, the inevitability of gradualness cannot fail to be appreciated.
1923 Labour Party Conference, 26 Jun.

Weber, Max 1864–1920

German sociologist and economist.

67 In Baxter's view, the care of external goods should only lie on the shoulders of the 'saint like a light cloak, which can be thrown aside at any moment.' But fate decreed that the cloak should become an iron cage.
1904–5 *The Protestant Ethic and the Spirit of Capitalism* (translated by Talcott Parsons, 1930), ch.5. Richard Baxter (1615–91) was an eminent Puritan, chaplain of Cromwell's army.

68 The impulse to acquisition, pursuit of gain, of money, of the greatest possible amount of money, has in itself nothing to do with capitalism. This impulse exists among waiters, physicians, coachmen, artists, prostitutes, dishonest officials, soldiers, nobles, crusaders, gamblers, and beggars. One may say that it has been common to all sorts and conditions of men at all times and in all cultures of the earth, wherever the objective possibility of it is or has been given.
1904–5 *The Protestant Ethic and the Spirit of Capitalism* (translated by Talcott Parsons, 1930).

69 Capital accounting in its formally most rational shape…presupposes *the battle of man with man*.
1922 Collected in Guenther Roth and Claus Wittich (eds) *Economy and Society* (1978), ch.1.

70 However many people may complain about the 'red tape', it would be sheer illusion to think for a moment that continuous administrative work can be carried out in any field except by means of officials working in offices… The choice is only that between bureaucracy and dilettantism in the field of administration.
1922 Collected in Guenther Roth and Claus Wittich (eds) *Economy and Society* (1978), ch.3.

Webster, Daniel 1782–1852

US lawyer and statesman, one of the greatest of US orators. As Secretary of State (1840–3) he negotiated the Webster–Ashburton treaty with Great Britain. A supporter of free trade, nationality and established institutions, he was unwilling to break the Union to abolish slavery.

71 [Alexander Hamilton] smote the rock of the national resources, and abundant streams of revenue gushed forth. He touched the dead corpse of the public credit, and it sprang upon its feet.
1831 Speech, New York, 10

72 There is always room at the top.
On being advised against joining the overcrowded legal profession, attributed.

Webster, John c.1580–c.1625

English dramatist. He collaborated with Dekker, Drayton, Marston and others. He is best known for two great tragedies, *The White Devil* (1612) and *The Duchess of Malfi* (1623).

73 Fortune's a right whore:
If she give aught, she deals it in small parcels,
That she may take away all at one swoop.
1612 *The White Devil*, act 1, sc.1.

74 All the damnable degrees
Of drinking have you staggered through.
1612 *The White Devil*, act 1, sc.1.

75 Perfumes, the more they are chafed, the more they render
Their pleasing scents; and so affliction
Expresseth virtue fully.
1612 *The White Devil*, act 1, sc.1.

76 Oh, they are politic: they know our desire is increased by the difficulty of enjoying, whereas satiety is a blunt, weary, and drowsy passion.
1612 Of women. *The White Devil*, act 1, sc.1.

77 See, the curse of children!
In life they keep us frequently in tears,
And in the cold grave leave us in pale fears.
1612 *The White Devil*, act 1, sc.2.

78 'Tis just like a summer birdcage in a garden; the birds that are without despair to get in, and the birds that are within despair, and are in a consumption, for fear they shall never get out.
1612 *The White Devil*, act 1, sc.2.

79 Lust carries her sharp whip
At her own girdle.
1612 *The White Devil*, act 2, sc.1.

80 See, a good habit makes a child a man,
Whereas a bad one makes a man a beast.
1612 *The White Devil*, act 2, sc.1.

81 A mere tale of a tub, my words are idle.
1612 *The White Devil*, act 2, sc.1.

82 Only the deep sense of some deathless shame.
1612 *The White Devil*, act 2, sc.1.

83 Find me but guilty, sever head from body,
We'll part good friends.
1612 *The White Devil*, act 3, sc.2.

84 For your names
Of whores and murderers, they proceed from you,
As if a man should spit against the wind;
The filth returns in's face.
1612 *The White Devil*, act 3, sc.2.

85 Sum up my faults, I pray, and you shall find,
That beauty, and gay clothes, a merry heart,
And a good stomach to a feast, are all,
All the poor crimes that you can charge me with.
1612 *The White Devil*, act 3, sc.2.

86 VITTORIA: A rape! a rape!
MONTICELSO: How!
VITTORIA: Yes, you have ravished justice,
Forced her to do your pleasure.
1612 *The White Devil*, act 3, sc.2.

87 Woman to man
Is either a God or a wolfe.
1612 *The White Devil*, act 4, sc.2.

88 For your gifts,
I'll return them all; and I do wish
That I could make you full executor
To all my sins.
1612 *The White Devil*, act 4, sc.2.

89 He could not have invented his own ruin,
Had he despaired, with more propriety.
1612 *The White Devil*, act 5, sc.1.

90 They that sleep with dogs shall rise with fleas.
   1612 *The White Devil*, act 5, sc.1.

91 O, the rare tricks of a Machiavellian!
   He doth not come, like a gross plodding slave,
   And buffet you to death; no, my quaint knave,
   He tickles you to death, makes you die laughing.
   1612 *The White Devil*, act 5, sc.3.

92 Call for the robin-red-breast and the wren,
   Since o'er shady groves they hover,
   And with leaves and flowers do cover
   The friendless bodies of unburied men.
   1612 *The White Devil*, act 5, sc.4.

93 I have heard grief named the eldest child of sin.
   1612 *The White Devil*, act 5, sc.4.

94 Are you grown an atheist? Will you turn your body,
   Which is the goodly palace of the soul,
   To the soul's slaughter-house? Oh, the cursèd devil,
   Which doth present us with all other sins
   Thrice-candied o'er.
   1612 *The White Devil*, act 5, sc.6.

95 Oh, yes, thy sins
   Do run before thee to fetch fire from hell,
   To light thee thither.
   1612 *The White Devil*, act 5, sc.6.

96 I myself have heard a very good jest, and have scorned to
   seem to have so silly a wit as to understand it.
   1623 *The Duchess of Malfi*, act 1, sc.1.

97 Then the law to him
   Is like a foul black cobweb to a spider;
   He makes it his dwelling, and a prison
   To entangle those shall feed him.
   1623 *The Duchess of Malfi*, act 1, sc.1.

98 DUCHESS: Diamonds are of most precious value
   They say, that have passed through most jewellers'
   hands.
   FERDINAND: Whores, by that rule, are precious.
   1623 *The Duchess of Malfi*, act 1, sc.1.

99 Wisdom begins at the end.
   1623 *The Duchess of Malfi*, act 1, sc.1.

1 DUCHESS: What do you think of marriage?
   ANTONIO: I take't, as those that deny purgatory,
   It locally contains or heaven, or hell;
   There's no third place in't.
   1623 *The Duchess of Malfi*, act 1, sc.2.

2 Ambition, madam, is a great man's madness,
   That is not kept in chains, and close-pent rooms,
   But in fair lightsome lodgings, and is girt
   With the wild noise of prattling visitants,
   Which makes it lunatic beyond all cure.
   1623 *The Duchess of Malfi*, act 1, sc.1.

3 I have long served virtue,
   And never ta'en wages of her.
   1623 *The Duchess of Malfi*, act 1, sc.1.

4 The misery of us, that are born great,
   We are forced to woo because none dare woo us.
   1623 *The Duchess of Malfi*, act 1, sc.1.

5 I hope in time 'twill grow into a custom
   That noblemen shall come with cap and knee
   To purchase a night's lodging of their wives.
   1623 *The Duchess of Malfi*, act 3, sc.2.

6 I would sooner swim to the Bermudas on
   Two politicians' rotten bladders, tied
   Together with an intelligencer's heartstring,
   Than depend on so changeable a prince's favour.
   1623 *The Duchess of Malfi*, act 3, sc.2.

7 A politician is the devil's quilted anvil,
   He fashions all sins on him, and the blows
   Are never heard.
   1623 *The Duchess of Malfi*, act 3, sc.2.

8 Love mixed with fear is sweetness.
   1623 *The Duchess of Malfi*, act 3, sc.2.

9 That curious engine, your white hand.
   1623 *The Duchess of Malfi*, act 3, sc.2.

10 Why should only I…
   Be cased up, like a holy relic? I have youth
   And a little beauty.
   1623 *The Duchess of Malfi*, act 3, sc.2.

11 You have shook hands with Reputation
   And made him invisible.
   1623 *The Duchess of Malfi*, act 3, sc.2.

12 Her melancholy seems to be fortified
   With a strange disdain.
   1623 *The Duchess of Malfi*, act 4, sc.1.

13 Other sins only speak; murder shrieks out.
   1623 *The Duchess of Malfi*, act 4, sc.2.

14 What's this flesh? A little crudded milk, fantastical puff-
   paste.
   1623 *The Duchess of Malfi*, act 4, sc.2. crudded = curdled.

15 What would it pleasure me, to have my throat cut
   With diamonds? Or to be smothered
   With cassia? Or to be shot to death, with pearls?
   1623 *The Duchess of Malfi*, act 4, sc.2.

16 O, that it were possible,
   We might but hold some two days' conference
   With the dead!
   1623 *The Duchess of Malfi*, act 4, sc.2.

17 I am Duchess of Malfi still.
   1623 *The Duchess of Malfi*, act 4, sc.2.

18 I know death hath ten thousand several doors
   For men to take their exits.
   1623 *The Duchess of Malfi*, act 4, sc.2.

19 FERDINAND: Cover her face; mine eyes dazzle: she died
   young.
   BOSOLA: I think not so; her infelicity
   Seemed to have years too many.
   1623 *The Duchess of Malfi*, act 4, sc.2.

20 Physicians are like kings,—they brook no contradiction.
   1623 *The Duchess of Malfi*, act 5, sc.2.

21 We are merely the stars' tennis-balls, struck and bandied
   Which way please them.
   1623 *The Duchess of Malfi*, act 5, sc.4.

Webster, Margaret   1905–72

US actress and director.

22 You must not wear your heart on your sleeve for daws to
   pick at.
   c.1940 To Tennessee Williams on the out-of-town closing of his
   first professionally produced play *Battle of Angels*. Recalled by
   Williams in the *New York Times*, 17 Mar 1957.
   ➤ See *Shakespeare* 758:50.

Wei Jingsheng 1950–

Chinese dissident, considered one of the fathers of the Chinese dissident movement, released in 1993 after serving a 14-year jail sentence for his role in the Democracy Wall Movement. He was arrested again in April 1994 and was released in 1997.

23 No leader deserves the unconditional confidence of his people.
1979 Part of a statement appearing on Democracy Wall under the pseudonym 'Voice of Today'. Quoted in Uli Franz *Deng Xiaoping* (1988).

Weighell, Sidney 1922–2002

British trade union leader. He was General Secretary of the National Union of Railwaymen (1975–83) and a member of the Trades Union General Council (1975–83). He joined the LNER in 1938 and became a full-time union official in 1954.

24 If you…believe in the philosophy of the pig trough—that those with the biggest snouts should get the largest share—I reject it.
1978 Labour Party Conference, 10 Apr.

25 I don't see how we can talk with Mrs Thatcher… I will say to the lads, 'Come on, get your snouts in the trough.'
1979 Speech, London, 10 Apr.

Weil, Simone 1909–43

French philosophical writer and mystic, who undertook manual labour to experience working-class life and served as a Republican in the Spanish Civil War (1936). A mystic Catholic who distrusted organized religion, she worked for the Free French in London, and starved herself to death in sympathy with the victims of war. Her works include *La Pesanteur et la Grâce* (*Gravity and Grace*, 1947) and *Attente de Dieu* (*Waiting for God*, 1950).

26 To us, men of the West, a very strange thing happened at the turn of the century; without noticing it, we lost science, or at least the thing that had been called by that name for the last four centuries. What we now have in place of it is something different, radically different, and we don't know what it is. Nobody knows what it is.
1941 *On Science, Necessity and the Love of God*, 'Classical Science and After' (translated by Richard Rees, 1968).

27 Science is voiceless; it is the scientists who talk.
1941 *On Science, Necessity and the Love of God* (translated by Richard Rees, 1968).

28 The future is made of the same stuff as the present.
1941 *On Science, Necessity, and the Love of God* (translated by Richard Rees, 1968).

29 *Tous les péchés sont des tentatives pour combler des vides.*
All sins are attempts to fill voids.
La Pesanteur et la Grâce (published 1947).

30 The beauty of the world is almost the only way by which we can allow God to penetrate us…the beauty of the world is the commonest, easiest and most natural way of approach.
Attente de Dieu (translated as *Waiting for God*, 1951).

31 Bourgeois society is infected by monomania: the monomania of accounting. For it, the only thing that has value is what can be counted in francs and centimes. It never hesitates to sacrifice human life to figures which

look well on paper, such as national budgets or industrial balance sheets.
La condition ouvrière, 'La rationalisation' (published 1951).

32 One might lay down as a postulate: All conceptions of God which are incompatible with the movement of pure charity are false.
Letter to a Priest (translated by A F Wills, published 1954).

33 The word 'revolution' is a word for which you kill, for which you die, for which you send the labouring masses to their deaths; but which does not contain any content.
Oppression and Liberty (translated by A F Wills and J Petrie, published 1958).

Weinberger, Caspar Willard 1917–

American politician. A former lawyer, he was state finance director of California when Ronald Reagan was Governor (1968–9), served in the administrations of Presidents Nixon and Ford, then became Secretary of Defense under President Reagan (1981–87).

34 Wishful thinking is equally as effective for arms control as it is for birth control.
1986 In *USA Today*, 6 Oct.

Weizsäcker, Richard Freiherr, Baron von 1920–

German politician. A member of the conservative Christian Democratic Union, he served as CDU Deputy Chairman (1972–9) and Mayor of West Berlin (1981–4) until being elected President of the Federal Republic of Germany (1984, re-elected 1989). In 1990 he signed the treaty that reunited East and West Germany. He served as President of Germany from 1990 to 1994.

35 There were many ways of not burdening one's conscience, of shunning responsibility, looking away, keeping silent. When the unspeakable truth of the Holocaust became known at the end of the war, all too many of us claimed that they had not known anything about it, or even suspected anything… Whoever refuses to remember the inhumanity is prone to new risks of infection… Seeking to forget makes exile all the longer; the secret of redemption lies in remembrance.
1985 On the 40th anniversary of the end of World War II, in the *New York Times*, 12 May.

Weldon, Fay *originally* *Franklin Birkinshaw* 1931–

English writer, an advertising copywriter before turning to novels and screenplays. She is best known for her fiction, which deal with recurring themes, including the nature of women's sexuality and experience in a patriarchal world. Her works include *Female Friends* (1974), *The Life and Loves of a She-Devil* (1983), *The Cloning of Joanna May* (1989) and *The Bulgari Connection* (2001).

36 Go to work on an egg.
1957 Advertising slogan for the British Egg Marketing Board.

37 The Life and Loves of a She-Devil.
1983 Title of novel.

38 It will do us no harm to retool our imaginations. AIDS is a major revolution in how writers write… Our heroes and heroines will have to change. The only thing AIDS is good for is fiction. Writers will have to think differently.
1987 In *The Guardian*, 7 Mar.

39 Pride comes before a fall; a sense of sisterhood with sad experience.
1987 *The Heart of the Country*, 'Chomp, Chomp, Grittle-Grax, Gone!'

40 Christianity is really a man's religion: there's not much in it for women except docility, obedience, who-sweeps-the-room-as-for-thy-cause, downcast eyes and death in childbirth. For the men it's better: all power and money and fine robes, the burning of the heretics—fun, fun, fun!—and the Inquisition fulminating from the pulpit.
1987 *The Heart of the Country*, 'Love Your Enemy'.

41 To journey is better than to arrive—or so say those who have already arrived.
1987 *The Heart of the Country*, 'Doing It All Wrong'.

42 It's full time work being on social security. They really make you earn your living.
1987 *The Heart of the Country*, 'Driven Mad'.

43 Men are so romantic, don't you think? They look for a perfect partner when what they should be looking for is perfect love.
1987 In the *Sunday Times*, 6 Sep.

44 I didn't set out to be a feminist writer. I just look at the sheep out of the window and watch their behaviour.
1989 In the *Observer*, 30 Apr.

45 I think if you had ever written a book you were absolutely pleased with, you'd never write another. The same probably goes for having children.
1991 In *The Guardian*, 28 Nov.

46 Nature's only interest is in having you procreate, then it throws you away.
1992 In *The Guardian*, 15 Jan.

Welland, Colin 1934–

British actor and writer. Best known for his screenplays for *Yanks* (1979, with Walter Bernstein) and *Chariots of Fire* (1981), for the second of which he won an Academy Award.

47 The British are coming.
1982 At the Academy Award ceremony in Los Angeles, 29 Mar.

Welles, (George) Orson 1915–85

US director and actor. He is best known for his radio production of H G Wells's *The War of the Worlds* (1938), and for the films *Citizen Kane* (1941), a masterpiece of cinema technique, and his adaptation of Booth Tarkington's *The Magnificent Ambersons* (1942).

48 In Italy for thirty years under the Borgias they had warfare, terror, murder, bloodshed—they produced Michelangelo, Leonardo da Vinci and the Renaissance. In Switzerland they had brotherly love, five hundred years of democracy and peace, and what did they produce? The cuckoo clock.
1949 Harry Lime's speech to Holly Martins as he leaves the great wheel, *The Third Man*. This phrase was added to the script by Welles who played Harry Lime.

49 A film is never really good unless the camera is an eye in the head of a poet.
1958 'Un ruban de rêves' in *L'Express*, 5 Jun. Reprinted in English in *International Film Annual*, no.2.

50 A typewriter needs only paper; a camera uses film, requires subsidiary equipment by the truckload and

several hundreds of technicians. That is always the central fact about the filmmaker as opposed to any other artist: he can never afford his own tools.
1958 Letter in the *New Statesman*.

51 I started at the top and worked down.
Attributed.

52 Every actor in his heart believes everything bad that's printed about him.
Attributed.

Wellington, Arthur Wellesley, 1st Duke of 1769–1852

British soldier and statesman. He was made a duke after his defeat of French forces in the Peninsular War, and took command of British forces again after Napoleon's escape from Elba in 1815. After victory at Waterloo, he went into politics, becoming Prime Minister in 1828. His dispatches and other papers were published in three series (1834–80).

53 As Lord Chesterfield said of the generals of his day, 'I only hope that when the enemy reads the list of their names, he trembles as I do'.
1810 Letter, 29 Aug, during the Peninsular War. Collected in *Supplementary Despatches* (1860).

54 We have in the service the scum of the earth as common soldiers.
1813 Comment 21 Jun, before the Battle of Vitoria. Quoted in Elizabeth Longford *Wellington: The Years of the Sword*, p.321.

55 Hard pounding this, gentlemen, let's see who will pound longest.
1815 At the Battle of Waterloo, 18 Jun. Quoted in Sir Walter Scott *Paul's Letters* (1816), letter 8.

56 Up guards and at them!
1815 Attributed shout at the Battle of Waterloo, 18 Jun.

57 It has been a damned serious business—Blucher and I have lost 30,000 men. It has been a damned nice thing—the nearest run thing you ever saw in your life… By God! I don't think it would have done if I had not been there!
1815 Comment to Thomas Creevey at Brussels, 19 Jun, the day after the Battle of Waterloo. Quoted in Sir Thomas Creevey *The Creevey Papers* (edited by Sir H Maxwell, 1904), p.142.

58 Napoleon did not manoeuvre at all. He just moved forward in the old style, in columns, and was driven off in the old style.
1815 Letter to Sir William Beresford, 2 Jul.

59 Next to a battle lost, the greatest misery is a battle gained.
1815 Of the Battle of Waterloo. Comment to Lady Shelley, Jul. Quoted in Richard Edgecumbe (ed) *The Diary of Frances, Lady Shelley* (1912), vol.1, ch.9, p.102.

60 The history of a battle is not unlike the history of a ball. Some individuals may recollect all the little events of which the great result is the battle won or lost; but no individual can recollect the order in which, or the exact moment at which, they occurred, which makes all the difference.
1815 Of the Battle of Waterloo. Letter, 8 Aug.

61 Beginning reform is beginning revolution.
1830 Attributed remark, 7 Nov.

62 I used to say of him that his presence on the field made the difference of 40,000 men.
1831 Of Napoleon. Comment, 2 Nov. Quoted in Philip Henry Stanhope *Notes of Conversations with the Duke of Wellington* (1888).

63 Our course in the House of Lords ought to be very firm and uncompromising but moderate…an example of what has since been called the politics of the extreme centre.
1832 Conduct of Opposition speech, Dec.

64 There is no such thing as a little war for a great nation.
1838 House of Lords, 16 Jan.

65 All the business of war, and indeed all the business of life, is to endeavour to find out what you don't know by what you do; that's what I call 'guessing what was at the other side of the hill'.
Quoted in John Wilson Croker *The Croker Papers* (edited by Bernard Pool, 1885), vol.3, ch.28.

66 Don't quote Latin; say what you have to say, and then sit down.
Advice to a new member of Parliament.

67 The Battle of Waterloo was won on the playing fields of Eton.
Attributed, and probably apocryphal. Quoted in Count Charles de Montalembert *De l'Avenir politique de l'Angleterre* (1856), ch.10: 'C'est ici qu'a été gagné la bataille de Waterloo'.

68 There is no mistake; there has been no mistake, and there shall be no mistake.
Quoted in William Fraser *Words on Wellington* (1889).

69 Publish and be damned.
To the publisher of the *Memoirs* of the courtesan Hariette Wilson, attempting blackmail. Attributed.

70 If you believe that, you'll believe anything.
Attributed.

Wells, H(erbert) G(eorge) 1866–1946

English writer and Fabian, best known for his scientific fantasies *The Time Machine* (1895) and *The War of the Worlds* (1898). He also wrote popular comic novels, notably *Kipps* (1905) and *The History of Mr Polly* (1910), and socio-political works on science and world peace (*The Outline of History*, 1920 and *The Work, Wealth and Happiness of Mankind*, 1931).

71 He was a practical electrician but fond of whisky, a heavy, red-haired brute with irregular teeth. He doubted the existence of the Deity but accepted Carnot's cycle, and he had read Shakespeare and found him weak in chemistry.
1894 'The Lord of the Dynamos'.

72 Bah! the thing is not a nose at all, but a bit of primordial chaos clapped on to my face.
1895 *Select Conversations with an Uncle*, 'The Man with a Nose'.

73 Yet, across the gulf of space, minds that are to our minds as ours are to the beasts that perish, intellects vast and cool and unsympathetic, regarded this earth with envious eyes, and slowly and surely drew their plans against us.
1898 *The War of the Worlds*, bk.1, ch.1.

74 At times I suffer from the strangest sense of detachment from myself and the world about me; I seem to watch it all from the outside, from somewhere inconceivably remote, out of time, out of space, out of the stress and tragedy of it all.
1898 *The War of the Worlds*, bk.1, ch.7.

75 The Social Contract is nothing more or less than a vast conspiracy of human beings to lie to and humbug themselves and one another for the general Good. Lies

are the mortar that bind the savage individual man into the social masonry.
1900 *Love and Mrs Lewisham*, ch.23.

76 Notice the smug suppressions of his face. In his mouth are Lies in the shape of false teeth.
1900 *Love and Mrs Lewisham*, ch.23.

77 In the country of the blind, the one-eyed man is king.
1904 'The Country of the Blind', collected in *The Country of the Blind and Other Stories* (1911).

78 Of course we can Learn even from Novels, Nace Novels that is, but it isn't the same thing as serious reading.
1905 *Kipps*, bk.2, ch.2.

79 He found that a fork in his inexperienced hand was an instrument of chase rather than capture.
1905 *Kipps*, bk.2, ch.7.

80 'I expect,' he said, 'I was thinking jest what a Rum Go everything is.'
1905 *Kipps*, bk.3, ch.3.

81 'You're a Christian?' 'Church of England,' said Mr Polly. 'Mm,' said the employer, a little checked. 'For good all round business work, I should have preferred a Baptist.'
1909 *The History of Mr Polly*, ch.3, pt.2.

82 Arson, after all, is an artificial crime… A large number of houses deserve to be burnt.
1909 *The History of Mr Polly*, ch.10, pt.1.

83 Once they heard someone call for 'Snooks'. 'I always thought that name was invented by novelists,' said Miss Winchelsea. 'Fancy! Snooks. I wonder which is Mr. Snooks?' Finally they picked out a stout and resolute little man in a large check suit. 'If he isn't Snooks, he ought to be,' said Miss Winchelsea.
1913 *Tales of Life and Adventure*, 'Miss Winchelsea's Heart'.

84 The War that will End War.
1914 Title of book.

85 Moral indignation is jealousy with a halo.
1914 *The Wife of Sir Isaac Harman*, ch.9.

86 The uglier a man's legs are, the better he plays golf. It's almost a law.
1915 *Bealby*.

87 He had the face of a saint, but he had rendered this generally acceptable by growing side-whiskers.
1915 'The Story of The Last Trump'.

88 Cynicism is humour in ill-health.
1915 'The Story of The Last Trump'.

89 Human history becomes more and more a race between education and catastrophe.
1920 *The Outline of History*, vol.2, ch.41.

90 Now it is on the whole more convenient to keep history and theology apart.
1922 *A Short History of the World*, ch.37.

91 I am reported to be 'pessimistic' about broadcasting… [The] truth is that I have anticipated its complete disappearance—confident that the unfortunate people, who must now subdue themselves to 'listening-in', will soon find a better pastime for their leisure.
1928 *The Way the World is Going*.

92 In England we have come to rely upon a comfortable time-lag of fifty years or a century intervening between the perception that something ought to be done and a serious attempt to do it.

1931 *The Work, Wealth and Happiness of Mankind*, ch.2.

93 The Shape of Things to Come.
1933 Title of book.

94 If his thinking has been sound, then this world is at the end of its tether. The end of everything we call life is close at hand and cannot be evaded.
1945 *Mind at the End of Its Tether*, ch.1.

Welsh, Irvine 1958–

Scottish writer. He scored a major critical success with his first novel, *Trainspotting* (1993, filmed 1995).

95 I grew up in what was not so much a family as a genetic disaster.
1995 *Marabou Stork Nightmares*, ch.2.

96 A symbol of all that's perfectly hideous about Scotland
1996 On the poet Hugh MacDiarmid. In *Scotland on Sunday*, 28 Jan.

97 There's fuck-all to say about my books other than what's written in them.
Quoted in Annalena McAfee *Lives and Works: Profiles of Leading Novelists, Poets and Playwrights* (2002).

Welty, Eudora 1909–2001

US novelist and short-story writer. She wrote five novels, set in her native Mississippi, and several collections of short stories, issued as *Collected Stories* (1981).

98 I have been told, both in approval and accusation, that I seem to love all my characters. What I do in writing of any character is to try to enter into the mind, heart, and skin of a human being who is not myself. Whether this happens to be a man or a woman, old or young, with skin black or white, the primary challenge lies in making the jump itself. It is the act of a writer's imagination that I set most high.
1981 *The Collected Stories of Eudora Welty*, preface.

99 It had been startling and disappointing to me to find out that story books had been written by *people*, that books were not natural wonders, coming up themselves like green grass.
1984 *One Writer's Beginnings*, I. 'Listening'.

1 The events in our lives happen in a sequence in time, but in their significance to ourselves they find their own order, a timetable not necessarily—perhaps not possibly—chronological… It is the continuous thread of revelation.
1984 *One Writer's Beginnings*, II. 'Learning to See'.

2 A sheltered life can be a daring life as well. For all serious daring starts from within.
1984 *One Writer's Beginnings*, III. 'Finding a Voice'.

Wenger, Arsène 1949–

French footballer and football manager. He has been manager of Arsenal since 1996.

3 A football team is like a beautiful woman. When you do not tell her so, she forgets she is beautiful.
2002 In *The Times*, 28 Dec.

Wentworth, Peter 1530–96

English parliamentarian. He was a prominent Puritan in the reign of Elizabeth I, to whom he presented challenges on the issues of religion and royal succession. He supported the liberties of parliament against encroachments by Elizabeth I. His speech to Parliament in 1576 was examined by the Star Chamber and he was sent to the Tower of London for it. He was imprisoned twice more, and it is thought he never regained his freedom the second time.

4 In this House, which is termed a place of free speech, there is nothing so necessary for the preservation of the Prince and State as free speech; and without it, it is a scorn and a mockery to call it a Parliament House, for in truth it is none but a very school of flattery and dissimulation, and so fit a place to serve the devil and his angels in, and not to glorify God and benefit the Commonwealth.
1576 House of Commons, 8 Feb.

Wentworth, William Charles 1790–1872

Statesman and explorer, born aboard a convict ship on which his mother was being transported for theft. One of the first to explore successfully beyond the Blue Mountains, he established the first Australian newspaper and was one of the founders of Sydney University. His *Australasia* (1823) was the first book of verse by a native-born Australian.

5 Illustrious Cook, Columbus of our shore,
To whom was left this unknown world t'explore,
Its untraced bounds on faithful chart to mark,
And leave a light where all before was dark.
1823 *Australasia*.

Werefkin, Marianne 1860–1938

Russian-born painter who emigrated to Germany just before 1900. She was a founding member of the Blaue Reiter group in Munich.

6 Art is not made only one way, art is a point of view… Rembrandt in our days would be Rembrandt again, because the work of the master is his self. But in order to be Rembrandt in our days he would have used new ways that would give a new culture.
1902 *Lettres à un Inconnu* (1901–05). Translated by Mara R Witzling (ed) in *Voicing Our Visions: Writings by Women Artists* (1992).

7 There is no history of art—there is the history of artists.
1905 *Lettres à un Inconnu* (1901–05). Translated by Mara R Witzling (ed) in *Voicing Our Visions: Writings by Women Artists* (1992).

Wesker, Arnold 1932–

English playwright.

8 And then I saw the menu… It said 'Chips with everything'. Chips with every damn thing. You breed babies and you eat chips with everything.
1962 *Chips with Everything* act 1, sc.2.

Wesley, Charles 1707–88

English Methodist hymn writer and preacher, brother of John Wesley.

9 Long my imprisoned spirit lay
Fast bound in sin and nature's night;
Thine eye diffused a quickening ray—
I woke, the dungeon flamed with light,
My chains fell off, my heart was free,

I rose, went forth, and followed thee.
1738 Hymn. 'And Can it Be'.

10 Hark! how all the welkin rings,
Glory to the King of kings.
Peace on earth and mercy mild,
God and sinners reconciled.
1739 'Hymn for Christmas'. In *Hymns and Sacred Poems*. The first two lines were changed to 'Hark! the herald-angels sing/ Glory to the new born king' in Whitfield's *Hymns for Social Worship* (1753).

11 Jesu, lover of my soul,
Let me to thy bosom fly,
While the nearer waters roll,
While the tempest still is high;
Hide me, O my Saviour, hide,
Till the storm of life is past;
Safe into the haven guide,
O receive my soul at last.
1740 'In Temptation', collected in *Hymns and Sacred Poems*.

12 Gentle Jesus, meek and mild,
Look upon a little child;
Pity my simplicity,
Suffer me to come to thee.
1742 'Gentle Jesus', collected in *Hymns and Sacred Poems*.

13 Rejoice, the Lord is King!
Your Lord and King adore;
Mortals, give thanks and sing,
And triumph evermore:
Lift up your heart, lift up your voice;
Rejoice, again, I say rejoice.
1746 'Rejoice, the Lord is King'. In *Hymns for our Lord's Resurrection*.

14 Love divine, all loves excelling,
Joy of heav'n, to earth come down,
Fix in us thy humble dwelling,
All thy faithful mercies crown.
Jesu, thou art all compassion,
Pure unbounded love thou art;
Visit us with thy salvation,
Enter every trembling heart.
1747 'Love Divine', collected in *Hymns for those that seek…Redemption*.

15 Forth in thy name, O Lord, I go,
My daily labour to pursue.
Thee, only thee, resolved to know,
In all I think or speak or do.
1749 'Forth in Thy Name', collected in *Hymns and Sacred Poems*.

16 Lo! He comes with clouds descending,
Once for favoured sinners slain;
Thousand thousand Saints attending
Swell the triumph of His train.
1758 'Lo! He Comes'. In *Hymns of Intercession for all Mankind*.

Wesley, John 1703–91

English evangelist, preacher and writer. Although he himself remained loyal to the Church of England, he is recognized as the principal founder of Methodism. He published his *Rules* for the Methodist Societies in 1743.

17 I felt my heart strangely warmed. I felt I did trust in Christ, Christ alone for salvation; and an assurance was given me that he had taken away *my* sins, even *mine*, and saved

me from the law of sin and death.
1738 Journal entry, 24 May.

18 Thou hidden love of God, whose height,
Whose depth unfathomed no man knows,
I see from far thy beauteous light,
Only I sigh for thy repose.
1738 *A Collection of Psalms and Hymns*, 'Divine Love'.

19 I look upon all the world as my parish.
1739 Journal entry, 11 Jun.

20 Do all the good you can
By all the means you can
In all the ways you can
In all the places you can
To all the people you can
As long as ever you can.
1743 'Rules of Conduct'.

21 Lord, let me not live to be useless!
1763 Journal entry, 22 Dec.

22 Sure a more consummate coxcomb never saw the sun! How amazingly full of himself! Whatever he speaks, he pronounces as an oracle.
1770 Of Rousseau. Journal entry, 3 Feb.

23 I have none of the infirmities of old age, and have lost several I had in my youth. The grand cause is, the good pleasure of God, who does whatever pleases him. The chief means are: 1. My constantly rising at four, for about fifty years. 2. My generally preaching at five in the morning; one of the most healthy exercises in the world. 3. My never travelling less, by sea or land, than four thousand five hundred miles in a year.
1774 Journal entry, 28 Jun.

24 I spent two hours with that great man, Dr Johnson, who is sinking into the grave by a gentle decay.
1783 Journal entry, 18 Dec.

25 The best of all is, God is with us!
1791 Quoted in *John Wesley's Journal*, edited by Robert Backhouse (1993), p.256.

26 Beware you be not swallowed up in books! An ounce of love is worth a pound of knowledge.
Quoted in R Southey *Life of Wesley* (1820), ch.16.

West, Benjamin 1738–1820

US painter who spent most of his working life in England.

27 Always remember, sir, that light and shadow never stand still.
Advice to the young John Constable, attributed in C R Leslie *Memoirs of the Life of John Constable* (1845).

West, Mae 1893–1980

US vaudeville and film actress born in Brooklyn, New York. She wrote many of the plays she starred in, including *Sex* (1929) and *Diamond Lil* (1928) later filmed as *She Done Him Wrong* (1933). Other films included *I'm No Angel* (1933) and *My Little Chickadee* (1940).

28 'Goodness what beautiful diamonds!'
'Goodness had nothing to do with it.'
1932 *Night After Night* (screenplay by Vincent Lawrence).

29 Why don't you come up sometime, see me?
1933 As Lou in *She Done Him Wrong*. The line is popularly rendered 'Come up and see me sometime.'

30 When I'm good I'm very very good, but when I'm bad I'm better.
1933 *I'm No Angel.*

31 Beulah, peel me a grape.
1933 *I'm No Angel.*

32 A man has one hundred dollars and you leave him with two dollars, that's subtraction.
1940 Line spoken in *My Little Chickadee.*

33 Lieutenant, is that your sword, or are you just glad to see me?
1944 Ad-libbed when her stage lover in *Catherine Was Great* became entangled with his sword scabbard as he attempted to embrace her. Attributed.

34 Catherine had three hundred lovers. I did the best I could do in a couple of hours.
1944 Curtain speech at the end of her play *Catherine Was Great.* Attributed.

35 I've been in Who's Who and I know what's what, but it's the first time I ever made the dictionary.
Reputedly said on learning that a life jacket was to be named after her.

36 It isn't what I do, but how I do it.
It isn't what I say, but how I say it—
And how I look when I do and say it.
Attributed.

West, Nathanael *pseudonym of* **Nathan Wallenstein Weinstein** 1903–40

US novelist, who lived for two years in Paris. After he wrote his most famous novel *Miss Lonelyhearts*, he spent his last five years writing scripts for a Hollywood film studio, which provided the material for a final masterpiece, *The Day of the Locust* (1939, filmed 1975).

37 Prayers for the condemned man will be offered on an adding machine. Numbers constitute the only universal language.
1933 *Miss Lonelyhearts.*

West, Dame Rebecca *formerly* **Cecily Isabel Fairfield** 1892–1983

Anglo-Irish novelist, journalist, biographer and critic. She trained for the stage but her involvement with the suffragettes led her into journalism, and her studies arising out of the Nuremberg war trials include *The Meaning of Treason* (1947) and *A Train of Powder* (1955). She bore a son to H G Wells during an affair which lasted 10 years.

38 Women know the damnation of charity because the habit of civilisation has always been to throw them cheap alms rather than give them good wages.
1912 'The Personal Service Association: Work for Idle Hands to Do', in *The Clarion*, 13 Dec.

39 Antifeminists, from Chesterton down to Dr Lionel Tayler, want women to specialise in virtue. While men are rolling round the world having murderous and otherwise sinful adventures of an enjoyable nature, in commerce, exploration or art, women are to stay at home earning the promotion of the human race to a better world.
1912 'The Personal Service Association: Work for Idle Hands to Do', in *The Clarion*, 13 Dec.

40 I saw in my own education some of the things which eat the power out of women.

1913 'Training in Truculence: The Working Women's College', in *The Clarion*, 14 Feb.

41 We have asked men for votes, they have given us advice. At present they are also giving us abuse.
1913 'The Sex War: Disjointed Thoughts on Men', in *The Clarion*, 18 Apr.

42 I have horrible nightmares of Sir Almwroth Wright's limp sentences wandering through the arid desert of his mind looking for dropped punctuation marks.
1913 'Lynch Law: The Tragedy of Ignorance', in *The Clarion*, 17 Oct. Almwroth Wright was one of the most vocal opponents of women's suffrage.

43 Who is there in that lot one would want as a father, except perhaps Mrs Thatcher? That choice would be irregular but safe.
1982 Of British Prime Ministers. *1900*, introduction.

44 There is, of course, no reason for the existence of the male sex except that one sometimes needs help with moving the piano.
Attributed.

Wharton, Edith Newbold *née* **Jones** 1861–1937

US novelist. She wrote more than 50 books in all, but is best known for her sophisticated novels of manners, which include *The House of Mirth* (1905) and *The Age of Innocence* (1920).

45 I despair of the Republic!… What a horror it is for a whole nation to be developing without a sense of beauty, and eating bananas for breakfast.
1904 On the US. Letter to Sara Norton, 19 Aug.

46 If I were shabby no one would have me: a woman is asked out as much for her clothes as for herself.
1905 *The House of Mirth*, bk.1, ch.1.

47 She was like a disembodied spirit who took up a great deal of room.
1905 *The House of Mirth*, bk.1, ch.2.

48 Of course, being fatally poor and dingy, it was wise of Gerty to have taken up philanthropy and symphony concerts.
1905 *The House of Mirth*, bk.1, ch.8.

49 Miss Farish, who was accustomed, in the way of happiness, to such scant light as shone through the cracks of other people's lives.
1905 *The House of Mirth*, bk.1, ch.14.

50 She keeps on being Queenly in her own room, with the door shut.
1905 *The House of Mirth*, bk.2, ch.1.

51 Paying for what she doesn't get rankles so dreadfully with Louisa; I can't make her see that it's one of the preliminary steps to getting what you haven't paid for.
1905 *The House of Mirth*, bk.2, ch.2.

52 Almost everyone in the neighbourhood had 'troubles', frankly localized and specified; but only the chosen had 'complications'. To have them was in itself a distinction, though it was also, in most cases, a death warrant. People struggled on for years with 'troubles', but they almost always succumbed to 'complications'.
1911 *Ethan Frome*, ch.7.

53 Mrs Ballinger is one of the ladies who pursue Culture in bands, as though it were dangerous to meet it alone.
1916 *Xingu and Other Stories*, 'Xingu'.

54 An unalterable and unquestioned law of the musical world required that the German text of French operas sung by Swedish artists should be translated into Italian for the clearer understanding of English speaking audiences.
1920 *The Age of Innocence*, bk.1, ch.1.

55 What can you expect of a girl who was allowed to wear black satin at her coming-out ball?
1920 *The Age of Innocence*, bk.1, ch.5.

56 Blessed are the pure in heart for they have so much more to talk about.
1932 In *John O'London's Weekly*, 10 Apr.

57 There is no such thing as old age, there is only sorrow.
1934 *A Backward Glance*, 'A First Word'.

Whately, Richard 1787–1863

English scholar and prelate, Archbishop of Dublin (1831), writer of treatises on logic and rhetoric. A founder of the Broad Church party, he supported Catholic emancipation and rejected sectarianism, but his caustic wit and outspokenness made him unpopular.

58 Preach not because you have to say something, but because you have something to say.
1854 *Apophthegms*.

59 Happiness is no laughing matter.
1854 *Apophthegms*.

Whistler, James (Abbott) McNeill 1834–1903

US artist, who moved to Paris and later London, where he was controversially received. He is best known for his 'nocturnes', including *Old Battersea Bridge* (1872–5, Tate, London), and the portrait of his mother (*The Artist's Mother*, 1871–2, Louvre, Paris).

60 I am not arguing with you—I am telling you.
1890 *The Gentle Art of Making Enemies*.

61 A picture is finished when all trace of the means used to bring about the end has disappeared.
1890 *The Gentle Art of Making Enemies*.

62 A life passed among pictures makes not a painter—else the policeman in the National Gallery might assert himself.
1890 *The Gentle Art of Making Enemies*.

63 To say to the painter, that Nature is to be taken as she is, is to say to the player, that he may sit on the piano.
1890 *The Gentle Art of Making Enemies*.

64 The imitator is a poor kind of creature. If the man who paints only the tree, or a flower, or other surface he sees before him were an artist, the king of artists would be the photographer.
1890 *The Gentle Art of Making Enemies*.

65 Art should be independent of all clap-trap—should stand alone, and appeal to the artistic sense of eye or ear, without confounding this with emotions entirely foreign to it, as devotion, pity, love, patriotism and the like. All these have no kind of concern with it; and that is why I insist on calling my works 'arrangements' and 'harmonies'.
1890 *The Gentle Art of Making Enemies*.

66 Poor lawyers, like poor paintings, are dear at any price.
On the cost and quality of some of the lawyers he had hired. Quoted in Arthur Jerome Eddy *Recollections and Impressions of J.A.M. Whistler* (1903).

Whitbread, Samuel 1758–1815

English radical Whig politician, founder of the famous brewing firm. The intimate friend of Fox, under Pitt he was Leader of the Opposition, and in 1805 headed the attack on the treasurer of the navy, Viscount Melville.

67 The nation suspects that the regular ministerial majorities in Parliament are bought, and that the Crown has made a purchase of the House with the money of the people. Hence the ready, tame and servile compliance to every royal verdict issued by Lord North… It is almost universally believed that this debt has been contracted in corrupting the representatives of the people.
1777 House of Commons, 16 Apr.

68 In a political point of view, nothing can possibly afford greater stability to a popular Government than the education of the people.
1807 House of Commons, 19 Feb.

White, Andrew Dickson 1832–1918

US educationalist. President of Cornell University.

69 I will not permit thirty men to travel four hundred miles to agitate a bag of wind.
On refusing permission for a team from Cornell University to visit Michigan to play a game of American football. Quoted in D Wallechinsky *The People's Almanac* (1975).

White, Edmund 1940–

US writer. His sensitive assessments of gay life have appeared in novels including *A Boy's Own Story* (1982) and *The Beautiful Room Is Empty* (1988), as well as in his essays.

70 In fact, they are the classic scapegoats. Our old fears about our sissiness, still with us though masked by the new macho fascism, are now located, isolated, quarantined through our persecution of the transvestite.
1980 *States of Desire: Travels in Gay America*, ch.2.

71 Those who believe machismo reeks of violence alone choose to forget it once stood for honor as well.
1980 *States of Desire: Travels in Gay America*, ch.5.

72 The AIDS epidemic has rolled back a big rotting log and revealed all the squirming life underneath it, since it involves, all at once, the main themes of our existence: sex, death, power, money, love, hate, disease and panic. No American phenomenon has been so compelling since the Vietnam War.
1986 'Afterword—AIDS: An American Epidemic', added to later editions of *States of Desire: Travels in Gay America*.

73 Paris is a city where even the most outrageous story of incest and murder is greeted with a verbal shrug: 'Mais c'est normal!'
2001 In *The Flâneur*.

White, E(lwyn) B(rooks) 1899–1985

US essayist, children's novelist, poet and parodist. He was closely associated with the rise and development of the *New Yorker* magazine.

74 MOTHER: It's broccoli, dear.
CHILD: I say it's spinach, and I say the hell with it.
1928 Cartoon caption, in the *New Yorker*, 8 Dec.

75 All poets who, when reading from their own works, experience a choked feeling, are major. For that matter,

all poets who read from their own works are major, whether they choke or not.
1939 *Quo Vadimus?*, 'How To Tell A Major Poet From A Minor Poet'.

76 It is easier for a man to be loyal to his club than to his planet; the by-laws are shorter, and he is personally acquainted with the other members.
1942 *One Man's Meat*, 'One Man's Meat'.

77 The duty of a democracy is to know then what it knows now.
1942 *One Man's Meat*, 'One Man's Meat'.

78 A poet's pleasure is to withhold a little of his meaning, to intensify by mystification. He unzips the veil from beauty, but does not remove it.
1942 *One Man's Meat*, 'Poetry'.

79 Democracy is the recurrent suspicion that more than half the people are right more than half the time.
1944 In the *New Yorker*, 3 Jul.

80 You can see in pantomime the puppets fumbling with their slips of paper…see them pick up their phone…see the noiseless, ceaseless capital of memoranda, in touch with Calcutta, in touch with Reykjavik, and always fooling with something.
1949 On office windows at twilight. *Here Is New York*.

81 I'm less than two months old and I'm tired of living.
1952 Wilbur the pig. *Charlotte's Web*, ch.3.

82 I can surely fool a man. People are not as smart as bugs.
1952 Charlotte. *Charlotte's Web*, ch.10.

83 It was the best place to be, thought Wilbur, this warm delicious cellar, with the garrulous geese, the changing seasons, the heat of the sun, the passage of swallows, the nearness of rats, the sameness of sheep, the love of spiders, the smell of manure, and the glory of everything.
1952 *Charlotte's Web*, ch.22.

84 It is not often that someone comes along who is a true friend and a good writer. Charlotte was both.
1952 *Charlotte's Web*, ch.22.

85 The time not to become a father is eighteen years before a war.
1954 *The Second Tree from the Corner*, 'The Second Tree from the Corner'.

86 Thurber did not write the way a surgeon operates, he wrote the way a child skips rope, the way a mouse waltzes.
1961 In the *New Yorker*, 11 Nov. Tribute to James Thurber.

87 A man who publishes his letters becomes a nudist—nothing shields him from the world's gaze except his bare skin.
1975 Letter to Corona Macheiner, 11 Jun.

88 She would write 8 or 10 words, then draw her gun and shoot them down.
1979 On his wife and fellow editor Katharine S White. *Onward and Upward in the Garden*.

89 Commuter—one who spends his life
In riding to and from his wife;
A man who shaves and takes a train,
And then rides back to shave again.
1982 *Poems and Sketches*, 'The Commuter'.

White, George Malcolm 1920–

US architect, designer of the Capitol, Washington.

90 The fact that you don't buy a teenager new clothes doesn't mean he isn't going to grow.
1987 On the need for a fourth Senate office building. In *Connoisseur*, Apr.

White, Patrick Victor Martindale 1912–90

Australian novelist, born in London, who went to Australia as an infant and settled there after World War II. He received the Nobel prize for literature in 1973, and numerous other awards, particularly for *Voss* (1957).

91 She would imprison the child in her house by the force of love.
1955 *The Tree of Man*, ch.7.

92 So that in the end there were the trees. The boy walking through them with his head drooping as he increased in stature. Putting out shoots of green thought. So that, in the end, there was no end.
1955 *The Tree of Man*, ch.26.

93 The mystery of life is not solved by success, which is an end in itself, but in failure, in perpetual struggle, in becoming.
1957 *Voss*, ch.10.

94 Perhaps true knowledge only comes of death by torture in the country of the mind.
1957 *Voss*, ch.16.

95 There is nothing like a rain of bombs to start one trying to assess one's own achievement.
1958 Essay on his literary career, in *Australian Letters*, 'The Prodigal Son', vol.1, no.3, Apr.

96 In all directions stretched the Great Australian Emptiness, in which the mind is the least of possessions…and the march of material ugliness does not raise a quiver from the average nerves.
It was the exaltation of the 'average' that made me panic most.
1958 Essay on his literary career, in *Australian Letters*, 'The Prodigal Son', vol.1, no.3, Apr.

97 Above all I was determined to prove that the Australian novel is not necessarily the dreary, dun-coloured offspring of journalistic realism.
1958 Essay on his literary career, in *Australian Letters*, 'The Prodigal Son', vol.1, no.3, Apr.

White, Theodore H(arold) 1915–86

US journalist and political commentator. His *The Making of the President, 1960* (1961), with its characteristic reportage style, won a Pulitzer Prize in 1962.

98 Chafing in action when his nature yearned to act, conscious of indignities real and imagined, Johnson went through three years of slow burn.
Of Lyndon B Johnson as John F Kennedy's Vice President. Quoted in Arthur M Schlesinger, Jr *A Thousand Days* (1965).

99 The best time to listen to a politician is when he is on a street corner, in the rain, late at night, when he's exhausted. Then he doesn't lie.
1969 In the *New York Times*, 5 Jan.

1 He was almost a force of nature, like a slumbering volcano, wreathed in clouds, occasionally emitting smoke which soothsayers attempted to interpret.
1969 Of Nelson Rockefeller. *The Making of the President, 1968*.

2 The epitaph on the Kennedy administration became

Camelot—a magic moment in American history, when gallant men danced with beautiful women, when great deeds were done, when artists, writers and poets met at the White House and the barbarians beyond the walls were held back.
1978 *In Search of History.*

3 Eisenhower has…a magic in American politics that is peculiarly his: he makes people happy.
Of Dwight D Eisenhower's appearances during Richard M Nixon's 1960 presidential campaign. Quoted in Michael R Beschloss *Eisenhower* (1990).

White, Thomas 1550–1624

English Puritan.

4 The cause of plagues is sin, if you look to it well; and the cause of sin are plays; therefore the cause of plagues are plays.
Attributed.

Whitehead, Alfred North 1861–1947

English mathematician and philosopher. He taught at Imperial College London and later at Harvard University. With his former pupil Bertrand Russell he wrote *Principia Mathematica* (1910–13).

5 It is a safe rule to apply that, when a mathematical or philosophical author writes with a misty profundity, he is talking nonsense.
1911 *Introduction to Mathematics.*

6 Knowledge does not keep any better than fish.
1916 'The Aims of Education; a plea for reform', address as president of the Mathematical Association.

7 Familiar things happen, and mankind does not bother about them. It requires a very unusual mind to undertake the analysis of the obvious.
1925 *Science and the Modern World.*

8 Religion is something which stands beyond, behind, and within the passing flux of immediate things; something which is real, and yet waiting to be realized; something which is a remote possibility, and yet the greatest of present facts; something that gives meaning to all that passes, and yet eludes apprehension; something whose possession is the final good, and yet is beyond all reach; something which is the ultimate ideal, and the hopeless quest.
1925 *Science and the Modern World.*

9 The worship of God is not a rule of safety—it is an adventure of the spirit, a flight after the unattainable. The death of religion comes with the repression of the high hope of adventure.
1925 *Science and the Modern World.*

10 Mathematics is thought moving in the sphere of complete abstraction from any particular instance of what it is talking about.
1925 *Science And the Modern World.*

11 Religion is what a man does with his solitariness.
1926 *Religion in the Making.*

12 The safest general characterization of the European philosophical tradition is that it consists of a series of footnotes to Plato.
1929 *Process and Reality*, pt.2, ch.1, section 1.

13 The power of Christianity lies in its revelation in act, of that which Plato divined in theory.
1938 *Adventures of Ideas.*

14 The essence of Christianity is the appeal to the life of Christ as a revelation of the nature of God and of his agency in the world. The record is fragmentary, inconsistent and uncertain… But there can be no doubt as to the elements in the record that have evoked the best in human nature. The Mother, the Child and the bare manger: the lowly man, homeless and self-forgetful, with his message of peace, love and sympathy: the suffering, the agony, the tender words as life ebbed, the final despair: and the whole with the authority of supreme victory.
1938 *Adventures of Ideas.*

15 What is morality in any given time or place? It is what the majority then and there happen to like, and immorality is what they dislike.
1941 Conversation, 30 Aug. Collected in *Dialogues* (1954).

Whitehead, Hal

Canadian marine biologist.

16 'Scientific whaling' is like the prostitution of the profession: using the name of science for a totally bogus purpose.
2004 *New Scientist*, May.

Whitehorn, Katharine 1926–

English journalist.

17 Hats divide generally into three classes: offensive hats, defensive hats, and shrapnel.
1963 *Shouts and Murmurs.*

Whitelaw, William Stephen Ian, 1st Viscount 1918–99

Scottish Conservative politician, Leader of the House of Commons (1970–2), Secretary of State for Northern Ireland (1972–3) and Employment (1973–4) and Home Secretary (1979–83). Loyal to Heath and then Thatcher, he led the House of Lords until 1988.

18 I do not intend to prejudge the past.
1973 On arriving in Ulster for the first time as Secretary of State for Northern Ireland, 2 Dec.

19 He is going round the country stirring up apathy.
1974 Of Harold Wilson during the general election campaign. Attributed.

20 A short, sharp shock.
1979 At the Conservative Party Conference, 10 Oct, on the need for more effective treatment of young offenders.
➤ See *Gilbert 355:25.*

Whiteman, Paul 1891–1967

US bandleader. A pioneer of 'sweet style' jazz in the 1920s, he recruited such talents as trumpeter Bix Beiderbecke. He developed Gershwin's 'symphonic jazz' experiments, commissioning *Rhapsody in Blue* in 1924.

21 Jazz came to America three hundred years ago in chains.
1926 *Jazz.*

Whiteread, Rachel 1963–

English sculptor. In 1993 she came to prominence when she made a cast of an entire disused house in East London. She won the 1993 Turner Prize.

22 When I visited concentration camps, I was more interested in how people responded to the camps than in the actual places. I watched kids picnicking on the ovens and other people stricken with grief.
2001 From an interview on www.guggenheim.org, 18 Apr.

Whiting, George   1884–1943

US songwriter.

23 When You're All Dressed Up and Have No Place To Go.
1912 Title of song (music by Newton Harding).

Whitlam, (Edward) Gough   1916–

Australian politician, leader of the Labor Party from 1967 and Prime Minister (1972–5). He resigned in 1978 to move into academia. His works include *The Italian Inspiration in English Literature* (1980).

24 The importance of an historical event lies not in what happened but in what later generations believe to have happened.
1973 Speech at Ballarat, Victoria, 3 Dec.

25 I do not mind the Liberals, still less do I mind the Country party, calling me a bastard. In some circumstances, I am only doing my job if they do. But I hope that you will not publicly call me a bastard, as some bastards in the Caucus have.
1974 Speech to the Australian Labor Party, 9 Jun.

26 We may say 'God Save the Queen', because nothing will save the Governor-General… Maintain your rage and your enthusiasm for the election now to be held and until polling day.
1975 On the Governor-General Sir John Kerr's action in dissolving the Australian Parliament, 11 Nov. Whitlam lost the subsequent election.

Whitman, Christine Todd   1947–

US Republican politician, Governor of New Jersey (1994–2001), she is a former freeholder in Somerset County, New Jersey and a former president of the State Board of Public Utilities.

27 The states are the laboratories of democracy.
1995 In the *New York Times*, 29 Jan.

Whitman, Walt(er)   1819–91

US poet. He was editor of the *Brooklyn Eagle* and worked as a nurse during the Civil War. His poetry reflected his mystical faith in democracy and was attacked for indecency because it addressed many taboo subjects. It is collected in *Leaves of Grass* (1855–92).

28 The Americans of all nations at any time upon the earth have probably the fullest poetical nature. The United States themselves are essentially the greatest poem.
1855 *Leaves of Grass*, preface.

29 As soon as histories are properly told there is no more need of romances.
1855 *Leaves of Grass*, preface.

30 I celebrate myself, and sing myself,
And what I assume you shall assume,
For every atom belonging to me as good belongs to you.
1855 *Leaves of Grass*, 'Song of Myself', section 1.

31 All goes onward and outward, nothing collapses,

And to die is different from what any one supposed, and luckier.
1855 *Leaves of Grass*, 'Song of Myself', section 6.

32 I believe a leaf of grass is no less than the journey-work of the stars.
1855 *Leaves of Grass*, 'Song of Myself', section 31.

33 I think I could turn, and live with animals, they are so placid and self-contain'd.
1855 *Leaves of Grass*, 'Song of Myself', section 32.

34 I have said that the soul is not more than the body,
And I have said that the body is not more than the soul,
And nothing, not God, is greater to one than one's self is.
1855 *Leaves of Grass*, 'Song of Myself', section 48.

35 Do I contradict myself?
Very well then I contradict myself,
(I am large, I contain multitudes.)
1855 *Leaves of Grass*, 'Song of Myself', section 51.

36 I too am not a bit tamed, I too am untranslatable,
I sound my barbaric yawp over the roofs of the world.
1855 *Leaves of Grass*, 'Song of Myself', section 52.

37 How beggarly appear arguments before a defiant deed!
1855 Leaves of Grass, 'Broad-Axe Song', later 'Song of the Broad-Axe' (from 1867).

38 If anything is sacred the human body is sacred.
1855 *Leaves of Grass*, 'Children of Adam', 'I Sing the Body Electric', section 8.

39 I do not think seventy years is the time of a man or woman,
Nor that seventy millions of years is the time of a man or woman,
Nor that years will ever stop the existence of me, or any one else.
1855 *Leaves of Grass*, 'Autumn Rivulets', 'Who Learns My Lesson Complete?'

40 Henceforth I whimper no more, postpone no more, need nothing,
Done with indoor complaints, libraries, querulous criticisms,
Strong and content I travel the open road.
1856 *Leaves of Grass*, 'Song of the Open Road', section 1.

41 What can ever be more stately and admirable to me than mast-hemm'd Manhattan?
1856 *Leaves of Grass*, 'Crossing Brooklyn Ferry', section 8.

42 He or she is greatest who contributes the greatest original practical example.
1856 *Leaves of Grass*, 'By Blue Ontario's Shores', section 13.

43 And I will show that nothing can happen more beautiful than death.
1860 *Leaves of Grass*, 'Proto-Leaf', later renamed 'Starting From Paumanok' (from 1867).

44 I hear it was charged against me that I sought to destroy institutions,
But really I am neither for nor against institutions.
1860 *Leaves of Grass*, 'Calamus', 'I Hear It Was Charged Against Me'.

45 Camarado, this is no book,
Who touches this touches a man.
1860 *Leaves of Grass*, 'Songs of Parting', 'So Long!'

46 O Captain! my Captain! our fearful trip is done,
The ship has weather'd every rack, the prize we sought is won,

The port is near, the bells I hear, the people all exulting.
1865 *Leaves of Grass*, 'Memories of President Lincoln', 'O Captain! My Captain!'

47 When lilacs last in the dooryard bloom'd,
And the great star early droop'd in the western sky in the night,
I mourn'd, and yet shall mourn with ever-returning spring.
1865–66 *Leaves of Grass*, 'Memories of President Lincoln', 'When Lilacs Last in the Dooryard Bloom'd', section 1.

48 Come lovely and soothing death,
Undulate round the world, serenely arriving, arriving,
In the day, in the night, to all, to each,
Sooner or later delicate death.
1865–66 *Leaves of Grass*, 'Memories of President Lincoln', 'When Lilacs Last in the Dooryard Bloom'd', section 14.

49 The Past—the dark unfathom'd retrospect!
The teeming gulf—the sleepers and the shadows!
The past! the infinite greatness of the past!
For what is the present after all but a growth out of the past?
1871 *Passage to India*, opening verse.

50 Political democracy, as it exists and practically works in America, with all its threatening evils, supplies a training-school for making first-class men. It is life's gymnasium, not of good only, but of all.
1871 *Democratic Vistas*.

51 In this broad earth of ours,
Amid the measureless grossness and the slag,
Enclosed and safe within its central heart,
Nestles the seed perfection.
1874 *Leaves of Grass*, 'Birds of Passage', 'Song of the Universal', section 1.

52 After you have exhausted what there is in business, politics, conviviality, love, and so on—and found that none of these finally satisfy, or permanently wear—what remains? Nature remains.
1876–77 *Specimen Days*, 'New Themes Entered Upon'.

53 Youth, large, lusty, loving—youth full of grace, force, fascination,
Do you know that Old Age may come after you with equal grace, force, fascination?
1881 *Leaves of Grass*, 'Youth, Day, Old Age and Night', stanza 1.

54 Have you not learn'd great lessons from those who reject you,
and brace themselves against you? or who treat you with
contempt, or dispute the passage with you?
1888 Leaves of Grass, 'Sands at Seventy', 'Stronger Lessons'.

55 No one will get at my verses who insists upon viewing them as a literary performance.
1888 'A Backward Glance O'er Travel'd Roads'.

Whittier, John Greenleaf 1807–92

US poet and abolitionist. A Quaker, he devoted himself to the cause of emancipation. His ballads and sentimental poems, such as 'Barbara Freitchie', which was included in *In War Time* (1864), were extremely popular in their day. His best work is the nostalgic narrative poem, *Snow-Bound* (1866).

56 When the care-wearied man seeks his mother once more,

And the worn matron smiles where the girl smiled before,
What moistens the lip and what brightens the eye?
What calls back the past, like the rich Pumpkin pie?
1844 'The Pumpkin', stanza 3.

57 When faith is lost, when honor dies,
The man is dead!
1850 'Ichabod', stanza 8.

58 Beneath her torn hat glowed the wealth
Of simple beauty and rustic health.
1854 'Maud Muller', l.3–4.

59 For of all sad words of tongue or pen,
The saddest are these: 'It might have been!'
1854 'Maud Muller', l.105–6.

60 The age is dull and mean. Men creep,
Not walk.
1855 'Lines, Inscribed to Friends Under Arrest for Treason Against the Slave Power', stanza 1.

61 Up from the meadows rich with corn,
Clear in the cool September morn.
1863 'Barbara Frietchie', opening lines.

62 'Shoot, if you must this old grey head,
But spare your country's flag,' she said.
1863 'Barbara Frietchie', l.35–36.

63 Dear Lord and Father of mankind,
Forgive our foolish ways!
Re-clothe us in our rightful mind,
In purer lives thy service find,
In deeper reverence praise
1872 'The Brewing of Soma'.

Whitton, Charlotte 1896–1975

Canadian politician, Mayor of Ottawa (1951–6, 1960–4), the first woman to serve as mayor of a Canadian city.

64 Whatever women do they must do twice as well as men to be thought half so good…luckily, it's not difficult.
1963 In *Canada Month*, Jun.

Whymper, Edward 1840–1911

English wood-engraver and mountaineer. In 1860–9 he conquered several hitherto unscaled peaks of the Alps, including the Matterhorn. He later published several books based on his travels in the Alps and elsewhere.

65 Do nothing in haste, look well to each step, and from the beginning think what may be the end.
1871 *Scrambles Amongst the Alps*.

Widdecombe, Anne 1947–

English Conservative politician and novelist.

66 He has something of the night in him.
1997 Of fellow Conservative Michael Howard. In the *Sunday Times*, (electronic edition) 11 May.

Wiener, Norbert 1894–1964

US academic, who studied mathematics with Bertrand Russell and taught at MIT. His work contributed to the development of the understanding of information systems. He coined the word *cybernetics* to describe the science of feedback control in systems.

67 The automatic machine, whatever we think of any

feelings it may or may not have, is the precise economic equivalent of the slave.
1949 *The Human Use of Human Beings*.

68 The new industrial revolution is a two-edged sword. It may be used for the benefit of humanity, assuming that humanity survives long enough to reach a period in which such a benefit is possible. If, however, we proceed along the clear and obvious lines of our traditional behavior, and follow our traditional worship of progress and the fifth freedom—the freedom to exploit—it is practically certain that we shall have to face a decade or more of ruin and despair.
1949 *The Human Use of Human Beings*.

69 Scientific discovery consists in the interpretation for our own convenience of a system of existence which has been made with no eye to our convenience at all.
1949 *The Human Use of Human Beings*.

Wilberforce, Samuel 1805–73

English prelate, Canon of Winchester, later Dean of Westminster and Bishop of Oxford.

70 If I were a cassowary
On the plains of Timbuctoo,
I would eat a missionary,
Cassock, band, and hymn-book too.
Attributed.

Wilbur, Richard 1921–

US poet. He taught at Harvard and Wesleyan Universities, and wrote a significant body of poems. He also contributed lyrics to Leonard Bernstein's opera, *Candide* (1957).

71 We milk the cow of the world, and as we do
We whisper in her ear, 'You are not true.'
1950 *Ceremony and Other Poems*, 'Epistemology'.

72 Forgive the hero, you who would have died
Gladly with all you knew; he rode that tide
To Ararat; all men are Noah's sons.
1950 *Ceremony and Other Poems*, 'Still, Citizen Sparrow'.

73 Outside the open window
The morning air is all awash with angels.
1956 *Things of This World*, 'Love Calls Us to the Things of This World'.

74 The soul shrinks
From all that it is about to remember,
From the punctual rape of every blessèd day
1956 *Things of This World*, 'Love Calls Us to the Things of This World'.

75 Columbus and his men, they say,
Conveyed the virus hither
Whereby my features rot away
And vital powers wither;
Yet had they not traversed the seas
And come infected back,
Why, think of all the luxuries
That modern life would lack.
1957 'Pangloss's Song', from *Candide*.

76 It is not tricks of sense
But the time's fright within me which distracts
Least fancies into violence
1969 *Walking to Sleep*, 'On the Marginal Way'.

77 All night, this headland

Lunges into the rumpling
Capework of the wind.
1976 *The Mind Reader*, 'Sleepless at Crown Point'.

78 Writing is…waiting for the word that may not be there until next Tuesday.
1987 In the *Los Angeles Times*, 13 Oct.

79 Most women know that sex is good for headaches.
1987 Quoted in the *Observer*, 1 Nov.

Wilcox, Ella Wheeler 1850–1919

US poet who wrote over 30 volumes of sentimental verse. Her temperance poems were collected in *Drops of Water* (1872). *Poems of Passion* (1883) was attacked for its immorality.

80 Laugh, and the world laughs with you:
Weep, and you weep alone;
For the sad old earth must borrow its mirth,
It has trouble enough of its own.
1883 *Poems of Passion*, 'Solitude'.

Wilde, Jane Francesca née *Elgee* 1826–96

Irish Poet and folklorist, mother of Oscar Wilde. She was an ardent nationalist and contributed verse and prose to the *Nation* under the pen name 'Speranza'.

81 'Tis midnight, falls the lamp-light dull and sickly
On a pale and anxious crowd,
Through the court, and round the judges thronging thickly,
With prayers they dare not speak aloud—
Two youths, two noble youths, stand prisoners at the bar—
You can see them through the gloom—
In the pride of life and manhood's beauty, there they are
Awaiting their death-doom.
'The Brothers'.

82 Weary men, what reap ye?—Golden corn for the stranger.
What sow ye?—Human corpses that wait for the avenger.
Fainting forms, hunger stricken, what see ye in the offing?
Stately ships to bear our food away, amid the stranger's scoffing.
There's a proud array of soldiers—what do they round your door?
They guard our master's granaries from the thin hands of the poor.
Pale mothers, wherefore weeping? Would to God that we were dead—
Our children swoon before us, and we cannot give them bread.
'The Famine Year'.

Wilde, Oscar Fingal O'Flahertie Wills 1854–1900

Anglo-Irish poet and dramatist, renowned for his wit and flamboyant lifestyle. His works include *The Picture of Dorian Gray* (1891), *Lady Windermere's Fan* (1892), *An Ideal Husband* (1895), *The Importance of Being Earnest* (1895) and *The Ballad of Reading Gaol* (1898). He was ruined by a trial arising from his homosexual relationships.

83 To make a good salad is to be a brilliant diplomatist—the problem is entirely the same in both cases. To know

exactly how much oil one must put with one's vinegar.
1880 *Vera, or The Nihilists*, act 2.

84 I have nothing to declare except my genius.
1882 On passing through US customs on a lecture tour. Quoted in F Harris, *Oscar Wilde* (1918), p.75.

85 Over the piano was printed a notice: 'Please do not shoot the pianist. He is doing his best.'
1883 *Impressions of America: Leadville*.

86 What captivity was to the Jews, exile has been to the Irish: America and American influence have educated them. Their first practical leader is an Irish-American.
1889 Of Charles Stewart Parnell. 'The Two Chiefs of Dunboy: or, an Irish Romance of the Last Century' in *Pall Mall Gazette*, 13 Apr.

87 Books of poetry by young writers are usually promissory notes that are never met. Now and then, however, one comes across a volume that is so far above the average that one can hardly resist the fascinating temptation of recklessly prophesying a fine future for its author. Such a book Mr Yeats's *Wanderings of Oisin* certainly is. Here we find nobility of treatment and nobility of subject-matter, delicacy of poetic instinct and richness of imaginative resource.
1889 In the *Pall Mall Gazette*, 12 Jul.

88 Newspapers have degenerated. They may now be absolutely relied upon.
1889 'The Decay of Lying', first published in the *Nineteenth Century Review*.

89 Art never expresses anything but itself.
1889 'The Decay of Lying', first published in the *Nineteenth Century Review*.

90 After playing Chopin, I feel as if I had been weeping over sins that I had never committed.
1891 *Intentions*, 'The Critic as Artist'.

91 Every great man nowadays has his disciples, and it is always Judas who writes the biography.
1891 *Intentions*, 'The Critic as Artist'.

92 Meredith is a prose Browning, and so is Browning.
1891 *Intentions*, 'The Critic as Artist'.

93 The one duty we owe to history is to rewrite it.
1891 *Intentions*, 'The Critic as Artist'.

94 It is through Art, and through Art only, that we can realise our perfection; through Art, and through Art only, that we can shield ourselves from the sordid perils of actual existence.
1891 *Intentions*, 'The Critic as Artist'.

95 All art is immoral.
1891 *Intentions*, 'The Critic as Artist'.

96 A little sincerity is a dangerous thing, and a great deal of it is absolutely fatal.
1891 *Intentions*, 'The Critic as Artist'.

97 Modern journalism justifies its own existence by the great Darwinian principle of the survival of the vulgarest.
1891 *Intentions*, 'The Critic as Artist'.

98 All that I desire to point out is the general principle that Life imitates Art far more than Art imitates Life.
1891 *Intentions*, 'The Decay of Lying'.

99 There is no such thing as a moral or an immoral book. Books are well written, or badly written.
1891 *The Picture of Dorian Gray*, preface.

1 The nineteenth century dislike of Realism is the rage of

Caliban seeing his own face in the glass.
1891 *The Picture of Dorian Gray*, preface.

2 The moral life of man forms part of the subject matter of the artist, but the morality of art consists in the perfect use of an imperfect medium.
1891 *The Picture of Dorian Gray*, preface.

3 There is only one thing in the world worse than being talked about, and that is not being talked about.
1891 *The Picture of Dorian Gray*, ch.1.

4 A man cannot be too careful in the choice of his enemies.
1891 *The Picture of Dorian Gray*, ch.1.

5 I like Wagner's music better than anybody's. It is so loud that one can talk the whole time without other people hearing what one says.
1891 *The Picture of Dorian Gray*, ch.4.

6 If one hears bad music, it is one's duty to drown it by one's conversation.
1891 *The Picture of Dorian Gray*, ch.4.

7 A cigarette is the perfect type of a perfect pleasure. It is exquisite, and it leaves one unsatisfied. What more can one want?
1891 *The Picture of Dorian Gray*, ch.6.

8 It is better to be beautiful than to be good. But…it is better to be good than to be ugly.
1891 *The Picture of Dorian Gray*, ch.17.

9 Anybody can be good in the country.
1891 *The Picture of Dorian Gray*, ch.19.

10 Murder is always a mistake… One should never do anything that one cannot talk about after dinner.
1891 *The Picture of Dorian Gray*, ch.19.

11 As for the virtuous poor, one can pity them, of course, but one cannot possibly admire them.
1891 'The Soul of Man under Socialism'.

12 Democracy means simply the bludgeoning of the people by the people for the people.
1891 'The Soul of Man under Socialism'.

13 I can resist everything except temptation.
1892 Lord Darlington. *Lady Windermere's Fan*, act 1.

14 Many a woman has a past, but I am told that she has at least a dozen, and that they all fit.
1892 Said by Duchess of Berwick. *Lady Windermere's Fan*, act 1.

15 Do you know, Mr Hopper, dear Agatha and I are so much interested in Australia. It must be so pretty with all the dear little kangaroos flying about. Agatha has found it on the map. What a curious shape it is! Just like a large packing case.
1892 Duchess of Berwick to Mr Hopper. *Lady Windermere's Fan*, act 2.

16 We are all in the gutter, but some of us are looking at the stars.
1892 Said by Lord Darlington. *Lady Windermere's Fan*, act 3.

17 There is nothing in the whole world so unbecoming to a woman as a Nonconformist conscience.
1892 Cecil Graham. *Lady Windermere's Fan*, act 3.

18 A man who knows the price of everything and the value of nothing.
1892 Lord Darlington's definition of a cynic. *Lady Winderemere's Fan*, act 3.

19 Experience is the name everyone gives to their mistakes.

1892 Dumby. *Lady Windermere's Fan*, act 3.

20 The play was a great success, but the audience was a disaster.

1892 Attributed comment after the poor reception of *Lady Windermere's Fan*.

21 LORD ILLINGWORTH: The Book of Life begins with a man and a woman in a garden.

MRS ALLONBY: It ends with Revelations.

1893 *A Woman of No Importance*, act 1.

22 The English country gentleman galloping after a fox – the unspeakable in full pursuit of the uneatable.

1893 Lord Illingworth. *A Woman of No Importance*, act 1.

23 MRS ALLONBY: They say, Lady Hunstanton, that when good Americans die they go to Paris.

LADY HUNSTANTON: Indeed? And when bad Americans die, where do they go to?

LORD ILLINGWORTH: Oh, they go to America.

1893 *A Woman of No Importance*, act 1.

24 The youth of America is their oldest tradition. It has been going on now for three hundred years.

1893 Lord Illingworth. *A Woman of No Importance*, act 1.

25 One should never trust a woman who tells one her real age. A woman who would tell one that, would tell one anything.

1893 Lord Illingworth. *A Woman of No Importance*, act 1.

26 Children begin by loving their parents; after a time they judge them; rarely, if ever, do they forgive them.

1893 Lord Illingworth. *A Woman of No Importance*, act 2.

27 After a good dinner one can forgive anybody, even one's own relations.

1893 Lady Caroline. *A Woman of No Importance*, act 2.

28 GERALD: I suppose society is wonderfully delightful!

LORD ILLINGWORTH: To be in it is merely a bore. But to be out of it is simply a tragedy.

1893 *A Woman of No Importance*, act 3.

29 No woman should have a memory. Memory in a woman is the beginning of dowdiness.

1893 Lord Illingworth. *A Woman of No Importance*, act 3.

30 You should study the Peerage, Gerald… It is the best thing in fiction the English have ever done.

1893 Lord Illingworth. *A Woman of No Importance*, act 3.

31 A man who can dominate a London dinner-table can dominate the world.

1893 Lord Illingworth. *A Woman of No Importance*, act 3.

32 I'm afraid I play no outdoor games at all, except dominoes. I have sometimes played dominoes outside a French café.

1895 Quoted by Gelett Burgess in 'A Talk with Mr Oscar Wilde' in *The Sketch*, 9 Jan.

33 JACK: I think Jack, for instance, a charming name.

GWENDOLEN: Jack?… No, there is very little music in the name Jack, if any at all, indeed. It does not thrill. It produces absolutely no vibrations… I have known several Jacks, and they all, without exception, were more than usually plain. Besides, Jack is a notorious domesticity for John! And I pity any woman who is married to a man called John. She would probably never be allowed to know the entrancing pleasure of a single moment's solitude. The only really safe name is Ernest.

1895 *The Importance of Being Earnest*, act 1.

34 Really, if the lower orders don't set us a good example, what on earth is the use of them?

1895 Algernon. *The Importance of Being Earnest*, act 1.

35 It is very vulgar to talk like a dentist when one isn't a dentist. It produces a false impression.

1895 Jack. *The Importance of Being Earnest*, act 1.

36 The truth is rarely pure, and never simple.

1895 Algernon. *The Importance of Being Earnest*, act 1.

37 In married life three is company and two none.

1895 Algernon. *The Importance of Being Earnest*, act 1.

38 Ignorance is like a delicate exotic fruit; touch it and the bloom is gone. The whole theory of modern education is radically unsound. Fortunately, in England, at any rate, education produces no effect whatsoever.

1895 Lady Bracknell. *The Importance of Being Earnest*, act 1.

39 To lose one parent, Mr Worthing, may be regarded as a misfortune; to lose both looks like carelessness.

1895 Lady Bracknell. *The Importance of Being Earnest*, act 1.

40 All women become like their mothers. That is their tragedy. No man does. That's his.

1895 Algernon. *The Importance of Being Earnest*, act 1, also in *A Woman of No Importance* (1893), act 2.

41 The good ended happily, and the bad unhappily. That is what fiction means.

1895 Miss Prism. *The Importance of Being Earnest*, act 2.

42 The chapter on the fall of the Rupee you may omit. It is somewhat too sensational.

1895 Miss Prism. *The Importance of Being Earnest*, act 2.

43 I hope you have not been leading a double life, pretending to be wicked and being really good all the time. That would be hypocrisy.

1895 Said by Cecily. *The Importance of Being Earnest*, act 2.

44 Charity, dear Miss Prism, charity! None of us are perfect. I myself am peculiarly susceptible to draughts.

1895 Dr Chasuble. *The Importance of Being Earnest*, act 2.

45 CECILY: When I see a spade I call it a spade.

GWENDOLEN: I am glad to say that I have never seen a spade.

1895 *The Importance of Being Earnest*, act 3.

46 Thirty-five is a very attractive age. London society is full of women of the very highest birth who have, of their own free choice, remained thirty-five for years.

1895 Lady Bracknell. *The Importance of Being Earnest*, act 3.

47 She wore far too much rouge last night, and not quite enough clothes. That is always a sign of despair in a woman.

1895 Lord Goring. *An Ideal Husband*, act 2.

48 Nothing is so dangerous as being too modern. One is apt to grow old-fashioned quite suddenly.

1895 Lord Markby. *An Ideal Husband*, act 2.

49 Fashion is what one wears oneself. What is unfashionable is what other people wear.

1895 Lord Goring. *An Ideal Husband*, act 3.

50 If one could only teach the English how to talk, and the Irish how to listen, society here would be quite civilised.

1895 Mrs Cheveley speaking. *An Ideal Husband*, act 3.

51 If this is the way Queen Victoria treats her prisoners she doesn't deserve to have any.

1895 On being obliged to stand in the rain as he awaited transport to take him to prison. Attributed.

52 He did not wear his scarlet coat,
For blood and wine are red,
And blood and wine were on his hands
When they found him with the dead.
1898 The Ballad of Reading Gaol, pt.1, stanza 1.

53 I never saw a man who looked
With such a wistful eye
Upon that little tent of blue
Which prisoners call the sky.
1898 The Ballad of Reading Gaol, pt.1, stanza 3.

54 Yet each man kills the thing he loves,
By each let this be heard,
Some do it with a bitter look,
Some with a flattering word.
The coward does it with a kiss,
The brave man with a sword!
1898 The Ballad of Reading Gaol, pt.1, stanza 7.

55 The Governer was strong upon
The Regulation Act:
The Doctor said that Death was but
A scientific fact:
And twice a day the Chaplain called,
And left a little tract.
1898 The Ballad of Reading Gaol, pt.3, stanza 3.

56 Something was dead in each of us,
And what was dead was Hope.
1898 The Ballad of Reading Gaol, pt.3, stanza 31.

57 And the wild regrets, and the bloody sweats,
None knew so well as I:
For he who lives more lives than one
More deaths than one must die.
1898 The Ballad of Reading Gaol, pt.3, stanza 37.

58 I know not whether Laws be right,
Or whether Laws be wrong;
All that we know who lie in gaol
Is that the wall is strong;
And that each day is like a year,
A year whose days are long.
1898 The Ballad of Reading Gaol, pt.5, stanza 1.

59 How else but through a broken heart
May Lord Christ enter in?
1898 The Ballad of Reading Gaol, pt.5, stanza 14.

60 I am dying, as I have lived, beyond my means.
1900 Accepting a glass of champagne shortly before his death. Attributed.

61 Either that wallpaper goes or I do.
1900 As he lay dying in a Paris hotel bedroom. Attributed.

62 Football is all very well as a game for rough girls, but it is hardly suitable for delicate boys.
Quoted in Alvin Redman The Epigrams of Oscar Wilde (1952).

63 The only possible form of exercise is to talk, not to walk.
Quoted in Alvin Redman The Epigrams of Oscar Wilde (1952).

64 Mr Bernard Shaw has no enemies, but is intensely disliked by all his friends.
Quoted in W B Yeats Autobiographies (1955).

65 It requires one to assume such indecent postures.
His reason for not playing cricket. Quoted in Bloomsbury Thematic Dictionary of Quotations (1988).

66 Work is the curse of the drinking classes.
Attributed.

67 Henry James wrote fiction as if it were a painful duty.
Attributed.

68 The three women I have admired most are Queen Victoria, Sarah Bernhardt and Lillie Langtry. I would have married any one of them with pleasure.
Attributed.

Wilder, Billy (Samuel) 1906–2002

Austrian-born writer and director who moved to Hollywood in 1934. He won Academy Awards for *The Lost Weekend* (1945), *Sunset Boulevard* (1950) and *The Apartment* (1960). Other successes include *Double Indemnity* (1944), *The Seven Year Itch* (1955) and *Some Like It Hot* (1959).

69 Johnny, keep it out of focus. I want to win the foreign picture award.
1950 Remark to cameraman John Seitz during the making of Sunset Boulevard.

70 Making a picture with Marilyn Monroe was like going to the dentist. It was hell at the time, but after it was all over it was wonderful.
Quoted in Doug McClelland Star Speak (1987).

71 No one ever leaves a star.
1950 Sunset Boulevard.

72 Fasten your cigarettes.
1972 Avanti (with I A L Diamond).

73 I don't object to foreigners speaking a foreign language; I just wish they'd all speak the same foreign language.
1972 Avanti (with I A L Diamond).

74 Hindsight is always twenty-twenty.
Attributed.

Wilder, Thornton Niven 1897–1975

US playwright and novelist. His most successful plays included *Our Town* (1938) and *The Skin of Our Teeth* (1942), while his other writings included the novel *The Bridge of San Luis Rey* (1927). His play *The Matchmaker* (1954) provided the basis for the hit musical *Hello, Dolly!*

75 From what human ill does not dawn seem to be an alleviation.
1927 The Bridge of San Luis Rey, ch.3.

76 Most everybody in the world climbs into their graves married.
1938 Our Town, act 2.

77 Marriage is a bribe to make a housekeeper think she's a householder.
1939 The Merchant of Yonkers, act 1.

78 The fights are the best part of married life. The rest is merely so-so.
1939 The Merchant of Yonkers, act 2.

79 My advice to you is not to inquire why or whither, but just enjoy your ice-cream while it's on your plate,—that's my philosophy.
1942 The Skin of Our Teeth, act 1.

80 When you're at war you think about a better life; when you're at peace you think about a more comfortable one.
1942 The Skin of Our Teeth, act 1.

81 We'll trot down to the movies and see how girls with wax faces live.
1942 The Skin of Our Teeth, act 3.

82 I've never forgotten for long at a time that living is a struggle. I know that every good and excellent thing in the world stands moment by moment on the razor-edge of danger and must be fought for—whether it's a field, or a home, or a country.
1942 *The Skin of Our Teeth*, act 3.

83 Literature is the orchestration of platitudes.
1953 In *Time*, 12 Jan.

84 A living is made, Mr Kemper, by selling something that everybody needs at least once a year. Yes, sir! And a million is made by producing something that everybody needs every day. You artists produce something that nobody needs at any time.
1954 *The Matchmaker*, act 1.

85 Ninety-nine percent of the people in the world are fools, and the rest of us are in great danger of contagion.
1954 *The Matchmaker*, act 1.

86 Never support two weaknesses at the same time. It's your combination sinners—your lecherous liars and your miserly drunkards—who dishonour the vices and bring them into bad repute.
1954 *The Matchmaker*, act 3.

87 But there comes a time in everybody's life when he must decide whether he'll live among human beings or not—a fool among fools or a fool alone.
1954 *The Matchmaker*, act 4.

88 I am not interested in the ephemeral—such subjects as the adulteries of dentists. I am interested in those things that repeat and repeat in the lives of the millions.
1961 In the *New York Times*, 6 Mar.

89 The less seen, the more heard. The eye is the enemy of the ear in real drama.
1961 In the *New York Times*, 6 Nov.

90 The process of learning is accompanied by alternations of pain and brief quickenings that resemble pain.
1967 *The Eighth Day*.

Wilding, Michael 1912–79

English actor. He is usually remembered for his performances in such films as *Piccadilly Incident* (1946) and *Spring in Park Lane* (1948).

91 You can pick out actors by the glazed look that comes into their eyes when the conversation wanders away from themselves.
Attributed.

Wilhelm II, Kaiser 1859–1941

Kaiser and King of Prussia 1888–1918. Dismissed Bismarck in 1890, beginning a long period of personal rule. Although his bellicosity contributed to the origins of World War I, he became a figurehead during the course of it. He abdicated at the end of the war and settled in the Netherlands.

92 We have…fought for our place in the sun and have won it. It will be my business to see that we retain this place in the sun unchallenged.
1901 Speech in Hamburg, 18 Jun. Quoted in *The Times*, 20 Jun.

93 You will be home before the leaves have fallen from the trees.
1914 Address to German troops leaving for the Front, Aug.

94 We draw the sword with a clean conscience and with clean hands.
1914 Address from the throne, Berlin, 4 Aug.

95 The machine is running away with him as it ran away with me.
1939 Of Adolf Hitler at the start of World War II, said to Sir Robert Bruce-Lockhart, 27 Aug.

Wilkinson, Anne 1910–61

Canadian poet. One of the founders of the important literary magazine, *The Tamarack Review*, she published poetry (*Counterpoint to Sleep*, 1951, and *The Hangman Ties the Holly*, 1955), a family history (*Lions in the Way*, 1956) and a children's book. Her collected poems were published in 1968.

96 Fabulous the insects
Stud the air
Or walk on running water,
Klee-drawn saints
And bright as angels are.
1955 *The Hangman Ties the Holly*, 'In June and Gentle Oven'.

97 Our hearts, unrisen, yield a heavy bread.
1955 *The Hangman Ties the Holly*, 'Topsoil to the Wind'.

Wilkinson, Jonny 1979–

English rugby player, member of the successful England Rugby World Cup team (2003).

98 The first game I ever played I scored a goal from the halfway line. Didn't have a clue what I was doing. Ball just came to me, so I whacked it.
2002 On his childhood attempts to play football. Quoted in *The Guardian*, 28 Jan.

99 I play with the fear of letting people down. That's what motivates me.
2004 Quoted on www.bbc.co.uk.

Will, George

1 What the federal government does basically is borrow money from people and mail it to people.
1993 Of entitlement programs. ABC TV broadcast, 19 Sep.

William of Poitiers 11c.

French chronicler of the life of William the Conqueror.

2 A strange manner of battle, where one side works by constant motion and ceaseless charges, while the other can but endure passively as it stands fixed to the sod. The Norman arrow and sword worked on: in the English ranks the only movement was the dropping of the dead: the living stood motionless.
c.1071 Of the Battle of Hastings, 14 Oct 1066. *Gesta Guillelmi ducis Normannorum et regis Anglorum* (edited by R Foreville, 1952).

William of Wykeham 1324–1404

Bishop of Winchester and Chancellor of England.

3 Manners makyth man.
Proverb common from the 14th century and said to be Wykeham's motto.

William III *also called William of Orange* 1650–1702

Dutch-born King of Great Britain (1689–1702), and Stadholder of the United Provinces (1672–1702). Husband of Mary, daughter of James II, he was invited by Protestant elements to assume the throne in the Glorious Revolution of 1688.

4 People in Parliament occupy themselves with private animosities and petty quarrels, and think little of the national interest. It is impossible to credit the serene indifference with which they consider events outside their own country.
1699 Letter, Jan.

5 The eyes of all England are on this Parliament. If you do in good earnest wish to see England hold the balance of Europe and to be indeed at the head of the Protestant interest, it will appear by your right improving the present opportunity.
1701 At the State Opening of Parliament, Dec.

6 Every bullet has its billet.
Quoted by John Wesley, journal entry, 6 Jun 1765.

Williams, (Hiram) Hank 1923–53

US country singer, the 'Father of Country Music'. His hits include 'Lovesick Blues', 'Hey, Good Lookin'', 'Jambalaya' and 'Your Cheatin' Heart'. His death was the result of alcoholism and drug abuse.

7 You got to have smelt a lot of mule manure before you can sing like a hillbilly.
Quoted in *Rolling Stone*, 1969.

Williams, Harry Abbott 1919–

English cleric and scholar, a member of the Anglican Community of the Resurrection. In his theological writings he combines theology with insights from psychology.

8 The prelude to resurrection as we experience it in this life is always powerlessness. We cannot raise ourselves by our own bootstrings.
1972 *The True Resurrection*.

Williams, Raymond 1921–88

Welsh critic and novelist. He is best known for his works mixing socio-cultural and literary criticism, including *The Long Revolution* (1966) and *The Country and the City* (1973).

9 The human crisis is always a crisis of understanding: what we genuinely understand we can do.
1958 *Culture and Society*, ch.3.

10 When art communicates, a human experience is actively offered and actively received. Below this activity threshold there can be no art.
1966 *The Long Revolution*, pt.1, ch.1.

Williams, Robin 1952–

US comedian and film actor. He starred in the TV series *Mork and Mindy* (1970s) and in such films as *The World According to Garp* (1982), *Good Morning, Vietnam* (1987), *Dead Poets Society* (1989), *The Fisher King* (1991), *Mrs Doubtfire* (1993), *The Birdcage* (1995) and *Good Will Hunting* (1997).

11 I thought lacrosse was what you find in la church.
1982 Interview in *Playboy*.

12 Cricket is baseball on valium.
Quoted in Colin Jarman *The Guinness Dictionary of Sports Quotations* (1990).

Williams, Shirley Vivien Teresa Brittain Williams, Baroness 1930–

English politician, a Labour MP from 1964. She lost her seat in 1979, co-founded the Social Democratic Party in 1981 and became its first elected MP. She lost her seat in 1983 but remained as SDP President (1982–8), and supported the merger with the Liberal Party in 1988. A professor at Harvard University, she remains active in British politics.

13 The British Civil Service…is a beautifully designed and effective braking mechanism.
1980 Speech at the Royal Institute of Public Administration, 11 Feb.

Williams, Tennessee Thomas Lanier 1911–83

US playwright. He won recognition as a leading contemporary writer with his play *The Glass Menagerie* (1945), which was followed by such intense, atmospheric and often brutal dramas as *A Streetcar Named Desire* (1947), *The Rose Tattoo* (1951), *Cat On A Hot Tin Roof* (1955), *Suddenly Last Summer* (1958) and *The Night of the Iguana* (1962).

14 In memory everything seems to happen to music.
1945 Tom. *The Glass Menagerie*, sc.1.

15 I didn't go to the moon, I went much further—for time is the longest distance between two places.
1945 Tom. *The Glass Menagerie*, sc.7.

16 I can't stand a naked light bulb, any more than I can a rude remark or a vulgar action.
1947 Blanche. *A Streetcar Named Desire*, sc.3

17 I have always depended on the kindness of strangers.
1947 Blanche. *A Streetcar Named Desire*, sc.11.

18 The only thing worse than a liar is a liar that's also a hypocrite!
1951 Rosa. *The Rose Tattoo*, act 3.

19 It is a terrible thing for an old woman to outlive her dogs.
1953 *Camino Real*, prologue.

20 Caged birds accept each other but flight is what they long for.
1953 Marguerite. *Camino Real*, block 7.

21 Bohemia has no banner. It survives by discretion.
1953 Marguerite. *Camino Real*, block 7.

22 We have to distrust each other. It's our only defence against betrayal.
1953 Marguerite. *Camino Real*, block 10.

23 We're all of us guinea pigs in the laboratory of God. Humanity is just a work in progress.
1953 The Gipsy. *Camino Real*, block 12.

24 Some mystery should be left in the revelation of character in a play, just as a great deal of mystery is always left in the revelation of character in life, even in one's own character to himself.
1955 *Cat on a Hot Tin Roof*, stage direction.

25 What is the victory of a cat on a hot tin roof?—I wish I knew… Just staying on it, I guess, for as long as she can.
1955 Maggie. *Cat on a Hot Tin Roof*, act 1.

26 You can be young without money but you can't be old without it.
1955 Maggie. *Cat on a Hot Tin Roof*, act 1.

27 A drinking man's someone who wants to forget he isn't still young an' believing.
1955 *Cat on a Hot Tin Roof*, act 2.

28 BRICK: Well, they say nature hates a vacuum, Big Daddy.

BIG DADDY: That's what they say, but sometimes I think that a vacuum is a hell of a lot better than some of the stuff that nature replaces it with.

1955 *Cat on a Hot Tin Roof*, act 2.

29 Mendacity is a system that we live in. Liquor is one way out an' death's the other.

1955 Brick. *Cat on a Hot Tin Roof*, act 2.

30 At the age of 14 I discovered writing as an escape from…being called a sissy by the neighborhood kids, and Miss Nancy by my father.

1957 In the *New York Times*, 17 Mar.

31 The world is a funny paper read backwards. And that way it isn't so funny.

1957 In the *Observer*, 7 Apr.

32 Don't look forward to the day you stop suffering, because when it comes you'll *know* you're dead.

1958 In the *Observer*, 26 Jan.

33 We're all of us sentenced to solitary confinement inside our own skins, for life!

1958 Val. *Orpheus Descending*, act 2, sc.1.

34 It haunts me, the passage of time. I think time is a merciless thing. I think life is a process of burning oneself out and time is the fire that burns you. But I think the spirit of man is a good adversary.

1958 In the *New York Post*, 30 Apr.

35 He was meddling too much in my private life.

1961 Explaining why he had dispensed with the services of his psychoanalyst. Attributed.

36 All cruel people describe themselves as paragons of frankness!

1963 Mrs Goforth. *The Milk Train Doesn't Stop Here Anymore*, sc.1.

37 Life is all memory except for the one present moment that goes by you so quick you hardly catch it going.

1963 Mrs Goforth. *The Milk Train Doesn't Stop Here Anymore*, sc.3

38 We all live in a house on fire, no fire department to call; no way out, just the upstairs window to look out of while the fire burns the house down with us trapped, locked in it.

1963 Chris. *The Milk Train Doesn't Stop Here Anymore*, sc.6.

Williams, Venus 1980–

US tennis player. Her first Grand Slam singles victory came in 2000 when she won the Wimbledon title. As well as other singles titles, she has won numerous doubles titles with her sister Serena.

39 I guess there's always going to be jobs that pay more than others, and I suppose I have one of those.

2002 In the *Observer*, 9 Jun.

Williams, William Carlos 1883–1963

US poet, a paediatrician as well as a writer. His poetry and objectivist aesthetic made him a major Modernist figure. He also wrote novels, stories, plays, literary and cultural essays and memoirs.

40 I will teach you my townspeople
how to perform a funeral
for you have it over a troop
of artists—

unless one should scour the world—
you have the ground sense necessary.

1917 *Al Que Quiere!*, 'Tract'.

41 Covertly the hands of a great clock
go round and round! Were they to
move quickly and at once the whole
secret would be out and the shuffling
of all ants be done forever.

1921 *Sour Grapes*, 'Overture to a Dance of Locomotives'.

42 Lifeless in appearance, sluggish
dazed spring approaches—

They enter the new world naked,
cold, uncertain of all
save that they enter.

1923 *Spring and All*, 'Spring and All'.

43 One by one the objects are defined—
It quickens: clarity, outline of leaf

But now the stark dignity of
entrance—Still, the profound change
has come upon them: rooted, they
grip down and begin to awaken.

1923 *Spring and All*, 'Spring and All'.

44 so much depends
upon

a red wheel
barrow

glazed with rain
water

beside the white
chickens.

1923 *Spring and All*, 'The Red Wheelbarrow'.

45 —through metaphor to reconcile
the people and the stones.

1944 *The Wedge*, 'A Sort of Song'.

46 Is it any better in Heaven, my friend Ford,
Than you found it in Provence?

1944 *The Wedge*, 'To Ford Madox Ford in Heaven'.

47 To make a start,
out of particulars
and make them general, rolling
up the sum, by defective means—
Sniffing the trees, just another dog
among a lot of dogs. What
else is there? And to do?

1946 *Paterson*, bk.1, preface.

48 For the beginning is assuredly
the end—since we know nothing, pure
and simple, beyond
our own complexities.

1946 *Paterson*, bk.1, preface.

49 Minds like beds always made up
(more stony than a shore)
unwilling or unable.

1946 *Paterson*, bk.1, preface.

50 Say it, no ideas but in things.

1946 *Paterson*, bk.1, 'The Delineaments of the Giants', 1.

51 Divorce is
the sign of knowledge in our time.
1946 Paterson, bk.1, 'The Delineaments of the Giants', 2.

52 Without invention nothing is well-spaced.
1948 Paterson, bk.2, 'Sunday in the Park', 1.

53 Unless there is
a new mind there cannot be a new
line, the old will go on
repeating itself with recurring
deadliness:
1948 Paterson, bk.2, 'Sunday in the Park', 1.

54 Beyond the gap where the river
plunges into the narrow gorge, unseen

—and the imagination soars, as a voice
beckons, a thundrous voice, endless
—as sleep: the voice
that has ineluctably called them—
that unmoving roar!
1948 Paterson, bk.2, 'Sunday in the Park', 1.

55 For what we cannot accomplish, what
is denied to love,
what we have lost in the anticipation—
a descent follows,
endless and indestructible.
1948 Paterson, bk.2, 'Sunday in the Park', 1.

56 For there is a wind or a ghost of wind
in all books echoing the life
there, a high wind that fills the tubes
of the ear until we think we hear a wind,
actual.
1949 Paterson, bk.3, 'The Library'.

57 and there grows in the mind
a scent, it may be, of locust blossoms
whose perfume is itself a wind moving
to lead the mind away.
1949 Paterson, bk.3, 'The Library'.

58 It isn't what he says that counts as a work of art, it's what
he makes with such intensity of perception that it lives
with an intrinsic movement of its very own to verify the
authenticity.
Of the poet. Quoted by Richard Eberhart in the *New York Times*,
17 Dec 1950.

59 I have never been one to write by rule, not even by my
own rules.
1954 Letter to Richard Eberhart, 23 May.

60 Love is that common tone
shall raise his fiery head
and sound his note.
1954 The Desert Music, 'The Orchestra'.

61 All writing is a disease. You can't stop it.
Quoted in *Newsweek*, 7 Jan 1957.

62 Nothing whips my blood like verse.
Quoted in John Thirlwall (ed) *The Selected Letters of William
Carlos Williams* (1957).

63 Though he is approaching death he is possessed by
many poems.
1958 Paterson, bk.5.

64 Anything is good material for poetry. Anything.
1958 Paterson, bk.5.

Williamson, Roy 1937–90

Scottish folksinger and musician, a partner in the Corries with
Ronnie Browne from 1961, and composer of 'Flower of Scotland',
adopted by many as an unofficial Scottish national anthem.

65 O flower of Scotland, when will we see your like again,
That fought and died for your wee bit hill and glen
And stood against him, proud Edward's army,
And sent him homeward tae think again.
1968 'Flower of Scotland', stanza 1.

Willis, Bruce 1955–

US actor. He has appeared in a number of action-man roles in
such films as *Die Hard* (1988) and its sequels, as well as taking
character parts.

66 Frankly, reviews are mostly for people who still read. Like
most of the written word, it is going the way of the
dinosaur.
1997 In *Time*, 19 May.

Willkie, Wendell Lewis 1892–1944

US politician, Republican candidate for the presidency (1940).

67 Any man who is not something of a Socialist before he is
forty has no heart. Any man who is still a Socialist after he
is forty has no head.
Quoted in Richard Norton Smith *Thomas E. Dewey and his Times*
(1982), p.294.
➤ *See* Twain 872:35.

Wilmer, Val(erie) 1941–

English writer and photographer. Her books on jazz include
Jazz People (1970), *As Serious As Your Life* (1977) and the
autobiographical *Mama Said There'd Be Days Like This* (1989).

68 A rather bitter British musician once remarked sourly to a
friend of mine: 'Oh, all *she* knows about music she
learned in bed with musicians.' To that, I can only add,
what better place to learn?
1989 Mama Said There'd Be Days Like This, ch.3.

Wilson, A(ndrew) N(orman) 1950–

English writer. He has written novels, criticism, journalism and
biography, including the controversial *Jesus* (1992).

69 It had never occurred to Giles that there was something
perfectly sensible about wanting to hold onto
innocence. He had always gone in for the idea that since
we only pass this way once, *experience* counts for
everything.
1982 Wise Virgins, ch.6.

70 Religion is the tragedy of mankind… But I do know, from
the inside as well as from personal observation, that
religion appeals to something deep and irrational and
strong within us, and that is what makes it so dangerous.
1991 Against Religion, no.19.

71 I should prefer to have a politician who regularly went to
a massage parlour than one who promised a laptop
computer for every teacher.
1999 In the *Observer*, 21 Mar.

Wilson, Sir Angus Frank Johnstone 1931–91

English writer. He wrote literary criticism, short stories and a
play, but was best known for his novels including *Anglo-Saxon*

Attitudes (1956) and *The Old Men in the Zoo* (1961).

72 'God knows how you Protestants can be expected to have any sense of direction,' she said. 'It's different with us, I haven't been to mass for years, I've got every mortal sin on my conscience, but I know when I'm doing wrong. I'm still a Catholic, it's there, nothing can take it away from me.' 'Of course, duckie,' said Jeremy…'once a Catholic always a Catholic.'
1949 *The Wrong Set*, 'Significant Experience'.

73 She was more than ever proud of the position of the bungalow, so almost in the country.
1957 'A Flat Country Christmas'.

74 All fiction is for me a kind of magic and trickery—a confidence trick, trying to make people believe something is true that isn't.
1957 In *The Paris Review*, no.17.

75 The impulse to write a novel comes from a momentary unified vision of life.
1963 *The Wild Garden*.

76 I have no concern for the common man except that he should not be so common.
1967 *No Laughing Matter*.

77 My theme is always *humanistic*. Life today is junglelike…it is complex, it is inhuman in its materialism.
1972 Letter to David Farrer, his publisher, Jul. Quoted in Margaret Drabble *Angus Wilson—A Biography* (1995).

78 All are deceptions, substitutes for the hard job of using reason and industry and intuition and compassion to solve even a little bit of the muddle with humaneness and awe for the natural world and the complexity of human beings.
1972 Letter to David Farrer, his publisher, Jul. Quoted in Margaret Drabble *Angus Wilson—A Biography* (1995).

79 People are able to live with only half a heart, to live without real compassion, because they are able to use words that are only forms.
1972 Interview in *Iowa Review*, no.3, Fall.

80 The novelist must be his own most harsh critic and also his own most loving admirer—and about both he must say nothing.
1976 Author's comment in D L Kirkpatrick (ed) *Contemporary Novelists*.

Wilson, Charles *called 'Engine Charlie'* 1890–1961

President of General Motors and Secretary of Defense. He was nicknamed 'Engine Charlie' to distinguish him from 'Electric Charlie' Wilson, president of General Electric.

81 For years I thought what was good for our country was good for General Motors, and vice versa. The difference did not exist. Our company is too big. It goes with the welfare of the country.
1953 Statement to US Senate, Committee on Armed Services, Jan.

Wilson, David Gordon

English-born US mechanical engineer and bicycling enthusiast.

82 You must invent because you enjoy it.
2004 On making his first recumbent bicycle in 1955.

Wilson, Edmund 1895–1972

US literary critic, social commentator, and novelist. Although his own fiction, plays and poems are now little read, he was an influential critic with a wide-ranging perspective on art, history and society.

83 In a sense, one can never read the book that the author originally wrote, and one can never read the same book twice.
1938 *The Triple Thinkers*, introduction.

84 Of all the great Victorian writers, he was probably the most antagonistic to the Victorian age itself.
1941 Of Dickens. *The Wound and the Bow*, 'Dickens: The Two Scrooges'.

Wilson, Edward O(sborne) 1929–

US biologist, Professor of Entomology at Harvard University. His works include *Insect Societies* (1971), *Sociobiology: The New Synthesis* (1975) and *Biophilia* (1984).

85 It came by a lightning flash like knowledge from the gods.
1975 On the 1953 discovery of the DNA molecule. *Sociobiology*.

86 Important science is not just any similarity glimpsed for the first time. It offers analogies that map the gateways to unexplored terrain.
1984 *Biophilia*.

87 To a considerable degree science consists in originating the maximum amount of information with the minimum expenditure of energy.
1984 *Biophilia*.

Wilson, Ernest 1876–1930

English plant hunter.

88 Smoke That Thunders.
1927 Book title, referring to Victoria Falls.

Wilson of Rievaulx, (James) Harold Wilson, Baron 1916–95

English Labour politician and Prime Minister (1964–70, 1974–6). A renowned debater, his economic plans were hampered by a balance of payments crisis. He faced too the problems of Rhodesian independence, opposition to Britain's proposed entry into the Common Market, and conflict within the Party. After a third general election victory, he resigned in 1976.

89 The school that I went to in the north was a school where more than half the children in my class never had any boots or shoes to their feet. They wore clogs, because they lasted longer than shoes of comparable price.
1948 Speech, Birmingham, 28 Jul.
➤ *See Bulmer-Thomas 166:55*.

90 All the little gnomes in Zurich and other finance centres.
1956 Speech, House of Commons, 12 Nov.

91 Every time that Mr Macmillan comes back from abroad, Mr Butler goes to the airport and grips him warmly by the throat.
1957 Attributed.

92 We are redefining and restating our socialism in terms of the scientific revolution… The Britain that will be forged in the white heat of this revolution will be no place for restrictive practices or outdated methods on either side of industry.

1963 Labour Party Conference, 1 Oct. His phrase has since been memorably rendered as 'the white heat of the technological revolution'.

93 The Labour Party is a moral crusade, or it is nothing.
1964 Scottish Labour Party conference, 5 Sep.

94 A week is a long time in politics.
1964 Comment to lobby correspondents, Oct. As such meetings are off the record, there is no exact source for this famous phrase.

95 Given a fair wind, we will negotiate our way into the Common Market, head held high, not crawl in… Negotiations? Yes. Unconditional acceptance of whatever terms we are offered? No.
1966 Speech, Bristol, 20 Mar.

96 In a recent interview, I was asked what, above all, I associated with socialism in this modern age. I answered that if there was one word I would use to identify modern socialism, it was 'Science'.
1967 Speech, 17 Jun.

97 From now on the pound abroad is worth 14 per cent or so less in terms of other currencies. That does not mean, of course, that the pound here in Britain—in your pocket or purse, or in your bank—has been devalued.
1967 National broadcast, 19 Nov. The speech gave rise to the well-known phrase, 'the pound in your pocket'.

98 We are creating a Britain of which we can be proud, and the world knows it. The world's tourists are coming here in their millions…because the new Britain is exciting. Yes, Britain with a Labour Government is an exciting place.
1969 Speech, Labour Party Conference, 30 Sep.

99 One man's wage rise is another man's price increase.
1970 In the *Observer*, 11 Jan.

1 Have you ever noticed how we only win the World Cup under a Labour government?
1971 Quoted in Peter Ball and Phil Shaw *The Book of Football Quotations* (1989).

2 The greatest asset that a head of state can have is the ability to get a good night's sleep.
1975 BBC Radio 4 broadcast, 16 Apr.

3 The party must protect itself against the activities of small groups of inflexible political persuasion…having in common only their arrogant dogmatism… I have no wish to lead a party of political zombies.
1975 Labour Party Conference, 30 Sep.

4 The main essentials of a successful Prime Minister are sleep and a sense of history.
1976 *The Governance of Britain*.

5 A constant effort to keep a party together, without sacrificing either principle or the essentials of basic strategy, is the very stuff of political leadership. Macmillan was canonized for it.
1979 *Final Term: The Labour Government 1974–76*.

Wilson, Michael 1937–

Canadian Minister of Finance in the 1980s.

6 No matter how we define the term, Canada has an acute shortage of rich people.
1985 Giving one reason why taxing the wealthy would not ensure the continuation of Canada's social programs, at the Canadian Economics Association, Montreal, 30 May.

Wilson, (Thomas) Woodrow 1856–1924

US statesman and 28th President (1913–21). He was twice elected Democratic President. His administration was chiefly remembered for Prohibition, woman's suffrage, US entry into World War I, and his championing of the League of Nations. He was awarded the Nobel peace prize (1919).

7 The feelings with which we face this new age of right and opportunity sweep across our heartstrings like some air out of God's own presence, where justice and mercy are reconciled, and the judge and the brother are one.
1913 Inaugural address, 4 Mar.

8 Human rights, national integrity, and opportunity as against material interests…are the issues that we now must face. I take this occasion to say that the United States will never again seek one additional foot of territory by conquest.
1913 Speech, Alabama, 27 Oct.

9 The people of the United States are drawn from many nations, and chiefly from the nations now at war. Some will wish one nation, others another, to succeed in this monumental struggle. I venture to speak a solemn word of warning. The United States must be neutral in fact as well as in name during these days that are to try men's souls. We must be impartial in thought as well as in action.
1914 Message to the Senate, 19 Aug.

10 There is such a thing as a man being too proud to fight; there is such a thing as a nation being so right that it does not need to convince others by force that it is right.
1915 Speech in Philadelphia, 10 May.

11 We are constantly thinking of the great war…which saved the Union…but it was a war which did a great deal more than that. It created in this country what had never existed before—a national consciousness.
1915 Memorial Day Address at Arlington National Cemetery, Virginia, 31 May.

12 America cannot be an ostrich, with its head in the sand.
1916 Speech, New Mexico, 1 Feb.

13 Nations should with one accord adopt the doctrine of President Monroe as the doctrine of the world; that every people should be left free to determine its own policy, its own way of development, unhindered, unthreatened, unafraid—the little along with the great and powerful. Those are American principles, American policies. We could stand for no others. They are also the principles of mankind, and must prevail.
1917 Speech to the Senate, 22 Jan.

14 Armed neutrality is ineffectual enough at best.
1917 Speech before a joint session of Congress, 2 Apr, to request a declaration that a state of war exists between Germany and the US.

15 The world must be made safe for democracy. Its peace must be planted on the tested foundations of political liberty.
1917 Speech before a joint session of Congress, 2 Apr, to request a declaration that a state of war exists between Germany and the US.

16 It is not an army that we must train for war; it is a nation.
1917 Speech, Washington, 12 May.

17 In this war, we demand nothing that is peculiar to ourselves; only that the world be made fit and safe to live

in. The programme of the world's peace, therefore, is our programme.
1918 The 'Fourteen Points' speech to Congress, 8 Jan.

18 People and provinces must not be bartered about from sovereign to sovereign as if they were chattels, or pawns in a game. Self-determination is not a mere phrase. It is an imperative principle, which statesmen will henceforth ignore at their peril.
1918 Address to Congress, 11 Feb.

19 People call me an idealist. That is how I know that I am an American. America is the only idealistic nation in the world.
1919 Speech, Sioux Falls, 8 Sep.

Wimperis, Arthur 1874–1953

British screenwriter. He provided the screenplays for such movies as *The Private Life of Henry VIII* (1932) and *Mrs Miniver* (1942).

20 My dear fellow, a unique evening! I wouldn't have left a turn unstoned.
After watching a vaudeville show. Quoted in E Short *Fifty Years of Vaudeville* (1946).

Winchell, Walter 1897–1972

US theatre critic and actor. His publications included *Broadway Thro'a Keyhole* (1933).

21 A newspaperman, whose sweetheart ran away with an actor.
Defining a drama critic. Attributed.

Winfrey, Oprah 1954–

US actress, talk-show host and businesswoman. She was the first woman to own and produce her own talk show and the first African-American to own a large television studio.

22 I am a product of every other black woman before me who has done or said anything worthwhile. Recognizing that I am part of history is what allows me to soar.
Quoted in Brian Lanker *I Dream a World: Portraits of Black Women Who Changed America* (1989).

Winkworth, Catherine 1827–78

English hymn writer and translator.

23 Now thank we all our God,
With heart and hands and voices,
Who wondrous things hath done,
In whom his world rejoices;
Who from our mother's arms
Hath blessed us on our way
With countless gifts of love,
And still is ours to-day.
1858 *Lyra Germanica* (translated from the original German of Martin Rinkart 'Nun danket alle Gott', c.1636).

Winner, Langdon

US academic and social critic with an interest in issues relating to technology and society.

24 The map of the world shows no country called Technopolis, yet in many ways we are already its citizens.
1986 *The Whale and the Reactor.*

Winner, Michael 1935–

British director. Credits include *Chato's Land* (1972), *Death Wish* (1974) and *The Wicked Lady* (1983).

25 Who says that actors are cattle? Show me a cow who can earn a million dollars a film.
Quoted by David Lewin in *Cinema Today*, 1 Jul 1970.

26 Keeping awake for ten weeks at a stretch.
1970 When asked what is the hardest part of directing. John Player Lecture, London, Sep.

27 A writer of talent needs only a typewriter and paper, a painter only needs brushes, canvas and paint, but I need a million dollars or more to be in business. That's a hell of a business to be in.
1974 In the *Observer Magazine*, 7 Jul.

28 I don't go to restaurants, I go to tables.
2004 In the *Observer*, 25 Jan.

29 A team effort is a lot of people doing what I say.
Attributed.

Winterson, Jeanette 1959–

English novelist. Her autobiographical first novel, *Oranges Are Not the Only Fruit* (1985), described her upbringing as an Evangelical Pentecostalist and her subsequent realization of her homosexuality. Subsequent novels include *Sexing the Cherry* (1989), *Written on the Body* (1992), *Art and Lies* (1994) and *The. PowerBook* (2000).

30 I asked why he was a priest and he said that if you have to work for anybody an absentee boss is best.
1987 *The Passion*, ch.1.

31 Adults talk about being happy because largely they are not.
1987 *The Passion*, ch.1.

32 I call him Jordan and it will do. He has no other name before or after. What was there to call him, fished as he was from the stinking Thames? A child can't be called Thames, no and not Nile either, for all his likeness to Moses. But I wanted to give him a river name, a name not bound to anything, just as the waters aren't bound to anything.
1989 *Sexing the Cherry.*

33 I have met a great many people on their way towards God and I wonder why they have chosen to look for him rather than themselves.
1989 *Sexing the Cherry.*

34 I don't hate men, I just wish they'd try harder. They all want to be heroes and all we want is for them to stay at home and help with the housework and the kids. That's not the kind of heroism they enjoy.
1989 *Sexing the Cherry.*

35 When I was born, my father wanted to drown me, but my mother persuaded him to let me live in disguise, to see if I could bring any wealth to the household.
2000 *The. PowerBook.*

36 In this life you have to be your own hero.
2000 *The. PowerBook.*

Wisdom, Norman 1915–

English comedian, born in London. He made his stage debut in 1946 and his first film appearance in *Trouble in Store* (1953). This was followed by a string of successes including *Man of the Moment* (1955), *Just My Luck* (1958) and *Follow a Star* (1959).

37 They don't seem to realize that I have grown up and can get laughs without falling downstairs.
1991 Quoted in Richard Dacre *Trouble in Store: Norman Wisdom, a Career in Comedy* (1991).

Witte, Sergei Yulevich 1849–1915

Russian politician. As Minister of Finance (1892) he encouraged capitalism and industrialization, making Russia a leading industrial power. He became first Prime Minister (1905–6) in the Revolution of 1905, but was unable to satisfy either conservatives or liberals.

38 The world is in flames today for a cause that interests Russia first and foremost; a cause that is essentially the cause of the Slavs, and which is of no concern to France or to England.
1914 Said to the French Ambassador, 10 Sep.

Wittgenstein, Ludwig Josef Johann 1889–1951

Austrian-born British philosopher who became one of the most influential and charismatic figures in British philosophy in this century. He was Professor of Philosophy at Cambridge (1939–47), and published only one book in his lifetime, the *Tractatus Logico-Philosophicus* (1921). Of his many posthumous publications, by far the most important is the *Philosophical Investigations* (1953).

39 *Was sich überhaupt sagen lässt, lässt sich klar sagen; und wovon man nicht reden kann, darüber muss man schweigen.*
What can be said at all can be said clearly; and whereof one cannot speak thereof one must be silent.
1921 *Tractatus Logico-Philosophicus*, preface (translated by Frank Ramsey).

40 *Die Welt ist alles, was der Fall ist.*
The world is all that is the case.
1921 *Tractatus Logico-Philosophicus*, prop.1 (translated by Pears and McGuinness).

41 *Die Welt ist die Gesamtheit der Tatsachen, nicht der Dinge.*
The world is the totality of facts, not of things.
1921 *Tractatus Logico-Philosophicus*, prop.1.1 (translated by Pears and McGuinness).

42 *Der Tod ist kein Ereignis des Lebens. Den Tod erlebt man nicht.*
Death is not an event in life: we do not live to experience death.
1921 *Tractatus Logico-Philosophicus*, prop 6.4311 (translated by Pears and McGuinness).

43 *Die Probleme werden gelöst, nicht durch Beibringen neuer Erfahrung, sondern durch Zusammenstellung des längst Bekannten. Die Philosophie ist ein Kampf gegen die Verhexung unseres Verstandes durch die Mittel unserer Sprache.*
The problems are solved, not by giving new information, but by arranging what we have always known. Philosophy is a battle against the bewitchment of our intelligence by means of language.
1945 *Philosophische Untersuchungen* (*Philosophical Investigations*), section 109 (translated by G E M Anscombe).

44 *Ein philosophisches Problem hat die Form: 'Ich kenne mich nicht aus'.*

A philosophical problem has the form: 'I don't know my way about'.
1945 *Philosophische Untersuchungen* (*Philosophical Investigations*), section 123 (translated by G E M Anscombe).

45 *Der Philosoph behandelt eine Frage wie eine Krankheit.*
The philosopher's treatment of a question is like the treatment of an illness.
1945 *Philosophische Untersuchungen* (*Philosophical Investigations*), section 255 (translated by G E M Anscombe).

46 *Was ist dein Ziel in der Philosophie?—'Der Fliege den Ausweg aus dem Fliegenglas zeigen'.*
What is your aim in philosophy?—To show the fly the way out of the fly-bottle.
1945 *Philosophische Untersuchungen* (*Philosophical Investigations*), section 309 (translated by G E M Anscombe).

47 *Ein 'innerer Vorgang' bedarf äußerer Kriterien.*
An 'inner process' stands in need of outward criteria.
1945 *Philosophische Untersuchungen* (*Philosophical Investigations*), section 580 (translated by G E M Anscombe).

48 *Wenn ein Löwe sprechen könnte, wir könnten ihn nicht verstehen.*
If a lion could talk, we could not understand him.
1945 *Philosophische Untersuchungen* (*Philosophical Investigations*), pt.2, section 11 (translated by G E M Anscombe).

Wittig, Monique 1935–2003

French feminist novelist who questioned traditional gender stereotypes in her writing.

49 *L'expérience…d'une femme écrivain est complètement schizophrénique. Il faut toujours faire coupure entre les deux: d'une part, employer un langage qui n'est pas le nôtre…et la lutte qu'on mène sur un autre plan, qui tend à casser tout ça, à essayer de faire à travers et dans le langage autre chose.*
The experience…of the woman writer is completely schizophrenic. One is always torn between two approaches: on the one hand, to use a language that is not ours…and on the other, the battle one fights to break all this up, in order to do something else through and in language.
Quoted in Jean-François Josselin 'Lettre à Sapho' in *Le Nouvel Observateur* (1973).

Wodehouse, Sir P(elham) G(renville) *also known as Plum* 1881–1975

Anglo-American writer, renowned for his humorous stories of the English country aristocracy. He lived in the US after World War II, taking citizenship in 1955, but never shed his quintessential Englishness.

50 An English peer of the right sort can be bored nearer to the point where mortification sets in, without showing it, than anyone else in the world.
1915 *Something Fresh*, ch.3.

51 She fitted into my biggest arm-chair as if it had been built round her by someone who knew they were wearing arm-chairs tight about the hips that season.
1919 *My Man Jeeves*, 'Jeeves and the Unbidden Guest'.

52 What with excellent browsing and sluicing and cheery conversation and what-not, the afternoon passed quite happily.
1919 *My Man Jeeves*, 'Jeeves and the Unbidden Guest'.

53 'What ho!' I said.
'What ho!' said Motty.
'What ho! What ho!'
'What ho! What ho! What ho!'
After that it seemed rather difficult to go on with the conversation.
1919 *My Man Jeeves*, 'Jeeves and the Unbidden Guest'.

54 In this matter of shimmering into rooms the chappie is rummy to a degree… He moves from point to point with as little uproar as a jellyfish.
1919 *My Man Jeeves*, 'Jeeves and the Hard-Boiled Egg'.

55 Chumps always make the best husbands. When you marry, Sally, grab a chump. Tap his forehead first, and if it rings solid, don't hesitate. All the unhappy marriages come from the husbands having brains. What good are brains to a man? They only unsettle him.
1920 *The Adventures of Sally*, ch.10.

56 I turned to Aunt Agatha, whose demeanour was now rather like that of one who, picking daisies on the railway, has just caught the down express in the small of the back.
1923 *The Inimitable Jeeves*, ch.4.

57 Jeeves coughed one soft, low, gentle cough like a sheep with a blade of grass stuck in its throat.
1923 *The Inimitable Jeeves*, ch.13.

58 As a rule, you see, I'm not lugged into Family Rows. On the occasions when Aunt is calling to Aunt like mastodons bellowing across the primeval swamps…the clan has a tendency to ignore me. It's one of the advantages I get from being a bachelor—and, according to my nearest and dearest, practically a half-witted bachelor at that.
1923 *The Inimitable Jeeves*, ch.16.

59 It was my Uncle George who discovered that alcohol was a food well in advance of medical thought.
1923 *The Inimitable Jeeves*, ch.16.

60 'Alf Todd,' said Ukridge, soaring to an impressive burst of imagery, 'has about as much chance as a one-armed blind man in a dark room trying to shove a pound of melted butter into a wild cat's left ear with a red-hot needle.'
1924 *Ukridge*, ch.5.

61 Honoria…is one of those robust, dynamic girls with the muscles of a welter-weight and a laugh like a squadron of cavalry charging over a tin bridge.
1925 *Carry On, Jeeves*, 'The Rummy Affair of Old Biffy'.

62 He looked haggard and careworn, like a Borgia who has suddenly remembered that he has forgotten to shove the cyanide in the consommé, and the dinner-gong due any moment.
1925 *Carry On, Jeeves*, 'Clustering Around Young Bingo'.

63 To my daughter Leonora without whose never-failing sympathy and encouragement this book would have been finished in half the time.
1926 *The Heart of a Goof*, dedication.

64 The Right Hon was a tubby little chap who looked as if he had been poured into his clothes and had forgotten to say 'When!'
1930 *Very Good, Jeeves*, 'Jeeves and the Impending Doom'.

65 I have at last come to a momentous decision. I am going to give up my press-clippings agency. I find that even a

favourable notice makes me feel sick nowadays, while an unfavourable one, even from a small provincial newspaper, puts me off my work for days.
1934 Letter to Denis Mackail, 15 Oct.

66 Into the face of the young man…had crept a look of furtive shame, the shifty, hangdog look which announces that an Englishman is about to talk French.
1935 *The Luck of the Bodkins*, ch.1.

67 It is never difficult to distinguish between a Scotsman with a grievance and a ray of sunshine.
1935 *Blandings Castle and Elsewhere*, 'The Custody of the Pumpkin'.

68 I can't do with any more education. I was full up years ago.
1938 *The Code of the Woosters*, ch.1.

69 He spoke with a certain what-is-it in his voice, and I could see that, if not actually disgruntled, he was far from being gruntled.
1938 *The Code of the Woosters*, ch.1.

70 Slice him where you like, a hellhound is always a hellhound.
1938 *The Code of the Woosters*, ch.1.

71 Roderick Spode? Big chap with a small moustache and the sort of eye that can open an oyster at sixty paces?
1938 *The Code of the Woosters*, ch.2.

72 He felt like a man who, chasing rainbows, has had one of them suddenly turn and bite him in the leg.
1940 *Eggs, Beans and Crumpets*, 'Anselm Gets His Chance'.

73 My war history has been a simple one. I have just sat in my chair and written all the time.
1946 Letter to Ira Gershwin, 24 Jan.

74 Ice formed on the butler's upper slopes.
1952 *Pigs Have Wings*, ch.5.

75 Has anyone ever seen a dramatic critic in the daytime? Of course not. They come out after dark, up to no good.
1955 In the *New York Mirror*, 27 May.

76 There'll always be an England, but who wants an England full of morons reading the *Express*?
1959 Letter to Denis Mackail, 22 Apr.

Wogan, Terry 1938–

Irish broadcaster and writer.

77 People confuse longevity with merit. Look at Cliff Richard.
2004 In the *Observer*, 28 Mar.

78 Ah, to be able to recognise when the tide is going out, when to get off the beach.
2004 On deciding when to retire. In the *Observer*, 28 Mar.

Wolf, Naomi 1962–

US writer; she was a Rhodes Scholar in 1986. *The Beauty Myth* (1990) and *Fire with Fire* (1993) examine the relationship between patriarchal power and female beauty.

79 The more legal and material hindrances women have broken through, the more strictly and heavily and cruelly images of female beauty have come to weigh upon them.
1990 *The Beauty Myth*, ch.1, 'The Beauty Myth'.

80 'Beauty' is a currency like the gold standard. Like any economy it is determined by politics, and in the modern age in the West it is the last, best belief system that keeps male domination intact.

1990 *The Beauty Myth*, ch.1, 'The Beauty Myth'.

81 When women breached the power structure in the 1980s…two economies finally merged. Beauty was no longer just a symbolic form of currency: it literally *became* money.

1990 *The Beauty Myth*, ch.2 'Work'.

Wolfe, James 1727–59

English general. He fought against the Jacobites at Culloden and was sent to Canada in 1756. Promoted to general after his prominence in the capture of Louisberg, he commanded the British force which took Quebec.

82 Gentlemen, I would rather have written those lines than take Quebec tomorrow.

1759 To his troops, 12 Sep, after reciting Thomas Gray's 'Elegy, Written in a Country Churchyard' the evening before storming the ramparts of Quebec and dying a hero's death on the Plains of Abraham the following day. Quoted in Francis Parkman *Montcalm and Wolfe* (1884).

83 Now God be praised, I will die in peace.

1759 Last words, on hearing of the defeat of the French at Quebec. Quoted in J Knox *Historical Journal of the Campaigns in North America* (1909), ch.17.

Wolfe, Thomas Clayton 1900–38

US novelist. Unsuccessful in drama, he wrote a series of sprawling, uneven but often powerful novels, two of which were published posthumously.

84 Most of the time we think we're sick, it's all in the mind.

1929 *Look Homeward, Angel*, pt.1, ch.1.

85 'Where they got you stationed now, Luke?'… 'At the p-p-p-present time in Norfolk at the Navy base,' Luke answered, 'm-m-making the world safe for hypocrisy.'

1929 *Look Homeward, Angel*, pt.3, ch.36.

86 My efforts to cut out 50,000 words may sometimes result in my adding 75,000.

1929 Letter to his editor, Maxwell Perkins.

87 If a man has a talent and cannot use it, he has failed. If he has a talent and uses only half of it, he has partly failed. If he has a talent and learns somehow to use the whole of it, he has gloriously succeeded, and won a satisfaction and a triumph few men ever know.

The Web and the Rock (published 1939), ch.29.

88 It was a cruel city, but it was a lovely one, a savage city, yet it had such tenderness, a bitter, harsh, and violent catacomb of stone and steel and tunnelled rock, slashed savagely with light, and roaring, fighting a constant ceaseless warfare of men and machinery; and yet it was so sweetly and so delicately pulsed, as full of warmth, of passion, and of love, as it was full of hate.

1939 *The Web and the Rock* (published 1939), ch.30.

89 You Can't Go Home Again.

Title of novel (published 1940).

Wolfe, Tom (Thomas Kennerley) 1931–

US journalist and novelist. He was a leading proponent of the New Journalism, with a propensity for a racy style and attention-grabbing titles. His book on the astronauts, *The Right Stuff* (1979), was filmed, as was his novel *The Bonfire of the Vanities* (1987).

90 The Electric Kool-Aid Acid Test

1968 Title of book.

91 Radical chic invariably favors radicals who seem primitive, exotic and romantic.

1970 *Radical Chic*.

92 Not 'Seeing is Believing', you ninny, but 'Believing is Seeing'. For modern art has become completely literary: the paintings and other works exist only to illustrate the text.

1975 *The Painted Word*, ch.1.

93 The idea was to prove at every foot of the way up…that you were one of the elected and anointed ones who had the right stuff and could move higher and higher and even—ultimately, God willing, one day—that you might be able to join that special few at the very top, that elite who had the capacity to bring tears to men's eyes, the very Brotherhood of the Right Stuff itself.

1979 *The Right Stuff*.

94 A cult is a religion with no political power.

1980 *In Our Time*, ch.2.

95 From Bauhaus to Our House.

1981 Title of book.

96 Today educated people look upon traditional religious ties—Catholic, Episcopal, Presbyterian, Methodist, Baptist, Jewish—as matters of social pedigree. It is only art that they look upon religiously.

1984 'The Worship of Art: Notes on the New God', in *Harper's*, Oct.

97 Yes, the labour movement was truly religious, like Judaism itself. It was one of those things you believed in for all mankind and didn't care about for a second in your own life.

1987 *The Bonfire of the Vanities*, ch.8.

98 A liberal is a conservative who has been arrested.

1987 *The Bonfire of the Vanities*, ch.24.

99 Pornography was the great vice of the Seventies; plutography—the graphic depiction of the acts of the rich—is the great vice of the Eighties.

1988 In the *Sunday Times Magazine*, 10 Jan.

1 The Versailles of American corporate culture.

1992 Of Manhattan's Four Seasons restaurant, in the *New York Times*, 14 Nov.

2 In the year 2000, a Tolstoy or a Flaubert wouldn't have stood a chance in the United States.

2000 *Hooking Up*.

Wollstonecraft, Mary *also known as* **Mrs Godwin** 1759–97

Anglo-Irish feminist and writer. Her *Vindication of the Rights of Man* (1790) was followed by *Vindication of the Rights of Woman* (1792), advocating gender equality. After bearing an illegitimate daughter to Captain Gilbert Imlay (1794) she married political writer William Godwin (1797) but died on the birth of their daughter, Mary Wollstonecraft Shelley.

3 I now speak of the sex in general. Many individuals have more sense than their male relatives; and…some women govern their husbands without degrading

themselves, because intellect will always govern.
1792 *A Vindication of the Rights of Woman*, introduction.

4 Men, in general, seem to employ their reason to justify prejudices, which they have imbibed, they can scarcely trace how, rather than root them out.
1792 *A Vindication of the Rights of Woman*, pt.1, ch.1.

5 Men, indeed, appear to me to act in a very unphilosophical manner when they try to secure the good conduct of women by attempting to keep them always in a state of childhood.
1792 *A Vindication of the Rights of Woman*, pt.1, ch.2.

6 Strengthen the female mind by enlarging it, and there will be an end to blind obedience; but as blind obedience is ever sought for by power, tyrants and sensualists are in the right when they endeavour to keep women in the dark, because the former only want slaves, and the latter a play-thing.
1792 *A Vindication of the Rights of Woman*, pt.1, ch.2.

7 Gentleness, docility, and a spaniel-like affection are, on this ground, consistently recommended as the cardinal virtues of the sex; and, disregarding the arbitrary economy of nature, one writer has declared that it is masculine for a woman to be melancholy. She was created to be the toy of man, his rattle, and it must jingle in his ears, whenever, dismissing reason, he chooses to be amused.
1792 *A Vindication of the Rights of Woman*, pt.1, ch.2.

8 Liberty is the mother of virtue, and if women be, by their very constitution, slaves, and not allowed to breathe the sharp invigorating air of freedom, they must ever languish like exotics, and be reckoned beautiful flaws in nature.
1792 *A Vindication of the Rights of Woman*, pt.1, ch.2.

9 The *divine right* of husbands, like the divine right of kings, may it is to be hoped, in this enlightened age, be contested without danger.
1792 *A Vindication of the Rights of Woman*, pt.1, ch.3.

10 A king is always a king—and a woman always a woman; his authority and her sex, ever stand between them and rational converse.
1792 *A Vindication of the Rights of Woman*, pt.1, ch.4.

11 I do not wish them to have power over men; but over themselves.
1792 Of women. *A Vindication of the Rights of Woman*, pt.1, ch.4.

12 Necessity never makes prostitution the business of men's lives; though numberless are the women who are thus rendered systematically vicious.
1792 *A Vindication of the Rights of Woman*, pt.1, ch.4.

13 Let woman share the rights and she will emulate the virtues of man, for she must grow more perfect when emancipated.
1792 *A Vindication of the Rights of Woman*, pt.1, ch.13.

Wolpert, Lewis 1929–

British developmental biologist.

14 The physics of motion provides one of the clearest examples of the counter-intuitive and unexpected nature of science.
1992 *The Unnatural Nature of Science*.

Wolstenholme, Kenneth 1920–2002

English football commentator. He broadcast for the BBC from 1948 to 1971, covering 22 FA Cup finals and five World Cups.

15 There are people on the pitch…they think it's all over…it is now!
1966 Radio commentary on the last goal of the World Cup final, in which England beat West Germany at Wembley.

Wood, Victoria 1953–

English playwright, lyricist and comedienne. Her comic plays include *Talent* (1979) and *Happy Since I Met You* (1981), and her television work is collected in *Mens Sana in Thingummy Doodah* (1991).

16 Jogging is for people who aren't intelligent enough to watch Breakfast TV.
1989 *Victoria Wood*, television series. Published in *Mens Sana in Thingummy Doodah* (1991).

17 LILL: My massage was marvellous. I feel really relaxed. And my masseur, Harold—
VICTORIA: You can't have a masseur called Harold. It's like having a member of the Royal Family called Ena.
1989 *Victoria Wood*, television series. Published in *Mens Sana in Thingummy Doodah* (1991).

Woodcock, George 1912–95

Canadian writer, poet, social critic and biographer. He also wrote several travel books. He has been described as a philosophical anarchist.

18 Well-founded fear, which takes one through the valley of the shadow of death without abandoning one there, is what makes the worst of worse journeys; the situation is made all the more intense when the fear is somehow mingled with delight.
'My Worst Journeys', collected in Keath Fraser (ed) *Worst Journeys: The Picador Book of Travel* (1991).

Woodman, Marion 1928–

Canadian therapist and author.

19 To strive for perfection is to kill love because perfection does not recognize humanity.
1982 *Addition to Perfection: The Still Unravished Bride*.

Woodroofe, Thomas 1899–1978

British naval officer.

20 The whole fleet's lit up. When I say 'lit up', I mean by fairy lamps.
1937 BBC radio commentary of the Spithead review, 20 May, Britain's first live outside broadcast. 'Lit up' was a common euphemism for 'drunk'.

Woods, Donald 1933–2001

South African editor and Black civil rights campaigner.

21 When I left South Africa, I arrogantly predicted that within seven years, apartheid would be gone. It has taken a bit longer than that.
1991 BBC TV broadcast, Feb.

Woods, Tiger 1975–

US golfer. He has won numerous events, including the US

Masters (1997, 2001, 2002), the British Open (2000) and the US Open (2000, 2002).

22 Growing up, I came up with this name: I'm a Cablinasian.
1997 Explaining his dissatisfaction with the term 'African-American' to describe his own Caucasian, African-American, Native American, Chinese and Thai ancestry. In an interview with Oprah Winfrey, 21 Apr.

23 My dad once told me: no matter what anyone says or writes, really, none of those people have to hit your four-foot putt. You have to go do it yourself.
2001 *Quotable Tiger*.

Woodsworth, James Shaver 1874–1942

Canadian politician, socialist and pacifist. An MP from 1921, in 1932 he founded the Co-operative Commonwealth Federation, serving as its chairman and parliamentary leader.

24 I take my place with the children.
1939 Casting the sole dissenting voice to ratify Canada's entry into World War II, in the House of Commons, Ottawa, 9 Sep.

Wooldridge, Adrian 1959–

English journalist with *The Economist* (London).

25 America has mitigated poverty by massively increasing pauperism.
1995 'Damned Statistics', in the *Wall Street Journal*, 27 Jul.

Woolf, (Adeline) Virginia née *Stephen* 1882–1941

English novelist, critic and essayist. Daughter of Sir Leslie Stephen and sister of Vanessa Bell, she married Leonard Woolf and in 1917 they formed the Hogarth Press. Her experimental novels include *Mrs. Dalloway* (1925) and *To the Lighthouse* (1927). *A Room of One's Own* (1929) is a feminist classic. She committed suicide by drowning.

26 Life…is a luminous halo, a semi-transparent envelope surrounding us from the beginning of consciousness to the end.
1919 'Modern Fiction'.

27 Each had his past shut in him like the leaves of a book known to him by heart; and his friends could only read the title.
1922 *Jacob's Room*, ch.5.

28 It's not catastrophes, murders, deaths, diseases, that age and kill us; it's the way people look and laugh, and run up the steps of omnibuses.
1922 *Jacob's Room*, ch.6.

29 Never did I read such tosh.
1922 On James Joyce's *Ulysses*. Letter to Lytton Strachey, 24 Apr.

30 I believe that all novels…deal with character, and that it is to express character—not to preach doctrines, sing songs, or celebrate the glories of the British Empire, that the form of the novel, so clumsy, verbose, and undramatic, so rich, elastic, and alive, has been evolved.
1924 'Mr Bennett and Mrs Brown'.

31 Life itself, every moment of it, every drop of it, here, this instant, now, in the sun, in Regent's Park, was enough. Too much, indeed.
1925 *Mrs Dalloway*.

32 It is vain and foolish to talk of knowing Greek.
1925 *The Common Reader*, 'On Not Knowing Greek'.

33 The interest in life does not lie in what people do, nor even in their relations to each other, but largely in the power to communicate with a third party, antagonistic, enigmatic, yet perhaps persuadable, which one may call life in general.
1925 *The Common Reader*, 'On Not Knowing Greek'.

34 For the self-centred and self-limited writers have a power denied the more catholic and broad-minded… Nothing issues from their minds which has not been marked with their own impress.
1925 *The Common Reader*, 'Jane Eyre and Wuthering Heights'.

35 A good essay must have this permanent quality about it; it must draw its curtain round us, but it must be a curtain that shuts us in not out.
1925 *The Common Reader*, 'The Modern Essay'.

36 We are nauseated by the sight of trivial personalities decomposing in the eternity of print.
1925 *The Common Reader*, 'The Modern Essay'.

37 *Middlemarch*, the magnificent book which with all its imperfections is one of the few English novels for grown up people.
1925 *The Common Reader*, 'George Eliot'.

38 London is enchanting. I step out upon a tawny coloured magic carpet, it seems, and get carried into beauty without raising a finger… People pop in and out, lightly, divertingly like rabbits; and I look down Southampton Row, wet as a seal's back or red and yellow with sunshine, and watch the omnibuses going and coming and hear the old crazy organs. One of these days I will write about London, and how it takes up the private life and carries it on, without any effort.
1926 Diary entry, 26 May.

39 So that is marriage, Lily thought, a man and a woman looking at a girl throwing a ball.
1927 *To the Lighthouse*, pt.1, ch.13.

40 She faded…became more inconspicuous than ever, in her little grey dress.
1927 *To the Lighthouse*, pt.1, ch.17.

41 One cannot think well, love well, sleep well, if one has not dined well.
1929 *A Room of One's Own*, ch.1.

42 A woman must have money and a room of her own if she is to write fiction.
1929 *A Room of One's Own*, ch.1.

43 Women have served all these centuries as looking-glasses possessing the magic and delicious power of reflecting the figure of man at twice its natural size.
1929 *A Room of One's Own*, ch.2.

44 I would venture to guess that Anon, who wrote so many poems without signing them, was often a woman.
1929 *A Room of One's Own*, ch.3.

45 Literature is strewn with the wreckage of men who have minded beyond reason the opinion of others.
1929 *A Room of One's Own*, ch.3.

46 It is obvious that the values of women differ very often from the values which have been made by the other sex… Yet it is the masculine values that prevail.
1929 *A Room of One's Own*, ch.4.

47 We think back through our mothers if we are women.
1929 *A Room of One's Own*, ch.4.

48 For there is a spot the size of a shilling at the back of the

head which one can never see for oneself. It is one of the good offices that sex can discharge for sex—to describe that spot.
1929 *A Room of One's Own*, ch.5.

49 For all the dinners are cooked; the plates and cups washed; the children sent to school and gone out into the world. Nothing remains of it all. All has vanished. No biography or history has a word to say about it.
1929 *A Room of One's Own*, ch.5.

50 I am not trying to tell a story. Yet perhaps it might be done in that way. A mind thinking. They might be islands of light—islands in the stream that I am trying to convey; life itself going on.
1929 Diary entry, 28 May.

51 Killing the Angel in the House was part of the occupation of a woman writer.
1931 'Professions for Women', lecture to the National Society for Women's Service, 21 Jan. Woolf's solution was to throw the inkpot at the Angel (the embodiment of stereotyped Victorian femininity) whenever she appeared.

52 Things have dropped from me. I have outlived certain desires; I have lost friends, some by death—Percival—others through sheer inability to cross the street.
1931 *The Waves*.

53 Yes, always keep the Classics at hand to prevent flop.
1937 Diary entry, 23 Jun.

54 Somewhere, everywhere, now hidden, now apparent in whatever is written down, is the form of a human being. If we seek to know him, are we idly occupied?
The Captain's Death Bed, 'Reading' (published 1950).

55 The poet gives us his essence, but prose takes the mould of the body and mind entire.
The Captain's Death Bed, 'Reading' (published 1950).

Woollcott, Alexander Humphreys 1887–1943

US critic, writer, actor and broadcaster. He became theatre critic for the *New York Times* in 1914 and subsequently became one of the celebrated Algonquin Round Table of wits and literary figures. Noted for his biting humour, he was the inspiration for Kaufman and Hart's play *The Man Who Came to Dinner*.

56 She is so odd a blend of Little Nell and Lady Macbeth. It is not so much the familiar phenomenon of a hand of steel in a velvet glove as a lacy sleeve with a bottle of vitriol concealed in its folds.
1934 Of Dorothy Parker. *While Rome Burns*, 'Our Mrs Parker'.

57 I have no need of your God-damned sympathy. I only wish to be entertained by some of your grosser reminiscences.
1942 Letter to Rex O'Malley. Quoted in Samuel Adams *Alexander Woollcott* (1945), ch.34.

58 A broker is a man who takes your fortune and runs it into a shoestring.
Quoted in Samuel Adams *Alexander Woollcott* (1945), ch.15.

59 Harold Ross…had a contempt for anything he didn't understand, which was practically everything.
Quoted in James Thurber *The Years With Ross* (1959), ch.15.

60 All the things I really like to do are either illegal, immoral or fattening.
Quoted in R Drennan *Wit's End* (1968).

61 The play left a taste of lukewarm parsnip juice.
Play review. Quoted in H Techmann *Smart Alex* (1976).

62 My doctor forbids me to play, unless I win.
Of croquet. Quoted in Colin Jarman *The Guinness Dictionary of Sports Quotations* (1990).

63 It is no game for the soft of sinew and the gentle of spirit. The higher and dirtier croquet-player can use the guile of a cobra and the inhumanity of a boa constrictor.
Quoted in Colin Jarman *The Guinness Dictionary of Sports Quotations* (1990).

64 Always a godfather, never a god!
On serving as godfather at a christening celebration for the 19th time. Attributed.

65 Just what God would do if he had the money.
On being shown round Moss Hart's splendid country retreat. Attributed.

66 The scenery was beautiful, but the actors got in front of it.
Play review.

Wordsworth, William 1770–1850

English poet. At first given to agnosticism and a revolutionary passion for social justice, he then turned to exploring the lives of humble people living in contact with nature. He succeeded Robert Southey as Poet Laureate in 1843.

67 Now, in this blank of things, a harmony,
Home-felt, and home-created, comes to heal
That grief for which the senses still supply
Fresh food.
1786 'Calm is all nature as a resting wheel', l.7–10. Published in the *Morning Post*, 13 Feb. 1802.

68 In this universe,
Where the least things control the greatest, where
The faintest breath that breathes can move a world.
1795–6 Oswald. *The Borderers*, act 3, l.1562–4 (published 1842).

69 These beauteous forms,
Through a long absence, have not been to me
As is a landscape to a blind man's eye:
But oft, in lonely rooms, and 'mid the din
Of towns and cities, I have owed to them,
In hours of weariness, sensations sweet,
Felt in the blood, and felt along the heart.
1798 'Lines composed a few miles above Tintern Abbey, on revisiting the banks of the Wye', l.22–8.

70 That best portion of a good man's life,
His little, nameless, unremembered, acts
Of kindness and of love.
1798 'Lines composed a few miles above Tintern Abbey, on revisiting the banks of the Wye', l.33–5.

71 For I have learned
To look on nature, not as in the hour
Of thoughtless youth; but hearing often-times
The still, sad music of humanity,
Nor harsh nor grating, though of ample power
To chasten and subdue. And I have felt
A presence that disturbs me with the joy
Of elevated thoughts; a sense sublime
Of something far more deeply interfused,
Whose dwelling is the light of setting suns,
And the round ocean and the living air,
And the blue sky, and in the mind of man.
1798 'Lines composed a few miles above Tintern Abbey, on

72 Therefore am I still
A lover of the meadows and the woods,
And mountains; and of all that we behold
From this green earth; of all the mighty world
Of eye, and ear,—both what they half create
And what perceive.
1798 'Lines composed a few miles above Tintern Abbey, on revisiting the banks of the Wye', l.102–6.

73 Away we go—and what care we
For treasons, tumults, and for wars?
We are as calm in our delight
As is the crescent moon so bright
Among the scattered stars.
1798 'Peter Bell', prologue, stanza 5 (published 1819).

74 Books! 'tis a dull and endless strife:
Come, hear the woodland linnet
How sweet his music! on my life
There's more of wisdom in it.
1798 'The Tables Turned', stanza 3.

75 One impulse from a vernal wood
May teach you more of man,
Of moral evil and of good,
Than all the sages can.

Sweet is the lore which Nature brings;
Our meddling intellect
Mis-shapes the beauteous forms of things:—
We murder to dissect.

Enough of science and of art;
Close up those barren leaves;
Come forth and bring with you a heart
That watches and receives.
1798 'The Tables Turned', stanzas 6–8.

76 I heard a thousand blended notes,
While in a grove I sate reclined,
In that sweet mood when pleasant thoughts
Bring sad thoughts to the mind.
1798 'Lines Written in Early Spring', stanza 1.

77 To her fair works did Nature link
The human soul that through me ran;
And much it grieved my heart to think
What man has made of man.
1798 'Lines Written in Early Spring', stanza 2.

78 She dwelt among the untrodden ways
Beside the springs of Dove,
A maid whom there were none to praise
And very few to love:

A violet by a mossy stone
Half hidden from the eye!
—Fair as a star, when only one
Is shining in the sky.

She lived unknown, and few could know
When Lucy ceased to be;
But she is in her grave, and, oh,
The difference to me!
1799 'She dwelt among the untrodden ways', complete poem (published 1800).

79 Three years she grew in sun and shower,

The Nature said, 'A lovelier flower
On earth was never sown;
This Child I to myself will take;
She shall be mine, and I will make
A Lady of my own.'
1799 'Three Years she grew in sun and shower', stanza 1 (published 1800).

80 A slumber did my spirit seal;
I had no human fears:
She seemed a thing that could not feel
The touch of earthly years.

No motion has she now, no force;
She neither hears nor sees;
Rolled round in earth's diurnal course
With rocks, and stones and trees.
1799 'A slumber did my spirit seal', complete poem (published 1800).

81 Physician art thou?—one, all eyes,
Philosopher!—a fingering slave,
One that would peep and botanize
Upon his mother's grave?
1799 'A Poet's Epitaph', stanza 5 (published 1800).

82 One to whose smooth-rubbed soul can cling
Nor form, nor feeling, great or small;
A reasoning, self-sufficing thing,
An intellectual All-in-all!
1799 'A Poet's Epitaph', stanza 8 (published 1800).

83 Shut close the door; press down the latch;
Sleep in thy intellectual crust;
Nor lose ten tickings of thy watch
Near this unprofitable dust.
1799 'A Poet's Epitaph', stanza 9 (published 1800).

84 In common truths that round us lie
Some random truths he can impart,—
The harvest of a quiet eye
That broods and sleeps on his own heart.
1799 'A Poet's Epitaph', stanza 13 (published 1800).

85 Wisdom and Spirit of the universe!
Thou soul, that art the eternity of thought,
And giv'st to forms and images a breath
And everlasting motion.
1799 'Influence of Natural Objects', l.1–4 (published in *The Friend* 28 Dec 1809).

86 Leaving the tumultuous throng,
To cut across the reflex of a star;
Image that, flying still before me, gleamed
Upon the glassy plain.
1799 'Influence of Natural Objects', l.49–52 (published in *The Friend* 28 Dec 1809).

87 When we had given our bodies to the wind,
And all the shadowy banks on either side
Came sweeping through the darkness, spinning still
The rapid line of motion, then at once
Have I, reclining back upon my heels,
Stopped short; yet still the solitary cliffs
Wheeled by me—even as if the earth had rolled
With visible motion her diurnal round!
1799 'Influence of Natural Objects', l.53–60 (published in *The Friend* 28 Dec 1809).

88 Oh there is blessing in this gentle breeze,
A visitant that while it fans my cheek

Doth seem half conscious of the joy it brings
From the green fields, and from yon azure sky.
Whate'er its mission, the soft breeze can come
To none more grateful than to me; escaped
From the vast city, where I long had pined
A discontented sojourner: now free,
Free as a bird to settle where I will.
1799–1805 *The Prelude*, bk.1, l.1–9 (published 1850).

89 I, methought, while the sweet breath of heaven
Was blowing on my body, felt within
A correspondent breeze, that gently moved
With quickening virtue, but is now become
A tempest, a redundant energy,
Vexing its own creation.
1799–1805 *The Prelude*, bk.1, l.33–8 (published 1850).

90 Either still I find
Some imperfection in the chosen theme,
Or see of absolute accomplishment
Much wanting, so much wanting, in myself,
That I recoil and droop, and seek repose
In listlessness from vain perplexity,
Unprofitably travelling towards the grave.
1799–1805 *The Prelude*, bk.1, l.261–7 (published 1850).

91 Fair seed-time had my soul, and I grew up
Fostered alike by beauty and by fear.
1799–1805 *The Prelude*, bk.1, l.301–2 (published 1850).

92 Dust as we are, the immortal spirit grows
Like harmony in music; there is a dark
Inscrutable workmanship that reconciles
Discordant elements, makes them cling together
In one society.
1799–1805 *The Prelude*, bk.1, l.340–4 (published 1850).

93 Then, the calm
And dead still water lay upon my mind
Even with a weight of pleasure, and the sky,
Never before so beautiful, sank down
Into my heart, and held me like a dream.
1799–1805 *The Prelude*, bk.2, l.70–4 (published 1850).

94 I was taught to feel, perhaps too much,
The self-sufficing power of Solitude.
1799–1805 *The Prelude*, bk.2, l.76–7 (published 1850).

95 Science appears but what in truth she is,
Not as our glory and our absolute boast,
But as a succedaneum, and a prop
To our infirmity.
1799–1805 *The Prelude*, bk.2, l.212–15 (published 1850).

96 That false secondary power
By which we multiply distinctions, then
Deem that our puny boundaries are things
That we perceive, and not that we have made.
1799–1805 *The Prelude*, bk.2, l.216–19 (published 1850).

97 A babe, by intercourse of touch
I held mute dialogues with my Mother's heart.
1799–1805 *The Prelude*, bk.2, l.267–8 (published 1850).

98 From my pillow, looking forth by light
Of moon or favouring stars, I could behold
The antechapel where the statue stood
Of Newton with his prism and silent face,
The marble index of a mind for ever
Voyaging through strange seas of Thought alone.
1799–1805 *The Prelude*, bk.3, l.58–63 (published 1850).

99 There's not a man
That lives who hath not known his god-like hours.
1799–1805 *The Prelude*, bk.3, l.190–1 (published 1850).

1 Visionary power
Attends the motions of the viewless winds,
Embodied in the mystery of words.
1799–1805 *The Prelude*, bk.5, l.595–7 (published 1850).

2 Even forms and substances are circumfused
By that transparent veil with light divine,
And, through the turnings intricate of verse,
Present themselves as objects recognised,
In flashes, and with glory not their own.
1799–1805 *The Prelude*, bk.5, l.601–5 (published 1850).

3 An open place it was, and overlooked,
From high, the sullen water far beneath,
On which a dull red image of the moon
Lay bedded, changing oftentimes its form
Like an uneasy snake.
1799–1805 *The Prelude*, bk.6, l.703–7 (published 1850).

4 In the very world, which is the world
Of all of us,—the place where, in the end,
We find our happiness, or not at all!
1799–1805 *The Prelude*, bk.11, l.142–4 (published 1850).

5 I shook the habit off
Entirely and for ever, and again
In Nature's presence stood, as now I stand,
A sensitive being, a *creative* soul.
1799–1805 *The Prelude*, bk.12, l.204–7 (published 1850).

6 A balance, an ennobling interchange
Of action from without and from within;
The excellence, pure function, and best power
Both of the object seen, and eye that sees.
1799–1805 *The Prelude*, bk.13, l.375–8 (published 1850).

7 The thought of death sits easy on the man
Who has been born and dies among the mountains.
c.1800 The Priest. 'The Brothers', l.182–3.

8 The moving accident is not my trade;
To freeze the blood I have no ready arts:
'Tis my delight, alone in summer shade,
To pipe a simple song for thinking hearts.
1800 'Hart-Leap Well', part 2, l.97–100.

9 I travelled among unknown men
In lands beyond the sea;
Nor England! did I know till then
What love I bore to thee.
1801 'I Travelled Among Unknown Men', stanza 1 (published 1807).

10 Poetry is the spontaneous overflow of powerful feelings: it takes its origin from emotion recollected in tranquillity.
1802 Preface to *Lyrical Ballads* (2nd ed. 1802; *Lyrical Ballads* first published 1798, preface added 1800, enlarged 1802).

11 Milton! thou shouldst be living at this hour:
England hath need of thee: she is a fen
Of stagnant waters: altar, sword and pen,
Fireside, the heroic wealth of hall and bower,
Have forfeited their ancient English dower
Of inward happiness. We are selfish men;
Oh! raise us up, return to us again;
And give us manners, virtue, freedom, power.
Thy soul was like a star, and dwelt apart;

Thou hadst a voice whose sound was like the sea:
Pure as the naked heavens, majestic, free,
So didst thou travel on life's common way,
In cheerful godliness; and yet thy heart
The lowliest duties on herself did lay.
1802 'Milton! thou shouldst be living at this hour', complete
poem (published 1807).

12 Thrice welcome, darling of the Spring
Even yet thou are to me
No bird, but an invisible thing,
A voice, a mystery.
1802 'To the Cuckoo', stanza 4 (published 1807).

13 It is a beauteous evening, calm and free,
The holy time is quiet as a nun
Breathless with adoration; the broad sun
Is sinking down in its tranquillity;
The gentleness of heaven broods o'er the sea:
Listen! the mighty being is awake,
And doth with his eternal motion make
A sound like thunder—everlastingly.
1802 'It is a beauteous evening calm and free', l.1–8 (published
1807).

14 With little here to do or see
Of things that in the great world be,
Sweet Daisy! oft I talk to thee
For thou art worthy,
Thou unassuming commonplace
Of Nature, with that homely face,
And yet with something of a grace
Which love makes for thee!
1802 'To the Daisy', stanza 1 (published 1807).

15 My heart leaps up when I behold
A rainbow in the sky:
So was it when my life began;
So is it now I am a man;
So be it when I shall grow old,
Or let me die!
The Child is father of the Man;
And I could wish my days to be
Bound each to each by natural piety.
1802 'My heart leaps up when I behold', complete poem
(published 1807).

16 My whole life have I lived in pleasant thought,
As if life's business were a summer mood;
As if all needful things would come unsought
To genial faith, still rich in genial good.
1802 'Resolution and Independence', stanza 6 (published 1807).

17 I thought of Chatterton, the marvellous boy,
The sleepless soul that perished in his pride.
Of him who walked in glory and in joy
Following his plough along the mountainside:
By our own spirits are we deified.
We poets in our youth begin in gladness;
But thereof comes in the end despondency and
madness.
1802 Of the poet Thomas Chatterton, who committed suicide at
the age of 17. 'Resolution and Independence', stanza 7
(published 1807).

18 The fear that kills;
And hope that is unwilling to be fed.
1802 'Resolution and Independence', stanza 17 (published
1807).

19 Earth hath not anything to show more fair:
Dull would he be of soul who could pass by
A sight so touching in its majesty:
This City now doth like a garment wear
The beauty of the morning; silent, bare,
Ships, towers, domes, theatres, and to the sky;
All bright and glittering in the smokeless air.
Never did sun more beautifully steep
In his first splendour, valley, rock, or hill;
Ne'er saw I, never felt, a calm so deep!
The river glideth at his own sweet will;
Dear God! the very houses seem asleep;
And all that mighty heart is lying still!
1802 Of London. 'Composed upon Westminster Bridge',
complete poem. (Published 1807).

20 Once did she hold the gorgeous East in fee,
And was the safeguard of the West: the worth
Of Venice did not fall below her birth,
Venice, the eldest child of Liberty.
1802 Of Venice. 'On the Extinction of the Venetian Republic',
l.1–4 (published 1807).

21 There was a time when meadow, grove, and stream,
The earth, and every common sight,
To me did seem
Apparelled in celestial light,
The glory and the freshness of a dream.
It is not now as it hath been of yore;—
Turn whereso'er I may,
By night or day,
The things which I have seen I now can see no more.
c.1802–1803 'Ode. Intimations of Immortality from
Recollections of Early Childhood', stanza 1 (published 1807).

22 Thou Child of Joy,
Shout round me, let me hear thy shouts.
c.1802–1803 'Ode. Intimations of Immortality from
Recollections of Early Childhood', stanza 3 (published 1807).

23 But there's a tree, of many, one,
A single field which I have looked upon,
Both of them speak of something that is gone:
The pansy at my feet
Doth the same tale repeat:
Whither is fled the visionary gleam?
Where is it now, the glory and the dream?
c.1802–1803 'Ode. Intimations of Immortality from
Recollections of Early Childhood', stanza 4 (published 1807).

24 Our birth is but a sleep and a forgetting:
The soul that rises with us, our life's star,
Hath had elsewhere its setting,
And cometh from afar:
Not in entire forgetfulness
And not in utter nakedness,
But trailing clouds of glory do we come
From God, who is our home:
Heaven lies about us in our infancy!
Shades of the prison-house begin to close
Upon the growing boy,
But he beholds the light, and whence it flows,
He sees it in his joy;
The youth, who daily farther from the east
Must travel, still is nature's priest,
And by the vision splendid
Is on his way attended;

At length the man perceives it die away,
And fade into the light of common day.
c.1802–1803 'Ode. Intimations of Immortality from Recollections of Early Childhood', stanza 5 (published 1807).

25 O joy! that in our embers
Is something that doth live,
That nature yet remembers
What was so fugitive!
c.1802–1803 'Ode. Intimations of Immortality from Recollections of Early Childhood', stanza 9 (published 1807).

26 Those obstinate questionings
Of sense and outward things,
Fallings from us, vanishings;
Blank misgivings of a creature
Moving about in worlds not realised,
High instincts before which our mortal nature
Did tremble like a guilty thing surprised.
c.1802–1803 'Ode. Intimations of Immortality from Recollections of Early Childhood', stanza 9 (published 1807).

27 Our noisy years seem moments in the being
Of the eternal silence: truths that wake,
To perish never:
Which neither listlessness, nor mad endeavour,
Nor man nor boy,
Nor all that is at enmity with joy,
Can utterly abolish or destroy!
Hence in a season of calm weather,
Though inland far we be,
Our souls have sight of that immortal sea
Which brought us hither,
Can in a moment travel thither,
And see the children sport upon the shore,
And hear the mighty waters rolling evermore.
c.1802–1803 'Ode. Intimations of Immortality from Recollections of Early Childhood', stanza 9 (published 1807).

28 Though nothing can bring back the hour
Of splendour in the grass, of glory in the flower;
We will grieve not.
c.1802–1803 'Ode. Intimations of Immortality from Recollections of Early Childhood', stanza 10 (published 1807).

29 Thanks to the human heart by which we live,
Thanks to its tenderness, its joys, and fears,
To me the meanest flower that blows can give
Thoughts that do often lie too deep for tears.
c.1802–1803 'Ode. Intimations of Immortality from Recollections of Early Childhood', stanza 11 (published 1807).

30 Let beeves and home-bred kine partake
The sweets of Burn-mill meadow;
The swan on still St Mary's Lake
Float double, swan and shadow!
We will not see them; will not go,
To-day, nor yet to-morrow;
Enough if in our hearts we know
There's such a place as Yarrow.

Be Yarrow stream unseen, unknown;
It must, or we shall rue it:
We have a vision of our own,
Ah! why should we undo it?
The treasured dreams of times long past,
We'll keep them, winsome Marrow!
For when we're there, although 'tis fair,

'Twill be another Yarrow!
1803 'Yarrow Unvisited', stanzas 6–7 (published 1807).

31 For thou wert still the poor man's stay,
The poor man's heart, the poor man's hand;
And all the oppressed, who wanted strength,
Had thine at their command.
1803 'Rob Roy's Grave', l. 109–12 (published 1807).

32 Thy friends are exultations, agonies,
And love, and man's unconquerable mind.
1803 'To Toussaint L'Ouverture', l.13–14 (published in the *Morning Post* 2 Feb).

33 What, you are stepping westward?
1803–5 'Stepping Westward', l.1 (published 1807).

34 Behold her, single in the field,
Yon solitary Highland Lass!
Reaping and singing by herself;
Stop here, or gently pass!
1803–5 'The Solitary Reaper', l.1–4 (published 1807).

35 She was a Phantom of delight
When first she gleamed upon my sight;
A lovely apparition sent
To be a moment's ornament.
1804 'She was a Phantom of delight', l.1–4 (published 1807).

36 And now I see with eye serene
The very pulse of the machine;
A being breathing thoughtful breath,
A traveller between life and death;
The reason firm, the temperate will,
Endurance, foresight, strength, and skill;
A perfect woman, nobly planned,
To warn, to comfort, and command.
1804 'She was a Phantom of delight', l.21–8 (published 1807).

37 Chains tie us down by land and sea;
And wishes, vain as mine, may be
All that is left to comfort thee.
1804 'The Affliction of Margaret', stanza 8 (published 1807).

38 My apprehensions come in crowds;
I dread the rustling of the grass;
The very shadows of the clouds
Have power to shake me as they pass.
1804 'The Affliction of Margaret', stanza 10 (published 1807).

39 Oh! pleasant exercise of hope and joy!
For mighty were the auxiliars which then stood
Upon our side, we who were strong in love!
Bliss it was in that dawn to be alive,
But to be young was very heaven!
1804 'The French Revolution as it appeared to enthusiasts at its commencement', l.1–5 (published in *The Friend*, 26 Oct. 1809).

40 I wandered lonely as a cloud
That floats on high o'er vales and hills,
When all at once I saw a crowd,
A host, of golden daffodils;
Beside the lake, beneath the trees,
Fluttering and dancing in the breeze.
1804 'I wandered lonely as a cloud', stanza 1 (published 1807).

41 Continuous as the stars that shine
And twinkle on the milky way
They stretched in never-ending line
Along the margin of a bay:
Ten thousand saw I at a glance,
Tossing their heads in sprightly dance.

1804 'I wandered lonely as a cloud', stanza 2 (published 1807).

42 The waves beside them danced; but they
Out-did the sparkling waves in glee:
A poet could not but be gay,
In such a jocund company:
I gazed—and gazed—but little thought
What wealth the show to me had brought.
1804 'I wandered lonely as a cloud', stanza 3 (published 1807).

43 For oft, when on my couch I lie
In vacant or in pensive mood,
They flash upon that inward eye
Which is the bliss of solitude;
And then my heart wih pleasure fills,
And dances with the daffodils.
1804 'I wandered lonely as a cloud', stanza 4 (published 1807).

44 If mine had been the painter's hand,
To express what then I saw; and add the gleam,
The light that never was, on sea or land,
The consecration, and the poet's dream.
1805 'Elegiac Stanzas: suggested by a picture of Peele Castle in a storm', stanza 4 (published 1807).

45 Not for a moment could I now behold
A smiling sea, and be what I have been.
1805 'Elegiac Stanzas: suggested by a picture of Peele Castle in a storm', stanza 10 (published 1807).

46 The world is too much with us; late and soon,
Getting and spending we lay waste our powers:
Little we see in nature that is ours;
We have given our hearts away, a sordid boon!
The sea that bares her bosom to the moon;
The winds that will be howling at all hours,
And are up-gathered now like sleeping flowers;
For this, for everything, we are out of tune;
It moves us not.—Great God! I'd rather be
A pagan suckled in a creed outworn;
So might I, standing on this pleasant lea,
Have glimpses that would make me less forlorn;
Have sight of Proteus rising from the sea;
Or hear old Triton blow his wreathèd horn.
1806 'The world is too much with us; late and soon', complete poem (published 1807).

47 Two voices are there; one is of the sea,
One of the mountains; each a mighty voice:
In both from age to age thou didst rejoice,
They were thy chosen music, Liberty!
1807 'Thought of a Briton on the Subjugation of Switzerland', l.1–4.

48 These people in the senseless hurry of their idle lives do not *read* books, they merely snatch a glance at them that they may talk about them. And even if this were not so, never forget what I believe was observed by Coleridge, that every great and original writer, in proportion as he is great or original, must himself create the taste by which he is to be relished.
1807 Letter to Lady Beaumont, 21 May, on his *Poems in Two Volumes* (1807). In *The Letters of William Wordsworth* edited by Alan G Hill (1984).

49 Surprised by joy—impatient as the wind
I turned to share the transport—Oh! with whom
But thee, deep buried in the silent tomb,
That spot which no vicissitude can find?
c.1812 'Surprised by joy—impatient as the wind', l.1–4

(published 1815). The poet's second daughter, Catherine, who died in June 1812, is the 'thee' referred to in the poem.

50 On Man, on Nature, and on Human Life,
Musing in solitude, I oft perceive
Fair trains of images before me rise,
Accompanied by feelings of delight
Pure, or with no unpleasing sadness mixed.
1814 'The Excursion', preface, l.1–5.

51 Not Chaos, not
The darkest pit of lowest Erebus
Nor aught of blinder vacancy, scooped out
By help of dreams—can breed such fear and awe
As fall upon us often when we look
Into our Minds, into the Mind of Man—
My haunt, and the main region of my song.
1814 'The Excursion', preface, l.35–41.

52 What soul was his, when, from the naked top
Of some bold headland, he beheld the sun
Rise up, and bathe the world in light!
He looked—
Ocean and earth, the solid frame of earth
And ocean's liquid mass, in gladness lay
Beneath him:—Far and wide the clouds were touched,
And in their silent faces he could read
Unutterable love.
1814 'The Excursion', bk.1, l.198–205.

53 This dull product of a scoffer's pen.
1814 Of Voltaire's novel *Candide*. 'The Excursion', bk.2, l.484.

54 Compassed round by pleasure, sighed
For independent happiness; craving peace,
The central feeling of all happiness,
Not as a refuge from distress or pain,
A breathing-time, vacation, or a truce,
But for its absolute self.
1814 'The Excursion', bk.3, l.380–5.

55 Society became my glittering bride,
And airy hopes my children.
1814 'The Excursion', bk.3, l.735–6.

56 'To every Form of being is assigned,'
Thus calmly spake the venerable Sage,
'An *active* Principle:—howe'er removed
From sense and observation, it subsists
In all things, in all natures.'
1814 'The Excursion', bk.9, l.1–5.

57 For all the startled scaly tribes that slink
Into his coverts, and each fearless link
Of dancing insects forged upon his breast.
1820 *The River Duddon*, no.28, 'Journey Renewed', l.6–8.

58 Still glides the stream, and shall for ever glide;
The Form remains, the function never dies;
While we, the brave, the mighty, and the wise,
We Men, who in our morn of youth defied
The elements, must vanish;—be it so!
1820 *The River Duddon*, no.34, 'After-Thought', l.5–9.

59 Enough, if something from our hands have power
To live, and act, and serve the future hour;
And if, as toward the silent tomb we go,
Through love, through hope, and faith's transcendent dower,
We feel that we are greater than we know.
1820 *The River Duddon*, no.34, 'After-Thought', l.10–14.

60 Ethereal minstrel! pilgrim of the sky!
　　Dost thou despise the earth where cares abound?
　　Or, while the wings aspire, are heart and eye
　　Both with thy nest upon the dewy ground?
　　1825 'To a Skylark', l.1–4 (published 1827).

61 Type of the wise who soar, but never roam;
　　True to the kindred points of Heaven and Home!
　　1825 'To a Skylark', l.11–12 (published 1827).

62 But who is innocent? By grace divine,
　　Not otherwise, O Nature! we are thine.
　　1834 'Evening Voluntaries', no.4, l.16–17 (published 1835).

63 Even so for me a vision sanctified
　　The sway of death; long ere my eyes had seen
　　Thy countenance—the still rapture of thy mien—
　　When thou, dear Sister! wert become death's bride:
　　No trace of pain or languor could abide
　　That change—age on thy brow was smoothed—thy cold
　　Wan cheek at once was privileged to unfold
　　A loveliness to living youth denied.
　　Oh! if within me hope should e'er decline,
　　The lamp of faith, lost Friend! too faintly burn;
　　The may that heaven-revealing smile of thine,
　　The bright assurance, visibly return:
　　And let my spirit in that power divine
　　Rejoice, as, through that power, it ceased to mourn.
　　1836 'November 1836', complete poem (published 1837).

64 The softest breeze to fairest flowers gives birth:
　　Think not that Prudence dwells in dark abodes,
　　She scans the future with the eye of gods.
　　1837 'At Bologna, In Remembrance of the Late Insurrections:
　　Continued', l.12–14 (published 1842).

65 Before us lay a painful road,
　　And guidance have I sought in duteous love
　　From Wisdom's heavenly Father. Hence hath flowed
　　Patience, with trust that, whatsoe'er the way
　　Each takes in this high matter, all may move
　　Cheered with the prospect of a brighter day.
　　1839–40 Sonnets upon the Punishment of Death, no.14, 'Apology',
　　l.9–14 (published in the Quarterly Review 1841).

66 With what nice care equivalents are given,
　　How just, how bountiful, the hand of Heaven.
　　1840 'Poor Robin', l.35–6 (published 1842).

67 That to this mountain-daisy's self were known
　　The beauty of its star-shaped shadow, thrown
　　On the smooth surface of this naked stone!
　　1844 'So fair so sweet', stanza 2 (published 1845).

68 21st May—a glorious day for beauty. I wish you could see
　　how lovely our country is at this fine season.
　　1846 Letter to William Boxall, 21 May.

Worley, Helen

69 Dance, little words, on the end of your string. I can make
　　you do most anything I want to. I can hide anywhere and
　　watch you say the things I would never dare.
　　1982 The Soul Survivor, 'Puppetry and Poetry'.

Wotton, Sir Henry 1568–1639

English traveller, diplomat, scholar and poet. A trusted
ambassador of James I and VI, he served in Venice and
Germany. His tracts and letters were collected as Reliquiae
Wottonianae (1651).

70 An ambassador is an honest man sent to lie abroad for
　　the good of his country.
　　Quoted in Izaak Walton's Life (1651).

Wragg, Ted (Edward) Conrad 1938–

English educator, a Professor of Education at the University of
Exeter.

71 Nobody loves a bad teacher.
　　1986 Education: an Action Guide for Parents.

Wright, Sir Almroth Edward 1861–1947

English bacteriologist and Professor of Experimental
Pathology, known for his work on parasitic diseases. A vocal
opponent of the suffragettes, he wrote The Unexpurgated Case
against Woman Suffrage (1913).

72 The recruiting field for the militant suffragists is the
　　million of our excess female population—that million
　　which had better long ago have gone out to mate with its
　　complement of men beyond the sea.
　　1912 Letter to The Times, 28 Mar.

73 The primordial argument against giving woman the
　　vote is that that vote would not represent physical
　　force.
　　1913 The Unexpurgated Case against Woman Suffrage, pt.2.

74 The woman voter would be pernicious to the State not
　　only because she could not back her vote by physical
　　force, but also by reason of her intellectual defects.
　　1913 The Unexpurgated Case against Woman Suffrage, pt.2.

75 Practically every man feels that there is in woman…an
　　element of unreason which, when you come upon it,
　　summarily puts an end to purely intellectual intercourse.
　　1913 The Unexpurgated Case against Woman Suffrage, pt.5.

Wright, Betsey

Aide to President Clinton.

76 Bimbo eruptions.
　　1994 On an explosion of charges of sexual harassment against
　　President Clinton. In the Washington Post, 30 May.

Wright, Frank Lloyd 1867–1959

US architect, known for his original and controversial designs
exploiting modern technology and cubist spatial concepts.
His works include the Imperial Hotel, Tokyo (1916–20) and the
Guggenheim Museum of Art, New York (1959).

77 Architecture is man's great sense of himself embodied in
　　a world of his own making. It may rise as high in quality
　　only as its source because great art is great life.
　　1930 In Frederick Gutheim (ed) Frank Lloyd Wright on
　　Architecture: selected writings (1894–1940).

78 I know we can't have a great architecture while it is only
　　for the landlord.
　　1932 In Frederick Gutheim (ed) Frank Lloyd Wright on
　　Architecture: selected writings (1894–1940).

79 The physician can bury his mistakes, but the architect
　　can only advise his client to plant vines.
　　1953 In the New York Times, 4 Oct.

Wright, James C, Jr 1922–

US Congressman, former speaker of the US House of
Representatives.

80 The boiling, churning caldron of America.
1987 On the House of Representatives. In *Life*.

81 I know how that pancake feels when you pour the syrup all over it.
1991 Of his official portrait, unveiled two years after he was forced to resign. In the *International Herald Tribune*, 12 Jul.

Wright, Judith Arundell *also known as* Judith Wright McKinney 1915–2000

Australian poet and conservationist, whose awards include the Robert Frost Memorial Prize (1976). Selected works have been published in *A Human Pattern* (1990).

82 The easy Eden-dreamtime then
in a country of birds and trees
made me your shadow-sister, child,
dark girl I couldn't play with.
1990 *A Human Pattern*, 'Two Dreamtimes', stanza 14. The poem is dedicated to Kath Walker (now Oodgeroo Noonuccal).

83 I am born of the conquerors,
you of the persecuted.
Raped by rum and an alien law,
progress and economics,

are you and I and a once-loved land
peopled by tribes and trees;
doomed traders and stock-exchanges,
bought by faceless strangers.
1990 *A Human Pattern*, 'Two Dreamtimes', stanzas 17–18. The poem is dedicated to Kath Walker (now Oodgeroo Noonuccal).

Wright, Kenyon 1932–99

Scottish Methodist minister, General Secretary of the Scottish Council of Churches since 1981, and Executive of the Scottish Constitutional Convention (1989–99).

84 What if that other single voice we know so well responds by saying, 'We say no, and we are the State'? Well, we say yes—and we are the people.
1989 Calling for a Scottish Parliament. Speech at the inaugural meeting of the Scottish Constitutional Convention, 30 Mar. The 'single voice' is that of Prime Minister Margaret Thatcher.

Wright, Orville and Wright, Wilbur 1871–1948, 1867–1912

Born in Dayton, Ohio, early mechanics and tinkerers, and eventually self-taught aviation engineers.

85 SUCCESS FOUR FLIGHTS THURSDAY MORNING ALL AGAINST TWENTY-ONE MILE WIND STARTED FROM LEVEL WITH ENGINE POWER ALONE AVERAGE SPEED THROUGH AIR THIRTY-ONE MILES LONGEST 59 SECONDS INFORM PRESS HOME CHRISTMAS.
1903 Telegram from the brothers at Kitty Hawk, North Carolina to their father, 17 Dec.

Wriston, Walter Bigelow 1919–

US banker. He joined Citibank in 1946 and worked his way up to chairman (1970–84).

86 Our banking system grew by accident; and wherever something happens by accident, it becomes a religion.
1975 In *Business Week*, 20 Jan.

87 When you retire…you go from who's who to who's that.
1985 In the *New York Times*, 21 Apr.

88 If you put a floor under wages and a ceiling over prices, a free man cannot long stand erect.
1986 *Risk and Other Four-Letters Words*.

89 The Doomsayers have always had their uses, since they trigger the coping mechanism that often prevents the events they forecast.
1986 *Risk and Other Four-Letter Words*.

90 Our current tendency to take our economic blood pressure every few minutes…obfuscates thought on many problems.
1986 *Risk and Other Four-Letter Words*.

91 Banking is a branch of the information business.
1986 *Risk and Other Four-Letters Words*.

92 It is a maxim of cryptology that what one man can devise, another can unravel. This principle keeps armies of tax lawyers and accountants employed, but adds nothing to our national productivity.
1986 *Risk and Other Four-Letters Words*.

93 Rising prices or wages do not cause inflation; they only report it. They represent an essential form of economic speech, since money is just another form of information.
1986 *Risk and Other Four-Letter Words*.

94 Every line in the government's budget has its own constituency.
1986 *Risk and Other Four-Letter Words*.

95 It's a Texas wrestling match with a new team against you every night.
1993 On life as a chief executive officer. In the *New York Times*, 25 Apr.

Wu-ti 157–87 BC

Chinese emperor of the Han dynasty who became its sixth ruler at the age of 16. The Han dynasty saw the Chinese expanding their political power westwards into Central Asia.

96 Autumn wind rises; white clouds fly.
Grass and trees wither; geese go south.
c.127 BC 'The Autumn Wind' (translated by Arthur Waley). The poem is a lament on leaving his mistress behind while he travelled on official business.

Wyatt, Sir Thomas (the Elder) 1503–42

English courtier and poet under Henry VIII. Twice imprisoned on capital offences—on charges of adultery with Anne Boleyn and for treason—he was twice released. Many of his poems were published in *Tottel's Miscellany* (1557). He is credited with introducing the sonnet form to English; many of his are translations from Petrarch.

97 In lusty leas at liberty I walk.
1536 'Mine Own John Poins'.

98 But here I am in Kent and Christendom,
Among the Muses, where I read and rhyme.
1536 'Mine Own John Poins'.

99 Farewell, Love, and all thy laws forever,
Thy baited hooks shall tangle me no more.
1557 'Farewell, Love'.

1 And graven with diamonds in letters plain
There is written, her fair neck round about:
Noli me tangere, for Caesar's I am,
And wild for to hold, though I seem tame.
1557 'Whoso List to Hunt'. The subject of the poem is thought to be Anne Boleyn.
➤ See Bible 118:23.

2 My lute, awake! Perform the last
Labour that thou and I shall waste,
And end that I have now begun;
For when this song is sung and past,
My lute, be still, for I have done.
1557 'My Lute, Awake!'

3 They flee from me, that sometime did me seek,
With naked foot, stalking in my chamber.
I have seen them gentle, tame, and meek,
That now are wild, and do not remember
That sometime they put themselves in danger
To take bread at my hand; and now they range,
Busily seeking with a continual change.
1557 'They Flee from Me'.

4 But all is turned, through my gentleness,
Into a strange fashion of forsaking.
1557 'They Flee from Me'.

Wycherley, William   c.1640–1716

English dramatist. Educated at Oxford and Middle Temple. Although a successful playwright who garnered attention and support from both Charles II and James II, his fortunes were unsteady. Plays include *The Gentleman Dancing-Master* (1672), *Love in a Wood* (1671), *The Country Wife* (1675) and *The Plain Dealer* (1677), the last two of which were based on plays by Molière.

5 Fy! madam, do you think me so ill bred as to love a husband?
1671 *Love in a Wood*, act 3, sc.4.

6 A good name is seldom got by giving it one's self.
1675 *The Country Wife*, act 1, sc.1.

7 A mistress should be like a little country retreat near the town, not to dwell in constantly, but only for a night and away.
1675 *The Country Wife*, act 1, sc.1.

8 Your virtue is your greatest affectation.
1675 *The Country Wife*, act 1, sc.1.

9 Women serve but to keep men from better company.
1675 *The Country Wife*, act 1, sc.1.

10 Mistresses are like books. If you pore upon them too much, they doze you, and make you unfit for company; but if used discreetly, you are the fitter for conversation by 'em.
1675 *The Country Wife*, act 1, sc.1.

11 'Tis as hard to be a good fellow, a good friend, and a lover of women, as 'tis to be a good fellow, a good friend, and a lover of money.
1675 *The Country Wife*, act 1, sc.1.

12 Wine gives you liberty, love takes it away.
1675 *The Country Wife*, act 1, sc.1.

13 For my part, I will have only those glorious manly pleasures of being very drunk and very slovenly.
1675 *The Country Wife*, act 1, sc.1.

14 Wit is more necessary than beauty; and I think no young woman ugly that has it, and no handsome woman agreeable without it.
1675 *The Country Wife*, act 1, sc.1.

15 He's a fool that marries; but he's a greater that does not marry a fool.
1675 *The Country Wife*, act 1, sc.1.

16 Poetry in love is no more to be avoided than jealousy.
1675 *The Country Wife*, act 3, sc.2.

17 I love to be envied, and would not marry a wife that I alone could love; loving alone is as dull as eating alone.
1675 *The Country Wife*, act 3, sc.2.

Wycliffe, John   c.1330–1384

English religious reformer. His many popular vernacular tracts attacked Church hierarchy, priestly powers, and the doctrine of transubstantiation, and he issued the first English translation of the Bible. Although condemned, his teaching was influential in its insistence on inward religion instead of formalism. His followers were derisively known as 'Lollards'.

18 Christ during His life upon earth was of all men the poorest, casting from Him all worldly authority. I deduce from these premises…that the Pope should surrender all temporal authority to the civil power and advise his clergy to do the same.
1384 Dismissing an order to appear before the Papal Court.

Wyeth, Andrew Newell   1917–

US painter, known for his meticulous depictions of the Pennsylvanian and Maine countryside. His most famous work is *Christina's World* (1948).

19 I get excited by the shape of a person's nose, the tone of their eyes, or the way their back looks when they're turned away from me. That's my reason for painting.
1991 In *National Geographic*, Jul.

Wylie, Betty Jane   1931–

Canadian dramatist and writer.

20 First deal with your own tears; tomorrow do something about acid rain.
1986 *Successfully Single*.

21 There are all kinds of ways of being unfaithful, not the worst of them with your body.
1988 *All in the Family: A Survival Guide for Living and Loving in a Changing World*.

22 Listening is one of the lesser-known skills that mistresses offer.
1988 *All in the Family: A Survival Guide for Living and Loving in a Changing World*.

23 There is a line between sexuality and promiscuity, and the line is closer to celibacy than not.
1988 *All in the Family: A Survival Guide for Living and Loving in a Changing World*.

24 Poverty isn't being broke; poverty is never having enough.
1989 *Everywoman's Money Book* (with Lynne MacFarlane).

Wyman, Jane   *originally Sarah Jane Fulks*   1914–

First wife of Ronald Reagan and best known as a film actress, she married Reagan (her second husband) in 1940 and divorced in 1948. She won an Academy Award for *Johnny Belinda* (1948).

25 Ask him what time it is and he'll tell you how the watch was made.
Of Ronald Reagan. Quoted in Jack Finney *From Time to Time* (1995).

Xenophon   c.435–c.354 BC

Athenian historian and soldier.

26 *Thalatta! Thalatta!*
The sea! The sea!
Anabasis bk. 4, 24. Shouted by the Greek soldiers from the Expedition of Cyrus in 401 BC when they reached the sea after months inland.

Yarborough, Ralph   1903–96

US liberal politician and Governor of Texas (1957–71).

27 It is the only case on record of a man swimming toward a sinking ship.
1973 On former Texas Governor John B Connally's switch from Democratic to the Republican party in his bid for the presidential nomination. Quoted in the *Washington Post*, 18 Jan 1988.

Yeats, Georgie *née Hyde–Lees*   1892–1968

Wife of Irish poet W B Yeats. Her attempts at automatic writing on their honeymoon in 1917 profoundly influenced Yeats' subsequent writing.

28 After your death people will write of your love affairs, but I shall say nothing, because I will remember how proud you were.
Quoted in Richard Ellman *A Long the Riverrun: Selected Essays* (1988), p.253.

Yeats, W(illiam) B(utler)   1865–1939

Irish poet. He was a prolific writer influenced by Irish mythology and by his close relationships with a number of women, eventually evolving his own system of symbolism which underlies much of his work. He also edited many books, including the controversial *Oxford Book of Modern Verse* (1936), and served as a Senator of the Irish Free State (1922–9).

29 Down by the salley gardens my love and I did meet;
She passed the salley gardens with little snow-white feet.
She bid me take love easy, as the leaves grow on the tree;
But I, being young and foolish, with her would not agree.

In a field by the river my love and I did stand,
And on my leaning shoulder she laid her snow-white hand.
She bid me take life easy, as the grass grows on the weirs;
But I was young and foolish, and now am full of tears.
1888 'Down by the Salley Gardens', complete poem. Collected in *Crossways*.

30 I will arise and go now, and go to Innisfree,
And a small cabin build there, of clay and wattles made:
Nine bean-rows will I have there, a hive for the honey-bee,
And live alone in the bee-loud glade.

And I shall have some peace there, for peace comes dropping slow,
Dropping from the veils of the morning to where the cricket sings;
There midnight's all a-glimmer, and noon a purple glow,
And evening full of the linnet's wings.
1888 'The Lake Isle of Innisfree', stanzas 1–2. Collected in *The Rose* (1893).

31 O Oisin, mount by me and ride
To shores by the wash of the tremulous tide,
Where men have heaped no burial-mounds,
And the days pass by like a wayward tune.
1889 'The Wanderings of Oisin', l.80–3.

32 The brawling of a sparrow in the eaves,
The brilliant moon and all the milky sky,
And all that famous harmony of leaves,
Has blotted out man's image and his cry.
1891 'The Sorrow of Love', stanza 1. Collected in *The Rose* (1893).

33 When you are old and grey and full of sleep,
And nodding by the fire, take down this book,
And slowly read, and dream of the soft look
Your eyes had once, and of their shadows deep;

How many loved your moments of glad grace,
And loved your beauty with love false or true,
But one man loved the pilgrim soul in you,
And loved the sorrows of your changing face;

And bending down beside the glowing bars,
Murmur, a little sadly how Love fled
And paced among the mountains overhead
And hid his face amid a crowd of stars.
1891 'When You Are Old', complete poem. Collected in *The Rose* (1893).

34 Rose of all Roses, Rose of all the World!
The tall thought-woven sails, that flap unfurled
Above the tide of hours, trouble the air,
And God's bell buoyed to be the water's care.
1891 'The Rose of Battle', l.1–4. Collected in *The Rose* (1893).

35 Out-worn heart, in a time out-worn,
Come clear of the nets of wrong and right;
Laugh, heart, again in the grey twilight,
Sigh, heart, again in the dew of the morn.
1893 'Into the Twilight', stanza 1. Collected in *The Wind Among the Reeds* (1899).

36 And walk among long dappled grass,
And pluck till time and times are done
The silver apples of the moon,
The golden apples of the sun.
1897 'The Song of Wandering Aengus', l.21–4. Collected in *The Wind Among the Reeds* (1899).

37 Half close your eyelids, loosen your hair,
And dream about the great and their pride;

They have spoken against you everywhere,
But weigh this song with the great and their pride;
I made it out of a mouthful of air,
Their children's children shall say they have lied.
1898 'He Thinks of Those who have Spoken Evil of His Beloved', complete poem. Collected in *The Wind Among the Reeds* (1899).

38 Had I the heavens' embroidered cloths,
Enwrought with golden and silver light,
The blue and the dim and the dark cloths
Of night and light and the half-light,
I would spread the cloths under your feet:
But I, being poor, have only my dreams;
I have spread my dreams under your feet;
Tread softly because you tread on my dreams.
1899 'He Wishes for the Cloths of Heaven', complete poem. Collected in *The Wind Among the Reeds* (1899).

39 You have disgraced yourselves again. You are rocking the cradle of a new masterpiece.
1907 Addressing the rioting audience at Dublin's Abbey Theatre at the première of J M Synge's *The Playboy of the Western World*.

40 What could have made her peaceful with a mind
That nobleness made simple as a fire,
With beauty like a tightened bow, a kind
That is not natural in an age like this,
Being high and solitary and most stern?
Why, what could she have done, being what she is?
Was there another Troy for her to burn?
1908 'No Second Troy', l.6–12. Collected in *The Green Helmet and Other Poems* (1910).

41 You say, as I have often given tongue
In praise of what another's said or sung,
'Twere politic to do the like by these;
But was there ever dog that praised his fleas?
1909 'To a Poet, who would have me Praise certain Bad Poets, Imitators of His and Mine', complete poem. Collected in *The Green Helmet and Other Poems* (1910).

42 I have made my song a coat
Covered with embroideries
Out of old mythologies
From heel to throat;
But the fools caught it,
Wore it in the world's eyes
As though they'd wrought it.
Song, let them take it,
For there's more enterprise
In walking naked.
1912 'A Coat', complete poem. Collected in *Responsibilities* (1914).

43 Romantic Ireland's dead and gone,
It's with O'Leary in the grave.
1913 'September 1913', refrain. Collected in *Responsibilities* (1914).

44 I have met them at close of day
Coming with vivid faces
From counter or desk among grey
Eighteenth-century houses.
1916 'Easter, 1916', l.1–4. Collected in *Michael Robartes and the Dancer* (1921).

45 The horse that comes from the road,
The rider, the birds that range
From cloud to tumbling cloud,
Minute by minute they change;
A shadow of cloud on the stream
Changes minute by minute;
A horse-hoof slides on the brim,
And a horse plashes within it;
The long-legged moor-hens dive,
And hens to moor-cocks call;
Minute by minute they live:
The stone's in the midst of all.
1916 'Easter 1916', l.45–56. Collected in *Michael Robartes and the Dancer* (1921).

46 Too long a sacrifice
Can make a stone of the heart.
1916 'Easter 1916', l.57–8. Collected in *Michael Robartes and the Dancer* (1921).

47 There's nothing but our own red blood
Can make a right Rose Tree.
1917 'The Rose Tree', stanza 3. Collected in *Michael Robartes and the Dancer* (1921).

48 I know that I shall meet my fate
Somewhere among the clouds above;
Those that I fight I do not hate,
Those that I guard I do not love.
1918 'An Irish Airman Foresees his Death', l.1.–4. Collected in *The Wild Swans at Coole* (1919).

49 Very nice, but if I had rehearsed you it would have been much better.
1919 Of Lady Gregory's title-role performance in his *Kathleen Ni Houlihan*. Recorded in Lady Gregory's journal, entry for 19 Mar.

50 Turning and turning in the widening gyre
The falcon cannot hear the falconer;
Things fall apart; the centre cannot hold;
Mere anarchy is loosed upon the world,
The blood-dimmed tide is loosed, and everywhere
The ceremony of innocence is drowned;
The best lack all conviction, while the worst
Are full of passionate intensity.
1919 'The Second Coming', l.1–8. Collected in *Michael Robartes and the Dancer* (1921).
➤ *See Achebe 2:18.*

51 And what rough beast, its hour come round at last,
Slouches towards Bethlehem to be born?
1919 'The Second Coming', l.21–2. Collected in *Michael Robartes and the Dancer* (1921).

52 An aged man is but a paltry thing,
A tattered coat upon a stick, unless
Soul clap its hands and sing, and louder sing
For every tatter in its mortal dress.
1926 'Sailing to Byzantium', stanza 8. Collected in *The Tower* (1928).

53 O chestnut tree, great-rooted blossomer,
Are you the leaf, the blossom, or the bole?
O body swayed to music, O brightening glance,
How can we know the dancer from the dance?
1927 'Among School Children', stanza 8. collected in *The Tower* (1928).

54 Never to have lived is best, ancient writers say;
Never to have drawn the breath of life, never to have
looked into the eye of day;
The second best's a gay goodnight and quickly turn
away.
1927 'From Oedipus at Colonnus', stanza 4. Collected in *The Tower* (1928).

55 The innocent and the beautiful
Have no enemy but time.
1927 'In Memory of Eva Gore-Booth and Con Markiewicz', l.24–5. Collected in *The Winding Stair and Other Poems* (1933).

56 If I make the lashes dark
And the eyes more bright
And the lips more scarlet,
Or ask if all be right
From mirror after mirror,
No Vanity's displayed:
I'm looking for the face I had
Before the world was made.
1928 'A Woman Young and Old', part 2 'Before the World was Made', stanza 1. Collected in *The Winding Stair and Other Poems* (1933).

57 A starlit or a moonlit dome disdains
All that man is,
All mere complexities
The fury and the mire of human veins.
1930 'Byzantium', stanza 1. Collected in *The Winding Stair and Other Poems* (1933).

58 Marbles of the dancing floor
Break bitter furies of complexity,
Those images that yet
Fresh images beget,
That dolphin-torn, that gong-tormented sea.
1930 'Byzantium', stanza 5. Collected in *The Winding Stair and Other Poems* (1933).

59 Only God, my dear,
Could love you for yourself alone
And not your yellow hair.
1930 'For Anne Gregory', l.16–18. Collected in *The Winding Stair and Other Poems* (1933).

60 Grant me an old man's frenzy.
Myself I must remake
Till I am Timon and Lear
Or that William Blake
Who beat upon the wall
Till Truth obeyed his call.
1936 'An Acre of Grass', stanza 3. Collected in *New Poems* (1938).

61 John Bull has gone to India
And all must pay him heed
For histories are there to prove
That none of another breed
Has had a like inheritance,
Or sucked such milk as he,
And there's no luck about a house
If it lacks honesty.
The ghost of Roger Casement
Is beating on the door.
1936 'The Ghost of Roger Casement', stanza 3. Collected in *New Poems* (1938).

62 Now that my ladder's gone,
I must lie down where all the ladders start,
In the foul rag-and-bone shop of the heart.
1937–8 'The Circus Animals' Desertion', part 3, l.6–8. Collected in *Last Poems* (1939).

63 Our master Caesar is in the tent
Where the maps are spread,
His eyes fixed upon nothing,
A hand under his head.

Like a long-legged fly upon the stream
His mind moves upon silence.
1938 'Long-Legged Fly', l.5–10. Collected in *Last Poems* (1939).

64 When Pearse summoned Cuchulain to his side,
What stalked through the Post Office? What intellect,
What calculation, number, measurement, replied?
We Irish, born into that ancient sect
But thrown upon this filthy modern tide
And by its formless spawning fury wrecked,
Climb to our proper dark, that we may trace
The lineaments of a plummet-measured face.
1938 'The Statues', stanza 4. Collected in *Last Poems* (1939).

65 Swear by what the sages spoke
Round the Mareotic Lake
That the Witch of Atlas knew,
Spoke and set the cocks a-crow.
1938 'Under Ben Bulben', stanza 1. Collected in *Last Poems* (1939).

66 Under bare Ben Bulben's head
In Drumcliffe churchyard Yeats is laid,
An ancestor was rector there
Long years ago; a church stands near,
By the road an ancient Cross.
No marble, no conventional phrase,
On limestone quarried near the spot
By his command these words are cut:
Cast a cold eye
On life, on death.
Horseman, pass by!
1938 'Under Ben Bulben', stanza 6. Collected in *Last Poems* (1939). The last three lines were used as his epitaph.

67 Propinquity had brought
Imagination to that pitch where it casts out
All that is not itself. I had grown wild
And wandered murmuring everywhere, 'My child, my child.'
1939 'A Bronze Head', l.18–21. Collected in *Last Poems* (1939).

68 OLD MAN: Do not let him touch you! It is not true
That drunken men cannot beget,
And if he touch he must beget
And you must bear his murderer.
Deaf! Both deaf!
1939 *Purgatory*.

Yellen, Jack 1892–1991

US lyricist.

69 Happy Days are Here Again.
1930 Title of song. It became linked with US Democrat campaigns.

Yeltsin, Boris 1931–

President of Russia. He graduated as a construction engineer in 1955 and entered work for the Communist Party. Called to Moscow in 1985 by Gorbachev, he was sacked in 1987 and against Gorbachev's wishes became Chairman of the Russian Parliament. He was elected President in 1991. His programme for a rapid transition to a market economy, support for other republics to be treated equally, and for multiparty democracy, helped him survive the following politicially tumultuous years, but his policies have caused much domestic criticism. He resigned in 1999 and was replaced by Vladimir Putin.

70 The West has not lived through totalitarianism, with a

single ideology for 70 years. We are escaping from the burden of the past, and only after we have done that will we be ready to integrate with Europe—and Europe needs Russia.
1991 Addressing socialist MPs in Strasbourg, 15 Apr.

71 I ask you to forgive me for not fulfilling some hopes of those people who believed that we would be able to jump from the totalitarian past into a bright, rich and civilized future in one go.
2000 On his retirement. In the *Observer*, 2 Jan.

Yevtushenko, Yevegeny Aleksandrovich 1933–

Russian poet. He emerged as a poet representing the young post-Stalin generation with such works as *The Third Snow* (1955), *Chausée Eutuziastov* (1956) and *The Promise* (1957). Later works have included *Babi Yar* (1962), concerning anti-Semitism in Russia, *Love Poems* (1977), *Ivan the Terrible and Ivan the Fool* (1979) and the novel *Berries* (1981).

72 I love sport because I love life, and sport is one of the basic joys of life.
1966 In *Sports Illustrated*, 19 Dec.

Yokoi, Shoichi 1915–97

Japanese corporal who emerged from the jungles of Guam in 1972 after hiding for 28 years. He was obeying his commanding officer's 1944 order to evade capture by the enemy.

73 I am deeply ashamed at my failure to serve His Majesty.
1972 Announcement to journalists at Tokyo airport, 2 Feb. Quoted in Edward Behr *Hirohito*, epilogue.

York, Sarah, Duchess of 1959–

English Duchess and children's author, ex-wife of Prince Andrew, Duke of York.

74 Women leave the Royal Family in only one mode—with their heads cleaved from the shoulders.
1997 *My Story*.

Yost, Elwy 1925–

Canadian television personality.

75 If you work very hard, and give life everything you've got, you may not quite make it.
1990 Comment, 17 Jan.

Young, Arthur 1741–1820

British agriculturalist and writer.

76 Give a man the secure possession of a bleak rock, and he will turn it into a garden; give him a nine years' lease on a garden, and he will convert it into a desert… The magic of PROPERTY turns sand to gold.
1787 Journal entries, 30 Jul and 7 Nov, published in *Travels in France and Italy* (1794).

Young, Brigham 1801–77

US Mormon leader.

77 This is the place!
1847 On first seeing Great Salt Lake Valley, Utah, 24 Jul.

Young, Douglas 1913–73

Scottish poet, scholar and nationalist. He was jailed for refusing

to serve in the British Army in 1941. After the war he taught classics at universities in Scotland, Canada and the US.

78 The Minister said it wald dee,
the cypress-buss I plantit.
But the buss grew til a tree,
naething dauntit.

It's growan, stark and heich,
derk and straucht and sinister,
kirkyairdielike and dreich.
But whaur's the Minister?
1943 *Auntran Blads*, 'Last Lauch'.

Young, Edward 1683–1765

English poet, tragedian and cleric, best known for his satires, *The Love of Fame, the Universal Passion* (1725–8) and the remarkable *Complaint, or Night Thoughts on Life, Death and Immortality* (1742–5), written on the death of his wife.

79 Some, for *renown*, on scraps of learning doat,
And think they grow immortal as they *quote*.
1725 *The Love of Fame, the Universal Passion* 'Satire 1'.

Yourcenar, Marguerite *pseudonym of* **Marguerite de Crayencour** 1903–87

French novelist. Born into aristocracy, she spent her childhood travelling in Europe and in 1937 left for the US, taking dual US–French nationality. She is best known for her historical novel *Mémoires d'Hadrien* (Memoirs of Hadrian, 1951), and for being the first woman elected to the Académie Française.

80 *Un homme qui lit, ou qui pense, ou qui calcule,*
appartient à l'espèce et non au sexe; dans ses meilleurs
moments, il échappe même à l'humain.
A person who reads or thinks or calculates, belongs to a kind and not to a gender; in his or her best moments, he or she escapes being human.
1951 *Mémoires d'Hadrien*.

81 *Les trois quarts de nos exercices intellectuels ne sont plus*
que broderies sur le vide.
Three quarters of our intellectual performances are no more than decorations over a void.
1951 *Mémoires d'Hadrien*.

82 *Tout bonheur est un chef-d'œuvre: la moindre erreur le*
fausse, la moindre hésitation l'altère, la moindre lourdeur
le dépare, la moindre sottise l'abêtit.
Happiness is always a work of art: the least fault distorts it, the least hesitation changes it, a little dullness spoils it, the smallest foolish act makes it idiotic.
1951 *Mémoires d'Hadrien*.

83 *Entre le rôle de sauveur et celui de complice du*
bourreau, j'aperçois tout au plus l'incommode emploi de
victime.
Between the role of saviour and that of butcher's accomplice, all I see left for you is the unsavoury role of victim.
1963 *Qui n'a pas son Minotaure?*, pt.3.

84 *Que le Dieu qui nous tue nous vienne en aide!*
God who kills us, come to our rescue!
1963 *Qui n'a pas son Minotaure?*, pt.3.

85 ARIANE: *Tu n'es que la réponse la plus courte qu'on puisse*
faire aux questions des hommes.
DIEU: *En sais-tu de meilleur?*

ARIANE: *Oui. Le mot rien est aussi court que le mot Dieu.*
ARIADNE: You are only the shortest possible answer to all the questions of men.
GOD (BACCHUS): Do you know a better one?
ARIADNE: Yes, the word no is just as short as the word God.
1963 *Qui n'a pas son Minotaure?*, pt.9.

86 Out of the debris of a statue thoroughly shattered a new art work is born: a naked foot unforgettably resting on a stone; a candid hand; a bent knee which contains all the speed of the foot race; a torso which has no face to prevent us from loving it.
Quoted in the *New York Times*, 10 May 1992.

Yüan Mei 1716–98

Chinese poet who was a magistrate for six years before retiring to live off his writings. Unorthodox and hedonistic, he also championed women poets.

87 If I can rejoice for a moment,
Death at an early age would still be a long life.
c.746 Collected in *A Book of Chinese Verse* (translated by N L Smith and R H Kotewall).

Z

Zangwill, Israel 1864–1926

English writer and leading Zionist, known for his novels on Jewish themes including *Children of the Ghetto* (1892) and *Ghetto Tragedies* (1894). Other works include the early collections of witty tales *The Bachelors' Club* (1891) and *The Old Maids' Club* (1892), and the plays *The Melting Pot* (1908) and *We Moderns* (1925).

88 America is God's Crucible, the great Melting Pot where all the races of Europe are melting and re-forming… God is making the American.
1908 *The Melting Pot.*

Zatopek, Emil 1922–2000

Czech athlete and middle-distance runner. He won the gold medal for the 10,000 metres at the 1948 Olympics in London and subsequently broke 13 world records as well as gold medals in the 10,000 metres and 5,000 metres events at the Helsinki Olympics in 1952.

89 An athlete cannot run with money in his pockets. He must run with hope in his heart and dreams in his head.
Quoted by Christopher Brasher in the *Observer*, 12 Sep 1982.

90 You can't climb up to the second floor without a ladder. When you set your aim too high and don't fulfil it, then your enthusiasm turns to bitterness. Try for a goal that's reasonable, and then gradually raise it. That's the only way to get to the top.
Quoted in Colin Jarman *The Guinness Dictionary of Sports Quotations* (1990).

Zeldin, Theodore

Historian and writer

91 Brilliant lecturers shouldn't be wasted in lecture rooms: they should appear on TV. We need black market universities, in which people just help each other, and which don't leave out the poor.
1995 Quoted in Christina Hardyment 'Zeldin and the art of human relationships', in *Oxford Today*, vol.7, no.2, Hilary Issue.

Zel'dovich, Yakov 1914–87

Russian astrophysicist.

92 Without publicity there is no prosperity.
Quoted by Tony Rothman in *Bostonia*, summer 1993, p.58.

Zhang, Jie 1937–

Chinese writer whose first short story appeared in 1978 and whose writing often sets romantic themes in the contemporary Chinese world of rapid modernization.

93 When we reach communism, will there still be cases of marriage without love?
1979 'Love Must Not Be Forgotten', in *Seven Contemporary Women Writers* (1982).

94 To live single is not such a fearful disaster. I believe it may be a sign of a step forward in culture, education and the quality of life.
1979 'Love Must Not Be Forgotten', in *Seven Contemporary Women Writers* (1982).

Zhao, Zhenkai pen name *Beo Dao* 1949–

Chinese writer who has written poetry and fiction and was associated with China's Democracy Movement. He is currently living in Norway. The use of pen names dates back to the Cultural Revolution when secrecy was often essential.

95 They say the ice age ended years ago.
Why are there icicles everywhere?
c.1989 'Answer', collected in Donald Finkel *A Splintered Mirror* (1991).

96 Freedom is only the distance
between the hunter and his prey.
c.1989 'Answer', collected in Donald Finkel *A Splintered Mirror* (1991).

Zhivkov, Todor 1911–98

Bulgarian statesman, part of the Communist coup d'état of 1944. Prime Minister from 1962 and Chairman of the Council of State from 1971, he was effectively President of the Republic. Conservative and unquestioningly loyal to the USSR, he was ousted in 1989 and expelled from the Party, charged with nepotism, corruption and abuse of power.

97 If I had to do it over again, I would not even be a communist. And if Lenin were alive today, he would say the same thing.
1990 In the *Sunday Times*, 9 Dec.

Zhou Enlai or *Chou En–Lai* 1898–1975

Chinese Communist Party leader, Prime Minister of the People's Republic from its creation in 1949 until his death. Under Mao Zedong he became the Party's chief negotiator and diplomat, and vastly increased China's international influence. In the Cultural Revolution (1966–76), he worked to preserve national unity.

98 For us, it is all right if the talks succeed; and it is all right if they fail.
1971 On President Nixon's visit, 5 Oct.

Zia Ul-Haq, Mohammed 1924–88

Pakistani soldier and politician. He led the military coup against Zulfikar Ali Bhutto (1977), becoming President a year later. He introduced a new policy of Islamization and freer-market economic programme, finally lifting martial law in 1985. He was killed in an aircrash.

99 Cricket can be a bridge and a glue… Cricket for peace is my mission.

Quoted in Helen Exley *Cricket Quotations* (1992).

Zidane, Zinedine 1972–

French footballer, Fifa World Player of the Year in 1998, 2000 and 2003.

1 Every day I think about where I come from and I am still proud to be who I am: first, a Kabyle from La Castellane, then an Algerian from Marseille, and then a Frenchman.

2004 Explaining his identity—his father was a Berber from the Kabylie region of Algeria and Zidane grew up in the Marseille suburb of La Castellane. In the *Observer*, 4 Apr.

Zoeller, Fuzzy 1951–

US golfer, his wins include the US Masters (1979) and the US Open (1984).

2 Even on the mornings when I creak out of bed, I still get pumped up about hitting that silly little white ball.

2001 In *Golf World*, 13 Apr.

Zola, Émile 1840–1902

French novelist, a pioneer of naturalism. His novels include *Thérèse Raquin* (1867) and the great series called *Les Rougon-Macquart*, which depicts all aspects of society under the Second Empire. After impeaching the military authorities over the Dreyfus case, Zola was sentenced to imprisonment (1898),

but escaped for a year to England, and was welcomed back as a hero. He died in Paris, accidentally suffocated by charcoal fumes.

3 *J'accuse.*
I accuse.

1898 Title of open letter to the President of France regarding the Dreyfus case.

4 A dead reign…a strange epoch of folly and shame.

On the France of the Second Empire. Quoted in Joanna Richardson *La Vie Parisienne* (1971), p.276.

Zolotow, Maurice

5 There is no more offensive act of theatrical rudeness than coming late to a performance.

1958 In *Theater Arts*, Feb.

Zuckerman, Solly Zuckerman, Baron 1904–84

South African-born English scientist, zoologist and educator, the author of several studies of primate behavior.

6 Science creates the future without knowing what the future will be. If scientists knew tomorrow's discovery they would make it.

1964 In the *Daily Mirror*.

Zwerin, Mike 1930–

US writer and musician. He plays trombone, and has written extensively on jazz.

7 Jazz musicians have some outlaw in them somewhere if they are serious about this music… There is no valid motivation for it other than love—outlaw motivation in a profit-motivated society.

1985 *La Tristesse de Saint Louis: Swing Under the Nazis*, ch.4.

INDEX

A

Aaron A. shall bear the judgment — BIBLE 89:25
rod of A. — BIBLE 89:38
abandon A. all hope — DANTE 252:94
a. established stereotypes — GORB 363:3
A. yourself to Nature's truths — RABE 676:78
don't a. it even now — KAFKA 454:25
want her to a. herself — LACL 484:85
with a. or not at all — VAN 877:33
abandoned What God a. — HOUS 416:80
What is not a. — SCHI 718:5
abandonment organized a. — MILL 572:6
abase humbly a. yourselves — PARN 639:92
Abba A., Father — BIBLE 120:74
ABC Learn the A. of science — PAVL 644:79
abdicate Better to a. — FULL 341:59
abducted A. by a French Marquis! — GRAH 365:36
Abe converting A. into a…saint — MENC 566:84
abecedary characters…form the a. — DOMI 278:19
abed in England now a. — SHAK 746:62
Abednego Meshach, and A. — BIBLE 106:95
Abel Where is A. thy brother? — BIBLE 86:59
Aberdour Half-owre, half-owre to A. — BALL 56:87
Aberfeldey birks of A. — BURNS 171:94
aberration not a temporary a. — JAMES 433:32
aberrations nineteenth-century a. — SMALL 796:21
abhorrent The more a. a news item — FOWL 332:70
war a. to all real women — FOWL 332:67
abhors two things it a. most — HAZL 387:70
abide A. with me — LYTE 524:17
Shall I a. — SHAK 765:51
abiding there is none a. — BIBLE 92:40
abilities A. of a brain surgeon — BRES 151:19
born with instincts and a. — BALZ 58:21
people according to their a. — MAIN 541:69
uncommon a. — BAGE 52:96
ability a. nor interest — MORE 596:57
a. to examine systematically — MARC 549:36
a. to express them — KRAUS 480:9
a. to get a good night's sleep — WILS 916:2
a. to get to the verge — DULL 293:90
a. to think in quotations — DRAB 286:87
each according to his a. — MARX 558:14
eliminate his a. to communicate — SCHW 721:65
exults in his physical a. — POE 656:17
famous without a. — SHAW 777:67
lost your a. — GONC 363:94
abjure a. all roofs — SHAK 763:69
ablaze set the world a. — GILB 354:14
able-bodied every a.-b. man — DORAM 282:1
abnormal if everybody is a. — HUTC 424:53
Living is a. — IONE 430:76
nothing a. about…homosexuality — PROU 671:76
abnormality riveted by Jewish a. — ROTH 699:26
abode come to your happy a. — LAUD 492:65
Divides a. with me — DICK 273:76
live in a numble a. — DICK 269:68
abodes aiming at the blest a. — POPE 660:12
Prudence…in dark a. — WORD 929:64
abolished state is not 'a.' — ENGE 314:66
abolition a. of all classes — MARX 558:16
a. of control — TOLK 862:96
a. of poverty — HOOV 411:58
A. of private property — MARX 558:3
a. of the slave trade — PITT 653:45
abominable a. no-man — ANON 24:15
are altogether become…a. — BOOK 142:41
abomination Electric guitars…a. — SEGO 726:74
Great desolation of a. — COBB 223:49
abominations A. Of The Earth — BIBLE 127:73
commit…all a. — BARN 60:63
Abora Singing of Mount A. — COLE 226:14
aboriginal a. and savage singer — CHOC 214:17
A. writer is a Janus-type — NARO 608:74
Aborigine alcohol to an A.? — NOON 617:57
abortions Misbegotten a. — VAUG 877:40
about minded what they were a. — STER 817:67
above either a. or below it — GILL 356:44
Unless a. himself he can — DANI 252:90
Abraham carried…into A.'s bosom — BIBLE 116:54
God of A. — PASC 641:39
Abram when A. was ninety years old — BIBLE 87:6
abrasive brash and a. — MAHA 539:29
abreast gaps even two can pass a. — FROST 338:84
a-brewing some ill a.-b. — SHAK 740:60
abroad A. is bloody — GEOR 349:20

A. is unutterably bloody — MITF 589:9
a., you almost feel…a statesman — MACM 536:70
before he goes a. — STER 818:90
don't hold with a. — CRISP 245:54
haven't been a. in so long — BENC 74:99
honest man sent to lie a. — WOTT 929:70
lov'd at home, rever'd a. — BURNS 170:70
No more. I will a. — HERB 398:9
scattereth a. — BIBLE 111:40
to go a. for ayre — PEPYS 647:42
walked a. in the shower — THOM 852:76
Weather a. — RICH 685:41
whole business a. — MONT 591:67
without suspicion tell a. — SPEN 809:92
would never go a. — SMOL 801:28
Absalom O my son A. — BIBLE 91:6
absence A. diminishes…passions — LARO 491:15
a. is no longer a felt…weight — STEI 816:46
A. is to love what wind is to fire — BUSSY 176:29
a. of the real thing — BERG 79:2
a. seemed my flame to qualify — SHAK 773:46
cry of A., A., in the heart — RANS 679:25
dote on his very a. — SHAK 739:49
every a. which follows it — STER 818:93
fit of a. of mind — SEEL 726:72
like a winter hath my a. been — SHAK 772:39
marked by an a. of crises — PECK 645:7
presence of a. — BERG 79:2
shoot me in my a. — BEHAN 70:4
takes place in your a. — RUSH 703:87
Through a long a. — WORD 923:69
world, which in thy a. — SHAK 765:51
absent a. are always in the wrong — DEST 264:28
a. from us long so — SCOTT 725:56
a. one from another — BIBLE 87:91
From you have I been a. — SHAK 772:40
If to be a. — LOVE 519:11
live in you…when you are a. — SCEVE 717:93
love the a. — BEHN 71:21
think of one's a. love — TROL 866:83
absentee a. boss is best — WINT 917:30
absenteeism persistent a. — SAMU 712:77
absentees those cruel a.! — EDGE 299:3
absent-minded motive of the a.-m. — BELL 74:89
absents often say, endear A. — LAMB 486:47
absolute a. rest is death — PASC 640:15
content so a. — SHAK 759:75
If a. sovereignty be not necessary — ASTE 36:23
Reaching no a. — GUNN 375:40
absolutely A. 100 per cent — SIMP 793:49
absolutes damn, damn all a.! — LAWR 494:17
absolutism A. moderated — MUNS 604:91
absolve History will a. me — CAST 199:75
Who shall a. the foulness — SASS 717:76
abstainers burden of…prudent a. — QUINE 675:52
abstinence almost a sin of a. — DRYD 292:49
praise of his a. — MILT 579:77
total a. is easier — AUGU 41:40
abstract A. Expressionists — WARH 889:64
A. painting…confronts you — POLL 657:38
contain any a. reasoning — HUME 422:15
ideological, or the a. — ROTH 699:28
is the a. spirit — KAND 454:35
Literature is not an a. science — QUIL 674:45
pictures known…as Cubist and A. — DAVIS 256:63
test of an a. picture — BETJ 83:86
there exists none which is a. — HEIN 391:54
abstraction Art is an a. — GAUG 347:67
death…like a cold a. — MILL 572:5
thought moving in…complete a. — WHIT 904:10
abstracts a. and brief chronicles — SHAK 753:65
abstruseness a. in their language — GOWE 365:29
absurd A. in form — GOET 360:12
a. is born of…confrontation — CAMUS 187:88
a. is the fundamental idea — CAMUS 187:86
a. to regard non-existence — SCHO 719:31
attacked as a. — JAMES 434:72
nothing so a. that it has not been said — CICE 218:24
something rather a. about the past — BEER 69:69
war abhorrent…and a. — FOWL 332:67
absurdist A. plays…in No Man's Land — ADAM 3:60
absurdity a. of being in love — LACL 484:80
a., only you are pure — VALL 876:19
fear of being an a. — FIND 323:60
abundance shall have a. — BIBLE 113:90
sound of a. of rain — BIBLE 92:20
abundant life more a. — MILL 573:41

abuse a.—I thrive on it — DOUG 283:28
a. of metaphors — PALM 635:19
a. the King — SHAK 769:49
also giving us a. — WEST 901:41
Bad language or a. — GILB 353:92
contempt, a. and wrong — MILT 586:47
if it is a. — SHER 788:59
more dangerous is the a. — BURKE 168:6
only offer a. — GALL 344:15
Whipping and a. — STOWE 826:75
abuses correction of private a. — PEEL 646:8
abusing old a. of God's patience — SHAK 743:68
abyss a. of time? — SHAK 774:77
brink of the final a. — MOUN 601:39
brooding on the vast a. — MILT 580:93
cradle rocks above an a. — NABO 606:29
facing a deep a. — HUSS 423:41
mother's heart is an a. — BALZ 58:17
plunge into a bottomless a. — SUN 829:28
riding into the bottomless a. — WALEY 885:91
rope over an a. — NIET 615:12
secrets of th'a. to spy — GRAY 370:38
unbottomed infinite a. — MILT 581:28
abysses whatsoever a. Nature leads — HUXL 426:6
Abyssinian In a vision…an A. maid — COLE 226:14
academic a. atmosphere — STEA 813:78
term of reproach in a. discussions — BERG 79:92
academies A. of Science — FRAN 335:17
academy groves of their a. — BURKE 169:84
accelerator press the a. to the floor — VUKO 883:62
accent a. of the place — LARO 491:54
Can you lose the a.? — MCGR 532:93
English without an a. — BENC 74:99
Scots a. of the mind — STEV 823:24
stresses of a. — SAND 713:15
with a strong English a. — SAKI 710:32
with a swaggering a. — SHAK 757:86
accents a. yet unknown! — SHAK 748:58
I hear in a. low — GRAY 369:7
I know noble a. — STEV 819:23
accentuate a. the existing inequities — HARDY 381:46
accept worse…having to a. it — FAUL 318:65
acceptable become a. tomorrow — HELL 392:67
no longer a. — CLIN 222:10
see the a. face of capitalism — HEATH 390:21
acceptance a. of a task — GIDE 353:84
broad a. of whatever — RUSS 705:55
deserves respect if not enthusiastic a. — ANGE 17:35
access a. to a better life…denied — ANGE 17:42
doesn't give you special a. — REAG 680:53
accession a. of Commodus — GIBB 351:52
accessories vital a. to my work — BAIN 52:12
accident a. happened to the rector — TROL 866:84
a. of sex — GILM 356:54
a., sickness, justice — NEME 610:38
a. that puts a stop to it — VALE 876:13
automobile a. — GIBB 352:67
Body-line…was not an a. — JAMES 433:32
entire universe…is Pure A. — OATES 620:91
God enlightens men…purely by a. — CYRA 250:60
happens by a.…becomes a religion — WRIS 930:86
have it found out by a. — LAMB 487:63
moments of magical a. — THOM 853:98
moving a. is not my trade — WORD 925:8
old age, a., sickness — LLOY 513:98
sometimes it's more of an A. — MILNE 574:81
accidents A.…in the best-regulated families — DICK 269:75
a. will happen — NORTH 618:69
chapter of a. is a very long one — CHES 210:36
Omissions are not a. — MOORE 595:36
Omissions are not a. — MOORE 595:42
problem of habitual a. — BENC 74:2
runs into a. — MARQ 554:31
accommodation warmth and a. — NUTT 619:83
a. these aims — UNIT 873:63
For what we cannot a. — WILL 914:55
real thing they a. — MORE 597:64
accomplishment absolute a. — WORD 925:90
a. of modern science — GALB 343:96
a. of what we can do — AGAS 8:65
knighthood as a social a. — NAIP 606:51
only a. my education ever bestowed — DRAB 286:87
accomplishments ahead of his a. — STEI 815:31
reasonable quantity of a. — AUST 43:85
accord comes of his own a. — TOCQ 861:87
accordion A.…in harmony — BIER 128:11

account a. for what we do	FENT 320:89
even when you take into a.	HOFS 406:54
faithful a. of men and things	ELIOT 303:76
most precise a.	TRIL 866:66
thy name in high a.	SCOTT 723:95
accountable a. for its exercise	DISR 275:35
accountants a. and solicitors	TAYL 837:21
accounting a. department	STEA 813:79
Capital a. in…rational shape	WEBER 894:69
monomania of a.	WEIL 896:31
accounts everyone's a. but their own	ARON 34:76
accuracy grace of a.	LOWE 521:62
no fineness or a. of suppression	BELL 73:70
accurate more a. in the beginning	JONS 450:61
neither clear-sighted nor a.	TROL 867:7
scrupulously a. instrument	ERNST 315:90
accursed bless th'a.	SHAK 762:48
think themselves a.	SHAK 746:62
accusation both in approval and a.	WELTY 899:98
mutual a. spent	MILT 585:19
accuse a. 'em of not having any faces	PRIE 668:25
I a.	ZOLA 937:3
justice enough to a.	GOLD 361:45
accused before you be a.	CHAR 206:28
persons who are a.	DENM 262:98
accustomed It is an a. action	SHAK 768:32
start to get a. to it	RIMS 688:99
torpor of the a.	WARR 889:77
ace an a. of joy up his sleeve	ONDA 625:85
someone else was about to play the a.	FIELD 322:31
ache a. to utter	SAND 712:90
still have that a.	UTTL 875:10
achieve I can a. it	JACK 431:8
those who a. something	HUXL 424:63
wish to a. the best	RUNGE 702:77
achievement a. its nothingness	HAMM 379:11
a. suffer from any taint	KNOX 476:21
Art…the supreme a.	POUND 665:66
assess one's own a.	WHITE 903:95
dote on past a.	HAZL 388:82
lowest…human a.	CART 198:49
one a. of Man	THUR 859:34
perpetuating its highest a.	SHAW 778:96
Poetry is the a.	SAND 713:1
tarnish the a.	THES 851:51
achievements a.…in a…fog	CONR 235:19
most enormous a.	THOR 858:10
Where be the brave a.	SPEN 808:90
achiever a. brings home	SHAK 744:82
Achilles see the great A.	TENN 840:66
acid Electric Kool-Aid A. Test	WOLFE 920:90
misses the hiss of a.	LEHM 501:65
tomorrow do…a. rain	WYLIE 931:20
acids A. stain you	PARK 638:65
acini a. degenerate leaving Islets	BANT 59:41
acknowledge a. and bewail	BOOK 141:2
In all thy ways a. him	BIBLE 98:9
acorns hundred a. are planted	CARL 192:17
acquaintance friend…first an a.	CHEK 209:12
good creditable a.	SWIFT 830:63
make a new a.	JOHN 446:68
not make a new a.	JOHN 442:36
of the deep a.	UPDI 875:97
repented of having sought his a.	BIRD 130:58
Should auld a. be forgot	BURNS 171:98
acquainted a. with all my ways	BIBLE 98:99
a. with the night	FROST 339:99
constituents with which we are a.	RUSS 705:43
when we were first a.	BURNS 171:10
acquiesce a. with silence	JOHN 442:43
acquisition a.…of positive knowledge	SART 715:40
by the a. of wealth	MONT 593:97
acquisitiveness jealousy, and a.	JAMES 434:66
acres few paternal a. bound	POPE 659:78
acrimony a. of the last election	DICK 268:26
acrobat poet like an a.	FERL 321:11
Acropolis A., where our Christmas	MOYN 601:41
acrostic province in A. Land	DRYD 289:50
act a. a gridiron	CLIVE 222:14
A. in such a way	KANT 455:45
a. like a lady	SIMON 792:36
a. of a writer's imagination	WELTY 899:98
a. of balancing	SPEN 807:62
a. of defending us	STEV 820:43
A. of Parliament to save…the nation	CONG 231:28
a. of putting two and two	KOES 477:32
a. of the servant	LEON 503:8

A. One, Scene One	HART 384:14
a. so brave and daring	ROCH 691:62
a. without benefit of experience	MILL 573:45
any evil or base a.	PLATO 655:93
Between the motion And the a.	ELIOT 306:71
cut…The second a.	COWA 240:26
don't have to a. with me	FURT 342:72
every a. of the authorities	REED 682:88
first a. on entering this world	BOYD 147:44
how to a. like a Congressman	KENN 464:47
I can't a.	HARD 381:43
indispensable a. of policy	PITT 653:45
itself almost an a.	ROSS 698:3
joyous and responsible human a.	FRIE 337:61
last a. crowns the play	QUAR 674:37
last a. harsh, and violent	DONNE 279:32
last a. is bloody	PASC 640:20
living a., the undoubted deed	MELV 564:30
nature yearned to a.	WHITE 903:98
not to be caught in the a.	STEN 816:53
ought never to a.	KANT 455:44
painting that is an a.	ROSE 697:64
second a. and the ending	ANON 24:41
something for the Third A.	ANON 24:31
tells you how to a.	UPDI 874:72
To a.…according to virtue	SPIN 810:31
to a. with your eyes	BONH 139:55
Troops always ready to a.	FRED 335:32
Whether you compose or a.	DIDE 273:87
who doth a. amiss	RALE 677:1
acta A. est fabula	AUGU 42:48
acted a. disinterestedly	LIPP 512:73
a. so tragic	HARG 382:78
acting a. and frequenting	PRYN 672:93
a. in its purest form	BONH 139:55
A. is therefore the lowest	MOORE 595:23
a. of a dreadful thing	SHAK 747:83
a. on what just finished	KESEY 465:73
convey when you are a.	BARR 61:91
danger chiefly lies in a. well	CHUR 215:51
important thing in a.	GOLD 362:90
Method a.?	BARR 61:98
robs the mind of all its powers of a.	BURKE 167:99
when he was off he was a.	GOLD 362:71
action a. and passion	CARL 192:15
a. from without and from within	WORD 925:6
A. is consolatory	CONR 234:7
a. is not sister	BAUD 64:64
a.…most dangerous thing	CLOU 223:31
a. of some sort, any sort	POUND 665:44
a. of the tiger	SHAK 746:42
a. planned at the beginning	MYRD 605:26
a. takes place in Poland	JARRY 435:89
an accustomed a.	SHAK 768:32
by a., not…contemplation	BRON 154:68
call his muscles into a.	POE 656:17
Chafing in a.	WHITE 903:98
deterrent out of an incredible a.	MCNA 537:94
do good a. by stealth	LAMB 487:63
doubt…be removed except by A.	CARL 192:98
Drama is a., sir	PIRA 652:24
end of man is an a.	CARL 192:96
every a.…is thought to aim	ARIS 29:50
every a. there is	NEWT 612:72
glorious in its a.	BYRON 181:57
If ever I do a mean a.	STER 818:2
impartial in thought as well as in a.	WILS 916:9
in a. how like an angel	SHAK 752:57
keep step with the a.	RIMB 687:93
lose the name of a.	SHAK 753:74
made to follow a course of a.	CONF 230:87
Makes it and th'a. fine	HERB 397:93
months of a. worse than inactivity	BYRON 179:4
moves great masses of men to a.	BOUL 146:22
Neither a. nor style	ACHE 2:37
Never confuse movement with a.	HEMI 395:27
No unchaste a.	SHAK 762:54
parents…snap into a.	ALLEN 12:50
precondition to meaningful a.	BART 62:13
representation of an a.	ARIS 29:54
right a. is freedom	ELIOT 308:33
sworn to a.	SASS 716:60
taking…a. to stop small ones	EDEN 299:90
than a single lovely a.	LOWE 520:35
That a. is best	HUTC 424:52
Thought is the child of A.	DISR 275:34
true men of a.	AUDEN 41:20

truth in a.	DISR 276:60
vice sometime's by a. dignified	SHAK 736:56
victim and slave of his a.	EMER 313:35
wheeled into a.	STEV 820:53
Youth, beauty, graceful a.	DRYD 290:90
actionable only a. one we can call	SALI 711:64
actions a. and counsels	LEST 505:48
a. are questions	LECA 499:21
a. are right in proportion	MILL 570:70
a. of two bodies	NEWT 612:72
A. receive their tincture	DEFOE 258:17
advantage…in practical a.	DRAKE 286:93
conscious of their a.	SPIN 810:25
consequences of certain a.	KISS 475:89
goal of our a.	MORE 597:69
Great a. are not…true sons	BUTL 177:46
honour and good a.	BACON 49:32
important legislative a.	JEVO 438:48
invades all gestures and a.	PIGL 651:14
man's critical a.	ELIOT 303:77
Men's a. are too strong	EMER 313:35
my a. are my Ministers'	CHAR 207:33
poor centre of a man's a.	BACON 49:21
practical a. we undertake	MILLS 574:70
Strong reasons make strange a.	SHAK 739:29
tend to justify our a.	MCNA 537:96
active a. and creative world	SPEN 807:65
a. child do deeds of youth	SHAK 711:67
resignation is a.	FITZ 325:17
take an a. part	JOHN 438:55
activities consequences of their a.	HOBS 405:32
human a. which are truly cumulative	SART 715:40
activity a. of soul exhibiting excellence	ARIS 29:51
a. of the very highest	RUSS 705:46
Imagination…into a separate a.	DUDEK 293:83
life was one round of a.	LEAC 496:64
moral a. which disentangles	POE 656:17
No physical a. is so vain	MAIL 540:59
one exclusive sphere of a.	MARX 557:99
untidy a. continues	BISH 131:76
act of God A. o. G. was defined	HERB 397:81
actor a. everywhere but upon the stage	CHES 211:39
a. giving positive criticism to a director	MULL 602:70
a. has a natural animosity	BROO 156:29
a. in his heart believes	WELL 897:52
a. is a kind of guy	BRAN 150:90
a great a. or a household word?	OLIV 624:66
as evidently an a.	WALP 887:27
better the a. the more stupid	CAPO 189:34
decent a. waiting for a chance	FLYNN 328:78
decision to become an a.	MCKE 534:16
every a. in Hollywood	GIEL 353:86
Every writer is a frustrated a.	STER 817:64
face of a moving-picture a.	MENC 566:86
For an a., it is…essential	MORL 598:87
great a.…walking down the street	COPL 237:66
greatest vice in an a.	HAZL 387:66
If an a. reads it out	SALI 711:57
Like a dull a.	SHAK 769:70
main problem of the a.	OLIV 624:71
never was an a.	MATU 561:75
sweetheart ran away with an a.	WINC 917:21
actors A. are cattle	HITC 404:16
a. got in front of it	WOOL 923:66
a. or spectators?	SHEL 785:98
A. who have tried to play Churchill	MANC 544:43
Authors are a.	STEV 820:42
best a. in the world	SHAK 753:62
come across a lot with a.	GRANT 366:49
delinquents are frustrated a.	MULL 602:7
Natural politicians are skilled a.	MARA 548:23
pick out a. by	WILD 911:91
pick out stage a. at the Oscars	MCKE 534:17
says that a. are cattle?	WINN 917:25
troupes of a. slaughtered	STOP 825:62
actress a. in motion pictures	DAVIS 255:52
aim of any a.	DAVIS 255:53
For an a. to be a success	BARR 61:94
Next worse to an a.	CARY 199:64
schooling any a. needs	GING 357:58
actresses bosoms of your a.	JOHN 441:22
acts all your a. are queens	SHAK 770:87
comedy in one hundred different a.	LAFO 485:12
five a. of Shakespeare's tragedy	FIELD 322:31
how their a. are defined	SZASZ 834:62
little, nameless, unremembered, a.	WORD 923:70
put your a. together	THOM 855:45

trouble with our a.   KRON 481:22
Unregarded a. in corners thrown   SHAK 749:37
violence and ferocity of our a.   JAMES 433:32
wait on wrinkled a.!   SHAK 733:62
what man's a. is like   DENH 261:95
when a., Disease, or sorrow strike   CLOU 222:26
When you're my a.   GIEL 353:85
When you've reached my a.   EPST 315:84
woes that wait on a.?   BYRON 179:17
world's great a. begins anew   SHEL 786:21
aged An a. man   YEATS 933:52
feet of the a.   BIBLE 108:57
granted to the a. or the young   LAUR 492:69
introduced to the A.   DICK 271:33
neither do the a. understand   BIBLE 93:67
so deliciously a. and sad   SHAW 777:48
ageing A....the only available way   AUBER 38:65
agency a. in the world   WHIT 904:14
Ladies' Detective A.   SMITH 798:57
agenda any item of the a.   PARK 639:85
agent a. of the largest   HAIG 376:65
agents A. do nothing for   TAYL 837:21
detest life-insurance a.   LEAC 496:57
employed a. to help me   MENC 565:63
language...we're its slavish a.   MATH 560:58
night's black a.   SHAK 768:16
people...would not need a.   CHAN 205:89
salon for his a.   BYRON 183:10
workers, with responsible a.   LENIN 502:82
age-old a.-o. and age-thick   POUND 664:39
ages a. and a. hence   FROST 338:89
doubt not through the a.   TENN 841:83
How many a. hence   SHAK 748:98
This is for the a.   PEI 646:13
Three poets, in three distant a.   DRYD 291:24
Throughout the a.   ALAN 9:85
wisest of men in all a.   STER 817:70
aggrandisement imperial a.   CHUR 216:72
aggravates It a. 'em   LEE 500:36
aggravating an a. child   BELL 73:59
aggregate a. of all the recipes   VALE 876:14
modified a. of external forces   SPEN 806:41
aggression female emotions of a.   LESS 505:40
menace of a.   ASQU 36:9
veto upon any mere a.   LEES 500:50
aggressive inherently a.   PALM 636:23
aggressor ranged against an a.   ATTL 37:40
aggressors a. got away with it   SMUTS 802:32
God loves not the a.   KORAN 477:45
agitators cared for, not by the labor a.   BAER 51:78
Agnes St. A.' Eve   KEATS 458:30
agnostic appropriate title of 'a.'   HUXL 426:7
agnosticism that is all that a. means   DARR 253:8
agony a. we cannot feel   MILL 572:5
Birth was Hard and bitter a.   ELIOT 306:74
only a., and that has ending   BROO 156:9
soul in a.   SHAK 734:92
agree All colours will a.   BACON 47:77
with her would not a.   YEATS 932:29
agreeable a. person...agrees with me   DISR 277:77
a. to strangers   SHAW 779:30
few hours in life more a.   JAMES 433:37
power to be a.   SWIFT 831:85
so charming and a.   ETHE 315:95
agreed except they be a.   BIBLE 106:7
agreeing A. or disagreeing?   AUDEN 41:32
agreement able to reach an a.   KENN 463:34
A. reached by the negotiators   SHUL 789:90
a. signed last night   CHAM 204:62
a. that satisfies us both   FRED 336:36
draft an international a.   TRUM 868:34
full a. with Government policy   HOWE 417:97
tacit a. to call all...by one name   CARL 191:70
we shall be in full a.   DAYAN 256:82
with hell are we at a.   BIBLE 103:27
agreements A. in likes and dislikes   CATI 200:96
agrees nobody a. with you   STEIN 815:15
agriculture bullfighting does to a.   HUBB 418:10
Ahab ran before A.   BIBLE 92:22
ahem poets get a quizzical a.   FULL 341:58
Ahithophel A. saw that his counsel   BIBLE 91:5
aid a. or advice on any matter   DISR 277:73
Alliteration's artful a.   CHUR 215:50
but for the a. of the book   PROU 671:92
doth come mine a.   SCOT 726:65
in straits a present a.   SCOT 725:62
lend us Thine a.!   HEBER 390:32

Without our a. he did us make   SCOT 725:64
Aïda can't judge Egypt by A.   FIRB 323:73
AIDS A....a classic own-goal   ANNE 18:54
A., cancer, nuclear war, pollution   MAMET 544:34
A. epidemic   WHITE 902:72
A. is a major revolution   WELD 896:38
I have A.   BROD 153:48
One has A.   GORB 363:4
stop them catching A.   CURR 249:43
ail what can a. thee   KEATS 458:17
ailments our a. are the same   SWIFT 830:61
aim a. in philosophy   WITT 918:46
a. of any actress   DAVIS 255:53
a. of every artist   FAUL 319:70
a. of science   JAMES 434:62
a. of the school of business   DEMI 261:83
a....the pursuit of truth   DESC 263:19
grand a. of all science   EINS 302:46
not make thoughts your a.   KIPL 473:67
our being's end and a.   POPE 660:23
rivalry of a.   ADAMS 4:81
set your a. too high   ZATO 936:90
strikes...as an ultimate a.   ENGE 314:67
aiming Pride still is a.   POPE 660:12
two things worth a. for   HIND 403:98
aims accomplish these a.   UNIT 873:69
modern life...divided a.   ARNO 32:22
real and...declared a.   ORWE 628:62
air a. all our compulsions meet   LARK 490:27
a. a solemn stillness holds   GRAY 369:10
a. becomes uranious   LEHR 502:72
a., earth, or sea   MILT 585:35
a. is all awash with angels   WILB 907:73
a. is not so full of motes   DONNE 281:87
a....kept in its proper place   MACA 525:35
a. moves like a river   LEON 503:14
a. of a man   ADDI 6:15
a. of delightful studies   MILT 578:61
a. of the Enchanted island   MERE 567:96
a. out of God's own presence   WILS 916:7
a. pollution and...artificial light   MATT 561:71
a. shall note her soft   DONNE 279:34
a. that inhabits you   ATWO 38:59
a. that kills   HOUS 415:59
a. too poor to rob   MORG 597:30
a. which is now thoroughly small   ELIOT 306:79
a. with barbarous dissonance   MILT 577:39
all the untilled a.   AUDEN 41:25
among the crowded a.   DICK 272:55
apocalyptic horsemen in the a.   MARC 548:26
arrow into the a.   LONG 516:51
ashes, strew them in the a.   MONT 593:5
babbling gossip of the a.   SHAK 756:59
beyond it, the deep blue a.   LARK 491:43
blue dome of a.   SHEL 783:41
Bounded by the vaporous a.   SHEL 783:28
breathe his native a.   POPE 659:78
breathe in that fine a.   TENN 846:23
breathing English a.   BROO 156:6
breath of wild a.   MERE 567:12
Brightness falls from the a.   NASHE 609:18
caste up in the a.   ANON 19:80
Castles in the a.   IBSEN 428:35
Clear the a.!   ELIOT 307:5
cloud-encircled meteor of the a.   SHEL 784:66
corrupt my a.   SHAK 769:66
Courage is in the a.   FROST 339:16
crisp morning a.   VERL 879:70
dove descending breaks the a.   ELIOT 309:70
Dust in the a.   ELIOT 309:41
Eating the a.   SHAK 742:44
enmity o'th' a.   SHAK 763:69
feet...in the a.   ROOS 696:47
fire-folk sitting in the a.!   HOPK 412:88
flies through the a.   LEYB 508:11
fog and filthy a.   SHAK 766:65
foolscaps of a.   AVIS 44:6
fresh a. and royalties   ASHF 35:97
From the a., fast down   OWENS 632:67
glittering in the smokeless a.   WORD 926:19
Gods, that wanton in the a.   LOVE 519:9
high thin a.   PIER 651:7
his happy good-night a.   HARDY 382:70
I eat men like a.   PLATH 654:68
Inebriate of A.   DICK 272:57
instead of the Hawaii a. route   ROCK 692:80
invigorating a. of freedom   WOLL 921:8

left the vivid a.   SPEN 807:47
mild as yellow a.   RANS 679:23
mouthful of a.   YEATS 932:37
music in the a.   ELGAR 302:68
natural as the a. we breathe   COLE 225:75
Now a. is hushed   COLL 228:47
poetry on the a.   ORWE 629:79
prevent the a.   THOR 858:11
pure a. and water   REES 682:89
purged the a. of pestilence   SHAK 755:47
raptures were All a. and fire   DRAY 287:5
redesigned everything but the a.   CALD 184:34
room full of good a.   LEAC 496:61
sails...trouble the a.   YEATS 932:34
second place of a. and light   FRAME 333:80
sightless couriers of the a.   SHAK 767:87
smote the a.   SHAK 774:96
soft summer a.   FOST 332:61
sound...circles in the a.   LEON 504:20
spells into the spongy a.   MILT 577:30
Stud the a.   WILK 911:96
such a conscience-stricken a.?   HOUS 416:89
sweetness fell from the a.   MACL 535:45
the a. is calm   PAST 642:42
The a. Nimbly and sweetly   SHAK 767:85
The a. so thick   THOM 856:63
The pure marble a.   MILT 582:50
Through high still a.   SNYD 802:47
to go abroad for a.   PEPYS 647:42
too professional a.   MCCA 537:26
to the fainting a.   SHEL 785:85
to warm the a.   SWIFT 831:81
Trifles light as a.   SHAK 760:91
unhealthy for want of a.   DICK 269:81
vomit forth into the a.   MARL 553:7
was there like food or a.   ROCK 692:74
web of sunny a.   BRON 154:76
what are names but a.?   COLE 226:98
where a. might wash   SWIN 833:24
Wild a., world-mothering a.   HOPK 412:1
With its sweet a.   SHAK 774:82
with my bottom in the a.   PIGG 651:12
without the help of the a.   ETHE 315:98
yelling through the troublous a.   COLL 228:48
aircraft A. I loved   LIND 510:43
Loud fluttering a. slope above   FULL 341:57
unsinkable a.-c. carrier   MACA 524:24
air force naval and a. f.   ROOS 696:51
airplane artist...flown in an a.   DAVIS 255:62
airplanes a....do not make...happier   DE 257:91
aphorisms that, like a.   NABO 606:27
airport pretty as an a.   ADAMS 4:69
airs a. from heaven   SHAK 751:25
killing a. and gases were bricked in   DICK 270:4
Naiad a. have brought me home   POE 656:22
Sound, and sweet a.   SHAK 774:92
whistle all the a.   GILB 354:1
airt plaidie to the angry a.   BURNS 173:54
airts Of a' the a.   BURNS 171:3
airy A., fairy Lilian   TENN 838:39
so a. and light a quality   SHAK 752:55
aitches nothing to lose but our a.   ORWE 628:47
aits among green a. and meadows   DICK 269:79
alack A., 'tis he!   SHAK 763:86
alacrity kind of a. in sinking   SHAK 743:79
modicum of a.   RYLE 707:80
Alan A. like the flowing on   FARJ 318:48
alarm spread a.   PENI 646:21
alarming what is a. in the doctrine   SART 715:47
alarms confused a. of struggle   ARNO 31:94
dwell in the midst of a.   COWP 241:54
marriage its a.   LAFO 485:6
alas A., a., how easily a priest   SMITH 801:10
May say A. but cannot help   AUDEN 39:86
albatross I shot the A.   COLE 225:82
Albert A. married beneath him   COWA 239:23
Prince A....discovered the impotence   CANN 188:8
albinos a., bonded in their flick   AVIS 44:6
Alcestis A. from the grave   MILT 580:89
A. rises from the shades   LAND 488:78
alchemist astrologer and the a.   MACA 526:59
alchemy all wealth a.   DONNE 279:42
alcohol a. is a...deadening force   WEBB 893:63
A. is a very necessary article   SHAW 780:42
A. is the prince of liquids   BRIL 153:38
a. made the present enough   GEE 348:93
a. produces a delightful social   BENN 76:48

a. to an Aborigine?	NOON 617:57
discovered that a. was a food	WODE 919:59
help of opium or a.	HERZ 400:55
Mere a. doesn't thrill me	PORT 663:3

alcoholic about stray a. drinks — HOOV 411:61
a. has been lightly defined — BARA 59:42
keys…to a confirmed a. — BALL 55:62
Alcoholics Anonymous A. A. might have
  worked for me — BEST 82:70
Alcoran Talmud, and the A. — BACON 48:94
Aldershot burnish'd by A. sun — BETJ 83:87
ale a.'s the stuff to drink — HOUS 415:65
bliss in a. — CRAB 242:81
drink your a. — HOUS 416:73
fed purely upon a. — FARQ 318:55
Loveth well good a. — ANON 20:3
milk and a. — SKEL 795:90
no more cakes and a.? — SHAK 756:63
send thee good a. — ANON 20:1
spicy nut-brown a. — MILT 576:9
ale-house A.-h. is healthy — BLAKE 135:63
alembic From an antique a. — DOYLE 286:83
Aleppo husband's to A. gone — SHAK 766:67
alert Must be on the a. — SPARK 806:22
Alexander A.'s Ragtime Band — BERL 79:11
Dost thou think A. — SHAK 755:32
if I were not A. — ALEX 11:18
Quhen A. oure kyng — ANON 19:84
Alexandrian A. lighthouses — GILL 355:38
Alger succession and Horatio A. — MAMET 544:35
alibi always has an a. — ELIOT 308:11
Alice A Town like A. — SHUTE 790:94
alien a. people clutching their gods — ELIOT 306:74
a. planet is Earth — BALL 57:99
democratic principles as a. — AUNG 42:49
nothing that is human a. — TERE 848:76
thou art an a. — AESC 8:63
alienated a. establishment of human — MARX 557:97
alienation Without a….no politics — MILL 572:9
alienists few professional a. — DOCT 277:2
alive a. for evermore — BIBLE 126:46
born into the world a. — GILB 354:13
created for people a. — HERN 399:26
half dead and half a. — BETJ 83:77
he is no longer a. — BENT 77:75
in Christ shall all be made a. — BIBLE 121:14
it's exhilarating to be a. — RICH 685:48
many ways…of being a. — DAWK 256:74
need'st not strive…to keep a. — CLOU 223:37
not just to be a. — MART 555:50
not life-like; it is a. — CECIL 201:22
only fault is that I am a. — MAP 548:20
only mission…to come down a. — HELL 392:59
Sex…keeps us all a. — EWART 316:24
was I dead before I was a. — BROW 158:78
wish they were the only one a. — AUDEN 41:19
Words are taken a. — CIXO 219:37
all A. are needed by each — EMER 312:4
a. for love — SPEN 808:84
A. for one — DUMAS 294:92
a. have to go through it — JERO 437:29
a. is always now — ELIOT 307:1
a. of that and more — SCHW 721:67
a. shall be well — JULI 452:5
a. shall die — SHAK 743:54
A. the Way with LBJ — HOLT 408:6
A. things perish — KEMP 461:88
a. things to a. men — BIBLE 121:99
America I've given you a. — GINS 357:64
Christ is a., and in a. — BIBLE 123:67
feared…by a.! — SIXT 794:88
Goodbye to A. That — GRAV 367:65
If it is for a. — SCHO 719:27
nothing, and yet possessing a. — BIBLE 122:30
silent question—'Is this a.?' — FRIE 337:59
That's a. folks! — FREL 336:46
would that you were a. to me — BROW 161:59
Allah A. is great — CLOU 223:33
allegations scandalous a. — PROF 670:59
allegiance a. to one Crown — GEOR 349:19
flag…has not pledged its a. — BALD 54:39
allegorical all the a. paintings — JOHN 447:73
allegories a. are so much lettuce — GINS 357:60
allegory cordially dislike a. — TOLK 862:99
great a.…the world — MELV 564:44
alley dropped it into the a. — CHAN 205:94
alley cat zest of the a. c. — MARQ 554:27

alleys lowest and vilest a. in London — DOYLE 285:67
not worry about the blind a. — FEYN 322:24
one of the blind a. — WAUGH 892:19
alleyways a. and drug fiends — LIND 510:46
all-forgiving God who is a.-f. — SMITH 799:64
alliance A….union of two thieves — BIER 128:14
steer clear of permanent a. — WASH 890:87
allies a. are too frightened — TALL 836:85
no eternal a. — PALM 636:22
alligator Been eaten by an a. — NASH 608:91
alligators A. have the right idea — MACD 531:62
all-in-all intellectual A.-in-a.! — WORD 924:82
alliteration A.'s artful aid — CHUR 215:50
alliterations drone of a. — BROY 163:98
allotment capable of digging an a. — DORAM 282:1
allowance a. made for their doubting — KIPL 473:67
all right make it a. r. — HAMM 380:22
all-round wonderful a.-r. man — BEER 70:90
All-Souls Christ-Church and A.-S. — JOHN 444:87
allure If parts a. thee — POPE 660:26
to a. by denying — TROL 867:96
allurement a. of private interest — STEU 819:9
allurements What a. she used — SIDN 790:2
alluring little scorn is a. — CONG 232:40
nothing is more a. — CONG 232:44
ally a. of the people — DODD 278:5
help of any a. — GARI 346:47
Her faithful a. — SITW 794:80
infamy of betraying an a. — CECIL 202:27
treacherous desertion of an a. — CHUR 216:61
almighty A. has placed your hand — CURZ 249:53
A. hearkens unto him — FRIE 337:67
A.'s orders to perform — ADDI 5:5
A. would answer me — BIBLE 93:66
find out the A. unto perfection? — BIBLE 93:57
Truth is strong next to the A. — MILT 579:71
work of an A. hand — ADDI 6:26
almond cut an a. rod — BRON 154:76
almonds rod of Aaron…yielded a. — BIBLE 89:38
almost-instinct a.-i. almost true — LARK 490:30
alms A. for oblivion — SHAK 757:5
so give a. — SHAK 770:87
throw them cheap a. — WEST 901:38
when thou doest thine a. — BIBLE 109:96
aloe a. seemed to ride — MANS 547:91
alone A. went she — KING 469:48
All we ask is to be let a. — DAVIS 255:57
A. and palely loitering — KEATS 458:17
A. I did it — SHAK 770:73
a. in a way that no earthling has ever been — COLL 228:38
a. in the desert — SAINT 709:16
a. on earth — BYRON 179:17
A….The word is life — SASS 716:74
A. until she dies — THOM 853:89
a. when he falleth — BIBLE 100:73
a. with his laughter — KAFKA 454:29
and a.; on shore — TENN 839:63
and live a. — YEATS 932:30
Antony…did sit a. — SHAK 765:24
been, shalt be, art, a. — ARNO 33:33
But wherefore thou a.? — MILT 583:75
find himself left a. — JOHN 442:36
Hell is a. — ELIOT 309:54
I am a. — GOET 360:26
imagination never lets him a. — SHAW 779:30
least unpleasant…to live a. — BERN 81:41
lie down a. — HOUS 416:84
live for years a. — AUDEN 40:94
loving a. is as dull as eating a. — WYCH 931:17
may not find myself a. — ROSE 696:62
mortal millions live a. — ARNO 32:9
never to be a. — BALL 55:63
no one exists a. — AUDEN 40:8
not good that the man should be a. — BIBLE 86:46
not sufficiently a. — VALE 876:15
One man a. ain't got — HEMI 394:13
or a fool a. — WILD 911:87
to be let a. — SUMN 828:20
totally a. with oneself — MODE 589:24
travels fastest who travels a. — KIPL 470:79
want to be a. — GARBO 345:38
when we are a. — GRIS 373:20
you a. are you? — SHAK 772:34
You'll never walk a. — HAMM 379:17
aloof a. in pride of distinction — SAND 713:4
alp an a. of unforgiveness — PLOM 656:8
Alph A., the sacred river — COLE 226:9

alpha A. and Omega — BIBLE 125:44
alpine streams along the A. height — BYRON 180:33
Alps A. and their people — RUSK 703:5
beneath some snow-deep A. — ELIOT 306:3
crossing the A. — WALP 887:21
Alsatians dislike…all dogs, but A. — LEVIN 506:63
altar a., sword and pen — WORD 925:11
broken A. — HERB 397:89
Ever at Thy glowing a. — CULL 247:95
on his own strange a. — SWIN 834:52
socks on the a. — NERU 611:62
altarpieces almost sacred a. — ROSE 697:71
altars even thine a., O Lord — BIBLE 96:45
wings display and a. raise — DRYD 289:50
altar-stairs great world's a.-s. — TENN 843:44
alteration alters when it a. finds — SHAK 773:48
alterations a. on the map of Europe — CHUR 216:59
alternative accept that there is no a. — THAT 850:19
a.' modes of living — SELF 727:81
an a. should not be discarded — PECK 645:5
Life. Consider the a. — MCLU 536:63
alternatives a. that are not their own — BONH 140:61
choice between two a. — MORAN 596:56
ends which have a. uses — ROBB 689:14
exhausted all other a. — EBAN 298:70
ignorance of a. — ANGE 17:32
always a. has to be somebody else — SMITH 800:4
we are a. dying — PETR 649:85
what is a. — VINC 881:14
am I am still proud to be who I am — ZIDA 937:1
I a. that I a. — BIBLE 88:12
I a. what I a. — BIBLE 121:12
know not where I a. — SHAK 729:42
Amalek A. prevailed — BIBLE 88:22
amalgamation out of adhesion a. — BRON 155:87
amaranth fields of a. — LAND 488:81
Amarantha A. sweet and fair — LOVE 519:12
amaranthus a. all his beauty shed — MILT 578:54
Amaryllis A. in the shade — MILT 578:49
kind A., the wanton country maid — CAMP 186:78
amateur a. status — GRAV 367:76
sign of an a. is too much detail — BURG 167:88
amateurs disease that afflicts a. — CHES 211:54
Hell is full of musical a. — SHAW 778:90
that we are a nation of a. — ROSE 696:61
a-Maying met her once a.-M. — MILT 576:5
amazement A. is the thing — REID 682:95
often met with a. — ANGE 17:35
Amazon She was an A. — BLAN 136:87
ambassador a. is an honest man — WOTT 929:70
a. that beds a queen — CLEV 221:85
no a. would ever be relieved — HEAN 389:14
ambassadors a. for Christ — BIBLE 122:28
Diplomatic problems…discussed by a. — ACHE 2:22
amber a. to observe the forms — POPE 661:36
of A. Snuff-box — POPE 659:76
turn those a. locks to grey — DRAY 286:99
unzipped fly caught in forever a. — COND 230:83
Amberley Lady A. ought to get — VICT 880:83
Ambersons Magnificent A. — TARK 836:96
ambiguities Resolve me of all a. — MARL 552:98
ambiguity Seven Types of A. — EMPS 313:60
ambiguous a….in his opinions — MCFA 531:70
ambition all that a….could effect — PITT 653:47
A….desire to be vilified — BIER 128:15
A., Distraction, Uglification — CARR 195:79
a. enough to be employed — LOCKE 514:16
A….great man's madness — WEBS 895:2
a. has been growing steadily — DALI 251:69
A. if it feeds at all — SONT 804:69
a. is that men should have — LAUR 492:72
a. merely to descry — SELF 727:80
a. of an old man — CHUR 215:56
a. of so airy and light — SHAK 752:55
A.'s debt is paid — SHAK 747:95
A. should be made of sterner stuff — SHAK 748:6
attempt something of a. — KUSH 482:43
avarice, lust and a. — LEWIS 507:73
brutal in its a. — NORR 618:65
Ill-weaved a. — SHAK 742:35
in those days a. — LAGE 485:20
Let not A. mock — GRAY 369:14
lilies of a. — DOUG 283:22
meaner things To low a. — POPE 660:6
no desire to gratify a. — PEEL 646:9
no other a. in the world — SHIP 789:77
not without a. — SHAK 766:81

brave A. all	DICK 273:81
drunks and A.	MOYN 601:44
good A. die they go to Paris	WILDE 909:23
Good A., when they die	APPL 27:24
If…A. do not succeed in engineering	LARD 490:15
Irish A. are about as Irish	GELD 348:95
majority of my fellow A.	NIXON 617:44
married to A.	WALP 887:32
To A., English manners	JARR 435:83
What makes war interesting for A.	DALL 251:75
whether A. are to be freemen	WASH 890:83
which amazes A.	GALL 344:15
amethyst ruby and a. eyes	BRAS 150:94
silver cross soft a.	KEATS 459:37
amiable good, a., or sweet!	MILT 584:14
how a. are thy dwellings	BOOK 143:62
In Claude's landscape all is…a.	CONS 235:25
amiss little disdain is not a.	CONG 232:40
ammunition pass the a.	FORGY 330:25
political a. runs low	STEV 820:53
amnesiacs red a. of autumn	PURDY 673:17
amoeba squashed a.	THER 851:49
amor Salud, Dinero, A.…y Tiempo	ANON 26:91
amorous As a. of their strokes	SHAK 764:23
be a., but be chaste	BYRON 179:98
excite my a. propensities	JOHN 441:22
amorousness a.…is rooted in	SCHO 719:33
amour beginning of an A.!	BEHN 71:17
amphibious a. ill-born mob	DEFOE 258:14
Amphitrite A. sails thro' myrtle	POPE 659:95
A.'s destined halls	SHEL 783:28
ample A. make this Bed	DICK 272:67
amplitude action…of some a.	ARIS 29:54
amputate Thank God they had to a.!	SASS 716:58
amuse created to a.	UPDI 874:86
amused a. by its presumption	THUR 859:26
instructed and a.	ATLAS 37:38
People muth be a.	DICK 270:7
We are not a.	VICT 880:88
amusement for the a. of women	MONT 591:66
I write for the general a.	SCOTT 725:41
very pleasant a.	JOHN 447:77
work is less boring than a.	BAUD 65:80
amusements less difficult than our a.	LOUI 518:96
we have no a.	SMITH 801:23
amuses a. the people of England	JOHN 443:61
amusing I am generally rather a.	BEER 69:71
previously a. human beings	COUP 239:1
torture and death…is a.	FROU 339:21
Amynta give A. so much freedom	BEHN 71:14
anabaptist a.…I am not a member	FLEM 327:62
anachronistic a., feudal institution	ACHE 2:23
Everything a. is obscene	BART 62:24
anaemia a sort of emotional a.	POUND 664:29
anagram mild a.	DRYD 289:50
analogies a. that map the gateways	WILS 915:86
analogue no a. in space	EDDI 298:83
analysis a., all architecture	NUTT 619:83
a. of the obvious	WHIT 904:7
intelligence and a.	LYND 524:15
in the last a.	PLAN 654:59
method of a.	TROT 868:20
analyst a. in…moral activity	POE 656:17
analytic skilled in a.	BUTL 177:40
analytics Sweet A., 'tis thou	MARL 552:93
analyzer I am an a.	BECK 68:46
anapaestic rolling a. Curled	BROW 159:2
Anarch Thy hand, great A.!	POPE 662:83
anarchic been, basically a.	LEGU 501:58
anarchist an aspirant a.	MORR 598:95
To a real a. a poke in the eye	CARY 199:65
anarchy A. and competition	RUSK 704:19
call it a.	HOBB 404:28
Freedom…cure of a.	BURKE 168:13
Mere a. is loosed	YEATS 933:50
more and more to a.	TOLK 862:96
anatomize Let them a. Regan	SHAK 763:80
anatomy A. is destiny	FREUD 337:54
portions of the human a.	HELP 393:89
ANC A. is a Government in waiting	MAND 544:47
ancestors a. had…nuclear power	LAMB 487:65
Bequeathèd down from many a.	SHAK 762:34
form of our primitive a.	MILL 573:59
more…favourable…than your a.	ADAMS 3:82
most obscure of all classes, our a.	CHES 211:61
never look backward to their a.	BURKE 168:30
of life than our a.	STEV 821:79

princes my a. followed	ORAH 626:20
spirits of our a.	RED 681:71
vices of his a.	FAUL 318:62
wild trick of his a.	SHAK 742:30
ancestral A. voices prophesying war!	COLE 226:13
ancestry delusion about its a.	INGE 429:54
reminds the world of its dark a.	BETH 83:76
whole female line of a.	EDGE 299:7
anchorage hope her a. maintain	SMART 797:31
anchored eternally a.	MILL 573:52
anchorite saintship of an a.	BYRON 179:7
anchors A. on Isabel	SHAK 758:30
ancient an a. aspect	STEV 819:25
a. and prophetic fame	MILT 581:25
A. of Days	GRANT 366:52
A. of Days	SMITH 801:26
a. past?	GARC 345:42
A. Person, for whom I	ROCH 692:71
a. saying is no heresy	SHAK 740:64
a. Spanish historians of America	ECHE 298:76
a. writers	YEATS 933:54
came to the A. of days	BIBLE 106:99
Europe of the a. parapets	RIMB 687:89
Even in a. days	TOLK 862:1
held sway since a. days	AESC 8:58
poetry…in a. items	DARIO 252:2
saying of an a. philosopher	ADDI 6:16
That is the a. secret	PRAT 667:99
What Art was to the A. world	DISR 276:47
With the a. is wisdom	BIBLE 93:59
Anderson John A. my jo	BURNS 171:10
androids Do A. Dream	DICK 265:58
anecdotage man fell into his a.	DISR 277:74
anemones amethyst eyes of a.	BRAS 150:94
Aneurin A. and Taliesin, cruel owls	BUNT 166:62
Anfield bad times at A.	PAIS 635:1
angel an a.'s stare	TATE 837:5
a. and a madman	THOM 852:66
a. came in unto her	BIBLE 114:21
a. departed from her	BIBLE 114:22
a. is like you, Kate	SHAK 746:66
A. of Death has been abroad	BRIG 152:30
a. of the Lord	BIBLE 115:26
a. of the Lord appeared	BIBLE 88:8
a. watching an urn	TENN 845:82
a. will be there	GUST 375:47
battleground for a dark a.	LENG 502:81
being and as an a.	MUIR 602:67
better a. is a man	SHAK 773:55
bored of everything, my A.	LACL 484:88
By Jupiter, an a.	SHAK 774:71
clip an A.'s wings	KEATS 458:25
drawing like an a.	NEVE 611:48
Drew one a.	BROW 162:67
drive an a. from your door	BLAKE 134:36
form, so a. fair	BRON 154:71
golden hours, on a. wings	BURNS 171:5
If an a. were ever	LICH 509:17
in action how like an a.	SHAK 752:57
ineffectual a.	ARNO 34:67
in his motion like an a.	SHAK 741:86
is man an ape or an a.?	DISR 276:69
it's like an a.	SART 715:43
Killing the A. in the House	WOOLF 923:51
Look homeward A.	MILT 578:56
Lost A. of a ruined Paradise!	SHEL 785:94
madman bum and a.	GINS 357:61
Man is neither a. nor beast	PASC 641:31
man nor a. can discern	MILT 582:51
may not be an a.	DUBIN 292:68
ministering a. thou!	SCOTT 723:1
O my love half a.	BROW 162:82
O, speak again, bright a.	SHAK 736:46
pause…for an a. to pass	FIRB 323:61
send down some a.	SMITH 799:64
She drew an a. down	DRYD 291:40
something of the a.…in him	ETHE 315:95
splendid a., newly drest	KEATS 459:37
tarantula on a slice of a. food	CHAN 204:74
the Recording A.	STEV 822:88
to act the a.	PASC 641:31
What a. wakes me	SHAK 738:3
White as an a. is the English child	BLAKE 134:30
woman yet think him an a.	THAC 849:2
wrestled…as the A. did with Jacob	WALT 888:45
angelfish opulent calm of a.	ALLEN 12:35
angel-infancy Shined in my A.-i.	VAUG 878:44

Angelo designs by Michael A.	TWAIN 870:77
angels air is all awash with a.	WILB 907:73
all the holy a. with him	BIBLE 113:91
A. affect us oft	DONNE 280:49
A. along that soar above	LOVE 519:10
a.…ascending and descending	BIBLE 87:88
A. can fly	CHES 211:63
a. gave the sign	ROSS 698:85
a. play unto Bach	BARTH 62:8
a., progeny of light	MILT 583:81
a.…singing out of tune	BYRON 183:4
a. to be lookers on	BACON 46:47
A. were, but with clothes	LOVE 519:15
as the a. of God	BIBLE 113:81
beggar died, and was carried by the a.	BIBLE 116:54
bright as a. are	WILK 911:96
Desolation A.	KERO 464:66
entertained a. unawares	BIBLE 124:3
flights of a. sing	SHAK 755:44
given her to…the a.	FERRE 321:19
Help, a.!	SHAK 754:2
If men were a.	MADI 538:21
invite God, and his A.	DONNE 281:90
joy in the presence of the a.	BIBLE 116:45
kreated a little lower than the a.	BILL 130:147
little lower than the a.	BIBLE 94:87
Liveried A. robed in green	LAND 488:84
makes the a. weep	SHAK 758:26
Men would be a., a.…gods	POPE 660:12
murderous a. in his head	DEVL 264:32
Not Angles, but a.	GREG 372:93
People are not fallen a.	LAWR 494:91
plead like a.	SHAK 767:87
serve the devil and his a.	WENT 899:4
skull that housed white a.	SASS 717:78
they breathe in me as a.	RICH 685:54
tongues of men and of a.	BIBLE 121:7
very phrase of a.	NASHE 609:11
where a. fear to tread	POPE 658:63
Where a. tremble	GRAY 370:38
with a., and archangels	BOOK 141:5
Ye holy a. bright	GURN 375:45
angel-visits Like a.-v., few and far	CAMP 186:69
anger a. about religion	HALI 378:90
A. and jealousy can no more	ELIOT 303:86
A. and tenderness	RICH 685:54
a. from the nineteenth century	LESS 505:35
A. invests with such a lovely grace	SIDN 790:13
A. is never without	HALI 378:86
a. is outrageous	BIBLE 100:57
a. of men who have no opinions	CHES 211:55
A.'s my meat	SHAK 769:68
contempt and a. of his lip!	SHAK 756:78
grievous words stir up a.	BIBLE 99:30
monstrous a. of the guns	OWEN 632:51
more In sorrow than in a.	SHAK 751:12
Never a.	SHAK 765:41
on me let thine a. fall	MILT 582:46
outer life of telegrams and a.	FORS 331:35
sense by…degrees of a.	EVANS 316:20
slow to a.	BIBLE 97:63
strike it in a.	SHAW 778:11
Touch me with noble a.	SHAK 763:70
Your a. was a climate	PIER 651:7
Angkor A.…greatest of Man's	TOYN 864:29
our people can build A. Wat	POL 657:42
angle any man may a. to	BERN 81:49
in every a. greet	MARV 556:67
angler An excellent a.	WALT 888:50
honest a.	WALT 888:47
well-governed a.	WALT 888:52
anglers a.…honest, civil quiet men	WALT 888:51
angles a. of their bodies	ANGE 17:47
auspicious a. have been polished	DOUG 283:31
Not A., but angels	GREG 372:93
Anglesea A. is the Mother of Wales	FULL 341:61
angling A. is somewhat like poetry	WALT 888:48
A.…like mathematics	WALT 888:53
a. or float fishing	JOHN 447:77
art of a.	WALT 888:49
Science is a. in the mud	HUXL 425:86
Anglo-Saxon an A.-S. Messenger	CARR 197:17
natural idol of the A.-S.	BAGE 51:85
angry 50s face was a.	WATE 890:93
a. only when I hit my thumb	AMIS 14:91
a. with my friend	BLAKE 135:59
A. Young Man	PAUL 643:74

Be ye a., and sin not	BIBLE 122:47
Golf…makes me so damned a.	GEOR 349:18
reconnected with the a. middle?	ANON 25:68
whosoever is a. with his brother	BIBLE 109:88
Angst kein Gemüt, sondern A.	FRIS 338:78
anguish a….at Rome	AUGU 42:43
In a. we uplift	DAVI 254:24
In our a. we struggle	AUDEN 40:12
love is the…remedy for a.	LEBO 499:18
pain and a. wring the brow	SCOTT 723:1
world's a. is caused by people	FAUL 318:66
animal all female life, a. and human	STAN 812:67
a. magnetism drew thee and me	BRON 155:88
a. pleasure of travelling	LIVI 512:83
a. trainer…knows	RYLE 707:80
Are you a.—or vegetable	CARR 197:18
Be a good a.	LAWR 493:87
between a. and Superman	NIET 615:12
characterizes the a. world	MILL 573:43
climbed down from this a.	MACA 525:37
committee is an a.	LECA 499:20
essentially the imitative a.	JAMES 434:66
feminine spouse to the masculine a.	DIAZ 265:50
making man a political a.	ARIS 29:57
man…a political a.	ARIS 29:57
Man is a noble a.	BROW 159:92
mystical drama of the a. life	AMIS 14:97
No a. ever invented anything	CHES 212:66
no such a. by animals	LAWR 495:25
only a. in the world to fear	LAWR 494:10
Only A. that Blushes	TWAIN 872:23
peasantry its pack a.	TROT 867:17
political a. can be defined	STEG 814:7
vegetable, and mineral	GILB 354:99
animals All a. are equal	ORWE 629:75
all a., except man, know	BUTL 178:70
animal by a. who are merely	LAWR 495:25
a. could be made human	HEINE 391:48
a. grow and live	LINN 511:63
a….on British television screens	ATTE 37:39
a….perfectly designed pieces of machinery	DAWK 256:71
a. seldom or never err	LICH 509:21
a. were already…builders	RUDO 701:61
a. will not look	AUDEN 39:86
best subjects…are a. and plants	HEIN 391:53
could turn, and live with a.	WHIT 905:33
distinguishes man from a.	OSLER 630:15
distinguish us from other a.	BEAU 66:4
fabulous a….who used to sing	DICK 268:33
footprints of weird a.	PATE 642:56
greater than…any other a.	MENC 566:78
human beings and a.	MOOR 596:55
leave off eating a.	THOR 857:80
Love the a.	DOST 283:11
Men are the only a.	MENC 566:79
paragon of a.!	SHAK 752:57
production of the higher a.	DARW 253:11
reason men are greater than a.	ELLI 311:85
short-lived weak a. men	MONT 591:64
understood by children and a.	STRA 826:90
unique among the a.	BRON 154:70
use a. to educate people	LAFO 485:96
Wild a. never kill	FROU 339:21
wildest of all the wild a.	KIPL 473:46
animate a. the whole	SMITH 801:20
animosities private a.	WILL 912:4
animosity actor has a natural a.	BROO 156:29
ankle down-gyvèd to his a.	SHAK 752:40
Anna Here thou. great A.	POPE 659:71
annals short and simple a.	GRAY 369:14
writ your a. true	SHAK 770:73
Annapurna A., to which we had gone	HERZ 401:59
Anne think that you are A.'s suitor	SHAW 778:88
Annie held awa to A.	BURNS 170:82
annihilating A. all that's made	MARV 556:75
annihilation a. of one of us	SHEL 782:12
No a. without representation	TOYN 864:26
anniversary a. of the first request	DARM 253:6
as an a. present	SHAN 776:32
anno domini a. d….most fatal	HILT 403:96
taste my A. D.	FARQ 318:54
announcer voice of a ball-park a.	KINS 470:72
announcers voices of its a.	ORWE 628:63
annoyance a. of a good example	TWAIN 872:18
Shadow of a.	SHEL 784:60
annuity Buy an a. cheap	DICK 268:39

annus horribilis 1992…has turned out to be an a. h.	ELIZ 310:67
anointed balm from an a. king	SHAK 735:15
elected and a. ones	WOLFE 920:93
anomaly singular a.	GILB 355:22
Anon A….was often a woman	WOOLF 922:44
another a. one walking beside you	ELIOT 306:65
do we look for a.?	BIBLE 111:32
from which a. has been evicted	PARN 639:91
Never loved a. one	PARK 637:43
one damned thing after a.	HUBB 417:6
answer all Call and A.	LAWR 494:8
already know the a.	JONG 448:3
an a. came directed	PATE 642:55
a.: because it was he	MONT 592:74
a. for but three things	WASH 890:82
a. me declined	SHAK 765:39
a. so many questions	RUSS 705:40
a. that became famous in Deptford	DAVI 254:40
a. to his simple question	GRAV 368:86
A. to the Great Question	ADAMS 4:66
a. to the Irish Question	SELL 727:83
Beauty was their a.	BRID 152:27
cast down wi' the first rough a.	SCOTT 724:38
charm…a way of getting the a. yes	CAMUS 187:98
copying the a. out	KIER 467:8
find the a. to that	HAWK 386:32
give a.!	KIPL 471:99
how ye ought to a. every man	BIBLE 123:69
men were the a.	BARN 60:71
more than the wisest man can a.	COLT 228:55
only way to a.	TRUM 868:30
on-the-one-hand…a.	BLIN 136:95
on the way to a pertinent a.	BRON 154:69
Pilate…would not stay for an a.	BACON 47:71
Puzzle me the right a.	HEAN 389:9
right a. to the wrong question	CHRI 215:40
shortest possible a.	YOUR 935:85
silver a. rang	BROW 159:4
soft a. turneth away wrath	BIBLE 99:30
So what's the a.?	NAUG 610:26
Speak now, and I will a.	HOUS 415:58
The a. is…to be both	MACH 533:98
uncle Toby would never offer to a.	STER 817:74
what a. should I give?	TENN 842:13
What is the a.?	STEIN 815:26
your final a.?	TARR 836:98
answered a. best with silence	JONS 448:17
Tell them I came, and no one a.	DELA 260:64
answering don't even remember a.	HAMM 379:9
answers a. as ask the right questions	LEVI 506:67
a. to its questions	RUSS 705:42
a. were meant ironically	TRIL 865:65
firm a. to questions	KUHN 481:35
give my friends the incorrect, absurd a.	ELLI 311:89
learned the a.	MACL 535:39
looking to other lives for a.	BRAU 150:97
questions, not a.	LECA 499:21
resist the easy and preferred a.	BLOOM 137:3
set of ready-made a.	ROBI 690:39
successive a. to questions	PAST 642:44
ant a.'s a centaur in his…world	POUND 665:59
Go to the a.	BIBLE 99:15
men of experiment are like the a.	BACON 47:60
antagonism a. between Russia	CECIL 202:33
Antarctica inform you proceeding A.	AMUN 15:12
antecedents a. are rum, Romanism	BURC 167:80
antechamber a. of perdition	SHAW 781:1
antechapel a. where the statue	WORD 925:98
antennae Artists are the a.	POUND 665:63
anthologies a. will…continue	JANE 435:76
anthology well-chosen a.	GRAV 368:82
Anthony St. A. of Padua	MCFA 531:74
anthropological a. malady	VAN 876:22
anthropologists a., or whatever	STARK 813:72
anthropophagi A., and men	SHAK 759:61
anti-abortion goal of the a.-a. forces	LEGU 501:50
Antichrist Rome to chase the A.	LESL 504:30
anticipation dead a.	VALE 875:12
intelligent a. of the facts	CURZ 249:52
lost in the a.	WILL 914:55
anticipations parts of their a.	BAGE 51:93
anti-classic A.-c. art	INGR 429:63
anti-climax a.-c. in the English	THUR 859:43
curious a.-c.	KAZIN 456:71
everything afterward savors of a.-c.	FITZ 325:93
antics Woven with a.	SPEN 808:83

antidote a. against the opium of time	BROW 159:90
Science is the great a.	SMITH 798:53
sweet oblivious a.	SHAK 768:38
antidotes a. are poison	SHAK 762:50
anti-Fascism cause of a.-f.	SPEN 807:66
antifeminists A., from Chesterton	WEST 901:39
anti-government a.-g. at the same	TSON 869:55
anti-intellectual Science…is really a.-i.	MENC 565:73
antipathy a. to the noisy Plebeian	CHES 211:41
strong a. of good to bad	POPE 661:61
antipodes slightest errand now to the A.	SHAK 744:95
antiquated as a. as a duel	GOOCH 363:97
antique more an a. Roman	SHAK 755:40
nude and a.	SWIN 833:26
traveller from an a. land	SHEL 784:49
Where is the a. glory	SPEN 808:90
antiquities A. are history defaced	BACON 46:42
museum of a.	ENGE 314:68
antiquity A….clichéd and boring	FLAU 326:41
controversy in a.	GERA 350:26
enforced to awake all a.	BACON 46:39
great art of a.	KLEE 475:6
man who goes to a.	BAUD 64:68
rejected all respect for a.	DISR 276:44
anti-Semitism prejudice of a.-S.	POUND 665:65
antithesis one vile a.	POPE 661:41
true a. to knowledge	DE 262:8
Antonio A., I am married	SHAK 740:82
O my A.	SHAK 739:38
Antony A. should conquer A.	SHAK 765:49
A., who lost the world	DRYD 292:57
Emperor A.	SHAK 755:55
oblivion is a very A.	SHAK 764:20
ants a. in the gleam	TENN 848:73
Call country a. to harvest offices	DONNE 279:41
shuffling of all a.	WILL 913:41
anvil devil's quilted a.	WEBS 895:7
England's on the a.	KIPL 474:85
anxiety free-floating a.	LURIE 522:91
Inconstancy, boredom, a.	PASC 640:14
no comfort, only a.	FRIS 338:78
taboo'd by a.	GILB 354:15
anxious more a. to please	SAND 712:84
most a. for its welfare	BURKE 168:2
pleasing a. being	GRAY 369:22
woman who is very a.	FREUD 337:53
anybody A. on for a game	SHAW 780:60
anything A. scares me	STEIN 815:18
ask for a. more	GERS 350:38
did not say a.	HEMI 393:97
nobody tells me a.	GALS 344:22
now, God knows, A. goes	PORT 663:4
our people…can do a.	POL 657:42
People will do a.	PERCY 648:50
think that science can do a.	RAY 680:40
apace ready man who write a.	BROW 161:50
apartheid a. would be gone	WOODS 921:21
closed the book on a.	DE 260:65
don't want a. liberalized	TUTU 870:71
apartments painting…to decorate a.	PICA 650:98
apathetic never flustered, never a.	AURE 42:55
apathy a. in education	FORS 331:38
shake off its a.	RENAN 683:98
stirring up a.	WHIT 904:19
ape achievement for the neotenic a.	ALDI 10:12
a. his cubs	MORE 596:58
a. in man	MCCA 528:9
glassy essence, like an angry a.	SHAK 758:26
How like us is…the a.!	ENNI 314:71
is man an a. or an angel?	DISR 276:69
Jesus and a nameless a.	MACD 529:37
played the sedulous a.	STEV 823:25
story of an a.	HARL 383:83
apertures a. have all been stopped up	LEON 503:13
apes anthropoid a. and human beings	LORE 517:89
called the a. of God	LEWIS 508:1
cargo of ivory, And a.	MASE 559:26
scourge those a.	JONS 448:8
Tarzan of the A.	BURR 173:56
aphorism may marry' is an a.	MITF 589:10
aphorisms A….more for your time	DUDEK 293:78
a. that, like epigrams	NABO 606:27
one of his questionable a.	ELIOT 303:93
translate a. into continuous prose	FRYE 340:38
aphrodisiac Fame is a powerful a.	GREE 371:63
Power is the ultimate a.	KISS 475:91
truffle is not a true a.	BRIL 152:37

used for artificial excitement and a. purpose BLISS 136:96
apocalyptic a. horsemen in the air MARC 548:26
Apollo A. and the sweet Muses RUSK 704:38
A.'s laurel bough MARL 553:9
call the A. a fancy piece? EMER 312:20
Yea, is not even A. SWIN 833:34
young A., golden-haired CORN 237:68
Apollos A. watered BIBLE 121:93
apologies My sincere a. LEES 501:51
apology a. for the Devil BUTL 178:78
A. is only egotism HOLM 408:94
made a combative a. SHUL 789:84
miles of…self-a.. RICH 686:70
My conduct shrieks aloud for a. BEER 69:73
Never make…an a. CHAR 206:28
no business to make any a. ROCHE 690:45
apostle a. of the Philistine ARNO 33:42
A.'s advice to use wine BERN 80:30
apostles a. of equality ARNO 33:55
A. would have done as they did BYRON 181:66
Cristes lore, and his a. twelve CHAU 208:76
least of the a. BIBLE 121:12
apostolic Holy Catholic and A. TEMP 838:34
through his a. skin BYRON 183:5
apparel a. oft proclaims the man SHAK 751:20
As men their best a. do BUTL 177:38
fashion wears out more a. SHAK 745:15
rich in a. TROL 866:74
apparent It is now a. PITT 652:37
me and the a. lovers REED 681:79
apparition a. of these faces POUND 664:28
a., sole of men SHEL 784:69
as if I had seen an a. DEFOE 258:18
lovely a. WORD 927:35
mere moral a. MENC 566:84
appeal books are of…universal a. FORD 330:3
He has a gay a. COWA 239:15
appeals system of a. that pervades CAPO 189:24
appear merely as I a. to myself KANT 454:40
wish to a. considerable JOHN 444:93
appearance according to a. alone LAFO 485:14
an a. of solidity ORWE 629:91
a. of…greater genius RUSS 705:46
attractive about her was not her a. BROO 156:28
gods…what they are like in a. PROT 670:65
images in a. remote from each other JOHN 441:25
man looketh on the outward a. BIBLE 91:90
not considered apart from her a. DE 257:94
appearances contrary to all a. GOWE 365:28
depends…upon their personal a. HAGG 376:60
explain their a. NEWT 612:71
Keep up a. CHUR 215:47
appears but by what a. HARDY 382:59
since so plainly it a. CRUZ 246:88
appeasement stench of a. THAT 850:32
appeaser a.…feeds a crocodile CHUR 217:4
appendix makes man its a. FROMM 338:82
appetite A. comes with eating RABE 676:67
a. is keen EMER 312:24
a. may sicken SHAK 755:45
but 'tis the a. SUCK 828:9
gallant a. for Meat PENE 646:19
have an a. for submission ELIOT 303:2
hungry edge of a. SHAK 734:4
men in a. BACON 49:48
Nature or unrestrainèd a. CAREW 190:58
satisfying a voracious a. FIEL 322:42
sickly a. to please SHAK 773:56
vaster the a. for more LEGU 501:55
will into a. SHAK 757:93
appetites a. as apt to change DRYD 289:63
more dinners than a. CHAM 204:69
Subdue your a. DICK 267:2
applaud A.…the comedy is over BEET 70:99
come to a. their money HIRS 403:8
Fish don't a. HOPE 411:76
applause amidst rounds of a. SOME 803:67
a., delight, the wonder JONS 449:43
A. is almost a duty CHAN 205:4
A. is a receipt SCHN 719:19
A.…the echo of a platitude BIER 128:16
a. which he cannot keep JOHN 441:46
expect any a. from it MONT 591:66
food and shelter and a. JARR 435:86
her own a. JONS 450:49
If met with a. MAIM 541:68
purred a. GRAY 368:98

apple Adam ate the a. HUGH 419:45
And for an a. damn'd OTWAY 630:23
a. a day ANON 26:83
a.…better than an insipid peach HUNT 423:31
a. blossoms fill the air SEEG 726:70
a. of his eye BIBLE 106:16
a. of his eye BIBLE 90:56
a. of the eye BIBLE 94:93
a. pressed with specious cant HOOD 410:44
a. that isn't young anymore GARBO 345:39
easy under the a. boughs THOM 852:71
goodly a. rotten at the heart SHAK 739:52
luckless a. did we taste MARV 556:80
millionaires love a baked a. FIRB 323:63
rind of one a. tasted MILT 579:65
apple-pickers the a.-p. missed it SAPP 714:28
apple-pie make an a.-p. FOOTE 329:94
apples a. are overripe MAMET 544:34
a. began to be golden-skinned DAVI 254:26
a. drop about my head MARV 556:74
a. of gold in pictures of silver BIBLE 100:50
as a tree bears a. EMER 313:42
Benes and baken a. LANG 489:97
Cézanne liked a. LIPP 511:64
small choice in rotten a. SHAK 732:27
Stolen, stolen, be your a. HUNT 423:29
The silver a. YEATS 932:36
appliances all a. and means to boot SHAK 743:53
application a. of human ingenuity NUTT 619:83
a. of science PARS 640:1
a. of them that is human PAINE 634:97
Art is not the a. of a canon PICA 650:97
novel is conscientious a. NEME 611:39
applications only a. of science PAST 642:45
appointed a. unto men once to die BIBLE 124:93
appointment a. by the corrupt few SHAW 778:5
we have kept our a. BECK 68:39
appraisal a. of the drift of public DAFOE 250:62
rough a., but curiously true ACHE 2:31
appreciate a. his efforts KENN 463:29
appreciated More loved and a. ELLI 311:89
appreciation object of aesthetic a. BARR 60:77
apprehension a. of perfection NIEB 614:98
articulate a. GERH 350:35
in a. how like a god SHAK 752:57
Religion…eludes a. WHIT 904:8
apprehensions a. come in crowds WORD 927:38
apprentice time…to become an a. BEAV 67:26
apprenticeship a. for freedom BARA 59:45
at the very beginning of the a. CIXO 219:40
wonderful a. JAMES 434:57
writing…take your a. in it PORT 663:9
approach a. and depart HERA 396:66
a. to the meaning ELIOT 308:30
two-track a. MCNA 537:95
approbation a. and consent POWE 667:94
gives manhood more a. SHAK 757:86
appropriate a. act of creation FEIN 319:85
a. one to apply SIMON 792:37
appropriation with this a. comes PAGE 633:78
approval a. of a course already decided BIER 129:23
carries no hint of a. HEND 395:35
people will not buy…without my a. BERE 78:89
approve I see…and a. OVID 631:45
approximation picture is only an a. MOTH 600:33
reasonable a. to it KEYN 465:85
April A., 1920 LEWIS 505:62
A. is the cruellest month ELIOT 305:52
bright cold day in A. ORWE 629:97
day in A. SHAK 740:65
flag to A.'s breeze unfurled EMER 312:2
glory of an A. day SHAK 729:26
lovely A. of her prime SHAK 770:1
Men are A. SHAK 750:79
Now that A.'s there BROW 160:30
of A. in Seventy-five LONG 516:62
Of A., May, of June HERR 399:33
proud-pied A. SHAK 772:40
smells A. and May SHAK 743:76
that A. morn BRID 152:25
well-apparell'd A. on the heel SHAK 735:36
Whan that A. with CHAU 208:66
apron crackling white a. TRAV 865:48
aprons made themselves a. BIBLE 86:50
apt how a. the poor are SHAK 756:76
Aquarius the age of A. RADO 677:89
Arabia spell of far A. DELA 260:66

Arabian A. fleet GIBB 351:57
A. Nights entertainment OSLER 630:18
to the A. desert to collect THES 851:51
Arabs dirty and ragged little street A. DOYLE 285:56
Jews and A. should settle AUST 44:5
joined with the A., by cracky! ACHE 3:48
Like the A. KAUF 455:57
up their tents like A. LONG 516:50
Aral stars…shine upon the A. Sea ARNO 32:28
Ararat rode that tide To A. WILB 907:72
arbeit A. macht frei ANON 22:60
arbiter a. Chance governs all MILT 581:32
a. of taste TACI 835:75
arbitrary accusation of being a. JAMES 433:41
sociology ruthlessly attaches the adjective 'a.' ARON 34:75
arch all experience is an a. TENN 839:63
a. Of the ranged empire fall SHAK 764:12
a. to build on ADAMS 4:76
forgot the a. DICK 266:66
like an a., is faith MILL 573:39
night's black a. BURNS 172:20
St Louis…golden a. MAIL 540:15
archaeologists a. twitter MACA 525:36
gangrene of professors, a. MARI 550:54
archangel A. a little damaged LAMB 486:35
A. Gabriel, madam MENZ 566:90
archangels with angels, and a. BOOK 141:5
archbishop a. had come to see me BURG 167:91
sense of purpose…from their a. MACM 537:82
archbishops a. and field marshals MURR 604:7
Archer make…Jeffrey A. rich BRAD 148:67
archer laughs at the a. BAUD 64:51
archers A. stand there on MUIR 601:54
as for you, a., soldiers JOAN 438:52
arches a. of the years THOM 855:36
Underneath the A. FLAN 325:20
Archimedes A. was not free MACA 526:61
architect a. is only really a glorified tailor TERRY 849:81
architect a.…advise his client WRIG 929:79
a. of his own fate CLAU 220:64
a.'s ability to build ROGE 694:10
a. who didn't build St Paul's THOR 858:10
Art and Assistance of the A. ALBE 10:99
dialogue between client and a. STERN 817:65
I would not be an a. OUD 631:36
painter can be an a. RUSK 703:8
position of the modern a. BETJ 83:95
architects A. cannot work ROGE 694:11
a., engineers and builders BIRNS 131:72
a. of our republic KING 468:35
great a. or great architecture LUTY 523:2
role of a. MURP 604:4
architectural great a. secret TROL 866:74
respectable a. man-milliner RUSK 704:25
architecture analysis, all a. NUTT 619:83
A. cannot be understood CASS 199:72
A.…how to waste space JOHN 441:5
A. is an art MALL 542:98
A. is man's great sense of himself WRIG 929:77
A. is the…mirror of life PEI 646:15
a. is the organization JOHN 440:99
A. is the will of the age MIES 569:50
a. of the world MARL 551:75
a. or revolution LECO 499:28
A. provides the framework LECO 499:30
art of a. JOHN 440:98
can't have a great a. WRIG 929:78
can't learn a. JOHN 440:1
co-creator of a social a. BEUYS 84:13
cuckoo clock style of a. HEMI 393:92
Fashion is a. CHAN 205:2
Fujiyama of A. MUMF 603:76
good a. if it works JOHN 440:99
great architects or great a. LUTY 523:2
history of City a. JOHN 441:2
learn from a. RUDO 701:62
New styles of a. AUDEN 39:76
phenomenon of a. ALLS 13:64
preoccupying myself with a. SELF 727:82
rectangular a. TOYN 864:29
rise and fall of English a. BETJ 83:80
role of a. MURP 604:4
views of a. WAGN 884:64
arctic Inarticulate, a. SCOTT 722:78
seven months of A. weather ANON 21:34
two kinds of A. problems STEF 814:3

Arcturi daisies, those pearled A.   SHEL 787:24
Ardenne Now I am in A.   SHAK 749:42
ardent children a. for…glory   OWEN 632:57
ardently great mind loves a.   PASC 640:8
ardour a. to improve society   SMALL 796:20
  There shall be no a.   SMITH 799:65
are know what we a.   SHAK 754:17
  what we truly a.   SCHI 718:4
  where you a.   ELIOT 308:20
area consciousness is a staging a.   BELL 74:91
  must not become the new a.   KENN 462:17
  studio is a torture a.   LIBE 509:15
arena a. in which to act   ROSE 696:63
  binary political a.   LEHM 501:69
Arethusa like the river A.   BROW 158:60
Argante A. the queen, an elf   LAYA 496:47
Argie Kill an A.   PRIV 670:57
argosy a. of crocs and dragons   AMIS 15:99
argue A. for your limitations   BACH 46:30
  a. freely according   MILT 579:68
  a. from what has been done   ATTL 38:42
  can't a. with a river   ACHE 3:42
  enemies of freedom do not a.   INGE 429:52
argues a. by increments of noise   BYATT 178:91
arguing In a. too   GOLD 361:55
  much a., much writing   MILT 579:66
  not a. with you   WHIS 902:60
argument All a. is against it   JOHN 445:28
  an impression, not an a.   HARDY 382:64
  any other kind of a.   STER 817:74
  a. against giving woman the
    vote   WRIG 929:73
  a. concerns no ordinary topic   PLATO 655:94
  a. with men a woman   MILT 586:57
  a. with people   KIRK 474:86
  can't have the a. both ways   SHAW 778:1
  detected…use of an a.   BENN 76:46
  essence of an a.   SCHL 718:11
  first a. that is brought against   STAMP 812:60
  found you an a.   JOHN 446:65
  good life is a main a.   JONS 450:53
  highth of this great a.   MILT 580:93
  metre-making a., that makes a poem   EMER 312:23
  never without an a.   HALI 378:86
  nice knock-down a. for you!   CARR 197:15
  not good at precise, coherent a.   BENN 76:36
  only a. available   LOWE 520:38
  sharpest men in a.   HOLM 407:80
  staple of his a.   SHAK 734:87
  supporting their guesses by a.   BAGE 51:93
  Whigs admit no force but a.   BROW 159:98
  you and love are still my a.   SHAK 772:31
arguments a. in favor of it   JAMES 434:74
  a. on both sides   SWIFT 831:73
  a. which are brought   JOHN 443:67
  beggarly appear a.   WHIT 905:37
  intellectual A.   PETTY 650:86
  start a.   RUSH 703:88
  tolerate unlikely a.   FORD 330:14
aria sing an a. for him?   LOUIS 518:7
Ariadne Since A. was a vintager   KEATS 457:5
arias Clear a. of light   DAY 257:84
Ariel Caliban casts out A.   POUND 664:38
arise A., shine   BIBLE 104:61
  I will a. and go now   YEATS 932:30
  let us a.   STEV 823:21
  Napoleons will duly a.   HUXL 425:84
aristocracy a. in a republic   MITF 589:13
  a. means government   CHES 213:97
  A. of the Moneybag   CARL 192:13
  a. preserves us   BAGE 51:85
  a. the most democratic   MACA 526:76
  Bunyip a.   DENI 261:96
  Chinese are the a.   MAUG 561:79
  Clover…is a.   DICK 273:75
  displeased with a.   HOBB 404:28
  Ireland…an absentee a.   DISR 276:50
  moneyed a.   BLEST 136:99
  possession of a bourgeois a.   ENGE 314:65
  relief for the a. of Great Britain   BRIG 152:31
  The true a.   BLIX 137:2
aristocrat A., democrat, autocrat   TENN 845:84
  a. is the democrat ripe   EMER 313:36
Aristotle Every Poet his own A.   BYRON 181:74
  follow this counsel of A.   ASCH 35:79
  lantern of A.'s brain   RALE 677:2
arithmetic different branches of A.   CARR 195:79

ark like the A. of the Covenant   JEFF 437:21
  Noe entered into the a.   BIBLE 113:87
  two and two unto Noah into the a.   BIBLE 86:64
  when he made mention of the a.   BIBLE 91:85
  won't start with Noah's A.   ECHE 298:76
Arlott hear John A.'s voice   THOM 852:77
arm a. of the Lord revealed?   BIBLE 104:50
  a. the weak   FRAN 333:91
  a. to a.   PEEL 646:10
  auld moon in her a.   BALL 56:85
  cam an a. and an honde   MALO 543:11
  gather the lambs with his a.   BIBLE 103:37
  given my right a. to be a pianist   ROBS 690:44
  Heston thinks America should a. its
    teachers   RUSH 703:94
  his reared a.   SHAK 766:56
  Human on my faithless a.   AUDEN 40:6
  Look at my a.!   TRUTH 869:52
  made bare his holy a.   BIBLE 104:48
  one a. bent   SASS 716:67
  strong a. of England   PALM 636:24
  such an a. for a bandage   SHER 787:45
  take the skin from the a.   ELIOT 307:5
  weak of will, the strong of a.   MAST 560:52
  wound them on his a.   MARL 553:15
  your a., old toad   LARK 491:34
Armada English against the A.   CUOMO 248:30
Armageddon A. will be at our door   MACA 524:23
armaments piling up national a.   ATTL 37:40
armchair a. theorists   ASHD 35:91
  a. which provides relaxation   MATI 560:63
  drivelling reader curled up in his a.   SARD 714:29
arm-chair a. fitted into my biggest a.-c.   WODE 918:51
armed a. attempt to impose the views   SCHL 718:10
  a. force shall not be used   UNIT 873:69
  a. with the liberty of the Press   SHER 788:69
  defended by her a. sons   REDM 681:72
armies a. swore terribly in Flanders   STER 818:81
  ignorant a. clash by night   ARNO 31:94
  land a. in China   MONT 593:1
  no invincible a.   STAL 812:57
  plenty of money and large a.   ANOU 26:4
  two equally matched a. meet   LAO 490:13
  whose fingers are ten a.   GINS 357:62
armistice a. for twenty years   FOCH 328:81
armour a. of light   BOOK 141:85
  no a. against fate   SHIR 789:83
  Put on the whole a. of God   BIBLE 122:52
armoury castle without an a.   GEOF 349:9
arms a. and the man   ANON 18:65
  A., and the man I sing   DRYD 292:42
  a. do flourish   BACON 50:59
  a. hang down to laugh   ELIOT 305:37
  a. of my true love   TENN 845:93
  buried in those monumental a.   WALL 886:15
  chess with a. and legs   BARZ 63:37
  clad in my longing a.   SURR 829:34
  clasped in my longing a.   ROCH 691:50
  Come to my a., my beamish boy   CARR 195:91
  Cromwell took up a.   STAL 812:55
  effective for a. control   WEIN 896:34
  Emparadised in one another's a.   MILT 583:66
  For the theatre one needs long a.   BERN 81:51
  freeing his a.   JOYCE 452:83
  from our mother's a.   WINK 917:23
  green a. round the bosom   SHEL 786:23
  history of a. control   ADEL 7:46
  hug it in mine a.   SHAK 758:35
  if my love were in my a.   ANON 20:99
  I never would lay down my a.   PITT 653:44
  in the a. of a chambermaid   JOHN 445:35
  laid down his a.!   HOOD 410:34
  lay down their a.   GOEB 359:8
  Lending a.   TAFT 835:76
  lord of folded a.   SHAK 733:76
  lore of a.   ANON 19:90
  more strong than traitors' a.   SHAK 748:11
  muscles of his brawny a.   LONG 515:44
  Of seeming a.…a short essay   DRYD 292:52
  once more in mine a.   SHAK 755:34
  outspread a. is equal   LEON 504:18
  prize Of wit or a.   MILT 576:10
  Rank'd a. and crested heads   SMART 797:29
  sap claws up through our a.   RILKE 687:86
  soldiers without a.   PAST 642:47
  strong a. be our conscience   SHAK 732:21
  take a. against a sea of troubles   SHAK 753:74

  take me in thy a.   MARL 552:88
  took her up in his a.   RIDGE 687:77
  took the ball in his a.   ANON 21:26
  To war and a. I fly   LOVE 519:13
  underneath are the everlasting a.   BIBLE 90:59
  very long a.   HALI 378:87
  Weep me not dead, in thine a.   DONNE 280:51
  what a. have lain   MILL 571:85
  why did we take up a.   CROM 245:71
  With a., legs, lips   ROCH 691:50
  wither slowly in thine a.   TENN 846:25
  world in a.   MACA 526:71
army accompanied by all the a.   GRAY 368:91
  affairs of the a.   JAUR 435:95
  a. has had…victory   MARL 551:67
  a. hurrying into battle   ORWE 627:35
  a. marches on its stomach   NAPO 607:65
  a. of unalterable law   MERE 567:8
  a. that we must train for war   WILS 916:16
  a. that will be able   TROT 867:15
  a. would be a base rabble   BURKE 168:15
  backbone of the A.   KIPL 472:19
  conduct of this a.   WASH 890:83
  conventional a. loses   KISS 475:90
  efficiency of an a.   JAY 436:98
  honour of the…British A.   CHUR 217:84
  hum of either a.   SHAK 746:46
  proud Edward's a.   WILL 914:65
  to maintain an a.   MORE 597:62
  were a self-centred a.   LAWR 495:39
  world proletarian a.   LENIN 502:84
aroint A. thee, witch   SHAK 766:67
arrange make Him a. it earlier   RULFO 702:66
arrangement a. into three reigns   GUED 374:27
arranging a. what we have always known   WITT 918:43
arrant he's an a. knave   SHAK 752:36
Arras slogged up to A.   SASS 716:63
arrest neither a. nor movement   ELIOT 307:95
arrested exercises in a. development   SELF 727:81
arrive a. where we started   ELIOT 309:48
  persisting, safe a.   MILT 582:44
  rather than striving to a.   HILL 402:90
arriving always a. and departing   MILL 573:52
arrogance do not accept his a.   VASC 877:39
  power leads man towards a.   KENN 463:36
arrogant most a. and invincible   JONS 449:31
  not often to the a.   JEFF 436:8
arrow a. into the air   LONG 516:51
  a. that flies feels   LONG 516:65
  a. that flieth by day   BIBLE 96:53
  draw an a. arbitrarily   EDDI 298:83
  in my heart his iron a.   SPEN 808:79
  killed by the a.   KELL 460:76
  shot an a.   HAMER 378:95
  Swifter than a.   SHAK 738:5
arrows a. of desire!   BLAKE 135:84
  a. of outrageous fortune   TWAIN 871:7
  As a. are in the hand   BIBLE 98:93
arse Kiss my a.!   PEPYS 647:25
  politician is an a.   CUMM 248:16
arson A.…artificial crime   WELLS 898:82
art abstract a.'s appearance   MOTH 600:31
  adventures…in great works of a.   FRAN 333:83
  adventures of…a.   WEST 901:39
  Affords this a.   MARL 552:95
  Aims of A.   KIPL 473:64
  All a. is immoral   WILDE 908:95
  All a. is solitary   LIBE 509:15
  All great a. is born   POUND 664:25
  all mediums of a.   PISS 652:35
  all the adulteries of a.   JONS 449:25
  American a.   ADAMS 4:85
  anything other than ideal a.   BAUD 64:68
  a.…achievement of stillness   BELL 73:75
  A. among a religious race   FUSE 342:75
  A. and Assistance of the Architect   ALBE 10:99
  a. and literature are left   LEWIS 507:88
  a. and morals   MURD 604:93
  A. and Religion…two roads   BELL 71:28
  A. and Science cannot exist   BLAKE 135:73
  a. can make us see   MACL 535:43
  A.…cannot avoid cheating   RIDI 687:75
  A. cannot be made…to please   DEGAS 259:31
  A. cannot hold its breath   ANTH 27:5
  A. comes to you proposing   ANON 24:30
  A.…communication that insinuates   CALAS 184:33
  a. constantly aspires   PATER 642:52

a. continue to follow nature — MOND 590:51
A. derives a considerable part — JAMES 433:40
A. does not expand — DEGAS 259:27
A. does not reproduce — KLEE 476:10
a. doesn't dare — HUST 424:49
A.…excludes all competition — FUSE 342:73
A. for a.'s sake — CONS 235:29
A. for a.'s sake — FORS 331:50
A. for a.'s sake — SAND 712:89
a. for practitioners and readers — LEAV 498:1
A., Glory, Freedom fail — BYRON 179:16
a. has no place in…life — RODC 693:87
A. has to move you — HOCK 405:40
A., if you like — LARK 490:22
a., in London — DRYD 288:40
A. is a game — PIER 651:9
A. is a jealous mistress — EMER 313:41
A. is an abstraction — GAUG 347:67
A. is a point of view — WERE 899:6
A. is dedicated echo — SANT 714:23
A. is history's nostalgia — WALC 885:80
A. is like Creation — KLEE 475:9
a. is long — CARM 193:47
A. is long, and time — LONG 515:42
A. is not a brassière — BARN 60:69
A. is not…a canon of beauty — PICA 650:97
A. is nothing without form — FLAU 326:29
a. is not…merely a skill — FRIE 337:70
A. is not truth — PICA 650:2
A. is only a means to life — MILL 573:41
a. is only possible — BEUYS 84:13
a. is pursued with a view to money — BUTL 178:76
A. is significant deformity — FRY 340:33
a. is the child — KAND 454:37
A. is the only work — GRAY 368:89
a. is the perfection of nature — BROW 158:68
a. is the retelling — LUCAS 522:80
a.…life imitates it — LEBO 499:10
A. may make a suit — HUME 422:10
A. most cherishes — BROW 162:65
a. museums to worship dead works — MAYA 562:92
A. must take reality by surprise — SAGAN 709:7
A. never expresses anything — WILDE 908:89
a., not chance — POPE 658:59
A. of all periods — RUNGE 702:74
a. of angling — WALT 888:49
a. of architecture — JOHN 440:98
a. of balance, of purity — MATI 560:63
a. of drawing — LIEB 509:26
a. of getting drunk — JOHN 445:36
a. of government — SHAW 778:4
a. of inexactitude — MURR 605:12
a. of losing — BISH 131:80
a. of making the most — SHAW 779:14
a. of newspaper paragraphing — MARQ 554:34
a. of our necessities — SHAK 763:75
a. of painting cannot be…judged — DURER 295:28
a. of perceiving — DICK 270:8
a. of pleasing — HAZL 387:68
a. of poetry — MACL 535:51
A. of Scratch — RUSK 704:30
a. of systematic over-simplification — POPP 663:2
a. of the masses — HALL 378:92
a. of the past — LEWI 508:8
a. of the writer — APOL 27:15
A. pales when compared — AQUI 28:31
A. produces ugly things — COCT 224:61
a. reverenced the while — JONS 449:36
a. should be a monster — TZARA 873:59
A. should be independent — WHIS 902:65
A.'s subject is the human clay — AUDEN 39:85
a. that conceals a. — HARDY 382:56
a. that helps old ladies — OLDE 624:62
a. that is interested in itself — SANT 714:24
a., that monopolizes — DUDEK 293:83
A.—the one achievement — THUR 859:34
A.…the supreme achievement — POUND 665:66
A. to fold her hands — ROSS 698:98
a. united with prophecy — NISB 616:39
A. was made to disturb — BRAQ 150:92
A.…will have a country — APOL 27:19
A. will liberate itself — MARC 548:27
a. world is a jungle — HAMM 379:12
as in a., dependent — RUSS 705:46
assaying of tea is an a. — MO 589:21
As the a. of reading — JAMES 434:65
attempt to realize A. — HOLM 408:95

Ausonia, skilled in every a. — BYRON 179:1
a very pretty a. — PEPYS 647:34
a wife in this a. of mine — MICH 568:35
beauty has in a. — DIDE 273:85
became an expert's a. — RUDO 701:62
become human is a. — NOVA 619:76
beginning and end of a. — HEIN 391:52
better teachers of the A. of Painting — DURER 295:29
betwixt Nature and A. — PRIOR 669:41
black a. to dispense — VAUG 878:45
boundaries between politics and a. — DANG 252:86
Bullfighting is the only a. — HEMI 394:5
burglar who respects his a. — OHEN 623:58
clever, but is it A.? — KIPL 471:4
conceptual a. the idea — LEWI 508:7
concern itself with a. — KLEE 475:7
condition of a. — CONR 234:94
corner-stones of literary a. — DUDEK 293:78
corrupt a. is the sentimental — PISS 652:32
counts as a work of a. — WILL 914:58
Dalí's importance…for a. historians — SCHW 721:60
Decorative a. does not exist — ROUA 700:38
delights of a. satisfy me — FUEN 340:41
demonstrates the a. of measuring — NEWT 612:73
destroy genius and a. — HAZL 388:94
deviating from the rules of a. — ADDI 7:41
difference between…true a. — CAPO 189:29
difficulty of a. — CHAR 206:25
Dress is a form of visual a. — HOLL 407:68
drunk we like our a. — LUCAS 522:77
Dying, Is an a. — PLATH 654:67
emotion of a. — ELIOT 305:45
end and test of a. — POPE 658:53
enemy of good a. — CONN 233:69
Europe had plenty of a. — BEHR 71:23
ever seen in A. or Nature — WAUGH 892:37
Every a.…is thought to aim — ARIS 29:50
Every true work of a. — FRIE 337:72
expressing emotion in the form of a. — ELIOT 305:47
Faustus, leave this damnèd a. — MARL 552:4
Film a. has a greater influence — BALA 53:26
final purpose of a. — MAIL 539:41
find in a. and science — HALD 377:76
Fond without a. — DRYD 289:64
for a shilling…conflict and a. — PRIE 668:17
fruits of speaking a.? — SIDN 790:3
future of a. — FLAU 326:31
give their lives to a. and science — EINS 301:33
glory and good of A. — BROW 162:89
goal of a. is almost divine — HUGO 420:63
good is always a product of a. — BAUD 65:73
great a. is great life — WRIG 929:77
Great a. is the contempt — FITZ 325:15
great a. of antiquity — KLEE 475:6
Happiness is always a work of a. — YOUR 935:82
hating, my boy, is an a. — NASH 608:83
hide…their want of a. — POPE 658:55
History…is an a. — FRAN 333:90
If a. does not enlarge…sympathies — ELIOT 303:84
If a work of a. is to be truly immortal — CHIR 213:15
If it is a. — SCHO 719:27
if it may even be called an a. — INGR 429:63
In a. economy is always beauty — JAMES 433:51
In a. one is — MODE 589:24
in a. the best is good enough. — GOET 360:14
in a. we have to follow — MOND 590:52
industry without a. — RUSK 704:29
informing them as a. — BLOOM 137:4
In Spenser, and in Jonson, A. — DENH 261:94
In sweet music is such a. — SHAK 775:13
In sweet music is such a. — SHAK 775:15
iron palaces of A. — HUGH 419:30
Isherwood became…a work of a. — BURU 174:84
Italy…home Of all A. — BYRON 180:32
it's only a. — CHAP 206:13
knows what a work of a. is — FRY 340:32
last and greatest a. — POPE 661:55
least realistic of a. forms — MAMET 544:38
leave a. to us — EPST 314:75
let it be an a. — SHAK 770:99
Life does not imitate a. — ALLEN 12:59
Life imitates A. far more — WILDE 908:98
Like a. and politics — DOCT 278:4
Literature…is an A. — QUIL 674:45
Literature is the a. of writing — CONN 233:65
lost, for a., at Sarajevo — LEWIS 508:4
Love…is also an a. — BALZ 57:15

love of a. for its own sake — PATER 642:53
masterpiece of a. has…a fixed place — EMER 312:20
men who have failed in…a. — DISR 277:76
modern a.…completely literary — WOLFE 920:92
Modern a. does not — ROSE 697:66
Modern A. no longer — ROSE 697:65
Modern a. tends towards — BAUD 65:74
morality of a. — WILDE 908:2
More matter with less a. — SHAK 752:43
more than Wisdom, A., or Nature — HERR 399:39
My religion and my a. — JOHN 439:67
nation's a. is greatest — HOPP 413:14
Nature in him was almost lost in A. — COLL 228:40
nature is the a. of God — BROW 158:69
nature's handmaid is. — DRYD 287:20
Nature that is above all a. — DANI 252:91
never know all about a. — OLSEN 625:77
new a. to them is natural — DAVI 254:33
new a. work is born — YOUR 936:86
next to Nature, A. — LAND 488:83
no a. which one government — SMITH 798:54
no a. without practice — PROT 670:64
no boundary line to a. — PARK 637:40
no history of a. — WERE 899:7
no one will take to a. — BELL 71:30
no such thing as authentic a. — CUMM 247:99
not as an a. form — TZARA 873:60
not the courtier's a. — DRYD 290:53
Not to admire, is all the a. — POPE 661:59
of ev'ry a. the soul — POPE 659:94
oldest a. in the world — CHAP 206:9
only a. that they look upon — WOLFE 920:96
perception of works of a. — DEWEY 264:44
perfection in a new kind of a. — RUNGE 702:75
photography…stand in for a. — BAUD 64:97
Poetry…is an a. of imitation — SIDN 791:19
Poetry is the a. of understanding — MACL 535:50
Politics is the a. of — VALE 876:16
pop a. and fine a. — MACI 533:5
Posing is a performing a. — SCHW 721:61
power of all true a. — EINS 301:37
preoccupying myself with…a. — SELF 727:82
pretty, but is it A.? — KIPL 471:3
procrastination is the a. — MARQ 554:23
profuse strains of unpremeditated a. — SHEL 784:54
Protestant form of a. — ORWE 628:56
purpose of a. — GOULD 364:21
reactions to a. or to music — COLE 225:76
reading…itself an a. — CARY 198:59
Religion and a.…from the same root — CATH 200:14
revenge of the intellect upon a. — SONT 804:70
rid of the element of a. in their being — CHES 211:54
says I know the a. — SPEN 809:97
schoolman's subtle a. — POPE 661:42
seven…exhibitions of modern a. — DUNL 295:16
sharp compassion of the healer's a. — ELIOT 308:21
shouldn't talk about a. — JOHN 440:1
spare…patience towards…music or a. — GLEN 359:4
specialized form of a. — PRIT 669:47
spit in the face of A. — MILL 572:15
start on all this A. — HERB 397:76
sweet music is such a. — SHAK 775:13
sweet music is such a. — SHAK 775:15
symbol of Irish a. — JOYCE 452:85
Teaching is not a lost a. — BARZ 63:32
than when A. — HERR 400:50
The a. of war — SUN 828:24
the dead a. of poetry — POUND 664:35
the end of A. — TURN 870:68
the necessary a. — DULL 293:90
There is no abstract a. — PICA 650:96
third great form of a. — HUGO 420:74
Though a.'s hid causes — JONS 449:25
through A.…realise our perfection — WILDE 908:44
Today a. is moving — MARC 548:26
trade and a. is to live — MONT 592:79
transformed into comic a. — ROTH 699:22
truth of a. should never be — HUGO 420:62
ultimate in a. — RUNGE 702:76
unattainable by the highest a. — STRA 826:80
undreamed-of collection of a. — SAAR 707:81
want that glib and oily a. — SHAK 762:54
What a. can wash her guilt — GOLD 361:47
What A. was to the ancient world — DISR 276:47
What is a. is not likely to be decided — COND 230:84
When a. communicates — WILL 912:10
where the a. resides — SCHN 719:18

Why shouldn't a. be pretty?	RENO 683:11	marriages, where both or one is an a.	SPARK 806:33	Oak, and A., and Thorn	KIPL 473:59
without the idea of a.	VIDAL 881:5	might as well be an a.	STOP 825:65	Out of the a.	PLATH 654:68
work of a.	NABO 606:40	More glutton than a.	PARK 637:48	There grows the wild a.	CALL 185:43
work of a., and as life	MILL 573:44	most American a. of all	ADLER 7:49	**ashamed** a. at my failure to serve	YOKOI 935:73
writer's only responsibility is to his a.	FAUL 318:68	Never trust the a.	LAWR 494:14	a. of one another	CONG 232:45
year of a. and dissipation	MOORE 595:22	not up to the a.…to find	GENET 348:4	a. to be my father's child!	SHAK 740:58
You talk of a.	SHAW 781:93	only become a good a.	INGR 429:64	feel a. of home	DICK 271:31
arterial it is a. blood	KEATS 460:65	pain that the a. feels	REDON 681:73	more things a man is a. of	SHAW 778:82
arteriosclerosis a. of culture	MILL 573:59	Portrait of the A. as	THOM 852:69	not…afraid of death, as a.	BROW 158:73
art-form a.-f.…invented in England	BEER 70:92	product of the a.	MAMET 543:26	not a. of…the American dream	SHUL 790:93
artful No a. wildness to perplex	POPE 659:95	qualities essential for the a.	DIDE 274:99	not a. to fail	JOHN 441:10
arthritis man who owns up to a.	NASH 608:82	Remember I'm an a.	CARY 199:64	seldom a.…that he cannot love	ELIOT 304:12
Arthur A.'s sword snatched	MUNRO 603:84	reward one should offer an a.	RENO 683:8	something he is a. of	SHAW 778:78
A. the firste syght of queene	MALO 542:4	special kind of a.	GILL 356:43	**Ashbourn** native of A., Derbyshire	ANON 21:29
courte of kynge A.	MALO 542:7	subject matter of the a.	WILDE 908:2	**ashbuds** More black than a.	TENN 840:69
kynge A. ys nat dede	MALO 543:12	to be lonely as an a.	THOM 852:68	**ashes** a. all my lust	MARV 556:63
named hym A.	MALO 542:2	what an a. does, is fail	BART 62:15	A. and sparks, my words	SHEL 783:48
Speak for England, A.!	AMERY 14:79	what style is to an a.	BUEC 165:43	a. of an oak	DONNE 281:79
article affect a singularity in that a.	SHER 787:38	writer of a.	STEV 824:40	a. taken to Australia	ANON 21:33
Alcohol is a very necessary a.	SHAW 780:42	**artiste** a. with short arms	BERN 81:51	a. to a.	BOOK 142:35
a. which nobody wants	HONE 409:27	**artistic** A. growth…a refining of the sense	CATH 200:86	a. under Uricon	HOUS 415:56
desireus of being the correct a.	ASHF 35:98	a. sense of eye or ear	WHIS 902:65	beauty for a.	BIBLE 104:62
For a slashing a.	THAC 849:99	a. temperament is a disease	CHES 211:54	burnt to a.	GRAH 365:35
In fact, the finished a.	RUSS 706:67	departure for our a. creation	WAGN 884:64	handful of grey a.	CORY 237:75
ordinary home-made a.	DICK 270:97	slightly a.	KENN 462:2	men and women…shall pass to a.	SAND 713:93
single sentence in a routine a.	MEYER 568:30	**artistry** invention or true a.	POUND 665:60	past is a bucket of a.	SAND 713:94
articles a. published in scientific	FEYN 322:24	**artists** are not savages a.	MACKE 533:18	repent in dust and a.	BIBLE 94:79
exchanging a.	RUSK 704:35	A. and poets	ANON 25:58	sat down among the a.	BIBLE 93:50
These a. subscribed	CONG 232:46	A. are the antennae	POUND 665:63	Scatter my a.	MONT 593:5
articulate a. and complete	STEV 820:31	A. are the only people	SLOAN 796:18	sour grapes and a.	ASHF 35:99
neither a. or worshipful	SNYD 803:51	a. go potty as they get older	BLAIR 133:20	splendid in a.	BROW 159:92
articulation A. is the tongue-tied's fighting	HARR 384:1	A.…if you copy others	BERN 81:46	tarnished with a. and soot	MOORE 594:18
artifice Art…through a.	RIDI 687:81	a. must break a hole	HALE 377:79	**ashore** perilous excursion a.	LEWIS 507:87
to conceal his a.	OGIL 623:41	a. produce something that	WILD 911:84	water comes a.	FROST 339:2
without a., I…work	ARET 29:42	a. took to the road	ROCK 693:84	**ashtrays** a. will become as obsolete	BLACK 132:90
artificer an a.…who formed it	PALEY 635:16	a. try to break your heart	RAUS 679:34	**Asia** dusty catastrophe of A.	BROD 153:53
single a. of the world	STEV 819:27	a. will…instruct us	OLSEN 625:77	from the furthest inch of A.	SHAK 744:95
The great a.	STEV 823:34	a.… want to become inhuman	APOL 27:13	in A. as elsewhere	BALD 54:49
artificial All things are a.	BROW 158:69	best subjects for a.	HEIN 391:53	pampered Jades of A.	MARL 552:83
arrest motion…by a. means	FAUL 319:70	conceived…by unknown a.	BART 62:18	seven churches which are in A.	BIBLE 125:42
artillery Our light a.	GILB 354:16	English a. are…ruined	RUSK 704:32	seven churches which are in A.	BIBLE 125:44
rusty a. of abuse	STEV 820:53	Great a. impose their	MAUP 561:85	Sitting as huge as A.	BARK 59:54
Th'a. of words	SWIFT 830:50	history of a.	WERE 899:7	stabilisation of East A.	HIRO 403:3
artisan promised to the studious a.!	MARL 552:96	Horrible as successful a.	JONG 448:1	**Asian** what A. boys ought	JOHN 440:83
artist aim of every a.	FAUL 319:70	If we…do not support our a.	MART 554:42	**aside** all gone a.	BIBLE 94:89
A more ideal A.	TENN 840:69	New York Pop a.	LIPP 511:64	**ask** again we a. aloud	KEATS 458:26
And so great an a.	NERO 611:41	no one wants Fine A.	FULL 341:50	A., and it shall be given you	BIBLE 110:7
a. absolute beauty	HALD 377:76	over a troop of a.	WILL 913:40	a. for my money back	HUXL 425:79
a. best serves his nation	KENN 463:35	poet shares with other a.	SPEN 807:60	a. less than one?	JONS 450:48
a. does not start with nothing	PERCY 648:51	position of the a. of Wales	THOM 853:97	A. me no more	TENN 842:13
a. does not tinker	MILL 572:23	style of most a. and all humbugs	CONN 233:73	a. not what your country	KENN 462:13
a.…driven by demons	FAUL 318:67	Summoning a. to participate	FROST 339:15	a. the hard question	AUDEN 39:79
a. has followed the rules	TINT 861:78	ten great a.	GREE 370:48	If you still have to a.	ARMS 30:75
a. is a spectator	ERNST 315:89	too difficult for a.	SCHN 719:23	intend to a. of them	KENN 462:9
a. is extremely lucky	BERR 82:68	What do these so-called a.	INGR 429:62	then you can a. me	KING 468:25
a. is in danger of death	HEMI 394:5	**arts** are the books, the a.	SHAK 734:86	what you a. them to do	WALD 885:87
a. is making something exist	BURR 173:62	a. are taught by degrees	THEO 851:39	**askew** come in a.	HEAT 390:26
a., like the idiot	SITW 794:84	a. babblative and scribblative	SOUT 805:11	**asking** a. too much	CANN 188:14
a. man and the mother woman	SHAW 778:84	a. of war	MORE 596:57	a. 'Who came second?'	REAR 681:69
a. must possess the courageous soul	CHOP 214:24	brought the a. into rustic Latium	HORA 414:29	You a. me the way?	KAFKA 454:29
a. needs but a roof	RYDER 707:76	elegant a. are unknown here	BROO 155:1	**asleep** Fall a., or hearing die	SHAK 775:15
A. of the Floating World	ISHI 431:92	finest of the A.	MERE 567:6	Fall a., or hearing, die	SHAK 775:13
a.'s first responsibility is to himself	DAVIS 255:58	France, famed in all great a.	ARNO 31:92	fast a. and weary	BIBLE 90:67
a. should fear	RYDER 707:77	France, mother of a.	BELL 72:38	happiest moment…falling a.	SCHO 719:34
a. should not only paint	FRIE 337:71	Greece, mother of a.	MILT 586:42	Not to fall a. is distinguished	BELL 74:83
a. who has travelled on a steam train	DAVIS 255:62	idea of an a. ghetto	HARR 384:3	thought me a.	PATM 643:59
a. who seeks dignity	ALBE 10:97	inglorious a. of peace	MARV 555:54	too young to fall a.	SASS 716:68
a. will be judged only by…solitude	CONN 233:86	In the a. of life	SHAW 778:93	we are a. in this world	BORG 145:92
a. with true feelings	FRIE 337:67	In the a. of peace	SHAW 778:94	**asp** a. doth on his feeder feed	LOVE 519:16
biography of the a.	ROSE 697:64	lowest of the a.	MOORE 595:23	child shall play on the hole of the a.	BIBLE 102:19
critic when he cannot be an a.	FLAU 326:30	mechanical a. and merchandise	BACON 50:59	small whisper of the a.	BYRON 180:36
dedication of an a.	SPARK 806:32	mind with a. improve	DONNE 279:43	**asparagus** a. of the poor	FRAN 333:92
eighteenth century a.	LEGER 501:53	Murder…One of the Fine A.	DE 262:9	grow a.	WADD 884:63
expect the a. to have more to say	CALAS 184:33	no A.; no Letters	HOBB 404:27	mention A. and it appeared	DICK 270:13
filmmaker…other a.	WELL 897:50	no ready a.	WORD 925:8	oysters and a. and good wines	SAKI 710:40
function of the a.	BETH 83:76	progress of the a. and the sciences	MAO 548:12	**aspect** evident a. of things	HEID 391:44
God is…another a.	PICA 650:1	servant of…the a.	BAUD 64:67	**aspects** a. of human life	POPP 662:92
greatest a. can conceive	MICH 568:33	so far advanced in the A.	HAZL 388:82	**aspen** a. good for staves	SPEN 808:73
half complete as a.	THUR 860:60	turn a. education into a system	HUGH 419:35	By the light quivering a. made	SCOTT 723:1
I am an a.	FUEN 340:41	**ascend** a. it then with religion	JONS 449:27	**aspens** a. quiver	TENN 838:43
if a great a. says	SELF 727:80	**Ascendancy** o the English A.	MACD 530:47	**Asperges** A. me hyssopo	BIBLE 127:87
innovative and important a.	DAVIS 255:59	**ascent** nobility of a.	POTT 664:20	**asphalt** only monument the a. road	ELIOT 307:88
joy of the a.	MILL 573:34	**asceticism** out of a.	MCCA 528:97	**aspic** old purpose done up in a.	LAWR 494:2
king of a.…photographer	WHIS 902:64	**Asclepius** offer a cock to A.	PLATO 655:31	**aspidistra** Keep the A. Flying	ORWE 627:34
life of the a. sufficiently miserable	BELL 71:30	**ash** alone as a mountain a.	DAY 257:86	**aspiration** thought and a.	ROSS 698:3
make himself an a.	SASS 717:79	a. for nothing ill	SPEN 808:73	**aspirations** a. that weren't realized	KISS 475:95
man who never…is no a..	BLAKE 135:77	Oak, and A., and Thorn	KIPL 473:58	poetry of our a.	CUOMO 248:31

young have a.   SAKI 710:33
aspire a. to give…a faithful account   ELIOT 303:76
bade me gaze, and there a.   ARNO 32:30
light, and will a.   SHAK 732:52
what else was there to a. to?   ROCK 692:82
aspirin both just a.   VIDAL 881:2
Asquith affair between Margot A.   PARK 637:45
Herbert A.'s clarity   BALF 55:57
ass am such a tender a.   SHAK 738:8
back of an a. to bear all   NASHE 609:19
braying like an a.   SITW 793:62
broaden your a. if not your mind   HEMI 394:19
Cover your a.   SAFI 708:98
enamoured of an a.   SHAK 738:10
Hood an a. with reverend purple   JONS 448:13
law is a a.   DICK 267:96
law is such an a.   CHAP 206:22
like an a. whose back   SHAK 758:33
Lord opened the mouth of the a.   BIBLE 89:40
making him egregiously an a.   SHAK 760:77
part man, part horse's a.   ACHE 2:31
Preposterous a.   SHAK 732:36
scoreboard is an a.   CARD 190:46
this a. o'er-offices   SHAK 755:29
thrice-double a.   SHAK 775:2
what an a. am I?   SHAK 753:80
With the jawbone of an a.   BIBLE 90:74
assailant vengeance on the a.   TROL 866:88
assailed a. by eyes   JAMES 434:64
assassin a.'s bullet   PARK 639:89
forgot…the a.   SAND 713:95
in harmony…sentiments of an a.   BIER 128:11
saviour or a.   MURP 604:4
assassinated until he's a.   KAUF 455:54
assassination A. has never changed   DISR 276:70
moderated by a.   MUNS 604:91
assassins because you are bullied by a.   LLOY 513:5
assault a.'on the mountain   CRAN 243:31
instance of a direct a.   SUMN 828:18
assaulting bees are a.…the flowers   REED 681:78
assay Help, angels! make a.   SHAK 754:2
assent ever given his a.   HUXL 424:64
expressions of a.   WAUGH 892:30
asserted a. itself in her   HARDY 382:57
assertions falsehood of his a.   JOHN 445:44
asses come out A.   BURNS 170:63
given to them by the Prize A.   SMITH 800:96
led by th' nose As a.   SHAK 759:72
asset greatest a. any country can have   CHUR 217:89
greatest a.…good night's sleep   WILS 916:2
assets assessing the value of a.   PAVL 644:80
complaining about loss of a.   ROTH 700:36
no longer liabilities but a.   SCHL 718:14
assimilation avenue of a. into society   DOCT 278:4
assistance Art and A. of the Architect   ALBE 10:99
conscious and creative a.   ROBBE 688:10
association free and equal a.   ENGE 314:68
newspaper represents an a.   TOCQ 861:85
Out of a. grows adhesion   BRON 155:87
associations all these accumulated a.   MELV 564:32
assonance adroit a.   UNTE 874:71
assume A. a virtue   SHAK 754:13
what I a. you shall a.   WHIT 905:30
assumption more powerful a.   SOLOW 803:61
assumptions a. of the ordinary man   ATTL 38:42
basic beliefs and a.   MILL 571:1
Mistaken in its a.   REGAN 682:93
assurance a. was given me   WESL 900:17
bright a.   WORD 929:63
diminish the dogmatic a.   RUSS 705:42
old house carried an a.   ACHE 2:25
on whom a. sits   ELIOT 306:60
some a. of grace   NIEB 614:97
the consoling a. of grace   NIEB 614:98
assurances greatest a. of safety   ACHE 3:51
assure a. the survival   KENN 462:12
assured ignorant of what he's most a.   SHAK 758:26
Assyrian oiled and curled A. Bull   TENN 845:81
asteroid an a. hitting the planet   KING 468:24
Astolat lily maid of A.   TENN 846:15
astonish A. me!   DIAG 265:46
astonished As many were a. at thee   BIBLE 104:49
a. at my own moderation!   CLIVE 222:16
beyond measure a.   BIBLE 114:14
suddenly a.   HEYE 410:71
astonishment not so much a.   SARG 714:31
the a. of loving   REID 682:95

truth which still fills me with a.   DAWK 256:72
your a.'s odd   ANON 22:51
astound startle well, but not a.   MILT 577:32
astounding seek for…the a.   BORG 144:89
astray sheep who've gone a.   KIPL 470:80
taking quite a liberty in going a.   ELIOT 303:72
astrologer gibberish of the a.   MACA 526:59
astronauts A.! Rotarians in space!   VIDAL 880:92
astronomer no a. can find   HUGH 419:50
astronomy A. teaches the correct   LEAC 496:59
asunder let no man put a.   BOOK 142:29
let not man put a.   BIBLE 113:71
asylum America is an insane a.   POUND 665:68
as though I were in a lunatic a.   CONA 230:80
ataxia beginnings of a.   SILVA 792:34
Ate with A. by his side   SHAK 748:2
Athalus craftier to pley…Than A.   CHAU 208:53
atheism a. is against…our reason   BURKE 169:38
Every luxury…a., breast-feeding   ORTON 627:30
inclineth Man's mind to a.   BACON 48:95
religion, and not a., is the true remedy   BURKE 168:13
When a. wants martyrs   SADE 708:94
atheist an embittered a.   ORWE 627:33
a.…no invisible means of support   BUCH 164:29
daylight a.   BEHAN 70:8
grown an a.?   WEBS 895:94
Sally said I was a sacrilegious a.   SALI 711:60
Thanks be to God, I am still an a.   BUNU 166:64
atheists A., fools, and madmen!   ONEI 625:99
should make men a.   CAREW 190:59
Athens A. arose!   SHEL 786:20
A., the eye of Greece   MILT 586:42
Burn, with A.   CAMP 186:59
Who brings owls to A.?   ARIS 29:45
Ye men of A.   BIBLE 119:48
athlete American a. is superior   CALI 184:36
a. cannot run with money   ZATO 936:89
I'm not an a.   BRYA 163:10
athletes All pro a. are bilingual   HOWE 417:98
athletics regard all a. as inferior   WAUGH 891:18
Athlone Great Gun of A.   ANON 21:37
Atkins Thank you, Mister A.   KIPL 471:90
Atlanta In A., the first question   BERE 78:88
Atlantic A. to the Pacific   CHUR 216:71
crosses the A.   MCCA 528:95
Irish…other side of the A.   WAUGH 892:38
sailed across the A.   BEHAN 70:5
steep A. stream   MILT 577:27
stormy North A. Ocean   LARD 490:14
this A. generation   KENN 463:30
atlas bicycle and an a.   MURP 604:99
discumbered A. of the state   COWP 240:50
Witch of A.   YEATS 934:65
atmosphere academic a.   STEA 813:78
a. favorable to the
   extraordinary   PAZ 644:89
brought up in an a.   SPEN 807:63
delightful social a.   BENN 76:48
general a. of unreality   QUEN 674:39
human creatures breathe an a.   DICK 271:17
placed in the luminous a.   LEON 504:20
atmospheric a. billboard   THOR 858:11
atom a. bombs are piling up   ORWE 629:83
a.…breathed before   BRON 154:66
conceal the power of the a.   COLE 225:73
every a. belonging to me   WHIT 905:30
Herman Melville who split the a.   LODGE 514:23
knowledge of the a.   EDDI 298:84
mystery of the a.   BRAD 149:73
no evil in the a.   STEV 820:52
atomic end up with the a. bomb   PAGN 634:86
forces a. energy on us   FROMM 338:82
form of a. blackmail   KENN 462:16
given us the a. bomb   KING 468:40
Hibakusha, a. victims   GEE 348:92
since the a. bomb   VREE 883:60
way it was with the a. bomb   OPPE 626:13
atoms air is not so full…of a.   DONNE 281:87
A. or systems into ruin hurled   POPE 660:9
fortuitous concourse of a.   FISKE 324:80
fortuitous concurrence of a.   PALM 636:25
Let onion a. lurk   SMITH 801:20
Nothing exists except a.   DEMO 261:84
smash to a.…everything he had learnt   ORTE 627:28
atomsmashers half a dozen a.   PERE 648:57
atom-streams saw the flaring a.-s.   TENN 847:33
atone pictures for the page a.   POPE 662:69

atonement This is the day of a.   RICH 685:56
atrocious a. crime of being…young   PITT 652:36
A. in content   GOET 360:12
atrocities a. that horrified us   HELL 392:67
atrophy a. of the imagination   GELL 348:98
music begins to a.   POUND 665:52
attach Where people wish to a.   AUST 44:93
attack a.…economic legends   GALB 343:93
a. is particularly wounding   THAT 850:25
French want to a.   ANON 25:74
lead such dire a.   MACA 526:65
plan of a.   SASS 716:63
serious a. upon morality   ORWE 628:65
attacks a. from outlaw states   REAG 680:60
attain cannot here a. unto them   HOOK 410:55
if we could a. it   TROL 867:3
attained only wisdom ever to be a.   PRAT 667:99
attainments a. are the lot of all   TOCQ 861:80
attempt a. at deliberate evasion   JONES 447:70
die in the a.   HELL 392:59
fearing to a.   SHAK 757:17
vain a. to subdue   GILL 356:41
attempts a. to display qualities   JOHN 441:26
attend Another to a. him   HERB 398:5
attendant a. and…inmate   CONA 230:80
attended When neither is a.   SHAK 741:91
attention an awful a.   SHER 788:65
a. on a particular aspect   ROBB 689:14
by paying a.   HUXL 425:89
distract our a.   THOR 857:84
drawing your a.   LEWIS 508:1
enough to get any child's a.   BAIL 52:3
fix our a. out of ourselves   HUME 422:3
husbands…cannot give their entire a.   BENN 76:44
more a. paid to them   JOHN 445:16
paying a. to them   SONT 804:79
socks compelled one's a.   SAKI 710:41
something worthy of a.   DARW 253:9
undivided a.…of the entire nation   BORAH 144:87
attentions pleasing a.   AUST 42:64
superior a. in little points   LAMB 486:44
attic A. boy to hunt   MILT 577:20
little brain a.   DOYLE 285:66
mellow glory of the A. stage   ARNO 31:91
O A. shape!   KEATS 459:54
speech as…pliant as A.   QUIL 674:44
attics shabby bums living in a.   LEWIS 507:88
attire a. be comely   LYLY 523:6
a. for a gentleman   SHAR 776:40
rich a. creeps rustling   KEATS 459:38
attitude don't like that a.   SHAN 776:28
elitist a. is basically suspicious   KRIS 481:17
enchantingly wavering a.   FITZ 324:89
end up with the a.   JACK 432:11
Fair a.!   KEATS 459:54
not my aptitude but my a.   JACK 431:8
scientific a. of mind   RUSS 705:48
attitudes a. and movements   LEON 503:16
in-office a. and behavior   COUP 238:93
number of conflicting a.   ALTH 13:70
paid to have a. toward things   HEMI 393:94
attorney Even an a. of modest talent   CAPO 189:24
gentleman is an a.   JOHN 444:92
in love with a rich a.'s…daughter   GILB 353:89
office boy to an a.'s firm   GILB 353:89
attorneyship dealt in by a.   SHAK 729:50
attracted a. by God, or by Nature   INGE 429:51
attraction A. and repulsion   BLAKE 134:37
by sure a. led   POPE 662:72
attractions register competing a.   KNIG 476:14
attractive a. about her was not her
   appearance   BROO 156:28
a. to the half-baked mind   FORS 331:32
When I find a woman a.   SAINT 709:93
attractiveness peculiar a. of each child   ACHE 2:20
attribute a. to God himself   SHAK 740:80
important a. of a lawyer   KENN 464:59
true a. of the soul   STAEL 812:54
attributes consisting in infinite a.   SPIN 811:36
attribution a. of false motives   BALD 54:51
Auburn Sweet A., loveliest village   GOLD 361:50
auction a joke were a charity a.   MCIL 533:1
auctions stands…between a.   RAUS 679:33
audacity punished for their a.   CABE 183:16
tactful in a.   COCT 224:57
Auden A. ran it   BOWL 147:35
I think I'm A.   EWART 316:26

W.H. A., a sort of gutless Kipling — ORWE 628:44
audience Ambushing the a. — STOP 825:67
and looks at the a. — STOC 824:53
a. look to their eyes — SHAK 737:88
a.…put up its umbrellas — BEER 69:73
a.'s power of judgement — HARD 381:43
a. was a disaster — WILDE 909:20
a. would immediately be looking — HITC 404:13
a. yelled, 'You're sublime' — HARG 382:78
awful attention in the a. — SHER 788:65
best a.…a little drunk — BARK 60:57
End without a. — SHAK 733:57
hold the a. — UPDI 874:86
if I don't practise…the a. knows — PADE 633:76
inviting his a. to discard him — ANNAN 17:51
keep the a. awake — OLIV 624:71
must have a London a. — AUST 43:78
seeking empathy with his a. — SAFI 708:1
spirits of the a. — BIER 129:40
two kinds of a. — SCHN 719:20
your a. is conjectural — ORWE 629:78
audiences a. come to hear — FREE 336:39
auditorium hidden a. of his skull — STER 817:64
I remember the a. — POWE 666:90
August A. for the people — AUDEN 39:84
winter…To recommence in A. — BYRON 182:95
august a. occasions of the state — FROST 339:15
Augusta A.…grandmother's maiden name — BERE 78:88
Augustus A. was a chubby lad — HOFF 406:51
auld a. lang syne! — BURNS 171:98
aunt A. is calling to A. — WODE 919:58
A. Jane observed — GRAH 365:33
A. Sally she's going to adopt — TWAIN 871:12
Her A.…from her Earliest Youth — BELL 73:58
said my a. Dot — MACA 525:37
Auntie Whenever A. moves around — STEV 823:15
aunts a. and uncles were legion — SHAW 781:1
cousins, and his a.! — GILB 353:93
her husband, her a. — RANS 679:21
play bridge with my old maid a. — FIEL 323:47
aura a. of one who knows — BANKS 58:36
Aurora rising with A.'s light — SWIFT 832:96
See how A. throws her fair — HERR 400:43
Zephyr with A. — MILT 576:5
Ausonia let A., skilled in every art — BYRON 179:1
Austen Jane A.…only novelist — BANKS 59:38
austere strode on a. — THOM 856:64
austerity high a. to delight — FREE 336:44
Austerlitz Pile the bodies…at A. — SAND 713:96
Australia always last year in A. — THER 851:50
ashes taken to A. — ANON 21:33
Being lost in A. — CHAT 208:50
camped in the centre of A. — STUA 827:97
colour in A. is gold — STRE 827:92
cricket tour in A. — LARW 491:55
Dead Heart of A. — GREG 372:97
housemaid…the best in A. — MELBA 563:15
indifference of…golden A. — LAWR 494:7
like A. less and less — LAWR 494:97
postmodern, multicultural A. — NARO 608:74
so much interested in A. — WILDE 908:15
Spirit of A. — FIELD 322:30
the other in A. — GAY 347:74
Australian A. be equal to…a Briton — PARK 638:83
A. literature — STEW 824:42
A. novel is not…dreary — WHITE 903:97
first and foremost…an A. — MELBA 563:15
proud that I am an A. — FRAN 335:22
spirit of an A. — FRAN 335:21
stretched the Great A. Emptiness — WHITE 903:96
Australians A. inherited the British mentality — PACK 633:73
Austria A. is a little world — HEBB 390:38
born in A. — SIMON 792:38
Austrian A. Empire did not exist — PALA 635:6
authenticity verify the a. — WILL 914:58
author a. and finisher of our faith — BIBLE 124:99
a. and giver of all good things — BOOK 141:88
a. because you like his books — LINK 511:61
a. is the first to go — COLL 227:34
a. of peace — BOOK 140:73
a. of the play — GILB 355:36
A. of the Whole escape — POPE 662:81
a.'s fairy godmother — LUCAS 522:78
a.'s mind — GAUG 347:68
a. spoils everything — LAFO 485:13
a. today proclaims — ROBBE 688:10

a. who speaks about his own books — DISR 277:80
a. writes with a misty profundity — WHIT 904:5
choose an a. — DILL 275:16
confession…of its a. — NIET 615:18
Corrected…By its A.! — FRAN 334:6
every other a. may aspire to praise — JOHN 442:38
expected to see an a. — PASC 640:12
fine future for its a. — WILDE 908:87
first-rate a. wants an exquisite heroine — FITZ 325:16
from the a.'s soul — HUXL 425:66
go to the a. — RUSK 704:23
Hunting the a., painter and musician — SITW 794:87
improved by its a.'s explanations — MACL 535:40
in Search of an A. — PIRA 652:23
Literature…depends…on the a.'s skill — QUIL 674:45
more than wit to make an a. — LA 483:57
no a. today — SARR 715:37
not only as an a. — GRASS 367:59
role of the a. — DIDE 274:92
sending the a. some small cash token — CONN 233:67
shrimp of an a. — GRAY 370:43
This is indeed to be an a.! — HAZL 388:83
truth about its a. — CHES 211:53
What I like in a good a. — SMITH 800:87
what the a. promised — JOHN 442:35
wish the a.…was a terrific friend — SALI 710:52
write like a distinguished a. — NABO 606:46
authoress dared to be an a. — AUST 43:79
authoritarian perpetuate a. rule — AUNG 42:49
authoritarianism 1984 a. — GINS 357:70
authorities a.…we do not control — CONN 233:85
between the issues and the highest a. — SHUL 790:91
every act of the a. — REED 682:88
If civil a. legislate — JOHN 438:56
authority a man under a. — BIBLE 110:14
a., either academic or worldly — MENC 565:60
A. forgets a dying king — TENN 847:47
a. in the affairs of the church — BECK 68:49
a. of a belief — KRIS 480:14
a. of supreme victory — WHIT 904:14
base a. from others' books — SHAK 733:69
combat general a. — DRYD 288:44
Dressed in a little brief a. — SHAK 758:26
enjoying such a. and prestige — BERE 78:89
established by the said a. — HOWA 417:94
exercises a. over beggars — MORE 597:63
for their robbery have a. — SHAK 758:28
hardly an a. upon anything — DAFOE 250:62
high a. of the self — TRIL 866:71
his a. and her sex — WOLL 921:10
I have disliked A. always — MORR 598:95
no one has the a. — KELM 461:79
O, what a. — SHAK 745:19
stamp of his a. — LAMB 486:43
takes on an a. — BAIL 52:99
those in a. — KELM 461:78
vices of a. — BACON 48:6
you hate a. — BAIL 52:99
authors ancient a. — BACON 46:39
A. and uncaptured criminals — LINK 511:55
A. are actors — STEV 820:42
a. of simile and metaphor — NASH 609:3
from English a. their copyrights — TROL 867:8
inability of their a. — NISB 616:38
invades a. like a monarch — DRYD 288:26
let great a. have their due — BACON 46:36
our a. make a doubt — BUTL 176:37
we a. repeat ourselves — FITZ 325:5
when two or three a. meet — PRIT 669:51
your taste in a. — ONEI 625:99
authorship popular a. — TROL 867:1
products…rather than of a. — WALD 885:85
autobiographies A. tell more lies — BYATT 178:90
autobiography age to write an a. — WAUGH 893:54
a. is an obituary — CRISP 245:59
a. is only 'a sort of life' — GREE 371:67
a. writ large — LEWO 508:10
deepest part of a. — WARR 889:75
rage for confession, a. — MANS 547:89
told it's a. — ROTH 699:30
write an a. is only to open — MELBA 563:15
autocracy communism as Tsarist a. — HERZ 400:56
principle of a. — NICH 613:84
autocrat Aristocrat, democrat, a. — TENN 845:84
rebel…turning into an a. — DURR 296:39
autographs write for a. — GILB 355:21
automate a.—or evaporate! — MERR 567:16

automatic a. machine — WIEN 906:67
balancing seemed rather a. — SPEN 807:62
automation patterns latent in a. — MCLU 536:60
automatons intelligently run by a. — MUMF 603:78
automobile artist…driven an a. — DAVIS 255:62
a. accident — GIBB 352:67
a. has practically reached the limit — ANON 22:45
a. is the greatest catastrophe — JOHN 441:2
a.…object of aesthetic appreciation — BARR 60:77
poorhouse in an a. — ROGE 695:23
autonomous the a. individual — ORWE 628:56
autonomy new conception of a. — GEOR 349:19
self-employment and artistic a. — MCLU 536:60
autumn a. and the falling fruit — LAWR 495:31
A. is desolation — TATE 837:4
A.'s pleasant weather — BURNS 170:85
A. wind rises — WU 930:96
breath of A.'s being — SHEL 783:43
carry well this A. night — BUNT 166:62
descends the a. evening — ARNO 33:52
happy a.-f. — TENN 842:6
harmony In a. — SHEL 782:21
O A., laden with fruit — BLAKE 133:25
old A. in the misty morn — HOOD 410:33
red amnesiacs of a. — PURDY 673:17
rose in rainy a. — THOM 852:76
sallow A. fills thy lap — COLL 228:48
Slow sobs…of a. — VERL 879:64
south, where there is no a. — LAWR 494:15
Thursday…in a. — VALL 876:20
autumnal pox of her a. face — JONS 449:24
auxiliars mighty were the a. — WORD 927:39
Auxiliary I was undone by my A. — STEE 814:97
avail good income is of no a. — SMITH 799:75
Avalun will fare to A. — LAYA 496:47
avant-garde chamber of the A.-G. — HUGH 419:30
one thing constant…is the a.-g.. — JOUV 451:75
There is no a.-g. — VARE 877:35
avant-gardism therapeutic a.-g. — HUGH 419:36
avarice a.: it increases its thirst — MONT 593:97
a., lust and ambition — LEWIS 507:73
gratify a., and extend corruption — JOHN 442:57
root of Evil, A. — MAND 545:54
take up with a. — BYRON 182:76
Ave-Maries A.-M. on his beads — SHAK 730:52
avenge shalt not a. — BIBLE 89:35
avenger still the enemy and the a. — BIBLE 94:86
wait for the a. — WILDE 907:82
avenue a. I'm taking you to — DUBIN 292:64
a. of assimilation into society — DOCT 278:4
average children are above a. — KEIL 460:69
there shall be the a. — SMITH 799:65
aversion gentleman's park is my a. — CONS 235:24
Those…fellows are my a. — STEE 814:1
with preference and a. — SHER 787:35
aviary an a. overstocked with jays — OHEN 623:55
avidity Beast ravens in its own a.? — EBER 298:74
Avilion island-valley of A. — TENN 847:52
avoid a. what is to come — SHAK 754:11
manages to a. them — HEIS 391:57
avoided what cannot be a. — SHAK 731:85
avoiding a. non-being — TILL 860:67
Avon Sweet Swan of A.! — JONS 449:46
awake a. for sake of Song! — FERG 320:5
a. in another one — BORG 145:92
A. my soul — KEN 461:93
Keeping a. for ten weeks — WINN 917:26
let me be a., my God! — COLE 226:94
rather sleep…than stay a. — ALBEE 10:95
trying to a. — JOYCE 452:87
When you're lying a. — GILB 354:15
awaken begin to a. — WILL 913:43
awakened a. from the dream of life — SHEL 786:3
awakening a time of a. consciousness — RICH 685:48
single a. — MARI 550:58
awakenings dream between two a. — ONEI 625:93
aware a. that one's mother — JARRY 435:93
I'm more a. — REAG 680:52
awareness a. of that revelation — FRYE 340:35
a. that words can outlive us — PLOUT 656:10
delicate a. of unreasoning things — DARK 253:5
terms of the human a. — LEAV 498:1
awash Washington is a. — SCHR 720:45
away A. we go — WORD 924:73
Come, dear children, let us a. — ARNO 31:82
People who never get carried a. — FORB 329:95
take that a. from me — GERS 351:40

take that a. from me — GERS 351:41
Take the soup a.! — HOFF 406:51
awe a. for the natural world — WILS 915:78
ever new and increasing admiration and a. — KANT 455:47
Exempt from a., worship, degree — SHEL 785:81
fear and a. — WORD 928:51
feelings of a. and respect — DICK 266:23
In a. of…myself — SHAK 747:75
Make this Bed with A. — DICK 272:67
no longer…stand rapt in a. — EINS 301:37
Stand in a. — BIBLE 94:85
The plan is called 'shock and a.' — ANON 26:82
With a.…I tread — CRAB 242:82
awful Anything a. makes me laugh — LAMB 486:33
How a. to reflect — SMITH 799:74
awfulness by its very a. — STEV 821:85
awkward I'm just an a. old maid — RENO 683:99
awkwardness regret The a. — HEAN 389:11
awoke a. in the capital — KAIKO 454:33
a. one morning — KAFKA 454:26
So I a. — BUNY 166:73
awry Gang aft a.-g. — BURNS 170:72
axe a.'s edge did try — MARV 555:55
a. will fall when they raise me — LEAC 497:72
let the great a. fall — SHAK 755:24
Many strokes…with a little a. — SHAK 730:72
sound of the white soldier's a. — RED 681:71
spinning wheel and the bronze a. — ENGE 314:68
stone than with an a. — JOHN 445:34
swinging his a. — BUNT 166:63
axe-blade a.-b. infinitely sharp — PRATT 667:1
axes two a. of the world — FRAN 333:85
axiom a. enforced by…experience — CONN 233:88
A.: Hatred of the bourgeois — FLAU 326:38
a. of politics — TOCQ 861:83
a. of sports — FRAY 335:30
long been an a. of mine — DOYLE 285:60
that was a general a. — SPARK 806:25
axioms hypotheses or a. — EINS 302:46
axis constitute an a. of evil — BUSH 175:10
under-belly of the A. — CHUR 217:88
axle glowing a. doth allay — MILT 577:27
axletree fly sat upon the a. — BACON 50:58
Ayatollah A.'s money to support — NORTH 618:71
I'm the A. Khomeini of Serbia — MILO 575:91
Ayr A.…ne'er a town surpasses — BURNS 172:14
Azcan A. in caftan — STEV 819:20
Azores At Flores in the A. — TENN 848:60
azure out the a. main — THOM 856:52
overgrown with a. moss — SHEL 783:45
rock inlaid with a. glaciers — BENU 78:85

B

Baal if B., then follow him — BIBLE 92:18
Babbitt name was George F. B. — LEWIS 507:86
To George F. B. — LEWIS 507:87
babblative arts b. and scribblative — SOUT 805:11
babbler What will this b. say? — BIBLE 119:47
babbling b. rhyme — SHAK 745:24
babe b., by intercourse of touch — WORD 925:97
Coleridge lull the b. at nurse — BYRON 179:2
find the b. wrapped — BIBLE 115:26
his b. in the nest — TENN 841:2
laid her b. to rest — MILT 576:1
naked new-born b. — SHAK 767:87
woo not like a b. — SHAK 732:31
Babel name of it called B. — BIBLE 87:71
babes As newborn b. — BIBLE 125:23
B. reduced to misery — BLAKE 134:55
even the b. in arms — THOM 852:56
Out of the mouth of b. — BIBLE 94:86
Tears, then, for b. — SHAK 730:73
babies b.…come into the world — MENC 566:80
b. like such toys — MORE 597:68
b. who rush at me — MANS 546:83
bit the b. in the cradles — BROW 160:26
hates dogs and b. — ROST 699:10
having b. without chloroform — BARB 59:50
long hours spent as b. — BRAD 148:56
only washing. And b. — THOM 853:91
Other people's b. — HERB 397:77
putting milk into b. — CHUR 217:89
You breed b. and you eat chips — WESK 899:8
Bab-lock-hithe Crossing…at B.-l.-h. — ARNO 32:18
baboon humanity with a b. — SHAK 759:69
morals of a b. — CAPO 189:33

baby b., assailed by eyes — JAMES 434:64
B. in an ox's stall — BETJ 84:99
b. is God's opinion — SAND 713:9
b. made in a test tube — MAIL 540:57
blind boy, Venus' b. — SPEN 809:2
don't be stingy b. — MARI 550:55
Every b. born into the world — DICK 267:10
Hasta la vista, b. — SCHW 721:63
little b. thing — MACD 530:56
mother laid her b. — ALEX 11:24
no more…than a man can have a b. — DRAP 286:95
no rhyme to 'lady' but 'b.' — SHAK 745:24
slept like a b. — DOLE 278:13
When the first b. laughed — BARR 61:81
Where did you come from, b. dear? — MACD 530:55
who gives a b. birth — MASE 559:35
why…name your b. 'John' — GOLD 362:82
Babylon B. be thrown down — BIBLE 127:74
B. The Great — BIBLE 127:73
By the rivers of B. — BIBLE 98:98
By the waters of B. — WALP 887:30
Ere B. was dust — SHEL 784:69
London is a modern B. — DISR 276:59
through the walls of B. — COMN 229:67
Baca through the valley of B. — BIBLE 96:46
Bacall hint of B.'s slinkiness — ALLEN 12:38
Bacchus B. hath drowned more men — FULL 341:62
Bach angels play only B. — BARTH 62:8
B. on the wrong notes — PROK 670:60
not B. or Schubert — MCCU 529:23
play B. your way — LAND 488:86
bachelor b., a solicitor, a Freemason — DOYLE 285:74
B. who has…experience — RIDGE 687:77
half-witted b. — WODE 919:58
he was a b. — SYMI 834:54
makes Legree a b. — CHES 210:24
married or a b. — ADDI 6:9
Never trust a…b. too near — ROWL 701:51
wise in the b. — STEV 821:87
bachelors reasons for b. to go out — ELIOT 303:92
where the b. sit — SHAK 744:91
back and they stared b. — GILL 355:39
at my b. in a cold blast — ELIOT 306:59
B. and side go bare — ANON 20:1
b. the masses — GLAD 359:93
b. to nature — GOTT 364:19
b. us or sack us — CALL 185:41
b. with ingots bows — SHAK 758:33
beast on my b. — DOUG 283:21
behind his b. — JOHN 444:92
coming b. seems possible — DICK 273:79
Dost thou look b. — TENN 843:48
down express in the small of the b. — WODE 919:56
flying b. and forth — PLATH 654:73
good coat upon his b. — JOHN 443:66
hangs upon thy b. — SHAK 737:79
I'll be b. — SCHW 721:62
it will come drifting b. — HAWES 385:30
lean'd my b. unto an aik — BALL 56:94
my b. I always hear — MARV 556:62
never turned his b. — BROW 163:95
not easy to call them b. — SAND 713:98
sit on a man's b. — TOLS 862:6
stab me in the b. — LAMP 487:71
stabs you in the b. — SNOW 802:40
thumps upon your b. — COWP 241:60
wallet at his b. — SHAK 757:5
way their b. looks — WYETH 931:19
Will ye no come b. again — NAIR 607:55
backbone b. of the Army — KIPL 472:19
backgammon sport I mastered…b. — JERR 438:43
backhand make her hit b. volleys — KING 468:26
wonderful b. drive — BETJ 83:84
backlash b. against women's rights — FALU 317:42
finding of limited use to b. publicists — FALU 317:41
backs b. to the wall — HAIG 376:66
on the b. of his friends — HUGH 419:26
when our b. are turned — CRISP 245:54
backshop reserve a b. — MONT 592:76
backside moral b. — LICH 509:16
skelp across her b. — ANON 21:73
backward b. motion — FROST 339:1
B. ran sentences — GIBBS 352:73
dark b. and abyss of time? — SHAK 774:77
fell from off the seat in — BIBLE 91:85
too far b. — THUR 859:32
when you look b. — ORWE 628:57

backwards life must be understood b. — KIER 467:12
memory that only works b. — CARR 196:5
rapidly b. and forwards — REED 681:78
backwoods b. of Canada — MOOD 594:8
back-yard squabble in your b.-y. — SYNGE 834:59
backyards American b. — MAIL 540:58
Bacon dig up B. — GILB 355:36
Bacon their lordships asked B. — BENT 78:81
think how B. shined — POPE 660:26
bacon bring home the b. — ONEI 626:3
bacon man who never ate b. — HATT 385:26
bad almost as b., good-mother — SHAK 754:6
as b. as b. can be — JOHN 446:61
b., and like to coins — TENN 847:42
b. book is as much — HUXL 425:66
b. die late — DEFOE 258:12
B. laws are the worst sort of tyranny — BURKE 168:25
b. poets deface — ELIOT 305:49
b.'s the best of us — FLET 328:69
b. unhappily — WILDE 909:61
because they are so b. — TROL 867:97
believe a thing to be b. — MILN 575:89
better than b. strokes — SHAK 748:19
bring them into b. repute — WILD 911:86
but some b. man — HERB 398:15
can't be all b. — FIEL 323:53
everything b. that's printed — WELL 897:52
good and b. of every land — BAIL 52:5
good Compensate b. in man — BROW 162:86
good or they were b. — TRAV 865:47
how b. you used to be — KNUD 476:25
How sad and b. and mad — BROW 162:77
If we live inside a b. joke — RABAN 675:59
Mad, b., and dangerous to know — LAMB 486:25
make b. good — SHAK 758:14
might also be very b. — HOCK 405:39
never was…a b. peace — FRAN 334:15
No man…irreclaimably b. — CARL 192:89
nothing either good or b. — SHAK 752:53
nothing so b. or so good — SHAW 777:65
not really b. at heart — BELL 73:91
not that we are so b. — NIGH 616:32
obstinacy in a b. one — STER 817:72
people…not good or b. enough — COMP 230:72
perhaps I was the least b. — SIHA 791:30
put up with b. things — TROL 866:80
strong antipathy of good to b. — POPE 661:58
sure it is b. morality — SKEL 795:96
that I have b. dreams — SHAK 752:54
think something is good or b. — STEV 820:58
though it be from b. to worse — IRVI 430:84
was b., she was horrid — LONG 516:61
we're not doing too b. — DICK 265:57
what is frankly b. — STEIN 815:24
what you feel b. after — HEMI 394:4
When b. men combine — BURKE 168:4
when I'm b. I'm better — WEST 901:30
Where everything is b. — BRAD 149:72
world is b. enough — CLOU 222:25
baddish Gilbert had a b. streak — QUIL 674:46
badge b. of all our tribe — SHAK 739:53
b. of authority — HERB 399:24
b. of lost innocence — PAINE 634:90
Red B. of Courage — CRANE 243:27
soldier wears a b. — READ 680:48
badgers When b. fight — CLARE 219:42
badminton art of b. is to deceive — THOM 854:22
bads goods…jointly with b. — BOUL 146:24
Baedeker B. is astonishingly — LEVIN 506:64
never Mr B. — HERB 397:79
baffled b. to fight better — BROW 163:91
bag agitate a b. of wind — WHITE 902:69
in a b. all sorts of seeds — SPEN 809:15
into a b. with holes — BIBLE 106:14
Tuppence a B.! — TRAV 865:49
upsetting of a b. of nails — RUSK 704:36
with nothing but a carpet b. — MELV 564:42
bagatelle vive la b.! — STER 818:3
bagel after another like a b. — IGNA 428:41
baggage believe the b. loves me — CONG 230:94
bagpipe Twelve Highlanders and a b. — ANON 26:87
when the b. sings i'th' nose — SHAK 740:77
bagpiper laugh like parrots at a b. — SHAK 739:35
bags picking up my b. — NEVI 611:49
thousand douche b. — LOWRY 521:66
Bah 'B.!' said Scrooge — DICK 268:27
Baiae in B.'s bay — SHEL 783:45

bairn bonnie broukit b.! — MACD 529:26
bairnie Singin' till a b. — MACD 529:29
bairnies waefu' wife and b. three — BALL 56:79
bairns when they werena gude b. — SCOTT 724:35
bait Roots ripe as old b. — ROET 694:2
baiting b. a mouse-trap with cheese — SAKI 710:48
  b. place of wit — SIDN 790:10
baker b. rhymes for his pursuit — BROW 162:92
  B. Street irregulars — DOYLE 285:56
Bakewell every fool in B. at Buxton — RUSK 704:38
Balaam ass…said unto B. — BIBLE 89:40
balance b., an…interchange — WORD 925:6
  b. between the hands employed — STEU 819:8
  b. of actual forces — NAPO 607:61
  bodies out of their natural b. — LEON 503:12
  causes, the b. sheet — MO 589:22
  ecological b. of the planet — SONT 804:73
  false b. is abomination — BIBLE 99:21
  held in b. only by the miracle — HONE 409:29
  hold the b. of Europe — WILL 912:5
  redress the b. of the Old — CANN 188:15
  sane b. of values — POUND 665:56
  scale…in nice b. — POPE 662:65
  the b. of power — PALM 636:26
balances checks and b. — ANON 24:33
  weighed in the b. — BIBLE 106:98
balancing b. an egg on a spoon — HILL 402:87
  b. seemed rather automatic — SPEN 807:62
balconies prams on concrete b. — BETJ 83:96
bald b. as an egg — CHEE 209:5
  b. as the bare mountain tops — ARNO 34:71
  brow is b. — BURNS 171:10
  fierce and b. — SASS 716:61
  fight between two b. men — BORG 145:94
  Go up, thou b. head — BIBLE 92:30
  Slightly b. — ANON 22:55
  young, b. Leader of the Opposition — KINN 470:71
baldness b. full of grandeur — ARNO 34:71
  far side of b. — SMITH 799:77
bale think upon my bitter b. — SPEN 808:79
bales down with costly b. — TENN 840:81
Balkans B. export…history — LEACH 496:53
  One of nature's B. — CURR 249:38
  some damned silly thing in the B. — BISM 131:87
ball after I have delivered the b. — BARR 61:89
  as round as a b. — SPEKE 806:36
  b. made of Krazy Putty — LODGE 514:24
  bowler and the b. — LANG 488:90
  chaperoning a b. — GILL 356:40
  coming-out b.? — WHAR 902:55
  cry Play B.! — NASH 609:5
  Death's unerring b. — EGAN 301:24
  each b. a potential crisis — TREV 865:58
  Every b. is…the first b. — BRAD 149:78
  Find out where the b. is — RANJ 678:17
  Games played with the b. — JEFF 437:22
  Gave up his bat and b. — EGAN 301:24
  girl throwing a b. — WOOLF 922:39
  gown for a dancing-school b. — HUME 422:11
  history of a b. — WELL 897:60
  history of bat and b. — ARLO 30:62
  impell'd the flying b. — BYRON 179:95
  I worship the b. — PELE 646:18
  killer with the b.' — LARW 491:56
  one b. left! — JOHN 447:80
  Play b.! — RICE 685:39
  real leather b. — UTTL 875:10
  red b. of fire — AGAWA 8:71
  roll…up into one b. — MARV 556:65
  Ruddy B. has taken flight — THOM 855:41
  secret of managing a b. club — STEN 816:54
  sight To such a tender b. — MILT 586:48
  silly little white b. — ZOEL 937:2
  'Sphere of Influence'—the cricket b. — ANON 21:35
  swing at the b. — DIMA 275:18
  that portion of the b. — POPE 662:71
  took the b. in his arms — ANON 21:26
  watch…hirelings kick a b. — PRIE 668:17
  what to do with the b. — SHAN 776:31
  wind it into a b. — BLAKE 135:74
ballad love a b. in print — SHAK 770:94
ballads b., songs and snatches — GILB 355:19
  refrain of one of the most popular b. — MACA 524:26
Ballinger Mrs B. is one of the ladies — WHAR 901:53
balloon if the moon's a b. — CUMM 247:6
  up like a b. — TRAV 864:45
balloons toes grow…as b. — THOM 853:95

balls elliptical billiard b. — GILB 355:28
  golden b. whirring through indigo — AVIS 44:6
  hear the bump of the b. — JOYCE 451:82
  hustling over large b. — EDWA 300:15
  matched our rackets to these b. — SHAK 745:30
  moment the first b. are bowled — HOWE 417:96
  only three b. and no one watches it — DAVIS 255:61
  thousand lost golf b. — ELIOT 307:88
  Why, these b. bound — SHAK 761:30
balls-up it was just a b.-u. — ORWE 628:54
balm b. from an anointed king — SHAK 735:15
  b. in Gilead — BIBLE 105:74
  b. of woe — SIDN 790:10
  B. to fester'd wounds — MILT 586:51
  b. upon the world — KEATS 458:16
  pity hath been b. — SHAK 730:83
balmy With b. hands his wounds — COLL 228:44
baloney it's still b. — SMITH 798:56
Baltimore B.…like dull diamonds — MAIL 540:55
bamboo Learn about…a b. stalk — BASHO 63:45
ban B. the Bomb — ANON 23:74
bananas b. republic — KEAT 456:75
  eating b. for breakfast — WHAR 901:45
  Yes, We Have No B. — DORG 282:2
band b. begins to play — KIPL 471:90
  cassock, b., and hymn-book — WILB 907:70
  go tell the b. — GERS 350:39
  humbler b. of duodecimos — CRAB 242:83
  mighty folios…a lordly b. — CRAB 242:83
bandage don't come to me for a b. — THAT 850:26
  such an arm for a b. — SHER 787:45
Bandersnatch frumious B. — CARR 195:90
bands b. of twelfth men — STOP 825:62
  fantastic b. — CRAS 244:40
  strong as iron b. — LONG 515:44
bandy not for me to b. civilities — JOHN 443:85
  will b. with thee in faction — SHAK 750:84
bane Deserve the precious b. — MILT 581:16
Banff Mein B. — MCNE 538:14
bang Not with a b. but a whimper — ELIOT 306:72
banish B. not him — SHAK 742:16
  I b. you — SHAK 769:66
banished b. from myself — PINT 652:22
  moral in it will be b. — TWAIN 871:93
bank and shoal of time — SHAK 767:86
  b. president finish the script — EPST 315:85
  b. where the wild thyme blows — SHAK 737:97
  beastly to the B. of England — CRIT 245:63
  cried all the way to the b. — LIBE 509:14
  easiest way to steal from a b. — KORT 480:3
  governor of the B. of England — KORDA 480:99
  however you b. your screw — LARK 491:42
  lay on Huntlie b. — BALL 56:89
  like a cheque drawn on a b. — POUND 665:48
  moonlight sleeps upon this b.! — SHAK 740:85
  officials with too many b. accounts — DOSP 282:3
  O waly, waly up the b. — BALL 56:94
  pregnant b. swelled up — DONNE 280:57
  shelving b. of turf — SHEL 786:23
  upon a b. of violets — SHAK 755:45
  vice presidents a b. has? — ROGE 694:13
banker A 'sound' b., alas! — KEYN 465:83
  B.' genes — THOM 854:24
  become a central b. — GREE 372:81
  Inside every b. — KORDA 480:99
bankers Bats have no b. — BERR 82:65
  mercy of b. and tripe sellers — MENC 565:60
Bankhead Tallulah B. barged — BROWN 157:43
  Tallulah B. on the stage — CAMP 185:54
bank-holiday jolly b.-h. — GILB 354:6
banking B. is a branch — WRIS 930:91
  b. system grew by accident — WRIS 930:84
banknotes fill old bottles with b. — KEYN 466:88
bankrupt B. of life — DRYD 290:78
bankruptcy Capitalism without b. — BORM 145:96
banks b. and braes o' bonie Doon — BURNS 172:26
  b. of every computer — GIBS 353:76
  b. were conservative — THOM 854:24
  bonnie b. o' Loch Lomond — ANON 20:20
  burnis hurlis all their b. doun — DOUG 283:17
  lifts me to my b. — DRYD 289:61
  On the b. of Rubicon — MACN 538:7
  on the bonnie b. o' Clyde — LAUD 492:64
  shadowy b. on either side — WORD 924:87
  so are b., so is cotton — DICK 268:26
banner b. over me was love — BIBLE 101:97
  b. with a strange device — LONG 516:48

blazoned b. we unfold — RUSS 706:63
  doth his b. rest — SURR 829:34
  fight under his b. — BOOK 141:12
  raising high the b. which reads — MERT 568:24
  royal b., and all quality — SHAK 760:94
  star-spangled b. — KEY 465:76
  trails like a b. in defeat — JEFF 436:6
banners b. set high on the poops — ROBE 689:17
  society inscribe on its b. — MARX 558:14
banquet b. of happiness — HUGO 420:71
  Before we begin our b. — ROWL 701:54
  words are a very fantastical b. — SHAK 744:4
banqueting me to the b. house — BIBLE 101:97
bantering this whole matter of b. — ISHI 431:94
Bapaume riddled corpses round B. — SASS 716:57
baptism Sadducees come to his b. — BIBLE 108:76
  suffering may well be called a b. — ELIOT 303:81
Baptist should have preferred a B. — WELLS 898:81
baptized Jesus, when he was b. — BIBLE 108:77
bar Back of the b. — SERV 728:3
  b. against your cruelty — LANY 489:6
  b. association meetings — SUTH 830:43
  b. himself in — BIRN 131:70
  B. of the House — RUSH 703:96
  gold b. of Heaven — ROSS 698:86
  I have crossed the b. — TENN 848:70
  prisoners at the b. — WILDE 907:81
  sat at the cocktail b. — WAUGH 892:43
  went to the B. — GILB 354:12
Barabbas B. was a publisher — CAMP 186:74
  crowd will always save B. — COCT 224:59
barajar paciencia y b. — CERV 203:48
Barbadoes sell themselves to the B. — SWIFT 831:92
barbarian betwixt an erring b. — SHAK 759:71
  He is a b. — SHAW 777:77
barbarians b. beyond the walls — WHITE 903:2
  B., Philistines, and Populace — ARNO 33:53
  excuse all…Irish b. — OROU 627:22
  Fit only for the b. — FULL 341:59
  rockets used by the b. — KISH 475:88
  without any b.? — CAVA 201:15
  young b. all at play — BYRON 180:39
barbaric b. yawp — WHIT 905:36
  people which…becomes b. — ELIOT 307:84
barbarism b. to decadence — CLEM 221:78
  b.…visited on the Irish — OROU 627:22
  civilization against b. — ROOS 696:59
  drift is always towards b. — REAG 681:68
  pure return of b. — LEVI 506:61
  wall…separates civilisation from b. — BUCH 164:24
barbarisms colloquial b. — JOHN 441:28
barbarities b. by the Irish — OROU 627:22
barbarity b. of tyrants — SMITH 801:7
barbarous b. feeling of nationality — SENI 728:98
  b. traffic in slaves — PITT 653:45
  Fashion is something b. — SANT 714:18
  rank me with the b. multitudes — SHAK 740:62
barber b.'s man hath been seen — SHAK 745:13
  imprudently married the b. — FOOTE 329:94
  must to the b.'s — SHAK 738:8
Barca to B. flowers — POPE 662:66
Barchester table in B. Towers — BROY 163:99
bard voice of the B.! — BLAKE 134:50
Bardie certain B.'s rantin, drinkin — BURNS 170:78
bards last of all the B. — SCOTT 722:84
  paint it, and as b. will not — CRAB 242:88
  writers and the b. — FERG 321:9
bare art stripped b. — MOTH 600:31
  B. like nude — SPEN 807:55
  made b. his holy arm — BIBLE 104:48
  so b. and full of wretchedness — SHAK 737:79
bareback rode the…hills b. — THOM 853:2
barefaced With b. power — SHAK 768:12
bargain Curse…science into the b. — COOK 235:33
  Necessity never made a good b. — FRAN 334:9
  never was a better b. driv'n — SIDN 790:4
  Will anyone be satisfied with the b.? — COLL 227:37
bargain-basement b.-b. Boadicea — HEAL 389:1
bargains Queens never make b. — CARR 197:26
  rule for b. — DICK 268:38
barge The b. she sat in — SHAK 764:23
barges b. as solemn as Barons — WALP 887:23
bark B. when their fellows do — SHAK 775:11
  come out as I do, and b. — JOHN 446:55
  heard a seal b.! — THUR 859:18
  swell billow, and swim b. — SHAK 748:20
Barkis B. is willin' — DICK 269:64

barks in their b. my thoughts	SHAK 749:54
barley among the bearded b.	TENN 839:45
b. and of rye	TENN 838:42
Corn rigs, an' b. rigs	BURNS 170:84
fill his barn with wheat or b.	BUNY 167:78
taste the b. bree	BURNS 171:6
Barleycorn John B. should d.	BURNS 171:93
barley-sheaves between the b.-s.	TENN 839:48
Barlow His b. Hornby and my B.	THOM 855:39
barn fill his b. with wheat or barley	BUNY 167:78
men from the b. and the forge	HOUS 415:54
stack or the b. door	MILT 576:7
Barnet old B., the minister's man	HOGG 406:59
barns gathered into b.	TRUTH 869:52
barometer poet...used as a b.	TRIL 866:70
baronet lily-handed b. he	TENN 841:99
barons b. and their supporters	INNO 430:71
knights and b. bold	MILT 576:10
barque Though his b. cannot be lost	SHAK 766:68
barrel buy ink by the b.	KIRK 474:86
dribble...like a leaky b.	ELIOT 303:79
out of the b. of a gun	MAO 548:7
barrel-load save them by the b.-l.	THOM 855:40
barrel-organ kind of human b.-o.	DICK 269:55
barren a b. bride	POPE 661:45
b. thing this Conservatism	DISR 276:46
Be she b.	SWIFT 832:12
breed for b. metal	SHAK 739:54
from Dan to Beersheba...'tis all b.	STER 818:99
make b. our lives	SWIN 833:30
small model of the b. earth	SHAK 735:19
Speech is often b.	ELIOT 303:97
Barrets didn't like about The B. of Wimpole	PARK 637:49
barricade some disputed b.	SEEG 726:70
barriers break down b.	GING 357:59
impenetrable b. of our prison	EDGE 299:1
barrows grassy b.	TENN 846:27
Barrymore B.'s acting till the cows	NATH 609:22
No B. would allow	BARR 61:96
bars b. a thousand harms	SHAK 732:25
b. of Madras, Oregon	SNYD 803:53
Between their silver b.!	FLEC 327:52
Bolts and b. will not	MOLI 589:28
half a dozen b. of Lillabullero	STER 817:74
look out through the same b.	LANG 488:92
Nor iron b. a cage	LOVE 519:10
no voluntary b.	PATM 643:63
Stare out between the b.	SACK 708:90
weary of these worldly b.	SHAK 747:81
bartender By the time a b. knows	MARQ 554:35
good drunk...a good b.	BISH 131:81
bartered People...must not be b.	WILS 917:18
base b. football player	SHAK 762:58
Joy without Labour is b.	RUSK 704:26
Majors at the B.	SASS 716:61
peace, be it never so b.	CROM 245:71
replaced it on its b.	NAPO 607:71
baseball B....collective chess	BARZ 63:37
b....free of chivalry	BROUN 157:37
B. has the great advantage	SHAW 781:94
B. is a Lockean game	NOVAK 618:72
better learn b.	BARZ 63:36
Cricket is b. on valium	WILL 912:12
things you can do in a b. game	STEN 816:55
unaware that b. was a Republican sport	ROBB 689:16
baseballs batting b.	THUR 859:39
baseness dignity or b. of a person	CHRI 215:37
basenesses b. are plainer to no eye	CARL 191:74
basest b. of all things	FAUL 318:63
bashfulness in England a particular b.	ADDI 6:25
Basil steal my B.-pot away	KEATS 458:29
sweet B. evermore	KEATS 458:28
basis laughter is the b. of humankind	RABE 676:64
on the b. of our splendid failure	FAUL 319:71
science has for its b.	PAINE 634:97
whole b....of architecture	WAGN 884:64
basked b. him in the sun	SHAK 749:46
basket egg heads are in one b.	ANON 23:87
like wet crabs in a b.	DURR 296:38
lived to be carried in a b.	SHAK 743:79
set the b. umbilicus-high	NASH 609:8
basketball B., a game	NASH 609:8
I'm the black, b.-playing Nietzsche	ONEAL 625:86
interest in b.	NASH 609:5
bass sustained b. part	KIER 467:15
basset-horn melodious b.-h.	MORG 597:78
basset-hounds yellow-bosomed b.	MORG 597:78
Bast got with child by Leonard B.	MANS 546:85
bastard all my eggs in one b.	PARK 638:71
Daddy, daddy, you b.	PLATH 654:70
knocked the b. off!	HILL 403:92
no matter how big a b.	SALI 711:59
publicly call me a b.	WHIT 905:25
bastards gods, stand up for b.!	SHAK 762:56
unless the b. have the courage	STEI 815:36
We are b. all	SHAK 773:62
bastinado or in b., or in steel	SHAK 750:84
bastion like a b.'s mole	SMART 797:28
bat batsman and the b.	LANG 488:90
b. that you were kind	MANN 546:79
b. with tears in your eyes	BRAD 149:75
black b., night	TENN 845:89
Bradman, with the b.	LARW 491:56
click of the b.	COOKE 236:42
come to see me b.	GRACE 365:32
Gave up his b. and ball	EGAN 301:24
history of b. and ball	ARLO 30:62
think he's going to b. on	JOHN 447:80
Twinkle, twinkle, little b.!	CARR 195:72
weak-eyed b....flits by	COLL 228:47
bath b. by the beach	REID 682:96
B. twice a day	BURG 167:83
long to take a b.	UPDI 874:88
nymph to the b. addressed	SHEL 785:85
soaping her breasts in the b.	EWART 316:23
steamed like a b.	JONS 448:20
test my b. before	NASH 609:98
wrote...on his b. tub	POUND 665:62
bathes b. daily in a running	MOORE 594:12
bathing-caps two b.-c.	TRAV 864:42
bathroom as he goes to the b.	BLYT 138:23
revolutionary in a b.	LINK 511:59
baths B. that made him young	HERR 399:34
two walking b.	CRAS 244:37
bats archaeologists...like b.	MACA 525:36
b. have been broken	HOWE 417:96
B. have no bankers	BERR 82:65
covered with the skins of b.	DRAY 287:7
sad b. wheel about the steeple	DEBU 258:3
Suspicions...like b.	BACON 49:34
batsman B. of the Dawn	THOM 855:41
b.'s Willey	JOHN 447:79
b. thinks he's bowled	LANG 488:90
Cricket is a b.'s game	BENA 74:96
ghostly b. plays	THOM 855:39
premium on temperament for a b.	BRAD 149:76
batsmen sending your opening b.	HOWE 417:96
The really great b.	TRAV 864:40
battalions big b.	VOLT 883:50
dreams in pale b.	SORL 804:90
sorrows come...in b.	SHAK 754:19
batter put the b. off his stride	SHAW 781:96
batteries shot from one of the b.	MACA 527:78
battery make no b.	SHAK 733:54
batting W.G. discovered b.	RANJ 678:16
battle army hurrying into b.	ORWE 627:35
b. against yourself	KILLY 467:16
B. decide everything	CLAU 220:65
b. for precedence	SITW 794:74
b. for the mind	NOON 617:55
b. for your all	AESC 8:59
B. Hymn of the Republic	OBRI 621:8
b. is not yours, but God's	BIBLE 93:44
b. of man with man	WEBER 894:69
b. of Waterloo	WELL 898:67
b. of Waterloo was won	ORWE 628:61
b....to break all this up	WITT 918:49
b. to the strong	BIBLE 101:85
b. to the strong	DAVI 254:24
B....untying with the teeth	BIER 128:17
Ben B. was a soldier bold	HOOD 410:34
better in b. than in bed	STER 818:86
borne the b.	LINC 510:41
brave that die in the b.	CLOU 223:35
drunk delight of b.	TENN 839:63
field of b.	STEV 821:86
fights no uphill b.	HAZL 388:78
forefront of the hottest b.	BIBLE 91:1
Goddess of the B.	BARK 60:56
half the b.	GOLD 362:67
history of a b.	WELL 897:60
invincible in b.	SOPH 804:86
lines of b. wind	MACG 531:76
lit the b.'s wreck	HEMA 393:91
most serious things...in a b.	CARR 196:3
Next to a b. lost	WELL 897:59
noise of b. rolled	TENN 847:45
on the field of b.	PAST 642:47
out of b. I escaped	OWEN 632:87
prepared for the b.	HUSS 424:43
See the front o' b. lour	BURNS 173:41
sent it into b.	KENN 463:24
sent it into b.	MURR 605:10
sent ten thousand men to b.	SITT 793:56
smelleth the b. afar off	BIBLE 93:75
strange manner of b.	WILL 911:2
strife is o'er, the b. done	POTT 663:17
This b. fares like	SHAK 730:74
trumpets which sing to b.	SHEL 786:17
Tweedledum...agreed to have a b.	CARR 196:97
we never won a b.	DAVIS 256:65
who shall prepare himself to the b.?	BIBLE 121:10
battlefield b. of Vietnam	MCLU 536:64
brave on a b.	MITC 588:97
or the b. we die	SULL 828:17
soldier dying on the b.	BISM 131:85
battle-flags b.-f. were furled	TENN 840:81
battleground b. for a dark angel	LENG 502:81
battlehorse painting...a b.	DENIS 262:97
battles b. and death	GARI 346:48
b., heroic actions	POUS 666:75
b....were but desparate and vain appeals	CHUR 216:68
b. with the immortals	HOMER 409:16
Dead b.	TUCH 869:57
exercises are unbloody b.	JOSE 451:73
fought his b.	BUNY 167:77
hell her b. wage	POPE 662:68
in a hundred b.	SUN 829:27
mother of all b.	HUSS 424:42
not called to win b.	JENK 437:25
O God of b.	SHAK 746:53
pitched in India	MACA 526:58
quarrel and have b.	MACM 537:78
where be the b.	SPEN 808:90
battleship like...launching a b.	OSBO 630:11
battlewagon like a venerable b.	TIME 860:72
bauble fool's b.	CROM 246:75
prettiest b. you ever saw	WALP 887:23
Baudelaire B....Whoremongers	ONEI 625:99
Like Shelley and like B.	ISHE 430:90
bauhaus From B. to Our House	WOLFE 920:95
bawcock King's a b.	SHAK 746:49
bawdry so without b.	SHAK 770:91
Baxter In B.'s view	WEBER 894:67
bay curve of a blue b.	LOWE 519:25
in Baiae's b.	SHEL 783:45
like a green b.-tree	BOOK 143:47
margin of a b.	WORD 927:41
planted a green B.-tree	BETH 82:73
Somebody bet on de b.	FOST 332:59
Bayleys B., and your Bests	MACA 525:38
bayonet b. is a weapon	ANON 22:58
force of the b.!	MIRA 587:76
bayonets grass of silver b.	MACG 531:76
throne of b.	INGE 428:50
BBC B. Radio is a never-never land	SAFER 708:95
B. 'set its house in order'	CRIT 245:63
the B....is very truthful	ORWE 628:63
be can b. but What we are	SHIR 789:81
For what shall b.—yes!	HAMM 379:5
How can I b. who I am?	JORD 450:64
Must it be? It must be!	BEET 70:97
only thing I'd really like to b.	SALI 711:61
only way one can b.	BECK 68:45
or not to b.	TWAIN 871:7
thou shouldst cease to b.	SHEL 782:23
To b., or not to b.	SHAK 753:74
What is there to b.	EMPS 314:64
What we appear to b.	SCHI 718:4
what we may b.	SHAK 754:17
you should not b.?	GRAV 367:67
beach Along the hidden b.	KIPL 473:51
dry shell on the b.	DU 294:97
marks of fishermen on the b.	NAIP 606:50
On the B. is a story	GARD 345:43
wood found on a b.	ROSE 697:65
beaches fight on the b.	CHUR 216:76
Beachy Birmingham by way of B. Head	CHES 212:86
beadle b. on boxin' day	DICK 266:79
Thou rascal b.	SHAK 763:92

beadroll Fame's eternal b.   SPEN 809:6
beads jewels for a set of b.   SHAK 735:22
  number Ave-Maries on his b.   SHAK 730:52
beak b. of preposterous widthlessness   CUMM 247:97
  thy b. from out my heart   POE 656:24
beaker b. full of the warm South   KEATS 459:58
beaks kites to whet their b.   RANS 679:24
beam b. that is in thine own eye?   BIBLE 110:5
  B. us up, Mr Scott   RODD 693:90
  eyes at the full midday b.   MILT 579:82
beaming b. soul   POPE 662:77
beams b. may not dissolve the ice   SURR 829:40
  b. of science fall   POPE 662:71
  little candle throws his b.   SHAK 741:89
  splendour of his mid-day b.   HERR 399:38
  way your smile just b.   GERS 351:41
bean Boston...home of the b.   BOSS 145:8
  Nine b.-rows   YEATS 932:30
  stale b.-soup, of college yells   MENC 566:87
beanbag b. of a heart   NOON 617:56
beanfields smell of the b.   CHAT 207:49
beans b. and peason put within   ANON 19:80
  determined to know b.   THOR 858:96
  hill of b.   GARN 346:52
  hill of b. in this crazy world   EPST 314:79
bear b. any burden   KENN 462:12
  b. fruit—or wither   JAY 436:98
  B. of Very Little Brain   MILNE 574:79
  bush supposed a b.!   SHAK 738:13
  every b. that ever there was   BRAT 150:96
  Exit, pursued by a b.   SHAK 770:81
  furry as a b.   SITW 794:71
  Grizzly b. is huge   HOUS 416:88
  hardest thing to b.   JUVE 453:16
  If you b. your cross   KEMP 461:91
  last b., shot drinking   CRANE 243:16
  many things to say...ye cannot b.   BIBLE 118:13
  more sorrow than they could b.   REST 683:16
  out of the paw of the b.   BIBLE 91:93
  Puritan hated b.-baiting   MACA 526:77
  rode on the back of a b.   LEAR 498:93
  tree could b. no more   FROST 338:92
  Wedged B. in Great Tightness?   MILNE 574:78
  Who can b. the Gracchi   JUVE 453:15
beard b. the lion in his den   SCOTT 723:98
  By thy long grey b.   COLE 225:80
  Com'st thou to b. me   SHAK 753:63
  endure a husband with a b.   SHAK 744:90
  even Aaron's b.   BIBLE 98:96
  hairs in the b.   GOYA 365:30
  have a b. coming   SHAK 737:89
  Loose his b., and hoary hair   GRAY 370:29
  off the Great Cham's b.   SHAK 744:95
  Old Man with a b.   LEAR 497:75
  send there a b.   SHAK 756:74
  singeing of the King of Spain's b.   DRAKE 286:92
  To shave the b. is a sin   IVAN 431:99
  without singeing someone's b.   LICH 509:20
bearded b. like a man!   DICK 273:78
beards b. forbid me to interpret   SHAK 766:71
  their long b.   SWIFT 831:88
bearing b. what is laid upon us   ELIOT 303:89
bear-like But b.-I. I must fight   SHAK 769:43
bears beat out tunes for b.   FLAU 326:34
  habitation for b. and wolves   SCHAW 717:96
  sympathise with the b.   MUIR 602:66
  the English and the b.   THOM 853:2
beast And what rough b.   YEATS 933:51
  b. imbued with such immortal fire?   BYRON 179:12
  b. on my back   DOUG 283:21
  B. ravens in its own avidity?   EBER 298:74
  Better B. and know your end   DEVL 264:32
  Blatant b.   SPEN 809:8
  call this b. to mind   BELL 72:47
  chase had a b. in view   DRYD 292:63
  Cocoa is a vulgar b.   CHES 212:80
  deem himself a god, or b.   POPE 660:16
  even-tempered the b.   TRUD 868:23
  huge inarticulate b.   HOFS 406:55
  I hold a b.   THOM 852:66
  makes a man a b.   WEBS 894:80
  making the b. with the two backs   SHAK 759:53
  Man is neither angel nor b.   PASC 641:31
  man who lay with a b.   HELL 392:66
  marks of the b.   HARDY 382:58
  night out for man or b.   FIEL 323:48
  number of the b.   BIBLE 126:67

  often acts the b.   PASC 641:31
  snorts like a great b.   SMITH 801:25
  Tam mounts his b.   BURNS 172:20
  tilt their aggregate b.   MACN 538:1
  Unto some brutish b.   MARL 553:8
  who worship the b.   BIBLE 126:68
  wild b., or a god   BACON 49:28
beastie Wee, sleeket, cowrin...b.   BURNS 170:71
beastly b. to the Bank of England   CRIT 245:63
  B. to the Germans   COWA 239:21
beasts all manner of fourfooted b.   BIBLE 119:39
  Among the b. no mate   MILT 584:5
  b. are our masters   FLET 328:70
  b. of the intellectual domain   HOLM 407:77
  b. on each other prey   ROCH 691:58
  brute b. that have no understanding   BOOK 142:20
  droop men and b.   NASHE 609:16
  fled to brutish b.   SHAK 748:7
  keeping b. of burden patient   KING 469:59
  man's distinctive mark...not the b.   BROW 162:74
  minds...to the b. that perish   WELLS 898:73
  Music might tame...wild b.   GAY 348:88
  Nature teaches b.   SHAK 769:58
  round about the throne, were four b.   BIBLE 126:53
  small and great b.   BIBLE 97:69
  wild b. and Lord man   MUIR 602:66
  wild b. ate it   BAUD 64:60
beat b. Mr Turgenev   HEMI 394:18
  b. my people to pieces   BIBLE 102:9
  b. them now and gain   THOM 853:80
  b. them today   STARK 813:76
  bloody b. them again   RAMS 678:9
  Don't b. me, pa!   JOYCE 451:80
  figure to get b. some time   LOUIS 518:5
  if we b. West Germany   RAMS 678:8
  One man...can always b. ten   SHAW 781:88
  this is really a b. generation   KERO 464:65
  To the b. of the measure   POUND 665:53
beaten No Englishman is...fairly b.   SHAW 781:82
  The b. road   SHEL 786:9
  You've b. them once   RAMS 678:9
beatificate translate And b.   QUIL 674:47
beating driven by b.   ASCH 35:80
  hear the b. of his wings   BRIG 152:30
beatings dread of b.!   BETJ 84:12
Beatles Chatterly ban And the B.   LARK 491:37
Beatrice B. like a lapwing runs   SHAK 744:9
beauteous B. the fleet   SMART 797:29
  b. things for which   CORY 238:77
  How b. mankind is!   SHAK 775:1
beautied b. with impermanence   SCOTT 722:76
  b. with plast'ring art   SHAK 753:73
beauties b. of the fute-ball   ANON 20:5
  B....their pretty eyes may roll   POPE 659:77
  concealed in b.   ADDI 6:18
  no matter what b. I saw   PRIOR 669:42
  pale, unripened b.   ADDI 6:33
  saved by b. not his own   POPE 662:69
  Thy b., yet could write   JONS 450:50
beautified b.' is a vile phrase   SHAK 752:44
beautiful appear b. outward   BIBLE 113:84
  art for the sake of...the b.   SAND 712:89
  b. and death-struck year   HOUS 415:61
  b. and frozen, I preserve you   ATWO 38:57
  B. and the Damned   FITZ 324:91
  b., and therefore to be wooed   SHAK 729:48
  b. as a wreck   SHEL 786:11
  B.! B.!   ALDR 11:16
  b. countenance   BIBLE 91:91
  B. dreamer   FOST 332:62
  B. for situation   BIBLE 95:27
  b. is always shocking   BAUD 65:70
  b. only when she is loved   EPST 315:82
  b. passionate body   SWIN 833:29
  b. sentiments   GIDE 353:83
  b., the tender, the kind   MILL 571:89
  b. things made by renunciation?   DEGAS 259:29
  b. woman...qualities of a gentleman   LABR 483:58
  beginning of a b. friendship   WALL 887:20
  better to be b. than to be good   WILDE 908:8
  Black is b.   ANON 23:96
  deal of scorn looks b.   SHAK 756:78
  desired all b. things   CHES 212:68
  feathers are more b.?   SHAK 732:43
  football team is like a b. woman   WENG 899:3
  For she was b.   SHEL 785:88
  Fowey Is a b. spot   QUIL 674:42

  grave hides all things b.   SHEL 785:74
  ground is like a b. woman   SNOW 802:45
  House B. is...lousy   PARK 637:50
  How b. the Republic was   DURR 296:37
  How b. upon the mountains   BIBLE 104:47
  if they are to seem b.   SCHO 720:36
  Life...is a b. thing   BURT 174:67
  make anything b. or desirable   STOWE 826:72
  more b. than death   WHIT 905:43
  most b. sight in orbit   SCHW 721:69
  most b. things on earth   ISAA 430:86
  most b. works   FLAU 326:31
  never have a mistress as b.   ARLT 30:66
  only b. if it has good grass   BUTL 177:63
  only hope of creating something b.   FLAU 326:36
  pard-like Spirit, b. and swift   SHEL 785:99
  perpetual hunger to be b.   RHYS 684:24
  picture that is b.   FRAN 334:4
  pleasure...because it is b.   POIN 657:34
  saddest and most b. sight   DALG 251:68
  science is very b.   OPPE 626:16
  silence makes a woman b.   SOPH 804:81
  small is b.   SCHU 720:51
  The innocent and the b.   YEATS 934:55
  things that are b.   DEBU 258:5
  too b. to live   DICK 267:4
  travel...to find the b.   EMER 312:19
  two most b. words   JAMES 434:54
  ugly things...frequently become b.   COCT 224:61
  When a woman isn't b.   CHEK 209:13
  worshipped because they are b.   RUSS 705:47

beauty absolute b.   HALD 377:76
  abuse and destroy b.   PORT 663:10
  ache of b.   UTTL 875:10
  all that b....e'er gave   GRAY 369:14
  And order, truth, and b. range   SMART 796:27
  Art is not...a canon of b.   PICA 650:97
  autumnal face, her pieced b.!   JONS 449:24
  b., and gay clothes   WEBS 894:85
  B. and the lust for learning   BEER 69:79
  b. beat on his conceits   MARL 551:78
  B....became money   WOLF 920:81
  b. can lie...in days   FOWL 332:71
  b. cold and austere   RUSS 705:39
  b. depended most on poetry   SIDN 791:17
  b. faded   PHIL 650:90
  b. for ashes   BIBLE 104:62
  b. from the light retir'd   WALL 886:13
  b. has in art   DIDE 273:85
  B. has only one form   HUGO 420:59
  b. hath ensnared thee   SHAK 733:63
  b. in the works of a great genius   ADDI 7:41
  b. is a guarantee of happiness   PROU 671:81
  b. is a joy for ever   KEATS 457:1
  B. is all very well   SHAW 778:2
  B. is as summer-fruits   BACON 49:42
  B. is a witch   SHAK 744:93
  B. is only sin deep   SAKI 710:30
  B. is the first test   HARDY 381:45
  B. is the lover's gift   CONG 231:34
  B. is truth, truth b.   KEATS 459:56
  b. is vain   BIBLE 100:64
  b. like a tightened bow   YEATS 933:40
  B....like the gold standard   WOLF 919:80
  B. lives though lilies die   FLEC 327:45
  b. made The bright world dim   SHEL 785:88
  b. of creatures   AQUI 28:27
  b. of holiness   BIBLE 97:59
  b. of inflections   STEV 819:22
  b. of its...shadow   WORD 929:67
  b....of life   ALLEN 12:39
  b. of marrow   SITW 794:66
  b. of sense objects   AQUI 28:30
  b. of speed   MARI 550:52
  b. of speed   MARI 550:53
  b....of the buildings we burnt   ELGIN 302:69
  b. of their s.   TENN 841:97
  b. of the morning   WORD 926:19
  b. of the world   SHAK 752:57
  b. of the world   WEIL 896:30
  b. of thy mind   SHAK 772:28
  B. pains   HAAS 376:52
  B. provoketh thieves   SHAK 749:32
  b.'s charming   SCOTT 724:40
  B....should not be wasted   SHAK 732:50
  b. so old and so new   AUGU 41:37

B.'s princely majesty	SHAK 729:47
b.'s self she is	ANON 20:8
b. than existed before	RUNGE 702:75
b., though injurious	MILT 586:59
B. too rich for use	SHAK 736:42
b. vanishes; b. passes	DELA 260:67
B., virtue, happiness	BERN 81:43
b. was rather for use	PRIOR 669:34
B. was their answer	BRID 152:27
befriended us with b.	CAVE 201:20
behold the b. of the Lord	BIBLE 95:7
best part of b.	BACON 49:44
cannot write of b.	BELL 72:41
carried into b.	WOOLF 922:38
day for b.	WORD 929:68
Death is a name for b.	LAYT 496:48
decay…of b.	CONG 231:29
dedicated to force and to b.	RIMB 688:98
desire of b.…has most	PATER 642:53
divers schedules of my b.	SHAK 756:58
doth b. beauteous seem	SHAK 771:19
equal in b. to	KORN 480:2
Euclid alone Has looked on B.	MILL 571:88
fading b.	WALL 886:18
fatal gift of b.	BYRON 180:34
Fostered…by b.	WORD 925:91
ghosts of B. glide	POPE 661:50
hardships into forms of b.	CAMP 186:61
her…unconventional b.	SCHL 718:14
Honesty coupled to b.	SHAK 750:67
If you get simple b.	BROW 161:38
images of female b.	WOLF 919:79
imagination seizes as b.	KEATS 457:89
In art economy is always b.	JAMES 433:51
in victory, there is no b.	LAO 490:11
I sat b. on my knees	RIMB 688:96
Is there in truth no b.?	HERB 398:6
judge the b. of life	LAUT 493:80
June for b.'s heightening	ARNO 33:44
Kindness is worth more than b.	ARRAS 34:77
Knowledge of ideal b.	BLAKE 135:79
lady of b. and high degree	RANS 679:21
Life, force and b.	POPE 658:53
light…From her own b.	SHEL 785:87
Look on b.	SHAK 740:71
loved your b.	YEATS 932:33
manhood's b.	WILDE 907:81
March with b.	SHAK 770:86
most radiant b.	EINS 301:37
nation…without a sense of b.	WHAR 901:45
no b. that we should desire him	BIBLE 104:50
not b. because it is not nature	CONS 235:24
On her b. I'll gaze	ROCH 691:67
pale court in b. and decay	SHEL 785:92
peace nor b.	LAWR 494:4
power of b.	SHAK 753:76
saw true b. till this night	SHAK 736:43
She walks in b.	BYRON 181:53
simple b. and rustic health	WHIT 906:58
since their b. passed	THOM 854:8
some sort of order (or b.)	POUND 665:66
soul of her b.	SHEL 785:85
Strength and b.	DEMO 261:85
Such seems your b. still	SHAK 772:42
the b. of the thing	GALL 344:19
There is only b.	MALL 542:89
things of b.	CRUZ 246:87
Tisn't b., so to speak	KIPL 473:56
trouble with b.	BAZE 63:39
turns all things to b.	JOHN 438:58
unmask her b. to the moon	SHAK 751:15
unzips the veil from b.	WHITE 903:78
What is b.	MARL 551:77
What is b.	VIEI 881:12
where all is order and b.	BAUD 64:61
where B. was	GALS 344:25
whose b. is past change	HOPK 412:86
why talk of b.	CUMM 247:0
wildest b. in the world	OWEN 632:60
Wit is more necessary than b.	WYCH 931:14
world is richer for a new b.	MARI 550:52
write the b. of your eyes	SHAK 771:4
youth and a little b.	WEBS 895:10
Youth, b., graceful action	DRYD 290:90
Beaverbrook B.…like the town tart	BAXT 65:88
papers conducted by…Lord B.	BALD 54:46
because B. it's there	MALL 542:99

Becher's deeper foreboding than…B.	FRAN 334:99
beck more offences at my b.	SHAK 753:78
become What's b. of me or you?	EMPS 314:64
bed A b., a b.	BALL 55:71
Ample make this B.	DICK 272:67
And so to b.	PEPYS 647:26
As to a lover's b.	SHAK 765:47
b. fell on my father	THUR 859:22
b. Of crimson joy	BLAKE 134:54
b. of daffodil sky	TENN 845:89
b.…the cold, cold grave	BALL 55:72
B.…the poor man's opera	HUXL 425:95
Best bloody place is bloody b.	BLAIR 132:98
better in battle than in b.	STER 818:86
bounced out of b.	MILNE 574:76
Chairman…lying on his death b.	MIN 587:69
comforts of the early morning b.	SHIP 789:77
Creep into thy narrow b.	ARNO 33:51
cry in my b.	AGUS 9:76
dark beside my b.	MACN 538:10
deck both b. and bower	SPEN 808:86
destroyed in b.	SKEL 795:8
die—in b.	SASS 716:62
early to b.	THUR 859:29
Early to b., early to rise	RODR 693:95
Every b. is narrow	MILL 571:83
get me to b.	SCOTT 725:59
go to b. by day	STEV 822:11
go to b. early	WAUGH 892:20
go to b. exhausted	ROTH 699:25
go to b. sober	FLET 328:68
haste me to my b.	SHAK 771:13
husbands lie snoring in b.	MORE 597:65
ideal companion in b.	DAVI 255:45
in b. with musicians	WILM 914:68
in love with my b.	SHAK 729:27
in my b. againe	ANON 20:99
lie diagonally in his b.	STER 818:89
lie down on my b.	HILL 403:95
lie o' both sides of the b.	DEKK 259:52
Lies in his b.	SHAK 738:25
Lying in b.	CHES 212:67
Lying in b.	WATE 890:91
lying in b. counting sheep	SIEG 791:24
lying in b., thinking	GINS 357:71
made his pedant b.	SHAK 767:85
make my b. in hell	BIBLE 98:1
manger for his b.	ALEX 11:24
mind is not a b.	AGATE 8:68
mostly sent to b.	LAND 488:80
mother, mother, mak my b.	BALL 55:65
Must we to b. indeed?	STEV 823:21
never…made my own b.	PU 673:22
not a b. of roses	STEV 821:86
not mount the marriage b.	JONS 449:27
now 'tis your b. time	DONNE 279:35
pillow on a b.	DONNE 280:57
preparing for b. with the shades up	STARR 813:77
rouse them from their lowly b.	GRAY 369:12
royal b. of Denmark	SHAK 752:33
sinners are still in b.	RUNY 703:85
sitting at the edge of a hotel b.	CHEE 209:3
spit-spot into b.	TRAV 864:41
stay in b. all day	BENC 74:2
still keeping open b.	HUXL 424:59
Strangle her in her b.	SHAK 760:99
sweat of an enseamèd b.	SHAK 754:10
take up thy b., and walk	BIBLE 117:86
this b.-presser	SHAK 742:15
under the b. for Communists	FOOT 329:91
wakes me from my flow'ry b.?	SHAK 738:3
Welcome to your gory b.	BURNS 173:41
When Harriet goes to b.	BROY 163:1
Who goes to b. with whom	SAYE 717:88
would 'twere b.-time	SHAK 742:26
you see that great b.	ONAS 625:80
bedchamber calls on my b. less	HILL 403:95
bedclothes little harm, save to his b.	SHAK 762:37
bedeck b. and bedrape us	SWIN 833:26
bedevilment Of man's b.	HOUS 416:76
bedfellows strange b.	SHAK 774:87
bedpan b. by a stranger	KUHN 481:34
bedrape bedeck and b. us	SWIN 833:26
bedroom b. in a Brussels hotel	THOM 855:34
doesn't matter what you do in the b.	CAMP 185:53
Lincoln's b.!	ONAS 625:80
spy in his b.	TOYN 864:33

trying on ties in his b.	CURT 249:47
what belongs in the b.	GOLD 362:83
bedrooms b. of the nation	TRUD 868:22
beds all snug in their b.	MOORE 594:15
hussies in your b.	SHAK 759:73
made the b., shopped for groceries	FRIE 337:59
Minds like b.	WILL 913:49
bedspreads b. according to rule	LEVE 506:60
bee as lightly as the B.	JONS 450:48
b. takes a middle course	BACON 47:60
b. with honied thigh	MILT 577:21
Pedigree…Does not concern the B.	DICK 273:75
sting like a b.	ALI 12:33
Where the b. sucks	SHAK 775:99
beech moss-grown b.	GRAY 369:4
warlike b.	SPEN 808:73
Beecham B.'s Pills are just the thing	BEEC 69:60
beef B. and a sea-coal fire	OTWAY 631:33
b., pork, and mutton	KIPL 474:71
great eater of b.	SHAK 756:51
roast b. of England	FIEL 322:37
beefsteak as English…as a b.	HAWT 386:53
beehive Fascist…b.	ORWE 628:66
been For what has b.—thanks!	HAMM 379:5
It might have b.!	WHIT 906:59
might have b.	HARTE 385:19
what hath b.	TENN 843:48
Where I have b.	GURN 375:43
beer B. and Britannia	SMITH 801:9
b. corrodes it	TWAIN 870:91
B., tobacco, and music	MANN 545:64
b. was strong	PRIOR 669:39
colour-bar and b.	NOON 618:59
embodied spirit of b.	BENN 76:51
ever taste b.?	DICK 267:19
faint stale smells of b.	ELIOT 305:28
felony to drink small b.	SHAK 730:63
Life isn't all b. and skittles	HUGH 420:54
muddy ecstasies of b.	CRAB 242:81
not all B. and Skittles	STEV 823:29
no wine or good b.	GORO 364:15
only a b. teetotaller	SHAW 777:59
only here for the b.	LEVE 506:54
Pints and quarts of Ludlow b.	HOUS 415:66
teach the Irish to drink b.	EDGE 299:98
Beersheba from Dan to B.	STER 818:99
bees a grave injustice to b.	ORWE 628:46
angry hive of b.	SHAK 730:58
B. are sometimes drowned	HAWT 386:37
Books are the b.	LOWE 520:34
early b. are assaulting	REED 681:78
Forget not b. in winter	SACK 708:87
hive of silvery B.	LEAR 497:81
innumerable b.	TENN 842:17
Keep b.	WADD 884:63
these are the wrong sort of b.	MILNE 574:77
bees-winged b.-w. eyes?	BETJ 83:81
Beethoven as B. was born for music	PELE 646:17
B. always sounds	RUSK 704:36
B. came with music	NEVE 611:48
B.'s Fifth Symphony	FORS 331:31
difference between B. and Mahler	COPL 237:66
From you, B., Bach, Mozart	SASS 716:65
how much I appreciate B.	HEIF 391:45
Roll over B.	BERRY 82:59
beetle b. wheels his droning flight	GRAY 369:10
b. winds His small but sullen horn	COLL 228:47
into a large brown b.	KAIKO 454:33
poor b. that we tread	SHAK 758:34
beeves Let b. and home-bred kine	WORD 927:30
before B., behind, between, above, below	DONNE 279:36
B. Thee in humility	HAMM 379:7
beset me behind and b.	BIBLE 98:99
those things which are b.	BIBLE 123:58
beg b. in the streets	FRAN 333:93
should not b. in vain	JONS 450:48
beget if he touch he must b.	YEATS 934:68
Is there no way to b.	HERR 399:34
never to b.	HOPK 413:7
begetter proclaimed its b.	MEYER 568:30
beggar a b. before you	ORAH 627:21
b. begrudges b.	HESI 401:64
b. by banqueting upon borrowing	BIBLE 108:53
b. died, and was carried by the angels	BIBLE 116:54
b. is still a man	MORI 598:83
b. who suns himself	SMITH 797:37

black boundin' b.	KIPL 471:94
whiles I am a b.	SHAK 738:21
beggared B. by fools	DRYD 290:89
beggars b….too professional air	MCCA 528:96
exercises authority over b.	MORE 597:63
pays us poor b. in red	KIPL 471:97
tiresome Serbia b. belief	MARY 558:17
When b. die	SHAK 747:87
beggar-woman b.-w. and single	ELIZ 309:55
beggary b. in the love	SHAK 764:11
Contempt and b. hangs	SHAK 737:79
begging nor his seed b. bread	BIBLE 95:17
begin B. at the beginning	CARR 195:86
b. from the subjective	SART 715:48
b. to dress ourselves	RICH 685:50
But let us b.	KENN 462:11
time to b. a new	DRYD 292:63
To b. at the beginning	THOM 853:85
worst of all is to b.	BART 62:12
beginner man ceases to be a b.	COLL 227:33
mere b.	HUGH 418:14
beginning as he was at the b.	HICKS 402:80
As it was in the b.	BOOK 140:69
As it was in the b.	RHYS 684:28
b., a middle, and an end	ARIS 29:55
b., a muddle, and an end	LARK 491:46
b. and end of art	HEIN 391:52
b. is assuredly the end	WILL 913:48
b. is often the end	ELIOT 309:49
b. of everything	REAG 680:59
b.' of feminism	ROWB 701:49
b. of the end	TALL 835:84
b. of wisdom	BIBLE 97:75
coming up b.	MUIR 602:61
each venture…a new b.	ELIOT 308:23
end of the b.	CHUR 217:86
end precedes the b.	ELIOT 307:1
from the b. think	WHYM 906:65
In my b. is my end	ELIOT 308:13
In the b. God created	BIBLE 85:37
In the b. was the Word	BIBLE 117:71
In the b. was the Word	ELIOT 305:36
more accurate in the b.	JONS 450:61
most important…is the b.	PLATO 655:96
my end is my b.	MARY 558:18
Never ending, still b.	DRYD 291:38
pleasure can be the b. of beauty	PROU 671:81
sort of a bad b.	DICK 265:57
urge in the b.	SAND 713:14
voted to make a new b.	CLIN 221:89
beginningless b., endless, topless,	
bottomless	RUSK 704:37
beginnings b. of ataxia	SILVA 792:34
ends by our b. know	DENH 261:95
mighty things from small b.	DRYD 287:20
begins Fashion constantly b. and ends	HAZL 387:70
where…the Church of England b.	PRIE 668:26
begot b. in fear	GRAV 367:67
when they b. me	STER 817:67
begotten B., not made	BOOK 141:95
beguiled B. again	HART 384:12
thou art b.	SKEL 795:92
Behan My name is B.	BEHAN 70:5
behave in excess except	LACL 484:82
How well I did b.	HOUS 414:47
must b. accordingly	KISS 475:92
things they b. sensibly about?	SHAW 777:56
behaving better b. themselves	SZASZ 834:62
expedient in the way of our b.	JAMES 434:73
behaviour abdication…Makes the B.	DICK 273:73
certain kinds of b.	ROBB 689:14
constitutes unacceptable b.	LEBO 499:5
decency and discretion in their b.	BACON 46:38
evoking a new b.	MERT 568:22
Fearful and hostile b.	FULB 341:45
guided my b.	MACL 534:29
in-office attitudes and b.	COUP 238:93
knowing…their b. very well	THOM 853:80
man's b. be quite harmless	SHAW 780:50
my b. full of rigor	BROW 158:54
Puritanism names the b.	SPEN 807:63
quality of moral b.	HUXL 425:87
social b. displays many features	HOMA 408:8
watch their b.	WELD 897:44
Whatever his private b.	MEYER 568:30
behaviourism Of course, B. 'works'	AUDEN 41:29
beheaded imprisoned…b. others	STAL 812:55

one of our kings who was b.	APPL 27:22
to see the King b.	PEPYS 647:28
behemoth Behold now b.	BIBLE 93:76
Black Mrs B.	SITW 794:65
behind b. your scenes	JOHN 441:22
beset me b. and before	BIBLE 98:99
it will be b. me	REGER 682:94
no bosom and no b.	SMITH 800:94
one must ride b.	SHAK 745:18
turn thee b. me	BIBLE 92:33
behold B. and see	SHAK 764:10
beholder cheer to its b.	ROCK 692:75
impossible that Grace	SIDN 791:21
beholders awe into the b.	SWIFT 831:77
beige B.! Just my color	DE 265:45
Beijing say here in B.	CLIN 222:10
being A b. darkly wise	POPE 660:16
at the edge of B.	SPEN 807:51
b. absolutely infinite	SPIN 811:36
b. always with myself	GIRO 358:84
b. and as an angel	MUIR 602:67
B. and Ideal Grace	BROW 160:9
b. and our birth	SHAK 769:51
B. is the great explainer	THOR 857:69
b. is to be perceived	BERK 79:5
b. who…need not even exist	BAUD 65:75
breath of Autumn's b.	SHEL 783:43
by avoiding b.	TILL 860:67
chain of b.	EMER 312:20
concerns thee and thy b.	MILT 584:98
creation, development and b.	HUMB 421:2
how such a b. could exist	ANDR 16:24
intellectual b.	MILT 581:22
live, and move and have our b.	BIBLE 119:50
man is the b. who wills	SCHI 718:2
mighty b. is awake	WORD 926:13
most prostituted b.	BAUD 65:83
part of our very b.	GAND 345:35
persist in its own b.	SPIN 810:28
pleasing anxious b.	GRAY 369:22
poem…once it is in b.	FROST 339:7
preserve one's b.	SPIN 810:31
presuppose a Supreme B.	DOUG 284:33
reason for b.	FRAN 333:88
sensitive b., a creative soul	WORD 925:5
that is the essence of our b.	BUSH 176:25
They had their b. once	PURDY 673:19
Unbearable Lightness of B.	KUND 482:36
very bottom of her b.	ADAMS 4:70
wheels of B. slow	TENN 843:39
beings b. brighter than have been	BYRON 181:55
b. which are impossible	REDON 681:74
evidence of supernatural b.	STEI 816:47
in his stomach more animated b.	SMITH 801:11
other b. in the zoological scale	CARB 189:39
three respectable b.	BAUD 65:82
Beirut If you liked B.	HEMP 395:32
beleaguered sense of being b.	RABAN 675:58
Belgium B. recovers in full measure	ASQU 36:9
B.'s capital had gathered	BYRON 179:23
Belial B. with words clothed	MILT 581:23
forth the sons of B.	MILT 581:10
belief abandoned a b. in God	STEV 820:41
abdication of b.	DICK 273:73
any unwarrantable b.	RICH 686:62
assert my b. that	ROOS 696:43
authority of a b.	KRIS 480:14
b. and hope had gone	RUSS 706:61
B. consists in affirming	EMER 312:28
b….founded upon my experience	DOYLE 285:67
b. in…human beings	ORWE 628:50
b. in luck	OATES 620:90
b. in their sincerity	TWAIN 870:76
b. is for it	JOHN 445:28
b. is made religious	CUPI 248:34
b. of truth	BACON 47:72
b. that we can start	POPP 662:93
b. which may be right	FORS 331:32
commit…to any religious b.	WAUGH 892:21
decline of religious b.	FREUD 337:56
do not believe in B.	FORS 331:51
epoch of b.	DICK 271:19
Faith…an illogical b.	MENC 565:58
firm b. in the justice of our cause	WASH 890:82
firm b. that everybody could write	BAIN 52:27
first expounder of our religious b.	SPEKE 806:35
impress the people…with a b.	PEEL 646:9

inherited this b.	MILL 571:96
last, best b. system	WOLF 919:80
leading to the b.	KAUF 456:60
lose b. in this truth	DU 293:74
My b. is that in life	TROL 866:86
national b.	MCCA 528:98
proportions his b. to the evidence	HUME 422:14
prospect of b.	SHAK 766:73
Rome…trades on b.	BURG 167:84
tiresome Serbia beggars b.	MARY 558:17
beliefs All known religious b.	DURK 296:35
b., traditions and aspirations	DURK 296:34
b….we hold sacred	ARON 34:75
different people, different b.	CART 198:46
discuss your b.	HELL 392:73
Home of…forsaken b.	ARNO 33:39
reverse important basic b.	MILL 571:1
someone's mistaken b.	ELLI 311:89
strong b. wounded	BROO 156:26
two contradictory b.	ORWE 630:3
believe b. also in me	BIBLE 118:8
b. and rejoice in Christ	LUTH 523:94
b., because they so were bred	DRYD 291:21
B. false teachers	SHAK 774:66
b. in ideas and die for them	ANOU 26:97
b. of my own stories	IRVI 430:83
B. one who has experienced it.	VIRG 882:26
b. what we choose	NEWM 612:64
cease to b.	HAMM 379:6
devils also b.	BIBLE 124:10
don't b. in preachers	BENE 75:8
Except I shall see…I will not b.	BIBLE 118:24
few will consent to b.	KENN 461:96
For those who b. in God	SEAT 726:69
fun to b. them	BACH 46:31
If you b. that	WELL 898:70
If you don't b. it	AUGU 42:44
live by what they b.	HAMP 380:26
mix what they b.	UPDI 874:73
Never b.	SKEL 795:99
never b. again	TOML 863:11
those who b.	WALK 885:1
Those who b. that they are	GRANT 424:63
what we ourselves b.	GRANT 366:48
willing to b. what they wish	CAES 184:23
believer b. will fight another	GREE 371:74
In a b.'s ear!	NEWT 613:78
make the b.'s leap	RABAN 675:61
believers objectionable types of b.	BORN 145:97
believes one b., then miracles occur	MILL 573:39
thinks he b. only what he sees	SANT 714:22
what an Englishman b.	SHAW 781:83
What your government b.	KENN 463:41
believing B. is Seeing	WOLFE 920:92
better at b. than at seeing	SANT 714:22
eating that's b.	THUR 859:47
pleasure of b. what we see	SHEL 782:24
torture them, into b.	NEWM 612:64
We are born b.	EMER 313:42
Belinda B. smiled, and all the world	POPE 659:69
belittlement all our injured b.	RABAN 675:58
belittling not b. the brave pioneer men	FERB 320:93
bell B., book, and candle	SHAK 738:24
b. rings and the widow weeps	SHAK 745:25
b.-rope that gathers God	CRANE 243:26
binkledy-winkled a b.	LEAR 498:88
double and the single b.	SLES 796:15
for whom the b. is tolling	NASH 609:5
for whom the b. tolls	DONNE 281:85
God's b. buoyed	YEATS 932:34
hear the surly sullen b.	SHAK 772:29
lifted, rough-tongued b.	LARK 490:22
like b.-bottoms and W.C. Fields	HAWES 385:30
silver-voiced b.-birds	KEND 461:95
tangles Of b.-flowers	SITW 793:63
The b. invites me	SHAK 767:96
Time and the b.	ELIOT 307:98
tolling b. Measures time	ELIOT 308:29
Twilight and evening b.	TENN 848:70
word is like a b.	KEATS 460:64
Bellamy one of B.'s veal pies	PITT 653:50
belle my time, my b. époque	HOLL 407:69
young b. of old Natchez	NASH 608:89
bellicose querulous and b.	MENC 565:55
bellies evil beasts, slow b.	BIBLE 124:87
studious for their b.	SAND 713:17
belligerent looked so b.	KARSH 455:52

belligerents Police...separate the b.   EDEN 299:90
bellman B. would cry: CARR 197:30
bellows flatt'ry is the b.   SHAK 769:49
bells beaten b.   STEV 824:38
  b. I hear   WHIT 905:46
  B. in your parlours   SHAK 759:73
  b. off San Salvador   CRANE 243:10
  b. of Shandon   MAHO 539:35
  B., the poor man's only music   COLE 226:96
  b. they sound so clear   HOUS 415:51
  church b. hollowing out   BETJ 84:10
  floating many b. down   CUMM 248:19
  lin-lan-lone of evening b.   TENN 848:71
  mortals who ring b.   MANN 545:69
  name is like a ring of b.   BETJ 83:94
  none of your ribbons and b.   MARQ 554:27
  Oh, noisy b., be dumb   HOUS 415:53
  passing-b. for these who die   OWEN 632:51
  Ring out, wild b.   TENN 844:60
  ring the b. of heaven   HODG 405:46
  ring their b.   WALP 887:39
  sleigh b. in the snow   BERL 80:16
  tall building, with a tower and b.   CRAB 242:95
belly b....send thee good ale   ANON 20:1
  b. was bitter   BIBLE 126:64
  bitter b.-tension   GIBB 352:72
  does not mind his b.   JOHN 443:74
  everything, except this perpetual B.   EMER 312:31
  filled his b. with the husks   BIBLE 116:47
  Gun Fired in the Pope's B.   ANON 21:37
  No b. and no bowels   RANS 679:28
  pour...by the b. full   SPEN 809:4
  upon thy b. thou shalt go   BIBLE 86:53
  whose God is their b.   BIBLE 123:59
belong b. to Britain   GERA 350:26
  Go where you b.   TROT 867:13
  really b.   GREE 371:55
  To betray, you must first b.   PHIL 650:88
belonging greatest sense of b.   ROTH 699:14
belongings b. of others   SALL 711:71
  b. on show   JOYCE 452:95
beloved b. is mine, and I am his   BIBLE 101:1
  Cry, the B. Country   PATON 643:69
  Dearly b., we are gathered together   BOOK 142:19
  more b. for the imperfections   RUSK 703:7
  the kiss to one's b.   ONEI 625:92
below either above or b. it   GILL 356:44
  He lies b.   PARK 638:62
belt could not see a b.   ASQU 36:14
belted Though I've b. you   KIPL 471:96
Ben bare B. Bulben's head   YEATS 934:66
  B. Hur translated into Irish   STEW 824:43
bench designed a b. in a few moments   BELL 72:44
  fluttering to a b.   SACK 708:88
  murd'rous hand a drowsy b. protect   CRAB 242:91
benches though we cropen under b.?   LANG 489:95
bend b. but do not break   LAFO 485:2
  b. to the wind   BUCK 165:39
  right on round the b.   LAUD 492:65
bending nations now b. under...tyranny   PITT 653:47
beneath B. is spread like a green sea   SHEL 783:28
  B. the visiting moon   SHAK 765:52
  see b. both beauty and ugliness   ELIOT 307:86
Benedick Nobody marks you.   SHAK 744:86
benedicte B., omnia opera Domini   BIBLE 128:97
benediction clouds in b.   DAY 257:84
beneficial harmless and even b.   SHAW 780:50
  Jogging is very b.   SCHU 720:49
benefit familiar one of social b.   HUGH 419:36
  owes a return for the b.   MILL 570:64
  what b. to the soul   HONO 409:32
  without the b. o' the Clergy   CONG 231:12
benefits disable all the b.   SHAK 750:75
  so many people...for material b.   COLU 229:62
  Who b.?   CICE 218:22
benefitted b. from prolonged warfare   SUN 829:26
benevolence b. of the butcher   SMITH 797:39
benevolent what is inexhaustible is b.   FRYE 340:39
Bengal tiger of B. crouches   MELV 564:38
benighted b. masses   QUINE 675:52
  must be b. and superstitious   JAMES 434:74
benign under the b. sky   BRON 155:99
benison b. of hot water   BROO 156:5
Benlomond o'er the lofty B.   TANN 836:91
bent Still B. to make some port   ARNO 32:8
  those with an academic b.   MAMET 543:32
Bentham B. held no post   MENC 565:60

benumbed faculties of the mind are b.   BROO 155:1
bequeathèd B. down from many   SHAK 762:34
bereft b. me of all words   SHAK 740:74
berhymed never so b.   SHAK 749:59
Berkeley fell to earth in B. Square   HAMER 378:95
Berlin Be off with your Irving B.!   GERS 350:39
  B. by Christmas   ANON 22:47
  Isherwood...find himself in B.   BURU 174:84
  Let them come to B.!   KENN 463:31
  New Frontier was closed by B.   MCGO 532:92
  soldiers drilling in B.   MORI 598:83
Berliner Ich bin ein B.   KENN 463:33
Berlitz glibness of the B.-school   FIRB 323:71
Berlusconi B. is unfit to lead Italy   ECON 298:82
Bermudas swim to the B.   WEBS 895:6
Bernard B....was rather pious   ASHF 35:95
Bernhardt admired most...Sarah B.   WILDE 910:68
berries b. harsh and crude   MILT 578:45
berry God could have made a better b.   BUTL 178:86
berserk Sex suppressed will go b.   EWART 316:24
beryl colour of a b.   BIBLE 105:84
beseech b. thee, shew me thy glory   BIBLE 89:31
  humbly do b. you   SHAK 760:88
beside Paul, thou art b. thyself   BIBLE 119:56
besieging who are b. Orleans   JOAN 438:52
best All is for the b.   VOLT 882:38
  Always to be b.   HOMER 409:18
  b. actors in the world   SHAK 753:62
  b. and the worst of this   SWIN 833:38
  b. cannot be expected   JOHN 446:67
  b. ends by the b. means   HUTC 424:51
  b. is like the worst   KIPL 471:88
  b. is yet to be   BROW 162:69
  b. lack all conviction   YEATS 933:50
  b. married that dies married young   SHAK 737:77
  b. minds in the world   ACHE 3:52
  b. of all possible worlds   CABE 183:18
  b. of all things   HUXL 426:15
  b. of the rich   SPARK 806:25
  b. that an American   KENN 461:96
  b. that has been known   ARNO 34:59
  b. that is known   ARNO 33:40
  B. thing in eird   HENR 396:53
  b. thing to be up and go   EMPS 314:63
  b....to do what the mob do   DICK 266:73
  B., to forget!   BROW 162:93
  Competition brings out the b.   SARN 714:33
  doing our b. to re-establish peace   ELIZ 310:66
  do our b. to reward your faith   SMITH 799:71
  do the b. you can   OBRI 620:5
  Drinking the b. tea   SNOW 802:35
  English are b.!   FLAN 326:25
  He is doing his b.   WILDE 908:85
  hope for the b.   SMITH 801:13
  It is b. to live   SOPH 804:89
  last b. friend   SOUT 805:10
  learn, at b. and worst   RABAN 675:59
  mediocrity...always at its b.   BEER 70:91
  most of everything and the b. of nothing   CHAN 205:84
  Mother Knows B.   FERB 320:92
  My God must have my b.   HERB 398:82
  Never to have lived is b.   YEATS 933:54
  one of the very b. means   HUXL 426:14
  people are at their b.   GRAY 368:88
  record of the b....moments   SHEL 786:16
  said against the b.   MILL 570:73
  serves his party b.   HAYES 387:63
  That action is b.   HUTC 424:52
  The b....enemy of the good   VOLT 883:47
  The b. is the b.   QUIL 674:43
  the b. words in the b. order   COLE 227:21
  very b. and the very worst   FORD 330:3
  What America does b.   FUEN 340:42
  Why not the b.?   CART 198:44
bestial what remains is b.   SHAK 760:78
bestride b. the narrow world   SHAK 747:76
bestseller B. is the gilded tomb   SMITH 800:84
best-sellers in all of the great b.-s.   PRIT 669:45
bet b. you, Ziggie, a hundred bucks   DILL 275:15
  if I would b. with other people   ROCH 691:49
  important matter as a b.   VERNE 879:71
beteem b. the winds of heaven   SHAK 751:7
Bethel O God of B.!   DODD 278:8
Bethlehem But thou, B.   BIBLE 106:12
  Christ is born in B.   CASW 199:82
  Let us now go even unto B.   BIBLE 115:26
  Slouches towards B.   YEATS 933:51

  when Jesus was born in B.   BIBLE 108:72
betide God's peace b. the souls   RANS 679:27
betray b. them both   WALC 884:70
  cruel brother will you b.   BALL 55:74
  finds too late that men b.   GOLD 361:47
  savage man alone does man b.   ROCH 691:58
  To b., you must first belong   PHIL 650:88
betrayal defence against b.   WILL 912:22
betrayed Betrothed, betrayer, and b.!   SCOTT 725:50
  but by ourselves, b.   CONG 230:95
  by luxury b.   GOLD 361:58
  democratic people b.   ATTL 37:41
  those that are b.   SHAK 774:67
betrayer Betrothed, b., and betrayed!   SCOTT 725:50
betraying b. my country and b. my friend   FORS 331:52
betrothed B., betrayer, and betrayed!   SCOTT 725:50
better B. a witty fool   SHAK 756:54
  b. future and a brighter day   SMUTS 802:31
  B. if he had said   HILL 403:93
  b. man than I am   KIPL 471:96
  b. than bad strokes   SHAK 748:19
  b. than light   HASK 385:25
  b. that some should   JOHN 445:21
  b. to dwell in a corner   BIBLE 100:45
  B. to use force   SHUL 789:89
  b. world than this   SHAK 749:29
  change for the b.   STEI 816:39
  don't know any b.   KENN 462:1
  Every day...I am getting b.   COUE 238:87
  far b. without the others   SIEY 791:26
  for b. for worse   BOOK 142:26
  from worse to b.   JOHN 442:37
  give place to b.   SHAK 748:15
  He is no b.   AUST 44:2
  I see the b. things   OVID 631:45
  kiss you take is b.   SHAK 757:10
  Love...unsought, is b.   SHAK 756:79
  no b. than you should be   BEAU 67:18
  no b. than you should be   THOM 853:92
  not sure I was much b.   SIHA 791:30
  took the best for thy b.   SHAK 754:7
  way to the B. there be   HARDY 382:71
  When you meet someone b.   CONF 230:88
  would be b. than nothing   KEYN 466:88
betters lord it...above their b.   OTWAY 631:28
between try to get b. them   STRA 826:86
Bevan nurses and Nye B.   HALD 377:77
beverage revolting b. in itself   STEV 821:76
beware all should cry, B.! B.!   COLE 226:55
  B. of anything that promises   SNYD 803:52
  B. Of entrance to a quarrel   SHAK 751:18
  B. of men   SPARK 806:29
  B. of over-great pleasure   FULL 341:47
  B. of quotations in Latin   FLAU 327:43
  B. of the man   SHAW 779:12
  B. of the man   SHAW 779:25
  B. of those who are homeless   SOUT 805:7
  B. the ides of March   SHAK 747:72
  O. b., my lord   SHAK 760:86
bewildered b. like an old lady   ACHE 3:40
  by the unprincipled to the utterly b.   CAPP 189:35
  without finally getting b.   HAWT 386:41
bewilderment sense of b. and terror   LEE 500:43
  wandering in delighted b.   OFAO 622:33
bewitch Do more b. me   HERR 400:50
bewitched b., bothered...am I   HART 384:12
  b. for ever   SACK 708:89
  b. with some ill charms   WALL 886:15
  b. with the rogue's company   SHAK 741:7
bewitching his wine's sae b.!   BURNS 173:55
bewitchment battle against the b.   WITT 918:43
bewrayed man by nothing is so well b.   SPEN 809:12
beyond the range of language   REID 682:95
  He hath been b.-sea   JONS 448:9
  is there anything b.?   BROO 156:17
  stands b., behind, and within   WHIT 904:8
bias History must not be written with b.   BETJ 84:97
biases bundle of b.   BALL 57:4
Bible B. as...a constable's handbook   KING 469:59
  B. said that nothing was permanent   FRAME 333:82
  cursing the bloody b.   HEMI 393:96
  do you ever read the B.?   CHAN 204:82
  He knows...his B.   ARNO 34:58
  Jacobean...who translated the B.   ACHE 2:24
  knowledge of the B., Shakespeare   WAUGH 893:55
  li'ble To read in the B.   HEYW 402:74
  quotations from the B.   LAWR 495:23

bit mouth…held in with b. — BIBLE 95:11
  though he had b. me — SHAK 764:96
bitch called John a Impudent B. — FLEM 327:59
  four-kind son-of-a-b. — ROBB 689:13
  old b. gone in the teeth — POUND 665:40
  she's kind of a b. — PAGL 634:83
  worst son of a b. — PARK 638:78
  you've got to have a son of a b. — BRIC 152:24
bitches Fare ye a' weel, ye b.! — KAME 454:34
bite b. some of my other generals — GEOR 349:11
  b. the hand that fed them — BURKE 169:48
  Color and b. permeate a language — SAFI 708:97
  hate to b. — HEAN 389:11
  rainbows…turn and b. — WODE 919:72
  smaller fleas to b. 'em — SWIFT 832:2
bitelbrowed b. and baberlipped — LANG 489:96
biting His b. is immortal — SHAK 766:59
bitter Because it is B. — OATES 620:94
  belly was b. — BIBLE 126:64
  be not b. against them — BIBLE 123:68
  b. cosmic joke — GELL 348:98
  b. furies — YEATS 934:58
  b. God to follow — SWIN 833:34
  B. is the knowledge — BAUD 64:66
  b. to thee — SWIN 834:49
  Death's b. cup — ABU 1:12
  How b. a thing it is — SHAK 750:86
  I found her b. — RIMB 688:96
  It is b.—b. — CRANE 243:28
  misfortunes more b. — BACON 48:85
  pleasant or b. — MART 555:51
  sour with the b. — GOLD 362:89
  with a b. look — WILDE 910:54
bitterness b. in our laughter — EMER 313:37
  b. of his soul — BIBLE 107:42
  drinking from the cup of b. — KING 468:37
  enthusiasm turns to b. — ZATO 936:90
  filled his life with b. — TWAIN 870:85
  no hatred or b. towards anyone — CAVE 201:18
  nor grief b. — LYLY 523:11
  sweet full of b. — LYLY 523:9
bivouac b. for corpses — MUSS 605:15
black All was b. — THOM 856:63
  Any color—so long as it's b. — FORD 330:8
  because I is b. — COHEN 224:67
  between b. and white — THOR 858:9
  B. America — JORD 450:64
  b. and blacker — STEV 823:29
  b. and white entwine — NOON 618:58
  b. as our loss — SITW 794:73
  B.…Baltic deep — TENN 846:99
  b. face — GIOV 357:76
  B. is beautiful — ANON 23:96
  B. love — GIOV 357:73
  b. man or a fair man — ADDI 6:9
  b. market universities — ZELD 936:91
  B. Mrs Behemoth — SITW 794:65
  B. people possess the secret of joy — WALK 885:1
  b. people with Jesus — GIOV 357:75
  B. power — ANON 23:97
  b. promise — HOLM 407:73
  B.'s not so b. — CANN 188:12
  b. statement of pistons — SPEN 807:54
  born in America with a b. skin — MALC 541:85
  called the chess-board…b. — BROW 161:49
  chose my b. people — SENG 727:94
  climb b. branches — FROST 338:92
  cold and tarnished b. — SITW 794:82
  devil damn thee b. — SHAK 768:36
  don't believe ye b. majority rule — SMITH 799:69
  either b. or white — TRAV 865:47
  fact parts in b. ink — BOWEN 147:29
  fought against b. domination — MAND 544:46
  he was a b. Irish type — PRIE 668:24
  I always wanted to be b. — RHYS 684:25
  I am B. — JORD 450:67
  I am b.…my soul is white — BLAKE 134:30
  I'm the b., basketball-playing Nietzsche — ONEAL 625:86
  instructed me to hate b. girls — ANON 18:63
  Irish as B. Americans are African — GELD 348:95
  Japan is like the b. hole — UMAS 873:62
  man has a b. face — EDWA 300:18
  More black, and b. and grey — GREE 371:76
  not be b. because I was — MORR 599:7
  product of every other b. woman — WINF 917:22
  purchased by the b. man's misery — DOUG 284:35
  regal b. Women — CULL 247:92

Southern B. girl — ANGE 17:31
  strength…in b. women — ANGE 17:38
  suits of solemn b. — TWAIN 871:7
  the linear b. — HEAN 389:11
  those of you watching in b. and white — MOTS 601:38
  unnatural red and b. — DICK 270:3
  When life looks b. — OBRI 620:5
  white men cheat b. men — LEE 500:38
  White shall not neutralize the b. — BROW 162:86
  Why do you wear b. — CHEK 209:9
  Wishing He I served were b. — CULL 247:95
  young, gifted and b. — HANS 380:34
blackberries reasons…plentiful as b. — SHAK 741:14
blackbird B. has spoken — FARJ 318:47
  b. is involved — STEV 819:23
  minute a b. sang — THOM 854:7
  the b. whistling — STEV 819:22
Blackfeet B., lying low — LIND 511:53
blackguard b. whose faulty vision — BIER 129:25
  Sesquipedalian b. — CLOU 222:17
blackletter b. man may be — HOLM 408:2
blackmail form of atomic b. — KENN 462:16
Blackman history of Mr. B. — NGU 613:79
blackness poverty of b. — DANG 251:85
blacks B.…used to play whites — ANGE 17:47
  don't ask employers…to like b. — BORO 145:2
  It's the same with B. — BIKO 129:46
  the b. in America — OROU 627:22
  want to be called b. — FEIF 319:84
  whites…ignorant of b. — ANGE 17:46
blackshirts armed camp of B. — MUSS 605:15
bladder bet my b. against — KIRK 474:86
  get the b. and blow it great — ANON 19:80
  wind out of the b. — ANON 21:24
bladders rotten b., tied Together — WEBS 895:6
blade B. on the feather — CORY 238:78
  b. struck the water — COKE 224:71
  drive the b. a little forward — CURZ 249:53
  gild the b. if you will — QUIN 675:53
  ranting roving b. — ANON 20:13
  taken up the broken b. — DE 259:36
  Whereat with b. — SHAK 738:16
blades b. pricked the mud — BROW 161:44
Blair B. is very convincing — CHIR 213:13
  I'm just Tony B. — BLAIR 132:6
  It will be B., B., B. — BENN 75:20
  Tony B. its Kubla Khan — RAWN 680:39
Blake B. once wildly muttered — SASS 716:75
  Till I am…William B. — YEATS 934:60
blame b. it on the other party — ANON 24:21
  b. thee now to weep — SHAK 732:38
  Dispraise, or b., nothing — MILT 587:65
  Do not b. me, madam — LABE 482:54
  freeze the heart as much as b. — BUCK 165:38
  grief as his b. — AYTO 45:15
  moved with the slightest touch of b. — EDGE 299:93
  neither is most to b. — SWIN 833:38
  nobody is to b. for anything — AMIS 15:7
  no one can really b. him — KEYN 465:83
  only the Master shall b. — KIPL 472:20
  take all the b. — ASTU 37:31
  yet he was most to b. — LANY 489:4
blanched b. with fear — SHAK 768:18
blancmange equivalent of b. — LEVIN 506:62
bland Cruel, but composed and b. — ARNO 32:29
  demeanour nobly b. — GILB 355:33
blank benign b.—a decent — MENC 566:86
  b. Of nature's work — MILT 582:38
  no blot for us Nor b.; — BROW 161:39
  practically b. as snow — HARDY 382:62
  this b. of things — WORD 923:67
blanket America is not like a b. — JACK 431:7
  four bare legs under a b. — DAVI 254:39
  right side of the b. — ASHF 35:98
  takes her wet b. with her — BROY 163:1
blankets rough male kiss of b. — BROO 156:4
blanks historians left b. — POUND 665:46
blare amid the b. of trumpets — EUDA 315:3
blasphemies great truths begin as b. — SHAW 781:78
blasphemy All manner of sin and b. — BIBLE 111:41
blast at my back in a cold b. — ELIOT 306:59
  b. of war blows — SHAK 746:42
  Striding the b. — SHAK 767:87
  wert thou in the cauld b. — BURNS 173:54
blasts b. from hell — SHAK 751:25
  B. of January — SHAK 770:85
  many b. to shake them — SHAK 731:6

blatant in a b. land — TENN 845:84
blaze b. of branch, or brazier — ELIOT 309:38
  broader still became the b. — MACA 526:70
  out into sudden b. — MILT 578:49
  trillion; but the b. — LOWE 520:41
blazon final b., and to prove — LARK 490:30
bleed breaks…and then we b. — SHEL 787:28
  do we not b.? — SHAK 740:68
  no time to b. — SHAK 734:96
bleeding Beneath the b. hands — ELIOT 308:21
  b. piece of earth — SHAK 748:1
  fell a-b. on Black Monday — SHAK 740:59
blemish lamb shall be without b. — BIBLE 88:15
  no b. but the mind — SHAK 757:88
blemishes tapes, b. and all — NIXON 617:48
blend strange b. of the commercial — STAP 813:70
bless attend and b. — GILB 354:18
  except thou b. me — BIBLE 87:92
  Lord b. thee, and keep thee — BIBLE 89:36
blessed b. and admit me to Paradise — ROSS 698:4
  B. are the dead — BIBLE 126:69
  B. are the pure in heart — WHAR 902:56
  b. be the evergreen Pine! — SCOTT 723:5
  b. be the name of the Lord — BIBLE 93:48
  B. is he who — VIRG 882:32
  B. is the almost insensitive tree — DARIO 252:4
  b. them unaware — COLE 225:88
  b. with a woman's brain — RICH 686:64
  b. with such happy manners — AUST 43:65
  b. you out of the house — BIBLE 97:79
  does not make a man b. — ARIS 29:51
  more b. to give than to receive — BIBLE 119:53
  wife seems more b. — HELO 393:86
blessèd Most b., most glorious — SMITH 801:26
blessedness happiness or b. of man — SPIN 811:34
blesses nation b. what undoes it — HUGO 421:81
blessing b., even life for evermore — BIBLE 98:96
  b. like experiencing madness — LISP 512:75
  b. of God Almighty — BOOK 141:10
  continual dew of thy b. — BOOK 140:75
  for the which b. — SHAK 744:90
  If this is a b. — CHUR 217:91
  most need of b. — SHAK 767:1
  Oh there is b. — WORD 924:88
  pour you out a b. — BIBLE 106:20
  proceedeth b. and cursing — BIBLE 125:14
  Prosperity is the b. — BACON 47:80
  steal immortal b. from her lips — SHAK 736:65
  Sweet was its b. — COCK 224:54
  system, and actually a b. — LIVI 512:83
  taken away thy b. — BIBLE 87:87
  thou shalt be a b. — BIBLE 87:72
  to delight…paid thy utmost b. — DELA 260:72
  to us a national b. — HAMI 379:98
  truly it's a b. — CLOU 222:25
blessings all the b. of this life — BOOK 141:84
  b. of a good thick skirt — KING 469:62
  b. of marriage — SHAW 778:1
  b. of youth — DEMO 261:85
  b. on your frosty pow — BURNS 171:10
  Free trade, one of the greatest b. — MACA 525:39
  from whom all b. flow — KEN 461:94
  glass of b. standing by — HERB 398:16
  Life is the greatest of b. — HEINE 391:47
blest be for ever b. — HOW 416:92
  still be very b. — GOLD 362:61
blew B. hither — HOUS 415:57
  b. man was born for — HOPK 412:95
blight b. man was born for — HOPK 412:95
Blimber Doctor B.'s assistant — DICK 269:55
blind all…are born b. — OKRI 624:61
  birth and growth…ubiquitous and b. — DILL 274:13
  b. and naked Ignorance — TENN 846:13
  b. as any noonday owl — TENN 847:43
  B. as the…nails — SITW 794:73
  b. boy, Venus' baby — SPEN 809:2
  b. dates are a way of life — EPST 315:84
  b., despised, and dying king — SHEL 783:34
  b. fury of creation — SHAW 778:83
  b. hysterics of the Celt. — TENN 844:62
  b. in the end — BERR 82:61
  b. lead the b. — BIBLE 112:59
  b. life within the brain — TENN 847:51
  B., old and lonely — SHEL 785:91
  b. receive their sight — BIBLE 111:33
  b. with smoke — SASS 716:59
  brave sun Die b. — JEFF 436:5
  but unbelief is b. — MILT 577:37

chance he might go b. — GREG 372:96
check the eyes and call them b. — MIDD 569:41
conversation of the b. — MOORE 595:27
country of the b. — WELLS 898:77
drawing back the b. — KIPL 473:61
eyes of the b. shall be opened — BIBLE 103:33
Fortune…she be b. — BACON 49:41
glass so gay, that it can b. — SPEN 809:11
Grief for a while is b. — SHEL 784:71
In the country of the b. — ERAS 315:86
it is the b. watchmaker — DAWK 256:73
I was b., now I see — BIBLE 118:99
love is b. — SHAK 740:61
Love, knocking its b. forehead — SAND 712:82
mathematician is a b. man — DARW 253:18
not worry about the b. alleys — FEYN 322:24
one-armed b. man — WODE 919:60
one of the b. alleys — WAUGH 892:19
Passions can…never b. me — LAFA 484:94
religion without science is b. — EINS 301:36
right to be b. — NELS 610:33
splendid work for the b. — SASS 716:64
through its own internal lighting b. — SHEL 784:66
Was b., but now I see — NEWT 613:76
will not make us b. — RUSH 703:89
winged Cupid painted b. — SHAK 737:86
Ye b. guides — BIBLE 113:83
blinded b. by the external tools — REYES 684:21
blindness 'eathen in 'is b. — KIPL 472:18
'eathen in 'is b. — KIPL 472:19
first love's impassioned b. — PEAC 645:96
blinds a drawing-down of b. — OWEN 632:52
b. let through the day — HOUS 416:77
blindworms Newts and b. — SHAK 737:98
blink at an e b. — DOUG 283:16
blinkard Thou b. blowboll — SKEL 795:93
bliss Almost the highest b. — KEATS 457:81
b. in ale — CRAB 242:81
B. in our brow's bent — SHAK 764:17
B. it was…to be alive — WORD 927:39
b. of solitude — WORD 928:43
deprived of everlasting b.! — MARL 552:99
domestic b. — PATM 643:68
Everywhere I see b. — SHEL 782:13
excels all other b. — DYER 296:50
faded b., faded so soon — MILT 581:27
fill Of b. on b. — MILT 583:66
gate of b. — CRAS 244:38
ignorance is b. — GRAY 368:95
never…parted, b. or woe — MILT 585:15
promise of pneumatic b. — ELIOT 305:35
thou hast not thy b. — KEATS 459:53
wingèd hours of b. — CAMP 186:69
blissful experience is not always b. — HUXL 425:94
blisters shoes…gave her b. — BAIN 52:8
blithe b. wi' Comrades dear — BURNS 170:83
No b. Irish lad was so happy — CAMP 186:65
blitz b. of a boy — CAUS 201:13
block big black b. — GILB 355:25
changes with the next b. — SHAK 744:84
chip off the old b. — BURKE 168:26
the biggest coal b. — HEAN 389:15
blockade Navy will run the b. — ANDE 15:15
blockhead bookful b. — POPE 658:62
No man but a b. — JOHN 445:20
blockheads b. of all ages — CONG 231:28
The b. talk — SCOTT 725:57
the greatest b. — MONT 591:67
blocks hew b. with a razor — POPE 659:88
spell God with the wrong b. — ROBI 690:33
You b., you stones — SHAK 746:71
bloke b. fer showin' off — DENN 262:1
blokes b. retire to the…pub — NEVI 611:49
blond like a b. satan — HAMM 380:21
more b. than you — CUMM 248:12
blonde b. to make a bishop kick — CHAN 204:75
in love with a beautiful b. — FIEL 323:52
blondes Gentlemen Prefer B. — LOOS 517:72
Gentlemen…seem to remember b. — LOOS 517:75
blood always worked with my b. — KOLL 477:39
angry up the b. — PAIGE 634:87
billet-doux written in cold b. — ETHE 315:93
B., all price excelling — AQUI 28:28
b. and other vital fluids — STER 818:85
B. and revenge…in my head — SHAK 731:90
b. and spirit together — MARI 550:57
b. and water — BIBLE 118:20

b. and wine are red — WILDE 910:52
b.-bedecked halls of their revel — POE 656:19
b. Come gargling — OWEN 632:57
b. enough upon your penal code — BYRON 179:4
b. from head to foot — MACL 535:31
b. in torrents pour — DAVI 254:25
b. is settled, and her joints — SHAK 737:76
b. is strong — GALT 344:29
B. may be thicker than water — SOME 803:66
b. [may lose] its fire — BYRON 180:37
b. mixed with wasted gold — KING 469:64
b. of all the martyrs — IVAN 431:99
b. of grape — BLAKE 133:25
B. of our Lord Jesus — BOOK 141:9
b. of patriots and tyrants — JEFF 436:15
b. of the Christians — TERT 849:82
b. of the new testament — BIBLE 114:96
b.-red blossom — TENN 846:99
b.-red flower of revolution — RAND 678:15
b. rolled out — HUGH 418:23
b.'s a rover — HOUS 414:44
b. speaks to you in my veins — SHAK 740:74
B. sport…in the gossip columns — INGH 429:58
b., toil, tears and sweat — CHUR 216:75
b. was cold — SCOTT 722:86
b. was shed for me — ELLI 310:79
b. was sprinkled on the wall — BIBLE 92:37
b. will be ready — SADE 708:94
b. with guilt is bought — SHEL 785:72
b. with the thought of dying — MASE 559:40
blow in cold b. — SHAW 778:11
brand sae drap wi' b. — BALL 56:76
by man shall his b. be shed — BIBLE 87:68
caked in b. — JOHN 439:72
Christ's b. streams in the firmament! — MARL 552:6
cinema in their b. — RICH 686:65
clouds as actual b. — MUNCH 603:80
conjure up the b. — SHAK 746:42
cooling the b. — FLAN 326:22
dark b. dammed within — CULL 247:94
daughter to his b. — SHAK 740:58
dogs licked the b. of Naboth — BIBLE 92:26
drink his b. — BOOK 141:7
dripping b. our only drink — ELIOT 308:22
economic b. pressure — WRIS 930:90
effusion of…human b. — OCON 621:20
enough of b. and tears — RABIN 676:80
Every drop of my b. — GAND 345:32
faints at the sight of b. — BETJ 83:95
faith melteth into b. — SHAK 744:93
find so much b. — SHAK 757:82
Fire, B., and Famine — HENR 395:45
first b. shed in revenge — PEPYS 647:28
flesh and b. — THOR 857:79
flesh and b. — THAC 849:85
freeze thy young b. — SHAK 752:28
glories of our b. and state — SHIR 789:83
glory smeared in dust and b. — SHAK 730:84
great effusion of b. — STUB 827:3
happit flesh and b. — FERG 321:9
heart's b. dyed — CONN 232:55
heyday in the b. — SHAK 754:8
I am in b. — SHAK 768:19
ice was in the b. — PIER 651:7
If b. be the price — KIPL 472:15
in place and b. — TENN 844:61
In whose cold b. — SHAK 730:69
iron and b. — BISM 131:83
joys are more to flesh and b. — DRYD 291:20
know the colour of that b. — KEATS 460:65
laws for the b. — SHAK 739:44
laws…writ in b. — MARL 552:83
liquors in my b. — SHAK 749:39
looked kneaded up with b. — BROW 161:44
look like flesh and b. — MOORE 595:24
love respects no b. — DEKK 259:47
May their b. cease to flow! — DAVIS 256:64
men are flesh and b. — SHAK 747:93
Moloch whose b. is running — GINS 357:62
More b.! More b.! — CRON 246:77
not…a question of birth or b. — OBRI 620:98
Nothing like b., sir — THAC 849:91
not shed her b. — SHAK 761:7
of British b.? — TENN 844:69
one drop of negro b. — HUGH 418:24
one of the b.-suckers — FRAN 335:22
O, the b. more stirs — SHAK 741:4

our own red b. — YEATS 933:47
poet's feverish b. — ARNO 32:7
poison the whole b. stream fills — EMPS 313:61
Politics is a b. sport — BEVAN 85:24
redness which affrights in b. — MELV 564:32
Resign your heart's b. — SHEL 782:14
Senator, it is American b. — MACA 524:28
sensations…Felt in the b. — WORD 923:69
sheds his b. with me — SHAK 746:61
show-business with b. — BELA 71:24
slaked the light with b. — TENN 848:69
smell the b. of a British man — SHAK 763:79
so much b. in him? — SHAK 768:33
so much b. in him? — SHAK 757:82
stained with b.? — SHAK 738:17
Stir the Vikings' b. — KING 469:49
streams of British b. — SCHAW 717:96
sweat and b. and souls — FRAN 335:22
talk about their Pilgrim b. — LOWE 520:28
the circulation of their b. — SMITH 799:72
this is my b. — BIBLE 114:96
Tiber foaming with much b. — POWE 667:93
To freeze the b. — WORD 925:8
tomahawks, wi' b. red-rusted — BURNS 172:22
too much b. — SHAK 757:11
voice of thy brother's b. — BIBLE 86:59
washed in the b. of the Lamb? — LIND 510:45
washed in the b. of the Lamb? — LIND 510:46
wash this b. Clean — SHAK 767:5
Waste of B. — STUD 827:4
water and the b. — TOPL 863:15
We be one b. — KIPL 471:10
welt'ring in his b. — DRYD 291:36
What case of flesh and b. — ROCH 691:55
When b. is nipped — SHAK 734:94
When the b. burns — SHAK 751:23
when the b. creeps — TENN 843:39
whips my b. like verse — WILL 914:62
win…By b. or ink — BYRON 181:70
with hands b. stained — ORTE 627:28
with his own b. he bought — STONE 825:57
Without shedding of b. — BIBLE 124:92
would draw b. — DUNC 295:14
written in letters of b. — STRA 826:89
Young b. must have its course — KING 469:53
bloodguiltiness Deliver me from b. — BIBLE 95:31
bloodless b. substitute for life — STEV 822:96
bloodmoney Dr B. — DICK 265:56
bloods mingle our b. together — SHAK 769:51
our two b. mingled be — DONNE 280:52
bloodshed Politics is war without b. — MAO 548:6
blood-thirsty b.-t. and deceitful man — BOOK 142:37
bloody battles b. exercises — JOSE 451:73
Be b., bold, and resolute — SHAK 768:23
b. beat them again — RAMS 678:9
B. instructions which, being taught — SHAK 767:86
greet you with b. hands — CORW 237:73
head is b. but unbowed — HENL 395:38
horrid malicious b. flame — PEPYS 647:47
My b. thoughts — SHAK 760:96
On the same b. morning — SCOTT 724:16
Walk! Not b. likely — SHAW 780:68
War's a b. game — SASS 716:70
Bloom Leopold B. ate with relish — JOYCE 452:92
bloom As well as any b. — THOM 854:18
b. is shed — BURNS 172:19
b. of that valley shall — MOORE 596:47
b. sae fresh and fair — BURNS 172:26
Charm…it's a sort of a b. — BARR 61:84
Each opening sweet of earliest b. — COLL 228:41
hung with b. along the bough — HOUS 414:41
look at things in b. — HOUS 414:43
Our b. is gone — STEV 819:25
risk of spoiling its b. — CONR 235:21
terrible and splendid b. — RAND 678:15
touch it and the b. is gone — WILDE 909:38
vernal b., or summer's rose — MILT 582:38
with the b. go I — ARNO 33:45
blooms b. each thing, then maids — NASHE 609:15
bloomy all the b. beds — SMART 797:29
blossom Are you…the b. — YEATS 933:53
b. by b. the spring begins — SWIN 832:19
b. in purple and red — TENN 845:92
b. of war — TENN 846:99
full spring-tide of b. — BETJ 83:89
last b. is the first b. — MACN 538:12
saft faulding b. — TANN 836:91

there is a b. about me — BOSW 145:9
Under the b. — SHAK 775:99
blossomer great-rooted b. — YEATS 933:53
blossoms art of orange b. — PISS 652:32
boughs do laughing b. bear — SPEN 809:92
cherry b. in the spring — ANON 22:67
million b. springing — MACG 531:76
of locust b. — WILL 914:57
rod of Aaron…bloomed b. — BIBLE 89:38
strange odours of b. — CONR 234:4
tender leaves…tomorrow b. — SHAK 775:20
blot And blackens every b. — TENN 846:5
b. on the fair face of creation — BRON 155:79
b. upon my pride — SHAK 735:17
It is no vicious b. — SHAK 762:54
text that looks a little b. — TENN 846:14
the art to b. — POPE 661:55
This world's no b. — BROW 161:39
blotched b. out beyond — STEV 819:24
blotted man will be b. out — JEFF 436:5
never b. out a line — JONS 450:55
blouse b. out and her nails grimed — MANS 546:82
blow bless the hand that gave the b. — DRYD 290:4
B. him again to me — TENN 841:2
b. in cold blood — SHAW 778:11
b. of a loy — SYNGE 834:59
b. over the face — AUBR 39:69
b., thou winter wind — SHAK 749:52
B., winds — SHAK 763:71
b. you through and through — SHAK 770:85
Death unfailing will strike the b. — CURR 249:40
first b. is half the battle — GOLD 362:67
Liberty's in every b. — BURNS 173:42
man who does not return your b. — SHAW 779:25
must strike the b.? — BYRON 179:14
put your lips together—and b. — FURT 342:72
receive a knock-down b. — HUNT 423:24
terrible b. — HAMER 378:96
that relaxed alluring b. — HEAN 389:15
until I b. up! — THOM 853:96
blowboll Thou blinkard b. — SKEL 795:93
blowing furious winter b. — RANS 679:25
blown to have b. up the King — HOBY 405:36
blows allured…without b. — STEE 814:1
b. and revenge for me! — SHAK 730:73
fled step-dame Study's b. — SIDN 790:8
It b. so hard — HOUS 415:56
stories And not by his b. — LAFO 485:8
when most she offers b. — SHAK 765:37
Blucher B. and I have lost — WELL 897:57
bludgeoning b. of the people — WILDE 908:12
blue b. and white young man — GILB 354:7
B., darkly, deeply — SOUT 805:2
b.-gum nigger — BENET 75:11
b. is all in a rush — HOPK 412:87
b.…Of night — YEATS 933:38
b. ribbon of the turf — DISR 276:63
chic old b.-haired ladies — CAPO 189:32
in yonder living b. — TENN 844:64
naked frosty b. — THOM 854:12
no b. without yellow — VAN 877:28
ocean b. or smoke b. — GALE 343:5
The b. deep — SHEL 784:55
The b. Mediterranean — SHEL 783:45
those b. remembered hills — HOUS 415:59
bluebell Mary, ma Scotch B. — LAUD 492:63
bluejay b. in peacock feathers — LAFO 485:9
bluejays shoot all the b. — LEE 500:34
blues blue-gum nigger to sing me b. — BENET 75:11
No white man ever had the b. — LEAD 497:74
soul keeps a singin' the b. — BERRY 82:59
Sweet b.! — HUGH 418:18
bluest b. veins to kiss — SHAK 765:31
bluff no matter how charming a b. — FITZ 325:7
blunder frae monie a b. free us — BURNS 170:81
so grotesque a b. — BENT 78:80
Youth is a b. — DISR 276:45
blundered Some one had b. — TENN 844:76
blundering b. will live on — SAND 713:2
blunders b.…shape history — TAYL 837:11
scapegoats for our b. — TWAIN 872:30
woman…Nature's agreeable b. — COWL 240:36
blur in retrospect…all a b. — SCHL 718:13
blush At first b. a new idea — MILL 571:1
b. at your faults — FLET 328:71
bring a b. into the cheek — DICK 271:43
knew by the b. — SOME 803:65

not b. to be admir'd — WALL 886:13
pass my name…I b. — TREE 865:53
with a b. retire — DICK 272:50
blushes B..Or needs to. — TWAIN 872:23
Who b. at the name? — INGR 429:59
blushing b.…a sign of guilt — CONG 231:31
Religion b. veils — POPE 662:82
sacrifice other people without b. — SHAW 779:26
without lowering her eyes and b. — SARR 715:37
Blyton Enid B. of economics — HOLME 407:71
boa reach for my feather B. — GINS 357:66
Boadicea bargain-basement B. — HEAL 389:1
board bred in a B.-School — KIPL 472:28
ideal b. of directors — DOCH 277:99
moving a single b. — SNYD 803:50
boarding-house landlady of a b.-h. — LEAC 496:58
boarding-school old-fashioned B.-s. — AUST 43:81
boards he who treads the b. — BISH 131:74
boar-pig Bartholomew b.-p. — SHAK 743:50
boast B. not thyself of tomorrow — BIBLE 100:56
b. of heraldry — GRAY 369:14
Boston…hast naught to b. — ANON 20:22
Britain, could you ever b. — SWIFT 832:95
empty b. of flesh — HABI 376:53
How many people can b. as much — BECK 68:39
Let no man b. himself — TROL 866:76
our absolute b. — WORD 925:95
Such is the patriot's b. — GOLD 361:40
boastful b. men so oft abashed — SPEN 808:90
boasting No b. like a fool — SHAK 768:25
boat beautiful pea-green b. — LEAR 497:83
b.…had the goods of a house — PEPYS 647:48
b. wallows in the sea — IGNA 428:42
came and found a b. — TENN 839:51
glass-bottomed b. — MIZN 589:7
intellectually promising b. — VAN 876:23
soul is an enchanted b. — SHEL 785:80
Speed, bonnie b. — BOUL 146:26
While his b. hastens — KEATS 457:82
boathook diplomatic b. — CECIL 202:29
boating Jolly b. weather — CORY 238:78
boatman B., do not tarry — CAMP 186:70
boatmen puny b. do not know how — HERZ 400:54
boats b. against the current — FITZ 325:2
b. began to near the winning post — COKE 224:71
b. or ships came near — LEAR 498:88
b. were tossed — LOWE 520:42
fooling among b.? — STEV 821:70
messing about in b. — GRAH 365:37
running into b. — PEPYS 647:46
bob b.-tail nag — FOST 332:59
meek with thirty b. a week — DAVI 253:22
bobolink B. for a Chorister — DICK 272:59
bobtailed b. Hob — SITW 794:67
Boche stab…A well-killed B. — READ 680:45
bodies actions of two b. — NEWT 612:72
adorning their b. — SMOL 801:28
angles of their b. — ANGE 17:47
b. are buried in peace — BIBLE 108:67
b. are under our wheels — SHAW 778:87
b. in space — MANN 546:71
b. measure out their place — MARV 556:78
b. of the living — SPEN 807:65
b. of those bones — DOMI 278:19
concern not for your b. — PLATO 654:78
embraces of our b. taste — CAREW 190:56
grave keeps b. — DONNE 281:78
house their b. — GIBR 352:74
inexhaustible b. — TATE 837:4
may have civilized b. — MELV 564:23
other heated b. — WATT 891:2
our dead b. — SCOTT 722:81
Pile the b. high — SAND 713:96
present your b. a living sacrifice — BIBLE 120:80
scent of unwashed b. — ACKR 3:54
scorn their b. — BAST 63:47
souls out of men's b.? — SHAK 744:5
souls…to your scattered b. go — DONNE 280:66
the structure of our b. — STOP 825:58
three b. no sensible man — MACM 536:77
well-developed b. — FORS 331:46
women's b. are more delicate — CHRI 215:38
bodily Close your b. eye — FRIE 337:69
Thanks to his b. form — REDT 681:76
bodkin that is the bare b. — TWAIN 871:7
With a bare b.? — SHAK 753:74
body air and water to the human b. — REES 682:89

as it is for the b. — HUXL 425:71
as well as of the b. — HAZL 388:93
beautiful passionate b. — SWIN 833:29
best marriage…of mind and b. — FOWL 332:71
b. able to endure — MARL 552:92
b. and material substance — CARL 193:34
B. and soul — JORD 450:64
b. and substance of his works — COLE 227:26
b. away to barter — NGU 613:79
b. between your knees — CORY 238:78
b. continues in its state — NEWT 612:69
b. could reform — TWAIN 871:97
b. is a machine for living — TOLS 862:4
b. is the temple — BIBLE 121:55
b. like a wardrobe. — THOM 853:93
b. like mine! — ATLAS 37:36
b. meet a b. — BURNS 173:49
b. of a cobbler — LOCKE 514:19
b. of a weak…woman — ELIZ 309:60
b. of Benjamin Franklin — FRAN 334:6
b. of…generalizations — FRIE 337:62
b. of its womanhood — SCHR 720:43
B. of our Lord Jesus — BOOK 141:8
b. of this death? — BIBLE 120:71
b. of truth and the b. — LIPP 511:71
b.'s harmony — POPE 662:77
b.…straight as Circe's wand — MARL 553:12
b.'s work's expired — SHAK 771:13
b. that will go on circulating — STEG 814:7
b. was as round — SPEKE 806:36
b. will be guarded — LOWE 519:23
brief loan of his own b. — CABE 183:14
bury my b. in Sussex grass — BENET 75:12
children of my b. — KOLL 477:38
commit his b. to the deep — BOOK 143:73
commit his b. to the ground — BOOK 142:35
damned of b. and soul — KIPL 471:1
dignity or baseness…not in their b. — CHRI 215:37
ease of b. — SMITH 797:37
Fleas…upon the b. — LAND 488:77
for the relief of the b. — RICH 685:47
get rid of the b. — PLATO 655:90
gun gives you the b. — THOR 858:2
had tasted her sweet b. — SHAK 760:94
Happiness is healthy for the b. — PROU 671:89
harmonies of the b. — BERN 81:42
head belongs to a b. — ROSSO 698:6
Health and an able b. — FLET 328:73
Her b. a bulb — PLATH 652:77
human b. is sacred — WHIT 905:38
I knew her b. there — CRANE 243:18
in time leaves the b. — SMOL 801:29
keep your b. white — STEV 823:32
knit together into one b. politic — HENR 395:46
labour of his b. — LOCKE 514:14
lack of health in the b. — PLATO 655:85
language is…the b., of thought — CARL 192:95
liberation of both b. and mind — BANN 59:40
little b. with a mighty heart — SHAK 745:33
live in company with a b. — DELA 260:59
looking for a b. in the coach — HITC 404:13
mans b. both for power — SPEN 808:85
mind, in b. strong! — MILT 586:46
mind or b. grieved — CAMP 187:81
mind or b. to prefer — POPE 660:19
more…Africa than my own b. — ORTON 627:29
most erotic part of the b. — BART 62:21
mystery…Of the glorious B. — AQUI 28:28
Naught broken save this b. — BROO 156:9
not a single molecule of my b. — DIDE 274:35
not be sound…in b. or mind — LLOY 513:96
nothing…but my b.'s length — SHAK 730:84
not of her flesh and b. — KEYN 465:80
not that thy whole b. should be cast — BIBLE 109:90
O b. swayed to music — YEATS 933:53
one b. and one heart — DOUG 283:20
onnable b.'d be safe? — LOWE 520:30
Over my dead b. — KAUF 456:62
own your own b. — JONG 448:96
patch up thine old b. — SHAK 743:50
prefer shifting my whole b. — HERZ 400:55
prose takes the mould of the b. — WOOLF 920:55
Prostitution. Selling one's b. — MACK 534:18
Punish a b. — DRYD 290:78
renders the b.…more perfect — PIUS 653:55
resurrection of the b. — BOOK 143:73
see…my b. without disgust — BAUD 64:65

service of the b.	MORE 597:67	bombs atom b. are piling up	ORWE 629:83

service of the b. — MORE 597:67
sever head from b. — WEBS 894:83
shaped my b. so — SHAK 731:87
soul is not more than the b. — WHIT 905:34
sound mind in a sound b. — JUVE 453:20
sound mind in a sound b. — LOCKE 514:20
Take, eat: this is my b. — BIBLE 121:6
temple, called his b. — THOR 857:79
that b. of men — STEE 814:94
the gigantic b. — MACA 525:54
this b. did contain a spirit — SHAK 742:35
this is my b. — BIBLE 121:6
this is my b. — BIBLE 114:96
time by how a b. sways — ROET 694:6
too violent for the b. — JEFF 437:22
toughness the b. will find — WAVE 893:58
turning the whole b. — PLATO 655:1
turn your b. — WEBS 895:94
Upon my buried b. lay — BEAU 67:13
use of my b. — BECK 68:42
vital fluids of the b. — STER 818:85
well proportioned b. — AUBR 39:68
what exercise is to the b. — STEE 814:95
Whether I was in my b. — HAND 380:31
whose b. is this? — RODR 694:97
Whose b., Nature is — POPE 660:14
witches that deform the b. — SHAK 733:59
with my b. I thee worship — BOOK 142:28
work of b. or mind — MILT 583:67
yer b. will disappear — KELM 461:80
You are the b. — SCEVE 717:94
Your b. rocking! — CRANE 243:12
bodyguards Bush has 100 b. — GORB 363:4
bodyline B. was devised to stifle — LARW 491:56
B. was not an incident — JAMES 433:32
Boer before the B.War — ORWE 628:53
Bognor Bugger B. — GEOR 349:16
bogs Brown b. with black water — COLUM 229:60
find a way out of the b. — MAIL 540:66
melancholy of the b. — WAUGH 892:38
bogus science, even b. science — PRIT 669:46
Bohemia B. has no banner — WILL 912:21
boil b. at different degrees — EMER 313:49
War That Would Not B. — TAYL 837:10
boils satan has not geven me b. — FLEM 327:58
bold Be b., be b. — SPEN 809:94
be b., it will not burst thee — BIBLE 108:56
hath made me b. — SHAK 767:97
He was a b. Man — SWIFT 832:7
lover b. and free — CLEV 221:84
solid, or b. — STRA 826:85
Virtue is b. — SHAK 758:39
want of cunning made me b. — SPEN 809:2
boldness Boldness…always b.! — DANT 252:1
b. is a child of ignorance — BACON 48:7
b. to wealth — HESI 401:66
differ chiefly in the b. — JEVO 438:47
in a young woman, it is b. — HUGO 421:94
bole Are you…the b.? — YEATS 933:53
Boléro toward the beginning of B. — LAMB 487:67
Bolingbroke this canker, B.? — SHAK 741:2
Bolivia and B. 1949 — THER 851:50
bollocks who would kick your b. — LOFT 515:31
Boloigne hadde been, and at B. — CHAU 208:74
Bolshevik B. tyranny is the worst — CHUR 216:61
Bolsheviks B. are sincere — DRIB 287:10
bolshevism b. run mad — SNOW 802:46
bolt b. is shot back — ARNO 31:99
b. of Cupid fell — SHAK 737:94
bolts and the b. are hurled — TENN 839:57
B. and bars will not — MOLI 589:28
bomb Americans want to b. — ANON 25:74
Ban the B. — ANON 23:74
B. brought peace — CHUR 217:90
b. the knot off a tree — JENS 437:27
end up with the atomic b. — PAGN 634:86
How We Got Along After The B. — DICK 265:56
hydrogen and napalm b. — ROUS 700:39
Long after the b. falls — JANO 435:77
production of the fission b. — FROMM 338:82
the way it was with the atomic b. — OPPE 626:13
word 'Now' is like a b. — MILL 572:3
bombardment fury of aerial b. — EBER 298:73
bombast swelling into b. — DRYD 288:25
bombed glad we've been b. — ELIZ 310:68
protect him from being b. — BALD 54:47

bombs atom b. are piling up — ORWE 629:83
b. and missiles lie…buried — RAND 678:14
B. away — ANON 23:99
b. bursting in air — KEY 465:76
Come, friendly b. — BETJ 83:83
construction of…powerful b. — EINS 301:35
Ears like b. — CAUS 201:13
rain of b. — WHITE 903:95
the roar of b. — ORWE 628:51
whiskered men with b. — TOLK 862:96
bonbon pink b. stuffed with snow — DEBU 258:6
bond According to my b. — SHAK 762:52
Let him look to his b. — SHAK 740:67
neither b. nor free — BIBLE 122:36
trust man on his oath or b. — SHAK 762:43
bondag Marriage…only actual b. — MILL 571:78
bondage b. of certain ribbons — SHAK 770:93
damn'd to the b. be? — HABI 376:54
from the b. of sins — BHAG 85:36
hold another in b. — FULL 341:48
in the house of b. — MACA 525:42
out of the house of b. — BIBLE 88:23
queen in b. — SHAK 729:49
spirit of b. — BIBLE 120:74
That sweet b. — SHEL 782:16
bonds draw tight the b. — CHAM 203:56
garters to be b. and shackles — BACON 48:88
bondsmen Hereditary b.! — BYRON 179:14
bone b.-ache disquietude of life — ALLEN 12:39
b. and muscle of my nation — FRAN 335:22
b. of my bones — BIBLE 86:47
B. of my b. thou art — MILT 585:15
Break the b. — RABE 676:66
cricket goes to the b. — ARLO 30:64
dog…with a juicy b. — AUDEN 40:89
every b. a-stare — BROW 161:44
touch his b. and his flesh — BIBLE 93:49
boneless b. wonder — CHUR 216:69
bones all my b. are out of joint — BIBLE 94:99
bodies of those b. — DOMI 278:19
b. are coral made — SHAK 774:83
b. are smitten asunder — BOOK 143:49
b. live to learn — ROET 694:6
brittle strength of b. — MILT 581:9
broken spirit drieth the b. — BIBLE 99:39
can these b. live — BIBLE 105:92
childish; only b. abide — LOWE 520:42
conjuring trick with b. — JENK 437:24
full of dead men's b. — BIBLE 113:84
Hope sleeps in our b. — PIER 651:10
interrèd with their b. — SHAK 748:5
lay his weary b. — SHAK 775:23
like the b. of dinosaurs — RAND 678:14
maketh the b. fat — BIBLE 99:34
massy chine b. — MUNDY 603:82
never mended no broken b. — DICK 265:62
New Zealand is in my very b. — MANS 547:96
O'er his white b. — BALL 55:94
our small b. — THOM 854:25
O ye dry b. — BIBLE 105:93
paste and cover to our b. — SHAK 735:19
Picked his b. — ELIOT 306:62
rattle of the b. — ELIOT 306:59
Rest of their b. — DONNE 281:67
rottenness in his b. — BIBLE 99:23
rotting b. of ten thousand — TS 869:53
Smash the scaffold of the b. — HUID 421:99
spewed Nantucket b. — LOWE 520:43
the tongue breaketh the b. — BIBLE 108:58
town of monks and b. — COLE 227:23
until your b. are clean — ADCO 5:99
valley which was full of b. — BIBLE 105:91
your b. are very brittle — STEV 823:19
bonfire th'everlasting b. — SHAK 767:7
bonhomie overcame his natural b. — BENT 78:78
bonjour B. tristesse — ELUA 312:98
bonkers stark, staring b. — HAIL 377:70
bonnet b. of Bonny Dundee — SCOTT 725:58
bonnie b. banks o' Loch Lomond — ANON 20:20
b., b. broom — BALL 55:70
b. brow was brent — BURNS 171:10
B. lassie will ye go — BURNS 171:93
b. mill-dams o' Binnorie — BALL 55:67
brisk and a b. lad — ANON 20:13
corn rigs are b. — BURNS 170:82
corn rigs are b. — BURNS 170:84
gin love be b. — BALL 56:94

service to my b. lassie — BURNS 171:2
bonny B. Dundee — SCOTT 724:28
B. Dundee — SCOTT 725:58
honest men and b. lasses — BURNS 172:14
no a b. fighter? — STEV 823:23
bons trucs b. t.…annihilated — CUMM 247:99
boo 18,000 people b. — PLAN 654:61
boobs girl with big b. — KING 468:26
booby who is not, at bottom, a b. — MENC 565:54
booh Sing 'B. to you— — GILB 354:5
book A good b. — MILT 579:64
as kill a good b. — MILT 578:62
as much a trade to write a b. — LA 483:57
bad b. is as much — HUXL 425:66
Bell, b., and candle — SHAK 738:24
betray me to a lingering b. — HERB 397:95
b.…a kind of optical instrument — PROU 671:92
b. and a head collide — LICH 509:18
b. and me together — BROW 161:61
b.…finished in half the time — WODE 919:63
b. in the ordinary sense — MILL 572:15
b. is not harmless — ELIOT 307:90
b. of knowledge — MILT 582:38
b. of life — BIBLE 127:78
b.…of my secret soul — SHAK 756:52
b. of road maps — STEI 893:75
b. out of which a people — LIPP 511:67
b. this learning mayst — SHAK 772:33
b.…you're all done reading — SALI 710:52
burn a b. — RUSH 703:89
by the b. — SHAK 750:91
called the b. Men Without Women — HEMI 393:96
commonplace b. be full — SWIFT 830:56
cover of an old b. — FRAN 334:6
dainties…bred in a b. — SHAK 733:79
damned, thick, square b.! — GLOU 359:5
difference between writing a b. — MAIL 540:57
dirty b. worth reading — POUND 665:67
do not throw this b. about — BELL 72:45
drown my b. — SHAK 775:98
Each creature…Is as a b. — ALAN 9:82
essence of a b. — NABO 606:41
Europe…a hardcover b. — DELI 260:75
ever written a b. — WELD 897:45
Every b. is like a purge — DU 294:97
face…is as a b. — SHAK 766:83
find one English b. — ARNO 33:36
Finishing a b. — CAPO 189:31
from the b. of honour razèd — SHAK 771:12
frowst with a b. — KIPL 472:37
Go little b. — SPEN 808:67
greatest b. he had ever read — STEIN 815:13
He is like a b. in breeches — SMITH 801:17
ideal companion…a good b. — DAVI 255:45
In the Penguin b. — HEAN 389:11
in thy b. all my members — BIBLE 98:2
little black b. with two players in — CHAR 207:46
little b. out of the angel's hand — BIBLE 126:64
Louvre is the b. — CEZA 203:52
make one b. — JOHN 444:7
man the index of that b. — DONNE 282:95
May my b. teach — GIDE 353:79
men with b. learning — RAMOS 678:6
mind afterwards—over a b. — LAMB 486:48
mine adversary had written a b. — BIBLE 93:66
Mona Lisa seem an open b. — LEAC 496:63
moral or an immoral b. — WILDE 908:99
nature's infinite b. of secrecy — SHAK 764:13
never call myself a b. lover — LARK 491:40
never read the same b. twice — WILS 915:83
nice new little b. — CATU 200:4
no instruction b. came with it — FULL 341:55
of the b. of war — MONT 593:1
old address b. — MCCU 529:22
oldest rule in the b. — CARR 195:87
one-b. novelist — ROTH 699:14
only one b. in them — BARN 60:75
only trouble with this b. — LEHM 501:70
past…like the leaves of a b. — WOOLF 922:27
possession of a b. — BURG 167:87
praise a b. too highly — MILL 573:56
private b. to prove — STEV 822:5
profession of b. writing — STEI 816:40
Publishing a b. is…like — ATWO 38:64
readers who are pleased with a b. — CONN 233:67
reading of a b.! — THOR 857:77
read one b. in my life — MITF 589:8

school history b. GLAS 359:99
seal the b. BIBLE 106:1
seldom peruses a b. ADDI 6:9
sell a man a b. MORL 598:86
sour misfortune's b. SHAK 737:80
take down this b. YEATS 932:33
take them out of this b. STER 817:75
tastes no wise b.-maker LUCAS 521:73
The B. of Life WILDE 909:21
then shut the b. PATM 643:58
Things in b.'s clothing LAMB 487:60
This b. is not about heroes OWEN 632:54
this b. is not concerned with Poetry OWEN 632:55
this is no b. WHIT 905:45
This little b. contains STIL 824:47
throw the entire b. in the fire SAND 712:86
To produce a mighty b. MELV 564:35
to write a really funny b. HEMI 393:93
To write the essential b. PROU 671:91
truly good b. THOR 857:75
understand that b. but fail NICO 614:96
until he has written a b. JOWE 451:78
when you read a b. GAUG 347:68
Who is worthy to open the b. BIBLE 126:56
word for word without b. SHAK 755:48
Would you read a Sustaining B. MILNE 574:78
write a b. a year TARTT 836:1
writing a b. GERA 350:25
Writing a b. of poetry MARQ 554:33
book-case red mahogany b.-c. BETJ 83:82
Bookie snatch B. Bob RUNY 702:79
book-keeping double-entry b.-k. MULL 602:72
book-learning b.-l. in monasteries GALL 344:19
books All b. are the Book of Job ELKIN 310:69
all my b. are botches MELV 564:43
all the b. you can export CHIS 213:16
archives of his b. RODC 693:87
are the b., the arts SHAK 734:86
author because you like his b. LINK 511:61
author who speaks about his own b. DISR 277:80
base authority from others' b. SHAK 733:69
Before high-piled b. KEATS 457:93
be not swallowed up in b.! WESL 900:26
bibliobuli...who are...drunk on b. MENC 565:74
B. and the man I sing POPE 662:64
B. are a load of crap LARK 491:32
B. are cold and certain HUGO 421:86
b. are divided RUSK 704:22
b. are either dreams LOWE 519:22
B. are good enough STEV 822:96
b. are more than b. LOWE 519:21
B. are theatres STEV 820:42
B. are the bees LOWE 520:34
b....are the nearest to us CONR 234:10
B. are the opium FRAN 333:84
B. are written by martyr-men CARL 193:30
b., convention and cliché POUND 664:24
B. do furnish a room POWE 666:81
b. echoing the life WILL 914:56
B. from Boots BETJ 83:85
B. have had their day BENN 77:58
b. have their own fate TERE 849:80
B. have to teach RUSH 703:91
b....how many of them I could avoid MACA 525:33
b. in the running brooks SHAK 749:34
B., like men SWIFT 830:54
B. make sense of life BARN 60:70
B. must follow sciences BACON 50:66
B. of poetry...promissory notes WILDE 908:87
b. one reads in childhood ORWE 629:81
b. promiscuously read MILT 579:73
B....propose to instruct DE 262:8
b. teach them GARC 345:42
b. that have a lot of dreck BART 62:10
b. that influence us FORS 332:56
b. that wound KAFKA 453:24
B. think for me LAMB 487:59
B.! 'tis a dull...strife WORD 924:74
b. to blisse ne to joye LANG 489:98
b. were read BELL 73:66
b. which do not have facts VIDAL 881:4
b. which you do not understand VIAN 880:77
b. written by Europeans NAIP 606:50
borrowers of b. LAMB 487:52
British...taste for bad b. BRAD 148:61
cannot learn men from b. DISR 275:34
Deep-versed in b. MILT 586:43

everybody could write b. BAIN 52:7
factory of b. SMITH 799:66
First to possess his b. SHAK 774:90
forefathers had no other b. SHAK 730:66
Forsake thy b., and mateless play BRON 155:91
Friends To borrow my b. ROBI 690:29
fuck-all to say about my b. WELSH 899:97
Give me b., fruit, french wine KEATS 458:13
God has written all the b. BUTL 178:78
Good travel b. RABAN 675:60
haven't read any of your b. JOYCE 452:2
If my b. had been any worse CHAN 204:79
In b. lies the soul of the whole Past CARL 193:34
indiscriminate reviewing of b. ORWE 629:82
in Germany, b. STAEL 812:52
I've read all the b. MALL 542:92
Keepers of b. MACL 535:41
let my b. be...eloquence SHAK 771:10
luminous plectrum of b. BELLI 72:42
Mistresses are like b. WYCH 931:10
more b. one reads MAO 548:17
more b. we read CONN 233:75
never yet was put into words or b. MELV 564:36
of making many b. there is no end BIBLE 101:93
old b. GOLD 362:62
people...do not read b. WORD 928:48
pictures of obscene b.! ARLT 30:66
reading of good b. DESC 263:17
Read the best b. first THOR 857:72
so charming as b. SMITH 801:12
Some b. accrete things HOLM 407:74
some b. are deemed most baneful MELV 564:46
Some b. are lies BURNS 170:67
Some b. are to be tasted BACON 50:53
Some b. are undeservedly forgotten AUDEN 41:18
spacious highways of b. SAND 713:13
spectacles of b. DRYD 288:25
story b....written by people WELTY 899:99
study of mankind is b. HUXL 424:56
trees shall be my b. SHAK 749:54
true University...is a collection of b. CARL 193:35
turned o'er many b. SHAK 740:78
two classes of b. FORD 330:3
who has written fine b. GARR 346:54
worse crimes than burning b. BROD 154:58
Writing b. is the closest men MAIL 540:49
booksellers bold b. SHER 788:63
embolden b. WAUGH 891:6
boomerang b. No more spear NOON 618:59
boon for heaven's grace and b. KEATS 459:37
Of neither would I ask the b. SHEL 786:18
recipients of the b. of liberty MAMET 543:25
sordid b.! WORD 928:46
boot b. in the face, the brute PLATH 654:69
imagine a b. stamping ORWE 630:4
power of your b. MOTI 600:35
Then hey for b. and horse KING 469:53
booted always be b. and spurred MONT 592:72
Booth B. died blind LIND 510:47
B. led boldly LIND 510:45
bootless spends a b. grief SHAK 759:67
boots a pair of b. TRAV 864:42
asleep in his b. STEV 819:26
before the truth has got its b. on CALL 185:40
children...never had any b. WILS 915:89
elastic-sided b. SHAR 776:40
It b. not to resist SHAK 730:81
look at his b. SHAW 780:62
pantheon of b. and overalls DUNN 295:17
truth is pulling its b. on SPUR 811:41
wear long b., hard b. SAND 713:98
went to school without any b. BULM 166:55
when I take my b. off DICK 269:60
bootstraps raise ourselves by our own b. WILL 912:8
booty none left to play b. DICK 266:90
booze B., of course, and then curtains AMIS 14:94
feeding on b. and spaghetti LEWIS 507:88
man shouldn't fool with b. FAUL 319:76
boozer clown, the b., the fighter? MAST 560:52
boozes tell a man who b. BURT 174:65
bop Playing b. is like playing Scrabble ELLI 310:73
Boralaski as Count B.'s wife SCOTT 723:14
bordello doorkeeper of a b. TOSC 863:18
border across the b. to get a drink ANON 22:49
chuck them over the b. WALE 885:90
Night Mail crossing the b. AUDEN 39:81
o'er the B. and awa' SCOTT 724:23

sung of B. chivalry SCOTT 722:84
Through all the wide B. SCOTT 723:96
borders b., beds and shrubberies KIPL 474:72
invade the b. of my realm ELIZ 309:60
no walls, no b. ATWO 38:50
tyranny whose b. are undefined MAIL 540:44
bore A colossal b. MERI 567:13
beside a muzzled b. STEP 817:59
complaints are a b. ACHE 2:36
Every hero becomes a b. EMER 313:33
healthy male adult b. UPDI 874:74
If your husband is a b. BELL 73:80
in it is merely a b. WILDE 909:28
is an old b. TREE 865:65
merely the Club B. SAKI 710:47
People find ideas a b. POUND 665:54
unless it becomes a b. POUND 664:32
bored better that aged diplomats be b. AUST 44:4
b. nearer to...mortification WODE 918:50
I am heavy b. BERR 82:63
leaving because I am b. SAND 713:16
nearly b. GOSSE 364:17
Never to be b. BALL 55:63
People do not read to be b. BEAV 67:27
Punctuality...virtue of the b. WAUGH 892:48
so b. with it all CHUR 218:12
boredom b. and pain of it BUEC 165:44
b., and the horror ELIOT 307:86
b. makes you old CAST 199:74
effect of b. on a large scale INGE 429:53
Here b. reaches its peak MILL 573:36
Inconstancy, b., anxiety PASC 640:14
Life is first b. LARK 491:35
not waiting for them to die of b. BLAN 136:89
Symmetry is b. HUGO 421:87
what makes a journey...horrible is b. GELL 348:1
bores B. and Bored BYRON 182:96
B. bore each other MARQ 554:34
B. have succeeded to dragons DISR 276:37
Borgia B. who has suddenly WODE 919:62
Borgias dining with the B. tonight BEER 70:88
thirty years under the B. WELL 897:41
boring Antiquity...clichéd and b. FLAU 326:41
Life...is b. BERR 82:62
previously amusing...become b. COUP 239:1
something curiously b. HUXL 424:55
work is less b. than amusement BAUD 65:80
born all b. and must die MATAK 560:55
as a poet...not b. yet THOM 854:28
as if I had insisted on being b. DICK 271:27
as natural...to be b. BACON 47:75
as soon as we were b. BIBLE 107:34
because you were b. in it? SHAW 781:76
bird b. in a cage SHAW 780:56
blight man was b. for HOPK 412:95
b....among the mountains WORD 925:7
b. and dying, dying MISH 587:84
b., And he had reasons ROBI 690:30
b. below par to the extent MONT 592:69
B. but to die POPE 660:16
b. free as Caesar SHAK 747:75
b. in a merry hour SHAK 744:98
b. in Canada JOHN 440:94
b. in the minds of a few KISS 475:93
b. into music SIMO 792:41
b. into the world alive GILB 354:13
B. of the sun SPEN 807:47
b. of woman TWAIN 870:81
b. out of due time BIBLE 121:12
b. to know you ELUA 311:97
b. to run SPRI 811:40
b. to set it right STRA 826:81
b....when wits were fresh and clear ARNO 32:22
b. where my father lived SITT 793:56
b. with an unreasonably large stock SHAW 781:1
b....with ready-made parents FRAME 333:81
b. with two things TEMP 838:35
Bred en b. in a brier-patch HARR 383:91
British Bourgeoisie Is not b. SITW 794:79
can't be b., unless it's...in DICK 269:76
Else, wherefore b.? TENN 847:58
engaged, married, or b. GALS 344:23
Every moment one is b. TENN 841:91
Except a man be b. again BIBLE 117:79
fashion is b. by small facts SCHI 718:98
If...b. were being invented DOYLE 286:83
if he had happened to be b....there FRIE 337:64

If Joan of Arc had been b. SIMON 792:38
in dying that we are b. FRAN 334:98
I've been b., and once ELIOT 307:82
I was b. on a day VALL 876:18
less than to be b. BEAU 67:9
misery of us, that are b. great WEBS 895:4
none of woman b. SHAK 768:23
not a single molecule…when b. DIDE 274:93
not b. a parasite FRAN 335:22
not b. under a rhyming planet SHAK 745:24
Not to be b. is the best AUDEN 39:87
One is not b. a woman DE 257:92
powerless to be b. ARNO 32:31
remember where I was b. BENET 75:10
Sociology was b. SMALL 796:20
Some men are b. kings SHAW 781:84
That ever I was b. SHAK 752:39
time to be b. BIBLE 100:70
to be b., to live and to die LABR 483:72
to the manner b. SHAK 751:24
We are all b. crazy BECK 68:40
We are b. believing EMER 313:42
When I was b. WINT 917:35
When we are b. SHAK 764:94
where I was b. SALI 710:51
why wasn't I b. old DICK 267:24
borne hath b. me on his back SHAK 755:31
borogove All mimsy were the b. CARR 195:90
boroughs bright b. HOPK 412:88
borrow know well enough to b. from BIER 128:12
poets…beg, b., or steal POUND 666:73
borrowed B. garments never fit FULL 341:63
b. time, b. money CALL 184:38
borrower b. of the night SHAK 768:11
Neither a b. nor a lender be SHAK 751:21
borrowing banqueting upon b. BIBLE 108:53
b. foolishly spent DUNC 295:10
borrowings b. cheap and the notes LUCAS 521:75
bosom Amputate my freckled B.! DICK 273:78
borne, see, on my b.! BROW 162:67
b. is actually a millstone GREER 372:86
b. of the great English ARNO 33:38
b. of the lake TENN 842:14
b. of the sea SHAK 730:61
b. of the stream SHEL 786:23
b. the bright waters meet MOORE 596:47
breaks in our b. SHEL 787:28
Can a man take fire in his b. BIBLE 99:17
charge within the b. DICK 272:54
Cleanse the fraught b.? SHAK 768:38
Close b.-friend KEATS 459:48
dear to this b. TANN 836:91
from the b. of the morn MARV 555:57
great within my b. SHAK 732:22
guardage to the sooty b. SHAK 759:56
Here in my b. JONS 449:39
in your fragrant b. dies CAREW 190:61
Let me to thy b. fly WESL 900:11
no b. and no behind SMITH 800:94
not a b. to repose upon DICK 270:11
sea that bares her b. WORD 928:46
shall men give into your b. BIBLE 115:31
tribes…slumber in its b. BRYA 163:12
will leave Thy b. MILT 582:46
bosoms b. of your actresses JOHN 441:22
hang and brush their b.? BROW 161:42
Quiet to quick b. is a hell BYRON 180:25
boss absentee b. is best WINT 917:30
b.…a comforting thought MARQ 554:32
talk to a b. MAMET 544:39
will always be his b. RAVI 679:38
Boston B. has become Urban Renewal MAIL 540:55
B.…hast naught to boast ANON 20:22
B.…home of the bean and the cod BOSS 145:8
B. is a state of mind APPL 28:25
B. man is the east wind APPL 28:26
B. State-House is the hub HOLM 408:85
bottle of B. sea BENET 75:11
Boswell B. was one of the smallest MACA 525:53
botanize peep and b. WORD 924:81
botched Presidents…have b. up ONAS 625:81
bother 'b. it' I may Occasionally say GILB 353:92
don't b. much about dress SHAW 777:62
bothered buzzard…is never b. FAUL 319:72
bothersome Life is short and b. LABR 483:69
Botticelli B. isn't a wine PUNCH 673:15
bottle a little for the b. DIBD 265:53

b. of Boston sea BENET 75:11
b. of salvation RALE 677:99
b. of the best STEV 821:73
brandish anything but my b. SHAK 742:41
cantaloupe in a coke b. JONES 448:93
desire to b. SHAK 738:9
fly the way out of the fly-b. WITT 918:46
ginger-beer b. STEV 822:99
leave the b. on the chimley-piece DICK 268:40
like magic in a pint b. DICK 270:13
Poetry in a b. FADI 317:38
scorpions in a b. OPPE 626:19
terrible than an empty b. LOWRY 521:65
vintage wine from a musty old b. BOYLE 148:49
bottles B. of Ring-Bo-Ree LEAR 497:81
fill old b. with banknotes KEYN 466:88
new wine into old b. BIBLE 111:21
bottom at the b. of a' the mischief SCOTT 724:33
b. of my grief? SHAK 736:72
b. stir The hell MILT 582:52
going to hit the b. MOND 590:49
I'm the b., you're the top PORT 663:5
old mad scientist at b. PERE 648:57
They have…middle and b. EMER 313:38
very b. of her being ADAMS 4:70
will reach the b. first GRAH 365:34
with my b. in the air PIGG 651:12
bottomless b., topsiturviest RUSK 704:37
Law is a b. pit ARBU 28:32
bottoms b. of my trousers rolled ELIOT 304:24
bough Apollo's laurel b. MARL 553:9
blossom that hangs on the b. SHAK 775:99
b. from Virginia's aged tree RANS 679:22
bread beneath the b. FITZ 324:83
Petals on a wet, black b. POUND 664:28
boughs b. do laughing blossoms bear SPEN 809:92
b. more silent than before MILL 571:86
b. off many a tree HERB 397:92
Green b. LORCA 517:85
lowest b. and the brushwood sheaf BROW 160:30
those b. which shake SHAK 772:30
bouillabaisse B. is only good DOUG 283:23
bouillon good poem is like a b. cube DOVE 284:39
boulders spills the upper b. FROST 338:84
bounce no more b. than…potato PORT 663:12
bounces bigger because of the b. MILNE 575:84
bound b. for the same bourn HOUS 415:61
b. to give it honestly JOHN 444:99
stream, confined in narrow b. CRAB 242:1
tall buildings in a single b.! SIEG 791:25
too small a b. SHAK 742:35
tranced woman, b. and stark FREE 336:43
boundaries b. between politics DANG 252:86
b. of the soul HERA 396:68
cannot remain within their b. DANTE 252:97
Deem that our puny b. WORD 925:96
few landmarks and no b. MCMU 537:89
step over the b. HIRST 404:11
boundary b. of the march PARN 639:93
no b. line to art PARK 637:40
bounded b. in a nutshell SHAK 752:54
boundless b., as we wish our souls SHEL 782:34
b., endless, and sublime BYRON 180:46
Is b. better, b. worse TENN 841:89
there is b. theft SHAK 762:49
bounds Eternity as if it had b. DUNC 295:13
flaming b. of place and time GRAY 370:38
is out of b. now LOWE 520:50
living know No b.? SHIR 789:79
thus far thy b. MILT 584:92
untraced b. WENT 899:5
wider shall thy b. be set BENS 77:61
bountiful How just, how b. WORD 929:66
nature…careless as it is b. DILL 274:31
bounty b. is as boundless SHAK 736:52
b. of God BLAKE 134:44
those his former b. fed DRYD 291:36
bouquets b. keep pouring in FREUD 336:51
Bourbon B. family is a dagger QUIN 675:53
bourbon sound of pouring b. MCCU 529:23
this b. is good TRUM 869:46
bourgeois astound the b. BAUD 65:86
beastly the b. is LAWR 495:26
b. always bounces up CONN 233:63
B. society is infected WEIL 896:31
English proletariat…more b. ENGE 314:65
Hatred of the b. FLAU 326:38

narrow horizon of b. MARX 558:14
person of b. origin ORWE 627:38
small-town b. at heart NABO 606:47
sordid b. world MISH 587:82
bourgeoisie b. in the long run TROT 867:17
b. of all classes, who deny tragedy BLIX 137:2
Discreet Charm of the B. BUNU 166:65
fine nervous flower of the b. BOGAN 138:32
For generations the British b. WAUGH 891:14
The b.'s weapon STEV 824:40
The British B. SITW 794:79
wanted to make the b. a class HUGO 421:92
Bournemouth B. is one of the few BETJ 83:93
Bovary Madame B. MCCA 528:8
bovine cow is of the b. NASH 608:75
bow Ane b. that is ay bent HENR 396:52
arrow from the Tartar's b. SHAK 738:5
B., b., ye lower middle classes! GILB 354:10
b. of burning gold! BLAKE 135:84
B. themselves when he did sing SHAK 775:12
b. to everyone SKEL 795:6
b. was made in England DOYLE 285:57
breaketh the b. BIBLE 95:26
breaketh the b. BOOK 143:51
drew a b. at a venture BIBLE 92:27
made-up b. ties SHAR 776:40
set my b. in the cloud BIBLE 87:69
Thou shalt not b. down thyself BIBLE 88:23
tightened b. YEATS 933:40
bowels b. of Christ CROM 245:72
b. of compassion BIBLE 125:37
b. were moved for him BIBLE 102:4
melted in the midst of my b. BIBLE 94:99
molten b. BOTT 146:17
No belly and no b. RANS 679:28
bower b. quiet for us KEATS 457:1
deck both bed and b. SPEN 808:86
flower perfumes the b. SCOTT 725:45
hâll and b. WORD 925:11
sought her baith by b. and ha' SCOTT 724:23
twa sisters in a b. BALL 55:67
bowers built upon the b. of paradise PAINE 634:90
cedar and sycamore b. KEND 461:95
bowl b. of night FITZ 324:82
child drinking a b. of milk SAND 713:12
Come, dear b. BARL 60:58
great b. of the sky MCMU 537:87
honey set in a green b. SMITH 799:61
I b. so slow BARR 61:89
love in a golden b. BLAKE 133:27
lurk within the b. SMITH 801:20
softly in the brimming b. JOYCE 451:82
bowled darned near b. him LARW 492:57
bowler b.'s Holding JOHN 444:79
b. thinks he bowls LANG 488:90
difference between a fast b. TRUE 868:26
bowling b. lobs and slow twisters JOYCE 451:82
bowls bowler thinks he b. LANG 488:90
B. is a young man's game BRYA 163:11
b. of fierce desire CRAS 244:43
Fill our b. once more SHAK 765:40
playing b. upon a splitting wreck DAVI 254:23
bow-shot A b.-s. from her TENN 839:48
bowstring thrice cut Cupid's b. SHAK 745:11
bow-wow Big B.-w. strain SCOTT 725:54
box B. about AUBR 39:69
b. and the puppets THAC 849:94
b. that fennel Grows around RANS 679:27
father gave him a b. MACN 538:13
jack in the b. ELKIN 310:70
Pit, b., and gallery POPE 661:34
rattle of the money b. LABO 483:55
time…kept in a b. RAINE 677:95
boxer b. never sees the big one FORE 330:24
With a nation, as with a b. ACHE 3:51
boxes banging down their bits of b. OSBO 630:11
Neat in their b. ROET 694:98
boxing activity is so vain as b. MAIL 540:59
b. is everything HEMI 395:31
B. is show-business with blood BELA 71:24
b. really combines LONS 517:69
I have covered b. GALL 344:14
Squash is b. BARR 61:92
boy any b.…become president STEV 821:69
As a b. HATT 385:26
Attic b. to hunt MILT 577:20

blind b., Venus' baby	SPEN 809:2
blitz of a b.	CAUS 201:13
b. always rose again	MAP 548:19
B. Meets Girl in Winnipeg	MACL 535:53
b. playing on the sea	NEWT 612:74
b.'s ideal of a manly career	DISR 276:52
b. stood on the burning deck	HEMA 393:91
b.'s will is the wind's	LONG 516:58
b. walking…head drooping	WHITE 903:92
b. with his father	IHIM 428:43
can't expect a b. to be vicious	SAKI 710:36
changed into a b.	KEIL 460:74
Chatterton, the marvellous b.	WORD 926:17
down to talk poetry, my b.	DICK 266:79
every b. and every gal	GILB 354:13
genuine b. is a rebel	MILL 573:50
Give to your b.	DRYD 289:56
growing b.	WORD 926:24
hating, my b., is an art	NASH 608:83
Her little b. weeping sought	BLAKE 134:35
How dost, my b.?	SHAK 763:75
if they like a b.	SALI 711:59
imagination of a b.	KEATS 457:99
Little B. kneels at the foot	MILNE 574:75
little tiny b.	SHAK 757:92
Mad about the b.	COWA 239:15
many a b. here	SHER 788:72
modest, good-humoured b.	BEER 69:72
My b.,' he says	RUNY 702:78
never was a b.	MILL 570:74
no b.…allured to letters	STEE 814:1
not the Model B.	TWAIN 870:83
office b.	GILB 353:94
parent who could see his b.	LEAC 497:66
plump and hearty, healthy b.	HOFF 406:51
purblind, wayward b.	SHAK 733:76
read to by a b.	ELIOT 305:39
remain a fifteen-year-old b.	ROTH 699:18
Robin was a rovin' B.	BURNS 171:92
salesman is got to dream, b.	MILL 571:95
Selwyn MacGregor, the nicest b.	SPARK 806:18
sensitive b.'s humiliations	SHAW 778:85
Speak roughly to your little b.	CARR 195:69
speak to your little b.	BLAKE 134:34
Than when I was a b.	HOOD 410:38
The b.'s mouth	TWAIN 871:13
this b. will be surrounded	HARD 381:39
to be a little b.	THUR 860:60
to be b. eternal	SHAK 770:74
What a wonderful b. he is!	HOGG 406:59
When I was a b.	SITT 793:56
When I was a b.	THOM 853:2
While yet a b.	SHEL 782:20
with our precious b.	DICK 268:43
You are a human b.	DICK 270:90
boyfriend and have a French b.	HEPB 396:58
boyhood characters of my b.	STEV 821:77
lost b. of Judas	RUSS 706:62
boys As flies to wanton b.	SHAK 763:84
Beautiful b. with bright red guitars	HENRI 395:41
b. are not going to be sent	ROOS 696:48
B. do now cry	PEPYS 647:25
B.' hate was dangerous	MUNRO 603:84
b. in their happy play	SCHR 720:40
b. late at their play!	ARNO 33:52
breaks are beating the b.	GIPP 357:77
By office b. for office b.	SALI 711:70
Christian b. I can scarcely hope	ARNO 34:72
elders, and fought by b.	LIVE 512:79
English…half-little b.	CELJ 202:40
give the b. a little tea	ANDE 16:22
Give them the cold steel, b.!	ARMI 30:70
good old b. was drinkin'	MCLE 534:26
hardly suitable for delicate b.	WILDE 910:62
lightfoot b. are laid	HOUS 415:64
loaded guns with b.	CRAB 242:6
only know two sorts of b.	DICK 267:94
other girls and b.	STEV 823:14
school b. or scholarship	LITT 512:77
The b. are dreaming wicked	THOM 853:87
three wild lads…brave b.	SCOTT 724:19
Till the b. come Home	FORD 330:20
what Asian b. ought	JOHN 440:83
Young b. would talk about it	STEI 816:44
bra Burn your b.!	ANON 24:11
braccia twelve b. across	LEON 503:13
bracelet diamond and safire b.	LOOS 517:79

braces liquid which rots b.	MORT 600:22
bracing Skegness is so b.	ANON 22:44
Bradford silk hat on a B. millionaire	ELIOT 306:60
Bradman B.'s batting genius	LARW 491:56
Bradyism B.…multisibling sensibility	COUP 239:98
brae waly, waly doun the b.	BALL 56:94
braes among thy green b.	BURNS 171:4
banks and b. o' bonie Doon	BURNS 172:26
b. o' Killiecrankie	BURNS 172:11
by yon bonnie b.	ANON 20:20
brag Men would b.	STEI 816:44
Brahmin Men are the B.	STAN 812:64
braid badge of tarnished b.	READ 680:48
b. to bind your hair	SCOTT 724:22
O' gude B. Claith	FERG 320:6
thy brow to b.	SCOTT 723:11
brain are the b. of heaven	MERE 567:8
blessed with a woman's b.	RICH 686:64
blind life within the b.	TENN 847:51
Bracing b. and sinew	KING 469:49
b. has Corridors	DICK 272:65
b. may devise laws	SHAK 739:44
b. of feathers	POPE 662:70
b. stops criticising	SLOAN 796:17
B.…wider than the Sky	DICK 272:63
B.…with which we think	BIER 128:19
children of an idle b.	SHAK 736:40
cobweb of the b.	BUTL 177:50
Dilutes with drivel every drizzly b.	BYRON 179:6
dislocate my B.!	DICK 273:78
draughts intoxicate the b.	POPE 658:54
dry b. in a dry season	ELIOT 305:43
Dwell in some idle b.	MILT 576:12
emptying the native's b.	FANON 317:44
gladness…thy b. must know	SHEL 784:63
gleaned my teeming b.	KEATS 457:93
I feared it might injure the b.	CARR 194:67
in my b. I sing it	BROW 162:67
lantern of Aristotle's b.	RALE 677:2
lenses through which the b. explores	DOUG 283:21
let the b. lie also	BROW 161:61
little b. attic	DOYLE 285:66
madness…should possess a poet's b.	DRAY 287:5
messages go quicker to the b.	SPARK 806:20
no one's b. rejects it	BACON 50:71
not for the weary b.	THOM 856:61
painting is done with the b.	MICH 568:34
passion of the b.	BURT 174:81
petrifactions of a plodding b.	BYRON 179:99
phonographs of hades in the b.	CRANE 243:25
phrases in his b.	SHAK 733:73
Purple haze is in my b.	HEND 395:36
puzzle their b.	GOLD 362:64
rafters of the b.	HUID 421:99
Relaxing your b. is fatal	MOSS 600:29
shifting my b.	HERZ 400:55
so small his b.	BUTL 176:37
studies of the b.	PENF 646:20
toil of b., or toil of hands	MELV 564:24
too little b.	SHAK 757:11
troubles of the b.	SHAK 768:38
unquiet heart and b.	TENN 842:23
What's in the b.	SHAK 773:45
whimsy heaped in his own b.	ROCH 691:56
work like madness on the b.	COLE 226:7
brainpower using their b.	MCDO 530:52
brains big feet and no b.	HAGEN 376:56
blow out your b.	KIPL 471:93
Blows out his b. upon the flute	BROW 162:92
B. are not everything	SHAW 777:71
b. get buried	ROTH 699:20
b. go to his head	ASQU 36:16
b. knocked out by them	SHEL 783:35
b. of Minerva	BARR 61:94
b. wuz to settle	LOWE 520:30
but extra b.	TRUE 868:26
clears the b.	PENE 646:19
feet instead of their b.	SOUSA 804:92
gentleman said a girl with b.	LOOS 517:73
had to use my b.	SHAN 776:35
have my b. ta'en out and buttered	SHAK 743:79
steal away their b.!	SHAK 760:80
such seething b.	SHAK 738:12
Through lovers' b.	SHAK 736:39
tormenting of the b.	MONT 591:64
What good are b. to a man?	WODE 919:55
with no b. at all	HERB 397:74

young man who has b.	STEV 822:94
brake small but workable b.	MURR 605:9
bramble-dew eyes of gold and b.-d.	STEV 823:34
brambles like the b. in a wild field	DIDE 274:3
branch accomplished in any b.	MARX 557:99
blaze of b., or brazier	ELIOT 309:38
b. of…antediluvian families	CONG 231:17
B. shall grow out of his roots	BIBLE 102:18
Cut is the b.	MARL 553:9
Lone on the fir-b.	MERE 566:93
lops the mouldered b. away	TENN 848:66
neither root nor b.	BIBLE 106:22
pluck an ivy b. for me	ROSS 697:77
reddens on the high b.	SAPP 714:28
tip of every b.	PLATH 654:72
branches b. of government	MILL 570:66
climb black b.	FROST 338:92
most lucrative of its b.	PAINE 634:93
poetry does not swing from the b.	CHOC 214:17
retain their b.	SOPH 804:85
branch-strained b.-s. metaphor	MOORE 595:41
brand b. him either a failure	HOLM 407:72
b. sae drap wi' bluid	BALL 56:76
brandy b. of the damned	SHAW 778:90
must drink b.	JOHN 445:37
neat b.	STEV 821:76
brash when it is b. or noisy	AUDEN 41:26
brashness a certain b.	GALB 343:93
brass belly and his thighs of b.	BIBLE 105:94
bound him with fetters of b.	BIBLE 90:75
B. Money	ANON 21:37
b., nor stone, nor earth	SHAK 772:25
evil manners live in b.	SHAK 775:24
feet like unto fine b.	BIBLE 120:65
nor walls of beaten b.	SHAK 747:81
serpent of b.	BIBLE 89:39
sounding b.	BIBLE 121:9
think gold that is b.	SPEN 809:11
brass-collar letter'd, braw b.-c.	BURNS 170:74
brassière Art is not a b.	BARN 60:69
brat you horrid b.	BEME 74:95
brattle Wi' bickering b.!	BURNS 170:71
brave act so b. and daring	ROCH 691:62
b. and battered sisters	PRIE 668:19
b. and meek with thirty bob a week	DAVI 253:22
b., generous…warm-hearted race	BUCH 164:27
b. man with a sword	WILDE 910:54
b. master was no more	MACA 527:78
B. men are a city's strongest tower	ALCA 13:37
b. on a battlefield	MITC 588:97
b. resistance	WASH 890:83
b. that die in the battle	CLOU 223:35
Fortune favours the b.	TERE 848:77
home of the b.?	KEY 465:76
How sleep the b.	COLL 228:42
instead of b. and fine	NOON 618:58
intelligent, the witty, the b.	MILL 571:89
make one b. push	STEV 822:2
makes e'en the valiant more b.	DIBD 265:54
Many b. men lived before	HORA 413:25
more b. than me	CUMM 248:12
Neither a wise man nor a b. man	EISE 302:50
noble race and b.	SIGO 791:28
None but the b. deserves the fair	DRYD 291:33
O b. new world	SHAK 775:1
That's a b. fellow	SHAK 769:61
the b., the mighty	WORD 928:58
this is most b.	SHAK 753:69
To fight aloud, is very b.	DICK 272:54
What's b., what's noble	SHAK 765:53
braver b. in another language	BROO 156:24
bravery b. of his grief	SHAK 755:38
braw that was b.	BURNS 171:47
brawling b. of a sparrow	YEATS 932:32
braying light is b.	SITW 793:62
brazen [Nature's] world is b.	SIDN 791:18
brazier blaze of branch, or b.	ELIOT 309:38
Brazil Science fiction, like B.	DISCH 275:30
Brazilian a B. without land or mone	STING 824:49
Brazilification B.…widening gulf	COUP 238:92
breach endure not yet A b.	DONNE 280:55
more unto the b.	SHAK 746:42
bread After b.	JOHN 440:88
b. and butter	MACK 534:19
b. and butter	MACD 530:47
b. and butter	SWIFT 832:6
b. and games	JUVE 453:19

b. and meat	STEV 821:76
b. and your butter	KIPL 474:71
b. beneath the bough	FITZ 324:83
b. eaten in secret	BIBLE 99:19
b. for the family	LEWIS 507:84
b. I dip in the river	STEV 823:30
b.-sauce of the happy ending	JAMES 433:47
b. to the wise	BIBLE 101:85
b. which strengtheneth	BIBLE 97:67
b. with the salt of tears	KAIKO 454:32
cannot give them b.	WILDE 907:82
cast my b. on the waters	JACK 431:5
Cast thy b. upon the waters	BIBLE 100:70
Cast your b. upon	HAGG 376:57
Content…To eat dusty b.	BOGAN 138:30
crust of b.	RYDER 707:76
cutting b. and butter	THAC 849:5
did eat of my b.	BIBLE 95:19
earn my b.	FRAN 335:22
eat b. to the full	BIBLE 88:21
eat the b. of sorrows	BIBLE 98:92
eat thy b. with joy	BIBLE 101:83
eat thy b. with quaking	BIBLE 105:87
give him b. to eat	BIBLE 100:52
Give us this day our daily b.	BIBLE 110:98
half a loaf was better than no b.	CHES 212:70
having looked to government for b.	BURKE 169:48
I am the b. of life	BIBLE 117:90
if his son ask b.	BIBLE 110:8
Jesus took b.	BIBLE 114:96
Jesus…took b.	BIBLE 121:6
lives not upon b. alone	STEV 822:89
man doth not live by b. only	BIBLE 89:47
Man shall not live by b. alone	BIBLE 109:78
meat, and cursed the b.	ROBI 690:28
nor his seed begging b.	BIBLE 95:17
offered a piece of b. and butter	MACK 534:19
People who eat white b.	VREE 883:61
ravens brought him b.	BIBLE 92:17
science as well as b.	JAMES 434:59
servants…have b. enough	BIBLE 116:47
shalt thou eat b.	BIBLE 86:56
Some gave them white b.	CARR 197:16
spend money for that which is not b.?	BIBLE 104:53
spoiled the b. and spilled the wine	PATM 643:57
steal b.	FRAN 333:93
take b. at my hand	WYATT 931:3
that b. should be so dear	HOOD 410:47
touch of his b.	SHAK 750:68
Who never ate his b. in sorrow	GOET 360:15
With the b. eaten	CERV 203:45
yield a heavy b.	WILK 911:97
breadlines b. continue	SKEL 795:1
breadwinner b. and a crosspatch	SMITH 800:92
break bend but do not b.	LAFO 485:2
B., b., b.	TENN 840:67
b. earth's sleep	OWEN 632:64
b. my staff	SHAK 775:98
B. the bone	RABE 676:66
but they never b.	BUCK 165:39
Never Give…an Even B.	FIEL 323:51
sex rules…I b.	SALI 711:53
those that will not b.	HEMI 394:99
Thou thyself must b.	ARNO 33:51
time to b. down	BIBLE 100:70
Words…sometimes b.	ELIOT 307:2
breaker b. of proverbs	SHAK 741:99
breaker-beaten b.-b. coast	BYRON 182:78
breakers angry b. roar	LEAR 497:76
like b. cliffward leaping!	CRANE 243:22
Set keel to b.	POUND 665:45
breakfast bananas for b.	WHAR 901:45
b., dinner, lunch, and tea	BELL 73:55
B. is the one meal	VAND 876:24
cooking b. this morning	SCHR 720:44
eat Rockefellers for b.	KENN 464:54
Hope is a good b.	BACON 47:70
hypothesis every day before b.	LORE 517:88
impossible things before b.	CARR 196:7
Where shall we our b. take	BALL 56:91
breakfasts b. on…frosty mornings	GRAH 366:39
breakfast-table well-provisioned b.-t.	HAWT 386:44
breakfast-time critical period…is b.-t.	HERB 397:84
breakneck riding at b. speed	BLAN 136:87
bream Backed lyke a b.	BERN 81:48
breast boiling bloody b.	SHAK 738:16

b. high amid the corn	HOOD 410:39
b. Still tender	HOPE 411:72
broods with warm b.	HOPK 412:84
buckles on his b.	SHAK 764:9
charms to soothe a savage b.	CONG 231:22
craving void…aching in the b.	POPE 659:82
creating in every English b.	MANC 544:44
creep into my b.	BEAU 67:16
crimson…robin's b.	TENN 840:75
deeply implanted in the human b.	DICK 267:92
depth of her glowing b.	SHEL 785:85
forged upon his b.	WORD 928:57
fresh, green b. of the new world	FITZ 325:1
heart leap in my b.	SAPP 714:27
hundred to adore each b.	MARV 556:62
in her red-berried b.	THOM 853:94
Leaning her b.	GIBB 352:68
light within his own clear b.	MILT 577:35
marched b. forward	BROW 163:95
milk in an old b.	MANS 546:83
miss the white b.	JEFF 436:10
moon on the b.	MOORE 594:16
my speaking b.	SHAK 771:10
Not a hook in all my b.	VAUG 878:48
nunnery Of thy chaste b.	LOVE 519:13
On her left b.	SHAK 773:59
on Madeleine's fair b.	KEATS 459:37
on mother's b.	TENN 841:2
peace in thy b.	SHAK 736:54
pepper-pot b. of thrush?	FRAME 333:79
seat within my captive b.	SURR 829:34
shining b.	GORD 363:6
shot…in our b.	ARNO 31:99
soft as the b. of doves	CORN 237:69
spirit in a loyal b.	SHAK 734:99
sweetness fills the b.	CASW 199:80
Tibbald's-monster-breeding b.	POPE 662:68
toss him to My b.	HERB 398:17
Truth hath a quiet b.	SHAK 734:1
twining in his speckled b.	MARV 556:69
tyrant of the throbbing b.	GRAY 370:35
wail Or knock the b.	MILT 587:65
what a panic's in thy b.!	BURNS 170:71
whose b. is a cannibal dynamo	GINS 357:62
windows to my b.	SHAK 771:11
Within whose b. did boil	SURR 829:38
wounds are in his b. and face	DAVIS 256:67
breastbone your white b.	CAUS 201:12
breast-feeding atheism, b.-f.	ORTON 627:30
breastplate b. of righteousness	BIBLE 122:52
put in the b. of judgment	BIBLE 89:25
Unpin that spangled b.	DONNE 279:35
What stronger b.	SHAK 730:59
breasts bore within their b. the grief	AYTO 45:18
b. are like two young roes	BIBLE 101:2
b. are under our foot	SHAW 778:87
b., the hallmark of our culture	DONA 278:21
clos'd within each other's b.	DRYD 289:60
could feel my b.	JOYCE 452:96
In living b.	SPEN 808:89
let her b. satisfy thee	BIBLE 99:14
prodigious b.	SWIN 834:48
soaping her b. in the bath	EWART 316:23
then her b. are dun	SHAK 773:51
Warring within our b.	MARL 551:75
breath a b. to forms	BYRON 181:55
air my quiet b.	KEATS 460:62
Art cannot hold its b.	ANTH 27:7
before thou giv'st them b.	SHAK 760:84
borne my b. away!	HOOD 410:37
b. And everlasting motion	WORD 924:85
b. can make them	GOLD 361:52
breathed into his nostrils the b. of life	BIBLE 86:43
breathes with human b.	TENN 841:90
b. goes now	DONNE 280:54
breathing a small b.	ROET 694:2
breathing thoughtful b.	WORD 927:36
b. of a buffalo in the winter	HAGG 376:58
b. of Autumn's being	SHEL 783:43
b. of degradation	BYRON 181:57
b. of Heav'n fresh-blowing	MILT 586:44
b. of kings	BURNS 170:70
b. of life	YEATS 933:54
b. Of the night-wind	ARNO 31:93
B.'s a ware	HOUS 414:44
b. that from my mistress reeks	SHAK 773:51
b. were as terrible	SHAK 744:94

b. will carry it	SPUR 811:41
call the fleeting b.?	GRAY 369:15
Clothed with his b.	TENN 847:48
cry that was no more than a b.	CONR 234:99
discernible from his b.	WALL 886:4
draw thy b. in pain	SHAK 755:41
endures for a b.	SWIN 833:22
fluttered and failed for b.	ARNO 32:14
having lost her b.	SHAK 765:25
healthy b. of morn	KEATS 459:44
last b. I drew in	LAMB 487:64
little b.	AURE 42:52
love thee with the b.	BROW 160:10
malice in my b.	SHAK 769:60
Meistersinger…set b. in steel	CRANE 243:23
morn and evening b.	BLAKE 133:23
must take the b.	MANS 546:84
O, for b. to utter	SHAK 742:15
own b. in our own nostrils	MACD 530:54
serpents of explosive b.	MARI 550:53
short of b.	SASS 716:61
sweet b. of heaven	WORD 925:89
tainting of the b.	LEWIS 508:59
taxed the b.	THOM 852:62
The faintest b.	WORD 923:68
Th'endeavour of this present b.	SHAK 733:67
use your b.	FLET 328:67
wait with bated b.	THAT 850:20
while there's b. of life	BISH 131:78
whose b. I hate	SHAK 769:66
with her thick b.	JONS 448:20
with low last b.	ROSS 698:97
breathe as though to b.	TENN 839:63
cannot see, nor b.	MASE 559:33
can't even hear people b.	CRON 246:80
they b. in me as angels	RICH 685:54
thought I could not b.	TENN 846:23
When…lapdogs b. their last	POPE 659:75
breathes B. there the man	SCOTT 723:91
hell itself b. out	SHAK 754:97
breathing b. in their faces	SHAK 774:96
B. like one that hath	TENN 839:53
Closer is He than b.	TENN 847:36
does not love b.	LEE 500:33
health, and quiet b.	KEATS 457:1
sound his b. kept	SHEL 785:76
Trick is to Keep B.	GALL 344:17
breathing-space want a little b. s.	MARP 553:18
breathing-time b.-t….or a truce	WORD 928:54
breathless B. and bewildered	ACHE 3:40
B., we flung us	BROO 155:2
bred B. en bawn in a brier-patch	HARR 383:91
Bredon summertime in B.	HOUS 415:51
bree A little aboon her b.	BALL 56:88
breeches He is like a book in b.	SMITH 801:17
render my leather b. incapable	SHER 787:37
breed b. apart from…humanity	MANK 545:62
b. for barren metal	SHAK 739:54
B. never dies	BENN 76:27
dogs I b. and sell	GRAV 367:78
none of another b.	YEATS 934:61
not b. one work	HOPK 413:10
Where they most b.	SHAK 767:85
breeder b. of sinners	SHAK 753:77
breeding formed by a different b.	DISR 276:53
guilt, or of ill b.	CONG 231:31
true b. of a gentleman	BYRON 182:86
breeds see what b. about her heart	SHAK 763:80
breeks b. aff a Hielandman	SCOTT 724:30
breeze b. of morning moves	TENN 845:89
b. of song	TENN 844:51
correspondent b.	WORD 925:89
dancing in the b.	WORD 927:40
Each b. from foggy mount	BYRON 179:6
flag to April's b. unfurled	EMER 312:2
fragrance was borne upon the b.	DICK 268:42
gentle b.	WORD 924:88
hay-harvest b.	CORY 238:78
planted…by some unnoticed b.	CARL 192:17
softest b….gives birth	WORD 929:64
The b. is on the sea	SCOTT 725:45
tossing b.	ARNO 33:45
wings of the b.	BRON 154:72
breezes little b. dusk	TENN 838:43
Brendan Saint B….Irish boats	BEHAN 70:5
brent bonie brow was b.	BURNS 171:10
Brer Fox en B. F., he lay low	HARR 383:90

brethren b. to dwell together — BIBLE 98:96
mother and my b.! — BIBLE 112:46
one of the least of these my b. — BIBLE 113:93
presence of all his b. — BIBLE 87:75
sent his b. away — BIBLE 88:4
Breughel B. of the 20th century — ADLER 7:49
brevity B. is the sister of talent — CHEK 209:8
B. is the soul — SHAK 752:42
B. is the soul of lingerie — PARK 637:41
b. of human life — PROT 670:65
first to complain of its b. — LABR 484:78
its body b. — COLE 226:6
brew b. that is true — PANA 636:27
brewery bladder against a b. — KIRK 474:86
brews peer of England b. — HOUS 415:65
briars blinding with b. my joy — BLAKE 138:57
bribe man who offers a b. — GREE 371:65
Marriage is a b. — WILD 910:77
Too poor for a b. — GRAY 370:42
bribes by b. to please — DYER 297:53
How many b. he had taken — BENT 78:81
brick carried a b. in his pocket — JOHN 443:79
men…expect b. — ASTE 36:21
on solid b. — POPE 662:74
palace built of squarèd b. — SPEN 808:75
piece of b. in his pocket — SWIFT 831:74
threw it a b. at a time — HARG 382:78
throw a b.…hitting the niece — ORWE 627:40
town of red b. — DICK 270:3
bricks Great poets seldom make b. — POUND 666:73
bridal b. of the earth and sky — HERB 398:14
bride a barren b. — POPE 661:45
as a b. adorned for her husband — BIBLE 127:79
b. and my darling to be? — BALL 56:80
b. of a ducal coronet — DICK 268:49
b. that cairries the bunch — MACD 529:39
death's b. — WORD 929:63
encounter darkness as a b. — SHAK 758:35
jealousy to the b. — BARR 61:80
missed his loving b. — NASH 608:91
my glittering b. — WORD 928:55
Passionless b. — TENN 847:35
read about his widowed b. — MCLE 534:25
So though a virgin, yet a b. — CAREW 190:63
to be his holy b. — STONE 825:57
took the b. about the neck — SHAK 732:40
unravished b. of quietness — KEATS 459:50
virgin-widow…mourning b. — DRYD 292:60
ye sall be his b. — SCOTT 724:21
bridegroom b. in my death — SHAK 765:47
b. little dreids — MACD 529:39
funeral train which the b. sees — CLOU 223:32
Like a b. from his room — AYTO 45:17
bride-grooms Of b.-g., brides — HERR 399:33
bridge Beautiful Railway B. — MCGO 531:78
b. and not a goal — NIET 615:13
b. between the world — RUSS 705:56
brought his b. technique with him — CECIL 202:25
cavalry charging over a tin b. — WODE 919:61
Cricket can be a b. — ZIA 937:99
cross the river by an Irish b. — STEW 824:44
Faith…the Pierless B. — DICK 272:69
Horatius kept the b. — MACA 526:68
keep the b. with me? — MACA 526:64
mime can be a b. between — MARC 549:30
play b. with my old maid aunts — FIEL 323:47
promise to build a b. — KHRU 466:1
rude b. that arched the flood — EMER 312:2
small b. in time — STEI 816:39
that great B. — CRANE 243:23
Venice, on the B. of Sighs — BYRON 180:31
bridges sleep under b. — FRAN 333:93
bridle b. and rudder of painting — LEON 504:17
b. reins a shake — BURNS 173:53
b. to her wanton will — SPEN 808:87
held in with bit and b. — BIBLE 95:11
Brie-cheese B.-c. poisoning — ADLER 7:50
brief b. as I have known a play — SHAK 738:15
b. quickenings that resemble pain — WILD 911:90
hold no b. for private enterprise — BURT 174:66
site, a b. and finance — ROGE 694:11
Tis b., my lord — SHAK 754:90
briefcase lawyer with a b. can steal — PUZO 673:24
briefcases in their b. is terrifying — KHRU 467:5
briefing B. for a Descent — LESS 505:41
brier How sweet is the b. — TANN 836:91
instead of the b.…the myrtle — BIBLE 104:58

brier-patch Bred en bawn in a b.-p. — HARR 383:91
brigade chiefs of the Irish B. — DAVIS 256:66
No tin hat b. — LEWIS 507:83
Viva la the New B.! — DAVIS 256:68
brigand I am a b. — SHAW 778:89
Briggs Matilda B.…was a ship — DOYLE 286:82
Bright I have B.'s disease — PERE 648:53
young lady named B. — BULL 165:52
bright b. as angels are — WILK 911:96
b. day that brings forth — SHAK 747:82
forgetting the b. speed — ARNO 32:28
leaden interfolds are b. — FREE 336:44
torches to burn b.! — SHAK 736:42
westward…the land is b. — CLOU 222:22
brightened b. by a smile — SAINT 709:18
brighter better future and a b. day — SMUTS 802:31
brightest B. and best of the sons — HEBER 390:32
part with their b. hour — HELL 392:80
wisest, b., meanest of mankind — POPE 660:26
bright-eyed b.-e. Mariner — COLE 225:81
brightness b. of his glory — BIBLE 124:89
b. of this vision — RAND 678:15
b. to hold in trust — SPEN 807:49
Leaking the b. away — SPEN 807:48
long the b. of the west — BRON 154:77
no b. in it? — BIBLE 106:10
provides the moon with its b. — ANAX 15:13
purest sky with b. — SPEN 808:75
transcendent b. didst outshine — MILT 580:98
Brighton Like B. Pier — KINN 470:68
Brignal B. banks are wild and fair — SCOTT 723:10
brilliance of a lightning storm — FLAU 326:33
brilliant b. moon — YEATS 932:32
everything b. and virgin — DAY 257:86
far less b. pen than mine — BEER 69:70
brillig Twas b., and the slithy toves — CARR 195:90
brim but sparkles near the b. — BYRON 179:20
full to the b. — DICK 270:1
brimstone b. and fire — BIBLE 87:79
brink scared to go to the b. — DULL 293:90
brisking counteracts…by b. about — SMART 796:26
Bristol not the Member for B. — BURKE 168:7
Britain an end to the old B. — BROWN 157:40
a stronger, fairer B. — BROWN 157:39
Backing B. — ANON 23:3
belong to B. — GERA 350:26
best built city in B. — DEFOE 258:23
B. absorbs and adapts — COOK 235:36
B. a fit country — LLOY 513:4
B. and for the hell of it — NOBLE 617:52
B., could you ever boast — SWIFT 832:95
B. had a savage culture — BANDA 58:24
B. has lost an Empire — ACHE 2:29
B. is a Morris Minor country — ANON 24:25
B. must…stand shoulder-to-shoulder — BLAIR 133:10
B.…on borrowed time — CALL 184:38
B.'s comparative performance — MISH 587:79
B. set the world ablaze — GILB 354:14
B.'s New Political Order — MITC 588:89
B.'s true national dish — COOK 235:36
B. was conquered — TACI 835:71
B. will not be involved in…war — DAILY 250:64
end of B. — GAIT 343:89
freedom of the press in B. — ORWE 628:48
Graces…not…natives of Great B. — CHES 210:33
Hath B. all the sun — SHAK 774:68
inability in B. to comprehend — HAUG 385:28
journalism…in B. — SAMP 712:76
lead B. and her fading empire — MANC 544:44
leads a country such as B. — THAT 850:30
most urgent tasks in B. — BEVE 85:27
new B. is exciting — WILS 916:98
Only in B. — MAJOR 541:72
precipitous decline for B. — MCFA 531:71
When B. first — THOM 856:52
Britannia beer and B. — SMITH 801:9
B., rule the waves — THOM 856:52
shouted 'Rule B.' — KIPL 472:27
British A B. officer — PANG 636:28
anything except the B. War Office — SHAW 777:70
as…rude as the B. — GALL 344:15
Australians inherited the B. mentality — PACK 633:73
B-b-b. object — MALO 543:14
beneath the B. flag — JOHN 440:94
B. are an aggressive nation — ABSE 1:9
B. are coming — WELL 897:47
B. bulldog into a Reagan poodle — STEEL 814:87

B. Civil Service — WILL 912:13
B. Empire has advanced — GEOR 349:19
B.…gluttons for satire — LODGE 514:22
B. had no way of knowing it — VONN 883:56
B. have more heritage than is good — BRYS 164:16
B. music…perpetual promise — BEEC 69:64
B. public falls for this — HAIL 377:70
B. soldier can stand up to anything — SHAW 777:70
B. 'Sphere of Influence' — ANON 21:35
B. subject, in whatever land — PALM 636:24
B.…taste for bad books — BRAD 148:61
B. want…another meeting — ANON 25:74
B. won't fight — GALT 345:30
broke a B. square! — KIPL 471:94
But B., no, the name's not right — HEAN 389:11
Come you back, you B. soldier — KIPL 470:85
Conversation is never easy for the B. — BRAD 148:64
deal with the IRA or the B. government — PAIS 635:3
decent, serious B. filth — OSBO 630:13
Dirty B. coaster — MASE 559:27
Dress B., look Irish — KOFF 477:34
face a B. Government — TUCH 869:58
fear that the B. electorate — WEBB 893:66
fleet of B. ships — NELS 610:32
For generations the B. bourgeoisie — WAUGH 891:14
greatness of the B. Nation — ADDI 6:21
Hitler never understood…the B. — BULL 166:54
impose the views…on the B. — SCHL 718:10
invade B. territory — HUNT 423:38
irritation with the word B. — BUFO 165:46
manly, B. game! — LOVE 518:8
Most B. statesmen…drunk too much — GEOR 350:23
no B. government — MACM 536:73
of B. blood? — TENN 844:69
old B. style of teaching — NEWM 612:60
planted the B. flag there — STUA 827:91
rather be B. than just — PAIS 635:2
rather bitter B. musician — WILM 914:68
ridiculous as the B. — MACA 525:48
ridiculous as the B. public — MACA 525:48
smell the blood of a B. man — SHAK 763:79
stony B. stare — TENN 845:87
streams of B. blood — SCHAW 717:96
supported by…the B. people — LAW 493:84
The B. Bourgeoisie — SITW 794:79
the B. public have no regard — EMIN 313:57
typical of the B. way of war — WAVE 893:45
United States and the B. — CHUR 217:93
Well, B. Public — BROW 162:79
Britisher healthy and childish B. — MACL 535:52
Briton Australian be equal to…a B. — PARK 638:83
better class of B. — BRAD 148:65
free-born B. — THAC 849:87
Britons B. alone use 'might' — WAUGH 892:34
Brixton shoddy streets of B. — ABSE 1:9
broadcasting essential that b. — THOR 858:11
In b. your audience is conjectural — ORWE 629:74
never-never land of b. — SAFER 708:95
'pessimistic' about b. — WELLS 898:91
broaden b. your ass if not your mind — HEMI 394:19
broadsword save his good b. — SCOTT 723:96
Broadway Has had B. — DAVIS 255:52
Lullaby of B. — DUBIN 292:69
music of B. — GERS 350:39
sinners on this part of B. — RUNY 703:85
sunny street as this B.! — DICK 267:25
walking down B. — WARH 889:64
brocade moth-eaten musical b. — LARK 491:45
stain…her new b. — POPE 659:70
broccoli It's b., dear — WHITE 902:74
brogues not fit to tie his b. — SCOTT 725:57
broke it bow'd, and syne it b. — BALL 56:94
Poverty isn't being b. — WYLIE 931:24
'Tis true, I'm b.! — JONS 450:52
When time is b. — SHAK 735:31
broken b. for you — BIBLE 121:6
b. to shivers — BIBLE 126:49
b. with the storms of state — SHAK 775:23
Is it not b.? — SHEL 785:99
jungle has b. down — JUMB 453:7
made to be b. — SWIFT 832:11
Our hearts are b. — GIUL 358:88
staff of this b. reed — BIBLE 103:35
we don't want it b. — QIAN 674:33
What is b. is b. — MITC 588:1
brokenhearted bind up the b. — BIBLE 104:62
broken-hearted both b.-h. — SWIN 833:37

ne'er been b.-h.	BURNS 172:29	**brotherhoods** b. of cedars	BROW 160:20	b. starts here	GREE 372:82
broker b....takes your fortune	WOOL 923:58	**brothers** All men are b.	POWE 666:80	The b. stops here	TRUM 869:45
honest b.	BISM 131:86	b. be, for a' that	BURNS 173:48	**bucket** not her b. bring	PRIOR 669:43
bronchitis unless he or she has b.	AGATE 8:69	B. of the Cosine	ROOS 696:58	past is a b. of ashes	SAND 713:94
bronze art b., oil portraits	RODC 693:87	b. on that bright loveliness	MACL 535:46	**buckets** b. into empty wells	COWP 241:73
B. cloud-waves	FREE 336:45	b. won't mind	COLUM 229:59	**Buckingham** changing...at B. Palace	MILNE 574:74
more lasting than b.	HORA 413:24	happy few, we band of b.	SHAK 746:60	**buckler** b. of the people's cause	DRYD 290:80
things of b. and stone	RUNY 703:86	So the two b.	KEATS 458:27	shield and b.	BIBLE 96:53
brooches I will make you b.	STEV 823:32	Working for Warner B.	MIZN 589:16	**buckles** b. on his breast	SHAK 764:9
brood b. over a full nest	ELIOT 303:97	**brothers-in-law** they aren't all b.-i.-l.	POWE 666:80	**bucks** bet you, Ziggie, a hundred b.	DILL 275:15
that thy b. is flown	TENN 842:10	**brow** bonie b. was brent	BURNS 171:10	**bud** be a b. again	KEATS 459:39
brooders Irishmen born b.	OBRI 620:99	brotherhoods of cedars on its b.	BROW 160:20	b. of the spring	DONNE 281:88
broods b. with warm breast	HOPK 412:84	B., bay and tray	DAVI 254:27	b. of thought	DARIO 252:3
Brook B. never succeeded	LEVE 506:53	b. is wet with	LONG 516:45	like a worm i' th' b.	SHAK 756:68
brook b. where you had often fished	COWL 240:40	b. so grim	ELIOT 307:6	thrusts a scaled b.	MANS 547:89
covert by some b.	MILT 577:21	Flushing his b.	KEATS 458:34	**Buddha** The B., the Godhead, resides	PIRS 652:25
drank of the b.	BIBLE 92:17	Ida's shady b.	BLAKE 133:21	**Buddhism** Christianity or B.	SAKI 710:42
five smooth stones out of the b.	BIBLE 91:94	lifted...her white b.	FREE 336:45	**Buddhist** Canadian Hinayana B.	GINS 357:68
never-failing b.	GOLD 361:51	meet my Maker b. to b.	CORN 237:71	**budge** You shall not b.	SHAK 754:4
where the b. is deep	SHAK 730:56	On his b. this mark	SHEL 783:37	**budget** figures...such as national b.	WEIL 896:31
willow grows aslant a b.	SHAK 755:25	pain and anguish wring the b.	SCOTT 723:1	forming the B.	LLOY 513:97
woodland b. he bounding crossed	SCOTT 723:88	rugged mountain's b.	GRAH 365:34	size of its military b.	BENN 75:17
Brooklyn over the B. Bridge	BISH 131:77	speech in that victorious b.	ARNO 31:90	**buds** darling b. of May	SHAK 771:5
brooks books in the running b.	SHAK 749:34	sweat of my b.	FRAN 335:22	rod of Aaron...brought forth b.	BIBLE 89:38
b., and rivers wide	MILT 576:8	sweat of one's b.	LIVI 512:83	sacrificing the early b.	ROCK 692:75
b. of Eden	TENN 847:29	thy b. to braid	SCOTT 723:11	**buffalo** breath of a b. in the winter	HAGG 376:58
b., On whose fresh lap	MILT 578:53	thy b. was smoothed	WORD 929:63	solidity of a water b.	PERE 648:58
b. too broad for leaping	HOUS 415:64	wrinkle deeper on the b.?	BYRON 179:17	where the b. roam	HIGL 402:86
golden sands, and crystal b.	DONNE 280:53	**brown** hard, b., nutlike word	BART 62:11	**Buffalo Bill** B. B.'s defunct	CUMM 247:4
sing of b.	HERR 399:33	have baked me too b.	CARR 195:84	**buffalos** flower-fed b.	LIND 511:52
Broom Beggarly B.	ANON 23:72	sinewy b. men	PRIE 668:28	**buffets** Fortune's b. and rewards	SHAK 754:88
broom b. of Cowdenknowes	BALL 55:70	**Browning** Meredith is a prose B.	WILDE 908:92	**buffoon** chemist, fiddler...and b.	DRYD 290:88
bright blows the b.	STEV 823:32	quotations from the Bible, B.	MCFA 531:73	**bugger** We done the b.!	TENZ 848:75
pods went pop on the b.	DAVI 254:26	safety catch on my B.!	JOHST 447:81	**bughtin-time** b.-t. is near	BURNS 172:39
Take a b. and clean	THER 851:43	**brows** b. full sternly bent	SPEN 809:15	**bugle** Blow, b.; answer	TENN 841:3
broomstick man is a b.	SWIFT 830:60	Gathering her b.	BURNS 172:13	Blow, b.; answer	TENN 841:4
broth cooks spoil the b.	ANON 20:12	not seen in either of our b.	DRAY 287:6	Blow, b., blow	TENN 841:3
brothel couldn't score in a b.	DOCH 277:1	pallor of girls' b.	OWEN 632:52	like an ivory b.	THOM 854:12
brothels b. with bricks of Religion	BLAKE 134:42	purple b. of Olivet	TENN 843:35	**bugles** Blow out, you b.	BROO 156:8
Of stews and b. only knew	HERB 398:18	unwrinkled b. in passport offices	STARK 813:72	b. of social change	HANDY 380:32
brother Am I my b.'s keeper?	BIBLE 86:59	**browsing** b. and sluicing	WODE 918:52	**bugs** People are not as smart as b.	WHITE 903:82
At the hand of every man's b.	BIBLE 87:68	**Bruce** Scots, wham B. has aften led	BURNS 173:41	**Buick** fawn, crossed with a B.	NICH 614:89
Be my b., or I kill you	CHAM 204:71	**bruise** parmacity for an inward b.	SHAK 741:1	**build** b. and never give war	LEE 500:40
BIG B. IS WATCHING YOU	ORWE 629:98	shalt b. his heel	BIBLE 86:53	b. himself a throne	INGE 428:50
b. came with subtilty	BIBLE 87:87	tread on it and b. it	TROL 866:87	but not I b.	HOPK 413:10
B. can you spare a dime?	HARB 380:35	**bruised** b. for our iniquities	BIBLE 104:51	If you b. it, he will come	KINS 470:72
b., in one night	LUMI 522:88	b. in a new place	IRVI 430:84	life it pretends to b. on	PRIT 669:47
b. in Shropshire	BARR 61:91	b. reed shall he not break	BIBLE 111:39	never ask why b.	SEXT 728:15
b. is born for adversity	BIBLE 99:38	b. reed shall he not break	BIBLE 103:43	No more to b.	FROST 338:93
b.'s name	SWIN 834:50	**brush** b. should not see better	GOYA 365:30	one that you b.	RYBC 707:74
B., thy tail hangs	KIPL 471:11	work with so fine a b.	AUST 43:88	so easy to b., too	IBSEN 428:35
B. to Death	DANI 252:88	**brushwood** boughs and the b. sheaf	BROW 160:30	think that we b.	RUSK 703:3
B. to Death	FLET 328:66	**brutality** without art is b.	RUSK 704:29	time to b. up	BIBLE 100:70
b. was dead, and is alive again	BIBLE 116:49	**Brute** Et tu, B.?	CAES 184:27	**builder** b. of a temple	THOR 857:79
darker b.	HUGH 418:16	Et tu, B.?	SHAK 747:94	can only be a b.	RUSK 703:8
Eat-well is drink-well's b.	FULL 341:64	**brute** B. heart of a b. like you	PLATH 654:69	**builders** b. have laboured in vain	BIBLE 127:93
every man against his b.	BIBLE 106:19	Chuck him out, the b.!	KIPL 471:92	Now we are the b.	BEVAN 84:15
friend that sticketh closer than a b.	BIBLE 99:41	creatures...Irrational and b.	MILT 586:55	**building** b. is good architecture	JOHN 440:97
genuine b. Jonathan	MOOD 594:7	heavy, red-haired b.	WELLS 898:71	b. of God	BIBLE 122:25
how oft shall my b. sin	BIBLE 113:70	lord of the fowl and the b.	COWP 241:54	b. without ornamentation	SANT 714:25
I am like no b.	SHAK 731:87	never saw a b. like that	BROW 161:45	b....with tomorrow inside	AKERS 9:79
I am sworn b.	SHAK 735:26	that ugly b., the ape!	ENNI 314:71	dedicating a new b.	ROCK 692:81
judge and the b. are one	WILS 916:7	treated as a b.	EDWA 300:18	first glimpse of the b.	POE 656:16
kynges court, my b.	CHAU 208:77	Whatever b. and blackguard	HOUS 416:72	ken by the b. o't	ANON 20:14
Life is very sweet, b.	BORR 145:3	**brutes** because the b. are dumb?	ELIOT 303:74	My name is on the b.	FORD 330:10
lo'ed him like a vera b.	BURNS 172:16	Exterminate all the b.!	CONR 234:98	opening the door of the b.	AREN 28:41
love God, and hateth his b.	BIBLE 125:41	one with the b.	HUXL 426:10	question of b.	LECO 499:28
marry with his b.	SHAK 754:6	**Brutus** B. is an honourable man	SHAK 748:5	tall b., with a tower and bells	CRAB 242:95
more close than a b.	KIPL 474:69	B.' will start a spirit	SHAK 747:77	very old b.	OSBO 630:12
mote that is in thy b.'s eye	BIBLE 110:5	no orator as B. is	SHAK 748:13	Victorians expected every b.	CASS 199:73
my b. had one	UTTL 875:10	Poor B., with himself at war	SHAK 747:73	wouldn't leave a burning b.	VAN 877:34
my fellow man—my b.	BAUD 64:53	You too, B.?	CAES 184:27	**buildings** Able to leap tall b.	SIEG 791:25
Nor a sister, nor a b.	MARG 549:37	**Bubber** B. was the first man	ELLI 310:75	b. of Hong Kong	BOOTH 144:82
scan your b. Man	BURNS 171:87	**bubble** break, like a b.	HOLM 408:83	cast your eyes on b.	PEI 646:15
seeth his b. have need	BIBLE 125:37	b. burst, and now a world	POPE 660:9	magnificence of the b. we burnt	ELGIN 302:69
Shall be my b.	SHAK 746:61	b. on the fountain	SCOTT 723:8	**built** And therefore b. for ever	TENN 847:59
Still to my b. turns	GOLD 361:39	glory a b.	SHEL 782:15	b. immovable cathedrals	GIDE 353:78
went in unto his b.'s wife	BIBLE 88:96	Honour but an empty b.	DRYD 291:38	b. in such a logical way	HOLM 408:89
whosoever is angry with his b.	BIBLE 109:88	Seeking the b. reputation	SHAK 749:50	b. to envious show	JONS 449:36
younger b. popped on to his throne	STOP 825:61	world's a b.	BACON 50:65	not what they b.	FENT 320:87
brotherhood Bawling B.	GRAND 366:45	**bubbles** beaded b. winking	KEATS 459:58	wait for schools to be b.	QABO 674:32
b. of men-at-wars	PAZ 644:89	dramatic criticism...tattoo soap b.	BROWN 157:44	**bulb** Her body a b.	PLATH 654:71
B. of the Right Stuff	WOLFE 920:93	earth hath b.	SHAK 766:74	naked light b.	WILL 912:16
crown thy good with b.	BATES 64:49	no harm as b.	KEYN 466:87	**bulk** wonder at his enormous b.	LEAC 496:63
Love the b.	BIBLE 125:25	**bubbling** with b. groan	BYRON 180:45	**Bull** John B. has gone to India	YEATS 934:61
men in b. combine	NOON 618:58	**Buck** poor Pearl B.!	PORT 663:12	**bull** gone to milk the b.	JOHN 443:68
table of b.	KING 468:39	**buck** b. doesn't even pause here	REGAN 682:91	In time the savage b.	KYD 482:45

take the b. GOLD 362:81
taking the b. by both horns ASHF 35:1
you b.'s pizzle SHAK 742:15
bull-baiting place of b.-b. SITW 794:87
Buller Captain B. broke a window JOYCE 452:94
bullet assassin's b. PARK 639:89
b....done the job five years ago COLL 227:37
b. through his head ROBI 690:28
b. through his heart THAC 849:90
Each b. has got its commission DIBD 265:55
Every b. has its billet WILL 912:6
Faster than a speeding b.! SIEG 791:25
one b. in ten thousand SPEN 807:57
bullet-headed the b.-h. many POUND 665:63
bullets Better b. than yours JEFF 436:10
b. made of platinum BELL 72:48
use psychic b. MAIL 540:47
where the b. all go in CAUS 201:12
bullfighting B. is the only art HEMI 394:5
that b. does to agriculture HUBB 418:10
bullfights Spain gets b. JONG 448:5
bullfrog eyes like a b. DAVIS 255:55
bullies b. you on manly principles SHAW 777:65
bull-rushes Divine...in b.-r. FRIE 337:68
bulls b. and foxes dine very well JUST 453:12
the ploughman of b. PROP 670:61
bull's-eyes three perfect b.-e. OFAO 622:34
bully If the President has a b. pulpit REAG 680:51
let a b. come into JOHN 440:82
love the lovely b. SHAK 746:49
most heinous b. HAIG 376:65
bullying 'b.'...not to his taste ANON 21:30
bum madman b. and angel GINS 357:61
somebody—instead of a b. SCHU 720:47
bumblebee b. can fly MAMET 543:32
bumf In b. lay salvation WAUGH 892:45
bump don't b. into people COWA 239:22
bumper b. of good liquor SHER 787:46
bums millionaires and b. taste MARQ 554:24
shabby b. living in attics LEWIS 507:88
bunches b. of clingy sob sisters PAGL 634:82
Buncombe speaking...to B. CARL 193:42
bundle b. of biases BALL 57:4
bungalow position of the b. WILS 915:73
There is our little b. REAG 681:65
bungler Man is a b. SHAW 778:94
poor magnificent b.! BAKER 53:22
bunk captain is in his b. SHAW 781:76
Exercise is b. FORD 330:9
History is more or less b. FORD 330:7
bunyip B. Aristocracy DENI 261:96
Buonarotti B. commended it VASA 877:38
burden bear the b. ARNO 32:4
b. is light BIBLE 111:38
escaping from the b. of the past YELT 934:70
heavy b. of responsibility EDWA 300:20
lay the b. equally CHUR 216:63
lighten the tax b. QUINE 675:52
music is a gift and a b. SIMO 792:41
not so heavy a b. EISE 302:52
President bears the b. KENN 462:22
realize what a b. MITC 588:95
Revolutions...never lightened the b. SHAW 778:3
what b. then.? MILT 582:54
White Man's b. KIPL 472:24
womanhood is a heavy b. DANG 251:85
Words strain...under the b. ELIOT 307:2
burdened present is b. too much HAWT 386:50
burdens b....and at my back LINK 511:60
b. on the broadest shoulders LLOY 513:97
burdocks With b., hemlock, nettles SHAK 763:86
bureaucracy B. defends the status PETER 649:77
B. is not an obstacle SCHU 721:58
B., the rule of no one MCCA 528:4
choice...b. and dilettantism WEBER 894:70
bureaucrat b.'s method of protecting SAFI 708:98
something about a b. VIDAL 881:93
bureaucratic b. or plain idiotic TUCH 869:59
b. society TREV 865:63
bureaucrats dictators nor the b. ORWE 629:83
burgeoned b. without...directors GLEI 359:2
Burger King B. K. and Dairy Queen HUXT 427:17
burgesses with staring b. STEV 821:81
burglar b. who respects his art OHEN 623:58
burgundy claret and b. in Scotland? SMITH 798:48
naïve domestic B. THUR 859:26
burial-mounds no b.-m. YEATS 932:31

buried b. in a good old age BIBLE 87:74
b. in so sweet a place SHEL 785:89
b. under the shale of eras RAND 678:14
b. with me HEWE 401:70
not b. me deep enough? TENN 845:96
not mind its being b. HOPK 413:7
Upon my b. body lay BEAU 67:13
when they b. him TENN 847:31
buries universal darkness b. all POPE 662:83
Burma Nothing happens in B. THER 851:46
There's a B. girl KIPL 470:85
burn better to marry than to b. BIBLE 121:96
b. and rave at close of day THOM 853:81
B., baby, b. ANON 23:1
B., with Athens CAMP 186:59
B. your bra! ANON 24:11
but b., b., b. KERO 464:62
three years of slow b. WHITE 903:98
burned bush b. with fire BIBLE 88:8
clothes not be b.? BIBLE 99:17
got myself b. or hanged JERO 437:36
shalt not be b. BIBLE 103:44
burnie whare the b. rowes BURNS 173:45
burning b. a farthing candle JOHN 443:72
b. and gassing people SIHA 791:29
B. dinner PIER 651:6
B. for b. BIBLE 89:24
b. of the leaves BINY 130:53
Castletown's b. HOGG 406:58
guardianship...against b. PATR 643:71
Lady's not for B. FRY 340:25
burnish thoughts began to b. HERB 398:7
Burn-mill B.-m. meadow WORD 927:30
Burns kens a wurd B. MACD 529:30
burns b. hurlis all their bankis DOUG 283:17
Not she which b. in't SHAK 770:80
burn-side waly, waly yon b.-s. BALL 56:94
burnt had to be b. down JOHN 441:4
burst b. into...bloom RAND 678:15
B. smilingly SHAK 764:4
burthen their b. to the ground TENN 846:25
Burton why was B. built on Trent? HOUS 415:65
bury b. for nothing DICK 268:44
b. them at suitable depths KEYN 466:88
b. whom he helped to starve POPE 661:39
good day to get out anything we want
to b. MOORE 595:25
went to b. her BIBLE 92:38
We will b. you KHRU 466:99
bus Hitler...missed the b. CHAM 204:66
no bloody b. BLAIR 132:97
tread in the b. on my toes? AUDEN 40:93
tumbled off a b. GRAH 365:33
buses men are like bloody b. COPE 237:61
Bush B. has 100 bodyguards GORB 363:4
How B. and his junta LECA 499:27
President B....seems to think CUOMO 248:29
the criminal, reckless little B. HUSS 424:45
The devil B. HUSS 424:42
We are against this war, Mr B. MOORE 596:45
bush Bed in the b. STEV 823:30
burdened licorice b. BETJ 84:6
b. afire with God BROW 160:14
b. burned with fire BIBLE 88:8
b. supposed a bear! SHAK 738:13
child of the mighty b. FRAN 335:22
good wine needs no b. SHAK 751:94
miracle of the lit b. THOM 855:32
Mother-b. that bore you! LAWS 496:46
passion in every b. LEE 500:45
seen the b. by moonlight LAWS 496:46
sun...on the...Australian b. LAWS 495:43
Sweet Robin sits on the b. SCOTT 724:39
thick b. that proved THOM 854:27
Thorough b., thorough brier SHAK 737:92
bushel a b. of Corn PETTY 649:84
put it under a b. BIBLE 109:85
bushels two b. of chaff SHAK 739:41
business advertising b....illusions QUEN 674:39
aim of the school of b. DEMI 261:83
an ethical b. ORWE 629:70
anon we shall dote on b. ETHE 315:96
any man in b. can afford STOWE 826:73
any other decent b. man LEWIS 507:88
broker who really intends to do b. BISM 131:86
B. at the end of its journey LLOYD 513:91
B. carried on as usual CHUR 216:59

B. first; pleasure afterwards THAC 849:6
b., industrial and commercial CARN 193:49
b. in great waters BIBLE 97:71
b. institution in the world ROGE 694:13
b. is to appraise DEWEY 264:44
b. is very simple GATES 347:62
b. meetings...supply people BOYD 147:41
b. of a comic poet CONG 231:5
b. of a statesman STEU 819:9
b. of the American people is b. COOL 236:46
b. of the day DRYD 292:52
b. of war GERB 350:29
b. practices would improve
immeasurably RODD 693:91
b. that we love SHAK 765:42
but a damn bad b. ROLL 695:32
buy many b. executives FORB 329:96
called away by particular b. SHER 788:52
Canada was open for b. ATWO 38:1
Corruption...is Chinese b. life ECON 298:80
damned serious b. WELL 897:57
dare to tell me that b. STEV 821:70
do your own b. BIBLE 123:70
end of this day's b. SHAK 748:22
ever-haunting importunity Of b. LAMB 486:39
exhausted what there is in b. WHIT 906:52
good all round b. work WELLS 898:81
growth of a large b. ROCK 692:75
heat of the b. is over! ETHE 315:93
hell of a b. to be in WINN 917:27
He which hath b. DONNE 280:50
horse racing...a solid, stable b. STEI 816:40
If everybody minded their own b. CARR 195:68
In civil b.; What first? BACON 48:7
is the world's b. KENN 463:41
It is good b. SKEL 795:96
jungles of b. HAMM 379:12
know...about b. cycles BECK 67:30
lawyer...swallowed up with b. WALT 888:52
life...is a dreary b. PERCY 648:70
life's b....a summer mood WORD 926:16
main b. of socialist parties KING 468:27
make b. for itself DICK 270:96
Men of b. BAGE 51:93
minding my own b. COOL 236:48
more b. after dinner SWIFT 831:71
my b. to see that we retain WILH 911:92
new rule for b. GATES 347:64
No B. Like Show B. BERL 80:17
no b., no income GALS 344:22
no concern with b. KIPL 470:83
none of your damn b. STIL 824:47
no other b. which government PAINE 634:91
No praying, it spoils b. OTWAY 631:32
Not slothful in b. BIBLE 120:81
over here it's a b. ROGE 695:26
paper of b. HAZL 388:77
people without b. DEFOE 258:22
Pleasure is a thief to b. DEFOE 258:24
principal b. of life is to enjoy BUTL 178:70
publicity agent of big b. ORWE 627:32
remained in the b. TWAIN 870:88
retail b. all over again NEME 611:39
robs you on b. principles SHAW 777:65
servant or has b. LAW 493:85
servants of b. BACON 48:99
strange, horrible b. VICT 880:86
successful in b. GILL 356:49
The b. of a general SUN 829:29
The rest is not our b. ELIOT 308:24
to do the b. THAC 849:88
true b. precept DICK 268:38
way that b. has structured itself HARV 385:23
We can do b. together THAT 850:23
What b. have you, miss SHER 787:35
whatever my b. PEPYS 647:45
What's your b. BERE 78:88
What was everybody's b. SMUTS 802:32
whin B. gets above sellin' tinpinny DUNNE 295:22
businessman prominent b. GALB 343:90
businessmen b....take on a science ASIM 35:6
like many b. of genius PUZO 673:25
message to the b. CURR 249:43
more businesslike than b. FROST 338:94
busk b. my heid BALL 56:94
buskins With b. shortened to descry HERR 400:41
busses trolley b. hissing BETJ 84:2

bust animated b. — GRAY 369:15
Uncorseted, her friendly b. — ELIOT 305:35
busy b. and insinuating rogue — SHAK 760:4
b., and the tired — FITZ 325:96
b. man who can keep up — STARR 813:77
important is keepin' b. — MOSES 600:25
Lord! Thou knowest how b. — ASTL 37:27
Nowher so b. a man — CHAU 208:73
busyness Extreme b. — STEV 822:97
but-an-ben wee b.-a.-b. — MORR 599:2
butcher benevolence of the b. — SMITH 797:39
Hog B. for the World — SAND 712:91
son of a first rate b. — ASHF 35:98
the consent of every b. — SHER 787:44
want to know a b. paints — BROW 162:92
When a b. tells you — JOHN 443:61
butchered B. to make a…holiday — BYRON 180:39
butchers gentle with these b. — SHAK 748:1
sadists…become policemen or b. — CONN 233:66
shepherds and b. — VOLT 883:51
Butler Mr B.…grips him warmly — WILS 915:91
butler A'great' b. can only be — ISHI 431:93
Ice formed on the b.'s upper slopes — WODE 919:74
butlers vagaries of b. — ACHE 2:26
butter a pound of melted b. — WODE 919:60
between b. and yoghurt — TRIL 865:64
bread and b. — MACK 534:19
bread and b. — MACD 530:47
bread and b. — SWIFT 832:6
bread and your b. — KIPL 474:71
b. in a lordly dish — BIBLE 90:68
b. nor shoes nor poetry — LEWIS 507:86
crush these men of b.? — ALBA 9:86
cutting bread and b. — THAC 849:5
King said 'B., eh?' — MILNE 574:76
loved…bread and b. — LEE 500:45
manage without b. — GOEB 359:7
offered a piece of bread and b. — MACK 534:19
rather have b. or guns? — GOER 359:10
steak spread with b. — KURO 482:41
buttercup I'm called little B. — GILB 353:91
buttered b. on both sides — JACK 431:5
butterflies case of b. so rich it looks — LARK 490:23
unsympathetic as b. — ELIOT 303:75
butterfly breaks a b. upon a wheel? — POPE 661:40
breathing incense into b.'s wings — BASHO 63:43
b. poised on a pigtailed ocean — SITW 793:59
b. upon the road — KIPL 470:73
Float like a b. — ALI 12:33
guts of a b. — CAPO 189:33
sharp wings of a b. — HARR 384:99
butterscotch sun poured in like b. — MITC 588:90
buttocks Miss Universe's b. — BENE 75:8
button b., hook, and lace — LOWE 519:23
But we don't care a b.! — LEAR 497:80
fourth waistcoat b. — LICH 509:19
little round b. at top — FOOTE 329:94
wad na gie a b. — BURNS 172:32
we are not the very b. — SHAK 752:51
buttons in his b. he will carry't — SHAK 743:76
taken of his b. off — KIPL 471:89
buxom b. are and prone — SPEN 808:88
Buxton every fool in Bakewell at B. — RUSK 704:38
buy b. his work — RENO 683:8
b. it of thee — BIBLE 90:77
can't b. many business executives — FORB 329:96
farm to b. my crown — SHAK 746:67
I will b. with you — SHAK 739:50
more to make than to b. — SMITH 798:48
no man might b. or sell — BIBLE 126:67
What can you b. — TOWNE 863:19
buyer If I…found a b. — RICH 685:58
buzzard come back as a b. — FAUL 319:72
buzzing b. about between right — HUXL 426:15
by-and-by lest we should be b.-a.-b. — ALDR 11:14
bygone Her b. simplicity — HARDY 382:56
bygones In commerce b. are for
ever b. — JEVO 438:46
by-laws b.-l. are shorter — WHITE 903:76
by-product something…as a b.-p. — HUXL 425:70
Byron B. bore, with haughty scorn — ARNO 33:32
B. is only great as a poet — GOET 360:23
the poetry of Lord B. — MACA 525:52
bystanders b.…hope that he will die — EMER 313:40
byway and the b. nigh me — STEV 823:30
byword Israel…a proverb and a b. — BIBLE 91:11

C

cabal killed by the usual c. — DAVI 255:43
cabbage c.-stumps of quotations — LAWR 495:23
cabbage-leaf cut a c.-l. — FOOTE 329:94
cabbages like their c. spherical — BOYD 147:45
Of c.—and kings — CARR 196:2
those who plant c. — RABE 676:75
while I am planting c. — MONT 592:73
cabin a small c. build — YEATS 932:30
sleep…in a log c. — BIRD 130:59
willow c. at your gate — SHAK 756:59
cabinet colleagues in the Truman c. — REST 683:13
Crossed in his C. — DISR 276:65
mislead the C. — ASQU 36:11
cable c. Hitler and ask him — GOLD 362:77
cables also the rudder c. — THOM 854:24
cabooses c. of collier-brigs — DICK 269:79
Cabots Lowells talk to the C. — BOSS 145:8
Cacaliban 'Ban, 'ban, C. — SHAK 774:88
cackle c. w'en he fine a wum — HARR 383:93
cackling when it takes to c. — ELIOT 303:97
cactus garden of c. and sour grapes — MERR 567:17
This is c. land — ELIOT 306:70
cad Flopshus C. — KIPL 472:28
cadence c., a quality of voice — CATH 200:95
golden c. of poesy — SHAK 733:80
cadillac See that gold C. — TRUMP 869:49
Cadogan One-eighty-nine C. Square — BETJ 83:85
cads c. of the most unscrupulous — FRY 339:22
Cadwallader C. and all his goats — SHAK 746:65
Cadwallon Cold is C.'s tongue — GRAY 370:30
Caesar As C. loved me — SHAK 748:4
born free as C. — SHAK 747:75
C. is more dangerous — SHAK 747:90
C., now be still — SHAK 748:24
C.'s I am — WYATT 930:1
C.'s spirit, ranging — SHAK 748:2
C.'s wife must be above suspicion — CAES 184:26
decree from C. Augustus — BIBLE 115:24
doth this our C. feed — SHAK 747:78
Either C. or nothing — BORG 145:95
envy of great C. — SHAK 748:25
from C.'s laurel crown — BLAKE 135:69
Imperial C. — SHAK 755:33
in the coffin there with C. — SHAK 748:8
noble C. saw him stab — SHAK 748:11
O mighty C.! — SHAK 748:99
Our master C. — YEATS 934:63
Religion C. never knew — COWP 241:52
Render therefore unto C. — BIBLE 113:80
speak in C.'s funeral — SHAK 748:5
that C. might be great! — CAMP 186:68
that I loved C. — SHAK 748:3
Then fall C. — SHAK 747:94
what should be in that 'C.' — SHAK 747:77
word of C. — SHAK 748:9
your boy, your C. — DRYD 289:56
Caesars Compare with C. — SHAK 743:49
We were C. — RADI 677:88
worship the C. and Napoleons — HUXL 425:84
café dominoes outside a French c. — WILDE 909:32
In the Garden City C. — BETJ 84:7
cafés shops and third-rate c. — LESS 505:37
caftan Azcan in c. — STEV 819:20
cage bird born in a c. — SHAW 780:56
born within the c. — TENN 843:33
c. like grots — SITW 794:69
c. they were tricked into entering — SNYD 803:52
no more natural…than a c. — SHAW 780:53
Nor iron bars a c. — LOVE 519:10
Over the c. floor — HUGH 419:38
put in a c. if…any sign of fierceness — CARB 189:39
relentless c. of routine — PLATH 654:62
robin red breast in a c. — BLAKE 135:67
cages not in making c. — SWIFT 831:70
Cain before she conceived of C. — BROW 158:78
C.…dwelt in the land of Nod — BIBLE 86:62
conceived and bare C. — BIBLE 86:58
first city C. — COWL 240:34
Had C. been Scot — CLEV 221:81
land God gave to C. — CART 198:54
Lord set a mark upon C. — BIBLE 86:61
tragedy and destiny of C. — JOHN 439:61
cairney ayont the c. — MACD 529:29
cajolery No amount of c. — BEVAN 84:17
cake have your c. and eat it — BARN 60:67

icing that detracts from the c. — AUCH 39:74
layer c. or a road — MILL 572:8
only a certain sized c. — CRIP 244:50
cakes after tea and c. and ices — ELIOT 304:19
c.…looked green with worry — FIRB 323:69
no more c. and ale? — SHAK 756:63
preoccupying myself with…Jane
Asher's c. — SELF 727:82
Calabria C. death — VIRG 882:33
Calais C.' lying in my heart — MARY 559:19
left C. on Monday — MACA 525:45
shew light at C. — JOHN 443:72
calamities Among the c. of War — JOHN 442:51
C. are of two kinds — BIER 129:20
calamity faint flicker of c. — HOLL 407:69
forced…into…belief is a c. — RICH 686:62
makes c. of so long life — TWAIN 871:7
something more than a public c. — SOUT 805:9
calamus c. saevior ense patet — BURT 174:72
calcine C. its clods — BROW 161:43
calculated c. to lighten the tax burden — QUINE 675:52
calculation c. shining out — DICK 268:91
essential elements in the c. — THOR 857:78
What c., number, measurement — YEATS 934:64
when a c. is made — JOHN 444:6
calculators Electronic c. can solve — KRUT 481:28
sophisters, economists, and c. — BURKE 169:34
Calcutta in touch with C. — WHITE 903:80
Caledonia O C.! stern and wild — SCOTT 723:92
calendar kind of Newgate c. — IRVI 430:78
calf bring hither the fatted c. — BIBLE 116:48
c. and the young lion — BIBLE 102:19
lion and the c. shall lie down — ALLEN 12:44
molten c. — BIBLE 89:26
When he killed a c. — AUBR 39:70
Caliban C. casts out Ariel — POUND 664:38
California C.'s power to cloud — BAKER 53:24
C., the department-store state — CHAN 205:84
From C. to the New York Island — GUTH 375:48
Caligula Emperor C.'s Habits — LONG 515:38
call All C. and Answer — LAWR 494:8
c. it the stream of thought — JAMES 434:63
c. me Newt — GING 357:59
c. the shots — IACO 427:30
c. the whole thing off — GERS 351:42
dead men's fingers c. them — SHAK 755:25
true c. of the desert — STARK 813:73
What do you c. the play? — SHAK 754:94
Whatever they c. him — TENN 845:84
wild c. and a clear c. — MASE 559:22
You could never c. — SITW 793:60
called Come when you're c. — EDGE 299:99
how things are c. — HOBB 404:22
I'm c. little Buttercup — GILB 353:91
calling c. him Smith — HOLM 408:91
can't hear you c. — SAND 713:98
high c. of God — BIBLE 123:58
mercenary c. — HOUS 416:79
nimble in the c. — LEWIS 507:86
callisthenics c. with words — PARK 638:69
calm a c. so deep — WORD 926:19
A vast and tender C. — VERL 879:65
c. in our delight — WORD 924:73
c. simmer gloamin' — TANN 836:91
Cruel…but c. and strong — SHEL 784:70
flat c. with drizzling rain — BOWEN 147:30
for a c. unfit — DRYD 289:76
I am not c. — KENN 462:5
in the c. bent up we grow — ANON 20:4
Lush, c. and voluptuous — BAUD 64:61
no joy but c.! — TENN 839:55
Nor peace within nor c. around — SHEL 783:32
opulent c. of angelfish — ALLEN 12:35
something…to c. her down — JAGG 432:17
there was a great c. — BIBLE 110:18
tumult dwindled to a c. — BYRON 183:6
with a stoic c. — SOME 803:67
Women are supposed to be very c. — BRON 154:78
world's best moment is a c. hour — ABU 1:11
calmness smallest space of c. — BEDE 68:54
calumnies C. are answered best — JONS 448:17
calumny loud roar of foaming c. — BYRON 180:36
calves c. of the stall — BIBLE 106:22
peculiarly susceptible to c. — HUXL 425:68
Calvin that land of C. — SMITH 801:14
Calvinists Commercial C. — MACD 530:47
Camacho C. was very nearly illiterate? — VARG 877:36

camaraderie c. does not hold — HUGH 419:43
Cambodia C. was not a mistake — SHAW 782:6
humble people of C. — SIHA 791:30
Cambridge C. has always tried — ANON 23:76
C. ladies…furnished souls — CUMM 247:3
C. people rarely smile — BROO 156:13
difficult feat for a C. male — PLATH 654:64
either Oxford or C. — SNAG 802:33
Oxford…more attractive than C. — BAED 51:77
to C. books he sent — BROW 159:98
Ye fields of C. — COWL 240:31
came angel c. — GUST 375:47
c., saw, and overcame — SHAK 743:62
c. to those who knew Him not — SCHW 721:70
I c., I saw — JOHN 438:59
I c., I saw, God conquered — CHAR 207:35
I c., I saw, I conquered — CAES 184:25
know not whence you c. — FITZ 324:85
where we c. from — HORN 414:36
camel c. has a single hump — NASH 608:87
C. humphed himself — KIPL 473:39
c. is a horse — ISSI 431:97
c.'s hump — KIPL 472:36
easier for a c. to go — BIBLE 113:74
raiment of c.'s hair — BIBLE 108:75
swallow a c. — BIBLE 113:83
Take my c., dear — MACA 525:37
Camelot Kennedy…became C. — WHITE 903:2
looked down to C. — TENN 839:50
lost…like C. — THAT 850:15
many-towered C. — TENN 838:42
never be another C. — ONAS 625:83
rode down to C. — TENN 839:49
to towered C. — TENN 839:45
camels distrust c. and anyone — LEWIS 507:82
camembert c. of time and space — DALI 251:72
camera c. can be the…weapon — PARK 639:89
c. is an eye in the head — WELL 897:49
c. makes everyone a tourist — SONT 804:74
c. relieves…burden of memory — BERG 79:96
c. uses film — WELL 897:50
got back to my c. — KARSH 455:52
I am a c. — ISHE 430:89
cameras pictures with c. — NEWM 612:59
camp armed c. of Blackshirts — MUSS 605:15
From c. to c. — SHAK 746:46
happy if the general c. — SHAK 760:94
never fortified a c. — CHRI 214:34
opposed c. of the empiricists — MERT 568:24
campaign after a bloody c. — HAYD 387:58
c. for birth control — MUNRO 603:85
defeat comparable to…military c. — EDIN 300:9
defiant c. of civil disobedience — CHUR 216:70
prospect of another c. — JOHN 439:73
campaigner congenital c. — MARA 548:25
camp-bedstead folding c.-b. — TRAV 864:42
Campbell C.'s Hippocrene — BYRON 182:75
do not Maister or C. me — SCOTT 724:32
Campbell-Bannerman Henry C.-B. — BENT 78:82
Campbells C. are comin' — ANON 20:17
camps When I visited concentration c. — WHIT 905:22
campus students on c. — NABO 606:33
world is a global c. — LODGE 514:25
can fill the c. — TENN 841:91
He who c., does — SHAW 778:7
Pass me the c., lad — HOUS 415:70
queerer than we c. suppose — HALD 377:74
Canaan land of C. — BIBLE 87:77
Canada as the enemy to C. — MOOD 594:10
backwoods of C. — MOOD 594:8
born in C. — JOHN 440:94
C. could have enjoyed — COLO 228:51
C.…hardly exists — BORG 145:93
C. has an acute shortage of rich — WILS 916:6
C. is not really a place — DAVI 255:44
C. is paranoid schizophrenia — ATWO 38:52
C. moved from colony to nation — INNIS 429:67
C. only needs to be known — HOPK 413:13
C.…the only country — MCLU 536:62
C. was open for business — ATWO 38:61
genius of C. — MORR 598:94
graduate from C. — FULF 341:46
independent Quebec…united C. — DESC 264:27
more than C. itself is worth — VOLT 882:41
not got much to say about C. — THOR 858:1
One foot in C. — GAY 347:74
symbol for C.…Survival — ATWO 38:54

two languages in C. — SAINT 709:27
Vive le C. français! — DE 259:41
Canadian C. kid who wants — RICH 686:73
C.…make love in a canoe — BERT 82:69
I'm a C. — CRON 246:78
in Paris, I remained a C. — RICH 686:72
Canadians C.…held together — ACHE 3:44
My generation of C. — FULF 341:46
special task, as French C. — BOUR 146:27
canal fell into the Grand C. — MORR 598:93
yesterdays, for the C. Zone — PARF 637:37
Canalettos C. go — MACM 537:79
canals unreal realms of the c. — MCCA 528:2
canaries song of c. — NASH 608:76
cancer AIDS, c., nuclear war — MAMET 544:34
C. can be rather fun — HALD 377:77
c.…close to the presidency — DEAN 257:88
dying of throat c. — BECK 68:48
political c. — ANON 25:49
white race is the c. — SONT 804:73
candid be c. where we can — POPE 660:7
save me, from the c. friend — CANN 188:13
candidate c. of probity and integrity — HAGUE 376:62
c. who can whistle Dixie — OBRI 621:8
potato c. — ANON 25:61
candidates boys or scholarship c. — LITT 512:77
checks go to c. — ANON 24:33
locked c. into ridiculous positions — DANF 251:84
candied Of c. apple, quince — KEATS 459:40
candle Bell, book, and c. — SHAK 738:24
burning a farthing c. — JOHN 443:72
day light such a c. — LATI 492:61
delight for being the c. — WEBB 893:62
democracy is but a flickering c. — MACK 534:21
fire or c. for warmth — MCLU 536:60
light a c., and sweep the house — BIBLE 116:45
little c. throws his beams — SHAK 741:89
Neither do men light a c. — BIBLE 109:85
candle-ends friends called him 'C.-e.' — CARR 197:29
candle-flame feel the steady c.-f. — BROW 161:33
candle-light dress by yellow c.-l. — STEV 822:11
Fire and fleet and c.-l. — BALL 56:81
candles c. are all out — SHAK 767:93
c. burns at both ends — MILL 571:81
c. burn their sockets — HOUS 416:77
extinguishes the c. and kindles fire — LARO 491:53
Night's c. are burnt out — SHAK 736:69
candlestick-maker C.-m. much — BROW 162:92
acquaints
candlesticks midst of the seven c. — BIBLE 125:45
candy C. Is dandy — NASH 608:80
cane nice Conduct of a clouded C. — POPE 659:76
canem Cave c.! — ANON 18:58
cankered cross-grained and the c. — MACD 530:48
cankerworm c., and the caterpillar — BIBLE 106:4
cann come fill up my c. — SCOTT 724:28
canned C. music is like…wallpaper — COOKE 236:43
Cannes C.…is 10,000 people — ANON 24:29
cannibal Better sleep with a sober c. — MELV 564:26
cannibals c., And Trojan Greeks? — SHAK 743:49
cannon C. to right of them — TENN 844:76
Even in the c.'s mouth — SHAK 749:50
mouth of the c. — RUSK 703:99
cannonball c. took off his legs — HOOD 410:34
cannon-ball hatched from a c.-b. — NAPO 607:70
cannot He who c., teaches — SHAW 778:7
canoe make love in a c. — BERT 82:69
canoes light c. have vanished — SIGO 791:28
canon Art is not…a c. of beauty — PICA 650:97
c. 'gainst self-slaughter! — SHAK 751:5
most inhibited sin in the c. — SHAK 761:24
canonization sort of natural c. — HAZL 388:81
canonized c. on earth — BROW 158:72
Macmillan was c. — WILS 916:5
canopy most excellent c. the air — SHAK 752:56
rich embroidered c. — SHAK 730:77
cant clear your mind of c. — JOHN 446:60
Cricket…sentimentalism and c. — CARD 190:45
cantaloupe put a c. in a coke bottle — JONES 448:93
Canterbury compass of his C. Tales — DRYD 292:45
cantos c. of unvanquished space — CRANE 243:21
cants c.…canted in this canting world — STER 818:83
canty wad na bean sae c. — BURNS 172:11
canvas c. a sentence or paragraph — MOTH 600:33
c. is to the painter — BRIL 152:36
c. was always saying no — BEAR 66:92
certain moment the c. — ROSE 696:63

crowd your c. — TENN 848:72
put Freud on c. — SCHW 721:60
see and imitate on c. — CUMM 247:99
cap but in a fool's c. — HOPK 412:79
c. in hand the day — SMITH 801:25
flap of my fur c. — STEV 821:76
Green jacket, red c. — ALLI 13:61
On Fortune's c. — SHAK 752:51
capability Negative C. — KEATS 457:91
capable anyone who was c. — KING 470:65
c. of an infinite diversity — REDT 681:76
c. of choosing a president — STEIN 815:28
c. of higher things — FORS 331:48
capacities vulgar sort of c. — BACON 46:38
capacity c. for innocent enjoyment — GILB 354:3
c. for seeing nothing — DUDEK 293:85
c. to do — FAUL 318:66
How large is the c. of man — AUGU 41:42
infinite c. for taking pains — ACHE 2:38
infinite c. for taking things — HUXL 425:91
caparisons lay his gay c. apart — SHAK 765:39
Capernaum heard done in C. — BIBLE 115:29
capers He c., he dances — SHAK 743:76
capework rumpling C. of the wind — WILB 907:77
capital awoke in the c. — KAIKO 454:33
c. development — KEYN 466:87
c. is become an overgrown monster — SMOL 801:29
c. of memoranda — WHITE 903:80
c. punishment tend to the security of the people — FRY 340:30
condition of c. and population — MILL 570:57
consumes intellectual c. — KISS 475:97
controversy over c. punishment — FISH 324:75
empty c. snorts — SMITH 801:25
exploited by American c. — INNIS 429:67
fine thing c. punishment is — DICK 266:90
If c. is growing — MARX 558:6
pandemonium, the high c. — MILT 581:17
To that high C. — SHEL 785:92
capitalism aberrations of…c. — SMALL 796:21
acceptable face of c. — HEATH 390:20
acceptable face of c. — HEATH 390:21
accuser of c. — MACL 535:31
Can c. survive? — SCHU 721:55
C. only works well — SWEE 830:46
C. requires people to be pious souls — CHER 210:22
c. without bankruptcy — BORM 145:96
c. with the gloves off — STOP 825:64
communism versus c. — NGUY 613:81
definition of c. — HAMP 380:27
evils of c. — KINN 470:66
nothing to do with c. — WEBER 894:68
old-fashioned free-market c. — GLEI 359:2
The tombstone of c. — STILL 824:46
unacceptable face of c. — HEATH 390:20
where c. is advanced — TROT 868:19
capitalist against their c. exploiters — LENIN 502:84
any major crisis of the c. system — EAGL 297:66
c. achievement — SCHU 721:56
forbid c. acts — NOZI 619:80
gulf that divides him from the c. — MARX 558:6
patching up the c. system — CONN 233:90
substance, of c. production — MARX 558:11
worker is the slave of c. society — CONN 234:91
capitals C. are increased — SMITH 798:46
New York is one of the c. — MAIL 540:55
Capitol ruins of the C. — GIBB 352:63
capitulate will not c. — JOHN 446:69
capon cold c.'s leg? — SHAK 741:98
caprice rule by whim or c. — DOUG 284:32
Capricorn Lady C., he understood — HUXL 424:59
caps always holding their c. — DUNN 295:18
They threw their c. — SHAK 769:57
captain broken…by the team c. — HOWE 417:96
c. is in his bunk — SHAW 781:76
c. of a mine-sweeper — CATTO 200:3
C. of the Gate — MACA 526:63
c. over his people — BIBLE 91:88
c.'s heart — SHAK 764:9
got the C.…on his back — RANS 679:24
O C.! my C.! — WHIT 905:46
plain, russet-coated C. — CROM 245:69
well-bred C. of the Pinafore! — GILB 353:92
captains All my sad c. — SHAK 765:40
c. and the kings — KIPL 472:21
C. of Industry — CARL 193:39
Star c. glow — FLEC 327:21

captivate law of love is to c. — SCEVE 717:92
captive both the captor and the c. — WAITE 884:68
  c. talk of chains — MILT 583:74
captives proclaim liberty to the c. — BIBLE 104:62
  serve your c.' need — KIPL 472:24
captivity c. thence captive, us to win — SPEN 809:96
  c. thence captive, us to win — SPEN 809:99
  led c. captive — BIBLE 96:39
  nothing beyond c. and depression — HARD 381:41
  What c. was to the Jews — WILDE 908:86
captor both the c. and the captive — WAITE 884:68
captors with the c. — WAITE 884:68
capture chase rather than c. — WELLS 898:79
Capulet no longer be a C. — SHAK 736:47
car bend…with thine iron c. — BLAKE 133:26
  buy a used c. — ANON 23:81
  can't drive the c. — TYNAN 872:47
  c. and ambulance — LEBO 499:14
  c. has become an article of dress — MCLU 536:59
  Carol like a rolling c. — FARJ 318:48
  drive his c. at you at 95 mph — BOYC 147:40
  gilded c. of day — MILT 577:27
  landscape…traversed in a c. — LEGER 501:53
  Microsoft were a c. — MURR 605:9
  motor c. was poetry — LEWIS 507:87
  over a cliff in your c. — VENA 879:59
  step out in front of a moving c. — DICK 265:60
  work hard and save hard to own a c. — HAGUE 376:63
  you only have one c. — MART 555:53
caravan Put up your c. — HODG 405:42
carbuncle monstrous c. on the face — CHAR 207:39
carbuncular young man c. — ELIOT 306:60
carcase c. of an old song — THOM 854:26
carcass c. and a skeleton — TRAH 864:37
  c. fit for hounds — SHAK 747:84
  c. seemed to be made of iron — MENC 566:85
carcasses c. of old policies — CECIL 202:30
  dead c. of unburied men — SHAK 769:66
card American Express c. — LODGE 514:25
  cheery old c. — SASS 716:63
  time c. office hours — BAND 58:25
cardinal unbecoming for a c. — JOHN 439:60
card-indexes memories are c.-i. — CONN 233:85
cards c. are ill shuffled — SWIFT 832:14
  c. as a substitute — ALBEE 9:88
  Never play c. with…Doc — ALGR 11:29
  old age of c. — POPE 661:50
  patience, and shuffle the c. — CERV 203:48
  tythe o' what ye waste at c. — BURNS 170:66
Cardus reading Neville C. — THOM 852:77
care agonizing c. — NIGH 616:29
  better c. of myself — BLAKE 133:19
  boots it with uncessant c. — MILT 578:49
  c. and not to c. — ELIOT 307:80
  c. beyond to-day — GRAY 368:94
  c. for the elderly — FIELD 322:34
  c. is like my shadow — ELIZ 309:59
  C. keeps his watch — SHAK 736:57
  c. killed a cat — SHAK 745:22
  c. less and less — SAYE 717:88
  c. lost Went all his fear — MILT 581:20
  c. of external goods — WEBER 894:67
  c. of this world — BIBLE 112:48
  Casting all your c. upon him — BIBLE 125:29
  cat that was ever killed by C. — ROBI 690:37
  dark forgetting of my c. — DANI 252:88
  despair and sceptred c. — GRAY 370:36
  entrust the c. of freedom — EISE 302:53
  greatest c. must be taken — STEU 819:8
  Have little c. that Life is brief — CARM 193:47
  Killing c. and grief — SHAK 775:13
  Killing c. and grief — SHAK 775:15
  lawyers who don't c. — RENO 683:1
  life…full of c. — DAVI 255:48
  neat, clean…and I didn't c. — CHAN 204:72
  neither of them c. for — HALI 378:90
  Nor for itself hath any c. — BLAKE 134:51
  past redress…past c. — SHAK 734:14
  people which ceases to c. — ELIOT 307:84
  ravelled sleave of c. — SHAK 767:2
  sicklied o'er with c. — TWAIN 871:7
  sought it with c. — CARR 197:32
  take c. of everybody — FULL 341:56
  Take c. to get — SHAW 779:24
  the water's c. — YEATS 932:34
  took a certain amount of c. — KING 469:61
  weary fu' o' c.! — BURNS 172:26

With what nice c. — WORD 929:66
career boy's ideal of a manly c. — DISR 276:52
  c.…product of that simple observation — BEHR 71:23
  c. structure for poets — TOWN 863:22
  c. was a text book example — TIME 860:74
  close my military c. — MACA 524:27
  design c. is a process of learning — BELL 72:43
  details…of man and c. — ELTON 311:95
  for c. advancement — GRANT 366:49
  my c., my brilliant c.! — FRAN 335:20
  Poetry is not a c. — ELIOT 307:85
  points clearly to a political c. — SHAW 780:44
  satisfying c. choice — COUP 238:89
careerism vulgar c. — GRAV 368:83
careers People don't choose their c. — DOSP 282:4
careful Be c. for nothing — BIBLE 123:60
  c. in the choice of his enemies — WILDE 908:4
  c. not to drink too much — HAMM 380:23
  So c. of the type — TENN 843:43
carefulness c. bringeth age — BIBLE 108:59
careless c. people — FITZ 325:99
  So c. of the single life — TENN 843:43
  The more c. — SWIFT 832:5
carelessness back into their…vast c. — FITZ 325:99
  looks like c. — WILDE 909:39
cares all your c. beguile — DRYD 291:28
  c. and pleasures — GIBB 351:54
  c. no more for one place — SOUT 805:7
  c., that infest the day — LONG 516:50
  flesh without c. — CIXO 219:38
  soil of his shallow c.! — BRON 155:97
  where c. abound — WORD 929:60
caress can c. or tickle — MITC 588:88
  curse sound like a c. — FOOT 329:90
careworn haggard and c. — WODE 919:62
cargo c. of ivory, And apes — MASE 559:26
caricatures c.…most penetrating — HUXL 425:69
caring C. is the greatest thing — HUGEL 418:13
Carle C., now the King's come! — SCOTT 725:44
Carlyle C. has led us all out — CLOU 222:19
  let C. and Mrs C. marry — BUTL 177:67
  our best men are dead! C. — PUNCH 673:14
carnage c. drear — SCOTT 723:3
carnal heathen in the c. part — POPE 661:44
carnation could never abide c. — SHAK 745:37
carnations musk c. break and swell — ARNO 33:46
Carol C. like a rolling car — FARJ 318:48
carol fluting a wild c. — TENN 847:53
Carolina So little cause for c. — HARDY 382:70
carollings So little cause for c. — HARDY 382:70
carpe C. diem — HORA 413:19
carpenter Walrus and the C. — CARR 196:1
carpenters Like c. they want to know — SEXT 728:15
  Politicians…are professionals, like c. — EICH 301:29
carpentry junkyards of secular c. — ROSE 697:71
carpet c. on the floor — JOHN 440:88
  grazes over the c., lowing — RAINE 677:93
  Neapolitan c. cleaner — CHEE 209:5
  tawny coloured magic c. — WOOLF 922:38
carpets long c. rose along — KEATS 459:42
carriage c. held but just Ourselves — DICK 272:66
  sent a c. to bring you back — CH 213:9
  window of the railroad c. — LEGER 501:53
carrion c. comfort — HOPK 412:2
  green-sickness c. — SHAK 736:71
carrots overdo it with your c.. — BECK 68:38
carry c. all he knew — GOLD 361:55
  c. knowledge with him — JOHN 445:31
  c. us not up hence — BIBLE 89:30
  must c. it with us — EMER 312:19
  Science may c. us to Mars — REPP 683:12
cars armoured c. of dreams — BISH 131:75
  c. and sleeping pills — HALD 377:77
  C.…supreme creation of an era — BART 62:18
  crazy about c. — SALI 711:58
  finned c. nose forward — LOWE 520:49
  like armoured c. — JANO 435:77
cart carrier's c. at the age of three — LEE 500:43
  c. with the home packed — COLL 227:36
  coaxes the built c. out — PATC 642:48
  Owl, and a useful C. — LEAR 497:81
Carterhaugh come or gae by C. — BALL 56:88
Carthage C. must be destroyed — CATO 200:1
cartons slag-heap covered in…c. — DRAB 286:91
cartridges carry pistols and c. — SHAW 777:52
Caruso C. came with a voice — NEVE 611:48
  when somebody insulted C. — LOUIS 518:7

carve c. him as a dish — SHAK 747:84
  c. on every tree — SHAK 749:55
carver was the c. happy — RUSK 703:1
carving c. and colouring of a thought — SITW 794:85
  C. is interrelated masses — HEPW 396:61
Casbah Come with me to the C. — BOYER 148:47
case c. me in leather — SHAK 733:60
  c.…not entirely devoid of interest — DOYLE 285:62
  c. of butterflies so rich it looks — LARK 490:23
  c. of petty right — THOM 854:10
  c. sae hard is — FERG 321:9
  doctors know a hopeless c. — CUMM 248:18
  enclosing it in a c. of wood — WATT 891:2
  find in fact to be the c. — HOMA 408:9
  heart in a c. o'gowd — BALL 57:95
  Just like a large packing c. — WILDE 908:15
  make the best of the c. — UPDI 874:80
  making a c. — KESEY 465:74
  presentation of your fraudulent c. — ADAMS 5:95
  put under a glass c. — KING 469:63
  slavery…condemned…in one c. — ASTE 36:24
  strong c. — BAIL 52:1
  Suitable C. for Treatment — MERC 566:91
  terrible c. of the Fountainblues — HUXT 426:16
  test c. of US capacity — MCNA 537:91
  victorious c. pleased — LUCAN 521:69
  When a lady's in the c. — GAY 347:78
  world is all that is the c. — WITT 918:40
Casement The ghost of Roger C. — YEATS 934:61
casement All night has the c. — TENN 845:90
  c. high and triple-arched — KEATS 459:36
  c. slowly grows — TENN 842:8
  Lethe flows beneath your c. — RANS 679:26
  on this c. shone — KEATS 459:37
  out at the c. — SHAK 750:80
cases assess the two c. — PASC 641:21
  only two types of c. — BENN 76:29
Casey Mr C., freeing his arms — JOYCE 452:83
cash c. cows to feed your pigs — ANDE 15:16
  C. for trash — CLIN 221:87
  c. payment…sole nexus — CARL 193:28
  pay you c. to go away — KIPL 474:70
  playing cricket for hard c.! — MITF 588:4
  sold myself for very little c. — CARL 191:71
cashing C. in. That's what — NOFZ 617:53
cash-value practical c.-v. — JAMES 434:71
casino activities of a c. — KEYN 466:87
  law courts…as a c. — INGR 429:60
casket C. of My soul — KEATS 458:8
cassia smothered With c.? — WEBS 895:15
Cassius C. has a lean…look — SHAK 747:79
cassock c., band, and hymn-book — WILB 907:70
cassowary If I were a c. — WILB 907:70
cast c. fear out — GRAV 367:67
  friends of the c. — HIRS 403:8
  in no wise c. out — BIBLE 117:91
  pale c. of thought — SHAK 753:74
  shadows that were c. — SASS 716:73
  shrieks to…heav'n are c. — POPE 659:75
caste chair is not a c. — HUGO 421:92
  thralldom of a military c. — LLOY 513:2
castle batailled as it were a c. wal — CHAU 209:95
  c. brown as owls — THOM 852:75
  c. hath a pleasant seat — SHAK 767:85
  c. without an armoury — GEOF 349:9
  falls on c. walls — TENN 841:3
  Look owre the c. Doune — BALL 55:69
  man's house is his c. — COKE 224:70
  rich man in his c. — ALEX 11:23
  swimming through an aquarian c. — ALLEN 12:35
  through his c. wall — SHAK 735:20
Castlereagh mask like C. — SHEL 783:36
castles C. in the air — IBSEN 428:35
  neurotic builds c. — ANON 22:59
  War to the c. — CHAM 204:68
Castletown C.'s burning — HOGG 406:58
castor-oil c. o. of the Palestinian — ANON 25:63
castrate delights of the flesh c. me — FUEN 340:41
casts plaster c. of footprints — PATE 642:45
casualty first c. when war comes — JOHN 439:78
casuists soundest c. doubt — POPE 659:1
Casy maybe like C. says — STEI 815:34
cat Aunt Jobiska's Runcible C. — LEAR 498:89
  a wild c.'s left ear — WODE 919:60
  black c. which isn't there — DARW 253:18
  care killed a c. — SHAK 745:22
  c. in profound meditation — ELIOT 307:10

gown and mossy c.	MILT 577:23
kill each other c. by c.	MAIL 540:47
madman in his padded c.	NABO 606:32
Minister's room is like a padded c.	CROS 246:84
outside of this c.	PUIG 672:1
tight hot c. of their hearts	BOGAN 138:30
cellar born in a c.	CONG 231:13
warm delicious c.	WHITE 903:83
cello An electric c.?	SEGO 726:74
C. players, like other great athletes	LLOY 514:10
cells These little grey c.	CHRI 214:32
Celt hysterics of the C.	TENN 844:62
celtic C. Demos rose a Demon	TENN 848:69
C. genius of Wales	ARNO 33:49
chair of C.	ARNO 33:50
Rangers and C. had both lost	DODD 278:6
cement c. of the universe	SELF 727:80
floor the meadows with c.	MACL 535:45
cemented c. with tears	HERB 397:89
cemeteries buried in...two great c.	SHAW 781:1
Corde avoided c.	BELL 74:88
cemetery allot a portion...as a c.	HAWT 386:39
c. is an open space	SHEL 785:89
c. of dead ideas	UNAM 873:65
Help me down C. Road	LARK 491:34
new plot in the c.	DAY 256:80
only place...is a c.	GENET 349:7
Running a c.	ANON 25:67
cenotaph laugh at my own c.	SHEL 783:41
censor ask the writer to c.	KELM 461:78
c. foreign news	WALEY 885:91
c. the gleam in my eye	LAUG 492:67
censorious c. said that she slept	SAKI 710:38
censors c. are paid	TREV 865:59
censorship instead of...'c.'	MAMET 543:22
censure every trade Save c.	BYRON 179:97
exposed to c.	JOHN 442:38
shame or c. free	JOHN 441:14
Take each man's c.	SHAK 751:19
census c. taker	TALLY 836:86
Irish C.	MACR 538:18
centaur ant's a c. in his...world	POUND 665:59
real C.	ACHE 2:31
centaurs They're c., though women	SHAK 763:89
centipede c. was happy quite	CRAS 244:44
Central Mount Stuart name it 'C.M.S.'	STUA 827:97
centre at their hearts the fire's c.	SPEN 807:47
c., and enjoy bright day	MILT 577:35
C. and soul of every sphere	HOLM 408:97
c. cannot hold	YEATS 933:50
c. is giving way	FOCH 328:80
c. of true religiousness.	EINS 301:37
From the c....to the sea	COWP 241:54
hid...Within the c.	SHAK 752:46
muddy c. before we breathed	STEV 820:31
poor c. of a man's actions	BACON 49:21
proclaiming himself the c.	ATWO 38:50
real c. of the household	SHAW 781:74
self-balanced on her c.	MILT 584:93
slightly left of c.	FRYE 340:40
system of which they were the c.	DICK 268:51
centrelight see the blue c. pop	KERO 464:62
cents forty c. a flask	LEAC 496:55
owe me ten c., sir	NABO 606:48
Today I feel like thirty c.	ADE 7:45
wouldn't give you two c.	BUCH 164:32
centuary strange thing...turn of the c.	WEIL 896:26
centuries All c. but this	GILB 355:22
c. of rebelliousness behind him	PRIE 668:24
country 'tis of c.	CUMM 247:8
customs...evolved over the c.	POWE 667:94
forty c. look down	NAPO 607:58
how I shall lie through c.	BROW 161:33
in process of c.	QUIL 674:44
One three c. removed	CULL 247:93
Through what wild c.	DELA 260:62
Weary wi c.	SMITH 801:25
well-wrought c.	ARLO 30:62
while c. fled?	SASS 716:73
centurion c. answered and said	BIBLE 110:14
c., which stood over against him	BIBLE 114:19
century absolve this end of the c.	LEVI 506:61
American nineteenth c.	THUR 859:49
anger from the nineteenth c.	LESS 505:35
born in this c.	KENN 462:12
Britisher...early 19th c.	MACL 535:52
c. of active service	MOUN 601:39

c. of the common man	ROUS 700:39
c. on which we are entering	WALL 886:9
c. that began with a golden age	VIDAL 881:5
guard for half a c.	MOLT 590:47
horror of the Twentieth C.	MAIL 540:56
intellectual life of our c.	ARNO 33:39
In the later nineteenth c.	GILL 355:38
into the 20th c.	STEV 820:62
man...walks across his c.	LEAC 496:56
new c. begins	MANN 545:69
nineteenth c.	MCLU 536:61
nineteenth c. is great	HUGO 421:95
No writer before the...19th c.	WAUGH 893:53
problem of the twentieth c.	DU 292:70
social problem of the twentieth c.	SMALL 796:21
Sociology...in the last half c.	VAN 876:23
twentieth c. had a wonderful capacity	DUDEK 293:85
working for 16th C. Fox	RENO 683:5
Cerberus C. and blackest midnight	MILT 576:4
damn them with King C.	SHAK 743:49
cerebrums c. and smaller adrenal	MENC 566:80
ceremonial refined, restricted, c.	REAG 680:51
ceremonies c. never wear shorts	MURR 604:7
ceremonious c. politeness	TWAIN 870:76
ceremony C., circus, farce	SCHL 718:12
C. is an invention	LAMB 486:44
c. known as afternoon tea	JAMES 433:37
c. of innocence is drowned	YEATS 933:50
depending on the c.	JOHN 440:99
that reverend c.	JONS 449:27
Ceres C. will join in the dance	SITW 794:66
laughing C. re-assume the land	POPE 659:97
certain c. because it is impossible	TERT 849:83
c. leisure of study	GERB 350:29
c....something to be sincere about	DRIB 287:10
Death...is c. to all	SHAK 743:54
laws of mathematics...are not c.	EINS 302:47
nothing can be said to be c.	FRAN 335:18
nothing is c.	BINY 130:55
certainties man will begin with c.	BACON 46:37
certainty C..C.. Feeling. Joy	PASC 641:39
c. of power	DAY 257:83
no longer wish to have c.	KAFKA 454:28
certificate need a medical c.	LLOY 513:96
Cervantes C....puts me to sleep	GONZ 363:96
cervix os c. of woman	SCHR 720:43
cesspool c. deep	CHAP 206:24
leaving you...in this sweet c.	SAND 713:16
London, that great c.	DOYLE 284:46
cetacean Noble and generous c.	KIPL 472:33
Cézanne All C.'s apples I would give	AUDEN 39:85
c. liked apples	LIPP 511:64
chafe c. and toss in the spray	ARNO 31:83
chaff see that the c. is printed	HUBB 417:9
two bushels of c.	SHAK 739:41
ungodly...are like the c.	BIBLE 94:81
chaffinch c. sings on the orchard	BROW 160:30
chagrin of c. at his own	RYLE 707:80
chain adds a link to my c.	ROCH 691:67
c. I forged in life	DICK 268:28
c. of being	EMER 312:20
c. of gold	SCOTT 724:22
c. of strong necessity?	SPEN 808:78
hanging in a golden c.	MILT 581:35
lengthening c.	GOLD 361:39
Such words as 'c.' or 'train'	JAMES 434:63
tuppence for your old watch c.	COLL 227:35
chains bind our souls with secular c.	MILT 580:87
Bound by gold c.	TENN 847:51
captive talk of c.	MILT 583:74
C. and Slaverie!	BURNS 173:41
c. fell off	WESL 899:9
c. of one's own transient desires	EINS 301:33
c. of slavery	GRIL 373:13
c. of the sea	WALC 884:78
C. tie us down	WORD 927:37
clock with weights and c.	COLUM 229:61
everywhere he is in c.	ROUS 700:41
forever in c.	PAZ 644:88
gilded c. and sordid affluence	PITT 653:42
in c., in pains	STUA 827:99
Jazz...in c.	WHIT 904:21
Man...held only by the slightest c.	EDGE 299:94
Newspapers...everywhere are in c.	SCOTT 722:79
nothing to lose but their c.	MARX 558:5
not kept in c.	WEBS 895:2
not so heavy...as a prisoner's c.	EISE 302:52

safer to be in c.	KAFKA 454:27
self-fashioned c. of slavery	MANS 546:81
Shake your c.	SHEL 783:38
woman must wear c.	FARQ 318:57
worse than a c., Dungeon	MILT 586:47
chair age of the editorial c.	MCLU 536:61
a too easy c.	POPE 662:80
c. is not a caste	HUGO 421:92
c....judged by one's pants	ANON 23:78
edge of the c. of Literature	THUR 859:21
Jumping from the c.	HUNT 423:35
knocks over a c.	TOYN 864:27
passed up towards the C.	RUSH 703:96
sat in my c. and written	WODE 919:73
seated in a c.	VALE 875:12
sunny c.	STEV 819:17
tears, and a sedan c.	DICK 266:82
The C. she sat in	ELIOT 306:56
chairman Asked by the c.	STRA 826:86
C. looked dissatisfied	MIN 587:69
c. of the Senate Ethics Committee	BRYAN 163:7
chairmen hooligans...92 club c.	CLOU 223:41
chaise-longue hurly-burly of the c.-l.	CAMP 185:52
chalice c. from the palace	PANA 636:27
chalk c. cliffs of Dover	BALD 54:48
challenge guts to take on a big c.	RODG 693:93
What a difficult c.!	PEI 646:14
challenged c. you to...leap	RABAN 675:61
If one is c.	GALB 343:90
challenges is a set of c.	KENN 462:9
chamber c. of my soul	SHAR 776:37
in the c. of consciousness	JAMES 433:42
many a listening c.	SHEL 782:20
nimbly in a lady's c.	SHAK 731:99
One need not be a C.	DICK 272:65
retired into a c.	AUBR 39:71
stalking in my c.	WYATT 931:3
throw myself down in my C.	DONNE 281:90
Chamberlain less than Wilt C.	PACK 633:75
Neville C. had greatness	CANN 188:9
chambermaid in the arms of a c.	JOHN 445:35
chambermaids worms that are thy c.	SHAK 737:81
chambers c. of the East	BLAKE 133:21
whispering c. of Imagination	DICK 268:48
chameleon c. on plaid	HOOV 411:65
free to be a c.	SART 715:41
chameleons C. feed on light	SHEL 784:64
champ C. and chafe	ARNO 31:83
champagne c. and the stars	FITZ 325:96
C.!...one deserves it	POL 657:43
c. that has stood for five days	ATTL 38:47
drink c. all night and not get drunk	BOHL 138:36
Fighting is like c.	MITC 588:97
I get no kick from c.	PORT 663:3
know about c. and caviar	FERB 320:95
like c. or high heels	BENN 76:43
not a c. teetotaller	SHAW 777:59
sufficient c.	PARK 638:57
champion siding c. conscience	MILT 577:32
this pretended c.	PARN 639:92
champions mould-breaking c.	THOM 855:42
Champmédy bury my tongue at C.	BENET 75:12
chance ain't got...no c.	HEMI 394:13
All c., direction	POPE 660:15
arbiter C. governs all	MILT 581:32
art, not c.	POPE 658:59
c. as a one-armed blind man	WODE 919:60
c. favours only	PAST 642:43
c. of being drowned	JOHN 443:59
c. to read them at all	THOR 857:72
decent actor waiting for a c.	FLYNN 328:78
either in nativity, c., or death	SHAK 744:80
element of c....is expelled	FISKE 324:80
entirely a matter of c.	AUST 42:63
Fate, Time, Occasion, C.	SHEL 785:79
From c., and death, and mutability	SHEL 785:81
game of c.	CAPO 189:24
had our last c.	MACA 524:23
haven't got a c.	FIEL 323:47
honest...sometimes by c.	SHAK 770:95
I decided to c. it	PRIE 668:24
If I c. to talk	SHAK 775:8
in contempt of c. happenings	RABE 676:76
mixture of c. and choice	FRIE 337:64
my c. to see the King beheaded	PEPYS 647:28
Necessity and c. Approach	MILT 584:91
No gifts from c.	ARNO 31:87

No girls, no legs...no c.   ANON 22:66
now to prove our c.   DRAY 286:1
only c. of eminence   SHAW 781:86
skirts of happy c.   TENN 843:48
through change and c.   BRID 152:26
time and c. happeneth   BIBLE 101:85
Under the bludgeonings of c.   HENL 395:38
various turns of c. below   DRYD 291:37
will never abolish c.   MALL 542:97
chancellor C. of the Exchequer   HOWE 417:96
king, and a c., and parliament-men   SCOTT 724:35
Lord High C. in his High Court   DICK 269:79
Chancery C. Lane young man   GILB 354:8
chances take c. for peace   DULL 293:90
chandeliered mute c. isolation   CAPO 189:32
change beyond her c. of life   HOPE 411:72
birth is...incipient c.   OVID 631:47
bugles of social c.   HANDY 380:32
Busily seeking with a continual c.   WYATT 931:3
can't c.   GUIR 374:33
certain relief in c.   IRVI 430:84
c., but I cannot die   SHEL 783:41
c., continuing c., inevitable c.   ASIM 35:6
C. in a trice   SWIN 833:27
c. is always nice   EURI 316:14
C. is not made without   JOHN 442:37
c. minds   KING 468:27
c. my state with kings'   SHAK 771:14
c. of consciousness   GINS 357:70
C. proves true   ICHI 428:38
continual occupation and c.   AUST 44:96
didn't come into politics to c. the
   Labour Party   BLAIR 132:2
ever-whirling wheel Of C.   SPEN 809:14
fundamental c.   GORB 363:1
great, growing engine of c.   TOFF 862:92
how nigh Your c.   MILT 583:64
leave it to a torrent of c.   CHES 211:62
Life may c.   SHEL 786:19
more things c....stay the same   KARR 455:51
nature's law to c.   ROCH 692:69
necessary not to c.   FALK 317:39
Neither to c., nor falter, nor repent   SHEL 785:83
not the man we have to c.   PRICE 668:15
once that c. is effected   ORWE 628:55
O the heavy c.   MILT 578:47
people c. and forget   HELL 392:77
protest against c.   STEI 816:39
realise...they can't c.   STEIN 815:15
religion, knavery, and c.   BEHN 71:13
ringing grooves of c.   TENN 841:87
Speech is the small c.   MERE 567:98
state without the means of some c.   BURKE 168:29
the many c. and pass   SHEL 786:7
Things c.   VIAN 880:75
through change and chance   BRID 152:26
thrown about loosely, like small c.   MENC 565:59
Time, Occasion, Chance, and C.?   SHEL 785:79
too much c. in too short a time   TOFF 862:91
until I c.d myself I could not c. others   MAND 544:50
which involves a great c.   TROL 867:99
wonderful c. from wives and work   EWART 316:24
changed Are we correct to have c.   ASAHI 34:78
c. upon a blue guitar   STEV 819:28
not c. overnight   KAIKO 454:33
Nothing has c. since   HUGH 419:40
physicists have c. our world   SNOW 802:43
shall all be c.   BIBLE 121:19
changelessness [God's] c. means   TAYL 838:25
changes cause of as many c.   RUSS 705:45
c. in circumstances   FRIE 337:62
c. we fear   JOHN 442:43
c. we think we see   FROST 338:83
c. within a biologic system   SELYE 727:86
c. with the next block   SHAK 744:84
Do not...make any c.   ANON 23:84
don't drop...make c.   SHAN 776:29
endure sudden c.   RABE 676:70
Enormous C.   PALEY 635:9
Her plot hath many c.   QUAR 674:37
monthly in her circled orb   SHAK 736:51
with foreseeing c. in the   KEYN 466:86
world's a scene of c.   COWL 240:29
changing constant in a c. world   JOUV 451:75
loved to be c.   DRAY 287:3
Chankly Hills of the C. Bore   LEAR 497:76
channel Butting through the C.   MASE 559:27

going to watch the shopping c.   COUP 239:1
hot slimy c. slowly glide   CRAB 242:99
channels forced into c. of evil   FAUL 318:66
narrow straight c.   RANJ 678:16
run freely through its c.   STER 818:85
chant c., ye little birds   BURNS 172:26
chaos begged God to have retained C.   EVANS 316:17
Be no longer a c.   CARL 192:1
bit of primordial c.   WELLS 898:72
born to make c. cosmic   BEER 69:74
C., a rough unordered mass.   OVID 631:42
c. is a science   GLEI 359:1
C. is come again   SHAK 760:83
C. is the score   MILL 572:16
c. of human experience   MACL 535:51
C. often breeds life   ADAMS 4:79
c. of the mind   SNYD 803:49
c. of vacancy   DELA 260:70
c. remembered in tranquillity   THUR 860:53
C. umpire sits   MILT 581:32
God dawned on C.   SHEL 785:96
means of overcoming c.   RICH 686:63
must have c. in one   NIET 615:14
Not C., not The darkest pit   WORD 928:51
reduce a c. of experience   GREE 371:68
reign of c. and old Night   MILT 581:12
stillness in the midst of c.   BELL 73:75
thy dread empire, C.!   POPE 662:83
wish for nothing but c.   HITL 404:18
chap Big c. with a small moustache   WODE 919:71
c. seems bent on cheatin'   HALI 378:83
c. who doesn't care much   WAUGH 892:32
common old working c.   FYFFE 342:78
decent c. never lets his public down   FLYNN 328:77
My dear c.!   GILB 355:37
tubby little c.   WODE 919:64
chapel c. was built in the midst   BLAKE 134:56
Devil always builds a c. there   DEFOE 258:13
finished that c. I was painting   MICH 568:32
chapels all the churches or c. in New York   BENN 77:58
chaperoning implacably c. a ball   GILL 356:40
chaplain twice a day the C. called   WILDE 910:55
chaplet So rich a c....to weave   MARV 556:69
Chapman Colonel C.'s adventures   WAVE 893:59
chappie c. is rummy   WODE 919:54
chappit Dinna be c. back   SCOTT 724:38
chaps biography is about C.   BENT 77:74
chapter approach c. One each year   FRAN 334:99
c. of accidents   CHES 210:36
c. on the fall of the Rupee   WILDE 909:42
now read another c.   MACH 532:96
chapters Whole c....one paragraph   CHAN 204:82
character all novels...deal with c.   WOOLF 922:30
American c.   MCCA 528:96
As the c. is   AELI 8:54
begin to think him a c.   LEAC 496:63
Being another c.   GIEL 353:87
by the content of their c.   KING 468:33
c. and compassion   NEWM 612:67
c....bearing a child alone   QUAY 674:38
c. in them that bear rule   POTT 664:20
c. is a...cultivated will   NOVA 619:74
c. is destiny   ELIOT 303:93
c. it gives of itself   HAZL 388:76
c. like Samson, Hercules   SIEG 791:24
c. of a family   STER 817:73
c. of those who handle it   AUST 43:84
c....sagacious blue-stocking   MACA 526:71
c. so entirely distorted   MILL 570:75
c. undecided   KEATS 457:99
c. who would sell his grandmother   GRANT 366:49
contempt for my c. and opinions   SHAW 778:81
dignity of soul and c.   CARL 191:84
do justice to my c.   EMMET 313:59
effect on the Parisian c.   HAZL 388:79
emerges a formidable c.   ANGE 17:35
even in one's own c. to himself   WILL 912:24
for our c.   PITT 653:46
hate and c. assassination   SMITH 800:88
hundred pounds...bad for my c.   CONN 233:67
ideas disintegrate, his c. changes   DIDE 274:3
identity with the c.   HAZL 387:66
leave my c. behind me   SHER 788:52
man of good c.   SHAW 780:64
man's c....abused   THAC 849:88
moral c....was full of promise   DICK 268:35
more c. than the combined heroes   BROY 163:99

more powerful...than the worth of c.   ALCO 10:5
my c. I despare for   FLEM 327:61
my thoughts I'll c.   SHAK 749:54
one c. in literature   PAGE 633:77
perfection of c.   AURE 42:55
problems with your main c.   ANON 24:41
reputation, c., person   LOVE 519:17
simplification of the human c.   FORS 331:45
Sports do not build c.   BROUN 157:38
stable ego of the c.   LAWR 494:90
stamp no c. on the mind   JEFF 437:22
style' to one's c.   NIET 615:10
tell a lot about a fellow's c.   REAG 680:56
think ourselves wise about his c.   ELIOT 303:77
to her possession of c.   MERE 567:11
true index of a man's c.   CONN 233:83
Virtue...is a state of c.   ARIS 29:52
want of c.   SHAW 777:72
weak spot or two in a c.   HOLM 408:93
well as the main c.   ROBBE 688:8
Whatever its position or c.   SCOTT 722:75
What is c.   JAMES 433:44
when it most reflects the c.   HOPP 413:14
without...stain upon your c.   ADAMS 3:76
women have no c.   POPE 661:43
writing of any c.   WELTY 899:98
characteristic c. of philosophy   RUSS 705:41
c. of the design   LEWO 508:9
c. of the really great novelist   BENN 76:38
nothing so c. as its hat   HOLM 408:88
one commanding c.   DISR 277:82
one common c.   DURK 296:33
characteristics c. of the present age   DISR 276:67
characterization safest general c.   WHIT 904:12
characters Absurdist plays...two c.   ADAM 3:60
altogether new c.   TROL 867:98
C. in Search of an Author   PIRA 652:23
c. of hell to trace   GRAY 370:32
c. will step out of it   PROU 670:68
comedy paints c.   HUGO 420:74
consideration of c.   JOHN 444:15
engraved in...unerasable c.   LAUT 493:75
four c. wide   CHAP 206:24
give wit to your c.   DIDE 273:83
great c. are formed   ADAMS 4:62
high c. are drawn   POPE 661:30
I describe imperfect c.   BRON 155:84
immense number of their c.   JOHN 445:34
learn from those c.   DOMI 278:19
most dissimilar c.   SMITH 797:40
Too many c.   AUST 43:75
void of all c.   LOCKE 514:17
Charadrius Jemuel rejoice with C.   SMART 796:23
charcoal drew...with a piece of c.   VASA 877:37
Philosophy...kind of c. appetite   CLEV 221:83
charge c. that an idea is radical   GALB 343:90
meant to c. me   GERH 350:33
most serious c.   KRUT 481:29
One c. alone we give   RUSS 706:63
One thing alone I c. you   DU 293:74
that is the c....kissing!   PACK 633:74
this exorbitant c.   KEMB 461:82
charges ceaseless c.   WILL 911:2
revolutionary cavalry c.   PAVL 644:82
Charing Cross I went out to C.C.   PEPYS 647:28
chariot Bring me my c. of fire!   BLAKE 135:84
burneth the c. in the fire   BIBLE 95:26
c. is an empty hazelnut   SHAK 736:39
c. of fire   BIBLE 92:28
first Sunday in a new c.   CONG 232:45
gal in a bang-up c.   DICK 272:48
Time's winged c.   LINK 511:60
Time's winged c.   MARV 556:62
Why is his c. so long in coming?   BIBLE 90:68
chariots burneth the c. in the fire   BOOK 143:51
Some trust in c.   BIBLE 94:96
chariot-wheel axletree of the c.-w.   BACON 50:58
charisma C. without substance   CAMP 185:50
charitable single men...more c.   BACON 48:04
charities cold c. of man to man   CRAB 242:90
some thirty c.   TENN 841:99
charity called c., the soul   MILT 585:35
c. for all   LINC 510:41
C. is the power of defending   CHES 211:51
c. of its silence   EMMET 313:59
c. shall cover the multitude of sins   BIBLE 125:28
damnation of c.   WEST 901:38

Do not ask me for c.	ADCO 5:99
greatest of these is c.	BIBLE 121:9
little earth, for c.	SHAK 775:23
lives in a spirit of c.	ROOS 696:44
mankind's concern is c.	POPE 660:21
Miss Prism, c.!	WILDE 909:44
movement of pure c.	WEIL 896:32
What is that c. worth	MARI 550:63
who has great c.	KEMP 461:84
Charles grand to hear Baby C.	SCOTT 725:43
[Prince C.] is entitled to be	JAY 436:2
Charlie C. he's my darling	BURNS 173:50
Charlotte love for C.	THAC 849:5
charm c. from every pore	LERN 504:26
c....getting the answer yes	CAMUS 187:98
c. he never so wisely	BOOK 143:55
C....it's a sort of a bloom	BARR 61:84
C. never made a rooster	ACHE 3:49
c. of all power is modesty	ALCO 10:3
c. of novelty	FLAU 326:35
Completing the c.	ELIOT 307:8
Discreet C. of the Bourgeoisie	BUNU 166:65
impregnated by Brownie Vernon's c.	QUIR 675:57
Music oft hath such a c.	SHAK 758:41
no c. to me	PERTH 648:70
paused on every c.	GOLD 361:51
What c. can soothe	GOLD 361:47
woman loses a c.	JOYCE 452:93
charmer Were t'other dear c. away!	GAY 347:87
charming beauty's c.	SCOTT 724:40
c. people have something to conceal	CONN 233:70
c. thing to meet	JAMES 433:39
c. to totter into vogue	WALP 887:26
no matter how c. a bluff	FITZ 325:7
so c. and agreeable	ETHE 315:95
so c. as books	SMITH 801:12
charms Against whose c.	SHAK 744:93
bewitched with some ill c.	WALL 886:15
c. are all o'erthrown	SHAK 775:3
C. strike the sight	POPE 659:77
Do not all c. fly	KEATS 458:25
fields and flocks have c.	CRAB 242:87
Music alone with sudden c.	CONG 232:48
O Solitude! where are the c.	COWP 241:54
still thy verse has c.	SCOTT 723:95
With all thy c.	MILT 577:41
chart enigma of the fever c.	ELIOT 308:21
on faithful c. to mark	WENT 899:5
charter c. of thy worth	SHAK 772:35
condemn the c.	INNO 430:71
chartered through each c. street	BLAKE 135:58
Chartres best friend at C.	LEWIS 507:78
C., our Notre Dame	RODR 693:96
Chartreuse produced...green C.	SAKI 710:31
chase had a beast in view	DRYD 292:63
c. rather than capture	WELLS 898:79
creatures of the c.	TENN 841:97
chaser c. of white and blue	ACHE 2:33
chasm nuance...is a wide c.	COND 230:82
save himself from the c.	BANN 59:39
chaste be amorous, but be c.	BYRON 179:98
c., and unexpressive she	SHAK 749:55
c. as unsunned snow	SHAK 773:63
c. goddess	ROMA 695:34
C. to her husband	POPE 661:45
English text is c.	GIBB 352:64
Never shall be free, Nor ever c.	DONNE 281:71
what is c. in Constantinople	FORD 329:2
chastity c. of honour	BURKE 169:35
c.'s the jewel	SHAK 762:34
clothed on with c.	TENN 840:71
Grant me c.	AUGU 41:35
chat had a c. with him	ROGE 694:19
wish we could c. longer	TALLY 836:87
Chatfield bloody ships today, C.	BEAT 66:97
Chattanooga C. Choo-choo	GORD 363:8
chattels Look to my c.	SHAK 745:38
chatter insignificant c. of the world	TROL 866:78
Women should...avoid idle c.	ANON 31:79
chattering Where the satyrs are c.	SITW 794:66
Chatterly C. ban And the Beatles	LARK 491:37
Chatterton C., the marvellous boy	WORD 926:17
Chaucer c., well of English undefiled	SPEN 809:6
exuberance of C.	HAMER 378:97
old famous poet C.	SPEN 808:70
chauffeur could have elected my c.	KENN 463:45
chauffeurs simply as our c.	SUN 829:33

cheap doesn't mean you're not c.	SEIB 726:75
flesh and blood so c.!	HOOD 410:47
life...so astonishingly c.	DILL 274:13
cheat c. at cards genteelly	BOSW 146:12
c. you yet	BURNS 170:78
fancy cannot c. so well	KEATS 460:64
Honesty was a c.	OTWAY 631:28
if both sides agree to c.	FRY 339:23
it's so lucrative to c.	CLOU 223:39
nothing so monosyllabic as to c.	FRY 340:28
sweet c. gone	DELA 260:70
To c. a man is nothing	GAY 347:86
cheated feeling you've been c.?	ROTT 700:37
pleasure...Of being c.	BUTL 177:55
cheating bent on c. himself	HALI 378:83
c. their master	KIER 467:8
cheats all c. and liars	JONES 447:90
c. of the movie screen	MAIL 539:38
checked Be c. for silence	SHAK 761:21
checkerboards Dallas naught but c.	MAIL 540:55
checks c. and balances in government	ANON 24:33
cheek bring a blush into the c.	DICK 271:43
c. of night	SHAK 736:42
c. wistfully pressed against the pane	SCHR 720:40
chorus, c. to c.	ROET 694:5
Feed on her damask c.	SHAK 756:68
gentle breeze...fans my c.	WORD 924:88
harlot's c.	SHAK 753:73
hollow c. or faded eye	TENN 842:13
slapped us on our c.	KHRU 467:4
smite thee on thy right c.	BIBLE 109:91
tears down Pluto's c.	MILT 576:18
thy cold Wan c.	WORD 929:63
withered c.	SCOTT 722:84
cheeks c. and eyes as bright	ROSS 697:74
c. are covered with paint	NASH 608:79
compare the c....to a rose	DALI 251:71
crack your c.!	SHAK 763:71
Famine is in thy c.	SHAK 737:79
Fat, ruddy c. Augustus had	HOFF 406:51
mask...hides our c.	DUNB 294:98
natural ruby of your c.	SHAK 768:18
purs lolled his c.	LANG 489:96
roses see I in her c.	SHAK 773:51
stain my man's c.	SHAK 763:70
tears run down her c.	ANON 20:3
cheels Facts are c.	BURNS 170:79
cheer be of good c.	BIBLE 118:14
c. up immensely	THAT 850:25
C. up—the worst	JOHN 440:95
drink wine, and eat good c.	MIDD 569:39
Greet the unseen with a c.!	BROW 163:96
piped with merry c.	BLAKE 133:28
scarce forbear to c.	MACA 526:67
cheerful C. as when she tortured	ROBI 690:37
far more c. and hopeful	HOLM 408:99
God loveth a c. giver	BIBLE 122:31
merry heart maketh a c.	BIBLE 99:31
cheerfulness c. fixed and permanent	ADDI 6:20
c. was always breaking in	EDWA 300:22
cheeriness chintzy c.	BETJ 83:77
cheerio C., here I go	PARR 639:95
cheerleader a c. for selfishness	ONEI 626:9
cheerly But c., c.	KEATS 457:6
cheers give three c.	GILB 353:92
sounds no worse than c.	HOUS 415:49
two c. for democracy	FORS 332:53
cheer-up Music is the great c.-u.	ODETS 622:30
cheese 246 different types of c.	DE 259:37
apples and c.	KIPL 474:71
baiting a mouse-trap with c.	SAKI 710:48
Botticelli's a c.!	PUNCH 673:15
C. for dessert	BRAC 148:50
C., milk's leap toward immortality	FADI 317:36
I do not like green c.	CHES 213:98
I've dreamed of c.	STEV 822:9
maggot...born i' the rotten c.	ELIOT 303:78
no end of Stilton C.	LEAR 497:81
cheeses ate the c. out of the vats	BROW 160:26
Cheevy Miniver C., born too late	ROBI 690:32
Miniver C., child of scorn	ROBI 690:30
chef celestial c.	MACB 527:82
Chekhov C. of the suburbs	LEON 503:3
the Russians have C.	DUVA 296:44
What C. saw in our failure	PRIT 669:52
Chelsea was a C. morning	MITC 588:90
chemise Petticoat said to the C.	PARK 637:41

chemist c., fiddler, statesman	DRYD 290:88
physician and c. are soldiers	PAST 642:47
sold at ev'ry c.	FORM 331:27
chemistry by c. and machinery	SHAW 778:93
C. followed in the wake of physics	CRIC 244:46
resort to physics and c.	MENC 566:77
Shakespeare...weak in c.	WELLS 898:71
Chens C. had been living in the UK	MO 589:19
cheque c. and the postal order	AUDEN 39:81
general statement is like a c.	POUND 665:48
cheques alive and writing c.	MONT 592:70
cherish love, c., and to obey	BOOK 142:27
to love and to c.	BOOK 142:26
cherished c. and hoarded	MENC 565:59
fox...so c. and locked up	SHAK 742:30
cheroot whackin' white c.	KIPL 471:87
cherries c., hairshirts, pinks	LOWE 521:58
c....which none may buy	CAMP 187:80
Cherrill marriages is like a c.	NIVEN 617:40
cherry c. blossoms in the spring	ANON 22:67
c. now Is hung	HOUS 414:41
early c.	JONS 449:37
see the c. hung with snow	HOUS 414:43
taste the ripened c.	CAREW 190:57
cherry-stones carve heads upon c.-s.	JOHN 446:63
cherub Proud limitary c.	MILT 583:74
cherubin heaven's c., horsed	SHAK 767:87
cherubs poor black c.	CULL 247:91
Cheshire cosmic C. cat	HUXL 426:4
chess C. is the gymnasium	LENIN 502:87
c. tournament disguised	CONN 233:70
go mad; but c. players do	CHES 211:58
idea of a contact sport was c.	HUGH 419:37
kind of collective c.	BARZ 63:37
Life's too short for c.	BYRON 183:9
populations about like c. pieces	MILL 572:26
Soviet game is c.	SHUL 789:88
win gracefully at c.	MILNE 574:73
chessboard world...a c.	ORWE 628:43
chess-board called the c.-b. white	BROW 161:49
chessman way you'd look at a c.	JARR 435:84
chest best jewel from time's c.	SHAK 772:25
childhood is a locked c.	MISH 587:81
dead man's c.	STEV 822:7
His c. against	SMART 797:28
no medals on my c.	EISE 302:60
Chesterton Antifeminists, from C.	WEST 901:39
chestnut O c. tree	YEATS 933:53
showers betumble the c. spikes	HARDY 382:76
spreading c.-tree	LONG 515:44
chestnuts c. in her lap	SHAK 766:67
Chevalier Charlie...the young C.	BURNS 173:50
Chevy Drove my C.	MCLE 534:26
chewing gum like lending c. g.	TAFT 835:76
Chianti a nice C.	TALLY 836:86
four bottles of C.	SHAF 729:21
chiaroscuro c. of romance	MAUG 561:78
chic c. is a convent	BROY 163:2
Radical c.	WOLFE 920:91
Chicago C. is a great American city	MAIL 540:55
now it's on to C.	KENN 464:51
Sexual Perversity in C.	MAMET 543:20
stock-yards at C.	HEMI 393:97
chicken c. whose head has	MITF 589:31
Gin and c. helpless	BARK 59:54
Mere c. feed	MARX 557:84
Some c., some neck!	CHUR 217:82
chickens beside the white c.	WILL 913:44
c. are coming home	MACA 524:30
Curses are like young c.	SOUT 805:4
more troublesome and costly than c.	SHAW 780:55
Our semantic c.	MAMET 543:28
chid you'll never be c.	EDGE 299:99
chide almost c. God	SHAK 750:75
channerin' worm doth c.	BALL 57:98
snarling trumpets 'gan to c..	KEATS 458:31
will not always c.	BIBLE 97:63
chief Hail to the C.	SCOTT 723:5
sinners; of whom I am c.	BIBLE 123:73
chiefs c. of the Irish Brigade	DAVIS 256:66
Confederated C.	DEKA 259:45
chieftain c. to the Highlands bound	CAMP 186:70
Great C. o' the Puddin-race!	BURNS 171:88
chiels couthy c. at e'ening meet	FERG 321:8
Chigwell first sense...of God...at C.	AUBR 39:71
child A C. will make two Dishes	SWIFT 832:94
active c. do deeds of youth	SHAK 771:17

am but a little c. — BIBLE 91:10
an aggravating c. — BELL 73:59
as a grown c. — POUND 664:30
ashamed to be my father's c.! — SHAK 740:58
be a very wicked little c. — DICK 267:18
before fact as a little c. — HUXL 426:6
Better is a poor and a wise c. — BIBLE 100:75
Can a woman forget her suckling c. — BIBLE 104:46
care for the c.'s rattle — JOHN 443:84
Cheevy, c. of scorn — ROBI 690:30
c. a mandrake root — DONNE 279:39
c. cannot possibly go on — KEMB 461:83
c. comes to know evil — MITC 588:85
C.! do not throw this book about — BELL 72:45
c. from the womb — SHEL 783:41
c. has a first claim — JUVE 453:21
C., if it were thine error — TENN 842:18
c. imposes on the man — DRYD 291:21
C. is father of the Man — WORD 926:15
c. is grown, and puts away — MILL 571:92
c. of eight is many-sided — DOUG 283:31
c. of forty years ago — THOM 852:55
c. of its time — KAND 454:37
c. of our grandmother Eve — SHAK 733:74
c. of the mighty bush — FRAN 335:22
C. on earth for me — BETJ 84:99
c. ought to be of the party — AUST 42:59
C. Roland to the dark tower — SHAK 763:79
c.'s a plaything for an hour — LAMB 486:32
c. should always say — STEV 822:12
c. was dear — COLE 225:78
c. was delyverd unto Merlyn — MALO 542:2
c. whose parent is unkent — SPEN 808:67
Come close to me, my darling c. — BRON 155:91
communism is the illegitimate c. — ATTL 38:45
Credulity…the c.'s strength — LAMB 487:54
devoured the infant c. — HOUS 416:88
difference between conceiving a c. — MAIL 540:57
draw nearer to…the mind of a c. — CHIR 213:15
eldest c. of sin — WEBS 895:93
Elephant's C. — KIPL 473:41
enough to get any c.'s attention — BAIL 52:3
every c. born therein — RUSK 704:28
father of the c. cried out — BIBLE 114:16
fixity of a thoughtful c.'s — HARDY 382:65
Go c. — SEXT 728:11
God bless the c. — HOLI 407:64
good habit makes a c. a man — WEBS 894:80
Half devil and half c. — KIPL 472:25
have a thankless c. — SHAK 762:63
have no other c. — SHAK 759:65
heart…that of a little c. — THAC 849:44
Heaven born c. — MILT 575:93
Helen was got with c. — MANS 546:85
hideous when…in a c. — SHAK 762:62
I am to have his c. — BURG 167:82
If you strike a c. — SHAW 778:11
imprison the c. in her house — WHITE 903:91
Invention, Nature's c. — SIDN 790:8
is it well with the c.? — BIBLE 92:31
I was a c. and very lonely — RHYS 684:30
Jesus Christ her little c. — ALEX 11:24
keeps a secret like a c. — HUGO 421:89
knows his own c. — SHAK 739:56
land that's governed by a c. — SHAK 731:9
lay down my life…for a c. — CLOU 223:30
like a c. waking — KIER 467:13
like an old c. — BEET 70:98
Lillian as a c. — FEIB 319:82
listens like a three years' c. — COLE 225:81
little c. shall lead them — BIBLE 102:19
Look upon a little c. — WESL 900:12
Lord B.…is a c. — GOET 360:23
Love is like a c. — SHAK 729:35
lullay, lullay, like a c. — SKEL 795:92
Magus Zoroaster, my dead c. — SHEL 784:69
make the c. a man — SHAK 733:64
making love is c.'s play — MITF 588:6
mid-May's eldest c. — KEATS 460:61
most blissful dream as a c. — SHIP 789:78
mother…chose to smother the c. — MCGO 532:86
murmuring…'My c., my c.' — YEATS 934:67
naked c. against hungry wolf — DAVI 254:23
nurse for a poetic c.! — SCOTT 723:92
Ocean's c., and then his queen — SHEL 783:29
old Adam in this C. — BOOK 141:11
On a cloud I saw a c. — BLAKE 133:28

one for a c. — BEEC 69:60
perfect for me this c. — HEAN 389:5
presence of the cherished c. — ELIOT 303:83
promise kept, And a c. — NEME 610:38
receive one such little c. — BIBLE 112:67
receive this C. — BOOK 141:12
refuse in respect of our c. — BIBLE 107:28
room up of my absent c. — SHAK 738:25
saddling of the right to a c. — SHAW 780:54
saw the young c. — BIBLE 108:73
seem to hear a c. weeping — DYSON 297:64
send the c. a errand — DICK 268:43
Set his c. — TENN 842:12
simpering, whimpering c. again — HART 384:12
simple dignity of a c. — SAND 713:12
solitary c. and solitary man — ACKR 3:56
something better—their c. — SHEL 782:10
spare the rod, and spoil the c. — BUTL 177:52
speak like a c. — NABO 606:46
successful parent…raises a c. — EPHR 314:74
sweet c. is the sweetest thing — LAMB 486:42
that every c. may reach — JONS 449:37
There is a man c. conceived — BIBLE 93:51
This C. I to myself will take — WORD 924:79
Thou C. of Joy — WORD 926:22
thought as a c. — BIBLE 121:9
took a c. out in the yard — CAPO 189:31
Train up a c. — BIBLE 100:46
unsatisfied c. — GRAV 368:86
unto us a c. is born — BIBLE 102:17
use of a new-born c.? — FRAN 335:19
virgin shall be with c. — BIBLE 108:71
weep like a c. for the past — LAWR 494:94
what a c. takes in — LAWR 495:34
what it is like to be a c. — JARR 435:88
When Israel was a c. — BIBLE 106:3
when I was a tiny c. — ROTH 699:17
White as an angel is the English c. — BLAKE 134:30
who gives a c. a treat — MASE 559:35
Who shows a c. — RILKE 687:87
wondering as a c. — BARB 59:47
wretched c. expires — BELL 73:55
wrote the way a c. skips — WHITE 903:86
young healthy C. — SWIFT 831:93
childbearing closest…to c. — MAIL 540:49
childbirth death in c. — WELD 897:40
taxes and c.! — MITC 588:99
childhood about my hard c. — GIOV 357:73
books one reads in c. — ORWE 629:81
c.…cannot remain a fairy-land — BOGAN 138:31
C. is measured out — BETJ 84:11
C. is not from birth — MILL 571:92
c., my youth, my entire life — SABA 707:82
c. shows the man — MILT 586:40
c. trees were green — MACN 538:9
clear space opened to her c. — THOM 852:55
doing things in c. — GONC 363:94
dreams of our c. — THOR 857:68
England…in my c. — ORWE 628:51
everything is as it was in my c. — EBER 298:72
experience of c. — LIVE 512:80
From his c. onward — HARD 381:39
glistening galaxy of c. — MATT 561:71
I in c. sweetly slept — CLARE 219:46
in the custody of c. — MISH 587:81
keep them always in a state of c. — WOLL 921:5
memories of earliest c. — MANS 547:89
miserable Irish Catholic c. — MCCO 528:17
Old age is second c. — ARIS 29:46
one moment in c. — GREE 371:52
prayed to rediscover my c. — RILKE 687:84
prefer to return to c.? — DESAI 262:12
privatize the cost of c. — HEWE 401:71
Remember your own c. — CAMP 186:75
secret of his c. — ACKR 3:55
'Tis the eye of c. — SHAK 767:4
what my lousy c. was like — SALI 710:51
where c. had strayed — RUSS 706:62
wove a web in c. — BRON 154:76
write about their c. — PARK 638:70
childhoods c. are sowing the wind — ELLI 311:86
instead of happy c. — HERR 399:30
childish c. weakness to lament — SHAK 731:85
either knavish or c. — JOHN 445:38
It was a c. ignorance — HOOD 410:38
my c. years did pass — SURR 829:37
put away c. things — BIBLE 121:9

childishness Second c.…oblivion — SHAK 749:51
What c. is it — BISH 131:78
childlike keep that c. creativity — HIRS 403:9
children account…c.…as bills — BACON 48:87
airy hopes my c. — WORD 928:55
All God's C. got Rhythm — KAHN 454:31
Americans do not rear c. — JARR 435:86
anxious to get c. — FREUD 337:53
Are not c. more creative — MACKE 533:14
asking a man to list his c. — ACHE 2:20
become as little c. — BIBLE 112:66
Being constantly with c. — BAIN 52:8
borne thirteen c. — TRUTH 869:52
bourgeois…reappears in your c. — CONN 233:63
breeds contempt—and c. — TWAIN 872:19
buried her c. — SYNGE 834:57
c. ardent for…glory — OWEN 632:57
c. are above average — KEIL 460:69
c. are a kind of discipline — BACON 48:90
c. are an heritage of the Lord — BIBLE 98:93
C. are dumb to say — GRAV 367:64
C. are haughty, disdainful, angry — LABR 483:73
c. are instructed — MCCA 528:3
c. are more troublesome — SHAW 780:55
c. aren't happy — NASH 608:85
C. begin by loving their parents — WILDE 909:26
C. being now come to the years — BOOK 142:17
c. being taught mathematical — GIBS 353:76
c. fear to go in the dark — BACON 47:73
c. from utter degradation — LOVE 519:17
c.…gone out into the world — WOOLF 923:49
c. have lost their innocence — GREER 372:89
C. have neither past nor future — LABR 483:74
C. have never been very good — BALD 53:33
C.…have no use for psychology — SING 793:52
c. I might have had — LOWRY 521:66
c. inter their parents — HERO 399:29
c. kind and natural — SHAK 745:33
c., let us shut — THAC 849:94
c. like olive plants — BIBLE 98:94
c. love you and are learning — ANON 23:84
c.…never had any boots — WILS 915:89
c.…not returnable — CRISP 244:52
c. of an idle brain — SHAK 736:40
c. of God — BIBLE 120:74
c. of God — BIBLE 109:83
c. of immigrants — RUSS 705:49
c. of men put their trust — BIBLE 95:14
c. of my body — KOLL 477:38
c. of the devil — TENN 848:61
c. of the kingdom — BIBLE 110:15
c. of the poor — DICK 270:85
c. of the revolution — LEGU 501:62
c. of your Father — BIBLE 109:94
c. one's 'mature' critics often are — WALK 885:94
C.'s c. are the crown — BIBLE 99:37
c. shall be the works — MICH 568:35
C. should acquire their heroes — AUDEN 41:27
c. sport upon the shore — WORD 927:27
C.'s talent to endure — ANGE 17:32
C. sweeten labours — BACON 48:85
C., to be illustrious — NEME 610:37
c. were nested all snug — MOORE 594:15
c. who leave home — SLOVO 796:19
c. will one day live — KING 468:33
C., you are very little — STEV 823:19
Come, dear c., let us away — ARNO 31:82
curse of c.! — WEBS 894:77
devour each of her c. — VERG 879:63
disappointment to their c. — POWE 666:76
distinction between c. and adults — BART 62:9
examine the throat…in c. — OSLER 630:17
exercise the rights of c. — COWP 241:66
father pitieth his c. — BIBLE 97:65
first class, and with c. — BENC 74:97
For all our c.'s fate — KIPL 474:76
for my c.'s c., the power — MATT 561:71
for the procreation of c. — BOOK 142:21
give good gifts unto your c. — BIBLE 110:8
give them to the c. — MORE 597:68
'God's police'—wives and little c. — CHIS 213:16
happy home and c. — PLATH 654:72
hates c. and dogs — FIEL 323:53
having c. — WELD 897:45
heart of the c. — BIBLE 107:23
He has no c. — SHAK 768:30
how easily a priest begets c. — SMITH 801:10

hundreds of c. to death	MAXT 562:88	chill bitter c. it was!	KEATS 458:30
impression made upon c.	BRYAN 163:9	c. down the spine	COOKE 236:42
In cradle clothes our c.	SHAK 741:93	November's sky is c.	SCOTT 723:93
in sorrow thou shalt bring forth c.	BIBLE 86:54	wind is c.	SCOTT 723:97
interfering with c.	RUSS 705:51	chilli c. was something cool	THAC 849:85
justified of her c.	BIBLE 111:37	society women never serve c.	RAYB 680:43
kill more women and c.	BALD 54:47	chills Of c. and fever she died	RANS 679:21
known as the C.'s Hour	LONG 516:61	Chilterns C., the North Downs	FORS 331:28
laughing stock of c.	SIDN 790:16	chime began to whirr and c.	AUDEN 40:92
learn a lot from their c.	SPARK 806:17	higher than the sphery c.	MILT 578:44
Let our c. grow tall	THAT 850:11	let your silver c.	MILT 576:97
like c.—talk to themselves	ONEI 625:92	that harmonious c.	DONNE 279:35
Literature…about having c.	LODGE 514:21	chimera Peace without honour…c.	CECIL 202:26
little c. died	AUDEN 40:98	chimeras wild impossible c.	SWIFT 831:82
little c.…Round his feet	SHEL 783:35	chimes c. ring out with a carol gay	BOND 139:52
Looking after c.	MCEW 587:66	heard the c. at midnight	SHAK 743:55
man shall be known in his c.	BIBLE 107:48	chimley bottle on the c.-piece	DICK 268:40
man…successful with his c.	EURI 316:15	chimney by the c. with care	MOORE 594:15
marry for c.	SHAW 780:52	oak in the c.	DONNE 281:79
Men are as chancy as c.	KIPL 472:31	old men from the c. corner	SIDN 791:20
Men are but c.	DRYD 289:63	smoke out at the c.	SHAK 750:80
misfits and precocious c.	MANK 545:62	chimney-piece upon the c.-p.	SCOTT 723:14
mother who talks about her own c.	DISR 277:80	chimneys Your c. I sweep	BLAKE 134:33
multitude of unprofitable c.	BIBLE 108:52	chimney-sweep there was a little c.-s.	KING 469:51
must become c. again	RUNGE 702:77	chimney-sweepers c.-s., come to dust	SHAK 774:74
No c. run to lisp their sire's return	GRAY 369:13	chimpanzee girl…turned into a c.	PERE 648:57
nor do his c. prattle about	HOMER 409:16	vase in the hands of a c.	WAUGH 893:57
not always favourable to the c.	MONT 593:98	chin obliterated the unimportant c.	CUMM 247:97
Novelists…are also c.	DE 264:34	one neck, one c.	SHAK 756:58
Our c., and our sins	SHAK 746:52	Take it on the c.	NAIP 606:52
Our c. swoon before us	WILDE 907:82	up to the c. in heaven	MIDD 569:45
parents kept me from c.	SPEN 807:52	China C. asked for a sword	BRID 152:28
peacemakers…the c. of God	BIBLE 109:83	C. has stood up	MAO 548:8
poisoning three little c.	DOYLE 285:52	C.? There lies a sleeping	NAPO 607:79
poor get c.	KAHN 454:30	from C. to Peru	JOHN 441:16
provoke not your c. to wrath	BIBLE 122:50	In C., even one million people	DENG 261:90
put to Dickens as c.	BENN 76:31	In C. the bat is a symbol	LAWR 494:96
Rachel weeping for her c.	BIBLE 105:78	land armies in C.	MONT 593:1
reasons for having c.	RUSS 706:60	outer C. 'crost the Bay!	KIPL 470:86
rich don't have c.	NEWM 612:68	than eat C.'s all our lives	HO 405:38
secrets…must be kept from c.	DRYD 287:21	the Wall of C.	PATM 643:67
send his c. away to school	BRAD 148:65	Till C. and Africa meet	AUDEN 40:91
sins of the fathers upon the c.	BOOK 141:93	yesterday in C.	GORD 364:10
spending my c.'s inheritance	ANON 25:69	Chinatown Forget it, Jake, it's C.	TOWNE 863:20
started life as c.	AMIS 14:90	Chinese as much C. as French	FLAU 326:27
STRANGELOVE REPRODUCTION:…c.	COUP 239:99	brought the C. people cannons	PEOP 647:24
Suffer little c.…to come unto me	BIBLE 113:72	C. are the aristocracy	MAUG 561:79
Suffer the little c. to come unto me	BIBLE 114:17	C. cheap labour	HARTE 384:17
take my place with the c.	WOOD 922:24	C. nurse with green trousers	MANS 546:83
tale which holdeth c.	SIDN 791:20	C. woman's foot fits her shoe	SCHR 720:40
Teach the c. under the…tree	QABO 674:32	Corruption…is C. business life	ECON 298:80
that their c. are naïve	NASH 608:92	courage in C. culture	MO 405:90
their c.'s c.	YEATS 932:37	difficult to trust the C.	DALAI 250:67
the nurture of c.	PALEY 635:12	heathen C. is peculiar	HARTE 384:16
They were privileged c.	BROO 156:25	no one can destroy the C. people	BUCK 165:39
thou shalt have c.	BOOK 143:50	typical C. wishes	RUSS 705:45
tiresome for c.	SAINT 709:15	We said to the C.	PALM 635:21
Today, c., I am	NGU 613:79	chintzy c. cheeriness	BETJ 83:77
too easy for c.	SCHN 719:23	chip c. off the old block	BURKE 168:26
To rescue our c.	JORD 450:66	chips C. with everything	WESK 899:8
trade union for pensioners and c.	HEATH 390:18	chivalrous from all c. actions	ANON 19:90
understood by c. and animals	STRA 826:90	chivalry age of c. is gone	BURKE 169:34
unto us and our c. for ever	BIBLE 90:53	age of c. is past	DISR 276:37
victory of the c. of light	BEND 74:7	baseball…free of c.	BROUN 157:37
Wars are fought by c.	LIVE 512:79	Belgium's…beauty and her c.	BYRON 179:23
We have c.	TENN 848:63	may be seen noble c.	MALO 543:13
Well, c., whar dar is	TRUTH 869:51	nine-tenths of the law of c.	SAYE 717:83
what is he doing with the c.	CAUS 201:14	noble acts of c.	CAXT 201:21
what will your c. see?	BETJ 83:96	noblesse and of c.	SPEN 808:67
when I look at my c.	CART 198:53	sung of Border c.	SCOTT 722:84
when mum…looks after the c.	FALU 317:41	Chloe speak, my fair C.	PRIOR 669:41
whom the lips of c.	NEALE 610:27	what can C. want?	POPE 661:46
wife and c.	BACON 48:86	chloroform having babies without c.	BARB 59:50
wife and c.	BACON 48:87	chocolate cake of c.	STEV 821:76
wife and c.	BACON 48:90	c. cream soldier!	SHAW 777:53
wife is beautiful and his c.	MENC 566:75	entire box of c. liqueurs	CAPO 189:23
will not teach their c.	SHAW 780:61	chocolates c., cherries, hairshirts	LOWE 521:58
wiser than the c. of light	BIBLE 116:50	choice and you takes your c.	PUNCH 672:6
Women…fought…for their c.	PANK 636:32	any c. in the matter	JOHN 444:15
Women's love…not for their c.	EURI 316:7	character concerned with c.	ARIS 29:52
words, like c.	NOON 617:56	c. between staying married	REAR 681:70
world…begat more c.	BACON 49:37	c. between two alternatives	MORAN 596:56
world in which c. have their existence	DICK 271:29	c. does not interfere	KENN 463:27
Yes, Sir…many c.	JOHN 443:62	c. virtues only gods	ROET 694:5
Young c. [are] sooner allured	ASCH 35:80	c. would be irregular but safe	WEST 901:43
Your c. are not your c.	GIBR 352:74	Each to his c.	KIPL 473:53
Chile in C. everything yields	BLEST 136:93	feeling of c.	VIDAL 881:2

freedom of c.	GITL 358:86		
homeless by c.	SOUT 805:7		
if one had no c.	ANGE 17:34		
just another lifestyle c.	QUAY 674:38		
Life's business…the terrible c.	BROW 162:86		
measure and the c.	JOHN 441:20		
mixture of chance and c.	FRIE 337:64		
only one c.—to be strong	MISH 587:83		
small c. in rotten apples	SHAK 732:27		
while he doth make his c.	SHAK 740:69		
choices equipped to make c.	LURIE 522:89		
free to make c.	THAT 850:13		
sum of all the c. gone before?	DIDI 274:5		
choir c. of saints	DONNE 281:80		
member of the c.	LOOS 517:82		
sing in the c.	KINN 470:67		
choirboy when raping a c.	PROU 671:84		
choirs Bare ruined c.	SHAK 772:30		
last c., last sounds	STEV 820:33		
choke doth c. the feeder	SHAK 734:7		
poets…whether they c. or not	WHITE 902:75		
choked experience a c. feeling	WHITE 902:75		
choleric mild or c. disposition	ADDI 6:9		
choose c. between betraying	FORS 331:52		
c. what many men desire	SHAK 740:62		
C. you…whom ye will serve	BIBLE 90:66		
do not c. our problems	FROMM 338:82		
free, therefore c.	SART 716:54		
not c. not to be	HOPK 412:2		
spirit, free to c.	ROCH 691:55		
They cannot c.	THOM 854:17		
thou canst not c.	SHAK 774:79		
woman can hardly ever c.	ELIOT 303:98		
would a man c.	JOHN 446:57		
choosing just c. so	BROW 162:76		
reason is but c.	MILT 579:74		
Chopin After playing C.	WILDE 908:90		
chopped c. up in bits	JAMES 434:63		
chopper cheap and chippy c.	GILB 355:25		
chopsticks pair of c.…in harmony	MIN 587:68		
chord just as they do in a c.	HONO 409:31		
pick a c., go twang	VICI 880:82		
struck one c. of music	PROC 670:58		
chords c. in the human mind	DICK 270:91		
c. of summer	DAY 257:84		
vasectomy of the vocal c.	ALTH 13:69		
chores do celestial c.	CULL 247:91		
chorister Bobolink for a C.	DICK 272:59		
chorus c. of indolent reviewers	TENN 847:30		
like a c. girl's tights	LAWR 495:36		
chorus-ending c.-e. from Euripides	BROW 161:48		
chosen c. and male	KENN 462:2		
doorman, was the one c.	AREN 28:41		
lesser should always be c.	KEMP 461:92		
ye are a c. generation	BIBLE 125:24		
Christ all at once what C. is	HOPK 413:8		
ambassadors for C.	BIBLE 122:28		
believe and rejoice in C.	LUTH 523:94		
bowels of C.	CROM 245:72		
certainly have despised C.	GREE 371:70		
C. being raised from the dead	BIBLE 120:68		
C., borne in to virgynyte	ANON 19:84		
C. comes to the oppressed	RUET 701:63		
C. died for us	BIBLE 120:65		
C. follows Dionysus	POUND 664:38		
C. had not been crucified?	USTI 875:5		
C. if my love were in my armes	ANON 20:99		
C. is all, and in all	BIBLE 123:67		
C. is born in Bethlehem	CASW 199:82		
C. laughed or played	FORS 332:57		
C. may dwell in your hearts	BIBLE 122:45		
C.…of all men the poorest	WYCL 931:18		
C. receive thy saule	BALL 56:81		
C. risen from the dead	BIBLE 121:14		
C.'s blood streams in the firmament!	MARL 552:6		
C.'s blood was shed for thee	BOOK 141:93		
C.'s lore, and his apostles twelve	CHAU 208:76		
C., the leader of the sect	TACI 835:74		
C.…the self-confession	FEUE 321:21		
C. the tiger	ELIOT 305:40		
C. was betrayed	RUSS 706:62		
C.! What are patterns for?	LOWE 519:23		
C. will perhaps be a female	NIGH 616:34		
C. with me	PATR 643:71		
C. wole we claym of him	CHAU 209:86		
churches have killed their C.	TENN 845:95		
civil wars as that of C.	MONT 593:89		

come, C. ANON 20:15
do all things through C. BIBLE 123:63
faith of C. BOOK 141:12
followed before C. died ORAH 626:20
Hold to C. BUTT 178:87
Jesus C., her Lord STONE 825:57
Jesus C. his only Son our Lord BOOK 140:71
Jesus C.…Word of God BARTH 62:4
life of C. as a revelation WHIT 904:14
May Lord C. enter in? WILDE 910:59
Must then a C. perish SHAW 781:85
new illnesses brought by C. GAUT 347:69
O C., O God HOPK 412:82
Ring in the C. TENN 844:61
Saviour C. again to Earth MASE 559:35
Saviour, which is C. the Lord BIBLE 115:26
So Judas did to C. SHAK 735:23
speechless it SWIN 833:43
the South is hardly C.-centred OCON 622:24
trust in C. WESL 900:17
unsearchable riches of C. BIBLE 122:44
uphold the C. TENN 846:21
whole state of C.'s Church BOOK 141:98
words our Saviour C. saith BOOK 141:3
Christ-Church light in C.-C. hall ARNO 32:20
study at C.-C. JOHN 444:87
Christendom C. ought to feel joyful COLU 229:62
in C. where is the Christian? EMER 312:6
Kent and C. WYATT 930:98
live in any place of C. ELIZ 309:56
prettiest Kate in C. SHAK 732:33
two lights of C. PIUS 653:52
christened arrived…already c. SAKI 710:37
c. with a hundred NASHE 609:10
christening Like a c., a wedding COOKE 236:41
Christian As with the C. religion ORWE 627:41
C. gospel is the knowledge NIEB 614:98
C. ideal has not been tried CHES 212:69
C. on a Pound a Week? HARD 381:40
C. that is in health LAW 493:85
every C. in Hitler's Europe FACK 317:31
forgive them as a C. AUST 43:70
form C. men ARNO 34:72
fraud of the C. system PAINE 634:97
fruits of C. civilisation BIRD 130:61
honourable style of a C. BROW 158:53
in Christendom where is the C.? EMER 312:6
in what peace a C. can die ADDI 7:43
lawful for C. men BOOK 144:77
no C. ear can endure SHAK 730:66
persuadest me to be a C. BIBLE 119:57
sad, good C. at her heart POPE 661:44
same…as a C. is? SHAK 740:68
than a drunken C. MELV 544:43
tiger that hadn't got a C. PUNCH 673:12
took her for a C. Scientist MITF 589:7
What being a C. means PECK 645:5
You're a C.? WELLS 898:81
Christianity C. has taught us HUGEL 418:13
C. is the most materialist TEMP 838:33
C.…man's religion WELD 897:40
decay of C. SAKI 710:31
essence of C. WHIT 904:14
fundamental doctrines of C. LAW 493:86
gap in C. FORS 332:57
go first, rock and roll or C. LENN 502:89
grave of C. ELIOT 307:91
He who begins by loving C. COLE 226:19
His C. was muscular DISR 277:87
If religion is only a garment of C. BONH 140:59
like C. without hell BORM 145:96
local thing called C. HARDY 382:73
nothing in C. or Buddhism SAKI 710:42
power of C. WHIT 904:13
Christians blood of the C. TERT 849:82
C. are frightened BARTH 62:7
C. are not called JENK 437:25
C. deified death STAEL 811:48
C. have burnt each other BYRON 181:66
C. that travel in Turkey BUTL 176:36
C. will hence have refreshment COLU 229:62
dreams of Jews, Muslims and C. CLIN 221:91
Jews and Arabs…like good C. AUST 44:5
misbeseeming C. PRYN 672:93
obstructed by the lives of C. JOHN 442:57
profess and call themselves C. BOOK 141:83
Christian Science C. S. explains all

cause and effect EDDY 299:87
Christmas At C. I no more desire SHAK 733:71
Berlin by C. ANON 22:47
C. should fall out ADDI 6:17
C.-tree decorated by a Pre-Raphaelite BEER 70:93
C. tree is lighted MOYN 601:41
C. without any presents ALCO 10:2
dreaming of a White C. BERL 80:16
football is proposed at C. ANON 21:30
Happy C. to all MOORE 594:19
inform press home C. WRIG 930:85
keep our C. merry still SCOTT 723:97
Love came down at C. ROSS 698:85
night before C. MOORE 594:14
One C. was much like another THOM 853:1
Christopher Robin C. R. Has Fallen MORT 600:21
C. R. is saying his prayers MILNE 574:75
C. R. went down with Alice MILNE 574:74
Christ's College lady of C.C. AUBR 39:68
chronicle Pride…his own c. SHAK 757:98
chronicles c. of the time SHAK 753:65
chryselephantine A c. poem POUND 664:32
chubby Augustus was a c. lad HOFF 406:51
chuck C. him out, the brute! KIPL 471:92
chuckle c.…from ear to ear ELIOT 306:59
irritating c. GILB 354:17
reading of a white man's c. ANGE 17:47
chum Nationalism, and its c. DUNN 295:20
chumps C.…the best husbands WODE 919:55
church a c. stands near YEATS 934:66
all the c. did echo SHAK 732:40
authority in the affairs of the c. BECK 68:49
before his c. affiliation LEWIS 507:84
believe in the C. TEMP 838:34
Broad of C. BETJ 83:79
Brought you to c. well-dressed HERB 398:18
build my c. BIBLE 112:62
came to the village c. TENN 845:82
C. ain't shucks TWAIN 870:87
C.…asks God only for peace BONH 139:56
C. clock at ten to three? BROO 156:15
c. for his mother CYPR 250:56
c. he…did not attend AMIS 14:89
C. is cold BLAKE 135:63
c. is my text BROW 158:56
c. is of mercies DONNE 281:87
c. must be reminded KING 468:41
C. of England ROYD 701:58
C. of England WELLS 898:81
c. to God BYRON 183:10
C. which abandons KUNG 482:37
churchyard into the c. DONNE 281:79
Come all to c. HOUS 415:53
decent c. GOLD 361:51
discipline of our holy C. OCON 621:19
excommunicated by the medieval c. ANON 25:59
fain would kill their c. TENN 845:95
figure in a country c. SWIFT 830:62
found God in c.? WALK 885:99
goes to c. as he goes to the bathroom BLYT 138:23
great period in his c. MILT 579:81
Here's a c.! DICK 271:36
high c. for the true mediocre MAIL 540:48
holy Catholick C. BOOK 140:71
huge c. above…village WALC 885:80
In C. your grandsire SWIFT 831:75
into his c. lewd hirelings MILT 582:58
Ireland…an alien C. DISR 276:50
keep the Sabbath going to C. DICK 272:59
MCC ends and the C. PRIE 668:26
nearer the C. ANDR 16:28
neither despair in the c. FACK 317:31
next to the C. HOOV 411:67
no government, c., corporation OAKE 619:86
no salvation outside the c. CYPR 250:57
noticed…since I have been in the C. WAUGH 891:17
officially named by the c. MCFA 531:74
'oly as a c. STRA 826:82
one Catholick and Apostolick C. BOOK 141:97
over the sea wet c. THOM 852:75
Paris to Saint Peter's C. SHAK 736:71
prayers of the c., to preserve SWIFT 832:9
respectable as the C. of England STEV 821:71
rice in a c. LENN 503:96
see a c. by daylight SHAK 744:92
sight of a white c. LOWE 519:25
some to c. repair POPE 658:58

State is the C. SHAW 779:37
suffer nobody to sleep in…[the c.] ADDI 6:14
taught respect for the c. NERU 611:43
The C.'s one foundation STONE 825:57
true C. …lies in the Editors CARL 191:76
Unto him be glory in the c. BIBLE 122:46
What is a c.? CRAB 242:95
what you find in la c. WILL 912:11
Where do you go to c.? BERE 78:88
Where Peter is…is the C. AMBR 13:75
whole state of Christ's C. BOOK 141:98
churches all the c. or chapels in New York BENN 77:58
all the c. you can build CHIS 213:16
c. and dry-goods stores MCMU 537:86
C. built to please the Priest BURNS 170:73
c. have killed their Christ TENN 845:95
In general the c. UPDI 874:81
intolerable Mischiefes to C. PRYN 672:93
seven c. which are in Asia BIBLE 125:42
seven c. which are in Asia BIBLE 125:44
Churchill Actors…tried to play C. MANC 544:43
C. once sponsored the…idea GALB 343:90
C. on top of the wave BEAV 67:19
inaccurate to say that C. MANC 544:45
opinion of Winston C. ELTON 311:95
quotations from…C. MCFA 531:73
Randolph C. went into hospital WAUGH 890:14
trousers of Winston C. BREZ 152:22
churchman As for the British c. BLYT 138:23
'Modern C.' WAUGH 892:21
churchmen the c. fain would kill TENN 845:95
churchyard church into the c. DONNE 281:79
c. full of sailor's graves BETJ 84:2
In Drumcliffe c. YEATS 934:66
nowhere worse taste, than in a c. JOWE 451:79
palsy-stricken, c. thing KEATS 453:95
churchyards When c. yawn SHAK 754:97
When c. yawn TWAIN 871:7
Chutzpah C.—that quality LEVA 506:52
Chuzzlewit C. suggested 'Swans' DICK 268:33
cicadae host of giant c. beat ROBE 689:18
cicadas c. have been screaming BOWL 147:34
Cicero C., citing Cato KNIG 476:15
cigar c. out of his mouth KARSH 455:52
substitute out of c. stumps DOUG 283:23
then the long c. TIME 860:72
cigarette c. is the perfect…pleasure WILDE 908:7
cigarettes best c. in my experience STEV 821:76
Fasten your c. WILD 910:72
cigars I'd like…to smoke c. DIAZ 265:50
roller of big c. STEV 819:84
Cimber C. should be banished SHAK 747:93
cinder how dry a c. this world is DONNE 281:77
scorched my intellect into a c. CARL 191:72
Cinderella If I made C. HITC 404:13
wand of C.'s Fairy Godmother DIOR 275:24
cinema c. in their blood RICH 686:65
C. is a matter of SCOR 722:73
c. is any kind of force LOACH 514:11
c. is built along 19th-century models GREE 370:46
c. is truth GODA 359:6
c. was…a new era QUIR 675:57
invented the c. LUMI 522:88
cinnamon c. and cloves ANON 20:9
Spicy grove, c. tree CULL 247:93
Circe body…straight as C.'s wand MARL 553:12
elegance of C.'s hair POUND 664:36
circle c. of its influence POTT 664:20
c. of the golden year TENN 841:94
c. of the heroic STOWE 825:71
c. round the globe MUNDY 603:83
come full c. MOYN 601:41
firmness makes my c. just DONNE 280:56
forms…an untranscendable c. SCHR 720:43
narrow c. of strikes ENGE 314:67
Round and round the c. ELIOT 307:8
Sorrow comes as in a c. CH 213:10
square the c. HEAN 389:5
Weave a c. round him thrice COLE 226:15
What other planets c. other suns POPE 660:8
wheel is come full c. SHAK 764:3
circles centre and cause of many c. LEON 504:20
c. of which we are the centres TROL 866:78
mind skating c. FROST 339:18
sweep in ever-widening c. HUXL 426:5
circling c. in his desire FLAU 326:39
circuit short c. in his identity ROTH 699:14

Success in C. lies — DICK 273:71
circuits c. of a digital computer — PIRS 652:25
circulation she has a good c. — RENO 683:7
 the c. of their blood — SMITH 799:72
 work, leisure, c. — LECO 499:30
circumcised c. people — GIBB 351:57
 C. the eighth day — BIBLE 123:56
circumcision very luxury…c. — ORTON 627:30
circumference just c., O world — MILT 584:92
circumlocution C.…literary trick — BIER 129:21
 C.Office — DICK 270:8
circumstance blows of c. — TENN 843:48
 escape from c. to ecstasy — BELL 71:28
 foresee no c. — HESE 401:61
 In the fell clutch of c. — HENL 395:38
 suspect such a c. — AUST 43:80
circumstances cheated by c. — LESS 504:34
 difficult to think of any c. — OAKE 620:87
 If c. lead me — SHAK 752:46
 more serious…in my present c. — SIDN 790:98
 pain of particular c. — CART 198:39
 things in terrible c. — MO 589:23
circumstantial How c. reality is! — UPDI 874:88
 no further than the Lie C. — SHAK 750:90
circus ain't shucks to a c. — TWAIN 870:87
 celebrated Barnum's c. — CHUR 216:69
 chess tournament disguised as a c. — CONN 232:51
 c. remains the same — ASHD 35:90
 gets the c. it deserves — JONG 448:5
 no right in the c. — MAXT 562:89
cirrhosis end up with c. of the liver — EAGL 297:65
cistern wheel broken at the c. — BIBLE 101:92
cisterns broken c. — BIBLE 105:68
citadel Coketown…ugly c. — DICK 270:4
 Troy's sacred c. — HOMER 409:24
cithera universe is arranged like a c. — HONO 409:31
cities American life, in large c. — MCCA 528:97
 c. and their civilities — PATM 643:67
 c. are divided into two parts — BROW 160:16
 c. of men — TENN 839:63
 c., throbbed the true life — NORR 618:65
 c. will have no rest from evils — PLATO 655:98
 do not look in great c. — AUST 43:74
 founder of c.! — COLUM 229:58
 friends…are in c. — SNYD 802:47
 great kings and fine c. — CATU 201:9
 hum Of human c. torture — BYRON 180:26
 impure love for c. — CASAL 199:68
 inquire of all the C. — ALBE 10:99
 In today's c.…on the outskirts — GENET 349:7
 Islanded by c. fair — SHEL 783:28
 Of towns and c. — WORD 923:69
 protect American c. — SCHL 718:16
 prowling through the c. — ORWE 629:83
 ruined c. of Germany — ORWE 629:80
 seek a livelihood…in c. — CANT 188:16
 Soveraign of c. — DUNB 294:5
 streets of a hundred c. — HOOV 411:57
 sung women in three c. — POUND 664:23
 Towered c. pleased — MILT 576:10
 whose c. he saw — HOMER 409:24
citizen am to become a private c. — EISE 302:59
 c. of life — SASS 716:58
 c. of no mean city — BIBLE 119:54
 c. of the proudest country — PARK 638:83
 c. of the world — BOSW 146:11
 I am a Roman c. — CICE 218:25
 liberty that the c. enjoys — SPEN 807:43
 No cold relation is a zealous c. — BURKE 169:43
 not lay aside the c. — WASH 890:81
 Sophia Loren is not a c. — GRAMM 366:43
 transformed…into the perfect c. — DOUG 283:31
citizens all c. should be free — MORE 597:67
 beat to death those c. — MAMET 543:23
 c. dream of the south and west — HARDY 382:76
 c. of Berlin — KENN 463:33
 c. of death's grey land — SASS 716:60
 c. of that other place — SONT 804:77
 fat and greasy c. — SHAK 749:35
 Healthy c. are the greatest asset — CHUR 217:89
 prosperous c. of Zenith — LEWIS 507:87
 State, or of c. — RUSK 704:17
 universality of c. speaking — MAZZ 562:2
citizenship more onerous c. — SONT 804:77
 union, before his c. — LEWIS 507:84
city amid the c.'s jar — ARNO 31:2
 balloon, coming out of a keen c. — CUMM 247:6

Beautiful c.! — ARNO 33:39
belonging to a race…a c., a group — DUDEK 293:81
Brave men are a c.'s strongest tower — ALCA 10:1
citizen of no mean c. — BIBLE 119:54
c.…is a human zoo — MORR 598:92
c. is built to music — TENN 847:59
C. now doth like a garment wear — WORD 926:19
c. of all time — HAWT 386:52
C. of London…clearing-house — CHAM 203:58
C. of perspiring dreams — RAND 679:29
C. of the Big Shoulders — SAND 712:91
c.…out of step with the century — CHEE 209:98
c. shoulderingly upwards — CUMM 247:1
c. that is set on an hill — BIBLE 109:85
c. there is a group — LESS 505:36
c. was on one side — MUNCH 603:80
c. where most people live — GRAY 368:90
c. will follow you — CAVA 201:17
decline and fall of the C. — GIBB 352:63
depart out of that house or c. — BIBLE 111:25
died…in sight of the c. — MACA 527:78
escaped From the vast c. — WORD 924:88
Every c. has a sex and age — BERG 79:1
except the Lord keep the c. — BIBLE 98:92
fall in love with a c. — MORR 599:4
felled a c. — THOM 852:62
first c. Cain — COWL 240:34
fishbone in the c.'s throat — LOWE 520:48
forbid…in the c. in future — EDWA 300:15
great noise in the c. — EDWA 300:15
hard-boiled c. — CHAN 205:85
heart of the c. — MOYN 601:41
Hell is a c. — SHEL 784:51
history of C. architecture — JOHN 441:2
How doth the c. sit solitary — BIBLE 105:79
if you would know…live in a c. — COLT 229:56
in the c. of our God — BIBLE 95:27
Like c. lights, receding — GIBS 353:76
looking over harbor and c. — SAND 713:92
make glad the c. of God — BIBLE 95:25
man whom the c. sets up — SOPH 804:84
men that make a c. — NICI 614:91
modern c., it takes on — RODR 693:96
New York was no mere c. — DIDI 274:6
O c. of God — BIBLE 96:48
Of two f's…is this c. — MATOS 561:66
Once in royal David's c. — ALEX 11:24
on the field and c. — THAC 849:90
Paris is a beast of a c. — HAZL 388:79
play-going in any large c. — TYNAN 872:44
precipitous c. — STEV 824:38
prepared for them a c. — BIBLE 124:97
private individual or for a c. — PLATO 655:3
realm, nation, or c. — KNOX 476:18
roofs of this distracted C. — CARL 192:7
run about through the c. — BOOK 143:56
sacred c. of the mind — CAMP 186:59
streets of the c. — MCCA 527:88
Sun-girt c., thou hast been — SHEL 783:29
that sweet C. — ARNO 33:44
The C. is of Night — THOM 856:61
The C. is of Night — THOM 856:62
The C.'s voice — SHEL 783:30
thin trees in a c. square — LOWE 519:25
This rortie wretched c. — SMITH 801:25
took the c. — BIBLE 90:64
Towery c. — HOPK 412:91
Unless the Lord guards the c. — BIBLE 127:93
Unreal C. — ELIOT 305:54
vastly overrated c. — BURG 167:84
very fine c. — DEFOE 258:23
Without a c. wall — ALEX 11:25
Zion, c. of our God! — NEWT 613:77
civet Give me an ounce of c. — SHAK 763:89
civil as for its c. use — MONT 593:98
 assault on our c. liberties — GORE 364:12
 British C. Service — WILL 912:13
 c. and obliging young woman — AUST 42:57
 c., political, and religious — JUNI 453:11
 c. servant doesn't make jokes — IONE 430:75
 c. servant lyricism — BAND 58:25
 C. Service is profoundly deferential — CROS 246:84
 c. To everyone — SISS 793:55
 C. war is impossible — PAVL 644:81
 c. war obstructs the crusade — INNO 430:1
 corresponding c. society — MARX 557:1
 dire effects from c. discord flow — ADDI 7:39

Here lies a c. servant — SISS 793:55
He was very c., 'Masa — DAVI 254:40
horror of c. war — HOMER 409:21
How can I be c. — GERS 350:39
In a c. war, a general must know — REED 682:84
In c. business; What first? — BACON 48:7
Pray, good people, be c. — GWYN 375:51
too c. by half — SHER 787:42
civilities bandy c. with my sovereign — JOHN 443:85
 cities and their c. — PATM 643:67
civility Scotch c. — ROCH 691:54
 see a wild c. — HERR 400:50
civilization advance the cause of c. — BRIL 153:39
 All c. has from time to time — ELLIS 311:82
 all of c.'s obstacles — SAND 712:82
 amenities of c. — MACD 530:48
 as c. spreads — TOCQ 861:80
 centers of European c. — TOLS 863:8
 c. and profits — COOL 236:44
 c. don't advance — ROGE 695:21
 C. has made the peasantry — TROT 867:17
 C. is a conspiracy — BUCH 164:25
 C. is a movement — TOYN 864:28
 c. is based on the…materialistic — BONA 139:51
 c.…is coupled with death — MILL 573:55
 c. is essentially one of property — EMER 313:37
 C. itself is a…balance — POUND 665:56
 c. of one epoch — CONN 233:80
 c. works its miracles — TOCQ 861:81
 continuity of c. — ORWE 629:80
 curriculum vitae of C. — ANDR 16:25
 depart from that c. — LISP 512:74
 destroying the c. — LIND 510:43
 Every c. that has ever existed — KISS 475:94
 fall of the last c. — READ 680:49
 farmyard c. of the Fabians — INGE 429:53
 fate of human c. — LOVE 519:18
 For a botched c. — POUND 665:40
 fruits of Christian c. — BIRD 130:61
 great movements of…human c. — BENN 77:58
 green end of one of c.'s hardest winters — FOWL 332:68
 habit of c. — WEST 901:38
 highest standard of c. — LLOY 513:1
 incompatible with c. — COOP 236:52
 inheritors of an old c. — REYES 684:21
 life-blood of real c. — TREV 865:57
 long last night over c. — MAIL 540:50
 mark of high c. — BERL 80:21
 passive, receptive side of c. — SPEN 807:65
 principal task of c. — FREUD 336:52
 quarrel of c. against — ROOS 696:59
 rottenness of our c. — READ 680:47
 saddest object in c. — STEV 824:41
 stupid of modern c. — KNOX 476:23
 sweetness of present c. — HUGO 421:97
 they maintain c. — TOCQ 862:88
 to imbue c. — JOHN 438:51
 undeniable pretensions as c. — PITT 653:45
 under our existing c. — STAN 812:64
 vulgar sort of c. — BURG 167:85
 wall…separates c. from barbarism — BUCH 164:24
 What do I think of Western c.? — GAND 345:36
 whole history of c. — JAMES 434:66
 without the usual interval of c. — CLEM 221:78
civilizations autonomous c. — SONT 804:73
 c. that abandon the quest for knowledge — LOVE 519:19
civilize adopt me and c. me — TWAIN 871:12
 allowed she would c. me — TWAIN 871:94
civilized c. human life — TRUM 868:34
 contact with the more c. — THOR 857:80
 highly c. human beings — ORWE 628:58
 I have become c. — BIRD 130:59
 society here would be quite c. — WILDE 909:50
 the more c.…the people — DIDE 273:89
civilizers two c. of man — DISR 277:78
civil-suited c.-s. Morn — MILT 577:20
clack whet their beaks c. — RANS 679:24
claim c. on your respect — JUVE 453:21
 c. those f. — TROL 866:79
 if the c. were broken — SHAW 778:1
 no human c.…significance — OATES 620:95
 on every beauty's c.? — CRUZ 246:87
claimant failed to embarrass the c. — STRA 826:86
clairvoyant Hate is always more c. — LACL 484:86
 People also claim to be c. — BOWL 147:38
clamorous with such a c. smack — SHAK 732:40
clamours c. soars and shrills — ROBE 689:18

clan Against the c. M'Tavish	AYTO 45:16	**Clavering** C., and Havering	LEVE 506:58
c. has a tendency to ignore me	WODE 919:58	**Claver'se** 'twas C. who spoke	SCOTT 725:58
Clancy C., of the Overflow'	PATE 642:55	**claw** red in tooth and c.	TENN 843:36
clanjamfrie haill c.	MACD 529:27	red in tooth and c.	TENN 843:45
clannish exceedingly c. family	SHAW 781:1	**claws** c. that catch	CARR 195:90
clap Don't c. too hard	OSBO 630:12	neatly spreads his c.	CARR 194:65
trees of the field shall c.	BIBLE 104:57	pair of ragged c.	ELIOT 304:21
Clapham safe back to C. Junction?	BUTL 178:74	**clay** Art's subject is the human c.	AUDEN 39:85
claret c. and burgundy in Scotland?	SMITH 798:48	C. blurs the whitewash	AVIS 44:6
C. is the liquor	JOHN 445:37	c. grew tall	OWEN 632:64
C. on my Tomb	KEATS 458:12	C. lies still	HOUS 414:44
clarets racehorses and the cheaper c.	SAKI 710:34	compounded am with c.	SHAK 772:29
clarions Great winds Thy c.	ELLE 310:71	dead and turned to c.	SHAK 755:33
clarity c. is a great liability	BALF 55:57	feet…of iron and part of c.	BIBLE 105:94
C. of mind results in	PASC 640:8	from gold and c.	SHEL 786:10
universal and unbounded c.	JOHN 441:9	Honouring itself the c. rears up	BARK 59:55
clark c. ther was of Oxenford	CHAU 208:71	loam, or painted c.	SHAK 734:99
clash c. together again	TENN 847:33	made of c.	GERS 351:45
class c. lies late and snores	CULL 247:91	of c. and wattles	YEATS 932:30
c. of declassed women	DUMAS 294:94	out of the miry c.	BIBLE 95:18
c. struggle…leads to the dictatorship	MARX 558:16	Potter and c. endure	BROW 162:70
could have had c.	SCHU 720:47	power over the c.	BIBLE 120:79
decay of ability in the ruling c.	ORWE 628:61	pure c. of time's mud	MALA 541:84
educated c.…hate us	CHEL 210:16	shall the c. say to him	BIBLE 103:45
Every known c. of refusal	SOME 803:67	**clean** Bath twice…to be really c.	BURG 167:83
every other c. in the community	RICA 685:35	C. from my hand?	SHAK 767:5
he gave her c.	HEPB 396:60	c. hands	GALS 344:26
history of c. struggles	MARX 558:2	grew more c. and white	BROW 159:8
like any other c.	TAWN 837:8	one more thing to keep c.	FRY 340:26
lowest c. is literary footmen	HAZL 388:90	Then I was c. and brave	HOUS 414:47
make the bourgeoisie a c.	HUGO 421:92	thugh dirty is c.	FLEM 327:62
men of any other c.	LODGE 515:29	trying to play c.	PARK 637:39
no other c. of dependants	MILL 570:75	until your bones are c.	ADCO 5:99
one c. is made to feel	DOUG 284:37	upbringings that were so c.	COUP 238:97
prosperity…through every c.	BRYAN 163:8	vanished c.	GURN 375:43
raise them as a c.	SMIL 797:34	will these hands ne'er be c.?	SHAK 768:34
sector of the liberal middle c.	EAGL 297:66	Wondrously c.	WALP 887:27
sinking middle c.	ORWE 628:47	**cleaners** father had a chain of dry c.	BENN 76:35
spokesman of a c.	CHAM 203:57	**cleanest** c. and beautifullest	DEFOE 258:23
very low c. among the European states	GEOR 349:12	**cleaning** Yesterday, We had daily c.	REED 681:77
We are talking c.	KILP 467:19	**cleanliness** C. is next to Godliness	DICK 271:26
Yuppies as a c.	ADLER 7:50	c. of…backyards	MAIL 540:58
classes All c. of society	JEVO 438:47	**clear** c., attentive mind	SNYD 802:48
c. of people	GARL 346:49	free and c. from any image	SHAK 757:87
c. within c. in Peckham	SPARK 806:19	how thin and c.	TENN 841:4
Comfort came in with the middle c.	BELL 71:31	might be too c.	GREE 372:84
curse of the drinking c.	WILDE 910:66	not immediately c.	THUR 859:45
disappearance of the middle c.	COUP 238:92	so c. and distinct	HUXL 426:8
divided into two c.	RUSK 704:22	unduly c.	GREE 372:81
equally on all c.	CHUR 216:63	want to make that very c.	ROMN 695:36
gathered together in c.	SMITH 800:96	**cleared** not matter how carefully c.	SHUL 789:90
General Strike has taught the working c.	BALF 54:55	**clearer** see a little c.	BRAC 148:51
Let the ruling c.	MARX 558:5	**clear-eyed** c.-e. adjustments	DAY 256:76
lower c. had such white skins	CURZ 250:54	**clearing-house** c.-h. of the world	CHAM 203:58
masses against the c.	GLAD 359:93	**clears** water c. us of this deed	SHAK 767:6
patsies for the ruling c.	HELL 392:79	**clear-sighted** c.-s. nor accurate	TROL 867:7
prove that the existence of c.	MARX 558:10	not the c.-s. who rule the world	CONR 235:19
Society is composed of two large c.	CHAM 204:69	**cleavage** c. contributes to narrow	ROSS 697:72
sports for the old ruling c.	HOBS 405:35	**cleft** c. for me	TOPL 863:15
the privileged c.?	SIEY 791:26	**clefts** narrow the cross c.	ROSS 697:72
To prove the upper c.	COWA 239:18	**clench** can c. and fight	MITC 588:88
two c. in good society	SHAW 781:73	**clenched** held my flower in a c. fist	HOFF 406:48
two c. of books	FORD 330:3	**clenches** wit degenerating into c.	DRYD 288:25
two c. of travel	BENC 74:97	**Cleopatra** C.'s morality	LAUT 493:78
wrote about the working c.	WAUGH 893:53	C.'s nose: if it had been shorter	PASC 640:17
classic A c.	TWAIN 872:33	down the Nile last night as C.	BROWN 157:43
No c. resembles any previous c.	HEMI 394:23	gone to gaze on C.	SHAK 765:24
tread on c. ground	ADDI 5:2	in the bed of C.	BROW 159:97
classical c. era was epic	HUGO 420:60	not…less than C.	DRYD 289:56
c. music and jazz	PREV 667:9	**clergy** all the c. you can despatch	CHIS 213:16
c. music of now	MCCA 528:12	c. were beloved	SWIFT 832:13
c. period was healthy	GOET 360:22	without the benefit o' the C.	CONG 231:12
C. quotations is the parole	JOHN 446:51	**clergyman** salary of a beneficed c.	WAUGH 892:21
classics bellyful of the c.	MILL 572:17	**clergymen** men, women, and c.	SMITH 801:16
c. are only primitive literature	LEAC 497:65	**clerical** features of c. cut	ELIOT 307:6
keep the C. at hand	WOOLF 923:53	**clerk** an unmannerly fat c.	SHER 787:44
the c. in paraphrase!	POUND 664:37	both the priest and c.?	SHAK 735:23
used to be c.	WAUGH 892:40	grete c. of nygromancye	MALO 542:1
classification c. of all things	DURK 296:33	small c. of some hotel	MANS 547:87
find fault with a c.	MILL 570:73	small house agent's c.	ELIOT 306:60
classless c. society	MARX 558:16	was the best c..	MACA 524:29
classroom Socrates in every c.	GRIS 373:18	**clerks** c. been noght wisest men	CHAU 209:84
clatter c. of high voices	DOYLE 285:56	**clever** c., but is it Art?	KIPL 471:4
draws the curtains…with a great c.	OSBO 630:11	c. enough to get all that money	CHES 212:88
Claudius Emperor C.	LONG 515:39	c. to a fault	BROW 161:50
clause but this one c.	RABE 676:73	Everything c. has been thought	GOET 360:18
Clavell How to frighten Miss C.	BEME 74:94	manage a c. man	KIPL 470:75

too c. by half	MAJOR 541:72	
cleverness The obstinancy of c.	STOWE 826:78	
cliché books, convention and c.	POUND 664:24	
c. and an indiscretion	MACM 536:68	
c. of whites being ignorant	ANGE 17:46	
clichés half-truths and c.	TOOLE 863:12	
click constant c. and kissing	BETJ 84:2	
clicking c. with the subject	EISE 302:65	
client c. is fain to hire a lawyer	BUTL 176:36	
c. must be led to safety	MORT 599:13	
dialogue between c. and architect	STERN 817:65	
serving the c.	JOHN 440:98	
venomous, and ungrateful c.	UPDI 874:80	
cliff drive over a c.	VENA 879:59	
edge of some crazy c.	SALI 711:61	
far from c. and scar	TENN 841:4	
In a coign of the c.	SWIN 834:51	
lawyers going over a c.	HUNT 423:23	
like jumping off a c.	BRYAN 163:7	
off the edge of the c.	MOND 590:49	
cliffs chalk c. of D.	BALD 54:48	
c. of fall	HOPK 413:5	
rubies in certain c.	MORE 597:68	
yet still the solitary c.	WORD 924:87	
climate c. allows him no chance	KIPL 470:82	
c. is bracing	MCGO 531:79	
c. of a perpetual Turkish bath	SWET 830:47	
c. of Manitoba	ANON 21:34	
c. suspends…understanding	BROO 155:1	
cloudy c.	BYRON 181:60	
common where the c.'s sultry	BYRON 181:65	
enquiries about the UK c.	SAMU 712:81	
fertile c. dwell	SHAK 759:51	
in love with a cold c.	SOUT 805:95	
not so much the result of c.	FUSE 342:74	
our chilling c.	SWIFT 832:95	
spring in their c.	DOUG 283:22	
whole c. of opinion	AUDEN 40:99	
Your anger was a c.	PIER 651:7	
climates and manners, c., council	TENN 839:63	
climax cap and c. of…years	PEARY 645:1	
flaming, fatal c.	SASS 716:60	
works its way up to a c.	GOLD 362:84	
climb teach ye how to c.	MILT 578:44	
climbing c. a birch tree	FROST 338:92	
c. into jobs	REST 683:16	
C. over rocky mountain	GILB 354:96	
clime born in the same c.	BYRON 182:83	
Love…no season knows, nor c.	DONNE 279:41	
sweet golden c.	BLAKE 134:53	
visit our c.	BLAKE 133:23	
climes styles for different c.	BROD 153:47	
clinging c. blindly to the vices	FAUL 318:62	
clingy bunches of c. sob sisters	PAGL 634:82	
Clinton classic Bill C., sincere	MARA 548:22	
C., the one indispensable…nation	VIDAL 881:9	
give C. his due	VIDAL 881:8	
Hillary C. is responsible	MCCU 529:24	
impeachment against William Jefferson C.	ANON 25:80	
Mr C.…is our first black President	MILL 572:13	
President C. returned today	DOWD 284:40	
cloak c.…an iron cage	WEBER 894:67	
knyf under the c.	CHAU 208:81	
cloaks c. for untidy minds	MOND 590:50	
display of rich c.	DICK 267:25	
clock Church c. at ten to three?	BROO 156:15	
c. is always slow	SERV 728:4	
c. with weights and chains	COLUM 229:61	
hands of a great c.	WILL 913:41	
I open with a c. striking	SHER 788:65	
produce? The cuckoo c.	WELL 897:48	
putting the c. on half an hour	KIER 467:14	
regard the hand of the c.	LECO 499:29	
time runs, the c. will strike	MARL 552:6	
watch the c. for you	SHAK 771:23	
wind up the c.	STER 817:68	
clockmakers Swiss c.	STRA 826:91	
clocks all the c. in the city	AUDEN 40:92	
c. the tongues of bawds	SHAK 741:94	
c. were striking thirteen	ORWE 629:97	
morning c. will ring	HOUS 414:45	
Stop all the c.	AUDEN 40:89	
clockwork c. orange	BURG 167:81	
every 30 years like c.	SIMON 792:40	
clod turned her into the c.	ALTH 13:71	
clods Calcine its c.	BROW 161:43	
c. and trampled earth	MUIR 602:56	

clog c. the foot of a flea SHAK 757:82
clogs age to quit their c. MILT 579:83
c....lasted longer than shoes WILS 915:89
c....which else might oversoar SHEL 785:81
clumping...all in c. ORWE 627:35
To hang c. on 'em SHAK 759:65
cloister c. without a library GEOF 349:9
in the court a c. AELR 8:55
studious c.'s pale MILT 577:22
cloisters quiet collegiate c. CLOU 223:34
clones c. have hung HUGH 419:34
Clootie Satan, Nick, or C. BURNS 170:77
Cloots auld C., I ken ye're thinkan BURNS 170:78
close c. of day YEATS 933:44
C. the play KAUF 456:61
day must have its c. STOWE 826:76
ineffective from c. up SCHO 720:36
live too c. to each other GOLD 360:32
still hasten to a c. COWP 240:47
closes c. Saturday night KAUF 455:55
or flowered c. SWIN 833:39
closest human beings who seem c. PRIE 668:22
closet forth the c. brought a heap KEATS 459:40
I'll to thy c. SHAK 731:94
put me in the C. DICK 272:62
when thou prayest, enter into thy c. BIBLE 110:97
closets Out of the c. ANON 23:9
closing opening and c. of a door SAND 713:99
you have a hell of a c. REAG 681:67
cloth Fine c. is never out of fashion FULL 341:65
new c. unto an old garment BIBLE 111:21
On a c. untrue GILB 355:28
clothe c. my naked villainy SHAK 731:7
clothed C. with his breath TENN 847:48
c. with the heavens TRAH 864:39
clothes Angels were, but with c. LOVE 519:15
as if she were taking off all her c. COLE 227:28
as much for her c. as for herself WHAR 901:46
being to buy new c. MONT 591:67
brand-new suit of c. HERB 399:24
buy a teenager new c. WHITE 903:90
c. and hair were neat GUNT 375:41
C. are our weapons CART 198:37
c. easy to copy SCHI 718:98
C. make the poor invisible HARR 383:89
c. off and hang her up NATI 610:25
c. possess an influence ALCO 10:5
c. were all tarnished MOORE 594:18
covered him with c. BIBLE 91:8
don't design c., I design dreams LAUR 492:68
earthly interests...held up, by C. CARL 192:93
Englishwoman's c. SITW 794:74
Fine c. are good JOHN 445:17
Good c. open all doors FULL 341:67
good smell of old c. BROO 156:5
Italy been a dealer in second-hand c. MARI 550:54
Kindles in c. a wantonness HERR 400:50
liars in old c. MARQ 554:38
liquefaction of her c. HERR 400:49
make a suit of c. HUME 422:10
married, not unto my c. SHAK 732:39
musty odour of old c. ACKR 3:54
not quite enough c. WILDE 909:47
Old C. are not venerable CARL 192:2
old c. know who's master SHER 787:37
On the state of her c. NASH 608:89
out of these wet c. ANON 22:54
politics with the c. off BRAD 148:62
poured into his c. WODE 919:64
require new c. THOR 857:88
soul...is his c. SHAK 761:31
take the girl's c. off CHAN 205:90
taste for French c. SCHL 718:14
the c. don't wear her QUANT 674:34
time when you have to let your c. MIDL 569:49
walked away with their c. DISR 276:56
wears her c. as if SWIFT 832:4
Who touched my c.? BIBLE 114:13
witnesses laid down their c. BIBLE 119:35
wore torn c. SPEN 807:52
clothing Be courtly ay in c. DUNB 294:4
c. affords a glimpse BART 62:21
c. for the soul divine BLAKE 135:68
c. of a manservant HUGO 421:77
Gave thee c. of delight BLAKE 133:29
Things in book's c. LAMB 487:60
cloths embroidered c. YEATS 933:38

cloud a fair luminous c. COLE 226:3
avails a storm c. RYDER 707:77
black c. carries the sun away ELIOT 307:98
c. instead, and ever-during MILT 582:38
c. in trousers! MAYA 562:91
From c. to tumbling c. YEATS 933:45
great c. came over me FOX 333:77
he melted like a c. TENN 848:60
If a c. knew loneliness RICH 685:56
kerchiefed in a comely c. MILT 577:20
Like a fiend hid in a c. BLAKE 135:60
little c. out of the sea BIBLE 92:21
moon on this c. sea SCOTT 722:77
motions of wind and c. LEE 500:45
no silver lining...without its c. STER 817:62
On a c. I saw a child BLAKE 133:28
peaks of c. CIAR 218:13
pillar of a c. BIBLE 88:19
set my bow in the c. BIBLE 87:69
She faded, like a c. SHEL 785:94
so great a c. of witnesses BIBLE 124:99
some gilded c. VAUG 878:44
Stooping through a fleecy c. MILT 576:16
The flying c. TENN 844:60
wandered lonely as a c. WORD 927:40
wild geese lost in c. BASHO 63:44
yon labouring c. MARL 553:7
cloud-capped c.-c. towers SHAK 774:94
clouded if your life should become c. OVID 631:48
cloud-encircled c.-e. meteor SHEL 784:66
cloudiness full of frost...and c.? SHAK 745:26
clouds After the greatest c. ALAN 9:83
all the c. that lowered TWAIN 871:7
carries the c. with it LEON 503:14
c. are deep FREE 336:44
c. are lightly curled TENN 839:57
c. do often rest MILT 576:8
c. of his own glory GREE 370:50
c. of the table above MONRO 591:58
c., or mud or like places LEON 504:19
c. takes all away SHAK 729:26
c. that blinded PIER 651:7
c. the c. chase MERE 567:12
c. turning blood red MUNCH 603:80
c. were touched WORD 928:52
cometh with c. BIBLE 125:43
dying c. contend SHAK 730:74
gloom of c. ADDI 6:20
heaven but the c. RUSK 703:5
Heaven is free From c. BYRON 180:33
He comes with c. descending WESL 900:16
left the red c. TANN 836:91
let the c. rain down BIBLE 128:96
Never doubted c. would break BROW 163:95
no pity sitting in the c. SHAK 736:72
nor the c. return after the rain BIBLE 101:92
O c., unfold! BLAKE 135:84
O'er which c. SHEL 784:56
piled gold c. LARK 491:33
prince of the c. BAUD 64:55
raise the wind, or rend the c. MARL 552:97
shadows of the c. WORD 927:38
sit in the c. SHAK 742:47
slow movement of c. DAY 257:84
Somewhere among the c. YEATS 933:48
the poor Indian...Sees God in c. POPE 660:11
Through the dark c. FORD 330:20
tossing sea of c. BENU 78:85
trailing c. of glory WORD 926:24
When c. are cursed by thunder THOM 852:65
white c. floating MCMU 537:87
white c. fly WU 930:96
White c. on the wing ALLI 13:62
wreathed in c. WHITE 903:1
cloud-topped Behind the c.-t. hill POPE 660:11
cloud-waves Bronze c.-w. FREE 336:45
Clough poet named C. SWIN 833:46
clout hit her a great c. STRO 827:95
cloven espied his c. foot BALL 55:73
clover c. and timothy-tops ROBE 689:18
C....is Aristocracy DICK 273:75
cloverleaf flower is the concrete c. MUMF 603:77
cloves cinnamon and c. ANON 20:9
Clovis aunt of C. SAKI 710:37
clown c., the boozer, the fighter? MAST 560:52
like the idiot or c. SITW 794:84
clowns those that play your c. SHAK 754:87

club any c. that will accept me MARX 557:91
belong to the most exclusive c. NASH 608:88
best c. in London DICK 272:46
far from the c. house LINK 511:54
harte in one hand and a c. in the other BILL 130:49
I am the C. Liar SAKI 710:47
man...loyal to his c. WHITE 903:76
No c. has been good enough BUSBY 175:87
savage wields his c. HUXL 426:13
secret of managing a ball c. STEN 816:54
clue Singularity...invariably a c. DOYLE 285:58
Clunton C. and Clunbury HOUS 415:57
clusters c. and constellations of data GIBS 353:76
Where we such c. had HERR 400:51
clutch Come, let me c. thee SHAK 767:54
clutching c. the inviolable shade ARNO 32:23
Clyde on the bonnie banks o' C. LAUD 492:64
coach generals are in my c. MARL 551:67
hold back against the c. TROL 867:99
looking for a body in the c. HITC 404:13
politics is like...a football c. MCCA 527:92
rattling of a c. DONNE 281:90
Up, and by c. PEPYS 647:39
coaches c. shall be scrap SAND 713:93
coachmaker o' mind the fairies' c. SHAK 736:39
coal Affection is a c. SHAK 733:53
c. to kindle fleshly flame SPEN 808:87
island is made mainly of c. BEVAN 84:16
it is a c. PEELE 646:12
like a c. SMART 797:36
live c. in his hand BIBLE 102:12
the biggest c. block HEAN 389:15
With England's own c. KIPL 474:71
coalition You may call it c. PALM 636:25
coalitions England does not love c. DISR 276:62
coalminers keep the c. off the streets BRES 151:19
coalmines in disused c. KEYN 466:88
coals all eyes else, dead c.! SHAK 770:96
Can one go upon hot c. BIBLE 99:17
c. thereof are c. of fire BIBLE 102:6
eyes that stare like c. RANS 679:27
gang to the c. i' the morning SKIR 795:14
heap c. of fire upon his head BIBLE 100:52
piles of dry wood with red-hot c. CISN 218:30
coarse c. emotion of mankind ELIOT 304:9
c. warty hands DONO 282:98
such a c. pattern HARDY 382:62
coast c. where souls are lost ANON 20:22
last train for the c. MCLE 534:27
look'd towards the French c. STER 818:90
near the shadowy c. THOM 855:39
People can't die, along the c. DICK 269:76
round the c. the languid air TENN 839:53
scarcely visited any c. JOHN 442:57
wild and breaker-beaten c. BYRON 182:78
you c. for a while REAG 681:67
coaster dirty British c. MASE 559:07
coat brown c., the...stockings MACA 525:54
c., and I have given that KRUG 481:23
c. Covered with embroideries YEATS 933:42
c. of many colours BIBLE 87:93
did not wear his scarlet c. WILDE 910:52
eternal Footman hold my c. ELIOT 304:22
for a riband to stick in his c. BROW 160:28
good c. upon his back JOHN 443:66
Grab your c. FIEL 323:46
have a good c. STAN 813:69
iron c. all overgrown SPEN 808:83
love that loves a scarlet c. HOOD 410:36
tattered c. YEATS 933:52
coats gold c. spots you see SHAK 737:92
cobbler body of a c. LOCKE 514:19
c. stick to his last APEL 27:11
cobble-stones On c.-s. I lay FLAN 325:20
cobblestreets the c. silent THOM 853:85
Cobleigh sounds like Uncle Tom C. THOM 852:77
Uncle Tom C. and all BALL 57:96
cobra guile of a c. WOOL 923:63
cobweb c. of the brain BUTL 177:50
foul black c. WEBS 895:97
cobwebs Laws are like c. SWIFT 830:58
reasoners...make c. BACON 47:60
weave fine c. BUTL 177:43
Coca-Cola billboards did to C.-C. UPDI 874:81
cocaine C. habit-forming? BANK 58:27
cock Before the c. crow BIBLE 116:62
C. and a Bull STER 818:94

c. doth craw — BALL 57:98
c. may craw — BURNS 171:6
c.'s shrill clarion — GRAY 369:12
c. who thought the sun had risen — ELIOT 303:80
c. with lively din — MILT 576:7
c. won't fight — BEAV 67:21
louder a c. can crow — TROL 867:90
Nationalism is a silly c. — ALDI 10:9
offer a c. to Asclepius — PLATO 655:92
this night, before the c. crow — BIBLE 114:97
with my old c. linnet — COLL 227:36
cockade lad wi' his white c. — ANON 20:13
cockatoo cage…to a c. — SHAW 780:53
green freedom of a c. — STEV 819:17
cockatrice hand on the c.' den — BIBLE 102:19
cockerel calls with a c.'s tongue — LEE 500:42
cockle like him that soweth c. — BUNY 167:78
Cockney much of C. impudence — RUSK 704:34
cockroaches c. will still be here — JANO 435:77
cocks drowned the c.! — SHAK 763:71
set the c. a-crow — YEATS 934:65
cocksure c.…as Tom Macaulay — MELB 563:18
cocktail c. is to…wine — CLAU 220:63
pause…known as the c. hour — DE 264:35
weasel under the c. cabinet — PINT 652:21
cock-up wash-out of a c.-u. — ANON 25:50
cocoa C. is a cad — CHES 212:80
rather have a nice cup of c. — COWA 240:28
cocoon c. of its own thoughts — LOWE 520:36
people live wrapped tight in a c. — CARR 194:56
Cocqcigrues coming of the C. — KING 469:58
Cocteau C. thinks that I am a poor thief — GENET 348:3
cod Boston…home of…the c. — BOSS 145:8
O bely! O stynkyng c. — CHAU 209:91
code c.…for those who oppose us — EISE 302:56
rigid c. of immorality — BRAD 148:53
trail has its own stern c. — SERV 728:2
codes rape us with…their c. — FREN 336:48
codfish taste of c. in it — GRIEG 373:10
Codrus peals of laughter, C.! — POPE 661:34
coelacanth like the c. — HOGG 406:61
coffee c. and doughnuts — DAVI 254:42
c. and oranges — STEV 819:17
measured out my life with c. spoons — ELIOT 304:20
morning cup of c. — HOLM 408:1
Rock 'n' roll is instant c. — GELD 348:96
wear c. as a perfume — VAN 877:27
went on drinking c. — GREE 370:51
coffee-house some obscure c.-h. — MONT 591:67
coffer litel gold in c. — CHAU 208:72
coffin Bring out the c. — AUDEN 40:89
heart is in the c. — SHAK 748:8
Shaped like a c. — MACN 538:13
silver plate on a c. — CURR 249:42
turns in his c. — GILB 355:36
coffins c. were looking up — DICK 266:89
cogent equally c. — GASK 346:58
cogging Some c., cozening slave — SHAK 760:4
cogitations c. still amaze — ELIOT 305:32
cogito c., ergo sum — DESC 263:21
coherence all c. gone — DONNE 281:76
coign In a c. of the cliff — SWIN 834:51
coil shuffled off this mortal c. — SHAK 753:74
coin single c. to medicine — VALLE 876:17
smallest current c. — BIER 128:13
coinage powerful c. — PLOUT 656:10
coiner c. of sweet words! — ARNO 32:24
coins and like to c. — TENN 847:42
barter it for silver c. — NGU 613:79
glory in large c. — HUGO 421:82
silver c. multiplying — WALC 884:78
coition trivial and vulgar way of c. — BROW 159:81
Coke cantaloupe in a C. bottle — JONES 448:93
C. bottles…great modern things — WARH 889:64
coke Happiness is like c. — HUXL 425:70
Coketown C.…ugly citadel — DICK 270:4
cold being white is c. and sad — RHYS 684:25
blood was c. — SCOTT 722:86
blow in c. blood — SHAW 778:11
called a c. a c. — BENN 76:42
Came in from the C. — LECA 499:19
careful c. beginneth — SPEN 808:79
c. and certain friends — HUGO 421:86
c. as truth — RHYS 684:27
c. coming they had of it — ANDR 16:27
c. coming we had of it — ELIOT 306:73
c. doesn't crouch over one — LAWR 494:15

C. doth not sting — NASHE 609:15
C. in the earth — BRON 155:93
c. o' the moon — BROW 162:75
c. reaches of the universe — KENN 462:17
c. roads…c. news — SCOTT 725:51
c., uncertain of all — WILL 913:42
comfort me with c. — SHAK 739:33
dressed ever caught in a c.? — NIET 616:26
Europe catches c. — METT 568:26
feel hot and think c. — CARY 198:61
foot and hand go c. — ANON 20:1
Give them the c. steel — ARMI 30:70
glass…hard, c. and misted over — RHYS 684:30
going down and becoming c. — SMITH 800:99
have to do that c. — HEMI 394:11
heart grown c. — SHEL 786:4
hot temper leaps o'er a c. decree — SHAK 739:44
ink in my pen ran c. — WALP 887:24
in love with a c. climate — SOUT 805:95
in the c. grave leave — WEBS 894:77
in the darkness and the c. — STEV 823:37
makes c. weather — SHAK 775:7
my boy? Art c.? — SHAK 763:75
naked in the dark and c. — LEGU 501:54
neither c. nor hot — BIBLE 126:51
No worse than a bad c. — MARX 557:93
silver thimble lies c. — SITW 794:82
'Tis bitter c. — SHAK 751:95
too c. always — SMITH 800:97
too c. for hell — SHAK 767:7
too c. for the spectators — SMITH 800:90
wert thou in the c. blast — BURNS 173:54
what I got…was a c. — THOR 858:1
wind was c. — SCOTT 722:84
yet so warm, and yet so c. — LAWS 496:46
colder even c. war — KENN 462:17
coldness heat full of c. — LYLY 523:9
colds c. a forward spring remove? — DONNE 280:44
Coleridge C.…has lately taken wing — BYRON 181:62
C. lull the babe at nurse — BYRON 179:2
Cultivate simplicity, C. — LAMB 486:27
indulgences of C. — THUR 859:49
observed by C. — WORD 928:43
shut up, like C. — QUIL 674:48
You will see C. — SHEL 784:66
Coliseum While stands the C. — BYRON 180:41
collage C. is a supersensitive — ERNST 315:90
collapse Agreement…starts to c. — SHUL 789:90
all his plans c. — JOSE 451:71
When I see my friends c. — SKEL 795:95
collapses nothing c. — WHIT 905:31
collar Malachi wore the c. — MOORE 596:48
shirt or c. ever comes back — LEAC 497:69
collarbone silly old c.'s bust — BETJ 84:9
collar-rolls In velvet c.-r. — KIPL 473:64
collaterals I detest c. — SOME 803:66
colleagues former c. are to be believed — HOWE 417:97
for myself and my c. — PEEL 646:8
most eminent of his c. — DISR 276:65
Most of my c. were -ists — HUXL 426:7
Smarter than most of his c. — REST 683:13
collecting what c. is all about — ANNE 18:55
collection c. of unrealistic goals — LURIE 522:91
extraordinary c. of talent — KENN 462:20
collections those mutilators of c. — LAMB 487:52
collective c. opinion…make history — SAFI 708:2
collectors great c. before me — DOUG 283:22
one-night stands in c.' homes — RAUS 679:33
college at school or c. — STEV 822:97
endow a c., or a cat — POPE 659:2
Fellows of another c. — LITT 512:77
Magdalen C. — GIBB 352:60
suppress each cathedral and c. — MACA 525:45
This great C. — HOUS 415:69
collie tither was a ploughman's c. — BURNS 170:75
collier-brigs cabooses of c.-b. — DICK 269:79
Collins if you do not marry Mr C. — AUST 43:66
colloquial clear it from c. barbarisms — JOHN 441:28
colloquialisms c., its humour — ROLL 695:33
collusive the puff c. — SHER 788:61
Cologne wash your city of C. — COLE 227:23
Colombia last optimist left in C. — GARC 345:41
colonel c. comes from Brian's race — DAVIS 256:67
For the C.'s Lady — KIPL 472:17
colonial have to be c. to know — WALC 884:73
large sections of the c. population — SCHL 718:10
colonialism C. forces the people — FANON 317:45

C. is not satisfied — FANON 317:44
colonies finest C. under the Crown — STUA 827:98
In the c. the economic substructure — FANON 317:43
products of all the c. — SITW 794:74
this realm, its c. — QUIL 674:44
colonists Roman c. settled in Britain — HYDE 427:21
colonization c. by any European — ADAMS 5:93
c. planted the seeds — MARI 549:48
colonized among c. people — SART 716:55
Colonus Singer of sweet C. — ARNO 31:91
colony an economic c. — TSON 869:54
brown men from a distant c. — PRIE 668:28
Crown C. system — KING 469:63
founders of a new c. — HAWT 386:39
from c. to nation to c. — INNIS 429:67
Colossus Like a C. — SHAK 747:76
Milton…could cut a C. from a rock — JOHN 446:63
colour abominable c. of his hair — HOUS 416:90
altered the c. of my mind — BRON 155:94
Any c.—so long as it's black — FORD 330:8
Beige! Just my c. — DE 265:45
between the mind and the c. — HEPW 396:61
burned gold was his c.? — CHAU 209:95
cast thy nightly c. off — SHAK 751:2
citizens of c. are concerned — KING 468:35
C. and bite permeate a language — SAFI 708:97
c. is a means of exerting — KAND 454:38
c. is the goal — HEIN 391:52
C. is the ultimate — RUNGE 702:76
c. I want those handrails — TRUMP 869:49
c. of a beryl — BIBLE 105:84
c. of my soul is iron-grey — DEBU 258:3
c. of one's skin — BALD 53:31
c. of sand — ASHB 35:83
c. of shadows — WALC 884:78
c. of their skin — KING 468:33
c. of the sky — CRANE 243:29
C. possesses me — KLEE 475:8
c. shrieked — MUNCH 603:80
c. to that of the Senses — MATI 560:64
exact c. and shape — MONET 591:53
formal principle of its c. — SHEL 786:13
for the c. of his hair — HOUS 416:89
heart never knows the c. of the skin — GEOR 349:21
know the c. of that blood — KEATS 460:65
know the c. rose — ABSE 1:6
life is c. and warmth — GREN 373:2
loses c. with the slightest — VIEI 881:12
Nature's scheme of c. — STRE 827:92
No c., only nuance! — VERL 879:68
paint the c. of the wind — BODE 138:28
problem of race and c. — DU 293:75
problem of the c. line — DU 292:70
relationships of c. or form — ROTH 700:34
see a man…not a c. — STEV 820:63
subtle spies Of c. — FREE 336:44
'tis a c. she abhors — SHAK 756:72
'twas a c. he never liked — SHAK 745:37
What c. is your parachute? — BOLL 139:46
yearned for warmth and c. — TENN 846:23
colour-bar c.-b. and beer — NOON 618:59
colour-blind wise person is c.-b. — SCHW 721:71
coloured For c. girls — SHAN 776:27
makes a man c. — HUGH 418:24
Negroes…replaced c. people — FEIF 319:84
shadow over the c. — BUCK 165:35
colouring c. of a thought — SITW 794:85
colourists Painters who are not c. — DELA 260:61
colours All c. will agree — BACON 47:77
coat of many c. — BIBLE 89:93
c. don't quite match your face — ASHF 35:94
c. laid so thick — DRYD 287:15
composition of c. — THEO 851:39
flat surface covered with c. — DENIS 262:97
fresh c. deck the wanton prime — SPEN 809:92
Fresh-quilted c. through the air — HERR 400:43
howl of unnerving c. — TZARA 873:58
I had shown my c. — ACHE 2:33
Lentil-soup c. — HUGH 419:28
more c. in these ten minutes — DICK 267:25
Scents, c., and sounds — BAUD 64:56
see the difference of the c. — MELV 564:47
table of c. — GALE 343:5
troop their c. — BAIN 52:11
colts play left-guard for the C. — BRES 151:19
columbine pink and purple c. — SPEN 808:98
Columbus C. and his men — WILB 907:75

C. of our shore WENT 899:5
first carnival person was Christopher C. COLE 225:72
my youth in C., Ohio THUR 859:22
column The fifth c. MOLA 589:25
thunderhead-like c. AGAWA 8:71
urn Throws up a steamy c. COWP 241:76
columns c. of the old rain forest AMIS 15:99
Greeks were hiding behind their c. DE 260:56
moved…in c. WELL 897:58
coma eight-year c. BENT 78:83
keep the mothers in a state of c. DAVI 254:30
comb fight between two bald men over a c. BORG 145:94
c. my hair BALL 56:94
combat c. the monster BALZ 57:6
naval c. GIBB 351:57
set a c. them between BALL 55:74
combative made a c. apology SHUL 789:84
combats causes them to hide their c. BALZ 57:13
comber c. wind-hounded? KIPL 473:50
combination c. of half-truths TOOLE 863:12
c. of outward with inward facts ELIOT 303:77
c. that is necessary ROOS 696:57
constant and uniform c. SMITH 797:43
exquisite c. TROL 866:82
unbeatable c. ANGE 17:33
combinations irregular c. JOHN 441:28
combine C. your hearts in one SHAK 746:69
sure to c. JAMES 434:61
combustion ruin and c. down MILT 580:95
come Art thou he that should c. BIBLE 111:32
avoid what is to c. SHAK 754:11
c. again with rejoicing BIBLE 98:91
C. and take them LEON 504:22
C., seeling night SHAK 768:15
C. what c. may SHAK 766:77
hands…remembered to c. with him PRIT 669:48
know not how to…c. in BIBLE 91:10
let him c. out JOHN 446:55
One to c., and one to go CARR 197:19
shape of things to c. WELLS 899:93
Surely I c. quickly BIBLE 127:85
Then c. on, c. on HERR 400:47
was, and is, and is to c. BIBLE 126:54
comedian test of a real c. NATH 609:21
comedians being c. GREE 371:66
comedies c. are ended BYRON 182:85
comedy All I need to make a c. CHAP 206:10
Applaud…the c. is over BEET 70:99
at a c. we only look HUXL 425:92
both c. and tragedy THUR 860:52
c. in one hundred different acts LAFO 485:12
C. is an imitation SIDN 791:21
C. is a very serious thing GARR 346:55
C.…is harder to do MALA 541:82
C. is if I walk into an open sewer BROO 157:31
C. is more like coke IZZA 431:4
c. paints characters HUGO 420:74
c. tells us GORM 364:13
Farce is nearer tragedy…than c. COLE 227:25
happier still is that musical c. AGATE 8:67
make in som c.! CHAU 208:64
Most Lamentable C. SHAK 737:87
rules c. can tolerate THUR 860:56
Talking of the C. JOHN 446:64
world is a c. WALP 887:31
Writers of c. have outlook THUR 860:55
comeliness no form nor c. BIBLE 104:50
comely boast themselves more c. MILT 577:26
Sae c. to be seen SCOTT 724:21
Comet On, C.! On, Cupid! MOORE 594:17
comet come like a daytime c. BISH 131:77
Woman is thought to be a C. MAKIN 541:76
comets Old men and c. SWIFT 831:88
there are no c. seen SHAK 747:87
comfort Be c. to my age SHAK 749:38
before providing c. MARI 550:63
beg cold c. SHAK 739:33
carrion c. HOPK 412:2
catechism of c. BENE 75:8
c. across many a…night NIET 615:21
C. came in with the middle classes BELL 71:31
c. comes too late SHAK 775:25
c. myself when SURR 829:40
c. of thy worth and truth SHAK 771:17
c. serves in a whirlwind HOPK 413:6
C.'s in heaven SHAK 734:11
c. to shift one's position IRVI 430:84

c. ye my people BIBLE 103:36
c. your bed SHAK 747:85
C. yourself PASC 641:37
dear husband for a c. SMITH 800:92
hobbit-hole, and that means c. TOLK 862:95
in comparative c. KING 469:62
loves…of c. and despair SHAK 773:55
Money is a c. ANON 18:74
mutual society, help, and c. BOOK 142:22
no c. like…having deserved it SHER 788:56
no c., only anxiety FRIS 338:78
not another c. like to this SHAK 759:75
not ecstasy but it was c. DICK 270:13
Nothing else will give you any c. SCOTT 725:60
only c. about being a woman STARK 813:71
receives c. like cold porridge SHAK 774:85
seeketh in society c. BACON 46:54
sees too deep for c. FADI 317:37
sense of inward c. AUBR 39:71
Society is no c. SHAK 774:73
Such c. as do lusty young men SHAK 735:36
tell you naught for your c. CHES 212:72
This must my c. be SHAK 734:2
Thou art all the c. SHAK 774:69
willing to live in c. DU 293:75
comfortable c. years allowed to man! SASS 716:58
Exploring…is not c. BUTL 177:65
palace more c. HOOV 411:64
something more c. HARL 383:84
think about a more c. one WILD 910:80
When people are too c. RICH 686:68
comforted Lord hath c. his people BIBLE 104:48
refused to be c. BIBLE 105:78
refused to be c. BIBLE 87:95
comforter C., where, where HOPK 413:4
comforters miserable c. are ye all BIBLE 93:62
comforting c.…to be the recipient FOWL 332:70
comfortless c., and worn, and old ROSS 697:76
comforts adversity is not without c. BACON 47:81
c. we despise SHAK 765:45
disregard for the sublime c. SHIP 789:77
helpers fail and c. LYTE 524:17
King of c. VAUG 878:48
loves and c. should increase SHAK 759:76
comic c. writers to have a hate figure TOWN 863:23
encouragement of c. strips UPDI 874:86
comical often think it's c. GILB 354:13
comics c.…great modern things WARH 889:64
coming cold c. we had of it ELIOT 306:73
c.! He is c.! AYTO 45:17
going out and thy c. in BIBLE 97:87
Welcome the c. POPE 659:87
command at your c. GRAV 367:63
basic c. of religion TOYN 864:32
c. me any service SHAK 744:95
c. of that vital sea CHUR 217:88
c. what you will AUGU 41:38
Had thine at their c. WORD 927:31
singular c., I do not understand AUDEN 41:32
The c. 'Thou shalt not kill' JOHN 439:61
wide as his c. DRYD 289:69
wisdom bears c. MILT 586:46
commanded Have I not c. thee? BIBLE 90:62
commanders of legions JUVE 453:19
C.…should die with troops CHUR 217:84
commandment c. on the pulse of life? SHAK 739:32
c. that states, 'Thou shalt fly' CLEE 220:72
first and great c. BIBLE 113:82
indivisibility, the first c. ROTH 699:29
new c. I give unto you BIBLE 118:7
Science knows only one c. BREC 151:11
This is my c. BIBLE 118:12
commandments Christian c. KIER 467:14
c. in your face SHAK 730:53
keep his c. BIBLE 101:94
love me and keep my c. BOOK 141:93
two great c. were MACA 525:52
write poetical c. BYRON 181:74
commands obedient to their c. SIMO 792:42
commemorative cold c. eyes ROSS 698:2
commendable silence is only c. SHAK 739:40
commendation beautiful face is a dumb c. PUBL 672:95
greater c. DRYD 288:25
man's c. with woman SHAK 757:87
commended highly c. of all BUNY 166:75
comment C. is free SCOTT 722:74

commentary c. on that cry KAZA 456:70
proliferating c. GRASS 367:60
commentators As learned c. view SWIFT 832:97
C. quote economic studies SAMU 712:80
commerce adventures…in c. WEST 901:39
c.…enhanced by success TREV 865:63
form of c. and consumption MARX 557:1
heaven fill with c. TENN 840:81
In c. bygones are for ever bygones JEVO 438:46
increase of riches and c. HUME 422:12
In matters of c. CANN 188:14
obstructed interstate c. HOOV 411:69
poets of c. GRAY 373:9
trade and c. HALL 378:91
commercial among a c. one FUSE 342:75
blend of the c. traveller STAP 813:70
c. society TREV 865:63
concern for c. viability MAMET 543:22
phonograph…is not of any c. value EDIS 300:12
safe haven from c. considerations SAFER 708:95
commercials 30-second c. DANF 251:84
commission c. you to carry out GOER 360:11
Each bullet has got its c. DIBD 265:55
commitment C. to the poor JOHN 439:63
with a three-ocean c. HAYW 387:64
committee c. is an animal LECA 499:20
horse designed by a c. ISSI 431:97
written by a c. GRIS 373:19
commodities c. derive their…value RICA 684:34
into the c. market TYSON 873:52
levied upon c. JOHN 442:45
commodity C. fetishism TATE 837:7
c. of good names SHAK 741:96
infinitely small amount of c. JEVO 438:45
worker becomes…cheaper c. MARX 557:95
Commodus accession of C. GIBB 351:52
common call not thou c. BIBLE 119:40
c. cry of curs SHAK 769:66
c. good to all SHAK 748:25
c. interest always will prevail DRYD 290:90
c. is the commonplace TENN 843:24
C. Law of England HERB 397:83
c. people swarm SHAK 730:78
c. property of the nation TIMES 861:77
c. prudence, and c. sense SMITH 801:7
concerns the c. weal GEOR 349:19
Crime is c. DOYLE 285:68
dream of a c. language RICH 685:52
he should not be so c. WILS 915:76
insipid c. sense SALI 711:68
leapt straight past the c. cold AYRES 45:14
lose their c. sense STEIN 815:22
loves not the c. people SHAK 769:61
make it too c. SHAK 742:42
man of c. opinion BAGE 52:96
man of great c. sense SHAW 778:79
nor lose the c. touch KIPL 474:68
praise that as c. sense THOR 858:98
speak as the c. people ASCH 35:79
still be c., dear RATT 679:32
surpass C. revenge MILT 581:26
the man is a c. murderer SAKI 710:45
those of c. sense HUXL 426:13
Tom Paine's c. sense ADAMS 5:91
trained and organized c. sense HUXL 426:13
way into the C. Market WILS 916:95
What [existentialists] have in c. SART 715:48
commonalty dog to the c. SHAK 769:55
commonplace c. young man GILB 354:6
great minds in the c. HUBB 417:7
Nature is c. STEIN 815:23
never yawn or say a c. thing KERO 464:62
Nothing is so c. HOLM 408:90
nothing so unnatural as the c. DOYLE 285:61
unassuming c. of Nature WORD 926:14
commons c., like an angry hive SHAK 730:58
Lords and C. of England MILT 579:80
commonwealth c. in which work SHAW 779:37
C. is fixed and stable BURKE 168:23
glorify God and benefit the C. WENT 899:4
head of the C. ACHE 2:29
service and conduct of the c. BURKE 168:5
vision of the C. MACM 536:67
commonwealths great c. collapse HOPE 411:71
raise up c. DRYD 289:74
communal experiment…in c. living BOWL 147:35
we're such a c. society SPIE 810:19

communicate c. with…emotions ROTH 700:34
eliminate his ability to c. SCHW 721:65
Genuine poetry can c. ELIOT 306:77
power to c. with a third party WOOLF 922:33
communication c. Of the dead ELIOT 309:40
evasion…rather than c. JONES 447:90
In terms of c. UMAS 873:62
public opinion and mass c. MERT 568:24
Thank you for your c. ELLI 310:80
communications c. system HAYEK 387:60
C. today puts a special RUSK 703:98
divine c. AUBR 39:71
Evil c. corrupt BIBLE 121:17
communicator Great C. ANON 24:24
communion C. of Saints BOOK 140:71
communism beginning…of c. HERZ 400:56
C.…bores them OROU 627:23
C. fits Germany STAL 812:58
c. is a dead dog SOLZ 803:64
C. is like prohibition ROGE 695:20
C. is the opiate LUCE 522:81
c. versus capitalism NGUY 613:81
consistent opponent of C. CHUR 217:81
how good c. is! MAO 547:2
Russian c. is the illegitimate child ATTL 38:45
socialism and c. MORR 598:99
spectre of c. MARX 558:4
USSR to reject C. KHRU 466:90
When we reach c. ZHANG 936:93
communist Catholic and the C. ORWE 629:92
C. must grasp the truth MAO 548:7
C. 'war of liberation' MCNA 537:91
Every c. has a fascist SPARK 806:27
fully-fledged c. CAST 199:79
government of Vietnam is C. GELL 348:2
higher phase of c. society MARX 558:14
In c. society MARX 557:99
member of the C. Party THOM 854:21
non-Communist premier BOHL 138:35
tremble at a c. revolution MARX 558:5
Vietnam took the c. road NGUY 613:82
would not even be a c. ZHIV 936:97
communists looking…for C. FOOT 329:91
theory of the C. MARX 558:3
communities c.…slightly removed COOP 236:52
filthier and filthier c. GARD 346:46
half-civilized c. BAGE 51:94
community c. consisting of a master BIER 129:34
c. is a fictitious body BENT 77:64
c. lacks goods CHUR 216:62
c. of Europe GLAD 359:94
c. of thought ADAMS 4:81
interests of the c. TOCQ 861:84
interests of…the c. RICA 685:35
involved as a c. GINS 357:70
member of a civilized c. MILL 570:62
no finer investment for any c. CHUR 217:89
not life that is not in c. ELIOT 307:89
not of war…but of…c. CHILD 213:8
part of the c. of Europe SALI 711:69
rule of any modern c. KEYN 466:91
scientific c. thinks KUHN 481:15
well-conducted c. CHIS 213:16
commuter C.—one who spends his life WHITE 903:89
compact c. of fire SHAK 732:52
companies busy c. of men MARV 556:72
great joint-stock c. MILL 570:66
U.S.A. is a group of holding c. DOSP 282:3
companion dear c. of my soul MIDD 569:40
found the c. THOR 858:95
gave him a c. VALE 876:15
happiness of finding a c. BERN 81:41
ideal c. in bed DAVI 255:45
silent c., exacting and eternal DELA 260:59
companionable c. as solitude THOR 858:95
companionless Wandering c. SHEL 787:30
companions All her lovely c. MOORE 596:50
c. for middle age BACON 48:91
keep pace with his c. THOR 858:30
company Banish not…Harry's c. SHAK 742:16
because we have c.? JARRY 435:90
c. breaks up CERV 203:45
c. of paper-blurrers SIDN 791:22
c. of the like-minded DELI 261:79
crowd is not c. BACON 49:29
enjoying their c. RUSS 705:51
frolicsome c. had begun SCOTT 724:20

from mine own c. SHAK 738:7
Good c., good wine, good welcome SHAK 775:6
In c. with several other old ladies DICK 270:10
In such a jocund c. WORD 928:42
leave all this constant c. DONNE 279:28
live in c. with a body DELA 260:59
man in a jail has…better c. JOHN 443:59
My idea of good c. AUST 44:95
only c. whose assets all walk MAYER 562:95
Our c. is too big WILS 915:81
provoked and have asked the c. SNOW 802:37
tell a man who boozes by the c. BURT 174:65
three is c. and two none WILDE 909:37
to shine in c. SWIFT 831:85
Vandyke is of the c. GAIN 342:86
When c. comes HUGH 418:16
When c. comes HUGH 418:17
with all the c. of heaven BOOK 141:5
worst of the c. SWIFT 830:63
your bill of c. SWIFT 830:65
compare c. to a stick and a string JOHN 447:77
C. with Caesars SHAK 743:49
Shall I c. thee SHAK 771:5
comparison c. in point of beauty MOORE 595:26
experience and c. JOHN 445:44
in c. to the infinite PASC 641:28
involuntary c. becomes a bore HORN 414:37
read…partly for c. SCHL 718:11
comparisons C. are odorous SHAK 745:16
compass c. of his Canterbury Tales DRYD 292:45
in that narrow c. HUME 422:3
shorts in this c.? MURR 604:7
compasses took the golden c. MILT 584:92
compassion bowels of c. BIBLE 125:37
character and c. NEWM 612:67
c. and sacrifice FAUL 318:63
c. and sacrifice FAUL 318:64
c. may become a justice JONS 449:33
c. on the son of her womb? BIBLE 104:46
c. to solve even a little WILS 915:78
crumbs of c. TUTU 870:70
heavenly c. in your hearts DICK 270:98
his father saw him, and had c. BIBLE 116:48
Jesu, thou art all c. WESL 900:14
live without real c. WILS 915:79
Mercy, pity, and justice WAITE 884:67
Samaritan…had c. on him BIBLE 115:38
sharp c. of the healer's art ELIOT 308:21
compassionate to be generous and c. THAT 850:13
compassions c. fail not BIBLE 105:82
compensations c. for growing older SKIN 795:12
competition Art…excludes all c. FUSE 342:73
c. between expert KEYN 466:86
C. brings out the best SARN 714:33
c. the Laws of Death RUSK 704:19
don't meet c. REVS 684:19
free c. of the market RICA 684:33
free c. was wasteful PUZO 673:25
law [of c.] may be sometimes hard CARN 193:49
tradition…Approves all forms of c. CLOU 223:40
your only c. is idiots MANK 545:60
complacence thou My sole c.! MILT 582:47
complacent hauf o't smug, c. SMITH 801:25
shake the c. pillars BETH 83:76
complain But do not c. HAMM 379:10
farmers…flourish and c. CRAB 242:94
musn't c. too much GREE 371:66
Never c. and never explain BALD 54:51
to whom to c. FIRB 323:62
complainers loudest c. BURKE 168:2
complains No one ever c. SELF 727:80
complaint borne…without c. ACHE 2:36
most fatal c. of all HILT 403:96
complement inevitable c. SCHU 721:58
mate with its c. of men WRIG 929:72
complete And in herself c. MILT 584:3
articulate and c. STEV 820:31
C. disillusionment STEIN 815:15
c. sentences GASS 346:61
Experience…is never c. JAMES 433:42
made the pile c. TENN 843:41
most c. and free STEV 821:78
completion c. of socialism MORR 598:99
time available for its c. PARK 639:84
complex c. and irregular SOLOW 803:60
military-industrial c. EISE 302:58
religious beliefs…simple or c. DURK 296:33

complexion bad c. GILB 354:98
c. of them all SHAK 740:66
c. we were not to spoil SCHR 720:40
different c.…than ourselves CONR 234:96
gold c. dimmed SHAK 771:5
thet depends on c. LOWE 520:30
complexities All mere c. YEATS 934:57
beyond our own c. WILL 913:48
complexity didn't grasp his own c. ELLI 311:91
possibility, and difficulty TRIL 866:66
reduce c. to simplicity JAMES 434:62
respect for the c. of learning JOVA 451:72
Unthinkable c. GIBS 353:76
compliance by a timely c. FIEL 322:40
c. with my wishes CHUR 217:9
tame and servile c. WHIT 902:67
complicated any problem, however c. ANDE 16:21
arrived in at a c. manner SAND 712:88
pattern more c. ELIOT 308:25
Things become c. MOYN 601:42
When a guy gets too c. he's unhappy CHAN 204:80
complications mysteries and c. GELL 348:97
one of the worst c. AGNEW 9:75
piling up of c. of every sort JAMES 434:56
complicity our tribe's c. HEAN 389:9
complies He that c. against his will BUTL 177:60
compliment empty c. GILB 355:20
greater c. than to be loved MACD 530:58
take it as a c. HAIG 376:65
compliments c. reaching the proper KIPL 470:74
c. to the purist CHAN 204:81
comply If you don't c. KELM 461:78
compose Before I c. a piece SATIE 717:81
feel the urge to c. BRAH 149:86
Never c. anything HOLST 408:5
Whether you c. or act DIDE 273:87
write, c. or paint GREE 371:72
composed c. as a conference report? GRIS 373:19
c. too much DVOR 296:49
c. wholly of constituents RUSS 705:43
Cruel, but c. and bland ARNO 32:25
composer demands of a c. HONE 409:30
limit to the c…time a c. LAMB 487:67
modern c. is a madman HONE 409:27
writer, the c., the artist KENN 463:35
composers advise all sensitive c. WALT 888:54
Not many c. have ideas GERS 350:56
works by contemporary c. HEIF 391:45
composing C. is not a profession HONE 409:28
in c. a work PASC 640:17
composition a style, not c. MORT 599:19
c. must be more accurate JONS 450:61
c. of colours THEO 851:39
c.…of tried medicines BACON 47:57
estimating my c. AUST 43:78
One c. is meagre DIDE 274:1
pure-painting c. MALE 542:88
compositions Read over your c. JOHN 444:98
compound urban c. MCLU 536:56
comprehensible world…is c. EINS 301:44
comprehension c. of the layman GOWE 365:29
devices of mere c. HOLM 407:74
comprehensions Wider c. FERG 320:5
compression c. is the first grace MOORE 595:30
compromise C. makes a good LOWE 520:39
C. used to mean CHES 212:70
English love of c. CARD 190:44
every prudent act…founded on c. BURKE 168:17
idea of a c. HUGH 420:55
would not tolerate c. on goals DULL 294:91
compulsion c. doth in music lie MILT 577:24
freely grows in deep c. SMITH 799:63
Give you a reason on c.? SHAK 741:14
ne'er can be…happy by c. COLE 226:5
stern hand of C. THUR 860:50
compulsions all our c. meet LARK 490:27
c., the fantasies LEGU 501:56
computer banks of every c. GIBS 353:76
circuits of a digital c. PIRS 652:25
c. is a fast idiot AMER 13:76
c. must be questioned MUMF 603:78
do not write on a c. OROU 627:26
most extraordinary c. of all KENN 463:26
no c. will ever ask HOPP 413:17
computer-age c.-a. journalists MCFA 531:74
computers c. are…stupid STER 817:61
world market for…five c. WATS 890:98

comrade c. with the wolf and owl — SHAK 763:69
Never leave a fallen c. — ANON 25:60
stepping where his c. stood — SCOTT 723:2
comrades blythe wi' C. dear — BURNS 170:83
c. apparently find it hard — GORB 363:99
help our French c. — KITC 475:4
con great pains to c. it — SHAK 756:57
Thanks I must you c. — SHAK 762:49
concave hell's c., and beyond — MILT 581:12
conceal duty…to c. his artifice — OGIL 623:41
Fate tried to c. him — HOLM 408:91
concealed utterly c. all — THOM 854:16
concealment c., like a worm — SHAK 756:68
conceit all his c. taken out of him — HOLM 407:79
As for c. — TROL 866:81
c. o' bein' richt — MACD 529:31
C. spoils the finest genius — ALCO 10:3
in his own c. — GREE 371:80
never forgive any c. — DRYD 292:48
only a c. — KAVA 456:67
self and vain c. — SHAK 735:20
so to his whole c. — SHAK 753:67
conceited say he's c. — SALI 711:59
very c. scurvy one — JONS 449:29
who is not c.? — TROL 866:81
conceits Be not wise in your own c. — BIBLE 120:83
c. as clownage keeps — MARL 551:70
Some people…run to c. — BART 62:11
conceive whatever we c. very clearly — DESC 263:22
conceived nothing…c. without God — SPIN 810:23
There is a man child c. — BIBLE 93:51
would seem to be well c. — GALB 343:99
concentrate c. to truth and liberty — SHEL 782:23
concentrated c. and it nourishes you — DOVE 284:39
concentrates c. his mind — JOHN 445:26
concentration c. camp is the final — MILL 572:6
open-ended stay in a c. camp — JOHN 439:73
When I visited c. camps — WHIT 905:22
concept abstruse and even partial c. — MILL 571:1
c. of God — BALD 54:37
c., structure, and style — POUS 666:75
conception false c. come true — MERT 568:22
questions enlarge our c. — RUSS 705:42
sorrow and c. — BIBLE 86:54
Yet her c. of God — STRA 826:83
conceptions All c. of God — WEIL 896:32
concepts metaphysical c. — STEI 816:47
mythical c., sun-gods and the like — FRYE 340:36
up the stairs in c. — STEI 815:31
conceptual c. art the idea — LEWI 508:7
concern c. not for your bodies — PLATO 654:78
c. was speech — ELIOT 309:43
life and its largest c. — ARNO 34:62
no c. for the common man — WILS 915:76
no c. with business — KIPL 470:83
no kind of c. with it — WHIS 902:65
two things that c. them — JUVE 453:19
concerned being ultimately c. — TILL 860:69
concerns first step that c. me — KENN 464:52
futile his c. — SIMO 792:43
concert Christmas c. by Pavarotti — BURKE 169:58
c. is dead — GOULD 364:20
shot fired in…a c. — STEN 816:50
concerts don't write little c. — MERW 568:25
concessions c. of the weak — BURKE 168:8
conciet glutted with c. — MARL 552:98
newness, the democratic c. — LAWR 494:97
conclaves Kingly c. stern and cold — SHEL 785:72
conclusion assume…powerful c. — SOLOW 803:61
cannot come to any c. — SACK 708:91
c.: life is something — LEBO 499:8
c. must be very scientific — JAMES 434:74
c. no one has yet dared — NIET 615:5
c. that sex is a sublimation — LODGE 514:26
c. that they are élitist — LODGE 515:28
denoted a foregone c. — SHAK 760:95
economists…would not reach a c. — SHAW 781:99
glorious c. — HUSS 424:43
impelled to the c. — JERO 437:31
laugh together over so odd a c. — EDDI 298:85
Ninety-nine times, the c. is false — EINS 301:34
other is a c. — JOHN 442:35
Reasoning draws a c. — BACON 50:73
three days to reach its c. — STOP 825:68
what better c. — TATE 833:8
conclusions draw the correct c. — KISS 475:89
Prime Minister reading out the c. — HESE 401:60

reach their c. about life — KIER 467:8
wrong c. at which mankind arrive — PALM 635:19
wrong in its c. — REGAN 682:93
concoct c. oneself — DOYLE 286:83
concord c. of sweet sounds — SHAK 741:88
lover of c. — BOOK 140:73
oft in pleasing c. end — MILT 586:60
Sinews of c. — FORD 330:12
concrete city is not a c. jungle — MORR 598:92
flower is the c. cloverleaf — MUMF 603:77
prams on c. balconies — BETJ 83:96
concubine c. or whore — HELO 393:86
too good to be your c. — SHAK 730:79
concupiscence wanderings of c. — BIBLE 107:33
concurrence fortuitous c. of atoms — PALM 636:25
condamné c. à faire libre — SART 715:51
condemn cannot c. it — DURK 296:32
c. it as an improbable fiction — SHAK 757:84
thoughtless to c. them — BRON 154:78
condemnation c. is the favourite — NIET 615:22
no c. to them which are in Christ — BIBLE 120:72
condemned behaviour which is c. — SPEN 807:63
c. for what we are — FENT 320:89
c. to be free — SART 715:51
c. to repeat it — SANT 714:19
Grudge not…lest ye be c. — BIBLE 125:17
Prayers for the c. man — WEST 901:37
condensation clever c. — PULI 672:4
condescend c. to men of low estate — BIBLE 120:83
condition average c. of the people — MILL 570:60
bettering our c. — SMITH 798:47
c.…of the Working Class — CARL 192:23
c. By which all mortal — MILT 578:42
c. left to women — LEGU 501:57
c. of art — CONR 234:94
c. of being human — ANOU 26:1
c. of capital and population — MILL 570:57
c. of the cases, was supernatural — MILL 570:72
c. rather than a profession — GRAV 367:73
c. that things resound — MARI 550:58
c. upon which God hath given liberty — CURR 249:41
economic c. has…improved — KRIS 481:16
Equality of c. is incompatible — COOP 236:52
excellence of his physical c. — NIVEN 617:40
fools decoyed into our c. — PEPYS 647:44
fugitives are of that c. — BACON 48:89
he knows his c. — PASC 641:32
looking as cheerfully…in that c. — PEPYS 647:28
Man's c.. Inconstancy — PASC 640:14
movement and not a c. — TOYN 864:28
perfect c. of slavery — ASTE 36:24
rises above the human c. — PAZ 644:89
towards the c. of music — PATER 642:52
War is a c. of progress — RENAN 683:98
whole human c. — HOPP 413:15
conditioned I'm exhausted, or c. — PUIG 672:1
conditions Bad as our urban c. — HALD 377:73
c. that are unspiritual — MARX 557:94
establish c. — UNIT 873:69
mirror of social c. — LIPP 511:70
play under bad c. — KAUF 455:56
social c. take recognizable — LIPP 511:71
they are only its c. — HEINE 391:49
under c.…unpropitious — ELIOT 308:24
condo forcing them to go c. — OROU 627:25
conduct C. is…our life — ARNO 34:62
c. of every private family — SMITH 798:48
its National c. — PULI 672:3
judgements on political c. — NEW 612:58
My c. shrieks aloud for apology — BEER 69:73
nice C. of a clouded Cane — POPE 659:76
observe a certain line of c. — MILL 570:64
one code of international c. — EISE 302:56
secure the good c. of women — WOLL 921:5
strange c. — ASTE 36:25
cone country…is an inverted c. — JOHN 445:30
sweet volcanic c. — LOWE 521:56
treat nature by…the c. — CEZA 203:51
Coney Island C. I. of the Mind — FERL 321:10
confection c. of tried medicines — BACON 47:57
confer c. with thee somewhat — NASHE 609:13
conference c.With the dead! — WEBS 895:16
naked into the c. chamber — BEVAN 85:22
No grand idea…born in a c. — FITZ 325:13
rather than hold three words'c. — SHAK 744:95
sales c. resembles a Passion play — SCRI 726:66
to hear our c. — SHAK 744:9

confess cannot c. them — SHAW 778:85
C. yourself to heaven — SHAK 754:11
If we c. our sins — BIBLE 125:34
truer than tongue c. — HOPK 412:82
wiser world doth greater thee c. — CAREW 190:50
confessed before the world c. — HOW 416:92
confession c.…of its author — NIET 615:18
greatest c. of its failure — STEV 824:41
making my Easter c. — JOSE 451:70
rage for c., autobiography — MANS 547:89
silence is your c. — EURI 316:11
sweetness of c. — FIRB 323:65
confide c. freely in death — ANOU 26:96
seldom c. in those who are better — CAMUS 188:1
confidence a c. trick — WILS 915:74
C. in an unfaithful man — BIBLE 100:51
fight with growing c. — CHUR 216:76
in quietness and in c. — BIBLE 103:30
Show your c. — GIUL 358:87
something like c. — GOOCH 363:97
suaveness isn't born of c. — HYDE 427:24
unconditional c. of his people — WEI 896:23
confident c. I can do very well — JOHN 442:35
in this will I be c. — BIBLE 95:7
confiding c., the intimate — MACD 530:48
confinement c.'s lingering hour — BYRON 179:95
sentenced to solitary c. — WILL 913:33
confirmation c. of truth — MILT 579:73
conflagrations c.…at Rome — AUGU 42:43
conflict brought into c. — BRIG 152:33
c. of its elements — BYRON 181:57
lexicon of c. and drama — SAFI 708:96
Never in the field of human c. — CHUR 216:78
too weak the c. to support — SHAK 764:4
We are in armed c. — EDEN 299:91
conflicts internal c. — ROSS 697:72
conformity c. of the image — DIDE 273:85
reward for c. — BROWN 157:50
confounds not the deed C. us — SHAK 767:98
confrontation born of this c. — CAMUS 187:88
confronts c. man with…choice — SART 715:47
confused c. the free — STEV 820:61
confusing c., disorienting — RICH 685:48
confusion all a c. — SCHL 718:13
C. now hath made his masterpiece — SHAK 767:9
c. of goals — EINS 301:39
C. on thy banners wait — GRAY 370:27
except my own c. — KERO 464:63
great blooming, buzzing c. — JAMES 434:64
let me never be put to c. — BIBLE 96:40
levee from a couch in some c. — CONG 232:44
confute how to c. him — SELD 726:78
congestion TB…that is the c. — ALLEN 12:43
Congo C., creeping through — LIND 511:48
congratulate sometimes c. ourselves — HAWT 386:35
congratulations C.…keep pouring — FREUD 336:51
congregation C. of Christ's flock — BOOK 141:12
Devil…hast the largest c. — DEFOE 258:13
landlord to the whole c. — ADDI 6:14
congress C. makes no progress — LIGNE 509:28
c. of stinks! — ROET 694:2
congressman easier…than…'C.' — GING 357:59
how to act like a C. — KENN 464:47
conjectural your audience is c. — ORWE 629:78
conjoined always c. together — HUME 422:4
conjunction epithalamic c. — ANDR 16:25
conjure c. up the blood — SHAK 746:42
conjuring c. trick with bones — JENK 437:24
conjuror level of the stage c. — MOORE 595:24
connect drive to c. — RICH 685:52
mystery of how they c. nouns — SAND 713:8
Only c.! — FORS 331:36
connection cannot find any artistic c. — KLEE 475:6
no c. worth speaking of — GALS 344:22
connections expresses the sum of c. — MARX 558:9
connoisseur c. of tame excitement — MOORE 595:38
connoisseurs c. of bread and butter — MACD 530:47
conquer able to fight and c. — TROT 867:15
Antony should c. Antony — SHAK 765:69
cannot c. America — PITT 653:43
die here, and we will c. — BEE 69:55
easier to c. it — WALP 887:28
England that was wont to c. — SHAK 734:9
In this sign thou shalt c. — CONS 235:30
resolve to c. or die — WASH 890:83
conquered c. and peopled — SEEL 726:72
C. people tend to be witty — BELL 73:78

God c.   JOHN 438:59
nation…perpetually to be c.   BURKE 168:9
Nothing can save the c.   VIRG 882:20
Romans c. the world   SWEE 830:45
same thing as the c.   ALEX 11:19
Thou hast c.   SWIN 833:35
will be c.   JOHN 446:69
conquering not c. but fighting well   COUB 238:86
worked too hard in c.   NAPO 607:69
conqueror commercial traveller…
missionary…barbarian c.   STAP 813:70
Love is a cruel c.   LAFO 485:8
overcame her savage c.   HORA 414:29
proud foot of a c.   SHAK 739:34
conquerors born of the c.   WRIG 930:83
laurel, meed of mighty c.   SPEN 808:73
conquers Love c. all things   VIRG 882:30
ruling passion c. reason   POPE 660:3
conquest c. of an unknown country   HEDIN 390:37
c. of the earth   CONR 234:96
end and object of c.   ALEX 11:19
fanned by C.'s crimson wing   GRAY 370:27
nature of c.   SHAK 743:61
never again seek…territory by c.   WILS 916:8
shameful c. of itself   SHAK 734:9
without threat of c.   RODO 693:94
conquests all the c.   SPEN 808:90
all thy c., glories, triumphs, spoils   SHAK 748:99
conquistador by temperament…c.   FREUD 336:50
conquistadores c. stole a page   MARTI 555:44
conscience binding on the c.   JOHN 439:61
catch the c. of the King   SHAK 753:72
c., above all liberties   MILT 579:68
c.…accomplishment of man's rest   BACON 48:5
c. ain't got no sense   TWAIN 871:10
c. ain't got no sense   TWAIN 871:11
C. always has   ROBI 690:37
c. clear my chief defence   DYER 297:53
c. does make cowards   SHAK 753:74
c. fools my wit!   JONS 448:18
C. has no more to do with gallantry   SHER 787:47
C. is a coward   GOLD 361:45
C. is but a word   SHAK 732:21
c. of the state   KING 468:41
C.: the inner voice   MENC 565:53
c. wakes despair   MILT 582:53
c. with injustice is corrupted   SHAK 730:59
dilemmas of c.   SNOW 802:36
exact a survey of his c.   DONNE 282:94
free c. from the paw   MILT 580:87
go against c.   LUTH 523:93
good digestion depends upon a good c.   DISR 276:36
good music and a clean c.   HIND 403:98
however strict their social c.   SMITH 799:81
In my c.…the baggage loves me   CONG 230:94
just as much c.   STOWE 826:73
keeper of his c.   DAVI 255:43
live with a good c.   SMITH 799:79
mortal sin on my c.   WILS 915:72
Neither c. nor sanity   MCNA 537:92
Nobody has any c.   HAWT 386:51
not burdening one's c.   WEIZ 896:35
O coward c.   SHAK 731:16
People talk about the c.   JAMES 433:49
policy sits above c.   SHAK 762:46
rule is a person's c.   LEE 500:35
Science without c.   RABE 676:62
siding champion c.   MILT 577:32
still and quiet c.   SHAK 775:19
sword with a clean c.   WILH 911:94
testimony of a good c.   KEMP 461:89
their c. as their King   TENN 846:21
the republic of c.   HEAN 389:13
to irritate your c.   OHEN 623:56
torn c. brings about   HUGO 421:87
umpire c., whom if   MILT 582:44
will not cut my c.   HELL 392:75
wound My c.   VAUG 878:45
consciences c. about doing evil   MORE 597:64
c. of the citizens   JOHN 438:56
conscious always c. of an inferiority   JOHN 445:22
c. of an uncomfortable sensation   DICK 269:84
c. of their actions   SPIN 810:25
Doth seem half c.   WORD 924:88
first I was scarcely c.   RUSS 705:56
To become c.   SAINT 709:24
tyranny of c. thought   BEEC 69:65

consciousness African national c.   MACM 536:71
Allow but a little c.   ELIOT 307:96
a time of awakening c.   RICH 685:48
building…part of the American c.   BUSH 175:88
chamber of c.   JAMES 433:42
change of c.   GINS 357:70
C., her awful Mate   DICK 272:68
c. is a staging area   BELL 74:91
c. is the only form you need   SARO 714:35
c. of myself   KANT 454:40
c. of science   DEWEY 264:43
c. of the limits   NIEB 614:99
c. that I have exercised the powers   PEEL 646:9
C., then, does not appear   JAMES 434:63
Cosmic c.   BUCKE 165:40
c. is a staging area   WILS 916:11
divinity…place in the human c.   DURK 296:34
from the beginning of c. to the end   WOOLF 922:26
habit of one's c.   MALE 542:88
in our ordinary c.   MOND 590:52
lopped off…your c.   ORWE 628:45
moral c. of people   MAIL 539:41
morning comes to c.   ELIOT 305:28
multiplicity of agreeable c.   JOHN 443:82
one-eighth part c.   GERH 350:35
states of c.   MOORE 594:21
stream of thought, of c.   JAMES 434:63
sublime c. of striving   HUMB 421:2
consecration c., and…dream   WORD 928:44
consensus C. Terrorism   COUP 238:93
consent approbation and c.   POWE 667:94
colonized people with their c.   SART 716:55
c. of all great men   RUSK 704:14
c. to the separation   GEOR 349:13
c.…under that Government   RAIN 677:92
engineering of c.   BERN 81:47
like enough to c.   SHAK 750:76
man without that other's c.   LINC 510:33
will ne'er c.   BYRON 181:68
consented Your father hath c.   SHAK 732:34
consenting between c. adults   NOZI 619:80
consequence as far as national c.   SCOTT 725:52
cause is the c.   FANON 317:43
c. of leaving one's home   LEBO 499:16
mistake subsequence for c.   JOHN 441:8
really a direct c.   PAST 642:46
trammel up the c.   SHAK 767:86
ultimate c.   MILL 572:6
consequences c. of changes   FRIE 337:62
damn the c.   MILN 575:89
In nature…only c.   VACH 875:11
In nature…there are c.   INGE 429:57
knowledge of c.   HOBB 404:24
of history and its c.   OBRI 620:99
social c. of their activities   HOBS 405:32
teach the c.   KISS 475:89
consequent c. to a time of war   HOBB 404:27
conservation C. of one resource   HERF 399:25
in favor of c.   TAFT 835:77
state…without the means of its c.   BURKE 168:29
conservatism barren thing this C.   DISR 276:46
c. and progress   TROL 866:82
C. discards Prescription   DISR 276:44
c. is based upon the idea   CHES 211:62
What is c.?   LINC 510:37
conservative banks were c.   THOM 854:24
called the C. party   CROK 245:65
C. Backbench MPs   BAKER 53:20
C.…enamoured of existing evils   BIER 129:22
C. government is…hypocrisy   DISR 276:50
C. ideal of freedom   MADAN 538:19
c. is a man   ROOS 696:47
C. Party at prayer   ROYD 701:50
leader of the C. Party   BEAV 67:20
leadership of the C. Party   HESE 401:61
make me c. when old   FROST 339:6
Metternich…was so c.   EVANS 316:17
most c. man in the world   BEVIN 85:29
Or else a little C.!   GILB 354:13
small c. majority   TYNAN 872:43
The Republic will be c.   THIE 851:52
the true C.   TENN 848:66
conservatives c. and reactionaries   VIDAL 881:3
C., as being by the law   MILL 570:67
C. base their…approach
to politics   HEATH 390:23
C. do not believe   HAIL 377:68

Life's better with the C.   ANON 23:77
terrible night for the C.   PORT 663:16
conserve to c. it, we must love it   MONT 593:93
consider C. anything, only don't cry!   CARR 196:6
c. the end in everything   LAFO 485:7
considerable wish to appear c.   JOHN 444:93
considerate if he were wisely c.   STEV 822:1
consideration c. of characters   JOHN 444:15
others worthy of c.   BLOOM 137:3
turns on moral c.   NAPO 607:67
con-si-de-ra-tion For a c.   SCOTT 725:42
considerations dictated by military c.   MCCA 528:10
considering c. how well they sell   JOYCE 452:2
consistency foolish c.   EMER 312:8
Too much c. is as bad   HUXL 425:71
consolatory mind C. food can find   SMART 797:31
console be consoled as to c.   FRAN 334:98
generally c. them   STEV 822:91
Knowledge…will not c. me   PASC 641:30
consolidation indissoluble c.   ROTH 699:29
consommé cyanide in the c.   WODE 919:62
consonants Only c. and vowels   RANS 679:28
shifting of vowels and c.   UNTE 874:71
thud of c.   BROY 163:98
consort But I c. with   KIPL 473:64
c. as they keep   MILT 577:21
conspiracies All professions are c.   SHAW 780:49
conspiracy Civilisation is a c.   BUCH 164:25
c. against the public   SMITH 798:44
c. is everything that ordinary life   DELI 261:80
c. of human beings   WELLS 898:75
c. to make you happy   UPDI 874:84
c. to oppress   DOUG 284:37
in a c. to under value them   JAMES 433:35
Indecency's c. of silence   SHAW 779:19
universal c. of silence   JAUR 435:95
vast right-wing c.   CLIN 222:12
conspirators All the c.   SHAK 748:25
C. have a logic   DELI 261:80
conspire stick'st not to c.   SHAK 770:3
constable Bible…c.'s handbook   KING 469:59
constabulary c. duty's to be done   GILB 354:3
constancy but c. in a good [cause]   BROW 158:70
C. alone is strange   ROCH 692:69
c. lives in realms above   COLE 226:7
c. of its vows   SHAW 778:1
no object worth its c.?   SHEL 787:30
constant c. as the Northern Star   SHAK 747:93
c. in a wondrous excellence   SHAK 773:43
C. you are   SHAK 741:33
more c. than a wife   RICK 686:75
No species remains c.   OVID 631:47
nothing in this world c.   SWIFT 830:59
one thing c.   JOUV 451:75
so c. to me   KEATS 457:6
To one thing c. never   SHAK 744:6
were man But c.   SHAK 729:41
Constantine walled by C. the Great   BAIL 52:42
Constantinople what is chaste in C.   FORD 329:2
constellation Los Angeles is a c.   MAIL 540:55
sets him in his c.   RILKE 687:87
constellations c. of data   GIBS 353:76
c. of feeling   DOUG 283:21
consternation returned in c.   SOME 803:67
constituencies elements in their c.   LIPP 512:72
go back to your c.   STEEL 813:86
constituency c. is the desperate   JACK 431:6
Every line in…budget has its own c.   WRIS 930:94
would not be in my c.   MENZ 566:90
constituents composed wholly of c.   RUSS 705:43
constitution abusing the best C.   FRAN 334:14
chief aim of their c.   MORE 597:67
corresponding social c.   MARX 557:1
country has its own C.   MUNS 604:91
free c.   GIBB 351:53
In the name of the C.   STAL 812:55
Like the British c.   CARD 190:42
pale of the C.   GLAD 358:89
parchment of a c.   TROT 867:44
parliamentary C. is not favourable   DISR 277:82
part of an Englishman's c.   AUST 43:77
The C. has never greatly bothered   BIDD 128:9
to our ancient C.   SWIFT 831:78
words of the C.   KING 468:35
constitutions men look at C.   JEFF 437:21
most unlikely c.   DICK 271:17
political C., are not our Life   CARL 192:18

constraint c., and sad occasion dear — MILT 578:45
constraints c. aping marriage — UPDI 874:77
construct c. a decoration — TROL 866:74
constructed peace must be c. — UNES 873:68
rightly c. boy's life — TWAIN 870:84
construction c. of…bombs — EINS 301:35
lifelong c. — GOULD 364:21
who comprehended its c. — PALEY 635:16
consul born when I was c. — CICE 218:28
consult C. the genius — POPE 659:93
C.…To seek another's approval — BIER 129:23
consume Rot, and c. themselves — SHAK 732:50
consumed bush was not c. — BIBLE 88:8
c. by use — GILL 356:49
consumer A person who is capable — STEIN 815:28
c. isn't a moron — OGIL 623:42
c.…is the king — SAMU 712:79
state for a potential c. — LURIE 522:91
consuming doubled their means of c. — MILL 570:59
consummation c.…wished — TWAIN 871:7
consumption balance of…c. — MALT 543:19
birds…in a c. — WEBS 894:78
c. is polarized — ILLI 428:46
C. is the sole end — SMITH 798:51
c. of valuable goods — VEBL 878:56
form of commerce and c. — MARX 557:1
galloping c. — GAND 345:33
no remedy against this c. — SHAK 742:43
not increase its c. — KEYN 466:91
universal c. — ILLI 428:45
contact Fly hence, our c. fear! — ARNO 32:22
removed from c. with…life — PRIT 669:47
voters have no c. — PRICE 668:14
contagion breathes forth c. — TWAIN 871:7
c. from her sable wings — MARL 552:85
c. in the tears — DRYD 289:54
c. of the world's slow stain — SHEL 786:4
C. to this world — SHAK 754:97
c., when it has once made head — DICK 271:17
great danger of c. — WILD 911:85
Rot inwardly, and foul c. — MILT 578:52
contain stating what it is to c. — JOHN 442:35
contaminated c. by…an identity — HAZL 387:66
contaminates lack of love c. — GUNN 375:39
contemplating c.…poetry — RICH 685:52
contemplation action, not by c. — BRON 154:68
Beneath thy c. — NEALE 610:28
best nurse c. — MILT 577:35
c. he and valour formed — MILT 583:62
c.…more than his reading — AUBR 39:67
c. of created things — MILT 583:79
mind…in a rapt c. — ELIOT 307:10
sitting apart in silent c. — GRAND 366:45
sundry c. of my travels — SHAK 750:72
youngling in the c. of evil — MILT 579:72
contemporary c. and future society — MURP 604:4
works by c. composers — HEIF 391:45
contempt breeds c.—and children — TWAIN 872:19
c. and anger of his lip! — SHAK 756:78
C. and beggary hangs — SHAK 737:79
c. for an arrant shit — JOSE 451:70
c. for anything he didn't understand — WOOL 923:59
c. for my character and opinions — SHAW 778:81
C. for the poor — OCON 622:28
c. for the poor performances — RYLE 707:80
c. of a great man — FITZ 325:15
c. of shame — JOHN 442:54
excites their c. — REED 682:88
for c. too high — COWL 240:35
greatest c. for novels — FORD 330:6
held in c. by those — GOLD 361:37
hold writers in c. — BELL 73:76
in c. of chance happenings — RABE 676:76
inward and secret c. — BACON 48:96
not for such c. — SHAK 731:3
Object of C. — AUST 42:57
pour c. on all my pride — WATTS 891:3
so great and general a c. — PEPYS 647:25
treat you with c. — WHIT 906:54
weakness, no c. — MILT 587:65
contend what it is we have to c. for — PITT 653:46
contender could have been a c. — SCHU 720:47
content beautiful…have the least c. — FLAU 326:31
contain any c. — WEIL 896:33
c. myself with wishing — PITT 652:36
c., retirement — THOM 856:54
C.'s a kingdom — HEYW 402:75

c. thyself to be…good — ADDI 7:37
c. to be such a one — SIDN 791:21
c. with his common humanity — SHAW 780:57
draw upon c. — GOLD 361:44
emptying…of all form and c. — FANON 317:44
full flavour of their c. — MILL 572:19
land of lost c. — HOUS 415:60
learned…to be c. — BIBLE 123:62
Looking back, I am c. — STEV 820:51
Must make c. with his fortunes — SHAK 763:76
Nor that c. surpassing wealth — SHEL 783:32
Nothing less will c. me — BURKE 168:10
Poor and c. is rich — SHAK 760:87
religious, not so much by its c. — CUPI 248:34
soul hath her c. — SHAK 759:75
Strong and c. I travel — WHIT 905:40
contented c. sort of discontent — KEATS 458:24
scarce be a c. woman — ROCH 691:66
we are c. — SCHR 720:40
contentedness procurer of c. — WALT 888:49
contention brawling, c. — STUB 827:3
Let the long c. cease! — ARNO 33:51
contentment C. and fulfilment — TROL 867:12
enjoying, what c. find? — MILT 584:1
Preaches c. to that toad — KIPL 470:73
contents c. worn out — FRAN 334:6
contest c. between agreeable fancy — STEV 820:59
counted the cost of this c. — DICK 273:82
end a c. quicker — SHER 787:46
pissing c. with that skunk — EISE 302:54
contests What mighty c. rise — POPE 658:64
continence perversion known as c. — HUXL 424:58
what c. to forbear — MILT 579:67
continent blowing through this c. — MACM 536:71
c. a new nation — LINC 510:39
C., I do not believe…exists — COOK 235:32
c. of energetic mongrels — FISH 324:77
C. people have good food — MIKES 569:51
c.'s violent requiem — DUNC 295:12
C. will not suffer England — DISR 276:42
descended across the C. — CHUR 217:92
deserted c. which gave me birth — MELBA 563:15
every man is a piece of the c. — DONNE 281:84
in the presence of this c. — FITZ 325:1
like having a c. disappear — JARR 435:79
part of our European c. — TOLS 863:8
That means on our c. — LEAC 497:72
U.S.A. is the slice of a c. — DOSP 282:3
continentals c. think life is a game — MIKES 569:52
continents dotted with c. and islands — MUIR 602:65
less difficult to join both c. — BOLI 139:45
contingent c. and the unforeseen — FISH 324:76
nothing c. is granted — SPIN 810:24
continually c. with thee — BIBLE 96:43
continuance felicity and long c. — BACON 50:67
continue c. in this quarter — SHAK 768:32
I intend to c. — THAT 851:33
we c.…a barbarous traffic — PITT 653:45
continuity c. of civilization — ORWE 629:80
contraception If you won't have c. — OBRI 620:1
contraceptive The C. Problem — DALY 251:78
contraceptives little use for c. — SHAR 776:40
contract c.…between those two — SMITH 797:43
c. theory in ritual form — NOVAK 618:72
Every law is a c. — SELD 726:77
Social C. is nothing more — WELLS 898:75
Society is indeed a c. — BURKE 169:39
verbal c. — GOLD 362:85
contracted happen to have c. it — JONES 447:89
more c. that power is — JOHN 445:30
contracts c. with the people — TRUM 868:35
Like all other c. — RICA 684:33
write enough to sign c. — GING 357:58
contradict c. myself? — WHIT 905:35
nobody to c. us — RADI 677:88
contradiction brook no c. — WEBS 895:20
c. in terms — SHAW 781:83
c., that New Orleans — MORT 599:19
fundamental c.…between socialism — DENG 261:89
locked…in this impossible c. — EAGL 297:65
risings…on c. that they grow — EMPS 314:63
spirit of c. — MACL 534:29
Whoever fears c. — SAINT 709:25
Woman's at best a c. — POPE 661:51
contradictions c., of the grotesque — TZARA 871:3
reconcile these c. — CARL 191:74
contradictory holding two c. beliefs — ORWE 630:3

contrapuntist c. is only a post-horse — MOZA 601:46
contraries Without c. — BLAKE 134:37
contrary c. to nature, c. to life — HUXL 425:71
c. to that order — JOHN 438:56
Hail Mary, quite c.! — GREE 371:61
not c. to reason — HUME 422:8
On the c.! — IBSEN 428:36
contribution c. to reality — THOM 853:99
editor…accepts with joy the c. — CANN 188:10
Man's c. to human history — JIANG 438:50
contrition a devout act of c. — OBRI 621:11
contrivance c. enough — JOHN 443:59
c. to raise prices — SMITH 798:44
Sexually, Woman is Nature's c. — SHAW 778:96
control campaign for birth c. — MUNRO 603:85
C. over behavior — LEGU 501:59
c. that which he produces — NGUGI 613:80
c. the meaning of words — DICK 265:61
history of arms c. — ADEL 7:46
in c. here — HAIG 376:64
knows how to c. or direct — MUGG 601:50
methods of c. — KEYN 465:85
sceptre to c. the world — SHAK 731:89
think you c. it — STEI 816:38
white people who were in c. — DAVIS 255:59
wrong members in c. — ORWE 628:60
controversy c. over capital — FISH 324:75
c. over freedom of speech — ORWE 629:93
great c. in antiquity — GERA 350:26
convalescence c.…makes illness — SHAW 781:79
convenience C. next suggested — COWP 241:67
elbow-chairs — BROY 163:2
convent c. for unloved women — POUND 664:24
convention books, c. and cliché — PAGL 634:81
Social c. is irrelevant — SCOTT 725:58
To the Lords of c. — KEYN 465:83
conventional c. and orthodox way — KISS 475:90
C. army loses — OBRI 620:4
C. life and c. people — NABO 606:47
c. way to rise above the c. — STAMP 812:60
proposal departing from c. lines — BRON 155:82
conventionality C. is not morality — LEWI 508:8
conventions c. of the present — ELIOT 304:6
convergence c. of human lots — POE 656:27
conversant c. with a Man's heart — AUST 44:95
conversation a great deal of c. — ACHE 2:18
Among the Ibo the art of c. — WODE 918:52
cheery c. and what-not — SMITH 798:44
c. ends in a conspiracy — BROW 158:54
c. I do acknowledge austere — LODGE 514:24
C. is like playing tennis — JONES 447:90
C. is more often — BRAD 148:64
C. is never easy for the British — MOORE 595:27
c. of the blind — WILD 911:91
c. wanders away from themselves — LEWIS 507:78
c. with my best friend — DESC 263:17
c. with the best men — STER 818:77
different name for c. — WODE 919:53
difficult to go on with the c. — WILDE 908:6
drown it by one's c. — WYCH 931:10
fitter for c. by 'em — CURT 249:47
In private c. — STERN 817:65
intimate as any c. — SAMP 712:76
journalism…as an extension of c. — SMITH 801:18
make his c. perfectly delightful — JOHN 442:52
materials for c. — OAKE 619:85
politics…are a c. — HOLM 407:76
stick on c.'s burrs — HUNT 423:37
support a flagging c. — SASS 716:75
conversational shallow c. ends — LINK 511:57
conversations c., and even a soliloquy — THOM 856:58
converse hold high c. — KEATS 457:81
sweet c. of an innocent — WOLL 921:10
them and rational c. — FORS 331:32
conversion believed in sudden c. — BIBLE 112:66
converted Except ye be c. — BIBLE 95:30
sinners shall be c. unto thee — EMER 313:53
convertible rogue…is still c. — PERE 648:62
upholstery of a Packard c. — ASHB 35:84
convex Self-portrait in a C. Mirror — POUND 665:52
conviction author's c. on this day — YEATS 933:50
best lack all c. — KUNI 482:39
c. is to report that dialogue — MEDA 563:5
c. that a hypothesis — STEAD 813:81
damnable iteration…of earnest c. — BROUN 157:36
every c. begins as a whim — JOHN 441:24
striking c. of the vanity —

what is called c. — HUNT 423:24
convictions c. are hills — FITZ 324:87
C. are more dangerous — NIET 615:4
feelings and c. — MORI 598:83
Stevenson's c. — LEHM 501:69
convenient any c. time for — MITC 588:99
convince labouring to c. — JOHN 443:67
persuading others, we c. — JUNI 453:10
works harder to c. himself — FRAS 335:27
convincing thought of c. — GOLD 362:70
conviviality taper of c. — DICK 267:14
convulsion wilful c. — STEV 824:39
convulsions groans and c. — STER 818:86
in c. hurled — POPE 661:34
Cook Illustrious C. — WENT 899:5
cook C. is a little unnerved — BETJ 84:5
c. was a good c. — SAKI 710:35
good c. is like a sorceress — SCHI 718:99
'Tis an ill c. — SHAK 737:74
very uncommon c. — SAKI 710:45
wanted to be a c. — DALI 251:69
Cooke-ham Farewell (sweet C.-h.) — LANY 489:7
cookery c. do! — MERE 567:97
cookie grandmother…like a c. — BAIL 52:3
cooking C. is like love — VAN 877:33
Good painting is like good c. — VLAM 882:35
offers succulent c. — POUND 665:43
Spare me from c. — PLATH 654:62
cooks bad female c. — NIET 615:23
c., physicians, carpenters — SUN 829:33
devil sends c. — FULL 341:66
not the c. — HARI 382:79
Skinny c. can't be trusted — ANON 24:36
the Devil sends c. — GARR 346:54
Too many c. — ANON 20:12
Whoso has sixpence…commands c. — CARL 192:92
cool chilli was something c. — THAC 849:45
C. is hot — WASH 890:89
c. of the day — BIBLE 86:50
c. white dress — FIRB 323:65
intellects vast and c. — WELLS 898:73
Keep c. — EMER 312:30
More than c. reason — SHAK 738:12
cooled coal that must be c. — SHAK 733:53
C. a long age — KEATS 459:58
Coolibah shade of a C. tree — PATE 642:54
Coolidge Nero fiddled, but C. — MENC 565:65
coomb stag in the Priory c. — DAVI 254:26
Coonardoo C. they called it — PRIC 668:16
Cooper make Jilly C.…rich — BRAD 148:67
rooting for Gary C. — BALD 54:39
cooperate C. on move one — RAPO 679:30
co-operating c.-o. and so self-moving. — RYLE 707:80
c.-o. in all that concerns — GEOR 349:19
co-operation c.-o. in their mutual — NOVAK 618:72
Government and c.-o. — RUSK 704:19
coot haunts of c. and hern — TENN 846:2
cop c. beatin' up a guy — STEI 815:34
Cope Hey, Johnnie C. — SKIR 795:14
Copernican universe is C. — PHIL 650:94
copier mere c. of nature — REYN 684:22
copies Make c., young man, many c. — INGR 429:64
coping c. with life — SPARK 806:17
trigger the c. mechanism — WRIS 930:89
Copper When Lord C. was right — WAUGH 892:30
copper c. into gold — SENG 727:95
Irishman is lined with c. — TWAIN 870:91
Copperfield that David C. kind of crap — SALI 710:51
copperheads forgot the c. — SAND 713:95
coppers c. hot — ADE 7:45
old time 'c.' — COLL 227:36
coppice love of field and c. — MACK 533:15
copulate people who can c. — MACD 529:40
copulating two skeletons c. — BEEC 69:63
copulation Birth, and c., and death — ELIOT 307:82
Let c. thrive — SHAK 763:88
Wit…is the unexpected c. of ideas — JOHN 441:25
copy all very well to c. — DEGAS 259:32
if you c. others — BERN 81:46
copying c. the answer out — KIER 467:8
copyists shortened the labour of c. — CARL 192:90
copyrights Take away…their c. — TROL 867:8
coral bones are c. made — SHAK 774:83
India's c. strand — HEBER 390:34
Japonica Glistens like c. — REED 681:77
corbies twa c. making a mane — BALL 56:92
cord threefold c. — BIBLE 100:74

Corde C. avoided cemeteries — BELL 74:88
cordiale entente c. — LOUIS 518:1
cords c. that hold India — CURZ 249:51
core compact c. — LENIN 502:82
heart and c. of ages — LOWE 519:21
In my heart's c. — SHAK 754:89
red ball of fire at its c. — AGAWA 8:71
Corinna Come, my C., come — HERR 400:44
Corinth Not everyone can sail to C. — ANON 18:59
cork pop the c. — STEV 822:99
tossed like a c. — HUGH 420:58
corked c. up for iver — ELIOT 303:79
corkscrew Bring in…a c. — DICK 267:11
corkscrews crooked as c. — AUDEN 39:87
Corky And C.'d protested — OATES 620:96
cormorant c. devouring time — SHAK 733:67
Sat like a c. — MILT 582:58
corn amid the c. — HOOD 410:39
c. rigs are bonie — BURNS 170:82
c. rigs are bonie — BURNS 170:84
Golden c. for the stranger — WILDE 907:82
golden ears of c. — HERR 400:47
graves…ploughed for c. — RED 681:71
In our sustaining c. — SHAK 763:86
meadows rich with c. — WHIT 906:61
produce a bushel of C. — PETTY 649:84
raise less c. and more hell — LEASE 498:97
there was c. — HERB 398:10
two ears of c. — SWIFT 831:80
yellow like ripe c. — ROSS 698:87
Corneille C. is…a clipped hedge — JOHN 447:74
Cornelius To you, C. — CATU 200:4
corner buy one on a c. — DAY 256:80
drives into a c. — JOHN 446:55
future…just around the c. — LESS 505:37
head stone of the c. — BIBLE 97:78
House at Pooh C. — PARK 637:47
into every penetrable c. — MACA 525:34
Joy shivers in the c. — ROBI 690:37
only one c. of the universe — HUXL 425:88
pointed out one c. of a square — CONF 230:89
some c. of a foreign field — BROO 156:6
spanked and stood in the c. — LEGU 501:63
turn a c. jinkan — BURNS 170:78
wake in a c. — KELM 461:80
what lay round the c. — KAVA 456:69
corners lounge at c. of the street — SPEN 807:50
obscure c. in one's own mind — HUXL 426:14
planes and the c. of rooms — MALL 542:98
round earth's imagined c. — DONNE 280:66
Unregarded age in c. thrown — SHAK 749:37
corner-stones c.-s. of literary art — DUDEK 293:78
cornfield o'er the green c. — SHAK 750:88
Cornpone C. and…Porkchop — ONAS 625:84
cornucopia brown paper c. — DUNNE 295:22
corollary C.—The history of science — SART 715:40
coronation Bring c., and sops — SPEN 808:68
coroner like the c.'s inquest — CONG 231:25
coronet bride of a ducal c. — DICK 268:49
coronets hearts are more than c. — TENN 840:74
corporal although this c. rind — MILT 577:41
UncleToby, interrupting the c. — STER 818:92
corporation C.…ingenious device — BIER 129:24
St Louis…arch of the c. — MAIL 540:55
corporations c. and local boards — MILL 570:66
great c. — GLEI 359:2
great modern c. — JAY 436:97
corps effete c. of impudent snobs — AGNEW 8:73
corpse before me is its c. — MAZZ 562:1
c. of the public credit — WEBS 894:71
fingers of cold are c. fingers — LAWR 494:15
good wishes to the c. — BARR 61:80
greeting a c. would give — BALD 54:42
hardly was the c. cold — STOP 825:61
I'll show you a c. — PUZO 673:26
make a lovely c. — DICK 268:45
more complete than a c. — VIAN 880:78
resuscitated c. — JENK 437:24
surgeon dissects a c. — APOL 27:14
corpses bivouac for c. — MUSS 605:15
c.…their unimportant look — DAVI 254:41
mock the riddled c. — SASS 716:57
corpulence burdenous c. my love — DONNE 280:61
correct about to c. themselves — BRADY 149:83
Are we c. to have changed — ASAHI 34:78
blot out, c., insert — SWIFT 832:96
do the perfectly c. thing — SHAW 780:71

moral is always c. — BART 62:17
not a c. deduction — KEYN 465:84
Protocoligorically c. — SHER 788:71
corrected C. and amended — FRAN 334:6
correcteth Lord loveth he c. — BIBLE 99:10
correction c. of private abuses — PEEL 646:8
look you, under your c. — SHAK 746:45
correctitude feather-bed of c. — BENN 76:51
Correggio corregiescity of C. — STER 818:82
correlative objective c. — ELIOT 305:47
correspondence c. was something like a duet — DONA 278:22
corridors admit princes to the c. — DOUG 283:21
brain has C. — DICK 272:65
c. of power — ALLEN 12:35
History has many…contrived c. — ELIOT 305:41
corrupt a people generally c. — BURKE 168:20
appointment by the c. few — SHAW 778:5
Beauty…easy to c. — BACON 49:42
c. my air — SHAK 769:66
daft or c. — FULL 341:59
should c. the world — TENN 847:62
corrupted c. by money — GREE 371:54
froth-c. lungs — OWEN 632:57
corrupter power a c. — SHEL 782:15
corruptible 'mongst things c. — MIDD 569:48
corruption c. in any government — BRUN 163:4
C. is more than a poison — ECON 298:80
c. of power — BRON 154:67
C., the most infallible symptom — GIBB 351:55
gratify avarice, and extend c. — JOHN 442:57
Louisianans don't tolerate c. — ANON 25:70
of dong and of c.! — CHAU 209:91
Stewed in c. — SHAK 754:10
suffer thine Holy One to see c. — BIBLE 94:92
corruptions man's c. — OTWAY 630:21
most pernicious C. — PRYN 672:93
corruptly Were not derived c. — SHAK 740:63
corset c. is…a mutilation — VEBL 878:54
Cory C., one calm summer — ROBI 690:28
Corydon Time, not C. — ARNO 33:47
cosine Brothers of the C. — ROOS 696:58
cosmetics c. and the silks — SEXT 728:91
factory, we make c. — REVS 684:20
cosmic bitter c. joke — GELL 348:98
born to make chaos c. — BEER 89:7
C. consciousness — BUCKE 165:40
cosmology problem of c. — POPP 663:95
cosmos c. has forgiven you — MAIL 540:62
push and pressure of the c. — JAMES 434:69
cossack c.'s whip — TROT 867:14
cost and counteth the c. — BIBLE 116:43
as though hate has no c. — SAND 713:4
c. of freedom — KENN 462:21
c. to freedom of opinion — SCHL 718:10
counted the c. of this contest — DICK 273:82
greatest c., namely time — ANTI 27:10
not apt to c. him — RUNY 702:80
that which dost c. me nothing — BIBLE 91:7
costly C. thy habit — SHAK 751:20
how c. summer was — SHAK 740:65
costs C. merely register — KNIG 476:14
Love c. us nothing — RICK 686:76
subtract the c. — GATES 347:62
whatever it c. them — UPDI 874:82
what everything really c. — SMITH 797:42
costume cardinal points of c. — MURR 604:57
c. will be Indecent — LAVER 493:81
national c., architecture — BIRD 130:62
cot paint the c. — CRAB 242:88
sheltered c. — GOLD 361:51
cottage before his c. door — SOUT 805:98
no cheerful c. has blest my eyes — SCHAW 717:96
removed like a c. — BIBLE 102:23
Wherever there's a c. small — PARK 638:81
cottages march in c. of…weeds — MARL 551:78
peace to the c. — CHAM 204:68
cottar stirk from a c. — SCOTT 723:13
cotton c. flowers of her dress — THOM 853:94
c. is high — HEYW 402:73
four c. ones — TRAV 864:42
so are banks, so is c. — DICK 268:26
world wrapped up in…jeweller's c. — DICK 269:81
cotton-town Lancashire c.-t. — ORWE 627:40
couch century of the psychiatrist's c. — MCLU 536:91
c. for luxury — SHAK 752:33
hidden c. — GORD 363:6

soul of man is a far c. — THOM 852:56
spirit of our c. — CHEE 209:4
stamp out literature in the c. — WAUGH 892:26
struggle for…my c.'s cause — OCON 621:20
sunlight falls across the c. — IHIM 428:43
the pride of my c. I sang — OBRU 621:12
the religion of the c. — SWIFT 832:13
this c. safe to work in — THAT 850:14
This was my c. — BLUN 137:15
to all the c. dear — GOLD 361:53
to be had in the c. — HAZL 387:67
to die for one's c. — HORA 413:23
took away their c. — SHER 787:33
totalitarianism in this c. — ORWE 629:94
to your own c. — JOAN 438:52
undiscovered c. — TWAIN 871:7
United States is the only c. — ROGE 695:23
unmapped c. within us — ELIOT 304:15
unsubduable c. — GILL 356:41
virtues! they've undone his c. — ADDI 7:35
vow to thee, my c. — SPRI 811:39
war rather than a c. — PILG 651:16
we shall liberate this c. — MAND 544:51
when our c. was born — INOU 430:72
Where is the c., my friend? — ARGU 29:43
who serves his c. best — HAYES 387:63
Who slights his c. thus — INGR 429:59
wild unexplored c. — LIVI 512:83
young c. is a real heritage — MANS 547:96
Your c. is more precious — PLATO 655:82
Your c. needs you! — ANON 22:46
countryman c. must have praise — BLYT 138:24
countrymen sacrifices of our fellow c. — EISE 302:64
steady his fellow c. — MURR 605:10
countryside c. is the colour of a lion — BOWL 147:34
disappeared from the c. — MACL 535:45
smiling and beautiful c. — DOYLE 285:67
well-farmed c. was their favourite — TOLK 862:1
counts grooves that c. — ANON 26:85
county Emeralds big as half a c. — LAND 488:84
married with the C. — SHAK 737:73
couple fool…in every married c. — FIEL 323:45
price paid for becoming a c. — COUP 239:1
couples happy c. in the face — STEV 821:82
courage as good a c….father had — ELIZ 309:56
Be strong and of a good c. — BIBLE 90:62
c. and faith and zest — KENN 463:23
'C.!' he said — TENN 839:53
c. holds firm — ANON 18:69
C. in your own — GORD 363:5
C. is a moral quality — MORAN 596:56
C. is in the air — FROST 339:16
C. is not simply one — LEWIS 507:77
C. is the most important — KENN 464:49
c. mounteth with occasion — SHAK 738:20
c. never to submit or yield — MILT 580:1
c. of the Negro — PHIL 650:95
c. prove my title — SHAK 766:61
C., rashness, and rebellion — MARI 550:52
c. the greater — ANON 18:76
c. to change the things — NIEB 614:1
c. to follow the talent — JONG 448:95
c. to give you unqualified praise — STEI 815:36
c. to know — KANT 455:42
c. to live out — MILL 573:32
c. to love — TROL 866:77
c. to ride a horse — LEAC 496:55
endurance, and c. — SCOTT 722:81
gently raised Their fainting c. — MILT 581:11
give me…the c. — BAUD 64:65
home…saved by his c. — MACA 527:78
it is not man Made c. — POUND 665:59
journey that required c. — MURP 604:3
Kindness and c. — MUIR 602:59
manly c. — PEEL 646:10
must have the c. to dare — DOST 282:7
my C. and Skill — BUNY 167:77
Nature all c. me denyis — DUNB 294:8
Neither fear nor c. saves — ELIOT 305:42
never to let…your c. grow dim — CURZ 249:53
on the c. and conduct — WASH 890:83
people who have the c. — MUSS 605:18
Red Badge of C. — CRANE 243:27
Screw your c. — SHAK 767:90
sheer c. and endurance — WAVE 893:58
Take c., my friend — READE 680:50
the matter of c. — SONT 804:80

void of c. — MAIL 540:52
Why, c., then — SHAK 731:85
With constant c. — JONS 448:8
without originality or moral c. — SHAW 778:79
with the c. of their race — SULL 828:17
courageous C. and loyal to the tips — ACHE 3:39
faith…creative and c. — CUPI 248:35
couriers sightless c. of the air — SHAK 767:87
course c. already decided upon — BIER 129:23
c. of a dishonest life — FRAS 335:27
c. of true love — SHAK 737:84
c. till I had ended — MUNDY 603:83
c. was unjustified — HIRO 403:5
earth's diurnal c. — WORD 924:80
face forward his c. — ANON 20:15
finish my earthly c. — BEET 70:98
golf c. is the epitome — GIRA 358:80
have finished my c. — BIBLE 124:86
held in the true c. — CARL 193:27
played on a five inch c. — JONES 447:85
take the wrong c. — KENN 462:22
Take you a c. — DONNE 279:43
There is no other c. — HUSS 424:43
things take their c. — MACA 526:73
Time rolls his ceaseless c. — SCOTT 723:6
courses in a series of c. — GOLD 361:35
miss out on any of the c. — RUSS 706:68
court air of the c. — ETHE 315:98
c. an amorous looking-glass — SHAK 731:99
c. as an orphan — LEVA 506:52
c. he practised — DRYD 290:93
c. is only as sound — LEE 500:37
c. of kynge Arthure — MALO 542:7
dreary length before the c. — DICK 269:80
fill the c. with quarrels — SHAK 775:5
in the c. a cloister — AELR 8:55
Keeps his pale c. — SHEL 785:92
kynges c., my brother — CHAU 208:77
taller…than any of his c. — SWIFT 831:77
threshold of Jove's c. — MILT 577:25
Through the c. — WILDE 907:81
To the Tennis C. — PEPYS 647:38
whole C. of Parliament — HENR 395:46
courted c. by an Italian — HEPB 396:58
courteous first, the Retort C. — SHAK 750:91
So c., so kind — SKEL 795:91
courtesan c. is a myth — FLAU 326:32
when the c. farts — ANON 20:10
courtesans crowd of c. — DUMAS 294:94
courtesies c. that raise me — BROW 159:1
small sweet c. of life — STER 818:4
courtesy breeds patience and c. — MUIR 602:59
defence like elaborate c. — LUCAS 521:74
second time do such a c. — SHAK 742:32
the greater c. — TENN 847:57
courthouse c. pacing up and down — LIND 511:50
court-huntsmen tell c.-h. — DONNE 279:41
courtier c. grave and serious — GILB 355:33
not the c.'s art — DRYD 290:93
courtings rhetorical c. — CLEV 221:82
courtliness c., and…fame — TENN 846:22
courtly Be c. ay in clething — DUNB 294:4
courtmartialled c. in my absence — BEHAN 70:4
courts about her c. were seen — LAND 488:84
brawling c. — TENN 844:55
C. for Cowards were erected — BURNS 170:73
c. of Europe are a jungle — BOLT 139:50
day in thy c. — BIBLE 96:47
decision of the c. — LEAC 497:67
forbidden by the c. — STIG 824:45
not enough c. — HUMP 422:17
courtship blindness of c. — LOWE 521:58
brash c. of the muse — THOM 854:28
C. to marriage — CONG 231:4
c. was so much as thought on — LAMB 486:43
cousin little c. is dead — RANS 679:22
cousins c., and his aunts! — GILB 353:93
c. as the sands of the sea — SHAW 781:1
couth such a thing as too much c. — PERE 648:61
couturiers c. the last possessors — DIOR 275:24
covenant c. between me — BIBLE 87:69
c. between me — BIBLE 87:77
c. from the beginning is — BIBLE 108:51
c. of our fathers? — BIBLE 106:19
c. with death — BIBLE 103:27
establish my c. — BIBLE 87:77
Coventry into a moral C. — PARN 639:91

cover c. of an old book — FRAN 334:6
C. your ass — SAFI 708:98
I c. all — SAND 713:96
on the c. of every issue — WAUGH 891:6
paste and c. to our bones — SHAK 735:19
they were just a c. — RAMOS 678:6
time to run for c. — ASHD 35:91
covering hair is given her for a c. — BIBLE 121:5
covers c. are too close together — LEHM 501:70
covert c. from the tempest — BIBLE 103:32
covertousness bereave him of his c. — MILT 579:78
cover-up c.-u., or anything else — NIXON 617:46
covet sin to c. honour — SHAK 746:55
Thou shalt not c. — BIBLE 88:23
Thou shalt not c. — CLOU 223:40
covetous Every c. and avaricious man — INNO 429:69
cow c. from a Lowland strath — SCOTT 723:13
c. is of the bovine — NASH 608:75
Kiss till the c. comes home — BEAU 67:11
Knowledge is a sacred c. — SZENT 834:65
milk the c. of the world — WILB 907:71
saddle fits a c. — STAL 812:58
show me a c. who can earn — WINN 917:25
steals a c. from a poor widow — SCOTT 723:13
The Red C. — TRAV 865:47
Truth, Sir, is a c. — JOHN 443:68
Coward I love you—Noël C. — COWA 239:19
coward Conscience is a c. — GOLD 361:45
c. does it with a kiss — WILDE 910:54
c. in the presence of — STAN 812:61
c. in thine own esteem — SHAK 767:88
Fore God I am no c. — TENN 848:60
gift of a c. — SHAK 755:49
coward just a c. — HEMI 394:15
The sea hates a c.! — ONEI 625:97
This sanguine c. — SHAK 742:15
cowardice admit the c. — SHAW 778:95
C., as distinguished from panic — HEMI 394:15
Nine times out of ten it is c. — SIDM 790:96
surest is c. — TWAIN 872:26
cowardly c. way to score — PELE 646:6
cowards conscience does make c. — SHAK 753:74
Courts for C. were erected — BURNS 170:73
C. die many times — SHAK 747:88
fools and c. might sit safe — OTWAY 631:28
goes to the heads of c. — MITC 588:97
learn'd are c. — DRYD 289:67
Tho' c. flinch — CONN 232:55
When c. mock the patriot's fate — INGR 429:59
coward-slave c.-s., we pass him by — BURNS 173:46
cowbind Green c. — SHEL 787:25
cowboy last true c. in America — HEAT 390:30
cowboys c. had lived for months — MCMU 537:87
Cowdenknowes broom of C. — BALL 55:70
Cowley Who now reads C.? — POPE 661:52
cow pat humble violet under a c. p. — BARN 60:65
cows Barrymore's acting till the c. — NATH 609:82
cash to feed your pigs — ANDE 15:16
dance with you till the c. — MARX 557:87
To be contented…that's for the c. — CHAN 205:3
cowshed smelling of the c. — THOM 853:89
cowslip C.…like tethered foam — CRANE 243:22
In a c.'s bell I lie — SHAK 775:99
I'th' bottom of a c. — SHAK 773:59
cowslip-banks sit on c.-b. — WALT 888:52
cowslips c., and kingcups — SPEN 808:68
c. wan that hang — MILT 578:54
cow-woman c.-w. and the scum-woman — GRAND 366:45
coxcomb c. ask two hundred guineas — RUSK 704:34
more consummate c. — WESL 900:22
coxcombs some made c. — POPE 658:51
cozenage town is full of c. — SHAK 733:59
Crabbe With C. it may be difficult — BYRON 182:75
crabbedness not the result of mere c. — FADI 317:37
crabs like wet c. in a basket — DURR 296:38
roasted c. hiss in the bowl. — SHAK 734:95
crab-tree schoolboys…climb a c.-t. — ROCH 691:63
crack c. your cheeks! — SHAK 763:71
hear the mighty c. — POPE 661:34
heaven's vault should c. — SHAK 764:5
no c. in a fortress — MILL 571:98
will sure c. both — SHAK 769:52
would c. in the flame — JEFF 436:10
crackling c. of thorns under a pot — BIBLE 101:77
generous with the c. — MACB 527:82
cracks c. of other people's lives — WHAR 901:49
cracky joined with the Arabs, by c.! — ACHE 3:48

cradle c. of a new masterpiece	YEATS 933:39
c. of Spanish walnut	PLATH 654:71
c. rocks above an abyss	NABO 606:29
c. to the grave	ANON 25:57
from the c. to the grave	SHEL 785:82
hand that rocks the c.	WALL 886:10
high mountain c. in Pamere	ARNO 32:28
In c. clothes our children	SHAK 741:93
Out of the c.	GRIF 373:12
Thou shalt not c.	BREC 151:8
cradled c. into poetry	SHEL 783:27
cradles bit the babies in the c.	BROW 160:26
craft Between c. and credulity	BURKE 168:18
cloakèd c. their store of skill	DYER 297:52
continued with my c.	JAMES 434:57
c. be best to lerne?	LANG 489:99
C. is the handprint	ANON 25:76
c. so long	HIPP 403:1
c. so long to lerne	CHAU 208:54
mere c. and cozenage	JONS 450:53
writing is a c.	PORT 663:9
crafts C. which require the most Time	CANT 188:17
craftsman produce the perfect c.	VITR 882:34
craftsmen c. share a knowledge	SACK 708:88
crag clasps the c.	TENN 844:68
cragged huge hill, C., and steep	DONNE 279:31
crags among these barren c.	TENN 839:62
craigs bizzing c. and mous to weet	FERG 321:8
cram C. as much pleasure as you can into life	MACG 532:90
cramp drugs cause c.	PARK 638:65
cranberries man wrapping c.	DOLE 278:14
Rice, and a C. Tart	LEAR 497:81
crane protection of the whooping c.	BRIN 153:42
Tall as a c.	SITW 794:70
Cranford here at C.	GASK 346:58
crank c. is a small engine	SHEE 782:7
c. until the idea succeeds	TWAIN 872:25
serve…apprenticeship as a c.	BROUN 157:36
crap David Copperfield kind of c.	SALI 710:51
crape saint in c. is twice	POPE 661:30
crash the c. is coming	PARK 638:68
thoughts of the c.	THOM 854:24
crave mind forbids to c.	DYER 296:50
the more you c.	POPE 661:57
craved c. no crumb	GILB 355:31
craves c. wary walking	SHAK 747:82
craving c. to risk death	FOWL 332:65
full as c.	DRYD 289:63
Crawford best time…with Joan C.	DAVIS 255:54
crawling c. between heaven	SHAK 753:79
maybe she will do the c.	FAUL 319:73
crazed c. with the spell	DELA 260:66
crazy all going to go c.	KRAM 480:5
c. about cars	SALI 711:58
c. for love	BART 62:9
C. Like A Fox	PERE 648:54
edge of some c. cliff	SALI 711:61
grow a little c.	GOLD 360:32
I suppose all writers are c.	CHAN 205:93
Orr was c.	HELL 392:60
that's what is c.	JONAS 447:84
unless I'm c.	HEMI 394:18
We are all born c.	BECK 68:40
would end by becoming c.	MAUP 562:87
cream cat to steal c.	SHAK 742:24
c. rises until it sours	PETER 649:76
queen of curds and c.	SHAK 770:88
cream-faced c.-f. loon!	SHAK 768:36
create absence of the urge to c.	MAMET 543:27
anything he might c.	MAMET 543:26
c. and keep quiet	FLAU 326:37
c., if it concerns poetry	HUGO 420:63
c. in our minds the very things	ABER 1:5
desire to c. something	PRIE 668:23
know, to kill and to c.	BAUD 65:82
To c. is…to destroy	CUMM 247:99
to c. jazz	GILL 356:48
created C. half to rise	POPE 660:17
c. the poodle	THUR 860:52
wealth that you never c.	TSON 869:55
creating envisioning all without c.	GORO 364:14
let us start c.	ANON 23:4
Shopping is Not C.	COUP 238:95
creation all of your soul in c.!	HUGO 420:72
appropriate act of c.	FEIN 319:85
Art is like C.	KLEE 475:9

artistic c. is modern life	WAGN 884:64
Back of every c.	MILL 573:39
between human c.	MILL 573:34
bless thee for our c.	BOOK 141:84
blind fury of c.	SHAW 778:83
blot on the fair face of c.	BRON 155:79
c. first brought forth	MILT 585:34
c. of images	HOLL 407:68
c. of the heavens and the earth	KORAN 477:43
C.'s tears in shoulder blades	STEV 820:44
deepest mysteries of c.	SHEL 782:11
Did ever woman, since the c.	STER 817:68
fairest of c.	MILT 584:14
from that equal c.	JEFF 436:12
horror of C.	HUGH 419:48
inexhaustible fullness of c.	HUMB 421:2
jazz…process of c.	LIEB 509:27
Love all God's c.	DOST 283:11
love C.'s final law	TENN 843:36
love C.'s final law	TENN 843:45
morning of his c.	HUXL 425:93
participate in the c.	ROBBE 688:10
parts of the C.	HALES 377:81
present at the C.	EVANS 316:17
she is his new c.	STONE 825:57
speak before you think c.'s [motto]	FORS 332:54
spelled out the history of c.	FISKE 324:80
spilled…hate into his dearest c.	BURG 167:93
supreme c. of an era	BART 62:18
think more of the c.	GAUG 347:67
through a limitless c.	HUXL 426:5
tire of all c.	HOLM 408:85
took the whole of C.	HUGH 419:39
Vexing its own c.	WORD 925:89
warrants the c.	FIELD 322:30
whole c. groaneth	BIBLE 120:75
whole c. moves	TENN 844:67
woman a mere after-thought in c.	STAN 812:67
world was before the c.	BROW 158:78
creations c. of a poet	SHEL 786:13
human c. mechanical	LEGER 501:52
like all original c. of the human spirit	DYSON 297:63
creative active and c. world	SPEN 807:65
always being c.	CANT 189:20
beautiful, c. and good	MING 587:70
C. Endeavour lost	WAUGH 892:25
c. gift	HOPK 413:11
c. people hate mathematics	ISSI 431:95
c. talent…drained off	RICH 686:65
reading…highly c.	CARY 198:59
satisfies the human c. instinct	QUEN 674:39
victim of c. suffering	KING 468:38
creativity angel of c. wrestling	LENG 502:81
c. comes to an end	ROTH 699:14
C. in science	KOES 477:32
dimensions of thought and c.	STEI 816:46
keep that childlike c.	HIRS 403:9
sex and c. are often seen	JONG 448:96
creator all-wise C.	HALES 377:81
c. from his work returned	MILT 584:94
c. in the year 1902	MORT 599:19
C.'s power display	ADDI 6:26
endowed by their C.	STAN 812:62
God, C. wise	MILT 585:27
greater glory of his C.	PIUS 653:55
my c., detest and spurn me	SHEL 782:12
Remember now thy C.	BIBLE 101:92
served the creature more than the C.	BIBLE 120:59
the C. made Italy	TWAIN 870:77
creators c. of odd volumes	LAMB 487:52
creature c. driven by demons	FAUL 318:67
c. here Beast, bird, insect	MILT 583:70
c. of the common streets	DICK 270:97
c.'s at his dirty work	POPE 661:35
Dear is the helpless c.	BYRON 181:70
Deformèd c.	SPEN 808:76
Each c. of the world	ALAN 9:82
every c. in a cave	SNYD 803:52
every c. shall be	MARL 552:1
God's first C.	BACON 50:61
imitator is a poor kind of c.	WHIS 902:64
in Christ, he is a new c.	BIBLE 122:2
kills a reasonable c.	MILT 578:62
lone lorn c.	DICK 269:61
Lovely c. in scarlet	GEOR 350:24
Man is a c. who	STEV 822:89
Man is a history-making c.	AUDEN 41:21

Man is the only c.	ORWE 629:72
No c. loves an empty space	MARV 556:78
no c. loves me	SHAK 731:19
No c. smarts so little	POPE 661:34
Not a c. was stirring	MOORE 594:14
proves, that every c.	SWIFT 832:1
ravished this fair c.	FIEL 322:40
served the c. more than the Creator	BIBLE 120:59
sigh of the oppressed c.	MARX 557:94
small c. of the night	AMIS 14:82
so good a c.	GALT 344:28
some new and wondrous c.	DARW 253:9
sort of c. that can't die	THER 851:49
thy c., to whom thou art bound	SHEL 782:12
Y'are the deed's c.	MIDD 569:47
creatures All c. great and small	ALEX 11:22
all c. here below	KEN 461:94
births of living c.	BACON 49:24
breastless c. under ground	ELIOT 305:34
countless joyful c. sing	KIER 467:15
c. give out a smell	LEES 500:48
c. in warmer countries	GUY 375:50
c.…looked from pig to man	ORWE 629:76
c. of commanding sadness	LEE 500:45
c. there Live	MILT 584:98
disagree Of c. rational	MILT 581:30
distinguished from all other c.	ADDI 6:30
fair c. of an hour	KEATS 457:94
frustrated c. we were	MILL 572:26
home, you idle c.	SHAK 746:70
human c. breathe an atmosphere	DICK 271:17
lawful lords of earthly c.	DAVI 254:33
meanest of his c.	BROW 162:66
Men are very fragile c.	STEP 817:60
no better than c.	JOHN 444:11
obedience of c.	HOOK 410:54
orders and inferior c.	MILT 586:55
race of upstart c.	MILT 581:34
rarest of political c.	MCFA 531:69
shining c. of the chase	TENN 841:97
solidarity with other isolated c.	BELL 74:85
spiritual c. walk the earth	MILT 583:69
These Ibsen c.	ANON 21:38
widows…the most perverse c.	ADDI 6:19
worst sin towards our fellow c.	SHAW 777:66
credentials There are no c.	LLOY 513:96
credit corpse of the public c.	WEBS 894:71
c. cards cancelled	ANON 25:59
c. goes to the man	DARW 253:19
c. to a Trappist nun	SHAR 776:41
faces as thin as c. cards	AMIS 14:99
From your fair c.	FLET 328:75
get c. for anything	JOHN 440:89
impossible to c.	WILL 912:4
I will take the c. for	BEVIN 85:33
more c. than they deserved	REST 683:16
Of c. lost	JONS 450:52
physicians…take the c.	BURG 167:86
seek to take the c.	PARK 637:46
the c. of our…government	STEE 814:94
to give them c.	USTI 875:3
world will give thee c.	CHUR 215:47
creditors gaping c.	OTWAY 631:26
credulities c. of mankind	CONR 234:16
credulity Between craft and c.	BURKE 168:18
interest dictates and c. encourages	JOHN 442:55
present age is craving c.	DISR 276:67
credulous men are the most c.	POPE 659:92
creed c. and particular reality	MUNCH 603:81
c. of a second-rate man	BAGE 51:95
c. of different parties	TOCQ 861:84
c. which accepts	MILL 570:70
establishing your c.	BAGE 51:79
got the better of his c.	STER 818:79
need…shapes a human c.	CULL 247:96
Non-violence…last article of my c.	GAND 345:34
pagan suckled in a c. outworn	WORD 928:46
shrieked against his c.	TENN 843:36
shrieked against his c.	TENN 843:45
solemn c. with solemn sneer	BYRON 180:28
underlies every c.	BLAV 136:91
unionism is stronger than c.	LAWS 495:44
creeds dust of c. outworn	SHEL 785:75
keys of all the c.	TENN 843:31
our casual c.	ARNO 32:21
second of man's c.	LAWR 495:39
than in half the c.	TENN 844:57

c. fighting c. minds · MUIR 602:58
c. shall be made straight · BIBLE 103:36
c. timber of humanity · KANT 455:43
c. winding ways · HERB 398:11
shortest line…may be the c. one · BREC 151:10
crop A runnable stag, a kingly c. · DAVI 254:27
crops among the gradual c. · SMITH 799:64
c. of love and hate · MUIR 602:63
with increasing c. · SHAK 733:64
croquet good game of C. · REID 682:96
higher and dirtier c.-player · WOOL 923:63
cross an ancient C. · YEATS 934:66
bear your c. willingly · KEMP 461:91
cling to the old rugged c. · BENN 75:23
C. alone has flown the wave · CRANE 242:8
c. be uncrossed · ELIOT 307:8
c. is God's truth · BONH 140:57
c. of the Legion of Honour · TWAIN 870:90
C. to be Borne · SMITH 800:92
endured the c. · BIBLE 124:99
grace without the c. · BONH 140:58
houses marked with a red c. · PEPYS 647:40
In the c. is salvation · KEMP 461:90
let him now come down from the c. · BIBLE 114:3
little marble c. below the town · HAYES 387:62
orgasm has replaced the c. · MUGG 601:48
shouldered high his voluntary C. · CAMP 186:61
sign of the C. · BOOK 141:12
stone remains, and the c. · MACC 527:84
survey the wondrous C. · WATTS 891:3
taketh not his c. · BIBLE 111:30
take up his c….and follow me · BIBLE 115:33
take up his c. daily · BIBLE 115:33
Upon the c. · SITW 794:73
win the Holy C. · MALO 543:12
cross-bow With my c.-b. I shot · COLE 225:82
cross-breed unhappy c.-b. · DISR 276:46
crossed c. in love · AUST 43:68
crosses between the c. · MCCR 529:19
nothing lives but c., cares, and griefs · SHAK 734:11
cross-gartered c.-g….she detests · SHAK 756:72
crossness make c. and dirt succeed · FORS 331:45
crossroads c. of all the evil · GENET 348:5
mankind faces a c. · ALLEN 12:56
crossword skill of a solved c. puzzle · SAND 713:15
crotch c. of this fig-tree · PLATH 654:72
crouch c., swivel, tug · OBRI 621:10
make c. beneath his foot · BROW 162:85
crow cock doth c. · BALL 57:98
c. doth sing as sweetly · SHAK 741:91
c. loves his fledglings · MORE 596:58
c. Makes wing · SHAK 768:16
dog bark at a c. · SHAK 744:88
louder a crow can c. · TROL 867:90
milk-white feather in a c. · CAMP 186:60
sun had risen to hear him c. · ELIOT 303:80
upstart c. · GREE 371:80
crowbar straightened out for a c. · HOLM 408:85
crowd c. begins to pour in · ROST 699:8
c. flowed over London Bridge · ELIOT 305:54
c. is not company · BACON 49:29
c. laughs with you always · VIDOR 881:11
c. of courtesans · DUMAS 294:94
c. will always save Barabbas · COCT 224:59
c. without singeing someone's beard · LICH 509:20
faces in the c. · POUND 664:28
Far from the madding c.'s · GRAY 369:20
flock of sheep…can make a c. · BEER 69:82
I saw a c. · WORD 927:40
jocosity catches the c. · MARQ 554:26
Out of the c. a mistress · SHEL 786:8
pale and anxious c. · WILDE 907:81
something about a c. · WALL 886:11
Will she pass in a c. · SWIFT 830:62
crowded marriage…was a bit c. · DIANA 265:48
crowds apprehensions come in c. · WORD 927:38
c., her beloved smoke · LAMB 486:29
enterprising firm that supplies c. · SIMP 792:45
talk with c. · KIPL 474:68
crow-flowers Of c.-f., nettles, daisies · SHAK 755:25
crown allegiance to one C. · GEOR 349:19
both divide the c. · DRYD 291:40
cause Against the c. · DRYD 290:80
c. enchased with pearl · MARL 551:74
c. enough to virtue · JONS 450:49
C. has made a purchase · WHIT 902:67
c. of a stranger · MOORE 596:48

c. of our life · SWIN 833:30
c. of sorrow · TENN 840:78
c. of twelve stars · BIBLE 126:65
Ere the King's c. shall fall · SCOTT 725:58
exchange it some day for a c. · BENN 75:23
farm to buy my c. · SHAK 746:67
fill me from the c. to the t. · SHAK 766:82
finest Colonies under the C. · STUA 827:98
from Ceasar's funeral c. · BLAKE 135:69
From the c. of his head · SHAK 744:10
fruition of an earthly c. · MARL 551:75
give there a c. of life · BIBLE 126:48
hairy gold c. · KIPL 471:97
head that wears a c. · SHAK 743:53
impious hand to the C. of Thorns · BRON 155:82
influence of the C. · DUNN 295:25
King his c. and dignity · SHAK 730:66
Lion and the Unicorn…for the c. · CARR 197:16
Put on my c. · SHAK 766:60
Scepter and c. must tumble down · SHIR 789:83
set the c. upon a stock · HOWA 417:94
strike his father's c. · SHAK 745:30
to wear a c. · ELIZ 310:62
undoubted right of the c. of England · COVE 239:6
virtuous woman is a c. · BIBLE 99:23
wear that c. · HEYW 402:75
within the hollow c. · SHAK 735:20
Word climbs upward into Its c. · DUNC 295:13
worn the c. · BIBLE 107:47
crowned c. knot of fire · ELIOT 309:51
C. with rank fumitor · SHAK 763:86
crowning moment of the Queen's c. · DIMB 275:20
crowns Cast their c. before · BIBLE 126:55
climb soonest unto c. · SHAK 730:82
Give c. and pounds and guineas · HOUS 414:46
last act v. the play · QUAR 674:37
crows roused the ribald c. · SHAK 757:9
thought to keep out the c. · MILT 579:63
crow-toe c.-t., and pale gessamine · MILT 578:54
crucible America is God's C. · ZANG 936:88
cast a violet into a c. · SHEL 786:13
man in a c. · ELKIN 310:70
crucibles agony dancing in his c. · THOM 853:95
crucified choose who is to be c. · COCT 224:59
c. Jesus…picture of God · BAKER 53:15
not been c.? · USTI 875:5
was c., dead, and buried · BOOK 140:71
crucifixion c….accuses human · BUTT 178:88
get in a whole C. · HUGH 419:33
crucify people would not even c. him · CARL 193:46
crudities c., doubts, and confusions · THOM 853:82
c. of his period · HAMER 378:97
cruel All c. people · WILL 913:36
bottom of the sea is c. · CRANE 243:9
c. brother will you betray · BALL 55:74
C., but composed and bland · ARNO 32:29
C. he looks · SHEL 784:70
c. men of Rome · SHAK 746:71
her c. sports · SPEN 809:14
single men…are more c. · BACON 48:90
The man…was essentially c. · QUIL 674:46
crueller nothing c. or more vain · JONG 448:1
cruellest The c. lies · STEV 822:90
cruelty bar against your c. · LANY 489:6
C. is the law · HARDY 382:68
c. is the primary feeling · SADE 708:93
c. without incentive · JOHN 442:57
Hanging is too good…said Mr C. · BUNY 166:70
neither kindness nor c. · ALBEE 9:87
top-full Of direst c. · SHAK 766:82
cruise all on our last c. · STEV 822:92
crumb craved no c. · GILB 355:31
crumble the Rockies may c. · GERS 351:45
when I c., who will remember · DELA 260:67
crumbled Hispanic world never c. · REYES 684:21
crumbs c….from the rich man's table · BIBLE 116:53
c. of compassion · TUTU 870:70
dogs eat of the c. · BIBLE 112:60
not worthy…to gather up the c. · BOOK 141:7
crumpet C. Baking…Company · DICK 267:98
crumpets buttered scones and c. · ELIOT 305:44
crusade moral c., or it is nothing · WILS 916:93
Presidents start out pretending to run a c. · COOKE 236:39
crusaders C. have multiplied · BERN 80:33
Crusades triumphs of the C. · RUNC 702:73
crush competition…I c. it · REVS 684:19

crust c. of an unfinished earth · KURA 482:40
Sleep in thy intellectual c. · WORD 924:83
crutches Time goes on c. · SHAK 744:3
cry and a c. before · TENN 847:48
answer to 'Hi!' or to any loud c. · CARR 197:28
Consider anything, only don't c. · CARR 196:94
c. I can no more · HOPK 412:2
c. in my bed · AGUS 9:76
c. of Absence…in the heart · RANS 679:25
c. or sing, justice must · MARIE 550:50
c. that was no more than a breath · CONR 234:99
c. that we are come · SHAK 764:94
C., the Beloved Country · PATON 643:69
c. with you for only a day · VIDOR 881:11
dying, if we could not c. · MAUP 562:87
empty compliment to c. · GILB 355:20
entire soul is a c. · KAZA 456:70
great c. in Egypt · BIBLE 88:17
heard my c. · BIBLE 95:18
hounds are in c. · SCOTT 723:9
If something makes you c. · CLIN 221:94
Need a body c.? · BURNS 173:49
new orphans c. · SHAK 768:28
no language but a c. · TENN 843:42
none to hear my c. · GILM 356:56
nor uttered c. · TENN 842:11
not to be obliged to c. · BEAU 64:94
tears which I made her c. · RACI 676:84
to c. it up · SWIFT 832:99
To c. to thee · HERB 398:13
What shall I c.? · BIBLE 103:36
your bald c. · PLATH 654:65
crying all the way that wild high c. · MASE 559:40
c. all the time · PRES 667:4
then not hear it c.! · HERB 398:13
cryptograph experience is like a c. · SCHO 719:30
cryptology Maxim of c. · WRIS 930:92
crystal as much as a plant or a c. · EMER 312:20
C. sincerity · HOPK 412:79
ego that can crack c. · CHEE 209:6
glass like unto c. · BIBLE 126:53
hold my lady's head like a c. · HEAN 389:7
crystalline his c. streams · SHEL 783:45
crystallization c….in a poem · UPDI 874:87
crystals teeth of splintered c.? · BROW 162:60
ten million little ice c. · SCHW 721:69
Cuba C. is always the best · GUIL 374:31
Havana, C….high society · CABR 183:19
whirlpool of C.'s political crisis · CAST 199:79
Cubans when C. get together · LEZA 508:12
cube c. is the basis of architecture · MALL 542:98
divide a c. into two other c.s · FERM 321:15
cubic Picasso paints…a c. shape? · MARC 548:29
cubist pictures known…as C. · DAVIS 256:63
cubists C., or Octagonists · ROOS 696:58
cubits c. this way and that · LAUR 492:70
cubs ape his c. · MORE 596:58
Cuchulain Pearse summoned C. · YEATS 934:64
cuckoldom c. be a discredit · CONG 232:42
cuckoo c. clock style · HEMI 393:92
C., jug-jug, pu-we · NASHE 609:15
c.'s parting cry · ARNO 33:45
hear the pleasant c. · DAVI 255:50
hedge-sparrow fed the c. · SHAK 762:60
Lhude sing c.! · ANON 19:83
merry c., messenger of Spring · SPEN 809:98
One flew over the c.'s nest · KESEY 465:70
produce? The c. clock · WELL 897:48
rainbow and a c.'s song · DAVI 255:49
Responsive to the c.'s note · GRAY 369:3
weather the c. likes · HARDY 382:76
cuckoo-echoing c.-e., bell-swarmèd · HOPK 412:91
cuckoos Of owls and c., asses · MILT 579:83
cucumber c. is added to it · MACK 534:19
c. narrow · SITW 794:76
c. should be well sliced · JOHN 444:3
cucumbers sun-beams out of c. · SWIFT 831:81
cuddled Who c. you when? · THOM 853:93
cue With a twisted c. · GILB 355:28
cuff Anything said off the c. · SKEL 795:2
Cuinchy C….was a slaughter yard… · BLUN 137:11
cuinsque Mens c. is est · CICE 218:27
cuisine c. here in America · CHIR 213:14
cully Man was…Woman's c. · CONG 230:95
culpable How c. was he · HEAN 389:9
culprit Stirs the c. · DICK 272:53
culprits better to choose the c. · PAGN 634:84

cult c. is a religion with no — WOLFE 920:94
c. of truth — PIER 651:5
What's a c.? — ALTM 13:72
cultivate C. simplicity, Coleridge — LAMB 486:27
cultivated C. Underrated Nobleman — GILB 355:32
cultivation structure of her c. — AUCH 39:74
cultural c. and historical role — SMITH 799:62
C. Cringe — PHIL 650:93
C. literacy is the oxygen — HIRS 403:6
fight for c. space — NARO 608:74
personalities and c. traditions — WATS 890:97
physical and c. distance — VAN 876:22
culture all kinds of mental c. — MILL 570:57
America is…rooted in Negro C. — ROLL 695:33
arteriosclerosis of c. — MILL 573:55
as some immense yeast c. — BOYD 147:43
breasts, the hallmark of our c. — DONA 278:21
Britain had a savage c. — BANDA 58:24
Canada…enjoyed…French c. — COLO 228:51
courage in Chinese c. — MO 589:20
C.…acquainting…with the best — ARNO 34:59
c. and my language — KELM 461:79
C. is dead — ANON 23:4
C. is the passion for sweetness — ARNO 34:60
C. may…be described simply — ELIOT 309:52
c. of modern painting — MOTH 600:32
elaborate defence of c. — ARNO 34:58
evidence of a nation's c. — THUR 859:44
evolution of c. — LOOS 517:71
excellence proper to c. itself — REYES 684:21
flourishing c. in our land — MAO 548:12
Football is…more central to our c. — GREER 372:92
genius of American c. — RODR 693:95
handprint of all c. — ANON 25:76
hear anyone talk of c. — JOHST 447:81
integral part of c. — GOULD 365:25
marketers in our c. — GITL 358:86
men of c. — ARNO 33:55
Modern European c. — SUN 829:32
new ways…give a new c. — WERE 899:6
no c. of the earth — HOBB 404:27
only place in our c. — STEI 816:45
pursue C. in bands — WHAR 901:53
sacred cow of American c. — HUGH 419:35
sad fact about our c. — AUDEN 41:16
salvage Europe's c. — ADEN 7:47
society and its c. — TRIL 866:71
Speeches in our c. — GALB 343:4
Tigers…but no c. — MACL 534:30
tools that go together with c. — REYES 684:21
unparalleled elsewhere in our c. — SHAP 776:36
various grades of c. — NIET 616:28
vast intuitive c. — SHAF 729:21
Versailles of American corporate c. — WOLFE 920:1
cultures all c. of the earth — WEBER 894:68
curiosity about alien c. — BOWL 147:36
cumbersome c. unwieldiness — DONNE 280:61
cumulative truly c. and progressive — SART 715:40
cunning c. known — POPE 661:31
c. men pass for wise — BACON 49:19
need have much c. — BACON 50:54
want of c. made me bold — SPEN 809:2
what pleated c. hides — SHAK 762:55
cup Come fill up my c. — SCOTT 724:28
c. is the new testament — BIBLE 121:6
c. of bitterness — KING 468:37
c. of full wine — FLET 328:72
c. of hot wine — SHAK 769:59
c. o' kindness — BURNS 175:59
c. runneth over — BIBLE 94:2
death in the c. — BURNS 173:55
Death's bitter c. — ABU 1:12
Fill the c. — TENN 841:91
gold c. won by the worst horse — MASE 559:39
heaven in our c. has thrown — ROCH 691:59
kiss but in the c. — JONS 449:40
League and C. double — BUSBY 175:87
let this c. pass from me — BIBLE 114:98
life's enchanted c. — BYRON 179:20
my c. shall be full — BOOK 143:44
no more personality than a paper c. — CHAN 205:85
Perfect the c. as planned — BROW 162:71
remove this c. from me — BIBLE 116:61
snow-water from a tin c. — SNYD 802:47
Socrates empties the c. of poison — FEUE 321:21
still foul the c. — GREY 373:5
cupboard no c. should be barer — LLOY 513:97

wicked man in the bathroom c. — EWART 316:23
cupboards c. bursting with skeletons — ORWE 628:59
Cupid bolt of C. fell — SHAK 737:94
thrice cut C.'s bow-string — SHAK 745:11
winged C. painted blind — SHAK 737:86
cups c. make any guilty men — JONS 449:35
c., That cheer but not inebriate — COWP 241:76
in kitchen c. — STEV 819:14
in their flowing c. — SHAK 746:59
pour not by c. — SPEN 809:4
cur 'bout the ears of the old c. — BUTL 177:48
curate average c. at home — FIRB 323:70
shabby c. who has strayed — AUDEN 41:20
sit upon the c.'s knee — CHES 212:92
curates abundant shower of c. — BRON 155:83
c. lean, and rectors fat — MACA 525:38
C., long dust, will come — BROO 156:11
curb use the snaffle and the c. — CAMP 186:56
curd c. of ass's milk — POPE 661:40
soother than the creamy c. — KEATS 459:40
curds concupiscent c. — STEV 819:14
queen of c. and cream — SHAK 770:88
cure as much for prevention as c. — GRAV 368:82
be no more; sad c. — MILT 581:22
cause or c.! — GOLD 361:42
c. except as a guillotine — LUCE 522:81
c. for it is occupation — SHAW 780:69
c. for this ill — KIPL 472:37
c. him for you — JUNG 453:9
c. of the id — ANON 22:50
c. the disease and kill the patient — BACON 49:31
labour against our own c. — BROW 159:82
love's malady without a c. — DRYD 292:55
Love…the longest to c. — LABR 483:64
lunatic beyond all c. — WEBS 895:2
no c. for this disease — BELL 72:54
no hope for a c. — AUST 43:73
nothing…a little money will not c. — DURA 295:27
palliate what we cannot c. — JOHN 442:43
sin the double c. — TOPL 863:15
there is no c. — HOME 409:13
think they can c. them — VOLT 883:42
will c. epilepsy — THEO 851:40
cures happy…in their c. — BACON 47:57
If a lot of c. are suggested — CHEK 209:14
seeker for c. — RICH 685:55
curfew c. tolls the knell — GRAY 369:10
curiales Quot c., tot tyranni — SALV 712:75
curiosities c. would be quite forgot — AUBR 39:66
curiosity c. about alien cultures — BOWL 147:36
c. becomes a sin — FRAN 333:89
c. is the life-blood — TREV 865:57
c. of an angel's stare — TATE 837:5
die when c. goes — SWIFT 830:49
hungry c. — GREE 371:68
Love, c., freckles — PARK 637:58
Newspapers always excite c. — LAMB 486:38
'satiable c. — KIPL 473:41
when one has lost all c. — WAUGH 893:54
curious c. in unnecessary matters — BIBLE 107:39
What a c. shape it is! — WILDE 908:15
curiouser 'C. and c.!' cried Alice — CARR 194:64
curl Who had a little c. — LONG 516:67
Curle C.…has been writing letters — ARBU 28:34
curlew I could hear a c. — HEAN 389:13
curls held c. to be effeminate — TWAIN 870:85
curragh got into…a c. — BEHAN 70:5
currency Beauty…form of c. — WOLF 920:81
debauch the c. — KEYN 465:79
new stamped with their c. — LAMB 486:43
passed from c. — UPDI 875:96
current boats against the c. — FITZ 325:2
c. to the source — FROST 339:1
c. under sea — ELIOT 306:62
giving a c. to the whole — HOPK 412:98
misleading guide to c. affairs — KEYN 465:81
currents their c. turn awry — TWAIN 871:7
curriculum vitae c. v. of Civilization — ANDR 16:25
curry hotter than the c. — THAC 849:85
curs cast away upon c. — SHAK 749:30
common cry of c. — SHAK 769:66
like to village c. — SHAK 775:11
curse America as a black c. — MILL 572:21
blessing, is to me a c. — MASS 560:50
bless them that c. you — BIBLE 109:93
common c. of mankind — SHAK 757:97
c. be ended — ELIOT 307:8

c. begins to act — SCHR 720:40
c. God, and die — BIBLE 93:50
c. I must send you — SIDN 791:23
c. is come upon me — TENN 839:50
C. not the king — BIBLE 101:89
c. of children! — WEBS 894:77
c. of Europe — SENI 728:98
c. of hell upon the sleek — RANS 679:24
c. of me and my nation — POUND 665:44
c. of Scottish literature — MUIR 601:52
C. on his virtues! — ADDI 7:35
c. sound like a caress — FOOT 329:90
C. the blasted, jelly-boned — LAWR 493:88
c. thee to thy face — BIBLE 93:49
c. upon your whunstane hearts — BURNS 170:66
c. when one works for God — LIVI 512:83
Empty C. — FRAN 334:12
Ignorance is the c. — SHAK 730:67
know how to c. — SHAK 774:80
real c. of Eve — RHYS 684:24
smite the earth a c. — BIBLE 107:23
the c. has come upon us — OBRI 621:7
the c. of a prose — STEP 817:59
the c. of disobedience — OTWAY 631:25
cursed c. above all cattle — BIBLE 86:53
c. is the ground for thy sake — BIBLE 86:55
I who have c. — WALC 884:70
We are c., Waldo — SCHR 720:39
curses C. are like young chickens — SOUT 805:4
c.…on each gashed head — SORL 804:90
c. on my head? — MILT 586:38
cursing began c. the bloody bible — HEMI 393:96
c. his staff — SASS 716:63
I have set…blessing and c. — BIBLE 90:54
proceedeth blessing and c. — BIBLE 125:14
curtain as if the c. never rose — DIDE 273:87
cloud c. of the future — CARL 191:78
c. call! — BARR 61:99
c. was up — KAUF 455:56
essay…must draw its c. round us — WOOF 922:35
prospectors who can't carry a c.? — DOUG 283:14
slamming down his silly c. — SALI 711:66
Thy hand…lets the c. fall — POPE 662:83
When the final c. comes down — MAJOR 541:73
curtains Booze, of course, and then c. — AMIS 14:94
bottoms of c. — STER 818:86
c. are drawn with care — MONRO 591:57
c., never meant to draw — POPE 660:5
draw the c. — SHAN 776:30
graves…like drawn c. — RALE 677:1
Let fall the c. — COWP 241:76
people…behind those clean lace c. — CHRI 214:27
she…draws the c. back — OSBO 630:11
shower c.…great modern things — WARH 889:64
Through windows, and through c. — DONNE 279:41
curtsey C. while you're thinking — CARR 196:92
curve c. of a blue bay — LOWE 519:25
curveship of the c. lend a myth — CRANE 243:14
Curzon met C. in Downing Street — BALD 54:42
cushion c. and soft Dean invite — POPE 659:96
cuspid c.'s last stand — PERE 648:59
cuss bloody town's a bloody c. — BLAIR 132:97
cussing c. and swearin' — STRA 826:82
custard every joke is…a c. pie — ORWE 628:65
custody in the c. of childhood — MISH 587:81
custom c.…of readers…pleased with a
book — CONN 233:67
c. has rendered necessary — DICK 266:87
C. is the most certain — JONS 450:60
C. reconciles us to everything — BURKE 168:1
C. that is before all law — DANI 252:91
justify a traditional c. — TWAIN 870:86
lest one good c. — TENN 847:50
Malay religion and c. — PANG 636:28
more than c. has pronounced — BRON 154:78
nor c. stale — SHAK 765:26
Rather than c. — LEZA 508:12
Render…c. to whom c. — BIBLE 120:86
rule by c. not by force — LEGU 501:58
tea and scandal…ancient c. — CONG 231:6
till c. make it — SHAK 758:18
'twill grow into a c. — WEBS 895:5
customers raising up a people of c. — SMITH 798:50
skinning your c. — KHRU 467:5
customs c. of his tribe — SHAW 777:77
c.…we hold sacred — ARON 34:75
habits and c. of the people — RICA 684:31

ill c. influence my very senses	ETHE 315:98	
laws and c....evolved	POWE 667:94	
such a part of our c.	ALME 13:65	
way to keep up old c.	BAGE 51:79	
ut c. it off, and...kill it	POWE 666:89	
C. me to pieces	SHAK 770:73	
c. out of anything	THUR 860:61	
efforts to c. out 50,000 words	WOLFE 920:86	
most unkindest c. of all	SHAK 748:11	
pay me the c.	GOMEZ 362:92	
should have been c.	COWA 240:26	
soon c. off	BIBLE 96:51	
uts c. off twenty years of life	SHAK 747:97	
uttlefish like c. squirting out ink	ORWE 628:62	
utty sarks c. s. run in your mind	BURNS 172:25	
yberspace C....hallucination	GIBS 353:76	
C. is the funhouse mirror	STER 817:63	
C. is where you are	GIBS 353:77	
ycle C. and epicycle, orb in orb	MILT 584:97	
decided to c. to India	MURP 604:99	
Life is a c.	MARC 549:30	
ycle-clips c.-c. in awkward reverence	LARK 490:26	
ycles know enough about business c.	BECK 67:30	
ylinder C. in common fire engines	WATT 891:2	
treat nature by the c.	CEZA 203:51	
ymbal talk but a tinkling c.	BACON 49:29	
tinkling c.	BIBLE 121:9	
ymbals c. glorious	MAHO 539:34	
ymbry Mon Mam C.	FULL 341:61	
yme What rhubarb, c.	SHAK 769:40	
ymric Clear C. voices	BUNT 166:62	
ynic C....A blackguard	BIER 129:25	
ynical c. gestures of the poor	SPEN 807:50	
ynicism C. is an unpleasant way	HELL 392:72	
C. is humour in ill-health	WELLS 898:88	
C. is intellectual dandyism	MERE 567:5	
the worst c.	OATES 620:90	
ynthia round Of C.'s seat	MILT 575:96	
ypress correct in c. wood	PARK 638:62	
c.-buss I plantit	YOUNG 935:78	
c. funeral	SPEN 808:73	
Nor waves the c.	TENN 842:14	
yprian forsake her C. groves	DRYD 291:27	
yril Nice one, C.	ANON 24:14	
ytherean throned C. be fallen	SWIN 833:36	
zechoslovakia dealing with C.	LLOY 513:7	

)

ad fuck you up, your mum and d.	LARK 491:38	
girls in slacks remember d.	BETJ 84:98	
talk to your d.	BUSH 175:99	
that person is d.	FALU 317:41	
ada D. began not as	TZARA 873:60	
D. D. D., a howl	TZARA 873:58	
D. means nothing	TZARA 873:57	
mama of d.	FADI 317:35	
addy Are you lost d.	LARD 490:16	
D., d., you bastard	PLATH 654:70	
knocked his D. down	HUGH 419:49	
aemon divine d. is absolute	BELL 71:30	
affadillies d. fill their cups	MILT 578:54	
affadowndillies Strew me...with d.	SPEN 808:68	
affodil bed of d. sky	TENN 845:89	
shining d. dies	TENN 845:98	
affodils D....before the swallow	SHAK 770:86	
dances with the d.	WORD 928:43	
host, of golden d.	WORD 927:40	
what d. were for Wordsworth	LARK 491:47	
aft ae...thinks the tither d.	SCOTT 725:48	
d. or corrupt	FULL 341:59	
agger d. drew and died	SHAK 738:16	
d....in the heart of France	QUIN 675:53	
d. which I see before me	SHAK 767:94	
Distress with d. keen	COLL 228:44	
aggers d. in men's smiles	SHAK 768:10	
Give me the d.	SHAK 767:4	
laid their d. ready	SHAK 767:99	
speak d. to her	SHAK 754:98	
aily cancer...growing d.	DEAN 257:88	
Yesterday, We had d. cleaning	REED 681:77	
ainties never fed of the d.	SHAK 733:79	
spiced d., every one	KEATS 459:40	
ais From high on the d.	VIRG 882:18	
aises Meadows trim with d.	MILT 576:8	
aisies covered...with violets and d..	SHEL 785:89	
d., those pearled Arcturi	SHEL 787:24	

picking d. on the railway	WODE 919:56	
picks a posy of d.	THOM 853:89	
Daisy Sweet D.! oft I talk to thee	WORD 926:14	
daisy D. and Lily	SITW 794:72	
Not yellow like a d.	TRUMP 869:49	
Dakotas D., I am for war	RED 681:71	
last bear, shot drinking in the D.	CRANE 243:16	
dale through the lonely d.	BLAKE 134:35	
Through wood and d.	COLE 226:13	
Dali D. is...disgusting	ORWE 630:9	
Dalí D.'s importance for the Surrealists	SCHW 721:60	
D.'s nature to play Gilbert	RUSS 706:65	
When D. hallucinated	RUSS 706:66	
dalliance primrose path of d.	SHAK 751:16	
silken d. in the wardrobe	SHAK 745:32	
dam d. it up	ACHE 3:42	
leave the d.	SHAK 740:66	
damage pay for the d.	STIG 824:45	
Damascus travelled the road to D.	ASHD 35:89	
damask Feed on her d. cheek	SHAK 756:68	
dame dance in the old d. yet	MARQ 553:21	
La belle d.	KEATS 459:41	
La belle D. sans merci	KEATS 458:19	
sulky sullen d.	BURNS 172:13	
this looser d. did skill	SPEN 808:87	
dames Ah! gentle d.!	BURNS 172:15	
laughing d. in who he did delight	BYRON 179:7	
O happy d.	SURR 829:39	
struts his d. before	MILT 576:7	
dammed only saved by being d.	HOOD 410:42	
damn d. by rule	OTWAY 630:22	
D. the torpedoes!	FARR 318:59	
D. you!	SHAW 777:75	
dear, I don't give a d.	MITC 588:1	
devil d. thee black	SHAK 768:36	
don't give a d.	SALI 711:56	
one d. thing over and over	MILL 571:90	
public doesn't give a d.	BEEC 69:62	
save those who d. them	HUGO 421:78	
damnable d. degrees Of drinking	WEBS 894:74	
d. woman's trick	SHAW 778:87	
this d. war	ACHE 3:52	
damnation blasted to eternal d.!	SHAW 781:81	
critical d.	WALT 888:54	
d. of almost everybody	INGE 429:55	
deep d. of his taking-off	SHAK 767:87	
which road leads to d.	DYSON 297:63	
damnations Twenty-nine distinct d.	BROW 160:21	
damned always those d. dishes	FREN 336:47	
among the d. already	SHAW 777:75	
And d. be him	SHAK 769:46	
Another d., thick, square book!	GLOU 359:5	
Beautiful and the D.	FITZ 324:91	
brandy of the d.	SHAW 778:90	
Cromwell, d. to everlasting fame!	POPE 660:26	
D. from here to eternity	KIPL 470:80	
d. long, dark...dangerous way	GOLD 362:66	
d. nice thing	WELL 897:57	
If I were d.	KIPL 471:1	
must be d. perpetually!	MARL 552:6	
the desperate, the d.	JACK 431:6	
damozel blessed d. leaned out	ROSS 698:86	
damp poisonous d. of night	SHAK 765:43	
damsel d. with a dulcimer	COLE 226:14	
d. woll come to you anone	MALO 542:5	
Dan from D. to Beersheba	STER 818:99	
dance best d. e'er cam to the Land	BURNS 172:38	
Can d. a little	ANON 22:55	
Ceres will join in the d.	SITW 794:66	
D., and Provençal song	KEATS 459:59	
d. has begun	BETJ 83:88	
d. in the old dame yet	MARQ 553:21	
d. is a measured pace	BACON 46:46	
d. is a poem	DIDE 273:86	
D., little words	WORL 929:69	
D. on this ball-floor	BLUN 137:13	
d. round in a ring	FROST 339:11	
d. round to all Eternity	FLET 327:64	
d. the dullest beanbag	NOON 617:56	
d. while you can	AUDEN 39:87	
daughters of the year shall d.!	BLAKE 133:25	
Drink and d.	PARK 638:61	
face the music and d.	BERL 79:15	
Learn then to d.	DAVI 254:33	
Let's have a d.	SHAK 745:27	
music...too far from the d.	POUND 665:52	
returning lightly d.	THOM 854:19	

spectral d., before the dawn	BROO 156:11	
sprightly d.	WORD 927:41	
teach an elephant to d.	MOSS 600:28	
the d. and war	STEIN 815:21	
the dancer from the d.	YEATS 933:53	
the d. was long	DOWS 284:44	
there the d. is	ELIOT 307:95	
time to d.	BIBLE 100:70	
To d. is to discover	SENG 727:97	
walk...before they d.	POPE 661:58	
When you do d.	SHAK 770:87	
Will you, won't you...join the d.?	CARR 195:82	
You expect to leave the d.	AGAS 8:64	
danced d. down the street	KERO 464:62	
d. his did	CUMM 248:19	
d. with a man	FARJ 318:49	
David d. before the Lord	BIBLE 91:99	
ye have not d.	BIBLE 111:36	
dancer Curled minion, d.	ARNO 32:24	
How can we know the d.	YEATS 933:53	
move...like a d.	ELIOT 309:44	
Now, D.! Now, Prancer	MOORE 594:17	
dancers d. dancing in tune	TENN 845:90	
d. quick and quicker flew	BURNS 172:23	
Like d. on the ropes	ETHE 315:92	
dances doesn't think she d.	GILB 355:22	
He capers, he d.	SHAK 743:76	
dancing as d. is to walking	WAIN 884:66	
Ask Nureyev to stop d.	KING 468:25	
D. is a frenzy and a rage	DAVI 254:31	
D. is a wonderful training	MORL 598:85	
d. is love's proper exercise	DAVI 254:32	
mature women, d.?	FRIEL 338:74	
mourning into d.	BIBLE 95:8	
pair Of d. pumps	MIDD 569:42	
past our d. days	SHAK 736:41	
stillness the d.	ELIOT 308:14	
the d. floor	YEATS 934:58	
very merry, d., drinking	DRYD 292:61	
dancing-master manners of a d.-m.	JOHN 442:30	
dandelions D. were either sweet	TRAV 865:47	
Sheaves of drooping d.	BETJ 83:92	
smell of the d.	COOKE 236:42	
dandruff cure for d.	LUCE 522:81	
dandy d. must aspire to be sublime	BAUD 65:78	
dandyism Cynicism is intellectual d.	MERE 567:5	
Dane never get rid of the D.	KIPL 474:71	
Roman than a D.	SHAK 755:40	
Dane-geld paying the D.-g.	KIPL 474:70	
danger best way to avoid d.	ROCHE 691:48	
bright face of d.	STEV 823:28	
but what is d.?	HAWT 386:34	
buzzard...is never...in d.	FAUL 319:72	
d. in touching	BURNS 173:55	
d. is always that...he will not recognize	AUCH 39:73	
d. is that gauge	LESS 505:36	
D. knows full well	SHAK 747:90	
d. of being torn with violence	ROSS 697:72	
d. of coming back prodigies	AUST 43:81	
d. of desire	SHAK 751:14	
d. of its tricking the writer	SAND 713:14	
D., the spur	CHAP 206:20	
d. to all Christendom	INNO 430:71	
d. to speak true	JONS 449:41	
doctors are the greater d.	JONS 448:15	
foresees d. and avoids it	KEYN 465:83	
great d. of contagion	WILD 911:85	
grouse are in no d.	EDIN 300:11	
I realized there was a measure of d.	EARH 297:67	
life from grief or d. free	JOHN 441:17	
measure of d.	GREE 371:58	
never be in d. of Popery	ADDI 6:21	
no d. in sweetness and youth	ROCH 691:67	
Out of this nettle d.	SHAK 741:10	
Pleased with the d.	DRYD 289:76	
political d.	GLAD 358:89	
razor-edge of d.	WILD 911:82	
rest in d. are	ETHE 315:92	
run into any kind of d.	BOOK 140:74	
The d. is past	POE 657:30	
united under the threat of d.	DE 259:37	
What d. will it be	SHAK 749:32	
When in d., ponder	WAGN 884:65	
would be in less d.	NASH 608:78	
dangerous Caesar is more d.	SHAK 747:90	
d. to climb a mountain	HAWT 386:34	
d. to meet it alone	WHAR 901:53	

d. to pay it off — SELL 727:84
delays are d. — DRYD 288:33
dirty, d. way — GOLD 362:66
Facility is a d. thing — SLOAN 796:17
generalizations are d. — DUMAS 294:95
have I something in me d. — SHAK 755:35
how d. everything is — STEIN 815:18
Mad, bad, and d. to know — LAMB 486:25
mad, then d. — BENN 75:19
makes it so d. — WILS 914:70
more d. is the abuse — BURKE 168:6
more d. than a mud-puddle — STEIN 815:10
most d. duo — SCAR 717:90
Nothing is more d. — ALAIN 9:81
Nothing is so d. — WILDE 909:48
potentially d. — JONES 447:89
Science becomes d. — SHAW 780:47
Sentiment was the more d. — GREE 371:54
sincerity is a d. — WILDE 908:96
some inquiries are too d. — SAGAN 708:4
such men are d. — SHAK 747:79
dangers appalling d. of family life — HUXL 425:76
d. thou canst make us scorn! — BURNS 172:21
limit the d. of this age — KENN 463:34
loved me for the d. — SHAK 759:63
perils and d. of this night — BOOK 140:77
Daniel D. come to judgement — SHAK 740:81
Dante D. makes me sick — VEGA 879:57
D. or Michelangelo — MULL 602:72
D. turned round violently — JOYCE 452:83
D., who loved well — BROW 162:63
dapper d. from your napper — COLL 227:35
dappled for d. things — HOPK 412:85
long d. grass — YEATS 932:36
dare art doesn't d. you — HUST 424:49
bear to live, or d. to die — POPE 660:23
d. lift a hand — JOHN 440:94
d. to eat a peach? — ELIOT 304:25
d., to slay Owen Roe O'Neil? — DAVIS 256:64
helps those who d. — VIRG 882:25
must have the courage to d. — DOST 282:7
Nobody'll d. — HUGH 418:17
They wouldn't d. — BARR 61:95
what others only d. to think — CHAR 206:27
dared never d. be radical — FROST 339:6
dares Who d., wins — ANON 22:61
daring d. of a moment's surrender — ELIOT 306:67
D. Young Man — SARO 714:34
dash of d. — SNOW 802:34
serious d. starts from within — WELTY 899:2
dark all aroun' in the d. — STEI 815:34
all before was d. — WENT 899:5
Between the d. and the daylight — LONG 516:61
blind man in a d. room — DARW 253:18
children fear to go in the d. — BACON 47:73
children talking...in the d. — DE 264:34
Climb to our proper d. — YEATS 934:64
colours will agree in the d. — BACON 47:77
come out after d. — WODE 919:75
d. and stormy night — BULW 166:57
D. as the Grave — LOWRY 521:68
D. as the world of man — SITW 794:73
d. backward and abyss of time? — SHAK 774:77
d. in light expos'd — MILT 586:47
D. is Light Enough — FRY 340:29
d....Of night — YEATS 933:38
d. place where it leads — JONG 448:95
d. time of the year — ELIOT 309:38
d. was talking to the dead — MACN 538:10
d. with something more than night — CHAN 205:96
Death...drop from the d. — ROSE 697:70
don't be afraid of the d. — HAMM 379:17
drawing you fall over in the d. — HIRS 403:7
For d. hour or twain — SHAK 768:11
naked in the d. and cold — LEGU 501:54
never to refuse a drink after d. — MENC 565:67
night...like a great d. wing — RAND 678:13
O d. d. d. — ELIOT 308:19
one tunnel, d. and solitary — SABA 707:82
on that d. earth — TENN 846:26
Out in the d. — THOM 854:20
real d. night of the soul — FITZ 325:9
round from the d. and the light — SWIN 833:47
sinks his ship in the d. — CORN 237:72
the d. well — PRIC 668:16
very d., and no brightness — BIBLE 106:10
Walk between d. and d. — GRAV 367:66

ways that are d. — HARTE 384:16
we are for the d. — SHAK 766:57
what d. days seen. — SHAK 772:39
what in me is d. Illumine — MILT 580:93
when it was yet d. — BIBLE 118:21
With d. forgetting — DANI 252:88
work in the d. — JAMES 433:46
darken days d. round me — TENN 847:49
darkies colored people...replaced d. — FEIF 319:84
darkling here as on a d. plain — ARNO 31:94
darkness called you out of d. — BIBLE 125:24
cast away the works of d. — BOOK 141:85
cast out into outer d. — BIBLE 110:15
children of d. — BEND 74:7
d. again and a silence — LONG 516:64
d. and silence reign — LEAR 497:76
d. beautiful with thee — TENN 844:50
D. came down — THAC 849:90
d. comprehended it not — BIBLE 117:72
d. crumbles away — ROSE 697:67
d. falls at Thy behest — ELLE 310:72
D. falls like a wet sponge — ASHB 35:82
d. from light — BROW 162:73
d. he called Night — BIBLE 85:39
d. of the grave — MILL 571:89
d. ridged the riven dark — FREE 336:43
d. shall be the light — ELIOT 308:14
d. shot with lightning — OFAO 622:33
d....sifts through your hand — ASHB 35:83
D. spreads his...wings — MILT 576:4
d. takes the edge off daylight — MOTI 600:34
d. visible Served only — MILT 580:97
d. was upon the face of the deep — BIBLE 85:37
Dawn on our d. — HEBER 390:32
day of the Lord be d. — BIBLE 106:10
design of d. — FROST 339:5
during the days of d. — PETA 649:75
first place of liquid d. — FRAME 333:80
Flags wearily through d. — SHEL 784:66
goeth in the d. — BIBLE 107:25
Go out into the d. — HASK 385:25
he counteracts the powers of d. — SMART 796:26
Hell's d. under his feet — CARL 193:37
him who gropes painfully in d. — CARL 192:98
horror of outer d. — GORD 363:7
In that d. camaraderie — HUGH 419:43
in the d. and the cold — STEV 823:37
in the d. bind them — TOLK 862:98
Is d., the fruit — SWIN 833:30
Lighten our d. — BOOK 140:77
Light out of d.! — MILT 585:34
light out of d. — DONNE 281:88
lots o'd. — MACD 529:36
make d. more visible — EDGE 299:1
men loved d. — BIBLE 117:82
minute of d. — RUSH 703:89
no d. but ignorance — SHAK 757:89
not d. but shadow — FRYE 340:39
Of d. till it smil'd — MILT 577:34
Of now done d. — HOPK 413:3
people that walked in d. — BIBLE 102:16
people which sat in d. — BIBLE 109:81
profounder the surrounding d. — HUXL 424:61
rear of d. thin — MILT 576:7
Ring out the d. — TENN 844:61
season of D. — DICK 271:19
seen in the d. — FRIE 337:69
shades of d. — DELA 260:71
Shares the d. — MILL 571:83
Surely the d. shall cover me — BIBLE 98:1
Swaddled with d. — ELIOT 305:40
sweeping through the d. — WORD 924:87
there's d. — SHAK 763:89
to d., on extended wings — STEV 819:19
torrent of d. — NOYES 619:78
turned around from d. to light — PLATO 655:1
two eternities of d. — NABO 606:29
universal d. buries all — POPE 662:83
Where there is d. — FRAN 334:98
darling bride and my d. to be? — BALL 56:80
Charlie he's my d. — BURNS 173:50
d. buds of May — SHAK 771:5
getting someone to call you d. — BARN 60:74
darlings d. of daytime! — KEND 461:95
darts fiery d. of the wicked — BIBLE 122:52
Darwinian D. principle — WILDE 908:97
dash d. away! Dash away! — MOORE 594:17

d. of daring — SNOW 802:3
d. of waves — ARNO 32:2
d. themselves to pieces — SHAK 731:
data constellations of d. — GIBS 353:7
graphical representation of d. — GIBS 353:7
date all too short a d. — SHAK 771:
arrive but at the d. — WALL 886:1
born...out of d. — POUND 664:3
d. which will live in infamy — ROOS 696:5
doubles your chances for a d. — ALLEN 12:4
merely a d. on a page — THOM 854:2
Name and d. — BUNT 166:6
out of d., obsolete — STEV 819:1
they d. from it — TWAIN 871:9
dated might become d. for a while — HAWES 385:3
dates blind d. are a way of life — EPST 315:8
ripping out the d. — LEAC 496:5
daughter begins to think of the d. — EDGE 299:
dance like a plumber's d. — MIDD 569:3
d. and the Moor — SHAK 759:5
d. loved a man — SHAK 756:6
d. of a hundred Earls — TENN 840:7
d. of Earth and Water — SHEL 783:4
d. of the gods — TENN 838:4
d. of the Southern Cross — FRAN 335:2
d. to his blood — SHAK 740:5
Don't put your d. on the stage — COWA 239:1
Elderly, ugly d. — GILB 353:8
Filled her with a d. — MILT 576:
Gigantic d. of the West — TENN 844:6
King o' Spain's d. — COLUM 229:6
kyngis d. of the londe — MALO 542:
lost your d. to...men — FERRE 321:1
loves my d. — SHAK 770:9
loveth son or d. — BIBLE 111:3
marry My d. Jill — NASH 608:9
Nokomis bore a d. — LONG 516:5
Squire's own d. — GRAV 368:8
Thou art thy father's d. — SHAK 749:3
To my d. Leonora — WODE 919:6
youngest d. does not love thee — SHAK 762:5
daughters d. are inclined to love — MONT 591:6
d. of her daughter — SHAK 733:6
d. of Jerusalem — BIBLE 101:9
d. of musick shall be brought low — BIBLE 101:9
d. of the year shall dance! — BLAKE 133:2
Earth's heedless sons and — BLUN 137:1
love among the d. — BIBLE 101:9
outraging their wives and d. — GENG 349:9
sons and d. of Life's longing — GIBR 352:7
sons and your d. shall prophesy — BIBLE 106:
wives and d. chaste — MOLI 589:2
Your d....will be married — WALP 887:3
Daumier one small Goya or a D. — AUDEN 39:8
dauntless d. in war — SCOTT 723:9
dauphin Daylight's d. — HOPK 412:8
David born this day in the city of D. — BIBLE 115:2
D. danced before the Lord — BIBLE 91:9
D. his ten thousands — BIBLE 91:9
D. was old and stricken in years — BIBLE 91:
once in royal D.'s city — ALEX 11:2
Philistine said unto D. — BIBLE 91:9
upon the throne of D. — BIBLE 102:1
daVinci d.V. and the Renaissance — WELL 897:4
Davy D. Abominated gravy — BENT 78:7
dawn brown fog of a winter d. — ELIOT 305:5
d. broke like a face — SASS 716:5
d. comes up like thunder — KIPL 470:8
d. in the mountains — MURP 604:
d. of intellectual enlightenment — CURZ 249:5
d. seem to be an alleviation — WILD 910:7
day doth d. — BALL 57:9
fight it at the d. — BALL 55:7
gathers God at d. — CRANE 243:2
grey d. breaking — MASE 559:2
grey d. of the morning after — ADE 7:4
I said to D. — THOM 855:3
I saw d. upon them — RAND 678:1
Lasses a-lilting before the d. — ELLI 310:7
magic of its d. — RUSS 706:6
Near the face of d. — MERE 566:9
No d.—no dusk — HOOD 410:5
peep of d. — GRAY 369:2
prays...that the d. may ripen — CARL 192:9
ray, and find no d. — MILT 582:3
redemption's happy d. — CASW 199:8
see by the d.'s early — CUMM 247:

d. go by, I remain — APOL 27:17
d. grow short — ANDE 16:20
d.…like a wayward tune — YEATS 932:31
d. of glory — PETA 649:75
d. of long ago — LIND 511:52
d.…of my pilgrimage — BIBLE 88:5
d. of my youth — SOUT 805:97
d. short — ANDR 16:27
d. that are no more — TENN 842:6
d. that are no more — TENN 842:7
d. that are no more — TENN 842:8
d. that are to try men's souls — WILS 916:9
d. that have gone by — FLEC 327:50
d. that make us happy — MASE 559:37
d. were our mechanics — LEUP 505:49
d. when work was scrappy — CHES 212:93
death my d. should expiate — SHAK 771:8
dirk and drublie d. — DUNB 294:8
drawing d. out — SHAK 747:96
E're half my d. — MILT 580:88
Even as our d. do grow — SHAK 759:76
few the d. are that hold — MILL 572:3
fifteen or twenty d. longer — PERTH 648:70
For forty d. — SITW 794:83
for the rest of my d. — PLATH 654:73
friends of other d. — ROBI 690:35
full of d., riches, and honour — BIBLE 92:41
genius of our d. — LARI 490:19
glamour Of childish d. — LAWR 494:94
glorious d. — GILB 354:14
good d. speed and depart — MART 555:49
Happy D. are Here Again — YELL 934:69
high, clear d. — CHAT 207:49
if ever come perfect d. — LOWE 520:31
In bygone d., Morag — LAUR 492:71
In olden d. a glimpse — PORT 663:4
in the d. of villainy? — SHAK 742:23
In the future d. — ROOS 696:50
in these last d. — BIBLE 124:89
in those d. ambition — LAGE 485:20
Length of d. is in her right hand — BIBLE 99:12
live laborious d. — MILT 578:49
Newgate in our schoolboy d. — DICK 266:63
nights and down the d. — THOM 855:36
number of my d. — BOOK 143:48
one of my well-looking d. — GOLD 362:63
remember the d. of Old — MOORE 596:48
salad d. — SHAK 764:22
seemed unto him but a few d. — BIBLE 87:90
seven d. war — MUIR 602:62
siege of battering d. — SHAK 772:25
Six d. of the week it soils — LARK 490:28
somewhat troublesome d. — FOST 332:58
Talk of our enlightened d. — MANS 546:81
teach us to number our d. — BIBLE 96:52
Ten D. That Shook — REED 682:87
the d. dividing — SWIN 832:19
though fall'n on evil d. — MILT 583:89
three whole d. together — SUCK 828:13
Time in hours, d., years — VAUG 878:49
walking for d., for months — ROBBE 688:9
was a habit in those d. — ROGE 695:24
What are d. for? — LARK 490:21
what dark d. seen. — SHAK 772:39
wi' her a'my simmer d. — SOUT 805:94
young d. of gathering flowers — PEAC 645:96
day-spring d.-s. born; here leave — MILT 586:44
day-star d.-s. in the ocean bed — MILT 578:57
daytime never met in the d. — THUR 860:63
deacons jawbones of d. — THOM 853:2
dead Adonais—he is d.! — SHEL 785:90
all d. men — BIBLE 88:18
as good as d. — EINS 301:37
being d. is hard work — RILKE 687:85
Bene they all d. — SPEN 808:90
better to be d. — NASH 608:82
Blessed are the d. — BIBLE 126:69
bring the d. to life — GRAV 367:70
brother was d., and is alive again — BIBLE 116:49
Bunny had been d. for several weeks — TARTT 836:96
But he's d., but he's d. — DAVIS 256:65
but in fact it is d. — MITF 589:13
By his d. smile — OWEN 632:59
Christ being raised from the d. — BIBLE 120:68
Christ risen from the d. — BIBLE 121:14
Come not, when I am d. — TENN 842:18
Come up and be d.! — DICK 272:47

communication Of the d. — ELIOT 309:40
communism is a d. dog — SOLZ 803:64
concert is d. — GOULD 364:20
conference With the d.! — WEBS 895:16
converse with the mighty d. — THOM 856:58
Culture is d. — ANON 23:4
dark was talking to the d. — MACN 538:10
d. and gone — YEATS 933:43
d. and gone, lady — SHAK 754:16
d. and half alive — BETJ 83:77
D.! and so great — NERO 611:41
d. and turned to clay — SHAK 755:33
d. are living — MACM 536:76
d. are raised up — BIBLE 111:33
d. bury their d. — BIBLE 110:17
d., but in the Elysian fields — DISR 277:83
d. come loupin' owre — MACD 529:28
d. don't die — LAWR 494:13
D. for a ducat, d. — SHAK 754:5
d. have come to take the living — DELI 261:81
D. Heart of Australia — GREG 372:97
d. know not any thing — BIBLE 101:82
d. level of provincial existence — ELIOT 303:90
D., long dead — TENN 845:94
d. man is the best fall guy — CHAN 205:91
d. man without…the panoply — DAVI 254:41
d. many times — PATER 642:51
D. men are serious — FIND 323:59
D. men never repent — DICK 266:90
d. might as well speak to the living — CATH 200:88
d. more than half — MILT 586:47
d. of winter — ELIOT 306:73
d. one lay moaning — SMITH 800:97
D. perfection, no more — TENN 845:78
d. reign — ZOLA 937:4
d. returning lightly — THOM 854:19
d. shall be raised incorruptible — BIBLE 121:19
d. shall not have died — LINC 510:39
D. shepherd — SHAK 750:71
d. to sin — BIBLE 120:67
d. which he slew at his death — BIBLE 90:76
d., who will not fight — GREN 373:2
D., your Majesty — DICK 270:98
Death will come when thou art d. — SHEL 786:18
deeper insights to the d. belong — FERG 320:5
democracy of the d. — CHES 211:61
distance that the d. have gone — DICK 273:79
dropping of the d. — WILL 911:2
dry and d. — SNYD 803:49
Either he's d. or my watch — MARX 557:89
ended and d. — GLAS 359:99
England mourns for her d. — BINY 130:51
enough room…to bury your d. men — CORW 237:73
fain to carry the d. — PEPYS 647:42
fairy…falls down d. — BARR 61:82
Faith without works is d. — BIBLE 124:11
fear of the d. — ACKR 3:56
fell as his feet as d. — BIBLE 125:45
food that d. men eat — DOBS 277:97
fool than to be d. — STEV 822:93
for the d. remeid is none — DUNB 294:7
found him with the d. — WILDE 910:52
globe of d. — THOM 852:62
healthy and wealthy and d. — THUR 859:29
hear the D. March play — KIPL 471:89
Heraclitus, they told me you were d. — CORY 237:74
Here Vaughan lies d. — SASS 717:77
heroic happy d. — CUMM 247:9
her warrior d. — TENN 842:11
Hitler was d. — SCHA 717:95
home among the d. — SHEL 786:9
house where there was not one d. — BIBLE 88:17
if this is pleasure we'd rather be d. — COWA 239:8
imagined for the mighty d. — KEATS 457:2
immortal spirit of the d. — SPEN 807:65
in the den…nine d. men — BALL 55:75
Joe, long d. — SLES 796:15
judge the quick and the d. — BOOK 140:71
just as easy for your d. to visit you — BELL 74:88
just at this d. hour — SHAK 751:96
kissed by the English d. — OWEN 632:53
lain for a century d. — TENN 845:92
lasting mansions of the d. — CRAB 242:82
law hath not been d. — SHAK 758:23
literature…very d. — LEWIS 507:90
little cousin is d. — RANS 679:22
live a life half d. — MILT 586:49

liveth, and was d. — BIBLE 126:46
living and the d. — CIXO 218:33
Lycidas is d., d. ere — MILT 578:45
main thing…is that he be d. — HONE 409:30
make sure he was d. — GOLD 362:91
make the d. live — KNEL 476:13
marks our English d. — KIPL 472:14
may be d. ground — REED 681:79
might as well be bloody d. — BLAIR 132:98
millions of the mouthless d. — SORL 804:90
Mindful of the unhonoured d. — GRAY 369:23
more to say when I am d. — ROBI 690:34
most of 'em d. — SASS 716:63
most of my friends are d. — FENT 320:88
Most of the d. were poor — THOM 852:56
Most people my age are d. — STEN 817:51
Most poets are d. — GRAV 368:83
mother…must be d. — AUST 42:15
Naked and the D. — MAIL 539:36
networks of d. speech — STARK 813:73
not D., but feed the grass — TATE 837:4
not for the d. — HERN 399:26
not the one d. — FROST 338:93
novel is d. — DELI 261:77
Now thou art d. — CAREW 190:51
of the happier d. — TENN 846:27
only d. thing that — THOM 854:14
only good Indian is a d. Indian — SHER 787:32
Over my d. body — KAUF 456:62
over the rich D.! — BROO 156:8
pattern…Of d. and living — ELIOT 308:25
praise the d. which are already d. — BIBLE 100:72
Private Means is d. — SMITH 800:3
quite for ever d.! — CONG 231:24
raise the d. — BIBLE 111:24
raise the d. — BIBLE 100:72
rather be d. — HAMI 379:2
recently-d. fish — ORWE 628:67
Remember me when I am d. — DOUG 283:19
remind me of the d. — SASS 716:68
rescue the d. — IGNA 428:42
risen from the d. — BIBLE 121:14
Sabbath of the d. — MACL 535:35
salutation of the d. — ROBI 690:35
savaged by a d. sheep — HEAL 388:99
saw the d., small and great — BIBLE 127:78
Sea shall give up her d. — BOOK 143:73
She munched, half d. — SMITH 799:64
She, she is d. — DONNE 281:77
Shone round him o'er the d. — HEMA 393:91
shrouded oft our martyred d. — CONN 232:55
Some people are better off d. — CHAN 205:87
Something was d. in each of us — WILDE 910:56
soul so d. — SCOTT 723:91
speak for sixty thousand d.! — HUGH 420:57
still as the d. — BLUN 137:10
stopped d. at the critical point — SOME 803:67
strike me d. — SHAK 765:48
The man is d.! — WHIT 906:57
the president is d. — ODON 622:31
The sleeping and the d. — SHAK 767:4
they're a'd. — ANON 21:25
This is the d. land — ELIOT 306:70
thou being d. art God — SWIN 833:36
though he were d., yet shall he live — BIBLE 118:3
'tis Death is d. — SHEL 786:5
to be said For being d. — BENT 77:75
tombs of its illustrious d. — HOWE 417:99
took their wages and are d. — HOUS 416:79
to the d. we owe…truth — VOLT 883:49
town…buried its d. — SHAW 781:1
two d. and the other dying — DOCH 277:99
two worlds, one d. — ARNO 32:31
unheroic D. who fed the guns? — SASS 717:76
until he's read…After that it's d. — WAUGH 892:32
upon all the living and the d. — JOYCE 451:81
useless to the d. — RICH 685:46
vastly more ways of being d. — DAWK 256:74
voice of the d. — TENN 847:32
wakes or sleeps with the enduring d. — SHEL 786:2
walking d. man — ANON 25:66
was I d. before I was alive — BROW 158:78
was living is now d. — ELIOT 306:64
we are all d. — KEYN 465:81
Weep when we not d. — DONNE 280:51
what we call d. is only changed — CARL 192:8
When I am d. — BELL 73:66

When I am d.	ROSS 697:83
When I am d. and opened	MARY 559:19
When I do not write…I'm d.	CIXO 219:39
when she was d.	GOLD 361:38
Why seek ye…among the d.?	BIBLE 116:67
withered heart was d.	SCOTT 722:86
with the departed d.	SHEL 782:20
word is d.	DICK 273:72
world of the d.	FORS 331:49
you'll know you're d.	WILL 913:32
youth stone d.	SASS 716:62
dead-born fell d.-b. from the press	HUME 422:16
deadliest endured the d.	RUSK 704:37
deadlines I love d.	ADAMS 4:71
deadliness d. of…purely scientific	GILL 356:45
recurring d.	WILL 914:53
deadlock Holy D.	HERB 397:80
deadly more d. in the long run	TWAIN 870:79
Deadwood D. and Lost Mule Flat	BENET 75:9
deaf At once is d. and loud	SHEL 784:65
d. adder that stoppeth her ears	BOOK 143:55
D.! Both d.!	YEATS 934:68
d. hear	BIBLE 111:33
d., how should they know	SORL 804:90
d. to hear	BIBLE 114:14
delightful period…if one was d.	LARW 491:55
dialogue of the d.	HOWE 417:95
ears of the d. shall be unstopped	BIBLE 103:33
husband who may be d.	OBRI 621:11
What d.…murderer	SHEL 786:1
deafanddumb language even d.	CUMM 247:8
deafening silence was d.	KARSH 455:52
Deal D. is a most villainous place	COBB 223:49
Deal faith-healer of D.	ANON 22:53
deal d. with them constantly	SHUL 789:87
ease some d.	SHAK 731:92
Fair D.	TRUM 868:29
deal good d. of a big-bug	TWAIN 871:96
great d. has been lost	WALL 886:8
New D. was ended by World War II	MCGO 532:92
stand for the square d.	ROOS 696:55
dealer agricultural implement d.	MENC 566:86
dealers d. and collectors	HAMM 379:12
dealing d. in facts, not realities	GOLD 362:88
d. with a woman	JACO 432:15
dealings d. with young men	PO 656:15
dean the cushion and soft D. invite	POPE 659:96
deans dowagers for d.	TENN 841:95
dear dangerously d.	BYRON 181:51
d., I don't give a damn	MITC 588:1
D. is the helpless creature	BYRON 181:70
d., My no longer cherished	MILL 571:84
d. to me as are the ruddy drops	SHAK 747:86
d. to me as life	SHAK 740:82
everything d. and valuable	PITT 653:46
for earth too d.	SHAK 736:42
My d. hands	RACH 676:81
Plato is d. to me	ARIS 29:61
that bread should be so d.	HOOD 410:47
too d. for my possessing	SHAK 772:35
dearer d. was the mother	COLE 225:78
dearest d. thing he owed	SHAK 766:78
d. to the world	SHAK 774:89
dearheart Make up your mind d.	OLIV 624:66
dearie kind D., O	BURNS 173:40
o'er me and my D.	BURNS 171:5
thinkin on my D.	BURNS 171:7
death 25 years after his d.	BEAV 67:23
absolute rest is d.	PASC 640:15
after d. God knows	ROSS 698:97
After the first d.	THOM 852:73
After your d. people will write	YEATS 932:28
all Life d. does end	HOPK 413:6
allotted d. and hell	MARL 553:7
all stories…end in d.	HEMI 394:7
Angel of D. has been abroad	BRIG 152:30
announcement of my d.	BROD 153:51
Any man's d. diminishes me	DONNE 281:85
Any woman's d.	RICH 685:51
arise From d.	DONNE 280:66
artist is in danger of d.	HEMI 394:5
battles and d.	GARI 346:48
beauty of life through d.	LAUT 493:80
Be thou faithful unto d.	BIBLE 126:48
Better passion and d.	LAWR 494:2
better than the most glorious d.	EURI 316:12
between life and d.	WORD 927:36
Birth, and copulation, and d.	ELIOT 307:82
blaze forth the d. of princes	SHAK 747:87
bleeding to d. of time	GRAV 367:77
body of this d.?	BIBLE 120:71
bores them to d.	OROU 627:23
bowl'd out by D.'s unerring ball	EGAN 301:24
bridegroom in my d.	SHAK 765:47
Brother to D.	DANI 252:88
buffet you to d.	WEBS 895:91
built your ship of d.	LAWR 495:31
Calabria d.	VIRG 882:33
Capital, where kingly D.	SHEL 785:92
ceaseth only in d.	HOBB 404:26
certain as d. and taxes	DEFOE 258:25
Chairman…lying on his d. bed	MIN 587:69
Christians deified d.	STAEL 811:48
'civilization'…is coupled with d.	MILL 573:55
competition the Laws of D.	RUSK 704:19
concerns himself with d.	MANN 545:68
condemn you to d.	CARR 194:66
consent to my own d.	RODR 694:97
consideration of d.?	STEV 822:1
could not stop for D.	DICK 272:66
courting d. to be our friend	PHIL 650:91
covenant with d.	BIBLE 103:27
craving to risk d.	FOWL 332:65
crushed him to d.!	JOYCE 452:83
daily walk with d.	WEBB 893:64
danger of violent d.	HOBB 404:27
darker than d. or night	SHEL 785:83
day of his d.	AUDEN 40:1
dead, a living d.	MILT 586:49
dead which he slew at his d.	BIBLE 90:76
d. after life	SPEN 808:81
D.…a good for all	BERN 81:45
d. and division	SWIN 833:30
D. and I Am found eternal	MILT 585:26
d. and I will coquette	MARQ 553:21
d. and life attonce	SPEN 809:93
D. and pain dominate	LEVE 506:60
d. and taxes	FRAN 335:18
d. and taxes	MITC 588:99
d. and the sole d.	BROW 162:73
d., a necessary end	SHAK 747:89
D. approaches with little delay	ORAH 626:20
D. at an early age	YUAN 936:87
d. being contrary to their principles	GALS 344:23
d. be not one stroke	MILT 585:26
D. be not proud	DONNE 281:67
d.…can be done as easily	ALLEN 12:51
D. cancels everything but truth	HAZL 388:81
d. closes all	TENN 840:66
D. comes to everyone	BERG 79:99
d. cometh soon	MACA 526:63
D. complete the same!	BROW 162:71
D. could drop	ROSE 697:70
D. destroys a man	FORS 331:37
D. devours all lovely things	MILL 571:83
d. had taken Mr Melchisedec	MERE 567:99
d. had undone so many	ELIOT 305:54
d. has a useful function	LABR 483:71
D. has made	TENN 844:50
d. hath no more dominion	BIBLE 120:68
d. hath…several doors	WEBS 895:18
D. his court	SHAK 735:20
d. in childbirth	WELD 897:40
d. in my hand	SHAK 731:90
d. instead of 'human rights'	PEOP 647:24
d. in the cup	BURNS 173:55
d. in the hunting	MORT 599:14
d. into the world	BIBLE 107:30
D. is a dialogue	DICK 273:70
D. is an acquired trait	ALLEN 12:48
D. is a name for beauty	LAYT 496:48
d. is as a lover's pinch	SHAK 766:62
d. is but a moment	SCHI 718:6
D.…is certain to all	SHAK 743:54
D. is…degrading punishment	BREN 151:17
D. is not an event in life	WITT 918:42
D.…is nothing	DRYD 288:42
D. is nothing at all	HOLL 407:67
D. is not soft-mouthed	BROD 153:50
D. is only for the mediocre	JARRY 435:91
d. is the cure of all diseases	BROW 159:82
D. is the end of life	TENN 839:56
d. is the national spectacle	LORCA 517:86
D. is the only mystery	SKEL 795:98
D. is the only pure	LAWR 494:1
D. is the remedy	CHAM 204:70
D. is the romantic	NOVA 619:73
d. is the supreme festival	BONH 140:60
d. is to lose belief	DU 293:74
D. is to Poetry	ABSE 1:8
d. i' the other	SHAK 747:74
D. lays his icy hand	SHIR 789:83
D. lies dead	SWIN 834:52
D. lies on her like	SHAK 737:76
d.…like a cold abstraction	MILL 572:5
D.…like a gas bill	BURG 167:89
D., like the quintessence	BURG 167:95
d. means little	CELI 202:36
d. my days should expiate	SHAK 771:8
D. never hurts. D. is sweet	ANOU 26:96
d.…of a beautiful woman	POE 656:25
d. of Domitian	GIBB 351:52
d. of his fellow-creatures	FROU 339:21
d. of his saints	BIBLE 97:77
d. of Nelson	SOUT 805:9
d. of one so young	SPEN 807:57
d. of religion	WHIT 904:9
d. of some of her	MASE 559:33
d. of the kindest owner	STOWE 826:72
D.…openeth the gate	BACON 47:76
D. opens unknown doors	MASE 559:32
d. reveals the eminent	SHAW 779:70
d. robs it of everything	VIEI 881:12
D.'s a great disguiser	SHAK 758:45
'D.,' said Mark Staithes	HUXL 425:81
D.'s artifact	ABSE 1:7
D.'s bitter cup	ABU 1:12
d.'s dark vale	SCOT 725:61
d.'s grey land	SASS 716:60
d. shall all the world subdue	SPEN 809:1
D. shall be no more	DONNE 281:68
d. shall have no dominion	THOM 852:61
D. should be a long	TZARA 873:56
D.'s second self	SHAK 772:30
D.'s shadow at the door	BLUN 137:9
D. stands above me	LAND 488:82
d. the journey's end	DRYD 292:59
d. the worst of evils	HEINE 391:47
D. to life is crown	MILT 586:63
D. tramples it to fragments	SHEL 786:7
d.…tyrant has in common	BROD 153:52
d.…under the power of language	CIXO 218:32
D. unfailing will strike the blow	CURR 249:40
D. unloads thee	SHAK 758:33
D. was the only absolute	GREE 371:59
d. was there relief	MOOR 596:55
d., where is thy sting?	BIBLE 122:20
d., where is thy sting?	BUNY 167:77
D. who comes at last	SCOTT 723:94
d., who had the soldier singled	DOUG 283:20
D. will come when thou art dead	SHEL 786:18
d. will have his day	SHAK 735:18
d. Will seize the doctor too	SHAK 774:75
d. without the responsibility	LEBO 499:7
defend to the d.	VOLT 883:55
deflow'red, and now to d.	MILT 584:14
delivered my soul from d.	BIBLE 97:76
Desire is d.	SHAK 773:56
Desire paces Eternity…craving d.	DUNC 295:13
die the d.	BIBLE 108:51
done to d. by Lenin	CHUR 216:61
do not see why d.	NABO 606:35
doomed to d.	DRYD 291:14
draw near unto the gates of d.	BIBLE 97:70
dull cold ear of D.?	GRAY 369:15
either in nativity, chance, or d.	SHAK 744:80
end thereof are the ways of d.	BIBLE 99:27
enormously improved by d.	SAKI 710:46
ere her d., Ruffles her	TENN 847:53
eternal: this is d.	LOWE 520:41
Every soul shall taste of d.	KORAN 478:50
Fear of d. and fear of life	MENC 566:76
fear of something after d.	TWAIN 871:7
fed on the fullness of d.	SWIN 833:35
feet go down to d.	BIBLE 99:13
first day of our Jubilee is d.	BROW 158:76
For all the d., we…die unrehearsed	MURR 604:8
foretaste of d.	SCHO 720:37
frightened of d.	DONL 279:24
from famine and d.	DARW 253:11
Glad to d.'s mystery	HOOD 410:49

go on living even after d. FRANK 334:2
hand in hand to d. ROSS 698:99
hard at d.'s door BOOK 143:68
I am become d. OPPE 626:14
if ought but d. part thee and me BIBLE 90:79
If people knew there'd be less d. MALA 541:79
If they were drowning to d. KROC 481:19
In every parting…an image of d. ELIOT 303:71
in love with easeful D. KEATS 460:62
in most cases, a d. warrant WHAR 901:52
in that sleep of d. SHAK 753:74
in the arts of d. SHAW 778:93
in their d. they were not divided BIBLE 91:98
In the ranks of d. MOORE 596:49
Into the jaws of D. TENN 845:77
invincible in his d. GIBB 351:56
is not d. at watch BLUN 137:12
isn't sex but d. SONT 804:72
Judge none blessed before his d. BIBLE 107:48
keep a league till d. SHAK 735:26
keys of hell and of d. BIBLE 126:46
kisses after d. TENN 842:8
land of the shadow of d. BIBLE 102:16
last enemy…is d. BIBLE 121:15
law of d. ANON 21:29
law of sin and d. WESL 900:17
Lead him to d. ROCH 691:57
leads through d. MANN 545:67
led all that way for Birth or D.? ELIOT 306:74
legions with the ways of D. LIND 510:46
let D. wreck all his rage MILT 582:46
libraries of d. DOMI 278:19
life, d., and that vast for-ever KING 469:50
Life, the shadow of d. SWIN 833:22
life to d. SHAK 743:59
life was d. ROSS 698:96
lively form of d. KYD 482:47
lost friends, some by d. WOOLF 923:52
Love is strong as d. BIBLE 102:6
lovely and soothing d. WHIT 906:48
love…put it to a violent d. ETHE 315:97
love thee better after d. BROW 160:10
make d. proud SHAK 765:53
masters the fear of d. BACON 47:74
matter of life and d. SHAN 776:28
May they walk in living d. DAVIS 256:64
Men fear d. BACON 47:73
men would take the d. sentence LAWR 495:40
midst of life we are in d. BOOK 142:34
misery, suffering and d. HARD 381:41
moment after d. HAWT 386:35
more beautiful than d. WHIT 905:43
more d. in it than Rubens HUGH 419:33
mortal taste Brought d. MILT 580:91
most uninspired form of d. VALE 875:12
mourned…not at his d. MONT 593:90
much of life and d. SHEL 782:18
much possessed by d. ELIOT 305:34
My name is D. SOUT 805:10
my sister D. FRAN 334:97
mysterious East…silent like d. CONR 234:5
name that sat on him was D. BIBLE 126:57
nearness of d. PAZ 644:89
necessity of d. HAWT 386:36
neither d., nor life BIBLE 120:78
new terrors of D. ARBU 28:34
Night; perchance of D. THOM 856:62
no drinking after d. FLET 328:67
no lonelier man in d. HEMI 394:6
no more d. BIBLE 127:80
Nor shall d. brag SHAK 771:5
not d.…which is terrible FIEL 322:44
nothing but d. UNAM 873:63
nothing…our own but d. SHAK 735:19
not so much afraid of d. BROW 158:73
obedient unto d. BIBLE 123:54
obey in life and in d. BARTH 62:4
Oh, world, Oh, d.? SPEN 807:57
one in love with d. SHEL 785:89
one medicine is D. ABU 1:13
On his d. bed poor Lubin PRIOR 669:40
only d. can stop it HEMI 394:24
only ending is d. GRAY 368:88
only nervousness or d. LEBO 499:5
Our own d. wish PUZO 673:27
owe God a d. SHAK 743:56
pale d. your vital twist shall sever DAVI 254:33

panoply of d. DAVI 254:41
Photography…flirting with d. BERG 79:98
plucked, for d. mature MILT 585:31
Poets after my d. KEATS 457:98
poor…whose d. interests no one CELI 202:39
power in the day of d. BIBLE 101:80
power of life and d. BIBLE 107:36
prepare as though for d. MANS 547:95
presence of the Red D. POE 656:19
quiet us in a d. so noble MILT 587:65
reflections on life and d. HERN 399:26
refusal of language is a d. BART 62:20
region and shadow of d. BIBLE 109:81
remedy for everything except d. CERV 203:46
rendezvous with D. SEEG 726:70
report of my d. TWAIN 872:31
riddles of birth and d. FRYE 340:39
room…we take up in d. SHIR 789:79
secret house of d. SHAK 765:46
seek D., or he not MILT 585:28
sense of d. is most SHAK 758:34
sentence of d. with a stay CARS 197:35
set before you life and d. BIBLE 90:54
shadow of d. BROW 159:94
shew the Lord's d. till he come BIBLE 121:6
shot to d., with pearls? WEBS 895:15
since by man came d. BIBLE 121:14
six months' oblivion…newspaper d. ADAMS 4:83
sleep and d. differ TRAH 864:37
so many years of fearing d. SHAK 747:97
sorrow flouted at is double d. SHAK 731:92
soul beneath the ribs of d. MANC 544:44
spy sent…by the forces of d. BOWL 147:33
starving to d. PLATH 654:72
stories of the d. of kings SHAK 735:20
stream He met his d. in DEVL 264:32
studied in his d. SHAK 766:78
suffers upon d. LABR 483:72
swallow up d. in victory BIBLE 103:24
Swarm over, D.! BETJ 83:83
sway of d. WORD 929:63
talk of the d. of God FACK 317:31
that stroke of d. JOHN 446:47
theft with a fine, not d. MORE 596:61
The way to dusty d. SHAK 769:42
this morning I signed my d. warrant COLL 227:37
Though he is approaching d. WILL 914:63
thought of d. sits easy WORD 925:7
till d. us do part BOOK 142:26
Till life and d. remember SWIN 832:16
time and d. pinned human FRAME 333:79
time come after d. GINS 357:61
'tis D. is dead SHEL 786:5
to be carnally minded is d. BIBLE 120:73
To muddy d. SHAK 755:26
tragedies are finished by a d. BYRON 182:85
translate thy life into d. SHAK 750:84
triumph over d. and sin SPEN 809:96
triumph over d. and sin SPEN 809:99
true knowledge only comes of d. WHITE 903:94
truly longed for d. TENN 841:90
ugly d. within my eyes SHAK 731:8
Under the ribs of D. MILT 577:40
up the line to d. SASS 716:61
valiant…taste of d. but once SHAK 747:88
valley of d. TENN 844:75
valley of D. TENN 844:76
valley of…d. BIBLE 94:2
vasty hall of d. ARNO 32:14
victory of sterility and d. BELL 73:69
virtues carry with it life and d. MARL 551:74
wages of sin is d. BIBLE 120:69
walk with D. TENN 842:16
wast not born for d. KEATS 460:63
watch the night and d. APOL 27:12
welter of bloodshed and d. LLOY 513:2
what we fear of d. SHAK 758:38
When d. approached GIBB 352:68
who is stronger than d.? HUGH 419:47
whole world is frightened to d.! SHER 788:73
Who owns all of space? D. HUGH 419:46
Why fear d.? FROH 338:81
with the rich in his d. BIBLE 104:52
women for escape from this d. NIGH 616:33
worm of d. GRAV 367:72
worst friend and enemy is but D. BROO 156:9
would burn you to d.! MERM 567:15

would like d. MONT 592:73
deathbed D. utterances PLOUT 656:10
death-dance d.-d. of our times CHES 212:81
death-doom Awaiting their d.-d. WILDE 907:81
deathless d. friends SASS 716:75
sense of some d. shame WEBS 894:82
death-rate d.-r. meant…supply SHAW 781:1
infantile d.-r. HALD 377:73
deaths d. column brought good HAMER 378:96
feigned d. to die. DONNE 279:40
labouring masses to their d. WEIL 896:33
many times before their d. SHAK 747:88
more d. than one must die. WILDE 910:57
ready for more d. GREE 370:50
wars and sudden d. do HUGH 418:25
death-warrant blood is my d.-w. KEATS 460:65
debasement d. of the human mind CHAN 205:86
debate This leads to a d. MACH 533:98
debauch d. his friend's wife genteelly BOSW 146:12
d. the currency KEYN 465:79
debauchery lead him into d. and sin OFLA 622:35
debonair buxom, blithe, and d. MILT 576:5
debris d. of a statue YOUR 936:86
debt Ambition's d. is paid SHAK 747:95
national d. HAMI 379:98
old d. for a borrowing DUNC 295:10
pay a d. to pleasure too? ROCH 691:51
promise made is a d. unpaid SERV 728:2
debtors D. can't be leaders IACO 427:30
debts D. are becoming BALZ 58:23
forgive us our d. BIBLE 110:98
our d., our care-full wives SHAK 746:52
pays all d. SHAK 774:91
unpaid d. HALD 377:77
Words pay no d. SHAK 757:2
decade before this d. is out KENN 462:14
d. or more of ruin WIEN 907:68
decadence absence…is d. MAMET 543:27
barbarism to d. CLEM 221:78
describe as 'Puritan d.' SPEN 807:63
decay after first d. SPEN 808:86
All human things are subject to d. DRYD 288:47
All things are in d. HERB 398:3
always looked upon d. MILL 573:42
bring either d. or explosion RUSS 705:53
by a gentle d. WESL 900:24
d. of ability in the ruling class ORWE 628:61
d. of Christianity SAKI 710:31
d. of parts CONG 231:29
d. Of that colossal wreck SHEL 784:50
D. with imprecision ELIOT 307:2
falling to d. WALP 887:22
found its d. COCK 234:34
Fretting for their d. ROSE 697:69
inferno of insipidity and d. LEWIS 508:6
introduced disease and d. SHER 787:33
less apt to d. JOHN 442:39
like to this d. SPEN 809:1
many men's d.? SPEN 809:14
men d. GOLD 361:52
pale court in beauty and d. SHEL 785:92
The woods d. TENN 846:25
decayed d. in his intellects JOHN 446:58
decaying we are but d. HERR 400:44
decays d. in the face BEHN 71:20
deceased name of the late d. KIPL 471:5
deceit by d. to breed offence DYER 297:53
kind without d. DRYD 289:64
neither was any d. in his mouth BIBLE 104:52
not up to small d. HARTE 384:15
shocked by honesty…few by d. COWA 239:20
deceitful blood-thirsty and d. man BOOK 142:37
heart is d. BIBLE 105:76
deceitfulness Cat of such d. ELIOT 308:11
deceits d. are strong MUIR 602:57
home to many d. POUND 664:39
deceive d. and delude mankind EPHO 314:73
practise to d.! SCOTT 723:99
sweet to d. the deceiver LAFO 485:5
deceived Like a d. husband SHAK 772:36
thou kind d.! LAFO 485:5
deceiver sweet to deceive the d. DRYD 289:65
deceivers Men were d. SHAK 744:6
wicked race of d. MILT 579:79
deceiving Seeing is d. THUR 859:47
December as short as D. SHAK 770:76
D. when they wed SHAK 750:79

From May to D. ANDE 16:20
made D. June TENN 844:58
decencies content to dwell in d. POPE 661:47
decency D. is indecency's conspiracy SHAW 779:19
d. of human beings ORWE 628:50
done in the name of 'd.' LEWIS 508:96
fail to observe d. and discretion BACON 46:38
ultimate d. of things STEV 823:29
want of d. DILL 275:17
with such spirit and d. PITT 652:36
decent d. godless people ELIOT 307:88
d. people live beyond their incomes SAKI 710:43
most d. nation BUSH 175:91
no use to d. people SHAW 780:51
decentralization technology of d. MURP 604:4
deception warfare is based on d. SUN 829:25
deceptions All are d. WILS 915:78
decide If I had to d. GRAMM 366:41
You'll have to d. DYLAN 297:55
decided d. by a person's thoughts KIM 467:20
d. never to be afraid KAVA 456:68
deciduous d. language THOM 855:31
deciphering philosophy is like the d. SCHO 719:30
decision a d. to be made PECK 645:5
a very deliberate d. POIN 657:35
by d. more embroils MILT 581:32
come to a very important d. MILNE 574:77
d. makers face each other SHUL 790:91
d. of the courts LEAC 497:67
Drug misuse…is a d. DICK 265:60
I made the d. long ago RENO 683:3
music that changed a man's d. SCHN 719:21
never try to make a right d. ONEI 626:4
right of ultimate d. MUMF 603:78
specific d. TUCH 869:58
wrong d. can make…miserable DENN 262:99
decisions are made beforehand LEWI 508:7
d. to become mothers FRIE 337:61
learn how to make a d. KISS 475:97
wartime d. TRUM 868:39
decisive so grave and d. STEV 821:85
deck boy stood on the burning d. HEMA 393:91
d. of the Titanic MORT 600:23
fall…on the d. DAVI 254:23
decks rose upon their d., and he cried TENN 848:64
turtle…'twixt plated d. NASH 608:81
declaration D. of Independence KING 468:35
d. will inspire irony GISC 358:85
declension D. looks from our land RANS 679:23
fall with the d. SMITH 798:45
declensions under a lot of d. BURG 167:85
decline preserve…from d. STEU 819:8
went into a bit of a d. ADAMS 4:67
writing the d. and fall GIBB 352:63
declined answer me d. SHAK 765:39
declining d. age of a state BACON 50:59
decompose d. in a barrel of porter DONL 279:25
decorations d.…of the embassy MACI 533:3
d. over a void YOUR 935:81
such gaudy d. MORE 597:68
decorative be d. and to do right! FIRB 323:68
decorum hunt D. down BYRON 179:1
sacrifices too much to d. HAZL 387:66
trousers of d. LICH 509:16
decoy fashion's brightest arts d. GOLD 361:56
decrease I must d. BIBLE 117:83
decree d. from Caesar Augustus BIBLE 115:24
hot temper leaps o'er a cold d. SHAK 739:44
decrees Levitical d. ROCHE 691:46
decrepit d. father takes delight SHAK 771:17
d., without being venerable HAWT 386:45
dedicated fanatically d. to…dogmas PIRS 652:26
dedication d. of an artist SPARK 806:32
deduction as much d. as you please DARW 253:17
logical d. from…hypotheses EINS 302:46
not a correct d. KEYN 465:84
deductions d. for the modern BROW 159:1
Dee sands of D. KING 469:48
dee diddle, we take it, is d. SWIN 834:53
deed A bloody d. SHAK 754:6
blow the horrid d. SHAK 767:87
By thought, word, and d. BOOK 141:2
Crime lies not in the d. HELO 393:88
d. dying tongueless SHAK 770:75
d. I'll do before SHAK 768:25
d. without a name SHAK 768:22
defiant d.! WHIT 905:37

dirty d. SYNGE 834:59
foul d. shall smell SHAK 748:2
good d. in a naughty world SHAK 741:89
living act, the undoubted d. MELV 564:30
may do the d. KEATS 457:83
my d. to my most painted word SHAK 753:73
one good d. in all my life SHAK 731:97
right d. for the wrong reason ELIOT 307:4
Th'attempt and not the d. SHAK 767:98
there is no glory in that d. READ 680:48
water clears us of this d. SHAK 767:6
whatever time the d. took place ELIOT 308:11
Y'are the d.'s creature MIDD 569:47
deeds better d. than words SHAK 729:28
D. are nothing BALZ 58:18
d. determine us ELIOT 303:77
d. left undone STOWE 826:77
D., not words EDGE 299:4
d. of youth SHAK 771:17
d. Shall be in water writ BEAU 67:10
ends all other d. SHAK 765:54
gentle mind by gentle d. SPEN 809:12
Glorious d. are not embraced PIUS 653:53
good d. are gone JANO 435:77
great d. were done WHITE 903:2
measure by thy d. SHAK 772:28
nameless in worthy d. BROW 159:91
these unlucky d. relate SHAK 761:19
Words to the heat of d. SHAK 767:96
worse d. worse suffering MILT 582:53
wrong and d. malign NOON 618:58
years of noble d. TENN 846:22
deedy haven't been at all d. COMP 230:77
deep beauty is only sin d. SAKI 710:30
Black…Baltic d. TENN 846:99
clouds are d. FREE 336:44
commit his body to the d. BOOK 143:73
d. beyond d. BETJ 84:10
D. calleth unto d. BIBLE 95:22
d., yet clear DENH 261:92
dive into the bottom of the d. SHAK 741:5
eye that sees too d. FADI 317:37
From the great d. TENN 847:40
heard the d. behind him TENN 847:48
lowest d. a lower d. MILT 582:55
Not d. the Poet sees ARNO 31:86
remorseless d. Clos'd o'er MILT 578:48
secrets of the d. MILT 585:35
singularly d. young man GILB 354:4
so d. a measure does it have HERA 396:68
thunders of the upper d. TENN 838:36
too d. for his hearers GOLD 362:70
Two voices…one is of the d. STEP 817:58
unfathomable d. forest THOM 854:17
where the brook is d. SHAK 730:56
wonders in the d. BIBLE 97:71
writers…do not seem so d. LAND 488:76
deeper d. than did ever plummet SHAK 775:98
deeps d. are cold HUGH 419:43
deep-versed D.-v. in books MILT 586:43
deer d. from the hill SCOTT 723:13
d., is in the wood of Hallaig MACL 535:34
d. sweeps by SCOTT 723:9
heart…chasing the d. BURNS 171:77
time's d. is slain MUIR 601:54
where the d. and the antelope play HIGL 402:86
Deever they're hangin' Danny D. KIPL 471:89
deface d. the image of man IVAN 431:99
defeat a refusal…to give in and admit d. MEDA 563:7
Champagne…in d. POL 657:43
country of d. PURDY 673:18
In d.: defiance CHUR 216:60
In d. unbeatable CHUR 217:5
laughing soldiers fought to their d. FENT 320:88
pleasure of the d. LACL 484:81
possibilities of d. VICT 880:85
scorn for d. TWAIN 872:28
snatching glory out of d. PRIE 668:19
suffering a national d. EDIN 300:9
through d. and humiliation SMUTS 802:31
victory turns into a d. DE 257:95
we know we should d. you KIPL 474:70
defeated destroyed but not d. HEMI 394:21
Down with the d. LIVY 513:88
Down with the d.! BREN 151:18
History to the d. AUDEN 39:86
meaning shows in the d. MASE 559:38

you will never be d. SUN 829:27
defect chief d. of Henry King BELL 72:53
d. of nature FRAN 333:86
fatal d. of current principles SIMON 792:37
make d. perfection SHAK 765:25
some affliction or d. BEER 70:85
that which depends on d. ARIS 29:52
defective d. in its evidence REGAN 682:93
defects all these d. came WEBB 893:62
by reason of her intellectual d. WRIG 929:74
Mencken's d. were commonplace MEYER 568:30
defence awake endeavour for d. SHAK 738:20
cheap d. of nations BURKE 169:35
conscience clear my chief d. DYER 297:53
d. against betrayal WILL 912:22
d. like elaborate courtesy LUCAS 521:74
d. of one's country HOMER 409:22
d. of the indefensible ORWE 629:87
d. that will protect SCHL 718:16
die in d. of their rights PITT 653:42
England's chief d. PHIL 650:89
greatest D. lay in the Art ALBE 10:99
Immodest words admit of no d. DILL 275:17
In cases of d. SHAK 745:40
in her d. GARI 346:47
intelligent means of d. KENT 464:58
interpret my d. THAT 850:12
make a pitiful d. SIDN 790:16
my rock…my d. BIBLE 96:34
Never make a d. CHAR 206:28
only d. is in offence BALD 54:47
tower of d. ALCA 10:1
defences and no d. GOLD 360:31
defend ourselves with guns GOEB 359:7
d. to the death VOLT 883:55
d. us against nature FREUD 336:52
let it d. itself TOLS 862:4
defended d. by her armed sons REDM 681:72
defenders surprising the d. MANC 544:41
defense painting is…for attack and d. PICA 650:98
strategy of d. GALB 343:90
defer D., d. GILB 355:23
defiance act of wilful d. SASS 716:56
bold d. with his prince DRYD 290:80
defiant before a d. deed WHIT 905:37
It is d. READ 680:47
deficiencies d. of fortune GOLD 361:44
deficiency d. in the graces JOHN 445:23
deficient very d. in means KISH 475:88
deficit Olympics…d. DRAP 286:95
Park Avenue…trade d. BART 63:26
defile neither shall ye d. yourselves BIBLE 89:33
presumed to d. DREN 287:8
define cannot d. the real problem FEYN 322:25
d. her feelings in language HARDY 381:53
d. jazz satisfactorily KING 470:65
ought to d. a man's income HICKS 402:80
to d. is to eliminate QUINE 675:51
defines he who d. himself LAO 489:10
definite d. maybe GOLD 362:86
like d. form STEV 821:77
no d. answers can RUSS 705:42
definition d. of a free society STEV 820:54
d. of a 'hero' FIND 323:58
d. of a horse DICK 270:2
d. of a specialist MAYO 562:97
d. of happiness KENN 463:38
d. of utter waste HUNT 423:23
d. of what a nurse NIGH 616:35
D.—Science is systematized SART 715:40
incapable of any d. MOORE 594:20
ultimate d. of this uniqueness COUS 239:3
want a d. of poetry THOM 853:79
definitions exact d. can be applied QUIL 674:45
which…they call D. HOBB 404:23
deflationary essentially a d. genius MORR 598:94
deflowered At last you are d. COWA 239:19
deformed how d. dost thou look! SHAK 733:78
None can be called d. SHAK 757:88
what a d. thief SHAK 745:14
deformity Art is significant d. FRY 340:33
mine own d. SHAK 731:2
Degas remember D. PISS 652:34
degenerate creative protests to d. KING 468:37
degradation breath of d. BYRON 181:57
children from utter d. LOVE 519:17
consent to such d. OCON 621:19

means of increasing her d. — STAN 812:65
sense of intellectual d. — JAMES 433:27
degree d. and a quality of trust — SHAP 776:36
d. of a person's intelligence — ALTH 13:70
d. of certainty — RUSS 705:54
d. of 'grand old man' — LEAC 497:72
d. of serenity — NIEB 614:97
didn't get a d. — DOWD 284:40
in however slight a d. — RYLE 707:80
lady of beauty and high d. — RANS 679:21
with d. dispense — JONS 449:38
degrees 105 d. in Saigon — ANON 26:84
arts are taught by d. — THEO 851:39
boil at different d. — EMER 313:49
by d. learn to work at all things — CARL 193:38
Crime…has its d. — RACI 677:86
d. of anger — EVANS 316:20
d. of communism and d. — NGUY 613:81
d. off east longitude — MUNDY 603:83
heal but by d.? — SHAK 760:82
thirty d. below zero — MOOD 594:7
will name you the d. — SHAK 750:91
dehumanize d., not just the slaves — MORR 599:6
deities d. of his own invention — PLATO 654:77
Deity doubted…the D. — WELLS 898:71
deity believe in a personal d. — HAMM 379:6
D. and the Drains — STRA 826:83
d. when Cubans get together — LEZA 508:12
Half dust, half d. — BYRON 181:57
Prosperity…not a d. — COOL 236:47
Dekanahwideh D., and…Chiefs — DEKA 259:45
delay reluctant amorous d. — MILT 583:63
We safely may d. — BRON 154:77
why shou'd we d.? — WALL 886:14
delayed it has been d. — JOHN 442:34
delays d. are dangerous — DRYD 288:33
delegate When in trouble, d. — WAGN 884:65
delicate d. death — WHIT 906:48
rich and d. English language — WAUGH 893:57
sufficiently d. — KEYN 465:85
The air is d. — SHAK 767:85
delicately d. as possible — RUSS 705:45
delicates fruits and princely d. — MARL 552:98
delicious d. dinner of too much — JOHN 439:71
d., nourishing, and wholesome — SWIFT 831:93
magic and d. power — WOOLF 922:43
wine…heavenly and d. — RABE 676:65
With most d. poison — SHAK 764:21
delight anyone's afflictions…source of
delight — LUCR 522:83
bind another to its d. — BLAKE 134:52
calm in our d. — WORD 924:73
decrepit father takes d. — SHAK 771:17
d. in simple things — KIPL 473:63
d. is in the law of the Lord — BIBLE 94:81
d. of her husband — RANS 679:21
d. themselves in…peace — BIBLE 95:16
D. thyself also in the Lord — BIBLE 95:15
do ill our sole d. — MILT 580:3
Energy is Eternal D. — BLAKE 134:38
feelings of d. — WORD 928:50
filled with such d. — SASS 716:69
gift, my ever new d. — MILT 583:76
give d. and hurt not — SHAK 774:92
go to't with d. — SHAK 765:42
harmony or true d.? — MILT 584:2
high austerity to d. — FREE 336:44
If you d. not in man — SHAK 753:59
inordinate sensual d. — BAXT 65:90
Love and d. are better teachers — DURER 295:29
makes eating a d. — SUCK 828:9
mixed profit with pleasure — HORA 414:33
nursed by d. — LYLY 523:9
Phantom of d. — WORD 927:35
simple human d. — BARB 59:48
source of little visible d. — BRON 155:96
succession of d. — SMART 797:31
the fruit of your d. — SURR 829:39
'Tis my d., alone in summer shade — WORD 925:8
to d.…paid thy utmost blessing — DELA 260:72
Too bright for our infirm D. — DICK 273:71
to teach and d. — SIDN 791:7
true spirit of d. — RUSS 705:44
unrest which men miscall d. — SHEL 786:4
various objects of d. — MILT 586:47
what d. we…have — PEPYS 647:44
What worlds d. — SPEN 808:79

delighted cruel, and d. in cruelty — QUIL 674:46
d. particularly in quotations — SCHL 718:11
only too d. to have been born — STRA 826:81
primary object…to be d. — CECIL 201:23
delightful d. to be a woman — SCHR 720:38
make his conversation perfectly d. — SMITH 801:18
society is wonderfully d.! — WILDE 909:28
two most d. things in it? — WALP 887:33
delights all d. my fortune — JONS 448:12
d. of a pantomime — DICK 267:97
d. of the flesh castrate me — FUEN 340:41
d.Will vanish — MILT 583:64
mind religiously affected d. — HOOK 411:56
Of the d. of this world — TWAIN 872:36
O love, for d.! — BIBLE 102:5
permissible d. of the soul — BACH 46:25
To scorn d., and live — MILT 578:49
violent d. have violent ends — SHAK 736:60
delineation d. of that which appeals — HUMB 421:1
happiest d. of its varieties — AUST 43:91
delinquencies indulge in a few d. — ELIOT 303:72
delinquents d. are frustrated actors — MULL 602:71
deliquescent d. leaves of paper — ANDR 16:25
delirium and one d. tremens — TWAIN 871:1
in such pleasant d. — ELIOT 303:75
may attack you in d. tremens — OBRI 621:11
delitabill Storyss to rede ar d. — BARB 59:51
deliver come down to d. them — BIBLE 88:11
let him d. him — BIBLE 94:98
sacrifice them all…to d. you — SHAK 740:82
who shall d. me — BIBLE 120:71
deliverance songs of d. — BIBLE 95:10
delivered d. me from all my fears — BIBLE 95:12
deliverer No d. ever rose — MORG 597:81
delivery Punctual D. Company — DICK 267:98
dell pure as the lily in the d. — LAUD 492:63
Delors UP YOURS D. — SUN 828:22
delph dresser filled with shining d. — COLUM 229:61
deluded Gods and men, we are all d. — SHEL 787:28
deluge After us the d. — POMP 658:46
delusion d. that macro-economics — HAYEK 387:61
d. that one likes oneself — DIDI 274:4
give up their liberties…under some d. — BURKE 168:27
nothing…but that addled d. — ELIOT 303:97
progress is utter d. — MILL 572:26
Trial…will be a d. — DENM 262:98
united by a d. — INGE 429:54
delusions mocked by d. — EMER 313:37
demagogue d. is a person — MARQ 554:37
demand d. disturbs the happy — BRON 155:85
d. for their labour — STEU 819:8
d. the time of the day — SHAK 741:94
d. this…for the race — SCHR 720:42
immeasurable or insolent d. — WALP 887:41
we d. the excellence — REYES 684:21
demands d. of a composer — HONE 409:30
d. that form the habit — TUCH 869:59
De Maupassant beat Mr D. M. — HEMI 394:18
demeanour d. nobly bland — GILB 355:33
demesne private pagus or d. — AUDEN 41:25
demi-god magician is a d.-g. — MARL 552:97
demigods musicians are not d. — TURN 870:67
demi-monde d.-m. does not represent — DUMAS 294:94
democracies D. must try to find ways — THAT 850:24
d. of the west — MASA 559:20
not embraced by d. — PIUS 653:53
tendency of d.…to mediocrity — COOP 236:51
democracy crisis of Western d. — LIPP 511:65
d. and peace — WELL 897:48
D. and proper drains — BETJ 83:85
D.! Bah! — GINS 357:66
D.…by the uneducated — CHES 213:97
d. is but a flickering candle — MACK 534:21
d. is just a slogan — GORB 363:99
D. is not a polite employer — HOOV 411:63
D. is supposed to give — VIDAL 881:2
D. is the recurrent suspicion — WHITE 903:79
D. is the theory — MENC 565:52
d. is the worst form of Government — CHUR 217:94
d.; it's the counting — STOP 825:63
D. means government by discussion — ATTL 38:46
D. means simply — WILDE 908:12
d. must remain at home — BORAH 144:87
d. of the dead — CHES 211:61
D. substitutes election — SHAW 778:5
D. was renewed in Scotland — DEWAR 264:41

duty of a d. — WHITE 903:77
experience of d. is like…life — CART 198:48
full-blooded and unconditional d. — GORB 363:2
great arsenal of d. — ROOS 696:49
grieved under a d. — HOBB 404:28
ideal form of d. — BEUYS 84:13
In a d. — FULB 340:44
laboratories of d. — WHIT 905:27
little less d. to save — ATKI 37:33
Love of d. is love — MONT 593:94
make d. stable — SKEL 795:94
modern d. is a tyranny — MAIL 540:44
obstacle to d. — SCHU 721:58
odyssey toward liberty, d. — MAIL 540:52
our d. was — MACA 526:76
political aspirant under d. — MENC 565:64
Political d.…in America — WHIT 906:50
priestly offices in a d. — LIPP 511:67
property-owning d. — SKEL 795:94
talk…about d. — ROOS 695:38
Television has made…d. unbearable — PERES 648:63
thanks to wine-less and d. — BROW 162:90
trouble in modern d. — BEVE 85:25
two cheers for d. — FORS 332:53
uncrowned king of an educated d. — STEAD 813:82
voice, of the d. — STEAD 813:80
We are a d. — PULI 672:3
Why D. means — HUGH 418:19
world must be made safe for d. — WILS 916:15
worst thing I can say about d. — BEVAN 84:14
democrat Aristocrat, d., autocrat — TENN 845:84
aristocrat is the d. ripe — EMER 313:36
d. only on principle — TWAIN 872:32
free man…and a D. — JOHN 440:80
democratic D. idea — BRYAN 163:8
D. Intellect — DAVIE 254:28
d. parliaments of tricks — WEBB 893:64
denouncing liberal d. principles — AUNG 42:49
Fig leaves of d. procedure — KENN 462:98
ideals of a d.…society — MAND 544:46
market is so vulgarly d. — KRIS 481:17
The D. Party has succeeded — ONEI 626:11
towards the d. powers — MASA 559:20
whole new d. world — CARL 192:90
democrats D. are fleeing — SHEV 788:74
demography nothing to do with d. — BERG 79:1
demolished d. or rebuilt — BOOTH 144:82
demolition Slated for d. — ASHB 35:85
demon Celtic Demos rose a D. — TENN 848:69
demonic tends towards the d. — BAUD 65:74
demon-lover wailing for her d.-l. — COLE 226:10
demons artist…driven by d. — FAUL 318:87
demonstration logic of d. — NISB 616:38
Spontaneous D. — ORWE 629:74
Demosthenes when D. spoke — OGIL 623:41
demur If I d. — HEAN 389:10
demurest D. of the tabby kind — GRAY 368:37
den beard the lion in his d. — SCOTT 723:98
from the d. — SMART 797:30
in the d.…nine dead men — BALL 55:75
Deng revisionist clique of D. — JIANG 438:31
deniability some future d. — POIN 657:35
denial timid requests, invites d. — SENE 727:93
denied but half d. — BUTL 177:58
Denmark beard me in D.? — SHAK 753:63
example of the king of D. — FACK 317:31
look like a friend on D. — SHAK 751:27
rotten in the state of D. — SHAK 751:27
royal bed of D. — SHAK 752:33
storks on the spires of D. — DOYLE 286:83
throne of D. to thy father — SHAK 751:98
villain dwelling in all D. — SHAK 752:36
denominator lowest common d. — JARR 435:87
lowest common d. of human — CART 198:49
no common d. — AUDEN 41:23
denote things which they d. — JOHN 442:39
dens d. of robbery and murder — NATI 610:25
dentist dread this like the d. — AUDEN 39:85
like going to the d. — WILD 910:70
smiling…like a clumsy d. — MANS 547:92
sooner go to my d. — WAUGH 892:28
talk like a d. when one isn't — WILDE 909:35
dentists adulteries of d. — WILD 911:88
d. ride roughshod — PERE 648:59
denunciation d. of the young — SMITH 799:72
deny cannot but d. them — SHAW 778:85
dare d. that the Third Estate — SIEY 791:26

D. it to a king? — SHAK 743:53
d. knowledge — KANT 455:46
d. me thrice — BIBLE 116:62
d. me thrice — BIBLE 114:97
neither…palliate nor d. — PITT 652:36
reason down the d. of everything — EMER 312:31
denying to allure by d. — TROL 867:96
deoch-an-doris Just a wee d.-a.-d. — MORR 599:2
deodar smell of d. wood burning — CHAT 207:49
deodorant Success is a great d. — TAYL 837:18
depart D.,—be off — HOLM 408:92
d. in God's name — JOAN 438:52
D., I say — AMERY 14:80
D., I say, and let us have done — CROM 246:74
Let him d. — SHAK 746:56
departed d. was a 'Roman' — LAWS 495:44
departing always arriving and d. — MILL 573:52
department d. of psychology — AYER 45:12
d. stores…like museums — WARH 889:65
fair sex is your d. — DOYLE 285:75
material in every d. — BEAV 67:27
not to a functionary or d. — STEAD 813:84
State D. — MCCA 527:93
departments public d. — DICK 270:8
department-store d.-s. state — CHAN 205:84
departure d. from this world — EMMET 313:59
function is d. can depart — LISP 512:74
grant them a fair d. — SHAK 739:49
possible point of d. — WAGN 884:64
dependence d. of one fact — HOBB 404:24
not subsist without D. — STEE 814:97
total d. on the appreciation of others — CONN 233:70
dependencies colonies and wide d. — QUIL 674:44
deplore d. but was powerless — LEAC 496:64
D. what is to be deplored — MORG 597:79
though still I do d.? — DONNE 281:81
depository d. of power — DISR 276:48
depressed no one d. in this house — VICT 880:85
depression d., combined with — LURIE 522:91
D. is when you lose — REAG 680:55
d. when you lose yours — TRUM 868:38
deprivation D. is…daffodils — LARK 491:47
deprived needy, I was d. — FEIF 319:83
violated and the d. — JORD 450:65
depriving chief means of d. them — HALL 378:91
de profundis D. P. clamavi ad te — BIBLE 128:94
Deptford famous in D. — DAVI 254:40
depth d. of her glowing breast — SHEL 785:85
d. unfathomed no man knows — WESL 900:18
in the d. be praise — NEWM 612:66
love thee to the d. — BROW 160:9
depths d. of every heart — HAWT 386:47
d. where her marvels are manifest — GORD 363:6
Out of the d. have I cried — BIBLE 98:95
people…out of their d. — FITZ 325:7
unfathomable d. of his…mind — COLE 227:26
Up from the d. I have cried to thee — BIBLE 128:94
deputy books…may be read by d. — BACON 50:53
if you and your d. will go back — ANDE 15:15
De Quincey Coleridge and D. Q. — THUR 859:49
Derby back streets of D. — CHRI 214:28
deride do not d. the fears — JORD 450:65
derision Lord shall have them in d. — BIBLE 94:83
old days to d. — SWIN 833:30
derivative but what is only d. — MILT 580:86
d. from this pure activity — LEWIS 508:95
descendants only chance for their d. — DAVI 254:30
descent claims of long d. — TENN 840:74
no nobility of d. — POTT 664:20
describe do not d. it fitly — JAMES 434:63
do nothing but d. — GRAY 369:8
poet's business is not to d. — ABER 1:5
description d. of a happy state — LOCKE 514:20
d. of the…Rhodes Scholar — MARA 548:24
d. of the rising sun — SHER 788:65
gay D. Aegypt glads — POPE 662:20
It beggared all d. — SHAK 764:23
picture that requires any d. — HOMER 409:26
truth of d. and the sentiment — SCOTT 725:54
descriptions d. of scenery — LEVIN 506:64
Desdemona love the gentle D. — SHAK 759:55
Othello subject D. — KOES 477:30
desert alone in the d. — SAINT 709:16
arid d. of his mind — WEST 901:42
call of the d. — STARK 813:73
came through the d. — THOM 856:63
Carlyle has led us all out into the d. — CLOU 222:19

company of d. people — THES 851:51
d. in a dry frigid weather — PIER 651:7
D. Storm — SCHW 721:67
d. were my dwelling-place — BYRON 180:42
Down my d. rhyme — CRAIK 242:7
Even in thy d. — BYRON 180:32
every man after his d. — SHAK 753:66
found him in a d. land — BIBLE 90:56
garden…into a d. — YOUNG 935:76
gardens of the D. — BRYA 164:13
knowledge…areas of d. — CHAN 205:83
legs of stone…in the d. — SHEL 784:49
Nothing went unrewarded, but d. — DRYD 290:89
pained d. lion — ARNO 32:25
pain in the d. — MOOR 596:55
power to make the world a d. — STEV 820:52
shores, and d. wilderness — MILT 577:31
streams in the d. — BIBLE 103:33
to say the d. is stingy — HEAT 390:28
waste its sweetness on the d. air — GRAY 369:17
went out into the d. — SITW 794:83
Zuleika, on a d. island — BEER 69:75
desertion treacherous d. of an ally — CHUR 216:61
deserts D. are there — SACK 708:90
d. of America — JOHN 442:57
d. of the heart — AUDEN 40:5
D. of vast eternity — MARV 556:62
Or his d. are small — MONT 593:4
Story is just just d. — ELKIN 310:70
deserve advertising we d. — SAYE 717:87
Something you…haven't to d. — FROST 338:87
deserved more credit than they d. — REST 683:16
never have d. it — SATIE 717:82
punished himself…if he d. it — ELIOT 303:85
deserving d. to do it — GRAY 368:88
lost without d. — SHAK 760:79
design according to the same d. — VIAN 880:80
any d. that you wish to give them — VAZD 878:53
characteristic of the d. — LEWO 508:9
d. career is a process of learning — BELL 72:43
d. of darkness — FROST 339:5
don't d. clothes, I d. dreams — LAUR 492:68
ill d. is most ill — HESI 401:65
only its d. The hand — MICH 568:33
when…dull there is a d. — STEE 814:91
designed deliberately d. — HAYEK 387:60
d. to show those — KEIL 460:72
designing d. for obsolescence — ISSI 431:96
designs d. were strictly honourable — FIEL 322:43
desirability d.…of telling lies — ORWE 629:93
desirable d.…be pretty — LAMB 486:42
produce that anything is d. — MILL 570:71
desire admitted d. to dress — LIN 510:32
all a wonder and a wild d. — BROW 162:82
animated by a sincere d. — PEEL 646:9
ardently d. that our country — PANK 636:33
arrows of d.! — BLAKE 135:84
At Christmas I no more d. — SHAK 733:71
a' the learning I d. — BURNS 170:64
bowls of fierce d. — CRAS 244:43
bred by d. — LYLY 523:9
bred in me a d. — MUNDY 603:83
Can one d. too much — SHAK 750:78
circling in hot d. — FLAU 326:39
crime is due to the repressed d. — WAUGH 892:23
danger of d. — SHAK 751:14
d. for food and sex — TOOLE 863:13
d.…is a tree of life — BIBLE 99:12
d.…is a tree of life — BIBLE 99:25
d. is increased by the difficulty — WEBS 894:76
d. is, that the Almighty — BIBLE 93:66
d. more love and knowledge — SHAK 749:29
d. not to be impinged upon — BERL 80:21
D. not to be rinsed with wine — HOPK 412:81
d. of beauty…has most — PATER 642:53
d. of bettering our condition — SMITH 798:47
d. of satisfying a voracious appetite — FIEL 322:42
D. paces Eternity — DUNC 295:13
d. shall fail — BIBLE 101:92
d. to be rich — BAGE 51:92
d. to create something — PRIE 668:23
d. to do right — DICK 271:41
d. to have all the fun — SAYE 717:83
d. to integrate into society — SARR 715:39
d. to know — RUSS 705:48
d. to know causes — HAZL 388:87
d. to make money — VAN 876:26

d. to objectify — MOORE 595:35
d. to take medicine — OSLER 630:15
d. to touch the truth — PACH 633:69
d. to win — CONN 233:61
d. what we do not have — LABR 483:69
few things to d. — BACON 49:17
flaming in d. — ROCH 691:50
forced by d. — RICH 686:62
Free from d. — LAO 489:9
fruitless d. — BINY 130:54
gave to the queen of Sheba all her d. — BIBLE 92:42
horizontal d. — SHAW 781:92
impersonation of d. — BROO 156:27
Is it not strange that d. — SHAK 743:51
is the prompting of d. — LEHM 501:67
lit my pinnacled d. — SASS 716:65
lost the d. to lead anyone — BEVE 85:25
love beyond d. — ELIOT 309:46
man's d. — HABI 376:54
man's d. is for the woman — COLE 227:22
mixing Memory and d. — ELIOT 305:52
naught for your d. — CHES 212:72
no longer d. happiness — SHAW 777:60
nothing like wealth for dulling d. — MCGU 532:94
objects of d. — RICA 684:34
one d. in life — SHAW 778:87
questioning them was my mind's d. — BRID 152:27
raging d. — TWAIN 870:89
restless d. of power — HOBB 404:26
singularity in a d. — DONNE 281:93
strange d. to seek power — BACON 48:1
this fond d. — ADDI 7:38
To d. immortality — SCHO 719:32
vain d. at last — ROSS 698:99
what I've tasted of d. — FROST 338:97
what many men d. — SHAK 740:62
Which of us has his d.? — THAC 849:94
yearning in d. — TENN 840:64
youth pined away with d. — BLAKE 134:53
desired I have d. to go — HOPK 412:78
not one to be d. — TENN 840:73
You who d. so much — CRANE 243:15
desires all d. known — BOOK 141:92
all holy d. — BOOK 140:76
d. in the interest — RUSS 705:48
d. of the heart — AUDEN 39:87
give thee the d. of thine heart — BIBLE 95:15
He who d. and acts not — BLAKE 134:40
increase Of my d. — SURR 829:35
infinite in its d. — NORR 618:65
lay lime to tangle her d. — SHAK 729:38
lopping off our d. — SWIFT 831:69
means…to satisfy our d. — PREV 668:12
murder…than nurse unacted d. — BLAKE 134:45
one's own transient d. — EINS 301:33
outlived certain d. — WOOLF 923:52
pimps for ill d. — DRYD 289:73
thoughtless youth…with vain d. — DRYD 291:6
two d. toss about — ARNO 32:7
unrealistic goals and d. — LURIE 522:91
desk but d. to write upon — BUTL 177:51
d. is a dangerous place — ANON 24:28
From counter or d. — YEATS 933:44
votary of the d. — LAMB 486:49
Desmond Wildly o'er D. — MCCA 527:88
desolate All is now d.…ambushed — MACA 525:36
None are as d. — BYRON 179:10
desolation D. Angels — KERO 464:66
D. in immaculate public — ROET 694:98
Great d. of abomination — COBB 223:49
love in d. masked — SHEL 785:99
made a d. they called it a peace — BURG 167:85
Magnificent d. — ALDR 11:16
perfect d. — FIELD 322:30
witnesses to the d. of war — GEOR 349:14
despair Be thine d. — GRAY 370:36
birds…without d. — WEBS 894:78
conscience wakes d. — MILT 582:53
D., not feast on thee — HOPK 412:2
d. of crystal brilliance — MACN 537:98
D. yawns — HUGO 421:88
dungeon of d. — CESA 203:49
filled me with a kind of d. — KAVA 456:66
final d.…supreme victory — WHIT 904:14
forerunner of d. — KENN 462:3
from d. Thus high — MILT 581:18
Giant D. had a wife — BUNY 166:71

Happiness…in savouring their d.   GENG 349:8
hurries me back to d.   COWP 241:56
iron-clasped volume of d.   POE 656:27
It was begotten by D.   MARV 556:66
Look on my works…and d.   SHEL 784:50
loves…of comfort and d.   SHAK 773:55
made D. a smilingness assume   BYRON 179:22
my charecter I d. for   FLEM 327:61
My meer d.   VAUG 878:43
needst not then d.!   ARNO 31:97
neither d. in the church   FACK 317:31
One path leads to d.   ALLEN 12:56
perplexed, but not in d.   BIBLE 122:24
quality of his d.   CONN 233:86
racked with deep d.   MILT 580:2
resolution from d.   MILT 580:5
ruin and d.   WIEN 907:68
Should all d.   SHAK 770:77
sign of d. in a woman   WILDE 909:47
Slimness Of D.   NICH 613:86
Snobbery…a form of d.   BROD 153:55
some divine d.   TENN 842:6
Symphony or give in to d.   ROY 701:57
through darkness and d.   SHEL 784:66
Where there is d.   FRAN 334:98
Where there is d.   THAT 850:16
winter of d.   DICK 271:19
work…out of d.   BAUD 65:80
despairer Too quick d.   ARNO 33:46
desperado 'd.'…all over him   BIRD 130:58
desperate constituency is the d.   JACK 431:6
d. act of men   READ 680:47
desperation hunger, poverty, d.   MARS 554:39
lives of quiet d.   THOR 857:83
despise comforts we d.   SHAK 765:45
d. the uninitiated mob   HORA 413:22
d. yourself too much   KAVA 456:67
government I d.   KEYN 465:77
live and d. writing   SMITH 800:1
more things to admire…than to d.   CAMUS 187:93
they that d. me   BIBLE 91:80
to hate and to d. myself   HAZL 388:85
despised blind, d., and dying king   SHEL 783:34
certainly have d. Christ   GREE 371:70
d. and rejected of men   BIBLE 104:50
d. of the people   BIBLE 94:98
despond Slough of D.   BUNY 166:67
despondency d. and madness   WORD 926:17
spread alarm and d.   PENI 646:21
despot country governed by a d.   JOHN 445:30
d. whom the wise ridicule and obey   BIER 129:30
despotism d. tempered by epigrams   CARL 192:12
enemy to d.   GARI 346:47
handed over to a ruthless d.   ATTL 37:41
modern form of d.   MCCA 528:4
dessert Cheese for d.   BRAC 148:50
now she could eat d.   ALTH 13:68
destination all signpost and no d.   KRON 481:22
d. is never a place   MILL 573:52
physical d.   GRAT 367:61
destinies recognised, and robed as d.   LARK 490:27
destiny Anatomy is d.   FREUD 337:54
by d., rather than choice   KENN 463:40
cannot escape d.   ROBBE 688:6
character is d.   ELIOT 303:93
d. demands and keep   NAPO 607:60
d. is to keep down   DOUG 283:14
d. obscure   GRAY 369:41
d. to wear a skirt in all countries   IZZA 431:3
escape his d.   PLATO 655:86
great hour of d.   SASS 716:60
Hanging and marriage…go by d.   FARQ 318:53
Hanging and wiving goes by d.   SHAK 740:64
historic d. of the Irish   WAUGH 892:38
imagine a d.   FIED 322:29
man…looking for his own d.   SAINT 709:23
measure up to their d.   APOL 27:18
naturally, it's d.   BAUD 65:73
part of the d.   THOR 857:80
riddles of…future d.   FRYE 340:39
shears of d.?   SHAK 739:32
stream of d.   SPEN 808:78
'Tis my d.   FORD 330:15
what I took to be our d.   LEWIS 507:78
who can deceive his d.   SPEN 809:91
destroy chose to d. themselves   HOYLE 417:4
D. his fib…in vain   POPE 661:35

d. ourselves due to atrophy   GELL 348:98
d. the law   BIBLE 109:86
d. the town   ANON 23:2
impatient to d.   JOHN 441:18
To create is…to d.   CUMM 247:99
write to d.   ROBBE 689:12
destroyed d. her man   SYNGE 834:51
everything…has been d.   FENT 320:88
man can be d.   HEMI 394:21
many a good tall fellow had d.   SHAK 741:1
More dreams are d.   SKEL 795:8
more easily it is d.   JOHN 445:30
once d., can never be supplied   GOLD 361:52
What's not d. by Time   BRAM 150:88
destroyer D. and preserver   SHEL 783:44
Is my d.   THOM 852:57
Time the d.   ELIOT 308:31
destruction dark angel of d.   LENG 502:81
d. of all justice   MORE 597:70
d. of human life   HARDY 381:46
d. of the whole world   HUME 422:8
d. that wasteth at noonday   BIBLE 96:53
D. with d. to destroy   MILT 585:28
for d. ice   FROST 338:97
going from us to be utter d.   BIBLE 107:31
Hell and d. are never full   BIBLE 100:60
most frightful form of d.   MACA 527:78
on the side of d.   KEYN 465:79
Pride goeth before d.   BIBLE 99:36
redeemeth thy life from d.   BIBLE 97:62
soul…startles at d.   ADDI 7:38
way, that leadeth to d.   BIBLE 110:9
Whose end is d.   BIBLE 123:59
destructive d. and often malign   MUGG 601:50
to the d. element submit yourself   CONR 234:2
desuetization d. of Scottish life   MACD 530:47
detachment strangest sense of d.   WELLS 898:74
detail become the slave of d.   RYDER 707:77
emotion, d. and image   BRAU 150:4
frittered away by d.   THOR 857:92
Retail is d.   SCHU 720:48
details deal with many d.   MILLS 574:70
d.…of man and career   ELTON 311:95
particular features or d.   GOYA 365:30
detection D. is…an exact science   DOYLE 285:51
d. of…human woes   DEWEY 264:43
detective d. novel…form of art   PRIT 669:47
Ladies' D. Agency   SMITH 798:57
writing a d. story   JAMES 434:57
determination d. of incident?   JAMES 433:44
determinism retrospective d.   BEND 74:7
deterrent credible d.   MCNA 537:94
d. would continue to deter   MACM 536:72
detest my creator, d. and spurn me   SHEL 782:12
detestation show him your d.   PARN 639:91
Detroit D. is a one-trade town   MAIL 540:55
deuce how the d. they ever could   BYRON 181:67
devaluation d. of the human   MARX 557:95
devastation d.…at Rome   AUGU 42:43
developed all this will have to be d.   ISHE 430:89
development arrested our d.   MILL 573:59
continuous and healthy d.   PARS 640:1
creation, d. and being   HUMB 421:2
d. in the productive facilities   MARX 557:1
d. itself ceases   PEAR 645:97
d. of mankind   NIET 615:23
human history and cosmic d.   BELL 74:83
if we approve of the d.   BEND 74:7
limit of its d.   ANON 22:45
own way of d.   WILS 916:13
phases of its d.   ERNST 315:89
process of historical d.   ROBI 690:40
progressive d.   GORB 363:1
symptomatic of…arrested d.   DISCH 275:29
truism in technological d.   STER 817:62
device miracle of rare d.   COLE 226:12
devices d. still are overthrown   SHAK 754:91
devil any sort of d. and the deep blue sea   RATT 679:31
apology for the D.   BUTL 178:78
as though some poor d.   SKIN 795:11
break a man's spirit is d.'s work   SHAW 777:57
But the D. whoops   KIPL 471:4
can the d. speak true?   SHAK 766:75
children of the d.   TENN 848:61
cleft the D.'s foot   DONNE 279:39
cursèd d.   WEBS 895:94
D. always builds a chapel   DEFOE 258:13

d., as a roaring lion   BIBLE 125:30
d. be in my feet   SCOTT 724:29
d. cam fiddlin thro' the town   BURNS 172:37
d. can cite Scripture   SHAK 739:52
d. damn thee black   SHAK 768:36
d. dancing in me glorious   MASE 559:34
d. had done for the rest   STEV 822:7
D. himself cannot make   MELV 564:42
D. howling 'Ho'   SQUI 811:42
d. is dead!   READE 680:50
D. is forever grinning in upon me   MELV 564:42
D. is still at hand   DRYD 289:73
d. made himself a woman   HUGO 421:79
d.…on the side of the learned   FRAN 333:89
D. out of hell!   JOYCE 452:83
d.'s awa wi' th' Exciseman   BURNS 172:38
d. sends cooks   FULL 341:66
d. sends cooks   GARR 346:54
d. should have all the good tunes   HILL 402:89
d.'s sooner raised   SHER 787:50
d.'s walking parody   CHES 211:42
d. taketh him up   BIBLE 109:80
d. understands Welsh   SHAK 742:20
d. will come, and Faustus   MARL 552:6
D. with d. damned   MILT 581:30
D. with perhaps   MUGG 601:37
d. won't turn them   SCOTT 725:53
envy of the d.   BIBLE 107:30
face the d.!   BURNS 172:21
favourable reference to the D.   CHUR 217:97
fears a painted d.   SHAK 767:4
fight…against…the d.   BOOK 141:12
given up believing in the d.   KNOX 476:23
give the d. his due   SHAK 741:99
go, poor d., get thee gone   STER 818:90
Half d. and half child   KIPL 472:25
heaviest stone that the d. can throw   HAZL 388:91
he counteracts the D.   SMART 796:26
how the D. they got there   POPE 661:36
If the d. doesn't exist   DOST 283:9
know he is a d.   ETHE 315:95
laughing d. in sneer   BYRON 181:48
May be the d.   SHAK 753:71
Nazarite conjured the d. into!   SHAK 739:50
old serpent, called the D.   BIBLE 126:66
opportunity for attacking the d.!   STEAD 813:85
plain to see, the D. walks   BETJ 84:4
politician is the d.'s quilted anvil   WEBS 895:7
poor d. has ended   BROW 161:47
Pope Fired in the D.'s belly   ANON 21:37
renounce the d. and all his works   BOOK 142:13
Resist the d., and he will flee   BIBLE 125:15
sacrifice…of the d.'s leavings   POPE 659:91
sacrifice them all…to this d.   SHAK 740:82
said the D.   WALL 886:5
saint when most I play the d.   SHAK 731:7
servant to the d.   SISS 793:55
serve the d. and his angels   WENT 899:4
shame the d.   SHAK 742:31
Tell us, pray, what d.   FORD 330:19
tempted of the d.   BIBLE 109:78
that d.'s madness—War   SERV 728:5
The d.!   ONEI 625:94
The d. Bush   HUSS 424:42
Till the D. whispered   KIPL 471:3
truth and shame the d.   LIPP 511:66
wiles of the d.   BIBLE 122:52
with you the d. will fly away   OCON 621:31
devil-born doubt is D.-b.   TENN 844:56
devildoms d. of Spain   TENN 848:60
devilish most D. thing   FLEM 327:54
devil-porter I'll d.-p. it no further   SHAK 767:7
devils casteth out d.   BIBLE 111:22
cast out d.   BIBLE 111:16
d. also believe   BIBLE 124:10
d. as tiles   SHAK 759:73
d. being offended   MAIL 540:46
d. to contest his vision   SHAK 745:37
foreign d. have made   ORAH 627:21
innumerable monsters and d.   LUTH 523:99
more d. than vast hell   SHAK 738:13
said they were d. incarnate   SHAK 745:37
devise what one man can d.   WRIS 930:92
Devon D., glorious D.!   BOUL 146:25
devotee great d. of the Gospel   SHAW 777:76
devotees most d. arrive   UPDI 875:92
devotion d. and our prayers   FRIE 337:70

d. of the wind and seas — LANC 487:72
hate with greater d. — SHAK 769:62
intelligence that moves, d. is — DONNE 282:96
object of universal d. — IRVI 430:85
passion for abstracted d. — JOHN 443:83
promote my invisible d. — BROW 158:54
with evergreen d. — BIRN 131:71
devour seeking whom he may d. — BIBLE 125:30
shed tears when they would d. — BACON 49:23
devoured could have d. me — KARSH 455:52
has d. the infant child — HOUS 416:88
devourer Time the d. — OVID 631:46
dew as sunlight drinketh d. — TENN 838:41
As the d. of Hermon — BIBLE 98:96
continual d. of thy blessing — BOOK 140:75
Debauchee of D. — DICK 272:57
d. her orbs upon the green — SHAK 737:92
d. of heaven — FORD 330:11
d. on the mountain — SCOTT 723:8
Drop down d. — BIBLE 128:96
fades awa' like morning d. — BALL 56:94
fresh with blooming d. — MERE 566:94
honey wild, and manna d. — KEATS 458:18
in the d. of the morn — YEATS 932:35
meet the morning d. — ARNO 33:48
Orient d., Shed from — MARV 555:57
pastures…washed with d. — SASS 717:77
rained a ghastly d. — TENN 840:81
resolve itself into a d. — SHAK 751:5
roses washed in d. — MILT 576:5
sea of d. — FIELD 322:32
speech shall distil as the d. — BIBLE 90:55
wave glittered the d. — MANS 547:91
wet with the d. of heaven — BIBLE 106:96
who hath begotten the drops of d.? — BIBLE 93:72
your chains to earth like d. — SHEL 783:38
dewdrop fragile d. — KEATS 457:82
globe as one great d. — MUIR 602:65
Starlight and d. — FOST 332:62
dewdrops seek some d. here — SHAK 737:92
showers and d. wet — ROSS 697:83
Dewey D. has no inner reserve — HOOV 411:68
dewfall d. at night — STEV 823:32
dew-like d.-l. steel — BRAU 150:4
dew-pearled hill-side's d.-p. — BROW 160:19
dews drinker of d. — DOYLE 286:83
night d. on still waters — TENN 839:54
dewy-feathered d.-f. Sleep — MILT 577:21
dhoti Mahatma's cotton d. — MURR 604:7
diabetes Politics is like having d. — JONES 447:89
diagnose able to d. — KEYN 465:79
diagnostician One finger…d. — OSLER 630:17
dial d.'s shady stealth — SHAK 772:33
needle on a d. — STEV 820:58
ride upon a d.'s point — SHAK 742:31
dialect d. I understand very little — PEPYS 647:37
purify the d. of the tribe — ELIOT 309:43
use of d. words — HARDY 382:58
dialogue And the d.! — CHAN 204:82
conviction is to report that d. — KUNI 482:39
Death is a d. — DICK 273:70
d. between client and architect — STERN 817:65
film script…without d. — MAMET 544:37
settlement through genuine d. — AUNG 42:50
unending d. between the present — CARR 194:52
dialogues d. with my Mother — WORD 925:97
dials carve out d. — SHAK 730:75
d. the signs — SHAK 741:94
diamond d. and safire bracelet — LOOS 517:79
d.…has scarce any value in use — SMITH 797:41
find a d. or a pearl — VAN 877:30
immortal d. — HOPK 413:8
more of rough than polished d. — CHES 210:33
soul…like a rough d. — DEFOE 258:1
diamonds d. and rubies — MORE 597:68
D. are of most precious value — WEBS 895:98
d. in the smog of…Megalopolis — MAIL 540:55
give him d. back — GABOR 342:82
Goodness what beautiful d.! — WEST 900:28
graven with d. in letters plain — WYATT 930:1
put d. on the floor — RIVE 688:4
throat cut With d.? — WEBS 895:15
Diana awf'lly bad luck on D. — BETJ 84:8
break D.'s law — POPE 659:70
legs were such D. shows — HERR 400:41
diaries good girls keep d. — BANK 58:30
wrote in my d. about…meals — BUSH 175:89

diary life of every man is a d. — BARR 61:79
more important than…d. — SASS 716:71
Secret D. of Adrian Mole — TOWN 863:21
The d. will…tell people who you are — FOWL 332:72
dice A throw of the d. — MALL 542:97
d. of God — EMER 312:11
[God] does not play d. — EINS 301:32
God not only plays d. — HAWK 385:31
heraldic equivalent of…furry d. — ANON 25:53
If the iron d. roll — BETH 83:75
dichotomy D. = operation — TYNAN 873:51
Dick D., I don't know how — NIXON 617:42
D. the shepherd blows — SHAK 734:94
Dickens D., Tolstoy, Hugo — LESS 505:35
D.…unremitting humanity — BENN 76:31
D. was not the first — PRIT 669:50
rewritten by Charles D. — COOKE 236:40
Thackeray and D. — STEV 822:1
dickens what the d. his name is — SHAK 743:75
dictates d. of reason — DICK 271:27
dictation told at d. speed — AMIS 14:93
dictator I am not a d. — PINO 652:19
not a director, he's a d. — MONR 591:59
dictators d. nor the bureaucrats — ORWE 629:83
personal contact with the d. — CHAM 204:64
seen by d. as subversive — JONG 448:96
dictatorship class struggle…d. — MARX 558:16
decapitated him from the d. — POWE 666:87
d. is beginning — SHEV 788:74
establish a d. — ORWE 630:5
nakedness of Stalinist d. — KENN 462:98
Television has made d. impossible — PERES 648:63
dictatorships bringing down d. — OROU 627:25
dictionaries D. are like watches — JOHN 446:67
To make a d. is dull work — JOHN 442:44
writer of d. — JOHN 442:38
writer of d. — JOHN 442:38
writer of d. — JOHN 442:46
dictionary d. of popular usage — GREE 371:64
except in the d. — KIMB 467:21
father still reads the d. — SCAR 717:89
first time I ever made the d. — WEST 901:35
Like Webster's d. — BURKE 169:54
outside of a d. — LODGE 514:23
sensible as a d.! — CARR 196:93
set him upon his d. — STEV 822:1
the metre of the d.? — THOM 852:64
diddle d., we take it, is dee — SWIN 834:53
die After I d. — TOSC 863:18
all shall d. — SHAK 743:54
and let him d. — TENN 844:60
appetite may sicken and so d. — SHAK 755:45
appointed unto men once to d. — BIBLE 124:93
as in Adam all d. — BIBLE 121:14
asleep, or hearing, d. — SHAK 775:13
as natural to d. — BACON 47:75
bear to live, or dare to d. — POPE 660:23
Beauty lives though lilies d. — FLEC 327:45
before I d. — MARTI 555:45
believe in ideas and d. for them — ANOU 26:97
blithe earth d. — JEFF 436:5
Born but to d. — POPE 660:16
break it must d. — KIPL 471:12
but nobody wants to d. — LOUIS 518:4
but they d. — UPDI 875:94
but to d., and go we — SHAK 758:37
but to do and d. — TENN 844:76
can't d., along the coast — DICK 269:76
change, but I cannot d. — SHEL 783:41
content to d. — BROWN 157:42
Cowards d. many times — SHAK 747:88
Created to pretend we never d. — LARK 491:45
curse God, and d. — BIBLE 93:50
Death, thou shalt d.! — DONNE 281:68
d. after having lived this way — LABR 483:68
d. and be a riddance! — DICK 269:63
d. at the age of thirty-seven — WALT 888:54
d. but once to serve our country — ADDI 7:36
d. dishevelled and soft — LOWE 521:53
d. each time — HEMI 394:14
d. fighting for his country — HOMER 409:23
D. for adultery! — SHAK 763:88
d. for free — VALLE 876:17
d. for my country? — SITT 793:56
d. happy — FOX 333:76
d. if you let it loose — SHAW 780:56
d. in errancy — ABU 1:10

d. in exile — GREG 372:95
d. in harness — AMIS 14:86
d. in the Lord — BIBLE 126:69
d. is better than length of days — AESC 8:60
d. is cast — CAES 184:24
D.? I should say not — BARR 61:96
d. laughing — WEBS 895:91
d. on your feet — IBAR 427:31
d. or get kicked out — HOOV 411:63
d. so young — AUDEN 40:94
d. the death — BIBLE 108:51
d. when curiosity goes — SWIFT 830:49
d. while you're still productive — BROD 153:49
d. without having played — BORO 145:99
Don't d. of ignorance — ANON 24:38
do or d.! — BURNS 173:42
do we not d.? — SHAK 740:68
Easy live and quiet d. — SCOTT 724:40
either love, or I must d. — FORD 330:15
Even if I d. — GAND 345:32
every man…born to d. — DRYD 292:59
Export or d. — ANON 22:62
Fall asleep, or hearing d. — SHAK 775:15
fated not to d. — DRYD 291:14
fear'st to d.? — SHAK 737:79
fight and d. for your country — GOLD 362:76
For all the death, we…d. unrehearsed — MURR 604:8
For another thing, they d. earlier — MENC 565:70
For thou must d. — HERB 398:14
for tomorrow we d. — BIBLE 121:16
For tomorrow we shall d.! — PARK 638:61
God does not d. — HAMM 379:6
Good Americans, when they d. — APPL 27:24
good d. early — DEFOE 258:12
have the power to d. — TENN 846:27
hazard of the d. — SHAK 732:24
Hope I d. before — TOWN 864:24
hope that he will d. — EMER 313:40
I clasp them…because they d. — CORY 238:77
idea d. instead of you — LEWIS 508:94
If I d., avenge me — MUSS 605:16
If I shall d. here — MATAK 560:55
if I shall d. — BROO 156:6
If I were now to d. — SHAK 759:75
I must d. — KEATS 460:65
in a month you've got to d. — GILB 355:20
in what peace a Christian can d. — ADDI 7:43
Is not born…does not d. — SITW 794:79
I, too, will d. by violence — MALC 541:86
I will d. in Paris — VALL 876:20
I will d. in peace — WOLFE 920:83
I will not have thee d.! — TENN 842:13
John Barleycorn should d. — BURNS 171:93
lerne to d. gladly — ANON 19:91
let it d. with thee — BIBLE 108:56
Let us determine to d. here — BEE 69:55
Live and Let D. — FLEM 327:54
live forever or d. in the attempt — HELL 392:59
live, I d. — LABE 482:53
love one man till I d. — HAMM 379:14
make a malefactor d. sweetly — DRYD 291:30
man can d. but once — SHAK 743:56
memory d. from the earth — SIDN 791:23
men to d. — BARK 60:56
most grand to d. — MASE 559:32
must men kill and d.? — SHEL 786:22
must needs d. — BIBLE 91:4
never can he d. — SPEN 809:93
not d. when the trees were green — CLARE 219:47
not made to d. — TENN 842:20
not so difficult to d. — BYRON 181:61
not that I'm afraid to d. — ALLEN 12:45
O, I d., Horatio! — SHAK 755:42
One should d. — PLATO 655:91
only d. once — MOLI 589:26
opponents eventually d. — PLAN 654:60
Or let me d.! — WORD 926:15
parting was to d. — TENN 844:58
people only d. at the last moment — CELI 202:38
pleasant thing to d. like this — BOUC 146:19
rather d. than not do so — BOUL 146:21
regret can d.! — TENN 844:52
religious system…can never really d. — SAKI 710:31
requested…that he might d. — BIBLE 92:23
resolve to conquer or d. — WASH 890:83
see my funeral before I d. — EDGE 299:97
smile can make one d. — SAINT 709:18

something he will d. for — KING 468:34
teach the rustic moralist to d. — GRAY 369:21
that I Must d. — DONNE 279:40
they only let Him d. — STUD 827:5
those that do d. — SHAK 766:59
thou shalt surely d. — BIBLE 86:45
Thus will I d. — DYER 297:53
time to d. — BIBLE 100:70
to choose life and d. — LOWE 520:50
toddle safely home and d. — SASS 716:62
to d. for one's country — HORA 413:23
to d. in dust — SPEN 809:1
to d. is different — WHIT 905:31
to d. is gain — BIBLE 123:53
To d. is nothing — ANOU 26:2
To d., to sleep — SHAK 753:74
to d. upon a kiss — SHAK 761:20
To d. will be an awfully big adventure — BARR 61:83
To-morrow let us do or d.! — CAMP 186:72
to morrow we shall d. — BIBLE 102:22
To triumph, and to d. — GRAY 370:36
we d. in earnest — RALE 677:1
weep or she will d. — TENN 842:11
we shall d....'tis but the time — SHAK 747:96
we who are about to d. — ANON 18:62
What 'tis to d. — BEAU 67:9
when I came to d. — THOR 857:91
When I d. — DONL 279:25
When I d. people will say — COMP 230:75
Where thou diest, will I d. — BIBLE 90:79
Whether we live...or d. — BIBLE 120:89
why will ye d. — BIBLE 105:90
with us, or we d. — KEATS 457:3
wit may wander ere he d. — TENN 847:39
word...for which you d. — WEIL 896:33
would surely d. — HELL 392:66
Ye shall not surely d. — BIBLE 86:49
You and I ought not to d. — ADAMS 5:90
You know when I need to d.? — ARMS 30:72
died all summer settled then and d. — LARK 490:23
d. amidst your dying country's cries — GRAY 370:31
d. as he had lived — CLEM 220:74
d. As one that had been studied — SHAK 766:78
d....before his birth — THUR 860:62
D., has he? — LOUIS 518:99
d. to save us all — ALEX 11:25
friends who d. — SASS 716:66
Just before she d. — STEIN 815:26
like saying that the patient d. — JACO 432:12
Men have d. from time to time — SHAK 750:77
Mithridates, he d. old — HOUS 415:68
mother-in-law d. — JERO 437:32
my people d. to build this country — ROBE 689:22
question why we d. — KIPL 474:81
She should have d. hereafter — SHAK 769:42
sweet dove d. — KEATS 457:87
when a Forsyte d. — GALS 344:23
When I d. — JARR 435:80
would God I had d. for thee — BIBLE 91:6
Would to God we had d. — BIBLE 88:21
Yes. As I d. — HEMI 394:14
dies Breed never d. — BENN 76:27
d. among the mountains — WORD 925:7
d. married young — SHAK 737:77
each day d. with sleep — HOPK 413:6
erect...his own tomb ere he d. — SHAK 745:25
He that d. — SHAK 774:91
how a man d. — JOHN 444:89
kingdom where nobody d. — MILL 571:92
man marries, d., or turns Hindoo — SHEL 784:67
something in me d. — VIDAL 881:96
soul...languishes and d. — ROCH 692:70
spectre-thin, and d. — KEATS 460:59
that little flame which never d. — RENO 683:10
then he d. — KIPL 470:82
when the Poet d. — SCOTT 723:90
who d. fighting has increase — GREN 373:2
worm that never d. — BROO 156:19
diet adoption of vegetable d. — SHEL 782:17
d. unparalleled — DICK 267:99
Give it a d. — DONNE 280:61
gods will d. me with — SHAK 774:69
immortal d. — RALE 677:99
In D., Furniture and Dress — MAND 545:54
twelfth day of my d. — PIER 651:8
differ d. chiefly in the boldness — JEVO 438:47
d. from those of common sense — HUXL 426:13

difference biggest d....she was taller — FEIB 319:82
country saves the d. — BAGE 51:87
crucial d. between — NISB 616:38
d. between a dog and a man — TWAIN 871:17
d. between burning and gassing — SIHA 791:29
d. between most people — TUCH 869:60
d. between one young woman — SHAW 780:45
d. between the most dissimilar — SMITH 797:40
d. between unethical and ethical — STEF 814:4
d. is...that of the living and the dead — CIXO 218:33
d. of 40,000 men — WELL 897:62
d. that makes a d. — BATE 64:50
don't make no d. — TWAIN 871:10
don't make no d. — TWAIN 871:11
love...Cares not for d. — DEKK 259:47
made all the d. — FROST 338:89
more d. within the sexes — COMP 230:74
only d. between us — BIRK 130:65
shade of d. — GREE 371:74
That's the d. between us — SHAW 781:93
The d. to me! — WORD 924:78
trust the very d. — JORD 450:66
differences cannot now end our d. — KENN 463:27
d. one finds among men — PASC 641:26
Jews and Arabs...settle their d. — AUST 44:5
little d. of speed — PRATT 667:1
National d. consist — NIET 616:28
open exchange of major d. — AUNG 42:50
different d. kinds of things sound — HONO 409:31
D. living is not living — SPEN 807:56
d. waters flow — HERA 396:66
do not feel greatly d. — BEAV 67:26
How d., how very d. — ANON 21:39
once you're hungry, you're d. — HUNT 423:22
saying something d. — HAVEL 385:29
differently they do things d. there — HART 385:20
difficult childhood...is just as d. — RILKE 687:84
D. do you call it — JOHN 447:71
d. not to write satire — JUVE 453:14
Endure what is d. to endure — HIRO 403:4
found d.; and left untried — CHES 212:69
living up to it that is d. — THAC 849:1
more d. from its rudeness — JOHN 445:34
others extremely d. — JOHN 446:56
still more d. question — GRAV 368:86
too d. for artists — SCHN 719:23
very d., maybe impossible — SOLOW 803:60
When a piece gets d. — SCHN 719:22
writing a good play is d. — PRIE 668:27
difficulties d. in providing — COMM 229:65
d. which have...amused philosophers — BERK 79:4
political and practical d. — KEYN 466:88
difficulty complexity, and d. — TRIL 866:66
if it had much d. — JOHN 445:41
diffidence and her name was D. — BUNY 166:71
dig d. and heap — ARNO 32:4
D. for Victory — DORAM 282:1
d. with it — HEAN 389:3
digamma simple d. in Homer — QUIL 674:47
digest inwardly d. them — BOOK 141:86
shall d. it — SHAK 740:76
digestion Few radicals have good d. — BUTL 178:80
good eater must have a good d. — DISR 276:36
man...think...about his d. — LEWIS 507:79
to facilitate d. — VOLT 883:52
diggeth d. a pit — BIBLE 101:87
dignities by indignities...to d. — BACON 48:2
peace above all earthly d. — SHAK 775:19
dignity assumption of d. — GALT 345:31
confers d. on a picture — ALBE 10:97
declares his d. — MILT 583:67
d. and worth — UNIT 873:69
d. in tilling a field — WASH 889:78
d. or baseness of a person — CHRI 215:37
imperishable d. of man — CARL 191:87
love was of that d. — SHAK 752:31
Official d. tends to increase — HUXL 425:80
penumbra of somber d. — ATLAS 37:37
sense of...moral d. — CURZ 249:5
simple d. of a child — SAND 713:12
stark d. of entrance — WILL 913:43
to give it possibility, scope, even d. — MACL 535:47
walk with sincerity and d. — WAITE 884:68
with silent d. — GROS 374:24
dildos delicate burdens of d. — SHAK 770:91
dilemmas d. of conscience — SNOW 802:36
dilettante d. looks only for pleasure — REDON 681:73

snowy-banded, d. — TENN 845:83
dilettantism bureaucracy and d. — WEBER 894:70
dilly-dally Don't d.-d. on the way — COLL 227:36
dilute d. it by voting for anyone — ONAS 625:82
dim d....Of night — YEATS 933:38
Pinnacled d. in the intense inane — SHEL 785:81
so d. and they're so smart — ROTH 699:30
dime can you spare a d.? — HARB 380:35
still don't have a d. — FEIF 319:83
dimension extra d. of feeling — FOWL 332:67
dimensions certain d. of thought — STEI 816:46
d. of a man's self — LAMB 487:55
d. of a man's self — LAMB 487:57
Time has three d. — HOPK 412:98
dimes come here bright as d. — LOWE 521:53
diminished national dividend is d. — PIGOU 652:15
rights of every man are d. — KENN 463:28
what to make of a d. thing — FROST 338:91
diminution increase or d. — RICA 685:36
diminutive man is a d. to nothing — DONNE 281:82
dimples hair and d. is coming — MOORE 595:24
din louder still the d. — MACA 526:70
'mid the d. Of towns and cities — WORD 923:69
music's d. — GILB 354:1
will not be heard above the d. — READ 680:49
dine bulls and foxes d. very well — JUST 453:12
d. with some men — BENT 78:76
English would manage to meet and d. — JERR 437:42
heroes to d. with us — TROL 867:97
tempt me to d. with him — SWIFT 830:65
dined if one has not d. well — WOOLF 922:41
diner Dinner in the d. — GORD 364:9
philosophic d.-out — BROW 162:78
dinero Salud, D., Amor...y Tiempo — ANON 26:91
diners feeding the poop back to d. — COUP 238:94
laughing in the d. — SAND 713:93
locations such as d. — COUP 238:91
dines say something when he d. — HUNT 423:36
dingy fatally poor and d. — WHAR 901:48
dining thought of d. — GOLD 362:70
dinner After a good d. — WILDE 909:27
After d. to the Duke's house — PEPYS 647:36
At a d. party one should — MAUG 561:73
best number for a d. party — GULB 374:35
Burning d. — PIER 651:6
criticize after d. — MARX 557:99
delicious d. of too much — JOHN 439:71
D. in the diner — GORD 364:9
d. of herbs where love is — BIBLE 99:40
D. parties are for eating — FERB 320:99
d. party of more than two — MENC 566:78
D....possessed...two dramatic features — POWE 666:79
expect if we haven't any d. — LEAR 498:91
expect our d. — SMITH 797:39
get it down onto the d. table — BONA 139:51
I managed at d. — RIDGE 687:80
mak our d. sweet — BALL 56:92
man should have d. — LEMAY 502:76
more business after d. — SWIFT 831:91
Music with d. is an insult — CHES 213:3
old friend for d. — TALLY 835:5
one cannot talk about after d. — WILDE 908:10
re-union d. — PARK 638:82
revolution is not a d. party — MAO 547:3
sinner...with no d. — RANS 679:28
three hours' march to d. — HAZL 387:75
too hungry for d. at eight — HART 384:11
whatever one had got for d. — RUSK 704:31
dinners all the d. are cooked — WOOLF 923:49
housewife's badly-cooked d. — BEET 70:2
more d. than appetites — CHAM 204:69
dinner-table dominate a...d.-t. — WILDE 909:31
dinosaurs like the bones of d. — RAND 678:14
dint d. of pity — SHAK 748:12
Diogenes would be D. — ALEX 11:18
Dionysus Christ follows D. — POUND 664:38
dip Leaning over...a lucky d. — DAY 257:86
diphtheria d. restored the status — HAMER 378:96
diploma d. is a lighted match — KOCH 476:27
diplomacy D....patriotic art of lying — BIER 129:26
Megaphone d. — HOWE 417:95
Rolls Royce d. — ANON 24:25
superstition of an antiquated d. — CECIL 202:33
underrated aspects of d. — SHUL 789:85
When d. fails — CHEN 210:19
diplomat A d. these days — USTI 875:4
d. is a deaf Trappist — LECA 499:22

diplomatic D. problems ACHE 2:22
putting out a d. boathook CECIL 202:29
diplomatist salad…brilliant d. WILDE 907:83
diplomats better that aged d. AUST 44:4
D. and protocols are…good PALM 635:20
D. lie to journalists KRAUS 480:11
direction any sense of d. WILS 915:72
blowing the new d. of Time LAWR 494:93
d. of our fears BERR 82:60
d. of society TOCQ 861:80
d. of the right line NEWT 612:70
d., which thou canst not see POPE 660:15
going in the opposite d. NICO 614:96
I have not settled in which d. BEAV 67:26
lines running in every d. ROSS 697:72
looking together in the same d. SAINT 709:12
new d. to technological SCHU 720:51
one positive pitch or d. HOPK 412:98
our ways and our d. THAT 850:15
precisely in the same d. PEARY 645:2
step in the wrong d. LEVA 505:51
directions moving in opposite d. SMITH 801:19
not equally stupid in all d. BELL 73:77
rode madly off in all d. LEAC 496:62
director actor giving positive criticism
to a d. MULL 602:70
d. makes only one film in his life RENO 683:4
no one but the d. POLA 657:36
not a d., he's a dictator MONR 591:59
telephone call from a d. PORT 663:7
directors ideal board of d. DOCH 277:99
direful something d. in the sound AUST 43:86
dirge knell is rung…their d. is sung COLL 228:43
dirt As ignorant as d.! SHAK 761:15
d. doesn't get any worse CRISP 245:56
d. kept breathing ROET 694:2
d., or grubs, or worms POPE 661:36
Huddled in d. ROCH 691:57
If d. were trumps LAMB 487:56
Instead of d. and poison SWIFT 830:53
make crossness and d. succeed FORS 331:45
mix sentences with d. BRAU 150:1
out of the d. ALTH 13:71
reputation for d. THOR 858:4
turn to d. SHAK 774:72
dirty big words…about d. things DOCT 277:2
d. son-of-a-bitch STEI 815:33
D., ugly, disagreeable DICK 270:97
d., wet hole TOLK 862:95
the d. weekend SMITH 799:62
this d., despicable little island WALP 887:32
thugh d. is clein FLEM 327:62
dirty-mindedness journalistic d.-m. LAWR 495:23
disabled trade union for the d. HEATH 390:18
disadvantage d. of being a hog MORT 600:20
disagree when doctors d. POPE 659:1
disagreeable not d. to him JOHN 446:49
such a d. man GILB 354:17
when she stoops to be d. AUST 43:87
disagreement absence of d. testifies MERT 568:23
disagrees a country that d. RUMS 702:68
can't find anyone who d. BENN 75:19
disappear like having a continent d. JARR 435:79
want to d. HUGO 420:75
disappointed haven't been d. GRAMM 366:42
disappointing war is somewhat d. GRIF 373:11
disappointment D. all I endeavour HOPK 413:9
parents…sometimes a d. POWE 666:76
without a feeling of d. LAMB 486:38
disappointments hard work, d. PEARY 645:1
disapprove d. of what you say VOLT 883:55
something of which you d. FIND 323:58
disarm d. the strong FRAN 333:91
disarmament Iraq appears not to have
come to a genuine acceptance…of…d. BLIX 136:98
disaster a glimpse of such a d. ORWE 628:50
audience was a d. WILDE 909:20
d. until it is finally manifest MURP 604:1
genetic d. WELSH 899:95
loss is no d. BISH 131:80
meet with Triumph and D. KIPL 473:67
recent d. at Rome AUGU 42:43
road to d. LLOY 513:7
single…not such a fearful d. ZHANG 936:94
worst d. since my election BROWN 157:47
disasters children…notorious d. EURI 316:15
day's d. in his morning face GOLD 361:54

d. of the world CONN 233:81
make guilty of our d. SHAK 762:57
disastrous d. and the unpalatable GALB 343:94
d. Presidents and Prime Ministers ONAS 625:81
to win a war is as d. as to lose CHRI 214:35
disbelief willing suspension of d. COLE 226:17
discerning Gives genius a better d. GOLD 362:64
discharge d. of any profession JOHN 444:6
no d. in that war BIBLE 101:80
disciple d. is not above his master BIBLE 111:27
d. who does not excel LEON 503:15
disciples d. came to him BIBLE 110:18
d. rebuked them BIBLE 113:72
d. saw him walking on the sea BIBLE 112:56
followers of Jesus…his d. JOHN 441:9
gave it to the d. BIBLE 114:96
hand toward his d. BIBLE 112:46
know that ye are my d. BIBLE 118:7
Likewise also said all the d. BIBLE 114:97
nowadays has his d. WILDE 908:91
discipleship grace without d. BONH 140:58
discipline d. of a monastery AELR 8:55
d. of humanity BACON 48:90
d. of our holy Church OCON 621:19
habit of d. TUCH 869:59
Life has no other d. MILL 572:25
Nature's stern d. DOBZ 277:98
scientist may find his d. severe CORN 237:72
testifies to a developing d. MERT 568:23
disciplines deeply biting of social d. LAWR 495:42
disclosure a short story is always a d. PRIT 669:55
Discobbolos Till Mrs D. said LEAR 497:82
discomfort d., fatigue, strain in large
amounts GELL 348:1
d. of…self-examination PECK 645:4
disconnect d. it from the rest of them FITZ 324:90
discontent contented sort of d. KEATS 458:24
divine d. KING 469:60
fruitful source of family d. BEET 70:2
winter of our d. SHAK 731:98
discontented hundred men d. LOUI 518:94
discontinuity d. within ROTH 699:14
discord All d., harmony POPE 660:15
dire effects from civil d. ADDI 7:39
Harmony in d. HORA 414:28
Melodious d. SHAK 733:55
Where there is d. THAT 850:16
discourage d. the composer HEIF 391:45
d. them from…attempts STEV 822:91
discouraged do not be d. HEMI 394:23
discourse Bid me d. SHAK 732:51
d. of the elders BIBLE 107:43
d. was about hunting PEPYS 647:37
fittest for d. DRYD 290:7
political or the scientific d. LEGU 501:63
provisions for d. AUST 42:59
Read not to…find talk and d. BACON 50:52
subtle and sinewy to d. MILT 579:80
discourses all d. but mine JONS 449:26
discover anxious to d. RUSS 705:54
d. what we ourselves believe GRANT 366:48
Man…can only d. PAINE 634:97
often d. what will do SMIL 797:35
should not d. GORD 363:6
To dance is to d. SENG 727:97
discoverers They are ill d. BACON 46:45
discoveries consequence of d. BACON 47:61
d. made FRAN 335:17
more important than their d. BRON 154:64
discovering Writing a poem is d. FROST 339:12
discovery d. aside MUNRO 603:86
D. consists of seeing SZENT 834:64
d. of some occult relation JOHN 441:25
If scientists knew tomorrow's d. ZUCK 937:6
logic of d. NISB 616:38
make room for d. APOL 27:21
medicinal d. AYRES 45:14
moral d.…the object of every tale CONR 234:12
never made a d. SMIL 797:35
new theory…a d. POPP 662:89
portals of d. JOYCE 452:90
Scientific d. and…knowledge PLAN 653:58
discreet whose ways are all d. PARK 637:43
discretion attain years of d. RUSK 704:28
better part of valour is d. SHAK 742:36
D. is the better part of Valerie MCGO 532:82
d. that would have done credit SHAR 776:41

fail to observe decency and d. BACON 46:38
now come to the years of d. BOOK 142:17
reached the height of d. BENN 76:51
survives by d. WILL 912:21
That which love worst endures, d. DONNE 280:61
discrimination D. is a hellhound KING 468:42
discussion after reasonable d. CHUR 217:9
Democracy means government by d. ATTL 38:46
d. of any subject SHEL 782:14
opportunity cost of economic d. GALB 343:98
discussions hate d. of feminism FREN 336:47
disdain d. the future now KENN 463:30
fall from her d. KYD 482:45
fortified with a strange d. WEBS 895:12
gifts increased by d. SURR 829:36
little d. is not amiss CONG 232:40
love or more d. CAREW 190:62
What, my dear Lady D.! SHAK 744:87
disdainful d. wave of a white ANGE 17:47
disease All writing is a d. WILL 914:61
artistic temperament is a d. CHES 211:54
biggest d. today THER 851:41
cause of my d. SURR 829:35
cure the d. and kill the patient BACON 49:31
democratic d. MILL 573:47
desperate d.…dangerous remedy FAWK 319:45
d. is incurable CHEK 209:14
d. is incurable SHAK 742:43
d. will spread with…malignity DICK 271:17
d. you don't look forward to MANK 545:57
Drug misuse is not a d. DICK 265:60
elimination of some d. SUTH 830:45
free from bad news and d. BIOY 130:56
Hypochondria is the only d. ANON 24:18
I have Bright's d. PERE 648:53
introduced d. and decay SHER 787:33
Life is an incurable d. COWL 240:32
Life is a sexually transmitted d. ANON 24:64
longer nurseth the d. SHAK 773:56
name any d. after two guys PUZO 673:28
national d. MCCU 529:21
no cure for this d. BELL 72:54
no d., bodily or mental SHEL 782:17
Progress is a comfortable d. CUMM 248:17
rarer forms of d. HARV 385:22
Red-and-gold d. MUSC 605:13
remedy is worse than the d. BACON 49:31
scars of d. MACA 525:54
shapes of foul d. TENN 844:61
strange d. of modern life ARNO 32:22
suffering from the particular d. JERO 437:31
Tedium is the worst d. POMP 658:47
There is one d. which is widespread MAIM 541:68
wasting d. of the frontal lobes ALBEE 10:93
while Nature cures the d. VOLT 883:54
worse d., t'escape JONS 448:15
diseased romantic d. GOET 360:22
When love grows d. ETHE 315:97
diseases death is the cure of all d. BROW 159:82
healeth all thy d. BIBLE 97:62
lists of fatal d. HELL 392:62
painful, chronic d. JONES 447:89
remedy to all d. BURT 174:77
scientific treatment for all d. SHAW 780:48
sneezes spread d. ANON 22:64
subject to the same d. SHAK 740:68
talk of d. is…entertainment OSLER 630:18
vulnerable to infectious d. KOES 477:31
diseconomies hit d. of scale early MCDO 530:52
disembodied d. and…murdered SHAR 776:45
disfigurement perceive their foul d. MILT 577:26
disgrace d. to the English nation INNO 430:71
d. to the planet STONE 825:56
d. to the playing fields FRY 339:22
Even to a full d. SHAK 769:70
Peace without honour is not only a d. CECIL 202:26
retreats without fearing d. SUN 829:30
disgraced dies rich…dies d. CARN 193:48
d., impeached, and baffled SHAK 734:97
wrongfully d. SHAK 772:26
You have d. yourselves YEATS 933:39
disgressions D.…sunshine STER 817:75
disgruntled if not actually d. WODE 919:69
disguise better go in d. BRAT 150:96
d. of determined hostility SHER 788:63
naked is the best d. CONG 231:11
disguised certainly very well d. CHUR 217:91

d. as insoluble problems GARD 346:45
disguiser Death's a great d. SHAK 758:45
disgust but as a d. TZARA 873:60
d. is reason's proper response PAGL 634:80
Loves die from d. LABR 483:65
Mummy, I'm sick with d. BETJ 84:9
see…my body without d. BAUD 64:65
touch a newspaper without d. BAUD 65:84
dish butter in a lordly d. BIBLE 90:68
discovery of a new d. BRIL 152:35
d. fit for the gods SHAK 747:84
here's a d. I love not SHAK 744:96
some d. more sharply spiced PATM 643:68
dishclout Romeo's a d. to him SHAK 737:73
dishes Are these the choice d. GARR 346:54
child will make two D. SWIFT 832:94
d. were ill-sorted DRYD 292:48
Home-made d. that drive HOOD 410:43
who does the d. FREN 336:47
dishonour d. the vices WILD 911:86
in d. stood TENN 846:19
dishonourable indecent and d. HELL 392:74
disillusionment D. in living STEIN 815:15
this age of d.? SHIP 789:78
disillusionments d. in the lives SAKI 710:34
disinfectant Sunlight is the best d. KENN 462:7
disintegrate People who d. AUST 44:44
disinterested meant to be d., pure SELF 727:80
dislike d.…at first sight STEE 814:99
like or d. them FORS 331:40
disliked d. by all his friends WILDE 910:64
disloyalty not like subversion or d. HELL 392:74
dismal d. grew his countenance BALL 55:73
dismay avoid us with d. TOLK 862:1
flies about in d. KIER 467:13
dismayed Be not afraid nor d. BIBLE 93:44
neither be thou d. BIBLE 90:62
dismissed fifty men d.? SHAK 763:69
dismount picking the place to d. BALL 55:61
Disney D. probably has the right idea HITC 404:16
disobedience campaign of civil d. CHUR 216:70
curse of d. OTWAY 631:25
disorder last d. mortal GOLD 361:38
sweet d. in the dress HERR 400:50
disorders common mental d. GRAV 368:82
disorientation stress and d. TOFF 862:91
disorienting d., and painful RICH 685:48
disparities not for such large d. KEYN 466:93
disparity d. between things ALBEE 9:89
dispatch Spaniards'd. ROCH 691:54
dispensation in the old d. ELIOT 306:74
dispiriting cannot but be d. SMITH 800:1
displaced I feel d. when I'm back in
America HYNDE 427:25
displacement d. is the rust ANGE 17:31
displeasing which is not d. LARO 491:49
dispone for dede d. DUNB 294:7
disposes God d. KEMP 461:86
disposition d. of the Working Class CARL 192:23
d. that I owe SHAK 768:18
goes so heavily with my d. SHAK 752:56
his goatish d. SHAK 762:57
liveliness of my d. FRED 335:32
mild or choleric d. ADDI 6:9
strong d. in youth POWE 666:77
dispositions d.…loved in private BURKE 168:5
d. of…mankind BURKE 168:3
disproof d. is turned aimlessly aside EDDI 298:85
disproven Nor yet d. TENN 848:68
disputants d. put me in mind ADDI 6:29
disputation that's a feeling d. SHAK 742:19
disputations d. of Plato HONO 409:32
Doubtful d. BIBLE 120:88
dispute D. it like a man SHAK 768:30
Shakespeare–Bacon d. GILB 355:36
disputes international d. EISE 302:57
lay your d. a' aside SKIN 795:13
left to their d. MILT 584:71
traditional d. of philosophers AYER 44:8
disquieted why art thou d. in me? BIBLE 95:21
disquietude bone-ache d. of life ALLEN 12:39
disregard d. for the sublime comforts SHIP 789:77
entire life in its flagrant d. MILI 569:54
dissatisfaction well-modulated d. TAAF 835:68
dissemble If you d. sometimes BACON 49:36
dissembling killed by d. LYLY 523:9
dissent d. is an act of faith FULB 340:44

in the name of d. SNOW 802:41
limit our expression of d. MAMET 543:22
Protestantism…is a sort of d. BURKE 168:11
successive waves of d. SCHO 719:24
dissenter d. is every human being MACL 535:42
dissidence d. of dissent BURKE 168:11
dissipated still keep looking so d. BENC 74:3
dissipation d. of energy begin? KELV 461:81
year of art and d. MOORE 595:22
dissociation d. of sensibility ELIOT 305:50
dissolve I d. it in rain SHEL 783:39
dissonance air with barbarous d. MILT 577:39
dissonant No sound is d. COLE 225:79
distance apparent from this d. THUR 859:38
At d. I forgive thee MILT 586:58
d. between your ears JONES 447:85
d. does not matter DEFF 258:10
d. lends enchantment to the view CAMP 186:66
d. that the dead have gone DICK 273:79
does not hold it at a d. SENG 727:96
emergency happening at a d. BARZ 63:38
for long d. after I hit it TREV 865:62
Freedom is only the d. ZHAO 936:96
In notes by d. made more sweet COLL 228:49
knack of judging a d. REED 681:79
love of grey-blue d. MACK 533:15
There's a hell of a d. PARK 638:69
time is the longest d. WILL 912:15
Tyranny of D. BLAI 132:95
viewed from a d. SCHO 720:36
worth of d. run KIPL 474:68
distances decussated at equal d. JOHN 442:47
letting go of d. STORR 825:70
distant We were d. JOHN 439:75
distaste d. for fishing STEI 815:35
distillation final d. of self DELI 261:78
distinction d. among her companions AUST 43:68
d. between children and adults BART 62:9
d. between virtue and vice JOHN 443:65
d. in the intellectual powers DARW 253:15
few escape that d. TWAIN 870:90
great d. between the sexes FOWL 332:67
no useful d. can be made GALB 343:92
one pre-eminent d. POTT 664:20
only real d. BELL 74:83
pride of d. SAND 713:4
without reaching such d. HUME 422:16
distinctions multiply d. WORD 925:96
trigger-fine d. LOWE 521:57
distinguished be d. above the rest HOMER 409:18
d. by your enemies HOOV 411:70
d. thing! JAMES 434:55
more d. than the generality of mankind BOSW 145:9
distorted facts and places were d. PACH 633:69
distorts d., disfigures and destroys FANON 317:44
distraction create some d. HERN 399:26
distress Dear d., and joy allied CULL 247:94
D. with dagger keen COLL 228:44
happy at another's d. LABR 484:75
refuge from d. WORD 928:54
those who are in d. VIRG 882:17
distresses insurmountable d. JOHN 442:43
distressing most d. thing HUXL 425:96
distribution arbitrary…d. KEYN 466:90
d., at fittest time RUSK 704:17
d. of uncertainty among economists STEIN 815:29
Laws…of D. MILL 570:56
district ye can ramble over the d. MCGO 531:79
districts d.…like squares of wheat LARK 491:36
distrust d. a man that says HAMM 380:23
d. each other BRAD 148:59
d. of its own vision JEFF 436:18
have to d. each other WILL 912:22
disturbances The Little D. of Man PALEY 635:8
ditch both shall fall into the d. BIBLE 112:59
lay distracted in a d. CRAS 244:44
ditches his windmills are d. USTI 875:7
ditch-water drinking bottled d.-w. SHAW 781:76
ditties Pipe to the spirit d. KEATS 459:52
ditty played an ancient d. KEATS 459:41
diversion merriment and d. SMITH 798:44
more fond of that d. MELV 564:33
turned a tax into a d. STEE 814:94
diversity d. in the faculties of men MADI 538:20
infinite d. of movement REDT 681:76
reduction of…d. HUXL 426:1
world safe for d. KENN 463:27

divide D. not nationally STRA 826:88
d. people into two groups HAMP 380:26
People sometimes d. others SPEN 807:64
divided in…death…not d. BIBLE 91:98
dividend national d. is diminished PIGOU 651:15
no d. from time's to-morrows SASS 716:60
dividing line d. the state GALB 343:95
divine all humanity d. SHAW 779:37
Could show me so d. MARV 556:66
d. and human history GARC 345:42
'd.' creation MILL 573:34
D. is everywhere FRIE 337:68
d. mystery in things DOST 283:11
double sacrilege on things d. DRYD 291:13
far-off d. event TENN 844:67
hand that made us is d. ADDI 6:27
image of the d. beauty AQUI 28:27
look d. as you advance NASH 608:94
lovely, Love D. ROSS 698:85
necessity of d. nature SPIN 810:24
political meetings…at a d. level ACHE 2:22
prohibition so d. SHAK 774:65
religion would still be holy and d. BAUD 65:75
Right D. of Kings POPE 662:76
some are fou o' love d. BURNS 170:69
soul so near d. BRON 154:71
to forgive, d. POPE 658:60
divineness participation or d. BACON 46:43
voice of the people hath some d. BACON 47:66
diviner glad d.'s theme DRYD 290:82
divines Doubts 'mongst d. SPEN 809:95
little statesmen and philosophers and d. EMER 312:8
divinest two d. things this world has HUNT 423:27
divinity d. and in humanity BACON 46:39
d. has provided mortals GERB 350:28
d.…in…human consciousness DURK 296:34
d. in odd numbers SHAK 744:80
d. or school metaphysics HUME 422:15
d. that shapes our ends SHAK 755:37
d. that stirs within us ADDI 7:38
piece of d. in us BROW 159:83
Pure Accident, pure d. OATES 620:91
Seal of D. and Immortality AUBR 39:71
such d. doth hedge a king SHAK 754:21
What is d. STEV 819:18
divinityship Plato…with all his d. STER 818:88
division absurd d. into sexes WAUGH 892:22
alone in the third d. NORTH 618:68
d. in our…prosperous society MACM 537:78
d. is a thread BUCH 164:24
d. of labor…social functions DURK 296:31
d. of labour is nothing MARX 557:97
effects of the d. of labour SMITH 797:38
heated d. of opinion TYNAN 872:43
Irish experience…one of d. DONO 282:97
music of d. RALE 677:1
The deep d. SWIN 834:48
divisions d. and precisions ELIOT 305:29
divorce D. is the sign of knowledge WILL 914:51
D.…political MONT 593:98
lifelong relationship…d. will never MORR 599:10
with success come drugs, d. HELL 392:64
Dixie whistle D. while humming OBRI 621:8
dizzy I left the theatre, d. and pale QUIR 675:57
DNA the salt of deoxyribose nucleic
acid (D.) WATS 890:96
do as they d. what I say THAT 850:29
capacity to d. FAUL 318:66
d. for your country KENN 462:13
Do not d. unto others SHAW 779:27
don't have to d. anything FURT 342:72
don't know what to d. ERTZ 315:91
d. or die! BURNS 173:42
d. the perfectly correct thing SHAW 780:71
d. what he got to d. STEI 815:32
d. what I please FRED 336:36
D.WHAT YOU WISH RABE 676:73
George—don't d. that GREN 372:99
How Not To D. It DICK 270:8
if we but know what to d. EMER 312:3
isn't what I d., but how I d. it WEST 901:36
know not…what I d. SHAK 729:42
Love only what you d. RICH 685:42
often discover what will d. SMIL 797:35
That thou doest, d. quickly BIBLE 118:6
This will never d. JEFF 437:23
will d. anything, Nerissa SHAK 739:48

Doasyouwouldbedoneby Mrs D.   KING 469:56
docile warriors…prefer them d.   ANDR 16:25
docility d.…cardinal virtues   WOLL 921:7
   d. in the pupil   RYLE 707:80
   except d., obedience   WELD 897:40
dock bringing the judge…into the d.   ALGR 11:31
   dull, dark d.   GILB 355:25
   put you in the d.   ADAMS 5:95
   you may now leave the d.   ADAMS 5:96
docks No one on the d.   AMADO 13:74
doctor death Will seize the d. too   SHAK 774:75
   d. advised him not to   GREG 372:96
   D., d., what do you say   ROTH 699:19
   d. forbids me to play   WOOL 923:62
   d.…has mistaken his profession   SHAW 780:59
   D. is said also   MORT 600:22
   D. said that Death   WILDE 910:55
   don't accept any d.   VALLE 876:17
   drinks more than his own d.   BARA 59:42
   Even if the d.   STEV 822:2
   fee the d. for a nauseous draught   DRYD 292:53
   I am a D.   ALBEE 10:93
   interview with a d.   JAMES 433:27
   keeps the d. away   ANON 26:83
   man, not even a d.   NIGH 616:35
   O master d., he is past   MASS 560:48
   pass for a cathedral d.   JONS 448:13
   take off your clothes for the d.   CAUS 201:12
   thank God, D.   STAN 812:61
   The d. found   GOLD 361:38
doctors d. considering it doubtful   DICK 267:5
   d., judges…beadles   MARX 557:96
   d. of profound wisdom   DICK 266:87
   d. say this is no time   SHAK 734:96
   if you believe the d.   SALI 711:68
   Most of your d.   JONS 448:15
   We d. know   CUMM 248:18
   when d. disagree   POPE 659:1
doctrine against any country or d.   MARS 554:39
   d. of President Monroe   WILS 916:13
   d. of 'separate but equal'   WARR 889:68
   d. of those who desire   INGR 429:63
   d. shall drop as the rain   BIBLE 90:55
   d.…that each one should select   SHEL 786:8
   keep out evil d.   MILT 579:63
   Sa lyis thair ane d. wyse   HENR 396:51
   to church…not for the d.   POPE 658:58
   United States to the Monroe D.   ROOS 696:53
   what is alarming in the d.   SART 715:47
   women's eyes this d.   SHAK 734:86
   world more than d.   MILL 572:24
doctrines all d. plain and clear   BUTL 177:57
   d. and practice of Socialism   MORR 598:98
   d. chiefly vouched for   JAMES 434:74
   fundamental d. of Christianity   LAW 493:86
   seven great facts and d.   HUGEL 418:12
dodge trying to d. it   TREE 865:54
Dodhead Jamie Telfer o' the fair D.   BALL 56:79
doe with the fallow d.   THOM 854:20
doers d.…not hearers only   BIBLE 124:7
   not of d.   HAZL 388:82
does He who can, d.   SHAW 778:7
   look for what she d.   GOET 360:13
dog A d.'s obeyed in office   SHAK 763:92
   always be a lost d. somewhere   ANOU 26:95
   Am I a d.   BIBLE 91:95
   Artist as a Young D.   THOM 852:69
   as though my d. has just died   WATE 890:92
   be a d., a monkey, or a bear   ROCH 691:55
   better than his d.   TENN 840:77
   Beware of the d.!   ANON 18:58
   circumcisèd d.   SHAK 761:19
   communism is a dead d.   SOLZ 803:64
   country to heel like a d.   LESS 504:33
   D. eat d.   CUOMO 248:33
   d. goes, intently haphazard   LEVE 506:57
   d. has a keener nose   SNYD 803:52
   d. is full of fleas   ACHE 3:50
   d. is turned to his own vomit   BIBLE 125:31
   d. licked me   SIMON 792:39
   d. returneth to his vomit   BIBLE 100:53
   D. returns to his vomit   KIPL 474:84
   d. that praised his fleas?   YEATS 933:41
   d. to the commonalty   SHAK 769:55
   d. will have his day   SHAK 755:36
   every d. his day   KING 469:53
   give them to a d.   SHAK 743:79

   giving your heart to a d.   KIPL 473:65
   grin like a d.   BOOK 143:56
   Holdfast is the only d.   SHAK 745:38
   hot d. without the mustard   CHAR 207:44
   I am his Highness' d.   POPE 662:84
   if a man bites a d.   BOGA 138:34
   If I had a yaller d.   TWAIN 871:10
   I've been working like a d.   LENN 503:94
   just another d.   WILL 913:47
   large, friendly d.   TOYN 864:27
   Like a d., he hunts   TENN 840:79
   like a d. walking   JOHN 443:73
   living d. is better than a dead lion   BIBLE 101:82
   Love is a D. from Hell   BUKO 165:50
   Mine enemy's d.   SHAK 764:96
   No d. can go as fast   FLAN 325:21
   nothin' but a hound d.   PRES 667:4
   not the lead d.   ANON 25:65
   paint…a d. as Picasso   MARC 548:29
   pancreatic ducts of a d.   BANT 59:41
   pick up a starving d.   TWAIN 871:17
   police of a d. that I know   FADI 317:37
   portrait of a d. that I know   JOHN 447:73
   Prevent the d. from barking   AUDEN 40:89
   rather have a man d.   FLEM 327:60
   rather hear my d. bark   SHAK 744:88
   tail must wag the d.   KIPL 471:4
   Thou art a beaten d.   POUND 665:61
   tongue like the tail of a d.   NASHE 609:19
   work like a d.   SIMON 792:36
dogged It's d. as does it   TROL 867:91
dogma d. of the Ghost   RYLE 707:78
dogmatic erect, elegant, d.   REST 683:14
dogmatism arrogant d.   WILS 916:3
   the greater the d.   OSLER 630:14
dogs bang these d. of Seville   TENN 848:61
   dancing d. and bears   HODG 405:46
   dislike almost all d.   LEVIN 506:63
   d. barking idiotically through   MENC 566:87
   d. called Spot   AMIS 14:97
   d. came and licked his sores   BIBLE 116:53
   d. eat of the crumbs   BIBLE 112:60
   d. had eaten the upholstery   PERE 648:62
   d. licked the blood of Naboth   BIBLE 92:26
   d. of Europe bark   AUDEN 40:4
   d. shall drink 'em 'till they burst   POPE 660:4
   D. with broken legs   PATC 642:49
   Don't let's go to the d.   HERB 397:73
   fought the d.   BROW 160:26
   gaze of d.   CALV 185:46
   hates children and d.   FIEL 323:53
   hates d. and babies   ROST 699:10
   holy unto the d.   BIBLE 110:6
   hosses, d., and men   THAC 849:91
   how it feels about d.   HAMP 380:28
   keep parrots or puppy d.   CAMP 186:64
   let slip the d. of war   SHAK 748:2
   like dancing d.   JOHN 444:11
   mad and hungry d.   MCKA 533:11
   Mad d. and Englishmen   COWA 239:13
   'Orses and d. is some men's fancy   DICK 269:71
   outlive her d.   WILL 912:19
   show d. I breed   GRAV 367:78
   sleep with d.   WEBS 895:90
   Throw physic to the d.   SHAK 769:39
   woman who is really kind to d.   BEER 69:78
Dogstar D. prancing   LAWR 494:5
   The D. rages!   POPE 661:33
doing d. it, actually d. it   KELM 460:77
   d. what is given us to do   ELIOT 303:89
   what everyone is d.   HERB 397:5
   what they should be d.   FULL 341:50
doing-good As for D.-g.   THOR 857:87
doleful dreamed a d. dream   BALL 56:57
doll d. in the d.'s house   DICK 272:49
dollar almighty d.   IRVI 430:85
   d. in another man's hands   OHEN 623:54
   life…printed on d. bills   ODETS 622:29
   one d., one vote   KRIS 481:17
   thousand d. suit   ANON 25:64
dollars D. damn me   MELV 564:43
   I feel like a thousand d.   OCON 622:27
   leave him with two d.   WEST 901:32
   looks like a million d.   LINK 511:58
   million d. to make a picture   TAYL 837:17
   poor race in a land of d.   DU 293:71
   What's a thousand d.?   MARX 557:84

   wuth eight hund'd d.   TWAIN 871:3
dolls false pretences on d.   RUNY 702:83
Dolores splendid and sterile D.   SWIN 833:28
dolorous d. midland sea   SWIN 833:42
dolphin-torn That d.-t.…sea   YEATS 934:58
domain beasts of the intellectual d.   HOLM 407:77
   outside the d. of political   MARX 557:96
Dombey made for D. and Son   DICK 268:51
dome blue d. of air   SHEL 783:41
   D. is a lemon   TOYN 864:34
   d. of the Pantheon   BRAM 150:87
   Life, like a d.   SHEL 786:7
   Millennium D. was intended to be New
     Labour's Xanadu   RAWN 680:39
   moonlit d.   YEATS 934:57
   Orchard, for a D.   DICK 272:59
   under the starry d.   MACN 538:4
domes d. and riggings and crooked   MORR 598:93
   d. and statues, spires   LARK 491:33
   shape of d.   GILL 355:38
   Ships, towers, d.   WORD 926:19
domestic d. industry of women   GILM 356:53
   d. life   GIBB 351:54
   d. servants at home   MAUG 561:81
   great safeguard…of d. life   ELIOT 303:1
   respectable d. establishment   BENN 75:25
   When d. servants are treated   SHAW 778:10
domesticate To marry is to d.   STEV 822:88
domesticated become d. too   GREE 371:62
dominant d.'s persistence   BROW 161:40
dominate d. a…dinner-table   WILDE 909:31
domination d. by fat-minded men   ARNO 34:74
   fought against white d.   MAND 544:46
   keeps male d. intact   WOLF 919:80
   military d. of Prussia   ASQU 36:9
dominion death hath no more d.   BIBLE 120:68
   death shall have no d.   THOM 852:61
   d. of the sea   COVE 239:6
   d., or empire above   KNOX 476:18
   d. over the works of thy hands   BIBLE 94:87
   equal d. is given to woman   STAN 812:66
   never consent…to English d.   ANON 19:86
   women have d. over you   BIBLE 107:25
dominions increase in its d.   ADDI 5:7
   Majesty's d.   NORTH 618:66
dominoes d. outside a French café   WILDE 909:32
   row of d. set up   EISE 302:55
   set of d.   TRAV 864:42
dominus Qualis d. talis est servus   PETR 649:83
Domitian death of D.   GIBB 351:52
done as soon as I d. it   SAND 713:3
   discovers has to be d.   HUXL 425:89
   D. because we are too menny   HARDY 382:69
   d. it very well   JOHN 444:97
   d. when 'tis d.   SHAK 767:86
   I go, and it is d.   SHAK 767:96
   it is not what was d.   HELO 393:88
   Love…not what you have d.   RICH 685:42
   So much has been d.   SHEL 782:11
   that which is d.…shall be d.   BIBLE 100:67
   that which they have d.   TENN 840:81
   things d. that he wants d.   SAMU 712:79
   What have I d. for you   HENL 395:40
   what's been d. before them?   SKIN 795:13
   What's d. is d.   SHAK 768:13
   When all is said and d.   SASS 716:71
Dong D.!—the D.!   LEAR 497:77
Donne Anne D., Un-done   DONNE 280:64
doom and the d. assigned   TENN 846:1
   crashing onwards irresistibly to d.   BOLD 139:41
   d. is, to be sifted by the wind   BUNT 166:59
   forfeit to a confined d.   SHAK 773:44
   God would have changed his d.   CLEV 221:81
   regardless of their d.   GRAY 368:94
   scaffold and the d.   AYTO 45:17
   the d. of man   JOHN 441:17
   this black d.   ORAH 627:21
   to the edge of d.   SHAK 773:48
   tragedy, ecstasy, d.   ROTH 700:34
doomed d., conscripted, unvictorious
     ones?   SASS 717:76
   d. to death   DRYD 291:14
   Literature is d.   ORWE 629:95
   story is ephemeral and d.   FAUL 318:63
dooms grandeur of the d.   KEATS 457:2
doomsayers D. have…their uses   WRIS 930:89
doomsday postpone d.   CAPO 189:24

Then is d. near — SHAK 752:52
Doon banks and braes o' bonie D. — BURNS 172:26
door another iron d. — SPEN 809:94
Armageddon will be at our d. — MACA 524:23
At the d. Dante turned — JOYCE 452:83
before his cottage d. — SOUT 805:98
big front d. — GILB 353:94
coming in at one d. — BEDE 68:54
Devil…holding the d. ajar — MELV 564:43
d. flew open — HOFF 406:53
d. has a creaking latch — POUND 665:43
d. of my flesh — BRID 152:27
d. of necessity — DEFOE 258:20
d. of the private whore — PARK 638:78
d. opens — GREE 371:52
d. out of the dungeon of self — MACD 530:54
d. to their own lives — AREN 28:41
d. we never opened — ELIOT 307:93
drive an angel from your d. — BLAKE 134:36
Drive out prejudices through the d. — FRED 336:34
exceed in interest a knock at the d. — LAMB 487:53
face…in a jar by the d. — LENN 503:96
Get up and bar the d. — BALL 56:77
grass beyond the d. — ROSS 698:94
hard at death's d. — BOOK 143:68
Holds fast the d. — CRAS 244:38
keep the d. of my lips — BIBLE 98:4
knocking at Preferment's d. — ARNO 32:17
Knocking on the moonlit d. — DELA 260:63
lamp beside the golden d. — LAZA 496:51
leaning on the john d. — OHARA 623:46
Lock the d., Lariston — HOGG 406:58
love shut his d. on me — SMITH 799:80
not being able to close his d. — STEN 816:52
off my d.! — POE 656:24
open d., and no man can shut it — BIBLE 126:50
opening and closing of a d. — SAND 713:99
over that same d. was likewise writ — SPEN 809:94
send thee out of d. — BRAD 149:79
Shut close the d. — WORD 924:83
shut the d. — POPE 661:33
Shut the d. after you — EDGE 299:99
soldiers…round your d. — WILDE 907:82
stairs and a deal d. — DICK 266:81
stand at the d., and knock — BIBLE 126:52
steps outside my d. — HILL 403:95
trundle…through the d. — STEV 823:15
whining of a d. — DONNE 281:90
Will it knock on my d. — AUDEN 40:93
with the d. shut — WHAR 901:50
doorkeeper d. of a bordello — TOSC 863:18
rather be a d. — BIBLE 96:47
doorman d. discovered…his tasks — AREN 28:41
doors all the d. were shut — HUSS 423:41
bar thine adamantine d. — BLAKE 133:26
behind the d. of yesterday — HYDE 427:19
death hath…several d. — WEBS 895:18
Death opens unknown d. — MASE 559:32
d. of perception — BLAKE 134:46
d. shall be shut in the streets — BIBLE 101:92
d. upon a woman's wit — SHAK 750:80
D., where my heart — TENN 843:27
ears yielding like swinging d. — DOUG 283:21
fresh air should be…out of d. — MACA 525:35
Good clothes open all d. — FULL 341:67
if there are no d. — MALA 541:80
Let the d. be shut — SHAK 753:80
Life, within d. — HAWT 386:44
little music out of d. — KEATS 458:13
Men shut their d. — SHAK 762:44
my d. are hateful — OTWAY 631:26
nailed…the d. of Parliament — MUSS 605:15
pictures out of d. — SHAK 759:73
red cross upon the d. — PEPYS 647:40
shut d. — GIDE 353:81
slamming d. and slopping water — MANS 546:82
taxi-cab with both d. open — HUGH 418:15
To live out of d. — STEV 821:78
To love is to…open d. — PAZ 644:88
Within d., or without — MILT 586:47
ye everlasting d. — BIBLE 94:4
doorstep worry on the d. — FIEL 323:46
dooryard in the d. bloom'd — WHIT 906:47
Dorcas D…full of good works — BIBLE 119:38
Dorsey Tommy D. breathed — SINA 793:51
dose double the d. — STOWE 826:75
dossier preparation of the d. — GILL 356:50

Dostoevsky D., and a dozen others — LESS 505:35
dote d. on his very absence — SHAK 739:49
dots hurrying d. which are men — CUMM 247:1
those damned d. — CHUR 215:57
double D., d., toil and trouble — SHAK 768:20
Global d. zero — ANON 24:37
leading a d. life — WILDE 909:43
double-bed deep peace of the d.-b. — CAMP 185:52
doubled found myself d. over — IGNA 428:41
doublet Lord Hamlet, with his d. — SHAK 752:40
doublethink D. means the power — ORWE 630:3
doubt clouded with a d. — TENN 847:52
curiosity, freckles, and d. — PARK 637:58
Decide this d. for me — COWP 240:42
d. about…civilization — ORWE 629:80
d. and to be ignorant — UNAM 873:66
d.…cannot be removed — CARL 192:98
D. everything at least once — LICH 509:24
d. His infinite goodness — WALL 886:3
D. is a necessary precondition — BART 62:13
d. is Devil-born — TENN 844:56
d. is in our passion — JAMES 433:46
d. of future foes — ELIZ 309:57
D. thou the stars — SHAK 752:45
d. whether one may not — HAWT 386:48
for her, d. — BALZ 57:14
fouk wou'd hae a d. on — FERG 320:6
he was prey to d. — CHAT 208:52
Horror and d. distract — MILT 582:52
I d. some foul play — SHAK 751:13
imagine the least d. — DESC 263:19
in d. to act or rest — POPE 660:16
itself and d. of itself — TILL 860:68
Life is d. — UNAM 873:63
life of d. — BROW 161:49
more faith in honest d. — TENN 844:57
new philosophy calls all in d. — DONNE 281:74
no d. as to the elements — WHIT 904:14
prolonged neurotic d. — BARZ 63:38
science teaches us to d. — BERN 81:38
sunnier side of d. — TENN 848:68
though we oft d. — MILT 587:66
troubled with religious d. — CHES 212:92
what you cannot d. — SKEL 795:99
when all men d. you — KIPL 473:67
When in d. — BLASS 136:90
When in d. — ITO 431:98
when in d., mumble — WAGN 884:65
When in d., shout — HARD 381:44
When in d., tell the truth — TWAIN 872:21
When in D.—Wash — GALL 344:13
When in d., win — HOYLE 417:3
Where there is d. — FRAN 334:98
Where there is d. — THAT 850:16
Why do you d. — JONS 450:48
wisdom, dying in d. — LOWE 520:52
doubted cannot reasonably be d. — HUME 422:11
that they cannot be d. — HUXL 426:8
doubter d. fights only with himself — GREE 371:74
doubtful d. dreams of dreams — SWIN 833:33
doubts content to begin with d. — BACON 46:37
d. are traitors — SHAK 757:17
D. 'mongst divines — SPEN 809:95
from these dead d. — MELV 564:27
my d. are done — DRYD 291:16
paint and have no d. — MICH 568:34
dough-baked d.-b. prose — CAREW 190:52
doughnuts coffee and d. — DAVI 254:42
Douglas doughty D. — BALL 55:66
D. in his hall? — SCOTT 723:98
Doune Look owre the castle D. — BALL 55:69
dove Beside the springs of D. — WORD 924:78
burnished d. — TENN 840:75
d. came to him in the evening — BIBLE 87:66
d. complaining — DAY 257:85
d. descending breaks the air — ELIOT 309:47
d. found no rest — BIBLE 87:65
gently as any sucking d. — SHAK 737:91
Oh that I had wings like a d.! — BIBLE 96:32
She is coming, my d. — TENN 845:92
silly, harmless, household d. — DRYD 289:64
Spirit of God descending like a d. — BIBLE 108:77
sweet d. died — KEATS 457:87
wings like a d. — BOOK 143:53
dove-like wings outspread D.-l. — MILT 580:93
Dover candle at D., to shew light — JOHN 443:72
chalk cliffs of D. — BALD 54:48

dinner at D. — MACA 525:45
doves d.' eyes — BIBLE 101:2
harmless as d. — BIBLE 111:26
seats of them that sold d. — BIBLE 113:79
soft as the breast of d. — CORN 237:69
The moan of d. — TENN 842:17
dovish don't consider myself d. — SCHW 721:66
dowagers d. for deans — TENN 841:95
dowdiness beginning of d. — WILDE 909:29
dowdy D…1 year after — LAVER 493:81
dower ancient English d. — WORD 925:11
Faith's transcendent d. — WORD 928:57
for deathless d. — ROSS 698:94
dowered d. with a sense of humour — SOME 803:67
dowf sae d. and weary — BURNS 172:39
dowie d. houms o' Yarrow — BALL 55:54
d. houms o' Yarrow — BALL 55:75
down brought d. — HAIL 377:69
death…done as easily lying d. — ALLEN 12:51
D., d. to hell — SHAK 731:86
D. on your knees — SHAK 750:69
D. she came and found a boat — TENN 839:51
D. with purists! — BAND 58:25
fear of letting people d. — WILK 911:99
had me d. — GERS 351:43
He that is d. needs fear no fall — BUNY 167:76
looked d. upon in our old age? — SCHU 721:57
never let you d. — WAUGH 891:11
nobody wants you to put it d. — RUCK 701:60
set me d. again — FROST 338:92
started at the top and worked d. — WELL 897:51
what they knocked d. — FENT 320:87
Why art thou cast d. — BIBLE 95:21
wish to level d. — JOHN 443:71
downfall d. of the British Empire — CHUR 216:65
down-gyvèd d.-g. to his ankle — SHAK 752:40
downhill going d. ever since — SHAR 776:43
Downing from Germany to D. Street — CHAM 204:63
met Curzon in D. Street — BALD 54:42
downpour d. of apologies — BEER 69:73
downs carved upon her d. — HEAN 389:7
fair on the dewy d. — TENN 845:98
o'er unhabitable d. — SWIFT 832:90
sun behind the D. — BETJ 84:4
downsitting knowest my d. — BIBLE 98:99
downstairs d. from their Ivory Towers — SMITH 799:82
why did you kick me d.? — BICK 128:8
down-to-earth people could be d.-t.-e. — SHUL 790:90
downturns market d. predicted — SAMU 712:80
downwards look no way but d. — BUNY 166:74
dowry your d. 'greed on — SHAK 732:34
dowser d. and not a navvy — LEAV 498:3
Dowson D…degenerates! — ONEI 625:99
dozen d. times and he is great — JARR 435:81
she has at least a d. — WILDE 908:14
Dracula night I finished D. — SAGE 709:9
draft d. an international agreement — TRUM 868:34
happy d. surpassed the image — DRYD 290:12
drafted didn't get d. — DOWD 284:40
draftsman d. of words — CUMM 248:23
drag time did d. along — TWAIN 871:2
dragging D. the whole sky — FROST 338:86
keeps d. me along — SEVI 728:10
dragnet swept like a d.-n. — DRYD 292:48
dragon ant…in his d. world — POUND 665:59
d., a symbol — MOORE 595:37
flagon with the d. — PANA 636:27
laid hold on the d. — BIBLE 127:77
Michael…fought against the d. — BIBLE 126:76
dragonfly d. Hangs — ROSS 698:94
dragons argosy of crocs and d. — AMIS 15:99
Bores have succeeded to d. — DISR 276:37
d. of Laune and Lane — ORAH 626:20
habitation of d. — BIBLE 103:33
spleen of fiery d. — SHAK 732:22
drain d. him dry as hay — SHAK 766:68
From this foul d. — TOCQ 861:81
put it down the d. — HERB 397:78
drains Deity and the D. — STRA 826:83
Drake Hutton and Betsy D. — NIVEN 617:40
drake neckyd lyke a d. — BERN 81:48
dram Tak aff your d.! — BURNS 170:76
drama A good d. critic — TYNAN 872:48
D. is a complete meal — IZZA 431:4
D. is action, sir — PIRA 652:24
D. is the third great form — HUGO 420:74
d.'s patrons give — JOHN 441:15

enemy of the ear in real d. — WILD 911:89
episode in a general d. — HARDY 382:60
exact past d. — PRIT 669:54
lexicon of conflict and d. — SAFI 708:96
marvel at the d. — SCRI 726:66
Mistaken Identity is to D. — ABSE 1:8
mystical d. of the animal life — AMIS 14:97
nodus of a d. — CARL 192:7
one character in literature or d. — PAGE 633:77
respond to a d. — MAMET 543:21
talent for d. — VIDAL 880:89
Viewed as a d. — GRIF 373:11

dramatic d. criticism…tattoo — BROWN 157:44
four most d. words — HART 384:14
modern era is d. — HUGO 420:60
thirty-seventh d. situation — JARRY 435:93

drank d. my ale — FARQ 318:55
d. without the provocation — SWIFT 831:84

drappie d. in our e'e — BURNS 171:6

draught for a d. of vintage! — KEATS 459:58
nauseous — DRYD 292:53
nauseous d. of life — ROCH 691:59

draughts great d. of time — BERR 82:61
peculiarly susceptible to d. — WILDE 909:44
shallow d. intoxicate — POPE 658:54

draughtsman Dali is a good d. — ORWE 630:9

draw d. first, to cultivate the Spirit — MATI 560:64
D. more and more often — PISS 652:34
d. something every day — CENN 203:42
d. upon content — GOLD 361:44
d. what you see only in memory — DEGAS 259:32
seemed to, the same way — HIRS 403:9

drawback d. of all sea-side places — DOUG 283:27

drawbacks everything has its d. — JERO 437:32

drawer Feminism…vegetable d. — PAGL 634:82

drawers d….of political cancer — ANON 25:49

drawing art of d. — LIEB 509:26
D. is not the form — DEGAS 259:30
D. is only a necessary evil — HEIN 391:52
growing old in d. nothing up! — COWP 241:73
three-dimensional d. — HIRS 403:7

drawing-down a d.-d. of blinds — OWEN 632:52

drawing-room magnificent in a d.-r. — THUR 859:17
Suez canal…through my d.-r. — EDEN 299:92

drawl quickest on the d.? — NEW 612:57

drawling-master D.-m….conger-eel — CARR 195:80

drayhorse greatness is only the d. — PATC 642:48

dread close your eyes with holy d. — COLE 226:15
d. of something after death — SHAK 753:74
every reason to d. — JORD 450:65
greatest d. of all — BETJ 84:12
secret d., and inward horror — ADDI 7:38
silence…fills me with d. — PASC 640:18
walk in fear and d. — COLE 225:90

dreadful d. to look on — HAGG 376:60

dream And d. about the great — YEATS 932:37
as a d. doth flatter — SHAK 772:35
as thou mightst in d. — SHEL 786:23
Because thou must not d. — ARNO 31:97
behold it was a d. — BUNY 166:73
behold, it was a d. — BIBLE 88:98
better to d….than to live — PROU 670:70
consecration, and the poet's d. — WORD 928:34
corresponds to our d. life — MAMET 543:21
deep d. of peace — HUNT 423:33
draw nearer to d. — CHIR 213:15
d. about the future — HAMM 379:11
d. comes to an end — GIRO 358:84
dreamed a dolefu' d. — BALL 55:75
dreamed of was a d. — ROSS 697:76
d. freely — GAUG 347:68
d. my d.s away — FLAN 325:20
d. of a common language — RICH 685:52
d. of being dressed in Paris — ANON 22:52
D. Of Electric Sheep? — DICK 265:58
d. of Home — FORD 330:20
d. of independent power — JAY 435:96
d. of Jeannie — FOST 332:61
d. of life — JARR 435:80
d. of life — SHEL 786:3
d. of money-bags — SHAK 740:60
d. of revolution — STOP 825:62
d. of social justice — NGUY 613:82
d. of the soft look — YEATS 932:33
d. that I am home again! — FLEC 327:50
d. that they clarify — HERN 399:26
d. things that never were — SHAW 781:2

Everlasting peace is a d. — MOLT 590:46
freshness of a d. — WORD 926:21
glory and the d. — WORD 926:23
golden d. of love and friendship — DRYD 289:66
have had a d. past — SHAK 738:11
held me like a d. — WORD 925:93
If you can d. — KIPL 473:67
I have a d. — KING 468:33
I have a d. — KING 468:39
In a d. — SEXT 728:14
In a d. of passion — SHAK 753:67
Liberals can d. — MACL 536:54
life be but a d. — PRIOR 669:44
Life is…a bad d. — ONEI 625:93
Life is but a D. — LI 509:13
Lives in a d. — LENN 503:96
man that is born falls into a d. — CONR 234:2
men d., but not equally — LAWR 495:38
most blissful d. as a child — SHIP 789:78
must we d. our d.s — BISH 131:79
new pictures as in a d. — MARC 548:26
old men's d.! — DRYD 290:82
old men shall d. d.s — BIBLE 106:5
one that hath a weary d. — TENN 839:53
Out of a misty d. — DOWS 284:45
perchance to d. — SHAK 753:74
phantasma or a hideous d. — SHAK 747:83
pictures come to me as if in a d. — VAN 877:29
quiet sleep and a sweet d. — MASE 559:23
shining and perishable d. — DIDI 274:6
silence of a d. — ROSS 697:74
sister to the d. — BAUD 64:64
Soft, I did but d. — SHAK 731:16
something…to d. about — FORD 330:23
So runs my d. — TENN 843:42
Success is the American D. — LEGU 501:36
To d. is happiness — HUGO 420:70
too old to d. — HAMM 379:16
vanished like a d. — CARL 193:34
waking from a troubled d. — HAWT 386:35
We live, as we d. — CONR 234:97
What happens to a d. deferred? — HUGH 418:20
wrecks of a dissolving d. — SHEL 786:21

dreamed at night he d. of it — GREE 371:53

dreamer Beautiful d. — FOST 332:62
Behold, this d. cometh — BIBLE 87:94
d. of dreams — BIBLE 89:49
poet and the d. — KEATS 458:31

dreamers d. of the day — LAWR 495:38
Soldiers are d. — SASS 716:60
We have been the d. — BEVAN 84:15

dreamest What d. thou, drunkard — SKEL 795:93

dreaming boys are d. wicked — THOM 853:87
D. like a love-adept — SHEL 785:76
d. of a White Christmas — BERL 80:16
d. spires — ARNO 33:44
while d. before it — GAUG 347:67

dreamlike a fact…so d. — RICH 685:44

dreams according to his d. — HUGO 421:91
advertising…dealt in…fugitive d. — QUEN 674:39
armoured cars of d. — BISH 131:75
awoke…from uneasy d. — KAFKA 454:26
books are either d. — LOWE 519:22
City of perspiring d. — RAND 679:29
Come to me in my d. — ARNO 31:1
different hopes, different d. — CART 198:46
doubtful d. of d. — SWIN 833:33
dreamer of d. — BIBLE 89:49
D. and drives — RODG 693:92
d., and our hopes — POPP 663:97
d. are all egocentric — WAUGH 893:50
d….are infanticiddle — NASH 608:93
d. be tossed and blown — HAMM 379:17
d. do show thee me — SHAK 771:18
D. have only the pigmentation — BARN 60:64
d. in pale battalions — SORL 804:90
d. of a poet — JOHN 442:42
d. of our childhood — THOR 857:68
d. of perfection — FAUL 319:71
d. of the participation — NICH 613:84
d. that have stayed with me — BRON 155:94
Fanatics have their d. — KEATS 458:14
Full of sweet d. — KEATS 457:1
had dreamed d. — THOM 852:56
have no d. — VREE 883:61
have only my d. — YEATS 933:38
he hunts in d. — TENN 840:79

help of d. — WORD 928:51
he pulls the legs of his d. — THOM 853:90
his summer d. — SHEL 783:45
history of irresponsible d. — POPP 663:98
hopes and d. of the Future — FRAME 333:81
if empty d. so please — HERR 399:35
in d. behold the Hebrides — GALT 344:29
In my d. is a country — SHAW 779:37
interpretation of d. — FREUD 336:51
in that sleep of death what d. — SHAK 753:74
I talk of d. — SHAK 736:40
life together with your d. — MOORE 594:13
Made holy by their d. — GIBS 352:75
More d. are destroyed — SKEL 795:8
never overstepped it save in d. — FROST 338:95
Out of d., songs — HERZL 401:57
Real are the d. of Gods — KEATS 458:21
shadows and in d. — STEV 819:18
steeple of my d. — DEBU 258:3
substance of my d. — SASS 716:65
such stuff As d. are made — SHAK 774:95
talking about d. — STERN 817:65
that I have bad d. — SHAK 752:54
The quick D. — SHEL 785:93
The way you haunt my d. — GERS 351:41
treasured d. — WORD 927:30
with their mothers in d. — SOPH 804:89

dreamt d. I went to Manderley again — DU 294:96
d. of in our philosophy — SHAK 752:38
d. there was an Emperor — SHAK 765:55
often d. of unhappiness — SHAK 744:1

dreamtime easy Eden-d. — WRIG 930:82

dreariness just to escape this d. — PERCY 648:50
unredeemed d. of thought — POE 656:16

dreary All seems d., savage — SCHAW 717:96

dregs drain not to its d. the urn — SHEL 786:22
d. of life — DRYD 288:43

dreich kirkyairdielike and d. — YOUNG 935:78

drenching in for a thorough d. — BEER 69:73

dress begin to d. ourselves — RICH 685:50
car has become an article of d. — MCLU 536:59
cool white d. — FIRB 323:65
cotton flowers of her d. — THOM 853:94
crocus d. — JOYCE 452:95
Diet, Furniture and D. — MAND 545:54
d. according to your age — DISR 277:88
d. and manners in England — SHAW 777:62
d. by yellow candle-light — STEV 822:11
D. is a form of visual art — HOLL 407:68
d. is very independent — GASK 346:58
d. me In borrowed robes? — SHAK 766:76
d. of thought — POPE 658:56
d….the badge of lost innocence — PAINE 634:90
Fond Pride of D. — FRAN 334:12
fop values himself upon his d. — CHES 210:26
glory of man is his d. — ANON 18:67
Heaven…how they d.! — DICK 267:25
in a last month's d. — NASH 608:82
its mortal d. — YEATS 933:52
make their d. a principal part — HAZL 387:72
man cannot d. — STER 818:95
noble youth did d. — SHAK 743:48
no such thing as a moral d. — CHUR 215:54
not a woman's d….a man's d. — BOWIE 147:31
Peace, the human d. — BLAKE 134:31
sweet disorder in the d. — HERR 400:50
this fleshly d. — VAUG 878:45
To d., to darn, to flower — LEWIS 507:81
whose d. no one observes — TROL 867:4
Women fond of d. — DE 257:93

dressed all D. Up — BURT 174:64
d. exactly like her — NASH 609:6
d. for this short comedy — RALE 677:1
d. in Paris — ANON 22:52
good spirits…when he's well d. — DICK 268:34

dresser d. filled with shining delph — COLUM 229:61

dresses d. make a curious sound — STEV 823:15
silk d. out of worms — STEV 820:40

dressmaker ask for…your d. — DACHE 250:61

drift d. is always towards barbarism — REAG 681:68
twas Peter's d. — SHEL 784:52

driftwood found out about the d.. — ROSE 697:66

drill d. to the tooth of America — CLIN 221:92

drill-sergeant d.-s. or animal trainer — RYLE 707:80

drink abolition of strong d. — MCGO 532:80
any little delicate thing to d. — DICK 270:13
as oft as ye d. it — BIBLE 121:6

be sure to d. it — TAO 836:92
better to d. than to fight — KING 469:61
careful not to d. — HAMM 380:23
damn the d. they'll swally — OBRI 621:7
D. a health to — SYNGE 834:58
d. all the d. — KEEN 460:68
D. and dance — PARK 638:61
D. deep, or taste not — POPE 658:54
d. for a living — KERR 465:67
D.! for you know not — FITZ 324:85
D.…is stronger than unionism — LAWS 495:44
d. life to the lees — TENN 839:63
D. not the third glass — HERB 397:88
d. one another's healths — JERO 437:30
d. sooner than pray — SHAK 741:6
d. takes the man — LEWIS 508:93
D. this in remembrance — BOOK 141:9
d. thy wine with a merry heart — BIBLE 101:83
d. to her as long — SHAK 755:50
D. to me, only — JONS 449:40
d. to obliviate that decent actor — FLYNN 328:78
d. unto one of these little ones — BIBLE 111:31
d. when we are not thirsty — BEAU 66:4
dripping blood our only d. — ELIOT 308:22
drove me to d. — FIEL 323:52
Eat, d., and love — BYRON 183:2
every creature d. but I — COWL 240:33
first d. on a Sunday morning — MCCU 529:23
follow strong d. — BIBLE 102:10
garments, heavy with their d. — SHAK 755:26
go a week without a d. — LEWIS 507:82
good as d. — CHES 212:66
has taken to d. — TARK 836:95
I am…a little in d. — STEE 814:90
Let others d. thee freely — HERR 400:40
let us eat and d. — BIBLE 121:16
let us eat and d. — BIBLE 102:22
Love…is not meat nor d. — MILL 571:91
meaning is my meat and d. — BROW 161:39
Nor any drop to d. — COLE 225:85
not eat with you, d. with you — SHAK 739:50
Now is the time to d. — HORA 413:20
One more d. — PARK 638:73
rule never to d. by daylight — MENC 565:67
spent $3m on d. — DALY 251:77
taste any d. once — CABE 183:13
taste who always d. — PRIOR 668:30
teach you to d. deep — SHAK 751:9
That I might d. — KEATS 459:58
The more you d. — POPE 661:57
they gave me vinegar to d. — BOOK 143:60
they take to it like d. — HAZZ 388:96
think that I can d. — ANON 20:2
this calls for a d. — THUR 859:48
those who don't d. — KEIL 460:72
to eat and to d. — GUIL 374:31
too early for a d.? — GORD 364:10
wants but little d. below — HOLM 407:75
we d. too much tea — PRIE 668:21
We d. to thee — TENN 844:69
what d. a man will have — MARQ 554:35
Whene'er to d. you are inclin'd — BURNS 172:25
wittles and d. to me — DICK 269:71
drinker first great…literary d. — THUR 859:49
drinkers moderate d. both — SHAW 779:16
drinking A d. man's someone — WILL 912:27
curse of the d. classes — WILDE 910:66
damnable degrees Of d. — WEBS 894:74
decided to stop d. — CONN 232:60
D. in the morning — RABE 676:69
D. is the soldier's pleasure — DRYD 291:35
d. out of spittoons — HEMI 394:20
d.…sobers us again — POPE 658:54
D. the best tea — SNOW 802:35
D., to engender wit — ROCH 692:68
from robbing…next to d. — DE 262:10
give up smoking, d. and loving — FREUD 336:49
hae been merry d. — BURNS 170:83
kept on d. — ROBI 690:32
much d., little thinking — SWIFT 831:71
no d. after death — FLET 328:67
redfaced from eating and d. — ABBO 1:1
red-hot with d. — SHAK 774:96
there's nothing like d. — DIBD 265:54
very merry, dancing, d. — DRYD 292:61
drinks couple of d. on a Saturday — FYFFE 342:78
he d. no wine — SHAK 743:63

He that d. fast — FRAN 334:8
drink-well Eat-well is d.-w.'s brother — FULL 341:64
drive d. and make love — MOSS 600:30
d. fast and furious — ABSE 1:9
d. one from home — HOOD 410:43
drivel Dilutes with d. — BYRON 179:6
when hearing this d.? — GERS 350:39
drivelling occupy some d. reader — SARD 714:29
driven writer is d. out far — HEMI 394:22
driver Do people…Wave at the d. — MCGO 532:85
hitting the d. so good — TREV 865:62
in the d.'s seat — BEAV 67:24
drivers d. of negroes — JOHN 444:12
driving like the d. of Jehu — BIBLE 92:34
dromedary d., two; Or else — NASH 608:87
drone d. of alliterations — BROY 163:98
droop begin to d. and drowse — SHAK 768:16
D. in a hundred A.B.C.'s — ELIOT 305:44
fortunes Will ever after d. — SHAK 774:78
drop don't d. players — SHAN 776:29
d. of a bucket — BIBLE 103:39
d. of hatred in your soul — MUNRO 603:88
d. serene hath quenched — MILT 582:37
Every d. of ink — WALP 887:24
last d. into that…glass — FITZ 325:97
Nor any d. to drink — COLE 225:85
one d. of negro blood — HUGH 418:24
One d. would save my soul — MARL 552:6
Raineth d. and staineth slop — POUND 664:27
That cordial d. — ROCH 691:59
droppeth d. as the gentle rain — SHAK 740:79
dropping d. in a very rainy day — BIBLE 100:59
drops dear to me as are the ruddy d. — SHAK 747:86
like d. of water — JOYCE 451:82
These are gracious d. — SHAK 748:12
dross the rest is d. — POUND 665:58
drought Such thirst will argue d. — CAREW 190:49
droughts d. and flooding rains — MACK 533:15
drove lifts a d. from a Sassenach — SCOTT 723:13
drown d. my book — SHAK 775:98
drowned d. a blind bitch's puppies — SHAK 743:79
d. in the honey — HAWT 386:37
lies d. with us — HERR 400:44
photograph…after I d. — ATWO 38:48
went and d. themselves — ANON 21:38
drowning guardianship…against d. — PATR 643:71
like death by d. — FERB 320:98
not waving but d. — SMITH 800:97
drowns With too much labour d. — SHAK 733:65
drowsy dull ear of a d. man — SHAK 739:26
drudge harmless d. — JOHN 442:46
drudgery Makes d. divine — HERB 397:93
drug alleyways and d. fiends — LIND 510:46
D. misuse is not a disease — DICK 265:60
Everything is a dangerous d. — CONN 233:79
most powerful d. used — KIPL 474:83
Poetry's a mere d. — FARQ 318:50
rape, sodomy and d. addiction — COOK 235:35
what purgative d. — SHAK 769:40
drugging not d., not robbing — PACK 633:74
drugs d. cause cramp — PARK 638:65
Sex 'n'd. 'n'rock 'n'roll — DURY 296:43
taken illegal d. — JOHN 439:69
with success come d. — HELL 392:64
druid same old d. Time — ROSE 697:67
drum Dumb as a d. — DICK 266:77
trumpet and the steady d. — MCCA 527:91
with his big brass d. — LIND 510:45
with muffled d. — AUDEN 40:89
Drumcliffe In D. churchyard — YEATS 934:66
drummer hears a different d. — THOR 858:97
drums are your d. a-beating yet? — SKIR 795:14
d. begin to roll — KIPL 471:91
Of guns, and d., and wounds — SHAK 741:1
Still, like muffled d. — LONG 515:42
trumpets, beat the d.! — MORE 597:74
drunk art of getting d. — JOHN 445:36
Be not d. with wine — BIBLE 122:49
best audience…a little d. — BARK 60:57
d. and asleep — STEV 819:26
d. his fill — SCOTT 723:4
D. many times a day — SHAK 758:44
d. we like our art — LUCAS 522:77
d. with sight of power — KIPL 472:22
getting over a four-day d. — HELL 393:83
good d.…a good bartender — BISH 131:81
got d. at onch — LONG 515:38

hasten to be d. — DRYD 292:52
I d. him to his bed — SHAK 765:30
Man…must get d. — BYRON 182:80
My mother, d. or sober — CHES 211:46
not genteel when he gets d. — BOSW 146:12
not so think as you d. — SQUI 811:43
Of course I'm d. — RUSS 706:70
Often d., and seldom sober — FULL 341:70
seen Wordsworth d. — HOUS 415:69
That which hath made them d. — SHAK 767:97
this meeting is d. — DICK 266:80
very d. and very slovenly — WYCH 931:86
way that a d. uses lamp-posts — LANG 488:89
drunkard d., my navigator — SEXT 728:12
earth shall reel…like a d. — BIBLE 102:23
rolling English d. — CHES 212:85
take this d. for a god — SHAK 775:2
What dreamest thou, d. — SKEL 795:93
drunkards as d. sing and vomit — CARRA 194:59
have to become d. first — JONES 447:88
miserly — WILD 911:86
drunken d. officer of British rule — WALC 884:70
not true that d. men cannot beget — YEATS 934:68
stagger like a d. man — BIBLE 97:72
drunkenness anything so bad as d. — CHES 212:66
d. expands — JAMES 434:68
D. is a joy reserved — CABE 183:16
D. is his best virtue — SHAK 762:37
man that is given to d. — BIBLE 108:54
time for d. — BAUD 65:69
drunks d. and Americans — MOYN 601:44
for two d. — TWAIN 871:1
Drury I did in D. Lane see — PEPYS 647:40
dry d. brain in a d. season — ELIOT 305:43
hearts very d. and tough — HOOK 411:56
held out to d. — REAG 680:61
in a d. and thirsty land — BIBLE 96:35
into a d. Martini — ANON 22:54
let us assemble, d., gray, spare — RANS 679:23
Like giving d. birth — SIMP 792:46
Sierras Will be d. — SNYD 803:49
within the womb is d. — HOPE 411:72
Yankees, feeling very d. — ANON 22:49
Dryad light-winged D. of the trees — KEATS 459:57
Dryden D. fails to render him — ARNO 33:34
D., Pope, and all their school — ARNO 34:69
Ev'n copious D. — POPE 661:55
dry-goods churches and d.-g. stores — MCMU 537:86
dual as antiquated as a d. — GOOCH 363:97
Everyone…holds d. citizenship — SONT 804:77
dualism d. which now weighs — DEWEY 264:43
Dublin features of the D. style — KENN 463:29
served in all the pubs in D. — DONL 279:25
ducat Dead for a d., dead — SHAK 754:5
Duchess D. of Malfi still — WEBS 895:17
in the arms…of a D. — JOHN 445:35
duck forgot to d. — DEMP 261:86
forgot to d. — REAG 680:57
O dainty d. — SHAK 738:17
ducks Four d. on a pond — ALLI 13:62
ducts pancreatic d. of dog — BANT 59:41
due give the devil his d. — SHAK 741:99
to every one his d. — JUST 453:13
duelling My soul's a trampled d. ground — RICK 686:75
dues Render…to all their d. — BIBLE 120:86
duet d. between a tuba and a piccolo — DONA 278:22
d. of two nightingales — STEV 820:44
dugs old man with wrinkled d. — ELIOT 306:60
Duke will make the D. say — SHAK 737:90
duke D. of Plaza-Toro! — GILB 355:32
D. takes a town — POMP 658:45
everybody praised the D. — SOUT 805:1
to the D.'s house — PEPYS 647:36
with the D. in Flanders — LOWE 519:23
dukes drawing room full of d. — AUDEN 41:20
dulce D. et decorum est — HORA 413:23
D. et decorum est — OWEN 632:57
pro patria, non 'd.' — POUND 664:39
dulcimer damsel with a d. — COLE 226:14
dull But you are d. — MIDD 569:38
d. and mean — WHIT 906:60
d., insipid thing is a billet-doux — ETHE 315:93
first requirement…be d. — ACHE 2:35
found it so intolerably d. — DARW 253:13
I am always deadly d. — BEER 69:71
In this d. world — SHAK 765:51
Like a d. actor — SHAK 769:70

not stupid, but...very d. — BEAV 67:20
recognize when he is d. — AUCH 39:73
To make dictionaries is d. work — JOHN 442:44
dullard d.'s envy of brilliant men — BEER 69:76
dullest d. person in the world — BENS 77:62
dullness cardinal sin is d. — CAPRA 189:36
everyday life, with its...deadly d. — EINS 301:33
invincible d. — JONS 449:31
little d. spoils it — YOUR 935:82
reconciliation with d. — LOWE 521:59
'tis a good d. — SHAK 774:79
dumb because the brutes are d.? — ELIOT 303:74
cannot be absolutely d. — FORD 329:1
deaf to hear, and the d. to speak — BIBLE 114:14
D. as a drum — DICK 266:77
d., dark, dull, bitter belly-tension — GIBB 352:72
d. enough to turn it down — TAYL 837:17
D., inscrutable and grand — ARNO 32:29
d. to say how hot — GRAV 367:64
Homage to plain d. luck — ACHE 3:47
if you cant be d. — OHARA 623:48
Our D. Friends — PARK 638:68
So d. he can't fart — JOHN 440:86
tongue of the d. sing — BIBLE 103:33
dump What a d.! — COFF 224:63
Dunblane flower o' D. — TANN 836:91
Duncan D. is in his grave — SHAK 768:14
Hear it not, D. — SHAK 767:96
wake D. with thy knocking — TWAIN 871:7
dunce amiable d. — CLIF 221:86
because...you're a d. — JOHN 446:53
d. that has been sent to roam — COWP 241:63
D. the second reigns — POPE 662:64
d. with wits — POPE 662:73
dunces A wit with a d. — POPE 662:73
d. are all...against him — SWIFT 830:67
Dundee bonnet of Bonny D. — SCOTT 725:58
piper o' D.? — ANON 20:16
stay langer in Bonny D.! — SCOTT 724:28
Dunfermline king sits in D. — BALL 56:84
dung better to sniff France's d. — HO 405:38
floors of plaister, and the walls of d. — POPE 660:5
more reeking the d. — INNO 429:70
of d. and of corrupcioun! — CHAU 209:91
dungeon door out of the d. of self — MACD 530:54
d. flamed with light — WESL 899:9
d. horrible, on all sides — MILT 580:97
d. of despair — CESA 203:49
d. of self — CONN 233:84
Himself is his own d. — MILT 577:35
imprisonment! The D. of — MILT 586:50
Nor airless d. — SHAK 747:81
prisoner in his d. — FLAU 326:39
worse than chains, D. — MILT 586:47
dunghill cock crowing on its own d. — ALDI 10:9
This enormous d. — VOLT 883:48
Upon the d. — SHAK 763:82
Dunkirk from D. to Belgrade — DAVIS 256:66
the epic of D. — PRIE 668:19
Dunsinane do come to D. — TWAIN 871:7
duo most dangerous d. — SCAR 717:90
duodecimos humbler band of d. — CRAB 242:83
dupes If hopes were d. — CLOU 222:21
dusk each slow d. — OWEN 632:52
for a moment in the d. — BROW 160:20
In the d. — GILB 353:90
dust a handful of d. — TENN 845:94
But what is D. — SITW 794:80
chimney-sweepers, come to d. — SHAK 774:74
comprehended the d. of the earth — BIBLE 103:38
darkened with filthy d. — SPEN 808:83
dialogue between The Spirit and the D. — DICK 273:70
D. as we are — WORD 925:92
d. forbids the birds — SITW 794:68
D. in the air — ELIOT 309:41
d., in the cool tombs — SAND 713:95
d. of creeds outworn — SHEL 785:75
d. of the churchyard — DONNE 281:79
d. on the nettles — THOM 854:18
d. returneth to d. again — GORD 363:7
d. return to the earth — BIBLE 101:92
d. shall be the serpent's meat — BIBLE 104:66
d. shalt thou eat — BIBLE 86:53
d. thou art, and unto d. — BIBLE 86:56
d. to d. — BOOK 142:35
D. to the d.! — SHEL 786:2
d. would hear her — TENN 845:92

Ere Babylon was d. — SHEL 784:69
Excuse My D. — PARK 637:42
fear in a handful of d. — ELIOT 305:53
fine d. — KELM 460:77
first raised a d. — BERK 79:4
formed man out of the d. — BIBLE 86:43
frame was D. — DICK 273:74
glory smeared in d. and blood — SHAK 730:84
Guilty of d. and sin — HERB 397:98
Half d., half deity — BYRON 181:57
heat of life in the handful of d. — CONR 234:6
In that rich d. a richer d. — BROO 156:6
in the d. be equal made — SHIR 789:83
isn't just d. — MACA 524:28
leaves...turning to d. — ANON 18:72
like d. that is blown away — BIBLE 107:34
little d. of praise — TENN 844:51
noble father in the d. — SHAK 751:2
not without d. and heat — MILT 579:70
O'er English d. — MACA 526:72
pays us but with age and d. — RALE 677:3
piles of dry d. — GLAS 359:99
proud and angry d. — HOUS 416:73
provoke the silent d. — GRAY 369:15
recover once my d. — MONT 593:5
remembereth that we are d. — BIBLE 97:65
repent in d. and ashes — BIBLE 94:79
save from d. — SPEN 807:49
shouldst give d. a tongue — HERB 398:13
this unprofitable d. — WORD 924:83
Time, a maniac scattering d. — TENN 843:39
To die in d. — SPEN 809:1
vex the unhappy d. — TENN 842:18
we're only made out of d. — DICK 265:57
what a d. do I raise — BACON 50:58
what is this quintessence of d.? — SHAK 752:57
when this d. falls — VAUG 878:46
You are not worth the d. — SHAK 763:85
dustbin d. upset in a high wind — GOLD 360:29
dustheap d. of history — TROT 867:13
dusty d. to the grave — STEV 821:87
Dutch D. may have their Holland — JOHN 440:94
fault of the D. — CANN 188:14
flowered once for D. sailors' eyes — FITZ 325:1
Dutchman icicle on a D.'s beard — SHAK 756:80
duties brace ourselves to our d. — CHUR 216:77
d. as King — EDWA 300:20
d. of the physician — OSLER 630:16
If I had no d. — JOHN 445:25
lowliest d. on herself — WORD 925:11
No d., only opportunities — ANON 24:42
Property has its d. — DRUM 287:13
duty absolved from all d. — PEAC 645:94
act...of d. and of justice — PITT 653:45
bounds of their d. — RICH 686:68
crimes committed in the name of d. — SNOW 802:41
declares that it is his d. — SHAW 778:78
done my d. as a man — TENN 848:64
do our d. as such — GLAD 359:94
Do the D. which lies nearest thee — CARL 192:98
do your d. — BADEN 51:74
d. as we understand it — LINC 510:38
d. in that state of life — BOOK 142:15
d. is to arouse the sleeper — BETH 83:76
d. laid down upon us by God — CARY 198:60
d. of a democracy — WHITE 903:77
d. of a journalist — STEAD 813:83
d. of an opposition — CHUR 215:58
d. of a serious biographer — TOYN 864:33
d. of being happy — STEV 822:98
d. of government — PAINE 634:91
d. of the writer — KENN 463:35
d., patriotism...clad — LLOY 513:99
d. that Mr Bulstrode rarely shrank — ELIOT 304:7
d. to have reported it — HELL 392:74
d. to the Queen — MARL 551:67
d. to try to prevent it — MILN 575:89
d....to wield the sword of France — DE 259:36
d., your reward, your destiny — HAMM 379:11
every man will do his d. — NELS 610:34
Every subject's d. — SHAK 746:50
fattening is the first d. — SPEKE 806:36
fiction...painful d. — WILDE 910:67
first d....is not to be poor — SHAW 779:38
first d. of a state — RUSK 704:28
first d. of the press — TIMES 861:77
first d. to serve society — JOHN 443:83

God, I have done my d. — NELS 610:36
health is a d. — SPEN 806:40
in d. both equally bound — STER 817:67
little d. and less love — SHAK 729:46
must do our d. — CECIL 202:32
my d. to have loved — TENN 846:24
one d. we owe to history — WILDE 908:93
one's d. to drown it — WILDE 908:6
our d. to follow — PALM 636:22
our only d. — GERG 350:32
perceive here a divided d. — SHAK 759:64
professional d. of the...agent — OGIL 623:41
religious sense of d. — DICK 271:41
Self-development is a higher d. — STAN 812:68
service is the common d. — ROCK 692:77
stage of d. run — KEN 461:93
stirring of d. — CURZ 249:53
terrible notions of d. — CLOU 223:31
tried to do his d. — MACA 524:27
urge thy d. — SHAK 748:18
whole d. of man — BIBLE 101:94
dwarf giant d., Dan Cupid — SHAK 733:76
dwarfish Upon a d. thief — SHAK 768:35
dwarfs D. standing on the shoulders — BERN 80:29
dwell at ease for aye to d. — TENN 839:59
D. I but in the suburbs — SHAK 747:85
means to d. therein — HERB 398:3
upon the logic...that you should d. — DOYLE 285:68
dwellers d. in different zones — DISR 276:53
dwelling d. place in all generations — BIBLE 96:49
thy humble d. — WESL 900:14
whimsical d. — CONG 232:39
Whose d. is the light — WORD 923:71
dwelling-place desert were my d.-p. — BYRON 180:42
How lovely is thy d.-p. — SCOT 725:63
dwellings how amiable art thy d. — BOOK 143:62
dwells In me there d. — TENN 846:17
dwindle d. into wife — CONG 232:46
Shall he d., peak, and pine — SHAK 766:68
dye behint yon auld fail d. — BALL 56:92
dying act of d. — JOHN 444:89
After d. has stopped — HOUS 415:49
An old, mad...and d. king — SHEL 783:34
behold you again in d. — STEV 823:36
blood with the thought of d. — MASE 559:40
born and d., d. — MISH 587:84
didn't mind d. — GLEN 359:3
d., and, behold, we live — BIBLE 122:30
d., bless the hand — DRYD 290:4
d., if we could not cry — MAUP 562:87
D., is an art — PLATH 654:67
d. is merely to quit — OVID 631:47
d....is terrible — FIEL 322:44
d. man's room — STER 818:86
d. now and done for — BETJ 84:3
d. pray at the last — DILL 275:14
d. tongueless — SHAK 770:75
D., we live — BROW 162:93
habit of living indisposeth us for d. — BROW 159:86
Here am I, d. — POPE 662:89
hold its breath...without d. — ANTH 27:7
I am d. — WILDE 910:60
idea of d. is worse than d. — PROU 671:83
If this is d. — STRA 826:87
immortality...through not d. — ALLEN 12:49
in d. that we are born — FRAN 334:98
instead of d., he sings — BENC 74:6
It was in d. — THOM 855:30
living a little more or d. — MAIL 539:42
love to those of the d. — LOWRY 521:67
men that are d. — JEFF 436:8
so many ways of us d. — BAIN 52:9
We are d. continuously — PETR 649:81
worth fighting for, worth d. — MITC 588:93
Dylan Never mind D. and the Dead — MACG 532:89
dynamic a play is a d. thing — TYNAN 872:45
class people as static and d. — WAUGH 892:22
strong and d. — GAND 345:32
world is...in d. unbalance — BART 62:16
dynamite did and it is d. — TRUM 869:43
dynamo cannibal d. — GINS 357:62
dynasty not respect for a d. — LOUIS 518:2

E

eager less e....to marry — FALU 317:40
eagle as an e. toward heaven — BIBLE 100:47

E. has landed — ALDR 11:15
e. know what's in the pit — BLAKE 133:27
e. mewing her mighty youth — MILT 579:82
e. or the snake — KIPL 471:7
e. suffers little birds — SHAK 731:96
e. was killed by the arrow — KELL 460:76
Fearless the e. — MCCA 527:88
hooded e. among blinking owls — SHEL 784:66
like an e. in a dove-cot — SHAK 770:73
youth is renewed like the e.'s — BIBLE 97:62
eagles More rapid than e. — MOORE 594:17
mount up with wings as e. — BIBLE 103:42
swifter than e. — BIBLE 91:98
Where are the e. — ELIOT 305:44
Where his e. never flew — COWP 241:52
eaglet space, an e.'s wing — CRANE 243:18
ear age shall see the golden e. — POPE 659:97
artistic sense of eye or e. — WHIS 902:65
beat upon my whorled e. — HOPK 412:80
by the hearing of the e. — BIBLE 94:79
Christ in every e. — PATR 643:71
chuckle…from e. to e. — ELIOT 306:59
close at the e. of Eve — MILT 583:73
e. becomes more Irish — BYRON 182:89
e. for her music — DAY 257:84
e. is much enamoured — SHAK 738:4
e. is not sensitive enough — MAHL 539:33
e. of a merchant — NASHE 609:19
E.'s deep-sweet music — SHAK 733:55
enchant thine e. — SHAK 732:51
enemy of the e. — WILD 911:89
Even one e. is more — ROTH 699:25
flattery lost on poet's e. — SCOTT 723:89
flea in mine e. — NASHE 609:12
Give every man thine e. — SHAK 751:19
Good music…penetrates the e. — BEEC 69:59
Hark in thine e. — SHAK 763:91
have no e. — LAMB 486:46
heart was piercèd through the e. — SHAK 759:68
history's e., already listening — SAMU 712:78
hollow of thine e. — SHAK 736:68
horrid stillness first invades the e. — DRYD 287:14
In a believer's e.! — NEWT 613:78
In Reason's e. they all rejoice — ADDI 6:27
in your husband's e. — GROM 374:21
Jacobites…give an e., give an e. — BURNS 172:31
jest's prosperity lies in the e. — SHAK 734:93
know not what into my e. — LAND 488:82
lark to shepherd's e. — SHAK 737:85
lend an e. to Plato — TENN 847:34
meant than meets the e. — MILT 577:19
Not to the sensual e. — KEATS 459:52
o'er my e. like the sweet sound — SHAK 755:45
Of eye, and e. — WORD 924:72
penetrated into the e. of man — FORS 331:31
pistol let off at the e. — LAMB 487:62
planted the e. — BIBLE 96:56
presented to the eye or e. — CRAB 242:1
purse out of your wife's e. — MORT 600:20
rich jewel in an Ethiope's e. — SHAK 736:42
Stop thine e. against the singer — SCOTT 724:40
telescope to his e. — SMITH 797:36
there reaches my e. — PAST 642:42
to the E. of Kings — POPE 662:64
tubes of the e. — WILL 914:56
Vexing the dull e. — SHAK 739:26
was all e. — MILT 577:40
whisper in her e. — WILB 907:71
whom he whispers in the e. — BROW 162:68
whose e. is a smoking tomb — GINS 357:62
world-deafened e. — ARNO 31:99
earl As far as the fourteenth e. — HOME 409:10
e. and a knight of the garter — ATTL 38:44
E. of Dudley and was beheaded — MILLS 574:72
Oh I see said the E. — ASHF 35:96
slain the E. of Murray — BALL 55:68
Earls daughter of a hundred E. — TENN 840:73
early always either too late or too e. — SART 715:44
e. will I seek thee — BIBLE 96:35
had it been e. — JOHN 442:34
However monstrously e. — SHIP 789:77
too e. for a drink? — GORD 364:10
try to be e. — DAY 256:77
vain for you to rise up e. — BIBLE 98:92
Woe unto them that rise up e. — BIBLE 102:10
earn e. it by enjoying such authority — BERE 78:89
e. that I eat — SHAK 749:57

e. your living — WELD 897:42
earnest impotence of being e. — CANN 188:8
in good e. wish — WILL 912:5
valuable or even e. — THOR 857:86
we die in e. — RALE 677:1
ears and hedges e. — SWIFT 831:90
blast of war…in our e. — SHAK 746:42
bless our human e. — MILT 576:97
Creep in our e. — SHAK 740:85
distance between your e. — JONES 447:85
dying has stopped the e. — HOUS 415:49
e. fall off like figs — THOM 853:95
e. he likes to bathe in sound — BROWN 157:45
E. like bombs — CAUS 201:13
e. like errant wings — CHES 211:42
e. of every one…shall tingle — BIBLE 91:83
e. of jet — GRAY 368:98
e. of the deaf shall be unstopped — BIBLE 103:33
e. that…hear one's secrets — ONEI 625:92
e. that hear the soft rain — RICK 686:74
e. to hear, let him hear — BIBLE 114:10
e. to hear, let him hear — BIBLE 111:35
e. yielding like swinging doors — DOUG 283:21
eyes and hearts e. — LYLY 523:9
fume of space foams in our e. — CRANE 243:20
golden e. of corn — HERR 400:47
Harrovian pricks up his e. — ANON 21:30
He that hath e. to hear — BIBLE 114:10
He that hath e. to hear — BIBLE 111:35
if men had e. — BYRON 182:99
In the porches of mine e. — SHAK 752:32
lend me your e. — SHAK 748:5
let thine e. be attentive — BIBLE 98:95
make the fur Fly 'bout the e. — BUTL 177:48
my e. drumming — SAPP 714:27
never mentions Hell to e. polite — POPE 659:96
noise of waters in my e. — SHAK 731:8
Pour oil into their e. — JONS 448:14
reaching the proper e. — KIPL 470:74
Rome about your e. — SHAK 769:69
seven thin e. — BIBLE 88:98
shout about my e. — CHES 211:43
That man's e. make — HUGH 418:15
thumbs vary…like e. — SHAW 781:90
To dying e. — TENN 842:8
two ambitious e. — JONS 448:13
up to the e. in love — STER 818:88
Walls have e. — ANON 22:63
Walls have e. — LINK 511:57
With ravished e. — DRYD 291:34
earth air, e., or sea — MILT 585:35
alien planet is E. — BALL 57:99
all cultures of the e. — WEBER 894:68
All people that on e. — SCOT 725:64
all the corners of the e. — BOOK 143:64
all the e. o'erwhelm them — SHAK 751:13
All the gold upon the e. — PLATO 655:87
alone on e. — BYRON 179:17
although the e. remove — SCOT 725:62
any man that breathes on e. — MARL 552:2
anything on e. can mend — MANN 546:79
anywhere else on e. — GURN 375:42
as if the e. had rolled — WORD 924:87
As if this e….were breathing — COLE 226:11
at any time upon the e. — WHIT 905:28
attempt to create heaven on e. — BORO 145:1
back to e. as the doorkeeper — TOSC 863:18
back to the nourishing e. — SAND 713:2
beauty fed my common e. — MASE 559:33
believe that the e. is flat — DRIB 287:10
belonging as much to sky as to e. — CARR 194:54
bleeding piece of e. — SHAK 748:1
blithe e. die — JEFF 436:5
Born for us on e. below — CASW 199:82
bowels of the harmless e. — SHAK 741:1
break e.'s sleep — OWEN 632:64
bridal of the e. and sky — HERB 398:14
brilliant light on e. — HUSS 424:43
call heaven and e. to witness — BIBLE 89:44
Canst work i'th'e. so fast? — SHAK 752:37
Can the e. do to us — BROW 159:6
care for no man on e. — DICK 271:23
certain fathoms in the e. — SHAK 775:98
Child on e. for me — BETJ 84:99
clear, and the e. sure — DONNE 279:34
clods and trampled e. — MUIR 602:56
cloud Enveloping the E. — COLE 226:3

comprehended the dust of the e. — BIBLE 103:38
conquest of the e. — CONR 234:96
cool flowery lap of e. — ARNO 31:3
crawling between heaven and e.? — SHAK 753:79
crust of an unfinished e. — KURA 482:40
daughter of E. and Water — SHEL 783:41
daughters of e. — JOHN 442:39
did thee feel the e. move? — HEMI 394:14
dominion…over all the e. — BIBLE 85:41
earned here on e. — THAT 850:18
e. abideth for ever — BIBLE 100:65
e. able to sustain — ASIM 35:3
e., and heav'n, and hell — POPE 662:68
e. and the heaven fled away — BIBLE 127:78
e.…Apparelled in celestial light — WORD 926:21
e. as we now see it — MACL 535:46
e. beneath her — GORD 363:6
E. cares for her own ruins — BINY 130:55
e. doth like a snake renew — SHEL 786:21
E. felt the wound — MILT 584:13
E. has waited — ROSE 697:69
e. hath bubbles — SHAK 766:74
e. hath not anything to show — WORD 926:19
e. in an earthly bed — TENN 845:96
e. in travail and in pain — LONG 516:59
e. is but an echo of the spheres — BYRON 182:99
e. is full of his glory — BIBLE 102:13
e. is hell when — NASHE 609:16
E. is here so kind — JERR 437:39
e. is nobler than the world — PRIE 668:18
e. is nothing very special — HOYLE 417:4
e. is still going round the sun — ORWE 629:83
e. is the Lord's — BIBLE 121:4
e. its dower of river — KEATS 457:4
E., lie heavily — ROSS 697:80
e. must borrow its mirth — WILC 907:80
e. of majesty — SHAK 734:38
e. peopled as ever by the inept — REPP 683:12
E. receive an honoured guest — AUDEN 40:3
e. savage, e. broken — COLUM 229:58
E.'s crammed with heaven — BROW 160:14
e. self-balanced — MILT 584:93
e. shall be full of the knowledge — BIBLE 102:19
e. shall reel to and fro — BIBLE 102:23
E.'s heedless sons — BLUN 137:12
E.'s shadows fly — SHEL 786:7
e. stood hard as iron — ROSS 697:84
e. the legend of the Gael — RUSS 706:61
E., thou bonnie — MACD 529:26
e. to e. — BOOK 142:35
e. to love — KIPL 473:52
e. was made for Dombey and Son — DICK 268:51
e. where cares abound — WORD 929:60
every man upon this e. — MACA 526:63
exalted in the e. — BIBLE 95:26
eyes…throughout the whole e. — BIBLE 92:43
feels the attraction of e. — LONG 516:65
fell to e. — HAMER 378:95
fell to e. — LONG 516:51
fifth part of the E. — FIELD 322:30
first man is of the e. — BIBLE 121:18
fixed upon the e. — MARL 551:72
for e. too dear — SHAK 736:42
For, heaven to e. — SHAK 742:32
foundations of the e.? — BIBLE 103:41
foundations of the e.? — BIBLE 93:69
From e.'s wide bounds — HOW 417:93
From sullen e. — SHAK 771:14
from which e., and grave — RALE 677:3
furniture of the e. — BERK 79:5
gazing on the e. — SHEL 787:30
get off the e.? — SAND 713:4
girdle round about the e. — SHAK 737:95
glance from heaven to e. — SHAK 738:13
globe of the e. — MUNDY 603:83
God…craves the e. — SEXT 728:20
God created the heaven and the e. — BIBLE 85:37
going to and fro in the e. — BIBLE 93:47
good men…make the e. wholesome — EMER 312:32
hallowed piece of e. — CLIN 221:91
happiest marriages on e. — DE 264:33
heaven and e. in…uniòn — MILT 575:96
Heaven and e. shall pass away — BIBLE 113:86
Heaven in E. — CRAS 244:34
heaven on e. — FORD 330:12
heaven on e. I have won — SHAK 762:35
heav'n and e. hath made — SCOT 726:65

Hell as well as on e. — LEWIS 507:72
hell on e. — SHAW 778:80
Hold off the e. — SHAK 755:34
How on e. can you privatize — PAVL 644:80
inherit the e. — BIBLE 95:16
inherit e. — BIBLE 109:83
in the deep-delved e. — KEATS 459:58
in the lowest parts of the e. — BIBLE 98:2
Johannesburg is needed upon the e. — PATON 643:70
judged the e. flat — UPDI 874:79
Judge of all the e. — BIBLE 87:78
kingly joys in e. — MARL 551:74
Kings are e.'s gods — SHAK 769:48
lap of e. — GRAY 369:25
last sound on the worthless e. — FAUL 319:75
let the e. be opened — BIBLE 128:96
lie with his mother e.? — SHAK 748:27
Lightly gentle e. — BEAU 67:13
little e., for charity — SHAK 775:23
longer than the e. — BIBLE 93:57
loose to play upon the e. — MILT 579:69
love…good tilled e. — TOLK 862:1
loves but half of E. — QUIL 674:40
low as where this e. — ROSS 698:88
make the e. my hell — SHAK 731:13
Man marks the e. with ruin — BYRON 180:44
meek shall inherit the e. — BIBLE 95:16
meek shall inherit the e. — BIRK 130:64
meek shall inherit the e. — DU 293:73
memory die from the e. — SIDN 791:23
Men are like the e. — SCHR 720:41
men call e. — MILT 577:25
men from the planet E. — ANON 23:10
men walk proudly through the e. — RAND 678:14
mingle our bloods…in the e. — SHAK 769:51
more nearer e. — SHAK 761:11
more things in heaven and e. — MAMET 543:32
more things in heaven and e. — SHAK 752:38
most beautiful things on e. — ISAA 430:86
most decent nation on…e. — BUSH 175:91
moved e. and hearth — TENN 840:66
much less grief on e. — BROD 153:57
must have a touch of e. — TENN 846:16
new heaven and a new e. — BIBLE 127:79
new heavens and a new e. — BIBLE 104:65
night close down on the e. — RAND 678:13
no culture of the e. — HOBB 404:27
none upon e. that I desire — BIBLE 96:43
no power on e. — BALD 54:47
no such thing on e. — CHES 211:49
no supporter but the huge firm e. — SHAK 738:23
not in e. or time recoverable — PURDY 673:17
nought…on…the e. doth live — SHAK 736:55
novelty on e., this fair defect — MILT 585:27
Ocean and e. — WORD 928:52
old in the e. — BRON 155:93
ominously upon the e. — GRAV 367:68
on e. a vicious weed — DRYD 290:84
on e. do dwell — KETHE 465:75
on e. I wait forlorn — ARNO 32:31
on e. no track — THOM 856:63
on that dark e. — TENN 846:26
On the bare e. expos'd — DRYD 291:36
On the e. he strowèd — SPEN 809:15
oppressions of this e. — SHEL 783:26
other nations of the e. — JAMES 433:35
our moment upon the e. — MANS 547:89
our room on this e. — GREN 373:3
paleyce as ony on e. — MALO 542:5
passenger on the spaceship, E. — FULL 341:54
Peace on e. and mercy mild! — BEEC 69:60
peace upon the e. — MILT 575:94
pearled Arcturi of the e. — SHEL 787:24
place among the nations of the e. — EMMET 313:59
portion of the e. — NAIP 606:49
present life of men on e. — BEDE 68:54
rapture the e. and the seas — BRON 154:72
regarded this e. with envious eyes — WELLS 898:73
returning him safely to e. — KENN 462:14
revealed Not of e. — MILT 584:98
round e.'s imagined corners — DONNE 280:66
salt of the e. — BIBLE 109:84
salt of the e. — SHEL 784:66
Saviour Christ again to E. — MASE 559:35
scatter them abroad…all the e. — BIBLE 87:71
scum of the e. — CHES 212:78
scum of the e.…soldiers — WELL 897:54

send peace on e. — BIBLE 111:29
serious house on serious e. — LARK 490:27
shall move the e. — ARCH 28:39
shall not perish from the e. — LINC 510:39
shortest-lived profession on e. — ROGE 695:28
Silver out of the E. in Peru — PETTY 649:84
Sing…all the e. — BIBLE 127:89
Six miles from e. — JARR 435:80
sleepers in that quiet e. — BRON 155:99
small model of the barren e. — SHAK 735:19
smell above the e. — SHAK 748:2
smite the e. a curse — BIBLE 107:23
Spaceship E. — FULL 341:55
spiritual creatures walk the e. — MILT 583:69
Standing on e., not rapt — MILT 583:89
strangers and pilgrims on the e. — BIBLE 124:96
sun is coming down to e. — MERE 567:96
sun went around the e. — ARNO 34:73
surface of the e. — SWIFT 831:79
temples of the e. — DIDE 274:96
that e. lie light — WALL 886:15
Things learned on e. — BROW 162:65
this broad e. of ours — WHIT 906:51
this e. of ours — DE 262:6
this green e. — WORD 924:72
thought about…the whole e. — BYRON 181:67
though the e. be removed — BIBLE 95:24
three nights in the heart of the e. — BIBLE 111:43
through heav'n and e. — MILT 582:51
through my lips to unawakened e. — SHEL 783:48
throw e. over your head — PASC 640:20
Thy will be done in e. — BIBLE 110:98
Till e. and sky — KIPL 470:81
tread on E. — ARNO 31:90
treasures upon e. — BIBLE 110:99
two paces of the vilest e. — SHAK 742:35
uttermost part of the e. — BIBLE 118:27
uttermost parts of the e. — BIBLE 111:44
uttermost parts of the e. — BIBLE 94:84
wall as solid as the e. — BUCH 164:24
way of all the e. — BIBLE 90:65
way of all the e. — BIBLE 91:9
we are on the e. — SHAK 734:11
what on e. is the use of them — WILDE 909:34
Wherewith to scorn the e. — MILT 585:18
While e.'s foundations stand — HOUS 416:86
whole e. as their memorial — PERI 648:64
whole face of the e. — PASC 640:17
whole rainy, stony e.? — HUGH 419:46
whole round e. — TENN 847:51
why e. loves e. — ANON 19:93
Yours is the E. — KIPL 474:68
earthling alone in a way that no e. — COLL 228:38
earthly all e. things above — SPRI 811:39
an e. song — TENN 843:46
e. immortality — FORD 330:12
e. paragon — SHAK 774:71
ne'er touched e. faces — SHAK 771:4
Off e. thingis name may bettir be — DUNB 294:2
too well for any e. use — FROST 338:95
earthquake e. swallows us — STEV 822:99
e. was really too much — LIGNE 509:29
e. were to engulf England — JERR 437:42
haven't had an e. lately — MILNE 575:83
Lord was not in the e. — BIBLE 92:24
not smiling back—that's an e. — MILL 571:94
shaken with an e. — ADDI 5:8
starts with an e. — GOLD 362:84
takes an e. to remind us — KURA 482:40
the gloom of e. — SHEL 783:33
to play golf during an e. — STAL 812:59
win a war than…win an e. — RANK 679:20
earthquakes e.…bright weather — CARL 192:5
famines, and pestilences, and e. — BIBLE 113:85
thought of e., and of wars — BYRON 181:67
ease Are you at e. now? — FLET 328:75
as in a doubtful e. — SURR 829:35
done with so much e. — DRYD 289:70
E. after war — SPEN 808:81
e. of body — SMITH 797:37
e. some deal — SHAK 731:92
for another gives its e. — BLAKE 134:51
health and perfect e. — DYER 297:85
heart's first e. — DAY 257:85
hours of e. — SCOTT 723:1
ignoble e., and peaceful sloth — MILT 581:23
interpose a little e. — MILT 578:55

Joys in another's loss of e. — BLAKE 134:52
man is most at e. — ALLS 13:63
no longer at e. here — ELIOT 306:74
prodigal of e.? — DRYD 290:78
Studious of laborious e. — COWP 241:75
True e. in writing — POPE 658:59
easel bread, and his e. — RYDER 707:76
easier e. to conquer it — WALP 887:28
e. with practice — GREE 371:71
how much e. — HALI 378:84
I am e. to be played on — SHAK 754:96
upon e. terms — JOHN 446:62
easing E. the spring — REED 681:78
east aristocracy of the E. — MAUG 561:79
As far as the e. is from the west — BIBLE 97:64
chambers of the E. — BLAKE 133:21
determined to go E. — MAIL 540:65
E. is E — KIPL 470:81
e. wind made flesh — APPL 28:26
e. wind prevails over the west — MAO 548:13
hold the gorgeous E. in fee — WORD 926:20
Hunter of the E. — FITZ 324:82
inscrutability of the E. — STARK 813:75
lands of the E. — GILL 356:48
look the E. End in the face — ELIZ 310:68
mysterious E., perfumed — CONR 234:5
politics in the E. — DISR 276:39
sigh of the e. on my face — CONR 234:4
There is no silence in the E. — MAUG 561:77
three kings into the e. — BURNS 191:93
tried to hustle the E. — KIPL 471:5
when the wind blew due E. — CARR 197:31
wind's in the e. — DICK 269:84
Easter frome Candylmas untyll E. — MALO 542:10
making my E. confession — JOSE 451:70
Eastern save in E. clime — BURG 167:98
eastern Come o'er the e. hills — BLAKE 133:23
Eastertide Wearing white for E. — HOUS 414:41
Easthampstead on E. Plain — KING 469:55
easy depending upon shock…is e. — PRIE 668:27
Difficult or e. — MART 555:51
e.—terribly e.? — SHAW 777:57
Life is not e. — SAIF 709:10
Life is not meant to be e. — FRAS 335:29
take life e. — YEATS 932:29
too e. for children — SCHN 719:23
eat all I had to e. — STEV 821:76
be able to e. less — PAVA 644:77
best place to e. — GUIL 374:31
but I will not e. with you — SHAK 739:50
buzzard…can e. anything — FAUL 319:72
couldn't e. — GREE 370:51
do not e. for the good of living — EMER 312:24
earn that I e. — SHAK 749:57
e. all the food — KEEN 460:68
e. and sleep and choose a wife — SASS 716:58
e. as much as a man — TRUTH 869:52
E., drink, and love — BYRON 183:2
e.…drink, and to be merry — BIBLE 101:81
e. in safety — SHAK 775:26
e. my ale — FARQ 318:55
e. the power out of women — WEST 901:40
e. thy bread with joy — BIBLE 101:83
e. to live — MOLI 590:38
e.…with a glum urge — FISH 324:79
e.…this do in remembrance — BIBLE 121:6
hoping…he will e. you last — REAG 680:54
I did e. — BIBLE 86:52
I e. what I see — CARR 195:71
kill, and e. — BIBLE 119:39
let us e. and drink — BIBLE 121:16
let us e. and drink — BIBLE 102:22
neither should he e. — BIBLE 123:72
Never e. at…Mom's — ALGR 11:29
So I did sit and e. — HERB 398:99
some wad e. that want it — ANON 21:23
Take, e.: this is my body — BIBLE 121:6
Tell me what you e. — BRIL 152:34
than e. China's all our lives — HO 405:38
To e., to survive — STAN 813:69
eaten e. me out of house — SHAK 742:46
has been e. by the bear — HOUS 416:88
never e. bread — KAIKO 454:32
eater good e. must be a good man — DISR 276:36
great e. of beef — SHAK 756:51
Out of the e. came forth meat — BIBLE 90:71
eating Appetite comes with e. — RABE 676:67

e. paté — SMITH 801:22
E. people is wrong! — FLAN 326:23
e. that's believing — THUR 859:47
E. the air — SHAK 742:44
for e., not mating — FERB 320:99
good news is that he's e. less — JACO 432:12
Lawful as e. — SHAK 770:99
loving alone is as dull as e. alone — WYCH 931:17
redfaced from e. and drinking — ABBO 1:1
subject of e. — HUNT 423:37
While someone else is e. — AUDEN 40:90
eats e. up himself — SHAK 757:98
Man is what he e. — FEUE 322:23
way that he e. jelly beans — REAG 680:56
Young misses whut e. — MITC 588:94
eat-well E.-w. is drink-well's brother — FULL 341:64
eaves sparrow in the e. — YEATS 932:32
upon her gilded e. — TENN 842:9
ebb ne'er e. to humble love — SHAK 760:96
ebony nine e. spikes — KING 469:62
eccentricity reputation for e. — SHAR 776:45
ecclesiastical interest in e. — WAUGH 891:17
ecclesiologist keen e. — BETJ 83:79
echo all the church did e. — SHAK 732:40
Art is dedicated e. — SANT 714:23
co-opted and obliterated e. — HEAN 389:15
e. began in some indescribable way — FORS 331:43
E., sweetest nymph — MILT 577:33
Scents, colours, and sounds e. — BAUD 64:56
sound must seem an e. — POPE 658:59
there reaches…the e. — PAST 642:42
waiting for the e. — MARQ 554:33
echoes all their e. mourn — MILT 578:47
Dead e.! But I knew her body — CRANE 243:18
e., dying, dying, dying — TENN 841:3
e., dying, dying, dying — TENN 841:4
e. of fear — EVANS 316:20
Our e. roll — TENN 842:5
state-controlled manufactory of e. — DOUG 283:29
wild e. flying — TENN 841:3
eclipse earthquake and e. — SHEL 783:33
eclipses modus of lunar e. — POUND 664:34
ecological e. balance of the planet — SONT 804:73
economic accepted e. legends — GALB 343:93
an e. colony — TSON 869:54
chief source of e. insecurity — ELLW 311:92
cold metal of e. theory — SCHU 721:54
Commentators quote e. studies — SAMU 712:80
e. condition has…improved — KRIS 481:16
e. equivalent of the slave — WIEN 906:67
e. factors in society — GILM 356:52
e. ones are incomprehensible — HOME 409:11
E. policy is random — STEIN 815:30
e., political, and social life — LEWIS 507:83
e. services that it can render — DURK 295:30
e. status of women — GILM 356:51
e. substructure — FANON 317:43
e. value of…women — GILM 356:53
engineering an e. revival — LARD 490:15
essential form of e. speech — WRIS 930:93
forces of e. law — KEYN 465:79
industrial and e. status — SKEL 795:94
In e. terms — GLEI 359:2
more effective e. service — TAWN 837:8
much of e. theory — HICKS 402:82
normal e. system works — SALT 711:74
not the e. index — MARC 549:35
opportunity cost of e. discussion — GALB 343:98
take our e. blood pressure — WRIS 930:90
talented e. theorists — TOBIN 861:79
understand the e. system — ROBI 690:40
When I read e. documents — HOME 409:12
economical e. with the truth — ARMS 30:80
economically e. backward — TROT 868:19
economics basic law of e. — HARR 384:5
branch of e. — STIG 824:45
E. and art are strangers — CATH 200:94
E. as a positive science — FRIE 337:62
E. as if People Mattered — SCHU 720:50
E., if it is to be — JEVO 438:44
E. is all about…choices — DUES 293:87
E. is the science — ROBB 689:14
e. suggests that they — MISH 587:79
Enid Blyton of e. — HOLME 407:71
from the Principles of E. — KEYN 465:84
master of e. — HOLM 408:2
purpose of studying e. — ROBI 690:39

economies few factors help…e. — MCDO 530:52
two e. finally merged — WOLF 920:81
economist a one-handed e. — TRUM 868:42
death of a political e. — BAGE 51:80
e. is someone who — HELL 392:71
world's greatest e. — SCHU 721:53
economists among professional e. — HAYEK 387:61
a very large number of e. — GALB 343:99
classical e. — VINER 881:15
deceived by e. — ROBI 690:39
distribution of uncertainty among e. — STEIN 815:29
e., and…economic theorists — KNIG 476:15
e. are…disinclined to publish — CANN 188:10
e. hardly know enough — BECK 67:30
E. have the least influence — BLIN 136:94
E. set themselves — KEYN 465:81
ideas of e. — KEYN 466:89
If all the e. in the world — SHAW 781:99
sophisters, e., and calculators — BURKE 169:34
economy arbitrary e. of nature — WOLL 921:7
Beauty…like any e. — WOLF 919:80
complex…as a modern e. — SOLOW 803:60
different schemes of e. — STEU 819:9
e. is based on planned obsolescence — STEV 819:10
E. is the art — SHAW 779:14
e. of a manufacture — BABB 45:19
e. of these people — SMOL 801:28
e., stupid! — ANON 25:54
her industry and e. — STAN 812:65
In art e. is always beauty — JAMES 433:51
in favour of general e. — EDEN 299:89
In the interests of e. — MAXT 562:88
its e. is in difficulty — WALE 885:90
No e. ever stands still — HARR 384:6
People want e. — IACO 427:28
performance of the American e. — STEIN 815:30
Political e. — RUSK 704:17
Political e. thus does — MARX 557:96
Political e. traces — BAGE 51:92
seeds of the spirit and e. — MARI 549:48
socialism and a market e. — DENG 261:89
working e. in the world — MARS 554:39
wrote 'Principles of Political E.' — BENT 78:78
ecstasies muddy e. of beer — CRAB 242:81
ecstasy bells of E. — GINS 357:69
e. of love — SHAK 752:41
e. Of sun-fed wine — NEIL 610:31
escape from circumstance to e. — BELL 71:28
immobility, e., and sleep — MARI 550:52
not e. but it was comfort — DICK 270:13
seraph-wings of e. — GRAY 370:38
think thereof without an e.? — BROW 158:65
What wild e.? — KEATS 459:51
ecstatic the e. and the bilious — ELIOT 303:73
ectoplasms Hollywood-movie e. — ELLI 311:88
Ector bare it forth unto syre E. — MALO 542:2
eczema Style…too often hides e. — CAMUS 187:97
eddy action's dizzying e. — ARNO 31:88
Eden birds of E. sang? — CULL 247:92
brooks of E. mazily murmuring — TENN 847:29
east of E. — BIBLE 86:62
easy E.-dreamtime — WRIG 930:82
E., demi-paradise — SHAK 734:8
E.'s green and gold — KIPL 471:3
E., shall enjoy their fill — MILT 583:66
E. took their solitary way — MILT 586:37
foot in E. — MUIR 602:63
garden eastwards in E. — BIBLE 86:44
out of the Garden of E. — MUGG 601:49
put him into the garden of E. — BIBLE 86:45
sent him forth from the garden of E. — BIBLE 86:57
when from E. we take — MACN 538:12
woe, With loss of E. — MILT 580:91
edge at the e. of Being — SPEN 807:51
e. of a new frontier — KENN 462:9
e. of some crazy cliff — SALI 711:61
e. of the stage — DIDE 273:87
e. of the world — SITW 794:84
e. to the superstitious tale — PRIT 669:46
Fills and trembles at the e. — ROET 694:1
hand…cutting e. of the mind — BRON 154:68
if they have a cutting e. — MURR 605:12
own folly, go over the e. — MOUN 601:39
push men over the e. — ROTH 699:16
edges octaves of its parallel e. — CUMM 247:1
Stain all your e. — SHAK 770:73
edify all things e. not — BIBLE 121:3

Edina E.! Scotia's darling seat — BURNS 171:90
Edinburgh E. will not disagree — STEEL 814:88
Ye E. Gentry! — BURNS 170:66
editing final e. down — DELI 261:78
products of e. — WALD 885:85
edition new e. of human nature — HAZL 388:83
new…more beautiful e. — FRAN 334:6
not in the latest e. — GREE 371:64
editor E.: a person employed — HUBB 417:9
e. is the uncrowned king — STEAD 813:82
e. must always be with the people — BENN 76:56
e. of an important magazine — CANN 188:10
e. of a village journal — MOOD 594:10
e. who cannot contemplate it — JOVA 451:76
Procrustes was an e. — SKEL 795:5
Show me a contented newspaper e. — CHRI 214:29
the one that the e. gives to the worms — MACH 532:95
Trust your e. — CHEE 209:7
editorial age of the e. chair — MCLU 536:61
This is the e. age — BENN 77:57
editors some newspaper e. — CHOP 214:25
true Church of England…in the E. — CARL 191:76
educability His whole e. — JAMES 434:66
educate e. the masses — OSLER 630:16
got to e. him first — SAKI 710:36
educated another sun to the e. — HERA 396:69
clothed, fed and e. — RUSK 704:28
'e.' people…come to the front — ORWE 627:38
government by the badly e. — CHES 213:97
instructed and amused…is e. — ATLAS 37:38
liberally e. person — BLOOM 137:3
never preach, but to the e. — AUST 43:78
stamps a man…as an e. gentleman — SHAW 779:39
that is e. — HAMI 379:1
thought highly e. — SNOW 802:37
uncrowned king of an e. democracy — STEAD 813:82
education American e. — ADAMS 4:85
apathy in e. — FORS 331:38
best kind of e. — BUCH 164:28
By e. most have been misled — DRYD 291:21
can't do with any more e. — WODE 919:68
e. and whisky the price it is — WAUGH 891:15
E. consists mainly — TWAIN 872:29
E.…discloses to the wise — BIER 129:27
E. in science and technology — HUXL 426:1
E.…in so much higher a degree — AUST 44:97
e. is a little too pedantic — CONG 231:19
E. is another sun — HERA 396:69
E. is a state-controlled — DOUG 283:29
E. is…hanging around — FROST 339:17
E. is impossible without love — DESB 262:13
e.…is mere sheep-herding — POUND 665:51
E. is the taming — BLOOM 137:4
E. is what remains — EINS 301:42
E. is what survives — SKIN 795:9
e. of the people — DISR 277:81
e. of the people — MILL 570:61
e. of the people — WHIT 902:68
e. produces no effect — WILDE 909:38
e. to eliminate the influence — MUSG 605:14
field of public e. — WARR 889:68
finished his e. till after — HAYD 387:58
good e.…to sustain a failure — BELL 71:26
Harvard e. consists of what you learn — CONA 230:81
have no e. — SMOL 801:28
having no e. — SHAN 776:35
hope to agree about e. — RUSS 705:52
If you think e. is expensive — BOK 139:39
lacking any mathematical e. — HAYEK 387:61
man of any e. — JOHN 445:23
man's e. begins — ROUS 700:44
Movies, and that is e. — ROGE 695:25
only accomplishment my e. — DRAB 286:87
part of every Englishman's e. — HUGH 420:54
priorities for Government…e., e. and e. — BLAIR 132:3
race between e. and catastrophe — WELLS 898:89
same relation to e. — HUBB 418:10
saw in my own e. — WEST 901:40
scramble themselves into a little e. — AUST 43:81
Soap and e. — TWAIN 870:79
So long as e. is not provided — DAVI 254:29
test and use of man's e. — BARZ 63:33
unblunted by formal e. — ANGE 17:33
value of a liberal e. — BREW 151:21
educational modern e. theorists — RUSS 705:51
political and e. status — SKEL 795:94
social and e. patterns — MCLU 536:60

educators priests and e.   NGU 613:79
Edward Prayer Book of E.VI   ACHE 2:24
   proud E.'s army   WILL 914:65
   proud E.'s power   BURNS 173:41
   winding-sheet of E.'s race   GRAY 370:32
eel adder better than the e.   SHAK 732:43
   funeral march of a fried e.   SHAW 781:91
eels small e. that left the deeper way   CRAB 242:99
   topped with good, rich, broiled e.   KURO 482:41
Eeyore snowing still,' said E.   MILNE 575:83
effacement brought full e.   RANS 679:26
effanineffable ineffable effable E.   ELIOT 307:10
effect all that…despotism could e.   PITT 653:47
   approaches the e. of painting   MICH 569:37
   e. on other people   SART 715:41
   instrument that has a good moral e.   ARIS 29:59
   minimum effort for maximum e.   HIRST 403:10
   Nature…a name for an e.   COWP 241:80
   notion of cause and e.   HUME 422:4
   poetry administers to the e.   SHEL 786:14
   win an e.   UPDI 874:73
effective Being e. is more important   BECK 68:31
effects dire e. from civil discord   ADDI 7:39
   e. deprave forever   BRON 155:89
   e. of the division of labour   SMITH 797:38
   grind out the true causes and e.   CARL 191:86
   not in its taste, but its e.   FULB 340:44
   slow preparation of e.   ELIOT 304:6
effectual any more e. way   TROL 866:87
effeminate held curls to be e.   TWAIN 870:85
efficiency competitive race for e.   ARNO 34:74
   e. and inefficiency   SHAW 779:36
   E.…is measured   JAY 436:98
   industrial e. consists   ROBI 689:24
   Practical e. is common   ROOS 696:57
efficient E. organization is one   STEA 813:79
   kept e. by the persistent absenteeism   SAMU 712:77
Effie E. M. was a monster   LEE 500:44
effigies e. of gods and goddesses   GILL 355:38
effluence e. of bright essence increate   MILT 582:36
effort e. to keep a party together   WILS 916:5
   e. very nearly killed her   BELL 73:58
   enjoyment of successful e.   SHIP 789:76
   Evil is done without e.   BAUD 65:73
   feeling that lures us on…to vain e.   CONR 234:6
   form of moral e.   LEAC 497:67
   main e.…has been a critical e.   ARNO 33:35
   minimum e. for maximum effect   HIRST 403:10
   not the e. or the failure   EMPS 313:61
   only e. worth making   BOWL 147:39
   steadily decreasing amount of e.   SCHU 721:56
   team e. is a lot of people   WINN 917:29
   unusually obstinate e.   JAMES 434:60
   worth every e.   THES 851:51
   years of e., hard work   PEARY 645:1
efforts appreciate his e.   KENN 463:29
   e. to understand…nature   BUSH 176:24
   excuse to cease all e.   ANGE 17:42
   field for their e.   BRON 154:78
effusion e. of…human blood   OCON 621:20
effusions liveliest e. of wit   AUST 43:91
egalitarian e.…should be élitist   LODGE 515:28
   more e. than it wants   SWEE 830:46
egg balancing an e. on a spoon   HILL 402:87
   bald as an e.   CHEE 209:5
   broody hen sitting on a china e.   FOOT 329:92
   e. heads are in one basket   ANON 23:87
   e. is full of meat   SHAK 736:61
   e. production in this country   CURR 249:45
   e.'s way of making another e.   BUTL 177:66
   hen's e. don't turn into a crocodile   KING 469:58
   It's very provoking…to be called an e.   CARR 196:8
   Killers from the e.   HUGH 419:41
   lay a tit's e.   MACD 530:50
   like eating an e.   KIPL 470:78
   No goose, no golden e.   TSON 869:55
   Remorse, the fatal e.   COWP 241:61
   See this e.   DIDE 274:96
   sitting on one addled e.   ELIOT 303:97
   to work on an e.   WELD 896:36
   when one is eating a demnition e.   DICK 267:7
egghead way of the e. is hard   STEV 820:56
eggheads E. are terrible Philistines   NABO 606:44
   E. of the world unite   STEV 820:55
eggs all my e. in one bastard   PARK 638:71
   as a weasel sucks e.   SHAK 749:44
   boil e. in your shoes   LEAR 498:94

Do you like green e. and ham?   SEUSS 728:8
   helps scenery like ham and e.   TWAIN 870:80
   roast their e.   BACON 49:22
   ways to dress e.?   MOORE 596:54
eglantine lush e.   SHEL 787:25
ego e. that can crack crystal   CHEE 209:6
   have a bit of an e.   HOPK 411:77
egocentric dreams are all e.   WAUGH 893:50
ego-games religion without e.-g.   REED 682:86
egomaniacs of neurotics, e.   MANK 545:62
egos E.…setting themselves apart   BUBER 164:22
   individual e., crazy for love   BART 62:9
egotism Apology is only e.   HOLM 408:94
   dilemmas of conscience and e.   SNOW 802:36
egotist E.…person of low taste   BIER 129:28
egregiously making him e. an ass   SHAK 760:77
Egypt against all the firstborn of E.   SHAK 749:45
   ancient E. persisted   RUSS 705:53
   beauty in a brow of E.   SHAK 738:13
   broken reed, on E.   BIBLE 103:35
   brought thee out of…E.   BIBLE 88:23
   brought thee out of…E.   BIBLE 96:44
   called my son out of E.   BIBLE 106:3
   can't judge E. by Aïda   FIRB 323:73
   died…in the land of E.   BIBLE 88:21
   good of the land of E.   BIBLE 88:3
   great cry in E.   BIBLE 88:17
   Jewish Queen of E.   TAYL 837:16
   not at war with E.   EDEN 299:91
   painting was brought to E.   VASA 877:37
   pass through the land of E.   BIBLE 88:16
   this bruised reed, even upon E.   BIBLE 92:39
Egyptian as thou killedst the E.?   BIBLE 88:7
   imagined…ancient E. princess   CASS 199:70
Egyptians E. were urgent upon the people   BIBLE 88:18
   E.…worship an insect   DISR 276:64
Eiffel stick them up your E. Tower   JAY 435:96
eight E. is a good time   STEV 822:8
eighteen E. is a good time   GOLD 360:31
   knew almost as much at e.   JOHN 443:70
eighteenth E.-century houses   YEATS 933:44
eighties vice of the E.   WOLFE 920:99
eighty you are never e.   SEXT 728:14
Eildon down by the E. Tree   BALL 56:89
Einstein As E. once said   PERCY 648:50
   Let E. be!   SQUI 811:42
eird Best thing in e.   HENR 396:53
Eisenhower E.…magic   WHITE 904:3
elaborate suggests an e. hobby   PRIE 668:23
Elaine Daintily alights E.   BETJ 84:1
   E. the fair   TENN 846:15
elasticity maximum e. for our minds   BUTT 178:87
elbow man demanding e. room   WAUGH 892:44
   seated e. to e.   GILL 356:40
   smokes on one e.   MORG 597:80
elbow-chairs Convenience…e.-c.   COWP 241:67
elbows Mr E. and Knees   ANON 24:40
elder e. man not at all   BACON 48:92
elderly care for the e.   FIELD 322:34
   e. man of 42   ASHF 35:93
   nightmare of e. white males   ABBO 1:1
elders discourse of the e.   BIBLE 107:43
   listening to their e.   BALD 53:33
   Nat of oure e.   CHAU 209:86
   party taken over by the e.   FITZ 325:4
eldritch e. light of sundown   DAY 257:85
elect e., the elected   LOWE 521:53
   not…who you are.   THOM 856:47
elected could have e. my chauffeur   KENN 463:45
   e. and anointed ones   WOLFE 920:93
   help them get e.   TAYL 837:19
   plebiscite e. generals   JUVE 453:19
election 11.30pm on e. night   MOND 590:49
   acrimony of the last e.   DICK 268:26
   Democracy substitutes e.   SHAW 778:5
   e. but the making of   NEW 611:51
   e. by the incompetent many   SHAW 778:5
   e. is coming   ELIOT 303:96
   enthusiasm for the e.   WHIT 905:26
   fictitious e. results that elect a fictitious
   president   MOORE 596:45
   Labour Party's e. programme   SNOW 802:46
   worst disaster since my e.   BROWN 157:47
elections leader who could…win e.   MCFA 531:69
   won the e.   SOMO 804:68
electorate province of a despicable e.   PITT 652:37
   What the e. gives   BLAIR 132:5

electors ever put before the e.   SNOW 802:46
Electra Mourning becomes E.   ONEI 625:96
electric Along the e. wires   AUST 44:2
   E. guitars are an abomination   SEGO 726:74
   E. Kool-Aid Acid Test   WOLFE 920:90
   married to an e. light   DIMA 275:19
electrician practical e.   WELLS 898:71
electricity E. is of two kinds   LEAC 496:60
   e. was dripping   THUR 859:23
   think that science is e.   GOUR 365:27
electrons same number of e.   EDDI 299:86
elegance e. is a state of mind   CASS 199:71
   E. is good taste   SNOW 802:34
   e. of Circe's hair   POUND 664:36
   her…un-American e.   SCHL 718:14
   outdone your e.   POUND 665:60
elegancy e., facility…of poesy   SHAK 733:80
elegant erect, e., dogmatic   REST 683:14
   Shakespeherian Rag…so e.   ELIOT 306:57
elegy e. To crown thy hearse?   CAREW 190:51
element can its native e.   MARV 555:57
   e. of fire is quite put out   DONNE 281:74
   e. within us   MURP 604:2
   Of all sweet sounds the life and e.!   COLE 226:3
   random e. in the world   EDDI 298:83
   to the destructive e. submit yourself   CONR 234:2
   yield their names to the e.   TATE 836:3
elementary 'E.', said he   DOYLE 285:71
elements among the e.   PLATH 654:65
   conflict of its e.   BYRON 181:57
   discordant e.   WORD 925:92
   e. and an angelic sprite   DONNE 281:72
   e. are cricket's presiding geniuses   CARD 190:48
   e. in their constituencies   LIPP 512:72
   e. in the record…evoked   WHIT 904:31
   e. of air and earth   SHAK 756:59
   framed us of four e.   MARL 551:75
   Men…defied The e.   WORD 928:58
   mirror of the universal e.   STEI 814:9
   our e., these piercing fires   MILT 581:24
elephant Aida's Child   KIPL 473:41
   e. sings deep in the forest-maze   HUGH 419:50
   e. which brought us hither   MUNDY 603:82
   God…invented…the e.   PICA 650:1
   masterpiece, an E.   DONNE 280:47
   shot an e. in my pyjamas   MARX 557:85
   sleeping with an e.   TRUD 868:23
   teach an e. to dance   MOSS 600:28
   thought he saw an E.   CARR 197:33
elephants e. for want of towns   SWIFT 832:98
   True philosophers are like e.   FONT 329:87
   Women are like e.   FIEL 323:49
elevation scoured us to an e.   LLOY 513:99
eleventh about the e. hour he went   BIBLE 113:77
elf deceiving e.   KEATS 460:64
   queen, an e. most fair   LAYA 496:47
Elfland horns of E.   TENN 841:4
Elginbrodde Martin E.   MACD 530:53
Eli Let E. rejoice   SMART 796:23
   ran unto E.   BIBLE 91:81
Elijah E.…cast his mantle   BIBLE 92:25
   E.…girded up his loins   BIBLE 92:22
   E. went up by a whirlwind   BIBLE 92:28
   send you E. the prophet   BIBLE 107:23
   spirit of E. doth rest on Elisha   BIBLE 92:29
eliminate e. his ability   SCHW 721:65
   e. the unnecessary   HOFF 406:50
   To define is to e.   QUINE 675:51
elimination e. of some disease   SUTH 830:43
Eliot George E.'s husband   MORR 598:93
   How unpleasant to meet Mr E.!   ELIOT 307:36
   T. S. E.'s mother-in-law   BENN 76:37
Elisha spirit of Elijah doth rest on E.   BIBLE 92:29
élites right of colonial é.   ILLI 428:45
Eliza so did take E.   JONS 449:46
Elizabeth God save E.   ANON 20:7
   Queen E. owned silk stockings   SCHU 721:56
   saying…ascribed to Queen E.   ADDI 6:16
Ellie So Tom went home with E.   KING 469:58
elliptics glassy pinnacles correct e.   BISH 131:73
elm tall e.'s shadow   THOM 854:9
   vine-prop e.   SPEN 808:73
elms Behind the e.   PRIOR 669:37
   Beneath those rugged e.   GRAY 369:12
   e., Fade into dimness   ARNO 33:52
   immemorial e.   TENN 842:17
elm-tree round the e.-t. bole   BROW 160:30

elm-trees e.-t. in the…meadows KING 469:52
elopement as if you worked…an e. DOYLE 285:51
eloquence e. in speaking MARIE 550:49
  e., native to famous wits MILT 586:42
  E. should persuade PASC 641:27
  more e. in a sugar touch SHAK 746:68
  splendour of his e. HUME 422:11
  Take e. and break its neck! VERL 879:69
  True e. has no time for e. PASC 640:10
eloquent not e., but he talks well BEAV 67:20
El Salvador peasants in E. S. OROU 627:22
else Who E. but Nelse? ANON 23:5
Elsinore wild and stormy steep, E.! CAMP 186:71
elusive Endings are e. BART 62:12
elves And the e. also HERR 400:48
  spite of all the criticizing e. CHUR 215:46
Elvis ate America BONO 140:64
  finding E. on Mars JOHN 439:70
Elysian dead, but in the E. fields DISR 277:83
emanation genius is a pure e. HAZL 388:84
emancipated more perfect when e. WOLL 921:13
emancipation e. of women MILL 570:77
  understand by e. GREER 372:88
  war for the e. LLOY 513:2
emancipator e.…as a crank BROUN 157:36
embalmer triumph of the e.'s art VIDAL 881:98
embarrass failed to e. the claimant STRA 826:86
  never e. my family JOHN 439:69
embarrassed e. by the words HEMI 393:97
embarrassment e. for those who benefit MARI 550:61
  E. of Riches ALLA 12:34
embassies e.…were everywhere HEAN 389:14
embassy e. of a nation about to go into…
  liquidation MACI 533:8
embers dead man's e. GRAV 367:70
  e. through the room MILT 576:17
  O joy! that in our e. WORD 927:25
emblem e. of ignorance ATAT 37:32
emblems scarves and e. BAIN 52:11
embodiment Law is the true e. GILB 354:11
embody e. the Law GILB 354:11
embrace close clinging to e. ROCH 691:50
  e. me she enclin'd MILT 580:90
  e. of the Venus de Milo DARIO 252:3
  endure, then pity, then e. POPE 660:18
  I e. the purpose of God TENN 846:1
  If I e. my rival RACI 677:85
  none I think do there e. MARV 556:63
  snug e. of the TIME 860:74
  that may e. SURR 829:39
  time to e. BIBLE 100:70
  will be guarded by e. LOWE 519:23
embraced would have e. him STAN 812:61
embraces age in her e. passed ROCH 692:70
  sleepy, soft e. GORD 363:6
embroidered e. cloths YEATS 933:38
embroideries Covered with e. YEATS 933:42
embroidery flower that sad e. wear MILT 578:54
emerald defile…the E. Isle DREN 287:8
  e. eyes GRAY 368:98
  e. twinkles in the grass TENN 845:88
  see the E. Drop RHYS 684:29
emeralds E. big as half a county LAND 488:84
emergency compelled by e. TROL 867:5
  e. happening at a distance BARZ 63:38
  Microscopes…In an E. DICK 272:56
  one e. following upon another FISH 324:76
  Whatever the e. GILB 353:92
emigration e. is…necessity MOOD 594:9
eminence higher e. in whatever DARW 253:15
  only chance of e. SHAW 781:86
  raised To that bad e. MILT 581:18
eminent death reveals the e. SHAW 779:20
Emmanuel call his name E. BIBLE 108:71
emotion coarse e. of mankind ELIOT 304:9
  conveying an e. HEPW 396:61
  degree of my aesthetic e. BELL 71:29
  e. of art ELIOT 305:45
  e. recollected in tranquillity WORD 925:10
  expressing e. in the form of art ELIOT 305:47
  for it is an e. GOLD 360:33
  language concentrating e. BRAU 150:4
  less bounding at e. new ARNO 33:48
  morality touched with e. ARNO 34:61
  plastic e. requires it BOCC 138:27
  Poetry….an escape from e. ELIOT 305:46
  Science…a source of strong e. BARZ 63:35

tranquillity remembered in e. PARK 638:66
  undercurrent of e. UPDI 875:97
  under stress of e. POUND 666:72
  Undisciplined squads of e. ELIOT 308:23
emotional e. depth of woman SCHR 720:43
  e. withdrawal in…overcrowding COUP 239:98
  Humour…is e. chaos THUR 860:53
  physical and e. sides BURG 167:93
emotionally e. I know she is better LEWIS 507:91
emotions basic human e. ROTH 700:34
  e. as palpable and as true HOLM 407:70
  e. entirely foreign WHIS 902:65
  e. of the everydayness STEI 814:9
  grounds for the noble e. RUSK 703:9
  mother of our e. KAND 454:37
  purgation of such e. ARIS 29:54
  raised e. both of rage and fear BYRON 181:48
  see his e. the sport HARDY 381:50
  used his e. even a little SAND 712:84
  world of the e. COLE 227:29
emparadised E. in one another's arms MILT 583:66
empathy politician seeking e. SAFI 708:1
Emperor E. Caligula's Habits LONG 515:38
  E. Claudius LONG 515:39
emperor dey makes you E. ONEI 625:88
  dreamt there was an E. SHAK 765:55
  e. of ice-cream STEV 819:15
  revived and was an e. SHAK 737:78
emperors e. and kings MARL 552:97
  Even e. cannot do it all BREC 151:13
emphasis e. is on the former KUNI 482:38
  e. on what happens next RUSK 703:98
  erotic e. upon it UPDI 874:91
empire all the rule, one e. MILT 585:35
  arch Of the ranged e. fall SHAK 764:12
  bounds of human E. BACON 50:62
  bounds of human E. BACON 47:68
  Britain has lost an E. ACHE 2:29
  British E. GEOR 349:19
  British E. and its Commonwealth CHUR 216:77
  brooders…build the E. OBRI 620:99
  downfall of the British E. CHUR 216:65
  e. is…power in trust DRYD 290:85
  e. must extend, so let extend MILT 586:40
  e. wilderness of freight and rails CRANE 243:17
  German E. arose? HERZL 401:57
  good…for the E. REDM 681:72
  government is…an E. ONEI 625:87
  great e. and little minds BURKE 168:16
  heavily thickening to e. JEFF 436:3
  hold a vaster E. MORR 598:97
  honour of the British E. CHUR 217:84
  How beautiful…under the E. DURR 296:37
  If the Austrian E. did not exist PALA 635:6
  lead Britain and her fading e. MANC 544:44
  liquidation of the British E. CHUR 217:87
  Lo! thy dread e., Chaos! POPE 662:83
  loungers and idlers of the E. DOYLE 284:46
  Mother E. stands splendidly isolated FOST 332:58
  not…Roman or an E. VOLT 883:45
  Pageant of E. SITW 794:74
  play the old Glasgow E. DODD 278:6
  To found a great E. SMITH 798:50
  whole Moghul E. is in our power CLIVE 222:15
  Without the E. HUGH 420:58
empires day of E. has come CHAM 203:59
  don't seek e. RUMS 702:70
  E. and old women BACON 47:57
  faiths and e. gleam SHEL 786:21
  ridiculous e. break like biscuits FULL 341:57
  Vaster than e. MARV 556:62
empirical e. system to be refuted POPP 662:87
  greatest number of e. facts EINS 302:46
empiricist e.…thinks he believes SANT 714:22
empiricists opposed camp of the e. MERT 568:24
employ e. their whole industry SMITH 798:48
employed mind is actually e. JOHN 444:6
  so innocently e. JOHN 444:5
employee In a hierarchy every e. PETER 649:76
employees e. of the government TOOLE 863:14
  love e. and TSON 869:55
employer not a polite e. HOOV 411:63
employers despise e. TSON 869:55
  don't ask e.…to like blacks BORO 145:2
  human e. quite literally MUMF 603:78
  other side of their e. DONO 282:98
employment choosing for e. SWIFT 831:82

e. by authors of simile NASH 609:3
  e. for his idle time WALT 888:49
  e. of the poor in roads MALT 543:19
  engaged in his e. GILB 354:3
  have to seek…gainful e. ACHE 2:21
  Hunting is not a proper e. ADDI 7:44
  lower e. of life JOHN 442:38
  maintain continuous full e. KEYN 465:85
  provide for full e. KEYN 466:90
  Wants steady e. in Hollywood DAVIS 255:52
employs e. the whole mind QUEN 674:39
emptiness Swinburne is just e. to me QUIL 674:48
empty are e. sounds JOHN 442:40
  Art for art's sake is an e. phrase SAND 712:89
  carriage…went e., and e. it returned CH 213:9
  country…disappointingly e. BARN 60:66
  e. as paper SCOTT 722:78
  e. of all human substance SAINT 709:20
  his head be e. SWIFT 830:56
  if e. dreams so please HERR 399:35
  philosophy is virtually e. AYER 45:13
  rich he hath sent e. away BIBLE 115:23
  rich he hath sent e. away BIBLE 128:99
empty-hearted e.-h. whose low sound SHAK 762:53
empty-vaulted through the e.-v. night MILT 577:34
emulation pale and bloodless e. SHAK 757:94
emulsion feeling of e. PERE 648:55
enamoured e. of an ass SHAK 738:10
enchant e. thine ear SHAK 732:51
enchanted holy and e. COLE 226:10
enchanter ghosts from an e. fleeing SHEL 783:43
enchanting What music is more e. SMITH 799:78
enchantment distance lends e. CAMP 186:66
  e.—what a great epoch LARI 490:19
enchilada He's the Big E. EHRL 301:27
enclosure what more magnificent e. JOHN 440:99
encomiast e. always knows JOHN 445:44
encounter free and open e. MILT 579:69
  turf-dances of human e. ALLEN 12:36
encourage to e. the others VOLT 882:37
encouragement e. of comic strips UPDI 874:86
  never-failing sympathy and e. WODE 919:63
encroachment gradual e. of ideas KEYN 466:89
encroachments e. on their property GALS 344:23
encyclopedia E. behind…world LAMB 486:41
end all the economists…laid e. to e. SHAW 781:99
  always treat humanity…as an e. KANT 455:45
  around at the e. to know KENN 464:53
  beginning, a muddle, and an e. LARK 491:46
  beginning is assuredly the e. WILL 913:48
  beginning is often the e. ELIOT 309:49
  beginning of the e. TALL 835:84
  Better Beast and know your e. DEVL 264:32
  Better is the e. of a thing BIBLE 101:78
  blessed the latter e. of Job BIBLE 94:80
  came to an e. all wars LLOY 513:3
  come to a bad e. BEER 69:76
  consider the e. in everything LAFO 485:7
  Consumption is the sole e. SMITH 798:49
  death, a necessary e. SHAK 747:89
  death…puts an e. to old age LABR 483:71
  dream comes to an e. GIRO 358:84
  e. a contest quicker SHER 787:46
  e. and object of conquest ALEX 11:19
  e. cannot justify the means HUXL 425:82
  e. is bitter as wormwood BIBLE 99:13
  e. is not yet BIBLE 113:85
  e. may justify the means TROT 868:21
  e. more than in the beginning JONS 450:61
  e. of all our exploring ELIOT 309:48
  e. of ane auld sang OGIL 623:43
  e. of a perfect day BOND 139:52
  e. of Britain GAIT 343:89
  e. of everything we call life WELLS 899:94
  e. of man is an action CARL 192:96
  e. of May HOUS 415:70
  e. of the beginning CHUR 217:86
  e. of the fight KIPL 471:5
  e. of this day's business SHAK 748:22
  e. precedes the beginning ELIOT 307:1
  e. thereof are the ways of death BIBLE 99:27
  e. where 'e began KIPL 472:19
  e., where I begun DONNE 280:56
  e. which is a piece of propaganda JOYCE 452:97
  e. which was no part SMITH 798:49
  E. without audience SHAK 733:51
  fight on until the e. HAIG 376:66

fresh, usual words to the e.	FORD 330:4	e. passively	WILL 911:2
go on till you come to the e.	CARR 195:86	e., then pity, then embrace	POPE 660:18
great e. comes slowly	DU 293:74	E. what is difficult to e.	HIRO 403:4
great enterprises seldom e.	ELIZ 310:66	life…difficult to e.	LABR 483:70
In my beginning is my e.	ELIOT 308:13	man will not merely e.	FAUL 318:64
in the e., there was no e.	WHITE 903:92	**enemies** Against his e.	SAINT 709:14
It hath no e.	SHAK 769:47	all e. under his feet	BIBLE 121:15
laid e. to e.	PARK 637:54	all the e. that I hated	BUCH 164:30
let me know mine e.	BOOK 143:48	Blind among e.	MILT 586:47
lies frae e. to e.	BURNS 170:67	bring our e. to justice	BUSH 175:8
Mankind must put an e. to war	KENN 462:18	careful in the choice of his e.	WILDE 908:4
means used to bring about the e.	WHIS 902:61	distinguished by your e.	HOOV 411:70
minutes hasten to their e.	SHAK 772:24	e. of freedom do not argue	INGE 429:52
my e. is my beginning	MARY 558:18	e. of truth than lies	NIET 615:4
no happy e. to it	HEMI 394:6	e. to Ireland	EDGE 299:3
not a means, it is an e.	ORWE 630:5	forget to hate your e.	ROGE 695:30
Now the e., I take it	MONT 592:75	giving his e. the slip	STER 817:71
only e. of writing	JOHN 442:51	Happiness…conquering one's e.	GENG 349:8
our being's e. and aim!	POPE 660:23	If laws are their e.	BURKE 168:22
poem…whose e. I knew	FROST 339:12	inherited 100 per cent of his e.	BUSH 175:94
purpose is beyond the e.	ELIOT 309:39	in the presence of mine e.	BIBLE 94:2
recurrent e. of the unending	ELIOT 309:42	love your e.	BIBLE 109:93
see what the e. is	ANON 18:66	make thine e. thy footstool	BIBLE 97:73
should make an e.	JONS 450:57	many e. that know not	SHAK 775:11
simplicity of their e.	FUSE 342:74	mausoleums for his e.	LINK 511:56
something ere the e.	TENN 840:66	mine e. that trouble me	BOOK 143:49
sorrow without e.	AESC 8:60	naked to mine e.	SHAK 775:21
source and e.…of art	POPE 658:53	no perpetual e.	PALM 636:22
speaking picture, with this e.	SIDN 791:19	only e. accidentally	ROUS 701:48
the e. of the way	PAST 641:41	rescues your estate from your e.	BROU 157:33
there's an e. on't	JOHN 444:88	scourge of his e.	GIBB 351:56
think what may be the e.	WHYM 906:65	Shaw has no e.	WILDE 910:64
this day to e. myself	TENN 847:34	speak with the e. in the gate	BIBLE 98:93
This is not the e. of anything	REAG 680:59	telling it gains you e.	RUIZ 702:65
thoughts to an e.	SMITH 800:2	through his e.	HUGH 419:26
triumphantly until the e.!	STEV 822:1	**enemy** afraid of his e.	PLUT 656:11
understood I their e.	BIBLE 96:42	as the e. to Canada	MOOD 594:10
unimproved e.	THOR 857:84	death is no such terrible e.	BACON 47:74
Waiting for the e.	EMPS 314:64	defense against the e.	PICA 650:98
War that will E. War	WELLS 898:84	despised the armed E.	ALBE 10:99
Whose e. is destruction	BIBLE 123:59	e. and your friend	TWAIN 872:27
Wisdom begins at the e.	WEBS 895:99	e. came and sowed tares	BIBLE 112:50
endanger e. my soul gratis?	SHAK 743:71	e. faints not	CLOU 222:20
endearment Terms of E.	MCMU 537:85	e.—for friendship's sake	BLAKE 135:81
endears all the more e.	TENN 841:1	e. half a mile away	MUIR 602:55
endeavour awake e. for defence	SHAK 738:20	E. has been here	HOBB 404:30
Creative E. lost	WAUGH 892:25	e. hath done this	BIBLE 112:51
disinterested e. to learn	ARNO 33:40	e. into a friend	KING 468:44
e. to find out	WELL 898:65	e. more mighty than he seems	SHAK 745:40
e., wish, desire, or long for	SPIN 810:29	e. of clear language	ORWE 628:62
listlessness, nor mad e.	WORD 927:27	e. of clear language	ORWE 629:89
lost faith in individual e.	CARL 191:83	e. of good art	CONN 233:69
Virtue…too painful an e.	POPE 661:47	e. of liberty	ROOS 696:59
endeavours e. are unlucky explorers	DOUG 283:22	e. of life	SPEN 808:77
e., in all branches of knowledge	ARNO 33:35	e. of the good	VOLT 883:47
ended e. by your inability	GONC 363:94	e. of the human race	MILL 572:17
griefs are e.	SHAK 759:66	e. reads the list of their names	WELL 897:53
no sooner was it e.	GLAS 359:99	e. to despotism	GARI 346:47
Endellion St E.…ring of bells	BETJ 83:94	e. to human happiness	JOHN 446:56
ending bread-sauce of the happy e.	JAMES 433:47	friends, but above all an e.	MULR 602:73
got your happy e.	MILE 569:53	great e. of clear language	ORWE 628:62
Never e., still beginning	DRYD 291:38	great e. of clear language	ORWE 629:89
second act and the e.	ANON 24:41	hands of the e.	ANON 25:60
endings E. are elusive	BART 62:12	Have no e.	YEATS 934:55
endless e. and indestructible	WILL 914:55	I am the e. you killed	OWEN 632:61
humility is e.	ELIOT 308:18	If thine e. be hungry	BIBLE 100:52
nowhere, and is e.	LARK 491:43	invasion of a common e.	KITC 475:4
end-run trying to e.-r. him	REAG 680:52	kill more…than the e.	BALD 54:47
ends actually deteriorated e.	HUXL 425:83	kisses of an e. are deceitful	BIBLE 100:58
all the e. of the earth shall see	BIBLE 104:48	Know the e.	SUN 829:27
burnt-out e. of smoky days	ELIOT 305:27	last e.…is death	BIBLE 121:15
But for his own e.	BEAU 67:17	man is e. to every man	HOBB 404:27
constantly begins and e.	HAZL 387:70	Man is not the e. of Man	PAINE 634:92
divinity that shapes our e.	SHAK 755:37	Mine e.'s dog	SHAK 764:96
e. at half past five	EWART 316:24	O mine e.?	BIBLE 92:26
e. by our beginnings know	DENH 261:95	put an e. in their mouths	SHAK 760:80
e. I think criminal	KEYN 465:77	Show me an e. of literature	HAMI 379:4
e. of the earth	KIPL 470:81	sincere friend or a sincere e.	HUGO 420:66
pursuing of the best e.	HUTC 424:51	speed toward the e.	HALS 378:94
shallow conversational e.	SASS 716:75	still the e.	BIBLE 94:86
violent delights have violent e.	SHAK 736:60	strike the e.	PANK 636:31
endurance e., and courage	SCOTT 722:81	sweet e., France	SIDN 790:11
e., science, temper	LONS 517:69	The eye is the e.	WILD 911:89
serenity essential to e.	ACHE 2:36	Thinking is the great e. of perfection	CONR 235:18
sheer courage and e.	WAVE 893:58	unrelenting e.	WASH 890:83
endure better to e. it	JOHN 442:51	with the wrong e.	BRAD 149:74
cannot e. my Lady Tongue	SHAK 744:96	worst friend and e. is but Death	BROO 156:9

energies all the e. of his life	PIER 651:5
e. and skills	KEYN 466:86
religious principles and e.	BERD 78:87
energy convert weaknesses…into	
burnable e.	BELL 74:92
deprive the soul of its e.	BLOOM 137:4
dissipation of e. begin?	KELV 461:81
E. is Eternal Delight	BLAKE 134:38
e. of a whole generation	THOM 855:43
e. of mighty rivers	MILL 572:26
e. stored up	GERS 350:37
every e. he may put forward	CURZ 249:51
Force is…an invisible e.	LEON 503:12
lakes of mental e.	GREER 372:91
managed to exude e.	SHAR 776:42
minimum expenditure of e.	WILS 915:85
reason and e.…are necessary	BLAKE 134:37
Science is an all-pervasive e.	BARZ 63:35
tempest, a redundant e.	WORD 925:89
time and e. from	MORE 597:67
enfant terrible free to be an e. t.	SART 715:41
engaged When a Forsyte was e.	GALS 344:23
engaging Sex is e.	JIANG 438:49
engendered e. by honesty	MURP 604:4
engine curious e.	WEBS 895:9
greatest e. of temporary opinion	HAZL 388:76
great, growing e. of change	TOFF 862:92
in dirt, the reasoning e. lies	ROCH 691:57
science is a two-handed e.	MONT 591:62
small e. that causes revolutions	SHEE 782:7
steam…work the e.	WATT 891:2
this formidable e.	COOP 236:54
throw herself in front of the e.	SHAW 778:87
two-handed e. at the door	MILT 578:52
engineer glorified sanitary e.	STRA 826:83
engineering e. of consent	BERN 81:47
engineers e. and physicists	KRUT 481:28
look out for e.	PAGN 634:86
today are our e.	LEUP 505:49
engines by our resistless e.	CARL 191:81
e. based on mechanical	LEUP 505:49
e. to play a little on our own	BURKE 168:28
so noiseless when the e. stopped	HEAN 389:13
England amuses the people of E.	JOHN 443:61
any village in E.	TROL 866:88
art-form…invented in E.	BEER 70:92
a town in the South of E.	ORWE 627:40
Be E. what she will	CHUR 215:52
between France and E.	JERR 437:41
bow was made in E.	DOYLE 285:57
Church of E.	ROYD 701:58
common law of E.	HERB 397:83
continent will not suffer E.	DISR 276:42
death of Nelson was felt in E.	SOUT 805:9
deep, deep sleep of E.	ORWE 628:51
defence of E.	BALD 54:48
describing E. in a phrase	ORWE 628:60
dress and manners in E.	SHAW 777:62
dull mercantile E.	BUCH 164:27
earthquake were to engulf E.	JERR 437:42
east longitude from E.	MUNDY 603:83
E. and America	GREN 373:4
E. and America	SHAW 781:98
E. and Saint George!	SHAK 746:44
E. are a good cricket team	SMITH 798:58
E.…comfortable time-lag	WELLS 898:92
E. does not love coalitions	DISR 276:62
E. full of morons	WODE 919:76
E. has greater counties	CRIP 244:49
E. has saved herself	PITT 653:49
E.…in my childhood	ORWE 628:51
E. invented the phrase	BAGE 51:82
E.…is a fen	WORD 925:11
E. is a garden	KIPL 474:72
E. is a garden	KIPL 474:73
E. is a great…nation	GARI 346:47
E. is a nation	NAPO 607:68
E. is not ruined	PRIE 668:28
E. is not the jewelled isle	ORWE 628:59
E. is one of the greatest	PALM 636:26
E. is the mother of Parliaments	BRIG 152:32
E. is the paradise of women	FLOR 328:76
E. is unrivalled for two things	DISR 277:95
E. mourns for her dead	BINY 130:51
E., my E?	HENL 395:40
E. people have good table manners	MIKES 569:51
E.'s chief defence	PHIL 650:89

E. was niver improved	DUNNE 295:23
genial E.	TENN 841:99
Give but an E. his whore	OTWAY 631:33
impossible for an E.	SHAW 780:61
last great E. is low	TENN 844:70
man, nay, even more, an E.	MORI 598:83
No E. is ever fairly beaten	SHAW 781:82
not one an E.	WALP 887:38
one E. could beat three Frenchmen	ADDI 6:21
part of an E.'s constitution	AUST 43:77
part of every E.'s education	HUGH 420:54
powerful image to your average E.	SMITH 799:62
remains an E.!	GILB 354:95
Remember that you are an E.	RHOD 684:23
rights of an E.	JUNI 453:11
takes off his hat to God's E.	SHAW 779:32
the Irishman turned E.	OBRI 620:99
vain, ill-natured thing, an E.	DEFOE 258:14
what an E. believes	SHAW 781:83
Englishmen absurd nature of E.	PEPYS 647:33
damned mischievous E.	SCOTT 725:55
Englishman does not travel to see E.	STER 818:98
E. act better than Frenchmen	BENN 76:40
E. are born gloaters	OBRI 620:99
E....nervously excitable race	DAVI 254:30
E. never will be slaves	SHAW 778:91
find E. doing it	SHAW 777:65
first to his E.?	MILT 579:81
love of E.	THOM 854:10
Mad dogs and E.	COWA 239:13
our very name as E.	PITT 653:46
When two E. meet	JOHN 442:53
Englishwoman E. is so refined	SMITH 800:94
E.'s clothes	SITW 794:74
Englishwomen better than E.	BENN 76:40
engraving E. then, is, in brief	RUSK 704:30
engulf chasm that threatens to e. him	BANN 59:39
enigma e. of the fever chart	ELIOT 308:21
mystery inside an e.	CHUR 216:73
enjoy did e. the music	JOHN 441:4
do not e. it	JULI 452:6
e. their triumph	HAMM 379:8
here e. the shade	JONS 450:51
highly taught and yet not to e.	ELIOT 304:11
impossible to e. idling	JERO 437:28
learnt to e. them	MORT 599:18
liberty, that we'll e.	JONS 449:35
principal business of life is to e.	BUTL 178:70
enjoyed e. talking to her	SITW 794:76
enjoying world...worth e.	DRYD 291:38
enjoyment done with e.	RUSK 703:1
essence of Toryism is e.	BAGE 51:79
innocent e.	GILB 354:3
more ascetic reason than mere e.	STARK 813:72
receives as complete e.	HUME 422:11
retrospective e. of successful effort	SHIP 789:76
enjoys Englishman never e. himself	HERB 397:85
enlarge e., diminish, interline	SWIFT 832:96
E. my life	JOHN 441:18
enlargement e. of the language	JOHN 442:41
enlightenment herald of e.	BOOK 144:79
intellectual e.	CURZ 249:53
literature...as transcendent e.	COND 230:84
motto of e.	KANT 455:42
promises freedom or e.	SNYD 803:52
enmities e. between nations	KENN 463:27
enmity at e. with joy	WORD 927:27
e. between thy seed	BIBLE 86:53
e. o'th' air	SHAK 763:69
enormity e. of the task	ACHE 2:34
enormous Like an e. yes	LARK 490:25
The E. Room was the greatest book	STEIN 815:13
enough E., if something from our hands	WORD 928:59
e., now, O Lord	BIBLE 92:23
first cries 'Hold, e.!'	SHAK 769:46
if we only get e. of them	JAMES 434:61
not e. jails	HUMP 422:17
poverty is never having e.	WYLIE 931:24
rainbow is e.	SHAN 776:27
seen e. of one war	JEFF 436:17
Two cheers are quite e.	FORS 332:53
enquire E., define, distinguish	ROCH 691:53
enquiries e. about the UK climate	SAMU 710:81
enrich how to e. a new nation	STIG 824:45
ense calamus saevior e. patet	BURT 174:72
enshrined e. in 10,000 indexes	ALLEN 12:37
ensigns ships and their e.	ROBE 689:17
enslave No woman shall ever e. me	SHAW 778:87
enslaved either free or e.	GRIL 373:13
e. as farm stock	SHAW 780:55
ensnared beauty hath e. thee	SHAK 733:63
ensure e. summer in England	WALP 887:29
entangle e. those shall feed	WEBS 895:97
entente e. cordiale	LOUIS 518:1
enter e. most intimately into	HUME 422:5
Let no-one e.	ANON 26:86
save that they e.	WILL 913:42
enterprise e. of martial kind	GILB 355:32
for or against their e.	DICK 268:51
hazard in the glorious e.	MILT 580:99
hold no brief for private e.	BURT 174:66
If E. is afoot	KEYN 465:82
leave it to private e.	KEYN 466:88
most important stage of any e.	PLATO 655:96
nurse of...heroic e.	BURKE 169:35
private e.	GALB 343:95
steady stream of e.	KEYN 466:87
system of soft e.	ARNO 34:74
there's more e.	YEATS 933:42
enterprises e. that require	THOR 857:88
great e. seldom end	ELIZ 310:66
entertain better to e. an idea	JARR 435:85
entertaining more e. than...boats	STEV 821:70
entertainment at an E. for Friends	SWIFT 832:94
craving e.; volatile	FERB 320:94
exotic and irrational e.	JOHN 446:46
proffered e.	TROL 866:84
regard literature as e.	COND 230:84
That's E.	DIETZ 274:10
under the head of E.	BEAV 67:27
we've dominated e.	JOHN 439:77
what lantern e.	SHAK 753:59
enthral Except You e. me	DONNE 281:71
enthrall Till they e. themselves	MILT 582:43
enthralled e. as I am	SHAK 770:93
free, but to thyself e.	MILT 583:85
enthroned E. i'th' market-place	SHAK 765:24
enthusiasm as e. would permit	GOSSE 364:17
E. is nothing	MILL 573:39
e. turns to bitterness	ZATO 936:90
fired with e.	LOMB 515:34
For sportswriters...it's the e.	FRAY 335:30
never to let your e. be soured	CURZ 249:53
Nothing great...without e.	EMER 312:18
Once we have made e. ridiculous	STAEL 811:47
play with manic e.	LYTT 524:18
poison of e. and superstition	SMITH 798:53
rage and your e. for the election	WHIT 905:26
Whatever...my e. or impatience	SHIP 789:77
entire e. and whole and perfect	SPRI 811:39
entirety man in his e.	BECK 68:33
entities What are the fundamental e.	KUHN 481:35
entitlement E. spending	ARMEY 30:69
entity not an animate e.	OBRI 620:3
entomologists ready labelled as e.	STARK 813:72
entrails yearn to crush out their e.!	BRON 155:98
entrance e. to a quarrel	SHAK 751:18
From my first e. in	HERB 397:98
grace the e. to Paradise	MICH 569:36
men have one e. into life	BIBLE 107:35
entrances e. of this world	BIBLE 107:26
exits and their e.	SHAK 749:48
entrepreneur brain of a Yankee e.	ONET 626:12
e. is no longer the bold	ROBI 690:38
entrepreneurs e. who have the guts	RODG 693:93
entrepreneurship E. can be learned	DRUC 287:17
entry value on e. into England	STEN 816:49
envelope semi-transparent e.	WOOLF 922:26
envenomed delusive and e. pleasure	BRON 155:89
envies e., all of them sad	AUDEN 40:13
envious e. at the foolish	BIBLE 96:41
silence e. tongues	SHAK 775:22
environment e. and its teaching	LAWR 495:34
forced...through e. and pressures	FAUL 318:66
humdrum issues like the e.	THAT 850:21
luxury of a peacetime e.	TRUM 868:39
moral e.	HAVEL 385:29
possible in his e.	RUSS 705:45
so well adjusted to his e.	JARR 435:82
We accept...great inequality of e.	CARN 193:49
envy Death...extinguisheth e.	BACON 47:76
E. and calumny and hate and pain	SHEL 786:4
E. and wrath shorten the life	BIBLE 108:59
E. bark at thee	SPEN 808:67
e....is force t'admire!	DANI 252:89
E. itself, and Vanity	MAND 545:54
e. no man's happiness	SHAK 749:57
e. of brilliant men	BEER 69:76
e. of great Caesar	SHAK 748:25
e. of the devil	BIBLE 107:30
e. oft his shadow be	JONS 450:51
e. of those of others	RYLE 707:80
e. of thy happy lot	KEATS 459:57
e. prevails	WALL 886:16
From e., hatred, and malice	BOOK 140:81
he of e. could obtain	SURR 829:36
I shall never attain: E.	PARK 638:75
mixture of e., vindictiveness	DISR 277:82
prisoners of e.	ILLI 428:47
Too low for e.	COWL 240:35
who is able to stand before e.?	BIBLE 100:57
enwrought e. with golden	YEATS 933:38
ephemeral not interested in the e.	WILD 911:88
story is e. and doomed	FAUL 318:63
Ephratah Bethlehem, E.	BIBLE 106:12
epic classical era was e.	HUGO 420:60
the e. of Dunkirk	PRIE 668:19
thundrous E. lilted out	TENN 841:96
epicure the e. would say	SMITH 801:21
epidemic Aids e.	WHITE 902:72
living this e. every minute	KRAM 480:5
epidemics Fashions...induced e.	SHAW 780:46
epididymis psyches...tied to their e.	STEP 817:60
epigram Impelled to try an e.	PARK 637:46
purrs like an e.	MARQ 554:34
What is an E.	COLE 226:6
epigrams Aphorisms and e.	DUDEK 293:78
despotism tempered by e.	CARL 192:12
epigraph for want of an e.	SIDN 791:23
epilepsy will cure e.	THEO 851:40
epilogue good play needs no e.	SHAK 751:94
episcopalian I am a E. just now	FLEM 327:62
episode e. in the life of a man	STAEL 811:44
epitaph are no e. of that oak	DONNE 281:79
e. drear	KIPL 471:5
e. on the Kennedy administration	WHITE 903:2
e. to be my story	FROST 339:10
Let no man write my e.	EMMET 313:59
that may be his e.	STEV 823:27
epitaphs nice derangement of e.	SHER 787:40
epithalamic e. conjunction	ANDR 16:25
epitome all mankind's e.	DRYD 290:88
between an e. and a parody	ISAA 430:87
golf course is the e.	GIRA 358:80
epoch civilization of one e.	CONN 233:80
e. of folly and shame	ZOLA 937:4
e. unrivalled in world history	LARI 490:19
great e. in our lives	MOOD 594:6
most memorable e.	ADAMS 5:89
equal all men are created e.	JEFF 436:12
as men become more e.	TOCQ 861:85
but which is e. to anything	LEAC 496:58
e. before a fish	HOOV 411:62
e. dominion is given to woman	STAN 812:66
e. rights of men and women	UNIT 873:69
e. to all things	GOLD 362:70
E., unclassed, tribeless	SHEL 785:81
except that of being e. to us	TRIL 866:68
in the dust be e. made	SHIR 789:83
maintenance of an e. number	SMITH 798:46
men and women are created e.	STAN 812:62
more e. than others	ORWE 629:75
never be completely e.	CUNN 248:26
reason, is naturally e. in all men	DESC 263:18
relatively e.	TOOLE 863:13
sees with e. eye, as God	POPE 660:9
separate but e.	WARR 889:68
ta'en with e. thanks	SHAK 754:88
That all men are e.	HUXL 424:64
turn your thoughts to becoming his e.	CONF 230:88
With e. mind	DRYD 292:59
equality apostles of e.	ARNO 33:55
democracy is love of e.	MONT 593:94
E. of condition is incompatible	COOP 236:52
E. of opportunity	KENN 463:25
E. would be a heaven	TROL 867:3
first e. is equity	HUGO 421:93
freedom and e.	ROUS 700:43
general state of e.	JOHN 445:21
Liberty, E., Adultery	BELL 73:79
Liberty, E., Fraternity!	LAMA 486:24

majestic e. of laws — FRAN 333:93
make some headway towards e. — FALU 317:42
never be complete e. — ANTH 27:9
really great in favour of e. — SHAW 781:86
equalize attempt to level…never e. — BURKE 168:31
e. before the others have scored — BLAN 136:88
equalized expectation is e. — ILLI 428:46
equally comes e. to us all — DONNE 281:79
henceforth be bestowed e. — SHAK 748:26
not e. happy — JOHN 443:82
equals 2 times 2 e. 13 — LICH 509:17
e., free from tyranny? — LANY 489:6
far from being our e. — NAPO 607:64
First among E. — ARCH 28:36
little friendship…between e. — BACON 50:50
Republic of e. — BABE 45:22
equation e. will come out at last — MACN 538:7
Equator disrespectfully of the E.! — SMITH 801:15
equestrian e. classes — SHAW 781:73
equilibrium functions…in e. — SPEN 806:41
human psychic e. — MAMET 544:33
point of e. will be known — JEVO 438:45
equinoctial beams under the e. — BURT 174:79
equipment e. by the truckload — WELL 897:50
shabby e. always deteriorating — ELIOT 308:23
survive with that e. — DAVIS 255:55
equity first equality is e. — HUGO 421:93
of all e. and justice — KNOX 476:18
principles of e. and justice — PEEL 646:9
equivalent musical e. of the towers — BEEC 69:61
United Nations is not…internal e. — EDEN 299:90
equivalents e. are given — WORD 929:66
era dated a new e. — THOR 857:77
ending of an historic e. — NEHRU 610:29
new e. is upon us — MACA 524:23
primitive e. was lyrical — HUGO 420:60
eras buried under the shale of e. — RAND 678:14
Erebus pit of lowest E. — WORD 928:51
erect e., elegant, dogmatic — REST 683:14
e.…his own tomb — SHAK 745:25
forms of virtue are e. — FUSE 342:76
free man cannot long stand e. — WRIS 930:88
Unless…he can E. himself — DANI 252:90
erections E., Ejaculations — BUKO 165:49
Erin when for E. dear we fall — SULL 828:17
Ernest only really safe name is E. — WILDE 909:33
erotic E. practices…diversified — BELL 74:90
most e. part of the body — BART 62:21
not more e. emphasis — UPDI 874:91
err fools shall not e. therein — BIBLE 103:34
Kings and Governments may e. — HERB 397:79
Man will e. — GOET 360:16
mortal, and may e. — SHIR 789:82
most may e. — DRYD 290:91
reas'ning but to e. — POPE 660:16
they do not e. — SCOTT 723:90
To e. is human — ANON 24:21
To e. is human — POPE 658:60
errancy die in e. — ABU 1:10
errand in thy joyous e. — FITZ 324:86
send the child a e. — DICK 268:43
slightest e. now to the Antipodes — SHAK 744:95
erred have e. exceedingly — BIBLE 91:97
while I e. — GOET 360:26
error commonest e. in politics — CECIL 202:30
discharge from sin and e. — ELIOT 309:47
E. is all around it — NICO 614:94
E.…never approached — METT 568:29
e. of his way — BIBLE 125:20
e.'s fenny bogs — ROCH 691:56
e. to imagine the loudest — BURKE 168:2
full of natural e. — PASC 640:13
grave e. to believe — PISS 652:35
judge of truth, in endless e. — POPE 660:17
myopia makes all e. mortal — LOWE 521:57
not a disease but an e. of judgement — DICK 265:60
not wholly free from e. — VINER 881:15
obstinacy, and of e. — POPP 663:98
only one inborn e. — SCHO 719:35
perpetuate an e. for ever — SCHO 719:32
persistent leaning towards e. — CONR 234:10
response to e. that counts — GIOV 357:72
Where there is e. — THAT 850:16
errors common e. of our life — SIDN 791:21
containing the grossest e. — TOLS 863:7
e. are volitional — JOYCE 452:90
E., like straws — DRYD 289:51

E. look so very ugly — ELIOT 303:72
e. of the rich — CHES 211:52
knowledge…mixed with our e. — POPP 663:97
less e. of fact — GREE 371:67
multitude of e. — DESC 263:23
point out other people's e. — ELIOT 304:7
reasoned e. — HUXL 426:12
some female e. — POPE 658:68
tares of spiritual e. — HOBB 404:30
erudition e. and his historic impact — NISB 616:39
eruptions Bimbo e. — WRIG 929:76
Esaias spoken of by the prophet E. — BIBLE 108:74
Esau E. despised his birthright — BIBLE 87:85
E.…is a hairy man — BIBLE 87:86
E. sells his birthright — BIBLE 87:83
E. was a cunning hunter — BIBLE 87:84
escalating both sides e. — KENN 464:52
escalator e. from the Social — HUXL 425:75
Escalus thing to be tempted, E. — SHAK 758:19
escape Author of the Whole e. — POPE 662:81
from which he made his e. — MILL 573:43
never quite e. — SMITH 799:60
No man should e. — OPPE 626:17
No one can e. — PLATO 655:86
nothing to e. from — ELIOT 309:54
Poetry…an e. from emotion — ELIOT 305:46
poor…can hardly ever e. — FORS 331:34
women cannot e. it — GIBB 352:70
writing as an e. from — WILL 913:30
escapist e. fiction — GALB 343:3
escarpments screes on her e. — HEAN 389:7
eschew e. the little turf-dances — ALLEN 12:36
escort burning building without an e. — VAN 877:34
Eskimo Hottentot and every E. — LEHR 502:72
Esmé For E. — SALI 711:63
esoteric e. matters — GOWE 365:29
especial Sweet e. rural scene — HOPK 412:92
espionage no place where e. is not — SUN 829:31
espoused fairest, my e. — MILT 583:76
essay e. on 'self-indulgence' — WAUGH 891:13
good e.…must draw its curtain — WOOLF 922:35
Of seeming arms…a short e. — DRYD 292:52
essays greatest of Man's e. — TOYN 864:29
not much good at e. — BETJ 83:95
essence effluence of bright e. increate — MILT 582:36
e. and quintessence — LOWE 519:21
e. of a book — NABO 606:41
e. of an argument — SCHL 718:11
e. of Christianity — WHIT 904:14
e. of freedom — ASTE 36:31
e. of inhumanity — SHAW 777:66
e. of music is revelation — HEINE 391:49
e. of real human love — ELIOT 303:83
e. of technology — HEID 391:43
e. of Toryism — BAGE 51:79
e. of war is violence — MACA 526:56
existence comes before e. — SART 715:48
existence precedes e.? — SART 715:49
glassy e., like an angry ape — SHAK 758:26
poet gives us his e. — WOOLF 923:55
poetry is the e. — STEV 820:41
uncompounded is their e. — MILT 581:9
very e. of phenomena — PAST 642:44
with our mixed e. — BYRON 181:57
essential e. oneness of mankind — STEI 814:9
Secrecy is the first e. — RICH 686:67
that something is e. — RENO 683:6
what is e. is invisible — SAINT 709:17
essentiality eternal and infinite e. — SPIN 811:36
essentials e. of a…Prime Minister — WILS 916:4
Essex fog on the E. marshes — DICK 269:79
In E. seek them all — CRIP 244:49
establishment found a handsome e. — DICK 270:14
the American e. — TIME 860:74
estate comfortable e. of widowhood — GAY 347:83
e. of the realm — MACA 525:49
Fallen from his high e. — DRYD 291:36
fourth e. in the politics — HAZL 388:80
grown to man's e. — STEV 823:14
in low e. began — TENN 843:48
ordered their e. — ALEX 11:23
out of my e. the sum of £50,000 — CHES 211:38
relieving the human e. — DEWEY 264:43
rescues your e. from your enemies — BROU 157:33
they had his e. — DRYD 290:89
estates live upon their own e. — EDGE 299:2
O, that e., degrees, and offices — SHAK 740:63

residents from raw e. — LARK 491:33
esteem come to e. the universe — FONT 328:85
coward in thine own e. — SHAK 767:88
e. not of that obedience — MILT 579:77
expressions of e. for Mr Boss — BAND 58:25
far above him…my e. — DRYD 289:62
higher e. among the gods — PLATO 655:82
lessened my e. of a king — PEPYS 647:30
object of love and e. — LAMB 486:44
esteemed more e. in Russia — SNOW 802:42
not with me e. — SHAK 740:82
shall be lightly e. — BIBLE 91:80
estimate know'st thy e. — SHAK 772:35
estimation highest e. of learning — SIDN 790:16
estranged e. from myself — HUGO 420:68
esurientes E. implevit bonis — BIBLE 128:99
eternal blasted to e. damnation! — SHAW 781:87
Death and I Am found e. — MILT 585:26
e. incognito — BARN 60:63
e., inexorable lapse — STOWE 826:76
e. monotony of passion — FLAU 326:35
e. not ourselves — ARNO 34:63
E. Passion! — ARNO 32:17
e. reciprocity of tears — OWEN 632:66
e. want of pence — TENN 841:92
Hope springs e. — POPE 660:20
idea alone is e. — FLAU 326:28
no e. allies — PALM 636:22
not for spreading e. truths — BLISS 136:96
not so much e. vigilance — ORWE 627:39
portion of the E. — SHEL 786:2
Primary word addresses the e. Thou — BUBER 164:23
prompts th'e. sigh — POPE 660:23
society as something e. — ORWE 628:54
summer is e. — GUY 375:50
to be boy e. — SHAK 770:74
trust was with the e. — MILT 581:20
variations on the e. struggle — LIN 510:32
eternities starlit with e. unknown — SASS 717:77
eternity are from e. — HOUS 416:73
As doth e. — KEATS 459:55
at last e. changes him — MALL 542:96
certain species of e. — SPIN 810:27
circular e. may seem atrocious — BIOY 130:56
dance round to all E. — FLET 327:64
day joins the past e. — BYRON 180:33
Deserts of vast e. — MARV 556:62
Desire paces E. — DUNC 295:13
e. in an hour — BLAKE 135:66
E. is in love — BLAKE 134:41
'E.' is there — DICK 273:76
e.…of life — ALLEN 12:39
e. of nothing — RUSK 704:37
E. of pleasures — FORD 330:12
e. of print — WOOLF 922:36
e. of thought — WORD 924:85
E. shut in a span — CRAS 244:84
E.! thou pleasing, dreadful thought! — ADDI 7:38
E. was in our lips — SHAK 764:17
E. was in that moment — CONG 231:81
e. without a solecism — BROW 158:65
feel a trace of e. — RILKE 687:85
From Here to E. — JONES 447:87
From here to e. — KIPL 470:80
from the soul's e. — ROSS 698:92
heirs of all e. — SHAK 733:67
image of e. — BYRON 180:46
in view of God and e. — CAVE 201:18
is the e. that awaits you — THOM 855:32
Lives in E.'s sunrise — BLAKE 134:48
radiance of e. — CLAR 220:60
saw E. the other night — VAUG 878:49
shadows of e. — VAUG 878:44
Silence is deep as E. — CARL 192:22
silence of e. — STEV 822:4
sing of Time or E. — TENN 846:28
speculations of e. or infinitude — ADDI 6:22
teacher affects e. — ADAMS 4:80
Through all E. to Thee — ADDI 6:24
thyself to all e. — ROSS 698:97
To know e.? — ROET 694:6
wander through e. — MILT 581:22
white radiance of E. — SHEL 786:7
Why didn't E. have this…age — KRAUS 480:8
ethereal blue e. sky — ADDI 6:26
e. mountain — BENU 78:85
etherized patient e. upon a table — ELIOT 304:17

ethic e. is not an e.   KOHL 477:37
ethical certain e. suspension   DIDI 274:9
  e. reality of the individual   KIER 467:10
  unethical and e. advertising   STEF 814:4
ethics can not conflict with e.   POIN 657:32
  drew a system of e.   MACA 525:52
  E. are no more a part   STEV 820:39
  e., as a branch of knowledge   AYER 45:12
  not aesthetics but e.   ROGE 694:12
Ethiope rich jewel in an E.'s ear   SHAK 736:42
Ethiopian Can the E. change   BIBLE 105:75
Etna sight of E. at sunset   WAUGH 892:37
Eton E. man…turns up his nose   ANON 21:30
  feelings on leaving E.   CONN 233:74
  holidays from E.   SITW 794:81
  on the playing-fields of E.   ORWE 628:61
  playing fields of E.   WELL 898:67
eucalypt tattered host of e.   ADAMS 4:63
Euclid E. alone Has looked   MILL 571:88
  fifth proposition of E.   DOYLE 285:51
  liquid E.s in foolscaps of air   AVIS 44:6
eunuch between a e. and a snigger   FIRB 323:70
  kind of moral e.   SHEL 784:52
  prerogative of the e.   STOP 825:60
  strain, Time's e.   HOPK 413:10
  time's e.   HOPK 413:7
eunuched e. with formality   CLEV 221:84
eunuchs Critics are like e.   BEHAN 70:7
  e. are on strike   ROTH 700:36
  e. of literature   HEMI 393:94
  two or three e.   BIBLE 92:36
Euphrates Nile or E.   GIBB 351:57
eureka E., E.!   ARCH 28:40
Europe all over E.   GREY 373:7
  alterations on the map of E.   CHUR 216:59
  best negotiators in E.   NELS 610:32
  Better fifty years of E.   TENN 841:88
  claim…to make in E.   HITL 404:20
  community of E.   GLAD 359:94
  courts of E. are a jungle   BOLT 139:50
  curse of E.   SENI 728:98
  dogs of E. bark   AUDEN 40:4
  Don Quixotes of E.   COBD 223:53
  England still stands outside E.   KEYN 465:80
  E. and…the future   MARI 549:48
  E. catches cold   METT 568:26
  E. from the thralldom   LLOY 513:2
  E. had arrived at a point   GREY 373:8
  E. had plenty of art   BEHR 71:23
  E. is a continent of   FISH 324:77
  E. is our common home   BREZ 152:23
  E. needs Russia   YELT 934:70
  E. rock and sway   LLOY 513:99
  E. should know   CONG 231:28
  E. was rich   IRVI 430:79
  ever another war in E.   BISM 131:87
  every Christian in Hitler's E.   FACK 317:31
  Furnished as all E. is   FRAN 335:17
  glory of E. is extinguished   BURKE 169:34
  greatest in E. for Riches and Greatness   BAIL 52:4
  guilty secrets of E.   DUNN 295:19
  hold the balance of E.   WILL 912:5
  If E. is wise and just   LAMA 486:24
  I long for E.   RIMB 687:89
  in E. nothing goes   ROTH 699:24
  intellect of E.   ARNO 33:35
  in the interest of E.   PALA 635:6
  It broke E.   MORR 599:6
  last gentleman in E.   LEVE 506:56
  leading journal of E.   HAZL 388:76
  map of Africa lies in E.   BISM 131:88
  nationalities of E.   ASQU 36:9
  nations of E. and outside   LEES 500:50
  noblest river in E.   ADDI 6:21
  no nation on the continent of E.   BRIG 152:33
  now afoot in E.   GUST 375:46
  part of the community of E.   CECIL 202:32
  part of the community of E.   SALI 711:69
  Prince of E., should dare to invade   ELIZ 309:60
  races of E. are melting   ZANG 936:88
  regard for the liberties of E.   BRIG 152:31
  salvage E.'s culture   ADEN 7:47
  save E. by her example   PITT 653:49
  slain this year in E.   WALP 887:38
  spectre is haunting E.   MARX 558:4
  splendidly isolated in E.   FOST 332:58
  territories of E.   GOER 360:11

that's old E.   RUMS 702:37
This going into E.   THOM 855:34
Through E. to the Aetolian shore   ARNO 33:32
tomorrow in E.   GORD 364:10
torch of war in E.   HITL 404:18
travellers in E.   MELV 564:42
trip to E. would be superfluous   SAAR 707:81
valuation of E.   JAMES 433:33
European Britain…E. state   GAIT 343:89
  Britain will not be…in a E. war   DAILY 250:64
  centers of E. civilization   TOLS 863:8
  colonisation by any E. powers   ADAMS 5:93
  E. football without the English   CHAR 207:44
  E. harmonies   GILL 356:48
  E. philosophical tradition   WHIT 904:12
  E. societies…moneyed aristocracy   BLEST 136:93
  first time a E.…sets foot   STEF 814:5
  greater humanity than the E.   MCCA 528:96
  happy…is not a characteristic of a E.   CHAN 205:3
  Latin America owes…to the E.   VASC 877:39
  Modern E. culture   SUN 829:32
  not a E. thing   NOLAN 617:54
  policy of E. integration   KOHL 477:36
  Unlike the classical E.   SENG 727:96
  very low class among the E. states   GEOR 349:12
Europeans books written by E.   NAIP 606:50
  E. have scarcely visited any coast   JOHN 442:57
  hearten those E.   MURR 605:10
evangelical but he is most e.   BEAV 67:20
Evangelist honour unto Luke E.   ROSS 698:98
evaporate automate—or e.!   MERR 567:16
evasion attempt at deliberate e.   JONES 447:90
  has not wit enough to invent an e.   CONG 231:30
Eve Adam and E. were dispossessed   BOUL 146:25
  Adam and E. were turned out   MUGG 601:49
  Adam knew E.   BIBLE 86:58
  all the fair daughters of E.   EDGE 299:93
  child of our grandmother E.   SHAK 733:74
  close at the ear of E.   MILT 583:73
  E. ate Adam   HUGH 419:45
  E. made Adam sin   MARG 549:39
  E. miscarried of me   BROW 158:78
  E. the rites Mysterious   MILT 583:71
  E., whose fault it was only   LANY 489:5
  fallen sons of E.   CHES 212:83
  I span and E. span   GILM 356:55
  meekest E.!   COLL 228:48
  mother E., who tasted   LANY 489:3
  real curse of E.   RHYS 684:24
  son of Adam and of E.   PRIOR 668:31
  When Adam delved and E. span   BALL 55:64
  When E. upon the first   HOOD 410:44
eve Be sudden—to E.   THOM 855:37
  from e. and morning   HOUS 415:57
  stag at e. had drunk   SCOTT 723:4
  St. Agnes' E.   KEATS 458:30
  were not sure, this e.   BROW 160:23
even get e.   KENN 463:46
evening at e., casual flocks   STEV 819:19
  Come in the e.   DAVIS 256:69
  couthy chiels at e. meet   FERG 321:8
  delight in the e.   PRIOR 669:42
  descends the autumn e.   ARNO 33:52
  e. cup of tea   HOLM 408:1
  e. full of the linnet's wings   YEATS 932:30
  e. is spread out against the sky   ELIOT 304:17
  e. meal   BARL 60:58
  e. quickens in the street   DE 264:35
  e. sees it close   LONG 516:46
  e. the strange horses   MUIR 602:62
  go to and fro in the e.   BOOK 143:56
  green chiffon e. gown   THAT 850:12
  It is a beauteous e.   WORD 926:13
  It was a summer e.   SOUT 805:98
  Late at e., drinkin' the wine   BALL 55:74
  lengthen, and the e. comes   NEWM 612:63
  mists of e. lie   BETJ 83:90
  morning wore to e.   TENN 843:25
  quiet-coloured end of e.   BROW 161:37
  rear cattle in the e.   MARX 559:89
  shadow at e. rising to meet you   ELIOT 305:53
  Soup of the e.   CARR 195:83
  stronger scent towards e.   STAEL 831:43
  there morning and e.   RUSK 704:38
  unique e.   WIMP 917:20
  welcome peaceful e. in   COWP 241:76
  window in the autumn e.   MORG 597:78

winter e. settles down   ELIOT 305:27
evenings known for e.   ELIOT 304:20
event Does arbitrate the e.   MILT 577:36
  enviable, boast-worthy, masculine e.   STEI 816:44
  e. at an obvious place   LIPP 511:69
  genuine imaginative e.   ROTH 699:28
  greatest e.…that ever happened   FOX 332:74
  horror…was the size of each e.   MAIL 540:56
  importance of an historical e.   WHIT 905:24
  news is to signalize an e.   LIPP 511:71
  no e. so commonplace   BUEC 165:44
  not a picture but an e.   ROSE 696:63
  outstanding e. was the doing   CARR 194:53
  to celebrate the e.   JERR 437:42
  vertical in the tumultuous e.   CESA 203:50
eventful the past was not more e.   ORWE 628:57
eventide fast falls the e.   LYTE 524:17
events All strange and terrible e.   SHAK 765:45
  e., mostly unimportant   BIER 129:32
  E., not books, should be forbid   MELV 564:76
  e. of life   SARO 714:35
  e. overlapping each other   DURR 296:38
  In all the e. of life   HUME 422:51
  irresistible march of e.   NAPO 607:60
  seek to fashion e.   NAPO 607:72
  three great e. for a person   LABR 483:72
  where there used to be e.   PIGL 651:14
eventualities e. in the future   MURP 604:4
ever For I go on for e.   TENN 846:3
  fall asleep for e.   SASS 716:68
  For e. and e. by   TENN 845:84
evergreen with e. devotion   BIRN 131:71
  even from e. to e.   BIBLE 96:49
  E. had not fixed   SHAK 751:5
  with an e. love   BIBLE 105:77
everlastingness shoots of e.   VAUG 878:45
evermore Name Liveth for E.   KIPL 474:80
Everton If E. were playing   SHAN 776:30
everybody E. but me   HUGH 418:19
  E. cries   STIPE 824:50
  E. gets so much information   STEIN 815:22
  e. is as nasty as himself   SHAW 777:50
  E. lies about sex   SEIN 726:76
  Most e. in the world   WILD 910:76
  take care of e.   FULL 341:56
  think of e. else as native   STEIN 815:17
  To e.'s prejudice   GILB 354:17
  What was e.'s business   SMUTS 802:32
  when e. is somebody   HUTC 424:53
everyday E. young man!   GILB 354:6
  ordinary, e.-d. people   DRUC 287:12
everydayness e. of life   STEI 814:9
everyman E., I will go with thee   ANON 19:97
everyone bow to e.   SKEL 795:6
  equally unsound to trust e.   SENE 727:89
  E. can master a grief   SHAK 745:12
  E. feels it   TROL 867:9
  E.…holds dual citizenship   SONT 804:77
  E. o. is more or less mad   KIPL 470:76
  E. suddenly burst out singing   SASS 716:69
  e. will say   GILB 354:4
  stop e. from doing it   HERB 397:75
everything against e. all the time   KENN 464:50
  beginning of e.   REAG 680:59
  boxing is e.   HEMI 395:31
  Brains are not e.   SHAW 777:71
  devourer of e.   OVID 631:46
  E. clever has been thought   GOET 360:18
  e. could be known and forgiven   GEE 348:93
  E.…endeavours to persist   SPIN 810:28
  e. except space and light   HEAT 390:28
  e. had to swing   ELLI 310:75
  E. has been discussed   ALEM 11:17
  E. has been done   INGR 429:62
  E. has been said   LABR 483:56
  E. has been written   FERN 321:18
  e. includes itself in power   SHAK 757:93
  e. I never wanted   GARD 346:44
  e. in its place   BEET 70:3
  e. is allowed   AMIS 15:7
  E. is decided   KIM 467:20
  e. is great   PASC 640:6
  E. presses on   STER 818:93
  e. that he can come by   SHAK 729:35
  E. we see   TOML 863:10
  e. would be done far better   SIEY 791:26

one year's e. 30 times — CARR 194:55
optimist...never had much e. — MARQ 554:25
philosophy teaching by e. — CARL 192:19
Some by e. find those words — CONG 231:2
store of e. — FRAME 333:81
stream of your e. — JAMES 434:71
substitute for a real e. — ALBEE 9:88
system to be refuted by e. — POPP 662:87
terminate in sensory e. — ELIOT 305:47
that hopeless wisdom of e. — ONEI 625:92
triumph of hope over e. — JOHN 444:91
try a new e. — SHAW 780:52
Twenty years e. as an actress — DAVIS 255:52
very little e. of self-government — EDIN 300:8
war...we don't have direct e. — DALL 251:75
When one does not e. it — SARR 715:38
women offer our e. — LEGU 501:61
world is diminished by the e. — SHAW 782:6
world...we don't have to e. — FRIS 338:76
worth a life's e. — HOLM 408:96
Your e. will be a lesson — AMIN 14:81
experiences categories in which e. — MANN 546:78
e. of life — NIEB 614:98
wisdom...after e. — PROU 671:75
experiment e....in communal living — BOWL 147:35
good e. lasts forever — KAPI 455:48
men of e. — BACON 47:60
Pure poetry is pure e. — SANT 714:26
reasoning to the test of e. — LAVO 493:83
wherever the e. has been fairly tried — SHEL 782:17
experimental All poetry is e. — STEV 820:38
e. reasoning concerning matter — HUME 422:15
experimentation spirit of e. — FRAN 335:17
experiments inquiries and e. — MENC 565:60
not necessarily...physical e. — CONN 233:87
expert An e. is someone — HEIS 391:57
became an e.'s art — RUDO 701:62
never trust an e. — MAMET 543:32
expertness unaccountable e. — THUR 859:20
experts divine right of e. — MACM 536:66
e. as stately and grand presidents — SUN 829:33
you should never trust e. — SALI 711:68
expiate death my days should e. — SHAK 771:8
something to e.; A pettiness — LAWR 494:9
expiring e., do foretell of him — SHAK 734:5
explain and which never e. — THOM 855:43
best way to e. it — CARR 195:89
e. to Her Majesty — KEMB 461:82
Never complain and never e. — BALD 54:51
You e. nothing, O poet — CLAU 220:62
explained painting...cannot be e. — RENO 683:6
Science has 'e.' nothing — HUXL 424:61
Shut up he e. — LARD 490:16
explainer Being is the great e. — THOR 857:69
said he was a village e. — STEIN 815:27
explanation devil...is the only e. — KNOX 476:23
explain his e. — BYRON 181:62
no e. is necessary — SEAT 726:69
saves tons of e. — SAKI 710:49
unless there is a verbal e. — COLE 225:76
explanations author's e. — MACL 535:40
explicable all things become e. — CLAU 220:62
explode Or does it e.? — HUGH 418:21
point where they e. — HENZE 396:57
exploit composed and high e. — MILT 581:21
e. of that gallant man — MILT 579:63
exploitation e. of their adult slave — GREER 372:89
exploiters against their capitalist e. — LENIN 502:84
exploiting a heavenly gift — QUIL 674:48
exploration e. was a...venture — THES 851:51
shall not cease from e. — ELIOT 309:48
explore happy nature to e. — POPE 660:19
irresistible need to e. — BRON 154:64
let us e. the stars — KENN 462:10
explorers endeavours are unlucky e. — DOUG 283:22
exploring E. is delightful — BUTL 177:65
explosion at the centre of an e. — ORWE 628:49
bring...decay or e.? — RUSS 705:53
hell of an e. — CATTO 200:3
export attempt to e. revolution — STAL 812:56
E. or die — ANON 22:62
expose don't let me e. myself — SCOTT 725:59
expositions e. of the doctrines — MORR 598:98
ex post referred to as e. p. — MYRD 605:26
exposure unseemly e. of mind — HAZL 388:93
expounder e. of our religious belief — SPEKE 806:35
ex-presidency directly to the e.-p. — MANN 546:77

ex-president great e.-p. — MANN 546:77
Express morons reading the E. — WODE 919:76
express e. in the small of the back — WODE 919:56
how e. and admirable — SHAK 752:57
little I can e. — NABO 606:38
never keen to e. themselves — BRAD 148:64
one's happiness to e. — MOORE 595:35
expressed could no otherwise be e. — MONT 592:74
that which cannot be e. otherwise — DELI 261:82
expression define an e....is to eliminate — QUINE 675:51
desire for aesthetic e. — WAUGH 892:23
E., for me, does not reside — MATI 560:62
e. for the inner sound — KAND 454:36
e. in English — ARNO 33:41
e. in vain — HEMI 393:97
E. is the dress — POPE 658:56
e. is to the thought — FLAU 326:31
e. may often be called bald — ARNO 34:71
e. of a people reflected — ROCK 692:83
e. of falling gravely downstairs — CUMM 247:97
e. of human separateness — MILL 572:6
e. of life as growth — MILL 573:42
e. of our...state of mind — FEIN 319:85
e. of the will to power — PAZ 644:90
e. which the few desire — PARE 636:36
first man I heard use the e. — ELLI 310:75
gave her the e. — THUR 859:41
Italy is a geographical e. — METT 568:27
most perfect e. of scorn — SHAW 781:80
my effort is their self e. — THOM 852:66
official e. of civil society — MARX 557:1
others by their hunted e. — LEWIS 507:75
Perhaps it was the right e. — WATE 890:93
perpendicular e. — SHAW 781:92
right to any mode of e. — POUND 664:33
sufficient power of e. — CHES 211:54
supreme e. of the mediocrity — TROT 867:16
vulgar e. of the passion! — CONG 231:7
expressions e. of esteem for Mr Boss — BAND 58:25
feeling...about some religious e. — RABI 676:79
pure e. of feeling — AYER 45:11
expressly we are told e. — SWIFT 831:68
express-train e.-t. drew up there — THOM 854:6
exquisite e., and...unsatisfied — WILDE 908:7
extemporanea medley of e. — PARK 638:60
exterminate e. a nation — SPOCK 811:38
extermination weapons of mass e. — RUSS 705:57
external idea of an e. cause — SPIN 810:30
impressions of e. things — RUSK 704:10
extinct labelled 'E.' — KING 469:63
extinction doomed to e. — POUND 665:55
presage of e. — SCOTT 722:76
sure e. that we travel to — LARK 491:44
extinguish e. hell — REED 681:81
e. the light of my mind — CRUZ 246:89
extinguished assimilated...never e. — DOUG 284:36
Nature is...seldom e. — BACON 49:39
extra add some e., just for you — LARK 491:38
always pay it e. — CARR 196:12
extraction e. of surplus labour — MARX 558:11
extra-marital e.-m. relationships — ALLEN 12:55
extraordinary E. how potent — COWA 239:11
interested in the e. — HUBB 417:7
work of one e. man — HUBB 417:8
extras No e., no vacations — DICK 267:99
extravagance with e. goes...waste — DILL 274:13
extravagances look upon all his e. — STEV 821:73
extravagant e. and irrational — SWIFT 831:82
e. with his own — SALL 711:71
extreme politics of the e. centre — WELL 898:63
take things to e. — KLEIN 476:11
extremes be whaur E. meet — MACD 529:31
E. meet — HOOD 410:41
measured at the e. — JAY 436:98
two e. of passion — SHAK 764:4
woman did not fly to e. — CRISP 245:53
Women are all in e. — LABR 483:59
extremism E. in the defence — GOLD 362:73
extremities e. of her corollaries — OCON 621:21
leave the body and e. — SMOL 801:29
extremity E. of griefs — SHAK 731:95
exuberance e. of his own verbosity — DISR 277:86
exultations friends are e. — WORD 927:32
eye Affection beaming in one e. — DICK 268:36
an e. simply — DOYLE 286:83
apple of his e. — BIBLE 106:16
apple of his e. — BIBLE 90:56

artistic sense of e. or ear — WHIS 902:65
as it were in the e. — MILT 578:62
ball as th' e. confin'd? — MILT 586:48
Bear welcome in your e. — SHAK 766:84
brought an e. for all — TENN 844:55
But with his leener e. — MARV 555:55
camera is an e. in the head — WELL 897:49
Care...in every old man's e. — SHAK 736:57
Cast a cold e. — YEATS 934:66
censor the gleam in my e. — LAUG 492:67
Christ in every e. — PATR 643:71
corner of your e. — NEW 611:52
curious hand or e. — LOVE 519:12
dark time the e. — ROET 694:7
drappie in our e. — BURNS 171:6
drown an e. — SHAK 771:15
drumlie grew his e. — BALL 55:87
every e. shall see him — BIBLE 125:43
e. did see Olivia — SHAK 755:47
e. diffused a quickening ray — WESL 899:9
e....ear...tongue of the people — STEAD 813:80
e. enthralled to thy shape — SHAK 738:4
e. for an e. — BIBLE 109:91
E. for e. — BIBLE 89:24
e. has permitted no change — HUGH 419:40
e. hath caught new pleasures — MILT 576:8
e. is the hammer — KAND 454:38
E. Nature's walks — POPE 660:7
e. never sees outlines — GOYA 365:30
e. of Almighty God — GLAD 358:91
e. of American man — BARR 60:77
e. of gods — WORD 929:64
e. of my understanding — JULI 452:4
e. of the big wind — MAIL 539:39
e. on the object — ARNO 33:34
e. on the prize — ANON 24:35
e. on the right hand — RUSH 703:96
e. that cannot be turned around — PLATO 655:1
e. that can open an oyster — WODE 919:51
e. that sees too deep — FADI 317:37
e. to e. — PEEL 646:10
e. to see nor tongue — LENT 503:2
e. was backward cast — SPEN 808:80
e....with thy nest — WORD 929:60
Fair nature's e., rise — MARL 552:6
ferlie he spied wi' his e. — BALL 56:89
fettered to her e. — LOVE 519:9
find a friend...close one e. — DOUG 283:30
Foley, I have only one e. — NELS 610:33
formed the e. — BIBLE 96:56
God finally caught his e. — KAUF 456:57
God with his mercyful e. — ANON 19:87
guide them with mine e. — BIBLE 95:11
had but one e. — DICK 267:1
Half hidden from the e.! — WORD 924:78
harvest of a quiet e. — WORD 924:84
hath closèd Helen's e. — NASHE 609:18
hollow cheek or faded e. — TENN 842:13
horrid deed in every e. — SHAK 767:87
human e. could see — TENN 840:81
if thine e. offend thee — BIBLE 112:68
if thy right e. offend thee — BIBLE 109:90
I have a good e., uncle — SHAK 744:92
in the twinkling of an e. — BIBLE 121:19
invisible to the e. — SAINT 709:17
In woman's e. the unanswerable — BYRON 181:51
Is thine e. evil — BIBLE 113:78
Its e. is always open — TOCQ 861:84
its e. is pasted. — MCCA 528:1
judgement of the e. — LEON 504:21
less in this than meets the e. — BANK 58:26
like a joyless e. — SHEL 787:36
long grey beard and glittering e. — COLE 225:80
looked into the e. — YEATS 933:54
look into a human e. — MELV 564:40
may charm our e. — COLL 228:46
mine e. seeth thee — BIBLE 94:79
Monet is only an e. — CEZA 203:53
more than meets the e. — KIPL 474:72
mote that is in thy brother's e. — BIBLE 110:5
nimble jugglers that deceive the e. — SHAK 733:59
no e. to our convenience — WIEN 907:69
no profaner e. may look — MILT 577:21
No shape to feed each gazing e. — DYER 297:51
object seen, and e. that sees — WORD 925:6
objects seen by the e. — PIERO 651:11
Of e., and ear — WORD 924:72

F

nocht but f.   BARB 59:51
vnder ane fenyeit f.   HENR 396:51
fables f. in the legend
old wives' f.   BIBLE 123:75
fabric f. of America   MCCA 527:91
f. of the heavens   MILT 584:97
monotonous f. of life   MILL 573:36
pull of a f. is governed   MOORE 595:40
face 50s f....60s f....70s f.   WATE 890:93
a beautiful f. is a dumb commendation   PUBL 672:95
acceptable f. of capitalism   HEATH 390:20
acceptable f. of capitalism   HEATH 390:21
Accustomed To Her F.   LERN 504:25
Am I in f. to-day?   GOLD 362:63
at their f. value   TAWN 837:8
autumnal f., her pieced beauty!   JONS 449:24
Before I knew thy f.   DONNE 280:49
before my f. the great increase   SURR 829:35
bend down my strange f.   SEXT 728:13
blot on the fair f. of creation   BRON 155:79
blow over the f.   AUBR 39:69
boot in the f., the brute   PLATH 654:69
boot stamping on a human f.   ORWE 630:4
born with a different f.?   BLAKE 135:65
bright f. of danger   STEV 823:28
cannot f. it steadily   ELIOT 308:32
canst not see my f.   BIBLE 89:32
cause his f. to shine upon us   BIBLE 96:37
chaos clapped on to my f.   WELLS 898:72
colors don't quite match your f.   ASHF 35:94
commandments in your f.   SHAK 730:53
Cover her f.   WEBS 895:19
curse thee to thy f.   BIBLE 93:49
dar'st not see my f.?   BEAU 67:16
decays in the f.   BEHN 71:20
Do thou amend thy f.   SHAK 742:22
draw a full f.   DRYD 291:29
each f. was turned   VIRG 882:18
earn the f. you have at fifty   CHAN 205:1
everybody's f. but their own   SWIFT 830:52
f. a British Government   TUCH 869:58
f....in a jar by the door   LENN 503:96
f....is so peculiarly unpleasant   SNOW 802:39
f....like a wedding-cake   AUDEN 41:34
f. ne'er shows   HERR 399:36
f. of American literature   PORT 663:11
f. of a moving-picture actor   MENC 566:86
f. of a saint   WELLS 898:87
F. of a traitor!   HUGO 420:76
f. of night is fair   TENN 845:98
f. of the world   LAUT 493:78
f. of Venus   BARR 61:94
f. softly made up   THAT 850:12
f. that launched a thousand ships   MARL 552:5
f. the man of the time   STEV 820:29
f. the music and dance   BERL 79:15
F. to f., silent   BROW 159:6
f. to the light   SASS 716:64
f. turned to the past   NARO 608:74
f. wearing the fixity   HARDY 382:65
f. with an undaunted tread   STEV 823:21
f. with blinking eyes   SASS 716:59
f. would be hardly observed   MONT 591:65
fall flat on your f.   THUR 859:32
False f. must hide   SHAK 767:92
famine in his f.   CHUR 215:43
Fanny Kelly's divine plain f.   LAMB 486:37
fell on his f.   BIBLE 114:98
filth returns in's f.   WEBS 894:84
first time...I saw your f.   MACC 528:16
garden in her f.   CAMP 187:80
gave his whole f. the expression   CUMM 247:97
give me a f.   JONS 449:25
glimpse of His bright f.   VAUG 878:44
God has given you one f.   SHAK 753:81
golden f. the meadows green   SHAK 771:16
good f. is a letter of recommendation   ADDI 6:16
hairy about the f.   SHAK 738:8
hand...goes over the f.   GARBO 345:39
Has he not a rogue's f.?   CONG 231:12
heart in's f.   SHAK 770:78
herds, of human f. divine   MILT 582:38
Her f. was lovely   SPEKE 806:36
Her fist of a f.   THOM 852:67
hides a smiling f.   COWP 240:45
hid the f.   DRYD 287:15
homely f.   GILB 354:98

honest, sonsie f.   BURNS 171:88
How my f., your flower   BROW 160:23
How unlike marble was that f.   KEATS 459:46
I have a grumpy f.   PINO 652:19
Intellectuals take apart her f.   SAINT 709:13
Jezebel...painted her f.   BIBLE 92:35
keeping your f. or your figure   CART 198:55
King's real. or his stamped f.   DONNE 279:43
kissed her...dainty f.   ASHF 35:1
like a f. full of character   MAUG 561:80
looked him honestly in the f.   DAVI 254:40
looking for the f.   YEATS 934:56
Look in my f.   ROSS 698:1
look on Helen's f. in hell   PARK 637:56
Look on her f.   POPE 658:68
look the East End in the f.   ELIZ 310:68
Lord spake unto Moses f. to f.   BIBLE 89:29
loss made one side of the f. repulsive   BIRD 130:58
love's f. May still seem love   SHAK 772:36
lying on his f.   THAC 849:90
make his f. shine upon thee   BIBLE 89:36
man has a black f.   EDWA 300:18
mannish manner of mind and f.   CARY 198:61
mark in every f. I meet   BLAKE 135:58
met him f. to f.   SULL 828:17
mind's construction in the f.   SHAK 766:79
mist on the sea's f.   MASE 559:21
monstrous carbuncle on the f.   CHAR 207:39
morning f.   GOLD 361:54
Moses hid his f.   BIBLE 88:10
most kiss-worthy f.   SIDN 790:13
my pilot f. to f.   TENN 848:70
never see my f. again   TENN 847:51
Newton with...silent f.   WORD 925:98
no f., only two profiles   ASQU 36:18
not recognize me by my f.   TROL 867:6
oft in my f.   SURR 829:34
oil to make his f. to shine   BIBLE 97:67
only f. I like to see   CAMP 186:57
on the f. of the globe   SMITH 801:11
painted f. of a savage   DICK 270:3
paint in the public's f.   RUSK 704:34
paradise...in his f.   DRYD 289:71
passions glowing in a human f.   MATI 560:62
people whom a fair f.   MAIL 540:66
Pity a human f.   BLAKE 134:31
plummet-measured f.   YEATS 934:64
poster with the enormous f.   ORWE 629:98
praised him to his f.   TENN 848:64
prayed for in our f.   BROW 160:11
proved to thy f.   SHAK 730:66
red in the f.   BENT 78:81
Royalty puts a human f.   RUNC 702:71
rude wind Blows in your f.   SHAK 763:85
sages have seen in thy f.?   COWP 241:54
saw the f. of God   MARL 552:99
seeing his own f. in the glass   WILDE 908:1
Sex Life in Ancient Rome f.   AMIS 14:83
She has a lovely f.   TENN 839:52
shining morning f.   SHAK 749:49
sigh of the east on my f.   CONR 234:4
sing in the robber's f.   JUVE 453:18
smug suppressions of his f.   WELLS 898:76
stamping on someone's f.   OSBO 630:11
stand f. to f.   KIPL 470:81
staring me in the f.   THUR 859:46
straight in the f.   GILL 355:39
Strike heaven on the f.   SHAK 768:28
string to each side of its f.   LEAC 496:54
such a f. should bear   SHAK 733:66
such a February f.   SHAK 745:26
sullen cold Exhausted f.?   SASS 716:67
surgeon...responsible for this f.   CUOMO 248:28
tears run...down my f.   OBRI 621:9
that homely f.   WORD 926:14
the f. he deserves   ORWE 630:7
the huge massy f.   MACA 525:54
three have changed the whole f.   BACON 47:61
thy classic f.   POE 656:22
Thy f. is valanced   SHAK 753:63
torso which has no f.   YOUR 936:86
truth has such a f.   DRYD 291:15
turn away thy f.   SHAK 748:23
turning my f. towards home   PARK 637:38
unacceptable f. of capitalism   HEATH 390:20
unclouded f. of Truth   SCOTT 722:74
until you're blue in the f.   NEWM 612:60

upon the night's starred f.   KEATS 457:94
up to the f. of a nation   ROCK 692:83
Vice...familiar with her f.   POPE 660:18
view our inner f.   GREG 372:94
Visit her f. too roughly!   SHAK 751:7
way plain before my f.   BOOK 142:38
wear one f. to himself   HAWT 386:41
white f.   GIOV 357:76
whole f. of the earth   PASC 640:17
whole life shows in your f.   BACA 45:23
whole world in the f.   LONG 516:45
woman's f. with nature's own hand   SHAK 771:7
wounds are in his breast and f.   DAVIS 256:67
your changing f.   YEATS 932:33
Your f., my thane   SHAK 766:83
faces almost everywhere two f.   DRYD 288:39
among so many millions of f.   BROW 158:80
breathing in their f.   SHAK 774:96
clouds...silent f.   WORD 928:52
f....a gallery of pictures   KNIG 476:15
f. as thin as credit cards   BACON 49:29
f. in the crowd   AMIS 14:96
f. of most American women   POUND 664:28
f. was that same immemorial look   FITZ 325:11
God...looks on shock-pried f.   LESS 505:35
hid...our f. from him   SWIN 832:18
know the f. I shall see   EBER 298:73
lords and owners of their f.   BIBLE 104:50
make f.   ROSS 698:97
make f.   SHAK 772:37
men with ugly f.   JOHN 444:11
Mild monastic f.   SCHN 719:22
most other people have f.   MASE 559:39
ne'er touched earthly f.   CLOU 223:34
plain men have rosy f.   TOOLE 863:51
probed their f.   SHAK 771:4
seen better f. in my time   STEV 823:33
strange f., other minds   ANGE 17:47
take their f. from 'em   SHAK 763:66
unidentifiable flying f.   TENN 847:49
With f. new   PRIE 668:25
with vivid f.   MCGO 532:85
  LOWE 520:40
  YEATS 933:44
facilitates be admitted that it f. much   LACL 484:84
facility F. is a dangerous thing   SLOAN 796:17
fact a f....so dreamlike   RICH 685:44
apparent statements of f.   AYER 44:10
believe that any f.   VIDAL 880:91
by an ugly f.   HUXL 426:9
can't figure him out like a f.   SHUL 790:93
conceal from ourselves the f.   PASC 640:9
concerning matter of f.   HUME 422:15
dependence of one f.   HOBB 404:24
disagreeable f.   STEV 820:59
drinking at the fountain of f.   PIER 651:5
every f....has been examined   PEAR 645:97
evil comes from this f.   GIRA 358:83
f. and fiction shouldn't be mixed   BOWEN 147:29
F. is stranger than fiction   GERV 351:47
f. is, you got to   WALK 885:98
f. of the artist   MAMET 543:26
f., propaganda, rumor   LIPP 511:67
f. that it is the...expression   PAZ 644:90
Frenchman is a f.   FRIE 337:66
grim f., however, is   PEAR 645:98
important f. regarding Spaceship Earth   FULL 341:55
indisputable f. that Americans   JAMES 433:35
in one f. can all agree   CLOU 222:24
knife-edge of mere f.   RICH 685:43
knocking your head against a f.   HUXL 426:15
man's religion is the chief f.   CARL 193:31
Matters of F.   HUME 422:13
national consciousness is a political f.   MACM 536:71
need only one f.   THOR 857:78
or records a f.   RUSK 703:2
pigmentation of f.   BARN 60:64
production of objective f.   MENC 565:73
reaching after f.   KEATS 457:91
Sit down before f.   HUXL 426:6
SPACE...the central f.   OLSEN 624:74
The f. is   STEV 821:79
where the idea and the f. collided   MCIL 533:2
Womanhood is the great f.   STAN 812:63
faction by f. cry'd up   PRIOR 669:34
f. is the worst of all parties   BOLI 139:44
From f.; for none sure   MILT 581:19

made them a f.   MACA 526:74
no leader, f., party or 'class'   OAKE 619:86
Two evils—greed and f.   MORE 597:70
factions leaders of white-mouse f.   MACD 530:47
factitious tremble for something f.   CLOU 223:31
factor dominant f. in our society   ASIM 35:6
factories bombs are…in the f.   ORWE 629:83
dynamiting f.   TOLK 862:97
living f. of the soul   MAYA 562:92
poems…in the f. and fields   MACD 530:43
factory f. of books   SMITH 799:66
in the f., he serves a machine   MARX 558:13
In the f., we make   REVS 684:20
prefers…to a concrete f.   WALC 885:80
truck passing by a f.   CAGE 184:28
within the reach of f. girls   SCHU 721:56
facts abandoned the f.   WATE 890:91
all the f. are known   FORD 330:22
begin with a good body of f.   DARW 253:17
beings loaded up with f.   UNAM 873:67
bring to light the hidden f.   LIPP 511:71
deadlier f., not dreams   MELV 564:46
dominant f. in English life   ORWE 628:61
F. alone are wanted in life   DICK 270:99
f., and the general laws of nature   BURB 167:79
F. are cheels   BURNS 170:79
f. are f.   JAMES 434:61
F. are generally overesteemed   UPDI 874:79
F. are like   UPDI 874:88
f. are lost forever   MAIL 539:43
f. are sacred   SCOTT 722:74
F. are ventriloquist's dummies   HUXL 425:90
f. do not cease   HUXL 424:62
f. don't mean a thing   ONEI 625:98
f., not realities   GOLD 362:88
f. we know about a man   LAWR 494:6
F.…were distorted   PACH 633:69
f., with the specific   ROTH 699:28
False f. are highly injurious   DARW 253:14
government and report the f.   ROGE 695:29
greatest number of empirical f.   EINS 302:46
ignoring the f.   ADAMS 4:84
imperial gallons of f.   DICK 270:1
intelligent anticipation of the f.   CURZ 249:52
knowledge of relevant f.   JAY 436:98
manners, and even f.   TROL 867:7
mixture of f. and truths   FRAME 333:80
not for the f. they elicited   INOU 430:73
obvious f. about grown-ups   JARR 435:88
outward with inward f.   ELIOT 303:77
Particular f. are never scientific   BERN 81:39
plainly evident f.   TOBIN 861:79
Religion…greatest of present f.   WHIT 904:8
rude f. at your feet   RABAN 675:61
Science is f.   POIN 657:33
seven great f.   HUGEL 418:12
severe f. of life   ELIOT 304:5
simultaneously the two f.   ORWE 630:9
small f., trends, or even politics   SCHI 718:98
That's all the f.   ELIOT 307:82
the f. of life   PARK 638:79
trust to nothing but f.   LAVO 493:83
when the external f.…are given   ELIOT 305:47
world is the totality of f.   WITT 918:41
faculties according to his f.   BAKU 53:25
borne his f. so meek   SHAK 767:87
diversity in the f. of men   MADI 538:20
dull and half-dead f.   ALBEE 10:94
dull f. can comprehend   EINS 301:37
experience and of general f.   MILL 570:76
f. have departed   THUR 859:17
f. of the mind…benumbed   BROO 155:1
mind fully develops its f.   STAEL 811:45
need exercise for their f.   BRON 154:78
faculty f. of laughter   ADDI 6:30
f. of seeing   SPEN 807:60
how infinite in f.   SHAK 752:57
fad Psychoanalysis is a permanent f.   DE 264:38
fade f. as a leaf   BIBLE 104:63
f. away into the forest   KEATS 459:58
F. far away   KEATS 460:59
flourish or may f.   GOLD 361:52
just f. away   MACA 524:26
just f. away   MACA 524:27
Nothing of him that doth f.   SHAK 774:84
old soldiers…just f. away   MACA 524:26
faded She f.…in her little grey dress   WOOLF 922:40

She f., like a cloud   SHEL 785:94
fading f. in music   SHAK 740:69
faery relish in the f. power   KEATS 457:94
fags f. and cabbage-stumps   LAWR 495:23
fail all right if they f.   ZHOU 936:98
f. a bit less   NICK 614:93
f. as a woman   FRID 337:57
f. conventionally   KEYN 466:92
f. to find thee   TENN 847:35
greatness may not f.   TENN 848:67
Guaranteed never to f.   FORM 331:27
not ashamed to f.   JOHN 441:10
Others must f.   VIDAL 881:97
Screw your courage…we'll not f.   SHAK 767:90
system in which no one can f.   HUGH 419:35
Try again…F. again   BECK 68:47
what an artist does, is f.   BART 62:15
will not f. thee   BIBLE 90:61
failing f. just when…succeeding   REST 683:16
principal f. occurred in the sailing   CARR 197:31
fails if another f.   BROW 160:21
not what she f. to do   GOET 360:13
When State Magic f.   REED 682:85
failure can stand anything but f.   COMD 229:63
confession of its f.   STEV 824:41
either a f. or madman   HOLM 407:72
enables him to sustain a f.   BELL 71:26
f., in perpetual struggle   WHITE 903:93
f. is ignominious   MENC 565:64
f. of feeling   STEV 820:34
f., or misfortune, or imprudence   STOWE 826:72
f. to communicate   PRIT 669:52
f. to provide for   KEYN 466:90
grant me a f. like that!   GOUN 365:26
no fear of any f.   FAWC 319:80
nothing like the f. of a close friend   CAREY 191:67
not the effort or the f.   EMPS 313:61
political lives…end in f.   POWE 667:95
redeems from utter f.   FIELD 322:30
splendid f. to do the impossible   FAUL 319:71
triumph of f.   RYAN 706:73
With f. comes f.   HELL 392:64
Women can't forgive f.   CHEK 209:10
failures f. are almost as important   AGAS 8:65
f. are ultimately f.   MURD 604:92
fain Where f., f. I would sleep?   BALL 55:72
faineant A f. government   TROL 867:93
faint f. at best, the beams   POPE 662:71
f. in the day of adversity   BIBLE 100:49
f. in the light   TENN 845:89
Felt f.—and never dared uplift   SHEL 784:52
They f. on hill   TENN 842:5
faint-hearted Farewell, f.…king   SHAK 730:69
fainting F. in coils   CARR 195:80
fair a F. Deal   TRUM 868:29
all the rest, though f. and wise   SHEL 786:8
as f. a name   SHAK 747:77
black man or a f. man   ADDI 6:9
cheating is f.   FRY 339:23
come in for the f.   HOUS 415:54
Disguise f. nature   SHAK 746:42
f. and f., and twice so f.   PEELE 646:11
f. and free competition   RICA 684:33
f. art thou   BURNS 173:44
F., fat, and forty   SCOTT 725:46
f. friend, you never can be old   SHAK 772:42
F. is foul, and foul is f.   SHAK 766:65
f., my love   BIBLE 101:2
f. sex is your department   DOYLE 285:75
F. stood the wind for France   DRAY 286:1
f. terms and a villain's mind   SHAK 739:55
f., the chaste   SHAK 749:55
f. to everybody   APPL 27:22
f. words…in foulest letters?   SHAK 743:64
got by f. means or foul   ORWE 627:32
held to the f.   BURNS 171:96
How f. and how pleasant   BIBLE 102:5
how sweet and f.   WALL 886:12
if it prove f. weather   SUCK 828:13
in the f. and the market place   PARN 639:91
lot is fallen unto me in a f. ground   BOOK 142:42
Ludlow f.   HOUS 415:66
most divinely f.   TENN 838:40
never yet f. woman   SHAK 763:73
None but the brave deserves the f.   DRYD 291:33
no one more f. and excellent   SPEN 808:85
Nothing is f. or good alone   EMER 312:4

Outward be f.   CHUR 215:47
remained at 'set f.'   BENN 76:41
Say, lingering f.!   CRAS 244:39
settle what's right and f.   HUGH 420:55
so f. that they called him the lady   AUBR 39:68
The rose looks f.   SHAK 771:20
Though this was f.   BURNS 173:43
fair-and-square stole it f. a. s.   HAYA 387:56
fairies beginning of f.   BARR 61:81
f. at the bottom of our garden   FYLE 342:79
I don't believe in f.   BARR 61:82
large sale among the f.   HEMI 393:96
fairin thou'll get thy f.!   BURNS 172:24
fairness Nocht is your f.   HENR 396:55
fairy Airy, f. Lilian   TENN 838:39
as if a passing f. had hiccuped   DICK 268:42
By f. hands their knell is rung   COLL 228:43
calls up the realms of f.   BYRON 182:90
Come not near our F. Queen   SHAK 737:98
f. kind of writing   DRYD 291:25
I mean by f. lamps   WOOD 921:20
moral tests and tasks set in f. tales   ELKIN 310:69
night-tripping f. had exchanged   SHAK 741:93
no one ever marries in a f. tale   KING 469:58
serve the F. Queen   SHAK 737:92
ugliest f. in the world   KING 469:56
fairy-godmother author's f. g.   LUCAS 522:78
fairy-gold We dealt in f.-g.   QUEN 674:39
fairyland childhood…f.-l.   BOGAN 138:31
everybody's got a F.   TRAV 864:44
faith add f., Add virtue, patience   MILT 585:35
America…was an object of f.   RABAN 675:61
author and finisher of our f.   BIBLE 124:99
basis of true f.   VIDAL 881:99
By f., and f. alone   TENN 842:19
comes i' f. full sail   CONG 231:35
died in f.   BIBLE 124:96
dissent is an act of f.   FULB 340:44
Draw near with f.   BOOK 141:99
dying for a f.   THAC 849:1
f., and…fire   ARNO 32:30
F.…belief without evidence   BIER 129:29
F. comprises   TILL 860:68
F. consists in believing   VOLT 883:46
f. finally free itself   CUPI 248:35
F. gives new light   TAYL 837:23
f., hope, charity   BIBLE 121:9
F., I have been a truant   SHAK 729:44
f. in fundamental human rights   UNIT 873:69
f. in the difficultest points   BROW 158:63
f. in the imperishable dignity of man   CARL 191:87
f. in the magic of official forms   WAUGH 892:45
F.' is a fine invention   DICK 272:56
f. I search for   SAND 712:89
F. is the state of   TILL 860:69
f. is the substance of things   BIBLE 124:95
F., like a jackal   MELV 564:27
F. may be defined briefly   MENC 565:58
f. melteth into blood   SHAK 744:93
f. of a Tory   POWE 667:94
f. of Christ   BOOK 141:12
f., so that I could remove mountains   BIBLE 121:9
F.'s transcendent dower   WORD 928:59
f. that right makes might   LINC 510:38
F., that's as well said   SWIFT 832:8
F.…the Pierless Bridge   DICK 272:69
f. unfaithful kept   TENN 846:19
f.…we can make it   DICK 265:57
F. without doubt   UNAM 873:63
F. without works is dead   BIBLE 124:11
For him, f.   BALZ 57:14
fought for Queen and F.   TENN 848:64
Found f. in me   DRAY 287:3
fright my f.   DRYD 291:16
future states…are left to f.   BYRON 182:85
genial f.   WORD 926:16
gift of f.   JOHN 438:55
good fight of f.   BIBLE 124:80
have f. as a grain of mustard   BIBLE 112:65
have kept the f.   BIBLE 124:86
heresies…explosions of f.   BREN 151:15
impossibilities…for an active f.   BROW 158:62
increase Catholic f.   VAZD 878:53
In f. and hope   POPE 660:21
inmost f. is overthrown   SASS 716:74
just shall live by f.   BIBLE 119:58
kept f. with me   HARDY 382:77

lamp of f. — WORD 929:63
life of doubt diversified by f. — BROW 161:49
like an arch, is f. — MILL 573:39
losing or regaining f. — FITZ 324:89
lost f. in individual endeavour — CARL 191:83
make room for f. — KANT 455:46
man's f. in himself — SHAW 777:57
may we bring f. — THAT 850:16
more f. in honest doubt — TENN 844:57
my cast-iron f. — STEV 823:29
My f. shall wax — DANI 252:87
My staff of f. — RALE 677:99
necessary…he hold the Catholic F. — BOOK 140:78
no f. in human perfectibility — POE 656:21
no f. in physic — JONS 448:15
no need for the f. — HOFF 405:47
Non-violence…first article of my f. — GAND 345:34
not an amiable f. — CARL 192:25
not f., but mere Philosophy — BROW 158:76
not found so great f. — BIBLE 110:14
O thou of little f. — BIBLE 112:57
O ye of little f.? — BIBLE 110:18
reward your f. in us — SMITH 799:71
Science…a f. as fanatical as any — BARZ 63:35
sea of f. — ARNO 31:93
shield of f. — BIBLE 122:52
simple f. than Norman blood — TENN 840:74
stand fast in the f. — BIBLE 122:21
still by f. he trod — LIND 510:47
suspension of disbelief…poetic f. — COLE 226:17
take thy word for f. — SHAK 769:52
test of our f. — LLOY 513:1
there is no f. — KIER 467:9
there is yet f. — ELIOT 308:14
times of f. as best — SMITH 800:98
triumphs of f. — RUNC 702:73
truth of our f. — JOHN 439:62
turning…people to our holy f. — COLU 229:62
unshakeable f. in…enterprise — BURT 174:66
walk by f., not by sight — BIBLE 122:26
was of the f. — AMIS 14:89
wears his f. but as the fashion — SHAK 744:84
When f. is lost — WHIT 906:57
Where there is doubt, f. — FRAN 334:98
With Punic f. — SALL 711:73
with Thee in f. — HAMM 379:7
faithful Be thou f. unto death — BIBLE 126:48
called F. and True — BIBLE 127:75
f. friend is the medicine — BIBLE 107:41
f. in that which is least — BIBLE 116:52
f. over a few things — BIBLE 113:89
f. to thee, Cynara! — DOWS 284:44
give…a f. account of men — ELIOT 303:76
moderately f. wife — SHAW 779:16
So f. in love — SCOTT 723:96
Translations…are seldom f. — CAMP 186:63
faithfulness great is thy f. — BIBLE 105:82
faith-healer f.-h. of Deal — ANON 22:53
faithless Be not f., but believing — BIBLE 118:25
faiths f. and empires gleam — SHEL 786:21
fanatically dedicated to…religious f. — PIRS 652:26
men's f. are wafer-cakes — SHAK 745:38
fake can't f. quality — BURR 173:60
freedom…was…a f. — ORWE 628:48
learned to f. that — GOLD 362:90
fakir posing as a f. — CHUR 216:70
falcon be a f. and go free — DUNC 295:14
dapple-dawn-drawn F. — HOPK 412:89
f. cannot hear the falconer — YEATS 933:50
Gentle as f. — SKEL 795:91
Falklands F. held a mirror up — RABAN 675:58
F. thing…fight between two bald men — BORG 145:94
fall Another thing to f. — SHAK 758:19
by dividing we f. — DICK 273:81
Created…half to f. — POPE 660:17
dead man is the best f. guy — CHAN 205:91
decline and f. — GIBB 352:63
despairing posture of his f. — POE 656:19
dew shall weep thy f. tonight — HERB 398:14
do not want to f. — HUGO 420:75
f., and not rise again — BIBLE 102:23
f. flat on your face — THUR 859:32
f. half in love — SALI 711:54
f. of a prince — ANON 18:70
f. of the last civilization — READ 680:49
f. out with those we love — TENN 841:1
f. through the air — GOLD 360:28

F. to thy prayers — SHAK 743:67
fear no f. — BUNY 167:76
great was the f. of it — BIBLE 110:13
haughty spirit before a f. — BIBLE 99:36
If he f. in — SHAK 741:3
If only we might f. — ANON 22:67
less likely to f. — GAY 347:79
Life is a horizontal f. — COCT 224:60
meditated on the F. — BETJ 84:7
No paradise, no f. — SNYD 803:49
nowhere to f. — ALAN 9:84
pride comes before a f. — WELD 897:39
Rome alone can make Rome f. — BELL 72:37
should happen to f. — SCOTT 724:15
Soar not too high to f. — MASS 559:43
some by virtue f. — SHAK 758:22
take heed lest he f. — BIBLE 121:2
though free to f. — MILT 582:41
voices dying with a dying f. — ELIOT 304:20
we f. and get crushed — DAY 256:76
fallacies science is…exploded f. — RAND 678:10
fallacy f.…about winning — BLAN 136:89
f. of retrospective determinism — BEND 74:7
Pathetic F. — RUSK 704:10
principle…suspect some f. — DARW 253:17
fallen f. from grace — BIBLE 122:37
Greece…though f., great! — BYRON 179:13
How are the mighty f. — BIBLE 91:98
How art thou f. — BIBLE 102:21
falling feeling I'm f. — FERL 321:12
Part of a moon was f. — FROST 338:86
without f. over — FREE 336:39
fallows Russet lawns and f. grey — MILT 576:8
Falls foaminess of the F. — SALA 710:50
false Believe f. teachers — SHAK 774:66
be not f. to others — BACON 49:20
Beware of f. prophets — BIBLE 110:10
Ere I am f. to you — OHAG 623:44
every individuality is…a f. step — SCHO 719:32
Everything is f. — BECK 68:43
f. definition of the situation — MERT 568:22
F. face must hide — SHAK 767:92
f. gallop of verses — SHAK 749:58
f. ideas prevail as to woman — STAN 812:63
f. of heart — SHAK 773:46
f. sincere — POPE 661:31
f. to any man — SHAK 751:22
Followed f. lights — DRYD 291:16
idle and most f. imposition — SHAK 760:79
If she be f. — SHAK 760:90
In friendship f. — DRYD 290:79
man who is f. to his friends — BERK 79:10
Ninety-nine times…is f. — EINS 301:34
origin of all f. science — HAZL 388:87
prov'd true before, Prove f. again — BUTL 177:57
reject as if absolutely f. — DESC 263:19
reject it as being f. — AYER 44:10
Ring out the f. — TENN 844:60
they have committed f. report — SHAK 745:23
thoughts dally with f. surmise — MILT 578:55
true poet…from the f. — POUND 666:71
trying to think everything f. — DESC 263:20
with love f. — YEATS 932:33
falsehood category of truth and f. — AYER 45:11
cuts f. like a knife — GURN 375:44
distinguishing truth from f. — DESC 263:18
f., cowardice, and poor descent — SHAK 729:37
Let her and F. grapple — MILT 579:69
strife of Truth with F. — LOWE 519:27
to express lying or f. — SWIFT 831:83
unfurnish'd Of f. — DRYD 289:64
what a goodly outside f. hath! — SHAK 739:52
falsehoods f. to deceive the public — STEF 814:4
f. which interest dictates — JOHN 442:55
falseness f. in all our impressions — RUSK 704:10
salutary pleasure in proving their f. — DARW 253:14
falser f. than vows made in wine — SHAK 750:70
falsetto curious f. voice — STRA 826:86
falsifiable statement…must be f. — POPP 663:96
falsity regions of sin and f. — MILT 579:73
falter hesitate and f. life away — ARNO 32:21
fame advances without coveting f. — SUN 829:30
ancient and prophetic f. — MILT 581:25
by verse seek f. — SIDN 790:15
claim to literary f. — BENN 76:37
Cromwell, damned to everlasting f.! — POPE 660:26
F. and rumour — JONS 449:21

F. and tranquillity are two — MONT 592:78
f. can never heal — AYTO 45:18
f. did not delay — DRAY 286:2
F. is a food — DOBS 277:97
F. is a powerful aphrodisiac — GREE 371:63
F. is based on what people say — DUDEK 293:79
f. is in the song — CARM 193:47
f. is no plant — MILT 578:50
f. is shrewdly gored — SHAK 757:8
F. is the spur — MILT 578:49
f., of valour — MARL 551:78
F.'s eternal beadroll — SPEN 809:6
F.'s luscious pot — RICK 686:76
Fareweel to a' our Scottish f. — BURNS 172:34
first alike in f.! — LOVE 518:8
frailty hath thy f. — NASHE 609:14
gate to good f. — BACON 47:76
general achieves f. — TS 869:53
genius…not to purchase f. — DRYD 289:50
great was his f. — EGAN 301:24
grow great in f. — DIBD 265:52
Let f., that all hunt — SHAK 733:67
live by f. — SPEN 809:1
Long life to thy f. — SCOTT 725:57
love and f. to nothingness so sink — KEATS 457:94
Man dreams of f. — TENN 846:11
no one shall work for f. — KIPL 472:20
Physicians of the utmost f. — BELL 72:54
pursued f. always in the hope — STAEL 811:46
Rather use than f. — TENN 846:12
servants of f. — BACON 48:99
that is f. — BERR 82:66
the desire of f. — TENN 846:22
verse the f. enrols — DONNE 281:78
write for money or f. — MOORE 595:35
famed As she is f. to do — KEATS 460:64
familiar Don't let us be f. or fond — CONG 232:45
F. in his mouth — SHAK 746:59
familiarity F. breeds contempt — TWAIN 872:19
families and there are f. — THAT 850:28
begin our public affection in our f. — BURKE 169:43
best-regulated f. — DICK 269:75
branch of…antediluvian f. — CONG 231:17
but two f. in the world — CERV 203:47
F.! I hate you! — GIDE 353:81
happy f. resemble each other — TOLS 862:5
in the best-regulated f. — NORTH 618:69
Mothers of large f. — BELL 72:49
sensibility…from…large f. — COUP 239:98
setteth the solitary in f. — BIBLE 96:38
family appalling dangers of f. life — HUXL 425:76
beautiful f. talk — COMP 229:70
be so in a f.? — ASTE 36:23
bread for the f. — LEWIS 507:84
brought up a large f. — GOLD 361:43
character of a f. — STER 817:73
conduct of every private f. — SMITH 798:48
each member of the f. — FRAME 333:81
every f. in America — JOHN 440:88
exceedingly clannish f. — SHAW 781:1
f. as an institution — MILLS 574:69
f. denied both stories — SAKI 710:38
f. does not need to do — ROCK 692:73
f. from sinking their property — MOOD 594:8
F. indivisibility — ROTH 699:29
f. joke that when — ROTH 699:17
f. life is all the life she knows — SHAW 780:56
f.—that dear octopus — SMITH 799:60
F.!… the home of all social evil — STRI 827:94
f. with the wrong members — ORWE 628:60
fine a f. he comes from — LEE 500:38
fruitful source of f. discontent — BEET 70:2
incest holds the f. together — INNIS 429:68
influence…than that of our own f. — CHUR 215:41
insecurity…in a single-parent f. — ELLW 311:92
member of the f.…is happier — FALU 317:41
not lugged into F. Rows — WODE 919:58
not of war…but of f. — CHILD 213:8
organisation of the f. — MARX 557:1
other members of the f. — OZICK 632:60
Others have their f. — CATH 200:93
patriarchy's…institution is the f. — MILL 574:62
sell members of my f. — ANNE 18:56
study of f. portraits — DOYLE 285:73
stuffy Victorian f. — ORWE 628:59
tense and peculiar f. — BEER 70:94
we, your blood f. — SPEN 806:37

F....goes as it must	ANON 18:68
F. hath held sway	AESC 8:58
f. in what I cannot fear	ROET 694:3
f. of human civilization	LOVE 519:18
f. of poetry	WALC 885:82
F. often preserves the undoomed	ANON 18:69
f. of this country depends	DISR 277:81
f. of those who toil	JOHN 442:38
f. of unborn millions	WASH 890:83
f. so enviously debars	MARV 556:67
F.'s such a shrewish thing	CHAP 206:17
F., Time, Occasion, Chance	SHEL 785:79
F. tried to conceal him	HOLM 408:91
F. wrote her a...tragedy	BEER 69:68
fears his f. too much	MONT 593:4
fits for f.	DRYD 291:23
For all our children's f.	KIPL 474:76
forced by f.	DRYD 292:42
foulness of their f.	SASS 717:76
full measure of their f.	CRANE 243:19
Happiness was my f.	RIMB 688:98
has no ill f.	WALL 886:18
I hold f.	FORD 330:17
In case it tempted F.	MCGO 532:84
It's a complex f.	JAMES 433:33
Jove and F. require	POPE 662:64
limits of a vulgar f.	GRAY 370:40
made weak by time and f.	TENN 840:66
makers of our f.	POPP 662:91
master of his f.	TENN 846:6
master of my f.	HENL 395:39
matter what f. befalls me	MILNE 575:87
meet my f.	YEATS 933:48
men cannot suspend their f.	DEFOE 258:12
meteor Ever hung my f.	MIDD 569:48
mock the patriot's f.	INGR 429:59
modern poet's f.	HOOD 410:53
my life, my f.	TENN 845:92
no armour against f.	SHIR 789:83
no f. that cannot be surmounted	CAMUS 187:89
No gifts...have conquered f.	ARNO 31:87
our pride, our folly, or our f.	DENH 261:93
Politics and the f. of mankind	CAMUS 187:85
power above The stars and f.	BUTL 177:62
proclaimed the f. that smote	ROBE 689:18
Read your f.	THOR 858:94
scorn of f.	DRYD 289:61
stern hand of f.	LLOY 513:99
torrent of his f.?	JOHN 441:19
when f. summons	DRYD 288:47
why should they know their f.?	GRAY 368:95
will...overruled by f.	MARL 553:13
won't triumph over his f.	KOES 477:30
fates F., we will know your pleasures	SHAK 747:96
hostages to the f.	LUCAN 521:71
masters of their f.	SHAK 747:96
O f., come, come	SHAK 738:17
What f. impose	SHAK 730:81
wills and f....contrary run	SHAK 754:91
fathead F.-h. poet that nobody reads	CHES 213:99
fatheaded f....wash-out of a cock-up	ANON 25:50
fatheads famous f., old wives	MACD 530:47
father a f., that's what matters most	BROWN 157:41
After the funeral, my f.	LAWR 494:18
ascend unto my F.	BIBLE 118:23
ashamed to be my f.'s child!	SHAK 740:58
ashes of his f.	MACA 526:63
As my poor f. used to say	HERB 397:76
As the F. knoweth me	BIBLE 118:2
bed fell on my f.	THUR 859:22
better off dead...your wife and my f.	CHAN 205:87
born where my f. lived	SITT 793:56
boy with his f.	IHIM 428:43
cannot have God for his f.	CYPR 250:56
children of your F.	BIBLE 109:94
Church which prays 'Our F.'	BONH 139:56
decrepit f. takes delight	SHAK 771:17
Deny thy f.	SHAK 736:47
draft-dodging f.	ROTH 699:12
electrical display of God the F.	ONEI 625:95
even as a f.	BIBLE 99:10
f. before him	SYMI 834:54
f....did not have the time	CIXO 218:34
f. drove them out	LOUI 518:91
F.! f.! where are you going?	BLAKE 134:34
F., forgive them	BIBLE 116:63
f. gave him a box	MACN 538:13

f. had a chain of dry cleaners	BENN 76:35
f. had a daughter	SHAK 756:67
f. hath chastised you with whips	BIBLE 92:15
F. in Heaven	KIER 467:13
F., into thy hands	BIBLE 116:66
F. is rather vulgar	DICK 271:16
f. lived his soul	CUMM 248:15
f. moved through dooms of love	CUMM 248:14
f., nor a mother	MARG 549:37
f. of English criticism	JOHN 445:43
f. of his people	GIBB 351:56
f. of knowledge	HIPP 403:2
f. of lights	BIBLE 124:6
f. of many nations	BIBLE 120:64
f. of our dramatic poets	DRYD 288:31
F. of Peace	DODD 278:10
f. of psychoanalysis	GREER 372:87
f. of the child cried out	BIBLE 114:16
f. of the fatherless	BIBLE 96:38
f. or my mother	STER 817:67
f. should be as a god	SHAK 737:83
f. sold me	BLAKE 134:33
F., Son and Holy Ghost	MCLE 534:27
f.'s sword he has girded	MOORE 596:49
f. still reads the dictionary	SCAR 717:89
f., the chariot of Israel	BIBLE 92:28
F....thou hadst none	BRAD 149:79
f....throwing rocks at the stork	BREC 150:5
f. used to say	MOORE 595:31
f. was self-made	ATWO 38:63
f. watched him across	MARQ 553:19
F. which is in heaven	BIBLE 110:12
F. which is in heaven	BIBLE 112:46
F. which is in heaven	BIBLE 109:85
F. which is in heaven	BIBLE 109:94
F. which is in heaven give good things	BIBLE 110:8
F. which is in heaven is perfect	BIBLE 109:95
F. will come	TENN 841:2
f. worked with a horse-plough	HEAN 389:4
Full fathom five thy f. lies	SHAK 774:83
glorify your F. which is in heaven	BIBLE 109:85
God...an exalted f.	FREUD 337:55
had a pig-headed f.	POUND 664:30
had it from my f.	SHAK 775:8
Hath the rain a f.?	BIBLE 93:72
Have we not all one f.	BIBLE 106:19
heavenly F. feedeth them	BIBLE 110:2
his f. saw him, and had compassion	BIBLE 116:48
Honour thy f. and thy mother	BIBLE 88:23
How like f.	BARR 61:99
I am like no f.	SHAK 731:87
inherited...melancholy from my f.	JOHN 444:1
it is I, your f.	BELL 71:25
Labour is the F....of Wealth	PETTY 650:85
Lead us, Heavenly F.	EDME 300:14
Like as a f. pitieth	BIBLE 97:65
Lord and F. of mankind	WHIT 906:63
loveth f. or mother	BIBLE 111:30
lusts of the f. ye will do	BIBLE 117:98
man leave his f. and his mother	BIBLE 86:47
mighty God, The everlasting F.	BIBLE 102:17
murdered his mother and f.	LEVA 506:52
My f. is deceased	MARL 552:88
My f. was a slave	ROBE 689:22
my f. wept	BLAKE 135:60
My noble f.	SHAK 759:64
Neither f. nor lover	ROET 694:4
no man cometh unto the F.	BIBLE 118:10
O my F., if it be possible	BIBLE 114:98
one way to speak to my f.	SAINT 709:27
one would want as a f.	WEST 901:43
on the ground without your F.	BIBLE 111:28
Our F. which art in heaven	BIBLE 110:98
Our F. who art	PARRA 639:94
person cannot choose his f.	FRIS 338:79
Praise F., Son, and Holy Ghost	KEN 461:94
pray to thy F.	BIBLE 110:97
proceedeth from the F. and Son	BOOK 141:96
record...of our mother and f.	FRAME 333:81
remembered dead f.	NICH 613:84
resembled My f.	SHAK 767:99
Seek for the noble f.	SHAK 751:2
Singing to F., Son	HOW 417:93
stopped loving my f.	NIN 616:37
tenderness of a f.	MORE 596:61
Thou art thy f.'s daughter	SHAK 749:31
though her f. be very rich	SHAK 732:26

throne of Denmark to thy f.	SHAK 751:9
Thus his f. wept	BIBLE 87:9
time not to become a f.	WHITE 903:8
To be a successful f.	HEMI 395:2
'twill come to my f. anon	AUBR 39:6
What would f. say	MANS 547:9
where's their f. live	THOM 853:9
who my f. was	SEXT 728:1
will of my F.	BIBLE 110:12
will of my F.	BIBLE 112:46
will of my F. which is in heaven	BIBLE 110:12
will of my F. which is in heaven	BIBLE 112:46
Wisdom's heavenly F.	WORD 929:6
wise f. that knows	SHAK 739:5
wise son heareth his f.'s instruction	BIBLE 99:2
without f. bred	MILT 576:12
You are old. F. William	SOUT 805:9
Your f. hath consented	SHAK 732:3
your f., whom you love, dies	STOP 825:6
fatherland There we have the F.!	MANN 545:6
fatherless fields of the f.	BIBLE 100:4
for the f., and for the widow	BIBLE 89:5
visit the f. and widows	BIBLE 124:9
fathers common revolt against the f.	COWL 240:38
f....are incurable	DAVI 254:3
f. brought forth upon	LINC 510:3
f. had a Paris	HUGO 420:69
f., provoke not your children	BIBLE 122:5
f. that begat us	BIBLE 108:66
f. would never...have dreamed	MARC 548:2
glory of children are their f.	BIBLE 99:37
God of our F.	MILT 586:55
Hast all our f. led	DODD 278:8
Instead of thy f.	BOOK 143:50
learned of their f.	BIBLE 107:43
men liking their f.	BRAD 148:57
My f. can have it	THOM 853:83
not better than my f.	BIBLE 92:23
Our f. have...provided	QUIL 674:44
revolts against its f.	MUMF 603:74
scenes his f. loved	CULL 247:93
slept with his f.	BIBLE 92:16
so did their f. to the false prophets	BIBLE 115:30
turn the heart of the f.	BIBLE 107:23
visit the sins of the f.	BOOK 141:93
fathom canst not f. it	TENN 838:38
Full f. five	SHAK 774:83
them that sleep...many a f. deep	CAMP 186:71
fathoms certain f. in the earth	SHAK 775:98
fifty f. deep	BALL 56:87
fatigue F. makes women talk	LEWIS 507:76
f. of adjectives	BROY 163:98
lover...dies from...f.	BART 62:22
physical f. than the painter	LEON 503:9
the f. of judging for themselves	SHER 788:62
fatigued chanced to be f.	FORS 331:43
fatness covered with f.	BIBLE 90:57
f. of these pursy times	SHAK 754:12
let your soul delight itself in f.	BIBLE 104:53
fattening f. is the first duty	SPEKE 806:36
illegal, immoral or f.	WOOL 923:60
fatter f. man trying to close in	AMIS 14:88
fatuity f. of idiots	SMITH 801:7
fatuous one term is as f. as another	ROOS 696:58
fatus Better an ignis f.	DICK 273:73
Faulkner read...Proust, F., Joyce	VARG 877:3
fault clever to a f.	BROW 161:50
Every man has his f.	SHAK 762:45
f. being greater	LANY 489:4
f....is not in our stars	SHAK 747:76
Faultless to a f.	BROW 162:84
f. of our politicians	TROL 867:93
f. of the Dutch	CANN 188:14
f. though great, yet he	LANY 489:4
Find not f. with one another	KORAN 479:88
had only one f.	THUR 860:64
He is all f.	TENN 846:16
hide the f. I see	POPE 662:63
hint a f.	POPE 661:38
His worst f.	SHAK 743:69
least f. distorts it	YOUR 935:82
never needs to admit a f.	BALZ 57:8
no kind of f.	GILB 354:11
only f. is that I am alive	MAP 548:20
suffer through no f. of their own	ELIZ 310:66
Whose f.? Whose but his	MILT 582:4
faultless Faultily f.	TENN 845:78

faults America has colossal f.   CUMM 247:10
  blush at your f.   FLET 328:71
  England…With all her f.   CHUR 215:52
  England, with all thy f. I love thee   COWP 241:70
  f. it has not strength enough   GOLD 361:45
  f. of a Government   ROOS 696:44
  f. of the economic society   KEYN 466:90
  fill you with the f. they had   LARK 491:38
  Jesus! with all thy f.   BUTL 178:84
  Neebours' f. an folly   BURNS 170:86
  private school has all the f.   CONN 233:72
  repair time's f.   MUIR 602:59
  Sum up my f., I pray   WEBS 894:85
  to her f. a little blind   PRIOR 669:32
  world of vile ill-favoured f.   SHAK 743:77
faun important senior f.   ANON 23:94
Faustus F., it is not half so fair   MARL 552:2
  F., leave this damnèd art   MARL 552:4
  F. like a foggy mist   MARL 553:7
  F. may…save his soul!   MARL 552:6
favour courtesan farts…as a f.   ANON 20:10
  depend on…prince's f.   WEBS 895:6
  F. is deceitful   BIBLE 100:64
  f. to men of skill   BIBLE 101:85
  feel so strongly in f.   BALC 53:28
  never get f. for lacking skill   SIDN 791:23
  undoubtedly continue in f.   JANE 435:76
  without her f.   JONS 450:54
favourite f. has no friend!   GRAY 368:1
  which among my novels is my f.   ACHE 2:20
favours felt all its f.   COCK 224:54
  Fortune, that f. fools   JONS 449:28
  willing to exchange…their f.   ANDR 16:25
fawn f., crossed with a Buick   NICH 614:89
fawning How like a f. publican   SHAK 739:51
fawns fallow f. invisible go   THOM 854:20
FBI F. are powerless to act   HOOV 411:69
  Texas, the F., and hunting trophies   KENN 463:42
fear abolition of poverty and f.   HOOV 411:58
  Ah F.! Ah frantic F.!   COLL 228:45
  arming me from f.   BRON 155:92
  As if his f. still followed   SPEN 808:80
  blanched with f.   SHAK 768:18
  by means of pity and f.   ARIS 29:54
  care lost Went all his f.   MILT 581:20
  concessions of f.   BURKE 168:8
  contempt of f.   JONS 448:8
  do it with no show of f.   SHAK 745:39
  editor…need f. nothing   BENN 76:56
  'ergophobia', meaning 'f. or hatred of
    work'   TYNAN 872:50
  every day surmount a f.   EMER 313:46
  fate in what I cannot f.   ROET 694:3
  f. a day whose evil is upon the wing   KORAN 479:91
  f. and awe   WORD 928:51
  f. attends her not   SHAK 745:39
  f. before him   BIBLE 97:59
  F.…helps you to race longer and live
    longer   SENNA 728:99
  f. in a handful of dust   ELIOT 305:53
  f. intensified the love   JACK 433:30
  f. is f. itself   ROOS 696:43
  F. is the great mover   BART 62:13
  f. it would make me conservative   FROST 339:6
  f. no ill   SCOT 725:61
  f. of being an absurdity   FIND 323:60
  f. of every man   JONS 450:57
  F. of Fifty   JONG 448:7
  f. of finding something worse   BELL 73:56
  f. of letting people down   WILK 911:99
  f. of little men   ALLI 13:61
  f. of one evil   BOIL 138:38
  f. of Political economy   SELL 727:84
  f. of something after death   TWAIN 871:7
  f. of suffering injustice   LARO 491:48
  f. of the dead   ACKR 3:56
  f. of the Lord is the beginning   BIBLE 97:75
  f. rationalized away   MAIL 540:52
  f. that the British electorate   WEBB 893:66
  f. that the Russian government   HERZ 400:56
  f. the birds of prey   SHAK 758:18
  f. thy nature   SHAK 766:80
  f. to hate   SHAK 735:27
  f. toward me is taught   BIBLE 103:29
  f.…we know not what   DRYD 288:42
  F. ye not therefore   BIBLE 111:28
  first boredom, then f.   LARK 491:35

flight and f.   MCCA 527:87
Fly hence, our contact f.!   ARNO 32:22
for f.…never get out   WEBS 894:78
Fostered…by f.   WORD 925:91
freedom from f.   ROOS 696:50
hate that which we often f.   SHAK 764:16
haunts of horror and f.   TENN 845:97
heart shall not f.   BIBLE 95:7
hope could have no f.   THOM 856:64
In f. begotten   GRAV 367:67
In Place of F.   BEVAN 84:18
let thy wiseness f.   SHAK 755:35
little with the f. of the Lord   BIBLE 99:32
Love mixed with f.   WEBS 895:8
Mankind, f. your Lord   KORAN 478:52
many things to f.   BACON 49:17
masters the f. of death   BACON 47:74
Men f. death   BACON 47:73
mercy toward them that f. him   BIBLE 97:64
Neither f. nor courage saves   ELIOT 305:42
never f., man   HOUS 416:91
never negotiate out of f.   KENN 462:10
no f. of any failure   FAWC 319:80
No passion so effectually…than f.   BURKE 167:99
no want to them that f. him   BIBLE 95:13
O believers, f. God   KORAN 478:67
perfect love casteth out f.   BIBLE 125:40
Pity is lost in rage and f.   CARL 192:11
pleasant situation of having no f.   CUMM 247:98
poise of hope and f.   MILT 577:36
Render…f. to whom f.   BIBLE 120:86
salvation with f. and trembling   BIBLE 123:55
self-examination with…f.   ICHI 428:39
sense by…echoes of f.   EVANS 316:20
so long as they f.   ACCI 1:16
strange that men should f.   SHAK 747:89
The f. that kills   WORD 926:18
There is a lurking f.   SAGAN 708:4
there is not a word of f.   LAND 488:82
those with an irrational f. of life   CONN 233:66
'Tis time to f.   SHAK 769:50
walk in f. and dread   COLE 225:90
weakness to lament or f.   SHAK 731:85
Well-founded f.   WOOD 921:18
what we f. of death   SHAK 758:38
whom shall I f.   BIBLE 94:6
whom shall I f.   BIBLE 127:86
whom shall I f.?   BIBLE 94:6
whom shall I f.?   BIBLE 127:86
who will not f.?   BIBLE 106:8
Why f. death?   FROH 338:81
with religion and f.   JONS 449:27
feared f. by Spain, by France   SIXT 794:88
  is it better to be loved than f.   MACH 533:98
  they that f. the LORD   BIBLE 106:21
fearful F. and hostile behavior   FULB 341:45
  f. thing to fall into the hands   BIBLE 124:84
  goodness never f.   SHAK 758:39
  O f. meditation!   SHAK 772:25
  Upon a f. summons   SHAK 751:97
  Why are ye f.   BIBLE 110:18
fearing f. to attempt   SHAK 757:17
fearless But thou liv'st f.   HERR 399:36
  F. minds climb   SHAK 730:82
fears delivered me from all my f.   BIBLE 95:12
  direction of our f.   BERR 82:60
  dispelled their f.   MILT 581:11
  f. do make us traitors   SHAK 768:26
  f. may be liars   CLOU 222:21
  F., prejudices, misconceptions   LLOY 513:6
  f. shall be in the way   BIBLE 101:92
  f. that I may cease to be   KEATS 457:93
  fifty hopes and f.   BROW 161:48
  Humanity with all its f.   LONG 516:54
  its joys and f.   BROW 161:34
  leave us in pale f.   WEBS 894:77
  longer shivering under f.   MILT 585:28
  nightly f.   GRAY 370:28
  no human f.   WORD 924:80
  nostalgic about old f.?   ACKR 3:57
  old f. about our sissiness   WHITE 902:70
  producing f. and anxieties   KING 468:40
  Prosperity is not without many f.   BACON 47:81
  secret…griefs and f.   BACON 48:84
  To him that ever f.   SHAK 760:87
  when f.…were rife   VAUG 878:48
  Whoever f. contradiction   SAINT 709:25

Who f. to speak of Ninety-Eight?   INGR 429:59
feasibility barest requirements of f.   MCEW 531:66
feast f. his neighbours   SHAK 746:57
  f. is made for laughter   BIBLE 101:88
  f. of experience   GOLD 361:35
  going to a f.   JONS 449:25
  Goldsmith's fine f.   GARR 346:54
  imagination of a f.   SHAK 734:4
  improper mating is a perpetual f.   SMITH 799:76
  Liberty's a glorious f.!   BURNS 170:73
  When I would make a f.   HARI 382:79
feasting f. with your ealdormen   BEDE 68:54
feasts public f.…public rout   DAVI 254:36
feat difficult f. for a…male   PLATH 654:64
  empty f.…to cheat   CLOU 223:39
feather Blade on the f.   CORY 238:78
  each f.   HUGH 419:39
  f. footed through   WAUGH 892:31
  f. to tickle the intellect   LAMB 487:62
  f. will turn the scale   SHAK 758:42
  light as a f.   SPUR 811:41
  milk-white f. in a crow   CAMP 186:60
  never moults a f.!   DICK 267:14
  reach for my f. Boa   GINS 357:66
  snug as a f. mattress   ANGE 17:40
  white owl's f.   ALLI 13:61
  winged with its own f.   KELL 460:76
  wit's a f.   POPE 660:25
feather-bed f.-b. of correctitude   BENN 76:51
feathers beautified with our f.   GREE 371:80
  bluejay in peacock f.   LAFO 485:9
  brain of f.   POPE 662:70
  cover thee with his f.   BIBLE 96:53
  f. are more beautiful?   SHAK 732:43
  f. will soon soak through   HOLM 407:79
  'Hope' is the thing with f.   DICK 272:58
  plumes her f.   MILT 577:35
  sad Time his f. move!   SPEN 809:5
feature f. of the Rugby game   ANON 21:26
  f. of this institution   DICK 268:26
  immortal f. of loveliness   MILT 579:79
  original f. of any religion   PAINE 634:94
  show virtue her own f.   SHAK 754:86
features best f. of that…form   SHAW 781:94
  commanding f.   HUNT 423:26
  D.…possessed…two dramatic f.   POWE 666:79
  F. are an index   DICK 268:41
  f. from behind the unreasoning   MELV 564:30
  f. gets on your mind   LEAC 496:63
  f. of clerical cut   ELIOT 307:6
  many f. at the same time   HOMA 408:8
  my f. rot away   WILB 907:75
  One of the saddest f.   ECON 298:81
February not Puritanism but F.   KRUT 481:29
  such a F. face   SHAK 745:26
fecundity what it is about f.   DILL 274:13
federal f. government   WILL 911:1
  so poor a record…as the F. Reserve   FRIE 337:65
federation F. of the world   TENN 840:81
fee hold the gorgeous East in f.   WORD 926:20
  set my life at a pin's f.   SHAK 751:26
  soul moves in his f.   JONS 449:22
feeble resource of the f.   GIBB 352:58
  weak and f. woman   ELIZ 309:60
feed f. he must and will   EMER 312:31
  f. myself With…poison   SHAK 764:21
  f. on him in thy heart   BOOK 141:8
  throw a f. into her   RUNY 702:81
  Will you still f. me   LENN 503:98
Feeder Mr F., B.A.   DICK 269:55
feeder doth choke the f.   SHAK 734:7
feeding starve with f.   SHAK 769:68
feel begins to f. unwell   KIPL 470:82
  dislike what I fancy I f.   ANON 22:53
  don't f. like going into it   SALI 710:51
  don't know how to f.   KENN 462:5
  Englishman…afraid to f.   FORS 331:47
  f. good after   HEMI 394:4
  f. hot and think cold   CARY 198:61
  f. keenly and strongly   STAEL 812:51
  f. not what they inspire   SHEL 786:17
  f. with them   BENN 76:56
  f. you've done something   HEMI 393:95
  make him f. that way   TWAIN 871:5
  No comfortable f.   HOOD 410:52
  Now does he f.   SHAK 768:35
  power…to make you f.   CONR 234:95

something more to do than f.	LAMB 486:26
that matters is whether you f. it	COLE 225:76
though you f. nothing	JULI 452:6
thow shalt nat f.	CHAU 208:55
women f. just as men f.	BRON 154:78
feeling All violent f.	RUSK 704:10
art must express a distinct f.	FRIE 337:72
barbarous f. of nationality	SENI 728:98
Certainty. F. Joy	PASC 641:39
constellations of f.	DOUG 283:21
cruelty is the primary f.	SADE 708:93
extra dimension of f.	FOWL 332:67
failure of f.	STEV 820:34
f....came as a...surprise	LESS 505:40
f. I'm falling	FERL 321:12
f. of all happiness	WORD 928:54
f. of emulsion	PERE 648:55
f. of Sunday	RHYS 684:28
f. of vengeance	DREN 287:8
F. teaches much more	DU 293:77
f. that here it is 11 o'clock	BRAN 150:89
f. that lures us on to joys	CONR 234:6
f. that you can't make it	POWE 666:90
f. which we derive from knowing	LAMB 486:44
f. you've been cheated?	ROTT 700:37
formal f. comes	DICK 272:60
generous and honest f.	BURKE 168:5
High mountains are a f.	BYRON 180:26
imprecision of f.	ELIOT 308:23
inner experience and inner f.	LAWR 495:30
keen vision and f.	ELIOT 304:8
lie down until the f. passes	HUTC 424:54
lonely f., but euphoric, too	CAMP 186:75
lost pulse of f.	ARNO 31:99
Love is not only a f.	BALZ 57:15
more true f.	JOWE 451:79
must not think that f. is everything	FLAU 326:29
Nor form, nor f.	WORD 924:82
not merely as f.	PLATH 654:64
obsessed by the f.	SPEN 807:66
profound f. of the power	NORTH 618:68
pure expressions of f.	AYER 45:11
purely personal F.	CUMM 247:99
that's a f. disputation	SHAK 742:19
true writers have experienced this f.	SARR 715:38
without a f. of disappointment	LAMB 486:38
feelings Aren't our best f.	BALZ 58:19
artist with true f.	FRIE 337:67
can't put them out of his f.	CARY 199:62
define her f. in language	HARDY 381:53
f. and convictions	MORI 598:83
f. of awe and respect	DICK 266:63
f. of human beings	JAMES 434:74
f. of liberty	PITT 652:40
f. of Sophia	AUST 42:56
f. on leaving Eton	CONN 233:74
f. prey upon us	AUST 44:96
f. these dull scenes produce	CRAB 242:1
f. you haven't really got	LAWR 495:24
get human f. right	HUTC 424:50
Irish f. and sensitivities	HAUG 385:28
keeping f. at bay	BROO 156:23
language of our f.	FRIE 337:70
no room for new f.	ELIOT 303:88
no spontaneous f.	ORWE 629:82
some of the uneasy f.	HUXL 426:14
feels f. it all as one	JAMES 434:64
fees answered, as they took their f.	BELL 72:54
f. are sufficient punishment	BAIL 52:2
very fat f.	BURG 167:86
feet aching hands and bleeding f.	ARNO 32:4
all enemies under his f.	BIBLE 121:15
all things under his f.	BIBLE 94:87
at a funeral and knew their f.	MAUG 561:75
beneath a monarch's f.	BURNS 171:90
black f. of the night	GILM 356:56
blooming round our f.	BETJ 84:6
both f. off the ground	JOHN 440:81
bound...about the f. of God	TENN 843:31
cloths under your f.	YEATS 933:38
credit...sprang upon its f.	WEBS 894:71
crowes f. be growen	CHAU 208:56
cutting off our f.	SWIFT 831:69
dapper from your napper to your f.	COLL 227:35
delivered...my f. from falling	BIBLE 97:76
die on your f.	IBAR 427:31
direct your f.	FIEL 323:46

down at her f.	TRAV 864:43
due f. never fail	MILT 577:22
exertions of your hands and f.	CONR 234:2
f. began to stutter	BURT 174:65
f. go down to death	BIBLE 99:13
f. in ancient time	BLAKE 135:82
f. like unto fine brass	BIBLE 125:45
f. of him that bringeth good tidings	BIBLE 104:47
f....of iron and part of clay	BIBLE 105:94
f. of the aged	BIBLE 108:57
f. on the ground	FERL 321:12
f. planted firmly	ROOS 696:47
f. planted on level ground	GOHE 360:27
f. shod with the preparation	BIBLE 122:52
f. thy tribute bring	LYTE 524:16
f. were almost gone	BIBLE 96:41
fog comes on little cat f.	SAND 713:92
get a democracy on its f.	PULI 672:3
goat f. dance an antic hay	MARL 552:89
hear a horse's f.	KIPL 473:61
hear it through their f.	SOUSA 804:92
Hell's darkness under his f.	CARL 193:37
herb at your f.	TROL 866:87
I have deserted...sighing at your f.	CONG 232:43
Its f. were tied	KEATS 457:87
Keep Thou my f.	NEWM 612:62
lamp unto my f.	BIBLE 97:84
lantern to my f.	SHAK 730:55
leaves the marks of his f.	LEAC 496:56
let my f. spend...time	OWENS 632:67
like hinds' f.	BIBLE 94:95
little children...Round his f.	SHEL 783:35
little snow-white f.	YEATS 932:29
meet those dancing f.	DUBIN 292:64
moon under her f.	BIBLE 126:65
nearer than hands and f.	TENN 847:36
nice f. and plenty of money	ASHF 35:2
not on its f.	HEMP 395:33
of my f. and my nails	NERU 611:42
palms before my f.	CHES 211:43
pansy at my f.	WORD 926:23
polished with the tread of f.	DICK 267:25
room at your f.?	BALL 55:72
rude facts at your f.	RABAN 675:61
Scots lords at his f.	BALL 56:87
set my f. upon a rock	BIBLE 95:18
shake off the dust of your f.	BIBLE 111:25
shoes from off thy f.	BIBLE 88:9
shoes on your f.	BIBLE 88:16
shoes right off its f.	DICK 268:43
skull, and the f.	BIBLE 92:38
slippered f.	GRAH 366:39
swift pattering of naked f.	DOYLE 285:56
tempt with wand'ring f.	MILT 581:28
things before his f.	ENNI 314:70
through the head down to the f.	ANGE 17:38
thy holy f.	BLAKE 133:23
tremble under her f.	TENN 845:92
walks with aimless f.	TENN 843:41
What stranger's f.	HOUS 416:81
wind's f. shine	SWIN 833:24
feigning Most friendship is f.	SHAK 749:53
truest poetry is f.	SHAK 750:66
felicity Absent thee from f.	SHAK 755:41
bliss and sole f.	MARL 551:75
f. in such government a rarer thing	BACON 50:67
more f. on the far side	SMITH 799:77
none can boast sincere f.	DRYD 292:59
optics of these eyes to behold f.	BROW 158:74
fell book be f.	SWIFT 830:55
instant that he f.	SCOTT 723:2
stood, and f. who f.	MILT 582:42
fellers f....kick your bollocks	LOFT 515:31
fellow damned f.-feeling	MACD 530:48
f. ain't got a soul	STEI 815:34
f. of a good respect	SHAK 748:23
f. that is neither a wit...nor a fool	CONG 231:18
Hail f., well met	SWIFT 831:91
hard to be a good f.	WYCH 931:11
hook-nosed f. of Rome	SHAK 743:62
no f. in the firmament	SHAK 747:93
other f. just blinked	RUSK 703:97
perfect citizen may be a fine f.	DOUG 283:31
Promise to forget this f.	SHER 787:34
respect the other f.'s religion	MENC 566:75
That f. seems...to possess	JOHN 444:90
That's a brave f.	SHAK 769:61

this f. doesn't know	TRUM 868:33
touchy, testy, pleasant f.	ADDI 6:13
fellow-citizen As f.-c.	GILB 355:20
fellow-creature esteem with a f.-c.	LAMB 486:44
fellow-creatures torture...of his f.-c.	FROU 339:21
fellowmen majority of their f.	DU 293:75
fellow-men f.-m. can do little	EMER 313:53
one that loves his f.-m.	HUNT 423:34
fellow-rover laughing f.-r.	MASE 559:23
fellows Bark when their f. do	SHAK 775:11
f. of another college	LITT 512:77
f....the flood could not wash away	CONG 231:17
f. were practising	JOYCE 451:82
level of his humble f.	HUXL 426:10
mighty fine f. nowadays	STEV 822:3
Nature hath framed strange f.	SHAK 739:35
Nay, droop not, f.	MASS 560:46
some o' them low f.	DICK 266:79
ten good f. and one good day	MILNE 575:87
Those grave f.	STEE 814:2
What should such f. as I do	SHAK 753:79
fellowship f. that they may never	MALO 542:7
he that hath f.	BIBLE 107:49
no f. with one that is mightier	BIBLE 108:50
pass through in His f.	SCHW 721:70
right hands of f.	BIBLE 122:35
felon When a f.'s not engaged	GILB 354:3
felt could not portray all I f.	HOLM 407:70
Genius is f.	DIDE 273:88
female adult American Negro f.	ANGE 17:35
all f. life...unclean	STAN 812:67
bad f. cooks	NIET 615:23
cast on f. wits	BRAD 149:80
child of our grandmother Eve, a f.	SHAK 733:74
chosen and f. shall be homely	KENN 462:2
Christ will perhaps be a f.	NIGH 616:34
fashionable f. life	SPEKE 806:36
f. emotions of aggression	LESS 505:40
f. of the species	KIPL 474:82
f. principle	LEGU 501:58
f. worker is the slave	CONN 234:91
images of f. beauty	WOLF 919:79
lay down my life for the British f.?	CLOU 223:30
male and f. created he them	BIBLE 85:41
neither male nor f.	BIBLE 122:36
our excess f. population	WRIG 929:72
sea...is a mighty f.	SEXT 728:17
Strengthen the f. mind	WOLL 921:6
two and two...male and the f.	BIBLE 86:64
unprotected f. travelling	BUTL 178:74
vindictiveness of the f.	CONN 233:77
What f. heart can gold despise?	GRAY 368:99
whole f. line of ancestry	EDGE 299:7
females imbecility in f.	AUST 44:93
make no fuss about f.	CAMPO 187:83
feminine beautiful f. tissue	HARDY 382:62
distinctively f.	HARDY 382:57
f. half of the world	MERE 567:11
f. in the man	KENT 464:59
Success is f.	FAUL 319:73
tired of being the f. spouse	DIAZ 265:50
who is her life, is f.	PATM 643:64
femininity handicraft of f.	OLIP 624:64
feminism 'beginning' of f.	ROWB 701:49
brief flowerings of f.	FALU 317:42
cardinal tenets of f.	LYND 524:15
F. has become a...vegetable drawer	PAGL 634:82
hate discussions of f.	FREN 336:42
feminist f. writer	WELD 897:44
I am a f.	JORD 450:67
fen England...is a f.	WORD 925:11
plashy f.	WAUGH 892:31
fence Hussein...is the f.	ANON 25:73
If the f. is strong enough	SMITH 798:50
old mare might droop across a f.	SMITH 799:64
fender propped on the f.	GRAH 366:39
Fenianism guilty authors of F.	ARNO 33:50
fennel box that f. Grows around	RANS 679:27
fens f. of jargon?	BAKER 53:23
reek o'th' rotten f.	SHAK 769:66
ferlie f. he spied wi' his e'e	BALL 56:89
fermentation requires long f.	CAPO 189:30
fern sparkle out among the f.	TENN 846:2
the f.-dark indifference	LAWR 494:7
ferret-faced f.-f., white-eyed boys	STEV 821:81
ferry row us o'er the f.	CAMP 186:70
fertile ambrosial and f.	THOR 857:75

f. pedant	WALP 887:37
such a fix to be so f.	NASH 608:81
fertilize f. the whole world	TOCQ 861:81
fervent f. in spirit	BIBLE 120:81
festal line of f. light	ARNO 32:20
fester Lilies that f.	SHAK 772:38
festina F. lente	AUGU 42:47
festival cannot woo in f. terms	SHAK 745:24
Death is the supreme F.	BONH 140:60
night before some f.	SHAK 736:64
Something like a f.	ANGE 17:39
fetishism Commodity f.	TATE 837:7
fettered so oft has f. me	HERR 400:46
You are f.	DICK 268:28
fetters bound him with f. of brass	BIBLE 90:75
F. of gold are still f.	ASTE 36:22
feud Fhairshon swore a f.	AYTO 45:16
feudal anachronistic, f. institution	ACHE 2:23
feuds f., and jealousies, and sorrows	SASS 716:60
Forget all f.	MACA 526:72
fever bred a f.	THOM 852:63
enigma of the f. chart	ELIOT 308:21
f. called 'Living'	POE 657:30
life's fitful f.	SHAK 768:14
Of chills and f. she died	RANS 679:21
youth is bent by...wintry f.	THOM 852:57
feverish over trembly and f.	TWAIN 871:6
fever-trees set about with f.-t.	KIPL 473:42
Février Janvier and F.	NICH 613:83
few appointment by the corrupt f.	SHAW 778:5
expression which the f. desire	PARE 636:36
f. and evil have the days...been	BIBLE 88:5
Gey f., and they're a' deid	ANON 21:25
grinders cease because they are f.	BIBLE 101:92
hated the ruling f.	BENT 77:71
owed by so many, to so f.	CHUR 216:78
There are not f.	JONS 449:41
We f., we happy f.	SHAK 746:60
where f. have been	KENN 461:96
fez necessary to abolish the f.	ATAT 37:32
Fhairshon F. swore a feud	AYTO 45:16
fib Destroy his f....in vain	POPE 661:35
fibre flesh and bone, f. and liquids	ELLI 311:88
fibres f. of England	FORS 331:28
fickle all men call thee f.	SHAK 736:70
and f. is the South	TENN 842:9
Whatever is f.	HOPK 412:86
Woman is often f.	FRAN 334:95
fiction AIDS is good for is f.	WELD 896:38
All f. is for me	WILS 915:74
best thing in f.	WILDE 909:30
biography is ultimately f.	MALA 541:84
But in a f.	SHAK 753:67
condemn it as an improbable f.	SHAK 757:84
don't make for very good f.	TROL 867:12
escapist f.	GALB 343:3
every 'I' is a f.	WALC 884:76
fact and f. shouldn't be mixed	BOWEN 147:29
Fact is stranger than f.	GERV 351:47
fascinating f.	BANKS 59:38
f. is a necessity	CHES 211:44
f....makes justice	PALEY 635:10
F. should render...morals	FORD 330:6
great temple of f.	UPDI 875:92
happiness ever been the subject of f.?	UPDI 875:1
heroes and villains from f.	AUDEN 41:27
in f. as in life	AUCH 39:72
Isherwood became a f.	BURU 174:84
money...to write f.	WOOLF 922:42
more lies than...self-indulgent f.	BYATT 178:90
newspapers...continuous f.	BEVAN 85:23
not an easy country for a f.-writer	UPDI 875:98
Poetry is a...piece of f.	MENC 565:57
Poetry is the supreme f.	STEV 819:13
Poetry is the supreme f.	STEV 820:47
police dog of American f.	FADI 317:37
predilection for genre f.	DISCH 275:29
Science f., like Brazil	DISCH 275:30
Stranger than f.	BYRON 182:97
That is what f. means	WILDE 909:41
to writing f.	UPDI 874:85
traditional f.	GALB 343:95
write f. and I'm told	ROTH 699:30
wrote f. as if it were	WILDE 910:67
fictions As a maker of f.	LECA 499:26
Perhaps we are all f.	GREE 371:73
Who says that f. only	HERB 398:6

fictitious f. election results that elect a	
f. president	MOORE 596:45
fiddle F., we know, is diddle	SWIN 834:53
good tune...on an old f.	BUTL 178:75
hog that could f.	ROCH 691:64
important beyond all this f.	MOORE 595:29
Music...plays second f. to none	ELLI 310:77
sell his f.	BURNS 171:96
trissyllables are f. rhymes	SMART 796:24
fiddle-de-dee French for f.-d.-d.?	CARR 197:26
fiddler f., and consequently a rogue	SWIFT 830:64
Fidele fair F.'s grassy tomb	COLL 228:41
fidelity books...our f. to truth	CONR 234:10
disparagements of his wife's f.	SHAW 781:96
gossamer f. of mere Man	POE 656:20
scrupulous f. to the truth	CONR 235:17
stone f. They hardly meant	LARK 490:30
fidget moved by little f. wheels	SLES 796:15
fie F., fo, and fum	SHAK 763:79
field as a flower of the f.	BIBLE 97:66
be on the f. of play	MILNE 575:87
beside a f. of grain	PARK 638:81
big f. of rye	SALI 711:61
death in the hunting f.	MORT 599:14
dignity in tilling a f.	WASH 889:78
every other f. has left nature	MOND 590:51
f. for their efforts	BRON 154:78
f. is full of shades	THOM 855:39
f. of social organization	MENC 565:60
Flodden's fatal f.	SCOTT 723:3
Happy f. or mossy cavern	KEATS 457:92
hill or f. or river	TENN 842:5
In a f. by the river	YEATS 932:29
In love's f.	CRAS 244:42
It is that cricket f.	POWYS 667:97
leave the whole f.	HELL 392:63
left on the f. not a few	DAVIS 256:66
like the brambles in a wild f.	DIDE 274:3
love of f. and coppice	MACK 533:15
man of the f.	BIBLE 87:84
market, hearth and f.	KIPL 474:75
on the f. and city	THAC 849:90
on the f. of battle	PAST 642:47
presence on the f.	WELL 897:62
rushed into the f.	BYRON 180:24
single f.	WORD 926:23
single in the f.	WORD 927:34
some corner of a foreign f.	BROO 156:6
tills the f.	TENN 846:25
What though the f.	MILT 580:1
whether it's a f.	WILD 911:82
Fields like...W.C. F. movies	HAWES 385:30
say about W C F.	ROST 699:10
fields At Play In The F.	MATT 561:70
blown f. or	SWIN 833:39
blue f. of heaven	KEATS 456:78
broken head in Cold Bath F.	MACA 526:58
dead, but in the Elysian f.	DISR 277:83
disgrace to the playing f.	FRY 339:22
farmer without f.	PARK 639:88
f. and flocks have charms	CRAB 242:87
f. and the waters shout	MERE 567:96
f. of amaranth	LAND 488:81
f. of barley and of rye	TENN 838:42
f. of millions of farms	HOOV 411:57
f. that their fathers have tilled	CHUR 217:81
f. that we have planted	MUIR 602:63
f. where Troy once was	OVID 631:41
fight in the f.	CHUR 216:76
flowering of His f.	TENN 847:44
flowerless f. of heaven	SWIN 832:17
foreign f., from Dunkirk	DAVIS 256:66
From the green f.	WORD 924:88
In f. where roses fade	HOUS 415:64
fields look on the f.	BIBLE 117:85
Low over dim f.	MERE 566:94
no definite...meaning in other f.	SART 715:40
poems...in the factories and f.	MACD 530:43
Poetic f. encompass me around	ADDI 5:2
rush through the f. in trains	CHES 213:99
sharp light the f. did lie	FREE 336:43
Strawberry f. forever	LENN 503:99
To f. where flies no...hail	HOPK 412:78
unshorn f., boundless and beautiful	BRYA 164:13
walk through the f.	CORN 237:69
What f.	SHEL 784:59
whispering of f. unsown	OWEN 632:62

fiend Beneath is all the f.'s	SHAK 763:89
dreadful f. of gods	SPEN 809:8
f. for becoming a torrent	LIGNE 509:29
F. walked up and down	MILT 582:48
frightful f....behind him tread	COLE 225:90
Like a f. hid in a cloud	BLAKE 135:60
marble-hearted f.	SHAK 762:62
fiends alleyways and drug f.	LIND 510:46
f. that plague thee	COLE 225:82
f. will snatch at it	SHAK 761:17
fierce f. and bald	SASS 716:61
That bright and f.	TENN 842:9
fierceness cage if...any sign of f.	CARB 189:39
swalloweth the ground with f.	BIBLE 93:75
fiere my trusty f.!	BURNS 171:1
Fife Thane of F.	SHAK 768:34
fife Elephant, That practised on a f.	CARR 197:33
fifth And he came f.	JOYCE 452:89
f. of the people	KENN 464:50
f. part of the Earth	FIELD 322:30
plead the F. Amendment	NIXON 617:46
The f. column	MOLA 589:25
fifty At f. you have the choice	CART 198:55
difficult thing is to have it at f.	DEGAS 259:33
Fear of f.	JONG 448:7
won't speak to me for f. minutes	DOYLE 285:63
fig an Olive, and a Turkey F.	BETH 82:73
don't care a f.!	LEAR 497:80
f. for those by law protected	BURNS 170:73
F. leaves of democratic	KENN 462:98
like a f. purple f.	PLATH 654:72
sewed f. leaves together	BIBLE 86:50
fight able to f. and conquer	TROT 867:15
a harder matter to f.	TENN 846:4
bear-like I must f.	SHAK 769:43
beautifully the English f.!	NAPO 607:63
believer will f. another	GREE 371:74
better to f. for the good	TENN 846:1
British won't f.	GALT 345:30
cannot f. against the future	GLAD 358:90
cannot f. for love	SHAK 737:96
can we f. with fifty-three?	TENN 848:60
clouds of the f.	KEY 465:76
cock won't f.	BEAV 67:21
couldn't begin to f.	TAYL 837:19
day we started to f.	ANON 24:35
Don't give up the f.	MARL 551:68
don't want to f.	HUNT 422:21
easier to f. for principles	STEV 820:49
f. and die for your country	GOLD 362:76
f. and f. again	GAIT 342:87
f. begins within himself	BROW 161:51
f. between two bald men	BORG 145:94
f. for freedom and truth	IBSEN 428:34
f. for mankind	SAINT 709:14
F. for our National Intelligence	CATT 200:2
f. for the right	CURZ 249:53
f. for your country	HOMER 409:20
f. in defence of one's country	HOMER 409:22
f. is bigger than life itself	KING 468:29
f. it out	GRANT 366:55
f. on the beaches	CHUR 216:76
f. on until the end	HAIG 376:66
F. the good f.	BIBLE 124:80
f. them, and pursue them	JOAN 438:52
fought a good f.	BIBLE 124:86
friendly kind of f.	STUB 827:2
Go I to f.	SHAK 734:1
great f. did win	SOUT 805:1
I shall f.	THAT 851:34
life be not a real f.	JAMES 434:67
lost, lost f., for the cause	CLOU 223:35
man...too proud to f.	WILS 916:10
man who runs away will f.	MENA 565:50
never a moment ceased the f.	TENN 848:62
no stomach to this f.	SHAK 746:56
not yet begun to f.	JONES 447:91
only the f. to recover	ELIOT 308:24
recalls...a f.	AMADO 13:74
those that fly, may f. again	BUTL 177:59
Those that I f.	YEATS 933:48
thou fought the better f.	MILT 583:83
To f. aloud	DICK 272:54
too frightened to f.	TALL 836:85
Ulster will f.	CHUR 215:55
we began this f.	GALS 344:26
We will f. them on the streets	HUSS 424:47

when you f.	HEMI 394:11
Wherever they's a f.	STEI 815:34
will not cease from mental f.	BLAKE 136:85
fighter clown, the boozer, the f.?	MAST 560:52
left to the f.'s honor	HEMI 394:5
no a bonny f.?	STEV 823:23
fighters nightmare f.	JARR 435:80
fighting f. against a superstitious	JAMES 433:33
f. amongst one and another	CLARK 219:54
f. for one thing—money	DEMP 261:87
F. is like champagne	MITC 588:97
F. still, and still destroying	DRYD 291:38
first twenty days of f.	CHUR 216:68
Football causeth f.	STUB 827:3
foremost f., fell	BYRON 180:24
formed through f.	MUSS 605:22
not conquering but f. well	COUB 238:86
period…between two periods of f.	BIER 129:38
tongue-tied's f.	HARR 384:1
twelve thousand f. men	SHAK 735:16
What are We f. for?	SERV 728:5
What is the use of f.	PANK 636:33
When there was any f.	GILB 355:32
when wilt thou leave f.	SHAK 743:50
who dies f. has increase	GREN 373:2
worth f. for, worth dying	MITC 588:93
fights f.…best part of married life	WILD 910:78
f. historical	GILB 354:99
f. you on patriotic principles	SHAW 777:65
knows what he f. for	CROM 245:69
scuffles of great f.	SHAK 764:9
figs better than f.	SHAK 764:14
ears fall off like f.	THOM 853:95
fig-tree green f.-t. in the story	PLATH 654:72
Train up a f.-t.	DICK 269:57
figurative f.…metaphorical God	DONNE 281:86
figure baby f. of the giant	SHAK 757:96
built about a mythical f.	HERB 397:83
can't f. him out	SHUL 790:93
f. in a country church	SWIFT 830:62
f. of Juno	BARR 61:94
f. which is as familiar to us	MACA 525:54
keeping your f. after 55	CART 198:55
masculine f. created by a woman	MENC 565:54
mourning f. walks	LIND 511:50
not a f. in the landscape	BRON 154:70
oblong angular f.	LEAC 496:58
passing away of a great f.	NEHRU 610:29
walk around a f.	ROSSO 698:7
figures f. fail you	ARLO 30:62
f. which do not exist for political	MARX 557:96
mystery is why we…collect these f.	BART 63:26
One composition…has many f.	DIDE 274:1
place occupied by the f.	MATI 560:62
prove anything by f.	CARL 192:24
traduce those f.	LEWIS 508:1
Fiji Golf is to F. what cricket is to America	SINGH 793:53
files foremost f. of time	TENN 841:86
filial untie the f. band	SCOTT 723:92
fill drunk his f.	SCOTT 723:4
much less f. them	ISAA 430:88
fillets pink f.	MACB 527:82
fillip rest's not worth a f.	BYRON 183:2
film a f. of mine that wasn't the director's cut	ALTM 13:73
A good f. script	MAMET 544:37
average…f. star	HEPB 396:58
director makes only one f. in his life	RENO 683:4
earn a million dollars a f.	WINN 917:25
F. art has a greater influence	BALA 53:26
F. Industry…Monarchy	MAMET 544:35
f. is never really good	WELL 897:49
F. is the least realistic	MAMET 544:38
greatest f. in the world	COPP 237:67
I always direct the same f.	FELL 319:86
only a good f.	BENN 76:32
right place to f. it	GARD 345:43
would get the f. made	OLDM 624:63
filmmaker central fact about the f.	WELL 897:50
film-makers few great f.-m.…might have	
been good novelists	RUSH 703:93
tell the younger f.-m.	SCOR 722:72
filmmaking no rules in f.	CAPRA 189:36
film-making fatal to good f.-m.	CHAN 205:88
films best f. are the best because	POLA 657:36
f. of one's own country	ANDE 16:18
hope to build a house with my f.	FASS 318:60
most f. are about one guy with a gun	LOACH 514:11

output of f. was prodigious	NIVEN 617:40
paintings and f.	WARH 889:62
seldom go to f.	BERR 82:64
started off in f. as a king	MORL 598:89
worst f. were always bad	NORM 618:61
filth f. and the sordidness	DONO 282:98
f. returns in's face	WEBS 894:84
hairy American f.	OSBO 630:13
remove f. and foulness	ABEL 1:3
so is f.	FORS 331:43
filthy all together become f.	BIBLE 94:89
f., sturdy, unkillable infants	POUND 664:29
not greedy of f. lucre	BIBLE 123:74
righteousnesses are as f. rags	BIBLE 104:63
fin winks the gold f.	TENN 842:14
final f. pleasure left to man	SNOW 802:35
I must bring out my Late Night F.	BEAV 67:25
My Indecision is F.	EBER 298:75
not f. because we are infallible	JACK 432:10
When the f. curtain comes down	MAJOR 541:73
your f. answer?	TARR 836:98
finality F. is not the language	DISR 276:66
finance functions of national f.	CHUR 216:62
site, a brief and f.	ROGE 694:11
Finchley Catherine the Great of F.	HEAL 389:2
find cannot f. it myself	KAFKA 454:29
ere you f. them	SHAK 739:41
f. information upon it	JOHN 444:9
to f. where you are going	STEI 816:37
with men I f. Him not	TENN 847:44
finding f. myself everyday	GIRO 358:84
f. of limited use to backlash	FALU 317:41
fine F. art is that in which	RUSK 704:12
f. wine leaves you with	AMER 14:77
May will be f. next year	HOUS 416:71
no one wants F. Artists	FULL 341:50
Old Cary Grant f.	GRANT 366:47
pop art and f. art	MACI 533:6
theft with a f., not death	MORE 596:61
think is particularly f.	JOHN 444:98
fineness no f. or accuracy	BELL 73:70
finer nothing could be f.	GORD 364:9
finery not bedizened with f.	TROL 866:74
finger bandaged f.	KIPL 474:84
Between my f. and my thumb	HEAN 389:3
chills the f. not a bit	NASH 609:98
clean f. nails	MORT 599:12
f. on the trigger	MACM 536:72
From the red gold keep thy f.	SCOTT 724:40
God's f. touched him	TENN 844:54
her choppy f. laying	SHAK 766:71
little f. shall be thicker	BIBLE 92:15
moving f. writes	FITZ 324:84
One f. in the…rectum	OSLER 630:17
pointed to with the f.	CICE 218:27
rugged f. to Heaven	LLOY 513:99
scratching of my f.	HUME 422:8
smile upon his f.'s end	SHAK 745:36
stick a f. into	SAFER 708:95
that lanky Yankee f.	CONN 232:54
Whose f.…on the trigger?	DAILY 250:66
fingers came forth f. of a man's hand	BIBLE 106:97
cannot lick his own f.	SHAK 737:74
dead men's f. call them	SHAK 755:25
f. of cold are corpse f.	LAWR 494:15
forc'd f. rude	MILT 578:45
judged…by the hovering f.	ANON 23:78
Just as my f.	STEV 819:21
kissed The f.	BROW 159:8
loyal to the tips of his stubby f.	ACHE 3:39
my f. wandered idly	PROC 670:58
nimble f. are no more	SITW 794:82
separate as the f.	WASH 889:79
staining of white f.	LEWIS 508:96
time that we pulled our f. out	EDIN 300:9
Until the F. Begin to Bleed	BUKO 165:51
whose f. are ten armies	GINS 357:62
With f. weary and worn	HOOD 410:45
work of thy f.	BIBLE 94:87
world…slipping through your f.	SHAW 781:72
finger-stalls fit—less f.-s.	GILB 355:28
finish start together and f. together	BEEC 69:62
test…is that you f. it	BENN 76:47
work is the f.	PEARY 645:1
finished f. in the first 100 days	KENN 462:11
It is f.	BIBLE 118:19
what just f. happening	KESEY 465:73

finite f. number of heart-beats	ARMS 30:79
Infinite…bury under the F.	CARL 192:99
Finland too late with F.	LLOY 513:7
Finn book…called Huckleberry F.	HEMI 394:10
Finnegans F. Wake took…years	PRIE 668:23
Joyce's F. Wake	NICO 614:96
fir f. that weepeth still	SPEN 808:73
Instead of the thorn…the f. tree	BIBLE 104:58
fire Absence is to love what wind is to f.	BUSSY 176:29
adamantine chains and penal f.	MILT 580:95
against my f.	SHAK 764:96
a light f. runs beneath my skin	SAPP 714:27
am on f. and I drown	LABE 482:53
at their hearts the f.'s centre	SPEN 807:47
beast imbued with such immortal f.?	BYRON 179:12
Beef and a sea-coal f.	OTWAY 631:33
believe that f. warms	HUME 422:6
brimstone and f.	BIBLE 87:79
Bring me my chariot of f.!	BLAKE 136:84
broad gate and the great f.	SHAK 762:39
bush burned with f.	BIBLE 88:8
Can a man take f. in his bosom	BIBLE 99:17
can't stand f.?	GALS 344:26
chariot of f.	BIBLE 92:28
cloven tongues like as of f.	BIBLE 119:29
compact of f.	SHAK 732:52
crowned knot of f.	ELIOT 309:51
different as…frost from f.	BRON 155:95
Don't f. unless fired upon	PARK 638:80
Doubt thou the stars are f.	SHAK 752:45
dropping-wells of f.	TENN 844:53
equally inspired with eager f.	ROCH 691:50
extinguishes candles and kindles f.	LARO 491:53
eyes were as a flame of f.	BIBLE 125:45
fell in the f.	GRAH 365:35
fetch f. from hell	WEBS 895:95
F. and fleet and candle-lighte	BALL 56:81
F., Blood, and Famine	HENR 395:45
F. burn, and cauldron bubble	SHAK 768:20
f. can burn	DANI 252:87
F..God of Abraham	PASC 641:39
f., is an excellent servant	COOP 236:54
f. is quite put out	DONNE 281:74
f. most pure	DONNE 279:34
F. Next Time	BALD 54:38
f. of s.	DICK 267:14
f. of sacrifice	ROCK 692:77
f. shall heat the deep	TENN 838:37
f. was furry	SITW 794:71
F. which Prometheus filch'd	BYRON 181:71
glass mingled with f.	BIBLE 126:70
God is a consuming f.	BIBLE 124:2
hath given me f.	SHAK 767:97
heap coals of f. upon his head	BIBLE 100:52
heaped-up sods upon the f.	COLUM 228:61
heart of f.	TENN 846:99
help to quench the f.	PRIOR 669:43
heretic that makes the f.	SHAK 770:80
hold a f. in his hand	SHAK 734:4
how great a matter a little f. kindleth	BIBLE 124:12
immortal f.	AUDEN 40:10
inspiration, 'sacred f.'	MOND 590:50
it is a f.	PEELE 646:12
kindle f. with snow	SHAK 729:33
kindly f. was fled	SCOTT 722:86
lake of f.	BIBLE 127:78
let them go to the f.	BINY 130:54
Like a cloud of f.	SHEL 784:55
Lord was not in the f.	BIBLE 92:24
melt in her own f.	SHAK 754:9
Most sacred f.	SPEN 808:89
neighbour's house is on f.	BURKE 168:28
nodding by the f.	YEATS 932:33
no wind, but pentecostal f.	ELIOT 309:38
O for a muse of f.	SHAK 745:29
Oft is without smoke	SPEN 808:74
on f. with the ships	ROBE 689:17
or ashes of a f.	LEON 504:19
Persons grouped around a f.	MCLU 536:60
philosophy puts out the f.	VOLT 883:43
pillar of f.	BIBLE 88:19
played with f.	VAUG 878:25
prepared to carry f.	PARN 639:92
raptures were All air and f.	DRAY 287:5
red ball of f.	AGAWA 8:71
restored by that refining f.	ELIOT 309:44
right Promethean f.	SHAK 734:86

flash came by a lightning f.   WILS 915:85
f. that brings good fortune   RHYS 684:29
Life…a f. of a firefly   HAGG 376:58
Mirth is like a f. of lightning   ADDI 6:20
that seeming bang and f.   ORWE 628:49
flashes like f. of lightning   SCHO 719:29
objects recognised, In f.   WORD 925:2
occasional f. of silence   SMITH 801:18
saw the f.   SZIL 834:66
some f. of genius   BYRON 181:52
flask forty cents a f.   LEAC 496:55
flat back to the gentleman's f.   MANS 547:93
believe that the earth is f.   DRIB 287:10
fictional characters are f.   WAUGH 893:52
He is many times f.   DRYD 288:25
Strike f. the thick rotundity   SHAK 763:72
teach it round or f.   JOHN 440:90
theorists who declare…world is f.   CANN 188:10
Very f., Norfolk   COWA 239:10
flatter abuse the King that f.   SHAK 769:49
F. the mountain tops   SHAK 771:16
Hope…dost thou f. me?   SIDN 790:12
flatterer f. does not have a good opinion   LABR 484:77
flattering nymphs with their f.   SITW 794:46
flattery care a bit for f.   MERE 567:6
care nothing for f.   CURZ 249:53
Dismiss…your f.   SHAK 733:54
f. is the bellows   SHAK 769:49
f. lost on poet's ear   SCOTT 723:89
f. of one's peers   LODGE 515:27
F. soothe…Death?   GRAY 369:11
guilt of f.   JOHN 445:44
Imitation is the sincerest form of f.   COLT 228:54
paid with f.   JOHN 442:49
questions…under the guise of f.   CHOP 214:25
school of f. and dissimulation   WENT 899:4
When f. soothes   DRYD 290:83
flatware look at f. catalogs   COUP 239:1
Flaubert a Tolstoy or a F.   WOLFE 920:2
His true Penelope was F.   POUND 664:36
shut up about F.   AMIS 14:95
flaunt got it, f. it   ANON 23:7
If you've got it, f. it   BROO 157:30
flavour faint f. of toast   TRAV 865:48
f. as hickory smoke   MUMF 603:79
full f. of their content   MILL 572:19
give f. to his tickled vanity   WEBB 893:62
high celestial f.   BYRON 182:83
ignorant of f.   FISH 324:79
spice…That gives it all its f.   COWP 241:72
flaw china jar receive a f.   POPE 659:70
fault or f.   GILB 354:11
flawed His f. heart   SHAK 764:4
We are the f. ones   DELI 261:80
flaws beautiful f. in nature   WOLL 921:8
hundred thousand f.   SHAK 763:70
We all have f.   THUR 859:42
flax smoking f. shall he not quench   BIBLE 111:39
smoking f. shall he not quench   BIBLE 103:43
flayed saw a woman f.   SWIFT 830:57
flaying f. would be fair   HOUS 416:90
flea between a louse and a f.   JOHN 446:59
clog the foot of a f.   SHAK 757:82
English literature's performing f.   OCAS 621:17
f. in mine ear   NASHE 609:12
Mark but this f.   DONNE 280:52
naturalists observe, a f.   SWIFT 832:2
volume can ever be written on the f.   MELV 564:35
fleas dog is full of f.   ACHE 3:50
f. that tease   BELL 73:65
F.…upon the body   LAND 488:77
praised his f.?   YEATS 933:41
rise with f.   WEBS 895:90
fled left his garment…and f.   BIBLE 88:97
lovers f. away   KEATS 459:43
fledglings crow loves his f.   MORE 596:58
flee They f. from me   WYATT 931:3
fleece f. was white as snow   HALE 377:80
forest f.   HOUS 415:55
won the Golden F.   BELL 72:39
fleet Arabian f.   GIBB 351:57
Beauteous the f.   SMART 797:29
Fire and f. and candle-lighte   BALL 56:81
f. of stars is anchored   FLEC 327:51
that is not also f.   THOM 854:14
Third F.'s sunken   HALS 378:94
took care of our f.   ADDI 6:21

who can be dull in F. Street   LAMB 486:28
whole f.'s lit up   WOOD 921:20
fleets Ten thousand f. sweep over   BYRON 180:44
flesh all f. shall see it together   BIBLE 103:36
All f. waxeth old   BIBLE 108:51
bloody f. our only food   ELIOT 308:22
bread and f. in the morning   BIBLE 92:17
delicate white human f.   FIEL 322:42
door of my f.   BRID 152:27
east wind made f.   APPL 28:26
empty boast of f.   HABI 376:53
errors of the f.   THOM 854:27
feel new gods in the f.   LAWR 494:4
few blows are struck into f.   MAIL 540:47
f. and blood   THOR 857:79
f. and blood   THAC 849:85
f. and blood so cheap!   HOOD 410:47
f. and my heart faileth   BIBLE 96:43
f.; but in what shape   MILT 581:9
f. is as grass   BIBLE 125:22
f. is sad, alas!   MALL 542:92
f. is weak   BIBLE 114:99
f. longeth for thee   BIBLE 96:35
F. of f., Bone   MILT 585:15
f. of her f.   BINY 130:51
F. Of Hope   NICH 613:86
f. of mine might be   SWIN 833:24
f. of my f.   BIBLE 86:47
f. of thy dear Son   BOOK 141:7
f. profiteth nothing   BIBLE 117:93
f. sinks downward   SHAK 735:32
F. was the reason   DE 260:57
f. which walls   SHAK 735:20
f. without cares   CIXO 219:38
From this world-wearied f.   SHAK 737:81
give them an heart of f.   BIBLE 105:86
give us hearts o' f.!   OCAS 621:14
happit f. and blude   FERG 321:9
heart and my f. crieth out   BIBLE 96:45
hollow prison of my f.   SHAK 731:93
horror of the word 'f.'   RENO 683:7
huge hill of f.   SHAK 742:15
in my f. shall I see God   BIBLE 93:64
Is my somber f. and skin   CULL 247:54
joys are more to f. and blood   DRYD 291:20
Let's press the f.   JOHN 440:87
little f.   AURE 42:52
look false f. and blood   MOORE 595:24
maketh marks in the f.   BIBLE 108:58
make your f. creep   DICK 266:72
marriage makes man and wife one f.   CONG 231:8
material is our own f.   THOR 857:79
men are f. and blood   SHAK 747:34
more fatal than painted f.   MACN 537:98
Mrs Forthby in the f.   SHAR 776:41
Neither f. nor fleshless   ELIOT 307:95
not of her f. and body   KEYN 465:80
outlive all f.   BYRON 181:55
pleasure of the f.   FUEN 340:41
poem…dream made f.   MILL 573:44
so much f.…so much nimbleness   DEKK 259:51
Take thou thy pound of f.   SHAK 740:83
they shall be one f.   BIBLE 86:47
things of the f.   BIBLE 120:73
this circle of f.   BROW 158:74
thorn in the f.   BIBLE 122:33
too solid f. would melt   SHAK 751:5
touch his bone and his f.   BIBLE 93:49
trees were surfaced like f.   LEE 500:45
vacations of the f.   TZARA 873:56
walk not after the f.   BIBLE 120:72
we are one, One f.   MILT 585:16
What case of f. and blood   ROCH 691:55
What's this f.?   WEBS 895:14
when we sat by the f. pots   BIBLE 88:21
Word was made f.   BIBLE 117:74
your despicable and rotten f.   MARQ 553:20
Fletcher gave Shakespeare and F. all   DENH 261:94
fleur f. de France as perdut   ANON 18:77
flew One f. over the cuckoo's nest   KESEY 465:70
something f. between me and the sun   BLUN 137:15
flexibility latter has f. of thought   PASC 640:5
flexible f. at all times   DIRK 275:26
flexitime F. is the essence of respect   PACK 633:70
flick bonded in their f. and flow   AVIS 44:6
flies As f. to wanton boys   SHAK 763:84
Dead f. cause the ointment   BIBLE 101:86

Eyes and Reason…to study F.   POPE 662:81
f. on summer eves   KEATS 460:61
f. when I pursue it   ELIZ 309:59
may catch small f.   SWIFT 830:58
Plague him with f.   SHAK 759:51
swarm like summer f.   SHAK 730:78
these summer f.   SHAK 734:91
Unfading moths, immortal f.   BROO 156:19
flight alarms of struggle and f.   ARNO 31:94
as immutable as those of f.   HEMI 394:17
day of their f.   MACA 526:55
Explores his solitary f.   MILT 581:31
f. is what they long for   WILL 912:20
f. of angels sing   SHAK 755:44
spread his aery f.   MILT 581:28
Swift be thine approaching f.   SHEL 786:18
Swift be thy f.!   SHEL 787:29
tiptoe for a f.   KEATS 457:79
flights four f. Thursday morning   WRIG 930:85
flighty f. as birds   DAY 257:86
flint snore upon the f.   SHAK 774:70
wait for the great f.   BIRN 131:70
Flintstones like relying on the F.   ARMEY 30:68
flip the rest is not worth a f.   BRON 155:79
flirtation bit of f. with missy   SPEKE 806:36
float English policy is to f. lazily   CECIL 202:29
F. like a butterfly   ALI 12:33
floating Artist of the F.World   ISHI 431:92
floats f. with the tide   HAZL 388:77
flock Christ's f.   BOOK 141:12
Fed the same f.   MILT 578:46
feed his f. like a shepherd   BIBLE 103:37
keeping watch over their f. by night   BIBLE 115:2
silent was the f.   KEATS 458:30
We are his f.   SCOT 725:64
flock-bed once a f.-b., but repaired   POPE 660:5
flocks fields and f. have charms   CRAB 242:87
f., or herds, of human   MILT 582:38
nibbling f. do stray   MILT 576:8
sang of f. and farms   VIRG 882:33
shepherds feed their f.   MARL 553:37
Flodden F.'s fatal field   SCOTT 723:3
flogging f. me constantly   TROL 867:6
flood across the f.   TENN 844:69
and takes the f.   TENN 847:53
broad f. behind   MACA 526:66
days that were before the f.   BIBLE 113:87
f. could not wash away   CONG 231:17
f. may bear me far   TENN 848:70
f. of remembrance   LAWR 494:94
f. that does not flow   SLES 796:15
not properly born, till f.   DICK 269:76
passage to the fallen f.   CRAB 242:99
rude bridge that arched the f.   EMER 312:2
taken at the f.   SHAK 748:16
telegraph poles above a f.   NICO 614:96
Thorough f., thorough fire   SHAK 737:75
tide…taken at the f.   BYRON 182:91
trees that yield to the f.   SOPH 804:85
years before the f.   MARV 555:61
floods f. of great waters   BIBLE 95:10
rain descended, and the f. came   BIBLE 110:13
floor beneath the watery f.   MILT 578:57
Clatter across the f.   MACC 527:83
f. under wages and a ceiling   WRIS 930:84
Look how the f. of heaven   SHAK 741:84
man has just waxed the f.   NASH 608:95
oiled his way around the f.   LERN 504:26
On the f. I am…at ease   POLL 657:34
put diamonds on the f.   RIVE 688:4
repeat that on the Golden F.!   HOUS 416:87
rose along the gusty f.   KEATS 459:42
swept the f.   GILB 353:94
three skips on the f.   BALL 56:77
trail…up the f.   STEV 823:39
women…kick the f.   OSBO 630:11
floors f. of memory   ELIOT 305:29
f. of plaister, and the walls of dung   POPE 660:5
f. of silent seas   ELIOT 304:21
flop Classics…prevent f.   WOOLF 923:53
f. in favour of your husband   DICK 271:22
f. is a f.   PAGL 634:81
total wreck, a f.   PORT 663:5
flops F. are a part of life   RUSS 706:68
Flora if he had married F.   SCOTT 723:14
Tasting of F.   KEATS 459:58
floral F. fascism   INDE 428:48

Florence maid called F.? SAKI 710:37
Rode past fair F. KEATS 458:27
Flores At F. in the Azores TENN 848:60
Florida Her name is F. SAKI 710:37
flotilla old f. lay KIPL 470:86
flounder f., the air ATWO 38:49
flour Finer than f., alive ROET 694:99
flourish f. or may fade GOLD 361:52
Human nature will not f. HAWT 386:38
No more doth f. SPEN 808:86
tidy and satisfactory f. ELIZ 310:66
flourishing fat and f. BIBLE 96:55
flow bonded in their flick and f. AVIS 44:6
flower About the f. disguised MARV 556:69
as a f. of the field BIBLE 97:66
bar the f. away ANON 19:82
bear no f. SHEL 786:13
Beauty is but a f. NASHE 609:18
blood-red f. of revolution RAND 678:15
bloom upon a f. THOM 854:18
blushing f. shall rise POPE 658:50
bot ane faiding f. HENR 396:55
Buddha…in the petals of a f. PIRS 652:25
constellated f. that never sets SHEL 787:24
creep from f. to f. SHEL 782:19
drives the f. THOM 852:57
fell upon a little western f. SHAK 737:94
f. amang them a' BALL 55:69
f. is born to blush unseen GRAY 369:17
f. is the concrete cloverleaf MUMF 603:77
f. of France is lost ANON 18:77
f. of old age DEMO 261:85
f. of Scotland WILL 914:65
f. that sad embroidery wears MILT 578:54
f. thereof falleth away BIBLE 125:22
glory in the f. WORD 927:28
grass withereth, the f. fadeth BIBLE 103:36
held my f. in a clenched fist HOFF 406:48
Here is the f. that you MEIL 563:10
How my face, your f. BROW 160:23
insect moves toward its f. BALZ 58:16
learning lightly like a f. TENN 844:66
look like the innocent f. SHAK 766:84
loved a tree or f. MOORE 596:53
lovelier f.…was never sown WORD 924:79
Man…cometh forth like a f. BIBLE 93:61
meanest f. that blows WORD 927:29
mysterious East, perfumed like a f. CONR 234:5
nayles whitter than the lylye f. CHAU 209:95
Nobody sees a f. OKEE 623:59
orange f. perfumes the bower SCOTT 725:45
pluck this f. safety SHAK 741:10
Poetry…the f. of…experience HUNT 423:30
same f. that smiles to day HERR 400:45
see…heaven in a wild f. BLAKE 135:56
seize the f. BURNS 172:19
shakes the f. free MANS 547:89
some gilded…f. VAUG 878:44
stem of the contained f. ROET 694:1
stronger than a f.? SHAK 772:25
sweetest f. for scent SHEL 785:86
sweetest f. of all the field SHAK 737:76
This midsummer f. SKEL 795:91
this the noble f. DONNE 281:79
to darn, to f. or knit LEWIS 507:81
touch his f. JONS 450:48
Wearing the white f. TENN 846:5
white rose and bean f. FRAME 333:79
whose fair f. SHAK 756:65
ys the f. of chevalry MALO 542:7
flower-bell fancy from a f.-b. BROW 161:48
flowering f. of His fields TENN 847:44
flowerings brief f. of feminism FALU 317:42
flowerless f. fields of heaven SWIN 832:17
f. rocks of hell SITW 793:59
flowers And it won't be f. AUDEN 39:80
azure moss and f. SHEL 783:45
bees are assaulting…the f. REED 681:78
better than a bunch of f. CARY 199:65
blushing f. POPE 658:50
brought…cannons rather than f. PEOP 647:24
but as a bed of f. DONNE 281:89
enjoy the spring f. SU 828:6
fairest f. WORD 929:64
Fair f. that are not gathered SHAK 732:50
f. begotten SWIN 832:19
f. come in stony places MASE 559:39

F. of all hue MILT 582:60
f. of the forest COCK 224:55
f. of the forest ELLI 310:78
f. the tenderness OWEN 632:52
f. to strew Thy way HERB 397:92
gathers its material from the f. BACON 47:60
Gave…her f. to love BROO 156:6
glass f. at Harvard MOORE 595:31
ground with vernal f. MILT 578:53
honey of all f. NASHE 609:11
hundred f. blossom MAO 548:12
immortal f. of poesy MARL 551:77
into foam of f. SWIN 833:24
intuitively in f. RUNGE 702:76
leaves and f. do cover WEBS 895:92
like f., a stronger scent STAEL 811:49
love…as the f. do RILKE 687:3
love to the f. KEND 461:95
lusty song of fruits and f. BLAKE 133:25
memories of f. and grass ROBE 689:19
men bearing f. SPARK 806:29
one which gathering f.…fears a DONNE 279:32
Our f. are merely—f. POE 656:23
Overlook a space of f. TENN 839:44
play with f. SHAK 745:36
prairie f. lie low LIND 511:52
sleeping f. WORD 928:46
That f. would bloom KEATS 457:4
the f. anew PHIL 650:90
thy garden f. JONS 449:37
to Barca f. POPE 662:66
tomb-stones where f. should be BLAKE 134:57
too soon for f. DELA 260:73
Until the f. are fragrant TOJO 862:94
Where have all the f. gone? SEEG 726:71
With other f. HERR 400:46
young days of gathering f. PEAC 645:96
flowery cool f. lap of earth ARNO 31:3
wakes me from my f. bed? SHAK 738:3
flowing longer f., longer free HERR 400:46
fluctuations mysterious f. of trade ELIOT 303:87
fluffy But f., just f. HERB 397:74
fluidity terrible f. of self-revelation JAMES 434:52
fluids blood and other vital f. STER 818:85
flush f. of a new-born sun KIPL 471:3
flustered never f., never apathetic AURE 42:55
flute brains upon the f. BROW 162:92
f.…is too exciting ARIS 29:59
gauger played the f. STEV 821:72
The sound of the f. will cure THEO 851:40
flutes to the tune of f. kept stroke SHAK 764:23
flutter f. far more, than leaves CENN 203:43
fluttering f. to a bench SACK 708:88
flux All is f., nothing is stationary HERA 396:64
passing f. of momental things WHIT 904:8
fly as great a f. as Cassio SHAK 759:74
cut off, and we f. away BIBLE 96:51
f. in his hand STER 818:78
f.…may sting JOHN 441:55
f. sat upon the axletree BACON 50:58
I cannot f. SHAK 769:43
Indoor f. casting NASH 609:5
like a f. crawling INGR 429:66
long-legged f. YEATS 934:63
noise of a f. DONNE 281:90
show the f. the way out WITT 918:46
solitary f.! GRAY 369:7
those that f., may fight again BUTL 177:59
'Thou shalt f.' CLEE 220:72
unzipped f. caught in forever amber COND 230:83
we cannot f. EMPS 314:63
will f. no more HOLM 407:79
wisdom made the f. NASH 609:2
wouldn't hurt a f. LEAC 497:71
fly-fishing F. f. may be…pleasant JOHN 447:77
flying Armstrongs are f. HOGG 406:58
f. in the face of presumptions JAMES 433:40
f. through space forever GAGA 342:84
growing, f., happening REID 682:95
shot one bird f. HEMI 394:3
foam Cowslip…like tethered f. CRANE 243:22
f. on the river SCOTT 723:8
into f. of flowers SWIN 833:24
wind…wild and dank with f. KING 469:48
foaminess f. of the Falls SALA 710:50
focus Johnny, keep it out of f. WILD 910:69
foe angry with my f. BLAKE 135:59

Call no man f. BENS 77:63
erect and manly f. CANN 188:13
everyone's a f. CLARE 219:42
find a f. PARK 638:64
f. oft-times having the f. in sight DONNE 279:35
furnace for your f. SHAK 775:4
never made a f. TENN 846:20
our sneaking f.? SITW 794:80
overcome but half his f. MILT 581:14
perhaps a jealous f. SHEL 786:9
wild unsated f.! COLL 228:44
foes against the f. SMART 797:28
doubt of future f. ELIZ 309:57
f., and oh, my friends MILL 571:81
judge a man by his f. CONR 234:3
loins of these two f. SHAK 735:33
neither f. nor loving friends KIPL 474:68
new f. arise Threatening to MILT 580:87
Set upon the f.! SHAK 732:22
slay their f. MACD 530:56
thirty thousand f. MACA 526:66
Words…the great f. of reality CONR 234:13
fog achievements…in a blessed, warm f. CONR 235:19
A f., miss DICK 269:82
brown f. of a winter dawn ELIOT 305:54
f. comes on little cat feet SAND 713:92
F. everywhere DICK 269:79
f. is rising DICK 273:80
Hover through the f. SHAK 766:65
like a cold f. ACHE 2:30
natural f. of the good man's mind BROW 161:36
trying to sculpture f. LEHM 501:68
foggy f. day in London Town GERS 351:43
fogs rising f. prevail upon the day DRYD 288:49
foil golden f. all over them SPEN 808:75
shining from shook f. HOPK 412:83
foining f. o'nights SHAK 743:50
fold f. after f., to the fainting air SHEL 785:85
f. my tens KAUF 455:57
if your name's above the f. LANCE 487:73
Now I f. you down SEXT 728:12
one f., and one shepherd BIBLE 118:2
tangl'd in the f. MILT 586:64
folders manila f. and mucilage ROET 694:98
foliage love for Linton is like the f. BRON 155:96
stillness of the buried f. HOLM 407:70
Folies-Bergère F.-B. and looks at STOC 824:53
folio whole volumes, in f. SHAK 733:75
folios mighty f.…a lordly band CRAB 242:80
folk All music is f. music ARMS 30:76
f. begin to tak the gate BURNS 172:12
F. music…fat people DYLAN 297:61
f. to goon on pilgrimages CHAU 208:67
f. wou'd hae a doubt on FERG 320:6
itinerant f. artists ROCK 693:84
just look at all the f. LAUD 492:62
matches of the Southron f. THOM 855:39
novels are strange f. LUCAS 520:17
'the Big F.', as they call us TOLK 862:1
trouble with a f. song LAMB 487:68
Wee f., good f. ALLI 13:61
we theatre f. MANK 545:62
folks bunch of f. hoping WALK 885:99
Don't let the old f. know HERB 397:72
eat, good f. PRIOR 669:38
F. don't like to have somebody LEE 500:36
f. eat the stuff they raise STEI 815:34
hand f. over to God's mercy ELIOT 303:82
my f. were growing old STEV 823:37
nor any of my f. MITC 588:96
That's all f.! FREL 336:46
What signifies't for f. to chide SKIN 795:13
When f. git ole HARR 383:95
where the old f. stay FOST 332:60
follies charming f. GILL 355:38
f. of this dull age CAREW 190:49
f. which a man regrets most ROWL 701:53
indulge in a few f. PROU 670:72
point out to us our f. TROL 866:79
Pour her exotic f. o'er the town BYRON 179:1
pretty f. that themselves commit SHAK 740:61
vices and f. of human kind CONG 231:5
whose f. cease with their youth PITT 652:36
follow f. me GARI 346:48
F. thou me! SCHW 721:70
he saith unto them, F. me BIBLE 109:82
horrid thing to f. JAMES 433:39

I f. the worse	OVID 631:45
In following him I f.	SHAK 758:49
Jesus said unto him, F. me	BIBLE 110:17
saith unto him, F. me	BIBLE 111:19
where few can f.	KENN 461:96
follower misguided f. climbs	ROCH 691:56
followers f. of Jesus	JOHN 441:9
vice promises to her f.	MILT 579:72
followship practising f.	THAT 851:36
folls Deal round to happy f.	BYRON 180:36
folly Age from f.	SHAK 764:19
All my joys to this are f.	BURT 174:68
brood of f.	MILT 576:12
curse of mankind, f. and ignorance	SHAK 757:97
darling F., Fickleness	MAND 545:54
epoch of f. and shame	ZOLA 937:4
Fashion, though F.'s child	CRAB 242:84
f....has a certain stamp	GERH 350:34
f. him that is in reputation	BIBLE 101:86
f. in that of a great kingdom	SMITH 798:48
f. is not always f.	AUST 43:84
f. of 'Women's Rights'	VICT 880:83
f. to be wise	GRAY 368:95
fool returneth to his f.	BIBLE 100:53
in their f. not less blind	HOPE 411:71
knavery and f. to excuse	CHUR 215:44
like f. shows	MILT 584:4
lovely woman stoops to f.	AUST 43:87
lovely woman stoops to f.	GOLD 361:47
make good their own f.	BACON 48:93
most loving, mere f.	SHAK 749:53
moved to f. by a noise	LAWR 495:41
Neebours' fauts an f.	BURNS 170:86
noise of f.	MILT 576:15
obstinacy of f.	STOWE 826:78
our pride, our f., or our fate	DENH 261:93
rather of their f.	ELIOT 308:17
shoot F. as it flies	POPE 660:7
such gratuitous f.	HUXL 425:74
too presumptuous f.	HARTE 385:18
uses his f. like a stalking-horse	SHAK 751:93
whirled into f. and vice	TENN 845:79
fond f. thing vainly invented	BOOK 144:75
F. without art	DRYD 289:64
never prove so f.	SHAK 762:43
rarity which I cannot but be f. of	ROCH 691:64
so f. of one another	SWIFT 830:61
Fonstein F....advanced category	BELL 74:92
font in the porphyry f.	TENN 842:14
food America, bring your own f.	LEBO 499:15
and the f. a tragedy	POWE 666:79
As I do live by f.	SHAK 749:46
bloody flesh our only f.	ELIOT 308:22
Continent people have good f.	MIKES 569:51
desire for f. and sex	TOOLE 863:13
discovered that alcohol was a f.	WODE 919:59
enough f. for eight	MOLI 590:37
estimated even in f. and necessaries	RICA 684:31
every mouthful of f.	FORD 329:98
Fame is a f.	DOBS 277:97
fed by a different f.	DISR 276:53
fed with the same f.	SHAK 740:68
finds its f. in music	LILLO 510:31
f. and not fine words	MOLI 590:42
F. comes first	BREC 151:7
f. for worms!	FRAN 334:6
f. is love	SHEL 784:64
f. of love	SHAK 755:45
f. out of the earth	BIBLE 97:67
give them f. and shelter	JARR 435:86
glum urge for f. to fill us	FISH 324:79
Hard f. for Midas	SHAK 740:72
having f. and raiment	BIBLE 123:78
junk f.	GASS 346:60
knowledge is as f.	MILT 583:90
libraries are f.	TUCH 869:61
love of f.	SHAW 778:86
man in a jail has...better f.	JOHN 443:59
more delicate the f.	INNO 429:70
music, moody f.	SHAK 765:28
nourishing, and wholesome F.	SWIFT 831:93
perpetual struggle for room and f.	MALT 543:17
problem is f.	DONL 279:24
quantity of f. required	RICA 684:32
senses...supply Fresh f.	WORD 923:67
Sharing f....an intimate act	FISH 324:78
ships to bear our f. away	WILDE 907:82

taste for...French f.	SCHL 718:14
think they're still getting real f.	COUP 238:94
was there like f. or air	ROCK 692:74
With eager feeding f.	SHAK 734:7
Women Whose Lives Are F.	OATES 620:92
fool A f., a f., I met a f.	SHAK 749:46
Any f. can be brave	MITC 588:97
Any f. may write a...book	GRAY 370:44
any man is so very a f.	SHAK 732:26
appear a f., a blockhead, or a knave	DRYD 291:29
becomes a f. and jester!	SHAK 743:67
Better a witty f.	SHAK 756:54
better to be a f.	STEV 822:93
blundering f. may	MORT 600:20
Busy old f.	DONNE 279:41
but in a f.'s cap	HOPK 412:79
can love like a f.	NASH 608:83
damn f. if he doesn't	FAUL 319:76
every f. in Buxton	RUSK 704:38
f. among fools	WILD 911:87
f. at the other	JOHN 447:77
f. consistent	POPE 661:31
f. doth think he is wise	SHAK 750:83
f. has a lot to teach	RABE 676:74
f. hath said in his heart	BIBLE 94:88
f. his whole life long	LUTH 523:1
F. in every man's mouth	BUNY 166:75
f....in every married couple	FIEL 323:45
f., In power of others	MILT 586:47
f. in the eye of the world	CONG 231:18
f. is happy	POPE 660:19
f. is love that in your will	SHAK 771:23
F.: it is you who are pursued	SHAW 778:88
f. lies here	KIPL 471:5
f. o'th' other senses	SHAK 767:95
f. returneth to his folly	BIBLE 100:53
'F.,' said my muse to me	SIDN 790:8
f.'s bauble	CROM 246:75
f. some of the people	LINC 510:35
f....that first invented kissing!	SWIFT 832:10
f. to make me merry	SHAK 750:74
f. too large for it	CHES 212:75
f. too many of the people	THUR 859:33
f. uttereth all his mind	BIBLE 100:61
f., who trusts a man	MARIE 550:51
greatest f. may ask more	COLT 228:55
have played the f.	BIBLE 91:97
He's a f. that marries	WYCH 931:15
human and makes me a f.	LEGU 501:64
I'd be a damn' f.	THOM 853:82
idle f.	FORD 330:16
Into a strumpet's f.	SHAK 764:10
knaves do work with, called a f.	BUTL 176:37
laughter of a f.	BIBLE 101:77
learned f. is more	MOLI 590:43
Let me play the f.	SHAK 739:37
like a musical f.	HUGH 418:18
little else than a f.	MCGO 532:80
Love's not time's f.	SHAK 773:48
make a f. of himself!	STEV 822:94
manage a f.	KIPL 470:75
man and wife make one f.	JONS 449:30
maxim is worthy of the f.	MACA 525:43
more of the f. than of the wise	BACON 48:8
Napoleon thinks that I am a f.	ALEX 11:20
No boasting like a f.	SHAK 768:25
Oh heav'nly f.	SIDN 790:13
patriot...a f.	DRYD 290:95
play the f....in's own house	SHAK 753:80
power to do any damn f. thing	FULB 340:43
prove one's self a f.	HAWT 386:48
resolv'd to live a f.	BEAU 66:6
Satisfy anyone but a damned f.	BART 62:11
'school' 'f.', a babbling rhyme	SHAK 745:24
smarts so little as a f.	POPE 661:34
Socrates...than a f. satisfied	MILL 570:69
surely f. a man	WHITE 903:82
the more f. I	SHAK 749:42
time to f. with politics	ROGE 695:26
To please a f.	CONG 232:38
What f. is not so wise	SHAK 733:82
whether he is a wise man or a f.	BLAKE 135:75
whosoever shall say, Thou f.	BIBLE 109:88
works is a f.	MORL 598:90
worship this dull f.	SHAK 775:2
wretched, rash, intruding f.	SHAK 754:7
foolery more hateful form of f.	BROW 162:78

fooling always f. with something	WHITE 903:80
foolish Better...than a f. wit	SHAK 756:54
disguises from the f.	BIER 129:27
envious at the f.	BIBLE 96:41
f., fond old man	SHAK 764:98
F. the man who trusts her	FRAN 334:95
f. thing was but a toy	SHAK 757:92
f. thing well done	JOHN 444:97
Forgive our f. ways	WHIT 906:63
God hath chosen the f. things	BIBLE 121:92
I, being young and f.	YEATS 932:29
likened unto a f. man	BIBLE 110:13
never said a f. thing	ROCH 692:72
not such a f. thing	ISHI 431:94
old and f. king	BIBLE 100:75
Only the f. are punished	MARG 549:40
saying a f. thing	STER 818:92
smallest f. act makes it idiotic	YOUR 935:82
These F. Things	MARV 557:82
foolishly don't think f.	JOHN 446:60
foolishness age of f.	DICK 271:19
f. of preaching	BIBLE 120:91
fools all the f. in town	TWAIN 871:9
Atheists, f., and madmen!	ONEI 625:99
Be friends, you English f.	SHAK 746:5
Beggared by f.	DRYD 290:89
busy f. may be stopped	DONNE 279:35
called the Paradise of F.	MILT 582:49
exportation of f.	CONG 231:28
Fashion...guide of f.	CRAB 242:84
f. and cowards might sit safe	OTWAY 631:28
F. are as like husbands	SHAK 756:73
f. are in a...majority	IBSEN 428:33
F. are my theme	BYRON 179:96
f. by heavenly compulsion	SHAK 762:57
F.! For I also had my hour	CHES 211:43
f. rush in	POPE 658:63
f. shall not err therein	BIBLE 103:34
For...government let f. contest	POPE 660:20
Fortune, that favours f.	JONS 449:28
great stage of f.	SHAK 764:94
I am two f.	DONNE 280:48
If honest Nature made you f.	BURNS 170:62
make f. of themselves about	SHAW 777:56
many f. at a university	GERH 350:34
marriage...leaves 'em still two f.	CONG 231:33
more f. than wise	GIBB 352:68
Nature meant but f.	POPE 658:51
none but f. would keep	SHAK 758:32
pair of credulous f.	SHIR 789:81
people in the world are f.	WILD 911:85
play the f. with the time	SHAK 742:47
please the f.	DRYD 289:75
poor f. decoyed	PEPYS 647:44
proved plain f.	POPE 658:51
secrets...must be kept...from f.	DRYD 287:21
shoal of f. for tenders	CONG 231:35
soldiers, mostly f.	BIER 129:32
suffer f. gladly	BIBLE 122:32
the f. caught it	YEATS 933:42
there are two kinds of f.	MORR 598:96
Thus may poor f.	SHAK 774:66
Tories remained f.	WALP 887:35
traps for eager and clever f.	SNYD 803:52
twenty-seven millions mostly f.	CARL 193:42
virtue of f.	BACON 47:67
What f. middle-class girls are	DRAB 286:89
what f. these mortals be!	SHAK 738:6
wise men follow f.	BACON 49:15
With the flannelled f.	KIPL 473:54
world is made up...of f. and knaves	BUCK 165:42
foolscaps f. of air	AVIS 44:6
foot And the Forty-second F.!	HOOD 410:35
blood from head to f.	MACL 535:31
breasts are under our f.	SHAW 778:87
caught my f.	GROS 374:24
cleft the Devil's f.	DONNE 279:39
'eathen idol's f.	KIPL 471:87
Englishman, sets f. on it	STEF 814:5
espied his cloven f.	BALL 55:73
f. and hand go cold	ANON 20:1
f. for f.	BIBLE 100:51
f. in Eden	MUIR 602:63
f. is on my native heath	SCOTT 724:32
f. less prompt	ARNO 33:48
f. out of joint	BIBLE 100:51
f. upon the stirrup	DELA 260:65

from head to f.	TENN 843:31
from head to f.	TENN 845:87
from his head to his f.	MOORE 594:18
his f. is guilty	BECK 68:33
hold Creation in my f.	HUGH 419:39
Leave not a f. of verse	POPE 662:74
length of Prester John's f.	SHAK 744:95
madly squeeze a right-hand f.	CARR 197:23
make crouch beneath his f.	BROW 162:85
never place their second f.	FONT 329:87
no man's f. can pass	BOTT 146:16
nor can f. feel	HOPK 412:83
no rest for the sole of her f.	BIBLE 87:65
One f. he centred	MILT 584:92
One f. in Canada	GAY 347:74
One f. in sea	SHAK 744:6
One square f. less	BENC 74:1
print of a man's naked f.	DEFOE 258:18
proud f. of a conqueror	SHAK 739:34
set her f. upon thy substance	BIBLE 107:45
sole of his f.	SHAK 744:10
speed of the f. race	YOUR 936:86
stick out a f.	ADLER 7:48
Th'inaudible and noiseless f.	SHAK 762:41
trodden under f. of men	BIBLE 109:84
trode her under f.	BIBLE 92:37
walked with willing f.	STEV 821:72
will not suffer thy f. to be moved	BIBLE 91:87
wished myself on f.	MUNDY 603:82
with shining f. shall pass	FITZ 324:86
football All…I owe to f.	CAMUS 188:5
base f. player	SHAK 762:58
bewteis of the f.-b.	ANON 20:5
College f.	GALL 344:12
College f. is a sport	HUBB 418:10
concentrate on f.	NICH 613:88
concerning f. playing	STUB 827:2
disregard for the rules of f.	ANON 21:26
European f. without the English	CHAR 207:44
F. causeth fighting	STUB 827:3
f. field is a place	ROUS 700:39
F. hooligans	CLOU 223:41
F.…is a grand game	BADEN 51:75
F. is all very well as a game	WILDE 910:62
F. is like a religion	PELE 646:18
F. is…more central to our culture	GREER 372:92
f. is proposed at Christmas	ANON 21:30
F.…keep the coalminers off the streets	BRES 151:19
f. magazines in their hands	BECK 67:29
f. team is like a beautiful woman	WENG 899:3
f.—the most exhilarating game	GOOD 363:98
F. then was fighting sorrow	HOUS 415:50
geriatric f. in the winter	KINN 470:67
good of f.	TAYL 837:21
ideal day for f.	SMITH 800:90
In f. it is widely acknowledged	FRY 339:23
kick it about all day like a f.	HOLM 408:83
life is…a game of f.	SCOTT 724:15
like a f. you do spurn me	SHAK 733:60
married during the f. season?	SHAN 776:32
more politics in f. than in politics	ERIK 315:88
No f. player…within the City	ELIZ 309:58
politics is like…a f. coach	MCCA 527:92
seeing some sexy f.	GULL 375:37
Some people think f.	SHAN 776:28
talk about f. or women	BERL 80:26
there be used F.-b., Golfe	JAME 432:22
To watch a f. game	BARZ 63:38
footballer no longer a f.	CRUY 246:86
footballs street being full of f.	PEPYS 647:39
footfalls F. echo in the memory	ELIOT 307:93
foothold f. in the narrow strip of land	BAKER 53:20
footing how…honesty, got f.	OTWAY 631:27
lived on a friendly f.	LAMB 486:43
foot-in-the-grave F.-i.-t.-g. young man!	GILB 354:9
foot-landrakers joined with no f.-l.	SHAK 741:6
footman eternal F. hold my coat	ELIOT 304:22
footmen But of all f.	HAZL 388:90
footnote greatness…soon be a f.	THAT 850:15
footnotes series of f.	NABO 606:36
series of f. to Plato	WHIT 904:12
serried f. to man	GRASS 367:60
footpath jog on, the f. way	SHAK 770:83
footprint looking for a man's f.	BEER 69:75
footprints f. of a gigantic hound!	DOYLE 285:72
F. on the sands of time	LONG 515:43
plaster casts of f.	PATE 642:56

footsoles midwife slapped your f.	PLATH 654:65
footsteps f. made no noise	DICK 267:20
home his f.…turned	SCOTT 723:91
plants his f. in the sea	COWP 240:43
poor slaves with weary f.	SHEL 786:9
footstool make thine enemies thy f.	BIBLE 97:73
fop f. in my heart	ETHE 315:98
man of sense and a f.	CHES 210:26
foppery f. of freedom	SHAK 757:16
forbear F. to judge	SHAK 730:60
forbid expressly to f. you	LOUI 518:92
f. the King to keep it	INNO 430:71
therefore I f. my tears	SHAK 755:27
forbidden wicked and to be f.	STUB 827:1
force alcohol is a…deadening f.	WEBB 893:63
All governments use f.	PARE 636:36
back her vote by physical f.	WRIG 929:74
Better to use f.	SHUL 789:89
combination of skill and f.	BURKE 168:32
dedicated to f. and to beauty	RIMB 688:98
disputes…settled by using f.	EISE 302:57
envy…is f. t'admire!	DANI 252:89
evil…a f. in the world	CHUR 215:42
F. is the same throughout	LEON 503:12
F. made the first slaves	ROUS 700:42
f. maintaining…the world	DOST 283:8
f. of honesty	SHAK 753:76
f. of the bayonet!	MIRA 587:76
f. that propels	KAND 454:35
Life, f. and beauty	POPE 658:53
lost faith…in natural f.	CARL 191:83
May the F.	LUCAS 522:79
motive f. impressed	NEWT 612:70
No f. to win the victory	DYER 297:51
no motion…no f.	WORD 924:80
not by f. but by understanding	BRON 154:65
not need to convince…by f.	WILS 916:10
only f. capable	KING 468:44
Other nations use 'f.'	WAUGH 892:34
out by f. of arms	LOUI 518:91
patience…achieve more than our f.	BURKE 169:41
persuade gently, not by f.	PASC 641:27
real revolutionary f.	OROU 627:25
spent its novel f.	TENN 840:77
supreme arbitrament of f.	CHUR 215:55
The f. that through	THOM 852:57
Tonality is a natural f.	HIND 403:97
unofficial f.—the Baker Street	DOYLE 285:56
use of f. alone is but temporary	BURKE 168:9
Who overcomes By f.	MILT 581:14
with an irresistible f.	HEDIN 390:37
worth more than f. and rage	LAFO 485:4
forced f.—by what?	FROMM 338:82
f.…into any…belief	RICH 686:62
f. to like what you get	SHAW 779:24
forces acknowledge the spiritual f.	MOORE 595:28
balance of actual f.	NAPO 607:61
centrifugal f. which are	NASH 609:7
communicate with his f.	SCHW 721:65
enhances the f. of the mind	PROU 671:89
f., although small	MAO 547:4
f. impressed thereon	NEWT 612:69
f. which must bring	RUSS 705:53
f. working in inverse order!	CARL 192:8
modified aggregate of external f.	SPEN 806:41
'targeted' by powerful f.	BELL 74:91
Ford Jerome to F. Madox F.	COLE 225:74
my friend F.	WILL 913:46
Nixon…gave us General F.	ABZUG 1:15
Our F.…had been the first	HUXL 425:76
ford bridge the f.	KIPL 472:13
Fords swarming in F.	FERB 320:94
fore at the f.	GILB 355:32
foreboding I am filled with much f.	POWE 667:93
with a deeper f.	FRAN 334:99
forecast even the weather f.	LODGE 514:22
prevents the events they f.	WRIS 930:89
forecastle crew is gambling in the f.	SHAW 781:76
forefathers f. had no other books	SHAK 730:66
genealogy of his f.	ECHE 298:76
Our f. would have died	OCON 621:19
recover it from all his f.	BUTL 178:85
rude f. of the hamlet	GRAY 369:12
simple f. would kill	MONT 592:70
Whatever our f. were	OVER 631:38
forefinger f. of all Time	TENN 841:96
f. of an alderman	SHAK 735:38

forehead Flames in the f.	MILT 578:57
He tapped his f.	CHRI 214:32
Love, knocking its blind f.	SAND 712:82
middle of her f.	LONG 516:67
Tap his f. first	WODE 919:55
with unbashful f. woo	SHAK 749:39
foreheads f. nobility is engraved	LAUT 493:75
foreign attacking the F. Secretary	BEVAN 85:21
courtly f. grace	TENN 848:64
defended…from f. invasion	REDM 681:72
do in f. affairs	JOHN 440:89
emancipating themselves from a f.	MAZZ 562:99
F. Secretary…naked	BEVAN 85:22
f. troop…in my country	PITT 653:44
in spite of…its f. propaganda	ORWE 628:63
knew a lot about f. affairs	REST 683:17
life is a f. country	KERO 464:61
loans…to f. nations	BAGE 51:94
No f. policy	KISS 475:93
past is a f. country	HART 385:20
portion of the f. world	WASH 890:87
sent into any f. wars	ROOS 696:48
speaking a f. language	WILD 910:73
win the f. picture award	WILD 910:69
worst of the F.…Office	CRIT 245:63
foreigner dagger which the f. left	QUIN 675:53
f. should in any respect	TROL 866:79
foreigners don't object to f.	WILD 910:73
f. always spell better	TWAIN 870:75
f. are fiends	MITF 589:9
f. could more easily	NGU 613:79
f. speak English	CRISP 245:54
forerunner f. of despair	KENN 462:3
foreseen What I had not f.	SPEN 807:48
foresight urge…to aftersight and f.	ELIOT 309:43
forest as a…hedge is to a f.	JOHN 447:74
behind it rose the f.	LONG 516:56
chose the f. path	FAWC 319:79
Dong through the f. goes	LEAR 497:77
even as the f. is	SHEL 783:47
flowers of the f.	COCK 224:55
flowers of the f.	ELLI 310:78
f. fleece	HOUS 415:55
F., where all must lose	THOM 854:17
f. with a golden track	LIND 511:48
Glimpse of the f.	SITW 794:66
into the f. dim	KEATS 459:58
lost to the f.	SCOTT 723:7
Marxism…like finding a map in a f.	CAST 199:79
met a fool i'th' f.	SHAK 749:46
paint a f. or a horse	MARC 548:27
redwood f.	GUTH 375:48
spark can start a f. fire	MAO 547:4
take a tree from the f.	SCOTT 723:13
the f.'s ferny floor	DELA 260:63
This is the f. primeval	LONG 516:52
thru the graveyard f.	PURDY 673:17
undulating tropical rain f.	BOYD 147:42
whole f. echoes	CARL 192:17
forests Among the f.	THOM 855:31
F. of middle-aged men	ABBO 1:1
f. of the night	BLAKE 135:61
f. where they roamed	SIGO 791:28
green days in f.	STEV 823:32
sole king of f. all	SPEN 808:73
foresworn Necessity will make us all f.	SHAK 733:72
foretaste f. of death	SCHO 720:37
foretold f. the rest	ELIOT 306:60
forever experiment lasts f.	KAPI 455:48
flying through space f.	GAGA 342:84
it lives f.	UPDI 874:90
talked on f. e.	HAZL 387:69
that vast f.	KING 469:50
forfeit f. of their name	HABI 376:54
forfended music of f. spheres	PATM 643:67
forget Best, to f.	BROW 162:93
cause us to f. their existence	HAWT 386:47
either f. right away	BECK 68:37
far worse than to f.	BENU 78:86
f. because we must	ARNO 31:98
F. it, Jake	TOWNE 863:20
f. me not	GINS 357:63
f. so much	DAVI 254:34
f. that words	JOHN 442:39
f. to tell each other	HELL 392:77
f. yourself in the park?	TAYL 837:15
glad to have humanity f.	HOOV 411:61

f. with us upon Saint Crispin's day — SHAK 746:62
lads who f. — SASS 716:66
met and f. with outright — TENN 846:4
That f. and died for — WILL 914:65
'Tis better to have f. and lost — CLOU 222:27
what they f. each other for — SOUT 805:99
foul dead, by f. subtraction — RANS 679:22
  doubt some f. play — SHAK 751:13
  Fair is f., and f. is fair — SHAK 766:65
  f. and pestilent congregation — SHAK 752:56
  F. deeds will rise — SHAK 751:13
  giving hand, though f. — SHAK 733:77
  got by fair means or f. — ORWE 627:32
  however f. within — CHUR 215:47
  in the less, f. profanation — SHAK 758:27
  Murder most f. — SHAK 752:29
  nipped, and ways be f. — SHAK 734:94
  still f. the cup — GREY 373:5
fouled Hath f. me — TENN 847:56
foulest fair words...in f. letters? — SHAK 743:64
foulness f. of their fate — SASS 717:76
  no vicious blot, murder, or f. — SHAK 762:54
  remove filth and f. — ABEL 1:3
found f. and lost again — ELIOT 308:24
  f. Him in — TENN 847:44
  f. myself — GRIL 373:15
  f. you an argument — JOHN 446:65
  Hast thou f. me — BIBLE 92:26
  I f. it! — ARCH 28:40
  if the ways be f. — JONS 449:32
  lost, but now am f. — NEWT 613:76
  To f. a great Empire — SMITH 798:50
foundation corner stone, a sure f. — BIBLE 103:28
  destroyed the f. of the organization — EISE 302:57
  end of our f. is...knowledge — BACON 50:62
  end of our f. is...knowledge — BACON 47:68
  f. of all good things — BURKE 169:44
  f. of morals, Utility — MILL 570:70
  f. of your ideas and phrases — LAUT 493:77
  laid the f. of the earth — BIBLE 97:61
  on the same f. — SWIFT 831:82
  The Church's one f. — STONE 825:57
  unassailable f. — ASQU 36:9
foundations again from the very f. — DESC 263:23
  firmest f. — GLAD 358:92
  f. of political liberty — WILS 916:15
  laid the f. of the earth? — BIBLE 93:69
  peaks, whose f. — LLOY 513:99
  visible F. in Nature — PETTY 650:86
  when earth's f. fled — HOUS 416:79
  While earth's f. stand — HOUS 416:86
founder f. of civil society — ROUS 700:40
founders f. of a new colony — HAWT 386:39
fount f. of pride — CULL 247:94
fountain back to the burning f. — SHEL 786:2
  broke into a f. — HARR 384:99
  bubble on the f. — SCOTT 723:8
  drinking at the f. of fact — PIER 651:5
  F., never to be play'd — POPE 659:95
  f. of all goodness — BOOK 142:32
  f. of good sense — DRYD 292:46
  f. of living waters — BIBLE 105:68
  f. of the water of life — BIBLE 127:81
  f. of vice as idleness — MONT 591:66
  f. sealed — BIBLE 102:3
  f. send forth at the same place — BIBLE 125:14
  f., shade, and rill — MILT 578:46
  f., spouting through his heir — POPE 660:4
  Let the healing f. start — AUDEN 40:5
  Let thy f. be blessed — BIBLE 99:14
  long-abused sight at the f. — MILT 579:82
  mighty f. momently was forced — COLE 226:11
  pitcher be broken at the f. — BIBLE 101:92
  rivulet and f. — GILB 354:96
  Sang with a f.'s panache — DAY 257:86
  summer-dried f. — SCOTT 723:7
  voice rise like a f. — TENN 847:51
  water in a f. — JOYCE 451:82
Fountainblues terrible case of the F. — HUXT 426:16
fountains Afric's sunny f. — HEBER 390:34
  f. are within — COLE 226:2
  f. fraught with tears — KYD 482:47
  f. mingle with the river — SHEL 783:42
  f. of timber — MUIR 602:64
  in great f. — GALE 343:5
  inscriptions on public f. — FLAU 327:43
  two faithful f. — CRAS 244:37

What objects are the f.? — SHEL 784:59
  writers, like clear f. — LAND 488:76
four F. be the things — PARK 637:58
  two and two are f. — HOUS 416:78
fourscore F. and upward — SHAK 764:98
  if...they be f. years — BIBLE 96:51
four-wheeled f.-w. part of him — JOHN 441:3
Fowey O the Harbour of F. — QUIL 674:42
fowl f., blinking at you — ELIOT 303:97
  lord of the f. — COWP 241:54
  small f. singis on the spray — DOUG 283:18
  You elegant F.! — LEAR 497:84
fowler from the snare of the f. — BIBLE 96:53
fowlers Watchful as f. — OTWAY 631:26
fowls F. are to the kitchen — BRIL 152:36
  f. of the air — BIBLE 110:2
  f. of the air — BIBLE 119:39
fox beset the historical f. — HUXL 426:7
  Crazy Like A F. — PERE 648:54
  f. barks not when he would — SHAK 730:57
  f. in the streets — MCCA 527:88
  galloping after a f. — WILDE 909:22
  kill a f. or the pheasant — SHAW 781:95
  trusted like the f. — SHAK 742:30
  Virginia f. hunt — WASH 890:84
  working for 16th Century F. — RENO 683:5
foxes bulls and f. dine very well — JUST 453:12
  f. have holes — BIBLE 110:16
  f....prolonging the lives — ELIOT 303:96
fox-hunting inferior forms of f.-h. — WAUGH 891:16
  prefer f.-h. — HAIL 377:68
foxlike Or f. in the vine — TENN 842:16
foxy 70s face was f. — WATE 890:93
fragile essentially f. — BAIN 52:9
  Men are very f. — STEP 817:60
fragments Death tramples it to f. — SHEL 786:7
  f. I have shored — ELIOT 306:68
  ideas, in f. — MILL 572:18
  Live in f. no longer — FORS 331:36
fragrance f. was borne upon the breeze — DICK 268:42
  Has she f.? — CAUL 201:11
  Isles of f. — POPE 662:78
  splendor and f. — ROCK 692:75
  sweetest f. from the herb — TROL 866:87
frailties draw his f. — GRAY 370:26
frailty F., thy name is woman — SHAK 751:8
  human f., folly, also crime — BYRON 182:83
  human f. will have it so — ETHE 315:96
  noblest f. of the mind — DRYD 287:17
frame all the human f. requires — BELL 73:55
  another f. of things — TENN 847:33
  an utterly exhausted f. — DOYLE 285:76
  calm and heav'nly f. — COWP 240:46
  f. of mind — FRIE 337:70
  f. perish...in conquering pain — BYRON 180:37
  f. was Dust — DICK 273:74
  in his bodily f....his lowly origin — DARW 253:16
  knoweth our f. — BIBLE 97:65
  oddest f. of sense — SHAK 758:46
  sensuous f. — TENN 843:39
  solid f. of earth — WORD 928:52
  spangled heavens, a shining f. — ADDI 6:26
  this goodly f., the earth — SHAK 752:56
  universal f. is without a mind — BACON 48:94
  Whatever stirs this mortal f. — COLE 226:99
  wield The mighty f. — MILT 584:97
framed have it f. and glazed — WALP 887:29
framework f. for a civilization — LECO 499:30
France always be the sister of F. — HUGO 420:67
  best soldiers F. ever had — PHIL 650:95
  better to sniff F.'s dung — HO 405:38
  between F. and England — JERR 437:41
  Cam ye ower frae F.? — ANON 20:18
  chased the English out of F. — LOUI 518:91
  dagger...in the heart of F. — QUIN 675:53
  duty...to wield the sword of F. — DE 259:36
  fair stood the wind for F. — DRAY 286:1
  fight in F. — CHUR 216:76
  find your people in F. — JOAN 438:52
  five in F. — THER 851:50
  flower of F. is lost — ANON 18:77
  follow them to F. — LESL 504:30
  F....a despotism...tempered — CARL 192:12
  F., famed in all great arts — ARNO 31:92
  F. had shown a light — TENN 848:69
  F. has lost a battle! — DE 259:35
  F. has more need of me — NAPO 607:62

F. in 1830 — LOUIS 518:2
  F. is adequately assured — ASQU 36:9
  F. is revolutionary — LAMA 485:23
  F., mother of arts — BELL 72:38
  Here lies F. — BISM 131:88
  if Jack were President of F. — ONAS 625:78
  inadequate for getting to F. — KINN 470:68
  in F....play a set — SHAK 745:30
  In F., they study men — STAEL 812:52
  In F....words reign over ideas — SAND 712:83
  insert...spirit of Christian F. — BOUR 146:27
  nineteenth-century F. — HELL 392:79
  no concern to F. — WITTE 918:38
  order...this matter better in F. — STER 818:97
  own F., a country — MORL 598:87
  singer in F. — SWIN 833:42
  sweet enemy, F. — SIDN 790:11
  swum from F. — MARL 552:88
  the roads lead to F. — THOM 854:19
  Vive la F.! — DE 259:41
  want to know what F. thinks — DE 259:42
  You're thinking of Europe as Germany
   and F. — RUMS 702:37
Francesca F. di Rimini, miminy — GILB 354:7
Francis I think I'm St F. of Assisi — PARK 638:68
  More than F. of Assisi — PACK 633:75
  St. F. de Sales — MATS 531:74
frank f. to all beside — POPE 661:45
Frankenstein media a F. monster — MUGG 601:50
  soul of F. — SHEL 782:11
frankincense gold, and f. — BIBLE 108:73
  hill of f. — BIBLE 101:2
Franklin body of Benjamin F. — FRAN 334:6
frankness paragons of f. — WILL 913:36
fraternity Liberty, Equality, F.! — LAMA 486:24
fraud daily f., contempt — MILT 586:47
  f. of the Christian system — PAINE 634:97
  one f., the other fornication — MATOS 561:66
  Style is a f. — DE 260:56
frauds to point at f. — RUSH 703:88
fray Fought was this noble f. — DRAY 286:2
  f. By which he reigns — MILT 581:32
freckles love, curiosity, f. — PARK 637:58
Freddy See F. before he sees you! — ANON 24:26
Frederic Stay, F., stay! — GILB 354:2
free advantage of not being f. — SNOW 802:42
  A F. Man is he — HOBB 404:29
  as a f. man — KENN 463:33
  be a falcon and go f. — DUNC 295:14
  born f. as Caesar — SHAK 747:75
  breed f. men? — HOPE 411:71
  cleanly I myself can f. — DRAY 287:6
  Comment is f. — SCOTT 722:74
  condemned to be f. — SART 715:51
  either f. or enslaved — GRIL 373:13
  every people should be left f. — WILS 916:13
  exertions of a f. people — PITT 653:47
  first people to demand f. speech — BISS 132:89
  f. and clear from any image — SHAK 757:87
  f. and easy — STEV 820:61
  f. and equal association — ENGE 314:68
  f., and f. they must remain — MILT 582:43
  f. as nature first made man — DRYD 288:35
  f. as the road — HERB 398:9
  f., but to thyself enthralled — MILT 583:85
  f. competition of the market — RICA 684:33
  f. constitution — GIBB 351:53
  f. from guilt or pain — SHEL 785:81
  f. from interest or prejudice — REES 682:89
  f. from...nationalism — ORWE 629:77
  f. lunch has still to be invented — GREE 372:85
  F. man! — BAUD 64:58
  f. man cannot long stand erect — WRIS 930:88
  f. man thinks of nothing less — SPIN 811:33
  f. nations are peaceful nations — BUSH 176:18
  f. of the networks — STARK 813:73
  f. their minds of...rubbish — DUDEK 293:82
  f., therefore choose — SART 716:54
  f. to do whatever the Government — SHAW 778:91
  f. to wander where I liked — SHIP 789:78
  F. trade...blessings — MACA 525:39
  f. world and the Communist — KENN 463:31
  give me the f. 'n' easy — GERS 350:39
  he is f. — SOLZ 803:62
  I am a f. man — ARET 29:42
  If the Son...shall make you f. — BIBLE 117:97
  in the cause of the f. — BINY 130:51

I was f. born — BIBLE 119:55
keep your fancy f. — HOUS 414:46
know our will is f. — JOHN 444:88
let me gae f. — SCOTT 724:28
live f. and uncommitted — THOR 857:90
longer f. — HERR 400:46
lover bold and f. — CLEV 221:84
lover...noble and f.? — EMER 312:21
makes the mind very f. — ELIOT 303:89
man is either f. — BARA 59:45
men naturally were born f. — MILT 580:85
mistaken in thinking themselves f. — SPIN 810:25
most complete and f. — STEV 821:78
Mother of the F. — BENS 77:61
music is really a f. thing — COLE 225:75
neither bond nor f. — BIBLE 122:36
never shall be f. — DONNE 281:71
Newspapers are born f. — SCOTT 722:79
No f. man shall be taken or imprisoned — MAGN 539:27
No one can be perfectly f. — SPEN 806:38
no such thing as a f. lunch — FRIE 337:63
our dear country had been f. — DAVIS 256:65
people are as f. as they want — BALD 54:35
permanently half-slave and half-f. — LINC 510:34
place of f. speech — WENT 899:4
poet must be f. — SART 715:41
princes should be f. — SHAK 729:49
prisoners were left f. to choose — SHAW 778:1
product of the f. mind — ORWE 628:56
pursuit...by f. men — WARR 889:69
safer...than to be f. — KAFKA 454:27
Shall the sex f. — HABI 376:54
So f. we seem — BROW 161:54
So long as man remains f. — DOST 283:10
someone to tell them they are f. — LAYT 496:50
spirit, f. to choose — ROCH 691:55
struggling to be f. — SHAK 754:2
Teach the f. man — AUDEN 40:5
Thou art f. — ARNO 31:89
tied the f. And holy-day...spirit — LAMB 486:39
to set me f. — STUA 827:99
to want to be f. — JONAS 447:84
truth shall make you f. — BIBLE 117:96
uphold me with thy f. spirit — BIBLE 95:30
Was he f.? — AUDEN 40:96
wholly slaves or wholly f. — DRYD 291:18
Who would be f. — BYRON 179:14
Writing f. verse — FROST 339:4
yearning to breathe f. — LAZA 496:51
ye shall be f. indeed — BIBLE 117:97
You who are f. — IGNA 428:42
free-born as only a f.-b. Briton — THAC 849:87
freed f. from his religion — SAINT 709:21
freedom and that is f. — MACA 525:42
army...devoted to f. — LAWR 495:39
Art, Glory, F. fail — BYRON 179:16
bird that will live in f. — MEIL 563:9
bondage which is f.'s self — SHEL 782:16
breathed the air of f. — WALE 885:88
cause of f. — SPEN 807:66
cherish f. — SCHI 718:8
conception of autonomy and f. — GEOR 349:19
Conservative ideal of f. — MADAN 538:19
controversy over f. of speech — ORWE 629:93
cost of f. is always — KENN 462:21
cost to f. of opinion — SCHL 718:10
could not give me f. — SHAK 764:19
does not come from f. — GIDE 353:84
dreaming of f. — SMITH 801:25
easy to suppose in a time of f. — FRAS 335:26
entrust the care of f. — EISE 302:53
Extreme f....to extreme slavery — PLATO 655:3
fight for f. and truth — IBSEN 428:34
fit to use their f. — MACA 525:43
foppery of f. — SHAK 757:16
f. and culture — MORE 597:67
f. and equality — ROUS 700:43
F. and WHISKY gang thegither — BURNS 170:76
F....cure of anarchy — BURKE 168:13
F. doth with degree — JONS 449:38
f. in my love — LOVE 519:10
f. is a noble thing! — BARB 59:52
f. is beautiful — BUSH 175:15
F. is not an ideal — STEV 820:60
F. is only the distance — ZHAO 936:96
f. is slavery — ORWE 629:99
f. is something people take — BALD 54:35

f. is...supremely valuable — HUXL 426:98
F. is the f. to say — ORWE 630:2
F. is the right — MONT 593:96
f. of choice — GITL 358:86
f. of choice — MILL 572:7
F. of men under government — LOCKE 514:15
f. of my mind — MILT 577:41
f. of religion — JEFF 437:19
f. of speech — BLACK 132:92
f. of the press — TOCQ 861:82
f. of the press and popular — MILL 570:66
f. of the press in Britain — ORWE 628:48
f. of those weakened — CESA 203:49
F. shrieked — CAMP 186:67
f. to exploit — WIEN 907:68
f. to marry — WARR 889:69
F., what liberties...in thy name! — GEOR 350:22
F. which in no other land — DRYD 290:11
gave him f. to choose — MILT 579:74
give another joyous f. — SCEVE 717:92
give you your name: F. — ELUA 311:97
greatest f. — BANN 59:40
guarantee f. — TOCQ 862:88
have a new birth of f. — LINC 510:39
have so much more f. — JOHN 445:16
History may be f. — ELIOT 309:45
honour, f. and curteisie — CHAU 208:68
if f. fall? — KIPL 474:77
illusions that restrict f. — FRYE 340:39
invigorating air of f. — WOLL 921:8
kept in their full f. — BAIL 52:6
Let the f. ring — SMITH 800:91
live in f. and hell — MAIL 540:52
love of f. — GLAD 358:92
manners, virtue, f., power — WORD 925:11
must not confuse with f. — STEV 820:58
'Neath every one a f. — LOWE 520:40
None can love f. heartily — MILT 580:84
nor even f. from pain — LAWR 494:4
out of servitude into f. — EMER 313:45
particular f. and a general orderliness — CARD 190:44
perfect f. — HUGEL 418:12
Perfect f. is reserved for the man — COLL 227:32
portal of f. — EISE 302:64
power of the hope of f. — BUCK 165:36
prisoned birds must find in f. — SASS 716:69
promises f. or enlightenment — SNYD 803:52
questions of f. — JORD 450:64
right action is f. — ELIOT 308:33
salvation of f. — STEV 820:57
satisfy our thirst for f. — KING 468:37
science...restricting human f. — BOOK 144:79
so close to f. — TWAIN 871:6
supreme Festival on the road to f. — BONH 140:60
there is no liberty or f. — NASHE 609:19
the secret of its f. — OAKE 619:86
They lyve in f. — JAME 432:21
To earn you f. — LAWR 495:37
unlimited idea of f. — BACH 46:28
voice of f. — SHAR 776:37
what f. really is — MITC 588:95
What's f. for? — ROET 694:6
Where F. slowly broadens — TENN 841:93
whose service is perfect f. — BOOK 140:73
wind of nationalism and f. — BALD 54:49
With a great sum obtained I this f. — BIBLE 119:55
zest for f. — KENN 463:23
freedom-for-all democracy and f.-f.-a. — MAIL 540:52
freedoms F. you'll not to me allow — BEHN 71:14
upon four essential f. — ROOS 696:50
freeman symbol of a f.'s power — BIER 129:45
freemasonry bitter f. — BEER 69:77
freemen happy f., are the only slaves — MASS 560:50
freer I feel strangely f.! — JOHN 439:74
free will cannot deprive...man of his f. w. — CONF 230:90
freeze f. thy young blood — SHAK 752:28
freezing Between melting and f. — ELIOT 309:38
freezings What f. have I felt — SHAK 772:39
frei Arbeit macht f. — ANON 22:60
freight Nation's F. Handler — SAND 712:91
wilderness of f. and rails — CRANE 243:17
French as much Chinese as F. — FLAU 326:27
As the F. say — SMITH 801:16
Englishman is about to talk F. — WODE 919:66
F. are a logical people — MORL 598:87
F. are nice people — MAZA 562:98
F. are polite — TWAIN 870:76

F. are wiser than they seem — BACON 49:27
F. Canadian Hinayana Buddhist — GINS 357:68
F. clothes and F. food — SCHL 718:14
F....differs in nothing from prose — GRAY 368:96
F. had a more martial air — HAYD 387:58
F. is not a static language — HUGO 420:65
F. king, admittedly — MORL 598:89
F. operas sung by Swedish — WHAR 902:54
F. Radicals...German — MARX 558:4
F. Revolution is merely the herald — BABE 45:22
F. she spak ful faire — CHAU 208:70
F. want to attack — ANON 25:74
F. will only be united — DE 259:37
Germans classify...the F. arrange — CATH 200:90
get all the F.-f. — GORE 364:11
good because cooked by the F. — DOUG 283:23
help our F. comrades — KITC 475:4
Imagine the Lord talking F. — DAY 256:78
improved her F. — GRAH 365:36
look'd towards the F. coast — STER 818:90
New Orleans...past the F. Quarter — MAIL 540:55
not that the F. are not profound — BROO 157:32
professor of F. letters — JOYCE 452:91
scrofulous F. novel — BROW 160:22
serve the F. in place of a state religion — BIER 129:35
seventeen million F. women — GISC 358:85
Speak in F. — CARR 196:95
special task, as F. Canadians — BOUR 146:27
speech...precise as F. — QUIL 674:44
to men [I speak] F. — CHAR 207:37
tongues of the F. Council — SHAK 746:68
we die F. — WAUGH 892:46
We have F. quarrels — SHAK 746:51
What are we learning F....for — OBRI 621:11
What's the F. for fiddle-de-dee? — CARR 197:26
wine...some are fond of F. — MASE 559:29
Frenchman to be a F. — FRIE 337:66
Frenchmen act better than F. — BENN 76:40
one Englishman could beat three F. — ADDI 6:21
Frenchwomen F. better — BENN 76:40
frenzy an old man's f. — YEATS 934:60
Dancing is a f. and a rage — DAVI 254:31
frequency tragedy...very fact of f. — ELIOT 304:9
frère mon f.! — ELIOT 306:55
fresh f. air and royalties — ASHF 35:97
f. and vigorous enough — WARD 888:58
F. as the air — JONS 449:37
f. colours deck the wanton prime — SPEN 809:92
how quick and f. — SHAK 755:46
So sad, so f. — TENN 842:7
freshness f. of a dream — WORD 926:21
fret Living, we f. — BROW 162:54
fretted so f. fast we are — BROW 161:54
Freud F....dramatis personae — THOM 852:54
F. has often stated — RODG 693:92
F. is the father — GREER 372:87
F. would have his revenge — DOCT 277:2
funny when F. died — JARR 435:79
If F. had worn a kilt — BURG 167:34
put F. on canvas — SCHW 721:60
trouble with F. — DODD 278:6
friars barefooted f. — GIBB 352:63
Fribsbi fatal man, Madame F. — THAC 849:96
friction f. of the whole machine — CLAU 220:56
internal f. and strife — ROTH 699:29
produce the least f. — LEUP 505:50
Friday call this F. good — ELIOT 308:22
man F. — DEFOE 258:19
friend ain't no f. of mine — PRES 667:4
angry with my f. — BLAKE 135:59
as you choose a f. — DILL 275:16
A woman can become a man's f. — CHEK 209:12
best f. I could ever have — KARL 455:49
choose between...betraying my f. — FORS 331:52
confide...in a f. — ANOU 26:96
conversation with my best f. — LEWIS 507:78
courting death to be our f. — PHIL 650:91
enemy and your f. — TWAIN 872:27
enemy into a f. — KING 468:44
every f. we lose — POPE 659:99
Everyone calls himself a f. — LAFO 485:10
fair f., you never can be old — SHAK 772:42
Faithful are the wounds of a f. — BIBLE 100:58
Faithful f. is the medicine — BIBLE 107:41
favourite has no f.! — GRAY 368:1
Forsake not an old f. — BIBLE 107:46
for the f. of mankind — MOLI 590:35

Forth reaching to the f.	MILT 584:13	for the f. of the thing	DOUG 283:24	one great f. flamed	MILT 580:97
f. in old age	BIBLE 96:55	f. for…thick-skinned grown-ups	SHAW 778:85	thrown alive into the f.	BELL 74:87
f. of memory	CONR 235:21	F. is f. but no girl	LOOS 517:80	furnaces Your worship is your f.	BOTT 146:17
f. of our labour	MONT 591:64	f. to believe them	BACH 46:31	furnish f. forth the marriage tables	SHAK 751:10
f. Of that forbidden tree	MILT 580:91	f. where I've found it	KIPL 472:16	f. the pictures	HEAR 389:17
f. of the Spirit	BIBLE 122:38	f. you think they had	JONG 448:2	furnished F. as all Europe is	FRAN 335:17
globed f.	MACL 535:36	make f. of people	GARC 345:40	furnishings f. of each Was-land	FRAME 333:81
green f. would swell	KEATS 457:4	mirth and f. grew fast	BURNS 172:23	furniture brain…with all the f.	DOYLE 285:66
Is darkness, the f.	SWIN 833:30	more f. to punt	SAYE 717:83	Diet, F. and Dress	MAND 545:54
like ripe f. thou drop	MILT 585:31	most f.…without laughing	ALLEN 12:53	f. on the deck	MORT 600:23
long for the f. at last	SHER 787:36	no reference to f.	HERB 397:82	f. that used to be in the salon	MACM 537:79
medlar being a f.	MACD 530:47	watch a game, it's f.	HOPE 411:74	nature's pride and richest f.!	MARL 551:72
O Autumn, laden with f.	BLAKE 133:25	what…was all the f. for	BETJ 84:3	No f. so charming	SMITH 801:12
ripest f. of all	MARL 551:75	function death has a useful f.	LABR 483:71	useless and cumbersome f.	TREE 865:54
tasting this fair f.	MILT 585:17	f. is to create…feeling of solidarity	DURK 295:30	furrow Between the shafts and the f.	HEAN 389:4
the f. of your delight	SURR 829:39	f. of a writer	CONN 233:75	leaves a shining f.	TENN 842:14
To f. or shade	HERB 397:97	f. of criticism	DEWEY 264:44	plough my own f.	ROSE 696:62
took of the f.	BIBLE 86:50	f. of kings	LOUI 518:96	furrows The sounding f.	TENN 840:65
Too late for f.	DELA 260:73	f. of literature	TRIL 866:71	furry fire was f.	SITW 794:71
venturing their necks for f.	ROCH 691:63	f. of news	LIPP 511:71	furtive f. tear	ROMA 695:35
With f. the vines	KEATS 459:48	f. of poetry	GRAV 367:74	look of f. shame	WODE 919:66
fruitcake it's f. weather!	CAPO 189:25	happiness is a by-product of f.	BURR 173:63	fury Allaying…their f.	SHAK 774:82
fruitcakes Bring on the f.	PARR 639:98	own no other f.	SHAK 770:87	blind f. of creation	SHAW 778:83
fruitful she'll be f.	SWIFT 832:12	proper f. of women	ELIOT 303:92	formless spawning f.	YEATS 934:64
fruitfulness f. and…enjoyment	NIET 615:9	pure f., and best power	WORD 925:6	full of sound and f.	SHAK 769:42
mellow f.	KEATS 459:48	society cannot f. properly	PARS 640:1	f., and rage of mortal men	BURT 174:79
fruition f.'s dull, and spoils	SUCK 828:10	special f. is departure	LISP 512:74	f., like a woman scorned	CONG 231:23
fruits by their f. ye shall know them	BIBLE 110:11	the f. never dies	WORD 928:58	f. of aerial bombardment	EBER 298:73
drop like the f. of the tree.	MERE 567:12	functionary not to a f.	STEAD 813:84	f. of a patient man	DRYD 290:97
f. and princely delicates	MARL 552:98	functioning f. out of ignorance	DENG 261:90	f. of the winter	BEDE 68:54
f. of Christian civilisation	BIRD 130:61	functions division of labor…social f.	DURK 296:31	F. with th'abhorred shears	MILT 578:49
f. of knowledge	FREUD 337:56	expedition…performed its f.	SPEKE 806:35	Great f., like great whisky	CAPO 189:30
f. of speaking art?	SIDN 790:3	f.…most nearly in equilibrium	SPEN 806:41	like a f. takest us out	BIBLE 108:69
gives to Zembla f.	POPE 662:66	In her f. weary	MILT 586:53	no f. like an ex-wife	CONN 233:76
Here are f., flowers	VERL 879:67	where it f. best	THAT 850:21	sit and watch the f. pass	ROBE 689:19
immortal f. of joy and love	MILT 582:39	fund f. for the maintenance	SMITH 798:46	The f. and the mire	YEATS 934:57
No f., no flowers	HOOD 410:52	fundament frigid upon the f.	NASH 609:98	furze stepped…over the f.	SOME 803:67
Of f., and flowers	KEATS 459:36	fundamental f.…liberties	PITT 653:42	fuse Each one of you is a f.	KOCH 476:27
twelve manner of f.	BIBLE 127:84	f. postulate that there	MONOD 591:56	through the green f.	THOM 852:57
under their f. load	SPEN 809:92	f. question of philosophy	CAMUS 187:87	fused f. together	GUST 375:46
frustrated never to be f.	BALL 55:63	f. things apply	HUPF 423:40	fuss f. about sleeping together	WAUGH 892:28
fry F. me!	CARR 197:28	funds providing the f.	STEW 824:42	make no f. about females	CAMPO 187:83
marked among the f.	THOM 856:59	funeral After the f., my father	LAWR 494:18	without more f.	SPEN 807:54
fuck Fish f. in it	FIEL 323:54	at a f. and knew their feet	MAUG 561:75	fustian whose f.'s so sublimely bad	POPE 661:37
f. you up, your mum and dad	LARK 491:38	cypress f.	SPEN 808:73	futile f. his concerns	SIMO 792:43
zipless f. is absolutely pure	JONG 448:97	for the f. expenses	JERO 437:32	future a receding f.	THOM 855:32
fucked constantly getting f.	MAMET 544:36	f. baked meats	SHAK 751:10	arrow is pointing towards the f.	EDDI 298:83
fudge two-fifths sheer f.	LOWE 520:32	f. marches around your heart	MILL 571:97	better f. and a brighter day	SMUTS 802:31
fudging f. and nudging	OWEN 632:49	F. marches to the grave	LONG 515:42	Children have neither past nor f.	LABR 483:74
fuel bury their radioactive f.	LAMB 487:65	f. march of a fried eel	SHAW 781:91	choose its own f.	KENN 463:27
fugitive f. and cloistered virtue	MILT 579:70	f. sermon…which was long	BELL 73:60	cloud curtain of the f.	CARL 191:78
thou art…a f.	AESC 8:63	f. song	GIBB 351:56	conceive extravagant hopes of the f.	BURKE 168:3
fugitives f. are of that condition	BACON 48:89	f. train which the bridegroom sees	CLOU 223:32	concerned about our f.	RODO 693:94
fugue hum a f.	GILB 354:1	how to perform a f.	WILL 913:40	controls the f.	ORWE 629:1
fugues f. and symphonies	SASS 716:66	low on his f. couch	GRAY 370:33	dipped into the f.	TENN 840:81
fulfil f. ourselves outside of [society]	SARR 715:39	or at a f.	TWAIN 871:95	disdain the f. now	KENN 463:30
fulfilled f. a long time	BIBLE 107:33	present is the f. of the past	CLARE 219:44	dream about the f.	HAMM 379:11
till all be f.	BIBLE 109:86	see my f. before I die	EDGE 299:97	drowned the F.	THOM 854:11
fulfilment altered in f.	ELIOT 309:39	seen a costlier f.	TENN 847:31	Europe and…the f.	MARI 549:48
Before f. is	BARK 59:55	showed up at his f.	GOLD 362:91	eventualities in the f.	MURP 604:4
Contentment and f.	TROL 867:12	two-thirds of the f.	LAWS 495:44	fight against the f.	GLAD 358:90
f. only a step	LEGU 501:55	victory…celebrated with the f. rite	LAO 490:12	forbid…in the city in f.	EDWA 300:15
full All then is f., possessing	POPE 659:82	funerals go to other men's f.	DAY 256:79	For the f. I cease	ORAH 626:20
f. as craving…f. as vain	DRYD 289:63	he does better f.	VIDAL 881:8	From past and f.	ELIOT 308:33
F. many a glorious morning	SHAK 771:16	steady supply of f.	SHAW 781:1	f. ain't what it used to be	ANON 24:32
f. of love and honesty	SHAK 760:84	fungus f. or a lichen	THOR 857:75	f. generations	TOLS 863:8
f. stop…at the right place	BABEL 45:21	funhouse Cyberspace is the f. mirror	STER 817:63	f.…has a voice	OAKE 619:36
f. up years ago	WODE 919:68	funny Be f. on a golf course?	SILV 792:35	f. in which our country	KENN 463:37
lived his life to the f.	RAND 678:11	first f. thought	TRAV 864:45	f. is made of the same stuff	WEIL 896:28
live it to the f.	SPARK 806:22	f. as long as it is happening	ROGE 694:17	f. is the man of statistics	HOLM 408:2
Serenely t., the epicure would say	SMITH 801:21	f. is subversive	ORWE 628:65	f. of art	FLAU 326:31
so f. of unmannerly sadness	SHAK 739:46	f. paper read backwards	WILL 913:31	f. of humanity is uncertain	LEVI 506:61
was na f.	BURNS 170:68	F. peculiar, or f. ha-ha?	HAY 386:54	f.'s bright	ANON 25:57
fuller Money…the true f.'s earth	GAY 347:82	f. when Freud died	JARR 435:79	f. shock…disorientation	TOFF 862:91
fullers f. and their wailing	ANON 18:65	F. without being vulgar	GILB 355:35	F.…That period of time	BIER 129:31
fullness earth…and the f. thereof	BIBLE 94:3	F. you should ask	CECIL 202:24	f. that will live up to my past	BENN 76:34
earth…and the f. thereof	BIBLE 121:4	knowing what's f. is one of them	AMIS 14:92	f. they dreamed of	LESS 505:37
filled with all the f. of God	BIBLE 122:45	less f. and lasts longer	ANOU 26:2	f. was a mystery	CHOP 214:22
fullstoppers f. and semicolonials	JOYCE 452:99	Life was a f. thing	CRISP 245:57	f. while existing	NARO 608:74
fumble f. with the sheets	SHAK 745:36	to write a really f. book	HEMI 393:93	Germany was afraid of the f.	GREY 373:8
fumbling f. the flowers	REED 681:78	fur dressed all in f.	MOORE 594:18	great f. behind him	CART 198:42
fume captured f. of space	CRANE 243:20	I'll make the f.	BUTL 177:48	great f. behind him	MARA 548:24
fumes of tobacco and liquors	LEWIS 508:96	furbelows little pleats and f.	SCHI 718:98	great soul in f.	EMER 313:43
fumitor Crowned with rank f.	SHAK 763:86	furies Break bitter f.	YEATS 934:58	happiness that the f. offers	DESB 262:14
fun Ain't we got f.	KAHN 454:30	ye f. fell	SHAK 738:17	have seen the f.	STEF 814:6
Cancer can be rather f.	HALD 377:77	furious grew fast and f.	BURNS 172:23	hope increasingly in the f.	MAJOR 541:70
do things for f.	STARK 813:72	furnace Heat not a f.	SHAK 775:4	hopes and dreams of the F.	FRAME 333:81

hopes of f. years	LONG 516:54
I have seen the f.	TOYN 864:30
in f. look upon me	KEMB 461:82
In the f. everybody	WARH 889:63
lets the f. in	GREE 371:52
liberation From the f.	ELIOT 309:46
nations of the f.	CURZ 249:53
no preparation for the f.	DISR 276:44
one no longer believes in the f.	COUP 239:99
onward into its uncertain f.	HOFS 406:55
orgiastic f.	FITZ 325:2
past and f....conquered	ELIOT 308:36
past and f. were comprehended	GEE 348:93
people who will run the f.	JONES 448:93
picture of the f.	ORWE 630:4
preparing students for the f.	DEMI 261:83
present in time f.	ELIOT 307:92
present or any f. writer	MILL 570:58
present, past and f. sees	BLAKE 134:50
prophesying a fine f.	WILDE 908:87
Prudence...scans the f.	WORD 929:64
Science creates the f.	ZUCK 937:6
security for the f.	TROL 866:82
seen the f.	HALB 377:72
The f. belongs to the bridge-builders	MCAL 524:20
The f., Mr Gittes	TOWNE 863:19
too eager for the f.	LARK 490:20
train of the f. to run over him	EISE 302:50
will be in the f.	KIPL 474:84
wonderful f. beckoned	PLATH 654:72
futurelessness so free of f.	COUP 238:97
futurism we establish F.	MARI 550:54
futurist I am a f. today	OGDEN 622:36
futurity f. casts upon the present	SHEL 786:17
no reference to f.	JOHN 445:25
walk on into f.	THOR 858:94
Fuzzy-Wuzzy 'ere's to you, F.-W.	KIPL 471:94

G

Gael legend of the G.	RUSS 706:61
Gaelic Michael read the G. scroll	RUSS 706:61
gage hope's true g.	RALE 677:99
gags no g., no chance	TODD 862:89
gaiety eclipsed the g. of nations	JOHN 446:47
g., the intrigue and the anguish	SCHL 718:12
gain farmers...with constant g.	CRAB 242:94
g. and loss involved	PASC 641:21
g. by marriage	DICK 270:14
g. I count but loss	WATTS 891:3
his own g.	SMITH 798:49
loss comes...from his g.	BROW 162:73
love of g.	SOPH 804:82
neither g. nor loss	ELIOT 308:24
neither g. nor loss of utility	JEVO 438:45
no g.	ANON 23:71
no war for...material g.	CHUR 216:72
pursuit of g.	WEBER 894:68
to g. applause	JOHN 441:26
to speculate is a g.	COUS 239:3
weather that bringeth no g.	DEKK 259:46
what do you g.?	CRUZ 246:87
what things were g. to me	BIBLE 123:57
gained something is eternally g.	JAMES 434:67
gains Light g. make heavy purses	BACON 50:56
gait forced g. of a shuffling nag	SHAK 742:18
gaiters All is gas and g.	DICK 267:12
gal every boy and every g.	GILB 354:13
slap-up g.	DICK 272:48
galaxy bathe them in the g.	LOVE 519:15
g. is one of billions	BRAUN 150:98
glistening g. of childhood	MATT 561:71
gale before the g.	SMART 797:29
fart in a g. of wind	BARN 60:65
g., it plies the saplings	HOUS 415:56
war-cries...on the g.	MCCA 527:87
gales cool g. shall fan the glade	POPE 658:50
g. shall fan the glade	POPE 658:50
Galice G. at Seint-Jame	CHAU 208:74
Galilean Among the G. mountains	CRAS 244:37
G., thy dead shall go down	SWIN 833:36
O pale G.	SWIN 833:35
Galilee like the Sea of G.	HOPK 412:98
Ye men of G.	BIBLE 119:28
Galileo like G. going before the Inquisition	LIVI 512:85
status of G.	GOULD 365:23
gall pigeon-livered and lack g.	SHAK 753:68

They gave me g. to eat	BOOK 143:60
wormwood and the g.	BIBLE 105:81
gallant g., civilized...people	ATTL 37:41
He was a braw g.	BALL 55:69
Sade, the g. marquis	RICK 686:75
Where is this young g.	SHAK 748:27
gallantry no more to do with g.	SHER 787:47
What men call g.	BYRON 181:65
gallants Travelled g.	SHAK 775:5
galleon g. tossed upon cloudy seas	NOYES 619:78
Stately as a g.	GREN 372:1
galleries g. of the house	MUNDY 603:82
gallery faces...a g. of pictures	BACON 49:29
g. in which the reporters sit	MACA 525:49
machine-gun to a shooting g.	OFAO 622:34
Pit, box, and g.	POPE 661:34
gallimaufry g. or hodgepodge	SPEN 808:71
gallon dying for $1.50 a g. oil	POWE 666:88
gallons imperial g. of facts	DICK 270:1
gallop false g. of verses	SHAK 749:58
G. about doing good	SMITH 800:6
g. and g. about?	STEV 822:13
galloped g., Dirck	BROW 160:27
gallowglass Bonnought and g.	MCCA 527:87
gallows g. in my garden	CHES 212:94
High upon the g. tree	SULL 828:17
see nothing but the g.	BURKE 169:36
world's going to be...one huge g.	BRAU 150:2
gallows-tree Below the g.-t.	BURNS 171:95
Jack on the g.-t.!	SCOTT 724:19
galoshes on his g. as he passes	LEAC 496:56
gals No g., no gags	TODD 862:89
galumphing G. Goodness!	TRAV 865:46
gambit by ploy or g.	POTT 664:22
gambler A g. is someone	TRUMP 869:48
Show me a g.	PUZO 673:26
Time, that tireless g.	BAUD 64:63
whore and g.	BLAKE 135:70
gambling g. in human lives	DYSON 297:63
Inside every b....a g. streak	KORDA 480:99
spent...$3m on g.	DALY 251:77
women, and technicians	POMP 658:48
game Anybody on for a g.	SHAW 780:60
any g. in the world	TRUE 868:25
Art is a g.	PIER 651:9
Athalus, that made the g.	CHAU 208:53
Baseball is a Lockean g.	NOVAK 618:72
best g. in the world to watch	TREV 865:58
Bowls is a young man's g.	BRYA 163:11
continentals think life is a g.	MIKES 569:52
Cricket...is a manly g.	ANNE 17:52
cricket is just another g.	EDIN 300:10
Cricket is the greatest g.	WARN 889:67
Cricket...the g. of games	FOWL 332:71
enough to take up the g.	ROGE 695:30
far more than a g., this cricket	CARD 190:47
Fashion should be a g.	QUANT 674:35
food is love and g.	SHEL 784:64
Football...is a grand g.	BADEN 51:75
forbid...such g.	EDWA 300:15
fowlers when their g.	OTWAY 631:26
g. called Poohsticks	MILNE 575:86
g. for rough girls	WILDE 910:62
g....is never lost till won	CRAB 242:4
g. is so full of plot-interest	FRY 339:24
g. is too hard	JAMES 433:24
g. of catch-as-catch-can	FOOTE 329:94
g. of golf...played on a Sunday	LEAC 497:67
g. of life seriously	LEARY 498:95
g. of no use	BACON 46:53
g. of the most terrifying stresses	ARLO 30:65
g. your country loves	RICE 685:39
g....at which to be bad	MILNE 575:88
giving over of a g.	BEAU 67:9
golf g. went bad	TREV 865:60
good g. of Croquet	REID 682:96
great g. to see	SYNGE 834:57
how you played the g.	RICE 685:37
If you watch a g.	HOPE 411:74
inside g., cold, sure, undistracted	DELI 261:80
is surely his g.	ROUS 700:39
it is a good g.	HICKS 402:82
It's the g. that calls me	MILNE 575:87
kids playing some g.	SALI 711:61
killing the g. with this phoney mystique	BRES 151:19
know the g.	MCCA 527:92
Love is a g.	ROBBE 688:11

manly, British g.!	LOVE 518:8
more than a g.	HUGH 420:56
most exhilarating g.	GOOD 363:98
nature of my g.	JAGG 432:18
Never change a winning g.	TILD 860:66
no better than a g.	JAMES 434:67
nobly did he play the 'noble g.'	EGAN 301:24
no g. for the soft of sinew	WOOL 923:63
no hunter's g.	JEFF 436:10
parody is a g.	NABO 606:43
play with him at any g.	SHAK 765:27
Poetry...a mug's g.	ELIOT 307:85
poetry a pedant's g.	BUNT 166:62
present rules of the g.	ROOS 696:55
ruin your g. in no time	BOTH 146:14
Science...is not a g.	PAUL 644:76
Soccer is a man's g.	CHAR 207:45
Socratic method is not a g.	BEER 70:83
some g. on these lone heaths	HAZL 387:75
Soviet g. is chess	SHUL 789:88
take seriously a g.	STOP 825:68
The g.'s afoot	SHAK 746:43
They talk a good g.	BECK 67:30
things you can do in a baseball g.	STEN 816:55
time to win this g.	DRAKE 286:94
Truth is...the g. of the few	BERK 79:9
War's a bloody g.	SASS 716:70
war's a g.	COWP 241:77
What a polite g. tennis is	BARR 61:90
When's the g. itself	MARX 557:92
woman is his g.	TENN 841:97
gameboard steeplechase and g.	ELKIN 310:69
games best and loveliest of g.	CARD 190:46
bread and g.	JUVE 453:19
dread of g.!	BETJ 84:12
G. played with the ball	JEFF 437:22
I play no outdoor g.	WILDE 909:32
like an aptitude for g.	MORAN 596:56
Most g. are skin-deep	ARLO 30:64
or any sinful g.	HARTE 384:15
playing at children's g.	CHES 211:47
gamester sly g.	BEHN 71:14
gammon sucking pig and thick g.	MACB 527:82
world of g. and spinnage	DICK 269:74
gamut Hepburn runs the g.	PARK 637:52
Gandhi odious to see Mr G.	CHUR 216:70
gang Bush and his treacherous g.	HUSS 424:42
g. should mismanage the country	MARQ 554:37
Ganges by the Indian G.	MARV 555:61
gangrene smelly g. of professors	MARI 550:54
gangsterism g. is a...assimilation	DOCT 278:4
gangsters always acted like g.	KUBR 481:32
glorified g.	MACD 530:47
gaol snail...the world's thy g.	DONNE 280:62
who lie in g.	WILDE 910:58
gap Beyond the g. where	WILL 914:54
bridge the g. between the two	CHUR 216:62
duty is to bridge the g.	KISS 475:98
g. between brute power	COMM 229:66
g. in Christianity	FORS 332:57
g. in the hills	ANON 22:42
great g. between	SYNGE 834:59
made a g. in nature	SHAK 765:24
gaps g. even two can pass abreast	FROST 338:84
garb words clothed in reason's g.	MILT 581:23
garbage g. heap	GARD 346:46
G. in, g. out	ANON 23:83
garden alone in a g.	ROSSO 698:6
bleak rock...into a g.	YOUNG 935:76
Come into the g., Maud	TENN 845:89
England is a g.	KIPL 474:72
England is a g.	KIPL 474:73
everyone with a g.	DORAM 282:1
gallows in my g.	CHES 212:94
g. eastwards in Eden	BIBLE 86:44
g. hard by Heaven	BOUL 146:25
g. inclosed is my sister	BIBLE 102:3
g. in her face	CAMP 187:80
g. of cactus and sour grapes	MERR 567:17
G. of Love	BLAKE 134:50
g. of the world	MARV 556:80
g.'s umbrage mild	SMART 797:29
ghost of a g.	SWIN 834:51
Glory of the G.	KIPL 474:72
Glory of the G.	KIPL 474:74
God Almighty first planted a g.	BACON 49:46
God's Heart in a g.	GURN 375:42

God the first g. made — COWL 240:34
God walking in the g. — BIBLE 86:50
happy g. placed — MILT 582:39
have a g. of my own — MARV 555:60
I have the whole g. — HAMM 379:13
imperfection of my g. — MONT 592:73
into the g. to cut — FOOTE 329:94
jungles here are a well-kept g. — BOLT 139:50
like a…birdcage in a g. — WEBS 894:78
man and a woman in a g. — WILDE 909:21
Muses' g. — CAREW 190:54
Nothing grows in our g. — THOM 853:91
Our England is a g. — KIPL 474:72
Our England is a g. — KIPL 474:73
out of the G. of Eden — MUGG 601:49
playing down at the bottom of my g. — SHAN 776:30
rosebud g. of girls — TENN 845:91
Sensitive Plant in a g. grew — SHEL 785:84
we must cultivate our own g. — VOLT 882:39
gardener Adam was a g. — KIPL 474:74
Adam was a g. — SHAK 730:65
bad for God's g. — HARDY 382:66
supposing him to be the g. — BIBLE 118:23
gardeners g., ditchers — SHAK 755:28
which our wills are g. — SHAK 759:70
gardening G.…most underrated — SHUL 789:85
gardens bodies are our g. — SHAK 759:70
Down by the salley g. — YEATS 932:29
g. of the Desert — BRYA 164:13
g. of the West — CONN 233:86
g., wine, and delicate — MONT 591:64
g. without sorrows — CIXO 219:38
in all of the neighbouring g. — REED 681:77
In his blue g. — FITZ 325:94
men Leaving the g. — LARK 490:31
ordered woods and g. — MACK 533:15
sweetest delight of g. — BROW 159:97
variety of g., meadows — MOORE 595:26
garden-state that happy g.-s. — MARV 556:76
gargling blood come g. — OWEN 632:57
garland immortal g. is to be — MILT 579:70
garlanded g. with carven imag'ries — KEATS 459:36
garlands crowning…with g. — COUB 238:85
Therewith fantastic g. did she make — SHAK 755:25
weave the g. of repose — MARV 556:71
you may gather g. there — SCOTT 723:10
garlic G. to mend her kissing — SHAK 770:89
garment caught him by his g. — BIBLE 88:97
City now doth like a g. wear — WORD 926:19
every new and eagerly expected g. — DICK 271:32
g. has looked very different — BONH 140:59
g. out of fashion — SHAK 773:64
g. that made skiing — ANON 23:86
Language is called the g. of thought — CARL 192:95
new cloth unto an old g. — BIBLE 111:21
Non-violence is not a g. — GAND 345:35
waxeth old as a g. — BIBLE 108:51
garments Borrowed g. never fit — FULL 341:63
g. too good For thee — CRAS 244:36
g. were always in patchez — NASH 608:89
Her g., heavy with their drink — SHAK 755:26
keepeth his g. — BIBLE 127:71
Kiss thy perfumed g. — BLAKE 133:23
part my g. among them — BIBLE 94:1
garners Hold like rich g. — KEATS 457:93
garret precious jewels into a g. — BACON 47:69
Garrick as evidently an actor as G. — WALP 887:27
garter earl and a knight of the g. — ATTL 38:44
George and G. dangling — POPE 660:5
garters girdles and g. to be bonds — BACON 48:88
thine own heir-apparent g.! — SHAK 741:9
gas All is g. and gaiters — DICK 267:12
G. smells awful — PARK 638:65
where you put in the g. — TAYL 838:26
gaseous God…a g. vertebrate — HAEC 376:55
gases killing airs and g. — DICK 270:4
gash g. in its throat — HUGH 419:42
gaslamps light coming from g. — CASAL 199:68
gasp made one G. and Stretch one's Eyes — BELL 73:58
gassing burning and g. people — SIHA 791:29
gate A-sitting on a g. — CARR 197:22
by shutting the park g. — MILT 579:63
Captain of the G. — MACA 526:63
Death…openeth the g. — BACON 47:76
g. of bliss — CRAS 244:38
g. of paradise — SHAW 781:1
g. of the year — HASK 385:25

gazed upon the g. — BYRON 183:5
guards at the g. — SUN 829:33
here at the g. alone — TENN 845:89
hobbled…through the garden g. — SASS 716:58
house with the narrow g. — SHAK 762:39
Hun is at the g. — KIPL 474:76
lark at heaven's g. — SHAK 773:61
matters not how strait the g. — HENL 395:39
passing through this G. — SASS 717:76
passion-flower at the g. — TENN 845:92
poor man at his g. — ALEX 11:23
watchful at his g. — DODD 278:9
wide is the g. — BIBLE 110:9
gates Come open your g. — SCOTT 724:28
g. of pearl and topaz — LAUR 492:70
g. of the world — HARDY 382:61
g.…shall not be shut — BIBLE 127:83
g. to the glorious — FORS 331:30
heaven's g. she claps — LYLY 523:8
iron g. of life — MARV 556:65
Lift up your heads, O ye g. — BIBLE 94:4
Nor g. of steel so strong — SHAK 772:25
Open the temple g. — SPEN 809:3
shut the g. of mercy — GRAY 369:19
Sprouting…at area g. — ELIOT 305:33
Such are the G. of Paradise — BLAKE 134:47
Through g. of pearl — HOW 417:93
towards the g. of hell — MILT 581:31
gateways g. of the mind — SASS 717:78
g. to unexplored terrain — WILS 915:86
gather G. ye rose-buds — HERR 400:45
g. you out of the countries — BIBLE 105:89
go and g. them up? — BIBLE 112:51
gaucho really a g. — GUIR 374:33
gaudy one other g. night — SHAK 765:40
rich not g. — SHAK 751:20
gauge danger is that g. — LESS 505:36
gauger Master G. play — STEV 821:72
Gaul G.…is divided into three parts — CAES 184:22
Gaullist G. only little by little — DE 259:39
gauntlet g. with a gift in't — BROW 160:11
take up the g. — BROW 158:58
gavottes birds sing g. — SITW 794:69
gay all the world was g. — POPE 659:69
assume everyone is g. — FIER 323:56
Being black is warm and g. — RHYS 684:25
chimes ring out with a carol g. — BOND 139:52
g. Description Aegypt glads — POPE 662:66
G. gilded scenes — ADDI 5:2
g. goodnight — YEATS 933:54
g. nature — SMART 797:31
G. rich and Rich g. — ANON 20:19
glass so g. — SPEN 809:11
He has a g. appeal — COWA 239:15
impiously g. — CRAB 242:85
It will be a g. world — READ 680:49
lay his g. caparisons apart — SHAK 765:39
lord and lady g. — SCOTT 722:85
poet could not but be g. — WORD 928:42
verse again shall…make them g. — DRAY 286:99
Gaza brought him down to G. — BIBLE 90:75
Eyeless in G. at the mill — MILT 586:45
gaze fixed in steadfast g. — MILT 575:95
g. of dogs — CALV 185:46
gone to g. on Cleopatra — SHAK 765:24
medium's g. is brief — IGNA 428:40
seal's wide spindrift g. — CRANE 243:11
shields him from the world's g. — WHITE 903:87
star of Truth…bade me g. — ARNO 32:30
gazed still they g. — GOLD 361:55
gazelle nursed a dear g. — MOORE 596:53
gazers eyes the g. strike — POPE 658:67
gazes For him that g. — CRAB 242:87
Gazette I inclose the G. — STEE 814:89
Pall Mall G. is written — THAC 849:98
gazing love does not consist in g. — SAINT 709:12
gear Time's…chariot changing g. — LINK 511:60
women and g. are at the bottom — SCOTT 724:33
geese garrulous g. — WHITE 903:83
G. are swans — ARNO 33:51
g. go south — WU 930:96
Like g. about the sky — AUDEN 40:91
More g. than swans — GIBB 352:68
take their g. for swans — BROO 157:32
wild g. lost in cloud — BASHO 63:44
Gehenna Down to G. — KIPL 470:79
gem every tear a g. — SHEL 783:35

Full many a g. — GRAY 369:17
g. of the western world — MOORE 596:48
treat it like a precious g. — PELE 646:18
gendarme United States…global g. — MCNA 537:92
gender tired of the g. of things — SEXT 728:16
to a kind and not to a g. — YOUR 935:80
genealogy g. of his forefathers — ECHE 298:76
general business of a g. — SUN 829:29
g. has no friends — LEMAY 502:76
g. must know — REED 682:84
g.'s disdained — SHAK 757:94
g. who advances — SUN 829:30
g. who does not believe — NATH 610:24
good for G. Motors — WILS 915:81
imperator and great g. — SHAK 733:76
'Twas caviare to the g. — SHAK 753:64
victorious g. — SUN 829:28
generalization g. can establish science — BERN 81:39
generalizations can be no g. — FISH 324:76
g. are dangerous — DUMAS 294:95
g. of science sweep — HUXL 426:5
tentatively accepted g. — FRIE 337:62
generals bite some of my other g. — GEOR 349:11
g. are in my coach — MARL 551:67
g. of his day — WELL 897:53
G., right-wing politicians — STEI 816:44
like dead g. — TUCH 869:57
most people and G. — TUCH 869:60
plebiscite elected g. — JUVE 453:19
Russia has two g. — NICH 613:83
soldiers, her g. too. — MERE 567:10
too serious…to be left to g. — CLEM 220:73
Whitehall g. — ASHD 35:91
generation all a lost g. — STEIN 815:12
energy of a whole g. — THOM 855:43
Every g. laughs — THOR 857:89
Every g. revolts — MUMF 603:74
every new idea…takes a g. or two — FEYN 322:25
every single g. gone — MACL 535:35
evil and adulterous g. — BIBLE 111:43
feminism divided my g. — LYND 524:15
for the next g. of men — LOWE 519:24
g. has come to know — TIME 860:72
G. x — COUP 238:88
grieved with this g. — BIBLE 97:58
ills of an entire g. — ISHE 430:90
in this g. — KENN 463:40
is a g. of men — HOMER 409:17
meaning of the Lost G. — KERO 464:65
men and women of this g. — LLOY 513:99
men in every g. — MILL 573:38
My g. of Canadians — FULF 341:46
new g.…every 30 years — COWL 240:38
new g. grows up — PLAN 654:60
new g. of Americans — KENN 462:12
new g. would take over — THOM 854:24
O g. of vipers — BIBLE 111:42
O g. of vipers — BIBLE 108:76
one g. sacrificing for the next — MAYH 562:96
our g., though not indifferent — CECIL 202:27
poets of each g. — DAY 256:75
refuge from one g. to another — BOOK 143:63
remind one g. — JEVO 438:48
sad for my g. — SAINT 709:20
second g. has no time — BALD 53:30
Seldom is it given to one g. — SARN 714:32
third and fourth g.…that hate me — BIBLE 88:23
This g. shall not pass — BIBLE 113:86
To my g. — AUDEN 41:30
unto this wicked g. — BIBLE 111:45
With each g. — SCHR 720:43
ye are a chosen g. — BIBLE 125:24
generations dwelling place in all g. — BIBLE 96:96
future g. — TOLS 863:8
g. believe to have happened — WHIT 905:24
G. have trod — HOPK 412:93
save succeeding g. — UNIT 873:69
shadows upon two g. — LLOY 513:2
through centuries of g. — MARQ 553:20
generosity luxury of g. — DICK 270:86
generous have more g. sentiments — JOHN 443:69
to be g. and compassionate — THAT 850:13
genes selfish molecules known as g. — DAWK 256:72
Wall St. g. — THOM 854:24
Genesis first chapter of G. — ACHE 2:34
G. was to be believed — SHAR 776:43
Genet G. had been right — ANGE 17:47

genetics G. is Important and Difficult — PARE 636:35
Geneva rules…from Rome or G. — BROW 158:56
Genghis G. Khan has arrived — THUR 860:65
genitals very different attitude to g. — BURG 167:94
genius 25-year old g. — GREE 372:83
  absolute g. for malingering — PROU 671:78
  appearance of…greater g. — RUSS 705:46
  attributes of g. — MOND 590:50
  Bradman's batting g. — LARW 491:56
  Celtic g. — ARNO 33:49
  cocker up my g. — JONS 448:12
  Conceit spoils the finest g. — ALCO 10:3
  destroy g. and art — HAZL 388:94
  dispenses with the need for g. — GALB 343:96
  each…be considered a g. — BERG 79:95
  Every age has a…universal g. — DRYD 288:23
  everything but g. and virtue — HAZL 388:81
  G. and regularity are utter Enemies — GAIN 342:85
  g. for painting, poetry, music — EMER 313:41
  g. found respectable? — BROW 160:13
  g. is an enormous littleness — PATC 642:48
  g. is enough — ARET 29:42
  G. is felt — DIDE 273:88
  G. is one per cent inspiration — EDIS 300:13
  g. lies in taking…ordinary people — BANKS 59:38
  g. makes no mistakes — JOYCE 452:90
  g.…not to purchase fame — DRYD 289:50
  g. of Canada — MORR 598:94
  g. of our days — LARI 490:19
  g. of the place — POPE 659:93
  g. that could cut a Colossus — JOHN 446:63
  g. to correct them — TELL 838:31
  g. was too sullen — DRYD 288:29
  G. will never mount high — BROO 155:1
  Gives g. a better discerning — GOLD 362:64
  In every work of g. — EMER 312:5
  interest to the fire of g. — LINC 510:36
  in theory if g. had not proved — LESS 505:44
  like many businessmen of g. — PUZO 673:25
  lot of time to be a g. — STEIN 815:19
  man of g. — POUND 664:33
  men of g. — CONA 230:79
  men of g. — DELA 260:58
  mind and g. — STEN 816:49
  monotony of g. — HAZL 387:65
  neither g. nor knowledge — JOHN 442:54
  neurotic can…be a literary g. — AUCH 39:73
  no interest in anything but g. — LAGN 489:1
  no man of g. — BEER 70:85
  nothing to declare except my g. — WILDE 908:84
  nourished all its g. — SMITH 801:25
  Philistine of g. in religion — ARNO 34:65
  Political g. — HEGEL 391:42
  some flashes of g. — BYRON 181:52
  stereotype of rejected g. — HUGH 419:31
  taking pains…said to be g. — ACHE 2:38
  talent instantly recognises g. — DOYLE 285:78
  that is the way of g.! — MANN 545:67
  the g. of the…press — BENN 77:59
  thing demanded of g. — GOET 360:21
  think like a g. — NABO 606:46
  Though taste, though g. bless — COLL 228:46
  Three-fifths of him g. — LOWE 520:32
  true g. appears — SWIFT 830:67
  true g. is…large general powers — JOHN 445:42
  vital g. — GOUR 365:27
  Work of Staggering G. — EGGE 301:25
  works of a great g. — ADDI 7:41
geniuses cricket's presiding g. — CARD 190:48
  G. are the luckiest — AUDEN 41:24
  One of the greatest g.…Shakespeare — WALP 887:25
genocide g. is being carried out — JOHN 439:64
genres these g. still hold — UPDI 874:86
gent knight was…a valiant G. — EVEL 316:21
genteel avoid is the 'shabby g.' — DISR 277:89
  not g. when he gets drunk — BOSW 146:12
  truly g. — HARDY 382:58
gentes G. and laitymen — JOYCE 452:99
gentile isolation to g. hostility — ROTH 699:29
Gentiles boasting as the G. use — KIPL 472:22
  G.' Lord and King — AQUI 28:28
  G., which have not the law — BIBLE 120:60
  preach among the G. — BIBLE 122:44
gentility I expected kindness and g. — PERE 648:61
  Money and g. — MITF 588:4
  Shabby g. has nothing — HOLM 408:88
  What's g. worth — GALS 344:26

gentle As g. and as jocund — SHAK 734:1
  carry g. peace — SHAK 775:22
  Do not go g. — THOM 853:81
  g. and respectful ways — FENW 320:91
  G. as falcon — SKEL 795:91
  g. mind by g. deeds — SPEN 809:12
  g., yet not dull — DENH 261:92
  I have seen them g. — WYATT 931:3
  love, so g. in his view — SHAK 735:34
gentleman act the g. — TAFT 835:78
  ask the honourable g. — ROCHE 691:47
  attire for a g. — SHAR 776:40
  back to the g.'s flat — MANS 547:93
  beautiful woman…qualities of a g. — LABR 483:58
  chance of becoming a g. in it — LAMM 487:70
  fashionable g. — ALSOP 13:67
  g. an' scholar — BURNS 170:74
  g. is an attorney — JOHN 444:92
  g.…loves to hear himself talk — SHAK 736:59
  g. on whom I built — SHAK 766:79
  g. poet — JOYCE 452:88
  g. to be the best dressed — TROL 867:4
  Gladstone…never a g. — DISR 277:82
  He's a g. — SHAW 780:62
  honourable g. caught the Whigs — DISR 276:56
  honourable g.'s poodle — LLOY 513:95
  I am a g. — SHAW 778:89
  king…cannot make a g. — BURKE 169:47
  last g. in Europe — LEVE 506:56
  legal g. who rescues your estate — BROU 517:33
  lovely g.! — SHAK 737:73
  man was apparently a g. — RIDGE 687:78
  no g. could…give offence — ROCHE 690:45
  No real English g. — BAGE 51:80
  Once a g. — DICK 271:18
  reputability to the g. of leisure — VEBL 878:56
  serving a great g. — ISHI 431:93
  So this g. said a girl — LOOS 517:73
  stamps a man…as an educated g. — SHAW 779:39
  that which you call a G. — CROM 245:69
  this venerable old g. — LEAC 497:72
  too pedantic for a g. — CONG 231:19
  true breeding of a g. — BYRON 182:86
  unable to describe a g. — TROL 867:11
  use of a g. in travelling — LOWE 519:20
  When a g. is disposed — SHAK 773:58
  Who was then a g. — BALL 55:64
gentleman-drover he…is a g.-d. — SCOTT 723:13
gentlemen American g. are the best — LOOS 517:79
  ask you g. — RODR 694:97
  creates good g. — MUGA 601:47
  difficult to behave like g. — MACK 534:20
  G. do not take soup — CURZ 250:55
  g. in England now abed — SHAK 746:62
  g.…in the same Lobby — PALM 636:25
  G. know that fresh air — MACA 525:35
  g.…possess only strength and valour — BRON 155:79
  G. Prefer Blondes — LOOS 517:72
  G.-rankers out on the spree — KIPL 470:80
  G.…seem to prefer blondes — LOOS 517:74
  G., you can't fight in here — KUBR 481:31
  Hard pounding this, g. — WELL 897:55
  ladies and g., last night — NATH 609:22
  male officers are g. — CARD 183:20
  most of the g. — WAUGH 891:9
  no ancient g. but gardeners — SHAK 755:28
  no salvation for g. — MOLI 589:27
  patriots…not to forget we are g. — BURKE 168:5
  since g. came up. — SHAK 730:62
  spoken of themselves as g. — WAUGH 891:14
  Tea…Is a g. — CHES 212:80
  'Then, g.,' said Redgauntlet — SCOTT 725:49
  two very civil g. — SHER 788:60
  When G. can see — DICK 272:56
  while the G. go by! — KIPL 473:61
  written by g. for g. — THAC 849:98
gentleness all…through my g. — WYATT 931:4
  Crist…we claym of him oure g. — CHAU 209:86
  G.…cardinal virtues — WOLL 921:7
  g. of heaven — WORD 926:13
gentles It's weel wi' you g. — SCOTT 724:26
gentlest fittest may also be the g. — DOBZ 277:98
gentlewoman cut out for a G. — SWIFT 832:4
  talk so like a waiting g. — SHAK 741:1
gently persuade g., not by force — PASC 641:27
gentry Ye Enbrugh G.! — BURNS 170:66
genuine place for the g. — MOORE 595:29

genuineness g. of apparent statements — AYER 44:10
  G. only thrives in the dark — HUXL 424:60
geographers So g., in Afric-maps — SWIFT 832:98
geography different from G. — BENT 77:74
  g. of one's own nature — BOWL 147:39
  like trying to stop G. — MONT 592:87
  too much g. — KING 469:47
geology reduced easily to basic g. — HILL 402:91
geometrician God is a g. — PLATO 655:4
géométrie Vanité de la g. — FRED 336:35
Geometry G. is that part — NEWT 612:73
geometry does not know his g. — ANON 26:86
  g. in the humming of the strings — PYTH 673:31
  G. is not true — PIRS 652:29
  G. is to sculpture — APOL 27:15
  G.…the only science — HOBB 404:23
  g. was degraded — MACA 526:61
  Night G. — KENN 462:99
  no 'royal road' to g. — EUCL 315:2
Geordie Jingling G. — SCOTT 725:43
George Amelia was praying for G. — THAC 849:90
  England and Saint G.! — SHAK 746:44
  fair Saint G. — SHAK 732:22
  G. and Garter dangling — POPE 660:5
  G.—don't do that — GREN 372:99
  G. III…consecrated obstruction — BAGE 51:90
  G. the Third — BENT 78:80
  G. who discovered that alcohol — WODE 919:59
  great G. weighs twenty stone — BYRON 182:92
  King G.'s glorious days — GILB 354:14
Georgian G. Silver goes — MACM 537:79
geranium madman shakes a dead g. — ELIOT 305:30
Géricault G. corpses, or Picasso — LIPP 511:64
germ very g. and first upgrowth — KING 469:60
German G. Empire arose? — HERZL 401:57
  G. memory was like…tongue — BURU 174:86
  G. people will turn — LENIN 502:84
  G. police spies — MARX 558:4
  G. text of French operas — WHAR 902:54
  like G. opera — WAUGH 892:36
  saw a G. soldier — STRA 826:86
  Should the G. people lay down — GOEB 359:8
  two literatures [French and G.] — ARNO 33:35
  under G. influence — GOER 360:11
  wee, wee G. lairdie! — CUNN 248:25
Germans Beastly to the G. — COWA 239:21
  G.…are going to pay — GEDD 348:91
  G. classify…the French arrange — CATH 200:90
  I hate not G. — THOM 854:10
  let the G. win the war — MILE 569:53
  problem of the Sudeten G. — HITL 404:21
Germany Communism fits G. — STAL 812:58
  country is at war with G. — CHAM 204:65
  every country except G. — GREY 373:8
  from G. to Downing Street — CHAM 204:63
  G. has become a menace — ROOS 696:59
  in G., books — STAEL 812:52
  ruined cities of G. — ORWE 629:80
  You're thinking of Europe as G. and France — RUMS 702:37
germinates g. and gestates by itself — HUST 424:49
germs Trap the g. — ANON 22:64
Gershwin G. died last week — OHARA 623:47
  G. keeps pounding on tin — GERS 350:39
Gerty G.…taken up…concerts — WHAR 901:48
gessamine crow-toe, and pale g. — MILT 578:54
gesture army without parade or g. — LAWR 495:39
  never make a fine g. — BERN 81:51
gestures cynical g. of the poor — SPEN 807:50
  parody…implods all g. — PIGL 651:14
get g. away inwardly — HERZ 400:55
  G. up, g. up for shame — HERR 400:42
  time to g. — BIBLE 100:70
  will never g. it — WEAT 893:61
getting g. over a four-day drunk — HELL 393:83
  Let's be g. at them — GRACE 365:31
  with all thy g. get understanding — BIBLE 99:11
Gettysburg G. address was so short — HEMI 394:17
gewgaw This g. world — DRYD 289:56
ghastly grave is g. — ANON 18:75
  more g. a business — HARDY 382:72
ghetto idea of an arts g. — HARR 384:3
  radio is a g. of good taste — KEIL 460:71
ghost Ay, thou poor g. — SHAK 752:34
  bowling of a g. — THOM 855:39
  cease to be g. — PAZ 644:88
  dogma of the G. — RYLE 707:78
  Father, Son and Holy G. — MCLE 534:27

gave up the g. BIBLE 114 , 118:19
gave up the g. BIBLE 116:66
g. from the tomb SHEL 783:41
g. of a garden SWIN 834:51
g. of a great house LEVE 506:58
g. of wind WILL 914:56
g. stories…for ghosts ALDI 10:10
g. will walk BROW 161:56
given up the g. BIBLE 93:56
mind full of g. MANS 546:82
peacock like a g. TENN 842:14
The g. of Roger Casement YEATS 934:61
thought to please my g. MENC 565:56
yielded up the g. BIBLE 114:5
ghosts ambushed with g. MACA 525:36
g. of beauty glide POPE 661:50
haunted by the g. SHAK 735:20
I sought for g. SHEL 782:20
like g. from an enchanter fleeing SHEL 783:43
rain Is full of g. MILL 571:85
ghoul g. of literature DELI 261:77
giant As when a g. dies SHAK 758:34
chalk g. HEAN 389:7
G. Despair had a wife BUNY 166:71
g. girls that have no secret SPEN 807:55
g. refreshed with wine BOOK 143:61
G.'s Causeway worth seeing? JOHN 445:39
lies a sleeping g. NAPO 607:59
like a g.'s robe SHAK 768:35
'This is I, the g.' MAST 560:54
To have a g.'s strength SHAK 758:25
upon the body of a g. LAND 488:77
giantism To go for g. SCHU 720:51
giants G. in physical power CARL 191:85
g., the sons of Anak BIBLE 89:37
like precocious g. PEAR 645:98
standing on the shoulders of g. BERN 80:29
Gibraltar G. may tumble GERS 351:45
giddy g., shallow, humorous youth SHAK 745:39
Gideon sword of the Lord, and of G. BIBLE 90:69
gier-eagle Strong, the g.-e. SMART 797:28
gift Beauty is the lover's g. CONG 231:34
cause of this fair g. SHAK 772:35
chance g. of nature MORAN 596:56
creative g. HOPK 413:11
destroying her g. by maiming BACON 50:70
Every good g….is from above BIBLE 124:6
exploiting a heavenly g. QUIL 674:48
for a New Year's g. SHAK 743:79
gauntlet with a g. in't BROW 160:11
g. half understood ELIOT 308:35
g. of a coward SHAK 755:49
g. of God is eternal life BIBLE 120:69
g. of tears SWIN 832:21
g. of vanity and pride GRIL 373:14
g. or trust MCCA 528:99
Heav'n's last best g. MILT 583:76
love is the g. of oneself! ANOU 26:3
love, or g., which is MILT 579:77
Madness is a g. PALEY 635:13
make the g. rich TROL 867:96
music is a g. and a burden SIMO 792:41
naught her priceless g. PATM 643:57
only g. is a portion of thyself EMER 312:25
other than the g. of life KOSI 480:4
problem without a g. BACH 46:29
speech, that supremely human g. MATH 560:57
When God hands you a g. CAPO 189:28
gifted divinely g. man TENN 843:48
g. individuals manage to do both SAKI 710:43
young, g. and black HANS 380:34
gift horse Always look a g. h. RABE 676:68
gifts cannot recall their g. TENN 846:26
countless of love WINK 917:23
diversities of g. BIBLE 121:8
even when bearing g. VIRG 882:19
For your g. WEBS 894:88
g. may henceforth be bestowed SHAK 748:26
give good g. unto your children BIBLE 110:58
great g. with one hand SNOW 802:40
man's work or his own g. MILT 580:88
No g. from chance ARNO 31:87
offer g. to people one knew DE 257:97
presented unto him g. BIBLE 108:73
rarer g. than gold BROO 156:8
received g. for men BIBLE 96:39
received g. for men BOOK 143:59

Rich g. wax poor SHAK 753:75
Rich men deal g. SHAK 762:51
Spend not then his g. JONS 449:21
stars were the g. MACC 528:16
whose heavenly g. SURR 829:36
Win her with g. SHAK 729:34
Gilbert G. had a baddish streak QUIL 674:46
G. to someone else's Sullivan RUSS 706:65
laid down by G. and Sullivan HUTC 424:53
verse again shall g. DRAY 286:99
gilded vegetables too g. GIRA 358:82
gilding g. of setting sun GARL 346:50
gile thai er ful of g. MINOT 587:71
Gilead balm in G. BIBLE 105:74
gillyflowers With g. SPEN 808:68
gimble Did gyre and g. CARR 195:90
gimcrack how g. a place LAUR 492:70
gin for a g. and for a snare BIBLE 102:15
G. and chicken helpless BARK 59:54
G. by pailfuls SCOTT 724:19
G. was mother's milk SHAW 780:67
Of all the g. joints EPST 314:76
proper union of g. and vermouth DE 264:33
receptacle for Gilbey's g. CHEE 209:3
sooner we can get out the g. REED 682:83
ginger empty g. ale bottles THUR 859:20
Nutmegs and g. ANON 20:9
Gipper win…one for the G. GIPP 357:77
gipsy Time, you old g. man HODG 405:42
giraffe God…invented the g. PICA 650:1
Swelling to maculate g. ELIOT 305:37
giraffes G.!—a People CAMP 186:62
man who believes in g. MITC 588:87
return the g. to the zoo NASH 609:8
gird g. up the loins of your mind BIBLE 125:21
girders Rumbling under blackened g. BETJ 83:91
girdle At her own g. WEBS 894:79
folds of a bright g. ARNO 31:93
g. round about the earth SHAK 737:95
g. when your hips stick NASH 609:4
leathern g. about his loins BIBLE 108:75
Off with that g. DONNE 279:35
the g. do the gods inherit SHAK 763:89
girdles g. and garters to be bonds BACON 48:88
girl Boy Meets G. in Winnipeg MACL 535:53
can't get no g. reaction JAGG 432:16
dark g. I couldn't play with WRIG 930:82
do a g. in ELIOT 307:83
doubt whether any g. TROL 866:83
first rock at a g. like I LOOS 517:82
forget myself with that g. TAYL 837:15
Fun is fun but no g. LOOS 517:80
g. in our town ANON 21:28
g. I saw was myself RHYS 684:30
g. likes to be crossed in love AUST 43:68
g….marries a literary man CHEE 209:2
g. must marry for love GABOR 342:83
g. solid with yearning LOWE 521:62
g. throwing a ball WOOLF 922:39
g. to miss out on any RUSS 706:68
g….turned into a chimpanzee PERE 648:57
g., unschooled, unpractisèd SHAK 740:73
g., who's danced with the Prince FARJ 318:49
g. whose cheeks NASH 608:79
g. who was a lady LOOS 517:77
g. with big boobs KING 468:26
Give me a g. SPARK 806:23
great mountainous sports g. BETJ 83:84
Home is the g.'s prison SHAW 779:21
I am a material g. MADO 538:22
I'm not a g. MANS 546:83
like a chorus g.'s tights LAWR 495:36
Look like a g. SIMON 792:36
maddest fantasticalest g. DEKK 259:51
nice g. should only fall SPARK 806:26
Oh, she's a splendid g. HUXL 425:77
Poor Little Rich G. COWA 239:7
pretty g. is like a melody BERL 79:12
quite loved by a g. TROL 867:95
Since I was a little g. ROTH 699:15
So this gentleman said a g. LOOS 517:73
There's a Burma g. KIPL 470:85
There was a little g. LONG 516:67
What can you expect of a g. WHAR 902:55
where the g. smiled before WHIT 906:56
wink your eye at some…g. MENC 565:56

young g.'s skin RENO 683:7
young g. stood beside NEIL 610:30
girlfriend going to visit our g. f. MAMET 544:39
girl-graduates sweet g.-g. TENN 841:95
girlie here and tell me, g. NASH 608:97
girls all the g….were laid PARK 637:54
Always be civil to the g. MITF 589:10
Anyone who marries three g. STEIN 815:25
Dancing…training for g. MORL 598:85
For coloured g. SHAN 776:27
game for rough g. WILDE 910:62
giant g. that have no secret SPEN 807:55
g. aren't ignorant COOP 236:56
G. aren't like that AMIS 14:84
G. are so queer ALCO 10:6
g. in slacks remember dad BETJ 84:98
g. so constantly do this TROL 866:84
g. suffered during this month BERR 82:67
g. think that they can do so TROL 867:98
g.' thin laughter RICK 686:74
g. were no longer to be treated LEE 500:45
g. with wax faces WILD 910:81
Golden lads and g. SHAK 774:74
good g. keep diaries BANK 58:30
It was the g. I liked BAIL 52:97
lads for the g. HOUS 415:54
lovely, gifted g. GRAV 367:79
make passes At g. PARK 638:63
Many g. have not the advantage FLEM 327:58
men and g. came and went FITZ 325:94
mill g. clumping ORWE 627:35
Most plain g. are virtuous ANGE 17:36
No g….no chance ANON 22:66
other g. and boys STEV 823:14
pallor of g.' brows OWEN 632:52
process whereby American g. turn HAMP 380:27
robust, dynamic g. WODE 919:61
rose-lipt g. HOUS 415:64
save women and g. WEBB 893:63
Secrets with g….are never valued CRAB 242:6
thing about g. SALI 711:54
to g. and boys HORA 413:22
Treaties are like g. DE 259:38
trouble with g. SALI 711:59
twelve little g. in two straight lines BEME 74:93
two g. had me buried! MANS 547:94
What do g. do ALCO 10:7
What fools middle-class g. are DRAB 286:89
what some g. marry ROWL 701:50
where g. might be sent AUST 43:81
within the reach of factory g. SCHU 721:56
Gittes The future, Mr G. TOWNE 863:19
give G., and it shall be given BIBLE 115:31
G. it up! G. it up! KAFKA 454:29
G. what you command AUGU 41:38
If she g. aught WEBS 894:73
more blessed to g. than to receive BIBLE 119:53
giver God loveth a cheerful g. BIBLE 122:31
givers when g. prove unkind SHAK 753:75
giving in g. that we receive FRAN 334:98
glaciers rock inlaid with azure g. BENU 78:85
glad g. grace YEATS 932:33
g. mad brother's name SWIN 834:50
g. of another death ELIOT 306:74
g. when they said unto me BIBLE 98:88
g. with all my heart DRAY 287:6
g. you like adverbs JAMES 434:53
heart was g. FOX 333:77
just g. to see me WEST 901:33
glade cool gales shall fan the g. POPE 658:50
gales shall fan the g. POPE 658:50
in the bee-loud g. YEATS 932:30
gladiators G. fight, or die, in flow'rs POPE 659:95
gladness excitement and g. BUEC 165:44
girded me with g. BIBLE 95:8
half with melancholy, half with g. LUGO 522:86
in heill wes and g. DUNB 294:6
poets…begin in g. WORD 926:17
serve the Lord with g. BIBLE 127:89
serve the Lord with g. BOOK 143:66
stale is their g. HARP 383:86
Teach men half the g. SHEL 784:63
Without g. availis no tresour DUNB 294:3
Gladstone G., like Richelieu DISR 277:84
Like G. speaking to Victoria MANC 544:45
Mr G. read Homer CHUR 216:66
unprincipled maniac G. DISR 277:82

G. not only plays dice.	HAWK 385:31	heavens declare the glory of G.	BOOK 142:43	my G. what an eye!	CEZA 203:53
G. of Abraham	PASC 641:39	hidden love of G.	WESL 900:18	my G., why hast thou forsaken me?	BIBLE 114:4
G. of love!	DODD 278:10	holy Lamb of G.	BLAKE 135:82	my G., why hast thou forsaken me?	BIBLE 94:97
G. of Love…Beteth his wynges	CHAU 209:87	honest G. is the noblest work	INGE 429:56	My Lord and my G.	BIBLE 118:25
G. of our Fathers	MILT 586:55	honour of G.	BACH 46:25	my spirit hath rejoiced in G.	BIBLE 115:23
G. of things as they are!	KIPL 472:20	hope thou in G.	BIBLE 95:21	my spirit hath rejoiced in G.	BIBLE 128:98
G. on his side	DYLAN 297:55	household of G.	BIBLE 122:43	nature of G.	WHIT 904:14
G. only, she for G. in him	MILT 583:62	how can he love G.	BIBLE 125:41	neither doth G. respect any person	BIBLE 91:4
G. ordered motion	VAUG 878:50	How could G.	LOUI 518:95	noblest work of G.	POPE 660:25
G. owns heaven	SEXT 728:20	how dwelleth the love of G. in him?	BIBLE 125:37	noble work of G.	BURNS 170:70
G. passes through the thicket	JOHN 438:58	How odd Of G.	EWER 316:28	no power but of G.	BIBLE 120:85
G. personally responsible	CHAP 206:23	I am a G.	SHEL 785:74	not afraid of G.	POPE 661:62
G. planted a garden	BIBLE 86:44	I am G., and King, and Law	SHEL 783:37	not…a supremely good G.	DESC 263:24
G. recognizes I will do that	CART 198:47	I came, I saw, G. conquered	JOHN 438:59	not G., is greater	WHIT 905:34
G. rest his soul	SMITH 800:3	if a G. there be	SWIN 833:44	Not only is there no G.	ALLEN 12:42
G.'s a good man	SHAK 745:18	If G. be for us	BIBLE 120:77	not that we loved G.	BIBLE 125:39
G. said…I am that I am	BIBLE 88:12	if G. choose	BROW 160:10	not three G.s: but one G.	BOOK 140:79
G. save Elizabeth	ANON 20:7	If G. did not exist	VOLT 883:53	not yet G.	THOR 857:70
G. save me from…adventures	BYRON 183:11	If G. had meant us to have group sex	BRAD 148:60	now with G.	WALT 888:50
G. save me from being 'nice'	LAWR 495:20	If G.…has any validity	BALD 54:37	obedience to G.	DAVI 256:70
G. save thee, ancient Mariner!	COLE 225:82	If, knowing G.	TENN 847:51	O believers, fear G.	KORAN 478:67
G. save the king	BIBLE 91:87	if this manifest G. enlightens men	CYRA 250:60	obey G. rather than men	BIBLE 119:33
G. save the king	SHAK 735:23	ignorance G. winked at	BIBLE 119:51	observed by Yours faithfully, G.	ANON 22:51
'G. save the Queen'	KIPL 472:27	image of man created by G.	IVAN 431:99	O Christ, O G.	HOPK 412:82
'G. save the Queen'	WHIT 905:26	imitate G.	FLAU 326:37	O city of G.	BIBLE 96:48
G. saw that it was good	BIBLE 85:40	immortal, invisible, G.	SMITH 801:26	Of all G.'s works	SPEN 808:85
G. sends meat	FULL 341:66	impulse which G. has	CRUZ 246:89	O G. in Heaven	ANON 19:96
G. send thee good ale	ANON 20:1	Inclines to think there exists a G.	CLOU 222:26	O G. of battles	SHAK 746:53
G.'s eternal store	MILT 584:92	indurate heart against G.	KNOX 476:19	O G. of Bethel!	DODD 278:9
G.'s finger touched him	TENN 844:54	infants are trying to spell G.	ROBI 690:33	O G.! Put back	JONES 447:86
G.'s first Creature	BACON 50:61	in favour with G. and man	BIBLE 115:28	Oh G.! that man	MELV 564:39
G. shall be my hope	SHAK 730:55	In G. 'tis glory	DRYD 290:84	Oh, G.! that men would see	BRAC 148:51
G. shall help her	BIBLE 95:25	in my flesh shall I see G.	BIBLE 93:64	oily man of G.	THOM 856:59
G. shall supply all your need	BIBLE 123:64	in science there exists no G.	STEI 816:47	old abusing of G.'s patience	SHAK 743:68
G. shall wipe away all tears	BIBLE 126:60	intellectual love of G.	SPIN 811:35	O Lord my G., I hope	STUA 827:99
G. shall wipe away all tears	BIBLE 127:80	interpret G.'s will	RUNC 702:72	O my G., Take the gentle path	HERB 398:19
G. shed His grace	BATES 64:49	in the minds of G.	GREE 371:73	One G., one law	TENN 844:67
G.'s in His heaven	BROW 160:19	In the name of G., go!	AMERY 14:80	One man with G.	KNOX 476:20
G.'s police	CHIS 213:16	Invisible, except to G. alone	MILT 582:51	one that would circumvent G.	SHAK 755:29
G.'s querulous calling	HUGH 419:45	Is G. by definition indifferent	EBER 298:74	Only G., my dear	YEATS 934:59
G.'s the theme	SMART 797:30	It is G. who splits the grain	KORAN 478:61	only make a sacrifice to G.	POPE 659:91
G. summons to the Abode of Peace	KORAN 478:68	I would to G.	SHAK 741:96	only men could serve G.	STEI 816:44
G. tells me how	TOSC 863:17	jealous G.	BIBLE 88:23	order of G. and of nature	MANN 546:80
G. tempers the wind	STER 818:6	jealous G.	BIBLE 89:46	Our G., our help	WATTS 891:5
G. that made the world	BIBLE 119:49	Jesus never claims to be G.	ROBI 690:42	out of the mouth of G.	BIBLE 109:78
G. that maketh men to be	BOOK 143:57	Just are the ways of G.	MILT 586:52	owe G. a death	SHAK 743:56
G., the best maker	SHAK 746:69	just die, G. willing	RULFO 702:66	paltered with Eternal G.	TENN 844:74
G. the first garden made	COWL 240:34	justify G.'s ways to man	HOUS 415:65	person to worship G.	ROOS 696:50
G. their severance ruled	ARNO 32:10	justify the ways of G. to men	MILT 580:93	play only Bach in praising G.	BARTH 62:8
G. the Omnipotent!	ELLE 310:71	Just what G. would do	WOOL 923:65	pleased G. hitherto to bestow	HOBB 404:23
G. therefore let him free	MILT 579:77	kick in the pants to G.	MILL 572:15	Praise belongs to G.	KORAN 477:40
G. the soul	POPE 660:14	kills the image of G.	MILT 578:62	Praise G., from whom	KEN 461:94
G. thi makere	CHAU 208:64	kingdom of G. is within you	BIBLE 116:56	prepare to meet thy G.	BIBLE 106:9
G. to send us a merry meeting	LANC 487:72	know that I am G.	BOOK 143:51	presume not G. to scan	POPE 660:16
G. to trust in	MARG 549:37	know the mind of G.	HAWK 386:32	prey I G. that non	CHAU 208:65
G. unmakes but to remake the soul	BROW 162:88	label men for G.	THOM 855:40	prime work of G.	MILT 586:47
G. was good on the physical	BURG 167:93	laboratory of G.	WILL 912:23	Prompt me, G.	THOM 855:29
G. was sick	VALL 876:18	Lamb of G., I come!	ELLI 310:79	prove G. statistically	GALL 344:21
G., who does whatever pleases him	WESL 900:23	lay wrestling with…my G.	HOPK 413:3	prove that G. does not exist	LABR 484:79
G., who is able to prevail	WALT 888:45	leap up to my G.!	MARL 552:6	pure in heart…shall see G.	BIBLE 109:83
G. who is all-forgiving	SMITH 799:64	lend a myth to G.	CRANE 243:14	Put your trust in G.	BLAC 132:93
G., who is her life	PATM 643:64	let me be awake, my G.!	COLE 226:94	reason and the will of G.	ARNO 33:54
G., who is our home	WORD 926:24	light…the shadow of G.	BROW 159:94	reason, it is playing G.	LEGU 501:63
G. who kills us	YOUR 935:84	like a G. in pain	KEATS 458:33	recognize G. without Jesus	PASC 641:75
G. who let us prove	BONH 140:62	living G. who made all things	FOX 333:77	remembered my G.!	SOUT 805:97
G. who Looks after	KIPL 473:57	Lord G. made them all	ALEX 11:22	reserved only for G.	BACON 46:47
G. who made him	KIPL 474:74	Lord G. of Hosts	KIPL 472:21	riddles of…the purposes of G.	FRYE 340:39
G. who made thee mighty	BENS 77:61	Lord G. of Sabaoth	BOOK 140:70	rouse G. to relent	EBER 298:73
G. will forgive me	HEINE 391:51	Lord G., we ha' paid	KIPL 472:15	Rowing Toward G.	SEXT 728:19
G. will provide himself a lamb	BIBLE 87:82	Lord is G. indeed	SCOT 725:64	same G. which worketh in all	BIBLE 121:8
G. will recognize his own	ARNA 31:81	Lord thy G. am a jealous G.	BOOK 141:93	same relation to G.	UPDI 874:81
G. with his mercyful iye	ANON 19:87	Lord thy G. is a jealous G.	BIBLE 89:46	saw the face of G.	MARL 552:99
G. won't, and we can't mend it	CLOU 222:24	love of Man, and in praise of G.	THOM 853:82	saw the Spirit of G.	BIBLE 108:77
G. would have changed his doom	CLEV 221:81	love the Lord Thy G.	BIBLE 113:82	security…in our relationship with G.	EDDI 298:85
G. wrongs not men anything	KORAN 478:69	madness…to believe oneself to be G.	FOUC 332:64	sees…as G. of all	POPE 660:9
go to your G.	KIPL 471:93	man G. hates	DOWL 284:42	Servant of G., well done	MILT 583:83
greatest good…knowledge of G.	SPIN 811:32	man's bedevilment and G.'s	HOUS 416:76	servant of the Living G.	SMART 796:25
Great G.!	SCOTT 722:80	man's distinctive mark…Not G.'s	BROW 162:74	shalt not tempt the Lord thy G.	BIBLE 109:79
Great G.!	STEN 816:51	Man's word is G. in man	TENN 847:31	sinning against G.	BOTHA 146:13
ground G.'s-Acre	LONG 516:49	may G. help us	BETH 83:75	sufficiency is of G.	BIBLE 122:22
Had I but served my G.	SHAK 775:21	may G. set me there	JOAN 438:53	suppose even G. was born	LOWE 520:52
hand folks over to G.'s mercy	ELIOT 303:82	May G. wither up their hearts!	DAVIS 256:64	sword without G.'s authority	LUTH 523:96
hand of G.	BIBLE 107:31	men that G. made mad	CHES 212:73	talk of the death of G.	FACK 317:31
hand of G.	HASK 385:25	mercy o' my soul, Lord G.	MACD 530:53	Teach me, my G. and King	HERB 397:94
hand of G.	MARA 548:21	more just than G.?	BIBLE 93:53	thank G.	THOM 853:92
hath not one G. created us?	BIBLE 106:19	My G. and King	HERB 397:91	thank G., Doctor	STAN 812:61
Have G. to be his guide	BUNY 167:76	My G. must have my best	HERB 398:18	thank G. for my sanguine	MURP 604:1

god

thank G. that he has spared me	BELL 72:52
that is really your G.	LUTH 523:98
their English G. is not so dominant	CARR 194:57
There G. is dwelling too	BLAKE 134:32
There is no G.	BIBLE 94:88
There is no G.	CLOU 222:25
there is no G.!	ONEI 625:90
thinks little of G.	PLUT 656:11
this man was the Son of G.	BIBLE 114:19
Those who know G.	PATM 643:65
Those who marry G.	GREE 371:62
Those whom G. hath joined	BOOK 142:29
thou art G.	BIBLE 96:49
Thou shalt have one G. only	CLOU 223:36
three-personed G.	DONNE 281:70
through darkness up to G.	TENN 843:44
Thus G. and nature linked	POPE 660:22
thy G. my G.	BIBLE 90:79
To G. belong the Names Most Beautiful	KORAN 478:66
To G. I speak Spanish	CHAR 207:37
to G. Or to each other	MILT 585:21
To The Unknown G.	BIBLE 119:48
To whom…will ye liken G.?	BIBLE 103:40
trust G.	BROW 162:69
trust in G.	DENN 262:99
trust in G.	SMITH 801:13
unknown to anyone but G.	PLATO 655:80
Unlike G. the artist	PERCY 648:51
unto G. the things that are G.'s	BIBLE 113:80
up to Nature's G.	POPE 660:27
Verb is G.	HUGO 421:83
Very G. of very G.	BOOK 141:95
vindicate the ways of G. to man	POPE 660:7
vision of the holiness of G.	BLOOM 137:5
voice of G.	ALCU 10:8
voice of G.	POPE 661:53
wait at G.'s right hand	GURN 375:45
walking…and praising G.	BIBLE 119:31
was G. out there	LEIS 502:73
waste of G.	STUD 827:4
weigh your G. and you	KIPL 472:26
We need to find G.	THER 851:44
Whatever is, is in G.	SPIN 810:23
What G. abandoned	HOUS 416:80
What G. hath cleansed	BIBLE 119:40
what G. hath given us	TAYL 837:23
what G. would have done	KAUF 455:58
What hath G. wrought!	BIBLE 89:42
what is a mind without G.?	PRAT 667:98
What therefore G. hath joined	BIBLE 113:71
What was good for G.'s birds	HARDY 382:66
When G. at first made man	HERB 398:16
When G. hands you a gift	CAPO 189:28
When G. hath made	TENN 843:41
Where G.'s presence is no longer	STEI 816:46
Where is now thy G.?	BOOK 143:49
White people…deal more with G.	GIOV 357:75
whose G. is their belly	BIBLE 123:59
Who trusted G.	TENN 843:36
Who trusted G.	TENN 843:45
why G. created women?	WALL 886:3
wild G. of the world	JEFF 436:8
will of G.	JOHN 438:56
wind thrashes G.	HUID 421:99
with G. all things are possible	BIBLE 113:75
with G.'s favour	WALT 888:44
words which he of G.	LANY 489:5
Word was with G.	BIBLE 117:71
works of G. in heav'n	MILT 585:35
worship of G.	WHIT 904:9
worship Sunday, not G.	BLYT 138:25
worship the Lord thy G.	BIBLE 109:80
would G. this flesh	SWIN 833:24
Would to G. that we were dead	WILDE 907:82
ye believe in G.	BIBLE 118:8
Yellow G. forever gazes down	HAYES 387:62
Yet her conception of G.	STRA 826:83
You don't fire G.	KENN 463:43
Zion, city of our G.!	NEWT 613:77

god Assumes the g. — DRYD 291:34

before the g. of science	KING 468:40
beneficent but implacable g.	LECO 499:29
could have been a g.	CHRI 215:36
Cry aloud: for he is a g.	BIBLE 92:19
cyclical economic g.	CUOMO 248:29
deem himself a g., or beast	POPE 660:16
either a g. or a wolf	WEBS 894:87
extemporal g. of rhyme	SHAK 733:75
g. going thro' his world	BROW 160:20
g. is not so glorious	MARL 551:74
g. of contemporary man's	MONT 591:62
g. self-slain	SWIN 834:52
if g. be pleased	EDWA 300:16
immortal g. of harmony	BEET 70:95
never a g.	WOOL 923:64
never make a g. out of form	KAND 454:36
next to of course g.	CUMM 247:8
Now the melancholy g.	SHAK 756:66
presents the g. unshorn	HERR 400:42
thank we all our G.	WINK 917:23
the g. pursuing	SWIN 832:20
to be like a g.	CATU 201:8
told me of my g.	BRID 152:27
to the g. he worships	THOR 857:79
treat it like a g.	PELE 646:18
triangles had made a g.	MONT 593:91
turning into a g.	VESP 880:73
wild beast, or a g.	BACON 49:28
Yblessed be g.	CHAU 209:85

God-conditioned G.-c. forms — MANN 545:46

goddess blind g. in the lottery — ASTU 37:31

Chaste g.	ROMA 695:34
g. is better than no g.	WARN 889:66
G. of the Battle	BARK 60:56
G. sage and holy	MILT 576:13
never saw a g. go	SHAK 773:51

godfather always a g. — WOOL 923:64

God-gifted G.-g. organ-voice — TENN 846:28

god-given g.-g. (though not to me) — PALEY 635:13

godhead the G. — PIRS 652:25

g. in which all life is human — SHAW 779:37

godless decent g. people — ELIOT 307:88

God-like G.-l. erect, with native — MILT 582:61

godlike anything G. about God — MILL 573:35

dictates of his g. mind	OTWAY 630:21
endurance is g.	LONG 516:53
one of their g. qualities	MENC 566:79

god-like g.-l. hours — WORD 925:99

godliness Cleanliness is next to G. — DICK 271:26

continual g.	BOOK 141:90
exercise which withdraweth from g.	STUB 827:1
In cheerful g.	WORD 925:11

godmother Cinderella's Fairy G. — DIOR 275:24

gods against all the g. of Egypt — BIBLE 88:16

alien people clutching their g.	ELIOT 306:74
Allotted by the g.	TENN 847:34
angels would be g.	POPE 660:12
As flies…are we to th' g.	SHAK 763:84
By the nine g. he swore	MACA 526:62
Concerning the g.	PROT 670:65
daughter of the g.	TENN 838:40
dish fit for the g.	SHAK 747:84
do not know much about g.	ELIOT 308:27
dreadful fiend of g.	SPEN 809:8
effigies of g. and goddesses	GILL 355:38
even the g. themselves struggle	SCHI 718:9
eye of g.	WORD 929:64
feel new g. in the flesh	LAWR 494:4
fit love for g.	MILT 584:12
Give, you g.	DRYD 289:56
G. and men, we are all deluded	MACN 538:4
g. are absent	BIBLE 119:42
g. are come down to us	SHAK 764:2
g. are just	LOWE 521:57
g., employed to	SHAK 750:65
g. had made thee poetical	PLATO 654:77
g. recognized by the state	LOVE 519:9
G., that wanton in the air	RUSK 704:38
g. there morning	SHAK 774:69
g. will diet me with	PLATO 655:82
higher esteem among the g.	COND 230:82
In Mexico the g. ruled	SAINT 709:21
inspired by the g. inside	CABE 183:16
joy reserved for the G.	SHAK 769:48
Kings are earth's g.	WILS 915:85
knowledge from the g.	BYRON 179:15
Land of lost g.	TENN 839:57
like G. together	MARL 551:72
looks…dare the g.	MONT 592:81
makes G. by the dozen	MAIL 540:46
man who would argue with the g.	DUNN 295:17
masculine invisibility makes g.	TENN 840:66
men that strove with g.	SHAK 731:88

nature of the g.?	SHAK 731:88
no other g. before me	BIBLE 88:23
Now g., stand up for bastards!	SHAK 762:56
one day become a g.	MILL 572:30
only g. should speak	ROET 694:5
Real are the dreams of G.	KEATS 458:21
reflected in its g.	SCHI 718:1
respect the same g. as themselves	DRAB 286:89
Sees G. with Daemons	POPE 662:68
Shall g. be said to thump	THOM 852:65
shall not go after other g.	BIBLE 89:46
sinned against my g.	FORD 330:6
superior to the G.	CATU 201:8
tempest of the g.	MARL 551:78
The g. themselves	TENN 846:26
The g. thought otherwise	VIRG 882:21
there are innumerable g.	BURR 173:58
These be thy g., O Israel	BIBLE 89:26
these that were G.	SWIN 833:36
utterance of the early G.	KEATS 459:47
What men or G. are these?	KEATS 459:21
what the g. had given him	BEER 70:85
When G. were young	THOM 853:24
When men make g.	ONEI 625:90
whom G. love dies young	MENA 565:49
Whom the g. wish to destroy	CONN 233:68
will of the g.	AESC 8:58
ye g., you make the weak	SHAK 747:81
ye shall be as g.	BIBLE 86:49
your g. or your vegetables	GIRA 358:82

Goebbels inferno depicted by Dr G. — ORWE 628:59

going g. out and thy coming in — BIBLE 97:87

lead by g.	KESEY 465:74
long and loath at g.	RANS 572:25

goings established my g. — BIBLE 95:18

gold All the g. upon the earth — PLATO 655:87

apples of g. in pictures of silver	BIBLE 100:50
Beauty…like the g. standard	WOLF 919:80
blood mixed with wasted g.	KING 469:64
bought and sold for English g.	BURNS 172:36
bow of burning g.!	BLAKE 135:84
burned g. was his colour	CHAU 209:95
but litel g. in cofre	CHAU 208:72
chain of g.	SCOTT 724:22
colour in Australia is g.	STRE 827:92
copper into g.	SENG 727:95
differs from g.	SHEL 786:10
envelopèd with g.	SPEN 808:83
eyes of g. and bramble-dew	STEV 823:34
Fetters of g.	ASTE 36:22
fly to India for g.	MARL 552:94
fly to India for g.	MARL 552:98
From the red g. keep thy finger	SCOTT 724:40
gild refinèd g.	SHAK 739:30
Glory, the grape, love, g.	BYRON 182:80
g., and frankincense, and myrrh	BIBLE 108:73
g. and silver	SHAK 738:24
g. and silver becks me	SHAK 738:24
g. an' velvet	ANON 21:28
G..Cadillac G.	TRUMP 869:49
g. doth more than either	KYD 482:46
G. is the gift	GRIL 373:14
g. wes changyd in to lede	ANON 19:84
green tigering the g.	HUGH 419:41
Gross g. from them runs	MARL 553:16
head was of fine g.	BIBLE 105:94
He who hath the g.	ANON 25:51
If g. ruste	CHAU 208:75
Like to airy thinness beat	DONNE 280:55
must be propped with g.	MAST 560:53
narrowing lust of g.	TENN 844:61
never have too much g.	MORE 597:62
never owned his g.	LAFO 485:11
next, my g.!	JONS 448:10
Nor all that glisters g.	GRAY 368:2
patens of bright g.	SHAK 741:86
property turns sand to g.	YOUNG 935:76
provoketh thieves sooner than g.	SHAK 749:32
pure g. flows	TOCQ 861:81
rain of g.	DAY 257:85
rarer gifts than g.	BROO 156:8
religion of g.	BAGE 51:85
sand and ruin and g.	SWIN 833:42
Silver and g. have I none	BIBLE 119:30
street of the city was pure g.	BIBLE 127:82
There is g.	SHAK 765:31

think g. that is brass SPEN 809:11
Thou gaudy g. SHAK 740:72
tipped with g. for this JONS 449:23
travell'd in the realms of g. KEATS 456:76
wear g. on your hair BALL 56:88
Wedges of g., great ouches SHAK 731:8
What is bettre than g.? CHAU 209:93
what's become of all the g. BROW 161:42
What use…the g. place FRAME 333:79
When g. becomes her object! SHAK 743:65
With g….cover ev'ry part POPE 658:55
golden cats with g. eyes SACK 708:90
circle of the g. year TENN 841:94
g. age in all the arts VIDAL 881:5
g. and silver YEATS 933:38
g. bowl be broken BIBLE 101:92
g. cadence of poesy SHAK 733:80
g. ear POPE 659:97
g. foil all over them SPEN 808:75
G. lads and girls SHAK 774:74
g. rules for an orchestra BEEC 69:62
g. years return SHEL 786:21
In the g. lightning SHEL 784:56
Kissing with g. face SHAK 771:16
poets only deliver a g. SIDN 791:18
west to the G. Gate KIPL 474:78
golden-calf g.-c. of self-love CARL 192:14
Goldengrove Over G. unleaving? HOPK 412:93
golden-haired young Apollo, g.-h. CORN 237:68
Goldsmith G. tells us AUST 43:87
Here lies Nolly G. GARR 346:53
Swift is more Irish than G. OBRI 620:98
goldsmith not in g.'s ware MIDD 569:38
Goldwyn You talk of art Mr G. SHAW 781:93
golf American people than G. has ROGE 694:18
Be funny on a g. course? SILV 792:35
better he plays g. WELLS 898:86
Fute-ball, G., or uther sik JAME 432:22
get it on the g. course SKEL 795:95
g. course is the epitome GIRA 358:80
g. game went bad TREV 865:60
G. is a game JONES 447:85
G. is a good walk spoiled TWAIN 872:40
G. is in the interest TAFT 835:78
G. is like life CLIN 221:2
G. is not…a fair game NICK 614:92
G. is so popular MILNE 575:88
G. is to Fiji what cricket is to America SINGH 793:53
G.…makes me so damned angry GEOR 349:18
g. may be played on a Sunday LEAC 497:67
g.…way of playing marbles CHES 213:4
great game of g. CROS 246:81
intrepid hunters of g. balls SMITH 799:65
mind off everything like g. ROGE 695:30
picking up the wrong g. ball LEMM 502:79
Playing polo is like…to play g. STAL 812:59
thousand lost g. balls ELIOT 307:88
unforgiving as g. greens ELKIN 310:69
when one is playing g. LYND 523:14
work at it, it's g. HOPE 411:74
golfer Actually, I am a g. MATU 561:72
gymnast and g., soldered together BRYA 163:10
make a g. out of him HAGEN 376:56
Goliath Nobody roots for G. CHAM 204:67
Gomorah rained upon…G. BIBLE 87:79
gondola What else is like the g.? CLOU 222:23
you have swam in a g. SHAK 750:75
gone all is g. HOOD 410:53
And they are g. KEATS 459:43
dead and g. YEATS 933:44
dead and g., lady SHAK 754:16
g., and for ever! SCOTT 723:8
g. without a word? SHAK 729:28
Now thou art g. MILT 578:47
Or that when I am g. LOVE 519:11
They're all g. now SYNGE 834:56
gongs struck regularly, like g. COWA 239:12
gong-tormented g.-t. sea YEATS 934:58
good aim at some g. ARIS 29:50
all men's g. TENN 848:69
all men's g. TENN 841:94
All partial evil, universal g. POPE 660:15
all things work together for g. BIBLE 120:76
and when she was g. LONG 516:67
Anybody can be g. in the country WILDE 908:9
Any g. thing GREL 372:98
art for the sake of the g. SAND 712:89

Be a g. man SCOTT 725:60
beautiful, creative and g. MING 587:70
because they are so g. TROL 867:97
because we deem it g. SPIN 810:29
being really g. all the time WILDE 909:43
Beneath the g. how far GRAY 370:40
better to be g. than to be ugly WILDE 908:8
between g. and evil HUSS 424:47
but to be g. STEV 822:88
common g. to all SHAK 748:25
constitutes its highest g. RUSS 705:42
content…to be obscurely g. ADDI 7:37
Do all the g. you can WESL 900:20
does not do much g. GILM 356:57
do him little g. JOHN 443:64
dull prospect of a distant g. DRYD 291:20
enemy of the g. VOLT 883:47
every evil, like every g. SCHO 719:31
every g. and excellent thing WILD 911:82
Every soul pursues the g. PLATO 655:99
evil seek to bring forth g. MILT 580:4
evil turn to g. MILT 585:34
For g. ye are and bad TENN 847:42
for the general G. WELLS 898:75
for the g. or evil side LOWE 519:27
Gallop about doing g. SMITH 800:6
General G. is the plea BLAKE 135:73
glory and g. of Art BROW 162:89
God saw that it was g. BIBLE 85:40
God-willing, I will make g. HITL 404:20
g. almost kill a man as kill MILT 578:62
g. and bad of every land BAIL 52:5
g., and had no power to see LANY 489:3
g. and ill together SHAK 762:36
g. both going and coming back FROST 338:92
G., but not religious-good HARDY 381:48
G. company, g. wine, g. welcome SHAK 775:6
g. Compensate bad in man BROW 162:86
g. day to get out anything we want to bury MOORE 595:25
g. die early DEFOE 258:12
g. ended happily WILDE 909:41
g. fast bowler TRUE 868:26
g. For which to strive MILT 581:19
g. for your legs SCHU 720:49
G., great and joyous SHEL 785:83
G. grows with her SHAK 775:26
g. honest and painful PEPYS 647:29
g. in everything SHAK 749:34
g. is always a product of art BAUD 65:73
G. isn't the word GILB 355:37
g. man to do nothing BURKE 169:52
g. men starve DRYD 290:9
g. must associate BURKE 168:4
g. never will be our task MILT 580:3
g. news baits MILT 586:62
g. of the land of Egypt BIBLE 88:3
g. of the people CICE 218:20
g. or they were bad TRAV 865:47
G., pleasure, ease, content POPE 660:23
g. that I would I do not BIBLE 120:70
G. Time was Had By All SMITH 800:93
G., to forgive BROW 162:93
g. to know the worst BRAD 149:72
g. to some man SHAW 777:73
g. to talk HOSK 414:39
g. turns out to be ARIS 29:51
g. we oft might win SHAK 757:17
greatest g. of the mind SPIN 811:32
great harm and great g. HESI 401:66
great instrument of moral g. SHEL 786:14
hear all the g. things said about ye BOUC 146:19
hear more g. HAZL 387:73
heav'n sees g. MILT 577:41
He wos wery g. to me DICK 270:88
hold fast that which is g. BIBLE 123:71
if we were very g. FULF 341:46
If ye think g. BIBLE 106:18
intuitive knowledge of G. SPIN 811:34
It does g. though JULI 452:6
It is always g. BEAU 67:8
it must be g. HOCK 405:39
it would be a g. idea GAND 345:36
kills the very g. HEMI 394:99
knowing g. and evil BIBLE 86:49
knowing the g. GRIS 373:20
knowledge of g. and evil MILT 579:65

knowledge of g. and evil MILT 579:67
Knowledge of g. bought dear MILT 582:59
learning things that are g. HERN 399:28
'Leave…while you're looking g..' LOOS 517:75
lies precisely the greatest g. ROUS 700:43
lives not three g. men SHAK 741:13
make bad g. SHAK 758:41
Man is neither g. nor evil BALZ 58:21
men most g. SHAK 739:27
never had it so g. MACM 536:69
never known much g. done SMITH 798:49
noble type of g. LONG 516:60
no for ony g. or ill BURNS 170:65
no g. in arguing LOWE 520:38
none that doeth g. BIBLE 94:89
none that doeth g. BOOK 142:41
not g. enough GALS 344:24
not g. enough yourself TROL 866:86
nothing either g. or bad SHAK 752:53
nothing g. to be had HAZL 387:67
Nothing is fair or g. alone EMER 312:4
nothing so bad or so g. SHAW 777:65
not necessary…that the world is g. CONR 234:9
not quite so g. GALT 344:28
only one g., knowledge SOCR 803:58
only read what is truly g. STEIN 815:24
only time it isn't g. for you HEMI 394:11
overcome evil with g. BIBLE 120:84
O ye wha are sae g. BURNS 170:86
preferred to be g. SALL 711:72
remained Stupidly g. MILT 584:11
rise on the evil and on the g. BIBLE 109:94
shall he not make it g.? BIBLE 89:41
shall not want any g. thing BIBLE 95:13
sick one gets of being 'g.' JAMES 433:26
single thing that is g. GALL 344:14
some g. thing comes tomorrow SHAK 743:60
some special g. doth give SHAK 736:55
something g. about someone LONG 517:68
still rich in genial g. WORD 926:16
strong antipathy of g. to bad POPE 661:61
suffer for the G. KIER 467:11
teach…of g. WORD 924:75
tell someone how g. KNUD 476:25
That is indeed very g. HOUS 416:87
That was very g. of him KAUN 456:65
The g. want power SHEL 785:73
the national g. PANK 636:33
They love the G. BROO 156:14
think something is g. or bad STEV 820:58
To believe in 'the greater g.' DIDI 274:9
too much of a g. thing? SHAK 750:78
what g. came of it SOUT 805:1
What's the g. of a home GROS 374:23
what we like is not necessarily g. BELL 71:32
what were g. to be done SHAK 739:43
what you feel g. after HEMI 394:4
When I'm g. WEST 901:30
When I'm g., I can be really g. DETT 264:29
When it sounds g., it is g. ELLI 310:74
where g. men rest FLEC 327:45
whoso hath this world's g. BIBLE 125:37
ye're just no a g. man KELM 461:80
You're g., you're real g. HUST 424:48
goodbye as you wave me g. PARR 639:95
G. Mr Zanuck RENO 683:5
G. to All That GRAV 367:65
good-for-nothing g.-f.-n. woman SHAW 779:30
Good Friday soldest him on G. F. SHAK 741:98
good-looking all the men are g.-l. KEIL 460:69
goodly g. to look to BIBLE 91:91
goodman g. of the house BIBLE 113:88
good-morning G.-m.; g.-m.! SASS 716:63
good-morrow bade g.-m. KEATS 457:6
good-mother almost as bad, g.-m. SHAK 754:6
good-nature keep her g.-n. SCOTT 725:52
goodness all my g. pass before thee BIBLE 89:32
crownest the year with thy g. BIBLE 96:36
distinguished from ordinary g. STOWE 825:71
fountain of all g. BOOK 142:32
Galumphing G.! TRAV 865:46
g. and mercy shall follow me BIBLE 94:2
g. infinite, g. immense! MILT 585:34
g. in things evil SHAK 746:48
g. never fearful SHAK 758:39
g. of your mechanics MOORE 595:33
G. what beautiful diamonds! WEST 900:28

If g. lead him not	HERB 398:17	best politics is good g.	STEV 821:66	studied as a branch of g.	JAY 436:97
odor…from g. tainted	THOR 857:82	British g. and…colonial population	SCHL 718:10	take from such G.	PAINE 634:93
The powerful g. want	SHEL 785:73	Canada…enjoyed: English g.	COLO 228:51	The foundation of the g.	SUN 829:33
Wealth does not bring g.	PLATO 654:78	checks and balances in g.	ANON 24:33	The object of g.	BEVE 85:26
goodnight gay g.	YEATS 933:54	corruption in any g.	BRUN 163:4	three main priorities for G.	BLAIR 132:3
G.-n. Ensured release	HOUS 416:86	Democracy…g. by the uneducated	CHES 213:97	two ideas of g.	BRYAN 163:8
say g.-n. till it be morrow	SHAK 736:53	Democracy means g. by discussion	ATTL 38:46	want of g. is any new kind of g.	HOBB 404:28
till our last g.	PEAC 645:96	Do not criticize your G.	CHUR 218:10	whatever the G. and public allow	SHAW 778:91
goods all my g. to feed the poor	BIBLE 121:9	duty of g.	PAINE 634:91	What your g. believes	KENN 463:41
Bill of G.	MORR 599:1	employees of the g.	TOOLE 863:14	who understands g.	TRUM 868:37
boat…had the g. of a house	PEPYS 647:48	Every line in the g.'s budget	WRIS 930:94	wish the G. would put a tax	SITW 794:78
community lacks g.	CHUR 216:62	every man…under a G.	RAIN 677:92	worst form of G.	CHUR 217:94
consumption of valuable g.	VEBL 878:56	expect from his G.	TRUM 868:29	would be great in our little g.	ROCH 691:63
g. and trappings of your life	MOORE 594:13	face a British G.	TUCH 869:58	**governmental** g. machinery	SPEN 807:43
g. do not spontaneously present	ECON 298:81	faineant g.	TROL 867:93	**governments** All g. use force	PARE 636:36
g.…procured by labour	RICA 684:34	false system of g.	PAINE 634:92	climates, council, g.	TENN 839:63
g.…produced jointly with bads	BOUL 146:24	faults of a G.	ROOS 696:44	G. care for…security of property	PANK 636:31
Labour does not only create g.	MARX 557:95	fear that the Russian g.	HERZ 400:56	g. have never learned anything	HEGEL 391:41
power of purchasing other g.	SMITH 797:41	federal g. does basically	WILL 911:1	G. need…shepherds	VOLT 881:5
with all my worldly g.	BOOK 142:28	feeble g.	JOHN 441:11	Kings and G. may err	HERB 397:79
good-tempered g.-t.…young woman	AUST 42:57	first object of g.	MADI 538:20	most despotic of infidel G.	BYRON 179:4
goose every g. a swan	KING 469:53	form of native g.	ONEI 625:87	nothing new in Third World g.	AUNG 42:49
g. because you like pâté	LINK 511:61	Freedom of men under g.	LOCKE 514:15	not to form g.	KING 468:27
No g., no golden egg	TSON 869:55	frightening views of g.	INOU 430:73	strong mutually antagonistic g.	WAUGH 892:29
on the ground at G. Green	KINN 470:69	G.…contrivance of human wisdom	BURKE 168:33	**governor** advising the…g. of Florida	BUSH 175:90
goosecap g. and…no judgement	NASHE 609:13	giving money to the G.	HERB 397:78	Can't afford them, G.	SHAW 780:65
goose-hiss dumb g.-h. of the wives	THOM 853:93	G. and co-operation	RUSK 704:19	G. of the Bank of England	HOWE 417:96
goosie Ridin' on a g.?	ANON 20:18	g. and report the facts	ROGE 695:29	G. of the Bank of England	KORDA 480:99
Gorbachev G. has 100…advisers	GORB 363:4	g. and the people	MILL 569:55	G. was strong upon	WILDE 910:55
I like Mr G.	THAT 850:23	G.…a necessary evil	PAINE 634:90	I'd be a terrific g.	CLIN 222:9
gore g. no more, they bellow	LIND 511:53	G. cannot endure…half-slave	LINC 510:34	moved honord words to be your g.	SCHW 721:64
mayn't be human g.	DICK 267:21	g. doesn't work	OROU 627:24	**Governor-General** save the G.-G.	WHIT 905:26
gored fame is shrewdly g.	SHAK 757:8	g. funding for…comic strips	UPDI 874:86	**governors** whereof ye are the g.	MILT 579:80
tossed and g. several persons	BOSW 145:10	G. has no other end	LOCKE 514:13	**governs** see how well she g.	SIXT 794:80
gorge into the narrow g., unseen	WILL 914:54	g. I despise	KEYN 465:77	**gowd** man's the g.	BURNS 173:46
My g. rises at it	SHAK 755:31	g. is far funnier than we are	BUCH 164:33	**gowk** be a conceited g.	HOGG 406:59
gorgon taught his g. destinies to sing	CAMP 186:61	G. is like everything	MONT 593:93	**gown** dressed in a new g.	HUME 422:11
gorgonised G. me from head	TENN 845:87	G. looks with favour	BALF 54:54	ease a heart Like a satin g.	PARK 637:44
gorry by g. by jingo by gee	CUMM 247:8	g. may…withdraw…troops	REDM 681:72	for an almsman's g.	SHAK 735:22
gory Never shake Thy g. locks	SHAK 768:17	G.…must fall	DRYD 290:92	g. and mossy cell	MILT 577:23
gospel based on the G.	JOHN 439:63	g. of a woman	BACON 50:67	g. of glory	RALE 677:99
Christian g. is the knowledge	NIEB 614:98	g. of laws	ADAMS 5:87	wrap me in a g.	HERB 397:95
G. of Getting On	SHAW 777:76	g. of the people	LINC 510:39	**gowns** priests in black g.	BLAKE 134:57
light of the g.	JOHN 442:57	G. of the strongest interests	CALH 184:35	**Goya** one small G.	AUDEN 39:85
preached a G.	TENN 848:69	G. of which Harrow	BALD 54:52	**Gracchi** Who can bear the G.	JUVE 453:15
preach the g.	BIBLE 114:20	g.…reflections on human nature	MADI 538:21	**grace** Amazing G.! How sweet	NEWT 613:76
receptive to the g.	RUET 701:63	g. representatives in the affairs	NICH 613:84	Being and Ideal G.	BROW 160:9
spirit of the g.	JOHN 438:55	g. shall be upon his shoulder	BIBLE 102:17	better deeds…to g. it	SHAK 729:28
wolves whose g.	MILT 580:87	g. subsidized commission	KRUT 481:28	but for the g. of God, goes God	CHUR 218:11
gospels canonical g. do not record	FORS 332:57	g. subsidy	ANON 25:57	by g. divine	WORD 929:62
teachings of the G.	KHRU 467:4	g. which imprisons any	THOR 857:71	by the g. of God I am	BIBLE 121:12
gossip Blood sport…in the g. columns	INGH 429:58	g. without newspapers	JEFF 436:13	Cheap g. is g. without discipleship	BONH 140:58
G. is a sort of smoke	ELIOT 304:13	greatest blessings which a g.	MACA 525:39	deprived me of your g. and favour	SHAK 762:54
G. is the opiate	JONG 448:99	having looked to g. for bread	BURKE 169:48	divine g. cleansed…me	ABEL 1:3
juicy piece of g.	HELL 392:73	help from a g. agency	STEIN 815:28	except through g.	PASC 640:13
pines are g. pines	FLEC 327:49	highest form of g.	SPEN 807:44	fallen from g.	BIBLE 122:37
roving woman gives rise to g.	ANON 18:73	husband, like a g.	BALZ 57:8	for heaven's g. and boon	KEATS 459:37
gossiping telling jokes or g.	CABR 183:19	influence of a g.	REES 682:89	full of g. and truth	BIBLE 117:74
gothic G. cathedrals…supreme creation	BART 62:18	In the councils of g.	EISE 302:58	glad g.	YEATS 932:33
G. structure, the impenetrable	EDGE 299:1	kept in sober g.	SPEN 808:85	God shed his g.	BATES 64:49
old one of G. windows	KORN 480:2	land of settled g.	TENN 841:93	G. be unto you	BIBLE 125:42
gout chide my palsy, or my g.	DONNE 279:43	live under one form of g.	JOHN 444:94	g. beyond recognition	REID 682:95
govern administer is to g.	MIRA 587:77	machinery of G.	MONT 591:61	g. did much more abound	BIBLE 120:66
have to g. afterwards	HUGH 419:26	meddling with the g.	LEST 505:48	G. from that g.	LANY 489:7
He that would g. others	MASS 559:42	monarchy…intelligible g.	BAGE 51:89	G. is given of God	CLOU 222:18
intellect will always g.	WOLL 920:3	most important job in G.	GARN 346:51	g. is sufficient for thee	BIBLE 122:34
Right…of Kings to g.	POPE 662:76	no art which one g.	SMITH 798:54	g. of accuracy	LOWE 521:62
Those that g. most	SELD 726:79	no British g. should be brought	MACM 536:73	g. of its external	VIEI 881:12
governance g. of Ronald Reagan	BAKER 53:24	No G. can be long secure	DISR 276:43	g. of our Lord Jesus Christ	BIBLE 127:85
governed g. by no other sway	MONT 593:3	no g. can stand	CONF 230:91	g. of Terpsichore	BARR 61:94
g. by the mob	GREN 373:4	no g., church, corporation	OAKE 619:86	g. under pressure	HEMI 394:1
g. by the pull	MOORE 595:40	No g. has the right	BROWN 157:48	g. us in the disgrace	SHAK 733:67
one of the most g. people	EDIN 300:8	No g. is going to take from me	MACL 535:31	g. was wasn't	PRIOR 669:39
governess woman who cannot be a g.	OLIP 624:64	not one that g. can indulge in	RENO 683:2	grows eke greater g.	SPEN 808:82
governesses If neither g. or mothers	DAVI 254:29	only good g.…is a bad one	CARY 199:66	had at least the g.	BENT 78:81
government 25 years of Labour g.	BEVAN 84:15	only two kinds of g.	DAFOE 250:63	If I am not in g.	JOAN 438:53
administration of the g.	SWIFT 831:78	operations of g.	RUNC 702:71	into g. againe	FLET 328:74
against every G. on earth	JEFF 436:16	prepare for g.	STEEL 813:86	inward and spiritual g.	BOOK 142:16
agencies of central g.	HUXL 425:97	pretend to obey a G.	RUSS 705:57	it is not man…made g.	POUND 665:59
All forms of g. fall	LEWIS 507:84	prying meddlesome G.	MACA 526:73	lend her g.	TENN 839:52
all g.…founded on compromise	BURKE 168:17	relations of a weak G.	REED 682:88	life itself is g.	BUEC 165:44
all g. without the consent	SWIFT 831:73	republican model of g.	WASH 890:85	means of g.	BOOK 141:84
all of them branches of g.	MILL 570:66	revolution than a g.	MARC 549:31	motions all accompanied with g.	DRYD 289:71
ANC is a G. in waiting	MAND 544:47	see the g. get out of the war	HELL 392:63	nature and the living g.	POPE 658:55
art of g.	SHAW 778:4	sister is given to g.	DICK 271:28	Never mind my g., lassie	SCOTT 724:37
ask me what a free g. is	BURKE 168:21	so pleased to be in the G.	BAXT 65:88	novel…it's a g.	MAIL 540:62
At the head of the G.	PETA 649:75	stability to a popular G.	WHIT 902:68	Observe his honour, or his g.	DONNE 279:43

O mickle is the powerful g.   SHAK 736:55
pity g. obtain   SIDN 790:7
something of a g.   WORD 926:14
such a lovely g.   SIDN 790:13
sweet attractive g.   MILT 583:62
tabernacles of thy g.   SCOT 725:63
To win her g.   MILT 576:10
unbought g. of life   BURKE 169:35
what g. he throws   FLEC 327:47
wordy of a g.   BURNS 171:88
graces deficiency in the g.   JOHN 445:23
G....not...natives of Great Britain   CHES 210:33
g. slighted, blossom on the tomb   CRAB 242:96
no time for the fine g.   SMITH 799:63
number all your g.   SHAK 771:4
gracious Oh, my G., Glorious   TRAV 865:46
grades various g. of culture   NIET 616:28
gradual Was the g. day   SPEN 807:48
gradualness inevitability of g.   WEBB 893:66
graduate g. from Canada   FULF 341:46
than to be a g.   HARDY 382:67
graft opportunity for g.   BIRNS 131:72
Grafton Hungry G.   ANON 23:72
grain amber waves of g.   BATES 64:49
beside a field of g.   PARK 638:81
Divine...in a g. of sand   FRIE 337:68
full ripened g.   KEATS 457:93
g. of sense   DRYD 290:9
guano and on g.   TENN 841:99
Rot half a g. a day   SHAK 761:14
the g. and hammer   HEAN 389:15
well meant for g.   TENN 843:24
which g. will grow   SHAK 766:72
grains two g. of wheat   SHAK 739:41
grammar don't want to talk g.   SHAW 780:63
down to posterity talking bad g.   DISR 277:92
erecting a g. school   SHAK 730:66
g. is to the art of the writer   APOL 27:15
kings must bow to g.   MOLI 590:41
mystical g. of amorous glances   CLEV 221:82
never made a mistake in g.   SAND 713:3
Once the g. has been learnt   BAIN 52:7
readers must take such g.   MACA 525:51
Religious law is like...g.   SACKS 707:84
To be loose with g.   EDWA 300:23
Why care for g.   WARD 888:59
With g., and nonsense   GOLD 362:64
grammars What sairs your G.   BURNS 170:62
gramophone puts a record on the g.   ELIOT 306:61
granaries guard our master's g.   WILDE 907:82
grand but never g.   HEAT 390:29
g., the barbarous, the savage   DIDE 274:90
petal down the G. Canyon   MARQ 554:33
the g. manner   POUS 666:75
grandchild little g.Wilhelmine   SOUT 805:98
grandeur baldness full of g.   ARNO 34:71
g. in this view of life   DARW 253:11
g. of the dooms   KEATS 457:2
g. that was Rome   POE 656:22
G....with a disdainful smile   GRAY 369:14
little bit of g. is gone   ANON 23:89
old Scotia's g.   BURNS 170:70
sort of g. creeps into it   MENC 566:87
with the g. of God   HOPK 412:83
grandfather who his g. is   WALC 884:72
grandfathers friends with its g.   MUMF 603:74
grandma g.'s maiden name   BERE 78:88
grandmama dear G. died   GEOR 349:15
grandmother child of our g. Eve   SHAK 733:74
day my g. exploded   BANKS 58:35
g. actually smelled like a cookie   BAIL 52:3
have become a g.   THAT 850:31
look...back to the g.   EDGE 299:7
may not marry his G.   BOOK 144:78
sell his g.   GRANT 366:49
grandmothers careful g.   DICK 266:87
grandsire heard my g. say   SHAK 731:95
your g. cut his throat   SWIFT 831:75
grandstands retire to the g.   GERG 350:32
granite monoliths made of g.   MENC 566:85
Of shadowy g.   TENN 839:54
Grannie G. remarked   FRAN 335:21
Grant Old Cary G. fine   GRANT 366:47
granted as God g. it   QUIL 674:41
taking things for g.   HUXL 425:91
grape blood of g.   BLAKE 133:25
Glory, the g., love, gold   BYRON 182:80

no g. that's kindly ripe   SUCK 828:11
peel me a g.   WEST 901:31
grapes sour g. and ashes   ASHF 35:99
where the g. of wrath   HOWE 417:1
grapeshot car...seems to ride on g.   MARI 550:53
whiff of g.   CARL 192:6
graphical g. representation of data   GIBS 353:76
grapple G. them to thy soul   SHAK 751:17
grasp should exceed his g.   BROW 161:55
grass a blade of g. stuck   WODE 919:57
books...like green g.   WELTY 899:99
burn the old g.   POL 657:41
causeth the g. to grow   BIBLE 97:67
dappled g.   YEATS 932:36
days are as g.   BIBLE 97:66
destroy a blade of g.   BOTT 146:16
eateth g. as an ox   BIBLE 93:76
eat g. as oxen   BIBLE 106:96
emerald twinkles in the g.   TENN 845:88
fall on g.   MARV 556:74
g., and a hare sitting up   LAWR 494:95
G. and trees wither   WU 930:96
g. grew longer   LEE 500:45
g. grows on the weirs   YEATS 932:29
g. is singing   ELIOT 306:36
g. is soft as...doves   CORN 237:69
g., it grew as scant   BROW 161:44
g., so springlike   ABSE 1:6
g. will grow in the streets   HOOV 411:57
g. withereth   BIBLE 125:22
g. withereth   BIBLE 103:36
g. withereth, the flower fadeth   BIBLE 103:36
green g. above me   ROSS 697:83
greenness of the g.   MARV 556:70
happy as the g. was green   THOM 852:71
heard by snakes in the g.   MO 589:18
hearing the g. grow   ELIOT 304:8
I am the g.   SAND 713:96
indicates that...g. is green   STEP 817:58
isn't g. to graze a cow   BETJ 83:83
kissed the lovely g.   BROO 155:2
know the g. beyond   ROSS 698:91
moonlight lying on the g.   THOM 854:9
not Dead, but feed the g.   TATE 837:4
only beautiful if it has good g.   BUTL 177:63
Pigeons on the g.   STEIN 815:14
Please Walk on the G.   THOM 856:49
rustling of the g.   WORD 927:38
sallower than g.   SAPP 714:27
showers upon the g.   BIBLE 90:55
snake lurks in the g.   VIRG 882:27
soft wind breathing through the g.   BRON 155:99
splendour in the g.   WORD 927:28
star-scattered on the g.   FITZ 324:86
the g. the polyanthus cheques   SMART 796:27
thin g. clothed them   THOM 854:25
two blades of g.   SWIFT 831:80
wan g. sea   SITW 794:72
grass-growing silent g.-g. mood   MELV 564:43
grasshopper afraid as a g.?   BIBLE 93:74
g. shall be a burden   BIBLE 101:92
grasshoppers g. with triumphing   ROBE 689:18
in our own sight as g.   BIBLE 89:37
grateful g. at last for a little thing   TENN 845:97
g. to the CLF   STEW 824:42
none more g.   WORD 924:88
revolution must be g.   LEGU 501:62
gratification g. of your wishes   SHEL 782:9
gratify g. some people   TWAIN 872:34
gratis endanger my soul g.?   SHAK 743:71
gratitude g. is a species   JOHN 441:23
G. looks to the past   LEWIS 507:73
vulgar g. to you   DICK 270:86
gratuitous prophecy is the most g.   ELIOT 304:4
grave Alcestis from the g.   MILT 580:89
amaranth on this side of the g.   LAND 488:81
A Page, a G.   POPE 662:74
bed...the cold, cold g.   BALL 55:72
birth astride of a g.   BECK 68:41
bring down my gray hairs...to the g.   BIBLE 88:1
broken-hearted woman tends the g.   HAYES 387:62
cold in the dreary g.!   BRON 155:93
cradle to the g.   ANON 25:57
cradle to the g.   BREC 151:8
Dark as the G.   LOWRY 521:68
darkness of the g.   MILL 571:89
dig the g. and let me   STEV 822:10

Duncan is in his g.   SHAK 768:14
dusty to the g.   STEV 821:87
even the g. yawns for him   TREE 865:52
foolish tears upon my g.   TENN 842:18
from the cradle to the g.   SHEL 785:82
Funeral marches to the g.   LONG 515:42
gift of a g.   SHAK 755:49
go down into the g....mourning   BIBLE 87:95
g. and serious   GILB 355:33
g. is ghastly   ANON 18:75
g. is not its goal   LONG 515:41
g. keeps bodies   DONNE 281:78
g. of Christianity   ELIOT 307:91
g.'s a fine and private   MARV 556:63
g.'s narrowness   GRAV 367:66
G. where is thy Victory?   BUNY 167:77
g., where is thy victory?   BIBLE 122:20
heaped its g.   CRANE 242:8
humours, whether g. or mellow   ADDI 6:13
in the cold g. leave   WEBS 894:77
in the dark and silent g.   RALE 677:3
jealousy is cruel as the g.   BIBLE 102:6
large kingdom for a little g.   SHAK 735:22
learned the secrets of the g.   PATER 642:51
Longfellow's g. or the glass   MOORE 595:31
lower me into the g.   LEE 500:41
made his g. with the wicked   BIBLE 104:52
made me a g. so rough   TENN 845:96
Marriage is the g. or tomb of wit   CAVE 201:19
mysterious East...dark like a g.   CONR 234:5
No repose...but in the g.   SCOTT 725:59
now in his colde g.   CHAU 208:82
no work...in the g.   BIBLE 101:84
O'Leary in the g.   YEATS 933:43
on that g. where English oak   HARTE 385:18
on the way to the g.   CRISP 245:57
Over this damp g.   ROET 694:4
paths of glory lead but to the g.   GRAY 369:14
Peace is in the g.   SHEL 785:74
pompous in the g.   BROW 159:92
profound as the g.   ADAMS 4:83
put on the g. of Gomer Owen   THOM 853:89
receive no letters in the g.   JOHN 447:70
she is in her g.   WORD 924:78
sinking into the g.   WESL 900:24
So pleasant this side of the g.   DIBD 265:54
sunk into the g.   JOHN 442:40
take me out o'th' g.   SHAK 764:97
that dark inn—the G.!   SCOTT 724:16
this side of the g.   PITT 653:46
thy humble g. adorned   POPE 665:99
till we go into the g.   SMITH 798:47
travelling towards the g.   WORD 925:90
Upon his mother's g.?   WORD 924:81
vast and wandering g.   TENN 843:26
Victorious o'er the g.   DODD 278:10
vortex of our g.   CRANE 243:11
within the g.'s brink   ANON 19:93
Without a g., unkindled   BYRON 180:45
gravemakers ditchers, and g.   SHAK 755:28
graves Arise from their g.   BLAKE 134:53
bloody hands and hospitable g.   CORW 237:73
climbs into their g. married   WILD 910:76
filled with g.   BLAKE 134:57
find ourselves dishonourable g.   SHAK 747:76
g. of the best soldiers   PHIL 650:95
g. of the martyrs   STEV 823:35
g. of the martyrs   STEV 823:36
g. that hide us   RALE 677:1
g. were opened   BIBLE 114:5
g. will give thee memory   SHAK 772:33
here about the g.   STEV 823:35
never went near the g. of his parents   BELL 74:88
Over the tumbled g.   ELIOT 306:66
sacred g. to be ploughed   RED 681:71
tears shed over g.   STOWE 826:77
gravestones Black village of g.   HUGH 419:51
graveyard thru the g. forest   PURDY 673:17
gravity governed by g.   MOORE 595:40
impulsive g. of head   POPE 662:72
natural force, like g.   HIND 403:97
Playing in musicked g.   AVIS 44:6
gravy No g. and no grub   RANS 679:28
Sir Humphrey Davy Abominated g.   BENT 78:77
slip with the g.   MACB 527:82
graze Could neither g. nor pierce   SHAK 760:1
grazes vacuum cleaner g.   RAINE 677:93

Graziano G. speaks…of nothing	SHAK 739:41	Captive G.	HORA 414:29
grease slides by on g.	LOWE 520:49	Fair G.! sad relic	BYRON 179:13
greasy fat and g. citizens	SHAK 749:35	glory that was G.	POE 656:22
g. Limpopo River	KIPL 473:42	G., Italy, and England did adorn	DRYD 291:24
great A being…rudely g.	POPE 660:16	G. might still be free	BYRON 182:87
All things both g. and small	COLE 225:92	summoned G. to arms	MARL 551:79
anyone among the g. men	INGR 429:61	**greed** G. begins where poverty ends	BALZ 58:22
dream about the g.	YEATS 932:37	g. is only one of them	VAN 876:26
far above the g.	GRAY 370:40	politics of g.	ARMEY 30:69
fears of being g.	TENN 848:67	socially commendable form of g.	SCHW 721:59
g. and almost only comfort	STARK 813:71	writer's g. is appalling	BALD 53:32
g. is thy faithfulness	BIBLE 105:82	**greedy** Be not g. to add money	BIBLE 107:28
G. men are not always wise	BIBLE 93:67	G. for the belongings of others	SALL 711:71
g. men have…elements of comicality	JENK 437:26	not g. of filthy lucre	BIBLE 123:74
g. men have their poor relations	DICK 270:94	thank goodness, I am g.	PUNCH 673:13
g. men…in politics	ELTON 311:95	**Greek** By dint o' G.	BURNS 170:63
G. men may jest	SHAK 758:27	G. and Roman poets	PRIOR 669:44
g. minds in the commonplace	HUBB 417:7	G. of today is essentially	MILL 572:29
g. To do that thing	SHAK 765:54	he could speak G.	BUTL 177:39
g. was his fame	EGAN 301:24	imitator of G. forms	MACKE 533:14
he is always g.	DRYD 288:25	neither G. nor Jew	BIBLE 123:67
He is truly g.	KEMP 461:84	neither Jew nor G.	BIBLE 122:36
how g. a matter a little fire kindleth	BIBLE 124:12	ne of G.	SPEN 809:95
How indigent the g.!	GRAY 369:5	poets who grew up on G.	ROET 694:5
in order to be g.	HOPK 413:13	questioned him in G.	CARR 197:34
leave g. things undone	GLAS 359:97	say a word against G.	SHAW 779:39
Madness in g. ones	SHAK 754:84	small Latin, and less G.	JONS 449:44
makes every man feel g.	CHES 211:56	talk of knowing G.	WOOLF 922:32
Man is only truly g.	DISR 276:49	Things in G. are not read	ANON 19:81
Minds that are g.	JONS 450:49	**Greeks** ethnic connection between the	
never produces anything g.	REYN 684:22	G. and me	MICH 568:31
Nothing g.…without enthusiasm	EMER 312:18	G. Had a Word for It	AKINS 9:80
Nothing g.…without g. men	DE 259:34	G.…hiding behind their columns	DE 260:56
qualities in a g. King	RICH 686:66	I fear the G.	VIRG 882:19
really g. in favour of equality	SHAW 781:86	make way, G.!	PROP 670:62
some g. man	HOOV 411:60	superiority of the G.	FUSE 342:74
ten g. artists	GREE 370:48	with cannibals, And Trojan G.?	SHAK 743:49
that Caesar might be g.!	CAMP 186:68	**green** believed in the g. light	FITZ 325:2
the g. crime	PACH 633:69	cakes…looked g. with worry	FIRB 323:69
the g. have kindness	POPE 661:39	fairest shepherd on our g.	PEELE 646:11
this g.…kingdom	PITT 652:37	fresh and g. they look	THAC 849:85
those who were truly g.	SPEN 807:46	frock of frolic g.	DRAY 286:96
Thou wouldst be g.	SHAK 766:81	golden face the meadows g.	SHAK 771:16
To be g.	EMER 312:9	g. and yellow melancholy	SHAK 756:69
We live in the g. indoors	RAINE 677:93	G. cowbind	SHEL 787:25
when the One G. Scorer comes	RICE 685:37	g. earth's end	MILT 578:43
works of a g. genius	ADDI 7:41	g. flash that brings good fortune	RHYS 684:29
world's g. men	HOLM 408:86	G. how I love you g.	LORCA 517:85
would be g. in our little government	ROCH 691:63	g. in judgement	SHAK 764:22
Great Britain G. B. calls the Far East	MENZ 566:89	g. only on the banner	BROD 153:53
G. B. is going to make war	BETH 82:74	g. thought in a g. shade	MARV 556:75
imperial might of G. B.	STEW 824:43	honey set in a g. bowl	SMITH 799:61
Metropolis of G.-B.	BAIL 52:4	In pastures g.	SCOT 725:61
Russia and G. B.	CECIL 202:33	In thy g. lap	GRAY 370:37
greater Four things g. than all	KIPL 471:98	June…in g. leaves	SPEN 810:16
g., broader and fuller life	DU 293:74	laid him on the g.	BALL 55:68
g. cannot be thought	ANSE 26:6	leaves are g.	ANON 18:72
lesser life shall be as the g.	GORD 363:7	leaves are g.	ANON 20:7
Something made g. by ourselves	ANGE 17:44	Make it a g. peace	DARN 253:7
the g. the differences	PASC 641:26	margent g.	MILT 577:33
greatest as well as the g. He	RAIN 677:92	passport's g.	HEAN 389:10
g. thing in the world	FORS 331:39	sees a g. light everywhere	SCHW 721:71
I am the g.!	ALI 12:32	smooth-shaven g.	MILT 576:16
least…control the g.	WORD 923:68	sported on the g.	SOUT 805:98
nation's art is g.	HOPP 413:14	What use…the g. river	FRAME 333:79
great-grandmothers g.-g. dread	BATT 64:52	Where I used to play on the g.	BLAKE 134:56
great-great-grandchildren our g.-g.-g.,		whiten the g. plains	SHEL 783:39
when they learn	PRIE 668:19	**greenery-yallery** g.-y., Grosvenor	GILB 354:9
great-great-grandfather in any one's		**green-eyed** g.-e. monster	SHAK 760:86
g.-g.-g.	SOME 803:66	**greengrocers** lying in the rain outside g.	BRAD 148:56
greatness certain g. in her	ELIOT 304:12	**Greenland** G.'s icy mountains	HEBER 390:34
far-off touch of g.	TENN 846:17	**greens** g.…that screeeeeeam	CARRA 194:58
glory and its g.	GAIT 342:87	healing g.	ABSE 1:6
greatest in Europe for Riches and G.	BAIL 52:4	**Greensleeves** to the tune of 'G.'	SHAK 744:81
g. is a-ripening	SHAK 775:20	**greenstone** lighting up the g. years	IHIM 428:43
g. of the British Nation	ADDI 6:21	**greenwood** in the good g.	SCOTT 723:9
g. thrust upon him	CANN 188:9	Under the g. tree	SHAK 749:43
highest point of all my g.	SHAK 775:18	**greet** it gars me g.	BURNS 172:15
himself attain g.	POE 657:29	**greeted** expect to be g. with smiles	BROO 156:25
Man's unhappiness…comes of his g.	CARL 192:99	**greeting** g. a corpse would give	BALD 54:42
Men…who have g. within them	CAMUS 187:85	**grenadiers** Pensions and G.	STER 818:84
moment of my g. flicker	ELIOT 304:22	**Grenville** Sir Richard G. lay	TENN 848:60
our g. as a nation	THAT 850:15	**Greta** G. woods are green	SCOTT 723:10
some achieve g.	SHAK 756:71	**grey** among g.…houses	YEATS 933:44
strength and the g. of England	CURZ 249:51	black and g.	GREE 371:76
great-rooted g.-r. blossomer	YEATS 933:53	death's g. land	SASS 716:60
Greece Athens, the eye of G.	MILT 586:42	few locks…are g.	SOUT 805:96

g. twilight	YEATS 932:35		
head grown g. in vain	SHEL 786:44		
in her little g. dress	WOOLF 922:40		
instead of the general g.	MILL 572:3		
Into their g.	FREE 336:44		
old and g.	YEATS 932:33		
question of it being g.	TRAV 865:47		
turn those amber locks to g.	DRAY 286:99		
two horrible shades of g.	THOR 858:71		
withered weak and g.	MILT 585:31		
grey-bearded g.-b. and wrinkled	HAWT 386:45		
greybeards g. call divine	SHAK 731:87		
grey-green great g.-g., greasy	KIPL 473:42		
greyhound g.…heeded lyke a snake	BERN 81:48		
greyhounds stand like g.	SHAK 746:43		
greyness Bright g.	GUNT 375:41		
gridiron act a g.	CLIVE 222:14		
grief acquainted with g.	BIBLE 104:50		
As is my g.	SHAK 731:87		
between g. and nothing	FAUL 318:61		
bore within their breasts the g.	AYTO 45:18		
bottom of my g.?	SHAK 736:72		
bravery of his g.	SHAK 755:38		
Each substance of a g.	SHAK 734:10		
foundation of g.	HUGO 421:88		
Fretting g. the enemy	SPEN 808:77		
g. and sin of idleness	MELV 564:24		
G. fills the room	SHAK 738:25		
g. flieth to it	BACON 47:74		
G. for a while is blind	SHEL 784:71		
g. forgotten	SWIN 832:19		
G. is a species of idleness	JOHN 444:96		
G. is carried off by the wings	LAFO 485:15		
G. is itself a med'cine	COWP 241:57		
g. is proud	SHAK 738:22		
g. itself be mortal	SHEL 785:97		
G. never mended	DICK 265:62		
g. of heart	SHAK 775:13		
g. of heart	SHAK 775:15		
g. returns with the revolving year	SHEL 785:95		
g.…upon the heels of pleasure	CONG 231:1		
g. with a glass	SWIN 832:21		
heard g. named the eldest	WEBS 895:93		
in much wisdom is much g.	BIBLE 100:68		
life from g. or danger free	JOHN 441:17		
long g. and pain	TENN 845:93		
make less the depth of g.	SHAK 730:73		
master a g.	SHAK 745:12		
much less g. on earth	BROD 153:57		
My g.'s so great	SHAK 738:23		
No man can cause more g.	FAUL 318:62		
nor g. bitterness	LYLY 533:81		
Oh my g.	SYNGE 834:60		
or grey g.	SWIN 833:39		
Pale G. and pleasing Pain	GRAY 370:35		
particular g. Is of so	SHAK 759:57		
part my g. have eas'd	MILT 586:47		
pitch of g.	HOPK 413:4		
quickened so with g.	GRAV 367:62		
silent manliness of g.	GOLD 361:59		
Smiling at g.	SHAK 756:69		
sounds of g. and mourning	DICK 267:20		
spends a bootless g.	SHAK 759:67		
That g. for which the senses	WORD 923:67		
the g. I feel	TENN 842:23		
The theme…is g., sheer g.	GOLD 360:33		
Thine be the g.	AYTO 45:15		
Till g. did tell me roundly	HERB 397:96		
wish to drown your g.	MCGO 537:19		
with a mother's g.	TRUTH 869:52		
griefs Extremity of g.	SHAK 731:95		
[Friendship]…cutteth g. in half	BACON 49:30		
g. are ended	SHAK 759:66		
g. which bow	ARNO 31:90		
oldest g. of summer	RICK 686:74		
tales of others' g.	SHAK 769:53		
grievance g. for the day	MANS 547:90		
grievances not magnifying g.	RIDGE 687:79		
redress of real g.	PEEL 646:0		
grieve Nor joy nor g. too much	DRYD 292:59		
thou leavest me to g.	SHEL 782:23		
We will g. not	WORD 927:28		
grieves gay nature g.	SMART 797:31		
g. that menial needs	HYDE 427:23		
grieving Margaret, are you g.	HOPK 412:93		
thought it died of g.	KEATS 457:87		
grievous most g. to him	TROL 867:92		

grills As long as mixed g. JANE 435:76
grim brow so g. ELIOT 307:6
the g....to prove himself PAGL 634:81
grin g. and fine intelligence NEW 611:51
G.Will Win ANON 24:16
How cheerfully he seems to g. CARR 194:65
it vanished…ending with the g. CARR 195:70
malevolent aged g. HUGH 419:41
Nature wears one universal g. FIEL 322:38
with a lipless g. ELIOT 305:34
grind g. in the prison house BIBLE 90:75
g. the faces of the poor? BIBLE 102:9
life is one demd horrid g.! DICK 267:13
grinders forty teeth…twenty-four g. DICK 270:2
g. cease because they are few BIBLE 101:92
gringo According to a g. GUIL 374:31
grip g. down and begin WILL 913:43
holding a people in its g. FANON 317:44
holds us in an iron g. FRID 337:57
in their dead g. TUCH 869:57
groan Condemned alike to g. GRAY 368:95
hear each other g. KEATS 460:59
thousands counted every g. ARNO 33:32
with bubbling g. BYRON 180:45
groaneth that which g. to be so HERB 397:90
groans g. and convulsions STER 818:86
g. of love LOWRY 521:67
Warring sighs and g. BURNS 172:28
grocer g. puts a pound weight SPEN 807:62
Grogan as old mother G. said JOYCE 452:86
Gromboolian great G. plain LEAR 497:76
grooves in the g. that those who rob CONN 233:89
what's in the g. ANON 26:85
grope g. about in the labyrinth SCHO 719:29
gross Not g. to sink SHAK 732:52
November, he full g. and fat SPEN 810:17
grossness measureless g. WHIT 906:51
vice…losing all its g. BURKE 169:35
Grosvenor G.Gallery GILB 354:9
grotesque became a g. ANDE 16:23
fashions strike us as g. VEBL 878:55
from the g. to the horrible DOYLE 285:81
grots cage like g. SITW 794:69
ground at length it stands the g. DRYD 290:98
both feet off the g. JOHN 440:81
can't keep on the g. TRAV 864:45
clearing g. a little LOCKE 514:16
Close by the g. SHAK 744:9
commit his body to the g. BOOK 142:35
cursed is the g. for thy sake BIBLE 86:55
dead g. in between REED 684:74
dewy g. WORD 929:60
Exiled to the g. BAUD 64:55
feet planted on level g. GOHE 360:27
fertile g. he caused to grow MILT 582:59
found a watch upon the g. PALEY 635:16
generally loses g. STEV 821:64
good for the g. SCHU 720:49
g. is like a beautiful woman SNOW 802:45
g. itself is falling FERL 321:12
g. with vernal flowers MILT 578:53
grow upon a spot of g. SWIFT 831:80
If that plane leaves the g. EPST 314:80
In his own g. POPE 659:78
inlay Broidered the g. MILT 583:70
kamikaze g. staff PARK 638:82
knit hands, and beat the g. MILT 577:29
know you by your g. BLUN 137:11
leaves…fall to the g. ANON 18:72
let us sit upon the g. SHAK 735:20
little time on the g. OWENS 632:67
lot is fallen unto me in a fair g. BOOK 142:42
lying on the g. ALAN 9:84
Marching o'er the metric g. CRAIK 242:7
most at ease on the g. ALLS 13:63
on the g. at Goose Green KINN 470:69
place…is holy g. BIBLE 88:9
Resources left in the g. are saved BRODY 154:61
second foot on the g. FONT 329:87
seven feet of English g. HARO 383:85
spilled it on the g. BIBLE 88:96
Stand your g. PARK 638:80
stone falls to the g. THOR 858:99
swalloweth the g. BIBLE 93:75
tears have overflowed his g.? DONNE 280:44
that never left the g. LOWE 520:52
their burthen to the g. TENN 846:25

they plopped to the g. PLATH 654:72
till the g. from whence he was taken BIBLE 86:57
till thou return to the g. BIBLE 86:56
tread on classic g. ADDI 5:2
unhurried G. swell ELIOT 308:29
when he has reached g. JOHN 442:34
when he hit the g. HUGH 419:49
when I was on the g. SIMON 792:39
grounds beautify their g. MALT 543:19
noble g. for the noble RUSK 703:9
group characterizes…minority g. MAIL 540:53
g. of other people ROSSO 698:6
g. of the unwilling HARK 383:82
nation or g. RUNC 702:72
only exploited g. in the world JONG 448:6
place in any political g. HELL 392:75
sobs from among the g. DICK 267:20
groupies don't get g. STIPE 824:51
groups divide people into two g. HAMP 380:26
g. of inflexible political persuasion WILS 916:3
g. who question that status MAMET 543:23
marginal g. who RUET 701:63
split into two polar g. SNOW 802:38
grouse g. are in no danger EDIN 300:11
grove deep windings of the g. BEAT 66:96
G. nods at g., each a mirror POPE 659:95
meadow, g., and stream WORD 926:21
While in a g. I sate WORD 924:76
grovelled he g. before him THAC 849:87
groves g. of their academy BURKE 169:36
o'er shady g. they hover WEBS 895:50
will seek the g. ROSS 698:90
grow For sure then I should g. HERB 397:97
g. for ever TENN 842:5
How do poems g.? WARR 889:74
isn't going to g. WHITE 903:90
its radiance would g. RAND 678:15
more we g. in numbers TERT 849:82
my wrath did g. BLAKE 135:59
some skin on to g. KHRU 467:2
which grain will g. SHAK 766:72
grow'd I 'spect I g. STOWE 826:74
growing ever grew anything worth g. SAND 713:4
g., bodily that is THOM 854:28
g., flying, happening REID 682:95
G. old is like being…penalised POWE 666:82
g….when ye're sleeping SCOTT 724:36
growing up I wasn't good At g. up FANT 318:46
growl sit and g. JOHN 446:55
grown now g. up to riper age BRON 154:76
grown-up people's feet STEV 822:11
Lillian as a g.-u. FEIB 319:82
take seriously…g.-u. women STEI 816:45
grown-ups obvious facts about g.-u. JARR 435:88
ordinary thick-skinned g.-u. SHAW 778:85
grows box that fennel G. around RANS 679:27
g. daily worse and worse SPEN 809:9
What g. by the words? SIDN 790:3
growth birth and g….are ubiquitous DILL 274:13
children of a larger g. DRYD 289:63
expression of life as g. MILL 573:49
for the g. of any and everything STUA 827:98
g. in the individual SMIL 797:32
g. is a leap in the dark MILL 573:45
g. of this nation GAND 345:32
growths sun-searched g. ROSS 698:94
grow up country safe to g. u. in THAT 850:14
g. u. to be Prime Minister RICH 686:73
grub No gravy and no g. RANS 679:28
old ones, g. SHAW 777:52
poor g., poor pay LOND 515:37
sphere of use…in the g. state DOUG 283:14
grudge g. against the children BIBLE 89:35
G. not one against another BIBLE 125:17
took it as a personal g. OHEN 623:54
grudges all their ancient g. WAUGH 892:38
don't hold no g. KENN 464:56
Grundy What will Mrs G. say? MORT 600:24
grunt every twitch and g. TRUD 868:23
gruntled far from being g. WODE 919:69
guarantee beauty is a g. of happiness PROU 671:81
each will g. all LEES 500:50
Englishman as a g. SHAW 779:34
guaranteed G. never to fail FORM 331:27
guard Alice is marrying one of the g. MILNE 574:74
g. against…unwarranted influence EISE 302:58
g. of the world proletarian army LENIN 502:84

Made good g. for itself SHAK 765:41
Those that I g. YEATS 933:48
guarded G. by timeless principalities GRAV 367:72
guardian g. angels sung this strain THOM 856:52
guardianship Christ for my g. PATR 643:71
guards Brigade of G. MACM 536:77
g. at the gate SUN 829:33
G. die but do not surrender CAMB 185:47
Up g. and at them WELL 897:56
guardsman g.'s cut and thrust differ HUXL 426:13
guerdon fair g. when we hope MILT 578:49
guerre mais ce n'est pas la g. BOSQ 145:7
guerrilla cardinal maxims of g. war KISS 475:90
Insurrection—by means of g. bands MAZZ 562:99
guess g. about what is seen SAND 713:99
venture A g. REED 681:79
you can perhaps g. why SEVI 728:10
guesses everybody g. ELIOT 308:35
secrets everybody g. SHAW 777:74
supporting their g. by argument BAGE 51:93
guest as a g. thanks his host DILL 275:14
awaited the expected g. ELIOT 306:60
Earth receive an honoured g. AUDEN 40:3
g. of one's time KENN 462:97
remembrance of a g. that tarrieth BIBLE 107:34
speed the parting g. POPE 659:87
guests g. should praise it HARI 382:79
Jews are hosts, and not g. SACH 707:83
the g. star-scattered FITZ 324:86
two great classes: hosts and g. BEER 70:87
Unbidden g. TENN 829:43
what…other g. thought of him SKIN 795:11
guidance act under the g. of reason SPIN 810:31
g. have I sought WORD 929:65
guide be thy g. ANON 19:97
except some man should g. me? BIBLE 119:36
g. informed him later NASH 608:91
g. of life HUME 422:9
g. thee with mine eye BIBLE 95:11
Have God to be his g. BUNY 161:76
infallible critical g. AUDEN 41:17
None need a g. POPE 662:72
place within them as a g. MILT 582:44
probability…very g. of life BUTL 176:31
without a g.…I…work ARET 29:42
guides Ye blind g. BIBLE 113:83
Guildford G….the most agreeable COBB 223:50
guile g. of a cobra WOOL 923:63
Of g., of hate, of envy MILT 584:11
packed with g. BROO 156:13
guillotine cure except as a g. LUCE 522:81
guilt blood with g. is bought SHEL 785:72
blushing…a sign of g. CONG 231:31
difference between politics and g. CLIN 221:94
free from g. or pain SHEL 785:81
g. and power TOPL 863:15
G. in his heart CHUR 215:43
g. of dissimulation SCOTT 725:43
g. of flattery JOHN 445:44
industry is g. RUSK 704:29
one g., one crime MILT 585:17
sense of g., which he denies LESS 504:32
servitude…the punishment of his g. CURR 249:41
she trembles with g. OCON 621:21
suspicious of g. in myself HELL 393:82
What art can wash her g. GOLD 361:47
guiltier G. than him they try SHAK 758:20
guiltless Lord will not hold him g. BIBLE 88:23
guilty 100 per cent not g. SIMP 793:49
better that ten g. persons escape BLAC 132:94
cups make any g. men JONS 449:35
feel somehow g. GRASS 367:59
Find me but g. WEBS 894:83
g. never escape unscathed BAIL 52:2
g. of corrupting…the young PLATO 654:25
G. of dust and sin HERB 397:98
g. spice to this recreation WAUGH 892:35
g. when they read VIDAL 881:4
his foot is g. BECK 68:33
innocent while g. BELL 74:89
like a g. thing surprised WORD 927:26
make g. of our disasters the sun SHAK 762:57
rich, deep, and g. CHAN 205:6
started like a g. thing SHAK 751:97
when one loves a g. person? CYRA 250:37
guinea but the g.'s stamp BURNS 173:46
force of the g. RUSK 704:16

g. pigs in the laboratory of God   WILL 912:23
jingling of the g.   TENN 840:80
guinea-coast G.-c. slavery   MELV 564:41
guineas g. for flinging a pot of paint   RUSK 704:34
twenty g. per annum   DICK 267:99
Guinevere delyverd hys doughtir G.   MALO 542:6
syght of queene G.   MALO 542:4
Guinness G. on a sunny day   GREE 370:49
guise no newe g. that it nas old   CHAU 208:78
guitar sang to a small g.   LEAR 497:83
What seems to pass for g.   POP 658:49
will break their g.   MIRO 587:78
You have a blue g.   STEV 819:28
guitars boys with bright red g.   HENRI 395:41
corpses, or Picasso g.   LIPP 511:64
gulf across the g. of space   WELLS 898:73
g. of mutual incomprehension   SNOW 802:38
G.War was like teenage sex   HARK 383:81
peace and civil order in the G.   ELIZ 310:66
social g. that divides him   MARX 558:6
teeming g.   WHIT 906:49
there is a great g. fixed   BIBLE 116:55
turning of the G. crisis   HUSS 423:41
walking on a string across a g.   DAVI 254:23
widening g. between the rich   COUP 238:92
gulfs g. will wash us down   TENN 840:66
gull g. sees farthest   BACH 46:27
g.'s way and the whale's way   MASE 559:23
image of the Great G.   BACH 46:28
gull-marked shining g.-m. mud   LARK 491:33
gulls does not even require g.   KEYN 466:86
gum can't fart and chew g.   JOHN 440:86
gun double-barrelled g. and pointers   KING 469:55
draw her g.   WHITE 903:88
give up my g.   HEST 401:68
Great G. of Athlone   ANON 21:37
g. gives you the body   THOR 858:2
likes to shoot his g.   COBA 223:46
Maxim G.   BELL 72:51
nice guy if you have a g.   KOCH 476:26
no g., but I can spit   AUDEN 41:25
out of the barrel of a g.   MAO 548:7
state where g. control   SIMP 792:47
gunfire g....sounded unreal   USTI 875:6
Gunga Din than I am, G.D.!   KIPL 471:96
gunner And the g. said   TENN 848:63
gunpowder g. and printer's ink   KRAUS 480:12
g. ran out of the heels   FOOTE 329:94
printing, g. and the magnet   BACON 47:61
guns but for these vile g.   SHAK 741:1
defend ourselves with g. not butter   GOEB 359:7
G. aren't lawful   PARK 638:65
g. begin to rattle   BARK 60:56
g. begin to shoot   KIPL 471:92
heard amid the g.   MCCR 529:19
hundred men with g.   PUZO 673:24
loaded g. with boys   CRAB 242:6
monstrous anger of the g.   OWEN 632:51
not found any smoking g.   BLIX 136:97
Of g., and drums, and wounds   SHAK 741:1
rather have butter or g.?   GOER 359:10
slaught'rin g.   BURNS 170:85
spring-g. in the realm   LOWE 519:26
unheroic Dead who fed the g.?   SASS 717:76
when the g. begin   SASS 716:60
gunshot g. is the perfect way   KENN 463:44
gust g. he hath in quarrelling   SHAK 755:49
gusts explanation of our g.   ELIOT 304:15
Gutenburg G. made everybody   MCLU 536:65
gut-feel g.-f. of the 55-year old   GREE 370:58
guts g. of a butterfly   CAPO 189:33
I'll lug the g.   SHAK 754:14
gutter born in the g.   KIPL 472:28
I lay down in the g.   BURT 174:65
straight into the g.   SMITH 799:82
We are all in the g.   WILDE 908:16
gutterals world of g.   STEV 819:16
guy Ah! County G.   SCOTT 725:45
average g. who could carry a tune   CROS 246:82
cop beatin' up a g.   STEI 815:34
dresses like a g.   GILB 355:22
g. that plays the kettle drums   SALI 711:60
kind of g. that wouldn't talk   SALI 711:55
nice g. if you have a gun   KOCH 476:26
no matter how nice a g.   SALI 711:57
optimist is a g.   MARQ 554:25
snatching a hard g.   RUNY 702:79

guys five g. who hate you   STEN 816:54
g. using false pretences   RUNY 702:83
name any disease after two g.   PUZO 673:28
Nice g. finish last   DURO 296:35
unmarried g. in New York suck   BUSH 176:26
gwine G. to run all night   FOST 332:59
Gyges G. of Lydia   VASA 877:37
gymnasium g. of the mind   LENIN 502:87
life's g.   WHIT 906:50
gymnast g. and golfer, soldered   BRYA 163:10
Gyn/Ecologists recommended by G.   DALY 251:78
Gypsies fat of rendered Jews and G.   VONN 883:56
gypsy Two-wheeled g. queen   DYLAN 297:58
vagrant g. life   MASE 559:23
gyre Did g. and gimble   CARR 195:90
turning in the widening g.   YEATS 933:50

H

habeas corpus protection of the h. c.   JEFF 437:19
habit because it was a h.   ROGE 695:24
becomes a h.   LOMB 515:35
breed a h. in a man!   SHAK 729:40
Costly thy h.   SHAK 751:20
country h. has me   SACK 708:89
gentlemen are in the h.   PALM 636:25
Getting to be a H. with Me   DUBIN 292:65
good h. makes a child a man   WEBS 894:80
h. cannot be tossed   TWAIN 872:42
h., custom and education   SMITH 797:40
h. in writing articles   FEYN 322:24
h. of civilisation   WEST 901:38
h....of correcting things   BRADY 149:83
h. of discipline   TUCH 869:59
h. of disgruntled men   TOLK 862:97
h. of profound reflection   CONR 235:18
h. of revelation   SKEL 795:7
H....the test of truth   CRAB 242:98
instinct; the h. is already old   LAWR 494:16
in the h. of flogging   TROL 867:6
monster that devours everything: h.   BALZ 57:6
order breeds h.   ADAMS 4:79
remnants of such a beautiful h.   ALME 13:65
shook the h. off   WORD 925:5
taste of lies...a h.   GELL 348:99
Television has spread the h.   SCHL 718:15
habitat native h. was hot water   ANON 24:34
habitation Deep-founded h.   BLAKE 133:26
God in his holy h.   BIBLE 96:38
h. for bears and wolves   SCHAW 717:96
h. of dragons   BIBLE 103:33
Lord...thy h.   BIBLE 96:54
none doth build a stately h.   HERB 398:3
world Of destined h.   MILT 584:95
habitations brick shops and h.   THOR 858:7
miles of human h.   CONR 235:20
receive you into everlasting h.   BIBLE 116:51
habitis prelatis in h. clericall   DUNB 294:5
habits each other's h., thoughts   DISR 276:53
first h. of intimacy   LAMB 486:43
h. and customs of the people   RICA 684:31
h. are geared towards   LIVE 512:81
h. of metaphoric thought   FRYE 340:36
h. of peace and patience   WALT 888:49
Pick up bad h. of expectancy   LARK 490:20
superficial h. of 'good citizenship'   WAUGH 892:38
habitual that which has become h.   ARIS 29:60
Habsburg H. monarchy   TAAF 835:68
hackles of tan with henna h.   STEV 819:20
hackneyed h. jokes from Miller   BYRON 179:97
hades phonographs of h. in the brain   CRANE 243:25
haemophilia kind of psychological h.   CURR 249:39
haft change the h. if you please   QUIN 675:53
hag h. obscene, and grisly phantom   BEAT 66:96
you...equiangular old h.!   OCON 621:21
haggard h. and careworn   WODE 919:62
h. and lank   GILB 354:9
Haggards the H. Ride no more   STEP 817:59
haggis Gie her a H.!   BURNS 171:89
haggling still h. at the price   GRAV 367:80
hags secret, black, and midnight h.   SHAK 768:22
ha-ha Funny peculiar, or funny h.-h.?   HAY 386:54
hail beaten dog beneath the h.   POUND 665:61
H.Caesar, we...salute you   ANON 18:62
H. fellow, well met   SWIFT 831:91
H. Mary, quite contrary!   GREE 371:61
H. nothing full of nothing   HEMI 394:2

h. shall sweep away the refuge   BIBLE 103:28
H. to the Chief   SCOTT 723:5
lashing h.   SHEL 783:39
say a H. Mary for you   JOYCE 451:80
such a h. of words   JONS 448:20
Where falls not h.   TENN 847:52
Hailsham Lord H. said   MONT 591:61
hair backward by the h.   BROW 159:4
braided her yellow h.   BALL 56:88
braid to bind your h.   SCOTT 724:22
ceases to alter...her h.   AUST 44:3
dressing their h.   SMOL 801:28
each particular h. to stand on end   SHAK 752:28
elegance of Circe's h.   POUND 664:36
fair h. gently waved   THAT 850:12
fictions only and false h.   HERB 398:6
for the colour of his h.   HOUS 416:89
h. a glory like a saint   KEATS 459:37
h. and dimples is coming   MOORE 595:24
h. and harpstring of gold   SWIN 833:34
h. as white as gin   CAUS 201:14
h. has become very white   CARR 194:67
h. is as a flock of goats   BIBLE 101:2
h. More black than ashbuds   TENN 840:69
h. off the Great Cham's beard   SHAK 744:95
h. that lay along   ROSS 698:87
h. 'twixt south and southwest side   BUTL 177:40
his floating h.!   COLE 226:15
hoary h.   GRAY 370:29
If a man have long h.   BIBLE 121:5
if my h. do but tickle   SHAK 738:8
in politics...with that h.   ASTOR 37:30
in their golden h.   TENN 841:95
I rise with my red h.   PLATH 654:68
kame my h.   BALL 56:94
lass wi' tousled h.   MACD 529:29
letters...serve one to pin up one's h.   CONG 232:36
light brown h.   FOST 332:61
lodestone of live h.   MACN 537:98
long h....is a glory to her   BIBLE 121:5
long, limp h.   DAVIS 255:55
loosen your h.   YEATS 932:37
loses his h.   DIAZ 265:50
man of your head and h.   JONS 449:27
must sugar my h.   CARR 195:84
My h. has been in training   SHER 787:37
never hurt a h. of him   STUD 827:5
no more that shining h.   LOVE 519:01
not hurt a h.   STER 818:78
one strangling golden h.   ROSS 698:95
pin up your h.   CONG 232:37
reft the jewels from her h.   HYDE 427:23
ruddy limbs and flourishing h.   BLAKE 133:24
scant as h. in leprosy   BROW 161:44
smoothes her h.   ELIOT 306:61
snow-white h. who has kept out   LEAC 497:72
space...laid on her h.   CRANE 243:18
stars in her h.   ROSS 698:86
such a head of h.   HOUS 416:90
tangles of Neaera's h.?   MILT 578:49
Thy hyacinth h.   POE 656:22
watching myself brush my h.   RHYS 684:30
wear gowd on your h.   BALL 56:88
weave the sunlight in your h.   ELIOT 305:31
When I lie tangled in her h.   LOVE 519:9
Wi' ribbons in her h.   BALL 56:82
woman, with such h.   BROW 161:42
you have lovely h.   CHEK 209:13
your yellow h.   YEATS 934:59
haircut rather bad h.   MCCA 528:96
hairs bring down my gray h.   BIBLE 88:1
few, sad, last grey h.   KEATS 460:59
five grey h.   DONNE 279:43
Had all his h.   SHAK 761:9
h. of your head are all numbered   BIBLE 111:28
h. were grown like eagles' feathers   BIBLE 106:96
h. were white like wool   BIBLE 125:45
How ill white h. becomes   SHAK 743:67
If h. be wires   SHAK 773:51
when my h. be grey   SURR 829:40
hairy Esau...is a h. man   BIBLE 87:86
h. American filth   OSBO 630:13
Haiti Go to H. and stand   PHIL 650:95
hale You are h., Father William   SOUT 805:96
half advantage...is h. the victory   DRAKE 286:93
fall h. in love   SALI 711:54
H. of them don't know   QUINN 675:54

h. of the nation is mad	SMOL 801:27
h. o't smug, complacent	SMITH 801:25
h. the battle	GOLD 362:67
h. the people are right	WHITE 903:79
h. was not told me	BIBLE 92:13
image of myself and dearer h.	MILT 583:77
live with only h. a heart	WILS 915:79
longest h. of your life	SOUT 805:8
loves but h. of Earth	QUIL 674:40
No, but h. a one	JONS 449:30
not told even the h.	POLO 657:40
The ae h. of the warld	SCOTT 725:48
to be thought h. so good	WHIT 906:64
half-baked attractive to the h.-b.	FORS 331:32
half-believers h.-b. in our…creeds	ARNO 32:21
half-brother America, thou h.-b.	BAIL 52:5
half-creature h.-c. of the Senate	MANS 547:98
half-dark From h.-d. to h.-d.	POUND 665:53
half-hour h.-o. to Aberdour	BALL 56:87
half-hung with mat h.-h.	POPE 660:5
half-light and the h.-l.	YEATS 933:38
half-naked striding h.-n. up the steps	CHUR 216:70
half-traitor never be h.-t.	HUGO 420:66
half-truths speak no more than h.-t.	LINK 511:57
half-workers women Must be h.-w.?	SHAK 773:62
Hall I have seen…Thomas H.	SMART 796:23
hall Douglas in his h.?	SCOTT 723:98
filled our h. like	RIVA 688:1
grey assembly h.	MUSS 605:15
H. or Terrace	LEAR 497:77
hire a h.	BELL 74:88
I knew that sullen h.	OWEN 632:59
kindest in the h.	DAVIS 256:65
logs into the h.	SHAK 734:94
skittish Fortune's h.	SHAK 757:4
sparrow should fly…into the h.	BEDE 68:54
vasty h. of death	ARNO 32:14
waited in our tutor's h.	BYRON 179:95
wealth of h. and bower	WORD 925:11
Halliag will go down to H.	MACL 535:35
hallmark h. of our culture	DONA 278:21
hallowed H. be thy name	BIBLE 110:98
halls Amphitrite's destined h.	SHEL 783:28
blood-bedecked h. of their revel	POE 656:19
h. of the White House	JOHN 439:74
through Tara's h.	MOORE 596:51
hallucinated when Dalí h.	RUSS 706:66
hallucination A consensual h.	GIBS 353:76
hallways along these same h.	ROBBE 688:9
enclosed h.	GIDE 353:81
halo jealousy with a h.	WELLS 898:85
Life…is a luminous h.	WOOLF 922:26
What…Is a h.?	FRY 340:26
halt h. ye between two opinions?	BIBLE 92:18
make it h. behind her	SHAK 774:93
halycon first h. period	WALT 888:54
ham Do you like green eggs and h.?	SEUSS 728:8
helps scenery like h. and eggs	TWAIN 870:80
Hambledonians last of H.	EGAN 301:24
hambre La mejor salsa…el h.	CERV 203:44
hamburgers future and it is h.	HALB 377:72
Hamelin H. town's in Brunswick	BROW 160:25
Hamilton [H.] smote the rock	WEBS 894:71
Marie H.'s to the kirk gane	BALL 56:82
Hamlet Could H. have been written	GRIS 373:19
get Tree to recite H.	GILB 355:36
H. is so much paper and ink	PRIE 668:17
H. Prince of Denmark	EVEL 316:22
H. with no rehearsal than TV golf	LEMM 502:78
Lord H., with his doublet	SHAK 752:40
No! I am not Prince H.	ELIOT 304:23
hammer an also dropped h.	RUSK 704:36
beating as hard as my h.	SCOTT 724:26
eye is the h.	KAND 454:38
hit my thumb with a h.	AMIS 14:91
the grain and h.	HEAN 389:15
thunderous h. shall drive thee	BLAKE 135:75
took an h. in her hand	BIBLE 90:67
with the h. she smote Sisera	BIBLE 90:68
hammers hear the h. ring	KIPL 474:85
hammock safety-net, not a h.	ANON 25:71
slept in a h.	SAKI 710:38
slow movement of a tropical h.	CHOC 214:17
hammock-shroud heavy-shotted h.-s.	TENN 843:26
Hampton-court servant…got to H.-c.	STEE 814:89
hand admire his sleight of h.	BUTL 177:55
beloved h. is laid	ARNO 31:99

bishops eat from my h.	DUPL 295:26
bite the h. that fed them	BURKE 169:48
bless the h. that gave the blow	DRYD 290:4
bringing me up by h.	DICK 271:30
by whose h.…people still are fed	DODD 278:8
came forth fingers of a man's h.	BIBLE 106:97
cap in h. the day	SMITH 801:25
Clean from my h.?	SHAK 767:5
cravens my weak h.	SHAK 774:65
curious engine, your white h.	WEBS 895:9
darkness…sifts through your h.	ASHB 35:83
death in my h.	SHAK 731:90
Devil is still at h.	DRYD 289:73
disdainful wave of a white woman's h.	ANGE 17:47
Don't let the h. fall	SLOAN 796:17
end…is close at h.	WELLS 899:94
Even there shall thy h. lead me	BIBLE 98:1
Eve's fair h., as from a…book	LANY 489:5
eye on the right h.	RUSH 703:96
fans into their h.	BALL 56:86
fate carries in her other h.	LAWR 495:40
fearful h. in felling quake	DONNE 279:32
fear thy skinny h.!	COLE 225:36
Fed with cold and usurous h.?	BLAKE 134:55
flame…one holds in the h.	MARG 549:45
fly in his h.	STER 818:78
foot and h. go cold	ANON 20:1
fork in his inexperienced h.	WELLS 898:79
Give me thy h.	SHAK 737:80
giving h., though foul	SHAK 733:77
great gifts with one h.	SNOW 802:40
h.…cutting edge of the mind	BRON 154:68
h. for h.	BIBLE 89:24
h. from day to day	MACN 538:3
h.…goes over the face	GARBO 345:39
h. in all things	WASH 889:79
h. in h., on the edge	LEAR 498:86
h. in h. to death	ROSS 698:99
h. in h. to hell	SHAK 732:21
h. in h. with Plenty	TENN 842:16
h. in h. with wand'ring	MILT 586:37
h.-in-h. even with the vow	SHAK 752:31
h. in too many pies	MENC 565:60
handle toward my h.?	SHAK 767:94
h. more instrumental to the mouth	SHAK 751:98
h. of God	BIBLE 107:31
h. of God	MARA 548:21
h. of Heaven	WORD 929:66
h. of steel in a velvet glove	WOOL 923:56
h. on the throat of Venice	TOME 863:9
h. so various	MILT 586:55
h. that follows intellect	MICH 568:33
h. that holds dominion	THOM 852:63
h. that kings Have lipped	SHAK 765:31
h. that made us is divine	ADDI 6:27
h. that rocks the cradle	WALL 886:10
h. that signed the paper	THOM 852:62
h. that writ it	SHAK 772:29
h., the head	RUSK 704:12
h. under his head	YEATS 934:63
h. wherewith I write	BROW 159:8
h. will be against every man	BIBLE 87:75
hard h. of…need	OTWAY 631:25
Have still the upper h.	COWA 239:18
have the use…but of my left h.	MILT 578:60
held her in its golden h.	GEE 348:93
hold a fire in his h.	SHAK 734:4
holden me by my right h.	BIBLE 96:43
if they want a h.	GERS 350:39
if thy right h. offend thee	BIBLE 109:90
infinity in the palm of your h.	BLAKE 135:66
In his h. are all the corners	BOOK 143:64
in his h. a spade	SPEN 809:15
in the palm of my h.	JULI 452:4
In this close h. of love	BROW 159:7
in thy h. a withered spray	ARNO 32:19
Into thine h. I commit my spirit	BIBLE 95:9
invisible h. of some…god	CUOMO 248:29
Jesus stretched forth his h.	BIBLE 112:57
join h. in h.	DICK 273:81
keep the Classics at h.	WOOLF 923:53
Keep your left h. high	ONEI 626:10
kissed her slender h.	TENN 845:86
kissed the h. and by the h. led	BLAKE 134:35
kissing your h.	LOOS 517:79
kiss thy h. to bid adieu	STER 818:93
laid her snow-white h.	YEATS 932:29

laid thine h. upon me	BIBLE 98:99
lay his h. on his heart	STRA 826:89
lays his h. on his heart	BEER 69:73
lays his icy h. on kings	SHIR 789:83
led by an invisible h.	SMITH 798:49
left h. is my thinking h.	HEPW 396:63
lest he put forth his h.	BIBLE 86:57
let not man have the upper h.	BOOK 142:40
let not thy left h. know	BIBLE 109:96
Let your h. slip	MACB 527:82
lilies in her h.	ROSS 698:86
little cloud…like a man's h.	BIBLE 92:21
made by the h. which feels	HEPW 396:61
magic h. of chance	KEATS 457:94
makes…with the things at h.	PERCY 648:51
make your h. so unsteady	CENN 203:43
man with heart, head, h.	TENN 845:84
mine…the painter's h.	WORD 928:44
Moses held up his h.	BIBLE 88:22
murd'rous h. a drowsy bench protect	CRAB 242:91
my h. a needle better fits	BRAD 149:80
my hat, and h.	BROW 158:54
My times be in Thy h.!	BROW 162:71
Nature's own h. painted	SHAK 771:7
nectar from his h.	MARL 553:12
of one whose h.	SHAK 761:19
Old Hodge stays not his h.	RANS 679:27
on each h. the flames	MILT 580:6
openest thine h.	BIBLE 98:5
other h. full of seas	HYDE 427:21
other h. held a weapon	BIBLE 93:45
Our times are in His h.	BROW 162:69
Poetry is an extra h.	MITC 588:88
poor man's h.	WORD 927:31
pure h. can touch a newspaper	BAUD 65:84
put forth thine h. now	BIBLE 93:49
put in his h. by the hole	BIBLE 102:4
put your h. into the h. of God	HASK 385:25
quality…made…by the human h.	CATH 200:91
rare fine h. at that	MANS 546:85
rash h. in evil hour	MILT 584:13
regard the h. of the clock	LECO 499:29
right h. of the Majesty	BIBLE 124:89
sandwich in her h.	DICK 266:66
shake your h. and help you	LOFT 515:31
show her the back of your h.	FAUL 319:73
Sit thou at my right h.	BIBLE 97:73
soon as I get hold of a h.	FITZ 324:90
stand on either h.	MACA 526:64
stern h. of Compulsion	THUR 860:50
stern h. of fate	LLOY 513:99
supplication of a dead man's h.	ELIOT 306:70
tennis-girl's h.!	BETJ 83:88
the kindlier h.	TENN 844:61
there's a h., my trusty fiere!	BURNS 171:1
this is my lady's h.	SHAK 756:70
this unworthy h.!	CRAN 243:32
thrust my h. into his side	BIBLE 118:24
Thy h., great Anarch!	POPE 662:83
till I have a good h.	SWIFT 832:14
time is now near at h.	WASH 890:83
tiny h. is frozen	GIAC 351:51
touch of a vanished h.	TENN 840:68
waiting for a h.	TENN 843:27
walking close at h.	CARR 196:1
wander h. in h.	NOYES 619:77
waters in the hollow of his h.	BIBLE 103:38
What immortal h. or eye	BLAKE 135:61
what mortal h.	SCOTT 723:92
Whatsoever thy h. findeth	BIBLE 101:84
what strong h. can hold	SHAK 772:25
with as delicate a h.	BUTL 177:43
with automatic h.	ELIOT 306:61
Women…tricks by sleight of h.	CONG 231:16
work of an Almighty h.	ADDI 6:26
written…with mine own h.	BIBLE 122:41
wrote it with a second h.	SPEN 809:1
Your h., your tongue	SHAK 766:84
handbag hitting it with her h.	CRIT 245:63
handbook Bible as…a constable's h.	KING 469:59
handclasp h.'s a little stronger	CHAP 206:11
handcuffs with the h. on his wrist?	HOUS 416:89
Handel H. is so great and so simple	BUTL 178:79
wisdom; H. sings it	EMER 313:47
handful fear in a h. of dust	ELIOT 305:53
give the barest h.	KIPL 472:28
h. of grey ashes	CORY 237:75

handicraft primitive and original h.   OLIP 624:64
handicrafts manufacture and in h.   MARX 558:13
handiwork sheweth his h.   BOOK 142:43
handkerchief feels like a damp h.   MACK 534:19
  germs in your h.   ANON 22:64
  without wetting his h.   LASS 492:60
handkerchiefs in the house wi' h.   SCOTT 724:26
  waistcoats and moral pocket h.   DICK 266:78
handle h. toward my hand?   SHAK 767:94
  h. which fits them all   HOLM 408:84
handles no h. to a horse   LEAC 496:54
handmaid h. of the Lord   BIBLE 114:22
  h. to religion   BACON 46:50
  nature's h. art   DRYD 287:20
  Riches are a good h.   BACON 47:65
handmaiden low estate of his h.   BIBLE 115:23
handmaidens five h., whose names   ROSS 698:90
  War has three h.   HENR 395:45
handprint h. of all culture   ANON 25:76
handrails color I want those h.   TRUMP 869:49
hands aching h. and bleeding feet   ARNO 32:4
  additional number of productive h.   SMITH 798:46
  a lot of intelligence in the h.   WAITS 884:69
  And then take h.   SHAK 774:81
  and with clean h.   WILH 911:94
  Art to fold her h.   ROSS 698:98
  Beneath the bleeding h.   ELIOT 308:21
  big h. and big feet   HAGEN 376:56
  bind the h. of…rogues   OTWAY 631:28
  blood and wine were on his h.   WILDE 910:52
  both grasp h.   STAN 812:61
  both h. in the pocket   SATIE 717:81
  By fairy h. their knell is rung   COLL 228:43
  By foreign h. thy dying eyes   POPE 671:81
  Cease to use your h.   ORWE 628:45
  cheap seats clap their h.   LENN 502:88
  clasping his h. together   SCOTT 725:49
  clean h.   GALS 344:26
  coarse warty h.   DONO 282:98
  cold immortal h.   SWIN 833:32
  Come; let us squeeze h.   MELV 564:37
  dirty h., the nails bitten   MACA 525:54
  dollar in another man's h.   OHEN 623:54
  done with the brain, not the h.   MICH 568:34
  Droops on the little h.   MILNE 574:75
  education…should be in State h.   MILL 570:61
  engraft our h.   DONNE 280:59
  exertions of your h. and feet   CONR 234:2
  Farewell, my poor h.   RACH 676:81
  Father, into thy h.   BIBLE 116:66
  flabby h.   GILB 355:21
  folding of the h. to sleep   BIBLE 99:16
  fortune…with both h. full   SHAK 743:64
  free heart from its own h.!   CRAS 244:40
  greet you with bloody h.   CORW 237:73
  h. are blue   LEAR 497:79
  h. employed in work   STEU 819:8
  h. guiding where I stumble   SASS 716:75
  h. his office on ourselves   MILT 585:28
  h. of the enemy   ANON 25:60
  h. of the living God   BIBLE 124:94
  H. of the surgeon   MAP 548:18
  h. of those who implement   SHUL 789:90
  H. that led me to the limelight   HEAN 389:1
  h. themselves do reach   MARV 556:74
  h. upon their hearts   HOUS 416:74
  hath no h.?   BIBLE 103:45
  Hath not a Jew h., organs   SHAK 740:68
  heart and h. and voices   WINK 917:23
  heavens are the work of thy h.   BIBLE 97:61
  his restless h.   PRIT 669:48
  Holding h. at midnight   GERS 351:44
  h….that would light the world   MILL 571:96
  in his h. the print of the nails   BIBLE 118:24
  Into thy h. I commend   BOOK 143:45
  keep my h. from picking   BOOK 142:14
  knit h., and beat the ground   MILT 577:29
  language that…spits on its h.   SAND 713:10
  large and sinewy h.   LONG 515:44
  License my roving h.   DONNE 279:36
  lift not h. of prayer   TENN 847:51
  made with our h.   SWIN 833:47
  man's fortune is in his own h.   BACON 49:40
  man's h. empty   WALC 884:79
  murders sticking on his h.   SHAK 768:35
  nearer than h. and feet   TENN 847:36
  not into the h. of Spain   TENN 848:63

  only one of the h. tends to get quoted   BLIN 136:95
  prize-fighters shaking h.   MENC 565:68
  puny h. Of heroes   COWP 241:77
  right h. of fellowship   BIBLE 122:35
  rise and shake h. with me   SPEKE 806:36
  Rose-bloom fell on her h.   KEATS 459:37
  seem thus washing her h.   SHAK 768:32
  Shake h. forever   DRAY 287:6
  shook h. with Reputation   WEBS 895:11
  shook h. with time   FORD 330:13
  slipping from our h.   LOWE 521:60
  Soon my h., on the sunken fosse   HEAN 389:7
  soul clap its h.   YEATS 933:52
  Strength without h.   SWIN 833:22
  stretch forth thy h.   BIBLE 118:26
  such small h.   CUMM 248:11
  Take h. and dance there   BROW 161:48
  temples made with h.   BIBLE 119:49
  thin h. of the poor   WILDE 907:82
  thought it out with both h.   SAYE 717:84
  through most jewellers' h.   WEBS 895:98
  tides of men into my h.   LAWR 495:37
  toil of brain, or toil of h.   MELV 564:24
  washed his h. before the multitude   BIBLE 114:2
  washes his h.   SHAK 741:12
  wash your h. and pray   KIPL 474:74
  what h. you would hold!   LAMB 487:56
  will these h. ne'er be clean?   SHAK 768:34
  with crooked h.   TENN 844:68
  with h. blood stained   ORTE 627:28
  work of his h.   LOCKE 514:14
  work with your own h.   BIBLE 123:70
  world's great h.   HUNT 423:28
  wringing their h.   WALP 887:39
handsaw know a hawk from a h.   SHAK 753:61
handsome as h. as my sister   KING 469:56
  Looks h. in three hundred pounds   SHAK 743:77
  once h. and tall as you   ELIOT 306:63
  present fashion is always h.   FULL 341:69
handy-dandy change…and h.-d.   SHAK 763:91
hang all h. together   FRAN 335:16
  as much as the half of a h.   OBRU 621:12
  cowslips wan that h.   MILT 578:54
  H. my Hat is Home   JERO 437:37
  h. no longer on me   SHAK 765:43
  H. on thy walls   JONS 449:37
  h. them on the horns   SHAK 769:57
  H. thyself   SHAK 741:9
  let him h. there   EHRL 301:28
  to have done is to h.   SHAK 757:6
hangdog shifty, h. look   WODE 919:66
hanged got myself burned or h.   JERO 437:36
  h. for stealing horses   HALI 378:85
  h., if some eternal villain   SHAK 760:4
  h. in a fortnight   JOHN 445:26
  I'll be h.   SHAK 741:7
  we shall be h.   CROM 245:71
hanging H. and marriage…go by destiny   FARQ 318:53
  H. and wiving goes by destiny   SHAK 740:64
  h. for the colour that it is   HOUS 416:90
  H. is too good for him   BUNY 166:70
  h. on with one hand   HYDE 427:21
  nane the waur o' a h.   MACQ 538:16
  plain piece of work, a bare h.   DRYD 291:30
  they're h. Danny Deever   KIPL 471:89
hangman little h. dare not shoot   SHAK 745:11
  naked to the h.'s noose   HOUS 414:45
hangover a bad reputation is like a h.   PRES 667:8
  what a h. is like   KEIL 460:72
hangs h. before her all the year   TENN 839:46
hangups everybody else's h.   BRAU 150:2
hanky panky no h. p. in the Tardis   BAKER 52:16
Hannibal how to gain a victory, H.   MARH 549:47
Hanover By famous H. city   BROW 160:25
Hansard H. is history's ear   SAMU 712:78
happen Can't H. Here   LEWIS 508:92
  even if it didn't h.   KESEY 465:71
  h. later to h.   NICH 613:87
  too much seems to h.   COUP 238:90
  Whatever must h. ultimately   KISS 475:1
happened fact that it had h. elsewhere   FOWL 332:70
  reminiscences of what never h.   SAKI 710:33
happenings contempt of chance h.   RABE 676:76
happens not what h. to a man   HUXL 425:73
  When something h. to me   KENN 462:5
happier four times h. than the rest   RABE 676:75
  member of the family…is h.   FALU 317:41

happiest best and h. moments   SHEL 786:16
  h. Africans in the world   SMITH 799:68
  h. moment of the happy man   SCHO 719:34
  H. when he is trying   LEHM 501:68
  h. women…have no history   ELIOT 303:91
happiness accustomed, in…h.   WHAR 901:49
  annual expenditure…result h.   DICK 269:67
  banquet of h.   HUGO 420:71
  bat is a symbol of h.   LAWR 494:96
  beauty is a guarantee of h.   PROU 671:81
  beginnings of the people's h.   STRA 826:89
  best recipe for h.   AUST 43:76
  consume h. without producing it   SHAW 777:55
  definition of h.   KENN 463:38
  does more for the h. of mankind   BRIL 152:35
  dower Of inward h.   WORD 925:11
  enemy to human h.   JOHN 446:56
  envy no man's h.   SHAK 749:57
  Greatest H. Principle   MILL 570:37
  greatest obstacle to h.   FONT 329:88
  H. consists in the multiplicity   JOHN 443:82
  H. engulfs our strength   BALZ 57:11
  h. ever been the subject of fiction?   UPDI 875:1
  H. in marriage   AUST 42:63
  H. is always a work of art   YOUR 935:2
  h. is assured   BIER 129:31
  H. is full of strife   ANOU 26:98
  H. is healthy for the body   PROU 671:89
  H. is like coke   HUXL 425:70
  H. is no laughing matter   WHAT 902:59
  H. lies in conquering one's enemies   GENG 349:8
  H. Makes up in Height   FROST 339:3
  h. mankind can gain   DRYD 287:19
  h. of an individual   JOHN 444:94
  h. of finding a companion   BERN 81:41
  h. of his humble home   GLAD 358:91
  h. of knowing   FRAN 335:17
  h. of the common man   BEVE 85:26
  h. of the greatest number   BENT 77:65
  h. of the next w.   BROW 159:85
  h. or blessedness of man   SPIN 811:34
  h. that the future offers   DESB 262:14
  h. through another man's eyes   SHAK 750:86
  h. too swiftly flies   GRAY 368:95
  H. was my fate   RIMB 688:98
  however uncertain of giving h.   AUST 43:67
  independent h.   WORD 928:54
  In love, h. is abnormal   PROU 670:71
  jealous possessions of h.   GIDE 353:81
  lifetime of h.!   SHAW 778:80
  lives in sin and looks for h.   BUNY 167:78
  longing for h.   CAMUS 187:88
  lost h. and lasting pain   MILT 580:96
  magic lore of h.   RIMB 687:95
  Man's h.   GIDE 353:84
  meaning…We can assign to h.   ELIOT 308:30
  money does not bring h.   LACL 484:84
  nearly like h.   GREE 370:51
  no h. within this circle of flesh   BROW 158:74
  no longer desire h.   SHAW 777:60
  not his own h.   SAINT 709:23
  Oh H.! our…end and aim!   POPE 660:23
  paint the memory of h.   SAIF 709:10
  Perfect h., by princes sought   CHAP 206:16
  private h. of the nation   JOHN 443:86
  procures the greatest h.   HUTC 424:52
  promised…either peace or h.   LEBON 498:4
  pursuit of h.   JEFF 436:12
  pursuit of h.   STAN 812:62
  science…can give no h.   POIN 657:32
  seemed to teach that h.   HARDY 382:60
  seize more of h.   ANON 19:89
  Simply seek h.   PECK 645:6
  somebody else's h.   HUXL 424:55
  so much h. is produced   JOHN 444:14
  sorceress who dispenses h.   SCHI 718:99
  sound off about h.   ICHI 428:37
  such a short-liv'd h.   BEHN 71:21
  To dream is h.   HUGO 420:70
  too happy in thine h.   KEATS 459:57
  Virtue is simply h.   BURR 173:63
  what is commonly called h.   SCHO 719:28
  where…We find our h.   WORD 925:4
  white man's h.   DOUG 284:35
happy Adults talk about being h.   WINT 917:31
  all be as h. as kings   STEV 823:18
  all the while I was quite h.   GIOV 357:73

all who are h.   JOHN 443:82
Anyone h. in this age   FULL 341:59
bread-sauce of the h. ending   JAMES 433:47
conspiracy to make you h.   UPDI 874:84
die h.   FOX 333:76
difficult…to be h. with someone!   LABR 483:66
duty of being h.   STEV 822:98
Eisenhower…makes people h.   WHITE 904:3
exist in order to be h.   SCHO 719:35
Forgive and be h.   PRAT 667:99
Getting up…does not make you h.   RABE 676:69
happiest moment of the h. man   SCHO 719:34
h. as the grass was green   THOM 852:71
H. Days are Here Again   YELL 934:69
h. families resemble each other   TOLS 862:5
H., h., h., pair!   DRYD 291:33
h….is not a characteristic   CHAN 205:3
H. is the country   AGATE 8:67
H. is the man   BIBLE 99:12
H. is the man   BIBLE 127:90
H. is the man   BIBLE 98:93
H. is the man that findeth wisdom   BIBLE 99:12
h. land   GOLD 361:57
H….like Ulysses   BELL 72:39
h. man inevitably confines   HAWT 386:46
h. much of the time   PECK 645:6
H. those early days   VAUG 878:44
h. through science   POIN 657:32
H. till I woke again   HOUS 415:67
h. time when one is in misery   DANTE 252:95
h.…we are not over-h.   SHAK 752:51
h. who have called thee so   SOUT 805:5
have been very h.   ATTL 38:43
How h. I could be   GAY 347:87
human race was most h.   GIBB 351:52
if life is…h.   LABR 483:70
If the prisoner is h.   SHAW 778:1
If you are as h.   BUCH 164:31
in nothing else so h.   SHAK 734:13
I've had a h. life   HAZL 388:88
I were but little h.   SHAK 744:97
keep me h. all the day   STEV 823:16
Let us all be h.   WARD 888:57
look these h. couples   STEV 821:82
make men h.   POPE 661:59
Marriages would…be as h.   JOHN 444:15
no h. end to it   HEMI 394:6
none should be h.   JOHN 445:21
no one can be perfectly h.   SPEN 806:38
nor as h. as one hopes   LARO 491:50
not a h. one   GILB 354:3
not a h. prospect   THOM 856:46
now to be most h.   SHAK 759:75
one of those h. places   THOR 858:8
one of those h. souls   SHEL 784:66
one should feel h.   SARR 715:38
only one thing to make me h.   HAZL 388:89
prevent me being h.   ANOU 26:95
remote from the h..   AUDEN 40:11
shame…from being h.   LABR 484:75
so few h. marriages   ASTE 36:25
so few marriages are h.   SWIFT 831:70
so h. as to sigh for   BEAU 67:7
So, I'm h. tonight   KING 468:43
someone, somewhere, may be h.   MENC 565:71
strangely h. with myself   IGNA 428:41
think themselves h.   BACON 48:3
This is the h. warrior   READ 680:46
thy h. strain?   SHEL 784:59
too h. in thine happiness   KEATS 459:57
twentieth will be h.   HUGO 421:95
unfurnish'd Of falsehood to be h.   DRYD 289:64
Was he h.?   AUDEN 40:96
When I am h. I live   SMITH 800:1
whether you are h. or not   SHAW 780:69
Which of us is h.   THAC 849:94
wretched…once to have been h.   BOET 138:29
Happy Isles touch the H. I.   TENN 840:66
harbour a voyage and not a h.   TOYN 864:28
h. and neighbour wood   THOM 852:74
h. without ships   DEFOE 258:22
looking over h. and city   SAND 713:92
O the H. of Fowey   QUIL 674:42
rain over the dwindling h.   THOM 852:75
hard game is too h.   JAMES 433:24
gave me the h. shoulder   HENRI 395:43
h. and practical man   HOYLE 417:4

h. on His Majesty's Opposition   HOBH 405:31
'H.,' replied the Dodger   DICK 267:91
h. rhyme   SHAK 745:24
h. to be room-mates   SALI 711:56
h. to be sought out   HERA 396:70
no success without h. work   SOPH 804:87
powerful h. thing   CONN 234:92
read very h.   JOHN 443:70
The woman is so h.   TENN 841:98
when the times were not h.   EMER 313:50
where a heart is h.   SHAK 733:54
hardcover Europe…a h. book   DELI 260:75
harden H. not your heart   BIBLE 97:58
harder they would be h. to them   TROL 866:89
hardest h. thing to bear   JUVE 453:16
h. thing to do   HEMI 394:9
hardhearted more cruel and h.   BACON 48:90
hard-hearts nature…makes these h.-h.   SHAK 763:80
hardship experience nothing but h.   BELL 72:41
meet any h.   KENN 462:12
teacheth him wholesome h.   LASS 492:60
hardships disappointments, h.   PEARY 645:1
h. of an emigrant's life   MOOD 594:6
very bottom of h.   DU 293:71
Hardy either 29 or Thomas H.   PARK 638:76
Kiss me, H.   NELS 610:35
hare covers…the h. and the hunter   PATC 642:48
grass, and a h. sitting up?   LAWR 494:95
h. limped trembling   KEATS 458:30
o'er the timid h.!   THOM 856:56
start a h.!   SHAK 741:4
hare-bells heath and h.-b.   BRON 155:99
hare-brained every h.-b. nut   SAFER 708:95
harem like eunuchs in a h.   BEHAN 70:7
hares h. have no time to read   BROO 156:21
little hunted h.   HODG 405:46
hark H.! ah, the Nightingale!   ARNO 32:12
H., h., the lark   SHAK 773:61
H.! how all the welkin rings   WESL 900:10
H. in thine ear   SHAK 763:91
Harlem like…a son of H.   OBRI 620:99
harlot h.'s cheek   SHAK 753:73
h.'s cry from street   BLAKE 135:70
he that cleaveth to h.   BIBLE 108:55
Portia is Brutus' h.   SHAK 747:85
prerogative of the h.   BALD 54:46
harlots Mother Of H.   BIBLE 127:3
Harlow t is silent, as in H.   ASQU 36:17
harm does h. to my wit   SHAK 756:51
does men great h.   HESI 401:66
does no h.   GILM 356:57
don't think it does any h.   THOM 852:68
Fate cannot h. me   SMITH 801:21
fear we'll come to h.   BALL 56:85
good provoke to h.   SHAK 758:41
How can it h. you   CRUZ 246:87
in his sleep he does little h.   SHAK 762:37
may do great h.   SHAW 780:50
no h. to retool our imaginations   WELD 896:38
Shall h. Macbeth   SHAK 768:23
Whoop, do me no h., good man   SHAK 770:91
harmful may be more h.   HUXL 426:12
who say it is h.   CRUZ 246:89
harming perpetual h. of somebody   FORD 329:98
harmless book is not h.   ELIOT 307:90
h. and even beneficial   SHAW 780:50
h. as doves   BIBLE 111:26
harmonies European h.   GILL 356:48
h. are concealed from me   FISH 324:76
h. of the body   BERN 81:42
inventor of h.   TENN 846:28
tranquil h.   GAUG 347:66
tumult of thy mighty h.   SHEL 783:47
harmony All discord, h., not understood   POPE 660:15
body's h.   POPE 662:77
h. comes…as a shock   RAINE 677:97
h.…comes to heal   WORD 923:67
h. for the honour of God   BACH 46:25
H.! H.!   SCHO 719:25
h. In autumn   SHEL 782:21
H. in discord   HORA 414:28
h. or true delight?   MILT 584:2
immortal god of h.   BEET 70:95
in h. with the sentiments of an assassin   BIER 128:11
knew such h. alone   MILT 575:96
Like h. in music   WORD 925:92
may we bring h.   THAT 850:16

ninefold h.   MILT 576:97
notions of law and h.   THOR 857:78
other h. of prose   DRYD 292:43
ravish like enchanting h.   SHAK 733:73
Sentimentally…disposed to h.   LAMB 486:45
that famous h.   YEATS 932:32
untaught h. of spring   GRAY 369:3
what hope of h.?   SHAK 730:54
harms bars a thousand h.   SHAK 732:25
harness die in h.   AMIS 14:86
joints of the h.   BIBLE 92:27
Harold a masseur called H.   WOOD 921:17
harp h., his sole remaining joy   SCOTT 722:84
h. that once through   MOORE 596:51
No h….could so cheerily play   CAMP 186:65
played everything but the h.   BARR 61:1
wild h. slung behind   MOORE 596:49
Harper H. smiled, well pleased   SCOTT 723:89
harps h. upon the willows   BIBLE 98:98
harpstring hair and h. of gold   SWIN 833:34
harpy conference with this h.   SHAK 744:95
harried h. man I think I be!   BALL 56:79
Harris the present Mrs H.   THUR 859:19
Harrison if Rex H. doesn't   GRANT 366:46
to see…H. hanged   PEPYS 647:28
Harrovian H. pricks up his ears   ANON 21:30
Harrow H. would not be ashamed   BALD 54:52
harrow beneath the h. knows   KIPL 470:73
H. the house of the dead   AUDEN 39:76
h. up thy soul   SHAK 752:28
Harry Banish not…H.'s company   SHAK 742:16
England breed again…a King H.?   DRAY 286:2
grunted H. to Jack   SASS 716:63
Know what I mean, H.?   BRUNO 163:6
little touch of H.   SHAK 746:47
harsh seem h., impertinent   JONS 449:26
harshness h. which resides in your heart   LABE 482:51
no h. gives offence   POPE 658:59
Hart one H. that you will not leave   HART 384:8
hart As the h. panteth   BIBLE 95:20
Harvard chair at H. or Princeton   MENC 565:60
didn't go to H.   JOHN 440:89
glass flowers at H.   MOORE 595:31
graduate of H. or not   JOHN 440:97
H. education consists of what   CONA 230:81
Yale College and my H.   MELV 564:28
harvest And it is h.   RANS 679:23
continual spring, and h.   SPEN 809:92
h. is past   BIBLE 105:73
h. of a quiet eye   WORD 924:84
laughs with a h.   JERR 437:39
Raymond like the H. Moon   FARJ 318:48
seedtime and h.   BIBLE 87:67
sheaves in h.   DONNE 281:88
When thou cuttest down thine h.   BIBLE 89:50
white already to h.   BIBLE 117:85
harvested heart has been h.   BAUD 64:59
harvesting h. from existence   NIET 615:9
harvests bad h., and…fluctuations   ELIOT 303:87
h. bury all his pride has planned   POPE 659:97
hash product is a final h.   MELV 564:43
hashish puffed h….didn't inhale   RICH 686:72
hasta H. la vista, baby   SCHW 721:63
haste Do nothing in h.   WHYM 906:65
eat it in h.   BIBLE 88:16
h. now to my setting   SHAK 775:18
life and light, with envious h.   ROCH 692:70
make what h. I can to be gone   CROM 246:76
Married in h.   CONG 231:1
marry in h.   CABE 183:15
Men love in h.   BYRON 182:94
repent in h.   CONG 231:2
send them out of the land in h.   BIBLE 88:18
shall not make h.   BIBLE 103:28
such h. to be doing   STEV 822:4
hasty let not thine heart be h.   BIBLE 101:76
man is ever h.   KORAN 479:75
need na start awa sae h.   BURNS 170:71
hasty-pudding sweets of h.-p.   BARL 60:58
hat All h. and no cattle   CONN 232:53
as is the h. of a soldier   HERB 399:24
Beneath her torn h.   WHIT 906:58
can't think without his h.   BECK 68:35
coat and top h.   LAVER 493:82
fashion of his h.   SHAK 744:84
from whose h.   KIPL 473:40
get your h.   FIEL 323:46

deserts of the h.	AUDEN 40:5
desires of the h.	AUDEN 39:87
desperateness of man's h.!	BUNY 166:66
dialogues with my Mother's h.	WORD 925:97
Did not our h. burn	BIBLE 117:69
directly to the h.	POE 656:20
Don't search…for my h.	BAUD 64:60
dried up your h.	FLAU 326:26
drink thy wine with a merry h.	BIBLE 101:83
ease a h. Like a satin gown	PARK 637:44
entered into my h.	HOLM 407:70
Enter every trembling h.	WESL 900:14
every Russian's inmost h.	PUSH 673:20
fade from my h.	MOORE 596:47
false h. doth know	SHAK 767:92
Fare thee well, great h.	SHAK 742:35
feed on him in thy h.	BOOK 141:8
felt my h. strangely warmed	WESL 900:17
figure of my h.	SHAK 758:50
finite number of h.-beats	ARMS 30:79
flesh and my h. faileth	BIBLE 96:43
fop in my h.	ETHE 315:98
for such a kind h.	SHAK 743:78
foul…shop of the h.	YEATS 934:62
free, the larger h.	TENN 844:61
from my h. the strings do break	CAMP 186:77
full h. Remains in use	SHAK 764:18
funeral marches around your h.	MILL 571:97
gambled my h. and lost	RIVE 688:3
gay clothes, a merry h.	WEBS 894:85
give thee the desires of thine h.	BIBLE 95:15
give them an h. of flesh	BIBLE 105:86
give them one h.	BIBLE 105:86
giving your h. to a dog	KIPL 473:65
glad with all my h.	DRAY 287:6
great flint…singing into his h.	BIRN 131:70
grief of h.	SHAK 775:13
grief of h.	SHAK 775:15
Guilt in his h.	CHUR 215:43
Harden not your h.	BIBLE 97:58
harshness which resides in your h.	LABE 482:51
has ached with a h.!	SWIN 833:29
haven't the h.	GRAH 365:35
haven't the h. to take a minute	CARA 189:38
have the h. to stay	BUTL 177:61
h. aches	KEATS 459:57
h., all mad with misery	SHAK 731:93
h. and core of ages	LOWE 519:21
h. and mind of America	BARZ 63:36
h. and my flesh crieth out	BIBLE 96:45
h. and stomach of a king	ELIZ 309:60
h. as big as Waterloo Station	AGATE 8:70
h. as sound as a bell	SHAK 745:11
h. be full of the spring?	SWIN 832:15
h. blackening	JEFF 436:5
h. bleeds for his country	JOHN 443:61
h. broken even more surely	LESS 505:43
h. but one	BOUR 147:28
h. dies within me	SCHAW 717:96
h. distrusting asks	GOLD 361:56
h. either breaks or boldens	BALZ 57:10
h. enough to begin to live	STEV 822:1
h. grown cold	SHEL 786:4
h. has been harvested	BAUD 64:59
h. has its reasons	PASC 641:23
h. hath ne'er within him burned	SCOTT 723:91
h. in a case o' gowd	BALL 57:95
h. in hiding	HOPK 412:90
h. in's face	SHAK 770:78
h. into my mouth	SHAK 762:52
H. Is A Lonely Hunter	MCCU 529:20
H. Is A Lonely Hunter	SHARP 776:38
h. is deceitful	BIBLE 105:76
h. is Highland	GALT 344:29
h. is in the coffin	SHAK 748:8
h. is in their boots	CHES 212:82
h. is in the right place	LIVI 512:83
h. is like wax	BIBLE 94:99
h. knocked in its cage	GREE 371:69
h. leap in my breast	SAPP 714:27
h. less bounding	ARNO 33:48
'h.' lies much lower	LICH 509:19
h. lies plain	ARNO 31:99
h. lingered so far	MOOD 594:6
h. love till now?	SHAK 736:43
h. never knows the colour of the skin	GEOR 349:21
h. of a brute like you	PLATH 654:69

h. of a man	ROUS 700:46
h. of a man…lodged in a woman	CONG 232:39
H. of England	DRAY 287:4
h. of fire	TENN 846:99
h. of lead	POPE 662:70
h. of man…dignity	TATE 837:6
h. of man go together	RUSK 704:12
h. of man has long been sore	HOUS 416:78
h. of our island	FORS 331:28
h. of standing	EMPS 314:63
h. of the city	MOYN 601:41
h. of the North is dead	LAWR 494:15
h. of woman	SHAK 747:92
h. on your sleeve	THAT 850:27
h. responsive swells	BYRON 181:49
h.'s beatin' rhythm	BERRY 82:59
h.'s deep-sore wounding	SHAK 733:55
h.'s first ease	DAY 257:85
h. shall break	SHAK 763:70
h. Shall break into	SHAK 763:70
h. shall not fear	BIBLE 95:7
h.'s in the Highlands	BURNS 171:9
h.'s so full of joy	DRYD 289:59
h.'s stalled motor	MAYA 562:93
h.…that of a little child	THAC 849:4
h. that swells	DRYD 289:61
h. that watches and receives	WORD 924:75
h. that with every year grows dim	CONR 234:6
h. the keener	ANON 18:76
h. untravelled	GOLD 361:39
h. was free	WESL 899:9
h. was glad	FOX 333:77
h. was one of those	BYRON 181:59
h. was to thy rudder	SHAK 765:36
h. was used to beat	TENN 843:27
h. which beats only for you	VERL 879:67
h. why do you pound	APOL 27:12
h. will break in twa	NAIR 607:55
h.…with thy nest	WORD 929:60
h. with usury to such scenes?	LAMB 486:29
heaven-entreated h.	CRAS 244:38
heavenly and hidden h.	BUEC 165:44
hedgehog of the h.	LOWE 521:58
His flawed h.	SHAK 764:4
history…begins in the h.	CATH 200:83
holiness of the h.'s affections	KEATS 457:89
Hope deferred maketh the h. sick	BIBLE 99:25
How irksome…to my h.!	SHAK 730:54
human h. is slightly left of centre	FRYE 340:40
humble and a contrite h.	KIPL 472:21
hurt you to the h.	TWAIN 872:27
index to the h.	DICK 268:41
indurate h. against God	KNOX 476:19
in his painted h.	KEATS 458:34
in his private h.	TWAIN 872:24
In its secret h.	SMITH 801:25
in my h. his iron arrow	SPEN 808:79
In my h.'s core	SHAK 754:89
in our h. we know	WORD 927:30
Into my h. an air	HOUS 415:59
into the bell of her h.	THOM 853:94
into the h. of man	SWIFT 831:82
into the world with your h.	SHEL 782:14
In your h.	GOLD 362:74
Irishman's h. is nothing	SHAW 779:31
Is your h. at rest?	FLET 328:75
Keep the free h.	CRAS 244:40
kid…about her h. condition?	SILV 792:35
king's h. is in the hand	BIBLE 99:43
know in my h. of h.s	STARK 813:72
knowledge of the h.	JOHN 444:95
know my h.	BIBLE 98:3
know not the h.	SHAK 771:11
land of their h.'s hope	DAVIS 256:66
language of the h.	POPE 661:42
larger was his h.	DRYD 290:93
laughing h.'s long peace	BROO 156:9
lay his hand on his h.	STRA 826:89
lays his hand on his h.	BEER 69:73
Left my H. in San Francisco	CROSS 246:83
Let every h. exult with joy	DODD 278:7
let not thine h. be hasty	BIBLE 101:76
Let not your h. be troubled	BIBLE 118:11
Let not your h. be troubled	BIBLE 118:8
Lift up your h.	WESL 900:13
light h. lives long	SHAK 734:89
like a h. in reserve	CESA 203:50

Like music on my h.	COLE 225:91
listened at his h.	FROST 338:93
little body with a mighty h.	SHAK 745:33
Little skill, a little h.	ROSS 698:4
live in my h.	HAMM 379:16
live with only half a h.	WILS 915:79
long let your h. be strong	LAUD 492:65
look in thy h., and write	SIDN 790:8
loosed our h. in tears	ARNO 31:3
Lord looketh on the h.	BIBLE 91:90
lotion of the h.	PARK 639:89
Lourd on my h.	MACD 529:41
love which is inside his h.	LAWR 494:6
love you with all my h.	ROCH 691:49
Made of a h.	HERB 397:89
made tender to the h.	PROU 671:79
Mad with much h.	DONNE 279:33
make this h. rejoice or ache	COWP 240:42
malpractice of the h.	CLOU 223:31
man after his own h.	BIBLE 91:88
man's h. is small	KIPL 473:52
man with h., head, hand	TENN 845:84
mean to a tired h.	BOND 139:52
mechanical in…h.	CARL 191:83
meek and lowly in h.	BIBLE 111:38
Mercy has a human h.	BLAKE 134:31
merry h. doeth good	BIBLE 99:39
merry h. goes all the day	SHAK 770:83
merry h. maketh a cheerful	BIBLE 99:31
merry h. with small possessioun	HENR 396:53
mind and in the h.	LARO 491:54
mind, h.…not myself	WELTY 899:98
more native to the h.	SHAK 751:98
mother's h. is an abyss	BALZ 58:17
much against my h.	PATM 643:62
much it grieved my h.	WORD 924:77
Must my h. grow sick	CULL 247:95
My h. has made its mind up	COPE 237:62
my h. is a handful of dust	TENN 845:94
my h. is glad	ANON 20:13
My h. leaps up	WORD 926:15
my h. remembers how!	STEV 823:35
My h. would hear her	TENN 845:92
my old bitter h.	ORAH 627:21
nation…had the lion h.	CHUR 217:3
naughtiness of thine h.	BIBLE 91:92
nearly breaks my h.	JERO 437:33
no iron can stab the h.	BABEL 45:21
No nearer the h. than the lip	ANON 19:98
No pitying h.	GRAY 370:33
not in the h. or in the saliva	ARGU 29:43
not my h.	JONS 449:25
not really bad at h.	BELL 73:59
not wear your h. on your sleeve	WEBS 895:22
not your h. away	HOUS 414:46
ocean or the human h.?	LAUT 493:74
oft…my h. to ache	BLAKE 135:81
O my little h.!	SHAK 733:76
one body and one h.	DOUG 283:20
Only with the h.	SAINT 709:17
open a window into one's h.	MELBA 563:15
Open not thine h.	BIBLE 107:44
opens the h. and lungs	STER 818:85
Open your h.	BROW 161:57
O pure of h.	COLE 226:4
O tiger's h.	SHAK 730:70
Out-worn h.	YEATS 932:35
own the h. and stool	COLUM 229:61
pageant of his bleeding h.	ARNO 33:32
passionate h. of the poet	TENN 845:79
Pass on, weak h.	TENN 842:18
Pitee…in gentil h.	CHAU 208:80
place that's broken my h.	BAUG 65:87
poor man's h.	WORD 927:31
Pourest thy full h.	SHEL 784:54
Praise…can freeze the h.	BUCK 165:38
Presume not on thy h.	SHAK 771:9
Pride leaves the h.	GAUT 347:71
produces a sadness of h.	MORSE 599:11
quickening of the h.	AUDEN 39:82
red red vitals of his h.	RANS 679:24
Religion's in the h.	JERR 437:38
removed their h. far from me	BIBLE 103:29
revolting and a rebellious h.	BIBLE 105:70
Rise in the h.	TENN 842:46
road to the h.	BALZ 58:16
roaming with a hungry h.	TENN 839:91

round his h. one…hair ROSS 698:95
ruddy drops that warm my h. GRAY 370:31
Sacred H. o' Jesus OCAS 621:14
sad, good Christian at her h. POPE 661:44
safe within its central h. WHIT 906:51
said to H., 'How goes it?' BELL 73:62
sank down Into my h. WORD 925:93
seat…in the h. GAND 345:35
see my h.…without disgust BAUD 64:65
see what breeds about her h. SHAK 763:80
self-destruction enter the h. CHEE 209:99
sensations…felt along the h. WORD 923:69
set the h. on fire SHAK 733:53
sick at h. SHAK 751:95
sickening of the h. POE 656:16
Sink h. and voice NEALE 610:28
sleeps on his own h. WORD 924:84
some h. did break TENN 843:25
souls Of the pure in h. RANS 679:27
spring of love gushed from my h. COLE 225:88
stone of the h. YEATS 933:46
straightest road to a man's h. FERN 321:17
strings…in the human h. DICK 267:23
struggle…fill a human h. CAMUS 187:90
stuffed roast h. JOYCE 452:92
take from them all…hardness of h. BOOK 141:87
take their h. in one hand BILL 130:49
temples th'upright h. and pure MILT 580:93
than a h. untainted? SHAK 730:59
Thanks to the human h. WORD 927:29
that mighty h. is lying still! WORD 926:19
That the bruised h. SHAK 759:68
the fart Of every h. SUCK 828:12
them whose h. is perfect BIBLE 92:43
there will your h. be also BIBLE 110:99
The tears fall in my h. VERL 879:66
the waters of the h. THOM 852:58
thoughts, and h. enlarges MILT 584:5
thou hast my h. PRIOR 669:41
through a broken h. WILDE 910:59
Thy rebuke hath broken my h. BOOK 143:60
tiger's h. GREE 371:80
to each loving h. how near! HOLM 408:97
Toyshop of their h. POPE 658:66
tragic h. BENET 75:13
triumph of his h. ADDI 6:21
true love hath my h. SIDN 790:4
trust not the h. of that man CARL 192:2
truths of the h. FAUL 318:63
turn the h. of the fathers BIBLE 107:23
united in one h. WALT 888:44
United to a h. like thine BRON 154:71
unpack my h. with words SHAK 753:69
unquiet h. and brain TENN 842:23
utmost passion of her h. HAWT 386:40
Vacant h., and hand, and eye SCOTT 724:40
Vengeance is in my h. SHAK 731:90
verses from my h. MARTI 555:45
visit my sad h. SHAK 747:86
walk in the ways of thine h. BIBLE 101:91
weather in the h. RICH 685:41
were my dear h.-strings SHAK 760:89
whan every lusty h. MALO 542:10
Whatever your h. LUTH 523:98
What female h. can gold despise? GRAY 368:99
where a h. is hard SHAK 733:54
where my h. is turning FOST 332:60
Where the h. lies BROW 161:61
wine that maketh glad the h. BIBLE 97:67
with a hopeful h. LAWR 495:22
withered h. was dead SCOTT 722:86
with its h. cut out STEG 814:7
With rue my h. is laden HOUS 415:63
woman touches another's h. LACL 484:89
word have I hid in mine h. BIBLE 97:81
wound my h. VERL 879:64

heart-ache h. and the…shocks SHAK 753:74
heart attack the occasional h. a. CHEN 210:17
heartbeats slow h. GRAV 367:77
heartbreak feel the h. GIBS 352:75
  h.-b. in the heart of things? GIBS 352:75
  h., hatred blind NOON 618:58
  H. Hotel PRES 667:5
heart-easing tell the most h.-e. things KEATS 457:85
heartening h. and the strong reply EMPS 314:63
hearth as from an unextinguished h. SHEL 783:48
  By this still h. TENN 839:62

cricket on the h. MILT 576:17
drive hunger from the h. LLOY 513:98
h. of television NEW 611:55
moved earth and h. TENN 840:66
hearth-fire h.-f. and the home-acre KIPL 473:60
heartiness h. that compels belief TWAIN 870:76
heartland from the h. of the country SHUL 790:93
heartless appallingly h. thing to do MANS 547:94
heartlessness the h. of human beings OKRI 624:61
heart-of-gold bawcock and a h.-o.-g. SHAK 746:69
hearts all that human h. endure GOLD 361:42
  any trace of it in their h. REDON 681:75
  apply our h. unto wisdom BIBLE 96:52
  broke the h. WAUGH 892:38
  cannot find it in our h. GELL 348:2
  carry in their h. LLOY 513:99
  clasp we to our h. ROSS 698:94
  Combine your h. in one SHAK 746:69
  Content in the…cell of their h. BOGAN 138:30
  curse upon your whunstane h. BURNS 170:66
  day with…brave h. CLIN 221:89
  dealt in hides, but never in h. DICK 268:52
  devices and desires of our own h. BOOK 140:66
  enthronèd in the h. of kings SHAK 740:80
  ever grow in our h. JOHN 439:65
  evil lurks in the h. of men? ATWO 38:62
  eyes and h. ears LYLY 523:9
  free h., free foreheads TENN 840:66
  given our h. away WORD 928:46
  hands upon their h. HOUS 416:74
  harden not your h. BOOK 143:65
  H. after them tangled MILT 586:39
  h. all rocky BYRON 180:37
  h. and hands and voices WINK 917:23
  H. and minds ANON 23:93
  h. are more than coronets TENN 840:74
  h. are yearning FORD 330:20
  h. be frolic GREE 371:79
  h. of men…have melted SHAK 735:28
  h., though stout LONG 515:42
  h. very dry and tough HOOK 411:56
  H. wound up with love SPEN 807:58
  Heaven in our h. NIGH 616:31
  heavenly compassion in your h. DICK 270:98
  if our h. were beating SCOTT 724:26
  In h. at peace BROO 156:7
  in our h. either to marry STEV 821:79
  in the gentlest h. SPEN 808:88
  in the imagination of their h. BIBLE 115:23
  keep your h. and minds BIBLE 123:60
  keep your h. and minds BOOK 141:10
  lighten our own h. SHAK 745:27
  Lord pondereth the h. BIBLE 99:44
  May God wither up their h.! DAVIS 256:64
  modern life…inspired h. ARNO 32:22
  Of finite h. that yearn BROW 161:60
  Our h. are broken GIUL 358:88
  our h. are great TENN 846:7
  Our h., unrisen WILK 911:97
  our h. were fulfilled SWIN 833:47
  O, you hard h. SHAK 746:71
  queen in people's h. DIANA 265:49
  sing to find your h. FLEC 327:45
  song for thinking h. WORD 925:8
  steel my soldiers' h. SHAK 746:53
  still can pierce our h. MUIR 602:61
  stout h. and stout swords BIRK 130:63
  sweetness…inspired their h. MARL 551:77
  take away our h. o' stone OCAS 621:14
  take them with our h. NEWM 612:59
  tempts your…heedless h. GRAY 368:2
  thousand h. are great SHAK 732:22
  thousand h. beat happily BYRON 179:23
  touching their h. TROL 866:87
  two h. beating each to each! BROW 161:34
  undeveloped h. FORS 331:46
  unto whom all h. be open BOOK 141:92
  Where men with Splendid H. BROO 156:12
  with beating h. STOWE 826:72
  wore at their h. SPEN 807:47
  wot's hidden in each other's h. DICK 268:46
heartstring intelligencer's h. WEBS 895:6
heartstrings playeth with your h. LYLY 523:11
  sweep across our h. WILS 916:7
hearty h. old man SOUT 805:96
heat ally the h. BLAKE 133:24
  bear…the h. ARNO 32:4

but he gat no h. BIBLE 91:8
can't stand the h. TRUM 868:32
false of h. SHAK 773:46
fantastic summer's h.? SHAK 734:4
h. full of coldness LYLY 523:9
H. not a furnace SHAK 775:4
h. of life CONR 234:6
h. of the business is over! ETHE 315:93
h. o'th' sun SHAK 774:74
In my limbs their former h.? HERR 399:34
in temperate h. SURR 829:40
not without dust and h. MILT 579:70
of h. or cold HUME 422:5
stirs up the Native H. PENE 646:19
transmit h. slowly WATT 891:2
trellises Of the h. SITW 793:63
voice of high midsummer's h. ROBE 689:18
white h. of this revolution WILS 915:92
heath foot is on my native h. SCOTT 724:32
  Land of brown h. SCOTT 723:92
  likewise a wind on the h. BORR 145:3
  moths fluttering among the h. BRON 155:99
Heathcliff Nelly, I am H. BRON 155:96
heathen break the h. TENN 846:21
  h. in 'is blindness KIPL 472:18
  h. in 'is blindness KIPL 472:19
  exalted among the h. BIBLE 95:26
  h. Chinee is peculiar HARTE 384:16
  h. for thine inheritance BIBLE 94:84
  h. in the carnal part POPE 661:44
  h. so furiously rage BOOK 142:36
  In h., Turk or Jew BLAKE 134:32
  in soul a h. DICK 270:97
  Why do the h. rage BIBLE 94:82
heather pore benighted h. KIPL 471:94
  pu'd the h. green BALL 55:75
  sweet as the h. LAUD 492:63
  tumble on the h. SCOTT 724:15
  whare the h. grows BURNS 173:45
heaths some game on these lone h. HAZL 387:75
heats give your h. to SHAK 775:9
  h. which my veins fill DONNE 280:44
heaven accusing…h. CAMUS 188:99
  after H.'s own heart DRYD 289:69
  airs from h. SHAK 751:25
  All this, and h. too! HENRY 396:47
  all we know of h. DICK 273:77
  and approving H. THOM 856:54
  any thing that is in h. above BIBLE 88:23
  are the brain of h. MERE 567:8
  as high as h. BIBLE 93:57
  as near to h. GILB 353:88
  as the h. is high BIBLE 97:64
  at h.'s command THOM 856:52
  awful rainbow once in h. KEATS 458:25
  beteem the winds of h. SHAK 751:7
  blue fields of h. KEATS 456:78
  breath of H. fresh-blowing MILT 586:44
  brightest h. of invention SHAK 745:29
  build haunted h. STEV 819:13
  But was a race of h. SHAK 764:17
  By h., I do love SHAK 733:81
  By h., methinks it were SHAK 741:5
  call h. and earth to witness BIBLE 89:44
  choir of h. BERK 79:5
  climb…Toward h. FROST 338:92
  Comfort's in h. SHAK 734:11
  Confess yourself to h. SHAK 754:11
  conquer H. also CARL 191:85
  contains a h., or hell WEBS 895:1
  crawling between h. and earth? SHAK 753:79
  day when h. was falling HOUS 416:79
  dew of h. FORD 330:11
  Did h. look on SHAK 768:30
  don't believe in h. GALL 343:9
  Down from the verge of h. MILT 583:88
  Down on your knees…thank h. SHAK 750:69
  earth and the h. fled away BIBLE 127:78
  Earth's crammed with h. BROW 160:54
  Elijah went up…into h. BIBLE 92:28
  enter into the kingdom of h. BIBLE 110:12
  enter into the kingdom of h. BIBLE 112:66
  enter into the kingdom of h. BIBLE 109:87
  Equality would be a h. TROL 867:3
  eternal joys of h. MARL 552:99
  Even if h. were real LAUR 492:70
  ever-moving spheres of h. MARL 552:6

hedgehog h. of the heart	LOWE 521:58
hedgehogs Thorny h., be not seen	SHAK 737:98
hedges and h. ears	SWIFT 831:90
hedge-sparrow h.-s. fed the cuckoo	SHAK 762:60
heed take h. lest he fall	BIBLE 121:2
heel From h. to throat	YEATS 933:42
In the h. of	KIPL 471:7
lifted up his h. against me	BIBLE 95:19
long thrust of his h.	HUGH 419:38
on the boldest h.	CRANE 243:23
shalt bruise his h.	BIBLE 86:53
well-apparell'd April on the h.	SHAK 735:36
heels At his h. a stone	SHAK 754:16
double-crossing of a pair of h.	HART 384:10
grief...treads upon the h. of pleasure	CONG 231:1
grow out at h.	SHAK 763:67
gunpowder ran out of the h.	FOOTE 329:94
lighten...our wives' h.	SHAK 745:27
like champagne or high h.	BENN 76:43
reclining back upon my h.	WORD 924:87
Heffalump H., a Horrible H.	MILNE 574:80
Hegel H. says somewhere	MARX 558:7
heifer plowed with my h.	BIBLE 90:72
heigh H. ho, h. ho	MOREY 597:75
With h.-ho	SHAK 763:76
height arms is equal to his h.	LEON 504:18
climbed up a h.	SUN 829:29
father moved through depths of h.	CUMM 248:14
Happiness Makes up in H.	FROST 339:8
Holiest in the h.	NEWM 612:66
kindred spider to that h.	FROST 339:5
love will be seen at its h.	FORS 331:36
None can usurp this h.	KEATS 458:15
performed...to such an h.	DRYD 288:29
heights brood on the towering h.	LEAR 497:76
struggle...towards the h.	CAMUS 187:90
heinous what h. sin	SHAK 740:58
heir h. of all things	BIBLE 124:89
h. to an inheritance	OAKE 620:88
I the h. of all the ages	TENN 841:86
never comes but brings an h.	SHAK 769:54
sole h. of the whole world	TRAH 864:39
son of memory, great h.	MILT 576:2
spouting through his h.	POPE 660:4
you are his h.	STOP 825:61
heiress American h.	MCCA 528:95
heirs children; they have h.	NEWM 612:68
if children, then h.	BIBLE 120:74
held H. we fall to rise	BROW 163:95
I'm being h. out to dry	REAG 680:61
Helen hath closèd H.'s eye	NASHE 609:18
H., did Homer never see	JONS 450:50
H., make me immortal	MARL 552:5
H.'s beauty in a brow	SHAK 738:13
H., whose beauty summoned	MARL 551:79
look on H.'s face in hell	PARK 637:56
Past ruined Ilion H. lives	LAND 488:78
where H. lies	BALL 56:78
Helena dross that is not H.	MARL 552:5
Helicon watered our houses in H.	CHAP 206:18
hell allotted death and h.	MARL 553:7
all the tribes of h.	SHAK 759:71
all we need of h.	DICK 273:77
America...may be going to H.	CUMM 247:10
And shall I couple h.?	SHAK 752:34
ane to heaven, an' ten to h.	BURNS 170:65
art as black as h.	SHAK 773:56
believe myself to be in h.	RIMB 688:97
blasts from h.	SHAK 751:25
Came not all h. broke loose?	MILT 583:75
cannot commit evil in h.	GENET 348:5
carried H. about with him	GREE 371:53
characters of h. to trace	GRAY 370:32
charm thy soul to h.	MARL 552:4
childhood prolonged...h.	BOGAN 138:31
claim in h. Precédence	MILT 581:19
contains or heaven, or h.	WEBS 895:1
curse of h. upon the sleek	RANS 679:24
deeper than h.	BIBLE 93:57
Descent into H.	LESS 505:41
Devil Fired into H.	ANON 21:37
Down, down to h.	SHAK 731:86
earth, and heav'n, and h.	POPE 662:68
earth is h. when	NASHE 609:16
England...the h. of horses	FLOR 328:76
extinguish h.	REED 681:81
fetch fire from h.	WEBS 895:95

flowerless rocks of h.	SITW 793:59
focus...on reducing the h.	BORO 145:1
foul as h. within	SHAK 773:49
gates of h. shall not prevail	BIBLE 112:62
good...definition of h.	SHAW 780:70
go to h. like lambs	CHES 212:82
Go to h.. Yours sincerely	ELLI 310:80
great painter of American h.	ALLEN 12:39
hand in hand to h.	SHAK 732:21
having harrowed h.	SPEN 809:96
having harrowed h.	SPEN 809:99
heaven in h.'s despair	BLAKE 134:51
heav'n of h., a h. of heav'n	MILT 580:7
he descended into h.	BOOK 140:71
H. a fury, like a woman scorned	CONG 231:23
H. and destruction are never full	BIBLE 100:60
H. as well as on earth	LEWIS 507:72
h. at the time	WILD 910:70
h. delivered up the dead	BIBLE 127:78
H. followed with him	BIBLE 126:57
H. grant what Love	MILT 576:18
H. hath no limits	MARL 552:1
h. in heaven's despite	BLAKE 134:52
H. is a city	SHEL 784:51
H. is being trapped	JOHN 440:92
H. is full of musical amateurs	SHAW 778:90
H. is murky	SHAK 768:33
H. is other people	SART 715:46
H....is to no longer love	BERN 80:28
h. itself breathes out	SHAK 754:97
h. itself cannot encroach	BAUD 64:54
h. lay about him	GREE 370:50
H. lies about us	MITC 588:85
h. make crooked	SHAK 731:87
h.; myself am h.	MILT 582:55
h. of a good universe	CUMM 248:18
h. of an explosion	CATTO 200:3
h. of an opening	REAG 681:67
h. on earth	SHAW 778:80
h.'s concave, and beyond	MILT 581:12
H.'s darkness under his feet	CARL 193:37
h. should bar the way	NOYES 619:79
h., than serve in heav'n	MILT 580:8
h. they made unmade	MORG 597:81
h. within him, for within him h.	MILT 582:52
her steps take hold on h.	BIBLE 99:13
holiday...excursion to h.	PRIE 668:19
hot from h.	SHAK 748:2
hotter name Than any in h.	SHAK 769:44
how the h. I ever got here	TRUM 868:28
If Hitler invaded H.	CHUR 217:97
I'm neurotic as h.	PLATH 654:73
I myself am h.	LOWE 520:46
In h. they'll roast thee	BURNS 172:24
injured lover's h.	MILT 583:78
in the interests of H.	FORS 331:45
Into the mouth of H.	TENN 845:77
keys of h. and of death	BIBLE 126:46
lead apes in h.	SHAK 732:30
leadest to the gates of h.	BIBLE 107:36
liar gone to burning h.	SHAK 761:13
like Christianity without h.	BORM 145:96
like that in Milton's h.	NERV 611:44
live in freedom and h.	MAIL 540:52
look on Helen's face in h.	PARK 637:56
Love is a Dog from H.	BUKO 165:50
make my bed in h.	BIBLE 98:1
make the earth my h.	SHAK 731:13
man who lives in h.	GALL 343:9
married to h.?	SHAK 732:26
more devils than vast h.	SHAK 738:13
never give them h.	TRUM 868:36
never know where the h. you are	SALI 711:53
never married, and that's his h.	BURT 174:74
never mentions H. to ears polite	POPE 659:96
night seems termless h.	THOM 856:61
No h. below us	LENN 503:91
Oh H.!	SNYD 803:49
out of h. leads up to light	MILT 581:29
passed a h. of time	SHAK 773:50
paving stones for H.	KING 469:64
Pequod packing off to h.	OBRI 621:6
Pope told us all to go to h.	LOWE 520:43
Prompted...by heaven and h.	SHAK 753:69
Quiet to quick bosoms is a h.	BYRON 180:25
readiest way to H.?	ROCH 691:65
riches grow in h.	MILT 581:16

road to h. is paved	ROTH 699:23
save more from H.	BENN 77:58
set on fire of h.	BIBLE 124:13
sounds frae h.	FERG 320:7
tell them the truth and they think it's h.	KEANE 456:74
There is h. as well	HUXL 425:94
there must be h.	BROW 161:35
There's a h. of a distance	PARK 638:69
There's h.	SHAK 763:89
'To h. with ye!' says she	STRO 827:95
too cold for h.	SHAK 767:7
towards the gates of h.	MILT 581:31
walked eye-deep in h.	POUND 664:39
war...is all h.	SHER 788:72
ways of saying 'To h. with you'	FENW 320:91
we stood in h.	OWEN 632:59
What is h.?	ELIOT 309:54
when H. shall be set blazing	KORAN 479:93
whole body...cast into h.	BIBLE 109:90
whose entrance leads to H.	MILT 577:37
Why, this is h.	MARL 552:99
wilt not leave my soul in h.	BIBLE 94:92
with h. are we at agreement	BIBLE 103:27
without a thought of Heaven or H.	BROW 158:75
write about h.	FIEN 323:55
write of H.	HERR 399:32
Hellenism Hebraism and H.	ARNO 34:57
Hellespontus over H. swam	SPEN 809:15
hellfire eyes to be cast into h. f.	BIBLE 112:68
in danger of h. f.	BIBLE 109:88
hellhound Discrimination is a h.	KING 468:42
h. is always a h.	WODE 919:70
hellish whole of the H. nation	SITW 793:60
hello H. sadness	ELUA 312:98
helm at the h. of our country	HOOV 411:60
helmet h. and the h.-feather	TENN 839:49
h. of salvation	BIBLE 122:52
saw the h. and the plume	TENN 839:50
help another h. there's none	HODG 405:45
another to h. him up	BIBLE 100:73
best way to h. the poor	HANC 380:29
can't h. people against their will	FREE 336:41
encumbers him with h.?	JOHN 442:34
from whence cometh my h.	BIBLE 97:87
give them h.	GELL 348:2
h. and support of the woman I love	EDWA 300:20
H., angels!	SHAK 754:2
h. from a government agency	STEIN 815:28
h. him to do it	HALI 378:83
h. me heaven	FIRB 323:68
h. of any ally	GARI 346:47
h. of his countenance	BIBLE 95:21
h. our French comrades	KITC 475:4
h. thou my unbelief	FORS 331:51
How shall I h. you	HOUS 415:58
I get by with a little h.	LENN 503:97
look on and h.	LAWR 494:13
make him an h. meet for him	BIBLE 86:46
mutual h....as often as warfare	DOBZ 277:98
mutual society, h., and comfort	BOOK 142:22
no h. for it	AUBER 38:65
seeking h. from none	GORD 363:5
Since there's no h.	DRAY 287:6
there is no h. in them	BOOK 143:72
they cannot h. him	SHAK 761:28
very present h. in trouble	BIBLE 95:24
where no one can h. him	HEMI 394:22
who can h. it?	ETHE 315:96
without the h. of the air	ETHE 315:98
helper mother's little h.	JAGG 432:17
helpers h. fail and comforts	LYTE 524:17
helping h. every feeble neighbour	GORD 363:5
helpless H., naked, piping loud	BLAKE 135:60
Must h. man	JOHN 441:19
hem h. of Nature's shift	SHEL 784:52
Hemingway back to H.'s work	COWL 240:40
H., remarks are not literature	STEIN 815:13
marriage to Ernest H.	BARR 61:78
hemisphere crystals...in a h.	SCHW 721:69
gilding the eastern h.	SHER 788:65
In the western h.	ROOS 696:53
western to the eastern h.	PEARY 645:2
hemlock h. I had drunk	KEATS 459:57
hen h. is only an egg's way	BUTL 177:66
nought worth a h.	DUNB 294:4
Royal Commission is a broody h.	FOOT 329:92
Two Owls and a H.	LEAR 497:75

hence going h....coming hither · SHAK 764:99
Hendrix H. could do so much better · COST 238:82
H. had both · POP 658:49
hen-pecked have they not h.-p. · BYRON 181:63
Henry H. the Eighth Took a thuctheththion · BENT 78:79
H.VIII....ideal · MACK 534:23
without strict doubt a Hoorah H. · RUNY 702:84
hens h. to moor-cocks call · YEATS 933:45
Hepburn H. runs the gamut · PARK 637:52
Heraclitus H., they told me · CORY 237:74
herald perfectest h. of joy · SHAK 744:97
Revolution is merely the h. · BABE 45:22
heraldic h. equivalent of...furry dice · ANON 25:53
heraldry boast of h. · GRAY 369:14
heralds Nobles and h. · PRIOR 668:31
herb dew-bespangling h. and tree · HERR 400:43
h. for the service of man · BIBLE 97:67
h. that sips the dew · MILT 577:23
light on such another h. · SHAK 762:38
small rain upon the tender h. · BIBLE 90:55
some single h. or tree · MARV 556:71
herbs dinner of h. where love is · BIBLE 99:32
greatest among h. · BIBLE 112:52
In plants, h., stones · SHAK 736:55
spinneys of murdering h. · THOM 853:95
Hercules character like Samson, H. · SIEG 791:24
Let H. himself · SHAK 755:36
herd h. instinct in the individual · NIET 615:7
more numerous was the h. · DRYD 290:87
resigns momentarily from the h. · MACL 535:42
unique to the level of the h. · MILL 573:47
herds h., of human face divine · MILT 582:38
here From H. To Eternity · JONES 447:87
H. am I · BIBLE 102:12
H. am I · BIBLE 91:81
H. am I; send me · BIBLE 102:12
h. and now · HAMM 379:11
h. and now cease to matter · ELIOT 308:26
h. it is at last · JAMES 434:55
H. we are again! · GRIM 373:16
one-tenth H. and Now · SWIFT 830:48
We're h., We're queer · ANON 24:48
Where is h.? · FRYE 340:37
would...never happen h. · FOWL 332:70
hereafter heaven...points out an h. · ADDI 7:38
hereditary peers, and they are h. · LLOY 513:6
heresies begin as h. · HUXL 426:11
hateful h. · SPEN 809:95
h....explosions of faith · BREN 151:15
h. perish not with their authors · BROW 158:60
most interesting ideas are h. · SONT 804:76
heresy ancient saying is no h. · SHAK 740:64
this hidden h. · RAHN 677:91
what an Englishman believes be h.? · SHAW 781:83
widespread modern h. · DRIB 287:10
heretic h. that makes the fire · SHAK 770:80
lawyer and politician and a h. · MENC 565:60
revolutionary ends as...a h. · CAMUS 187:96
heretics burning of the h. · WELD 897:40
heritage British have more h. than is good · BRYS 164:16
children are an h. · BIBLE 98:93
goodly h. · BIBLE 94:91
I have a goodly h. · BOOK 142:42
proud of our ancient h. · KENN 462:12
thy true h. · POUND 665:58
young country is a real h. · MANS 547:96
hermaphrodites Nor even h. · LAUT 493:75
hermit dwell a h. anywhere · LOWE 520:36
In habite an h. unholy · LANG 489:93
hermitage Find out the peaceful h. · MILT 577:23
palace for a h. · SHAK 735:22
That for a h. · LOVE 519:10
Hermon As the dew of H. · BIBLE 98:96
hern haunts of coot and h. · TENN 846:2
hero American history as a great h. · MENC 565:66
Being a h. is about · ROGE 695:28
be your own h. · WINT 917:36
conquering h. comes! · MORE 597:74
definition of a 'h.' · FIND 323:58
Every h. becomes a bore · EMER 313:33
Forgive the h. · WILB 907:72
h. from his prison · AYTO 45:17
h. is a man who would argue · MAIL 540:46
h. is a sneaking piece · SCOTT 723:14
h. of his own life story · BARTH 61:2
h. perish, or a sparrow fall · POPE 660:9
H., Venus' nun · MARL 553:11

memory of a h. · GIBB 351:56
no such thing as a h. · MO 589:23
one murder...millions a h. · PORT 663:13
Show me a h. · FITZ 325:14
Show me a h. · PUZO 673:26
to his very valet seemed a h. · BYRON 181:58
truth about its h. · CHES 211:53
who aspires to be a h. · JOHN 445:37
Herod Oh, for an hour of H.! · HOPE 411:73
heroes become statesmen and h. · WARD 888:56
cowards as quickly as of h. · MITC 588:97
fit country for h. to live in · LLOY 513:4
h. and heroines will have to change · WELD 896:38
h. and villains from fiction · AUDEN 41:27
h. of three recent novels · BROY 163:99
h. to dine with us · TROL 867:97
h. were made · RUSS 706:62
I'll follow the h. · ORAH 626:20
land that has need of h. · BREC 151:9
land that has no h. · BREC 151:9
men...want to be h. · WINT 917:34
past h. of production · LOWE 521:63
puny hands Of h. · COWP 241:77
risk of being h. · BOLT 139:49
sang of...farms and h. · VIRG 882:33
speed glum h. · SASS 716:61
This book is not about h. · OWEN 632:54
Weird h. · THOM 855:42
heroic h., or epic · ROUA 700:38
How h. to be able to · JAMES 433:24
obstacle to being h. · HAWT 386:48
of h. hearts · TENN 840:66
our Ministry is not h. · CECIL 202:27
persons of h. stature · AMIS 15:9
running something much less h. · COOKE 236:39
heroine When a h. goes mad · SHER 788:67
heroines h. will have to change · WELD 896:38
start with plain h. · FITZ 325:16
heroism h. is to resist the doubt · HAWT 386:48
h. of Johnson · STEV 822:1
not the kind of h. they enjoy · WINT 917:34
Unnatural vices...fathered by our h. · ELIOT 305:42
heron h. priested shore · THOM 852:74
reminded me of a h. · BANKS 58:36
herring A plague o' these pickle h.! · SHAK 756:66
roast thee like a h.! · BURNS 172:24
herrings as pilchards are to h. · SHAK 756:73
'New h., new!' · NASHE 609:10
Herzog thought Moses H. · BELL 73:73
hesitate h. and falter life away · ARNO 32:21
h. dislike · POPE 661:38
hesitates He who h. · THUR 859:40
hesitation H. increases in relation · HEMI 395:28
least h. changes it · YOUR 935:82
hest broke your h. to say so! · SHAK 774:89
Heston H. thinks America should arm
its teachers · RUSH 703:94
heterosexual no sensitive h. · MAIL 539:40
hew h. blocks with a razor · POPE 659:88
h. him as a carcass · SHAK 747:84
hey With a h., and a ho. · SHAK 750:88
heyday h. in the blood · SHAK 754:8
hibakusha H., atomic victims · GEE 348:92
hibernation long h. · GRAV 367:72
people live in h. · OHARA 623:50
Hibernia H.'s Land · JOHN 441:13
hick Sticks nix h. pix · ANON 22:57
hickory flavor as h. smoke · MUMF 603:79
hid Where truth is h. · SHAK 752:46
hidden h. even as a strange tongue · DURER 295:28
H. in wonder · SCOTT 722:78
the h. persuaders · PACK 633:71
this h. heresy · RAHN 677:91
hide False face must h. · SHAK 767:92
h. his two ambitious ears · JONS 448:13
h. is sure to flatten 'em · BELL 72:48
h. myself in T. · TOPL 863:15
h. of a rhinoceros · BARR 61:94
h. us from the face · BIBLE 126:58
not smart enough to h. it · REST 683:13
run, but he can't h. · LOUIS 518:3
wrapped in a woman's h.! · SHAK 730:70
hideous always seemed...quite h. · BAUD 65:79
hated because they are h. · RUSS 705:47
h. when...in a child · SHAK 762:62
hides H. from himself · JOHN 441:18
often dealt in h. · DICK 268:52

hiding heart in h. · HOPK 412:90
h. place from the wind · BIBLE 103:32
Thou art my h. place · BIBLE 95:10
waters shall overflow the h. place · BIBLE 103:28
hiechts down frae its auld h. · SMITH 801:25
hierarchy In a h. every employee · PETER 649:76
Hierocles like the pedant in H. · JOHN 443:79
hieroglyphs Words...are but dead h. · MILL 573:51
hierophants Poets are the h. · SHEL 786:17
high ascended on h. · BIBLE 96:39
being h. and solitary · YEATS 933:40
between the h. and low · SIDN 790:10
Chancellor in his H. Court · DICK 269:79
for contempt too h. · COWL 240:35
h. and lifted up · BIBLE 102:11
h. heels are most agreeable · SWIFT 831:78
h. in poor countries · SMITH 798:45
h. Roman fashion · SHAK 765:53
I get h. with a little help · LENN 503:97
return from H. Mass · MACA 525:37
setteth me upon my h. places · BIBLE 94:95
stayed in the h. room · SPEN 807:59
tabernacles of the most H. · BIBLE 95:25
Way up h. · HARB 381:38
highballs Three h. and I think · PARK 638:68
higher capable of h. things · FORS 331:48
Swifter, h., stronger · ANON 22:93
highest h. form of government · SPEN 807:44
h. point of all my greatness · SHAK 775:18
sees farthest who sees h. · BACH 46:27
highflyer h. at Fashion · DICK 271:39
highland between lowland and h. · SWIN 834:51
heart is H. · GALT 344:29
prescribed H. manner · BURG 167:94
solitary H. Lass · WORD 927:34
Highlander no H. need...shame · SCOTT 723:13
highlanders Twelve H. and a bagpipe · ANON 26:87
highlands chieftain to the H. · CAMP 186:70
de-Tibetanization of the H. · MACD 530:47
gang to the H. wi' me? · BALL 56:80
heart's in the H. · BURNS 171:9
In the h. · STEV 823:33
in the Scottish H. · STEV 821:74
Ye H. and ye Lawlands · BALL 55:68
high-minded not an h.-m. · BOOK 143:58
high-water h.-w. mark of my youth · THUR 859:22
The h.-w. mark...of...literature · ORWE 628:44
highway broad h. of the world · SHEL 786:9
h. for our God · BIBLE 103:36
h. shall be there · BIBLE 103:34
make seas our smooth h. · CARL 191:81
highwayman h. came riding · NOYES 619:78
highways happy h. · HOUS 415:60
spacious h. of books · SAND 713:13
hijackers starve...the h. · THAT 850:24
hilarity h. was like a scream · GREE 371:56
sinking flame of h. · DICK 267:15
Hilary I like H. · PAGL 634:83
hill All, all, are sleeping on the h. · MAST 560:52
as it trundles down the h. · TROL 867:99
Behind the cloud-topped h. · POPE 660:11
city that is set on an h. · BIBLE 109:85
climbed a h. as light fell short · HODG 405:43
deer from the h. · SCOTT 723:13
dwell in thy holy h.? · BIBLE 94:90
flung us on the windy h. · BROO 155:2
God's h. · BOOK 143:58
green h. far away · ALEX 11:25
haven under the h. · TENN 840:68
h. of beans · GARN 346:52
h. of beans in this crazy world · EPST 314:79
h. of frankincense · BIBLE 101:2
h. or field or river · TENN 842:5
h. will not come to Mahomet · BACON 48:5
huge h., Cragged, and steep · DONNE 279:31
huge h. of flesh · SHAK 742:15
hunter home from the h. · STEV 822:10
hunts on a lonely h. · SHARP 776:38
meadow and the h. · ROBE 689:19
o'er the h. the eastern star · BURNS 172:39
Over h., over dale · SHAK 737:92
rolls down a h. · TAKU 835:80
round it was, upon a h. · STEV 819:12
Shepherd, from the h. · ARNO 32:15
sit upon a h. · SHAK 730:75
sleep upon his h. · LIND 511:51
stood upon that silent h. · HODG 405:44

war h....simple one WODE 919:73
War makes rattling good h. HARDY 382:74
way of indicating how h. MALA 541:81
We make h. REAG 680:62
What is h., in fact IRVI 430:78
What will H. say? SHAW 777:69
whole of contemporary h. ROY 701:56
Who owns h.? NEW 611:50
You appear before h. CLEM 220:75
hit A h., a very palpable h. SHAK 755:39
can't think and h. BERRA 82:57
get there; h. it RANJ 678:17
h. a ball further PRIE 668:28
h. at all if it can be avoided ROOS 696:56
h. that stride and keep it SAND 713:13
hither transported h. and thither OVID 631:47
Hitler at least H. was mad LIVI 512:87
cable H. and ask him GOLD 362:77
destruction of H. CHUR 217:97
every Christian in H.'s Europe FACK 317:31
German Chancellor, Herr H. CHAM 204:62
grew up scared of H. BAIL 52:98
Herr H. and Signor Mussolini HALI 378:84
H. attacked the Jews NIEM 614:3
H. had already found ROBI 690:41
H.'s gas chambers MEIR 563:12
H. showed surprising loyalty BULL 166:53
H. was a Jeanne d'Arc POUND 665:57
H. was dead SCHA 717:95
H....missed the bus CHAM 204:66
Like kissing H. CURT 249:49
marches with H. CHUR 217:81
people H. never understood BULL 166:54
Was not H. a paper tiger MAO 548:11
When I go to see Herr H. HEND 395:35
hits go to see h. JOUR 451:74
hive angry h. of bees SHAK 730:58
bitter h. to grope for honey SPEN 809:2
h. for the honey-bee YEATS 932:30
in the h. of home MACN 538:4
hives fill our h. with honey SWIFT 830:53
hoard Our h. is little TENN 846:7
To h. is...villainous RABE 676:71
Hoare Samuel H. was the pygmiest BOOT 144:83
hoary h. hills are seen POPE 662:66
Hobbes H. clearly proves SWIFT 832:1
hobbit in the ground there lived a h. TOLK 862:95
hobbit-hole h.-h....comfort TOLK 862:95
hobbits H. are an unobtrusive TOLK 862:1
hobby suggests an elaborate h. PRIE 668:23
hobby-horse man rides his H.-H. STER 817:70
hobgoblin h. of little minds EMER 312:8
hobnailed That h. goblin SITW 794:67
hobo-trekkers H.-t. that forever CRANE 243:17
hock sipped at the weak h. BETJ 83:81
hodgepodge h. of all other speeches SPEN 808:71
hoe But to take a large h. KIPL 472:37
tickle her with a h. JERR 437:39
Hofstadter H.'s Law HOFS 406:54
hog disadvantage of being a h. MORT 600:20
H. Butcher for the World SAND 713:?
h. that could fiddle ROCH 691:64
mere h. at his trough HUNT 423:36
put lipstick on a h. RICH 686:60
talk h. and hominy FERB 320:95
hogamus H., higamous JAMES 434:75
hogs Fattenin' h. ain't in luck HARR 383:94
fatting h. of late SPEN 810:17
let it not be like h. MCKA 533:11
Holbein H. of Jell-O ads ADLER 7:49
hold first cries 'H., enough!' SHAK 769:46
h. down one thing BELL 73:70
h. fast that which is good BIBLE 123:71
H. fast the form of sound words BIBLE 124:83
H., h., my heart SHAK 752:34
H. on, h. on! ANON 24:35
H. them cheap HOPK 413:5
H. then my sword SHAK 748:23
like to h. it back SEVI 728:10
To have and to h. BOOK 142:26
undermine her h. on life FORS 331:43
Holding bowler's H. JOHN 447:79
hole decayed h. among the mountains ELIOT 306:66
dry, bare, sandy h. TOLK 862:95
flame creeps in at every h. PEELE 646:12
h. in the ground TOLK 862:95
h. in the subconscious HALE 377:79

h. that allows the mouse in JACO 432:13
kick a h. in a stained glass window CHAN 204:75
Might stop a h. SHAK 755:33
not enough...to be h. BRAT 150:95
sphere into an inaccessible h. CHUR 217:8
holes into a bag with h. BIBLE 106:14
holiday His first h. BOUC 146:20
h. steamers made an excursion PRIE 668:19
in a h. humour SHAK 750:76
perpetual h. is a good...definition SHAW 780:70
regular h. to them DICK 266:85
Roman h. BYRON 180:39
two years in H. Inns MOND 590:48
holidays h. from Eton SITW 794:81
h....interfere with one's work EDWA 300:21
H....learning experience OGDEN 622:38
Term, h., term, h. LEWIS 507:78
holier h. lot to be unknown HOPK 412:96
h. than thou BIBLE 104:64
In h. shapes SHAK 762:49
holiness beauty of h. BIBLE 97:59
h. of always being the injured party ANGE 17:42
mind is bent to h. SHAK 730:52
vision of the h. of God BLOOM 137:5
way of h. BIBLE 103:34
Holland Dutch may have their H. JOHN 440:94
H....lies so low HOOD 410:42
hollow Down to the h. FLAN 326:22
h., heartless, mirthless THUR 860:51
h. of thine ear SHAK 736:68
waters in the h. of his hand BIBLE 103:38
We are the h. men ELIOT 306:69
hollow-headed h.-h. mediocrity MENC 566:86
hollowness h. disappoints at the time BRON 155:89
Reverb no h. SHAK 762:53
hollows bowery h. crowed TENN 847:52
Hollywood America gets H. JONG 448:5
Americans...considered H. MAMET 543:30
average H. film star HEPB 396:58
every actor in H. GIEL 353:86
Hooray for H. MERC 566:92
Inside this H. playboy FLYNN 328:78
I should not have been invited to H. CHAN 204:79
not very keen on H. COWA 240:28
vote for H. as a Republican WALL 886:2
Wants steady employment in H. DAVIS 255:52
holme carver h. SPEN 808:73
Holmes H. remarked, impatiently DOYLE 285:77
John Clellon H....and I KERO 464:65
To Sherlock H. she is always DOYLE 285:64
Holocaust truth of the H. WEIZ 896:35
holsters inside of his h. SHAW 777:52
holy be h....with impunity? RACI 677:87
called the H. Roman Empire VOLT 883:45
cased up, like a h. relic WEBS 895:10
coming to that h. room DONNE 281:80
discipline of our h. Church OCON 621:19
give solemn thanks to the H. Trinity COLU 229:62
great source of the h. river SPEKE 806:35
h. alliance to exorcise MARX 558:4
h. and enchanted COLE 226:10
H. Catholic and Apostolic TEMP 838:34
H. Deadlock HERB 397:80
H., divine, good MILT 584:14
h.; for I am h. BIBLE 89:33
H., h., h. BIBLE 126:54
H., h., h. BOOK 141:5
H., h., h., is the Lord BIBLE 102:11
H., H., H.! Lord God Almighty! HEBER 390:35
h. hush STEV 819:17
h. nation BIBLE 125:24
h. place of the tabernacles BIBLE 95:25
h. rest, and peace NEWM 612:63
h. Satan DAMI 251:79
h. thing to see BLAKE 134:55
h. unto the dogs BIBLE 110:6
Made h. by their dreams GIBS 352:75
Nothing but h., pure, and clear HERB 397:90
place...is h. ground BIBLE 88:9
proofs of h. writ SHAK 760:91
religion would still be h. and divine BAUD 65:75
Sabbath...making it h. WALK 885:97
Sae pious and sae h. BURNS 170:86
suffer thine H. One BIBLE 94:92
thy h. feet BLAKE 133:23
touch of h. bread SHAK 750:68
holy-day free And h.-d....spirit LAMB 486:39

Holy Ghost Because the H.G. HOPK 412:84
blasphemy against the H.G. BIBLE 111:41
but by the H.G. BIBLE 121:7
filled with the H.G. BIBLE 119:29
Have ye received the H.G.? BIBLE 119:52
H.G. is come upon you BIBLE 118:27
I believe in the H.G. BOOK 140:71
I believe in the H.G. BOOK 141:96
John Wesley and the H.G. MENC 566:84
pretending to...gifts of the H.G. BUTL 176:32
temple of the H.G. BIBLE 121:95
who was conceived by the H.G. BOOK 140:71
Holy Grail see the H.G. MALO 542:9
There lies the H.G. MACA 524:22
Holy See insult to the H.S. INNO 430:71
Holy Spirit H.S....invisible TAYL 838:34
inspiration of thy H.S. BOOK 141:92
holy-water h.-w. death MCGO 532:81
homage both an h. and a critique MOTH 600:32
h. of a tear BYRON 179:10
H. to plain dumb luck ACHE 3:47
involuntarily pay h. POTT 664:20
home advocating for H. Rule MCGO 532:80
against books the H. Secretary WAUGH 892:26
airs have brought me h. POE 656:22
ALL parts and none are h. MAIL 540:65
always a bad sign, at h. MITF 589:12
and I am far from h. NEWM 612:62
and returning h. BUCH 164:31
Are they being...too much at h.? COLE 225:74
At h., whispering OWEN 632:62
At h., you always have to be MACM 536:70
best country ever is, at h. GOLD 361:40
blest by suns of h. BROO 156:6
both h. runs and strike outs RODG 693:93
call the cattle h. KING 469:48
came h., h. to a lie POUND 664:39
Can't Go H. Again WOLFE 920:89
cart with the h. packed COLL 227:36
chickens have come h. to roost MAMET 543:28
children who leave h. SLOVO 796:19
Comes h. again SHAK 772:35
consequence of leaving one's h. LEBO 499:16
could have stayed h. CLIN 222:8
domestic servants at h. MAUG 561:81
dream of going 'h.' PARK 638:83
dream of H. FORD 330:20
dream that I am h. again! FLEC 327:50
drive one from h. HOOD 410:43
dunce that has been kept at h. COWP 241:63
E.T. phone h. MATH 560:60
everything off and went h. SZIL 834:66
Family!... the h. of all social evil STRI 827:94
feel ashamed of h. DICK 271:31
field, or a h. WILD 911:82
friends, and native h. MILT 577:26
gat him h. to his house BIBLE 91:5
get h. from work PARKS 639:90
give me a h. HIGL 402:86
God, who is our h. WORD 926:24
Hang my Hat is H. JERO 437:37
Heaven and H. WORD 929:61
hills of h.! STEV 823:36
h. among the dead SHEL 786:9
h. and put a bullet ROBI 690:28
'h.'—a real life MANS 546:83
h. his footsteps...turned SCOTT 723:91
h., in a flood of tears DICK 266:82
H. is heaven NASH 608:86
H. is the girl's prison SHAW 779:71
H. is the place FROST 338:87
H. is where one starts from ELIOT 308:25
H. I would go OTWAY 631:26
H. James HILL 403:94
H. life as we understand it SHAW 780:53
h. life of our own dear Queen ANON 21:39
H. of lost causes ARNO 33:39
h. of the brave? KEY 465:76
h. of the scorpion SNYD 803:49
h. of the weird LAWS 495:43
h....saved by his courage MACA 527:78
H.'s h. ARBU 28:33
H. they brought TENN 842:11
h. to...Jews, Muslims and Christians CLIN 221:91
h., you idle creature SHAK 746:70
House is not a H. ADLER 7:52
humble h. GLAD 358:91

husbands to stay at h. ELIOT 303:92
I can get all that at h. COOK 235:35
if they go from h. GASK 346:58
in my bosom, and at h. JONS 449:39
in the hive of h. MACN 538:4
into the h.—where it belongs HITC 404:14
isn't much to write h. about HYDE 427:22
it never is at h. COWP 240:49
keep the Sabbath…staying at H. DICK 272:59
Kiss till the cow comes h. BEAU 67:11
last night the cows came h. NATH 609:22
live at h., quiet, confined AUST 44:96
lov'd at h., rever'd abroad BURNS 170:70
luminous h. of waters ARNO 32:28
Lurching to…'H. sweet H.' SASS 716:57
man who thinks to found a h. DOUG 283:26
merely ready to go h. KAIKO 454:33
merriest when they are from h. SHAK 745:31
milk comes frozen h. SHAK 734:94
My h. policy? I wage war CLEM 221:76
national h. for the Jews BALF 54:54
never felt myself from h. BOSW 146:11
never to attempt to make at h. SMITH 798:48
Next to a letter from h. DOOL 282:99
not a thing remains at h. BELLI 72:42
not yet gone h. THUR 859:17
ocean…was his h. BYRON 179:21
our eternal h. WATTS 891:5
out of house and h. SHAK 742:46
problems of running a h. THAT 850:17
refuge from h. life SHAW 777:63
Rowing h. to haven MASE 559:26
small places, close to h. ROOS 695:39
snail…is at h. DONNE 280:62
sons, her h., her food NATI 610:25
stay at h. and help WINT 917:34
stay at h., my noble lord BALL 55:74
Stay h. and cause no trouble AESC 8:61
They should go back h. BLUN 137:21
thou art my h. PRIOR 669:42
till the cows come h. MARX 557:87
toddle safely h. and die SASS 716:62
to go h. in the dark OHEN 623:57
to the mountains is going h. MUIR 602:64
turning my face towards h. PARK 637:38
unconquerable…the American h. SELZ 727:87
was just that I was leaving h. STEV 823:37
welcome h. to me! BURNS 171:97
What's the good of a h. GROS 374:23
When I was at h. SHAK 749:42
when mum stays h. FALU 317:41
who gives a child a h. MASE 559:35
woman's true position in the h. STAN 812:63
women are to stay at h. WEST 901:39
you can't go h. again BRYS 164:15
You will be h. before WILH 911:93
home-acre hearth-fire and the h.-a. KIPL 473:60
homecoming h. of…companions HOMER 409:24
home-fires Keep the H.-f. burning FORD 330:20
home-keeping H.-k. youth SHAK 729:23
homeland h. is sweet to him HUGH 418:14
live in his h. BELL 72:39
PLO is a h. NEW 611:53
homeless fine for the h. VAN 877:32
h. and self-forgetful WHIT 904:14
h. by choice SOUT 805:7
h. man in a thousand dollar suit ANON 25:64
h., tempest-tossed LAZA 496:51
homely female shall be h. KENN 462:2
h. slighted Shepherd's trade MILT 578:49
home-made H.-m. dishes HOOD 410:43
Homer a simple digamma in H. QUIL 674:47
blind H. sing to me? MARL 552:3
Helen, did H. never see JONS 450:50
H.…chronicled the siege of Troy CUOMO 248:30
H. invariably composes ARNO 33:34
H.…Never existed. FLAU 327:42
in H. than H. knew SWIFT 832:97
Mr Gladstone read H. CHUR 216:66
never read a line of H. MILL 572:29
Shakespeare was the H. DRYD 288:31
Virgil and H. DRYD 288:45
when the worthy H. nods HORA 414:34
homes firelit h., clean beds and wives SASS 716:60
h. of silent prayer TENN 843:37
stately h. of England COWA 239:18
stately h. of England HEMA 393:90

homesteads carry fire…into your h. PARN 639:92
homeward Look h. Angel MILT 578:56
sent him h. tae think again WILL 914:65
homewards Most roads lead men h. MASE 559:30
homey taste of lies was h. GELL 348:99
hominy Mrs H.…slowly up it DICK 268:47
talk hog and h. FERB 320:95
homme h. n'est rien d'autre SART 715:50
h. n'est rien d'autre SART 715:52
homo Ecce h. BIBLE 128:4
h. sapiens, a vertebrate mammal CARB 189:37
neotenic ape, species h. sapiens ALDI 10:12
homos stately h. of England CRISP 245:58
homosexuality H. was the badge EAGL 297:65
preoccupied with his latent h. MAIL 539:40
honest any h. man's GILB 354:3
both h. and intelligent ORWE 629:92
for h. Poverty BURNS 173:46
good h. and painful PEPYS 647:29
hated…when I tried to be h. ELLI 311:89
h. God INGE 429:56
h. man's the noble work of GOD BURNS 170:70
h. men and bonny lasses BURNS 172:14
h., old-fashioned Boarding-school AUST 43:81
h., sonsie face BURNS 171:88
hope to remain h. HOWE 417:2
in a general h. thought SHAK 748:25
like an h. man SHAK 744:4
looking for an h. man DIOG 275:22
man who lies…is an h. man SAFI 708:99
moderately h. man SHAW 779:16
most of us are h. all the time MATH 560:59
not h.…but he is most evangelical BEAV 67:20
not naturally h. SHAK 770:95
obscure things that are h. BIBLE 107:33
one of the few h. people FITZ 325:95
people…are least h. AUST 43:72
To be h. SHAK 752:47
whatsoever things are h. BIBLE 123:61
world's grown h. SHAK 752:52
writer overwhelmingly h. MOORE 595:39
write straight h. prose HEMI 394:9
honestly deal with each other h. CHAN 205:89
honesty Art, whose h. must work RIDI 687:81
brings more h. and care WEBB 893:64
full of love and h. SHAK 760:84
h. be no puritan SHAK 761:27
H. coupled to beauty SHAK 750:67
h. is a good thing MARQ 554:29
h. is his SHAK 762:45
h. is not to be based RUSK 704:27
H. was a cheat OTWAY 631:28
it lacks h. YEATS 934:61
most important thing…is h. GOLD 362:90
people are shocked by h. COWA 239:20
perilous to a man's h. TROL 867:95
so rich as h. SHAK 761:32
that damn'd…quality call'd h. OTWAY 631:27
transform h. from what it is SHAK 753:78
Wisdom without h. JONS 450:53
writers…have a terrible h. CHAN 205:93
honey Believe me, h. TUCK 870:62
bitter hive to grope for h. SPEN 809:2
buzzes in the h. there THOM 853:94
Come Back…Huck H.! FIED 322:28
drowned in the h. HAWT 386:37
eat my peas with h. NASH 609:9
fill our hives with h. SWIFT 830:53
flowing with milk and h. BIBLE 88:11
h., and plenty of money LEAR 497:83
h. a sauce to sugar SHAK 750:67
h. of all flowers NASHE 609:11
h. of poison-flowers TENN 845:80
h. pot for every scholar SAFER 708:95
h. wild, and manna dew KEATS 458:18
how can I be h. now? OLSEN 624:73
in my mouth sweet as h. BIBLE 126:64
is there h. still for tea? BROO 156:15
locusts and wild h. BIBLE 108:75
milk and h. blessed NEALE 610:28
Money…sweeter than H. FRAN 334:10
Pedigree of H. DICK 273:75
Reach me a rose, h. FITZ 325:97
scoop of pure h. SMITH 799:61
summer's h. breath SHAK 772:25
sweeter than h. BIBLE 97:83
honey-bee hive for the h.-b. YEATS 932:30

honeycomb gave him…an h. BIBLE 117:70
lips…drop as an h. BIBLE 99:13
honey-dew he on h.-d. hath fed COLE 226:15
honeymoon H.'s over…get married EPST 315:83
Hong Kong buildings of H. K. BOOTH 144:82
honour All h.'s mimic DONNE 279:42
as an h. to Shakespeare JONS 450:55
Can H.'s voice provoke GRAY 369:15
Cavalier who loves h. SCOTT 725:58
chastity of h. BURKE 169:35
Chief who in h. advances! SCOTT 723:5
clear h.…purchased by the merit SHAK 740:63
crowned him with glory and h. BIBLE 94:87
for the h. of England CONG 231:28
fount whence h. springs MARL 551:76
from the book of h. raze'd SHAK 771:12
full of days, riches, and h. BIBLE 92:41
Giving h. unto the wife BIBLE 125:27
glory, laud and h. NEALE 610:27
goblin H. which the world adores CAREW 190:59
had the h. to be TILL 860:70
he was valiant, I h. him SHAK 748:4
his h. and his quality taken BLUN 137:16
His h. rooted TENN 846:19
H. all men BIBLE 125:25
h. and good actions BACON 49:32
h. aspireth to it BACON 47:74
H. but an empty bubble DRYD 291:38
h. cuts falsehood GURN 375:44
h. did but jest GREE 371:78
h., duty, patriotism LLOY 513:99
h., fredom and curteisie CHAU 208:68
h., her reputation, and her person GOTT 364:18
h. is a private station ADDI 7:37
H. is like a match PAGN 634:85
h. is my life SHAK 734:99
H. is not the exclusive property HOOV 411:66
h., it is no longer peace RUSS 706:64
h. lies in killing men MARG 549:43
h., love, obedience SHAK 768:37
h. May privilege more sins SHIR 789:80
h. of God BACH 46:25
h. of the British Empire CHUR 217:84
H. pricks me on SHAK 742:27
h. turn to dust MARV 556:63
h. unto Luke Evangelist ROSS 698:98
h. would thee do SHAK 745:33
how I do h. thee! SHAK 740:81
hurt that H. feels TENN 840:80
If I lose mine h. SHAK 765:33
If your h. disna ken SCOTT 724:29
in her left hand riches and h. BIBLE 99:12
It is not for me, Your H. BIRK 130:66
Jealous in h. SHAK 749:50
Keeps h. bright SHAK 757:6
leave not a stain in thine h. BIBLE 108:63
left to the fighter's h. HEMI 394:5
Legion of H. TWAIN 870:90
louder he talked of his h. EMER 313:44
Loved I not h. more LOVE 519:14
mace of h. MANC 544:44
make one vessel unto h. BIBLE 120:79
no spark of h. bides SHAK 730:69
Observe his h. DONNE 279:43
Of power, of h. MARL 552:96
once stood for h. WHITE 902:71
only h. and life…spared FRAN 333:94
peace, I hope, with h. DISR 277:85
Peace without h. CECIL 202:26
pension list…a roll of h. CLEV 221:80
pluck bright h. SHAK 741:5
prophet is not without h. BIBLE 112:54
Render…h. to whom h. BIBLE 120:86
reputation for wisdom and h. BIBLE 101:86
Set h. in one eye SHAK 747:74
signed with their h. SPEN 807:47
sin to covet h. SHAK 746:55
some smatch of h. SHAK 748:23
staff of h. for mine age SHAK 731:89
stain her h., or…brocade POPE 659:70
symbol of national h. KRUG 481:26
them that h. me I will h. BIBLE 91:80
this journey…and the h. thereof EDWA 300:16
To h. his own words TENN 846:21
Upon my h. PARK 638:78
when h. dies WHIT 906:57
with native h. clad MILT 582:61

with wealth and h. blest	DRYD 290:78
honourable Brutus is an h. man	SHAK 748:5
designs were strictly h.	FIEL 322:43
intentions are perfectly h.	SHAW 779:34
most h.…was to steal	RABE 676:63
surrender…was as h. as resistance	ANGE 17:34
true and h. wife	SHAK 747:86
whatever is sweet, and h.	MELV 564:32
honoured but h. of them all	TENN 839:63
H. and bless'd be	SCOTT 723:5
h. by your friends	HOOV 411:70
More h. in the breach	SHAK 751:24
honouring wirschep and great h.	DUNB 294:2
honours bears his blushing h.	SHAK 775:20
neither h. nor wages	GARI 346:48
talk of high h.	TS 869:53
hood him that wears a h.	ANON 20:2
racing car whose h.	MARI 550:53
wear the h.	DUNC 295:14
Hoo-doo H.-d.…unorganized	REED 682:86
hoods gaudy h. and linings!	DICK 267:25
hoofs plunging h. were gone	DELA 260:65
hook button, h., and lace	LOWE 519:23
by h. or by crook	MORE 596:57
draw out leviathan with an h.?	BIBLE 94:78
head down on the h.	JUST 453:12
Not a h. in all my breast	VAUG 878:48
hookers played so many h.	MACL 534:24
hook-nosed h.-n. fellow of Rome	SHAK 743:62
hooks baited h. shall tangle	WYATT 930:99
With silken lines, and silver h.	DONNE 280:53
hooligans Football h.?	CLOU 223:41
hoops pot shall have ten h.	SHAK 730:63
with h. of steel	SHAK 751:17
hooray Dear Mrs A, H., h.	COWA 239:19
H. for Hollywood	MERC 566:92
hooter because the h. hoots	CHES 212:82
Hoover H. with a smile	ONEI 626:9
hop H. forty paces	SHAK 765:25
hope Abandon all h.	DANTE 252:94
against h. believed in h.	BIBLE 120:64
belief and h. had gone	RUSS 706:61
Can something, h.	HOPK 412:2
do not h. to turn	ELIOT 306:78
exercise of h.	WORD 927:39
fair exchange when we h.	MILT 578:49
faith, h., charity	BIBLE 121:9
feeble H. could ne'er	MARV 556:66
Flesh Of H..	NICH 613:86
fruitful of nourishment	SPEN 809:15
gathers her most vital h.	MELV 564:27
God shall be my h.	SHAK 730:55
high h. of adventure	WHIT 904:9
high uplifted beyond h.	MILT 581:18
H., art thou true	SIDN 790:12
h. could have no fear	THOM 856:64
H. deferred maketh the heart sick	BIBLE 99:25
H., for a season	CAMP 186:67
h. for the best	SMITH 801:13
h. full of immortality	BIBLE 107:31
H. guides us by her star	BRON 155:86
h. has often caused	SOPH 804:82
h. in Christ	BIBLE 121:13
H. is a good breakfast	BACON 47:70
H. is the power of being cheerful	CHES 211:51
'H.' is the thing with feathers	DICK 272:58
h., love of finished years	ROSS 697:74
H. may vanish	SHEL 786:19
h. never comes That comes to all	MILT 580:97
h. of glory	BOOK 141:84
h. of instant results	SCHL 718:15
h. of science	INGE 429:55
h. of winning her love	STAEL 811:46
h., once crushed	ARNO 33:48
h. on God is founded	BRID 152:26
h. sleeps in our bones	PIER 651:10
h. so transcendent	LAWR 495:39
H. springs eternal	POPE 660:10
h.'s true gage	RALE 677:99
h. that he will die	EMER 313:40
h. thou in God	BIBLE 95:21
h. to get one every 30 years	SIMON 792:40
H. to joy is little less	SHAK 734:12
h.…unwilling to be fed	WORD 926:18
H. ushers in a Revolution	CARL 192:5
H. withering fled	BYRON 181:48
Idle to h.	REED 681:81

if…h. should e'er decline	WORD 929:63
I h. in thee	STUA 827:99
illusions that…limit h.	FRYE 340:39
in the store we sell h.	REVS 684:20
in trembling h. repose	GRAY 370:26
Is it too much to h.	REDM 681:72
Land of H. and Glory	BENS 77:61
land of their heart's h.	DAVIS 256:66
lined himself with h.	SHAK 742:44
living h. rose in me	FOX 333:77
Love without h.	GRAV 368:87
Maybe all one can do is h.	MILL 572:11
may be brought to h.	TROL 867:92
may we bring h.	THAT 850:16
miserable have…only h.	SHAK 758:31
must run with h.	ZATO 936:89
Nature to his h. has giv'n	POPE 660:11
no h. of finding ourselves	MILL 572:27
nor h. nor health	SHEL 783:32
no very lively h.	SMITH 801:24
one more rich h.	SHAK 771:14
only h. of creating something	FLAU 326:36
others have to h. for heaven	SLOAN 796:18
Our h. for years to come	WATTS 891:5
place where sanity and h.	ROUS 700:39
poise of h. and fear	MILT 577:36
power of the h. of freedom	BUCK 165:36
Rootless h.	BINY 130:54
Some blessed H.	HARDY 382:70
spring of h.	DICK 271:19
strength and my h. is perished	BIBLE 105:81
this pleasing h.	ADDI 7:38
Through love, through h.	WORD 928:59
triumph of h.	JOHN 444:91
True h. is swift	SHAK 731:14
unconquerable h.	ARNO 32:23
wait without h.	ELIOT 308:14
Whatever h. is yours	OWEN 632:60
what h. of harmony?	SHAK 730:54
what was dead was H.	WILDE 910:56
What…we may gain from h.	MILT 580:5
Where there is despair, h.	FRAN 334:98
who can h.	WALL 886:16
wish for what I faintly h.	DRYD 287:16
woes which H. thinks infinite	SHEL 785:83
hopeful To be h. in an artistic sense	CONR 234:9
hopelessness h. of knowing	LEAC 496:63
hopes airy h.	WORD 928:55
all h. to disappear	GILB 354:98
clues, h., and fears	LIPP 511:67
Cricket is…full of forlorn h.	ORWE 629:70
day with high h.	CLIN 221:89
different yearnings, different h.	CART 198:46
fifty h. and fears	BROW 161:48
fondest h. decay	MOORE 596:53
forgive me for not fulfilling some h.	YELT 935:71
h. and dreams of the Future	FRAME 333:81
h. and h. to fears	SHAK 773:49
h. and prayers of liberty-loving people	EISE 302:49
h. of future years	LONG 516:54
How strangely h. delude men	MASS 560:49
If h. were dupes	CLOU 222:21
late on h. depended	SHAK 759:66
nor as happy as one h.	LARO 491:50
shipwrecking all their h.	MOOD 594:8
tender leaves of h.	SHAK 775:20
To sympathy with h. and fears	SHEL 784:58
vanity of human h.	JOHN 441:24
hoping go truly h. to find adventure	HEAT 390:27
h.…someone will make things right	REAG 680:54
Hopper Do you know, Mr H.	WILDE 908:15
H. is the great painter	ALLEN 12:39
hoppy H., Croppy, Droppy	ELLIS 311:81
hop-yards for what were h.-y. meant	HOUS 415:65
Horatio more things…H.	SHAK 752:38
O, I die, H.!	SHAK 755:42
Horatius H. kept the bridge	MACA 526:68
out spake brave H.	MACA 526:63
stood brave H.	MACA 526:66
horde language of the h.	MALL 542:95
Society is now one polished h.	BYRON 182:96
horizon always somebody else's h.!	GRAH 366:38
h. of daily environment	EINS 301:33
multiplying on the sold h.	WALC 884:78
narrow h. of bourgeois	MARX 558:14
neither h., cloud, nor sound	CARR 194:54
pressing up over the h.	TIME 860:72

workhouse from the h.	LLOY 513:98
horizons h. come	HUGH 419:38
sorrow's h. are vague	MCMU 537:89
horizontal h. desire	SHAW 781:92
your position would be h.	OHARA 623:49
horn blind H.'s hate	KIPL 474:78
h., the h., the lusty h.	SHAK 750:82
hunter's h. is ringing	SCOTT 723:9
if we can pick up a h.	FREE 336:39
it won't come out of your h.	PARK 637:40
keys of a postboy's h.	BENET 75:10
Poured thro' the mellow h.	COLL 228:49
'scorn' 'h.', a hard rhyme	SHAK 745:24
small but sullen h.	COLL 228:47
wreathèd h.	WORD 928:46
Hornby my H. and my Barlow	THOM 855:39
hornets wasps and h. break through	SWIFT 830:58
Hornie Auld H., Satan, Nick	BURNS 170:77
hornpipes h. and strathspeys	BURNS 172:38
horns got to draw in their h.	LEMAY 502:75
h. of cockled snails	SHAK 733:83
h. of Elfland	TENN 841:4
keeping clear of her h.	SZENT 834:65
Morning on the silver h.	TENN 842:16
on the h. o'th' moon	SHAK 769:57
pulled in their h.	JUVE 453:19
taking the bull by both h.	ASHF 35:1
With its h. through mist	THOM 852:75
horny-handed H.-h. sons of toil	SALI 711:67
horrible grotesque to the h.	DOYLE 285:81
It is h., yet fascinating	DOYLE 285:76
people were so h.	AMIS 14:90
to not feel any, that is h.	VIAN 880:79
horribly h. in love with her	SHAK 744:8
horrid h. malicious bloody flame	PEPYS 647:47
h. thing, a very h. thing	BUTL 176:32
h. thing to follow	JAMES 433:39
was bad, she was h.	LONG 516:67
horror beauty…watch it only full of h.	VIEI 881:12
boredom, and the h., and the glory	ELIOT 307:86
define your own h. journey	GELL 348:1
haunts of h. and fear	TENN 845:97
H. and doubt distract	MILT 582:52
h.…for a whole nation	WHAR 901:45
h. of civil war	HOMER 409:21
h. of Creation	HUGH 419:48
h. of outer darkness	GORD 363:7
h. of the Twentieth Century	MAIL 540:56
H., tyrant of the throbbing breast	GRAY 370:35
I have a h. of the word	RENO 683:7
in the midst of h.	ANGE 16:30
no imagination…no h.	DOYLE 285:48
one expanding h. in American life	MAIL 540:52
secret dread, and inward h.	ADDI 7:38
The h.! The h.!	CONR 234:99
horrors Congenial h., hail!	THOM 856:57
I have supped full with h.	SHAK 769:41
horse Always look a gift h.	RABE 676:68
behold a pale h.	BIBLE 126:57
behold a white h.	BIBLE 127:75
between a rider and his h.	SURT 829:42
Be ye not as the h.	BIBLE 95:11
camel is a h.	ISSI 431:97
courage to ride a h.	LEAC 496:55
cup won by the worst h.	MASE 559:39
dearer than his h.	TENN 840:77
definition of a h.	DICK 270:2
duchess-faced h.	THOM 853:2
even do for a h.	NIGH 616:35
flung himself upon his h.	LEAC 496:62
fond of a h.	HALI 378:82
for want of a h.	FRAN 334:13
Give me another h.!	SHAK 731:16
given the h. strength?	BIBLE 93:74
Go not my h. the better	SHAK 768:11
hear a h.'s feet	KIPL 473:61
h. came spurring in	MACA 526:70
h. drench to bring 'em off	LAMB 486:36
h. in the silence champed the grasses	DELA 260:63
h. is drawn by the cart	KIPL 471:4
h. on the mountain	LORCA 517:85
H. riding is a perfect comparison	
with singing	PAVA 644:78
kingdom for a h.!	SHAK 732:23
leene was his h. as is a rake	CHAU 208:71
never heard no h. sing	ARMS 30:76
never look at another h.	MARX 557:90

no handles to a h. — LEAC 496:54
No h.'s cry was that — ARNO 32:25
nothing but talk of his h. — SHAK 739:45
One h. endeavoured to climb — SOME 803:67
One stiff blind h. — BROW 161:44
paint a forest or a h. — MARC 548:27
part man, part h.'s ass — ACHE 2:31
rather have a goddam h. — SALI 711:58
ridden the passions…magnificent h. — BROY 163:97
sightless h. — WALEY 885:91
sting a stately h. — JOHN 441:29
strong as a farm h. — LEE 500:44
The h. loves the hound — SURT 829:41
The h. that comes — YEATS 933:45
Then hey for boot and h. — KING 469:53
thrown from his h. — ANON 20:15
to my h.[I speak]German — CHAR 207:37
true as truest h. — SHAK 738:2
two men ride of a h. — SHAK 745:18
where's the bloody h.? — CAMP 186:56
Why does a hearse h. snicker — SAND 713:97
horseback as long as I live on h. — BIRD 130:59
horse-backbreaker this h.-b. — SHAK 742:15
horseguards can be in the H. — RATT 679:32
horsehair settee of the h. sea! — SITW 793:57
horse-hoof A h.-h. slides — YEATS 933:45
horseless-carriage h.-c.…a luxury — ANON 21:41
horseman H., pass by! — YEATS 934:66
world's greatest h. — SCHU 721:53
horsemen apocalyptic h. in the air — MARC 548:26
chariot of Israel, and the h. thereof — BIBLE 92:28
horse-plough worked with a h.-p. — HEAN 389:4
horsepond celibacy is…a muddy h. — PEAC 645:92
horse-racing makes h. r.…stable — STEI 816:40
horses as fed h. in the morning — BIBLE 105:69
best carriage h. — TROL 867:99
Bring on the empty h.! — CURT 249:50
But so are h. — GILM 356:52
cannot ride two h. — MAXT 562:89
Come saddle my h. — SCOTT 724:28
Don't Spare the H. — HILL 403:94
England…the hell of h. — FLOR 328:76
evening the strange h. — MUIR 602:62
frighten the h. — CAMP 185:53
generally given to h. — JOHN 442:48
hanged for stealing h. — HALI 378:85
heaven…filled—with h. — DUDEK 293:80
h. of instruction — BLAKE 134:43
h. o' Kansas — KIPL 472:23
h. who had never seen a man — BRIN 153:41
hurdling the meter like tired h. — BROY 163:98
in h., dawgs, and men — THAC 849:91
love of h. — FIND 323:60
never know what Trojan h. — BEVIN 85:30
H. and dorgs is some men's fancy — DICK 269:71
what they value in their h. — EMER 313:38
wild white h. play — ARNO 31:83
Women and H. — KIPL 471:98
horticulture You can lead a h. — PARK 638:72
hosanna Glorious h. — SMART 797:30
hosannas make sweet h. ring — NEALE 610:27
hose put a h. in their mouth — KROC 481:19
hospital I was in h. once — BECK 68:48
Randolph Churchill went into h. — WAUGH 893:56
hospitality old Irish h. — EDGE 299:96
host a h., of golden daffodils — WORD 927:40
as a guest thanks his h. — DILL 275:14
Guarded…as by an h. — BYRON 182:78
met a h., and quelled it — PEAC 645:95
O all you h. of heaven! — SHAK 752:34
soundless-clapping h. — THOM 855:39
streams in the countless h. — HOW 417:93
tattered h. of eucalypt — ADAMS 4:63
Though an h. should encamp — BIBLE 95:7
under the h. — PARK 638:73
hostage h. to hostage-takers — INOU 430:74
other guy is called a h. — IACO 427:30
hostages Freeing h. is like — WAITE 884:68
h. to fortune — BACON 48:86
h. to the fates — LUCAN 521:71
hostile cannot let…rogue nations hold
this nation h. — BUSH 175:7
Fearful and h. behavior — FULB 341:45
morally h. — THUB 858:15
regarded…as a h. regime — BUSH 175:9
hostilities prevent a resumption of h. — EDEN 299:90
hostility the disguise of determined h. — SHER 788:63

hosts armed h. dog thefts — TOOLE 863:13
God of H., be with us — KIPL 472:21
Lord of h., to me! — SCOT 725:63
two great classes: h. and guests — BEER 70:87
university where…the Jews are h. — SACH 707:83
hot beat the iron while it is h. — DRYD 292:41
Can one go upon h. coals — BIBLE 99:17
Cool is h. — WASH 890:89
don't understand too h. — SALI 711:53
feel h. and think cold — CARY 198:61
for your foe so h. — SHAK 775:4
H. and rebellious liquors — SHAK 749:39
H. as any hottentot — SITW 793:58
h. as molten lead — SHAK 742:33
h. as the steam — WATT 891:2
h. from hell — SHAK 748:2
h. temper leaps o'er a cold decree — SHAK 739:44
how h. the day is — GRAV 367:64
If it be a h. day — SHAK 742:41
while the strike is h. — ANON 24:47
hot-bloods h.-b. between fourteen — SHAK 745:14
hotel great advantage of a h. — SHAW 777:63
man comes into a great h. — MILL 571:99
open to all—like the Ritz H. — MATH 560:56
small clerk of some h. — MANS 547:87
hotel-keepers Swiss are inspired h.-k. — MONT 592:70
that h.-k. continue — TROL 866:80
hotels all stuck over with large brown h. — HEMI 393:92
h. will…have disappeared — LEVIN 506:64
Hotspur H. of the North — SHAK 741:12
Hottentot H. and every Eskimo — LEHR 502:72
might as well have been H. — LAWR 494:18
hottentot Hot as any h. — SITW 793:58
hotter call'st thyself a h. name — SHAK 769:44
houms dowie h. o' Yarrow — BALL 55:74
dowie h. o' Yarrow — BALL 55:75
hound footprints of a gigantic h.! — DOYLE 285:72
hawk, his h., and his lady fair — BALL 56:92
mettled h. — SCOTT 724:22
slepyng h. to wake — CHAU 208:57
The horse loves the h. — SURT 829:41
hounding World, in h. me — CRUZ 246:87
hounds carcass fit for h. — SHAK 747:84
h. are in cry — SCOTT 723:9
keep…any racehorse or pack of h. — CHES 211:38
like fell and cruel h. — SHAK 755:47
When the h. of spring — SWIN 832:18
hour arrival of an h. — SHAK 742:31
At such an h. the sinners — RUNY 703:85
Awaits alike th' inevitable h. — GRAY 369:14
awful quarters of an h.! — ROSS 698:5
books of the h. — RUSK 704:22
but one bare h. to live — MARL 552:6
child's a plaything for an h. — LAMB 486:32
companioned inarticulate h. — ROSS 698:94
dead deathless h. — ROSS 698:92
Do not expect again a phoenix h. — DAY 257:85
during that h.…I forgot — ATWO 38:60
eternity in an h. — BLAKE 135:66
falling h. by h. — MACN 538:3
For dark h. or twain — SHAK 768:11
from childhood's h. — MOORE 596:53
great h. of destiny — SASS 716:60
h. ago since it was nine — SHAK 749:47
h. approaches Tam maun ride — BURNS 172:20
h. be but A year — MARL 552:6
h. for getting up — SHIP 789:77
h. is not far off — LENIN 502:84
h. is upon her again — GIBB 352:70
h. of my death — KEATS 458:11
h. Of thoughtless youth — WORD 923:71
h. or a day — NASHE 609:12
h.'s come, but not the man — SCOTT 724:34
h. when earth's foundations fled — HOUS 416:79
How many makes the h. — SHAK 730:76
humblest h. is when he compares — BARR 61:79
I also had my h. — CHES 211:43
I Have known the lightning's h. — DAY 257:83
its h. come round — YEATS 933:51
just at this dead h. — SHAK 751:96
known as the Children's H. — LONG 516:61
meaning of this happy h. — KLEE 475:8
mine h. is not yet come — BIBLE 117:77
Not an h. more nor less — SHAK 764:98
nothing can bring back the h. — WORD 927:28
now's the h. — BURNS 173:41
Of a ship's h. — SLES 796:15

Of thee one h. — DONNE 280:60
Oh, for an h. of Herod! — HOPE 411:73
pause…known as the cocktail h. — DE 264:35
rash hand in evil h. — MILT 584:13
ring out the h. — APOL 27:17
serve the future h. — WORD 928:59
Some luckless h. — BURNS 170:78
take an h.'s leisure — STARK 813:74
the h. is nigh — SCOTT 725:45
their finest h. — CHUR 216:77
This is the exquisite h. — VERL 879:65
Time and the h. runs — SHAK 766:77
to serve the h. — TENN 844:74
to the h. its solitude — STEV 819:27
uncertain h. before the morning — ELIOT 309:42
watch at that midnight h. — LEAR 497:77
weight of the superincumbent h. — SHEL 785:94
world's best moment is a calm h. — ABU 1:11
world-without-end h. — SHAK 771:23
hour-glass still as the h.-g. — ROSS 698:93
hours best…in a couple of h. — WEST 901:34
crime…The h. are good — ALLEN 12:41
ever-rolling silent h. — PEAC 645:96
few h. in life more agreeable — JAMES 433:37
few h. of giving his enemies — STER 817:71
fruitless h., but neither — MILT 585:19
glare Of the interminable h. — ARNO 31:99
golden H., on angel wings — BURNS 171:5
hath not known his god-like h. — WORD 925:99
h. are made for men — RABE 676:72
h., days, months…rags of time — DONNE 279:41
h. of weariness — WORD 923:69
h. they know not how to employ — MONT 591:66
h. were cups of sack — SHAK 741:94
h. will take care of themselves — CHES 210:29
How slowly do the h. — SPEN 809:5
I was in Tennessee 24 h. — RAY 680:41
march of only a few h. — PEARY 645:2
sweetest h. that e'er I spend — BURNS 170:60
talk its pensive h. away — BRON 155:91
the darksome h. — GOET 360:15
The pitiless h. — THOM 856:61
three and a half h. long — CHAP 206:24
Three h. a day — TROL 867:10
tide of h. — YEATS 932:34
time card office h. — BAND 58:25
Time in h., days, years — VAUG 878:49
Upon the h. and times — SHAK 771:23
Work eight h. — PICK 651:3
house About the lilting h. — THOM 852:71
allegations…repeated outside the H. — PROF 670:59
All my h. — JONS 448:20
approbation of this H. — WALP 887:40
as for me and my h. — BIBLE 90:66
bawdy h. is to a cathedral — MENC 565:62
boat…had the goods of a h. — PEPYS 647:48
brawling woman in a wide h. — BIBLE 100:45
built his h. upon a rock — BIBLE 110:13
called a woman in my own h. — WAUGH 892:33
clean someone's h. — THER 851:43
corrupt and servile H. of Commons — SHER 788:69
dark h. and a whip — SHAK 750:34
Dark h., by which — TENN 843:27
depart out of that h. or city — BIBLE 111:25
doll in the doll's h. — DICK 272:49
dwell in the h. of the Lord — BIBLE 94:2
dwell in the h. of the Lord — BIBLE 95:7
even in the h. of worship — PARN 639:91
Except the Lord build the h. — BIBLE 98:92
far from the club h. — LINK 511:54
From Bauhaus to Our H. — WOLFE 920:95
full h. — MACA 524:31
galleries of the h. — MUNDY 603:82
gat him home to his h. — BIBLE 91:5
ghost of a great h. — LEVE 506:58
go into the h. of the Lord — BIBLE 98:88
gone tiptoe in this h. — MILL 571:97
great h. of our humanity — DUNC 295:15
great h. of Tarquin — MACA 524:62
Harrow the h. of the dead — AUDEN 39:76
hauf-way h. — MACD 529:31
H.…a place of free speech — WENT 899:4
h. as nigh heaven — MORE 597:51
H. at Pooh Corner — PARK 637:47
H. Beautiful is…lousy — PARK 637:50
h.…become a den of robbers — BIBLE 105:72
h. divided against itself — LINC 510:34

h. fell upon the lords BIBLE 90:76
h. in the world RYBC 707:74
H. is not a Home ADLER 7:52
H. is pleased to direct me LENT 503:2
h. not made with hands BIBLE 122:25
H. of Lords WELL 898:63
H. of Lords, an illusion STOP 825:60
H. of Lords in his own head LLOY 513:6
H. of Lords is a model FIELD 322:34
H. of Lords is like a glass ATTL 38:47
H. of Lords must be the only institution SAMU 712:77
H. of peers GILB 354:14
h. rose like magic HARG 382:78
h. that has got over JERO 437:35
h. to be broken up BIBLE 113:88
h. was filled with smoke BIBLE 102:11
h. wherein our Life is led CARL 192:18
h. where I was born HOOD 410:37
h. where there was not one dead BIBLE 88:17
h., which I have hallowed BIBLE 91:11
h. with the narrow gate SHAK 762:39
imprison the child in her h. WHITE 903:91
In my Father's h. are many mansions BIBLE 118:9
in the h. of bondage MACA 525:42
In the h. of Life THUR 859:21
invisibly all over the h. THUR 859:23
jewel of our h. SHAK 762:34
just moved into the chicken h. MACA 524:30
Killing the Angel in the H. WOOLF 923:51
labor of keeping h. MCCA 528:6
Leader of the H. of Commons DISR 276:64
live in a h. on fire WILL 913:38
Looking around the H. THOR 858:13
love the H. of Commons so passionately CHAN 205:7
luck about a h. YEATS 934:61
magic h. of glass ROBE 689:19
Majesty entered the H. RUSH 703:96
'Make my h. your inn.' MOORE 595:32
man…in the way in the h. GASK 346:59
man's h. is his castle COKE 224:70
Marriage is not a h. ATWO 38:51
meanest member of the H. HENR 395:46
Members of this H. BAXT 65:89
mind to sell his h. SWIFT 831:74
mistress of every h. MILL 571:78
moat defensive to a h. SHAK 734:8
moderately healthy h. SHAW 779:16
neighbour's h. is on fire BURKE 168:28
no one depressed in this h. VICT 880:85
offered his h. to sale JOHN 443:79
office of the White H. MENC 565:72
Oh, to have a little h.! COLUM 229:61
old h. carried an assurance ACHE 2:25
one-man H. of Commons MANC 544:45
One need not be a H. DICK 272:65
on the front porch of the h. LANCE 487:73
out of h. and home SHAK 742:46
out of the h. of the Lord BIBLE 97:79
Peace be to this h. BIBLE 115:35
Peace be to this h. BOOK 142:31
play the fool…in's own h. SHAK 753:80
regulates the size of the h. LECO 499:29
return into my h. BIBLE 111:45
secret h. of death SHAK 765:46
serious h. on serious earth LARK 490:27
set a h. on fire BACON 49:22
seven pillared worthy h. LAWR 495:37
sharing the h. with a disembodied SHAR 776:45
sit in the h. wi' handkerchers SCOTT 724:26
snail…Carrying his own h. DONNE 280:62
sneak into the h. in her train LAMB 486:43
sparrow hath found an h. BIBLE 96:45
Speaker of the H. GARN 346:51
still more honourable H. ROCHE 691:47
talking about building a h. STERN 817:65
tell you your h. is burning MUNRO 603:87
Tenants of the h. ELIOT 305:43
thief breaks into my h. PAINE 634:89
this is no my ain h. ANON 20:14
to clean h. THUR 860:50
to the Duke's h. PEPYS 647:36
Unless the Lord has built the h. BIBLE 127:93
venal H. of Peers SHER 788:69
What h. more stately HERB 398:3
when all through the h. MOORE 594:14
Wisdom hath builded her h. BIBLE 99:18
women in the h. GILM 356:52

young and inexperienced h. JERO 437:35
You take my h. SHAK 740:84
housed h., clothed, fed RUSK 704:28
household a great actor or a h. word? OLIV 624:66
Her h. to me HERB 397:97
h. features her person PRIOR 669:34
h. of God BIBLE 122:43
keep thy h. the Church BOOK 141:90
My name…a h. word ASHB 35:87
not a member of the h. KENN 462:97
our names…as h. words SHAK 746:59
put his h. in order BIBLE 91:5
real centre of the h. SHAW 781:74
woman, than to study h. MILT 584:9
Yiddish is a h. tongue OZICK 632:68
housekeeper a man marries his h. PIGOU 651:15
h. think she's a householder WILD 910:77
housekeeping H. ain't no joke ALCO 10:4
housemaid If I'd been a h. MELBA 563:17
nice to the second h. JAMES 433:49
housemaids damp souls of h. ELIOT 305:33
houses big h. sat in…propinquity GILL 356:40
calling of selling h. LEWIS 507:86
cry in strangers' h. MANS 547:93
Eighteenth-century h. YEATS 933:44
few of his friends' h. JOHN 446:57
going on inside their h. ALME 13:65
h. are made of stones POIN 657:33
h. deserve to be burnt WELLS 898:82
h. just as big SMITH 799:81
h. marked with a red cross PEPYS 647:40
h. there wear verandahs MURR 604:6
live in the h. they build STEI 815:34
narrow streets, old h. THOR 858:5
not the h. FENT 320:87
pigeons…loath to leave their h. PEPYS 647:46
plague o' both your h. SHAK 736:62
round their golden h. TENN 839:57
sandstone apartment h. CHEE 209:46
sensible to build h. KEYN 466:88
seven o'clock from the h. REED 681:79
staying in their h. PEPYS 647:46
studios, and in the workers' h. MAYA 562:92
The trees and the h. THOM 856:60
the very h. seem asleep WORD 926:19
towns or h. raised by poetry COWL 240:30
ugly h. stand MILL 571:82
unessential h. began to melt FITZ 325:1
housetops lowered o'er our h. TWAIN 871:7
housewife busy h. ply her evening care GRAY 369:13
h.'s badly-cooked dinners BEET 70:2
Many a h. GREER 372:90
mock the good h. Fortune SHAK 748:26
scholar or a complete h. PLATH 654:63
the h. that's thrifty SHER 788:54
housework help with the h. WINT 917:34
no need to do any h. CRISP 245:56
Houston oil depletion…makes H. MAIL 540:55
how H. you? GRANT 366:47
person who knows 'h.' RAVI 679:38
Howard Then sware Lord Thomas H. TENN 848:60
how-de-do Here's a h.-d.-d.! GILB 355:26
Howell H. & James young man GILB 354:9
howl H., h., h., h.! SHAK 764:5
New widows h. SHAK 768:28
howling h. commercial success GREE 371:70
howls h. on for more SHEL 784:65
hub h. of the solar system HOLM 408:85
hubris H. clobbered by Nemesis ALDI 11:13
Hudson Close by the H. HUGH 419:30
hue innermost idea of this h. MELV 564:32
most lily-white of h. SHAK 738:2
native h. of resolution SHAK 753:74
of dazzling h. KEATS 458:20
hues all one's favourite h. DOYLE 286:83
Rainbow…left thee all her lovely h. DAVI 255:47
huffing h. of hyphenated words BROY 163:98
huffy Not h., or stuffy HERB 397:74
hugged h. the offender, and forgave DRYD 292:51
hulk stoop-shouldered h. TIME 860:72
hum h. a fugue GILB 354:1
h. of either army SHAK 746:46
h. Of human cities BYRON 180:26
mist and h. ARNO 32:27
pilgrim borne in heedless h. COLL 228:47
propels the h. KAND 454:35
human accusing…the h. race CAMUS 188:99

all female life, animal and h. STAN 812:67
All h. things are subject to decay DRYD 288:47
All must love the h. form BLAKE 134:32
all that h. hearts endure GOLD 361:42
All that is h. GIBB 352:59
all the months of h. birth MASE 559:33
animals could be made h. HEINE 391:48
application of h. ingenuity NUTT 619:83
articulate h. relationships VIDAL 880:89
as h. eye could see TENN 840:81
awing the h. mind JEFF 436:18
basic h. emotions ROTH 700:34
become h. is art NOVA 619:76
Being h., she must KIPL 472:29
belief in h. liberty MACL 535:49
believe in taking h. life NATH 610:24
between h. creation MILL 573:34
bless our h. ears MILL 576:97
boot stamping on a h. face ORWE 630:4
bounds of h. Empire BACON 50:62
bounds of h. Empire BACON 47:68
breathes with h. breath TENN 841:90
But h. creatures' lives! HOOD 410:46
but it's greater to be h. ROGE 695:27
call the sciences h. invention PAINE 634:97
cancer of h. history SONT 804:73
can no longer bear to be h. BECK 68:32
care for far more than h. life PANK 636:31
chaos of h. experience MACL 535:51
chords in the h. mind DICK 270:91
city is…a h. zoo MORR 598:92
civilized h. life TRUM 868:34
collection…of h. knowledge KENN 462:20
condition of being h. ANOU 26:1
condition of the h. race GIBB 351:52
considerers of h. things MILT 579:76
constituting of h. virtue MILT 579:73
contribution to h. history JIANG 438:50
could be the whole h. condition HOPP 413:15
death instead of 'h. rights' PEOP 647:24
degraded h. life MARX 558:3
destiny of the h. race THOR 857:80
destruction of h. life HARDY 381:46
devaluation of the h. world MARX 557:95
development of h. destinies FISH 324:76
does a h. form display BLAKE 136:86
do h. rights begin ROOS 695:39
enemy of the h. race MILL 572:17
escapes being h. YOUR 935:80
essence of real h. love ELIOT 303:83
establishment of h. activity MARX 557:97
every h. has a finite number ARMS 30:79
experience of being h. LEWO 508:10
fight for their own h. rights PANK 636:32
forget the h. race BYRON 180:42
For insight into h. affairs DYSON 297:62
form of h. reason LEVI 506:66
forms of h. knowledge MANN 545:66
frightened by my h. impossibility ANDR 16:24
from any h. experience JAMES 433:27
From what h. ill WILD 910:75
get h. feelings right HUTC 424:50
giving life in h. fashion REDON 681:74
godhead in which all life is h. SHAW 779:37
greatest thing a h. soul RUSK 704:33
greatness of the h. soul ROCK 692:77
herds, of h. face divine MILT 582:38
histories…of h. life POPP 662:92
history of the h. race HARL 383:83
Hope…in the h. breast POPE 660:10
horse is at least h. SALI 711:58
h. activity that takes TRIL 866:66
h. affairs would never improve ORWE 627:33
h. being and fish can coexist peacefully BUSH 175:2
H. blunders usually TAYL 837:11
h. body is sacred WHIT 905:38
h. creation mechanical LEGER 501:52
h. desire for food TOOLE 863:13
Humane, but not h. CUMM 248:22
h. employers quite literally MUMF 603:78
h. enterprise GOULD 365:24
h. experience is actively offered WILL 913:62
h. history GARC 345:42
H. history…a race WELLS 898:89
h. intellectual tradition GOULD 365:25
h. kind Cannot bear…reality ELIOT 307:94
H. life is but a series NABO 606:36

wisdom of h.	ELIOT 308:18
humorist know I was a h.	JERO 437:36
humorists difficulty with h.	UPDI 874:73
H. are not happy men	CONN 233:71
not an easy time for h.	BUCH 164:33
humorous 'tis no marvel, he is so h.	SHAK 742:20
humour dowered with a sense of h.	SOME 803:67
effusions of wit and h.	AUST 43:91
have a good sense of h.	SALI 711:56
h. in ill-health	WELLS 898:88
H.…is emotional chaos	THUR 860:53
h., its music	ROLL 695:33
h. of a scholar	BACON 50:51
in a holiday h.	SHAK 750:76
lack of a sterner kind of h.	WEBB 893:62
malignity…in a piece of h.	STEE 814:2
no h. to marry	DEKK 259:52
no sense of h.	ALBEE 9:91
people…have…in common…hatred	
and h.	PRYOR 672:94
sufficient sense of h.	HALD 377:77
warn't in a good h.	TWAIN 871:98
woman in this h. wooed?	SHAK 731:4
humours h. of the whole English	DRYD 292:45
h., whether grave or mellow	ADDI 6:13
in all h. sportively I range	DRAY 286:97
hump camel has a single h.	NASH 608:87
camel's h.	KIPL 472:36
husband who may…have a h.	OBRI 621:11
without a positive h.	THAC 849:86
humph H. yourself!	KIPL 473:39
Hun H. is at the gate	KIPL 474:76
hundred As long as one h.…remain	ANON 19:86
be all one a h. years hence	EMER 312:30
dying of a h. good symptoms	POPE 662:85
h. judges have declared	QUIL 674:43
h. pound on't	SHAK 773:57
h. years later	FAUL 319:70
Rode the six h.	TENN 844:75
Rode the six h.	TENN 844:76
Rode the six h.	TENN 845:77
steal more than a h. men	PUZO 673:24
trade a h. contemporary readers	KOES 477:29
hundredth h. time I am right	EINS 301:34
hung who ne'er h. there	HOPK 413:5
Hungarian not enough to be H.	KORDA 480:1
Hungary sons of H.	GILB 354:18
hunger against h., poverty	MARS 554:39
bodily h. in his eyes	SHAW 780:41
drive h. from the hearth	LLOY 513:98
Fainting forms, h. stricken	WILDE 907:82
fed your h. like an endless task	CRANE 243:15
he that cometh to me shall never h.	BIBLE 117:90
H. allows no choice	AUDEN 40:8
H. and love	FRAN 333:85
h. for recognition and money	SELF 727:80
H. is the best sauce	CERV 203:44
h. no more	BIBLE 126:60
h., thirst…and death	GARI 346:48
idle if h. didn't pinch him	ELIOT 303:99
kill this whole assembly with h.	BIBLE 88:21
O sacred h.	SPEN 809:7
perish with h.!	BIBLE 116:47
perpetual h. to be beautiful	RHYS 684:24
present to plese with H.	LANG 489:97
suffered thee to h.	BIBLE 89:47
hungred h., and ye gave me meat	BIBLE 113:92
hungry ate when we were not h.	SWIFT 831:84
feed the h. on statistics	LLOY 513:94
fight so h. people can eat	STEI 815:34
filled the h. with good things	BIBLE 115:23
filled the h. with good things	BIBLE 128:99
I am not h.	PUNCH 673:13
if ever thou art h.	KIPL 471:10
If thine enemy be h.	BIBLE 100:52
known what it was like to be h.	LARD 490:17
lean and h. look	SHAK 747:79
never going to be h. again	MITC 588:96
once you're h., you're different	HUNT 423:22
rare and h.	STEV 821:76
small h. shivering self	ELIOT 304:11
Huns H.…chanted a funeral song	GIBB 351:56
hunt h., and vote, and raise the price	BYRON 183:7
h. in fields, for health	DRYD 292:53
H., shoot, and fight	BRON 155:79
people who h.	SHAW 781:77
To H. an 'assault'	CRAN 243:31

You will see H.	SHEL 784:66
hunter between the h. and his prey	ZHAO 936:96
covers…the hare and the h.	PATC 642:48
Esau was a cunning h.	BIBLE 87:84
Heart Is A Lonely H.	MCCU 529:20
Heart Is A Lonely H.	SHARP 776:38
h. home from the hill	STEV 822:10
H. of the East	FITZ 324:82
h.'s horn is ringing	SCOTT 723:9
h.'s javelin in his side	ARNO 32:25
Man is the h.	TENN 841:97
mighty h. before the Lord	BIBLE 87:70
Miss Joan H. Dunn	BETJ 83:88
no h.'s game	JEFF 436:10
rings on h.'s shout	SIGO 791:28
without ever becoming h.	MARX 557:99
hunters intrepid h. of golf balls	SMITH 799:65
hunting call h. one of them	JOHN 447:75
discourse was about h.	PEPYS 647:37
English counties like h.-tunes	BENET 75:10
hound is to the h. gane	BALL 56:92
h. he loved	SHAK 732:49
H. is not a proper employment	ADDI 7:44
H. the author, painter and musician	SITW 794:87
I went h. wild	OWEN 632:60
passion for h.	DICK 267:92
tuckt up she a h. goes	HERR 400:41
we must have h.	JOHN 440:93
hunting-frock cashier the h.-f.	SHER 787:37
hunting-grounds h.-g. for the poetic	ELIOT 304:3
Huntlie lay on H. bank	BALL 56:89
hunts he h. in dreams	TENN 840:79
hurled Atoms or systems into ruin h.	POPE 660:9
Swift to be h.	HOOD 410:49
hurly-burly h.-b. of the chaise	CAMP 185:52
hurrah The Last H.	OCON 622:22
hurricane America is a h.	MAIL 539:39
crazy-eyed H. blowing	KIPL 473:50
heard there was a h. on the way	FISH 324:74
Irish h., a flat calm	BOWEN 147:30
Let the h. drag the pieces	HUID 421:99
hurricanoes You cataracts and h.	SHAK 763:71
hurroosh h. that follows	CRIT 245:62
hurry H. slowly	AUGU 42:47
Liberals in a h.	SAINT 709:28
modern life…sick h.	ARNO 32:22
senseless h.	WORD 928:48
So who's in a h.?	BENC 74:4
there will be no special h.	HEMI 394:99
hurt done the lover mortal h.	DOUG 283:20
give delight and h. not	SHAK 774:92
helped and h. us	MILL 571:96
h. one till one sweats	HALD 377:77
h. that Honour feels	TENN 840:80
I h. her	RIMB 688:96
it will do no h.	SHAK 761:27
never h. a hair of him	STUD 827:5
Nothing doth more h.	BACON 49:19
shall not h. nor destroy	BIBLE 102:19
shall not h. nor destroy	BIBLE 104:66
stomach that they mayn't h.	LAMB 486:36
they had never h. us	GELL 348:2
what you said h. me	LIBE 509:14
Wrath brings…gravest h.	EURI 316:13
hurting instead of h.	HUME 422:12
You are h. be!	KIPL 473:43
husband at all times your faithful h.	STEE 814:90
attempting to cuckold a h.	JONG 448:97
back of her h.'s newspaper	GREER 372:90
Chaste to her h.	POPE 661:45
dear h. for a comfort	SMITH 800:92
Dear h.! I take shame	MOOD 594:6
delight of her h.	RANS 679:21
established for the h. and wife	MONT 593:98
finding a h. for one's mistress	COOP 236:57
flop in favour of your h.	DICK 271:22
Get thee a good h.	SHAK 761:25
good works in her h.	MILT 584:9
hands of the h.	ADAMS 3:61
has an ideal h.	TARK 836:97
h. and a happy home	PLATH 654:72
h. be a man	LAMB 486:43
h. frae the wife despises!	BURNS 172:15
h. held her upright	SMITH 799:64
H., I come	SHAK 766:61
h. is a whole-time job	BENN 76:44
h. is thy lord	SHAK 732:46

h. is torn from her	NATI 610:25
h. is what is left of the lover	ROWL 701:52
h., like a government	BALZ 57:8
h. pays for all	DUNB 294:4
h.…shall rule over thee	BIBLE 86:54
h. wears a mask	MARI 550:59
if she loses her h.	EURI 316:6
If your h. is a bore	BELL 73:80
in her h.'s heart	SHAK 756:64
in your h.'s ear	GROM 374:21
is it well with thy h.?	BIBLE 92:31
life her h. makes for her	ELIOT 304:10
light wife doth make a heavy h.	SHAK 741:92
Like a deceived h.	SHAK 772:36
makes a bad h.	EMER 313:41
man…makes the best h.	NORR 618:64
most indulgent h.	DICK 270:13
must have a h.	SHAK 732:30
My H. and I	ELIZ 310:65
Never trust a h. too far	ROWL 701:51
nothing but his being my h.	CONG 231:20
send me no h.	SHAK 744:90
so ill bred as to love a h.	WYCH 931:5
So may my h.	SHAK 758:48
to vote for one's h.	ONAS 625:82
to yourself, that h.	JAMES 433:25
unbelieving h. is sanctified	BIBLE 121:11
We have to…grimace for a h.	OBRI 621:11
husbandry h. in heaven	SHAK 767:93
husbands bad h.…good wives	BACON 48:93
Chumps…make the best h.	WODE 919:55
divine right of h.	WOLL 921:9
doan never ketch h.	MITC 588:94
Fools are as like h.	SHAK 756:73
h. lie snoring in bed	MORE 597:65
H., love your wives	BIBLE 123:68
h. to stay at home	ELIOT 303:92
Let h. know Their wives	SHAK 761:6
reformed rakes make the best h.	BRON 154:74
some women govern their h.	WOLL 920:3
When h.…breathe their last	POPE 659:75
women…succeed in spite of their h.	LEE 500:47
hush A brooding h.	THOM 856:63
h. with the setting moon	TENN 845:90
somebody ought to have said 'h.'	CAMP 185:52
hushed h. and anxious hours	HOOV 411:60
hushed-up like wrongs h.-u.	OWEN 632:65
husk h. of meaning	ELIOT 309:39
Hussein deflecting America's anger	
from Bin Laden to Saddam H.	LECA 499:27
H. isn't just sitting	ANON 25:73
not going after Saddam H.	SCHW 721:65
hussies h. in your beds	SHAK 759:73
hustle tried to h. the East	KIPL 471:5
hut Love in a h.	KEATS 458:22
hyacinth h. with rich inlay	MILT 583:70
Thy h. hair	POE 656:22
hyacinths h. and biscuits	SAND 713:1
Hyades rainy H. vext the dim sea	TENN 839:63
hybreds h. and lubberds!	JOYCE 452:99
hydrogen h. bomb	FROMM 338:82
hyena wolf, the h., and the skunk?	BRYAN 163:9
hygiene H. is the corruption	MENC 565:61
h. of older people	SMITH 799:72
hymns brought home to me by the h.	LAWR 495:34
Singing h. unbidden	SHEL 784:58
Sing on, with h. uproarious	BETJ 83:87
sings h. at heaven's gate	SHAK 771:14
hyperbole encourage unedifying h.	DUNN 295:20
scarcely h. to say	CLIVE 222:15
speaking in perpetual h.	BACON 48:97
hyperboles Three-piled h.	SHAK 734:91
hyphenate Everybody else has to h.	MORR 599:57
hypochondria H. is the only disease	ANON 24:18
hypochondriacs h. of history	AGNEW 8:74
hypocrisy H. is a tribute	LARO 491:52
H. is the most difficult…vice	MAUG 561:76
H., the only evil	MILT 582:51
m-m-making the world safe for h.	WOLFE 920:85
old-fashioned American h.	GALL 344:12
organized h.	DISR 276:57
That would be h.	WILDE 909:43
the Pharisees' h.	PAST 641:41
hypocrite first bolt-hole of the h.	BRAGG 149:84
h. lecteur!	ELIOT 306:55
H. reader	BAUD 64:53
liar that's also a h.	WILL 912:18

No man is a h. — JOHN 446:66
hypocrites cant of h. — STER 818:83
  h. austerely talk — MILT 583:71
  h....in the synagogues — BIBLE 109:96
  scribes and Pharisees, h.! — BIBLE 113:84
  tongue and soul...be h. — SHAK 754:98
  ye h., ye can discern — BIBLE 112:61
hypotheses smallest number of h. — EINS 302:46
hypothesis character...to an h.? — STER 817:73
  conviction that a h. — MEDA 563:5
  discard a pet h. — LORE 517:88
  endeavour to construct a h. — HARDY 381:54
  nature of an h. — STER 818:80
  slaying of a beautiful h. — HUXL 426:9
hyssop Purge me with h. — BIBLE 95:29
  sprinkle me with h. — BIBLE 127:87
Hyssopps H. of the Glen — ASHF 35:98
hysteria therapy of h. — FREUD 336:51
hysterics blind h. of the Celt — TENN 844:62

I

iacta I. est alea — CAES 184:24
Iago I.'s soliloquy — COLE 227:27
  yet the pity of it, I. — SHAK 760:98
iambics In keen i. — DRYD 289:50
Iban The I., when they decide — OHAN 623:45
Ibo Among the I....conversation — ACHE 2:18
Ibsen Nietzsche, I....madmen! — ONEI 625:99
  These I. creatures — ANON 21:38
ice bloody i. on bloody head — BLAIR 132:98
  cracked i. crunching — STEV 820:44
  Glitt'ring with i. — POPE 662:66
  good to break the i. — BACON 49:18
  hot i. and wondrous...snow — SHAK 738:14
  i. age ended years ago — ZHAO 936:95
  I. formed on the butler — WODE 919:74
  i. of its own indifference — ROOS 696:44
  i. on a hot stove — FROST 339:7
  i. was in the blood — PIER 651:7
  may not dissolve the i. — SURR 829:40
  skating on very thin i. — CAMP 185:54
  skating over thin i. — EMER 312:16
  sunny pleasure-dome with caves of i.! — COLE 226:12
  talent, a glass, and some cracked i. — BARR 61:98
  To curle on the i. — PENE 646:19
  To smooth the i. — SHAK 739:30
  world will end...in i. — FROST 338:97
iceberg portent of an i. — BROW 162:64
  The i. rises — BISH 131:74
icebergs like i. in the ocean — GERH 350:35
icecaps blue i. on the mountains — CHAT 207:49
ice-cream emperor of i.-c. — STEV 819:15
  enjoy your i.-c. — WILD 910:79
Iceman The I. Cometh — ONEI 626:2
ice pick Baby LeRoy with an i. p. — ROST 699:10
ices after tea and cakes and i. — ELIOT 304:19
ice-scratched I.-s. slabs — SNYD 803:49
ichor perspiration was but i. — BYRON 183:5
icicle hang like an i. — SHAK 756:80
icicles When i. hang by the wall — SHAK 734:94
  White night of i. — MALL 542:94
  Why are there i. everywhere? — ZHAO 936:95
iciness an i., a sinking — POE 656:16
icing i. that detracts from the cake — AUCH 39:74
id cure of the i. — ANON 22:50
Ida I.'s shady brow — BLAKE 133:21
idea absurd is the fundamental i. — CAMUS 187:86
  Alligators have the right i. — MACD 531:62
  always gone in for the i. that — WILS 914:69
  Between the i. And the reality — ELIOT 306:71
  charge that an i. is radical — GALB 343:90
  controlling i. that holds us — FRID 337:57
  Dying for an i. — LEWIS 508:94
  endowed with the i. of God — DESC 263:25
  entertain an i. — JARR 435:85
  every new i....takes a generation — FEYN 322:25
  failure is not in the i. — MCGO 532:92
  first i. was not our own — STEV 820:30
  For an i. ever to be fashionable — SANT 714:20
  general i., of course — LEAC 497:69
  good i. but it won't work — ROGE 695:20
  had the wrong i. first — FEYN 322:24
  Hang your i. on a peg — BRIS 153:44
  hate the i. of causes — FORS 331:52
  his every i. rationalized — PIER 651:5
  i. alone is eternal — FLAU 326:28

i.-bound in the past — LAWR 494:99
  i. for which I can live — KIER 467:7
  i....has still not been said enough — DELA 260:58
  i. of an external cause — SPIN 810:30
  i. of a system — GEOR 349:19
  i. of death saves him — FORS 331:37
  i. of dying is worse — PROU 671:83
  i. of elder wisdom — UPDI 875:96
  i. of liberty — SPIN 810:25
  i. of weapons — RUSS 705:57
  i. or concept — LEWI 508:7
  i. that they are going to live — DAVIS 255:51
  innermost i. of this hue — MELV 564:32
  it would be a good i. — GAND 345:36
  let the i. soak in — MILL 572:31
  new i....close to insanity — MILL 571:1
  nice place, inside an i. — MCIL 533:2
  No grand i. was ever born — FITZ 325:13
  Nothing is more dangerous than an i. — ALAIN 9:81
  possess but one i. — JOHN 444:90
  sacrificed...for...an i. — MILL 573:57
  shoot his like in the name of an i. — BROD 153:57
  slightest i. what they should be doing — FULL 341:50
  teach the young i. — THOM 856:53
  the i. of death must be born — MACH 532:96
  The man with a new i. — TWAIN 872:25
  to whom the i. first occurs — DARW 253:99
  Whatever is...perceived is an i. — BERK 79:6
  What redeems it is an i. only — CONR 234:96
  when a politician does get an i. — MARQ 554:30
ideal American is an i. — FRIE 337:66
  An i. wife — TARK 836:97
  boy's i. of a manly career — DISR 276:52
  Christian i. has not been tried — CHES 212:69
  Conservative i. of freedom — MADAN 538:19
  Freedom is not an i. — STEV 820:60
  i. day for football — SMITH 800:90
  i. which I hope to live for — MAND 544:46
  i. would be to belong to none — DUDEK 293:81
  ideas, or on an i. — LAWR 494:98
  my song has an i. — CHOC 214:17
  nearer today to the i. — HOOV 411:58
  not charmed with the i. of life — MILL 570:59
  Religion...ultimate i. — WHIT 904:8
  softly sleeps the calm I. — DICK 268:48
idealism grips with so-called i. — MENC 566:81
  i. is not uncommon — ROOS 696:57
  I. is the noble toga — HUXL 426:2
idealistic America...only i. nation — WILS 917:19
  our i. pretensions — OBRI 620:2
idealists I. are very apt to walk — SMITH 799:82
idealized i. into powerlessness — JONG 448:6
idealizer Sorrow, the great i. — LOWE 520:37
ideals forever hallowed by the i. — EISE 302:64
  i. and visions to the past — KENN 463:30
  i. of a democratic...society — MAND 544:46
  i....painters' techniques — RENO 683:9
  men without i. — CAMUS 187:85
  tell the i. of a nation — DOUG 283:25
  white man's superior i. — VASC 877:39
ideas addiction...to the i. — GALB 343:91
  alter and exchange our i. — BERN 81:36
  believe in i. and die for them — ANOU 26:97
  borrowed i. — CALL 184:38
  cemetery of dead i. — UNAM 873:65
  dreams that have...changed my i. — BRON 155:94
  false i. prevail as to woman's — STAN 812:63
  find really marvellous i. — LEON 504:19
  foundation of your i. and phrases — LAUT 493:77
  founded not upon visionary i. — GLAD 358:92
  great i. are hogwash — NABO 606:41
  Great people talk about i. — LEBO 499:12
  i. about the nation — LESS 504:31
  I. are born from hatred — GENET 348:6
  i. begin to destroy sex in America — DOCT 277:2
  i. get cloath'd — STER 818:95
  i. must be as broad as Nature — DOYLE 285:50
  i. of economists — KEYN 466:89
  i., or on an ideal — LAWR 494:98
  i. take their beginnings — LOCKE 514:18
  Innate i. are in every man — BLAKE 135:79
  isolate him, and his i. disintegrate — DIDE 274:3
  live in the mind, in i. — MILL 572:18
  machine for transmission of i. — BOWL 147:33
  most interesting i. — SONT 804:76
  new i. or fresh outlooks — MACK 533:10
  no i. and the ability — KRAUS 480:9

no i. but in things — WILL 913:50
  Not many composers have i. — GERS 350:36
  of nasty i. — SWIFT 831:87
  our i. that make us — UNAM 873:64
  People find i. a bore — POUND 665:54
  publishing of his i. — KAZIN 456:71
  realm of i. — MILL 571:1
  Relations of I. — HUME 422:13
  share no one's i. — TURG 870:65
  signs of i. — JOHN 442:39
  two i. are more inseparable — SMITH 801:9
  two i. in her head — LINK 511:58
  two i. of government — BRYAN 163:8
  two opposed i. in the mind — FITZ 325:8
  unexpected copulation of i. — JOHN 441:25
  vehicle for conveying i. — MACB 527:81
  without any i. — LOCKE 514:17
  words reign over i. — SAND 712:83
identical exist, but are i. — FORS 331:43
identity live without an i. — MCLU 536:62
  mistaking...similarity for real i. — PALM 635:19
  questions of freedom and i. — JORD 450:64
  sense of personal i. — STEV 822:97
  short circuit in his i. — ROTH 699:14
ideological i., or the abstract — ROTH 699:28
ideologies i. and inventions — SONT 804:73
  not to have i. — HOFS 406:56
ideology an i. that is warlike — OBRI 620:2
  more important than i. — NEWM 612:67
  single i. for 70 years — YELT 934:70
ides Beware the i. of March — SHAK 747:72
idiocy facilitate the infection of i. — BIER 129:33
  human...potential for i. — ONET 626:12
idioms licentious i. — JOHN 441:28
  long words and exhausted i. — ORWE 628:62
idiot artist, like the i. — SITW 794:84
  computer is a fast i. — AMER 13:76
  good loser...an i. — DURO 296:36
  i. who praises — GILB 355:22
  law is...a i. — DICK 267:96
  possibly an i. — DALI 251:71
  tale Told by an i. — SHAK 769:42
idiotism hundred new titles of i. — NASHE 609:10
idiots fatuity of i. — SMITH 801:7
  I. are always in favour — SHAW 781:86
  play the i. in her eyes — SHAK 757:4
  village i., policemen — MACD 530:47
  your only competition is i. — MANK 545:60
idle all be i. if we could — JOHN 445:19
  all the day i.? — BIBLE 113:77
  As i. as a painted ship — COLE 225:84
  be not i. — BURT 174:83
  happiest when I am i. — WARD 888:58
  I. to hope — REED 681:81
  If you are i. — JOHN 445:40
  many a one who would be i. — ELIOT 303:99
  merely the art of the i. — INGR 429:63
  most i. and unprofitable — GIBB 352:60
  Most 'scruciating i. — KIPL 472:38
  Reputation is an i....imposition — SHAK 760:79
  such i. fellows as I — AUBR 39:66
idleness faculty for I — STEV 822:97
  grief and sin of I. — MELV 564:24
  Grief is a species of i. — JOHN 444:96
  I., which is often becoming — STEV 821:87
  pains and penalties of i. — POPE 662:80
  reading is not i. — SPEN 807:65
idlers loungers and i. of the Empire — DOYLE 284:46
idling enjoy i. thoroughly — JERO 437:28
idol ancient i., on his base again — BROW 161:48
  celestial and my soul's i. — SHAK 752:44
  'eathen i.'s foot — KIPL 471:87
  God...would be an i. — BONH 140:62
  i. to offend the national religion — BENT 77:68
  natural i. of the Anglo-Saxon — BAGE 51:85
  one-eyed yellow i. — HAYES 387:62
  plaything and their i. — SHEL 782:10
idolatry contemporary man's i. — MONT 591:62
  on this side i. — JONS 450:55
  organization of i. — SHAW 778:4
  stubbornness is as iniquity and i. — BIBLE 91:89
idols i. of consumption' — LOWE 521:63
  like old i. — BOTT 146:17
if 'i.' is the only peacemaker — SHAK 751:92
Iffucan Chieftain I. of Azcan — STEV 819:20
ignis fatuus Reason, an i. f. — ROCH 691:56
ignoble made i. talk — TENN 846:20

travel…engages the i.   CELI 202:35
truth of the i.   KEATS 457:89
Were it not for i.   JOHN 445:35
whispering chambers of I.   DICK 268:48
woman indulges her i.   NATH 609:20
imaginations jumbled…in our i.   AUST 43:69
perish through their own i.   BOOK 142:39
imaginative genuine i. event   ROTH 699:28
richness of i. resource   WILDE 908:87
the truly i….analytic   POE 656:18
imagine i. a boot stamping   ORWE 630:4
i. a destiny   FIED 322:29
Try to i.   THUR 859:45
young men can possibly i.   SMITH 799:77
imagined i., not recalled?   LOWE 521:61
imbecility i., extravagance and political
hysteria   CHUR 215:56
i. in females   AUST 44:93
reduce women of a certain age to i.   BROO 156:27
sneaking piece of i.   SCOTT 723:14
imbrown golden ear I. the slope   POPE 659:97
imitate i. the action of the tiger   SHAK 746:42
never failed to i. them   BALD 53:33
imitated Genius…is not i.   DIDE 273:88
who has not i.?   INGR 429:61
imitation Comedy is an i.   SIDN 791:21
I. is more interesting   STEIN 815:23
i….is the easiest   CONF 230:86
I. is the sincerest form of flattery   COLT 228:54
Poetry…is an art of i.   SIDN 791:19
servile i. thrown away   CAREW 190:54
What is the beauty of i.?   DIDE 273:85
imitator i. is a poor kind of creature   WHIS 902:64
Immanuel call his name I.   BIBLE 102:14
immensity I. cloistered   DONNE 280:65
in that enormous i.   BRAUN 150:98
immigrants all i. to this place   ATWO 38:53
children of i.   RUSS 705:49
immoral All art is i.   WILDE 908:95
illegal, i. or fattening   WOOL 923:60
i. is what you feel bad after   HEMI 394:4
moral or an i. book   WILDE 908:99
not considered i., or even bad form   CECIL 202:25
people looked on it as i.   GALS 344:25
self-assertion as i.   KURO 482:42
immorality i. is what they dislike   WHIT 904:15
old i. condoned   SHAW 782:5
rigid code of i.   BRAD 148:53
smacks of levity, i. almost   STARK 813:72
immortal Being a thing i.   SHAK 751:26
cold i. hands   SWIN 833:32
dim night of this i. day   SHEL 785:82
grow i. as they quote   YOUNG 935:79
His biting is i.   SHAK 766:59
human spirit is i.   MURP 604:2
i….because he has a soul   FAUL 318:64
i. diamond   HOPK 413:8
i. diet   RALE 677:99
i. god of harmony   BEET 70:95
I., invisible, God   SMITH 801:26
I. longings in me   SHAK 766:60
i. part of myself   SHAK 760:78
i. spirit of the dead   SPEN 807:65
I. youth to mortal maids   LAND 488:78
lifting…into i. sunlight   CUMM 247:1
long i. dream   KEATS 458:21
Sire of an i. strain   SHEL 785:91
son who…would make you i.   MARQ 553:20
taken an i. wound   FROST 339:19
This little steamer…is i.   PRIE 668:19
What i. hand or eye   BLAKE 135:61
immortality angling for i.   HUXL 425:86
belief in i.   DOST 283:8
cannot bear the sight of your i.   MARQ 553:20
earthly i.   FORD 330:12
hope full of i.   BIBLE 107:31
i….through not dying   ALLEN 12:49
I….to such as are fit for it   EMER 313:43
just Ourselves—And I.   DICK 272:66
longing after i.?   ADDI 7:38
milk's leap toward i.   FADI 317:36
millions long for i.   ERTZ 315:91
no i., no soul or mind   STEI 816:47
only cruel i.   TENN 846:25
permanence, for i.   NUTT 619:83
Seal of Divinity and I.   AUBR 39:71
To desire i.   SCHO 719:32

immortals battles with the i.   HOMER 409:16
Francis Parkman and other i.   PRIAL 668:13
President of the i.   HARDY 382:63
verbal portraits…of the i.   CHUR 215:41
immunity shield of congressional i.   SMITH 800:88
Sleep demands…guilty i.   BARN 60:63
immutable Few things are as i.   GALB 343:91
laws of prose writing are as i.   HEMI 394:17
perfect, not i.   MILT 583:80
imp i. of fame   SHAK 746:49
impact historic i. upon the social
judgement that makes an i.   NISB 616:39
  LEAV 498:2
impartial i. in thought as well   WILS 916:9
impartiality I. is an acquired taste   RIFK 687:82
Protestations of i. I shall make none   COBB 223:47
impassioned i., at the birth   ERNST 315:89
impatience time…ticking with i.   RAINE 677:95
Whatever…my enthusiasm or i.   SHIP 789:77
impatient i. as the wind   WORD 928:49
i. to see him   SMITH 800:2
so i. of inferiority   JOHN 441:23
impeachment i. against William Jefferson
Clinton   ANON 25:80
impediment know cause or just i.   BOOK 142:18
impediments free of all i.   MARP 553:18
impenetrable what is i….really exists   EINS 301:37
imperfect abhor the i.   CURZ 249:53
I describe i. characters   BRON 155:84
i. is all our knowledge!   DONNE 281:91
perfect use of an i. medium   WILDE 908:2
thereby be i. in all   PLATH 654:63
imperfection hold on to my i.   FRAN 333:88
still I find Some i.   WORD 925:90
imperfections dwell rather upon…i.   ADDI 6:18
means of seeing one's i.   NIEB 614:98
more beloved for the i.   RUSK 703:7
imperial enslaves you on i. principles   SHAW 777:65
imperialism i. would be razed   MAO 548:10
US i.   MAO 548:11
imperialistic We're not i.   RUMS 702:70
imperialists i. brought…cannons   PEOP 647:24
impermanence beautied with i.   SCOTT 722:76
impersonation i. of desire   BROO 156:27
impertinent Ask an i. question   BRON 154:69
impinged desire not to be i. upon   BERL 80:21
impious i. men bear sway   ADDI 7:37
implacable i. in hate   DRYD 290:79
implanted God has i. in me   CRUZ 246:89
implausible no matter how i.   SHAR 776:44
implication idiomatical kind of i.   STER 818:88
implore I adore thee, i. thee   STUA 827:99
importance attach too much i.   RUSS 705:51
diminish the i. [of newspapers]   TOCQ 862:88
inverse ratio to the i.   HUXL 425:80
little of his own i.   GREE 371:65
important i. while they're doing it   MITC 588:92
little things are infinitely the most i.   DOYLE 285:87
living well…most i.   PLATO 655:81
look i. and to say   KIPL 474:70
more i. than keeping a good diary   SASS 716:71
most i. of all the lessons   HUXL 426:99
most i. single thing   JOVA 451:76
most i. thing in acting   GOLD 362:90
most i. thing in life   PASC 641:29
most i. thing in the world   SHAW 777:47
Paintin's not i.   MOSES 600:75
Personal relations are the i. thing   FORS 331:35
seen to be so i.   JAMES 434:72
think that's pretty i.   KING 468:31
importation i. of all foreign wines   SMITH 798:48
importune too proud to i.   GRAY 370:42
imposition idle and most false i.   SHAK 760:79
impossibility frightened by my human i.   ANDR 16:24
i….to prove that God does not exist   LABR 484:79
Upon I.   MARV 556:66
impossible beings which are i.   REDON 681:74
certain because it is i.   TERT 849:83
frontiers of the i.   KILLY 467:16
i. that any beholder   SIDN 791:21
i. to find out who was…leaking   REAG 681:66
i….its open his mouth   SHAW 780:67
i. to repeat in one period   RENO 683:9
i….will be done   CALO 185:45
Loving your neighbour…bloody i.   CLEE 220:72
nothing shall be i. unto you   BIBLE 112:65
one can't believe i. things   CARR 196:7
peaceful revolution i.   KENN 462:19

scientist…states that something is i.   CLAR 220:59
splendid failure to do the i.   FAUL 319:71
think on things i.   DRYD 287:16
very difficult, maybe i.   SOLOW 803:60
when you have eliminated the i.   DOYLE 285:54
wish it were i.   JOHN 447:71
works at the i.   STEI 816:41
imposters treat those two i.   KIPL 473:67
impotence cases of wrongdoing or i.   ROOS 696:53
i. of being earnest   CANN 188:8
wasn't i. that led me in to a reclusive
existence   ROTH 700:32
impotent An i. people   THOM 854:26
i. as a beached whale   TIME 860:73
impoverishment increase…in i.   HARR 383:88
imprecision Decay with i.   ELIOT 307:2
i. of feeling   ELIOT 308:23
impress marked with their own i.   WOOLF 922:34
impression change…the received i.   PRICE 668:15
conveyed much the same i.   SIMON 792:38
figure to receive an i.   ROSSO 698:7
first i. pleases   TINT 861:78
i. is of a slightly   NICO 614:95
i. you produce   ROSSO 698:6
naive i. of the scene   MONET 591:53
novel is an i.   HARDY 382:64
produce an i. on the reader   BENN 76:53
produces a false i.   WILDE 909:35
impressionable girl at an i. age   SPARK 806:23
impressions falseness in all our i.   RUSK 704:10
few true i.   BELL 74:86
imbued with two deep i.   PAST 642:46
most striking of all the i.   MACM 536:71
occupation and change…weaken i.   AUST 44:96
one hundred times more i.   LEGER 501:53
weaving and unweaving of false i.   ELIOT 303:70
imprison i. the child in her house   WHITE 903:91
Take me to You, i. me   DONNE 281:71
imprisoned i. some, and beheaded   STAL 812:55
No free man shall be taken or i.   MAGN 539:27
Which i. you   HUGH 419:53
imprisonment i.! The Dungeon of   MILT 586:50
morality of i.   SHAK 757:16
on pain of i.   EDWA 300:15
upon pain of i.   ELIZ 309:58
improbabilities adding to the i.   HAWT 386:51
improbable occurrence of the i.   MENC 565:58
improbity guards against i.   BENT 77:70
impromptu preparing his i. speeches   BIRK 131:69
improper conceal something i.   FLAU 327:43
impropriety I. is the soul of wit   MAUG 561:74
no i….with Miss Keeler   PROF 670:59
without i.   GILB 354:15
improve can't i. something   TUTU 870:71
done to i. it   KEIL 460:70
i. the means for achieving   HUXL 425:83
improved Englishman was niver i.   DUNNE 295:23
enormously i. by death   SAKI 710:46
i. her French   GRAH 365:36
i. out of all knowledge   SITW 794:74
improvement i. in the productive   SMITH 797:38
in its gradual i.   THOR 857:80
only i. she could detect   ALTH 13:68
or i. than population   MILL 570:60
improvements no i….introduced   ANON 22:45
improving an i., an advancing   DONNE 281:93
certain of i.   HUXL 425:88
improvisation i. of human existence   MCCU 529:22
impudence much of Cockney i.   RUSK 704:34
starve for want of i.   DRYD 290:9
impudent i. mountebank who sold pills   ADDI 5:8
silly things…in an i. way   AUST 43:84
impulse i. from a vernal wood   WORD 924:75
i. of the moment   AUST 42:64
i. to acquisition   WEBER 894:68
i. to punish is powerful   NIET 615:16
i. to write a novel   WILS 915:75
i. without purpose   BIER 129:44
narrative i. is always with us   COOV 236:58
natural i. which God   CRUZ 246:89
owes all its onward i.   HAWT 386:46
rooted in the sexual i.   SCHO 719:33
their wonted i. give   COLE 226:1
impulses manipulation of his own i.   MILL 573:34
impunity holy…with i.?   RACI 677:87
with strict i.   TATE 836:3
impure To the Puritan all things are i.   LAWR 495:32

impurity bring i. much rather · MILT 579:70
imputation i. of this idiot · NASHE 609:14
inability historic i. in Britain · HAUG 385:28
  i. to cross the street · WOOLF 923:52
  i. to put on your socks · GONC 363:94
inaccuracy little i. sometimes saves · SAKI 710:49
inaction i. of those who could · HAILE 377:67
inadequate i. for getting to France · KINN 470:68
inane Pinnacled dim in the intense i. · SHEL 785:81
inanimate stupidity of the i. · STER 817:61
inanity folly and i. · STOWE 826:78
inarticulate I., arctic · SCOTT 722:78
  raid on the i. · ELIOT 308:23
inattention same i. is discovered · JOHN 446:58
inbreeding sick with i. · THOM 854:26
Inca sensuous and elegant I. · DARIO 252:2
  Who was our first I.? · GARC 345:42
incantation overlay of priestly i. · GALB 343:1
incantations Whispering lunar i. · ELIOT 305:29
incapacitated man who is not…i. · GLAD 358:89
incapacity i. is worse · JEFF 436:7
incarnate Jesus Christ, living and i. · BONH 140:58
  world is order i. · MILL 573:33
incarnation gift…is I. · ELIOT 308:35
  i. of this verse · SHEL 783:48
  nearest thing in i. to…God · OLIV 624:70
incense morning i. · BARL 60:58
  Orchid—breathing i. · BASHO 63:43
  stupefying i.-smoke · BROW 161:33
incentive cruelty without i. · JOHN 442:57
incentives might reduce i. · KRUG 481:25
inceptions multiplying of former i. · DONNE 281:93
incest i. holds the family together · INNIS 429:68
  luxury and damnèd i. · SHAK 752:33
inch cubic i. of some stars · MACC 527:85
  every i. a king · SHAK 763:87
  Not an i. of our territory · FAVRE 319:78
inch-rule his own i.-r. of taste · ADAMS 4:78
incident Body-line was not an i. · JAMES 433:32
  determination of i.? · JAMES 433:44
incidental wifehood…but i. · STAN 812:63
incidents i. well linked · COWP 240:47
incisions Underneath their fine i. · DICK 272:53
incite do not rear children, you i. · JARR 435:86
incivility sabbath-breaking…to i. · DE 262:10
inclination as i. leads him · JOHN 443:64
  do not check their i. · MONT 591:66
  door of i. · DEFOE 258:20
  general i. of all mankind · HOBB 404:26
  i. of my nature · ELIZ 309:55
  who have no i. for either · LESS 505:46
  wicked i. in most people · JOHN 446:58
inclinations highest i. of a man · LONS 517:69
  multitude of perverse i. · SHAR 776:41
  our i. daily alter · ETHE 315:96
include I. me out · GOLD 362:87
incognito eternal i. · BARN 60:63
income Annual i. twenty pounds · DICK 269:67
  as a source of i. · KEMB 461:82
  define a man's i. · HICKS 402:80
  good i. is of no avail · SMITH 799:75
  I. Tax return has made · ROGE 694:18
  in favour of inequality of i. · SHAW 781:86
  large i. is the best recipe · AUST 43:76
  lottery…yields public i. · QUINE 675:52
  real i. is increased · KEYN 466:91
  real i. of the community · KEYN 466:88
  rises to meet i. · PARK 639:87
  that sort of i. bracket · MORL 598:89
incomes inequalities of i. and wealth · KEYN 466:93
  live beyond their i. · SAKI 710:43
incompetence not i. but war · PIER 651:6
  rise to his level of i. · PETER 649:76
incompetent election by the i. many · SHAW 778:5
  i. as the average male · CUNN 248:26
  i. swine · SASS 716:63
  tax on pianos for the i. · SITW 794:78
incomplete i. self · GASS 346:61
  judge yourself i. · NERVO 611:47
incomprehension gulf of mutual i. · SNOW 802:38
inconsistencies searches out any i. · RUSS 705:41
inconstancy I., boredom, anxiety · PASC 640:14
  infidelity is not i. · LACL 484:87
  Man with that i. was born · BEHN 71:21
  nothing…constant, but i. · SWIFT 830:59
inconstant i., uncertain, unknown · LOCKE 514:15
incontinence turpitude of i. · SCOTT 725:43

inconvenience adventure is…i. · CHES 211:65
  i. is often considerable · AUST 43:85
  not made without i. · JOHN 442:37
inconveniences free…of all i. · MARP 553:18
  i. attend play-going · TYNAN 872:44
inconvenient cause may be i. · BENN 76:43
  i. to be poor · COWP 241:58
incorruptible seagreen I. · CARL 192:10
increase another man's price i. · WILS 916:99
  God gave the i. · BIBLE 121:93
  He must i. · BIBLE 117:83
  i. in inverse ratio · HUXL 425:80
  i. of riches and commerce · HUME 422:12
  not i. its consumption · KEYN 466:91
  without either i. or diminution · RICA 685:36
increases What judgement I had i. · DRYD 292:43
incredulity epoch of i. · DICK 271:19
increments i. of noise · BYATT 178:91
indebted I. and discharged · MILT 582:54
  thing I'm i. to her for · FIEL 323:52
indecency I.'s conspiracy of silence · SHAW 779:19
indecent I.…10 years before · LAVER 493:81
  i. behaviour · WAUGH 891:9
  inhuman and i. and dishonorable · HELL 392:74
  name itself as i. · SPEN 807:63
  to assume such i. postures · WILDE 910:65
indecision My I. is Final · EBER 298:75
indefensible defence of the i. · ORWE 629:87
  defending…i. · CHES 211:51
indemnity Double I. · CAIN 184:32
independence chief virtue…is its i. · SCOTT 722:75
  for our i. · PITT 653:46
  new electronic i. · MCLU 536:58
  war for i. · SCHL 718:10
  willing to grant America i. · GEOR 349:12
independent Britain as an i. European state · GAIT 343:89
  free and i. condition · ADAMS 5:93
  I. existence—so called · HUXL 425:75
  i. of the vagaries · ACHE 2:26
indestructible endless and i. · WILL 914:55
  We, i.! · GRASS 367:60
indeterminate Science rejects the i. · BERN 81:37
index i. of a feeling mind · CRAB 242:5
  i. of output per capita · MISH 587:79
  i. of this country · MARC 549:35
  i. to the heart · DICK 268:41
  man the i. of that book · DONNE 282:95
  marble i. of a mind · WORD 925:98
  true i. of a man's character · CONN 233:83
indexes enshrined in 10,000 i. · ALLEN 12:37
  Wall Street i. predicted · SAMU 712:80
India decided to cycle to I. · MURP 604:99
  Englishman's justification in I. · CURZ 249:53
  fly to I. for gold · MARL 552:94
  fly to I. for gold · MARL 552:98
  From I.'s coral strand · HEBER 390:34
  gone to I. · YEATS 934:61
  in twentieth-century I. · FRIE 337:64
  loss of I. · CHUR 216:65
  money in I. · KIPL 472:32
  Nothing in I. is identifiable · FORS 331:42
  pitched battles in I. · MACA 526:58
  realize what I. is · CURZ 249:51
  So far I like I. · MAIL 540:67
Indian history of the I. Ocean · NAIP 606:50
  likely to be an I. · HEAT 390:30
  Like the base I. · SHAK 761:19
  Lo! the poor I. · POPE 660:11
  only good I. · SHER 787:32
  poetry…in the legendary I. · DARIO 252:2
  Shadow…an old I. name · AMIS 14:97
  treated like an I. widow · MITF 589:10
Indians I. are you · BALD 54:39
  I., if we last another twenty years · MCMU 537:86
  I. singing the…requiem · DUNC 295:12
  reading Neville Cardus to the I. · THOM 852:77
Indies carry the wealth of the I. · JOHN 445:31
indifference heresy in the form of i. · RAHN 677:91
  i., a physical i. · LAWR 494:3
  i. of those · HAILE 377:67
  i.—the fern-dark i. · LAWR 494:7
  pass over youth in dull i. · CONG 231:32
  serene i. · WILL 912:4
  superb i. to mortal · STEV 822:1
  there shall be i. · SMITH 799:65
indifferent delayed till I am i. · JOHN 442:34
  i.…at the birth of his work · ERNST 315:89

i. judge · SIDN 790:10
  Is God by definition i. · EBER 298:74
  worst sin…to be i. · SHAW 777:66
indifferentism rather than i. · NIGH 616:51
indifferently look on both i. · SHAK 747:74
indigenous intrinsic, i., something · MORR 599:7
indigent How i. the great! · GRAY 369:5
indigestion morale and high i. · MURK 604:98
indignation Moral i. · WELLS 898:85
  noble and terrific i. · LESS 505:35
  wrath and i. against us · BOOK 141:2
indignations books…contain…our i. · CONR 234:10
indignities by i.…to dignities · BACON 48:2
  i. real and imagined · WHITE 903:98
indignity God…spared me the i. · BELL 72:52
  held himself free from i. · PALM 636:24
  ultimate i. is to be given · KUHN 481:37
indirection sense by i. · EVANS 316:20
indiscretion cliché and an i. · MACM 536:68
  i. without temptation · BIER 129:41
individual and every i. · TRUM 868:29
  And the i. withers · TENN 841:84
  bestowed on the i. · MCCA 528:99
  capacity for i. enterprise · WAVE 893:58
  debased of style, not i. · MAIL 540:52
  definition of an i. · KOES 477:28
  difficult…for the i. · HAYEK 387:59
  economic liberties of the i. · KRIS 480:15
  ethical reality of the i. · KIER 467:10
  Every form is i. · HEIN 391:54
  Every i.…intends only · SMITH 798:49
  faith in i. enterprise · BURT 174:66
  feeling i. appeared weak · BELL 74:85
  for a private i. or for a city · PLATO 655:3
  force…the i. to believe · PENF 646:20
  growth in the i. · SMIL 797:32
  happiness of an i. · JOHN 444:94
  herd instinct in the i. · NIET 615:7
  idea…extinguished in i. minds · DURK 296:34
  immortality for the i. · SCHO 719:32
  i., and only the i. · NABO 606:40
  i. features are portrayed · HUMB 421:5
  i. is a minority · ELLI 311:90
  i. is no longer to be sovereign · DOUG 284:34
  i. men and women · THAT 850:28
  i. opinions are not colorful · SAFI 708:2
  i. profit without i. responsibility · BIER 129:24
  Insists I too am an i. · LARK 490:22
  law [of competition]…hard for the i. · CARN 193:49
  life style…destructive of the i. · HARV 385:23
  moral i. courage in Chinese · MO 589:20
  no i. can recollect the order · WELL 897:60
  of the ignorant i. · KEYN 466:86
  only done by one i. · MACH 533:99
  oppressed or obscure i. · HAZL 388:78
  ordinary in the i. · MANN 546:74
  the autonomous i. · ORWE 628:56
  the i. and…the state · PLATO 654:27
  wanted to be an i. · GULL 375:36
  what any i. thinks · PETE 649:78
  work of the i. · SIKO 791:32
individualism aberrations of i. · SMALL 796:21
  American system of rugged i. · HOOV 411:59
individuality i. is…special error · SCHO 719:32
  I.…the aim of political liberty · COOP 236:53
  i.…the weakness of our race · DELA 260:59
  men without i. have no taste · BENN 76:52
individuals gifted i. manage · SAKI 710:43
  hostile behavior…to i. · FULB 341:45
  i. are always right · VIAN 880:76
  I. pass like shadows · BURKE 168:23
  i. when they make up · KEYN 465:84
  negotiation between i. · MUNCH 603:81
  not consist of i. · MARX 558:74
  satisfactory to i. inside · BIOY 130:56
  set of atomic i. · NOVAK 618:72
  worth of the i. composing · MILL 570:68
Indochina jungles of I. · MCGO 532:92
  passed in I. · GREE 371:57
indoctrination substituting i. · PETE 649:78
indoor Done with i. complaints · WHIT 905:40
indoors We live in the great i. · RAINE 677:93
indubitable absolutely i. · DESC 263:19
inducement if…i. were offered · KING 469:61
indulge i. in a few follies · PROU 670:72
  naturally i. in a few delinquencies · ELIOT 303:72
  not one that government can i. in · RENO 683:2

indulgence i. encourages us — COWP 241:66
i. to sit in a room — HELL 392:73
kind protection and i. — STOWE 826:72
indulgences i….never change — BEAU 66:2
industrial advanced i. society — HAYEK 387:60
i. and economic status — SKEL 795:94
i. balance sheets — WEIL 896:31
i. worker would sooner have…£5 — BLYT 138:24
new i. revolution — WIEN 907:68
The I. Revolution — TOYN 864:25
industrially they who rule i. — CONN 233:88
industrious man who…is i. — DICK 269:78
industry British i. — HEATH 390:20
Captains of I. — CARL 193:39
employ their whole i. — SMITH 798:48
grip upon i. — TAWN 837:8
her i. and economy — STAN 812:65
I am an i. — CRUY 246:86
I. and all the virtues — HUXL 425:67
i. and intuition — WILS 915:78
i. can't take you — UPDI 874:75
i. that…needs better people — DRUC 287:12
Life without i. — RUSK 704:29
literary i. would not exist — LESS 505:42
Ministers of I. — MAND 545:54
re-equipping of British i. — BEVE 85:27
stream of human i. — TOCQ 861:81
subsidy to the high technology i. — CHOM 214:20
there is no place for i. — HOBB 404:27
War is the national i. — MIRA 587:75
whole field to private i. — HELL 392:63
inedible i. raised to the unspeakable — BASK 63:46
ineffable as an i. mystery — SCHW 721:70
i. effable — ELIOT 307:10
ineffective i. from close up — SCHO 720:36
inefficiency efficiency and i. — SHAW 779:36
inept earth peopled as ever by the i. — REPP 683:12
inequalities significant i. of incomes — KEYN 466:93
inequality great i. of environment — CARN 193:49
in favour of i. of income — SHAW 781:86
saddest sight…fortune's i. exhibits — CARL 193:26
inevitable arguing with the i. — LOWE 520:38
foresee the i. — ASIM 35:4
have a suspicion it's i. — LEAC 497:73
i. the Titanic was going to set sail — HAGUE 376:61
violent revolution i. — KENN 462:19
inexhaustible what is i. is benevolent — FRYE 340:39
inexpressible expressing the i. — HUXL 425:72
infallible i. criterion of wisdom — BURKE 169:45
i. symptom — GIBB 351:55
not final because we are i. — JACK 432:10
infamous acting…unlawfull, i. — PRYN 672:93
infamy I.! I.! — ROTH 700:35
old lies and new i. — POUND 664:39
infancy about him in his i. — GREE 370:50
dug a spring in i. — BRON 154:76
Heaven…in our i. — WORD 926:24
i. of our poetry — DRYD 292:44
In unexperienc'd i. — TRAH 864:35
Irish…in the i. of the race — OFAO 622:33
lies about us in our i. — MITC 588:85
Women are from their very I. — ASTE 36:21
infant an i. of three — RANS 679:21
describe the i. phenomenon — DICK 267:8
head of the human i. — SCHR 720:43
i. breaks its rattle — SADE 708:93
i. crying for the light — TENN 843:42
i. whose middle — NASH 608:93
Sooner murder an i. — BLAKE 134:45
to a little i. — BACON 47:75
infantile i. death-rate — HALD 377:73
infants filthy, sturdy, unkillable i. — POUND 664:29
i. are trying to spell God — ROBI 690:33
Sustenance for their helpless I. — SWIFT 831:92
infect she would i. to the North Star — SHAK 744:94
infected come i. back — WILB 907:75
infection difficult to stay a moral i. — DICK 271:17
facilitate the i. of idiocy — BIER 129:33
for fear of the i. — PEPYS 647:43
i. and the hand of war — SHAK 734:8
i. of politics — BRON 154:67
i. of the common sky — GRAV 367:68
new risks of i. — WEIZ 896:35
infelicity her i.…years too many — WEBS 895:19
inference i….watch…had a maker — PALEY 635:16
inferior becomes the i. — GREE 371:65
i. to most civilised ages — CARL 191:84

not to be i. to…nature — PERI 648:65
Switzerland as an i. — SMITH 801:8
Titles…are disgraced by the i. — SHAW 778:9
inferiority always conscious of an i. — JOHN 445:22
lie of their i. — KING 468:42
preserved from a state of i. — GEOR 349:12
say he has an i. complex — SALI 711:59
inferno i. depicted by Dr Goebbels — ORWE 628:59
moronic i. — BELL 74:82
moronic i. of insipidity — LEWIS 508:6
infidelity I. does not consist — PAINE 634:98
i. is not inconstancy — LACL 484:87
infield No reason why the i. — SHAW 781:96
infinite being absolutely i. — SPIN 811:36
Canna see the i. — MACD 529:38
everything would appear…i. — BLAKE 134:46
for both are i. — SHAK 736:52
Her i. variety — SHAK 765:26
his passion is I. — PARK 638:59
how i. in faculty — SHAK 752:57
in comparison to the i. — PASC 641:28
i. can never meet — MARV 556:67
i. choice — GITL 358:86
i. diversity of movement — REDT 681:76
i. number of possibilities — GREE 371:69
man and the i.! — MACD 529:32
striving toward the i. — HUMB 421:2
there is an I. in him — CARL 192:99
To feel the i. — STAEL 812:54
zero and the i. — JARRY 435:92
infinitely i. large and i. small — LEVI 506:61
i. small amount of commodity — JEVO 438:45
infinities arise…you numberless i. — DONNE 280:66
infinitive split an i….stay split — CHAN 204:81
split i. is always wrong — THUR 860:59
infinitude speculations of eternity or i. — ADDI 6:22
infinity i. in the palm of your hand — BLAKE 135:66
infirm I. of purpose! — SHAK 767:4
Minstrel was i. and old — SCOTT 722:84
infirmities i. of old age — WESL 900:23
infirmity feblit with i. — DUNB 294:6
i. of noble mind — MILT 578:49
propTo our i. — WORD 925:95
inflammation i. of the sentence — THUR 859:46
inflation Having a little i. — HEND 395:34
not just i….or stagnation — MACL 536:55
Rising prices…do not cause i. — WRIS 930:93
Steel prices cause i. — BLOU 137:8
inflexible i. political persuasion — WILS 916:3
inflict i. myself on the public — MORL 598:90
influence auspicious star, whose i. — SHAK 774:78
books that i. us — FORS 332:56
bright eyes Rain i. — MILT 576:10
British 'Sphere of I.' — ANON 21:35
clothes possess an i. — ALCO 10:5
direct i. upon the soul — KAND 454:38
Film art has a greater i. — BALA 53:26
guard against…unwarranted i. — EISE 302:58
i. of a government — REES 682:89
i. of a nation — BENN 75:17
i. of…Milton and Dryden — ELIOT 305:50
i….of our own family — CHUR 215:41
i. of the Crown — DUNN 295:25
i. them from within — JOHN 438:55
i. which is moved not — SHEL 786:17
no i. on the future value — JEVO 438:46
often malign i. — MUGG 601:50
save…from its i. — WEBB 893:63
think I can i. them slightly — THOM 853:80
two points of i. — ARNO 34:57
where his i. stops — ADAMS 4:80
influences i. them in proportion — TOCQ 861:85
intellectual i. — KEYN 466:89
thousand i. constantly press — ORWE 627:37
influenza call it i. if ye like — BENN 76:42
information armed with the same i. — MISH 587:80
branch of the i. business — WRIS 930:91
dispersed i. — HAYEK 387:60
Everybody gets so much i. — STEIN 815:22
find i. upon it — JOHN 444:9
haphazard heap of i. — TOLS 863:7
I. is any difference — BATE 64:50
I….necessary to the human mind — REES 682:89
i. vegetable, animal and mineral — GILB 354:99
knowledge…lost in i.? — ELIOT 307:87
maximum amount of i. — WILS 915:87
money is just another form of i. — WRIS 930:93

not by giving new i. — WITT 918:43
only ask for i. — DICK 269:72
pure i. — GOULD 365:24
read partly for i. — SCHL 718:11
Withholding i. from someone — KLINE 476:12
woman of…little i. — AUST 42:62
informed but far better i. — BIRK 130:67
desire to be i. — BROW 158:57
informer i….cannot be a soldier — FLAU 326:30
informing i. them narrowly — GALB 343:96
ingenious i. are always fanciful — POE 656:18
no matter how i. — KISS 475:93
ingots back with i. bows — SHAK 758:33
i., like in each respect — MARL 553:13
ingrateful for the multitude to be i. — SHAK 769:63
On her i. top! — SHAK 763:68
ingratitude As man's i. — SHAK 749:52
buried by i. — LYLY 523:9
I. is monstrous — SHAK 769:63
I., more strong than traitors' arms — SHAK 748:11
I., thou marble-hearted fiend — SHAK 762:62
ingredients the very i. of virtue — MILT 579:75
ingress i. into the world — LONG 516:63
inhabitant i. of the North of England — FORD 329:1
ordinary i. is incomprehensible — STARK 813:75
inhabitants i. not…grow old — CONN 233:81
i. of different planets — DISR 276:53
i. of myth — FIED 322:29
landscape and its i. — UPDI 875:97
shared among its i. — SIDG 790:95
such uncomely i. — WALP 887:21
inhale as if she would i. them — FIRB 323:72
but I didn't i. — RICH 686:72
didn't i. — DOWD 284:40
To i. Paris — HUGO 421:90
inherent i. in the human situation — GREE 371:72
inherit all which it i. — SHAK 774:94
inheritance care for its literary i. — ELIOT 307:84
Has had a like i. — YEATS 934:61
have our i. — SMITH 799:65
heathen for thine i. — BIBLE 94:84
heir to an i. — OAKE 620:88
how my i. was proceeding — HAMER 378:96
spending my children's i. — ANON 25:69
inheritor succeed as his i. — SHAK 769:54
inheritors i. of an old civilization — REYES 684:21
inhibition I. is no good provider — HESI 401:66
inhibitions cultivate a few i. — LOOS 517:81
inhuman artists…want to become i. — APOL 27:13
i. and indecent and dishonorable — HELL 392:74
i. in its materialism — WILS 915:77
inhumanity essence of i. — SHAW 777:66
i. of a boa constrictor — WOOL 923:63
Man's i. to Man — BURNS 170:80
refuses to remember the i. — WEIZ 896:35
rewarded with i. — ROLL 695:33
iniquities bruised for our i. — BIBLE 104:51
forgiveth all thine i. — BIBLE 97:62
If thou, Lord, shouldest mark i. — BIBLE 98:95
rewarded us according to our i. — BIBLE 97:63
iniquity hated i. — GREG 372:95
infamous seminary of i. — CHES 211:38
i. is taken away — BIBLE 102:12
shapen in i. — BIBLE 95:28
stubbornness is as i. — BIBLE 91:89
tongue is…a world of i. — BIBLE 124:13
visiting i. of the fathers — BIBLE 88:23
initiation i. into a new state — ELIOT 303:81
injured always being the i. party — ANGE 17:42
forgiveness to the i. — DRYD 288:36
injuries i. sustained in his native town — ANON 21:29
poisons and awkward i. — ANOU 26:96
take revenge for slight i. — MACH 533:97
injurious highly i. to the poor — HALL 378:91
injury height without sustaining i. — LEON 503:13
i. is much sooner forgotten — CHES 210:28
i. would vex a very saint — SHAK 732:38
members from i. and molestation — MILL 570:64
result of a critical i. — RUSS 705:41
Where there is i. — FRAN 334:98
injustice cruel i. if you deny it — CARL 193:30
fear of suffering i. — LARO 491:48
grave i. to bees — ORWE 628:46
I. anywhere is a threat — KING 468:32
i. of taking a speck for the whole — EDGE 299:5
I….prevents my doing it — BUTL 178:77
nothing so finely perceived…as i. — DICK 271:29

protect him against i. — PALM 636:24
superior to i. — PLATO 655:95
injustices i. are sanctioned — FRAN 333:91
ink 12 ounces of paper and i. — MORL 598:86
black i. in white milk — MUNRO 603:88
brain that i. may character — SHAK 773:45
buy i. by the barrel — KIRK 474:86
cuttlefish squirting out i. — ORWE 628:62
Every drop of i. — WALP 887:24
gunpowder and printer's i. — KRAUS 480:12
Hamlet is so much paper and i. — PRIE 668:17
hath not drunk i. — SHAK 733:79
I....A villainous compound — BIER 129:33
i....tempered with love's sighs — SHAK 734:85
medium is printer's i. — KRAUS 480:8
mix...water with their i. — GOET 360:20
Rorschach i. blots — LICH 509:25
spend time and i. — GALS 344:24
win...By blood or i. — BYRON 181:70
inmate who is...the i. — CONA 230:80
inn best in every i. — STEV 821:73
brought him to an i. — BIBLE 115:38
Do you remember an I. — BELL 73:65
In the worst i.'s worst room — POPE 660:5
no room for them in the i. — BIBLE 115:25
that dark i.—the Grave! — SCOTT 724:16
world's an i. — DRYD 292:59
inn-door up to the old i.-d. — NOYES 619:78
inner i. process — WITT 918:47
strengthened...in the i. man — BIBLE 122:45
innings life was like his i. — EGAN 301:24
Innisfree go to I. — YEATS 932:30
innocence ceremony of i. is drowned — YEATS 933:50
end of i. — GOLD 360:28
first state of i. — BEHN 71:18
Ignorance is not i. — BROW 162:91
i. and even the right — RODR 693:95
I. ends when one is stripped — DIDI 274:4
I. is a science of the sublime — CIXO 219:40
i. should be bold — MASS 560:46
I. thy Sister dear! — MARV 556:72
lost their i. — GREER 372:89
Never such i. — LARK 490:31
purity and place and i. — MILT 583:71
Some final i. — SPEN 807:49
spurious i. — BELL 74:89
though conscious of your i. — JOHN 445:18
wanting to hold onto i. — WILS 914:69
worthy of the joy of i. — OFLA 622:35
innocency state of i. Adam fell — SHAK 742:23
innocent 'baby', an i. rhyme — SHAK 745:24
But who is i.? — WORD 929:62
Can one be i. — CYRA 250:58
essential self is i. — UPDI 874:90
guilty until...proved i. — ORWE 630:6
i. as strawberries — THOM 852:70
i. of the charge — ARCH 28:37
look like the i. flower — SHAK 766:84
one i. suffer — BLAC 132:94
sleep'—the i. sleep — SHAK 767:2
sores on i. tongues — OWEN 632:57
The i. and the beautiful — YEATS 934:55
to hurt i. people — HELL 392:74
innocents We are...the i. — DELI 261:80
innovate I....or evaporate! — MERR 567:16
To i. is not to reform — BURKE 169:49
innovation Fashion...produces i. — SANT 714:18
I. most of the time — SCHM 719:17
innovations ill-shapen, so are all i. — BACON 49:24
innovator time is the greatest i. — BACON 49:25
inns i. of Molten Blue — DICK 272:57
two years in Holiday I. — MOND 590:48
innuendoes beauty of i. — STEV 819:22
in-office i.-o. attitudes and behavior — COUP 238:93
inquest like the Coroner's I. — CONG 231:25
inquire i. in his temple — BIBLE 95:7
I. often — PENN 647:23
not to i. why or whither — WILD 910:79
inquiries invited his i. — MENC 565:60
religious i. — GIBB 352:61
some i. are too dangerous — SAGAN 708:4
inquiry every i....is thought to aim — ARIS 29:50
i. of truth — BACON 47:72
Inquisition like Galileo going before the I. — LIVI 512:85
inquisition I....from the pulpit — WELD 897:40
To these I. dogs — TENN 848:60
inquisitiveness tribalism and i. — ALDI 10:12

inquisitors severe i. — BACON 48:90
inroad i. on the discipline — OCON 621:19
insane among the i. — DE 257:93
Man is quite i. — MONT 592:81
insanity new idea...close to i. — MILL 571:1
prelude to i. — WAUGH 891:17
So with sanity and i. — MELV 564:47
inscription i. on public fountains — FLAU 327:43
inscriptions In lapidary i. — JOHN 444:13
inscrutability i. of the East — STARK 813:75
inscrutable i. singular name — ELIOT 307:10
i. to the last — THUR 859:31
insect Egyptians came to worship an i. — DISR 276:64
i. moves toward its flower — BALZ 58:16
i. youth are on the wing — GRAY 369:6
into a gigantic i. — KAFKA 454:26
one is but an i. — JOHN 441:29
insects dancing i. — WORD 928:57
Fabulous the i. — WILK 911:96
I. are what neurosis — AMIS 15:8
keep down microscopic i. — DOUG 283:14
insecurity source of economic i. — ELLW 311:92
inseparable found i. — HUME 422:4
i. part — GAND 345:35
inside i. and an outside — HEPW 396:62
i. and strength were philosophy — SIDN 791:17
i. the tent pissing out — JOHN 440:84
insides rest of a person's i. — TWAIN 871:10
insight For i. into human affairs — DYSON 297:62
if it only added judgement to i. — FORS 331:39
i. I have gained from poker — MAMET 543:31
moment's i. — HOLM 408:96
most revolutionary i. of all — JONG 448:96
read...partly for i. — SCHL 718:11
insights deeper i. to the dead belong — FERG 320:5
i. of the Jewish prophets — NIEB 614:98
perceptions and i. — KISS 475:97
insignificance Men thin away to i. — HARDY 381:51
without losing their i. — BAXT 65:89
insignificant as i. as possible — GALT 345:31
obvious and i. — JAMES 434:72
see himself as both exceptional and i. — MAIL 540:53
insincerity clear language is i. — ORWE 628:62
clear language is i. — ORWE 629:89
enemy of...language is i. — ORWE 628:62
enemy of...language is i. — ORWE 629:89
insipid He is many times flat, i. — DRYD 288:25
i. thing is a billet-doux — ETHE 315:93
Simplicity...is wholly i. — HOGA 406:57
insipidity inferno of i. and decay — LEWIS 508:6
insolence i. is not invective — DISR 276:61
i. of wealth — JOHN 445:32
lazy i. of a shoe salesman — PERE 648:58
supports with i. — JOHN 444:29
insolencies i. of other Turks — BUTL 176:36
insolencies i. political ones are i. — HOME 409:11
science leads only to the i. — DISR 276:72
insolvency i. spelt glamour — HAMI 379:3
insomnia febrile i., mortal leaps — MARI 550:52
ideal i. — JOYCE 452:98
inspector An I. Calls — PRIE 668:20
great i., with a myriad eyes — STEAD 813:84
inspiration Genius is one per cent i. — EDIS 300:13
hierophants of an unapprehended i. — SHEL 786:17
My sole i. — PORT 663:7
scripture is given by i. — BIBLE 124:84
temperamental i. — MOND 590:50
inspire feel not what they i. — SHEL 786:17
i. free hearts — KENN 463:23
i. hopeless passion — THAC 849:96
your selves i. These...works — POPE 662:64
inspired i. by the gods inside — SAINT 709:21
inspirer poet is more the i. — ELUA 311:96
instalment last i. missing — CRISP 245:59
instant at that i. — KARSH 455:52
Before me at this i. — SHAK 763:66
be i. in season — BIBLE 124:85
i. that he fell — SCOTT 723:2
perish in the very i. — GRAY 368:91
instinct delicacy of poetic i. — WILDE 908:87
i. for being unhappy — SAKI 710:40
i. for contentment — KRIS 481:16
i. for not ruining...vision — BLUN 137:17
i. of mankind — TAWN 837:8
i.; the habit is already old — LAWR 494:16
i. told him that the best liar — BUTL 178:72
intimate with him by i. — AUST 43:77

Love has its own i. — BALZ 58:16
maternal i. — FRID 337:57
natural i. to abjure man — HARDY 381:55
nerve and i. is clamouring — LESS 504:34
rather of i. than of practice — REED 682:84
satisfies the human creative i. — QUEN 674:39
sublimation of the work i. — LODGE 514:26
what the i....can conceive — PICA 650:97
what we believe upon i. — BRAD 149:71
womanly i. that clothes possess — ALCO 10:5
instinctively what you know i. — BELL 72:43
instincts atheism is against...our i. — BURKE 169:38
born with i. and abilities — BALZ 58:21
High i. — WORD 927:26
i. already catered for — BENN 75:25
only trust our own i. — LAFO 485:97
true to your i.,' was his motto — LAWR 493:87
institution cannot see an i. — CRIT 245:63
deep stake...in such a glorious i. — BURKE 168:15
family as an i. — MILLS 574:89
feature of this i. — DICK 268:26
i. of the throne — ACHE 2:23
Is an i. always — JARR 435:87
It's an i. — HUGH 420:56
no major i. in the US — FRIE 337:65
only i. in the world — SAMU 712:77
partly of human i. — MILL 570:56
such as are in the i. — EMER 312:29
institutions destroy i. — WHIT 905:44
free i. can exist — MARS 554:39
i. are framed — TREV 865:63
i., civil and ecclesiastical — PEEL 646:8
i. presuppose a Supreme Being — DOUG 284:33
most licentious of human i. — SHAW 778:99
old i. entirely reformed — MACH 533:99
take the i. and liberties — POWE 667:94
walls of i. — ROET 694:99
instruct amuse and i. — UPDI 874:86
i. thee and teach thee — BIBLE 95:11
instructed i. and amused — ATLAS 37:38
instruction all the i. and knowledge — JAY 436:98
All true histories contain i. — BRON 154:73
horses of i. — BLAKE 134:43
i. in righteousness — BIBLE 124:3
i. without talent — VITR 882:34
no i. book came with it — FULL 341:55
instructions Bloody i. — SHAK 767:86
instructive something i. — KHOM 466:97
instrument great i. of moral good — SHEL 786:14
I am an i. — RICH 685:47
i. might be less — JOHN 442:39
i. of chase — WELLS 898:79
i. of Your peace — FRAN 334:98
i. plays itself — BACH 46:24
i. that has a good moral effect — ARIS 29:59
i. with which each learns — PLATO 655:1
more perfect i. of the soul — PIUS 653:55
most sensitive i. known to man — BEEC 69:66
old one-stringed i. — RANJ 678:16
painting...an i. of war — PICA 650:98
Polling is merely an i. — GALL 344:20
Prosperity is only an i. — COOL 236:47
supersensitive...i. — ERNST 315:90
The book...a kind of optical i. — PROU 671:92
tune the i. here at the door — DONNE 281:80
instruments all the i. agree — AUDEN 40:1
fit i. to make slaves — PITT 652:40
Furnished...with nice i. — FRAN 335:91
i. ill-adapted for the purpose — CHUR 217:8
i. of labour — MARX 558:12
i. of vengeance — DONO 282:98
I. of War — ALBE 10:99
i., strung to a vast precision — CRANE 243:16
i. to plague us — SHAK 764:2
lofty i. of war — SHAK 742:32
man, and not his i. — MO 589:21
insufferable Oxford...has made me i. — BEER 69:72
insufferables sovereign of i. — BIER 128:10
insult His presence here...an i. — RED 681:71
i. of each other's presence — ISHE 431:91
i. of each shabby skirt — DONO 282:98
i. to the Holy See — INNO 430:71
i....to the cook — CHES 213:3
much sooner forgotten than an i. — CHES 210:28
prolonged i. — MILL 572:15
ring of a really original i. — CARR 194:61
standing i. to sportsmen — FRY 339:22

i. is full of noises	SHAK 774:92
ship, an i., a sickle moon	FLEC 327:52
shores of this happy i.	GLAD 358:92
silent i. imbowers	TENN 839:44
this sceptred i.	SHAK 734:8
isles fished by obstinate i.	POUND 664:36
I. of fragrance	POPE 662:78
taketh up the i.	BIBLE 103:39
Venice…thron'd on her hundred i.!	BYRON 180:31
islets acini degenerate leaving I.	BANT 59:41
Islington from I. to Marybone	BLAKE 135:72
isolated splendidly i. in Europe	FOST 332:58
isolation mute chandeliered i.	CAPO 189:32
personal i. to gentile	ROTH 699:29
Israel bring you into the land of I.	BIBLE 105:89
chariot of I.	BIBLE 92:28
glory of thy people I.	BIBLE 115:27
God is good to I.	BIBLE 96:41
Hear, O I.	BIBLE 89:45
If he be the King of I.	BIBLE 114:3
In I. it's enough	ROTH 699:25
I. loved Joseph	BIBLE 87:93
I. shall be a proverb	BIBLE 91:11
I.'s head forlorn	LAZA 496:52
I.'s monarch	DRYD 289:69
judgment of the children of I.	BIBLE 89:25
lost sheep of the house of I.	BIBLE 111:23
no king in I.	BIBLE 90:77
no, not in I.	BIBLE 110:14
of the stock of I.	BIBLE 123:56
Palestinians in I.	OROU 627:22
ruler in I.	BIBLE 106:12
smote the king of I.	BIBLE 92:27
there is a prophet in I.	BIBLE 92:32
These be thy gods, O I.	BIBLE 89:26
When I. was a child	BIBLE 106:3
issue great i. between the free world	KENN 463:31
i. of that darling Plea	FLET 327:64
poverty, as an i.	KRUG 481:24
issues i. and the highest authorities	SHUL 790:91
truth about important i.	LEWO 508:10
isthmus this i. of a middle state	POPE 660:16
Italia I.! oh I.	BYRON 180:34
Italian cursed be the I.	GARI 346:47
expensive I. pictures	BERE 78:89
I. character has to	MUSS 605:22
speech…dulcet as I.	QUIL 674:44
to women [I speak] I.	CHAR 207:37
Italy Berlusconi is unfit to lead I.	ECON 298:82
evoke the soul of I.	MAZZ 562:1
from I. that we launch	MARI 550:54
graved inside of it, 'I.'	BROW 161:57
Greece, I., and England did adorn	DRYD 291:24
I.…garden of the world	BYRON 180:32
I. is a geographical expression	METT 568:27
made I. from designs	TWAIN 870:77
not been in I.	JOHN 445:22
opera houses in I.	JOHN 441:4
Paradise of exiles, I.!	SHEL 783:25
ruined by residence in I.	RUSK 704:32
Troy and reach I.	VIRG 882:16
itch disease…an i.	MUSC 605:13
i. all over	TWAIN 871:95
i. but a kind of colourable right	LEST 505:48
i. of praise?	CAREW 190:49
Mine eyes do i.	SHAK 761:5
poetry is like having an i.	WARR 889:73
poor i. of your opinion	SHAK 769:56
item any i. of the agenda	PARK 639:85
iteration damnable i. day after day	STEAD 813:81
i. of nuptials	CONG 232:47
Ithaka I. always in your mind	CAVA 201:16
itself Forever be I. again	GINS 357:69
i. and doubt of i.	TILL 860:68
itsy I. bitsy…Bikini	VANCE 876:21
Itylus half assured for I.	SWIN 832:18
ivory cargo of i., And apes	MASE 559:26
downstairs from their I. Towers	SMITH 799:82
i. on which I work	AUST 43:88
i. sun	PIER 651:7
ivy creeping i. clings to wood	COWP 241:62
dead walls…Their i. mantles	BYRON 180:38
like i. round a sapling	SHER 788:53
myrtle and i. of sweet	BYRON 183:3
myrtles brown, with i.	MILT 578:45
pluck an i. branch for me	ROSS 697:77
ivy-mantled yonder i.-m. tower	GRAY 369:11

J

Jabberwock Beware the J., my son!	CARR 195:90
Jack grunted Harry to J.	SASS 716:63
if J. were President	ONAS 625:78
J.…a charming name	WILDE 909:33
J.—I'm all right!	BONE 139:54
J. on the gallows-tree!	SCOTT 724:19
one vote—for J.	ONAS 625:82
sack-and-sugar J.?	SHAK 741:98
The days of you and J.	ONAS 625:81
This J., joke	HOPK 413:8
jack j. in the box	ELKIN 310:70
When I kissed the J.	SHAK 773:57
jackal Faith, like a j.	MELV 564:27
jackassonance derided as j.	UNTE 874:71
jackdaws mixed-media j.	BACON 50:68
Pig, and some green J.	LEAR 497:81
jacket Green j., red cap	ALLI 13:61
jack-in-a-box bounced up like a j.	HUGH 419:49
jack-knife Just a j.-k. has Macheath	BREC 151:6
Jacob God of J.	PASC 641:39
J. awaked out of his sleep	BIBLE 87:89
J. served seven years for Rachel	BIBLE 87:90
J. was a plain man	BIBLE 87:84
sold his birthright unto J.	BIBLE 87:85
wrestled…as the Angel did with J.	WALT 888:45
Jacobean J.…translated the Bible	ACHE 2:24
Jacobites either J. or became Whigs	WALP 887:35
Ye J. by name	BURNS 172:31
jade Let the galled j. wince	SHAK 754:95
jaded j. with the rush and glare	ARNO 31:99
jades hollow pampered j. of Asia	SHAK 743:49
pampered j. of Asia	MARL 552:81
Jael J.…took a nail	BIBLE 90:67
Jaguar park one j. and drive away	HAGUE 376:63
jaguar said Painted J.	KIPL 473:45
Jah by his name J.	BIBLE 96:38
jail being in a j.	JOHN 443:59
farm or the county j.	THOR 857:90
kept out of j. till eighty	LEAC 497:72
patron and the j.	JOHN 441:97
jailer brutal j. is strict	DELA 260:59
j. of your murderer	HUGH 419:53
jails not enough j.	HUMP 422:17
Jake Forget it, J.	TOWNE 863:20
jake If everything is simply j.	DONL 279:24
jam rule is, j. to-morrow	CARR 196:4
jamais j. triste archy j. triste	MARQ 554:28
James Henry J. wrote fiction	WILDE 910:67
J. II, and the old Pretender	GUED 374:27
name is Truthful J.	HARTE 384:15
read all of Henry J.	THUR 860:58
take Eliza, and our J.!	JONS 449:46
William J. could almost hear	LOWE 520:48
work of Henry J.	GUED 374:27
Jane got used to being called J.	SAKI 710:37
J., J.	SITW 794:70
Whatever Happened to Baby J.?	DAVIS 255:54
jangling I have long been j.	OTWAY 631:35
j. around gently	PAIGE 634:87
Janissaries forced to hire J.	BUTL 176:36
January Blasts of J.	SHAK 770:85
Janus by two-headed J.	SHAK 739:35
J. glance of…significant eye	BYRON 180:36
J. of poets	DRYD 288:39
J.-type figure	NARO 608:74
Janvier J. and Février	NICH 613:83
Japan Empire of J.	ROOS 696:51
ensure J.'s self-preservation	HIRO 403:3
island country of J.	TOJO 862:94
J. is like the black hole	UMAS 873:62
J. offers as much novelty	BIRD 130:60
J.'s manufacturing base	TSON 869:54
next week in J.	THER 851:50
Japanese J.…have a saying	MORR 598:96
J. have perfected good manners	THER 851:48
J.…rarely commit a solecism in taste	BIRD 130:62
J. see self-assertion	KURO 482:42
J. should have no concern	KIPL 470:83
J. young man	GILB 354:7
japonica J. Glistens like coral	REED 681:77
jar amid the city's j.	ARNO 31:2
Carry moonbeams home in a j.	BURKE 169:55
china j. receive a flaw	POPE 659:70
face…in a j. by the door	LENN 503:96
placed a j. in Tennessee	STEV 819:12

scent you pour in a j.	HORA 414:27
When such strings j.	SHAK 730:54
jargon fens of j.?	BAKER 53:23
Jarndyce J. and J. still drags	DICK 269:80
jasper What is bettre than j.?	CHAU 209:93
jaundice good for the j.	SMART 796:23
javelin hunter's j. in his side	ARNO 32:25
jaw j. is better than…war	CHUR 217:2
zebra stripes along his j.	ELIOT 305:37
jawbone With the j. of an ass	BIBLE 90:74
jaws finger their j. in painful	CIAR 218:14
gently smiling j.!	CARR 194:65
Into the j. of Death	TENN 845:77
j. that bite	CARR 195:90
ponderous and marble j.	TWAIN 871:7
stand at the j. of the cave	AMIS 15:98
jay j. more precious than the lark	SHAK 732:43
jays overstocked with j.	OHEN 623:55
jazz amateur j. musician	LYTT 524:18
define j. satisfactorily	KING 470:65
difference between classical…and j.	PREV 667:9
j.…artificial excitement	BLISS 136:96
J. came to America…in chains	WHIT 904:21
J. has always been	JONES 448:92
J. is an impure art	MELLY 563:21
J. is a small word	TEAL 838:27
J. is the result of…energy	GERS 350:37
J. music has haunted America	HOLM 407:73
J. musicians are	TURN 870:67
J. musicians have some outlaw	ZWER 937:7
j. performance centers	LIEB 509:27
J. will endure	SOUSA 804:92
New Orleans is the cradle of j.	MORT 599:19
Though the J. Age continued	FITZ 325:4
to create j.	GILL 356:48
jealous Art is a j. mistress	EMER 313:41
J. in honour	SHAK 749:50
J. souls will not be answered	SHAK 760:97
Lord thy God is a j. God	BIBLE 89:46
perhaps a j. foe	SHEL 786:9
jealousy ear of j.	BIBLE 107:29
j. can no more…lose sight	ELIOT 303:86
J. is all the fun	JONG 448:2
j. is cruel as the grave	BIBLE 102:6
j.…the green-eyed monster	SHAK 760:86
j. to the bride	BARR 61:80
j. with a halo	WELLS 898:85
Love…is full of j.	SHAK 729:31
Nor j. Was understood	MILT 583:78
Poetry…no more…than j.	WYCH 931:16
quiet resting from all j.	BEAU 67:9
tyrant J.	DRYD 291:32
weaned by j.	LYLY 523:9
Jeannie dream of J.	FOST 332:61
jeering j. at everything	PEPYS 647:33
jeers in the midst of j.	BAUD 64:55
Jeeves J. coughed…like a sheep	WODE 919:57
Jefferson when Thomas J. dined alone	KENN 462:20
Jehu driving of J.	BIBLE 92:34
Jellicoe J. was the only man	CHUR 216:64
jellies j. soother than the creamy	KEATS 459:40
jelly Out, vile j.!	SHAK 763:81
jelly beans way that he eats j. b.	REAG 680:56
jelly-bellied J.-b. Flag-flapper	KIPL 472:28
jellyfish little uproar as a j.	WODE 919:54
Jemuel Let J. rejoice	SMART 796:23
je-ne-sais-quoi j.-n.-s.-q. young man	GILB 354:7
Jenny J. kissed me	HUNT 423:35
Jeoffry my cat J.	SMART 796:23
Jericho from Jerusalem to J.	BIBLE 115:37
jerk turned with a sudden j.	KAFKA 454:29
jerkin with a buff j.?	SHAK 741:95
jerks bring me up by j.	DICK 271:30
jeroboams bad vats and j.	THOM 853:95
Jerome Said J. K. to Ford Madox	COLE 225:74
jerseys striped j. of one colour	ANON 21:32
Jerusalem Built in J.'s wall	BLAKE 135:74
certain man went down from J.	BIBLE 115:37
daughters of J.	BIBLE 101:98
from the east to J.	BIBLE 108:72
hadde she been at J.	CHAU 208:74
holy city, new J.	BIBLE 127:79
J. the golden	NEALE 610:28
Pray for the peace of J.	BIBLE 98:89
Sing through all J.	CASW 199:82
snare to the inhabitants of J.	BIBLE 102:15
Speak ye comfortably to J.	BIBLE 103:36

there J.'s pillars stood BLAKE 135:72
Till we have built J. BLAKE 136:85
To measure J. BIBLE 106:15
was J. builded here? BLAKE 135:83
waste places of J. BIBLE 104:48
jessamine casement j. stirred TENN 845:90
Jesse rod out of the stem of J. BIBLE 102:18
Jessie J., the flower o' Dunblane TANN 836:91
jest fellow of infinite j. SHAK 755:31
glory, j., and riddle POPE 660:17
heaven admits no j. FORD 330:14
He had his j. DRYD 290:89
honour did but j. GREE 371:78
j.'s prosperity lies in the ear SHAK 734:93
jocund as to j. SHAK 734:1
Life is a j. GAY 347:76
that's no j. RALE 677:1
they do but j., poison in j. SHAK 754:93
use myself in j. DONNE 279:40
very good j. WEBS 895:96
whole wit in a j. BEAU 66:6
jester becomes a fool and j.! SHAK 743:67
Jesu J., lover of my soul WESL 900:11
J., thou art all compassion WESL 900:14
Jesus all one in Christ J. BIBLE 122:36
around when J. Christ JAGG 432:18
black people with J. GIOV 357:75
call his name J. BIBLE 108:70
come, Lord J. BIBLE 127:85
crucified J....picture of God BAKER 53:19
dear Lord J., set me free STUA 827:99
followers of J. JOHN 441:9
for all cometh of J. LYDG 523:4
grace without J. Christ BONH 140:58
greatest Jew since J. Christ ROBB 689:13
If J. Christ were to come today CARL 193:46
J. and a nameless ape MACD 529:37
J. Christ her little child ALEX 11:24
J. Christ is a Democrat WALL 886:2
J. Christ...Word of God BARTH 62:4
J. cried with a loud voice BIBLE 114:4
J., here we are HILL 403:93
J....I love thee still BUTL 178:84
J. increased in wisdom BIBLE 115:28
J. led up of the Spirit BIBLE 109:78
J., meek and mild WESL 900:12
J. never claims to be God ROBI 690:42
J. of Nazareth was the most scientific man EDDY 299:88
J. saw it, he was much displeased BIBLE 114:17
J. shall reign where'er WATTS 891:4
J. stretched forth his hand BIBLE 112:57
J. the author and finisher BIBLE 124:99
J., the very thought of Thee CASW 199:80
J., 'tis such a vulgar expression CONG 231:7
J. took bread BIBLE 114:96
J....took bread BIBLE 121:6
J....took bread BIBLE 114:96
J. was a moderniser BLAIR 133:11
J. went into the temple of God BIBLE 113:79
J. went unto them BIBLE 112:56
J. wept BIBLE 118:4
J. wept HUGO 421:97
J., when he had cried again BIBLE 114:5
J., when he was baptized BIBLE 108:77
John seeth J. BIBLE 117:75
more popular than J. Christ LENN 502:89
No man can say that J. BIBLE 121:7
none but J. heard TRUTH 869:52
recognize God without J. PASC 641:34
Sacred Heart o' J. OCAS 621:14
Stand Up For J.! DUFF 293:88
sweet reasonableness of J. ARNO 34:64
sweet the name of J. NEWT 613:78
thing that J. really would've liked SALI 711:60
When J. came to Birmingham STUD 827:5
When J. heard it, he marvelled BIBLE 110:14
when J. was born in Bethlehem BIBLE 108:72
wrong to...blame J. BENN 75:16
Jesuses trained seals, creeping J. MACD 530:47
Jew eke most lovely J. SHAK 738:2
greatest J. since Jesus Christ ROBB 689:13
Hath not a J. eyes? SHAK 740:68
I'm not really a J....Just J.-ish MILL 573:58
In heathen, Turk or J. BLAKE 134:32
J. is only the name MILL 572:5
J. of Tarsus BIBLE 119:54
like an...assimilated J. OBRI 620:99

makes you a normal J. ROTH 699:26
neither Greek nor J. BIBLE 123:67
neither J. nor Greek BIBLE 122:36
States...the J. among the nations FERB 320:94
take my leave of the J. SHAK 740:57
jewel chastity's the j. SHAK 762:34
For your sake, j. SHAK 759:65
has yet one j. left MILT 579:78
j. in a...chest. SHAK 734:99
j. [judged] by the light ANON 23:78
j. of the kingdom SUN 829:30
j. that we find SHAK 758:21
precious j. in his head SHAK 749:33
rich j. in an Ethiope's ear SHAK 736:42
time's best j. SHAK 772:25
jewelled j. mass of millinery TENN 845:81
jewellers through most j.' hands WEBS 895:98
jewellery Don't ever wear artistic j. COLE 227:30
jewelry gigantic chunk of costume j. LAUR 492:70
hang on to her j. LOOS 517:77
rest...can rattle your j. LENN 502:88
jewels capital bosom to hang j. upon DICK 270:11
Dumb j....move a woman's mind SHAK 729:34
Health and...body are two j. FLET 328:73
j. five-words-long TENN 841:96
j. for a set of beads SHAK 735:22
precious j. into a garret BACON 47:69
reft the j. from her hair HYDE 427:23
unvalued j. SHAK 731:8
With gold and j. cover POPE 658:55
jewel-sea love her j.-s. MACK 533:15
Jewish insights of the J. prophets NIEB 614:98
J. family was an inviolate ROTH 699:29
J.. I don't work out RIVE 688:4
J. Puritan of the middle NEME 611:39
J. Queen of Egypt TAYL 837:16
solution of the J. question GOER 360:11
Jews All men are J. MALA 541:81
don't ask employers...to like...J. BORO 145:2
fat of rendered J. and Gypsies VONN 883:56
Have mercy upon all J. BOOK 141:87
Hitler attacked the J. NIEM 614:3
J., a headstrong...race DRYD 289:72
J. and Arabs should settle AUST 44:5
J. in Palestine OROU 627:22
J. lived by...insight SACKS 707:85
J. which believeth not BIBLE 119:45
King of the J. BIBLE 118:17
King of the J. BIBLE 108:72
national home for the J. BALF 54:54
noticed that J. shout? ROTH 699:25
The Irish and the J. have a psychosis BEHAN 70:9
the last J. to die without standing up MEIR 563:12
To choose The J. EWER 316:28
university where...the J. are hosts SACH 707:83
What captivity was to the J. WILDE 908:86
Jezebel J....painted her face BIBLE 92:35
jib cut of his j. DOUG 284:34
jilt cruel j. to me MORSE 599:11
jingle must j. in his ears WOLL 921:7
jingles trifles and j. BACON 49:38
jingling one j. padlock POPE 662:75
Jingo by J. if we do HUNT 422:21
jo For auld lang syne, my j. BURNS 171:99
John Anderson my j. BURNS 171:10
Joan If J. of Arc had been born SIMON 792:38
play Saint J. THOR 858:3
Job All books are the Book of J. ELKIN 310:69
blessed the latter end of J. BIBLE 94:80
J. open his mouth in vain BIBLE 93:68
poor as J. SHAK 742:40
job $60 GI j. EISE 302:60
difficultest j. a man can do DAVI 253:22
finish the j. CHUR 217:80
hard j. of using reason WILS 915:78
How would you like a j. PLAN 654:61
husband is a whole-time j. BENN 76:44
If they will only do their j. SELZ 727:88
It's a man's j. AESC 8:61
j., as I see it MACD 530:50
j. is likely to be ill-done KEYN 466:87
j. of the nurture of children PALEY 635:12
Keeping up...a full-time j. CRISP 244:51
loneliest j. in the world BALD 54:45
loses his j. TRUM 868:38
lost the j. JOYCE 452:89
man who wants to do a good j. ELIOT 308:12

most improper j. TOLK 862:96
Nae harder j. to mortals MACD 529:33
neighbour loses his j. REAG 680:55
only doing my j. if they do WHIT 905:25
our j. to make women unhappy PUCK 672:98
second most important j. GARN 346:51
since he has lost his j. MORG 597:80
social order...my j. to preserve FRAN 333:91
to do the j. too long SWIFT 831:75
whether my j. is a j. KNIG 476:15
will always have a j. RAVI 679:38
Jobiska Aunt J. made him drink LEAR 498:87
Aunt J.'s Runcible Cat LEAR 498:89
jobs climbing into j. REST 683:16
fewer the j. worth doing JAY 436:99
j. that pay more than others WILL 913:39
Mine is one of the j. WEAT 893:61
woman...not the top j. THAT 850:8
Jock J., when ye hae naething SCOTT 724:36
stop yer tickling, J.! LAUD 492:62
tears...For J. of Hazeldean SCOTT 724:21
Wi' J. of Hazeldean SCOTT 724:23
jocosity j. catches the crowd MARQ 554:26
jocund As gentle and as j. SHAK 734:1
j. day Stands tiptoe SHAK 736:69
Joe J., long dead SLES 796:15
Say it ain't so, J. ANON 22:48
jog As we j. on STER 817:69
J. on, j. on SHAK 770:83
jogging J. is for people WOOD 921:16
J. is very beneficial SCHU 720:49
Johannesburg No second J. PATON 643:70
John I J. saw the holy city BIBLE 127:79
J. Brown is stowed NASH 608:96
J. had his raiment of camel's hair BIBLE 108:75
J., like J. FARJ 318:48
J. seeth Jesus BIBLE 117:75
J. to the seven churches BIBLE 125:42
notorious domesticity for J. WILDE 909:30
shew J. again those things BIBLE 111:33
unto the multitudes concerning J. BIBLE 111:34
why...name your baby 'J.' GOLD 362:82
john leaning on the j. door OHARA 623:46
Johnny Little J. Head-in-Air HOFF 406:52
not despair For J. Head-in-Air PUDN 672:99
sleeps as sound As J. Underground PUDN 672:99
Johnson heroism of J. STEV 822:1
J. approached a...position MANC 544:41
J.'s morality HAWT 386:53
J. went through three years WHITE 903:98
that great man, Dr J. WESL 900:48
You are a philosopher, Dr J. EDWA 300:22
Johnsonian subtlety of J. strategy MANC 544:42
joined j. with no foot-landrakers SHAK 741:6
joiner imagination of a lodge j. MENC 566:86
j. with j. HESI 401:64
joint manacled with j. or limb MILT 581:9
The time was out of j. STRA 826:81
together every j. and member MILT 579:79
jointed It is nothing j.; it flows JAMES 434:63
joints between the j. of the harness BIBLE 92:27
fettle your fine j. SHAK 736:71
j. are stiff SHAK 737:76
joke bitter cosmic j. GELL 348:98
every j. is...a custard pie ORWE 628:65
family j. that when ROTH 699:37
funniest j. in the world SHAW 779:33
Housekeeping ain't no j. ALCO 10:4
if a j. were a charity auction MCIL 533:1
If we live inside a bad j. RABAN 675:59
j.'s a very serious thing CHUR 215:49
many a j. had he GOLD 361:54
our only j. BARR 61:87
jokes bad j. of history GUED 374:29
civil servant doesn't make j. IONE 430:75
difference of taste in j. ELIOT 304:14
don't make j. ROGE 695:29
hackneyed j. from Miller BYRON 179:97
Krishna's j. may be vapid FORS 332:57
my little j. on Thee FROST 339:13
no j....no chance ANON 22:66
no more j. in Music-halls SASS 716:57
shouldn't make j. CARR 196:96
telling j. back there KAUF 456:60
telling j. or gossiping CABR 183:19
joking My way of j. SHAW 779:33
jollier j. than the people LUCAS 521:72

greater j. shewn in deviating — ADDI 7:41
great J. seat — KIPL 470:81
green in j. — SHAK 764:22
He j. brings — OAKL 620:89
if it only added j. to insight — FORS 331:39
in danger of the j. — BIBLE 109:88
j. faileth me — KNOX 476:19
j. fouk wou'd hae a doubt on — FERG 320:6
j. frame By her…standard — POPE 658:53
j. is a mere lottery — DRYD 288:27
j. is…subject to affection — JOHN 445:44
j. Of all mankind — SCHI 718:4
j. of the great whore — BIBLE 127:72
j. that makes an impact — LEAV 498:2
j. that yourself arise — SHAK 771:22
j. what they see — MIDD 569:41
j. with this generation — BIBLE 111:44
last j. of mankind — FRYE 340:35
Last J.'s fire must cure this place — BROW 161:43
Men of business have a solid j. — BAGE 51:93
men of j. frame — MARL 552:84
Moral j. — NIET 615:22
neither do the aged understand j. — BIBLE 93:67
not a disease but an error of j. — DICK 265:60
notoriously unsound in j. — HOLM 407:80
O j.! thou art fled — SHAK 748:7
on whose j. they — TUCH 869:60
people's j. always true — DRYD 290:91
possessing j. — KEYN 466:86
power of j. — HARD 381:43
put in the breastplate of j. — BIBLE 89:25
reserve thy j. — SHAK 751:19
spirit and j. equal — MILT 586:43
still have j. here — SHAK 767:86
till J. Tide — KIPL 473:59
Too many…pass j. — TRUM 868:39
true j. day — ANON 20:15
vulgar…capacities do make a j. — BACON 46:38
wait till J. break — DICK 272:67
What j. I had increases — DRYD 292:43
would not give his j. rashly — ADDI 6:15
judgements Delivers brawling j. — TENN 846:13
j. below our own — BROW 158:57
j. of the English law — SYNGE 834:58
j. on political conduct — NEW 612:58
moral j. do not say anything — AYER 45:11
obstinate, ridiculous j. — MORE 596:59
sentinels unto our j. — MIDD 569:41
judges doctors, j.…beadles — MARX 557:96
hundred j. have declared — QUIL 674:43
hungry j. — POPE 659:73
j. thronging thickly — WILDE 907:81
threw me in front of the J. — BETJ 84:9
When j. steal themselves — SHAK 758:28
judging happy condition of j. — MELV 564:42
Heaven he j.…spectator — RALE 677:1
j. others according to — LAFO 485:14
j. the values of things — JEVO 438:46
knack of j. a distance — REED 681:79
the fatigue of j. for themselves — SHER 788:62
jug j., j., j., tereu — LYLY 523:7
Pap took the j. — TWAIN 871:1
w'en it git loose fum de j. — HARR 383:92
Juggins you J.! — PUNCH 673:15
juggler perceive a j.'s sleight — BUTL 177:55
jugglers nimble j. that deceive the eye — SHAK 733:59
juice j. of deliberate, journalistic — LAWR 495:23
lukewarm parsnip j. — WOOL 923:61
nor half so full of j. — SUCK 828:11
runnel of j. — RANS 679:23
whether there is enough j. — GEDD 348:91
juices Keep the j. flowing — PAIGE 634:87
sexual j. flow toward a painting — FUEN 340:41
juke j. box's blowin' a fuse — BERRY 82:59
Julia in silks my J. goes — HERR 400:49
thought of Donna J.'s eyes — BYRON 181:67
Julian remembered poor J. — HEMI 394:12
Juliet east, and J. is the sun — SHAK 736:45
J. and her Romeo — SHAK 737:82
Unless philosophy can make a J. — SHAK 736:66
July born on the fourth of J. — COHAN 224:65
J.'s day as short — SHAK 770:76
second day of J. 1776 — ADAMS 5:89
winter—ending in J. — BYRON 182:95
Jumblies lands where the J. live — LEAR 497:79
jump decide which way to j. — BOYC 147:40
J. her, and thump her — SHAK 770:91

j. the life to come — SHAK 767:86
j. with common spirits — SHAK 740:62
jumping j. over the moon — RAMS 678:7
June It was late J. — THOM 854:6
Jolly J., arrayed — SPEN 810:16
J. for beauty's heightening — ARNO 33:44
made December J. — TENN 844:58
newly sprung in J. — BURNS 173:44
rare as a day in J. — LOWE 520:31
jungle art world is a j. — HAMM 379:12
city is not a concrete j. — MORR 598:92
courts of Europe are a j. — BOLT 139:50
dangerous to explore a j. — HAWT 386:34
J. star or j. track — CULL 247:92
law of the j. — JUMB 453:7
Law of the J. — KIPL 471:12
Law of the J. — KIPL 471:9
Mumbo-Jumbo is dead in the j. — LIND 511:49
New York is a j. — AMIS 15:99
wise primitive in a giant j. — MAIL 539:37
jungles lost…in the j. of Indochina — MCGO 532:92
juniper sat down under a j. tree — BIBLE 92:23
white leopards sat under a j.-tree — ELIOT 307:81
junk j. food — GASS 346:60
junkyards j. of secular carpentry — ROSE 697:71
Juno figure of J. — BARR 61:94
haughty J.'s unrelenting hate — DRYD 292:42
Jupiter By J., an angel — SHAK 774:71
J. from above — OVID 631:40
temple of J. — GIBB 352:63
juries j. fill their stomachs — SYNGE 834:58
jurisprudence American j. — CAPO 189:24
jury acquitted by a Limerick j. — ADAMS 5:96
I'll be judge, I'll be j. — CARR 194:66
j. is only as sound — LEE 500:37
j. passing on the prisoner's life — SHAK 758:20
lawyer trying to pick a smart j. — BAIL 52:1
Press is the living J. — BENN 76:55
Trial by j. — DENM 262:98
tried before a j. — JOHN 445:18
jury-men that j.-m. may dine — POPE 659:73
just and I should be j. — HERB 397:97
Be j., my lovely swain — BEHN 71:14
cause is j. — DICK 273:82
Give it because it is j. — LLOY 513:5
gods are j. — SHAK 764:2
How j., how bountiful — WORD 929:66
it is our j. exaltation — PITT 653:47
j.…are not the leaders — CONR 234:14
j., gentle, wise — SHEL 785:81
j. people…are happier than unjust — PLATO 655:94
j. shall live by faith — BIBLE 119:58
rather be British than j. — PAIS 635:2
sendeth rain on the j. — BIBLE 109:94
Shall mortal man be more j. — BIBLE 93:53
soul of the j. — STAEL 811:49
Thou art indeed j., Lord — HOPK 413:9
thou art j. — TENN 842:20
whatsoever things are j. — BIBLE 123:61
justice act…of duty and of j. — PITT 653:45
ain't the shop for j. — DICK 267:95
bring our enemies to j. — BUSH 175:8
destruction of all j. — MORE 597:70
Die he or j. must — MILT 582:45
do j. to my character — EMMET 313:59
dream of social j. — NGUY 613:82
Equal and exact j. — JEFF 437:19
firm belief in the j. of our cause — WASH 890:82
have ravished j. — WEBS 894:86
humanity, reason, and j., tells me — BURKE 168:12
Injustice anywhere is a threat to j. — KING 468:32
j. and mercy are reconciled — WILS 916:7
J. is being allowed to do — BUTL 178:77
J. is doing one's work — PLATO 655:97
J. is such a fine thing — LESA 504:29
J. is superior — PLATO 655:95
J. is the constant — JUST 453:13
J. is the means — FRAN 333:91
J. is truth — DISR 276:60
j. must be carried out — MARIE 550:50
j., or happiness or prosperity — CURZ 249:53
J. should consider — HELO 393:88
J. should not only be done — HEWA 401:69
'J.' was done — HARDY 382:63
Let j. be done — FERD 320:1
Let j. be done — MANS 547:99
Let j. be done — WATS 891:1

Literature…makes j. — PALEY 635:10
love of j. in most men — LARO 491:48
may become a j. — JONS 449:33
Mercy…and j. come from God — WAITE 884:67
no business with the j. — JOHN 444:99
of all equity and j. — KNOX 476:18
Poetic j., with her lifted scale — POPE 662:65
Posterity will do j. to…Gladstone — DISR 277:82
price of j. is eternal publicity — BENN 76:50
principles of equity and j. — PEEL 646:9
Publicity is the very soul of j. — BENT 77:70
pursuit of j. — GOLD 362:73
quicker Than j., judge or vicar — SHER 787:46
Revenge is a kind of wild j. — BACON 47:78
rule of distributive j. — HOMA 408:59
seldom has j. enough to accuse — GOLD 361:45
small things and j. — SOPH 804:84
temper so J. with mercy — MILT 585:20
Thwackum was for doing j. — FIEL 322:41
To no man will we…deny…j. — MAGN 539:28
treat the films…with less than j. — ANDE 16:18
under which j. — UNIT 873:69
when I show j. — SHAK 758:24
When mercy seasons j. — SHAK 740:80
Where j. grows — SPEN 808:82
Where j. is denied — DOUG 284:37
which is the j. — SHAK 763:91
justification Englishman's j. in India — CURZ 249:53
j. in every line — CONR 234:94
social and psychological j. — KEYN 466:93
justifications power j. would go on — STEI 816:44
justified half as good as j. — BUTL 177:58
justifies that j. the end — TROT 868:21
justify end cannot j. the means — HUXL 425:82
'j.' and affirm…beliefs — ELLI 311:89
the less there is to j. — TWAIN 870:86
justifying better j. themselves — SZASZ 834:62
justitia Fiat j. — FERD 320:1
Fiat j. — WATS 891:1
Fiat j., pereat coelum — ADAMS 5:92
jutty No j., frieze — SHAK 767:85
juvescence j. of the year — ELIOT 305:40
juxtaposition Allah…and J. — CLOU 223:33

K

Kaa thou art hungry, O K. — KIPL 471:10
Kalashnikovs didn't have K. — BONO 140:63
kaleidoscope it's like a beautiful k. — COLE 225:77
kamikaze the k. ground staff — PARK 638:82
kangaroo K., K.! — FIELD 322:30
Tie Me K. Down, Sport — HARR 383:98
kangaroos little k. flying about — WILDE 908:51
Kansas farmers of K. — LEASE 498:97
horses o' K. think — KIPL 472:23
nights in K. City close early — MAIL 540:55
Kasper Old K.'s work was done — SOUT 805:98
Kate angel is like you, K. — SHAK 746:66
kiss me, K. — SHAK 732:35
kiss me, K. — SHAK 732:48
sometimes K. the curst — SHAK 732:33
Swear me, K. — SHAK 742:21
witchcraft in your lips, K. — SHAK 746:68
Kathmandu to the north of K. — HAYES 387:62
Kean K. is original — COLE 226:18
There is in K. — HAZL 387:65
keel Set k. to breakers — POUND 665:45
keener grows k. with constant use — IRVI 430:80
keep k., and pass, and turn again — EMER 313:39
k. our people in — KENN 463:32
k. the salary — GOMEZ 362:92
k. things like this — HUGH 419:40
love to k. it by me — JERO 437:33
may God k. me there — JOAN 438:53
time to k. — BIBLE 100:70
To k. him…two — DOUG 283:30
you can k. the lot — JAY 435:96
keeper Am I my brother's k.? — BIBLE 86:59
first lost k. — SEXT 728:12
k. of his conscience…k. of the stone — DAVI 255:43
Lord is thy k. — BIBLE 97:68
keepers k. of the house shall tremble — BIBLE 101:92
keeps gave it us for k. — AYRES 45:14
keepsake rope for a k. — TWAIN 872:22
Kelly Fanny K.'s divine plain face — LAMB 486:37
Kemble Mr K. sacrifices too much — HAZL 387:66
Kennedy epitaph on the K. — WHITE 903:2

Mrs K. is going to marry	JOHN 439:74	k., and eat	BIBLE 119:39
you're no Jack K.	BENT 78:84	k. a wife with kindness	SHAK 732:41
Kennedys we K., we eat Rockefellers	KENN 464:54	k. my mother	BOYD 147:44
Who killed the K.?	JAGG 432:19	k. sick people	MARL 552:86
kennel whips to k. The renegade	RANS 679:27	K. them all	ARNA 31:81
Kensal Paradise by way of K.	CHES 212:87	k. us for their sport	SHAK 763:84
Kent everyone knows K.	DICK 266:69	know, to k. and to create	BAUD 65:82
K. and Christendom	WYATT 930:98	mettle enough...to k. care	SHAK 745:22
Kentish courts of K. Town	BETJ 83:92	must men k. and die?	SHEL 786:22
fog on the K. heights	DICK 269:79	My k. shall be thy k.	KIPL 471:10
kept married women are k. women	SMITH 800:83	never k. for sport	FROU 339:21
kerchiefed k. in a comely cloud	MILT 577:20	no approaches, but to k.	JONS 450:52
Kern to K. or Cole Porter	GERS 350:39	No sportsman wants to k. a fox	SHAW 781:95
kernel Haldis the k., sueit	HENR 396:51	not catastrophes...k. us	WOOLF 922:28
k. is boredom	GELL 348:1	simply has to go out and k.	LEAC 497:71
k. scarcely compensates...cracking	BRON 154:73	The command 'Thou shalt not k.'	JOHN 439:61
kernels meagre hill of k.	RANS 679:23	Thou shalt not k.	BIBLE 88:23
Kerouac not even Mr K.	CAPO 189:22	Thou shalt not k.	CLOU 223:37
Ketch as Jack K.'s wife said	DRYD 291:30	time to k.	BIBLE 100:70
kettle different k. of fish	SHAR 776:41	to be professional, but to k. him	TYSON 873:55
guy that plays the k. drums	SALI 711:60	To wit, I k. thee	SHAK 750:84
how agree the k.	BIBLE 108:50	will not actually k. him	BERR 82:68
Polly put the k. on	DICK 267:22	word for which you k.	WEIL 896:33
speech is like a cracked k.	FLAU 326:34	**killed** don't mind your being k.	KITC 475:5
Kew his Highness' dog at K.	POPE 662:84	effort very nearly k. her	BELL 73:58
K. in lilac-time	NOYES 619:77	k. all the day long	BIBLE 95:23
key easy k., Dost open life	DRYD 289:65	k. in no time	DICK 266:87
Getting into the k. of C sharp	BUTL 178:74	k. not thee	SHAK 748:24
k. is Russian national interest	CHUR 216:73	kiss thee ere I k. thee	SHAK 761:20
k. of knowledge	BIBLE 115:41	Who k. the Kennedys?	JAGG 432:19
k. of the bottomless pit	BIBLE 126:62	would each have k. the other	KING 469:61
k. to human warmth	ISHI 431:94	**killer** k. with the ball	LARW 491:56
looking for the k.	BENN 75:24	lover and k. are mingled	DOUG 283:20
out of k. with his time	POUND 664:35	**killers** K. from the egg	HUGH 419:41
smile is often the k.	SAINT 709:18	**Killiecrankie** braes o' K.	BURNS 172:11
the k., the minor k., to existence	BLIX 137:2	**killing** if war did not include k.	ANGE 17:39
Turn the k. deftly	KEATS 458:8	K. care and grief	SHAK 775:13
keyboard Color is the k.	KAND 454:38	K. care and grief	SHAK 775:15
song along the k.	OHARA 623:46	**kills** cancer often k.	HALD 377:77
keyhole age has a k.	MCCA 528:1	it k. me	HOPK 413:7
out at the k	SHAK 750:80	k. life within himself	SAINT 709:25
Keynes cure...before K.	ROBI 690:41	k. me some six or seven dozen	SHAK 741:12
keys enter the names and hand the k.	MANS 547:87	k. the very good	HEMI 394:99
fingers on these k.	STEV 819:21	that k. and pains not?	SHAK 766:58
k. of all the creeds	TENN 843:31	Time k. us	SITW 794:86
k. of hell and of death	BIBLE 126:46	time quietly k. them	BOUC 146:18
k. of Paradise	DE 262:7	waste remains and k.	EMPS 313:61
k. of the kingdom of heaven	BIBLE 112:62	**kilt** k., the lava-lava	MURR 604:7
k. of the...liquor store	BALL 55:62	**kin** little more than k.	SHAK 751:99
Over the noisy k.	PROC 670:58	makes the whole world k.	SHAK 757:7
keystone night's black arch the k.-s.	BURNS 172:20	Religion and art...close k.	CATH 200:94
khaki gentleman in K.	KIPL 472:27	**kin and kith** own k. a. k.	NASH 608:78
zephyr and k. shorts	BETJ 83:84	**kind** children k. and natural	SHAK 745:33
Khan In Xanadu did Kubla K.	COLE 226:9	Earth is here so k.	JERR 437:39
kick If I can k. them four years	CHAR 207:46	euerich in his k.	JAME 432:21
I get no k. from champagne	PORT 663:3	finish...among k. people	BEET 70:98
k. against the pricks	BIBLE 119:37	for such a k. heart	SHAK 743:78
k. it about all day	HOLM 408:83	for the maiming of his k.	MACG 531:76
k. you out	WAUGH 891:11	I am one with my k.	TENN 846:1
sold...for 'one and a k.'	FORM 331:27	isolating him from his k.	PARN 639:91
watch...hirelings k. a ball	PRIE 668:17	K. is my love today	SHAK 773:43
kicked die or get k. out	HOOV 411:63	k. its caressing	COCK 224:54
get his head k. off	KHRU 467:4	k. without deceit	DRYD 289:64
kicking k. and screaming	STEV 820:62	more than kin and less than k.	SHAK 751:99
kid Here's looking at you, k.	EPST 314:78	one of their own k.	KORDA 480:99
leopard shall lie down with the k.	BIBLE 102:19	people will always be k.	SASS 716:64
when you have a k.	HEMI 395:29	romantic poet...no other k.	FROST 339:3
When you're a k.	ALBEE 9:88	should be pretty of its k.	LAMB 486:42
kiddies You k. have crumpled	BETJ 84:5	so constant...so k.	KEATS 457:6
kidnapped realize that I'm k.	ALLEN 12:50	So courteous, so k.	SKEL 795:91
kidney most unscrupulous k.	FRY 339:22	to a k. and not to a gender	YOUR 935:80
kidneys liked grilled mutton k.	JOYCE 452:92	woman who is really k. to dogs	BEER 69:78
kids cooking breakfast...for my k.	SCHR 720:44	your lack of k.	COLUM 229:59
don't have any k. yourself	LARK 491:39	**kinder** k. to the brutes	ELIOT 303:74
help with the housework and the k.	WINT 917:34	**kindergarten** kind of k.	ROBI 690:33
How many k. did you kill	ANON 23:95	**kindness** acts Of k.	WORD 923:70
k. playing some game	SALI 711:61	cup o' k.	BURNS 171:99
way k. laugh when they're hungry	STEI 815:34	husband's k. when it comes	BACON 48:93
Kildare broke a window in K.	JOYCE 452:94	I expected k. and gentility	PERE 648:61
kill almost k. a man as k.	MILT 578:62	kill a wife with k.	SHAK 732:41
As k. a king	SHAK 754:6	K. and courage	MUIR 603:59
canst thou k. me	DONNE 281:67	K. in another's trouble	GORD 363:5
cure the disease and k. the patient	BACON 49:31	K. is worth more than beauty	ARRAS 34:77
How many kids did you k.	ANON 23:95	k. of strangers	WILL 912:17
intendest thou to k. me	BIBLE 88:7	k. that human beings do not lose	LEGU 501:54
k. all the lawyers	SHAK 730:64	k. that I can show	GREL 372:98
k. a man than a hawk	JEFF 436:9	little bit of plain, ordinary k.	BUCH 164:32

Melting through k.	ROCH 691:50
milk of human k.	SHAK 766:80
neither k. or cruelty	ALBEE 9:87
place your k. there	ROCH 691:62
sheer k. and affection	TROL 866:84
the great have k.	POPE 661:39
thought of you with k.	PEAC 645:96
value on spontaneous k.	JOHN 446:54
kindred k. spider	FROST 339:5
kindreds all k. of the earth shall wail	BIBLE 125:43
all nations, and k.	BIBLE 126:59
kinds divided into two k.	HUME 422:13
Knowledge is of two k.	JOHN 444:9
There are two k.	SAINT 710:29
two k. of audience	SCHN 719:20
two k. of Methodists	ELIOT 303:73
two k. of mind	PASC 640:5
kine home-bred k.	WORD 927:30
King abuse the best k.	SHAK 769:49
abusing...the best k.	FRAN 334:14
a' for our rightfu' k.	BURNS 173:51
am I sent for to a k.	SHAK 735:23
Authority forgets a dying k.	TENN 847:47
balm from an anointed k.	SHAK 735:15
beat the K. ninety-nine times	CROM 245:71
be the favourite of a k.?	MARL 552:88
between the k. and the people	SELD 726:77
blind, despised, and dying k.	SHEL 783:34
bold K. of Sweden	LESL 504:30
born K. of the Jews?	BIBLE 108:72
Carle, now the K.'s come!	SCOTT 725:44
catch the conscience of the K.	SHAK 753:72
chief defect of Henry K.	BELL 72:53
could a Don K. happen	KING 468:28
Willie K. made up like Philip	NICO 614:95
king consumer...is the k.	SAMU 712:79
contrary to the k.	SHAK 730:66
Creston Clarke played K. Lear	FIELD 322:31
Curse not the k.	BIBLE 101:89
Deny it to a k.?	SHAK 743:53
did a k. to death	THOM 852:62
editor is the uncrowned k.	STEAD 813:82
England breed again...a K. Harry?	DRAY 286:2
every inch a k.	SHAK 763:87
example of the k. of Denmark	FACK 317:31
executed the k.	STAL 812:55
Exempt from awe...the k.	SHEL 785:81
faint-hearted and degenerate k.	SHAK 730:69
follow the k.	TENN 847:58
forbid on behalf of the K.	EDWA 300:15
forced from the k.	INNO 430:71
found in the k. a monk	AELR 8:55
Gentiles' Lord and K.	AQUI 28:28
Glory to the K. of k.s	WESL 900:10
God bless our good and gracious K.	ROCH 692:72
God save the K.	ANON 22:49
God save the K.	BIBLE 91:87
God's patience and the K.'s English	SHAK 743:68
go in unto the k.	BIBLE 93:46
hath not offended the k.	MORE 597:73
heart and stomach of a k.	ELIZ 309:60
Here lies a k.	CAREW 190:55
Honour the k.	BIBLE 125:25
If he be the K. of Israel	BIBLE 114:3
If the k. loves music	MENC 565:51
image of the K.	TENN 847:44
impossible for the K.	PEPYS 647:31
In sleep a k.	SHAK 772:35
is the year's pleasant k.	NASHE 609:15
kill a k. and marry	SHAK 754:6
k. borne of all Englond	MALO 542:3
K. George's glorious days	GILB 354:14
k. has no dignity	MORE 597:63
k. is always a k.	WOLL 921:10
k. is strongest	BIBLE 107:24
k. Lodgreaunce delyverd	MALO 542:6
k. may make a nobleman	BURKE 169:47
k. of codpieces	SHAK 733:76
K. of comforts, K. of life	VAUG 878:48
K. of glory, K. of peace	HERB 398:2
K. of Glory wore	MARV 556:69
k. of infinite space	SHAK 752:54
K. of K.s	BIBLE 127:76
K. of the Jews	BIBLE 118:17
K. of the Jews	BIBLE 108:72
k. of the world	CAME 185:48
K. of the world shall raise us	BIBLE 108:69

K. o' Spain's daughter	COLUM 229:60	God hath numbered thy k.	BIBLE 106:98
K.'s a bawcock	SHAK 746:49	His k. stretch	WATTS 891:4
K. said 'Butter, eh?'	MILNE 574:76	if a k. be divided against itself	BIBLE 114:9
K. shall answer and say unto them	BIBLE 113:93	jewel of the k.	SUN 829:30
k.'s heart is in the hand	BIBLE 99:43	k. against k.	BIBLE 113:85
k. sits in Dunfermline	BALL 56:84	k. for a horse!	SHAK 732:23
K.'s name is a tower	SHAK 731:15	k. for it was too small	SHAK 742:35
K.'s real, or his stamped face	DONNE 279:43	k. has ever been so	MONT 593:89
k.'s torch throws its light	CYRA 230:51	k. is as wide as the universe	FLAU 326:40
k. thought mair o' Marie	BALL 56:82	k. of God is within you	BIBLE 116:56
k. was much moved	BIBLE 91:6	k. of the well	SONT 804:77
K., who ordainest Great winds	ELLE 310:71	k. shall not continue	BIBLE 91:88
k. who wants to maintain	MORE 597:62	large k. for a little grave	SHAK 735:22
lad that's born to be k.	BOUL 146:26	mind to me a k. is	DYER 296:50
lessened my esteem of a k.	PEPYS 647:30	My k., safeliest when with one man	DONNE 279:36
Let a k. recall	ERAS 315:87	one end of the k. to the other	WEBB 893:66
like a tyrant or k.	PASC 641:27	palaces in K. come	MASE 559:35
looking for a k.	MACD 530:56	people of this k.	LOUI 518:90
Lord Lion K.-at-arms!	SCOTT 723:95	re-establishment of the laws of the k.	BLOOM 137:6
make us a k. to judge us	BIBLE 91:86	share the k. with	MARL 552:88
Man who Would be K.	KIPL 470:77	this formidable k.	PITT 652:37
mortal temples of a k.	SHAK 735:20	Thy k. come	BIBLE 110:98
my crowned K.	HOWA 417:94	vegetating k.	LOWE 520:47
My dead K.!	JOYCE 452:83	when thou comest into thy k.	BIBLE 116:64
My God and K.	HERB 397:91	yet thy k. shall pass	SWIN 833:36
name the k. would give it	PENN 646:22	**kingdoms** acquiring new k.	MORE 596:57
no k. in Israel	BIBLE 90:77	children of former k.	BACON 49:37
not so glorious as a k.	MARL 551:74	How many k.	PASC 640:19
old and foolish k.	BIBLE 100:75	kissed away K.	SHAK 765:34
once and future k.	MALO 543:12	returned to…these K.	ELIOT 306:74
one-eyed man is k.	ERAS 315:86	sheweth him all the k. of the world	BIBLE 109:80
one-eyed man is k.	WELLS 898:77	**kinged** England…is so idly k.	SHAK 745:39
O worship the K.	GRANT 366:52	**kingfisher** After the k.'s wing	ELIOT 307:99
Ozymandias, k. of k.s	SHEL 784:50	**kings** accounted poet k.	KEATS 457:85
passions of a k.	HUGO 421:77	all be as happy as k.	STEV 823:18
priests ruled, the k. interpreted	COND 230:82	axe to fell k.	BUNT 166:63
profits that an idle k.	TENN 839:62	breath of k.	BURNS 170:70
qualities in a great K.	RICH 686:66	But not of k.	MARL 552:90
Quhen Alysaunder oure k.	ANON 19:84	captains and the k. depart	KIPL 472:21
quietly along the K.'s highway	STER 817:70	change my state with k.'	SHAK 771:14
Reagan…hell of a k.	ONEI 626:7	divine right of k.	MACM 536:66
receive honour of the k.	BIBLE 108:64	enthronèd in the hearts of k.	SHAK 740:80
Rejoice, the Lord is K.!	WESL 900:13	function of k.	LOUI 518:96
ruthless K.!	GRAY 370:27	great k. and fine cities	CATU 201:9
saw the K. play at tennis	PEPYS 647:38	hand that k. Have lipped	SHAK 765:31
Say 'Pardon', k.	SHAK 735:29	K. and Desperate Men	KRON 481:21
served my K.	SHAK 775:21	K. and Governments may err	HERB 397:79
singeing of the K. of Spain's beard	DRAKE 286:92	K. are earth's gods	SHAK 769:48
smote the k. of Israel	BIBLE 92:27	K….began their reigns	GARC 345:42
soldier of the K.	KITC 475:4	k. break faith	SHAK 738:21
sole k. of forests all	SPEN 808:73	k. can cause or cure	GOLD 361:42
son of Heaven's eternal K.	MILT 575:92	K. for such a plot	MILT 576:3
soul, the K. of Heaven	LYTE 524:16	k. is mostly rapscallions	TWAIN 871:8
started off in films as a k.	MORL 598:89	K. may be blest	BURNS 172:18
still am I K. of those	SHAK 735:24	k. must bow to grammar	MOLI 590:41
subject's duty is the K.'s	SHAK 746:50	k. of the earth stand up	BOOK 142:36
substitute shines brightly as a k.	SHAK 741:90	k. shall shut their mouths	BIBLE 104:49
such a plain k.	SHAK 746:67	K. should not p.	COWP 241:77
such divinity doth hedge a k.	SHAK 754:21	k. that fear their subjects' treachery?	SHAK 730:77
supports his k. on loyal principles	SHAW 777:65	k. to mount guard	CARL 192:92
Tartars made them a K.	POLO 657:39	K. will be tyrants from policy	BURKE 169:37
Teach me, my God and K.	HERB 397:94	k., with standards	MOORE 596:48
Thee, Redeemer, K.	NEALE 610:35	know the k. of England	GILB 354:99
The K. dropp'd a tear	BLAKE 135:80	lays his icy hand on k.	SHIR 789:83
The K. makes no distinction	STRA 826:88	Many k. have sat down	BIBLE 107:47
The K. to Oxford sent a troop	BROW 159:98	Might first made k.	MARL 552:83
the K. will ride	DONNE 279:41	palaces of k. are built	PAINE 634:90
To be a K.	ELIZ 310:62	pale k., and princes	KEATS 458:19
To be a Pirate K.	GILB 354:97	Physicians are like k.	WEBS 895:20
To be k.	SHAK 766:73	powerful K. and…Queens	DONNE 281:89
to have blown up the K.	HOBY 405:36	power of k. and magistrates	MILT 580:86
To reverence the K.	TENN 846:21	pride of k.	POPE 660:6
to see the K. beheaded	PEPYS 647:28	Punctuality…of k.	LOUI 518:98
To the K.'s Theatre	PEPYS 647:32	raise up commonwealths and ruin k.	DRYD 289:74
Upon the k.	SHAK 746:52	security which k. are fighting for	SMITH 797:37
Wha…hae we got for a K.	CUNN 248:25	Some men are born k.	SHAW 781:84
What must the K. do now?	SHAK 735:22	statue of one of our k.	APPL 27:22
when we had a k.	SCOTT 724:35	stories of the death of k.	SHAK 735:20
Who…is a k. indeed	CHAP 206:15	such is the breath of k.	SHAK 734:3
Who is this K. of glory?	BIBLE 94:4	than that of most k.	HOOV 411:64
with a k.'s son my childish	SURR 829:37	three k. into the east	BURNS 171:93
worm that hath eat of a k.	SHAK 754:15	throne of k.	SHAK 734:8
		to the Ear of K.	POPE 662:64
kingdom best walls of this k.	COVE 239:6	Until philosophers rule as k.	PLATO 655:98
Childhood is the k.	MILL 571:92	Walk with k.	KIPL 474:68
children of the k.	BIBLE 110:15	War is the trade of k.	DRYD 291:26
Content's a k.	HEYW 402:75	what are k.	MARL 552:91
folly in that of a great k.	SMITH 798:48		

Kinnock K. has travelled the road	ASHD 35:89
Kipling a sort of gutless K.	ORWE 628:44
the boys, principally K.	HEMI 393:96
kirk k. or market	STEV 822:97
Marie Hamilton's to the k. gane	BALL 56:82
Kirkconnell On fair K. lea!	BALL 56:78
kirtle kilted her green k.	BALL 56:88
kiss about to k. your hand	GILB 355:33
Ae fond k.	BURNS 172:28
Anger's self I needs must k.	SIDN 790:13
best part of love is the k.	MANN 546:75
bluest veins to k.	SHAK 765:31
body k. a body	BURNS 173:49
can no more keep…a k. there	DE 264:36
clung to a k.	BYRON 182:81
cup…leaped to k. me	FLET 328:72
did never k. and greet?	KEATS 457:4
drew with one long k.	TENN 838:41
envied k. to share	GRAY 369:13
first k. is magic	CHAN 205:90
glowing k. had won	HOOD 410:39
heralded by a k.	DARIO 252:3
I tried to k. her	RHYS 684:30
k. again with tears!	TENN 841:1
k. but in the cup	JONS 449:40
k. her and mix her with me	SWIN 833:40
k. his dirty shoe	SHAK 746:49
k. is still a k.	HUPF 423:40
k. Long as my exile	SHAK 769:71
K. me as if you made	BROW 160:23
K. me, Hardy	NELS 610:35
k. me once again	JONS 450:48
k. my ass in Macy's window	JOHN 440:85
k. my parchèd lips	SHAK 739:33
k. thee ere I killed thee	SHAK 761:20
k. thy hand to bid adieu	STER 818:93
K. till the cow comes home	BEAU 67:11
k. you take is better	SHAK 757:10
let us k. and part	DRAY 287:6
make me immortal with a k.!	MARL 552:5
rough male k. of blankets	BROO 156:4
Salute…with an holy k.	BIBLE 120:90
saw you take his k.	PATM 643:59
took the k. sedately	TENN 845:86
visit with a wandering k.	CAREW 190:57
when tyrants seems to k.	SHAK 769:50
When women k.	MENC 565:92
whisper it in the k.	ONEI 625:92
With this k. I wed thee	HEYW 402:77
kissed had I wist, before I k.	BALL 57:95
how he k. me	JOYCE 452:96
Jenny k. me	HUNT 423:35
k. away Kingdoms and provinces	SHAK 765:34
k. by a man	KIPL 470:78
k. by the English dead	OWEN 632:53
k. her once by the pig-sty	THOM 853:89
k. her violently	ASHF 35:1
k. it and then fled	SHEL 786:23
When first we k.	BRID 152:25
When I k. the jack	SHAK 773:57
kisses Are not your k.…filthy	DONNE 279:32
a-wastin' Christian k.	KIPL 471:87
couches and k.	THOM 853:94
forgotten my k.	SWIN 833:38
how many k.	CATU 201:6
k. of an enemy are deceitful	BIBLE 100:58
littered with remembered k.	MACN 538:6
More than k.	DONNE 280:63
numbering of k.	CLEV 221:82
Of many thousand k.	SHAK 765:50
remembered k.	TENN 842:8
Stolen k. much completer	HUNT 423:29
understand thy k.	SHAK 742:19
kissing constant click and k.	BETJ 84:2
fool…that first invented k.!	SWIFT 832:10
Garlic to mend her k.	SHAK 770:89
I wasn't k. her	MARX 557:83
K. don't last	MERE 567:97
k. had to stop?	BROW 161:41
k. is as full of sanctity	SHAK 750:68
K. with golden face	SHAK 771:16
Like k. Hitler	CURT 249:49
lip…it was made For k.	SHAK 731:3
lipped, and trembled k.	SHAK 765:31
overeagerly k. women	PACK 633:74
Kissinger if Mr K. is a great writer	ANON 25:62
Nixon and K. began	PILG 651:17

kiss-worthy most k.-w. face   SIDN 790:13
kitchen better get out of the k.   TRUM 868:32
   Eat in the k.   HUGH 418:17
   Fowls are to the k.   BRIL 152:36
   history…through the k. window   CHILD 213:8
   in k. cups   STEV 819:14
   k. in the right place   JOHN 440:97
   lack of reason in the k.   NIET 615:23
   make my k.   STEV 823:32
   mischief in the k.   THUR 859:49
   Out of the k., to stew   ONEI 626:5
   perpetually clean k.   BUKO 165:47
   send me to eat in the k.   HUGH 418:16
Kitchener K.…a great poster.   ASQU 36:12
kitchens talked of warm k.   GRAH 366:39
kites k. to whet their beaks   RANS 679:24
kitten trouble with a k.   NASH 608:90
kittle place Ca'd the K. Housie?   ANON 20:18
knack k. of judging a distance   REED 681:79
   Technology…the k. of so arranging   FRIS 338:76
knave all a k. or half a slave   INGR 429:59
   he's an arrant k.   SHAK 752:36
   K. of Hearts   CARR 195:85
   my quaint k.   WEBS 895:91
knavery k. and folly to excuse   CHUR 215:44
   religion, k., and change   BEHN 71:13
knaves Bold k. thrive   DRYD 290:9
   K. and Knavery   ANON 21:37
   rulers, mostly k.   BIER 129:32
   to conclude, they are lying k.!   SHAK 745:23
   world is made up…of fools and k.   BUCK 165:42
knavish either k. or childish   JOHN 445:38
knee A little aboon her k.   BALL 56:88
   and bend my k.   SHAK 735:23
   child upon her k.   TENN 842:12
   civility of my k.   BROW 158:54
   every k. should bow   BIBLE 123:54
   k. which contains all the speed   YOUR 936:86
   noblemen…cap and k.   WEBS 895:5
   on bended k.   STUA 827:99
   Sitting on a wise man's k.   HUXL 425:90
   sit upon the curate's k.   CHES 212:92
   woman is as young as her k.   QUANT 674:36
knee-cap soul started at the k.-c.   LEWIS 508:2
kneel k. still with one little cheek   SCHR 720:40
   K. to nobody   SKEL 795:6
knees body between your k.   CORY 238:78
   climb upon her k.   GRAY 369:13
   creeps rustling to her k.   KEATS 459:38
   Down on your k.   SHAK 750:69
   just on its k.   HEMP 395:33
   live on your k.   IBAR 427:31
   Mr Elbows and K.   ANON 24:40
   not in the k.   JERR 437:38
   Sweeney spreads his k.   ELIOT 305:37
   upon my k. every morning   SHAK 744:90
   work is done upon his k.   KIPL 474:74
knell for it is a k.   SHAK 767:96
   k. Of a spent day   CRANE 243:26
   k. of parting day   GRAY 369:10
   sound strikes like a rising k.!   BYRON 179:23
knew Adam k. Eve   BIBLE 86:58
   I k. him, Horatio   SHAK 755:31
   k. almost as much at eighteen   JOHN 443:70
   k. a lot about foreign affairs   REST 683:17
   k. too well   FROST 338:95
   that he nothing k.   MILT 586:41
   those who k. Him not   SCHW 721:70
knickers k.…of crêpe-de-chine   MACN 538:2
   wearing calico k.   JAMES 433:29
knife carved upon it with a k.   SHAK 743:58
   crumbling…under the k.-e.   RICH 685:43
   cuts as keen as a k.   BAUG 65:87
   gave her a dull paring k.   BRID 152:28
   I had a k. and two forks   RIDGE 687:80
   keeps 'em on the k.   NASH 609:9
   k. is lost in it   SHEL 784:68
   k. through a layer cake   MILL 572:8
   sharpness like a clasping k.   BROW 159:7
   smylere with the k.   CHAU 208:81
   strike with our spirit's k.   SHEL 786:3
   Surgeons…take the k.!   DICK 272:53
   War to the k.   PALA 635:7
   wind's like a whetted k.   MASE 559:23
knight gentle k. was pricking   SPEN 808:72
   k. at arms   KEATS 458:17
   k. had made a sudden pause   CARR 197:21

   K. in the triumph   ADDI 6:21
   k. of the garter   ATTL 38:44
   k. to be their wooer   BALL 55:67
   k. was…a valiant Gent   EVEL 316:21
   name of ony k.   MALO 542:8
   never was k. like…Lochinvar   SCOTT 723:96
   new-slain k.   BALL 56:92
   parfit gentil k.   CHAU 208:69
   Poor K.!   NABO 606:28
   red-cross k.   TENN 839:48
   seyde that on k.   MALO 542:7
   shortest k. of the year   RICH 686:61
knight-errant masquerading k.-e.   PARN 639:92
knighthood k. as…accomplishment   NAIP 606:51
   never accept a k.   KENN 464:48
knights k. and barons bold   MILT 576:10
   K. of the Isosceles Triangle   ROOS 696:58
   k. used in those days   CAXT 201:21
   order of k.   GUIB 374:30
   Red-Branch K. to danger   MOORE 596:48
knit to darn, to flower or k.   LEWIS 507:81
knits k. me to thy rugged strand!   SCOTT 723:92
knitter beautiful little k.   SITW 794:76
knitting as if it were k.   GLAS 359:98
   woman still at her k.   PLATH 654:71
knock k., and it shall be opened   BIBLE 110:7
   k., breathe, shine, and…mend   DONNE 281:70
   k. over the first one   EISE 302:55
   none will hear the postman's k.   AUDEN 39:82
   right to k. him down   JOHN 446:48
   stand at the door, and k.   BIBLE 126:52
knocked k. the bastard off!   HILL 403:92
knocker Tie up the k.   POPE 661:33
knocks nature k. them all flat   RENO 683:6
   What really k. me out   SALI 710:52
knot bomb the k. off a tree   JENS 437:27
   certain k. of peace   SIDN 790:10
   crowned k. of fire   ELIOT 309:51
   k. be unknotted   ELIOT 307:8
   political k. that would not yield   BIER 128:17
   then all is a k.   JONS 450:62
know all ye need to k.   KEATS 455:94
   already k. the answer   JONG 448:3
   As I k. more of mankind   JOHN 446:62
   Be still, and k.   BIBLE 95:26
   by their fruits ye shall k. them   BIBLE 110:11
   can be said to k.   RUSS 705:54
   courage to k.   KANT 455:42
   do not k. who or what I am   SELL 727:85
   don't k. where you are   GROS 374:25
   Dost thou k. me?   SHAK 763:90
   full up with the things they k.   HERN 399:28
   general must k.   REED 682:84
   greatest virtue…is to k. God   SPIN 811:32
   hate any one that we k.   HAZL 387:74
   How did they k.?   PARK 637:51
   I do not k. myself   GOET 360:24
   I k. it well, your mishap   HEINE 391:50
   I k. not   HAND 380:31
   I k. thee well   SHAK 764:95
   K. all that there is to be knowed   GRAH 366:40
   k. I'm right   GOLD 362:74
   k. more than you think   SPOCK 811:37
   k. most of the rooms   FULL 341:60
   k. nothing whatever about you   DOYLE 285:74
   k. thee not, old man   SHAK 743:60
   k., to kill and to create   BAUD 65:82
   k. what to do with it   WALP 887:28
   k. what we are   SHAK 754:17
   k. without learning   INGR 429:63
   leader…must k. that he knows   RAND 678:12
   Let him not k.'t   SHAK 760:93
   let's learn not to k.   CRUZ 246:88
   Mistress, k. yourself   SHAK 750:69
   must k. where you are   STEI 816:37
   never k. what's hit you   KENN 463:44
   no one knows what he doesn't k.   CARY 199:67
   not stand to k. any more   MUNRO 602:84
   O that a man might k.   SHAK 748:22
   other half don't k. they don't k.   QUINN 675:54
   people k. what the land k.s   SAND 713:7
   pity those I do not k.   SHAK 758:24
   place thereof shall k. it no more   BIBLE 97:66
   reading might make her k.   SIDN 790:7
   report on what I k.   FRIS 338:75
   Scientists k. so much   SHAP 776:36
   something that you k.   HEMI 394:8

   the more we k.   HUXL 424:61
   thought to k. this   BIBLE 96:42
   We don't k. where that money   REAG 681:63
   what I do k. I k. better   AGATE 8:68
   what should they k. of England   KIPL 471:99
   what thou dost not k.   SHAK 741:11
   what you do not k.   ELIOT 308:20
   When will the world k.   WALP 887:33
   Yet I k. her for   SHAK 775:16
   You k. I k. you k.   GUNN 375:39
knowes Ca' the yowes to the k.   BURNS 173:45
knoweth be as one that k.   BIBLE 108:62
know-how American k.-h.   COLO 228:51
knowing art of k. what to overlook   JAMES 434:65
   k. there was no corner   KAVA 456:69
   k. what will be known   FRAN 335:17
   k. who we are is k.   MILL 572:5
   lust of k.   FLEC 327:46
   precisely in k. its limits   KANT 455:41
knowledge After such k., what
   forgiveness?   ELIOT 305:41
   all branches of k.   ARNO 33:35
   all k. and wonder   BACON 46:35
   all k. is human   POPP 663:97
   all k.…my province   BACON 46:32
   any addition to k.   DONNE 281:93
   a pound of k.   WESL 900:26
   because they lead to the k.   JONG 448:96
   best mode of k.   SENG 727:97
   Bitter is the k.   BAUD 64:66
   blocked up the way to k.   BERK 79:4
   by words without k.?   BIBLE 93:69
   Can k. have no bound   DENH 261:91
   carry k. with him   JOHN 445:31
   chapter of k. is very short   CHES 210:36
   civilizations that abandon the quest for k.   LOVE 519:19
   climbing after k.   MARL 551:75
   collection…of human k.   KENN 462:20
   craftsmen share a k.   SACK 708:88
   deny k.   KANT 455:46
   dissemble sometimes your k.   BACON 49:36
   enlightenment in all spheres of k.   BOOK 144:79
   ethics, as a branch of k.   AYER 45:12
   evergreen tree of diabolical k.   SHER 787:36
   ever to have pure k.   PLATO 655:90
   exactly of their own k.   MONT 591:63
   experience and intuited k.   MO 589:21
   father of k.   HIPP 403:2
   forms of human k.   MANN 545:66
   for want of better K.   PATE 642:55
   from k. ignorance   BROW 162:73
   fruits of k.   FREUD 337:56
   genius of k.   GOUR 365:27
   God has given k.   MARIE 550:49
   greatest good…is the k. of God   SPIN 811:32
   ignorance is never better than k.   FERMI 321:16
   imperfect is all our k.   DONNE 281:91
   impersonation…of secret k.   BROO 156:27
   improved out of all k.   SITW 794:74
   inner reserve of k.   HOOV 411:68
   intuitive k. of God   SPIN 811:34
   jazz, if one has the k.   MORT 599:19
   key of k.   BIBLE 115:41
   K. advances by steps   MACA 525:46
   k. and is not rejected   RUSS 705:55
   k. and love of God   BOOK 141:10
   K. and survey of vice   MILT 579:73
   k. and timber shouldn't   HOLM 408:87
   k. as collective k.   SHAP 776:36
   k.…at the center of true religiousness   EINS 301:37
   k. belongs to humanity   PAST 642:46
   k. can only be finite   POPP 663:1
   k. combined with that of other   GALB 343:96
   K. comes, but wisdom   TENN 841:84
   k. derived from experience   ELIOT 308:16
   k.…did ne'er unroll   GRAY 369:16
   K. dwells In heads   COWP 241:78
   k. for the sake of understanding   BUSH 176:25
   k. from the gods   WILS 915:85
   k. increaseth sorrow   BIBLE 100:68
   k. in her presence   MILT 584:4
   K. is a polite word   CUMM 248:20
   K. is a sacred cow   SZENT 834:65
   k. is as food   MILT 583:90
   k. is bought in the market   CLOU 222:18
   K. is of two kinds   JOHN 444:9
   k. is, ourselves to know   POPE 661:28

known

K. is power	BACON 46:33
K. is proud	COWP 241:79
K....keep any better than fish.	WHIT 904:6
k.....lost in information?	ELIOT 307:87
k. might become more clear	LANY 489:5
K. might pity win	SIDN 790:7
k. of causes	BACON 50:62
k. of causes	BACON 47:68
k. of good and evil	MILT 579:65
k. of good and evil	MILT 579:67
k. of its giant strength	NORR 618:65
k. of literate English...desert	CHAN 205:83
k. of man is as the waters	BACON 46:44
k. of oneself	MILL 573:40
k. of the Bible, Shakespeare	WAUGH 893:55
k. of the boundless skies	BYRON 181:67
k. of the heart	JOHN 444:95
k. of the stars	EDDI 298:84
k. originates in...experience	MAO 547:5
k....recorded experience	CARL 192:15
k. shall be increased	BIBLE 106:1
k....shall vanish away	BIBLE 121:9
k. that he lived in vain	BYRON 179:22
k. that since perfection	NIEB 614:98
k. that the soul	PATM 643:64
k. that you can have is inexhaustible	FRYE 340:39
k. that you'll grow out of it	DAY 256:81
K. the wing	SHAK 730:63
K....will not console me	PASC 641:30
Language and k.	SULL 828:16
larger the island of k.	MACI 533:9
Let k. grow	TENN 842:22
lies in the way to k.	LOCKE 514:16
limits of human k.	NIEB 614:99
love of Christ, which passeth k.	BIBLE 122:45
materials of reason and k.	LOCKE 514:17
men naturally desire k.	ARIS 29:48
more love and k. of you	SHAK 749:29
multiplieth words without k.	BIBLE 93:68
no k. of myself	KANT 454:40
no k. when the day was done	KEATS 458:28
nor k....in the grave	BIBLE 101:84
not be lessened by the k.	HUXL 426:10
Of k. there is no satiety	BACON 46:51
one who speaks, without k.	BIER 129:29
only one good, k.	SOCR 803:58
opinion...is but k.	MILT 579:66
ourselves, and our k.	POPP 663:95
Out-topping k.	ARNO 31:89
possession of k.	POPP 662:90
presupposition of the k.	HEID 391:44
progress of human k.	FRAN 335:17
province of k. to speak	HOLM 408:98
Science is k. arranged	BURB 167:79
Science is organized k.	SPEN 806:39
Science is systematized positive k.	SART 715:40
scientific k. have been achieved	PLAN 653:58
seek for k. and wisdom	SHEL 782:9
sign of k. in our time	WILL 914:51
small advances in k.	PROU 671:77
sociologists of k.	MERT 568:24
Sorrow is k.	BYRON 181:56
Such k. is too wonderful	BIBLE 98:99
Such k. is too wonderful	BOOK 143:70
things that are preventing k.	PROT 670:65
third kind of k.	SPIN 811:35
thorough k. of human nature	AUST 43:91
through their union can k. arise	KANT 454:39
time to close the five parts of k.	BROW 159:95
to follow k.	TENN 840:64
too much k.	POPE 660:16
tree of k.	BYRON 181:56
tree of k.	BYRON 181:71
Tree of K. grew fast	MILT 582:59
true antithesis to k.	DE 262:8
true k. only comes of death	WHITE 903:94
two modes of acquiring k.	BACON 50:73
Why seek for k.	EDGE 299:1
win k. of the causes	VIRG 882:32
without k. of the same	LEON 504:21

known

known be k., and not know	COLT 229:56
Canada only needs to be k.	HOPK 413:13
Have ye not k.?	BIBLE 103:41
k. them all already, k. them all	ELIOT 304:20
must have k. me	TROL 867:6
not meant 'to be k.'	SAGAN 708:4
than to be k.	HOPK 412:96

till I am k.	JOHN 442:34
knows going one k. not where	MASE 559:25
He k. nothing	SHAW 780:44
person who k. 'how'	RAVI 679:38
Knox Lady K....irrelevance	SOME 803:66
see John K. in Paradise	PARK 637:56
knuckle-end That k.-e. of England	SMITH 801:14
Köhln K., a town of monks	COLE 227:23
Ko-Ko If K.-K. tells us true	GILB 355:20
Koran interpretation of the K.	GIBB 351:57
Korea dust that is settling in K.	MACA 524:28
shall go to K.	EISE 302:51
Kosciusko as K. fell!	CAMP 186:67
Kosovo K. is not a part of Serbia	MILO 575:90
stop ethnic cleansing in K.	BLAIR 133:12
Kraken the K. sleepeth	TENN 838:36
Krazy ball made of K. Putty	LODGE 514:24
Krieg K. findet immer einen Ausweg	BREC 151:14
Krishna K.'s jokes may be vapid	FORS 332:57
Kruger finished killing K.	KIPL 472:27
kurrajong Under a k.	NEIL 610:31
Kurtz Mistah K.—he dead	CONR 234:1
kuwaiting We're k.	ANON 24:45
Kyle lad was born in K.	BURNS 171:91
Kyrie K. eleison	ANON 19:96

L

label l. our toys good and bad	DYSON 297:63
rag of a l. to cover himself	HUXL 426:7
labials heavenly l.	STEV 819:16
labor onward march of l.	LEWIS 507:83
laboratories Outside their l.	PAST 642:47
states are the l. of democracy	WHIT 905:27
laboratory Give me an...l.	PERE 648:57
hissing l. of his wishes	THOM 853:95
l. of God	WILL 912:23
laborious rising unto place is l.	BACON 48:2
Studious of l. ease	COWP 241:75
Labour only leaders L. loves	HARR 383:97
labour 25 years of L. Government	BEVAN 84:15
all ye that l.	BIBLE 111:38
applies himself to l. and exercise	CONF 230:92
as much of a l. to write	HUXL 425:66
Britain with a L. Government	WILS 916:98
British L. movement...strikes	ENGE 314:67
calamity of a L. Government	HESE 401:62
Chinese cheap l.	HARTE 384:17
common wages of l.	SMITH 797:43
daily l. to pursue	WESL 900:15
demand for their l.	STEU 819:8
dignify the l.	CRANE 243:15
division of l.	BABB 45:19
division of l. is nothing	MARX 557:97
division of l....social functions	DURK 296:31
don't let L. ruin it	ANON 23:77
do ye not l. and toil	BIBLE 107:25
Ease and alternate l.	THOM 856:54
example of unproductive l.	GRAY 368:91
extraction of surplus l.	MARX 558:11
fruit of our l.	MONT 591:64
Give us l.	SCHR 720:42
good reward for their l.	BIBLE 100:73
I in l. lie	DONNE 279:35
In all l. there is profit	BIBLE 99:29
In l. and trouble...more dignified	CHES 211:41
instruments of l.	MARX 558:12
intellectual l. (of science)	HUMB 421:2
l. and wages first	MANN 546:80
L. does not only create goods	MARX 557:95
l. going upstairs	MUNDY 603:82
L. government	GEOR 349:15
L. Governments in every country	GREY 373:6
l. in his vocation	SHAK 741:97
l. in the deep mid-ocean	TENN 839:58
l. in vain	BIBLE 98:92
L. isn't working	ANON 24:22
L. is the Father...of Wealth	PETTY 650:85
L. is the Party of law and order	BLAIR 132:99
L. leader	MCFA 531:69
L. movement was truly religious	WOLFE 920:97
L. of an age in piled stones	MILT 576:2
l. of his body	LOCKE 514:14
l. of keeping house	MCCA 528:6
l. of women	GILM 356:52
l. once spent	JEVO 438:36
L. Party is a moral crusade	WILS 916:93

L. Party's election programme	SNOW 802:46
L. Party, when...entrusted with power	WEBB 893:66
l. required to obtain...goods	RICA 684:34
l.-time necessary to reproduce	MARX 558:10
l....to pervert that end	MILT 580:4
l. until the evening	BIBLE 97:68
L. was the first p.	SMITH 797:42
l. weariness	LYLY 523:11
l. we delight in	SHAK 767:8
l. which he taketh under the sun?	BIBLE 100:65
L. without joy	RUSK 704:26
last L. that thou and I shall waste	WYATT 931:2
little effect after much l.?	AUST 43:88
many still must l. for the one	BYRON 181:47
more l. in hewing	JOHN 445:34
mountains are in l.	HORA 414:32
natural price of l.	RICA 684:31
natural price of l.	RICA 685:36
no time to l.	ROGE 695:26
performed much of the l.	STAN 812:65
performing any kind of l.	WARD 888:58
productive powers of l.	SMITH 797:38
product of mental l.	MARX 558:10
rest rather than l.	RICH 686:68
role of l. in society	NEVI 611:49
sacrifice of more and more l.	RICA 684:32
shortened the l. of copyists	CARL 192:90
Six days thou shalt l.	BIBLE 88:23
society do not want his l.	MALT 543:18
they that live l.	BIBLE 107:26
this waye to l.	ANON 19:80
To learn and l.	BOOK 142:15
true success is to l.	STEV 822:95
understood...the natural price of l.	RICA 684:31
With too much l. drowns	SHAK 733:95
yet is their strength l.	BIBLE 96:51
laboured l. to it without the reward	SCOTT 722:80
labourer employed as an under-l.	LOCKE 514:16
king's torch throws its light upon a l.	CYRA 250:60
l. is worthy of his hire	BIBLE 115:35
l. or a tradesman	LAW 493:54
l. to take his pension	RUSK 704:15
labourers enable the l....to subsist	RICA 685:36
take that of L.' Unions	RUSK 704:35
too many L. to cultivate the Lands	CANT 188:16
labouring A l. man that is given	BIBLE 108:54
l. swain	GOLD 361:50
Sleep is sweet to the l. man	BUNY 166:72
labours Children sweeten l.	BACON 48:85
from their l. rest	HOW 416:92
notice...of my l.	JOHN 442:34
One thousand l.	LABE 482:54
share of the l. and sacrifices	MILL 570:64
uncessant l. see	MARV 556:71
laburnums L., dropping-wells	TENN 844:53
labyrinth dreamt I was in the l.	MUIR 602:57
is in the l.	ROBBE 688:8
l. of our life	SCHO 719:29
peopled l. of walls	SHEL 783:45
labyrinthine down the l. ways	THOM 855:36
Lachlan I met him, down the L.	PATE 642:55
lack l. of many a thing	SHAK 771:15
l. their sacred poet	HORA 413:25
lacked If I l. any thing	HERB 397:98
lacrosse I thought l. was	WILL 912:11
lad brisk and a bonnie l.	ANON 20:13
l. does not care for	JOHN 443:94
l. of life	SHAK 746:49
l. that's born to be king	BOUL 146:26
l. was born in Kyle	BURNS 171:91
many a lightfoot l.	HOUS 415:63
myself a sterling l.	HOUS 415:67
Up, l.	HOUS 414:49
When I was a l.	GILB 353:94
ladder can't climb...without a l.	ZATO 936:90
kick away the l.	SUN 829:29
l. set up on the earth	BIBLE 87:88
Now that my l.'s gone	YEATS 934:62
raise a l. without a wall	HONE 409:29
rounds of society's l.	MOORE 595:22
with lantern and with l.	STEV 823:20
laden heart is l.	HOUS 415:63
ladies art that helps old l.	OLDE 624:62
by act of God, we are l.	CARD 183:20
Cambridge l....furnished souls	CUMM 247:3
chic old blue-haired l.	CAPO 189:32

delectable lusty l.   DUNB 294:5
Good l., help to fill   SURR 829:39
good night, sweet l.   SHAK 754:18
keep us from scaring the l.   MCMU 537:86
l....admitted on special days   WARN 889:66
l. and gentlemen, last night   NATH 609:22
l. apparently rolled along   HUXL 425:68
l. in very high positions   AMIN 14:81
l., just a little more virginity   TREE 865:51
l. that must be wooed   CAMP 186:78
l., whose bright eyes   MILT 576:10
l., yield to love   LYLY 523:11
lang may the l. sit   BALL 56:86
lion among l.   SHAK 737:1
old l. in tennis shoes   MOSK 600:27
old l. of both sexes   DICK 270:10
remember the l.   ADAMS 3:61
Sigh no more, l.   SHAK 744:6
worth any number of old l.   FAUL 318:69
ye lords of l. intellectual   BYRON 181:63
young l. spend their time   SWIFT 831:70
ads Golden l. and girls   SHAK 774:74
l. are far away   FORD 330:20
l. in their hundreds   HOUS 415:54
l. who fought   SASS 716:66
Then strip l.   SCOTT 724:15
three wild l. were we   SCOTT 724:19
Two l. that thought   SHAK 770:74
ady accomplished l.   SHAK 756:75
act like a l.   SIMON 792:36
behaved like a perfect l.   TRAV 865:47
cannot endure my L. Tongue   SHAK 744:96
certain little l. comes by   GAY 348:90
Come, l., let not this   MARL 551:71
coyness L. were no crime   MARV 555:61
dreamt my l. came   SHAK 737:78
Fair l., will you any?   LYLY 523:9
for the love of a l.!   GILB 355:31
girl who was a l.   LOOS 517:77
hawk, his hound, and his l. fair   BALL 56:92
Here lies a l. of beauty   RANS 679:21
hold my l.'s head   HEAN 389:7
l. as thou art   SHAK 742:21
l. from the provinces   GILB 355:22
l. in the wig   DICK 268:48
L., l., should you meet   PARK 637:43
l. novelist   GILB 355:22
l. of Christ's College   AUBR 39:68
L. of my own   WORD 924:79
L. of Shalott   TENN 839:44
L. of Shalott   TENN 839:47
L. of Shalott   TENN 839:50
L. of Shalott   TENN 839:51
L. of Shalott   TENN 839:52
L. of the Lake   MALO 542:5
l. of the West Country?   DELA 260:67
l. protests too much   SHAK 754:92
L.'s not for Burning   FRY 340:25
l. that's known as Lou   SERV 728:3
l. wants to be dressed   NASH 609:6
l. was not seen!   SCOTT 724:23
l. who found out   ROSE 697:66
L. with a Lamp   LONG 516:60
L. would be Queen   POPE 661:49
L. you deserve this state   MARV 556:62
like a dying l.   SHEL 787:31
lord and l. gay   SCOTT 722:85
lovely l., garmented in light   SHEL 785:87
Lydia The Tattooed L.   HARB 381:37
make a sweet l. sad   SHAK 757:99
manners of a l.   FRAN 335:21
No l. closer   SHAK 741:11
no rhyme to 'l.'   SHAK 745:24
not exactly a l.   RIDGE 687:78
Of many a l.   SPEN 808:86
O lang will his l.   BALL 55:59
old l. at a busy intersection   ACHE 3:40
quarrel for a l.   HALI 378:90
San Francisco is a l.   MAIL 540:55
saw a l. bright   BALL 56:89
talk like a l.   SHAW 780:63
the l. is a tramp   HART 384:11
'Twas a good l.   SHAK 762:38
When a l.'s in the case   GAY 347:78
wrong to strike a l.   THUR 860:59
You are the body, l.   SCEVE 717:94
lag with some l.   HOMA 408:9

lain l. for ages and will lie   TENN 838:37
l. with their mothers   SOPH 804:89
lair silence round about his l.   KEATS 455:44
laird l. o' Cockpen   NAIR 607:53
lifts a drove from a Sassenach l.   SCOTT 723:13
laity conspiracies against the l.   SHAW 780:49
tell the l. of our love   DONNE 280:54
laitymen Gentes and l.   JOYCE 452:99
lake beside a cold l.   SCOTT 722:77
bosom of the l.   TENN 842:14
daffodils...beside the l.   WORD 927:40
glitter like a l.   BYRON 182:78
I am in the l.   ATWO 38:48
l. I saw bass-viols   LEVE 506:58
l. is the great source   SPEKE 806:35
l. of fire   BIBLE 127:78
Maker, in that crimson l.   MONT 593:5
Marriage may...be a stormy l.   PEAC 645:92
middle of a stormy l.   EISE 302:62
real pitch l.   HUXL 425:79
Round the Mareotic L.   YEATS 934:65
lakes grass is green, l. damp   STEP 817:58
L., mountains, and rivers   AUST 43:69
shakes across the l.   TENN 841:3
Some people swim l.   WEBB 893:64
songs in its l.   SCOTT 722:78
lakeside by the l.   SCHW 721:70
lamb ape to Hazlitt, to L.   STEV 823:25
Behold the L. of God   BIBLE 117:75
brought as a l. to the slaughter   BIBLE 104:51
Did he who made the L. make thee?   BLAKE 135:62
Englishman...flattered, is a l.   CHAP 206:21
God will provide himself a l.   BIBLE 87:82
holy L. of God   BLAKE 135:82
L. of God   CASW 199:82
L. of God, I come!   ELLI 310:79
l. shall be without blemish   BIBLE 88:15
leads me to the L.!   COWP 240:46
Little l., who made thee?   BLAKE 133:29
Maria, to the shorn l.   STER 818:6
Mary had a little l.   HALE 377:80
one little ewe l.   BIBLE 91:2
Pipe a song about a l.!   BLAKE 133:28
washed in the blood of the L.?   LIND 510:45
washed in the blood of the L.?   LIND 510:46
when he would steal the l.   SHAK 730:57
wolf also shall dwell with the l.   BIBLE 102:19
wolf and the l. shall feed together   BIBLE 104:66
wolf and the l....united   ARIS 29:47
lambs gather the l. with his arm   BIBLE 103:37
go to hell like l.   CHES 212:82
l. end up head down   JUST 453:12
poor little l.   KIPL 470:80
lame l. man leap as an hart   BIBLE 103:33
l. man who keeps the right road   BACON 47:64
l. walk   BIBLE 111:33
made l. by...spite   SHAK 771:70
Science without religion is l.   EINS 301:36
lament childish weakness to l.   SHAK 731:85
l. of the poets   THOM 855:31
l. the past   BURKE 168:3
naught other to l.   PATM 643:61
lamentation l., and bitter weeping   BIBLE 105:78
lamented ye have not l.   BIBLE 111:36
Lammas It fell about the L. tide   BALL 55:66
It was upon a L. night   BURNS 170:82
lamp dying l., a falling shower   SHEL 785:99
Eternal l. of love!   HERR 399:38
Lady with a L.   LONG 516:60
l. beside the golden door   LAZA 496:51
l.-l. dull and sickly   WILDE 907:81
l. of day   DOUG 283:18
l. of faith   WORD 929:63
l. unto my feet   BIBLE 97:84
l. was dark   MACN 538:10
smell of the l.   HERR 400:40
smell too strong of the l.   STER 817:76
sovran vital l.   MILT 582:37
To keep a l. burning   THER 851:42
lamppost asking a l. how it feels   HAMP 380:28
leaning on a l.   GAY 348:90
lampposts way that a drunk uses l.   LANG 488:89
lamps I mean by fairy l.   WOOD 921:20
l. are going out   GREY 371:9
l. are guttering low   HOUS 416:91
l., by whose dear light   MARV 556:68
L. for my gloom   SASS 716:75

l. that shone o'er fair women   BYRON 179:23
lampshade a Nazi l.   PLATH 654:66
Lancashire In a L. cotton-town   ORWE 627:40
typical sound of L.   ORWE 627:35
Lancelot at that tyme sir L.   MALO 542:8
bold Sir L.   TENN 839:48
L. mused a little space   TENN 839:52
Not L., nor another   TENN 846:24
which I found in L.   TENN 846:23
lances Shall be our l.   GILB 354:16
lancet veins...to invite the l.   SHER 787:45
land across the other l.   MUIR 602:63
all that travel by l.   SWIFT 832:9
America...heroic, sentimental l.   RABAN 675:61
away into the silent l.   ROSS 697:78
best dance e'er cam to the L.   BURNS 172:38
best people never l.   MACN 538:11
brought me in to possess this l.   BIBLE 89:48
by l. and sea   WORD 927:37
by sea as by l.   GILB 353:88
clear the l. of evil   KIPL 472:13
clung...to the l.   MOOD 594:6
cut off Israel out of the l.   BIBLE 91:11
darkness of the l.   TENN 844:61
death's grey l.   SASS 716:60
doghter of the l. of Camylarde   MALO 542:4
England's green and pleasant l.   BLAKE 136:85
exact survey of the l.   DONNE 282:94
exiles from our fathers' l.   GALT 344:29
famine was sore in the l.   BIBLE 88:3
fat of the l.   BIBLE 88:3
flourishing culture in our l.   MAO 548:12
glorious l. above the sky   HILL 402:88
glorious l. of ours   FERB 320:93
good and bad of every l.   BAIL 52:5
happy l.   GOLD 361:57
harsh l.'s red and green   HYDE 427:23
his hands prepared the dry l.   BOOK 143:64
history of the l.   LONG 516:60
Ill fares the l.   GOLD 361:52
in a blatant l.   TENN 845:84
in a dry and thirsty l.   BIBLE 96:35
in a strange l.?   BIBLE 98:98
in the l. of the living   BIBLE 97:76
l. and ocean without rest   MILT 580:88
l. and the mind   NGU 613:79
l. flowing with milk and honey   BIBLE 88:11
l. God gave to Andy Stewart   SMITH 799:65
l. God gave to Cain   CART 198:54
L. is the only thing   MITC 588:93
l. lies desolate and stripped   ADAMS 4:63
l. may be said to be discovered   STEF 814:5
l. may vary more   FROST 339:2
L. of brown heath   SCOTT 723:92
L. of Calvin   SMITH 801:14
l. of cattle and sheep   LAWS 496:45
L. of hope and glory   BENS 77:61
l. of light and revelation   CLIN 221:91
l. of lost content   HOUS 415:60
L. of lost gods   BYRON 179:15
L. of Nod   BIBLE 86:62
L. of Nod at last   STEV 823:22
l. of our birth   KIPL 473:62
l. of sand and ruin   SWIN 833:42
l. of settled government   TENN 841:93
l. of the free   KEY 465:76
l. of their heart's hope   DAVIS 256:66
l. of the pilgrims'   CUMM 247:8
l. o' the leal   NAIR 607:54
l. stares at the sun   SCOTT 722:78
l. that has need of heroes   BREC 151:9
l. that has no heroes   BREC 151:9
l. that I heard of   HARB 381:38
l. wherein thou art a stranger   BIBLE 87:77
L. where my fathers died   SMITH 800:91
l. where the Bong-tree   LEAR 497:84
laughing Ceres re-assume the l.   POPE 659:97
length and breadth of the l.   MOOD 594:10
light across the l.?   TENN 841:94
Lilacs out of the dead l.   ELIOT 305:52
little wrong in the l.   MENC 565:51
love-sick l. that mourns for thee   BLAKE 133:23
loving the l.   MOORE 596:54
made our l. a tomb   ORAH 627:21
Maker's image through the l.   DRYD 289:69
Marched into their l.   AYTO 45:16
mist and hum of that low l.   ARNO 32:27

my own, my native l.! — SCOTT 723:91
nakedness of the l.. — BIBLE 88:99
narrow strip of l. — BAKER 53:20
Oh, thou dear l. — SCHAW 717:96
once-loved l. — WRIG 930:83
Only the weathering l. — SNYD 803:49
Past is a strange l. — THOM 854:5
Peace is…more precious than…l. — SADAT 708:92
people know what the l. knows — SAND 713:7
pocket of my l. — FRAME 333:79
pointed toward the l. — TENN 839:53
poor race in a l. of dollars — DU 293:71
Praise the sports of the l. — REID 682:96
publishes to every l. — ADDI 6:26
rich fruitful l. — BLAKE 134:55
rural virtues leave the l. — GOLD 361:60
security of the l. — COVE 239:6
She was our l. — FROST 339:9
Silence ruled this l. — DARK 253:5
sun rose and set on their l. — SITT 793:56
than ever before in any l. — HOOV 411:58
The l. of my fathers — THOM 853:83
the law of the l. — MAGN 539:27
there was no l. left — IHIM 428:44
think of my own native l. — COWP 241:56
This is the dead l. — ELIOT 306:70
This l. is your l. — GUTH 375:48
Thou on the l. — SCOTT 724:19
Thus fares the l. — GOLD 361:58
town surrounded by l. — MOORE 595:26
traveller from an antique l. — SHEL 784:49
truth is a pathless l. — KRIS 480:13
unto a l. that I will shew thee — BIBLE 87:72
want to build a better l. — CHRI 214:27
want to free this l. — MARI 550:54
westward…the l. is bright — CLOU 222:22
what shall this l. produce? — RANS 679:23
wide brown l. for me — MACK 533:15
windy sea of l. — MILT 582:48
with my native l. — TENN 846:1
Woe to that l. — SHAK 731:9
woman is a foreign l. — PATM 643:60
workman in the l. — LLOY 513:98
would be a grand l. — FREE 336:40
wrong throughout the l. — MUIR 601:53
Your l., your wealth — JAY 435:96
landing l. a man on the moon — KENN 462:14
landlady l. of a boarding-house — LEAC 496:58
landlord architecture…for the l. — WRIG 929:78
interest of the l. — RICA 685:35
l. does not intend to repair — ADAMS 5:94
l. to the whole congregation — ADDI 6:14
landlords before the l. of the country — PARN 639:92
l. and persons of property — MALT 543:19
landmark Remove not the old l. — BIBLE 100:48
removeth his neighbour's l. — BIBLE 90:52
landmarks l. that are scarcely more — HUBB 418:11
nomads, on a plain with few l. — MCMU 537:89
landmined l. and unforgiving — ELKIN 310:69
lands different from things in other l. — LAWS 495:43
envy of less happier l. — SHAK 734:8
forsake me, and of all my l. — SHAK 730:84
l. are the mother — PETTY 650:85
l. beyond the sea — WORD 925:9
l. where the Jumblies live — LEAR 497:79
satisfies the poor in other l. — HEGEL 391:40
sold your own l. — SHAK 750:73
songs of other l. — EVANS 316:19
Where are our l.? — SITT 793:56
landscape art of l. — RUNGE 702:75
Burning like a sunlit l. — MACD 530:49
half the l. is unavailable — DOUG 283:27
implacability of the l. — NOLAN 617:54
invention of the l. painter — FUSE 342:77
l. and its inhabitants — UPDI 875:97
l. broken into — LEGER 501:53
L. is to American painting — HUGH 419:32
l. round it measures — MILT 576:8
l. to a blind man's eye — WORD 923:69
shaper of the l. — BRON 154:70
the beauty of l. — HILL 402:91
landscapes fades the glimmering l. — GRAY 369:10
if l. were sold — STEV 821:77
l. of seas full of fish — CIXO 219:38
Someone said of his l. — HAZL 388:95
landslide Republican l. on Nov 8 — CUOMO 248:32
lane country l. — PARK 638:81

dragons of Laune and L. — ORAH 626:20
In an English l. — BROW 161:56
l. was made — DICK 268:47
walk down the l. — FREED 336:37
lanes green and shaded l. — MACK 533:15
language abstruseness in their l. — GOWE 365:29
American l. — ADAMS 4:85
any l. you choose — GILB 354:15
Bad l. or abuse — GILB 353:92
beyond the l. of the living — ELIOT 309:40
beyond the range of l. — REID 682:95
braver in another l. — BROO 156:24
certain mistress of l. — JONS 450:60
Color and bite permeate a l. — SAFI 708:97
confound the l. of all the earth — BIBLE 87:71
constantly changing l. of politics — SAFI 708:96
conveyed…in the best chosen l. — AUST 43:91
countries divided by a common l. — SHAW 781:98
deciduous l. — THOM 855:31
define her feelings in l. — HARDY 381:53
don't use whatever l. — KELM 461:78
dramatic words in the English l. — HART 384:14
dream of a common l. — RICH 685:52
enemy of clear l. — ORWE 628:62
enemy of clear l. — ORWE 629:89
English l. is nobody's…property — WALC 884:75
English l. readers — GISC 358:85
enlargement of the l. — JOHN 442:41
ere we learn the l. — THOR 857:68
every l. even deafanddumb — CUMM 247:8
Experience is…larger than l. — RICH 685:57
Finality is not the l. of politics — DISR 276:66
fine flow of l. — RIDGE 687:78
French is not a static l. — HUGO 420:65
from one l. to another — SHEL 786:13
fumbling with…English l. — WAUGH 893:57
gifted glassblower of l. — HERS 400:53
Great literature is simply l. — POUND 665:47
greed wrapped in the l. of love — ARMEY 30:69
inaccessible…except…their l. — FRAME 333:81
in a room with the English l. — HUTC 424:50
in the English l. — THUR 859:43
lack of a whole l. — MUIR 601:52
l. all nations understand — BEHN 71:12
L. and knowledge — SULL 828:16
l. an opera is sung in — APPL 27:23
l. concentrating emotion — BRAU 150:4
L. does not leave fossils — BRAU 150:99
L. grows out of life — SULL 828:15
l. has said that reason — MACL 535:32
l. have the right — KELM 461:79
l. he was the lodesterre — LYDG 523:3
L. is a form — LEVI 506:66
L. is a skin — BART 62:23
L. is only the instrument — JOHN 442:39
L. is the flesh-garment — CARL 192:95
L. is using us to talk — MATH 560:58
l. of our feelings — FRIE 337:70
l. of the age — GRAY 368:96
l. of the heart — POPE 661:42
l. of the horde — MALL 542:95
l. that can serve our purposes — MACD 530:49
l. that is not ours — WITT 918:49
L. was not powerful enough — DICK 267:8
l., which is what you use — MERW 568:25
law is like the grammar of l. — SACKS 707:84
learned l. — GIBB 352:64
Life is a foreign l. — MORL 598:84
life…under the power of l. — CIXO 218:32
Man's natural l. — FLAU 327:43
mobilized the English l. — KENN 463:24
mobilized the English l. — MURR 605:10
more learning in their [Chinese] l. — JOHN 445:34
most beautiful words in the…l. — JAMES 434:54
Music is the universal l. — LONG 515:40
must re-invent l. — IRIG 430:77
My l. fails! — BELL 73:57
my l. is plain — HARTE 384:16
natural l. of all religions — STAEL 812:53
neither speech nor l. — BOOK 142:43
no l. but a cry — TENN 843:42
No respect for their l. — SHAW 780:61
not…a question of…blood or l. — OBRI 620:98
no word in their l. — SWIFT 831:83
Numbers…universal l. — WEST 901:37
obligated to its l. — BROD 154:59
Only where there is l. — RICH 685:45

our l. fails — WALL 886:16
our l. grows — WALL 886:16
Ours is a precarious l. — THUR 860:54
people…of an hard l. — BIBLE 105:85
Poetry happens because of l. — OLIV 624:65
Poetry…through human l. — MALL 542:91
Political l. — ORWE 629:91
pure rhetoric of a l. — STEV 820:33
refine our l. — JOHN 441:28
refusal of l. is a death — BART 62:20
remains of the English l. — COUP 238:96
room for but one l. — ROOS 696:60
same forms and the same l. — FLAU 326:35
Slang is a l. — SAND 713:10
sociologists…I do not speak their l. — DYSON 297:62
sophisticated use of l. — KUNI 482:38
sorry when any l. is lost — JOHN 444:2
speak the same foreign l. — WILD 910:73
strange l. all I know — LAND 488:82
suicides have a special l. — SEXT 728:19
sure in l. strange she said — KEATS 458:18
taught me l. — SHAK 774:80
The l. plain — COWP 240:47
They are, after all, a l. — BANKS 58:32
unvisionary l. of farm, city and love — ENGLE 314:69
use in measured l. — TENN 842:23
Words are…from a defunct l. — CIXO 219:32
world understands my l. — HAYDN 387:52
writers…make their l. convey more — CONN 233:37
languages dictate the l. in which — BALL 57:2
Do you know L. — CARR 197:26
exchanged…in our respective l. — COOK 235:34
Fluent in all the l. — CURN 249:37
instructed in all l., living and dead — DICK 267:97
three or four l. — SHAK 755:48
thunder In such lovely l. — LAWR 495:28
two l. in Canada — SAINT 709:27
universal l.: love, music and sports — MOSES 600:26
wit in all l. — DRYD 288:24
woman speaks eighteen l. — PARK 637:53
langue au pouvoir de la l. — CIXO 218:32
languish l. like exotics — WOLL 921:8
Relieve my l. — DANI 252:88
languor L. cannot be — SHEL 784:60
pain or l. — WORD 929:63
languors lilies and l. of virtue — SWIN 833:27
lank haggard and l. young man — GILB 354:9
lanky that l. Yankee finger — CONN 232:54
lantern Hang a l. on your problem — MATT 561:62
hast no l. — JONS 449:36
l. of Aristotle's brain — RALE 677:2
l. on the stern — COLE 227:24
with l. and with ladder — STEV 823:20
lanterns jaunty gilded l. — GILL 355:38
Laocoön L.…made different? — EMER 312:20
lap brooks, On whose fresh l. — MILT 578:53
cool flowery l. of earth — ARNO 31:3
drop Into thy mother's l. — MILT 585:31
In thy green l. — GRAY 370:37
lap-dogs l.-d.…shake — POPE 658:65
lapidary In l. inscriptions — JOHN 444:13
laps tumbling into some men's l. — BACON 46:55
lapse l. of moments is ever — STOWE 826:76
l. of one lesser — CANM 188:2
lapwing Beatrice like a l. runs — SHAK 744:9
wanton l. — TENN 840:75
lard as fed with l. — SPEN 810:10
large l. as life — CARR 197:26
small thing…made l. — TWAIN 871:17
Lariston Lock the door, L. — HOGG 406:58
lark bisy l., messager of day — CHAU 208:78
jay more precious than the l. — SHAK 732:43
l. at break of day arising — SHAK 771:14
l. at heaven gate — SHAK 773:61
l.…sightless song — TENN 844:64
l.'s on the wing — BROW 160:51
More tuneable than l. — SHAK 737:85
nightingale, and not the l. — SHAK 736:68
sing as sweetly as the l. — SHAK 741:91
Waked by the l. — SHAK 757:7
larks Four L. and a Wren — LEAR 497:75
hear the l. so high — HOUS 415:52
imprisoned l. — GRAV 368:82
l.…singing the same five notes — CATH 200:84
larkspur The l. listens — TENN 845:92
lash bear de l. as well — TRUTH 869:52
Why dost thou l. that whore? — SHAK 763:92

lashes make the l. dark   YEATS 934:56
lass A l. unparalleled   SHAK 766:63
Drink to the l.   SHER 788:54
every l. a queen   KING 469:53
it came with a l.   JAME 432:23
l. wi' tousled hair   MACD 529:29
lover and his l.   SHAK 750:88
my bonie l.   BURNS 171:2
my bonie l.   BURNS 173:44
solitary Highland L.   WORD 927:34
lasses honest men and bonny l.   BURNS 172:14
L. a-lilting before the dawn   ELLI 310:78
lassie Bony l. will ye go   BURNS 171:94
love a l., a bonnie   LAUD 492:63
love she's but a l.   BURNS 171:8
Never mind my grace, l.   SCOTT 724:37
service to my bonie l.   BURNS 171:2
wae my l. by my side   LAUD 492:64
last cobbler stick to his l.   APEL 27:11
great thing is to l.   HEMI 394:8
here it is at l.   JAMES 434:55
l. best friend   SOUT 805:10
l. of all he was seen of me   BIBLE 121:12
l. of all the Bards   SCOTT 722:84
l. one is as good   HEMI 394:3
l. person to say anything   SAKI 710:48
l. shall be first   BIBLE 113:76
l. shall be first   BIBLE 113:78
l. to lay the Old aside   POPE 658:57
l.…will go over very quickly   EISE 302:55
l. word on nothing   HUGO 421:98
One of the l.   UPDI 874:83
She is the l. of lands   HOPE 411:72
sung her first and l.   GIBB 352:68
the l. act crowns the play   QUAR 674:37
lasting more l. than bronze   HORA 413:24
latch door has a creaking l.   POUND 665:43
press down the l.   WORD 924:83
late always either too l. or too early   SART 715:44
comfort comes too l.   SHAK 775:25
coming l. to a performance   ZOLO 937:5
Dread of being l.!   BETJ 84:12
five minutes too l.   COWL 240:37
L. have I loved you   AUGU 41:37
long choosing, and beginning l.   MILT 584:6
make sure of not being l.   KIER 467:14
people who are l.   LUCAS 521:72
sit up l.   BIBLE 98:92
soon or l.   THOM 854:17
unhappy day too l.   SHAK 735:16
wakest too l.   SKEL 795:93
we have come too l.   LABR 483:56
later l. than you think   SERV 728:4
Latin Don't quote L.   WELL 898:66
from the L. e, 'out'   LEAC 497:70
L. America owes its being   VASC 877:39
L.. Man's natural language   FLAU 327:43
more fanatical official than a L.   HAZZ 388:96
ne yet of L.   SPEN 809:95
small L., and less Greek   JONS 449:44
speech as…dignified as L.   QUIL 674:44
Latin America state of emergency has
   existed in L. A.   DEBR 257:99
latitude wishes to claim a certain l.   HAWT 386:42
Latium arts into rustic L.   HORA 414:29
latrine mouth…used as a l.   AMIS 14:82
latter l. stems from virtue   HELO 393:87
lattice cried through the l.   BIBLE 90:68
laudanum abuse…like l.   STOWE 826:75
laudate L. Dominum, omnes gentes   BIBLE 127:92
laugh And l. as I pass   SHEL 783:39
Anything awful makes me l.   LAMB 486:33
arms hang down to l.   ELIOT 305:37
But I l.   HUGH 418:16
Dinna mak' me l.   LAUD 492:62
do we not l.?   SHAK 740:68
Famous for his l.   FLAU 327:42
heard…a meaning l.   EWART 316:23
if I l. at any mortal thing   BYRON 182:88
If we didn't l.   LLOYD 513:93
l. all of the time   LOOS 517:80
l. and lie   PARK 638:61
l. at all you trembled at   COWP 241:64
l. at him before   NATH 609:21
l. at human actions   SPIN 810:22
l. at…l. with   SPEN 807:64
l. broke into a thousand pieces   BARR 61:81

L., heart   YEATS 932:35
l. is the best pesticide   NABO 606:45
l. like a squadron of cavalry   WODE 919:61
l. like parrots   SHAK 739:35
l. me to scorn   BIBLE 94:98
L. no man to scorn   BIBLE 107:42
l. of superiority   GREE 371:75
l. on that particular day   TRAV 864:45
L. to scorn   SHAK 768:23
l. uproariously in youth   BROO 156:14
L. where we must   POPE 660:7
l. with me, or at me   STER 817:69
lips that l. and hide   SWIN 832:20
man cannot make him l.   SHAK 743:63
more ridiculous than a ridiculous l.   CATU 201:7
not a thing to l. to scorn   SHAK 750:82
nothing more unbecoming…to l.   CONG 231:7
Poetry is what makes me l.   THOM 853:79
quick to l. at everything   BEAU 66:99
sitteth in the heavens shall l.   BIBLE 94:83
those whom I love…make me l.   AUDEN 41:23
way people look and l.   WOOLF 922:28
laughed Full well they l.   GOLD 361:54
I l. him out of patience   SHAK 765:30
l. and suffered at my side   SASS 716:66
speck ter be l. at   HARR 383:95
When he l.   AUDEN 40:98
laughing boughs do l. blossoms bear   SPEN 809:92
cannot forbear l.   PEPYS 647:33
l. in the diners   SAND 713:93
L., quaffing, and unthinking   DRYD 292:61
most fun…without l.   ALLEN 12:53
so filled with L. Gas   TRAV 864:45
waked herself with l.   SHAK 744:1
when I am l. at anyone   BEER 69:71
laughing stock l. s. of children   SIDN 790:16
laughs crowd l. with you always   VIDOR 881:11
get l. without falling   WISD 918:37
he l. longest who l. last   MASE 559:36
he who l. last   ALEX 11:20
irritating l.   GILB 355:21
l. with a harvest   JERR 437:39
world l. with you   WILC 907:80
laughter alone with his l.   KAFKA 454:29
better to write of l.   RABE 676:64
bitterness in our l.   EMER 313:37
faculty of l.   ADDI 6:30
feast is made for l.   BIBLE 101:88
girls' thin l.   RICK 686:74
'Homeric l.'   FLAU 327:42
illiberal and so ill-bred, as audible l.   CHES 210:32
inexhaustible source of l.   TOLS 863:8
kind of l. people laugh at   MCIL 533:1
l. at their quaint opinions   MILT 584:97
L. is a reward   CHAN 205:4
L. is pleasant   PEAC 645:93
l., It is mad   BIBLE 100:69
L. need not be cut out   THUR 860:61
l. of a fool   BIBLE 101:77
Let us have…mirth and l.   BYRON 182:79
listens to your sweet l.   CATU 201:8
love and l.   GORD 363:7
no time for mirth and l.   ADE 7:45
Our sincerest l.   SHEL 784:61
peals of l.…round thee   POPE 661:34
produce l.   JOHN 444:11
scattered l. in the rear   KAUF 456:60
seismic with l.   BARK 59:54
senators burst with l.   AUDEN 40:98
The l. of man   THUR 860:61
turns herself to l.   SPEN 809:97
under running l.   THOM 855:36
weeping and with l.   MACA 526:68
With mirth and l.   SHAK 739:37
laundries Land of l.   BETJ 83:91
laundry any first-class l.   LEAC 497:69
goes into the l.   KIPL 473:55
Laune dragons of L. and Lane   ORAH 626:20
Laura if L. had been Petrach's wife   BYRON 182:84
Rose-cheeked L.   CAMP 187:79
laurel l. for the perfect prime   ROSS 697:77
l., need of mighty conquerors   SPEN 808:73
laurels l. to paeans   CICE 218:26
'Tis sweet to win…one's l.   BYRON 181:70
worth all your l.   BYRON 183:3
ye l., and once more   MILT 578:45
lava walk on the l.…while it was cooling   PATE 642:56

lavatory men-servants' l.   WAUGH 892:27
lavender L. water tinged with pink   LEAR 498:87
Lavinian Italy, at its L. shore   VIRG 882:16
law All things, by a l. divine   SHEL 783:42
almost a l.   WELLS 898:86
Angel, it's a l. of nature   LACL 484:88
basic l. of economics   HARR 384:5
bondage known to our l.   MILL 571:78
both the l. and the gospel   JONS 450:54
break Diana's l.   POPE 659:70
breeds without the L.   KIPL 472:22
brilliance is needed in the l.   MORT 599:12
business of the l.   MACL 535:47
care for your l.   TRUM 869:46
come to destroy the l.   BIBLE 109:86
Conservatives, as being by the l.   MILL 570:67
Creation's final l.   TENN 843:36
Creation's final l.   TENN 843:45
criminal l. is no use   SHAW 780:51
Custom that is before all l.   DANI 252:91
dinna ken muckle about the l.   SCOTT 724:35
Every l. is a contract   SELD 726:77
Every l. is an evil   BENT 77:67
first is l.   DRYD 291:17
fulfilled the l.   BIBLE 120:86
game within the view of the l.   LEAC 497:67
goal of every system of l.   ROUS 700:43
God is thy l.   MILT 583:72
God's l. thet fetters   LOWE 520:30
good of the people is the chief l.   CICE 218:20
hang all the L. and the prophets   BIBLE 113:83
he whom l. calls yours   DRYD 289:62
higher l. in journalism   LIPP 511:66
Hofstadter's L.   HOFS 406:54
Ignorance of the l.   SELD 726:78
in his l. doth he meditate   BIBLE 94:81
internal equivalent of…rule of l.   EDEN 299:90
invariable l. of the newspaper   DANA 251:83
it is of no force in l.   COKE 224:68
judgments of the English l.   SYNGE 834:58
keepeth the l., happy is he   BIBLE 100:62
Keep ye the l.   KIPL 472:13
know the l. since I have spent   MILI 569:54
l. cannot make a man love   KING 468:31
l. has very wisely given   JOHN 443:76
l. hath not been dead   SHAK 758:23
l. is a ass   DICK 267:96
L. is a bottomless pit   ARBU 28:32
L. is naturally founded   MONT 593:92
l. is such an ass   CHAP 206:22
l. is the most powerful   GIRA 358:81
L. is the true embodiment   GILB 354:11
l. not supported by the people   HUMP 422:17
l. of academic life   LODGE 515:27
l. [of competition]…hard   CARN 193:49
l. of death   ANON 21:29
l. of God   MARG 549:43
l. of love   SCEVE 717:92
l. of Moses is harsh   MORE 596:61
l. of nature   HOOK 410:54
l. of the jungle   JUMB 453:7
L. of the jungle   KIPL 471:12
l. of the jungle   KIPL 471:9
l. of the musical world   WHAR 902:54
l. of the Yukon   SERV 728:1
l. pervading all nature   HARDY 382:68
l. seems like a sort of maze   MORT 599:13
l.'s their will   SHAK 769:48
l. to weed it out   BACON 47:78
l. unto themselves   BIBLE 120:60
l.…like a…black cobweb   WEBS 895:97
love is liberty, and nature, l.   POPE 659:82
love is the fulfilling of the l.   BIBLE 120:87
love thy l.   BIBLE 97:86
Men…have L. for their god   PLATO 655:83
moral l. within   KANT 455:47
mysterious l., true source   MILT 583:72
nine points of the l.   ANON 20:11
nine-tenths of the l. of chivalry   SAYE 717:83
no l. if we were to invoke one code   EISE 302:56
no l. to prevent us   SHAW 778:87
No man can point to any l.   DOUG 284:38
no right to transgress the l.   DOST 282:6
nor the world's l.   SHAK 737:79
not according to the l.   BIBLE 93:46
one l., one element   TENN 844:67
Order is heaven's first l.   POPE 660:24

l. so little	DAVI 254:34	deliquescent l. of paper	ANDR 16:25
l. to love by loving	HUXL 425:89	Falls like the l. in October	FULL 341:70
l. to pray	HERB 398:23	famous harmony of l.	YEATS 932:32
l. what not to play	GILL 356:46	flutter far more, than l. do	CENN 203:43
l. while they teach	SENE 727:91	fond of handling the l.	SHER 787:36
l....who He is	SCHW 721:70	golden dead l.	LEVE 506:58
let's l. not to know	CRUZ 246:88	June...in green l.	SPEN 810:16
men do not l. very much	HUXL 426:99	laughing l. of the tree	SWIN 832:20
Parents l. a lot	SPARK 806:17	l. and flowers do cover	WEBS 895:92
she may l.	SHAK 740:73	l. are green	ANON 18:72
To l. and labour	BOOK 142:15	l. are green	ANON 20:7
We live and l.	POMF 657:44	l. dead Are driven	SHEL 783:43
We live and l.	TILM 860:71	l. grow on the tree	YEATS 932:29
what you l....not studying	CONA 230:81	l. of myrtle	MARL 553:17
Where there is much to l.	MILT 579:66	l. of the tree...for the healing of the nations	BIBLE 127:84
you shall l. nothing	HUXL 426:6	l. to a tree	KEATS 457:95
learned devil...on the side of the l.	FRAN 333:89	Like that of l.	HOMER 409:17
Entrepreneurship can be l.	DRUC 287:11	lisp of l.	SWIN 832:18
For I have l.	WORD 923:71	long l. cover me	SWIN 833:2
l. are cowards	DRYD 289:67	noise among the l.	KEATS 456:78
L. men...do many times fail	BACON 46:38	only l. me fifty more	HOUS 414:42
l....to be content	BIBLE 123:62	on Severn snow the l.	HOUS 415:55
marries...hasn't l. much	STEIN 815:25	past...like the l. of a book	WOOLF 922:27
of the opinion with the l.	CONG 230:93	sewed fig l. together	BIBLE 86:50
one thing we l.	READ 680:48	Shatter your l.	MILT 578:45
who has l. well how to obey	KEMP 461:87	shows his hoar l.	SHAK 755:25
learning accuse him to have wanted l.	DRYD 288:25	spear through the dead l.	MANS 547:89
a' the l. I desire	BURNS 170:64	Tawny are the l.	RANS 679:23
attain good l.	ASCH 35:80	tender l. of hopes	SHAK 775:20
Beauty and the lust for l.	BEER 69:79	the falling l.	SMART 797:31
better than l. a lot of things	HERN 399:28	The riverbed...half full of l.	HEAN 389:12
can't be alwayth a l.	DICK 270:7	those barren l.	WORD 924:75
complexity of l.	JOVA 451:76	thou among the l.	KEATS 460:59
design career is a process of l.	BELL 72:43	to some, l. free to all	MILT 583:71
Hibernian l.	ROCH 691:54	Uneasily the l. fall	PURDY 673:17
highest estimation of l.	SIDN 790:16	What if my l. are falling	SHEL 783:47
just enough of l. to misquote	BYRON 179:97	yellow drifts Of withered l.	ARNO 33:52
know without l.	INGR 429:63	yellow l., or none	SHAK 772:30
l. and blundering will live on	SAND 713:2	**leave-taking** It is not worth l.-t.	SHAK 766:62
l. is...dangerous	POPE 658:54	**leaving** Dear World, I am l.	SAND 713:16
L., that cobweb of the brain	BUTL 177:50	his life...the l. of it	SHAK 766:78
l. what not to say	BAIN 52:7	L. reminds us	FORD 330:23
let all l. in	ANON 19:98	prevent them from l.	KENN 463:32
light of l.	RALE 677:2	**leavings** sacrifice...of the devil's l.	POPE 659:91
lost in their collected l.	HAWT 386:37	**Lebanon** cedared L.	KEATS 459:40
men with book l.	RAMOS 678:6	Irish...as the Shiites in L.	OROU 627:22
more l. in their [Chinese] language	JOHN 445:34	**Leben** L. ist Nur ein Moment	SCHI 718:6
much l. doth make thee mad	BIBLE 119:56	Mehr als das L.	SCHI 718:8
Of such deep l.	SPEN 809:95	**lechery** L., l., still	SHAK 757:12
on scraps of l. doat	YOUNG 935:79	**lecteur** hypocrite l.!	ELIOT 306:55
O this l.	SHAK 732:29	**lecture** classic l.	TENN 841:96
process of l. is accompanied	WILD 911:90	twilight from the l.	STEV 820:32
Reading is the basics for all l.	BUSH 175:98	**lecturers** l. shouldn't be wasted	ZELD 936:91
tough time l. how	KENN 464:47	**lectures** comes to hear your l.	BRAD 148:63
Wear your l., like your watch	CHES 210:31	l. & my poetry	BERR 82:67
where l. may be...impossible	OAKE 620:87	**lecturing** experience of popular l.	HUXL 426:14
learnt smash...everything he had l.	ORTE 627:28	**lederhosen** Metaphysical l.	ENRI 314:72
what has been l. has been forgotten	SKIN 795:9	**lee** between windward and l.	SWIN 834:51
leas In lusty l. at liberty	WYATT 930:97	dragons of Laune...and L.	ORAH 626:20
lease l. for a year	ANOU 26:94	**leek** l. is the asparagus	FRAN 333:92
summer's l.	SHAK 771:5	**leeks** eyes were green as l.	SHAK 738:18
without any predictable l.	KOSI 480:4	**leer** assent with civil l.	POPE 661:38
leash Mankind Under The L.	DISCH 275:28	fascinating l.	GILB 354:17
least l. of all saints	BIBLE 122:44	**lees** l. left by Bismarck	GREY 373:5
Where the l....control	WORD 923:68	**le Fey** third sister, Morgan l. F.	MALO 542:1
leather case me in l.	SHAK 733:60	**left** better to be l. than never...loved	CONG 231:33
Gave up...his l., wax and all	EGAN 301:24	Keep your l. hand high	ONEI 626:10
l....to a shoemaker	WAUGH 892:41	l. hand is my thinking hand	HEPW 396:63
little bit of l.	MITF 588:5	l. the room	GROS 374:24
real l. ball	UTTL 875:10	Let them be l.	HOPK 412:97
leave For who would l.	JOHN 441:13	liberal middle class will shift to the l.	EAGL 297:66
l. her far away	KEATS 457:6	not allowing his l. wing to see	ASQU 36:19
l. out of the definition	KING 470:65	slightly l. of centre	FRYE 340:40
l. some skin on	KHRU 467:2	**left-guard** play l.-g. for the Colts	BRES 151:19
not l. in San Francisco	HART 384:8	**leg** here I leave my second l.	HOOD 410:35
shall be happy to l.	BAUD 64:64	literary man—with a wooden l.	DICK 271:38
take my l. of the Jew	SHAK 740:57	sell his wooden l.	DICK 268:43
will take my l. of you	SHAK 752:50	which l. went after which	CRAS 244:44
will ye l. me thus?	HERB 398:18	**legacy** No l. is so rich	SHAK 761:32
leaves amongst the shady l.	SPEN 809:92	**legal** hasn't exactly got a l. mind	BETJ 83:95
Autumn fills thy lap with l.	COLL 228:48	judge in the l. and moral sense	DEWEY 264:44
before the l. have fallen	WILH 911:93	l. and material hindrances	WOLF 919:79
betweenThe sleeping l.	COWP 241:69	l. and moral responsibility	HAYD 387:58
burning of the l.	BINY 130:53	l. gentleman who rescues your estate	BROU 157:33
covered up in l.	KEATS 460:61	plethora of l. requirements	BIRNS 131:72
crowned with calm l.	SWIN 833:32	**legality** taint of l.	KNOX 476:21
dazzling through the l.	TENN 839:48	**legend** bloody tough being a l.	ATKI 37:35

fables in the l.	BACON 48:94		
l. of the Gael	RUSS 706:61		
past exudes l.	MALA 541:84		
legends accepted economic l.	GALB 343:93		
aged l. say	ROSS 698:98		
legion aunts and uncles were l.	SHAW 781:1		
L.: for we are many	BIBLE 114:12		
L. of Honour	TWAIN 870:90		
l. of the unremarked	SAFI 708:2		
refuse the L. d'Honneur	SATIE 717:82		
legions give me back my l.	AUGU 42:46		
l. with the ways of Death	LIND 510:46		
puissant l., whose exile	MILT 581:13		
leg-irons with tinkling l.-i.	WALC 884:78		
legislate If civil authorities l.	JOHN 438:56		
l. to make the well-to-do	BRYAN 163:8		
legislation foundation of...l.	BENT 77:65		
frame its l. upon...justice	PEEL 646:9		
L.'s sov'reign pow'rs	BURNS 171:90		
strength to influence l.	MURR 605:11		
legislative important l. actions	JEVO 438:48		
l. power	GIBB 351:53		
legislators unacknowledged l.	SHEL 786:17		
legislature constitution of the l.	MILL 570:66		
interference of the l.	RICA 684:33		
l. of this country	PITT 653:45		
l. was animated by a sincere desire	PEEL 646:9		
Legree makes L. a bachelor	CHES 210:24		
legs animal with four back l.	LECA 499:20		
asure were his l.	CHAU 209:95		
chess with arms and l.	BARZ 63:37		
could never have stood upon his l.	DICK 268:31		
Dogs with broken l.	PATC 642:49		
Four l. good	ORWE 629:73		
good for your l.	SCHU 720:49		
he pulls the l. of his dreams	THOM 853:90		
His l. bestrid the ocean	SHAK 766:56		
His l., perhaps, were shorter	STRA 826:84		
l. go first	FRAY 335:30		
l. ungainly huddled	SASS 716:67		
l. were such Diana shows	HERR 400:41		
more to marriage than four bare l.	DAVI 254:39		
no l....no chance	ANON 22:66		
not for your bad l.	ELIZ 310:61		
open my l.	HILL 403:95		
recuvver the use of his l.	DICK 267:5		
same old l.	GIRO 358:84		
see my l. when I take my boots off	DICK 269:60		
slimy things did crawl with l.	COLE 225:85		
strongest l. in Pontefract	BETJ 84:6		
two perfectly good l.	ROOS 696:47		
Two vast and trunkless l.	SHEL 784:49		
uglier a man's l. are	WELLS 898:86		
under his huge l.	SHAK 747:76		
walking on his hinder l.	JOHN 443:73		
walls of spiders' l.	DRAY 287:7		
Wooden l. are not inherited	CONK 232:50		
you have between your l.	BEEC 69:66		
Leibniz L. never married	FONT 329:89		
leisure At l. married	CONG 231:2		
better pastime for their l.	WELLS 898:91		
disguised l. are regarded	MISH 587:79		
Increased means and increased l.	DISR 277:78		
iron...polish it at l.	DRYD 292:41		
l. answers l.	SHAK 758:47		
l. of study	GERB 350:29		
l. ruined great kings	CATU 201:9		
l. to bother about	SHAW 780:69		
live at more l.	MONT 592:75		
Men...detest at l.	BYRON 182:94		
monotony, work or l.	POMP 658:47		
repeat at l.	CABE 183:15		
repeat at l.	CONG 231:1		
reputability to the gentleman of l.	VEBL 878:56		
take an hour's l.	STARK 813:74		
wisdom...by opportunity of l.	BIBLE 108:65		
LeMay Bombs away with Curtis L.	ANON 23:99		
lemon in a squeezing of a l.	GOLD 362:65		
squeezed as a l. is squeezed	GEDD 348:91		
the Dome is a l.	TOYN 864:34		
with a slice of l.	FLEM 327:56		
lend If thou wilt l. this money	SHAK 739:54		
L. less than thou owest	SHAK 762:59		
lender Neither a borrower nor a l. be	SHAK 751:21		
lendeth l. unto the Lord	BIBLE 99:42		
length drags its dreary l.	DICK 269:80		
nothing...but my body's l.	SHAK 730:84		

rules of ancient l. MILT 579:83
sacred fire of l. WASH 890:85
settle our true l. MONT 592:76
so easy as l. ASTE 36:22
soul of a journey is l. MARP 553:18
spirit of l. HAND 380:30
survival and success of l. KENN 462:12
Sweet land of l. SMITH 800:91
taking quite a l. in going astray ELIOT 303:72
there is no l. or freedom NASHE 609:19
thy chosen music, L.! WORD 928:47
thy l. into bondage SHAK 750:84
tree of l. must be refreshed JEFF 436:15
voices of l. be mute? CUMM 247:9
walking…with the Statue of L. CONR 235:23
When love is l. POPE 659:82
Wine gives you l. WYCH 931:12
yelps for l. JOHN 444:12
liberty-loving prayers of l.-l. people EISE 302:49
librarians l. are keepers MACL 535:41
libraries l. are food TUCH 869:61
L. are reservoirs of strength GREER 372:91
l. of death DOMI 278:19
l., querulous criticisms WHIT 905:40
When we run our l. HUME 422:15
library a circulating l. in a town SHER 787:36
cloister without a l. GEOF 349:9
damned l. of yours! ONEI 625:99
lumber room of his l. DOYLE 285:66
replaced the l. pass LODGE 514:25
smell of the l. ACKR 3:54
than a public l. JOHN 441:24
turn over half a l. JOHN 444:7
libre condamné à être l. SART 715:51
No vers is l. ELIOT 308:12
Vive le Québec l.! DE 259:41
libretto l. that should never THOM 857:66
Libya first triumph over L. PLUT 656:12
licence love not freedom, but l. MILT 580:84
scientist is given l. LISP 512:74
servitude and extreme l. TOCQ 861:82
TV l. THOM 856:65
license accord greater l. COOP 236:54
licensing l. and prohibiting MILT 579:69
licentious l. passages GIBB 352:64
Marriage is the most l. SHAW 778:99
licentiousness satisfy luxury and l. MORE 597:66
lichen fungus or a l. THOR 857:75
licker L. thats mighty loud HARR 383:92
licorice l. fields at Pontefract BETJ 84:6
lid down came the l. LEWIS 508:4
I dips me l. DENN 262:1
lids lift their heavy l. PATM 643:58
with thy vailèd l. SHAK 751:2
lie Art is a l. PICA 650:2
believe a l. TAYL 837:23
big l. is no worse ORWE 629:94
cannot tell a l. WASH 890:80
Don't l. SZIL 834:67
Dost thou l. so low? SHAK 748:99
every word she writes is a l. MCCA 528:11
fall victim to a big l. HITL 404:17
honest man sent to l. abroad WOTT 929:70
I mean, you l. SWIFT 832:3
isn't told a l. KIPL 473:61
know to be a l. HAMP 380:26
led to believe a l. BLAKE 135:71
l. can travel halfway round the world CALL 185:40
L. Circumstantial SHAK 750:90
l. down alone HOUS 416:84
l. down until the feeling passes HUTC 424:54
l. follows by post BERE 78:90
l. has become…a pillar SOLZ 803:63
l.…is a beautiful twilight CAMUS 188:4
l. is an abomination STEV 820:48
l. is the handle HOLM 408:84
L. not one to another BIBLE 123:67
l. of their inferiority KING 468:42
L. soft, sleep hard MIDD 569:39
l. to and humbug themselves WELLS 898:75
l. where I am and sleep SHIP 789:77
l. which is all a l. TENN 846:4
l. will go round the world SPUR 811:41
l. with his mother earth? SHAK 748:27
L. with me BIBLE 88:97
l. without moving RHYS 684:26
l. with your legs ungainly SASS 716:67

loves to l. with me SHAK 749:43
makes me down to l. SCOT 725:61
misleading impression, not a l. ARMS 30:80
Nature admits no l. CARL 193:41
not a man, that he should l. BIBLE 89:41
old L.: Dulce et decorum est OWEN 632:57
Parliaments are the great l. POBE 656:13
rather l. in the woollen SHAK 744:90
remedies oft in ourselves do l. SHAK 761:26
rule and dare not l. TENN 845:84
Science…is the great l. GOUR 365:27
sixth, the L. with Circumstance SHAK 750:91
Soul of my l. HERR 399:38
telling a big l. about you TRUM 868:30
truth of God into a l. BIBLE 120:59
Violence is a l. JOHN 439:62
what is a l.? BYRON 182:93
What's the good of a l. GREE 371:77
When he speaketh a l. BIBLE 117:98
when you come to l. here SCOTT 725:60
lied to women l. like a Cretan HARDY 381:52
lies all propaganda is l. ORWE 628:64
Autobiographies tell more l. BYATT 178:90
dashed and brewed with l. DRYD 289:75
desirability…of telling l. ORWE 629:93
don't deal in l. KIPL 473:67
English are polite by telling l. BRAD 148:58
Everybody l. about sex SEIN 726:76
few more l. eat into the seed MAIL 539:38
here he l. STEV 822:10
Here l. Nolly Goldsmith GARR 346:53
History is condemned…to l. FRAN 333:86
History, sir, will tell l. SHAW 777:69
how would l. resist passions? DIDE 273:84
L. and literature LAFO 485:3
L. are essential to humanity PROU 671:86
l. are invented BRAQ 150:93
l., damned l. and statistics DISR 277:93
l.…from the loudspeakers ORWE 629:83
l. one who meant well STEV 823:27
L. That Are My Life ELLI 311:87
l., thinking it is the truth SAFI 708:99
make l. sound truthful ORWE 629:91
Matilda told such Dreadful L. BELL 73:58
more readily swallow l. than truth GELL 348:99
old men's l. POUND 664:39
one of the social l. IBSEN 428:33
Plain l. are dangerous SAYE 717:85
Some books are l. BURNS 170:67
sweep away the refuge of l. BIBLE 103:28
telling l. and selling socks MERW 568:25
tell me no more unnecessary l. ADAMS 5:95
The cruellest l. STEV 822:90
truth to cover l. CONG 231:11
lieutenant died…like a second l. CLEM 220:74
life access to a better l.…denied ANGE 17:42
advances through l. JOHN 442:36
afraid of l. STEV 821:79
Alcohol…makes l. bearable SHAW 780:42
all female l.…unclean STAN 812:67
all his l.…in the wrong ROCH 691:57
all human l. is there! JAMES 433:36
all L. death does end HOPK 413:6
all my l. JOHN 444:1
all my l. JOHN 439:67
all the blessings of this l. BOOK 141:84
all the emergencies of l. FORS 331:33
all the energies of his l. PIER 651:5
amend my l. SHAK 742:22
American l. MAIL 540:52
American l. MCCA 528:97
American way of l. MENC 566:83
American writer…acquires a new l. AMIS 15:2
America's cultural l. ROCK 693:84
A missed l. HEINE 391:50
and for her l. he died STONE 825:57
And the l. everlasting BOOK 140:57
And this our l. SHAK 749:34
animal thirst for l. BANKS 58:37
Anythin' for a quiet l. DICK 266:86
appeal to the l. of Christ WHIT 904:14
a précis of l. FRIEL 337:73
Architecture is the…mirror of l. PEI 646:15
arena to which he devoted his l. LEHM 501:69
Art is only a mirror of l. MILL 573:41
as though my very l. JORD 450:67
At fifteen l. had taught me ANGE 17:34

Bankrupt of l. DRYD 290:78
beauty of l. through death LAUT 493:80
believe in l.! DU 293:74
believe in taking human l. NATH 610:24
be Queen for l. POPE 661:49
best of L. is but intoxication BYRON 182:80
best part of married l. WILD 910:78
better standards of l. UNIT 873:69
better to dream your l. PROU 670:70
better to enjoy l. JOHN 442:51
between l. and death WORD 927:36
birthday of my l. ROSS 697:73
bitter moments of l. POWYS 667:97
bitterness of l.! CARR 197:33
blind dates are a way of l. EPST 315:84
blood-thirsty clinging to l. ARNO 33:38
bone-ache disquietude of l. ALLEN 12:39
Book of L. WILDE 909:21
books echoing the l. WILL 914:56
Books make sense of l. BARN 60:70
books, they are the l. LOWE 519:21
born to eternal l. FRAN 334:98
bottom of l. WASH 889:78
breathed into his nostrils…breath of l. BIBLE 86:43
breath of l. YEATS 933:54
brevity of human l. PROT 670:65
brings about a disconnected l. HUGO 421:87
bring the dead to l. GRAV 367:70
brisking about the l. SMART 796:26
broke up their…habits of l. SHER 787:33
business of l. WELL 898:65
but once in my l. SAND 713:3
By my l. SHAK 756:70
calamity of so long l. TWAIN 871:7
care for far more than human l. PANK 636:31
careless of the single l. TENN 843:43
cause of a single l. is liberty BACON 48:88
cessation of individual l. HUXL 426:10
chain I forged in l. DICK 268:28
change…we see in l. FROST 338:83
Chaos often breeds l. ADAMS 4:79
choice, becomes a way of l. MILL 572:7
choose l. BIBLE 90:54
cities, throbbed the true l. NORR 618:65
citizen of l. SASS 716:58
civilized human l. TRUM 868:34
cold as l. RHYS 684:27
comes late in l. JERR 437:40
common errors of our l. SIDN 791:21
compensate for too little l. BURG 167:88
conclusions about l. KIER 467:8
consumed by the l. process MCCA 528:6
continentals think l. is a game MIKES 569:52
contrary to l. HUXL 425:71
cool sequestered vale of l. GRAY 369:20
coping with l. SPARK 806:17
corresponds to our dream l. MAMET 543:21
course of a dishonest l. FRAS 335:27
course to take in l. KURO 482:42
crown of our l. SWIN 833:30
cut off from real l. CROS 246:84
cuts off twenty years of l. SHAK 747:97
dangers of family l. HUXL 425:76
day's hard work in thy l. LAWR 494:18
dearly love in your l. TROL 867:97
dear to me as l. SHAK 740:82
dear to me as light and l. BURNS 171:5
death after l. SPEN 808:81
death and l. attonce SPEN 809:93
Death is not an event in l. WITT 918:42
Death to l. is crown MILT 586:63
dedicated my l. MAND 544:46
destruction of human l. HARDY 381:46
devoted the best years of his l. BIRK 131:69
differ as to the ends of l. RUSS 705:52
different ranks of l. SMITH 797:37
difficulties in providing for…l. COMM 229:65
diminish my l. RENO 683:3
discovered the secret of l. CRICK 244:47
does not care that l. HYDE 427:23
Does thy l. destroy BLAKE 134:54
domestic l. GIBB 352:51
dominant facts in English l. ORWE 628:61
done it all my l. NASH 609:9
don't want…more in your l. RHYS 684:26
Doth the winged l. destroy BLAKE 134:48
Do you believe in the l. to come? BECK 68:44

dark in l. expos'd — MILT 586:47
Dark is L. Enough — FRY 340:29
Darkness from l. — BROW 162:73
darkness shall be the l. — ELIOT 308:14
dawn's early l. — KEY 465:76
Dear as the l. — GRAY 370:31
dear to me as l. and life — BURNS 171:5
deriving l. from each other — BERL 80:24
dungeon flamed with l. — WESL 899:9
eldritch l. of sundown — DAY 257:85
entrance of thy words giveth l. — BIBLE 97:85
every ray of God's l. — DOST 283:11
everything except space and l. — HEAT 390:28
face to the l. — SASS 716:64
far from the l. of day — ORAH 626:20
fierce l. which beats — TENN 846:5
'Forward, the L. Brigade!' — TENN 844:76
from far thy beauteous l. — WESL 900:18
from fidelity to the l. — RODR 693:95
from those flames No l. — MILT 580:97
Give me a l. — HASK 385:25
gives a lovely l. — MILL 571:81
God called the l. Day — BIBLE 85:39
golden and silver l. — YEATS 933:38
Hail holy L. — MILT 582:36
hands…that would l. the world — MILL 571:96
happy realms of l. — MILT 580:98
Heaven's l. forever shines — SHEL 786:7
hours of l. return — ARNO 32:4
how my l. is spent — MILT 580:88
I am black…bereaved of l. — BLAKE 134:30
I am the l. of the world — BIBLE 117:95
infant crying for the l. — TENN 843:42
In l. inaccessible — SMITH 801:26
into his marvellous l. — BIBLE 125:24
jewel [judged] by the l. — ANON 23:78
lamps, by whose dear l. — MARV 556:68
land of l. — CLIN 221:91
last l. has gone — THOM 854:9
laws…of l. and shade — CAPO 189:27
Lead, kindly L. — NEWM 612:62
leave a l….before was dark — WENT 899:5
Let there be l. — BIBLE 85:38
Let there be l. — MACD 529:36
Let there be l.! — SHEL 786:20
level of the l. — FORD 330:6
life and l., with envious haste — ROCH 692:70
l. after l. well used — MILT 582:44
l. and shadow never stand still — WEST 900:27
l., and will aspire — SHAK 732:52
l. at the end — LOWE 521:60
l. beyond compare — NEALE 610:28
L. dies before thy…word — POPE 662:83
l. dissolved in star-showers — SHEL 783:31
l. falls and fills — ROET 694:1
l. fantastic round — MILT 577:29
l. gleams an instant — BECK 68:41
l. heart lives long — SHAK 734:89
l. in manners — ASCH 35:81
l. in the white mackerel sky — BISH 131:77
l. in the window — SPEN 807:59
l. is braying — SITW 793:62
l. is in the soul — MILT 586:48
l. is still — ELIOT 307:99
l. of learning — RALE 677:2
l. of my mind — CRUZ 246:89
l. of setting suns — WORD 923:71
l. of Terewth — DICK 270:92
l. of the bright world dies — BOUR 147:28
l. of the gospel — JOHN 442:57
l. of the world — BIBLE 109:85
l. of the world — BIBLE 117:95
l. of thought — SHEL 784:58
l. out for the territory — TWAIN 871:12
L. out of darkness! — MILT 585:34
l. out of darkness — DONNE 281:88
l. ranged in the non-space — GIBS 353:76
l., shade and perspective — CONS 235:27
l., she said, not of the sky — NEIL 610:30
l. shineth in darkness — BIBLE 117:72
l. that is love — KEND 461:95
l. that she loves — TENN 845:89
L. thickens — SHAK 768:16
l. to counterfeit a gloom — MILT 576:17
l. to lighten the Gentiles — BIBLE 115:27
l. to see that duty — MACA 524:27
l. to shine upon the road — COWP 240:46

l. unto my path — BIBLE 97:84
l. which experience gives — COLE 227:24
l. wife doth make a heavy husband — SHAK 741:92
l. within his own clear breast — MILT 577:35
L. wrestling…incessantly with l. — CRANE 243:12
like a shaft of l. — TENN 841:94
line of festal l. — ARNO 32:20
lived l. in the spring — ARNO 31:96
long l. shakes — TENN 841:3
Lord is my l. — BIBLE 94:6
lord of l. — DOUG 283:18
lost to l. for evermore — BYRON 181:49
lovely lady, garmented in l. — SHEL 785:87
making them see the l. — PLAN 654:60
married to an electric l. — DIMA 275:19
mellowed to that tender l. — BYRON 181:53
men loved darkness rather than l. — BIBLE 117:82
More l.! — GOET 360:25
morning l. creaks down again — SITW 794:70
mosquitoey summer night l. — ASHB 35:86
naked l. bulb — WILL 912:16
Night, the shadow of l. — SWIN 833:22
noose of l. — FITZ 324:82
Not l. them for themselves — SHAK 757:15
Of night and l. — YEATS 933:38
one day, the l. — MANS 547:89
On the l. fantastic — MILT 576:6
out of hell leads up to l. — MILT 581:29
passed away in colder l. — PEAC 645:96
passion for sweetness and l. — ARNO 34:60
poem is…a l. by which — WARR 889:72
poets…set their own inimitable l. — POUND 666:73
Prince of L. — MILT 575:94
pure and endless l. — VAUG 878:49
put out the l. — SHAK 761:7
quality of fiery aery l. — MACD 530:49
radiant l., though sun — MILT 577:35
realms of l. — GURN 375:45
reft the sonne his l. — CHAU 209:89
remember while the l. — SWIN 833:31
restore the l. — DANI 252:88
river of crystal l. — FIELD 322:32
round from the dark and the l. — SWIN 833:47
saw great l. — BIBLE 109:81
season of L. — DICK 271:19
second place of air and l. — FRAME 333:80
seen a great l. — BIBLE 102:16
sees a green l. everywhere — SCHW 721:71
severity of perfect l. — TENN 846:23
sharp l. the fields did lie — FREE 336:43
shed such l. before — MUNRO 603:90
shew l. at Calais — JOHN 443:72
slaked the l. with blood — TENN 848:69
so airy and l. a quality — SHAK 752:55
Some true, some l. — TENN 847:42
such scant l. — WHAR 901:49
sweetness and l. — SWIFT 830:53
that earth lie l. — WALL 886:15
That was the true L. — BIBLE 117:73
the frosty l. — TENN 844:60
The l. that loses — SWIN 832:19
The l. that never was — WORD 928:44
themes in a new l. — LUCAS 522:80
the way, the truth, and the l. — BIBLE 118:10
This l., this glory — COLE 226:4
To l. thee thither — WEBS 895:95
turned around from darkness to l. — PLATO 655:1
unchanged, and universal l. — POPE 658:53
University should be a place of l. — DISR 277:79
waited for the l. — ROBI 690:28
when my l. is low — TENN 843:39
where sweetness and l. failed — FORS 331:45
Where there is darkness, l. — FRAN 334:98
with a l. behind her! — GILB 353:90
within…all l. was contained — MARTI 555:44
world of l. — VAUG 878:51
lighten l. the tax burden — QUINE 675:52
 our own hearts — SHAK 745:27
lightest l. that wear most of it — SHAK 740:71
light-headed l.-h., variable men — STEV 821:85
light-hearted l.-h. way…he seduces — POMP 658:45
lighthouse Keeping a l.-h. with his eyes — CAMP 186:62
 sitivation at the l. — DICK 266:86
lighting Bring in the bottled l. — DICK 267:11
 through its own internal l. blind — SHEL 784:66
lightning beheld Satan as l. — BIBLE 115:36
 brilliance of a l. storm — FLAU 326:33

came by a l. flash — WILS 915:85
different as a moonbeam from l. — BRON 155:95
I Have known the l.'s hour — DAY 257:83
In the golden l. — SHEL 784:56
In thunder, l., or in rain? — SHAK 766:64
L. rods have had it better — NEW 612:56
like flashes of l. — SCHO 719:29
loosed the fatal l. — HOWE 417:1
Mirth is like a flash of l. — ADDI 6:20
O at l. and lashed rod — HOPK 412:82
rather be a l. rod — KESEY 465:72
reading Shakespeare by flashes of l. — COLE 226:18
struck by l. — ORWE 628:49
struck by l. five or six times — JARR 435:81
thunder and l. of Desert Storm — SCHW 721:67
tree On fire by l. — BYRON 180:27
light-o'-love watching his luck…his l.-o.-l. — SERV 728:3
lights always knew the l. were on — STARR 813:77
 an all-the-l.-on man — REED 681:82
 broken l. of thee — TENN 842:21
 carnival l. — GREE 371:69
 Father of l. — BIBLE 124:6
 Followed false l. — DRYD 291:16
 l. around the shore — ROSS 698:91
 l. begin to twinkle — TENN 840:66
 name Zimmermann in bright l.? — MERM 567:15
 spent l. quiver and gleam — ARNO 31:84
 There will be l. everywhere — READ 680:49
 though the l. — HAWT 386:47
 turn on the l. — GUIM 374:32
 Turn up the l. — OHEN 623:57
 two l. of Christendom — PIUS 653:52
like as she is, I do not l. her — SHAK 744:89
 Besides, I l. you not — SHAK 750:70
 does not mean that you l. him — CHUR 217:99
 Do I not l. that — TAYL 837:22
 don't l. something — GREE 370:47
 get what you l. — SHAW 779:24
 If we are l. you — SHAK 740:68
 l. enough to consent — SHAK 750:76
 l. it or not — THOM 856:48
 l. or dislike them — FORS 331:40
 more l. my own — HOPK 413:12
 nothing…made me l. him less — CONG 231:20
 shall not look upon his l. again — SHAK 751:11
 What I l. about Clive — BENT 77:75
 what is l. to thee? — BYRON 180:32
 whether I l. it — VAUG 877:41
 Whether you l. it not — KHRU 466:99
 woman whom you do not l. — ANOU 26:92
liked l. by only four people — HOCK 405:39
like-minded company of the l.-m. — DELI 261:79
likeness any l. of any thing — BIBLE 88:23
 l. and correct incidence of light — ALBE 10:98
 translate beauty into his l. — SHAK 753:76
likes Agreements in l. and dislikes — CATI 200:96
 everyone l. you except yourself — BROWN 157:50
liking Friendships begin with l. — ELIOT 304:16
 Thy lust and l. — SKEL 795:93
lilacs l. last…bloom'd — WHIT 906:47
 L. out of the dead land — ELIOT 305:52
lilac-time Kew in l.-t. — NOYES 619:77
Lilian Airy, fairy L. — TENN 838:39
lilies And a few l. blow — HOPK 412:78
 Beauty lives though l. die — FLEC 327:45
 Consider the l. of the field — BIBLE 110:2
 feedeth among the l. — BIBLE 101:1
 l. and languors of virtue — SWIN 833:27
 l. in her hand — ROSS 698:86
 l. of ambition — DOUG 283:22
 L. that fester — SHAK 772:38
 L. without, roses — MARV 555:59
 peacocks and l. — RUSK 703:4
 put thy pale, lost l. out of mind — DOWS 284:44
 roses overgrown, And l. — MARV 555:60
 Ye L. male! — CRAB 242:97
Lillabullero half a dozen bars of L. — STER 817:74
Lillian L. as a grown-up — FEIB 319:82
 L., you should have stayed a virgin — CART 198:53
Lilliput Swiftian L. — MCCA 528:2
lilting l. at our yowe-milking — ELLI 310:78
lily Daisy and L. — SITW 794:72
 How sweet the l. grows — HEBER 390:33
 l. all her sweetness — TENN 842:14
 l. of the valleys — BIBLE 101:96
 pure as the l. in the dell — LAUD 492:63
 splendid…glows the l. — FLEC 327:47

light heart l. long · SHAK 734:89
lived many l. · SLES 796:15
L. and Loves of a She-Devil · WELD 896:37
l. cease to be illumined · HAMM 379:6
l. have been given to find · MACD 530:49
l. not three good men · SHAK 741:13
L. of great men · LONG 515:43
l. of men and women · HOOV 411:58
l. of quiet desperation · THOR 857:83
l. of the medieval saints · SAKI 710:34
looking to other l. for answers · BRAU 150:97
Man l. by science · JAMES 434:59
man l. well · KIPL 470:82
Most people spend…their l. · LABR 484:76
music of men's l. · SHAK 735:31
ninety l. have been taken away · MCGO 531:78
no fish ye're buying—it's men's l. · SCOTT 724:25
Not a moment of your l. · BLUN 137:11
obstructed by the l. of Christians · JOHN 442:57
of all l. · STEV 821:78
other Annapurnas in the l. of men · HERZ 401:59
our l. are…dark interludes · ONEI 625:95
our l. resemble the stuff of…novels · AUST 44:1
Our l….shall end · PHIL 650:91
our l. would grow together · SWIN 833:39
political l….end in failure · POWE 667:95
poor l. we lead · NIGH 616:32
pounces upon it and l. · MILL 572:22
quintessence of their l. · LOWE 519:21
repeat in the l. of the millions · WILD 911:88
rest of their l. · TREE 865:54
some l. duller · TAKU 835:79
statements about the world and our l. · BOYD 148:46
their jumpsome l. · KIPL 473:48
Upon the King…our l. · SHAK 746:52
waking moment of their l. · KING 468:42
Where nothing l. but crosses · SHAK 734:11
Women Whose L. Are Food · OATES 620:92
writers' l. · GIBB 352:67
liveth l., and was dead · BIBLE 126:46
living act of l. had been enjoyable · BOWL 147:31
'alternative' modes of l. · SELF 727:81
Are you yet l.? · SHAK 744:87
be considerate to the l. · VOLT 883:49
Begin by l. · ANOU 26:2
better than l. badly? · CRIT 245:64
beyond the language of the l. · ELIOT 309:40
bodies of the l. · SPEN 807:65
by l. well · JONS 450:53
catch the Manners l. · POPE 660:7
cut off out of the land of the l. · BIBLE 104:52
dead might as well speak to the l. · CATH 200:88
difference is…that of the l. · CIXO 218:33
Different l. is not l. · SPEN 807:56
Disillusionment in l. · STEIN 815:15
do not eat for the good of l. · EMER 312:24
drink for a l. · KERR 465:67
equal dominion…over every l. thing · STAN 812:66
fever called 'L.' · POE 657:30
get mine own l. · BOOK 142:15
good l. and good poetry · LUCAS 521:76
in the land of the l. · BIBLE 97:76
l. a little more or dying · MAIL 539:42
l. and dying at once · KUNI 482:39
l. and partly l. · ELIOT 307:3
l. are dead · MACM 536:76
l. dead man · SHAK 733:61
l. dog is better than a dead lion · BIBLE 101:82
l. in sin · HERB 397:72
L. is abnormal · IONE 430:76
L. is an illness · CHAM 204:70
l. is made…by selling · WILD 911:84
l. know No bounds? · SHIR 789:79
l. next to you · TRUD 868:23
l. stood motionless · WILL 911:2
L., we fret · BROW 162:93
l. well…most important · PLATO 655:81
l. which are yet alive · BIBLE 100:72
long habit of l. · BROW 159:86
man to earn his own l. · MORE 596:60
miserable beyond all l. things · SHEL 782:12
New York…'l.' there · DIDI 274:6
no l. with thee · ADDI 6:13
no pleasure i' l. · ELIOT 303:79
partnership not only between…l. · BURKE 169:39
pattern…Of dead and l. · ELIOT 308:25
prospect of l. in it · JAY 436:2

realize Art in l. forms · HOLM 408:95
repetition of the wrong way of l. · DURR 296:41
scale of l. must be reduced · CHUR 216:63
still a l. lion · SOLZ 803:64
sure of l. forever · HAWT 386:36
they must hate to work for a l. · ROWL 701:50
tired of l. · WHITE 903:81
upon all the l. and the dead · JOYCE 451:81
was l. is now dead · ELIOT 306:64
wasted his substance with riotous l. · BIBLE 116:46
who l. had no note · GIBB 352:68
Why seek ye the l. among the dead? · BIBLE 116:67
world…does not owe us a l. · EDIN 300:9
living-room comfort of the l. r. · MCLU 536:64
Livingstone 'Dr L., I presume?' · STAN 812:61
wouldn't vote for Ken L. · SCAR 717:91
Lloyd L. George could not see a belt · ASQU 36:14
L. George spoke · BENN 76:46
lo L., thro' her works · SMART 797:31
load for her the heavier l. · BALZ 57:14
how to l. and bless · KEATS 459:48
like a heavy l. · HUGH 418:21
l. of sorrow · SHAK 745:20
taking home a 'l.' · BURT 174:65
under their fruits l. · SPEN 809:92
loaded dice of God are always l. · EMER 312:11
loads ploughs and borne our l. · MUIR 602:61
loaf half a l….better than no bread · CHES 212:70
l. to cast away my speech · THUR 859:35
loafed to have l. and lost · TEMP 838:32
loafing cricket as organized l. · SHAK 734:99
loam Men are but gilded l. · CRANE 243:22
rife as the l. Of prairies · CABE 183:14
loan brief l. of his own body · FERRE 321:19
God has us…on l. · FRAME 333:81
memories on l. · ELLI 310:78
loaning moaning on ilka green l. · BAGE 51:94
loans effect of the new l. of England · SHAK 756:57
loath l. to cast away my speech · RANS 679:25
long and l. at going · BIBLE 105:89
shall l. yourselves · BURNS 170:71
loathe l. to rin an' chase thee · TWAIN 870:83
loathed and l. him · MIDD 569:43
both loved and l. · SHAK 737:99
loathing deepest l. to the stomach · TWAIN 872:39
loathsome Exercise is l. · SHEL 785:81
l. mask has fallen · BIBLE 117:89
loaves five barley l. · BIBLE 112:55
five l., and two fishes · SHAK 730:63
l. sold for a penny · MALA 541:83
metaphor…provides two l. · RUNY 702:84
lob nothing but a l. · TYNAN 872:43
lobbies l. during the interval · PALM 636:25
lobby gentlemen…in the same L. · BALD 54:50
go into the l. against us · ALBEE 10:93
lobes disease of the frontal l. · CARR 195:84
lobster 'Tis the voice of the l. · MACM 536:67
local little l. difficulties · HARDY 382:73
l. thing called Christianity · ACHE 3:52
location worst possible l. in the world · COUP 238:91
locations visiting l. such as diners · ANON 20:20
loch bonnie banks o' L. Lomond · SCOTT 723:96
Lochinvar O, young L. · MILL 574:61
lock crying at the l. · HERB 398:15
Joy, I did l. thee up · GILB 355:25
life-long l. · HOGG 406:58
L. the door, Lariston · STER 818:93
twisting that l. · SHAW 778:1
why l. him in? · BURNS 170:71
lockèd l., letter'd, braw brass-collar · SOME 803:67
locket l. around his neck · SHAK 741:5
locks drownèd honour by the l. · SOUT 805:96
few l. which are left · SHAK 752:28
knotty and combinèd l. · BURNS 170:71
l. were like the raven · SHAK 768:17
Never shake Thy gory l. · MILT 579:82
shaking her invincible l. · DRAY 286:99
turn those amber l. to grey · DOUG 283:27
locomotion purposes of human l. · CANN 188:10
locomotive l….more efficient · SIEG 791:25
More powerful than a l.! · RIVE 688:2
rails are to a l. · KAFKA 454:25
up to the approaching l. · GINS 357:63
were never no l. · ANON 21:27
locomotives l. travelling twice as fast · LIND 511:52
where the l. sing · MCCA 527:87
Loc Suilig steed by L. S. · WILL 914:57
locust l. blossoms

years that the l. hath eaten · BIBLE 106:4
locusts famine grew, and l. came · THOM 852:63
meat was l. · BIBLE 108:75
lodestar his wife Is the l. · PARK 637:43
lodesterre language he was the l. · LYDG 523:3
lodge where thou lodgest, I will l. · BIBLE 90:79
lodging give us a safe l. · NEWM 612:63
l., wife, and children · DICK 269:71
lodgings fair lightsome l. · WEBS 895:2
pent up in frowzy l. · SMOL 802:30
loft in a l. in Salt Lake Farm · THOM 853:89
loftiness l. of thought · DRYD 291:27
log big rotting l. · WHITE 902:72
Blackened l. and stump · LAWS 496:46
logic as it isn't it ain't. That's l. · CARR 196:98
By a kind of perverted l. · FANON 317:44
Conspirators have a l. · DELI 261:80
Her l. was a combination · TOOLE 863:12
kind of internal l. · HONE 409:29
l. and rhetoric · BACON 50:55
L. doesn't apply to · MINS 587:74
L. is rare · DOYLE 285:68
l. of discovery · NISB 616:38
L.'s chiefest end? · MARL 552:35
logical fears…and remains l. · SAINT 709:25
l. deduction from…hypotheses · EINS 302:46
never met a steadily l. person · GELL 348:97
straightforward l. manner · WATS 890:97
logicians If we may believe our l. · ADDI 6:30
logic-mill Philosophers…sort of L.-m. · CARL 191:86
logs pile the l. · POUND 665:62
Tom bears l. · SHAK 734:94
loins Elijah…girded up his l. · BIBLE 92:22
fire of my l. · NABO 606:30
forth the fatal l. · SHAK 735:33
Gird up now thy l. · BIBLE 93:69
gird up the l. of your mind · BIBLE 125:21
leathern girdle about his l. · BIBLE 108:75
l. girt about with truth · BIBLE 122:52
thicker than my father's l. · BIBLE 92:15
with your l. girded · BIBLE 88:16
loitered l. my life away · HAZL 388:89
loiterers Liege of all l. · SHAK 733:76
Lolita L., light of my life · NABO 606:30
loll l. on velvet and satin · FRAN 335:22
Lombardy waveless plain of L. · SHEL 783:28
London All of L. littered · MACN 538:6
art, in L. · DRYD 288:40
As L. is to Paddington · CANN 188:11
at once removed…to L. · ANON 21:29
best built city…L. excepted · DEFOE 258:23
best club in L. · DICK 272:46
Cam ye doun by L.? · ANON 20:18
crowd flowed over L. Bridge · ELIOT 305:54
dependence of L. on Washington · BENN 75:18
do not live in L. · RICH 686:59
far from L.! · NOYES 619:77
foggy day in L. Town · GERS 351:43
gazed at the L. skies · BETJ 83:81
Hell is…much like L. · SHEL 784:51
If a man bring to L. · PETTY 649:84
impressions…since I left L. · MACM 536:71
journey from L. · TALB 835:81
L. Bridge was a greater piece of work · ADDI 6:21
L., hast thou accused · SURR 829:38
L. is a modern Babylon · DISR 276:59
L. is enchanting · WOOLF 922:38
L….Metropolis of Great-Britain · BAIL 52:4
L. money-dealers · BAGE 51:94
L. spread out in the sun · LARK 491:36
L., that great cesspool · DOYLE 284:46
L., that great sea · SHEL 784:65
L., thou art of townes · DUNB 294:5
longer to elect a Mayor for L. · WATE 890:94
lowest and vilest alleys in L. · DOYLE 285:67
man in L. · GALT 344:28
many MPs never see the L. · LIVI 512:84
must have a L. audience · AUST 43:78
my Acquaintance in L. · SWIFT 831:93
No foteball player…within…L. · ELIZ 309:58
out into the streets of L. · HICKS 402:78
rainy Sunday in L. · DE 262:6
rather live in lively L. · EWART 316:25
reach the length o' L. · SCOTT 724:35
scarce go to L. · LASS 492:60
stagecoach from L. to Oxford · HAZL 387:73
this is a L. particular · DICK 269:82

fasting, for a good man's l.	SHAK 750:69	If you don't l. life	CLARK 219:51
fault was only too much l.	LANY 489:5	I had definitely fallen in l.	BENU 78:85
favor mother l.	BRIN 153:42	I l. all waste	SHEL 782:24
fear intensified the l.	JACK 433:30	I l. metaphor	GASS 346:60
feeling that lures us on…to l.	CONR 234:6	I l. not hollow cheek	TENN 842:13
fell in l. with himself	POWE 666:78	immortal L.	TENN 842:19
Filled with her l.	DONNE 279:33	Imperious l. hath highest	SPEN 808:88
filled with l.	ROCH 691:50	impure l. for cities	CASAL 199:68
first l.'s impassioned blindness	PEAC 645:96	in business, politics…l.	WHIT 906:52
first two l. the third	WAXM 893:60	in l. as in sport	GRAV 367:76
fit l. for gods	MILT 584:12	In l., happiness is abnormal	PROU 670:71
fitter for me to l.	ROCH 691:61	In l.'s field	CRAS 244:42
flame of life and l.	LAWR 494:6	in l. with a beautiful blonde	FIEL 323:52
food is l.	SHEL 784:64	in l. with a cold climate	SOUT 805:95
food of l.	SHAK 755:45	in l. with a country	LESS 505:43
fool of l.	HAZL 388:85	in l. with American names	BENET 75:9
For liberation—not less of l.	ELIOT 309:46	in l. with easeful Death	KEATS 460:62
For L.'s sake	JONS 450:48	in l. with my bed	SHAK 729:27
for L. thou wakest not	FERG 320:5	in l. with seventeen million	GISC 358:85
for the l. he had to her	BIBLE 87:90	intellectual l. of God	SPIN 811:35
for the l. of a ladye!	GILB 355:31	In this close hand of l.	BROW 159:7
For thy sweet l. remembered	SHAK 771:14	Is first and passionate l.	BYRON 181:71
for your l. to her	SHAK 732:30	Is l. a tender thing?	SHAK 735:37
freedom in my l.	LOVE 519:10	I wish I were in l. again	HART 384:10
free to l. or hate	SART 715:41	jot of former l. retain	DRAY 287:6
Friendship and l.	GRIL 373:14	Kind is my l. today	SHAK 773:43
From Russia with L.	FLEM 327:55	know by l.	PATM 643:66
fruit of the Spirit is l.	BIBLE 122:38	knowledge and l. of God	BOOK 141:10
full of l. and honesty	SHAK 760:84	lack of l. contaminates	GUNN 375:39
Garden of L.	BLAKE 134:56	lack of l. from l.	BROW 162:73
Give me more l.	CAREW 190:62	Lassie I l. best	BURNS 171:3
give orders to l.	SAND 712:87	late remorse of l.	BYRON 180:37
give them your l.	GIBR 352:74	law of l.	SCEVE 717:92
give us thine own eternal l.!	OCAS 621:14	learn to l. by loving	HUXL 425:89
Glory, the grape, l., gold	BYRON 182:80	left thy first l.	BIBLE 126:47
God is l.	BIBLE 125:38	Lenten is come with l.	ANON 19:85
God is l.	KIER 467:15	Lerne to l.	LANG 489:99
God is l.	LEE 500:32	less skill to l.	SKEL 795:3
God of l.!	DODD 278:10	let me l.	DONNE 279:43
God of L.…Beteth his wynges	CHAU 209:87	let me sow l.	FRAN 334:98
golden dream of l. and friendship	DRYD 289:66	let us live and l.	CAMP 186:76
got to l. one man	HAMM 379:14	let us l.!	CATU 200:5
grace Which l. makes	WORD 926:14	Linked in l. so dear	MILT 585:17
Greater l. hath	THOR 858:12	little duty and less l.	SHAK 729:46
Greater l. hath no man	BIBLE 118:12	lived to l.	DESB 263:36
Greater l. than this	JOYCE 452:91	live in l.	SIDN 791:23
great, powerful souls l. life	HEINE 391:46	live with me and be my l.	MARL 553:17
greed wrapped in the language of l.	ARMEY 30:69	long-liv'd as present l.	WALL 886:18
groans of l.	LOWRY 521:67	looking for is perfect l.	WELD 897:43
hate all that don't l. me	FARQ 318:51	looks breed l.	MARL 551:74
hate me as much as you l. me	BECK 68:49	lost the world for l.	DRYD 292:57
hate the one, and l. the other	BIBLE 110:1	l. a bright particular star	SHAK 761:22
hath business, and makes l.	DONNE 280:50	l., all alike, no season knows	DONNE 279:41
Have I forgot, my only L.	BRON 155:93	l. all God's creation	DOST 283:11
have you left the ancient l.	BLAKE 133:22	l. all my characters	WELTY 899:98
Health, Wealth, L.…and Time	ANON 26:91	l. among the daughters	BIBLE 101:96
Hearts wound up with l.	SPEN 807:58	l., an abject intercourse	GOLD 361:48
Hell grant what L.	MILT 576:18	L. and delight are better teachers	DURER 295:29
Hell…is to no longer l.	BERN 80:28	L., and do what you like	AUGU 41:41
help and support of the woman I l.	EDWA 300:20	L. and friendship exclude	LABR 483:63
Herein is l.	BIBLE 125:39	L. and hate…are necessary	BLAKE 134:37
hidden l. of God	WESL 900:18	l. and honour and pity	FAUL 318:63
his l. made mine	DRYD 289:62	l. and joy that fights	MANS 546:83
His strange l. still admire	DONNE 281:69	l. and laughter	GORD 363:7
honeying and making l.	SHAK 754:10	l. and marriage rarely can combine	BYRON 182:83
hope nor l.	STEV 823:31	l. and murder will out	CONG 231:10
hope of winning her l.	STAEL 811:46	l. and mutual honour	MILT 584:96
horribly in l. with him	SHAK 744:8	l. and no sex if you're fat	GIOV 357:74
How dare he make l. to me	KRAS 480:6	L. and scandal	FIEL 322:35
How do I l. thee?	BROW 160:9	l., and she be fair!	KEATS 459:53
how dwelleth the l. of God in him?	BIBLE 125:37	l. and toil	KIPL 473:62
how to l. himself	SHAK 759:69	l. a quarrel	ETHE 315:94
Humanity i l. you	CUMM 247:5	l. as deep	SHAK 736:52
Hunger and l.	FRAN 333:85	l. at first sight	GRANT 366:51
I behold, in l.	STEV 819:25	l. a wench	SHIR 789:80
I do not l. thee, Dr Fell	BROWN 157:51	l. a womman that she woot it nought	CHAU 208:55
I do not l. you, Sabidius	MART 555:47	l. bade me welcome	HERB 397:98
I fell in l.…at once	THOM 853:80	l. betwixt us two?	COWL 240:31
If l. be a god	LYLY 523:10	l. be younger than thyself	SHAK 756:65
If l. be treasure	OTWAY 631:30	l. but only her!	BYRON 180:42
If l. remains	BROW 161:56	L. came down at Christmas	ROSS 698:85
if l. were all	COWA 239:9	l. can claim no place	ANDR 16:26
If l. were what the rose is	SWIN 833:39	l. can do with a twined thread	BURT 174:79
if my l. were in my armes	ANON 20:99	l.…can never go wrong	PARK 638:60
If thou beest l., begone	BEAU 67:16	l. carries within itself	NERVO 611:47
If thou must l. me	BROW 159:5	L. ceases to be a pleasure	BEHN 71:16
If two people l. each other	HEMI 394:6	l., cherish, and to obey	BOOK 142:27

l. colour the most	RUSK 703:6
L. comforteth…like sunshine	SHAK 733:56
L. conquers all things	VIRG 882:30
L. costs us nothing	RICK 686:76
l. Creation's final law	TENN 843:36
l. Creation's final law	TENN 843:45
L., curiosity, freckles	PARK 637:58
loved as to l.	FRAN 334:98
L. divine…excelling	WESL 900:14
l. does not consist in gazing	SAINT 709:12
l. endures no tie	DRYD 292:56
l. everything that's old	GOLD 362:62
l., excludes all competition	FUSE 342:73
l. for Linton is like the foliage	BRON 155:96
l., frendshyp, cowardyse	MALO 543:13
l. give me more such nights	HERR 399:35
l. has always mixed	LAFA 484:92
l. has its own instinct	BALZ 58:16
l. he laughed to scorn	SHAK 732:49
l. in a golden bowl	BLAKE 133:27
L. in a hut	KEATS 458:22
l. in desolation masked	SHEL 785:99
l. in public	DRYD 289:59
l. in shadow best is made	JONS 450:51
l. in summer's wonderland	NOYES 619:77
l. interests me more	LAUR 492:72
L. invincible in battle	SOPH 804:86
l. is a boy	BUTL 177:52
l. is a cruel conqueror	LAFO 485:8
l. is a Dog from Hell	BUKO 165:50
l. is a fanclub	HENRI 395:42
l. is a game	ROBBE 688:11
l. is a human emotion	BAKER 52:16
l. is always a liar	RUIZ 702:64
l. is a mystery	LAFO 485:18
l. is a payment	DUNC 295:10
l. is as a fever	SHAK 773:56
l. is a spirit	SHAK 732:52
l. is a universal migraine	GRAV 368:81
l. is a very papithatick thing	FLEM 327:63
l. is blind	SHAK 740:61
l. is come to me	ROSS 697:73
l. is ever rewarded	BACON 48:96
l. is for the particular	DUDEK 293:84
l.…is full of jealousy	SHAK 729:31
l. is here to stay	GERS 351:45
l. is just a system	BARN 60:74
l. is like a child	SHAK 729:35
l. is like any other luxury	TROL 867:2
l. is like the measles	JERO 437:29
l. is merely a madness	SHAK 750:64
l. is more cruel than lust	SWIN 833:30
l. is most nearly itself	ELIOT 308:26
l. is mutually feeding each other	HEAD 388:97
l. is not a flame	MARG 549:45
l. is nothing else than	SPIN 810:30
l. is not l.	SHAK 773:48
l.…is not meat nor drink	MILL 571:91
l. is not only a feeling	BALZ 57:15
l. is not secure	CHES 212:74
l. is of a birth	MARV 556:66
l. is off sae mekill mycht	BARB 59:53
l. is of the valley	TENN 842:16
l. is only one of many	JOHN 443:80
l. is secured by good nature	ROCH 691:79
l. is space and time	PROU 671:79
l. is strong as death	BIBLE 102:6
l. is that common tone	WILL 914:60
l. is the best thing in life	MANN 546:75
l. is the delusion	MENC 565:69
l. is the extremely	MURD 604:93
l. is the fart	SUCK 828:12
l. is the fulfilling of the law	BIBLE 120:87
l. is the gift of oneself!	ANOU 26:3
l. is the only force	KING 468:44
l. is the story	STAEL 811:44
l. is the whole	CUMM 248:15
L., knocking its blind forehead	SAND 712:82
l. leans through geranium windows	LEE 500:42
l. long life	SHAK 764:14
l. looks not with the eyes	SHAK 737:86
l. [looks] to the present	LEWIS 507:73
l. means not ever	SEGAL 726:73
l. men too little	BURKE 169:42
l. mixed with fear	WEBS 895:8
l. not a gaping pig	SHAK 740:77
l. not man less	BYRON 180:43

The more I l....I quarrel · MARG 549:38
then they dream of l. · SHAK 736:39
There is no l. · AUDEN 40:13
The wise want l. · SHEL 785:73
They l. us for it · TENN 841:97
thine inestimable l. · BOOK 141:84
think of one's absent l. · TROL 866:83
this l. of ours is immoderate · BURT 174:78
this l. of the land · MITC 588:93
this spring of l. · SHAK 729:26
this word, 'l.' · SHAK 731:87
those whom they want to l. · FORS 331:34
thoughts of l. · TENN 840:75
thousands...that l. me · BOOK 141:93
Through l., through hope · WORD 928:59
Thus did they l. · LOVE 519:15
till l. have all his rites · SHAK 744:3
time of our l. and pride · SU 828:6
time to l. · BIBLE 100:70
Time...weakens l. · LABR 483:62
'Tis l. in l. · SUCK 828:8
to be wroth with one we l. · COLE 226:7
to conserve it, we must l. it · MONT 593:93
to dissemble your l. · BICK 128:8
To live is like to l. · BUTL 178:82
To l., and bear · SHEL 785:83
to l. and to be wise · BACON 46:52
to l. and to cherish · BOOK 142:26
To l. is to be a fish · IGNA 428:42
touch of l. · SHAK 729:33
tragedy, l. and heroism · LEWIS 507:87
true l. hath my heart · SIDN 790:4
two Milwaukeeans in l. · HECHT 390:36
Uninterrupted joy, unrivalled l. · MILT 582:39
universal languages: l., music and sports · MOSES 600:26
unselfish and self-sacrificing l. · POE 656:20
unspoken l. · MORG 597:77
Unutterable l. · WORD 928:52
us that trade in l. · SHAK 765:28
vain in verse my l. to show · SIDN 790:7
vanity, sets l. a task · HUNT 423:32
vegetable l. should grow · MARV 556:62
visible world seems formed in l. · MELV 564:31
voice falls as they say l. · LARK 490:25
wait without l. · ELIOT 308:14
war, as in l. · NAPO 607:66
warrior that is rapt with l. · MARL 551:78
War springs from the l. · RUNC 702:72
was sick, in l. · POPE 661:29
we are always in l. · PASC 640:9
we don't accomplish our l. · RILKE 687:86
we l. thee best · TENN 844:69
we who were strong in l. · WORD 927:39
What is commonly called l. · FIEL 322:42
what is denied to l. · WILL 914:55
What is l. · SHAK 756:61
What l.? · SHEL 784:59
What l. he must have lost · SMITH 799:66
What l. I bore to thee · WORD 925:9
what manner of l. · BIBLE 125:36
What one gives in l. · DESB 263:15
what thing is l. · PEELE 646:12
What will survive of us is l. · LARK 490:30
when I l. thee not · SHAK 760:83
when I was in l. with you · HOUS 414:47
When l. grows diseased · ETHE 315:97
When l. is done · BOUR 147:28
When l. is liberty · POPE 659:82
Where I and my l. wont to gae · BALL 56:94
Where mercy, L. and Pity dwell · BLAKE 134:32
where there is no l. · BACON 49:29
which men call L. · SPEN 808:89
Whose l. is given · PARK 637:56
who's injured by my l.? · DONNE 280:44
wilder shores of l. · BLAN 136:87
will not be long, l. · COLUM 229:59
with an everlasting l. · BIBLE 105:77
with L. and Squalor · SALI 711:63
with l. false · YEATS 932:33
woman's friendship ever ends in l. · GAY 347:71
woman wakes to l. · TENN 846:11
Women...I. completely · BAIN 52:13
Women's l. is for their men · EURI 316:7
Women will l. her · SHAK 770:97
wondrous miracle did L. devise · DAVI 254:32
write of your l. affairs · YEATS 932:28
written for the l. of Man · THOM 853:82

wrong for me to l. my own? · SITT 793:56
yet His l. observes · AUDEN 40:12
yet to see the one she should l. · LABR 483:61
yield, that l. may win · CRAS 244:41
yield to l., ladies · LYLY 523:11
you and l. are still my argument · SHAK 772:31
you'll l. Mogadishu · HEMP 395:32
'You must sit down,' says L. · HERB 398:99
young things that marry for l. · SHAW 780:52
Youth means l. · BROW 162:81
love-adept Dreaming like a l.-a. · SHEL 785:76
love-broker no l.-b. in the world · SHAK 757:81
loved Alas! that all we l. of him · SHEL 785:97
As Caesar l. me · SHAK 748:4
beautiful only when she is l. · EPST 315:82
Be l. like Nature! · COLE 226:97
both l. and loathed · MIDD 569:43
Dante, who l. well · BROW 162:63
daughter l. a man · SHAK 756:67
didn't come...to be l. · GRAMM 366:42
each l. one blotted · BYRON 179:17
for she l. much · BIBLE 115:32
greater compliment than to be l. · MACD 530:58
Had we never l. sae kindly · BURNS 172:29
Hail, wedded l. · MILT 583:72
I have l. · SUCK 828:13
l l. even the tears · RACI 676:84
l l. him too much · RACI 676:82
is it better to be l. than feared · MACH 533:98
Late have I l. you · AUGU 41:37
l. her against reason · DICK 271:34
l. me for the dangers · SHAK 759:63
l. most living things · THOM 854:15
l. not at first sight? · MARL 553:13
l. not at first sight? · SHAK 750:71
l. righteousness · GREG 372:95
l. thee once · AYTO 45:15
l. the man · JONS 450:55
l. to be changing · DRAY 287:3
many l. your moments · YEATS 932:33
never been more l. · ELLI 311:89
no sooner looked but they l. · SHAK 750:85
Now thou hast l. me · DONNE 279:38
self and the l. one · PHIL 650:94
Sir, you and I have l. · SHAK 764:20
skill...to be l. · SKEL 795:3
thirst to be l. · RHYS 684:24
to be l. needs only to be seen · DRYD 291:15
to have l. and lost · TENN 843:34
To have l., to have thought · ARNO 31:96
Twice or thrice had I l. thee · DONNE 280:49
We l., sir · BROW 162:77
what thou and l Did, till we l.? · DONNE 279:37
love-in-idleness maidens call it l.-i.-i. · SHAK 737:94
loveliness Its l. increases · KEATS 457:1
l. to living youth denied · WORD 929:63
portion of the l. · SHEL 786:6
love-lorn By a l.-l. loon · GILB 355:31
lovely Her face was l. · SPEKE 806:36
How l. is thy dwelling-place · SCOT 725:63
In Claude's landscape all is l. · CONS 235:25
Look thy last on all things l. · DELA 260:72
more l. and more temperate · SHAK 771:5
once he made more l. · SHEL 786:6
whatsoever things are l. · BIBLE 123:61
woods are l., dark and deep · FROST 339:98
love-making l.-m., or wooing of it · BACON 47:72
love-quarrels L.-q. oft in pleasing · MILT 586:60
lover all affliction taught a l. · POPE 659:84
As to a l.'s bed · SHAK 765:47
Beauty is the l.'s gift · CONG 231:34
death is as a l.'s pinch · SHAK 766:62
dividing l. and l. · SWIN 832:19
ex-wife looking for a new l. · CONN 233:76
fause L. staw my rose · BURNS 172:27
fond l.? · SUCK 828:7
Give me a l. bold and free · CLEV 221:84
hard to be...a l. of women · WYCH 931:11
Have I a l. · EMER 312:21
Having a l. isn't much · HYDE 427:22
husband is what is left of the l. · ROWL 701:52
injured l.'s hell · MILT 583:78
l. and his lass · SHAK 750:88
l. and killer are mingled · DOUG 283:20
l., and the poet · SHAK 738:13
l. chosen · GRAV 367:75
l....of angling · WALT 888:49

l. of life · GORD 363:7
l. of men, the sea · SWIN 833:40
l. of the meadows · WORD 924:72
l.'s bad reputation · NAPO 607:67
l.'s quarrel with the world · FROST 339:10
l. who does not forget · BART 62:22
maner of l. spryngith · MALO 542:10
mankind love a l. · EMER 312:13
Neither father nor l. · ROET 694:4
place her l. as high as she · BALZ 57:5
Scratch a l. · PARK 638:64
sighed as a l. · GIBB 352:62
sweeter...will be the word l. · HELO 393:86
true l. of literature · SOUT 805:6
weary l. · GORD 363:6
Who can deceive a l.? · VIRG 882:23
woman loves her l. · BYRON 182:82
world's greatest l. · SCHU 721:53
Your passionate l. · STEE 814:89
lovers Catherine had...l. · WEST 901:34
Journeys end in l. · SHAK 756:60
L. and madmen · SHAK 738:12
l. be virtuous · LYLY 523:10
L. be war and tak gude heid · HENR 396:54
l. cannot see · SHAK 740:61
l. fled away · KEATS 459:43
l. lately wed · TENN 839:40
l. of the picturesque · MCGO 531:79
l. old are l and she · BROW 161:57
l.' perjury · DRYD 292:56
l. were all untrue · DRYD 292:63
me and the apparent l. · REED 681:79
Mirrors are the perfect l. · ATWO 38:56
Mitterrand has 100 l. · GORB 363:4
sleepless l....awake · POPE 658:65
star-crossed l. · SHAK 735:33
Though l. be lost · THOM 852:61
time becometh l. best · DRAY 286:98
to thy motions l.' seasons run? · DONNE 279:41
track for l. on the printed snow · CAREW 190:57
loves Anyone who l. his country · GARI 346:48
For who l. me must · TENN 846:16
from their l. receive · KEATS 458:32
game your country l. · RICE 685:39
He l. us not · SHAK 768:2
kills the thing he l. · WILDE 910:54
Let him that l. me · SHAK 765:48
Life and L. of a She-Devil · WELD 896:37
l. and comforts should increase · SHAK 759:76
l. but half of Earth · QUIL 674:40
L. die from disgust · LABR 483:65
l. me dearly · KEATS 459:5
l., must I remember them? · APOL 27:16
l. my daughter · SHAK 770:90
l. nothing but himself · SOUT 805:7
l. the horror · HOMER 409:21
l. to lie with me · SHAK 749:43
man swear he l. me · SHAK 744:88
one that l. his fellow-men · HUNT 423:34
pettiness ruins the greatest l. · ANOU 26:93
Seat of pleasures, and of l. · DRYD 291:27
true l. without suspicion · SPEN 809:92
Two l. I have · SHAK 773:55
when no one l. us · STAEL 811:50
whose l. I prize · SHAK 769:46
love-sick l.-s. land that mourns · BLAKE 133:23
lovest What thou l. well · POUND 665:58
love-story as if you worked a l.-s. · DOYLE 285:51
loveth He prayeth well, who l. well · COLE 225:92
Lord l. he chasteneth · BIBLE 124:1
l. father or mother · BIBLE 111:30
love-whispering L.-w. woods · POPE 662:79
loving but the astonishment of l. · REID 682:95
discharge for l. · MATL 560:65
For l., and for saying so · DONNE 280:48
give up smoking, drinking and l. · FREUD 336:49
Hated wickedness that hinders l. · BROW 162:63
l. alone is as dull as eating alone · WYCH 931:17
L. in truth · SIDN 790:7
L. not, hating not · BROW 162:76
most l., mere folly · SHAK 749:53
privilege...of l. longest · AUST 44:98
So l. to my mother · SHAK 751:7
stop l. ourselves · STAEL 811:50
loving-kindness crowneth...l. k. · BIBLE 97:62
low between the high and l. · SIDN 790:10
Dost thou lie so l.? · SHAK 748:99

en Brer Fox, he lay l.	HARR 383:90
had me l.	GERS 351:43
He that is l.	BUNY 167:76
Holland…lies so l.	HOOD 410:42
l. in rich…countries	SMITH 798:45
Sweet and l.	TENN 841:2
Too l. for envy	COWL 240:35
lowbrow l., a bit of a murderer	MILL 573:57
lowcut l., belongings on show	JOYCE 452:95
Lowells L. talk to the Cabots	BOSS 145:8
lower gittin a little l. ever since	BILL 130:47
if the l. orders don't	WILDE 909:34
l. middle classes!	GILB 354:10
no longer l. classes	TOCQ 861:80
lowing grazes over the carpet, l.	RAINE 677:93
lowland between l. and highland	SWIN 834:51
Ye Highlands and ye L.	BALL 55:68
low-pay l.-p., low-prestige	COUP 238:89
loy blow of a l.	SYNGE 834:59
loyal l. sport of love	ANON 19:90
l. to the tips of his stubby fingers	ACHE 3:39
supports his king on l. principles	SHAW 777:65
loyalties above all other l.	JAMES 433:25
Home of…impossible l.	ARNO 33:39
loyalty applauded…his l.	HATT 385:26
done by intrigue, not by l.	HUGO 421:80
I want l.	JOHN 440:85
love and l.	RUNC 702:72
l. and order	GLAD 358:92
l. to the United States	ROOS 696:60
l. to the world organization?	CHUR 217:93
l. we all feel	GREE 371:55
lucasta L. might I crave	LOVE 519:11
lucid l., inescapable rhythms	STEV 819:23
make a l. interval	DRYD 288:49
lucidity I have a terrible l.	VAN 877:29
Lucifer L., son of the morning!	BIBLE 102:21
luck always just my l.	PARK 637:57
belief in l.	OATES 620:90
Fattenin' hogs ain't in l.	HARR 383:94
Homage to plain dumb l.	ACHE 3:47
I never had bad l.	TRUM 868:31
L. is a dividend of sweat	KROC 481:18
l. o' the prize	BURNS 172:37
l. to be called upon	CHUR 217:3
man…down on his l.	DAVI 254:42
more l.…than any other game	ARLO 30:65
no l. about a house	YEATS 934:61
Oedipus he had the l.	HUGH 419:49
of that natural l.	SHAK 765:27
such a thing as l.	MAMET 543:31
Was there ever man had such l.?	SHAK 773:57
watching his l.	SERV 728:3
when he's unhappy—his l. runs out	CHAN 204:80
Wish me l., as you wave	PARR 639:95
worst l. any man could have	HEMI 394:15
your faltering l.	CIAR 218:13
luckier to die is different…and l.	WHIT 905:31
luckiest l. of mortals	AUDEN 41:24
lucky Do I feel l.	EAST 298:68
if we are too l.	JONG 448:4
L. is the man	EURI 316:15
My L. Star	FREED 336:38
lucrative most l. of its branches	PAINE 634:93
lucre not greedy of filthy l.	BIBLE 123:74
Lucy When L. ceased to be	WORD 924:78
ludicrous dignity becomes l.	GALT 345:31
rogue alive to the l.	EMER 313:53
Ludlow L. fair	HOUS 415:66
to L. come	HOUS 415:54
luely O l., I, cam she in	SOUT 805:93
Sae l., I., cam she in	SOUT 805:94
lug I'll l. the guts	SHAK 754:14
luggage Empty l. may be easier	NEW 611:54
look after the l.	LOWE 519:20
luggies jaups in l.	BURNS 171:89
lukewarm thou art l.	BIBLE 126:51
lullaby dreamy l.!	GILB 355:19
L. of Broadway	DUBIN 292:69
Once in a l.	HARB 381:38
Rock them, rock them, l.	DEKK 259:48
lullay l., l., like a child	SKEL 795:92
lullings l. and the relishes of it	HERB 398:1
lumber l. of the schools	SWIFT 830:51
l. room of his library	DOYLE 285:66
luminous l. home of waters	ARNO 32:28
lump l. of clotted nonsense	DRYD 288:41
L. the whole thing!	TWAIN 870:77
ugly l.	KIPL 472:36
lumps Go down like l. of lead	HODG 405:45
lunar Held in a l. synthesis	ELIOT 305:29
lunatic all in l. asylums	CHES 211:59
as though I were in a l. asylum	CONA 230:80
certified a l.	CROS 246:84
engagingly l. about Ralph	USTI 875:7
l., the lover	SHAK 738:13
lunatics if any l. were at large	ELIOT 303:1
L. are sincere	DRIB 287:10
lunch free l. has still to be invented	GREE 372:85
long-range planning is l.	OGDEN 622:40
naked l. is natural	GINS 357:60
no such thing as a free l.	FRIE 337:63
When he sat down to l.	LONG 515:38
wish the meeting…as the l.	CHRI 215:39
luncheon do not take soup at l.	CURZ 250:55
l. with a city friend	BELL 73:67
lunch-time Every l. t.	HAMER 378:96
lung have a l. removed	WAUGH 893:56
our left l.	GAND 345:33
lungs air ungainly in our new l.	ATWO 38:49
opens the heart and l.	STER 818:85
using your l. all the time	LEAC 496:61
lure swimming towards the l.	HEAN 389:8
wherever you may l. it	KAFKA 454:25
luscious Fame's l. pot	RICK 686:76
lush L., calm and voluptuous	BAUD 64:61
lust avarice, l. and ambition	LEWIS 507:73
Beauty and the l. for learning	BEER 69:79
hutch of tasty l.	HOPK 412:81
looked on a lot of women with l.	CART 198:47
looketh on a woman to l. after her	BIBLE 109:89
love is more cruel than l.	SWIN 833:30
L. carries her sharp whip	WEBS 894:79
l. of knowing	FLEC 327:46
l. of the goat	BLAKE 134:44
same rule applies for l.	MONT 593:97
Thy l. and liking	SKEL 795:93
weigh them pleasure by their l.	DYER 297:52
women's unnatural, unsatiable l.	BURT 174:80
lustre exceeding l. and the pure	SHEL 784:66
l. in its sky	SHEL 782:21
l. of it will never appear	DEFOE 258:11
l. of midday to objects	MOORE 594:16
Where is thy l. now?	SHAK 763:81
lusts l. of the father ye will do	BIBLE 117:98
prince's appetite And serve his l.	MASS 560:47
Thou hotly l.	SHAK 763:92
to satisfy men's carnal l.	BOOK 142:20
lusty am strong and l.	SHAK 749:39
In l. leas at liberty	WYATT 930:97
l. song of fruits	BLAKE 133:25
l. young men	SHAK 735:36
lute As her l. doth live	CAMP 186:71
little rift within the l.	TENN 846:9
l. its tones	KEATS 457:4
My l., awake!	WYATT 931:2
pleasing of a l.	SHAK 731:99
with his l. made trees	SHAK 775:12
lute-resounding l.-r. waves	POPE 662:79
Luther L.; the Philistine of genius	ARNO 34:65
Lutheran spleeny L.	SHAK 775:16
luxuries distinction…between l.	GALB 343:92
l. That modern life	WILB 907:75
l. to brood over in my walks	KEATS 458:11
luxury by l. betrayed	GOLD 361:58
couch for l.	SHAK 752:33
every l. was lavished on you	ORTON 627:30
'horseless-carriage' is at present a l.	ANON 21:41
Love is like any other l.	TROL 867:2
l. of a peacetime environment	TRUM 868:39
l. of doing good	CRAB 242:3
l. the accomplished sofa	COWP 241:67
satisfy l. and licentiousness	MORE 597:66
style is the only real l.	ARMA 30:67
whilst L. Employed	MAND 545:54
Lycid hearse where L. lies	MILT 578:54
Lycidas head of your lov'd L.	MILT 578:48
L. is dead, dead ere	MILT 578:45
L. your sorrow	MILT 578:57
Lydia L. The Tattooed Lady	HARB 381:37
lying l. for one's country	BIER 129:26
One of you is l.	PARK 638:59
putting away l.	BIBLE 122:47
smallest amount of l.	BUTL 178:72
subject…to this vice of l.!	SHAK 743:57
We've been l. so long	STEI 816:43
you can tell when a man is l.	BOHL 138:36
lynching keep him from l. me	KING 468:31
Lyndon L. gave me that instead	ROCK 692:80
lynx sharp as any l.	SITW 793:58
Lyons coming hither from L.	WALP 887:21
lyre Make me thy l.	SHEL 783:47
many-chorded l.	RANJ 678:16
my l. has a soul	CHOC 214:17
remembered tone of a mute l.	BYRON 180:37
lyric a'e gowden l.	MACD 530:42
O l. love	BROW 162:82
lyrical primitive era was l.	HUGO 420:60
lyricism sick of cautious l.	BAND 58:25

M

ma Look M.	CAGN 184:30
M.'s out, Pa's out	FLAN 326:24
Mabel Nay, M., nay!	GILB 354:2
macadam made of melting m.	AMIS 15:99
Macaulay cocksure…as Tom M.	MELB 563:18
M., Gibbon, Tolstoy	PRIAL 668:13
memory of M.	BARR 61:94
Philistine, Lord M.	ARNO 33:42
young M. or Ruskin	BARB 59:47
Macavity M., M.…no one like M.	ELIOT 308:11
Macbeth Little Nell and Lady M.	WOOL 923:56
M. does murder sleep	SHAK 767:2
M. shall sleep no more	SHAK 767:3
M. slurping your soup?	PAGE 633:77
My name's M.	SHAK 769:44
Shall harm M.	SHAK 769:23
Macduff Lay on, M.	SHAK 769:46
M. was from his mother's womb	SHAK 769:45
mace fool's bauble—the M.	CROM 246:75
m. of honor	MANC 544:44
m. to knock down the passengers	BENT 77:68
macerations Made way for m.	POUND 664:38
MacGregor name is M.!	SCOTT 724:32
Selwyn M., the nicest boy	SPARK 806:18
Macheath Just a jack-knife has M.	BREC 151:6
Machiavellian rare tricks of a M.	WEBS 895:91
machine A reading m.	LOWE 520:33
automatic m.	WIEN 906:67
body is a m. for living	TOLS 862:4
depressing the keys of the m.	BIER 129:40
friction of the whole m.	CLAU 220:66
Ghost in the M.	RYLE 707:78
m. for transmission of ideas	BOWL 147:33
m.-gun to a shooting gallery	OFAO 622:34
m. is running away with him	WILH 911:95
m. slipping from	LOWE 521:60
m. that makes the art	LEWI 508:7
m., the m. is necessary	MILL 571:99
m., the railway	NIET 615:5
man…a minutely set, ingenious m.	BLIX 137:1
[man] is a universal m.	REDT 681:76
muskets and m. guns	MUSS 605:19
not a man, you're a m.	SHAW 777:54
One m. can do the work	HUBB 417:8
Prayers…on an adding m.	WEST 901:37
pulse of the m.	WORD 927:36
pulverizing m.	BACON 50:36
machine-gunned wall and m.-g.	TAYL 837:21
machinery Age of M.	CARL 191:80
assume the form of m.	MARX 558:12
by chemistry and m.	SHAW 778:93
governmental m. that he lives under	SPEN 807:43
m. of Government	MONT 591:61
mind is pure m.	GINS 357:62
primitive m. and primitive music	LEAC 497:65
read somewhere that m.	MARI 550:56
warfare of men and m.	WOLFE 920:88
whole m. of the state	ENGE 314:68
machines begin with sewing m.	PAGN 634:86
m. and to be chosen	LEUP 505:50
M. are worshipped	RUSS 705:47
m. devised by mankind	BORE 144:88
m.…do not make men…happier	DE 257:91
m. for making more m.	BOTT 146:17
m. we worship	PRIE 668:22
problem is not whether m. think	SKIN 795:10
We are survival m.	DAWK 256:72
machismo m. reeks of violence	WHITE 902:71
macho the new m. fascism	WHITE 902:70

m. it to people WILL 911:1
Night M. crossing the border AUDEN 39:81
the multitudes in m. SMART 797:29
mails two weeks' delayed m. KIPL 473:57
main every man…part of the m. DONNE 281:84
hushed the stormy m. GRAY 370:30
owre the friendly m. NAIR 607:55
Maine inhabitant of…the State of M. FORD 329:1
mainstream gladly enter the m. COEN 224:62
main-travelled m.-t. road GARL 346:49
Maise Proud M. is in the wood SCOTT 724:39
maize with Plenty in the m. TENN 842:16
majestic m. river floated on ARNO 32:27
Majesty his M. hath determined SWIFT 831:78
M. entered the House RUSH 703:96
M.'s dominions NORTH 618:66
May it please your M. LENT 503:2
majesty appears to Your M.'s slave KISH 475:88
as his m. is BIBLE 107:38
Beauty's princely m. SHAK 729:47
certain alienated m. EMER 312:5
Dead, your M. DICK 270:98
explain to Her M. KEMB 461:82
first in loftiness…next in m. DRYD 291:24
his M.'s Opposition HOBH 405:31
love your m. SHAK 762:52
naked m. seemed lords of all MILT 582:61
paucity…imparts m. ALBE 10:97
right hand of the M. BIBLE 124:89
sight so touching in its m. WORD 926:19
suddenly recognised by His M. FREUD 336:51
major All poets who…are m. WHITE 902:75
books m. or minor SAND 713:13
major-general modern M.-G. GILB 354:99
majority big enough m. TWAIN 871:9
don't believe in black m. rule SMITH 799:69
Government of the absolute m. CALH 184:35
m.…happen to like WHIT 904:15
m. never has right IBSEN 428:33
m.…the best repartee DISR 276:58
no m., no government OAKE 619:86
One man with God is always a m. KNOX 476:20
poverty, ignorance…of the m. DU 293:75
Putting a m. together DOLE 278:14
small conservative m. TYNAN 872:43
majors live with scarlet M. SASS 716:61
make cannot m. a man love KING 468:31
cost him more to m. SMITH 798:48
may not quite m. it YOST 935:75
Scotsman on the m. BARR 61:85
maker appealing directly to my M. BRAH 149:86
best m. of all marriages SHAK 746:69
God thi m. CHAU 208:64
hope to meet my M. CORN 237:71
M., in that crimson lake MONT 593:5
m. of heaven and earth BOOK 140:71
m. of his own fortune STEE 814:93
M. of the stars and sea BETJ 84:99
ready to meet my m. CHUR 217:96
Scattered his M.'s image DRYD 289:69
serve therewith my M. MILT 580:88
shall a man be more pure than his m. BIBLE 93:53
striveth with his M.! BIBLE 103:45
the watch…had a m. PALEY 635:16
makers m. of our fate POPP 662:91
T'abhor the m. DRYD 291:22
making process of m. something else HUXL 425:70
somebody who is obsessed by M. CUMM 247:5
mal Honi soit qui m. y pense EDWA 300:17
Malacca Whoever is Lord of M. TOME 863:9
maladies all the m. of stinking states JOHN 441:11
call all sorts of m.…by one name CARL 191:70
malady Life is a m. ABU 1:13
love's a m. without a cure DRYD 292:55
malaria like m. in his veins GREE 371:53
Malay M. Peninsula…climate SWET 830:47
M. religion and custom PANG 636:28
Malaysia in M. 1937 THER 851:50
male chosen and m. shall go forth KENN 462:2
Especially the m. of the species LAWR 495:26
incompetent as the average m. CUNN 248:26
keeps m. domination intact WOLF 919:80
makes a m. healthy THUR 859:29
m. and female created he them BIBLE 85:41
m. officers are gentlemen CARD 183:20
m. quality HOPK 413:11
m. who enforces order LEGU 501:58

more deadly than the m. KIPL 474:82
neither m. nor female BIBLE 122:36
no reason for the existence of the m. WEST 901:44
rough m. kiss of blankets BROO 156:4
self-worship of the m. MILL 571:79
weapon of the m. CONN 233:77
Ye Lilies m.! CRAB 242:97
malefactor make a m. die sweetly DRYD 291:30
males Nothing but m. SHAK 767:91
six…left…all m. BENN 76:28
malevolent something m. CATH 200:89
thought a m. speech JONS 450:55
Malfi Duchess of M. still WEBS 895:17
malice crabbed m. DISR 276:65
From envy, hatred, and m. BOOK 140:81
m. in my breath SHAK 769:60
M. is of a low stature HALI 378:87
m. mingled with a little wit DRYD 291:19
m. toward none LINC 510:41
the wildest m. SITW 794:65
worst your m. can DRYD 289:62
malicious God is…not m. EINS 301:31
horrid m. bloody flame PEPYS 647:47
malignity m. and rapidity DICK 271:17
motiveless m. COLE 227:27
the m. of a lie STEE 814:2
malingering absolute genius for m. PROU 671:78
malleable speech as m. and pliant QUIL 674:44
malpractice m. of heart CLOU 223:31
malt m. does more than Milton HOUS 415:65
maltworms purple-hued m. SHAK 741:6
Malvernian That old M. brother BETJ 83:84
mama M. may have HOLI 407:64
m. of dada FADI 317:35
mamas Red-Hot M. TUCK 870:63
mamby-pambies outing for m.-p. CHAR 207:45
mammal You are…a vertebrate m. CARB 189:39
mammon cannot serve God and m. BIBLE 110:1
friends of the m. BIBLE 116:51
pale M. pine amidst his store POPE 660:4
man Account me m. MILT 582:46
all animals, except m., know BUTL 178:70
all that may become a m. SHAK 767:89
All visible objects, m. MELV 564:30
almost kill a m. as kill MILT 578:62
always a m.'s shadow JARR 435:87
an all-the-lights-on m. REED 681:82
And ah for a m. TENN 845:85
and all that makes m. TENN 846:22
an educated m. HEAN 389:9
Angry Young M. PAUL 643:74
An iron m. SHAK 743:59
an old m. young TENN 840:70
any m. is so very a fool SHAK 732:26
Any m.'s death diminishes me DONNE 281:85
any m. that breathes on earth MARL 552:2
any m. whatsoever TARK 836:95
anything said, ask a m. THAT 850:10
ape in m. MCCA 528:9
apparel oft proclaims the m. SHAK 751:20
architectural m.-milliner RUSK 704:25
arms and the m. ANON 18:65
Arms, and the m. I sing DRYD 292:42
Art…absorbs the m. FUSE 342:73
artist m. and the mother woman SHAW 778:84
as artist and as m. THUR 860:60
as good as life to a m. BIBLE 108:61
as if you were a simple m. PARRA 639:94
As m.'s ingratitude SHAK 749:52
as much as a m. TROL 867:10
as much as a m. TRUTH 869:52
Athwart m.'s noses SHAK 735:38
average m. sees woman MUIR 602:67
A was a m. SHAK 751:11
battle of m. with m. WEBER 894:69
Be a good m. SCOTT 725:60
before a m. knew how to sin BEHN 71:18
Behold the m. BIBLE 128:4
being more than m. RUSS 705:44
better angel is a m. SHAK 773:55
better m. than I am KIPL 471:96
between a m. and a woman GIBB 352:72
between m. and wife ANDR 16:26
bind the heart of m.! GILM 356:55
Books and the m. I sing POPE 662:64
Both m. and bird and beast COLE 225:92
bread to a m. LEWIS 507:84

breed a habit in a m.! SHAK 729:40
bring a m. peace BOOK 143:47
busy m. who can keep up STARR 813:77
call m. a little world DONNE 281:82
call up my m. SCOTT 724:28
Can a M. be a Christian HARD 381:40
cannot be abrogated by m. SUMN 828:19
cannot make a m. love KING 468:31
can throw at a m. HAZL 388:91
care for no m. on earth DICK 271:23
Care…in every old m.'s eye SHAK 736:57
care-wearied m. WHIT 906:56
celebration of m. THOM 852:78
century of the common m. ROUS 700:39
century of the common m. WALL 886:9
Chancery Lane young m. GILB 354:8
child…in the debased, degraded m. ELIOT 303:83
Child is father of the M. WORD 926:15
civilized m.…into a savage TOCQ 861:81
clever chiel', m. MACQ 538:16
cold charities of m. to m. CRAB 242:90
coloured m. MACI 533:7
comfortable years allowed to m.! SASS 716:58
comfort to each m. ANON 18:74
coming together of a m. and wife STOP 825:59
commonplace young m. GILB 354:6
confronts m. with…choice SART 715:47
conservative is a m. ROOS 696:47
contemporary m.'s idolatry MONT 591:62
conversant with a M.'s heart POE 656:27
covetous m. all his treasure MILT 579:78
create m. in our image BIBLE 85:41
creative nature of m. MILL 573:43
crime of being a young m. PITT 652:36
cultured modern m. RODC 693:87
Dark as the world of m. SITW 794:73
darkness of m.'s heart GOLD 360:28
dat m. of mine HAMM 379:14
dead m. leave to think! SHAK 737:78
dead m.'s embers GRAV 367:70
Dealing with a m. JACO 432:15
dear and valuable to m. PITT 653:46
Death destroys a m. FORS 331:37
deface the image of m. IVAN 431:99
degree of 'grand old m.' LEAC 497:72
Desiring this m.'s art SHAK 771:14
desperateness of m.'s heart! BUNY 166:66
dimensions of a m.'s self LAMB 487:55
dimensions of a m.'s self LAMB 487:57
Dispute it like a m. SHAK 768:30
distinguishes m. from animals OSLER 630:15
divinely gifted m. TENN 843:48
double minded m. is unstable BIBLE 124:5
dream past the wit of m. SHAK 738:11
drinking m. is never less LAMB 487:58
drive a m. out of his wits ALCO 10:6
dull ear of a drowsy m. SHAK 739:26
dying m.'s room STER 818:86
Each m. has his Jew MILL 572:5
each m. is alone BERG 79:94
Each m. is the architect CLAU 220:64
Ech m. for hymself CHAU 208:77
effect of travel on a m. LIVI 512:83
elderly m. of 42 ASHF 35:93
employment for a thinking m. ADDI 7:44
Enclosing every thin m. WAUGH 892:44
end of m.'s motion BACON 48:5
episode in the life of a m. STAEL 811:44
ever tasted M.? KIPL 472:33
every great m. nowadays WILDE 908:91
every m. against his brother BIBLE 106:16
every m. a liar BIBLE 120:61
every m. and nation LOWE 519:27
Every m. at every moment BAUD 65:91
every m.…born to die DRYD 292:59
Every m. has a right JOHN 446:48
Every m. has his fault SHAK 762:45
every m. is enemy to every m. HOBB 404:27
every m. is not a proper champion BROW 158:58
Every m. is the maker STEE 814:93
every m. is two men BORG 145:92
Every m. is wanted EMER 312:26
every m. must play a part SHAK 739:36
every m. of every nation THAC 849:1
Every m. over forty SHAW 779:22
every m. reclaimed his own property BUTL 178:85
every m. shall eat SHAK 775:26

Every m.'s own reason   BROW 158:59
every m. straight before him   BIBLE 90:64
every m....under a Government   RAIN 677:92
Every m. who is high up   BARR 61:87
every m. will do his duty   NELS 610:34
every m., woman and child   GOLD 362:78
every m. would lay his hand   STRA 826:89
Every moment dies a m.   TENN 841:91
everyone has sat except a m.   CUMM 248:16
Every time I leave the old m.   OCON 622:27
Every true m.'s apparel   SHAK 758:43
Every unjust m.   PLATO 655:88
Every wise m.'s son   SHAK 756:60
exploit of that gallant m.   MILT 579:63
eye of American m.   BARR 60:77
facts we know about a m.   LAWR 494:6
false to any m.   SHAK 751:22
fancy of m. has painted   LOCKE 514:17
fasting, for a good m.'s love   SHAK 750:69
Fathers, what is m.!   MILT 586:55
fear of every m.   JONS 450:57
feminine in the m.   KENT 464:59
final pleasure left to m.   SNOW 802:35
find a m.   PASC 640:12
fine m. who...knows nothing   EISE 302:62
first-class fightin' m.   KIPL 471:94
first enterprising m.   RUDO 701:61
first m. I heard use the expression   ELLI 310:75
first m. is of the earth   BIBLE 121:18
fog of the good m.'s mind   BROW 161:36
follies which a m. regrets most   ROWL 701:53
foolish, fond old m.   SHAK 764:98
Foolish the m. who trusts her   FRAN 334:95
fool, who trusts a m.   MARIE 550:51
For a m. to admit a distaste   STEI 815:35
For he owes not any m.   LONG 516:45
For m. will be blotted out   JEFF 436:5
formed m. out of the dust   BIBLE 86:43
For tribal m. space   MCLU 536:56
Free m.!   BAUD 64:58
free m.   JOHN 440:80
free m. thinks of nothing less   SPIN 811:33
friend of a m.   COLL 228:44
fury of a patient m.   DRYD 290:97
gave m. speech   SHEL 785:78
Get a new m.!   SHAK 774:88
ghastly to every m.   ANON 18:75
Give a m. the secure possession   YOUNG 935:76
Give every m. thine ear   SHAK 751:19
give it to the first m.   SCHR 720:38
Give me a m.   HAGEN 376:56
Give me that m.   SHAK 754:89
give the white m. nothing else   WALK 885:98
giving m. dominion over woman   STAN 812:66
glory of God is m.   ANON 18:67
God created m.   VALE 876:15
God hath given liberty to m.   CURR 249:41
God in M.   CRAS 244:34
God is a m.   GIRA 358:83
God is not a m.   BIBLE 89:41
God made himself a m.   HUGO 421:79
God, M., Destiny   MILL 572:15
God never made...for m. to mend   DRYD 292:53
good eater must be a good m.   DISR 276:36
good habit makes a child a m.   WEBS 894:80
good m.'s glory   KEMP 461:89
good to preserve the health of M.   BYRD 178:93
good to some m.   SHAW 777:73
gossamer fidelity of mere M.   POE 656:20
Go West, young m.   SOULE 804:91
Greater love hath no m.   BIBLE 118:12
greatest m. in the world   TRUM 868:40
great m. walking down the street   COPL 237:66
guess what a m.   MORL 598:85
had made her such a m.   SHAK 759:62
haggard and lank young m.   GILB 354:9
half a m. to suffer   LAWR 494:92
happiness of m.   PAINE 634:98
happiness or blessedness of m.   SPIN 811:34
happiness through another m.'s eyes   SHAK 750:86
Happy is the m.   BIBLE 99:12
Happy is the m.   BIBLE 127:90
Happy is the m.   BIBLE 98:93
harried m. I think I be!   BALL 56:79
hate a m. who swallows it   LAMB 486:40
hate a m. you have hurt   TACI 835:70
heaping obligations on a m.   SHAW 778:87

heart of a m.   ROUS 700:46
heart of a m....lodged in a woman   CONG 232:39
heart of m. go together   RUSK 704:12
hearty old m.   SOUT 805:96
hero is a m.   MAIL 540:46
holy m. to crysten hym   MALO 542:2
honest m.'s   GILB 354:3
honest m.'s the noblest   POPE 660:25
honest m.'s the noble work   BURNS 170:70
honest m. who married   GOLD 361:43
hour's come, but not the m.   SCOTT 724:34
how a m. dies   JOHN 444:89
However vast a m.'s spirit   PASC 640:7
how hard it is to become a m.   CARP 193:51
How many roads must a m. walk   DYLAN 297:54
husband be a m.   LAMB 486:43
hyest thyng that m. may kepe   CHAU 209:90
I am a free m.   ARET 29:42
I am a m.   SHAK 763:74
I am a m.   TERE 848:76
I am a sincere m.   MARTI 555:45
if a m. bites a dog   BOGA 138:34
If a m. does not make   JOHN 442:36
If a m. do not erect   SHAK 745:25
If a m. have a tent   LEON 503:13
If a m. have long hair   BIBLE 121:5
If a m. look sharply   BACON 49:41
if a m. should spit   WEBS 894:84
If a m. were called   GIBB 351:52
If a m. were sure of living   HAWT 386:36
If a m. write little   BACON 50:54
If any m. be in Christ   BIBLE 122:27
If any m. will come after me   BIBLE 115:33
If m. were anything   DONNE 281:75
If m. were robbed   FONT 328:84
if the Queen were a m.   VICT 880:84
If this young m.   GILB 354:4
If you delight not in m.   SHAK 753:59
If you hate a m.   CARL 191:73
If you would work any m.   BACON 49:49
Ignorance...excuses no m.   SELD 726:78
I got my m.   GERS 350:38
immense new powers on m.   CHUR 217:95
imperishable dignity of m.   CARL 191:87
Imprisoned in every fat m.   CONN 233:82
in a young m. is timidity   HUGO 421:94
inclinations of a m.   LONS 517:69
inestimable privilege of m.   SHEL 782:14
in favour with God and m.   BIBLE 115:28
injured no m.'s reputation   LOVE 519:17
Innate ideas are in every m.   BLAKE 135:79
in spirit she is a m.   GOTT 364:18
interrupt a m.   STER 817:68
in the image of God made he m.   BIBLE 87:68
in truth the m.   POPE 661:29
in youth m. is...depraved   MITC 588:85
I saw an aged, aged m.   CARR 197:22
is m. an ape or an angel?   DISR 276:69
It profits a m. nothing   BOLT 139:48
It's a m.'s job   AESC 8:61
Japanese young m.   GILB 354:7
Jewish m. with parents   ROTH 699:18
join together this m.   BOOK 142:19
justify God's ways to m.   HOUS 415:65
kill a m. than a hawk   JEFF 436:9
know thee not, old m.   SHAK 743:67
labouring m. that is given   BIBLE 108:54
large-hearted m.   BROW 159:99
last strands of m.   HOPK 412:2
laws of m.   HOUS 416:75
less m. has to do with...death   MELV 564:29
let him pass for a m.   SHAK 739:47
let not m. have the upper hand   BOOK 142:40
Life as a M.   ROTH 699:21
life of a m....heroic poem   CARL 192:21
life of every m.   MUIR 602:60
life of m.   BACON 50:65
like a m....chasing rainbows   WODE 919:72
like an honest m.   SHAK 744:4
Like master like m.   PETR 649:83
like unto the Son of m.   BIBLE 125:45
line where m. leaves off   FROST 338:95
Little m., little m.!   ELIZ 310:63
lonely m. is a lonesome thing   CHEE 209:3
looked from pig to m.   ORWE 629:76
looking for an honest m.   DIOG 275:22
Look out for this m.'s music   PARRY 639:99

love freedom...but good m.   MILT 580:84
love is a thing below a m.   STER 818:88
love not m. less   BYRON 180:43
love of m.   JEFF 436:4
lowly m.   WHIT 904:14
make a deal with one m.   DWOR 296:48
make a m. appear a fool   DRYD 291:29
make a m. blessed and happy   ARIS 29:51
make a m. by standing a sheep   BEER 69:82
make a monkey of a m.   BENC 74:98
make me bearded like a m.!   DICK 273:78
make me mistress to the m.   POPE 659:83
makes a m. stand straight   HELL 392:76
making of m.   SWIN 832:21
m. about whom all is forgotten   BENT 78:82
m. a child   SHAK 733:64
m. after his own heart   BIBLE 91:88
manage a clever m.   KIPL 470:75
m. a little pope of perfection   LAWR 494:97
m. alone can keep that peace   CHUR 217:90
m. alone does m. betray   ROCH 691:58
m. alone in a room   HUTC 424:50
m. also has his moral   LICH 509:16
M. always desires...happiness   ANON 19:89
M....always to be blest   POPE 660:10
m., a madyn, and a tre   ANON 19:94
m. and a woman in a garden   WILDE 909:21
m. and a woman looking at a girl   WOOLF 922:39
m. and his wine's sae bewitching!   BURNS 173:55
m. and his work existed   MEYER 568:30
m., and not his instruments   MO 589:21
m. and the infinite!   MACD 529:32
m. and the intention   LEON 503:16
m. and wife make one fool   JONS 449:30
M. appears to be the missing link   LORE 517:89
m. at the wheel   MARI 550:52
m. bears beliefs   EMER 313:42
M., being reasonable   BYRON 182:80
M. be my metaphor   THOM 852:59
m. body both for power   SPEN 808:85
m. booste of conning   LYDG 523:4
m. born in America   OLSEN 624:74
m. by nothing is so well bewrayed   SPEN 809:12
m. can be a parent   MUIR 602:68
m. can become famous   SHAW 777:67
m. can be destroyed   HEMI 394:21
m. can be so innocently employed   JOHN 444:5
m. can die but once   SHAK 743:56
m. can never elevate his mistress   BALZ 57:5
M....can not be happy   POIN 657:32
m. cannot be too careful   WILDE 908:4
m. cannot choose but pay   PATM 643:57
m. cannot dress   STER 818:95
m. cannot...hold another   FULL 341:48
M. cannot live   GILL 356:44
M. cannot live without seeking   BERL 80:22
m. cannot make him laugh   SHAK 743:63
M. cannot make principles   PAINE 634:97
m. ceases to be a beginner   COLL 227:33
M. comes and tills   TENN 846:25
m. comes around to needing   FULL 341:52
m. comes into a great hotel   MILL 571:99
m. couldn't wear a moustache   HOOV 411:68
M. delights not me   SHAK 752:58
m. desires to live long   SWIFT 831:86
m. die better   MACA 526:63
m. does not attain   GOULD 365:23
m. does not keep pace   THOR 858:97
M. does not live by bread alone   GILL 356:45
m. does what he likes   GILL 356:42
m. doth not live by bread only   BIBLE 89:47
m. doth seek a triple perfection   HOOK 410:55
m....down on his luck   DAVI 254:42
M. dreams of fame   TENN 846:11
m. enough for a woman   DEKK 260:53
m....even more, an Englishman   MORI 598:83
m. fallen among Fabians   LENIN 502:86
m. feels instinctively   LOWE 520:35
m. feel so lonely, alien   LAWR 494:5
m. feels that...in woman   WRIG 929:75
m. first of all exists   SART 715:49
M. for all seasons   BOLT 139:47
M. found his form   BERD 78:87
m. Friday   DEFOE 258:19
m. gets into the ring   MAIL 540:59
m. God hates   DOWL 284:42
m. goes in for politics   ROGE 695:26

M. goeth forth unto his work   BIBLE 97:68
m. goeth to his long home   BIBLE 101:92
m. got to do   STEI 815:32
M. hands on misery to m.   LARK 491:39
m. has a House of Lords   LLOY 513:6
m. has a property   LOCKE 514:14
m. has created him   DOST 283:9
m. has just waxed the floor   NASH 608:95
m. hasn't discovered   KING 468:34
m. has one hundred dollars   WEST 901:32
m. has to prove himself   PAGL 634:81
m. has two irons   BEAU 67:8
m. hates to be moved   LAWR 495:41
M. hath his daily work   MILT 583:67
M....held only by the slightest   EDGE 299:94
M., her last work   TENN 843:45
m. he was to all the country   GOLD 361:53
m. hurling himself at…chaos   POUND 665:66
m. in a frock coat   LAVER 493:82
m. in a large check suit   WELLS 898:83
m. in all the world's   SHAK 733:73
M. (in good earnest)   MONT 592:71
m. in higher rank   RUSK 704:15
m. in his entirety   BECK 68:33
m. in London   GALT 344:28
m. in the crucible   ELKIN 310:70
M. in the highest   SWIN 833:45
m. in the smoker   SAND 713:93
m. in the street   BALD 54:47
m....in the way in the house   GASK 346:59
m. invents nothing   SHAW 778:93
M. is a bungler   SHAW 778:94
m. is a common murderer   SAKI 710:45
M. is a creature who   STEV 822:89
M. is a history-making creature   AUDEN 41:21
M. is all symmetry   HERB 398:4
M. is a noble animal   BROW 159:92
M. is a rope, fastened   NIET 615:12
M. is a singular creature   BRON 154:70
M. is a tool-using animal   CARL 192:91
M. is a torch borne in the wind   CHAP 206:14
M. is a useless passion   SART 715:45
m. is a wolf   PLAU 655:5
m. is become as one of us   BIBLE 86:57
M. is born free   ROUS 700:41
M. is born to live in society   DIDE 274:3
m. is born unto trouble   BIBLE 93:54
m. is bound to rebel against   IBSEN 428:33
M. is by his constitution   BURKE 169:38
M. is condemned   SART 715:51
m. is distinguished   ADDI 6:30
m. is either free   BARA 59:45
M. is essentially the imitative   JAMES 434:66
m. is ever hasty   KORAN 479:75
m. is in substance   HUXL 426:10
m. is killing time   LOWE 520:51
m. is like a phonograph   SHAW 780:54
m. is m. and master   TENN 846:6
m. is most at ease   ALLS 13:63
M. is neither angel nor beast   PASC 641:31
M. is neither good nor evil   BALZ 58:21
M. is no other   SART 715:52
M. is nothing but a subject   PASC 640:13
M. is…not more happy   POE 656:21
m. is not 'taking'   JONG 448:97
M. is not the enemy of M.   PAINE 634:92
M....is of few days   BIBLE 93:61
M. is one world   HERB 398:5
M. is only a reed   PASC 641:24
M. is only truly great   DISR 276:49
M. is…over-complicated   POUND 665:55
M. is polygamous   JAMES 434:75
M. is quite insane   MONT 592:81
m. is something that   NIET 615:11
M. is still   KENN 463:26
m. is strong before he is moral   FAUL 318:66
m. is the being who wills   SCHI 718:2
M. is the hunter   TENN 841:97
M. is the measure of all things   PROT 670:63
M. is the Only Animal   TWAIN 872:23
M. is the only creature   ORWE 629:72
M. is the only one   FROU 339:21
M. is the shuttle   VAUG 878:50
M. is ungrateful to his Lord   KORAN 479:96
M. is what he eats   FEUE 322:23
M. is who he is   SAINT 709:22
m. keeps another person's secret   LABR 483:60

m. knows he is to be hanged   JOHN 445:26
m. knows that he is miserable   PASC 641:32
m. lay down his wife   JOYCE 452:91
m. lies late   MORG 597:80
M....little lower than the angells   BILL 130:47
M. lives by science as well   JAMES 434:59
m. lives well   KIPL 470:82
m. looketh on the outward   BIBLE 91:90
m....loyal to his club   WHITE 903:76
m. made the rest   KRON 481:20
m. made the town   COWP 241:68
M....makes of himself   SART 715:50
M. marks the earth with ruin   BYRON 180:44
m. married is…married   SHAK 761:30
m. marries his housekeeper   PIGOU 651:15
m. may be born a poet   SASS 717:79
m. may be brought to hope   TROL 867:92
m. may fish with the worm   SHAK 754:15
M. may not marry his Grandmother   BOOK 144:78
m. may write   JOHN 441:21
m....mere complexities   YEATS 934:57
m. must be sacrificed   LOWE 519:24
m. must have a rare recipe   LAMB 486:28
Manners makyth m.   WILL 911:3
m....never have attempted   THOM 857:66
m. nor angel can discern   MILT 582:51
m., not even a doctor   NIGH 616:35
m. of clay, son   MILT 584:8
m. of…comprehensive nature   DRYD 292:45
m. of genius   BEER 70:85
m. of genius   POUND 664:33
m. of giant stature   NEHRU 610:29
m. of good character   SHAW 780:64
m. of great common sense   SHAW 778:79
m. of great worth   POLO 657:39
m. of independent means   MENC 565:60
m. of many ways   HOMER 409:24
m. of my name   NAPO 607:73
m. of paradoxes   ROUS 700:45
m. of science   PIER 651:5
m. of sense and a fop   CHES 210:26
m. of sorrow who wins   LAO 490:13
m. of substance, of flesh and bone   ELLI 311:88
m. of the present   HOLM 408:2
m. of wealth and taste   JAGG 432:18
m. of yearning thought   ROSS 698:3
m. o'independent mind   SMITH 801:25
m. on the flying trapeze   LEYB 508:11
m. on the flying trapeze   SARO 714:34
M. on the moon   BAKER 53:22
m. or a woman   WELTY 899:98
M....political animal   ARIS 29:56
m. possesses nothing certainly   CABE 183:14
M. proposes   KEMP 461:86
m....proud and yet a wretched thing   DAVI 254:35
m., proud m.   SHAK 758:26
m. reaches old age   MAO 548:9
m.'s affection   GILB 354:98
m.'s a fool to look   MOODY 594:11
m.'s a m.   BURNS 173:47
m. says he likes a woman   HEPB 396:59
m. says what he knows   ROUS 700:47
m.'s behaviour…harmless   SHAW 780:50
m.'s boots   MACC 527:83
m.'s commendation with woman   SHAK 757:81
M.'s condition. Inconstancy   PASC 640:14
M.'s contribution to human history   JIANG 438:50
m.'s corruptions   OTWAY 630:21
m.'s critical actions   ELIOT 303:77
m.'s decision on how to vote   SCHN 719:21
m.'s desire is for the woman   COLE 227:22
m.'s dying   MANN 546:70
m....searches for recognition   MANN 546:74
m.'s education begins   ROUS 700:44
m.'s failures   WARR 889:70
m.'s fall made manifest   MILL 573:48
m.'s first disobedience   MILT 580:91
m.'s gotta do what a m.'s   LADD 484:91
m.'s got to figure   LOUIS 518:5
m. shall be as an hiding place   BIBLE 103:32
m. shall be known in his children   BIBLE 107:48
M. shall not live by bread alone   BIBLE 109:78
M.'s happiness   GIDE 353:84
m.'s heart good to hear   SHAK 737:90
m. should have dinner   LEMAY 502:76
m. should importune me   MONT 592:74
m. should know something   STER 818:90

m. should never be ashamed   POPE 659:89
m. should never think that   TROL 866:86
m. shouldn't fool with booze   FAUL 319:76
m. should rejoice in his own works   BIBLE 100:71
m. should think   MORE 596:58
m.'s image   YEATS 932:32
M.'s inhumanity to M.   BURNS 170:80
M.'s loneliness is but his fear   ONEI 625:91
M.'s love is…a thing apart   BYRON 181:73
M.'s love is of m.'s life   AMIS 14:84
M.'s lovely…power   LOWE 520:50
M.'s natural language   FLAU 327:43
m.'s natural qualities   SHER 788:55
m. so various   DRYD 290:88
M.'s power of selection   DARW 253:10
m.'s reach should exceed   BROW 161:55
m.'s strength is but little   SIMO 792:43
M. stands face to face   CAMUS 187:88
m.'s the gowd   BURNS 173:46
m....successful with his children   EURI 316:15
m.'s unhappiness   PASC 640:16
m. swear he loves me   SHAK 744:88
M.'s word is God in m.   TENN 847:31
m.'s work or his own gifts   MILT 580:88
m.'s worth something   BROW 161:51
m. takes a drink   LEWIS 508:93
m. taketh his sword   BIBLE 107:25
m. talks loudly against religion   STER 818:79
m. telling the truth   JONES 448:92
m. that could look no way   BUNY 166:74
m. that Fortune's buffets   SHAK 754:88
m. that gets drunk   MCGO 532:80
m. that hails you Tom or Jack   COWP 241:60
m. that hath friends   BIBLE 99:41
m. that hath no music   SHAK 741:88
m. that is born   TWAIN 870:81
m. that is born falls into a dream   CONR 234:2
M. that is born of a woman   BOOK 142:33
m. that meddles with cold iron!   BUTL 177:47
m. that men like   NORR 618:64
m. that says when   HAMM 380:21
m. that will nocht quhen he may   HENR 396:50
m. the index of that book   DONNE 282:95
m. the living sepulchre   CLARE 219:44
m. there walked without a mate   MARV 556:76
m. the wonderful   BYRON 181:67
m. to be in love   MORL 598:88
m. to create his own meaning   KUBR 481:33
m. to do nothing   BURKE 169:52
m. to earn his own living   MORE 596:60
m. to han ben in prosperitee   CHAU 208:50
m. to know that he is his own   MONT 592:77
M. to M. the warld o'er   BURNS 173:48
m....too proud to fight   WILS 916:10
m. to reduce women…to imbecility   BROO 156:27
m. to tell how human   MILT 584:99
m. under authority   BIBLE 110:14
M., unlike any other thing   STEI 815:31
m....up against Nature   GABOR 342:80
M. wants but little   HOLM 407:75
m. wants to murder a tiger   SHAW 779:29
m. wants what a woman has—sex   DWOR 296:46
m. was apparently a gentleman   RIDGE 687:78
M. was by Nature Woman's cully   CONG 230:95
M. was made for Joy and Woe   BLAKE 135:68
m. wastes part of his life   JOHN 441:26
m. way out there in the blue   MILL 571:94
m. who any woman might love   BIRD 130:57
m. who believes in giraffes   MITC 588:87
m. who boasts   MENC 565:59
m. who can dominate   WILDE 909:31
m. who can reason   LESS 505:46
m. who cares no more   SOUT 805:7
m. who comes to England   MANS 547:1
m. who conducts himself well   DICK 269:78
m. who didn't wax   KIPL 470:78
M. Who Died Twice   ROBI 690:36
m. who…dies among   WORD 925:7
m. who dies rich   CARN 193:48
m. who does not believe in human   CAST 199:78
m. who does not return   SHAW 779:25
m. who doesn't love oysters   SAKI 710:40
m. who goes to a psychiatrist   GOLD 362:79
m. who has acted   EMER 313:35
m. who has lived many years   HEMI 394:6
m. who has murdered   LEVA 506:52
m. who has no office   SHAW 777:49

sick m. must think — LEWIS 507:79
sick m.'s passport — MARL 552:85
since by m. came death — BIBLE 121:14
sit by and see the blind m. — WALEY 885:91
sit on a m.'s back — TOLS 862:6
slave themselves to m.'s desire — HABI 376:54
small m. can be — MILL 571:93
smith a mighty m. — LONG 515:44
so becomes a m. — SHAK 746:42
Soccer is a m.'s game — CHAR 207:45
solace to m. giffis — BARB 59:52
sole nexus of m. to m. — CARL 193:28
solitary child and solitary m. — ACKR 3:56
So long as m. remains free — DOST 283:10
some great m. — HOOV 411:60
Son of m. shall come in his glory — BIBLE 113:91
sorrow…for a vulgar m. — DRYD 289:57
So this is m. — TATE 837:6
soul of m. — AUBR 39:71
soul of this m. — SHAK 761:31
sovereign'st thing that any m. — SKEL 794:89
spake on that ancient m. — COLE 225:81
span of a m.'s…arms — LEON 504:18
special kind of m. — GILL 356:43
spirit of m. is a good adversary — WILL 913:34
sportsman is a m. who — LEAC 497:71
stamps a m. at once — SHAW 779:39
state of m. — SHAK 775:20
still at least a m. — SCOTT 724:27
straightest road to a m.'s heart — FERN 321:17
strange prodigious creatures, M. — ROCH 691:55
strange what a m. may do — THAC 849:2
strengthened…in the inner m. — BIBLE 122:45
strips a m. of everything — HAZL 388:81
strong m. after sleep — MILT 579:82
strong m. exults in his…ability — POE 656:17
stupid m. is doing something — SHAW 778:78
such a degradation of m.? — BRYAN 163:9
such a disagreeable m. — GILB 354:17
such another m.! — SHAK 765:55
Such was their awe of m. — MILT 583:70
superiority of one m.'s opinion — JAMES 433:45
surely fool a m. — WHITE 903:82
system…makes m. its appendix — FROMM 338:82
Take up the White M.'s burden — KIPL 472:24
teach a wise m. — RABE 676:74
Teach the free m. — AUDEN 40:5
thanks of m. and woman — PAINE 634:88
That m.'s silence — HARDY 381:49
That which once united m. — BOLD 139:41
The greater m. — TENN 847:57
their murdered m. — KEATS 458:27
The Little Disturbances of M. — PALEY 635:8
The m. is dead! — WHIT 906:57
Then a m. will say it — ANCO 15:14
The Reasonable M. — HERB 397:83
therefore the state of m. — MILT 579:67
There is a m. child conceived — BIBLE 93:51
There's not a m. That lives — WORD 925:99
there the m. are as mad — SHAK 755:30
There was an old m. — QUIL 674:47
There was once a m. — KNOX 476:22
thing civilized by M. — MERE 566:95
thinking m.'s television — HAMP 380:25
think like a m. — SIMON 792:36
thin m. inside every fat m. — ORWE 628:52
This m., Comrades — GROM 374:22
This was a m. — SHAK 748:25
Thou art the m. — BIBLE 91:3
Thou madest m. — TENN 842:20
till m. ceases to be — PEAR 645:97
time in a m.'s life — MALA 541:80
time of a m. or woman — WHIT 905:39
tired of being a m. — NERU 611:42
tireless m. of Marshall — ROBI 690:38
'Tis no sin for a m. — SHAK 741:97
To be a poor m. — DU 293:71
To cheat a m. is nothing — GAY 347:86
Toil is m.'s allotment — MELV 564:24
To no m. will we…deny…justice — MAGN 539:28
totality of m., sense — MARI 550:57
to the image, not to the m. — PRICE 668:14
to the last m. — HAIG 376:66
touches this touches a m. — WHIT 905:45
truth in no m. — BEAU 67:17
two civilizers of m. — DISR 277:78
two things no m. — MOSS 600:30

type of m. — TOYN 864:31
understand a m. better — HUGO 421:85
used car from this m.? — ANON 23:81
Use every m. — SHAK 753:66
'Vain m.,' said she — SPEN 809:1
value of a m. — ANON 24:17
value, or worth of a m. — HOBB 404:25
Victory switches from m. to m. — HOMER 409:19
vilify a great m. — POE 657:29
vindicate the ways of God to m. — POPE 660:7
walking dead m. — ANON 25:66
wants to buy a m. — MCCA 528:95
War is to m. — MUSS 605:21
was a self-made m. — HELL 392:58
was a spare m. — AUBR 39:68
Wash That M. — HAMM 380:18
Was m. made stupid — EBER 298:74
wasn't the m. who could do it — JOHN 439:76
Was there a m. dismayed? — TENN 844:76
Was there ever m. had such luck? — SHAK 773:57
watching a m. — BYATT 178:89
way to meet other queer m. — MCKE 534:16
wears m.'s smudge — HOPK 412:83
wed a fair young m. — CAMP 187:81
what a frugal m. annually saves — SMITH 798:46
what a m. does with his solitariness — WHIT 904:11
what a m. would like to be true — BACON 47:59
What a piece of work is a m.! — SHAK 752:57
what drink a m. will have — MARQ 554:35
Whatever each m. can…do — BURKE 168:32
What is great in m. — NIET 615:13
What is m. — BLIX 137:1
What is m. in nature? — PASC 641:28
What m., that thou art mindful — BIBLE 94:87
What m. has made of m. — WORD 924:77
what m. is there of you — BIBLE 110:8
What manner of m. is this — BIBLE 110:18
What m. that sees — SPEN 809:14
What m. thinks of changing — TROL 867:98
what m. will do any good — TROL 866:81
what one m. can devise — WRIS 930:92
whatsoever a m. soweth — BIBLE 122:39
When a m. marries — SHEL 784:67
when a m. should marry? — BACON 48:92
When a m. takes a farm — PARN 639:91
When God at first made m. — HERB 398:16
When I was a young m. — SCHU 721:53
When the military m. approaches — SHAW 778:97
Where m. has manned the trenches — MACG 531:76
where no m. has gone before — RODD 693:89
Where's the m. could ease — PARK 637:44
whether a m. is good or evil — BLAKE 135:75
white m. in Africa — LESS 504:32
whole duty of m. — BIBLE 101:94
whore-master m. — SHAK 762:57
Who's master, who's m. — SWIFT 831:91
Whoso would be a m. — EMER 312:7
wicked m. in the bathroom — EWART 316:23
wife full of words to a quiet m. — BIBLE 108:57
wise m. knows himself to be a fool — SHAK 750:83
within this learned m. — MARL 553:9
wit of m. — WARN 889:67
woman a m. loves — STEV 821:78
woman be more like a m.? — LERN 504:27
woman needs a m. — STEI 816:42
woman…sees much more than a m. — MILL 570:76
woman…to be the toy of m. — WOLL 921:7
woman to hold a m. — SPARK 806:16
Woman to m. — WEBS 894:87
wonderous and fearful in m. — MELV 564:36
working m. into a passive role — ORWE 627:37
work of one extraordinary m. — HUBB 417:8
world an honest m. — LICH 509:22
worm, and no m. — BIBLE 94:98
worst luck any m. could have — HEMI 394:15
Would this m.…ask why? — AUDEN 40:14
wrong m. the woman — HARDY 382:62
Yet each m. kills — WILDE 910:54
You'll be a m., my son! — KIPL 474:68
young m. at the age of twenty-three — DAMR 251:80
young m. cleanse his way? — BIBLE 97:80
young m. will be wiser — TENN 847:39

manage by those who m. it — JOHN 445:41
m. a clever man — KIPL 470:75
m. without butter — GOEB 359:7
managed world is disgracefully m. — FIRB 323:62
management m. can only be properly — JAY 436:97

m. of external things — CARL 191:84
Reagan…lacked m.…skills — ONEI 626:7
manager Want To See The M. — BURR 173:59
managers M.…do things right — BENN 77:60
m. to run their concerns — ROBI 690:38
Manchester M.…mere village — DEFOE 258:21
man-cub m.-c. is a m.-c. — KIPL 471:9
Mandalay Come you back to M. — KIPL 470:86
come you back to M.! — KIPL 470:85
M. has its name — MAUG 561:78
Mandarin great yellow M. — CHES 212:79
M. style — CONN 233:73
Mandelson M.…can skulk in broad
daylight — HOGG 406:63
Manderley went to M. again — DU 294:96
mandrake child a m. root — DONNE 279:39
manger laid him in a m. — BIBLE 115:25
m. for his bed — ALEX 11:24
Mother, the Child and the bare m. — WHIT 904:64
wrapped in the rude m. — MILT 575:93
mangle immense pecuniary M. — DICK 271:20
Manhattan in M.'s Town — HUGH 419:30
mast-hemm'd M. — WHIT 905:41
middle-management of M. — AMIS 14:96
statistics for M. Island — BART 63:26
manhood envied beginning of m. — STEI 816:44
envy men their m. — PANK 636:34
gives m. more approbation — SHAK 757:86
linger in m. — THOR 857:68
M. a struggle — DISR 276:45
m. is cast Down — LAWR 494:94
m., long misled — DRYD 291:16
m.'s beauty — WILDE 907:81
nobility of m. — HUXL 426:10
manhoods hold their m. cheap — SHAK 746:62
mania Composing…is a m. — HONE 409:38
m. for sentences — FLAU 326:26
maniacal mirthless, m. — THUR 860:51
manifest disaster until it is finally m. — MURP 604:1
It was m. to me — TROL 866:88
manifestation teabreaks and…m. — MISH 587:79
manifestations see only the m. — LAO 489:9
manifesto first powerful plain m. — SPEN 807:54
rely on some political m. — JOHN 439:63
upsetting incendiary m. — MARI 550:54
man-in-the-street To the m. — AUDEN 40:9
manipulation m. of…impulses — MILL 573:34
m. of the inventive — LEWIS 508:95
science…system of m. — BOOK 144:79
Manitoba climate of M. — ANON 21:34
mankind All the ills of m. — DUDEK 293:81
an apple damn'd m. — OTWAY 630:23
As I know more of m. — JOHN 446:62
benefit of m. — MACL 535:31
bestow on m. — HOBB 404:23
careless of m. — TENN 839:57
coarse emotion of m. — ELIOT 304:9
common curse of m. — SHAK 757:98
common duty of m. — ROCK 692:77
conclusions at which m. arrive — PALM 635:19
crimes that shame m. — NOON 618:58
deceive and delude m. — EPHO 314:73
deserve better of m. — SWIFT 831:80
destroy in m. the belief — DOST 283:8
development of m. — NIET 615:23
drug used by m. — KIPL 474:83
essential oneness of m. — STEI 814:9
evils m. had to fear — ELIOT 303:87
Example is the school of m. — BURKE 169:51
existence of m. in its power — ADAMS 4:74
Father of m. — WHIT 906:63
fight for m. — SAINT 709:14
for the friend of m. — MOLI 590:35
furnishing m. with the two — SWIFT 830:53
general inclination of all m. — HOBB 404:24
generality of m. — BOSW 145:9
giant leap forward for m. — ARMS 30:78
greatest of m. — DRYD 289:62
great mass of m. — HALL 378:91
half of m. died — MAO 548:10
happiness m. can gain — DRYD 287:19
How beauteous m. is! — SHAK 775:1
I am involved in m. — DONNE 281:85
instinct of m. — TAWN 837:8
judgement Of all m. — SCHI 718:4
last judgment of m. — FRYE 340:35
machines devised by m. — BORE 144:88

m. at least one lesson — MUMF 603:75
m. does not bother — WHIT 904:7
m. faces a crossroads — ALLEN 12:56
M., fear your Lord — KORAN 478:52
m. from superfluous ornament — LOOS 517:70
m. is divisible into two great classes — BEER 70:87
M. is resilient — HELL 392:67
m. love a lover — EMER 312:13
m. minus one — MILL 570:65
M. must put an end to war — KENN 462:18
m. rules its women — CATO 200:97
m.'s concern is charity — POPE 660:21
M. Under The Leash — DISCH 275:28
m., We have created you male and
female — KORAN 479:89
M. won — KHRU 467:3
mass massacre of m. — RUSS 705:57
mass of m. understand it — BAGE 51:89
miseries or credulities of m. — CONR 234:16
motto of m. — LAFO 485:1
my words among m. — SHEL 783:48
Nature has in store for m. — FERMI 321:16
novel of m. — GAUT 347:70
only the wisest of m. — SMITH 799:73
only two Of m. — MILT 582:39
peace for all m. — ANON 23:10
principles of m. — WILS 916:13
progress of m. — SART 715:40
proper study of m. is man — POPE 660:16
proper study of m. is science — RABI 676:79
ride m. — EMER 312:27
shut the gates of mercy on m. — GRAY 369:19
significance for m. — KRAUS 480:12
small step for m. — BROD 153:56
spark that moves m. — SIKO 791:32
Spectator of m. — ADDI 6:10
study of m. is books — HUXL 424:56
Survey m. — JOHN 441:16
tenth of m. — SHAK 770:77
There is no history of m. — POPP 662:92
Three quarters of m. — COTM 238:84
tragedy of m. — WILS 914:70
universal language of m. — LONG 515:40
untold sorrow to m. — UNIT 873:69
war that has ever scourged m. — LLOY 513:3
wisest, brightest, meanest of m. — POPE 660:26
manliness sense of m. — CURZ 249:53
silent m. of grief — GOLD 361:59
manly boy's ideal of a m. career — DISR 276:52
bullies you on m. principles — SHAW 777:65
glorious m. pleasures — WYCH 931:13
manna M. and dates — KEATS 459:40
m., which thou knewest not — BIBLE 89:47
tongue Dropped m. — MILT 581:21
We loathe our m. — DRYD 290:5
manner extraordinary m. — STOP 825:61
m. rude and wild — BELL 72:46
m. which will make — NICH 613:87
poetry is written in a m. — POUND 664:24
to the m. born — SHAK 751:24
treated in…unemotional m. — DOYLE 285:51
urbanity of m. — CHES 212:79
mannerly M. Margery — SKEL 795:90
manners bewrayed…by his m. — SPEN 809:12
blessed with such happy m. — AUST 43:65
catch the M. living — POPE 660:7
cities of men and m. — TENN 839:63
corrupt good m. — BIBLE 121:17
Country m. — MUNRO 603:87
describe morals, m. — TROL 867:7
dress and m. in England — SHAW 777:62
have books for good m. — SHAK 750:91
health and good m. — TAFT 835:78
in divers m. — BIBLE 124:89
Japanese have perfected good m. — THER 851:44
Leave off first for m.' sake — BIBLE 108:60
light in m. — ASCH 35:81
magic of m. — ALCO 10:5
m. and religion of m. — MONT 591:63
m. are far more frightening — JARR 435:83
M. makyth man — WILL 911:3
m. of a dancing master — JOHN 442:30
m. of a lady — FRAN 335:21
m.…of the whole English nation — DRYD 292:45
M.…the need of the plain — WAUGH 892:49
m., virtue, freedom, power — WORD 925:11
Men's evil m. — SHAK 775:24

Men's m. ne'er were viler — JONS 449:34
music marreth men's m. — GALE 343:6
not to his m. — SHAK 740:58
ordered by different m. — DISR 276:53
perfectly good m. — VAND 876:24
Scientists have odious m. — TWAIN 872:37
soften m., but corrupt the heart — BYRON 179:1
teach you better m. — PALM 635:21
Manning manned by M. — BROW 162:80
mannish m. manner of mind — CARY 198:61
manor He that purchases a m. — DONNE 282:94
manservant clothing of a m. — HUGO 421:77
mansion careless of its m. new — MARV 555:57
Jove's court My m. is — MILT 577:25
modest m. — GOLD 361:53
mansionry By his loved m. — SHAK 767:85
mansions Build…stately m. — HOLM 407:82
In my Father's house are many m. — BIBLE 118:9
lasting m. of the dead — CRAB 242:82
mantelpiece remained on the m. — MACN 538:13
mantle Elijah…cast his m. — BIBLE 92:25
m. o' green — TANN 836:91
thread from life's frayed m. — ABU 1:14
Thy m. good — SHAK 738:17
twitched his m. blue — MILT 578:59
mantles their rings or green m. — BALL 56:88
mantraps laws and sets m. — LOWE 519:26
Mantua M. brought me life — VIRG 882:33
manufacture economy of a m. — BABB 45:19
m. and in handicrafts — MARX 558:13
manufactures greater part of m. — HALL 378:91
manufacturing m. base — TSON 869:54
m. profits are lowered — RICA 684:32
persists in an article — HONE 409:27
manunkind this busy monster, m. — CUMM 248:17
manure civilization…the m. — CONN 233:80
m., lime, piled against — ROET 694:2
natural m. — JEFF 436:15
smell of m. — WHITE 903:83
smelt a lot of mule m. — WILL 912:7
manuscript chopped the m. — COWL 240:39
manuscripts Lenin's m. — MAO 548:15
many Done because we are too m. — HARDY 382:69
election by the incompetent m. — SHAW 778:5
m. be called, but few chosen — BIBLE 113:78
M. things are formidable — SOPH 804:83
not m. of your nation — SHAK 746:45
so much been owed by so m. — CHUR 216:78
the m. change and pass — SHEL 786:7
many-headed m.-h. monster — POPE 661:56
many-maned M.-m. scud-thumper — UPDI 874:74
map Agatha has found it on the m. — WILDE 908:15
creating in the mind a m. — SPEN 807:56
false m. of the world — ORWE 629:81
m. of the world shows no country — WINN 917:24
Marxism…m. in a forest — CAST 199:79
my head is a m. — FIEL 322:36
nor to make a m. — THES 851:51
on any m. of the world — ROOS 695:39
Roll up that m. — PITT 653:48
Sorrow…cannot be rolled up like a m. — CH 213:10
tide across a m. — LOWE 521:62
maple m. seldom inward sound — SPEN 808:73
maps all the m. change — LEGU 501:61
Geography is about M. — BENT 77:74
relief m. of…unhappiness — FITZ 325:11
the m. are spread — YEATS 934:63
mar did not make, and cannot m. — ARNO 31:2
Maradona with a ball M. could — PLAT 654:74
Marathon From M. to Waterloo — GILB 354:99
mountains look on M. — BYRON 182:87
trivial skirmish fought near M. — GRAV 367:71
marble Forget thyself to m. — MILT 576:14
Glowed on the m. — ELIOT 306:56
hammering m. instead — THOR 857:79
How unlike m. was that face — KEATS 459:46
made up of m. and mud — HAWT 386:43
m. block doth not confine — MICH 568:33
m. to retain — BYRON 181:59
modelled in m. — BIRD 130:58
Not m. nor the gilded — SHAK 771:21
ponderous and m. jaws — TWAIN 871:7
portrait in m. — BERN 81:52
The pure m. air — MILT 582:50
this in m. — BEAU 67:10
winged Lion's m. piles — BYRON 180:31
marble-hearted m.-h. fiend — SHAK 762:62

marbles golf…playing m. — CHES 213:4
M. of the dancing floor — YEATS 934:58
put away their rattles, m. — MORE 597:68
where they played m. — KIPL 472:28
March ashbuds in the front of M. — TENN 840:69
beware the ides of M. — SHAK 747:72
Channel in the mad M. days — MASE 559:27
droghte of M. — CHAU 208:66
M. is the month — KEIL 460:72
sturdy M. with brows — SPEN 809:15
winds of M. — SHAK 770:86
march m. of a nation — PARN 639:93
m. of intellect — SOUT 805:12
m. of only a few hours — PEARY 645:2
m. of stupidity — DELI 261:76
mare old m. might droop — SMITH 799:64
remember Tam o' Shanter's m. — BURNS 172:25
son of a m. — AIDAN 9:77
Though Patience be a tired m. — SHAK 745:34
Tom Pearce, lend me your grey m. — BALL 57:96
Mareotic Round the M. Lake — YEATS 934:65
Margaret As Merry M. — SKEL 795:91
It is M. you mourn for — HOPK 412:95
M., are you grieving — HOPK 412:93
M.…at her happiest confronting political
dragons — MAJOR 541:75
marge page having an ample m. — TENN 846:14
Margery Mannerly M. — SKEL 795:90
margin m. is too narrow — FERM 321:15
m. of a bay — WORD 927:41
meander through a meadow of m. — SHER 787:51
vanishes over the m. — TENN 848:72
whose m. fades — TENN 839:63
marginality epitomized m. — ECON 298:79
margins work in the m. — DELI 261:77
Marie I am M. of Roumania — PARK 638:60
king in M. Antoinette — MORL 598:89
marijuana experimented with m. — CLIN 221:88
marinated I am well m. — OLSEN 624:73
mariner It is an ancient M. — COLE 225:80
M. hath his will — COLE 225:81
mariners m. had fabled news — LOWE 520:42
My m. — TENN 840:66
not yet self-determined by White M. — ONEI 625:87
rest ye, brother m. — TENN 839:58
mark If you would hit the m. — LONG 516:65
m. of high civilisation — BERL 80:21
m.…of the beast — BIBLE 126:67
m. of the mint — CHES 212:93
m. of the philosopher — SOCR 803:55
m. upon Cain — BIBLE 86:61
press toward the m. — BIBLE 123:58
Progress, man's distinctive m. — BROW 162:74
Some m. of virtue — SHAK 740:70
this m. I saw — SHEL 783:37
marked in M. Harborough — CHES 213:2
She m. thee there — POPE 662:80
market black m. universities — ZELD 936:91
commodities m. — TYSON 873:52
free competition of the m. — RICA 684:33
In m., hearth and field — KIPL 474:75
kirk or m. — STEV 822:97
knowledge is bought in the m. — CLOU 222:18
m. is so vulgarly democratic — KRIS 481:17
no way…can buck the m. — THAT 851:35
offering them on the m. — PAVL 644:80
price that the m. sets — FRIE 337:64
studies alleging that m. downturns — SAMU 712:80
which we call the m. — HAYEK 387:60
You can't beat the m. — BART 63:25
market-days m.-d. are wearing late — BURNS 172:12
marketing M.…feeding the poop — COUP 238:94
market-place in the fair and the m. p. — PARN 639:91
markings treasured for their m. — RAINE 677:94
marks indelible m. of that mould — SCHR 720:43
leaves the m. of his feet — LEAC 496:56
M. of weakness, m. of woe — BLAKE 135:58
m. the first place — PARK 637:47
Signor Benedick. Nobody m. you — SHAK 744:86
terrible m. of the beast — HARDY 382:58
marksmen Men, you are all m. — PUTN 673:21
Marlbro M.'s mighty soul — ADDI 5:4
marlet temple-haunting m. — SHAK 767:85
Marlowe M., bathed in…springs — DRAY 287:5
marriage blessings of m. — SHAW 778:1
comedies are ended by a m. — BYRON 182:85
constraints aping m. — UPDI 874:77

masculine adoption of the m. — GREER 372:88
dignified as Latin, m. — QUIL 674:44
enviable, boast-worthy, m. event — STEI 816:44
feminine spouse to the m. animal — DIAZ 265:50
m. for a woman to be melancholy — WOLL 921:7
m. in the woman — KENT 464:59
m. values that prevail — WOOLF 922:46
say she has a m. mind — FULL 341:49
sombre-suited m. world — WARN 889:66
This m. invisibility — DUNN 295:17
mask husband wears a m. — MARI 550:59
loathsome m. has fallen — SHEL 785:81
m. like Castlereagh — SHEL 783:36
m. of a vulgar soul — MAUG 561:80
m. of prevailing morals — BEAU 66:2
monkey's m. reveals the monkey — BASHO 63:41
No m. like open truth — CONG 231:11
obliged to throw off the m. — PARN 639:92
pluck the m. from…face of the Pharisee — BRON 155:82
profound loves the m. — NIET 615:20
thousand-year-old m. — ROSE 697:65
We wear the m. that grins — DUNB 294:98
masked love in desolation m. — SHEL 785:99
masks are but as pasteboard m. — MELV 564:30
trying on gas-m. — CHAM 204:61
masochism spirit of national m. — AGNEW 8:73
masonry bind…into the social m. — WELLS 898:75
masons professionals, like…m. — EICH 301:29
masquerade miss a m. — POPE 659:70
truth in m. — BYRON 182:93
masquerading m. knight-errant — PARN 639:92
mass blessed mutter of the m. — BROW 161:33
broad m. of a nation — HITL 404:17
Chaos, a rough unordered m. — OVID 631:42
from its m.Walls — BYRON 180:40
go to M. every day — BELL 72:52
haven't been to m. for years — WILS 915:72
malicious…crapulous m. — ADAMS 5:91
m. of the nation — TWAIN 871:16
ocean's liquid m. — WORD 928:52
opium for every conceivable m. — KENN 462:4
The m. of men — THOR 857:83
We were one m. — DRYD 289:60
massacre mass m. of mankind — RUSS 705:57
not as sudden as a m. — TWAIN 870:79
Massermann M., the cat man — ANON 22:70
masses anything said about the m. — PRIE 668:25
art of the m. — HALL 378:92
back the m. — GLAD 359:93
benighted m. of wishful thinkers — QUINE 675:52
bow ye m.! — GILB 354:10
Carving is interrelated m. — HEPW 396:61
educate the m. — OSLER 630:16
gathered itself…into m. — CARL 191:82
Government…exasperates the m. — REED 682:88
intelligence of the great m. — MENC 565:63
make the m. prosperous — BRYAN 163:8
m. yearning to breathe — LAZA 496:51
paper which the m. call money — ANDR 16:25
philosopher should judge the m. — CYRA 250:59
The m. are wrong — VIAN 880:76
tumult of the m. — ALCU 10:8
wide support of the m. — LENIN 502:82
masseur m. called Harold — WOOD 921:17
Massey M. won't be satisfied — KAUF 455:54
mast bends the gallant m. — CUNN 248:24
master belonging to the m. — STOWE 826:72
brave m. was no more — MACA 527:78
condemned by a faceless m. — PAZ 644:88
disciple is not above his m. — BIBLE 111:27
does not excel his m. — LEON 503:15
do not M. or Campbell me — SCOTT 724:32
great M. so to sympathize — MILT 575:93
Has a new m. — SHAK 774:88
himself to be my m. — TUTU 870:70
In order to become the m. — DE 259:43
insufferable m. — JEFF 436:4
Like m. like man — PETR 649:83
man…becomes a m. in that science — COLL 227:33
Man…is m. of everything — MILL 573:37
Man is the m. of things — SWIN 833:45
marvel thy m. hath not — SHAK 734:88
m. a grief — SHAK 745:12
m., a mistress and two slaves — BIER 129:34
m. minds of all nations — TWAIN 871:16
m.-mistress of my passion — SHAK 771:7
M. morality — NIET 616:24

m. of himself — MASS 559:42
m. of his fate — TENN 846:6
m. of his trade — DRAY 287:7
m. or servant of the state — KING 468:41
M.: records prove the title — ARLO 30:62
maxim of every prudent m. — SMITH 798:48
no more subtle m. — TENN 846:22
not make dreams your m. — KIPL 473:67
O divine M. — FRAN 334:98
Oh my divine m.! — HUGO 420:73
old clothes know who's m. — SHER 787:37
O m. doctor, he is past — MASS 560:48
only the m. shall praise — KIPL 472:20
Our m.Caesar — YEATS 934:63
poet is a m. of the quotidian — PRIT 669:54
press…a terrible m. — COOP 236:54
Rabboni; which is to say, M. — BIBLE 118:23
slave has but one m. — LABR 483:67
village m. taught his little school — GOLD 361:54
when I hae a gude m. — SCOTT 724:29
which is to be m. — CARR 196:11
Who's m., who's man — SWIFT 831:91
Without a m.…I…work — ARET 29:42
work of the m. — LEON 503:8
world with her divine M. — MILT 579:79
mastered m. whatever was — LOWE 520:33
only athletic sport I m. — JERR 438:43
masterpiece cradle of a new m. — YEATS 933:39
driven to create a m. — SELF 727:80
friend…the m. of nature — EMER 312:14
function…is to produce a m. — CONN 233:75
great and glorious m. — MONT 592:85
knows, at first sight, a m. — POUND 665:41
m. of art has…a fixed place — EMER 312:20
Nature's great m. — DONNE 280:47
no m. can be anything — MARI 550:52
now hath made his m. — SHAK 767:9
obscure unfinished m. — NABO 606:36
masterpieces creation of genuine m. — DALI 251:73
m. having one-night stands — RAUS 679:33
masters any of those m. — MCCU 529:23
beasts are our m. — FLET 328:70
copying the m. — INGR 429:64
fall from their m.' table — BIBLE 112:60
made them slave m. — MORR 599:6
m. at the moment — SHAW 782:4
m. of different bits of man — LAWR 495:33
m. of their fates — SHAK 747:76
m.' thoughts — MARL 551:77
new m. — HALI 378:89
not m. of our own affections — ETHE 315:96
Old M.: how well they understood — AUDEN 40:90
people are the m. — BURKE 168:24
Power of new M. — ALBE 10:99
relations with their m. — MILL 570:75
serve two m. — BIBLE 110:1
The people are the m. — BLAIR 132:5
Unmarried men…best m. — BACON 48:89
mastery Love…constreyned by m. — CHAU 209:87
m. of the thing! — HOPK 412:90
m. of vocabulary and syntax — SAYE 717:86
mast-hemm'd m.-h. Manhattan — WHIT 905:41
mastiff trusty m. that is to watch — LLOY 513:95
mastodons calling to Aunt like m. — WODE 919:58
masturbation Don't knock m. — ALLEN 12:54
M. is the thinking man's television — HAMP 380:25
mat foot in the m. — GROS 374:24
worst room, with m. half-hung — POPE 660:5
match burnt m. skating in a urinal — CRANE 243:25
diploma is a lighted m. — KOCH 476:27
Honour is like a m. — PAGN 634:85
m. flickers — STEV 822:99
m. its military strength — KENN 463:37
strike a m. — AMIS 15:98
matchboxes substitute…empty m. — DOUG 283:23
matches as m. in the rough — DICK 268:43
extravagant m. — GILB 355:28
have to have a box of m. — HOME 409:12
little I repair to the m. — THOM 855:39
playing with a box of m. — HARL 383:83
With that stick of m. — MAND 544:51
mate Among the beasts no m. — MILT 584:5
Consciousness, her awful M. — DICK 272:62
lady's ta'en another m. — BALL 56:92
man there walked without a m. — MARV 556:76
m. with its complement of men — WRIG 929:72
Not…one solitary m. — EGAN 301:24

people should m. for life — ALLEN 12:55
shearing m. who wrote it — PATE 642:55
mated But we was badly m. — STRO 827:95
material basic m. a writer works with — CATH 200:92
body and m. substance — CARL 193:34
Corridors—surpassing M. Place — DICK 272:65
endowed m. forces with — MARX 558:8
external m. things — LOCKE 514:18
From a m. and spiritual terrain — FULL 341:59
gathers its m. from the flowers — BACON 47:60
good a m.…to build a life from — CAREY 190:65
good m. for poetry — WILL 914:64
living in a m. world — MADO 538:22
make its m.…interesting — BEAV 67:27
march of m. ugliness — WHITE 903:96
m.…and the moral — DEWEY 264:43
m. is our own flesh — THOR 857:79
m. position of the worker — MARX 558:6
moral or a m. one — ARNO 33:34
Nothing is m. in space — ROSSO 698:7
only objects in the m. universe — FORS 331:50
so many people…for m. benefits — COLU 229:62
universe…as a m. system — PAGE 633:79
world of m. life — ARNO 33:49
materialism deteriorate into m. — MOLT 590:46
inhuman in its m. — WILS 915:77
materialist m. of all great religions — TEMP 838:33
materials action…essential m.? — CARL 192:15
m. for conversation — JOHN 442:52
m. of reason and knowledge — LOCKE 514:17
raw m. out of which — TEMP 838:35
sculptor can use twenty different m. — BOCC 138:27
she begins to gather the m. — OCON 622:26
maternity m. to women — MUSS 605:21
woman…cursed in her m. — STAN 812:67
mates thuctheththion of m. — BENT 78:79
very popular among his m. — EWART 316:26
math be quite straightforward — GATES 347:62
M. was my worst subject — TRIL 865:65
Mathematica Principia M. — RUSS 705:56
mathematical m. concepts — GIBS 353:76
m. elegance — GREE 372:83
m. or philosophical author — WHIT 904:5
Moriarty of m. celebrity — DOYLE 285:70
must be a m. science — JEVO 438:44
one m., the other…intuitive — PASC 640:5
The m. is that evident aspect — HEID 391:44
mathematician m. is a blind man — DARW 253:18
trifles in which a m. — MACA 526:61
mathematicians m.…cabbages — BOYD 147:45
mathematics All science requires m. — BACON 50:71
Angling…like m. — WALT 888:46
Between the penis and m. — CELI 202:34
creative people hate m. — ISSI 431:95
extensive use of m. — HAYEK 387:61
laws of m.…are not certain — EINS 302:47
m. as surely as in poetry — RUSS 705:44
M. is the door — BACON 50:72
M. is thought moving — WHIT 904:10
m., orthography, geometry — DICK 267:99
M. possesses not only truth — RUSS 705:39
no one ignorant of m. — PLATO 654:75
of flight, of m., of physics — HEMI 394:17
order and mystical m. — BROW 159:96
secret of success in m. — LEHR 502:71
ugly m. — HARDY 381:45
Vanity of m.! — FRED 336:35
ways to teach m. — NEWM 612:60
maths M. is the purest science — BROW 160:17
Matilda a-waltzing M. with me — PATE 642:54
M. told such Dreadful Lies — BELL 73:58
mating for eating, not m. — FERB 320:99
matrimony argument in favour of m. — AUST 43:89
critical period in m. — HERB 397:84
holy estate of M. — BOOK 142:24
holy estate of M. — BOOK 142:25
in holy M. — BOOK 142:18
in holy M. — BOOK 142:19
m.…was also a legalized way of
committing assault — EMEC 312:99
more of love than of m. — GOLD 361:46
not be joined together in holy M. — BOOK 142:18
respectable as that of m. — TROL 866:75
safest in m.…a little aversion — SHER 787:35
Without thinking…of men or m. — AUST 43:67
matron sober-suited m. — SHAK 736:63
worn m. smiles — WHIT 906:56

matrons stout m. — GILL 356:40
matter Does it m.? — SASS 716:64
  doesn't so much m. what you do — JAMES 433:50
  few things m. at all — BALF 55:58
  here and now cease to m. — ELIOT 308:26
  here's no great m. — ELIOT 304:22
  if it is it doesn't m.! — GILB 355:30
  is no 'living m.' — MONOD 591:55
  least m. dear to Him — AUDEN 40:12
  living and non-living m. — PAGE 633:79
  Marriage is a m. — SHAK 729:50
  m. is the scaffolding — THOM 855:33
  m. of life and death — SHAN 776:28
  More m. with less art — SHAK 752:43
  no rights in this m. — ROET 694:4
  no subject m. — DAVIS 256:63
  not the m. of the work — GLAS 359:97
  obscurity of the m. — PROT 670:65
  order…this m. better — STER 818:97
  removing the m. of sin — MILT 579:76
  some arduous and difficult m. — SIDN 790:98
  straightforward a m. — RUSK 704:15
  subsists on the m. he destroys — BELL 74:92
  that great renovator of m. — OVID 631:47
  then he's full of m. — SHAK 749:36
  thet's wots the m. with you — SHAW 779:35
  this high m. — WORD 929:65
  throat of well-printed m. — MORR 598:98
  Vain m. is worse — BACON 46:40
  when all the m.'s spent — DANI 252:87
  Why, what's the m. — SHAK 745:26
matter-of-fact m.-o.-f. young man — GILB 354:6
matters m. just as little — SHAW 778:95
  m. not how a man dies — JOHN 444:89
  m. outside…everyday experience — CONR 235:17
  questions about the greater m. — ARIS 29:49
  read strange m. — SHAK 766:83
  suspect his taste in higher m. — LAMB 486:40
  What can I do that m.? — SPEN 807:53
  what m. in your life — RUSH 703:87
Matthew saw a man, named M. — BIBLE 111:19
  Sir M. left the room — LINK 511:56
mattress cold porridge on a damp m. — BRID 152:29
  gasping on a little flock m. — DICK 266:87
  snug as a feather m. — ANGE 17:40
mature have in our m. years — TROL 866:85
  m. imagination of a man — KEATS 457:99
  m. poets steal — ELIOT 305:49
maturity wisdoms of m. — LIVE 512:80
Maud M. is not seventeen — TENN 845:86
maul not afraid…of a 'm.' — ANON 21:30
maunder Let her m. and mumble — CARL 192:4
mausoleum mouth…as its m. — AMIS 14:82
mausoleums m. for his enemies — LINK 511:56
mavis m. and merle are singing — SCOTT 723:9
mawkishness thence proceeds m. — KEATS 457:99
maws feed the m. — KEYN 466:86
maxim essential m. of your liberties — PITT 653:42
  grounded m. So rife — MILT 586:56
  M. Gun — BELL 72:51
  m. is worthy of the fool — MACA 525:43
  m. of every prudent master — SMITH 798:48
  so useless as a general m. — MACA 525:44
  will that my m. — KANT 455:44
maxims cardinal m. of guerrilla war — KISS 475:90
  m., of self-justification — EDGE 299:93
maximum m. of temptation — SHAW 778:8
May 21st M.—a glorious day — WORD 929:68
  airiest M.? — GRAV 367:68
  at least the seventh of M. — TROL 866:76
  darling buds of M. — SHAK 771:5
  end of M. — HOUS 415:70
  From M. to December — ANDE 16:20
  Maids are M. — SHAK 750:79
  M.'s new-fangled shows — SHAK 733:71
  M. will be fine next year — HOUS 416:71
  mid-m.'s eldest child — KEATS 460:61
  moonlight-coloured m. — SHEL 787:25
  nightingale when M. is past — CAREW 190:60
  that the moneth of M. — MALO 542:10
  wife left you in M. — NORD 618:60
  world is white with M. — TENN 847:41
maybe definite m. — GOLD 362:86
May-day M.-d. freshness amidst — MORR 598:98
Maying let's go a M. — HERR 400:44
mayonnaise M.…One of the sauces — BIER 129:35
mayor longer to elect a M. for London — WATE 890:94

lord m. of Birmingham — LLOY 514:8
  my Lord M. commands — PEPYS 647:42
  tart who has…married the m. — BAXT 65:88
maypole where's the M. in the Strand — BRAM 150:88
May-poles sing of M.-p. — HERR 399:33
maze A mighty m.! — POPE 660:6
  every m. of quick — TENN 844:63
  law seems like a sort of m. — MORT 599:13
  Life is a m. — CONN 233:78
  Philosophy to him was…a m. — SANT 714:21
  the m. of schools — POPE 658:51
  through the watery m. — MARV 557:81
  wander in that golden m. — DRYD 287:16
MCC where the M. ends — PRIE 668:26
McCarthyism M. is Americanism — MCCA 527:94
McGrew dangerous Dan M. — SERV 728:3
Mcjob M.…no-future job — COUP 238:89
McLuhan M. put a telescope — SMITH 797:36
McNamara M.'s war — MCNA 537:90
McTavish Against the clan M. — AYTO 45:16
me gone up and met m. — HOFF 406:49
  I most delight in M. — CAMP 186:57
  M., evidently — HUGH 419:47
  not with m. is against m. — BIBLE 111:40
  soul is never required of m. — SMITH 800:4
  trouble with m. — SALI 711:57
mea see m. bat — GRACE 365:32
mead By the stream and o'er the m. — BLAKE 133:29
meadow a m. of margin — SHER 787:51
  Burn-mill m. — WORD 927:30
  in m. or plain — SWIN 832:18
  m., grove, and stream — WORD 926:21
  painted m., or a purling stream — ADDI 5:3
  Winter scourged the m. — ROBE 689:19
meadows among green aits and m. — DICK 269:79
  by-path m. — STEV 821:87
  enamelled m. with filigree hedges — WALP 887:23
  Fair these broad m. — GALT 344:29
  floor the m. with cement — MACL 535:45
  golden face the m. green — SHAK 771:16
  Golden lie the m. — MERE 567:96
  lover of the m. — WORD 924:72
  m. fresh and gay — MARV 556:70
  m. runnels — KEATS 457:4
  M. trim with daisies — MILT 576:8
  undulating green m. — HUXL 425:79
  Up from the m. — WHIT 906:61
  variety of gardens, m. — MOORE 595:26
meadowsweet timothy-tops and m. — ROBE 689:18
meagre m. hill of kernels — RANS 679:23
  One composition is m. — DIDE 274:1
meal Breakfast is the one m. — VAND 876:24
  can't fake…a good m. — BURR 173:60
  evening m. — BARL 60:58
  m. was large — PRIOR 669:39
  Salad is not a m. — LEBO 499:9
meals cooking three m. a day — PLATH 654:62
  good m. that I…am wearing — BUSH 175:89
  keep with you at m. — SHAK 747:85
  lessen thy M. — FRAN 334:7
mealy M. boys, and beef-faced boys — DICK 267:94
mean abhor…the m. — CURZ 249:53
  dull and m. — WHIT 906:60
  family talk, m. and worried — COMP 229:70
  Happy the golden m.! — MASS 560:50
  I m. what I say — CARR 195:71
  improved m. — THOR 857:84
  m. between nothing and everything — PASC 641:28
  m. between two vices — ARIS 29:52
  meanly admires m. things — THAC 849:95
  no m. city — BIBLE 119:54
  too m. to be your queen — SHAK 730:79
  woman of m. understanding — AUST 42:62
meaner m. things To low ambition — POPE 660:6
  She must take m. things — ELIOT 303:98
meanest wisest, brightest, m. — POPE 660:26
meaning control the m. of words — DICK 265:61
  experience but missed the m. — ELIOT 308:30
  Free from all m. — DRYD 290:99
  Has no m. — SNYD 802:48
  husk of m. — ELIOT 309:39
  Is there a m. to music? — COPL 237:65
  it lacks m. — PAZ 644:90
  language charged with m. — POUND 665:47
  man to create his own m. — KUBR 481:33
  m. is my meat and drink — BROW 161:39
  m., not to find yours — RUSK 704:23

m. of the Lost Generation — KERO 464:65
  no definite and unquestionable m. — SART 715:41
  precise m. of a word — BAND 58:25
  Religion…gives m. to all — WHIT 904:8
  richest without m. — RUSK 703:2
  to some faint m. make pretence — DRYD 288:49
  true m. of religion — ARNO 34:61
meaningless creative world…m. — SPEN 807:65
  half of what she wrote would be m. — CHAN 205:83
meaninglessness very m. of life — KUBR 481:33
meanings let my m. show — CAMP 186:60
  Minding our m. — AUDEN 40:12
  two m. packed up into one word — CARR 196:13
  VALUE…has two different m. — SMITH 797:41
  war…an openness about the m. — DALL 251:75
  wrestle…words and m. — ELIOT 308:15
meanness land of m. — BYRON 179:5
  vice of m. — THOM 856:50
meannesses assorted m. — GILL 355:39
means best ends by the best m. — HUTC 424:51
  by defective m. — WILL 913:47
  doubled their m. of consuming — MILL 570:59
  end may justify the m. — TROT 868:21
  good…By all the m. — WESL 900:20
  grant…that my m. may lie — COWL 240:35
  honestly and deeply m. — JAMES 434:69
  improve the m. — HUXL 425:83
  Increased m. and increased leisure — DISR 277:78
  m. employed determine the nature — HUXL 425:82
  m. nothing in this country — GOLD 361:34
  m. of grace — BOOK 141:84
  m. of increasing her degradation — STAN 812:65
  m. of procuring respect — JOHN 445:17
  m. of rising in the world — JOHN 444:10
  m.…to satisfy our desires — PREV 668:12
  m. which have never yet been tried — BACON 47:63
  never simply as a m. — KANT 455:45
  No one m. all he says — ADAMS 4:86
  Perfections of m. — EINS 301:39
  persons of small m. — ELIOT 303:72
  Power is not a m. — ORWE 630:5
  report what he m. — ANON 23:92
  Sceptical scrutiny is the m. — SAGAN 708:6
  take the m. whereby I live — SHAK 740:84
  took away…their m. of support — SHER 787:33
  unapproachable by any other m. — LEAV 498:98
  uniformity of their m. — FUSE 342:74
  We call that a man's m. — DONNE 282:94
meant it's what I m. — VAUG 877:41
  m. than meets the ear — MILT 577:19
  said what I m. — STEV 820:51
Meany M. could run for President — DOLE 278:11
measles Love is like the m. — JERO 437:29
  Love iz like the m. — BILL 130:50
  Love's like the m. — JERR 437:40
measure beyond m. astonished — BIBLE 114:71
  full m. of their fate — CRANE 243:19
  good m., pressed down — BIBLE 115:31
  Man is the m. of all things — PROT 670:65
  m. and the choice — JOHN 441:20
  m. by thy deeds — SHAK 772:28
  m. of love — LEWIN 507:69
  m. of public support — TIMES 861:76
  m. of the universe — SHEL 785:78
  m. shadows — HUBB 418:11
  m. still for m. — SHAK 758:47
  m. up to their destiny — APOL 27:18
  modernness is the m. of merit — EMER 313:34
  move in m. — ELIOT 309:44
  No one had any m. — PERK 648:67
  number, weigh and m. — HALES 377:81
  Number, Weight, or M. — PETTY 650:86
  Shrunk to this little m.? — SHAK 748:99
  There is a m. in things — HORA 414:35
  To the beat of the m. — POUND 665:53
  with what m. ye mete — BIBLE 114:11
  with what m. ye mete — BIBLE 110:4
measured m. at the extremities — JAY 436:98
  m. by his worth — SHAK 769:47
measurement ghostly errors of m. — HUBB 418:11
measurements terms of m. — MYRD 605:26
measures Better than all m. — SHEL 784:62
  In buskined m. move — GRAY 370:35
  not changed my m. — ANNE 17:53
  relax my expansionist m. — KEYN 465:85
measuring art of m. — NEWT 612:73
measuring-rod m.-r. of distance — RILKE 687:87

M. are born makers   WALC 884:79
M. are but children   DRYD 289:63
M. are but gilded loam   SHAK 734:99
m....are discriminated against   MEIR 563:13
m. are equal before a fish   HOOV 411:62
m. are good-looking   KEIL 460:69
m. are grown mechanical in head   CARL 191:83
M. are like the earth   SCHR 720:41
M. are lived over again   BROW 158:61
m. are merriest   SHAK 745:31
M. are mistaken   SPIN 810:25
m. are nearly always willing   CAES 184:23
m. are never so good   MACK 534:22
m. are not hanged   HALI 378:85
m. are not made for hours   RABE 676:72
m. aren't attracted to me   LEE 500:31
m. are rewarded   SZASZ 834:62
M. are so romantic   WELD 897:43
m. are still   MACN 538:4
m. are the Brahmin   STAN 812:64
M. are the only animals   MENC 566:79
m. are to wait for liberty   MACA 525:43
M. are very fragile   STEP 817:60
m. as angels without feminine   MILT 585:21
m. at sometime were masters   SHAK 747:76
m. at whiles are sober   HOUS 416:74
m. call earth   MILT 577:25
m. cannot suspend their fate   DEFOE 258:12
m. can tell me things   MITC 588:92
m....capable of every wickedness   CONR 234:15
M. creep, Not walk   WHIT 906:60
m. dare trust themselves   SHAK 762:42
m. decay   GOLD 361:52
m. do not learn very much   HUXL 426:99
M. don't and can't   RUSK 704:35
M. don't know women   TROL 866:89
m. dream, but not equally   LAWR 495:38
M....employ their reason   WOLL 921:4
M. enter local politics   PARK 639:86
m....expect brick   ASTE 36:21
M. fear death   BACON 47:73
m. feel a little more secure   MORE 597:64
M. first make slaves   DOUG 284:38
m. from the planet Earth   ANON 23:10
M. from whom my ways begin   BLUN 137:11
m. have a much better time   MENC 565:70
m. have died from time to time   SHAK 750:77
M. have every advantage   AUST 44:97
m. have lost their reason!   SHAK 748:7
m. have their price   WALP 888:42
M. ignorant of letters   SAND 713:17
m. ill at ease   HAWT 386:46
m. in appetite   BACON 49:48
m. in a smoke-filled room   SIMP 793:48
m. in brotherhood   NOON 618:58
m. in considerable number   MILL 570:77
m. in every generation   MILL 573:38
M. in great fortunes   BACON 48:4
M. in great place   BACON 48:99
m. in the habits of women   CHAR 207:31
m....in their old age   POPE 659:91
m. into their chief providers   MILLS 574:69
m. it hurt when it fell   DONNE 281:79
m. kill the fat swine   ANON 19:80
m. know so little of m.   DU 293:72
M. learn while they teach   SENE 727:91
m. Leaving the gardens   LARK 490:31
m. liked to put me down   OKEE 623:60
m., like satyrs grazing   MARL 552:89
m. liking their fathers   BRAD 148:57
m. loved darkness   BIBLE 117:82
M. love in haste   BYRON 182:94
m. may come   TENN 846:3
M. might as well project   LARD 490:14
m. mispronounce it   MORL 598:84
m. most good   SHAK 739:27
M. multiply like Mice   CANT 188:18
M. must endure   SHAK 764:99
M. must learn now   SHAK 762:46
m. must needs abide   SHAK 730:81
m. must walk   POPE 661:58
M., my brothers   TENN 840:81
m. naturally desire knowledge   ARIS 29:48
M. not afraid of God   POPE 661:62
M. of any other class   LODGE 515:29
M. of business   BAGE 51:93
m. of culture   ARNO 33:55

M. of England   SHEL 784:53
m. of experiment   BACON 47:60
m. of genius   DELA 260:58
m. of iron   ALBA 9:86
m. of judgement frame   MARL 552:84
m. of like passions   BIBLE 119:43
m. of measured merriment   LEWIS 507:89
m. of our time   MACA 525:40
M. of power   FOOT 329:93
m. of science   MILL 572:14
M. of sound sense   PLATO 655:83
m. of the hour   HAMM 379:8
m. of the present age   OVER 631:38
m. of the West   WEIL 896:26
m. of the world   DICK 266:83
m. only become great   DE 259:34
m. out of servitude   EMER 313:45
M. reverence one another   THOR 857:70
M. see objects   FOWL 332:67
M. seldom make passes   PARK 638:63
M.'s evil manners   SHAK 775:24
M. should be either treated   MACH 533:97
m. should have a...feeling   LAUR 492:72
m. should put an enemy   SHAK 760:80
M. shut their doors   SHAK 762:44
m. sit and hear   KEATS 460:59
M.'s manners   JONS 449:34
M., some to business   POPE 661:49
m. so old as we   SHAK 735:35
m....spread it around   BAIN 52:13
m. started at the intelligence   SOUT 805:9
m....succeed through the help of their wives   LEE 500:47
m.'s watch upon the world   MACL 535:41
M. talk of killing time   BOUC 146:18
m. that are dying   JEFF 436:8
m. that God made mad   CHES 212:73
m. that make a city   NICI 614:91
m. that strove with gods   TENN 840:66
m. that women marry   LONG 516:66
m., their rights and nothing more   ANTH 27:8
M.! The only animal   LAWR 494:10
m. there are love not a gaping pig   SHAK 740:77
M. thin away to insignificance   HARDY 381:51
m. too profoundly convinced   READ 680:47
m. to take their exits   WEBS 895:18
m. trying to be writers   JONES 447:88
m. walk proudly through the earth   RAND 678:14
m. were deceivers   SHAK 744:6
m. were only capable   MILL 572:31
m. were the answer   BARN 60:71
m. who are as various as the sands   FORS 331:46
m. who are not historians   FORS 331:49
m. who argues by increments   BYATT 178:91
m. who borrow   LAMB 487:51
m. who had never seen a horse   BRIN 153:41
m. who have minded   WOOLF 922:45
m. who live with   NIEB 614:97
m. who really believe in themselves   CHES 211:59
m. who say yes, lie   MELV 564:42
M.Whose Lives Are Money   OATES 620:92
m. who want to become inhuman   APOL 27:13
m. will boast of knowledge   LANY 489:5
m. will...do it for pay   MELV 564:48
m. wish to hear no stories   BERN 81:40
m. with book learning   RAMOS 678:6
m. with broken souls   PATC 642:49
m. without ideals   CAMUS 187:85
m. without imagination   PROU 671:85
M. with secrets   DELI 261:79
M. with sisters dear   HOOD 410:46
m. with the muck-rakes   ROOS 696:54
m. with ugly faces   MASE 559:39
m., women, and clergymen   SMITH 801:16
M. would be angels   POPE 660:12
m. would take the death sentence   LAWR 495:40
m. write in place lite   CHAU 208:63
M., you are all marksmen   PUTN 673:21
more animated beings than...m.   SMITH 801:11
more I admire m.   LEVIN 506:63
Most wretched m.   SHEL 783:27
music marreth m.'s manners   GALE 343:6
must judge m.   LICH 509:23
must m. kill and die?   SHEL 786:22
name all the m.   MCCA 527:93
Nearly all our best m. are dead!   PUNCH 673:14
Noble m. in the quiet of morning   DUNC 295:12

No m. who knows aught   MILT 580:85
not dreams of doting m.?   MELV 564:46
nothing noble-minded m.   KINC 468:22
not into the hands of m.   BIBLE 107:38
not permit thirty m.   WHITE 902:69
obey God rather than m.   BIBLE 119:33
of all m. most miserable   BIBLE 121:13
of war I have slain m.   SHAK 759:54
Old m. and comets   SWIFT 831:88
Old m. forget   SHAK 746:58
only m. like thee are fit   OTWAY 631:35
O shame to m.!   MILT 581:30
other m. are tempted   BUTL 177:54
pacific—and all his m.   KEATS 456:77
port, for m.   JOHN 445:37
powerful m. in our society   BELL 73:76
present life of m. on earth   BEDE 68:54
presumed to be what m.   LIPP 512:73
primitive m. are...credulous   POPE 659:92
problem is...whether m. do   SKIN 795:10
pursuit...by free m.   WARR 889:69
push m. over the edge   ROTH 699:16
quit you like me   BIBLE 122:21
quit yourselves like m.   BIBLE 91:84
rank of devoutly religious m.   EINS 301:37
reality on which m. can act   LIPP 511:71
reason m. are greater than animals   ELLI 311:85
reason why m. lived   LOWE 519:21
reputation of m.   MONT 591:66
resident in m.   SHAK 731:87
reverberates through m.'s history   KOES 477:33
Rich m. deal gifts   SHAK 762:51
rich m. rule the law   GOLD 361:41
rights as m., as free m.   PITT 653:42
robot mice and robot m.   BRAD 149:70
sardine m. crammed in   MACN 538:1
say best m. are moulded   SHAK 758:48
see m. as trees, walking   BIBLE 114:15
Sensible m. are all the same religion   DISR 277:90
sent ten thousand m. to battle   SITT 793:56
short-lived weak animals m.   MONT 591:64
should make m. atheists   CAREW 190:59
show m. energetically   GRAY 368:88
shows of love to other m.   SHAK 747:73
sinewy brown m.   PRIE 668:28
single m....more charitable   BACON 48:90
So long as m. can breathe   SHAK 771:5
So long as m. worship   HUXL 425:84
so many kinds of awful m.   COPE 237:60
Some m. are born kings   SHAW 781:84
Some m. creep in   SHAK 757:4
some m. who have their heads   HERN 399:28
something true about m.   JAMES 434:57
som m. say in many partys   MALO 543:12
sound as the m. who make it   LEE 500:37
Strong bronzed m.   CULL 247:92
stuffed shirts, hollow m.   MACD 530:47
substance of m.   SWIN 833:44
take a minute from the m.   CARA 189:38
taking ordinary m.   GALB 343:96
tale which holdeth...old m.   SIDN 791:20
talked about by m.   PERI 648:65
tall m. had ever very empty heads   BACON 47:69
ten thousand of those m.   SHAK 746:54
the purgatory of m.   FLOR 328:76
these m. paid their shillings   PRIE 668:17
think as wise m.   ASCH 35:79
thou hast m.   SHAK 730:66
thousand m. that fishes gnawed   SHAK 731:8
three m. I admired most   MCLE 534:27
tide in the affairs of m.   SHAK 748:16
tides of m. into my hands   LAWR 495:37
'Tis all m.'s office   SHAK 745:20
'Tis no shame for m.   SHIR 789:80
toil in other m.'s extremes   KYD 482:49
to m. [I speak] French   CHAR 207:37
torment, kill and damn m.   MARG 549:39
transform M. into Monsters   FORD 330:19
travelled among unknown m.   WORD 925:9
truthful towards m.   HARDY 381:52
trying to do with eight m.   ROBI 689:24
twelve thousand fighting m.   SHAK 735:16
twice as well as m.   WHIT 906:64
two m. look out   LANG 488:92
two m. stand together   WAVE 893:38
Two m. who differ   RUSS 705:52
two strong m.   KIPL 470:81

understanding better than other m.	DRYD 288:44
Unmarried m. are best friends	BACON 48:89
unmarried or childless m.	BACON 48:86
upon two generations of m.	LLOY 513:2
vain, unnecessary things are m.	ROCH 691:60
vast majority o' m.	MACD 529:31
vexes public m.	TENN 841:92
voices elected me of all m.	LEE 500:45
war between m. and women	THUR 859:24
war…between m. and women	LYND 524:15
war is obsolete or m. are	FULL 341:53
wasteful of promising young m.	HUGH 418:25
weak and miserable m.	CHOM 214:18
We are selfish m.	WORD 925:11
We are the hollow m.	ELIOT 306:69
Weary m., what reap ye?	WILDE 907:82
we've got the m.	HUNT 422:21
What all m. should avoid	DISR 277:89
What are m. to rocks	AUST 43:69
what many m. desire	SHAK 740:62
What m. or Gods are these?	KEATS 459:51
when all m. shall speak well	BIBLE 115:30
When m. make gods	ONEI 625:90
When m. reach…50	TEKA 838:30
when shall English m.	DRAY 286:2
where good m. rest	FLEC 327:45
where m. May read	SHAK 766:83
which all m. knew!	TENN 844:71
which m. call Love	SPEN 808:89
While m. are rolling round	WEST 901:39
white m. cheat black m.	LEE 500:38
Who, of m., can tell	KEATS 457:4
Wine and women will make m.	BIBLE 108:55
wise m. do not say	MART 555:46
Wise m. fish here	STEL 816:48
wisest of m. in all ages	STER 817:70
wisest of you m.	PLATO 654:76
With four-and-twenty m.	AYTO 45:16
with m.'s blood	KING 469:64
With m. this is impossible	BIBLE 113:75
Without thinking highly…of m.	AUST 43:67
Women…behave like m.	MACK 534:20
women…envy m.	PANK 636:34
Working m. of all countries	MARX 558:5
Would m.…distil it out	SHAK 746:48
Wrath brings mortal m.…hurt	EURI 316:13
Yes, Sir, many m.	JOHN 443:62
Yesterday's m.	ANON 24:12
you are m. of stones	SHAK 764:5
Young m. mend not their sight	DONNE 281:92
young m.'s vision	DRYD 290:82
young m. think it is	HOUS 416:85
menace against every form of m.	ROTH 699:29
m. of aggression	ASQU 36:9
public m.	BURG 167:83
men-children Bring forth m.-c.	SHAK 767:91
Mencken M.'s defects	MEYER 568:30
mend Garlic to m. her kissing	SHAK 770:89
God won't, and we can't m. it	CLOU 222:24
mendacities Better m.	POUND 664:37
mendacity M. is a system	WILL 913:29
mene M., M., Tekel, Upharsin	BIBLE 106:98
menopause going through the m.	WALT 888:43
menpleasers with eyeservice, as m.	BIBLE 122:51
Mensch M. ist das Wesen	SCHI 718:2
M. ist, was er isst	FEUE 322:23
menstrual m. years are vestigial	LEGU 501:57
menstruation m.…enviable	STEI 816:44
mental sort of m. rebellion	ORWE 628:65
mentality Australians inherited the British m	PACK 633:73
mentally m.…deadening force	WEBB 893:63
mentation forms of m.	KOES 477:31
mention recourse to the m. of it	JOHN 446:49
menu and then I saw the m.	WESK 899:8
full m. of rights	TUTU 870:70
part of life's m.	RUSS 706:68
Menuhin first choice…M.	ADLER 7:51
mercantile dull m. England	BUCH 164:27
Mercaptan M. went on to preach	HUXL 424:58
Mercator M.'s North Poles	CARR 197:30
Mercedes-Benz buy me a M.-B.	JOPL 450:63
merchandise mechanical arts and m.	BACON 50:59
merchant ear of a m.	NASHE 609:19
heaven is like unto a m.	BIBLE 112:53
What m.'s ships have my sighs	DONNE 280:44
merchants m. full of sybstaunce	
and myght	DUNB 294:5

m.…intent on profit	PIUS 653:53
m., who mind little	MONT 591:63
mercies All occasions invite his m.	DONNE 281:88
church is full of m.	DONNE 281:87
tender m.	BIBLE 97:62
thy faithful m. crown	WESL 900:14
merciful Blessed are the m.	BIBLE 109:83
Draw near…in being m.	SHAK 731:88
God be m. unto us	BIBLE 96:37
merciless sunlight streaming m.	ATWO 38:49
time is a m. thing	WILL 913:34
mercury M. with a Pitchfork	BRAU 150:3
mercy at the m. of the reflexes	BALD 53:31
easy in the m. of his means	THOM 852:72
entirely and helplessly at his m.	SHAW 778:87
God ha' m.	KIPL 470:80
God have m.	RANS 679:28
goodness and m. shall follow me	BIBLE 94:2
hand folks over to God's m.	ELIOT 303:82
have m., and not sacrifice	BIBLE 111:20
Have m. upon all Jews	BOOK 141:87
have m. upon us	BOOK 140:80
in wrath remember m.	BIBLE 106:13
justice and m. are reconciled	WILS 916:7
La belle dame sans m.	KEATS 459:41
Large and without m.	OLSEN 624:74
leaving m. to heaven	FIEL 322:41
'Lord have m. upon us'	PEPYS 647:40
merciful…shall obtain m.	BIBLE 109:83
M., compassion, and justice	WAITE 884:67
m. endureth for ever	BIBLE 98:97
M. has a human heart	BLAKE 134:31
m. is on them that fear him	BIBLE 115:23
m. show to me	POPE 662:63
M. sighed farewell!	BYRON 181:48
m. to forgive	DRYD 291:17
most tender m. is neglect	CRAB 242:91
Mother of M.	ROBI 690:27
new law of m.	MORE 596:61
Nothing emboldens sin…as m.	SHAK 762:47
Peace on earth and m. mild	WESL 900:10
Peace on earth and m. mild!	BEEC 69:60
plenteous m.	BIBLE 97:63
property is always to have m.	BOOK 141:7
quality of m. is not strained	SHAK 740:79
shewed m. on him	BIBLE 115:39
shewing m. unto thousands	BIBLE 88:23
shew m. unto thousands in them	BOOK 141:93
shut the gates of m.	GRAY 369:19
so great is his m.	BIBLE 97:64
so is his m.	BIBLE 107:38
still at the m. of words	THOM 853:80
temper so Justice with m.	MILT 585:20
When m. seasons justice	SHAK 740:80
Where m., Love and Pity dwell	BLAKE 134:32
Meredith M. is a prose Browning	WILDE 908:92
mergers m.-and-acquisitions	GLEI 359:2
meridian full m. of my glory	SHAK 775:18
merit confuse longevity with m.	WOGAN 919:77
greatest m. for the public	BACON 48:86
herein consisted his m.	MILT 579:77
How he esteems your m.	COWP 241:60
irrespective of any possible m.	WAUGH 891:13
M. and good works	BACON 48:5
m. of both sexes	LABR 483:58
m. of the wearer!	SHAK 740:63
m. wins the soul	POPE 659:77
modernness is the measure of m.	EMER 313:34
of rewarding m.	SWIFT 831:82
oft got without m.	SHAK 760:79
positive m. of enjoying	RUSS 705:51
merits m. of a classification	MILL 570:73
seek his m. to disclose	GRAY 370:26
meritus m., 'so he ought to be'	LEAC 497:70
merle mavis and m. are singing	SCOTT 723:9
Merlin child was delyverd unto M.	MALO 542:2
unto M., and the Table Rounde	MALO 542:6
mermaid Choicer…M. Tavern?	KEATS 457:92
Done at the M.!	BEAU 66:6
m.…tolled my son to shipwreck	DEKK 259:50
mermaids heard the m. singing	ELIOT 304:26
merriest m. men are m.	SHAK 745:31
merrily M., m. shall I live now	SHAK 775:99
merriment damn…measured m.	LEWIS 507:89
even for m. and diversion	SMITH 798:44
Frame your mind to…m.	SHAK 732:25
it is no m.	KORAN 479:95

merry As M. Margaret	SKEL 795:9
began to be m.	BIBLE 116:4
eat…drink, and to be m.	BIBLE 101:8
fool to make me m.	SHAK 750:7
Fortune is m.	SHAK 748:1
keep our Christmas m. still	SCOTT 723:9
Let us be m.	CURR 249:4
meet that we should make m.	BIBLE 116:4
m. as a marriage bell	BYRON 179:2
m. as the day is long	SHAK 744:9
m. cuckoo, messenger of Spring	SPEN 809:9
m. heart goes all the day	SHAK 770:8
m. heart maketh a cheerful	BIBLE 99:3
M. it is in the good greenwood	SCOTT 723:
m. songs of peace	SHAK 775:2
never m. when I hear	SHAK 741:8
to be m. best becomes you	SHAK 744:9
very m., dancing, drinking	DRYD 292:6
wine maketh m.	BIBLE 101:8
Meshach Shadrach, M.	BIBLE 106:9
mess don't m. with it	WALL 887:1
general m. of…feeling	ELIOT 308:2
God…has made an awful m.	BURR 173:5
Here's another fine m.	HARDY 381:4
let other people clean up the m.	FITZ 325:9
m. of pottage	BIBLE 87:8
unspeakable idiotic m.	ORWE 628:5
what we can make of the m.	ELIOT 307:
message may your m. be heard	WALL 886:
medium is the m.	MCLU 536:5
m. came…for me	PENI 646:2
m. of fear	MCCA 527:9
m. of peace to Ireland	ARNO 33:5
m. to the businessmen	CURR 249:4
Send them a m.	ANON 24:1
the m. came	AUST 44:
will never deliver the m.	MILL 571:9
messages m. go quicker to the brain	SPARK 806:2
messenger Anglo-Saxon M.	CARR 197:1
m. of Satan	BIBLE 122:3
m. of Spring	SPEN 809:9
says, I am a m.	MILL 571:9
wingèd m. of heaven	SHAK 736:4
messing m. about in boats	GRAH 365:3
m. with people's hands	HEND 395:3
mess-makers pioneers…m.-m.	PIRS 652:2
met way we m.	SWIN 833:3
when We innocently m.	JONS 449:3
metal breed for barren m.	SHAK 739:5
cold m. of economic theory	SCHU 721:5
forests of m.	THOM 855:3
metaphor All slang is m.	CHES 211:4
authors of simile and m.	NASH 609:
branch-strained m.	MOORE 595:4
Cricket…the great m.	FOWL 332:7
I love m.	GASS 346:6
I love m.	MALA 541:8
Man be my m.	THOM 852:5
No m. reinvents…nurture	PALEY 635:1
Science is all m.	LEARY 498:9
through m. to reconcile	WILL 913:4
whaling a universal m.	LODGE 514:2
metaphoric habits of m. thought	FRYE 340:3
metaphorical deeper than m. sense	CARL 191:8
metaphors abuse of m.	PALM 635:1
Curling with m.	HERB 398:
didn't have m. in my day	TRUE 868:2
handful of m.	BORG 144:9
m. by which it is most naturally	JAMES 434:6
sweet phrases, lovely m.	HERB 398:1
metaphysic high As m. wit can fly	BUTL 177:4
metaphysical M. in lederhosen	ENRI 314:7
M. questions and reflections	HERN 399:2
metaphysics divinity or school m.	HUME 422:1
Explaining m. to the nation	BYRON 181:6
m. is a branch of fantastic literature	BORG 144:8
M. is the finding of bad reasons	BRAD 149:7
M. means nothing but	JAMES 434:6
science of m.	MENC 567:7
small portion of m.	PLAN 653:5
meteor cloud-encircled m. of the air	SHEL 784:6
m. Ever hung my fate	MIDD 569:4
slides the silent m.	TENN 842:1
Streamed, like a m.	GRAY 370:2
methinks lady protests too much, m.	SHAK 754:9
method All m. is imperfect	NICO 614:9
anything other than…general m.!	BAUD 64:6

genius has invented a m.	RUSS 705:46	up agen m.-c. morality	SHAW 780:66
had a certain m.	RUSS 705:56	We of the sinking m. c.	ORWE 628:47
M. acting?	BARR 61:98	What fools m.-c. girls are	DRAB 286:89
m. and secret…of Jesus	ARNO 34:64	world is full of m.-c. people	SHAR 776:46
m. of assisting…pure science	CONA 230:79	middle classes lower m. c.	GILB 354:10
no objection to this m.	STER 817:76	Middle East America's dependence	
our m. of questioning	HEIS 391:55	on oil from the M. E.	KERRY 465:68
people and the m.	RYLE 707:79	progress in the M. E.	BLAIR 133:14
scientific m. has always been	PIRS 652:30	Middlemarch M….grown up	WOOLF 922:37
there is m. in't	SHAK 752:49	middles m. are nowhere to be found	BART 62:12
true m. of warfare	MAZZ 562:99	Middlesex All M. is ugly	COBB 223:48
You know my m.	DOYLE 285:55	midge lightly skims the m.	BETJ 83:90
You know my m.	DOYLE 285:59	like a fretful m.	ROSS 698:88
Methodist insufferable as a M.	MENC 566:88	mid-heaven prancing in m.-h.	LAWR 494:5
Methodists two kinds of M.	ELIOT 303:73	Midland M., bound for Cricklewood	BETJ 83:91
methods institution of the	UNIT 873:69	midlands living in the M.	BELL 73:63
m. are outdated and incorrect	ANON 23:84	south…north and m.	MACM 537:78
m. differ from those	HUXL 426:13	midnight Cerberus and blackest m.	MILT 576:4
m. of control	KEYN 465:85	gathered at m.	KEATS 458:7
other m. to stop them	KISH 475:88	heard the chimes at m.	SHAK 743:55
rule-of-thumb m.	MARX 558:12	Holding hands at m.	GERS 351:44
theory and m. of revolution	MAO 547:5	If you wake at m.	KIPL 473:61
You know my m.	DOYLE 285:55	Love, the reeling m. through	PARK 638:61
Methuselah days of M.	BIBLE 86:63	m., in our little town	LIND 511:50
metre hurdling the m. like tired horses	BROY 163:98	m. in the silence	BROW 163:94
m. of the dictionary?	THOM 852:64	m. never come	MARL 552:6
Time is the m.	WALC 884:77	m.'s all a-glimmer	YEATS 932:30
metres not m., but…argument	EMER 312:23	M. shakes the memory	ELIOT 305:30
Two m., or a little more	ROBBE 688:7	m. with no pain	KEATS 460:62
Metro Win a M.!	PRIV 670:57	mock the m. bell	SHAK 765:40
metropolis art is born of the m.	POUND 664:25	roused themselves at m.	TROL 866:88
M. of Great-Britain	BAIL 52:4	shadow of the m. hour	BYRON 180:38
Metternich M….so conservative	EVANS 316:17	stroke of m. ceases	HOUS 416:84
mettle m. enough in thee	SHAK 745:22	'Tis m., falls the lamp-light	WILDE 907:81
undaunted m. should compose	SHAK 767:91	troubled m. and the noon's repose	ELIOT 305:32
mettlesome m. women	ANDR 16:25	midst there am I in the m. of them	BIBLE 113:69
mew cat will m.	SHAK 755:36	through the m.	JONS 450:61
Mexican If I were a M.	CORW 237:73	midstream has to stop in m.	BAND 58:25
Mexico In M. the gods ruled	COND 230:82	midsummer high M. pomps	ARNO 33:46
Poor M., so far from God	DIAZ 265:51	saw M. Night's Dream	PEPYS 647:32
Micawber never will desert Mr M.	DICK 269:66	This m. flower	SKEL 795:91
mice as long as it catches m.	DENG 261:88	very m. madness	SHAK 757:83
best-laid schemes o' M. an' Men	BURNS 170:72	midwife fairies' m.	SHAK 735:38
Men multiply like M.	CANT 188:18	m. slapped your footsoles	PLATH 654:65
robot m. and robot men	BRAD 149:70	revolution was our m.	INOU 430:72
Michael M….against the dragon	BIBLE 126:66	so far like the m.	SOCR 803:54
M. read the Gaelic scroll	RUSS 706:61	midwinter M. Spring	ELIOT 308:37
Michelangelo Dante or M.	MULL 602:72	mien monster of so frightful m.	POPE 660:18
If M. were a heterosexual	BROWN 157:49	rapture of thy m.	WORD 929:63
women…Talking of M.	ELIOT 304:18	might as our m. lessens	ANON 18:76
mickle O m. is the powerful grace	SHAK 736:55	danced…with all his m.	BIBLE 91:99
microbe M. is so very small	BELL 72:50	do it with thy m.	BIBLE 101:84
microcosm m. of little world	BROW 159:83	duty past thy m.	SHAK 748:18
microphone paid for this m.	REAG 681:64	faith that right makes m.	LINC 510:38
microscopes magnifyin' gas m.	DICK 266:81	famousèd for m.	SHAK 771:12
M. are prudent	DICK 272:56	M. first made kings	MARL 552:83
Microsoft M. were a car	MURR 605:9	Not by m., nor by power	BIBLE 106:17
Midas Hard food for M.	SHAK 740:72	O tell of his m.	GRANT 366:53
midday walks under the m. sun	MILT 577:35	sovereign sway…dissolved by m.?	DRYD 290:91
middle honeyed m. of the night	KEATS 458:32	unbelief…no source of m.	MACD 530:57
In the m. ages	JERO 437:36	mightier m. and richer than thyself	BIBLE 108:50
live in the M. Ages	SMITH 800:98	mightily levis mirry…levis m.	DUNB 294:3
m.-management of Manhattan	AMIS 14:96	mighty God who made thee m.	BENS 77:61
m. of the journey of our life	DANTE 252:93	How are the m. fallen	BIBLE 91:98
moist his m.!	NASH 608:93	little body with a m. heart	SHAK 745:33
nuclear power in the m. ages	LAMB 487:65	Look on my works, ye M.	SHEL 784:50
politics the m. way	ADAMS 5:88	m. things from small beginnings	DRYD 287:20
reconnected with the angry m.?	ANON 25:68	more m. than he seems	SHAK 745:40
royal family in the m. ages	HALD 377:73	some have called thee M.	DONNE 281:67
safely by the m. way	OVID 631:43	the brave, the m.	WORD 928:58
Secret sits in the m.	FROST 339:11	with his m. talk	SYNGE 834:59
middle-age companions for m. a.	BACON 48:91	migraine Love is a universal m.	GRAV 368:81
frightening thing about m. a.	DAY 256:81	Mijor Earl M. E.'s Grendorter!	SHAW 780:43
mere m. a. snuffs out	HUGH 418:25	mild m. or choleric disposition	ADDI 6:9
m. a. of a state	BACON 50:59	milder Not m. is the general lot	ARNO 31:88
misspent youth and m. a.	THUR 860:58	mile braces at a distance of a m.	MORT 600:22
pleasures of m. a.	POUND 665:49	compel thee to go a m.	BIBLE 109:92
middle-aged m.-a. man can't	UPDI 874:87	enemy half a m. away	MUIR 602:55
nine m.-a. couples	THOM 855:34	mile-a sad tires in a m.-a.	SHAK 770:83
The M.-A. Man	THUR 859:25	miles end of evening smiles, M.	BROW 161:37
middle class great English m. c.	ARNO 33:38	first m. of the brief march	PEARY 645:2
M.C. was quite prepared	BELL 73:58	had gone m. away	HEAN 389:8
m.-c. woman	LURIE 522:89	Looking down for m.	SNYD 802:47
provincial, resolutely m.-c.	MCFA 531:70	lost in the m.	SCOTT 722:78
Puritan of the m. c.	NEME 611:39	m. of human habitations	CONR 235:20
symbol of an emerging m.-c. Briton	MCFA 531:72	m. to go before I sleep	FROST 339:98
true m.-c. unit	SHAW 779:16	Six m. from earth	JARR 435:80

Thousands of m. of wheat	RICH 686:70		
twenty m. a day?	MARL 552:81		
two m. more and then we rest!	BRON 154:77		
milestones m. into headstones	LOWE 520:40		
milieu writer from the m.	ROTH 699:14		
militant ceases to be m.	MORR 598:99		
military among a m. one, trophies	FUSE 342:75		
close my m. career	MACA 524:27		
defeat…lost m. campaign	EDIN 300:9		
defiance of m. authority	SASS 716:56		
hold the m. mind	TUCH 869:57		
m. and nuclear sense	WALE 885:90		
m. society	TREV 865:63		
m. struggle may frankly be regarded	SCHL 718:10		
m. success will have achieved	ELIZ 310:66		
m. system…subsidy	CHOM 214:20		
m. take positions	KENN 464:53		
M. Two-Step	GREN 372:1		
overseas m. commitments	FERG 320:3		
political and the other m.	MCNA 537:95		
race has no m. purpose	MOUN 601:39		
species of m. instinct	HAYD 387:58		
study of m. history	CLAU 220:66		
thralldom of a m. caste	LLOY 513:2		
When the m. man approaches	SHAW 778:97		
military-industrial m.-i. complex	EISE 302:58		
milk black ink in white m.	MUNRO 603:88		
child drinking a bowl of m.	SAND 713:12		
crudded m.	WEBS 895:14		
curd of ass's m.	POPE 661:40		
drunk the m. of Paradise	COLE 226:15		
end is moo, the other, m.	NASH 608:75		
find a trout in the m.	THOR 857:76		
flowing with m. and honey	BIBLE 88:11		
for water…brought him m.	BIBLE 90:68		
Gin was mother's m.	SHAW 780:67		
gone to m. the bull	JOHN 443:68		
how we can m. her	SZENT 834:65		
hubbies moaned in M.Wood	THOM 853:93		
m. and ale	SKEL 795:90		
m. and honey blessed	NEALE 610:28		
m., and not of strong meat	BIBLE 124:91		
m. and sperm of kindness	MELV 564:37		
m. and the yoghurt	MORT 599:15		
m. and toast and honey	MITC 588:90		
m. comes frozen home	SHAK 734:94		
m. in an old breast	MANS 546:83		
m. of human kindness	SHAK 766:80		
m.'s leap toward immortality	FADI 317:36		
m. the cow of the world	WILB 907:71		
putting m. into babies	CHUR 217:89		
sincere m. of the word	BIBLE 125:23		
sucked such m.	YEATS 934:61		
this m.-soup men call domestic bliss	PATM 643:68		
milk-white m.-w.; now, purple	SHAK 737:94		
milky called the M.Way	MARTI 555:44		
Far as the solar walk, or m. way	POPE 660:11		
m. sky	YEATS 932:32		
stars…on the m. way	WORD 927:41		
Mill John Stuart M….effort of will	BENT 78:78		
mill busy m.	GOLD 361:51		
Gaza at the m. with slaves	MILT 586:45		
God's m. grinds slow	HERB 398:22		
sallow for the m.	SPEN 808:73		
stomach is a m.	HUNT 423:39		
mill-dams bonnie m.-d. o' Binnorie	BALL 55:67		
millennium century and m.	LEVI 506:61		
M. Dome was intended to be New			
Labour's Xanadu	RAWN 680:39		
millinery jewelled mass of m.	TENN 845:81		
million a m. is made by producing	WILD 911:84		
looked like a m. dollars	CART 198:43		
m. dollars to make a picture	TAYL 837:57		
multitude of one m.	KOES 477:28		
patent double m.	DICK 266:81		
turn-up in a m.	BEVIN 85:32		
millionaire billionaire instead of a m.	WATE 890:95		
I am a m.	SHAW 779:40		
Who wants to be a m.?	PORT 663:85		
millionaires m. and bums taste	MARQ 554:24		
m. love a baked apple	FIRB 323:63		
millions 'as m. at 'ome	KIPL 471:97		
M. drew up before	NEW 611:55		
m. long for immortality	ERTZ 315:91		
m. of the mouthless dead	SORL 804:90		
m. which it is…sucking up	COBB 223:48		
probably been m. of earths	HOYLE 417:4		

repeat in the lives of the m.	WILD 911:88	extreme thoughts…in his m.	DIDE 274:3	m. is bent to holiness	SHAK 730:52
There are m. to be grabbed	MANK 545:60	face should bear a wicked m.	SHAK 733:66	m. is clouded	TENN 847:52
Three m. of people	PITT 652:40	facility for m. games	COUP 239:98	m. is its own place	MILT 580:7
What m. died	CAMP 186:68	fair terms and a villain's m.	SHAK 739:55	m. is maturing late	NASH 608:97
mills dark Satanic m.?	BLAKE 135:83	Farewell the tranquil m.	SHAK 760:94	m. is…more self-reliant	LIVI 512:83
m. of God grind slowly	LOGAU 515:32	favours only the prepared m.	PAST 642:43	m. is not a bed	AGATE 8:68
millstone bosom is actually a m.	GREER 372:86	features gets on your m.	LEAC 496:63	m. is pure machinery	GINS 357:62
m.…into the sea	BIBLE 127:74	feeble powers of my m.	SIDN 790:98	m. is ta'en up wi'	NAIR 607:53
m. were hanged about his neck	BIBLE 112:67	fit of absence of m.	SEEL 726:72	m. is the least of possessions	WHITE 903:96
Tradition…can be as much a m.	MACI 533:5	fog of the good man's m.	BROW 161:36	m. is the true self	CICE 218:27
millstones m.…about your neck	DAVI 254:23	frailty of the m.	CONG 232:41	m. makes us	GRIL 373:13
M. around our neck	DISR 277:94	frame of m.	FRIE 337:70	m. may loose its force	BYRON 180:37
tears…Turned to m.	SHEL 783:35	Frame your m. to mirth	SHAK 732:25	m. may rest on the intuition	BACON 50:73
mill-wheel millstone as a m.-w.	MACI 533:5	freedom of my m.	MILT 577:41	m. o'er all the world	MILT 586:40
Milton like that in M.'s hell	NERV 611:44	gateways of the m.	SASS 717:78	m. off everything like golf	ROGE 695:30
malt does more than M.	HOUS 415:65	gentle m. by gentle deeds	SPEN 809:12	m. of large general powers	JOHN 445:42
M., a name to resound	TENN 846:28	gird up the loins of your m.	BIBLE 125:21	m. of man	MARL 552:97
M.! thou shouldst be living	WORD 925:11	God…destroys their m.	DRYD 291:23	m. of man	WORD 923:71
M.…was a genius	JOHN 446:63	greatest good of the m.	SPIN 811:32	m. of Ronald Reagan	NOON 617:55
Some mute inglorious M.	GRAY 369:18	greatness of m.	MARC 549:36	m. or body grieved	CAMP 187:81
Thou shalt believe in M.	BYRON 182:75	green sickness of the m.	CLEV 221:83	m. or body to prefer	POPE 660:16
Milwaukeeans two M. in love	HECHT 390:36	gymnasium of the m.	LENIN 502:87	m. religiously affected	HOOK 411:56
mim All m. were the borogoves	CARR 195:90	hand…cutting edge of the m.	BRON 154:68	m.'s construction in the face	SHAK 766:79
mime m. can be a bridge between	MARC 549:30	has a vulgar m.	LEWIS 507:74	m. shuttles and reminds	ROTH 699:13
mimic All honour's m.	DONNE 279:42	having it affect his m.	HOOV 411:68	m. skating circles	FROST 339:18
mince m., and slices of quince	LEAR 498:86	heart and m. of America	BARZ 63:36	m. that has seen, and suffered	CARL 191:75
mincing M. poetry	SHAK 742:18	His m. moves	YEATS 934:63	m. that went into	GLAS 359:97
mind agree to be of one m.	BACON 47:66	hold the military m.	TUCH 869:57	m. to me a kingdom is	DYER 296:50
all in the m.	WOLFE 920:84	hold the m. in place	MILL 572:3	m. to prance	JOHN 444:87
altered the colour of my m.	BRON 155:94	homeland of the m.	NEW 611:53	m. was less difficult to develop	AUST 42:62
A man's m.	TROL 867:5	If I am out of my m.	BELL 73:73	m. was like a many-legged, wingless	
ambitious m. Will covet more	MILT 581:19	If the ocean was pure m.	PRAT 667:98	insect	UPDI 875:99
A m. thinking	WOOLF 923:50	ignis fatuus in the m.	ROCH 691:56	m. was once the true	MARV 556:70
And to my m.	SHAK 751:24	image in her m.	DRYD 290:12	m. was too wide for a professor	MENC 565:60
angling…rest to his m.	WALT 888:49	impotence of m.	MILT 586:46	m. watches itself	CAMUS 187:84
arid desert of his m.	WEST 901:42	improper m. is a perpetual feast	SMITH 799:76	m. with all your toys	MILT 576:72
assail his m. another while	MARL 552:92	index of a feeling m.	CRAB 242:5	m. with arts improve	DONNE 279:43
attracted to me by my m.	LEE 500:31	Indian, whose untutored m.	POPE 660:11	minister to a m. diseased	SHAK 768:38
attractive to the half-baked m.	FORS 331:32	infirmity of noble m.	MILT 578:49	mirrored themselves in my m.	ELIOT 303:76
author's m.	GAUG 347:68	in one's m. a…map	ORWE 629:81	miserable state of m.	BACON 49:17
awing the human m.	JEFF 436:18	Intense irradiation of a m.	SHEL 784:66	most personal state of m.	FEIN 319:85
A Woman seldom Writes her M.	STEE 814:98	interwoven with the highest m.	AGAS 8:66	move a woman's m.	SHAK 729:34
beauty of thy m.	SHAK 772:28	In youth open your m.	ANON 19:98	Music affects the human m.	KHOM 466:97
best marriage…of m. and body	FOWL 332:71	Ithaka always in your m.	CAVA 201:16	necessary to the human m.	REES 682:89
blessedness is…satisfaction of m.	SPIN 811:34	Jealousy…tyrant of the m.!	DRYD 291:32	never brought to m.?	BURNS 171:98
Boston is a state of m.	APPL 28:25	Keep violence in the m.	ALDI 10:11	noble m. is here o'erthrown!	SHAK 754:83
breast, and quiet m.	LOVE 519:13	known by the human m.	PAGE 633:79	no blemish but the m.	SHAK 757:88
brilliant m.	ASQU 36:15	know the m. of a woman	LAWR 494:19	noblest frailty of the m.	DRYD 287:17
broad of M.	BETJ 83:79	know the m. of God	HAWK 386:32	no grayness in the m.	GUNT 375:41
calming influence on the m.	MATI 560:63	lack of a whole m.	MUIR 601:52	non-space of the m.	GIBS 353:76
Calm of m., all passion	MILT 587:67	land and the m.	NGU 613:79	no passion in the m. of man	BACON 47:75
calm the troubled m.	CONG 232:48	leaves thy m.'s imprint	SHAK 772:33	not astound The virtuous m.	MILT 577:32
certain liveliness of m.	RABE 676:76	Let this m. be in you	BIBLE 123:54	not be sound…in body or m.	LLOY 513:96
certain unsoundness of m.	MACA 525:41	liberation of both body and m.	BANN 59:40	nothing unbends the m. like them	GAY 347:55
chaos of the m.	SNYD 803:49	light of my m.	CRUZ 246:89	not in my perfect m.	SHAK 764:98
chords in the human m.	DICK 270:91	lingers in the m.	LARO 491:54	not m. its being buried	HOPK 413:7
Clarity of m. results in	PASC 640:8	Little subconscious m.	ONEI 626:3	not yet of Percy's m.	SHAK 741:12
classical m. at work	PIRS 652:31	live in the m., in ideas	MILL 572:18	of a m.…that they cannot help	SHAK 761:28
clear, attentive m.	SNYD 802:48	long in your m.	HOLM 408:87	Of any good m.	JONS 449:41
clear your m. of cant	JOHN 446:60	Love looks…with the m.	SHAK 737:86	Of my own m.	THOM 855:36
concentrates his m. wonderfully	JOHN 445:26	made up my m.	LLOY 513:97	one-dimensional m.	RUSS 706:59
Coney Island of the M.	FERL 321:10	maintain a quiet m.	DYER 297:52	One man that has a m.	SHAW 781:88
conjunction of the m.	MARV 556:67	makes the m. very free	ELIOT 303:89	O the m., m. has mountains	HOPK 413:5
consistency is as bad for the m.	HUXL 425:71	Make up your m. dearheart	OLIV 624:66	our better m.	ARNO 33:50
constant still in m.	MACA 526:66	man but changed his m.	POPE 661:29	our rightful m.	WHIT 906:60
contracts the m.	THER 851:45	mannish manner of m.	CARY 198:61	out of his m.	SHAR 776:46
contradictory beliefs in one's m.	ORWE 630:3	man o'independent m.	SMITH 801:25	padlock—on her m.	PRIOR 669:32
converse of an innocent m.	KEATS 457:81	man's unconquerable m.	WORD 927:32	peace of m.	SMITH 797:37
corners in one's own m.	HUXL 426:14	masterpiece of art…in the m.	EMER 312:20	pendulum of the m.	JUNG 453:8
corridors into the m.	DOUG 283:21	measure what the m.	MILT 583:90	perversity of the human m.	TROL 867:92
corrupt and befool the m.	BAXT 65:90	might…be said to possess a m.	ELLI 311:88	philosophy inclineth Man's m.	BACON 48:95
couldn't make up my m.	PLATH 654:72	m. against speculation	RUSS 705:42	plastic state of m.	CARRA 194:59
country of the m.	WHITE 903:94	m. and genius	STEN 816:49	pleasure in the exercise of the m.	BARZ 63:33
creating in the m. a map	SPEN 807:56	m. be afterwards applied	THEO 851:39	poet represents the m.	STEV 820:43
crooked my m. to answer	SHAK 731:87	m. By owing owes not	MILT 582:54	poet's m. is perfectly equipped	ELIOT 305:51
culture of the m.	MORE 597:67	m. can make Substance	BYRON 181:55	pollen from one to another m.	LOWE 520:34
cutty sarks run in your m.	BURNS 172:25	m. can weave itself	LOWE 520:36	pray to have a sound m.	JUVE 453:20
debasement of the human m.	CHAN 205:86	m. charged with an eager purpose	ELIOT 303:88	presence of m.	LONS 517:69
depths of his own oceanic m.	COLE 227:26	m. doth serve for all	DYER 297:51	prodigious quantity of the m.	TWAIN 870:74
dictates of his godlike m.	OTWAY 630:21	m.…fixed on the horizon	EINS 301:33	product of the free m.	ORWE 628:56
does not m. his belly	JOHN 443:74	m. for ever Voyaging	WORD 925:98	proud m., a crafty wit	KNOX 476:19
don't not being President	KENN 462:6	m. full of ghosts	MANS 546:82	putting the m. to sleep	SLOAN 796:17
dribble your m. out	ELIOT 303:79	m. fully develops its faculties	STAEL 811:45	Put your brilliant m. to work	ONAS 625:78
elegance is a state of m.	CASS 199:71	m. has a thousand eyes	BOUR 147:28	raise and erect the m.	BACON 46:43
employs the whole m.	QUEN 674:39	m.…in a rapt contemplation	ELIOT 307:10	Reading is to the m.	STEE 814:95
enter into the m.…not myself	WELTY 899:98	m. is actually employed	JOHN 444:6	reconstruction of the m.	RICH 685:47
exist out of the m.	BERK 79:6	m. is a museum	RAINE 677:96	refresh the m. of man	SHAK 732:36

relationship between the m.	HEPW 396:61	infirm and baby m.	COWP 241:77
robs the m. of all its powers	BURKE 167:99	in the m. of God	GREE 371:73
sacred city of the m.	CAMP 186:59	keep your hearts and m.	BIBLE 123:60
Sa dois the m. that is ay diligent	HENR 396:52	keep your hearts and m.	BOOK 141:10
same m. animating them all	BROWN 157:46	Little things affect little m.	DISR 276:54
satisfied with her lover's m.	TROL 866:83	live…close to great m.	BUCH 164:28
say she has a masculine m.	FULL 341:49	marriage of true m.	SHAK 773:48
scientific attitude of m.	RUSS 705:48	maximum elasticity for our m.	BUTT 178:87
scientific m. does not	LEVI 506:67	m., and muses on	MARL 551:77
scorn…our m.	BAST 63:47	m. and soules of men	PRYN 672:93
Scots accent of the m.	STEV 823:24	m. grown crooked	MUIR 602:58
see in my m. a noble	MILT 579:82	m. innocent and quiet	LOVE 519:10
shackled the enquiring m.	HOPE 411:71	M. like beds	WILL 913:49
short neck denotes a good m.	SPARK 806:20	m. of American women	FRIE 337:59
sorcerers that change the m.	SHAK 733:59	m. so impatient	JOHN 441:23
sorrow which enhances…the m.	PROU 671:89	M. still passion-ridden	LIND 510:46
sound m. in a sound body	LOCKE 514:20	M. that are great	JONS 450:49
spirit…of a sound m.	BIBLE 124:81	m. that are to our m.	WELLS 898:73
stamp no character on the m.	JEFF 437:22	mislead their weak m.	SAYE 717:86
state of m. from which it springs	DURK 296:32	model the m. of his subjects	STEU 819:9
steal Fire from the m.	BYRON 179:20	most thoughtful m.	RUSK 703:6
stock my m.	CRUZ 246:87	Nothing issues from their m.	WOOLF 922:34
suffered to relax his m.	MACA 526:61	nurse and tutor of eccentric m.	LAWS 495:43
suppose the m. to be	LOCKE 514:17	one thing on their m.	EVANS 316:20
sweetest music to a woeful m.	SIDN 790:6	operations of our own m.	LOCKE 514:18
thanks to his m.	REDT 681:76	paid to have dirty m.	TREV 865:59
That m. and soul	TENN 842:22	power to cloud men's m.	BAKER 53:24
The m. continues free	PENF 646:20	praise effect in mighty m.	DRYD 290:83
The poem in the m.	THOM 855:30	Publishers can get their m.	LECA 499:24
the poet's m.	TENN 838:38	question…potential parents' m.	SCHU 721:57
there grows in the m.	WILL 914:57	Reason enslaves all whose m.	SHAW 779:18
thinks his m.…more clever	MAIM 541:68	reflection of your own m.	ASTE 36:20
To the noble m.	SHAK 753:75	Regimented m. cannot grasp	AUNG 42:50
touching a new m.	STEV 819:25	self-pleasing and humorous m.	BACON 48:88
tumours of a troubl'd m.	MILT 586:51	strange faces, other m.	TENN 847:49
two kinds of m.	PASC 640:5	such relationships as our m.	LEBON 498:4
Two things fill the m.	KANT 455:47	Superstition…religion of feeble m.	BURKE 169:40
unbent her m. afterwards	LAMB 486:48	take them with our m.	NEWM 612:59
undermine the simple m.	BIBLE 107:33	tenderness of patient m.	OWEN 632:52
universal frame is without a m.	BACON 48:94	thousand m. the same thought	TOCQ 861:86
Unless…new m.	WILL 914:53	virtue of weak m.	DRYD 287:18
unseemly exposure of m.	HAZL 388:93	want of congenial m.	MOOD 594:6
until reeled the m.	GIBBS 352:73	whose m. he learned of	HOMER 409:24
urge the m. to aftersight	ELIOT 309:43	Women never have young m.	DELA 260:74
Venice will linger in your m.	MORR 598:93	writers could live in their own m.	BRAD 148:66
very unusual m.	WHIT 904:7	mine You go Uruguay…I'll go m.	MARX 557:86
warriors of Eternal M.	RUSS 706:61	mineral vegetable, animal and m.	GILB 354:99
whatever in my m.	MORR 598:99	minerals M. grow, plants grow	LINN 511:63
white m.	GIOV 357:76	miners m. poured to war	MACA 526:69
Whitman's m. to be more like	HOPK 413:12	m. sweat their guts out	ORWE 627:36
whose m. is stayed on thee	BIBLE 103:25	Minerva brains of M.	BARR 61:94
with a quiet m.	BOOK 141:89	mine-sweeper captain of a m.-s.	CATTO 200:3
With equal m.	DRYD 292:59	mineworkers Union of M.	MACM 536:77
within thy m. rehearse	TENN 841:89	mingle m. it with the love of others	SHAW 777:58
words echo…in your m.	ELIOT 307:93	m. our bloods together	SHAK 769:51
work my m.	SHAK 771:13	miniature life in m.	ONEI 625:93
work of body or m.	MILT 583:67	mining snakeskin-titles of m.-claims	BENET 75:9
you put me in m. on't	SHER 788:66	minion Curled m.	ARNO 32:24
Your m. now, moldering	RICH 685:43	Mistress m., you	SHAK 736:71
minded m. what they were about	STER 817:67	morning's m.	HOPK 412:89
minds add to our m.	CRUZ 246:88	**minister** As a M.	TAAF 835:68
begin in the m. of men	UNES 873:68	fair spirit for my m.	BYRON 180:42
best m. in the world	ACHE 3:52	first M. in history	HOWE 417:97
born in the m. of a few	KISS 475:93	give the M. a venal House of Peers	SHER 788:69
Cambridge…comfortable m.	CUMM 247:3	King's First M.	CHUR 217:87
change m.	KING 468:27	M. said it wald dee	YOUNG 935:78
change the m. of others	SAFI 708:97	m. the like to you	SHAK 729:30
cloaks for untidy m.	MOND 590:50	m. to a mind diseased	SHAK 768:38
corrupting the m. of the young	PLATO 654:77	old Barnet, the m.'s man	HOGG 406:59
Danger, the spur of all great m.	CHAP 206:20	quotes from the…Prime M.	MCFA 531:73
discrimination of our m.	STEV 820:58	safety of a M.	WALP 887:40
dusty recesses of their m.	LAWR 495:38	Yes, M.! No, M.!	CROS 246:84
except in the m. of men	READ 680:49	**ministerial** regular m. majorities	WHIT 902:67
extinguished in individual m.	DURK 296:34	**ministering** m. angel thou!	SCOTT 723:1
fairly developed m.	FORS 331:46	**ministers** changed my M.	ANNE 17:53
far from their nasty little m.	DEBU 258:5	confirmed by the Council of M.	FREUD 336:51
Fearless m. climb	SHAK 730:82	Foreign M. were called	ACHE 2:22
free their m. of…rubbish	DUDEK 293:82	hard on His Majesty's M.	HOBH 405:31
from the closed m. of the many	ROBB 688:5	how much my M. talk	THAT 850:29
great empire and little m.	BURKE 168:16	M. fully design	MACA 525:45
great m. in the commonplace	HUBB 417:7	M. of Industry	MAND 545:54
happiest and best m.	SHEL 786:16	m. of Love	COLE 226:94
have aspiring m.	MARL 551:75	m. of the new testament	BIBLE 122:22
Hearts and m.	ANON 23:93	M. of thought	SHEL 785:93
hobgoblin of little m.	EMER 312:8	m. to consult the public good	SWIFT 831:87
hunger of ambitious m.	SPEN 809:7	my actions are my M.	CHAR 207:33
image…in the m. of others	AUDEN 41:22	permit his M. to serve him	RICH 686:66

ministration gentle m. of science	ARNO 33:50
ministries has made many m.	BAGE 51:83
ministry hireling of the M.	OCON 621:19
Miniver M. loved the Medici	ROBI 690:31
minnows this Triton of the m.?	SHAK 769:64
minor books major or m.	SAND 713:13
minorities m. who…suffer	ELIZ 310:66
we are all m. now	THOR 858:13
minority individual is a m.	ELLI 311:90
member of a m. group	MAIL 540:53
minstrel Ethereal m.!	WORD 929:60
fuller m. in	TENN 844:61
M. was infirm and old	SCOTT 722:84
wandering m.	GILB 355:19
minstrel-boy M.-b. to the war	MOORE 596:49
mint helps the m. and the thyme	VERL 879:70
mark of the m.	CHES 212:93
minute both in the same m.	KEATS 458:11
Changes at the Last M.	PALEY 635:9
do something phoney every m.	SALI 711:57
Even in a m.!	SHAK 755:46
fill the unforgiving m.	KIPL 474:86
Let there pass A m.	LOWE 520:41
m. bit of…Feeling	CUMM 247:99
M. by m. they change	YEATS 933:45
m. of darkness	RUSH 703:89
speak more in a m.	SHAK 736:59
sucker born every m.	BARN 60:76
take a m. from the men	CARA 189:38
minutes and m. capons	SHAK 741:94
forty-five m. of…privacy	PARK 638:74
how slowly m. roll	ROCH 692:70
m. hasten to their end	SHAK 772:24
m. how they run	SHAK 730:76
precious m. waste	SHAK 772:33
seem to do it every 10 m.	FULB 340:43
take care of the m.	CHES 210:29
Twenty three and a quarter m.	MITF 589:11
was fifteen m. before	TWAIN 871:5
watched for ten m.	SZIL 834:66
minx This m., of course	SITW 793:58
Mirabeau Under M. Bridge	APOL 27:16
miracle m. in me	DANI 252:87
m. is not the breaking of…laws	BLOOM 137:6
m., moment by moment	HUXL 425:93
m. of a kind of internal logic	HONE 409:29
m. of rare device	COLE 226:12
m. of the lit bush	THOM 855:32
no greater m.?	MARL 552:95
power of m.	FEUE 321:22
prays for a m.	TURG 870:66
sort of walking m.	PLATH 654:66
therein works a m. in nature	SHAK 740:71
to be rich…it's a m.	CONN 232:52
unless this m. have might	SHAK 772:25
wondrous m. did Love devise	DAVI 254:32
miracles civilization works its m.	TOCQ 861:81
m. are ceased	COWL 240:30
one believes, then m. occur	MILL 573:39
miraculous m. becomes the norm	MILL 572:28
reduce the m. to the mundane	DIDI 274:6
Miranda Admired M.!	SHAK 774:89
mire Sow returns to her M.	KIPL 474:84
The fury and the m.	YEATS 934:57
wallowing in the m.	BIBLE 125:31
mirror Art is…a m.	PIER 651:9
as in a m., we perceive	MARL 551:77
bevelled edge of a sunlit m.	ABSE 1:7
Cyberspace is the funhouse m.	STER 817:63
each a m. of the other	POPE 665:95
Each creature…a m.	ALAN 9:82
Falklands held a m. up.	RABAN 675:58
From m. after m.	YEATS 934:56
gilt-framed drawing room m.	ROCK 692:83
Hold…the m. up to nature	SHAK 754:86
like a m. which copies	LEON 504:21
live and sleep in front of a m.	BAUD 65:78
m. cracked from side	TENN 839:50
m. of and a connection	MILL 574:62
m. of the soul	QUIN 675:50
moving through a m. clear	TENN 839:46
news is not a m.	LIPP 511:70
not have a rear-view m.	MURR 605:9
oppose a m.	JONS 448:8
Photography was conceived as a m.	STEI 814:9
prince is like a m.	CHAR 207:36
scripture…like a m.	GREG 372:94

moan Listen to them m.   RAMS 678:8
   twa corbies making a m.   BALL 56:92
moaning m. on ilka green loaning   ELLI 310:78
moat m. defensive to a house   SHAK 734:8
mob amphibious ill-born m.   DEFOE 258:14
   best…to do what the m. do   DICK 266:73
   bibblebabbling m.   LEWIS 507:83
   despise the uninitiated m.   HORA 413:22
   governed by the m.   GREN 373:4
   m. of scribbling women   HAWT 386:49
   nose of a m. is…imagination   POE 657:28
   presence of such a m.   STAN 812:61
   whisper to a m.   HUNT 423:25
mobile M.…and more affable   DAVIS 255:52
mobility contributes…to our m.   STEV 820:58
mobilized m. the English language   KENN 463:24
mock m. the air with idle state   GRAY 370:27
   m. the good housewife Fortune   SHAK 748:26
   m. the midnight bell   SHAK 765:40
   m. the riddled corpses   SASS 716:57
   m. the time   SHAK 767:92
   Pray do not m.   SHAK 764:98
   sit in the clouds and m. us   SHAK 742:47
   to muddy or m.   PALEY 635:12
mocked God is not m.   BIBLE 122:39
   smiles…As if he m. himself   SHAK 747:80
mockery In monumental m.   SHAK 757:6
   Trial…will be…a m.   DENM 262:98
mockingbird sin to kill a m.   LEE 500:34
Moctezuma poetry in…great M.   DARIO 252:2
mode any m. of expression   POUND 664:33
   any m. to abolish war   PAINE 634:93
   broke up their m. of living   SHER 787:33
   m. of interestedness   UPDI 874:89
   m. of talking   JOHN 446:60
   m. of their times   DAY 256:75
model 1910 m. has a string   LEAC 496:54
   draw anything in the m. line   BRON 155:84
   House of Lords is a m.   FIELD 322:34
   m. for the New Woman   WARN 889:66
   m. of all the catastrophes   SONT 804:78
   m. our political systems   HAMI 379:99
   m. the minds of his subjects   STEU 819:9
   m. to thy inward greatness   SHAK 745:33
   not the M. boy   TWAIN 870:83
   pattern on which to m. themselves   CHAR 207:36
   small m. of the barren e.   SHAK 735:19
   take as your m.   ALBE 10:98
   very m.   GILB 354:99
   without a m.…I…work   ARET 29:42
modelling go after the m. like a fly   INGR 429:66
models Children…have no other m.   BALD 53:33
   m. destroy genius   HAZL 388:94
   not with women but with m.   BUSH 176:27
   writers…find them worth m.   COWL 240:38
moderate be in nothing so m.   JEFF 436:4
   uncompromising but m.   WELL 898:63
   under a m. weight of prose   LAND 488:85
moderation astonished…own m.!   CLIVE 222:16
   easier than perfect m.   AUGU 41:40
   I am still for m.   ANNE 17:53
   Let your m. be known   BIBLE 123:60
   m. in the pursuit of justice   GOLD 362:73
   m. in war is imbecility   MACA 526:56
   playful m. in politics   HUNT 423:25
modern being too m.   WILDE 909:48
   cultured m. man   RODC 693:87
   m. art tends towards   BAUD 65:74
   m. Churchman   WAUGH 892:21
   m. craze for regulating   WAVE 893:58
   m. democracy is a tyranny   MAIL 540:44
   m. era is dramatic   HUGO 420:60
   M. European culture   SUN 829:32
   m. hardback writer   MORT 599:15
   m. life would lack   WILB 907:75
   m. Major-General   GILB 354:99
   M. poets mix   GOET 360:20
   m. science and technology   GALB 343:96
   muse of m. literature   SONT 804:71
   My music is not m.   SCHO 719:26
   not be either m. nor art   ROSE 697:65
   our m. technic shows   OPPE 626:18
   point of departure…is m. life   WAGN 884:64
   Science is to the m.   DISR 276:47
   this filthy m. tide   YEATS 934:64
   triumph of m. science   WAUGH 893:56
   waste of m. tenements   THOR 858:6

moderniser Jesus was a m.   BLAIR 133:11
modernity frauds of m.   WAUGH 892:38
modernness Perpetual m.   EMER 313:34
modes m. of thinking are different   JOHN 446:50
modest M.? My word, no   REED 681:82
modesty charm of all power is m.   ALCO 10:3
   maintain a becoming m.   BOUL 146:22
   time to cultivate m.   SITW 794:75
modicum m. of alacrity   RYLE 707:80
modish the more m.   SWIFT 832:5
modus m. of lunar eclipses   POUND 664:34
Mogadishu you'll love M.   HEMP 395:32
Moghul M. Empire is in our power   CLIVE 222:15
mold work of…curious m.   SPEN 808:83
Mole Diary of Adrian M.   TOWN 863:21
mole like a bastion's.   SMART 797:28
   On her left breast A m.   SHAK 773:59
   Well said, old m.   SHAK 752:37
   wilt thou go ask the m.?   BLAKE 133:27
molecule not a single m. of my body   DIDE 274:93
molecules preserve the selfish m.   DAWK 256:72
molestation injury and m.   MILL 570:64
Molière advances…since M.   PROU 671:77
   the French M.   DUVA 296:44
Moloch M.…is pure machinery   GINS 357:62
mome m. raths outgrabe   CARR 195:90
moment at the last m.   GUIM 374:32
   awful daring of a m.'s surrender   ELIOT 306:67
   carefully choose one's m.   BECK 68:45
   Consider every m. past   ABU 1:14
   dangerous m. in human history   BELL 74:83
   Eternity was in that m.   CONG 231:98
   Every great mistake has a halfway m.   BUCK 165:37
   Every m. dies a man   TENN 841:91
   Every m. is a golden one   MILL 572:25
   exact m. at which   WELL 897:60
   force the m. to its crisis?   ELIOT 304:19
   happiest m. of the happy man   SCHO 719:34
   Life is but a m.   SCHI 718:6
   masters at the m.   SHAW 782:4
   m. after death   HAWT 386:35
   m. of joy is…harder to get   PO 656:14
   m. of my greatness flicker   ELIOT 304:22
   m.'s insight   HOLM 408:96
   m.'s ornament   WORD 927:35
   m. when curiosity becomes a sin   FRAN 333:89
   m. white   BURNS 172:19
   naked m. in politics   GERG 350:31
   No more distressing m.   TUCH 869:58
   Not for a m.   WORD 928:45
   of no m. to the happiness   JOHN 444:94
   one m. in childhood   GREE 371:52
   people only die at the last m.   CELI 202:38
   present m. that goes by   WILL 913:37
   public of the m.   LUCAS 522:80
   rejoice for a m.   YUAN 936:87
   stands m. by m.   WILD 911:82
   state of mind at that particular m.   FEIN 319:85
   suspension of disbelief for the m.   COLE 226:17
   there is only the unattended M.   ELIOT 308:34
   what is seen during a m.   SAND 713:99
   world's best m. is a calm hour   ABU 1:11
   worry and terror of the m.   MORR 598:98
momentariness delight in m.   GRAV 367:66
moments all m. are key m.   BUEC 165:44
   best and happiest m.   SHEL 786:16
   bitter m. of life   POWYS 667:97
   bright m. illuminate our path   SCHO 719:29
   brilliant frozen m.   LIVE 512:80
   designed a bench in a few m.   BELL 72:44
   highest quality to your m.   ANON 24:30
   m. of vision   BLUN 137:17
   pattern Of timeless m.   ELIOT 309:50
   pressing present m.   STUA 827:96
   quality to your m.   PATER 642:53
   such m. really mean   MUNRO 603:90
   There are no ordinary m.   MILL 574:67
   Wagner has good m.   ROSS 698:5
   worst m. into money   DONL 279:27
Mona Lisa lotta cats copy the M. L.   ARMS 30:77
   M. L. of the vegetable world   HUGH 419:34
   M. L. painted by a club?   GRIS 373:19
   M. L. seem an open book   LEAC 496:63
Monan danced the…on M.'s rill   SCOTT 723:4
monarch beneath a m.'s feet   BURNS 171:90
   invades authors like a m.   DRYD 288:26
   Israel's m.   DRYD 289:69

merry M., scandalous and poor   ROCH 691:52
modern constitutional M. exists no
   longer by right   HOGG 406:62
   m. of all I survey   COWP 241:54
   m. of the sea   GILB 353:93
   self-worship of the m.   MILL 571:79
   With a m.'s voice   SHAK 748:2
   With ravished ears The m. hears   DRYD 291:34
monarchies All the four M.   DONNE 281:89
   m. end by poverty   MONT 593:95
monarchs m. to choose favourites   SWIFT 831:82
   when fate summons, m. must obey   DRYD 288:47
monarchy discontented under m.   HOBB 404:28
   Film Industry is the American M.   MAMET 544:35
   Habsburg m.   TAAF 835:68
   m.…intelligible government   BAGE 51:89
   Than purest m.   MONT 593:3
monasteries some join m.   WEBB 893:64
monastery discipline of a m.   AELR 8:55
   Protective M. of Aesthetic Truth   MAMET 543:30
Monday Arriving M.   SWAN 830:44
   fell a-bleeding on Black M.   SHAK 740:59
   left Calais on M.   MACA 525:45
   worked M.…fired Wednesday   ALGR 11:30
Monet M. is only an eye   CEZA 203:53
money America had plenty of m.   BEHR 71:23
   America is so m.-hungry   TYSON 873:53
   Aphorisms…more for your…m.   DUDEK 293:77
   art…pursued with a view to m.   BUTL 178:76
   ask for my m. back   HUXL 425:79
   athlete cannot run with m.   ZATO 936:89
   authors…talking about m.   PRIT 669:51
   Ayatollah's m. to support   NORTH 618:71
   Beauty…became m.   WOLF 920:81
   blame someone…for making m.   ORWE 629:69
   borrowed time, borrowed m.   CALL 184:38
   borrow m. from people   WILL 911:1
   borrow m. off them   TWAIN 872:37
   borrow the m.   WARD 888:57
   Brass M.   ANON 21:37
   can be young without m.   WILL 912:26
   clever enough to get all that m.   CHES 212:88
   come to applaud their m.   HIRS 403:8
   corrupted by m.   GREE 371:54
   cost me much m.   PEPYS 647:27
   desire to make m.   VAN 876:26
   divided from…courtesans…by m.   DUMAS 294:94
   don't like m., actually   LOUIS 518:6
   Either your m.   WALK 885:98
   enough to get m. from it   LEAC 497:68
   except for m.   JOHN 445:20
   feeling they've wasted their m.   OLIV 624:71
   for…such sums of m.   SCHA 717:96
   giving m. to the Government   HERB 397:78
   goä wheer m. is!   TENN 847:54
   God would do if he had the m.   WOOL 923:65
   greatest possible amount of m.   WEBER 894:68
   greedy to add m. to m.   BIBLE 107:28
   happened to be a lot of m.   MERR 568:19
   hard to be…a lover of m.   WYCH 931:11
   hath no m.   BIBLE 104:53
   haven't got the m., so we've got to think   RUSH 706:72
   his private parts, his m.   BUTL 178:83
   honey, and plenty of m.   LEAR 497:83
   hunger for recognition and m.   SELF 727:80
   if he'd had the m.   KAUF 455:58
   If m. go before   SHAK 743:72
   If thou wilt lend this m.   SHAK 739:54
   If you can…count your m.   GETTY 351:49
   innocently employed…in getting m.   JOHN 444:5
   In the absence of m.   BALC 53:27
   leg for any m.   DICK 268:43
   licence to print m.   THOM 856:65
   little m., but not much   BEAV 67:20
   lost m. by underestimating   MENC 565:63
   love of m. is the root   BIBLE 124:79
   Make all the m.   SHAK 759:71
   makes the current m.   JONS 450:60
   make the white people…some m.   DAVIS 255:59
   making m. at the same time   BENN 77:58
   man's reputashun outlasts his m.   BILL 130:48
   marry for m. and comfort   SHAW 780:52
   Men Whose Lives Are M.   OATES 620:92
   m. and a room of her own   WOOLF 922:42
   M. and gentility   MITF 588:4
   m. answereth all things   BIBLE 101:88
   m. appears to vary   HUXL 426:3

m. can't buy me love   LENN 503:93
m. controls opinion   ORWE 628:48
M. couldn't buy friends   MILL 574:64
m. does not bring happiness   LACL 484:84
M. does not smell   VESP 879:72
m. from the pockets of the people   SMITH 798:54
m. has a power above   BUTL 177:62
m. has dissolved more worries   BLEST 136:93
M. is a comfort   ANON 18:74
M. is a good soldier   SHAK 743:73
M. is a kind of poetry   STEV 820:45
M. is better than poverty   ALLEN 12:52
m. is how we keep the score   CHAP 206:12
m. is just…information   WRIS 930:93
M. is like muck   BACON 49:12
m. is the standard   MORE 597:66
M.…is the true fuller's earth   GAY 347:82
m. manipulators and speculators   MAMET 544:35
m. on de bob-tail nag   FOST 332:59
M.'s a horrid thing   JAMES 433:39
M. speaks sense   BEHN 71:12
m…. Spend it, spend it   SHAK 743:74
M.…sweeter than Honey   FRAN 334:10
m.…that purchased that manor?   DONNE 282:94
M.…the most important thing   SHAW 777:47
M.…was exactly like sex   BALD 54:36
m. was not scarce?   EMER 313:50
m. you bet on him   FLAN 325:21
m. you save   LARK 491:42
most m. on a style   MING 587:70
Much discussion of m.   GALB 343:1
never been able to dominate m.   JOHN 439:77
nexus of all love and m. and power   DIDI 274:6
nice feet and plenty of m.   ASHF 35:2
no m. in poetry   GRAV 368:84
no m. in your purse   SHAK 749:41
no one shall work for m.   KIPL 472:20
nothing…a little m. will not cure   DURA 295:27
nothing left but m. and power   STAEL 811:47
original purchase m.   SMITH 797:42
paper which the masses call m.   ANDR 16:25
poet can earn much more m.   AUDEN 41:16
poisoning…for their insurance m.   DOYLE 285:52
possession of m.   KIPL 472:32
power and m. and fine robes   WELD 897:40
power of m. is…male power   DWOR 296:47
press…eagerly to pay m.   STEE 814:94
Prince calls in the good old m.   LAMB 486:43
put your m. in trust   HOLM 407:81
rattle of the m. box   LABO 483:55
ready m.   GRAMM 366:44
religion of m.   GAUT 347:72
retreated back into their m.   FITZ 325:99
rub up against m.   RUNY 702:78
runs into real m.   DIRK 275:27
Sex is like m.   UPDI 874:78
share out the little m.   MONT 592:70
side with plenty of m.   ANOU 26:4
sixty-three ways to find the m.   RABE 676:63
spent all the m.   JOHN 446:52
spent some of my own m.   KENN 464:47
state…master of m.   BEVE 85:28
take no m. of me   SHAK 770:93
tells you it is not a m. problem   CLIN 221:90
the act of marrying for m.   MAIL 540:63
Time is m.   FRAN 334:11
unlimited m.   CICE 218:23
voice is full of m.   FITZ 325:98
voter who uses his m.   SAMU 712:79
We're in the m.   DUBIN 292:66
we've got the m. too!   HUNT 422:21
What m. is better bestowed   THAC 849:3
what m. will do   PEPYS 647:45
what to do with their m.   BARA 59:44
when m. rolled in   HUGH 418:23
when you don't have any m.   DONL 279:24
where that m. came from   REAG 681:63
With the m. I spent   KENN 463:45
with the m. of the people   WHIT 902:67
women who have the most m.   GILM 356:53
worst moments into m.   DONL 279:27
write for m. or fame   MOORE 595:35
Yes, they have more m.   HEMI 394:12
You pays your m.   PUNCH 672:6
You talk of art…I think of m.   SHAW 781:93
moneybag Aristocracy of the M.   CARL 192:13
money-bags dream of m.-b.   SHAK 740:60

money-changers tables of the m.   BIBLE 113:79
moneys my m. and my usances   SHAK 739:53
Mongolia British Outer M.   BENN 75:15
mongrels continent of energetic m.   FISH 324:77
monitor sad m. scorning   CALL 185:43
monk a very political old m.   MURD 604:97
  found in the king a m.   AELR 8:55
  m. throwing himself   MAP 548:19
monkey make a m. of a man   BENC 74:98
  m.'s mask reveals the m.   BASHO 63:41
  M. with lollipop paws   LEAR 497:81
  never look long upon a M.   CONG 231:21
  no reason to attack the m.   BEVAN 85:21
monkeys Cats and m.   JAMES 433:36
  gave a million m. typewriters   HART 384:9
monks m.…lathy lot of thkunkth   BENT 78:79
  m.…naturally have a weak stomach   BERN 80:30
  town of m. and bones   COLE 227:23
monogamous Woman m.   JAMES 434:75
monoliths m. made of granite   MENC 566:85
monomania m. of accounting   WEIL 896:31
monopoly best of all m. profits   HICKS 402:79
  M. is Business   LLOYD 513:91
  M. power must be abused   SIMO 792:44
  newspaper is…a m.   SCOTT 722:74
  that efficient m.   PUZO 673:25
monosyllabic nothing so m.   FRY 340:28
monotonous becomes m.   TROL 866:83
  m., and wearisome   THOR 858:6
monotony articulate m.   STEP 817:58
  certain m. of genius   HAZL 387:65
  eternal m. of passion   FLAU 326:35
  m. of a watery surface   MOORE 595:26
  m. of marriage   GIBB 352:72
  m., work or leisure   POMP 658:47
Monroe doctrine of President M.   WILS 916:13
  making a picture with Marilyn M.   WILD 910:70
  Marilyn M. who was blonde   MAIL 540:58
  United States to the M. Doctrine   ROOS 696:53
monsieur m., for methinks   SHAK 738:8
monster art should be a m.   TZARA 873:59
  capital is become an overgrown m.   SMOL 801:29
  Effie M. was a m.   LEE 500:44
  Frankenstein m.   MUGG 601:50
  IS, the whited m.   LOWE 520:42
  jealousy…the green-eyed m.   SHAK 760:86
  make a m. of the multitude   SHAK 769:63
  many-headed m. of the pit   POPE 661:56
  m. that devours everything   BALZ 57:6
  m. was indeed the best   KARL 455:49
  m., which the Blatant beast men call   SPEN 809:8
  O thou m. ignorance   SHAK 733:78
  the m. there's no gagging   SHER 787:50
  this busy m., manunkind   CUMM 248:17
  Vice is a m.   POPE 660:18
monster-breeding m.-b. breast   POPE 662:68
monsters m. and devils   LUTH 523:99
  nocturnal m. that threaten   ROBBE 689:12
  stay out of politics or become m.   GINS 357:67
  transform Men into M.   FORD 330:19
  vile, unlovable, morbid m.   ANON 21:38
monstrous all that is m.   GOLD 360:32
  Ingratitude is m.   SHAK 769:63
  m. with politics   GINS 357:67
  seem a m. thing   FORD 329:2
  Two evils, m. either one   RANS 679:25
Montana M. skies seemed deeper   MCMU 537:87
Mont Blanc M. B. yet gleams   SHEL 782:18
Monte Testaceo its own M. T.   CLOU 222:28
Montgomery gie's a sang, M. cry'd   SKIN 795:13
  Robert M.'s genius   MACA 525:51
month April is the cruellest m.   ELIOT 305:52
  beginning of a new m. or year   MANN 545:69
  hesitates about a m.   STEV 822:2
  m. that God designed   KEIL 460:72
  old man in a dry m.   ELIOT 305:39
  one m. you have to live   GILB 355:20
  stand to in a m.   SHAK 736:59
  this is the m.   MILT 575:92
months all the m. of human birth   MASE 559:33
  few m. obliterate   BUNT 166:60
  first six m.   TRUM 868:28
  for m., for years   ROBBE 688:9
  go for m. on end   ORWE 627:40
  of the m. and stars   SWIN 832:17
  seven m. since she is gone   MILL 571:97
  think for m.   EINS 301:34

Monticelso M.: How!   WEBS 894:86
Montmorenci steep Of M.   KEATS 457:82
Montparnasse not rest quiet in M.   BENET 75:12
Montreal M. Olympics   DRAP 286:95
monument Builds his m. mockingly   JEFF 436:5
  built thyself a livelong m.   MILT 576:2
  like patience on a m.   SHAK 756:69
  live no longer in m.   SHAK 745:25
  m. of English prose   ELIOT 307:91
  m. of old Irish hospitality   EDGE 299:96
  m. sticks like a fishbone   LOWE 520:48
  m. to the man who did it   APPL 27:22
  not trying to make a m.   HARR 384:4
  only m. left of R.   BELL 72:36
  only m. the asphalt road   ELIOT 307:88
  sonnet is a moment's m.   ROSS 698:92
monumental buried in those m. arms   WALL 886:15
monuments nor the gilded m.   SHAK 771:21
mood In vacant or in pensive m.   WORD 928:43
  life's business…a summer m.   WORD 926:16
  m. will give us anything   SHAK 748:14
  silent grass-growing m.   MELV 564:43
  that sweet m.   WORD 924:76
moods envy not in any m.   TENN 843:33
  ever…changing m.   VIRG 882:24
moon an affair with the m.   STER 818:1
  and the m. was full   TENN 847:46
  apples of the m.   YEATS 932:36
  ask for the m.   ROBI 689:25
  beneath a waning m.   COLE 226:10
  Beneath the visiting m.   SHAK 765:52
  brilliant m.   YEATS 932:32
  broad m. rose circling into sight   BYRON 182:81
  calm…As is the crescent m.   WORD 924:73
  carry the m. in my pocket?   BROW 161:47
  cold o' the m.   BROW 162:75
  corners of the M.   MILT 578:43
  course of one revolving m.   DRYD 290:88
  danced by the light of the m.   LEAR 498:36
  danced the m.   SCOTT 723:4
  Daughter of the M.   LONG 516:56
  dull red image of the m.   WORD 925:3
  empty when the m. is full   BUTL 177:43
  even the m. is frightened   SHER 788:73
  from the dying m.   TENN 841:2
  honour from the pale-faced m.   SHAK 741:5
  How many miles the m. might   BYRON 181:67
  hush with the setting m.   TENN 845:90
  I didn't go to the m.   WILL 912:15
  if the m.'s a balloon   CUMM 247:6
  jumping over the m.   RAMS 678:7
  landing a man on the m.   KENN 462:14
  lovely m.—she lifted   FREE 336:45
  Man on the m.   BAKER 53:22
  melodious cats under the m.   HUXL 425:78
  m. and stars are set   STEV 822:13
  m. and the stars   MACC 528:16
  m.…in her silver shoon   DELA 260:69
  m. is up   BYRON 180:35
  m. of moons   DICK 270:92
  m. on the breast   MOORE 594:16
  m. on this cloud sea   SCOTT 722:77
  m. or favouring stars   WORD 925:98
  m.'s unclouded light   BURNS 170:82
  m. under her feet   BIBLE 126:65
  m. was a ghostly   NOYES 619:78
  m. was overhead   TENN 839:47
  m.…which thou hast ordained   BIBLE 94:87
  mortals call the M.   SHEL 783:40
  never gazed on the m.   SHAK 770:90
  new m. hangs   THOM 854:12
  nor the m. by night   BIBLE 97:87
  O more than m.   DONNE 280:51
  only a paper m.   HARB 380:35
  on the horns o'th' m.   SHAK 769:57
  O swear not by the m.   SHAK 736:51
  Part of a m.   FROST 338:86
  project a voyage to the m.   LARD 490:14
  Raymond like the Harvest M.   FARJ 318:48
  saucer like some full m.   MONRO 591:58
  saw the new m.   BALL 56:83
  Scotland kens beneath the m.   FERG 321:8
  set foot upon the m.   ANON 23:10
  shone the wintry m.   KEATS 459:37
  slow m. climbs   TENN 840:66
  sun and m. Were in   MILT 577:35
  sung to the m.   GILB 355:31

m. of many Socialists　ORWE 628:43
run the paper…with no other m.　BEAV 67:22
secret m. of the absent-minded　BELL 74:89
motives at the…bottom of their m.　ORWE 629:86
attribution of false m.　BALD 54:51
no corrupt or interested m.　PEEL 646:9
no man who knows my m.　EMMET 313:59
One of the strongest m.　EINS 301:33
motor before the m. car　THOM 853:2
heart's stalled m.　MAYA 562:93
Money…in m. racing nowadays　CHAP 206:12
m.…is the reader　CURT 249:46
M. racing is dangerous　HAWT 386:34
right is only a m. hand　HEPW 396:63
motorcycle m. black madonna　DYLAN 297:58
powerful m.-c.　USTI 875:7
motors good for General M.　WILS 915:81
motorway outside lane of a m.　BOYC 147:40
motto criticism's m.　FORS 332:54
jamais triste that is my m.　MARQ 554:28
Let their m. be:—Hunt, shoot　BRON 155:79
m. of everyone　DORAM 282:1
m. of mankind　LAFO 485:1
Nixon's m.　COUS 239:4
that's the m.　HARD 381:44
true to your instincts…was his m.　LAWR 493:87
With this for m.　TENN 846:12
woman's m.　STAN 812:68
mottoes m. on sundials　POUND 664:36
mould as through a m.　SCHR 720:43
broke the m.　ARIO 29:44
lips the m. falls close　ROSS 698:96
settles in the m.　JEFF 436:3
through the m.　MANS 547:89
mouldering m. like wedding-cake　RICH 685:43
Moulmein By the old M. Pagoda　KIPL 470:85
M. is situated　KIPL 470:84
moulting when they're m.　NASH 608:76
mount never climbed M. Fuji　MORR 598:96
O Oisin, m. by me　YEATS 932:31
There is a high m.　STUA 827:97
mountain 'assault' on the m.　CRAN 243:31
bare m. tops are bald　ARNO 34:71
Buddha…at the top of a m.　PIRS 652:25
chilly and inhospitable m.　KENN 461:96
climbed my last political m.　WALL 886:7
dangerous to climb a m.　HAWT 386:34
dew on the m.　SCOTT 723:8
Doing time is like climbing a m.　DEAN 257:89
ethereal m.　BENU 78:85
every m. and hill shall be made low　BIBLE 103:36
Flatter the m. tops　SHAK 771:16
from his m. walls　TENN 844:68
get me to the m. of myrrh　BIBLE 101:2
gone on the m.　SCOTT 723:7
heaping m. on m.　CARL 191:85
high m. cradle in Pamere　ARNO 32:28
horse on the m.　LORCA 517:85
in m. exploration　SHIP 789:76
Land of the m.　SCOTT 723:92
light atop the m.　POUND 666:73
m. and a national shrine　MUMF 603:76
m. of his holiness　BIBLE 95:27
m. outline varies　THOR 857:78
m. revealing its geologic　MILL 572:8
m. which is of no use for sheep　BUTL 177:63
mowing down m. ranges　MILL 572:26
one m., one sea, one river　BURT 174:73
purple m. majesties　BATES 64:49
ragged m. ranges　MACK 533:15
river jumps over the m.　AUDEN 40:91
robes the m. in its azure hue　CAMP 186:66
rocky m.　GILB 354:96
say unto this m.　BIBLE 112:65
somebody has shifted the m.　LEVIN 506:64
stood on more m. tops　THOR 858:10
Tching prayed on the m.　POUND 665:62
there stands One m.　BROW 160:20
Throng from each m.-pass!　MCCA 527:87
Up the airy m.　ALLI 13:61
wires that span the m. stream　CRANE 243:16
yonder m. height　TENN 842:15
mountain-daisy to this m.-d.　WORD 929:67
mountaineer On, every m.　MCCA 527:87
mountainous great m. sports girl　BETJ 83:69
mountains Among the Galilean m.　CRAS 244:37
Before the m. were brought forth　BIBLE 96:49

Before the m. were brought forth　BOOK 143:63
blue Friuli's m.　BYRON 180:33
blue icecaps on the m.　CHAT 207:49
born and dies among the m.　WORD 925:7
dawn in the m.　MURP 604:2
decayed hole among the m.　ELIOT 306:66
England's m. green?　BLAKE 135:82
faith, so that I could remove m.　BIBLE 121:9
grass is green…m. steep　STEP 817:58
Greenland's icy m.　HEBER 390:34
High m. are a feeling　BYRON 180:26
How beautiful upon the m.　BIBLE 104:47
intellects, like the tops of m.　MACA 526:59
mind has m.　HOPK 413:5
m. are stern teachers　TILM 860:71
M. are the beginning　RUSK 704:11
m. be carried into the…sea　BIBLE 95:24
m. by the winter sea　TENN 847:45
M. divide us　GALT 344:29
m. look on Marathon　BYRON 182:87
M. of whimsy　ROCH 691:56
M. on whose…breast　MILT 576:8
m.…shall break forth　BIBLE 104:57
m.…to him were friends　BYRON 179:21
m. were there　HERZ 401:58
remove m., and make seas　CARL 191:81
said to the m.…Fall on us　BIBLE 126:58
shadow of the blue m.　MELBA 563:15
skill to move m.　HOFF 405:47
There are new m.　LEGU 501:61
to the m. is going home　MUIR 602:64
true call…of the m.　STARK 813:73
voices…One of the m.　WORD 928:47
weighed the m. in scales　BIBLE 103:38
What are men to rocks and m.?　AUST 43:69
when the m. shall be set moving　KORAN 479:93
Woods, or steepy m.　MARL 553:17
mountainside along the m.　WORD 926:17
every m.　SMITH 800:91
mountain-spring Rivers and m.-s.　OAKL 620:89
mountain-stream in the fall of m.-s.　BEAT 66:96
m.-s. that ends　LOWE 520:28
mountain-top as on a m.-t.　HUXL 426:10
been to the m. t.　KING 468:43
mountaintops misty m.　SHAK 736:69
mountain-tops m. t. that freeze　SHAK 775:12
mountebank impudent m. who sold pills　ADDI 5:8
mere anatomy, a m.　SHAK 733:61
story of a m. and his zany　WALP 887:34
mountebanks m.…imitate　LEWIS 508:1
mounted always well m.　HALI 378:82
Mountjoy M. began to move　MACA 527:78
mourn Blessed are they that m.　BIBLE 109:83
countless thousands m.!　BURNS 170:80
Margaret you m. for　HOPK 412:95
m. a mischief that is past　SHAK 759:66
m. with ever-returning spring　WHIT 906:47
secure, and now can never m.　SHEL 786:4
time enough to m.　DANI 252:88
time to m.　BIBLE 100:70
mourned m. unto you　BIBLE 111:36
mourners let the m. come　AUDEN 40:89
m. go about the streets　BIBLE 101:92
mournful M. and Never-ending　POE 656:26
mourning in such very deep m.　AUST 42:58
M. becomes Electra　ONEI 625:96
m. for my life　CHEK 209:9
m. into dancing　BIBLE 95:8
M. is a hard business　MALA 541:79
mourns m. when many leave　OWEN 632:66
one m. alone　BERG 79:99
mouse absurd little m.　HORA 414:32
catch a m. or two (for form's sake)　GRAY 370:41
invention of a m.!　DISN 275:33
leave room for the m.　SAKI 710:48
m. in a mousehole　EISE 302:66
m. sticks in his sharp paw　ANON 18:71
not even a m.　MOORE 594:14
not the m. who is the thief　JACO 432:13
way a m. waltzes　WHITE 903:86
mouse-trap baiting a m.-t.　SAKI 710:48
The M.　SHAK 754:94
moustache Big chap with a small m.　WODE 919:71
couldn't wear a m. like that　HOOV 411:68
didn't wax his m.　KIPL 470:78
drawing a m. on a madonna　VENT 879:62
worn a m.　SIMON 792:38

moustaches Nothing…except m.　BROD 153:53
mouth Christ in the m.　PATR 643:71
doth become the m. as well　SHAK 747:77
draw near me with their m.　BIBLE 103:29
Even in the cannon's m.　SHAK 749:50
Familiar in his m.　SHAK 746:59
for an Englishman to open his m.　SHAW 780:61
gift horse in the m.　RABE 676:68
hand more instrumental to the m.　SHAK 751:98
have not found the m.　ACHE 2:19
heart into my m.　SHAK 762:52
In his m. are Lies　WELLS 898:76
in my m. sweet as honey　BIBLE 126:64
Into the m. of Hell　TENN 845:77
just whispering in her m.　MARX 557:83
keep your m. shut　ITO 431:98
laugh…before he opens his m.　NATH 609:21
m. and my breasts　SEXT 728:16
m. do crush their wine　MARV 556:74
m. is smoother than oil　BIBLE 99:13
m. it, as many of your players do　SHAK 754:85
m. must be held in　BIBLE 95:11
m. of a hog to eat　NASHE 609:19
m. of the cannon　RUSK 703:99
m. shall shew forth thy praise　BIBLE 95:31
m. so prim　ELIOT 307:6
m.…used as a latrine　AMIS 14:82
No M. And I Must Scream　ELLI 311:84
no m. to put it in　DICK 266:66
opened not his m.　BIBLE 104:51
open thy m. wide　BIBLE 96:44
out of his m. went a…sword　BIBLE 125:45
Out of the same m. proceedeth　BIBLE 125:14
purple-stained m.　KEATS 459:58
put a hose in their m.　KROC 481:19
put my words in thy m.　BIBLE 105:67
put one into her m.　THAC 849:85
rash with thy m.　BIBLE 101:76
satisfieth thy m. with good things　BIBLE 97:62
Set a watch…before my m.　BIBLE 98:4
slap-dash down in the m.　CONG 231:99
strawberries at the m. of their pot　ELIZ 310:64
tail in its m.　FERL 321:14
that which goeth into the m.　BIBLE 112:58
The boy's m.　TWAIN 871:13
When the m. says yes　HUGO 420:76
wine will burn our m.　EMER 313:37
with an open m.　STEV 821:67
with its tail in its m.　HOOD 410:41
z is keeping your m. shut　EINS 301:43
mouthful every m. of food　FORD 329:98
m. of air　YEATS 932:37
mouthless millions of the m. dead　SORL 804:90
mouth-organ Menuhin on the m.-o.　ADLER 7:51
mouths bizzing craigs and m. to weet　FERG 321:8
Blind m.! that scarce　MILT 578:51
from your smoky m.　MARL 553:7
made m. in a glass　SHAK 763:73
m. Of wisest men　MILT 586:56
'Pardon' for kings' m.　SHAK 735:29
put an enemy in their m.　SHAK 760:80
speaking truth, to m. like mine　BROW 162:89
move America is always on the m.　CUMM 247:10
feel the earth m.?　HEMI 394:14
if it made its own m.　JARR 435:84
in him we live, and m.　BIBLE 119:50
m. his hearers　FRAS 335:27
Sometimes you m. publicly　BAKER 53:18
moveables to my chattels and my m.　SHAK 745:38
moved Being m. is what collecting　ANNE 18:55
do not like being m.　CLOU 223:31
m. by what is not unusual　ELIOT 304:9
m., not only as an author　GRASS 367:59
not m. with concord　SHAK 741:88
shall not be m.　BIBLE 95:25
movement aggressive m.　MARI 550:52
infinite diversity of m.　REDT 681:76
joyful with swift m.　ANON 18:71
neither arrest nor m.　ELIOT 307:95
Never confuse m. with action　HEMI 395:27
only m.…dropping of the dead　WILL 911:2
Our m. took a grip　GOER 359:9
Our nature consists in m.　PASC 640:15
slow m. of clouds　DAY 257:84
ticking m. of the human timepiece　ASLET 36:8
movements m. of human thought　BENN 77:58
m. of the limbs　LEON 503:16

natural and ordinary m. — FONT 329:86
physical m. — GALS 344:24
mover Fear is the great m. — BART 62:13
moves it m. again since it is life — FAUL 319:70
Nevertheless, it m. — GALI 343:7
movie can't wait till the m. comes out — JACK 431:9
cheats of the m. screen — MAIL 539:38
Life in the m. business — MAMET 544:36
m.-makers…put more reality — HECHT 390:36
m., this is the way to do it — LANE 488:88
old m. plots — BAKER 53:24
only a m. of the past — KESEY 465:73
same m. could be seen — JORD 451:69
movies Adding sound to m. — PICK 651:4
Good m. make you care — KAEL 453:23
lesson in how not to write for the m. — CHAN 204:82
like pornographic m. — ROGE 695:31
M. are more likely…to reach deep
  feelings — MAIL 540:64
Thanks to the m. — USTI 875:6
the basic appeal of m. — KAEL 453:22
thing that can kill the M. — ROGE 695:25
trot down to the m. — WILD 910:81
violence in m. — TARA 836:93
W. C. Fields m. — HAWES 385:30
moving always already m. — HEID 391:44
face of a m.-picture actor — MENC 566:86
in form and m. — SHAK 752:57
lie without m. — RHYS 684:26
privilege of always m. — LEWIS 507:70
mowers m. in the hay — MUIR 602:55
Mowgli M. answered — KIPL 471:10
mown often as we are m. down — TERT 849:82
Mozart en famille they play M. — BARTH 62:8
sonatas of M. — SCHN 719:23
MP Being an MP feeds your vanity — PARR 639:97
goings-on of an unlucky MP — CRIT 245:62
MPs many M. never see the London — LIVI 512:84
much how m. unexpected, by so m. — SHAK 738:20
m. I want which most men have — DYER 296:50
m. to hear and see — SKEL 794:89
no man is named m. — EMER 312:26
muck in lovely m. I've lain — HOUS 415:67
Money is like m. — BACON 49:12
sing 'em m. — MELBA 563:14
when to stop raking the m. — ROOS 696:54
muckle M. he made o' that — MACQ 538:15
muckrake with a m. in his hand — BUNY 166:74
mud blades pricked the m. — BROW 161:44
clouds, or m. or like places — LEON 504:19
cover the universe with m. — FORS 331:45
gaping mussels, left upon the m. — CRAB 242:99
he was just all m. — TWAIN 871:99
He who slings m. — STEV 821:64
made up of marble and m. — HAWT 386:43
more dangerous than a m.-puddle — STEIN 815:10
M.! M.! Glorious m.! — FLAN 326:22
pure clay of time's m. — MALA 541:84
Science is angling in the m. — HUXL 425:74
sees the m., and…the stars — LANG 488:92
shining gull-marked m. — LARK 491:33
stream that ends in m. — LOWE 520:28
muddied The people m. — SHAK 754:20
muddle Ah, Rachel, aw a m.! — DICK 270:6
beginning, a m., and an end — LARK 491:46
intellectual m. early — MURD 604:95
meddle and m. — DERBY 262:11
solve…the m. with humaneness — WILS 915:78
muddy to m. or mock — PALEY 635:12
muffin Hot M….Company — DICK 267:98
mug Poetry…a m.'s game — ELIOT 307:85
muir-men m.-m. win their hay — BALL 55:66
mulberry tarrying in m. shade — SHAK 738:16
mule m. of politics — DISR 276:46
not as the horse, or as the m. — BIBLE 95:11
Sicilian m. was to me — GLAD 359:95
smelt a lot of m. manure — WILL 912:7
mules m….accustomed to burdens — RICH 686:68
multifarious another of the m. ways — SITW 794:86
multiplication m. of the fittest — SPEN 806:41
multiplied m. itself in broad ways — REYES 684:21
multiply be fruitful and m. — BIBLE 85:41
multitude another to the m. — HAWT 386:41
by reason of this great m. — BIBLE 93:44
cover the m. of sins — BIBLE 125:28
for the m. to be ingrateful — SHAK 769:63
From an exemplary m. — VIAN 880:81

hide a m. of sins — BIBLE 125:20
m. of one million — KOES 477:28
m. of perverse inclinations — SHAR 776:41
M. too familiar — LEST 505:48
m., which no man could number — BIBLE 126:59
sprung in affluent m. — TWAIN 871:16
stupidity of the m. — BAUD 64:67
washed his hands before the m. — BIBLE 114:2
multitudes I contain m. — WHIT 905:35
rank me with the barbarous m. — SHAK 740:62
seeing the m., he went up — BIBLE 109:83
Weeping, weeping m. — ELIOT 305:44
mum fuck you up, your m. — LARK 491:38
merryman moping m. — GILB 355:31
M., the Persil-user — BETJ 84:84
oafish louts remember M. — BETJ 84:98
when m. stays home — FALU 317:41
mumble Let her maunder and m. — CARL 192:4
m. with great coherence — GREE 372:81
when in doubt, m. — WAGN 884:65
mummies make the m. dance — LIND 510:44
mummy had his M.'s leave — KIPL 472:35
M., I'm sick with disgust — BETJ 84:9
munched And m., and m., and m. — SHAK 766:67
mundane miraculous to me — DIDI 274:6
mundus pereat m. — FERD 320:1
Munster sun that was M.'s glory — ORAH 627:21
mural purest…is the m. — OROZ 627:27
murals m. on the wall — BETJ 84:7
murder anyone meditating m. — FISH 324:75
brought back m. into the home — HITC 404:14
call it m. — MAXT 562:88
commit rape, m. — BARN 60:63
dens of robbery and m. — NATI 610:25
hard to tell it fr'm m. — DUNNE 295:22
in five years…ready to commit m. — DAMR 251:80
love and m. will out — CONG 231:10
Macbeth does m. sleep — SHAK 767:2
man indulges himself in m. — DE 262:10
man wants to m. a tiger — SHAW 779:29
met M. on the way — SHEL 783:36
Most sacrreligious m. — SHAK 767:9
m. and to ravish — AYTO 45:16
M. doesn't round out — HAMM 380:24
m., hate, vertue — MALO 543:13
m., homicide — STUB 827:3
M. is always a mistake — WILDE 908:10
M. is a unique crime — JAMES 434:58
M. most foul — SHAK 752:29
M….One of the Fine Arts — DE 262:9
m. shrieks out — WEBS 895:13
M., though it have no tongue — SHAK 753:70
m. to dissect — WORD 924:75
M. wol out — CHAU 209:96
no vicious blot, m. — SHAK 762:54
one m. made a villain — PORT 663:13
rape and m. — NOON 618:58
scymitars, wi' m. crusted — BURNS 172:22
Sooner m. an infant — BLAKE 134:45
took m. out of the Venetian vase — CHAN 205:94
Treason and m. — SHAK 745:35
warfare, terror, m. — WELL 897:48
war, I call it m. — LOWE 520:29
war…I think it m. — PAINE 634:89
murdered all that I had m. — SHAK 732:20
except the m.'s — HAMM 380:24
Glamis hath m. sleep — SHAK 767:3
m. them 0–0 — SHAN 776:34
one a m. self — ROSS 698:97
recently m. woman — SHAR 776:45
their m. man — KEATS 458:27
murderèd son of the dear m. — SHAK 753:69
murderer jailer of your m. — HUGH 419:53
m. for a fancy prose — NABO 606:31
m. from the beginning — BIBLE 117:98
m., to be a politician — MILL 573:57
sometimes the m.'s — HAMM 380:24
the man is a common m. — SAKI 710:45
you must bear his m. — YEATS 934:68
murderers of whores and m. — WEBS 894:84
murderous m. hate — SHAK 770:3
murders m. sticking on his hands — SHAK 768:35
murk only adds to the m. — MILL 573:54
murmur live m. of a summer's day — ARNO 32:16
m. about his name — RUSK 704:14
m. among the zealots — HUME 422:16
m., soon replies — MILT 580:88

murmurings noise of m. — BIBLE 107:29
murmurs In hollow m. died away — COLL 228:50
muscle m. of my nation — FRAN 335:22
not extra m. — TRUE 868:26
take the m. from bone — ELIOT 307:5
muscles call his m. into action — POE 656:17
girls with the m. of a welter-weight — WODE 919:61
m. of his brawny arms — LONG 515:44
relax your m. — MOSS 600:29
She had the rippling m. — PERE 648:58
muscular His Christianity was m. — DISR 277:87
muse brash courtship of the m. — THOM 854:28
'Fool,' said my M. to me — SIDN 790:8
invocation of the M. — GRAV 367:74
Let my M. — HERR 400:40
Livelier liquor than the M. — HOUS 415:65
loving a foreign m. — BENET 75:11
meditate the thankless m. — MILT 578:49
M. invoked — SWIFT 832:96
m. is…of the English strain — DRAY 286:97
m. of Moore — BYRON 182:75
M. shall sit, and think — GRAY 369:4
O for a m. of fire — SHAK 745:29
Perversity is the m. — SONT 804:71
provokes the snarling m. — JOHN 441:14
same soil as the M. — UNTE 874:71
shelter, and even m. — TUCH 869:61
spelt by the unlettered m. — GRAY 369:21
Tell me, M. — HOMER 409:24
The tenth M. — TROL 866:73
trivial people should m. and thunder — LAWR 495:28
Who loves not…the heavenly m. — DOWL 284:42
Why does my M. only speak — SMITH 800:1
muses Among the M. — WYATT 930:98
M.' garden — CAREW 190:54
m. gave their full consent — LANY 489:7
M. in striped trousers — ORWE 629:79
M. sing of happy swains — CRAB 242:86
priest of the M. — HORA 413:22
sweet M. of the Light — RUSK 704:38
who brings The Smithfield M. — POPE 662:64
museum in the South Kensington M. — KING 469:63
marble m. of the soul — RODR 693:96
mind is a m. — RAINE 677:96
m. of antiquities — ENGE 314:68
You're the Louvr' M. — PORT 663:6
museums art m. to worship dead works — MAYA 562:92
department stores…like m. — WARH 889:65
free her from the numberless m. — MARI 550:54
In all m. throughout the world — PATE 642:56
mush m. and slush — OWEN 632:96
mushroom I am…a m. — FORD 330:11
Life…too short to stuff a m. — CONR 235:22
m. which has poisoned — MILL 572:21
mushrooms Patriots…like m. — WALP 887:41
music advised to give her m. — SHAK 773:60
after the m. had finished — HELP 393:93
All m. is folk m. — ARMS 30:76
Appalling Popularity of M. — LAMB 487:66
as Beethoven was born for m. — PELE 646:17
Beer, tobacco, and m. — MANN 545:64
Bells, the poor man's only m. — COLE 226:96
Birds warbling all the m. — COWP 241:69
British m….perpetual promise — BEEC 69:64
by that m….embrace — SHAK 742:32
Canned m….audible wallpaper — COOKE 236:33
century…deserves its own m. — DEBU 258:7
city is built to m. — TENN 847:59
compulsion doth in m. lie — MILT 577:20
consume it in m. — MONT 591:64
creation of m. is…natural — COLE 225:71
daughters of m. shall be brought low — BIBLE 101:92
day the m. died — MCLE 534:25
day the m. died — MACL 534:27
did enjoy the m. — JOHN 441:9
doesn't want new m. — HONE 409:30
Do not take up m. — BOUL 146:21
Don't just move to the m. — MARL 551:69
don't know anything about m. — BEER 69:81
ear for her m. — DAY 257:84
Ear's deep-sweet m. — SHAK 733:55
English may not like m. — BEEC 69:57
essence of m. — MOZA 601:46
ethereal m. — GALL 344:19
everything seems to happen to m. — WILL 912:14
existence like a piece of m. — MACB 527:81
face the m. and dance — BERL 79:15

called them by wrong n. — BROW 161:52
calleth them all by their n. — BIBLE 98:6
cat must have Three Different N. — ELIOT 307:9
commodity of good n. — SHAK 741:96
enter the n. and hand the keys — MANS 547:87
five handmaidens, whose n. — ROSS 698:90
forgets words as one forgets n. — WAUGH 893:51
For your n. — WEBS 894:84
given their n. up to her — JONS 450:54
Home of…unpopular n. — ARNO 33:39
How can they use such n. — SASS 716:75
live like our n. — WALC 884:73
live so long in our n. — BROW 159:88
lost all the n. — JOHN 446:52
men's n. On sand — MILT 577:31
men whose n. you never knew — ARLO 30:62
n….associated…with racehorses — SAKI 710:34
n. in print — CHES 212:93
n. of dogs — AMIS 14:97
n. of those who in their lives — SPEN 807:47
n. to be mentioned — AUST 43:70
our n….as household words — SHAK 746:59
spare the grossness of the n. — DRYD 291:29
what are n. but air? — COLE 226:98
Naming n. of parts — REED 681:77
Nanda N. Devi Basin — SHIP 789:78
Nanki-Poo Long life to N.-P. — GILB 355:20
nanny n. seemed to be extinct — HOGG 406:61
Nantucket spewed N. bones — LOWE 520:43
nap short n. at sermon — ADDI 6:14
Naples now N. holds me — VIRG 882:33
See N. and die? — DEBR 257:1
Napoleon Maybe N. was wrong — STOP 825:66
N. did not manoeuvre — WELL 897:58
N. had commanded — ORWE 629:74
N. learned from the mistakes — TAYL 837:13
N. of crime — DOYLE 285:70
N. thinks that I am a fool — ALEX 11:20
signs of N.'s greatness — UNSE 874:70
wanted to be N. — DALI 251:69
Napoleons Caesars and N. — HUXL 425:84
napper from your n. to your feet — COLL 227:35
narcissistically reflecting…n. — TALE 835:82
narcotics Like dull n. — TENN 842:23
narration life as n. — MANN 545:66
time is the medium of n. — MANN 546:71
narrative construct a n. for ourselves — AUST 44:99
motive in this n. — TWAIN 871:93
n. impulse is always with us — COOV 236:58
no longer…fiction…only n. — DOCT 278:3
narratives conceive of our lives as n. — LEHM 501:66
narrow bestride the n. world — SHAK 747:76
cucumber n. — SITW 794:66
margin is too n. — FERM 321:15
n. straight channels — RANJ 678:16
path…sometimes 'tis too n. — DRYD 289:53
straight and n. as a tomb — SMITH 800:95
narrow-necked as with n.-n. bottles — POPE 659:90
narrow-souled It is with n.-s. people — POPE 659:90
Nasticreechia N. Krorluppia — LEAR 498:92
nastier anything n. to say — SAYE 717:84
Blood…a great deal n. — SOME 803:66
nasty everybody is as n. as himself — SHAW 777:50
far from their n. little minds — DEBU 258:5
how n. the n. people are — POWE 666:84
of n. ideas — SWIFT 831:87
Something n. in the woodshed — GIBB 352:71
Zip that turns n. — CHRI 214:33
nation affairs of the n. — AMERY 14:80
American n. will speak — ROOS 696:52
America…only idealistic n. — WILS 917:19
any n. where Christianity — SWIFT 832:13
any other n. may be its workshop — CHAM 203:58
arm the n. — MANC 544:44
as a n. taste-blind — FISH 324:79
as a n., we don't dress well — SHAW 777:62
asset for one n. — RUNC 702:72
be a n. of shopkeepers — PUNCH 672:7
bedrooms of the n. — TRUD 868:22
best serves his n. — KENN 463:35
Better one suffer, than a n. grieve — DRYD 290:86
bind up the n.'s wounds — LINC 510:41
British are an aggressive n. — ABSE 1:9
broad mass of a n. — HITL 404:17
build that n.'s fate — BLAKE 135:70
common property of the n. — TIMES 861:77
continent a new n. — LINC 510:39

credit of the n. — CONG 231:28
curse of me and my n. — POUND 665:44
darlings of our n. — SHAK 759:56
doing it to a whole n. — SIHA 791:29
engaged in n. building — GARV 346:56
every man and n. — LOWE 519:27
every man of every n. — THAC 849:1
existence as a n. — PITT 653:46
Explaining metaphysics to the n. — BYRON 181:62
exterminate a n. — SPOCK 811:38
fate as a n. — HOFS 406:56
fetishism…God of this n. — TATE 837:7
fourth-class n. — JAY 436:2
general synod of the n. — BAIL 52:6
government of a n. — SUN 829:33
great and powerful n. — GARI 346:47
great n. betrayed — INOU 430:74
half of the n. is mad — SMOL 801:27
happiness of the n. — JOHN 443:86
history of our n. — TOOLE 863:12
holy n. — BIBLE 125:24
in any one n. — HUME 422:12
influence of a n. — BENN 75:17
inspired the n. — CHUR 217:3
integrity of the Irish n. — REDM 681:72
I want to talk to a n. — PULI 672:2
little war for a great n. — WELL 898:64
living Jury of the N. — BENN 76:55
lowest rank of every n. — JOHN 443:60
make war on a kindred n. — BETH 82:74
most decent n. — BUSH 175:91
muscle of my n. — FRAN 335:22
n. about to go into…liquidation — MACI 533:8
n….against n. — BIBLE 113:85
n….against n. — BIBLE 102:8
n. is being so right — WILS 916:10
n. blesses what undoes it — HUGO 421:81
n. has always been committed — KENN 462:12
n. heaps its scorn — LAZA 496:52
n. is a rainbow — JACK 431:7
n. is a society united — INGE 429:54
n. is not governed — BURKE 168:9
n. is the universality — MAZZ 562:2
n. not slow and dull — MILT 579:80
n. of gentlemen — MUGA 601:47
n. of shopkeepers — NAPO 607:68
n. of shopkeepers — SMITH 798:50
n. of shopkeepers — STOP 825:66
n. of violence — JORD 450:65
n. ruled by swine — THOM 855:45
n….run by an old man — BROD 153:52
n. seems to slouch onward — HOFS 406:55
n.'s experience and his vision — KISS 475:98
N.'s Freight Handler — SAND 712:91
n. shall rise against n. — BIBLE 113:85
n. should commit itself — KENN 462:14
n. suspects…regular ministerial — WHIT 902:67
n.'s whole scale of living — CHUR 216:63
n. talking to itself — MILL 572:2
n., to remain healthy — MUSS 605:20
n. to the policy — ROOS 696:42
n. was ever blessed with — FRAN 334:14
n….without a sense of beauty — WHAR 901:45
needed to constitute a n.? — SIEY 791:26
nobility of descent in a n. — POTT 664:20
nobody…or I'm a n. — WALC 884:71
our greatness as a n. — THAT 850:15
parcel of rogues in a n.! — BURNS 172:35
parcel of rogues in a n.! — BURNS 172:36
personification of the n. — PAST 642:46
puissant n. rousing herself — MILT 579:82
realm, n., or city — KNOX 476:18
reform a n. — CARL 191:88
rich and lazy n. — KIPL 474:70
service of this n. — GAND 345:32
social life of our n. — LEWIS 507:83
tell the ideals of a n. — DOUG 283:25
that we are a n. of amateurs — ROSE 696:61
the one indispensable—or was it
   indisposable?—n. — VIDAL 881:9
things that matter for a n. — LLOY 513:99
thinking in terms of n. states — ADEN 7:47
to enrich a new n. — STIG 824:45
To every n. a term — KORAN 478:63
trade union for the n. — HEATH 390:18
train for war…a n. — WILS 916:16
Type of a coming n. — LAWS 496:45

up to the face of a n. — ROCK 692:83
We have, as a n. — MAMET 543:22
What ish my n.? — SHAK 746:45
what our N. stands for — BETJ 83:85
what stupid age or n. — BUTL 177:56
whole of the Hellish n. — SITW 793:60
who writes the n.'s laws — PERE 648:57
will make of thee a great n. — BIBLE 87:72
wise n. preserves its records — HOWE 417:99
With a n., as with a boxer — ACHE 3:51
Youth of a N. — DISR 276:55
national African n. consciousness — MACM 536:71
German N. Socialism — GOER 359:9
n. capacity for individual enterprise — WAVE 893:58
n. costume…architecture, or…art — BIRD 130:62
N. Debt is a very Good thing — SELL 727:84
n. dividend is diminished — PIGOU 651:15
our n. slogans — THUR 859:48
policeman in the N. Gallery — WHIS 902:62
rock of the n. resources — WEBS 894:71
suffering a n. defeat — EDIN 300:9
think little of the n. interest — WILL 912:4
nationalism also took…their n. — GOER 359:9
Canadian n. was systematically — INNIS 429:67
Current n. is merely — ILLI 428:45
dangerous being n. — RUNC 702:72
free from…n. — ORWE 629:77
N., and its chum, patriotism — DUNN 295:20
N. is a silly cock — ALDI 10:9
n….seen as a noble thing — BAKER 53:21
somewhat blatant n. — RUSS 705:49
wind of n. and freedom — BALD 54:49
nationalities smaller n. — ASQU 36:9
nationality barbarous feeling of n. — SENI 728:98
Other people have a n. — BEHAN 70:9
nations advantageous…to n. — PAINE 634:93
all n., and kindreds — BIBLE 126:59
Amid…the misery of n. — PITT 653:47
among 50 n. — TRUM 868:34
before him shall be gathered all n. — BIBLE 113:91
both rich and poor n. — ILLI 428:46
cheap defence of n. — BURKE 169:35
civilized n. of the world — PEARY 645:1
day of small n. has passed away — CHAM 203:59
dazzle and bewilder n. — MACA 525:42
dead n. never rise again — LONG 516:59
deceive the n. no more — BIBLE 127:77
different n. should do — MONT 593:92
enmities between n. — KENN 463:27
fierce contending n. — ADDI 7:39
free n. are peaceful n. — BUSH 176:18
great n. have always acted — KUBR 481:32
happiest n., have no history — ELIOT 303:91
hostile behaviour…to n. — FULB 341:45
intercourse with foreign n. — DECA 258:8
Jew among the n. — FERB 320:94
king to judge us like all the n. — BIBLE 91:86
language all n. understand — BEHN 71:12
League of n. — MACD 530:59
leave it to…foreign n. — BACON 50:60
leaves of the tree…for the healing of the n. — BIBLE 127:84
Levitical degrees between n. — ROCHE 691:46
living n. wait — AUDEN 40:4
loans…to foreign n. — BAGE 51:94
master minds of all n. — TWAIN 871:16
men and n. behave wisely — EBAN 298:70
most bourgeois of all n. — ENGE 314:65
n. and governments have never — HEGEL 391:41
n. are as a drop — BIBLE 103:39
n.; between whom…no intercourse — DISR 276:53
n. desirous of emancipating — MAZZ 562:99
n. into a new-made artificial state — POWE 667:94
n. large and small — UNIT 873:69
n. of Europe and outside — LEES 500:50
n. of the future — CURZ 249:53
n. that have prospered and declined — LARD 490:15
N. touch at their summits — BAGE 51:88
n. which spoiled you — BIBLE 106:16
N. would do well — COWP 241:77
not living n. but dead states — CHAM 203:56
no very good symptom…of n. — CARL 191:77
often that n. learn — KISS 475:89
other n. of the earth — JAMES 433:35
Other n. use 'force' — WAUGH 892:34
peace…with all n. — LINC 510:41
place among the n. of the earth — EMMET 313:59
Praise the Lord, all n. — BIBLE 127:92

O ruined piece of n.	SHAK 763:90
our mortal n.	WORD 927:26
Our n. consists	PASC 640:15
painter…must take n.	MALL 542:93
physicians…leave it to N.	BURG 167:86
poetical n.	WHIT 905:28
presented to us by N.	LAVO 493:83
primary feeling that n. imprints in us	SADE 708:93
pure mortal n.	CARL 191:84
renovator of matter N.	OVID 631:47
representations of general n.	JOHN 443:78
repugnant to n.	KNOX 476:18
rich in n.'s store	FORD 330:18
scientist does not study n.	POIN 657:34
scream passing through n.	MUNCH 603:80
secured by good n. and truth	ROCH 691:67
See how n.…grows in silence	THER 851:44
Sexually, Woman is N.'s contrivance	SHAW 778:96
she in spite of n.	SHAK 759:60
Simple N. is the most harmless	BEHN 71:19
simple N. to his hope has giv'n	POPE 660:11
singing is delightful to n.	BYRD 178:93
sketch from n.	CONS 235:26
spark o' N.'s fire	BURNS 170:64
spectacle of n.	ROUS 700:94
state of war by n.	SWIFT 832:1
struggles and strives against n.	INNO 429:69
subtlety of n.	BACON 47:58
suff'ring eye inverted N. sees	POPE 659:95
teach us the n. of the ties	PLATO 655:2
therein works a miracle in n.	SHAK 740:71
thou and n. can so gently part	SHAK 766:62
thro' N., up to N.'s God	POPE 660:27
Thus God and n. linked	POPE 660:22
To look on n.	WORD 923:71
too much after n.	GAUG 347:67
to see in paintings bits of n.	MALE 542:88
to sin our biased n. leans	DRYD 289:73
touch of n.	SHAK 757:7
trace The naked N.	POPE 658:55
travellers and wanderers by n.	FERB 320:94
treat n. by the cylinder	CEZA 203:51
true n. of poetry	RICH 685:52
true n. of the 'otherness'	NOLAN 617:54
ultimate mystery of n.	PLAN 654:59
Unerring n., still divinely bright	POPE 658:53
unrevealed glory of N.	SHIP 789:78
Verse hath a middle n.	DONNE 281:78
violates the order of n.	HERO 399:29
visible Foundations in N.	PETTY 650:86
voice the word 'n.'	REDON 681:75
Vows can't change n.	BROW 162:81
war of n.	DARW 253:11
war with rude N.	CARL 191:81
weakest in n.	PASC 641:24
Whatever N. has in store	FERMI 321:16
What is man in n.?	PASC 641:28
what n. itselfe cant endure	FLEM 327:57
whatsoever abysses N. leads	HUXL 426:6
what you have been given by n.	PERI 648:65
when n. is so beautiful	VAN 877:29
where man leaves off and n. starts	FROST 338:95
while N. cures the disease	VOLT 883:54
Whose body, N. is	POPE 660:14
Wise n. did never put her…jewels	BACON 47:69
wished to copy n.	CEZA 203:54
woman…N.'s agreeable blunders	COWL 240:36
workings of n.	AQUI 28:31
works of N. are…simple	BORE 144:88
writer…an outcast by n.	BARN 60:68
your divine n. is always free	PEACE 645:91
youth…is in n.'s priest	WORD 926:24
natures alien to their n.	HAZZ 388:96
n. that are mute!	MERE 567:2
Pleasures of worse n.	MASS 559:45
subsists…in all n.	WORD 928:56
naught falling into n.?	ADDI 7:38
haif n. quhen he wald	HENR 396:50
n. but jouissance	GREE 371:79
wear out to n.	SHAK 763:90
naughtiness bewitching of n.	BIBLE 107:33
n. of thine heart	BIBLE 91:92
naval n. and air force	ROOS 696:51
n. combat	GIBB 351:57
nave make a n. of it	STEV 819:13
walk down the n. of his abbey	HOME 409:14
navel soul…ended at the n.	LEWIS 508:2

steam comes…her n.	THOM 853:95
navies nations' airy n.	TENN 840:81
navigation employ steam n.	LARD 490:14
navigator drunkard, my n.	SEXT 728:12
navvy dowser and not a n.	LEAV 498:3
navy England's chief defence…the n.	PHIL 650:89
n. nothing but rotten timber	BURKE 168:15
N. will run the blockade	ANDE 15:15
one-and-a-half ocean n.	HAYW 387:64
put at the head of the n.	CARS 197:36
Queen's N.	GILB 353:93
Queen's N.	GILB 353:94
nay N., Mabel, n.!	GILB 354:2
yea be yea; and your n., n.	BIBLE 125:18
Nazareth any good…out of N.?	BIBLE 117:76
Nazarite your prophet the N.	SHAK 739:50
Nazi a N. lampshade	PLATH 654:66
give him the N. salute	HEND 395:35
Nazidom fights on against N.	CHUR 217:81
Neaera tangles of N.'s hair?	MILT 578:49
near as n. to heaven	GILB 353:88
come not n. to me	BIBLE 104:64
so n. and yet so far	TENN 844:59
nearer draw a little n.	BRAC 148:51
n. by not keeping still	GUNN 375:40
nearness n. of death	PAZ 644:89
neat n. as a furled umbrella	EMERY 313:55
n., clean, shaved and sober	CHAN 204:72
Still to be n.	JONS 449:25
You look n.	COLL 227:35
Nebraska skies of Texas or N.	MCMU 537:87
Nebuchadnezzar N.…was driven	BIBLE 106:96
necessaries required three n.	JONS 450:58
necessary absolutely n.	JOHN 442:54
love of life is n.	JOHN 441:27
n. for mortals to be worn	EURI 316:10
n. not to change	FALK 317:39
n. to the human mind	REES 682:89
no explanation is n.	SEAT 726:69
No more things…than is n.	OCCAM 621:18
Notes are often n.	JOHN 443:81
slavery…so n.	ASTE 36:24
so that the n. may speak	HOFF 406:50
that unnoticed and that n.	ATWO 38:59
The superfluous, a very n. thing	VOLT 882:36
whatever language is n.	KELM 461:78
necessities art of our n.	SHAK 763:75
distinction…luxuries and n.	GALB 343:92
earliest practical n.	HAWT 386:39
n. call out…virtues	ADAMS 4:62
simple n. of human life	COMM 229:65
necessity chain of strong n.?	SPEN 808:78
door of n.	DEFOE 258:20
fold Of dire n.	MILT 586:64
hard n. of bringing the judge	ALGR 11:31
intelligence and n.	ANGE 17:33
Liquor…sidestepping n.	FADI 317:34
N. and chance Approach	MILT 584:91
n. has induced…greater license	COOP 236:54
n. invented stools	COWP 241:67
N. never made a good bargain	FRAN 334:9
N. never makes prostitution	WOLL 921:12
n. of divine nature	SPIN 810:24
n. of doing so	GERH 350:33
n. of making things plain	HUXL 426:14
n. of stealing	MORE 596:60
N.'s sharp pinch!	SHAK 763:69
N. will make us all forsworn	SHAK 733:72
nothing stronger than N.	EURI 316:5
strong n. of time	SHAK 764:18
sworn…To grim n.	SHAK 735:26
neck clothed his n. with thunder?	BIBLE 93:74
eloquence and break its n.!	VERL 879:69
had but one n.!	CALI 184:37
his n. brake, and he died	BIBLE 91:85
left his straight n.	ROSS 698:95
locket around his n.	SOME 803:67
millstone around a woman's n.	GREER 372:86
millstones…about your n.	DAVI 254:23
Millstones around our n.	DISR 277:94
millstone were hanged about his n.	BIBLE 112:67
n. God made for other use	HOUS 414:45
n. is like the tower	BIBLE 101:2
n. like an ostrich	DAVIS 255:55
one n., one chin	SHAK 756:58
one washes one's n.	BARN 60:62
over my n. and eyes	STEV 821:76

rain on the n.	COOKE 236:42
short n. denotes a good mind	SPARK 806:20
Some chicken, some n.!	CHUR 217:82
sticks its n. out	ANON 25:56
took the bride about the n.	SHAK 732:40
necklaces with our n.	MAND 544:51
necks venturing their n. for fruit	ROCH 691:63
necktie left my n. God knows where	HOUS 415:66
necromancy grete clerke of n.	MALO 542:1
nectar as butterflies sipping n.	ELIOT 303:75
lie beside their n.	TENN 839:57
n. from his hand	MARL 553:12
nectarine n., and curious peach	MARV 556:74
need Deserted at his utmost n.	DRYD 291:36
evil…face of total n.	BURR 173:57
God shall supply all your n.	BIBLE 123:64
hand of a vexatious n.	OTWAY 631:25
human n. and…silence	CAMUS 187:88
human n. continues to grow	COMM 229:66
In thy most n.	ANON 19:97
Lord, forgive me if my n.	CULL 247:96
most n. of blessing	SHAK 767:1
N. and oppression starveth	SHAK 737:79
n. for a well-defined personal space	COUP 239:98
n. to look within	SNYD 803:51
n. was the sorest	SCOTT 723:7
no n. for the faith	HOFF 405:47
seeth his brother have n.	BIBLE 125:37
Will you still n. me	LENN 503:98
worse n. for them	SHEL 785:73
needed makes it feel n.	SCHU 720:49
needing n. what I've invented	FULL 341:52
needle my hand a n. better fits	BRAD 149:80
n. and the pen	LEWIS 507:81
n. is not worth the search	JACK 432:11
phonograph n.	GOLD 362:75
Plying her n. and thread	HOOD 410:45
reading of a n.	STEV 820:58
shove…with a red-hot n.	WODE 919:60
that poor little n.…of femininity	OLIP 624:64
through the eye of a n.	BIBLE 113:74
needs according to his n.	BAKU 53:25
each according to his n.!	MARX 558:14
menial n. and base	HYDE 427:23
must n. die	BIBLE 91:4
primary n.	GABOR 342:81
real n. of man	SCHU 720:51
tools, the ideals, the n.	RENO 683:9
needy provider for a n. man	HESI 401:66
wasn't poor, I was n.	FEIF 319:83
negation affirmation from n.	THUR 860:54
negative All satisfaction…always n.	SCHO 719:28
Electricity…positive and n.	LEAC 496:60
Great N.	ROCH 691:53
it was also n.	SNOW 802:37
N. Capability	KEATS 457:91
negativism nattering nabobs of n.	AGNEW 8:74
neglect easy to n.…the truth	CORN 237:72
most tender mercy is n.	CRAB 242:91
n. God and his Angels	DONNE 281:90
punished for n.	JOHN 442:38
sweet n. more taketh me	JONS 449:25
neglected n. and misunderstood	RABAN 675:58
negotiate If we are to n.	BISM 131:86
n.…into the Common Market	WILS 916:95
never n. out of fear	KENN 462:10
negotiation n. and society	MUNCH 603:81
negotiations opened n.	KISH 475:88
negotiators Agreement…by the n.	SHUL 789:90
best n. in Europe	NELS 610:32
negro all her n. train	SMART 796:22
America is…rooted in N. culture	ROLL 695:33
American N. female	ANGE 17:35
American N. problem	BALD 53:29
average N. could never hope to go	DAVIS 255:60
courage of the N.	PHIL 650:95
every Irishman would kill a n.	FREE 336:40
friend of the N. assumes	FULL 341:48
n. either didn't get in the pot	MARS 554:41
N. or saint	HOLM 407:72
N.…was never looked at	BALD 53:31
One drop—you are a N.!	HUGH 418:24
The past of…the N.	OBRI 620:99
negroes Afro-American…replaced N.	FEIF 319:84
bronze N. breathe	LOWE 520:48
drivers of n.	JOHN 444:12
gnaws at n.	KING 468:42

infant n. in the West Indies	DICK 266:78
neighbour covet thy n.'s wife	BIBLE 88:23
false witness against thy n.	BIBLE 88:23
guinea in your n.'s pocket	RUSK 704:16
into the n. room	SHAK 754:14
look his n. in the face	STEV 820:63
love thy n.	BIBLE 89:35
love thy n.	BIBLE 113:82
love thy n.	BIBLE 109:93
love thy n. as thyself	BIBLE 89:35
love thy n. as thyself	BIBLE 113:82
Loving your n. as much as yourself	CLEE 220:72
n. loses his job	REAG 680:55
n. loses his job	TRUM 868:38
policy of the good n.	ROOS 696:42
removeth his n.'s landmark	BIBLE 90:52
stare…at our unintroduced n.	ELIOT 304:6
to hate your n.	MACA 525:52
Whenever our n.'s house is on fire	BURKE 168:28
wrest the ball from your n.	ANON 21:32
neighbourhood everyone in the n.	WHAR 901:52
n. kids	WILL 913:30
neighbourly like to be n.	HALI 378:83
neighbours advantage over their n.	SMITH 798:48
as the n. described them	MIN 587:68
commerce of all its n.	HUME 422:12
common hatred of its n.	INGE 429:54
drouthy n.…meet	BURNS 172:12
feast his n.	SHAK 746:57
merry songs…to all his n.	SHAK 775:26
Sane people did what their n. did	ELIOT 303:1
sport for our n.	AUST 43:71
neighed n. after his neighbour's wife	BIBLE 105:69
Nell Little N. and Lady Macbeth	WOOL 923:56
Nelly Let not poor N. starve	CHAR 207:34
Nelson death of N.	SOUT 805:9
N. confides that every man	NELS 610:34
nemesis Hubris clobbered by N.	ALDI 11:13
neon something like n. signs	UREY 875:2
neotenic achievement for the n. ape	ALDI 10:12
nephew n.…propounded 'Oysters'	DICK 268:33
Neptune more than N.	FULL 341:62
Nerissa will do anything, N.	SHAK 739:48
Nero N. fiddled, but Coolidge	MENC 565:65
nerve Anatomised in every n.	JONS 448:8
every n. a man may strain	CURZ 249:51
n. and instinct is clamouring	LESS 504:34
n. o'er which do creep	SHEL 783:26
raw n. ends of humanity	ANON 25:58
nerves but it quiets my n.	LOUIS 518:6
n. out of the job in hand	MANS 546:82
n. prick and tingle	TENN 843:39
N. sit ceremonious	DICK 272:60
quiver from the average n.	WHITE 903:96
nerve-shaken n.-s., over-civilized	MUIR 602:54
nervos N. belli	CICE 218:23
nervous came the turn of the n. system	RAMO 678:5
'native' is a n. condition	SART 716:55
n. tics	UPDI 875:93
take your n. system seriously	LEARY 498:95
nest brood over a full n.	ELIOT 303:97
It's like building a n.	OCON 622:26
long since my n. is made	TENN 842:10
n. of singing birds	JOHN 441:7
n. upon the dewy ground	WORD 929:60
One flew over the cuckoo's n.	KESEY 465:70
swallow a n. for herself	BIBLE 96:45
nest-egg not a n.-e. person	JOHN 439:66
nestling N. me everywhere	HOPK 412:1
net admiration…crosses the n.	BARR 61:90
bring her to the n.	KING 468:26
goodness make the n.	SHAK 760:81
just get rid of the n.	HUGH 419:35
N.. Anything reticulated	JOHN 442:47
over the n. in a different shape	LODGE 514:24
stick it in the n.	SHAN 776:31
tennis with the n. down	FROST 339:4
Whizzing them over the n.	BETJ 83:84
nets fishery without n.	DEFOE 258:22
n. of wrong	YEATS 932:35
tangled in amorous n.	MILT 586:39
time in making n.	SWIFT 831:70
nettle Out of this n. danger	SHAK 741:10
nettles dust on the n.	THOM 854:18
network indispensable n.	GLEI 359:2
networks n. of dead speech	STARK 813:73
neuroses store their moldy n.	PAGL 634:82
neurosis N. has…genius	PROU 671:78
N. is the way of	TILL 860:67
what n. would sound like	AMIS 15:8
neurotic character…described as n.	PAGE 633:77
I'm n. as hell	PLATH 654:73
Makes cats n.	ANON 22:70
n. builds castles	ANON 22:59
n. can…be a literary genius	AUCH 39:73
person as n.	SZASZ 834:63
prolonged n. doubt	BARZ 63:38
the n. classes	SHAW 781:73
neurotics gatherings of n.	MANK 545:62
neutral United States must be n.	WILS 916:9
neutrality Armed n. is ineffectual	WILS 916:14
overwhelmingly for a policy of n.	BORAH 144:87
neutralizing n.…newspapers	TOCQ 861:83
never could n. tell why	GILB 353:91
everything I n. wanted	GARD 346:44
N. again	ANON 23:82
n., n. use	GILB 353:92
N.'s a hard call	VENA 879:60
N. to have lived	YEATS 933:54
This will n. do	JEFF 437:23
never-ending n.-e. Remembrance	POE 656:26
nevermore Quoth the raven, 'N..'	POE 656:24
never-never in the N.-N.	GUNN 375:38
Radio is a n.-n. land	SAFER 708:95
never-sere ivy n.-s.	MILT 578:45
new against the n. and untried	LINC 510:37
all things are become n.	BIBLE 122:27
brook the n.	FERG 321:9
discovery of the 'n.'?	INGR 429:62
draw n. mischief on	SHAK 759:66
feel comfortable in the n.	MO 589:19
find the old in the n.	MANN 546:74
I make all things n.	BIBLE 127:80
making something n.	GILL 356:47
n. and original plan	GILB 354:12
N. Deal for the American people	ROOS 695:41
N. Deal is ended by World War II	MCGO 532:92
n. every morning	BIBLE 105:82
n. heaven and a n. earth	BIBLE 127:79
N. to me	TRAH 864:34
Nothing…Which is not n.	FLET 328:74
not make a n. acquaintance	JOHN 446:68
put on the n. man	BIBLE 123:67
ring in the n.	TENN 844:60
Shock of the N.	DUNL 295:16
something impossibly n.	THARP 850:7
something n. to look forward to	FORD 330:23
the n. will grow	POL 657:41
things n. and curious	CUMM 247:1
New Age signs of a N. A. coming?	SMITH 800:99
new born pity, like a…n.-b. babe	SHAK 767:87
use of a n.-b. child?	FRAN 335:19
New England brought against N. E.	KRUT 481:29
Newfoundland Quoyle steered away to N.	PROU 670:69
Newgate gaze on the exterior of N.	DICK 266:63
kind of N. calendar	IRVI 430:78
New Jersey learned in N. J.	BALD 53:31
New Labour N. L. brand has been badly contaminated	GOULD 364:22
N. L.'s Xanadu	RAWN 680:39
saw 'N. L.' conceived	GALL 344:16
Newman new-manned By N.	BROW 162:80
Newmarket N., that infamous	CHES 211:38
newness conditioned to respect n.	UPDI 874:82
n., the democratic conceit	LAWR 494:97
New Orleans Hoo-doo…in N. O.	REED 682:86
N. O. is unremarkable	MAIL 540:55
news always n. to somebody	KAVA 456:68
a newspaper needs in its n.	PULI 672:4
brought bitter n. to hear	CORY 237:74
cold roads…cold n.	SCOTT 725:51
dog bites a man, that is not n.	BOGAN 138:34
Evil n. rides post	MILT 586:62
free from bad n. and disease	BIOY 130:56
get n.…from objective sources	BUSH 176:17
good n. is that he's eating less	JACO 432:12
good n. yet to hear	CHES 212:87
literature is n.	POUND 665:50
mariners had fabled n.	LOWE 520:42
master passion is the love of n.	CRAB 242:93
media for the dissemination of n.	CHRI 214:30
n.…and nothing but the n.	DANA 251:82
n. is not a mirror	LIPP 511:70
n. of the day	LIPP 511:67
n. or no n. to be	LEST 505:48
n. when there is no n.	ORWE 629:68
n.…would have made me sick	SHAK 742:81
not…different enough to make n.	SAFI 708:2
only n. until he's read it	WAUGH 892:32
primary office is the gathering of N.	SCOTT 722:74
suckers for good n.	STEV 820:59
Tell Tchaikovsky the n.	BERRY 82:59
The function of n.	LIPP 511:71
The more abhorrent a n. item	FOWL 332:70
today is no longer n.	RUSK 703:98
to get the n. to you	TWAIN 872:21
uncovers the run of the n.	LIPP 511:69
What's the n.?	SHAK 752:52
when I see the evening n.	CLIN 221:95
New South Wales govern N. S.W.	BELL 73:57
newspaper art of n. paragraphing	MARQ 554:34
daily n.…greatest organ	BENN 77:58
even from a small provincial n.	WODE 919:65
every word in…my n. must be clear	CHRI 214:27
good n., I suppose	MILL 572:2
hit a n. reader between the eyes	BRIS 153:43
invariable law of the n.	DANA 251:83
I will show you a bad n.	CHRI 214:29
n. is…a monopoly	SCOTT 722:74
n. is an adviser	TOCQ 861:87
n. represents an association	TOCQ 861:86
n.'s one and only aim	ORWE 627:90
oblivion amounts to n. death	ADAMS 4:83
Once a n. touches a story	MAIL 539:43
One of the virtues…of a n.	SCOTT 722:75
Only a n. can place	TOCQ 861:86
person employed by a n.	HUBB 417:9
reaches the n. office	LIPP 511:67
Reading someone else's n.	BRAD 148:54
stamp of a n.	KRAUS 480:8
subsist without a n.	JOHN 442:52
touch a n. without disgust	BAUD 65:84
What a n. needs	PULI 672:4
newspapers believe all you read in n.	MACA 524:24
importance (of n.)	TOCQ 862:88
I read the n. avidly	BEVAN 85:23
lies from the print of n.	MAIL 539:54
My approach to n.	CHRI 214:31
neutralising the effects of n.	TOCQ 861:83
N. always excite curiosity	LAMB 486:38
n. and dogeared historybooks	DOSP 282:3
N. are born free	SCOTT 722:79
n.…are the most villainous	SHER 788:58
N. have degenerated	WILDE 908:88
N.…inevitably reflect	LIPP 511:68
n.…querulous and bellicose	MENC 565:55
n. without a government	JEFF 436:13
not n. in the ordinary acceptance	BALD 54:46
other half doesn't read n.	VIDAL 881:6
Rage…writing columns for n.	BRES 151:20
to please n.	THOM 854:19
world mirrored in the n.	LESS 505:39
New Testament blessing of the 'N. T.'	BACON 47:80
blood of the N. T.	BIBLE 114:96
Could the N. T. have	GRIS 373:19
ministers of the N. T.	BIBLE 122:22
N. T. had not proved in time	GREE 371:70
N. T. in my blood	BIBLE 121:6
Newton N. with his prism	WORD 925:98
Shakespeare or Sir Isaac N.	FERG 320:6
newts N. and blindworms	SHAK 737:96
New Year on this day of N. Y.	POUND 665:2
New York a kind of N. Y.	USTI 875:8
all the churches or chapels in N. Y.	BENN 77:58
an aviary…called N. Y.	OHEN 623:55
In N. Y. people don't	JOUR 451:74
little trip to N.Y.	OHARA 623:54
N. Y. is a jungle	AMIS 15:99
N. Y. Island	GUTH 375:48
N. Y. is not the cultural centre	BELL 74:81
N. Y. is one of the capitals	MAIL 540:55
N. Y. is the meeting place	BARN 60:61
N. Y. Pop artists	LIPP 511:64
N. Y. State will decertify him	CUOMO 248:28
N. Y. theater has died	MILL 572:10
N. Y., thy name is irreverence	HUXT 427:18
N. Y. was no mere city	DIDI 274:6
New Yorkers busy N. Y. take time	OKEE 623:59
New Zealand I was born in N. Z.	MANS 547:96
next What time's the n. swan?	SLEZ 796:16

nexus n. of all love and money — DIDI 274:6
sole n. of man to man — CARL 193:28
NHS N. is quite like heaven — HALD 377:77
Nicaraguan N. resistance — NORTH 618:71
nice All the n. people — SPARK 806:25
But they sounded n. — RAMOS 678:6
change is always n. — EURI 316:14
don't try to make things n.! — IVES 431:2
e sae n. wi' Robin — BURNS 171:91
how nasty the n. people — POWE 666:84
Makes n. of no vile hold — SHAK 739:28
n. girl should only fall — SPARK 806:26
N. guys finish last — DURO 296:35
n. man — SWIFT 831:87
n. to the second housemaid — JAMES 433:49
someone wants to be n. to me — PUIG 672:1
Too n. for a statesman — GOLD 362:70
nicety sift…with the utmost n. — STEE 814:2
niche Madonna Standing in a n. — PARK 638:78
Nicholas St. N. soon would be there — MOORE 594:15
Nick Satan, N., or Clootie — BURNS 170:77
nickel if it doesn't make a n. — GOLD 362:58
nickname Everybody has a n. — AMADO 13:74
n. is the heaviest stone — HAZL 388:91
only one…that ain't got a n. — DICK 266:74
niece hitting the n. of a bishop — ORWE 627:40
nieces carrying of n. — RIDGE 687:77
Nietzsche I'm the black, basketball-playing N. — ONEAL 625:86
N.…fools, and madmen! — ONEI 625:99
Nigel dogs called N. — AMIS 14:97
Nigeria I am a daughter of N. — EMEC 312:1
nigger blue-gum n. to sing me blues — BENET 75:11
humble myself to a n. — TWAIN 871:5
just a red n. — WALC 884:71
niggers 'twixt de n. of de Souf — TRUTH 869:51
nigh Draw n. to God — BIBLE 125:15
night 11.30pm on election n. — MOND 590:49
ability to get a good n.'s sleep — WILS 916:2
acquainted with the n. — FROST 339:99
ain't a fit n. out — FIEL 323:48
All n. has the casement — TENN 845:90
All n. long in the dark — STEV 822:13
All n., this headland — WILB 907:77
all of n.'s pathways — AGUS 9:76
All the grey n. — DELA 260:70
al the n. with open ye — CHAU 208:67
armies clash by n. — ARNO 31:94
as a watch in the n. — BIBLE 96:50
As glorious to this n. — SHAK 736:46
ask of thee, belovèd N. — SHEL 786:18
Awoke one n. — HUNT 423:33
black as the hour of n. — OBRI 620:5
black bat, n. — TENN 845:89
black feet of the n. — GILM 356:56
borrower of the n. — SHAK 768:11
bowl of n. — FITZ 324:82
braw bricht moonlicht n. — MORR 599:2
brother, in one n. — LUMI 522:88
brothers…in the unending n. — MACL 535:46
bucking ranches of the n. — THOM 853:87
But peaceful was the n. — MILT 575:94
by and by black n. — SHAK 772:30
by n. in a pillar of fire — BIBLE 88:19
By n. or day — WORD 926:21
calmest and most stillest n. — SHAK 743:53
cheek of n. — SHAK 736:42
Closed his eyes in endless n. — GRAY 370:38
closes Saturday n. — KAUF 455:55
Come, civil n. — SHAK 736:63
come from n.…go into n. — FOWL 332:65
come like a thief in the n. — POE 656:19
comes at n. to die — ARNO 32:25
Come, seeling n. — SHAK 768:15
coming for us that n. — BALD 54:40
dark and stormy n. — BULW 166:57
darker than death or n. — SHEL 785:83
darkness he called N. — BIBLE 85:39
dark n. of tyranny — MURR 605:10
day and n. — SWIN 833:47
day and n. shall not cease — BIBLE 87:67
day brought back my n. — MILT 580:90
Day in N. — CRAS 244:34
Day's Journey into N. — ONEI 626:1
day will not follow in n. — TATE 837:6
death's dateless n. — SHAK 771:15
dim n. of this immortal day — SHEL 785:82

do the same things every n. — OSBO 630:11
dream by n. in the dusty recesses — LAWR 495:38
dreaming n. will hide — SHAK 757:9
dying in the n. — TENN 844:60
earned a n.'s repose — LONG 516:46
ending of interminable n. — ELIOT 309:42
ensnared thee to this n. — SHAK 733:63
every n. at tea-time — STEV 823:20
every n. to sit — ROCH 692:68
Every n., whisper 'Peace' — GROM 374:21
face of n. is fair — TENN 845:98
forests of the n. — BLAKE 135:51
foul womb of n. — SHAK 746:46
gentle into that good n. — THOM 853:81
genuine n. admits no ray — DRYD 288:49
get up at n. — STEV 822:11
gloomiest n. will wear on — STOWE 826:76
going to be a bumpy n. — MANK 545:61
Good n., ladies, good n. — SHAK 754:18
Good n., sweet prince — SHAK 755:44
Gwine to run all n. — FOST 332:59
hard day's n. — LENN 503:94
Harry in the n. — SHAK 746:47
haunts you n. and day — BERL 79:12
If he fall in, good n. — SHAK 741:3
in endless n. — HERR 400:44
infant crying in the n. — TENN 843:42
in the long n. — SURR 829:40
in the n., to all, to each — WHIT 906:48
invisible worm…flies in the n. — BLAKE 134:54
I often wish the n. — HOOD 410:37
I saw n. close down — RAND 678:13
Let n. come — APOL 27:17
Let no n. Seal thy sense — DELA 260:72
long n. settling in — MILL 572:21
loud even in the dead of n. — SHAK 756:59
Love [ruled] the n. — DRYD 292:62
middle of the n. — CARR 196:99
middle of the n. — KEATS 458:32
middle of the n. — THOM 854:24
middle of the n. — THUR 860:50
middle of the n. — TWAIN 871:7
moonless n. in the small town — THOM 853:85
moon Walks the n. — DELA 260:69
morn to n., my friend — ROSS 697:82
mosquitoey summer n. light — ASHB 35:86
museum to be looted at n. — RAINE 677:96
ne'er forget that happy n. — BURNS 170:84
N. and day on me she cries — BALL 56:78
n. before Christmas — MOORE 594:14
n. before some festival — SHAK 736:64
n. Darkens the streets — MILT 581:10
n. doth summon all to sleep? — DRAY 286:98
n.…filled with music — LONG 516:50
N. Geometry — KENN 462:99
n. has a thousand eyes — BOUR 147:28
N. hath a thousand eyes — LYLY 523:12
n. is beginning to lower — LONG 516:61
n. is dark, and I am — NEWM 612:62
n. is darkening round me — BRON 155:90
n. is long — SHAK 768:31
n. of our natural ignorance — HOBB 404:30
n. of this worrisome day — BERN 81:45
n. once more — BECK 68:41
n.'s black agents — SHAK 768:16
n.'s black arch — BURNS 172:20
N.'s candles are burnt out — SHAK 736:69
n. shineth as the day — BIBLE 98:1
n.'s lodging of their wives — WEBS 895:5
n. that numbers the leaf — STEV 820:44
n. that wins — SWIN 832:19
n., the shadow of light — SWIN 833:22
n. time I shall not forget — SWIN 833:31
n. to do with sleep? — MILT 577:28
n. when choice was any more — DIDI 274:5
n. will more than pay — ARNO 31:1
N., with all her negro train — SMART 796:22
n. with different stars — SACK 708:90
nothing but the n. — HOUS 416:91
Of n. and light — YEATS 933:38
one calm summer n. — ROBI 690:28
one n. certifieth another — BOOK 142:43
one other gaudy n. — SHAK 765:40
only for a n. and away — WYCH 931:7
on the n. before — SHIP 789:77
out-soared the shadow of our n. — SHEL 786:4
perfect day nor n. — SHAK 730:74

poisonous damp of n. — SHAK 765:43
politician…late at n. — WHITE 903:99
poor souls who dwell in n. — BLAKE 136:86
progresses…day and n. — MONT 592:87
raised many of them in one n. — WALP 887:41
real dark n. of the soul — FITZ 325:9
reign of chaos and old N. — MILT 581:12
returned on the previous n. — BULL 165:52
Revel the n. — SHAK 743:66
sat by n. — SCOTT 722:77
saw Eternity the other n. — VAUG 878:49
see another Saturday n. — MCNA 537:93
sense of a long last n. — MAIL 540:50
seye as it was n.! — CHAU 209:89
shades of n. — LONG 516:48
shadow of the silent n. — MARL 552:85
Ships that pass in the n. — LONG 516:64
silence of the n. — ROSS 697:74
sinning of the n. before — RUNY 703:85
sleep one ever-during n. — CAMP 186:76
slept the n. away — PRIOR 669:38
small creature of the n. — AMIS 14:82
Some n. you'll fail — BROW 161:58
something more than n. — CHAN 205:96
something of the n. in him — WIDD 906:66
son of the sable N. — DANI 252:88
Spirit of n.! — SHEL 787:29
studying all the summer n. — MARV 556:68
Tender is the N. — FITZ 325:6
Tender is the N. — KEATS 460:60
that n. I knew — SZIL 834:66
That n., that year — HOPK 413:3
The City is of N. — THOM 856:61
The City is of N. — THOM 856:62
there shall be no n. there — BIBLE 127:83
There's n. and day, brother — BORR 145:3
thief in the n. — BIBLE 125:33
This ae n., this ae n. — BALL 56:81
This n. shall thy soul — SMITH 800:4
this n. wi' mirth and glee — SKIN 795:13
thoughts that come in the n. — HEAT 390:26
through the empty-vaulted n. — MILT 577:34
torment of the n.'s untruth — DANI 252:88
upon the n.'s starred face — KEATS 457:94
walks in beauty like the n. — BYRON 181:53
watch the coming of the n. — MATT 561:71
watch the n. and death — APOL 27:12
western sky in the n. — WHIT 906:47
What he sall ken this n. — MACD 529:39
while the n. is gathering g. — BRON 155:91
white moth thither in the n.? — FROST 339:5
White n. of icicles — MALL 542:94
wide womb of uncreated n. — MILT 581:22
will not last the n. — MILL 571:81
witching time of n. — SHAK 754:97
with us perpetual n. — JONS 449:21
wonderful Southern n.-sky — LAWR 494:5
world's last n.? — DONNE 281:73
Would the n. were come — SHAK 751:13
write through the n. — PATC 642:49
night-clubbing for n.-c. souses — GERS 350:39
nightfall After n., I wouldn't leave V.S.N. — VAN 877:34 / WALC 884:74
night-gown in his n.-g. — MILL 574:61
night-gowns seven flannel n.-g. — TRAV 864:42
nightingale an 'twere any n. — SHAK 737:91
bright n. amorous — SWIN 832:18
for the sake of Miss N. — STRA 826:82
Hark! ah, the N.! — ARNO 32:12
little brown n. — HARDY 382:76
n., and not the lark — SHAK 736:68
N. begins its song — COLE 226:97
n. does sit so late — MARV 556:68
n. when May is past — CAREW 190:60
no music in the n. — SHAK 729:36
'tis the ravished n. — LYLY 523:7
nightingales duet of two n. — STEV 820:44
nightmare History…is an. — JOYCE 452:87
n. of elderly white males — ABBO 1:1
n. of the dark — AUDEN 40:4
nightmares horrible n. — WEST 901:42
n. of many — RODO 693:94
night-raven n.-r. sings — MILT 576:4
nights All days are n. — SHAK 771:18
dogs barking…through endless n. — MENC 566:87
fled Him, down the n. — THOM 855:36
long, long wintry n. — LEAR 497:76

On the 5th N. — HOBY 405:36
these N. skies — FREE 336:44
now all is always n. — ELIOT 307:1
fierce urgency of n. — KING 468:36
here and n. cease to matter — ELIOT 308:26
Live always in this paradisal n. — KHAY 466:95
must be a great soul n. — EMER 313:43
n. is the day of salvation — BIBLE 122:29
N. is the time to drink — HORA 413:20
N. what? — SARO 714:36
nowadays many left like him n. — WAUGH 891:15
nowhere From n. we came — HAGG 376:58
in other words, n. — JARRY 435:89
n. to fall — ALAN 9:84
you're n. — GROS 374:25
nowt Say n. — CLOU 223:42
nozzle hits the exit n. — SCHW 721:69
nuance No colour, only n.! — VERL 879:68
n. in an ideological difference — COND 230:82
nubbly Nice but n. — KIPL 472:33
nuclear AIDS, cancer, n. war — MAMET 544:34
ancestors had discovered n. power — LAMB 487:65
military and n. sense — WALE 885:90
n. arms race — MOUN 601:39
n. reaction in uranium — EINS 301:35
n. war survivors — COUP 238:96
so-called independent n. weapons — BENN 75:18
nude Bare like n. — SPEN 807:55
mistress is n. — KILP 467:19
n. and antique — SWIN 833:26
nudes madonnas and shameless n. — MALE 542:88
nudging fudging and n. — OWEN 632:49
nudism lyrical bit about n. — JOYCE 452:97
nudist becomes a n. — WHITE 903:87
nugget n. of the human condition — ACKE 3:53
nuisance n. for the few people — CHES 211:47
pleasant n. in not being able to walk — DARW 253:9
positive n. to you — HOLST 408:5
nuisances pestilential n. — GILB 355:21
null splendidly n. — TENN 845:78
number best n. for a dinner party — GULB 374:35
big positive n. — GATES 347:62
called the wrong n. — THUR 859:27
cousins…without n. — SHAW 781:1
express myself in Terms of N. — PETTY 650:86
finite n. of heart-beats — ARMS 30:79
ghost with a n. — PAZ 644:88
increase their n. — TOCQ 861:83
n. all your graces — SHAK 771:4
n. of syllables — SAND 713:15
n. of the beast — BIBLE 126:67
n. of the stars — BIBLE 98:6
n., weigh and measure — HALES 377:81
n. who can write — MACD 529:40
On this next n. — LENN 502:88
teach us to n. our days — BIBLE 96:52
numbers better than n. — CROM 245:68
brings home full n. — SHAK 744:82
By n. here from shame — JOHN 441:14
divinity in odd n. — SHAK 744:80
greatest happiness for the greatest n. — HUTC 424:52
hours their n. spend! — SPEN 809:5
more we grow in n. — TERT 849:82
no safety in n. — THUR 859:28
N.…universal language — WEST 901:37
n. which could call — COWL 240:30
politics of n. — TANA 836:89
write the beauty…in fresh n. — SHAK 771:4
numbness drowsy n. pains — KEATS 459:57
numerous more n. formerly — TOLK 862:1
nun credit to a Trappist n. — SHAR 776:41
Hero, Venus' n. — MARL 553:11
quiet as a n. — WORD 926:13
nunc N. dimittis — BIBLE 128:1
N. est bibendum — HORA 413:20
nunnery Get thee to a n. — SHAK 753:77
Get thee to a n. — TWAIN 871:7
n. Of thy chaste breast — LOVE 519:13
put to scole in a n. — MALO 542:1
nuptials iteration of n. — CONG 232:47
Nureyev Ask N. to stop dancing — KING 468:25
nurse best n. in contemplation — MILT 577:35
Chinese best n. with green trousers — MANS 546:83
definition of what a n. — NIGH 616:35
dirty n., Experience — TENN 847:56
keep a hold of N. — BELL 73:56
Nature's soft n. — SHAK 743:52

n. and tutor of eccentric minds — LAWS 495:43
n. for a poetic child! — SCOTT 723:92
n. of manly sentiment — BURKE 169:35
n. of ninety years — TENN 842:12
priest continues what the n. began — DRYD 291:21
nursery light in the night n. — MACN 538:4
nurses old men's n. — BACON 48:91
to be n. and pianists — ROTH 699:15
nursing n. the unconquerable hope — ARNO 32:23
nursling n. of the sky — SHEL 783:41
Ocean's n., Venice — SHEL 783:28
nurture job of the n. of children — PALEY 635:12
nut cracking the n. — BRON 154:73
every hare-brained n. — SAFER 708:95
heading into n. country — KENN 463:39
n. schell, thocht it be hard — HENR 396:51
nut-brown spicy n.-b. ale — MILT 576:9
nutlike hard, brown, n. word — BART 62:11
nutmegs N. and ginger — ANON 20:9
nutrition People in n. — DAVIS 255:51
nuts fearful…would go n. — CUMM 247:98
where the n. come from — DISCH 275:30
where the n. come from — THOM 852:53
nutshell bounded in a n. — SHAK 752:54
Nyasaland bring Stonehenge to N. — BANDA 58:24
nymph Echo, sweetest n. — MILT 577:33
n. shall break Diana's law — POPE 659:70
rose like a n. — SHEL 785:85
nymphs n. with their flattering — SITW 794:66
Where were ye N. — MILT 578:48
Ye N. that reign o'er sewers and sinks — COLE 227:23

O

oak ashes of an o. — DONNE 281:79
builder o., sole king — SPEN 808:73
charms to…bend a knotted o. — CONG 231:22
English o. and holly — HARTE 385:18
fells the hardest-timbered o. — SHAK 730:72
O., and Ash, and Thorn — KIPL 473:58
O., and Ash, and Thorn — KIPL 473:59
o.'s thick branches — GRAY 369:4
plant an o. in a flower-pot — BRON 155:97
wedges cleave the hardest o. — KYD 482:45
win the palm, the o. — MARV 556:71
Oakland having come from O. — STEIN 815:20
oaks Beneath our o. hast slept — BLAKE 133:24
oak-tree When the o.-t. is fallen — CARL 192:17
O altitudo reason to an O. a.! — BROW 158:64
oar wind and wave and o. — TENN 839:58
oars like a ship with the o. lifted — MANS 547:91
The o. were silver — SHAK 764:23
oat-cakes o.-c. and sulphur — SMITH 801:14
oath A terrible o. — SHAK 757:86
forced to swear an o. — MARG 549:46
good mouth-filling o. — SHAK 742:21
He who cheats with an o. — PLUT 656:11
If ever I utter an o. again — SHAW 781:81
lose an o. — SHAK 733:82
man is not upon o. — JOHN 444:13
neither by any other o. — BIBLE 125:18
not ask thine o. — SHAK 769:52
since I took the o. — MACA 524:26
sin to keep a sinful o. — SHAK 730:68
sworn a solemn o. — BURNS 171:93
trust man on his o. — SHAK 762:43
oaths for o. are straws — SHAK 745:38
o. are but words — BUTL 177:53
standers-by to curtail his o. — SHAK 773:58
'Tis not the many o. — SHAK 761:33
oats O. A grain…given to horses — JOHN 442:48
OBE stands for Old Big 'Ead — CLOU 223:43
obedience end to blind o. — WOLL 921:6
except docility, o. — WELD 897:40
infuses…that liberal o. — BURKE 168:15
in the name of duty and o. — SNOW 802:41
life of strict o. — DOST 282:6
O.…is Good Luck's mother — AESC 8:62
o. of creatures — HOOK 410:54
o. to God — DAVI 256:70
swift in all o. — KIPL 472:13
truth in no man, nor o. — BEAU 67:17
obedient o. to their commands — SIMO 792:42
o. unto death — BIBLE 123:54
obey easy enough to o. — TUCH 869:59
love, cherish, and to o. — BOOK 142:27
o. God rather than men — BIBLE 119:33

One must o. the man — SOPH 804:84
That can so well o. — MARV 555:56
to o. is better than sacrifice — BIBLE 91:89
to those who o. Him — SCHW 721:70
who has learned well how to o. — KEMP 461:87
wise ridicule and o. — BIER 129:30
obeyed God has more right to be o. — JOHN 438:56
o. as a son — GIBB 352:62
She who must be o. — HAGG 376:59
when to be o. — HAWT 386:48
obituary autobiography is an o. — CRISP 245:59
object America…an o. of faith — RABAN 675:61
B-b-british o. — MALO 543:14
chosen o., a definite task — POPP 663:94
desperately insignificant o. — DAVI 254:41
distinguish himself from an o. — SENG 727:96
end and o. of conquest — ALEX 11:19
'express' an o. — ROSE 696:63
let the form of an o. be what it may — CONS 235:27
most exalted o. — DARW 253:11
no o. worth its constancy? — SHEL 787:30
o. all sublime — GILB 355:27
o. behind that name — SPEN 807:63
o. from the crime — POPE 659:84
o.…is less discernible — LEGER 501:53
o. of aesthetic appreciation — BARR 60:77
O. of C. — AUST 42:57
o. of interest — RUSK 703:98
o. of love and esteem — LAMB 486:44
o. of universal devotion — IRVI 430:85
o. of war is not to die — PATT 643:73
o. quite forgotten — SHAK 729:32
o. seen, and eye that sees — WORD 925:6
o. strange and high — MARV 556:79
o. to seeing on the screen — GOLD 362:83
Picasso studies an o. — APOL 27:14
poem…is a physical o. — MACB 527:81
saddest o. in civilization — STEV 824:41
see the o. as in itself — ARNO 33:35
set before him a provoking o. — MILT 579:37
sex o. — GIOV 357:74
stimulus and o. of our meditation — MANN 545:63
utility of some particular o. — SMITH 797:41
When gold becomes her o.! — SHAK 743:65
why should…your team o.? — HEND 395:35
woman into a sex o. — MORG 597:82
objection no o. to this method — STER 817:76
objectionable O. in action — GOET 360:12
objections o. to this proposition — HOBH 405:31
objective achieve that o. — MCNA 537:96
final o. is not — LIEB 509:27
gained our first o. — SASS 716:59
o. by pretending — LEWO 508:10
o. correlative — ELIOT 305:47
o. was the world — DULL 294:91
production of o. fact — MENC 565:73
speak of the Fascist o. — ORWE 628:46
objectives limited o. he has now — OCON 622:25
objectivity slivers and shreds of o. — CUPI 248:35
objects All visible o., man — MELV 564:30
arranging any set of o. — MILL 570:73
bad poet dwells…in a world of o. — ELIOT 305:48
credit ordinary and visible o. — BROW 158:63
enjoyment of beautiful o. — MOORE 594:21
extracted from many o. — SHAK 750:72
forward the o. which we have — PLATO 655:2
lose sight of their o. — ELIOT 303:26
lustre of midday to o. — MOORE 594:16
Men see o. — FOWL 332:67
o. as I think them — PICA 650:99
o. of desire — RICA 684:34
o. of human reason — HUME 422:13
o. of Sensation — LOCKE 514:18
o. recognised, In flashes — WORD 925:2
o. seen by the eye — PIERO 651:11
One by one the o. — WILL 913:43
only o. in the material universe — FORS 331:50
ornament from utilitarian o. — LOOS 517:71
secure those important o. — PITT 653:45
too visible as sex o. — FRIE 337:60
try to forget what o. — MONET 591:53
obligated o. to Russia — BROD 154:73
obligation acknowledge no o. — GIBB 352:60
because o. is a pain — JOHN 441:23
not an o. but a joy — KILLY 467:16
o. of a more scrupulous fidelity — CONR 235:17

o. to become the servant SHAW 780:54
o. to which…we may hold a n. JAMES 433:41
pile o. on o. CHAM 203:56
politics is an o. ROGE 695:26
sense of o. CRANE 243:30
obligations honourable o. CHUR 216:71
Nobility brings o. LEVIS 506:65
o. arising UNIT 873:69
o. of man CAMUS 188:5
trick of heaping o. SHAW 778:87
obliging civil and o. young woman AUST 42:57
obliviate drink to o. FLYNN 328:78
oblivion Alms for o. SHAK 757:5
cold o. SHEL 786:8
memory be left in o. EMMET 313:59
o. amounts to newspaper death ADAMS 4:83
O, my o. is a very Antony SHAK 764:20
Second childishness and mere o. SHAK 749:51
oblong o. of pink MONET 591:53
obloquy greatest o. i' th' world SHAK 762:34
speechless o. BYRON 180:36
obnoxious o. to each carping tongue BRAD 149:80
obscene anachronistic is o. BART 62:24
pictures of o. books! ARLT 30:66
obscenity o., a depraved act CHOM 214:18
O. is a cleansing process MILL 573:54
o. is what happens RUSS 705:58
Sex and o. are not synonymous BREN 151:16
obscure getting more o. THOM 852:60
he who sits o. SHEL 784:66
through the palpable o. MILT 581:28
obscurity afraid of losing my o. HUXL 424:60
o. of a learned language GIBB 352:64
o. of our investigations SCHO 719:29
o. of the matter PROT 670:65
rest in o. and peace! EMMET 313:59
obsequies celebrates his o. SCOTT 723:90
tear to grace his o. GRAY 370:33
obsequiousness O. is glorified CHAO 205:8
observance breach than the o. SHAK 751:24
o. of trifles DOYLE 285:59
observation from personal o. WILS 914:70
Let o. with extensive JOHN 441:16
O. is always selective POPP 663:94
product of that simple o. BEHR 71:23
road of experiment and o. LAVO 493:83
Scientific o. is always a viewing HUXL 426:1
sense and o. WORD 928:56
things…worth their o. ADDI 6:18
Where o. is concerned PAST 642:43
observations pure o. alone POPP 662:93
what o. would lead him AYER 44:10
observe never can o. anything HUME 422:5
O. how system into system runs POPE 660:8
o.…just by watching BERRA 82:56
o. the best speakers JONS 450:58
You see, but you do not o. DOYLE 285:65
observed exists until…it is o. BURR 173:62
o. by Yours faithfully, God ANON 22:51
o. with sufficient closeness TROL 867:92
observer every o. necessarily suffers ORWE 629:93
keen o. of life AUDEN 40:9
o. of human nature DICK 266:67
social position of the o. MANN 546:78
obsessed o. by the feeling SPEN 807:66
obsolescence designing for o. ISSI 431:96
obsolete Either war is o. FULL 341:53
out of date, o. STEV 819:10
obstacle Bureaucracy is not an o. SCHU 721:58
gameboard and o. course ELKIN 310:69
greatest o. to being heroic HAWT 386:48
greatest o. to happiness FONT 329:88
obstacle-racing sport…is o.-r. TREE 865:54
obstacles all of civilization's o. SAND 712:82
raining down o. MANC 544:41
obstinacy o., and of error POPP 663:98
O. in a bad cause BROW 158:70
o. in a bad one STER 817:72
obstinate not because he is o. BLOOM 137:3
stricken with most o. love SIDN 790:1
obstructed o. interstate commerce HOOV 411:69
obstruction consecrated o. BAGE 51:90
obtain o. the largest measure TIMES 861:76
o. the reputation TROL 867:1
obviating o. of all future wars FORD 330:6
obvious afraid of the deafeningly o. KAVA 456:68
analysis of the o. WHIT 904:7

occasion constraint, and sad o. dear MILT 578:45
courage mounteth with o. SHAK 738:20
every possible o. LYTT 524:18
had frequent o. to test…friendship POE 656:20
man who never missed an o. SHAW 781:3
nations, and on this o. ROCHE 691:46
no o. to exert his understanding SMITH 798:52
o., catalyst, or tripwire ACKE 3:53
O., Chance, and Change? SHEL 785:79
o. is not merely NEHRU 610:29
occasions All o. invite his mercies DONNE 281:88
august o. of the state FROST 339:15
crowds for all o. SIMP 792:45
feeling…on rare o. FERL 321:12
o. and causes why SHAK 746:64
o. such as these MURP 604:1
Prose on certain o. LAND 488:85
occult some o. relation JOHN 441:25
occupation continual o. and change AUST 44:96
cure for it is o. SHAW 780:69
Every o.…is…absurd QUEN 674:39
golfer…my real o. MATU 561:72
no housewifery, nor…earthly o. SMOL 801:28
not quite the o. of an adult OLIV 624:67
pause in the day's o. DE 264:35
pause in the day's o. LONG 516:61
Sport…is an o. PIUS 653:55
occupations imaginable o. THUR 859:39
worse o. in this world STER 818:5
occurred never o. to him GARC 345:40
occur at the bottom of the o. RAND 678:14
butterfly poised on a pigtailed o. SITW 793:59
crossed an o. NICH 613:85
dark unfathomed caves of o. GRAY 369:17
day-star in the o. bed MILT 578:57
eye that sees on the o. MACL 535:33
from o.'s farthest coast HOW 417:93
His legs bestrid the o. SHAK 766:56
icebergs in the o. GERH 350:35
If the o. was pure mind PRAT 667:98
land and o. without rest MILT 580:88
lavished the o. on you in vain BORG 144:91
life at the o. bottom HECHT 390:36
Neptune's o. wash this blood SHAK 767:5
new joys to the mild o. MILT 575:94
O. and earth WORD 928:52
o. for orient pearl MARL 552:94
o. for orient pearl MARL 552:98
o. is flat again KEYN 465:81
o. of truth lay all NEWT 612:74
o. or the human heart? LAUT 493:74
o. protesting against separation GRAT 367:61
O. racing is like standing HEATH 390:25
O.'s child, and then his queen SHEL 783:29
O.'s nursling, Venice SHEL 783:28
o.…was his home BYRON 179:21
one-and-a-half o. navy HAYW 387:64
On one side lay the o. TENN 847:46
outstretch'd o. glitter BYRON 182:78
painted ship Upon a painted o. COLE 225:84
pores of the o. and shores SHEL 783:41
rivers with the o. SHEL 783:42
round o. WORD 923:71
sky…Spread like a rosy o. BYRON 182:81
So on the o. of life LONG 516:64
till the o. Is folded AUDEN 40:91
Tweed rins to the o. BURNS 172:35
oceans Portable and compendious o. CRAS 244:37
octaves o. of its parallel edges CUMM 247:1
octavos o. fill a spacious plain CRAB 242:83
October Falls like the leaves in O. FULL 341:70
fifteenth of O. 1764 GIBB 352:63
funny…month, O. NORD 618:60
leaf still in O. FLET 328:68
O.'s strife GURN 375:44
octopus o. is soft ARNO 34:74
odd cure of the id by the o. ANON 22:50
divinity in o. numbers SHAK 744:80
o. old ends, stol'n SHAK 731:7
people's voice is o. POPE 661:53
something o. about women BENN 76:30
odds beats thee 'gainst the o. SHAK 765:27
face the o. HOUS 416:76
ode O. on a Grecian Urn FAUL 318:69
odes quoted o. TENN 841:96
odi o. et amo CATU 201:10
odium He lived in the o. BENT 78:77

odorous Comparisons are o. SHAK 745:16
odour no o. so bad THOR 857:82
o. of sanctity WALL 886:4
o. of wine RABE 676:65
principle of its colour and o. SHEL 786:13
Stealing and giving o. SHAK 755:45
sweet o.…doth in it live SHAK 771:20
odours dirt and ill o. THOR 858:4
gentle o. led my steps SHEL 786:23
phoenix…Exhales her o. BYRON 179:3
probed…their o. ANGE 17:47
puff of wind…laden with strange o. CONR 234:4
Odysseus Like O., the President KEYN 465:78
odyssey long o. toward liberty MAIL 540:52
Oedipus O.…dripping PAGE 633:77
O. he had the luck HUGH 419:49
O. triumph over gravity KOES 477:30
reason is his best O. BROW 158:59
Oedipuses peculiar family, the O. BEER 70:94
off if honour prick me o. SHAK 742:27
Want To Get O. ANON 23:85
offal barrow of butcher's o. SHAK 743:79
offence After o. returning MILT 586:59
by deceit to breed o. DYER 297:53
forgave the o. DRYD 292:51
greatest o. against virtue HAZL 388:92
image of o. SHAK 757:87
like to give o. FROST 338:85
mean to give o. ROCHE 690:45
never resented for an o. SWIFT 830:55
no harshness gives o. POPE 658:59
O, my o. is rank! SHAK 754:99
only defence is in o. BALD 54:47
Shipton 'assault'…a criminal o. CRAN 243:31
sour o. SHAK 757:99
What dire o.…springs POPE 658:64
whatsoever o. or injury HENR 395:46
offences more o. at my beck SHAK 753:78
offend nothing shall o. them BIBLE 97:86
o., when 'tis let loose SUCK 828:12
offended I have o. reputation SHAK 765:35
no one is consciously o. ELIOT 307:90
This hath o.! CRAN 243:32
we are sharply o. TWAIN 872:24
offender hugged the o. DRYD 292:51
offenders society o. GILB 355:21
offensive It may sound o. STEV 821:76
someone else is being o. BROO 156:22
taking the o. PENI 646:21
offer intend to o. KENN 462:9
nothing to o. anybody KERO 464:63
o. he can't refuse PUZO 673:23
power to o.…love SHAW 777:58
offering delightest not in burnt o. BIBLE 95:31
lamb for a burnt o. BIBLE 87:82
o. too little CANN 188:14
offerings burnt o. BIBLE 91:7
burnt o. BIBLE 91:89
delight in burnt o. BIBLE 91:89
offers when most she o. blows SHAK 765:37
office A dog's obeyed in o. SHAK 763:92
By o. boys for o. boys SALI 711:70
don't have power…have o. TODD 862:90
Each in his turn o. DODD 278:9
eternal villain…to get some o. SHAK 760:4
fill a high o. LOUI 518:94
gainful employment…not…public o. ACHE 2:71
high officials leave o. KISS 475:97
in which the o. is held HUXL 425:80
man who has no o. SHAW 777:49
never pretend to any other o. HUME 422:7
never seen an o. STEV 821:70
not going to be in o. MOND 590:49
o. boy GILB 353:94
o. of respiration DICK 266:87
o. of the White House MENC 565:72
o. sanctifies the holder ACTON 3:59
o. to be new stamped LAMB 486:43
o. was his pirate ship LEWIS 507:87
primary o. is the gathering of News SCOTT 722:74
raised taxes before he took o. DOLE 278:15
reaches the newspaper o. LIPP 511:67
seven years in o. GISC 358:85
So clear in his great o. SHAK 767:87
they have once won o. GALB 343:91
'Tis all men's o. SHAK 745:20
vote somebody into o. GERG 350:32

officer

way out of elective o.   HOOV 411:63
officer British o.   PANG 636:28
officers o. and fellow-rankers said   SMITH 800:3
offices ants to harvest o.   DONNE 279:41
   go back to your o.   ANDE 15:15
   good o. that sex can discharge   WOOLF 922:48
   great o....give social prestige   BAGE 51:87
official more fanatical o.   HAZZ 388:96
   The o. world   SNOW 802:36
officials high o. leave office   KISS 475:97
   o. are the servants   GOWE 365:28
   o. working in offices   WEBER 894:70
   set of bigmouthed o.   DOSP 282:3
off-key sing...a little o.   MILL 572:15
   sing o. k.   GERS 351:41
offspring human o.   MILT 583:72
   o. of Heav'n first-born   MILT 582:36
   o. of journalistic realism   WHITE 903:97
   would not care about his o.   HAWT 386:36
often written so o.   GERG 350:30
oil America's dependence on o.   KERRY 465:68
   anointest my head with o.   BIBLE 94:2
   go out to an o. rig   HEATH 390:21
   how much o....with one's vinegar   WILDE 907:83
   in him we see O.   GOLD 362:69
   keep putting o. in it   THER 851:42
   mix like O. and Vinegar   GAIN 342:85
   mouth is smoother than o.   BIBLE 99:13
   o. can is mightier than the sword   DIRK 275:25
   o. depletion...makes Houston   MAIL 540:55
   o. to make his face to shine   BIBLE 97:67
   Pour o. into their ears   JONS 448:14
   Some people find o.   GETTY 351:50
   thou hast anointed my head with o.   BOOK 143:44
   Warren's blackin', or Rowland's o.   DICK 266:79
   where you put in the o.   TAYL 838:26
   why o. painting was invented   DE 260:57
   wine...sweeter...than o.   RABE 676:65
oily o. man of God   THOM 856:59
ointment Dead flies cause the o.   BIBLE 101:86
   like the precious o.   BIBLE 98:96
Oisin O O.   YEATS 932:31
   Wanderings of O.   WILDE 908:87
okie O. use' ta mean   STEI 815:33
Oklahoma Okie...from O.   STEI 815:33
old adherence to the o. and tried   LINC 510:37
   A human being is o.   FITZ 325:18
   And she, being o.   SMITH 799:64
   appeared o. unto me   BIBLE 105:77
   appearèd, to have been of o.   SPEN 808:83
   As an o. soldier   SHAW 778:95
   As you are o. and reverend   SHAK 762:61
   beauty so o. and so new   AUGU 41:37
   Behold, thou art o.   BIBLE 91:86
   Being an o. maid   FERB 320:98
   being o. is having lighted rooms   LARK 491:41
   be she o.   SWIFT 832:12
   boredom makes you o.   CAST 199:74
   born o. and ugly?   DICK 267:24
   brook the o.   FERG 321:9
   buried in a good o. age   BIBLE 87:74
   can't be o. without it   WILL 912:26
   chancèd in the times of o.   SHAK 731:94
   chilly and grown o.   BROW 161:42
   country safe to grow o. in   THAT 850:14
   crown of o. men   BIBLE 99:37
   die before I get o.   TOWN 864:24
   die or grow o.   MONT 591:64
   fat and grows o.   SHAK 741:13
   find the o. in the new   MANN 546:74
   folks git o. en strucken   HARR 383:95
   foolish, fond o. man   SHAK 764:98
   growing o. in drawing nothing up!   COWP 241:73
   Grow o. along with me   BROW 162:69
   how subject we o. men   SHAK 743:57
   If you're going to get o.   STEG 814:8
   I grow o....I grow o.   ELIOT 304:24
   ill and o. and terrified   BETJ 84:3
   I'm just an awkward o. maid   RENO 683:99
   insecurity in America...growing o.   ELLW 311:92
   know thee not, o. man   SHAK 743:67
   Long be it ere thou grow o.   ROCH 692:71
   love everything that's o.   GOLD 362:62
   make me conservative when o.   FROST 339:6
   more virtue than o. men   JOHN 443:69
   never can be o.   SHAK 772:42
   never too o.   THOR 858:3

   no fashion for the o.   CHAN 205:99
   no man would be o.   SWIFT 831:86
   now am not too o.   BLUN 137:16
   now am o.   BIBLE 95:17
   o. and stricken in years   BIBLE 91:8
   O. and young   STEV 822:92
   o. fashioned   ALLEN 12:55
   o., For a dream's sake   ROSS 697:76
   o. have reminiscences   SAKI 710:33
   o. heads on your young shoulders   SPARK 806:21
   o. immorality condoned   SHAW 782:5
   o., mad...dying king   SHEL 783:34
   o. man, and heavy   BIBLE 91:85
   o. man broken   SHAK 775:23
   o. man does not care for   JOHN 443:84
   o. man in a dry month   ELIOT 305:39
   O. Man with a beard   LEAR 497:75
   o. man with wrinkled dugs   ELIOT 306:60
   o. man young   TENN 844:60
   o. men shall dream   BIBLE 106:5
   o. [might as well speak] to the young   CATH 200:88
   o. people are square   SHAF 729:22
   o. people make so many journeys   BLYT 138:26
   o. ways are the safest   COKE 224:69
   our land, it is o.   RANS 679:23
   persuade you, young and o.   PLATO 654:78
   put off the o. man   BIBLE 123:67
   redress the balance of the O.   CANN 188:15
   remember the days of o.   MOORE 596:48
   Ring out the o.   TENN 844:60
   o. nose   GIRO 358:84
   Say I'm growing o.   HUNT 423:35
   she is not yet so o.   SHAK 740:73
   socialize the cost of growing o.   HEWE 401:71
   Some day before I'm o.!   KIPL 473:44
   suppose an o. man decayed   JOHN 446:58
   Tell me the o., o. story   HANK 380:33
   tell when one is getting o.   EDWA 300:21
   The o....talk to themselves   ONEI 625:92
   the o. will go on   WILL 914:53
   think he is growing o.   IRVI 430:82
   Though I look o.   SHAK 749:39
   times begin to wax o.   BIBLE 107:27
   'Tis well an o. age is out   DRYD 292:63
   to be forty years o.   HOLM 408:99
   too o. and intelligent   BRAD 148:65
   too o. to dream   HAMM 379:16
   warn you not to get o.   KINN 470:70
   We are o., we are o.   SMITH 800:99
   we grow o.   TENN 841:94
   whats the use of being o.   OHARA 623:48
   when he is o., he will not depart   BIBLE 100:46
   when they get to feeling o.   BROO 156:14
   when thou shalt be o.   BIBLE 118:26
   When you are o.   YEATS 932:33
   when you are o. sit   DICK 269:57
   you and I are o.   TENN 840:66
   youth, before I waxèd o.   SPEN 809:2
old age cold and forlorn o. a.   STEV 821:79
   death...puts an end to o. a.   LABR 483:71
   died in a good o. a.   BIBLE 92:41
   first sign of o. a.   HICKS 402:78
   flower of o. a.   DEMO 261:85
   fruit in o. a.   BIBLE 96:55
   infirmities of o. a.   WESL 900:23
   looked down upon in our o. a.?   SCHU 721:57
   man reaches o. a.   MAO 548:9
   men...in their o. a.   POPE 659:91
   o. a., accident, sickness   LLOY 513:98
   o. a. and experience   ROCH 691:57
   O. A. a regret   DISR 276:45
   O. a. hath yet his honour   TENN 840:66
   o. a. is always fifteen years older   BARU 63:31
   O. a. is second childhood   ARIS 29:46
   O. a....it's the only disease   MANK 545:57
   O. A. may come after you   WHIT 906:53
   o. a. of cards   POPE 661:50
   O. a. should burn and rave   THOM 853:81
   should accompany o. a.   SHAK 768:37
   son of his o. a.   BIBLE 87:93
Oldcastle Sweet Jack O.   SHAK 742:16
older As I get o.   FERL 321:14
   As I grow o.   SOLO 803:59
   As we get o.   REED 681:80
   As we grow o.   ELIOT 308:25
   enjoy getting o.?   CHER 210:20
   growing o. has served no purpose   RILKE 687:84

   grow o. and o.   SAYE 717:8
   man as he grows o.   STEI 816:3
   O. than love   SCOTT 722:7
   O. than the time of chronometers   ELIOT 308:2
   The o. I get   FRID 337:5
   was so much o. then   DYLAN 297:5
oldest o. hath borne most   SHAK 764:
old-fashioned apt to grow o.-f.   WILDE 909:4
   be always o.-f.   SANT 714:2
   make these products o.-f.   STEV 819:1
   o.-f. Boarding-school   AUST 43:8
   o.-f. Virginia fox hunt   WASH 890:8
Old Testament O. T. makes   STAN 812:6
   Prosperity...blessing of the O. T.   BACON 47:8
Old World eyes of the O.W.   MANS 546:8
O'Leary with O. in the grave   YEATS 933:4
oligarchy always an o. that governs   PARE 636:3
   call it o.   HOBB 404:2
olive an O., and a Turkey Fig   BETH 82:7
   children like o. plants   BIBLE 98:9
   fruitful o.   SPEN 808:7.
   o. leaf pluckt off   BIBLE 87:6
   Stretched under the o. trees   SPEN 807:5
Oliver difficulty in inducing O.   DICK 266:3
olives acquired taste, like o.   RIFK 687:8
Olivet brows of o.   TENN 843:3
Olympic O. games   COUB 238:8
   O. weight lifter   NIGH 616:2
Olympics Montreal O.   DRAP 286:9
omega Alpha and O.   BIBLE 125:4
omen One o. is best of all   HOMER 409:20
ominous is o.   SANT 714:20
omission art of o.   LIEB 509:2
   glaring sin of o.   OSLER 630:1
omissions O. are not accidents   MOORE 595:3
   O. are not accidents   MOORE 595:4
   o. of a Government   ROOS 696:4
omit o. to paint that which he sees   FRIE 337:7
omnibuses run up the steps of o.   WOOLF 922:2
omnipotence final proof of God's o.   DE 264:3
   honour, and o.   MARL 552:9
omnipotent God the O.   ELLE 310:7
   O. but friendless   SHEL 785:77
   Power, which seems o.   SHEL 785:8
omniscience his specialism is o.   DOYLE 285:7
Omnium Duke of O.   TROL 867:1
Onan O....spilled it on the ground   BIBLE 88:9
Onassis going to marry...O.!   JOHN 439:74
once O. upon a time   KING 469:5
once-bitten happily for the o.-b.   HOME 409:13
ondulous lifting with a great o. stride   CUMM 247:
one all but o.—shall live   SHAK 753:82
   all o. in Christ Jesus   BIBLE 122:3
   At o. with the O.   GREE 370:4
   being o. and not two   FLET 327:64
   forgive Thy great big o.   FROST 339:13
   hearts in o., your realms in o.   SHAK 746:9
   how to be o. up   POTT 664:2
   If ever two were o.   BRAD 149:8
   it ought to be Number O.   CARR 195:8
   it will be all o.   EMER 312:30
   not o. among them   SHAK 739:49
   o. bullet in ten thousand   SPEN 807:5
   o. for all   DUMAS 294:92
   o. in three   SHAW 779:37
   o. of the twenty   SHAK 739:43
   only o. to make a quarrel   INGE 428:49
   people arose as o. man   BIBLE 90:78
   souls in o. shall grow   PHIL 650:9
   The O. remains   SHEL 786:7
   Three in O.   ALEX 11:2
   Two are better than o.   BIBLE 100:7
one-and-twenty When I was o.-a.-t.   HOUS 414:46
one-armed o.-a. man   DOLE 278:14
one-dimensional o.-d. mind   RUSS 706:5
one-eyed o.-e. man is king   ERAS 315:86
   o.-e. man is king   WELLS 898:77
one-handed a o.-h. economist   TRUM 868:42
O'Neil slay Owen Roe O.   DAVIS 256:64
one-man o.-m. House of Commons   MANC 544:45
oneness essential o. of mankind   STEI 814:5
one-night o.-n. stands in collectors'   RAUS 679:33
onerous more o. citizenship   SONT 804:77
ones weaken the necessary o.   MONT 593:99
oneself delusion that one likes o.   DIDI 274:4
   Hell is o.   ELIOT 309:54
   left to o.   BERL 80:2

love is the gift of o.! — ANOU 26:3
what is useful to o. — SPIN 810:31
one-stringed old o.-s. instrument — RANJ 678:16
one-trade Detroit is a o.-t. town — MAIL 540:55
one-way o.-w. property of time — EDDI 298:83
onion Let o. atoms lurk — SMITH 801:20
tears live in an o. — SHAK 764:15
only O. in America — KING 468:28
o. things that are true — SHAW 777:56
onward o. and outward — WHIT 905:31
ooze present than in the o. — NABO 606:39
opal mind is a very o. — SHAK 756:66
open get these things out in the o. — PULI 672:3
getting out into the o. — KELM 460:77
keep the store o. nights — KAUF 456:61
Never lay yourself o. — HUNT 423:24
o. door, and no man can shut it — BIBLE 126:50
o. thy mouth wide — BIBLE 96:44
whole nation out in the o.? — SIHA 791:29
opening Eyes...go on o. — REID 682:95
hell of an o. — REAG 681:67
No better o. anywhere — DICK 269:78
o. and closing of a door — SAND 713:99
opening-night o.-n. audience — HIRS 403:8
opera born for o. buffa — ROSS 698:4
first rule in o. — MELBA 563:16
I am like an o. singer — MEAT 562:4
language an o. is sung in — APPL 27:23
like German's — WAUGH 892:36
No good o. plot — AUDEN 41:15
o....composed by God — CARD 190:43
o. isn't what it used to be — COWA 239:16
o....is to music — MENC 565:62
O. is where a guy gets stabbed — BENC 74:6
poor man's o. — HUXL 425:95
Some of the o. houses — JOHN 441:4
to the o. one goes either — VOLT 883:52
opera-glasses to view...take o.-g. — RIDGE 687:79
operas French o. sung by Swedish — WHAR 902:54
operation military-style o. — CRAN 243:31
o. of separating — JOHN 441:3
refused an o. — GREG 372:96
operations diversities of o. — BIBLE 121:8
field of o. — BELL 74:91
o. of government — RUNC 702:71
o. of our own minds — LOCKE 514:18
performing a few simple o. — SMITH 798:52
operator dial the o. — TREV 865:62
operators billions of legitimate o. — GIBS 353:76
Ophelia most beautified O. — SHAK 752:44
much of water hast thou, poor O. — SHAK 755:27
soft you, the fair O. — TWAIN 871:7
Ophir Nineveh from distant O. — MASE 559:26
opiate Communism is the o. — LUCE 522:81
emptied some dull o. — KEATS 459:57
o. of the oppressed — JONG 448:99
opinion almost of o. — MONT 591:64
better to have no o. of God — BACON 419:4
Busy o. — FORD 330:16
client asks his o. — JOHN 444:99
collective o....can make history — SAFI 708:2
combat...with particular o. — DRYD 288:44
cost to freedom of o. — SCHL 718:10
current o. — MCCA 528:99
Do not despise my o. — LEON 504:19
drift of public o. — DAFOE 250:62
engine of temporary o. — HAZL 388:76
everything else is o. — DEMO 261:84
flatterer does not have a good o. — LABR 484:77
fool gudgeon, this o. — SHAK 739:39
form a clear o. — BONH 140:61
gave it for his o. — SWIFT 831:80
give him my o. — DICK 270:93
God's o. that life should go on — SAND 713:9
guided by o. polls — THAT 851:36
have his every o. regenerated — PIER 651:5
heated division of o. — TYNAN 872:43
high in Mr Podsnap's o. — DICK 271:42
instrument for gauging public o. — GALL 344:20
laughter at their quaint o. — MILT 584:97
low o. of himself — TROL 866:81
mankind...of one o. — MILL 570:65
man of common o. — BAGE 52:96
money controls o. — ORWE 628:48
north of my lady's o. — SHAK 756:80
offer him an o. — SPEN 807:62
of his own o. still — BUTL 177:60

of the o. with the learned — CONG 230:93
o. breeds ignorance — HIPP 403:2
o. in good men — MILT 579:66
o. is about a woman — JAMES 433:45
o. of himself, having once risen — BENN 76:41
o. of our best friends — MARG 549:44
o. of Winston Churchill — ELTON 311:95
organization of public o. — LIPP 511:68
Party is organized o. — DISR 276:68
poor itch of your o. — SHAK 769:56
Prejudice...vagrant o. — BIER 129:42
public o. will sweep them away — PULI 672:3
reason the o. of others — WOOLF 922:45
recurring again to Plato's o. — STER 818:88
scorching world's o. — FLET 328:75
was ever of the o. — GOLD 361:43
whole climate of o. — AUDEN 40:99
wolf remains of a different o. — INGE 428:49
opinions as many o. as...people — TERE 848:79
borrow other men's o. — BACON 48:3
confirm and establish our o. — BROW 158:57
contempt for my character and o. — SHAW 778:81
don't care to give o. — HERN 399:27
How long halt ye between two o.? — BIBLE 92:18
Men...bad as their o. — MACK 534:22
men who have no o. — CHES 211:55
one truth, and many o. — KURZ 482:44
o. that they...entertain — PALM 636:25
o. were not acted on — ELIOT 303:1
private parts...and his religious o. — BUTL 178:83
Stiff in o. — DRYD 290:88
takes no notice of their o. — CROM 245:70
think his own o. — MORE 596:58
those who have certain o. — STEIN 815:29
what their o. make of them — LICH 509:23
wish to spread those o. — BUTL 177:64
Women were expected to have weak o. — ELIOT 303:1
opium against art, as against o. — RODC 693:87
antidote against the o. of time — BROW 159:90
help of o. or alcohol — HERZ 400:55
It is the o. of the people — MARX 557:94
just, subtle, and mighty o.! — DE 262:7
Music is no different from o. — KHOM 466:97
o. for every conceivable mass — KENN 462:4
o. has left the happiest memory — GREE 371:57
o. of the West — FRAN 333:84
opium-dose Bible as...an o.-d. — KING 469:59
opponent an o. cannot be...honest — ORWE 629:92
sound to his o. bitter — MILNE 574:73
tries to best his o. — PAUL 644:76
opponents pushed back...by their o. — PANK 636:30
trip, hack and push their o. — FRY 339:22
truth...convincing its o. — PLAN 654:60
opportunist rather be an o. and float — BALF 55:59
opportunities equal o. — MAND 544:46
No duties, only o. — ANON 24:42
o....thicker than anywhere else — BALD 53:30
series of great o. — GARD 346:45
wise man will make more o. — BACON 50:57
woman with fair o. — THAC 849:86
opportunity age of right and o. — WILS 916:7
build a society of o. — MAJOR 541:70
Equality of o. — KENN 463:25
existence and o. — TEMP 838:35
giving you the o. — DICK 270:86
improving the present o. — WILL 912:5
Know thine o. — PITT 653:51
least o. invades it — NICO 614:94
let slip an o. — SHAW 781:3
maximum of o. — SHAW 778:8
not time or o. — AUST 42:60
o. accorded him since Adam — MUGG 601:49
o. as against material interests — WILS 916:8
o. cost of economic discussion — GALB 343:98
o. for attacking the devil! — STEAD 813:85
o. for graft — BIRNS 131:72
O. makes a thief — BACON 46:34
o. to rise again — SARN 714:32
o. to serve our country — SMITH 799:71
scarcity of o. — ANGE 17:36
strong seducer, o.! — DRYD 288:37
substantial equality of o. — ROOS 696:55
unfettered o. — MADAN 538:19
opposèd o. may beware of thee — SHAK 751:18
opposite in justice and in its o. — SOPH 804:84
o. of talking — LEBO 499:13
opposition duty of an O. — CHUR 215:58

formidable O. — DISR 276:43
Her Majesty's O. — BAGE 51:82
His Majesty's O. — HOBH 405:31
Prime Minister or Leader of the O. — DISR 277:82
war of eternal o. — LYND 524:15
when it has a strong o. — SWEE 830:46
young, bald Leader of the O. — KINN 470:71
oppositions riven by a dozen o. — ROSS 697:72
oppress o., rob, and degrade them — DOUG 284:37
oppressed Christ comes to the o. — RUET 701:63
friend of the o. — GARI 346:47
opiate of the o. — JONG 448:99
o. can find...safety — ANGE 17:42
o., who wanted strength — WORD 927:31
past of the o. people — FANON 317:44
oppression Need and o. starveth — SHAK 737:79
often a mechanical o. — HEMI 394:11
o. he may heretofore have suffered — MANS 547:1
proud o. will not hear me — OTWAY 630:24
To make o. bitter — SHAK 753:68
oppressions o. of this earth — SHEL 783:26
oppressor confront the o. — MAKW 541:77
day o' the O. is ended — KIPL 472:23
revolutionary ends as an o. — CAMUS 187:96
The o.'s wrong — TWAIN 871:7
oppressors we may have our o. — PUIG 672:1
optical o. flecks — UPDI 875:93
o. form of thought — HUGO 420:64
optimism as agreeable as o. — BENN 76:49
optimist have to be an o. — SAND 713:1
last o. left in Colombia — GARC 345:41
o. after it, he knows too little — TWAIN 872:35
o. is a guy — MARQ 554:25
o. proclaims that we live in the best — CABE 183:18
o....sees a green light everywhere — SCHW 721:71
optimistic If I was not o. — OUD 631:36
make us o. or — UNAM 873:64
O. lies have...therapeutic value — SHAW 780:59
options discuss your o. afterwards — SHAN 776:31
opulent o. calm of angelfish — ALLEN 12:35
oracle pronounces as an o. — WESL 900:22
oracles o. are dumb — MILT 576:99
o. of God — BIBLE 124:91
orange clockwork o. — BURG 167:81
Orangeman Pocket of a Stout O. — ANON 21:37
oranges bowl of o., too — MITC 588:90
coffee and o. — STEV 819:17
orator An o. is a good man — CATO 200:98
greatest o., who triumphs — HUME 422:11
no o. as Brutus is — SHAK 748:13
oratory Poetry...not as o. — POUND 664:31
orb Cycle and epicycle, o. in o. — MILT 584:97
monthly changes in her circled o. — SHAK 736:51
There's not the smallest o. — SHAK 741:86
orbit most beautiful sight in o. — SCHW 721:69
orbits circled in their o. — DICK 268:51
orbs dew her o. upon the green — SHAK 737:92
o., Or dim suffusion veiled — MILT 582:37
orchard fair with o. lawns — TENN 847:52
hath thy o. fruit — JONS 449:37
O., for a Dome — DICK 272:59
orchards Not all do o. please — VIRG 882:28
orchestra for o. without music — RAVEL 679:37
golden rules for an o. — BEEC 69:62
plays the kettle drums in the o. — SALI 711:60
separates you from the o. — DIDE 273:87
orchestrated Three farts...o. — BARB 59:49
orchestration o. of platitudes — WILD 911:83
orchid O.—breathing incense — BASHO 63:43
ordeal o. of meeting me — CHUR 217:96
worst possible o. — BERR 82:68
order all in o. stand — CRAB 242:83
And o., truth, and beauty range — SMART 796:27
arranged them in alphabetical o. — HELL 392:62
been a rock of o. — METT 568:28
benevolence of the passive o. — MERE 567:3
change the social o. — FRAN 333:91
colours assembled in a certain o. — DENIS 262:97
decently and in o. — BIBLE 121:11
establishing a world o. — EISE 302:57
explain to our sense of o. — HARDY 382:62
fairest o. in the world — HERA 397:71
forces working in inverse o.! — CARL 192:8
Good o. is the foundation — BURKE 169:44
loyalty and o. — GLAD 358:92
new o. from the old — WEBB 893:65
old o. changeth — TENN 847:50

ordainer of o. BROW 159:96
o. breeds habit ADAMS 4:79
o. does not create life SAINT 709:19
O. is heaven's first law POPE 660:24
o. of Melchizedek BIBLE 97:74
o. of nature FONT 328:85
o. of the acts PAST 641:41
o. our lives more rationally LECO 499:29
possess internal o. FORS 331:50
precise idea of o. BERN 81:43
preponderantly geometric o. LEGER 501:52
recollect the o. in which WELL 897:60
re-establish peace and civil o. ELIZ 310:66
reminders of o. GREER 372:91
sense of o. ORWE 628:43
significance to ourselves…find…o. WELTY 899:1
society, social o. MUNCH 603:81
some sort of o. GREE 371:68
some sort of o. (or beauty) POUND 665:66
subversion of good o. KNOX 476:18
sudden light that shows new o. CORN 237:72
values o. without constraint LEGU 501:58
vast o. of the universe PAGE 633:79
where all is o. and beauty BAUD 64:61
words in their best o. COLE 227:21
world has not to be put in o. MILL 573:33
ordered You o..I obeyed BERN 80:33
orderliness freedom and a general o. CARD 190:44
orders Almighty's o. to perform ADDI 5:5
'E don't obey no o. KIPL 472:18
give o. to love SAND 712:87
Gordon should be under my o. CROM 245:66
in all his tinted o. FIRB 323:67
lower o. are seen unfavourably CHES 211:41
o. and inferior creatures MILT 586:55
organisation…of o. MARX 557:1
Reasonable o. are TUCH 869:59
willing to follow his o. BIBLE 127:90
ordinary all o. people CHEK 209:11
divided into 'o.' and 'extraordinary' DOST 282:6
I find the…the o. much more satisfying RAUS 679:34
o. affairs of o. people GOWE 365:29
o. in the individual MANN 546:74
O. life bypassed me OBRI 620:4
o. man and woman ATTL 38:42
o. people through o. situations BANKS 59:38
o. wine just leaves AMER 14:77
taking o. men GALB 343:96
There are no o. moments MILL 574:67
warn you not to be o. KINN 470:70
work of fiction o. men HUBB 417:8
ore slaves that dig the golden o. CRAB 242:89
organ Heaven's deep o. blow MILT 576:97
Seated one day at the o. PROC 670:58
With most miraculous o. SHAK 753:70
organ-grinder o. g. is present BEVAN 85:21
organism o. is preparing to rest MAMET 544:34
over-complicated o. POUND 665:55
organization appropriate o. GALB 343:96
bigger the o. JAY 436:99
destroyed the foundation of the o. EISE 302:57
efficient o. is one in which STEA 813:79
o. for pleasure JOHN 440:99
O. is alien to their natures HAZZ 388:96
o. is the greatest morale builder DOOL 282:99
o. of idolatry SHAW 778:4
o. of public opinion LIPP 511:68
systematic o. of hatreds ADAMS 4:75
organizations part in the various o. JOHN 438:55
organized highly o. part of it GALB 343:95
o. for that TOLS 862:4
organs given us all more o. BRAD 148:60
inner o. of beasts JOYCE 452:92
take your sense o. seriously LEARY 498:95
that o. that piss LAYT 496:49
orgasm o. has replaced the cross MUGG 601:48
orgy need an o., once NASH 608:86
Orient O. dew, Shed from MARV 555:57
slow revenge of the O. PRIE 668:21
oriental Tea, although an O. CHES 212:80
you are an O. FORS 331:40
orientation from the o. of a few ROBB 688:5
origin account for their own o. MILL 570:72
indelible stamp of his lowly o. DARW 253:16
Philosophy…has no other o. SOCR 803:55
takes its o. from emotion WORD 925:10
original curse Their frail o. MILT 581:27

greatest o. practical example WHIT 905:42
great O. proclaim ADDI 6:26
in order to imitate the o. BERN 81:52
line up to see the o. ARMS 30:77
new and o. plan GILB 354:12
She's the o. good time DAVIS 255:56
things counter, o., spare HOPK 412:86
thought is like o. sin LEBO 499:11
thought is often o. HOLM 407:78
originality All my o. consists REDON 681:74
Artistic o. has only NABO 606:42
o.…manner of thinking MAUP 561:83
result is his o. ROTH 699:14
without o. or moral courage SHAW 778:79
originals o. from whence all LOCKE 514:18
Orion loose the bands of O.? BIBLE 93:73
O. standing on his head LAWR 494:5
orisons his morning o. SMART 796:26
their hasty o. OWEN 632:51
Orkney In bloody O. BLAIR 132:97
In bloody O. BLAIR 132:98
Orlando Run, run, O. SHAK 749:55
Orleans who are besieging O. JOAN 438:52
ornament esteem'st the o. of life SHAK 767:88
mankind from superfluous o. LOOS 517:70
moment's o. WORD 927:35
old o. of his cheek SHAK 745:13
o. from utilitarian objects LOOS 517:71
o. which truth doth give SHAK 771:19
respecting all o. RUSK 703:1
used literature as an o. VARG 877:36
ornamentation building without o. SANT 714:25
ornaments hide with o. their…art POPE 658:55
orphan carried by an o. boy SCOTT 722:84
court as an o. LEVA 506:52
widow and his o. LINC 510:41
orphans new o. cry SHAK 768:28
Orpheus O. with his lute made trees SHAK 775:12
soul of O. sing MILT 576:18
orthodox certainly not o. STRA 826:83
orthodoxy 'o.'…no longer means CHES 211:48
O. or My-doxy CARL 192:9
unimpeachable o. RAHN 677:91
orthography now is he turned o. SHAK 744:4
Orwell episode out of George O. COOKE 236:40
O. told us we would MAMET 543:28
Oscar assume that O. said it PARK 637:46
Oscars pick out stage actors at the O. MCKE 534:17
Walk two O. behind WARR 889:71
Osiris mangled body of O. MILT 579:79
Out-glares the Heav'ns O. HERR 399:38
ostrich America cannot be an o. WILS 916:12
neck like an o. DAVIS 255:55
Othello O. subject Desdemona KOES 477:30
something like it in O. SHER 788:66
other think there is no o. SCHR 720:41
Were she o. than she is SHAK 744:89
otherness quintessence of o. BURG 167:95
visual form of the 'o.' NOLAN 617:54
others alone among o. SAINT 709:16
Do not do unto o. SHAW 779:27
liberty is the love of o. HAZL 387:71
love of o. SHAW 777:58
more pleasing to o. JOHN 445:33
o. were only my wives GUIT 374:34
pity o. had to leave KINN 470:69
ought It is, but hadn't o. to be HARTE 385:19
o. to flow through KIPL 470:84
what o. to be HOMA 408:9
what you o. to do SART 716:54
ounce o. of Silver out of the Earth PETTY 649:84
ourselves advance a step beyond o. HUME 422:3
do not talk of o. TROL 866:78
how to get rid of o. HORN 414:36
interplay between nature and o. HEIS 391:55
no hope of finding o. MILL 572:27
O. to end o. SHAK 765:44
power is the love of o. HAZL 387:71
stop loving o. STAEL 811:50
vainly conceal from o. PASC 640:9
out fall not o. by the way BIBLE 88:4
I don't have to go o. SMITH 800:86
Let me o.! ATWO 38:50
O., damned spot SHAK 768:33
O., vile jelly! SHAK 763:81
relevance…for what it leaves o. FERL 321:13
wit is o. SHAK 745:17

outcast writer…an o. by nature BARN 60:68
outcome o. of the struggle ANGE 17:35
outdated methods are o. ANON 23:84
outdoor I play no o. games WILDE 909:32
outfits bareleg o. MURR 604:7
outlaw attacks from o. states REAG 680:60
Jazz musicians have some o. ZWER 937:7
wandering o. of his…mind BYRON 179:19
outline drew his own o. VASA 877:37
mountain o. varies THOR 857:78
outlines eye never sees o. GOYA 365:30
outlive I o. you SEXT 728:37
many years o. performance? SHAK 743:51
outlook Writers of comedy have an o. THUR 860:55
outrage do o. to its…unity HOMA 408:8
Satire is moral o. ROTH 699:22
outrageous don't know how to be o. LEMMY 502:80
outside England…o. Europe KEYN 465:80
from the o. inwards FRIE 337:69
Give me the o. of all things LEWIS 508:3
I am just going o. OATES 620:97
o. pissing in JOHN 440:84
o. to every form HEPW 396:62
people who live o. SABA 707:82
watch…from the o. WELLS 898:74
we can get o. ourselves RABI 676:79
outsider can an o. understand KAFKA 454:25
outsiders imagined by o. WATS 890:97
o. do not understand MUNRO 603:89
war against the o. GARI 346:48
outstanding o. men become fewer TOCQ 861:80
outstrip o. all praise SHAK 774:93
outward inevitably turns o. UPDI 874:89
man looketh on the o. appearance BIBLE 91:90
need of o. criteria WITT 918:47
onward and o. WHIT 905:31
virtue on his o. parts SHAK 740:70
outworn free itself from all that is o. CUPI 248:35
out-worn o.-w. heart YEATS 932:35
Oval English cricket…died at the O. ANON 21:33
ovation Arrange o. SWAN 830:34
oven burn as an o. BIBLE 106:22
ovens gassing people in o. SIHA 791:29
over It ain't o. 'til it's o. BERRA 82:58
never get o. it FROST 339:19
O. after o. JOYCE 452:94
O. my dead body KAUF 456:62
O.paid, o.fed, o.sexed, and o. here TRIN 866:72
they think it's all o. WOLS 921:15
overalls pantheon of boots and o. DUNN 295:17
overboard propose to throw o. MANN 545:66
throw the occasional man o. GILM 356:57
overcoat meaning…only its o. CAREY 190:66
put on your o. LOWE 520:38
overcoats never taken off their o. THUR 859:21
overcrowding situations of o. COUP 239:98
oversteemed Facts are generally o. UPDI 874:79
overflow Clancy, of the O.' PATE 645:15
spontaneous o. WORD 925:10
overlook knowing what to o. JAMES 434:65
overpaid all that they are being o. for SELZ 727:88
O., overfed, oversexed, and over here TRIN 866:72
overpower She can o., astonish HUNT 423:26
overrated three most o. things KENN 463:17
override she will o. you FAUL 319:73
overrule threaten to o. him PAXM 644:84
oversexed Overpaid, overfed, o., and over here TRIN 866:72
over-shoes o.-s. in love SHAK 729:24
oversights mistakes and o. MURP 604:8
oversimplification O. is now BERG 79:92
over-simplification systematic o.-s. POPP 663:2
overstepped never o. it FROST 338:95
overstocked aviary o. with jays OHEN 623:55
overthrow think'st thou dost o. DONNE 281:67
over-well love is given o.-w. PARK 637:56
Ovid O., the soft philosopher DRYD 291:31
ovum Via o. cranium STEV 820:56
owe O. no man any thing BIBLE 120:86
o. no man hate SHAK 749:57
o. nothing to Women's Lib THAT 850:9
Owen grave of Gomer O. THOM 853:89
owl blind as any noonday o. TENN 847:43
comrade with the wolf and o. SHAK 763:69
moping o. GRAY 369:11
of the white o. sweeping MERE 566:93
O., and a useful Cart LEAR 497:81

O. and the Pussy-Cat · LEAR 497:83
o., for all his feathers · KEATS 458:30
singing o. · ROCH 691:64
sings the staring o. · SHAK 734:94
white o.'s feather · ALLI 13:61
owlish describe myself as o. · SCHW 721:66
owls castle brown as o. · THOM 852:75
hooded eagle among blinking o. · SHEL 784:66
Of o. and cuckoos, asses · MILT 579:83
Two O. and a Hen · LEAR 497:75
Who brings o. to Athens? · ARIS 29:45
own call my o. · DRYD 290:8
crisis…we can call our o. · SALI 711:64
prefer to o. slot machines · TRUMP 869:48
what isn't one's o. · PLATO 655:97
what you o. · ELIOT 308:20
wouldn't want to o. one · FIEL 323:49
own-alone All by my o.-a. self · HARR 383:96
owner rather o. be · DONNE 280:60
owners sons of former slave o. · KING 468:39
ownership importance of social o. · STRA 826:79
its source of power: o. · KINN 470:66
own-goal AIDS…a classic o.-g. · ANNE 18:54
owns Who o. all of space? · HUGH 419:46
ox Baby in an ox's stall? · BET] 84:99
eateth grass as an ox · BIBLE 93:76
shalt not muzzle the ox · BIBLE 90:51
stalled ox and hatred therewith · BIBLE 99:32
oxen eat grass as o. · BIBLE 106:96
o. frae the furrowed field · BURNS 172:39
Oxenford Clerk ther was of O. · CHAU 208:71
Oxford clever men at O. · GRAH 366:40
either O. or Cambridge · SNAG 802:33
Mussolini had been at O. · HALI 378:84
O.…has made me insufferable · BEER 69:72
O.…more attractive than Cambridge · BAED 51:77
poetry, which is in O. made · DRYD 288:40
schools of O. · GIBB 351:57
stagecoach from London to O. · HAZL 387:73
The King to O. sent a troop of horse · BROW 159:98
to found at O. a chair · ARNO 33:50
University of O. · GIBB 352:60
Oxfordshire all the birds Of O. · THOM 854:7
oxlips o. and the nodding violet · SHAK 737:97
Oxtail university of O. · JOYCE 452:91
Oxus O., forgetting the bright speed · ARNO 32:28
oxygen o. of publicity · THAT 850:24
o. of social intercourse · HIRS 403:6
oyster An o. may be crossed in love! · SHER 788:68
bold Man that first ate an O. · SWIFT 832:7
eye that can open an o. · WODE 919:71
No o. ever profited · THUR 859:36
o. of the old school · DICK 270:87
sympathetic unselfishness of an o. · SAKI 710:42
world's mine o. · SHAK 743:70
you can't enjoy an o. · CLARK 219:51
oyster-knife sneer…like an o.-k. · ANNAN 17:51
oysters But by no means unlike o. · DICK 268:33
eat my o. · SWIFT 832:12
man who doesn't love o. · SAKI 710:40
Poverty and o.…seem to go · DICK 266:76
Ozymandias My name is O. · SHEL 784:50

P

pa Don't beat me, pa! · JOYCE 451:80
Ma's out, Pa's out · FLAN 326:24
pace bloody thoughts with violent p. · SHAK 760:96
dance is a measured p. · BACON 46:46
jogging justling p. · MUNDY 603:82
know how to p. themselves · DIOR 275:23
not keep p. · THOR 858:97
one p. ahead of myself · MCGO 532:83
p. of science · FROMM 338:82
paces Hop forty p. · SHAK 765:25
three p. through the room · TENN 839:50
Time travels in divers p. · SHAK 750:63
paciencia p. y barajar · CERV 203:48
Pacific Atlantic to the P. · CHUR 216:71
star'd at the p. · KEATS 456:77
Pacioli heard of Fra Luca P. · MULL 602:72
pack changed the form of the p. · TROT 867:17
face the murderous cowardly p. · MCKA 533:12
God! I will p., and take a train · BROO 156:12
revenged on the whole p. · SHAK 757:91
soldier's p. is not so heavy · EISE 302:52
with rifle and p. · SASS 716:63

packages internationally marketed p. · ILLI 428:45
Packard upholstery of a P. · PERE 648:62
pack-horses Shall p.-h. · SHAK 743:49
pact I make a p. with you · POUND 664:30
pad dolor of p. · ROET 694:98
Paddington As London is to P. · CANN 188:11
paddle leave to p. · KIPL 472:35
paddles 'ear their p. chunkin' · KIPL 470:86
padlock clap your p. · PRIOR 669:32
one jingling p. on the mind · POPE 662:75
pads writing p., notebooks · RODC 693:87
Padua wive it wealthily in P. · SHAK 732:28
paeans laurels to p. · CICE 218:26
paga Non si p., non si p. · FO 328:79
pagan animals (p., I regret to say) · DICK 268:33
p. suckled in a creed · WORD 928:46
pagans example of the ancient p. · GUIB 374:30
P. deified life · STAEL 811:48
wild p. at the cash register · CHER 210:22
page A P., a Grave · POPE 662:74
blotted from life's p. · BYRON 179:17
cannot tear out a single p. · SAND 712:86
father struggled through half a p. · LAWR 494:18
looks well enough on the p. · BUNT 166:61
on a beautiful quarto p. · SHER 787:51
one sweet p. · PATM 643:58
p. having an ample marge · TENN 846:14
pictures for the p. atone · POPE 662:69
Rule 1, on p. 1 · MONT 593:1
sports p. records · WARR 889:70
stole a p. from the Universe! · MARTI 555:44
when you looked at the front p. · CHRI 214:31
pageant like this insubstantial p. · SHAK 774:94
P. of Empire · SITW 794:74
p. of his bleeding heart · ARNO 33:32
pages funny p. of the history books · DEAN 257:87
read the first 2 p. · JOYCE 452:97
pagoda old Moulmein P. · KIPL 470:85
pagus private p. or demesne · AUDEN 41:25
paid Ambition's debt is p. · SHAK 747:95
being p. in or p. out · HUXL 426:3
getting what you haven't p. for · WHAR 901:51
more women are p. · FALU 317:40
p. for a woman · GREE 371:65
p. for this microphone · REAG 681:64
p. the prices of life · GURN 375:44
p. with a smile · SAINT 709:18
p. with flattery · JOHN 442:49
these men p. their shillings · PRIE 668:17
you p. us more · HAMM 380:22
pail milk comes frozen home in p. · SHAK 734:94
pails ice crunching in p. · STEV 820:44
pain After great p. · DICK 272:60
alternations of p. · WILD 911:90
always in p. · BELL 72:41
and all the p. · SWIN 832:18
boredom and p. of it · BUEC 165:44
cause of all this p. · JULI 452:5
clenched on a round p. · THOM 852:67
delight in physics p. · SHAK 767:8
drama of p. · HARDY 382:60
draw thy breath in p. · SHAK 755:41
earth in travail and in p. · LONG 516:59
ease after p. · MILT 578:42
equal ease unto my p. · CAREW 190:62
Eternal P.! · ARNO 32:13
first feel p. yourself · HORA 414:31
forgets the p. · JEFF 436:11
forget the wandering and p. · FLEC 327:50
for quhome ye suffer p. · HENR 396:54
frame perish…in conquering p. · BYRON 180:37
hark—what p.! · ARNO 32:12
Infinite passion, and the p. · BROW 161:60
inflict p. upon oneself · MERE 567:3
Joy always came after p. · APOL 27:16
know the p. · WALC 884:73
lack the thing should rid my p. · SURR 829:35
Liberty's exquisite p. · BROW 159:3
life's a p. · DAVI 254:35
like a God in p. · KEATS 458:33
long grief and p. · TENN 845:93
lost happiness and lasting p. · MILT 580:96
midnight with no p. · KEATS 460:62
most intolerable p. · SHAW 779:13
narcotics, numbing p. · TENN 842:23
neither…any more p. · BIBLE 127:80
no greater p. than to remember · DANTE 252:95

no living thing to suffer p. · SHEL 784:71
no p. is greater than…being alive · DARIO 252:4
No p.—no gain · ANON 23:71
nor even freedom from p. · LAWR 494:4
obligation is a p. · JOHN 441:23
Oh p.! Oh p.! · BAUD 64:57
on p. of imprisonment · EDWA 300:15
Our Lady of P. · SWIN 833:28
owes its pleasure to another's p. · COWP 241:74
p. accompanied by the idea · SPIN 810:30
p. and anguish wring the brow · SCOTT 723:1
p. full of pleasantness · LYLY 523:9
p. in the desert · MOOR 596:55
p. in the soul · HAMM 379:11
p. is dreadful · CATU 201:10
p. isn't real · ANON 22:53
p. is perfect misery · MILT 583:86
p. is the one nobility · BAUD 64:54
p. is worse · JEFF 436:7
p. of particular circumstances · CART 198:39
p.…of their thorns · BERN 81:44
p. or languor · WORD 929:63
p. or pleasure · HUME 422:5
p. than paralysis! · NIGH 616:31
p. that the artist feels · REDON 681:73
Pale Grief and pleasing P. · GRAY 370:35
pleasure of my p. · SIDN 790:7
rest from p. · DRYD 287:19
startle this dull p. · COLE 226:1
studies or his usual p.? · SHAK 732:36
sufferance of your friendly p. · KYD 482:45
Superflux of p. · SWIN 833:25
Sweet is pleasure after p. · DRYD 291:35
tender for another's p. · GRAY 368:95
Though full of p. · MILT 581:22
threshold of p. · GELL 348:1
travaileth in p. · BIBLE 120:75
turns to pleasing p. · SPEN 809:93
unforgotten p. · ROSS 698:99
upon p. of imprisonment · ELIZ 309:58
wicked to deserve such p. · BROW 161:45
with a sob of p. · JOYCE 452:83
with ceaseless p. · GOLD 361:39
without one p. · TENN 847:35
With some p. is fraught · SHEL 784:61
world without our p. · LANY 489:6
would not give Him p. · STUD 827:5
painch P., tripe, or thairm · BURNS 171:88
Paine Tom P.'s common sense · ADAMS 5:91
painful as p. as the other · BACON 47:75
confusing, disorienting, and p. · RICH 685:48
good honest and p. · PEPYS 647:29
growing up is p. · ANGE 17:31
life of men is p. · EURI 316:9
p. warrior · SHAK 771:12
too p. for me · BIBLE 96:42
painkiller P. X and P. Y · VIDAL 881:2
pains at p. to attract · JOHN 446:54
Beauty p. · HAAS 376:52
by p. men come to greater p. · BACON 48:2
great p. to con it · SHAK 756:57
infinite capacity for taking p. · ACHE 2:38
Luff…all p. makis lycht · BARB 59:53
made my p. his prey · SPEN 809:1
many the p. he suffered · HOMER 409:24
Marriage has many p. · JOHN 443:58
Muses never knew their p. · CRAB 242:86
one thousand scathing p. · LABE 482:54
p. and penalties of idleness · POPE 662:86
p. a world of kisses · SHAK 759:62
P. of love · DRYD 288:34
p. the immortal spirit must endure · ARNO 31:90
pleasure in poetic p. · COWP 241:71
sympathize with people's p. · HUXL 424:55
that kills and p. not? · SHAK 766:58
too much p. to think · HUME 422:6
paint artist should not only p. · FRIE 337:71
cheeks are covered with p. · NASH 608:79
do not p. · GAUG 347:67
flinging a pot of p. · RUSK 704:34
I p. a portrait I lose a friend · SARG 714:30
keep her in p. and powder · NIMI 616:36
P. as they spoke in Sparta · DIDE 274:2
p. the living · KNEL 476:13
p. the memory of happiness · SAIF 709:10
showed the p. · DRYD 287:15
those who p. 'em truest · ADDI 5:6

worth more than the price of the p. — VAN 877:31
painted best picture that was ever p. — HEMI 394:26
have p. a picture — HOMER 409:26
Mona Lisa p. by a club? — GRIS 373:19
p. skin contents the eye? — SHAK 732:43
painter appear to one American p. — ROSE 696:63
best woman p. — OKEE 623:60
canvas is to the p. — BRIL 152:36
Every good p. — DALI 251:73
for the p., style is…vision — PROU 671:90
great p. of American hell — ALLEN 12:39
He that would be a p. — DURER 295:29
I am a p. — KLEE 475:8
invention of the landscape p. — FUSE 342:77
makes not a p. — WHIS 902:62
mine…the p.'s hand — WORD 928:44
not a great sculptor or p. — RUSK 703:8
p. carries the whole — MOTH 600:32
p. has two chief objects — LEON 503:11
p. only needs brushes — WINN 917:27
p. pursues his with greater — LEON 503:9
p. sketches A visible world — AUDEN 39:88
p. who draws by practice — LEON 504:21
picture-p. is indistinguishable — LEWIS 507:88
some great p. — SHEL 783:33
subject is to the p. — RIVE 688:2
Telling a p. — MALL 542:93
tools…or the p.' techniques — RENO 683:9
to say to the p. — WHIS 902:63
very great p. said to me — SITW 794:77
painters P.…dissipated — BLAKE 135:76
P. of history — KNEL 476:13
p. speak with works — CARR 194:60
p., thus unskilled to trace — POPE 658:55
P. who are not colourists — DELA 260:61
sculptors and p. — THOR 857:79
painting Abstract p.…confronts — POLL 657:38
Art of P. — BLAKE 135:78
art of p. cannot be truly judged — DURER 295:28
bridle and rudder of p. — LEON 504:17
culture of modern p. — MOTH 600:32
difference between p. and sculpture — LEON 503:9
excellent p. — ALBE 10:98
Good p. is like good cooking — VLAM 882:35
grasped what p. could be — MONET 591:54
I feel…part of the p. — POLL 657:37
Landscape is to American p. — HUGH 419:32
of poetry than…of p. — STEV 820:39
oil p., etchings — RODC 693:87
P. and Punctuality — GAIN 342:85
P.…art of protecting — BIER 129:36
P. has been a smiling — MORSE 599:11
p. is done with the brain — MICH 568:34
p.…is essentially a flat surface — DENIS 262:97
p. is merely the image — CELL 202:41
p. is not done to decorate — PICA 650:98
P. is poetry which is seen — LEON 503:11
P. is…representation — PIERO 651:11
p. of sounds, noises and smells — CARRA 194:58
p., poetry, music, architecture — EMER 313:41
p. should be considered excellent — MICH 569:37
P.'s not important — MOSES 600:25
p. that is an act — ROSE 697:64
p.…the presence of absence — BERG 79:2
p. was brought to Egypt — VASA 877:37
p. which cannot be explained — RENO 683:6
produce illumination and not p. — DELA 260:61
purest…form of p. — OROZ 627:27
reason for p. — WYETH 931:19
sense of music or of p. — JOHN 440:1
sexual juices flow toward a p. — FUEN 340:41
to achieve this total p. — CARRA 194:59
walks around a p. — ROSSO 698:7
when you are moved by a p. — ANNE 18:55
when you look at p. — GAUG 347:68
paintings accept p. and sculptures — CHUR 215:41
all the allegorical p. — JOHN 447:73
In judging p. — TINT 861:78
my p. do not sell — VAN 877:31
P. are Rorschach — LICH 509:25
p.…exist only to illustrate the text — WOLFE 920:92
poor lawyers, like poor p. — WHIS 902:66
surface of my p. — WARH 889:62
to see in p. bits of nature — MALE 542:88
paints artist with true feelings p. — FRIE 337:67
pair gentle p., ye little think — MILT 583:64
Happy, happy, happy, p.! — DRYD 291:33

p. of credulous fools — SHIR 789:81
p. of sparkling eyes — GILB 355:34
pairs like proverbs, they occur in p. — SIMON 792:37
pal Me p.…does the toff — DENN 262:1
palace chalice from the p. — PANA 636:27
hazards of the P. of Varieties — CRIT 245:62
in at the p. door — DICK 266:67
in the p.…a monastery — AELR 8:55
in the p. walk — TENN 842:14
left her p. bare — HYDE 427:23
Love in a p. — KEATS 458:22
p. and a prison on each hand — BYRON 180:31
p. built of squarèd brick — SPEN 808:75
p. built upon the sand — MILL 571:82
p. fit for you and me — STEV 823:32
p. more comfortable — HOOV 411:64
p. of the soul — WEBS 895:94
p. of wisdom — BLAKE 134:39
princely p. willed me to indite — LANY 489:7
purple-lined p. — KEATS 458:23
room of the p. — SITW 794:65
thine own p. — DONNE 280:62
palaces gorgeous p. — SHAK 774:94
iron p. of Art — HUGH 419:30
old p. — SHEL 783:45
p. in Kingdom come — MASE 559:35
p. of kings are built — PAINE 634:90
thy p. and tow'rs — BURNS 171:90
palate carries the p. to its highest — BRIL 153:38
gave to his p. — JOYCE 452:92
Glide o'er my p. — BARL 60:58
man's heart is through his p. — FERN 321:17
P., the hutch of tasty lust — HOPK 412:81
steps down the p. — NABO 606:30
palates p. both for sweet and sour — SHAK 761:6
pale Art thou p. for weariness — SHEL 787:30
I left the theatre, dizzy and p. — QUIR 675:57
In p. contented sort — KEATS 458:24
in sorrow p. — BLAKE 134:35
P., beyond porch — SWIN 833:32
p. of the Constitution — GLAD 358:89
p., unripened beauties — ADDI 6:33
started…and turned p. — SOUT 805:9
Why so p. and wan — SUCK 828:7
Palenke poetry…in P. and Uatlán — DARIO 252:2
Palestine establishment in P. — BALF 54:54
haven in sunny P. — MASE 559:26
Jews in P. — OROU 627:22
Palestinian P. peace movement — ANON 25:63
Palestinians P. in Israel — OROU 627:22
P., PLO is a homeland — NEW 611:53
palfrey p. fresh and fair — SCOTT 724:22
pall pallor…shall be their p. — OWEN 632:52
would p. a little — THUR 859:39
Palladium P. of all the civil — JUNI 453:11
palliate p. what we cannot cure — JOHN 442:43
palliative sleep…a p. — CHAM 204:70
pallid p. and thin young man — GILB 354:9
P., unshaved and thirsty — SASS 716:59
Palliser Mr P. was one of those — TROL 866:82
P., Duke of Omnium — TROL 867:11
Pall Mall P. M.Gazette is written — THAC 849:98
pallor p. of girls' brows — OWEN 632:52
palm where the p. tree grows — MARTI 555:45
wind is in the p. tree — KIPL 470:85
win the p., the oak — MARV 556:71
palm-oil proverbs are the p.-o. — ACHE 2:18
palms in their hands — BIBLE 126:59
the p. of her hands — BIBLE 92:38
palooka sobbed the panting p. — PERE 648:53
palpable very p. hit — SHAK 755:39
palsy chide my p., or my gout — DONNE 279:43
p. shakes a few — KEATS 460:59
strucken wid de p. — HARR 383:95
paltry man is but a p. thing — YEATS 933:52
Pam P., I adore you, P. — BETJ 83:84
Pamere high mountain cradle in P. — ARNO 32:28
pan fish that talks In the frying p. — DELA 260:68
panacea suffrage…is their p. — CARL 193:29
panache Sang with a fountain's p. — DAY 257:86
Panama Vietnam…near P. — ANON 23:6
pancake know how that p. feels — WRIG 930:81
pancreatic p. ducts of dog — BANT 59:41
pandemic AIDS p.…own-goal — ANNE 18:54
pandemonium p., the high capital — MILT 581:17
pandering p. to the public taste — BEAV 67:28
Pandora If you open that P.'s box — BEVIN 85:30

pane cheek…against the p. — SCHR 720:40
tap at the p. — BROW 161:34
panegyrics Coarse p. — GRAY 369:9
panes diamonded with p. — KEATS 459:36
pangs More p. will — HOPK 413:4
quietus which his p. might take — TWAIN 871:7
panic Don't P. — ADAMS 4:65
made me p. most — WHITE 903:96
p. in which the passenger is kept — HAZL 388:79
What a p.'s in thy breastie! — BURNS 170:71
Panjandrum Grand P. himself — FOOTE 329:94
panoply p. of death — DAVI 254:41
pansies p.; that's for thoughts — SHAK 755:23
pansy p. at my feet — WORD 926:23
pink, and the p. — MILT 578:54
pant I p., I sink — SHEL 786:12
Pantagruelism P. is…liveliness — RABE 676:76
pantheon dome of the P. — BRAM 150:87
p. of boots and overalls — DUNN 295:17
panther muscles of a p. — PERE 648:58
sofa upholstered in p. skin — PLOM 656:9
pantomime delights of a p. — DICK 267:97
in p. the puppets fumbling — WHITE 903:80
pantry stow'd his p. — BURNS 170:69
pants chair…judged by one's p. — ANON 23:78
in fast thick p. were breathing — COLE 226:11
kick in the p. to God — MILL 572:15
lower limbs in p. — NASH 608:94
secret of life in your p. — CUMM 247:5
Stretch p. — ANON 23:86
Pap P. warn't in a good humor — TWAIN 871:98
papa P.…gives a pretty form — DICK 271:16
p. may have — HOLI 407:64
paper 12 ounces of p. and ink — MORL 598:86
crawling over a piece of p. — INGR 429:66
deliquescent leaves of p. — ANDR 16:25
empty as p. — SCOTT 722:78
few sheets of p. — ARET 29:42
figures which look well on p. — WEIL 896:31
good manners to read the p. — VAND 876:24
grey p. with blunt type! — BROW 160:22
Hamlet is so much p. and ink — PRIE 668:17
hand that signed the p. — THOM 852:62
hath not eat p. — SHAK 733:79
here is the p. that bears his name — CHAM 204:62
I had the p. — HEMI 394:98
It is a commercial p. — HAZL 388:77
just for a scrap of p. — BETH 82:74
keepers of print and p. — MACL 535:41
loo p. gets thicker — MITF 589:12
needs only a typewriter and p. — WINN 917:27
only a p. moon — HARB 380:36
on passive p. — POPE 662:74
p. allegories but ill comprehended — MELV 564:44
P. blushes not — MIDD 569:46
p. it's written on — GOLD 362:85
puppets…with their slips of p. — WHITE 903:80
reactionaries are p. tigers — MAO 548:11
run the p. — BEAV 67:22
sheet of green p. — ATWO 38:50
talking on p. — BAIN 52:7
unpleasant'st words…blotted p. — SHAK 740:75
We set down on p. — TRUM 868:34
when…this p. appears dull — STEE 814:91
white p., void of all — LOCKE 514:17
word down on p. — MILL 573:32
Your eight-page p. — MAST 560:54
paperback America as the p. version — DELI 260:75
paper-blurrers company of p.-b. — SIDN 791:22
paper-mill thou hast built a p.-m. — SHAK 730:66
papers He's got my p. — PINT 652:20
what I read in the p. — ROGE 694:14
paper-weight pad and p.-w. — ROET 694:98
paperwork keep the p. down — ORTON 627:31
papist between Protestant and P. — STRA 826:88
P. have no right to complain! — OBRI 620:1
paprika splash of p. — VREE 883:59
parables end up writing p. — BERG 79:97
many things unto them in p. — BIBLE 112:47
parachute jumping out of a p. — MACL 534:28
What color is your p.? — BOLL 139:46
parade army without p. or gesture — LAWR 495:39
solemnised with pomp and p. — ADAMS 5:89
paradise be with me in p. — BIBLE 116:64
blessed and admit me to P. — ROSS 698:4
blundered into P. — THOM 855:40
built upon the bowers of p. — PAINE 634:90

called the P. of Fools — MILT 582:49
cheapened p. — PATM 643:57
Cheese for dessert…like P. Lost — BRAC 148:50
closest you can get this side of P. — BUEC 165:43
drunk the milk of P. — COLE 226:15
England is the p. of women — FLOR 328:76
fleeting joys Of P. — MILT 585:25
gate of p. — SHAW 781:1
grace the entrance to P. — MICH 569:36
heavenly p. is that place — CAMP 187:80
In P. of all things — MILT 583:72
keys of P. — DE 262:7
lay on nature is a p. — SHAK 758:38
Life's p. — FORD 330:12
Lost Angel of a ruined P.! — SHEL 785:94
my dying place was P. — BROW 158:78
No p., no fall — SNYD 803:49
P. by way of Kensal Green — CHES 212:87
p. for a sect — KEATS 458:14
p.…in his face — DRYD 289:71
P. of exiles — SHEL 783:25
p. of four seas — MARV 556:80
P. shall be the refuge — KORAN 479:92
possess A p. within — MILT 585:35
see John Knox in P. — PARK 637:56
serpent…in P. — HUGH 419:45
spindrift gaze toward p. — CRANE 243:11
Such as the Gates of P. — BLAKE 134:47
They paved p. — MITC 588:91
when P. shall be brought nigh — KORAN 479:92
wilderness is p. — FITZ 324:83
win a p.? — SHAK 733:82
wreck of P. — SHEL 786:11
paradises Two p. 'twere in one — MARV 556:77
paradox p. of high religion — NIEB 614:98
paradoxes man of p. — ROUS 700:45
paragon earthly p. — SHAK 774:71
p. of animals! — SHAK 752:57
paragons p. of frankness — WILL 913:36
paragraph canvas a sentence or p. — MOTH 600:33
most beautiful prose p. — BLOOM 137:7
paragraphing art of newspaper p. — MARQ 554:34
paragraphs hardening of the P. — THUR 859:46
parallel north of the 38th p. — MARS 554:40
speaks…of things without p. — BIER 129:29
there is no p. term — BERG 79:92
parallelism Friendship needs…p. — ADAMS 4:81
parallelogram landlady…is a p. — LEAC 496:58
paralyse p. it by encumbering — TOLS 862:4
paralysis pain than p.! — NIGH 616:31
paramedics run for the p. — SKEL 795:95
paramour her lusty p. — MILT 575:93
many a p. — SPEN 808:86
paramours willow worn of forlorn p. — SPEN 808:73
Worn of p. — SPEN 808:68
paraphrase soul in p. — HERB 398:12
the classics in p.! — POUND 664:37
parasite not born a p. — FRAN 335:22
parasols What various p.! — DICK 267:25
parcel p. of rogues — BURNS 172:35
p. of rogues — BURNS 172:36
parcels deals it in small p. — WEBS 894:73
parched p. ground…a pool — BIBLE 103:33
parchment p. of a constitution — TROT 867:14
pard freckled like a p. — KEATS 458:20
pard-like p.-l. Spirit, beautiful — SHEL 785:99
pardon beseech you of your p. — SHAK 760:88
bitter to thee, p. — SWIN 834:49
cannot help nor p. — AUDEN 39:86
I p. that man's life — SHAK 763:88
ne'er p., who have done the wrong — DRYD 288:36
O p. me — SHAK 748:1
p. after execution — SHAK 775:25
P. me boy — GORD 363:8
p. not that — SHAK 740:84
Say 'P.,' king — SHAK 735:29
Where there is injury, p. — FRAN 334:98
pardonable almost always p. — GRAV 367:75
pardoning in p. that we are — FRAN 334:98
parent child whose p. is unkent — SPEN 808:67
man can be a p. — MUIR 602:68
p. who could see his boy — LEAC 497:66
successful p.…raises a child — EPHR 314:74
To lose one p. — WILDE 909:39
parents avoid having p. — CRISP 245:55
be good to p. — KORAN 479:76
best friends and p. — MARG 549:44

born…with ready-made p. — FRAME 333:81
cannot get subsistence from his p. — MALT 543:18
children inter their p. — HERO 399:29
how my p. were occupied — SALI 710:51
influence of p. — MUSG 605:14
In mine it was the p. — SLOVO 796:19
Jewish man with p. — ROTH 699:18
joys of p. — BACON 48:84
loving their p. — WILDE 909:26
nobleman from surfeiting of his p. — LASS 492:60
No one understands their p. — FRIS 338:77
Of p. good — SHAK 746:49
p. can't take you — UPDI 874:75
p. don't have to say — MORE 597:68
p. kept me from children — SPEN 807:52
p. learn a lot — SPARK 806:17
p. lived like — MIN 587:68
p.…realize that I'm kidnapped — ALLEN 12:50
p.…sometimes a disappointment — POWE 666:76
p. were created for — NASH 608:85
p. won't slight you — COLUM 229:59
question…in many potential p. — SCHU 721:57
stranger to one of your p. — AUST 43:66
two first p. — MILT 582:39
web do p. weave — NASH 608:92
Pariahs women the P. — STAN 812:64
Paris As far as P. — JONS 448:9
dressed in P. — ANON 22:52
Fashion is more tyrannical at P. — CHES 210:35
frocks are built in P. — SAKI 710:32
good Americans die they go to P. — WILDE 909:23
in P., I remained a Canadian — RICH 686:72
I will die in P. — VALL 876:20
Nothing can compare to P. — DESC 263:26
old house in P. — BEME 74:93
Outside of P. — MOLI 589:27
P. is a beast of a city — HAZL 388:79
P. is a city where — WHITE 902:73
P. made of stone — HUGO 420:69
P. preserves the soul — HUGO 421:90
plant our religion in P. — LESL 504:30
When P. sneezes — METT 568:26
when they die, go to P. — APPL 27:24
parish all the world as my p. — WESL 900:19
consent of every butcher in the p. — SHER 787:44
p. of rich women — AUDEN 40:2
pension from his p. — RUSK 704:15
Park as Mungo P. once had to do — GALT 345:31
park All I need…is a p. — CHAP 206:10
don't want to come out to the p. — BERRA 82:54
gentleman's p. is my aversion — CONS 235:24
Over p., over pale — SHAK 737:92
P. Avenue…trade deficit — BART 63:26
Then over the p. — PEPYS 647:34
Parker Charlie P.…always filled — KAVA 456:66
When I first heard Charlie P. — GILL 356:47
parks mountain p. and reservations — MUIR 602:64
p., my walks, my manors — SHAK 730:84
parliament are on this P. — WILL 912:5
as in the time of P. — HENR 395:46
began our P. — HOBY 405:36
create a modern P. — CONN 232:56
Cromwell said to the Long P. — AMERY 14:80
dissolved P. — STAL 812:55
enables P. to do things — SHAW 780:42
in a 21st-century p. — ASHD 35:92
In the last P. — JOWE 451:77
Kiss my P.! — PEPYS 647:25
majorities in P. — WHIT 902:67
mockery to call it a P. House — WENT 899:4
nailed…the doors of P. — MUSS 605:15
P. is a deliberative assembly — BURKE 168:7
P. must lay the burden equally — CHUR 216:63
P. of England — BAIL 52:6
P. of man — TENN 840:81
P. speaking through reporters — CARL 193:42
People in P. — WILL 912:4
Scottish P.…hereby reconvened — EWING 316:29
set up an entire Scottish P. — WATE 890:94
There shall be a Scottish P. — DEWAR 264:40
two-thirds majority in P. — FREUD 336:51
parliamentarian pleasure for a p. — CRIT 245:62
parliaments democratic p. of tricks — WEBB 893:64
England is the mother of P. — BRIG 152:32
P. are the great lie — POBE 656:13
parlour perfumed p. snake — DUNNE 295:24
parlours farmhouse p. — THOM 853:2

Parma P.…should dare to invade — ELIZ 309:60
parmacity p. for an inward bruise — SHAK 741:1
Parnassus poor man's P. — EMER 313:54
to climb P. — BURNS 170:63
Parnell Poor P.! — JOYCE 452:83
parodies P. and caricatures — HUXL 425:66
parody between an epitome and a p. — ISAA 430:87
p. is a game — NABO 606:43
p.…replaced history — PIGL 651:14
parole p. of literary men — JOHN 446:51
parrot Sick as a p. — ANON 24:20
this p. what I have purchased — CLEE 220:70
with a p. and five companions — HEYE 401:72
parrots keep p. or puppy dogs — CAMP 186:64
laugh like p. — SHAK 739:35
Parsee There lived a P. — KIPL 473:40
parsimonious Nothing…more p. — SMOL 801:28
parsimony beggarly p. and ignoble — NASHE 609:12
Capitals are increased by p. — SMITH 798:46
parsley P. Is gharsely — NASH 609:1
parsnip lukewarm p. juice — WOOL 923:61
parson different cause, says p. Sly — PRIOR 669:40
drowns the p.'s saw — SHAK 734:95
If P. lost his senses — HODG 405:46
p. owned his skil! — GOLD 361:55
part bids me play my p. — SPEN 809:97
every man must play a p. — SHAK 739:36
every prudent p. — POPE 661:46
fifth p. of the Earth — FIELD 322:30
forgot my p. — SHAK 769:70
however and whenever we p. — DICK 268:30
know in p.…prophesy in p. — BIBLE 121:9
let us kiss and p. — DRAY 287:6
lose a p. of ourselves — POPE 659:99
no p. of his intention — SMITH 798:49
no p. with lads — SASS 716:66
Not a tolerable woman's p. — AUST 43:75
p. of all that I have met — TENN 839:63
P. of a moon — FROST 338:86
p. on better terms — OTWAY 631:35
p. with their brightest hour — HELL 392:80
play its…rational p. — LEWIS 507:83
principal p. of themselves — HAZL 387:72
see the inmost p. of you — SHAK 754:4
Sir, you and I must p. — SHAK 764:20
Some p. of us — SKEL 795:97
take your own p. — BORR 145:4
thou and nature can so gently p. — SHAK 766:62
we ourselves are p. of nature — PLAN 654:59
what we can p. with — FORD 330:23
white…yet a p. of me — HUGH 418:22
will more willingly p. withal — SHAK 752:50
parted measured swords, and p. — SHAK 750:90
the way we p. — SWIN 833:37
parterre nod on the p. — POPE 659:97
Parthenon though it were the P. — LOWE 519:25
Parthenons miniature P. — GILL 355:38
particel every p. and utensil — SHAK 756:58
participant point of view of p. — GALL 344:14
participate everybody is invited to p. — SCRI 726:66
p. in a tragedy — HUXL 425:92
participation dreams of the p. — NICH 613:84
particle catching every air-borne p. — JAMES 433:42
pushing young p. — GILB 354:9
particular Every p. Thou — BUBER 164:23
it's about everything in p. — SPARK 806:28
p. and universal — BERG 79:97
p. expenditure — EDEN 299:89
So singular in each p. — SHAK 770:87
particulars must do it in Minute P. — BLAKE 135:73
out of p. — WILL 913:47
parties both p. nobly are subdued — SHAK 743:61
contract…between those two p. — SMITH 797:43
cowardly, middle-class p. — GOER 359:9
creed of different p. — TOCQ 861:84
Dinner p. are for eating — FERB 320:99
Things must be done by p. — DISR 277:82
without the p. — JOHN 444:15
parting at our p. — JONS 449:35
Every p. is a foretaste — SCHO 720:37
In every p.…an image of death — ELIOT 303:71
P. is all we know — DICK 273:77
P. is such sweet sorrow — SHAK 736:53
true love p. — THOM 854:21
partitions thin p. do their bands — DRYD 290:77
partner look for a perfect p. — WELD 897:43
Sole p. and sole part — MILT 583:65

haunt of ancient P. — TENN 839:61
hold their p. — BIBLE 116:59
holy rest, and p. — NEWM 612:63
honey p. in old poems — JEFF 436:5
if one wishes to travel in p. — STARK 813:72
Imperishable p. — HOUS 416:86
inglorious arts of p. — MARV 555:54
In hearts at p. — BROO 156:7
In His will is our p. — DANTE 252:98
in p. and…in war — MONT 593:92
In p., children inter their parents — HERO 399:29
In p.: goodwill — CHUR 216:60
instrument of Your p. — FRAN 334:98
In the arts of p. — SHAW 778:94
in Thee in p. — HAMM 379:7
in what p. a Christian can die — ADDI 7:43
keep him in perfect p. — BIBLE 103:25
King of glory, King of p. — HERB 398:2
led forth with p. — BIBLE 104:57
Let him who desires p. — VEGE 879:58
lettest thou thy servant depart in p. — BIBLE 128:1
lettest thou thy servant depart in p. — BIBLE 115:27
let us make p. — CROM 245:71
live together in p. — UNIT 873:69
Love of P., and lonely musing — COLL 228:50
made a desolation they called it a p. — BURG 167:85
made a separate p. — HEMI 394:98
Make it a green p. — DARN 253:7
means of preserving p. — WASH 890:86
merry songs of p. — SHAK 775:26
message of p., love — WHIT 904:14
more p. and it is the holier — HOPK 412:96
more potent advocates of p. — GEOR 349:14
never…a bad p. — FRAN 334:15
no better p.-keepers — PALM 635:20
no p.…to the wicked — BIBLE 104:60
Nor for my p. — JONS 449:39
Nor p. within nor calm around — SHEL 783:32
no such thing as inner p. — LEBO 499:5
not a p. treaty — FOCH 328:81
Nothing can bring you p. — EMER 312:10
now do hold their p. — SURR 829:35
Now we have to win the p. — CLEM 221:79
Palestinian p. movement — ANON 25:63
p. above all earthly dignities — SHAK 775:19
p. among our peoples — KIPL 472:13
p. and propagation — WALP 887:33
p. and rest can never dwell — MILT 580:97
P.…a period of cheating — BIER 129:38
P. be to this house — BIBLE 115:35
P. be to this house — BOOK 142:31
p. betrayed us — MUIR 602:58
p. be unto you — BIBLE 128:2
P. cannot be built on exclusion — ADAMS 4:73
p. cannot be maintained — RUSS 706:64
P.; come away — TENN 843:46
p. comes dropping slow — YEATS 932:30
P., Enjoyment, Love and Pleasure! — BURNS 172:30
p. for our time — CHAM 204:63
peaceful sloth, Not p. — MILT 581:23
p. has been broken — ROOS 696:46
p. hath her victories — MILT 580:87
p. have they which love thy law — BIBLE 97:86
p., I hope, with honour — DISR 277:85
P. I leave with you — BIBLE 118:11
p. in Shelley's mind — SHEL 787:26
p. in thy breast — SHAK 736:54
P. is in the grave — SHEL 785:74
P. is…more precious than…land — SADAT 708:92
p. is of the nature — SHAK 743:61
P. is poor reading — HARDY 382:74
P. its ten thousands — PORT 663:14
p. makes plenty — ANON 19:95
p. nor beauty — LAWR 494:4
p. of each country — JOHN 438:57
P. of God, which passeth — BIBLE 123:60
P. of God, which passeth — BOOK 141:10
p. of mind — SMITH 797:37
P. on earth and mercy mild — BEEC 69:60
P. on earth and mercy mild — WESL 900:10
p.…on the tested foundations — WILS 916:15
P., p.; when there is no p. — BIBLE 105:71
P., the human dress — BLAKE 134:31
p. there's nothing — SHAK 746:42
P. to corrupt no less — MILT 585:33
p. to hers is small — CRIP 244:49
p. to him that is far off — BIBLE 104:59

p. to Ireland — ARNO 33:50
p. to the cottages — CHAM 204:68
p. to thy soul — SCOTT 725:57
p. to you which were afar off — BIBLE 122:42
p. which the world cannot give — BOOK 140:76
P. without honour — CECIL 202:26
piping time of p. — SHAK 731:2
Policemen…keepers of the p. — MAMET 543:23
poor, who will not fast in p. — CRAB 242:92
power, p. and healing — MATT 561:71
Pray for the p. of Jerusalem — BIBLE 98:89
Prince of P. — BIBLE 102:17
probabilities of p. or war — PALM 636:26
programme of the world's p. — WILS 916:17
promised…either p. or happiness — LEBON 498:4
publisheth p. — BIBLE 104:47
re-establish p. and civil order — ELIZ 310:57
rest in obscurity and p.! — EMMET 313:59
Rest in soft p. — JONS 449:42
send p. on earth — BIBLE 111:29
shall the Great P. be established — DEKA 259:45
should kneel for p. — SHAK 732:47
soft phrase of p. — SHAK 759:59
Stalin…lover of p. — NEHRU 610:29
take chances for p. — DULL 293:90
there abides a p. of thine — ARNO 31:2
they are in p. — BIBLE 107:31
they love p. and quiet — TOLK 862:1
thing fall down in p. — MAYB 562:94
though not its p. — GRAV 367:66
though sorrowing, yet in p. — MILT 585:29
thousand years of p. — TENN 844:61
time of p. — BIBLE 100:70
Universal p. is declared — ELIOT 303:96
universal p. lie — TENN 841:94
War is p. — ORWE 629:99
war is preferable to a shameful p. — TACI 835:73
war yield to p. — CICE 218:26
We came in p. — ANON 23:10
weeds of p.…triumphs — MILT 576:10
we prepare…for p. — PEAR 645:98
What hast thou to do with p.? — BIBLE 92:33
When there was p. — AUDEN 40:95
whisper 'P.' — GROM 374:21
wilderness and they call it p. — TACI 835:69
workshop for world p. — HARR 384:4
peaceful free nations are p. nations — BUSH 176:18
friendship is never p. — SEVI 728:9
On every p. home — KIPL 474:75
p. revolution impossible — KENN 462:19
What…made her p. — YEATS 933:40
peace-keepers no better p.-k. — PALM 635:20
peacemaker 'if' is the only p. — SHAK 751:92
peacemakers Blessed are the p. — BIBLE 109:83
peacetime p. environment — TRUM 868:39
where they're living it's p. — KRAM 480:5
peach better than an insipid p. — HUNT 423:31
dare to eat a p.? — ELIOT 304:25
nectarine, and curious p. — MARV 556:74
peacock bluejay in p. feathers — LAFO 485:9
droops the milk-white p. — TENN 842:14
Eyed like a p. — KEATS 458:20
pride of the p. — BLAKE 134:44
peacocks p. and lilies — RUSK 703:4
p. strutting by — KIPL 474:72
peak 17,000-foot p. — BENU 78:85
upon a p. in Darien — KEATS 456:77
peaks great p. we had forgotten — LLOY 513:99
Sundered by p. — TU 869:56
peal widest p. for years — HODG 405:46
peals p. of laughter…round thee — POPE 661:34
peanut P. butter has survived — KEIL 460:70
peanuts more salted p. consumed — SPIL 810:21
pea-pod povere peple tho p.-p. — LANG 489:97
pear know the taste of a p. — MAO 547:5
p. on top of two toothpicks — ACHE 2:28
pearl crown enchased with p. — MARL 551:74
find a diamond or a p. — VAN 877:30
gates of p. and topaz — LAUR 492:70
great ouches, heaps of p. — SHAK 731:8
ocean for orient p. — MARL 552:94
ocean for orient p. — MARL 552:98
p. in every cowslip's ear — SHAK 737:92
profited from its p. — THUR 859:36
tears to p. he turned — MARL 553:15
threw a p. away — SHAK 761:19
pearls Give p. away — HOUS 414:46

p. by the seashore — MORE 597:68
Scatter thy p. — BLAKE 133:23
search for p. — DRYD 289:51
seeking goodly p. — BIBLE 112:53
shot to death, with p.? — WEBS 895:15
Pearse P. summoned Cuchulain — YEATS 934:64
pear-tree glassy p.-t. — HOPK 412:87
peas eat my p. with honey — NASH 609:9
Here are sweet p. — KEATS 457:79
peasant p. and a philosopher — JOHN 443:82
thankful I am a p. — FRAN 335:22
peasantry bold p. — GOLD 361:52
p. its pack animal — TROT 867:17
peasants changed from p. — WAUGH 892:38
p. in El Salvador — OROU 627:22
p. now Resign their pipes — CRAB 242:86
p. should be killed — LUTH 523:96
peason beans and p. put within — ANON 19:80
pebble P. or a prettier shell — NEWT 612:74
p. Ruttled in dry ground — JEFF 436:11
Pebworth Piping P. — ANON 23:72
pecker p. in my pocket — JOHN 440:85
Peckham classes within classes in P. — SPARK 806:19
peculiar Funny p., or funny ha-ha? — HAY 386:54
p. people — BIBLE 125:24
pecuniam p. infinitam — CICE 218:23
pecuniary immense p. Mangle — DICK 271:20
pedagogic for p. and other purposes — GALB 343:99
pedal large gas p. — MURR 605:9
pedant fertile p. — WALP 887:21
like the p. in Hierocles — JOHN 443:79
poetry a p.'s game — BUNT 166:62
pedantic too p. for a gentleman — CONG 231:19
pedants P. may cry out loud — GONZ 363:96
pederast [Music] a p. might hum — PROU 671:85
pedestalled p. in triumph? — BROW 162:85
pedigree P. of Honey — DICK 273:75
religious ties…social p. — WOLFE 920:96
pedigrees p. of nations — JOHN 442:2
pedlar looked like a p. — MOORE 594:18
pee P., po, belly, bum, drawers — FLAN 326:24
peel p. me a grape — WEST 901:31
peep p. and botanize — WORD 924:81
p. through their eyes — SHAK 739:35
treason can but p. — SHAK 754:21
peeping p. Tom of the sciences — BISH 131:82
peepshow ticket for the p. — MACN 538:2
peer English p. of the right sort — WODE 918:50
Lycidas…not left his p. — MILT 578:45
Peerless P. — ROCH 691:65
peerage were I to be offered a p. — CHAN 205:7
You should study the P. — WILDE 909:30
peers flattery of one's p. — LODGE 515:27
House of p. — GILB 354:14
judged by our p. — BALZ 57:9
Of Satan and his p. — MILT 581:17
p., and they are hereditary — LLOY 513:6
peevish something p. that way — SHAK 743:69
temper…has become licentiously p. — DISR 276:65
Virginity is p., proud, idle — SHAK 761:24
peeweets the p. crying — STEV 823:36
peg Hang your idea on a p. — BRIS 153:44
Pegasus thought it P. — KEATS 457:84
peignoir Complacencies of the p. — STEV 819:17
Pele I was not the White P. — BEST 82:72
pellet p. with the poison — PANA 636:27
pelt wear my p. tanned — MIDD 569:42
pelting p. of this pitiless storm — SHAK 763:78
pen altar, sword and p. — WORD 925:11
Before my p. has gleaned — KEATS 457:93
Biting my truant p. — SIDN 790:8
could use the sword and p. — LAND 488:84
Devise wit, write p. — SHAK 733:75
drop of ink in my p. — WALP 887:24
far less brilliant p. than mine — BEER 69:70
garden with your p. — CAMP 186:58
hung up my p. — SIMON 792:40
needle and the p. — LEWIS 507:81
Never durst poet touch a p. — SHAK 734:85
p. but also with a blue pencil — LUCAS 522:78
p. has been in their hands — AUST 44:97
p. is mightier than the sword — BULW 166:58
p. is worse than the sword — BURT 174:72
p. refusing to draw anything — BRON 155:84
poet's p. all scorn — BRAD 149:80
poet's p. Turns them to shapes — SHAK 738:13
prevents his holding a p. — DICK 267:5

p. came to theirs — HODG 405:46
p. can be poor — OCON 622:28
p. can claim America — ROLL 695:33
p. change and forget — HELL 392:77
p. contend for their liberty — HALI 378:89
p. could be down-to-earth — SHUL 790:93
p. could neither see — JOHN 441:4
p. do actually desire it — MILL 570:71
P. do not change — VIAN 880:75
P. don't choose their careers — DOSP 282:4
p. don't go to the theater — JOUR 451:74
P. don't…like…beautiful — DEBU 258:5
P. don't resent having nothing — COMP 229:69
p.…don't trust their reactions — COLE 225:76
P. do what you pay — WALD 885:87
P. find ideas a bore — POUND 665:54
p. free from routine — LINK 511:55
p. getting into a state — GALS 344:24
p. have spoken — FITT 324:81
p. I hate — HART 384:11
P. in nutrition — DAVIS 255:51
p. in portraits are thinking — LIVE 512:78
P. in Power — PATC 642:50
p. in the back streets of Derby — CHRI 214:28
p. in the world are fools — WILD 911:85
P. in this country — RICH 686:65
p. know what the land knows — SAND 713:7
p. listen to you — SNOW 802:42
P. live within winter — MUNRO 603:89
p. look at the sea — FROST 339:2
p. love junk food — GASS 346:60
p. may be made to follow — CONF 230:87
p. may complain — WEBER 894:70
P. must learn to hate — MAND 544:49
P.…must not be bartered — WILS 917:18
P. must not do things for fun — HERB 397:82
P. mutht be amuthed — DICK 270:7
p. never give up their liberties — BURKE 168:27
p. not spoken about — GEE 348:92
p. of all sorts — APOL 27:18
p. of a strange speech — BIBLE 105:85
p. of Crete — SAKI 710:39
p. of his pasture — BOOK 143:64
p. of South Africa — SMUTS 802:31
P. of the same trade — SMITH 798:44
P. of the world, unite — MAO 548:14
p. of this country — PEEL 646:9
p. of whom we know nothing — CHAM 204:61
p. on their way towards God — WINT 917:33
p. on whom nothing is lost! — JAMES 433:43
p. ought to be free — MACA 525:43
P. out of work — EVANS 316:20
p. overlaid with taxes — BACON 49:33
p. say the president — MARC 549:32
p. seem to be divided — DOST 282:6
p.'s flag is deepest red — CONN 232:55
p. should mate for life — ALLEN 12:55
p. sinned against — COMP 230:76
p. sliding with their skates — PEPYS 647:34
P. sometimes divide others — SPEN 807:64
p. starved for self-definition — BURNS 169:59
p. struggled on for years — WHAR 901:52
p. supplied with electric light — MCLU 536:60
p.'s voice is odd — POPE 661:53
p.'s wery scarce — DICK 265:62
p.'s wrongs his own — DRYD 290:90
p. taut for war — THOM 854:25
p. that do err in their heart — BIBLE 97:58
p. that on earth — KETHE 465:75
p. that walked in darkness — BIBLE 102:16
p. that want to try a new experience — SHAW 780:52
p. to complexify them — MOYN 601:42
p. trying to convince themselves — SNYD 803:52
p. until they set the basket — NASH 609:8
p. want a sense of purpose — MACM 537:82
P. want economy — IACO 427:28
p. were a kind of solution — CAVA 201:15
p. were so horrible — AMIS 14:90
p. which ceases to care — ELIOT 307:84
P. who are always praising — SMITH 800:98
p. who are late — LUCAS 521:72
p. who are moral or immoral — CHUR 215:54
p. who are paid to have attitudes — HEMI 393:94
p. who are too busy — WAUGH 892:47
p. who belong somewhere else — STEIN 815:17
p. who called the Milky Way — MARTI 555:44
p. who can copulate — MACD 529:40

p. who can't get along — GRAY 368:89
p. who dare not assert — MUMF 603:78
p. who do not hear the sound — MAIL 539:39
p. who have been persecuted — KISS 475:2
p. who have flabby hands — GILB 355:21
p. who have no love — SHAW 777:58
p. who have read — HAYA 386:55
p. who have the courage — MUSS 605:18
p. who hire them — NEW 611:50
p. who hunt — SHAW 781:77
P. who leave their own time — MASE 559:84
p. who live outside — SABA 707:82
p. whom a fair face — MAIL 540:66
P. who never get carried away — FORB 329:95
p. who never trouble — STARK 813:75
P. who obtain power — VIDAL 881:94
p. who shoot grouse — EDIN 300:11
p. who want to do nothing — DODD 278:5
p. who wave at trains — MCGO 532:85
p. who were not as obsessed — LESS 505:39
p. who will run the future — JONES 448:93
p. will always be kind — SASS 716:64
P. will do anything — PERCY 648:50
p. will live on — SAND 713:2
p. will more readily swallow lies — GELL 348:99
P. wish to be settled — EMER 312:17
p. without business — DEFOE 258:22
P. without history — ELIOT 309:50
P. would rather sleep — ALBEE 10:95
p. you have seen — MURR 605:11
P. you know — LARK 491:41
persuade…half the p. — GAIT 343:88
photographing p. — EISE 302:65
platypus and p. — THUR 860:52
please all of the p. — CONN 234:92
pleasure of pleasing inferior p. — CLOU 223:29
poetry ignores most p. — MITC 588:86
poor little street-bred p. — KIPL 471:99
Poor p. staying — PEPYS 647:46
power over p. — SOLZ 803:62
Power to the p. — ANON 23:8
prayers of liberty-loving p. — EISE 302:49
Pray, good p., be civil — GWYN 375:51
present at gatherings of p. — SNOW 802:37
problems of three little p. — EPST 314:79
proud conceited ignorant p. — ANON 20:22
p.…shows that I communicate — ROTH 700:34
punching p. in the head — LEON 503:7
Quiet p. avoid the question — DICK 268:26
raising up a p. of customers — SMITH 798:50
really nice English p. — SHAW 781:74
rebellious p. — REED 682:88
religion of these p. — MONT 591:63
representatives of the p. — WHIT 902:67
resented by thousands more p. — ROCK 692:73
Respected p. are only rascals — STEN 816:53
sacrifice other p. without blushing — SHAW 779:26
self-help created among working p. — SMIL 797:34
shame more p. don't switch — PIRS 652:27
showing other p. where to dig — LEAV 498:3
slam at the p. — FITZ 325:12
smiles of the p. — MARC 549:35
snake about to devour p. — NIXON 617:41
society in which what p. fulfil — MAJOR 541:70
so long as the right p. get shot — EAST 298:69
so many p. — GALS 344:25
so many p. showed up — GOLD 362:91
some p. a bit behind — VARE 877:35
Some p. find oil — GETTY 351:50
Some p. read too much — MENC 565:74
Some p. swim lakes — WEBB 893:64
Some p. think football — SHAN 776:28
Soviet p. — GORB 363:2
speak as the common p. — ASCH 35:79
stiffnecked p. — BIBLE 89:27
struggle of the African p. — MAND 544:46
submitted…to the whole p. — STEAD 813:84
suicide kills two p. — MILL 572:4
Superior p. never make — MOORE 595:31
supported by…the British p. — LAW 493:84
Take most p. — SALI 711:58
tell p. what they do not want — ORWE 629:71
tells other p. what to do — BARA 59:44
TELL THE P.! — CHRI 214:30
The p. are the masters — BLAIR 132:5
The p. die so — PEPYS 647:42
The p. muddied — SHAK 754:20

These p. are good — VAZD 878:53
These p.…do not read books — WORD 928:48
things p. had once held against her — SCHL 718:14
thy p. shall be my p. — BIBLE 90:79
till p. behave themselves — KING 469:56
time changes p. — PROU 671:87
too many of the p. — THUR 859:33
trivial p. should muse and thunder — LAWR 495:28
two p. miserable instead of four — BUTL 177:67
two sorts of p. — SHAW 779:36
two types of p. — PASC 641:33
unconditional confidence of his p. — WEI 896:23
united p. — PARK 638:83
very ancient p. — TOLK 862:1
Very Decent to P. — ROTH 699:15
very few p. come this way — LEAR 498:90
views of the p. — GALL 344:20
voice of the p. — ALCU 10:8
voice of the p. — BACON 47:66
voice of the p. — PITT 652:39
voices of young p. — SMITH 799:78
Waldo is one of those p. — SAKI 710:46
way p. look and laugh — WOOLF 922:28
We are a religious p. — DOUG 284:33
we are the p. — WRIG 930:84
What kind of p. — CHUR 217:83
what other p. wear — WILDE 909:49
what p. have got against — HOPE 411:75
what p. say of us — SMITH 799:74
what the p. think it so — BURKE 168:21
When p. are too comfortable — RICH 686:68
When p. do not respect us — TWAIN 872:24
when you bore p. — KISS 475:99
wherever I find your p. — JOAN 438:52
whether just p.…are happier — PLATO 655:94
whole world is bereft of p. — LAMA 485:22
willing to see p. sacrificed — MILL 573:57
will of the p. — PARE 636:36
Win Friends and Influence P. — CARN 193:50
without other p. hearing — WILDE 908:5
Women…are invisible p. — FRIE 337:82
Words can keep p. apart — MARC 549:30
world empty of p. — LAWR 494:95
world is full of middle-class p. — SHAR 776:46
you too are p. — SAND 713:5
peopled earth p. as ever by the inept — REPP 683:12
p. half the world — SEEL 726:72
peoples meeting place of the p. — BARN 60:61
new-caught, sullen p. — KIPL 472:25
other p.' Kings — GARC 345:42
peace among our p. — KIPL 472:13
silent sullen p. — KIPL 472:26
We the P. — UNIT 873:64
pepper a little P. or Salt — SWIFT 832:94
cucumber…dressed with p. — JOHN 444:3
pepper-pot p.-p. breast of thrush? — FRAME 333:79
Pequod P. packing off to hell — LOWE 520:43
perceive nature of reason to p. things — SPIN 810:27
p. their foul disfigurement — MILT 577:26
perceived being is to be p. — BERK 79:5
percent Six p. unemployment — PASS 641:40
perception doors of p. — BLAKE 134:45
dullest p. always — THOR 858:98
intensity of p. — WILL 914:58
Japanese…destitute of p. — BIRD 130:62
mechanism of p. — SNYD 803:51
outside a central p. — DELI 261:97
p. that something ought to be done — WELLS 898:92
reeducation of p. — DEWEY 264:44
some particular p. or other — HUME 422:5
perceptions but those p. — HUME 422:3
perch p., and not their terror — SHAK 758:18
percussion Like a P. Instrument — BUKO 165:51
Percy not yet of P.'s mind — SHAK 741:12
perdition ante-chamber of p. — SHAW 781:77
P. catch my soul — SHAK 760:83
P. catch my soul — SHER 788:66
Science…is the soul's p. — RABE 676:62
son of p. — BIBLE 118:15
To bottomless p. — MILT 580:95
perestroika Russian word 'p.' — GORB 363:1
perfect be thou p. — BIBLE 87:76
Be ye therefore p. — BIBLE 109:95
Can a man be p. — FORS 332:57
constant, he were p.! — SHAK 729:41
end of a p. day — BOND 139:52
formal poetry p. only in form — SAND 713:15

God…had created a p. world SHAR 776:43
grow more p. when emancipated WOLL 921:13
gunshot is the p. way KENN 463:44
Heaven is being p. BACH 46:26
If thou wilt be p. BIBLE 113:73
most p. expression of scorn SHAW 781:80
most p. of Swiss clockmakers STRA 826:91
no knowledge comes to be p. DONNE 281:93
None of us are p. WILDE 909:44
no one is p. MAIN 541:69
Nothing is more p. VIAN 880:78
not in my p. mind SHAK 764:98
One p. limousine PARK 637:57
p. as much as we can SPIN 811:34
p. condition of slavery ASTE 36:24
p. in a short time BIBLE 107:33
p. republics are a p. nonsense FOWL 332:65
P. the cup as planned BROW 162:71
p. use of an imperfect medium WILDE 908:2
strength is made p. in weakness BIBLE 122:34
them whose heart is p. BIBLE 92:43
thought p. by every body AUST 43:80
three inches long, p. HUGH 419:41
union is p. DICK 273:82
We're not all p. PIZZ 653:56
when that which is p. is come BIBLE 121:9
would be the p. friend SMITH 799:80
perfectability no faith in human p. POE 656:21
perfection achieved p. HUGH 418:14
achieved some sort of p. HOYLE 417:4
Almighty unto p.? BIBLE 93:57
a placid p. unattainable STRA 826:80
confess p. so could err SHAK 759:60
Dead p., no more TENN 845:78
dreams of p. FAUL 319:71
friend who loved p. SMITH 799:80
got to be p. for me MELBA 563:17
make defect p. SHAK 765:25
man a little pope of p. LAWR 494:97
Nestles the seed p. WHIT 906:51
p. does not recognize humanity WOOD 921:19
p. in a new kind of art RUNGE 702:75
P. irritates AUCH 39:72
P., of a kind AUDEN 40:97
p. of behaviour CHRI 215:37
p. of character AURE 42:55
p. of the human race INGE 429:55
Pictures of p. AUST 43:90
pursuit of p. ARNO 33:54
Right p. SHAK 772:26
seek a triple p. HOOK 410:55
since p. is love NIEB 614:98
Thinking is the great enemy of p. CONR 235:18
through Art…realise our p. WILDE 908:94
What's come to p. perishes BROW 162:65
perfidious P. wretch! TREI 865:55
perfidy petty p. BYRON 180:36
performance any p. is discussable BURKE 169:57
been all words, And no p. MASS 559:44
brilliance in the p. HEMI 394:5
Britain's comparative p. MISH 587:79
coming late to a p. ZOLO 937:5
full of promise, but of no p. DICK 268:35
instant of their p. GRAY 368:91
jazz p. centers LIEB 509:27
literary p. WHIT 906:55
many years outlive p.? SHAK 743:51
music…greater than its p. PREV 667:9
p. of the American economy STEIN 815:30
p. of the life of man MUIR 602:60
p. of the task itself SHIP 789:76
resulting p. GALB 343:96
so poor a record of p. FRIE 337:65
the p. everything HUNT 423:31
performances intellectual p. YOUR 935:81
poor p. of others RYLE 707:80
performed be p. with tact JOHN 441:3
perfume all p. yes JOYCE 452:96
p. is itself a wind WILL 914:57
p. of a thousand roses BERN 81:44
wear coffee as a p. VAN 877:27
perfumes p.…are chafed WEBS 894:75
p. is there more delight SHAK 773:51
Pergo P. Park knew me LEVE 506:58
peril at his p. further go HERB 397:90
At the p. of its soul SCOTT 722:74
perilous no position more p. TROL 867:95

perils feeling that lures us on…to p. CONR 234:6
p. and dangers of this night BOOK 140:77
p. do environ BUTL 177:47
smile at p. past! SCOTT 723:12
sordid p. of actual existence WILDE 908:94
through the p. of winter TROL 866:76
period during this p. THUR 859:38
from an early p. MACA 526:76
lived in any other p. HAZL 388:84
p. in one's life LARW 491:55
p. in question MYRD 605:26
p. not to be judged LEVI 506:61
p. of cheating BIER 129:38
p., once past RUNGE 702:74
persist for a long p. RUSS 705:53
repeat in one p. RENO 683:9
periodical governs the p. press TROL 866:73
periods Art of all p. RUNGE 702:74
really had two p. NABO 606:28
periphery you most inimitable p. OCON 621:21
periphrastic p. study ELIOT 308:15
perish All things p. KEMP 461:88
hero p., or a sparrow fall POPE 660:9
If I had to p. twice FROST 338:97
if I p., I p. BIBLE 93:46
p. in the very instant GRAY 368:91
shall p. unconsoled LANG 488:90
those that offer resistance p. SOPH 804:85
perishing p. never entered my head DOUG 283:15
periwigs fashion…as to p. PEPYS 647:43
perjuries Jupiter…laughs at lovers' p. OVID 631:40
perjury lovers' p. DRYD 292:56
permanent cheerfulness fixed and p. ADDI 6:20
less p. than thought BUNT 166:59
P. crisis justifies p. control HUXL 425:97
p., like the things JOHN 442:39
The word p. FRAME 333:82
very small extent p. NIET 616:28
pernicious most p. race SWIFT 831:79
Perón see Eva P. as either MADO 539:23
perpendicular p. expression SHAW 781:92
perpetual light…seemed p. SPEN 807:59
no p. enemies PALM 636:22
p. holiday is a good…definition SHAW 780:70
p. hunger to be beautiful RHYS 684:24
steady and p. serenity ADDI 6:20
'Tis with us p. night JONS 449:21
perpetuate helps to p. it KING 468:30
p. an error for ever SCHO 719:32
perpetuated So they are p. GALB 343:93
perpetuating contrivance for p. SHAW 778:96
perplex wildness to p. the scene POPE 659:95
perplexed p., but not in despair BIBLE 122:24
perplexities obvious p. ARIS 29:49
perplexity listlessness from vain p. WORD 925:99
perquisites scorn of irregular p. WAUGH 891:14
persecute Why p. we him BIBLE 93:65
persecuted because he is p. GOULD 365:23
born…of the p. WRIG 930:83
p. for righteousness' sake BIBLE 109:83
persecution P. is a bad…way to plant religion BROW 158:71
P. is not an original feature PAINE 634:94
p. of the transvestite WHITE 902:70
P. produced its natural effect MACA 526:74
some degree of p. SWIFT 832:13
persecutions greatest of all p. PASC 641:36
perseverance by the name of p. STER 817:72
P., dear my lord SHAK 757:6
Persian p. pussy from over the sea MARQ 554:27
Persians Truth-loving P. GRAV 367:71
Persil Mum, the P.-user BETJ 84:4
persist p. in its own being SPIN 810:28
person advantage to take of a p. MANS 547:94
aggravates an earnest p. MELV 564:45
altered her p. SWIFT 830:57
Ancient P., for whom I ROCH 692:71
another p. in America NORTH 618:70
being in love with a p. LESS 505:43
but as a p. GRASS 367:59
can a p. see rightly SAINT 709:17
classify a p. SZASZ 834:63
demagogue is a p. MARQ 554:37
dullest p. in the world BENS 77:62
explain it to the average p. FEYN 322:26
For her own p. SHAK 764:23
his breath and p. WALL 886:4

household features her p. PRIOR 669:34
judged as done against our p. HENR 395:46
last p. to say anything SAKI 710:48
lifetime of one p. HORN 414:36
most pleasing p. in all the world LABR 483:58
My idea of an agreeable p. DISR 277:77
never met a steadily logical p. GELL 348:97
no more a p. AUDEN 40:99
no p. can be a poet MACA 525:41
no sane p. would do SHAW 780:42
not a political p. HELL 392:75
not at all the sort of p. CARL 191:69
not a well-rounded p. BELL 73:77
old p. of Ware LEAR 498:93
one p. were of the contrary opinion MILL 570:65
only in memory…same p. DIDE 274:35
only thing…is an uninterested p. CHES 211:49
p. bearing his share of the labours MILL 570:64
p. born who is so unlucky MARQ 554:31
p. can be fully involved MANN 546:73
p. can be truly affectionate PREV 668:11
p. cannot choose his father FRIS 338:79
p. concerns himself with life MANN 545:68
p. freed from his religion SAINT 709:21
P. from Porlock SMITH 800:2
p. seldom falls sick EMER 313:40
p. should be mourned MONT 593:90
p. to worship God ROOS 696:50
p. up early…is a Christian LAW 493:85
p. we were yesterday UPDI 875:94
p. who expects nothing from society SAND 712:85
p. who has used his emotions SAND 712:84
p. who is capable of choosing STEIN 815:28
p. who is not RUSK 703:8
p. who knows 'how' RAVI 679:38
p. who likes sports MENC 566:82
p. who lives for today BELL 72:40
p. who reads or thinks YOUR 935:80
poet is a p. FROST 339:3
politician is a p. LLOY 514:9
species of p. WAUGH 892:21
the only p. I know MONR 591:60
three great events for a p. LABR 483:72
Time, the world and the p. CIXO 219:35
umblest p. going DICK 269:68
unhappy p. seeks out another MARG 549:41
unmusical p. HENZE 396:56
when you live with a p. FORD 329:1
wish to absorb this p. MAMET 543:26
worse than killing a p. LAUR 492:71
wretched p.'s feelings MARI 550:63
personal ourselves and least p. MANS 547:89
p. and national morality SHAW 777:47
p. aspect of a thing RICH 686:64
P. relations are the important thing FORS 331:35
transcend the painfully p. SART 715:42
Vengeance is a p. reaction RENO 683:2
personalities all great events and p. MARX 558:7
original displaced p. MANK 545:62
People who disintegrate as p. AUST 44:99
p. and cultural traditions WATS 890:97
trivial p. decomposing WOOLF 922:36
personality discontinuity within his p. ROTH 699:14
had a lousy p. SALI 711:55
no more p. than a paper cup CHAN 205:85
P. is an unbroken series FITZ 325:92
P. Tithe: A price paid COUP 239:1
Poetry…an escape from p. ELIOT 305:46
persons civilized p. are willing DU 293:75
congratulation that p. MILL 570:59
divers paces with divers p. SHAK 750:63
God is no respecter of p. BIBLE 119:41
great p.…borrow BACON 48:3
interested in things, not in p. CURIE 249:36
neither p. nor property will be safe DOUG 284:37
Ordinary p. do not perceive PASC 641:26
P.…entering into relation BUBER 164:22
p. of small means ELIOT 303:72
p. using parties as tools DISR 277:82
p. who are accused DENM 262:98
p. who are considered…its members BENT 77:64
p. who fenced in…land ROUS 700:48
p. whom you cannot care for TROL 867:97
resentment towards p. NEWM 612:65
some have done in their p. BROW 159:88
which private p. ROUS 701:48
perspective everything in p. CEZA 203:51

light, shade and p.	CONS 235:27	
lovely thing this p.	UCCE 873:61	
P. is the bridle	LEON 504:17	
p. of a subway tunnel	TOOLE 863:12	
reality seen from the p. of reason	PAGE 633:79	
scenic p. suits it	HUGO 420:64	
Writing has laws of p.	CAPO 189:27	

perspiration Genius is…p. EDIS 300:13
  p. was but ichor BYRON 183:5
persuade p. gently, not by force PASC 641:27
  p.…half the people GAIT 343:88
  trying to p. you PLATO 654:78
persuaded p. that God hath shut RALE 677:2
persuaders hidden p. into the code KOES 477:31
  the hidden p. PACK 633:71
persuading By p. others JUNI 453:10
persuasion lexicon of…p. SAFI 708:96
  not faith but p. BROW 158:63
  P. is the resource of the feeble GIBB 352:58
persuasiveness personal p. QUIL 674:45
Peru Silver out of the Earth in P. PETTY 649:84
peruked p. sea whose swell SITW 793:59
perverse frown and be p. SHAK 736:50
  multitude of p. inclinations SHAR 776:41
  widows…the most p. creatures ADDI 6:19
perversion last great p. FOWL 332:65
  melancholy sexual p. HUXL 424:58
  War…the universal p. RAE 677:90
perversity P. is the muse SONT 804:71
  p. of the human mind TROL 867:92
  Sexual P. in Chicago MAMET 543:20
perverted I'm exhausted…or p. PUIG 672:1
pessimism P.…as agreeable BENN 76:49
pessimist p. before 48 TWAIN 872:35
  p. fears this is true CABE 183:18
  p. sees only the red SCHW 721:71
  what a p. is? SHAW 777:50
pessimistic optimistic or p. UNAM 873:64
  'p.' about broadcasting WELLS 898:91
pesticide laugh is the best p. NABO 606:45
pestilence noisome p. BIBLE 96:53
  purged the air of p. SHAK 755:47
  sooner caught than the p. SHAK 744:85
  who desires…breeds p. BLAKE 134:40
  winter, plague and p. NASHE 609:17
pestilences famines, and p. BIBLE 113:85
pests Rumour is of all p. the swiftest VIRG 882:22
petal dropping a rose p. MARQ 554:33
  sleeps the crimson p. TENN 842:14
petals Buddha…in the p. of a flower PIRS 652:25
  P. on a wet, black bough POUND 664:28
  pursed Its p. up BROW 160:23
  softer falls Than p. TENN 839:54
Peter other disciple did outrun P. BIBLE 118:22
  P., and upon this rock BIBLE 112:62
  P. chose from man to hide CRAB 242:99
  P. like a piper's tune FARJ 318:48
  P. remembered the word of the Lord BIBLE 116:62
  P. said unto him BIBLE 114:97
  P.'s drift SHEL 784:52
  Saint P.…pattered with his keys BYRON 183:5
  Where P. is…is the Church AMBR 13:75
  wholly in P. Pan ever since TYNAN 872:46
Peterkin Quoth little P. SOUT 805:1
petition circulating a p. STEG 814:7
petitioners save me…from my p. DRYD 290:96
Petrarch I do not…copy P. ARET 29:42
petrifactions p. of a plodding brain BYRON 179:99
petrol matches on a p. dump HARL 383:83
petticoat P. said to the Chemise PARK 637:41
  turned out of the realm in my p. ELIZ 309:56
petticoats perpendicular in p.! OCON 621:21
  red-flannel p. THOM 853:2
pettiness p. of those who should carry them BREC 151:13
  p. ruins the greatest loves ANOU 26:93
  something to expiate; A p. LAWR 494:9
petulance p. is not sarcasm DISR 276:61
pewter No p. and no pub RANS 679:28
phagocytes stimulate the p. SHAW 780:48
phallic P. and ambrosial POUND 664:38
phantasma Like a p. SHAK 747:83
phantom hag obscene, and grisly p. BEAT 66:96
  p. beings loaded up with facts UNAM 873:67
  P. of delight WORD 927:35
phantoms p. an unprofitable strife SHEL 786:3
Pharaoh P. awoke BIBLE 88:98

P. rose up in the night BIBLE 88:17
Pharisee pluck the mask from…face of the P. BRON 155:82
Pharisees P. said, He casteth out BIBLE 111:22
  righteousness of the scribes and P. BIBLE 109:87
  the P.' hypocrisy PAST 641:41
  when he saw many of the P. BIBLE 108:76
  Woe unto you, scribes and P. BIBLE 113:84
phase p. in a continuing process ROBI 690:40
  p. of…life PEAR 645:97
phases Humanity does not pass through p. LEWIS 507:70
  p. in the development MARX 558:16
  p. of its development ERNST 315:89
Phelps P. calls Medlar Novelists MACD 530:47
phenomena economic p. FRIE 337:62
  very essence of p. PAST 642:44
phenomenon Crime…not a natural p. PACK 633:72
  describe the infant p. DICK 267:62
  describe the opposite p. BERG 79:92
  Felicitous p.! MOORE 595:37
  one actual p. THOR 857:85
  p. has been so compelling WHITE 902:72
  present or past p. PEAR 645:97
  recurring p. FALU 317:42
phial take the p. cleanly DOYLE 286:83
Philadelphia P.…like dull diamonds MAIL 540:55
philanthropy p. and symphony WHAR 901:48
Philip Let us march against P. OGIL 623:41
  Willie King made up like P. NICO 614:95
Philippi meet them at P. SHAK 748:17
Philistine apostle of the P. ARNO 33:42
  P. of genius in religion ARNO 34:65
  P. said unto David BIBLE 91:95
Philistines angelic revenges on the P. ARNO 33:50
  Barbarians, P., and Populace ARNO 33:53
  Eggheads are terrible P. NABO 606:44
  Let me die with the P. BIBLE 90:76
  P. be upon thee BIBLE 90:75
  P. took him, and put out his eyes BIBLE 90:75
Philistinism P.!…we have not ARNO 33:41
Phillipines In the P., there are COWA 239:14
Phillis P., why shou'd WALL 886:14
philosopher For every p. SPAR 806:34
  he was a p. CHAU 208:72
  man of science is a poor p. EINS 301:40
  mark of the p. SOCR 803:55
  No p. now looks WEBB 893:65
  nothing so absurd…said by some p. CICE 218:24
  Ovid, the soft p. of love DRYD 291:31
  peasant and a p. JOHN 443:82
  P.!—a fingering slave WORD 924:81
  p. and a common street porter SMITH 797:40
  p., and the poet LAWR 495:33
  p. should judge the masses CYRA 250:59
  p.'s treatment of a question WITT 918:45
  properly to be called a p. PIER 651:5
  prove the weeping p. SHAK 739:46
  saying of an ancient p. ADDI 6:16
  There was never yet p. SHAK 745:21
  You are a p., Dr Johnson EDWA 300:22
philosophers amused p. BERK 79:4
  economists and political p. KEYN 466:89
  God of Jacob, not of the p. PASC 641:39
  little statesmen and p. and divines EMER 312:8
  or p. can judge THOM 854:10
  p. have not maintained SWIFT 831:82
  p.…interpreted the world MARX 557:98
  P.…stand among us CARL 191:86
  p. to teach him CARL 192:92
  traditional disputes of p. AYER 44:8
  True p. are like elephants FONT 329:87
  Until p. rule as kings PLATO 655:98
philosophic p. diner-out BROW 162:78
  p. republic of Mr de Valera STEW 824:43
  the p. mind SMART 797:31
philosophical European p. WHIT 904:12
  mathematical or p. author WHIT 904:5
  one p. problem POPP 663:95
  one truly serious p. problem CAMUS 187:87
  p. problem has the form WITT 918:44
  p., the ideological ROTH 699:28
philosophies all p. shall fail CHES 212:75
  point their blind P. ROCH 691:53
philosophizing p. or aestheticizing CABR 183:19
philosophy aim in p. WITT 918:46
  angel…tell…his p. LICH 509:17

any p. in thee, shepherd? SHAK 749:56
characteristic of p. RUSS 705:41
compound of poetry and p. MACA 525:47
destroy more prejudices than p. DIDE 273:84
dreamt of in our p. SHAK 752:38
from plumbing to p. LAUG 492:66
Hang up p.! SHAK 736:66
Histories make…natural p., deep BACON 50:55
History is p. CARL 192:19
if p. could find it out SHAK 753:60
in knowing its limits that p. consists KANT 455:41
inside and strength were p. SIDN 791:17
interest of p. POPP 663:95
mere touch of cold p.? KEATS 458:25
moral p.…handmaid to religion BACON 46:50
new p. calls all in doubt DONNE 281:74
Nice p. FORD 330:14
not confounded p. PIRA 652:21
not faith, but mere P. BROW 158:76
Not p., after all BEER 70:86
p. has hitherto been NIET 615:18
P.…has no other origin SOCR 803:55
P., if it cannot RUSS 705:49
p. inclineth Man's mind BACON 48:95
P.! In whose light NERV 611:44
P. is a battle against the bewitchment WITT 918:43
p. is like the deciphering SCHO 719:30
p. is this tyrannical NIET 615:19
p. is to be studied RUSS 705:42
P.…kind of charcoal appetite CLEV 221:83
p. of the pig trough WEIG 896:24
p. puts out the fire VOLT 883:43
P.…route of many roads BIER 129:39
P.! the lumber of SWIFT 830:51
P. to him was…a maze SANT 714:21
P. was wrong RANS 679:26
p. which is so important JAMES 434:69
p. will be replaced by poetry ARNO 34:68
Plain women…to be faced with p. ELIOT 304:5
political power and p. PLATO 655:98
science…blind without p. AYER 45:31
spoil you through p. BIBLE 123:65
that's my p. WILD 910:79
Three-fourths of p. SNYD 803:52
true business of p. BACON 47:60
truth in p. DIDE 273:85
universe which p. contemplates RUSS 705:42
what is p.? SPAR 806:34
years of analytical p. HARDY 382:62
Phlebas Consider P. ELIOT 306:63
Phoebus golden P. never be beheld SHAK 766:63
  P. gins arise SHAK 773:61
phoenix Do not expect…p. hour DAY 257:85
  P. builds her spicy nest CAREW 190:61
  p. midst her fires BYRON 179:3
phone answer the p. THUR 859:27
  call him up on the p. SALI 710:52
  P. for the fish knives BETJ 84:5
  pick up their p. WHITE 903:80
  put the p. down thoughtfully SHAR 776:45
phonemes morphemes and p. THOM 855:33
phoney going to do something p. SALI 711:57
phonograph man is like a p. SHAW 780:57
  p.…is not of any commercial value EDIS 300:12
  vaccinated with a p. needle GOLD 362:75
phonographs p. of hades CRANE 243:25
phosphorescence rubbing p. MACD 530:54
photograph like flames around a p. HOLL 407:69
  p.…after I drowned ATWO 38:48
  p. and be photographed! RODC 693:87
  p. of the Pope ANON 25:55
  signed p. of the Kaiser WAUGH 892:27
  took the p. KARSH 455:52
photographer p. without a magazine PARK 639:87
photographing p. people EISE 302:65
photographs p., of the immortals CHUR 215:41
  p. taken of him at work RODC 693:87
  use p.…literally BACON 50:68
photography If p. is allowed BAUD 64:67
  P. is truth GODA 359:6
  P.…stops the flow of life BERG 79:98
  p. takes on an authority BAIL 52:99
  P. was conceived as a mirror STEI 814:9
phrase beauty…in one tiny p. FOWL 332:71
  empty p. SAND 712:89
  I find the p. in Shakespeare SCOTT 725:57
  that's an ill p. SHAK 752:44

from foggy mount and marshy p.   BYRON 179:6
gleamed Upon the glassy p.   WORD 924:86
great Gromboolian p.   LEAR 497:76
heavens above that p.   THOM 856:60
Jacks…more than usually p.   WILDE 909:33
language is p.   HARTE 384:16
loveliest village of the p.   GOLD 361:50
Manners…need of the p.   WAUGH 892:49
Most p. girls are virtuous   ANGE 17:36
nomads, on a p.   MCMU 537:89
no p. women on television   FORD 329:97
octavos fill a spacious p.   CRAB 242:83
p. blunt man   SHAK 748:13
p. facts   THOM 855:33
p. single vow   SHAK 761:33
P. women…faced with philosophy   ELIOT 304:5
pricking on the p.   SPEN 808:72
speak p. and to the purpose   SHAK 744:4
such a p. king   SHAK 746:67
waveless p. of Lombardy   SHEL 783:28
plainness perfect p. of speech   ARNO 33:36
Your p. and your shortness   SHAK 732:44
plains land of sweeping p.   MACK 533:15
the green p.   SHEL 783:39
plan any p. for stopping it   PERK 648:67
don't have a moral p.   CRON 246:78
execution of his p.   STEU 819:9
isn't a very good p.   THAT 850:27
new and original p.   GILB 354:12
not without a p.   POPE 660:6
p. of attack   SASS 716:63
p. that we arrive here   VAZD 878:53
postulate that there is no p.   MONOD 591:56
rogue is outlining a treacherous p.   FRAS 335:27
save it, save the p.   NIXON 617:46
planarian cross-eyed p.   THER 851:49
plane If that p. leaves the ground   EPST 314:80
inclined p. of little vessels   DICK 270:1
landing by p.   MACL 534:28
p. of the picture   PIERO 651:11
p. with the general   NATH 610:24
We travel by p.   CHEE 209:4
planes p. which advance   GOYA 365:30
vertical and horizontal p.   MALL 542:98
planet After one look at this p.   BURR 173:59
alien p. is Earth   BALL 57:99
As the p. globalizes   OGDEN 622:37
creepers on a commodious p.   SAND 713:5
disgrace to the p.   STONE 825:56
ecological balance of the p.   SONT 804:73
excursion to another p.   BIRD 130:60
Given the state of the p.   CAREY 190:64
her in her cooling p.   EMPS 314:62
lifetime on this p.   KENN 462:11
loyal to his club than to his p.   WHITE 903:76
men from the p. Earth   ANON 23:10
nobody on the p.   GILL 356:47
not born under a rhyming p.   SHAK 745:24
Out of the Silent P.   LEWIS 507:71
Pity the p.   LOWE 521:56
p. of Love is on high   TENN 845:89
p. swims into his ken   KEATS 456:77
points about this p.   MACA 525:34
pushed around by a p.   PEACE 645:91
wandering p.'s course   MARL 551:75
planetary obedience of p. influence   SHAK 762:57
planets inhabitants of different p.   DISR 276:53
mind can…people p.   BYRON 181:55
Shall such high p.   SIDN 790:5
stars and p. circled   DICK 268:51
use of the sun and the p.   LEAC 496:59
What other p. circle other suns   POPE 660:8
plank thick as a p.   DIANA 265:47
planks piled against slippery p.   ROET 694:2
planner p. made lots of them   HOYLE 417:4
planners acting like socialist p.   GLEI 359:2
planning all p. and decisions   LEWI 508:7
my idea of long-range p.   OGDEN 622:40
p. any mischief   JUVE 453:21
the more difficult p. becomes   HAYEK 387:59
plans all his p. collapse   JOSE 451:71
drew their p. against us   WELLS 898:73
felonious little p.   GILB 354:3
finest p. have always been spoiled   BREC 151:13
hurled Their hopeful p.   HOUS 416:72
no place for women's p.   AESC 8:61
p. for remedying…human estate   DEWEY 264:43

plant as much as a p. or a crystal   EMER 312:20
fame is no p.   MILT 578:50
grow up…as a tender p.   BIBLE 104:50
I'd have been a p. somewhere   TREV 865:61
p. must spring again   SHEL 786:13
p. where savages are   BACON 49:38
Sensitive P. in a garden grew   SHEL 785:84
those who p. cabbages   RABE 676:75
time to p.   BIBLE 100:70
plantations new p….the children   BACON 49:37
planted I have p.   BIBLE 121:93
p. and replanted   HAWT 386:38
p. on level ground   GOHE 360:27
plants best subjects…animals and p.   HEIN 391:53
love the p.   DOST 283:11
Minerals grow, p. grow   LINN 511:63
talk to the p.   CHAR 207:40
to collect p.   THES 851:51
plashes horse p. within it   YEATS 933:45
plaster Paris made of p.   HUGO 420:69
plastering beautied with p. art   SHAK 753:73
plastic constellation of p.   MAIL 540:55
pictorial or p. art   TZARA 873:59
p. surgeon…responsible   CUOMO 248:28
platan p. round   SPEN 808:73
plate fed from a mashed p.   SMITH 799:64
ice-cream while it's on your p.   WILD 910:79
p. of meat   MACB 527:81
silver p. on a coffin   CURR 249:42
plates p. and cups washed   WOOLF 923:49
platform On the p….policeman   STEW 824:43
platforms Party p. are contracts   TRUM 868:35
platinum bullets made of p.   BELL 72:48
platitude Applause…echo of a p.   BIER 128:16
longitude with no p.?   FRY 340:27
p. is simply a truth   BALD 54:43
stroke a p. until it purrs   MARQ 554:34
platitudes orchestration of p.   WILD 911:83
slaughter of a thousand p.   ORTE 627:28
Plato disputations of P.   HONO 409:32
lend an ear to P.   TENN 847:34
P. divined in theory   WHIT 904:13
P.…in the body of his work   SIDN 791:17
P. is dear to me   ARIS 29:61
P., thou reason'st well!   ADDI 7:38
recurring again to P.'s opinion   STER 818:88
series of footnotes to P.   WHIT 904:12
platypus poodle, the p. and people   THUR 860:52
play admiration of each other's p.   BARR 61:90
author of the p.   GILB 355:36
band begins to p.   KIPL 471:90
Better than a p.   CHAR 207:32
boys in their happy p.   SCHR 720:40
boys late at their p.!   ARNO 33:52
Close the p.   KAUF 456:61
done your work and may go p.   ASTL 37:28
do not p. things as they are   STEV 819:28
Everything that heard him p.   SHAK 775:13
for fair p.   ROOS 696:55
Forsake thy books, and mateless p.   BRON 155:91
good p. needs no epilogue   SHAK 751:94
holdeth children from p.   SIDN 791:20
Judge not the p.   QUAR 674:37
learn what not to p.   GILL 356:46
life? a p. of passion   RALE 677:1
loved your p.   ANON 24:41
made to p. therein   BIBLE 97:69
Marry, our p. is   SHAK 737:87
mend My wretched p.   MANN 546:79
most insipid, ridiculous p.   PEPYS 647:32
Mr Puff's p. within a p.   SHER 788:66
nothing to do with fair p.   ORWE 630:8
Not only will I not p.   GRANT 366:46
our p. is played out   THAC 849:94
perfectly dreadful p.   BANK 58:29
p. a creative mixture   SHUL 789:88
p. a thing quickly   MOZA 601:45
P. ball!   RICE 685:39
p., I remember, pleased not   SHAK 753:64
p. is a dynamic thing   TYNAN 872:45
p. is life   SHAW 779:37
P. it!   EPST 314:77
p. it over again and p.   LAMB 487:68
p. left a taste of…parsnip   WOOL 923:61
p. lousy   PARK 637:37
p.…never really takes on   HART 384:13
p.…some ten words long   SHAK 738:15

p.'s the thing   SHAK 753:72
p. that after you've been   KEIL 460:73
p. the fools with the time   SHAK 742:47
p. under bad conditions   KAUF 455:56
p. well and lose   FULL 342:71
p. with him at any game   SHAK 765:27
p. without a woman   KYD 482:50
rest of the p.   PASC 640:20
Shakespeare set his p. writing aside   CUOMO 248:30
spoils the p. much more   SUCK 828:10
The action of the p.   ONEI 625:87
The p. is over   AUGU 42:48
The p. was a great success   WILDE 909:20
thing I didn't like about…the p.   PARK 637:49
unless the p. is stopped   KEMB 461:83
usually the p. itself   TYNAN 872:44
What do you call the p.?   SHAK 754:94
what's the p.?   BOOTH 144:81
will not let my p. run   DENN 262:2
witty prologue to a very dull p.   CONG 231:4
woman's part in the p.   AUST 43:75
writing a good p. is difficult   PRIE 668:27
y is p.   EINS 301:43
youths at cricks did p.   JOSE 451:72
playboy expected me to be a p.   FLYNN 328:77
Inside this Hollywood p.   FLYNN 328:78
P. of the Western World   SYNGE 834:60
played easier to be p. on   SHAK 754:96
how you p. the game   RICE 685:37
My music…is merely badly p.   SCHO 719:26
p. an ancient ditty   KEATS 459:41
p. on a five inch course   JONES 447:85
p. the way I would   KAVA 456:66
p. with both hands   SATIE 717:81
player as he a P. were   SPEN 810:16
not monstrous that this p. here   SHAK 753:67
raped…nothing a p.   MCEN 531:65
say to the p.   WHIS 902:63
walking shadow, a poor p.   SHAK 769:42
whatever the other p. did   RAPO 679:30
wrapped in a p.'s hide   GREE 371:80
players don't drop p.   SHAN 776:29
entertainment the p. shall receive   SHAK 753:59
I and the rest of the p.   QUIN 675:49
little black book with two p. in   CHAR 207:46
men and women merely p.   SHAK 749:48
mouth it, as many of your p. do   SHAK 754:85
p. have often mentioned   JONS 450:55
p. not to be too good   NICH 613:88
P., Sir!   JOHN 444:11
p. think of a football   PELE 646:18
too cold for the p.   SMITH 800:90
Will you see the p.   SHAK 753:65
playfield p. of Satan   NABO 604:60
play-going p.-g. in any large city   TYNAN 872:44
playing ask me to stop p.   KING 468:25
staying married and p. snooker   REAR 681:70
playing-fields p.-f. of Eton   ORWE 628:61
play-poets Profession of P.-p.   PRYN 672:93
plays Absurdist p….in No Man's Land   ADAM 3:60
All p. are about decay   MAMET 544:33
cause of sin are p.   WHITE 904:4
don't want to see p. about rape   COOK 235:35
English p.   GOET 360:12
Leave writing p.   DRYD 289:50
old p….disgust this refined age   EVEL 316:22
p. are suited to incoherent argument   BENN 76:36
p. can define a moment   HYTN 427:27
The proof is in his p.   ONEI 625:98
tremendous stage on which it p.   RABI 676:79
women's parts in p.   CHAR 207:31
write p. in our heads   MAMET 544:21
plaything literature was the best p.   GARC 345:40
p. and their idol   SHEL 782:10
sensualists…want…a p.   WOLL 921:6
plaything-house little p.-h.   WALP 887:23
playthings choice of p.   KIPL 472:31
playwright some p. was forever   SALI 711:66
Plaza-Toro Duke of P.-T.!   GILB 355:32
plea beauty hold a p.   SHAK 772:25
issue of that darling P.   FLET 327:64
without one p.   ELLI 302:19
plead But when I p.   SPEN 809:97
so what I p. is just   HOPK 413:9
pleasant fallen unto me in p. places   BIBLE 94:91
How fair and how p.   BIBLE 102:5
how p., Lord, they be!   SCOT 725:63

p. sits above conscience — SHAK 762:46
p. to keep all the nationalities — TAAF 835:68
tyrants from p. — BURKE 169:37
Wisdom and p. dictate — NAPO 607:60
polished p. up the handle — GILB 353:94
p. with the tread of feet — DICK 267:25
soul...must be p. — DEFOE 258:11
polite English are p. by telling lies — BRAD 148:58
imbues his p. things — TWAIN 870:76
never mentions Hell to ears p. — POPE 659:96
not a p. employer — HOOV 411:63
The French are p. — TWAIN 870:76
What a p. game tennis is — BARR 61:90
politeness ceremonious p. — TWAIN 870:76
Punctuality is the p. — LOUI 518:98
politic they are p. — WEBS 894:76
'Twere p. to do the like — YEATS 933:41
political addiction of p. groups — GALB 343:91
a very p. old monk — MURD 604:97
binary p. arena — LEHM 501:69
Britain's New P. Order — MITC 588:89
circulates p. life — TOCQ 861:84
climbed my last p. mountain — WALL 886:7
confronting p. dragons — MAJOR 541:75
Divorce...has a great p. — MONT 593:98
foundations of p. liberty — WILS 916:15
frightened by 'p.' sermons — BARTH 62:7
goal that supplies the p. magic — SCHL 718:16
half your p. life — THAT 850:21
lucky...discovered a p. theory — CAST 199:79
making man a p. animal — ARIS 29:57
model our p. systems — HAMI 379:99
My p. opinions — TOLK 862:96
national consciousness is a p. fact — MACM 536:71
not a p. person — HELL 392:75
particular p. conditions — MARX 557:1
points clearly to a p. career — SHAW 780:44
P. action is of second rank — MANN 546:76
p. ammunition runs low — STEV 820:53
p. and educational status — SKEL 795:94
p. and practical difficulties — KEYN 466:88
p. and social conditions — MARS 554:39
p. and the other military — MCNA 565:71
p. animal can be defined — STEG 814:7
p. aspirant under democracy — MENC 565:64
p. cancer — ANON 25:49
p. consequences — MANS 547:99
p. danger — GLAD 358:89
P. democracy...in America — WHIT 906:50
P. economy thus does — MARX 557:96
P. economy traces — BAGE 51:92
P. genius — HEGEL 391:42
p. gentlemen drape over — HUXL 426:2
p. in this country — TROL 867:99
p. meetings...at a divine level — ACHE 2:22
p. noncommitment — VAN 876:22
p. ones are insoluble — HOME 409:11
p. or constitutional history — JAY 436:97
p. or religious faiths — PIRS 652:26
p. point of view — WHIT 902:68
p. power grows out of the barrel — MAO 548:7
p. question is...a painful sight — LODGE 515:29
p. struggle — HAIL 377:68
p. zombies — WILS 916:3
reclaim these things—poetry, rock'n'roll,
   p. activism — SMITH 800:89
single p. argument left — THAT 850:25
stuff of p. leadership — WILS 916:5
Tears...can never be p. — BELL 74:87
third-rate p. wheel-horse — MENC 566:86
We are not a p. party — MAND 544:47
politically rule industrially...rule p. — CONN 233:88
politician At home, you always have to
   be a p. — MACM 536:70
consummate British p. — MCFA 531:72
lawyer and p. and a heretic — MENC 565:60
like a scurvy p. — SHAK 764:93
more of a missionary than a p. — CART 198:52
murderer, to be a p. — MILL 573:57
No man can be a p. — HARR 383:87
pate of a p. — SHAK 755:29
p. is a man — TRUM 868:37
p. is an arse — CUMM 248:16
p. is a person — LLOY 514:9
p. is a statesman who — STEV 821:67
p. is the devil's quilted anvil — WEBS 895:7
p. is trained — MURR 605:12

p....on a street corner — WHITE 903:99
p. poses as the servant — DE 259:43
p. rises on the backs — HUGH 419:26
p. seeking empathy — SAFI 708:1
prefer to have a p. — WILS 914:71
the kind of p. — STEV 821:68
when a p. does get an idea — MARQ 554:30
politicians always impress p. — HAYEK 387:61
fault of our p. — TROL 867:93
Few p. are good at taking the high
   ground — MAND 544:52
Natural p. are skilled actors — MARA 548:23
one of those p. — TROL 866:82
Outer Mongolia for retired p. — BENN 75:15
p. and scientists were lazier — WAUGH 892:47
P. are neither bad nor good — EICH 301:29
P. are the same all over — KHRU 466:1
p....enormous sexual pull — COND 230:85
P....entitled to change their minds — HATT 385:27
p. have had to listen — FITT 324:81
p....hold writers in contempt — BELL 73:76
P. neither love nor hate — DRYD 290:81
p. of our time — MACA 525:43
p. or philosophers — THOM 854:10
P. use statistics — LANG 488:89
race of p. put together — SWIFT 831:80
revolution to get the p. out — CAST 199:77
sense of purpose...not...from their p. — MACM 537:82
Successful p. — LIPP 512:72
too important to be left to the p. — DE 259:44
Two p. rotten bladders — WEBS 895:6
what p. are up to — HUMP 422:19
wind instead of the p. — WADD 884:63
politics American p. — GRAMM 366:44
American p. — WHITE 904:3
any more about p. — TRUM 868:33
axiom of p. — TOCQ 861:83
Beauty...determined by p. — WOLF 919:80
best p. is good government — STEV 821:66
boundaries between p. and art — DANG 252:86
choice in p. — THOR 858:9
commonest error in p. — CECIL 202:30
constantly changing language of p. — SAFI 708:96
contact I have had with p. — HEMI 394:20
cross current of world p. — HUGH 420:58
didn't come into p. to change the
   Labour Party — BLAIR 132:2
difference between p. and guilt — CLIN 221:94
Don't be 'practical' in p. — CONN 233:89
England is unrivalled for...p. — DISR 277:95
Finality is not the language of p. — DISR 276:66
get on in p. — BAKER 53:20
great men...in p. — ELTON 311:95
History is past p. — FREE 336:42
infection of p. — BRON 154:67
In p....anything said — THAT 850:10
In p., madame — MULR 602:73
In p....retreat is honorable — MCCA 528:10
Like art and p. — DOCT 278:4
long experience of p. — MACM 536:74
making p. a spectator sport — GERG 350:32
man goes in for p. — ROGE 695:26
matter of modern p. — ARNO 33:49
Men enter local p. — PARK 639:86
mistaken zeal in p. — JUNI 453:10
mixed with p. and p. — LAFA 484:92
more p. in football than in p. — ERIK 315:88
more than our p. and our laws — DEWAR 264:42
mule of p. — DISR 276:46
My p....is England — DISR 276:51
naked moment in p. — GERG 350:31
nature of p. — POWE 667:95
never get on in p. — ASTOR 37:30
no true friends in p. — CLARK 219:48
observe about this p. thing — ROGE 694:16
people who want to get on in p. — DEED 258:9
Philistine of genius in...p. — ARNO 34:65
playful moderation in p. — HUNT 423:25
poets should stay out of p. — GINS 357:67
P. and the fate of mankind — CAMUS 187:85
P. are much discussed — DICK 268:26
P. are now nothing more — JOHN 444:10
P., as a practice — ADAMS 4:75
P. as a profession — HOWE 417:2
P. come from man — WAITE 884:67
P. has got to be...fun — CLARK 219:49
p. in the East — DISR 276:39

P. is a blood sport — BEVAN 85:24
P. is a thing — AMIS 14:85
P. is just like show business — REAG 681:67
p. is like...a football coach — MCCA 527:92
P. is like having diabetes — JONES 447:89
P. is not an exact science — BISM 131:84
P. is not the art of the possible — GALB 343:94
P. is perhaps the only profession — STEV 822:6
P. is the art of preventing — VALE 876:16
P. is the art of the possible — BUTL 176:34
P. is the skilled use — PEAR 645:99
P. is too important — DE 259:44
P. is war — MAO 548:6
P. make you think — CAST 199:74
P. mixed with the imagination — STEN 816:50
p. of greed — ARMEY 30:69
p. of numbers — TANA 836:89
p. of the country — HAZL 388:80
p. of the extreme centre — WELL 898:63
p. than men of any other class — LODGE 515:29
p. the middle way — ADAMS 5:88
Practical p. consists in — ADAMS 4:84
secret springs of p. — TOCQ 861:84
sex is just p. — BRAD 148:62
society...think much about p. — LEWIS 507:79
some scheme of p. — MONT 591:64
South Africa, renowned...For p. — CAMP 185:55
sphere of practical p. — KING 469:63
the p. of our society — OAKE 619:85
There are times in p. — GALB 343:97
to blame...is p. — ANON 26:21
view of history...not of war and p. — CHILD 213:8
volunteer to go into p. — LEE 500:39
War...the continuation of p. — CLAU 220:67
week is a long time in p. — WILS 916:94
what p. is all about — TRUM 868:41
what there is in business, p. — WHIT 906:52
Without alienation...no p. — MILL 572:9
World-p. stepped in — LEWIS 508:4
You will find in p. — BALD 54:51
polkadot Yellow P. Bikini — VANCE 876:21
polkadots One week he's in p.-d. — DAVI 254:85
Poll talked like poor P. — GARR 346:53
poll p. results — GALL 344:20
pollen p. from one to another mind — LOWE 520:34
polling P. is merely an instrument — GALL 344:20
pollution air p. and...artificial light — MATT 561:71
p.–environmental problem — BOUL 146:24
universal p. — ILLI 428:45
pollutions p. of a great...city — DICK 269:79
Polly Hullo, P., my love — THOM 853:93
Mr P. — WELLS 898:81
polo Playing p. is like...golf — STAL 812:59
polyanthus grass the p. cheques — SMART 796:27
polyester P....most valuable word — ANON 25:52
polygamous Man is p. — JAMES 434:75
polygamy chaste p. — CAREW 190:63
p. was made a sin — DRYD 289:68
pomegranate sings on yon p. tree — SHAK 736:68
temples are like a piece of a p. — BIBLE 101:2
pomp grinning at his p. — SHAK 735:20
No princely p. — DYER 297:51
p. of power — GRAY 369:14
p. of the superfluous causes — NEWT 612:71
solemnised with p. and parade — ADAMS 5:89
Pompeius P....his first triumph — PLUT 656:12
Pompey Knew you not P.? — SHAK 746:71
pomps high Midsummer p. — ARNO 33:46
p. and vanity — BOOK 142:13
pond An old p. — BASHO 63:40
Four ducks on a p. — ALLI 13:62
have their stream and p. — BROO 156:17
In the p. beside the meadow — MACG 531:76
muddy p. of daily life — HERZ 400:54
ponder When in danger, p. — WAGN 884:65
poniards She speaks p. — SHAK 744:94
ponies p. have swallowed their bits — BETJ 84:8
Pontefract licorice fields at P. — BETJ 84:6
poodle bulldog into a Reagan
   created the p. — THUR 860:52
honourable gentleman's p. — LLOY 513:95
Pooh happy morning Being P. — MILNE 575:85
House at P. Corner — PARK 637:47
'I ought to say,' explained P. — MILNE 574:81
pooh P., p. to you — GILB 354:5
Poohsticks game called P. — MILNE 575:86
pool In a great p. a swan's nest — SHAK 774:68

Leaning over…a rock p.	DAY 257:86
rears from off the p.	MILT 580:6
pools Where the p. are bright	HOGG 406:60
poop feeding the p. back to diners	COUP 238:94
p. was beaten gold	SHAK 764:23
poops high on the p. of the ships	ROBE 689:17
poor annals of the p.	GRAY 369:14
as a p. woman	THAC 849:97
As for the virtuous p.	WILDE 908:11
asparagus of the p.	FRAN 333:92
backward steward for the p.	POPE 660:4
being p.	YEATS 933:38
being so p.	BLUN 137:9
Bells, the p. man's only music	COLE 226:96
bestow all my goods to feed the p.	BIBLE 121:9
best way to help the p.	HANC 380:29
Better is a p. and a wise child	BIBLE 100:75
Blessed are the p. in spirit	BIBLE 109:83
brings him into the world p.	INNO 429:69
children of the p.	DICK 270:85
Clothes make the p. invisible	HARR 383:89
Commitment to the p.	JOHN 439:63
cynical gestures of the p.	SPEN 807:50
destruction of the p. is their poverty	BIBLE 99:20
distance between the rich and the p.	CARL 191:82
don't leave out the p.	ZELD 936:91
Employed a Million of the P.	MAND 545:54
expensive…to be p.	BALD 54:34
Farewell, my p. hands	RACH 676:81
fatally p. and dingy	WHAR 901:48
first duty…is not to be p.	SHAW 779:38
Four spectres haunt the p.	LLOY 513:98
Give me your tired, your p.	LAZA 496:51
grind the faces of the p.?	BIBLE 102:9
gulf between the rich and the p.	COUP 238:92
high and low, rich and p.	MORI 598:83
high in p. countries	SMITH 798:45
houseless and unemployed p.	BRON 155:85
How p. are they	SHAK 760:82
If thou art rich, thou'rt p.	SHAK 758:33
If you're p.	MART 555:53
inconvenient to be p.	COWP 241:58
keep D.H. Lawrence p.	BRAD 148:67
kisses the p. last	SHAK 765:50
knew…that he was p.	DICK 273:74
Laws grind the p.	GOLD 361:41
life of the journalist is p.	GIBB 352:69
live by robbing the p.	SHAW 778:89
merry Monarch, scandalous and p.	ROCH 691:52
more p. than you think	MEIJ 563:8
murmuring p., who will not fast	CRAB 242:92
nice people were p.	SPARK 806:25
Nothing is so p. and melancholy	SANT 714:24
one of the undeserving p.	SHAW 780:66
Peace is p. reading	HARDY 382:74
pitiful defence of p. poetry	SIDN 790:16
pity upon the p.	BIBLE 99:42
plenty has made me p.	OVID 631:44
p. always with you	BIBLE 114:94
p. always ye have with you	BIBLE 118:5
P. and content is rich	SHAK 760:87
p. and the weary predominate	GARL 346:49
p. are to be proud!	SHAK 756:76
p. as Job	SHAK 742:40
p. cannot always reach	FORS 331:34
p. for a' that!	BURNS 173:46
p. get children	KAHN 454:30
p. have no right	RUSK 704:20
p.…have occasion for	HALL 378:91
p. have the gospel preached	BIBLE 111:33
p. in a loomp is bad	TENN 847:55
p. in spirit	SPARK 806:25
p. Ireland still continues p.?	BERK 79:8
p. is hated	BIBLE 99:28
P. Little Rich Girl	COWA 239:7
p. man at his gate	ALEX 11:23
p. man had nothing	BIBLE 91:2
p. man's opera	HUXL 425:95
p. man's Parnassus	EMER 313:54
p. man's wealth	SIDN 790:10
P. naked wretches	SHAK 763:78
p.'s decay	GOLD 361:57
p. silly-clever Irishman	SHAW 779:32
p. Sir Patrick	EDGE 299:95
p. slaves with weary footsteps	SHEL 786:9
p. to do him reverence	SHAK 748:9
p. virgin…an ill-favoured thing	SHAK 750:89
p.…whose death interests no one	CELI 202:39
p., yet making many rich	BIBLE 122:30
rich and I've been p.	TUCK 870:62
Rich And The P.	DISR 276:53
Rich gifts wax p.	SHAK 753:75
rich should become p.	ARIS 29:58
so p. a record of performance	FRIE 337:65
the p. are our equals	TRIL 866:68
The p. sleep little	OTWAY 631:34
thin hands of the p.	WILDE 907:82
Though very p.	GOLD 362:61
thousand p. musicians	VAUG 877:42
Thus may p. fools	SHAK 774:66
To be a p. man	DU 293:71
Too p. for a bribe	GRAY 370:42
to this day is every scholar p.	MARL 553:16
tragedy…not that men are p.	DU 293:72
unkillable infants of the very p.	POUND 664:29
used to think I was p.	FEIF 319:83
wealth…makes them doubly p.	CRAB 242:89
When that the p. have cried	SHAK 748:6
poorer for richer for p.	BOOK 142:26
poorest p. he that is in England	RAIN 677:92
p. of people believe	HEGEL 391:40
poorhouse p. in an automobile	ROGE 695:23
pop p. art and fine art	MACI 533:6
P. art is the inedible	BASK 63:46
P. artists did images	WARH 889:64
P. music…classical music of now	MCCA 528:12
popcorn Everything else is mere p.	BELL 74:83
pope ay, or a p.!	HARDY 382:67
Dryden, P., and all their school	ARNO 34:69
elected a President, not a P.	STRE 827:93
man a little p. of perfection	LAWR 494:97
not you who are p.	BERN 80:32
photograph of the P.	ANON 25:55
P. and Tsar, Metternich	MARX 558:4
P. composes with his eye	ARNO 33:34
P. is quite satisfied	MICH 568:32
P. should surrender…authority	WYCL 931:18
P. told us all to go to hell	OBRI 621:6
popery never be in danger of P.	ADDI 6:21
popes P. and Popery	ANON 21:37
popinjay Came the great P.	SITW 794:69
poplar p. never dry	SPEN 808:73
poplars white p. fluttering	CHAT 207:49
poppet no go my p.	MACN 538:3
poppies Flanders fields the p.	MCCR 529:19
pleasures are like p. spread	BURNS 172:19
Poppins Mary P. looked down	TRAV 864:43
poppy Not p. nor mandragora	SHAK 760:92
poppycock this is p.	JOHN 440:97
pops p. of Sillery	GILB 354:16
populace Barbarians…and P.	ARNO 33:53
factious P.	JOHN 441:51
give the name of P.	ARNO 33:56
popular Marriage is p.	SHAW 778:8
Nothing can render them p.	SWIFT 832:13
over-great pleasure in being p.	FULL 341:47
p. humanity is treason	ADDI 7:35
P. in our time	HUGH 419:31
very p. among his mates	EWART 316:26
why soap operas are…so p.	STEI 816:45
popularity Appalling P. of Music	LAMB 487:66
no easy p.	THAT 850:19
P.? It is glory	HUGO 421:82
population capital and p.	MILL 570:57
control the p. without…Herod?	OBRI 620:1
foreign p. must endeavour	RUSS 705:49
full half of the p.	MORE 597:56
immediate checks to p.	MALT 543:16
Ireland…a starving p.	DISR 276:50
only talked of p.	GOLD 361:43
P. EXPLOSION	BRUN 163:5
P.…increases in geometrical ratio	MALT 543:15
p. provides a subsidy	CHOM 214:20
segment of our p.	TRUM 868:29
populations moving whole p.	MILL 572:26
privileged p.	SONT 804:78
working p. of both countries	LOND 515:37
populous p. and smoky city	SHEL 784:51
p. railway town	THOR 858:7
porcelain rogue in p.	MERE 567:4
porch beyond p. and portal	SWIN 833:32
he'll be on your p.	JOHN 440:82
on the front p. of the house	LANCE 487:73
To the top of the p.!	MOORE 594:17
porches In the p. of mine ears	SHAK 752:32
porcupine dry birth to a p.	SIMP 792:46
key is to be a p.	MATT 561:68
like fucking a p.	MIZN 589:16
quill from a p.	MOORE 595:43
quills upon the fretful p.	SHAK 752:28
pore charm from every p.	LERN 504:26
pores came through the p.	GREE 370:51
p. of the ocean and shores	SHEL 783:41
pork Yes, to smell p.	SHAK 739:50
porkchop Uncle…and his Little P.	ONAS 625:84
Porlock a person on business from P.	COLE 226:8
Person from P.	SMITH 800:2
pornography give p. a bad name	BARN 60:60
P.…attempt to insult sex	LAWR 495:29
p. is really about	SONT 804:72
p. only adds to the murk	MILL 573:54
P.…vice of the Seventies	WOLFE 920:99
porphyry and polished p.	SMART 796:27
porpoise lively p. in a strong tide	DICK 266:7
p.…treading on my tail	CARR 195:81
porpoises sporting like p.	SITW 793:61
porridge lines falling like cold p.	BRID 152:29
receives comfort like cold p.	SHAK 774:85
sand in the p.	COWA 239:8
venomous p.	THOM 853:95
Porsches friends all drive P.	JOPL 450:63
Porson better poet than P.	HOUS 415:69
port brother…who drinks p.	BARR 61:91
p. after stormy seas	SPEN 808:81
p., for men	JOHN 445:37
p. is near	WHIT 905:46
p. without trade	DEFOE 258:22
ship in p. is safe	HOPP 413:18
Still bent to make some p.	ARNO 32:8
the little p.	TENN 847:31
There lies the p.	TENN 840:66
portal beyond porch and p.	SWIN 833:32
p. of freedom	EISE 302:64
well-marked front p.	UPDI 875:92
portals p. of discovery	JOYCE 452:90
portent p. of an iceberg	BROW 162:64
Self-parody is the first p.	MCMU 537:88
This is the best p.	HOMER 409:22
Porter to Kern or Cole P.	GERS 350:39
porter Ultimate P.	MANS 547:88
porter all p. and skittles	DICK 266:85
decompose in a barrel of p.	DONL 279:25
definition…for a p.	NIGH 616:35
mug of p. in the long nights	OBRI 621:7
philosopher and…p.	SMITH 797:40
Portia P. is Brutus' harlot	SHAK 747:85
porticos spitting on p.	NERU 611:43
portion no claim…to the smallest p.	MALT 543:18
only gift is a p. of thyself	EMER 312:25
p. for ever	BIBLE 96:43
p. is so small Of…pain	MILT 581:9
p. of the earth	NAIP 606:49
p. of the Eternal	SHEL 786:2
p. of the loveliness	SHEL 786:6
right to a fair p.	BURKE 168:32
That best p. of…life	WORD 923:70
that is his p.	BIBLE 100:71
that p. of the ball	POPE 662:71
the curse…all your p.	OTWAY 631:25
portmanteau p.…two meanings	CARR 196:13
portmanteaux people are like p.	MANS 547:88
portrait do not paint a p.	DALI 251:70
I paint a p. I lose a friend	SARG 714:30
make a p.	ROSSO 698:6
p. in marble	BERN 81:52
p. of a dog that I know	JOHN 447:73
p. of a trout	HUGH 419:33
P. of the Artist	THOM 852:69
two styles of p. painting	DICK 267:3
portraits accept the verbal p.	CHUR 215:41
people in p. are thinking	LIVE 512:78
p. I paint of women	LAUR 492:72
study of family p.	DOYLE 285:73
portray could not p. all I felt	HOLM 407:70
Portuguese assurance, typically P.	ACHE 2:25
pose combine a p. imperious	GILB 355:33
posies thousand fragrant p.	MARL 553:17
posing P. is a performing art	SCHW 721:61
position at the cost of his social p.	MARX 558:6
Every p. must be held	HAIG 376:66
get people into a p.	KAZIN 456:72

high p., but not a safe one BERN 80:31
if not impossible p. LEWO 508:10
in a p. to instruct us PEOP 647:24
lucidly justifying his p. AMERY 14:78
mathematical is this fundamental p. HEID 391:44
no p. more perilous TROL 867:95
only one p. for an artist THOM 853:97
p. at the summit of the world PEARY 645:2
p....epitomized marginality ECON 298:79
p., I'd have done the same NIXON 617:50
p. of the artists of Wales THOM 853:97
p. ridiculous CHES 211:40
rose to his p. TROT 867:16
Whatever its p. or character SCOTT 722:75
positions military take p. KENN 464:53
ridiculous p. DANF 251:84
positive All satisfaction...never p. SCHO 719:28
P....Mistaken at the top of one's voice BIER 129:41
something p. and precious PRIT 669:52
possess not enough to p. her LACL 484:85
possessed limited in order to be p. BURKE 168:19
p. by what is not LEGU 501:56
p. with murd'rous hate SHAK 770:3
possessing P. what one loves PROU 671:80
too dear for my p. SHAK 772:35
possession everlasting p. BIBLE 87:77
in the glad p. JONS 448:11
merry hart with small p. HENR 396:53
p. intended to last THUC 859:16
P. is nine points ANON 20:11
p. is the final good WHIT 904:8
p. of a bourgeois aristocracy ENGE 314:65
p. of that object conveys SMITH 797:41
secure p. of a bleak rock YOUNG 935:76
possessions concern not for...p. PLATO 654:78
for he had great p. BIBLE 113:73
jealous p. GIDE 353:81
mind is the least of p. WHITE 903:96
possessor libel on its p. SHEL 782:15
not profitable to its p. MARQ 554:29
possibilities p. of life LEAV 498:1
short of their inherent p. MUMF 603:75
To believe only in p. BROW 158:76
possibility How great a P. CARL 192:3
laws of p. REDON 681:74
life...to give it p. MACL 535:47
objective p. WEBER 894:68
p. of anybody getting me out BRAD 149:78
p. of human happiness ERNST 315:90
Religion...a remote p. WHIT 904:8
Violent, vivid and of infinite p. EBER 298:72
possible art of the p. GALB 343:94
if a thing is p. CALO 185:45
no explanation is p. SEAT 726:69
Politics is the art of the p. BUTL 176:34
p. is one of the provinces BAUD 65:71
scientist states that something is p. CLAR 220:59
thank all time who made this p. ANDR 16:29
wasn't p. for me or anyone KAVA 456:66
possum Honourable P. BERR 82:64
post boats...near the winning p. COKE 224:71
Lie follows by p. BERE 78:90
may not quit the p. TENN 847:34
p. of honour ADDI 7:37
stalked through the P. Office YEATS 934:64
postal cheque and the p. order AUDEN 39:81
desire to take p. courses BRAD 148:52
postboy keys of a p.'s horn BENET 75:10
postcard and a p. album TRAV 864:42
postcards have a set of p. printed ELLI 310:80
post-chaise driving briskly in a p.-c. JOHN 445:25
poster Kitchener...a great p. ASQU 36:12
live up to one's p. TREE 865:53
p. on the student's wall VETT 880:74
p. with the enormous face ORWE 629:98
posterior protecting his p. SAFI 708:98
posterity fear of vexing p.! ROCHE 691:47
footprints preserved for p. PATE 642:56
love of p. HAWT 386:36
People will not look forward to p. BURKE 168:30
p. be after him CROM 245:71
P. do something for us ADDI 7:40
p. talking bad grammar DISR 277:92
P. will do justice to...Gladstone DISR 277:82
protecting his posterior from p. SAFI 708:98
Thy p. shall sway COWP 241:52
To evoke p. GRAV 367:69

To invoke one's p. CELI 202:37
trustees of P. DISR 276:55
posters P. of the sea and land SHAK 766:69
post-horse contrapuntist...p. MOZA 601:46
postman hear the p.'s knock AUDEN 39:82
The P. Always Rings Twice CAIN 184:31
postmodern p....Australia NARO 608:74
postpone p. no more WHIT 905:40
postponement Life...one long p. MILL 573:46
posts sprinkle all the p. SPEN 809:4
postscript pith is in the p. HAZL 388:86
seldom Writes...but in her P. STEE 814:98
postulate lay down as a p. WEIL 896:32
p. of objectivity MONOD 591:56
Postumus Oh, my P., P. HORA 413:21
posture died each in the despairing p. POE 656:19
postures indecent p. WILDE 910:65
post-war awash in p.-w. testosterone SCHR 720:45
posy sprinkle a p. of daisies THOM 853:89
pot don't make them in the one p. JOYCE 452:86
Fame's luscious p. RICK 686:76
great Melting P. ZANG 936:88
Joan doth keel the p. SHAK 734:94
melting p. never worked MORR 599:3
not a melting p. CART 198:46
strawberries at the mouth of their p. ELIZ 310:64
three-hooped p. SHAK 730:63
potato any more than a p. HAWT 386:38
no more bounce than a boiled p. PORT 663:12
p. candidate ANON 25:61
You say p. GERS 351:42
potatoes Let the sky rain p. SHAK 744:81
Papa, p., poultry, prunes DICK 271:16
potent more p. than any other man STEAD 813:81
potential both as chaos and as p. POUND 665:66
p. for the disastrous rise EISE 302:58
potentialities puritanical p. LEWIS 508:96
potions p. have I drunk of siren tears SHAK 773:49
Potomac All quiet along the P. MCCL 528:15
potsherd Let the p. strive BIBLE 103:45
p. to scrape himself BIBLE 93:50
pottage bread and p. of lentiles BIBLE 87:85
mess of p. BIBLE 87:83
Potter Harry P. was a highly unusual boy ROWL 701:55
potter Hath not the p. power BIBLE 120:79
like a p.'s vessel BIBLE 94:84
P. and clay endure BROW 162:70
P. is piqued with p. HESI 401:64
poultry A p. matter MARX 557:84
foxes...prolonging the lives of the p. ELIOT 303:96
I hate pudgy p. PERD 648:52
Pound in Ezra P.'s term MACD 530:47
pound Christian on a P. a Week? HARD 381:40
give thee a silver p. CAMP 186:70
grocer puts a p. weight SPEN 807:62
hundred p. on't SHAK 773:57
pound P. a week and his keep LAWS 496:45
p....in your pocket WILS 916:97
Take thou thy p. of flesh SHAK 740:83
two thousand p. in lead MIDD 569:38
who will p. longest WELL 897:55
pounds Fifty p.! LAWR 494:18
p. will take care LOWN 521:64
three hundred p. a year! SHAK 743:77
weight in p., shillings MILNE 575:84
pour p. on him all we can HERB 398:16
poverty abolition of p. HOOV 411:58
against hunger, p., desperation MARS 554:39
America has mitigated p. WOOL 922:25
amidst its p. and squalor ARNO 33:56
best-dressed p. HARR 383:89
between the ignorance and p. WALP 887:22
destruction of the poor is their p. BIBLE 99:20
Greed begins where p. ends BALZ 58:22
hardest thing to bear in p. JUVE 453:16
hated p. JOHN 441:14
inhibition attaches to p. HESI 401:66
In honoured p. thy voice SHEL 782:23
In p., hunger, and dirt HOOD 410:45
marry the Irish...look for p. DONL 279:23
monarchies end by p. MONT 593:95
Money is better than p. ALLEN 12:52
no...crime so shameful as p. FARQ 318:56
P. and oysters...seem to go DICK 266:76
P. has a home in Africa HEAD 388:98
p., ignorance and disease DU 293:75
P. is a great enemy JOHN 446:56

P. is...blamed on anyone OCON 622:28
P. isn't being broke WYLIE 931:24
P. makes peace ANON 19:95
p. of blackness DANG 251:85
p.'s catching BEHN 71:11
prefer p. with liberty PITT 653:42
represent p. as no evil JOHN 443:67
So shall thy p. come BIBLE 99:16
struggled with p. BALD 54:34
terrible reality of p. LEGU 501:60
there for honest P. BURNS 173:46
trouble with p. KRUG 481:24
upon p., vice, and misery SUMN 828:18
where p. is enforced DOUG 284:37
worst of crimes is p. SHAW 779:38
pow blessings on your frosty p. BURNS 171:10
powder keep her in paint and p. NIMI 616:36
keep your p. dry BLAC 132:93
take a p. and they are gone ACHE 3:41
powdered Still to be p. JONS 449:25
powders P. and liquids DOYLE 286:83
rogue gives you Love P. LAMB 486:36
power above thy p. BIBLE 108:50
according to the p. that worketh BIBLE 122:46
add reach to p. ACHE 3:51
all p. is a trust DISR 275:35
Almighty p. Hurled MILT 580:95
antithesis...is not pleasure, but p. DE 262:8
apt words have p. MILT 586:51
awful shadow of some unseen P. SHEL 782:19
beauty...hath strange p. MILT 586:59
because they confer p. RUSS 705:47
because we had p. BENET 75:14
best in his p. TROL 867:94
Black p. ANON 23:97
brute p. and human need COMM 229:66
certainty of p. DAY 257:83
changing it is within our p. REAG 680:62
charm of all p. is modesty ALCO 10:3
conceal the p. of the atom COLE 225:73
conceive a dominant p. HARDY 381:54
constructs p. structures LEGU 501:58
corridors of p. ALLEN 12:35
corruption of p. BRON 154:67
cowards...sit safe in p. OTWAY 631:28
Creator's p. display ADDI 6:26
cult...religion with no political p. WOLFE 920:94
defy P., which seems omnipotent SHEL 785:83
delightful and delighting p. MITF 588:5
depository of p. DISR 276:48
descriptive p....literary style PULI 672:4
Desire of p. DRYD 290:84
desire of p. after p. HOBB 404:26
desire to seek p. BACON 48:1
devil hath p. SHAK 753:71
differences of speed And p. PRATT 667:1
drape over their will to p. HUXL 426:2
dream of independent p. JAY 435:96
drunk with sight of p. KIPL 472:22
During my tenure of p. PEEL 646:9
earthly p. doth then show SHAK 740:80
eat the p. out of women WEST 901:40
Eternal God of p. TENN 844:74
excessive love for the balance of p. BRIG 152:31
existence of mankind in its p. ADAMS 4:74
expression of the will to p. PAZ 644:90
fealty to those in p. MAMET 544:35
feel herself a source of p. BROO 156:27
fool, In p. of others MILT 586:47
Force is a spiritual p. LEON 503:12
fourth p....into two p.s FERM 321:15
friend in p. is a friend lost ADAMS 4:77
full of p. TENN 844:66
gauge of their real p. LESS 505:36
given women so much p. JOHN 443:76
God...loved the People in P. PATC 642:50
good, and had no p. to see LANY 489:3
guessing p. BAGE 51:93
guilt and p. TOPL 863:15
have the p. to die TENN 846:27
history of political p. POPP 662:92
hold on to p. until then WANG 888:55
if he had the p. MILL 570:65
its source of p. KINN 470:66
Knowledge is p. BACON 46:33
lawful p. is still superior DRYD 290:98
legislative p. GIBB 351:53

legislative p. vested — LOCKE 514:15
Literature is a p. line — CURT 249:46
love of p. — HAZL 387:71
magic and delicious p. — WOOLF 922:43
making our p. credible — KENN 462:15
manners, virtue, freedom, p. — WORD 925:11
mans body both for p. — SPEN 808:85
man's p. of selection — DARW 253:10
means most within our p. — MALT 543:19
measure the p. — MACC 527:85
Men of p. — FOOT 329:93
microscopes of hextra p. — DICK 266:81
mind...when it attacks p. — STAEL 811:45
Moghul Empire is in our p. — CLIVE 222:15
Monopoly p. must be abused — SIMO 792:44
more contracted that p. is — JOHN 445:30
most p. to hurt us — BEAU 67:14
must climb to p. — TAWN 837:8
name is in p. — NAPO 607:73
Never lacks p. to dismiss itself — SHAK 747:81
New nobility is but the act of p. — BACON 48:10
nexus of all love and money and p. — DIDI 274:6
no hope but from p. — BURKE 168:22
no man...hath p. over the spirit — BIBLE 101:80
none can call our p. to account? — SHAK 768:33
no p. game — JONG 448:97
no p. on earth — BALD 54:47
Not by might, nor by p. — BIBLE 106:17
nothing left but money and p. — STAEL 811:47
Now we have shown our p. — SHAK 769:67
obedience is ever sought for by p. — WOLL 921:6
Of p., of honour — MARL 552:96
Passion and the p. to roam — BYRON 179:21
People who obtain p. — VIDAL 881:94
political p. and philosophy — PLATO 655:98
pomp of p. — GRAY 369:14
p. a corrupter — SHEL 782:15
p. and his love — GRANT 366:52
p. and money and fine robes — WELD 897:40
p. and spirit of America — NORR 618:65
p., and the glory — BIBLE 110:98
P. and War — KIPL 471:98
p. attractive shines — MARL 551:74
p. can be...applied — LEUP 505:50
p. can be rightfully exercised — MILL 570:62
p. can get people — KAZIN 456:72
p. divine — WORD 929:63
p. divine...wash the river Rhine? — COLE 227:23
P. Girt round with weakness — SHEL 785:99
p. in small things — SOPH 804:84
P. into will — SHAK 757:93
P. is my mistress — NAPO 607:69
P. is not a means — ORWE 630:5
P. is the ultimate aphrodisiac — KISS 475:91
p. justifications would go on — STEI 816:44
p. of all true art — EINS 301:37
p. of asking questions — RUSS 705:40
p. of beauty — SHAK 753:76
p. of Christianity — WHIT 904:13
p. of holding...beliefs — ORWE 630:3
p. of its own — BACON 47:60
p. of judging well — DESC 263:18
p. of kings and magistrates — MILT 580:86
p. of life and death — BIBLE 107:36
p. of man — SHAK 768:23
p. of many — SHEL 782:18
p., Of many ways to die — MILT 585:28
p. of miracle — FEUE 321:22
p. of money is...male p. — DWOR 296:47
P. of new Masters — ALBE 10:99
p. of newspapers — TOCQ 861:85
p. of purchasing other goods — SMITH 797:41
p. of reasoned speech — ARIS 29:57
p. of science — SHAP 776:36
p. of Solidarity — WALE 885:88
p. of solitude — NORTH 618:68
p. of steady misrepresentation — DARW 253:12
p. of temptation — TROL 866:85
p. of the hope of freedom — BUCK 165:36
p. of the human intellect — LEWIS 508:95
p. of the will — MORAN 596:56
p. of the written word — CONR 234:95
p. or respect in the world — BAGE 51:92
p. over people — SOLZ 803:62
p. over women — LEGU 501:59
p., peace and healing — MATT 561:71
P. requires that one do — SART 715:41

P. tends to corrupt — ACTON 3:59
p. that can make us truthful — BONH 140:57
p. that created — THUR 860:52
p. that I have on you — SHAK 774:76
p. to add or detract — LINC 510:40
p. to ask for love — SHAW 777:58
p. To chasten and subdue — WORD 923:71
p. to cloud men's minds — BAKER 53:24
p. to communicate — WOOLF 922:33
p. to do any damn fool thing — FULB 340:43
p. to do me harm — SHAK 761:15
p. to end it — SASS 716:56
P....to him who dares — DOST 282:7
p. to hurt and will — SHAK 772:37
p. to learn — PLATO 655:1
p. To live, and act — WORD 928:59
p. to love, or hate — MARL 553:13
p. to make dance — NOON 617:56
p. to make the world a desert — STEV 820:52
p. to master words — SCAR 717:89
p. to shake me — WORD 927:38
P. to the people — ANON 23:8
p. to touch our senses — MILT 576:97
p. we embody — JORD 450:66
p. with our purpose — KENN 463:37
p. without responsibility — BALD 54:46
present possessors of p. — BURKE 168:3
proletarian can take p. — TROT 868:19
proud Edward's p. — BURNS 173:41
pure function, and best p. — WORD 925:6
Repentance...want of p. to sin — DRYD 292:58
responsibility without p. — STOP 825:60
satisfying exercise Of p. — MACB 527:80
self-limited writers have a p. — WOOLF 922:34
self-sufficing p. of Solitude — WORD 925:94
sheer joyous p. of song — BEER 70:35
slow-chapped p. — MARV 556:64
some P. the giftie gie us — BURNS 170:81
spirit...of p., and of love — BIBLE 124:81
spiritual will to p. — NIET 615:19
still and solemn p. — SHEL 782:18
such unlimited p. — ADAMS 3:61
that diffusion of p. — OAKE 619:86
That false secondary p. — WORD 925:96
the balance of p. — PALM 636:26
The good want p. — SHEL 785:73
The greater the p. — BURKE 168:6
The press has enormous p. — TOCQ 861:84
This beautiful and beauty-making p. — COLE 226:4
Thy p. to save — DODD 278:10
ungodly in great p. — BOOK 143:47
United States as an independent p. — GEOR 349:13
use of his p. — HOBB 404:25
vast amounts of p. could be released — EINS 301:55
Visionary p. — WORD 925:1
weakening of the royal p. — INNO 430:71
welcome, thou dread p.! — BYRON 180:38
what sustains interest...is p. — JIANG 438:49
When p. corrupts — KENN 463:36
When p. leads man — KENN 463:36
who will come to p. — SHEV 788:74
will to p. must increase — LEGU 501:55
With barefaced p. — SHAK 768:12
women breached the p. structure — WOLF 920:81
ye shall receive p. — BIBLE 118:27
You don't have p. if — TODD 862:90

powerful evil spirit...supremely p. — DESC 263:24
'It's p.,' he said — HUGH 418:24
more p. conclusion — SOLOW 803:61
More p. than a locomotive! — SIEG 791:25
p. hard thing — CONN 234:92
p. men in our society — BELL 73:76
preparedness makes us p. — GOER 359:10
republic has been much more p. — ADDI 5:7
this p....kingdom — PITT 652:37
two most p. poets — ELIOT 305:50
wealthier or more p. — HELO 393:87

powerless any other world p. — THUB 858:15
FBI are p. to act — HOOV 411:69
p. to be born — ARNO 32:31

powerlessness idealized into p. — JONG 448:6
resurrection...is always p. — WILL 912:8

powers all rest my p. defy — DONNE 279:35
all th' ethereal p. — MILT 585:35
distinction in the intellectual p. — DARW 253:15
exercised the p. committed to me — PEEL 646:9
explore unknown p. — SHEL 782:11

feeble p. of my mind — SIDN 790:98
full use of your p. — KENN 463:38
greatest p. of the world — PALM 636:26
immense new p. on man — CHUR 217:95
Legislation's sov'reign p. — BURNS 171:90
mind of large general p. — JOHN 445:42
p. of intelligence — LYND 524:15
p. of old Europe — MARX 558:4
p. of the state — GIBB 351:54
p. that be are ordained — BIBLE 120:85
productive p. of labour — SMITH 797:38
prostitute all their p.! — FORS 331:48
rise of misplaced p. — EISE 302:58
towards the democratic p. — MASA 559:20
vital p. wither — WILB 907:75
we lay waste our p. — WORD 928:46
with large p. and privileges — PENN 646:22
ye heavenly p. — GOET 360:15

pox p. of her autumnal face — JONS 449:24
practical as p. as the theory — OPPE 626:18
by p. achievements — TAWN 837:8
Don't be 'p.' in politics — CONN 233:89
For most p. purposes — UPDI 874:79
hard and p. man — HOYLE 417:4
might have a p. use — UREY 875:2
original p. example — WHIT 905:42
seeks after immediate p. utility — HELM 393:84

practice bloody or murmuring p. — STUB 827:2
doctrines and p. of Socialism — MORR 598:98
easier with p. — GREE 371:71
no p. without art — PROT 670:64
offending both legal and natural p. — STOP 825:61
Politics, as a p. — ADAMS 4:75
p....be greatly simplified — CARL 191:70
proved them wrong in p. — LESS 505:44
rather of instinct than of p. — REED 682:84
respiration—a troublesome p. — DICK 266:87
something which works in p. — HELL 392:71
stoop from speculation to p. — MACA 526:61
trainer...knows in his p. — RYLE 707:70

practices consists of p. of this kind — HEATH 390:20
no place for restrictive p. — WILS 915:92

practise p. to deceive! — SCOTT 723:99
practiser frequent p. of...angling — WALT 888:49
practising p. long shies — JOYCE 451:82
practitioners art for p. and readers — LEAV 498:1
many p. make a living — SUTH 830:43
prætorian P. here, p. there — SCOTT 724:24
prairie p. flowers lie low — LIND 511:52
prairies rife as the loam Of p. — CRANE 243:22
speech of England...The P. — BRYA 164:13

praise all other p. is shame — SIDN 790:15
community...lived in p. of God — ELIOT 307:89
counterpoise to unintelligent p. — WAUGH 892:42
countryman must have p. — BLYT 138:24
courage to give you unqualified p. — STEI 815:36
Damn with faint p. — POPE 661:38
garment of p. — BIBLE 104:62
girded with p. — GRANT 366:52
Give them not p. — SORL 804:90
giving hand...shall have fair p. — SHAK 733:77
guests should p. it — HARI 382:79
Heedless o' p. — MACD 529:35
His p. forth tell — KETHE 465:75
His p. forth tell — SCOT 725:64
if men withheld their p. — SHEEN 782:8
In deeper reverence p. — WHIT 906:63
In p. of what another's said — YEATS 933:41
itch of p.? — CAREW 190:49
knowledge and her p. — MILT 583:68
let all the people p. thee — BIBLE 96:37
let the song of p. be sung — POTT 663:17
little dust of p. — TENN 844:51
mouth shall shew forth thy p. — BIBLE 95:31
Never p. a sister — KIPL 470:74
only the master shall p. — KIPL 472:20
outstrip all p. — SHAK 774:93
paint 'em truest p. 'em most — ADDI 5:6
p. any man — SHAK 765:32
P....can freeze the heart — BUCK 165:38
p. effect in mighty minds — DRYD 290:83
p. for the singing! — FARJ 318:47
P.God, from whom — KEN 461:94
P. him — HOPK 412:86
p. him and exalt him — BIBLE 128:97
P. life, it deserves p. — JEFF 436:11
p. should sing — LYTE 524:16

P. the Lord	FORGY 330:25
P. the sports of the land	REID 682:96
P. to the Holiest	NEWM 612:66
pudding against empty p.	POPE 662:65
sing the p.	MARV 557:81
so long as it's unqualified p.	COWA 240:25
song in thy p.	BURNS 171:4
Teach the free man how to p.	AUDEN 40:5
the p. of his holy Name	BOOK 142:21
this rich p.	SHAK 772:34
unmerited p.	JOHN 445:44
utter all thy P.	ADDI 6:24
without hope of p.	JOHN 442:38
praised more in him to be p.	JONS 450:56
p. him to his face	TENN 848:64
p. the living God	FOX 333:77
praises high p. of God	BIBLE 98:7
sing p. lustily	BOOK 143:46
praising doing one's p. for oneself	BUTL 178:71
P. all alike, is p. none	GAY 347:75
P. what is lost	SHAK 762:40
walking, and leaping, and p. God	BIBLE 119:31
when I am p. anyone	BEER 69:71
pram enemy of good art...the p.	CONN 233:69
prams p. on concrete balconies	BETJ 83:96
prance mind to p.	JOHN 444:87
prater pert, prim P.	CHUR 215:43
pray drink sooner than p.	SHAK 741:6
dying p. at the last	DILL 275:14
fold her hands and p.	ROSS 698:98
learn to p.	HERB 398:23
nor p. with you	SHAK 739:50
P. do not mock.	SHAK 764:98
p. exclusively of others	WAUGH 893:50
p. for my soul	TENN 847:51
p. for you	SMITH 801:24
P.God our greatness	TENN 848:67
P. inwardly	JULI 452:6
P., love, remember	SHAK 755:23
'P., my dear'	STER 817:68
p. thee then	HUNT 423:34
p. to have a sound mind	JUVE 453:20
p. to thy Father	BIBLE 110:97
p. we have the wisdom	ALLEN 12:56
p. you do not fall in love	SHAK 750:70
wash your hands and p.	KIPL 474:74
Watch and p.	BIBLE 114:99
When I would p. and think	SHAK 758:30
prayer Conservative Party at p.	ROYD 701:58
fruitless p.	TENN 843:45
given to p.	SHAK 743:69
God erects a house of p.	DEFOE 258:13
homes of silent p.	TENN 843:37
house of p.	BIBLE 113:79
More things are wrought by p.	TENN 843:37
most perfect p.	LESS 505:45
people's p.	DRYD 290:82
P. Book of Edward VI	ACHE 2:24
p., observance, discipline	ELIOT 308:35
p. of a righteous man	BIBLE 125:19
Shakespeare and a p. book	BAIN 52:12
Thy wish nor p.	VAUG 878:43
wing and a p.	ADAM 5:98
wish for p.	BERN 80:27
wish her grateful' p.	BURNS 171:89
prayers added vexation of p.	TWAIN 870:84
Christopher Robin is saying his p.	MILNE 574:75
devotion and our p.	FRIE 337:70
Fall to thy p.	SHAK 743:67
Forgets her p.	SITW 793:60
Knelt down with angry p.	HODG 405:46
know whose p.	KIPL 471:1
not very addicted to p.	ASHF 35:95
P. for the condemned man	WEST 901:37
p. for the observers of his law	BACON 48:9
p. of liberty-loving people	EISE 302:49
p. of the church, to preserve	SWIFT 832:9
p. they dare not speak aloud	WILDE 907:81
set it in my p.	SHAK 774:89
solemn p. for the great exaltation	COLU 229:62
sudden on some p.	BROW 160:11
yet like his p.	SHAK 773:45
prayeth He p. well	COLE 225:92
praying No p., it spoils business	OTWAY 631:32
prays Whatever a man p.	TURG 867:66
preach could never p.	AUST 43:78
p. among the Gentiles	BIBLE 122:44

p. good tidings unto the meek	BIBLE 104:62
P. not because you have to say	WHAT 902:58
p. the discovery of the 'new'?	INGR 429:62
P. the word	BIBLE 124:85
preacher as the P. saith	HARDY 382:72
village p.'s modest mansion	GOLD 361:53
preachers don't believe in p.	BENE 75:8
pirates, p.	SYNGE 834:58
preaching Christian p.	BARTH 62:7
foolishness of p.	BIBLE 120:91
gone about p.	JERO 437:36
p....one of the most healthy exercises	WESL 900:23
p. point is not a meeting point	THER 851:43
woman's p. is like a dog	JOHN 443:73
preamble Pardon my long p.	LAWR 495:36
precautions take some elementary p.	LEVIN 506:64
take the necessary p.	CRISP 245:55
took p. against it	GALS 344:23
precedence battle for p.	SITW 794:74
believe I take p.	SAKI 710:47
claim in hell P.	MILT 581:19
precedency p. between a louse	JOHN 446:59
precedent From p. to p.	TENN 841:93
precedents there are no p.	DEBU 258:7
precept carry p. to the highest	BYRON 181:74
Let your p. be, Be Easy	STEE 814:96
p. must be upon p.	BIBLE 103:26
true business p.	DICK 268:38
very little p. and practice	EDGE 299:93
preceptions p. and insights	KISS 475:97
preceptor artist...p. of his time	BETH 83:76
precepts if one follows p.	SENE 727:90
precincts warm p. of the cheerful day	GRAY 369:22
precious all p. in God's sight	JACK 431:7
all that's p. in our joys	STER 818:7
how p. is frivolity!	FORS 331:48
Life is too p.	ELIOT 303:70
make vile things p.	SHAK 763:75
most p. to me	SHAK 768:30
my P., my P.?	TOLK 862:3
P. in the sight of the Lord	BIBLE 97:77
something positive and p.	PRIT 669:52
Thy words are too p.	SHAK 749:30
precipice On the summit of the p.	HOLM 407:70
precise too p. in every part	HERR 400:50
precisely Thinking p.	SOLOW 803:60
precision p. unapproachable	LEAV 498:98
strung to a vast p.	CRANE 243:16
precisions divisions and p.	ELIOT 305:29
precondition p. to meaningful action	BART 62:13
predecessors shoulders of their p.	RUSS 705:46
steal from their p.	POUND 666:73
predestination Social P. Room	HUXL 425:75
predicting better at p. events	STOP 825:69
prediction regardless of p.	RICH 685:41
predilection p. for genre fiction	DISCH 275:29
p....is with us	AUDEN 40:12
pre-eminence keep...the p.	BIBLE 108:63
preface P. to a...Suicide Note	BARA 59:43
prefer Did not p. You	DRAY 287:3
p. the destruction	HUME 422:8
preference P. and prejudice creep in	HILL 402:91
p. which it is forced	LAMB 486:44
with p. and aversion	SHER 787:35
work: if not by p.	BAUD 65:80
preferment knocking at P.'s door	ARNO 32:17
pregnancy avoid p....mathematics	MENC 566:77
pregnant finish...without getting it	ANON 24:39
like being a little p.	HEND 395:34
Like finding oneself p.	ACHE 2:32
mad'st it p.	MILT 580:93
strong pillars and p. supporters	BAIL 52:6
trying to stay half p.	BOHL 138:35
prejudice critic...without p.	NATH 610:24
free from interest or p.	REES 682:89
let no p....asperse them	EMMET 313:59
Preference and p. creep in	HILL 402:91
p. runs in favour of two	DICK 267:1
P....vagrant opinion	BIER 129:42
Race p....a shadow	BUCK 165:35
suburban p. of anti-Semitism	POUND 665:65
the p....run in favour of two	SHER 787:38
To everybody's p.	GILB 354:17
Travel is fatal to p.	TWAIN 870:78
prejudices Drive out p.	FRED 336:34
employ their reason to justify p.	WOLL 921:4
honest p....of a true Englishman	ADDI 6:21

our errors, our p., our dreams	POPP 663:97
paradoxes than of p.	ROUS 700:45
Passions destroy more p.	DIDE 273:84
p., misconceptions	LLOY 513:6
prelates p. in habitis clericall	DUNB 294:5
prelude p. to insanity	WAUGH 891:17
p. to resurrection	WILL 912:8
preludes p. to that eternal separation	STER 818:93
premium greater p. on temperament	BRAD 149:76
prentices schoolboys, and sour p.	DONNE 279:41
preoccupation chief p. to avoid	LESS 504:32
one constant p.	RUSS 705:54
preparation complete lack of p.	WAVE 893:59
no p. for the future	DISR 276:44
no p. is thought necessary	STEV 822:6
preparations all the p. with regard to	GOER 360:11
prepare p. for government	STEEL 813:86
p. to meet thy God	BIBLE 106:9
p. to shed them now	SHAK 748:10
prepared Be P.	BADEN 51:74
preparedness p. makes us powerful	GOER 359:10
preposterous p. troop of sons	SOME 803:66
Pre-Raphaelite decorated by a P-R.	BEER 70:93
prerogative first is law, the last p.	DRYD 291:17
p. of the eunuch	STOP 825:60
presage p. of extinction	SCOTT 722:76
presagers dumb p.	SHAK 771:10
Presbyterian P. at Kercaldy	FLEM 327:62
Presbyterians regarded by strict P.	THOM 856:51
prescription discards P.	DISR 276:44
prescriptions according to her p.	MORE 597:69
p. are not kept	SHAK 773:56
p. written by patients	KRAUS 480:7
rules and p.	NISB 616:38
presence castellated, shimmering p.	MORR 598:93
Cast me not...from thy p.	BIBLE 95:30
come before his p. with a song	BOOK 143:66
come before his p. with thanksgiving	BIBLE 96:57
feel the p. of the past	PEI 646:15
from whose unseen p.	SHEL 783:43
His p. here is...an insult	RED 681:71
horror that her p. excites	GRAV 367:74
If thy p. go not with me	BIBLE 89:30
insult of each other's p.	ISHE 431:91
majestic p.	HUNT 423:26
not often let their p. be known	DU 293:73
p. of a bad historian	ELTON 311:95
p. of absence	BERG 79:2
p. of the cherished child	ELIOT 303:83
p. of the Red Death	POE 656:19
Where God's p. is no longer	STEI 816:46
whither shall I flee from thy p.?	BIBLE 98:1
present afraid of the p.	GREY 373:8
alcohol made the p. enough	GEE 348:93
bitter birthday p.	DILL 274:12
Children...live in the p.	LABR 483:74
conventions of the p.	LEWI 508:8
dialogue between the p. and the past	CARR 194:52
die...when you are...p.	SCEVE 717:93
except for the one p. moment	WILL 913:37
finding myself at p.	MUNDY 603:83
Forsytes were p.	GALS 344:23
For the p. at any rate	ROSE 696:62
future...same stuff as the p.	WEIL 896:28
futurity casts upon the p.	SHEL 786:17
gave it me...for an un-birthday p.	CARR 196:10
give this p. to her dear	LANY 489:5
It is the p. that counts	CELI 202:37
love [looks] to the p.	LEWIS 507:73
man of the p.	HOLM 408:2
men of the p. age	OVER 631:38
more eventful than the p.	ORWE 628:57
no crime like the p.	WASH 890:90
no redress for the p.	DISR 276:44
not live in the p.	THOM 852:55
others, past and p.	NABO 606:42
Piers this p. to plese	LANG 489:97
politics is p. history	FREE 336:42
p. alone was significant	CHOP 214:22
p. at the Creation	EVANS 316:17
p. at their marriages	TROL 866:84
p....growth out of the past	WHIT 906:49
p....has a voice	OAKE 619:85
p. in time future	ELIOT 307:92
p. is an age of talkers	HAZL 388:82
p. is an important time	CARL 191:79
p. is burthened too much	HAWT 386:50

take p. in the words   KENN 463:33
the great and their p.   YEATS 932:37
the p. of my country I sang   OBRU 621:12
Thine eyes my p.   SIDN 790:15
time of our love and p.   SU 828:6
too much weakness for the stoic's p.   POPE 660:16
What argufies p. and ambition?   DIBD 265:55
will her p. deflower   SPEN 808:86
priest both the p. and clerk?   SHAK 735:23
came down a certain p.   BIBLE 115:37
Churches built to please the P.   BURNS 170:73
Delicate-handed p. intone   TENN 845:83
parish p. rebuked him   OFLA 622:35
p. begets children   SMITH 801:10
p. continues what the nurse began   DRYD 291:21
p. is given permission   LISP 512:74
p. is the worshipper   SHAW 779:37
p. of the Muses   HORA 413:22
p., warrior, poet   BAUD 65:82
rid me of this turbulent p.?   HENR 395:44
Thou art a p. for ever   BIBLE 97:74
why he was a p.   WINT 917:30
youth…is nature's p.   WORD 926:24
priestcraft ere p. did begin   DRYD 289:68
p. into a great religious   LEWIS 508:95
priesthood arcane p.   GOULD 365:25
one or another kind of p.   MILL 571:1
royal p.   BIBLE 125:24
priests invention of theologians or p.   NIEB 614:98
p. and educators   NGU 613:79
p. are only men   BROW 162:81
p. in black gowns   BLAKE 134:57
p. interpreted and interposed   COND 230:82
P., princes, women   POPE 661:31
p. very dear to the people   TROL 866:88
p. were infinitely more attentive   FITZ 324:89
seize our p.   ANON 19:96
women nor with p.   SOUT 805:3
primary cruelty is the p. feeling   SADE 708:93
p. requirement for a writer   STAEL 812:51
p. word addresses the eternal Thou   BUBER 164:23
primative wildly natural and p.   THOR 857:75
prime dead ere his p.   MILT 578:45
fresh colours deck the wanton p.   SPEN 809:92
gathered in their p.   SHAK 732:50
In the p. of your life   RICH 685:43
lovely April of her p.   SHAK 770:1
One's p. is elusive   SPARK 806:22
Prime Minister best P. M. we've got   BUTL 176:35
essentials of a successful P. M.   WILS 916:4
every p. m.…since
Balfour…died unhappy   HAIL 377:71
grow up to be P. M.   RICH 686:73
I forget I'm P. M.   BLAIR 132:6
last P. M. with jurisdiction in Ireland   ADAMS 4:72
man who nearly becomes P. M.   BUTL 176:33
My chances of being PM   JOHN 439:70
next P. M. but three   BELL 73:57
P. M. is the loneliest job   BALD 54:45
P. M. or Leader of the Opposition   DISR 277:82
P. M. reading out the conclusions   HESE 401:60
that the P. M.'s advisers are responsible
is absurd   FOLL 328:83
unknown P. M.   ASQU 36:10
would not want to be P. M.   THAT 850:8
Prime Ministers disastrous…P. m.   ONAS 625:81
primetime doesn't help…when p. TV   QUAY 674:38
primeval p. ooze to the stars   VIDAL 881:95
This is the forest p.   LONG 516:52
primitive comprehend…p. forms   EINS 301:37
most p. and most sophisticated   KUNI 482:38
p. era was lyrical   HUGO 420:60
p. form of cricket…Tip-and-Run   SHAW 781:94
p. men are…credulous   POPE 659:92
p. music and p. medicine   LEAC 497:65
radicals who seem p.   WOLFE 920:91
wise p. in a giant jungle   MAIL 539:37
primrose P. Hill and Saint John's Wood   BLAKE 135:72
p. path of dalliance   SHAK 751:16
p. that forsaken dies   MILT 578:54
p. way   SHAK 767:7
primroses Wan as p.   KEATS 458:7
prince Advise the p.   ELIOT 304:23
bold defiance with his p.   DRYD 290:80
danced with the P. of Wales   FARJ 318:49
Dread p. of plackets   SHAK 733:76
fall of a p.   ANON 18:70

Good night, sweet p.   SHAK 755:44
Here lies a p.   JOSE 451:71
His Weariness the P.   FIRB 323:67
preservation of the P. and State   WENT 899:4
P. calls in the good old money   LAMB 486:43
p. is like a mirror   CHAR 207:36
P. of Europe, should dare to invade   ELIZ 309:60
p. of glory died   WATTS 891:3
P. of Light   MILT 575:94
p. of the clouds   BAUD 64:55
p. of the devils   BIBLE 111:22
P., thou art sad   SHAK 745:28
safer for a p. to be feared   MACH 533:98
soothe the p.'s appetite   MASS 560:47
soul of a p.   LOCKE 514:19
Sweet p., I come   MARL 552:88
under the rank of a p.   KING 469:58
Were you with these, my p.   ADDI 6:33
Who made thee a p.   BIBLE 88:7
princedoms p., virtues, powers   MILT 583:81
princes admit p. to the corridors   DOUG 283:21
blaze forth the death of p.   SHAK 747:87
make p. in all lands   BOOK 143:50
'must' is not to be used to p.!   ELIZ 310:63
Of p. shall outlive   SHAK 771:21
pale kings, and p.   KEATS 458:19
Perfect happiness, by p. sought   CHAP 206:16
power…shines in p.' eyes!   MARL 551:74
P. and lords may flourish   GOLD 361:52
P. and lords…the breath of kings   BURNS 170:70
p. apply themselves   MORE 596:57
p. my ancestors followed   ORAH 626:20
p. should be free   SHAK 729:49
p. to know their true interest   SWIFT 831:82
put not your trust in p.   BOOK 143:72
She's all states, and all p.   DONNE 279:42
though p. rage   ANON 20:4
you that are p. born   DAVI 254:33
princess ancient Egyptian p.   CASS 199:70
great p.   FORD 330:12
p. among the provinces   BIBLE 105:79
the peoples' p.   BLAIR 132:7
Princeton chair at Harvard or P.   MENC 565:60
principalities timeless p.   GRAV 367:72
principle active p. of Wealth   PETTY 650:85
advocates no great p.   HAZL 388:78
aesthetic p. of our times   ROGE 694:10
an active P.   WORD 928:56
called this p.…Natural Selection   DARW 253:10
Cats seem to go on the p.   KRUT 481:30
Conservatism…shrinks from P.   DISR 276:44
does everything on p.   SHAW 777:65
facts and not…a p.   DARW 253:17
female p.   LEGU 501:58
first p. of existentialism   SART 715:50
formal p. of its colour   SHEL 786:13
Greatest Happiness P.   MILL 570:70
identifying oneself with a p.   HEGEL 391:42
It has no other p.   HAZL 388:77
on p., not by instinct   TWAIN 872:32
p. in life with me   SHAW 777:64
p. laid down by Gilbert   HUTC 424:53
p. of the English law   DICK 270:96
p. which…gives us a firm Rock   BUTT 178:87
p. which prompts to save   SMITH 798:47
rebels from p.   BURKE 169:37
romantic p. of life   NOVA 619:73
Self-determination…imperative p.   WILS 917:18
sensibility of p.   BURKE 169:35
snob…on p.   SHAW 780:58
tenth time, lack of p.   SIDM 790:96
principles acceptance of p.   UNIT 873:69
action of religious p.   BERD 78:87
based on mechanical p.   LEUP 505:49
betrayed the p.   INOU 430:74
civilization with sound p.   JOHN 438:55
contrary to their p.   GALS 344:23
current p. of administration   SIMON 792:37
denouncing liberal democratic p.   AUNG 42:49
easier to fight for p.   STEV 820:49
fights you on patriotic p.   SHAW 777:65
happily arrogating those p.   MAMET 543:25
if you surrender all your p.   TODD 862:90
man of fixed and unbending p.   DIRK 275:26
man without p.   FORD 329:99
morally acting on the highest p.   SHAW 780:50
mythical stories become structural p.   FRYE 340:36

Politicians…when they adjust their p.   HATT 385:27
p. are the same   JOHN 446:50
p. around my neck   BALF 55:59
p. employed in science   RUSS 705:41
p. form the bright constellation   JEFF 437:19
p. of a free constitution   GIBB 351:53
p. of equity and justice   PEEL 646:9
p. of mankind   WILS 916:13
p. which at first lead to scepticism   BERK 79:7
putting our p. into execution   WEBB 893:66
round certain p.   TOCQ 861:84
when the p. dissolve   MILL 572:3
wrote 'P. of Political Economy'   BENT 78:78
print definite…in p.   COMP 230:72
eternity of p.   WOOLF 922:36
keepers of p. and paper   MACL 535:41
love a ballad in p.   SHAK 770:94
names in p.   CHES 212:93
p. of a man's naked foot   DEFOE 258:18
put them into p.   LESS 505:40
we quarrel in p.   SHAK 750:91
when they see them in p.   KRAUS 480:11
printed chaff is p.   HUBB 417:9
developed, carefully p., fixed   ISHE 430:89
printing invented the art of p.   CARL 192:90
p., gunpowder and the magnet   BACON 47:61
restrained from p.   JOHN 443:86
Prior once was Matthew P.   PRIOR 668:31
priority without the reward of p.   SCOTT 722:80
priory stag in the P. coomb   DAVI 254:26
Prism Charity, dear Miss P.   WILDE 909:44
prism Newton with his p.   WORD 925:98
prison endure torture in p.   PANK 636:33
good friend…visits you…in p.   BRAD 148:63
hero from his p.   AYTO 45:17
his dwelling, and a p.   WEBS 895:97
hollow p. of my flesh   SHAK 731:93
Home is the girl's p.   SHAW 779:21
impenetrable barriers of our p.   EDGE 299:1
in p., and ye came unto me   BIBLE 113:92
opening of the p.   BIBLE 104:62
palace and a p. on each hand   BYRON 180:31
pestilential p.   GILB 355:25
portion as the site of a p.   HAWT 386:39
P., dungeons, blessed places   GENET 348:5
p. is to live without mirrors   ATWO 40:5
p. of his days   AUDEN 40:5
public school…at home in p.   WAUGH 892:24
put me in p.   ONDA 625:85
So cruel p. how could   SURR 829:37
souls' p. we call England   SHAW 781:75
Stone walls do not a p. make   LOVE 519:10
taking him to p.   HOUS 416:89
true place…also a p.   THOR 857:71
What is a ship but a p.?   BURT 174:76
worst of p. life   STEN 816:52
prisoned p. birds must find   SASS 716:69
prisoner passing on the p.'s life   SHAK 758:20
p. in his dungeon   FLAU 326:39
p.'s release   SIDN 790:10
sculpture is the p.   THOM 855:33
your being taken p.   KITC 475:5
prisoners p., be not despairit   ANON 20:4
p., handcuffed two   LESS 505:35
p.…I'll find them law   MACQ 538:17
p. of addiction   ILLI 428:47
p. out of captivity   BOOK 143:57
p. were left free to choose   SHAW 778:1
p. whom they hide   HAWT 386:47
Queen Victoria treats her p.   WILDE 909:50
stand p. at the bar   WILDE 907:81
which p. call the sky   WILDE 910:53
prison-house grind in the p. h.   BIBLE 90:75
secrets of the p.-h.   MOOD 594:8
Shades of the p.-h.   WORD 926:24
prisons disastrous policy in the p.   KENN 462:8
P. are built with stones   BLAKE 134:42
privacy P. is a privilege not granted   LAUR 492:69
undisturbed p.   PARK 638:74
private allurement of p. interest   STEU 819:9
am to become a p. citizen   EISE 302:59
better that we stay p. people   SART 715:1
his p. parts, his money   BUTL 178:83
hold no brief for p. enterprise   BURT 174:66
in his p. heart   TWAIN 872:24
making the p. world public   GINS 357:71
matter of p. gain   OROZ 627:27

p. depends on the unreasonable · SHAW 779:17
p. has no definite…meaning · SART 715:40
P. is a comfortable disease · CUMM 248:17
p.—is always revolutionary · POPP 662:89
p. is utter delusion · MILL 572:26
P., man's distinctive mark · BROW 162:74
p. of human knowledge · FRAN 335:17
p. of society and wealth · RICA 684:32
p. through the world · LONG 516:63
promote social p. · UNIT 873:69
same each time with p. · BENN 75:19
scientific and technical p. · JOHN 438:55
since Social P. began · KIPL 474:84
sing the p. · DONNE 280:46
skin of p. · SOYI 805:13
social p. · JOHN 438:57
speak…about making p. · POPP 663:98
swell a p. · ELIOT 304:23
thanking the God of P. · LEWIS 507:85
turtle…makes p. · ANON 25:56
War is a condition of p. · RENAN 683:98
When one hears of p. · SKEL 795:4
progression by gradual p. · ARIS 29:49
p. of exploded fallacies · RAND 678:10
Without contraries is no p. · BLAKE 134:37
progressive liberal and p. · TRIL 866:68
p. who is prudent · JOHN 440:81
truly cumulative and p. · SART 715:40
prohibiting licensing and p. · MILT 579:69
prohibition Communism is like p. · ROGE 695:20
p. so divine · SHAK 774:65
project p.…for…shopkeepers · SMITH 798:50
p. for extracting sun-beams · SWIFT 831:81
projected it's what's p. · PRICE 668:15
projections other figures…p. · ELIOT 309:54
pro-jobs cannot be p.-j. · TSON 869:55
proletarians p. have nothing to lose · MARX 558:5
proletariat dictatorship of the p. · MARX 558:16
English p.…more bourgeois · ENGE 314:65
p. can take power · TROT 868:19
the true p. · BLIX 137:2
prologue foolish thing…long p. · BIBLE 108:68
witty p. to a very dull play · CONG 231:4
prolonged War is being deliberately p. · SASS 716:56
prom libel on a Yale p. · PARK 637:54
Prometheus Fire which P. filch'd · BYRON 181:71
promiscuity emotional p. · MAIL 540:51
sexuality and p. · WYLIE 931:23
promise against reason, against p. · DICK 271:34
appalling p. · AUDEN 40:12
black p. of untrammeled joy · HOLM 407:73
Eating the air on p. · SHAK 742:44
full of p., but of no performance · DICK 268:35
full of youthful p. · IRVI 430:79
gaudy p. of what life ought to be · COOKE 236:41
p. kept, And a child · NEME 610:38
p. made is a debt unpaid · SERV 728:2
p. none relies on · ROCH 692:72
p. of fair weather · DICK 268:51
p. of pneumatic bliss · ELIOT 305:35
p. of their early years · POWE 666:76
p. to build a bridge · KHRU 466:1
state of perpetual p. · BEEC 69:64
promised p. to do when you are sick · SIGI 791:27
seen the p. land · KING 468:43
promises Don't ask me for p. · SHAW 777:51
failed p. of American life · GILL 355:39
not a set of p. · KENN 462:9
not having received the p. · BIBLE 124:96
P. and pie-crust · SWIFT 832:11
p. to keep · FROST 339:98
Wealth…made up largely of p. · POUND 666:74
young man of p. · BALF 54:56
promissory one long p. note · BEEC 69:64
signing a p. note · KING 468:35
promontory seems to me a sterile p. · SHAK 752:56
See one p. · BURT 174:73
promote he will p. himself · DUGO 293:89
promotion p. of the human race · WEST 901:39
sweat but for p. · SHAK 749:40
prompt I meant to be p. · DAY 256:77
pronounce frame to p. it right · BIBLE 90:70
p. it Vinchy · TWAIN 870:75
proof absence of any other p. · NEWT 613:75
admirable p. of this · FERM 321:15
exist as living p. · THOM 855:42
final p. of God's omnipotence · DE 264:37

flawless p. of the existence of God · EDDI 298:85
no need of formal p. · BOYD 148:46
p. that only men · STEI 816:44
p. through the night · KEY 465:76
The p. is in his plays · ONEI 625:98
tyrannous and rough in p. · SHAK 735:34
written for…narrative, not of p. · QUIN 675:56
proofs purist who reads your p. · CHAN 204:81
prop Science…a p. · WORD 925:95
you do take the p. · SHAK 740:84
propaganda all p. is lies · ORWE 628:64
engines of p. · BALD 54:46
full of p. · ACHE 3:50
in spite of…its foreign p. · ORWE 628:63
piece of p. in favour · JOYCE 452:97
p. arm of the American Dream · HASK 385:24
p., rumor, suspicion · LIPP 511:67
strikes…not as a means of p. · ENGE 314:67
propagandist p.'s purpose · HUXL 425:85
propagandists cleverest p. extant · BUCH 164:27
propagation peace and p. · WALP 887:33
Was all our p. · DONNE 280:59
propensities excite my amorous p. · JOHN 441:22
side of their natural p. · BURKE 169:50
propensity hereditary p. · EDGE 299:93
p. for being poor · AUST 43:89
property Abolition of private p. · MARX 558:3
any object of p. · BENT 77:68
bourgeois p. is…revolutionary · OROU 627:25
character, person, or p. · LOVE 519:17
civilization…of p., of fences · EMER 313:37
common p. of the nation · TIMES 861:77
consider himself as public p. · JEFF 437:20
destroys my p. · PAINE 634:89
every man reclaimed his own p. · BUTL 178:85
family from sinking their p. · MOOD 594:8
for our p. · PITT 653:46
Happiness…in taking their p. · GENG 349:8
landlords and persons of p. · MALT 543:19
magic of P. · YOUNG 935:76
misapplied is a'body's p. · MACD 529:30
neither persons nor p. will be safe · DOUG 284:37
one-way p. of time · EDDI 298:83
on their p. · GALS 344:23
preservation of p. · LOCKE 514:13
P. has its duties · DRUM 287:13
p. in his person · LOCKE 514:14
P. is theft · PROU 670:66
P. like incest · INNIS 429:68
p. of any political party · HOOV 411:66
p. of the rich · RUSK 704:20
rights of p. originate · MADI 538:20
sanctity of life and p. · SCHL 718:10
security of p. · PANK 636:31
Thieves respect p. · CHES 211:64
violent p. fordoes itself · SHAK 752:41
property-owning p.-o. democracy · SKEL 795:94
prophecies verification of…p. · TROL 867:94
prophecy art united with p. · NISB 616:39
p., and religion, all in one · RUSK 704:33
p. is the most gratuitous · ELIOT 304:4
self-fulfilling p. is · MERT 568:22
though I have the gift of p. · BIBLE 121:9
trumpet of a p.! · SHEL 783:48
urn Of bitter p. · SHEL 786:22
verses and the p. · WALL 886:16
prophesy hang out and p. · PALEY 635:15
P. upon these bones · BIBLE 105:93
who can but p.? · BIBLE 106:8
prophet banner of the P. · BROD 153:53
happen to a p. · HUXL 425:96
I am no p. · ELIOT 304:22
If there arise among you a p. · BIBLE 89:49
Juxtaposition his p. · CLOU 223:33
loathing Was p. to the rest · MIDD 569:48
Methinks I am a p. · SHAK 734:5
more than a p. · BIBLE 111:34
p. is not without honour · BIBLE 112:54
there is a p. in Israel · BIBLE 92:32
What-you-may-call-it is his p. · DICK 269:59
your p. the Nazarite · SHAK 739:50
prophetic like p. strain · MILT 577:23
O my p. soul! · SHAK 752:30
prophets Beware of false p. · BIBLE 110:10
destroy the land of p. · BIBLE 109:86
films of one's own country like the p. · ANDE 16:18
hang all the law and the p. · BIBLE 113:82

persecuted they the p. · BIBLE 109:83
so did their fathers to the false p. · BIBLE 115:30
spake by the P. · BOOK 141:96
prophilaxis wise course of p. · SILVA 792:34
propinquity P. had brought · YEATS 934:67
self-congratulatory p. · GILL 356:40
proportion bills! That's out of p. · LARK 490:28
in equal p. to age · HEMI 395:28
in inverse p. to the sum · PARK 639:85
innate sense of p. · HONE 409:29
no p. kept · SHAK 735:31
sense of wholesome p. · POWYS 667:97
soul refines…in p. · MARI 551:64
strangeness in the p. · BACON 49:45
proportions distorted…p. · MILL 570:75
exact p. · HALES 377:81
Fashion…is a matter of p. · CHAN 205:2
Full of p., one limb to another · HERB 398:4
p. are easily determined · HEIN 391:52
p., everything has its share · MATI 560:62
proposal every new p. · STAMP 812:60
propose We p. it, we massage it · CUOMO 248:27
proposes Man p., but God disposes · KEMP 461:86
proposition no longer a tenable p. · STEI 816:46
p. that all men are created · LINC 510:39
p. that two times two · LICH 509:24
p. which it purports to express · AYER 44:10
p. which we can understand · RUSS 705:43
self-evident p. · MACA 525:43
thinks over that p. · KIER 467:12
propositions central p.…are these · HUXL 426:8
p. would sound like · LICH 509:17
truth of P. · HOBB 404:22
proprietor hotel without a p. · MANS 547:87
propriety despaired, with more p. · WEBS 894:89
p. of thoughts and words · DRYD 288:46
proscription punished by p. · CHES 210:35
prose condescend to p. · BYRON 181:74
connect the p. and the passion · FORS 331:36
dough-baked p. · CAREW 190:52
fancy p. style · NABO 606:31
for discourse and nearest p. · DRYD 290:7
Gertrude Stein's p. song · LEWIS 508:98
Good p. is like a window · ORWE 629:85
In p., the worst thing · ORWE 629:90
laws of p. writing · HEMI 394:17
love thee in p. · PRIOR 669:41
'monument of English p.' · ELIOT 307:91
most beautiful p. paragraph · BLOOM 137:7
never pin up my hair with p. · CONG 232:37
not poetry, but p. run mad · POPE 661:37
other harmony of p. · DRYD 292:43
Poetry is to p. · WAIN 884:66
produce great p. · THOM 853:3
P. books are the show dogs · GRAV 367:78
P. is when all the lines · BENT 77:72
p. of the realities · CUOMO 248:31
P. on certain occasions · LAND 488:85
p. takes the mould of the body · WOOLF 923:55
P. = words in their best order · COLE 227:21
shut me up in P. · DICK 272:62
speaking p. for forty years · MOLI 590:40
straight honest p. · HEMI 394:9
translate aphorisms into…p. · FRYE 340:38
unattempted yet in p. or rhyme · MILT 580:92
well written as p. · POUND 664:26
prosecution attention in the p. · WASH 890:82
p. of any undertaking · JOHN 441:27
prospect dull p. of a distant good · DRYD 291:20
hold out a p. for nations · PITT 653:47
noblest p. · JOHN 443:63
p. from the watershed · STARK 813:74
p. of a brighter day · WORD 929:65
p. of another campaign · JOHN 439:73
p. of belief · SHAK 766:73
p. of reigning · JAY 436:2
p. of tackling an unsolved problem · SHIP 789:76
which…has the happier p. · PLATO 654:05
prospectors unoffending p. · DOUG 283:14
prospects few pleasanter p. · HAWT 386:44
gilded scenes and shining p. rise · ADDI 5:2
Wide and undetermined p. · ADDI 6:22
prosper keep it may p. · KIPL 471:12
p. that love thee · BIBLE 88:89
Treason doth never p. · HARI 382:80
prosperity Grit riches and p. · BROWN 158:52
jest's p. lies in the ear · SHAK 734:93

hat incredible thing, a p.	CRAW 244:45
rade for the p. good	SMITH 798:49
ribunal of p. opinion	TOCQ 861:84
rue to the p.	BERK 79:10
vexes p. men	TENN 841:92
Well, British P.	BROW 162:79
vhatever the…p. allow	SHAW 778:91
Whatever they may be in p. life	FREN 336:48
write for yourself and have no p.	CONN 233:62
ublic-address station p.-a. system	JAMES 433:29
ublican How like a fawning p.	SHAK 739:51
ublicists use to backlash p.	FALU 317:41
ublicity history of p.	LEAV 498:99
oxygen of p.	THAT 850:24
orice of justice is eternal p.	BENN 76:50
o. agent of big business	ORWE 627:32
P. is the very soul of justice	BENT 77:70
Without p.…no prosperity	ZELD 936:92
With p. comes humiliation	JANO 435:78
ublicly Sometimes you move p.	BAKER 53:18
ublic-school English p. s.	WAUGH 892:24
p.-s. system all over	WAUGH 891:11
ublish ask a superior to p.	HOPK 412:96
I'll p., right or wrong	BYRON 179:96
P. and be damned.	WELL 898:69
p.…what you actually did	FEYN 322:24
ublished never have been p.	MACL 535:40
ublisher Barabbas was a p.	CAMP 186:74
nad a p. shot	UNSE 874:70
o., to take writers seriously	POWE 666:85
Xerox makes everybody a p.	MCLU 536:65
ublishers fear…become p.	CONN 233:66
P. can get their minds	LECA 499:24
ublishing important…in p.	JOVA 451:76
p. of his ideas	KAZIN 456:71
ubs served in all the p. in Dublin	DONL 279:25
udding cold, black suet-p.	LEWIS 508:98
p. against empty praise	POPE 662:65
uddin-race Chieftain o' the P.-r.!	BURNS 171:88
uddle p. wonderful	CUMM 247:2
superficial as a p. in the sunlight	LEAC 496:63
uddling p. in a tub continually	PERTH 648:70
udenda vile members…called 'p.'	ABEL 1:3
uff friends all united to p.	SWIN 833:46
pipe with solemn interposing p.	COWP 240:48
the p. oblique, or p. by implication	SHER 788:61
uffed get one's self p.	TROL 867:1
uffing P. is of various sorts	SHER 788:61
uff-paste fantastical p.-p.	WEBS 895:14
uffs p. from the hookah-mouth	KIPL 471:98
ugh Mr P. minces among bad vats	THOM 853:95
ull tug, p. and plop	OBRI 621:10
ulp become so much p.	CAMP 185:49
If P. Fiction had been set	GRANT 366:50
ulpit If the President has a bully p.	REAG 680:51
Inquisition fulminating from the p.	WELD 897:40
ulsations translate p. into images	RICH 685:47
ulse feeling a woman's p.	STER 818:5
lost p. of feeling	ARNO 31:99
p. of life?	SHAK 739:32
p. of the machine	WORD 927:36
scene before him beat like a p.	AMIS 14:82
ulse-less p. lot…England	LAWR 493:88
ulses feeling of p. the physic of love	CLEV 221:82
umice Beside a p. isle	SHEL 783:45
polished with dry p.?	CATU 200:4
umpkin like the rich P. pie	WHIT 906:56
un p. is Pierian	UNTE 874:71
so vile a p.	DENN 262:3
through a pipe and exhaled in a p.	LAMB 487:64
unctual p. rape of every…day	WILB 907:74
unctuality Painting and P.	GAIN 342:85
P. is the politeness	LOUI 518:98
P. is the vice	PATR 643:72
P.…virtue of the bored	WAUGH 892:48
unctuation dropped p. marks	WEST 901:42
mix…the sun with p.	BRAU 150:1
Zero Tolerance Approach to P.	TRUSS 869:50
Punic With P. faith	SALL 711:73
unish impulse to p. is powerful	NIET 615:16
P. a body	DRYD 290:78
p. everyone who deserved it	ELIOT 303:85
unished p. not for what they do	SZASZ 834:62
unishment All p. is mischief	BENT 77:66
Death is…degrading p.	BREN 151:17
fees are sufficient as	BAIL 52:2
marked out for p.	BUCH 164:30
p. fit the crime	GILB 355:27
p. is greater than I can bear	BIBLE 86:60
P. is not for revenge	FRY 340:31
seek to convert by p.	MILL 573:40
servitude…the p. of his guilt	CURR 249:41
Some p. seems preparing	FRAN 334:14
take a lot of p. to write	HEMI 393:93
punishments charged with p.	HENL 395:39
neither rewards nor p.	INGE 429:57
Severe and terrible p.	MORE 596:60
punk Well do you p.?	EAST 298:68
punt more fun to p.	SAYE 717:83
slow p. swings round	ARNO 32:18
punters p. don't want to sleep	CURT 249:48
pupil p. is too young	RYLE 707:80
pupils p. are the crème de la crème	SPARK 806:21
p. might demonstrate	GIBB 351:57
teacher who does not equip his p.	PETE 649:78
puppets box and the p.	THAC 849:94
p.…with their slips of paper	WHITE 903:80
puppies drowned a blind bitch's p.	SHAK 743:79
puppy p.'s insolent yelp	ANON 19:98
purchase More in the cunning p.	JONS 448:11
water…will p. scarce any thing	SMITH 797:41
purchased see 'tis p. by the weight	SHAK 740:71
purchasers to encourage p.	SWIFT 831:74
pure Be warm, but p.	BYRON 179:98
blank virtue, not a p.	MILT 579:72
Blessed are the p. in heart	BIBLE 109:83
ever to have p. knowledge	PLATO 655:90
in gudis be a	DUNB 294:3
know nothing, p. and simple	WILL 913:48
Live p., speak true	TENN 847:58
meant to be disinterested, p.	SELF 727:80
more p. than his maker?	BIBLE 93:53
Nothing but holy, p., and clear	HERB 397:90
only you are p.	VALL 876:19
O p. of heart	COLE 226:4
prince whose intentions were p.	JOSE 451:71
p. air and water	REES 682:89
p. as the driven slush	BANK 58:28
p. science can flourish	STEA 813:78
souls Of the p. in heart	RANS 679:27
temples th'upright heart and p.	MILT 580:93
truth is rarely p.	WILDE 909:36
Unto the p. all things are p.	BIBLE 124:88
whatsoever things are p.	BIBLE 123:61
zipless fuck is absolutely p.	JONG 448:97
purest p. and most thoughtful	RUSK 703:6
purgation p. of such emotions	ARIS 29:54
purgatory England…p. of men	FLOR 328:76
no other p. but a woman	BEAU 67:12
those that deny p.	WEBS 895:1
purge Every book is like a p.	DU 294:97
P. me with hyssop	BIBLE 95:29
purify p. the dialect of the tribe	ELIOT 309:43
purists Down with p.!	BAND 58:25
puritan describe as 'P. decadence'	SPEN 807:63
honesty be no p.	SHAK 761:21
P. hated bear-baiting	MACA 526:77
P. of the middle class	NEME 611:39
To the P. all things are impure	LAWR 495:32
puritanism not P. but February	KRUT 481:29
P. names the behaviour	SPEN 807:63
P.. The haunting fear	MENC 565:71
purity preserve unblemished p.	ABEL 1:3
P. of race does not exist	FISH 324:77
purling p. stream	ADDI 5:3
purple Before, milk-white; now, p.	SHAK 737:94
pink and p. columbine	SPEN 808:68
P. haze is in my brain	HEND 395:36
p. wardrobe of thy side	CRAS 244:36
So cool a p.	KEATS 457:5
with reverend p.	JONS 448:13
purpose art achieves a p.	CONS 235:29
As if all this had some p.	SARD 714:29
before this p. cool	SHAK 768:21
called according to his p.	BIBLE 120:76
can cite Scripture for his p.	SHAK 739:52
devoted to a nobler p.	CURZ 249:51
end and p. of all production	SMITH 798:51
except for a noble p.	HERB 397:85
God, for some strong p.	SHAK 735:28
human autonomy, human p.	MUMF 603:78
impulse without p.	BIER 129:44
know how to live to p.	MONT 592:85
mind charged with an eager p.	ELIOT 303:88
Nature…nothing without some p.	ARIS 29:57
novels written with a p.	FORD 330:6
old p. done up in aspic	LAWR 494:2
one increasing p. runs	TENN 841:83
power with our p.	KENN 463:37
p. and determination	KENN 463:30
p. breaks…when it is fulfilled	ELIOT 309:39
p. of art	GOULD 364:21
p. so ravenous	LAWR 495:39
p. was less firm	MOOD 594:6
real p. of life	SCHO 719:32
set p. and…exhausted frame	DOYLE 285:76
speak plain and to the p.	SHAK 744:4
system which has no p.	FROMM 338:82
unconquerable p. shall be realized	LAMB 486:34
without any practical p.	PLAN 653:58
yoke-devils sworn to either's p.	SHAK 745:35
purposes Can execute their airy p.	MILT 581:9
p. to which it is instrumental	MILL 570:73
put it to useful p.	ACHE 3:42
riddles of…the p. of God	FRYE 340:39
purring p. of contented cats	GRAH 366:39
purse as thy p. can buy	SHAK 751:20
carrying a very heavy p.	ASCH 35:81
consult your P.	FRAN 334:12
consumption of the p.	SHAK 742:43
no money in your p.	SHAK 749:41
nothing in thy p.	BIBLE 108:53
p. is the mirror	QUIN 675:50
silk p. out of your wife's	MORT 600:20
steals my p. steals trash	SHAK 760:85
purses Light gains make heavy p.	BACON 50:56
pursue fight them, and p. them	JOAN 438:52
pursued only the p., the pursuing	FITZ 325:96
want to be p. by it	KAFKA 454:25
you who are p.	SHAW 778:88
pursuer you are the p.	SHAW 778:88
pursuit every action and p.	ARIS 29:50
p. of happiness	WARR 889:69
p. of pleasure	PROU 671:86
p. of sanity	BELL 73:72
p. of truth	DESC 263:19
p.…without any practical purpose	PLAN 653:58
spare no p.	DICK 271:17
What mad p.?	KEATS 459:51
pursuits dress according to…your p.	DISR 277:88
engaged in congenial p.	MOOD 594:6
pursy fatness of these p. times	SHAK 754:12
push p. may send him over it	SITW 794:84
total p. and pressure	JAMES 434:69
pussy Owl and the P.-Cat	LEAR 497:83
persian p. from over the sea	MARQ 554:27
P. said to the Owl	LEAR 497:84
putrefaction preserve it from p.	JOHN 446:64
puzzle Don't p. me	STER 818:91
p. all the wise	DRYD 289:75
puzzling But what's p. you	JAGG 432:18
pygmies like retarded p.	PEAR 645:98
Of all the p.	BOOT 144:3
p.…content to have our paper	MELV 564:44
pyjamas shot an elephant in my p.	MARX 557:85
pylons P., those pillars	SPEN 807:85
Pym Mr P. used to sit	RUSH 703:96
pyramid society was resembled a p.	NAPO 607:71
star-y-pointing p.?	MILT 576:2
unquestionable, like a p.	ORWE 628:54
pyramids p. of sweetmeats	DRYD 292:48
summit of these p.	NAPO 607:58
Pyramus Death of P. and Thisbe	SHAK 737:87
Most radiant P.	SHAK 738:2
scene of young P.	SHAK 738:14
Pyrenees tease in the High P.	BELL 73:65
Pythagoras never…since P.' time	SHAK 749:59
P.' metempsychosis	MARL 553:8
python shoes are made of p.	MACN 538:2

Q

quack potent q., long versed	CRAB 242:91
quad always about in the Q.	ANON 22:51
no-one about in the Q.	KNOX 476:22
quadrille q. in a sentry box	JAMES 433:48
quaffing q., and unthinking	DRYD 292:61
quails we long for q.	DRYD 290:5
quaint Q.…50 years after	LAVER 493:81
Quaker But I knaw'd a Q. feller	TENN 847:54
quaking eat thy bread with q.	BIBLE 105:87

spent lights q. and gleam · ARNO 31:84
Quixote Don Q. of Europe · COBD 223:53
quixotic Q. quality · USTI 875:7
quo Q. vadis · BIBLE 128:3
quotation Every q. contributes · JOHN 442:41
q. is a national vice · WAUGH 892:40
quotations ability to think in q. · DRAB 286:87
Classical q. is the parole · JOHN 446:51
delighted particularly in q. · SCHL 718:11
q. from the Bible · LAWR 495:23
q. from the Bible, Browning · MCFA 531:73
q. in Latin · FLAU 327:43
recommend him by select q. · JOHN 443:79
quote grow immortal as they q. · YOUNG 935:79
q. the fights historical · GILB 354:99
quotes q. from the shortstop · MCFA 531:73
quotidian poet is a master of the q. · PRIT 669:54

R

rabbits r. ruled by stoats · ORWE 628:46
rabble r. of the filthy…infants · POUND 664:29
Rabboni R.; which is to say, Master · BIBLE 118:23
Raca say to his brother, R. · BIBLE 109:88
race adroit and joyless r. · WAUGH 892:38
antennae of the r. · POUND 665:63
Art among a religious r. · FUSE 342:75
avoid a competitive r. · ARNO 34:74
brave, generous, humorous, talented,
  warm-hearted · BUCH 164:27
But was a r. of heaven · SHAK 764:17
colonel comes from Brian's r. · DAVIS 256:67
courage of their r. · SULL 828:17
demand this…for the r. · SCHR 720:42
destiny of the human r. · THOR 857:80
Englishmen…nervously excitable r. · DAVI 254:30
entire r. passes through · SCHR 720:43
hearted r. · BUCH 164:27
ills…spring from belonging to a r. · DUDEK 293:81
intent on my own r. · STEV 824:38
Irish…in the infancy of the r. · OFAO 622:33
Jews…murmuring r. · DRYD 289:72
law [of competition]…for the r. · CARN 193:49
like the rest of my r.? · BLAKE 135:65
men and women with our r. · KIPL 473:62
my second r. · VAUG 878:44
noble r. and brave · SIGO 791:28
No r. can prosper · WASH 889:78
northern r. · CHUR 215:43
nuclear arms r. · MOUN 601:39
Of some new r. called Man · MILT 581:25
perpetuate their r. · RICA 685:36
poor r. in a land of dollars · DU 293:71
pride of r. or spirit · SMITH 801:25
problem of r. and color · DU 293:75
Purity of r. does not exist · FISH 324:77
quiet, pilfering, unprotected r. · CLARE 219:43
r. between education · WELLS 898:89
r. is not to the swift · BIBLE 101:85
r. is to the swift · DAVI 254:24
r. of glory run · MILT 586:54
r. of upstart creatures · MILT 581:34
R. prejudice…a shadow · BUCK 165:35
r. that is set before us · BIBLE 124:99
r. which has become self-conscious · LAWR 494:99
rear my dusky r. · TENN 841:85
simple r.! · SCOTT 723:89
slinks out of the r. · MILT 579:70
Swift was the r. · DRYD 290:94
they which run in a r. · BIBLE 121:1
unbodied joy whose r. · SHEL 784:56
unto a savage r. · TENN 839:62
what avails the sceptred r.! · LAND 488:75
white r. does not really think · STEIN 815:17
white r. is the cancer · SONT 804:73
race horse think of a fine r. h. · MOZA 601:46
racehorse keep…any r. · CHES 211:38
racehorses associated…with r. · SAKI 710:34
races after they have won a few r. · DIOR 275:23
appointed you r. and tribes · KORAN 479:89
Brings forth its r. · LONG 516:59
composed of two distinct r. · LAMB 487:51
glory of rulers or of r. · BEVE 85:26
so-called white r. · FORS 331:41
war of r. · MUIR 602:66
worst horse at the r. · MASE 559:39
Rachel R. weeping for her children · BIBLE 105:78

seven years for R. · BIBLE 87:90
racial As a matter of r. pride · FEIF 319:84
r. antipathies…of the Old World · BORAH 144:87
racing Ocean r. is like standing · HEATH 390:25
r. car whose hood · MARI 550:53
rack Leave not a r. behind · SHAK 774:94
stretched on the r. · POPE 662:80
racket job or a r. · KNIG 476:15
ruins the whole r. · LOOS 517:84
whar dar is so much r. · TRUTH 869:51
rackets matched our r. to these balls · SHAK 745:30
Rackrent Sir Patrick R. lived · EDGE 299:96
racquets boxing with r. · BARR 61:92
radiance fountain itself of heavenly r. · MILT 579:82
its r. would grow · RAND 678:15
white r. of Eternity · SHEL 786:7
radiant cherry blossoms…r. · ANON 22:67
radical charge that an idea is r. · GALB 343:90
never dared be r. · FROST 339:6
R. chic · WOLFE 920:91
r. is a man · ROOS 696:47
radicalism feeling…R. cannot allay · CHES 211:41
radicals Few r. have good digestion · BUTL 178:80
French R. and German · MARX 558:4
radio BBC R. is a never-never land · SAFER 708:95
Down for a new r. · SNYD 803:51
everything you hear on the r. · MANK 545:59
largely on television and r. · HUMP 422:19
Public r. is a ghetto · KEIL 460:71
than ever existed in r. · SARN 714:32
radioactive bury their r. fuel · LAMB 487:65
radish like a forked r. · SHAK 743:58
Raffles 'Cricket,' said R. · HORN 414:37
raft Come Back To The R. · FIED 322:28
put to sea on a wooden r. · HEYE 401:72
rag that Shakespearian r. · BUCK 165:34
rage Dancing is a frenzy and a r. · DAVI 254:31
fury, and r. of mortal men · BURT 174:79
let Death wreck all his r. · MILT 582:46
Maintain your r. · WHIT 905:26
no r., like love to hatred turned · CONG 231:23
Pity is lost in r. and fear · CARL 192:11
R. is the only quality · BRES 151:20
r. of Caliban · WILDE 908:1
r. of competition · DYER 297:52
R., r. against the dying · THOM 853:81
repressed their noble r. · GRAY 369:16
Strong without r. · DENH 261:92
such an immodest r. · CAREW 190:49
void of noble r. · TENN 843:33
Why do the heathen r. · BIBLE 94:82
with hard-favoured r. · SHAK 746:42
worth more than force and r. · LAFO 485:4
ragged a r. virtue · OTWAY 631:29
If I was very r. and very jolly · DICK 268:34
raggedness looped and windowed r. · SHAK 763:78
rags no scandal like r. · FARQ 318:56
r., and hags, and hideous wenches · COLE 227:23
r. of time · DONNE 279:41
righteousnesses are as filthy r. · BIBLE 104:63
rows of disgusting old r. · LAWR 494:11
You had better be in r. · DISR 277:89
rag-time Lurching to r.-t. tunes · SASS 716:57
raid r. on the inarticulate · ELIOT 308:23
rail never…any body else to r. at me · CONG 230:94
r. against all the firstborn · SHAK 749:45
r. at the ill · TENN 846:1
railed r. on Lady Fortune · SHAK 749:46
railroad r.…you blasted its rocks · RUSK 704:38
ride on the r. · THOR 857:93
railroads country of r. · CHEE 209:4
Player with R. · SAND 712:91
rails r. are to a locomotive · RIVE 688:2
r. into the Grand Stand · SOME 803:67
wilderness of freight and r. · CRANE 243:17
railway climax to the r. age · TAYL 837:12
picking daisies on the r. · WODE 919:56
populous r. station · THOR 858:7
read out over a r. station · JAMES 433:29
threatened its life with a r.-share · CARR 197:32
raiment having food and r. · BIBLE 123:78
parted his r., and cast lots · BIBLE 116:63
thieves, which stripped him of his r. · BIBLE 115:37
rain after the r.…never a stain · SHEL 783:41
as the r. cometh down · BIBLE 104:56
As the r. over the town · VERL 879:66
cloud which had outwept its r. · SHEL 785:94

columns of the old r. forest · AMIS 15:99
continually wetted with r. · STEV 821:74
dissolve it in r. · SHEL 783:39
doctrine shall drop as the r. · BIBLE 90:55
drees the wind and r. · SMITH 801:25
droppeth as the gentle r. · SHAK 740:79
Dull roots with spring r. · ELIOT 305:52
fall like r. · AUDEN 39:80
flat calm with drizzling r. · BOWEN 147:30
glazed with r. water · WILL 913:44
hail, or r., or any snow · TENN 847:52
Hath the r. a father? · BIBLE 93:72
I saw r. falling · STEV 824:38
It can r. for 100 days · WAUGH 891:7
left Him in the r. · STUD 827:5
Let the sky r. potatoes · SHAK 744:81
like a drop of r. · BYRON 180:45
like sunshine after r. · SHAK 733:56
like wet sidewalks cause r. · BLOU 137:8
lying in the r. outside greengrocers · BRAD 148:56
nor the clouds return after the r. · BIBLE 101:92
not even the r. · CUMM 248:11
old man…waiting for r. · ELIOT 305:39
Only the r. never tires · HUGH 419:52
Pale r. over · THOM 852:75
politician…in the r. · WHITE 903:99
r. also filleth the pools · BIBLE 96:46
r. Is full of ghosts · MILL 571:85
r. is over and gone · BIBLE 101:99
r. of bombs · WHITE 903:95
r. of gold · DAY 257:85
r.…of the failing stars · RICK 686:74
r. on my bicycle · LEE 500:45
r. on the neck · COOKE 236:42
R., r., and sun! · TENN 847:39
R.! R.! R.! · KEATS 457:97
ripple of r. · SWIN 832:18
send my roots r. · HOPK 413:10
singin' in the r. · FREED 336:37
smale r. downe can r.? · ANON 20:99
sound of abundance of r. · BIBLE 92:20
stand out here in the r. · BRADY 149:82
Still falls the R. · SITW 794:73
sun and the r. are flying · STEV 823:35
through the drizzling r. · TENN 843:28
to command the r. · PEPYS 647:30
tomorrow…acid r. · WYLIE 931:20
volleying r. · ARNO 33:45
Weather and r. · KIPL 473:66
wedding-cake left out in the r. · AUDEN 41:34
wind and the r. · SHAK 763:76
wind and the r. · SHAK 757:92
rainbow and the r. drawn · STEV 824:38
another hue Unto the r. · SHAK 739:30
awful r. once in heaven · KEATS 458:25
light as the r. · HARR 384:99
nation is a r. · JACK 431:7
r. and a cuckoo's song · DAVI 255:49
R. gave thee birth · DAVI 255:47
r. in the sky! · TENN 847:39
r. is enuf · SHAN 776:27
r. of his will · LOWE 520:44
simple blessing of a r. · ABSE 1:7
Somewhere over the R. · HARB 381:38
when I behold A r. · WORD 926:15
Who in the r. can draw · MELV 564:47
rainbows like a man…chasing r. · WODE 919:72
r. gave them promise · DICK 268:51
raindrops fresh as the r. on a statue's · WALC 885:81
R. Keep Fallin' on my Head · DAVID 253:21
rainfall in r. at morning · STEV 823:32
rainforest burning the r. · STING 824:49
rainmakers sweating r. · AMIS 15:99
rains droughts and flooding r. · MACK 533:15
Every time it r., it r. · BURKE 169:53
winter's r. and ruins · SWIN 832:19
raise Still r. for good · JOHN 441:20
The Lord shall r. me up · RALE 677:3
raisin like a r. in the sun? · HUGH 418:20
rake leene was his hors as is a r. · CHAU 208:71
woman is at heart a r. · POPE 661:49
rakes reformed r.…husbands · BRON 154:74
rally language designed to r. · SAFI 708:97
ram old black r. Is tupping · SHAK 759:52
rode upon a r. · SPEN 809:15
we often have to r. it · CUOMO 248:27

Ramah voice was heard in R. — BIBLE 105:78
ramble joins me in my R. — DICK 273:76
  The social r. ain't restful — PAIGE 634:87
rampallion r., you fustilarian! — SHAK 742:45
ramparts O'er the r. — KEY 465:76
rams fat of r. — BIBLE 91:89
Ramsgate visit to R. — CHES 211:45
ran didn't know how it r. — TAYL 838:26
  door flew open, in he r. — HOFF 406:53
  r. a hundred years — HOLM 408:89
  r. away with me — WILH 911:95
  r. both together — BIBLE 118:22
random Economic policy is r. — STEIN 815:30
  heap of r. sweepings — HERA 397:71
  r. element in the world — EDDI 298:83
Rangers R. and Celtic had both lost — DODD 278:6
ranges Something lost behind the R. — KIPL 473:49
ranging for that I was r. — DRAY 287:3
Rangoon from R. to Mandalay? — KIPL 470:86
rank elevate his mistress to his r. — BALZ 57:5
  holds on his r. — SHAK 747:93
  keep no r. nor station — LOWE 520:45
  lowest r. of every nation — JOHN 443:60
  man in higher r. — RUSK 704:15
  O, my offence is r.! — SHAK 754:99
  Political action is of second r. — MANN 546:76
  r. is but the guinea's stamp — BURNS 173:46
  r. of devoutly religious men — EINS 301:37
  r. pride, and haughtiness of soul — ADDI 6:32
rankles r....with Louisa — WHAR 901:51
ranks different r. of life — SMITH 797:37
  even the r. of Tuscany — MACA 526:67
  In the r. of death — MOORE 596:49
  well-ordered r. maintain — CRAB 242:83
ransomed R., healed, restored — LYTE 524:16
ransoming this world's r. — AQUI 28:28
rape cocktail...as r. is to love — CLAU 220:63
  commit r., murder — BARN 60:63
  don't want to see plays about r. — COOK 235:35
  man...can steal it (r.) — DWOR 296:46
  principle of procrastinated r. — PRIT 669:45
  r. and murder — NOON 618:58
  r.! a r.! — WEBS 894:86
  r. of every blessèd day — WILB 907:74
raped R. by rum — WRIG 930:83
rapes holy r. upon our will — CAREW 190:53
  If there are armed r. — TOOLE 863:13
Raphael R. paints wisdom — EMER 313:47
Raphaels talked of their R. — GOLD 362:72
rapid progress...will be r. — FRAN 335:17
  R. Reaction Force — ANON 25:75
rapids while shooting the r. — HILL 402:87
rapist unsuccessful r. — HEMI 394:25
rapists all men are r. — FREN 336:48
rapscallions kings is mostly r. — TWAIN 871:8
rapture first fine careless r.! — BROW 160:31
  love, and r.'s due — ROCH 691:51
  r. on the lonely shore — BYRON 180:43
  still r. of thy mien — WORD 929:63
raptures frantic with thy r. — HERR 399:39
  r. and roses of vice — SWIN 833:27
  r. were All air and fire — DRAY 287:5
rare as r. things will, it vanished — BROW 162:62
  Logic is r. — DOYLE 285:68
  Nothing is thought r. — FLET 328:74
  O r. Ben Jonson — JONS 450:47
  r....after the fall of a prince — ANON 18:70
  r. as a day in June — LOWE 520:31
  r....to take writers seriously — POWE 666:85
rarest r. of all women — SHAK 770:97
rarity r....I cannot but be fond of — ROCH 691:64
rascal r. have not given me medicines — SHAK 741:7
  rather be called a r. — JOHN 445:23
  stretch-mouthed r. — SHAK 770:91
rascality effect of prudence on r. — SHAW 779:15
  shocked by its r. — MENC 566:81
rascals r. use me! — DENN 262:2
  R., would you live for ever? — FRED 335:33
  Respected people are only r. — STEN 816:53
rash Be not r. — BIBLE 101:76
  look rather r. my dear — ASHF 35:94
  not splenative and r. — SHAK 755:35
  r. of...American filth — OSBO 630:13
raspberry Three farts and a r. — BARB 59:49
rat Droll r., they would — ROSE 697:68
  How now, a r.? — SHAK 754:5
  like a r. without a tail — SHAK 766:67

ship...associated with the giant r. — DOYLE 286:82
Taylled lyke a r. — BERN 81:48
  tyranny of 'the r. race' — THOM 855:42
  used to be the r. race — HOUL 414:40
  was an Irish r. — SHAK 749:59
rate r. of profit — SMITH 798:45
  wages...above their actual r. — SMITH 797:43
ratio increases in geometrical r. — MALT 543:15
  inverse r. to the importance — HUXL 425:80
  inverse r. to the number — HUXL 425:87
rational disagree Of creatures r. — MILT 581:30
  fully r., fully men — BERL 80:24
  hostile behavior is not r. — FULB 341:45
  irrational is r. — STEV 820:32
  process of a r. mind — HELL 392:60
rationality Appeals to r. — MELL 563:20
rats nearness of r. — WHITE 903:83
rattle care for the child's r. — JOHN 443:84
  infant breaks its r. — SADE 708:93
  pleasure of hearing 'em r. a little — FARQ 318:57
  r. of a globe — DRYD 289:56
  r. of the bones — ELIOT 306:59
  silencer on its r. — ACHE 3:45
  spoilt his nice new r. — CARR 196:97
  stuttering rifles' rapid r. — OWEN 632:51
  woman...the toy of man, his r. — WOLL 921:7
rattles put away their r., marbles — MORE 597:68
rattlesnake r. with a silencer — ACHE 3:45
  thought he saw a r. — CARR 197:34
Ravel R. toward the end of La Valse — LAMB 487:67
ravelled not r. and perplexed — JONS 450:62
raven locks were like the r. — BURNS 171:10
  Poe, with his r. — LOWE 520:32
  Quoth the r. — POE 656:24
  sad presaging r. — MARL 552:85
  smoothing the r. down — MILT 577:34
ravens Beast r. in its own avidity? — EBER 298:74
  doth the r. feed — SHAK 749:38
  r. brought him bread — BIBLE 92:17
  three r. sat on a tree — BALL 56:91
ravish except You r. me — DONNE 281:71
  murder and to r. — AYTO 45:16
  r. like enchanting harmony — SHAK 733:73
ravished r. always with her love — BIBLE 99:14
  r. this fair creature — FIEL 322:40
  r. with the whistling of a name — POPE 660:26
ravishing dear r. thing — BEHN 71:17
raw price of r. produce — RICA 684:32
  r. nerve ends of humanity — ANON 25:58
ray down with a flaming r. — BOND 139:52
  every r. of God's light — DOST 283:11
  eye diffused a quickening r. — WESL 899:9
  genuine night admits no r. — DRYD 288:49
  r. from the infinite source — HUXL 426:10
  r. of rays — DICK 270:92
  To find thy piercing r. — MILT 582:37
ray-gun President R.-G. — SCAR 717:90
Raymond R. like the Harvest Moon — FARJ 318:48
rays last r. of feeling — MOORE 596:47
  splendour borrows all her r. — POPE 659:98
razor hew blocks with a r. — POPE 659:88
  r. ceases to act — HOUS 416:82
  r. that threatens the throat — ANGE 17:31
razor-edge r.-e. of danger — WILD 911:82
razors R. pain you — PARK 638:65
RCA windows of the R. Building — THUR 859:39
reach add r. to power — ACHE 3:51
  daring beyond our r. — DELI 261:80
  He disdains all things above his r. — OVER 631:37
  meaner things are within her r. — ELIOT 303:98
  out of humanity's r. — COWP 241:55
  Religion...beyond all r. — WHIT 904:8
  resources...within your r. — PIND 651:18
  truth...beyond our r. — POPP 663:97
  within the r. of factory girls — SCHU 721:56
reaching without any irritable r. — KEATS 457:91
reaction habit of instant r. — SCHL 718:15
  opposed an equal r. — NEWT 612:72
  Vengeance is a personal r. — RENO 683:2
reactionaries conservatives and r. — VIDAL 881:3
  r. are paper tigers — MAO 548:11
reactionary r. is a somnambulist — ROOS 696:47
read advised him not to r. — GREG 372:96
  books were r. — BELL 73:66
  cannot or will not r. — HAYA 386:55
  go r. with thee — SHAK 731:94
  hares have no time to r. — BROO 156:21

haven't r. any of your books — JOYCE 452:2
  if he r. little — BACON 50:54
  I r., and sigh, and wish — HERB 397:97
  little I can r. — SHAK 764:13
  man ought to r. — JOHN 443:64
  never loved to r. — LEE 500:33
  never r. so far — SHAK 732:36
  no time to r. — BROO 156:21
  only r. what is truly good — STEIN 815:24
  Pick up and r. — AUGU 41:36
  Pleasure might cause her r. — SIDN 790:7
  r. about the war — HEMI 394:98
  r. a novel...gravest sins — WAUGH 892:35
  r., mark, learn, and inwardly digest — BOOK 141:86
  R. not to contradict and confute — BACON 50:52
  r. only the kind — KAFKA 453:24
  R. over your compositions — JOHN 444:98
  r. partly for information — SCHL 718:11
  R. somewhat seldomer — BROW 161:50
  r. strange matters — SHAK 766:83
  r. that stuff by myself — SALI 711:57
  r. the best authors — JONS 450:58
  r. the first 2 pages — JOYCE 452:97
  r. very hard — JOHN 443:70
  slowly r. — YEATS 932:33
  Stand still, traveller, and r.! — ANON 26:90
  teach a child to r. — BUSH 175:4
  things I once r. — SNYD 802:47
  wants to have r. — TWAIN 872:33
  We are what we r. — MANG 545:55
  What do you r., my lord? — SHAK 752:48
  What people r. most of the time — CRIT 245:61
  when you r. — GAUG 347:68
  where I r. and rhyme — WYATT 930:73
  Who'll r. that sort of thing? — PERS 648:69
  writes as fast as they can r. — HAZL 388:83
reader anyone finishing...great r. — ANON 25:62
  average r. read a novel — OCON 622:25
  breaks it gently to the r. — BIER 129:21
  Far from neglecting him [the r.] — ROBBE 688:10
  Gutenburg made everybody a r. — MCLU 536:65
  In reality, each r. reads — PROU 671:92
  motor...is the r. — CURT 249:46
  not say so to the r. — LAUT 493:76
  not to inform the r. — ACHE 3:43
  one r. in a hundred years — KOES 477:29
  produce an impression on the r. — BENN 76:53
  r....does not view — ROBBE 688:8
  r. is important to me — NABO 606:40
  r. must conclude — STARR 813:77
  r. seldom peruses a book — ADDI 6:9
  reception of the r. — TERE 849:80
  right r. of a good poem — FROST 339:19
  That ideal r. — JOYCE 452:98
  Will you be a r. — THOR 858:94
readers addresses each of its r. — TOCQ 861:85
  art for practitioners and r. — LEAV 494:91
  imprinted on the minds of his r. — BOLD 139:42
  poets...give their r. sleep — POPE 662:67
  r. better to enjoy life — JOHN 442:51
  r. how to read them — RUSH 703:91
  r. who are pleased with a book — CONN 233:67
  r. will find it very French — GISC 358:85
  so few good r. — VIDAL 881:10
  to which so many of my r. belong — CHES 211:47
reading As the art of r. — JAMES 434:65
  careful r. between the lines — MARA 548:22
  choose...leaders on the basis of...r. — BROD 153:57
  contemplation...more than his r. — AUBR 39:67
  finish r. one — GERA 350:25
  inclined to love r. — MONT 591:66
  I prefer r. — SMITH 800:85
  no taste for r. — SMOL 801:28
  not to pretend that r. is...passive — CARY 198:59
  Peace is poor r. — HARDY 382:74
  Promiscuous r. is necessary — MILT 579:63
  r. all the novels — HUGH 419:27
  r. books — HAZL 388:89
  r. is not idleness — SPEN 807:65
  R. isn't an occupation — ORTON 627:31
  R. is the basics for all learning — BUSH 175:98
  R. is to the mind — STEE 814:95
  R. it, however — MOORE 595:29
  r. of a white man's chuckle — ANGE 17:47
  r., writing and 'rithmetic — DICK 269:71
  so much eager r. — BELLI 72:42
  soul of r. — STER 817:75

substitute for r. it — BURG 167:87
the endlessness of r. — MANG 545:55
time is spent in r. — JOHN 444:7
worse crime…is not r. them — BROD 154:58
reads r. Incessantly — MILT 586:43
ready books…or which we are r. — FORS 332:56
jobs before they were r. — REST 683:16
merely r. to go home — KAIKO 454:33
Rapid Reaction Force to be r. — ANON 25:75
R. writing makes — JONS 450:59
Reagan bulldog into a R. poodle — STEEL 814:87
glory of Ronald and Nancy R. — WARR 889:76
governance of Ronald R. — BAKER 53:24
had it better than Nancy R. — NEW 612:56
mind of Ronald R. — NOON 617:55
President R. is a rhetorical roundheels — SAFI 708:1
R….hell of a king — ONEI 626:7
to R. the main fact was a vision — SHUL 790:93
real any less r. and true — SHAW 777:56
imaginary are the most r. — STEF 814:3
other than oneself is r. — MURD 604:93
r., honest…Boarding-school — AUST 43:81
r. price of everything — SMITH 797:42
r. truths and made-up truths — BARRY 61:93
Religion…something which is r. — WHIT 904:8
realism dislike of R. — WILDE 908:1
offspring of journalistic r. — WHITE 903:97
realities facts, not r. — GOLD 362:88
prose of the r. — CUOMO 248:31
reality absolute r. — HUGO 420:62
aspect of r. — HART 384:13
awesome r. to Rent Day — ANGE 17:45
Between the idea And the r. — ELIOT 306:71
bring them back to r. — KLEIN 476:11
Cannot bear very much r. — ELIOT 307:94
can't face r. nor deal with it — SHAW 779:30
choice is not between dream and r. — BANKS 58:34
circumstantial r. is — UPDI 874:88
consecrated to r. — BYRON 183:10
contribution to r. — THOM 853:99
covered the world of r. — MILL 572:14
craftsmen…have held R. down — SACK 708:88
creed and particular r. — MUNCH 603:81
destroys the discovery of r. — KRIS 480:14
discovery of r. — MURD 604:93
do not refer to r. — EINS 302:47
ethical r. of the individual — KIER 467:10
In r., killing time — SITW 794:86
In r., who am I? — FANON 317:45
make a picture of r. — LIPP 511:71
make r. bearable — PROU 670:72
manipulation of r. — DICK 265:61
more r. into a picture — HECHT 390:36
mugged by r. — ADEL 7:46
politicians…recreating r. — MARA 548:23
R….doesn't go away — DICK 265:59
r….is unendurable — CONN 233:79
R. is what I see — BURG 167:92
r….over public relations — FEYN 322:27
'r.' transcending the limits — AYER 44:9
r. was no less wonderful — SHIP 789:78
regulate imagination by r. — JOHN 447:78
remove all traces of r. — PICA 650:96
rhetoric passed for r. — BENT 78:83
salt of r. — BELL 73:64
Science provides a vision of r. — PAGE 633:79
sense of ultimate r. — BELL 71:27
speaks about r. — POPP 663:96
straining against r. — MCCA 528:3
taming of r. — UPDI 875:95
terrible r. of poverty — LEGU 501:60
thoughts have any relation to r. — CHES 211:60
tourist in other people's r. — SONT 804:74
upon which r. is written — MILL 572:16
way of operating on r. — PAZ 644:90
we eat r. sandwiches — GINS 357:60
Words…the great foes of r. — CONR 234:13
realization makes this r. bearable — NIEB 614:98
r. that to be sporting — SKIN 795:12
r. that we have denied…reality — PAGE 633:78
With this r. we turn — HERZ 401:59
realize dare you to r. it — HUST 424:49
realm better to improve his r. — ERAS 315:87
corrupted the youth of the r. — SHAK 730:66
estate of the r. — MACA 525:49
in na place of the R. — JAME 432:22
In the r. of science — STEI 816:47

invade the borders of my r. — ELIZ 309:60
One r., one people, one leader — ANON 22:56
provided this r. — QUIL 674:44
ready to defend the r. — PHIL 650:89
r., nation, or city — KNOX 476:18
r. of free song — LOWE 519:26
r. of ideas — MILL 571:1
r. of the Spirit — MATI 560:64
this r., this England — SHAK 734:8
turned out of the r. in my petticoat — ELIZ 309:56
realms constancy lives in r. above — COLE 226:7
existed in different r. — MEYER 568:30
great Anna! whom three r. obey — POPE 659:71
happy r. of light — MILT 580:98
hearts in one, your r. in one — SHAK 746:69
travell'd in the r. of gold — KEATS 456:76
unreal r. of the canals — MCCA 528:2
whatever r. to see — GOLD 361:39
reap r. where he hath sown — KIPL 472:13
that shall he also r. — BIBLE 122:39
reapers r., reaping early — TENN 839:45
reaping r. something new — TENN 840:81
rear Americans do not r. children — JARR 435:86
r. of your affection — SHAK 751:14
surprising the defenders from the r. — MANC 544:41
reascend fail to r. Self-raised — MILT 581:13
reason act under the guidance of r. — SPIN 810:31
asked one another the r. — SHAK 750:85
atheism…against…our r. — BURKE 169:38
before reaching the age of r. — SADE 708:93
believing what r. cannot — VOLT 883:46
beyond all r. — HAMM 379:6
Blotting out r. — GRAV 368:81
boundaries our r. — RODO 693:94
but a woman's r. — SHAK 729:25
cleverness and r. — STOWE 826:78
dark of r. grows — BETJ 84:11
dictates of r., religion, and morality — DICK 271:27
disgust is r.'s proper response — PAGL 634:80
Eyes And R….to study Flies? — POPE 662:81
find out the r. for it — LECA 499:21
form of human r. — LEVI 506:66
for some specific r. — RUSS 705:55
Give you a r. on compulsion? — SHAK 741:14
God gave [Adam] r. — MILT 579:74
governments…founded on r. — PARE 636:36
great r. to be sad — SHAK 750:73
hearing all manner of r.? — MILT 579:73
How noble in r. — SHAK 752:57
Human r. won — KHRU 467:3
if it be against r. — COKE 224:68
ignorance, his r. such — POPE 660:16
in erring R.'s spite — POPE 660:15
In R.'s ear they all rejoice — ADDI 6:27
It is not, therefore, r. — HUME 422:9
kills r. itself — MILT 578:62
lack of r. in the kitchen — NIET 615:23
Let's r. with the worst — SHAK 748:21
let us r. together — BIBLE 102:7
live in a world ruined by R. — MAMET 543:29
longing…for r. — CAMUS 187:88
lost everything except his r. — CHES 211:57
loved her against r. — DICK 271:34
man who can r. — LESS 505:46
man who listens to R. — SHAW 779:18
materials of r. and knowledge — LOCKE 514:17
men have lost their r.! — SHAK 748:7
more ascetic r. than…enjoyment — STARK 813:72
More than cool r. — SHAK 738:12
Music says nothing to the r. — BURG 167:96
nature of r. to perceive things — SPIN 810:27
not contrary to r. — HUME 422:8
not from r. but from love — GIDE 353:80
not his r., but his passions — STER 818:79
not to r. why — TENN 844:76
Now tell me the r. — SOUT 805:96
objects of human r. — HUME 422:13
Only r. can convince us — BELL 71:32
produces innovation without r. — SANT 714:18
prose which knows no r. — STEP 817:59
pursue my r. to an O altitudo! — BROW 158:64
reality…from the perspective of r. — PAGE 633:79
r. against reading! — SHAK 733:70
r. and energy…are necessary — BLAKE 134:37
r. and the will of God — ARNO 33:54
R., an ignis fatuus — ROCH 691:56
r. doth buckle and bow — BACON 46:43

r. down or deny everything — EMER 312:31
r. for being — FRAN 333:88
r. for being a professional — ROST 699:11
r. for having children — RUSS 706:60
r. for my rhyme — SPEN 810:18
r. for rejecting them — RUSS 705:41
r. I escaped — DOUG 283:15
r. is best and pleasantest — ARIS 29:53
r. is equally cogent — GASK 346:58
r. I should be the same? — AYTO 45:15
r. is identical with love — MACL 535:32
r., is naturally equal in all men — DESC 263:18
r. is not the subversion — STEV 820:57
R. is…the slave of the passions — HUME 422:7
r. knows nothing — PASC 641:23
r. of the strongest — LAFO 485:98
r. so many people — GOLD 362:91
r. straightens it out — LAFO 485:16
R. thus with life — SHAK 758:32
R. to rule — DRYD 291:17
R. to rule all — AURE 42:52
r. why I loved him — MONT 592:74
r. with one another — MOLI 590:45
Respect and r. — SHAK 733:62
rest may r. and welcome — BROW 162:68
right deed for the wrong r. — ELIOT 307:4
ruling passion conquers r. — POPE 660:3
Science…distrusts pure r. — MENC 565:73
there is r. to hope — JOHN 442:57
There's r. good — JONS 449:34
to perfect…the intellect or r. — SPIN 811:34
triumph of human r. — HAWK 386:32
vaster r. — THOM 854:27
voice of r. is stifled — BURKE 168:18
war…for such a stupid r. — MARY 558:17
what humanity, r….tells me — BURKE 168:12
what's the r.? — HARI 382:80
where we go is r. — PATC 642:48
with how little r. — JOHN 441:9
without the use of r. — LEON 504:21
words clothed in r.'s garb — MILT 581:23
worse appear The better r. — MILT 581:21
reasonable Man, being r. — BYRON 182:80
no r. man could have expected — HERB 397:81
r. man adapts himself — SHAW 779:17
right than be r. — NASH 609:99
The R. Man — HERB 397:83
reasonableness sweet r. of Jesus — ARNO 34:64
reasoning contain any abstract r. — HUME 422:15
knowledge…by r. — BACON 50:73
r. and belief…essential materials? — CARL 192:15
r. comes down to…feeling — PASC 641:22
r. to the test of experiment — LAVO 493:83
What has R. to do with…Painting — BLAKE 135:78
reasons bad r. for what we believe — BRAD 149:71
born, And he had r. — ROBI 690:30
five r. why men drink — ALDR 11:14
function…to make r. for husbands — ELIOT 303:92
Good r. must…give place — SHAK 748:15
heart has its r. — PASC 641:23
r. are as two grains of wheat — SHAK 739:41
r. for making war — FRED 335:32
r. that I quit going to the theatre — SALI 711:66
Strong r. make strange actions — SHAK 739:29
there are no r. — MO 589:22
two very cogent r. — JOHN 446:52
rebel bound to r. against — IBSEN 428:33
boy is a r. and an anarch — MILL 573:50
r….turning into an autocrat — DURR 296:39
Showed like a r.'s whore — SHAK 766:66
very r. to my will — SHAK 765:43
What is a r.? — CAMUS 187:94
rebelled or him who hath r. — MILT 583:85
rebellion a sort of mental r. — ORWE 628:65
between sycophancy and r. — BAKER 53:20
Courage, rashness, and r. — MARI 550:52
If r. was the certain consequence — MANS 547:99
I incite this meeting to r. — PANK 633:1
little r. now and then — JEFF 436:14
r. against being what he is — CABE 183:17
R. against tyrants — DAVI 256:70
r. is as the sin of witchcraft — BIBLE 91:89
R. lay in his way — SHAK 742:25
Twelve Highlanders…make a r. — ANON 26:87
women are in furious secret r. — SHAW 780:54
rebellious for the r. also — BIBLE 96:39
Hot and r. liquors — SHAK 749:39

r. dwell in a dry land — BIBLE 96:38
r. people — REED 682:88
revolting and a r. heart — BIBLE 105:70
rebelliousness centuries of r. — PRIE 668:24
rebels Cheering.a rout of r. — SHAK 743:59
r. from principle — BURKE 169:37
rebuke Open r. is better — BIBLE 100:58
r. of his people shall he take away — BIBLE 103:24
scorner heareth not r. — BIBLE 99:24
Thy r. hath broken my heart — BOOK 143:60
recant will not r. anything — LUTH 523:93
receipt Applause is a r. — SCHN 719:19
receive in giving that we r. — FRAN 334:98
more blessed to give than to r. — BIBLE 119:53
r. no letters in the grave — JOHN 447:70
skill to give as…to r. — QUIL 674:45
those who r. it — GOLD 361:37
whosoever shall not r. you — BIBLE 111:25
reception meets with a better r. — JOHN 443:66
r. of the reader — TERE 849:80
recesses dusty r. of their minds — LAWR 495:38
recession R. is when your neighbour — REAG 680:55
r. when your neighbour — TRUM 868:38
recessions four out of the last five r. — SAMU 712:80
recipe best r. for happiness — AUST 43:76
man must have a rare r. — LAMB 486:28
recipes r. that are always successful — VALE 876:14
recipient comforting…to be the r. — FOWL 332:70
reciprocity eternal r. of tears — OWEN 632:66
reciproque rewarded…with the r. — BACON 48:96
reckon if you could tell how to r. — SHAK 746:51
reckoning make at your own r. — TROL 866:86
re-clothe r.-c. us in our rightful mind — WHIT 906:63
recognition books…deserve r. — VIAN 880:77
cannot force a r. — KISS 475:89
displaced by the r. — WAGN 884:64
grace beyond r. — REID 682:95
hunger for r. and money — SELF 727:80
recognize as if I should r. it — DOYLE 285:74
not r. me by my face — TROL 867:6
r. the honourable Member — CHUR 217:99
r. your prime — SPARK 806:22
recollect does not r. where — JOHN 446:58
r. all the little events — WELL 897:60
We must r. — PITT 653:46
recollection alas! r. at hand — COWP 241:56
recommendation letter of r. — ADDI 6:16
recommendations opposite r. — SIMON 792:37
recompense r. is a pleasure — JOHN 441:23
reconcilement never can true r. — MILT 582:57
reconciliation r. with dullness — LOWE 521:59
record artistic r. created — ROCK 693:84
dreadful r. of sin — DOYLE 285:67
I think that's the r. — THOM 853:84
Poetry is a r. — SHEL 786:16
puts a r. on the gramophone — ELIOT 306:61
r. is fragmentary — WHIT 904:14
r. of his triumphant passage — KENN 463:23
r.…of our mother and father — FRAME 333:81
searched the r. for years — MENC 565:63
set down the following r. — FRAME 333:80
to r. what you want — HOLI 407:65
recording r., not thinking — ISHE 430:89
records half-a-dozen r. — SHAW 780:57
r. for both home runs — RODG 693:93
r. of the human spirit — MACL 535:41
r. prove the title good — ARLO 30:62
wise nation preserves its r. — HOWE 417:99
recover what has been lost — ELIOT 308:24
seldom or ever r. — SHAK 766:59
recreation guilty spice to this r. — WAUGH 892:35
play or r. — STUB 827:2
recruiting r. field for the militant — WRIG 929:72
rector accident happened to the r. — TROL 866:88
An ancestor was r. — YEATS 934:66
rectors curates lean, and r. fat — MACA 525:38
rectum portion of the r. — BELLI 72:42
red An Admiral r. — SITW 793:59
crimson r., blood r., wine r. — GALE 343:5
fiction…printed in r. ink — BOWEN 147:29
keep the r. flag flying. — CONN 232:55
November's leaf is r. — SCOTT 723:93
pessimist sees only the r. — SCHW 721:71
r. in the face — BENT 78:81
r. like crimson — BIBLE 102:7
R. lips are not so r. — OWEN 632:53
r. r. vitals of his heart — RANS 679:24

r. wheel barrow — WILL 913:44
r. with mirth — SHAK 770:84
rose is r. — ANON 20:7
tawdry yellow strove with dirty r. — POPE 660:5
[The R. Flag] is the funeral march — SHAW 781:91
The r. rose cries — TENN 845:92
took their r. straight — ACHE 2:33
two r. eyes that stare — RANS 679:27
unnatural r. and black — DICK 270:3
When in doubt wear r. — BLASS 136:90
red-branch R.-B. Knights — MOORE 596:48
redeemed Fear not: for I have r. thee — BIBLE 103:44
not r. from time — ELIOT 309:50
redeemer know that my r. liveth — BIBLE 93:64
redemption life's r. — STEV 820:41
married past r. — DRYD 288:38
Our great r. — MILT 575:92
Poetry is a means of r. — STEV 820:35
secret of r. — WEIZ 896:35
redfaced r. from eating and drinking — ABBO 1:1
Redgauntlet 'Then…' said R. — SCOTT 725:49
red-haired R.-H. Man's Wife — CARL 191:68
red-hot Last of the R.-H. — TUCK 870:63
r.-h. with drinking — SHAK 774:96
rediscover r. their humanity — TUTU 870:69
redress no r. for the present — DISR 276:44
r. of real grievances — PEEL 646:8
Things past r. — SHAK 734:14
reds R.…that shouuuuuuut — CARRA 194:58
reed And night this toppling r. — BLUN 137:10
bruised r. shall he not break — BIBLE 111:39
bruised r. shall he not break — BIBLE 103:43
clasped a r. — SHEL 787:28
Man is only a r. — PASC 641:24
r. shaken with the wind — BIBLE 111:34
sighing of a r. — BYRON 182:99
staff of this broken r. — BIBLE 103:35
staff of this bruised r. — BIBLE 92:39
reeducation r. of perception — DEWEY 264:44
reefs collection of r., rocks — MORT 599:13
Reekie Auld R.! — FERG 321:3
reel beheaded in the third r. — MILLS 574:72
earth shall r. to and fro — BIBLE 102:23
r. to and fro — BIBLE 102:23
r. to and fro — BIBLE 97:72
world must r. — BERR 82:61
reeling Love, the r. midnight through — PARK 638:61
reels threesome r.…foursome r. — BURNS 172:38
refer r. to Rule 1 — ITO 431:98
reference favourable r. to the Devil — CHUR 217:97
no r. to fun in any Act — HERB 397:82
references R. upon request — DAVIS 255:52
refine correct, insert, r. — SWIFT 832:96
r. our language — JOHN 441:28
refined Englishwoman is so r. — SMITH 800:94
more r., restricted, ceremonial — REAG 680:51
R. himself to soul — DRYD 292:49
refinement r. on the principle — BURKE 168:11
reflect gave Leibniz time to r. — FONT 329:89
r. that what people say — SMITH 799:74
reflection after long r. — GALL 344:14
buildings…the r. of society — PEI 646:15
habit of profound r. — CONR 235:18
humiliating r. — FERN 321:17
Mental r. is…more interesting — PIRS 652:27
objects of R. — LOCKE 514:18
probably a r. — HOPP 413:15
r. of your own minds — ASTE 36:20
truth of a r. — MONT 591:65
reflections Mortifying R. — CONG 231:21
reflex r. of a star — WORD 924:86
reflexes r.…caused in other people — BALD 53:31
reform All r. except a moral one — CARL 193:45
Beginning r. — WELL 897:61
party of progress or r. — MILL 570:63
r. a world — CARL 191:88
r. the old man — TWAIN 871:97
r. this little piece — MILLS 574:70
spirit of the R. Bill — PEEL 646:8
To innovate is not to r. — BURKE 169:49
reformation plotting some new r. — DRYD 290:2
reforming of R. itself — MILT 579:81
reformers All R., however strict — SMITH 799:81
drifting social r. — STRA 826:79
martyrs or r.—or both — CHAR 206:27
R. are going into hiding — SHEV 788:74
we're law r. — HUMP 422:18

refrain still remember the r. — MACA 524:26
with a happy r. — FREED 336:37
refreshment R. after toil — MILT 578:42
refrigerator keep a martini in the r. — DE 264:36
refrigerators r.…great modern — WARH 889:64
refuge eternal God is thy r. — BIBLE 90:59
God is our r. — SCOT 725:62
God is our r. and strength — BIBLE 95:24
last r. of a scoundrel — JOHN 444:8
Lord, which is my r. — BIBLE 96:54
Paradise shall be the r. — KORAN 479:92
r. from distress — WORD 928:54
r. from home life — SHAW 777:93
r. open to every man — BABE 45:22
safe r. for the exile — GARI 346:47
so easy to take r. in — IBSEN 428:35
thou hast been our r. — BOOK 143:63
thy wings shall be my r. — BOOK 143:54
refugees Serbs out, Nato in, r. back — ROBE 689:21
refusal Every known class of r. — SOME 803:67
every r. to act — REED 682:88
r. of language is a death — BART 62:20
refuse an offer he can't r. — PUZO 673:21
I r. to become a seeker — RICH 685:55
I r. to send anyone else — RANK 679:19
large r. bin — BAIN 52:12
mind will very generally r. — TROL 867:5
no just government should r. — JEFF 436:16
people r. to see me — ELLI 311:88
r. in respect of our child — BIBLE 107:28
refute r. it thus — JOHN 443:75
regalia Great Queen in her r. — GAY 347:74
regard have as great a r. for religion — OCAS 621:16
r. the law courts — INGR 429:60
r. to their own interest — SMITH 797:39
Should be without r. — SHAK 768:13
Unconditional positive r. — ROGE 694:9
Victorian r. for the pride of people — PRIT 669:56
without r. to your happiness — PECK 645:6
regeneration r.…into a new state — ELIOT 303:81
Regent's Park in the sun, in R. P. — WOOLF 922:31
regime in love…a political r. — LESS 505:43
we enter a new r. — DOUG 284:34
regiment breasts for r. — MARL 551:58
kings, when r. is gone — MARL 552:01
led his r. from behind — GILB 355:32
Monstrous R. of Women — KNOX 476:17
r.'s in 'ollow square — KIPL 471:89
region airy r. thrilling — MILT 575:99
r. is facing a deep abyss — HUSS 423:41
r. where 'twas born — MARV 555:57
regions r. mild of calm and…air — MILT 577:25
r. of sin and falsity — MILT 579:73
r. of sorrow, doleful shades — MILT 580:97
unknown r. preserved — ELIOT 304:3
views…the r. of the sky — ENNI 314:70
register r. of the crimes and miseries — IRVI 430:78
regress r. is…downfall — BACON 48:2
regret at last and vain r. — ROSS 698:99
If that plane leaves…you'll r. it — EPST 314:80
Old Age a r. — DISR 276:45
one r. in life — ALLEN 12:47
only possible r. I have — BORO 145:99
only r. in the theatre — BARR 61:97
r. can die! — TENN 844:52
r. that I have but one — HALE 377:78
r. very much that — HOMER 409:26
said goodbye to without r. — HARD 381:41
seldom spoken with greater r. — BALD 54:50
wild with all r. — TENN 842:8
regrets Do I have r.? — CLIN 222:6
end up with the right r. — MILL 572:11
follies which a man r. most — ROWL 701:53
regular icily r. — TENN 845:78
regularity Genius and r. — GAIN 342:85
regulation The R. Act — WILDE 910:65
regulations cannot frame r. — HAWT 386:34
rehabilitation sad, refusing r. — KIRK 475:87
rehearsal Comedy of 'The R.' — JOHN 446:64
rehearsed if I had r. you — YEATS 933:49
Reich greater part of the R. — GOEB 359:8
reign called upon some day to r. — HARD 381:39
coined in some r. — LAMB 486:43
dead r. — ZOLA 937:4
govern is to r. — MIRA 587:77
lazy, long, lascivious r. — DEFOE 258:16
Omnipotent but friendless is to r. — SHEL 785:77

r. had here its last	MILT 575:96
r. in this horrible place	COWP 241:54
r. of chaos and old Night	MILT 581:12
reigning r. over a fourth-class nation	JAY 436:2
reigns arrangement into three r.	GUED 374:27
Dunce the second r.	POPE 662:64
reincarnated If I were r.	FAUL 319:72
reindeer Can R. Fly?	HIGH 402:84
sleigh, and eight tiny r.	MOORE 594:16
reinforcement r. of the State	CAMUS 187:95
reins try the r.	BIBLE 105:76
reinvent r. himself	BURU 174:84
reject those who r. you	WHIT 906:54
rejected despised and r. of men	BIBLE 104:50
rejection concise, slighting r. slip	HELL 392:68
eventual r.	LEBO 499:8
use the r. as an excuse	ANGE 17:42
rejoice before Him, and r.	KETHE 465:75
before him and r.	SCOT 725:64
fortunate, I r. at it	SHAK 748:4
I r. that America has resisted	PITT 652:40
R., and be exceeding glad	BIBLE 109:83
r. and be glad	BIBLE 97:78
r. for a moment	YUAN 936:87
R. in the Lord alway	BIBLE 123:60
R., O young man	BIBLE 101:91
R.! R.! R.!	HEATH 390:22
R., the Lord is King!	WESL 900:13
R. with them that do r.	BIBLE 120:82
that wanted to r.	SURR 829:39
rejoicing come again with r.	BIBLE 98:91
related men to whom they are r.	GILM 356:51
relation mental r. with a woman	LAWR 494:19
nobody like a r.	THAC 849:88
No cold r. is a zealous citizen	BURKE 169:43
poor r. is the most irrelevant	LAMB 487:61
some occult r.	JOHN 441:25
relations altering the old r.	CARL 191:82
even one's own r.	WILDE 909:27
great men have their poor r.	DICK 270:94
memory…all its clear r.	ELIOT 305:29
r. of…Government and…people	REED 682:88
unreasonably large stock of r.	SHAW 781:1
whatever their r. with men	FREN 336:48
relationship a r. with Ms Lewinsky	CLIN 221:98
if we have that r.	EDDI 298:85
lifelong r….divorce will never	MORR 599:10
outside this work r.	MARX 557:96
r. between man and man	ROUS 701:48
remains of the 'special r.'	BENN 75:18
special r.	CHUR 217:93
special r. with the United States	ACHE 2:29
their mutual association and r.	PLATO 655:2
women see the r. between objects	FOWL 332:67
relationships don't spend…in r.	BRAD 148:56
extra-marital r.	ALLEN 12:55
r. of color or form	ROTH 700:34
such r. as our minds	LEBON 498:4
sum of connections and r.	MARX 558:9
relative set out…In a r. way	BULL 165:52
Success is r.	ELIOT 307:7
relatives people your r. hate	HAMM 380:19
relativism R. implies…indifference	VAN 876:22
relaxation form of r. to me	HAMM 379:12
release illusory r.	UPDI 875:95
inescapable, imperative need for r.	FEIN 319:85
prisoner's r.	SIDN 790:10
relic cased up, like a holy r.	WEBS 895:10
rob the r.	DRYD 291:13
sad r. of departed worth!	BYRON 179:13
relics hallowed r.	MILT 576:2
R. from the past	CHEE 209:98
relief approaches the effect of r.	MICH 569:37
certain r. in change	IRVI 430:84
experience r. when one returns	COUP 238:91
for the r. of the body	RICH 685:47
For this r. much thanks	SHAK 751:95
great r. to reach this	SKIN 795:12
liquor is the only mechanical r.	HEMI 394:11
r. and depth	GOYA 365:30
sleep provides r.	CHAM 204:70
religion all the r. I want	HALD 377:76
anger about r.	HALI 378:90
any r., by any sect	KRIS 480:13
Art and R….two roads	BELL 71:28
As to r.	PAINE 634:91
as well as in r.	JUNI 453:10

As with the Christian r.	ORWE 627:41
basic command of r.	TOYN 864:32
belief imposed by r.	KRIS 480:14
black face and a different r.	EDWA 300:18
broken down by Age, Sex, and R.	MACR 538:18
brothels with bricks of R.	BLAKE 134:42
can't talk r. to a man	SHAW 780:41
Christianity…man's r.	WELD 897:40
Christianity was the r.	SWIFT 832:13
cult is a r. with no…power	WOLFE 920:94
do the same by their r.	DICK 271:26
drunk on whiskey or r.	MENC 565:74
each r. only one of the seven colours	BLAV 136:92
either on r. or policy	RUSK 704:27
established as a r.	LEWIS 508:96
Football is like a r.	PELE 646:18
For my r.	BROW 158:53
freed from his r.	SAINT 709:21
freedom of r.	JEFF 437:19
handmaid to r.	BACON 46:50
happens by accident…becomes a r.	WRIS 930:86
hearing about r. even more	MITF 589:7
Hoo-doo…was an unorganized r.	REED 682:86
If r. is only a garment	BONH 140:59
if R. were intended	BUTL 177:44
in both science and r.	SAGAN 708:6
indirect way to plant r.	BROW 158:71
In matters of r….I never give any advice	CHES 211:37
in the Roman Catholic r.	TROL 866:88
late to trust the old r.	LOWE 520:52
leave him for r.	SPARK 806:16
life smashes r.	NERU 611:43
literature is a substitute for r.	ELIOT 306:76
Malay r. and custom	PANG 636:28
manners and r.	MONT 591:63
man's r. is the chief fact	CARL 193:31
man talks loudly against r.	STER 818:79
Men will wrangle for r.	COLT 228:52
My r. and my art	JOHN 439:67
no reason to bring r. into it	OCAS 621:16
not impossibilities enough in r.	BROW 158:62
of any r., or party or profession	COLE 227:26
One r. is as true as another	BURT 174:82
original feature of any r.	PAINE 634:94
paradox of high r.	NIEB 614:98
Philistine of genius in r.	ARNO 34:65
philosophy bringeth…to r.	BACON 48:95
plant our r. in Paris	LESL 504:30
prophecy, and r., all in one	RUSK 704:33
Pure r. and undefiled	BIBLE 124:9
reject me on account of my r.	BELL 72:52
R. and art…from the same root	CATH 200:94
R. blushing veils	POPE 662:82
R. but a childish toy	MARL 552:82
R. Caesar never knew	COWP 241:52
R. does not banish mirth	WALT 888:53
r. has had its day	BENN 77:58
r., history…would be useless	BALZ 58:20
R. is far more acute than science	FORS 331:39
R. is something which stands	WHIT 904:8
R. is the sigh	MARX 557:94
r. is to do good.	PAINE 634:95
R. is what a man does	WHIT 904:11
r. is whatever…most interested in	BARR 61:88
r., knavery, and change	BEHN 71:13
r. most prevalent in our northern	BURKE 168:11
r….not simply morality	ARNO 34:61
r. of gold	BAGE 51:85
r. of money	GAUT 347:72
r. of science	LEWIS 508:95
R.'s in the heart	JERR 437:38
r. to make us hate	SWIFT 830:66
R….tragedy of mankind	WILS 914:70
r….true remedy for superstition	BURKE 168:13
r….will be replaced by poetry	ARNO 34:68
r. without science is blind	EINS 301:36
r. would still be holy and divine	BAUD 65:75
respect the other fellow's r.	MENC 566:75
revolution of 1789 is her political r.	LAMA 485:23
rules of my r. from Rome	BROW 158:56
rum and true r.	BYRON 182:77
Self-righteousness is not r.	BRON 155:82
Sensible men are all the same r.	DISR 277:90
serve the French in place of a state r.	BIER 129:35
snare to R.	TAYL 837:23
standard of r., intelligence, and virtue	SMIL 797:34
Superstition…r. of feeble minds	BURKE 169:40

That is my r.	SHAW 779:40
'Theosophy' is the essence of all r.	BLAV 136:91
this man's r. is vain	BIBLE 124:8
true r. of America	MAIL 540:60
when r. was strong	SZASZ 834:61
wisest r.	HAIL 377:68
with r. and fear	JONS 449:27
religions knit and break r.	SHAK 762:48
natural language of all r.	STAEL 812:53
of all great r.	TEMP 838:33
R. are kept alive by heresies	BREN 151:15
religious All known r. beliefs	DURK 296:33
Art among a r. race	FUSE 342:75
belief is made r.	CUPI 248:34
be virtuous—be r.	SCOTT 725:60
Casting a dim r. light	MILT 577:22
commit…to any r. belief	WAUGH 892:21
decline of r. belief	FREUD 337:56
feeling…about some r. expressions	RABI 676:79
first expounder of our r. belief	SPEKE 806:35
hope I will be r. again	FLEM 327:61
labour movement was truly r.	WOLFE 920:97
Man…a r. animal	BURKE 169:38
natural r. sense	LAWR 495:35
private parts…and his r. opinions	BUTL 178:83
r. inquiries	GIBB 352:61
R. law is like…grammar	SACKS 707:84
r. system…green Chartreuse	SAKI 710:31
r. ties…social pedigree	WOLFE 920:96
same r. experience	ROTH 700:34
seem to be r.	BIBLE 124:8
take an almost r. view	HOYLE 417:4
troubled with r. doubt	CHES 212:92
virtually r. prophecy	NISB 616:39
We are a r. people	DOUG 284:33
religious-good Good, but not r.-g.	HARDY 381:48
religiously follows r. the new	THOR 857:89
religiousness center of true r.	EINS 301:37
reliques religious race produces r.	FUSE 342:75
relish some r. of the saltness	SHAK 742:39
relishes lullings and the r. of it	HERB 398:1
reluctantly r., unexpectedly	MORT 599:17
remain but the rocks r.	HERB 397:87
days go by, I r.	APOL 27:17
nothing will r.	HOUS 415:48
'Shall r.'?	SHAK 769:64
so r. ignorant	GREG 372:96
south of us r.	JOHN 440:94
remains cut up what r.	KIPL 471:93
r. an Englishman!	GILB 354:95
remake Myself I must r.	YEATS 934:60
remark can't stand…rude r.	WILL 912:16
fowl, blinking at you without r.	ELIOT 303:97
Which I wish to r.	HARTE 384:16
remarkable nothing left r.	SHAK 765:52
r. thing about Shakespeare	GRAV 368:85
to wish to be r.	HOLM 408:90
remarks r. are not literature	STEIN 815:13
remedies encumbering it with r.	TOLS 862:4
not apply new r.	BACON 49:25
prescribes the r.	MOLI 590:45
r. oft in ourselves	SHAK 761:26
When r. are past	SHAK 759:66
remedy Auntie Maggie's…r.	FORM 331:27
Death is the r.	CHAM 204:70
desperate…dangerous r.	FAWK 319:81
for the deid r. is none	DUNB 294:7
know not how to r.	KYD 482:49
no r. against this consumption	SHAK 742:43
r. for everything except death	CERV 203:46
r. is worse than the disease	BACON 49:13
sought the r.	SHAK 750:85
Things without all r.	SHAK 768:13
What is the r.?	SHAK 757:95
remember Ah yes! I r. it well	LERN 504:24
cannot but r. such things	SHAK 768:30
cannot r. anyone ever asking	REAR 681:69
day I can already r.	VALL 876:20
if thou wilt, r.	ROSS 697:83
I r., I r., The fir trees	HOOD 410:38
I r., I r., The house	HOOD 410:41
I r. watching myself	RHYS 684:30
must r. this	HUPF 423:40
never r. whether it snowed	THOM 853:1
r. Degas	PISS 652:34
R. First to possess his books	SHAK 774:90
R. me when I am gone	ROSS 697:78

R. that you are an Englishman — RHOD 684:23
R. thee? — SHAK 752:34
R. the rights — GLAD 358:91
r. what is past — HALI 378:88
thou r. and I forget — SWIN 832:16
To r. is far worse — BENU 78:86
who I r. he was — SEXT 728:18
Who will r. — SASS 717:76
wrong people r. Vietnam — HERR 399:31
ye want to r. — KELM 461:80
remembered Campbell-Bannerman is
   r. chiefly — BENT 78:82
names…freshly r. — SHAK 746:59
r.…for the invention of a mouse! — DISN 275:33
r. poor Julian — HEMI 394:12
surest way not to be r. — MAIL 540:54
tranquillity r. in emotion — PARK 638:66
remembrance book of r. was written — BIBLE 106:21
first…to my r. I ever saw — PEPYS 647:40
flood of r. — LAWR 494:94
Makes the r. dear — SHAK 762:40
Mournful and never-ending R. — POE 656:26
My r. is very free — SHAK 757:87
r. of things past — SHAK 771:15
rosemary, that's for r. — SHAK 755:23
this do in r. of me — BIBLE 121:6
reminiscences old have r. — SAKI 710:33
R. make one feel — SHAW 777:48
some of your grosser r. — WOOL 923:57
remission Without…no r. — BIBLE 124:92
remnants r. of such a beautiful habit — ALME 13:65
remodified We can be r., changed — DOUG 284:36
remonstrance all complaint and r. — MACA 526:73
remorse hottentot, without r.! — SITW 793:58
r., my worm — RIMB 688:98
R., the fatal egg — COWP 241:61
What says Monsieur R.? — SHAK 741:98
with as little r. — SHAK 743:79
remorseless treacherous and r. — SHAW 778:84
remote inconceivably r. — WELLS 898:74
removed cannot be r., but abideth — BIBLE 98:90
It ought to be r. — BEEC 69:58
r. from contact with…life — PRIT 669:47
r. from the sphere — KING 469:63
remuneration r. for…footballer — ANON 21:36
renaissance antiquity and its R. — KLEE 475:6
Leonardo da Vinci and the R. — WELL 897:48
r. is a logical link — MASA 559:20
R. was simply the green end — FOWL 332:68
rend time to r. — BIBLE 100:70
render perfumes…more they r. — WEBS 894:75
r. to every one his due — JUST 453:13
rendezvous r. with Death — SEEG 726:70
renegade whips to kennel The r. — RANS 679:27
renewal Boston…Urban R. — MAIL 540:55
renovator that great r. of matter — OVID 631:47
renown high r., riches, and royaltie — DUNB 294:5
Some, for r., on scraps — YOUNG 935:79
rent like r. and wages — SMITH 798:45
r. everything — KOSI 480:4
r. out my room — ALLEN 12:50
r. we pay — GREN 373:3
to go on paying the r. — TURN 870:67
Rentacrowd R. Ltd. — SIMP 792:45
rent-day awesome reality to R. D. — ANGE 17:45
rentiers indistinguishable from r. — ROBI 690:38
renunciation act of r. — MORAN 596:56
beautiful things made by r. — DEGAS 259:29
repair friendship in constant r. — JOHN 442:36
reparation never make r. — JAMES 434:58
repartee majority…the best r. — DISR 276:58
repeal method to secure the r. — GRANT 367:56
repeat condemned to r. it — SANT 714:19
does no harm to r. — LESS 505:42
r. in one period — RENO 683:9
shall have to r. that — HOUS 416:87
those things that r. and r. — WILD 911:88
what they hear, they r.! — SITW 794:64
repel retard what we cannot r. — JOHN 442:43
repelled I am r. by those — REDON 681:75
only r. by man — INGE 429:51
repent all men every where to r. — BIBLE 119:51
Dead men never r. — DICK 266:90
It doth r. me — SHEL 784:71
r. at leisure — CONG 231:1
r. in dust and ashes — BIBLE 94:79
r. in haste — CONG 231:2

r. it from my very soul — SHAK 731:97
R. what's past — SHAK 754:11
R. ye: for the kingdom of heaven — BIBLE 108:74
   when one cannot r.? — SHAK 754:1
repentance R. is the virtue of weak — DRYD 287:18
R.…want of power to sin — DRYD 292:58
sinners to r. — BIBLE 111:20
sinners to r. — BIBLE 114:7
Try what r. can — SHAK 754:1
repetition r. of the wrong way — DURR 296:41
repetitions use not vain r. — BIBLE 110:97
reply heartening and the strong r. — EMPS 314:63
not to make r. — TENN 844:76
sportive kind r. — GRAY 369:7
third, the R. Churlish — SHAK 750:91
report composed as a conference r.? — GRIS 373:19
good r. maketh the bones fat — BIBLE 99:34
not too proud to r. — DANA 251:81
r. of an aspect — LIPP 511:70
r. of my death — TWAIN 872:31
r. of valour — SHAK 757:81
r. on what I know — FRIS 338:75
r. what he means — ANON 23:92
the right to r. events — ORWE 629:93
they have committed false r. — SHAK 745:23
Who hath believed our r.? — BIBLE 104:50
reporters gallery in which the r. sit — MACA 525:49
reports daily r. are submitted — STEAD 813:84
r., films, phonograph records? — RODC 693:87
r. that I took the loss badly — DOLE 278:13
repose appreciate the charm of r. — LIVI 512:83
give thy r. To the wet sea-boy — SHAK 743:53
hushed in grim r. — GRAY 370:34
In Claude's landscape all is…r. — CONS 235:25
No r. for Sir Walter — SCOTT 725:59
r. implicitly on — JEFF 436:18
r. is taboo'd — GILB 354:15
r. of a pacific station — ADAMS 4:62
seek r. In listlessness — WORD 925:90
sigh for thy r. — WESL 900:18
repositories r. of the marvellous — DIOR 275:24
representation Taxation without r. — OTIS 630:19
Tragedy is…a r. — ARIS 29:54
without r. — TOYN 864:26
representations just r. of general — JOHN 443:78
representative being your r. — BELL 72:52
most r., the physical scientists — SNOW 802:38
r. of wealth — MILL 570:59
representatives r. of the people — WHIT 902:67
repressed being persecuted and r. — ROLL 695:33
repression r. of the high hope — WHIT 904:9
reproach common r. is true — SOCR 803:53
common term of r. — BERG 79:92
escape r. — JOHN 442:38
lexicon of…ridicule and r. — SAFI 708:96
reproduce cannot be expected to r. — HOLM 408:1
reproduction Strangelove R. — COUP 239:99
reptile of the fish and r. — LOWE 520:47
reptiles fishes and r. — BRYAN 163:9
poisonous r. — GERA 350:26
republic architects of our r. — KING 468:35
At its birth, the r. — LAMA 486:24
despair of the R.! — WHAR 901:45
How beautiful the R. was — DURR 296:37
Love the Beloved R. — FORS 332:53
rarely happens that a r. — MACH 533:99
r. has been much more powerful — ADDI 5:7
R. has no need for scientists — COFF 224:64
r. of conscience — HEAN 389:13
R. of equals — BABE 45:22
The R. will be conservative — THIE 851:52
true R. — ANTH 27:8
republican on r. principles — SHAW 777:55
R. form of government — SPEN 807:44
R. landslide on Nov 8 — CUOMO 248:32
The R. Party — STEV 820:62
unaware that baseball was a
   R. sport — ROBB 689:16
vote for Hollywood as a R. — WALL 886:2
Republicans If R. will stop — STEV 820:50
its members are now R. — ONEI 626:11
R.…get elected — OROU 627:24
republics Large r. seem — PALM 636:23
Mischiefes to Churches, to R. — PRYN 672:93
perfect r. are a perfect nonsense — FOWL 332:65
R. end by wealth — MONT 593:95
repugnance historical r. to woman — PAGL 634:80

repulsion Attraction and r. — BLAKE 134:37
reputation At ev'ry word a r. dies — POPE 659:72
bad r. is like a hangover — PRES 667:8
better for the r. — KEYN 466:92
dignity has descended over his r. — ATLAS 37:37
her scandalous r. — SITW 793:60
I have offended r. — SHAK 765:35
injured no man's r. — LOVE 519:17
lover's bad r. — NAPO 607:67
made himself of no r. — BIBLE 123:54
man's r. outlasts his munny — BILL 130:48
purest treasure…Is spotless r. — SHAK 734:99
r. for being difficult — MATT 561:68
r. for eccentricity — SHAR 776:45
r. for honesty — JONS 450:53
r. for wisdom and honour — BIBLE 101:86
R. is an idle…imposition — SHAK 760:79
r. is at stake — SHAK 757:8
r. of five-and-twenty — DRYD 288:22
r. of having read — THUR 860:58
r. of understanding — DRYD 288:44
R., r., r.! — SHAK 760:78
Seeking the bubble r. — SHAK 749:50
shook hands with R. — WEBS 895:11
so high a public r. — FRIE 337:65
the r. of benevolence — SHER 788:57
unenviable r. — THOR 858:4
Until you've lost your r. — MITC 588:5
women as the r. of men — MONT 591:66
wrecks a woman's r. — COLE 227:30
reputations murdered r. of the week — CONG 231:25
true fuller's earth for r. — GAY 347:82
request first r. for my resignation — DARM 253:6
r.…at my departure — EMMET 313:59
requests let your r. be made known — BIBLE 123:60
timid r., invites denial — SENE 727:93
requiem continent's violent r. — DUNC 295:12
required r. neither genius nor knowledge — JOHN 442:54
that which is r. of him — GILL 356:42
requirement first r. of a statesman — ACHE 2:35
primary r. for a writer — STAEL 812:51
requirements meet the barest r. — MCEW 531:66
unfortunate r. — SHAR 776:41
requisite It is r. from time to time — JEVO 438:48
requite lest her r. thee — BIBLE 107:44
rescue come to our r. — YOUR 935:84
rescuers had to r. themselves — TIME 861:75
r. the dead — IGNA 428:42
To r. our children — JORD 450:66
rescuers r. had to rescue themselves — TIME 861:75
research design of scientific r. — LEWO 508:9
Effective r. scarcely begins — KUHN 481:35
supply plenty of r. — FALU 317:41
researches r. no end to our r. — MONT 592:83
r. in original sin — PLOM 656:9
resemblance r. to World War II — BARR 61:78
resemble r. thee in likeness — WALL 886:12
we will r. you in that — SHAK 740:68
resent r.…unless…biased — VORS 883:58
resentment r. and…the whip — LESS 504:32
r. towards persons — NEWM 612:65
reservation stick us on a r. — MCMU 537:86
reservations mountain parks and r. — MUIR 602:64
reserve kindness in r. — POPE 661:39
r. inventory of…thinking — RAND 678:11
reserves it was Rochdale r. — SHAN 776:32
reservoir inexhaustible r. of love — BAUD 65:83
r. on Forty-second Street — AUCH 39:75
r., to keep and spare — POPE 660:4
words drawn from the special r. — ACHE 2:24
reservoirs r. of strength — GREER 372:91
residence Ireland as a place of r. — SAKI 710:44
ruined by r. in Italy — RUSK 704:32
residencies Inns are not r. — MOORE 595:32
residents r. from raw estates — LARK 491:33
resignation admire their r. — MACD 529:25
first request for my r. — DARM 253:6
Please accept my r. — MARX 557:91
r. is active — FITZ 325:17
special excitement of a rumored r. — SHUL 789:86
resigned r.…in full agreement — HOWE 417:97
resist It boots not to r. — SHAK 730:81
r. everything except temptation — WILDE 908:13
r. only what is inevitable — MILL 573:53
R. the devil, and he will flee — BIBLE 125:15
respect only those who r. me — DE 259:40
resistance Americans…r. — TRIL 866:69

glory of the r. — LACL 484:81
ength of r. to which Ulster — LAW 493:84
ne of least r. — AMERY 14:78
passive r. — MELV 564:45
efinement on the principle of r. — BURKE 168:11
, in your listener — MILL 573:56
alvation along the lines of least r. — FORD 329:99
support the Nicaraguan r. — NORTH 618:71
surrender…was as honorable as r. — ANGE 17:34
hose that offer r. — SOPH 804:85
•sisted when it ought to be r. — HAWT 386:48
•solution could reach that great r. — BROW 158:75
native hue of r. — SHAK 753:74
native hue of r. — TWAIN 871:7
. from despair — MILT 580:5
hought and r. — TROL 866:85
•solutions great and mighty r. — BUTL 177:46
•solve fixed r. not to quit — MORAN 596:56
R. not to be poor — JOHN 446:56
R. to be thyself — ARNO 32:6
•solved inwardly r. — TWAIN 870:88
•sonance r. of his solitude — CONN 233:86
•sort various bustle of r. — MILT 577:35
•source r. of the feeble — GIBB 352:58
sacrifice of another r. — HERF 399:25
•sources between scarce r. — ROBB 689:14
confident of its own r. — LIVI 512:83
R. left in the ground are saved — BRODY 154:61
r.…within your reach — PIND 651:18
services of our r. — FRIE 337:64
you have no Inner R. — BERR 82:63
•spect due r. — STEE 814:94
English have no r. — SHAW 780:61
feelings of awe and r. — DICK 266:63
fellow of a good r. — SHAK 748:23
first claim on your r. — JUVE 453:21
guarded only by neighbourly r. — CHUR 216:71
hold them in r. — SAND 713:5
How I did r. you — TROL 866:89
how much I should r. myself — JAMES 433:26
means of procuring r. — JOHN 445:17
neither doth God r. any person — BIBLE 91:4
no r. of place, persons, nor time — SHAK 756:62
On both sides more r. — SHAK 769:65
only qualifications I really much r. — JAMES 434:53
poor but deserving of r. — OCON 622:28
R. and reason — SHAK 733:62
r. for anything — LOUIS 518:2
r. for the living symbol — LABO 483:55
r. if not enthusiastic acceptance — ANGE 17:35
r. must give us pause — TWAIN 871:7
r. only those who resist me — DE 259:40
that faint word, r.! — DRYD 289:58
treat him with priestly r. — OFLA 622:35
When people do not r. us — TWAIN 872:24
without losing one's r. — SAKI 710:41
•spectability R. is a very good thing — STEV 821:71
save a shred of its r. — READ 680:47
wife's fidelity and his mother's r. — SHAW 781:96
•spectable cannot make him r. — EMER 312:31
easy and r. — TROL 866:75
except to appear r. — STEV 822:5
from Madeira, but perfectly r. — SHAW 777:61
genius found r.? — BROW 160:13
highly r. — GILB 354:8
more r. he is — SHAW 778:82
those who aren't r. — SAKI 710:43
•spected R. people are only rascals — STEN 816:53
r.…through her toilette — DE 257:94
•spectful gentle and r. ways — FENW 320:91
•spiration it was artificial r. — BURG 167:82
•sponse disgust is reason's proper r. — PAGL 634:80
r. is to the image — PRICE 668:14
r. to error that counts — GIOV 357:72
r. will be adequate — FULL 341:56
•sponsibility allocate the r. — HIRO 403:5
artist's first r. is to himself — DAVIS 255:58
burden of r. — EDWA 300:20
death without the r. — LEBO 499:7
don't have the sole r. — DENN 262:99
equality of r. — KENN 463:25
heavy burden of r. — EDWA 300:20
legal and moral r. — HAYD 387:58
Liberty means r. — SHAW 778:6
no sense of r. — KNOX 476:24
power without r. — BALD 54:46
profit without individual r. — BIER 129:24

r. of society — PALEY 635:14
r. of the poet — PALEY 635:14
r. of the poet — PALEY 635:15
r. of the writer — ALGR 11:31
r. without power — STOP 825:60
sense of collective r. — ALDI 10:9
shunning r. — WEIZ 896:35
writer have a social r.? — NABO 606:48
writer's only r. — FAUL 318:68
responsible Being r., I will direct — PITT 652:39
r. and wrong — CHUR 217:98
rest absolute r. is death — PASC 640:15
accomplishment of man's r. — BACON 48:5
all r. my powers defy — DONNE 279:35
astonish the r. — TWAIN 872:34
command me to my r. — DRAY 286:98
die or r. at last! — SHEL 786:22
distinguished above the r. — HOMER 409:18
dove found no r. — BIBLE 87:65
far, far better r. that I go to — DICK 271:25
fly away, and be at r. — BIBLE 96:32
give thee r. — BIBLE 89:30
God…ordained no r. — VAUG 878:50
ill a-brewing towards my r. — SHAK 740:60
In returning and r. shall ye be saved — BIBLE 103:30
in which to r. — GUNN 375:40
Is your heart at r.? — FLET 328:75
long long ago at r. — CORY 237:75
needful hours of r.? — DRYD 290:78
no r. from evils — PLATO 655:98
Nothing is easier…than r. — ADAMS 4:83
One needs more r. — WAUGH 892:20
playing, to our latest r. — RALE 677:1
r. from pain — DRYD 287:19
r. from their labours — BIBLE 126:69
r. in danger are — ETHE 315:92
r. in obscurity and peace! — EMMET 313:59
r. not day and night — BIBLE 126:54
r. of them ever got here — TRUM 868:28
r. rather than labour — RICH 686:68
r. us here…relating tales — SHAK 769:53
seeking r., and findeth none — BIBLE 111:45
shall not r. quiet in Montparnasse — BENET 75:12
should not enter into my r. — BIBLE 97:58
Sleep and r. — TENN 841:2
weary be at r. — BIBLE 93:52
Where's the r. of me? — ROBI 689:26
will not let them r. — KEATS 458:15
restaurant always went right to a r. — LARD 490:17
restaurants don't go to r. — WINN 917:28
preoccupying myself with…r. — SELF 727:82
rested better r. than ordinarily — HEYE 401:72
resting-place find the necessary r.-p. — KIER 467:12
restless his r. hands — PRIT 669:48
its people…moving, shifting, r. — FERB 320:94
R., he rolls — ROCH 691:52
restoration not revolution but r. — HARD 381:42
worst of a revolution is a r. — FOX 333:75
restoratives No r. — FORD 330:12
restrain it is not possible to r. them — RICH 686:68
restraint free from this r. — CONG 232:49
praise the firm r. — CAMP 186:56
suffer from too rigid a r. — BRON 154:78
with our moral r. — KENN 463:37
would that r. upon us — JOHN 443:86
restraints paucity of r. — SPEN 807:43
restrictions r. on woman — FULL 341:48
restructuring whole world needs r. — GORB 363:1
result accomplished the r. — ACHE 2:37
how small a realized R. — CARL 192:3
our r. is vitiated — THOR 857:78
r. is the battle won or lost — WELL 897:60
r. looked rather like the Forth Bridge — BRIT 153:45
r. of my upbringing — DYSON 297:62
r. of the energy stored — GERS 350:37
satisfied with that r. — SCHW 721:65
secure and lasting r. — DESC 263:23
results hope of instant r. — SCHL 718:15
how many dangerous r. — LOUI 518:92
poll r. — GALL 344:20
r. dies with the worker — LEON 503:10
r. of thought and resolution — TROL 866:85
resurrection by man came also the r. — BIBLE 121:14
foretaste of r. — SCHO 720:37
I am the r., and the life — BIBLE 118:3
in the r. they neither marry — BIBLE 113:81
prelude to r. — WILL 912:8

reclaimed…property at the r. — BUTL 178:85
r. is rare — ADAMS 4:83
r. of the body — BOOK 143:73
R. to eternal life — BOOK 142:35
resuscitate r., if it concerns history — HUGO 420:63
retail R. is detail — SCHU 720:48
retard r. what we cannot repel — JOHN 442:43
reticence R., in three volumes — GLAD 359:96
retire being young until you r. — LARK 491:42
don't r. in this business — MITC 588:3
r., and in retiring draw — MILT 586:39
r.…from who's who to who's that — WRIS 930:87
r. to the grandstands — GERG 350:32
sign for him to r. — DISR 277:74
want to r. at 50 — KINN 470:67
retirement must be no r. — HAIG 376:66
short r. urges sweet return — MILT 584:10
retiring at high speed — HALS 376:74
retort first, the R. Courteous — SHAK 750:91
retreat If I r., kill me — MUSS 605:16
into which one can r. — ORWE 620:81
mistress…little country r. — WYCH 931:7
principle solitude and r. — MONT 592:76
r.…in his own soul — AURE 42:53
r. into advance — ROOS 696:43
retrograde r. if it does not advance — GIBB 352:59
retrospect dark unfathom'd r. — WHIT 906:49
in r.…all a blur — SCHL 718:13
we live in r. — HAZL 388:82
return alas! we r. — FORS 331:30
came through and…shall r. — MACA 524:21
day of their r. — MACA 526:55
r. no more — SWIFT 830:54
shall not r. unto me void — BIBLE 104:56
returnable children…are not r. — CRISP 244:52
returned r. from battle — HOMER 409:16
returning In r.…shall ye be saved — BIBLE 103:30
r. him safely to earth — KENN 462:14
R. were as tedious — SHAK 768:19
returns gives the basest r. — INNO 429:70
reunion every r. a foretaste — SCHO 720:37
re-union r.-u. dinner — PARK 638:82
reveal r. the appalling dangers — HUXL 425:76
something to r. — THOM 854:16
revealed those things which are r. — BIBLE 90:53
revel blood-bedecked halls of their r. — POE 656:19
R. the night — SHAK 743:66
revelation continuous thread of r. — WELTY 899:1
essence of music is r. — HEINE 391:49
few weeks ago I had a r. — STEIN 815:30
habit of r. — SKEL 795:7
inspired by divine r. — BACON 46:44
land of light and r. — CLIN 221:91
lies in its r. in act — WHIT 904:13
man's r. to man — FRYE 340:35
r. of character in a play — WILL 912:24
r. of Jesus Christ — BIBLE 125:21
r. of Mahomet — GIBB 351:57
r. of the nature of God — WHIT 904:80
r. of the sexual goings-on — CRIT 245:62
r. of Thought — EMER 313:45
revelations extraordinary r. — BUTL 176:32
heaven…measured as R. says — LAUR 492:70
It ends with R. — WILDE 909:21
sounded like the book of R. — JAMES 433:29
revelled fought as they r. — DAVIS 256:66
revellers one by one dropped the r. — POE 656:19
revelry sound of r. by night — BYRON 179:23
revenge Blood and r.…in my head — SHAK 731:90
blows and r. for me! — SHAK 730:73
Caesar's spirit, ranging for r. — SHAK 748:2
capable and wide r. — SHAK 760:96
favourite form of r. — NIET 615:22
first blood shed in r. — PEPYS 647:28
Freud would have his r. — DOCT 277:2
General Ford as his r. — ABZUG 1:15
harbour any thoughts of r. — JOSE 451:70
in r. I took her to pieces — CONG 231:26
kiss…sweet as my r.! — SHAK 769:71
little R. herself — TENN 848:65
On desperate r. — MILT 582:40
permanent…had its own kind of r. — FRAME 333:82
Prompted to my r. — SHAK 753:69
Punishment is not for r. — FRY 340:31
R. is a kind of wild justice — BACON 47:78
r. of the intellect upon art — SONT 804:70
R. triumphs over death — BACON 47:74

greatest in Europe for R.	BAIL 52:4
Grit r. and prosperitie	BROWN 158:52
hire old r.	CHAU 209:86
increase of r. and commerce	HUME 422:12
infinite r. in a little room	MARL 552:84
in her left hand r.	BIBLE 99:12
natural science accumulates new r.	ALEM 11:17
R. are a good handmaid	BACON 47:65
R. are for spending	BACON 49:32
r. certainly make themselves wings	BIBLE 100:47
r. fineless is as poor	SHAK 760:87
r. grow in hell	MILT 581:16
r. to men of understanding	BIBLE 101:85
r. where is my deserving?	SHAK 772:35
r. will leave us sick	EMER 313:37
unsearchable r. of Christ	BIBLE 122:44
world's r., which dispersèd lie	HERB 398:16
ichness all in a rush With r.	HOPK 412:87
r.; his double action	HUGEL 418:12
r….of existence	KENN 463:36
ickshaw no go the r.	MACN 538:2
ico is this the end of R.	ROBI 690:27
id harder it is to get r.	TWAIN 870:86
how to get r. of ourselves	HORN 414:36
idea of getting r. of it	JERO 437:33
r. of Paul Revere	LONG 516:62
time we got r. of Him	BALD 54:37
iddance die and be a r.!	DICK 269:63
iddle could not…expound the r.	BIBLE 90:71
glory, jest, and r.	POPE 660:17
had not found out my r.	BIBLE 90:72
How still the R. lies!	DICK 272:52
r. wrapped inside a mystery	CHUR 216:73
ide being taken for a r.	JOSE 451:70
mount by me and r.	YEATS 932:31
ticket to r.	LENN 503:95
two men r. of a horse	SHAK 745:18
we r. them down	TENN 841:97
ider between a r. and his horse	SURT 829:42
good r. may often be thrown	ANON 20:15
r. hanging like a locket	SOME 803:67
steed That knows his r.	BYRON 179:18
The r., the birds	YEATS 933:45
the r. was lost	FRAN 334:13
iders r. on the earth together	MACL 535:46
idicule wise r. and obey	BIER 129:30
idiculous fine sense of the r.	ALBEE 9:91
made r. by friends	BIER 128:15
makes men r.	JUVE 453:16
most r. and scornful sort	SIDN 791:21
R….20 years after	LAVER 493:81
step above the r.	PAINE 634:99
To the R.	GRAH 365:33
we have made enthusiasm r.	STAEL 811:47
iding keep on r.	TRUM 869:44
Ridley good comfort Master R.	LATI 492:61
rife r. as the loam Of prairies	CRANE 243:22
rifle a r….had gone off	ORWE 628:49
Let him who has a r.	HO 405:37
r. all the breathing spring	COLL 228:41
roll to your r.	KIPL 471:93
with r. and pack	SASS 716:63
rifles stuttering r.' rapid rattle	OWEN 632:51
rift little r. within the lute	TENN 846:9
rig Tato, R. and Scunge	MURR 604:7
Rigby Eleanor R. picks up the rice	LENN 503:96
right absolute and unlimited r.	BENT 77:68
age of r. and opportunity	WILS 916:7
All's r. with the world	BROW 160:19
Always do r.	TWAIN 872:34
as much r….as pigs have to fly	CARR 195:77
be decorative and to do r.!	FIRB 323:68
belief which may be r.	FORS 331:32
better to be approximately r.	BUFF 165:45
beyond doubt that they are r.	VAN 876:25
boldly speak in r.	OTWAY 630:24
born to set it r.!	SHAK 752:39
Brotherhood of the R. Stuff	WOLFE 920:93
desire to do r.	DICK 271:41
D. H. Lawrence was r.	GIBB 352:72
discussion of any subject is a r.	SHEL 782:14
divine r. of husbands	WOLL 921:9
editor…will always be r.	BENN 76:56
every man did that which was r.	BIBLE 90:97
exclusively in the r.	HUXL 424:63
fight for the r.	CURZ 249:53
Give it because it is r.	LLOY 513:5

great r. of an excessive wrong	BROW 162:83
have the r. to exist	KELM 461:79
her r. to…opinions	PALM 636:26
hundredth time I am r.	EINS 301:34
If the young fellow is r.	QUIN 675:49
if two wrongs don't make a r.	COUS 239:4
irresponsible and r.	CHUR 217:98
itch but a kind of colourable r.	LEST 505:48
it isn't enough to be r.	OATES 620:96
Judge of all the earth do r.	BIBLE 87:78
know I'm r.	GOLD 362:74
legal r. to say what you like	ORWE 628:48
Lenin was r.	KEYN 465:79
Let's do it r.	PEI 646:13
majority never has r.	IBSEN 428:33
may she always be in the r.	DECA 258:8
meet and r. so to do	BOOK 141:4
must also be r.	GOULD 365:23
My country r. or wrong	CHES 211:46
nation being so r.	WILS 916:10
nature's state, where all have r.	DRYD 290:92
neither r. nor safe	LUTH 523:93
never try to make a r. decision	ONEI 626:4
Next to being r.	HUXL 426:15
no claim of r.	MALT 543:18
No government has the r.	BROWN 157:48
no more r. to…happiness	SHAW 777:55
no r. to strike	COOL 236:45
no r. to transgress the law	DOST 282:6
not between r. and wrong	JUNG 453:8
novelist…does not have the r.	FLAU 326:37
one thing we did r.	ANON 24:35
on the r. side	GALB 343:97
people who hunt are the r. people	SHAW 781:77
petty r. or wrong	THOM 854:10
quite r. too	GREY 373:6
r. action is freedom	ELIOT 308:33
r. angle is necessary	MALL 542:98
R. as a Ribstone Pippin!	BELL 73:62
R. Divine of Kings	POPE 662:76
r. in his own eyes	BIBLE 99:44
r. in his own eyes	BIBLE 90:77
r. is not what someone gives you	CLARK 219:55
r. is only a motor hand	HEPW 396:63
r. is retreating	FOCH 328:80
r. not to understand	CALV 185:46
r. now is wrong	SPEN 809:10
r. out of wrong	JONS 449:32
R. perfection	SHAK 772:26
r. place to film it	GARD 345:43
r. to a fair portion	BURKE 168:32
r. to hear what other…human	CARL 193:30
r. to the property	RUSK 704:20
r. to utter what he thinks	JOHN 446:48
saddling of the r. to a child	SHAW 780:54
secure of private r.	DRYD 290:91
settle what's r. and fair	HUGH 420:55
Sit thou at my r. hand	BIBLE 97:73
solve it r. or wrong	WATS 891:99
someone will make things r.	REAG 680:54
sometimes in the r.	DRYD 288:27
Still in thy r. hand	SHAK 775:22
successful or otherwise, always r.	ADAMS 5:92
sure that it is r.	HAND 380:30
take from me my r. to speak	MACL 535:31
'the r.' is only the expedient	JAMES 434:73
the r. to report events	ORWE 629:93
the r. to tell people	ORWE 629:71
They can't all be r.	DRIB 287:10
things…will not come r.	OBRI 620:5
though r. were worsted	BROW 163:95
to be proved r.	HUXL 425:96
to get things r.	RYLE 707:80
turn'd him r. and round about	BURNS 173:53
Ulster will be r.	CHUR 215:55
undoubted r. of the crown	COVE 239:6
way which seemeth r.	BIBLE 99:27
whatever be his r. to it	STEV 823:26
what his r. wing was doing	ASQU 36:19
when ye turn to the r. hand	BIBLE 103:31
whether you do r.	TWAIN 871:10
whether you do r.	TWAIN 871:11
wrong and r.	YEATS 932:35
wrong because not all was r.	CRAB 242:2
wrong notes are r.	IVES 431:2
young and perhaps he is r.	MAHL 539:33
righted none that could be r.	JONAS 447:83

righteous came not to call the r.	BIBLE 114:7
I have seen the r. forsaken	BLUN 137:16
not come to call the r.	BIBLE 111:20
not seen the r. forsaken	BIBLE 95:17
r. runneth into it	BIBLE 99:40
r. with impunity?	RACI 677:87
souls of the r.	BIBLE 107:31
righteousness breastplate of r.	BIBLE 122:52
eternal…makes for r.	ARNO 34:63
feareth him, and worketh r.	BIBLE 119:41
For my r. the Lord hath brought	BIBLE 89:48
hunger and thirst after r.	BIBLE 109:83
kingdom of God, and his r.	BIBLE 110:3
let the clouds rain down r.	BIBLE 128:96
loved r.	GREG 372:95
paths of r.	BIBLE 94:2
paths of r.	SCOT 725:61
r. shall exceed the r. of the scribes	BIBLE 109:87
Sun of r. arise	BIBLE 106:22
things that we think are our r.	BUTT 178:88
what r. really is	ARNO 34:64
worketh r.	BIBLE 119:41
worketh r.	BIBLE 94:90
righteousnesses r. are as filthy rags	BIBLE 104:63
rights all a talkin' 'bout r.	TRUTH 869:51
backlash against women's r.	FALU 317:42
believe that they have r.	HEGEL 391:40
bill of r.	JEFF 436:16
certain inalienable r.	STAN 812:62
death instead of 'human r.'	PEOP 647:24
die in defence of their r.	PITT 657:42
discuss women's r.	CLIN 222:10
exercise for r. of children	COWP 241:66
fight for their own human r.	PANK 636:32
full menu of r.	TUTU 870:70
Human r., national integrity	WILS 916:8
Let woman share the r.	WOLL 921:13
maintenance of established r.	PEEL 646:8
men, their r. and nothing more	ANTH 27:8
Natural r. is simple nonsense	BENT 77:69
of all 'r. of man'	CARL 193:27
Property has…its r.	DRUM 287:13
r. inherent and inalienable	JEFF 436:12
r. of an Englishman	JUNI 453:11
r. of every man	KENN 463:28
r. of every other nation	PARN 639:92
r. of the individual	CHUR 216:72
r….of the laboring man	BAER 51:78
r. of the savage	GLAD 358:91
r. of the smaller nationalities	ASQU 36:9
r….on…basis of a physical	BOTHA 146:13
Stand up for your r.	MARL 551:68
the r. of the people	SUN 829:33
trenching on another's r.	BRON 155:89
vital personal r.	WARR 889:69
rill By cool Siloam's shady r.	HEBER 390:33
danced the moon on Monan's r.	SCOTT 723:4
gushing of a r.	BYRON 182:99
the descending r.	SMART 796:27
Rimbauds always chasing R.	PARK 194:61
ring clear, clean r. of…insult	CARR 194:61
dance round in a r.	FROST 339:11
fantastic r., Round	BROW 161:48
forms a r.	SCHR 720:43
four walls and a r.	HEAN 389:5
get me in any r. with Mr Tolstoy	HEMI 394:18
great r. of…light	VAUG 878:49
his luminous r.	TENN 839:60
jow or r.	FERG 320:7
man gets into the r.	MAIL 540:59
One R. to rule them all	TOLK 862:98
R. out the want	TENN 844:61
R. out, wild bells	TENN 844:60
This pretty r.	SCHR 720:38
unconquered in a r.	CHES 212:91
what shall we do for a r.?	LEAR 497:84
willing to sell…Your r.?	LEAR 498:85
with this r. I thee wed	BOOK 142:28
ringmaster r. has altered	ASHD 35:90
rings r., and things	SHAK 732:35
their r. or green mantles	BALL 56:88
Rio roll to R.	KIPL 473:44
riot blaze of r. cannot last	SHAK 734:5
He didn't r.	TEBB 838:28
ripe we r. and r.	SHAK 749:47
ripeness R. is all	EMPS 314:62
R. is all	SHAK 764:99

ripped Untimely r. — SHAK 769:45
ripples the infernal r. — POUND 664:34
rise but stoop to r. — MASS 559:43
Created half to r. — POPE 660:17
Early to r. — THUR 859:29
One man's wage r. — WILS 916:99
opportunity to r. again — SARN 714:32
R., take up thy bed — BIBLE 117:86
R. up, my love — BIBLE 101:99
Some r. by sin — SHAK 758:22
risen He is not here, but is r. — BIBLE 116:67
rising constantly r. at four — WESL 900:23
means of r. in the world — JOHN 444:10
ways of the bird r. — REID 682:95
risings r....on contradiction — EMPS 314:63
risk England...preferred the r. — CECIL 202:27
increases in relation to r. — HEMI 395:28
r. of becoming a subordinate species — SCOTT 725:52
r. of being heroes — BOLT 139:49
r. of maiming it for life — SHAW 778:11
Without r. there is no faith — KIER 467:9
risks one of the r. that he takes — STEV 821:69
suffering, and some r. — PEARY 645:1
rite fascination of an ancient r. — SAND 713:12
newer r. is here — AQUI 28:29
victory...celebrated with the funeral r. — LAO 490:12
rites body of organized r. — LEWIS 508:96
till love have all his r. — SHAK 744:3
ritual part of the Texas r. — FERB 320:95
rival If I embrace my r. — RACI 677:85
rivalry r. of aim — ADAMS 4:81
r.; sane and healthy — NORR 618:65
tendencies to r., jealousy — JAMES 434:66
rivals r. rail — JOHN 441:10
river air moves like a r. — LEON 503:14
Alph, the sacred r. — COLE 226:9
bread I dip in the r. — STEV 823:30
can't argue with a r. — ACHE 3:42
cross the r. by an Irish bridge — STEW 824:44
drinketh up a r. — BIBLE 93:77
either side the r. lie — TENN 838:42
foam on the r. — SCOTT 723:8
fog down the r. — DICK 269:79
fountains mingle with the r. — SHEL 783:42
great source of the holy r. — SPEKE 806:35
hill or field by the r. — TENN 842:5
In a field by the r. — YEATS 932:29
listening to a r. — HEAN 389:12
majestic r. floated on — ARNO 32:27
nature of a r. — BACON 46:41
not so much like any r. — HOPK 412:98
Ol' Man R. — HAMM 379:15
On a tree by a r. — GILB 355:29
one great winding r. — RANJ 678:16
pure r. of water of life — BIBLE 127:84
r....a strong brown god — ELIOT 308:27
r. glideth at his own sweet will — WORD 926:19
r. is within us — ELIOT 308:28
r. jumps over the mountain — AUDEN 40:91
r. of crystal light — FIELD 322:32
'r.' or a 'stream' are the metaphors — JAMES 434:63
r. remains unchanged — KIRK 475:87
r.'s slow presence — LARK 491:33
R. Tiber foaming with much blood — POWE 667:93
r. winding clearly — TENN 839:45
salmon from the r. — SCOTT 723:13
Sleepless as the r. — CRANE 243:14
snow falls in the r. — BURNS 172:19
Thames...the noblest r. — ADDI 6:21
up the mouth of a r. — KIPL 470:84
Up the r. and o'er the lea — HOGG 406:60
wanted to give him a r. name — WINT 917:32
waters Of the R. Lee — MAHO 539:35
What use the green r. — FRAME 333:79
where there is no r. — KHRU 466:1
where the r. plunges — WILL 914:54
white flows the r. — STEV 823:32
world's greatest r. — DOSP 282:3
riverbed cold fog over a r. b. — ACHE 2:30
The r., dried-up — HEAN 389:12
river-rounded rook-racked, r.-r. — HOPK 412:91
rivers All the r. run into the sea — BIBLE 100:66
as the r. of water: he turneth it — BIBLE 99:43
brooks, and r. wide — MILT 576:8
By shallow r. — MARL 553:17
By the r. of Babylon — BIBLE 98:98
energy of mighty r. — MILL 572:26

R. and mountain-spring — OAKL 620:89
R. and seas...to float their ships — DICK 268:51
R. are damp — PARK 638:65
r. flowing through it — JAMES 433:28
r. of water in a dry place — BIBLE 103:32
R. ran reid — DOUG 283:17
r....shall not overflow thee — BIBLE 103:44
step into the same r. — HERA 396:66
timber and irrigating r. — MUIR 602:64
washed by the r. — BROO 156:6
when r. are swollen — SOPH 804:85
river-slaying r.-s. as something worse — LAUR 492:71
rivets r....that join'd us — DRYD 289:60
rivulet neat r. of text — SHER 787:51
Skipping r. — GILB 354:96
rivulets Myriads of r. — TENN 842:17
road and the r. below me — STEV 823:31
artists took to the r. — ROCK 693:84
Before us lay a painful r. — WORD 929:65
drive the r. — KIPL 472:13
endless r. you tread — HOUS 416:91
every r. I wandered by — HOUS 415:61
Golden R. to Samarkand — FLEC 327:46
Help me down Cemetery R. — LARK 491:34
high r....to England — JOHN 443:63
horse...from the r. — YEATS 933:45
however long and hard the r. — CHUR 216:74
lame man who keeps the right r. — BACON 47:64
layer cake or a r. — MILL 572:8
life runs on, the r. — LOWE 520:40
light to shine upon the r. — COWP 240:46
look ahead up the white r. — ELIOT 306:65
main r. of procreation — WAUGH 892:19
make the whole r. — DEAN 257:87
merry r., a mazy r. — CHES 212:86
no expeditious r. — THOM 855:40
no 'royal r.' to geometry — EUCL 315:2
on a lonesome r. — COLE 225:90
only monument the asphalt r. — ELIOT 307:88
out on the r. — MASE 559:25
right on to the end of the r. — LAUD 492:65
r. along which — TAWN 837:8
r. is life — KERO 464:64
r. leads me forth — MASE 559:30
r. leads me seawards — MASE 559:31
r. lies long and straight — STEV 821:87
r. of excess — BLAKE 134:39
r. of experiment and observation — LAVO 493:83
r. of life — GARL 346:49
r. runs by — TENN 838:42
r. that we did not take — HUSS 423:41
r. to a knowledge of the stars — EDDI 298:84
R. to Heaven — BALL 56:90
r. to hell is paved — ROTH 699:23
r. to suns — SCOTT 722:77
r. to the heart — BALZ 58:16
r. to wealth — TROL 866:75
r. was a ribbon — NOYES 619:78
r. wind up-hill — ROSS 697:82
rolling English r. — CHES 212:85
shut the r. through the woods — KIPL 473:66
straightest r. to a man's heart — FERN 321:17
surpassed on the r. — HALI 378:82
takes no private r. — POPE 660:27
The beaten r. — SHEL 786:9
the middle of the r. — BEVAN 84:19
travel any r. a second time — IBN 427:32
travel the open r. — WHIT 905:40
turn of the r. — FAWC 319:79
various cause the same wild r. — SCOTT 724:16
watched the ads...not the r. — NASH 608:96
which r. leads to damnation — DYSON 297:63
Words spoken on the r. — MO 589:18
ye'll talk the high r. — ANON 20:20
yon braid, braid r. — BALL 56:90
road-maps book of r. m. — STEI 816:37
roads All r. lead to Rome — LAFO 485:19
Came through cold r. — SCOTT 725:51
dangerous to cross main r. — HAWT 386:34
employment of the poor in r. — MALT 543:19
How many r. must a man — DYLAN 297:54
lawless r. Ran wrong — MUIR 601:53
Most r. lead men homewards — MASE 559:30
Now all the r. lead — THOM 854:19
r. by which men escape — BELL 71:28
r. leading from nowhere — BIER 129:39
r. that turning always — MUIR 601:54

r., the railways, the banks — MILL 570:6
thousand r. lead to Rome — ALAN 9:8
three r. to ruin — POMP 658:4
Two r. diverged in a wood — FROST 338:8
wet, winding r. — COLUM 229:6
roadside must show him on the r. — PARN 639:9
roadway by the r. poplar-lined — MACG 531:7
roam power to r. — BYRON 179:2
Where'er I r. — GOLD 361:3
where'er we r. — GOLD 361:4
roar called upon to give the r. — CHUR 217:
Let him r. again — SHAK 737:9
melancholy, long, withdrawing r. — ARNO 31:9
r. Of...pained desert lion — ARNO 32:2
r....on the other side of silence — ELIOT 304:
that unmoving r.! — WILL 914:5
roars r. of infuriated spectators — ORWE 630:
roast r. beef of England — FIEL 322:37
rob peace to thy soul, R. Burns! — SCOTT 725:5
r. a lady of her fortune — FIEL 322:4
r., murder, and commit — SHAK 743:6
slays More than you r. — SHAK 762:5
those who r. you — CONN 233:8
time I began to r. — SITW 794:6
robbed He that is r. — SHAK 760:9
r. man of everything — SOLZ 803:6
sooner or later be r. — STEV 821:7
The r. that smiles — SHAK 759:6
We wuz r.! — JACO 432:1
robber sing in the r.'s face — JUVE 453:18
robbers den of r. in your eyes? — BIBLE 105:7
robbery dens of r. and murder — NATI 610:2
just a cover for r. — RAMOS 678:
r. to be equal with God — BIBLE 123:5
Thieves for their r. — SHAK 758:2
robbing not drugging, not r. — PACK 633:7
r. the rich — SHAW 778:8
think little of r. — DE 262:1
Robbins President R. was so well — JARR 435:8
robe Bring forth the best r. — BIBLE 116:4
falling...like a r. — FLAU 326:35
Give me my r. — SHAK 766:6
like a giant's r. — SHAK 768:3
r. is the light — GRANT 366:5
robes all her r. are gone — ANON 20:
dress me In borrowed r.? — SHAK 766:7
impatient child that hath new r. — SHAK 736:6
R. loosely flowing — JONS 449:2
R., Tato, dig — MURR 604:7
washed their r. — BIBLE 126:6
Winter...rudely rends thy r. — COLL 228:3
robin be sae nice wi' R. — BURNS 171:91
Call for the r.-red-breast — WEBS 895:9
Rantin' rovin' R. — BURNS 171:7
r. red breast in a cage — BLAKE 135:6
Sweet R. sits on the bush — SCOTT 724:3
robot r. mice and r. men — BRAD 149:7
r. vehicles blindly programmed — DAWK 256:7
robots not using these r. — ANGLE 17:5
technically efficient r. — CALL 185:3
work of r. — GOULD 365:2
robs r. himself that spends — SHAK 759:6
r. you on business principles — SHAW 777:65
robust too much attainted...to be r. — HOFS 406:5
Rochdale take my wife to see R. — SHAN 776:3
Rochefoucauld Duke of R.-Liancourt — LOUI 518:9
rock been a r. of order — METT 568:28
blue-black tooth of sheer r. — BENU 78:85
cut a Colossus from a r. — JOHN 446:63
don't have a r. voice — MEAT 562:4
first r. at a girl like I — LOOS 517:82
go first, r. and roll or Christianity — LENN 502:5
It's Only R. and Roll — JAGG 432:20
made himself the r. — SCHO 719:24
more women in the r. scene — HARV 385:21
my r. and my salvation — BIBLE 96:34
principle which...gives us a firm R. — BUTT 178:87
prisoner of the hard r. — THOM 855:33
reclaim these things—poetry, r.'n'roll, political activism — SMITH 800:89
Rhyme is the r. — DRYD 290:1
r. a quarter of a million miles up — BAKER 53:22
R. of Ages — TOPL 863:15
r. of offence — BIBLE 102:15
r. of the national resources — WEBS 894:71
r. that is higher than I — BIBLE 96:33
Safe upon solid r. — MILL 571:82

secure possession of a bleak r.	YOUNG 935:76	challenges: the R. Catholic	MACM 536:77	cat on a hot tin r.	WILL 912:25
set my feet upon a r.	BIBLE 95:18	departed was a 'R.'	LAWS 495:44	corrugated tin r.	BEEC 69:63
Sex 'n' drugs 'n' r. 'n' roll	DURY 296:43	fabulous yellow r. candles	KERO 464:62	good umbrella but a poor r.	LOWE 520:39
shadow of a great r.	BIBLE 103:32	Greek and R. poets	PRIOR 669:44	He has restored the r.!	BETJ 83:78
The poem in the r.	THOM 855:30	heard the snobbish R. say	BEER 70:88	high embowèd r.	MILT 577:22
three very simple r. and roll reasons	GELD 348:94	high R. fashion	SHAK 765:53	majestical r.	SHAK 752:56
truth is the uncharted r.	CORN 237:72	I am a R. citizen	CICE 218:25	prefers a thatched r.	WALC 885:80
rocked they r. the system	ROBI 690:43	in the R. Catholic religion	TROL 866:88	r., instead of slats	DRAY 287:7
Rockefellers eat R. for breakfast	KENN 464:54	Like the R., I seem to see	POWE 667:93	r. in words deceiving	MILT 576:99
rocket he rose like a r.	PAINE 634:96	Make way, R. writers	PROP 670:62	r. of gold	JONS 449:36
r.'s red glare	KEY 465:76	more an antique R.	SHAK 755:40	tiles on the r.	LUTH 523:95
rockets r. used by the barbarians	KISH 475:88	noblest R. of them all	SHAK 748:25	twigs into a leaky r.	RUDO 701:61
Rockies the R. may crumble	GERS 351:45	not…holy, or R.	VOLT 883:45	weeks of watching the r. leak	SNYD 803:50
rocking-chair always has the r.-c.	ROBI 690:37	R. holiday	BYRON 180:39	**roofs** abjure all r.	SHAK 763:69
rocking-horse about upon a r. h.	KEATS 457:84	since the R. colonists	HYDE 427:21	over the r. of the world	WHIT 905:36
rocks begin to twinkle from the r.	TENN 840:66	the R., in days of old	PALM 636:24	r. of this distracted City	CARL 192:7
but the r. remain	HERB 397:87	To-day the R. and his trouble	HOUS 415:56	Shake not thy r.	BLAKE 133:26
change the r. of Scotland	JOHN 441:13	Would that the R. people	CALI 184:37	slate r. in sun	DAY 257:86
charms…To soften r.	CONG 231:22	**romance** calls his work a R.	HAWT 386:42	**rooks** r. came home	HODG 405:43
father…throwing r. at the stork	BREC 150:5	chiaroscuro of r.	MAUG 561:78	The r. are blown about	TENN 843:29
flowerless r. of hell	SITW 793:59	cloudy symbols of a high r.	KEATS 457:94	**rooky** Makes wing to th' r. wood	SHAK 768:16
Guarded by shoals and r.	BYRON 182:78	fine r.	FIEL 323:47	**room** although the r. grows chilly	GRAH 365:35
heaven but the r.	RUSK 703:5	not a little given to r.	EVEL 316:21	always r. at the top	WEBS 894:72
hitting…bottles with small r.	THUR 859:20	There's r. for you!	MORR 598:93	being Queenly in her own r.	WHAR 901:50
Love…resembles the eternal r.	BRON 155:96	Utopian and revolutionary r.	WEBB 893:65	Books do furnish a r.	POWE 666:81
miraculously glide past the r.	CUOMO 248:29	while there's…love and r.	BERL 79:15	coming to that holy r.	DONNE 281:80
older than the r.	PATER 642:51	**romances** are like r. read	SUCK 828:10	dark r. where I began	MASE 559:33
railroad…you blasted its r.	RUSK 704:38	no more need of r.	WHIT 905:29	dog in a very small r.	TOYN 864:27
rifted r. whose entrance leads	MILT 577:37	**Romans** Friends, R., countrymen	SHAK 748:5	dying man's r.	STER 818:86
r. melt wi' the sun	BURNS 173:44	poverty of the present R.	WALP 887:22	embers through the r.	MILT 576:17
steering…for the r.	GILM 356:57	R. call it stoicism	ADDI 6:32	enough r. in your own country	CORW 237:73
Such uncouth r.	WALP 887:21	R. conquered the world	SWEE 830:45	flung himself from the r.	LEAC 496:62
walled round with r.	SWIN 834:51	west of Ireland, the R. had never	CHRI 214:34	framed…in a comfortable r.	WALP 887:29
What are men to r.	AUST 43:69	**romantic** defining a r. poet	FROST 339:3	Grief fills the r.	SHAK 738:25
will sit upon the r.	MARL 553:17	Men are so r.	WELD 897:43	Here in this r.	STEV 819:21
With r., and stones and trees	WORD 924:80	New York…an infinitely r. notion	DIDI 274:6	How little r.	SHIR 789:79
Rockwell Norman R., the Brueghel	ADLER 7:49	R….100 years after	LAVER 493:81	infinite riches in a little r.	MARL 552:84
rod chief a r.	POPE 660:25	r. awe of them	HEMI 394:12	in the morning r. reading	WAUGH 892:35
enforced by the r.	SPEKE 806:36	r. diseased	GOET 360:22	into the neighbour r.	SHAK 754:14
r. and staff me comfort still	SCOT 725:61	r. interest in our own sex	CONN 233:87	leave r. for the mouse	SAKI 710:48
r. and thy staff	BIBLE 94:2	R. Ireland's dead	YEATS 933:43	left the r.	GROS 374:24
r. out of the stem of Jesse	BIBLE 102:18	**romanticism** all else is grandiose r.	BUKO 165:48	lights in the r.	GUIM 374:32
rule them with a r. of iron	BIBLE 126:49	tinge it with r.	DOYLE 285:51	make r. for discovery	APOL 27:21
spare the r., and spoil the child	BUTL 177:52	**Rome** All roads lead to R.	LAFO 485:19	make r. for faith	KANT 455:46
spareth his r.	BIBLE 99:26	ascribed to the augurs of R.	KNIG 476:15	man in a jail has more r.	JOHN 443:59
steel r. runs right through	ANGE 17:38	At R. she hadde been	CHAU 208:74	men in a smoke-filled r.	SIMP 793:48
The r. of Aaron	BIBLE 89:38	Bishop of R. hath no jurisdiction	BOOK 144:76	Minister's r. is like a padded cell	CROS 246:84
Throw away thy r.	HERB 398:19	Burn, with Athens and with R.	CAMP 186:59	music from a farther r.	ELIOT 304:20
wisdom be put in a silver r.	BLAKE 133:27	cruel men of R.	SHAK 746:71	no r. for new feelings	ELIOT 303:88
rode Then she r. forth	TENN 840:71	deliberating in R.	LIVY 513:89	no r. in his workshop	FAUL 318:63
roe following the r.	BURNS 171:9	founded before the City of R.	BAIL 52:4	not r….to swing a cat	SMOL 802:30
loving hind and pleasant r.	BIBLE 99:14	grandeur that was R.	POE 656:22	only slipped away into the next r.	HOLL 407:67
roes breasts are like two young r.	BIBLE 101:2	hook-nosed fellow of R.	SHAK 743:62	our r. on this earth	GREN 373:3
Roger Sir R. is landlord	ADDI 6:14	Humorists…burn while R. fiddles	CONN 233:71	Paces about her r. again	ELIOT 306:61
steal from Samuel R.	BYRON 182:75	irreverential word of R.?	HAWT 386:52	parents…rent out my r.	ALLEN 12:50
rogue 100,100 thalers a r.	LICH 509:22	It was at R.	GIBB 352:63	perpetual struggle for r. and food	MALT 543:17
bewitched with the r.'s company	SHAK 741:7	Let R. in Tiber melt	SHAK 764:12	retired to my r.	STER 818:98
busy and insinuating r.	SHAK 760:4	Like R., Nkongsamba was built	BOYD 147:42	r. at your head	BALL 55:72
easy it is to call r.	DRYD 291:29	O lucky R.	CICE 218:28	r. full of good air	LEAC 496:61
fiddler, and consequently a r.	SWIFT 830:64	Only R. can resemble R.	BELL 72:37	r. in the west for wolves	BABB 45:20
Has he not a r.'s face?	CONG 231:12	on my way to R.	WAUGH 893:56	r. in this country	ROOS 696:60
O, what a r. and peasant slave	SHAK 753:67	out of R.	GARI 346:48	r. of her own	WOOLF 922:42
r. alive to the ludicrous	EMER 313:53	recent disaster at R.	AUGU 42:43	r. of the palace	SITW 794:65
r. gives you Love Powders	LAMB 486:36	R.!…city of the soul	BYRON 180:35	r. or on the street	ROSSO 698:6
r. in porcelain	MERE 567:4	R. immortal	GURN 375:44	r. to recognize him	BUEC 165:44
r. is outlining a treacherous plan	FRAS 335:27	R. is but a wilderness	SHAK 731:59	r. to swing a cat	DICK 269:77
wasna he a r.	ANON 20:16	R…is like its own Monte Testaceo	CLOU 222:28	R. with a View	FORS 331:29
rogues bold deserving r.	OTWAY 631:28	R….only monument left of R.	BELL 72:36	silence in the r.	KINS 470:72
parcel of r.	BURNS 172:35	R. shall perish	COWP 241:53	Sir Matthew left the r.	LINK 511:56
parcel of r.	BURNS 172:36	R. shall stand	BYRON 180:41	sit in the same r. with me	PARK 638:70
r. slighted me into the river	SHAK 743:79	R.'s just a city	BURG 167:84	Social Predestination R.	HUXL 425:75
you dissentious r.	SHAK 769:56	R. to chase the Antichrist	LESL 504:30	stayed in the high r.	SPEN 807:59
Roland Child R. to the dark tower	SHAK 763:79	rules of my religion from R.	BROW 158:56	stay quietly in his r.	PASC 640:16
role How do you approach a r.?	EVANS 316:18	see R. while it yet exists	WALP 887:22	that r.'s upper end	SPEN 809:94
masculine r.	GREER 372:88	serve not R.	KIPL 474:75	took up a great deal of r.	WHAR 901:47
play the r. of watchmaker	DAWK 256:73	Sex Life in Ancient R. face	AMIS 14:83	vilest earth Is r. enough	SHAK 742:35
r. is…filling vacuums	CART 198:51	shake your R.	SHAK 769:69	within a little r.	SMITH 800:95
r. of the poet to look	PRIT 669:53	that I loved R. more	SHAK 748:3	you shall keep your r.	STEV 823:32
subside into the r.	STRA 826:79	thousand roads lead to R.	ALAN 9:85	**room-mates** hard to be r.-m.	SALI 711:56
time that occupies the same r.	MCLU 536:56	Three nuncios from R.	MACA 525:45	**rooms** close-pent r.	WEBS 895:2
You have played out your r.	TROT 867:13	**Romeo** Juliet and her R.	SHAK 737:82	Know most of the r.	FULL 341:60
roll R. darkling down	JOHN 441:19	never will be R.	SHAK 736:49	lighted r. Inside your head	LARK 491:41
r. us shoreward soon	TENN 839:53	O R., R.	SHAK 736:47	Other Voices, Other R.	CAPO 189:21
roller basic white and with a r.	BROWN 157:49	**roof** artist needs but a r.	RYDER 707:76	People fill their r.	TREE 865:54
rolling r. down the street	IGNA 428:41	Beneath my shady r.	BLAKE 133:25	planes and the corners of r.	MALL 542:98
Rolls Royce R. R. diplomacy	ANON 24:25	Blown through the r.	THOM 854:27	shimmering into r.	WODE 919:54
roman Before the R. came to Rye	CHES 212:85	can't live under the same r.	MONT 592:78	**Roosevelt** answer that I will give…R.	CHUR 217:80

Politicians are the s.	KHRU 466:1	place where s. and hope	ROUS 700:39	date on S. night	ALLEN 12:46
reason I should be the s.?	AYTO 45:15	pursuit of s.	BELL 73:72	Glasgow Empire on a S. night	DODD 278:6
s. yesterday, and to day	BIBLE 124:4	restore themselves to s.	SMALL 796:21	see another S. night	MCNA 537:93
Two things are always the s.	STEIN 815:21	So with s. and insanity	MELV 564:47	Saturdays passionately, on…S.	SHER 787:48
sameness spotted wolf of s.	SOYI 805:13	There ain't no S. Claus	MARX 557:58	**Saturn** the Revolution may, like S.	VERG 879:63
sames s. of am	CUMM 248:14	**sans** S. teeth, s. eyes, s. taste	SHAK 749:51	**saturn** Sat gray-haired S.	KEATS 459:44
Samhain the long nights after S.	OBRI 621:7	**San Salvador** bells off S. S.	CRANE 243:10	while S. whirls	TENN 839:60
samite Clothed in white s.	TENN 847:38	**sanspareil** Cricket…the s.	FOWL 332:71	**satyrs** men, like s. grazing	MARL 552:89
Sammy What Makes S. Run?	SCHU 720:46	**Santa** S.'s grotto lies not in icy Lapland	HIGH 402:85	Where the s. are chattering	SITW 794:66
Samothrace Victory of S.	MARI 550:53	**Santa Claus** Nobody shoots S. C.	SMITH 798:55	**sauce** honey a s. to sugar	SHAK 750:67
Samsa S. awoke one morning	KAFKA 454:26	**sap** s. flows up through our arms	RILKE 687:86	Hunger…best s. in the world	CERV 203:44
Samson character like S., Hercules	SIEG 791:24	soul's s. quivers	ELIOT 309:38	**saucepans** ghosts of s.	MANS 546:82
Philistines be upon thee, S.	BIBLE 90:75	**sapient** s. sutlers of the Lord	ELIOT 305:36	**saucer** s. like some full moon	MONRO 591:58
S. said, Let me die	BIBLE 90:76	**saplings** gale, it plies the s.	HOUS 415:56	**saucy** no be half sae s.	BURNS 171:8
Samuel Lord called S.	BIBLE 91:81	**sapphire** s. melts into the sea	TENN 845:88	**Saul** S. and Jonathan were lovely	BIBLE 91:98
sanctify s. yourselves	BIBLE 89:33	**sapphire-blaze** throne, the s.-b.	GRAY 370:38	S. hath slain his thousands	BIBLE 91:96
sanction pile…s. on s.	CHAM 203:56	**Sappho** Call me S., Call me Chloris	COLE 226:98	S., S., why persecutest thou me?	BIBLE 119:37
sanctity kissing is as full of s.	SHAK 750:68	Dark S.!	BYRON 179:12	whose name was S.	BIBLE 119:35
odour of s.	WALL 886:4	**Sara** S. could commit adultery	CARY 199:63	**sausage** tin of Bologna s.	STEV 821:76
s.…in the state of victimization	ANGE 17:42	**Sarajevo** lost, for art, at S.	LEWIS 508:4	**savage** civilized man…into a s.	TOCQ 861:81
s. of life	GLAD 358:91	**sarcasm** Never use s. on players	FERG 320:2	manner in which a s. wields	HUXL 426:13
s. of life and property	SCHL 718:10	petulance is not s.	DISR 270:97	not a genuine foreign-grown s.	DICK 270:97
sanctuary inner s. of the Nanda	SHIP 789:78	**sardines** Life…like a tin of s.	BENN 75:24	painted face of the s.	DICK 270:3
shall be for a s.	BIBLE 102:15	**sark** S. rins o'er the Solway sands	BURNS 172:35	removed from the s. state	COOP 236:52
three classes which need s.	BALF 54:44	**sashes** nice new s.	GRAH 365:35	rights of the s.	GLAD 358:91
Until I went into the s.	BIBLE 96:42	**Sassenach** drove from a S. laird	SCOTT 723:13	s. individual man	WELLS 898:75
sand as a snowdrift on the s.	KHAY 466:94	**sat** s. down on the right hand	BIBLE 124:89	s. man…does man betray	ROCH 691:58
as tough a rope of s.	BUTL 177:43	you have s. too long here	CROM 246:74	s. place!	COLE 226:10
cathedrals In the s.	GIDE 353:78	**Satan** beheld S. as lightning	BIBLE 115:36	s. servility slides by	LOWE 520:49
colour of s.	ASHB 35:83	called the Devil, and S.	BIBLE 126:66	subtle, but s.	CAPO 189:29
die upon the s.	ARNO 32:25	diligence of S.	BUNY 166:66	take some s. woman	TENN 841:85
Divine…in a grain of s.	FRIE 337:68	Get thee behind me, S.	BIBLE 112:63	unto a s. race	TENN 839:62
edge of the s.	LEAR 498:86	Get thee hence, S.	BIBLE 109:80	wild…the noble s. ran	DRYD 288:35
every grain of s.	DOST 283:11	like a blond S.	HAMM 380:21	**savaged** s. by a dead sheep	HEAL 388:99
gasped upon the s.	MARL 552:88	Lord said unto S.	BIBLE 93:47	We s. them	GELL 348:2
I on the s.	SCOTT 724:19	Man, with his S.	SNYD 803:49	**savage-pictures** s.-p. fill their gaps	SWIFT 832:98
no bigger than a grain of s.	CHEE 209:99	messenger of S.	BIBLE 122:33	**savages** plant where s. are	BACON 49:38
ostrich, with its head in the s.	WILS 916:12	Of S. and his peers	MILT 581:17	**Savannah** In S.…drink?	BERE 78:88
palace built upon the s.	MILL 571:82	other toward S.	BAUD 65:81	**savannahs** s. grew lonely as the sea	HARR 384:99
print…plain to be seen in the s.	DEFOE 258:18	playfield of S.	NABO 606:37	**savant** Buddhist Beat Catholic s.	GINS 357:68
property turns s. to gold	YOUNG 935:76	S. exalted sat	MILT 581:18	**save** bit to s. humanity	HUGH 419:27
s. and ruin and gold	SWIN 833:42	s. has not geven me boils	FLEM 327:58	destroy the town to s. it	ANON 23:2
s. dunes the wind lifted	PIER 651:7	S., Nick, or Clootie	BURNS 170:77	himself he cannot s.	BIBLE 114:3
s. in the porridge	COWA 239:8	S. with thoughts inflamed	MILT 581:31	I can s. this country	PITT 652:38
see a world in a grain of s.	BLAKE 135:66	**satchel** schoolboy with his s.	SHAK 749:49	need not exist in order to s. us	DE 264:37
Such quantities of s.	CARR 196:1	**satiated** rather die s. than slim	PIER 651:8	nothing will s. the Governor	WHIT 905:26
throw the s. against the wind	BLAKE 135:64	**satiety** love's sad s.	SHEL 784:60	principle which prompts to s.	SMITH 798:47
waste of white barren s.	SCHAW 717:96	Of knowledge there is no s.	BACON 46:51	s. a shred of its respectability	READ 680:47
write in s.	WALL 886:17	s. is a blunt…passion	WEBS 894:76	s. everything that anyone else	DOWD 284:41
sandal massive s. set on stone	MILL 571:88	**satin** allowed to wear black s.	WHAR 902:55	S. something	ANON 24:31
sandals still in straw hat and s.	BASHO 63:42	ease a heart Like a s. gown	PARK 637:44	s. those that have no imagination?	SHAW 781:85
Sanders a bed…Clerk S. said	BALL 55:71	heroine…goes into white s.	SHER 788:67	s. those who damn them	HUGO 421:78
sandfly mosquito and s.	DOUG 283:14	loll on velvet and s.	FRAN 335:22	s. us from the power	JORD 450:66
sands Come unto these yellow s.	SHAK 774:81	Silk an' s.	ANON 21:28	**saved** is sometimes s.	THUR 859:40
cousins as the s. of the sea	SHAW 781:1	**satire** British…gluttons for s.	LODGE 514:22	name…whereby we must be s.	BIBLE 119:32
Footprints on the s. of time	LONG 515:43	difficult not to write s.	JUVE 453:14	only s. by being dammed	HOOD 410:42
golden s., and crystal brooks	DONNE 280:53	let s. be my song	BYRON 179:96	s. the sum of things	HOUS 416:80
lone and level s.	SHEL 784:50	s., being levelled at all	SWIFT 830:55	we are not s.	BIBLE 105:73
men's names On s.	MILT 577:31	s. costs a lot!	RICK 686:76	what must I do to be s.?	BIBLE 119:44
men who are as various as the s.	FORS 331:46	S. is a lesson	NABO 606:43	Whosoever will be s.	BOOK 140:78
s. of Africa	JOHN 442:57	S. is a sort of glass	SWIFT 830:52	Who then can be s.?	BIBLE 113:75
s. of Dee	KING 469:48	S. is dependent on strong beliefs	BROO 156:26	**saviour** a s. spring to life	BIBLE 128:96
s. o' life shall run	BURNS 173:44	S. is moral outrage	ROTH 699:22	Between the role of s.	YOUR 935:83
smoothed down like silly s.	BUNT 166:59	S. or sense, alas!	POPE 661:40	God my S.	BIBLE 115:23
steer too nigh the s.	DRYD 289:76	**satiric** have the s. temperament	BEER 69:71	God my S.	BIBLE 128:98
vision of the crowded, howling s.	CHES 211:41	**satisfaction** All s.…never positive	SCHO 719:28	Hark…The S. comes	DODD 278:7
sand-strewn S.-s. caverns	ARNO 31:84	cannot render s.	MIDD 569:40	Hide me, O my S.	WESL 900:11
sandwich raw-onion s.	BARN 60:72	can't get no s.	JAGG 432:16	in the city of David a S.	BIBLE 115:26
sandwiches other…eating s.	DICK 266:66	s. of human needs	NUTT 619:83	S. of 'is country	KIPL 471:92
we eat reality s.	GINS 357:60	What's the s.	HORN 414:37	s. or assassin	MURP 604:4
sane above all, of s. vitality	LUCAS 521:76	won a s. and a triumph	WOLFE 920:87	words our S. Christ saith	BOOK 141:3
Mahdi…is very s.	CECIL 202:31	**satisfied** and we must be s.	SYNGE 834:55	**savour** if the salt have lost his s.	BIBLE 109:84
no s. person would do	SHAW 780:42	eyes of man are never s.	BIBLE 100:60	s. like unto a blessed field	HERR 400:47
rewards for being s.	AMIS 14:92	forces s. mediocrity	RENAN 683:98	stinking s.	BIBLE 101:86
s. balance of values	POUND 665:56	having it, is s.?	THAC 849:94	very homely household s.	BYRON 182:83
S.…did what their neighbours	ELIOT 303:1	kisses…to make me fully s.?	CATU 201:6	with your sweet s.	BIBLE 105:89
Show me a s. man	JUNG 453:9	Massey won't be s.	KAUF 455:54	**savoury** meat is s.	EMER 312:24
they shall be s.	THOM 852:61	may be equally s.	JOHN 443:82	**saw** find thy s. of might	SHAK 750:71
San Francisco Heart in S. F.	CROSS 246:83	s. with her lover's mind	TROL 866:83	**sawdust** S. and spangles	CARD 189:41
not leave in S. F.	HART 384:8	s. with that result	SCHW 721:65	**sawed-off** as a s.-o. shotgun	PARK 638:77
S. F. is a lady	MAIL 540:55	way to be s.	BAGE 51:79	**Sawyer** Tom S. he says the same	TWAIN 871:10
sang s. and wallowed	THOM 853:2	**satisfy** delights of art s. me	FUEN 340:41	**saxophone** s. is the embodied spirit	BENN 76:54
s. his didn't	CUMM 248:19	none of these finally s.	WHIT 906:52	s. was…his key to the world	HOLM 407:72
s. themselves to sleep	HODG 405:43	s. our thirst for freedom	KING 468:37	**say** can s. only one thing at a time	HOMA 408:8
sanitary glorified s. engineer	STRA 826:83	those who are hardest to s.	DESC 263:68	don't have to s. anything	FURT 342:72
sanity fight…to bring back s.	GAIT 342:87	**saturated** too s. with it	DURK 296:32	have something to s.	WHAT 902:58
Neither conscience nor s.	MCNA 537:92	**Saturday** couple of drinks on a S.	FYFFE 342:78	I have so much more to s.	RAVEL 679:36

isn't what I s., but how I s. it — WEST 901:36
like to s. nothing — SOPH 804:88
little to s. — SKEL 794:89
many things to s. unto you — BIBLE 118:13
must s. something but not much — REAG 680:61
nothing at all to s. — SAINT 709:13
Nothing is easier to s. — TERE 848:78
nothing to s. — BALF 55:57
nothing to s., s. nothing — COLT 228:53
not moved to s. something — HUNT 423:36
O s., can you see — KEY 465:76
relevance for what it does not s. — FERL 321:13
s. nothing, do nothing, be nothing — ANON 25:72
S. not soft things — SORL 804:90
s. the perfectly correct thing — SHAW 780:71
s. what they please — FRED 336:36
s. what you have to s. — WELL 898:66
so much still to s. — BART 63:27
that's what I shall s.! — GILB 354:5
you should s. what you mean — CARR 195:71
saying ancient s. is no heresy — SHAK 740:64
do now remember a s. — SHAK 750:83
famous witty s. — THUR 859:45
lest a s. learnt — TENN 846:26
s. of an ancient philosopher — ADDI 6:16
This is a faithful s. — BIBLE 123:73
used to s. something different — HAVEL 385:29
sayings heareth these s. of mine — BIBLE 110:13
s. are generally like women's letters — HAZL 388:86
says Don't report what he s. — ANON 23:92
Who is it that s. most — SHAK 772:34
scabs Make yourselves s.? — SHAK 769:56
scaffold content to die…on the s. — BROWN 157:42
s. and the doom — AYTO 45:17
whether on the s. high — SULL 828:17
scaffolding s. of spirit — THOM 855:33
There is no s. — HONE 409:29
scald s. and viper through her — THOM 853:95
tears Do s. like molten lead — SHAK 764:97
scale judicious, is the s. — MILT 584:5
On every golden s.! — CARR 194:54
Poetic justice, with her lifted s. — POPE 662:65
s. doesn't matter — DONO 282:97
Scotland in true s. — MACD 529:38
something on the s. of the grand — DIDE 274:90
scales cannot balance tragedy in the s. — BENET 75:13
weighed the mountains in s. — BIBLE 103:38
scallop-shell s.-s. of quiet — RALE 677:99
scalpel intimacy of a surgeon's s. — ANGE 17:46
scan presume not God to s. — POPE 660:31
scandal Cut S.'s head off — SHER 787:50
divided…by public s. — DUMAS 294:94
Love and s. — FIEL 322:35
No s. about Queen Elizabeth — SHER 788:64
no s. like rags — FARQ 318:56
Retired to their tea and s. — CONG 231:6
s.…gives offence — MOLI 590:32
s. is often worse than the sin — MARG 549:42
s. of…exalted person's fall — CANM 188:7
scandalous Monarch, s. and poor — ROCH 691:52
scapegoat let him go for a s. — BIBLE 89:34
poor s. — HEAN 389:6
scapegoats s. for our blunders — TWAIN 872:30
they are the classic s. — WHITE 902:70
scar far from cliff and s. — TENN 841:4
scarce money was not s.? — EMER 313:50
s. a thing but is — MIDD 569:43
scarcity by the influence of s. — ROBB 689:14
from their s. and from…labour — RICA 684:34
s. of opportunity — ANGE 17:36
scarecrow s. of the law — SHAK 758:18
scared s. or too sulky — RYLE 707:80
scarf S. up the tender eye — SHAK 746:93
scarlet bind this line of s. thread — BIBLE 90:63
lips more s. — YEATS 934:56
live with s. Majors — SASS 716:61
Lovely creature in s. — GEOR 350:24
raise the s. standard — CONN 232:55
s. coat — WILDE 910:52
sins were s. — BELL 73:66
though your sins be as s. — BIBLE 102:7
scars My Marks and S. I carry — BUNY 160:71
scarred who carry our s. — GEE 348:92
s. that never felt a wound — SHAK 736:45
sleeve and show his s. — SHAK 746:58
scarves present them with s. — BAIN 52:11
scatter s. and gather — HERA 396:66

s. up and down — SHAK 730:58
scattered God blew and they were s. — ANON 20:6
scene Act One, S. One — HART 384:14
ask to see The distant s. — NEWM 612:62
breath, a little s. — SHAK 735:20
every day Speaks a new s. — QUAR 674:37
lofty s. be acted over — SHAK 748:98
naive impression of the s. — MONET 591:53
Of what s. — SHEL 785:98
preside o'er the s. — TANN 836:91
start a s. or two — ELIOT 304:23
Supporting…Unto the S. — DICK 272:69
Sweet especial rural s. — HOPK 412:92
this s. of man — POPE 660:6
Upon that memorable s. — MARV 555:55
waste his dearest s. — COLL 228:44
wildness to perplex the s. — POPE 659:95
scenery chew up the s. — PARK 637:48
end of all natural s. — RUSK 704:11
helps s. like ham and eggs — TWAIN 870:64
lovely descriptions of s. — BELL 72:35
S. is fine — KEATS 457:96
s. was beautiful — WOOL 923:66
scenes behind your s. — JOHN 441:22
feelings these dull s. produce — CRAB 242:1
From s. like these — BURNS 170:70
heart with usury to such s. — LAMB 486:29
s. his fathers loved — CULL 247:93
s. of our life — SCHO 720:36
s. where man hath never trod — CLARE 219:46
seldom…making love in any of his s. — DRYD 288:29
synthesizing the s. — MARA 548:23
scent first s. you pour — HORA 414:27
How hot the s. is — GRAV 367:64
s.…locust blossoms — WILL 914:57
s. of unwashed bodies — ACKR 3:54
s. survives their close — THOM 855:35
stronger s. towards evening — STAEL 811:49
sweetest flower for s. — SHEL 785:86
scents render Their pleasing s. — WEBS 894:75
sceptic knowledge for the s. side — POPE 660:16
scepticism if we start from s. — RUSS 705:55
preserve our s. — HUME 422:6
principles which at first lead to s. — BERK 79:7
sceptre S. and crown…tumble down — SHIR 789:83
s. as an emblem of royalty — BENT 77:68
s. for a palmer's…staff — SHAK 735:22
s. so fantastically borne — SHAK 745:39
s. to control the world — SHAK 731:89
sceptreless S., free…but man — SHEL 785:81
schedule s. is already full — KISS 475:96
Scheherazadesworth S. of stories — BARTH 62:3
Scheisskopf S. had the facts — HELL 392:61
scheme assist this detestable s. — MACA 525:45
interpret it as a rational s. — ROBI 690:40
s. by which the nations — LEES 500:50
s. of merriment — JOHN 442:56
Socialists and s. — MACL 536:54
stoical s. of supplying — SWIFT 831:69
schemes best-laid s. o' Mice — BURNS 170:72
expediency of different s. — STEU 819:9
s. for persuading monarchs — SWIFT 831:82
schizophrenia Canada is paranoid s. — ATWO 38:52
schizophrenic experience…is…s. — WITT 918:49
Schoenberg Why is S.'s Music — BERG 79:91
scholar better s. than Wordsworth — HOUS 415:69
gentleman an' s. — BURNS 170:74
humour of a s. — BACON 50:51
Like a dull s. — STEV 819:25
my honest s. — WALT 888:52
never be a complete s. — PLATH 654:63
s.'s life — JOHN 441:17
to this day is every s. poor — MARL 553:16
Zip, I am such a s.! — RODG 693:92
scholars nor its great s. great men — HOLM 408:86
philosophers and s. — PASC 641:39
scholarship boys or s. candidates — LITT 512:77
school aim of the s. of business — DEMI 261:83
at s. or college — STEV 822:97
Example is the s. of mankind — BURKE 169:51
explain s. to a higher intelligence? — MATH 560:61
for life, not for s. — SENE 727:92
get the feeling…you're not in s. — BRAN 150:89
growth of the Skyscraper S. — JOHN 440:96
kiddie in s. — NASH 608:83
no rhyme…for 's.' — SHAK 745:24
oyster of the old s. — DICK 270:87

playing fields of a public s. — FRY 339:22
private s. has all the faults — CONN 233:72
s. boys or scholarship — LITT 512:77
S. is where you go — UPDI 874:75
s. of flattery and dissimulation — WENT 899:42
s. that I went to in the north — WILS 915:89
s.…with tomorrow inside — AKERS 9:79
taught his little s. — GOLD 361:54
Three little maids from s. — GILB 355:24
till he's been to a good s. — SAKI 710:36
till we leave s. — LEWIS 507:78
truck passing by a music s.? — CAGE 184:28
went to s. without any boots — BULM 166:55
schoolboy Not the s. heat — TENN 844:62
what every s. knows — SWIFT 831:89
whining s. with his satchel — SHAK 749:49
schoolboys go chide Late s. — DONNE 279:41
like s. — KIER 467:8
s. who…climb a crab-tree — ROCH 691:63
schoolchildren What all s. learn — AUDEN 40:7
schoolgirl Pert as a s. — GILB 355:24
schooling finish my s. without — ANON 24:39
s. any actress needs — GING 357:58
school-inspector s.-i. of average — KING 469:57
schoolman s.'s subtle art — POPE 661:42
schoolmaster s.'s answer — GRAV 368:86
you'll be becoming a s. — WAUGH 891:99
schoolmasters all the s. you can — CHIS 213:16
Let s. puzzle their brain — GOLD 362:64
schools class s.…into four grades — WAUGH 891:10
endeavour, through its s. — RUSS 705:49
hundred s. of thought — MAO 548:12
in the maze of s. — POPE 658:51
lumber of the s. — SWIFT 830:51
s. are not much good — DRUC 287:11
s. for the imagination — GIRA 358:81
s. of Oxford — GIBB 351:57
s. of theology…are to be overturned — DIDE 274:96
Tedium…in s. — POMP 658:47
wait for s. to be built — QABO 674:32
schooner was the s. Hesperus — LONG 516:47
Schopenhauer S.…madmen! — ONEI 625:99
Schubert not Bach or S. — MCCU 529:23
sciatic cure epilepsy and s. gout. — THEO 851:40
S. fiction is no more…for scientists — ALDI 10:10
s. fiction is the apocalyptic literature — BALL 57:1
S. fiction writers foresee — ASIM 35:4
science Advertising…as the s. — LEAC 497:36
aim of s. is always — JAMES 434:62
All s. is cosmology — POPP 663:95
All s. requires mathematics — BACON 50:71
an art and not a s. — MO 589:21
and s. weak — SZASZ 834:61
application of natural s. — MARX 558:12
Art and S. cannot exist — BLAKE 135:73
a serious interest…in s. — PYKE 673:29
beams of s. fall — POPE 662:71
by s. as well as bread — JAMES 434:59
can s. flourish — PARS 640:1
consciousness of s. — DEWEY 264:43
create a whole s. — ROST 699:8
Creativity in s. — KOES 477:32
Detection is…an exact s. — DOYLE 285:51
early successes of s. — HUXL 425:83
Economics as a positive s. — FRIE 337:62
Economics is the s. — ROBB 689:14
Enough of s. — WORD 924:75
express themselves…upon the s. — MAIM 541:68
Fair S. frowned not — GRAY 369:24
find in art and s. — HALD 377:76
from s., is criticism — RUSS 705:41
Furnished…with Academies of S. — FRAN 335:17
generalizations of s. sweep — HUXL 426:5
give their lives to art and s. — EINS 301:33
god of s. — KING 468:47
grand aim of all s. — EINS 302:46
great man of s. — KING 469:58
great tragedy of S. — HUXL 426:9
hardest s. to forget — POPE 659:84
higher parts of his s. — MACA 526:61
History is not a s. — FRAN 333:90
history of s. reaches Alan Turing — HODG 405:41
history of s. shows — DARW 253:12
hope of s. — INGE 429:55
human s. is at a loss — CHOM 214:19
I am called s. — FLAU 326:40
if it is to be a s. — JEVO 438:44

try to walk s. STEV 823:19
sedge s. has wither'd KEATS 458:17
seditions surest way to prevent s. BACON 48:11
seduce s., bamboozle LIPP 512:72
seducer Thou strong s. DRYD 288:37
seduction ethical or social s. BEVAN 84:17
persuade her to give it away (s.) DWOR 296:46
see cannot s., and in the third NORTH 618:68
complain we cannot s. BERK 79:4
day…meant not to s. THAT 850:22
few…learn to s. OKRI 624:61
Helen, did Homer never s. JONS 450:50
In all things Thee to s. HERB 397:94
I s. what I eat CARR 195:71
I was blind, now I s. BIBLE 118:99
lovers cannot s. SHAK 740:61
much to hear and s. SKEL 794:89
neither s. nor hear JOHN 441:4
not that I did not s. HOLM 407:70
pleasure of believing what we s. SHEL 782:24
power…to make you s. CONR 234:95
s. and hear and understand HEMI 394:8
s. better than I do GOYA 365:30
S. one…s. all BURT 174:73
s. them as they are JOHN 447:78
s. things, and you say, 'Why?' SHAW 781:2
s. this day and live SHAK 746:57
still can't s. HUGH 418:19
stream…we s. ourselves in FROST 339:1
what we do not s. SHAK 758:21
what we s. is life WARR 889:72
won't even go to s. it GRANT 366:46
yet I s. thee still SHAK 767:94
You s., but you do not observe DOYLE 285:65
seed bearing precious s. BIBLE 98:91
blood…is the s. TERT 849:82
carrying your s. MARQ 553:20
democrat…gone to s. EMER 313:36
enmity between thy s. and her s. BIBLE 86:53
few more lies eat into the s. MAIL 539:38
Nestles the s. perfection WHIT 906:51
nor his s. begging bread BIBLE 95:17
received s. among the thorns BIBLE 112:48
received s. into the good ground BIBLE 112:49
s. its harvest KEATS 457:4
s. of knowledge BACON 46:35
s. should not be his BIBLE 88:96
sowed in youth a mustard s. BRON 154:76
spring again from its s. SHEL 786:13
thy s. may live BIBLE 90:54
weed…of celestial s. DRYD 290:84
seeds colonization planted the s. MARI 549:48
in a bag all sorts of s. SPEN 809:15
s. of time SHAK 766:72
some s. fell by the wayside BIBLE 112:47
seedtime s. and harvest BIBLE 87:67
seed-time Fair s.-t. WORD 925:91
seeing better at believing than at s. SANT 714:22
faculty of s. things SPEN 807:60
gave up s. years ago JOHN 441:4
Not 'S. is Believing' WOLFE 920:92
point is the s. REID 682:95
S. is deceiving THUR 859:47
s. on the screen GOLD 362:83
s. what Adam had seen HUXL 425:93
s. what everybody has seen SZENT 834:64
way of s. is also a way of not s. BURKE 169:57
way of s. them RUSK 704:13
Worth s.? JOHN 445:39
seek do not s. to understand ANSE 26:5
may not so much s. FRAN 334:98
not need to s. out TOCQ 861:87
s. all day SHAK 739:41
s., and ye shall find BIBLE 110:7
S. ye the Lord BIBLE 104:54
To strive, to s. TENN 840:66
Who s., who hope, who love SIDN 790:15
seeker s. for cures RICH 685:55
seemed s. well pleased, all s. MILT 583:82
seems know not 's.' SHAK 751:3
seen as I done it I s. it SAND 713:3
cannot be s. and sung ISAA 430:34
God whom he hath not s.! BIBLE 125:41
if it's s. through GREE 371:77
I've sometimes s. RIMB 687:88
much have I s. TENN 839:63
not having s. JOHN 445:22

s. enough of one war JEFF 436:17
s. for what one is DRAB 286:88
s. to be done HEWA 401:69
s. to want…certainly never get WEAT 893:61
The less s. WILD 911:89
Things that are s. JOHNS 439:68
things that I have s. POLO 657:40
to be loved needs only to be s. DRYD 291:15
vanity of being s. SMOL 801:28
what is s. during a moment SAND 713:99
where they cannot be s. HAWK 385:31
sees s. is truly seen SNYD 802:48
thinks he believes only what he s. SANT 714:22
segment s. of our population TRUM 868:29
segregation S. now, s. tomorrow WALL 886:6
Seine flows the S. APOL 27:16
seismograph Collage…a s. ERNST 315:90
lightning rod than a s. KESEY 465:72
seize S. the day HORA 413:19
seldom s. look at them MORT 599:18
select not to a s. committee PULI 672:2
Selection called this…Natural S. DARW 253:10
S. is the invention FUSE 342:77
selective even more s. GREE 371:67
Observation is always s. POPP 663:94
selects s. and omits STRA 826:80
self All by my own-alone s. HARR 383:96
Am I your s. SHAK 747:85
Anger's s. I needs must kiss SIDN 790:13
at once as Nature's s. BROW 161:48
Dearer than s. BYRON 179:10
door out of the dungeon of s. MACD 530:54
dungeon of s. CONN 233:84
fictitious s. CHOP 214:23
final distillation of s. DELI 261:78
for its absolute s. WORD 928:54
greater to one than one's s. WHIT 905:34
high authority of the s. TRIL 866:71
incomplete s. GASS 346:61
knowledge of the s. KANT 454:40
live without the s. ATWO 38:58
look within and examine your own s. CONF 230:88
mysterious belief in a s. MANS 547:89
s. as the window UPDI 875:93
s. cannot be escaped BART 62:14
s.…epicentre of the solar system PHIL 650:94
s. is now the sacred cow HUGH 419:35
s. persists like a dying star ROET 694:8
small hungry shivering s. ELIOT 304:11
that's your own s. HUXL 425:88
The essential s. UPDI 874:90
The s. is hateful PASC 641:25
thy s. present SPEN 808:67
to thine own s. be true SHAK 751:22
was his natural s. TWAIN 871:98
weave my s. into the sense HERB 398:8
Wisdom's s. Oft seeks MILT 577:35
write for the public and have no s. CONN 233:62
self-absorbed sign of the s.-a. RYBC 707:75
self-assertion Japanese see s.-a. KURO 482:42
self-assured s.-a. who strut HAMM 379:8
self-awareness highest state of s.-a. LARD 490:15
self-complacency s.-c. brought WEBB 893:62
self-condemning neither s.-c. MILT 595:70
self-confession Christ…the s.-c. FEUE 321:21
self-conscious most s.-c. people JAMES 433:35
race which has become s.-c. LAWR 494:99
self-consciousness writer's s.-c. UPDI 874:89
self-consumer s.-c. of my woes CLARE 219:45
self-contain'd placid and s.-c. WHIT 905:33
self-contradiction poet is a s.-c. FROST 339:3
self-control s.-c.…courage PEEL 646:10
self-definition starved for s.-d. BURNS 169:59
self-denial S.-d. is not a virtue SHAW 779:15
self-destruction beginnings of s.-d. CHEE 209:99
self-determination S.-d. is not WILS 917:18
self-development S.-d. is…duty STAN 812:68
self-devotion saved by his…s.-d. MACA 527:78
self-discovery s.-d. WALC 885:83
self-division man in s.-d.! SIDN 790:99
self-esteem s.-e. is sacrosanct HUGH 419:35
wiping out his s.-e. MARI 550:63
self-examination practise s.-e. ICHI 428:39
significant s.-e. PECK 645:4
self-fashioned s.-f. chains of slavery MANS 546:81
self-flagellation for s.-f. solely CAPO 189:28
self-fulfilling s.-f. prophecy MERT 568:22

self-government experience of s.-g. EDIN 300:8
self-help healthy spirit of s.-h. SMIL 797:34
spirit of s.-h. SMIL 797:32
spirit of s.-h. SMIL 797:34
self-image crippled s.-i. THOM 855:45
self-indulgence essay on 's.-i.' WAUGH 891:13
self-interest enlightened s.-i. KEYN 465:84
selfish s. molecules known as genes DAWK 256:72
s. propriety of civilized man MUIR 602:66
s. and s. STEV 821:80
selfishness a cheerleader for s. ONEI 626:9
dross of s. ROCK 692:77
S. must always be forgiven AUST 43:73
strongest protest against s. GOOD 363:98
self-justification habit…of s.-j. EDGE 299:93
self-love golden-calf of s.-l. CARL 192:14
life depends upon s.-l. JORD 450:67
s.-l. and social be the same POPE 660:22
s.-l. is always the beginning MANN 546:72
S.-l., my liege SHAK 746:41
S.-l.…often unrequited POWE 666:78
self-lovers nature of extreme s.-l. BACON 49:22
self-made was a s.-m. man HELL 392:18
self-neglecting vile a sin As s.-n. SHAK 746:41
self-parody S.-p. is the first portent MCMU 537:88
self-pity S.-p.…is as snug ANGE 17:40
self-portrait S.-p. in a Convex Mirror ASHB 35:84
self-presentation place for s.-p. RYBC 707:75
self-preservation ensure Japan's s.-p. HIRO 403:3
self-raised fail to reascend s.-r. MILT 581:13
self-removed must be s.-r. MANS 546:81
self-respect Being an MP…starves
your s.-r. PARR 639:97
self-love and s.-r. JORD 450:67
S.-r.…comes to us GRIS 373:20
self-restraint promotes s.-r. TAFT 835:74
self-revelation fluidity of s.-r. JAMES 434:52
self-righteousnes S.-r. is not religion BRON 155:82
self-sacrifice higher duty than s.-s. STAN 812:68
s.-s. as the sensible course KURO 482:42
S.-s. enables us to sacrifice SHAW 779:26
self-schooled s.-s., self-scanned ARNO 31:90
self-seeking in a less s.-s. age CECIL 202:27
self-slain god s.-s. SWIN 834:52
self-slaughter Against s.-s. SHAK 774:65
canon 'gainst s.-s.! SHAK 751:50
self-sufficing reasoning, s.-s. thing WORD 924:82
self-worship s.-w. of the monarch MILL 571:79
sell as if it were to s. HERB 398:7
buy with you, s. with you SHAK 739:50
how well they s. JOYCE 452:2
no man might buy or s. BIBLE 126:67
s. his grandmother GRANT 366:49
selling lives by s. something STEV 823:26
selves Anger and tenderness: my s. RICH 685:54
many…hundreds of s.? MANS 547:84
nor is it our s. UPDI 875:93
s. conditional UPDI 875:94
stronger, riskier s. MORR 599:4
the particularity of s. TRIL 866:71
semantic s. inversions MAMET 543:28
semblable mon s. ELIOT 306:55
semblance bore S. of worth MILT 581:14
semicolon not enough…to be s. BRAT 150:95
semicolony s. BRAT 150:95
seminars girls suffered…so did my s. BERR 82:67
sempiternal S. though sodden ELIOT 308:37
Sempronius we'll do more, s. ADDI 6:31
senate half-creature of the S. MANS 547:98
S. becomes the wife TAYL 837:19
tuned in the US S. BRIN 153:40
senator Korea, S.…American blood MACA 524:21
Time is the 101st S. DODD 278:5
United States S. JOHN 440:81
senators group of s. DAUG 253:20
burst with laughter AUDEN 40:98
send I refuse to s. anyone else RANK 679:19
not about to s. American boys JOHN 440:83
time for you to s. it back JACK 431:5
Whom shall I s. BIBLE 102:12
senility the prime of s. OTOO 630:20
senior s. years are reached RAND 678:11
sennights Weary s. nine times nine SHAK 766:68
sensation delightful s. FERB 320:98
objects of S. LOCKE 514:18
seat of this s. HOUS 416:8
s. is the same HEMI 394:3

s. of a short, sharp shock — GILB 355:25
sensational somewhat too s. — WILDE 909:42
sensations life of s. — KEATS 457:90
penultimate s. — GALS 344:24
secret of their s. — MACKE 533:14
s. sweet — WORD 923:69
truth of my own s. — CONR 235:17
sense afraid of losing your moral s. — STEIN 815:10
any s. of direction — WILS 915:72
art of making s. — MACL 535:51
beauty to my s. shall run — DONNE 279:34
Bereaving s., but endless — MILT 585:26
Bestow a purer s. — MALL 542:95
between s. and nonsense — JUNG 453:8
bring men back to common s. — BERK 79:7
common s., and relatively — MORT 599:12
common s. tells us — NABO 606:29
creeps after s. — DRYD 288:32
Decking the s. — HERB 398:7
deep s. of…shame — WEBS 894:82
Devoid of s. and motion — MILT 581:22
don't need so much s. — HERN 399:28
each other and with the s. — KUHN 481:35
echo to the s. — POPE 658:59
established s. it is socially nil — LAWR 494:3
fine s. of the ridiculous — ALBEE 9:91
fountain of good s. — DRYD 292:46
free of s. and restriction — HEAT 390:26
glorious s. of words — ACHE 2:24
Good s. is the most fairly — DESC 263:18
If that s. is lost — EMER 313:53
in a two-fold s. — MILL 573:44
integrated s. — THUR 860:52
it is not s. — CHUR 271:53
It is not tricks of s. — WILB 907:76
lose the sin, yet keep the s. — POPE 659:84
lost s. of Victorian regard — PRIT 669:56
man of s. and a fop — CHES 210:26
Men of sound s. — PLATO 655:83
more or less dumb s. — JAMES 434:69
Much S.—the starkest Madness — DICK 272:61
none in her s. — BEHN 71:20
oddest frame of s. — SHAK 758:46
one…of s. forlorn — COLE 225:93
poor toper whose untutored s. — CRAB 242:81
religious s. of duty — DICK 271:41
rough s. of the daily jostle — DELI 261:80
Seal thy s. in deathly slumber — DELA 260:72
s. and observation — WORD 928:56
s. and outward things — WORD 927:26
s. by indirection, degrees of anger — EVANS 316:20
s. from nonsense — THUR 860:54
s. is mocked in every thing — DAVI 254:35
s. of a long last night — MAIL 540:50
s. of being more — RUSS 705:44
s. of intellectual degradation — JAMES 433:27
s. of taste — BALL 57:4
's.' of what is going on — BART 62:10
s. of wonder — SOCR 803:55
s. sublime — WORD 923:71
Shadwell never deviates into s. — DRYD 288:49
shamefaced s. — MORE 597:68
sing good s. — LOUI 518:96
splendour borrows…from s. — POPE 659:98
Still follow s. — POPE 659:94
Take care of the s. — CARR 195:76
That it enchants my s. — SHAK 757:1
That the s. aches — SHAK 760:2
the ground s. necessary — WILL 913:40
the s. faints — SHEL 783:45
Through s. and nonsense — DRYD 290:99
to curb the s. — DRYD 292:49
Touch…most demystifying of all s. — BART 62:19
use only Arguments of S. — PETTY 650:86
want of s. — DILL 275:17
weave my self into the s. — HERB 398:8
without any sign of common s. — CHIR 213:15
without one grain of s. — DRYD 290:9
work upon the vulgar with fine s. — POPE 659:88
world of s. and the world — RUSS 705:56
sense-experience limits of…s.-e. — AYER 44:9
senseless worse than s. things! — SHAK 746:71
senses assault on the s. — MCCA 528:97
colour to that of the S. — MATI 560:64
come to my s. — GRAMM 366:41
disagreeable to all the s. — DICK 270:97
extensions of our s. — STEV 820:58

five s. within whose pentagon — BERG 79:94
fool o'th' other s. — SHAK 767:95
ill customs influence my very s. — ETHE 315:98
Let s. rule — SHAK 745:38
makes the s. rough — SHAK 729:47
Parson lost his s. — HODG 405:46
power to touch our s. — MILT 576:97
s. can think nothing — KANT 454:39
stuck to all my s. — MITC 588:90
subtlety of the s. — BACON 47:58
there are only five s. — PATM 643:65
the s. still supply — WORD 923:67
Unto our gentle s. — SHAK 767:85
use of the s. and hands — DARW 253:15
sensibilities as the s. decline — STOWE 826:75
middle-class people of nice s. — SHAR 776:46
one's own fine s. — HELL 393:82
sensibility Dear s.! — STER 818:7
dissociation of s. — ELIOT 305:50
Experience…an immense s. — JAMES 433:42
multisibling s. — COUP 239:98
self-confession of human s. — FEUE 321:21
s. of a male adolescent — AUDEN 41:30
s. of principle — BURKE 169:35
s. transformed into intelligence — GOUR 365:27
sensible Extremely s. — STEW 824:44
no s. man directly challenges — MACM 536:77
S. men are all the same religion — CARR 196:93
silly things…done by s. people — DISR 277:90
sing when they are feeling s. — AUST 43:84
sensitive s. boy's humiliations — AUDEN 41:15
s. man understands — SHAW 778:85
S. Plant in a garden grew — FRIE 337:67
sensitivities Irish feelings and s. — SHEL 785:84
sensual first a s. — HAUG 385:28
inordinate s. delight — HOOK 410:55
music and s. matters — BAXT 65:90
only s. pleasure without vice — KHOM 466:97
sensualists tyrants and s. — JOHN 447:72
sensuality s.…into sexual vanity — WOLL 921:6
sent Who s. you to me—God? — WEBB 893:62
sentence canvas a s. or paragraph — PUCC 672:97
declared meaning of a spoken s. — MOTH 600:33
hit…reader…with your first s. — CAREY 190:66
if this is slavery, give me a life s. — BRIS 153:43
judges soon the s. sign — CHAR 207:43
most important…the English s. — POPE 659:73
pronounced a more rounded s. — JOVA 451:76
pull of the s. — JOHN 446:64
S. first—verdict afterwards — MOORE 595:40
s. is a sound — CARR 195:88
s. is factually significant — FROST 338:88
s. structure — AYER 44:10
single s. in a routine article — THUR 859:46
sentences Backward ran s. — MEYER 568:30
complete s. — GIBBS 352:73
mania for s. — GASS 346:61
mix s. with dirt — FLAU 326:26
Mr. Blackman in three s. — BRAU 150:1
s., the structure — NGU 613:79
S. which simply express moral — MORR 599:7
silences between s. — AYER 45:11
sentiment corrupted by s. — LIND 510:42
nurse of manly s. — GREE 371:54
rich in s. — BURKE 169:35
s. jointly dictate — TENN 841:96
s. which I feel strongly — RODO 693:94
those who have no s. — SCOTT 725:57
truth of description and the s. — MAIL 540:51
sentimental America…s. land — SCOTT 725:54
corrupt art is the s. — RABAN 675:61
getting more s. as I get older — PISS 652:32
sentimentalism inclined towards s. — CART 198:41
S. is the working off — CARD 190:45
sentimentality S. is a failure — LAWR 495:24
S. is the emotional promiscuity — STEV 820:34
Sledgehammer s. — MAIL 540:51
sentimentering no time to be s. — KENT 464:60
sentiments beautiful s. — TWAIN 871:4
s. in the world — GIDE 353:83
Them's my s.! — LOWE 520:35
sentry quadrille in a s. box — THAC 849:89
stands a wingèd s. — JAMES 433:48
separated now we're s. — VAUG 878:47
separately all hang s. — STRO 827:95
separateness his weakness and his s. — FRAN 335:16

separation consent to the s. — BELL 74:85
preludes to that eternal s. — GEOR 349:13
protesting against s. — STER 818:93
s. breeds…regrets — GRAT 367:61
Six degrees of s. — CH 213:11
sepòlchered s. in such pomp — GUARE 374:26
September cool S. morn — MILT 576:3
sing in S. — WHIT 906:61
When you reach S. — KEND 461:95
sepulchre came first to the s. — ANDE 16:20
man the living s. — BIBLE 118:22
no man knoweth of his s. — CLARE 219:44
stone taken away from the s. — BIBLE 90:60
sepulchres like unto whited s. — BIBLE 118:21
sequence events…happen in a s. — BIBLE 113:84
sequential s., but memory — WELTY 899:1
sequestered Each s. in its hate — LIVE 512:81
one of those s. spots — AUDEN 40:4
Serbia I'm the Ayatollah Khomeini of S. — HARDY 382:61
Kosovo is not a part of S. — MILO 575:91
Serbs S. out, Nato in, refugees back — MILO 575:90
S. will follow me — ROBE 689:21
sere fall'n into the s. — MILO 575:91
serene more solemn and s. — SHAK 768:37
Serengeti six…left in the S. — SHEL 782:21
Serenissima pinnacles of the S. — BENN 76:28
serenity complaints…undermine the s. — MORR 598:93
steady and perpetual s. — ACHE 2:36
serf hands of a s. — ADDI 6:20
serfdom abolish s. from above — HYDE 427:23
serial obituary in s. form — ALEX 11:21
series in a s. of courses — CRISP 245:59
s. of great opportunities — GOLD 361:35
s. of undertakings — GARD 346:45
serious Comedy is a very s. thing — SART 715:52
Dead men are s. — GARR 346:55
from s. things — FIND 323:59
Make…the s. smile — THOR 857:84
more s. than I should be — POPE 659:86
much more s. than that — SIDN 790:98
Of all s. things — SHAN 776:28
position is s. — BEAU 66:3
s. attempt to do it — KEYN 466:87
s. reading — WELLS 898:92
tell when one is getting old and s. — WELLS 898:78
the s. and the smirk — EDWA 300:21
think of something s. — DICK 267:3
you are not s. — TRAV 864:45
You cannot be s.! — RIMB 687:91
seriousness wallowing in low s. — MCEN 531:64
sermon funeral s. — BELL 74:84
painful s. — BELL 73:60
preach a brilliant s. — PEPYS 647:29
rejected the S. on the Mount — HUXL 424:58
short nap at s. — BRAD 149:73
whole of her s. — ADDI 6:14
sermons frightened by 'political' s. — FORS 331:36
S. and soda water the day after — BARTH 62:7
S. in stones — BYRON 182:79
serpent dust shall be the s.'s meat — SHAK 749:34
find the s. old — BIBLE 104:66
old s., called the Devil — MARV 556:69
s. beguiled me — BIBLE 126:66
s. did not seduce Eve — BIBLE 86:52
s. of brass — HUGH 419:45
s. shall bite him — BIBLE 89:39
s. to sting you — BIBLE 101:87
s. under't — SHEL 782:9
s. was more subtil — SHAK 766:84
sharper than a s.'s tooth — BIBLE 86:48
Time like a s. — SHAK 762:63
venomous as the poison of a s. — CRANE 243:18
will he give him a s.? — BOOK 143:55
serpent-haunted s.-h. sea — BIBLE 110:8
serpents s. of explosive breath — FLEC 327:48
wise as s. — MARI 550:53
servant act of the s. — BIBLE 111:26
bid your s. once adieu — LEON 503:8
cast ye the unprofitable s. — SHAK 771:23
clever s. — BIBLE 113:90
good and faithful s. — JEFF 436:4
he is the s. of the Living God — BIBLE 113:89
looking-glass of a s. — SMART 796:25
Lord, thy s. rears — JOYCE 452:85
never leave to be Your humble s. — HERB 397:89
nor the s. above his lord — ROCH 691:61
now lettest thou thy s. — BIBLE 111:27
— BIBLE 128:1

now lettest thou thy s.	BIBLE 115:27
obligation to become the s.	SHAW 780:54
politician poses as the s.	DE 259:43
press...is an excellent s.	COOP 236:54
public s. who make it	NEW 611:50
S. of God, well done	MILT 583:83
s. of the sciences	BAUD 64:67
s. or has business	LAW 493:85
s. shall be healed	BIBLE 110:14
s. to be bred at an University	CONG 231:19
s. to the devil	SISS 793:55
s. with this clause	HERB 397:53
services of a menial s.	GRAY 368:91
Speak, Lord; for thy s. heareth	BIBLE 91:82
took upon him the form of a s.	BIBLE 123:54
wakes them himself, or sends his s.	ADDI 6:14
when ye hae a gude s.	SCOTT 724:29
whose s. I am	LENT 503:2
writer or a good public s.	MACM 537:83
servants as one of thy hired s.	BIBLE 116:47
domestic s. at home	MAUG 561:81
Give unto thy s. that peace	BOOK 140:76
reveal Himself to his s.	MILT 579:81
S. accumulate the privileges	DONO 282:98
s. of the public	GOWE 365:28
s. of the sovereign	BACON 48:99
Unmarried men...best s.	BACON 48:89
We are the s. of the people	BLAIR 132:5
When domestic s. are treated	SHAW 778:10
workmen and menial s.	MALT 543:19
Ye s. of the Lord	DODD 278:9
serve Choose you...whom ye will s.	BIBLE 90:66
Him s. with fear	KETHE 465:75
s. and obey them	HUME 422:7
Thee only we s.	KORAN 477:40
serves S. to say thus	SHAK 743:60
service abdicated the s. of it	PITT 652:39
any s. to the world's end?	SHAK 744:95
arrived in my s. already christened	SAKI 710:37
century of active s.	MOUN 601:39
did more s. than he	GOLD 361:43
do you...much s.	ASTE 36:20
do you that last good s.	ROCH 691:66
essential s. to his country	SWIFT 831:80
If I last in this s.	SHAK 733:60
in purer lives thy s. find	WHIT 906:63
in the s. the scum	WELL 897:54
no-future job in the s. sector	COUP 238:89
point to his ease of s.	ISHI 431:93
reward for equally good s.	ROOS 696:55
s. and the greater glory	PIUS 653:55
s., as to the Lord	BIBLE 122:51
s. is the common duty	ROCK 692:77
s. of my love	SPRI 811:39
s. of this nation	GAND 345:32
s. to my bonie lassie	BURNS 171:2
s. we render to others	GREN 373:3
shrink from the s. of his country	PAINE 634:88
soong the s. dyvyne	CHAU 208:70
whose s. is perfect freedom	BOOK 140:73
serviceable s. villain	SHAK 764:95
serviceman do not call a s.	BRIN 153:40
services commands Our s. a while	SHAK 764:18
if his s. are not recognised	DUGO 293:89
Nor s. to do	SHAK 771:23
price...on the s.	FRIE 337:64
s. of a menial servant	GRAY 368:91
serviettes crumpled the s.	BETJ 84:5
servile s. minds into terror	TZARA 873:59
servility slave in base s.	SHAK 729:49
serving s. the client	JOHN 440:98
servitude base laws of s.	DRYD 288:35
History may be s.	ELIOT 309:45
out of s. into freedom	EMER 313:45
s. and extreme licence	TOCQ 861:82
s. still can pierce	MUIR 602:61
s....the consequence of his crime	CURR 249:41
s....To serve th' unwise	MILT 583:85
sesquipedalian S. blackguard	CLOU 222:17
sessions of sweet silent thought	SHAK 771:15
set by God's grace, play a s.	SHAK 745:30
s. down This	ELIOT 306:74
turn on your s.	BRIN 153:40
Virtue is...best plain s.	BACON 49:43
Setebos S., S., and S.!	BROW 162:75
settee Lady Venus on the s.	SITW 793:57
setting Had elsewhere its s.	WORD 926:24
haste now to my s.	SHAK 775:18
s. which influences it	ROSSO 698:6
settle helped to s. this glorious land	FERB 320:93
less will you s. for one	KIPL 472:16
settlement political s. of this crisis	HUSS 423:41
s. through genuine dialogue	AUNG 42:50
settler maintained by the s.	SART 716:55
settlers When old s. say	LESS 504:31
seven hewn out her s. pillars	BIBLE 99:18
Jacob served s. years	BIBLE 87:90
s. great facts and doctrines	HUGEL 418:12
seventy times s.	BIBLE 113:70
seventh God blessed the s. day	BIBLE 85:42
opened the s. seal	BIBLE 126:61
seventies vice of the S.	WOLFE 920:99
seventy To be s. years young	HOLM 408:99
seventy-seven At s.-s. it is time	JOHN 444:4
severance God their s. ruled	ARNO 32:10
severe intentionally a little too s.	KIER 467:14
s. he was and stern to view	GOLD 361:54
severest s. writers of the s. age	DRYD 288:45
severity pure s. of perfect light	TENN 846:23
simplicity or with s.	ARNO 33:37
Summer...with its usual s.	COLE 227:20
Severn from the S. to the Tyne!	KIPL 474:85
on S. snow the leaves	HOUS 415:55
the S. fills	TENN 843:30
Seville dogs of S.	TENN 848:61
sew time to s.	BIBLE 100:70
Sewell S. & Cross young man	GILB 354:9
sewer filthy s. pure gold flows	TOCQ 861:81
sea is the universal s.	COUS 239:5
trip through a s.	MIZN 589:17
sewers Ye Nymphs that reign o'er s.	COLE 227:23
sex accident of s.	GILM 356:54
broken down by Age, S.	MACR 538:18
call you darling after s.	BARN 60:74
can either s. assume	MILT 581:9
cardinal virtues of the s.	WOLL 921:7
complete example of her s.	RUSS 706:67
desire for food and s.	TOOLE 863:13
destroy s. in America	DOCT 277:2
difference is not that of s. or age	CIXO 218:33
eclipses and predominates...her s.	DOYLE 285:64
equal, as their s. not equal	MILT 583:62
Everybody lies about s.	SEIN 726:76
Every city has a s. and age	BERG 79:1
fair s. is your department	DOYLE 285:75
Gulf War was like teenage s.	HARK 383:81
his authority and her s.	WOLL 921:10
If God had meant...group s.	BRAD 148:60
if S-E-X ever rears its ugly head	AYCK 44:7
In the s. war	CONN 233:77
isn't s. but death	SONT 804:72
Literature is...about having s.	LODGE 514:21
litigation takes the place of s.	VIDAL 881:1
money buys women, s., status	DWOR 296:47
Money...was exactly like s.	BALD 54:36
offices that s. can discharge for s.	WOOLF 922:48
one s. from another	THUR 860:54
Pornography...attempt to insult s.	LAWR 495:29
practically conceal its s.	NASH 608:81
privilege...for my own s.	AUST 44:98
Redeem the age and s.	PHIL 650:91
riding high on s. and self-esteem	HOLL 407:69
romantic interest in our own s.	CONN 233:87
run after by the other s.	SHAW 780:52
s. and creativity are often	JONG 448:96
S. and obscenity are not synonymous	BREN 151:16
S. had never before asserted	HARDY 382:57
S....I really don't understand	SALI 711:53
S. is engaging	JIANG 438:49
s. is good for headaches	WILB 907:79
s. is just politics	BRAD 148:62
s. is like money	UPDI 874:78
S. Life in Ancient Rome face	AMIS 14:15
S. 'n' drugs 'n' rock 'n' roll	DURY 296:43
s. object	GIOV 357:74
s. rears its ugly 'ead	ALLI 12:60
S....single-crop farming	BELL 74:90
S. suppressed will go berserk	EWART 316:24
s. was something no woman	MUNRO 603:85
S.! What is that but life	CHER 210:21
s. with someone I love	ALLEN 12:54
Shall the s. free	HABI 376:54
She gave him s.	HEPB 396:60
soft, unhappy s.	BEHN 71:22
talk on 'S. and Civics'	BETJ 84:7
too visible as s. objects	FRIE 337:60
weaker s., to piety more prone	ALEX 11:27
what s. and psychoanalysis are	HUGH 419:32
When you have money, it's s.	DONL 279:24
woman into a s. object	MORG 597:82
Women complain about s.	LAND 488:74
word s. in capital letters	WAUGH 891:6
sexes absurd division into s.	WAUGH 892:22
great distinction between the s.	FOWL 332:67
intellectual powers of the two s.	DARW 253:15
merit of both s.	LABR 483:58
more difference within the s.	COMP 230:74
old ladies of both s.	DICK 270:10
there are three s.	SMITH 801:16
wiser...of the two s.	GIBB 351:54
wives of both s.	MACD 530:47
sexologist kind of German s.	DOCT 277:2
sexophones s. wailed like...cats	HUXL 425:78
sexual felt s. urgings	COND 230:35
man cares most for s. intercourse	TWAIN 872:36
rooted in the s. impulse	SCHO 719:33
S. Etiquette	LOCH 514:12
s. juices flow toward a painting	FUEN 340:41
s. relations with that woman	CLIN 221:97
sublimated...into s. activity	BRAD 148:52
sexuality s. and promiscuity	WYLIE 931:23
s....suddenly recognised	FREUD 336:51
women's horrifying s.	MILL 572:12
sexy seeing some s. football	GULL 375:37
shabby If I were s.	WHAR 901:46
S. gentility has nothing	HOLM 408:88
shackles garters to be bonds and s.	BACON 48:88
Memories are not s.	BENN 75:26
s. of an old love	TENN 846:19
shad-blow s.-b., flaked	CRANE 243:32
shade alone in summer s.	WORD 925:8
Amaryllis in the s.	MILT 578:49
broader browner s.	GRAY 369:4
clutching the inviolable s.	ARNO 32:32
enjoy the s.	JONS 450:51
fleeting image of a s.	SHEL 785:88
fountain, s., and rill	MILT 578:46
his steadfast s.	TENN 839:60
laws...of light and s.	CAPO 189:27
light, s. and perspective	CONS 235:27
Lord is thy s. upon thy right hand	BIBLE 98:77
No s., no shine	HOOD 410:52
ragged penury of s.	ADAMS 4:63
returned that s.	KEATS 458:15
s. is on the brightest wing	SITW 794:68
s. of a great name	LUCAN 521:70
S. off the trees	CORY 238:78
shall crowd into a s.	POPE 658:50
sitting in the s.	KIPL 474:73
sit under the s. of it	DICK 269:57
Spring...with rustling s.	SEEG 726:70
Summer-house, that knows no s.	POPE 659:95
throw no one into the s.	BULOW 166:56
Under the s. of a Coolibah	PATE 642:54
variable as the s.	SCOTT 723:1
Within its s. we'll live	CONN 232:55
shades Alcestis rises from the s.	LAND 488:78
luminous s.	GORD 363:6
preparing for bed with the s. up	STARR 813:77
regions of sorrow, doleful s.	MILT 580:97
s. and wanton winds	MILT 578:53
s. of darkness	DELA 260:71
s. of humiliation	EVANS 316:20
shadow ancient s. and twilights	RUSS 706:62
awful s. of some unseen Power	SHEL 782:19
but a s.'s s.	SHAK 752:55
care is like my s.	ELIZ 309:59
days on the earth are as a s.	BIBLE 92:40
dream...of a s.	CHAP 206:14
Falls the s.	ELIOT 306:71
hair and my s.	NERU 611:42
have to vanquish his s.	NIET 615:6
I am your s.	SCEVE 717:94
I have a little s.	STEV 823:17
land of the s. of death	BIBLE 102:16
Life's but a walking s.	SHAK 769:42
light and s. never stand still	WEST 900:27
love in s. best is made	JONS 450:51
Man...fleeth also as a s.	BIBLE 93:61
merest s. line	THUR 860:54
neither s. of turning	BIBLE 124:6

No s. walks behind me JOHN 439:74
not darkness but s. FRYE 340:39
out-soared the s. of our night SHEL 786:4
s. at morning striding behind ELIOT 305:53
s. cast by the light of a fire VASA 877:37
s. of a great rock. BIBLE 103:32
S. of annoyance SHEL 784:60
s. of cloud YEATS 933:45
s. of the midnight hour BYRON 180:38
s. of the silent night MARL 552:85
s. over the colored BUCK 165:35
s. shortened in the sun JARR 435:87
S. That Comes in Sight AMIS 14:97
s. that runs across the grass HAGG 376:58
s. white as stone ROET 694:6
spy my s. SHAK 731:2
star-shaped s. WORD 929:67
swan and s. WORD 927:30
tall elm's s. THOM 854:9
The S. cloaked TENN 843:31
Time...a vast s. VAUG 878:49
under the s. of thy wings BIBLE 95:14
under the s. of thy wings BIBLE 94:93
under the s. of war SPEN 807:53
with the s. of his wings SHAK 731:96
you have got a s. FLET 328:75
shadowless Stand s. like Silence HOOD 410:33
shadows Cats...than their s. TESS 849:84
colour of s. WALC 884:78
Each substance...hath twenty s. SHAK 734:10
Earth's s. fly SHEL 786:7
fills the s. SWIN 832:18
half sick of s. TENN 839:47
illustrate a s. DONNE 281:88
individuals pass like s. BURKE 168:23
live to trace Their s. KEATS 457:94
make the s. visible NERV 611:44
measure s. HUBB 418:11
mirrors of the gigantic s. SHEL 786:17
s. among s. UPDI 874:79
s. have offended SHAK 738:19
s. in a sunshine day? MARL 552:91
s., not substantial things SHIR 789:83
s. of eternity VAUG 878:44
S. of the world appear TENN 839:46
s. upon two generations LLOY 513:2
shapes, and beckoning s. MILT 577:31
silent s. and in dreams? STEV 819:18
sleepers and the s. WHIT 906:49
their s. deep YEATS 932:33
the well in the s. PRIC 668:16
Types and s. have their ending AQUI 28:29
very s. of the clouds WORD 927:38
what is time but s. SASS 716:73
where the S. lie TOLK 862:98
shadow-sister your s.-s. WRIG 930:82
Shadrach S., Meshach BIBLE 106:95
Shadwell S. never deviates DRYD 288:49
S....of all my sons DRYD 288:48
shafts Between the s. and the furrow HEAN 389:4
birch for s. SPEN 808:73
shake seems to s. the spheres DRYD 291:34
s. a man's faith SHAW 777:57
s. off its apathy RENAN 683:98
s. your Rome SHAK 769:69
the rousing s. POPE 658:65
shaken S. and not stirred FLEM 327:56
Shakespeare as wise...As S. FERG 320:6
closest you can get to S. BUEC 165:43
compare [Jonson] with S. DRYD 288:30
complete S. and a prayer book BAIN 52:12
dig up S. and dig up Bacon GILB 355:36
five acts of S.'s tragedy FIELD 322:31
gave S. and Fletcher all DENH 261:94
good enough for S.'s day VICT 880:86
honour to S. JONS 450:55
I find the phrase in S. SCOTT 725:57
I hear S. think CALL 185:44
knowledge of the Bible, S. and Wisden WAUGH 893:55
read S. I am struck LAWR 495:28
remarkable thing about S. GRAV 368:85
s. and i are often low browed MARQ 554:26
S. by flashes of lightning COLE 226:18
S....eye of God OLIV 624:70
S. for his honoured bones MILT 576:2
S....had the largest and most
  comprehensive soul DRYD 288:25

S. is the great genius of the drama BENN 77:59
S. made use of it first SHER 788:66
S. one gets acquainted with AUST 43:77
S. set his play writing aside CUOMO 248:30
S.'s much-quoted passage ORWE 628:59
S.'s name...stands absurdly too high BYRON 181:52
S....wanted taste WALP 887:25
S. was an Irish Catholic ONEI 625:98
S. was the Homer DRYD 288:31
S....weak in chemistry WELLS 898:71
S....is...a forest JOHN 447:74
souls most fed with S.'s flame CHES 212:91
special reservoir...fed by S. ACHE 2:24
Stratford trades on S. BURG 167:84
The English have S. DUVA 296:44
three good sets of S. ONEI 625:99
tried...to read S. DARW 253:13
Whaur's yer Wullie S. noo? ANON 20:21
Shakespearian That S. rag BUCK 165:34
shall His absolute 's.'? SHAK 769:64
shallow s. conversational ends SASS 716:75
shallows bound in s. and in miseries SHAK 748:16
small eels...within the s. play CRAB 242:99
Shalott beside remote S. TENN 839:48
Lady of S. TENN 839:44
Lady of S. TENN 839:47
Lady of S. TENN 839:50
Lady of S. TENN 839:51
Lady of S. TENN 839:52
shame all other praise is s. SIDN 790:15
contempt of s. JOHN 442:54
epoch of folly and s. ZOLA 937:4
greater was the s. LANY 489:4
hangs his head for s.? INGR 429:59
look of furtive s. WODE 919:66
neither sin nor s. ROCHE 691:46
neither sin nor s. STER 818:1
noble s. KING 469:60
no love...no s. SHAW 777:58
no s. for a man to die HOMER 409:23
race of s. MILT 586:54
sense of...deathless s. WEBS 894:82
s....from being happy at another's distress LABR 484:75
S. is the most violent LAFA 484:95
S. of the versifying tribe! GRAY 369:8
s. on you ARMS 30:75
s. or censure free JOHN 441:14
s. the devil SHAK 742:17
s. will be too long SHAK 746:63
'Tis no s. for men SHIR 789:80
whose glory is in their s. BIBLE 123:59
shameful s. conquest of itself SHAK 734:9
vile members...called 'pudenda' ['s.'] ABEL 1:3
shameless S....5 years before LAVER 493:81
shamrock S. shine for ever new! DAVIS 256:68
shandeism True S....opens the heart STER 818:85
Shandon bells of S. MAHO 539:35
Shannon green banks of S. CAMP 186:65
shape art thou, execrable s.? MILT 581:33
assume a pleasing s. SHAK 753:71
com'st in such a questionable s. SHAK 751:25
exact colour and s. MONET 591:53
eyes have drawn thy s. SHAK 771:11
flesh; but in what s. they MILT 581:9
good s. for more sinning RUNY 703:85
gordian s. of dazzling hue KEATS 458:20
in the s. of a woman RICH 685:47
let it keep one s. SHAK 758:18
might be any s. CARR 196:9
most rational s. WEBER 894:69
nobler s. erect and tall MILT 582:61
No s. to feed each gazing eye DYER 297:51
O Attic s.! KEATS 459:54
over the net in a different s. LODGE 514:24
s. of things to come WELLS 899:93
share the selfsame s. MACD 529:37
some partial narrow s. POPE 662:81
stereotyped s. assumed LIPP 511:69
what s. it will take SHEV 788:74
who's in worse s. than MONR 591:60
shaper s. of the landscape BRON 154:70
shapes full of s. is fancy SHAK 755:46
horrid s., and shrieks MILT 576:4
immortal s. Of bright MILT 577:25
In holier s. SHAK 762:49
s., and beckoning shadows MILT 577:31
s. of rot PURDY 673:17

Turns them to s. SHAK 738:13
share biggest snouts...largest s. WEIG 896:24
s. the insult ISHE 431:91
to her s....errors fall POPE 658:68
shareholder large s. TANA 836:90
shareholders mass of inert s. ROBI 690:38
shares sell its s. DRUC 287:12
sharing not of war...but of...s. CHILD 213:8
S. a bed and a future FADI 317:32
shark oppose the man-eating s. BRIN 153:42
s. has pretty teeth, dear BREC 151:6
Sharon rose of S. BIBLE 101:96
sharp s. as any lynx SITW 793:58
s. be the weather SCOTT 724:15
short, s. shock WHIT 904:20
so s. the conquerynge CHAU 208:54
sharper s. than any two-edged sword BIBLE 124:90
s. than a serpent's tooth SHAK 762:63
sharpest s. men in argument HOLM 407:80
shatterday frightday, s. JOYCE 452:1
shave buy you more than a s. LARK 491:42
rides back to s. again WHITE 903:89
To s. the beard is a sin IVAN 431:99
shaving when I am s. of a morning HOUS 416:82
Shaw S. has no enemies WILDE 910:64
shay wonderful one-hoss s. HOLM 408:89
she great S.-who-must-be-obeyed HEAL 389:2
S. who must be obeyed HAGG 376:59
sheaf forgot a s. in the field BIBLE 89:50
shears Fury with th'abhorred s. MILT 578:49
resembles a pair of s. SMITH 801:19
s. of destiny? SHAK 739:32
sheath never s. the sword ASQU 36:9
you s. SHAK 742:15
sheaves bringing his s. BIBLE 98:91
s. in harvest DONNE 281:88
Sheba queen of S. BIBLE 92:42
queen of S. BIBLE 92:42
Solomon gave to the queen of S. BIBLE 92:42
she-bear s.-b. coming up the street FOOTE 329:2
shedding Without s. of blood BIBLE 124:92
She-Devil Loves of a S.-D. WELD 896:37
she-elephant great S.-e. HEAL 389:2
sheep All we like s. have gone astray BIBLE 104:51
an old half-witted s. STEP 817:58
as a s. before her shearers BIBLE 104:51
as s. going astray BIBLE 125:26
come to you in s.'s clothing BIBLE 110:10
counted as s. for the slaughter BIBLE 95:23
Dream Of Electric S.? DICK 265:58
erred and strayed...like lost s. BOOK 140:66
giveth his life for the s. BIBLE 118:2
go rather to the lost s. BIBLE 111:23
having an hundred s. BIBLE 116:44
hundred years as a s. MUSS 605:17
hungry s. look up MILT 578:52
land of cattle and s. LAWS 496:45
like a s. with a blade of grass WODE 919:57
little black s. KIPL 470:80
lying in bed counting s. SIEG 791:24
men better than s. TENN 847:51
mountain s. are sweeter PEAC 645:95
mountain which is of no use for s. BUTL 177:63
nation of panicked s. THOM 855:45
prize-oxen and of s. TENN 841:99
sameness of s. WHITE 903:83
savaged by a dead s. HEAL 388:99
s. go to a slaughter-house MACD 529:25
s. he doth us take SCOT 725:64
s. in s.'s clothing GOSSE 364:16
s. in the midst of wolves BIBLE 111:26
s. of his hand BOOK 143:64
s. on his right hand BIBLE 113:91
s. out of the window WELD 897:44
shepherds looking on their seely s. SHAK 730:77
shroudes as I a s. were LANG 489:93
standing a s. on its hind-legs BEER 69:82
strange that s.'s guts SHAK 744:5
teeth are like a flock of s. BIBLE 101:2
the shepherd his s. PROP 670:61
useless for the s. to pass INGE 428:49
with not many black s. ORWE 628:59
sheep-bells s.-b. and the ship-bells KIPL 473:51
sheepfold let the wolf into the s.! INGR 429:65
sheep-herding mere s.-h. POUND 663:51
sheep-hook how to hold A s.-h. MILT 578:51
sheepskins well down among the s. STEV 821:76

sheet causes, the balance s. — MO 589:22
great s. knit at the four corners — BIBLE 119:39
old England's winding s. — BLAKE 135:70
wet s. and a flowing sea — CUNN 248:24
sheets brother popped…into his s. — STOP 825:61
fumble with the s. — SHAK 745:36
Sheffield reminded him of S. United — HATT 385:26
shelf deepens like a coastal s. — LARK 491:39
Life…Behind the S. — DICK 272:64
stuffed ones on a s. — POUND 665:54
take the phial cleanly from its s. — DOYLE 286:83
shelf-life s. l. of the moral causes — IGNA 428:40
s. l. somewhere between — TRIL 865:64
shell dry s. on the beach — DU 294:97
pebble or a prettier s. — NEWT 612:74
s. of his victim — ANNAN 17:51
s.…of meaning — ELIOT 309:39
skin and s. of things — VAUG 878:43
Within thy airy s. — MILT 577:33
Shelley did you once see S. plain — BROW 161:53
Like S. and like Baudelaire — ISHE 430:90
peace in S.'s mind — SHEL 787:26
What S. shrilled — SASS 716:75
shells not the s. and rockets — KISH 475:88
shelter no s. but in a fool's cap — HOPK 412:79
Our s. from the stormy blast — WATTS 891:5
running for the s. — JAGG 432:17
s., and even muse — TUCH 869:61
s. thee, I'd s. thee — BURNS 173:54
s., warmth and accommodation — NUTT 619:83
shelves symmetry of s. — LAMB 487:52
shepherd any philosophy in thee, s.? — SHAK 749:56
as a s. divideth his sheep — BIBLE 113:91
Dead s. — SHAK 750:71
Dick the s. blows — SHAK 734:94
feed his flock like a s. — BIBLE 103:37
finding herself at S.'s Bush — BUTL 178:74
homely slighted S.'s trade — MILT 578:49
I am the good s. — BIBLE 118:2
Lord is my s. — BIBLE 94:2
Lord's my s. — SCOT 725:61
power by which our S. rose — DODD 278:10
Scythian s. — MARL 551:72
S. and Bishop of your souls — BIBLE 125:26
S., from the hill — ARNO 32:15
s., thee the woods — MILT 578:47
star that bids the s. — MILT 577:27
the fairest s. — PEELE 646:11
the s. his sheep — PROP 670:61
truth in every s.'s tongue — RALE 677:98
shepherds liberal s. — SHAK 755:25
s. abiding in the field — BIBLE 115:26
s. and butchers — VOLT 883:51
s. feed their flocks — MARL 553:17
s. looking on their seely sheep — SHAK 730:77
s., weep no more — MILT 578:57
warmth of s.' flames — MARL 551:78
What time the s. — SHAK 730:74
sherry have a sweet s. — BENN 76:33
mischief…with the cooking s. — THUR 859:49
unattainable soda and s. — SALA 710:50
very fond of brown s. — CHES 213:98
Shibboleth Say now S. — BIBLE 90:70
shield broken was her s. — SCOTT 723:3
lady in his s. — TENN 839:48
Our S. and Defender — GRANT 366:52
our sword and our s. — HUGH 420:58
s. me with shining breast — GORD 363:6
s. of congressional immunity — SMITH 800:88
s. of faith — BIBLE 122:31
s. ourselves from the sordid perils — WILDE 908:94
trusty s. and weapon — LUTH 523:97
truth shall be thy s. — BIBLE 96:53
where the s. and spear — SPEN 808:90
why should you want to s. him? — SAKI 710:45
shift let me s. for myself — MORE 597:72
shifty s., hangdog look — WODE 919:66
Shiites Irish…as the S. in Lebanon — OROU 627:22
shilling kindly drop a s. — KIPL 472:27
willing to sell for one s. — LEAR 498:85
shillings these men paid their s. — PRIE 668:17
weight in pounds, s. — MILNE 575:84
shimmering s. into rooms — WODE 919:54
shine Arise, s. — BIBLE 104:61
can give me a s. — GORD 363:8
every one doth s. — SHAK 747:93
No one could s. his shoes — ISAA 430:88

not to s. in use! — TENN 839:63
sun…shall s. on me — SHAK 734:2
To see him s. so brisk — SHAK 741:1
shingles naked s. of the world — ARNO 31:93
shining see it s. plain — HOUS 415:60
s. those who do not allow 's.' — ANON 21:30
shins not afraid of his s. — ANON 21:30
ship aloe…like a s. — MANS 547:91
As idle as a painted s. — COLE 225:84
being in a s. — JOHN 443:59
built your s. of death — LAWR 495:31
English s., they say — LOND 515:37
Matilda Briggs…was a s. — DOYLE 286:82
mildest…That ever scuttled s. — BYRON 182:86
Of a s.'s hour — SLES 796:15
office was his pirate s. — LEWIS 507:87
O S. of State — LONG 516:54
sail this new s. of mine? — BALL 56:84
s., an isle, a sickle moon — FLEC 327:52
s. has weather'd every rack — WHIT 905:46
s. in port is safe — HOPP 413:18
s. is always referred — NIMI 616:36
S. me somewhere — KIPL 471:88
s. [of state] will be saved — CUOMO 248:29
s. on the sea — LORCA 517:85
s.'s upon the sea — KIPL 471:7
s. would not travel due West! — CARR 197:31
Sink me the s. — TENN 848:63
steel s. loaded with monoliths — MENC 566:85
Swimming full upon the s. — BROW 162:64
swimming toward a sinking s. — YARB 932:27
tall s. and a star to steer — MASE 559:21
The s.'s ignored — BISH 131:74
truth…sinks his s. — CORN 237:72
went down to the s. — POUND 665:45
whale s. was my Yale College — MELV 564:28
What is a s. but a prison? — BURT 174:76
ship-bells sheep-bells and the s.-b. — KIPL 473:51
shipping fishes first to s. did impart — DRYD 287:20
tiers of s. — DICK 269:79
ships as s. on the foam — KIPL 471:97
boats or s. came near — LEAR 498:88
down to the sea in s. — BIBLE 97:71
drew a thousand s. — MARL 551:79
face that launched a thousand s. — MARL 552:5
fleet of British s. — NELS 610:32
harbour without s. — DEFOE 258:22
My experience of s. — BRAD 148:55
my s. are out of gear — TENN 848:60
my thoughts on white s. — COLUM 229:60
nor its s. empty of men — NICI 614:91
old s. sail like swans — FLEC 327:53
railways, magnificent s. — LARI 490:19
Rivers and seas…to float their s. — DICK 268:51
s. and stars and isles — FLEC 327:45
S. that pass in the night — LONG 516:64
S., towers, domes — WORD 926:19
something wrong with our bloody s. — BEAT 66:97
stately s. are twirled and spun — HODG 405:45
stately s. go on — TENN 840:68
Stately s. to bear our food — WILDE 907:82
sunken and damaged s. — HALS 378:94
There go the s. — BIBLE 97:69
Thracian s. and the foreign — SWIN 832:18
We've got the s. — HUNT 422:21
What merchant's s. have my sighs — DONNE 280:44
with the moving s. — SWIN 833:41
Shipton S. 'assault' — CRAN 243:31
shipwreck like s. — CATH 200:89
mermaid…tolled my son to s. — DEKK 259:50
s. of time — BACON 46:42
shipwrecking s. all their hopes — MOOD 594:8
shire s. which we…may call — DRAY 287:4
shires Round both the s. — HOUS 415:51
shirt sang the 'Song of the S.' — HOOD 410:45
s. or collar ever comes back — LEAC 497:69
shirts stuffed s., hollow men — MACD 530:47
than the coarse s. — THOM 854:25
shit contempt for an arrant s. — JOSE 451:70
give a s. what happens — NIXON 617:46
look and feel like s. — AMIS 15:6
whatta you do when you s.? — CARU 198:58
shivering S. and sighing — PARK 638:59
shivering-sweet s.-s. to the touch? — CORN 237:69
shivers broken to s. — BIBLE 126:49
shoals Guarded by s. and rocks — BYRON 182:78
shock depending upon s. tactics — PRIE 668:27

harmony comes…as a s. — RAINE 677:97
s. around the age of five — BALD 54:39
S. of the New — DUNL 295:16
short, sharp s. — GILB 355:25
short, sharp s. — WHIT 904:20
The plan is called 's. and awe' — ANON 26:82
shocking glimpse of stocking…s. — PORT 663:4
s., but not pathetic — HUGH 419:42
shock-pried s.-p. faces — EBER 298:73
shocks thousand natural s. — SHAK 753:74
shod with iron — DICK 270:2
shod s. with iron — DICK 270:2
shoe blaming his s. — BECK 68:33
Chinese woman's foot fits her s. — SCHR 720:40
for want of a s. — FRAN 334:13
Into a left-hand s. — CARR 197:23
lazy insolence of a s. salesman — PERE 648:58
Sailed off in a wooden s. — FIELD 322:32
smiled in the s. — TRAV 864:49
shoemaker leather…to a s. — WAUGH 892:41
shoes blue suede s. — PERK 648:66
boil eggs in your s. — LEAR 498:94
butter nor s. nor poetry — LEWIS 507:86
drunk its little s. — DICK 268:43
I can buy a new pair of s. — CHAR 207:47
make his own s. — SMITH 798:48
mind it wipes its s. — THOM 853:88
most s. wins — ANON 26:91
never even…tied my s. — PU 673:22
No one could shine his s. — ISAA 430:88
old ladies in tennis s. — MOSK 600:27
pinching of thin s. — DICK 267:35
put off thy s. — BIBLE 88:9
s.—and ships—and sealing-wax — CARR 196:2
s. are made of python — MACN 538:2
s.…expensive and too small — BAIN 52:8
s. on your feet — BIBLE 88:16
tips of his patent-leather s. — CHRI 214:34
when we want s. — SWIFT 831:69
Wooden S. — ANON 21:37
shoeshine on a smile and a s. — MILL 571:94
shoestring careless s. — HERR 400:50
runs it into a s. — WOOL 923:58
shoon moon…in her silver s. — DELA 260:69
shoot ask him to s. around you — GOLD 362:77
Do not s. — MALO 543:14
do not s. the pianist — WILDE 908:85
guns begin to s. — KIPL 471:92
idea how to s. — THOM 856:53
just need to s. straight — GOLD 362:76
s. his like in the name of an idea — BROD 153:57
S., if you must — WHIT 906:95
s. me in my absence — BEHAN 70:4
s. them down — WHITE 903:88
shout and they s. — INGE 429:52
When we're afraid we s. — SONT 804:75
shooting always helps my s. — HEMI 394:11
Nothing wrong with s. — EAST 298:94
shoots s. of everlastingness — VAUG 878:45
shop ain't for justice — DICK 267:95
foul rag-and-bone s. — YEATS 934:62
pops its head into the s. — FOOTE 329:94
talking s. in Strasbourg — BEVIN 85:31
shopkeepers be a nation of s. — PUNCH 672:7
nation of s. — NAPO 607:68
nation of s. — SMITH 798:50
nation of s. — STOP 825:66
shopping S. is Not Creating — COUP 238:95
watch the s. channel — COUP 239:1
shops hideous brick s. — THOR 858:7
men that run the s. — LEWIS 507:89
s. curiously low — THOR 858:5
sordid little s. — LESS 505:51
shopworn word…has become so s. — RENO 683:7
shore beat on the rocky s. — LEAR 497:76
Bequeath us no earthly s. — CRANE 243:11
broad sandy s. — BYRON 182:78
children sport upon the s. — WORD 927:27
control…Stops with the s. — BYRON 180:44
here is no s. — SCOTT 722:77
hugging the s. — UPDI 874:85
I linger on the s. — TENN 841:84
left the Trojan s. — DRYD 292:42
lights around the s. — ROSS 698:91
(more stony than a s.) — WILL 913:49
one on s. — SHAK 744:6
print…on the s. — DEFOE 258:18
rapture on the lonely s. — BYRON 180:43

reedy s.   GIBB 352:68
refuse of your teeming s.   LAZA 496:51
s. of Gitche Gumee   LONG 516:56
s. of the wan grass sea   SITW 794:72
s. Of the wide world   KEATS 457:94
small eels that left…For the warm s.   CRAB 242:99
some false impossible s.   ARNO 32:8
stretch from s. to s.   WATTS 891:4
This embattled s.   EISE 302:64
towards the pebbled s.   SHAK 772:24
unknown and silent s.   LAMB 486:30
Upon the Irish s.   BURNS 173:53
waves upon the s.   SHEL 783:31
shoreline longer the s. of wonder   MACI 533:9
shores bade betwixt their s.   ARNO 32:10
Desolate s.   KEATS 457:86
glide past the rocks to safer s.   CUOMO 248:29
many leave these s.   OWEN 632:66
s., and desert wildernesses   MILT 577:31
s. of morning   ATWO 38:49
s. of this happy isle   GLAD 358:92
To s. by the wash   YEATS 932:31
wilder s. of love   BLAN 136:87
short all too s. a date   SHAK 771:5
as s. as December   SHAK 770:76
Gettysburg address was so s.   HEMI 394:17
Let life be s.   SHAK 746:63
Life is s. and bothersome   LABR 483:69
Life is too s.   SCOTT 722:83
nasty, brutish and s.   HOBB 404:27
not so s. as sweet   SHAK 735:29
poor, nasty, brutish and s.   GIBB 352:69
s.…if one follows patterns   SENE 727:90
s. neck denotes a good mind   SPARK 806:20
s. one ready for my own   FROST 339:10
s., sharp shock   GILB 355:25
s., sharp shock   WHIT 904:20
s. story is always a disclosure   PRIT 669:55
time of life is s.   SHAK 742:31
shortage acute s. of rich people   WILS 916:6
s. of coal and…of fish   BEVAN 84:16
short-circuit poetic s.-c.   SENG 727:95
shortcut s. c. to everything   MILL 573:49
shortcuts but I know the s.   RULFO 702:66
shortest s. knight of the year   RICH 686:61
s. line between two points   BREC 151:10
s. way to do many things   SMIL 797:33
short-haired s.-h. joy and roughness   SNYD 803:53
shortness spend that s. basely   SHAK 742:31
Your plainness and your s.   SHAK 732:44
shorts s. and washing themselves   LINK 511:59
s. in this compass?   MURR 604:7
shot long shot…a very long s.!   DOYLE 285:69
Major Strasser has been s.   EPST 314:81
marvellously good s.   COWA 240:27
never s. anything   SITW 794:83
Out of the s.…of desire   SHAK 751:14
plot in it will be s.   TWAIN 871:93
s. an arrow   HAMER 378:95
s. at for sixpence   DIBD 265:52
s. fired in…a concert   STEN 816:50
s. from one of the batteries   MACA 527:78
s. heard around the world   EMER 312:2
s. one bird flying   HEMI 394:3
s. to death, with pearls?   WEBS 895:15
used to be a big s.   WALD 885:86
volley of words…quickly s. off   SHAK 729:29
when it pained most, I s.   HAAS 376:52
shotgun as a sawed-off s.   PARK 638:77
old man with a s.   TWAIN 871:97
shots but of the best s.   VOLT 883:50
shoulder on my leaning s.   YEATS 932:29
queer s.   GINS 357:65
shifted it to another s.   SHAW 778:3
S. the sky   HOUS 416:73
shrug of s.   SPEN 807:50
stand s. to s.   TALE 835:82
stands on any s.   SHAK 763:66
tears in s. blades   STEV 820:44
shoulders burdens the broadest s.   LLOY 513:97
City of the Big S.   SAND 712:91
grow beneath their s.   SHAK 759:61
head…little use without my s.   CARR 194:63
lie on the s. of the…saint   WEBER 894:67
old heads on your young s.   SPARK 806:21
s. globed   HEAN 389:4
s. held the sky suspended   HOUS 416:80

s. of their predecessors   RUSS 705:46
Square your s.   HOUS 416:91
standing on the s. of giants   BERN 80:29
shout rings no hunter's s.   SIGO 791:28
s. and they shoot   INGE 429:52
shouted with a great s.   BIBLE 90:64
s. that tore hell's   MILT 581:12
S. with the largest   DICK 266:73
Silent;—hardly a s.   ARNO 33:52
When in doubt, s.   HARD 381:44
shouting heavens fill with s.   TENN 840:81
S. is not a substitute   STEV 820:57
thunder of the captains, and the s.   BIBLE 93:75
tumult and the s. dies   KIPL 472:21
shouts let me hear thy s.   WORD 926:22
shovel s. also   KIPL 472:37
S. them under   SAND 713:96
show backers of the s.   HIRS 403:8
do it with no s. of fear   SHAK 745:39
in his simple s.   SHAK 730:56
Last Picture S.   MCMU 537:84
mock the time with fairest s.   SHAK 767:92
No Business Like S. Business   BERL 80:17
really a weird s.   LAWR 494:3
S. me a sane man   JUNG 453:9
that within which passeth s.   SHAK 751:4
the s. does not go on   PAGL 634:81
What wealth the s.…had brought   WORD 928:42
showbiz secondary s. nonsense   AMIS 15:1
show-business s.-b. with blood   BELA 71:24
showdown begun the great s.   HUSS 424:42
shower abundant s. of curates   BRON 155:83
dying lamp, a falling s.   SHEL 785:99
in sun and s.   WORD 924:79
like standing under a cold s.   HEATH 390:25
pierced with softest s.   KYD 482:45
Pope in the s.   ANON 25:55
s. of all my days   THOM 852:76
sweetness of a s.   THOM 854:18
turf such the honeyed s.   MILT 578:53
with a sudden s.   VALL 876:20
showers Aegypt glads with s.   POPE 662:66
s. betumble the chestnut spikes   HARDY 382:76
Small s. last long   SHAK 734:6
Spring shall pour his s.   COLL 228:48
showery S., Flowery, Bowery   ELLIS 311:81
showgirl out-of-work s.   CHAN 204:73
showing-up Eighty percent…is s.-u.   ALLEN 12:57
shows May's new-fangled s.   SHAK 733:71
shrapnel defensive hats, and s.   WHIT 904:17
shred save a s. of its respectability   READ 680:47
shreds s. of objectivity   CUPI 248:35
thing of s. and patches   GILB 355:19
shrew taming the savage s.   FERB 320:97
shriek bat With short shrill s.   COLL 228:47
shrieks louder s. to pitying heav'n   POPE 659:75
shrimp s. of an author   GRAY 370:43
until a s. learns to whistle   KHRU 466:98
shrine deface the s.!   DRYD 291:13
erect our national s.   FORS 331:28
mountain and a national s.   MUMF 603:76
United Nations…a s.   OBRI 620:3
shrines like vapour over s.   BROW 159:2
shrivelling s. away into nothingness   KELM 460:77
Shropshire brother in S.   BARR 61:91
shroud s. Of thoughts   BYRON 180:30
starched pleats of a s.   LEVE 506:60
stiff dishonoured s.   ELIOT 305:38
shrouds s. are put on us   SCHR 720:39
Shrovetide far back as S.   ANON 21:29
shrub-ruster s.-r., sky-mocker   UPDI 874:74
shrug borne it with a patient s.   SHAK 739:53
s. of shoulder   SPEN 807:50
shucks Church ain't s.   TWAIN 870:87
shut I wish he had just s. up   QUIL 674:48
who was…leaking and s. them up   REAG 681:66
shutter camera with its s. open   ISHE 430:89
not clicking the s.   EISE 302:65
shutters close the s. fast   COWP 241:76
we'd need keep the s. up   DICK 268:46
shuttle Man is the s.   VAUG 878:50
swifter than a weaver's s.   BIBLE 93:55
Welcome to s. diplomacy!   SISCO 793:54
shuttles s. again and rejoins   ROTH 699:13
shy I am terribly s.   CHAN 205:5
s. of 'the Big Folk'   TOLK 862:1
Sicilian S. mule was to me   GLAD 359:95

S. Muses, let us sing   VIRG 882:28
sick Dante makes me s.   VEGA 879:57
from my s. bed   LEE 500:41
get s. or die   HOOV 411:63
half my men are s.   TENN 848:60
Heal the s.   BIBLE 111:24
heart is s.   TENN 843:39
Hope deferred maketh the heart s.   BIBLE 99:25
How s. one gets of being 'good'   JAMES 433:26
if you are s.   FORD 330:9
kingdom of the s.   SONT 804:77
news…would have made me s.   SHAK 742:37
person seldom falls s.   EMER 313:40
promised to do when you are s.   SIGI 791:27
riches will leave us s.   EMER 313:37
s. and wicked   AUST 43:90
s., and ye visited me   BIBLE 113:92
S. as a parrot   ANON 24:20
s. at heart   SHAK 751:95
s. of both   JOHN 445:24
s. that surfeit with too much   SHAK 739:42
thcream until I'm s.   CROM 245:67
the s. may have liberty   PEPYS 647:42
they that are s.   BIBLE 111:20
they that are s.   BIBLE 114:7
when he is s.   JOHN 446:57
When I was s.   SHAK 729:30
When I was s.   STEV 823:16
sickening s. of the heart   POE 656:16
sickness breed a bloodless s.   CAMP 187:81
Fitter for s.   SHAK 729:45
green s. of the mind   CLEV 221:83
in s. and in health   BOOK 142:24
in s. and in health   BOOK 142:25
in s. and in health   BOOK 142:26
nature of the s.   SHAK 757:95
s., and unemployment   LLOY 513:98
s. enlarges the dimensions   LAMB 487:55
s. enlarges the dimensions   LAMB 487:57
trublit now with gret s.   DUNB 294:6
universal s.   TRIL 866:67
Sidcup If only I could get…to S.!   PINT 652:20
side Back and s. go bare   ANON 20:1
ever strong upon the stronger s.   HAZL 388:78
From thy riven s.   TOPL 863:15
go by thy s.   ANON 19:97
move over to the other s.   REED 682:84
on the right s.   GALB 343:97
on the s. of the underdog   PALEY 635:10
purple wardrobe of thy s.   CRAS 244:36
spear pierced his s.   BIBLE 118:20
suffered at my s.   SASS 716:66
this s. of the grave   PITT 653:46
this s. the tomb   BYRON 179:22
through a s. door   UPDI 875:92
thrust my hand into his s.   BIBLE 118:24
turn always one s.   SCHR 720:41
Walk on the Wild S.   ALGR 11:28
Who is on my s.?   BIBLE 92:36
Who is on the Lord's s.?   BIBLE 89:28
with Ate by his s.   SHAK 748:2
sides houseless heads and unfed s.   SHAK 763:78
much might be said on both s.   ADDI 6:15
On both s. more respect   SHAK 769:65
Poetry cannot take s.   SPEN 807:61
prick the s. of my intent   SHAK 767:87
room at your twa s.   BALL 55:72
to take s.   RUSH 703:88
work from the four s.   POLL 657:37
would have three s.   MONT 593:91
sidewalks like wet s. cause rain   BLOU 137:8
side-whiskers by growing s.-w.   WELLS 898:87
siege chronicled the s. of Troy   CUOMO 248:30
fallen by S. into the Power   ALBE 10:99
Sierras S. Will be dry   SNYD 803:49
sieve in a s. I'll thither sail   SHAK 766:67
Our S. ain't big   LEAR 497:80
sifted in my private s.   CAMPO 187:83
they went to sea in a s.   LEAR 497:78
they went to sea in a s.   LEAR 497:79
Washington is a s.   REAG 681:66
went to sea in a s.   LEAR 497:78
siftings let their liquid s. fall   ELIOT 305:38
sigh long-drawn s.   WALL 886:3
not spare a s.   HOPK 412:94
prompts th' eternal s.   POPE 660:23
shall I ever s. and pine?   HERB 398:9

s. for thy repose — WESL 900:18
S., heart — YEATS 932:35
s. is just a s. — HUPF 423:40
s. of the east on my face — CONR 234:4
s. still for the dark — LOWE 520:47
so happy as to s. for — BEAU 67:7
telling this with a s. — FROST 338:89
when I s. — SPEN 809:97

sighed even s. offensively — GERH 350:33
no sooner loved but they s. — SHAK 750:85
Or s. and looked — THOM 856:55
S. and looked, and s. again — DRYD 291:39
s. as a lover — GIBB 352:62

sighing Shivering and s. — PARK 638:59

sighs Before my s. did dry it — HERB 398:10
heaving copious s. — CHEE 209:3
ships have my s. drowned? — DONNE 280:44
Warring s. and groans — BURNS 172:28

sight all Wonders in one s.! — CRAS 244:34
at first s., a masterpiece — POUND 665:41
Beauty...at first s. — SHAW 778:2
blind the wisest s. — SPEN 809:11
can no more bear to lose s. — ELIOT 303:86
can to s. or thought — MILT 584:14
Charms strike the s. — POPE 659:77
dislike...at first s. — STEE 814:99
Does lecher in my s. — SHAK 763:88
ere he drove out of s. — MOORE 594:19
fell in love...at first s. — POWE 666:78
gleamed upon my s. — WORD 927:35
keen discriminating s. — CANN 188:12
keeps it out of s. — BREC 151:6
long-abused s. at the fountain — MILT 579:82
losing your s.? — SASS 716:64
lost s. — KISS 475:90
many a vanished s. — SHAK 771:15
most beautiful s. in orbit — SCHW 721:69
never to admit them in your s. — AUST 43:70
saddest s. that fortune's inequality — CARL 193:26
sad s. to me — PEPYS 647:40
sense of human s. — MILT 576:13
s....most magical — BART 62:19
s. of Proteus — WORD 928:46
s. of you alone — ROSSO 698:6
s. so touching in its majesty — WORD 926:19
s. to make an old man — TENN 840:70
s. To such a tender ball — MILT 586:48
someliest in s. — DUNB 294:5
sweep him from my s. — SHAK 768:12
thousand years in thy s. — BIBLE 96:50
trees of noblest kind for s. — MILT 582:59
walk by faith, not by s. — BIBLE 122:26
What a s. it were — JONS 449:46
with the blessing of s. — HOLM 407:70
wonderful s. — MACA 524:31
Young men mend not their s. — DONNE 281:92

sigh-tempests nor s.-t. move — DONNE 280:54

sights behold such s. — SHAK 768:18
come to such s. colder — HOPK 412:94
discover s. of woe — MILT 580:97
few more impressive s. — BARR 61:85
most poignant s. — JOHN 439:72
power of many s. — SHEL 782:18
seen some strange s. — HOUS 415:69
s. as youthful poets — MILT 576:11
sounds and smells And s. — BETJ 84:11

sign And it is a good s. — PARN 639:92
In this s. thou shalt conquer — CONS 235:30
it is a bad s. — SARR 715:38
know him by this s. — SWIFT 830:67
might be the s. of something — JENK 437:24
never give out my zodiac s. — PEACE 645:91
outward and visible s. — BOOK 142:16
s. for him to retire — DISR 277:74
s. of an ill-spent youth — SPEN 807:45
s. of an unconscious act — MOND 590:32
s. of the Cross — BOOK 141:12
s. of the self-absorbed — RYBC 707:75
s. or a wonder — BIBLE 89:49
s. that silence heaves — KEATS 456:78

signal Only a s. shown — LONG 516:64
really do not see the s. — NELS 610:33

signal-elm s.-e., that looks on — ARNO 33:43

signals receives s. — UMAS 873:62

significance literal s. — AYER 44:9

significations s. of their words — HOBB 404:23

signify What does it s. — GASK 346:58

signifying S. nothing — SHAK 769:42

signpost all s. and no destination — KRON 481:22

signs merely conventional s.! — CARR 197:30
S. are taken for wonders — ELIOT 305:40
s. might be permanent — JOHN 442:39
s. of a New Age coming? — SMITH 800:99
s. of our own time — CARL 191:79
something like neon s. — UREY 875:2

silence After s. — HUXL 425:72
all in s....stand — CRAB 242:83
answered best with s. — JONS 448:17
Be checked for s. — SHAK 761:21
charity of its s. — EMMET 313:59
conspiracy of s. — JAUR 435:95
darkness again and a s. — LONG 516:64
darkness and s. reign — LEAR 497:76
die in s. — PLATO 655:91
earth...in that eternal s. — MACL 535:46
Elected S., sing to me — HOPK 412:80
eternal s. — WORD 927:27
eternal s. of these...spaces — PASC 640:18
even s., is spray-gunned? — OLSEN 624:75
foster-child of s. — KEATS 459:50
God is the friend of s. — THER 851:44
grand talent pour le s. — CARL 193:33
great beauty of s. — CHAP 206:9
heart...trembles into s. — BYRON 181:49
Indecency's conspiracy of s. — SHAW 779:19
in that s. we the tempest fear — DRYD 287:14
land stares...in a huge s. — SCOTT 722:78
Learning to lie with s. — BYRON 180:36
midnight in the s. — BROW 163:94
most magical moment...is a s. — CRON 246:80
moves upon s. — YEATS 934:63
No voice, but oh! the s. sank — COLE 225:91
occasional flashes of s. — SMITH 801:18
often told in s. — STEV 822:90
pink, spread s. — CARR 194:54
private s. in which we live — PRIT 669:52
roar...on the other side of s. — ELIOT 304:8
sign that s. heaves — KEATS 456:78
s....does not necessarily brood — ELIOT 303:97
s. envious tongues — SHAK 775:22
s. has a sound — KOH 477:35
s. in heaven — BIBLE 126:61
s. in the hills — TENN 843:30
s. in the room — KINS 470:72
s. in the White House — ACHE 2:30
S. is become his mother tongue — GOLD 361:49
s. is most noble till the end — SWIN 833:23
s. is only commendable — SHAK 739:40
s. is the greatest of all persecutions — PASC 641:36
S. is the most perfect expression — SHAW 781:80
S. is the perfectest herald — SHAK 744:97
S. is the virtue of fools — BACON 47:67
s. is your confession — EURI 316:11
s. makes a woman beautiful — SOPH 804:81
S. more musical — ROSS 697:81
s. most offends me — SHAK 744:98
s. of eternity — STEV 822:4
s. of the night — ROSS 697:74
s. of the voice of justice — HAILE 377:67
S. round about his lair — KEATS 459:44
S. ruled this land — DARK 253:5
s. sounds no worse — HOUS 415:49
s. surged softly backward — DELA 260:65
s., told me truths — THOM 854:8
s. until any voice is heard — LEZA 508:12
s. was deafening — KARSH 455:52
small change of s. — MERE 567:98
soft grey s. — JOYCE 451:82
solemn s. — GILB 355:25
Sorrow and s. are strong — LONG 516:53
speak by s. — PATM 643:66
Stand shadowless like S. — HOOD 410:33
stones of s. — HEAN 389:6
Sunset and s.! — COLUM 229:58
That man's s. — HARDY 381:49
There is no s. in the East — MAUG 561:77
There is s. — BLUN 137:11
The rest is s. — SHAK 755:43
threatened to s. Father Fahrt — OBRI 621:6
Till a s. fell — TENN 845:90
time to keep s. — BIBLE 100:70
'Tis visible s. — ROSS 698:93
true call...is their s. — STARK 813:73
Under all speech there lies a s. — CARL 192:22

upon the wings Of s. — MILT 577:34
widening slowly s. all — TENN 846:9
Wildness and s. disappeared — MACL 535:45
you provide the s. — STOK 825:55

silencer rattlesnake with a s. — ACHE 3:45

silences s. between sentences — LIND 510:42
Success is in the s. — CARM 193:47

silencing no more be justified in s. — MILL 570:65

silent infinite spaces Are still s. — EBER 298:37
in the dark and s. grave — RALE 677:3
kingfisher's wing...is s. — ELIOT 307:99
not enough...to be s. — BRAT 150:35
Out of the S. Planet — LEWIS 507:71
should not be s. — MARIE 550:49
S.;—hardly a shout — ARNO 33:52
s. majority of my fellow Americans — NIXON 617:44
s. manliness of grief — GOLD 361:59
s. sullen peoples — KIPL 472:26
s. was the flock — KEATS 458:30
thereof one must be s. — WITT 918:39
They fell s. — VIRG 882:14
Thou, s. form — KEATS 459:55
t is s., as in Harlow — ASQU 36:17
ways of...keeping s. — WEIZ 896:35

silhouette s. of a brooding soul — SAND 712:90
the s. of greatness — TIME 860:72

silica more dangerous than s. — ROET 694:99

silk blue-shadowed s. — STEV 819:21
S. an' satin — ANON 21:28
s. dresses out of worms — STEV 820:40
s. stockings...within the reach — SCHU 721:56
s. suit — PEPYS 647:27
s., too often hides eczema — CAMUS 187:90
skein of s. — JONS 450:62
that thing of s. — POPE 661:40

silks rainbow s. and satins! — DICK 267:25
When as in s. my Julia goes — HERR 400:49

silkworm Heaven—of s. — MOORE 595:37

silly Lazy and s. — SITW 794:72
s. things do cease to be s. — AUST 43:84
so young and so s. — SPEN 807:57
You were s. like us — AUDEN 40:2

silly-clever poor s.-c. Irishman — SHAW 779:32

Siloam By cool S.'s shady rill — HEBER 390:33

silver apples of gold in pictures of s. — BIBLE 100:50
better than the merchandise of s. — BIBLE 99:12
Between their s. bars! — FLEC 327:52
breast and his arms of s. — BIBLE 105:94
fill it in a s. tassie — BURNS 171:2
Georgian S. goes — MACM 537:79
give thee a s. pound — CAMP 186:70
gold and s. — SHAK 738:24
gold and s. — SHAK 774:72
gold and s. becks me — SHAK 738:24
golden and s. — YEATS 933:38
Just for a handful of s. — BROW 160:28
no s. lining...without its cloud — STER 817:62
S. and gold have I none — BIBLE 119:30
s. cord be loosed — BIBLE 101:92
S. out of the Earth in Peru — PETTY 649:84
S. sails all out of the west — TENN 841:2
s. thimble lies cold — SITW 794:82
s. waves of thy sweet singing — SHEL 785:80
that s. sphere — SHEL 784:57
There's a s. lining — FORD 330:20
thirty pieces of s. — BIBLE 106:18
thirty pieces of s. — BIBLE 114:95
what woman having ten pieces of s. — BIBLE 116:45

Silvia S. in the night — SHAK 729:36
Who is S.? — SHAK 729:39

Simeon S.-quiet evensong — LEVE 506:58

similar s. to independent...states — JAY 436:97

similarity science is not just any s. — WILS 915:86

simile authors of s. and metaphor — NASH 609:3

simple as s. as possible — EINS 302:48
beliefs...whether s. or complex — DURK 296:33
business is very s. — GATES 347:62
good and s. — VAZD 878:53
Life was s. — HOPP 413:16
nature...runs on such s. things — FONT 328:85
no vice so s. — SHAK 740:70
pure and s., beyond — WILL 913:48
s. great ones gone — TENN 845:84
s. question — GRAV 368:86
S. truth — SHAK 772:27
spoil her s. plots — HOLME 407:71
Truth is too s. — SAND 712:88

truth…never s.   WILDE 909:36
understanding unto the s.   BIBLE 97:85
whether they be wise or s.   SCHW 721:70
simples compounded of many s.   SHAK 750:72
simpleton revolutionary s.   LEWIS 508:97
simplicities totalitarian s.   LYND 524:15
simplicity Cultivate s., Coleridge LAMB 486:27
die out for want of s.   POUND 665:55
hate American s.   JAMES 434:56
Her bygone s.   HARDY 382:56
makes s. a grace   JONS 449:25
miscalled s.   SHAK 772:27
reduce complexity to s.   JAMES 434:62
s. cannot endure for long   DELA 260:60
s. of their end   FUSE 342:74
s. of this clause of Catch-22   HELL 392:60
s. or with severity   ARNO 33:37
S., without variety   HOGA 406:57
Success…founded on s.   BEAV 67:28
simplification s. of the human   FORS 331:45
simplified my life is much s.   CHUR 217:97
simplifies s. and clarifies   STRA 826:80
simplify ability to s.   HOFF 406:50
s. the points to myself   HOME 409:12
simply play it s.   CHEK 209:11
simulacrum sun itself is but the dark s. BROW 159:94
simulation A good s., be it…myth   PAGE 633:78
simultaneity long sweetness of the s. ASHB 35:86
sin All manner of s.   BIBLE 111:41
All s. tends to be addictive   AUDEN 41:28
almost a s. of abstinence   DRYD 292:49
as a carnal s.   THOM 856:51
beauty is only s. deep   SAKI 710:30
before man knew how to s.   BEHN 71:18
bellows blows up s.   SHAK 769:49
Can cunning s. cover   SHAK 745:19
cause of plagues is s.   WHITE 904:4
curiosity becomes a s.   FRAN 333:89
discharge from s. and error   ELIOT 309:47
dreadful record of s.   DOYLE 285:67
eldest child of s.   WEBS 895:93
Eve made Adam s.   MARG 549:39
every mortal s.   WILS 915:72
Excepting Original S.   CAMP 186:73
fat cats…without s.   PECK 645:4
fight…against s.   BOOK 141:12
filth that attends conviction for s.   BUNY 166:67
glaring s. of omission   OSLER 630:17
grief and s. of idleness   MELV 564:24
Guilty of dust and s.   HERB 397:98
hate, vertue, and s.   MALO 543:13
Hatred is always a s.   MUNRO 603:88
He that is without s.   BIBLE 117:94
He that lives in s.   BUNY 167:78
hold it half a s.   TENN 842:23
how oft shall my brother s.   BIBLE 113:70
If any man s.   BIBLE 125:35
If it be a s.   SHAK 746:55
If we say that we have no s.   BIBLE 125:34
imagine to remove s.   MILT 579:76
in s. did my mother conceive me   BIBLE 95:28
Is it s. To ruin   SHAK 765:46
law of s. and death   WESL 900:17
lead him into debauchery and s.   OFLA 622:35
living in s.   HERB 397:98
lose the s., yet keep the sense   POPE 659:84
more unpopular forms of s.   BRIN 153:42
most inhibited s. in the canon   SHAK 761:24
neither s. nor shame   ROCHE 691:46
neither s. nor shame   STER 818:1
no s. but ignorance   MARL 552:82
no s. but to be rich   SHAK 738:21
not a s. to be rich   CONN 232:52
Nothing emboldens s. so much   SHAK 762:47
not so vile a s.   SHAK 746:41
only one real s.   LESS 505:38
palace of sweet s.   KEATS 458:23
patched with s.   SHAK 756:55
polygamy was made a s.   DRYD 289:68
real s. against life   PORT 663:10
regions of s. and falsity   MILT 579:73
Repentance…want of power to s.   DRYD 292:58
researches in original s.   PLOM 656:9
Ring out…the s.   TENN 844:61
scandal is…worse than the s.   MARG 549:42
several s. to every sense   VAUG 878:45
Shall we continue in s.   BIBLE 120:67

s. and inconvenience   WALK 885:95
s. and nothing more   SEXT 728:11
S. has many tools   HOLM 408:84
S. if thou wilt   CHUR 215:47
s. in private is not to s.   MOLI 590:32
s. is ever before me   BIBLE 95:28
s. is the cause   JULI 452:5
s., my soul. Lo-lee-ta   NABO 606:30
sinner and s. boldly   LUTH 523:94
s. of whisky   SPARK 806:18
s. purged   BIBLE 102:12
S.'s rotten trunk   COWP 241:62
s. the double cure   TOPL 863:15
s. to keep a sinful oath   SHAK 730:68
s. to kill a mockingbird   LEE 500:34
s. to swear unto a s.   SHAK 730:68
s. until I blow up!   THOM 853:96
s. which doth so easily beset us   BIBLE 124:99
s. which preaches virtue   MARI 550:62
s. will find you out   BIBLE 89:43
s.With statisticians   AUDEN 41:33
s. ye do by two and two   KIPL 471:6
Some rise by s.   SHAK 758:22
sometimes s. is a pleasure   BYRON 181:72
Stand in awe, and s. not   BIBLE 94:85
sulky lips were shaped for s.   BETJ 84:6
Sure it is no s.   SHAK 758:36
taketh away the s. of the world   BIBLE 117:75
that I might not s.   BIBLE 97:81
That noble S.   MAND 545:54
this ambrosial s.   BYRON 181:71
'Tis no s. for a man   SHAK 741:97
To shave the beard is a s.   IVAN 431:99
to s. our biased nature leans   DRYD 289:73
triumph over death and s.   SPEN 809:96
triumph over death and s.   SPEN 809:99
unconsciousness of s.   CHES 212:79
wages of s. is death   BIBLE 120:69
what heinous s.   SHAK 740:58
Where s. abounded   BIBLE 120:66
Wilt thou forgive that s.   DONNE 281:81
world, to offer for their s.   MARV 555:58
worst s. towards our fellow creatures SHAW 777:66
Sinatra ask S. to stop singing   KING 468:25
S.'s voice was highly valued   FRIE 337:64
sincere I am s.   SHAW 779:34
s. friend or a s. enemy   HUGO 420:66
sincerely Go to hell. Yours s.   ELLI 310:80
sincerity A little s. is a dangerous WILDE 908:96
belief in their s.   TWAIN 870:76
Crystal, s.   HOPK 412:79
S. is all that counts   DRIB 287:10
test of your s.   BENN 76:47
walk with s. and dignity   WAITE 884:68
sinecure gives no man a s.   POUND 665:42
sinew Bracing brain and s.   KING 469:49
sinews lay s. upon you   BIBLE 105:93
s., grow not instant old   SHAK 752:34
S. of concord   FORD 330:12
s. of war   CICE 218:23
Stiffen the s.   SHAK 746:42
sinewy s. brown men   PRIE 668:28
sinfulness saints aware of their own s. BLOOM 137:5
sing allow them to s. and to write MAZA 562:98
Bow themselves when he did s.   SHAK 775:12
Can't act. Can't s.   ANON 22:55
charmingly sweet you s.!   LEAR 497:84
crow doth s. as sweetly   SHAK 741:91
cry or s., justice must   MARIE 550:50
in ev'ry corner s.   HERB 397:91
Let me s. of thee   HUXT 427:17
let us s. unto the Lord   BIBLE 96:57
let us s. unto the Lord   BOOK 143:64
might not s. of Love?   SCOT 722:86
people do not s.   AUDEN 41:15
S.…Booh to you—   GILB 354:5
s., alang wi' me   SKIN 795:13
s.…a little off-key   MILL 572:15
s. both high and low   SHAK 756:60
s. giving opinions   HERB 399:27
s. in September   KEND 461:95
s. in the choir   KINN 470:67
S. joyfully to God   BIBLE 127:89
s. like a hillbilly   WILL 912:7
s. myself   WHIT 905:30
s. of brooks   HERB 399:33
s.…of Heaven   HERR 399:32

s. of Time or Eternity   TENN 846:28
S. on, with hymns   BETJ 83:78
S. to the Lord   SCOT 725:64
S. unto the Lord a new song   BOOK 143:46
suffers little birds to s.   SHAK 731:96
that in me s. no more   MILL 571:87
That s., and singing   MILT 578:58
The way yours s. off key   GERS 351:41
What are you going to s.?   MELBA 563:14
whereat I weep and s.   SURR 829:35
work goes on merrily, when folks s.   BICK 128:7
Yanks began to s.   ANON 22:49
Singapore S. you don't volunteer   LEE 500:39
singe That it do s.   SHAK 775:4
singeing s. of…Spain's beard   DRAKE 286:92
singer aboriginal…s. of America   CHOC 214:17
electric s.?   SEGO 726:74
I am like an opera s.   MEAT 562:4
none hear Beside the s.   LAND 488:79
Stop thine ear against the s.   SCOTT 724:40
There lived a s.   SWIN 833:42
singers have known s.   HERN 399:27
not the work of other s.   SINA 793:51
singing ask Sinatra to stop s.   KING 468:25
burst out s.   SASS 716:69
come before his presence with s.   BIBLE 97:60
delight in s., tho' none hear   LAND 488:79
Horse riding is a perfect comparison
  with s.   PAVA 644:78
Praise for the s.!   FARJ 318:47
silver waves of thy sweet s.   SHEL 785:80
s. aloud   SHAK 763:86
s. each morning out of each night   CUMM 248:14
s. in the rain   FREED 336:37
s. in the wilderness   FITZ 324:83
s. is delightful to nature   BYRD 178:93
S., it's the same thing   CARU 198:58
S. so rarely   SCOTT 724:39
s. still dost soar   SHEL 784:55
sweeter than s.   KEND 461:95
single become a s. war   GUST 375:46
beggar-woman and s.   ELIZ 309:55
come not s. spies   SHAK 754:19
continued s.   GOLD 361:43
Nothing in the world is s.   SHEL 783:42
s. in the field   WORD 927:34
s. man in possession   AUST 42:61
s.…not such a fearful disaster   ZHANG 936:94
single-parent s.-p. family   ELLW 311:92
sings instead of dying, he s.   BENC 74:6
waking till she s.   LYLY 523:8
singular Is it not s.   TROL 867:1
So s. in each particular   SHAK 770:78
singularity affect a s. in that article SHER 787:38
s. in a desire   DONNE 281:93
S. is almost invariably a clue   DOYLE 285:58
things it abhors most, s. and vulgarity HAZL 387:70
sinister derk and straucht and s.   YOUNG 935:78
s., the malignant   MACD 530:48
sink good night, or s. or swim   SHAK 741:3
Not gross to s.   SHAK 732:52
s. her, split her in twain!   TENN 848:63
sinkhole Hollywood…a s.   MAMET 543:30
sinking kind of alacrity in s.   SHAK 743:79
s., a sickening of the heart   POE 655:15
s. middle class   ORWE 628:47
swimming toward a s. ship   YARB 932:27
sinned have s.   BIBLE 120:62
have s. [Sind]   NAPI 607:57
More s. against   SHAK 763:74
people s. against   COMP 230:76
s. against my gods   FORD 330:6
would have s. incessantly   ROBI 690:31
sinner converteth the s.   BIBLE 125:20
dead s. revised and edited   BIER 129:43
make of…her a s.   CONG 232:49
please my ghost, forgive some s.   MENC 565:56
s. and sin boldly   LUTH 523:94
s.…with no dinner   RANS 679:28
who is that young s.   HOUS 416:89
sinners believe themselves to be s. PASC 641:33
combination s.   WILD 911:86
for favoured s. slain   WESL 900:16
for we are s. all   SHAK 730:60
God and s. reconciled   WESL 900:10
miserable s.   BOOK 140:80
s. before the Lord   BIBLE 87:73

s. that housed white angels — SASS 717:78
well-dressed s. — VIEI 881:12
Skullion S. had little use — SHAR 776:40
skunk blaming a s. for stinking — ORWE 629:69
pissing contest with that s. — EISE 302:54
wolf, the hyena, and the s.? — BRYAN 163:9
skuttle put me in mind of the s. fish — ADDI 6:29
sky About us in the s. — HOUS 415:52
above, the vaulted s. — CLARE 219:46
Above us only s. — LENN 503:91
and in the s. — MCCR 529:19
bed of daffodil s. — TENN 845:89
belonging as much to s. as to earth — CARR 194:54
blue ethereal s. — ADDI 6:26
blue s. of spring — ALLI 13:62
boats were tossed S.-high — LOWE 520:42
Brain...wider than the S. — DICK 272:63
bridal of the earth and s. — HERB 398:14
bright reversion in the s. — POPE 659:79
clean the s. — ELIOT 307:5
close against the s. — HOOD 410:38
color of the s. — CRANE 243:29
common s. — GRAV 367:68
die in yon rich s. — TENN 842:5
Dragging the whole s. — FROST 338:86
evening is spread out against the s. — ELIOT 304:17
flaming from th'ethereal s. — MILT 580:95
forehead of the morning s. — MILT 578:57
from yon azure s. — WORD 924:88
gaze into sea or s. — MELV 564:40
Give me the clear blue s. — HAZL 387:5
glorious land above the s. — HILL 402:88
great bowl of the s. — MCMU 537:87
held the s. suspended — HOUS 416:80
hollowing out the s. — BETJ 84:10
Is a golden s. — HAMM 379:17
isolation of the s. — STEV 819:19
keen city in the s. — CUMM 247:6
Let the s. rain potatoes — SHAK 744:81
light, she said, not of the s. — NEIL 610:30
lonely sea and the s. — MASE 559:21
lustre in its s. — SHEL 782:21
meet the s. — TENN 838:42
milky s. — YEATS 932:32
no bright sign in the s. — HUSS 424:43
No more to use the s. — JEFF 436:6
no s. could squeak through — PLATH 654:69
November's s. is chill — SCOTT 723:93
nursling of the s. — SHEL 783:41
obstacles...from the s. — MANC 544:41
purest s. with brightness — SPEN 808:75
rainbow in the s. — WORD 926:15
rainbow in the s.! — TENN 847:39
sent him down the s. — CORY 237:74
Shoulder the s., my lad — HOUS 416:73
s. cannot have two suns — CHIA 213:5
s. changes when they are wives — SHAK 750:79
s. grows darker — CHES 212:72
s. is darkening like a stain — AUDEN 39:80
s. is red — BIBLE 112:61
s. is the limit — SHUL 790:93
s., Never before so beautiful — WORD 925:93
s. no height above him — ATWO 38:50
s. snivels green snot — MITS 589:14
s....Spread like a rosy ocean — BYRON 182:81
stared into the s. — HODG 405:44
starry s. — GERS 351:44
star...shining in the s. — WORD 924:78
Sunset divides the s. — BYRON 180:33
there a glimpse of mystic s. — LAWS 496:46
The Sheltering S. — BOWL 147:32
the s. acutest at its vanishing — STEV 819:27
th'eternal spheres and lamping s. — SPEN 808:89
thread loosened from the s. — ROSS 698:94
to the wild s. — TENN 844:60
triple-towered s. — DAY 257:85
true as the s. — KIPL 471:12
turrets split the s. — LAND 488:84
under the benign s. — BRON 155:99
views...the regions of the s. — ENNI 314:70
walking down the s. — GILM 356:56
western s. in the night — WHIT 906:47
wheeling s. — SNYD 803:49
which prisoners call the s. — WILDE 910:53
wide and starry s. — STEV 822:10
will across the s. in stars — LAWR 495:37
wonderful Southern night-s. — LAWR 494:5

yon twelve-winded s. — HOUS 415:57
Skye over the sea to S. — BOUL 146:26
sky-mocker s.-m., rave! — UPDI 874:74
skyscraper growth of the S. School — JOHN 440:96
skyscrapers about four s. behind — JOHN 441:6
New glass s. — TALE 835:82
tops of s. — GILL 355:38
slab Beneath this s. — NASH 608:96
slabs Ice-scratched s. — SNYD 803:49
slack observing me grow s. — HERB 397:98
slacks girls in s. remember dad — BETJ 84:98
slag measureless grossness and the s. — WHIT 906:51
slag-heap post-industrial s.-h. — DRAB 286:91
slain he...that's s. — BUTL 177:59
O s. and spent — SWIN 833:43
s. the Earl of Murray — BALL 55:68
s. think he is s. — EMER 313:39
s. this year in Europe — WALP 887:38
Slaka In S., sex is just politics — BRAD 148:62
slam not a s. at you — FITZ 325:12
slamming s. down his silly curtain — SALI 711:66
slander civic s. — TENN 844:61
devised this s. — SHAK 760:4
one to s. you — TWAIN 872:27
s.'s venomed spear — SHAK 734:97
S.Valentine With falsehood — SHAK 729:37
To speak no s. — TENN 846:21
writs for libel and s. — PROF 670:59
slanders secondarily they are s. — SHAK 745:23
slang All s. is metaphor — CHES 211:45
S. is a language — SAND 713:10
S. is vigorous and apt — GALS 344:27
s....was...out of date — GREE 371:64
slant Truth...tell it s. — DICK 273:71
slap-dash s.-d. down in the mouth — CONG 231:99
slaps if someone s. you — KHRU 467:4
slate split in soft s. — BUNT 166:60
write his thoughts upon a s. — HOOD 410:53
slats roof, instead of s. — DRAY 287:7
slaughter counted as sheep for the s. — BIBLE 95:23
Cuinchy...was a s. yard — BLUN 137:14
face such s. — WALC 884:70
'I am going to s. you' — TRAV 864:40
like lions to the roaring s. — CUMM 247:9
one who delights in s. — LAO 490:11
perpetrators of Tuesday's s. — SONT 804:80
s. of a thousand platitudes — ORTE 627:28
s. of plague, pestilence and famine — SHAW 778:93
s. will resume — CONG 230:96
wade through s. to a throne — GRAY 369:19
war and mutual s. — MILT 583:87
slaughterhouse sheep go to a s.-h. — MACD 529:25
s. thoughts — SHAK 769:41
soul's s. — WEBS 895:94
slaughtering s. one another — GUIB 374:30
slaughters S. a thousand waiting — SHAK 770:75
slave act a s. to limit — SHAK 757:3
adult s. — GREER 372:89
Being your s. — SHAK 771:23
Be not the s. of words — CARL 192:94
economic equivalent of the s. — WIEN 906:67
greatest of mankind...my s. — DRYD 289:62
gross plodding s. — WEBS 895:91
has been s. to thousands — SHAK 760:85
made them s. masters — MORR 599:6
man...not passion's s. — SHAK 754:89
married woman is a s. — BALZ 57:7
My father was a s. — ROBE 689:22
noble and the s. — SCOTT 724:16
peasant s. am I! — SHAK 753:67
permanently half-s. and half-free — LINC 510:34
Philosopher!—a fingering s. — WORD 924:81
s. has but one master — LABR 483:67
S., I have set my life — SHAK 732:24
s. in base servility — SHAK 729:49
s. morality — NIET 616:24
s. of some defunct economist — KEYN 466:89
s. of the author's mind — GAUG 347:68
s. of the passions — HUME 422:7
S. to no sect — POPE 660:27
S. to Prodigality — MAND 545:54
Some cogging, cozening s. — SHAK 760:4
This yellow s. — SHAK 762:48
Throw this s. — SHAK 763:82
victim and s. of his action — EMER 313:35
worker is the s. of capitalist society — CONN 234:91
Your Majesty's s. — KISH 475:88

slavery administration of s. — STOWE 826:72
because they impose s. — RUSS 705:47
Chains and S.! — BURNS 173:41
chains of s. — GRIL 373:13
cowardice perpetuated s. — ROUS 700:42
definition of s. — SWIFT 831:73
escapes s. except by a...revolution — LACL 484:90
Extreme freedom...to extreme s. — PLATO 655:3
freedom is s. — ORWE 629:99
nothing so dreadful as voluntary s. — DICK 273:82
perfect condition of s. — ASTE 36:24
perished in hopeless s. — OCON 621:19
S. broke the world — MORR 599:6
S.'s a thing thet depends — LOWE 520:30
s. to a pattern — NIN 616:37
s. was originally established — DOUG 284:38
S....weed that grows — BURKE 168:14
sold off into s. — TRUTH 869:52
soon as they got out of s. — WALK 885:98
state of S. — GILL 356:42
thought s. tolerable — UPDI 874:79
worst possible kind of s. — BARA 59:46
slaves all women are born s. — ASTE 36:24
asking s. what was going on — ALME 13:65
barbarous traffic in s. — PITT 653:45
Britons never will be s. — THOM 856:52
Englishmen never will be s. — SHAW 778:91
Force made the first s. — ROUS 700:42
freemen or s. — WASH 890:83
Gaza at the mill with s. — MILT 586:45
happy freemen, are the only s. — MASS 560:50
impart to wives and s. — DRYD 289:69
intercourse between tyrants and s. — GOLD 361:48
martyred s. of Time — BAUD 65:69
only fit for the s. — FLET 328:65
our posterity made s. — CROM 245:71
poor s. with weary footsteps — SHEL 786:9
professional players are soccer s. — CHAR 207:43
remain no legal s. — MILL 571:78
ruling them like s. — SHEL 785:81
S. and Slavery — ANON 21:37
s. that dig the golden ore — CRAB 242:89
s. we'll ever be — DAVIS 256:65
sons of former s. — KING 468:39
soul of the s. — GILL 356:48
two kinds of s. — ILLI 428:47
tyrants...only want s. — WOLL 921:6
voluntarily to submit to be s. — PITT 652:40
wholly s. or wholly free — DRYD 291:18
women into darling little s. — MILLS 574:69
Slavs cause of the S. — WITTE 918:38
slay Though he s. me, yet will I trust — BIBLE 93:60
slayer red s. think he slays — EMER 313:39
slaying s. of a beautiful hypothesis — HUXL 426:9
slays s. More than you rob — SHAK 762:50
sleave ravelled s. of care — SHAK 767:2
sledgehammer S. sentimentality — KENT 464:60
sleek curse...upon the s. upstart — RANS 679:24
sleeket Wee, s., cowrin, tim'rous — BURNS 170:71
sleek-headed S.-h. men — SHAK 747:79
sleep ability to get a good night's s. — WILS 916:2
afford much comfort in s. — BROW 159:97
awaked out of his s. — BIBLE 87:89
azure-lidded s. — KEATS 459:40
battening...in his s. — TENN 838:37
bleary eyed for lack of s. — DAUG 253:20
borders of s. — THOM 854:17
break earth's s. — OWEN 632:64
Caged in its s. — SMITH 801:25
calf won't get much s. — ALLEN 12:44
Care-charming s. — FLET 328:66
Cervantes usually puts me to s. — GONZ 363:96
closes soft in s. — STEP 817:58
Come s., O s. — SIDN 790:10
country...going to s. — RENAN 683:98
deep, deep s. of England — ORWE 628:51
deep House of Commons s. — CHAN 205:6
dewy-feathered S. — MILT 577:21
doen they only s. — SPEN 808:90
dreamless, uninvaded s. — TENN 838:36
each day dies with s. — HOPK 413:6
endless—as s. — WILL 914:54
full of s. — YEATS 932:33
get a good night's s. — KEEN 460:68
giveth his beloved s. — BIBLE 98:92
go s. if I can — SHAK 749:45
grinning in their s. — LAWR 494:11

have a nice, quiet s. | CHAM 204:63
haven't been to s. for | WAUGH 892:20
immobility, ecstasy, and s. | MARI 550:52
inhibitions and get some s. | LOOS 517:81
in his cunning s. | THOM 853:90
in his s. he does little harm | SHAK 762:37
In s., afraid | ROET 694:8
in s. old palaces | SHEL 783:45
I shall s. | SWIN 833:41
I s. like a baby too | POWE 666:91
lack of s. | GOLD 360:32
lasting s. | BEAU 67:9
let me s. a little | MACN 538:5
let me s. alway | COLE 226:94
Lie soft, s. hard | MIDD 569:39
lie where I am and s., s., s. | SHIP 789:77
like unwilling s. | KEATS 457:80
miles to go before I s. | FROST 339:98
more in your life except to s. | RHYS 684:26
Murders the innocent s. | TWAIN 871:7
never s. with anyone | ALGR 11:29
night doth summon all to s.? | DRAY 286:98
night to do with s.? | MILT 577:28
of Night, but not of S. | THOM 856:61
One short s. past | DONNE 281:68
O partial s. | SHAK 743:53
O s., O gentle s. | SHAK 743:52
O S.! the friend of Woe | SOUT 805:5
O, such another s. | SHAK 765:55
poets…give their readers s. | POPE 662:67
poor Indian's s. | KEATS 457:82
putting the mind to s. | SLOAN 796:17
quiet s. and a sweet dream | MASE 559:23
rounded with a s. | SHAK 774:95
sang themselves to s. | HODG 405:43
shall not all s. | BIBLE 121:19
S. after toil | SPEN 808:81
s. and a forgetting | WORD 926:24
s. and a sense of history | WILS 916:4
s. and death differ | TRAH 864:37
S. and rest | TENN 841:2
S. demands…guilty immunity | BARN 60:63
S. dwell upon thine eyes | SHAK 736:54
s. Full of sweet dreams | KEATS 457:1
S. I can get nane | BURNS 171:7
S. is death without | LEBO 499:7
s. is sweet to the labouring man | BUNY 166:72
S. is when all the unsorted stuff | GOLD 360:29
S. no more | SHAK 767:2
S. no more | SHAK 767:3
s. out-of-doors | BIRD 130:59
s. provides relief | CHAM 204:70
S. shall neither night nor day | SHAK 766:68
S., son of the sable Night | DANI 252:88
S., that sometimes shuts | SHAK 738:7
s.…through life | ALBEE 10:95
S. to wake | BROW 163:95
s. under bridges | FRAN 333:93
s. upon ale | FARQ 318:55
s. when you ain't sleepy | TWAIN 871:95
S. will come when thou art fled | SHEL 786:18
s. with dogs | WEBS 895:90
s. with women we do not love | DIDE 274:97
softer than s. | TENN 839:61
Still it cried 'S. no more' | SHAK 767:3
stop it from going to s. | RUSH 703:88
such as s. o'nights | SHAK 747:79
The poor s. little | OTWAY 631:34
think of them that s. | CAMP 186:71
Thou art inclined to s. | SHAK 774:79
time enough to s. | HOUS 414:44
To die, to s. | SHAK 753:74
together out of s. | MARI 550:58
wake to s. | ROET 694:3
waking from its s. | KIER 467:13
when you s. you remind me | SASS 716:68
Where fain, fain I would s.? | BALL 55:72
Yet a little s. | BIBLE 99:16
sleeper duty is to arouse the s. | BETH 83:76
never a quiet s.? | TENN 845:96
sleepers in the diners and s. | SAND 713:93
s. in that quiet earth | BRON 155:99
sleepest Thou s. too long | SKEL 795:92
sleepeth s., and must be wakened | BIBLE 92:19
sleeping except s. and resting | TWAIN 872:39
growing…when ye're s. | SCOTT 724:36
I was s. with the President | REAG 680:53

The s. and the dead | SHAK 767:4
wake s., and sleep | MONT 592:82
sleepless S. as the river | CRANE 243:14
S. with cold | ROSS 698:2
sleeps never sad but when she s. | SHAK 744:1
sleep-time silence of the s.-t. | BROW 163:94
sleepwalker assurance of a s. | HITL 404:19
sleepy not s. and…no place | DYLAN 297:60
sleeve ace of joy up his s. | ONDA 625:85
heart on your s. | THAT 850:27
heart upon my s. | SHAK 758:50
lacy s. with a bottle of vitriol | WOOL 923:56
not wear your heart on your s. | WEBS 895:22
strip his s. | SHAK 746:58
sleeves language that rolls up its s. | SAND 713:10
s. rolled | MCCA 527:94
sleigh s., and eight tiny reindeer | MOORE 594:16
sprang to his s. | MOORE 594:19
sleight admire his s. of hand | BUTL 177:55
slender kissed her s. hand | TENN 845:86
slept and he s. | TENN 844:54
But while men s. | BIBLE 112:50
s. with his fathers | BIBLE 92:16
slew as he was ambitious, I s. him | SHAK 748:4
dead which he s. at his death | BIBLE 90:76
Who s. them? | SITT 793:56
slice people want a larger s. | CRIP 244:50
sliced they'd come up s. | TREV 865:60
slide We can s. it | REED 681:78
sliding hear time s. past you | RHYS 684:26
slight s. all that do | FARQ 318:51
Slightly S. in Peter Pan | TYNAN 872:46
slime slimier s.! | BROO 156:18
slimness S. Of Despair | NICH 613:86
slimy s. things did crawl with legs | COLE 225:85
thousand thousand s. things | COLE 225:87
slings s. and arrows | SHAK 753:74
slinkiness hint of Bacall's s.? | ALLEN 12:38
slip gave us all the s.? | BROW 160:24
giving his enemies the s. | STER 817:71
s. into something more comfortable | HARL 383:84
slippery real world…is s. | DAY 256:76
standing is s. | BACON 48:2
stands upon a s. place | SHAK 739:28
woman's brain: vague, s. | RICH 686:64
words are s. | ADAMS 4:86
slips like greyhounds in the s. | SHAK 746:43
slithy 'S.' means 'lithe and slimy' | CARR 196:13
slivers last s. and shreds of objectivity | CUPI 248:35
sloeblack s., slow, black | THOM 853:85
slog with a s. to square leg | JOYCE 452:94
slogan democracy is just a s. | GORB 363:99
s. than a genuine goal | LEGU 501:95
slogans our national s. | THUR 859:48
s.…confused with solutions | BENT 78:83
slogged s. up to Arras | SASS 716:63
slope golden ear Imbrown the s. | POPE 659:97
That s. through darkness | TENN 843:44
slopes butler's upper s. | WODE 919:74
sloppy prefer their English s. | SAYE 717:86
slot plays s. machines | TRUMP 869:48
sloth ignoble ease, and peaceful s. | MILT 581:23
too much time in studies is s. | BACON 50:51
when resty s. | SHAK 774:70
slothful Not s. in business | BIBLE 120:81
s. man saith | BIBLE 100:54
Slough friendly bombs…fall on S. | BETJ 83:83
slough S. of Despond | BUNY 166:67
slovenly very drunk and very s. | WYCH 931:13
slow but ain't it s.? | HERB 397:86
clock is always s. | SERV 728:4
come he s., or come he fast | SCOTT 723:94
drinks fast, pays s. | FRAN 334:8
each s. dusk | OWEN 632:52
grinds s., but sure | HERB 398:22
s. of speech | BIBLE 88:13
takes the music…too s. | SAINT 710:29
telling you to s. down | ANON 23:79
slowing s. down to get a good look | GIBB 352:67
slowly Hurry s. | AUGU 42:47
much easier…than to play it s. | MOZA 601:45
Wisely and s. | SHAK 736:58
sluggard Go to the ant, thou s. | BIBLE 99:15
slugs silver trails of inebriated s. | JAMES 433:28
sluice Grand S., and a high steeple | ANON 20:22
stop beside the opening s. | CRAB 242:1
sluicing browsing and s. | WODE 918:52

slum if you've seen one city s. | AGNEW 8:72
not a s. in the country | HALD 377:73
slumber neither s. nor sleep | BIBLE 97:87
Seal thy sense in deathly s. | DELA 260:72
s. did my spirit seal | WORD 924:80
s. is more sweet | TENN 839:58
softer than s. | KEND 461:95
slumbers Golden s. kiss your eyes | DEKK 259:48
unquiet s. | BRON 155:99
slums gay intimacy of the s. | WAUGH 892:24
slush mush and s. | OWEN 632:49
pure as the driven s. | BANK 58:28
slut be she s. | SWIFT 832:12
smack some s. of age in you | SHAK 742:39
Small Here lies…John S. | EGAN 301:24
small All things both great and s. | COLE 225:92
design…in a thing so s. | FROST 339:5
division in a country so s. | DONO 282:97
do s. things well | GLAS 359:97
Man is s. | SCHU 720:51
Microbe is so very s. | BELL 72:50
S. is Beautiful | SCHU 720:50
S. is Beautiful | SCHU 720:51
S. is the worth | WALL 886:13
s. thing…made large | TWAIN 871:51
so s. a thing | ARNO 31:96
still s. voice | BIBLE 92:24
smallest in the s. room of my house | REGER 682:94
small-talk s.-t. flows from lip | CRAB 242:97
small-talking s.-t. world | FRY 340:27
small-town s.-t. bourgeois at heart | NABO 606:47
smart Even s. girls do it | SALI 711:59
if we were…very s. | FULF 341:46
not s. enough to hide it | REST 683:85
One is s. | GORB 363:14
scorn which mocked the s. | ARNO 33:32
surety…shall s. | BIBLE 99:22
smarter S. than…his colleagues | REST 683:13
s. than you are | BART 63:25
Some are s. than others | MARC 549:34
thought themselves s. | ATTL 38:44
smarts tyrannizeth in the bitter s. | SPEN 808:88
smeddun the s. tane | SMITH 801:25
smell creatures give out a s. | LEES 500:48
oozy s. | TOLK 862:95
shares man's s. | HOPK 412:83
s. far worse than weeds | SHAK 772:38
s. of steaks | ELIOT 305:27
s. so sweet | SHAK 741:1
s. the blood of a British man | SHAK 763:79
s. too strong of the lamp | STER 817:76
sweet keen s. | ROSS 698:91
the s. of it | UTTL 875:10
What a lovely s. | SMITH 797:36
would s. as sweet | SHAK 736:48
Yes, to s. pork | SHAK 739:50
smells faint stale s. of beer | ELIOT 305:28
measured out by sounds and s. | BETJ 84:11
painting of sounds, noises and s. | CARRA 194:58
tell me it s. like roses | JOHN 445:3
smelt And s. so? Pah! | SHAK 755:32
smile by his s., I knew | OWEN 632:59
Cambridge people rarely s. | BROO 156:13
dismiss the past with a s. | LESS 504:33
every fascist a communist s. | SPARK 806:27
faint fleeting s. | THUR 859:31
has a nice s. | GROM 374:22
heaven-revealing s. | WORD 929:63
if I s. it happens | TRAV 864:45
last fading s. | HUXL 426:4
make a s. go on all fours | MACA 526:57
of that human s. | HUGO 421:97
on a s. and a shoeshine | MILL 571:37
should forget and s. | ROSS 697:79
simply watch her s. | SAINT 709:13
s. and s. and be a villain | SHAK 752:35
s. at perils past! | SCOTT 723:12
s. at the claims | TENN 840:74
s. I could feel in my hip pocket | CHAN 204:76
s. is often the key | SAINT 709:18
S. of heaven | SHAK 775:14
S. or sigh | BARK 60:56
So thou would'st s. | MARL 552:88
vain tribute of a s. | SCOTT 723:89
way your s. just beams | GERS 351:41
where the s. dwells a little longer | CHAP 206:11
with a heavenly s. | KIER 467:13

smiled At me you s.   TENN 840:73
  s. with…spontaneity   ACHE 2:27
  soldiers he s. at   SASS 716:63
smiler s. with the knyf   CHAU 208:81
smiles charmed it with s.   CARR 197:32
  daggers in men's s.   SHAK 768:10
  expect to be greeted with s.   BROO 156:25
  men with careful s.   LEWIS 507:89
  Nae mair your s. can cheer me   COCK 224:55
  Seldom he s.   SHAK 747:80
  S. awake you when you rise   DEKK 259:48
  s. of the people   MARC 549:35
  S., tears, of all my life!   BROW 160:10
  Their s.,Wan as primroses   KEATS 458:7
  The robbed that s.   SHAK 759:67
smiling S. at grief   SHAK 756:69
  villain with a s. cheek   SHAK 739:52
smilingness a s. assume   BYRON 179:22
smirk serious and the s.   DICK 267:3
  s. with his wife   MARI 550:59
smite s. once, and s. no more   MILT 578:52
Smith calling him S.   HOLM 408:91
  F E S. is very clever   ASQU 36:16
  name were John D S. IV   ROCK 692:78
  S….an over-dressed pirate   LEAC 496:63
  S., the name is so poetical   CHES 211:50
  smith s. a mighty man   LONG 515:44
Smithfield who brings The S. Muses   POPE 662:64
smithy village s. stands   LONG 515:44
smitten be s. against the other   BIBLE 108:50
  may be s., and die   BIBLE 91:1
  s. me these three times?   BIBLE 89:40
smog diamonds in the s.   MAIL 540:55
smoke Above the s. and stir   MILT 577:25
  blind with s.   SASS 716:59
  crowds, her beloved s.   LAMB 486:29
  don't s.   CURR 249:44
  flavor as hickory s.   MUMF 603:79
  Gossip is a sort of s.   ELIOT 304:13
  house was filled with s.   BIBLE 102:11
  middle page you said: 'Holy s.'   CHRI 214:31
  occasionally emitting s.   WHITE 903:1
  Oft fire is without s.   SPEN 808:74
  or a man who does not s.   STEV 821:84
  s. of their torment ascendeth   BIBLE 126:68
  s. out at the chimney   SHAK 750:80
  smudge of s.   TIME 860:72
smoke-filled men in a s.-f. room   SIMP 793:48
  s.-f. room in some hotel   DAUG 253:20
smoker bad taste of the s.   ELIOT 304:13
  man in the s.   SAND 713:93
smokes noises…throbbed with s.   CUMM 247:1
smoke-stack salt-caked s.-s.   MASE 559:27
smoking give up s., drinking and loving FREUD 336:49
  not found any s. guns   BLIX 136:97
  seed her first a-s.   KIPL 471:87
  sit placidly s. his pipe   SHIP 789:77
  s. flax shall he not quench   BIBLE 111:39
  s. flax shall he not quench   BIBLE 103:43
smooth I am a s. man   BIBLE 87:86
  prickly to the s.   MACD 530:48
  S. runs the water   SHAK 730:56
  true love never did run s.   SHAK 737:84
smudge wears man's s.   HOPK 412:83
Smudges wasn't it naughty of S.   BETJ 84:9
smug hauf o't s., complacent   SMITH 801:25
  s. suppressions of his face   WELLS 898:76
snaffle use the s. and the curb   CAMP 186:56
snail s.'s on the thorn   BROW 160:19
  s., which everywhere doth roam   DONNE 280:62
snails horns of cockled s.   SHAK 733:83
snake earth doth like a s. renew   SHEL 786:21
  gathering flowers…fears a s.?   DONNE 279:32
  greyhound…heeded lyke a s.   BERN 81:48
  Like an uneasy s.   WORD 925:3
  Once bitten by a s.   DALAI 250:67
  perfumed parlor s.   DUNNE 295:24
  s. about to devour people   NIXON 617:41
  s. lurks in the grass   VIRG 882:27
snakes heard by s. in the grass   MO 589:18
  s. with double tongue   SHAK 737:98
snakeskin s.-titles of mining-claims   BENET 75:9
snapper-up s.-u. of…trifles   SHAK 770:82
snare from the s. of the fowler   BIBLE 96:53
  I saw the s.   TENN 840:73
  s. to Religion   TAYL 837:23
  s. to the inhabitants of Jerusalem   BIBLE 102:15

Trial…will be…a s.   DENM 262:98
  wha can avoid the fell s.?   BURNS 173:55
snarling s. all before I came   SHAK 731:5
snaw-wreaths s.-w. in thaw   NAIR 607:54
sneaking 's.'…not to his taste   ANON 21:30
  s. piece of imbecility   SCOTT 723:14
sneer celebrated s.   GILB 354:17
  s….like an oyster-knife   ANNAN 17:51
  solemn creed with solemn s.   BYRON 180:28
  teach the rest to s.   POPE 661:38
sneering without s., teach the rest   POPE 661:38
sneeze it's like having a good s.   LAWR 494:89
sneezes beat him when he s.   CARR 195:69
  Coughs and s.   ANON 22:64
snigger between a eunuch and a s.   FIRB 323:70
  entertaining s.   GILB 354:17
snob admires mean things is a S.   THAC 849:95
  s….on principle   SHAW 780:58
snobbery S….a form of despair   BROD 153:55
  S. with Violence   BENN 76:27
snobs effete corps of impudent s.   AGNEW 8:73
snooker Billiards is very similar to s. DAVIS 255:61
  staying married and playing s.   REAR 681:70
snore s. upon the flint   SHAK 774:70
snorting S. and sporting   SITW 793:61
snot shy snivels green s.   MITS 589:14
snotgreen s. sea   JOYCE 452:84
snout as wise a s. on   FERG 320:6
snouts get your s. in the trough   WEIG 896:25
snow beautiful in their s.   RUSK 703:5
  bells, across the s.   TENN 844:60
  birds sit brooding in the s.   SHAK 734:95
  chaste as unsunned s.   SHAK 773:63
  cold climate, and frost and s.   SOUT 805:95
  dark over the s.   THOM 854:20
  deep s. piled above   BRON 155:93
  few acres of s.   VOLT 882:41
  hail, or rain, or any s.   TENN 847:52
  Hidden in wonder and s.   SCOTT 722:78
  ice and wondrous…black s.   SHAK 738:14
  icicles and bitter s.!   MALL 542:94
  If s. be white   SHAK 773:51
  kindle fire with s.   SHAK 729:33
  last streak of s.   TENN 844:63
  locks are like the s.   BURNS 171:10
  made whiter than s.   BIBLE 127:87
  'mid s. and ice   LONG 516:48
  new-fallen s.   MOORE 594:16
  pale virgin shrouded in s.   BLAKE 134:53
  pink bonbon stuffed with s.   DEBU 258:6
  See amid the winter's s.   CASW 199:82
  sleigh bells in the s.   BERL 80:16
  s. falling fastest   JOYCE 451:81
  s. falls in the river   BURNS 172:19
  S. fell, the trees stood   NEME 610:38
  S. had fallen, s. on s.   ROSS 697:84
  S. has begun to fall   DUNN 295:19
  s. in May's new-fangled shows   SHAK 733:71
  wallow naked in December s.   SHAK 734:4
  white as driven s.   SHAK 770:92
  white as s.   BIBLE 125:45
  white as s.   BIBLE 102:7
  whiter skin of hers than s.   SHAK 761:7
  whiter than s.   BIBLE 95:29
  whiter than s.   BIBLE 127:87
snowdrift as a s. on the sand   KHAY 466:94
snow-leopard like a s.-l. waiting   LAWR 494:15
snows frigid as then s.   BYRON 179:6
  season of s. and sins   SWIN 832:19
  where are last year's s.?   VILL 881:13
snowstorm watching a s.   ROTH 699:17
snow-water Drinking cold s.-w.   SNYD 802:47
snow-white little s.-w. feet   YEATS 932:29
  s.-w. trunk   FROST 338:92
snowy S., Flowy, Blowy   ELLIS 311:81
snuff only took s.   GOLD 362:72
  s., tobacker, and sleep   DICK 269:71
snuff-box of Amber S.-b.   POPE 659:76
soap S. and education   TWAIN 870:79
  What! no s.?   FOOTE 329:94
  why s. operas are…so popular   STEI 816:45
soap-boxes keep getting up on s.-b.   LOOS 517:84
soar s. where he is sitting now   SHEL 786:2
soaring S. ever singest   SHEL 784:55
  s. human boy!   DICK 270:90
sob S., heavy world   AUDEN 40:11
sober at least not s.   JOHN 444:1

be s., and hope to the end   BIBLE 125:21
  Be s., be vigilant   BIBLE 125:30
  during his s. intervals   LAMB 487:58
  go to bed s.   FLET 328:68
  if they were quite s.   SHAW 780:42
  kept in s. government   SPEN 808:85
  man must stay s.   DAY 256:76
  men at whiles are s.   HOUS 416:74
  Merely s.   BANKS 58:33
  My mother, drunk or s.   CHES 211:46
  Often drunk, and seldom s.   FULL 341:70
  one-third s.   BURT 174:65
  or when both were s.   THUR 860:63
  sedate, s., silent   HOOD 410:40
  s. as a Judge   FIEL 322:39
  stuff when I'm s.   RUSS 706:70
  Wordsworth drunk and Porson s.   HOUS 415:69
sober-suited s.-s. matron   SHAK 736:63
sobriety liquor traffic is to s.   TWAIN 872:20
  S. diminishes   JAMES 434:68
sobs life is made up of s.   OHEN 623:51
  s. from among the group   DICK 267:20
soccer I was born for s.   PELE 646:17
  professional players are s. slaves   CHAR 207:43
  S. is a man's game   CHAR 207:45
  s., of all sports   ROUS 700:39
  world's best s. teams   CALI 184:36
sociable To one not s.   SHAK 774:73
social at the cost of his s. position   MARX 558:6
  being on s. security   WELD 897:42
  commit A s. science   AUDEN 41:33
  corresponding s. constitution   MARX 557:1
  fitting for the s. scientist   BOUL 146:22
  how to apply s. theory   STIN 824:48
  impact upon the s. sciences   NISB 616:39
  importance of s. ownership   STRA 826:79
  moral and s. progress   MILL 570:57
  more hateful…The s. sage's   BROW 162:78
  No s. study   MILLS 574:68
  political and s. conditions   MARS 554:39
  political, and s. life   LEWIS 507:83
  self-love and s. be the same   POPE 660:22
  since S. Progress began   KIPL 474:84
  s. and educational patterns   MCLU 536:60
  s. consequences of their activities   HOBS 405:32
  S. Contract is nothing more   WELLS 898:75
  s. fabric would fly asunder   SHAW 778:1
  s. phenomenon   GOULD 365:24
  s. position of the observer   MANN 546:78
  s. problem of the twentieth century   SMALL 796:21
  s. problem solved   MACD 530:42
  s. progress   JOHN 438:57
  S. scientists could supply   FALU 317:41
  society, s. order   MUNCH 603:81
  things that are purely s.   WASH 889:79
  without s. advance   HARR 383:88
  works in the s. sciences   NISB 616:38
socialising better off not s.   WALK 885:92
socialism creeping s.-libertarianism   GINS 357:5
  doctrines and practice of S.   MORR 598:98
  identify modern s.   WILS 916:96
  meaning of s.   GOER 359:9
  nothing in S. that…will not cure   DURA 295:27
  proceed to the building of s.   LENIN 502:85
  restating our s.   WILS 915:92
  s. and a market economy   DENG 261:89
  s. and communism   MORR 598:99
  S. does not mean much   ORWE 628:42
  S. is neither Protestant nor Catholic   CONN 233:90
  This is not s.   SNOW 802:46
  worst advertisement for S.   ORWE 627:41
socialist America's leading s.   ECON 298:79
  main business of s. parties   KING 468:27
  mark…of S. literature   ORWE 628:44
  S. before he is forty   WILL 914:67
  S. papers…came out   MORR 598:98
  s. society   NOZI 619:80
  solid workingman's s.   MCFA 531:71
  sun of the s. revolution   LENIN 502:84
  world could become s.   MAO 544:99
socialists If s. lose sight   STRA 826:79
  motive of many S.   ORWE 628:43
  S. are Liberals   SAINT 709:28
  S. can scheme   MACL 536:54
socialize s. the cost of growing old   HEWE 401:71
societies marriage in most s.   DWOR 296:46
  s. which…cannot sustain   MO 589:20

troops, and sweet s. — MILT 578:58
society advanced industrial s. — HAYEK 387:60
All classes of s. — JEVO 438:47
altering the shape of s. — ORWE 628:55
as s. develops, its mythical stories — FRYE 340:36
avenue of assimilation into s. — DOCT 278:4
Bourgeois s. is infected — WEIL 896:31
build a s. of opportunity — MAJOR 541:70
buildings…the reflection of s. — PEI 646:15
carrying on in s. — PAIGE 634:87
certain types of s. — PARS 640:1
classless s. — MARX 558:16
cling together In one s. — WORD 925:92
comparatively prosperous s. — MACM 537:78
contemporary and future s. — MURP 604:4
declension, of the s. — SMITH 798:45
definition of a free s. — STEV 820:54
democratic and free s. — MAND 544:46
desire to integrate into s. — SARR 715:39
direction of s. — TOCQ 861:80
dominant factor in our s. — ASIM 35:6
economic factors in s. — GILM 356:52
every one of that s. — LOCKE 514:15
existing basis of s. — KEYN 465:79
faults of the economic s. — KEYN 466:90
first duty to serve s. — JOHN 443:83
founder of civil s. — ROUS 700:40
greater pest to s. — MACA 526:73
great safeguard of s. — ELIOT 303:1
Havana, Cuba…high s. — CABR 183:19
higher phase of communist s. — MARX 558:14
If the idea of s. were extinguished — DURK 296:34
In a consumer s. — ILLI 428:47
In communist s. — MARX 557:99
In our s. this person — MAMET 543:26
intellectual life…of western s. — SNOW 802:38
intersections within a s. — MILLS 574:68
In the affluent s. — GALB 343:92
just as s. ought to be — MORR 599:3
knowledge of the s. it serves — CASS 199:72
looking closely at s. — TRIL 866:69
loss of s. in which — MOOD 594:6
Man is born to live in s. — DIDE 274:3
Man seeketh in s. — BACON 46:54
member of s. — MORI 598:83
mirror of our own s. — STER 817:63
modern ardor to improve s. — SMALL 796:20
mutual s., help, and comfort — BOOK 142:22
negotiation and s. — MUNCH 603:81
no Arts; no Letters; no S. — HOBB 404:27
noble s. for providing — DICK 266:78
no importance…to s. — NABO 606:40
no one in our s. is allowed — OAKE 619:86
no such thing as s. — THAT 850:28
nothing to distinguish human s. — SHAW 780:55
pervading all nature and s. — HARDY 382:68
place in s. — NIGH 616:30
play a much larger part in s. — SNOW 802:42
poor s. — TAWN 837:9
powerful men in our s. — BELL 73:76
progress of s. and wealth — RICA 684:32
promotes that of the s. — SMITH 798:49
quarrel with its s. — TRIL 866:71
radical vision of s. — WALK 885:93
receives the protection of s. — MILL 570:64
responsibility of s. — PALEY 635:14
role of labour in s. — NEVI 611:49
rounds of s.'s ladder — MOORE 595:22
sick s. must think — LEWIS 507:79
socialist s. — NOZI 619:80
s. as something eternal — ORWE 628:54
S. became my…bride — WORD 928:55
s. distributes itself — ARNO 33:53
s. do not want his labour — MALT 543:18
s. has resembled a pyramid — NAPO 607:71
s. here would be quite civilised — WILDE 909:50
s. in which they live — JAMES 434:57
s. in which thought — RUSS 705:53
S. is all but rude — MARV 556:73
s. is an organized conspiracy — DOUG 284:37
S. is composed of two large classes — CHAM 204:69
s. is full of women — WILDE 909:46
s. is indeed a contract — BURKE 169:39
S. is no comfort — SHAK 774:73
S. is now one polished horde — BYRON 182:96
S. needs first of all — SUMN 828:20
s. offenders — GILB 355:21

S. requires…retrieve his fortunes — DICK 270:14
S. should not ask anything — SAND 712:85
s. that admires — LECA 499:23
s. that repressed — KRIS 480:15
s. that will organize production — ENGE 314:68
s.…they had emigrated — MO 589:19
s., where none intrudes — BYRON 180:43
s.…which is riven — ROSS 697:72
s., with all its…skill and force — BURKE 168:32
s. women never serve chilli — RAYB 680:43
solitude sometimes is best s. — MILT 584:10
suppose s. is wonderfully — WILDE 909:28
temptation to see all of s. — LEWO 508:10
the politics of our s. — OAKE 619:85
truth in the s. — KING 468:42
two classes in good s. — SHAW 781:73
unequals what s. — MILT 584:2
value judgments about the s. — VAN 876:22
very fabric of s. — JOHN 439:62
well adjusted members of s. — CALL 185:39
well-being of s. — ROOS 696:54
we're such a communal s. — SPIE 810:19
We want a s. in which — THAT 850:13
working s. — TREV 865:63
sociologist according to a s. — UNSE 874:70
was a s. — MURD 604:95
sociologists s. are akin to Marxists — ARON 34:76
s. of knowledge — MERT 568:24
sociology department of…s. — AYER 45:12
s.…attaches the adjective 'arbitrary' — ARON 34:75
S. is…about why they don't have — DUES 293:87
S. is a new science — GOWE 365:29
S. is the science of talk — KNIG 476:16
s., it is as an art — NISB 616:39
S. seems to have missed — VAN 876:23
S. was born — SMALL 796:20
What is it about s. — BAKER 53:23
sockets candles burn their s. — HOUS 416:77
socks inability to put on your s. — GONC 363:94
s. are loners — COPE 237:63
s. compelled one's attention — SAKI 710:41
s. on the altar — NERU 611:43
telling lies and selling s. — MERW 568:25
women who wear ankle s. — BENN 76:30
Socrates be S. dissatisfied — MILL 570:69
realized, like S. — PLATO 654:76
S. empties the cup of poison — FEUE 321:21
S. in every classroom — GRIS 373:18
S. is guilty — PLATO 654:77
Socratic S. method is not a game — BEER 70:83
sod prairies' dreaming s. — CRANE 243:14
stands fixed to the s. — WILL 911:2
withered in the s.? — BRON 154:76
soda heaven sent us S.Water — CHES 212:81
Sermons and s. water — BYRON 182:79
unattainable s. and sherry — SALA 710:50
sodden s. towards sundown — ELIOT 308:37
sodium having discovered s. — BENT 78:77
Sodom men of S. were wicked — BIBLE 87:73
rained upon S. and upon Gomorrah — BIBLE 87:79
sodomy rape, s. and drug addiction — COOK 235:35
sods flaming s., the snivelling — LAWR 493:88
heaped-up s. upon the fire — COLUM 229:61
sofa fainted alternately on the s. — AUST 42:56
luxury the accomplished s. — COWP 241:67
s., chair or a hot-water bottle — SMITH 800:92
s. upholstered in panther skin — PLOM 656:9
wheel the s. round — COWP 241:76
soft cushion and S. Dean invite — POPE 659:96
Her voice was ever s. — SHAK 764:6
meets me s. and supple — FLET 328:72
Say not s. things — SORL 804:90
wanted your s. verges — HENRI 395:43
softly but never hit s. — ROOS 696:56
Soho Perambulate in glamorous S. — HUGH 419:30
soil don't fight war on our s. — DALL 251:75
Foul as their s. — BYRON 179:6
grows on mortal s. — MILT 578:50
portion of the virgin s. — HAWT 386:39
same s. as the Muse — UNTE 874:71
same worn-out s. — HAWT 386:38
s. Is bare now — HOPK 412:83
s. may best Deserve — MILT 581:16
s. of his shallow cares! — BRON 155:97
texture of the s. — SMITH 799:63
soils Six days of the week it s. — LARK 490:28
sojourner discontented s. — WORD 924:88

sojourners s. and passing subjects — MUIR 602:59
solace s. to man giffis — BARB 59:52
solar hub of the s. system — HOLM 408:85
self…epicentre of the s. system — PHIL 650:94
sold s. and again s. — SAND 713:2
s. my farm — SHAK 746:67
s. your own lands — SHAK 750:73
think I've s. myself — CARL 191:71
would have s. London — RICH 685:58
soldier always tell an old s. — SHAW 777:52
As an old s. — SHAW 778:95
as is the hat of a s. — HERB 399:24
'A s.,' cried my Uncle Toby — STER 818:92
assumed the s. — WASH 890:81
Ben Battle was a s. bold — HOOD 410:34
British s. can stand up to anything — SHAW 777:70
Christ's faithful s. — BOOK 141:12
Come you back, you British s. — KIPL 470:85
death, who had the s. singled — DOUG 283:20
Drinking is the s.'s pleasure — DRYD 291:35
Every British and French s. killed — CHUR 216:61
For a s. I listed — DIBD 265:52
German s. trying to violate — STRA 826:86
glazed eyes of a s. dying — BISM 131:85
go to your Gawd like a s. — KIPL 471:93
honest man and a s. — SHAK 744:4
informer when he cannot be a s. — FLAU 326:30
like a s.'s ribbon — ABSE 1:15
Money is a good s. — SHAK 743:73
never expect a s. to think — SHAW 777:68
Not though the s. knew — TENN 844:76
ruffian soldier, and s. good — SCOTT 724:16
s. of the King — KITC 475:4
s.'s life is terribly hard — MILNE 574:71
s.'s pack is not so heavy — EISE 302:52
s. wears a badge — READ 680:48
sound of the white s.'s axe — RED 681:71
summer s. and the sunshine patriot — PAINE 634:88
the s. lists his wounds — PROP 670:61
Unknown S. — ASQU 36:10
very poor s. — SHAW 777:53
would himself have been a s. — SHAK 741:1
soldiers best s. France ever had — PHIL 650:95
black s. to death — LOWE 520:50
changed from peasants and s. — WAUGH 892:38
common s. — WELL 897:54
Countries that have s. in charge — MACK 534:21
if you believe the s. — SALI 711:68
ladder behind s. — SUN 829:29
laughing s. fought to their defeat — FENT 320:88
make his s. fight — SUN 829:28
men like s. may not quit — TENN 847:34
old s. never die — MACA 524:26
physician and chemist are s. — PAST 642:47
proud array of s. — WILDE 907:82
S. are citizens — SASS 716:60
s. drilling in Berlin — MORI 598:39
S. find wars — DONNE 280:44
s. he smiled at — SASS 716:63
S., I'm getting out — GARI 346:44
s., mostly fools — BIER 129:32
s.…of the Irish Brigade — DAVIS 256:66
s. of the ploughshare — RUSK 704:18
S., think that — NAPO 607:58
steel my s.' hearts — SHAK 746:53
sole no rest for the s. of her foot — BIBLE 87:65
s. cause of…unhappiness — PASC 640:16
s. evidence…possible — MILL 570:71
s. of his foot — SHAK 744:10
solecism eternity without a s. — BROW 158:65
Japanese…rarely commit a s. — BIRD 130:62
solemn more s. and serene — SHEL 782:21
s. creed with s. sneer — BYRON 180:28
s. gladness even crowned — TENN 843:35
s. slope of mighty limbs — SWIN 834:48
solicitor can only go to his s. — DISR 277:73
solicitors accountants and s. — TAYL 837:21
solid not s. at all, but a liquid — CAREY 190:65
only s.…reformation — CARL 191:88
s. pudding against empty praise — POPE 662:65
something s. and concrete — KELM 460:77
solidarity create…a feeling of s. — DURK 295:30
power of S. — WALE 885:88
s. with other isolated creatures — BELL 74:85
solidity an appearance of s. — ORWE 629:91
s. of a water buffalo — PERE 648:58
solids surfaces and s. — PIERO 651:11

sentence is a s.	FROST 338:88
sighing s., the lights	ROSS 698:91
Silence has a s.	KOH 477:35
S., and sweet airs	SHAK 774:92
's.' banker, alas!	KEYN 465:83
s. diffuses itself in circles	LEON 504:20
s. his breathing kept	SHEL 785:76
s. is forced	BLAKE 133:22
s. is gone out into all lands	BOOK 142:43
s. mind in a s. body	JUVE 453:20
s. must seem an echo	POPE 658:59
s. of abundance of rain	BIBLE 92:20
s. of a great amen	PROC 670:58
s. of drubbing and sobbing	SMITH 800:99
S. of Surprise	BALL 57:3
s. of the cricket bats	JOYCE 451:82
s. of the white soldier's axe	RED 681:71
s. of water's murmuring	SHEL 786:23
s. strikes like a rising knell!	BYRON 179:23
s., substantial flesh and blood	ELIOT 308:22
s. That saved a wretch	NEWT 613:76
s. together harmoniously	HONO 409:31
Sweet s every s.	TENN 842:17
sweet s....upon a bank of violets	SHAK 755:45
thinking has been s.	WELLS 899:94
thund'ring s.	GOLD 361:55
twelve great shocks of s.	TENN 840:72
typical s. of Lancashire	ORWE 627:35
what surge that s. can start	PUSH 673:20
wound...with a sinful s.	VAUG 878:45
soundbites can't speak in s.	CLAR 220:61
sounded But they s. nice	RAMOS 678:6
s. like the book of Revelations	JAMES 433:29
sounds better than it s.	TWAIN 872:38
concord of sweet s.	SHAK 741:88
doggerel of s.	RUSK 704:37
empty s.	JOHN 442:40
measured out by s.	BETJ 84:11
Music is the art of s.	BUSO 176:28
Not many s. in life	LAMB 487:53
Of all sweet s. the life and element!	COLE 226:3
painting of s., noises and smells	CARRA 194:58
power of...many s.	SHEL 782:18
Scents, colours, and s.	BAUD 64:56
self-same s.	STEV 819:21
s. frae hell	FERG 320:7
s. of their voices	ANGE 17:47
s. which oft have raised me	COLE 226:1
s. will take care of themselves	CARR 195:76
When it s. good	ELLI 310:74
soup Beautiful S.	CARR 195:83
Gentlemen do not take s.	CURZ 250:55
live upon s. and bouille	SMOL 801:28
Macbeth slurping your s.	PAGE 633:77
never let his s. get cold	HOFF 406:51
s. in Ireland	WAUGH 891:12
steam of the social s.	ACKR 3:54
thick giblet s.	JOYCE 452:92
soupkitchener Sao long, aol s.!	SHAW 780:43
sour fathers have eaten s. grapes	BIBLE 105:88
garden of cactus and s. grapes	MERR 567:17
gotta take the s.	GOLD 362:89
How s. sweet music is	SHAK 735:31
mixture of the sweet and the s.	LAFO 485:6
s. grapes and ashes	ASHF 35:99
s. misfortune's book	SHAK 737:80
s. offence	SHAK 757:99
sweet or s.	TRAV 865:47
source as a s. of income	KEMB 461:82
backward motion toward the s.	FROST 339:1
chief s. of economic insecurity	ELLW 311:92
great s. of the holy river	SPEKE 806:35
inexhaustible s. of laughter	TOLS 863:8
s. and end...of art	POPE 658:53
s....beyond all reason	HAMM 379:6
S. inexhausted of all	STER 818:7
s. of practically every good title	HEMI 393:96
sources from the most remote of s.	HEAT 390:26
invisible s. and echoes	HARR 384:99
s. of the Nile	ELIOT 304:3
ultimate s. of knowledge	POPP 663:97
sours world of sweets and s.	POE 656:23
souses night-clubbing s.	GERS 350:39
south a town in the S. of England	ORWE 627:40
fickle is the S.	TENN 842:9
full of the warm S.	KEATS 459:58
In the S., the war	TWAIN 871:92

must s. of us remain	JOHN 440:94
niggers of de S.	TRUTH 869:51
s., where there is no autumn	LAWR 494:15
The S. is avenged!	BOOTH 144:80
the S. is hardly Christ-centred	OCON 622:24
travelling due s.	PEARY 645:2
wanton in the S.	TENN 842:10
South Africa people of S. A.	SMUTS 802:31
S. A., renowned...For politics	CAMP 185:55
victory for all the people of S. A.	MAND 544:48
When I left S. A.	WOODS 921:21
South America flow through S. A.	KIPL 470:84
southern acquire the S. knack	STEV 823:24
daughter of the S. Cross	FRAN 335:22
S. Black girl	ANGE 17:31
S. Cross insignificantly mixed	LAWR 494:5
southerners S. can never resist	MITC 588:98
Southey S....so quaint	BYRON 182:75
South Pacific mask from the S. P.	ROSE 697:65
south-wind s.-w. rushing warm	TENN 840:81
sovereign bandy civilities with my s.	JOHN 443:85
called by my s.	PITT 652:39
Five s. fingers taxed	THOM 852:62
good service to his s.	SUN 829:30
individual is no longer to be s.	DOUG 284:34
servants of the s.	BACON 48:99
s., accompanied by all the army	GRAY 368:91
S. of cities	DUNB 294:5
s. of insufferables	BIER 128:10
s. of sighs and groans	SHAK 733:76
s. sway...dissolved by might?	DRYD 290:91
Whoso has sixpence is s.	CARL 192:92
with s. eye	SHAK 771:16
sovereignest s. thing that any man	SKEL 794:89
telling me the s. thing on earth	SHAK 741:1
sovereigns s. and magistrates	LUTH 523:96
we...its s.	BYRON 181:57
sovereignty challenge...no s.	LANY 489:6
If absolute s. be not necessary	ASTE 36:23
soviet all-eclipsing S. world	THUB 858:15
bully...S. Union	HAIG 376:65
Civil war...in the S. Union	PAVL 644:81
going on in the S. Union	GORB 363:1
S. game is chess	SHUL 789:88
S. Republic needs an army	TROT 867:15
S. Union remains a superpower	WALE 885:90
S. Union would be of enormous extent	GOEB 359:8
twenty years ago in the S. Union	THER 851:50
Soviets S. sought not...the sun	DULL 294:91
S....would occupy...Europe	GOEB 359:8
sow S. returns to her Mire	KIPL 474:84
s. that was washed	BIBLE 125:31
What s. ye?	WILDE 907:82
sower s. went forth to sow	BIBLE 112:47
soweth whatsoever a man s.	BIBLE 122:39
sown reap where he hath s.	KIPL 472:13
s. the tares of spiritual errors	HOBB 404:30
space across the gulf of s.	WELLS 898:73
any visitor from outer s.	BURR 173:59
Architecture...how to waste s.	JOHN 441:5
atoms and empty s.	DEMO 261:84
beyond S. and Time	BROO 156:18
bodies in s.	MANN 546:71
camembert of time and s.	DALI 251:72
captured fume of s.	CRANE 243:20
cemetery is an open s.	SHEL 785:89
everything except s. and light	HEAT 390:28
feel the same way about form and s.	DAVIS 255:62
flying through s.	MUIR 602:65
flying through s. forever	GAGA 342:84
gleaming cantos of unvanquished s.	CRANE 243:21
inner s....is the real subject	BALL 57:1
island rock in s.	CIAR 218:13
king of infinite s.	SHAK 752:54
Lancelot mused a little s.	TENN 839:52
laws of s. and time	CORY 238:77
Love is as s.	PROU 671:79
more s. where nobody s.	STEIN 815:16
need for a well-defined personal s.	COUP 239:98
no analogue in s.	EDDI 298:83
No creature loves an empty s.	MARV 556:78
Nothing is material in s.	ROSSO 698:7
o's. at aince	MACD 529:36
out of time, out of s.	WELLS 898:74
pleasure of enclosed s.	JOHN 440:99
poem full of s. and reverie	BAUD 65:85
puzzles me more than time and s.	LAMB 486:31

Rotarians in s.!	VIDAL 880:92
shining s.	GRAV 367:66
smallest s. of calmness	BEDE 68:54
s. in which to reproduce	ROSE 696:63
S. isn't remote	HOYLE 417:5
s....laid on her hair	CRANE 243:18
s. not to dwell in	GIRA 358:80
s. of life between	KEATS 457:99
S....the central fact	OLSEN 624:74
S.—the final frontier	RODD 693:88
start of s.	SCOTT 722:77
vacancy which occupies the s.	TOOLE 863:69
spaces figures...empty s. around	MATI 560:62
infinite s. Are still silent	EBER 298:73
silence of these infinite s.	PASC 640:18
s. between the houses	FENT 320:87
s. between the stars	HENRI 395:41
s. swarming with erotic bodies	CIXO 219:38
vacant interstellar s.	ELIOT 308:19
spaceship passenger on the s., Earth	FULL 341:54
S.-s. and time machines	KOES 477:30
trying to launch a homemade s.	FAUL 319:75
spacings s. of the spheres	PYTH 673:31
spade call a s. a s.	BURT 174:69
glad...never seen a s.	WILDE 909:45
poor crooked scythe and s.	SHIR 789:83
s. he also hent	SPEN 809:55
s. is never so merely a s.	FRY 340:28
truth calls a s.!	BROW 162:90
Write with your s.	CAMP 186:58
spades Let s. be trumps!	POPE 659:74
spaghetti feeding on booze and s.	LEWIS 507:88
you see I owe to s.	LOREN 517:87
Spain devildoms of S.	TENN 848:60
feared by S., by France	SIXT 794:88
In S., the priests ruled	COND 230:32
King o' S.'s daughter	COLUM 229:60
not into the hands of S.	TENN 848:63
not only S....will...have refreshment	COLU 229:62
Pretender in S.	SWIFT 831:92
singeing of the King of S.'s beard	DRAKE 286:92
slow old tunes of S.	MASE 559:28
S. gets bullfights	JONG 448:5
S. is the only country	LORCA 517:86
S.! renown'd, romantic land!	BYRON 179:11
S....should dare to invade	ELIZ 309:60
war in S. is over	MUSS 605:22
spam wanted steak...offered s.	MALA 541:78
span Contract into a s.	HERB 398:16
Eternity shut in a s.	CRAS 244:34
flung the s. on even wing	CRANE 243:23
I s. and Eve s.	GILM 356:55
Less than a s.	BACON 50:65
life's...but a s.	DAVI 254:35
should reach the s.	SASS 716:58
spangled s. heavens, a shining frame	ADDI 6:26
Unpin that s. breastplate	DONNE 279:36
spangles Sawdust and s.	CARD 189:41
stars were so many s.	ARNO 34:73
Spaniard S. brought to America	MARI 549:46
S. have his Spain	JOHN 440:94
Spaniards S. and other nations	GARC 345:42
S. seem wiser than they are	BACON 49:27
thrash the S. too	DRAKE 286:94
spaniel s. on those principles	LLOY 513:96
Spanish after the S. Empire fell	REYES 684:31
ancient S. historians of America	ECHE 298:76
fond of S. wine	MASE 559:29
S. ships of war at sea!	TENN 848:60
speech...sonorous as S.	QUIL 674:44
To God I speak S.	CHAR 207:37
spanner fished...with a s.	BETJ 84:8
spare can you s. a dime?	HARB 380:35
power...is to s. you	SHAK 774:76
was a s. man	AUBR 39:68
spark no s. of honour bides	SHAK 730:69
single s. can start a...fire	MAO 547:4
s. from heaven	ARNO 32:19
s. from heaven	ARNO 32:21
s. from heaven!	ARNO 32:21
s....of heavenly fire	DRYD 290:84
s. of humanity can tolerate	RUSS 705:57
s. of inextinguishable thought	SHEL 786:15
s. o' Nature's fire	BURNS 170:64
s. that moves mankind	SIKO 791:32
tiny s. of energy	MACC 527:85
sparkles Alive with s.	KEATS 459:9

echo of the s.   BYRON 182:99
moving as the restless s.   MARL 551:75
music in the spacings of the s.   PYTH 673:31
Ring out, ye crystal s.   MILT 576:97
seems to shake the s.   DRYD 291:34
s. of existence   ELIOT 308:36
s. were formed in fright   MELV 564:31
start from their s.   SHAK 752:28
spice Variety's the s. of life   COWP 241:72
spider foul black cobweb to a s.   WEBS 895:97
S., s., spin   MACN 538:5
s.'s touch, how exquisitely fine   POPE 660:13
What brought the kindred s.   FROST 339:5
spiders like s. across the stars   KERO 464:62
love of s.   WHITE 903:83
reasoners resemble s.   BACON 47:60
walls of s.' legs   DRAY 287:7
spider-web kind of huge s.-w.   JAMES 433:42
spies As if we were God's s.   SHAK 764:1
come not single s.   SHAK 754:19
German police s.   MARX 558:4
subtle s.   FREE 336:44
Ye are s.   BIBLE 88:99
spikes sitting on nine ebony s.   KING 469:62
s. and loops   UPDI 874:88
spin whether it would take s.   HOME 409:14
spinach it's s....the hell with it   WHITE 902:74
spin-doctors s.-d. in spin clinics   BENN 75:21
spindrift seal's wide s. gaze   CRANE 243:11
spine chill down the s.   COOKE 236:42
Sits on its craggy s.   SMITH 801:25
sunken fosse of her s.   HEAN 389:7
spinnage world of gammon and s.   DICK 269:74
spinning-wheel losing the s. w.   GAND 345:33
spinster live to hear myself called s.   SHER 787:44
lonelier than any s.   GREER 372:90
saved many an English s.   MITF 589:10
slightly bearded s.   NICO 614:95
spinsters insisted upon by s.   DALY 251:78
spires dreaming s.   ARNO 33:44
slope their pointing s.   MILT 580:6
s. and cranes cluster   LARK 491:33
storks on the s. of Denmark   DOYLE 286:83
What s., what farms   HOUS 415:59
Ye distant s.   GRAY 368:92
spirit adventure of the s.   WHIT 904:9
angry s.'s yell   BEAT 66:96
as the s. moves him   SART 715:41
be filled with the S.   BIBLE 122:49
blood and s. together   MARI 550:57
born of the S.   BIBLE 117:80
break a man's s.   SHAW 777:57
broken s. drieth the bones   BIBLE 99:39
'Brutus' will start a s.   SHAK 747:77
by my s., saith the Lord   BIBLE 106:17
cabined ample S.   ARNO 32:14
Caesar's s., ranging   SHAK 748:2
chiefly thou O s.   MILT 580:93
clear s. doth raise   MILT 580:57
commit my s.   BIBLE 95:9
disembodied s.   WHAR 901:47
diversities of gifts, but the same S.   BIBLE 121:8
dividing asunder of soul and s.   BIBLE 124:90
do the same things by The s.   BUTL 177:54
evil s....does his utmost to deceive   DESC 263:24
exasperated s. Proceeds   ELIOT 309:44
fair s. for my minister   BYRON 180:42
feel...the s. of a place   PEI 646:15
fervent in s.   BIBLE 120:81
fruit of the S.   BIBLE 122:38
full of the Great S.   MARTI 555:44
genial s. droop   MILT 586:53
gentlier on the s. lies   TENN 839:54
gloom pervaded my s.   POE 656:16
greatness of your s.   ROCH 691:62
Hail to thee, blithe S.   SHEL 784:54
hath not One s. to command   SHAK 774:90
haughty s. before a fall   BIBLE 99:36
healthy s. of self-help   SMIL 797:34
history of the human s.   ARNO 34:59
However vast a man's s.   PASC 640:7
human s. is immortal   MURP 604:2
I commend my s.   BOOK 143:45
immortal s. grows like harmony   WORD 925:92
immortal s. must endure   ARNO 31:90
immortal s. of the dead   SPEN 807:65
indifference to...soul or s.   LAWR 494:3

ingenious, and piercing s.   MILT 579:80
In one s. meet   SHEL 783:42
in s. she is a man   GOTT 364:18
in the S. on the Lord's day   BIBLE 125:44
into thy hands I commend my s.   BIBLE 116:66
is the abstract s.   KAND 454:35
It is a s.; and they cried out   BIBLE 112:56
It is the s. that quickeneth   BIBLE 117:93
Jesus led up of the S.   BIBLE 109:78
kill the s. here   MAIL 540:47
leap into s.   UPDI 874:91
let my s....rejoice   WORD 929:63
letter killeth, but the s. giveth life   BIBLE 122:22
life-blood of a master s.   MILT 579:64
like all...creations of the human s.   DYSON 297:63
Long my imprisoned s. lay   WESL 899:9
Love is a s.   SHAK 732:52
my s. hath rejoiced in God   BIBLE 115:23
my s. hath rejoiced in God   BIBLE 128:98
never approached my s.   METT 568:29
no man...hath power over the s.   BIBLE 101:80
not given us the s. of fear   BIBLE 124:81
not to disparage things of the s.   BUSH 176:23
nought...so much the s. calms   BYRON 182:77
o'ercrows my s.   SHAK 755:42
Of s. so still   SHAK 759:60
on my s. make a music, too   STEV 819:21
pard-like S., beautiful and swift   SHEL 785:99
pastures of the s.   SASS 717:77
patient in s. is better   BIBLE 101:78
poor in s.   SPARK 806:25
pour out my s.   BIBLE 106:5
power and s. of America   NORR 618:65
pride of race or s.   SMITH 801:25
pure s. shall flow   SHEL 786:2
put a new s. within you   BIBLE 105:86
question thee concerning the S.   KORAN 479:77
realm of the S.   MATI 560:31
renew a right s. within me   BIBLE 95:30
scaffolding of s.   THOM 855:33
seeds of the s. and economy   MARI 549:48
s. and judgement equal   MILT 586:43
S. and the Dust   DICK 273:70
s. burning but unbent   BYRON 181:50
s. capable of compassion   FAUL 318:64
s. could remain tinged   LOWE 521:55
s., free to choose   ROCH 691:55
S. gave them utterance   BIBLE 119:29
s. grew robust   DICK 273:74
s. hath rejoiced in God   BIBLE 115:23
s. hath rejoiced in God   BIBLE 128:98
s. I have seen   SHAK 753:71
s. in a loyal breast   SHAK 734:99
s. indeed is willing   BIBLE 114:99
s. in which it was done   HELO 393:88
s. is cuddled   JOHN 440:99
s. is soaring   BRON 154:72
S. of adoption   BIBLE 120:74
s. of an Australian   FRAN 335:21
S. of Australia   FIELD 322:30
s. of Elijah doth rest on Elisha   BIBLE 92:29
s. of experimentation   FRAN 335:17
s. of health   SHAK 751:25
s. of her s.   BINY 130:51
s. of liberty   HAND 380:30
s. of man is a good adversary   WILL 913:34
S. of Night!   SHEL 787:29
s. of our City   GIUL 358:88
s. of our country   CHEE 209:4
s. of self-help   SMIL 797:32
s. of self-help   SMIL 797:34
S. of the Age   HAZL 388:84
S. of the Age   VIDAL 880:91
S. of the Lord God is upon me   BIBLE 104:62
s. of the Reform Bill   PEEL 646:8
s. of wisdom and understanding   BIBLE 102:18
s. of youth in everything   SHAK 772:40
s. shall return unto God   BIBLE 101:92
s. that now resists   PITT 653:42
s. within it is tough   WAVE 893:58
S. with S. can meet   TENN 847:36
Stirs the dumb s.   ELIOT 309:38
strike with our s.'s knife   SHEL 786:3
sulky Scottish s.   SCOTT 725:53
sword of the s.   BIBLE 122:52
take not thy holy s. from me   BIBLE 95:30
the s. leaves his mortal body   BHAG 85:35

the S. wanders on to a new body   BHAG 85:34
things of the S.   BIBLE 120:73
this body did contain a s.   SHAK 742:35
this grey s.   TENN 840:64
to thee my true s.?   SHAK 773:45
to the strength of s.   SHAK 747:25
true s. of delight   RUSS 705:44
unclean s. is gone out of a man   BIBLE 111:45
uphold me with thy free s.   BIBLE 95:30
Whither shall I go from thy s.?   BIBLE 98:1
Wild S., which art moving   SHEL 783:44
Wisdom and S. of the universe!   WORD 924:85
with a joyful s.   TENN 848:64
with such s. and decency   PITT 652:35
worser s. a woman   SHAK 773:45
worship him in s. and in truth   BIBLE 117:84
spirits aerial s. live inspher'd   MILT 577:25
angling...a cheerer of his s.   WALT 888:49
By our own s. are we deified   WORD 926:17
Come, you s.   SHAK 766:52
disposition of the s.   BACON 50:64
For S. when they please   MILT 581:9
freeing s.   FLAU 326:40
frost-bound-blood, and s.   HERR 399:39
good s. and good temper   DICK 268:34
great and solemn s.   HUMB 421:2
jump with common s.   SHAK 740:62
Kate's s. sank to the very bottom   ADAMS 4:70
like two s.   SHAK 773:55
making the most of good s.   HARDY 381:51
on their softened s. sink   BYRON 180:37
s. fetch me what I   MARL 552:98
s. have forgot   ARNO 31:88
s. in heaven   RUSK 703:5
s. masculine, create   MILT 585:27
s. of our ancestors   RED 681:71
s. of the wise   SHAK 742:47
S. of well-shot woodcock   BETJ 83:82
s. rushed together   TENN 840:76
stillness where our s. walk   SASS 716:74
two kindred s. flee   KEATS 457:81
widowhood...keeps up a wife's s.   GAY 347:83
spiritual acknowledge the s. forces   MOORE 595:28
affliction...either physical or s.   BEER 70:85
Force is a s. power   LEON 503:12
From a material and s. terrain   FULL 341:59
large s. adventures   DAVI 255:44
lastly a s. and divine   HOOK 410:55
man with detestable s. qualities   BUKO 165:47
our only s. task   MALL 542:91
see...with the s. eye   FRIE 337:69
s. demands   TAWN 837:8
sustain them through any s.   WALK 885:1
spiritually Morally, s.   MILL 572:26
s. limited on those   NIET 615:22
spit distaff, or the s.?   LEWIS 507:81
gob of s. in the face   MILL 572:15
never s. white again   SHAK 742:41
s. against the wind   WEBS 894:84
spite beating myself for s.   SIDN 790:8
fortune's dearest s.   SHAK 771:17
O cursèd s.   SHAK 752:39
slander and the s.   TENN 844:61
s. of Pride, in erring Reason's s.   POPE 660:15
spit-spot s.-s. into bed   TRAV 864:41
spittoons drinking out of s.   HEMI 394:20
obsolete as s.   BLACK 132:90
spleen Kind pity chokes my s.   DONNE 279:30
s. of fiery dragons   SHAK 732:24
splenative not s. and rash   SHAK 755:35
splendid Oh, she's a s. girl   HUXL 425:77
s. and a happy land   GOLD 361:57
and sterile Dolores   SWIN 833:28
splendour Heaven's s. over his head   CARL 193:37
not be content with...present s.   CARL 191:78
Pavilioned in s.   GRANT 366:52
s. borrows all her rays from sense   POPE 659:98
s. in the grass   WORD 927:28
s. of a sudden thought   BROW 162:72
s. of his mid-day beams   HERR 399:38
sun...in his first s.   WORD 926:19
splinters teeth like s.   CAUS 201:13
Spode Roderick S.?   WODE 919:71
spoil Beware lest any man s. you   BIBLE 123:65
complexion we were not to s.   SCHR 720:40
s. our own   JERO 437:30
spoils loaded with s.   CARL 191:81

s. of time   GRAY 369:16
spoken Glorious things are s.   BIBLE 96:48
  have s. it   GRIS 373:20
  people not s. about   GEE 348:92
  s. lightly of my deathless friends   SASS 716:75
spokesmen find their own…s.   COWL 240:38
sponge Darkness falls like a wet s.   ASHB 35:82
  married to a s.   SHAK 739:48
spontaneity s. of a mechanical tiger   ACHE 2:27
spoof forecast…some kind of s.   LODGE 514:22
spook s.…who haunted…Poe   ELLI 311:88
spoon ate with a runcible s.   LEAR 498:86
  balancing an egg on a s.   HILL 402:87
  blindly searching the s.   SMITH 799:64
  traces of the…gold s.   DICK 270:5
  Why doesn't he use a s.?   DE 264:30
spoons faster we counted our s.   EMER 313:44
  let us count our s.   JOHN 443:65
  measured out my life with coffee s.   ELIOT 304:20
  s. and the pots   SEXT 728:16
  when you want his s.?   HORN 414:37
  world locks up its s.   SHAW 778:97
sport Detested us.   COWP 241:74
  ended his s. with Tess   HARDY 382:63
  fellowly s. or pastime   STUB 827:2
  good enough s.   HORN 414:37
  idea of a contact s. was chess   HUGH 419:37
  in love as in s.   GRAV 367:76
  In no s.…more humiliated   MAIL 540:59
  kill us for their s.   SHAK 763:84
  love s. because I love life   YEVT 935:72
  loyal s. of love   ANON 19:90
  made skiing a spectator s.   ANON 23:86
  make her more s.   MONT 592:80
  national s. of England   TREE 865:54
  never kill for s.   FROU 339:21
  no such s. as s. by s.   SHAK 734:90
  only athletic s. I mastered   JERR 438:43
  Our s., our studies, and our souls   BYRON 179:95
  Politics is a blood s.   BEVAN 85:24
  running people down is considered s.   FOST 332:63
  spectator s.   GERG 350:32
  s. for our neighbours   AUST 43:71
  S.…is an occupation   PIUS 597:68
  s.…is war minus the shooting   ORWE 630:8
  s. of a merry-go-round   HARDY 381:50
  s. that bears the same relation   HUBB 418:10
  submits to them in s.   EDGE 299:94
  Summer loves to s.   COLL 228:48
  that makes the s.   SUCK 828:8
  traditional and popular s.   SITW 794:87
sporting realization that to be s.   SKIN 795:12
  Snorting and s. like porpoises   SITW 793:61
sports axiom of s.   FRAY 335:30
  First of all S.!   LOVE 518:8
  hate all s. as rabidly   MENC 566:82
  her cruel s.   SPEN 809:14
  lawfullest of s.   BAXT 65:90
  Organised outdoor s.   HOBS 405:35
  Praise the s. of the land   REID 682:96
  private s. the stews would blush   MASS 559:45
  simple s.   TENN 844:55
  soccer, of all s.   ROUS 700:39
  S. do not build character   BROUN 157:38
  s. pages are strictly   NASH 609:5
  turn to the s. section   WARR 889:70
  universal languages: love, music and s.   MOSES 600:26
  uther sik unproffitable s.   JAME 432:22
  We've dominated s.   JOHN 439:77
sportsman he was never…A S.   SITW 794:83
  No s. wants to kill   SHAW 781:95
  s. is a man who   LEAC 497:71
sportsmanship S.…the Church   HOOV 411:67
sportsmen standing insult to s.   FRY 339:22
sportswriters s.…enthusiasm   FRAY 335:30
sportswriting thing that s. teaches   FORD 330:21
Sporus Let S. tremble   POPE 661:40
spot come to this hallowed s.   KING 468:36
  dear the schoolboy s.   BYRON 181:70
  dogs called S.   AMIS 14:97
  firm s. on which to stand   ARCH 28:39
  hit the sorest s.   CHES 210:24
  only one bright s.   TOLK 862:97
  Out, damned s.   SHAK 768:33
  pleasanter s. you never spied   BROW 160:25
  s. acclaimed by savant   HUGH 419:30
  s.…at the back of the head   WOOLF 922:48

s.…it can take out   GAY 347:82
s. which no vicissitude   WORD 928:49
stir of this dim s.   MILT 577:25
there is no s. in thee   BIBLE 101:2
tied to the s. by some…creature   DARW 253:9
trouble finding the sensitive s.   LACL 484:89
spotlight s. of public life   FOST 332:63
spots leopard his s.?   BIBLE 105:75
  making my s. ache   KIPL 473:45
  sequestered s.   HARDY 382:61
spouse Adam from his fair s.   MILT 583:71
  sister, my s.   BIBLE 102:3
  s. is in despair   PRIOR 669:40
  tired of being the feminine s.   DIAZ 265:50
spray in thy hand a withered s.   ARNO 32:19
  small fowlys singis on the s.   DOUG 283:18
  s. of Western pine!   HARTE 385:18
  toss in the s.   ARNO 31:83
spray-gunned even silence, is s.-g.?   OLSEN 624:75
spread not good except it be s.   BACON 49:12
sprig s. of bays   SWIFT 832:95
spring absent in the s.   SHAK 772:40
  Bare Winter…changed to S.   SHEL 786:23
  bear waiting for s.   PIER 651:10
  blue sky of s.   ALLI 13:62
  buffalos of the s.   LIND 511:52
  can S. be far behind?   SHEL 783:48
  cherry blossoms in the s.   ANON 22:67
  chilly fingered s.   KEATS 458:7
  colds a forward s. remove?   DONNE 280:44
  continual s., and harvest   SPEN 809:92
  Cowslip…bloomed that s.   CRANE 243:22
  darling of the S.   WORD 926:12
  dazed s. approaches   WILL 913:42
  dug a s. in infancy   BRON 154:76
  Easing the s.   REED 681:78
  enjoy the s. flowers   SU 828:6
  ever-returning s.   WHIT 906:47
  every winter change to s.   TENN 843:42
  found in the s. to follow?   SWIN 832:15
  from my native s.   DRYD 289:61
  honeyed s.   GRAY 369:6
  In the S. a livelier iris   TENN 840:75
  It is s., moonless night   THOM 853:85
  less quick to s. again   ARNO 33:48
  like a man taking his last s.   BANN 59:39
  lived light in the s.   ARNO 31:96
  messenger of S.   SPEN 809:98
  Midwinter S. is its own season   ELIOT 308:37
  only the certain s.   BINY 130:55
  play'd a s., and danc'd it round   BURNS 171:95
  rifle all the breathing s.   COLL 228:41
  second s.   PHIL 650:90
  seen…with his vision, S.   SACK 708:89
  severest winter…the s.   COWP 241:65
  songs of S.?   KEATS 459:49
  s. of love   COLE 225:88
  S. shall pour his showers   COLL 228:48
  s. summer autumn winter   CUMM 248:19
  S., the sweet s.   NASHE 609:15
  S. to the North   MACD 529:41
  s. when the world is puddle wonderful   CUMM 247:2
  Sweet lovers love the s.   SHAK 750:88
  taste not the Pierian s.   POPE 658:54
  the s. begins   SWIN 832:19
  thou have no s.   DONNE 281:88
  untaught harmony of s.   GRAY 369:3
  When S. comes round   SEEG 726:70
  When the hounds of s.   SWIN 832:18
  when their game will s.   OTWAY 631:69
  when the s. comes   GIBB 352:70
  wind that breathes the s.   MILT 576:5
  year's at the s.   BROW 160:19
springing Praise for them s.   FARJ 318:47
springs Beside the s. of Dove   WORD 924:78
  fifty s. are little room   HOUS 414:43
  four wanton s.   SHAK 734:3
  from the people…all s.   DISR 275:35
  Hope s. eternal   POPE 660:10
  Marlowe, bathed in the Thespian s.   DRAY 287:5
  no bitter s.   KIPL 473:63
  s. to catch woodcocks   SHAK 751:23
  take from seventy s. a score   HOUS 414:42
  weaker s. of the human character   HAMI 379:99
  Where s. not fail   HOPK 412:78
springtime In s.-t.…ring-time   SHAK 750:88
  s. of America's cultural   ROCK 693:84

sprinkle So shall he s. many nations   BIBLE 104:49
sprite elements and an angelic s.   DONNE 281:72
spur Danger, the s.   CHAP 206:20
  have no s.   SHAK 733:60
  keenest s. to exertion   BENT 77:70
spurn s. me hence…s. me hither   SHAK 733:60
spurred always be booted and s.   MONT 592:72
spurs suffre hym…to wynne his s.   EDWA 300:16
spurt blue s. of a lighted match   BROW 161:34
spy Here's none to s.   JONS 450:48
  not to play the s.   TOYN 864:33
  s. ring   MCCA 527:93
  s. sent into life   BOWL 147:33
  S. who Came in   LECA 499:19
  th'infected s.   POPE 658:61
spying S. on other people's lives   ALME 13:65
squabble s. in your back-yard   SYNGE 834:59
squadrons side of the big s.   BUSSY 176:30
  s. in Saimear's   MCCA 527:87
squads Undisciplined s. of emotion   ELIOT 308:23
squalid misfits…and s. criminals   REAG 680:60
  s. wretchedness   BYRON 179:4
squalor amidst its poverty and s.   ARNO 33:56
  with Love and S.   SALI 711:63
square broke a British s.!   KIPL 471:94
  grows a glimmering s.   TENN 842:8
  here is a little s. of blue   MONET 591:53
  honest, so thoroughly s.   LERN 504:27
  old people are s.   SHAF 729:22
  pointed out one corner of a s.   CONF 230:89
  run quite out of s.   SPEN 809:9
  slog to s. leg   JOYCE 452:94
  thin trees in a city s.   LOWE 519:25
squares about the flowering s.   TENN 844:63
squash S. is boxing   BARR 61:92
  S.…it's flagellation   COWA 239:24
squeaks Thin s. of radio static   CRANE 243:20
squeeze s. ourselves universally   MELV 564:37
squeezing in a s. of a lemon   GOLD 362:65
squire S.'s own daughter   GRAV 364:87
squires s. ride slowly towards the sea   CHES 212:90
squirrel joiner s. or old grub   SHAK 736:39
  s.'s heart beat   ELIOT 304:8
stab I saw him s. and s. again   READ 680:45
  noble Caesar saw him s.   SHAK 748:11
  s. me in the back   LAMP 487:71
  wound and s. us   KAFKA 453:24
stability s. or enlargement   JOHN 442:41
  s. to a popular Government   WHIT 902:68
stables s. are the real centre   SHAW 781:74
stack s. or the barn door   MILT 576:7
stadiums listen, at the s.   ABSE 1:9
staff break my s.   SHAK 775:98
  cursing his s.   SASS 716:63
  kamikaze ground s.   PARK 638:82
  My s. of faith   RALE 677:99
  rod and s. me comfort still   SCOT 725:61
  rod and thy s.   BIBLE 94:2
  s. in your hand   BIBLE 88:16
  s. of honour for mine age   SHAK 731:89
  s. of this broken reed   BIBLE 103:35
  s. of this bruised reed   BIBLE 92:39
staffocracy 's.' has been created   SHUL 790:92
stag s. at eve had drunk   SCOTT 723:4
  s. in the Priory coomb   DAVI 254:26
  s. of warrant   DAVI 254:27
stage actor everywhere but…s.   CHES 211:39
  All the world's a s.   SHAK 749:48
  As large as is the s.   JONS 448:8
  before we go quite off this s.?   POPE 659:99
  daily s. of duty   KEN 461:93
  Don't put your daughter on the s.   COWA 239:17
  edge of the s.   DIDE 273:87
  final s.   GARD 346:46
  frets his hour upon the s.   SHAK 769:42
  great s. of fools   SHAK 764:94
  mellow glory of the Attic s.   ARNO 31:91
  musty breezes of a bare s.   HART 384:13
  On the s. he was natural   GOLD 362:71
  On the s. of the universe   LAFO 485:12
  played upon a s.   SHAK 757:84
  putting up a s. set   WAITE 884:68
  science…has this tremendous s.   RABI 676:79
  Self-pity in its early s.   ANGE 17:40
  s. but echoes back   JOHN 441:15
  s. of wisdom   SKIN 795:12
  s. where every man must play   SHAK 739:36

s. where truth calls spade a spade! BROW 162:90
time to get off the s. MAJOR 541:73
to know the people…on the s. PAGE 633:77
United Nations…is…a s. OBRI 620:3
Where's the s. BOOTH 144:81
wonder of our s.! JONS 449:43
stagecoach s. from London to Oxford HAZL 387:73
travelling in a s. IRVI 430:84
stagecoaches twice as fast as s.? ANON 21:27
stages constantly and in their early s. SHUL 789:87
stagflation sort of s. situation MACL 536:55
staggered drinking have you s. WEBS 894:74
stagnate freedom to s. STEV 820:60
stagnation not just inflation…or s. MACL 536:55
too absolute a s. BRON 154:78
stain after the rain…never a s. SHEL 783:41
as with no s. SHEL 785:94
bright s. on the vision GRAV 368:81
sky is darkening like a s. AUDEN 39:80
S. all your edges SHAK 770:73
s.…it can take out GAY 347:82
s. like a wound BURKE 169:35
s. the stiff dishonoured shroud ELIOT 305:38
world's slow s. SHEL 786:4
stains Innumerable of s. KEATS 459:36
stair highest pavement of the s. ELIOT 305:31
one pair of s. by the waterside PEPYS 647:46
rising…by a winding s. BACON 48:98
rising…is by a winding s. BACON 48:98
structure in a winding s.? HERB 398:6
staircase S. wit DIDE 274:98
steps of a s. MALL 542:98
stairs Fallen Down S. MORT 600:21
naked feet upon the s. DOYLE 285:56
pushed her down the s. DAVIS 255:54
rat-riddled s.? BROW 161:47
see through a flight o' s. DICK 266:81
Up s. and doun s. MILL 574:61
up the s. of his concepts STEI 815:31
stake burnt at the s. SMITH 800:98
made life my common s. VAUG 878:52
parboiled head upon a s. MONT 593:5
reputation is at s. SHAK 757:8
s.…in such a glorious institution BURKE 168:15
tied me to a s. SHAK 769:43
Unless you s. your life HEIS 391:56
what it is we have at s. PITT 653:46
stale frizzled, s. and small LOWE 520:45
nor custom s. SHAK 765:26
s., a garment out of fashion SHAK 773:64
s. is their gladness HARP 383:86
Winter…hangs on until it is s. CATH 200:87
Stalin If S. had learned…cricket DOWN 284:43
S.…lover of peace NEHRU 610:29
that S. himself rose TROT 867:16
Stalinist nakedness of S. dictatorship KENN 462:98
stalk With martial s. SHAK 751:96
stalking s. in my chamber WYATT 931:3
stalking-horse folly like a s.-h. SHAK 751:93
Stalky this was S.'s contribution KIPL 472:28
stallion black s. on a field of snow CAMP 186:60
watersmooth-silver…s. CUMM 247:4
stallions bared teeth of s. CRANE 243:22
stalls Tank come down the s. SASS 716:57
stalwart three stout and s. sons BALL 57:97
stamina lowering a man's s. DOUG 283:15
stamp but the guinea's s. BURNS 173:46
indelible s. of his lowly origin DARW 253:16
physics or s. collecting RUTH 706:71
s. collection waits BETJ 83:82
s. makes the current money JONS 450:60
s. of his authority LAMB 486:43
s. of university training GERH 350:34
stand able to s. before thee BIBLE 90:61
By uniting we s. DICK 273:81
climb the rails into the Grand S. SOME 803:67
cuspid's last s. PERE 648:59
firm spot on which to s. ARCH 28:39
having done all, to s. BIBLE 122:52
If she can s. it, I can EPST 314:77
light and shadow never s. still WEST 900:27
makes a man s. straight HELL 392:76
no time to s. DAVI 255:48
not s. for WAUGH 892:33
s. a year or twa BURNS 171:8
s. like greyhounds SHAK 746:43
S. still, traveller, and read! ANON 26:90

S. Up! S. Up For Jesus! DUFF 293:88
s. up to anything SHAW 777:70
therefore I hope to s. WALP 887:40
They that s. high SHAK 731:6
who shall be able to s.? BIBLE 126:58
standard advancing s. of religion SMIL 797:34
her just s. POPE 658:53
raise the scarlet s. CONN 232:55
s. of…Red Hugh MCCA 527:87
Truth is its own s. SPIN 810:26
standardized he is s.; transformed DOUG 283:31
standards Advance our s.! SHAK 732:22
s. by which he lived CHRI 214:34
s. of green unfurled MOORE 596:48
standers-by not for any s.-b. SHAK 773:58
standing heart of s. EMPS 314:63
like to write s. up HEMI 394:19
s. is slippery BACON 48:2
s. on the edge SALI 711:61
tired with s. DONNE 279:35
standoffish Are they being s. COLE 225:51
standpoint s. of what it attains BURKE 169:57
stands No economy ever s. still HARR 384:6
s. an instant in the sun HYDE 427:23
s.…for something younger FIRB 323:64
strengthen whilst one s. ROSS 697:75
Stanford S. Rivers lost me LEVE 506:58
staple s. of his argument SHAK 734:87
Stapleford osier-beds, S. Abbots LEVE 506:58
star about its chilling s. BERR 82:61
Being a s. has made it possible DAVIS 255:60
birth to a dancing s. NIET 615:14
catch a falling s. DONNE 279:39
constant as the Northern S. SHAK 747:93
curb a runaway young s. BYRON 183:4
discovery of a s. BRIL 152:35
don't want to sleep with the s. CURT 249:48
dusk lit by one large s. MERE 566:93
every s. that heaven MILT 577:23
eve's one s. KEATS 459:44
Fair as a s. WORD 924:78
grapples with his evil s. TENN 843:48
great s. early droop'd WHIT 906:47
height, and at the s. MERE 567:8
Hitch your wagon to a s. EMER 313:48
Hope guides us by her s. BRON 155:86
In heaven no single s. THOM 856:63
in his separate s. KIPL 472:20
Jungle s. or jungle track CULL 247:92
Knew you, and named a s.! BROW 161:58
life hovers like a s. BYRON 182:1
like a sinking s. TENN 840:64
loftiest s. of unascended heaven SHEL 785:81
love a bright particular s. SHAK 761:22
merely the s.' tennis-balls WEBS 895:21
most auspicious s. SHAK 774:78
My Lucky S. FREED 336:38
No one ever leaves a s. WILD 910:71
not one s. of all FROST 338:96
o'er the hill the eastern s. BURNS 172:39
on the charge of a s.! SHAK 762:57
our life's s. WORD 926:24
Polar s. of poetry KEATS 457:88
put on the yellow s. FACK 317:31
reflex of a s. WORD 924:86
self persists like a dying s. ROET 694:8
soul was like a s. WORD 925:11
S. and angels ROSS 698:85
s. fall from heaven BIBLE 126:62
s. in the east BIBLE 108:72
S. kissing s. CRANE 243:12
s. of deathless and painless peace HUGH 419:50
s. of stars DICK 270:92
s. that bids the shepherd MILT 577:27
s. to every wand'ring SHAK 773:48
swart s. sparely looks MILT 578:53
tall ship and a s. to steer MASE 559:21
twinkle of a fading s. ELIOT 306:70
when the white s. hovers MERE 566:94
white s. of Truth ARNO 32:30
would you like to swing on a s. BURKE 169:55
stardom s.…gave me everything GARD 346:44
stare frozen s.…at…neighbour ELIOT 304:6
no time to stand and s.? DAVI 255:48
stony British s. TENN 845:87
two red eyes that s. RANS 679:27
When I do s. SHAK 763:88

with one bold s. ELIOT 306:60
Stark or Molly S.'s a widow STARK 813:76
stark tranced woman, bound and s. FREE 336:43
We are s. naught all FLET 328:69
starlight And s. wood SHEL 782:20
Into the frosty s. ARNO 32:27
moonlight and the s. LONG 516:55
S. and dewdrop FOST 332:62
starlit s. or a moonlit dome YEATS 934:60
s. with eternities unknown SASS 717:77
starry s. sky GERS 351:44
stars almost immense, with s. MILT 584:95
Among the scattered s. WORD 924:73
And she forgot the s. KEATS 458:28
and the s. came out TENN 848:62
as the s. are slow THOM 854:20
as the s. for ever and ever BIBLE 106:1
Beneath the s. MIDD 569:48
broad stripes and bright s. KEY 465:76
came forth to see the s. DANTE 252:96
champagne and the s. FITZ 325:94
chilly s. I can forgo CORY 237:76
Continuous as the s. WORD 927:41
crocus lustres of the s. CRANE 243:10
crowned with the s. TRAH 864:39
crown of twelve s. BIBLE 126:65
cubic inch of some s. MACC 527:85
Doubt thou the s. are fire SHAK 752:45
eyes were blind with s. HODG 405:44
Far beyond the s. VAUG 878:47
fault…is not in our s. SHAK 747:76
fiercer than s. BRAS 150:94
flag, the S. and Stripes ROOS 696:60
fleet of s. is anchored FLEC 327:51
have the s. ROBI 689:25
heaven And calculate the s. MILT 584:97
heaven without s. SANT 714:25
high time we relit the s. APOL 27:20
How strange the s. SCOTT 722:76
imitate the s. celestial DAVI 254:33
in his right hand seven s. BIBLE 125:45
journey-work of the s. WHIT 905:32
just as the s. do BELL 74:92
knowledge of the s. EDDI 298:84
let us explore the s. KENN 462:10
like never-ending s. BETJ 84:10
Look at the s.! HOPK 412:88
looker at s. DOYLE 286:83
men…dream of the s. ELLI 311:85
moon and s. are set STEV 822:13
moon and the s. MACC 528:16
moon or favouring s. WORD 925:98
More s. than…heaven DIETZ 274:11
morning s. sang together BIBLE 93:70
move the s. to pity FLAU 326:34
new-bathed s. ARNO 32:28
night with different s. SACK 708:90
number of the s. BIBLE 98:6
Of all the western s. TENN 840:66
of the months and s. SWIN 832:17
opposition of the s. MARV 556:67
Owl looked up to the S. LEAR 497:83
power above The s. and fate BUTL 177:62
primeval ooze to the s. VIDAL 881:95
rain…of the failing s. RICK 686:74
sees the mud, and one the s. LANG 488:70
seven s. go squawking AUDEN 40:91
shining of the s. TENN 847:44
shooting s. attend thee HERR 400:38
Sister of the s. PATM 643:63
spaces between the s. HENRI 395:41
splendid s. FLEC 327:52
s. all singing and shining MUIR 602:65
s. and planets circled DICK 268:51
s. are dead AUDEN 39:86
s. came otherwise BROW 162:75
s., democratically inconspicuous LAWR 494:5
s. in her hair ROSS 698:86
s. in our galaxy BRAUN 150:98
s. move still, time runs MARL 552:6
S. scribble on our eyes CRANE 243:21
S., s., And all eyes else SHAK 770:96
s. that have a different birth SHEL 787:30
s. that reigned at my nativity MARL 553:7
s. Thou knew'st by name MILT 585:35
s. threw down their spears BLAKE 135:62
s. to flight FITZ 324:82

s. were going out CLAR 220:57
s. were so many spangles ARNO 34:73
s. were suddenly for LEE 500:45
s., which thou hast ordained BIBLE 94:87
s. with deep amaze MILT 575:95
strives to touch the s. SPEN 808:69
sun, moon, and s., brother BORR 145:3
to you, you chaste s. SHAK 761:7
who didst the s....know ARNO 31:90
will across the sky in s. LAWR 495:37
yoke of inauspicious s. SHAK 737:81
star-shine and s.-s. at night STEV 823:32
star-showers light dissolved in s.-s. SHEL 783:31
star-spangled s.-s. banner KEY 465:76
start end is where we s. from ELIOT 309:49
forgiven you...so that you can s. MAIL 540:62
Nature got the s. DENH 261:94
s. again, somewhere else MAJOR 541:71
s. of space SCOTT 722:77
s. together and finish t. BEEC 69:62
Straining upon the s. SHAK 746:43
To make a s. WILL 913:47
started s. like a guilty thing SHAK 751:97
s. out very quiet HEMI 394:18
starter Few thought he was even a s. ATTL 38:44
starting consternation to the s.-point SOME 803:67
startled It s. him just to hear RAMOS 678:6
starts buck s. here GREE 372:82
everything by s. DRYD 290:88
s. with an earthquake GOLD 362:84
starvation degradation and s. LOVE 519:17
weapon is s. STEV 824:40
starve bury whom he helped to s. POPE 661:39
s. with feeding SHAK 769:68
they that s. with nothing SHAK 739:42
starveling 'Sblood, you s. SHAK 742:15
starving disdain if they were not s. ROCH 691:63
truly affectionate when he is s.? PREV 668:11
state assist the S. PITT 652:39
august occasions of the s. FROST 339:15
bestowed...by the s. MCCA 528:99
between S. and S. ROUS 701:48
beweep my outcast s. SHAK 771:14
body continues in its s. NEWT 612:69
Boston is a s. of mind APPL 28:25
California, the department-store s. CHAN 205:84
cannot...miss it in my weak s. COMP 229:70
desirable mental s. LURIE 522:91
difference of birth or s.? DEKK 259:47
discumbered Atlas of the s. COWP 240:50
dividing the s. from...private GALB 343:95
economy of a S. RUSK 704:17
Fascist...'beehive s.' ORWE 628:46
first duty of a s. RUSK 704:28
general S. education MILL 570:61
glories and my s. depose SHAK 735:24
glories of our blood and s. SHIR 789:83
gods recognized by the s. PLATO 654:77
Government, even in its best s. PAINE 634:90
greatest asset...head of s. can have WILS 916:2
happy s. in this world LOCKE 514:20
healthy s. of political life MILL 570:63
highest s. of self-awareness LARD 490:15
his nature to live in a s. ARIS 29:56
I am the S. LOUI 518:99
if marriage be such a blessed s. ASTE 36:25
independent European s. GAIT 343:89
individual and...the s. PLATO 654:78
initiation into a new s. ELIOT 303:81
interests coincide with the s.'s MUSS 605:23
In that s. I came, return VAUG 878:46
in whatsoever s. I am BIBLE 123:62
living symbol of the s. LABO 483:55
meetings have caused in my S. LOUI 518:92
mental s. MANN 546:76
mock the air with idle s. GRAY 370:27
naked s. MCCA 528:6
new-made artificial s. POWE 667:94
no such thing as the S. AUDEN 40:8
Nothing doth more hurt in a s. BACON 49:19
not necessary in a S. ASTE 36:23
Oh happy s.! POPE 659:82
O Ship of S. LONG 516:54
Our s. cannot be severed MILT 585:16
O wretched s. of man SIDN 790:99
pillar of the S. SOLZ 803:63
police s. GINS 357:70

portentous, and a thing of s. LIND 511:50
powers of the s. GIBB 351:54
reinforcement of the S. CAMUS 187:95
ruin or to rule the s. DRYD 290:79
sad obscure sequestered s. BROW 162:88
Scoffing his s. SHAK 735:20
Secrecy...in the affairs of S. RICH 686:67
servant of the s. KING 468:41
servants of the sovereign or s. BACON 48:99
ship [of s.] will be saved CUOMO 248:29
s....called the Holy Roman Empire VOLT 883:45
s., condition, or degree MILT 584:98
S. Department MCCA 527:93
s. has no place TRUD 868:22
s. Is kingly MILT 580:88
S. is responsible THAT 850:13
S. is the Church SHAW 779:37
s. lottery as a public subsidy QUINE 675:52
s. manifested by a specific syndrome SELYE 727:86
s....master of money BEVE 85:28
s. of innocency Adam fell SHAK 742:23
s. of man SHAK 775:20
s. of rut GALS 344:24
s. of war by nature SWIFT 832:1
s....takes no notice CROM 245:70
s. where gun control SIMP 792:47
s....withers away ENGE 314:66
s. without...some change BURKE 168:29
s. won't bother us anymore MAO 547:2
storms of s. SHAK 775:23
That s. is a s. of Slavery GILL 356:42
The more the s. 'plans' HAYEK 387:59
things o' the S. NAIR 607:53
this isthmus of a middle s. POPE 660:16
To preserve a trading s. STEU 819:8
vital importance to the s. SUN 828:24
voter...pernicious to the S. WRIG 929:74
we are the s. WRIG 930:84
When S. Magic fails REED 682:85
Where Venice sate in s. BYRON 180:31
whole machinery of the s. ENGE 314:68
whole worl's in a s. OCAS 621:13
With wealth your s....improve DONNE 279:43
women do not count in the S. DAVI 256:70
worst s. of affairs KLEE 475:7
worth of the S. MILL 570:68
youth of a s. BACON 50:59
state-controlled s.-c....echoes DOUG 283:29
stately grow great and s. STEV 823:19
more s. and admirable WHIT 905:41
one of the s. homos CRISP 245:58
she is tall and s. TENN 845:86
S. as a galleon GREN 372:1
s. homes of England COWA 239:18
statement Every scientific s. POPP 662:88
general s. is like a cheque POUND 665:48
least cheering s. LEBO 499:10
no s. which refers to a 'reality' AYER 44:9
scientific s. speaks POPP 663:96
sheer joy of felicitous s. SCHL 718:11
s. and a metaphorical way MALA 541:81
s. as an act of wilful defiance SASS 716:56
statements apparent s. of fact AYER 44:10
attacks from outlaw s. REAG 680:60
Have more s. perished HOPE 411:71
independent or semi-independent s. JAY 436:97
In s. unborn SHAK 748:98
She's all s. DONNE 279:42
s. of consciousness MOORE 594:21
stinking s. JOHN 441:11
thinking in terms of nation s. ADEN 7:47
statesman abroad, you almost feel...a s. MACM 536:70
agree with him, he is a s. LLOY 514:9
business of a s. STEU 819:9
constitutional s. is in general BAGE 52:96
definition of a constitutional s. BAGE 51:95
first requirement of a s. ACHE 2:35
politician is a s. who STEV 821:67
rule...for a s., a courtier, or a lover CHAR 206:28
s....enamoured of existing evils BIER 129:22
speculative s. ADDI 6:10
s. is a politician who TRUM 868:37
s. is preventing...plots WALT 888:52
s.'s duty is to bridge KISS 475:98
Too nice for a s. GOLD 362:70
statesmanship You call that s. BEVAN 85:22
statesmen adored by little s. EMER 312:58

Among modern s. CHES 212:70
become s. and heroes WARD 888:56
some are born s. SHAW 781:84
s....ignore at their peril WILS 917:18
s. of E. TAYL 837:12
s....take on a science fictional way ASIM 35:6
static A novel is a s. thing TYNAN 872:45
class people as s. and dynamic WAUGH 892:22
French...will never become s. HUGO 420:65
Thin squeaks of radio s. CRANE 243:20
station Eternity...as of a s. DICK 273:76
honour is a private s. ADDI 7:37
keep no rank nor s. LOWE 520:45
towers of St Pancras S. BEEC 69:61
Worked on Middleton's s. LAWS 496:45
stationary All is flux, nothing is s. HERA 396:64
stations train passes through s. LEWIS 507:70
statistic exchange rate is only a s. KRUG 481:26
statisticians sin With s. AUDEN 41:33
statistics feed the hungry on s. LLOY 513:94
lies, damned lies and s. DISR 277:93
man of s. HOLM 408:2
only tables and s. OPPE 626:15
Politicians use s. LANG 488:89
seemingly inanimate of s. MAMET 543:31
S. are designed DISKI 275:31
S. are the triumph BELL 73:69
s. for Manhattan Island BART 63:26
unless s. lie CUMM 248:12
statue s. inside every block ORWE 628:52
s. of one of our kings APPL 27:22
s.'s brow WALC 885:81
walk around a s. ROSSO 698:7
walking...with the S. of Liberty CONR 235:23
statues like sepulchral s. DONNE 280:59
Trees cut to S. POPE 659:95
With s. on the terraces KIPL 474:72
stature add one cubit unto his s.? BIBLE 110:2
increased in s. WHITE 903:92
Jesus increased in wisdom and s. BIBLE 115:28
Look not...on the height of his s. BIBLE 91:90
Malice is of a low s. HALI 378:87
man of giant s. NEHRU 610:29
mighty s. MILT 580:6
persons of heroic s. AMIS 15:9
status Bureaucracy defends the s. quo PETER 649:77
economic s. of women GILM 356:51
industrial and economic s. SKEL 795:94
Policemen so cherish their s. MAMET 543:23
restored the s. quo HAMER 378:96
restored the s. quo SQUI 811:42
s. and profits of war TREV 865:63
s. of a cathedral RODR 693:96
s. of Galileo GOULD 365:23
s. of 'native' SART 716:55
the quo has lost its s. PETER 649:77
statutes s. or usages therein obtaining MILL 570:56
staves aspen good for s. SPEN 808:73
comest to me with s.? BIBLE 91:95
stay My s., my guide, and lantern SHAK 730:55
poor man's s. WORD 927:31
S., Frederic, s.! GILB 354:2
s. in a concentration camp JOHN 439:73
Will you not s. HODG 405:42
Yet will not s. GRAV 367:63
stays Old Hodge s. not his hand RANS 679:27
steadiness s., self-control...courage PEEL 646:10
steady how s. you hold your weapon SIMP 792:47
s. and perpetual serenity ADDI 6:20
s. and stolid-y GILB 354:2
steak s. spread with butter KURO 482:41
wanted s. and they offered spam MALA 541:78
steaks smell of s. ELIOT 305:27
steal most honourable...was to s. RABE 676:63
poets...beg, borrow, or s. POUND 666:73
silently s. away KAUF 455:57
s. bread FRAN 333:93
S. me a while SHAK 738:7
s. my Basil-pot away KEATS 458:29
s. us from ourselves DRYD 289:65
Thou shalt not s. BIBLE 88:23
Thou shalt not s. CLOU 223:39
When judges s. themselves SHAK 758:28
steam powers of s. WATT 891:2
s. comes...navel THOM 853:95
s. of the social soup ACKR 3:54
steamer This little s....is immortal PRIE 668:19

steamers all you Big S.   KIPL 474:71
  Daily the s. sidle up   AUDEN 39:84
steed s. and the shrill trump   SHAK 760:94
  s. by Loc Suilig   MCCA 527:87
  s. was the best   SCOTT 723:96
  waves bound…as a s.   BYRON 179:18
steeds curb thy fierce s.   BLAKE 133:24
  mounting barbèd s.   SHAK 731:99
steel dew-like s.   BRAU 150:4
  Give them the cold s.   ARMI 30:70
  hand of s. in a velvet glove   WOOL 923:56
  him they feared to meet with s.   DAVIS 256:64
  locomotive of s.   KAFKA 454:25
  Meistersinger…set breath in s.   CRANE 243:23
  red line tipped with s.   RUSS 706:69
  s. my soldiers' hearts   SHAK 746:53
  S. prices cause inflation   BLOU 137:8
  s. rod runs right through   ANGE 17:38
  though locked up in s.   SHAK 730:59
  with hoops of s.   SHAK 751:17
  wounded surgeon plies the s.   ELIOT 308:21
steel-true S.-t. and blade-straight   STEV 823:34
Steemie S. lecturing   SCOTT 725:43
steep s. and thorny way   SHAK 751:16
steeple Grand Sluice, and a high s.   ANON 20:22
  in his own religious s.   CAMP 186:62
  in s. hing   FERG 320:7
  s. of my dreams   DEBU 258:3
steeplechase s. and gameboard   ELKIN 310:69
steeples In s. far and near   HOUS 415:51
  Till you have drenched our s.   SHAK 763:71
steering s. full speed ahead   GILM 356:57
Stein Gertrude S. said   STEIN 815:13
  Gertrude S.'s prose song   LEWIS 508:98
Stella S., think not that I   SIDN 790:15
stem s. of the contained flower   ROET 694:1
stems gold is on the pine-s.   MERE 567:96
stench s. of appeasement   THAT 850:32
stenches two and seventy s.   COLE 227:23
Stendhal fought two draws with S.   HEMI 394:18
step but one s. from…the horrible   DOYLE 285:81
  dare not take a s.   SHAW 778:87
  every individualis is…a false s.   SCHO 719:32
  first s. that counts   DEFF 258:10
  get up a s. that ain't there   JACO 432:15
  isn't the first s.   KENN 464:52
  look well to each s.   WHYM 906:65
  must go nowhere, s. out   LEWIS 508:99
  new theory…a…s. forward   POPP 662:89
  One S. Forward   LENIN 502:83
  small s. for a man   ARMS 30:78
  small s. for mankind   BROD 153:56
  s. in the wrong direction   LEVA 505:51
  varies with every s.   THOR 857:78
step-dame fled s.-d. Study's blows   SIDN 790:8
step-parents s.-p.…disappointment   POWE 666:76
stepping s. where his comrade   SCOTT 723:2
steps by backward s.   VAUG 878:46
  gentle odours led my s.   SHEL 786:23
  s. down the palate   NABO 606:30
  s. had well nigh slipped   BIBLE 96:41
  s. of a staircase   MALL 542:98
  s. take hold on hell   BIBLE 99:13
  treading the s. already marked   SHEL 782:11
stereotype s. of rejected genius   HUGH 419:31
stereotypes abandon established s.   GORB 363:3
sterile seems to me a s. promontory   SHAK 752:56
  splendid and s. Dolores   SWIN 833:28
  Truths discovered…are s.   FRAN 333:87
sterility victory of s.   BELL 73:69
stern Kingly conclaves s. and cold   SHEL 785:72
  lantern on the s.   COLE 227:24
  solitary and most s.   YEATS 933:40
  s., obdurate, flinty, rough   SHAK 730:71
sterner s. stuff   SHAK 748:6
Stevenson S.'s convictions   LEHM 501:69
stew soporific s. of every day!   SARD 714:29
steward backward s. for the poor   POPE 660:4
  lord commended the unjust s.   BIBLE 116:50
Stewart land God gave to Andy S.   SMITH 799:65
stewing no matter how much s.   CURT 249:48
stewpan others again that it is a s.   HUNT 423:39
stews Of s. and brothels only knew   HERB 398:18
  private sports the s. would blush   MASS 559:45
St Francis I'm S. F. of Assisi   PARK 638:68
stick coat upon a s.   YEATS 933:52
  fell like the s.   PAINE 634:96

give me my s.. I'll face it   LEAC 497:73
  heard his s. thumping   MANS 547:94
  scratched with a s.   KIPL 471:3
  Speak softly and carry a big s.   ROOS 696:52
  s. and a string   JOHN 447:77
  s. I am about to cut   BENT 77:68
  water curves a s.   LAFO 485:16
sticking-place courage to the s.-p.   SHAK 767:90
sticks like s. of sealing-wax   DICK 268:31
  Nothing s. to him   SCHR 720:44
  S. nix hick pix   ANON 22:57
  take up pick-axes and s.   HO 405:37
stiffen S. the sinews   SHAK 746:42
  time to s.   ORWE 628:67
stiffnecked s. people   BIBLE 89:27
stile-a merrily hent the s.-a.   SHAK 770:83
still America…isn't standing s.   CUMM 247:10
  Be s., and know   BIBLE 95:26
  commune…and be s.   BIBLE 94:85
  No economy ever stands s.   HARR 384:6
  not keeping s.   GUNN 375:40
  said to my soul, be s.   ELIOT 308:14
  s. and quiet conscience   SHAK 775:19
  S. falls the Rain   SITW 794:73
  s. small voice   BIBLE 92:24
  Sunday…standing s.   RHYS 684:28
  they liked me 's.'   DICK 272:62
stillness air a solemn s. holds   GRAY 369:10
  horrid s. first invades the ear   DRYD 287:14
  sense of rapacious s.   BANKS 58:36
  solemn s. of the buried foliage   HOLM 407:70
  s. can outlast   SASS 716:73
  s. in the midst of chaos   BELL 73:75
  s. where our spirits walk   SASS 716:74
  that s. ultimately best   CRANE 243:15
stilts nonsense upon s.   BENT 77:69
stimulus s. and object   MANN 545:63
sting care not who they s.   SHAK 730:58
  death, where is thy s.?   BIBLE 122:20
  it is a s.   PEELE 646:12
  s. a stately horse   JOHN 441:29
  s. like a bee   ALI 12:33
  that inwardly doth s.   SURR 829:35
stings s. in their tails   BIBLE 126:63
stink earth shall have a foul s.   ANON 19:93
stinker Outrageous S.   KIPL 472:28
stinks stenches…and several s.!   COLE 227:23
stint at pleasure s. their melody   SHAK 731:96
stipple s. leaves with sun   SACK 708:89
stir s. not up, nor awake my love   BIBLE 101:98
stirk s. from a cottar   SCOTT 723:13
stirks They gang in S.   BURNS 170:63
stirred Shaken and not s.   FLEM 327:56
  S. for a bird   HOPK 412:90
stirrup foot upon the s.   DELA 260:65
  sprang to the s.   BROW 160:27
stirrup-pump simple s.-p.   REED 681:81
stitch S.! s.! s.!   HOOD 410:45
St John Awake, my S. J.!   POPE 660:6
  Rev S. J. Froude put the phone down   SHAR 776:45
St Louis three girls from S. L.   STEIN 815:25
St Mary still S. M.'s Lake   WORD 927:30
stoats rabbits ruled by s.   ORWE 628:46
stock column of s. quotations   DOSP 282:3
  enslaved as farm s.   SHAW 780:55
  fight for that s.   HOWA 417:94
  impoverished the public s.   JOHN 446:47
  waste its s.   CRUZ 246:87
stocking glimpse of s.   PORT 663:4
stockings come to her in yellow s.   SHAK 756:72
  for the silk s.   JOHN 441:22
  her last…pair of s.   CHAN 204:73
  his s. fouled   SHAK 752:40
  pinking of thin s.   DICK 267:25
  Queen Elizabeth owned silk s.   SCHU 721:56
  s. were hung   MOORE 594:15
Stockport rubbish was sent to S.   ANON 26:89
stocks feet…hurt in the s.   BOOK 143:67
  reads 'storks' for 's.'   FREUD 337:53
  s. were sold   BELL 73:57
stoic Every S. was a S.   EMER 312:6
  weakness for the s.'s pride   POPE 660:16
  with a s. calm   SOME 803:67
stoicism Romans call it s.   ADDI 6:32
Stoics Let the S. say what they please   EMER 312:24
stole s. it fair and square   HAYA 387:56
  wonder where you s. 'em   SWIFT 831:76

stolen horses may not be s.   HALI 378:85
  not wanting what is s.   SHAK 760:93
  revolution has been s.   JIANG 438:51
  S., s., be your apples   HUNT 423:29
  S. waters are sweet   BIBLE 99:19
  They'll say it's s.   BRAD 149:80
stolid steady and s.-y   GILB 354:6
stolidity cinder of s.   CARL 191:72
stomach adventures on a drained s.   BYRON 183:11
  army marches on its s.   NAPO 607:65
  bring 'em off your s.   LAMB 486:36
  but a s., gentlemen, a s.   HUNT 423:87
  deepest loathing to the s.   SHAK 737:99
  good s. to a feast   WEBS 894:85
  Had s. for 'em all   SHAK 761:9
  healthy s. is…conservative   BUTL 178:85
  heart and s. of a king   ELIZ 309:60
  If your s. disputes you   PAIGE 634:87
  in his s. more animated beings   SMITH 801:11
  little wine for thy s.'s sake   BIBLE 123:77
  naturally have a weak s.   BERN 80:30
  no s. for such meat   DOBS 277:97
  no s. to this faith   SHAK 746:56
  pit of the s.   HOUS 416:83
  soul, of a s.   SAKI 710:40
  s. is not good   ANON 20:2
  s. sets us to work   ELIOT 303:99
  s. thinks her throat is cut   RUNY 702:81
  when you have a s. ache   GORO 364:15
stomachs juries fill their s.   SYNGE 834:58
St Omer old man of S.O.   QUIL 674:47
stone At his heels a s.   SHAK 754:16
  blessed is the hard s.   DARIO 252:4
  bomb them into the S. Age   LEMAY 502:75
  carved in s.   TENN 845:82
  creeping ivy clings to…s.   COWP 241:62
  cruelties of the S. Age   CHUR 217:85
  Here the s. images   ELIOT 306:70
  hurl a s. at   MOOD 594:10
  inside every block of s.   ORWE 628:52
  keeper of the s.   DAVI 255:43
  lay s. on s.   ARNO 32:4
  Leave not…a foot of s.   POPE 662:74
  let him first cast a s.   BIBLE 117:94
  Like a s.   TAKU 835:80
  lonely man…a s., a bone, a stick   CHEE 209:3
  massive sandal set on s.   MILL 571:88
  naked s.   WORD 929:60
  nickname is the heaviest s.   HAZL 388:91
  no bigger than an agate s.   SHAK 735:38
  no s. unturned   SHAR 776:39
  Paris made of s.   HUGO 420:69
  Saturn, quiet as a s.   KEATS 459:44
  Sculpture in s.   MOORE 595:24
  see and imitate…in s.   CUMM 247:99
  seventy years of s.   THOM 852:67
  shadow white as s.   ROET 694:6
  sound of iron on s.   DELA 260:65
  s. and earth is closer to the truth   HEAT 390:28
  s. besmeared with sluttish time   SHAK 771:21
  s. commemorates…Ellis   ANON 21:26
  s. falls to the ground   THOR 858:99
  s. fidelity They hardly meant   LARK 490:30
  s. flung into the water   LEON 504:20
  s. in my straw hat   STEV 821:76
  s. of our fortresses   FAVRE 319:94
  s. of stumbling   BIBLE 102:15
  s. of the heart   YEATS 933:46
  s. remains, and the cross   MACC 527:84
  s. set in the silver sea   SHAK 734:8
  s. taken away from the sepulchre   BIBLE 118:21
  s. than with an axe   JOHN 445:31
  s. that puts the stars to flight   FITZ 324:82
  s. the twenty-first   BROW 162:76
  S. walls do not a prison   LOVE 519:10
  s. was cut out without hands   BIBLE 105:94
  s. which the builders refused   BIBLE 97:78
  swerd of this s.   MALO 542:3
  sword…out of the s.   MUNRO 603:84
  take away our hearts o' s.   OCAS 621:14
  take the s. from the s.   ELIOT 307:5
  themselves as s.   SHAK 772:37
  The s.'s in the midst   YEATS 933:45
  things of bronze and s.   RUNY 703:86
  trunkless legs of s.   SHEL 784:49
  turn you like them to s.   TATE 837:5
  understanding of the S. Age   ARMEY 30:68

violet by a mossy s. — WORD 924:78
Virtue is like a rich s. — BACON 49:43
water upon the s. — STEAD 813:81
Wedding-Guest sat on a s. — COLE 225:81
weight which is the s. — HEPW 396:61
will he give him a s.? — BIBLE 110:8
written of me on my s. — FROST 339:10
Stonehenge bring S. to Nyasaland — BANDA 58:24
like a monogrammed S. — RIVA 688:1
stone-like Naked and s.-l. — FREE 336:43
stones could aye peeble them wi' s. — SCOTT 724:35
five smooth s. out of the brook — BIBLE 91:94
houses are made of s. — POIN 657:33
Inestimable s. — SHAK 731:8
on thy cold grey s. — TENN 840:67
pavements fang'd with murderous s. — COLE 227:23
pavement s. are polished — DICK 267:25
people and the s. — WILL 913:45
picked up with s. — FROST 338:96
raise a cone of s. — STUA 827:97
reconcile ourselves to the s. — MACD 530:45
red As the stained s. — OWEN 632:53
Sermons in s. — SHAK 749:34
s. be made bread — BIBLE 109:78
s. have stood for a thousand years — JEFF 436:5
s. into the Theban wall — COWL 240:30
s. of silence — HEAN 389:6
s. with little water drops — SHAK 733:64
s. would cry out — SHEEN 782:8
s. would immediately cry out — BIBLE 116:59
storm-sculptured s. — SASS 716:73
threw words like s. — SPEN 807:52
time to cast away s. — BIBLE 100:70
will move s. — SHAK 737:88
With rocks, and s. and trees — WORD 924:80
you are men of s. — SHAK 764:5
stonewall want you all to s. — NIXON 617:46
stood Freely they s. who s. — MILT 582:42
s. upon that silent hill — HODG 405:44
stool on his rickety s. — HUGH 418:18
own the hearth and s. — COLUM 229:61
stools necessity invented s. — COWP 241:67
stoop dares to s. — DOST 282:7
grief...makes his owner s. — SHAK 738:22
jewel...we s. and take — SHAK 758:21
stoops lovely woman s. to folly — GOLD 361:47
stop ask me to s. playing — KING 468:25
nobody's gonna s. them — BERRA 82:54
one approaches your s. — COPE 237:61
S. and consider! — KEATS 457:82
s. everyone from doing it — HERB 397:75
S. The World — ANON 23:85
Time...Must have a s. — SHAK 742:34
You can't s. it — WILL 914:61
stop-light sees only the red s.-l. — SCHW 721:71
store as large as s. — HERB 398:9
from great s. — KIPL 472:28
in the s. we sell hope — REVS 684:20
keep the s. open nights — KAUF 456:61
Laid up in s. for me — TRAH 864:36
no wealthy s. — DYER 297:51
pale Mammon pine amidst his s. — POPE 660:4
rich in nature's s. — FORD 330:18
s. of experience — FRAME 333:81
s. of skill — DYER 297:52
those who...behold her s. — CRAB 242:89
vast s. which the busy — LOCKE 514:17
Whatever Nature has in s. — FERMI 321:16
Who's minding the s.? — REAG 680:58
stored lay s. in me — RICH 685:55
stores department s....museums — WARH 889:65
stories added to his s. — STEIN 815:13
all s....end in death — HEMI 394:7
believe of my own s. — IRVI 430:83
copious s., oftentimes begun — SHAK 733:57
dead men never bring awkward s. — DICK 266:90
family denied both s. — SAKI 710:38
make up your own s. — WADD 884:63
mythical s. become structural — FRYE 340:36
new s. are born from old — RUSH 703:90
no invention as to s. — BYRON 181:52
pictures are the love s. — LAUR 492:72
s....about the great and powerful — BERN 81:40
Sad s. chancèd — SHAK 731:94
Scheherazades worth of s. — BARTH 62:3
s. And not by his blows — LAFO 485:8
s. of the death of kings — SHAK 735:20

S. to rede ar delitabill — BARB 59:51
tell ourselves s. — DIDI 274:7
there are only two or three human s. — CATH 200:84
turn to s. and poems — DYSON 297:62
stork throwing rocks at the s. — BREC 150:5
storks reads 's.' for 'stocks' — FREUD 337:53
s. on the spires of Denmark — DOYLE 286:83
storm At the end of the s. — HAMM 379:17
brows like gathering s. — BURNS 172:13
colour if the s. — RYDER 707:77
did na mind the s. — BURNS 172:17
driven away with the s. — BIBLE 107:34
fled away into the s. — KEATS 459:43
full of frost, of s. and cloudiness? — SHAK 745:26
infinite s. of beauty — MUIR 602:65
In the howling s. — BLAKE 134:54
pelting of this pitiless s. — SHAK 763:78
Rides...and directs the s. — ADDI 5:5
rides upon the s. — COWP 240:43
S. and stress — KAUF 456:64
s. is long past — KEYN 465:81
s. is up — SHAK 748:20
s. of life — WESL 900:11
swell before s. — KIPL 473:50
wings of the s. — GRANT 366:53
storm-clouds s.-c. brood — LEAR 497:76
the s.-c. thundrous melody — STEP 817:58
storms broken in on by the s. — ADAMS 5:94
explanation of our gusts and s. — ELIOT 304:15
haunts the s. — BAUD 64:55
He sought the s. — DRYD 289:76
raging s. movis us to shake — ANON 20:4
s. of state — SHAK 775:23
sudden s. are short — SHAK 734:6
weathered the severest s. — KENN 463:23
Where no s. come — HOPK 412:78
storm-sculptured s.-s. stones — SASS 716:73
stormy dark and s. night — BULW 166:57
s. and altogether warlike — LUTH 523:99
S., husky, brawling — SAND 712:91
story advantage...in telling their s. — AUST 44:97
any s. is ephemeral — FAUL 318:63
building...to tell a s. — CASS 199:73
epitaph to be my s. — FROST 339:10
Every fine s. must leave...pleasure — CATH 200:95
fool in the old s. — MACA 525:43
form of the short s. — SARO 714:35
gallous s. — SYNGE 834:59
going to tell a true s. — ECHE 298:76
green fig-tree in the s. — PLATH 654:72
Here then will we begin the s. — BIBLE 108:68
how he had started a s. — HEMI 394:12
involved in a s. — MANN 546:73
means to write one s. — BARR 61:79
Never was a s. — SHAK 737:82
no matter how implausible your s. — SHAR 776:44
No s. comes from nowhere — RUSH 703:90
not trying to tell a s. — WOOLF 923:50
novel tells a s. — FORS 331:44
Once a newspaper touches a s. — MAIL 539:43
On the Beach is a s. — GARD 345:43
our own s. — THUR 859:30
place where a s. ended — ELIOT 309:41
present moments in the s. — STUA 827:96
sacred s. of the soul's delight — LANY 489:7
Still is the s. told — MACA 526:68
s. books had been written by people — WELTY 899:99
s. for which the world — DOYLE 286:82
S. is just just deserts — ELKIN 310:70
s. of a mountebank and his zany — WALP 887:34
s. of an ape — HARL 383:83
s. of a woman's life — STAEL 811:44
s. of Colonel Chapman's — WAVE 893:59
s. of the soul — RUSS 706:61
s. of the unconquerable fortress — SELZ 727:87
s. shall the good man teach — SHAK 746:60
s. with a moral — OHEN 623:56
s. within yourself — KAFKA 454:25
summits old in s. — TENN 841:3
Tell me the old, old s. — HANK 380:33
tells a s. or records — RUSK 703:2
tell this s. as much — NORTH 618:70
this s. is unreal — PACH 633:69
To tell my s. — SHAK 755:41
truly be an extraordinary s. — STIPE 824:52
whatever s. you want — KELM 461:78
'what is all this s. about?' — STER 818:94

What we want is a s. — GOLD 362:84
when a scandalous s. is believed — SHER 788:56
story-teller no true s.-t. — HEMI 394:7
stout s. and resolute little man — WELLS 898:83
three s. and stalwart sons — BALL 57:97
stove ice on a hot s. — FROST 339:7
Stowe Mrs. S. did not hit — CHES 210:24
St Pancras towers of S. P. — BEEC 69:61
St Paul didn't quite build S. P.'s — THOR 858:10
I am designing S. P.'s — BENT 78:76
pray for you at S. P.'s — SMITH 801:24
straight crooked be made s. — ELIOT 307:8
don't need to be 's.' to fight — GOLD 362:76
every man s. before him — BIBLE 90:64
however s. or winding — THOM 854:17
makes a man stand s. — HELL 392:76
make s. in the desert — BIBLE 103:36
narrow s. channels — RANJ 678:16
no s. thing can ever — KANT 455:43
nothing ever ran quite s. — GALS 344:25
sets you all s. again — HUXL 426:15
s. and narrow as a tomb — SMITH 800:95
took their red s. — ACHE 2:33
straightfaced S. in his cunning — THOM 853:90
strain Big Bow-wow s. — SCOTT 725:54
dozing sages drop the drowsy s. — COWP 240:48
muse is...of the English s. — DRAY 286:97
s. of expectation — FIRB 323:69
s. on the affections — ELIOT 304:14
That s. again — SHAK 755:45
untarnished by its s.! — LOWE 521:55
straits echoing s. between us — ARNO 32:9
in s. a present aid — SCOT 725:62
strand Come sailing to the s.! — BALL 56:86
knits me to thy rugged s.! — SCOTT 723:92
left fair Scotland's s. — BURNS 173:51
name upon the s. — SPEN 809:1
Scotland for the S.? — JOHN 441:13
wandering on a foreign s. — SCOTT 723:91
where's the Maypole in the S. — BRAM 150:88
strands lost s. and weave — MCCA 527:91
these last s. of man — HOPK 412:2
strange acquaints a man with s. — SHAK 774:87
bedfellows — SHAK 765:45
All s. and terrible events — ROCH 692:69
Constancy alone is s. — SHAK 752:29
foul, s., and unnatural — BROW 161:53
How s. it seems, and new — SCOTT 722:76
How s. the stars — BIBLE 98:98
in a s. land? — SHAK 774:84
Into something rich and s. — CONG 232:45
Let us be very s. — SHAK 766:83
read s. matters — BIBLE 92:14
Solomon loved many s. women — TENN 842:8
So sad, so s. — TRAH 864:38
S. all, and New — GERS 350:36
s. instruments — THOM 854:5
s. land, most s. — SYNGE 834:59
s. man is a marvel — HOLL 407:69
s. one that summer — SHAK 747:89
s. that men should fear — SHAK 744:5
s. that sheep's guts — SHAK 768:18
You make me s. — COUP 239:99
Strangelove S. Reproduction — DOYLE 285:49
strangeness confound s. — BACON 49:45
no...beauty that hath not some s. — RUSS 705:40
s. and wonder lying — TRAH 864:38
stranger A S. here — KUHN 481:34
bedpan by a s. — MOORE 596:48
crown of a s. — BIBLE 89:50
for the s. — NASH 608:78
From the wiles of a s. — WILDE 907:82
Golden corn for the s. — SIMO 792:42
Go, s., and tell the Spartans — HOUS 416:76
I, a s. and afraid — PESS 649:72
I'm a s. here — BIBLE 87:77
land wherein thou art a s. — MILL 572:5
name we give to that s. — BENS 77:63
never love a s. — VIRG 882:17
No s. to trouble — BIBLE 113:92
s., and ye took me in — DICK 272:70
S., pause and ask thyself — MONT 592:70
s. strayed into...their valleys — BIBLE 88:23
s. that is within thy gates — AUST 43:66
s. to one of your parents — AUDEN 41:25
S., unless with bedroom eyes — BIBLE 99:22
surety for a s.

this emotion is a s. — EINS 301:37
What s.'s feet may find — HOUS 416:81
when a s. looks at it — FAUL 319:70
who is the smiling s. — CAUS 201:14
world becomes s. — ELIOT 308:25
strangers agreeable to s. — SHAW 779:30
bought by faceless s. — WRIG 930:83
Closest of S. — WASH 890:88
cry in s.' houses — MANS 547:93
desire we may be better s. — SHAK 750:62
Economics and art are s. — CATH 200:94
entertain s. — BIBLE 124:3
kindness of s. — WILL 912:17
loved s. and bread — LEE 500:45
shall we s. be — TU 869:56
s. and pilgrims on the earth — BIBLE 124:96
s. before thee — BIBLE 92:40
s. honoured, and by s. — POPE 659:81
s. to flight and fear — MCCA 527:87
s. to themselves — BACON 48:4
ye are no more s. — BIBLE 122:43
strangle it is to s. him — RACI 677:85
S. her in her bed — SHAK 760:99
strangling s. in a string — HOUS 414:45
Strasbourg S.—the Council — BEVIN 85:31
Strasser Major S. has been shot — EPST 314:81
stratagems policies, nor s. — MILT 579:71
strategists lesson here for s. — GLEI 359:2
strategy s. of defense — GALB 343:90
subtlety of Johnsonian s. — MANC 544:42
Stratford scole of S. atte Bowe — CHAU 208:70
S. trades on Shakespeare — BURG 167:84
strath cow from a Lowland s. — SCOTT 723:13
strathspeys hornpipes and s. — BURNS 172:38
Strato I prithee, S. — SHAK 748:23
Strauss symphony by S. — PORT 663:6
waltz must be S.'s! — GERS 350:39
Stravinsky no new music since S. — ELLI 310:76
straw couch of s. — THOM 853:89
expect brick where they afford no s. — ASTE 36:21
Headpiece filled with s. — ELIOT 306:69
headpieces stuffed with s. — MACD 530:47
Oft stumbles at a s. — SPEN 808:69
once a flock-bed, but repaired with s. — POPE 660:5
Pipes of wretched s. — MILT 578:52
sleep on s. — CHEE 209:7
still in s. hat and sandals — BASHO 63:42
s. for a bedding — BELL 73:65
Where is this s. — SHAK 763:75
strawberries innocent as s. — THOM 852:70
strawberry Like s. wives — ELIZ 310:64
S. fields forever — LENN 503:99
straws Errors, like s. — DRYD 289:51
stray never taught to s. — POPE 660:11
with me you'd fondly s. — GAY 347:84
streak Gilbert had a baddish s. — QUIL 674:46
s. of yellow — MONET 591:53
stream Against the s. — FROST 339:1
bosom of the s. — SHEL 786:23
By the s. and o'er the mead — BLAKE 133:29
cloud on the s. — YEATS 933:45
dark-lit s. — THOM 854:11
eves by haunted s. — MILT 576:11
glen with one thin s. — DEVL 264:32
have their s. and pond — BROO 156:17
leaves in the glassy s. — SHAK 755:25
make thy s. — DENH 261:92
meadow, grove, and s. — WORD 926:21
mountain-s. that ends — LOWE 520:28
painted meadow, or a purling s. — ADDI 5:3
paint with tinted s. — CONS 235:28
passed many a straunge s. — CHAU 208:74
poison the whole blood s. fills — EMPS 313:61
river bed where no s. runs — ACHE 2:30
rowing against the s. — SCOTT 725:41
running s. of sparkling joy — DICK 270:90
salt weed sways in the s. — ARNO 31:84
steady s. of enterprise — KEYN 466:87
s. bears us — JONS 450:61
s., confined in narrow bound — CRAB 242:1
s. of destiny — SPEN 808:78
s. of human industry — TOCQ 861:81
s. of thought, of consciousness — JAMES 434:63
s. of your experience — JAMES 434:71
sunlight on a s. — ROSS 697:74
Trailing in the cool s. — ARNO 32:18
wires that span the mountain s. — CRANE 243:16

streamers fan spread and s. out — CONG 231:35
streams abundant s. of revenue — WEBS 894:71
golden run the s. — MERE 567:96
lavish s. to quench a country's thirst — POPE 660:4
love of…Brown s. — MACK 533:15
mix'd, As meeting s. — DRYD 289:60
s. in the desert — BIBLE 103:33
these silver s. — WALT 888:52
winds and s. — GIBS 352:75
street clumping down the cobbled s. — ORWE 627:35
danced down the s. — KERO 464:62
don't do it in the s. — CAMP 185:53
drab s. — GREE 371:69
evening quickens in the s. — DE 264:35
Forty-Second S. — DUBIN 292:64
great man walking down the s. — COPL 237:66
harlot's cry from s. to s. — BLAKE 135:70
inability to cross the s. — WOOLF 923:52
lamp-post at the corner of the s. — GAY 348:90
long s. roars — TENN 844:65
long unlovely s. — TENN 843:27
looking in the s. — KIPL 473:61
once walked down a s. — KIPL 473:56
On the bald s. — TENN 843:28
Out into the s. I ran — MASE 559:34
passed down the s. — STUD 827:5
past me in the s. — STEV 822:11
politician…on a s. corner — WHITE 903:99
posting up the s. — STEV 823:20
pulled to the side of the s. — STEI 816:37
ring in Heaven's s. — MASE 559:35
room or on the s. — ROSSO 698:6
salmon sing in the s. — AUDEN 40:91
sawdust-trampled s. — ELIOT 305:28
she-bear coming up the s. — FOOTE 329:94
s. being full of footballs — PEPYS 647:39
s. of the city was pure gold — BIBLE 127:82
such a sunny s. — DICK 267:25
sunny side of the s. — FIEL 323:46
through the public s. — SHAK 765:25
wander through each charter'd s. — BLAKE 135:58
when they met on the s. — KNIG 476:15
wouldn't cross the s. for it — JONAS 447:84
streets beg in the s. — FRAN 333:93
Beside grain-scattered s. — LARK 491:33
creature of the common s. — DICK 270:97
Down these mean s. a man must go — CHAN 204:77
fox in the s. — MCCA 527:88
game to keep the coalminers off the s. — BRES 151:19
good-for-nothing woman on the s. — SHAW 779:30
in the s., in the trams — MAYA 562:92
in the s. of the town — PARN 639:91
into the s. — ANON 23:9
Martian met me in the s. — ANDR 16:24
night Darkens the s. — MILT 581:10
not the s. that exist — FENT 320:87
principal s. are the fairest — DEFOE 258:23
prowling the s. — JANO 435:77
s. of a hundred cities — HOOV 411:57
s. o' the toon? — MACD 530:43
s. were dark with something more — CHAN 205:96
town of narrow s. — THOR 858:5
uttereth her voice in the s. — BIBLE 98:8
wandering in the s. below — HUGH 419:30
strength all the necessary s. — GOLD 360:31
As thy days, so shall thy s. be — BIBLE 90:58
by reason of s. — BIBLE 96:51
deemed Equal in s. — MILT 581:20
devoured all our s. — LAWR 495:39
for thou hast a little s. — BIBLE 126:50
gentleman…possess only s. — BRON 155:79
give me the s. — BAUD 64:65
God is our refuge and s. — BIBLE 95:24
God is the s. of my heart — BIBLE 96:43
go from s. to s. — BIBLE 96:46
Happiness engulfs our s. — BALZ 57:11
ignorance is s. — ORWE 629:99
inadult'rate s. — HERR 400:40
in quietness…shall be your s. — BIBLE 103:30
inside and s. were philosophy — SIDN 791:17
knowledge of its giant s. — NORR 618:65
man's s. is but little — SIMO 792:43
military s. with our moral restraint — KENN 463:37
misdoubt her s. — MILT 579:69
name is a tower of s. — SHAK 731:15
no s. in unbelief — MACD 530:57
not now that s. — TENN 840:66

not s. enough to prevent — GOLD 361:45
not the s. to choose — CHEE 209:1
oppressed, who wanted s. — WORD 927:31
outlive Thy youth, thy s. — MILT 585:31
pleasure of the flesh robs s. — FUEN 340:41
present s. and best security — TROL 866:62
refuge and our s. — SCOT 725:62
rejoiceth in his s. — BIBLE 93:74
roll all our s. — MARV 556:65
shewed s. with his arm — BIBLE 115:23
size of…its industrial s. — BENN 75:17
S. and beauty — DEMO 261:85
s. and my hope is perished — BIBLE 105:81
s. and the greatness of England — CURZ 249:51
s. and weakness of human nature — MACA 526:71
s. is made perfect in weakness — BIBLE 122:24
s. is small — BIBLE 100:49
s. lined with tenderness — ANGE 17:33
s. might have refused — LANY 489:4
s. nor the will — WALE 885:90
s. of five — BETJ 83:84
s. of our salvation — BOOK 143:64
s. that is almost frightening — ANGE 17:38
s. to force the moment — ELIOT 304:19
s. to harvest your fruit — MURR 605:11
S. without hands to smite — SWIN 833:22
than what their own s. — HOBB 404:27
tower of s. — TENN 844:72
triumphant conviction of s. — CONR 234:6
what is s. without — MILT 586:46
what s. I have's mine — SHAK 775:3
which by his s. and wit — HOBB 404:29
with my utmost s. — VAUG 878:48
would but fain his s. renew — HERR 399:34
strengths make my s. — JONS 449:39
stress in times of s. — ORWE 627:38
Storm and s. — KAUF 456:64
s. and disorientation — TOFF 862:91
S. is the state — SELYE 727:86
under s. of emotion — POUND 666:72
stresses s. of accent — SAND 713:15
stretch S. pants — ANON 23:86
stricken s. with most obstinate love — SIDN 790:1
stricture intensiveness as s. — BURKE 169:57
stride poet is allowed the s. — SAND 713:13
put the batter off his s. — SHAW 781:96
strife dull and endless s. — WORD 924:74
Happiness is full of s. — ANOU 26:98
hear the silver s. — DICK 272:55
heavens free from s. — CORY 237:76
In Place of S. — CAST 199:75
internal friction and s. — ROTH 699:29
madding crowd's ignoble s. — GRAY 369:20
may be but sturt or s. — DUNB 294:1
none was worth my s. — LAND 488:83
no s. can grow up there — MILT 581:15
no talebearer, the s. ceaseth — BIBLE 100:55
on the verge of s. — CORN 237:68
pleasures with rough s. — MARV 556:65
put an end To s. — BYRON 181:70
root of s.? — SURR 829:38
some to public s. — POPE 661:49
S. discorde and waistis wanis — ANON 20:5
the stern s. — SCOTT 723:3
The s. is o'er — POTT 663:17
With phantoms an unprofitable s. — SHEL 786:3
strike afraid to s. — POPE 661:38
By and by it will s. — SHAK 774:86
General S. has taught the working classes — BALF 54:55
If you s. a child — SHAW 778:11
I s. out three of them — BOIL 138:37
no right to s. — COOL 236:45
organise a formidable s. — HICKS 402:81
s. and sink and split — SHAW 781:76
s. it out — JOHN 444:98
s. sooner than speak — SHAK 741:6
s. with our spirit's knife — SHEL 786:3
that loves me s. me dead — SHAK 765:48
while the s. is hot — ANON 24:47
strikers longstaff sixpenny s. — SHAK 741:6
s. couldn't score in a brothel — DOCH 277:1
strikes narrow circle of s. — ENGE 314:67
string chewing little bits of s. — BELL 72:53
dullis on the s. — HENR 396:52
end of the golden s. — BLAKE 135:74
held together with s. — ACHE 3:44
Our eyes, upon one double s. — DONNE 280:58

individual s. — HORS 414:38
I never s. myself to hours — RABE 676:72
interested…not in its s. — SANT 714:24
introduce the s. of eating — HUNT 423:37
know a s. ourselves — JOHN 449:9
look like the s. — DALI 251:70
Math was my worst s. — TRIL 865:65
no s. of England — PITT 653:42
no such thing…as an uninteresting s. — CHES 211:49
see how the s. quakes! — SHAK 763:88
serious s. — ARNO 33:37
Spare…for his s.'s sake — COWP 241:59
Stick to your s. — CATO 200:99
s….concept, structure — POUS 666:75
s. full of natural error — PASC 640:13
s. is to the painter — RIVE 688:2
s. matter of the artist — WILDE 908:2
s. that should never — THOM 857:66
s. to the judgement — SCHI 718:4
s….to this vice of lying! — SHAK 743:57
theory of the s. is complete — MILL 570:58
this s. for heroic song — MILT 584:6
woman…a s. in marriage — STAN 812:67
worst mistakes…in his s. — HEIS 391:57
subjection As to woman's s. — STAN 812:66
attract Thy love, not thy s. — MILT 585:22
subjective begin from the s. — SART 715:48
subjectivity universe of human s. — SART 715:53
subject-matter nobility of s.-m. — WILDE 908:87
subjects best s. for artists — HEIN 391:53
ignorant, only on different s. — ROGE 694:15
model the minds of his s. — STEU 819:9
pray To several s. — SHAK 758:30
prosperous and happy s. — MORE 597:63
sojourners and passing s. — MUIR 602:59
S. choose me — MOORE 595:41
s. for a pair of…saints — SHAK 735:22
Talk about those s. — HOLM 408:87
tyrant has in common with his s. — BROD 153:52
Unmarried men…not always best s. — BACON 48:89
were their s. wise — COWP 241:77
sublimation s. of the work instinct — LODGE 514:26
sublime dandy must aspire to be s. — BAUD 65:78
Howls the s. — DICK 268:48
object all s. — GILB 355:27
science of the s. — CIXO 219:40
short from the S. — GRAH 365:33
step above the s. — PAINE 634:99
s. position, but not a secure one — BERN 80:31
s., there yet lurks — MELV 564:32
'the s.' In the old sense — POUND 664:35
torture into aught of the s. — POE 656:16
submerged s. beneath the surface — GERH 350:35
submission coy s., modest pride — MILT 583:63
have an appetite for s. — ELIOT 303:2
starving them into s. — MANC 544:41
submissive Remember to be s. — AESC 8:63
subordinate all other ends are s. — PIUS 653:55
subsequence s. for consequence — JOHN 441:8
subsidy government s. — ANON 25:57
public s. of intelligence — QUINE 675:52
subsist enable the labourers…to s. — RICA 685:36
subsistence not any s. without a mind — BERK 79:5
S….increases in arithmetical ratio — MALT 543:15
unlimited Means of S. — CANT 188:18
withdraw your means of s. — STEV 824:40
substance body and s. of his works — COLE 227:26
change of s. — MANN 545:65
Charisma without s. — CAMP 185:50
decision-making, not s. — KISS 475:97
Each s. of a grief — SHAK 734:10
empty of all human s. — SAINT 709:20
is the s. of men — SWIN 833:44
man of s. — ELLI 311:88
merchauntis full of s. — DUNB 294:5
My s. was not hid from thee — BIBLE 98:2
one s. with the Father — BOOK 141:95
one that sucks his s. — LAMB 486:49
renews and varies its s. — OVID 631:47
set her foot upon thy s. — BIBLE 107:45
s. consisting in infinite attributes — SPIN 811:36
s. of my dreams — SASS 716:65
suck out the very s. — RABE 676:66
summed with all his s. — CHAP 206:14
wasted his s. with riotous living — BIBLE 116:46
worth, not s. — MILT 581:11
substances Even forms and s. — WORD 925:2

substitute adequate s. for wit — PRIE 668:27
applied to some God s. — RUNC 702:72
bloodless s. for life — STEV 822:96
excellent and nutritious s. — DOUG 283:23
in creating a s. — PAGE 633:78
most flawless proof…is no s. — EDDI 298:85
no s. for talent — HUXL 425:67
no s. for victory — MACA 524:25
offer abuse as a s. — GALL 344:15
Shouting is not a s. — STEV 820:57
s. for a real experience — ALBEE 9:88
s. shines brightly as a king — SHAK 741:90
test is a mere s. — MUSS 605:18
substructure economic s. — FANON 317:43
subterfuge s. for hiding something — CALAS 184:33
subtle almost invariably s. — STRA 826:85
God is s. — EINS 301:31
know not well the s. ways — EMER 313:39
schoolman's s. art — POPE 661:42
serpent was more s. — BIBLE 86:48
s., but savage — CAPO 189:29
subtlest s. and most poetic — FOWL 332:71
subtleties I do not deal with s. — BIRK 131:68
s., not made to rule — MILT 586:46
subtlety brother came with s. — BIBLE 87:87
s. of nature — BACON 47:58
subtraction that's s. — WEST 901:32
suburban mowers on s. lawns — RICK 686:74
s. prejudice of anti-Semitism — POUND 665:65
suburbs Chekhov of the s. — LEON 503:3
Dwell I but in the s. — SHAK 747:85
subversion do not like s. or disloyalty — HELL 392:74
subversive funny is s. — ORWE 628:65
seen by dictators as s. — JONG 448:96
subway perspective of a s. tunnel — TOOLE 863:12
succedaneum Science…a s. — WORD 925:95
succeed all right if the talks s. — ZHOU 936:98
If at first you don't s. — HICK 402:83
not enough to s. — VIDAL 881:97
s. as his inheritor — SHAK 769:54
s. unconventionally — KEYN 466:92
succeeded only thing we haven't s. in — HUXL 425:81
succeeding just when they were s. — REST 683:16
success any chance of s. — KISS 475:93
argue…after…your technical s. — OPPE 626:13
Eighty percent of s. — ALLEN 12:57
For an actress to be a s. — BARR 61:94
gained for the universe by s. — JAMES 434:67
harness of their s. — HAMM 379:8
hope of s. — SMITH 801:24
howling commercial s. — GREE 371:70
If A is s. in life — EINS 301:45
it deifies us. — TWAIN 872:28
May all s. — GILB 354:18
no s. without hard work — SOPH 804:87
not in mortals to command s. — ADDI 6:31
not solved by s. — WHITE 903:93
owed his lack of s. to nobody — HELL 392:58
religion…is S. — BARR 61:88
S. and failure are both difficult — HELL 392:64
s. and miscarriage — JOHN 442:40
s. comes before work — KIMB 467:21
s. four flights — WRIG 930:85
s. happens to an English writer — AMIS 15:2
S. hath made me — JONS 448:19
s. hide its emptiness — HAMM 379:11
S. in Circuit lies — DICK 273:71
S., instead of — MILL 572:7
s. in war — CHUR 216:79
S. is a great deodorant — TAYL 837:18
S. is counted sweetest — DICK 272:51
s. is disgraceful — MENC 565:64
S. is feminine — FAUL 319:73
S. is in the silences — CARM 193:47
s. isn't everything — HELL 392:76
S. is relative — ELIOT 307:7
S. is the American Dream — LEGU 501:60
S. never depended on pandering — BEAV 67:28
The play was a great s. — WILDE 909:20
triumphant with far-ranging s. — COMM 229:65
true s. is to labour — STEV 822:95
vanquished by his own s. — SCHI 718:7
With his surcease s. — SHAK 767:86
successes important…as his s. — AGAS 8:65
pleasure at his own s. — RYLE 702:80
successful He who is s. is good — ECO 298:77
Horrible as s. artists — JONG 448:1

no matter how s. — JOHN 440:89
or s. without love — TROL 867:9
S. crimes alone are justified — DRYD 290:6
s. in business — GILL 356:49
s. person is a sinner — ECO 298:77
The more s. the villain — HITC 404:15
To be a s. father — HEMI 395:29
too lucky or too s. — JONG 448:4
succession interminable s. — EINS 301:33
s. and Horatio Alger in one — MAMET 544:35
successor science the s. — RUSS 705:46
succinct try hard to be s. — HORA 414:30
succour for s. flee — SPEN 808:67
succumb too…resourceful to s. — HOFS 406:55
suck s. melancholy out of a song — SHAK 749:44
s. out the very substance — RABE 676:66
sucker Never Give a S. — FIEL 323:51
s. born every minute — BARN 60:76
suckers green s. of youth — SHER 788:53
sucklings mouth of babes and s. — BIBLE 94:86
sucks s. us all up — SEXT 728:17
Where the bee s., there suck I — SHAK 775:99
Sudan at your 'ome in the S. — KIPL 471:94
sudden all of a s. it hits me — SIEG 791:24
s., and quick in quarrel — SHAK 749:50
s. with summer — SCOTT 722:78
suede blue s. shoes — PERK 648:46
Suez somewhere east of S. — KIPL 471:88
S. canal…flowing through — EDEN 299:92
suffer Better one s. — DRYD 290:86
better to s. than to die — LAFO 485:1
But doth s. a sea-change — SHAK 774:84
does not the woman always s. — BALZ 57:14
don't have to s. to be a poet — CIAR 218:15
have courage to s. — TROL 866:97
if he makes others s. — SZASZ 834:63
if so be that we s. with him — BIBLE 120:74
leaders who make them s. — SIHA 791:30
Life…makes us s. — ANOU 26:91
make them s. before I pack…in — CHAR 207:46
prepared to s. for it — BENN 76:43
s. for the Good — KIER 467:17
s. from the strangest sense — WELLS 898:74
S. her self — WALL 886:13
s. hym…to wynne his spurres — EDWA 300:16
s. in one's whole self — LAWR 494:92
S. me to thee — WESL 900:12
s. through no fault of their own — ELIZ 310:66
s. what is difficult to us — HIRO 403:4
voice of those who s. — CESA 203:49
sufferance s. is the badge — SHAK 739:53
suffered greatly, have s. greatly — TENN 839:63
He who has s. much — ANON 18:78
s. at my side — SASS 716:66
s. in his spirit — HOMER 409:24
s….the neurotic ills — ISHE 430:90
women s. in the…United States — FRIE 337:59
sufferers We have been the s. — BEVAN 84:15
suffering About s….never wrong — AUDEN 40:90
by s. even animals could — HEINE 391:48
Deep, unspeakable s. — ELIOT 303:81
Doing or s. — MILT 580:3
Give us back our s. — NIGH 616:31
good time for s. — GOLD 360:31
learn in s. — SHEL 783:27
likely to lead to s. — BERL 80:23
loved the s. many — BENT 77:71
s., and some risks — PEARY 645:1
s. from galloping consumption — GAND 345:33
s. from the particular disease — JERO 437:31
s., the agony, the tender words — WHIT 904:31
tell of their s. — ACHE 2:19
the day you stop s. — WILL 913:32
To each his s. — GRAY 368:95
victim of creative s. — KING 468:38
You can't avoid s. — COOP 236:56
suffers every observer necessarily s. — ORWE 629:93
one who does, not s. wrong — SHEL 784:70
suffice ice…would s. — FROST 338:97
sufficiency An elegant s. — THOM 856:54
s. is of God — BIBLE 122:22
sufficient S. to have stood — MILT 582:41
Suffolk S. used to worship Sunday — BLYT 138:25
suffrage English are used to s. — CARL 193:29
Universal s. is counter-revolution — PROU 670:67
universal s. prevails — PARE 636:36
suffragists militant s. — WRIG 929:72

sugar against a pound of s. — SPEN 807:62
  honey a sauce to s. — SHAK 750:67
  more eloquence in a s. touch — SHAK 746:68
suggestion s., by the imagination — RUSK 703:9
suggestions absorb whispered s. — KOES 477:31
suicide depression, neurosis and s. — HELL 392:64
  except the s. — HEMI 394:6
  excessive tolerance of s. — DURK 296:32
  girls who have considered s. — SHAN 776:27
  human race commit s. — ADAMS 4:74
  not even s. — STEV 822:88
  s. 25 years after his death — BEAV 67:23
  s. is a great source — NIET 615:21
  s. is not a very intelligent — KENT 464:58
  s. kills two people — MILL 572:4
  s. notes — PLOUT 656:10
  S.: that mysterious route — HUGO 421:96
  Twenty Volume S. Note — BARA 59:43
  upright, or to commit s. — MISH 587:83
  war…it is s. — MACD 530:60
  who have considered s. — WEBB 893:64
suicides s. have a special language — SEXT 728:15
suit A silk s. — PEPYS 647:27
  fresh s. of bright white linen — HERB 399:24
  man in a large check s. — WELLS 898:83
  thousand dollar s. — ANON 25:64
suitcases s. are much better — SALI 711:56
suitor think that you are Ann's s. — SHAW 778:88
suits customary s. of solemn — TWAIN 871:7
  middle-aged men in dark s. — ABBO 1:1
  s. of woe — SHAK 751:4
  wear strange s. — SHAK 750:75
sulky s. Scottish spirit — SCOTT 725:53
sullen cope him in these s. fits — SHAK 749:36
  genius was too s. — DRYD 288:29
  I knew that s. hall — OWEN 632:59
  s. cold Exhausted face? — SASS 716:67
Sullivan Gilbert to someone else's S. — RUSS 706:65
sulphur oat-cakes and s. — SMITH 801:14
  Puffed its s. — BETJ 83:91
Sultan S.'s turret — FITZ 324:82
sultans Both S. of Swat — LARD 490:18
sultry where the climate's s. — BYRON 181:65
sum final s. never balances — MO 589:22
  proportion to the s. involved — PARK 639:85
  rolling up the s. — WILL 913:47
  s. and substance, of capitalist — MARX 558:11
  s. of all the choices gone before? — DIDI 274:5
  s. of the interests of…members — BENT 77:64
  the s. of all matter is constant — OVID 631:47
  worked out the s. for themselves — KIER 467:8
Sumatra giant rat of S. — DOYLE 286:82
summer after many a s. — TENN 846:25
  all s. settled there and died — LARK 490:23
  All through that s. — MUIR 602:55
  chords of s. — DAY 257:84
  dark s. dawns — TENN 842:8
  dead long s. days — BYRON 182:78
  dream On s. eves — MILT 576:11
  fantastic s.'s heat? — SHAK 734:4
  grace a s. queen — SCOTT 723:10
  guest of s. — SHAK 767:85
  how costly s. was — SHAK 740:65
  if it takes all s. — GRANT 366:55
  In s., quite the other way — STEV 822:11
  It was a s. evening — SOUT 805:98
  last rose of s. — MOORE 596:50
  last s. of its kind — HOLL 407:69
  like a s. birdcage — WEBS 894:78
  Like s. tempest — TENN 842:12
  live murmur of a s.'s day — ARNO 32:16
  love in s.'s wonderland — NOYES 619:77
  Made glorious s. — SHAK 731:98
  mosquitoey s. night light — ASHB 35:86
  no s. progress — ANDR 16:27
  oldest griefs of s. — RICK 686:74
  one swallow does not make a s. — ARIS 29:51
  reasonable s. weather — WAUGH 891:7
  same winter and s. — SHAK 740:68
  silent s. heaven — TENN 848:60
  Singest of s. — KEATS 459:57
  studying all the s. night — MARV 556:68
  sudden with s. — SCOTT 722:78
  S. afternoon—s. afternoon — JAMES 434:54
  s. all the year round — ORWE 628:53
  s. droops, droop men — NASHE 609:16
  S. in Winter — CRAS 244:34

s. is ended — BIBLE 105:73
  s. is eternal — GUY 375:50
  S. is icumen in — ANON 19:83
  s. loves to sport — COLL 228:48
  s. out of winter — DONNE 281:88
  s. sang in me — MILL 571:87
  s. soldier and the sunshine patriot — PAINE 634:88
  s. winds that creep — SHEL 782:19
  S.…with its usual severity — COLE 227:20
  sunlight of your s. day — ARLO 30:62
  thou, O S. — BLAKE 133:24
  thro endless s. days — DICK 272:57
  through the s. is not heard — SHEL 782:21
  through the s. suns — RICE 685:39
  waken from his s. dreams — SHEL 783:45
  way to ensure s. in England — WALP 887:29
  winter's big with s. — SACK 708:87
summer-dried s.-d. fountain — SCOTT 723:7
summer-fruits Beauty is as s.-f. — BACON 49:42
summer-gale sun and s.-g. — GRAY 370:37
summer-house S.-h…no shade — POPE 659:95
summers ninety s. had Death — EGAN 301:24
  raw inclement s. — SWIFT 831:81
  So many s. dry — SHAK 770:98
  thousand s. are over — SWIN 832:15
summertime In s. in Bredon — HOUS 415:51
summit ascend to its s. — PAVL 644:79
  at the s. of the world — PEARY 645:2
  made to rest on its s. — NAPO 607:71
  somebody thought of the s. meetings — ACHE 2:22
  s. of these pyramids — NAPO 607:58
summits Nations touch at their s. — BAGE 51:88
  snowy s. old — TENN 841:3
summons s. thee to heaven — SHAK 767:96
  Upon a fearful s. — SHAK 751:97
  when fate s., monarchs must obey — DRYD 288:47
sums size of s. of money — HUXL 426:3
sun After the greatest clouds, the s. — ALAN 9:83
  against a setting s. — SHAK 762:44
  Aldershot s. — BETJ 83:87
  all the s. that shines? — SHAK 774:68
  And I will sing of the s. — POUND 664:23
  And the s. went down — TENN 848:62
  apples of the s. — YEATS 932:36
  as the s. at noon — DONNE 281:88
  beauty of the s. — SHAK 729:26
  before you let the s. in — THOM 853:88
  beneath the s. — KIPL 473:58
  between me and the s. — BLUN 137:15
  black cloud carries the s. away — ELIOT 307:98
  blessed s. himself — SHAK 741:94
  Born of the s. — SPEN 807:47
  bosom-friend of the maturing s. — KEATS 459:48
  Bright as the s., her eyes — POPE 658:67
  broad s. Is sinking down — WORD 926:13
  Busy old fool, unruly s. — DONNE 279:41
  cannot make our s. — MARV 556:65
  chambers of the s. — BLAKE 133:21
  Close to the s. — TENN 844:68
  cock who thought the s. had risen — ELIOT 303:80
  Copper s. or scarlet sea — CULL 247:92
  countenance was as the s. — BIBLE 125:45
  Cricket…worship in the summer s. — BLUN 137:19
  dawn upon them like the s. — RAND 678:14
  description of the rising s. — SHER 788:65
  Doubt that the s. doth move — SHAK 752:45
  earth is still going round the s. — ORWE 629:83
  Education is another s. — HERA 396:69
  enjoyed the s. — ARNO 31:96
  eyes are nothing like the s. — SHAK 773:51
  flakes burn in the sinking s. — SHEL 782:18
  flush of a new-born s. — KIPL 471:3
  from the searching s. — RALE 677:1
  glory flames from s. and star — HOLM 408:97
  going down of the s. — BINY 130:52
  Go out in the midday s. — COWA 239:13
  heat of the s. — WHITE 903:83
  heavens' glorious s. — SHAK 733:68
  he beheld the s. — WORD 928:52
  in s. and shower — WORD 924:79
  in the s., in Regent's Park — WOOLF 922:31
  IT'S THE S.WOT WON IT — SUN 828:23
  ivory s. — PIER 651:7
  kiss of the s. — GURN 375:42
  labour which he taketh under the s.? — BIBLE 100:65
  land stares at the s. — SCOTT 722:78

Laughed in the s. — BROO 155:2
  like a raisin in the s.? — HUGH 418:20
  little window where the s. — HOOD 410:37
  live by an invisible s. — BROW 159:93
  London spread out in the s. — LARK 491:36
  love that moves the s. — DANTE 252:99
  love to all men 'neath the s.! — KIPL 473:63
  maketh his s. to rise — BIBLE 109:94
  meet the s. upon the upland lawn — GRAY 369:24
  mix…the s. with punctuation — BRAU 150:1
  Move him into the s. — OWEN 632:62
  neither shall the s. light on them — BIBLE 126:60
  Never did s. more beautifully steep — WORD 926:19
  no homage unto the s. — BROW 159:83
  no new thing under the s. — BIBLE 100:67
  No s.—no moon! — HOOD 410:51
  not a place in the s. — DULL 294:91
  observations of the s. — STUA 827:97
  on which the s. never sets — NORTH 618:66
  our own place in the s. — BULOW 166:56
  our place in the s. — WILH 911:92
  Our s. is one of 100 billion — BRAUN 150:98
  over the fjord—the s. — MUNCH 603:80
  pleasures Known under the s. — REID 682:96
  proudest country under the s. — PARK 638:83
  Quick-glancing to the s. — GRAY 369:6
  quietest places Under the s. — HOUS 415:62
  Rain, rain, and s.! — TENN 847:39
  rays of the s. — KIPL 473:40
  robbed even the s. — MCMU 537:87
  ruin any pastime under the s. — MITF 588:4
  sea escaping With the s. — RIMB 687:94
  see the s. the other way round? — BISH 131:78
  setting s. — GARL 346:50
  shadow in the s. — ELIZ 309:59
  shadow in the s. — SHAK 731:2
  sitting in the s. — SOUT 805:98
  softe was the s. — LANG 489:93
  stand out of my s. — DIOG 275:21
  stands an instant in the s. — HYDE 427:23
  stipple leaves with s. — SACK 708:89
  s. and moon Were in — MILT 577:35
  s. and summer-gale — GRAY 370:37
  s. and the rain are flying — STEV 823:35
  s. behind the Downs — BETJ 84:4
  s. came dazzling — TENN 839:48
  s. climbs slow — CLOU 222:22
  s. comes up with a word — CURN 249:37
  s. could not be reproduced — CEZA 203:54
  s. delights to peep — SHAK 771:11
  s. doth parch the green — SURR 829:40
  s. farthest off — ANDR 16:27
  s. go down upon your wrath — BIBLE 122:47
  s. has gane down — TANN 836:91
  s. has gone in — SMITH 800:86
  s. has gone to rest — LAUD 492:64
  s. has left the sky — STEV 823:20
  s. hums down — THOM 853:94
  s. is coming down to earth — MERE 567:96
  s. is daily new and old — SHAK 772:32
  s. is going down — SMITH 800:99
  s. is lost — DONNE 281:74
  s. itself is but the dark simulacrum — BROW 159:94
  s. loste his hewe — CHAU 209:89
  s., moon, and stars, brother — BORR 145:3
  S. of righteousness arise — BIBLE 106:22
  s. of suns — DICK 270:92
  s. of the socialist revolution — LENIN 502:84
  s.…on the…Australian bush — LAWS 495:43
  s. poured in like butterscotch — MITC 588:90
  s. provides the moon — ANAX 15:13
  s. Rises upon a world — HUGH 419:44
  s. rose and set on their land — SITT 793:56
  s. rose in your eyes — MACC 528:16
  s. shall not smite thee — BIBLE 97:87
  s. shines bright on Loch Lomond — ANON 20:20
  s. that lights the ages — CASAL 199:68
  s. that warms you — SHAK 734:2
  s. was darkened — BIBLE 116:65
  s. was shining on the sea — CARR 196:99
  s. was up, they were scorched — BIBLE 112:47
  s. went around the earth — ARNO 34:73
  s. will not rise — HOMER 409:25
  sweetheart of the s. — HOOD 410:39
  The kind old s. — OWEN 632:63
  the s.…has gone down — ORAH 627:21
  The s. has left the lea — SCOTT 725:45

the s. loves him SMART 796:26
tired the s. with talking CORY 237:74
too much i' th's. SHAK 751:1
to the rime-ringed s. KIPL 474:78
under the s. and moon GOLD 360:32
unwearied s. from day to day ADDI 6:26
upon the quickening s. DONNE 279:34
upper boulders in the s. FROST 338:84
use of the s. and planets LEAC 496:59
Vermeer gave to the s.'s LOWE 521:62
walks under the midday s. MILT 577:35
wanton with the s. MILT 575:93
watch the s. set again RHYS 684:29
We make guilty...the s. SHAK 762:57
When the s. goes down BOND 139:52
When the s. shall be darkened KORAN 479:93
where'er the s. WATTS 891:4
where no s. shines THOM 852:58
Wherever there is s. BEAU 67:15
While the s....be not darkened BIBLE 101:92
wind up the s. and moon BYRON 183:4
With the dying s. BOUR 147:28
with the s. KEN 461:93
with the s. to match BROW 162:75
woman clothed with the s. BIBLE 126:65
worlds...circle round the s. DICK 269:81
sunbeams extracting s.-b. SWIFT 831:81
fatuous s. toil OWEN 632:64
motes that people the s. MILT 576:12
s. dart through them SHEL 782:18
sunbonnet s. as well as the sombrero FERB 320:93
Sunday feeling of S. RHYS 684:28
first drink on a S. morning MCCU 529:23
first S. in a new chariot CONG 232:45
golf may be played on a S. LEAC 497:67
Here of a S. morning HOUS 415:52
married o' S. SHAK 732:35
rainy S. in London DE 262:6
smelt like S. afternoons THOM 853:2
than a pig on S. TRUM 868:33
worship S., not God BLYT 138:25
sundial I am a s. BELL 73:68
sundials mottoes on s. POUND 664:36
sundown eldritch light of s. DAY 257:85
sodden towards s. ELIOT 308:37
s. makes them mournful BLUN 137:9
sundry s. contemplation SHAK 750:72
sunflower s., weary of time BLAKE 134:53
S., you were a s. GINS 357:63
sung not worth being said is s. BEAU 66:98
s. her first and last GIBB 352:68
s. of Border chivalry SCOTT 722:84
sun-girt S.-g. city, thou hast been SHEL 783:29
sun-gods s.-g. and the like FRYE 340:36
sunlight brooks the s. worse JONS 450:51
fair s. of God MACD 530:54
s. falls across the country IHIM 428:43
S. is the best disinfectant KENN 462:7
s. of your summer day ARLO 30:62
s. on a stream ROSS 697:74
s. streaming merciless ATWO 38:49
superficial as a puddle in the s. LEAC 496:63
upwards into hard s. CUMM 247:1
weave the s. in your hair ELIOT 305:31
will be s. later MACN 538:7
sunny s. pleasure-dome COLE 226:12
s. side of the street FIEL 323:46
sunrise like s. from the sea SHEL 786:20
Lives in Eternity's s. BLAKE 134:48
s. Brings back the brightness BLUN 137:9
suns gleam of a million...s.? TENN 848:73
light of setting s. WORD 923:71
process of the s. TENN 841:83
remember through the summer s. RICE 685:39
road to s. SCOTT 722:77
sky cannot have two s. CHIA 213:5
S. that set may rise JONS 449:21
What other planets circle other s. POPE 660:8
sunset sail beyond the s. TENN 840:66
seen dawn and s. on moors MASE 559:28
shadow that...loses itself in the s. HAGG 376:58
sight of Etna at s. WAUGH 892:31
slow, exquisite coming of s. COOKE 236:42
sulphur to the s. BETJ 83:91
S. and silence! COLUM 229:58
S. divides the sky BYRON 180:33
s. fadeth in the west SHAK 772:30

urine dump at s. SCHW 721:69
sunset-touch there's a s.-t. BROW 161:48
sunshades Sit around under s. JOYCE 452:94
sunshine calm s. of the heart CONS 235:25
Digressions...are the s. STER 817:75
into adventure and s. FORS 331:30
Love comforteth...like s. SHAK 733:56
Scotsman...and a ray of s. WODE 919:67
shadows in a s. day? MARL 552:91
s. patriot will...shrink PAINE 634:88
the thunder and the s. TENN 840:66
sup upon myself SHAK 769:68
s. with him, and he with me BIBLE 126:52
superficiality discussed as s. BURKE 169:57
superfluous s. in me to point out ADAMS 4:64
s. to demand the time SHAK 741:94
The s., a very necessary thing VOLT 882:36
trip to Europe would be s. SAAR 707:81
superflux S. of pain SWIN 833:25
superhuman s. undertaking GIRA 358:79
superincumbent s. hour SHEL 785:99
superior ask a s. to publish HOPK 412:96
Justice is s. PLATO 655:95
lawful power is still s. DRYD 290:98
of the feudal s. MILL 571:79
relieved to find a s. TUCH 869:60
rise s. to all considerations STEV 821:71
s. creation HARD 381:39
s. persons can remain s. ORWE 627:36
s. to all...despotism PITT 653:47
s. to any imaginative exercise VIDAL 880:91
that is sick Of his s. SHAK 757:94
Titles...embarrass the s. SHAW 778:9
superiority laugh of s. GREE 371:75
s. of one man's opinion JAMES 433:45
s. of the Greeks FUSE 342:74
superiors counsels of their s. LEST 505:48
superlatives s....worn shoddy FITZ 325:16
superman between animal and S. NIET 615:12
teach you the S. NIET 615:11
supernatural by s. means HOOK 410:55
cases, was s. MILL 570:72
evidence of s. beings STEI 816:47
s. source of evil CONR 234:15
superpower resources of a s. SHAR 776:37
s. in the military and nuclear sense WALE 885:90
supersensitive s....instrument ERNST 315:90
superstition In all s. wise men BACON 49:15
poison of enthusiasm and s. SMITH 798:53
religion...true remedy for s. BURKE 168:13
s. in avoiding s. BACON 49:16
S. is the poetry of life GOET 360:19
S. is the religion of feeble minds BURKE 169:40
s. of an antiquated diplomacy CECIL 202:33
s. sets the...world in flames VOLT 883:43
superstitions end as s. HUXL 426:11
town whence s. comes LESL 504:30
superstitious edge to the s. tale PRIT 669:46
men of Athens...ye are too s. BIBLE 119:43
must be benighted and s. JAMES 434:74
superstructure dubiousness of...s. DESC 263:23
economic substructure is also a s. FANON 317:43
superwoman I am not s. BLAIR 132:96
supped I have s. full with horrors SHAK 769:41
supper After s. Pap took the jug TWAIN 871:1
Hope...is a bad s. BACON 47:70
know s.'s ready STEI 815:34
supple meets me soft and s. FLET 328:72
suppliant thus the s. prays JOHN 441:18
supplication s. of a dead man's hand ELIOT 306:70
s. to the rose FLEC 327:47
supplications voice of my s. BIBLE 98:95
supply promise of s. SHAK 742:44
see that the s. is not tainted SCOTT 722:74
steady s. of funerals SHAW 781:1
support ask for your s. NIXON 617:44
help and s. of the woman I love EDWA 300:20
mutually s. one another PARS 640:1
no invisible means of s. BUCH 164:29
prepared to s. them LAW 493:84
s. a flagging conversation HUNT 423:37
s. my cat GRAV 367:78
s. rather than illumination LANG 488:89
to have everybody's s. OLLI 624:72
what is low raise and s. MILT 580:93
without nourishment and s. SMOL 801:29
supporter no s. but the...earth SHAK 738:23

supporters pregnant s. BAIL 52:6
suppress easy to...s. the truth CORN 237:72
s. one's vanity JAMES 433:22
suppressed could not be generally s. HOOV 411:61
must be s. DENG 261:96
suppression no...accuracy of s. BELL 73:70
supreme presuppose a S. Being DOUG 284:33
sure Be s. your sin will find you out BIBLE 89:43
grinds slow, but s. HERB 398:22
hateth suretiship is s. BIBLE 99:22
make s. he was dead GOLD 362:91
surety s. for a stranger BIBLE 99:22
surface crawl upon the s. SWIFT 831:79
Errors...upon the s. flow DRYD 289:51
in the lake...under the s. ATWO 38:48
just below the s. RUSS 705:40
mind...looks dingy on the s. PIRS 652:31
monotony of a watery s. MOORE 595:26
painting...is essentially a flat s. DENIS 262:97
s. of articulate apprehension GERH 350:35
thrown On the smooth s. WORD 929:65
surfaces painterly s. POPO 662:86
representation of s. and solids PIERO 651:11
surfeit s. of the sweetest things SHAK 737:99
s. with too much SHAK 739:42
surge s....In every Russian's...heart! PUSH 673:20
surgeon abilities of a brain's. BRES 151:15
Hand of the s. MAP 548:18
intimacy of a s.'s scalpel ANGE 17:46
Picasso studies...like a s. dissects APOL 27:14
plastic s....responsible for this face CUOMO 248:28
poor s. hurts one person at a time BOYER 148:48
way a s. operates WHITE 903:86
wounded s. plies the steel ELIOT 308:21
surgeons S. must be very careful DICK 272:51
surgical s. war ASHD 35:91
surpassed pleasure of not being s. HALI 378:82
surplus-value production of s.-v. MARX 558:11
surprise perchance, with strange s. THOM 855:40
Sound of S. BALL 57:3
sure of a big s. BRAT 150:34
s. them out of KIPL 473:48
Truth's superb s. DICK 273:71
surprised Don't be s. HEAN 389:10
s. by joy WORD 928:49
s. they had remembered PRIT 669:48
s. to find it done at all JOHN 443:3
surprises S. are foolish things AUST 43:85
surrealism I am s. DALI 251:74
surrealists Dalí's...for the S. SCHW 721:60
surrender daring of a moment's s. ELIOT 306:67
Guards...do not s. CAMB 185:47
never s. CHUR 216:76
path of s. KENN 462:21
see the s. of Quebec MONT 592:86
shall never s. CHUR 216:76
s....was as honorable as resistance ANGE 17:34
unconditional and immediate s. GRANT 366:54
worst thing...is s. ORWE 629:90
surrendered never s. before NORM 618:63
Surrey full S. twilight! BETJ 83:88
surroundings see only my s. ELLI 311:88
surveillance keep me under s. WANG 888:55
survey exact s. of the land DONNE 282:94
S. mankind JOHN 441:50
s. of all the world SHAK 742:34
survival insures the s. of the fittest CARN 193:49
necessary for s. of the fittest PALEY 635:11
struggle for s. ROTH 699:21
s. had depended on...reading ANGE 17:47
s. of the fittest SPEN 806:41
s. of the fittest SUMN 828:39
s. of the vulgarest WILDE 908:97
We are s. machines DAWK 256:72
survive Can capitalism s.? SCHU 721:55
continue to s. TRUM 868:34
fitted to s. GOLD 360:30
s. with that equipment DAVIS 255:55
those will s. whose functions SPEN 806:40
To eat, to s. STAN 813:69
survived Peanut butter has s. KEIL 460:70
they who s. fought and drank DAVIS 255:66
survivor lone s. ANON 25:60
survivors are relentless s. BUCK 165:39
more the s.'affair MANN 546:75
nuclear war s. COUP 238:96
struggle won by s. ANGE 17:35

suspect no matter how s.	VIDAL 880:91
nothing makes a man s.	BACON 49:35
suspects Round up the usual s.	EPST 314:81
suspend s. my audience's power	HARD 381:43
s. the functioning of the imagination	HEMI 394:16
suspended Illinois...s. animation	OHARA 623:50
s. in me	ATWO 38:57
s. my religious inquiries	GIBB 352:61
suspenders must not forget the S.	KIPL 472:34
suspense more s., more dramatic torque	LANE 488:87
suspension willing s. of disbelief	COLE 226:17
suspicion banish squint s.	MILT 577:36
Caesar's wife must be above s.	CAES 184:26
Democracy is the recurrent s.	WHITE 903:79
have a s. it's inevitable	LEAC 497:73
rich with s.	RICH 685:43
s. that electricity	THUR 859:23
true loves without s.	SPEN 809:92
suspicions s. amongst thoughts	BACON 49:34
suspicious more s. of adjectives	SAND 713:8
Sussex bury my body in S. grass	BENET 75:12
S. by the sea!	KIPL 473:53
S. countryside	GRANT 366:50
sustenance S. for their helpless	SWIFT 831:92
sutlers sapient s. of the Lord	ELIOT 305:36
swaddled S. with darkness	ELIOT 305:40
swaddling-clothes him in s. c.	BIBLE 115:25
swagman once was a s. camped	PATE 642:54
swain Be just, my lovely s.	BEHN 71:14
labouring s.	GOLD 361:50
no better than a homely s.	SHAK 730:75
with my dear s.	BALL 55:70
swains all our s. commend her?	SHAK 729:39
Muses sing of happy s.	CRAB 242:86
swallow Daffodils...before the s.	SHAK 770:86
flies with s.' wings	SHAK 731:14
one s. does not make a summer	ARIS 29:51
O sister s.	SWIN 832:15
O tell her, S.	TENN 842:10
O tell her, S.	TENN 842:9
s. a nest for herself	BIBLE 96:45
s. twitt'ring	GRAY 369:12
s. up death in victory	BIBLE 103:24
swallowed or be s.	TRUM 869:44
swallow-flights Short s.-f. of song	TENN 843:38
swallows passage of s.	WHITE 903:83
swam think you have s. in a gondola	SHAK 750:75
swamps bellowing across the...s.	WODE 919:58
swan dies the s.	TENN 846:25
every goose a s.	KING 469:53
full-breasted s.	TENN 847:53
great pool a s.'s nest	SHAK 774:68
like a sleeping s.	SHEL 785:80
silver s.	GIBB 352:68
s. on...St Mary's Lake	WORD 927:30
Sweet S. of Avon!	JONS 449:46
wild s. of a world	JEFF 436:10
swan-bosomed s.-b. tree	SITW 794:72
Swanee down upon the S. River	FOST 332:60
swanlike he makes a s. end	SHAK 740:69
swans Chuzzlewit suggested 'S.'	DICK 268:33
old ships sail like s.	FLEC 327:53
s. are geese	ARNO 33:51
take their geese for s.	BROO 157:32
swarm S. over, Death!	BETJ 83:83
swarming s. in Fords, in ocean liners	FERB 320:94
swastika Not God but a s.	PLATH 654:69
sway How fit he is to s.	MARV 555:56
s. of death	WORD 929:63
swaying S. to and fro	HUGH 418:18
swear conscience...to s. by	STOWE 826:73
gentleman is disposed to s.	SHAK 773:58
man s. he loves me	SHAK 744:88
O s. not by the moon	SHAK 736:51
sin to s. unto a sin	SHAK 730:68
S. me, Kate	SHAK 742:21
S. not	BIBLE 125:18
s. to the Lord	HUGH 418:19
swearing cussin' and s.	STRA 826:82
take me up for s.	SHAK 773:57
swears Hardly ever s. a big, big D—	GILB 353:92
sweat In the rank s.	SHAK 754:10
In the s. of thy face	BIBLE 86:56
Luck is a dividend of s.	KROC 481:18
miners s. their guts out	ORWE 627:36
none will s. but for promotion	SHAK 749:40
perfection's s.	WALC 885:81

s. and blood and tears	
s. of my brow	FRAN 335:22
s. of one's brow	LIVI 512:83
s. pours down me	SAPP 714:27
wet through with s.	GREE 370:51
wet with honest s.	GREE 370:51
sweating s. it out again	WILDE 910:57
sweats the bloody s.	LESL 504:30
Sweden bold King of S.	WHAR 902:54
Swedish sung by S. artists	DESC 263:23
sweep need of making a clean s.	SHAK 768:12
s. him from my sight	HERA 397:71
sweeping heap of random s.	HERB 397:93
sweeps Who s. a room	JONS 449:25
sweet All is not s.	SHEL 785:89
buried in so s. a place	SHAK 740:65
day...never came so s.	THOM 854:14
dead thing that smells s.	ANOU 26:96
Death is s.	SHAK 771:14
For thy s. love remembered	KEATS 459:52
Heard melodies are s.	BROW 162:77
how it was s.!	SHAK 735:31
How sour s. music is	WALL 886:12
how s. and fair	BIBLE 97:83
How s. are thy words	HEBER 390:33
How s. the lily grows	SHAK 740:85
How s. the moonlight	SWIN 834:49
if s., give thanks	BIBLE 126:64
in my mouth s. as honey	SHAK 757:99
make a s. lady sad	LAFO 485:6
mixture of the s. and the sour	TENN 845:92
my own, my s.	BURT 174:68
Naught so s. as melancholy	SHAK 735:29
not so short as s.	SHAK 755:45
not so s. now	SPEN 809:92
shady leaves, their s. above	BRID 152:25
So s., love seemed	SHEL 783:45
So s., the sense faints	BIBLE 99:19
Stolen waters are s.	TENN 841:2
S. and low	HORA 413:23
s. and seemly thing	TENN 842:8
s. as those	SIDN 790:11
s. enemy, France	LYLY 523:9
s. full of bitterness	DRYD 291:35
S. is pleasure after pain	BYRON 181:69
S. is revenge	SHAK 775:13
s. music is such art	SHAK 775:15
s. music is such art	SHAK 771:20
s. odour...doth in it live	TRAV 865:47
s. or sour	STEV 820:44
s. pea, that has run wild	CORY 237:76
s., s. is this human life	SHEL 783:47
S. though in sadness	LOVE 519:13
Tell me not, S.	SHEL 782:16
That s. bondage	BYRON 181:70
'Tis s. to win	SHAK 736:48
would smell as s.	SAPP 714:28
sweet-apple Just as the s.-a. reddens	FIEL 322:35
sweeteners best s. of tea	SHEL 785:86
sweetest s. flower for scent	SIDN 790:6
s. music to a woeful mind	KIPL 471:7
s. way to me	HOOD 410:39
sweetheart Like the s. of the sun	WINC 917:21
s. ran away with an actor	DRYD 292:48
sweetmeats pyramids of s.	BELL 72:41
sweetness cannot write of s.	ASHB 35:86
long s. of the simultaneity	WEBS 895:8
Love...is s.	ROCH 691:67
no danger in s. and youth	BIBLE 90:71
out of the strong came forth s.	ARNO 34:60
passion for s. and light	ARNO 33:54
s. and light	SWIFT 830:53
s. and light	MACL 535:45
s. fell from the air	CASW 199:80
s. fills the breast	LYLY 523:11
s. never breedeth satiety	FIRB 323:65
s. of confession	GRAY 369:17
waste its s. on the desert air	FORS 331:45
where s. and light failed	HERB 397:92
sweets brought'st Thy s. along	CRIT 245:62
only safe pleasure...boiled s.	BARL 60:58
sing the s. I know	HUNT 423:29
Stolen s. are always sweeter	CIBB 218:18
Stolen s. are best	HUNT 423:35
S. into your list	WORD 927:30
s. of Burn-mill	CONG 231:32
s. of life	

S. with s. war not	DOUG 283:13
world of s. and sours	POE 656:23
swell And go to ev'ry s. affair	PORT 663:8
bones on the thrashed s.	LOWE 520:43
burnish, sprout, and s.	HERB 398:7
music...with its voluptuous s.	BYRON 179:23
peruked sea whose s.	SITW 793:59
unhurried Ground s.	ELIOT 308:29
Where the green s. is	HOPK 412:78
with its mighty s.	KEATS 457:86
swelling s. into bombast	DRYD 288:25
swerve s. neither to the right	CURZ 249:53
swerving most unnoble s.	SHAK 765:35
Swift S. is more Irish than Goldsmith	OBRI 620:98
swift race is not to the s.	BIBLE 101:85
race is to the s.	DAVI 254:24
S. was the race	DRYD 290:94
True hope is s.	SHAK 731:14
With s., slow	HOPK 412:86
swifter S., higher, stronger	ANON 22:43
Swiftian S. Lilliput	MCCA 528:2
swim good night, or sink or s.	SHAK 741:3
s. to the Bermudas	WEBS 895:6
swimmer excellence as a s.	BURKE 169:57
Like an unpractised s.	SHAK 733:65
Swinburne S....degenerates!	ONEI 625:99
S. is just emptiness to me	QUIL 674:48
swindler as if I were a s.	LAWR 494:18
swindles as all truly great s. are	OHEN 623:53
swine husks that the s. did eat	BIBLE 116:47
incompetent s.	SASS 716:63
men kill the fat s.	ANON 19:80
nation ruled by s.	THOM 855:45
on a filthy s.	SPEN 808:76
pearls before s.	BIBLE 110:6
s. to show you	ALBEE 10:92
swine-drunk for he will be s.-d.	SHAK 762:37
swines blasted, jelly-boned s.	LAWR 493:88
swing if it ain't got that s.	ELLI 310:75
if it ain't got that s.	MILLS 574:71
swinger s. of birches	FROST 338:92
swinging keep s. after the music	HELP 393:89
swings we pulls up on the s.!	CHAL 203:55
swiped s. all the good ones	HEMI 393:96
Swiss operated by the S.	USTI 875:8
S. are inspired hotel-keepers	MONT 592:70
S. clockmakers	STRA 826:91
switch We turned the s.	SZIL 834:66
Switzerland look upon S.	SMITH 801:8
S....had brotherly love	WELL 897:48
S. is a small, steep country	HEMI 393:92
swivel crouch, s., tug	OBRI 621:10
swollen udder a s. wobble	RAINE 677:93
when rivers are s.	SOPH 804:85
swoop take away all at one s.	WEBS 894:73
sword altar, s. and pen	WORD 925:11
Arthur's s. snatched	MUNRO 603:84
brave man with a s.	WILDE 910:54
came not to send peace, but a s.	BIBLE 111:29
carry fire and s.	PARN 639:92
caution of a s.	CLEV 221:85
China asked for a s.	BRID 152:28
could use the s. and pen	LAND 488:84
duty...to wield the s. of France	DE 259:36
fallen by the edge of the s.	BIBLE 108:58
father's s. he has girded	MOORE 596:49
flaming s.	BIBLE 86:57
gave them a s.	NIXON 617:50
Hold then my s.	SHAK 748:23
is that your s., or	WEST 901:33
It is at once our s.	HUGH 420:58
let him who has a s.	HO 405:37
lightnings Thy s.	ELLE 310:71
man taketh his s.	BIBLE 107:25
may gyff you that s.	MALO 542:5
My S., I give to him	BUNY 167:77
Negro's s.	PHIL 650:95
never sheath the s.	ASQU 36:9
Norman arrow and s.	WILL 911:2
Nor shall my s. sleep	BLAKE 136:85
oil can is mightier than the s.	DIRK 275:25
oyster...with s. will open	SHAK 743:70
peasants take up the s.	LUTH 523:96
pen is mightier than the s.	BULW 166:58
pen is worse than the s.	BURT 174:72
Plough...twin to the s.	COLUM 229:58
pulleth oute this s.	MALO 542:3

sharper than any two-edged s. | BIBLE 124:90
soldiers of the s. | RUSK 704:18
s. against s. | SHAK 765:39
s. has won in half a year | MOLT 590:47
s. of the Lord | BIBLE 90:69
s. of the Spirit | BIBLE 122:52
s. shall perish with the s. | BIBLE 114:1
threw the s. as farre | MALO 543:11
Turning the word to s. | SHAK 743:59
two-edged s. | WIEN 907:62
two-edged s. in their hand | BIBLE 98:7
watery if not flaming s. | MARV 556:80
We draw the s. | WILH 911:94
Wounds inflicted by the s. | RICH 686:69
sword-belt s.-b. upside down | LAWR 494:5
sword-pen raise my s.-p. | BURG 167:81
swords beat their s. into plowshares | BIBLE 102:8
Beat your plowshares into s. | BIBLE 106:6
so we measured s. | SHAK 750:90
stout hearts and stout s. | BIRK 130:63
s., our law | SHAK 732:21
sworn I am s. brother | SHAK 735:26
s. to action | SASS 716:60
sycophancy between s. and rebellion | BAKER 53:20
sycophants surrounded by s. | HARD 381:39
syllable first s. of…advice | THOR 857:86
last s. of recorded time | SHAK 769:42
syllables number of s. | SAND 713:15
symbiosis s. of architecture | MURP 604:4
symbol education on the s. level | HUXL 426:1
In China the bat is a s. | LAWR 494:96
respect for the living s. | LABO 483:55
see nothing without a visible s. | BAGE 51:84
s. for America | ATWO 38:54
s. of an emerging middle-class | MCFA 531:94
s. of Irish art | JOYCE 452:85
s. of national honor | KRUG 481:26
s. of the power | MOORE 595:37
what it is the s. of | JENK 437:24
symbolism handles s. rather like | NIGH 616:29
symbols cloudy s. of a high romance | KEATS 457:94
let us know…as s. do | MACC 527:84
s. effortlessly shared | UPDI 875:97
symmetry frame thy fearful s.? | BLAKE 135:61
Man is all s. | HERB 398:4
S. is boredom | HUGO 421:88
sympathetic s. unselfishness | SAKI 710:42
sympathies cosmopolitan s. | ROSE 697:68
sympathy a lot of s. with him | KINN 470:71
awakened my maternal s. | PERE 648:56
failed to inspire s. in men | BEER 69:79
God-damned s. | WOOL 923:57
never-failing s. and encouragement | WODE 919:63
no intercourse and no s. | DISR 276:53
s. for the selfish | MUIR 602:66
s. with freedom | GLAD 358:92
tea and s. | ANDE 16:22
To s. with hopes and fears | SHEL 784:58
writer…universal in s. | BARN 60:68
symphonies five swune s. | ROSS 698:90
fugues and s. have brought | SASS 716:66
symphony consort to th'angelic s. | MILT 576:97
orchestrating a s. of unhappiness | ROCK 692:79
philanthropy and s. concerts | WHAR 901:48
s. must be like the world | MAHL 539:31
write a s. like that | DAMR 251:80
write his Ninth S. | ROY 701:57
You're a melody from a s. | PORT 663:6
symptom first s. of true love | HUGO 421:94
infallible s. | GIBB 351:55
s. of a deficient vitality | STEV 822:97
s. of…emotional disturbances | VAN 876:26
symptoms hundred good s. | POPE 662:85
s. are similar | BANKS 58:33
syndrome manifested by…s. | SELYE 727:86
Synge persons…out of S.'s plays | OBRI 621:7
synod general s. of the nation | BAIL 52:6
synonym Violation is a s. | DWOR 296:49
syntax mastery of vocabulary and s. | SAYE 717:86
shackled by the rules of s. | MACA 525:51
S. and vocabulary | MATH 560:58
synthesis Held in a lunar s. | ELIOT 305:29
s. of forty-six years | STEIN 815:30
s. of hyacinths and biscuits | SAND 713:1
synthesizer Joyce was a s. | BECK 68:46
syphilis manage to avoid s. | SILVA 792:34
Syrian On arrival at a S. port | BAED 51:76

syrops lucent s. | KEATS 459:40
syrup pancake…when you pour the s. | WRIG 930:81
system American s. | HOOV 411:59
automatic s. | MUMF 603:78
came the turn of the nervous s. | RAMO 678:5
communications s. | HAYEK 387:60
empirical s. to be refuted | POPP 662:87
every computer in the human s. | GIBS 353:76
false s. of government | PAINE 634:92
got the North Pole out of my s. | PEARY 645:1
greater and more equitable s. | MACA 524:23
Love is just a s. | BARN 60:74
Observe how s. into system runs | POPE 660:8
patent s.…added | LINC 510:36
science has…a s. of principles | PAINE 634:7
self…epicentre of the solar s. | PHIL 650:94
s. is benign | CRISP 245:60
s. of existence…with no eye | WIEN 907:69
s. of soft enterprise | ARNO 34:74
s. of which they were the centre | DICK 268:51
s. that we live in | WILL 913:29
s. which has no purpose | FROMM 338:82
they rocked the s. | ROBI 690:43
tonic to the s. | LIVI 512:83
true s. of the world | ALEM 11:17
virtues of the s. | MCCA 528:3
systems After that, we had s. | HOPP 413:16
are living s. | MONOD 591:55
Atoms or s. into ruin hurled | POPE 660:9
Away with s. | MERE 567:96
number of symbol s. | HUXL 426:1
Our little s. | TENN 842:21

T

ta thousand ta's and Pardon's | BETJ 84:1
tabacco fumes of t. and liquors | LEWIS 508:96
going to leave off t.! | LAMB 486:34
tabby Demurest of the t. kind | GRAY 368:97
tabernacle who shall abide in thy t.? | BIBLE 94:90
tabernacles holy place of the t. | BIBLE 95:25
How amiable are thy t. | BIBLE 96:45
t. of thy grace | SCOT 725:63
Tabitha T.…called Dorcas | BIBLE 119:38
table behave mannerly at t. | STEV 822:12
clouds of the t. above | MONRO 591:58
gets down from the t. | SITW 793:60
In England…good t. manners | MIKES 569:51
Miss Bolo rose from the t. | DICK 266:82
patient etherized upon a t. | ELIOT 304:17
preparest a t. before me | BIBLE 94:2
reside at T. Mountain | HARTE 384:15
sit at the t. | HUGH 418:17
t. in a smoke-filled room | DAUG 253:20
t. in Barchester Towers | BROY 163:99
t. of brotherhood | KING 468:39
this thy T. | BOOK 141:7
Thou shalt prepare a t. | BOOK 143:44
thrown from the t. | TUTU 870:70
tableau t. of crimes and misfortunes | VOLT 883:44
tablecloth Oedipus…over your t. | PAGE 633:77
tables creatures set upon t. | JOHN 444:11
furnish forth the marriage t. | SHAK 751:10
leave the word of God, and serve t. | BIBLE 119:34
My t.—meet it is | SHAK 752:35
sit at rich men's t. | BROW 159:1
sitting at their dressing t. | OSBO 630:11
table-talk Let it serve for t.-t. | SHAK 740:76
taboo t. birth control method | DALY 251:78
Tabor King Lear at the T. Grand | FIELD 322:31
tacit t., but constant and uniform | SMITH 797:43
tacks when you come to brass t. | ELIOT 307:82
tacky defines t. for all time | ANON 25:52
Toady, perhaps, even t. | ACHE 3:48
tact affection and t. | RUSS 705:50
tactful t. in audacity | COCT 224:57
tactics tolerate…only on t. | DULL 294:91
taedium vitae keep off the t. v. | JOHN 443:61
taffeta changeable t. | SHAK 756:56
tail Improve his shining t. | CARR 194:65
Nor knowst'ou wing from t. | POUND 665:61
porpoise…treading on my t. | CARR 195:81
such a little t. | BELL 72:47
t. hangs down behind! | KIPL 471:11
t. in its mouth | FERL 321:14
t. must wag the dog | KIPL 471:4
Their t. the rudder | DRYD 287:20

vanished…end of the t. | CARR 195:70
wags its t. | TOYN 864:27
waving his wild t. | KIPL 473:47
with its t. in its mouth | HOOD 410:41
tailor t. does not attempt | SMITH 798:48
t. make thy doublet | SHAK 756:66
there lived a t. in Gloucester | POTT 664:19
you t.'s yard | SHAK 742:15
tailors carpenters, or t. | SUN 829:33
off the list of living t. | MERE 567:99
tails Brushin'off my t. | BERL 79:14
stings in their t. | BIBLE 126:63
trains will run over their t. | SITW 793:61
We of the long t.! | GRASS 367:60
take see that the supply is not t. | SCOTT 722:74
t. cannot, sir, t. from me anything | SHAK 752:50
can't t. that away | GERS 351:40
can't t. that away | GERS 351:41
Nay, t. my life and all | SHAK 740:84
t. away from our years | CRUZ 246:88
T. her up tenderly | HOOD 410:48
T. him for all in all | SHAK 751:11
t. the bull | GOLD 362:81
T. thou thy pound of flesh | SHAK 740:83
triple ways to t. | KIPL 471:7
taking t. them up one by one | HOMA 408:8
talcum t. is always walcum | NASH 608:77
tale brings in a several t. | SHAK 731:18
could a t. unfold | SHAK 752:28
edge to the superstitious t. | PRIT 669:46
had a t. to tell | SCOTT 722:81
History is a t. of efforts | KISS 475:95
marvelous t. | HAWT 386:51
mere t. of a tub | WEBS 894:81
moral discovery…object of every t. | CONR 234:12
most tremendous t. of all | BETJ 84:99
No t. ever happened | BART 62:17
recalls a t. | AMADO 13:74
sad t.'s best for winter | SHAK 770:79
same t. repeat | WORD 926:23
speak out a plain t. | SCOTT 724:37
t. of arms | VIRG 882:16
t. should be judicious | COWP 240:47
t. Told by an idiot | SHAK 769:42
tedious as a twice-told t. | SHAK 739:26
tell the t. that I heard | HOUS 415:68
thereby hangs a t. | SUCK 828:11
Trust the t. | LAWR 494:14
With a t. forsooth he cometh | SIDN 791:20
talebearer where there is no t. | BIBLE 100:55
talent Brevity is the sister of t. | CHEK 209:8
Children's t. to endure | ANGE 17:32
creative t.…drained off | RICH 686:66
Even an attorney of modest t. | CAPO 189:24
Everybody has t. at twenty-five | DEGAS 259:33
Everyone has t. | JONG 448:99
extraordinary collection of t. | KENN 462:20
extraordinary t. | GOET 360:13
gilded tomb of a mediocre t. | SMITH 800:84
grand t. pour le silence | CARL 193:33
has a t. and cannot use it | WOLFE 920:87
infinite variety of t. | HAZL 387:65
make do with t. | BALC 53:27
must have t. too | KORDA 480:1
no substitute for t. | HUXL 425:67
OK, if you like t. | MERM 567:14
one really notable t. | MENC 565:65
snuffs out ten times more t. | HUGH 418:25
t., a glass, and some cracked ice | BARR 61:98
T. comes from originality | MAUP 561:83
t. for drama | VIDAL 880:86
t. instantly recognises genius | DOYLE 285:78
t. like a uniform | AUDEN 40:94
t. of our English nation | DRYD 290:2
t. to amuse | COWA 239:9
t. which is death to hide | MILT 580:88
T. wins games | JORD 451:68
t. without instruction | VITR 882:34
what every actor…wants: t. | GIEL 353:86
woman's particular t. | HUGO 421:85
wonder how many people of t. | STEV 824:40
writer of t. needs only | WINN 917:27
talents applied his t. to serving | ISHI 431:93
God-given t. | LEON 503:7
small t. might have use | CRAB 242:97
t.…howe'er designed | POPE 662:75
tales full of runic t. | FLEC 327:49

natural fear…is increased with t.   BACON 47:73
T., marvellous t.   FLEC 327:45
t. of others' griefs   SHAK 769:53
whereof t. are told   JONS 449:36
words seemed to them as idle t.   BIBLE 117:68
Taliesin Aneurin and T., cruel owls   BUNT 166:62
talk Bad t. drives out good   KNIG 476:16
beautiful family t.   COMP 229:70
do not t. of ourselves   TROL 866:78
English t. is a quadrille   JAMES 433:48
exercise is to t.   WILDE 910:63
good to t.   HOSK 414:39
hear anyone t. of culture   JOHST 447:81
how much my Ministers t.   THAT 850:49
If a lion could t.   WITT 918:48
loves to hear himself t.   SHAK 736:59
nor good t.   KIPL 473:56
nothing but t. of his horse   SHAK 739:45
no time to t.   BALD 53:30
No use to t. to me   HOUS 414:46
one cannot t. about after dinner   WILDE 908:10
People t. about the conscience   JAMES 433:49
rather t. than work   BOYD 147:41
scientists who t.   WEIL 896:27
should be less t.   THER 851:43
shouldn't t. about art   JOHN 440:1
T. about those subjects   HOLM 408:87
t. a little wild   SHAK 775:8
t. but a tinkling cymbal   BACON 49:29
T.…commit an indiscretion   BIER 129:44
t. in this manner   JOHN 446:60
t. is of the weather   JOHN 442:53
t. like a lady   SHAW 780:63
t. slid north   KIPL 471:98
t. so like a waiting gentlewoman   SHAK 741:1
t.…tendeth only to penury   BIBLE 99:29
t. themselves mad   SHAK 744:2
t. too much   DRYD 290:87
t. to the young people   JONES 448:93
t. was endless, compulsive   COUP 238:96
t. well but not too wisely   MAUG 561:73
t. with you, walk with you   SHAK 739:50
very easy to t.   DICK 267:7
way not to be remembered is to t.   MAIL 540:54
wouldn't t. to you much   SALI 711:55
write or even to t.   THES 851:51
talked So much they t.   CHUR 215:45
t. about…not being t. about   WILDE 908:3
t. on for ever   HAZL 387:69
talkers present is an age of t.   HAZL 388:82
talking if you ain't t. about him   BRAN 150:90
opposite of t. is waiting   LEBO 499:13
stop people t.   ATTL 38:46
T. all the time   CABR 183:19
t. on paper   BAIN 52:7
tired the sun with t.   CORY 237:74
will still be t.   SHAK 744:86
talks all right if the t. succeed   ZHOU 936:98
dead man…never t. back   CHAN 205:91
Licker t. mighty loud   HARR 383:92
Who t. of my nation?   SHAK 746:45
tall divinely t.   TENN 838:40
Let our children grow t.   THAT 850:11
once handsome and t. as you   ELIOT 306:63
she is t. and stately   TENN 845:86
T. as a crane   SITW 794:70
t., impossibly t., incomparably t.   CUMM 247:1
Tallard Monsieur T.   MARL 551:67
taller biggest difference…she was t.   FEIB 319:82
t. than other men   HARO 383:85
tallow-face Out…You t.-f.!   SHAK 736:71
Tallulah T. never bored anyone   LOOS 517:83
Talmud T., and the Alcoran   BACON 48:94
Tam T. was glorious   BURNS 172:18
tamarisks lowly t.   VIRG 882:28
tambourine Hey! Mr T. Man   DYLAN 297:60
shilling in my little t.   KIPL 472:27
Tamburlaine T.!—A Scythian   MARL 551:72
tame fox…ne'er so t.   SHAK 742:30
gentle, t., and meek   WYATT 931:3
heyday in the blood is t.   SHAK 754:8
Lions make leopards t.   SHAK 734:98
no man ever learned to t.   MEIL 563:9
though I seem t.   WYATT 930:1
which thou canst not t.   HERB 397:88
tamed not a bit t.   WHIT 905:36
tan of t. with henna hackles   STEV 819:20

tane smeddum t.
tang t. of faintly scented urine   JOYCE 452:92
tangential God is the t. point   JARRY 435:92
tangere Noli me t.   BIBLE 128:5
tangled t. web we weave   SCOTT 723:99
tangles Pelt down through the t.   SITW 793:63
tangos sings outdated t.!   DIAZ 265:50
tank T. come down the stalls   SASS 716:57
tanks set the t. on them   MARC 549:32
wooden t. filled with water   GILL 355:38
tap on t., but not on top   CHUR 217:6
running t. of words   MOORE 594:12
tape complain about the 'red t.'   WEBER 894:70
leapt at the t.   BANN 59:39
taper t. of conviviality   DICK 267:14
tapes t., blemishes and all   NIXON 617:48
tapestry t. hanging on four…hooks   MILL 572:3
tape-tied t.-t. curtains   POPE 660:5
tapeworm t. in an intestine   GOLD 360:30
tappets t. that finally push men   ROTH 699:16
tar thumbnail dipped in t.   PATE 642:55
Tara T. rose so high   LAND 488:84
tarantula t. on a slice of angel food   CHAN 204:74
Tar-Baby T.-B., she stay still   HARR 383:90
tares sowed t. among the wheat   BIBLE 112:50
tarnish silver over this t.   LOWE 521:57
tarnished badge of t. braid   READ 680:48
man…who is neither t. nor afraid   CHAN 204:77
tarry Longer will t.   DRAY 286:1
why t. the wheels of his chariots?   BIBLE 90:68
Tarsus T.…no mean city   BIBLE 119:54
tart t. who has…married the mayor   BAXT 65:88
Tartar arrow from the T.'s bow   SHAK 738:5
Tartars T. made them a King   POLO 657:39
Tarzan T. of the Apes   MACM 536:73
task acceptance of a t.   GIDE 353:84
criticism that assumes this t.   DEWEY 264:44
definite t., an interest   POPP 663:94
Delightful t.!   THOM 856:53
enormity of the t.   ACHE 2:34
fed your hunger like an endless t.   CRANE 243:15
Good life be now my t.   DRYD 291:16
good never will be our t.   MILT 580:3
morning sees some t.   LONG 516:46
one t. for all   KIPL 474:77
performance of the t. itself   SHIP 789:76
sets love a t. like that   HUNT 423:32
t. begun so often   MACN 538:5
t. is smoothly done   MILT 578:43
t. is trying to determine   BART 63:25
t. of science can never end   PEAR 645:97
t. which I am trying to achieve   CONR 234:95
too useless a t.   KEYN 465:81
what he reads as a t.   JOHN 443:64
What is our t.?   LLOY 513:4
Women have but one t.   COUB 238:85
tasks have been my t.   KOLL 477:38
independent thoughts, or even t.   MCLU 536:60
sets us to the t.   SCHW 721:70
t. could not be limited   AREN 28:41
tassels fluttering of…silk t.   DICK 267:25
tassie fill it in a silver t.   BURNS 171:2
taste a matter of t.   STEV 821:71
arbiter of t.   TACI 835:75
bad t. of the smoker   ELIOT 304:13
but not t. thee   HERR 400:40
difference of t. in jokes   ELIOT 304:14
Ghastly Good T.   BETJ 83:80
ghetto of good t.   KEIL 460:71
Good t. is better than bad t.   BENN 76:52
How sweet are thy words unto my t.   BIBLE 97:83
Impartiality is an acquired t.   RIFK 687:82
no t. for reading   SMOL 801:28
nowhere worse t.   JOWE 451:79
once they get the t.   HAZZ 388:96
pandering to the public t.   BEAV 67:28
questions of t.   ADAMS 4:78
sense of t.   BALL 57:4
splash of bad t.   VREE 883:59
suspect his t. in higher matters   LAMB 486:40
t. and see that the Lord is good   BIBLE 95:13
t. as lightly as the Bee   JONS 450:48
t. for French clothes   SCHL 718:14
t. for simplicity cannot endure   DELA 260:60
t. my Anno Domini   FARQ 318:54

T. not when the wine-cup glistens   SCOTT 724:40
t. of codfish   GRIEG 373:10
t. of death but once   SHAK 747:88
t. the barley bree   BURNS 171:6
Though t., though genius bless   COLL 228:46
tolerate are those of t.   THUR 860:56
undoubtedly wanted t.   WALP 887:25
value is not in its t.   FULB 340:44
writer…must…create the t.   WORD 928:48
taste-blind as a nation t.-b.   FISH 324:79
tastes t. greatly alter   JOHN 443:84
t. its own innocence   UPDI 874:90
t. may not be the same   SHAW 779:27
t. no wise book-maker   LUCAS 521:73
tattered t. coat upon a stick   YEATS 933:52
tatters wallpaper…falling to t.   MILL 572:14
Tattle always despised Mr T.   CONG 231:20
tattoo t. soap bubbles   BROWN 157:44
tattooed Lydia The T. Lady   HARB 381:37
taught t. to be afraid   HAMM 380:19
what we call highly t.   ELIOT 304:11
tavern good t.   JOHN 444:14
t. for his friends   DOUG 283:26
taverns sat in t. while the tempest   HOUS 416:72
tawny T. are the leaves   RANS 679:23
tax argue for t. increases   KRUG 481:25
Bats…pay no t.   BERR 82:65
hateful t.   JOHN 442:45
keeps armies of t. lawyers   WRIS 930:92
lighten the t. burden   QUINE 675:52
put a t. on pianos   SITW 794:78
turned a t. into a diversion   STEE 814:94
taxation resists your t. in America   PITT 653:42
T. without representation   OTIS 630:19
taxed all the world should be t.   BIBLE 115:24
never t. for speech   SHAK 761:21
taxes certain as death and t.   DEFOE 258:25
death and t.   FRAN 335:18
death and t.   MITC 588:99
no new t.   BUSH 175:92
only President who raised t.   DOLE 278:15
Only the little people pay t.   HELM 393:85
people overlaid with t.   BACON 49:33
true…as t. is   DICK 269:73
taxi empty t. arrived at 10   CHUR 217:7
going in a t.   SHAW 780:68
taxicab ears make him look like a t.   HUGH 418:15
taxpayers only those t.   NUNN 619:82
Tay Bridge of the Silv'ry T.   MCGO 531:78
Tayler Chesterton down to…T.   WEST 901:39
TB TB or not TB   ALLEN 12:43
Tchaikovsky Tell T. the news   BERRY 82:59
Tching T. prayed on the mountain   POUND 665:62
tea afternoon or evening cup of t.   HOLM 408:1
after t. and cakes and ices   ELIOT 304:19
ain't going to be no t.   MANS 546:85
assaying of t. is an art   MO 589:21
best sweeteners of t.   FIEL 322:35
ceremony known as afternoon t.   JAMES 433:37
Drinking the best t.   SNOW 802:35
get a cup of t.   HYNDE 427:25
give the boys a little t.   ANDE 16:22
My t. is nearly ready   STEV 823:20
Retired to their t. and scandal   CONG 231:6
singles we played after t.   BETJ 83:87
sometimes counsel…sometimes t.   POPE 659:71
sooner the t.'s out of the way   REED 682:83
Take some more t.   CARR 195:73
T., although an Oriental   CHES 212:80
T. for two   CAES 183:21
t. is brought at five   MONRO 591:57
T. is like the East   CHES 212:79
t. is not healthy   GORO 364:15
The way you sip your t.   GERS 351:40
we drink too much t.   PRIE 668:21
we'll all have t.   DICK 267:22
When I makes t. I makes t.   JOYCE 452:86
woman is like a t. bag   ROOS 695:40
your t. you sip   CRAB 242:97
teabreaks t. and other manifestations   MISH 587:79
teach but t. high thought   TENN 846:22
can easier t. twenty   SHAK 739:43
fool has a lot to t.   RABE 676:74
how can they t.?   DAVI 254:29
I can t. thee   SHAK 742:17
in order to t. himself   KAZIN 456:71
learn what it had to t.   THOR 857:91

learn...to t. it well — RABAN 675:59
Never t. anyone anything — SALI 711:62
Nor at all can t. — TENN 847:34
Sensible men never t. — DISR 277:90
simply t. the most — KEATS 457:85
T. me, Muse — HOMER 409:24
T. me the old, old story — HANK 380:33
t. one that, would t. one anything — WILDE 909:25
To t. all would be — MAUP 561:84
you never can t. — SHAW 777:64
telling not arguing...I am t. you — WHIS 902:60
still t. what is told — SHAK 772:32
Why are you t. me this? — GALT 345:30
Tempe vale of T. — RUSK 704:38
temper good spirits and good t. — DICK 268:34
hot t. leaps o'er a cold decree — SHAK 739:44
Keep me in t. — SHAK 762:64
One equal t. — TENN 840:66
only keep your t. — STER 817:69
science, t. — LONS 517:69
tart t. never mellows — IRVI 430:80
t. changed Into their t. — MILT 581:24
t., naturally morose — DISR 276:65
undertaken in a friendly t. — PEEL 646:8
woman of...uncertain t. — AUST 42:62
temperament Artistic t. — LENG 502:81
by t....a conquistador — FREUD 336:50
greater premium on t. — BRAD 149:76
have the satiric t. — BEER 69:71
sanguine t. — MURP 604:1
temperaments Human t. — LUCAS 522:77
temperance less Her t. over appetite — MILT 583:90
t....the flower of old age — DEMO 261:85
virtue of prosperity, is t. — BACON 47:79
temperate in t. heat — SURR 829:40
more lovely and more t. — SHAK 771:5
t. affords me none — CAREW 190:62
temperature light t. when I set out — CECIL 202:24
t. not naturally its own — SCHU 721:54
t.'s risin' — BERRY 82:59
tempered t. with love's sighs — SHAK 734:85
tempest covert from the t. — BIBLE 103:32
here and there with a t. — BIBLE 107:34
homeless, t.-tossed — LAZA 496:51
t., a redundant energy — WORD 925:89
t. came her tears — TENN 842:12
t. of the gods — MARL 551:78
we the t. fear — DRYD 287:14
while the t. hurled — HOUS 416:72
While the t. still is high — WESL 900:11
tempests looks on t. — SHAK 773:48
tempest-tossed Yet it shall be t.-t. — SHAK 766:68
tempest-tost welcome to the t.-t. — BYRON 182:78
temple body is the t. — BIBLE 121:95
great t. of fiction — UPDI 875:92
inquire in his t. — BIBLE 95:7
Open the t. gates — SPEN 809:3
t. bells they say — KIPL 470:85
t., called his body — THOR 857:79
t. in which the priest — SHAW 779:37
t. of Jupiter — GIBB 352:63
The Lord's anointed t. — SHAK 767:9
train filled the t. — BIBLE 102:11
vault of the T. of Peace — BRAM 150:87
veil of the t. was rent — BIBLE 114:5
veil of the t. was rent — BIBLE 116:65
temples dwelleth not in t. — BIBLE 119:49
mortal t. of a king — SHAK 735:20
smote the nail into his t. — BIBLE 90:93
solemn t. — SHAK 774:94
t. are like a piece of a pomegranate — BIBLE 101:2
t. of his God — MACA 526:63
t. of the earth are to be overturned — DIDE 274:96
t. stood on two pillars — HUGH 419:36
t. th'upright heart and pure — MILT 580:93
tempora O t. — CICE 218:29
tempt shalt not t. the Lord thy God — BIBLE 109:79
T. me no more — DAY 257:83
temptation able...to resist t. — BRON 154:75
enter not into t. — BIBLE 114:99
indiscretion without t. — BIER 129:44
It is always t. — KIPL 474:70
last t. is the greatest treason — ELIOT 307:4
lead us not into t. — BIBLE 110:98
maximum of t. — SHAW 778:8
power of t. — TROL 866:85
prepare thy soul for t. — BIBLE 107:37

protections against t. — TWAIN 872:26
resist everything except t. — WILDE 908:13
say anything against t. — SAKI 710:48
t. beset me — FOX 333:77
t. in the wilderness — BIBLE 97:58
t. of recklessly prophesying — WILDE 908:87
t. to see all of society — LEWO 508:10
Why comes t. — BROW 162:85
temptations In spite of all t. — GILB 354:95
t. both in wine and women — KITC 475:4
t. of a monopoly — SCOTT 722:74
tempted one thing to be t. — SHAK 758:19
t. to refuse it — CHAN 205:7
When t. to say something — ITO 431:98
tempter when the t. came to him — BIBLE 109:78
ten In t. thousand years — SNYD 803:49
one bullet in t. thousand — SPEN 807:57
T. or twelve — HOPK 412:92
t. thousand of those men — SHAK 746:54
T. thousand saw I — WORD 927:41
there is enough for t. — MOLI 590:37
woman having t. pieces of silver — BIBLE 116:45
tenacity our evolutionary t. — BANKS 58:37
tenants T. of the house — ELIOT 305:43
Ten Commandments aren't no T. C. — KIPL 471:88
tendencies strong t. to rivalry — JAMES 434:66
two simultaneous t. — BAUD 65:81
tender beautiful, the t., the kind — MILL 571:89
made t. to the heart — PROU 671:79
men had grown more t. — STUD 827:5
such a t. voice — BLAKE 133:29
t. for another's pain — GRAY 368:95
T. is the Night — FITZ 325:6
t. is the North — TENN 842:9
t. leaves of hopes — SHAK 775:20
things that are t. — BACON 49:18
tender-minded T.-m. and tough — JAMES 434:70
tenderness Anger and t.: my selves — RICH 685:54
its t., its joys — WORD 927:29
knows not t. — DRYD 289:59
strength lined with t. — ANGE 17:33
t. gets no response — NERVO 611:47
t. is not so oft — BACON 48:90
t. of patient minds — OWEN 632:52
tenders shoal of fools for t. — CONG 235:89
tenement weak, frail, decayed t. — ADAMS 5:94
tenements waste of modern t. — THOR 858:6
Tennessee I was in T. 24 hours — RAY 680:41
placed a jar in T. — STEV 819:12
tennis already stuffed t. balls — SHAK 745:13
Anybody...for a game of t.? — SHAW 780:60
Conversation is like playing t. — LODGE 514:24
die without having played enough t. — BORO 145:99
old ladies in t. shoes — MOSK 600:27
saw the King play at t. — PEPYS 647:38
stars' t.-balls — WEBS 895:21
taken up t. — GULL 375:36
t. could be shorn — HUGH 419:35
T....game of no use — BACON 46:53
t. with the net down — FROST 339:4
two hundred asphalt t. courts — HUXL 425:79
What a polite game t. is — BARR 61:90
tennis-girl t.-g.'s hand! — BETJ 83:88
Tennyson dead!...T. — PUNCH 673:14
Lawn T. — JOYCE 452:88
tenor noiseless t. of their way — GRAY 369:20
tens fold my t. — KAUF 455:57
tension general sense of t. — MACM 537:78
t. all human energies — MUSS 605:18
Under the t., slip, slide, perish — ELIOT 307:2
tent Caesar is in the t. — YEATS 934:63
Came to my t. — SHAK 732:20
inside the t. — JOHN 440:84
little t. of blue — WILDE 910:53
not a house or even a t. — ATWO 38:51
t. made in linen — LEON 503:13
tentacles t. that stifle and suffocate — ARNO 34:74
tenth t. of mankind — SHAK 770:77
t. time, lack of principle — SIDM 790:96
tents dwelling in t. — BIBLE 87:84
dwell in the t. of wickedness — BIBLE 96:47
stately t. of war — MARL 551:70
up their t. like Arabs — LONG 516:50
tenure During my t. of power — PEEL 646:9
Teresa I'm not Mother T. — TYSON 873:54
term served a t. — GILB 353:94
T., holidays, t., holidays — LEWIS 507:78

To every nation a t. — KORAN 478:63
terminations terrible as her t. — SHAK 744:94
terms age conceived in spatial t. — MIES 569:50
contradiction in t. — SHAW 781:83
direct and unassuming t. — ROCK 693:84
fair t. and a villain's mind — SHAK 739:55
In good set t. — SHAK 749:46
No t. except...surrender — GRANT 366:54
part on better t. — OTWAY 631:35
silken t. precise — SHAK 734:91
T. of Endearment — MCMU 537:85
t. too deep for me — GILB 354:4
upon easier t. — JOHN 446:62
Terpsichore grace of T. — BARR 61:94
terrace sit on the t. remembering — SASS 716:64
T. or lofty Tower — LEAR 497:77
terraces statues on the t. — KIPL 474:72
terrain fought...for such barren t. — NOON 617:55
From a material and spiritual t. — FULL 341:59
terrible All strange and t. events — SHAK 765:45
dying...is t. — FIEL 322:44
it's got to be t.! — PUZO 673:28
It's sometimes t. — HUXL 425:94
t. is the place you hold — BERN 80:31
thee t. and dear. — SHEL 787:29
terrier toothless t. on Valium — SIKO 791:31
terrified t. and tight — BETJ 84:3
terrifying in their briefcases is t. — KHRU 467:5
territory all parts of this vast t. — TOCQ 861:84
better...than to increase his t. — ERAS 315:87
comes with the t. — MILL 571:95
invade British t. — HUNT 423:38
Not an inch of our t. — FAVRE 319:78
Over all this t....an iron curtain — GOEB 359:8
t. ahead of the rest — TWAIN 871:12
terror even t. of their lives — SHAR 776:39
flame of incandescent t. — ELIOT 309:47
I would be in t. — PRAT 667:98
no t., brother Toby — STER 818:86
Our war on t. is well begun — BUSH 175:11
perch, and not their t. — SHAK 758:18
servile minds into t. — TZARA 873:59
T....arises from...disestablishment — KING 469:45
t. by night — BIBLE 96:53
t. could it not repress — SURR 829:38
t. for lowering a man's stamina — DOUG 283:15
t. of his name — BEAU 67:15
t. of the world — GIBB 351:56
t. that paralyses — ROOS 696:43
Thy t., O Christ — KIPL 474:75
victory in spite of all t. — HOPK 412:82
warfare, t., murder — CHUR 216:74
terrorism any nation that continues to harbor...t. — BUSH 175:9
Consensus T. — COUP 238:93
make sure t. never prevails — BLAIR 133:10
terrorist cannot let t....nations hold this nation hostile — BUSH 175:7
One is a t. — GORB 363:4
righted by the t.'s program — JONAS 447:83
starve the t. — THAT 850:24
t....from the same basket — CONR 234:11
terrorists to get at t. — GORE 364:12
with us, or...with the t. — BUSH 175:9
terrors new t. of Death — ARBU 28:34
t. of the earth — SHAK 763:70
The Little T. — GAVA 347:73
Tess ended his sport with T. — HARDY 382:63
test Electric Kool-Aid Acid T. — WOLFE 920:90
end and t. of art — POPE 658:53
Habit...the t. of truth — CRAB 242:98
Martyrdom is the t. — JOHN 446:48
really decisive t. — JAY 436:98
t. is a new substitute — MUSS 605:18
t. of a real comedian — NATH 609:21
to a lie-detector t. — KOES 477:30
universal t. of travel — GELL 348:1
testament Than my T. fer that — LOWE 520:29
testaments last wills and t. — MELV 564:33
testimonies t. are my meditation — BIBLE 97:82
testimony t. of a good conscience — KEMP 461:89
testosterone awash in post-war t. — SCHR 720:45
tests moral t. and tasks — ELKIN 310:69
test tube baby made in a t. t. — MAIL 540:57
tether world is at the end of its t. — WELLS 899:94
Teutonic speech...free of T. guttural — QUIL 674:44

Texas deeper than the skies of T. — MCMU 537:87
part of the T. ritual — FERB 320:95
state of T. — KENN 463:42
T. wrestling match — WRIS 930:95
text enrich My t. with many things — BYRON 181:74
except the first t. — GIRA 358:78
German t. of French operas — WHAR 902:54
great t. in Galatians — BROW 160:21
holy t. around she strews — GRAY 369:21
listen to the wind's t. — THOM 854:27
neat rivulet of t. — SHER 787:51
paintings…to illustrate the t. — WOLFE 920:92
square of t. — TENN 846:14
t. book example — TIME 860:74
texts difference of t. — SPEN 809:95
texture closest, in t. — THOM 853:98
t. and tone — MORR 599:7
T. is the content — POPO 662:86
t. of the soil — SMITH 799:63
Thackeray T. and Dickens — STEV 822:1
T. settled like a meat-fly — RUSK 704:31
Thames Crossing the stripling T. — ARNO 32:18
fished…from the stinking T. — WINT 917:32
gaily as the sparkling T. — ARNO 32:22
mouth of the T. — GIBB 351:57
Sweet T., run softly — ELIOT 306:59
Sweet T., run softly — SPEN 809:13
T. is between me and the Duchess — WALP 887:23
T.…the noblest river — ADDI 6:21
thrown in the T. — SHAK 743:79
upon the banks of T. — JONS 449:46
where the charter'd T. does flow — BLAKE 135:58
youthful T. — ARNO 33:43
thane T. of Cawdor lives — SHAK 766:76
T. of Fife — SHAK 768:34
Your face, my t. — SHAK 766:83
thank not going to t. anybody — MILL 574:65
not please but t. you — DILL 275:14
only themselves to t. — SAYE 717:86
t. all those who made this possible — ANDR 16:29
t. me, love me, and reward me — SHAK 760:77
t. we all our God — WINK 917:23
thankful must be t. — HAMM 379:10
t. that I am here to welcome you — STAN 812:61
thankless have a t. child — SHAK 762:63
thanks give solemn t. — COLU 229:62
give t. unto thee — BOOK 143:71
give t. unto the Lord — BIBLE 98:97
ta'en with equal t. — SHAK 754:88
T. for All the Fish — ADAMS 4:68
T. for tomorrow — ATKI 37:34
t. to you all — KENN 464:51
to give t. is good — SWIN 834:49
thanksgiving come…with t. — BIBLE 96:57
With proud t. — BINY 130:51
Thatcher better prospect than Mrs T. — HESE 401:62
father, except perhaps Mrs T. — WEST 901:43
If Margaret T. wins — KINN 470:70
it was T., T., T. — BENN 75:20
nobody scared me as much as Mrs T — LIVI 512:86
plutonium blonde…T. — SCAR 717:90
reappeared in the shape of…T. — HOGG 406:61
talk with Mrs T. — WEIG 896:25
[T.] has been charging around — HEAL 389:1
[T.] has turned the…bulldog — STEEL 814:87
T. is a…tyrant — MACM 537:80
T. was perfect for me — TOWN 863:23
thawed t. and gone — KHAY 466:94
theatre devotes himself to the t. — BEAU 66:2
Execrable English T. — GOET 360:12
For the t. one needs long arms — BERN 81:51
go to the t. to be entertained — COOK 235:35
I left the t., dizzy and pale — QUIR 675:57
I like the t., but never come late — HART 384:11
in England nobody goes to the t. — AGATE 8:69
interview that turned towards the T. — PRIE 668:27
into the t. as a voyeur — FRIS 338:80
laughter in the rear of the t. — KAUF 456:60
most magical moment in the t. — CRON 246:80
only place…to construct a t. — GENET 349:7
only regret in the t. — BARR 61:97
people don't go to the t. — JOUR 451:74
quit going to the t. — SALI 711:66
remain in the t. — TYNAN 872:43
talent…drained off into t. — RICH 686:65
t. a place to scratch — MUSC 605:13
t.…can't and doesn't change society — HYTN 427:27

t. has always been essential — MAMET 544:33
t. has died in my lifetime — MILL 572:10
t. is irresistible — ARNO 34:66
t. is the primary evidence — THUR 859:44
t. of man's life — BACON 46:47
we t. folk — MANK 545:62
what is happening in the t. — TYNAN 872:48
what t. is all about — STOP 825:67
theatres books are t. — STEV 820:42
chain of moving picture t. — DOSP 282:3
t. have had their day. — BENN 77:58
towers, domes, t. — WORD 926:19
theatrical fail to find happiness in t. life — PAVL 644:83
theatricals game of private t. — JAMES 434:67
thee my little jokes on T. — FROST 339:13
Shakespeare—or t. — SCOTT 725:57
soul be required of t. — SMITH 800:4
theft Property is t. — PROU 670:66
there is boundless t. — SHAK 762:49
what would be t. in other poets — DRYD 288:26
them Let's be getting at t. — GRACE 365:31
theme Fools are my t. — BYRON 179:96
imperfection in the chosen t. — WORD 925:90
it is my t.! — DENH 261:92
must choose a mighty t. — MELV 564:35
My t. is always humanistic — WILS 915:77
so grave a t. — PRIOR 669:44
t., concept, structure — POUS 666:75
t. defeats structuralism — GOLD 360:33
t. too high doth seem — GURN 375:45
themes actions, and religious t. — POUS 666:75
leave great t. unfinished — MACB 527:80
muses on admirèdd t. — MARL 551:77
no transcendent t. in life — FORD 330:21
t. in a new light — LUCAS 522:80
t. men always have loved — DAY 256:75
themselves him rather than t. — WINT 917:33
ought to be doing for t. — JOHN 440:83
principal part of t. — HAZL 387:72
theologians if you believe the t. — SALI 711:68
invention of t. or priests — NIEB 614:98
theology hope of t. — INGE 429:55
keep history and t. apart — WELLS 898:90
schools of t.…are to be overturned — DIDE 274:96
t., philosophy, history, art — ARNO 33:35
T., sir, is a fortress — MILL 571:98
theorem T.—The acquisition — SART 715:40
theories come to nature with your t. — RENO 683:6
't.' and 'goals' — KIPL 473:64
theorist half-baked t. — TRUE 868:25
theorists armchair t. — ASHD 35:91
modern educational t. — RUSS 705:51
particularly economic t. — KNIG 476:15
talented economic t. — TOBIN 861:79
t. who can ruin your game — BOTH 146:14
theorize mistake to t. — DOYLE 284:47
theorizing t. about music — HEINE 391:49
theory All t.…is grey — GOET 360:17
Democracy is the t. — MENC 565:52
in t. if genius had not proved — LESS 505:44
life without t. — DISR 276:38
new t.…a discovery — POPP 662:89
new t. is attacked — JAMES 434:72
no good t. of what it is — MELL 563:20
not apply t. to history — STIN 824:48
nothing in the t. to indicate — SIMON 792:37
Plato divined in t. — WHIT 904:13
practical as the t. — OPPE 626:18
prop up their t. — TWAIN 872:37
t. and methods of revolution — MAO 547:5
T. is a good thing — KAPI 455:48
t. of modern education — WILDE 909:38
T. of Permanent Adolescence — CONN 233:74
t. of the Communists — MARX 558:3
t. of the subject is complete — MILL 570:58
t. that his wife is beautiful — MENC 566:75
without…a t. — POPP 662:93
wonders if it will work in t. — HELL 392:71
theosophy 'T.' is the essence — BLAV 136:91
T., on earth, is like — BLAV 136:92
therapy form of t. — GREE 371:72
psychoanalytic t. of hysteria — FREUD 336:51
there not t., t. is no t. t. — STEIN 815:20
thermodynamics Second Law of T. — SNOW 802:37
thermometer t. had been longer — MOOD 594:7
Thermopylae old man of T. — LEAR 498:94
The Scream This became T. S. — MUNCH 603:80

Thespian T. springs — DRAY 287:5
thick dashed through t. and thin — DRYD 290:99
grown t. — BIBLE 90:57
lay it on so t. — BUTL 178:71
T. and unwholesome — SHAK 754:20
t. as a plank — DIANA 265:47
thicker History gets t. and t. — TAYL 837:14
thicket t. of the world — JOHN 438:58
thick-jewelled t.-j. shone — TENN 839:49
thick-skinned t.-s. grown-ups — SHAW 778:85
writers…become t.-s. — WAUGH 892:42
thief apparel fits your t. — SHAK 758:43
come as a t. — BIBLE 125:33
come as a t. — BIBLE 127:71
come like a t. in the night — POE 656:19
cries out boldly — CONG 231:15
grand t. into God's fold — MILT 582:58
have a t. or two — SHAK 758:20
He that steals…is a t. — SCOTT 723:13
in what watch the t. would come — BIBLE 113:88
Jean Cocteau thinks that I am poor t. — GENET 348:3
not the mouse who is the t. — JACO 432:13
Opportunity makes a t. — BACON 46:34
Pleasure is a t. to business — DEFOE 258:24
rather have been the good t. — BROW 159:91
steals something from the t. — SHAK 759:67
t. breaks into my house — PAINE 634:89
t. cometh not, but for to steal — BIBLE 118:1
t. in the night — BIBLE 125:33
Upon a dwarfish t. — SHAK 768:35
what a deformed t. — SHAK 745:14
which is the t.? — SHAK 763:91
thieves Beauty provoketh t. — SHAK 749:32
best of t. — DRYD 289:65
fell among t., which stripped him — BIBLE 115:37
made it a den of t. — BIBLE 113:79
so much gained upon the t. — STEV 821:73
T. for their robbery — SHAK 758:24
T. for want of Work — SWIFT 831:92
T. out, profit in! — ANON 18:64
T. respect property — CHES 211:74
T. think that I am a poor writer — GENET 348:3
Twenty Thousand T. — JOYCE 452:3
union of two t. — BIER 128:14
when t. cannot be true — SHAK 741:8
where t. do not break through — BIBLE 110:99
you are t. professed — SHAK 762:49
thigh bee with honied t. — MILT 577:21
happy dawning of her t. — HERR 400:41
on his t. a name written — BIBLE 127:76
smote them hip and t. — BIBLE 90:73
thimble silver t. lies cold — SITW 794:82
thimbles sought it with t. — CARR 197:32
thin Enclosing every t. man — WAUGH 892:44
how t. and clear — TENN 841:4
in every fat man a t. one — CONN 233:82
No matter how t. — SMITH 798:56
pallid and t. young man — GILB 354:9
t.…as a furled umbrella — EMERY 313:55
thine only call me T. — COLE 226:98
thing any manner of creeping t. — BIBLE 89:33
Being a t. immortal — SHAK 751:26
dear ravishing t. — BEHN 71:17
design…in a t. so small — FROST 339:5
do a t. in Israel — BIBLE 91:83
do only one t. at once — SMIL 797:33
excellent t. in woman — SHAK 764:6
far, far better t. that I do — DICK 271:25
fond t. vainly invented — BOOK 144:75
getting on with the bloody t. — EVANS 316:18
great To do that t. — SHAK 765:34
if a t. is worth doing — CHES 212:71
if they have a good t. — SHAK 742:42
it don't mean a t. — ELLI 310:75
it don't mean a t. — MILLS 574:71
least t. contains something — MAUP 561:86
life is the t. — SMITH 800:85
local t. called Christianity — HARDY 382:73
most important t. in life — PASC 641:29
most important t. in the world — SHAW 777:47
no new t. under the sun — BIBLE 100:67
one damned t. after another — HUBB 417:6
one t. we did right — ANON 24:35
palsy-stricken, churchyard t. — KEATS 459:35
poor virgin…an ill-favoured t. — SHAK 750:89
prettier the kind of a t. — LAMB 486:42
say that the t. is good — MOORE 594:20

ought to do the right t.   MCNA 537:97
Technology…is a queer t.   SNOW 802:40
t. about girls   SALI 711:54
t. depicted is less stationary   LEGER 501:53
t. fall down in peace   MAYB 562:94
too much of a good t.?   SHAK 750:78
unlike any other t….in the universe   STEI 815:31
what t. is love   PEELE 646:12
what to make of a diminished t.   FROST 338:91
ings accept…the t. that cannot   NIEB 614:1
all mortal t. doth sway   SPEN 809:14
all needful t.   WORD 926:16
All other t. must   SCHI 718:2
all the t. thou canst desire   BIBLE 99:12
All t. are artificial   BROW 158:69
All t. are become new   BIBLE 122:27
All t. are lawful for me   BIBLE 121:3
All t. are literally better   RUSK 703:7
all t. be done decently   BIBLE 121:11
All t. began in order   BROW 159:96
All t. bright and beautiful   ALEX 11:22
All t., by a law divine   SHEL 783:42
all t. work together for good   BIBLE 120:76
By whom all t. were made   BOOK 141:95
do all t. through Christ   BIBLE 123:63
ear of jealousy heareth all t.   BIBLE 107:29
faculty of seeing t.   SPEN 807:60
fairest t. have fleetest   THOM 855:35
fanatic for the externality of t.   LEWIS 508:3
habit…of correcting t.   BRADY 149:83
he that contemneth small t.   BIBLE 108:54
higher order of t.   MILL 573:34
impressions of external t.   RUSK 704:10
In the nature of t.   SPIN 810:24
leave great t. undone   GLAS 359:97
Little t. affect little minds   DISR 276:54
Many t. are formidable   SOPH 804:83
Mind not high t.   BIBLE 120:83
more t. are shewed unto thee   BIBLE 107:39
more t. in heaven and earth   SHAK 752:38
mystery of t.   SHAK 764:1
new way of looking at t.   MILL 573:52
power in small t.   SOPH 804:84
present state of t.   BAGE 51:79
remembrance of t. past   SHAK 771:15
sad vicissitude of t.   STER 818:96
Say not soft t.   SORL 804:90
science…interested in t.   CURIE 249:36
secret t. belong unto the Lord   BIBLE 90:53
sorts of t.   RYLE 707:79
These Foolish T.   MARV 557:82
T. are the sons   JOHN 442:39
T. fall apart   YEATS 933:50
T. have dropped from me   WOOLF 923:52
T. I'd been better without   PARK 637:58
T. in book's clothing   LAMB 487:60
t. in the world   RUSK 703:4
t. I once read   SNYD 802:47
t. made matter very little   CUMM 247:7
t. people had once held against her   SCHL 718:14
t. people make fools of themselves   SHAW 777:56
T. that are seen   JOHNS 439:68
t. that are tender and unpleasing   BACON 49:18
t. which have never yet been done   BACON 47:63
T. without all remedy   SHAK 768:13
t. you can do in a baseball game   STEN 816:55
think on these t.   BIBLE 123:61
thou hast created all t.   BIBLE 126:55
totality of facts, not of t.   WITT 918:41
to whom such t. are nothing   SOPH 804:89
useful or pleasurable t.   RUSK 704:17
value of the world of t.   MARX 557:95
wanted to be three t.   SCHU 721:53
way of doing t. rightly   RUSK 704:13
What t. have we seen   BEAU 66:6
why and wherefore in all t.   SHAK 746:64
thingummy no…but T.   DICK 269:59
think begin to t. about it   HEYE 401:72
cannot t. well, love well   WOOLF 922:41
can't t. and hit   BERRA 82:57
can't t. for you   DYLAN 297:55
can't t. without his hat   BECK 68:35
don't t. foolishly   JOHN 446:60
don't t. much of it   STRA 826:87
effort to t. clearly   JAMES 434:60
feel hot and t. cold   CARY 198:61
fellows whom it hurts to t.   HOUS 415:65

greatly t. or bravely die?   POPE 659:79
haven't got the money, so we've got to t.   RUSH 706:72
I am inclined to t.   DOYLE 285:77
if they t., they fasten   HOUS 416:74
If you can t.   KIPL 473:67
know more than you t.   SPOCK 811:37
might as well t. big   TRUMP 869:47
more clearly than you t.   BAKER 53:17
never expect a soldier to t.   SHAW 777:68
not so t. as you drunk   SQUI 811:43
pains to t. otherwise   HUME 422:6
problem is not whether machines t.   SKIN 795:10
talk who never t.   PRIOR 668:30
t. and t. for months and years   EINS 301:34
t. back through our mothers   WOOLF 922:47
T. before you speak   FORS 332:54
t. by fits and starts   HOUS 416:74
t. continually of those   SPEN 807:46
t….exclusively of others   WAUGH 893:50
t. he is growing old   IRVI 430:82
t. him so…t. him so   SHAK 729:25
t. is to be full   KEATS 460:59
t. like a man   SIMON 792:36
T. not of them   KEATS 459:49
t. perhaps even less   BROW 161:50
t. so highly   STEV 822:99
t. that science can do anything   RAY 680:40
t. that we t.   BIER 128:19
t., therefore I am   DESC 263:21
t. too little   DRYD 290:87
t. with them   BENN 76:56
t. you are doing nothing   JULI 452:6
try to t. it again   GOET 360:18
What I t., I utter   SHAK 769:60
What will Mrs Grundy t.?   MORT 600:24
Whenever I t.   STEV 819:11
When I t., I must speak   SHAK 750:61
When I would pray and t.   SHAK 758:30
when we t. of thee, O America!   WALP 887:30
thinker incompleteness as a t.   WEBB 893:62
thinkers masses of wishful t.   QUINE 675:52
thinking and then to t.!   HAZL 387:75
cannot prevent people from t.   SCHI 718:3
employment for a t. man   ADDI 7:44
expedient in the way of our t.   JAMES 434:73
explicit in my t.   RUSS 705:56
feverish after so much t.   CARR 197:25
hearing, t., writing   HAZL 388:39
instead of t.   JOHN 447:78
inventory of unfinished t.   RAND 678:11
It ain't t. about it   TROL 867:91
I, who was t. this   DESC 263:20
left hand is my t. hand   HEPW 396:63
live no longer by t.   SHAK 750:87
modes of t. are different   JOHN 446:50
much drinking, little t.   SWIFT 831:71
not a substitute for t.   STEV 820:57
not merely as t.   PLATH 654:64
originality…manner of t.   MAUP 561:83
science…a refinement of everyday t.   EINS 301:41
science fictional way of t.   ASIM 35:6
T. is the great enemy of perfection   CONR 235:31
t. makes it so   SHAK 752:53
T. precisely and systematically   SOLOW 803:60
t. what nobody has thought   SZENT 834:64
t. what you really think   GINS 357:71
too busy t. about myself   SITW 794:75
usually a way of not t.   HELL 393:82
verbal t. is the most articulate   KOES 477:31
thinks person who reads or t.   YOUR 935:80
t. too much   SHAK 747:79
utter what he t. truth   JOHN 446:48
what his heart t.   SHAK 745:11
third deny that the T. Estate   SIEY 791:26
nothing new in T. World   AUNG 42:49
There is no t.!   SAINT 710:29
the t. day he rose again   BOOK 140:71
t. day comes a frost   SHAK 775:20
t. kind of knowledge   SPIN 811:35
t. who walks always beside you?   ELIOT 306:65
To make a t., she joined the…two   DRYD 291:24
third-rate what in the world is t.-r.?   HELL 392:65
thirst believeth…shall never t.   BIBLE 117:90
hunger, t….and death   GARI 346:48
man can raise a t.   KIPL 471:88
neither t. any more   BIBLE 126:60
nor a t. for water, but of hearing   BIBLE 106:11

pride which causes t.   DANTE 252:97
quench a country's t.   POPE 660:4
t. to be loved   RHYS 684:24
t. without quenching it   UPDI 874:81
without the provocation of t.   SWIFT 831:84
thirsteth Ho, every one that t.   BIBLE 104:53
thirstier t. than ever   SALA 710:50
thirsty t., and ye gave me drink   BIBLE 113:92
t. land springs of water   BIBLE 103:33
when I was t. they gave me vinegar   BOOK 143:60
thirteen clocks were striking t.   ORWE 629:97
T. wasted years   ANON 23:91
thirty American women over t.   FITZ 325:11
Between t. and forty   BENN 76:51
past t., and three parts iced   ARNO 32:11
t. pieces of silver   BIBLE 106:18
t. pieces of silver   BIBLE 114:95
t. years' experience   CARR 194:55
thirty-five between…t.-s. and forty   DIOR 275:23
thirty-seventh t.-s….situation   JARRY 435:93
Thisbe Death of Pyramus and T.   SHAK 737:87
love T.: very tragical   SHAK 738:14
thistle flew like the down of a t.   MOORE 594:19
t., O my soul   MACD 529:35
t. yet'll unite   MACD 529:32
thistles t. blinterin' white   MACD 529:39
thither transported hither and t.   OVID 631:47
Thomas John T. says goodnight   LAWR 495:22
T., because thou hast seen me   BIBLE 118:25
True T.   BALL 56:89
thorn Instead of the t….the fir tree   BIBLE 104:58
left the t. wi' me   BURNS 172:27
Oak, and Ash, and T.   KIPL 473:58
Oak, and Ash, and T.   KIPL 473:59
plant this t., this canker   SHAK 741:2
pricks like t.   SHAK 735:37
pull the t.   SCOTT 723:11
snail's on the t.   BROW 160:19
t. in the flesh   BIBLE 122:33
without t. the rose   MILT 582:60
thorns crackling of t. under a pot   BIBLE 101:77
impious hand to the Crown of T.   BRON 155:82
lily among t.   BIBLE 101:96
loops and t.   UPDI 874:88
no t. go as deep   SWIN 833:30
pain…of their t.   BERN 81:44
received seed among the t.   BIBLE 112:48
some fell among t.   BIBLE 112:47
t. of life   SHEL 783:46
thorny life is t.   COLE 226:7
t. way to heaven   SHAK 751:16
thoroughfare t. ful of wo   CHAU 208:83
thou eternal T.   BUBER 164:23
t. wilt not often be mistaken   PENN 647:23
Thus far t. shalt go   PARN 639:93
thought Action…the enemy of t.   CONR 234:7
All t., all passions, all delights   COLE 226:99
beautiful clean t.   LAWR 494:95
become our own t. police   MAMET 543:22
bud of t.   DARIO 252:3
but teach high t.   TENN 846:22
By t., word, and deed   BOOK 141:2
call it the stream of t.   JAMES 434:63
calmer of unquiet t.   WALT 888:49
can to sight or t.   MILT 584:14
carving and colouring of a t.   SITW 794:85
ceases to move in t.   ELIOT 307:84
certain dimensions of t.   STEI 816:46
closer the expression is to the t.   FLAU 326:31
community of t.   ADAMS 4:81
deep t., reason, or imagination   DARW 253:15
different from what we t.   HAVEL 385:29
dress of t.   POPE 658:56
end of man is…not a t.   CARL 192:96
Eternity!…dreadful t.!   ADDI 7:38
eternity of t.   WORD 924:85
Experience is the child of T.   DISR 275:34
greater cannot be t.   ANSE 26:6
great movements of human t.   BENN 77:58
habit of t.   SKEL 795:7
habits of metaphoric t.   FRYE 340:85
impartial in t. as well as in action   WILS 916:9
in a general honest t.   SHAK 748:25
inward world of t.   ARNO 33:49
Language is called the garment of t.   CARL 192:95
less permanent than t.   BUNT 166:59
liberty of t. perishes   ORWE 629:95

no enemy but t.	YEATS 934:55
no precious t. at all	SHAK 771:23
Not an easy t. for humorists	BUCH 164:33
nothing but T. destroys us	KORAN 479:87
no t. for eloquence	PASC 640:10
no t. for the fine graces	SMITH 799:63
no t. to bleed	SHAK 734:96
no t. to labour	ROGE 695:26
no t. to read	BROO 156:21
no t. to stand and stare?	DAVI 255:48
not in earth or t. recoverable	PURDY 673:17
not redeemed from t.	ELIOT 309:50
not t. or opportunity	AUST 42:60
now is the accepted t.	BIBLE 122:29
Old T. is still a flying	HERR 400:45
once our t. devour	MARV 556:64
on t.—No, you were late	LERN 504:24
out of key with his t.	POUND 664:35
out of t., out of space	WELLS 898:74
own t. out of their work	MASE 559:41
passage of t.	WILL 913:34
pass away the t.	SHAK 731:2
passed a hell of t.	SHAK 773:50
peace for our t.	CHAM 204:63
Plays...cut through t.	MILL 572:8
play the fools with the t.	SHAK 742:47
plenty of t. to win	DRAKE 286:94
point free in t.	DIDI 274:5
Popular in our t.	HUGH 419:31
pure clay of t.'s mud	MALA 541:84
puzzles me more than t. and space	LAMB 486:31
rags of t.	DONNE 279:41
really understands at the t.	THOM 855:43
Redeeming the t.	BIBLE 122:48
remember'd for a very long t.	MCGO 531:78
repair t.'s faults	MUIR 602:59
right notes at the right t.	BACH 46:24
saltness of t.	SHAK 742:39
same old druid T.	ROSE 697:67
same t. in a thousand minds	TOCQ 861:86
searched for myself across t.	CIXO 219:36
seeds of t.	SHAK 766:72
seen better faces in my t.	SHAK 763:66
see the t.'s deformity	JONS 448:8
sent before my t.	SHAK 731:1
sequence in t.	WELTY 899:1
She's the original good t.	DAVIS 255:56
shipwreck of t.	BACON 46:42
shook hands with t.	FORD 330:13
short the t. to run	DRYD 290:94
short t....does not make a man	ARIS 29:51
signs of our own t.	CARL 191:79
sing of T. or Eternity	TENN 846:28
slap t. on their wrists	KINC 468:22
slow and still the t.	TWAIN 871:2
small bridge in t.	STEI 816:39
something to do with the t.	ROGE 695:22
somewhat before his t.	HARDY 382:65
soul of the whole Past T.	CARL 193:34
sounds in the movement of t.	BUSO 176:28
Space-ships and t. machines	KOES 477:30
speech is shallow as T.	CARL 192:22
spend t. and ink	GALS 344:24
sphere of leisure t.	LOWE 521:63
spoils of t.	GRAY 369:16
stars move still, t. runs	MARL 552:6
strain, T.'s eunuch	HOPK 413:10
strong necessity of t.	SHAK 764:18
sunflower, weary of t.	BLAKE 134:53
supreme cause of our t.	SPEN 807:66
Suspended in t.	ELIOT 308:37
Take a little t.	DICK 270:9
tasks...to fulfil for our t.	SCHW 721:70
That passed the t.	BECK 68:36
That T. could turn up	HEYW 402:76
that t. of night	GINS 357:71
Then while t. serves	HERR 400:44
there...existed, at some t.	PALEY 635:16
there is t. for everything	BOLD 139:41
There was a t.	WORD 926:21
They reflect t.	FULL 341:58
think of having such a good t.	LOOS 517:77
this odd warp in t.	RICH 685:53
This t....is a very good one	EMER 312:3
thoughts are spurred on by t.	LECO 499:29
Through the cold t.	BIRN 131:71
through t. t. is conquered	ELIOT 307:97
tied to their t.	PISS 652:35
till t. and times are done	YEATS 932:36
T., a maniac scattering dust	TENN 843:39
t. and chance happeneth	BIBLE 101:85
t. and death pinned human	FRAME 333:79
t. and energy from	MORE 597:67
T. and the bell	ELIOT 307:98
T. and the hour runs	SHAK 766:77
t. appears to have been frozen	COUP 238:91
t. cannot destroy	MURP 604:2
t. changes people	PROU 671:88
t. Craves that we taste	GREE 371:79
t. enough for everything	GUNN 375:38
t. enough to sleep	HOUS 414:44
T. flies and takes me	SEVI 728:10
t. for such a word	SHAK 769:42
t. goes about its immemorial work	AMIS 15:6
T. goes on crutches	SHAK 744:3
t. goes...T. stays	DOBS 277:96
t. had come	PENI 646:21
t. has come...To talk of many things	CARR 196:2
T. has no divisions	MANN 545:69
T. has three dimensions	HOPK 412:98
T. has transfigured them	LARK 490:30
T. hath...A wallet	SHAK 757:5
T. held me green and dying	THOM 852:72
t. hovers o'er	JOHN 441:18
t. in everybody's life	WILD 911:87
T. in hours, days, years	VAUG 878:49
t. is all I lacked	DOUG 283:22
t. is eating away my life	BAUD 64:57
t. is long	DU 293:74
T. is money	FRAN 334:11
T. is no healer	ELIOT 308:32
t. is now near at hand	WASH 890:83
t. is on his side	BANKS 58:36
T. is on our side	GLAD 358:90
T. is our tedious is.	MILT 576:1
t. is out of joint	SHAK 752:39
T. is the 101st Senator	DODD 278:5
t. is the greatest innovator	BACON 49:25
T. is the great physician	DISR 276:40
t. is the longest distance	WILL 912:15
t. is the medium of narration	MANN 546:71
T. is the metre	WALC 884:77
t. is tied to the wrist	RAINE 677:95
T. kills us	SITW 794:86
t. like a serpent	CRANE 243:18
T., Love, Beauty	MILL 572:15
t. may cease	MARL 552:6
T., not Corydon, hath conquered	ARNO 33:47
t. not to become a father	WHITE 903:85
t. of a man or woman	WHIT 905:39
t. of awakening consciousness	RICH 685:48
t. of life is short	SHAK 742:31
t. of their growth	ROSE 697:69
T. past and t. future	ELIOT 307:96
T. present and t. past	ELIOT 307:92
t. remembered	SWIN 832:19
T. rolls	SCOTT 723:6
T.'s all-serving wave?	BRON 155:93
't.'s arrow'	EDDI 298:83
t.'s best jewel	SHAK 772:25
t.'s deer is slain	MUIR 601:54
T.'s devouring hand	BRAM 150:88
T. seemeth...of the nature	BACON 46:41
t.'s eternal motion	FORD 330:17
t.'s furrows I behold	SHAK 771:8
T. shall not lose	DONNE 279:34
T. shall turn those amber locks	DRAY 286:99
T. shall unfold	SHAK 762:5
t. sic causis has repairit	ANON 20:4
T.'s most lethal weapon	SITW 794:80
T. spent on any item	PARK 639:85
T.'s thievish progress	SHAK 772:33
T....strengthens friendship	LABR 483:62
T.'s wheels runs back	BROW 162:70
T.'s winged chariot	LINK 511:60
T. that is moved	SLES 796:15
T., that takes survey	SHAK 742:34
T., that tireless gambler	BAUD 64:63
t. that we are living in	TOML 863:10
t. that we love best	LAUD 492:64
t....the author of authors	BACON 46:36
T., the deer	MACL 535:34
T. the destroyer	ELIOT 308:31
T. the devourer	OVID 631:4
T., the world and the person	CIXO 219:
t. to cultivate modesty	SITW 794:
t. to do intensive...digging	LEAV 498
t. to every purpose	BIBLE 100:
t. to get married	EPST 315:
t. to make it shorter	PASC 641:
t. to think about it	FONT 329:
T. travels in divers paces	SHAK 750:
T. turns the old days	SWIN 833:
T. was away	MACN 538
t. was out of joint	STRA 826:
T. we may comprehend	BROW 158:
t. we shall not know	PEAC 645:
t. when all men walk proudly	RAND 845:
t. when the most powerful	MACA 526:
t. when thou mayest be found	BIBLE 95:
t. when too much seems to happen	COUP 238:
t. when you have to let your clothes	MIDL 569:
T., which takes...Our youth	RALE 677
T. will change it	BRON 155:9
T. will come when you will hear me	DISR 276:
T. will not be ours	JONS 449:
T. will run back	MILT 575:
t. with a gift of tears	SWIN 832:
t. ylost may nought recovered be	CHAU 208:
T., you old gipsy man	HODG 405:
t. you see him	RUNY 702:
T., you thief	HUNT 423:
'Tis t. to fear	SHAK 769:
to be t.'s eunuch	HOPK 413
To choose t. is to save t.	BACON 49:
to do with the t. of the day?	SHAK 741:9
to kill an admiral from t. to t.	VOLT 882:
tolling bell Measures t.	ELIOT 308:
took t. to realize	HYDE 427:
too much change in too short a t.	TOFF 862:
too much of the t.	THUR 859:
too much t. talking	THOM 853:
torments...may in length of t.	MILT 581:
Torture and T.	BYRON 180:
to the end of t.	GAIN 342:8
tower of my t.	NEME 610:
ugly things...beautiful with t.	COCT 224:
understood in t.	KIER 467:
wake us T. and t. over	LARK 490:
warn't no t. to be	TWAIN 871
wastes her t.	WALL 886:
weak by t. and fate	TENN 840:6
weight of this sad t.	SHAK 764
we shall die...'tis but the t.	SHAK 747:
whatever t. of your life	SPARK 806:2
what is t. but shadows	SASS 716:7
What, then, is t.?	AUGU 41:3
What t.'s the next swan?	SLEZ 796:
when his t. is come	TWAIN 872:2
When our t.'s come	DIBD 265:5
When t. is broke	SHAK 735:3
When t. was open-eyed	LOWE 520:4
when we meet at any t. again	DRAY 287:
whips and scorns of t.	SHAK 753:
whirligig of t.	SHAK 757:9
whole t. the engine is at work	WATT 891
witching t. of night	SHAK 754:9
world enough, and t.	MARV 555:6
writer's t. is spent	JOHN 444:
wrong most of the t.	KURZ 482:4
timebo quem t.	BIBLE 127:8
time-honoured t.-h. bread-sauce	JAMES 433:4
time-lag t.-l. of fifty years	WELLS 898:9
timepiece human t.	ASLET 36:
Times The T. every morning	KING 469:5
The T. is...entitled	HAZL 388:7
times There are t. in politics	GALB 343:5
The T. They Are A' Changing	DYLAN 297:5
tincture from the t.	DEFOE 258:1
What t.!	CICE 218:2
when the t. were not hard	EMER 313:5
times aesthetic principle of our t.	ROGE 694:1
All t. are his seasons	DONNE 281:8
all t. I have enjoyed	TENN 839:6
approaches recent t.	TAYL 837:
at all t. and in all cultures	WEBER 894:6
bad t. at Anfield	PAIS 635:
best of t....worst of t.	DICK 271:1
Different rhymes for different t.	BROD 153:4
different t. in the same country	RICA 684:3

iscern the signs of the t.? BIBLE 112:61
atness of these pursy t. SHAK 754:12
a all t. to come SMITH 798:46
a t. of crisis BALZ 57:10
ve in oppressive t. MAMET 543:22
node of their t. DAY 256:75
ot for the fashion of these t. SHAK 749:40
ot for you to know the t. BIBLE 118:27
lo t. were more dangerous INOU 430:72
ld t. GOLD 362:62
uins of forgotten t. BROW 159:84
hall there be womanly t.? MCEW 531:67
gn of knowledge in our t. WILL 914:51
undry t. and in divers manners BIBLE 124:89
are changed STEV 821:87
begin to wax old BIBLE 107:27
have become vulgar MOLI 590:29
long past WORD 927:30
of faith as best SMITH 800:98
of preservation SHAK 775:17
that try men's souls PAINE 634:88
ne-stricken t.-s. willow CALL 185:43
netable t. not necessarily WELTY 899:1
netables imposed...by railway t. TAYL 837:12
aid t. requests, invites denial SENE 727:93
nidity in a young man is t. HUGO 421:94
non Till I am T. YEATS 934:60
motheus Let old T. yield the prize DRYD 291:40
mothy T. Winters... CAUS 201:13
a cat on a hot t. roof WILL 912:25
orrugated t. roof BEEC 69:63
Gershwin keeps pounding on t. GERS 350:39
pened a t. STEV 821:76
acture Actions receive their t. DEFOE 258:17
age t. of tawny yellow SALA 710:50
agle ears of every one...shall t. BIBLE 91:83
aker do not matter a t.'s curse SHIN 789:75
akering first rule of intelligent t. EHRL 301:26
aklings drowsy t. GRAY 369:10
sel Titles are t. SHEL 782:15
at t. ends and the orange t. begins? MELV 564:47
ated in all his t. orders FIRB 323:67
nyTim none of us forget poor T. T. DICK 268:30
e school-boy's t. THAC 849:3
he t.'s a good one POUND 665:42
of every branch PLATH 654:72
aped t. with gold for this JONS 449:23
apenny Wi' t., we fear nae evil BURNS 172:21
as loyal to the t. of his stubby fingers ACHE 3:39
atoe t. on the misty mountaintops SHAK 736:69
ed busy, and the t. FITZ 325:96
Give me your t., your poor LAZA 496:51
nan is t. of London JOHN 445:27
oon get t. of them all SHAW 780:57
hou art t. ARNO 33:51
., above all GIRO 358:84
of being a woman SEXT 728:16
of knocking ARNO 32:17
of living WHITE 903:81
of the truth ALBEE 9:89
res rain never t. HUGH 419:52
resias I T., old man ELIOT 306:60
resome Love...troublesom & t. FLEM 327:63
for children SAINT 709:15
tan like thy glory, T. SHEL 785:83
tania moonlight, proud T. SHAK 737:93
tanic deck of the T. MORT 600:23
nevitable the T. was going to set sail HAGUE 376:61
tans we are T. CARL 191:85
he Personality T.: A price paid COUP 239:1
hes Bring ye all the t. BIBLE 106:20
tian cares much at heart about T. RUSK 704:14
le appropriate t. of 'agnostic' HUXL 426:7
ourage prove my t. SHAK 766:61
loes he feel his t. SHAK 768:35
riends could only read the t. WOOLF 922:27
guarantee of a t. LISP 512:74
ecords the t. good ARLO 30:62
of...significance LEVE 506:53
ain t. of Trades Unions RUSK 704:35
vhatever t. suit thee! BURNS 170:77
les because there were no t. in it HEMI 393:96
skin-titles BENET 75:9
undred new t. of idiotism NASHE 609:10
are tinsel SHEL 782:15
distinguish the mediocre SHAW 778:9
willow Willow, t., t.! GILB 355:29

Tlön metaphysicians of T. BORG 144:89
toad should I let the t. work LARK 490:28
simply talked to T. GRAH 366:39
Squat like a t. MILT 583:73
t. beneath the harrow KIPL 470:73
t. in fun CRAS 244:44
t. or adder to catch MUIR 602:56
t., ugly and venomous SHAK 749:33
your arm, old t. LARK 491:34
toady T., perhaps, even tacky ACHE 3:48
toast faint flavour of t. TRAV 865:48
let the t. pass SHER 788:54
milk and t. and honey MITC 588:90
my t. would be ADAMS 5:92
smell of buttered t. GRAH 366:39
t. of a' the town BURNS 173:43
t. with three times three GILB 355:20
Will Not Take this T. ANON 21:37
toasted t., and buttered on both sides JACK 431:5
toasted-cheese called him...'T.-c.' CARR 197:29
tobacco Beer, t., and music MANN 545:64
lives without t. MOLI 590:33
T., divine, rare, superexcellent t. BURT 174:77
tobacco-pipes dirty t.-p. ELIOT 304:13
Toby uncle T. would never offer STER 817:74
today All the poet can do t. OWEN 632:56
beat them t. STARK 813:76
down in the woods t. BRAT 150:96
here t., and gone to-morrow BEHN 71:15
Here t.—in next week tomorrow! GRAH 366:38
Kind is my love t. SHAK 773:43
live t. MART 555:46
Living for t. LENN 503:91
Maybe not t., maybe not tomorrow EPST 314:80
Never do t. what you can put off PUNCH 672:8
person who lives for t. BELL 72:40
such a day tomorrow as t. SHAK 770:74
technology of t. GABOR 342:81
t. hidden by science! NIET 615:85
t. I am fifty-five REED 681:80
T. if ye will hear his voice BOOK 143:65
t. is no longer news RUSK 703:98
T., t., unhappy day SHAK 735:16
T. we have naming of parts REED 681:77
vibrant and the beautiful t. MALL 542:90
Where are the warriors t.? SITT 793:56
wiser t. than he was yesterday POPE 659:89
toddle t. safely home and die SASS 716:62
toe t. of one shoe TRAV 864:43
t. to t. PEEL 646:10
Washington Post...with your big t. LANCE 487:73
toenails makes my t. twinkle THOM 853:79
toes Pobble who has no t. LEAR 498:87
stepping on your t. MOSS 600:67
t. grow big and black THOM 853:95
tread in the bus on my t.? AUDEN 40:93
turn out your t. as you walk CARR 196:95
toff Me pal...does the t. DENN 262:1
toga Idealism is the noble t. HUXL 426:2
t., the kilt MURR 604:7
together able to sit t. KING 468:39
all hang t. FRAN 335:16
Both bound t. WALL 886:16
looking t. in the same direction SAINT 709:12
toil cricket's manly t. BYRON 179:95
fatuous sunbeams t. OWEN 632:64
ferocious and endless t. GARL 346:50
Horny-handed sons of t. SALI 711:67
love and t. KIPL 473:62
mock their useful t. GRAY 369:14
more sweet than t. TENN 839:58
necessary...to be worn with t. EURI 316:10
Sleep after t. SPEN 808:81
smeared with t. HOPK 412:83
t. and trouble of acquiring it SMITH 797:42
T. conquered the world VIRG 882:31
t., envy, want JOHN 441:17
t. in other men's extremes KYD 482:49
t. its desolation HAMM 379:11
t. obscure, and a' that BURNS 173:46
t. Of dropping buckets COWP 241:73
t. that is destroyed MCCA 528:6
War...is t. and trouble DRYD 291:38
waste their t. SCOTT 723:89
Why t. to no avail? LI 509:13
with his t. he won DRYD 290:78
toiled forgot for which he t. SHAK 771:12

toilet can be read only in the t. MILL 572:19
toilette judged...through her t. DE 257:94
toils prudently their t. upbraid MARV 556:71
t., the conflicts, the sufferings SCHW 721:70
token sending...small cash t. CONN 233:67
told ate and drank as he was t. HOFF 406:51
not t. even the half POLO 657:40
the way it is t. here PACH 633:69
tolerable Not a t. woman's part AUST 43:75
scarcely t. and the...unbearable DAFOE 250:63
tolerance excessive t. of suicide DURK 296:32
t. as uncertainty BURKE 169:57
to practice t. UNIT 873:69
tolerate cannot t. them DE 259:40
Louisianans don't t. corruption ANON 20:76
t. unlikely arguments FORD 330:14
We are not going to t. REAG 680:60
toll t. me back KEATS 460:64
Tolstoy a T. or a Flaubert WOLFE 920:2
in any ring with Mr T. HEMI 394:18
T., Hugo, Dostoevsky LESS 505:35
Tom Every T., Dick and Harry GOLD 362:82
his name was T. KING 469:51
more...than in all T. Jones JOHN 444:95
SoT. went home with Ellie KING 469:58
T. bears logs SHAK 734:94
tomahawks t., wi' blude red-rusted BURNS 172:22
tomato You say t. GERS 351:42
tomatoes if I grew t. TREV 865:60
tomb a t. and a dungeon HAWT 386:47
best-seller is the gilded t. SMITH 800:84
buried in the silent t. WORD 928:49
Claret on my t. KEATS 458:12
erect...his own t. SHAK 745:25
fair Fidele's grassy t. COLL 228:41
ghost from the t. SHEL 783:41
graces...blossom on the t. CRAB 242:96
Kings for such a t. MILT 576:3
made our land a t. ORAH 627:21
Marriage is the grave or t. of wit CAVE 201:19
Pyramus, at Ninny's T. SHAK 738:2
smoking t. GINS 357:62
straight and narrow as a t. SMITH 800:95
this side the t. BYRON 179:22
this side the t. DAVI 255:49
t. remain uninscribed EMMET 313:59
totter towards the t. SAYE 717:88
toward the silent t. WORD 928:59
world would smell...a t. SHEL 784:66
tombs Faith...feeds among the t. MELV 564:27
Nerves sit...like T. DICK 272:60
rose from these stone t. MORG 597:81
shovelled into the t. SAND 713:95
upon our brazen t. SHAK 733:67
tombstone The t. of capitalism STILL 824:46
t. white KIPL 471:5
tomb-stones t.-s. where flowers BLAKE 100:97
Tommy O it's T. this KIPL 471:90
T. 'ow's yer soul? KIPL 471:91
tomorrow Boast not thyself of t. BIBLE 100:56
building...with t. inside AKERS 9:79
die for him t. BALL 55:65
for t. we die BIBLE 121:16
For t. we shall die! PARK 638:61
here to-day, and gone t.-m. BEHN 71:15
History...start again t. DURR 296:41
If scientists knew t.'s discovery ZUCK 937:6
Kill me t. SHAK 761:10
put off till t. PUNCH 672:8
some good thing comes t. SHAK 743:60
such a day t. as today SHAK 770:74
Thanks for t. ATKI 37:5
T., and t., and t. SHAK 769:42
T. country then RICH 686:71
t. is another day MITC 588:2
T. is Saint Crispian SHAK 746:57
T.-m. let us do or die! CAMP 186:72
t. morning, We shall have REED 681:77
T. shall we strangers TU 869:56
t.'s life's too late MART 555:46
t. that is the object RUSK 703:98
t. we shall die BIBLE 102:22
t. we will run faster FITZ 325:2
t....what he did today and yesterday LABR 483:68
T. when thou leav'st DONNE 279:38
what's going to happen t. QUINN 675:54
tomorrows time's t. SASS 716:60

tom-tit little t.-t. sang — GILB 355:29
tonality T. is a natural force — HIND 403:97
tone deep, autumnal t. — SHEL 783:47
  ditties of no t. — KEATS 459:52
tones noble t. — GAUG 347:66
  t. of a loved voice — ARNO 31:99
tongs t. and boniest doggerel — RUSK 704:37
tongue Before I taught my t. — VAUG 878:45
  bridleth not his t. — BIBLE 124:8
  bury my t. at Champmédy — BENET 75:12
  calls with a cockerel's t. — LEE 500:42
  cannot endure my Lady T. — SHAK 744:96
  citizens speaking the same t. — MAZZ 562:2
  Confounds the t. — SHAK 729:47
  daily changing t.? — WALL 886:16
  every t. should confess — BIBLE 123:54
  eye to see nor t. — LENT 503:2
  for mortal t. — GURN 375:45
  hearing not my t. — SHAK 758:30
  hidden even as a strange t. — DURER 295:28
  hold your t. — DONNE 279:43
  I have often given t. — YEATS 933:41
  In a neat's t. — SHAK 739:40
  knot that would not yield to the t. — BIER 128:17
  knoweth and yet holdeth his t. — BIBLE 108:62
  Lends the t. vows — SHAK 751:23
  Letting the rank t. blossom — BROW 162:75
  lost my t. from — NICH 613:85
  made our English t. — SPEN 808:71
  More than that t. — SHAK 771:10
  Murder, though it have no t. — SHAK 753:70
  music of his own vain t. — SHAK 733:73
  mysmetre for defaute of t. — CHAU 208:65
  my t. from…lying — BOOK 142:14
  my t., the mystery — AQUI 28:28
  never in the t. — SHAK 734:93
  obnoxious to each carping t. — BRAD 149:80
  of a slow t. — BIBLE 88:13
  relation between the human t. — WAXM 893:60
  sad words of t. or pen — WHIT 906:59
  sharp t. in your head — PERE 648:60
  sharp t. is the only — IRVI 430:80
  shouldst give dust a t. — HERB 398:13
  show you have a Scotch t. — SCOTT 724:37
  snakes with double t. — SHAK 737:98
  stick out your t. — MARQ 554:22
  still the t. is wagging — SHER 787:50
  stroke of the t. breaketh — BIBLE 108:58
  sweet English t. — FLEC 327:44
  thud of consonants in t. — BROY 163:98
  t. acquire the Southern — STEV 823:24
  t. and soul…be hypocrites — SHAK 754:98
  t. Could scarcely cry — BLAKE 134:33
  t. could utter — TENN 840:67
  t. Dropped manna — MILT 581:21
  t. is a fire — BIBLE 124:13
  t. is a little member — BIBLE 124:12
  t. is the clapper — SHAK 745:11
  t. like the tail of a dog — NASHE 609:19
  t. seeking out…a sore tooth — BURU 174:86
  t. shall sing aloud — BIBLE 95:31
  t.'s sweet air — SHAK 737:85
  t. taking a trip — NABO 606:30
  t.…tipped with gold — JONS 449:23
  trippingly on the t. — SHAK 754:85
  truth in every shepherd's t. — RALE 677:98
  use of my oracular t. — SHER 787:40
  when he's holding his t. — JAMES 433:38
  While I have a t. — OCON 621:21
  with stammering lips and another t. — BIBLE 103:26
  with your heart and t. — SHEL 782:14
  words of t. and pen — HARTE 385:19
  Wounds…inflicted by the t. — RICH 686:69
  write well in any t. — ASCH 35:79
  you dried neat's t. — SHAK 742:15
  Your hand, your t. — SHAK 766:84
tongued t. with fire — ELIOT 309:40
tongueless t. vigil and all the pain — SWIN 832:18
tongues all nations…and t. — BIBLE 126:59
  began to speak with other t. — BIBLE 119:29
  clocks the t. of bawds — SHAK 741:94
  Had I your t. and eyes — SHAK 764:5
  keep your t. well-omened — HORA 413:22
  silence enough t. — SHAK 775:22
  sores on innocent t. — OWEN 632:57
  terror…the t. declare — ELIOT 309:47
  though fallen, and evil t. — MILT 583:89

thousand several t. — SHAK 731:18
t. A dismal universal hiss — MILT 585:24
t. in trees — SHAK 749:34
t. of flame are in-folded — ELIOT 309:51
t. of men and of angels — BIBLE 121:9
t. of the French Council — SHAK 746:68
t. recant like beaten weather vanes — CRANE 243:24
t., that syllable men's — MILT 577:31
Walls have t. — SWIFT 831:90
we loose wild t. — KIPL 472:22
whispering t. can poison truth — COLE 226:7
tongue-tied t.-t.'s fighting — HARR 384:1
tonic hatred is a t. — BALZ 57:12
  t. to all save men — DOUG 283:28
tonight fixed it t. — SNYD 803:50
  soul be required of me t. — SMITH 800:4
  T. n. she'll hae but three — BALL 56:83
  T.—to you — NIXON 617:44
  T. we sleep — MACN 538:7
tons saves t. of explanation — SAKI 710:49
  weighs a hundred t. — MACC 527:85
Tony T. will go on and on and on — PRES 667:3
took person you and I t. me for — CARL 191:69
tool basic t. for the manipulation — DICK 265:61
  computer…only a t. — AMER 13:76
  fashioned it with a graving t. — BIBLE 89:26
  only edged t. — IRVI 430:80
  T. Maker, Stacker of Wheat — SAND 712:91
  worker uses a t. — MARX 558:13
tools filmmaker…afford his own t. — WELL 897:50
  Give us the t. — CHUR 217:80
  persons using parties as t. — DISR 277:82
  rudimentary t. to discover — PETE 649:78
  secrets are edged t. — DRYD 287:21
  Sin has many t. — HOLM 408:84
  t. of their t. — THOR 857:85
  t.…painters' techniques — RENO 683:9
  t. that go together with culture — REYES 684:21
  want to know which t. — SEXT 728:15
  Without t. he is nothing — CARL 192:91
tooth blue-black t. of sheer rock — BENU 78:85
  drill to the t. of America — CLIN 221:92
  like a broken t. — BIBLE 100:51
  moral truth is a hollow t. — MAST 560:53
  red in t. and claw — TENN 843:36
  red in t. and claw — TENN 843:45
  sharper than a serpent's t. — SHAK 762:63
  tongue seeking out…a sore t. — BURU 174:86
  t. for a t. — BIBLE 109:91
  t. for t. — BIBLE 89:24
toothache endure the t. patiently — SHAK 745:21
  Music helps not the t. — HERB 398:21
toothless t. terrier on Valium — SIKO 791:31
tooth-picker fetch you a t.-p. now — SHAK 744:95
toothpicks pear on top of two t. — ACHE 2:28
top always room at the t. — WEBS 894:72
  carefully cleared at the t. — SHUL 789:90
  dipped its t. — FROST 338:92
  from the naked t. — WORD 928:52
  from this t. Of speculation — MILT 586:36
  I'm the bottom, you're the t. — PORT 663:5
  On her ingrateful t.! — SHAK 763:68
  only way to get to the t. — ZATO 936:90
  on tap, but not on t. — CHUR 217:6
  started at the t. and worked down — WELL 897:51
  t. of admiration — SHAK 774:89
  t. of the greasy pole — DISR 276:71
  You're the t. — PORT 663:6
topaz gates of pearl and t. — LAUR 492:70
topee swell beneath a solar t. — HERB 399:24
toper poor t. whose untutored sense — CRAB 242:81
topic conflicting…on the same t. — ALTH 13:70
  constant t. — JOHN 443:86
  most poetical t. in the world — POE 656:25
  no ordinary t. — PLATO 655:94
topics have but two t. — JOHN 445:24
tops like whipping t. — HODG 405:45
  used to think their slender t. — HOOD 410:38
torch bear the t. of truth — LICH 509:20
  king's t. throws its light — CYRA 250:60
  lights the t. of war — HITL 404:18
  Man is a t. borne in the wind — CHAP 206:14
  science…the t. which illuminates — PAST 642:46
  t. has been passed — KENN 462:12
torches as we with t. do — SHAK 757:15
  one thousand burning t. — LABE 482:54
  O, she doth teach the t. — SHAK 736:42

toreador T., en garde! — MEIL 563
Tories potential T. — ORWE 628:
  sensible T. — WALP 887:
  T. own no argument but force — BROW 159:
torment Christ perish in t. — SHAW 781:
  major writer…required major t. — BERG 79
  More grievous t. — KEATS 458:
  more I feel T. within — MILT 58
  smoke of their t. ascendeth — BIBLE 126:
  t. for our crimes — CHES 252:
  t. of the night's untruth — DANI 252:
torments t.…may in length of time — MILT 581:
  will not have anybody's t. — CHES 211:
Toronto T. is a kind of — USTI 875
torpedoes Damn the t.! — FARR 318:
torpor woke me from the t. — WARR 889:
torrent fiend for becoming a t. — LIGNE 509:
torso background to a t. — AUDEN 39:
  t. which has no face — YOUR 936:
tortoise writing for the t. market — BROO 156:
torture Behaviourism…t. — AUDEN 41:
  endure t.…for the national good — PANK 636:
  human cities t. — BYRON 180:
  T. and Time — BYRON 180:
  t. in the country of the mind — WHITE 903:
  t. into aught of the sublime — POE 656:
  t. not again — SHEL 786
  t. of a lingering…passion — ETHE 315:
  t.…of his fellow-creatures — FROU 339:
  t. one poor word — DRYD 289:
Tory born a T.…die a T. — POWE 667:
  extinction of the T. Party — BEVAN 84
  hatred for the T. Party — BEVAN 84
  Let Whig and T. a' agree — SKIN 795:
  neither a Whig nor a T. — DISR 276:
  what is called the T. — CROK 245:
  wise T. and a wise Whig — JOHN 446:
Toryism essence of T. — BAGE 51:
tosh Never did I read such t. — WOOLF 922:
toss t. him to My breast — HERB 398:
  t. in the spray — ARNO 31:
tossed t. and gored several persons — BOSW 145:
totalitarian t. and corrupt tyrannies — MO 589:
  t. simplicities — LYND 524:
totalitarianism friends of t. — ORWE 629:
  West has not lived through t. — YELT 934:
totality t. that I cannot suppress — ROSSO 698
totter charming to t. into vogue — WALP 887:
  t. towards the tomb — SAYE 717:
touch dares not put it to the t. — MONT 593
  Do not let him t. you! — YEATS 934:
  Do not t. me — BIBLE 128
  exquisite t.…is denied to me — SCOTT 725:
  Gently its t. awoke him — OWEN 632:
  intercourse of t. — WORD 925:
  little t. of Harry — SHAK 746:
  mere t. of cold philosophy? — KEATS 458:
  Of t. or marble — JONS 449:
  shivering-sweet to the t. — CORN 237:
  T. me not — BIBLE 118:
  T. me with noble anger — SHAK 763:
  T.…most demystifying of all senses — BART 62:
  t. of earthly years — WORD 924:
  t. of holy bread — SHAK 750:6
  t. of love — SHAK 729:
  t. of nature — SHAK 757
  t., taste, smell your way — BUEC 165:
  wants the natural t. — SHAK 768:2
touches Nothing t. — HUGH 419:
  t. it, he fingers it, he feels it — SENG 727:9
touching danger in t. — BURNS 173:
touch-line kick…over the t.-l. — CHAR 207:4
touchstone t. of the highest — RUSS 705:4
tough bloody t. being a legend — ATKI 37:
  gets t., the t. get — ROCK 693:8
  She was too t. — TAYL 837:
  t. on crime — BLAIR 132:9
  Truth is t. — HOLM 408:8
tough-minded Tender…t.-m. — JAMES 434:7
toujours t. gai t. gai — MARQ 553:2
tour t. round the world — HARD 381:3
Tourane vulgar soul. Such is T. — MAUG 561:8
tourism T. is the march of stupidity — DELI 261:7
tourist camera makes everyone a t. — SONT 804:7
  t. is an ugly human being — KINC 468:8
tourists world's t. are coming here — WILS 916:9
tous T. pour un — DUMAS 294:9

trains Do people who wave at t. — MCGO 532:85
Fair t. of images — WORD 928:50
Garscadden T. — KENN 462:99
No bloody t. — BLAIR 132:97
rush through the fields in t. — CHES 213:99
t. will run over their tails — SITW 793:61
trait Death is an acquired t. — ALLEN 12:48
depend on this t. — JAMES 434:66
traitor Face of a t.! — HUGO 420:76
Thou art a t. — SHAK 731:11
t. Stands in worse — SHAK 774:67
traitors cowards flinch and t. sneer — CONN 232:55
doubts are t. — SHAK 757:17
fears do make us t. — SHAK 768:26
hate t. and the treason love — DRYD 291:22
more strong than t.' arms — SHAK 748:11
see a sort of t. — SHAK 735:25
t....are a unfortunate class — WARD 888:56
tramp why the lady is a t. — HART 384:31
trams in the streets, in the t. — MAYA 562:92
tramways t., buses, aeroplanes — LARI 490:19
trance in mad t. — SHEL 786:3
tranquil anchored in t. waters — KENN 463:23
tranquillity chaos...in t. — THUR 860:53
divine T. — TENN 847:35
emotion recollected in t. — WORD 925:10
sinking down in its t. — WORD 926:13
Sorrow is t. — PARK 638:66
transactions t....people expect — AUST 43:72
transcend write poems...to t. — SART 715:42
transcendent no t. themes in life — FORD 330:21
t. enlightenment — COND 230:84
t. passion — DRYD 289:57
transcendental T. Meditation — SHAR 776:42
transform t. honesty — SHAK 753:76
t. Men into monsters — FORD 330:19
transformation fluidity, t. — MARC 549:30
yearning for t. that underlies — MATH 560:57
transformed found himself t. — KAFKA 454:26
transgression where no law...no t. — BIBLE 120:63
transgressions acknowledge my t. — BIBLE 95:28
Remember not...my t. — BIBLE 94:5
so far hath he removed our t. — BIBLE 97:64
wounded for our t. — BIBLE 104:51
transgressors teach t. thy ways — BIBLE 95:30
transient Mirth is short and t. — ADDI 6:20
transitory t. in this vale of tears — FERRE 321:19
translate few...as cannot write, t. — DENH 261:93
t. beauty into his likeness — SHAK 753:76
t. pulsations into images — RICH 685:47
You've no right to t. — QUIL 674:47
translation book...merely needs t. — PROU 671:91
lose something in the t. — DRYD 288:24
T. is the paradigm — MATH 560:57
vanity of t. — SHEL 786:13
what is lost in t. — FROST 339:20
translations T....are seldom faithful — CAMP 186:63
translunary those brave t. things — DRAY 287:5
transmission gears of a cycle t. — PIRS 652:25
transport hours of t. we shall spend! — AUST 43:69
t. breaks upon the town — DICK 272:55
t. in Los Angeles — LEBO 499:14
turned to share the t. — WORD 928:49
yearn for the first available t. — GELL 348:1
transvestite about time a t. potter won — PERRY 648:68
persecution of the t. — WHITE 902:70
trap after leaving the t. — HUXL 426:7
T. of their own making — FLET 327:64
trapeze man on the flying t. — LEYB 508:11
man on the flying t. — SARO 714:34
man on the flying t. — THUR 25 859
trappings goods and t. of your life — MOORE 594:13
t. and the suits of woe — SHAK 751:4
Trappist credit to a T. nun — SHAR 776:41
diplomat is a deaf T. — LECA 499:22
traps t. for eager and clever fools — SNYD 803:52
trash Cash for t. — CLIN 221:87
white man is t. — LEE 500:38
travail earth in t. and in pain — LONG 516:59
travel all that t. by land — SWIFT 832:9
crime...you t. a lot — ALLEN 12:41
effect of t. on a man — LIVI 512:83
Good t. books — RABAN 675:60
I cannot rest from t. — TENN 839:63
if one wishes to t. in peace — STARK 813:73
Never to t. any road — IBN 427:32
not to t. but to love — AUGU 42:45

real way to t.! — GRAH 366:38
To t. hopefully — STEV 822:95
To t. is useful — CELI 202:35
t. for it too! — SHAK 750:74
t. forth so far! — SHAK 749:32
t. for t.'s sake — STEV 821:75
t. four hundred miles — WHITE 902:69
T. is fatal to prejudice — TWAIN 870:78
t., so broadening — THER 851:45
t. the open road — WHIT 905:40
t....the sweetest and most delightful — CORY 238:79
two classes of t. — BENC 74:97
universal test of t. — GELL 348:1
Writing and t. broaden your ass — HEMI 394:19
travelled care which way he t. — BEAV 67:24
He who has not t. — ANON 24:17
I t. among unknown men — WORD 925:9
took the one less t. by — FROST 338:89
traveller Farewell, Monsieur T. — SHAK 750:75
historian or a t. — HARR 383:87
If a t. were informed — DISR 276:64
'Is there anybody there?' said the T. — DELA 260:63
no t. returns — TWAIN 871:7
Stand still, t., and read! — ANON 26:90
to the t., a mountain — THOR 857:78
t. between life and death — WORD 927:36
t. from an antique land — SHEL 784:49
t. from the cradle to the grave — SHEL 785:82
t. is...recommended — BAED 51:77
t. must have the back — NASHE 609:19
t. must...make himself...useless — GALT 345:31
t.'s passport is sometimes asked for — BAED 51:76
t....you have great reason — SHAK 750:73
when the t. reaches it — STARK 813:74
Where the t.'s journey is done — BLAKE 134:53
travellers not be like other t. — AUST 43:69
sit outside at 'The T.' Rest' — HARDY 382:76
t. and wanderers by nature — FERB 320:94
t. can use...editions — LEVIN 506:64
t. in Europe — MELV 564:42
t., who make too short — MONT 591:63
travelling knowledge gained in t. — BAUD 64:66
never t. less — WESL 900:23
So it is in t. — JOHN 445:31
t. in a straight line — MAIL 540:44
t. induces a feeling — THER 851:45
use of t. — JOHN 447:78
travels In my t....never felt — BOSW 146:11
sundry contemplation of my t. — SHAK 750:72
talk of my t. was to tarnish — THES 851:51
t. fastest who t. alone — KIPL 470:79
treacherous none so t. — SHAW 778:84
treachers t. by spherical — SHAK 762:57
treachery mother of all t. — PAIS 635:4
tread All that t. — BRYA 163:12
face with an undaunted t. — STEV 823:21
heavy is the t. — THOM 854:31
so airy a t. — TENN 845:92
tawny t. sublime — CRAIK 242:7
We t. upon — SHAK 758:21
treason feel the t. sharply — SHAK 774:67
hate traitors and the t. love — DRYD 291:22
he harbours t. — SHAK 730:56
last temptation is the greatest t. — ELIOT 307:4
Music is a t. — KHOM 466:97
popular humanity is t. — ADDI 7:35
T. and murder — SHAK 745:35
t. can but peep — SHAK 754:21
T. doth never prosper — HARI 382:80
T. has done his worst — SHAK 768:14
T. is but trusted — SHAK 742:30
t. is not owned — DRYD 290:6
t. to his country — JOHN 442:50
treasons From plots and t. — DRYD 290:96
t., stratagems, and spoils — SHAK 741:88
what care we For t. — WORD 924:73
treasure covetous man all his t. — MILT 579:78
dig for hidden t. — TWAIN 870:89
great t. and trouble therewith — BIBLE 99:32
he that has stolen the t. — CONG 231:15
If love be t. — OTWAY 634:46
Preserve it as your chiefest t. — BELL 72:45
purest t. mortal times afford — SHAK 734:99
Rich the t. — DRYD 291:35
She is your t. — SHAK 732:30
Thine be ilka joy and t. — BURNS 172:30
t. in earthen vessels — BIBLE 122:23

t. in heaven — BIBLE 113:73
t. is their only trust — DYER 297:52
t. may be hard to find — BRON 154:73
t. on which we should live — HERZ 401:59
Without glaidnes availis no t. — DUNB 294:3
treasures accumulated t. of age — IRVI 430:79
Better than all t. — SHEL 784:62
Not all the t. of the world — PAINE 634:89
opened thee t. — BIBLE 108:73
Strange T. lodg'd — TRAH 864:38
t. upon earth — BIBLE 110:99
treasury cast into the t. — BIBLE 114:18
If the T. were to fill — KEYN 466:88
well-filled t. — FRED 335:32
wonder sitting on the T. Bench — CHUR 216:69
treat always t. humanity...as an end — KANT 455:45
If you t. her gently — SNOW 802:45
must t. them carefully — HIND 403:99
Talk about a t. — COLL 227:35
way to t. her — FAUL 319:73
who gives a child a t. — MASE 559:35
treaties arising from t. — UNIT 873:69
T. are like girls — DE 259:38
treatise T. of Human Nature — HUME 422:16
treatment diligent t. — PLATO 655:2
one sort of t. may serve for all — CARL 191:70
scientific t. for all diseases — SHAW 780:48
Suitable Case for T. — MERC 566:91
t. of a question is like — WITT 918:45
treaty hand that signed the t. — THOM 852:63
not a peace t. — FOCH 328:81
tree almost insensitive t. — DARIO 252:4
as a t. bears apples — EMER 313:42
billboard lovely as a t. — NASH 608:84
birds still hopping on the t. — STEV 822:1
bomb the knot off a t. — JENS 437:27
buss grew til a t. — YOUNG 935:78
But a t. chiefly — THOM 854:15
But there's a t., of many — WORD 926:23
carve on every t. — SHAK 749:55
Christmas t. is lighted — MOYN 601:41
climbing a birch t. — FROST 338:92
desire...a t. of life — BIBLE 99:12
desire...a t. of life — BIBLE 99:25
dew-bespangling herb and t. — HERR 400:43
each t....a tranced woman — FREE 336:43
evergreen t. of diabolical knowledge — SHER 787:36
every t. of the garden — BIBLE 86:45
Eve, who tasted of the t. — LANY 489:3
form as a t. has form — POUND 666:69
fruit Of that forbidden t. — MILT 580:91
gave me of the t. — BIBLE 86:52
golden t. of actual life — GOET 360:17
Hast thou eaten of the t. — BIBLE 86:51
hewing down a t. — JOHN 445:34
land where the Bong-t. — LEAR 497:84
laughing leaves of the t. — SWIN 832:20
leaves grow on the t. — YEATS 932:29
leaves to a t. — KEATS 457:95
live on this Crumpetty T. — LEAR 498:90
loved a t. or flower — MOORE 596:53
make a right Rose T. — YEATS 933:47
man, a madyn, and a t. — ANON 19:94
marked a t. — STUA 827:97
On a t. by a river — GILB 355:29
on the T. of Life — MILT 582:58
pine t. drops its dead — MERE 567:12
problems of a t. — MAMET 544:34
sat down under a juniper t. — BIBLE 92:23
sat under the T. — KIPL 471:3
shade of a Coolibah t. — PATE 642:54
shady cypress t. — ROSS 697:83
sings on yon pom'granate t. — SHAK 736:68
smell thee on the t. — SHAK 761:8
some single herb or t. — MARV 556:71
somewhere in the Orange T. — NEIL 610:30
spoils the growth of the t. — SHER 788:53
stands the lonely t. — MILL 571:86
sticking in a t. — SCOTT 724:36
swan-bosomed t. — SITW 794:72
take a t. from the forest — SCOTT 723:13
Teach...under the nearest t. — QABO 674:32
that's why the t. — ANON 22:51
thocht it was a trustie t. — BALL 56:94
three ravens sat on a t. — BALL 56:91
t., a house, a field — MONET 591:53
t. Continues to be — KNOX 476:22

War…is toil and t. — DRYD 291:38
When in t., delegate — WAGN 884:65
where all t. seems — SWIN 833:33
troubled Let not your heart be t. — BIBLE 118:11
Let not your heart be t. — BIBLE 118:8
t. on every side — BIBLE 122:24
troubles got over all its t. — JERO 437:35
help them through their t. — ALCO 10:7
take arms against a sea of t. — SHAK 753:74
t. are worse than your own — ALGR 11:29
t. of our proud and angry dust — HOUS 416:73
t. of the brain — SHAK 768:38
trough slip with the gravy t. — MACB 527:82
t. between the two world wars — LEWIS 508:6
trousers asked me for my t. — KRUG 481:23
bottoms of my t. rolled — ELIOT 304:24
Chinese nurse with green t. — MANS 546:83
cloud in t. — MAYA 562:91
covered…with the t. of decorum — LICH 509:16
involve taking the t. off — BENN 76:29
men's t.…great modern things — WARH 889:64
Muses in striped t. — ORWE 629:79
never have your best t. on — IBSEN 428:34
t., jackets, shoes — LARI 490:19
t. of Winston Churchill — BREZ 152:22
trout find a t. in the milk — THOR 857:76
portrait of a t. — HUGH 419:33
Where the grey t. lies — HOGG 406:60
trowel lays it on with a t. — CONG 231:9
Troy against our crumbling T. — MACN 538:1
fields where T. once was — OVID 631:41
Homer…chronicled the siege of T. — CUOMO 248:30
Priam's sons of T. — SURR 829:37
sail from the land of T. — VIRG 882:16
Scare T. out of itself — SHAK 757:14
T.'s Chieftain — VIRG 882:18
T.'s sacred citadel — HOMER 409:24
Was there another T. — YEATS 933:40
Where's T. — BRAM 150:88
truant Biting my t. pen — SIDN 790:8
every t. knew — GOLD 361:54
t. in the law — SHAK 729:44
truce vacation, or a t. — WORD 928:54
truck t., a producer or a critic — LEMM 502:77
t. passing by a factory — CAGE 184:28
truckload equipment by the t. — WELL 897:50
trudged t. along unknowing — DRYD 292:50
true accept…as being t. — AYER 44:10
admitted to be t. — JAMES 434:72
always say what's t. — STEV 822:12
And is it t.? — BETJ 84:99
any less real and t. — SHAW 777:56
Art for the sake of the t. — SAND 712:89
as long as it isn't t. — CAPO 189:26
as t.…as taxes is — DICK 269:73
be known to be t. — RUSS 705:42
Be so t. to thyself — BACON 49:20
brew that is t. — PANA 636:27
But a t. man — INGR 429:59
called Faithful and T. — BIBLE 127:75
can the devil speak t.? — SHAK 766:75
Change proves t. — ICHI 428:38
common reproach is t. — SOCR 803:54
dark and t. — TENN 842:9
don't know they're t. — BACH 46:31
equally happy, is not t. — JOHN 443:82
errors that I had accepted as t. — DESC 263:23
Every t. work of art — FRIE 337:72
expected to go quite t. — JOHN 446:67
false or t. — YEATS 932:33
friends are t. — BIER 129:31
Geometry is not t. — PIRS 652:29
Hope, art thou t. — SIDN 790:12
hope's t. gage — RALE 677:99
if I know what t. love is — TENN 846:18
If it be t. that good wine — SHAK 751:94
keep on saying…it will be t. — BENN 76:45
kept him falsely t. — TENN 846:19
let God be t. — BIBLE 120:61
Live pure, speak t. — TENN 847:58
no matter how t. — VIDAL 880:91
Nothing is t. — ANOU 26:99
nothing is t. except the exaggerations — ADOR 7:53
nothing more t. — LARK 491:44
old saying and a t. — SWIFT 831:71
remain t. to himself — KENN 463:35
ring in the t. — TENN 844:60

rough appraisal, but curiously t. — ACHE 2:31
said t. things…by wrong names — BROW 161:52
say something t. — JAMES 434:57
something is t. that isn't — WILS 915:74
Some t., some light — TENN 847:42
supposing thou art t. — SHAK 772:36
sure they are t. — SHAK 770:94
that which was prov'd t. before — BUTL 177:57
'The t.'…is only the expedient — JAMES 434:73
to haue t. lufe agane — HENR 396:54
to thine own self be t. — SHAK 751:22
t. and honourable wife — SHAK 747:86
t. attribute of the soul — STAEL 812:54
T. eloquence has no time — PASC 640:10
T. Love…differs from gold — SHEL 786:10
t. love hath my heart — SIDN 790:4
t. lover of literature — SOUT 805:6
t. nature of poetry — RICH 685:52
t. that sin is the cause — JULI 452:5
t., wise friend called Piggy — GOLD 360:28
t. wood, of yew wood — DOYLE 285:57
t. writers have experienced this feeling — SARR 715:38
what a man would like to be t. — BACON 47:59
whatever we conceive…is t. — DESC 263:22
what is t. cannot always be proven — HUMP 422:20
What I tell you three times is t. — CARR 197:27
what people say of us is t.! — SMITH 799:74
whatsoever things are t. — BIBLE 123:61
what we believe is not necessarily t. — BELL 71:32
when thieves cannot be t. — SHAK 741:8
which may be t. — HAWT 386:41
truest those who paint 'em t. — ADDI 5:6
t. poetry is the most feigning — SHAK 750:66
truffle t. is not a true aphrodisiac — BRIL 152:37
truffles where the t. are — ALBEE 10:92
truism t. in technological — STER 817:62
truisms box of t. — MACN 538:13
Truman colleagues in the T. cabinet — REST 683:13
Trump T. is the price of progress — KRUG 481:25
trump at the last t. — BIBLE 121:19
Lord with the sound of the t. — BOOK 143:52
trumpet Blow t. — TENN 847:41
do not sound a t. before thee — BIBLE 109:96
great voice, as of a t. — BIBLE 125:44
if the t. give an uncertain sound — BIBLE 121:10
novel was not a t. — LESS 505:40
Pride…his own t. — SHAK 757:98
shifted his t. — GOLD 362:72
t. and the steady drum — MCCA 527:91
t. is sounding — MCCA 527:87
t. of a prophecy! — SHEL 783:48
t. shall sound — BIBLE 121:19
t. shrill hath thrice — SPEN 809:98
trumpets blow Your t., angels — DONNE 280:66
eagles and the t. — ELIOT 305:44
eating…to the sound of t. — SMITH 801:22
never been amid the blare of t. — EUDA 315:3
priests blew with the t. — BIBLE 90:64
saith among the t., Ha, ha — BIBLE 93:75
silver, snarling t. — KEATS 458:31
thunderstorm or blare of t. — MANN 545:69
t., beat the drums! — MORE 597:74
T. sounded for him — BUNY 167:77
t. which sing to battle — SHEL 786:17
trumps If dirt were t. — LAMB 487:56
Let spades be t.! — POPE 659:74
truncheons extort their t. — COWP 241:77
trunk perish, t. and all — SOPH 804:85
Sin's rotten t. — COWP 241:62
So large a t. — BELL 72:47
trust absolute t. — SHAK 766:79
all power is a t. — DISR 275:35
brightness to hold in t. — SPEN 807:49
children of men put their t. — BIBLE 95:14
degree and a quality of t. — SHAP 776:36
does still my t. renew — BRID 152:26
do I put my t. — BIBLE 96:40
don't t. anybody — KAIKO 454:32
don't t. him, we are friends — BREC 151:12
empire is…power in t. — DRYD 290:85
equally unsound to t. everyone — SENE 727:89
gift or t. — MCCA 528:99
If you can t. yourself — KIPL 473:67
In America few people will t. — MAIL 540:45
knowing…about whom they can t. — SHAP 776:36
man assumes a public t. — JEFF 437:20
men dare t. themselves — SHAK 762:42

Never t. a husband too far — ROWL 701:5
never t. an expert — MAMET 543:3
never t. a woman who — WILDE 909:2
Never t. the artist — LAWR 494:1
only two lawyers…who t. each other — DOLE 278:1
pains that conquer t. — TENN 843:3
Put not your t. in money — HOLM 407:8
put not your t. in princes — BOOK 143:7
Quhome ye may t. — HENR 396:5
Time, which takes in t. — RALE 677:
treasure is their only t. — DYER 297:5
t. also in him — BIBLE 95:1
T. him as much as…a rattlesnake — ACHE 3:4
t. in Christ — WESL 900:1
t. in God — DENN 262:9
t. in God — SMITH 801:1
t. in him — BIBLE 103:3
t. in him — BIBLE 93:6
t. in the basic fairness — NIXON 617:4
T. in the Lord with all thine heart — BIBLE 98:
t. man on his oath — SHAK 762:4
t. me not at all — TENN 846:1
T. none, for oaths are straws — SHAK 745:3
T. not the physician — SHAK 762:5
t. that good shall fall — TENN 843:4
t. that somehow good — TENN 843:4
t. the very difference — JORD 450:6
without the t. of the people — CONF 230:9
trusted friend, in whom I t. — BIBLE 95:1
not to be t. when he does — HAMM 380:2
speaker is not to be t. — EUDA 315:
To be t. is a greater compliment — MACD 530:5
t. like the fox — SHAK 742:3
trustees t. of Posterity — DISR 276:5
trusting never extended to t. him — BULL 166:5
trusty T., dusky, vivid, true — STEV 823:3
truth absolute t. — HALD 377:7
Absolute t. is a very rare — THOM 855:4
absolute t. is not attainable — ORWE 629:9
absurd is…the first t. — CAMUS 187:8
accepted as t. — KING 468:4
according to t. — BURB 167:7
admitted the t. — LAUT 493:7
a little beyond exact t. — STEE 814:
Americans are polite by telling the t. — BRAD 148:5
And love of t. — TENN 846:2
And order, t., and beauty range — SMART 796:2
Art…cheating t. — RIDI 687:8
art is not t. — PICA 650:
astray as a premature t. — ROST 699:
authority and show of t. — SHAK 745:1
bear the torch of t. — LICH 509:2
Beauty is t., t. beauty — KEATS 459:5
before the t. has got its boots on — CALL 185:4
believe, falsely, to be the t. — HAMP 380:2
blaze of t. and liberty — MACA 525:4
books…contain…our fidelity to t. — CONR 234:1
bright countenance of t. — MILT 578:6
But it's the t. — KESEY 465:7
category of t. and falsehood — AYER 45:1
Celie, it's the t. — WALK 885:9
certain basis of t. — HERZ 400:5
Church which abandons the t. — KUNG 482:3
closer to the t. — HEAT 390:2
cold as t. — RHYS 684:2
comfort of thy worth and t. — SHAK 771:1
Communist must grasp the t. — MAO 548:
completely as too much t. — TWAIN 872:4
concentrate to t. and liberty — SHEL 782:2
confirmation of t. — MILT 579:7
cult of t. — PIER 651:
dared to speak the t. — TROL 866:8
dearer still is t. — ARIS 29:6
Death cancels everything but t. — HAZL 388:8
distinguishing t. from falsehood — DESC 263:7
do not seek for the t. — BORG 144:8
doubt about the t. — MARG 549:4
Doubt t. to be a liar — SHAK 752:4
economical with the t. — ARMS 30:8
enemies of t. than lies — NIET 615:
essence of all religion and of absolute t. — BLAV 136:9
experience as our t. — LEGU 501:6
fear mortal t. — POIN 657:3
fight for freedom and t. — IBSEN 428:3
first casualty…is t. — JOHN 439:7
French t. — ROCH 691:5
full of grace and t. — BIBLE 117:7

incapable of a t.   LAMB 486:45
lamentable t. is the sweetest music   SIDN 790:6
like a wayward t.   YEATS 932:31
melodie…sweetly play'd in t.   BURNS 173:44
Peter like a piper's t.   FARJ 318:48
sad raggy t.   HUGH 418:18
sudden springing of a t.   LOWE 519:25
Then murder's out of t.   SHAK 761:12
thunder to the t. of 'Greensleeves'   SHAK 744:81
we are out of t.   WORD 928:46
tunes all the good t.   HILL 402:89
beat out t. for bears   FLAU 326:34
only know two t.   GRANT 367:57
slow old t. of Spain   MASE 559:28
t. at which he was…working   DICK 269:55
tunic closest, all-concealing t.   SHEL 784:52
tunnel between two points was a t.   MANC 544:41
end of the t.   LOWE 521:60
one t., dark and solitary   SABA 707:82
On leaving the t.   LEVIN 506:64
perspective of a subway t.   TOOLE 863:12
some profound dull T.   OWEN 632:58
tunnels t. that re-wind themselves   CRANE 243:25
tuppence T. a Bag!   TRAV 865:24
t. for all of the rest!   FLAN 326:25
Wouldn't give you t.   COLL 227:35
turbid t. look the most profound   LAND 488:76
turbulent democracy…sometimes t.   CART 198:48
rid me of this t. priest?   HENR 395:44
turf At his head a grass-green t.   SHAK 754:16
blue ribbon of the t.   DISR 276:63
green t. beneath my feet   HAZL 387:75
pile of t. against the wall.   COLUM 229:61
shelving bank of t.   SHEL 786:23
t. such the honeyed showers   MILT 578:53
turf-dances t.-d. of…encounter   ALLEN 12:36
Turgenev beat Mr T.   HEMI 394:18
Turk In heathen, T. or Jew   BLAKE 134:32
malignant and a turbaned T.   SHAK 761:19
Turkey Christians that travel in T.   BUTL 176:36
In T. it was always 1952   THER 851:50
T. carpet bears to a picture   MACA 525:50
turkey It was a t.!   DICK 268:31
secure all the myrtle and t.   AUST 43:76
turkish perpetual T. bath   SWET 830:47
Turks like those wicked T.   DICK 269:59
turmoil with ceaseless t.   COLE 226:11
turn could t., and live with animals   WHIT 905:33
do not hope to t.   ELIOT 306:78
painter must have a natural t.   DURER 295:29
requite thee with a shrewd t.   BIBLE 107:44
t. away thy face   SHAK 748:23
t. from Africa and live?   WALC 884:70
t. of the road   FAWC 319:79
t. to little things   GIBS 352:75
wouldn't have left a t. unstoned   WIMP 917:20
You t. if you want to   THAT 850:20
Turnball Mr T. had predicted   TROL 867:94
Turner T. looks a bit shaky   JOHN 447:80
turning shadow of t.   BIBLE 124:6
take the wrong t.   CONN 233:78
The lady's not for t.   THAT 850:20
T. and t. in the widening gyre   YEATS 933:50
turnings all its narrow t.   DICK 270:96
t. intricate of verse   WORD 925:2
turnip noises like a t.   MACD 530:47
turnips type your t.   CAMP 186:58
turn-up t.-u. in a million   BEVIN 85:32
turpitude t. of incontinence   SCOTT 725:43
turret daily from the t. wall   MUIR 602:55
Sultan's t.   FITZ 324:82
washed me out of the t.   JARR 435:80
turrets gorgeous t.   MAHO 539:34
t. split the sky   LAND 488:84
turtle Behold the t.   ANON 25:56
traces of t. soup   DICK 270:5
t. lives 'twixt plated   NASH 608:81
tutor nurse and t. of eccentric minds   LAWS 495:43
TV lecturers…should appear on TV   ZELD 936:91
more interesting than TV   PIRS 652:27
TV licence   THOM 856:65
TV soap operas?   UPDI 874:86
twaddle better far write t.   MANS 547:97
Twain one book by Mark T.   HEMI 394:10
twain go with him t.   BIBLE 109:92
never the t. shall meet   KIPL 470:81
Tweed T. rins to the ocean   BURNS 172:35

Willie Wastle dwalt on T.   BURNS 172:33
tweed thread of good-class t.   BENN 76:27
Tweedledum T. and Tweedledee   CARR 196:97
Twelfth Night T. N.…a silly play   PEPYS 647:36
twelve in the sworn t.   SHAK 758:20
six nights when I was t.   THOM 853:1
There are only t. notes   HIND 403:99
twelvemonth t. after The seven days   MUIR 602:62
twenties dead by their late t.   GRAV 368:83
twentieth horror of the T. Century   MAIL 540:56
t. will be happy   HUGO 421:95
twentieth-century t.-c. Russia   HELL 392:79
twenty cuts off t. years of life   SHAK 747:97
first t. years are the longest   SOUT 805:8
first t. years…still growing   THOM 854:28
love…means t. things   BENN 76:39
one of the t.   SHAK 739:43
T. Thousand Thieves   JOYCE 452:3
T. Volume Suicide Note   BARA 59:43
T. will not come again   HOUS 414:42
twenty-four then we shall be t.-f.   HOUS 416:71
truth t.-f. times a second   GODA 359:6
twice gives the poor man t. as much   PUBL 672:96
victory is t. itself   SHAK 744:82
twice-told tedious as a t.-t. tale   SHAK 739:26
Twickenham T.…happy places   THOR 858:8
twigs man bent some t.   RUDO 701:61
twilight grey t. poured   TENN 839:61
in the grey t.   YEATS 932:35
lie…is a beautiful t.   CAMUS 188:4
pilots of the purple t.   TENN 840:81
Suspicions…fly by t.   BACON 49:34
T. and evening bell   TENN 848:70
t. from the lecture   STEV 820:32
t.'s last gleaming   KEY 465:76
twilights ancient shadows and t.   RUSS 706:62
twin ambition's ugly t.   KUSH 482:43
twinkle roguish t. in his eye   THOM 856:59
t. of a fading star   ELIOT 306:70
twinkling in the t. of an eye   BIBLE 121:19
Jew in the t.   SHAK 740:57
twins threw the t. she nursed   GRAH 365:34
two t. cleaving together   MILT 579:65
twist Let him t.…in the wind   EHRL 301:28
pale death your vital t. shall sever   DAVI 254:33
twitch affected by every t.   TRUD 868:23
twitter t. of sleepy canaries   GRAH 366:39
two being one and not t.   FLET 327:64
Can t. walk together   BIBLE 106:7
If ever t. were one   BRAD 149:81
must have t. you know   CARR 197:19
sin ye do by t. and t.   KIPL 471:6
think that t. and t. are four   HOUS 416:78
T. and t. is five   DOST 282:5
T. are better than one   BIBLE 100:73
t. for tea   CAES 183:21
t. ideas are more inseparable   SMITH 801:9
t. kinds of Arctic problems   STEF 814:3
T. lads that thought   SHAK 770:74
t. plus t. make four   ORWE 630:2
t. shall withstand him   BIBLE 100:74
T. things are always the same   STEIN 815:21
T. women placed together   SHAK 775:7
went in t. and t.   BIBLE 86:64
two-faced not t.-f.   SNOW 802:39
Tyburn has a damned T.-Face   CONG 231:12
Tyne from the Severn to the T.!   KIPL 474:85
type grey paper with blunt t.!   BROW 160:22
highest t. of human nature   SPEN 807:44
megaphone of big t.   MAST 560:54
T. of the wise   WORD 929:61
types certain t. of society   PARS 640:1
device of Movable T.   CARL 192:90
only two t. of cases   BENN 76:29
T. and shadows have their ending   AQUI 28:29
typewriter acquires a new t.   AMIS 15:2
needs only a t. and paper   WINN 917:21
t.…judged by…fingers   ANON 23:78
t. needs only paper   WELL 897:50
typical hardly find a t. American   BARN 60:61
more t. and less exotic   ANON 23:76
typing isn't writing…it's t.   CAPO 189:22
tyrannical most t. and oppressive   CALH 184:35
tyrannies totalitarian and corrupt t.   MO 589:20
tyrannous love…so t. and rough   SHAK 735:34
tyranny Bolshevik t. is the worst   CHUR 216:61
burden of t.   SHAW 778:3

call it t.   HOBB 404:28
dark night of t.   MURR 605:10
equals, free from t.?   LANY 489:6
expresses its t. by reducing   MILL 573:47
liberty against t.   ROOS 696:59
modern democracy is a t.   MAIL 540:44
slow t. of moonlight   CRANE 243:13
struggled against t.   TUTU 870:72
Taxation…is t.   OTIS 630:19
t. begins   PITT 653:41
t. of conscious thought   BEEC 69:65
T. of Distance   BLAI 132:35
t. of 'the rat race'   THOM 855:42
T. sets up…echo-chamber   CHAT 208:51
until this t. be over-past   BOOK 143:54
worst sort of t.   BURKE 168:25
yoke of t.   PITT 653:47
tyrant by force or like a t.   PASC 641:27
t. has in common   BROD 153:52
t. spell has bound me   BRON 155:90
t., t. Jealousy   DRYD 291:32
vengeful t. stricken   SULL 828:17
tyrants abject intercourse between t.
   and slaves   GOLD 361:48
all men would be t.   ADAMS 3:61
As many councillors, so many t.   SALV 712:75
barbarity of t.   SMITH 801:7
blood of patriots and t.   JEFF 436:15
Rebellion against t.   DAVI 256:70
stuff of which t. are made   BEAV 67:19
t. and sensualists are…right   WOLL 921:6
t. do defeat   SHAK 747:81
t. from policy   BURKE 169:37
T. seldom want pretexts   BURKE 169:46
when t. seems to kiss   SHAK 769:50
tyre Roosevelt's spare t.   GARN 346:52
tyres everything but the air in the t.   CALD 184:34
tythe t. o' what ye waste at cartes   BURNS 170:66

U

Ubu Mother U., you are very ugly   JARRY 435:90
udder u. a swollen wobble   RAINE 677:93
UFO convinced that U. exist   CART 198:45
ugliness march of material u.   WHITE 903:96
see beneath both beauty and u.   ELIOT 307:86
u. has a thousand   HUGO 421:94
u., vice and unhappiness   BERN 81:43
ugly All Middlesex is u.   COBB 223:48
Art produces u. things   COCT 224:54
better to be good than to be u.   WILDE 908:80
Mother Ubu, you are very u.   JARRY 435:90
not more u.   SHAK 753:73
so very u. in persons of small means   ELIOT 303:72
There is nothing u.   CONS 235:27
toad, u. and venomous   SHAK 749:33
tourist is an u. human being   KINC 468:23
u. mathematics   HARDY 381:45
u. woman is a blot   BRON 155:76
wish he were not so u.   BRON 154:74
UK enquiries about the UK climate   SAMU 712:81
Ulster resistance to which U.   LAW 493:84
U.'s honoured dead   PAIS 635:3
U. will be right   CHUR 215:55
Ulsterman armed Protestant U.   REDM 681:72
ulterior free of u. motives   JONG 448:97
ultimate u. mystery of nature   PLAN 656:33
Ulysses Happy…like U.   BELL 72:39
interest throughout U.   BOWL 147:38
nature of the sickness found, U.   SHAK 757:95
passages of U.   MILL 572:19
U.…is a dogged attempt   FORS 331:45
umbrella fatal forgotten u.   MANS 546:85
good u. but a poor roof   LOWE 520:39
neat as a furled u.   EMERY 313:55
you have got…an u.   FLET 328:75
umbrellas audience…put up its u.   BEER 69:73
umpire Never argue with an u.   BOTH 146:15
perched like an u.   AVIS 44:6
u., the pavilion cat   LANG 488:90
umpiring come to see you u.   GRACE 365:32
unable unwilling or u.   WILL 913:49
unacceptable u. face of capitalism   HEATH 390:20
unadmitted u. desire to undress   LIN 510:32
un-American Solitude is u.-A.   JONG 448:98
unapproachable u., the hard-bitten   MACD 530:48
unarmed rode all u.   SCOTT 723:96

unattainable flight after the u. WHIT 904:9
unattended only the u. Moment ELIOT 308:34
unbalance world is…in dynamic u. BART 62:16
unbearable expressing lightly the u. UPDI 875:95
tolerable and the absolutely u. DAFOE 250:63
U. Lightness of Being KUND 482:36
unbecoming nothing more u. CONG 231:7
u. for a cardinal JOHN 439:60
unbelief Because of your u. BIBLE 112:65
Blind u. is sure to err COWP 240:44
gained…by our u. BROW 161:49
help thou mine u. BIBLE 114:16
help thou my u. FORS 331:51
u., in denying them EMER 312:28
u. of what is false MACD 530:57
unbelievers money…has no u. GAUT 347:72
un-birthday u.-b. present CARR 196:10
unborn possible to talk to the u. BARZ 63:34
Ventriloquizing for the u. GRAV 367:69
uncertain u. business of war GERB 350:29
U., coy, and hard to please SCOTT 723:1
uncertainties capable of being in u. KEATS 457:91
uncertainty distribution of u. STEIN 815:29
tolerance as u. BURKE 169:57
u.? Even ignorance? NIET 615:17
uncharitableness malice, and all u. BOOK 140:81
uncivilized very u. to invade HUNT 423:38
uncle her u. once taught her HEAN 389:15
Mine u.? SHAK 752:30
My u. was famous SPEN 807:62
real live nephew of my U. Sam's COHAN 224:65
she wanted U. Tom LEE 500:44
U. Matthew was saying MITF 589:11
u. who could never walk down HOME 409:14
unclean all as an u. thing BIBLE 104:63
man of u. lips BIBLE 102:12
u. shall not pass BIBLE 103:34
unclubbable very u. man JOHN 443:77
uncomfortable when he is only u. SHAW 778:92
when it hardens does it become u. ANGE 17:40
uncommitted live free and u. THOR 857:90
uncommon u. abilities BAGE 52:96
very u. cook SAKI 710:45
unconceptualisable concrete and u. KELM 460:77
unconcern looks with u. JOHN 442:34
unconcerned Thou u. canst hear POPE 661:34
unconscious u.…interpreter—in the eye BRON 155:80
u. in us warns us MOND 590:52
u. unity with life MILL 573:43
unconventional completely u. life BIRD 130:59
uncouth Nothing…more u. DISR 277:84
U. unkist, said…Chaucer SPEN 808:70
undecided five who are u. STEN 816:54
undeniable u. pretensions PITT 653:45
under-belly u.-b. of the Axis CHUR 217:88
undercurrent u. of emotion UPDI 875:97
undercurrents imperceptible u. CUOMO 248:29
u., drifting, waiting MORG 597:77
u. of everlasting murmur RUSK 704:14
underdog can't teach an u. STEV 821:65
on the side of the u. PALEY 635:10
underdogs among the u. WAUGH 892:39
undergarments old-fashioned u. LEWIS 507:85
undergraduate first modern u. LEVE 506:53
undergraduates with the u. HAZL 387:73
underground best part of him is u. ANON 25:61
Give me an u. laboratory PERE 648:57
might well be u. GILB 355:21
not rest from taking u. FRAME 333:79
underlings we are u. SHAK 747:76
underlip u. protruded a little MANS 547:86
underpants word means u. MURR 604:7
underprivileged u. was over-used FEIF 319:83
understand Adults never u. anything SAINT 709:15
believe so that I may u. ANSE 26:5
contempt for anything he didn't u. WOOL 923:59
dogs who don't u. CALV 185:46
don't believe…won't u. AUGU 42:44
don't think I u. people FORS 331:40
hard to u. GORB 363:99
language I don't u. APPL 27:23
may not be made to u. it CONF 230:87
people…who u. pictures KIPL 471:2
really don't u. KENN 463:31
Sex…I really don't u. SALI 711:53
shewed unto thee than men u. BIBLE 107:39
striven…to u. them SPIN 810:22

talent is to u. a man HUGO 421:85
u. himself KAZIN 456:71
u. that a man TROL 867:92
u. that you experience KAFKA 454:25
u. thy kisses SHAK 742:19
understood as to u. FRAN 334:98
we could not u. him WITT 918:48
what they us. not SHEL 786:17
When I do not u. SOPH 804:88
wise enough to u. SCHW 721:66
Women…we should not u. CONG 231:16
understanding among men of u. PLATO 655:82
capable of u. each other BERL 80:24
declare, if thou hast u. BIBLE 93:69
experience and u. of life MILL 572:23
eye of my u. JULI 452:4
find you an u. JOHN 446:65
for the clearer u. of English WHAR 902:54
for thy more sweet u. SHAK 733:74
good u. with a new mistress ETHE 315:94
in length of days u. BIBLE 93:59
lack of u. BIER 129:27
lean not unto thine own u. BIBLE 98:9
learn u., and to give answer BIBLE 107:43
more u. than all my teachers BIBLE 97:82
no occasion to exert his u. SMITH 798:52
pains toward creating u. NEWM 612:60
passeth all u. BOOK 141:10
patient, sardonic u. LESS 505:35
pleasing to…the u. ADDI 6:22
presume yourself ignorant of his u. COLE 226:16
problem of u. the world POPP 663:95
reputation of u. DRYD 288:44
too much u. GOLD 360:32
u. can intuit nothing KANT 454:39
u. unto the simple BIBLE 97:85
with all thy getting get u. BIBLE 99:11
woman of mean u. AUST 46:62
women's…u. is freer and sharper CHRI 215:38
understatement That is an u. SAMU 712:80
understood have ye not u. BIBLE 103:41
life must be u. backwards KIER 467:12
never u. what music was FAURE 319:77
understudies slaughtered by their u. STOP 825:62
undertaker greeting…give an u. BALD 54:42
undertaking no such u. CHAM 204:65
prepared to join…the u. MILL 570:77
prosecution of any u. JOHN 441:27
undertakings series of u. SART 715:52
will to desperate u. SHAK 752:41
undervalue conspiracy to u. v. them JAMES 433:35
underwater u. hazards MORT 599:13
underwear in the rain in your u. BRADY 149:82
like…skid-marked u. COUP 238:97
u. first, last and all the time BREC 151:8
Wearing us. as formal HEMI 395:30
underwhelmed u. by the prospect JAY 436:2
underwood green u. and cover SWIN 832:19
underwrite u. it with their lives MILL 573:38
undisciplined U. squads of emotion ELIOT 308:23
undismayed go forth to meet him u. SHER 788:69
undoing u. of those human rights KENN 462:12
undone John Donne…U.-d. DONNE 280:64
leave great things u. GLAS 359:97
Woe is me! for I am u. BIBLE 102:12
undoomed u. warrior ANON 18:69
undulate forms of pleasure u. FUSE 342:76
undying his passion is Infinite, u. PARK 638:59
uneasy no u. feeling JOHN 443:61
U. lies the head SHAK 743:53
uneatable full pursuit of the u. WILDE 909:22
unemployed u.…do not have the skills CALL 185:39
unemployment creating u. ROBI 689:24
cure u. before Keynes ROBI 690:41
need be no more u. KEYN 466:88
reduce u. HEATH 390:19
u. only looks good PASS 641:40
unexamined u. life is not worth SOCR 803:57
unexpected By how much u. SHAK 738:20
expect the u. HERA 396:70
unexplored hitherto u. country SHIP 789:78
unexpressive the chaste, and u. she SHAK 749:55
unfairnesses u. that were explained GALL 344:18
unfaithful Confidence in an u. man BIBLE 100:51
ways of being u. WYLIE 931:21
unfashionable Fashion is…u. CHAN 205:94
u. is what other people wear WILDE 909:49

unfeathered u. two-legged thing DRYD 290:78
unfed calls us, still u. KIPL 472:14
unfeeling u. for his own GRAY 368:95
unfit picked from the u. HARK 383:82
u. for a nation of shopkeepers SMITH 798:50
u. for power FOOT 329:93
unfitness personal u. GLAD 358:89
unfittest survival of the u. SUMN 828:19
unforeseen contingent and the u. FISH 324:76
unforgetful teach the u. to forget? ROSS 698:99
unforgiveness an alp of u. PLOM 656:8
unfruitful he becometh u. BIBLE 112:48
unwarranted as they are u. AYER 44:8
ungartered U., and down-gyvèd SHAK 752:40
ungodly counsel of the u. BIBLE 94:81
the hope of the u. BIBLE 107:34
u. in great power BOOK 143:47
ungracious as some u. pastors do SHAK 751:16
unhandsome she were u. SHAK 744:89
unhanged not three good men u. SHAK 741:13
unhappiest u. moment SCHO 719:34
unhappiness cause of man's u. PASC 640:16
loyalty we shall feel to u. GREE 371:55
Man's u.…comes of his greatness CARL 192:99
unhappy each u. family TOLS 862:5
guy gets too complicated he's u. CHAN 204:80
if it makes you so u. CARR 196:96
instinct for being u. SAKI 710:40
keeps the u. from thinking DIBD 265:54
making one another u. MENC 566:79
never as u. as one thinks LARO 491:50
some should be u. JOHN 445:21
speak when she is u.? SMITH 800:1
These u. people SWIFT 831:82
unhappiest moment of the u. man SCHO 719:34
unhealthy u. for want of air DICK 269:81
unheard those u. Are sweeter KEATS 459:52
unholy Refrain from the u. pleasure BELL 72:45
sights u., Find out MILT 576:4
unicorn Lion and the U.…fighting CARR 197:16
rarer than the u. JONG 448:97
u. and lion wild SHAK 733:64
uniform gaunt u. ADAMS 4:63
good u. must work its way DICK 266:83
Should be more u. HOOD 410:36
talent like a u. AUDEN 40:94
u. 'e wore KIPL 471:95
uniformity manageable u. HUXL 426:1
u. of their means FUSE 342:74
uniforms buried in their u. DOSP 282:3
unimaginable nothing was u. DIDI 274:8
unimpeachable u. orthodoxy RAHN 677:91
uninformed most unlearned and u. AUST 43:79
uninstructed plain to u. people HUXL 426:14
union impossible u. ELIOT 308:36
National U. of Mineworkers MACM 536:77
Only through their u. KANT 454:39
proper u. of gin and vermouth DE 264:33
protesting against u. GRAT 367:61
remain in u. with England SCOTT 725:52
Sail on, O U. LONG 516:54
u., before his citizenship LEWIS 507:84
u. is perfect DICK 273:82
U. to be dissolved LINC 510:34
U. which never strikes HICKS 402:81
u. with the universe RUSS 705:42
war…which saved the U. WILS 916:11
unionism u. is stronger than creed LAWS 495:44
unions aggregations of trade u. DOSP 282:3
Hitler attacked the u. NIEM 614:3
unique Murder is…u. crime JAMES 434:58
sonatas of Mozart are u. SCHN 719:23
u. to the level of the herd…u. MILL 573:47
uniqueness poet reminds…u. COUS 239:3
unison in u. with this order MILL 573:33
unit true middle-class u. SHAW 779:16
united country needs to be u. JOHN 439:76
reminded him of Sheffield U. HATT 385:26
u. by nothing TOLS 863:7
u. in one person HESS 401:67
United Kingdom Ireland and…U.K. LLOY 513:5
United Nations If the U.N. once EISE 302:57
Peoples of the U.N. UNIT 873:69
The U.N. cannot do anything OBRI 620:3
turn the U.N. back into a talking shop BLAIR 133:14
U.N. is not in a position EDEN 299:90
When we started the U.N. HARR 384:4

United States defeat the U. S. aggressors MAO 548:14
friendship of the U. S. GEOR 349:13
have our U. S.-mania RODO 693:94
In the U. S....more space STEIN 815:16
In the U. S. there's a Puritan ethic ECO 298:77
lies about the U. S. STEV 820:50
loyalty to the U. S. ROOS 696:60
mental illness of the U. S. ATWO 38:52
no major institution in the U. S. FRIE 337:65
politics in the U. S. TOCQ 861:83
President of the U. S. UPDI 874:80
problem with the U. S. economy KRUG 481:25
prominent as the U. S. MUNCH 603:81
so close to the U. S. DIAZ 265:51
stand shoulder-to-shoulder with the
U. S. of America BLAIR 133:10
test case of U. S. capacity MCNA 537:91
The U. S. today is an empire FERG 320:4
the US edition of Time BRYS 164:20
U. S. imperialism MAO 548:11
U. S....is warm-hearted FERB 320:94
U. S. and the British CHUR 217:93
U. S., democratic and various UPDI 875:98
U. S....global gendarme MCNA 537:92
U. S....greatest poem WHIT 905:28
U. S. is the best and fairest BUSH 175:91
U. S. is the biggest business ROGE 694:13
U. S. is...the great melting pot MARS 554:41
U. S. is the only country ROGE 695:23
U. S. must be neutral WILS 916:9
U. S. of America ROOS 696:51
U. S....the Jew among the nations FERB 320:94
U. S. to the Monroe Doctrine ROOS 696:53
U. S. will never again seek WILS 916:8
Vice-President of the U. S. GARN 346:51
women in the U. S. BRYS 164:21
wouldn't have stood a chance in the U. S. WOLFE 920:2
unity dwell together in u.! BIBLE 98:96
rich, dark, organic u. HOMA 408:8
unconscious u. with life MILL 573:43
universal All partial evil, u. good POPE 660:15
and u. peace lie TENN 841:94
appetite, an u. wolf SHAK 757:93
books...of u. appeal FORD 330:3
'He never listens' is u. MACK 533:13
if it is not u. TOLK 862:97
[man] is a u. machine REDT 681:76
maxim should become a u. law KANT 455:44
mirror of the u. elements STEI 814:9
old u. truths FAUL 318:63
particular and u. BERG 79:97
reach the u. SART 715:42
u. as sea sickness SHAW 778:95
u. darkness buries all POPE 662:83
u. frame is without a mind BACON 48:94
u. languages: love, music and sports MOSES 600:26
u. pollution and u. frustration ILLI 428:45
u. sickness TRIL 866:67
u. suffrage prevails PARE 636:36
u. test of travel GELL 348:1
war tends to become u. DU 293:75
universals Myth deals in false u. CART 198:39
universe black hole of the u. UMAS 873:62
boundless u. TENN 841:89
by which the u. is regulated PAINE 634:97
cement of the u. SELF 727:80
circumscribe This u. MILT 584:92
cold reaches of the u. KENN 462:17
come to esteem the u. FONT 328:85
corner of the u. HUXL 425:88
cover the u. with mud FORS 331:45
entire u....is Pure Accident OATES 620:91
entities of which the u. is KUHN 481:35
explain the u. BERL 80:22
faintly through the u. JOYCE 451:81
galaxies populating the u. BRAUN 150:98
hell of a good u. next door CUMM 248:18
In this u. WORD 923:68
kingdom is as wide as the u. FLAU 326:40
laws and order of the U. HARDY 382:72
Life, the U. and Everything ADAMS 4:66
man said to the u. CRANE 243:30
many wonderful things...in the u. COLT 229:57
measure of the u. SHEL 785:78
Miss U.'s buttocks BENE 75:8
mock the u. ARET 29:42
no intention in the u. MONOD 591:56

no other u. except the human u. SART 715:53
Not for all the u. contains OCON 621:20
nothing dead in this U. CARL 192:8
nothing in the whole u. OVID 631:47
nothing is accidental in the u. OATES 620:91
of her myriad u. TENN 847:33
only objects in the material u. FORS 331:50
On the stage of the u. LAFO 485:12
otherwise kindly u. HARDY 381:55
phenomenon of [the] u. PEAR 645:97
plural, like the u. PESS 649:71
protons in the u. EDDI 299:86
Put back Thy u. JONES 447:86
stole a page from the U.! MARTI 555:44
sweet winds of the u. MACD 530:54
tinker with the u. MILL 572:23
transitory in the u. GIRA 358:80
u. appears as an infinite MUIR 602:65
u. had a beginning MILL 570:72
u. is arranged like a cithera HONO 409:31
u. is Copernican, not Ptolemaic PHIL 650:94
u. is not only queerer HALD 377:74
u. which philosophy contemplates RUSS 705:42
unlike any other thing...in the u. STEI 815:31
utmost limits of the u. HUME 422:3
vast order of the u. PAGE 633:79
Why does the u. go to...the bother of
existing? HAWK 386:33
Wisdom and Spirit of the u.! WORD 924:85
universities As to our u. LODGE 515:28
black market u. ZELD 936:91
critics are like American u. ALBEE 10:94
escape our u. OPPE 626:17
u., and the public charities MILL 570:66
university critic to the u. BRAD 148:68
dismissed from a German u. TILL 860:70
fools at a u. GERH 350:34
no u. could pay STIG 824:45
of that famous u. HAZL 387:73
servant to be bred at an U. CONG 231:19
this ancient U. HOUS 415:69
true U....is a collection of books CARL 193:35
u. has failed you GOHE 360:27
U. of Oxford GIBB 352:60
u. of Oxtail JOYCE 452:91
U. should be a place of light DISR 277:79
u. where he didn't inhale DOWD 284:40
u. where...the Jews are hosts SACH 707:83
unjust abhor...the u. CURZ 249:53
Every u. man PLATO 655:88
u. in the least BIBLE 116:52
unjustified course was u. HIRO 403:5
unkillable filthy, sturdy, u. infants POUND 664:29
unkind Midlands...sodden and u. BELL 73:63
None...deformed but the u. SHAK 757:88
position is admittedly u. STEV 821:71
Thou art not so u. SHAK 749:52
u. or irreverential word HAWT 386:52
when givers prove u. SHAK 753:75
unkindled u., uncoffined BYRON 180:45
unkindness by my u. shaken SHAK 773:50
unkist Uncouth u., said...Chaucer SPEN 808:70
unknown as One u. SCHW 721:70
bird rising, unnamed, u. REID 682:95
holier lot to be u. HOPK 412:96
let nothing...be u. to you RABE 676:78
route towards the u. HUGO 421:96
She lived u. WORD 924:78
To that u. and silent shore LAMB 486:30
tread safely into the u. HASK 385:25
uncertain, u., arbitrary rule LOCKE 514:15
u. Prime Minister ASQU 36:10
U., unkist, and lost CHAU 208:55
ways that are still largely u. REYES 684:21
unlearned most u. and uninformed AUST 43:79
what we have u. TWAIN 872:29
unlessoned u. girl, unschooled SHAK 740:73
unlucky U. the land BREC 151:9
u. to sound off ICHI 428:37
unmarried paid to them while u. JOHN 445:16
u. guys in New York suck BUSH 176:26
U. men are best friends BACON 48:89
unmask u. her beauty to the moon SHAK 751:15
unmeaning u. thing it is HAZL 388:79
unmentionable Everything was u. DIDI 274:8
unmourned are all u. and unknown HORA 413:25
unmoved u. this place leaves one SNYD 803:51

U. though witlings sneer JOHN 441:10
unmusical Nothing can be more u. DISR 277:84
no...u. person HENZE 396:56
unnatural both equally u. GRAT 367:61
everlastingly being u. MITC 588:92
foul, strange, and u. SHAK 752:29
nothing so u. as the commonplace DOYLE 285:61
U., he called them SHAR 776:40
unnebulous u. train of words BISH 131:71
unnecessary eliminate the u. HOFF 406:50
often utterly u. TOLS 863:7
thou u. letter SHAK 763:65
to do the u. HARK 383:82
uncomfortable, u., and...useless STEV 821:71
vain, u. things are men ROCH 691:60
unnoble most u. swerving SHAK 765:35
unnoticed that u. and that necessary ATWO 38:59
unofficial u. magic becomes stronger REED 682:85
unorthodox loopholes for an u. ORWE 628:48
unpack my heart with words SHAK 753:69
unpalatable disastrous and the u. GALB 343:94
unparalleled lass u. SHAK 766:63
u. elsewhere in our culture SHAP 776:36
unpleasant enough u. things RENO 683:11
face...is so peculiarly u. SNOW 802:39
How u. to meet Mr Eliot! ELIOT 307:6
u. way of saying the truth HELL 392:72
unplumbed u., salt, estranging sea ARNO 32:10
unpolished ignorant and u. people DICK 271:41
unpopular safe to be u. STEV 820:54
unpredictable never aim to be u. JAY 436:1
unpremeditated u. lay SCOTT 722:85
unprincipled sold by the u. CAPP 189:35
unprofitable most idle and u. GIBB 352:60
weary, stale, flat, and u. SHAK 751:6
unprovoked It seemed u. STEV 824:91
unquestionable one u. truth TOLS 863:7
unquestioned u. law WHAR 902:54
unravel can devise, another can u. WRIS 930:72
unreal gunfire...sounded u. USTI 875:6
this story is u. PACH 633:69
unreality general atmosphere of u. QUEN 674:39
unreason woman...element of u. WRIG 929:75
unreasonable u. one persists SHAW 779:17
unremarked legion of the u. SAFI 708:2
unrequited Self-love...often u. POWE 666:78
unrest root of the social u. LECO 499:28
u. which men miscall delight SHEL 786:4
unrighteousness cleanse...all u. BIBLE 125:34
mammon of u. BIBLE 116:51
unromantic u. poet FROST 339:3
unsaid that which is u. ANOU 26:99
unsatiable be not u. BIBLE 108:60
unsatisfied leaves one u. WILDE 908:7
unscathed guilty never escape u. BAIL 52:2
unscotch if you u. us SCOTT 725:55
unscrupulous most u. kidney FRY 339:22
unsearchable u. dispose Of highest MILT 587:66
unseen all-seeing but u. BYRON 180:38
Greet the u. BROW 163:96
O friend u., unborn, unknown FLEC 327:44
Of u. things above HANK 380:33
unselfish u....are not the leaders CONR 234:14
unselfishness u. of an oyster SAKI 710:42
unsex u. me here SHAK 766:82
unshackle u....transient desires EINS 301:33
unshorn presents the god u. HERR 400:42
unsightly grotesque, if not u. VEBL 878:55
unsinkable u. air-craft carrier MACA 524:24
unsophisticated u. can really go for AMIS 14:85
unsorted u. stuff GOLD 360:29
unsound notoriously u. HOLM 407:80
unspeakable inedible raised to the u. BASK 63:46
u. in full pursuit WILDE 909:22
unspiritual conditions that are u. MARX 557:94
unspontaneous I am u. KENN 462:5
unspotted keep himself u. BIBLE 124:9
unstable U. as water BIBLE 88:6
unstoned left a turn u. WIMP 917:20
unsubduable u. country GILL 356:41
unsympathetic u. as butterflies ELIOT 303:75
untalented product of the u. CAPP 189:35
untell To u. the days HEYW 402:76
unthinking Laughing...u. time DRYD 292:61
painful process of U. CUMM 247:99
untimely U. ripped SHAK 769:45
untired against the new and u. LINC 510:37

untouched expect to be u. by madness — BELL 73:72
untranslatable I too am u. — WHIT 905:36
untrodden among the u. ways — WORD 924:78
untrue blaming mirrors for being u. — LAFO 485:99
  man who's u. to his wife — AUDEN 40:9
untruth torment of the night's u. — DANI 252:88
  transfigured them into U. — LARK 490:30
  why not rather u.? — NIET 615:17
untruths they have spoken u. — SHAK 745:23
untwist Not u....these last strands — HOPK 412:2
unusual moved by what is not u. — ELIOT 304:9
unutterable looked u. things — THOM 856:55
  present u. things — THOR 857:77
unvisionary u. language of farm — ENGLE 314:69
unwanted feeling of being u. — THER 851:41
unwarrantable any u. belief — RICH 686:62
unwarranted u. as they are unfruitful — AYER 44:8
unwell begins to feel u. — KIPL 470:82
unwholesome u. in their thoughts — SHAK 754:20
unwieldiness cumbersome u. — DONNE 280:61
unwilling group of the u. — HARK 383:82
  u. or unable — WILL 913:49
unwise sight of the u. — BIBLE 107:31
unworldliness out of u. — MCCA 528:97
unworthy opinion...is u. of him — BACON 49:14
  U. was what he did — AESC 8:57
unwrung our withers are u. — SHAK 754:95
up cannot bear levelling up — JOHN 443:71
  curtain was up — KAUF 455:56
  more up and down than sideways — HEMI 393:92
  Up, all of us — PEPYS 647:41
  Up was the heartening — EMPS 314:63
  UP YOURS DELORS — SUN 828:22
upbringing result of my u. — DYSON 297:62
  the u. a nun would envy — ORTON 627:29
upbringings u. that were so clean — COUP 238:97
upgrowth germ and first u. — KING 469:60
upharsin Mene, Mene, Tekel, U. — BIBLE 106:98
upholding u. all things by the word — BIBLE 124:89
upholstery dogs had eaten the u. — PERE 648:62
  faded u. of loss — BROY 163:98
uplands thrilling over her u. — DAY 257:84
upon Either with it or u. it — ANON 18:57
upper Have still the u. hand — COWA 239:18
  no longer u. classes — TOCQ 861:80
uprising knowest...mine u. — BIBLE 98:99
uproar amidst that joy and u. — CAMP 186:71
  little u. as a jellyfish — WODE 919:54
  set all the city on an u. — BIBLE 119:45
upset not u., are you? — BANKS 58:33
upside autocracy turned u. down — HERZ 400:56
  turned the world u. down — BIBLE 119:46
upstairs labour going u. — MUNDY 603:82
  u. into the world — CONG 231:13
upstart curse...upon the sleek u. — RANS 679:24
  u. crow — GREE 371:80
upwardly-mobile all pigs are u.-m. — THOM 855:45
uranium nuclear reaction in u. — EINS 301:35
urban all u. and rural sounds — LAMB 487:53
  Boston has become U. Renewal — MAIL 540:55
  incomplete in the u. compound — MCLU 536:59
urchin ribald, inspired u. — DAY 257:86
urge absence of the u. to create — MAMET 543:27
  something other than the u. — SAND 713:14
  U. that impels women — THUR 860:50
urgency fierce u. of now — KING 468:30
  Life...having a sense of u. — BURT 174:67
urgent assurance...that nothing was u. — ACHE 2:25
  Egyptians were u. upon the people — BIBLE 88:11
urgings felt sexual u. — COND 230:85
Uriah Set ye U. in the forefront — BIBLE 91:1
Uricon ashes under U. — HOUS 415:56
Urim U. and the Thummim — BIBLE 89:25
urinal burnt match skating in a u. — CRANE 243:25
urine Cannot contain their u. — SHAK 740:77
  faintly scented u. — JOYCE 452:92
  red wine of Shiraz into u. — BLIX 137:1
  u. dump at sunset — SCHW 721:69
urn angel watching an u. — TENN 845:82
  bubbling and loud-hissing u. — COWP 241:76
  dust falls to the u. — VAUG 878:46
  Lean on a garden u. — ELIOT 305:31
  storied u. — GRAY 369:15
  u. Of bitter prophecy — SHEL 786:22
urs strew your pathway...dreadful u. — HOLM 407:76
us before they get at us — GRACE 365:31
usage dictionary of popular u. — GREE 371:64

usages statutes or u. therein obtaining — MILL 570:56
usances my moneys and my u. — SHAK 739:53
use consumed by u. — GILL 356:49
  designed its u. — PALEY 635:16
  for the u. of his power — HOBB 404:25
  how to make the best u. of it — SIMO 792:41
  keener with constant u. — IRVI 430:80
  little u. for contraceptives — SHAR 776:40
  no u. for the teachings — KHRU 467:4
  no u. save abuse — SIMO 792:44
  Remains in u. with you — SHAK 764:18
  skilled u. of blunt objects — PEAR 645:99
  u. alone that sanctifies expense — POPE 659:98
  U. every man — SHAK 753:66
  u. him as he uses thee — SHAK 761:25
  u. of a new-born child? — FRAN 335:19
  u. of travelling — JOHN 447:78
  value in u. — SMITH 797:41
used let them be well u. — SHAK 753:65
  shouldn't be much u. — HOLM 408:87
useful both viable and u. — HAYEK 387:61
  returns home wise and u. — BELL 72:39
  science is said to be u. — HARDY 381:46
  To be u....hideous — BAUD 65:79
  what is u. to oneself — SPIN 810:31
useless as u....as possible — GALT 345:31
  let me not live to be u.! — WESL 900:21
  Protestations...are always u. — COBB 223:47
  speech they know to be u. — ELIOT 303:94
  wars are u. — RICH 685:46
uses all the u. of this world! — SHAK 751:6
Usher's Well wife at U.W. — BALL 57:97
usquabae Wi' u., we'll face — BURNS 172:21
USSR Back in the U. — LENN 503:1
  for the U. to reject Communism — KHRU 466:98
usury u. age-old — POUND 664:39
utensil every particle and u. — SHAK 756:58
utilitarian our u. world — STARK 813:72
utility foundation of morals, U. — MILL 570:70
  immediate practical u. — HELM 393:84
  neither gain nor loss of u. — JEVO 438:45
  u. of some particular object — SMITH 797:41
  view to future u. — JEVO 438:46
utopia u. remains forever closed — MAIL 540:52
  view as an infernal U. — LEWIS 508:5
  whatever U. of human virtue — HAWT 386:39
utopian U....romance — WEBB 893:65
Utopias end all the static U. — INGE 429:53
utter ache to u. — SAND 712:90
  Thou wilt not u. — SHAK 741:11
  What I think, I u. — SHAK 769:60
utterance u. of the early Gods — KEATS 459:47
utterances by his own u. — PARN 639:92
  Deathbed u. — PLOUT 656:10
uttered u. it a hundred times — HOLM 407:78
U-turn catchphrase, the U.-t. — THAT 850:20
Uzziah year that king U. died — BIBLE 102:11

V

vacancy aught of blinder v. — WORD 928:51
  chaos of v. — DELA 260:70
  next v. for God — CIAR 218:14
  v. which occupies the space — TOOLE 863:14
  which but for v. — SHAK 765:24
vacant v. into the v. — ELIOT 308:19
vacation v., or a truce — WORD 928:54
vacations v. of the flesh — TZARA 873:56
vaccinated v. with a phonograph — GOLD 362:75
vacuum cannot work in a v. — ROGE 694:11
  nature hates a v. — WILL 913:28
  v. cleaner grazes over the carpet — RAINE 677:93
  v. that fills a v. — GALB 343:4
vacuums role is...filling v. — CART 198:51
vagaries correct the v. — KEYN 466:86
  v. of butlers — ACHE 2:26
vague woman's brain: v., slippery — RICH 686:64
vailèd with thy v. lids — SHAK 751:2
vain a' is done in v. — BURNS 173:52
  Call it not v. — SCOTT 723:90
  Destroy his fib...in v. — POPE 661:35
  full as v. — DRYD 289:63
  head grown grey in v. — SHEL 786:4
  He is so v. — DISR 277:82
  he seeks in v. — HELM 393:84
  imagine a v. thing? — BIBLE 94:82
  In v.—always in v. — DAVI 254:25

  in v. decry'd and curst — POPE 662:64
  name of the Lord thy God in v. — BIBLE 88:23
  nothing is in v. — HERB 397:87
  of Amber Snuff-box justly v. — POPE 659:76
  role of the author is v. enough — DIDE 274:92
  Say not...the wounds are v. — CLOU 222:20
  soul...made first in v. — BROW 162:88
  v. desire at last — ROSS 698:99
  v., giddy, shallow, humorous youth — SHAK 745:39
  v. in verse — SIDN 790:7
  v. man,' said she — SPEN 809:1
  V. matter is worse — BACON 46:40
  V. thy onset! — ARNO 33:51
  v. to mislike the current fashion — FULL 341:68
  v., unnecessary things are men — ROCH 691:60
  youth is v. — COLE 226:7
vainer role of the critic...is v. — DIDE 274:92
valanced Thy face is v. — SHAK 753:63
vale after I depart this v. — MENC 565:56
  cool sequestered v. of life — GRAY 369:20
  death's dark v. — SCOT 725:61
  i' th' midst a horrid v. — MILT 580:6
  Saimear's green v. — MCCA 527:87
  shady sadness of a v. — KEATS 459:44
  v. in whose bosom — MOORE 596:47
  v. of soul-making — KEATS 459:45
  v. of tears — FERRE 321:19
  v. of Tempe — RUSK 704:38
  V., the three lone weirs — ARNO 33:43
  violet-embroidered v. — MILT 577:33
Valentine Slander V. — SHAK 729:37
vales Making all the v. rejoice? — BLAKE 133:29
  o'er us and hills — WORD 927:40
valet to his very v. seemed a hero — BYRON 181:58
valiant As he was v., I honour him — SHAK 744:8
  makes e'en the v. more brave — DIBD 265:54
  Ring in the v. man — TENN 844:61
  v. and martial — BACON 49:33
  v., but not too venturous — LYLY 523:6
  v. man and true — TENN 848:64
  v. taste of death but once — SHAK 747:88
validity If...God has any v. — BALD 54:37
Valium Cricket is baseball on V. — WILL 912:12
  toothless terrier on V. — SIKO 791:31
valley bicker down a v. — TENN 846:2
  Every v. shall be exalted — BIBLE 103:36
  Green was my v. — LLEW 513:90
  hill can't be a v. — CARR 196:93
  in some such v. — SHIP 789:78
  journeys through the v. — LEE 500:45
  love is of the v. — TENN 842:16
  paweth in the v. — BIBLE 93:74
  V. and hamlet, sing! — OAKL 620:89
  v. between Buxton — RUSK 704:38
  v. is his golden cup — MERE 567:9
  v. of Death — TENN 844:75
  v. of Death — TENN 844:76
  v. of...death — BIBLE 94:2
  v. sheep are fatter — PEAC 645:95
  v. which was full of bones — BIBLE 105:91
  world a v. so sweet — MOORE 596:47
valleys below them in the v. — TENN 839:57
  descend into the v. again — LLOY 513:99
  listening V. hear — BLAKE 133:23
  Piping down the v. wild — BLAKE 133:28
  stranger strayed into...their v. — MONT 592:70
  That v., groves, hills — MARL 553:17
  thou who passest through our v. — BLAKE 133:24
  Ye v. low where — MILT 578:53
valour better part of v. — SHAK 742:36
  contemplation he and v. formed — MILT 583:62
  fame, of v. — MARL 551:78
  ideals, the v. and the sacrifices — EISE 302:64
  possess only strength and v. — BRON 155:79
  report of v. — SHAK 757:81
  So full of v. — SHAK 774:96
  wonder at the desperate v. — JONS 448:16
valuable everything dear and v. — PITT 653:46
  freedom is...supremely v. — HUXL 426:98
  v. or even earnest — THOR 857:86
valuation bias of v. — KEYN 466:86
  superstitious v. of Europe — JAMES 433:33
value any v. at all in the world — LACL 484:83
  consciousness of human v. — DEWEY 264:43
  Diamonds are of most precious v. — WEBS 895:98
  economic v. of...women — GILM 356:53

be v.—be religious　SCOTT 725:60
learn…to be v.　PROV 667:10
lovers be v.　LYLY 523:10
Most plain girls are v.　ANGE 17:36
the v. who believe themselves　PASC 641:33
v. man　GREE 371:53
v. men pass mildly away　DONNE 280:54
When men grow v.　POPE 659:91
virulent in its most v. form　JERO 437:31
virus Conveyed the v. hither　WILB 907:75
If this is what v. pneumonia does　COOP 236:50
visage all his v. wanned　SHAK 753:67
Melancholy, Whose saintly v.　MILT 576:13
v. was so marred　BIBLE 104:49
viscous thought is v.　ADAMS 4:86
visible All things v.　BOOK 141:94
Art…makes v.　KLEE 476:10
too v. as sex objects　FRIE 337:60
v. self as its medium　HOLL 407:68
vision Boy, I got v.　GOLD 361:36
brightness of this v.　RAND 678:15
cried in a whisper…at some v.　CONR 234:99
devils to contest his v.　MAIL 540:46
distrust of its own v.　JEFF 436:18
faulty v. sees things as they are　BIER 129:25
In a v. once I saw　COLE 226:14
keen v. and feeling　ELIOT 304:8
man…without some v.　LAWR 495:30
nation's experience and his v.　KISS 475:98
no v., no foresight, no sight at all　DAWK 256:73
Poetry—tries to tell you about a v.　ENGLE 314:69
powerful v., formal and austere　PAGE 633:79
President's v.　SCHL 718:16
Science provides a v. of reality　PAGE 633:79
serving his v.　KENN 463:35
skull that…had v.　SASS 717:78
tinkering with moments of v.　BLUN 137:17
to Reagan the main fact was a v.　SHUL 790:93
unified v. of life　WILS 915:75
v. of an America　RODO 693:94
v. of a time　RAND 678:14
v. of our own　WORD 927:30
v. of the Commonwealth　MACM 536:67
v. of the holiness of God　BLOOM 137:5
v. of the world　TENN 840:81
v. sanctified　WORD 929:63
v. splendid　WORD 926:24
v. to recognize it as such　MILL 572:25
Where there is no v.　BIBLE 100:62
with his v.　SACK 708:89
young men's v.　DRYD 290:82
visions appear in v.　AUDEN 40:10
history of great v.　ADEL 7:46
lost in stormy v.　SHEL 786:3
My Oberon, what v.　SHAK 738:10
screwy v.　BELL 73:79
seen v. and had amazing　THOM 852:56
these v. did appear　SHAK 738:19
v. for a simple human delight　BARB 59:48
v. of sugarplums danced　MOORE 594:15
young men shall see v.　BIBLE 106:5
visit ever paying you a v.　MORT 599:17
going to v. every country　KEEN 460:68
On every formal v.　AUST 42:59
visitant v. that…fans my cheek　WORD 924:88
visitation time of their v.　BIBLE 107:32
visiting-card v.-c. will answer　BAED 51:76
visitor any v. from outer space　BURR 173:59
caused the v.　KIPL 473:57
reels them off to every new v.　SHAW 780:57
subduing the impenitent v.　BIER 129:40
v. from Mars contemplating　LAVER 493:82
v. with a return ticket　GREE 371:58
visitors V. who wish to remain　LEBO 499:14
visits beauties…were but my v.　PRIOR 669:42
tendered their v.　JONS 450:54
vista at the end of every v.　BURKE 169:36
Hasta la v., baby　SCHW 721:63
visual v. aids, that sort of thing　NEWM 612:60
vitae V., non scholae discimus　SENE 727:92
vital No matter how v.　GLAS 359:99
vitality lowering the subject's v.　VEBL 878:54
not v. enough　JOHN 446:64
symptom of a deficient v.　STEV 822:97
V. in a woman　SHAW 778:83
vitalized highly v. persons　GALS 344:23
vitals red red v. of his heart　RANS 679:24

vitamins right proteins and v.　CART 198:56
vitriol lacy sleeve with a bottle of v.　WOOL 923:56
vituperation learn to accept v.　WAUGH 892:42
viva V. la the New Brigade!　DAVIS 256:68
vive V. l'amour!　STER 818:3
V. le Québec!　DE 259:41
vivid left the v. air　SPEN 807:47
vocabulary have a great v.　FEIF 319:83
mastery of v. and syntax　SAYE 717:86
Syntax and v.　MATH 560:58
to be a v.　UPDI 875:97
v. needs constant fertilizing　WAUGH 893:51
vocal vasectomy of the v. chords　ALTH 13:69
vocation dignity…the high v.　CARL 191:87
I have not felt the v.　CLOU 223:30
labour in his v.　SHAK 741:97
robs strength from my artistic v.　FUEN 340:41
'Tis my v., Hal　SHAK 741:97
vodka medium V. dry Martini　FLEM 327:56
vogue charming to totter into v.　WALP 887:26
voice as the v. of reason　LEGU 501:63
audible v. of the Past　CARL 193:34
broken v.　SHAK 753:67
certain what-is-it in his v.　WODE 919:69
confront the oppressor with one v.　MAKW 541:77
Conscience: the inner v.　MENC 565:53
echoes back the public v.　JOHN 441:15
every v. be song!　DODD 278:7
fill my mourning v.　SURR 829:39
gave v. to three words　LAMA 486:24
Give…few thy v.　SHAK 751:19
hard note crept into his v.　WALL 886:5
heard the still v. calling　LAWS 496:46
heard thy v. in the garden　BIBLE 86:51
Her v. was ever soft　SHAK 764:6
Imagination is the v.　MILL 573:35
In honoured poverty thy v.　SHEL 782:23
It was her v. that made　STEV 819:27
let thy v. rise　TENN 847:51
lift up your v.　WESL 900:13
Lord, hear my v.　BIBLE 128:94
Lord, hear my v.　BIBLE 98:95
make our v. audible　STEV 822:4
Methought I heard a v. cry　SHAK 767:2
Mistaken at the top of one's v.　BIER 129:41
moderate his v. at the same time　STER 817:68
Money speaks…with a male v.　DWOR 296:47
music…for the human v.　ANGE 17:48
No v., but oh! the silence sank　COLE 225:91
No v. or hideous hum　MILT 576:99
only v. I care to hear　CAMP 186:57
people's v. is odd　POPE 661:53
quality of v. that is…the writer's own　CATH 200:95
refuseth to hear the v. of the charmer　BOOK 143:55
reserve the more weighty v.　BACON 49:18
safe I sing with mortal v.　MILT 583:89
silence until any v. is heard　LEZA 508:12
Sink heart and v.　NEALE 610:28
sound of a v. that is still!　TENN 840:68
still small v.　BIBLE 92:24
such a tender v.　BLAKE 133:29
supplicating v.　JOHN 441:20
sweet and potent v.　COLE 226:3
Sweeter thy v.　TENN 842:17
sweet little rinky-dink of a v.　MAIL 540:58
The City's v.　SHEL 783:30
thundrous v.　WILL 914:54
till thou obey my v.　BLAKE 135:75
Today if ye will hear his v.　BOOK 143:65
tones of a loved v.　ARNO 31:99
top of your v.　BAKER 53:18
transmit the v. over wires　ANON 21:31
trick of that v.　SHAK 763:87
true v. arose in me　FOX 333:77
tune her sacred v.　JOHN 441:12
tune thy jolly v.　BLAKE 133:25
utter forth a glorious v.　ADDI 6:27
v., a mystery　WORD 926:12
v. as the sound of many waters　BIBLE 125:45
v. falls as they say love　LARK 490:25
v. in every wind　GRAY 368:93
v. in the darkness　LONG 516:64
v. is full of money　FITZ 326:98
v. less loud, through its joys　BROW 161:34
v.…like the sea　WORD 925:11
v. of dolorous pitch　HOOD 410:45
v. of freedom　SHAR 776:37

v. of high midsummer's heat　ROBE 689:18
v. of him that crieth　BIBLE 103:36
v. of the Bard!　BLAKE 134:50
v. of the dead　TENN 847:32
v., of the democracy　STEAD 813:80
v. of the people　ALCU 10:8
v. of the people　BACON 47:66
v. of the people　PITT 652:39
v. of those who suffer　CESA 203:49
v. said in mastery　BROW 159:4
v., so in a shapeless flame　DONNE 280:49
v. stunning as thunder　KINS 470:72
v. that tells him he is not　TRUM 868:40
v. the word 'nature'　REDON 681:75
v. which failed to sound　MILNE 574:73
With a monarch's v.　SHAK 748:2
with cheerful v.　KETHE 465:75
voiceless Science is v.　WEIL 896:27
voices Ancestral v. prophesying war!　COLE 226:13
Bubble their colourful v.　HUGH 419:44
clatter of high v.　DOYLE 285:56
Clear Cymric v.　BUNT 166:62
drowning out of false v.　DELI 261:78
English don't raise their v.　HELL 392:81
heart and hands and v.　WINK 917:23
hear v. in the air　KEYN 466:89
Moans round with many v.　TENN 840:66
Other V., Other Rooms　CAPO 189:21
soft v. die　SHEL 787:27
sounds of their v.　ANGE 17:47
Two v. are there　STEP 817:58
Two v. are there　WORD 928:47
unbearable v. of its announcers　ORWE 628:63
v. are heard among them　BOOK 142:43
v. dying with a dying fall　ELIOT 304:20
v. elected me of all men　LEE 500:45
v. of liberty be mute?　CUMM 247:9
v. of young people　SMITH 799:78
v. telling him that　TRUM 868:40
voice-trained v.-t. to speak　WATE 890:92
void All is without form and v.　HAZL 388:95
beating in the v.　ARNO 34:67
decorations over a v.　YOUR 935:81
No craving v.…in the breast　POPE 659:82
not enough…to be v.　BRAT 150:95
rubbish to the v.　TENN 843:41
shall not return unto me v.　BIBLE 104:56
terrors that flock to fill the v.　LEGU 501:56
v. in your life, fill it　NERVO 611:47
v. of noble rage　TENN 843:33
voids sins are attempts to fill v.　WEIL 896:29
volcanic v. landscapes a poor girl　CHEE 209:2
volcano erupt like a v.　MACD 530:50
like a slumbering v.　WHITE 903:1
volcanoes We are v.　LEGU 501:61
vole questing v.　WAUGH 892:31
volley fine v. of words　SHAK 729:29
volleys make her hit backhand v.　KING 468:26
Volsces Cut me to pieces, V.　SHAK 770:73
Voltaire always like V.　TALMA 836:88
mock on, V. Rousseau　BLAKE 135:64
Rousseau, V.…united in one person　HESS 401:67
V., Rousseau…fools, and madmen!　ONEI 625:99
V. smiled　HUGO 421:97
volume iron-clasped v. of despair　POE 656:27
take in our hand any v.　HUME 422:15
Twenty V. Suicide Note　BARA 59:43
v. can ever be written on the flea　MELV 564:35
v.…so far above the average　WILDE 908:87
world is a great v.　DONNE 282:95
volumes creators of odd v.　LAMB 487:52
Reticence, in three v.　GLAD 359:96
To their subsequent v.　SHAK 757:96
voluntary faith…become as fully v.　CUPI 248:35
volunteers brave York V.　BROCK 153:46
voluptuous Lush, calm and v.　BAUD 64:61
vomit dog is turned to his own v.　BIBLE 125:31
dog returneth to his v.　BIBLE 100:53
Dog returns to his v.　KIPL 474:84
giant pool of crapulous v.　BOYD 147:42
vortex bisection of a v.!　OCON 621:21
into the v. of immensity　DICK 268:48
v. of our grave　CRANE 243:11
vote against giving woman the v.　WRIG 929:73
Fifty per cent…won't v.　VIDAL 881:6
fighting for the v.　PANK 636:33
I cast only one v.　ONAS 625:82

man's decision on how to v. — SCHN 719:21
my hearty v. — SWIFT 831:75
one dollar, one v. — KRIS 481:17
One man shall have one v. — CART 198:57
v. for a woman — WATE 890:92
v. somebody into office — GERG 350:32
women…trying for the v. — PANK 636:29
working classes…given the v. — WAUGH 893:53
voter v. who uses his money — SAMU 712:79
what the v. receives — PRICE 668:15
woman v.…pernicious to the State — WRIG 929:74
voters v. have no contact — PRICE 668:14
votes asked men for v. — WEST 901:41
giving v. to the most obscure — CHES 211:61
speeches and majority v. — BISM 131:83
voting It's not the v. — STOP 825:63
vow v.…made to her in marriage — SHAK 752:31
v. that is vowèd true — SHAK 761:33
v. that to-morne — MALO 542:9
v. to thee, my country — SPRI 811:39
vowels Only consonants and v. — RANS 679:28
Scrabble with all the v. missing — ELLI 310:73
shifting of v. and consonants — UNTE 874:71
vows cancel all our v. — DRAY 287:6
constancy of its v. — SHAW 778:1
Dismiss your v. — SHAK 733:54
falser than v. made in wine — SHAK 750:70
he v. his passion — PARK 638:59
Lends the tongue v. — SHAK 751:23
They fulfil their v. — KORAN 479:91
V., oaths, and all — JONS 450:52
voyage long, beautiful v. — TZARA 873:56
v. and not a harbour — TOYN 864:28
v. is entirely imaginary — CELI 202:35
v. of their life — SHAK 748:16
v. of voyages — MUNDY 603:83
voyeur into the theatre as a v. — FRIS 338:80
voyeurs the lethal v. — RUSH 703:92
vulgar called wicked than v. — LEWIS 507:80
Father is rather v. — DICK 271:16
Funny without being v. — GILB 355:35
More is v. — SPARK 806:24
rude remark or a v. action — WILL 912:16
shallow and v. view — WEBB 893:62
times have become v. — MOLI 590:29
v. love…v. man — DRYD 289:57
v. sort of capacities — BACON 46:38
v. to talk like a dentist — WILDE 909:35
work upon the v. with fine sense — POPE 659:88
vulgarest survival of the v. — WILDE 908:97
vulgarities may have other v. — HELL 392:81
vulgarity mould of its v. — JEFF 436:3
singularity and v. — HAZL 387:70
vulgarizing succeeded in…v. — HUXL 425:81
vulnerable she is so v. — CURR 249:39
v. human beings — TURN 870:67

W

wabe gyre and gimble in the w. — CARR 195:90
wad leave him a w. — BALL 56:88
waddle flounce at a w. away — THOM 853:93
wade should I w. no more — SHAK 768:19
Wadman married to Mrs W. — STER 818:89
wag How now, mad w.? — SHAK 741:95
tail must w. the dog — KIPL 471:4
wage One man's w. rise — WILS 916:99
w. against the enmity — SHAK 763:69
w. no war with women — SOUT 805:3
wage-earner status of the w.-e. — SKEL 795:94
wager w. that he does exist — PASC 641:21
wages better w. and shorter h. — ORWE 627:42
common w. of labour — SMITH 797:43
earneth w. to put it into a bag — BIBLE 106:14
floor under w. and a ceiling — WRIS 930:88
Home…and ta'en thy w. — SHAK 774:74
labour and w. first — MANN 546:80
like rent and w. — SMITH 798:45
neither honours nor w. — GARI 346:48
never ta'en w. of her — WEBS 895:3
rather than give them good w. — WEST 901:38
rise of w. — RICA 684:32
took their w. — HOUS 416:79
w. may rise — MARX 558:6
w. of sin is death — BIBLE 120:69
w. should be left to…competition — RICA 684:33
waggon Hitch your w. to a star — EMER 313:48

Wagner like W.'s music better — WILDE 908:5
W. has good moments — ROSS 698:5
W.'s music is better — TWAIN 872:38
write music like W. — GOLD 362:80
wags how the world w. — SHAK 749:47
You w. that judge — OTWAY 630:22
wail suffice to w. their scorn — DANI 252:88
when I w. — SPEN 809:97
wailing fullers and their w. — ANON 18:65
in w. there's nought availing — CURR 249:40
wailsday tearsday, w. — JOYCE 452:1
waist from the w. They're centaurs — SHAK 763:89
fourth w. button — LICH 509:19
open your w. — HUNT 423:24
yolk runs down the w. — DICK 267:7
waistcoats w. and…handkerchiefs — DICK 266:78
wait I can w. — LISZT 512:76
must w. until a shrimp — KHRU 466:98
to w. is life — HUGO 420:70
w. and not be tired — KIPL 473:67
w. on wrinkled age! — SHAK 733:62
w., seated in a chair — VALE 875:12
w. until man comes around — FULL 341:52
w. upon the Lord — BIBLE 103:42
You just w. — THOM 853:96
waited w. patiently for the Lord — BIBLE 95:18
waiter damn good head w. — GULB 374:35
like the way a Swiss w. talks — CHAN 204:81
nothing but a head w. — USTI 875:4
waiters impulse exists among w. — WEBER 894:68
waiting pain of w. — GUY 375:50
The meaning is the w. — THOM 855:29
W. for the end — EMPS 314:64
wake doomed at last to w. — JOHN 442:42
w. from ignorance — JOHN 441:12
w. in a corner — KELM 461:80
w. sleeping, and sleep — MONT 592:82
w. slightly altered — UPDI 875:94
w. up one morning — HEYE 401:72
w. us Time and time over — LARK 490:21
we w. eternally — DONNE 281:68
when you w. in the morning — SAND 713:11
waked w. herself with laughing — SHAK 744:1
wakeful W. they lie — GRAV 367:77
wakened sleepeth, and must be w. — BIBLE 92:19
wakening w. and uprising prove — KEBLE 460:67
wakes He lives, he w. — SHEL 786:5
w. in our hearts — KIER 467:13
w. or sleeps with the enduring dead — SHEL 786:2
Walden To W. the saxophone was — HOLM 407:72
Waldo W. is one of those people — SAKI 710:46
We are cursed,W. — SCHR 720:39
Waldron a song…to Mal W. — OHARA 623:46
Wales Celtic genius of W. — ARNO 33:49
give his soul…But for W. — BOLT 139:48
influence of W. — WAUGH 891:16
Mother of W. — FULL 341:61
position of the artists of W. — THOM 853:97
there were wolves in W. — THOM 853:2
walk And w. among…grass — YEATS 932:36
before we have learnt to w. — CONN 233:78
closer w. with God — COWP 240:46
country safe to w. in — THAT 850:14
do not w. so fast — BLAKE 134:34
good w. spoiled — TWAIN 872:40
make running water w. — RAYB 680:42
Men creep, Not w. — WHIT 906:60
me to w. doth make — SCOT 725:61
never w. down the nave — HOME 409:14
rise up and w. — BIBLE 119:30
stray Far as the solar w. — POPE 660:11
take up thy bed, and w. — BIBLE 117:86
talk, not to w. — WILDE 910:63
those who like to w. — HILL 402:91
w., and not faint — BIBLE 103:42
w. before me — BIBLE 87:76
w.…before they dance — POPE 661:58
w. by faith, not by sight — BIBLE 122:26
W. by the shore — SITW 794:72
W. cheerfully — FOX 333:78
w. down the lane — FREED 336:37
W.! Not bloody likely — SHAW 780:68
w. off proud — SAND 713:98
W. on the Wild Side — ALGR 11:28
w. on, w. on — HAMM 379:17
w. round it several times — SATIE 717:80
w. through the storm — HAMM 379:17

W. two Oscars behind — WARR 889:71
w. ye in it — BIBLE 103:31
w. your mystic way — GILB 354:4
Will you w. a little faster? — CARR 195:81
walking are ye w. yet? — SKIR 795:14
as dancing is to w. — WAIN 884:66
craves wary w. — SHAK 747:82
hate w. — SMOL 801:28
just w. dully along — AUDEN 40:90
w., and leaping, and praising God — BIBLE 119:31
w. dead man — ANON 25:66
W. is a way of being somewhere — HILL 402:90
W. so early — SCOTT 724:39
walks luxuries…in my w. — KEATS 458:11
w. up and down with me — SHAK 738:25
wall auld grey w. — MACD 529:28
Before I built a w. — FROST 338:85
behind its great w. — THUR 860:65
daily from the turret w. — MUIR 602:55
had to put a w. up — KENN 463:32
hanging on the w. — BETJ 83:86
interesting as a w. can be — SHAW 781:89
Jackson…like a stone w. — BEE 69:55
leaped over a w. — BIBLE 94:54
lined up against a w. — TAYL 837:21
office of a w. — SHAK 734:8
picture on the w. — JOHN 440:80
pile of turf against the w. — COLUM 229:61
Something…that doesn't love a w. — FROST 338:84
stones into the Theban w. — COWL 240:30
To the top of the w.! — MOORE 594:17
to the w., dying, but fighting back! — MCKA 533:12
walks through a w. — MALA 541:80
w. as solid as the earth — BUCH 164:24
w. fell down flat — BIBLE 90:64
w. is strong — WILDE 910:36
W. of China — PATM 643:67
W. St. genes — THOM 854:24
W. Street indexes predicted — SAMU 712:80
w. which separates you — DIDE 273:87
Washes its w. on the southern side — BROW 160:25
Watch the w. — KIPL 473:61
were not the W. itself extant — ADDI 6:23
When icicles hang by the w. — SHAK 734:94
Without a city w. — ALEX 11:25
with stones to build a w. — FROST 338:96
wrote…upon the plaister of the w. — BIBLE 106:97
Wallace Scots, wha hae wi' W. bled — BURNS 173:41
wallet lump to my w. — WALL 886:11
Time hath…A w. — SHAK 757:5
walling w. in or w. out — FROST 338:61
wallow let us w. — FLAN 326:22
wallowing w. in low seriousness — BELL 74:84
wallpaper audible w. — COOKE 236:43
Either that w. goes — WILDE 910:61
w. with which the men — MILL 572:14
walls cell whose w. are mirrors — ONEI 625:89
dead w.…Their ivy mantles — BYRON 180:38
floors of plaister, and the w. of dung — POPE 660:55
four grey w. — TENN 849:55
four w. and a ring — HEAN 389:5
Four w. with tomorrow inside — AKERS 9:79
Hang on thy w. — JONS 449:37
look into the stains of w. — LEON 504:19
mute on Tara's w. — MOORE 596:51
noticed how many w. the room had — CHAN 205:92
no w., no borders — ATWO 38:50
on so many suburban w. — HUGH 419:34
on the w. of the world — KENN 463:40
peopled labyrinth of w. — SHEL 783:28
phosphorescence out of the w. — MACD 530:54
posts and w. with wine — SPEN 809:2
Stone w. do not a prison — LOVE 519:10
W. have ears — ANON 22:63
W. have ears — LINK 511:52
W. have tongues — SWIFT 831:9
w., nor its ships — NICI 614:91
w. of institutions — ROET 694:9
w. of spiders' legs — DRAY 287:2
W., palaces, half-cities — BYRON 180:40
w., the only sharers of secrets — AMMI 15:1
w. with the heads of Bison — MACN 538:2
Whose w. were high — SPEN 808:7
within thy wicked w. — SURR 829:3
wooden w. are the best — COVE 239:4
walnut cradle of Spanish w. — PLATH 654:7
walnuts you received 29 w. — STE 841:8

walrus W. and the Carpenter | CARR 196:1
Walter No repose for Sir W. | SCOTT 725:59
Sir W., being strangely surprised | AUBR 39:69
waltz w. that is Viennesey | GERS 350:39
waly O w., w. up the bank | BALL 56:94
wan w. grass sea | SITW 794:72
wand all I have of magic w. | HARR 384:2
body…straight as Circe's w. | MARL 553:12
last possessors of the w. | DIOR 275:24
stroke of the enchanter's w. | BYRON 180:31
wander w. in that golden maze | DRYD 287:16
wandered as I w. by the way | SHEL 786:23
we have w. all our ways | RALE 677:3
wanderer do not we,W., await it too? | ARNO 32:21
foiled circuitous w. | ARNO 32:28
wanderers As w. do | JONS 449:39
wandering forget the w. and pain | FLEC 327:50
W. between two worlds | ARNO 32:31
w. minstrel | GILB 355:19
wanders w. and loses himself | CONF 230:92
Wanstead W. drew me over | LEVE 506:58
want die out for w. of simplicity | POUND 665:55
for w. of better Knowledge | PATE 642:55
get what you w. | SMITH 799:73
giant evils of W. | BEVE 85:27
gittin all you w. | HARR 383:94
hide…their w. of art | POPE 658:55
if you w. it | WEAT 893:61
I w. it that way | IVES 431:2
no w. to them that fear him | BIBLE 95:13
pleasantest preservative from w. | AUST 43:67
signifies the w. of government | HOBB 404:28
w. as an armed man | BIBLE 99:16
w. of character | SHAW 777:72
w. that pinches | VIRG 882:31
w. to be alone | GARBO 345:38
w. to disappear | HUGO 420:75
What more can one w.? | WILDE 908:7
wanted Every man is w. | EMER 312:26
everything I never w. | GARD 346:44
never really w. to | KING 470:65
Not as we w. it | QUIL 674:41
unless he w. something off you | SALI 711:55
w. only one thing | HAZL 388:89
wanting Much w., so much w. | WORD 925:90
One being only is w. | LAMA 485:22
wanton As files to w. boys | SHAK 763:84
hath made me w. | JONS 448:19
wantonness in clothes a w. | HERR 400:50
wantons Sleep, pretty w. | DEKK 259:48
wants article which nobody w. | HONE 409:27
social w. of the people | CHIS 213:16
supplying our w. | SWIFT 831:69
to provide for human w. | BURKE 168:33
w. have no limits | FLAU 326:40
wanwordy W., crazy, dinsome thing | FERG 320:7
war After each w. | ATKI 37:33
against this they made w. | SHER 787:33
Ancestral voices prophesying w.! | COLE 226:13
army that we must train for w. | WILS 916:16
arts of w. | MORE 596:57
at w. over a few acres | VOLT 882:41
at w. you think about | WILD 910:80
'a w. to end w.' | LEWIS 508:4
beating of w. drums | KOES 477:33
Before the w. | ORWE 628:53
benefitted from prolonged w. | SUN 829:26
be prepared for w. | WASH 890:86
blast of w. blows | SHAK 746:42
blossom of w. | TENN 846:99
British ships of w. | NELS 610:32
British way of w. | WAVE 893:59
bungled, unwise w. | PLOM 656:8
business of w. | GERB 350:29
business of w. | WELL 898:65
calamities of W. | JOHN 442:55
cardinal maxims of guerrilla w. | KISS 475:90
cast all weapons of w. | DEKA 259:45
century…out of this w. | WALL 886:9
Civil w. is impossible | PAVL 644:81
cold w. is getting warmer | BARU 63:30
Communist 'w. of liberation' | MCNA 537:91
conscientious objection to w. | STRA 826:86
consequent to a time of w. | HOBB 404:27
convulsions of a great w. | LLOY 513:99
cruellest and most terrible w. | LLOY 513:3
Dakotas, I am for w. | RED 681:71

dance and w. | STEIN 815:21
dauntless in w. | SCOTT 723:96
declared w. on America | HIRO 403:3
delays…in w. | DRYD 288:33
desires peace prepare for w. | VEGE 879:58
done very well out of the w. | BALD 54:41
Don't mention the w. | CLEE 220:71
Ease after w. | SPEN 808:81
easier to make w. | CLEM 221:77
eighteen years before a w. | WHITE 903:85
Either w. is obsolete | FULL 341:53
essence of w. | MACA 526:56
European w. thrust upon us | MARY 558:17
even colder w. | KENN 462:17
ever another w. in Europe | BISM 131:87
everything possible to avoid w. | SCHW 721:66
Every time I have asked us to go to w. | BLAIR 133:12
everywhere, I wage w. | CLEM 221:76
first casualty when w. comes | JOHN 439:78
First World W. had begun | TAYL 837:12
France has not lost the w.! | DE 259:35
furnish the w. | HEAR 389:17
get out of the w. altogether | HELL 392:63
give a w. and nobody will come | SAND 713:6
good w. makes a good peace | HERB 398:20
government in peace and in w. | BEVE 85:26
green snot. There is w. | MITS 589:14
hashed over by nuclear w. | COUP 238:96
how we began this w. | PRIE 668:19
I can't go to w. | RANK 679:19
idealism, as in w. time | MENC 566:81
If there is w. | GREY 373:6
If the w. didn't…kill you | ORWE 628:54
if they mean to have a w. | PARK 638:80
if w. did not include killing | ANGE 17:39
In a civil w., a general must know | REED 682:84
In a pattern called a w. | LOWE 519:23
infection and the hand of w. | SHAK 734:8
in peace and…in w. | MONT 593:92
Instruments of W. | ALBE 10:99
in the midst of a cold w. | BARU 63:29
In the sex w. | CONN 233:77
In w.…all are losers | CHAM 204:60
In w.…no substitute for victory | MACA 524:25
In w.: resolution | CHUR 216:60
justice, w. and crime | NEME 610:38
killing men at w. | MARG 549:43
know the w. prepared | KIPL 474:75
laws…silent in time of w. | CICE 218:21
less than w. to waste | MILT 585:33
let the Germans win the w. | MILE 569:53
Like a…holy w., a revolution | COOKE 236:41
like to the morning's w. | SHAK 730:74
little w. for a great nation | WELL 898:64
living through w. | KRAM 480:5
lofty instruments of w. | SHAK 742:32
looks on w. as all glory | SHER 788:72
Lord is a man of w. | BIBLE 88:20
lose the w. in an afternoon | CHUR 216:64
magnificent, but it isn't w. | BOSQ 145:7
Make love, not w. | ANON 23:90
make w. on a kindred nation | BETH 82:74
Mankind must put an end to w. | KENN 462:18
McNamara's w. | MCNA 537:90
military struggle…a w. | SCHL 718:10
miners poured to w. | MACA 526:69
Minstrel-boy to the w. | MOORE 596:49
neither shall they learn w. | BIBLE 102:8
never to go to w. with one another | CHAM 204:62
never understood this liking for w. | BENN 75:25
never was a good w. | FRAN 334:15
no discharge in that w. | BIBLE 101:80
No less renowned then w. | MILT 580:87
not at w. with Egypt | EDEN 299:91
not be involved in a European w | DAILY 250:64
nothing of a sacredness of w. | BONH 139:56
not in fair w. | CHUR 216:61
no w. for domination | CHUR 216:72
object of w. is not to die | PATT 643:73
of the book of w. | MONT 593:1
of w. I have slain men | SHAK 759:54
once w. is over | BEVE 85:27
Our w. on terror is well begun | BUSH 175:11
painting…an instrument of w. | PICA 650:98
people taut for w. | THOM 854:25
permanently on a w. footing | HUXL 425:97
plumed w.-bonnet | BENET 75:9

Politics is w. | MAO 548:6
Poor Brutus, with himself at w. | SHAK 747:73
Power and W. | KIPL 471:98
probabilities of peace or w. | PALM 636:26
profits of w. or office | TREV 865:63
purposes of the w. | LEES 500:50
quickest way of ending a w. | ORWE 629:96
read about the w. | HEMI 394:98
reasons for making w. | FRED 335:32
responsibility for the w. | HIRO 403:5
scourge of w. | UNIT 873:69
seek to avoid w. | BLAIR 133:13
seek…to avoid w. | CHAM 204:64
seen enough of one w. | JEFF 436:17
seven days w. | MUIR 602:62
sinews of w. | CICE 218:23
single w. | GUST 375:46
some slain in w. | SHAK 735:20
Spanish ships of w. at sea! | TENN 848:60
Stand up and take the w. | KIPL 474:76
stately tents of w. | MARL 551:70
state of w. by nature | SWIFT 832:1
success in w. | CHUR 216:79
success in w. | CLARK 219:52
support an offensive w. | PAINE 634:89
surgical w. | ASHD 35:91
Sweets with sweets w. not | SHAK 770:2
take chances in w. | DULL 293:90
tell us all about the w. | SOUT 805:99
tempered by the w. | KENN 462:12
that first invented w. | MARL 551:73
The art of w. | SUN 828:24
They had lost a w. | CLAV 220:68
think hard before starting a w. | BISM 131:85
this country is at w. with Germany | CHAM 204:63
this damnable w. | ACHE 3:52
This is the w. room | KUBR 481:31
this is w. | ADAMS 4:64
Those who can win a w. well | CHUR 216:67
though w. should rise against me | BIBLE 95:7
throughout the w. | GILB 354:14
through the Second World W. | BUSH 176:24
time of w. | BIBLE 100:70
To offer w. | SHAK 732:47
torch of w. in Europe | HITL 404:18
To w. and arms I fly | LOVE 519:13
truth…known at the end of the w. | WEIZ 896:35
try to end the w. | EISE 302:51
under the shadow of w. | SPEN 807:53
used to w.'s alarms | HOOD 410:34
view of history…not of w. | CHILD 213:8
wage no w. with women | SOUT 805:3
wage w. against art | RODC 693:87
w. abhorrent to all real women | FOWL 332:67
w. against the outsiders | GARI 346:48
W. alone can carry | MUSS 605:18
w. always finds a way | BREC 151:14
w. and mutual slaughter | MILT 583:87
W., and the pity of W. | OWEN 632:55
w., as in love | NAPO 607:66
w. between civilised nations | GOOCH 363:97
w. between men and women | THUR 859:24
w. breeds w. again | DAVI 254:25
w. called murder | MACD 530:60
w. every twenty-five years | MUSS 605:20
w. for the emancipation | LLOY 513:2
W. has its own sweetness | LAFO 485:6
W. has three handmaidens | HENR 395:45
w. hath no fury | MONT 592:68
w. hath smoothed | SHAK 731:99
w. history…simple one | WODE 919:73
w., I call it murder | LOWE 520:29
w.…I hate w. | ROOS 696:45
w. in heaven | BIBLE 126:66
w. in Spain is over | MUSS 605:22
w. in Vietnam | MCCA 527:89
W. is a condition of progress | RENAN 683:98
W. is, after all | RAE 677:90
w. is a necessary part | MOLT 590:46
W. is being deliberately prolonged | SASS 716:56
W. is capitalism with | STOP 825:64
W.…is not a relationship | ROUS 701:48
W. is peace | ORWE 629:99
w. is preferable to…peace | TACI 835:73
w. is somewhat disappointing | GRIF 373:11
W. is the national industry | MIRA 587:75
W. is the trade of kings | DRYD 291:26

learn her wanton w. — ROET 694:6
Let me count the w.! — BROW 160:9
look both w. — EDDI 298:84
maintain mine own w. — BIBLE 93:60
Most sure in all His w. — NEWM 612:66
neither are your w. my w. — BIBLE 104:55
nine and sixty w. — KIPL 471:8
the w. of God to man — POPE 660:7
w. are not as theirs — HOUS 416:75
w. deep and the weather sharp — ELIOT 306:73
w. of saying 'To hell with you' — FENW 320:91
whose w. are all discreet — PARK 637:43

weak arm the w. — FRAN 333:91
concessions of the w. — BURKE 168:8
entrust...freedom to the w. — EISE 302:53
eyesight has always been w. — GREG 372:96
flesh is w. — BIBLE 114:99
God hath chosen the w. things — BIBLE 121:92
How w. a thing — SHAK 747:92
let the w. say, I am strong — BIBLE 106:6
to be w. is miserable — MILT 580:3
w. alone repent! — BYRON 181:50
w. always have to decide — BONH 140:61
w. and feeble woman — ELIZ 309:60
w. and miserable men — CHOM 214:18
W. shall perish — SERV 728:1
w. spot or two in a character — HOLM 408:93
w., still tremulous — LEVE 506:60

weaker One is never w. — OLLI 624:72
wife...the w. vessel — BIBLE 125:27

weakest w. in nature — PASC 641:24

weakness childish w. to lament — SHAK 731:85
felt only his own w. — BELL 74:85
Marks of w. — BLAKE 135:58
means of w. and debility — SHAK 749:39
Power Girt round with w. — SHEL 785:99
sought her w. to reprove — LANY 489:5
strength and w. of human nature — MACA 526:71
strength is made perfect in w. — BIBLE 122:34
though it be a w. — JONS 449:33
w. for the stoic's pride — POPE 660:16
w. offered, strength — LANY 489:4
w. of our race — DELA 260:59
w. which impairs — ARNO 31:90

weaknesses pity...weakens our w. — BALZ 57:12
support two w. at the same time — WILD 911:86
virtues of their w. — MENC 566:76
w....into burnable energy — BELL 74:92

Wealdstone W. turned to waves — BETJ 84:2

wealth all that w. e'er gave — GRAY 369:14
all w. alchemy — DONNE 279:42
as their w. increaseth — MARL 552:84
Black love is Black w. — GIOV 357:73
born into w. — ROCK 692:74
by the acquisition of w. — MONT 593:97
cannot redistribute w. — TSON 869:55
carry the w. of the Indies — JOHN 445:31
consume w. without producing it — SHAW 777:55
cunning purchase of my w. — JONS 448:11
distribution of w. — HARDY 381:46
distribution of w. and income — KEYN 466:90
everything yields to w. — BLEST 136:93
excessive w. a libel — SHEL 782:15
Health, W., Love...and Time — ANON 26:91
heroic w. — WORD 925:11
how much w....in a country — SIDG 790:95
I have had w. — ALBE 10:96
insolence of w. — JOHN 445:32
Labour is the Father...of W. — PETTY 650:85
Large was his w. — DRYD 290:93
Nor that content surpassing w. — SHEL 783:32
nothing like w. for dulling desire — MCGU 532:94
no w. but life — RUSK 704:21
poor man's w. — SIDN 790:10
prevents the rule of w. — BAGE 51:85
prodigal of its w. — NORR 618:65
produce more w. — GILM 356:52
progress of society and w. — RICA 684:32
representative of w. — MILL 570:59
Republics end by w. — MONT 593:95
rich man's w. is his strong city — BIBLE 99:20
road to w. — TROL 866:75
Science...casts its w. — HERZ 400:54
the skill—the w. — ROOS 696:49
w. abides not — EURI 316:16
w. accumulates and men decay — GOLD 361:52
W. accumulates whatever — KEYN 465:82

w. and a good name — WALT 888:44
W. cannot make a life — HERR 399:37
W. does not bring goodness — PLATO 654:78
W. has more and more increased — CARL 191:82
W. I ask not — STEV 823:31
W., in a commercial age — POUND 666:74
w. is distributed in...society — MILL 570:56
w. is health — DYER 297:53
w....makes them doubly poor — CRAB 242:89
w. Of simple beauty — WHIT 906:58
w. of steaming phrases — SCHU 721:54
w. with our wisdom — KENN 463:37
What w....to me had brought — WORD 928:42
with w. and honour blest — DRYD 290:78
With w. your state...improve — DONNE 279:43
worker...poorer the more w. — MARX 557:95

wealthier To be w. or more powerful — HELO 393:87
wealthy healthy and w. and dead — THUR 859:29
w. wife was she — BALL 57:97

weaned were we not w. till then? — DONNE 279:37
weans w. in their bed — MILL 574:61

weapon bayonet is a w. — ANON 22:58
how steady you hold your w. — SIMP 792:47
most deadly w. — PARK 639:89
nobler w. than a wound — CRAS 244:42
Nostalgia IS A W. — COUP 239:2
other hand held a w. — BIBLE 93:45
religious and political w. — LEWIS 508:95
thoughtlessness is the w. of the male — CONN 233:77
Time's most lethal w. — SITW 794:80
trusty shield and w. — LUTH 523:97
w. had none — SCOTT 723:96
w. is starvation — STEV 824:40
w. which will make war — MORT 600:22

weapons Clothes are our w. — CART 198:37
do not have w. of mass destruction — HUSS 424:46
fought with nuclear w. — MOUN 601:39
hurt with the same w. — SHAK 740:68
into the cavity...cast all w. — DEKA 259:45
Iraq probably has no w. of mass destruction — COOK 236:37
lawful...to wear w. — BOOK 144:77
not only with w. — MANC 544:44
prevent...nuclear w. — AMIS 15:4
seeking w. of mass destruction — BUSH 175:10
w. against their capitalist exploiters — LENIN 502:84
W. grow rusty — HICKS 402:81
w. of mass destruction — BUSH 175:10
w. of mass destruction — BUSH 176:18
w. of mass destruction...in Iraq — BLIX 136:99
w. of mass extermination — RUSS 705:57
w. of war perished! — BIBLE 91:98
women...dropping their w. — OSBO 630:11
women's w., water-drops — SHAK 763:70

wearer merit of the w.! — SHAK 740:63
new w. of clothes — THOR 857:88

weariness Art thou pale for w. — SHEL 787:30
His W. the Prince — FIRB 323:67
hours of w. — WORD 923:69
labour w. — LYLY 523:11
study is a w. — BIBLE 101:93
W. Can snore — SHAK 774:70
w., the fever, and the fret — KEATS 460:59
yet w. May toss him — HERB 398:17

wearing meals that I...am w. — BUSH 175:89
wearisome monotonous, and w. — THOR 858:6

weary faint and be w. — BIBLE 103:42
fast asleep and w. — BIBLE 90:67
great rock in a w. land — BIBLE 103:32
How w., stale, flat, and unprofitable — SHAK 751:6
In me or, most w. — HOPK 412:2
lay his w. bones — SHAK 775:23
Let him be rich and w. — HERB 398:1
Let us not be w. in well doing — BIBLE 122:40
poor and the w. predominate — GARL 346:49
sae dowf and w. — BURNS 172:39
Say I'm w. — HUNT 423:35
Waukin still and w. — BURNS 171:7
w. be at rest — BIBLE 93:52
w. lot is thine — SCOTT 723:11
w. of these worldly bars — SHAK 747:81

weasel as a w. sucks eggs — SHAK 749:44
w. under the cocktail cabinet — PINT 652:21
weather Autumn's pleasant w. — BURNS 170:85
blue unclouded w. — TENN 839:49
calm or stormy w. — ROSS 697:75
Cricket w. — JOYCE 452:94

dry frigid w. — PIER 651:7
earthquakes are preceded by bright w. — CARL 192:5
fair w.: for the sky is red — BIBLE 112:61
french wine and fine w. — KEATS 458:13
he is also part of the w. — TRIL 866:70
Hillary...responsible for the w. — MCCU 529:24
If it prove fair w. — SUCK 828:13
in clear w. — SURR 829:40
in red w. — STEV 819:26
it's fruitcake w.! — CAPO 189:25
Jolly boating w. — CORY 238:78
makes cold w. — SHAK 775:7
more w....than anywhere else — SAMU 712:81
possible combination of w. — LODGE 514:22
promise of fair w. — DICK 268:51
protecting flat surfaces from the w. — BIER 129:36
reasonable summer w. — WAUGH 891:7
sad or singing w. — SWIN 833:39
season of calm w. — WORD 927:27
seven months of Arctic w. — ANON 21:34
sharp be the w. — SCOTT 724:15
talk is of the w. — JOHN 442:53
waiting for the w. to break — PINT 652:20
ways deep and the w. sharp — ELIOT 306:73
W. abroad — RICH 685:41
W. and rain — KIPL 473:66
w. sharp — ANDR 16:27
w. that bringeth no gain — DEKK 259:46
w. the cuckoo likes — HARDY 382:76
won't hold up the w. — MACN 538:3

weave So did I w. my self — HERB 398:8
tangled web we w. — SCOTT 723:96
W. the warp — GRAY 370:32

weaving w. and unweaving — ELIOT 303:70

web as little w. as this — SHAK 759:74
She left the w. — TENN 839:50
tangled w. we weave — SCOTT 723:99
w. do parents weave — NASH 608:92
w. of our grand illusion — PAGE 633:78
w. of our life — SHAK 762:36
wove a w. in childhood — BRON 154:76

webs Theoretical w., dirty w. — KELM 460:87
With swarthy w. — TENN 847:53

Webster Like W.'s dictionary — BURKE 169:54

wed December when they w. — SHAK 750:79
w. a fair young man — CAMP 187:81
w. itself with Speech — TENN 843:32
w. ye to my youngest son — SCOTT 724:21
With this kiss I w. thee — HEYW 402:77

wedding barefoot on her w. day — SHAK 732:30
Be well ware of w. — ANON 19:92
bought her w. clothes — ADDI 6:28
face...like a w.-cake — AUDEN 41:34
Let's have a w. — DICK 271:36
moldering like w.-cake — RICH 685:43
till our w. day — COLUM 229:59
where a w. has been — LENN 503:96
white lies to ice a w. cake — ASQU 36:13

wedding-guest W.-G. stood still — COLE 225:81
weddings All w. are similar — BERG 79:99
wedlock together in holy w. — BOOK 142:30
W....hath oft compared been — DAVI 254:36
Wednesday blue and white W. heart — HATT 385:26
He that died o' W. — SHAK 742:29
worked Monday...fired W. — ALGR 11:30

weed on earth a vicious w. — DRYD 290:84
O thou w. — SHAK 760:2
salt w. sways in the stream — ARNO 31:84
weeds all the idle w. that grow — SHAK 763:86
grubbing w. from gravel paths — KIPL 474:73
keep w. from overwhelming you — SHUL 789:87
Long live the w. — HOPK 412:97
smell far worse than w. — SHAK 772:38
w. of peace...triumphs — MILT 576:10
w. will overrun the fields — HOOV 411:57
winter w. outworn — SHEL 786:21

week £1 per w. — ANON 21:36
accomplished in a w. — STEV 822:2
any crisis next w. — KISS 475:96
as much as a w. — TWAIN 870:74
but a w. married — SHAK 744:2
Christian on a Pound a W.? — HARD 381:40
Englishman...there only a w. — FRAS 335:28
go a w. without a drink — LEWIS 507:82
lease for a w. — ANOU 26:94
Middle of Next W. — CARR 197:34
once a w. there should be — ORWE 629:74

takes the rest of the w.	WALK 885:97	
That Was The W.	ANON 23:88	
tried…once a w.	JOHN 445:18	
w., a natural day	MARL 552:6	
w. is a long time in politics	WILS 916:94	
weekend the dirty w.	SMITH 799:62	
weekends plumber on w.	ALLEN 12:42	
weeks brief hours and w.	SHAK 773:48	
w. of watching the roof leak	SNYD 803:50	
weep better…to w. at joy	SHAK 744:83	
blame thee now to w.	SHAK 732:38	
No, I'll not w.	SHAK 763:70	
not to w. at them	SPIN 810:22	
O now you w.	SHAK 748:12	
O, w. for Adonais!	SHEL 785:90	
shepherds, w. no more	MILT 578:57	
That he should w. for her?	SHAK 753:67	
that I may not w.	BYRON 182:88	
time to w.	BIBLE 100:70	
To w. is to make less	SHAK 730:73	
w. and know why	HOPK 412:94	
w. for him	SHAK 748:4	
W. If you can	HAMM 379:10	
W. not for little Léonie	GRAH 365:36	
w. on your own grave	GRAV 367:69	
w. or she will die	TENN 842:11	
w. with them that w.	BIBLE 120:82	
w. with them that w.	SHAK 731:92	
when I w.	SPEN 809:97	
Why w. ye by the tide	SCOTT 724:21	
you w. alone	WILC 907:80	
weeping doth that bode w.?	SHAK 761:5	
full cause of w.	SHAK 763:70	
Her little boy w. sought	BLAKE 134:35	
joy at w.!	SHAK 744:83	
prove the w. philosopher	SHAK 739:46	
Rachel w. for her children	BIBLE 105:78	
w. and gnashing of teeth	BIBLE 110:15	
w. and gnashing of teeth	BIBLE 113:90	
w. over sins…never committed	WILDE 908:90	
weeps before we know…why he w.	DU 293:76	
Weetabix The W. Years	BENN 75:22	
weigh But w. this song	YEATS 932:37	
number, w. and measure	HALES 377:81	
'tis best to w.	SHAK 745:40	
weighs W. heavily on me	KEATS 457:80	
weight collapsed under the w.	CANN 188:9	
counter-opinion of…same w.	SPEN 807:62	
just w. is his delight	BIBLE 99:21	
Number, W., or Measure	PETTY 650:86	
'tis purchased by the w.	SHAK 740:71	
w. of the superincumbent hour	SHEL 785:99	
w. of this sad time	SHAK 764:8	
w. of womanhood	DANG 251:85	
w. were taken off the driving wheels	CANN 188:10	
weights clock with w. and chains	COLUM 229:61	
weighty drowneth that which is w.	BACON 46:41	
weird home of the w.	LAWS 495:43	
weirs grass grows on the w.	YEATS 932:29	
three lone w.	ARNO 33:43	
welcome And W. To It	THUR 859:37	
Bear w. in your eye	SHAK 766:84	
effusive w. of the pier	AUDEN 39:84	
rest may reason and w.	BROW 162:68	
terrible events are w.	SHAK 765:45	
thankful that I am here to w. you	STAN 812:61	
W. to shuttle diplomacy!	SISCO 793:54	
w. was not excessive	USTI 875:9	
welcomest often w. when…gone	SHAK 729:43	
welfare goes with the w.	WILS 915:81	
highest w. of your souls	PLATO 654:78	
most anxious for its w.	BURKE 168:2	
W. is hated by those	GOLD 361:37	
w.…of the Irish nation	REDM 681:72	
W. should be a safety-net	ANON 25:71	
w. will be a hand-up	BLAIR 133:9	
welkin bow'd w.…doth bend	MILT 578:43	
Hark! how all the w. rings	WESL 900:10	
let the w. roar	SHAK 743:49	
well All manner of thing shall be w.	ELIOT 309:51	
all shall be w.	JULI 452:5	
And did it very w.	GILB 354:14	
be alive, but to be w.	MART 555:50	
bed-time…and all w.	SHAK 742:26	
cannot think w., love w.	WOOLF 922:41	
confident I can do very w.	JOHN 442:35	
dark w.	PRIC 668:16	
do not feel quite w.	GALB 343:2	
don't dress w.	SHAW 777:62	
in some measure made me w.	SHAK 742:37	
Is it w. with thee?	BIBLE 92:31	
kingdom of the w.	SONT 804:77	
knew too w.	FROST 338:95	
like water in the w.	SMITH 799:63	
looks w. enough on the page	BUNT 166:61	
man lives w.	KIPL 470:82	
never speaks w. of me	CONG 230:94	
One's country is wherever one does w.	ANON 18:61	
valley of Baca make it a w.	BIBLE 96:46	
w. as long as I live on h.	BIRD 130:59	
when looking w. can't	SUCK 828:7	
when things are going w.	BEAU 66:1	
worth doing w.	CHES 210:27	
Would all do so w. as I!	DYER 297:53	
well-appointed w.-a. three-deckers	PALM 635:20	
well-being responsible for its w.-b.	PORT 663:10	
well-bred w.-b. Captain	GILB 353:92	
well-educated w.-e. young women	AUST 43:67	
well-fed 60s face was w.-f.	WATE 890:93	
Wellington shoot three W. College boys	KING 469:55	
well-killed stab…A w.-k. Boche	READ 680:45	
well-looking one of my w.-l. days	GOLD 362:63	
well-off Awrish people are too w.-o.	SHAW 779:35	
well-rounded not a w.-r. person	BELL 73:77	
wells buckets into empty w.	COWP 241:73	
go about and poison w.	MARL 552:86	
w. of salvation	BIBLE 102:20	
well-spaced nothing is w.-s.	WILL 914:52	
well-to-do w.-t.-d. prosper	BRYAN 163:8	
well-written w.-w. life is almost as rare	CARL 192:20	
Welsh devil understands W.	SHAK 742:20	
Welshmen W. [are] Taffies	PAXM 644:86	
wench besides, the w. is dead	MARL 552:87	
fair hot w.	SHAK 741:94	
love a w.	SHIR 789:80	
O ill-starred w.	SHAK 761:17	
stuff fit only for a w.	MASE 559:29	
w.…strays so from her kind	DEKK 259:50	
Wenonah called her name W.	LONG 516:55	
wept Caesar hath w.	SHAK 748:6	
He w. to hear	BLAKE 133:28	
I could have w.	HOLM 407:70	
Jesus w.	BIBLE 118:4	
Werther dies from excess…(like W.)	BART 62:22	
W. had a love	THAC 849:5	
Wesen Mensch ist das W	SCHI 718:2	
Weser river W., deep and wide	BROW 160:25	
Wesley W. and the Holy Ghost	MENC 566:84	
west As far as the east is from the w.	BIBLE 97:64	
blessed life was the W.'s future	TOLS 863:8	
daughter of the W.	TENN 844:69	
dearly like the W.	BURNS 171:3	
democracies of the w.	MASA 550:20	
east wind prevails over the w.	MAO 548:13	
falling down the w.	FROST 338:86	
for many people in the w.	SOLZ 803:64	
gardens of the W.	CONN 233:86	
Go W., young man	GREE 370:45	
Go W., young man	SOULE 804:91	
Iris of the W.	BYRON 180:33	
lady of the W. Country	DELA 260:67	
Lochinvar…out of the w.	SCOTT 723:96	
long the brightness of the w.	BRON 154:77	
men of the W.	WEIL 896:26	
oath on the plain at W. Point	MACA 524:26	
opium of the w.	FRAN 333:84	
planted another one down in the w.	BOUL 146:25	
room in the w. for wolves	BABB 45:20	
safeguard of the W.	WORD 926:20	
ship would not travel due W.!	CARR 197:31	
than they do in the W.	SNOW 802:42	
warm wind, the w. wind	MASE 559:24	
W. has not lived	YELT 934:70	
W. is W.	KIPL 470:81	
where the W. begins	CHAP 206:11	
who only the W. End know	POWE 667:96	
Westbury W.…nasty odious	COBB 223:51	
Westen Im W. nichts Neues	REMA 683:97	
western All Quiet on the W. Front	REMA 683:97	
intellectual life…of w. society	SNOW 802:48	
music of the W. Hemisphere	GILL 356:48	
we have the w.	DUVA 296:44	
w. is not only the history of this country	LANG 488:91	
w. part of our European	TOLS 863:8	
Wind of the w. sea	TENN 841:2	
written in by a W. Union boy	DOSP 282:3	
Westerner typical W. wishes	RUSS 705:45	
West Germany beat W.G.	RAMS 678:8	
West Indies an island in the W. I.	ONEI 625:87	
infant negroes in the W. I.	DICK 266:78	
Westminster the wine bars and brothels of W.	MVI 512:84	
westward stepping w.?	WORD 927:33	
Then w. ho!	SHAK 756:77	
w.…the land is bright	CLOU 222:22	
wet bereft Of w. and wildness?	HOPK 412:97	
in the dark and w.	STEV 822:13	
out of these w. clothes	ANON 22:54	
Petals on a w., black bough	POUND 664:28	
whacky Iraqi is really not w.	ACHE 3:48	
whale gull's way and the w.'s way	MASE 559:23	
impoTent as a beached w.	TIME 860:73	
'No,' said the W.	KIPL 472:33	
th'enormous w.	SMART 797:28	
three nights in the w.'s belly	BIBLE 111:43	
whaleroad and the w.	LOWE 520:43	
w. ship was my Yale College	MELV 564:28	
whiteness of the w.	MELV 564:32	
whaleroad w. and the whale	LOWE 520:43	
whales great w. come sailing by	ARNO 31:85	
tub of male w.	UPDI 874:74	
whaling 'Scientific w.' is like the prostitution	WHIT 904:16	
w. a universal metaphor	LODGE 514:23	
what I know w.'s w.	WEST 901:35	
knew W. was W.	TRAV 865:47	
Now w.?	SARO 714:36	
W. ho!	WODE 919:53	
what-is-it spoke with a certain w.-i.-i.	WODE 919:69	
whaups W. are crying	STEV 823:35	
wheat districts…like squares of w.	LARK 491:36	
fill his barn with w. or barley	BUNY 167:78	
separate the w. from the chaff	HUBB 417:9	
sowed tares among the w.	BIBLE 112:50	
Stacker of W.	SAND 712:91	
Thousands of miles of w.	RICH 686:70	
two grains of w.	SHAK 739:41	
w. is green	SHAK 737:85	
wheel before the w.	THOM 853:2	
ever-whirling w. of Change	SPEN 809:14	
every turn of the w.	BAUD 64:63	
Fortune from the w.	SHAK 748:26	
legalistic w. of fortune	CAPO 189:24	
man at the w.	MARI 550:52	
O, how the w. becomes it!	SHAK 755:22	
red w. barrow	WILL 913:44	
restoration of the w.	GAND 345:33	
shoulder to the w.	GINS 357:65	
spinning w. and the bronze axe	ENGE 314:68	
Upon a w. of fire	SHAK 764:97	
w. broken at the cistern	BIBLE 101:92	
w. in the middle of a w.	BIBLE 105:84	
w. is come full circle	SHAK 764:3	
w. of life	STER 818:85	
w.'s kick and the wind's song	MASE 559:21	
W. that turned the Trade	MAND 545:54	
whirlèd like a potter's w.	SHAK 729:42	
you who turn the w.	ELIOT 306:63	
wheeler-dealer called him a w.-d.	MANC 544:42	
wheel-horse third-rate…w.-h.	MENC 566:56	
wheels apparently rolled along on w.	HUXL 425:68	
bodies are under our w.	SHAW 778:87	
moved by little fidget w.	SLES 796:15	
Time's w. runs back	BROW 162:70	
use of w. within w.	MANC 544:42	
w. of Being slow	TENN 843:39	
w.…over my head	TENN 845:94	
whirligig w. of the train	SITW 793:61	
when distrust a man that says w.	HAMM 380:23	
forgotten to say 'W.!'	WODE 919:64	
whence W. are we	SHEL 785:98	
w., wherefore, whither	BRAH 149:86	
where never know w. you are	SALI 711:54	
W. is here?	FRYE 340:37	
w. I was born	SALI 710:51	
w. you are	GROS 374:25	
where'er w. you walk	POPE 658:50	
wherefore For every why he had a w.	BUTL 177:41	
why and w. in all things	SHAK 746:64	
whet kites to w. their beaks	RANS 679:24	
whiff w. of grapeshot	CARL 192:6	
whiffling make it the w.	HAZL 388:79	

look to w. — ELIOT 306:63
windy w. side of the law — SHAK 757:85
wine Apostle's advice to use w. — BERN 80:30
Be not drunk with w. — BIBLE 122:49
blood and w. are red. — WILDE 910:52
both in w. and women — KITC 475:4
Botticelli isn't a w. — PUNCH 673:15
buy w. and milk without money — BIBLE 104:53
cargo of…sweet white w. — MASE 559:26
cup of full w. — FLET 328:72
dark w. of Venice! — MORR 598:93
days of w. and roses — DOWS 284:45
Differs…as much as w. and water — MARL 553:14
Drinking the blude-red w. — BALL 56:84
drink thy w. with a merry heart — BIBLE 101:83
drink w., and eat good cheer — MIDD 569:39
Drink w.…as you please — BAUD 65:69
ecstacy Of sun-fed w. — NEIL 610:31
falser than vows made in w. — SHAK 750:70
fetch to me a pint o' w. — BURNS 171:2
Few things surpass old w. — BYRON 182:79
fine w. leaves you with — AMER 14:77
flask of w. — FITZ 324:83
flown with insolence and w. — MILT 581:10
fond of Spanish w. — MASE 559:29
french w. and fine weather — KEATS 458:13
From w.…friendship springs! — GAY 348:89
full of dewy w. — KEATS 460:61
giant refreshed with w. — BOOK 143:61
Good w., a friend — ALDR 11:14
good w. needs no bush — SHAK 751:94
have their strong w. diluted — SALI 711:68
he drinks no w. — SHAK 743:63
Here is w. — KEATS 457:5
last drops of vintage w. — BOYLE 148:49
Late at e'en, drinkin' the w. — BALL 55:74
like w. through water — BRON 155:94
lordliest in their w. — MILT 586:61
man and his w.'s sae bewitching! — BURNS 173:55
mouth do crush their w. — MARV 556:74
new friend is as new w. — BIBLE 107:46
new w. into old bottles — BIBLE 111:21
new w. intoxicated — MILT 585:18
Not given to w. — BIBLE 123:74
not look for w. — JONS 449:40
not to be rinsed with w. — HOPK 412:81
no w. or good beer — GORO 364:15
old w. — GOLD 362:62
out-did the frolic w. — HERR 400:51
pass the rosy w. — DICK 267:15
Pour out the w. without restraint — SPEN 809:4
press the rue for w.! — SCOTT 723:11
red w. had brought red ruin — CHES 212:81
red w. of Shiraz into urine? — BLIX 137:1
small people talk about w. — LEBO 499:12
sops in w. — SPEN 808:68
spiced in the w. of sadness — MALA 541:82
spoiled the bread and spilled the w. — PATM 643:57
Sure there was w. — HERB 398:10
Sweet is old w. in bottles — BYRON 181:70
till w. inflame them? — BIBLE 102:10
truth…credited to w. — PLIN 655:6
venison pies and good w. — LOUI 518:91
water…into the w. — CHES 212:77
water that was made w. — BIBLE 117:78
w. and wax — ANON 19:84
W. and women will make men — BIBLE 108:55
w., be sure to drink it — TAO 836:92
w. can…the wise beguile — POPE 659:86
w. does but draw forth — SHER 788:55
w. for thy stomach's sake — BIBLE 123:77
W. gives you liberty — WYCH 931:12
w. in rivers — SCOTT 724:19
W. is as good as life — BIBLE 108:61
W. is the strongest — BIBLE 107:24
W. makes a man better — JOHN 445:33
w. maketh merry — BIBLE 101:88
w., oh how much sweeter — RABE 676:65
w. that maketh glad — BIBLE 97:67
w. that tasted of the tar? — BELL 73:65
w. was a farce — POWE 666:79
w. was port — PRIOR 669:39
w. which overflows — MERE 567:9
w. will burn our mouth — EMER 313:37
with w. dispense — CRAB 242:81
woman, w. and song — LUTH 523:1
wine-cup when the w.-c. glistens — SCOTT 724:40

wine-less thanks to w.-l. — BROW 162:90
wine-pots castaway w.-p. — CLOU 222:28
wines importation of all foreign w. — SMITH 798:48
wine-vaults previously been to a w.-v. — DICK 268:42
wing After the kingfisher's w. — ELIOT 307:99
crept…on a broken w. — TENN 845:97
crow Makes w. — SHAK 768:16
flung the span on even w. — CRANE 243:23
insect youth are on the w. — GRAY 369:6
lark's on the w. — BROW 160:19
left w.…right w. — ASQU 36:19
night…like a great dark w. — RAND 678:13
Nor knowst'ou w. from tail — POUND 665:61
shade is on the brightest w. — SITW 794:68
space, an eaglet's w. — CRANE 243:18
weak-eyed bat…on leathern w. — COLL 228:47
White clouds on the w. — ALLI 13:62
w. and a prayer — ADAM 5:98
w. of friendship — DICK 267:14
w. of friendship — DICK 267:15
w. trails like a banner — JEFF 436:6
w. wherewith we fly to heaven — SHAK 730:67
with as inconstant w. — SHEL 782:19
winged w. messenger of heaven — SHAK 736:46
wings angel…in his foreign w. — SMITH 799:64
beating…his luminous w. — ARNO 34:67
carried off by the w. of time — LAFO 485:15
clip an Angel's w. — KEATS 458:25
cloudy w. expand — BYRON 180:31
contagion from her sable w. — MARL 552:85
Creative Endeavour lost her w. — WAUGH 892:25
deep-damasked w. — KEATS 459:36
dip their w. in tears — TENN 843:38
divinity…breeding w. — MILT 585:18
each one had six w. — BIBLE 102:11
flapped its tinsel w. — MARV 556:66
flies with swallows' w. — SHAK 731:14
full of the linnet's w. — YEATS 932:30
gates she claps her w. — LYLY 523:8
giant w. prevent him from walking — BAUD 64:55
God of Love…Beteth his w. — CHAU 209:87
golden hours, on angel w. — BURNS 171:5
healing in his w. — BIBLE 106:22
hear the beating of his w. — BRIG 152:30
indefatigable w. — MILT 581:28
lets grow her w. — MILT 577:35
Liberty lends us her w. — BRON 155:86
May cricket…spread its w. — BRAD 149:77
mechanical birds with many w. — RAINE 677:94
meer despair of w. — VAUG 878:43
mount up with w. as eagles — BIBLE 103:42
Oh that I had w. like a dove! — BIBLE 96:32
pair of fiery w. displayed — BEAU 67:16
pigeons…burned, their w. — PEPYS 647:46
Puts on swift w. — MILT 581:31
riches certainly make themselves w. — BIBLE 100:47
Save w., for heaven — KEATS 459:37
soul has w. — DELA 260:59
to darkness, on extended w. — STEV 819:19
under his w. shalt thou trust — BIBLE 96:53
under the shadow of thy w. — BIBLE 95:14
under the shadow of thy w. — BIBLE 94:93
under the shadow of thy w. — BOOK 143:54
Upon her w. presents — HERR 400:42
upon the w. Of silence — MILT 577:34
while the w. aspire — WORD 929:60
w. are no longer w. to fly — ELIOT 306:79
w. break into fire — BROW 159:6
w. display and altars raise — DRYD 289:50
w. like a dove — BOOK 143:53
w. of gentle flush — KEATS 457:79
w. of the breeze — BRON 154:72
w. of the morning — BIBLE 98:1
w. outspread Dove-like — MILT 580:93
w. with tireless feet — ROBE 689:18
with ah! bright w. — HOPK 412:84
with the shadow of his w. — SHAK 731:96
wingtip from w. to w. — BACH 46:28
winner crowning the w. — COUB 238:85
winners there are no w. — CHAM 204:60
where would the w. be? — STEN 817:56
winning fallacy…about w. — BLAN 136:89
If the world be worth thy w. — DRYD 291:38
Never change a w. game — TILD 860:66
not the w. that matters — COOKE 236:42
not w. but taking part — COUB 238:86
the question as to whether we are w. — RUMS 702:69

W. isn't everything — LOMB 515:33
W. isn't everything — PALM 635:17
w. man's affection — GILB 354:98
Winnipeg Boy Meets Girl in W. — MACL 535:53
winnowed deep thoughts can be w. — SAGAN 708:6
wins If Margaret Thatcher w. — KINN 470:70
one who w. — SEXT 728:17
teamwork w. championships — JORD 451:68
Who dares, w. — ANON 22:61
w. everyone's approval — HORA 414:33
winter age is as a lusty w. — SHAK 749:39
among the w. snows — GLAD 358:91
as w. changes the trees — BRON 155:96
as w. lies — MACD 529:41
Bare W.…changed to Spring — SHEL 786:23
bleak mid-w. — ROSS 697:84
Blow, blow, thou w. wind — SHAK 749:52
Christmas…in the Middle of W. — ADDI 6:17
covered in w. with violets — SHEL 785:89
dead of w. — ELIOT 306:73
do we believe in w.? — ROTH 699:17
English w. — BYRON 182:95
especially in W. — SWIFT 832:94
every w. change to spring — TENN 843:42
Forget not bees in w. — SACK 708:87
For w., spring, and summer — ANON 20:8
from w. going into w. — BEDE 68:54
furious w. blowing — RANS 679:25
furious w.'s rages — SHAK 774:74
heel Of limping w. — SHAK 735:36
How like a w. — SHAK 772:39
If W. comes — SHEL 783:48
In w. I get up at night — STEV 822:11
ninetieth w. came — EGAN 301:24
Now is the w. — SHAK 731:98
O W.! bar thine adamantine doors — BLAKE 133:26
People live within w. — MUNRO 603:89
poor as w. — SHAK 760:87
sad tale's best for w. — SHAK 770:79
same w. and summer — SHAK 740:68
severest w.…the spring — COWP 241:65
Summer in W. — CRAS 244:34
summer out of w. — DONNE 281:88
through the perils of w. — TROL 866:76
Thus in the w. stands — MILL 571:86
Twice a week the w. — HOUS 415:50
very dead of w. — ANDR 16:27
was the w. wild — MILT 575:93
when rivers were swollen in w. — SOPH 804:85
W. evening settles down — ELIOT 305:27
W. is come and gone — SHEL 785:95
W. is for women — PLATH 654:71
w. is past — BIBLE 101:99
W. lies too long — CATH 200:87
w. long, harsh w. — NASH 609:5
w., plague and pestilence — NASHE 609:17
W. scourged the meadow — ROBE 689:19
w.'s rains and ruins — SWIN 832:19
w. weeds outworn — SHEL 786:21
w., when men kill the fat swine — ANON 19:80
w. wind is loud and wild — BRON 155:91
W., yelling through the troublous air — COLL 228:48
Would seem a w.'s day — ROCH 692:70
winters Four lagging w. — SHAK 734:3
green end of one of civilization's hardest w. — FOWL 332:68
Of those four w. — GREE 371:57
sixteen w. cannot blow away — SHAK 770:98
wipe Gives it a w. — HOOD 410:53
wire fine w. around our s. — STEV 820:58
high w. of his own making — FERL 321:11
wireless message came on the w. — PENI 646:21
wires Along the electric w. — AUST 44:2
transmit the voice over w. — ANON 21:31
w. that span the mountain stream — CRANE 243:16
wisdom acquire that kind of w.? — ATWO 38:62
age of w. — DICK 271:19
apply our hearts unto w. — BIBLE 96:52
attained the sum Of w. — MILT 535:35
beginning of w. — LOWE 520:52
beginning of w. — BIBLE 97:75
beginning of w. — FLAU 326:38
but not to our w. — BANKS 58:37
but w. lingers — TENN 841:84
cannot myself give birth to w. — SOCR 803:54
contrivance of human w. — BURKE 168:33
dispose Of highest w. — MILT 587:66

Worship is transcendent w. — CARL 193:32
wondered w. why young women — JOHN 445:16
wonderful after…it was w. — WILD 910:70
most w. in the world — SIHA 791:30
name shall be called W. — BIBLE 102:17
O w., w., and most w. — SHAK 749:60
reality was no less w. — SHIP 789:78
What a w. boy he is! — HOGG 406:59
w. time—the War — HUGH 418:23
w. to listen to — HARDY 381:49
wondering w. what lay round — KAVA 456:69
w. whether it would take spin — HOME 409:14
wonders all W. in one sight! — CRAS 244:34
Everything has its w. — KELL 460:75
His w. to perform — COWP 240:43
left us surmising w. — QUIL 674:48
lost w. of the ancient world — AUCH 39:75
Of all the w. — SHAK 747:89
Seven W. of the World — ADDI 6:21
Signs are taken for w. — ELIOT 305:40
We carry with us the w. — BROW 158:66
w. in the deep — BIBLE 97:71
w. Of common things — MIDD 569:41
w. of the western world — SYNGE 834:58
wondrous we'll be w. rich — OTWAY 631:30
woo April when they w. — SHAK 750:79
cannot w. in festival terms — SHAK 745:24
Come, w. me, w. me — SHAK 750:76
forced to w. — WEBS 895:4
So thou wilt w. — SHAK 736:50
were not made to w. — SHAK 737:96
when a married man doth w. — DONNE 280:50
w. not like a babe — SHAK 732:31
wood bit about nudism in the w. — JOYCE 452:97
bows down to w. — KIPL 472:18
correct in cypress w. — PARK 638:62
courters'-and-rabbits' w. — THOM 853:85
creeping ivy clings to w. — COWP 241:62
dark impenetrable w. — SCOTT 723:2
enclosing it in a case of w. — WATT 891:2
Far off the w. — FREE 336:43
found myself in a dark w. — DANTE 252:93
goblets for a dish of w. — SHAK 735:22
harbour and neighbour w. — THOM 852:74
Heap on more w.! — SCOTT 723:97
impulse from a vernal w. — WORD 924:75
in the w. the furious winter — RANS 679:25
Land of…shaggy w. — SCOTT 723:92
maker of worn w. — UPDI 874:74
piles of dry w. with red-hot coals — CISN 218:30
Proud Maisie is in the w. — SCOTT 724:39
rooky w. — SHAK 768:16
Sit…in this w. — BRON 154:77
springth the w. nu — ANON 19:83
strange odours…of aromatic w. — CONR 234:4
that piece of w. — MANN 546:79
Through w. and dale — COLE 226:13
true w., of yew w. — DOYLE 285:57
two pieces of w. — MITF 588:5
Two roads diverged in a w. — FROST 338:89
violin is w. and catgut — PRIE 668:17
Where no w. is…the fire goeth out — BIBLE 100:55
whiffling through the tulgey w. — CARR 195:91
w. a Piggy-wig stood — LEAR 497:84
w. found on a beach — ROSE 697:65
w. of Hallaig — MACL 535:34
w.'s in trouble — HOUS 415:55
woodbine luscious w. — SHAK 737:97
well attir'd w. — MILT 578:54
w. spices are wafted — TENN 845:89
woodcock Spirits of well-shot w. — BETJ 83:82
woodcocks springes to catch w. — SHAK 751:23
wooden W. legs are not inherited — CONK 232:50
W. Shoes — ANON 21:37
woodland stands about the w. ride — HOUS 414:41
woodlands about the w. I will go — HOUS 414:43
wood-pigeons brassy w.-p. — HUGH 419:44
woods Enter these enchanted w. — MERE 567:7
Flow down the w. — SACK 708:89
for the w. against the world — BLUN 137:18
If you go down in the w. — BRAT 150:96
in the deep green w. — HOLM 407:70
in w. the noble savage ran — DRYD 288:35
let it loose in the w. — SHAW 780:56
Love-whispering w. — POPE 662:79
never knew the summer w. — TENN 843:33
ordered w. and gardens — MACK 533:15

pleasure in the pathless w. — BYRON 180:43
shepherd, thee the w. — MILT 578:47
shut the road through the w. — KIPL 473:66
these hoary w. are grand — GALT 344:29
The w. decay — TENN 846:25
through the Wet Wild W. — KIPL 473:47
Tomorrow to fresh w. — MILT 578:59
went to the w. — THOR 857:91
w. are lovely — FROST 339:98
w. as deep and cool — COWL 240:40
W., or steepy mountain — MARL 553:17
worked in the w. — SNYD 803:53
woodshed Something nasty in the w. — GIBB 352:71
wooed therefore to be w. — SHAK 729:48
woman in this humour w.? — SHAK 731:4
wooer knight to be their w. — BALL 55:67
wooing a fresh w. — STOP 825:59
won by w. thee — SHAK 762:35
Young men a w. — ANON 19:92
wool jeweller's cotton and fine w. — DICK 269:81
shall be as w. — BIBLE 102:7
Woolf afraid of Virginia W.? — ALBEE 9:90
woollen Odious! in w.! — POPE 661:32
rather lie in the w. — SHAK 744:90
word according to thy w. — BIBLE 128:1
according to thy w. — BIBLE 114:22
according to thy w. — BIBLE 115:27
according to thy w. — BIBLE 97:80
ages for the wrong w. — USTI 875:3
ancient w. of courage — SHAK 732:22
At ev'ry w. a reputation — POPE 659:72
bad-weather kind of w. — BUFO 165:46
before thy uncreating w. — POPE 662:83
Bilbo's the w. — CONG 230:96
bring out of each w. — JAMES 434:71
By any other w. — SHAK 736:48
By thought, w., and deed — BOOK 141:2
by water and the w. — STONE 825:57
cannot utter a w. — SHAW 777:58
changed…to past Without a w. — LARK 490:31
choke the w. — BIBLE 112:48
Conscience is but a w. — SHAK 732:21
contempt of thy w. — BOOK 141:87
discouraging w. — HIGL 402:86
eaten thee for a w. — SHAK 734:88
every w. has its marrow — SMART 796:24
every w. she writes is a lie — MCCA 528:11
every w. stabs — SHAK 744:94
every w. that proceedeth — BIBLE 89:47
every w. that proceedeth — BIBLE 109:78
falling cadence of the lovely w. — MAUG 561:78
final w., before I'm done — HALD 377:77
Fine w., 'legitimate' — SHAK 762:56
first w. on everything — HUGO 421:98
gone without a w.? — SHAK 729:28
Good isn't the w. — GILB 355:37
great actor or a household w.? — OLIV 624:66
great deal to make one w. mean — CARR 196:12
Greeks Had a W. for It — AKINS 9:80
hard, brown, nutlike w. — BART 62:11
hast kept my w. — BIBLE 126:50
have not the w. — ARNO 33:41
heareth the w. — BIBLE 112:48
heareth the w. — BIBLE 112:49
horror of the w. 'flesh' — RENO 683:7
How the w. rolls—Leonora — CRAIK 242:7
If thou hast heard a w. — BIBLE 108:56
In one w. — PASC 641:32
In one w. he told me the secret — LEHR 502:71
In the beginning was the W. — BIBLE 117:71
In the beginning was the W. — ELIOT 305:36
kens a w. Burns — MACD 529:30
leave the w. of God — BIBLE 119:34
Let the w. go forth — KENN 462:12
lies in one little w.! — SHAK 734:3
Lord's First W. — FARJ 318:48
Love in search of a w. — LANI 489:2
Man's w. is God in man — TENN 847:37
most important sense of the w. — MOORE 594:20
my most painted w. — SHAK 753:73
never will speak w. — SHAK 761:18
No man would set a w. — MILL 573:32
No simple w. — JONS 449:35
not one w. is said — STAN 812:66
no w. in their language — SWIFT 831:83
No w. like 'Pardon' — SHAK 735:29
Observant of the heavenly w. — DODD 278:9

ordinary sense of the w. — MILL 572:15
people answered him not a w. — BIBLE 92:18
pleynly, at a w. — CHAU 209:92
polite w. for dead…imagination — CUMM 248:20
Polyester…the most valuable w. — ANON 25:52
power of the written w. — CONR 234:95
Preach the w. — BIBLE 124:85
precise meaning of a w. — BAND 58:25
proud Victorian w. — PRIT 669:56
run to and fro to seek the w. — BIBLE 106:11
say a w. against G. — SHAW 779:39
single w. even may be a spark — SHEL 786:15
solemn w. of warning — WILS 916:9
So shall my w. be — BIBLE 104:56
speaks to us the same w. — SCHW 721:70
speak the w. only — BIBLE 110:14
spoken the foremost w. — BALL 56:77
sweeter…will be the w. lover — HELO 393:86
Taäke my w. for it — TENN 847:55
take thy w. for faith — SHAK 769:52
tears wash out a w. — FITZ 324:84
Tell them…I kept my w. — DELA 260:64
that w. 'hummy', my darlings — PARK 637:47
there is not a w. of fear — LAND 488:82
The w. is life — SASS 716:74
the w. of a noble Messenger — KORAN 479:94
The w.VALUE — SMITH 797:41
This is my final w. — BEAV 67:26
thru the nicht we spak nae w. — SOUT 805:93
torture one poor w. — DRYD 289:50
Turning the w. to sword — SHAK 743:59
unkind or irreverential w. — HAWT 386:52
unto me according to thy w. — BIBLE 114:22
upholding all things by the w. — BIBLE 124:89
use no w.…under stress — POUND 666:72
utter and see in w. — SAND 712:90
voice the w. 'nature' — REDON 681:75
What is honour? A w. — SHAK 742:28
When I hear that w. — GINS 357:66
whose lightest w. — SHAK 752:28
whose w. one cannot believe — VICT 880:84
with a flattering w. — WILDE 910:54
without adding a w. — TROL 867:1
w. alone shall fit — CHES 212:75
w. 'civilization' to my mind — MILL 573:55
W. climbs upward — DUNC 295:13
w. fitly spoken — BIBLE 100:50
w. for w. without book — SHAK 755:48
w. from the content — FLAU 326:31
W. has somehow got around — THUR 860:59
w. have I hid in mine heart — BIBLE 97:81
w. is a lamp — BIBLE 97:84
W. is but wynd — LYDG 523:5
w. is dead — DICK 273:72
w. is like a bell — KEATS 460:64
w. is the carving — SITW 794:85
w. is the Verb — HUGO 421:83
w.…means just what I choose — CARR 197:15
w. means underpants — MURR 604:7
w. 'Now' is like a bomb — MILL 572:3
w. of Caesar — SHAK 748:9
w. of God is quick — BIBLE 124:90
w. of our God shall stand for ever — BIBLE 103:36
w. of worlds — CURN 249:37
w.…out of a ladys lips — FLEM 327:59
w.'s anguish is caused by people — FAUL 318:66
w. spoken in due season — BIBLE 99:33
w. stung him — SITW 794:64
w. that may not be there — WILB 907:78
W. was made flesh — BIBLE 117:74
w. within the w. — ELIOT 305:40
wordless set of w. symbols — UPDI 875:97
words alms-basket of w. — SHAK 734:88
and aimable w. — TENN 846:22
any relation to the w. — ROSE 697:65
apt w. have power — MILT 586:51
ate and drank the precious W. — DICK 273:74
bad poet dwells…in a world of w. — ELIOT 305:48
believed not the w. — BIBLE 92:13
Be not the slave of w. — CARL 192:94
bereft me of all w. — SHAK 740:74
better deeds than w. — SHAK 729:28
big w. to talk about dirty things — DOCT 277:2
But w. are w. — SHAK 759:68
callisthenics with w. — PARK 638:69
can drug, with w. — LOWE 519:22
can express in w. — NABO 606:38

shall make my w. all sound — LAYA 496:47
the soldier lists his w. — PROP 670:61
too much attainted by w. — HOFS 406:55
With balmy hands his w. to bind — COLL 228:44
w. are in his breast and face — DAVIS 256:67
w. I had on Crispin's day — SHAK 746:58
W. inflicted by the sword — RICH 686:69
w. of deadly hate — MILT 582:57

woven Joy and Woe are w. fine — BLAKE 135:68
w. and held together — JACK 431:7

wrath chariots of w. — GRANT 366:53
Envy and w. shorten the life — BIBLE 108:59
eternal w. Burnt after them — MILT 583:88
give place unto w. — BIBLE 120:83
in w. remember mercy — BIBLE 106:13
my w. did end — BLAKE 135:59
Nursing her w. — BURNS 172:13
provoke not your children to w. — BIBLE 122:50
soft answer turneth away w. — BIBLE 99:30
sun go down upon your w. — BIBLE 122:47
sware in my w. — BIBLE 97:58
Throw away thy w. — HERB 398:19
tygers of w. — BLAKE 134:43
warned you to flee from the w. — BIBLE 108:76
w. and indignation against us — BOOK 141:2
W. brings…gravest hurt — EURI 316:13
W. is cruel — BIBLE 100:57
w. of the Lamb — BIBLE 126:58
w. of the lion — BLAKE 134:44
w. which thou condemnest — BLAKE 135:75

wreaths laurel w. entwine — HARTE 385:18
w. of fame and interest — MARV 556:69

wreck Amid the w.…of nations — PITT 653:47
decay Of that colossal w. — SHEL 784:50
From its own w. — SHEL 785:83
playing bowls upon a splitting w. — DAVI 254:23
rock on which thou art to w. — DRYD 290:1
worthless check, a total w. — PORT 663:5
w. and not the story of the w. — RICH 685:49
w. of Paradise — SHEL 786:11

wreckage w. of men — WOOLF 922:45

wrecks thousand fearful w. — SHAK 731:8
Vomits its w. — SHEL 784:65
w. of a dissolving dream — SHEL 786:21
w. will surface over the sea — EWART 316:27

Wren Sir Christopher W. said — BENT 78:76

wren Four Larks and a W. — LEAR 497:75
No, the w. goes to't — SHAK 763:88
robin-red-breast and the w. — WEBS 895:92

wrest w. the ball from your neighbour — ANON 21:32

wrestle w. not against flesh — BIBLE 122:52
w.…words and meanings — ELIOT 308:15

wrestling lay w. with…my God — HOPK 413:3
Light w. there incessantly with light — CRANE 243:12
Texas w. match — WRIS 930:95

wretch Excellent w.! — SHAK 760:83
My wife…poor w. — PEPYS 647:35
on a w. wilt thou be revenged? — SIDN 790:5
Perfidious w.! — TREI 865:55
poor w. whose one d. — SHAW 778:87
Pulled the poor w. — SHAK 755:26
Saucy pedantic w. — DONNE 279:41
saved a w. like me! — NEWT 613:76
sharp-looking w. — SHAK 733:61
W., under a comfort — HOPK 413:6
w. who supports — JOHN 442:49

wretched All men hate the w. — SHEL 782:12
how w. I should be — ALBE 10:96
make every one w. — JAMES 433:26
man…a w. thing — DAVI 254:35
Most w. men — SHEL 783:27
O w. state of man — SIDN 790:99
This rortie w. city — SMITH 801:25
w. man that I am! — BIBLE 120:71
w., rash, intruding fool — SHAK 754:7

wretchedness so bare and full of w. — SHAK 737:79
w. is irremediable? — EDGE 299:1

wretches Poor naked w. — SHAK 763:78
w. hang — POPE 659:73

Wright W.'s limp sentences — WEST 901:42

wring w. under the load of sorrow — SHAK 745:20

wrinkle out…with the first w. — DRYD 288:22
What stamps the w. — BYRON 179:17

wrinkles let old w. come — SHAK 739:37
w. will devour — NASHE 609:18

wrist time is tied to the w. — RAINE 677:95
tread her w. — DUNC 295:14

wrists slap time on their w. — KINC 468:22

writ censure this mysterious w. — DRYD 291:19
One w. with me — SHAK 737:80
stol'n forth of Holy W. — SHAK 731:7
w. your annals true — SHAK 770:73

write allow them to sing and to w. — MAZA 562:98
always w. of you — SHAK 772:31
as a man ought to w. — TROL 867:10
as much of a labour to w. — HUXL 425:66
better to w. of laughter — RABE 676:64
cause to w. about me — GIOV 357:73
difficult not to w. satire — JUVE 453:14
do not w. on a computer — OROU 627:26
Don't w. anything down — DOWD 284:41
Don't you like to w. letters? — HEMI 393:95
engender in those who w. — GOWE 365:29
few…as cannot w. — DENH 261:93
For a man to w. well — JONS 450:58
If a man w. little — BACON 50:54
invoked, sit down to w. — SWIFT 832:96
isn't much to w. home about — HYDE 427:22
I w. because — GALL 344:18
like to w. standing up — HEMI 394:19
look in thy heart, and w. — SIDN 790:8
make me w. too much — DANI 252:92
may w. at any time — JOHN 441:21
necessary to w. for oneself — FLAU 326:36
never w. another — WELD 897:45
No man can w. — FAUL 319:74
not easy to w. well — JAMES 434:57
number who can w. — MACD 529:40
people who do not w. — GREE 371:72
those who cannot w. — POPE 661:54
took him seventeen years to w. — PRIE 668:23
to w. a really funny book — HEMI 393:93
To w. music is to — HONE 409:29
to w. or even to talk — THES 851:51
try to w. as good — HEMI 394:26
watches over us when we w. — AMIS 15:5
What I feel most moved to w. — MELV 564:43
When I do not w. — CIXO 219:39
when you w. or when you fight — HEMI 394:11
would have liked to w. — KAVA 456:66
w. a book a year — TARTT 836:1
w. about it if I like — STEIN 815:20
w. against your name — RICE 685:37
w. enough to sign contracts — GING 357:58
w.…exclusively of others — WAUGH 893:50
w. for money or fame — MOORE 595:35
w. for the adults — WALK 885:94
W: for these words are true — BIBLE 127:80
w. his thoughts upon a slate — HOOD 410:53
W. me as one that loves — HUNT 423:34
w. music like Wagner — GOLD 362:80
w. of Hell — HERR 399:32
w. straight honest prose — HEMI 394:9
w. the beauty of your eyes — SHAK 771:4
w.…too early in your life — RILKE 687:83
w. whatever story — KELM 461:78
w. when I feel spiteful — LAWR 494:89
w. when there is something — HEMI 394:8
w. with no dinner — RANS 679:28
yet could w. of thee? — JONS 450:50

writer Aboriginal w. is a Janus-type — NARO 608:74
advertisement w. uses his mastery — SAYE 717:86
art of the w. — APOL 27:15
as a w. or artist — STEV 824:40
Asking a working w. — HAMP 380:28
ask the w. to censor — KELM 461:78
basic material a w. works with — CATH 200:92
being a professional w. — ROST 699:11
being a w. here means nothing — GOLD 361:34
concealed beauties of a w. — ADDI 6:18
danger of its tricking the w. — SAND 713:14
Detach the w. — ROTH 699:14
duty of the w. — KENN 463:35
Every w. is a frustrated actor — STER 817:64
experience…of the woman w. — WITT 918:49
For the w.…as for the painter — PROU 671:90
function of a w. — CONN 233:75
good w. always works — STEI 816:41
good w. is not…a good book critic — BISH 131:81
great and original w. — WORD 928:48
greatest part of a w.'s time — JOHN 444:7
great w.…always the plodder — POUND 666:70
great w. creates a world of his own — CONN 233:64
great w. does not…invent — PROU 671:91

housewife or a complete w. — PLATH 654:63
If any w. thinks — SHAR 776:46
If I were a w. — DELI 261:77
if Mr Kissinger is a great w. — ANON 25:62
it is the w. — ASIM 35:5
lesser w. may entice…for a moment — CONN 233:64
loopholes for an unorthodox w. — ORWE 628:48
major w.…required major torment — BERG 79:3
memorandum…to protect the w. — ACHE 3:43
modern hardback w. — MORT 599:15
No modern Irish w. — ORWE 629:77
not an easy country for a fiction-w. — UPDI 875:98
No w. before the…19th century — WAUGH 893:53
No w., sacred or profane — PATM 643:64
occupation of a woman w. — WOOLF 923:51
plain, rude w. — BURT 174:69
present or any future w. — MILL 570:58
primarily a w. — GENET 348:3
primary requirement for a w. — STAEL 812:51
responsibility of the w. — ALGR 11:31
role of the w. and critic divided — BRAD 148:68
something of the w. in the work — STIPE 824:52
stink…of the w.'s pride — SALI 711:65
success happens to an English w. — AMIS 15:2
To a w., madness is a final distillation — DELI 261:78
Too much importance is given the w. — BOWL 147:33
tragic w. does not have to believe — KRUT 481:27
true friend and a good w. — WHITE 903:84
understand a w.'s ignorance — COLE 226:16
vanity of the w. — REES 682:89
vicious…to be a creative w. — LAWR 495:20
When a w. calls his work — HAWT 386:42
wise w.…writes for the youth — FITZ 324:88
w. and nothing else — HUTC 424:50
w.…at the White House — WHITE 903:2
w. by profession — GRASS 367:58
w. enters into a structure — FRYE 340:36
w. has to rob his mother — FAUL 318:69
w. have a social responsibility? — NABO 606:48
w.…if you copy others — BERN 81:46
w. must eventually write — ROY 701:57
w. of dictionaries — JOHN 442:38
w. of dictionaries — JOHN 442:46
w. of talent needs only — WINN 917:27
w. or a good public servant — MACM 537:83
w. overwhelmingly honest — MOORE 595:39
w. risks sterility — HOLM 407:74
w.'s ambition — KOES 477:29
w.'s greed is appalling — BALD 53:32
w.'s only responsibility — FAUL 318:68
w. thinks from…cliché — POUND 664:24
w.…universal in sympathy — BARN 60:68
w. who has nothing to say — BIER 129:21
w. writes in order to teach — KAZIN 456:71

writers All w. are either 29 — PARK 638:76
All w. are vain — ORWE 629:86
ancient w. — YEATS 933:54
and of all w. — TIMES 861:76
as many good w. — VIDAL 881:10
bad w. must start with plain heroines — FITZ 325:16
cause of poets and of w. — SPEN 807:66
comic w. to have a hate figure — TOWN 863:23
Creative w. are always greater — FORS 332:55
Derivative w. seem — NABO 606:42
English…the best dull w. — CHAN 204:78
few w. can prostitute — FORS 331:48
give young w. advice — HELL 392:78
great Victorian w. — WILS 915:84
hold w. in contempt — BELL 73:76
I suppose all w. are crazy — CHAN 205:93
Make way, Roman w. — PROP 670:62
men trying to be w. — JONES 447:88
Most w. in…their careers — WAUGH 892:42
Most w. need a wound — AMIS 15:3
no different from other w. — BARN 60:75
rare…to take w. seriously — POWE 666:85
self-limited w. — WOOLF 922:34
severest w. of the severest age — DRYD 288:45
some w. are lost — HAWT 386:37
such great w. in the past — HEMI 394:22
true w. have experienced this feeling — SARR 715:38
w. and the bardies — FERG 321:9
W. are always envious — CAREY 191:67
W. are much more esteemed — SNOW 802:42
w. are there to overhear — BEAT 66:94
w. could live in their own minds — BRAD 148:66
w., like clear fountains — LAND 488:75